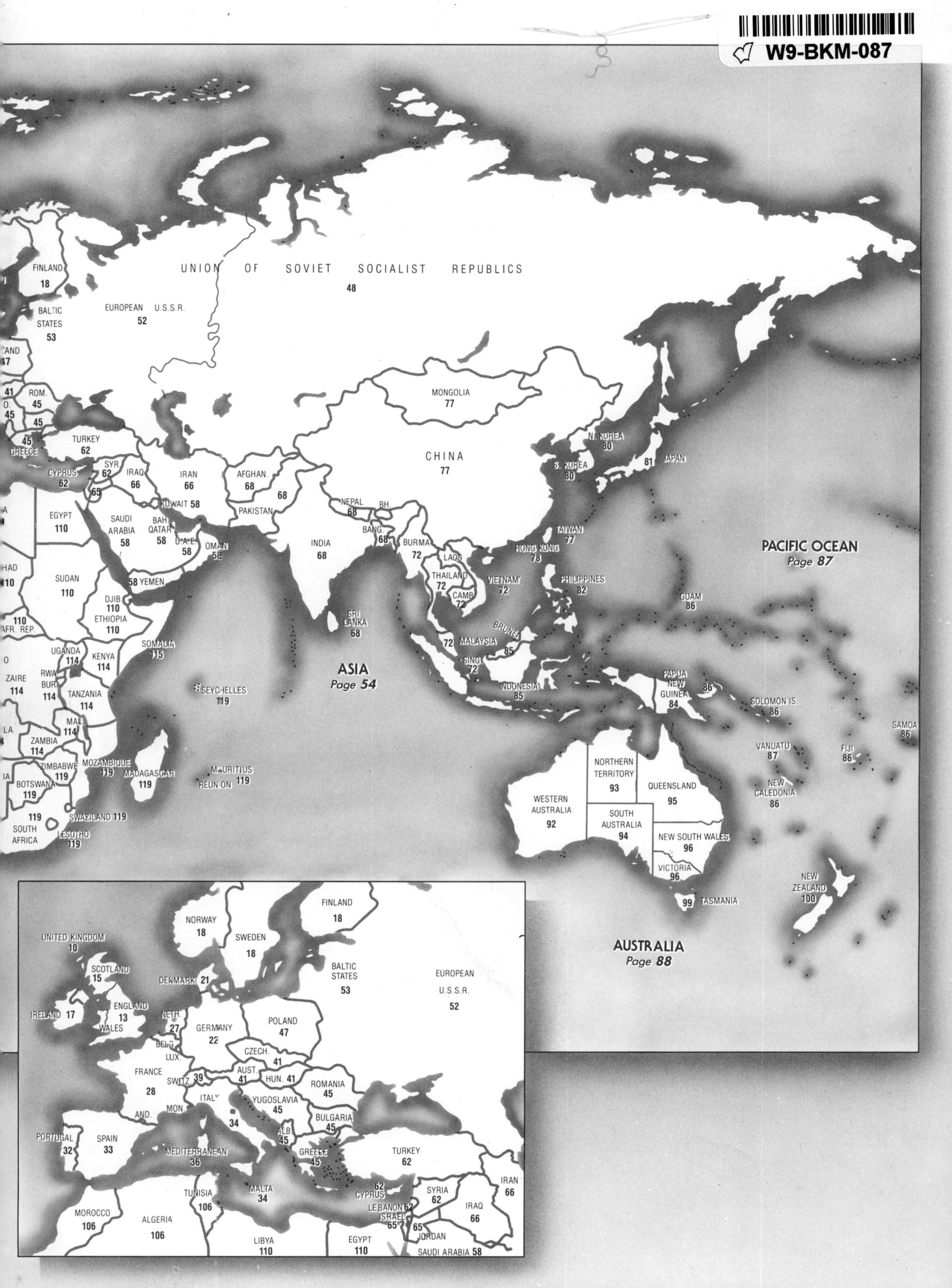

FINLAND
18

BALTIC
STATES
53

UNION OF SOVIET SOCIALIST REPUBLICS
48

EUROPEAN U.S.S.R.
52

ROM.
45

45

45
GREECE

MONGOLIA
77

TURKEY
62

CYPRUS
62

SYR.
62

IRAQ
66

IRAN
66

AFGHAN.
68

68

CHINA
77

N. KOREA
80

S. KOREA
80

JAPAN
81

EGYPT
110

SAUDI
ARABIA
58

KUWAIT 58

BAH.
QATAR
58

U.A.E.
58

OMAN
58

NEPAL
68

BH.

BANG.
68

PAKISTAN

INDIA
68

BURMA
72

LAOS

TAIWAN
77

HONG KONG
78

PACIFIC OCEAN
Page 87

SUDAN
110

YEMEN
58

DJIB.
110

ETHIOPIA
110

SRI
LANKA
68

THAILAND
72

CAMB.
72

VIETNAM
72

PHILIPPINES
82

GUAM
86

HAD
10

110
AFR. REP.

UGANDA
114

KENYA
114

SOMALIA
115

BRUNEI

MALAYSIA
85

SING.
72

ZAIRE
114

RWA.
114

BUR.

TANZANIA
114

SEYCHELLES
119

ASIA
Page 54

INDONESIA
85

PAPUA
NEW
GUINEA
84

86

SOLOMON IS.
86

SAMOA
86

MAL.
114

ZAMBIA
114

MOZAMBIQUE
119

MADAGASCAR
119

MAURITIUS
119

REUNION 119

VANUATU
87

FIJI
86

NEW
CALEDONIA
86

ZIMBABWE
119

BOTSWANA
119

119

SWAZILAND 119

SOUTH
AFRICA

LESOTHO
119

NORTHERN
TERRITORY
93

QUEENSLAND
95

WESTERN
AUSTRALIA
92

SOUTH
AUSTRALIA
94

NEW SOUTH WALES
96

VICTORIA
96

NEW
ZEALAND
100

TASMANIA

AUSTRALIA
Page 88

UNITED KINGDOM
10

NORWAY
18

SWEDEN
18

FINLAND
18

SCOTLAND
15

DENMARK 21

BALTIC
STATES
53

EUROPEAN
U.S.S.R.
52

IRELAND 17

ENGLAND
13
WALES

NETH.
27

GERMANY
22

POLAND
47

BEL.
LUX.

FRANCE
28

SWITZ. 39

CZECH.
41

AUST.
41

HUN. 41

ROMANIA
45

ITALY

YUGOSLAVIA
45

BULGARIA
45

AND.

MON.

34

ALB.
45

PORTUGAL
32

SPAIN
33

GREECE
45

TURKEY
62

IRAN
66

MEDITERRANEAN
36

CYPRUS
62

SYRIA
62

IRAQ
66

TUNISIA
106

MALTA
34

LEBANON 62
ISRAEL
65

65

JORDAN

MOROCCO
106

ALGERIA
106

LIBYA
110

EGYPT
110

SAUDI ARABIA 58

OPPORTUNITY

"The golden opportunity you are seeking is in yourself. It is not in your environment, it is not in luck or chance, or the help of others; it is in yourself alone."
                    --Orsion Swett Marden

The year of 1991 is behind us and we now go on to seek new opportunities and climb new mountains. Life is full of positive challenges and rewards if our vision allows it!

We hope that this World Atlas will foster your imagination of far away places and the challenges that others around the world face in your position daily.

We, at the Eastern Division, would like to take this opportunity to thank you for your contribution in making World Team Snap-on the success it is today. May 1992 hold a rewarding year for you and your family.

Sincerely,

Nicholas L. Loffredo
Vice President - Eastern Division

HAMMOND® WORLD ATLAS

HAMMOND® AMBASSADOR WORLD

ATLAS

HAMMOND INCORPORATED   MAPLEWOOD, NEW JERSEY 07040

Hammond Publications Advisory Board

Library of Congress Cataloging-in-Publication Data
Hammond Incorporated.
  Hammond ambassador world atlas.
    p. cm.
  Includes indexes.
  ISBN 0-8437-1292-9
  1. Atlases.   I. Title   II. Title:
Ambassador world atlas
G1021.H265   1991b   [G&M]
912–dc20   91-22994
                                      CIP
                                     MAP

Contents

GAZETTEER-INDEX I
GLOSSARY OF ABBREVIATIONS VI

Terrain Maps of Land Forms and Ocean Floors
Contents IX
Index VII

Thematic Maps— Global Relationships
Contents T1

World and Polar Regions
World 1
Arctic Ocean 4
Antarctica 5

Europe
Europe 6
United Kingdom and Ireland 10
Norway, Sweden, Finland,
    Denmark and Iceland 18
Germany 22
Netherlands, Belgium and Luxembourg 25
France 28
Spain and Portugal 31
Italy 34
Switzerland and Liechtenstein 37
Austria, Czechoslovakia and Hungary 40
Balkan States 43
Poland 46
Union of Soviet Socialist Republics 48

Asia
Asia 54
Near and Middle East 58
Turkey, Syria, Lebanon and Cyprus 61
Israel and Jordan 64
Iran and Iraq 66
Indian Subcontinent and Afghanistan 68
Burma, Thailand, Indochina and Malaya 72
China and Mongolia 75
Japan and Korea 79
Philippines 82
Southeast Asia 84

Pacific Ocean and Australia
Pacific Ocean 86

Australia 88
Western Australia 92
Northern Territory 93
South Australia 94
Queensland 95
New South Wales and Victoria 96
Tasmania 99
New Zealand 100

Africa
Africa 102
Western Africa 106
Northeastern Africa 110
Central Africa 113
Southern Africa 117

South America
South America 120
Venezuela 124
Colombia 126
Peru and Ecuador 128
Guianas 131
Brazil 132
Bolivia 136
Chile 138
Argentina 141
Paraguay and Uruguay 144

North America
North America 146
Mexico 150
Central America 153
West Indies 156

Canada
Canada 162
Newfoundland 166
Nova Scotia and Prince Edward Island 168
New Brunswick 170
Quebec 172
Ontario 175
Manitoba 178
Saskatchewan 180
Alberta 182
British Columbia 184
Yukon and Northwest Territories 186

United States
United States 188
Alabama 193

Alaska 196
Arizona 198
Arkansas 201
California 204
Colorado 207
Connecticut 210
Delaware 244
Florida 212
Georgia 215
Hawaii 218
Idaho 220
Illinois 222
Indiana 225
Iowa 228
Kansas 231
Kentucky 234
Louisiana 238
Maine 241
Maryland 244
Massachusetts 247
Michigan 250
Minnesota 253
Mississippi 256
Missouri 259
Montana 262
Nebraska 264
Nevada 266
New Hampshire 268
New Jersey 271
New Mexico 274
New York 276
North Carolina 279
North Dakota 282
Ohio 284
Oklahoma 287
Oregon 290
Pennsylvania 293
Rhode Island 247
South Carolina 296
South Dakota 298
Tennessee 234
Texas 301
Utah 304
Vermont 268
Virginia 306
Washington 309
West Virginia 312
Wisconsin 315
Wyoming 318
The Fifty States 320

World Index 325
GEOGRAPHICAL TERMS 474
MAP PROJECTIONS 475
WORLD STATISTICS 478
FOREIGN CITY WEATHER 480
U.S. CITY WEATHER 482
TABLES OF AIRLINE DISTANCES 484

Introduction to the World Atlas

Over 90 years ago, my great-grandfather, Caleb Stillson Hammond, had a vision for his newly born company. That vision was based upon integrity, accuracy, innovation and timeliness of the maps and atlases produced by the C.S. Hammond Map Company. In the spirit of that vision, Hammond Incorporated is proud to present a world atlas with the most up-to-date, beautifully rendered, accurate, easy-to-use map collection available. This is a reference volume that will be instrumental in helping the reader understand the issues that we all face in today's ever-changing, complex world.

The atlas you are holding is one of the very few on the market today that reflects the changes that have occurred worldwide, including the reunification of Germany and unification of Yemen. Our fully revised United States map collection now features state flags and final 1990 U.S. Census figures. In fact, there are thousands of revisions and enhancements that have been made throughout the atlas. These revisions echo the new nations, shifting boundaries and the fluid internal divisions of many countries. New communities generated by the opening up of resources in the developing nations are also noted. Up-to-date geographical information, both foreign and domestic, is received daily by our editors.

The current edition of the Hammond World Atlas introduces an outstanding new section devoted to the special features and issues of today's world–24 pages of thematic maps. These maps cover fundamental global relationships: political, natural, and cultural highlights as well as social and economic matters.

Our dramatic series of physical maps of landforms and ocean floors, in the section **The Physical World**, were originally produced as sculptured terrain models, thus simulating the earth's surface in a highly realistic manner. The three-dimensional effect is both instructive and pleasing to the eye.

As in previous editions, the atlas is organized to make the retrieval of information as simple and quick as possible. The guiding principle in organizing the atlas material has been to present separate subjects on separate maps. In this way, each individual map topic is shown with the greatest degree of clarity, unencumbered with extraneous information that is best revealed on separate maps. Of equal importance from the standpoint of good atlas design is the treatment of all current information on a given country or state as a single atlas unit. Thus, the basic reference map of an area is accompanied on adjacent pages by all supplementary information pertaining to that area. For example, the detailed index for a given map always appears on the same page as, or on the pages immediately following, the reference map. This same map index provides population data for the many cities, towns and villages shown on the map. Highlight information on the area, i.e., the total population and area, the capital, the highest point, is listed in the summary fact listings accompanying each unit. An adjacent locator map relates the subject area to the larger world beyond. A three-dimensional picture of the area is exhibited by means of the accompanying full-color topographic map. A separate economic map defines the vital agricultural, industrial and mineral resources of the area. In the case of the foreign maps, the flag of each independent nation appears on the appropriate page. Finally, certain country units contain special subject maps dealing with the history, climate, demography and vegetation of the area.

The back of the book contains a second type of index. This is a multi-paged "A-to-Z" index of all the world's places that appear on the maps. The use of this map index is essential when the name of a place is known but its country, state, or province is unknown.

In closing it may be said that the atlas has truly been designed for contemporary use. Just as the information presented on the following pages is as current and up-to-date as the editors and cartographers could issue it, so the design and organization has been as well planned as possible to create a work useful to present generations.

President
HAMMOND INCORPORATED

Introduction to the Maps and Indexes

The following notes have been added to aid the reader in making the best use of this atlas. Though the reader may be familiar with maps and map indexes, the publisher believes that a quick review of the material below will add to his enjoyment of this reference work.

Arrangement—The Plan of the Atlas. The atlas has been designed with maximum convenience for the user as its objective. Part I of the atlas is devoted to the physical world—terrain maps of land forms and the sea floor. Part II features thematic maps and diagrams on a wide variety of subjects such as climate, languages and energy. Part III contains the general political reference maps, area by area. All geographically related information pertaining to a country or region appears on adjacent pages, eliminating the task of searching throughout the entire volume for data on a given area. Thus, the reader will find, conveniently assembled, political, topographic, economic and special maps of a political area or region, accompanied by detailed map indexes, statistical data, and illustrations of the national flags of the area.

The sequence of country units in this American-designed atlas is international in arrangement. Units on the world as a whole are followed by a section on the polar regions which, in turn, is followed by pages devoted to Europe and its countries. Every continent map is accompanied by special population distribution, climatic and vegetation maps of that continent. Following the maps of the European continent and its countries, the geographic sequence plan proceeds as follows: Asia, the Pacific and Australia, Africa, South America, North America, and ends with detailed coverage on the United States.

Political Maps—The Primary Reference Tool. The most detailed maps in each country unit are the *political maps.* It is our feeling that the reader is likely to refer to these maps more often than to any other in the book when confronted by such questions as—Where? How big? What is it near? Answering these common queries is the function of the political maps. Each political map stresses *political* phenomena—countries, internal political divisions, boundaries, cities and towns. The major political unit or units, shown on the map, are banded in distinctive colors for easy identification and delineation. First-order political subdivisions (states, provinces, counties on the state maps) are shown, scale permitting.

The reader is advised to make use of the *legend* appearing under the title on each political map. Map *symbols,* the special "language" of maps, are explained in the legend. Each variety of dot, circle, star or interrupted line has a special meaning which should be clearly understood by the user so that he may interpret the map data correctly.

Each country has been portrayed at a *scale* commensurate with its political, areal, economic or tourist importance. In certain cases, a whole map unit may be devoted to a single nation if that nation is considered to be of prime interest to most atlas users. In other cases, several nations will be shown on a single map if, as separate entities, they are of lesser relative importance. Areas of dense settlement and important significance within a country have been enlarged and portrayed in inset maps inserted on the margins of the main map. The scale of each map is indicated as a fractional representation (1:1,000,000). The reader is advised to refer to the linear or "bar" scale appearing on each map or map inset in order to determine the distance between points.

The *projection* system used for each map is noted near the title of the map. Map projections are the special graphic systems used by cartographers to render the curved three-dimensional surface of the globe on a flat surface. Optimum map projections determined by the attributes of the area have been used by the publishers for each map in the atlas.

A word here as to the choice of place names on the maps. Throughout the atlas names appear, with a few exceptions, in their local official spellings. However, conventional Anglicized spellings are used for major geographical divisions and for towns and topographic features for which English forms exist; i.e., "Spain" instead of "España" or "Munich" instead of "München." Names of this type are normally followed by the local official spelling in parentheses. As an aid to the user the indexes are cross-referenced for all current and most former spellings of such names.

Names of cities and towns in the United States follow the forms listed in the *Post Office Directory* of the United States Postal Service. Domestic physical names follow the decisions of the Board on Geographic Names, U.S. De-

partment of the Interior, and of various state geographic name boards.

It is the belief of the publishers that the boundaries shown in a general reference atlas should reflect current geographic and political realities. This policy has been followed consistently in the atlas. The presentation of *de facto* boundaries in cases of territorial dispute between various nations does not imply the political endorsement of such boundaries by the publisher, but simply the honest representation of boundaries as they exist at the time of the printing of the atlas maps.

Indexes—Pinpointing a Location. Each political map is accompanied by a comprehensive index of the place names appearing on the map. If you are unfamiliar with the location of a particular geographical place and wish to find its position within the confines of the subject area of the map, consult the map index as your first step. The name of the feature sought will be found in its proper alphabetical sequence with a key reference letter-number combination corresponding to its location on the map. After noting the key reference letter-number combination for the place name, turn to the map. The place name will be found within the square formed by the two lines of latitude and the two lines of longitude which enclose the coordinates—i.e., the marginal letters and numbers. The diagram below illustrates the system of indexing.

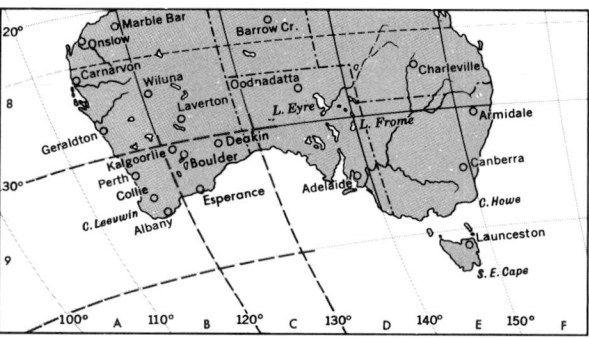

In the case of maps consisting entirely of insets, the place name is found near the intersection point of the imaginary lines connecting the coordinates at right angles. See below.

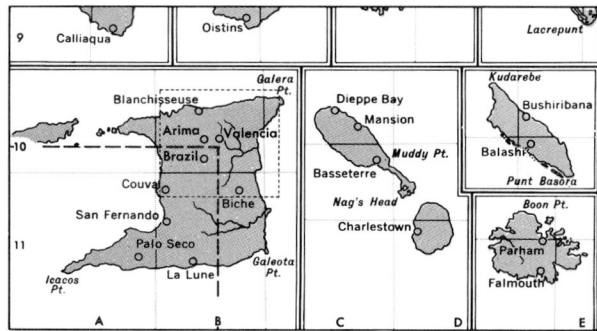

Where space on the map has not permitted giving the complete form of the place name, the complete form is shown in the index. Where a place is known by more than one name or by various spellings of the same name, the different forms have been included in the index. Physical features are listed under their proper names and not according to their generic terms; that is to say, Rio Negro will be found under Negro and not under Rio Negro. On the other hand, Rio Grande will be found under Negro and not under Rio Grande. Accompanying most index entries for cities and towns, and for other political units, are *population figures* for the particular entries. The large number of population figures in the atlas makes this work one of the most comprehensive statistical sources available to the public today. The population figures have been taken from the latest official censuses and estimates of the various nations. Dates and sources for the population figures are listed in the Gazetteer-Index of the World following this section.

Population and area figures for countries and major political units are listed in bold type *fact lists* on the margins of the indexes. In addition, the capital, largest city, highest point, principal languages and the prevailing religions of the country concerned are also listed. The Gazetteer-Index of the World on the following pages provides a quick reference index for countries and other important areas. Though population and area figures for each major unit are also found in the map section, the Gazetteer-Index provides a conveniently arranged statistical comparison contained in five pages. As mentioned, dates and sources of the population figures appearing in the country indexes are also listed in this section.

All index entries for cities and towns in the indexes accompanying individual state maps for the United States are preceded by a five-digit postal ZIP code number applying to the community. A dagger (†) designates those places that do not possess a post office. The ZIP code number listed in such cases refers to that of the nearest post office. An asterisk (*) marks those larger cities which are divided into multiple ZIP code areas. Using the single ZIP code number listed in such cases will direct your letter to the proper city with dispatch. However, if the precise ZIP code number of the address within the city is needed, it is suggested that the reader refer to the latest National ZIP Code Directory at his local post office. This detailed guide lists every street in a multiple ZIP code city with the proper ZIP code for the street.

Relief Maps. Accompanying each political map is a relief map of the area. The purpose of the relief map is to illustrate the surface configuration (TOPOGRAPHY) of the region. A shading technique in color simulates the relative ruggedness of the terrain—plains, plateaus, valleys, hills and mountains. Graded colors, ranging from greens for lowlands, yellows for intermediate evaluations to brown in the highlands, indicate the height above sea level of each part of the land. A vertical scale at the margin of the map shows the approximate height in meters and feet represented by each color.

Economic Maps—Agriculture, Industry and Resources. One of the most interesting features that will be found in each country unit is the economic map. From this map one can determine the basic activities of a nation as expressed through its economy. A perusal of the map yields a full understanding of the area's economic geography and natural resources.

The agricultural economy is manifested in two ways: color bands and commodity names. The color bands express broad categories of *dominant land use,* such as cereal belts, forest lands, livestock range lands or nonagricultural wastes. The red commodity names, on the other hand, pinpoint the areas of production of *specific* crops, i.e., wheat, cotton, sugar beets, etc.

Major mineral occurrences are denoted by standard letter symbols appearing in blue. The relative size of the letter symbols signifies the relative importance of the deposit.

The manufacturing sector of the economy is presented by means of diagonal line patterns expressing the various *industrial* areas of consequence within a country.

The fishing industry is represented by names of commercial fish species appearing offshore in blue letters. Major waterpower sites are designated by blue symbols.

The publishers have tried to make this work the most comprehensive and useful atlas available, and it is hoped that it will prove a valuable reference work. Any constructive suggestions from the reader will be welcomed.

Sources and Acknowledgements

A multitude of sources goes into the making of a large-scale reference work such as this. To list them all would take many pages and would consume space better devoted to the maps and reference materials themselves. However, certain general sources were very useful in preparing this work and are listed below.

STATISTICAL OFFICE OF THE UNITED NATIONS.
Demographic Yearbook. New York. Issued annually.

STATISTICAL OFFICE OF THE UNITED NATIONS.
Statistical Yearbook. New York. Issued annually.

THE GEOGRAPHER, U.S. DEPARTMENT OF STATE.
International Boundary Study papers. Washington. Various dates.

THE GEOGRAPHER, U.S. DEPARTMENT OF STATE.
Geographic Notes. Washington. Various dates.

UNITED STATES BOARD ON GEOGRAPHIC NAMES.
Decisions on Geographic Names in the United States. Washington. Various dates.

UNITED STATES BOARD ON GEOGRAPHIC NAMES.
Official Standard Names Gazetteers. Washington. Various dates.

CANADIAN PERMANENT COMMITTEE ON GEOGRAPHICAL NAMES.
Gazetteer of Canada series. Ottawa. Various dates.

UNITED STATES POSTAL SERVICE.
National Five Digit ZIP Code and Post Office Directory. Washington. Issued annually.

UNITED STATES POSTAL SERVICE.
Postal Bulletin. Washington. Issued weekly.

UNITED STATES DEPARTMENT OF THE INTERIOR. BUREAU OF MINES.
Minerals Yearbook. 4 vols. Washington. Various dates.

UNITED STATES GEOLOGICAL SURVEY.
Elevations and distances in the United States. Reston, Va. 1980.

CARTACTUAL.
Cartactual—Topical Map Service. Budapest. Issues bi-monthly.

AMERICAN GEOGRAPHICAL SOCIETY.
Focus. New York. Issued ten times a year.

THE AMERICAN UNIVERSITY.
Foreign Area Studies. Washington. Various dates.

CENTRAL INTELLIGENCE AGENCY.
General reference maps. Washington. Various dates.

A sample list of sources used for specific countries follows:

Afghanistan
CENTRAL STATISTICS OFFICE.
Preliminary Results of the First Afghan Population Census 1979. Kabul.

Albania
DREJTORIA E STATISTIKES.
1979 Census. Tiranë.

Argentina
INSTITUTO NACIONAL DE ESTADISTICA Y CENSOS.
Censo Nacional de Población y Vivienda 1980. Buenos Aires.

Australia
AUSTRALIAN BUREAU OF STATISTICS.
Census of Population and Housing 1981. Canberra.

Brazil
FUNDACAO INSTITUTO BRASILEIRO DE GEOGRAFIA E ESTATISTICA.
IX Recenseamento Geral do Brasil 1980. Rio de Janeiro.

Canada
STATISTICS CANADA.
1981 Census of Canada. Ottawa.

Cuba
COMITE ESTATAL DE ESTADISTICAS.
Censo de Población y Viviendas 1981. Havana.

Hungary
HUNGARIAN CENTRAL STATISTICAL OFFICE.
1980 Census. Budapest.

Indonesia
BIRO PUSAT STATISTIK.
Sensus Penduduk 1980. Jakarta.

Kuwait
CENTRAL OFFICE OF STATISTICS.
1980 Census. Al Kuwait.

New Zealand
DEPARTMENT OF STATISTICS.
New Zealand Census of Population and Dwellings 1981. Wellington.

Panama
DIRECCIÓN DE ESTADISTICA Y CENSO.
Censos Nacionales de 1980. Panamá.

Papua New Guinea
BUREAU OF STATISTICS.
National Population Census 1980. Port Moresby.

Philippines
NATIONAL CENSUS AND STATISTICS OFFICE.
1980 Census of Population. Manila.

Saint Lucia
CENSUS OFFICE.
1980 Population Census. Castries.

Singapore.
DEPARTMENT OF STATISTICS.
Census of Population 1980. Singapore.

U.S.S.R.
CENTRAL STATISTICAL ADMINISTRATION.
1979 Census. Moscow.

United States
BUREAU OF THE CENSUS.
1980 Census of Population. Washington.

Vanuatu
CENSUS OFFICE.
1979 Population Census. Port Vila.

Zambia
CENTRAL STATISTICAL OFFICE.
1980 Census of Population and Housing. Lusaka.

Gazetteer-Index of the World

This alphabetical list of continents, countries, states, possessions and other major geographical areas provides a quick reference to their area in square miles and square kilometers, population, capital or chief town, map page number and an index reference. The index reference indicates the square on the respective page in which the name may be found. The population figures used in each case are the latest reliable figures obtainable. The government listings are based primarily on the nomenclature contained in the World Factbook published by the CIA of the United States Government. Those governments currently unsettled or in transition are indicated with a † symbol.

Country	Square Miles	Area Square Kilometers	Population	Capital or Chief Town	Page and Index Ref.	Government or Ownership
*Afghanistan	250,775	649,507	15,814,000	Kabul	68/A 2	authoritarian
Africa	11,707,000	30,321,130	648,000,000	....	102/.......	
Alabama, U.S.	51,705	133,916	4,062,608	Montgomery	195/.......	state of the U.S.
Alaska, U.S.	591,004	1,530,700	551,947	Juneau	196/.......	state of the U.S.
*Albania	11,100	28,749	3,199,000	Tiranë	45/E 5	communist
Alberta, Canada	255,285	661,185	2,365,825	Edmonton	182/.......	province of Canada
*Algeria	919,591	2,381,740	22,971,000	Algiers	106/D 3	republic
American Samoa	77	199	32,297	Pago Pago	87/J 7; 86/.......	unincorporated, unorganized territory of the U.S.
Andorra	188	487	50,000	Andorra la Vella	33/G 1	co-principality (France and Spain)
*Angola	481,351	1,246,700	9,747,000	Luanda	114/C 6	Marxist people's republic
Anguilla, U.K.	35	91	6,519	The Valley	156/F 3	dependent territory of the U.K.
Antarctica	5,500,000	14,245,000	....		5/.......	....
*Antigua and Barbuda	171	443	76,000	St. John's	161/E 11; 156/G 3	parliamentary democracy
*Argentina	1,072,070	2,776,661	31,929,000	Buenos Aires	143/.......	republic
Arizona, U.S.	114,000	295,260	3,677,985	Phoenix	198/.......	state of the U.S.
Arkansas, U.S.	53,187	137,754	2,362,239	Little Rock	202/.......	state of the U.S.
Armenian S.S.R., U.S.S.R.	11,506	29,800	3,283,000	Erivan	52/F 6	Soviet republic
Aruba, Netherlands	75	193	66,790	Oranjestad	161/E 9	autonomous member of the Netherlands realm
Ascension Island, St. Helena	34	88	719	Georgetown	102/A 5	part of St. Helena
Ashmore & Cartier Islands, Australia	61	159	....	(Canberra, Austr.)	88/C 2	territory of Australia
Asia	17,128,500	44,362,815	3,176,000,000	....	54/.......	
*Australia	2,966,136	7,682,300	15,602,156	Canberra	88/.......	federal parliamentary state
Australian Capital Territory	927	2,400	221,609	Canberra	96/E 4	territory of Australia
*Austria	32,375	83,851	7,635,000	Vienna	40/B 3	federal republic
Azerbaidzhan S.S.R., U.S.S.R.	33,436	86,600	7,029,000	Baku	52/G 6	Soviet republic
Azores, Portugal	902	2,335	275,900	Ponta Delgada	32/.......	autonomous region of Portugal
*Bahamas	5,382	13,939	253,000	Nassau	156/C 1	independent commmonwealth
*Bahrain	240	622	489,000	Manama	58/F 4	traditional monarchy
Baker Island, U.S.	1	2.6	....	....	87/J 5	unincorporated territory of the U.S.
Balearic Islands, Spain	1,936	5,014	655,909	Palma	33/H 3	autonomous community of Spain
*Bangladesh	55,126	142,776	106,507,000	Dhaka	68/G 4	republic
*Barbados	166	430	256,000	Bridgetown	161/B 8	parliamentary democracy
*Belgium	11,781	30,513	9,883,000	Brussels	27/E 7	constitutional monarchy
*Belize	8,867	22,966	180,000	Belmopan	154/C 2	parliamentary
*Belorussian S.S.R., U.S.S.R.	80,154	207,600	10,200,000	Minsk	52/C 4	Soviet republic
*Benin	43,483	112,620	4,591,000	Porto-Novo	106/E 6	democratic reform†
Bermuda, U.K.	21	54	67,761	Hamilton	156/H 3	dependent territory of the U.K.
*Bhutan	18,147	47,000	1,483,000	Thimphu	68/G 3	monarchy
*Bolivia	424,163	1,098,582	7,193,000	La Paz; Sucre	136/.......	republic
Bonaire, Neth. Antilles	112	291	8,087	Kralendijk	161/E 9	part of Netherlands Antilles
Bophuthatswana, South Africa	15,570	40,326	1,200,000	Mmabatho	119/D 5	self-governing black African "homeland"
*Botswana	224,764	582,139	1,256,000	Gaborone	119/C 4	parliamentary republic
Bouvet Island, Norway	22	57	....	....	5/D 1	territory of Norway
*Brazil	3,284,426	8,506,663	150,368,000	Brasília	132/.......	federal republic
British Columbia, Canada	366,253	948,596	2,883,367	Victoria	184/.......	province of Canada
British Indian Ocean Terr.	29	75	2,000	(London, U.K.)	54/L 10	dependent territory of the U.K.
British Virgin Islands	59	153	11,006	Road Town	157/H 1	dependent territory of the U.K.
*Brunei	2,226	5,765	249,000	Bandar Seri Begawan	85/E 4	constitutional sultanate
*Bulgaria	42,823	110,912	8,981,000	Sofia	45/F 4	democratic reform†
*Burkina Faso	105,869	274,200	9,001,000	Ouagadougou	106/D 6	military
*Burma (Myanmar)	261,789	678,034	38,541,000	Rangoon	72/B 2	military
*Burundi	10,747	27,835	5,302,000	Bujumbura	114/E 4	republic
California, U.S.	158,706	411,049	29,839,250	Sacramento	204/.......	state of the U.S.
*Cambodia (Kampuchea)	69,898	181,036	8,055,000	Phnom Penh	72/E 4	in dispute
*Cameroon	183,568	475,441	11,540,000	Yaoundé	114/B 2	one-party republic
*Canada	3,851,787	9,976,139	25,309,331	Ottawa	162/.......	confederation with parliamentary democracy
Canary Islands, Spain	2,808	7,273	1,367,646	Las Palmas; Santa Cruz	32/B 4	autonomous community of Spain
Cape Province, South Africa	261,705	677,816	5,543,506	Cape Town	118/C 6	province of South Africa
*Cape Verde	1,557	4,033	347,000	Praia	106/B 8	republic
Cayman Islands, U.K.	100	259	18,000	Georgetown	156/B 3	dependent territory of the U.K.
Celebes, Indonesia	72,986	189,034	7,732,383	Ujung Pandang	85/G 6	part of Indonesia
*Central African Republic	242,000	626,780	2,740,000	Bangui	114/C 2	republic
Central America	197,480	511,475	28,296,000	....	154/.......	
*Chad	495,752	1,283,998	5,538,000	N'Djamena	111/C 4	republic
Channel Islands, U.K.	75	194	133,000	St. Helier; St. Peter Port	13/E 8	part of the United Kingdom
*Chile	292,257	756,946	12,961,000	Santiago	138/.......	republic
*China, People's Rep. of	3,691,000	9,559,690	1,133,682,501	Beijing	77/.......	communist party-led state
China, Republic of (Taiwan)	13,971	36,185	20,204,880	Taipei	77/K 7	one-party presidential regime
Christmas Island, Australia	52	135	3,184	Flying Fish Cove	54/M 11	territory of Australia
Ciskei, S. Africa	2,988	7,740	635,631	Bisho	119/D 6	self-governing black African "homeland"
Clipperton Island, France	2	5.2	....	....	146/H 8	possession of France
Cocos (Keeling) Islands, Australia	5.4	14	555	West Island	54/N 11	territory of Australia

*Member of the United Nations

Gazetteer-Index of the World

Country	Area Square Miles	Square Kilometers	Population	Capital or Chief Town	Page and Index Ref.	Government or Ownership
*Colombia	439,513	1,138,339	30,241,000	Bogotá	126/.......	republic
Colorado, U.S.	104,091	269,596	3,307,912	Denver	208/.......	state of the U.S.
*Comoros	719	1,862	484,000	Moroni	119/G 2	republic
*Congo	132,046	342,000	1,843,000	Brazzaville	114/B 4	people's republic
Connecticut, U.S.	5,018	12,997	3,295,669	Hartford	210/.......	state of the U.S.
Cook Islands, New Zealand	91	236	17,695	Avarua	87/K 7	self-governing in free association with New Zealand
Coral Sea Islands, Australia	8.5	22	....	....	88/J 3	territory of Australia
Corsica, France	3,352	8,682	289,842	Ajaccio; Bastia	28/B 6	part of France
*Costa Rica	19,575	50,700	2,959,000	San José	154/E 5	democratic republic
Côte d'Ivoire, see Ivory Coast						
*Cuba	44,206	114,494	10,617,000	Havana	158/.......	communist state
Curaçao, Neth. Antilles	178	462	145,430	Willemstad	161/G 7	part of Netherlands Antilles
*Cyprus	3,473	8,995	699,000	Nicosia	62/E 5	republic
*Czechoslovakia	49,373	127,876	15,679,000	Prague	41/C 2	republic
Delaware, U.S.	2,044	5,294	668,696	Dover	245/R 3	state of the U.S.
*Denmark	16,629	43,069	5,135,000	Copenhagen	21/.......	constitutional monarchy
District of Columbia, U.S.	69	179	609,909	Washington	244/F 5	district of the United States
*Djibouti	8,880	23,000	456,000	Djibouti	111/H 5	republic
*Dominica	290	751	81,000	Roseau	161/E 7	parliamentary democracy
*Dominican Republic	18,704	48,443	6,867,000	Santo Domingo	158/D 6	republic
*Ecuador	109,483	283,561	10,490,000	Quito	128/C 3	republic
*Egypt	386,659	1,001,447	53,080,000	Cairo	110/E 2	republic
*El Salvador	8,260	21,393	5,207,000	San Salvador	154/C 4	republic
England, U.K.	50,516	130,836	46,220,955	London	13/.......	part of the United Kingdom
*Equatorial Guinea	10,831	28,052	341,000	Malabo	114/A 3	republic
Estonian S.S.R., U.S.S.R.	17,413	45,100	1,573,000	Tallinn	52/C 3; 53/.......	Soviet republic
*Ethiopia	471,776	1,221,900	50,774,000	Addis Ababa	110/G 5	communist†
Europe	4,057,000	10,507,630	689,000,000	....	7/.......	
Falkland Islands & Dependencies, U.K.	6,198	16,053	1,813	Stanley	120/E 8; 143/D 7	dependent territory of the U.K.
Faroe Islands, Denmark	540	1,399	41,969	Tórshavn	21/B 2	self-governing overseas administrative division of Denmark
*Fiji	7,055	18,272	727,000	Suva	87/H 8; 86/.......	republic
*Finland	130,128	337,032	4,973,000	Helsinki	18/O 6	republic
Florida, U.S.	58,664	151,940	13,003,362	Tallahassee	212/.......	state of the U.S.
*France	210,038	543,998	56,160,000	Paris	28/.......	republic
French Guiana	35,135	91,000	90,000	Cayenne	131/E 3	overseas department of France
French Polynesia	1,544	4,000	137,382	Papeete	87/L 8	overseas territory of France
*Gabon	103,346	267,666	1,206,000	Libreville	114/B 4	republic
*Gambia	4,127	10,689	688,000	Banjul	106/A 6	republic
Gaza Strip	139	360	400,000	Gaza	65/A 4	occupied by Israel
Georgia, U.S.	58,910	152,577	6,508,419	Atlanta	217/.......	state of the U.S.
Georgian S.S.R., U.S.S.R.	26,911	69,700	5,449,000	Tbilisi	52/F 6	Soviet republic
*Germany	137,753	356,780	78,890,000	Berlin	22/.......	republic
*Ghana	92,099	238,536	13,391,000	Accra	106/D 7	military
Gibraltar, U.K.	2.28	5.91	31,000	Gibraltar	33/D 4	dependent territory of the U.K.
*Great Britain & Northern Ireland (United Kingdom)	94,399	244,493	57,236,000	London	10/.......	see United Kingdom
*Greece	50,944	131,945	9,983,000	Athens	45/F 6	presidential parliamentary republic
Greenland, Denmark	840,000	2,175,600	49,773	Nuuk (Godthåb)	4/B 12	self-governing overseas administrative division of Denmark
*Grenada	133	344	103,103	St. George's	161/D 9; 156/G 4	parliamentary democracy
Guadeloupe & Dependencies, France	687	1,779	328,400	Basse-Terre	161/A 5; 156/F 4	overseas department of France
Guam, U.S.	209	541	105,979	Agaña	87/E 4; 86/.......	organized, unincorporated territory of the U.S.
*Guatemala	42,042	108,889	9,197,000	Guatemala	154/B 3	republic
*Guinea	94,925	245,856	6,706,000	Conakry	106/B 6	republic
*Guinea-Bissau	13,948	36,125	943,000	Bissau	106/A 6	republic
*Guyana	83,000	214,970	1,024,000	Georgetown	131/B 3	republic
*Haiti	10,694	27,697	5,609,000	Port-au-Prince	158/C 5	republic
Hawaii, U.S.	6,471	16,760	1,115,274	Honolulu	218/.......	state of the U.S.
Heard & McDonald Islands, Australia	113	293	....	....	2/N 8	territory of Australia
Holland, see Netherlands						
*Honduras	43,277	112,087	4,951,000	Tegucigalpa	154/D 3	republic
Hong Kong, U.K.	403	1,044	5,761,000	Victoria	77/H 7; 78/.......	colony of the U.K.
Howland Island, U.S.	1	2.6	....	....	87/J 5	unincorporated territory of the U.S.
*Hungary	35,919	93,030	10,553,000	Budapest	41/D 3	republic
*Iceland	39,768	103,000	250,000	Reykjavík	21/B 1	republic
Idaho, U.S.	83,564	216,431	1,011,986	Boise	220/.......	state of the U.S.
Illinois, U.S.	56,345	145,934	11,466,682	Springfield	222/.......	state of the U.S.
*India	1,269,339	3,287,588	843,930,861	New Delhi	68/D 4	federal republic
Indiana, U.S.	36,185	93,719	5,564,228	Indianapolis	227/.......	state of the U.S.
*Indonesia	788,430	2,042,034	179,136,000	Jakarta	85/D 7	republic
Iowa, U.S.	56,275	145,752	2,787,424	Des Moines	229/.......	state of the U.S.
*Iran	636,293	1,648,000	55,208,000	Tehran	66/F 4	theocratic republic
*Iraq	172,476	446,713	16,335,000	Baghdad	66/C 4	republic
*Ireland	27,136	70,282	3,540,643	Dublin	17/.......	republic

Gazetteer-Index of the World

Country	Square Miles	Area Square Kilometers	Population	Capital or Chief Town	Page and Index Ref.	Government or Ownership
Ireland, Northern, U.K.	5,452	14,121	1,543,000	Belfast	17/F 2	part of the United Kingdom
Isle of Man, U.K.	227	588	64,000	Douglas	13/C 3	part of the United Kingdom
*Israel	7,847	20,324	4,625,000	Jerusalem	65/B 4	republic
*Italy	116,303	301,225	57,574,000	Rome	34/......	republic
*Ivory Coast (Côte d'Ivoire)	124,504	322,465	9,300,000	Yamoussoukro	106/C 7	republic
*Jamaica	4,411	11,424	2,392,000	Kingston	158/......	parliamentary democracy
Jan Mayen, Norway	144	373	....	....	6/D 1	territory of Norway
*Japan	145,730	377,441	123,116,000	Tokyo	81/......	constitutional monarchy
Jarvis Island, U.S.	1	2.6	....	....	87/K 6	unincorporated territory of the U.S.
Java, Indonesia	48,842	126,500	73,712,411	Jakarta	85/J 2	part of Indonesia
Johnston Atoll, U.S.	.91	2.4	327	....	87/K 4	unincorporated territory of the U.S.
*Jordan	35,000	90,650	2,779,000	Amman	65/D 3	constitutional monarchy
*Kampuchea (Cambodia)	69,898	181,036	5,200,000	Phnom Penh	72/E 4	in dispute
Kansas, U.S.	82,277	213,097	2,485,600	Topeka	232/......	state of the U.S.
Kazakh S.S.R., U.S.S.R.	1,048,300	2,715,100	16,538,000	Alma-Ata	48/G 5	Soviet republic
Kentucky, U.S.	40,409	104,659	3,698,969	Frankfort	237/......	state of the U.S.
*Kenya	224,960	582,646	24,872,000	Nairobi	115/G 3	republic
Kermadec Islands, New Zealand	13	33	5	....	87/J 9	part of New Zealand
Kingman Reef, U.S.	0.1	0.26	....	....	87/K 5	unincorporated territory of the U.S.
Kirgiz S.S.R., U.S.S.R.	76,641	198,500	4,291,000	Frunze	48/H 5	Soviet republic
Kiribati	291	754	64,000	Bairiki	87/J 6	republic
Korea, North	46,540	120,539	22,419,000	P'yŏngyang	80/D 3	communist
Korea, South	38,175	98,873	42,793,000	Seoul	80/D 5	republic
*Kuwait	6,532	16,918	2,048,000	Al Kuwait	58/E 4	constitutional monarchy
*Laos	91,428	236,800	3,721,000	Vientiane	72/D 3	communist
Latvian S.S.R., U.S.S.R	24,595	63,700	2,681,000	Riga	52/B 3; 53/......	Soviet republic
*Lebanon	4,015	10,399	2,897,000	Beirut	62/F 6	republic
*Lesotho	11,720	30,355	1,700,000	Maseru	119/D 5	military†
*Liberia	43,000	111,370	2,508,000	Monrovia	106/C 7	republic
*Libya	679,358	1,759,537	3,773,000	Tripoli	110/B 2	socialist people's (masses) state
*Liechtenstein	61	158	28,000	Vaduz	39/J 2	hereditary constitutional monarchy
Lithuanian S.S.R., U.S.S.R.	25,174	65,200	3,690,000	Vilnius	52/B 3; 53/......	Soviet republic
Louisiana, U.S.	47,752	123,678	4,238,216	Baton Rouge	238/......	state of the U.S.
*Luxembourg	999	2,587	378,000	Luxembourg	27/J 9	constitutional monarchy
Macau, Portugal	6	16	448,000	Macau	77/H 7	overseas territory of Portugal
*Madagascar	226,657	587,041	9,985,000	Antananarivo	119/H 3	republic
Madeira Islands, Portugal	307	796	262,800	Funchal	32/A 2	autonomous region of Portugal
Maine, U.S.	33,265	86,156	1,233,223	Augusta	243/......	state of the U.S.
*Malawi	45,747	118,485	8,022,000	Lilongwe	114/F 6	one-party state
Malaya, Malaysia	50,806	131,588	11,138,227	Kuala Lumpur	72/D 6	part of Malaysia
*Malaysia	128,308	332,318	17,377,000	Kuala Lumpur	72/D 6; 85/E 4	federated parliamentary democracy
*Maldives	115	298	206,000	Male	54/L 9	republic
*Mali	464,873	1,204,021	7,960,000	Bamako	106/C 6	republic
*Malta	122	316	353,000	Valletta	34/E 7	parliamentary democracy
Manitoba, Canada	250,999	650,087	1,063,016	Winnipeg	179/......	province of Canada
Marquesas Islands, French Polynesia	492	1,274	5,419	Atuona	87/N 6	part of French Polynesia
Marshall Islands	70	181	30,873	Majuro	87/G 4	constitutional; free association with the U.S.
Martinique, France	425	1,101	328,566	Fort-de-France	161/D 5	overseas department of France
Maryland, U.S.	10,460	27,091	4,798,622	Annapolis	245/......	state of the U.S.
Massachusetts, U.S.	8,284	21,456	6,029,051	Boston	249/......	state of the U.S.
*Mauritania	419,229	1,085,803	1,970,000	Nouakchott	106/B 5	military republic
*Mauritius	790	2,046	1,068,000	Port Louis	119/G 5	parliamentary democracy
Mayotte, France	144	373	47,300	Dzaoudzi	119/G 2	territorial collectivity of France
*Mexico	761,601	1,972,546	86,154,000	Mexico City	150/......	federal republic
Michigan, U.S.	58,527	151,585	9,328,784	Lansing	250/......	state of the U.S.
Micronesia, Federated States of	....	....	73,160	Kolonia	87/E 5	constitutional; free association with the U.S.
Midway Islands, U.S.	1.9	4.9	453	....	87/J 3	unincorporated territory of the U.S.
Minnesota, U.S.	84,402	218,601	4,387,029	St. Paul	255/......	state of the U.S.
Mississippi, U.S.	47,689	123,515	2,586,443	Jackson	256/......	state of the U.S.
Missouri, U.S.	69,697	180,515	5,137,804	Jefferson City	261/......	state of the U.S.
Moldavian S.S.R., U.S.S.R.	13,012	33,700	4,341,000	Kishinev	52/C 5	Soviet republic
Monaco	368 acres	149 hectares	27,063	....	28/G 6	constitutional monarchy
*Mongolia	606,163	1,569,962	2,070,000	Ulaanbaatar	77/E 2	socialist†
Montana, U.S.	147,046	380,849	803,655	Helena	262/......	state of the U.S.
Montserrat, U.K.	40	104	12,073	Plymouth	157/G 3	dependent territory of the U.K.
*Morocco	172,414	446,550	24,522,000	Rabat	106/C 2	constitutional monarchy
*Mozambique	303,769	786,762	15,326,000	Maputo	119/E 4	people's republic
Myanmar, see Burma						
*Namibia	317,827	823,172	1,818,000	Windhoek	118/B 3	republic
Natal, South Africa	33,578	86,967	5,722,215	Pietermaritzburg	119/E 5	province of South Africa
Nauru	7.7	20	9,000	Yaren (district)	87/G 6	republic
Navassa Island, U.S.	2	5	....	....	156/C 3	unincorporated territory of the U.S.
Nebraska, U.S.	77,355	200,349	1,584,617	Lincoln	264/......	state of the U.S.
*Nepal	54,663	141,577	18,442,000	Kathmandu	68/E 3	constitutional monarchy
*Netherlands	15,892	41,160	14,906,000	The Hague; Amsterdam	27/F 5	constitutional monarchy
Netherlands Antilles	390	1,010	246,000	Willemstad	156/E 4	autonomous member of the Netherlands realm
Nevada, U.S.	110,561	286,353	1,206,152	Carson City	266/......	state of the U.S.

Gazetteer-Index of the World

Country	Square Miles	Area Square Kilometers	Population	Capital or Chief Town	Page and Index Ref.	Government or Ownership
New Brunswick, Canada	28,354	73,437	709,442	Fredericton	170/.......	province of Canada
New Caledonia & Dependencies, France	7,335	18,998	133,233	Nouméa	87/G 8	overseas territory of France
Newfoundland, Canada	156,184	404,517	568,349	St. John's	166/.......	province of Canada
New Hampshire, U.S.	9,279	24,033	1,113,915	Concord	268/.......	state of the U.S.
New Jersey, U.S.	7,787	20,168	7,748,634	Trenton	273/.......	state of the U.S.
New Mexico, U.S.	121,593	314,926	1,521,779	Santa Fe	274/.......	state of the U.S.
New South Wales, Australia	309,498	801,600	5,401,881	Sydney	96/B 2	state of Australia
New York, U.S.	49,108	127,190	18,044,505	Albany	276/.......	state of the U.S.
*New Zealand	103,736	268,676	3,389,000	Wellington	100/.......	parliamentary democracy
*Nicaragua	45,698	118,358	3,384,000	Managua	154/D 4	republic
*Niger	489,189	1,267,000	7,250,000	Niamey	106/F 5	republic
*Nigeria	357,000	924,630	104,957,000	Lagos	106/F 6	military
Niue, New Zealand	100	259	3,578	Alofi	87/K 7	self-governing territory in free association with New Zealand
Norfolk Island, Australia	13.4	34.6	2,175	Kingston	88/L 5	territory of Australia
North America	9,363,000	24,250,170	427,000,000	....	146/.......	
North Carolina, U.S.	52,669	136,413	6,657,630	Raleigh	281/.......	state of the U.S.
North Dakota, U.S.	70,702	183,118	641,364	Bismarck	282/.......	state of the U.S.
Northern Ireland, U.K.	5,452	14,121	1,543,000	Belfast	17/F 2	part of the United Kingdom
Northern Marianas, U.S.	184	477	16,780	Capitol Hill	87/E 4	commonwealth associated with the U.S.
Northern Territory, Australia	519,768	1,346,200	154,848	Darwin	93/.......	territory of Australia
North Korea	46,540	120,539	17,914,000	P'yŏngyang	80/D 3	communist state
Northwest Territories, Canada	1,304,896	3,379,683	52,238	Yellowknife	187/G 3	territory of Canada
*Norway	125,053	323,887	4,242,000	Oslo	18/F 7	constitutional monarchy
Nova Scotia, Canada	21,425	55,491	873,176	Halifax	168/.......	province of Canada
Oceania	3,292,000	8,526,280	23,000,000	....	87/.......	
Ohio, U.S.	41,330	107,045	10,887,325	Columbus	284/.......	state of the U.S.
Oklahoma, U.S.	69,956	181,186	3,157,604	Oklahoma City	288/.......	state of the U.S.
*Oman	120,000	310,800	2,000,000	Muscat	58/G 6	absolute monarchy
Ontario, Canada	412,580	1,068,582	9,101,694	Toronto	175, 177/....	province of Canada
Orange Free State, South Africa	49,866	129,153	1,833,216	Bloemfontein	119/D 5	province of South Africa
Oregon, U.S.	97,073	251,419	2,853,733	Salem	291/.......	state of the U.S.
Orkney Islands, Scotland	376	974	17,675	Kirkwall	15/E 1	part of the United Kingdom
*Pakistan	310,403	803,944	112,050,000	Islamabad	68/B 3	parliamentary democracy
Palau	188	487	12,116	Koror	86/D 5	U.N. trusteeship administered by the U.S.
Palmyra Atoll, U.S.	3.85	1	....	....	87/K 5	unincorporated territory of the U.S.
*Panama	29,761	77,082	2,418,000	Panamá	154/G 6	centralized republic
*Papua New Guinea	183,540	475,369	3,593,000	Port Moresby	85/B 7; 87/E 6	parliamentary democracy
Paracel Islands, China	....	....	....	....	85/E 2	occupied by China; claimed by Taiwan and Vietnam
*Paraguay	157,047	406,752	4,157,000	Asunción	144/.......	republic
Pennsylvania, U.S.	45,308	117,348	11,924,710	Harrisburg	294/.......	state of the U.S.
*Peru	496,222	1,285,215	22,332,000	Lima	128/.......	republic
*Philippines	115,707	299,681	60,097,000	Manila	82/.......	republic
Pitcairn Islands, U.K.	18	47	54	Adamstown	87/O 8	dependent territory of the U.K.
*Poland	120,725	312,678	37,931,000	Warsaw	47/.......	democratic
*Portugal	35,549	92,072	10,467,000	Lisbon	32/B 3	republic
Prince Edward Island, Canada	2,184	5,657	126,646	Charlottetown	168/E 2	province of Canada
Puerto Rico, U.S.	3,515	9,104	3,522,037	San Juan	161/.......	commonwealth associated with the U.S.
*Qatar	4,247	11,000	422,000	Doha	58/F 4	traditional monarchy
Québec, Canada	594,857	1,540,680	6,532,461	Québec	172, 174/....	province of Canada
Queensland, Australia	666,872	1,727,200	2,587,315	Brisbane	95/.......	state of Australia
Réunion, France	969	2,510	570,000	St-Denis	119/F 5	overseas department of France
Rhode Island, U.S.	1,212	3,139	1,005,984	Providence	249/H 5	state of the U.S.
*Romania	91,699	237,500	23,249,000	Bucharest	45/F 3	democratic†
Russian S.F.S.R., U.S.S.R.	6,592,812	17,075,400	147,386,000	Moscow	48/D 4	Soviet republic
*Rwanda	10,169	26,337	6,274,000	Kigali	114/E 4	republic
Sabah, Malaysia	29,300	75,887	1,002,608	Kota Kinabalu	85/F 4	state of Malaysia
Saint Helena & Dependencies, U.K.	162	420	5,147	Jamestown	102/B 6	dependent territory of the U.K.
*Saint Kitts and Nevis	104	269	44,404	Basseterre	156/F 3; 161/C 11	constitutional monarchy
*Saint Lucia	238	616	148,000	Castries	161/G 6	parliamentary democracy
Saint Pierre & Miquelon, France	93.5	242	6,034	Saint-Pierre	166/C 4	territorial collectivity of France
*Saint Vincent & the Grenadines	150	388	124,000	Kingstown	161/A 8; 157/G 4	constitutional monarchy
Sakhalin, U.S.S.R.	29,500	76,405	655,000	Yuzhno-Sakhalinsk	48/P 4	part of U.S.S.R.
San Marino	23.4	60.6	23,000	San Marino	34/D 3	republic
*São Tomé and Príncipe	372	963	116,000	São Tomé	106/F 8	republic
Sarawak, Malaysia	48,202	124,843	1,294,753	Kuching	85/E 5	state of Malaysia
Sardinia, Italy	9,301	24,090	1,450,483	Cagliari	34/B 4	region of Italy
Saskatchewan, Canada	251,699	651,900	1,009,613	Regina	181/.......	province of Canada
*Saudi Arabia	829,995	2,149,687	14,435,000	Riyadh	58/D 4	monarchy
Scotland, U.K.	30,414	78,772	5,117,146	Edinburgh	15/.......	part of the United Kingdom
*Senegal	75,954	196,722	7,113,000	Dakar	106/A 5	republic
*Seychelles	145	375	67,000	Victoria	119/H 5	republic
Shetland Islands, Scotland	552	1,430	18,494	Lerwick	15/G 2	part of the United Kingdom
Siam, see Thailand						
Sicily, Italy	9,926	25,708	4,628,918	Palermo	34/D 6	region of Italy
*Sierra Leone	27,925	72,325	4,047,000	Freetown	106/B 7	one-party presidential republic
*Singapore	226	585	2,704,000	Singapore	72/F 6	republic
Society Islands, French Polynesia	677	1,753	117,703	Papeete	87/L 7	part of French Polynesia
*Solomon Islands	11,500	29,785	299,000	Honiara	87/G 6; 86/.......	parliamentary democracy

Gazetteer-Index of the World

Country	Area Square Miles	Square Kilometers	Population	Capital or Chief Town	Page and Index Ref.	Government or Ownership
*Somalia	246,200	637,658	7,339,000	Mogadishu	115/H 3	republic
*South Africa	455,318	1,179,274	34,492,000	Cape Town; Pretoria	118/C 5	republic
South America	6,875,000	17,806,250	297,000,000	....	120/	
South Australia, Australia	379,922	984,000	1,345,945	Adelaide	94/.......	state of Australia
South Carolina, U.S.	31,113	80,583	3,505,707	Columbia	296/.......	state of the U.S.
South Dakota, U.S.	77,116	199,730	699,999	Pierre	298/.......	state of the U.S.
South Korea	38,175	98,873	37,448,836	Seoul	80/D 5	republic
*Spain	194,881	504,742	39,328,000	Madrid	33/........	parliamentary monarchy
Spratly Islands	....	....	....	....	85/E 4	in dispute; claims by China, Malaysia, Philippines, Taiwan, Vietnam
*Sri Lanka	25,332	65,610	16,806,000	Colombo	68/E 7	republic
*Sudan	967,494	2,505,809	24,485,000	Khartoum	110/E 4	military
Sumatra, Indonesia	164,000	424,760	19,360,400	Medan	84/B 5	see Indonesia
*Suriname	55,144	142,823	400,000	Paramaribo	131/C 3	republic
Svalbard, Norway	23,957	62,049	3,431	Longyearbyen	18/C 2	territory of Norway
*Swaziland	6,705	17,366	681,000	Mbabane	119/E 5	monarchy
*Sweden	173,665	449,792	8,541,000	Stockholm	18/J 8	constitutional monarchy
Switzerland	15,943	41,292	6,647,000	Bern	39/.......	federal republic
*Syria	71,498	185,180	11,719,000	Damascus	62/G 5	military republic
Tadzhik S.S.R., U.S.S.R.	55,251	143,100	5,112,000	Dushanbe	48/G 6	Soviet republic
Tahiti, French Polynesia	402	1,041	95,604	Papeete	87/L 7	see French Polynesia
Taiwan	13,971	36,185	16,609,961	Taipei	77/K 7	one-party presidential regime
*Tanzania	363,708	942,003	24,802,000	Dar es Salaam	114/F 5	republic
Tasmania, Australia	26,178	67,800	436,353	Hobart	99/.......	state of Australia
Tennessee, U.S.	42,144	109,153	4,896,641	Nashville	237/.......	state of the U.S.
Texas, U.S.	266,807	691,030	17,059,805	Austin	303/.......	state of the U.S.
*Thailand	198,455	513,998	55,448,000	Bangkok	72/D 3	constitutional monarchy
Tibet, China	463,320	1,200,000	1,790,000	Lhasa	76/C 5	part of China
*Togo	21,622	56,000	3,296,000	Lomé	106/E 7	republic
Tokelau, New Zealand	3.9	10	1,575	Fakaofo	87/J 6	territory of New Zealand
Tonga	270	699	95,000	Nuku'alofa	87/J 8	constitutional monarchy
Transkei, South Africa	16,910	43,797	2,000,000	Umtata	119/D 6	self-governing black African "homeland"
Transvaal, South Africa	109,621	283,918	10,673,033	Pretoria	119/D 4	province of South Africa
*Trinidad and Tobago	1,980	5,128	1,212,000	Port-of-Spain	157/G 5; 161/A 10	parliamentary democracy
Tristan da Cunha, St. Helena	38	98	251	Edinburgh	2/J 7	see St. Helena
Tuamotu Archipelago, French Polynesia	341	883	9,052	Apataki	87/M 7	see French Polynesia
*Tunisia	63,378	164,149	7,465,000	Tunis	106/F 1	republic
*Turkey	300,946	779,450	56,741,000	Ankara	62/D 3	republican parliamentary democracy
Turkmen S.S.R., U.S.S.R.	188,455	488,100	3,534,000	Ashkhabad	48/F 6	Soviet republic
Turks and Caicos Islands, U.K.	166	430	7,436	Cockburn Town, Grand Turk	156/D 2	dependent territory of the U.K.
Tuvalu	9.78	25.33	9,000	Fongafale, Funafuti	87/H 6	democracy
*Uganda	91,076	235,887	17,804,000	Kampala	114/F 3	republic
*Ukrainian S.S.R., U.S.S.R.	233,089	603,700	51,704,000	Kiev	52/D 5	Soviet republic
*Union of Soviet Socialist Republics	8,649,490	22,402,179	286,730,817	Moscow	48/.......	socialist union
*United Arab Emirates	32,278	83,600	1,206,000	Abu Dhabi	58/F 5	federation of sheikdoms
*United Kingdom	94,399	244,493	57,236,000	London	10/.......	constitutional monarchy
*United States	3,623,420	9,384,658	249,632,692	Washington	188/....	federal republic
*Uruguay	72,172	186,925	3,077,000	Montevideo	145/.......	republic
Utah, U.S.	84,899	219,888	1,727,784	Salt Lake City	304/.......	state of the U.S.
Uzbek S.S.R., U.S.S.R.	173,591	449,600	19,906,000	Tashkent	48/G 5	Soviet republic
*Vanuatu	5,700	14,763	155,000	Vila	87/G 7	republic
Vatican City	108.7 acres	44 hectares	1,000	....	34/B 6	sacerdotal (priest-related) monarchy
Venda, South Africa	2,510	6,501	450,000	Thohoyandou	119/E 4	self-governing black African "homeland"
*Venezuela	352,143	912,050	19,246,000	Caracas	124/.......	republic
Vermont, U.S.	9,614	24,900	564,964	Montpelier	268/.......	state of the U.S.
Victoria, Australia	87,876	227,600	4,019,478	Melbourne	96/B 5	state of Australia
*Vietnam	128,405	332,569	64,412,000	Hanoi	72/E 3	communist state
Virginia, U.S.	40,767	105,587	6,216,568	Richmond	307/.......	state of the U.S.
Virgin Islands, British	59	153	11,006	Road Town	157/H 1	dependent territory of the U.K.
Virgin Islands, U.S.	132	342	96,569	Charlotte Amalie	161/A 4	organized, unincorporated territory of the U.S.
Wake Island, U.S.	2.5	6.5	302	Wake Islet	87/G 4	unincorporated territory of the U.S.
Wales, U.K.	8,017	20,764	2,790,462	Cardiff	13/D 5	part of the United Kingdom
Wallis and Futuna, France	106	275	9,192	Mata Utu	87/J 7	overseas territory of France
Washington, U.S.	68,139	176,480	4,887,941	Olympia	310/.......	state of the U.S.
West Bank	2,100	5,439	c. 800,000	....	65/C 3	occupied by Israel
Western Australia, Australia	975,096	2,525,500	1,406,929	Perth	92/.......	state of Australia
Western Sahara	102,703	266,000	174,000	....	106/B 3	occupied by Morocco
*Western Samoa	1,133	2,934	163,000	Apia	87/J 7	constitutional monarchy
West Virginia, U.S.	24,231	62,758	1,801,625	Charleston	312/.......	state of the U.S.
*White Russian S.S.R., see Belorussian S.S.R.						
Wisconsin, U.S.	56,153	145,436	4,906,745	Madison	317/.......	state of the U.S.
World	(land) 57,970,000	150,142,300	5,292,000,000	....	1,2/....	
Wyoming, U.S.	97,809	253,325	455,975	Cheyenne	319/.......	state of the U.S.
*Yemen	188,321	487,752	10,183,000	San'a	58/D 7	republic
*Yugoslavia	98,766	255,804	23,798,000	Belgrade	45/C 3	socialist federal republic
Yukon Territory, Canada	207,075	536,324	23,504	Whitehorse	186/E 3	territory of Canada
*Zaire	905,063	2,344,113	34,491,000	Kinshasa	114/D 4	republic
*Zambia	290,586	752,618	8,073,000	Lusaka	114/E 7	one-party state
*Zimbabwe	150,803	390,580	9,122,000	Harare	119/D 3	parliamentary democracy

Glossary of Abbreviations

A

A. A. F. — Army Air Field
Acad. — Academy
A. C. T. — Australian Capital Territory
adm. — administration; administrative
A. F. B. — Air Force Base
Afgh., Afghan. — Afghanistan
Afr. — Africa
Ala. — Alabama
Alb. — Albania
Alg. — Algeria
Alta. — Alberta
Amer. — American
Amer. Samoa — American Samoa
And. — Andorra
Ant., Antarc. — Antarctica
Ant. & Bar. — Antigua and Barbuda
Ar. — Arabia
arch. — archipelago
Arg. — Argentina
Ariz. — Arizona
Ark. — Arkansas
A. S. S. R. — Autonomous Soviet
    Socialist Republic
Aust. — Austria
Aust. Cap. Terr. — Australian Capital
    Territory
Austr., Austral. — Australian, Australia
aut. — autonomous
Aut. Obl. — Autonomous Oblast

B

B. — bay
Bah. — Bahamas
Barb. — Barbados
Battlef. — Battlefield
Bch. — Beach
Belg. — Belgium
Berm. — Bermuda
Bol. — Bolivia
Bots. — Botswana
Br. — Branch
Br. — British
Braz. — Brazil
Br. Col. — British Columbia
Br. Ind. Oc. Terr. — British Indian
    Ocean Territory
Bulg. — Bulgaria

C

C. — cape
Calif. — California
Can. — Canada
can. — canal
cap. — capital
Cent. Afr. Rep. — Central African
    Republic
Cent. Amer. — Central America
C. G. Sta. — Coast Guard Station
C. H. — Court House
chan. — channel
Chan. Is. — Channel Islands
Chem. Ctr. — Chemical Center
co. — county
C. of G. H. — Cape of Good Hope
Col. — Colombia
Colo. — Colorado
comm. — commissary
Conn. — Connecticut
cont. — continent
cord. — cordillera (mountain range)
C. Rica — Costa Rica
C. S. — County Seat
C. Verde — Cape Verde
Czech. — Czechoslovakia

D

D. C. — District of Columbia
Del. — Delaware
Dem. — Democratic
Den. — Denmark
depr. — depression
dept. — department
des. — desert
dist., dist's — district, districts
div. — division
Dom. Rep. — Dominican Republic

E

E. — East
Ec., Ecua. — Ecuador
elec. div. — electoral division
El Salv. — El Salvador
Eng. — England
Equat. Guinea, Eq. Guin — Equatorial
    Guinea

escarp. — escarpment
est. — estuary
Eth. — Ethiopia

F

Falk. Is. — Falkland Islands
Fin. — Finland
Fk., Fks. — Fork, Forks
Fla. — Florida
for. — forest
Fr. — France, French
Fr. Gui. — French Guiana
Fr. Poly. — French Polynesia
Ft. — Fort

G

G. — gulf
Ga. — Georgia
Game Res. — Game Reserve
Ger. — Germany
geys. — geyser
Gibr. — Gibraltar
glac. — glacier
gov. — governorate
Gr. — Group
Greenl. — Greenland
Gren. — Grenada
Gt. Brit. — Great Britain
Guad. — Guadeloupe
Guat. — Guatemala
Guinea-Biss. — Guinea-Bissau
Guy. — Guyana

H

har., harb., hbr. — harbor
hd. — head
highl. — highland, highlands
Hist. — Historic, Historical
Hond. — Honduras
Hts. — Heights
Hung. — Hungary

I

i., isl. — island, isle
I. C. — independent city
Ice., Icel. — Iceland
Ida. — Idaho
Ill. — Illinois
Ind. — Indiana
ind. city — independent city
Indon. — Indonesia
Ind. Res. — Indian Reservation
int. div. — internal division
inten. — intendency
Int'l — International
Ire. — Ireland
is., isls. — islands
Isr. — Israel
isth. — isthmus
Iv. Coast — Ivory Coast

J

Jam. — Jamaica
Jct. — Junction

K

Kans. — Kansas
Ky. — Kentucky

L

L. — Lake, Loch, Lough
La. — Louisiana
Lab. — Laboratory
lag. — lagoon
Ld. — Land
Leb. — Lebanon
Les. — Lesotho
Liecht. — Liechtenstein
Lux. — Luxembourg

M

Mad., Madag. — Madagascar
Man. — Manitoba
Mart. — Martinique
Mass. — Massachusetts
Maur. — Mauritania
Md. — Maryland
met. area — metropolitan area
Mex. — Mexico
Mich. — Michigan
Minn. — Minnesota
Miss. — Mississippi
Mo. — Missouri
Mon. — Monument
Mong. — Mongolia
Mont. — Montana

Mor. — Morocco
Moz., Mozamb. — Mozambique
mt. — mount
mtn. — mountain

N

N., No., North. — North, Northern
N. Amer. — North America
Nam., Namib. — Namibia
N. A. S. — Naval Air Station
Nat'l — National
Nat'l Cem. — National Cemetery
Nat'l Mem. Park — National Memorial
    Park
Nat'l Mil. Park — National Military
    Park
Nat'l Pkwy. — National Parkway
Nav. Base — Naval Base
Nav. Sta. — Naval Station
N. B., N. Br. — New Brunswick
N. C. — North Carolina
N. Dak. — North Dakota
Nebr. — Nebraska
Neth. — Netherlands
Neth. Ant. — Netherlands Antilles
Nev. — Nevada
New Bruns. — New Brunswick
New Cal., New Caled. — New Caledonia
Newf. — Newfoundland
New Hebr. — New Hebrides
N. H. — New Hampshire
Nic. — Nicaragua
N. Ire. — Northern Ireland
N. J. — New Jersey
N. Mex. — New Mexico
Nor. — Norway, Norwegian
North. — Northern
North. Terr., No. Terr. — Northern
    Territory
    (Australia)
N. S. — Nova Scotia
N. S. W., N.S. Wales — New South Wales
N. W. T., N. W. Terrs. — Northwest
    Territories
    (Canada)
N. Y. — New York
N. Z., N. Zealand — New Zealand

O

Obl. — Oblast
O. F. S. — Orange Free State
Okla. — Oklahoma
Okr. — Okrug
Ont. — Ontario
Ord. Depot — Ordnance Depot
Oreg. — Oregon

P

Pa. — Pennsylvania
Pak. — Pakistan
Pan. — Panama
Papua N. G. — Papua New Guinea
Par. — Paraguay
par. — parish
passg. — passage
P. E. I. — Prince Edward Island
pen. — peninsula
Phil., Phil. Is. — Philippines
Pk. — Park
pk. — peak
plat. — plateau
P. N. G. — Papua New Guinea
Pol. — Poland
Port. — Portugal, Portuguese
Pr. Edward I. — Prince Edward Island
pref. — prefecture
P. Rico — Puerto Rico
prom. — promontory
prov. — province, provincial
pt. — point

Q

Que. — Québec
Queens. — Queensland

R

R. — River
ra. — range
Rec., Recr. — Recreation, Recreational
reg. — region
Rep. — Republic
res. — reservoir
Res. — Reservation, Reserve
R. I. — Rhode Island
riv. — river
Rom. — Romania

S

S. — South
Sa. — Sierra, Serra
S. Afr., S. Africa — South Africa
salt dep. — salt deposit
salt des. — salt desert
S. Amer. — South America
São T. & Pr. — São Tomé
    and Príncipe
Sask. — Saskatchewan
Saudi Ar. — Saudi Arabia
S. Aust., S. Austral. — South Australia
S. C. — South Carolina
Scot. — Scotland
Sd. — Sound
S. Dak. — South Dakota
Sen. — Senegal
sen. dist. — senatorial district
Seych. — Seychelles
S. F. S. R. — Soviet Federated Socialist
    Republic
Sing. — Singapore
S. Leone — Sierra Leone
S. Marino — San Marino
Sol. Is. — Solomon Islands
Sp. — Spanish
Spr., Sprs. — Spring, Springs
S. S. R. — Soviet Socialist Republic
St., Ste. — Saint, Sainte
Sta. — Station
St. P. & M. — Saint Pierre and
    Miquelon
St. Vin. & Grens. — St. Vincent & The
    Grenadines
str., strs. — strait, straits
Sur. — Suriname
Swaz. — Swaziland
Switz. — Switzerland

T

Tanz. — Tanzania
Tas. — Tasmania
Tenn. — Tennessee
terr., terrs. — territory, territories
Tex. — Texas
Thai. — Thailand
trad. — traditional
Trin. & Tob. — Trinidad and Tobago
Tun. — Tunisia
twp. — township

U

U. A. E. — United
    Arab Emirates
U. K. — United Kingdom
Upp. Volta — Upper Volta
urb. area — urban area
Urug. — Uruguay
U. S. — United States
U. S. S. R. — Union of Soviet Socialist
    Republics

V

Va. — Virginia
Ven., Venez. — Venezuela
V. I. (Br.) — Virgin Islands (British)
V. I. (U. S.) — Virgin Islands (U. S.)
Vic. — Victoria
Viet. — Vietnam
Vill. — Village
vol. — volcano
Vt. — Vermont

W

W. — West, Western
Wash. — Washington
W. Aust., W. Austral. — Western
    Australia
W. Indies — West Indies
Wis. — Wisconsin
W. Samoa — Western Samoa
W. Va. — West Virginia
Wyo. — Wyoming

Y

Yugo. — Yugoslavia
Yukon — Yukon Territory

Z

Zim. — Zimbabwe

Index to Terrain Maps

on pages X through XXXII

This index contains only names of land and ocean physical features. Names of towns, internal divisions and countries are not included. The entry name is followed by a letter-number combination which refers to the area on the map in which the name will be found. The number following the map reference for the entry refers, not to the page on which the entry will be found, but to the map plate number.

Abitibi (riv.) E5/18
Aconcagua, Cerro (mt.) E4/16
Adare (cape) M7/1
Aden (gulf) A5-6/4
Adrar des Iforas (plat.) C4/12
Adriatic (sea) E6-7/3
Aegean (sea) E6/2
Agadir (canyon) B2-3/12
Aguja (pt.) A4/15
Agulhas (ridge) B-C6/13
Ahaggar (mts.) C3/12
Air (mts.) D4/12
Akimiski (isl.) E5/18
Alabama (riv.) H7/19
Aland (isls.) E3/3
Alaska (pen.) B8/19
Albany (riv.) E5/18
Aldabra (isls.) G2/13
Aldan (riv.) E3/4
Alejandro Selkirk (isl.) A6/14
Aleutian (isls.) A-B8/19
Aleutian (trench) E2-G1/10
Alexander (arch.) A3-4/18
Allegheny (riv.) K4/19
Alps (mts.) C-D6/3
Altai (mts.) D4/4
Altamaha (riv.) K6/19
Altay (mts.) C1-2/7
Altiplano (plat.) C6/15
Altun Shan (range) B-C2/7
Amazon (riv.) E3/15
Amery (ice shelf) J7/1
Amirante (trench) H1-2/13
Amudar'ya (riv.) B2/6
Amundsen (abyssal plain) C7/1
Amur (riv.) E3/4
Anambas (isls.) C4/8
Anatolia (plat.) B2/5
Ancohuma, Nevada (mt.) C5/15
Andaman (sea) A-B3/8
Andes (mts.) A1-B6/14
Andros (isl.) F3/20
Angara (riv.) D3/4
Angel (fall) D2/15
Angola (basin) B-C6/11
Annamese Cordillera (mts.) C2/8
Annobón (isl.) C6/12
Antarctic (pen.) E7/1
Anticosti (isl.) G5/18
Antigua (isl.) H4/20
Apennines (mts.) D6-E7/3
Apo (vol.) F4/8
Appalachian (mts.) J6-L2/19
Apurímac (riv.) B5/15
Aqaba (gulf) C3/5
Arabian (sea) B6/4
Arafura (sea) C6/10
Araguaia (riv.) F4/15
Arakan Yoma (mts.) B2/8
Araks (riv.) D2/5
Aral (sea) B4/4
Ararat (mt.) D2/5
Aravalli (range) C4/6
Ardennes (forest) C5/3
Arena (pt.) A4/19
Argentine (basin) E6/16
Argun (riv.) E1/7
Aripuanã (riv.) D4/15
Arkansas (riv.) G6/19
Arnhem Land (reg.) D1/9
Arno (riv.) D7/3
Aru (isls.) H5/8
Aruba (isl.) G5/20
Ascension (isl.) A6/11
Assiniboine (riv.) F2/19
Atacama (des.) A2-3/16
Atbara (riv.) F4/12
Athabaska (riv.) C4/18
Atka (isl.) A8/19
Atlas (mts.) B3-C2/12
Atrak (riv.) F2/5
Attu (isl.) A8/19
Austral (isls.) G7/10
Australian-Antarctic (basin) K-L7/1
Axel Heiberg (isl.) D1/18
Ayers (rock) C3/9
Azores (isls.) A1/12
Azov (sea) F5/2
Azuéro (pen.) E6/20
Babar (isls.) G6/8
Babuyan (isls.) E2/8
Back (riv.) D3/18
Baffin (isl.) E2/18
Bahamas (isls.) F3/20
Bahrain (isl.) E4/5
Bahr el Ghazal (riv.) D4/12
Balaton (lake) E6/3
Balearic (isls.) C7/3
Bali (isl.) E6/8
Balkan (mts.) E5/2
Balkhash (lake) C4/4
Balsas (riv.) B4/20
Baltic (sea) E4-3/3
Bananal (isl.) F5/15
Banda (sea) F-G5/8
Bandeira (mt.) F2/16
Bangka (isl.) C5/8
Bangweulu (lake) D2/13
Bani (riv.) B4/12
Banks (isl.) C2/18
Barbados (isl.) H5/20
Barbuda (isl.) H4/20
Barcoo (riv.) D4/9
Barents (sea) E1/2
Barisan (mts.) B-C5/8
Barkly Tableland (plat.) D2/9
Barlee (lake) B4/9
Barrow (pt.) C6/19
Bartle Frere (mt.) E2/9
Bassas da India (isl.) F3/13
Bathurst (isl.) D2/18
Batu (isls.) B5/8
Baykal (lake) D3/4
Beaufort (sea) B1/18
Belcher (isls.) E4/18
Bellingshausen (sea) C-D7/1
Ben Nevis (mt.) B4/3
Bengal (bay) D6-E7/6
Beni (riv.) C5/15
Benue (riv.) D5/12
Bering (sea) A7-B8/19
Bermejo (riv.) C3/16
Bermuda (isl.) G2/20
Bighorn (riv.) D3/19
Bihé (plat.) B-C2/13
Billiton (isl.) D5/8
Bioko (isl.) C6/12
Biscay (bay) B6/3
Bitteroot (range) C2-3/19
Black (hills) E3/19
Black (sea) E-F5/2
Blake (plat.) L7/19
Blanc (mt.) C6/3
Blanc (cape) A4/12
Blanco (cape) A3/19
Blue Nile (riv.) F4/12
Bobaomby (cape) G2/13
Bodélé (depr.) D4/12
Bo Hai (gulf) F3/7
Bohol (isl.) F3/8
Bojador (cape) A3/12
Bolivar (mt.) C2/15
Bon (cape) D2/12
Bonaire (isl.) G5/20
Bone (gulf) F5/8
Boothia (pen.) D2/18
Borneo (isl.) D5/8
Bornholm (isl.) D4/3
Bosporus (strait) B1/5
Bothnia (gulf) E2/3
Bougainville (isl.) G1/9
Bow (riv.) B5/18
Brahmaputra (riv.) E4/6
Branco (riv.) D3/15
Brazil (basin) E5/1
Brazilian (highlands) F5-G6/15
Brazos (riv.) F7/19
Brodeur (pen.) D2/18
Brooks (range) C7/19
Bruce (mt.) A3/9
Bug (riv.) F5/3
Buru (isl.) F5/8
Bylot (isl.) E2/18
Caatingas (forest) G4/15
California (gulf) A1-2/20
Cambay (gulf) B5/6
Cameroon (mt.) D5/12
Campeche (bay) C3/20
Campos (reg.) E1-2/16
Canada (basin) B-C1/18
Canadian (riv.) F6/19
Canary (isls.) A3/12
Canaveral (cape) K7/19
Caniapiscau (riv.) F4/18
Cantabrian (mts.) B7/3
Cape (basin) B6/13
Cape Breton (isl.) G5/18
Cape Fear (riv.) K5/19
Cape York (pen.) E1-2/9
Caribbean (sea) F-G4/20
Carlsberg (ridge) A-B6/4
Carnegie (lake) B3/9
Caroline (isls.) C5/10
Caroni (riv.) D2/15
Carpathian (mts.) F5-6/3
Carpentaria (gulf) H6/8
Cascade (range) B3/19
Caspian (sea) G4-H5/2
Cauca (riv.) B2/15
Caucasus (mts.) F-G5/2
Cayman (isls.) E4/20
Ceara (abyssal plain) G3/15
Cebu (isl.) F3/8
Celebes (isl.) E5/8
Celtic (shelf) A-B5/3
Central Indian (ridge) B7-8/4
Central Pacific (basin) E4-5/10
Ceram (isl.) G5/8
Ceylon (plain) C7/4
Chad (lake) D4/12
Chagos-Laccadive (ridge) B7-6/4
Challenger (deep) C4/10
Challenger (plat.) G5/9
Champlain (lake) L3/19
Chang (riv.) E4/7
Channel (isls.) B5/3
Chao Phraya (riv.) B2-3/8
Charlie Gibbs (fracture zone) E2/1
Chatham (rise) E8/10
Chattahoochee (riv.) J6/19
Chelyuskin (cape) D2/4
Chenab (riv.) B3/6
Chesapeake (bay) L5/19
Cheyenne (riv.) E3/19
Chidley (cape) F3/18
Chile (trench) B8/14
Chiloé (isl.) A6/16
Chimborazo (mt.) A3/15
Chin (hills) F5/6
Chindwin (riv.) C5/7
Choiseul (isl.) H1/9
Chonos (arch.) A6/16
Chota Nagpur (plat.) D5/6
Chubut (riv.) B6/16
Chukchi (sea) A2/1
Churchill (riv.), Labrador G4/18
Churchill (riv.), Man.-Sask. C4/18
Cimarron (riv.) F5/19
Citlaltépetl (vol.) C4/20
Clarion (fracture zone) H-J4/10
Clark Fork (riv.) C2/19
Clear (cape) A5/3
Clipperton (fracture zone) H5-J4/10
Coast (ranges) B4/17
Coats (isl.) E3/18
Cobourg (pen.) C1/9
Coco (riv.) E4/20
Cocos (basin) A5/8
Cocos (isl.) D6/20
Cod (cape) M3/19
Colombia (basin) F5/20
Colombian (trench) A2/15
Colorado (riv.), Argentina B5/16
Colorado (riv.), Texas F7/19
Colorado (riv.), Utah-Ariz. C5/19
Columbia (cape) D1/18
Columbia (riv.) B2/19
Communism (peak) C2/6
Comorin (cape) C7/6
Comoros (isls.) G2/13
Conception (pt.) A5/19
Congo (canyon) A1/13
Congo (Zaire) (riv.) D6/12
Connecticut (riv.) L3/19
Cook (isls.) F-G6/10
Coosa (riv.) J6/19
Coppermine (riv.) C3/18
Coral (sea) G-H2/9
Coroni (riv.) H6/20
Corrientes (cape) A3/20
Corsica (isl.) D7/3
Courantyne (riv.) D2/14
Cozumel (isl.) D4/20
Crete (isl.) A2/5
Crimea (pen.) F5/2
Cristóbal Colón (mt.) B1/15
Cuando (riv.) C3/13
Cuango (riv.) C6/11
Cuanza (riv.) B2/13
Cuba (isl.) E-F3/20
Cubango (riv.) C3/13
Coluene (riv.) E5/15
Cumberland (riv.) J5/19
Cumberland (sound) F3/18
Cunene (riv.) B3/13
Curaçao (isl.) G5/20
Cyprus (isl.) B2/5
Da Hingan Ling (range) E2-F1/7
Dahlak (arch.) C6/5
Dakar (canyon) A4/12
Dal (riv.) E3/3
Damavand (mt.) E2/5
Danube (riv.) E5/2
Dardanelles (strait) A1/5
Darling (range) A5/9
Darling (riv.) E4/9
Dasht-e Kavir (salt des.) E2/5
Dasht-e Lut (des.) F3/5
Davis (strait) F2/18
Dead (sea) C3/5
Death Valley (depr.) B5/19
Deccan (plat.) C5-6/6
Delagoa (bay) E4/13
Delaware (bay) L4/19
Delgado (cape) F2/13
Demerara (abyssal plain) F1/15
Denmark (strait) E2/1
Deseado (riv.) B6/16/
Des Moines (riv.) G4/19
Devon (isl.) D2/18/
Dezhnev (cape) E1/4/
Diamantina (fracture zone) A7-8/10
Dinaric Alps (mts.) E6-7/3/
Dnieper (riv.) E4/2
Dniester (riv.) E4/2
Doberai (pen.) G4/8
Dominica (isl.) H4/20
Don (riv.) F4/2
Dondra (head) D8/6
Dordogne (riv.) C6/3
Douro (riv.) B7/3
Dra, Wadi (dry riv.) B3/12
Drake (passg.) D7/1
Drakensberg (mts.) D5-E4/13
Dubawnt (riv.) D3/18
East (cape) H5/9
East China (sea) F-G4/7
Easter (isl.) K7/10
Eastern Ghats (mts.) C6-D5/6
East Pacific (rise) K5-8/10
East Siberian (sea) E1-2/4
Ebro (riv.) B7/3
Edith Ronne (ice shelf) D7/1
Edwards (plat.) E7/19
Elba (isl.) D7/3
Elbe (riv.) D5/3
Elbert (mt.) D4/19
El'brus (mt.) G5/2
Elburz (mts.) E2/5
Eleuthera (isl.) F3/20
Ellef Ringnes (isl.) D1/18
Ellesmere (isl.) D1/18
El Misti (mt.) C5/15
Emi Koussi (mt.) E4/12
Emperor Seamount (chain) E2/10
Ems (riv.) D5/3
Enderby (abyssal plain) G-H7/1
Engaño (cape) F6/7
English (chan.) B5/3
Erie (lake) J4/19
Essequibo (riv.) E2/15
Ethiopian (highlands) G5/12
Etna (vol.) E8/3
Etosha Pan (depr.) C3/13
Euboea (isl.) A1/5
Euphrates (riv.) D3/5
Everest (mt.) E4/6
Evvoia (isl.) E6/2
Eyre (lake) D4/9
Eyre (pen.) D5/9
Faeroe (isls.) B3/3
Falkland (isls.) C7/16
False Divi (pt.) D6/6
Farasan (isls.) C6/5
Farewell (cape), Greenland F2/17
Farewell (cape), New Zealand G5/9
Fear (cape) K5/19
Fiji (isls.) E6/10
Finisterre (cape) A6/3
Finland (gulf) E-F3/3
Fitzroy (riv.) B2/9
Flathead (lake) C-D2/19
Flattery (cape) A1/19
Flinders (riv.) E2/9
Flores (isl.) F6/8
Florida (straits) E3/20
Fly (riv.) H5/8
Fortescue (riv.) A3/9
Fort Nelson (riv.) B4/18
Fort Peck (lake) E2/19
Foxe (basin) E3/18
Franz Josef Land (isls.) H1/1
Fraser (riv.) B5/18
Fria (cape) B3/13
Frio (cape) F3/16
Frisian (isls.) C4/3
Frome (lake) E4/9
Fuji (mt.) H3/7
Fundy (bay) G5/18
Furneaux Group (isls.) E-F6/9
Gabon (canyon) C6/12
Galapagos (isls.) L5/10
Gallinas (pt.) B1/15
Galveston (bay) G7/19
Ganges (riv.) E5/6
Garonne (riv.) B6/3
Gaspé (pen.) G5/18
Georges (bank) M3/19
Georgia (basin) E7/16
Georgian (bay) E6/18
Georgina (riv.) D3/9
Gibraltar (strait) A8/3
Gibson (des.) B-C3/9
Gila (riv.) C6/19
Gilbert (isls.) E5/10
Glama (riv.) D3/3
Gobi (des.) D-E2/7
Godavari (riv.) C6/6
Good Hope (cape) C5/13
Gotland (isl.) E4/3
Gough (isl.) B8/11
Gracias a Dios (cape) E4/20
Gran Chaco (reg.) C2-3/16
Grand Bahama (isl.) F3/20
Grand Banks of Newfoundland (banks) G5/18
Grande (riv.), Brazil E2/16
Grande (riv.), Mexico C4/20
Grande de Santiago (riv.) B3/20
Grand Erg Oriental (des.) C3/12
Great (basin) B3-C4/19
Great (plains) D1-E7/19
Great Abaco (isl.) F3/20
Great Australian (bight) C5/9
Great Barrier (reef) E2-F3/9
Great Bear (lake) B3/18
Great Britain (isl.) F2/1
Great Dividing (range) E3-F5/9
Greater Antilles (isls.) E-G4/20
Great Exuma (isl.) F3/20
Great Inagua (isl.) F3/20
Great Indian (des.) B-C4/6
Great Karoo (reg.) C5/13
Great Khingan (range) E4/4
Great Salt (lake) C4/19
Great Sandy (des.) B-C3/9
Great Slave (lake) C3/18
Great Victoria (des.) C4/9
Green (riv.) D4/19
Greenland (isl.) E1-2/17
Greenland (sea) F-G1/1
Grenada (isl.) H5/20
Groote Eylandt (isl.) D1/9
Guadalcanal (isl.) H1/9
Guadalquivir (riv.) A8/3
Guadeloupe (isl.) H4/20
Guadiana (riv.) A7/3
Guajira (pen.) F5/20
Guam (isl.) C4/10
Guantanamo (bay) F4/20
Guaporé (riv.) D5/15
Guatemala (basin) C6/20
Guaviare (riv.) C2/15
Guayaquil (gulf) A3/15
Guiana (highlands) D2-E3/15
Guinea (gulf) C6/12
Gunong Tahan (mt.) B4/8
Guri (res.) D2/15
Hainan (isl.) E6/7
Halmahera (isl.) G4/8
Hamersley (range) A3/9
Han (riv.) E4/7
Harirud (riv.) A2/6
Hatteras (abyssal plain) F2-G3/20
Hatteras (cape) L5/19
Hawaii (isl.) B7/19
Hawaiian (isls.) F3-G4/10
Hay (riv.) B4/18
Hebrides (isls.) B3/3
Helmand (riv.) A3/6
Hiiumaa (isl.) E3/3
Himalaya (range) D3-E4/6
Hindu Kush (mts.) G-H2/5
Hispaniola (isl.) G4/20
Hokkaido (isl.) H1/7
Honshu (isl.) H2/7
Hood (mt.) B2/19
Hormuz (strait) F4/5
Horn (cape) B8/16
Howe (cape) F5/9
Huai (riv.) E4/7
Huang (Hwang) (riv.) E3/7
Huascaran (mt.) B4/15
Hudson (bay) E4/18
Hudson (riv.) L3/19
Huila, Nevada del (mt.) B3/15
Humboldt (riv.) B4/19
Huron (lake) J3/19
Iberian (pen.) B7/3
Ibiza (isl.) C7/3
Içá (riv.) C3/15
Iceland (isl.) B1/2
Iguaçu (riv.) D3/16
Iguazú (falls) D3/16
Ili (riv.) A1/7
Illinois (riv.) H4/19
Indus (riv.) B4/6
Ionian (sea) E8/3
Iowa (riv.) G4/19
Iran (plat.) E-F3/5
Ireland (isl.) F2/1
Irish (sea) B4/3
Irrawaddy (riv.) F5/6
Irtysh (riv.) C3/4
Ishim (riv.) H2/2
Issyk-kul (lake) C-D2/6
Itaipu (res.) D3/16
Izu-Ogasawara (trench) C3/10
Jamaica (isl.) F4/20
James (bay) E5/18
James (riv.), S. Dakota F3/19
James (riv.), Virginia K5/19
Jan Mayen (isl.) C1/3
Japan (basin) G2/7
Japan (sea) G2/7
Japurá (riv.) C3/15
Java (isl.) D6/8
Javari (riv.) B4/15
Jhelum (riv.) C3/6
Jos (plat.) C5/12
Juan de Fuca (strait) A1/19
Juan Fernández (isls.) A-B6/14
Jumna (riv.) C4/6
Jura (mts.) D6/3
Juruá (riv.) C4/15
Jutland (pen.) D4/3
Juventud (isl.) E3/20
K2/(Godwin Austen) (mt.) C3/6
Ka Lae (cape) B7/19
Kalahari (des.) C4/13
Kama (riv.) G3/2
Kamchatka (pen.) F2-3/4
Kangaroo (isl.) D5/9
Kansas (riv.) G5/19
Kapuas (riv.) D5/8
Kara (sea) C2/4
Kara-Bogaz (gulf) E1/5
Kara-Kum (des.) F1-2/5
Karakoram (range) C2-3/6
Kariba (lake) D3/13
Karimata (strait) C-D5/8
Kasai (riv.) C1/13
Kathiawar (pen.) B5/6
Kattegat (strait) D4/3
Kauai (isl.) A7/19
Kemi (riv.) E2/3
Kenai (pen.) C8/19
Kentucky (lake) H5/19
Kenya (mt.) G6/12
Kerguelen (plat.) J6/1
Kermadec (trench) F7/10
Kerulen (riv.) E2/7
Keweenaw (pen.) H2/19
Khanka (lake) G1/7
Khyber (pass) C3/6
Kilimanjaro (mt.) G6/12
Kimberley (plat.) B-C2/9
Kinabalu (mt.) D4/8
Kioga (lake) F6/12
Kistna (riv.) C6/6
Kivu (lake) F6/12
Kizilirmak (riv.) C2/5
Kjölen (mts.) D2-E1/3
Kodiak (isl.) C8/19
Kola (pen.) F1/3
Kolepom (isl.) H5/8
Kolguyev (isl.) F1/2
Kolyma (range) E2/4
Korat (plat.) C2/8
Korea (strait) G3/7
Kosciusko (mt.) F5/9
Kra (isthmus) B3/8
Kuban' (riv.) C1/5
Kunlun Shan (range) A-C3/7
Kura (riv.) D1/5
Kuria Muria (isls.) F5/5
Kuril (isls.) D2/10
Kutch (gulf) B5/6
Kuybyshev (res.) F3/2
Kwango (riv.) C1/13
Kyushu (isl.) G3/7
Kyzyl-Kum (des.) G1/5
Labrador (sea) G3/18
Laccadive (Cannanore) (isls.) B7/6
Lachlan (riv.) E5/9
Ladoga (lake) F3/3
Lake of the Woods (lake) D5/18
Lanai (isl.) A7/19
Lands End (prom.) B5/3
La Pérouse (strait) H1/7
Laptev (sea) D2/4
Laurentian (mts.) K-L2/19
Laurentian (plat.) C3-F5/18
Leeuwin (cape) A5/9
Lena (riv.) E2/4
Lesser Antilles (isls.) H4-5/20
Lesvos (isl.) E6/2
Leyte (isl.) F3/8
Liard (riv.) B3/18
Libyan (des.) E3/12
Ligurian (sea) D7/3
Limpopo (riv.) E4/13
Lincoln (sea) D1/4
Lindesnes (cape) C4/3
Line (isls.) G5/10
Lions (gulf) C7/3
Llano Estacado (plain) E6/19
Llanos (plain) C2/15
Llullaillaco (vol.) B3/16
Lofoten (isls.) D1/3

Index continued

Logan (mt.) A3/18
Loire (riv.) C6/3
Lomami (riv.) E6/12
Lombok (isl.) E6/8
Lomonosov (ridge) D1/4
Long (isl.), Bahamas F3/20
Long (isl.), U.S. L4/19
Lookout (cape) L4/19
Lop Nur (riv.) C2/7
Lopatka (cape) F3/4
Lord Howe (rise) D7/10
Louisville (ridge) F7-8/10
Lower California (pen.) A1-2/20
Lualaba (riv.) D4/11
Luangwa (riv.) E2/13
Lule (riv.) E2/3
Lulua (riv.) C1/13
Luzon (isl.) E2/8
Luzon (sea) E3/8
M'Clintock (chan.) D2/18
Máckay (lake) C2/9
Mackenzie (riv.) B3/18
Madagascar (isl.) G3/13
Madeira (isls.) A2/12
Madeira (riv.) C4/15
Madre Occidental, Sierra (mts.)
    B1-2/20
Madre Oriental, Sierra (mts.)
    C6-D7/20
Madre de Dios (riv.) C4/15
Madre del Sur, Sierra (mts.) B3-C4
    20
Madura (isl.) E6/8
Magdalena (riv.) B2/15
Magellan (strait) A-B7/16
Main (riv.) D4/3
Maisí (cape) F4/20
Majorca (isl.) C7/3
Makassar (strait) E4/8
Makgadikgadi Salt Pan (depr.)
    D3/13
Malacca (strait) B4/8
Malaita (isl.) H1/9
Malay (pen.) B-C4/8
Maldives (isls.) B8/6
Malpelo (isl.) A2/15
Malta (isl.) E8/3
Mamoré (riv.) D4/15
Man, Isle of (isl.) B4/3
Manitoba (lake) D4/18
Manitoulin (isl.) J3/19
Mannar (gulf) C7/6
Mar, Serra do (range) D-E3/16
Maracaibo (lake) C1/15
Marajó (isl.) F3/15
Marañón (riv.) B4/15
Margarita (isl.) H4/20
Margherita (mt.) F6/12
Mariana (isls.) C4/10
Mariana (trench) D4/10
Marmara (sea) B1/5
Maroni (riv.) E2/15
Marquesas (isls.) H6/10
Marra (mts.) E4/12
Marshall (isls.) D4/10
Martaban (gulf) F6/6
Martha's Vineyard (isl.) L3/19
Martinique (isl.) H4/20
Masbate (isl.) E3/8
Mascarene (plain) H3/13
Massif Central (plat.) C6/3
Mato Grosso (plat.) E4/15
Maui (isl.) B7/19
Mauna Kea (mt.) B7/19
Mauritius (isl.) H3/13
May (cape) L4/19
McKinley (mt.) C7/19
Mead (lake) C4/19
Mediterranean (sea) C-E2/12
Mekong (riv.) D6/4
Melanesian (basin) D4/10
Melville (isl.), Canada C2/18
Melville (isl.), Australia C1/9
Melville (pen.) E3/18
Mendeleyev (ridge) D1/4
Mendocino (cape) A3/19
Mergui (arch.) B3/8
Meta (riv.) C2/15
Meuse (riv.) C4/3
Mexico (gulf) D3/20
Michigan (lake) H3/19
Mid-Atlantic (ridge) E4-F4/1
Middle Loup (riv.) F4/19
Mid-Indian Ocean (basin) C7/4
Mid-Pacific (seamounts) D4/10
Milk (riv.) D2/19
Mindanao (isl.) F4/8
Mindoro (isl.) E3/8
Minnesota (riv.) G3/19
Minorca (isl.) C7/3
Mirim (lagoon) D4/16
Mississippi (riv.) H6/19
Missouri (riv.) G4/19
Mistassini (lake) F4/18
Mitchell (mt.) J4/19
Mitumba (range) D2/13
Mobutu Sese Seko (lake) F6/12
Mojave (des.) B4/19
Molokai (fracture zone) G-H3/10
Moluccas (isls.) F-G4/8
Mona (passg.) G4/20
Monterey (bay) A4/19
Morena, Sierra (range) A7/3
Mornington (abyssal plain) A8/14
Moro (gulf) F4/8
Moselle (riv.) C4/3
Mozambique (chan.) F3/13
Muchinga (mts.) E2/13
Murray (fracture zone) G-H3/10
Mweru (lake) D2/13
Namib (des.) B3-4/13
Nanda Devi (mt.) D4/6
Nansen (basin) D1-2/4

Nantucket (isl.) M3/19
Napo (riv.) B3/14/
Nares (abyssal plain) G-H3/20
Narmada (riv.) C4/6
Nasser (lake) F3/12
Nazca (ridge) L7/10
Nefud (des.) C-D3/5
Negrais (cape) F6/6/
Negro (riv.), Brazil D3/15
Negro (riv.), Argentina B4/15
Negros (isl.) E3/8
Nelson (riv.) D4/18
Nevada, Sierra (mts.) B4-4/19
New Caledonia (isl.) D6/10
Newfoundland (isl.) H4/18
New Georgia (isl.) H1/9
New Guinea (isl.) C4/10
New Hebrides (trench) E6/10
New Ireland (isl.) D4/10
New Siberian (isls.) D-E2/4
New Zealand (isls.) H6/9
Nias (isl.) B4/8
Nicaragua (lake) E4/20
Nicobar (isls.) F7/6
Niemen (riv.) E4/3
Niger (riv.) C4/12
Nile (riv.) F3/12
Ninety East (ridge) J4/1
Niobrara (riv.) F4/19
Nipigon (lake) E4/18
Nordkapp (cape) E1/3
North (cape) H4/9
North (isl.) H4/9
North (sea) C4/3
Northern Dvina (riv.) F2/2
North Platte (riv.) E4/19
North Saskatchewan (riv.) C4/18
North Scotia (ridge) D7/16
North West (cape) A3/9
Northwest Pacific (basin) D3/10
Norton (sound) B7/19
Norwegian (sea) C1-2/2
Novaya Zemlya (isl.) H1/1
Nubian (des.) F4/12
Nueces (riv.) F7/19
Nullarbor (plain) C4/9
Nyasa (lake) E2/13
Oahe (lake) F3/19
Oahu (isl.) A7/19
Ob' (riv.) C3/4
Occidental, Sierra Madre (mts.)
    C6/17
Ocmulgee (riv.) J6/19
Oconee (riv.) J6/19
Oder (riv.) E4/3
Ogaden (reg.) G4/12
Ogooue (riv.) D6/12
Ohio (riv.) H4/19
Ojos del Salado, Nevada (mt.)
    B3/16
Okeechobee (lake) K8/19
Okhotsk (sea) E3/4
Okinawa (isl.) G4/7
Okovanggo (basin) C3/13
Olwampi (cape) F4/7
Olympus (mt.) A1/5
Oman (gulf) F4/5
Ona (basin) C8/16
Onega (lake) E2/2
Ontario (lake) K3/19
Orange (riv.) C4/13
Ord (riv.) C2/9
Ordos (reg.) D3/7
Orhon (riv.) D1/7
Oriental, Sierra Madre (mts.) C6/17
Orinoco (riv.) D2/15
Orkney (isls.) C3/3
Orozco (fracture zone) A4/20
Ottawa (riv.) F6/18
Ouachita (riv.) G6/19
Owen (fracture zone) A-B6/4
Owyhee (riv.) B3/19
Ozark (plat.) G4/19
Pacaraíma, Sierra (mts.) H6/20
Pacific-Antarctic (ridge) A-B7/1
Padre (isl.) F8/19
Palau (isls.) G3/8
Palawan (isl.) E3/8
Palk (strait) C7/6
Palmas (cape) B4/12
Pamir (mts.) C2/6
Pamlico (sound) L4/19
Pampas (reg.) C4/16
Panama (gulf) E5-6/20
Panay (isl.) E3/8
Paraguay (riv.) C3/16
Parana (riv.) D2/16
Parece Vela (isl.) G1/8
Parnaíba (riv.) G4/15
Parry (chan.) D2/18
Passero (cape) E8/3
Patagonia (reg.) B5-7/16
Patos (lagoon) D4/16
Peace (riv.) B4/18
Pechora (riv.) F1/2
Pecos (riv.) E6/19
Pegu Yoma (mts.) F5-6/6
Peipus (lake) F3/3
Peloponnisos (pen.) F7/3
Pemba (isl.) F1/13
Penobscot (riv.) M2/19
Pennine Chain (range) B4/3
Penrhyn (basin) G4/10
Peribonca (riv.) F4/18
Persian (gulf) E4/5
Perth (basin) A7/10
Peru (basin) L6/10
Peru-Chile (trench) A3-6/16
Philippines (isls.) F4/8/
Phoenix (isls.) F4/10
Pikes (peak) E4/19
Pilcomayo (riv.) C3/16
Pitcairn (isl.) H7/10
Plata, Río de la (riv.) C4/16
Platte (riv.) F4/19

Po (riv.) D6/3
Pobeda (peak) D2/6
Pontic (mts.) C1/5
Poopó (lake) C4/16
Popocatépetl (vol.) B4/20
Porcupine (bank) A3/2
Potomac (riv.) K4/19
Powell (lake) C4/19
Poyang Hu (lake) F4/7
Prince Charles (isl.) E3/18
Prince Edward (P.E.I.) (isl.) G4/18
Prince Patrick (isl.) C1/18
Prince of Wales (isl.) D2/18
Prut (riv.) E4/2
Puerto Rico (isl.) G4/20
Puncak Jaya (peak) H4/8
Purus (riv.) D4/15
Putumayo (riv.) B3/15
Pyramid (lake) B4/19
Pyrenees (mts.) B-C7/3
Qaidam (basin) C3/7
Qattara (depr.) A3/5
Qinghai Hu (lake) C3/7
Qu'Appelle (riv.) E1/19
Queen Charlotte (isls.) A4/18
Queen Elizabeth (isls.) D1/18
Queensland (plat.) F2/9
Race (cape) G4/18
Rainier (mt.) B2/19
Ras al Hadd (cape) F4/5
Ras Aser (cape) H4/12
Ras Dashan (mt.) G4/12
Ravi (riv.) C3/6
Red (riv.), Texas-La. G7/19
Red (riv.), Vietnam C1/8
Red (sea) C4-4/5
Red Deer (riv.) D1/19
Red River of the North (riv.) F2/19
Reina Adelaida (arch.) A7/16
Reindeer (lake) D4/18
Republican (riv.) F4/19
Réunion (isl.) H4/13
Revillagigedo (isls.) A3/20
Reyes (pt.) A4/19
Reykjanes (ridge) F2/17
Rhine (riv.) D4/3
Rhodes (isl.) B2/5
Rhône (riv.) C6/3
Riga (gulf) E4/3
Rio Grande (fracture zone) A-B7/11
Rio Grande (riv.) F7/19
Roanoke (riv.) K4/19
Robinson Crusoe (isl.) B6/14
Rockall (isl.) A3/3
Rocky (mts.) B3-B6/17
Roggeveen (basin) K-L7/10
Romanche (fracture zone) F4/1
Roraima (mt.) D2/15
Ross (sea) M7/1
Rovuma (riv.) F2/13
Royale (isl.) H2/19
Rub' al Khali (des.) E-F4/5
Rufiji (riv.) F1/13
Ryukyu (isls.) G4/7
Saaremaa (isl.) E3/3
Sabine (riv.) G6/19
Sable (cape), Florida K8/19
Sable (cape), Nova Scotia G6/18
Sable (isl.) G4/18
Sacramento (riv.) A4/19
Saginaw (bay) J3/19
Saguenay (riv.) L1/19
Sahara (des.) B-E4/12
Saharian (seamounts) A3/11
Saint Christopher (isl.) H4/20
Saint George's (chan.) B4/3
Saint Helena (isl.) B6/11
Saint-Jean (lake) F4/18
Saint Johns (riv.) K7/19
Saint Lawrence (gulf) G4/18
Saint Lawrence (isl.) B7/19
Saint Lawrence (riv.) F4/18
Saint Lucia (isl.) H4/20
Saint Vincent (isl.) H4/20
Sakakawea (lake) F2/19
Sakarya (riv.) B2/5
Sakhalin (isl.) F3/4
Sala y Gomez (ridge) K-L7/10
Salado (riv.) B4/16
Salado del Norte (riv.) B3/16
Salmon (riv.) C2/19
Salton Sea (lake) B6/19
Salween (riv.) B2/7
Samar (isl.) F3/8
Samoa (isls.) F6/10
San Antonio (cape), Cuba E3/20
Sanga (riv.) D6/12
San Joaquin (riv.) A4/19
San Jorge (gulf) B6/16
San Lucas (cape) A3/20
San Matías (gulf) B6/16
San Salvador (isl.) M8/19
Santa Barbara (isls.) A4/19
Santa Isabel (isl.) H1/9
Santos (plat.) E4/14
São Francisco (riv.) H4/15
Saône (riv.) C6/3
São Roque (cape) H4/15
São Tomé (isl.) C6/12
São Vicente (cape) A8/3
Sardinia (isl.) D7/3
Saskatchewan (riv.) C4/18
Satpura (range) C4/6
Sava (riv.) E6/3
Savannah (riv.) K6/19
Schouten (isls.) H4/8
Scotia (sea) D8/14
Seine (riv.) C4/3
Selenge (riv.) D1/7
Selvas (forest) D4-E3/15
Semeru (peak) E6/3
Senegal (riv.) A4/12
Sevan (lake) D1/5
Severn (riv.), Ontario D4/18
Severnaya Zemlya (isls.) D2/4

Seward (pen.) B7/19
Seychelles (isls.) H1/13
Shan (plat.) C4/7
Shandong (Shantung) Bandao
    (pen.) F3/7
Shari (riv.) D4/12
Shasta (mt.) B3/19
Shebelle, Wadi (riv.) G4/12
Shetland (isls.) C3/3
Shikoku (isl.) G3/7
Siahan (range) A-B4/6
Siberia (reg.) D3-E2/4
Siberud (isl.) B4/8
Sicily (isl.) E8/3
Sidra (gulf) D-E2/12
Sierra Leone (basin) A4/11
Sierra Nevada (mts.) B4/17
Sigsbee (deep) D3/20
Simpson (des.) D3/9
Sinai (pen.) B3/5
Sittang (riv.) F6/6
Sjaelland (isl.) D4/3
Skagerrak (strait) D4/3
Smallwood (res.) E6/9
Smoky Hill (riv.) F4/19
Snake (riv.) C2/19
Sobradinho (res.) G4/15
Society (isls.) G6/10
Socotra (isl.) E6/5
Solomon (isls.) G-H1/9
Somali (basin) H4/11
Somerset (isl.) D2/18
Songhua (Sungari) (riv.) F1/7
Souris (riv.) F2/19
South (cape) E6/9
South (isl.) G6/9
Southampton (isl.) E3/18
South Australia (basin) C4/9
South China (sea) C4-E2/8
Southeast Indian (ridge) J6-M7/1
Southern Alps (mts.) G6/9
Southern Indian (lake) D4/18
South Georgia (isl.) E8/16
South Platte (riv.) E4/19
South Sandwich (trench) F6-7/1
South Saskatchewan (riv.) C4/18
Southwest Indian (ridge) G-H6/1
Southwest Pacific (basin) F7-G8/10
Spencer (gulf) D4/9
Sri Lanka (isl.) D7/6
Syr-Dar'ya (riv.) C4/4
Syrian (des.) C3/5
Tagus (abyssal plain) B2/12
Tagus (riv.) A7/3
Tahat (mt.) C3/12
Tahiti (isl.) G6/10
Tainaron (cape) F8/3
Taitao (pen.) A7/16
Taiwan (isl.) F4/7
Taklimakan (des.) B2/7
Talaud (isls.) F4/8
Tampa (bay) K7/19
Tana (lake) G4/12
Tana (riv.) G6/12
Tanami (des.) C2/9
Tanana (riv.) C7/19
Tanezrouft (des.) C3/12
Tanganyika (lake) E1/13
Tanimbar (isls.) G6/8
Tapajós (riv.) E4/15
Tapti (riv.) C4/6
Taranto (gulf) E7/3
Tarim (riv.) B2/7
Tarnak (riv.) G3/5
Tasman (sea) D7/10
Tasmania (isl.) E6/9
Taupo (lake) H4/9
Taurus (mts.) B-C2/5
Tehuantepec (isthmus) C4/20
Teles Pires (riv.) E4/15
Tennessee (riv.) H6/19
Terek (riv.) D1/5
Teulada (cape) D8/3
Texoma (lake) F6/19
Thailand (gulf) B3/8
Thames (riv.) C4/3
Tiber (riv.) D7/3
Tibesti (mts.) D-E3/12
Tibet (plat.) B3/7
Tien Shan (range) A-B2/7
Tierra del Fuego (isl.) B7/16
Tietê (riv.) E2/16
Tigris (riv.) D3/5
Tihama (reg.) C5-D6/5
Tiki (basin) H6/10
Timor (isl.) F6/8
Tinaca (pt.) F4/8
Tirich Mir (mt.) C2/6
Titicaca (lake) C4/15
Tobago (isl.) H4/20
Tobol (riv.) C3/4
Tocantins (riv.) F3/15
Tokelau (isls.) F6/10
Toledo Bend (res.) G7/19

Tombigbee (riv.) H6/19
Tomini (gulf) E-F4/8
Tonga (trench) F6/10
Tonkin (gulf) C2/8
Tonle Sap (lake) C3/8
Torawitan (cape) F4/8
Torne (riv.) E2/3
Torrens (lake) D4/9
Transkei (basin) D6/13
Tres Puntas (cape) B6/16
Trinidad (isl.) H4/20
Trinity (riv.) G7/19
Tristan da Cunha (isl.) B8/11
Tshuapa (riv.) E6/12
Tsimlyansk (res.) G4/2
Tuamotu (arch.) H6/10
Tucuruí (res.) F4/15
Tukangbesi (isls.) F4/8
Turkana (lake) G6/12
Turks and Caicos (isls.) G3/20
Tuz (lake) C2/5
Tyrrhenian (sea) D7/3
Ubangi (riv.) D6/12
Ucayali (riv.) B4/15
Uele (riv.) E4/12
Ulithi (isl.) H3/8
Umnak (isl.) B8/19
Unalaska (isl.) B8/19
Ungava (pen.) E4/18
Unimak (isl.) B8/19
Upper Klamath (lake) B3/19
Ural (mts.) G1-3/2
Urmia (lake) D2/5
Uruguay (riv.) C4/16
Ussuri (riv.) G1/7
Ust'-Urt (plat.) F1/5
Usumacinta (riv.) D4/20
Vaal (riv.) D4/13
Vaksh (riv.) H2/5
Valdés (pen.) C6/16
Vals (cape) G6/8
Van (lake) D2/5
Vancouver (isl.) A4/18
Vänern (lake) D3/3
Vardar (riv.) F7/3
Vättern (lake) D4/3
Vaupés (riv.) C3/15
Venezuela (gulf) C1/15
Verde (cape) A4/12
Vesteralen (isls.) D1/3
Vestfjord (fjord) D2-1/3
Victoria (falls) D3/13
Victoria (isl.) C2/18
Victoria (lake) F6/12
Vilyuy (riv.) E3/4
Vindhya (range) C4/6
Virgin (isls.) H4/20
Vistula (riv.) E4/3
Vityaz (trench) E6/10
Vohimena (cape) F4/13
Volga (riv.) G4/2
Volta (lake) B4/12
Wabash (riv.) H4/19
Wake (isl.) E4/10
Wallaby (plat.) A6/10
Walvis (ridge) C7/11
Warrego (riv.) E4/9
Warta (riv.) E4/3
Wasatch (range) C-D4/19
Weddell (sea) E7/1
Wei (riv.) D3/7
Weser (riv.) D4/3
Wessel (cape) D1/9
West (cape) G6/9
West Caroline (basin) H4/8
Western Dvina (riv.) F3/3
Western Ghats (mts.) C5-6/6
West Fiji (basin) E6/10
West Indies (isls.) G-H3/20
West Sheba (ridge) D-E6/5
Wetar (isl.) F6/8
White (sea) E2/2
White Nile (riv.) F4/12
Whitney (mt.) B4/19
Willamette (riv.) B2/19
Williston (lake) B4/18
Wilshaw (riv.) H3/13
Windward (passg.) F4/20
Winnebago (lake) H3/19
Winnipeg (lake) D4/18
Winnipegosis (lake) F1/19
Wisconsin (riv.) H3/19
Woods (lake) G2/19
Wrangel (isl.) M1/1
Wu (riv.) D4/7
Xi (riv.) D4/7
Xiang (riv.) E4/7
Xingu (riv.) E4/15
Yablonovvy (range) D4-E3/4
Yakhsh (riv.) C2/6
Yalong (riv.) D4/7
Yalu (riv.) F2/7
Yangtze (Chang) (riv.) E4/7
Yap (isl.) H3/8
Yarkant (riv.) A2/7
Yazoo (riv.) H6/19
Yellow (Huang) (riv.) E3/7
Yellow (sea) F3/7
Yellowstone (riv.) E2/19
Yellowstone (lake) D3/19
Yenisey (riv.) D3/4
Yobe (riv.) D4/12
York (cape) F2/9
Yuan (riv.) E4/7
Yucatán (pen.) D3-4/20
Yukon (riv.) B2/17
Zagros (riv.) E3/5
Zaire (Congo) (riv.) D6/12
Zambezi (riv.) E4/13
Zanzibar (isl.) F1/13
Zapiola (ridge) E6/16
Zaysan (lake) B1/7
Zhob (riv.) B3/6

HAMMOND®

THE PHYSICAL WORLD
Terrain Maps of Land Forms and Ocean Floors

CONTENTS

THE WORLD	X-XI
EUROPE	XII
WESTERN EUROPE	XIII
ASIA	XIV
SOUTHWEST ASIA	XV
SOUTHERN ASIA	XVI
EAST ASIA	XVII
SOUTHEAST ASIA	XVIII
AUSTRALIA AND NEW ZEALAND	XIX
PACIFIC OCEAN	XX-XXI
AFRICA	XXII
NORTHERN AFRICA	XXIII
SOUTHERN AFRICA	XXIV
SOUTH AMERICA	XXV
NORTHERN SOUTH AMERICA	XXVI
SOUTHERN SOUTH AMERICA	XXVII
NORTH AMERICA	XXVIII
CANADA	XXIX
UNITED STATES	XXX-XXXI
MIDDLE AMERICA	XXXII

RELIEF MODELS BY ERNST G. HOFMANN, ASSISTED BY RAFAEL MARTINEZ

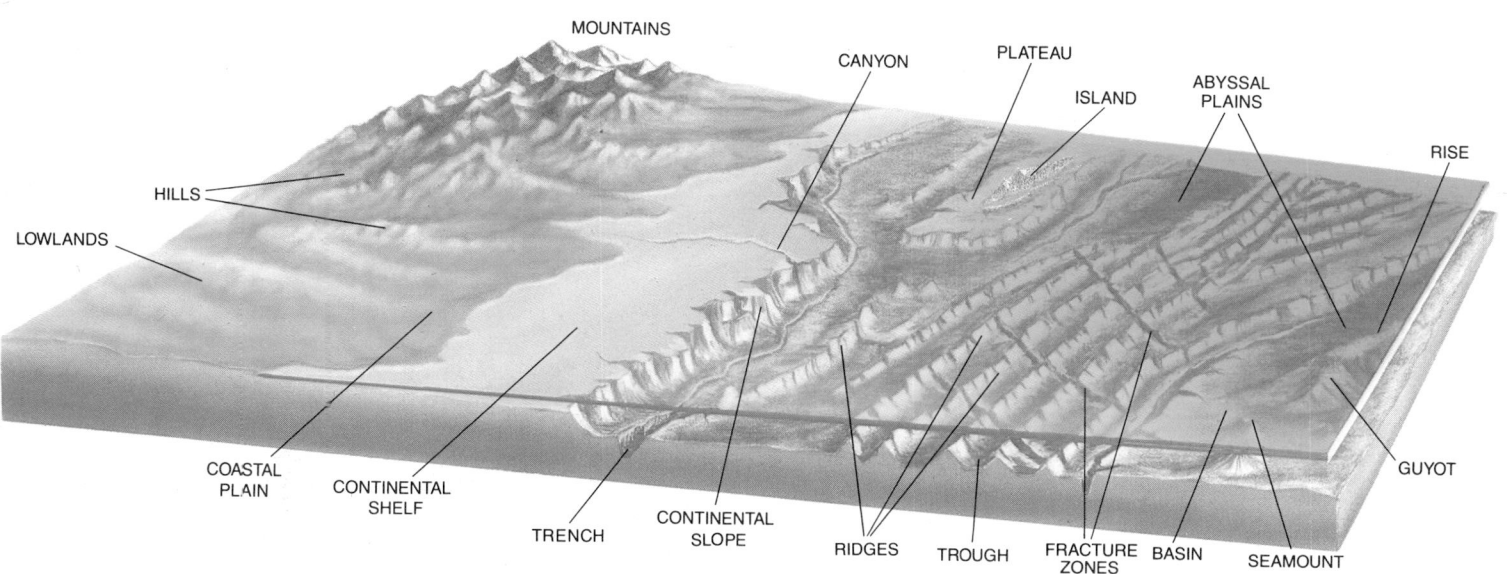

The oblique view diagram above is designed to provide a detailed view of the ocean floor as if seen through the depth of the sea. Graduating blue tones are used to contrast ocean floor depths: from light blue to represent shallow continental shelves to dark blues in the greater depths. Land relief is shown in conventional hypsometric tints.

In this dramatic collection of topographic maps of continents, oceans and major regions of the world, Hammond introduces a revolutionary new technique in cartography.

While most maps depicting terrain are created from painted artwork that is then photographed, Hammond now premiers the use of a remarkable sculptured model mapping technique created by one of our master cartographers.

The process begins with the sculpting of large scale three-dimensional models. Once physical details have been etched on the models and refinements completed, relief work is checked for accurate elevation based on a vertical scale exaggerated for visual effect.

Finished models are airbrushed and painted, then photographed using a single northwesterly light source to achieve a striking three-dimensional effect. The result is the dynamic presentation of mountain ranges and peaks on land, and canyons, trenches and seamounts on the ocean floor. Never before have maps conveyed such rich beauty while providing a realistic representation of the world as we know it.

ARCTIC OCEAN

CANADA
BASIN

QUEEN ELIZABETH
ISLANDS

Ellesmere

GREENLAND

Greenland
Sea

Wrangel
I.

Beaufort Sea

Banks
I.

Baffin

Baffin
Island

Bay

Arctic Circle

North

Chukchi
Sea

Pt. Barrow

Victoria
I.

Denmark St.

Iceland

Bering Sea

ALEUTIAN
BASIN

Yukon

Mt. McKinley

Gulf of Alaska

ROCKY

Great Bear
L.

NORTH

Great Slave
L.

Peace

Hudson

Bay

LABRADOR
BASIN

IRMINGER BASIN

ICELAND BASIN

Great
Britain

ALEUTIAN ISLANDS

ALEUTIAN TRENCH

Mackenzie

Mountains

AMERICA

Great
Lakes

Newfoundland

CHARLIE-GIBBS
FRACTURE ZONE

Ireland

MENDOCINO FRACTURE ZONE

C. Mendocino

Great Plains

Missouri

Ohio

C. Race

ATLANTIC

HAWAIIAN

HAWAIIAN RIDGE

ISLANDS

MOLOKAI FRACTURE ZONE

Tropic of Cancer

Colorado

Rio Grande

Lower
California

Mississippi

Gulf of
Mexico

Appalachian Mts.

C. Hatteras

MID-ATLANTIC RIDGE

Azores

WEST

Cuba

Caribbean
Sea

INDIES

O

C. Verde

CENTRAL

PACIFIC

CLIPPERTON FRACTURE ZONE

Equator

GUATEMALA
BASIN

Orinoco

Amazon

ROMANCHE FRACTURE ZONE

BASIN

PACIFIC

Negro

Madeira

C. de São Roque

BRAZIL

OCEAN

PERU

BASIN

Andes

PERU-CHILE TRENCH

SOUTH

São Francisco

BRAZIL

BASIN

OCEAN

TONGA
TRENCH

OCEAN

Tropic of Capricorn

NAZCA RIDGE

CHILE
BASIN

AMERICA

Paraná

MID-ATLANTIC RIDGE

KERMADEC
TRENCH

SOUTHWEST

PACIFIC

BASIN

PERU-CHILE TRENCH

Mountains

Cerro
Aconcagua

ARGENTINE

BASIN

EAST PACIFIC RISE

Falkland Is.

Tierra del Fuego

SOUTH
SANDWICH
TRENCH

C. Horn

Drake Passage

PACIFIC-ANTARCTIC RIDGE

AMUNDSEN ABYSSAL PLAIN

Antarctic
Peninsula

WEDDELL

Antarctic Circle

Bellingshausen

Sea

Weddell

ABYSSAL PLAIN

Sea

Ross Sea

ANTARCTICA

Ross Ice Shelf

Edith Ronne
Ice Shelf

0   500   1000   1500   2000   2500   3000 MILES at Equator

0   500 1000 1500 2000 2500   3000 KILOMETERS at Equator

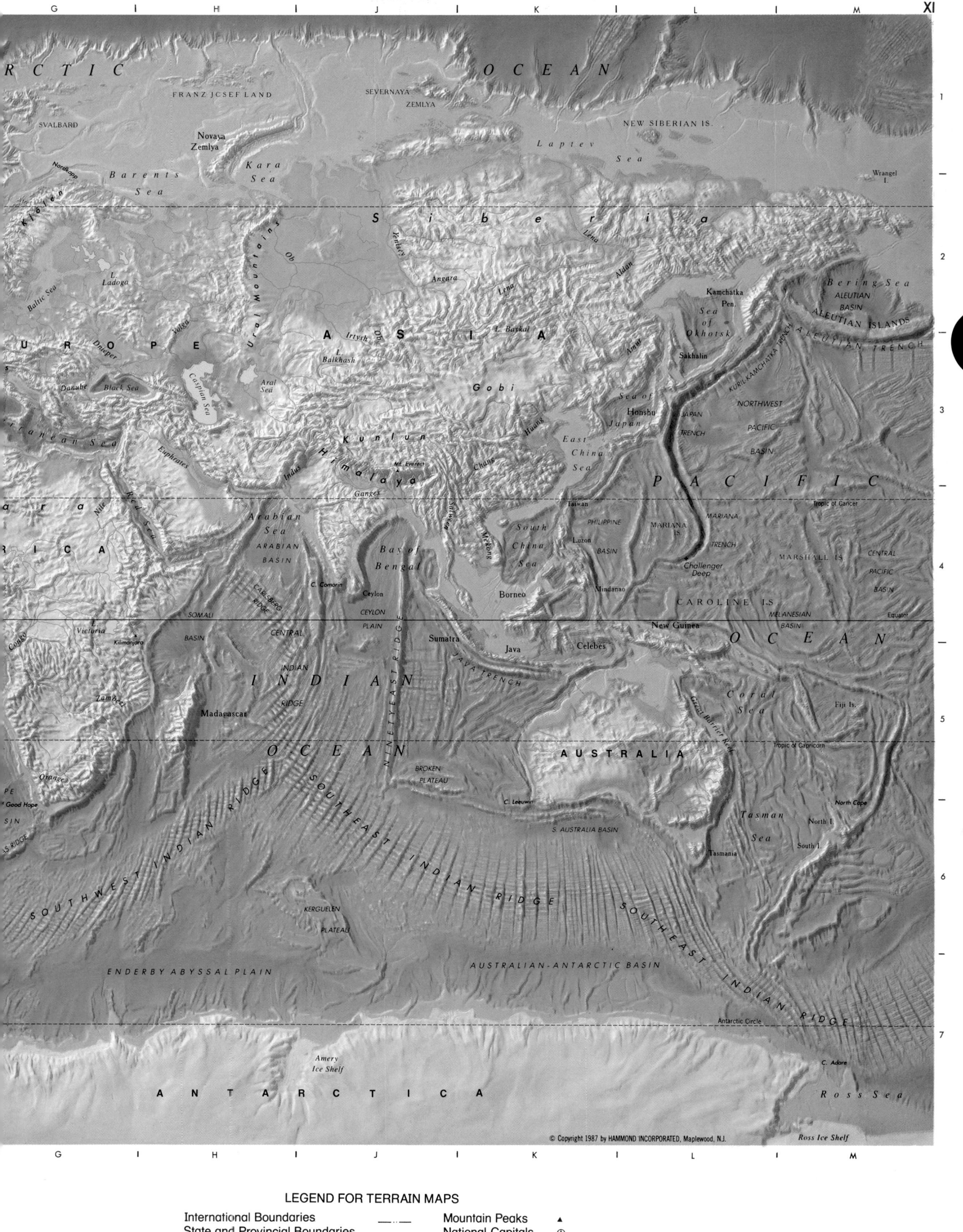

G   H   I   J   K   L   M

A R C T I C   O C E A N

FRANZ JOSEF LAND   SEVERNAYA
                                ZEMLYA   NEW SIBERIAN IS.

SVALBARD   Novaya   L a p t e v
                 Zemlya   S e a
Nordkapp   Kara
              B a r e n t s Sea   Wrangel
              S e a   I.
    Kjölen
                                    S   i   b   e   r   i   a

                                         Ural Mountains
                                                 Ob   B e r i n g S e a
L. Ladoga   Kamchatka   ALEUTIAN
                                                                             Pen.   BASIN
Baltic Sea   Irtysh   Angara   Lena   ALEUTIAN ISLANDS
                        A   Ob   Aldan   ALEUTIAN TRENCH
              Volga   S   I   A   Sea
U R O P E   L.   L. Baykal   Sakhalin of
              Dnieper   Balkhash   Okhotsk
Danube Black Sea   G o b i   Sea of
              Caspian Sea   Aral   Honshu Japan   NORTHWEST
terranean Sea   Sea   Huang Japan JAPAN   PACIFIC
                    Euphrates   K u n l u n   Chang East   TRENCH BASIN
ara   China
              Nile Red Sea   H i m a l a y a   Mt. Everest Chang Sea   KURIL KAMCHATKA TRENCH
I C A   Indus   Taiwan   Tropic of Cancer
              Arabian   Ganges   Salween   PHILIPPINE MARIANA MARIANA
              Sea   ARABIAN   Bay of   Mekong South Luzon BASIN IS. TRENCH
                     BASIN   Bengal   China   Challenger   MARSHALL IS CENTRAL
              C. Comorin   Sea Mindanao   Deep   PACIFIC
              CARLSBERG   Ceylon   Borneo   CAROLINE IS   BASIN
              RIDGE   CEYLON   MELANESIAN Equator
L. Victoria SOMALI   PLAIN   Sumatra Java   New Guinea   BASIN
Kilimanjaro BASIN CENTRAL   Java Celebes   O C E A N
              INDIAN   JAVA TRENCH   C o r a l   Fiji Is.
Zambezi   RIDGE I N D I A N   S e a
Madagascar   North Cape
PE   O C E A N   BROKEN   AUSTRALIA   Tasman
Good Hope   PLATEAU   S e a North I. Tropic of Capricorn
SIN   C. Leeuwin   Tasmania South I.
LS RIDGE   SOUTHWEST INDIAN RIDGE SOUTHEAST S AUSTRALIA BASIN
              NINETYEAST RIDGE   INDIAN RIDGE SOUTHEAST INDIAN RIDGE
              KERGUELEN
              PLATEAU
              ENDERBY ABYSSAL PLAIN   AUSTRALIAN-ANTARCTIC BASIN
                                                                        Antarctic Circle
              Amery   C. Adore
              Ice Shelf
A   N   T   A   R   C   T   I   C   A   R o s s S e a

© Copyright 1987 by HAMMOND INCORPORATED, Maplewood, N.J.   Ross Ice Shelf

G   H   I   J   K   L   M

LEGEND FOR TERRAIN MAPS

International Boundaries	_ . _	Mountain Peaks	▲
State and Provincial Boundaries	_ . _	National Capitals	⊛
Other Boundaries	_ _ _ _	Other Capitals	⊙
Boundaries Along Rivers	⌒	Canals	

WORLD | Plate 1

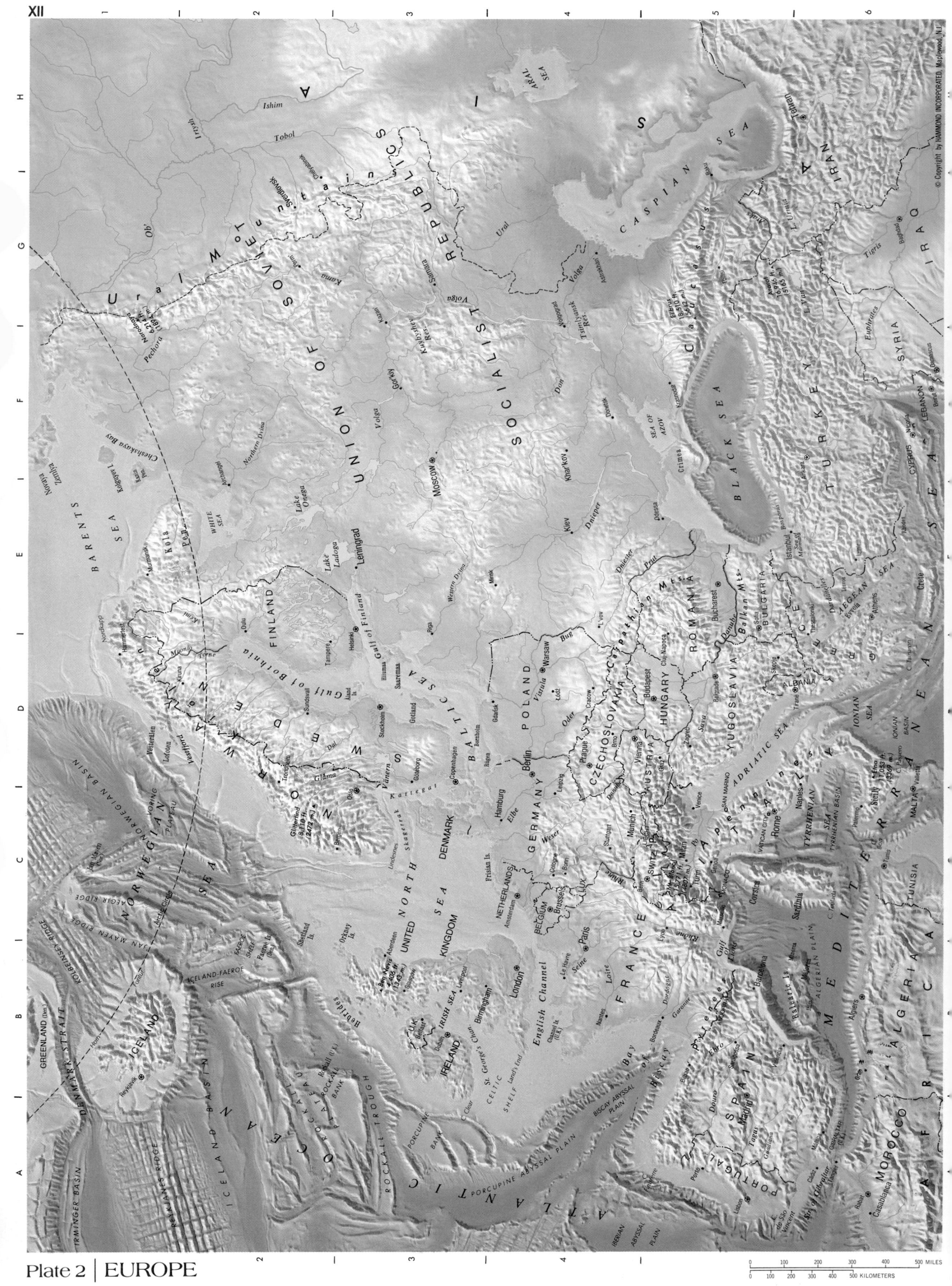

Plate 2 | EUROPE

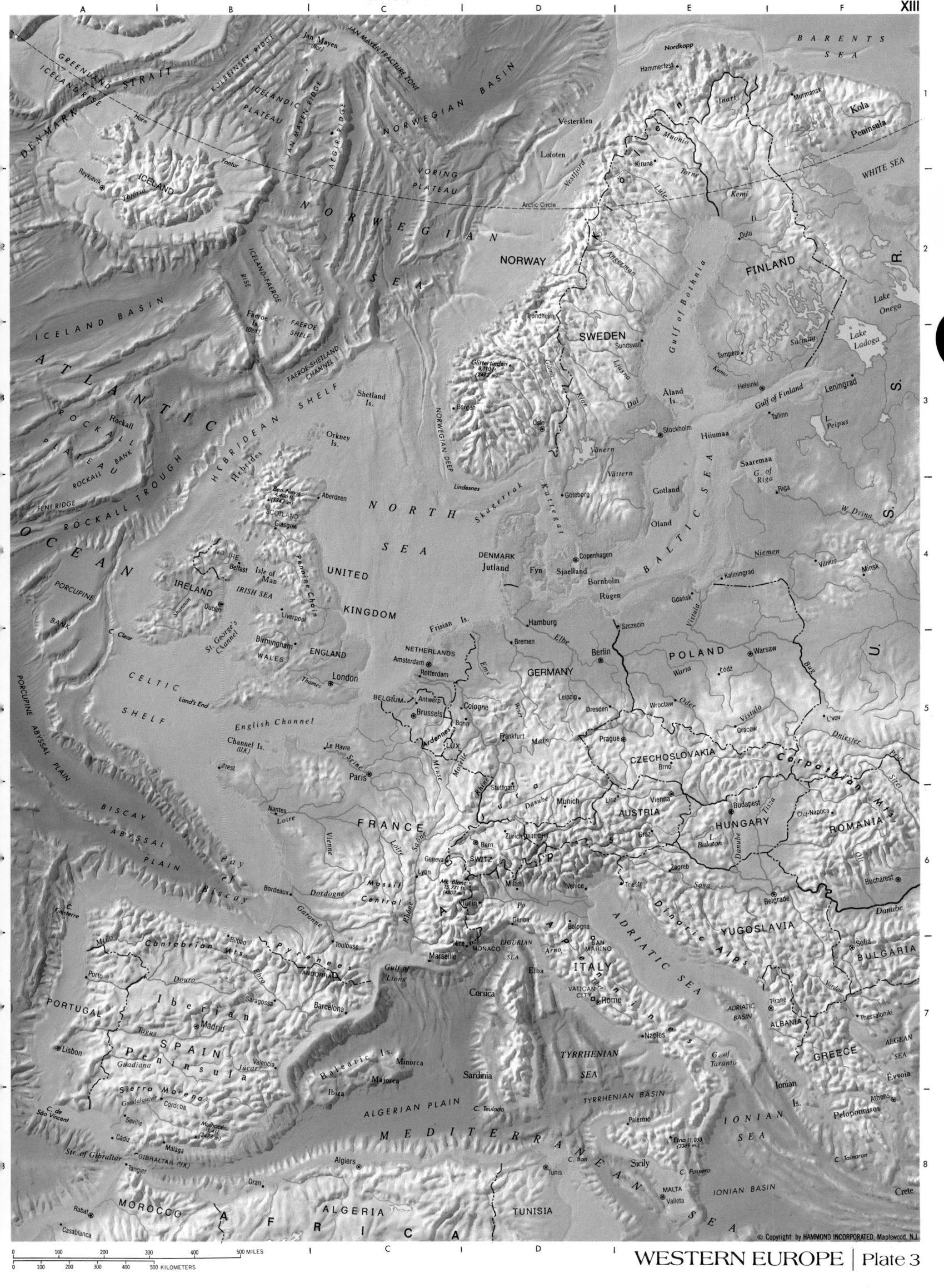

WESTERN EUROPE | Plate 3

A | B | C | D | E | F

GREENLAND

ATLANTIC OCEAN

ICELAND

ROCKALL ROUGH

BEAUFORT SEA

CANADA BASIN

Alaska
UNITED STATES

Kodiak

ALEUTIAN TRENCH

LINCOLN SEA

Pt. Barrow

ARCTIC

NORWEGIAN SEA

FAEROE

LOMONOSOV RIDGE

North Pole

MAKAROV BASIN

MENDELYEYEV RIDGE

Bering Str.

C. Dezhnev

IRELAND

UNITED KINGDOM

London

NORTH SEA

NORWEGIAN BASIN

SHELF

NANSEN BASIN

AMUNDSEN BASIN

OCEAN

EAST SIBERIAN SEA

BERING SEA

ALEUTIAN BASIN

SHIRSHOV RIDGE

Spitsbergen

Franz Josef

PORTUGAL

Paris

ABYSSAL PLAIN

BISCAY

ENGLISH CHANNEL

DEN.

SWEDEN

FINLAND

NORWAY

BARENTS SEA

Nordkapp

Novaya Zemlya

KARA SEA

LAPTEV SEA

New Siberian Is.

C. Chelyuskin

SPAIN

BAY OF BISCAY

GERMANY

POLAND

BALTIC SEA

Moscow

Volga

U

R

A

L

S

S

R

UNION OF SOVIET SOCIALIST REPUBLICS

S i b e r i a

Nizh.

Nordvik

Lena

Vilyuy

Yakutsk

SEA OF OKHOTSK

Sakhalin

PACIFIC

MEDITERRANEAN SEA

BLACK SEA

Caucasus

Volga

Ural

Sverdlovsk

Chelyabinsk

Tobol

Ob'

Omsk

Irtysh

Novosibirsk

Krasnoyarsk

Angara

L. Baykal

Yablonovyy Ra.

Amur

Harbin

KOREA

SEA OF JAPAN

KURIL BASIN

JAPAN TRENCH

CYPRUS

LEBANON

ISRAEL

JORDAN

Damascus

IRAQ

Baghdad

Tigris

Euphrates

IRAN

Tehran

CASPIAN SEA

ARAL SEA

Syr-Darya

Amu-Darya

Tashkent

Alma-Ata

Karaganda

L. Balkhash

Tien Shan

Ürümqi

Tarim

Taklimakan

A l t a i

Ulaanbaatar

MONGOLIA

G o b i

Great Khingan Ra.

Shenyang

Beijing

Dalian

S. KOREA

Seoul

JAPAN

Tokyo

SAUDI ARABIA

Riyadh

KUWAIT

Persian Gulf

BAHRAIN

QATAR

UAE

Gulf of Oman

Muscat

OMAN

YEMEN

Aden

Rub' al Khali

Karachi

PAKISTAN

Lahore

Delhi

New Delhi

Indus

Hindu Kush

AFGHANISTAN

Islamabad

Helmand

K2 Godwin Austen 28,250 ft. (8,611 m.)

K u n l u n

T i b e t

C e n t r a l

C H I N A

Lanzhou

Xi'an

Taiyuan

Huang

YELLOW SEA

Tianjin

EAST CHINA SEA

Nanjing

Shanghai

Chengdu

Wuhan

Chongqing

Chang

RED SEA

EGYPT

Cairo

ETHIOPIA

SOMALIA

Aden

Gulf of Aden

ARABIAN SEA

INDUS CONE

ARABIAN SEA BASIN

Bombay

Ahmadabad

Narbada

Godavari

Krishna

Hyderabad

Bangalore

Madras

INDIA

Mt. Everest 29,028 ft. (8,848 m.)

NEPAL

Kanpur

Ganges

H i m a l a y a

BHUTAN

Brahmaputra

BANGLADESH

Dhaka

Calcutta

BAY OF BENGAL

GANGES CONE

BURMA

Rangoon

THAILAND

Bangkok

HONG KONG U.K.

Guangzhou

Hainan

Taipei

Taiwan

RYUKYU TRENCH

Tropic of Cancer

PHILIPPINE SEA

WEST PHILIPPINE BASIN

PARECE VELA

KYUSHU-PALAU RIDGE

SOUTH CHINA SEA

PHILIPPINES

Manila

Luzon

SOMALI BASIN

CARLSBERG RIDGE

OWEN FRACTURE ZONE

WESTERN GHATS

Cochin

SRI LANKA (CEYLON)

Colombo

Comorin

MALDIVES

CHAGOS-LACCADIVE RIDGE

SEYCHELLES

MASCARENE PLATEAU

MASCARENE BASIN

MADAGASCAR

MAURITIUS

Réunion (Fr.)

Tropic of Capricorn

MADAGASCAR BASIN

CENTRAL INDIAN RIDGE

BRITISH INDIAN OCEAN TERR.

Equator

MID-INDIAN BASIN

NINETY EAST RIDGE

OCEAN BASIN

INDIAN OCEAN

CEYLON PLAIN

COCOS BASIN

Andaman Is.

ANDAMAN SEA

Nicobar Is.

Gulf of Thailand

CAMBODIA

VIETNAM

Ho Chi Minh City

Palawan

Kuala Lumpur

MALAYSIA

BRUNEI

SINGAPORE

SUNDA SHELF

Sumatra

SUNDA TRENCH

INVESTIGATOR RIDGE

JAVA TRENCH

Jakarta

Java

Surabaya

JAVA SEA

NORTH AUSTRALIA BASIN

EXMOUTH PLATEAU

Great Sandy Desert

AUSTRALIA

SULU SEA

SULU BASIN

Mindanao

CELEBES SEA

Celebes

Borneo

I N D O N E S I A

FLORES SEA

BALI

SUMBA

Lombok

SUMBAWA BASIN

SAVU BASIN

TIMOR

TIMOR SEA

New Guinea

PHILIPPINE TRENCH

PALAU TRENCH

1 | 2 | 3 | 4 | 5 | 6 | 7 | 8

Plate 4 | ASIA

© Copyright by HAMMOND INCORPORATED, Maplewood, N.J.

0   300   600   900   1200   1500 MILES

0   300   600   900   1200   1500 KILOMETERS

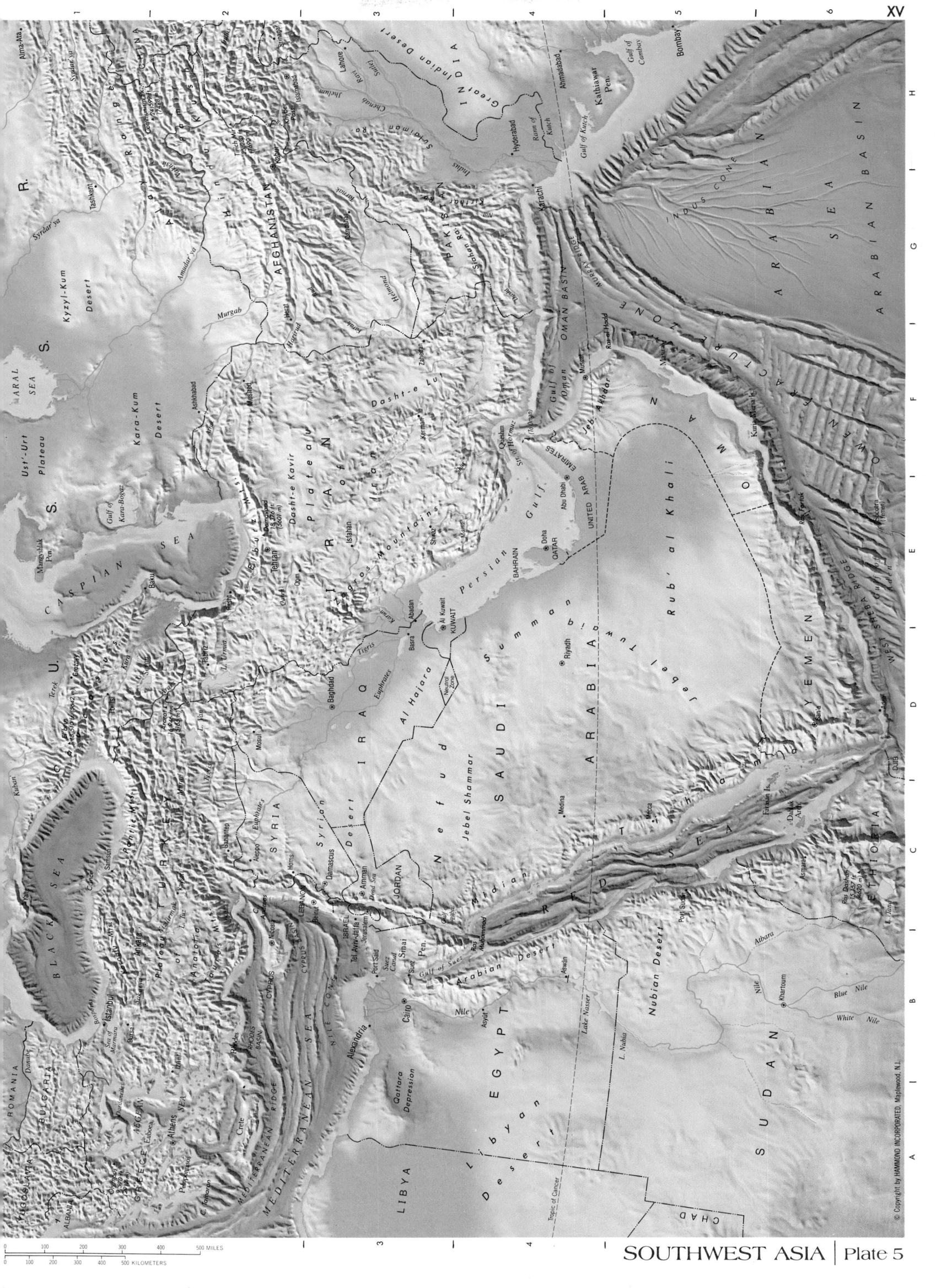

© Copyright by HAMMOND INCORPORATED, Maplewood, N.J.

0   100   200   300   400   500 MILES
0   100   200   300   400   500 KILOMETERS

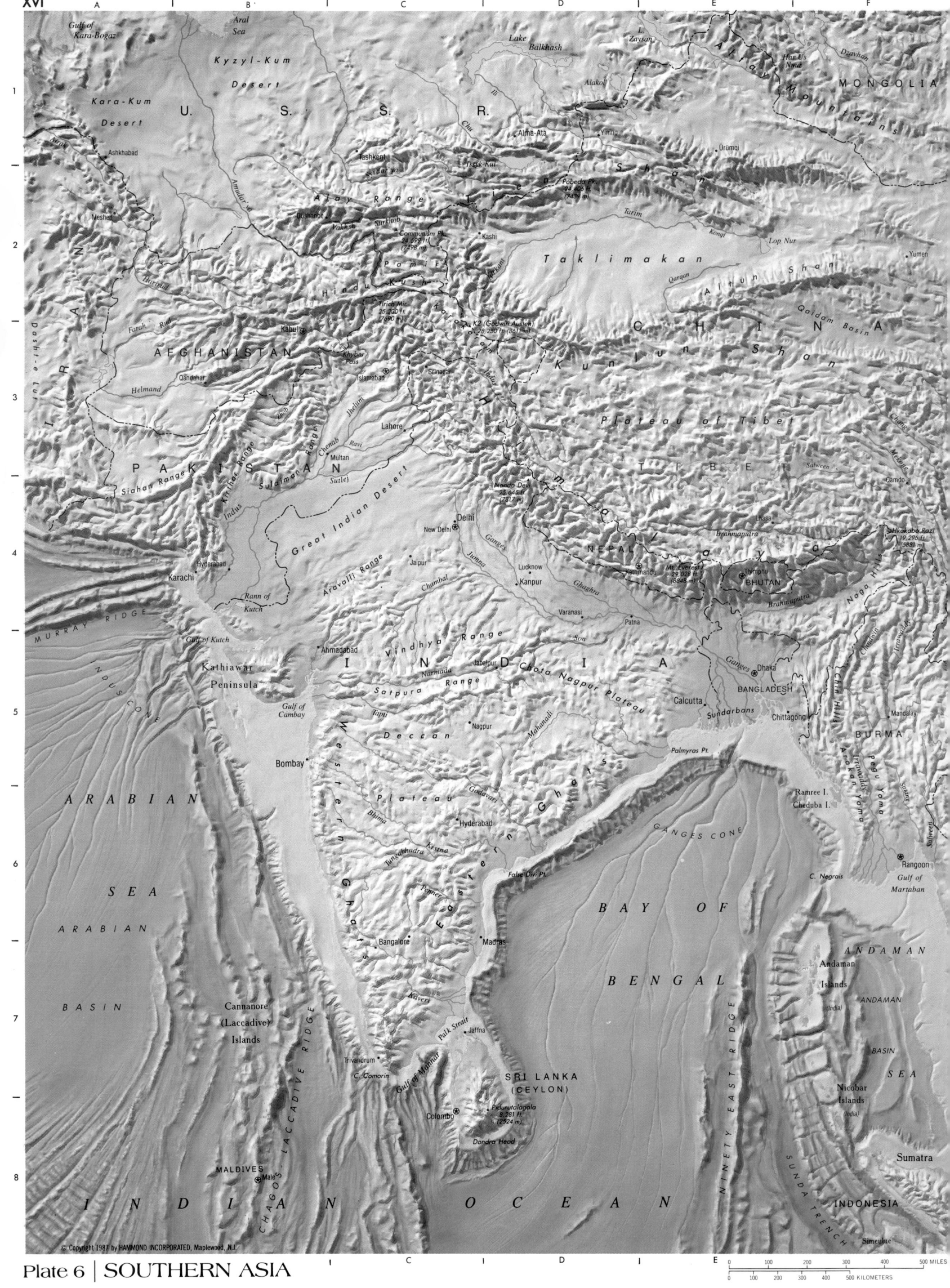

Plate 6 | SOUTHERN ASIA

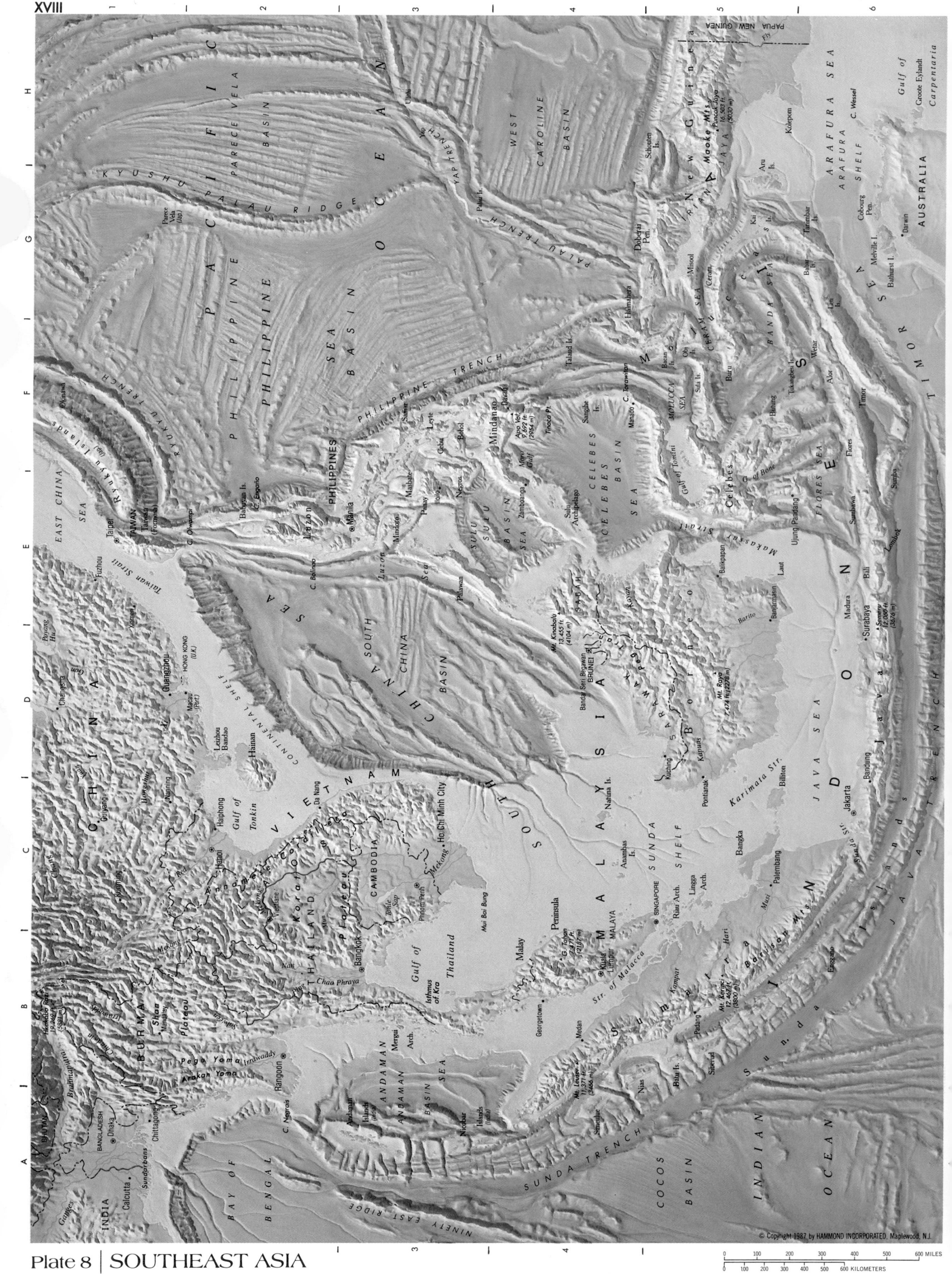

Plate 8 | SOUTHEAST ASIA

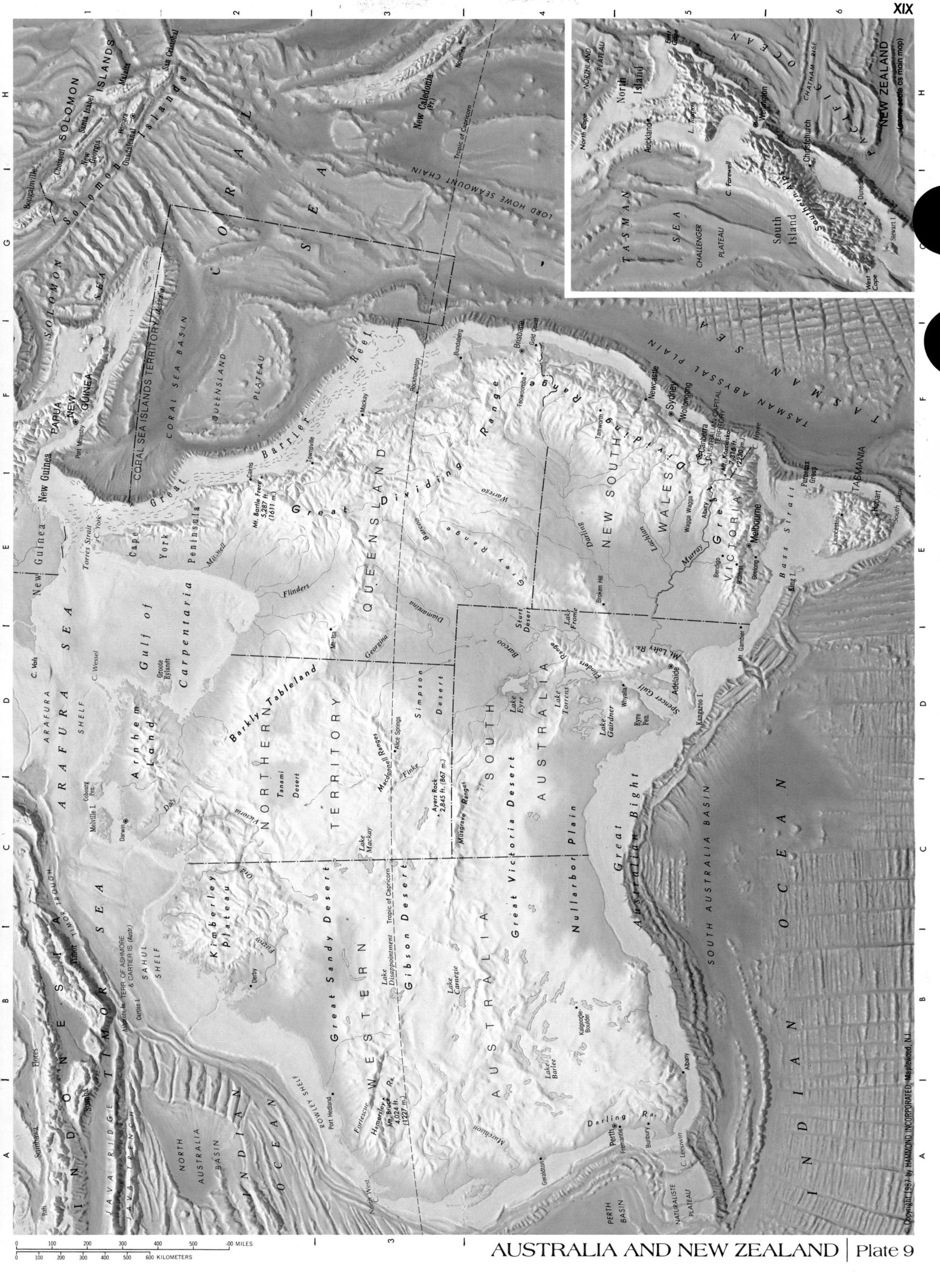

AUSTRALIA AND NEW ZEALAND | Plate 9

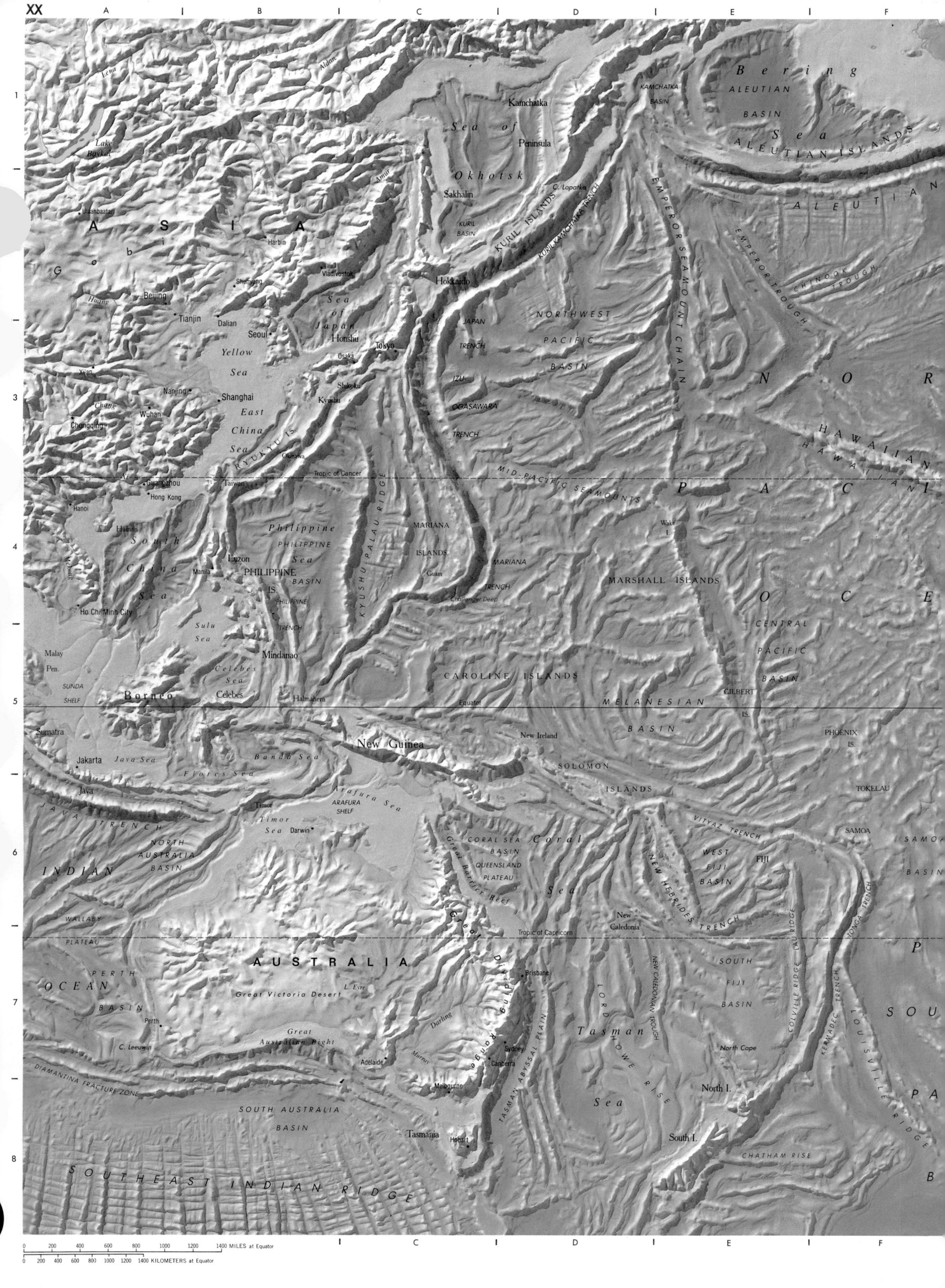

A I B I C I D I E I F

1

I

ASIA

G

2

3

4

5

6

7

8

Lena

Aldan

Lake
Baykal

Ulaanbaatar

ö b i

Harbin

Shenyang

Vladivostok

Sakhalin

Sea of

Okhotsk

Kamchatka

Peninsula

C. Lopatka

KAMCHATKA
BASIN

B e r i n g

ALEUTIAN

BASIN

S e a

ALEUTIAN ISLANDS

Huang

Beijing

Tianjin

Dalian

Seoul

Honshu

Osaka

Tokyo

Sea

of

Japan

Hokkaido

KURIL
BASIN

KURIL ISLANDS

KURIL-KAMCHATKA TRENCH

EMPEROR SEAMOUNT CHAIN

EMPEROR TROUGH

ALEUTIAN

CHINOOK
TROUGH

Xian

Nanjing

Shanghai

Chang

Wuhan

Chongqing

Yellow

Sea

East

China

Sea

Kyushu

Shikoku

JAPAN

TRENCH

IZU

OGASAWARA

TRENCH

NORTHWEST

PACIFIC

BASIN

N O R

HAWAIIAN

HAWAIIAN

RYUKYU IS.

Okinawa

Tropic of Cancer

MID-PACIFIC SEAMOUNTS

P A C I

Guangzhou

Taiwan

Hong Kong

Hainan

Philippine

PHILIPPINE

Sea

BASIN

MARIANA

ISLANDS

Guam

MARIANA

TRENCH

Challenger Deep

Wake
I.

MARSHALL ISLANDS

O C E

Hanoi

South

China

Sea

Luzon

Manila

PHILIPPINE

IS.

PHILIPPINE

TRENCH

Mindanao

Sulu
Sea

KYUSHU-PALAU RIDGE

CENTRAL

PACIFIC

BASIN

Ho Chi Minh City

Malay
Pen.

SUNDA
SHELF

Borneo

Celebes
Sea

Celebes

Halmahera

Equator

CAROLINE ISLANDS

MELANESIAN

GILBERT

IS.

BASIN

Sumatra

Jakarta

Java

Java Sea

Banda Sea

Flores Sea

New Guinea

New Ireland

SOLOMON

ISLANDS

PHOENIX
IS.

TOKELAU

JAVA TRENCH

Timor

Timor

Sea Darwin

ARAFURA
SHELF

Arafura Sea

NORTH

AUSTRALIA

BASIN

INDIAN

WALLABY

PLATEAU

AUSTRALIA

Great Victoria Desert

L. Eyre

CORAL SEA
BASIN

QUEENSLAND

PLATEAU

Great Barrier Reef

Great Dividing Range

Coral

Sea

VITYAZ TRENCH

NEW HEBRIDES

TRENCH

WEST
FIJI
BASIN

FIJI

SAMOA

SAMOA

BASIN

New
Caledonia

Tropic of Capricorn

P

OCEAN

PERTH

BASIN

Perth

C. Leeuwin

Great

Australian Bight

Adelaide

Darling

Murray

Brisbane

Sydney

Canberra

Melbourne

TASMAN ABYSSAL PLAIN

NEW CALEDONIAN TROUGH

LORD HOWE RISE

Tasman

Sea

SOUTH

FIJI

BASIN

North Cope

North I.

South I.

COLVILLE RIDGE

DAU RIDGE

KERMADEC TRENCH

LOUISVILLE RIDGE

TONGA TRENCH

S O U

P A

DIAMANTINA FRACTURE ZONE

Tasmania

Hobart

SOUTH AUSTRALIA

BASIN

CHATHAM RISE

B

S O U T H E A S T   I N D I A N   R I D G E

0   200   400   600   800   1000   1200   1400 MILES at Equator

0   200   400   600   800   1000   1400 KILOMETERS at Equator

A I B I C I D I E I F

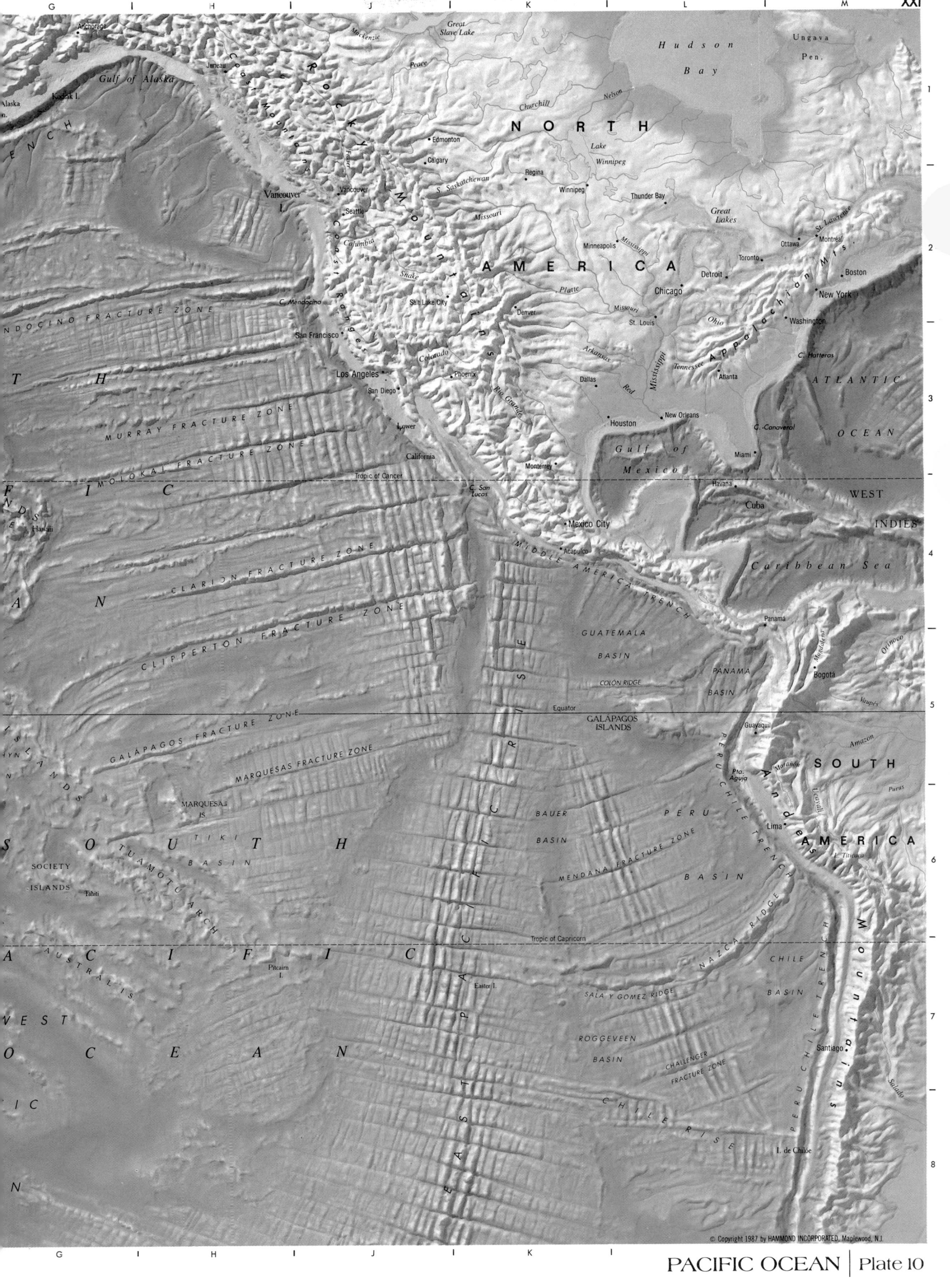

© Copyright 1987 by HAMMOND INCORPORATED, Maplewood, N.J.

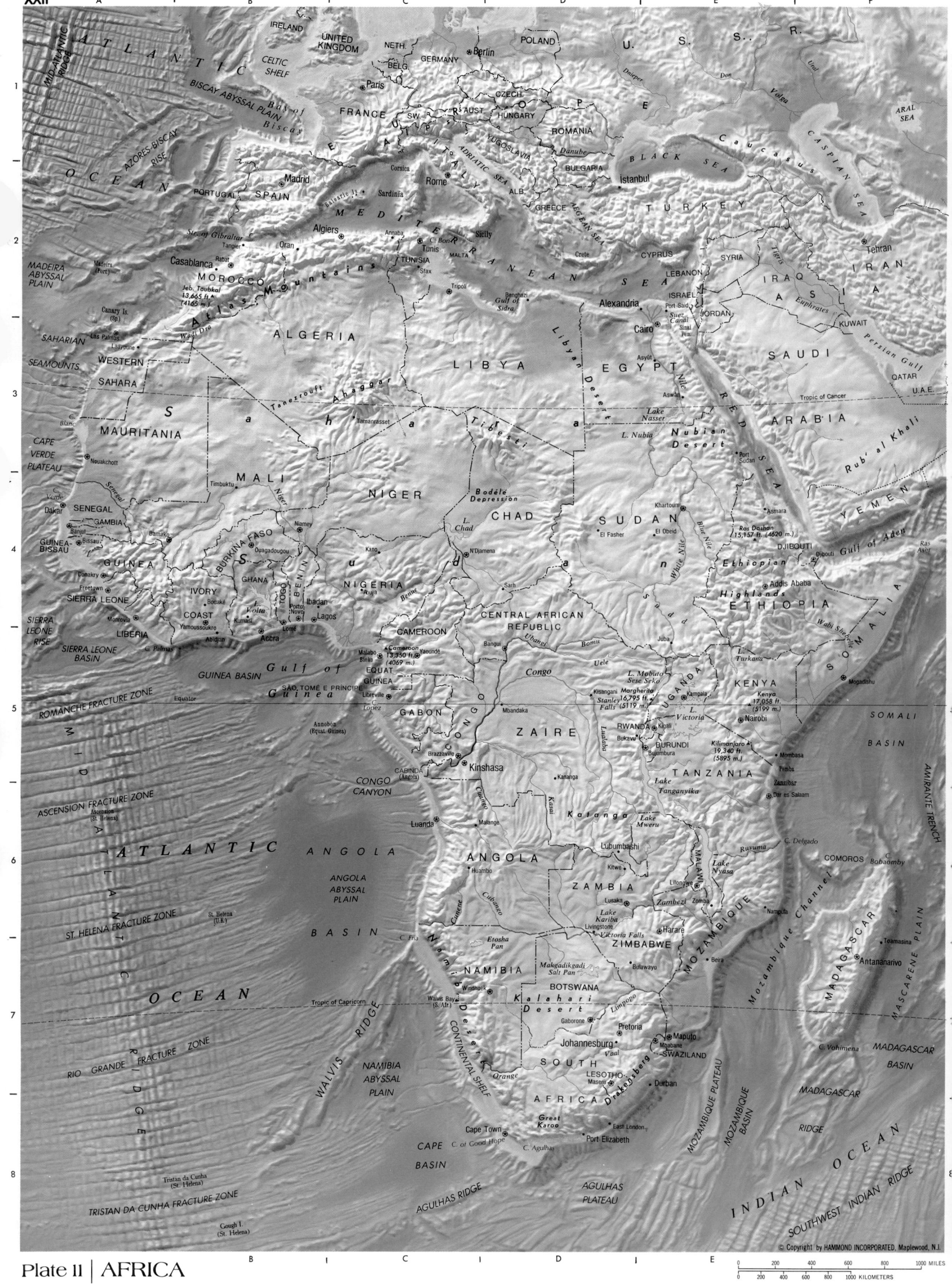

A   B   C   D   E   F

1

2

3

4

5

6

7

8

MID-ATLANTIC RIDGE
ATLANTIC
OCEAN
AZORES-BISCAY RISE
BISCAY ABYSSAL PLAIN
Bay of Biscay
CELTIC SHELF
IRELAND
UNITED KINGDOM
NETH.
BELG.
Paris
FRANCE
SW.
AUST.
GERMANY
Berlin
POLAND
CZECH
HUNGARY
ROMANIA
Danube
YUGOSLAVIA
BULGARIA
ITALY
ADRIATIC SEA
Rome
Corsica
Sardinia
Balearic Is.
SPAIN
PORTUGAL
Madrid
MADEIRA ABYSSAL PLAIN
Madeira (Port.)
Canary Is. (Sp.)
Las Palmas
SAHARIAN SEAMOUNTS
CAPE VERDE PLATEAU
Verde
Dakar
SENEGAL
GAMBIA
Banjul
Bissau
GUINEA-BISSAU
Conakry
Freetown
SIERRA LEONE
SIERRA LEONE RISE
SIERRA LEONE BASIN
Monrovia
LIBERIA
C. Palmas
Str. of Gibraltar
Tangier
Casablanca
Rabat
MOROCCO
Oran
Algiers
Annaba
Tunis
TUNISIA
Sfax
Tripoli
MEDITERRANEAN SEA
Sicily
MALTA
GREECE
AEGEAN SEA
Crete
ALB.
Istanbul
BLACK SEA
Caucasus
TURKEY
CYPRUS
SYRIA
LEBANON
ISRAEL
Alexandria
Cairo
Suez Canal
Port Said
Sinai Pen.
JORDAN
Dnieper
Don
Volga
Ural
U. S. S. R.
ARAL SEA
CASPIAN SEA
Tehran
IRAN
IRAQ
Euphrates
Tigris
KUWAIT
Persian Gulf
SAUDI ARABIA
QATAR
U.A.E.
Rub' al Khali
Tropic of Cancer
Jeb. Toubkal 13,665 ft. (4165 m.)
Atlas Mountains
Wadi Dra
WESTERN SAHARA
Laâyoune
Blanc
MAURITANIA
Nouakchott
MALI
Timbuktu
Senegal
Niger
Bamako
GUINEA
BURKINA FASO
Ouagadougou
IVORY COAST
GHANA
Bouaké
Kumasi
Yamoussoukro
Abidjan
Accra
L. Volta
TOGO
BENIN
Porto Novo
Lomé
Lagos
Ibadan
NIGERIA
Abuja
Kano
Niamey
ALGERIA
Tanezrouft
Ahaggar
Tamanrasset
S a h a r a
LIBYA
Gulf of Sidra
Benghazi
EGYPT
LIBYAN DESERT
Asyût
Aswân
Lake Nasser
L. Nubia
Tibesti
Bodélé Depression
NIGER
CHAD
L. Chad
N'Djamena
S u d a n
Sarh
Benue
CAMEROON
Cameroon 13,350 ft. (4069 m.)
Malabo
Bioko
Yaoundé
EQUAT. GUINEA
SÃO TOMÉ E PRÍNCIPE
Libreville
Lopez
GABON
Annobón (Equat. Guinea)
GUINEA BASIN
Gulf of Guinea
Equator
CENTRAL AFRICAN REPUBLIC
Bangui
Ubangi
Bomu
Uele
Congo
ZAIRE
Mbandaka
Kisangani
Margherita 16,795 ft. Stanley Falls (5119 m.)
L. Mobutu Sese Seko
UGANDA
Kampala
RWANDA
Kigali
BURUNDI
Bujumbura
Bukavu
L. Victoria
KENYA
Kenya 17,058 ft. (5199 m.)
Nairobi
Kilimanjaro 19,340 ft. (5895 m.)
Mombasa
Pemba
Zanzibar
Dar es Salaam
TANZANIA
Lualaba
Lake Tanganyika
Katanga
Kananga
Kasai
Lulua
Kwango
Kwilu
Brazzaville
Kinshasa
CONGO CANYON
CABINDA (Angola)
ASCENSION FRACTURE ZONE
Ascension (St. Helena)
ATLANTIC OCEAN
ANGOLA
ANGOLA ABYSSAL PLAIN
BASIN
St. Helena (U.K.)
ST. HELENA FRACTURE ZONE
Luanda
Malange
ANGOLA
Huambo
Cuanza
Cubango
Lake Mweru
Lubumbashi
Kitwe
Katanga
Lake Mweru
ZAMBIA
Lusaka
Zambezi
MALAWI
Lilongwe
Lake Nyasa
Ruvuma
C. Delgado
COMOROS
Bobaomby
Lake Kariba
Livingstone
Victoria Falls
ZIMBABWE
Harare
Zomba
MOZAMBIQUE
Nampula
Beira
MOZAMBIQUE CHANNEL
MADAGASCAR
Toamasina
Antananarivo
MASCARENE PLAIN
AMIRANTE TRENCH
SOMALI BASIN
SOMALIA
Mogadishu
Ras Aser
Gulf of Aden
DJIBOUTI
Djibouti
YEMEN
Ethiopian Highlands
ETHIOPIA
Addis Ababa
Ras Dashan 15,157 ft. (4620 m.)
Asmara
Khartoum
El Obeid
El Fasher
SUDAN
Blue Nile
White Nile
Sobat
Juba
Turkana
Wabi Shebelle
Port Sudan
Nubian Desert
RED SEA
MID-ATLANTIC RIDGE
WALVIS RIDGE
C. Fria
Namib Desert
NAMIBIA
Etosha Pan
Windhoek
Walvis Bay (S. Afr.)
NAMIBIA ABYSSAL PLAIN
Tropic of Capricorn
Cunene
ROMANCHE FRACTURE ZONE
Equator
RIO GRANDE FRACTURE ZONE
Tristan da Cunha (St. Helena)
TRISTAN DA CUNHA FRACTURE ZONE
Gough I. (St. Helena)
ATLANTIC OCEAN
CAPE BASIN
Cape Town
C. of Good Hope
C. Agulhas
AGULHAS RIDGE
AGULHAS PLATEAU
Great Karoo
SOUTH AFRICA
Port Elizabeth
East London
Durban
Drakensberg
Maseru
LESOTHO
Orange
Vaal
Johannesburg
Pretoria
Gaborone
BOTSWANA
Kalahari Desert
Makgadikgadi Salt Pan
Bulawayo
Limpopo
Maputo
Mbabane
SWAZILAND
CONTINENTAL SHELF
Namib Desert
MOZAMBIQUE PLATEAU
MOZAMBIQUE BASIN
MADAGASCAR RIDGE
MADAGASCAR
C. Vohimena
MADAGASCAR BASIN
INDIAN OCEAN
SOUTHWEST INDIAN RIDGE

© Copyright by HAMMOND INCORPORATED, Maplewood, N.J.

Plate 11 | AFRICA

0   200   400   600   800   1000 MILES
0   200 400 600 800 1000 KILOMETERS

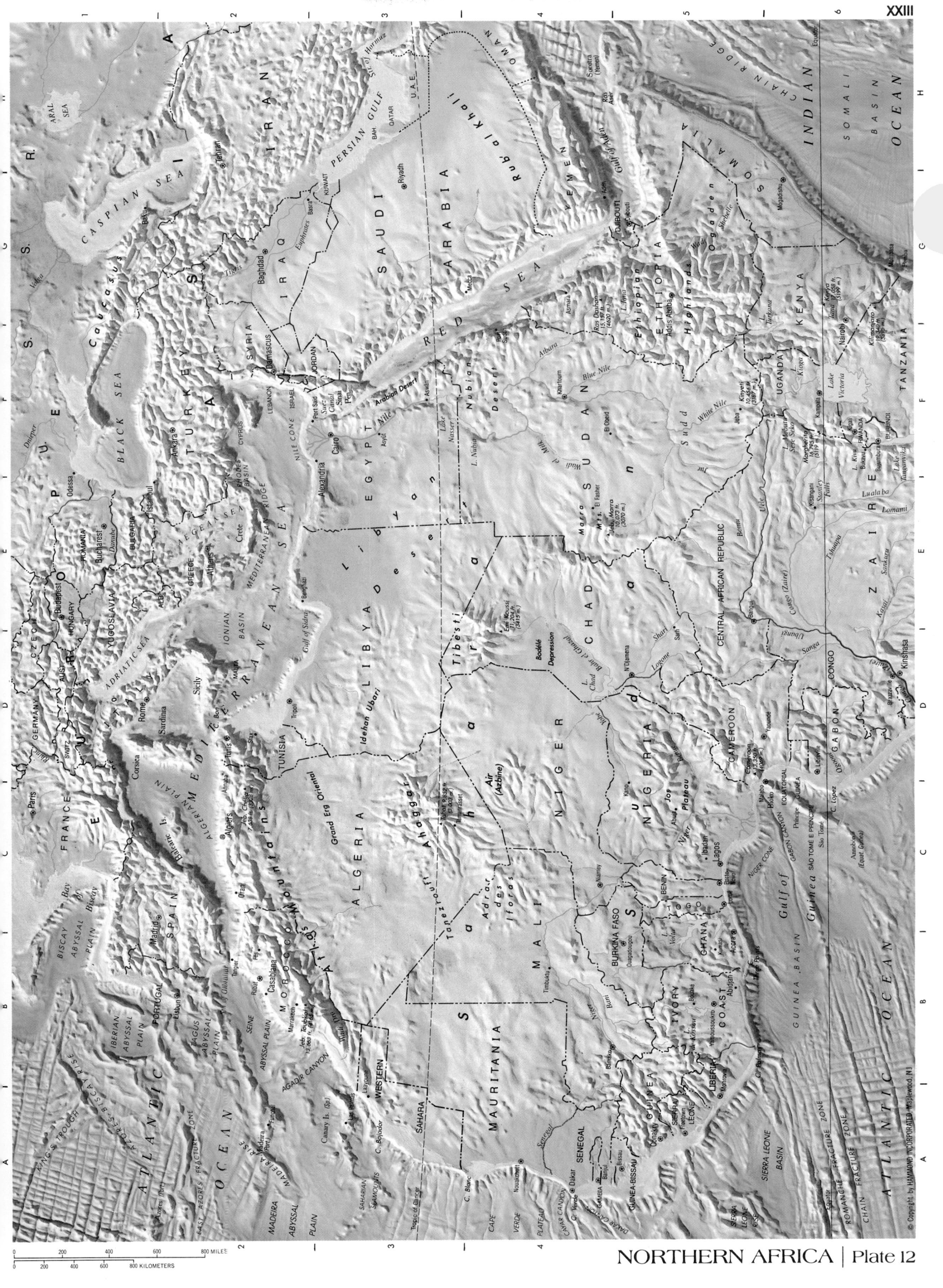

NORTHERN AFRICA | Plate 12

0   200   400   600   800 MILES
0   200   400   600   800 KILOMETERS

© Copyright by HAMMOND INCORPORATED, Maplewood, N.J.

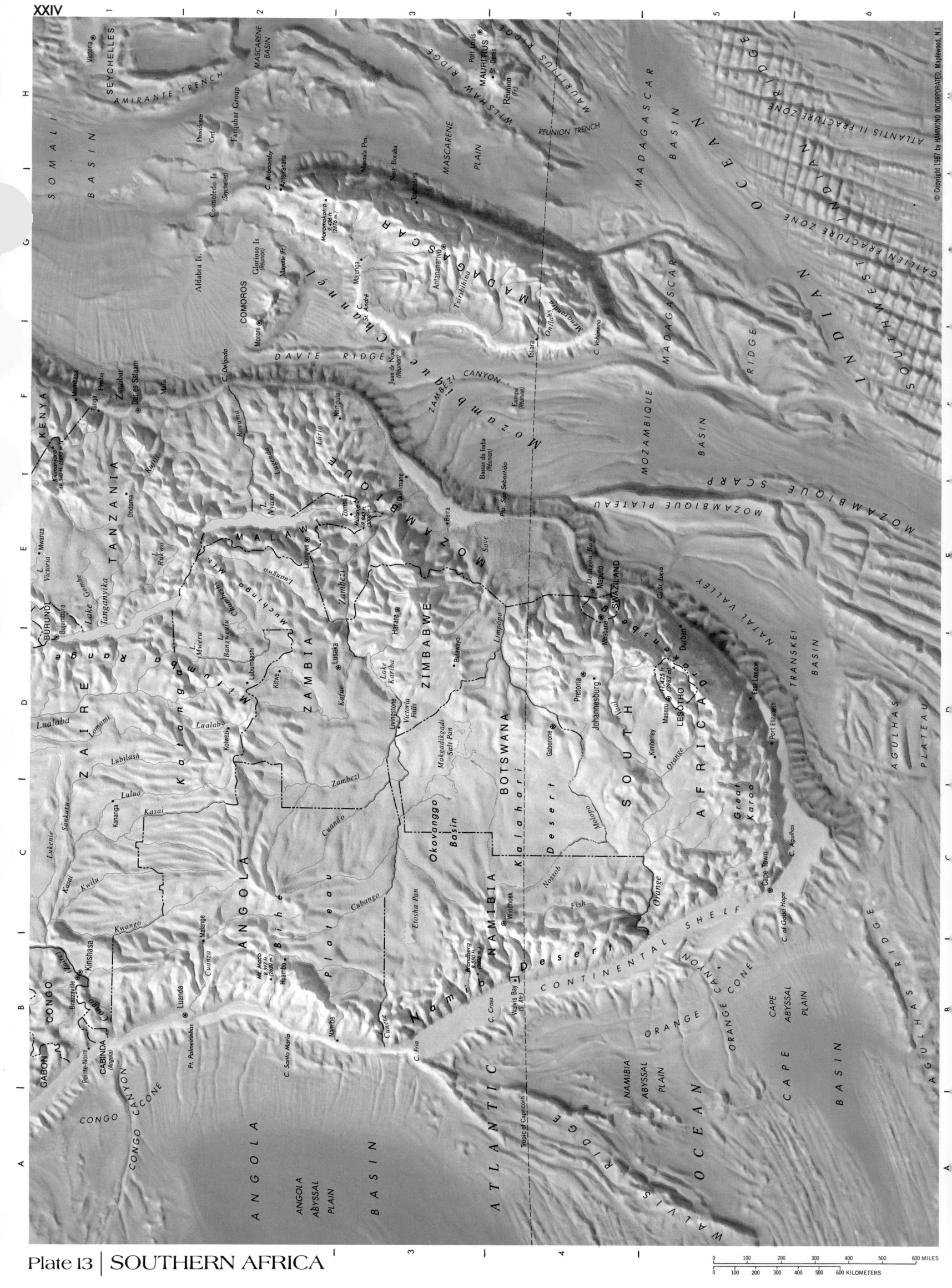

Plate 13 | SOUTHERN AFRICA

| 0 | 100 | 200 | 300 | 400 | 500 | 600 MILES |
| 0 | 100 | 200 | 300 | 400 | 500 | 600 KILOMETERS |

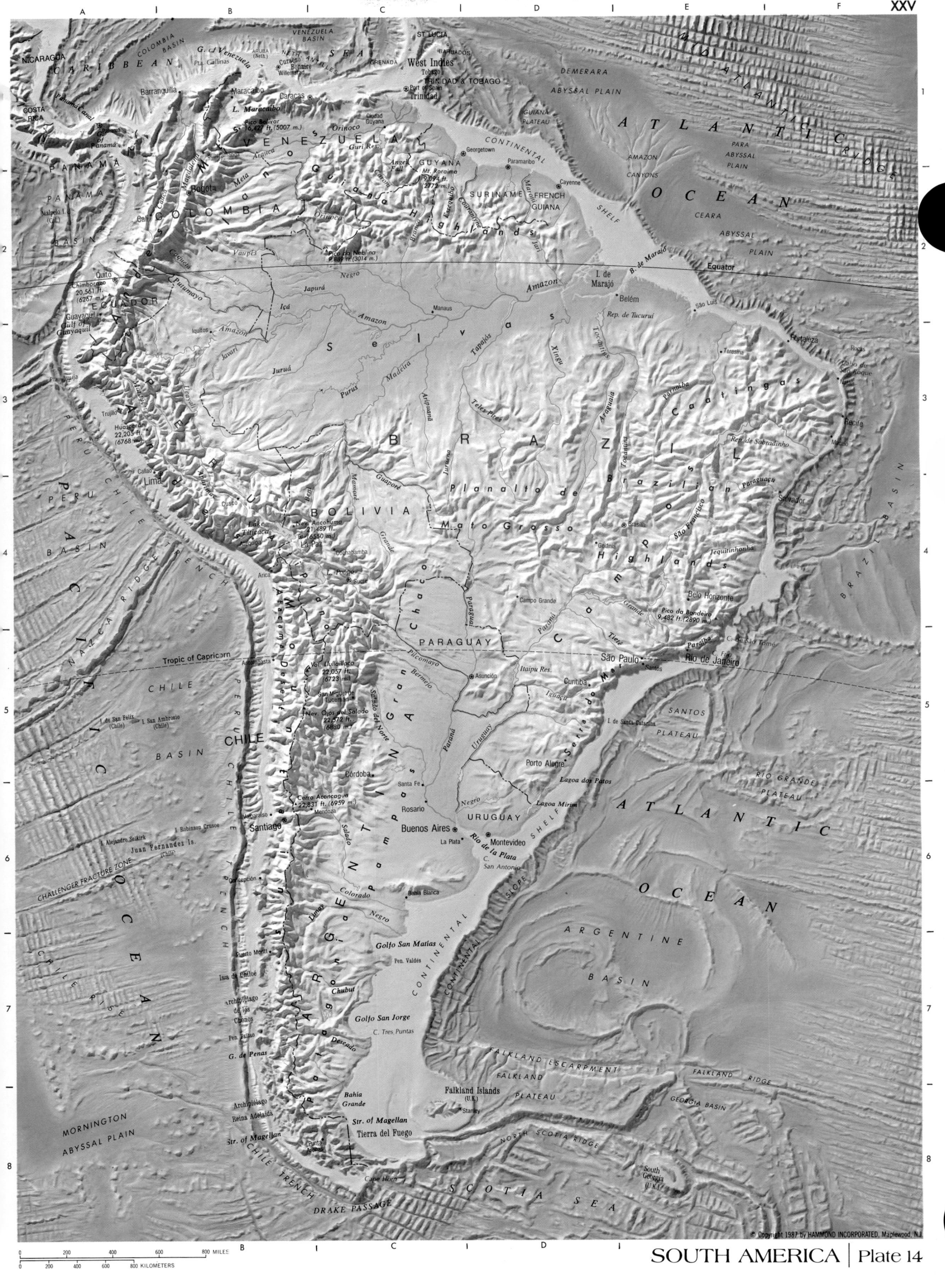

SOUTH AMERICA | Plate 14

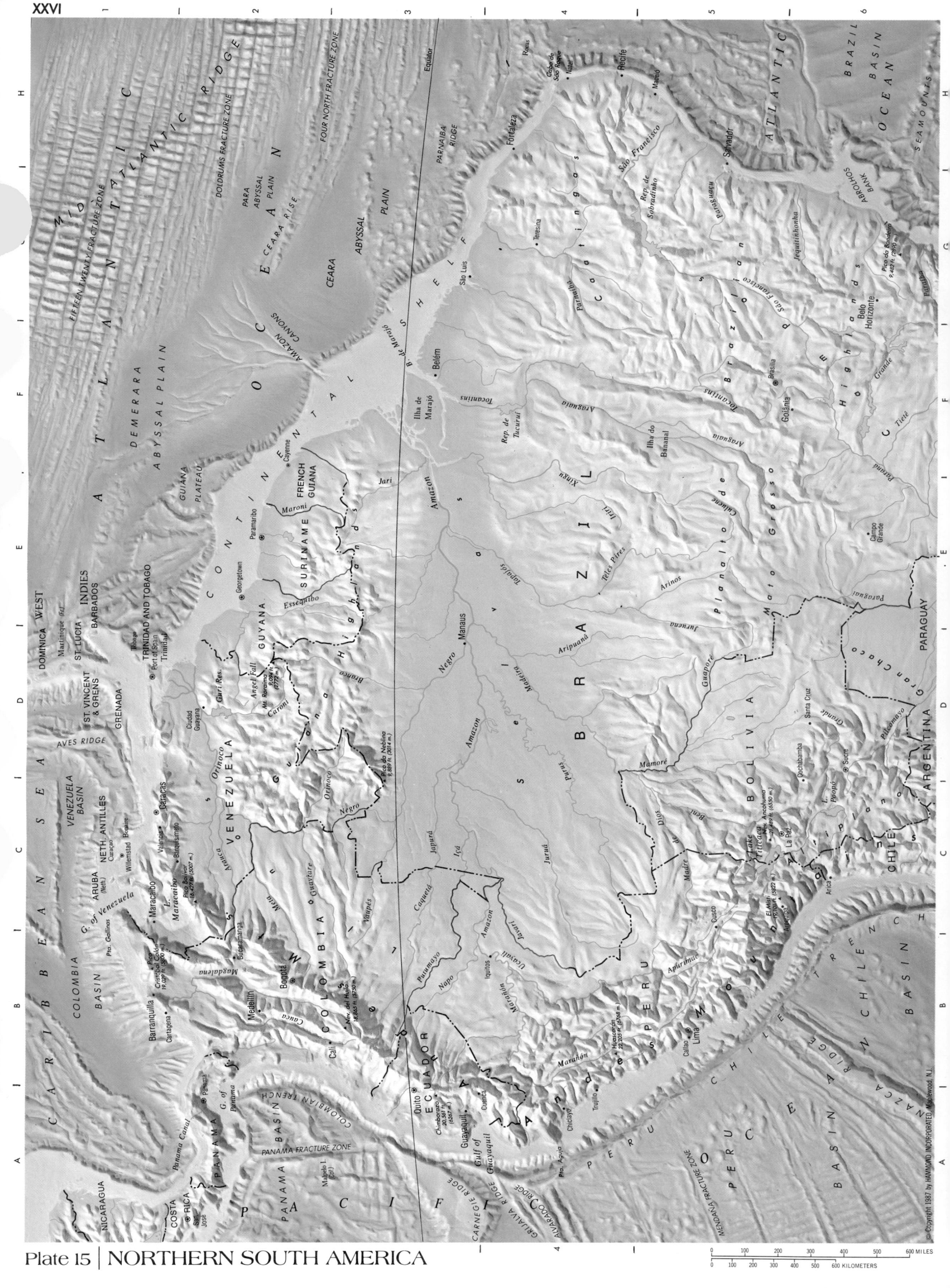

Plate 15 | NORTHERN SOUTH AMERICA

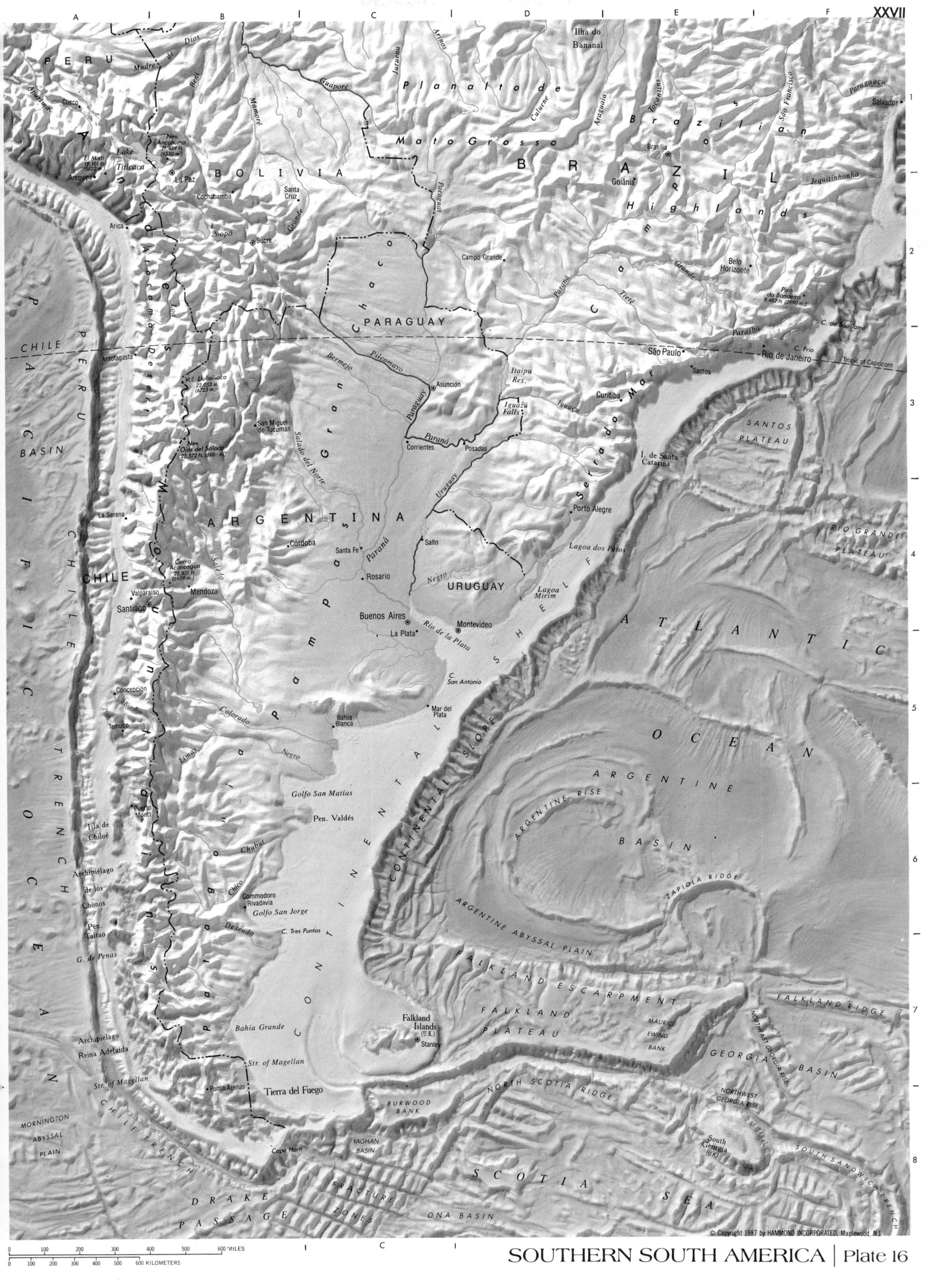

PERU

Dios
Madre de
Apurímac
Cusco
El Misti
19,101 ft.
(5822 m.)
Arequipa
Nev. Ancohuma
21,489 ft.
(6550 m.)
Lake
Titicaca
La Paz
Cochabamba

BOLIVIA
Santa Cruz
Grande
Sucre
Poopó

Arica

Beni
Mamoré
Guaporé

Planalto de

Mato Grosso

Ilha do
Bananal

Juruena
Araguaia

Paraguai

Brasília
Goiânia

B R A Z I L

Jequitinhonha
Salvador
Paraguaçu

Campo Grande

PARAGUAY
Asunción

Itaipú
Res.
Iguazú
Falls
Iguaçu
Paraná

Grande
Tietê

São Francisco

Belo
Horizonte
Pico
da Bandeira
9,482 ft. (2890 m.)
C. de São Tomé

São Paulo
Santos
Curitiba
I. de Santa
Catarina

Rio de Janeiro
C. Frio
Tropic of Capricorn

CHILE
PERU

Antofagasta

Vol. Llullaillaco
22,057 ft.
(6723 m.)

San Miguel
de Tucumán

Nev.
Ojos del Salado
22,572 ft. (6880 m.)

Salado del Norte

PACIFIC

BASIN

PERU

CHILE TRENCH

La Serena

Cerro
Aconcagua
22,831 ft.
(6959 m.)

Córdoba
Santa Fe

Rosario

Salto

Paraná

Negro

URUGUAY

Lagoa dos Patos

Porto Alegre

Serra do Mar

SANTOS
PLATEAU

RIO GRANDE
PLATEAU

A R G E N T I N A

Valparaíso
Santiago
Mendoza

Buenos Aires
La Plata

Montevideo

Río de la Plata

C.
San Antonio

Lagoa
Mirim

A T L A N T I C

Concepción
Bío-Bío
Temuco

Colorado

Negro
Limay

Golfo San Matías

Pen. Valdés

Bahía
Blanca

Mar del
Plata

O C E A N

ARGENTINE

BASIN

Puerto
Montt
Isla de
Chiloé

Archipiélago
de los
Chonos
Pen.
Taitao

G. de Penas

Chubut

Chico
Deseado

Commodoro
Rivadavia

Golfo San Jorge

C. Tres Puntas

CONTINENTAL SLOPE

CONTINENTAL

SHELF

ARGENTINE RISE

ZAPIOLA RIDGE

ARGENTINE ABYSSAL PLAIN

FALKLAND ESCARPMENT

FALKLAND
PLATEAU

MAURICE
EWING
BANK

FALKLAND RIDGE

NORTHEAST GEORGIA RISE

GEORGIA BASIN

Archipiélago
Reina Adelaida

Bahía Grande

Falkland
Islands
(U.K.)
Stanley

Str. of Magellan

Str. of Magellan

Punta Arenas

Tierra del Fuego

BURWOOD
BANK

NORTH SCOTIA RIDGE

NORTHWEST
GEORGIA RISE

South
Georgia
(U.K.)

SOUTH SANDWICH TRENCH

MORNINGTON
ABYSSAL
PLAIN

CHILE TRENCH

Cape Horn

YAGHAN
BASIN

S C O T I A   S E A

DRAKE
PASSAGE

FRACTURE
ZONES

ONA BASIN

© Copyright 1987 by HAMMOND INCORPORATED, Maplewood, N.J.

0   100   200   300   400   500   600 MILES
0   100   200   300   400   500   600 KILOMETERS

SOUTHERN SOUTH AMERICA | Plate 16

Plate 17 | NORTH AMERICA

ICELAND BASIN

ICELAND

Reykjavik

REYKJANES RIDGE

IRMINGER BASIN

OCEAN

DENMARK STRAIT

C. Farewell

Arctic Circle

GREENLAND
(Denmark)

Nuuk

DAVIS STRAIT

BAFFIN BAY

Disko Island

Baffin Island

LABRADOR BASIN

ATLANTIC

CONTINENTAL SHELF

GRAND BANKS OF NEWFOUNDLAND

C. Race
St. John's

Newfoundland

NOVA SCOTIA

Cape Breton I.

Sable I.

C. Sable

Halifax

Gulf of St. Lawrence

Ile d'Anticosti

P.E.I.

Charlottetown

NEW BR.

Fredericton

Saint John

Bay of Fundy

C. Cod

Boston

New York

Philadelphia

Pittsburgh

Hudson

Québec

L. St-Jean

Peribonca

Montréal

Ottawa

L. Ontario

Niagara Falls

Toronto

Hamilton

L. Erie

Cleveland

Detroit
Windsor

Lake Huron

Georgian Bay

Sudbury

Timmins

L. Nipigon

Sault Ste. Marie

Lake Superior

Thunder Bay

Lake Michigan

Milwaukee

Chicago

Minneapolis

Mississippi

Missouri

L. of the Woods

Winnipeg

Brandon

Lake Winnipeg

Red

Regina

L. Manitoba

Swift Current

Saskatoon

Prince Albert

Lethbridge

Calgary

Edmonton

Bow

Athabasca

L. Athabasca

Sask.

S. Sask.

Churchill

Reindeer L.

So. Indian L.

Nelson

Churchill

Rankin Inlet

HUDSON BAY

MANITOBA

SASKATCHEWAN

NORTHWEST TERRITORIES

ALBERTA

Great Slave Lake

Yellowknife

Great Bear Lake

Coppermine

Mackenzie

Inuvik

Hay

Liard

Ft. Nelson

Peace

BEAUFORT SEA

BEAUFORT SHELF

Pt. Barrow

Brooks Range

UNITED STATES

ALASKA

Fairbanks

Tanana

Mt. McKinley
20,320 ft.
(6194 m)

Alaska Range

Yukon

CHUKCHI SEA

USSR

Bering Strait

Nome

ARCTIC OCEAN

BASIN

CANADA BASIN

NORTHWIND RIDGE

QUEEN ELIZABETH ISLANDS

C. Columbia

Axel Heiberg Island

Ellesmere Island

Ellef Ringnes I.

N. Mag. Pole

Melville I.

Bathurst I.

Prince Patrick I.

Banks Island

Amundsen Gulf

Victoria Island

Cambridge Bay

M'Clintock Chan.

Pr. of Wales I.

Parry Channel

Devon I.

Brodeur Pen.

Somerset I.

Boothia Pen.

Gulf of Boothia

Bylot I.

Cumberland Sd.

Cumberland Pen.

Frobisher Bay

C. Chidley

Foxe Basin

Foxe Pen.

Pr. Charles I.

Melville Pen.

Southampton I.

Coats I.

Mansel I.

Belcher Is.

Ungava Bay

Ungava Peninsula

Hudson Strait

Koksoak

Labrador

Smallwood Res.

Churchill

Goose Bay

La Grande

Rupert

Mistassini

Caniapiscau

L. Mistassini

QUÉBEC
ONTARIO

Rouyn

Abitibi

Akimiski I.

James Bay

Albany

Severn

Kazan

Dubawnt

Back

Thelon

Peel

Pelly

YUKON TERRITORY

BRITISH COLUMBIA

Whitehorse

Teslin

Stikine

Skeena

Nass

Prince Rupert

Queen Charlotte Is.

Queen Charlotte Sd.

Alexander Archipelago

Gulf of Alaska

PACIFIC OCEAN

C. Mendocino

Great Salt Lake

Snake

Columbia

Yellowstone

Missouri

UNITED STATES

Rocky Mountains

Coast Mts.

Fraser

Williston L.

Columbia

Kootenay

Prince George

Vancouver

Vancouver I.

Victoria

C. Flattery

Seattle

Portland

Coast Ranges

CASCADE RANGE

BASIN

Laurentian Upland

Laurentian Mountains

LABRADOR

0   100   200   300   400   500   600 MILES

0   100   200   300   400   500   600 KILOMETERS

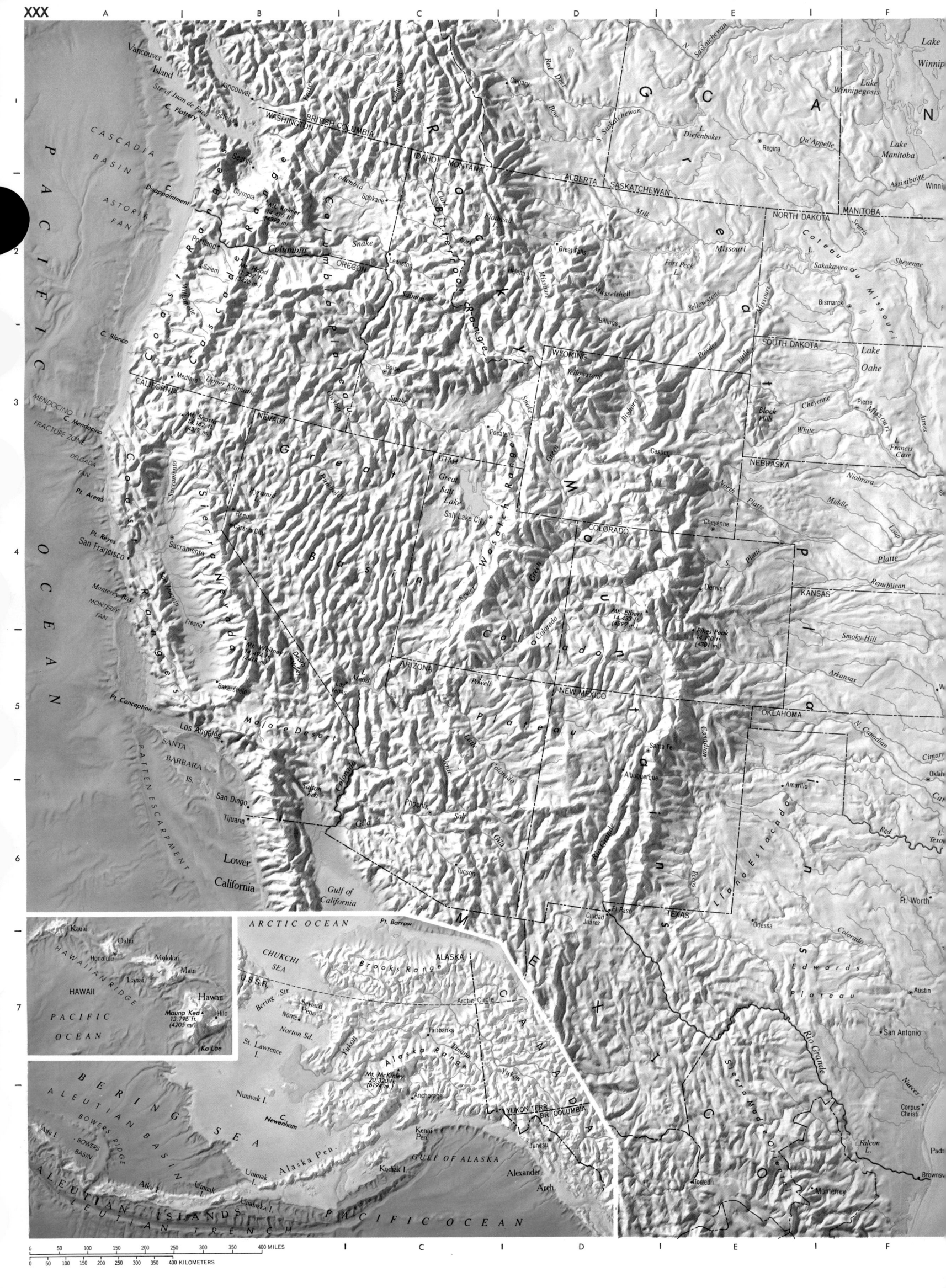

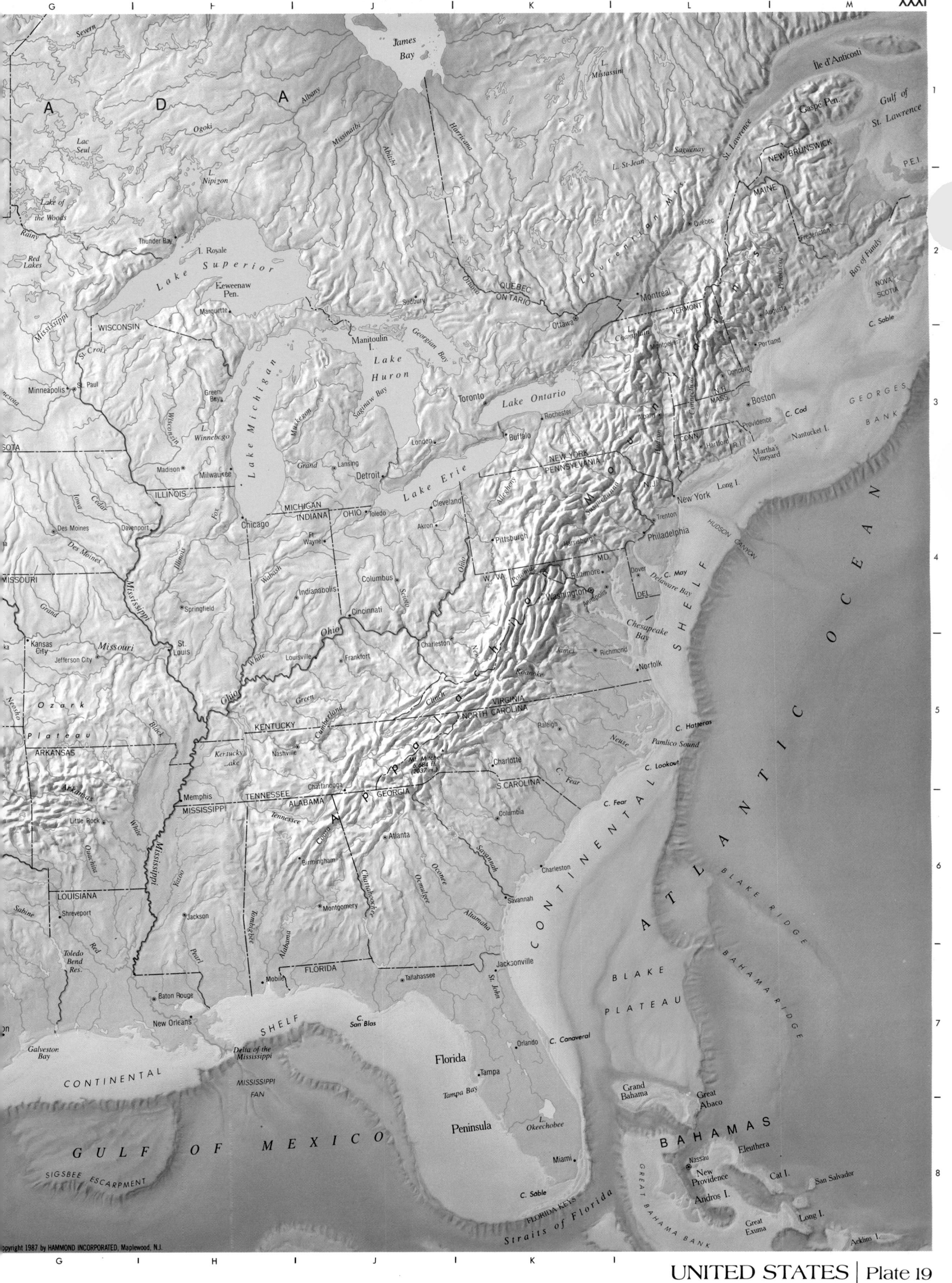

UNITED STATES | Plate 19

Plate 20 | MIDDLE AMERICA

| 0 | 100 | 200 | 300 | 400 | 500 | 600 MILES |
| 0 | 100 | 200 | 300 | 400 | 500 | 600 KILOMETERS |

GLOBAL RELATIONSHIPS

Contents

T-1   World–Structure
T-2   The Geologic Record
T-4   World–Climate
T-6   World–Vegetation and Soils
T-8   World–Population

T-10 World–Languages and Religions
T-12 World–Standards of Living
T-14 World–Agriculture and Fishing
T-16 World–Energy
T-18 World–Mineral Resources

T-20 World–Production: Agricultural Commodities
T-21 World–Production: Metals and Nonmetals
T-22 World–Transportation
T-23 World–Air Distances and Time Zones
T-24 World–Global Politics

GLO
REL

Plate Tectonics

Eurasian Plate · Arabian Plate · Philippine Plate · Pacific Plate · Juan de Fuca Plate · North American Plate · Caribbean Plate · Cocos Plate · Nazca Plate · South American Plate · African Plate · Indo-Australian Plate · Antarctic Plate · Scotia Plate

Kuril-Kamchatka Trench · Japan Trench · Ryukyu Trench · Mariana Trench · Philippine Trench · Java Trench · New Hebrides Trench · Tonga Trench · Kermadec Trench · Aleutian Trench · San Andreas Fault · Peru-Chile Trench · North Scotia Ridge · South Sandwich Trench

Reykjanes Ridge · Mid-Atlantic Ridge · Mid Atlantic Ridge · Carlsberg Ridge · Central Indian Ridge · Southwest Indian Ridge · Southeast Indian Ridge · Pacific Rise · East Pacific Rise · Pacific-Antarctic Ridge

Arctic Circle · Tropic of Cancer · Equator · Tropic of Capricorn

Plate Boundary ————
Uncertain Boundary – – – –
Direction of Plate Movement ——→

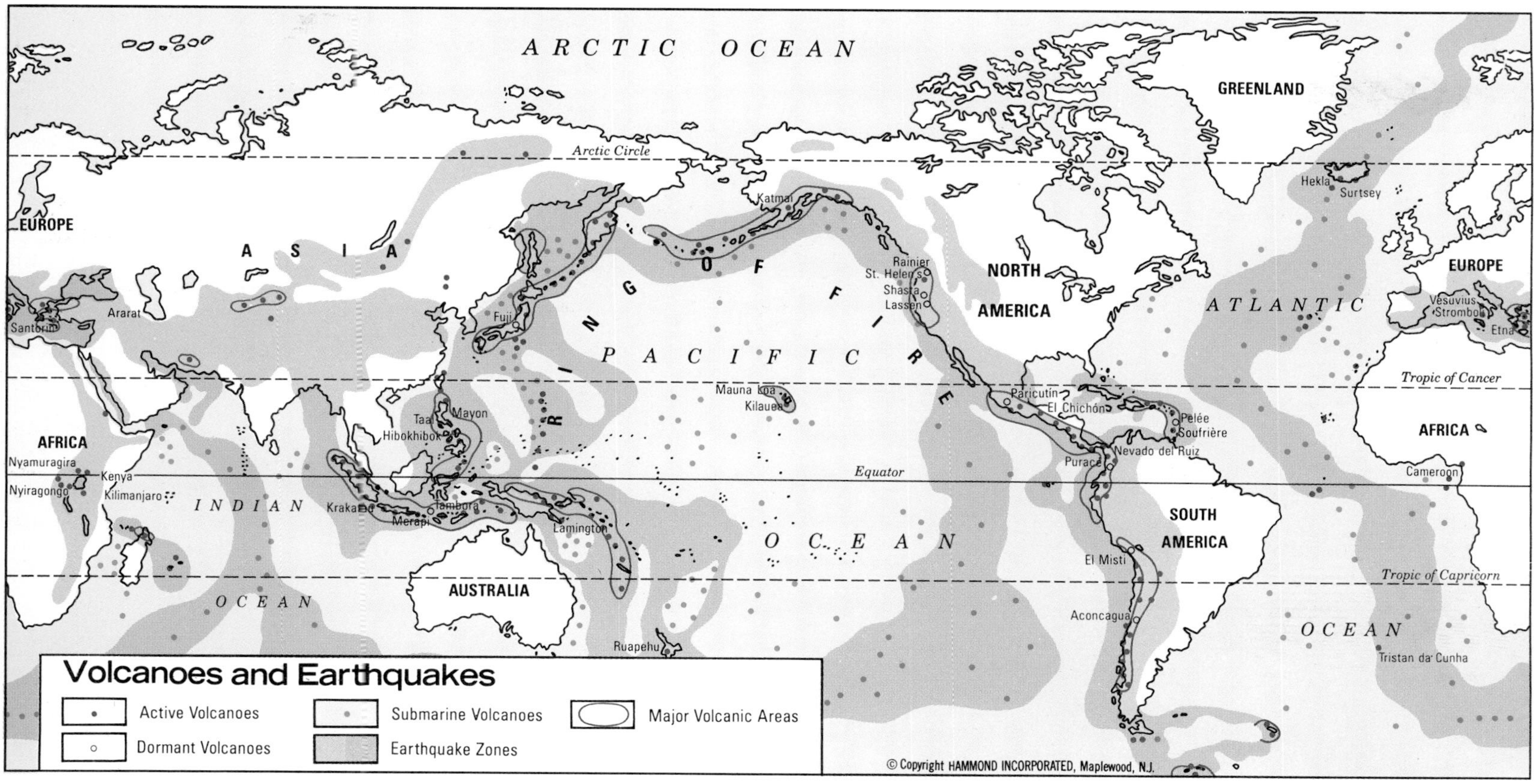

© Copyright HAMMOND INCORPORATED, Maplewood, N.J.

Volcanoes and Earthquakes

ARCTIC OCEAN · GREENLAND · EUROPE · ASIA · NORTH AMERICA · ATLANTIC · AFRICA · INDIAN OCEAN · PACIFIC OCEAN · AUSTRALIA · SOUTH AMERICA · RING OF FIRE

Hekla · Surtsey · Katmai · Rainier · St. Helens · Shasta · Lassen · Fuji · Mauna Loa · Kilauea · Taal · Mayon · Hibokhibok · Paricutin · El Chichón · Pelée · Soufrière · Nevado del Ruiz · Puracé · Vesuvius · Stromboli · Etna · Ararat · Santorini · Nyamuragira · Nyiragongo · Kenya · Kilimanjaro · Krakatoa · Tambora · Merapi · Lamington · Cameroon · El Misti · Aconcagua · Ruapehu · Tristan da Cunha

Arctic Circle · Tropic of Cancer · Equator · Tropic of Capricorn

• Active Volcanoes
○ Dormant Volcanoes
• Submarine Volcanoes
◯ Major Volcanic Areas
▒ Earthquake Zones

© Copyright HAMMOND INCORPORATED, Maplewood, N.J.

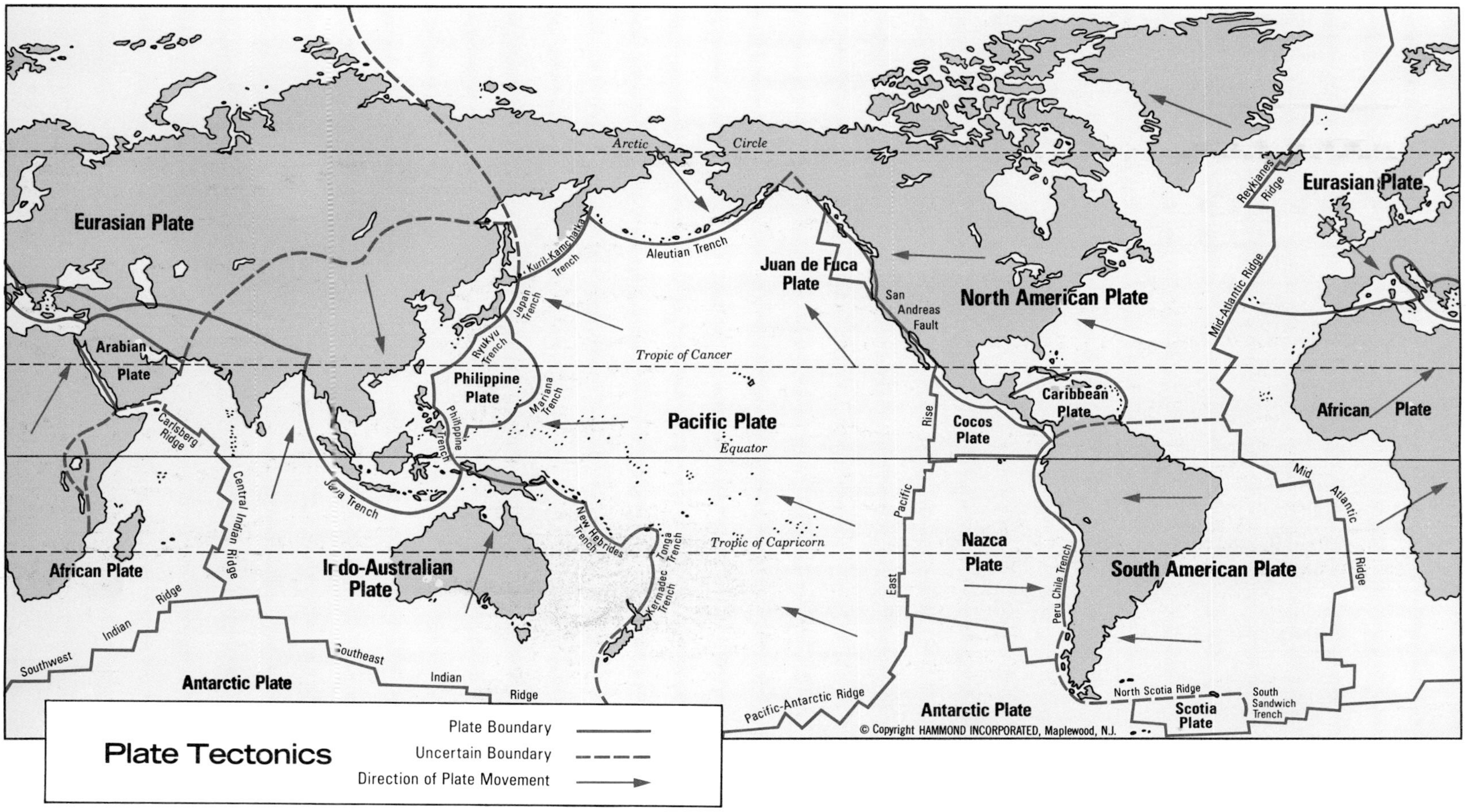

Geologic Time

TIME DIVISION			YEARS AGO	MAJOR GEOLOGIC DEVELOPMENTS
CENOZOIC ERA	QUATERNARY PERIOD	RECENT	10,000	GREAT LAKES NORWEGIAN FJORDS ICE AGES BLACK SEA CASPIAN SEA
CENOZOIC ERA	QUATERNARY PERIOD	PLEISTOCENE	1-2 million	
CENOZOIC ERA	TERTIARY PERIOD	PLIOCENE	11 million	
CENOZOIC ERA	TERTIARY PERIOD	MIOCENE	25 million	HIMALAYAS
CENOZOIC ERA	TERTIARY PERIOD	OLIGOCENE	40 million	ALPS
CENOZOIC ERA	TERTIARY PERIOD	EOCENE	60 million	
CENOZOIC ERA	TERTIARY PERIOD	PALEOCENE	70 million	ANDES MOUNTAINS ROCKY MOUNTAINS CHALK DEPOSITS
MESOZOIC ERA		CRETACEOUS PERIOD	135 million	COAST RANGES SIERRA NEVADA JURA MOUNTAINS
MESOZOIC ERA		JURASSIC PERIOD	180 million	NEW JERSEY PALISADES
MESOZOIC ERA		TRIASSIC PERIOD	225 million	CAUCASUS URAL MOUNTAINS APPALACHIAN MOUNTAINS
PALEOZOIC ERA		PERMIAN PERIOD	270 million	POTASH DEPOSITS
PALEOZOIC ERA		PENNSYLVANIAN PERIOD	300 million	COAL DEPOSITS
PALEOZOIC ERA		MISSISSIPPIAN PERIOD	350 million	ACADIAN MOUNTAINS
PALEOZOIC ERA		DEVONIAN PERIOD	400 million	
PALEOZOIC ERA		SILURIAN PERIOD	440 million	NIAGARA FALLS CAPROCK TACONIC MOUNTAINS
PALEOZOIC ERA		ORDOVICIAN PERIOD	500 million	LIMESTONE DEPOSITS VERMONT MOUNTAINS
PALEOZOIC ERA		CAMBRIAN PERIOD	600 million	ARIZONA MOUNTAINS
		PRE-CAMBRIAN		METALLIC ORE DEPOSITS LAURENTIAN MOUNTAINS ADIRONDACK MOUNTAINS

© Copyright HAMMOND INCORPORATED, Maplewood, N.J

Continental Drift

225 Million Years Ago

180 Million Years Ago

70 Million Years Ago

Present Time

→ Continuing Evolution
⊣ Point of Extinction

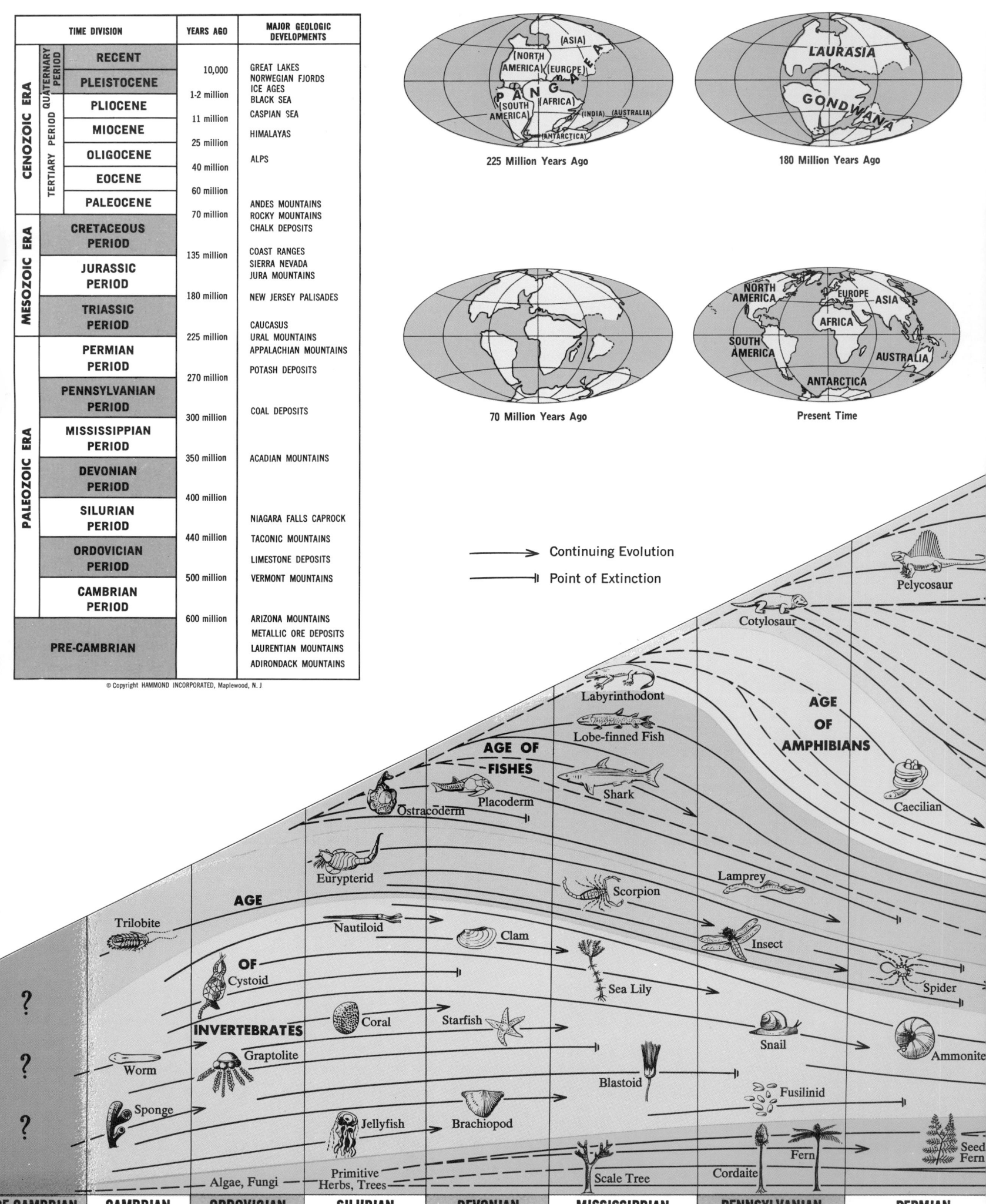

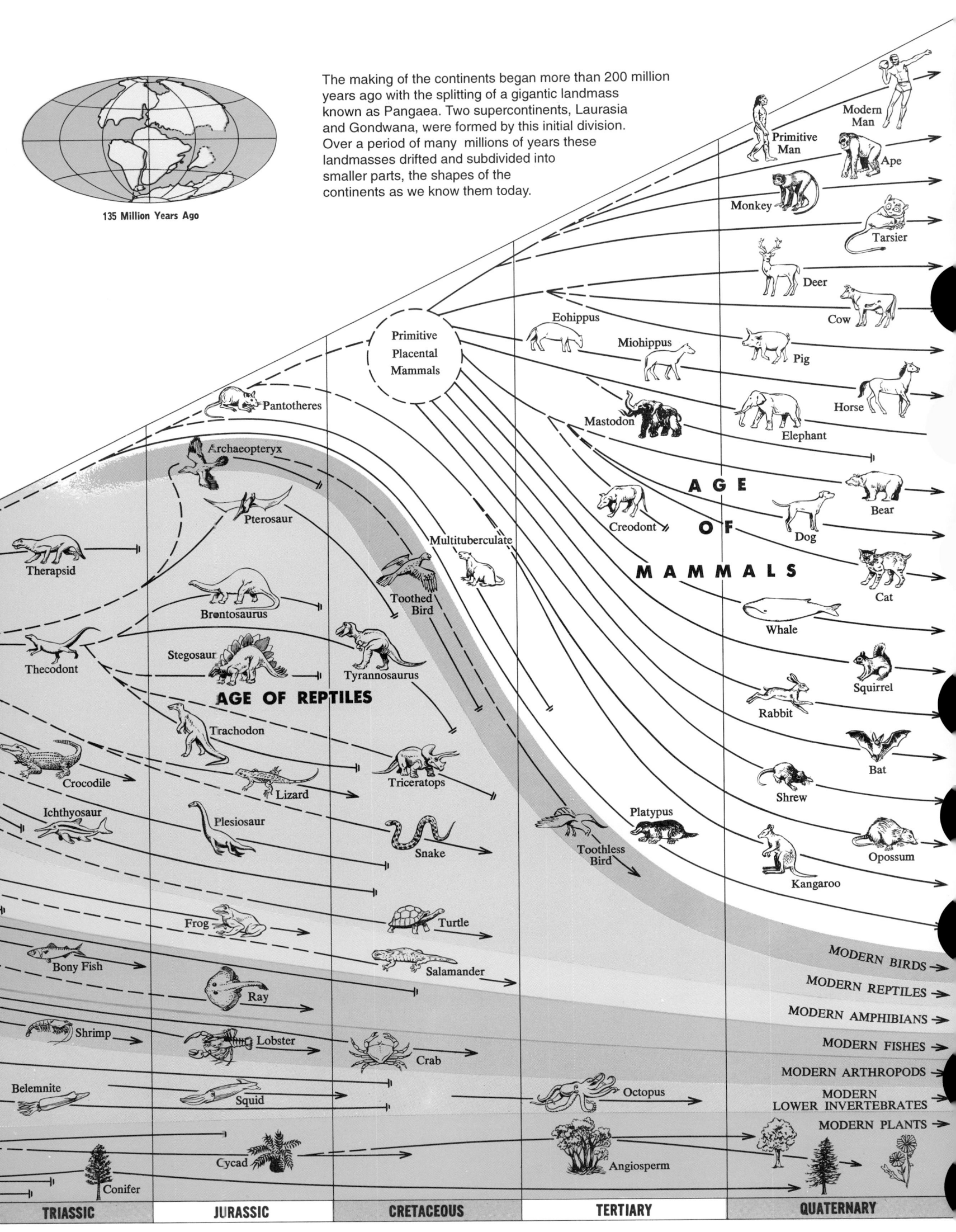

The making of the continents began more than 200 million years ago with the splitting of a gigantic landmass known as Pangaea. Two supercontinents, Laurasia and Gondwana, were formed by this initial division. Over a period of many millions of years these landmasses drifted and subdivided into smaller parts, the shapes of the continents as we know them today.

135 Million Years Ago

Modern Man

Primitive Man

Ape

Monkey

Tarsier

Deer

Cow

Eohippus

Miohippus

Pig

Horse

Primitive Placental Mammals

Mastodon

Elephant

Pantotheres

Archaeopteryx

A G E

Pterosaur

Creodont

Bear

O F

Dog

Multituberculate

M A M M A L S

Cat

Therapsid

Brontosaurus

Toothed Bird

Whale

Stegosaur

Tyrannosaurus

Thecodont

AGE OF REPTILES

Squirrel

Trachodon

Rabbit

Crocodile

Triceratops

Bat

Lizard

Platypus

Ichthyosaur

Shrew

Plesiosaur

Snake

Toothless Bird

Opossum

Kangaroo

Frog

Turtle

MODERN BIRDS

Salamander

MODERN REPTILES

Bony Fish

MODERN AMPHIBIANS

Ray

MODERN FISHES

Shrimp

Lobster

MODERN ARTHROPODS

Crab

MODERN LOWER INVERTEBRATES

Belemnite

Squid

Octopus

MODERN PLANTS

Cycad

Angiosperm

Conifer

| TRIASSIC | JURASSIC | CRETACEOUS | TERTIARY | QUATERNARY |

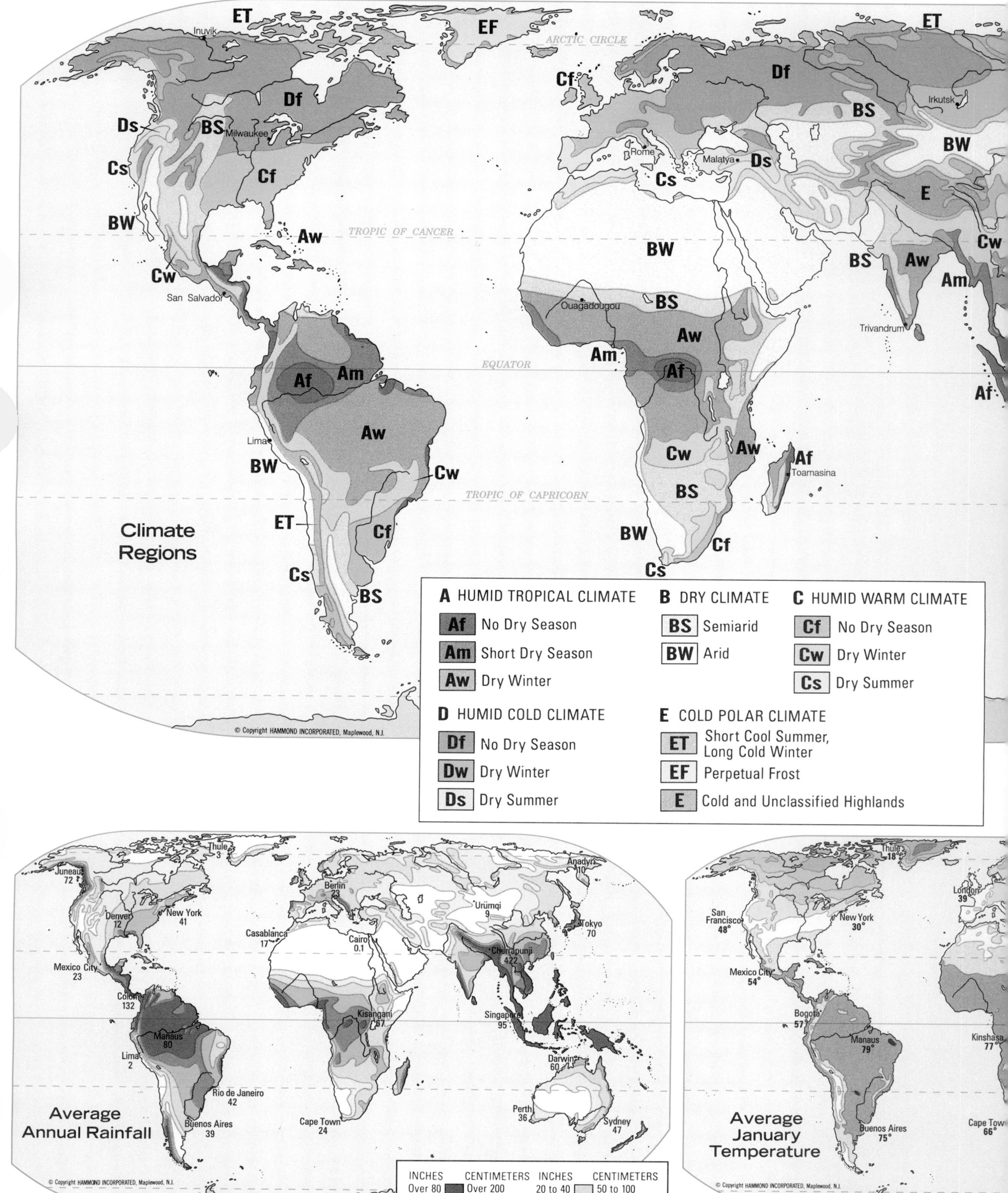

Climate Regions

© Copyright HAMMOND INCORPORATED, Maplewood, N.J.

A HUMID TROPICAL CLIMATE
- **Af** No Dry Season
- **Am** Short Dry Season
- **Aw** Dry Winter

B DRY CLIMATE
- **BS** Semiarid
- **BW** Arid

C HUMID WARM CLIMATE
- **Cf** No Dry Season
- **Cw** Dry Winter
- **Cs** Dry Summer

D HUMID COLD CLIMATE
- **Df** No Dry Season
- **Dw** Dry Winter
- **Ds** Dry Summer

E COLD POLAR CLIMATE
- **ET** Short Cool Summer, Long Cold Winter
- **EF** Perpetual Frost
- **E** Cold and Unclassified Highlands

Average Annual Rainfall

© Copyright HAMMOND INCORPORATED, Maplewood, N.J.

INCHES	CENTIMETERS	INCHES	CENTIMETERS
Over 80	Over 200	20 to 40	50 to 100
60 to 80	150 to 200	10 to 20	25 to 50
40 to 60	100 to 150	Under 10	Under 25

Average January Temperature

© Copyright HAMMOND INCORPORATED, Maplewood, N.J.

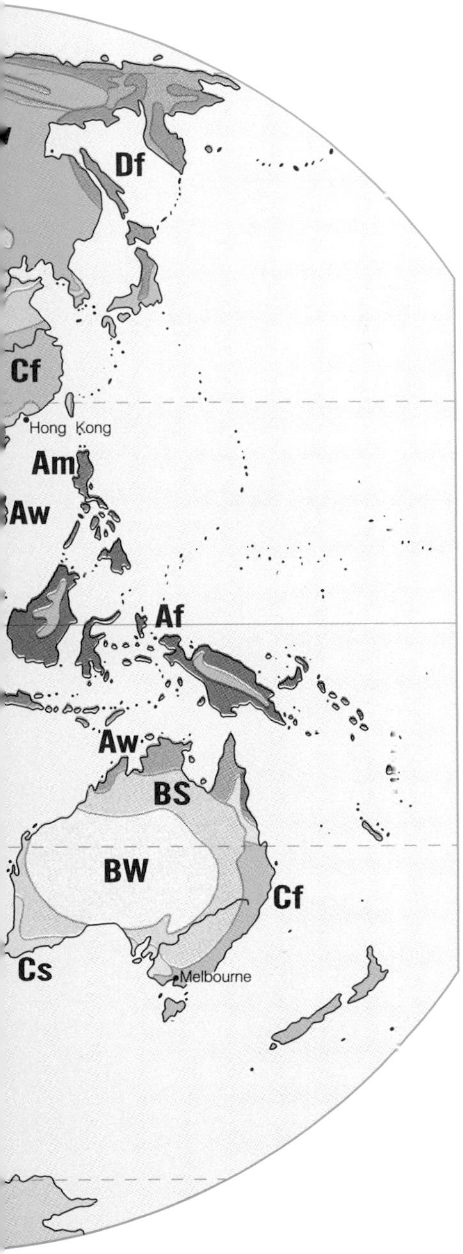

Selected Climate Stations

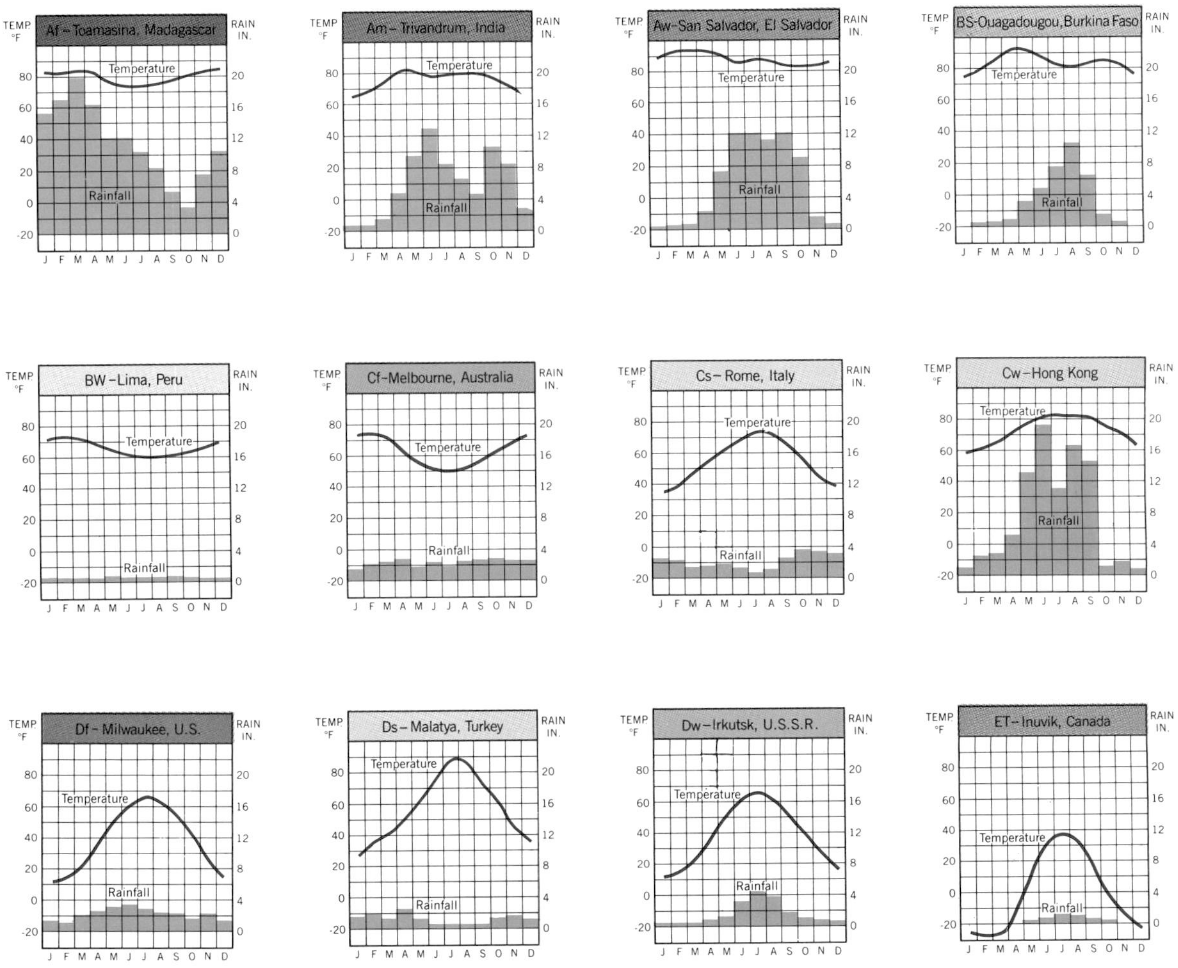

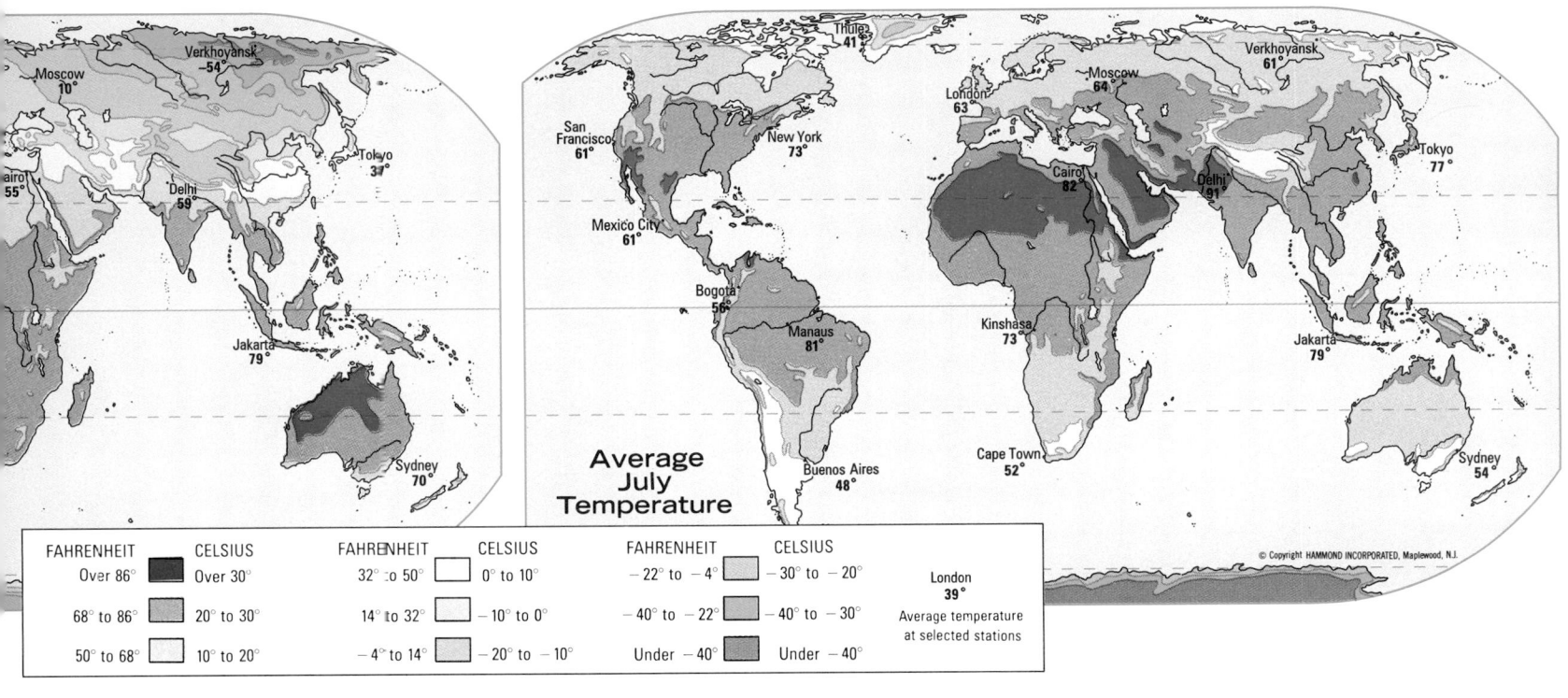

Af – Toamasina, Madagascar
TEMP °F — Temperature — RAIN IN.
Rainfall
J F M A M J J A S O N D

Am – Trivandrum, India
TEMP °F — Temperature — RAIN IN.
Rainfall
J F M A M J J A S O N D

Aw – San Salvador, El Salvador
TEMP °F — Temperature — RAIN IN.
Rainfall
J F M A M J J A S O N D

BS – Ouagadougou, Burkina Faso
TEMP °F — Temperature — RAIN IN.
Rainfall
J F M A M J J A S O N D

BW – Lima, Peru
TEMP °F — Temperature — RAIN IN.
Rainfall
J F M A M J J A S O N D

Cf – Melbourne, Australia
TEMP °F — Temperature — RAIN IN.
Rainfall
J F M A M J J A S O N D

Cs – Rome, Italy
TEMP °F — Temperature — RAIN IN.
Rainfall
J F M A M J J A S O N D

Cw – Hong Kong
TEMP °F — Temperature — RAIN IN.
Rainfall
J F M A M J J A S O N D

Df – Milwaukee, U.S.
TEMP °F — Temperature — RAIN IN.
Rainfall
J F M A M J J A S O N D

Ds – Malatya, Turkey
TEMP °F — Temperature — RAIN IN.
Rainfall
J F M A M J J A S O N D

Dw – Irkutsk, U.S.S.R.
TEMP °F — Temperature — RAIN IN.
Rainfall
J F M A M J J A S O N D

ET – Inuvik, Canada
TEMP °F — Temperature — RAIN IN.
Rainfall
J F M A M J J A S O N D

Df
Cf
Hong Kong
Am
Aw
Af
Aw
BS
BW
Cf
Cs
Melbourne

Moscow 10°
Verkhoyansk −54°
Tokyo 37°
Cairo 55°
Delhi 59°
Jakarta 79°
Sydney 70°

Thule 41°
Moscow 64°
Verkhoyansk 61°
London 63°
San Francisco 61°
New York 73°
Cairo 82°
Delhi 91°
Tokyo 77°
Mexico City 61°
Bogota 56°
Manaus 81°
Kinshasa 73°
Jakarta 79°
Cape Town 52°
Buenos Aires 48°
Sydney 54°

Average July Temperature

© Copyright HAMMOND INCORPORATED, Maplewood, N.J.

FAHRENHEIT	CELSIUS	FAHRENHEIT	CELSIUS	FAHRENHEIT	CELSIUS	
Over 86°	Over 30°	32° to 50°	0° to 10°	−22° to −4°	−30° to −20°	London 39°
68° to 86°	20° to 30°	14° to 32°	−10° to 0°	−40° to −22°	−40° to −30°	Average temperature at selected stations
50° to 68°	10° to 20°	−4° to 14°	−20° to −10°	Under −40°	Under −40°	

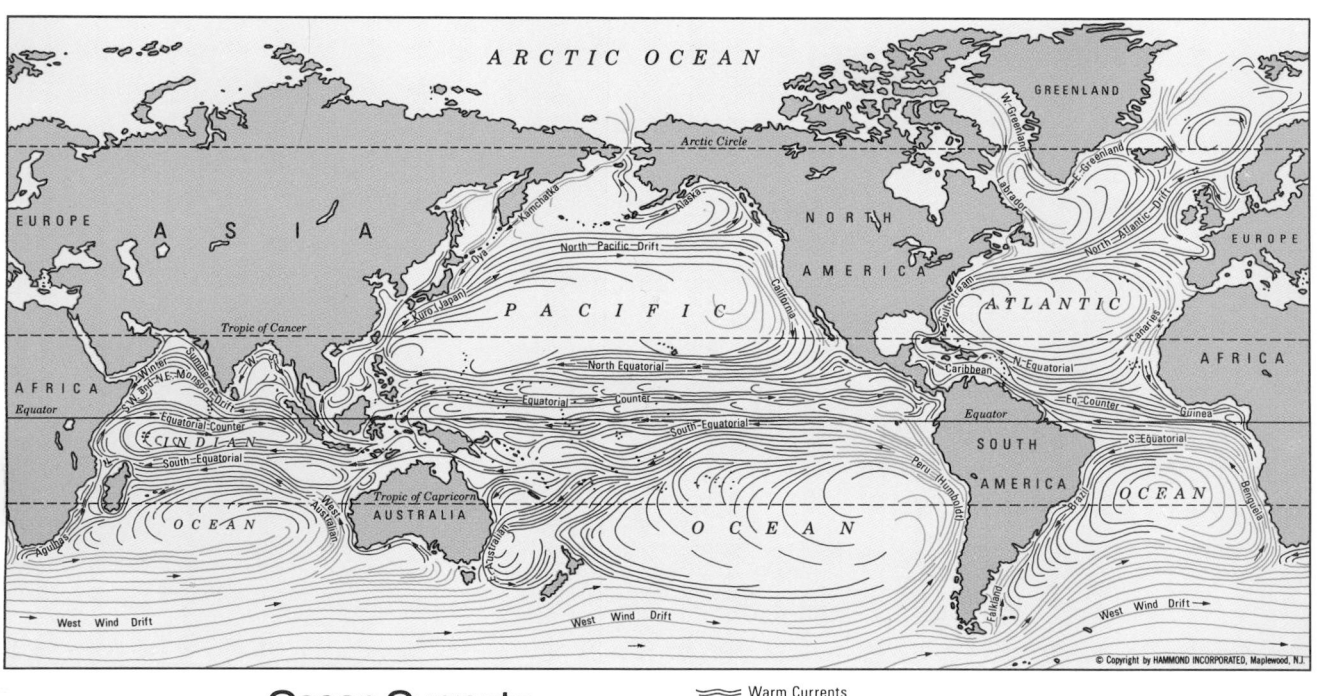

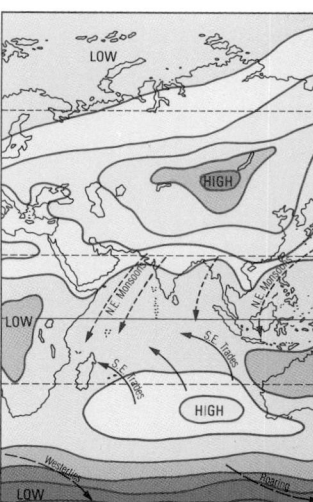

Ocean Currents

〰 Warm Currents
〰 Cold Currents
→ Direction of Flow

World—Vegetation and Soils

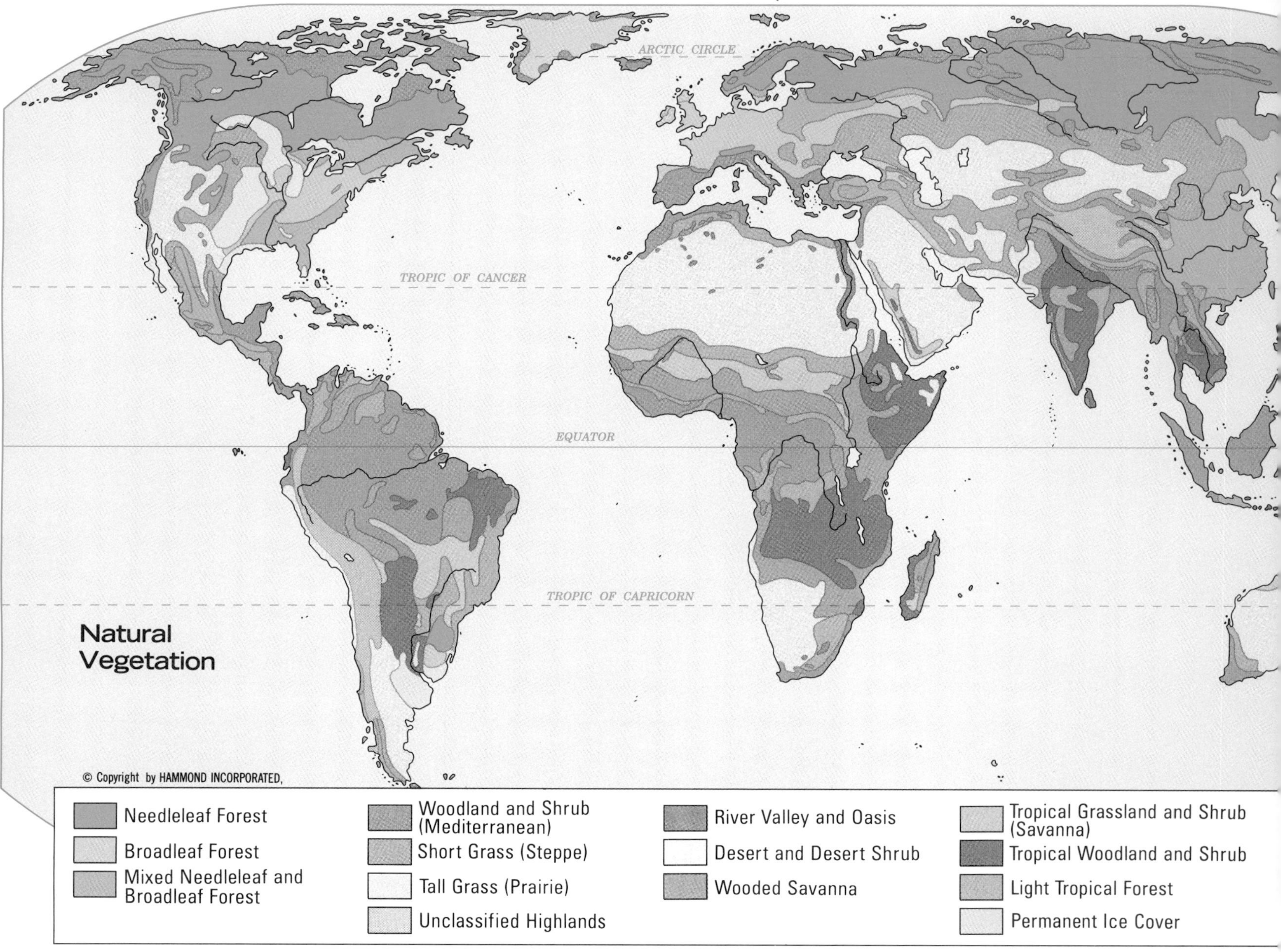

Natural Vegetation

© Copyright by HAMMOND INCORPORATED,

▪ Needleleaf Forest	▪ Woodland and Shrub (Mediterranean)
▪ Broadleaf Forest	▪ Short Grass (Steppe)
▪ Mixed Needleleaf and Broadleaf Forest	▪ Tall Grass (Prairie)
	▪ Unclassified Highlands
▪ River Valley and Oasis	▪ Tropical Grassland and Shrub (Savanna)
▪ Desert and Desert Shrub	▪ Tropical Woodland and Shrub
▪ Wooded Savanna	▪ Light Tropical Forest
	▪ Permanent Ice Cover

Air Pressure and Winds

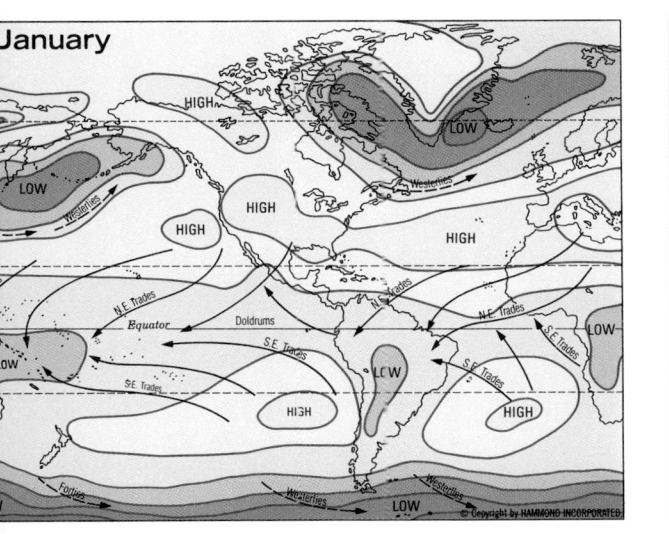

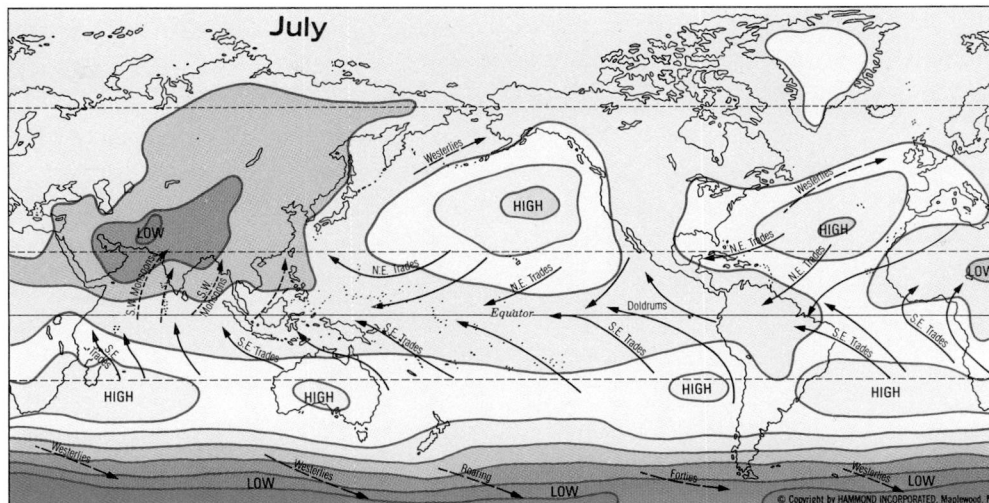

July

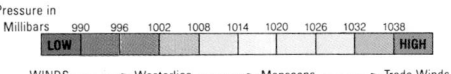

Pressure in
Millibars   990   996   1002   1008   1014   1020   1026   1032   1038

LOW   HIGH

WINDS ——→ Westerlies ------→ Monsoons ——→ Trade Winds

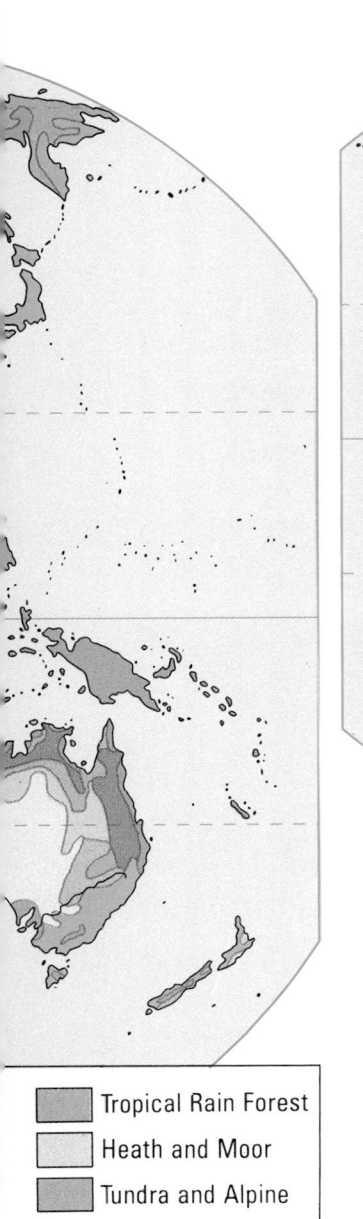

Tropical Rain Forest
Heath and Moor
Tundra and Alpine

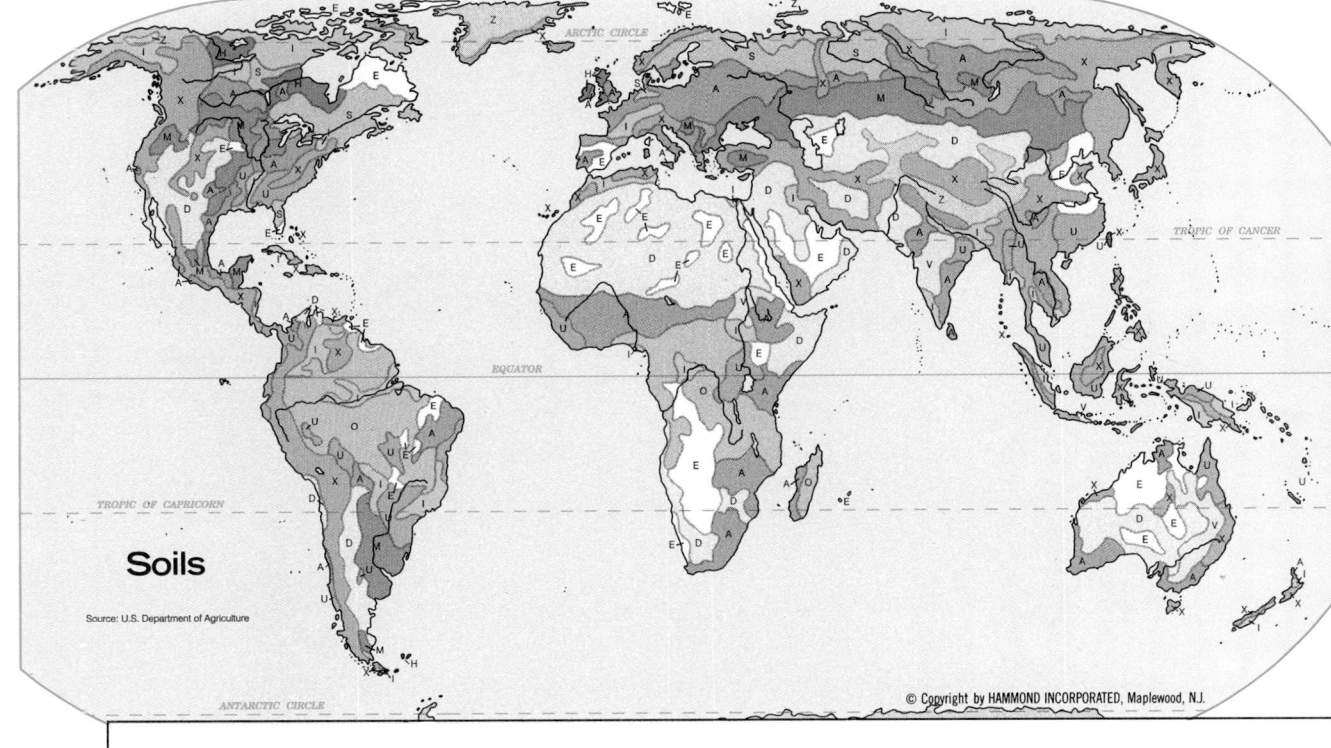

Soils

Source: U.S. Department of Agriculture

© Copyright by HAMMOND INCORPORATED, Maplewood, N.J.

A Alfisols – grey to brown surface soils, medium to high organic content	O Oxisols – tropical and subtropical highly–weathered soils
D Aridisols – dry or desert area soils, low in organic matter	S Spodosols – acidic, coarse–textured soils of well–watered regions
E Entisols – soils with little or no layered development	U Ultisols – like alfisols but more clayey and acidic
H Histosols – wet, highly organic (peat and muck) soils	V Vertisols – clayey soils that swell when wet, crack when dry
I Inceptisols – weak, slightly developed young soils	X Mountain Soils – mixed varieties of limited extent
M Mollisols – thick, dark, organic–rich soils	Z Little or No Soil

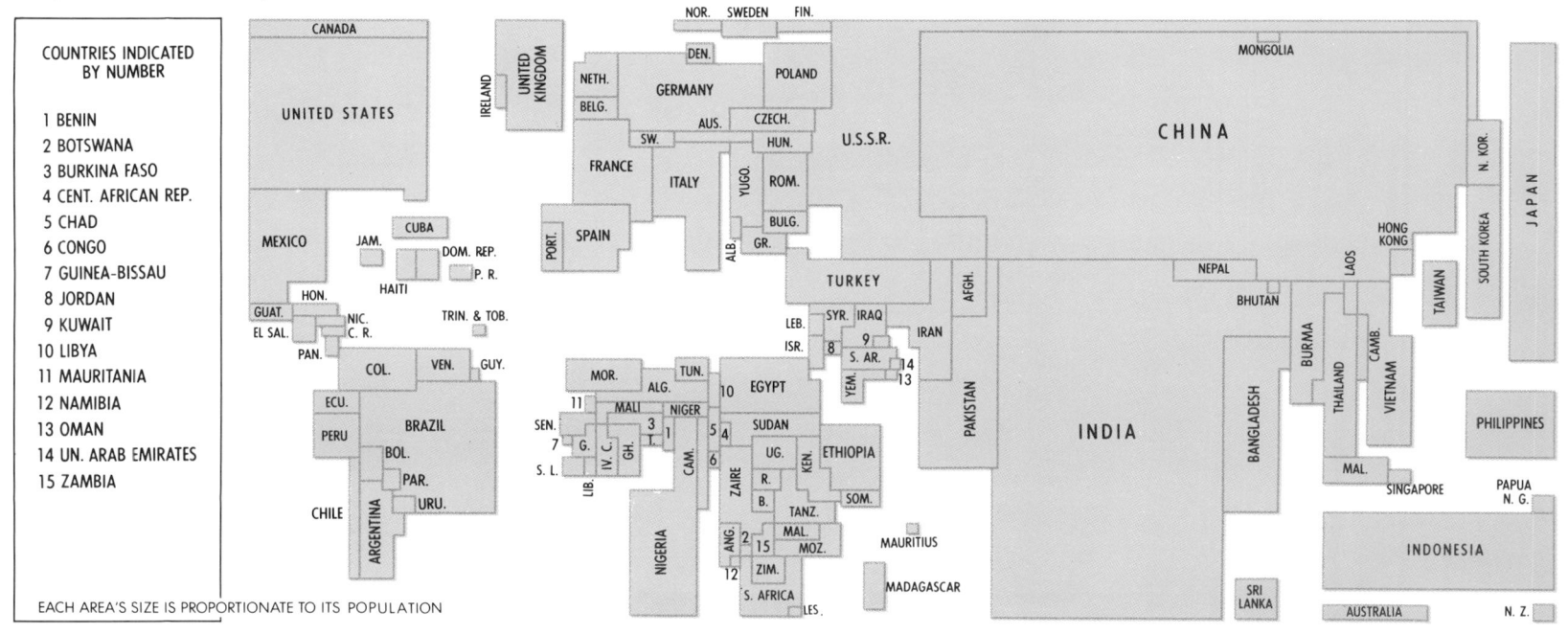

Population Distribution

Source: *United Nations*

© Copyright by HAMMOND INCORPORATED, Maplewood, N.J.

DENSITY PER SQ. KILOMETER:	Over 100	50–100	10–50	1–10	Under 1
SQ. MILE:	Over 260	130–260	25–130	3–25	Under 3

• Urban areas with over 6,000,000 inhabitants

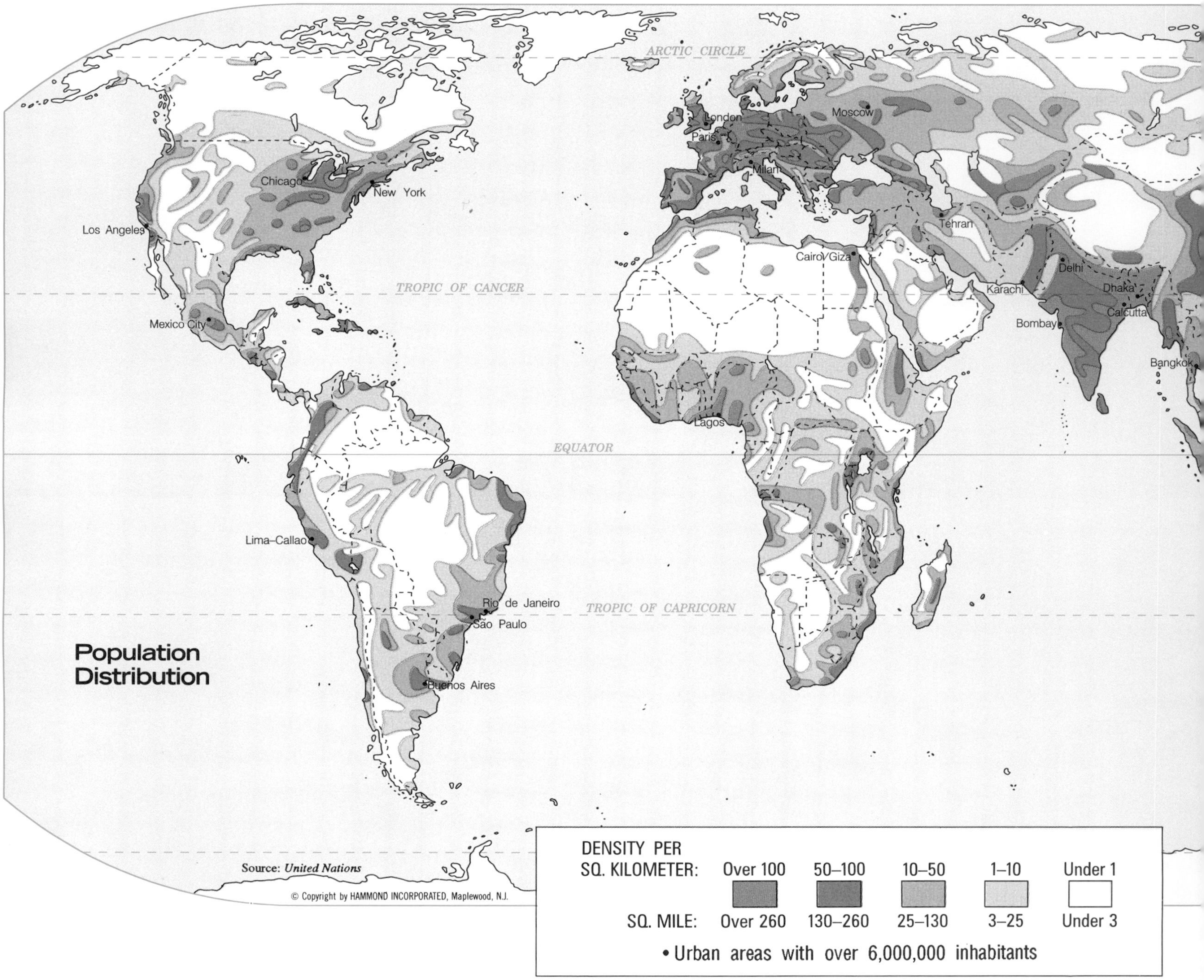

Population Comparisons

COUNTRIES INDICATED BY NUMBER

1 BENIN
2 BOTSWANA
3 BURKINA FASO
4 CENT. AFRICAN REP.
5 CHAD
6 CONGO
7 GUINEA-BISSAU
8 JORDAN
9 KUWAIT
10 LIBYA
11 MAURITANIA
12 NAMIBIA
13 OMAN
14 UN. ARAB EMIRATES
15 ZAMBIA

EACH AREA'S SIZE IS PROPORTIONATE TO ITS POPULATION

Great Cities

The World's Largest
Urban Areas

TOKYO/YOKOHAMA, Japan
MEXICO CITY, Mexico
SÃO PAULO, Brazil
NEW YORK, U.S.
SHANGHAI, China
CALCUTTA, India
BUENOS AIRES, Argentina
SEOUL, South Korea
RIO DE JANEIRO, Brazil
BOMBAY, India
LONDON, U.K.
LOS ANGELES, U.S.
OSAKA/KOBE, Japan
BEIJING, China
MOSCOW, U.S.S.R.
JAKARTA, Indonesia
CAIRO/GIZA, Egypt
PARIS, France

0   5   10   15   20
MILLIONS OF INHABITANTS   Source: *United Nations*

Town and Country

Urban and Rural Components of
the Populations of Selected Countries

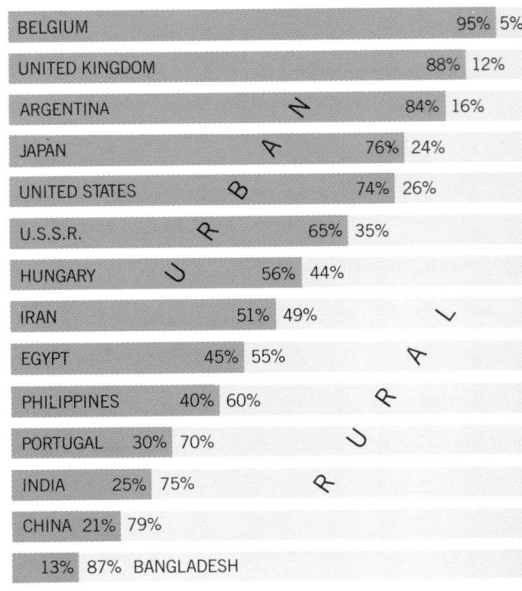

Country	Urban	Rural
BELGIUM	95%	5%
UNITED KINGDOM	88%	12%
ARGENTINA	84%	16%
JAPAN	76%	24%
UNITED STATES	74%	26%
U.S.S.R.	65%	35%
HUNGARY	56%	44%
IRAN	51%	49%
EGYPT	45%	55%
PHILIPPINES	40%	60%
PORTUGAL	30%	70%
INDIA	25%	75%
CHINA	21%	79%
BANGLADESH	13%	87%

Population Pyramids for Selected Countries

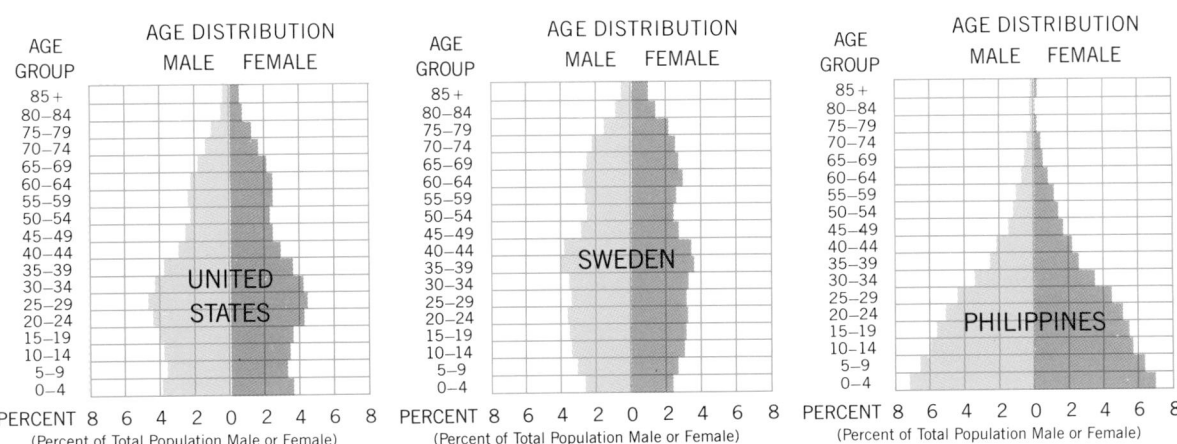

AGE GROUP — AGE DISTRIBUTION MALE FEMALE

85+, 80–84, 75–79, 70–74, 65–69, 60–64, 55–59, 50–54, 45–49, 40–44, 35–39, 30–34, 25–29, 20–24, 15–19, 10–14, 5–9, 0–4

UNITED STATES

SWEDEN

PHILIPPINES

PERCENT 8 6 4 2 0 2 4 6 8
(Percent of Total Population Male or Female)

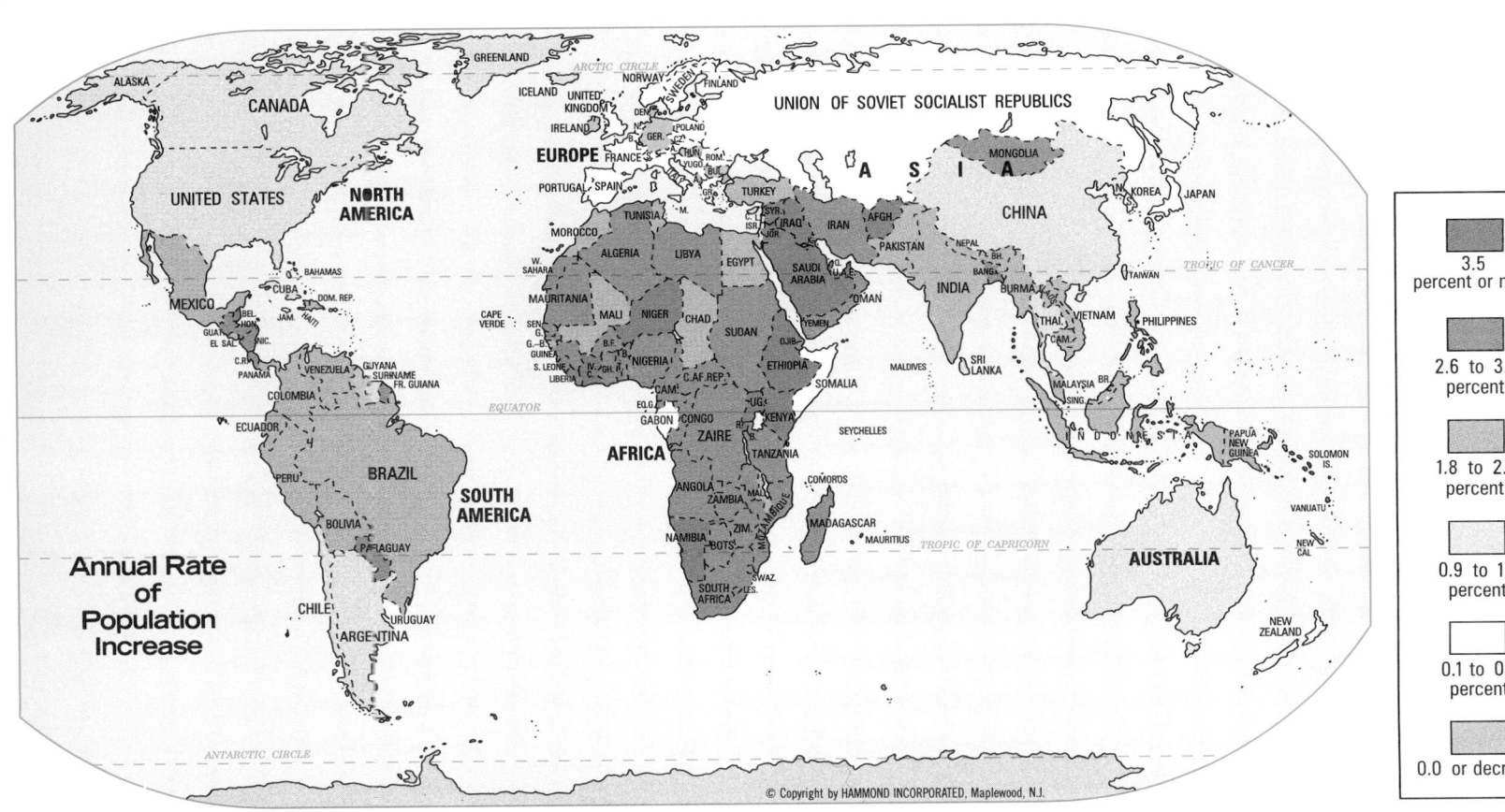

Annual Rate of Population Increase

3.5 percent or more

2.6 to 3.4 percent

1.8 to 2.5 percent

0.9 to 1.7 percent

0.1 to 0.8 percent

0.0 or decrease

© Copyright by HAMMOND INCORPORATED, Maplewood, N.J.

ARCTIC CIRCLE

INUPIK
23
INUPIK
INUPIK
ICELANDIC
CREE
FRENCH
NORWEGIAN
SWEDISH
FINNISH
LAPP
SAMOYED
KOMI
KHANTY
EVENK
YAKUT
RUSSIAN
1C
ENGLISH
1A
1E
POLISH
GERMAN
UKRAINIAN
1C
TATAR
10
RUSSIAN
KAZAKH
10
KHALKA MONGOL
10

E N G L I S H
1A

1B
FRENCH
SPANISH
PORTUGUESE
ITALIAN
1B
TURKISH
KURDISH
3
TURKMEN
UZBEK
TADZHIK
KIRGIZ UIGHUR
KHALKA MONGOL
10

TROPIC OF CANCER

S P A N I S H
23
1B
SPANISH
1B
1B
MAYAN
1A
1A
1A
1A
23

ARABIC
BERBER
ARABIC
A R A B I C
HEBREW
PERSIAN
PASHTO
BALUCHI
1J
PUNJABI
SINDHI
HINDI
1K
GUJARATI
MARATHI
TELUGU
BENGALI
BURMESE
TIBETAN
CHINE
12

ARABIC
5
TUAREG
TEDA
ARABIC
BEJA
6
AMHARIC
5

EQUATOR

SPANISH
1B
ENGLISH & HINDI
1A, & 1K
CARIB
23
23
WOLOF
FULANI
MANDINGO
MOSSI
HAUSA
5
AKAN
YORUBA
IBO
DINKA
AZANDE
GALLA
SOMALI
6
SINHALESE
1K
TAMIL
16

Q U E C H U A
23
23
1B
PORTUGUESE
FANG
MONGO
KONGO
BALUBA
SWAHILI
8
B A N T U
L A N G U A G E S
7

TROPIC OF CAPRICORN

S P A N I S H
GUARANI
23
MBUNDU
BEMBA
SHONA
MAKUA
MALAGASY
19
1B

SPANISH
1B
1A
8
TSWANA
ZULU 1A
AFRIKAANS
XHOSA
1A
ENGLISH
1A

Languages

23

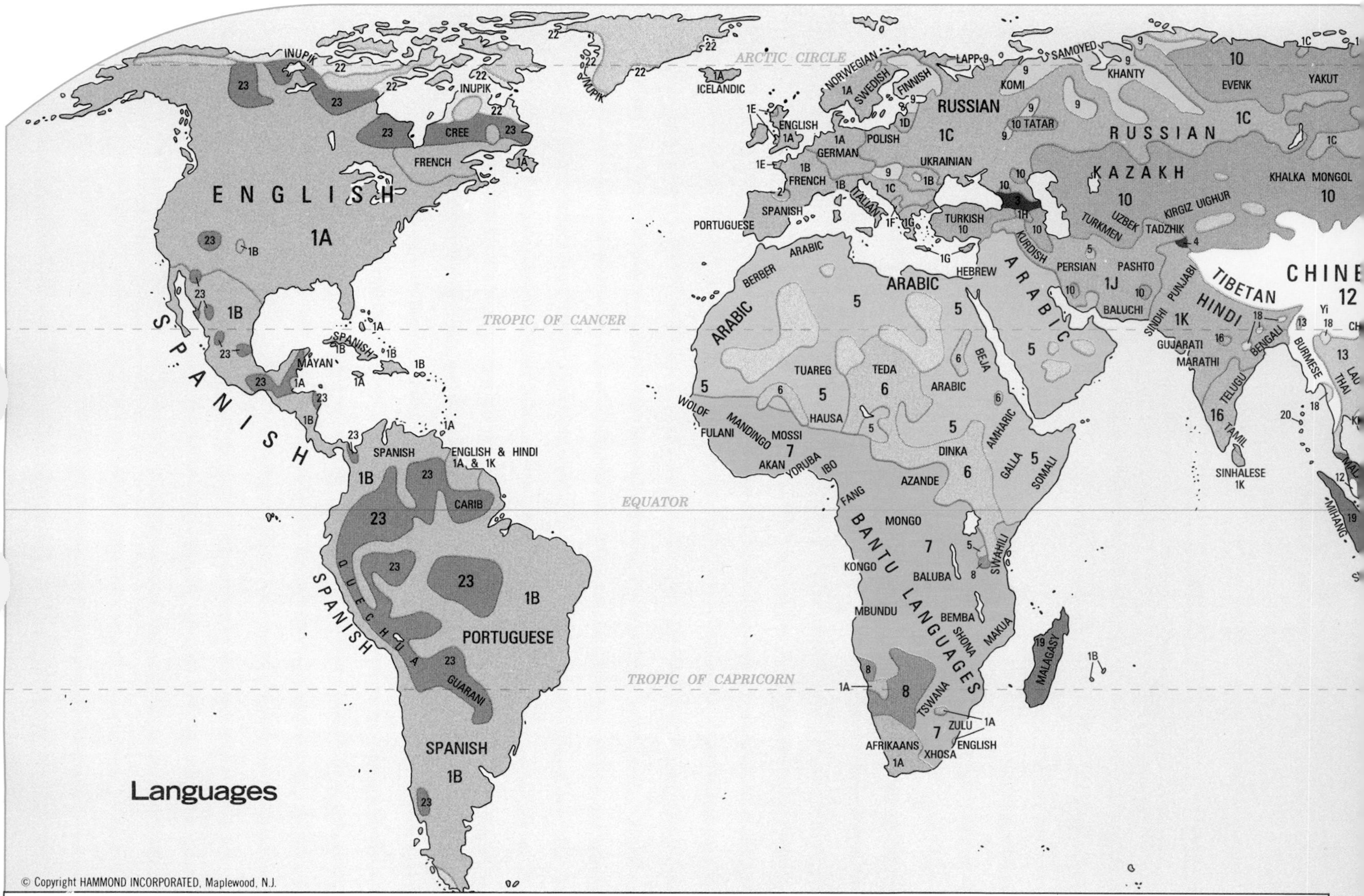

© Copyright HAMMOND INCORPORATED, Maplewood, N.J.

	LANGUAGE FAMILIES					
1 INDO-EUROPEAN	**5** AFRO-ASIATIC (HAMITO-SEMITIC)	**10** ALTAIC	**15** JAPANESE	**20** PAPUAN
1A—Germanic	**6** NILO-SAHARAN	**11** PALEO-SIBERIAN FAMILIES	**16** DRAVIDIAN	**21** AUSTRALIAN
1B—Romance				
1C—Slavic	**2** BASQUE	**7** NIGER-CONGO	**12** SINO-TIBETAN	**17** VIETNAMESE	**22** ESKIMO-ALEUT
1D—Baltic				
1E—Celtic	**3** CAUCASIAN FAMILIES	**8** KHOISAN	**13** THAI-KADAI	**18** AUSTRO-ASIATIC	**23** AMERICAN INDIAN FAMILIES
1F—Albanian				
1G—Greek　1J—Iranian	**4** BURUSHASKI	**9** URALIC	**14** KOREAN	**19** AUSTRONESIAN	UNPOPULATED AREAS
1H—Armenian　1K—Indo-Aryan				

Major Languages: Number of Speakers

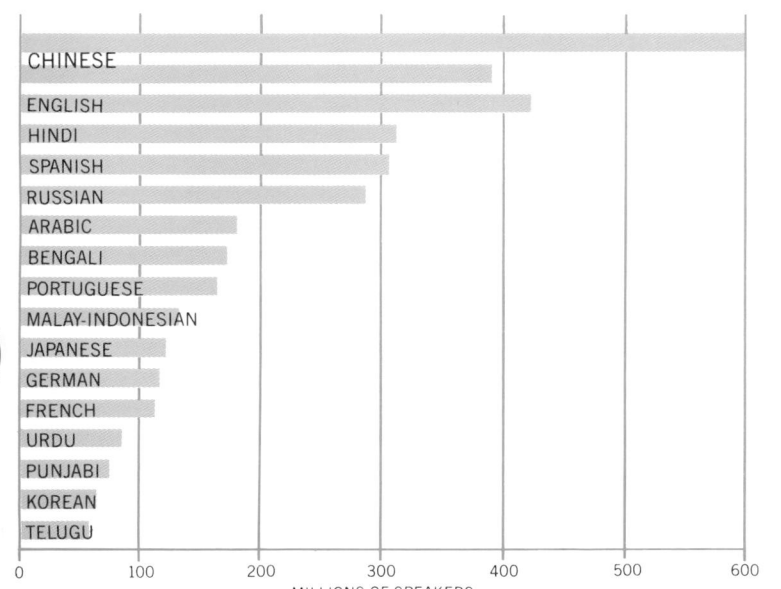

CHINESE
ENGLISH
HINDI
SPANISH
RUSSIAN
ARABIC
BENGALI
PORTUGUESE
MALAY-INDONESIAN
JAPANESE
GERMAN
FRENCH
URDU
PUNJABI
KOREAN
TELUGU

0　100　200　300　400　500　600
MILLIONS OF SPEAKERS

Major Religions: Membership

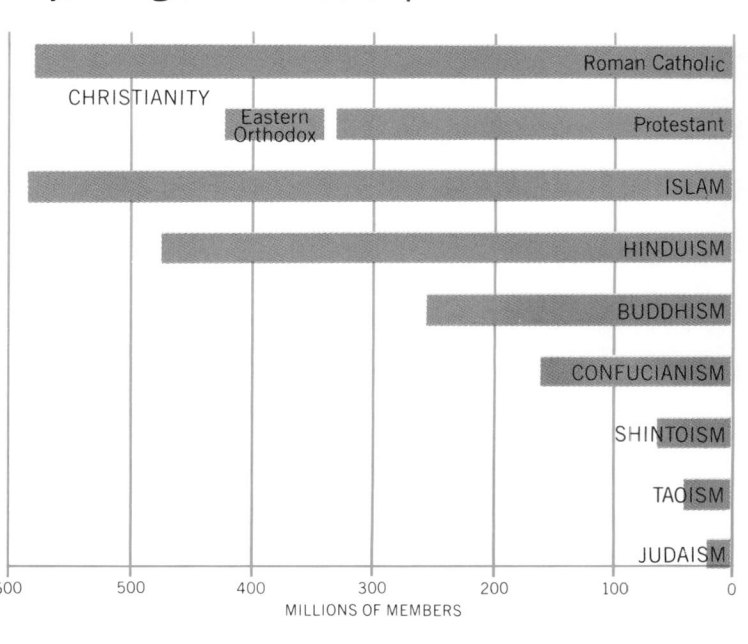

CHRISTIANITY
Roman Catholic
Eastern Orthodox
Protestant
ISLAM
HINDUISM
BUDDHISM
CONFUCIANISM
SHINTOISM
TAOISM
JUDAISM

600　500　400　300　200　100　0
MILLIONS OF MEMBERS

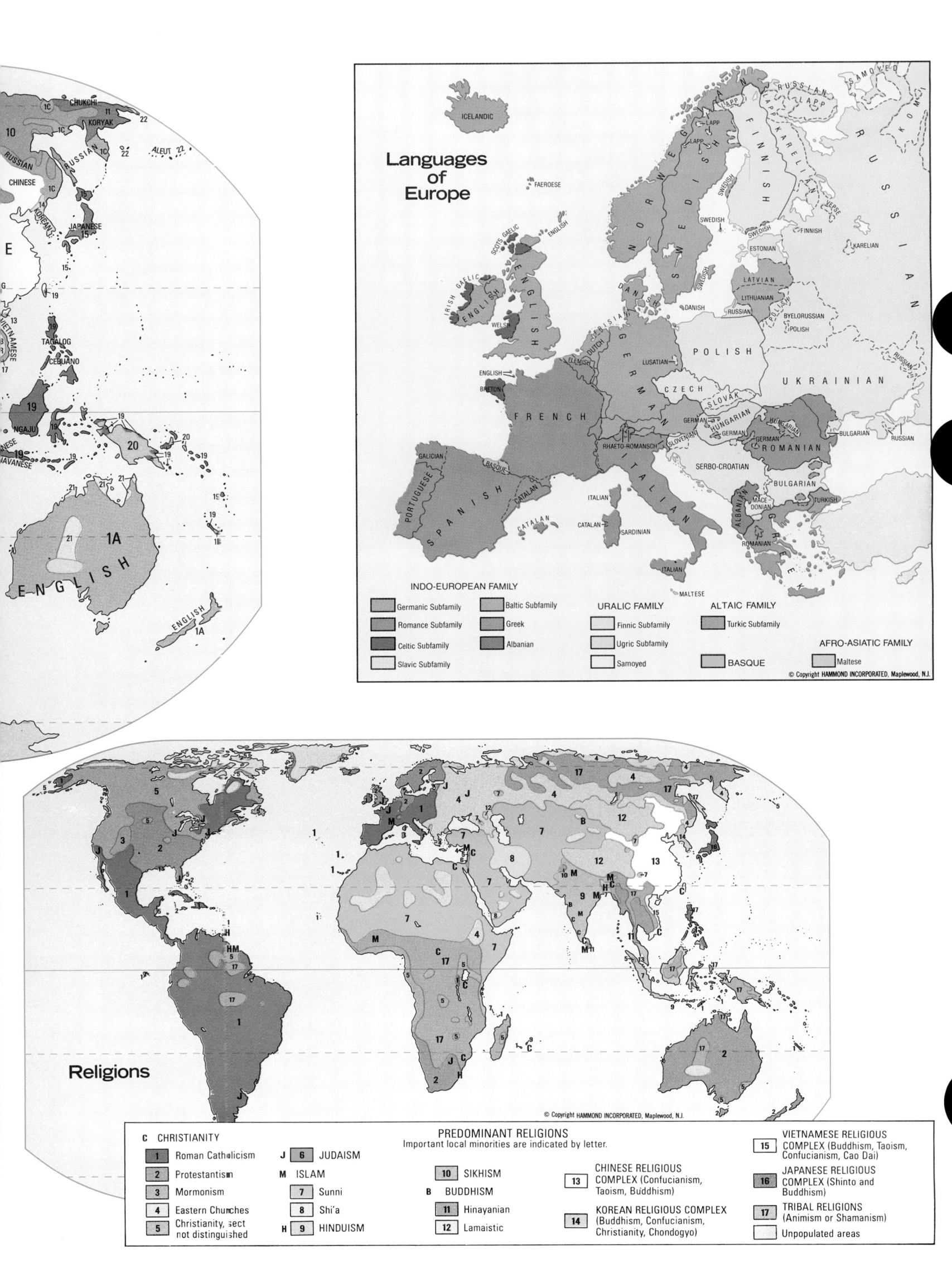

Languages of Europe

INDO-EUROPEAN FAMILY

- Germanic Subfamily
- Romance Subfamily
- Celtic Subfamily
- Slavic Subfamily
- Baltic Subfamily
- Greek
- Albanian

URALIC FAMILY

- Finnic Subfamily
- Ugric Subfamily
- Samoyed

ALTAIC FAMILY

- Turkic Subfamily

BASQUE

AFRO-ASIATIC FAMILY

- Maltese

© Copyright HAMMOND INCORPORATED, Maplewood, N.J.

Religions

© Copyright HAMMOND INCORPORATED, Maplewood, N.J.

PREDOMINANT RELIGIONS
Important local minorities are indicated by letter.

C CHRISTIANITY

1. Roman Catholicism
2. Protestantism
3. Mormonism
4. Eastern Churches
5. Christianity, sect not distinguished

J 6 JUDAISM

M ISLAM

7. Sunni
8. Shi'a

H 9 HINDUISM

10. SIKHISM

B BUDDHISM

11. Hinayanian
12. Lamaistic

13. CHINESE RELIGIOUS COMPLEX (Confucianism, Taoism, Buddhism)

14. KOREAN RELIGIOUS COMPLEX (Buddhism, Confucianism, Christianity, Chondogyo)

15. VIETNAMESE RELIGIOUS COMPLEX (Buddhism, Taoism, Confucianism, Cao Dai)

16. JAPANESE RELIGIOUS COMPLEX (Shinto and Buddhism)

17. TRIBAL RELIGIONS (Animism or Shamanism)

Unpopulated areas

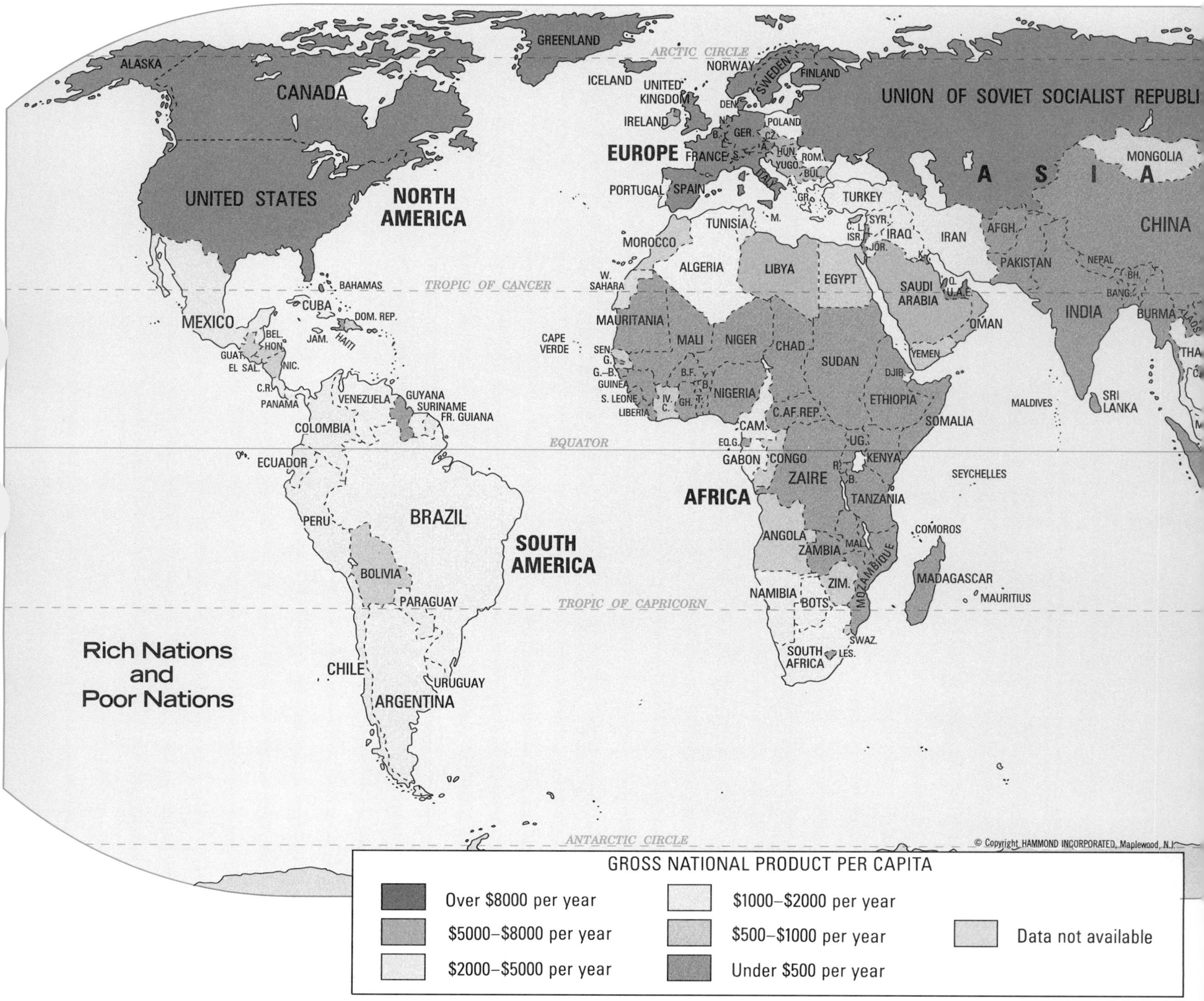

Gross National Product

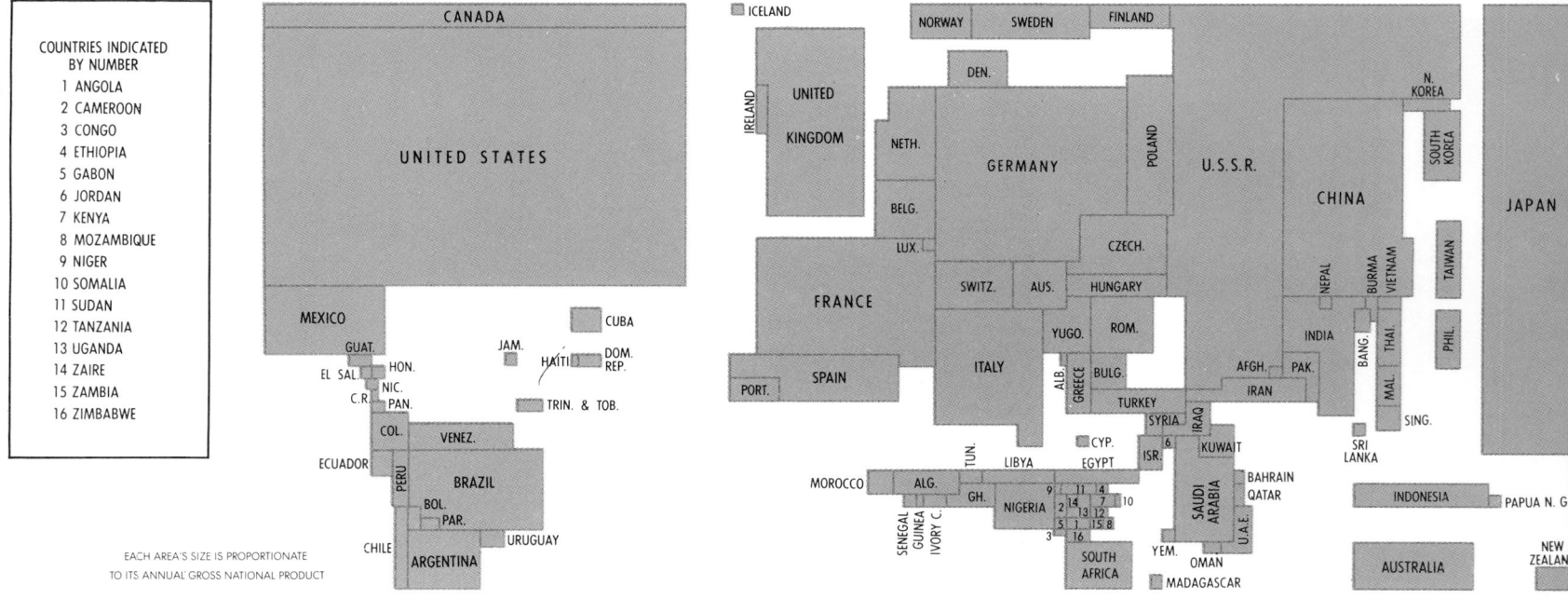

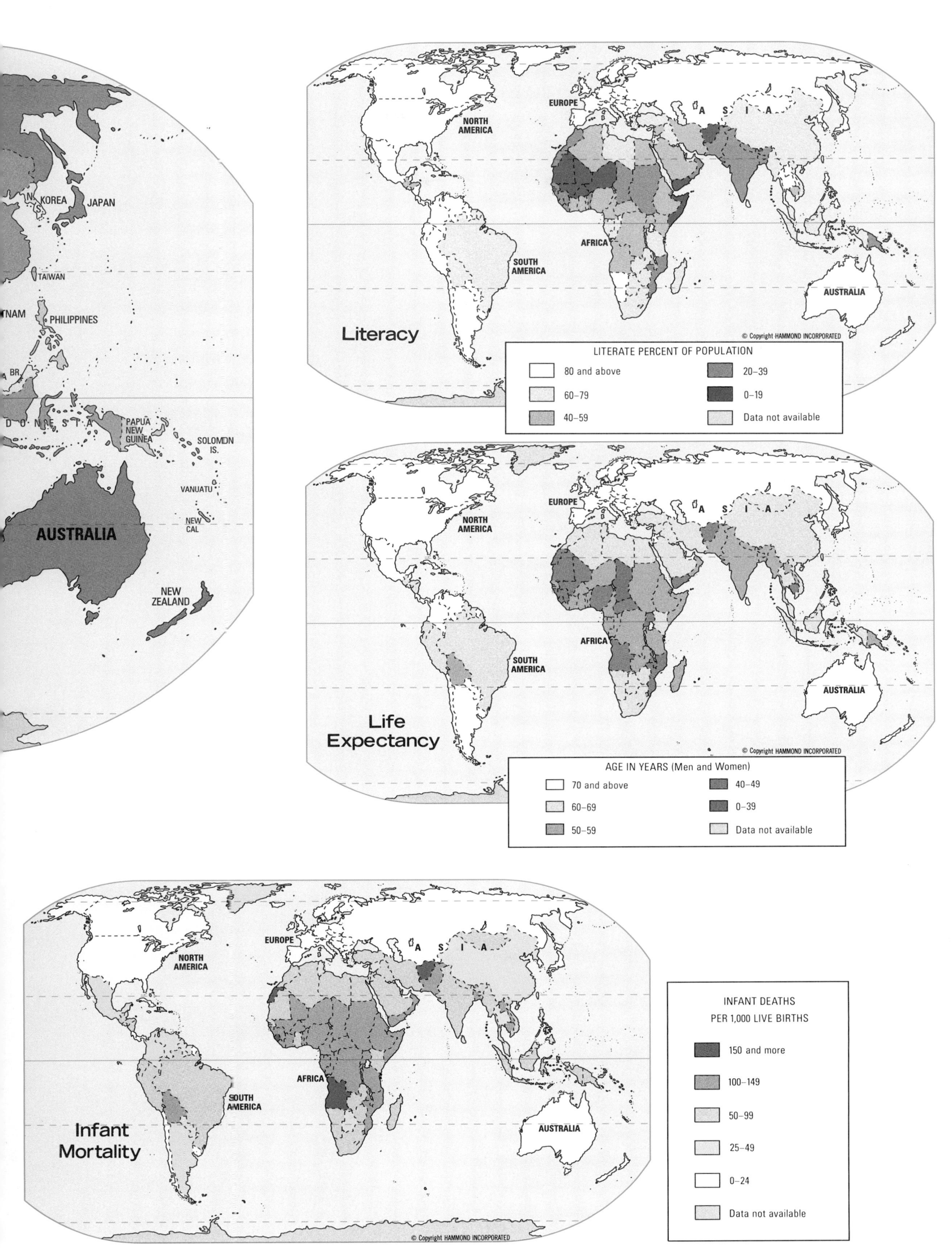

Literacy

© Copyright HAMMOND INCORPORATED

LITERATE PERCENT OF POPULATION

- 80 and above
- 60–79
- 40–59
- 20–39
- 0–19
- Data not available

Life Expectancy

© Copyright HAMMOND INCORPORATED

AGE IN YEARS (Men and Women)

- 70 and above
- 60–69
- 50–59
- 40–49
- 0–39
- Data not available

Infant Mortality

© Copyright HAMMOND INCORPORATED

INFANT DEATHS PER 1,000 LIVE BIRTHS

- 150 and more
- 100–149
- 50–99
- 25–49
- 0–24
- Data not available

KOREA JAPAN TAIWAN NAM PHILIPPINES BR INDONESIA PAPUA NEW GUINEA SOLOMON IS. VANUATU NEW CAL AUSTRALIA NEW ZEALAND

NORTH AMERICA EUROPE ASIA AFRICA SOUTH AMERICA AUSTRALIA

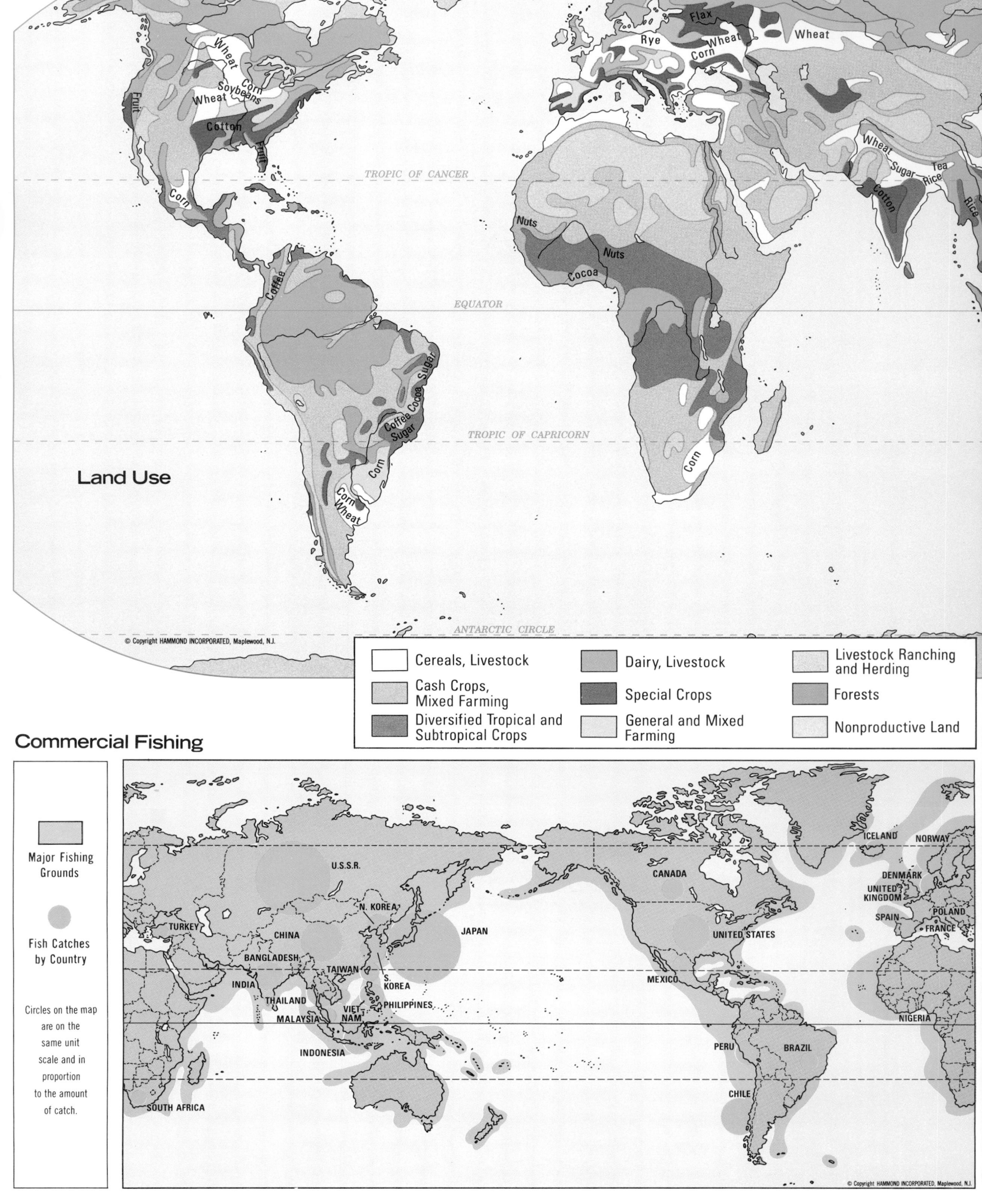

Land Use

© Copyright HAMMOND INCORPORATED, Maplewood, N.J.

	Cereals, Livestock		Dairy, Livestock		Livestock Ranching and Herding
	Cash Crops, Mixed Farming		Special Crops		Forests
	Diversified Tropical and Subtropical Crops		General and Mixed Farming		Nonproductive Land

Commercial Fishing

Major Fishing Grounds

Fish Catches by Country

Circles on the map are on the same unit scale and in proportion to the amount of catch.

© Copyright HAMMOND INCORPORATED, Maplewood, N.J.

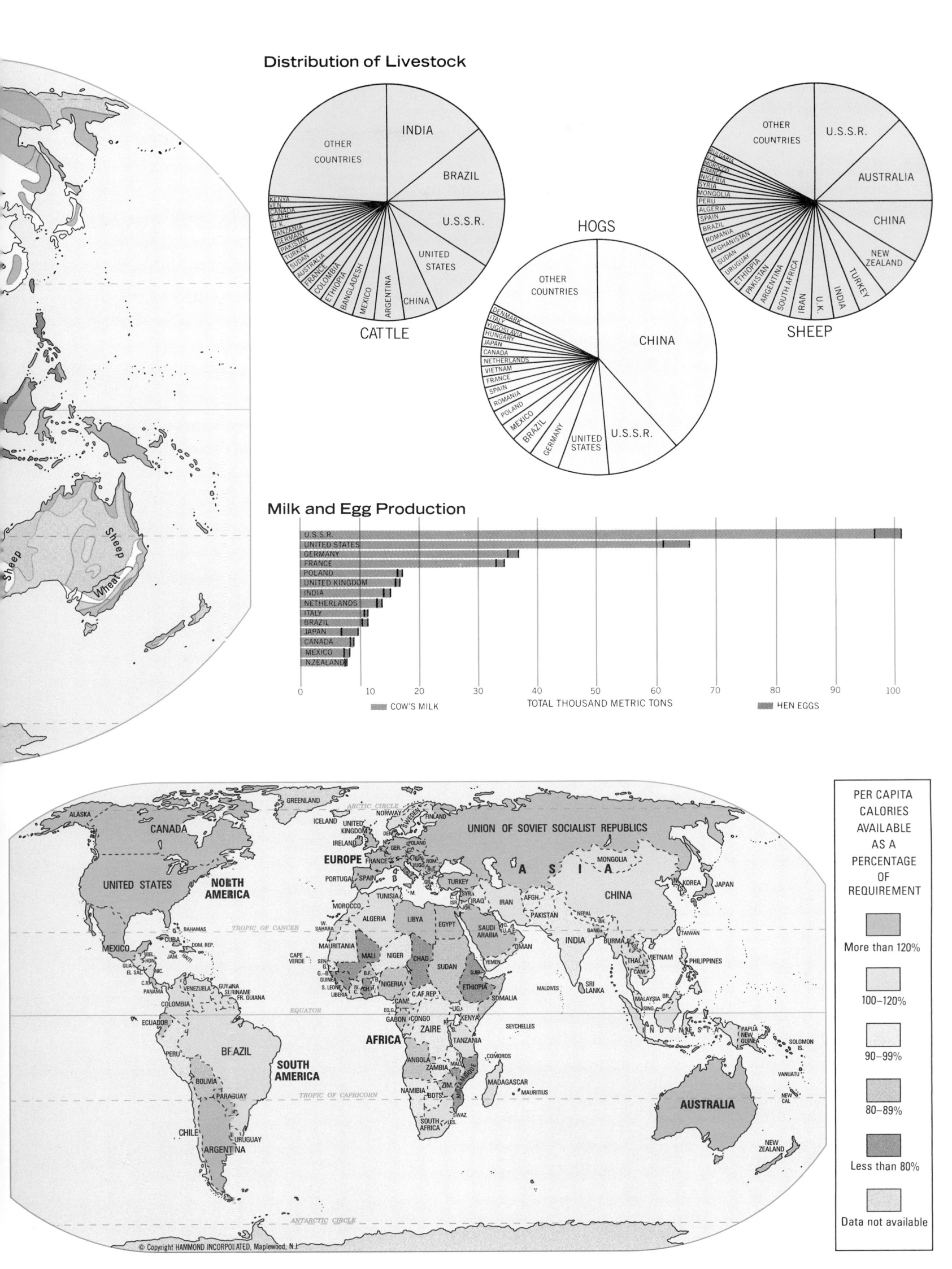

Distribution of Livestock

CATTLE
- INDIA
- BRAZIL
- U.S.S.R.
- UNITED STATES
- CHINA
- ARGENTINA
- MEXICO
- BANGLADESH
- ETHIOPIA
- COLOMBIA
- FRANCE
- AUSTRALIA
- SUDAN
- TURKEY
- PAKISTAN
- GERMANY
- TANZANIA
- U.K.
- S. AFR.
- CANADA
- VEN.
- KENYA
- OTHER COUNTRIES

HOGS
- CHINA
- U.S.S.R.
- UNITED STATES
- GERMANY
- BRAZIL
- MEXICO
- POLAND
- ROMANIA
- SPAIN
- FRANCE
- VIETNAM
- NETHERLANDS
- CANADA
- JAPAN
- HUNGARY
- YUGOSLAVIA
- ITALY
- DENMARK
- OTHER COUNTRIES

SHEEP
- U.S.S.R.
- AUSTRALIA
- CHINA
- NEW ZEALAND
- TURKEY
- INDIA
- U.K.
- IRAN
- SOUTH AFRICA
- ARGENTINA
- PAKISTAN
- ETHIOPIA
- URUGUAY
- SUDAN
- AFGHANISTAN
- ROMANIA
- BRAZIL
- SPAIN
- ALGERIA
- MONGOLIA
- SYRIA
- NIGERIA
- FRANCE
- MOROCCO
- BULGARIA
- OTHER COUNTRIES

Milk and Egg Production

Bar chart: TOTAL THOUSAND METRIC TONS (scale 0 to 100)

- U.S.S.R.
- UNITED STATES
- GERMANY
- FRANCE
- POLAND
- UNITED KINGDOM
- INDIA
- NETHERLANDS
- ITALY
- BRAZIL
- JAPAN
- CANADA
- MEXICO
- N.ZEALAND

Legend: ▓ COW'S MILK   ▓ HEN EGGS

PER CAPITA CALORIES AVAILABLE AS A PERCENTAGE OF REQUIREMENT

- More than 120%
- 100–120%
- 90–99%
- 80–89%
- Less than 80%
- Data not available

© Copyright HAMMOND INCORPORATED, Maplewood, N.J.

Mineral Fuels

Prudhoe Bay
Beaufort Sea
GREENLAND
ARCTIC CIRCLE
ALASKA
NORWAY
SWEDEN
U. S. S. R.
CANADA
S S
North Sea
UNITED KINGDOM
IRELAND
POL.
UNITED STATES
FRANCE
EUROPE
GER.
H. R.
Y.
ASIA
NORTH AMERICA
Sh Sh
PORT.
SP.
ITALY
GR.
TURKEY
SYR.
IRAN
AFGH.
CHINA
Sh Sh
ISR.
IRAQ
Persian Gulf
PAKISTAN
TROPIC OF CANCER
Gulf of Mexico
MOROCCO
TUN.
LIBYA
EGYPT
SAUDI ARABIA
U.A.E.
INDIA
CUBA
ALGERIA
OMAN
BURMA
MEXICO
NIGER
YEMEN
GUATEMALA
SUDAN
TRINIDAD & TOBAGO
VENEZUELA
IV. C. GH.
NIGERIA
C.AF.REP.
CAMEROON
COLOMBIA
SURINAME
EQUATOR
ECUADOR
Niger Delta
GABON
CONGO
ZAIRE
PERU
Sh   Sh
AFRICA
BRAZIL
BOLIVIA
SOUTH AMERICA
ANGOLA
MOZ.
MADAGASCAR
TROPIC OF CAPRICORN
NAMIBIA
Sh
Sh
SOUTH AFRICA
CHILE
ARGENTINA

© Copyright by HAMMOND INCORPORATED, Maplewood, N.J.

⬛ Oil Fields	+ Major Uranium Deposits
⬭ Natural Gas Fields	☐ Important Peat Deposits
○ Major Coal Deposits	Sh Oil Shale
S Oil Sands	

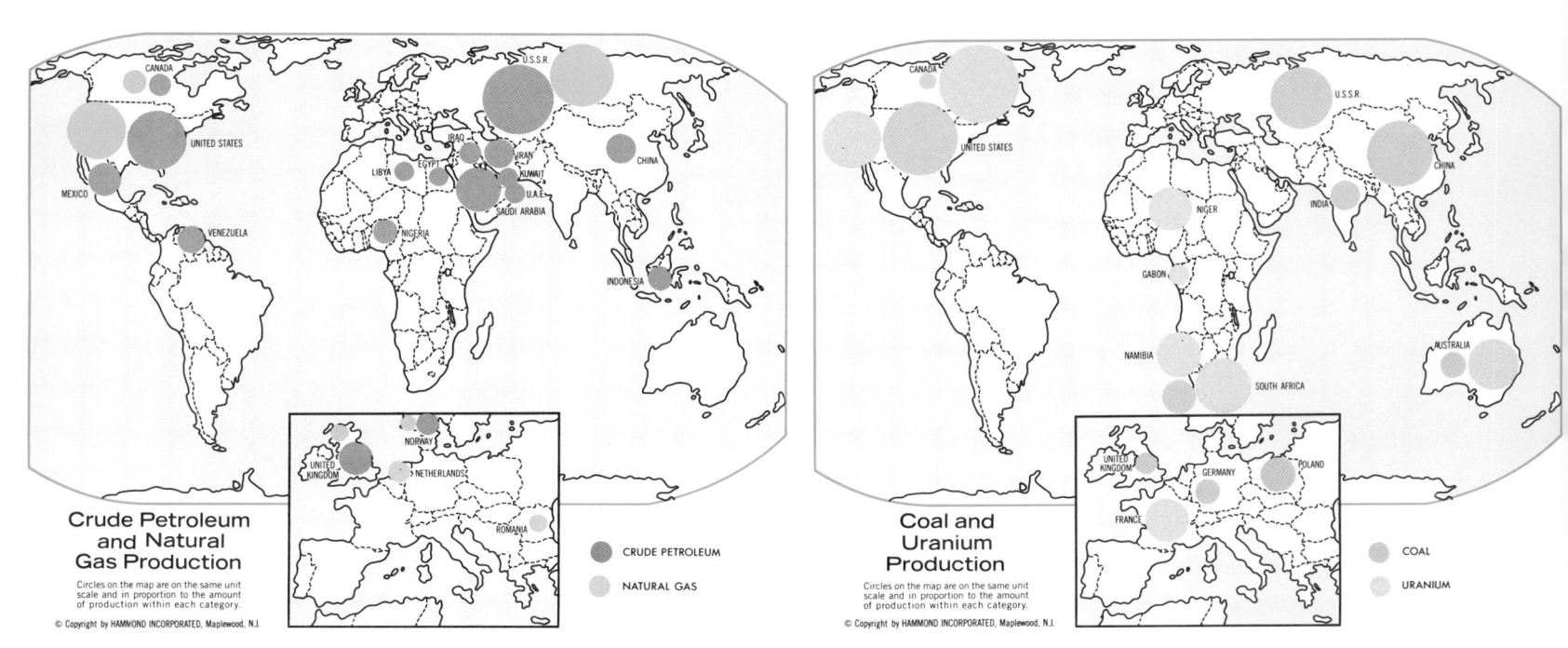

Crude Petroleum and Natural Gas Production

Circles on the map are on the same unit scale and in proportion to the amount of production within each category.

© Copyright by HAMMOND INCORPORATED, Maplewood, N.J.

● CRUDE PETROLEUM
● NATURAL GAS

CANADA
U.S.S.R.
UNITED STATES
IRAQ
EGYPT
IRAN
CHINA
MEXICO
LIBYA
KUWAIT
U.A.E.
VENEZUELA
NIGERIA
SAUDI ARABIA
INDONESIA

NORWAY
UNITED KINGDOM
NETHERLANDS
ROMANIA

Coal and Uranium Production

Circles on the map are on the same unit scale and in proportion to the amount of production within each category.

© Copyright by HAMMOND INCORPORATED, N.J.

● COAL
● URANIUM

CANADA
U.S.S.R.
UNITED STATES
CHINA
NIGER
INDIA
GABON
NAMIBIA
AUSTRALIA
SOUTH AFRICA

UNITED KINGDOM
GERMANY
POLAND
FRANCE

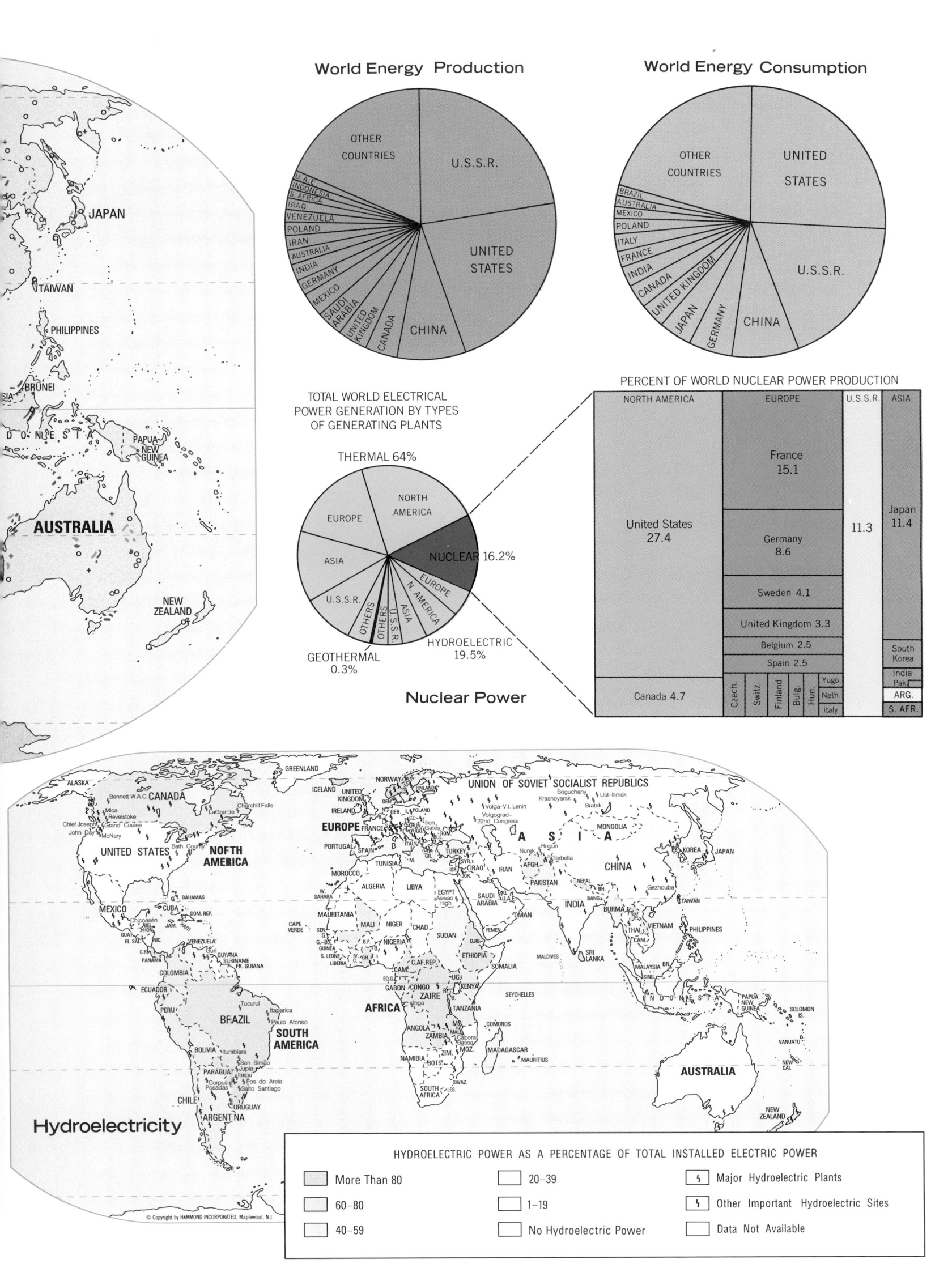

World Energy Production

OTHER COUNTRIES
U.S.S.R.
U.A.E.
INDONESIA
S. AFRICA
IRAQ
VENEZUELA
POLAND
IRAN
AUSTRALIA
INDIA
GERMANY
MEXICO
SAUDI ARABIA
UNITED KINGDOM
CANADA
CHINA
UNITED STATES

World Energy Consumption

OTHER COUNTRIES
UNITED STATES
BRAZIL
AUSTRALIA
MEXICO
POLAND
ITALY
FRANCE
INDIA
CANADA
UNITED KINGDOM
JAPAN
GERMANY
CHINA
U.S.S.R.

TOTAL WORLD ELECTRICAL POWER GENERATION BY TYPES OF GENERATING PLANTS

THERMAL 64%

NORTH AMERICA
EUROPE
ASIA
U.S.S.R.
OTHERS
OTHERS
U.S.S.R.
ASIA
N. AMERICA
EUROPE
NUCLEAR 16.2%
HYDROELECTRIC 19.5%

GEOTHERMAL 0.3%

Nuclear Power

PERCENT OF WORLD NUCLEAR POWER PRODUCTION

NORTH AMERICA	EUROPE	U.S.S.R.	ASIA
United States 27.4	France 15.1	11.3	Japan 11.4
	Germany 8.6		
	Sweden 4.1		
	United Kingdom 3.3		South Korea
	Belgium 2.5		India
	Spain 2.5		Pak.
Canada 4.7	Czech. Switz. Finland Bulg. Hun. Yugo. Neth. Italy		ARG. S. AFR.

Hydroelectricity

ALASKA
GREENLAND
Bennett W.A.C. CANADA
ICELAND
UNITED KINGDOM
NORWAY
FINLAND
UNION OF SOVIET SOCIALIST REPUBLICS
Boguchany
Ust-Ilimsk
Krasnoyarsk
Bratsk
Mica
Revelstoke
IRELAND
EUROPE
DEN.
POLAND
GER.
Volga-V.I. Lenin
Volgograd- 22nd Congress
MONGOLIA
Chief Joseph
Grand Coulee
John Day McNary
LaGrande
Churchill Falls
Iron Gates
YUGO.
ROM.
ASIA
Revelstoke
Bath County
UNITED STATES
NORTH AMERICA
PORTUGAL
SPAIN
FRANCE
ITALY
TURKEY
SYR.
IRAQ
IRAN
AFGH.
Nurek
Rogun
Tarbella
KOREA
JAPAN
CHINA
MEXICO
BAHAMAS
CUBA
DOM. REP.
Chicoasén
JAM.
HAITI
MOROCCO
TUNISIA
ISR.
JOR.
PAKISTAN
NEPAL
BH.
Gezhouba
TAIWAN
GUAT.
EL SAL.
C.R.
VENEZUELA
GUYANA
SURINAME
FR. GUIANA
W. SAHARA
ALGERIA
LIBYA
EGYPT
Aswan High
SAUDI ARABIA
U.A.E.
OMAN
INDIA
BURMA
THAI.
VIETNAM
PHILIPPINES
PANAMA
COLOMBIA
Guri
MAURITANIA
MALI
NIGER
CHAD
SUDAN
YEMEN
CAM.
SRI LANKA
MALAYSIA BR.
SING.
ECUADOR
SEN.
G.-B.
GUINEA
S. LEONE
LIBERIA
NIGERIA
C.AF.REP.
ETHIOPIA
SOMALIA
MALDIVES
PERU
Tucuruí
Itaparica
BRAZIL
Paulo Afonso
EQ.G.
GABON
CONGO
ZAIRE
UG.
KENYA
SEYCHELLES
PAPUA NEW GUINEA
SOLOMON IS.
BOLIVIA
Iturbiara
SOUTH AMERICA
ANGOLA
ZAMBIA
Cabora Bassa
COMOROS
TANZANIA
MADAGASCAR
MAURITIUS
VANUATU
San Simão
Jupia
Itaipu
PARAGUAY
Corpus Posadas
Fos do Areia
Salto Santiago
NAMIBIA
ZIM.
MOZ.
BOTS.
AUSTRALIA
NEW CAL.
CHILE
URUGUAY
SWAZ.
LES.
SOUTH AFRICA
ARGENTINA
NEW ZEALAND

© Copyright by HAMMOND INCORPORATED, Maplewood, N.J.

HYDROELECTRIC POWER AS A PERCENTAGE OF TOTAL INSTALLED ELECTRIC POWER

More Than 80
60–80
40–59
20–39
1–19
No Hydroelectric Power

⚡ Major Hydroelectric Plants
⚡ Other Important Hydroelectric Sites
Data Not Available

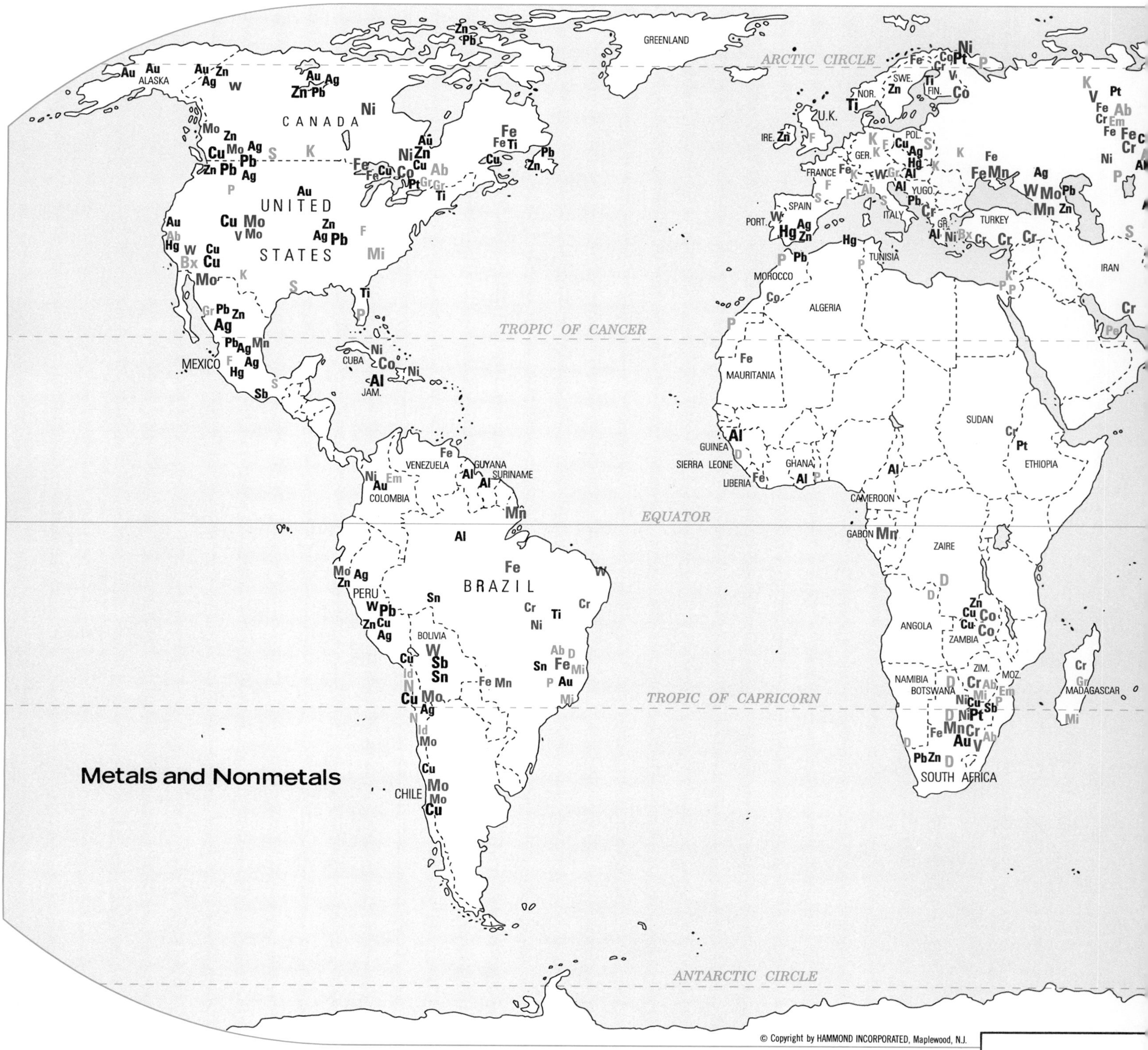

Metals and Nonmetals
ARCTIC CIRCLE
TROPIC OF CANCER
EQUATOR
TROPIC OF CAPRICORN
ANTARCTIC CIRCLE
GREENLAND
ALASKA
CANADA
UNITED STATES
MEXICO
CUBA
JAM.
VENEZUELA
GUYANA
SURINAME
COLOMBIA
PERU
BOLIVIA
BRAZIL
CHILE
IRE.
U.K.
NOR.
SWE.
FIN.
POL.
GER.
FRANCE
SPAIN
PORT.
ITALY
YUGO.
GR.
TURKEY
IRAN
MOROCCO
ALGERIA
TUNISIA
MAURITANIA
GUINEA
SIERRA LEONE
LIBERIA
GHANA
CAMEROON
GABON
SUDAN
ETHIOPIA
ZAIRE
ANGOLA
ZAMBIA
ZIM.
MOZ.
NAMIBIA
BOTSWANA
SOUTH AFRICA
MADAGASCAR

U.S. Imports of Selected Minerals and Metals

Percent of Apparent Consumption

PERCENT
Principal Foreign Suppliers named for each commodity.
100
90
80
70
60
50
40
30
20
10
0
ANTIMONY Mexico–China
ASBESTOS Canada–South Africa
BAUXITE & ALUMINA Australia–Guinea–Jamaica
CHROMIUM South Africa–Zimbabwe–Turkey
COBALT Zambia–Canada–Zaire
COPPER Canada–Chile
GOLD Canada–Switzerland
IRON ORE Canada–Venezuela–Liberia
MANGANESE Gabon–Brazil–Australia
MERCURY Spain–Turkey–China
MICA (SHEET) India–Germany–Belgium
NICKEL Canada–Norway–Australia
PLATINUM South Africa–United Kingdom–U.S.S.R.
SILVER Mexico–Canada
SULFUR Mexico–Canada
TIN Brazil–Malaysia–Bolivia–Indonesia–Thailand
TITANIUM Australia–Canada–South Africa
TUNGSTEN Bolivia–China–Peru
VANADIUM Canada–South Africa
ZINC Canada–Mexico–Peru

IRON AND FERROALLOY METALS

Co	Cobalt
Cr	Chromium
Fe	Iron Ore
Mn	Manganese
Mo	Molybdenum
Ni	Nickel
V	Vanadium
W	Tungsten

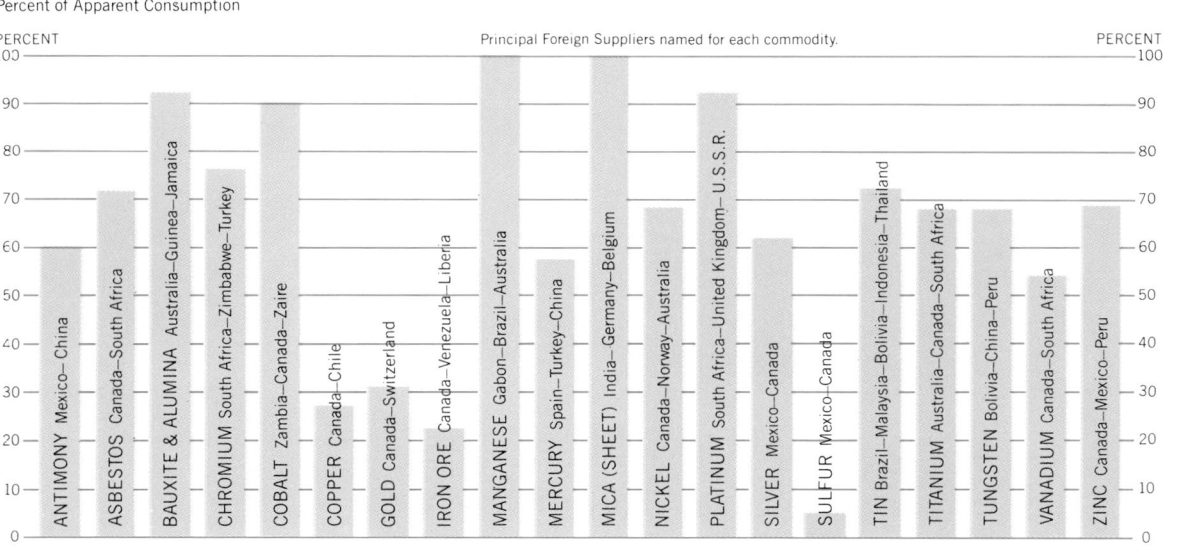

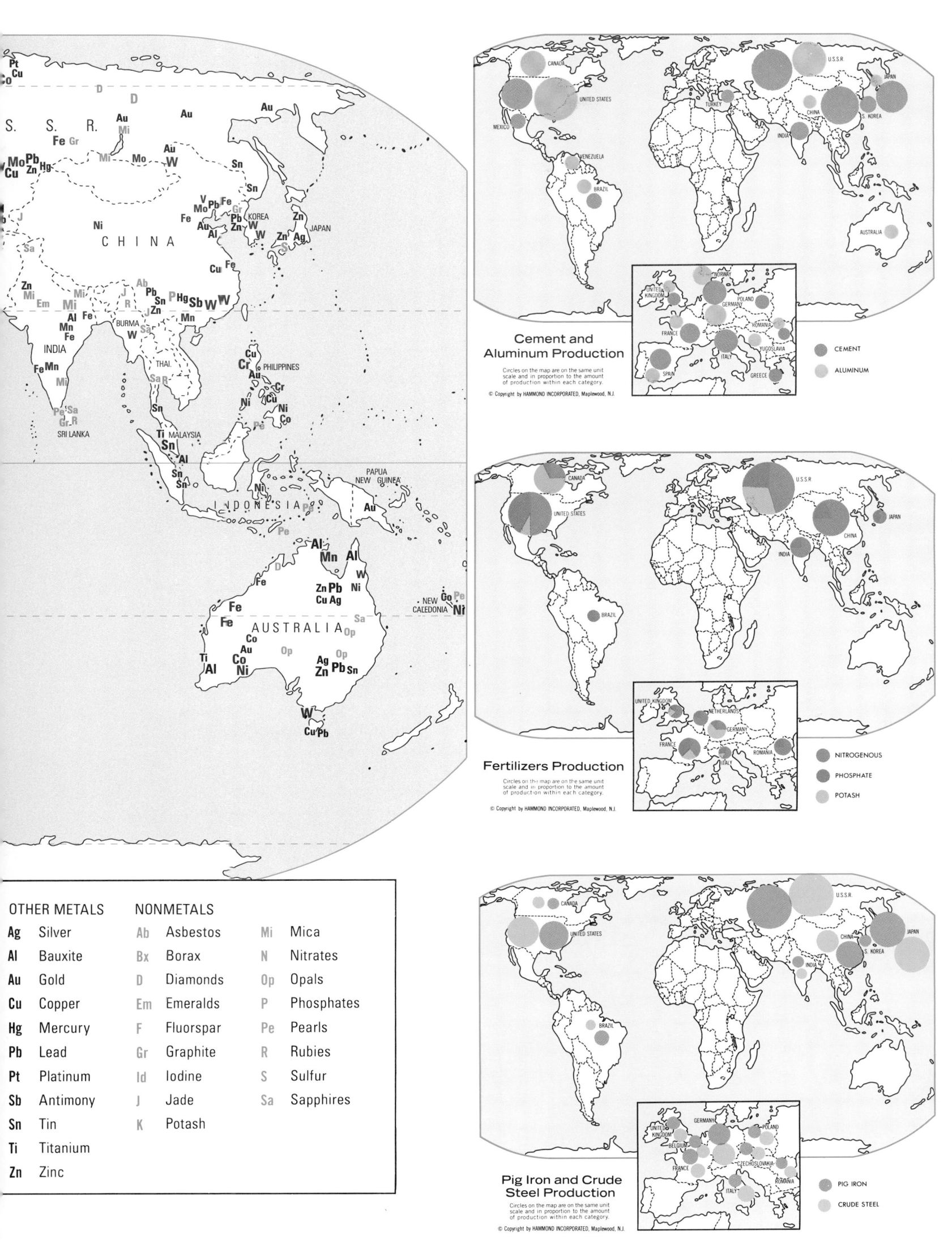

OTHER METALS

Ag	Silver
Al	Bauxite
Au	Gold
Cu	Copper
Hg	Mercury
Pb	Lead
Pt	Platinum
Sb	Antimony
Sn	Tin
Ti	Titanium
Zn	Zinc

NONMETALS

Ab	Asbestos	**Mi**	Mica
Bx	Borax	**N**	Nitrates
D	Diamonds	**Op**	Opals
Em	Emeralds	**P**	Phosphates
F	Fluorspar	**Pe**	Pearls
Gr	Graphite	**R**	Rubies
Id	Iodine	**S**	Sulfur
J	Jade	**Sa**	Sapphires
K	Potash		

Cement and Aluminum Production

Circles on the map are on the same unit scale and in proportion to the amount of production within each category.

© Copyright by HAMMOND INCORPORATED, Maplewood, N.J.

- CEMENT
- ALUMINUM

Fertilizers Production

Circles on the map are on the same unit scale and in proportion to the amount of production within each category.

© Copyright by HAMMOND INCORPORATED, Maplewood, N.J.

- NITROGENOUS
- PHOSPHATE
- POTASH

Pig Iron and Crude Steel Production

Circles on the map are on the same unit scale and in proportion to the amount of production within each category.

© Copyright by HAMMOND INCORPORATED, Maplewood, N.J.

- PIG IRON
- CRUDE STEEL

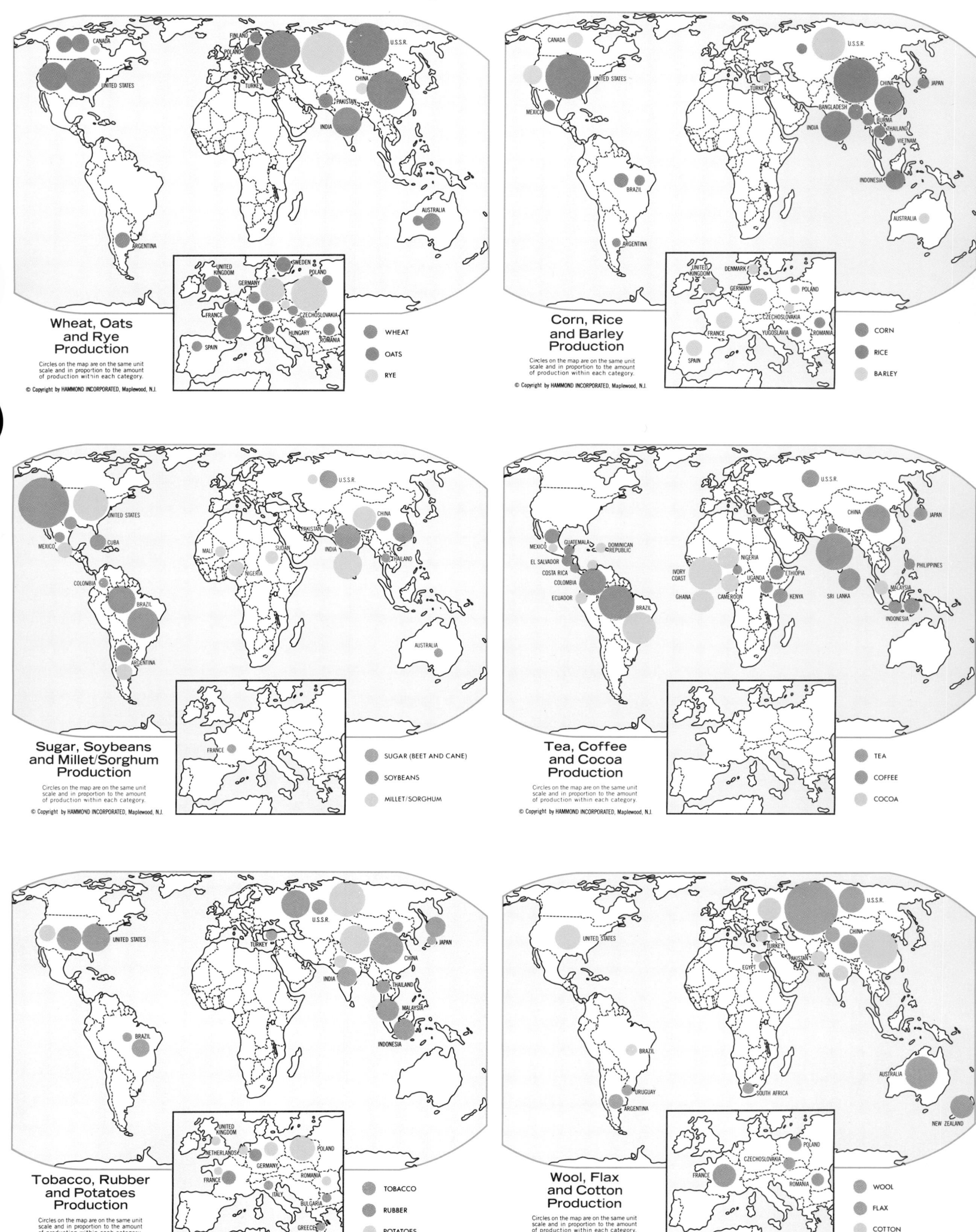

Wheat, Oats and Rye Production

Circles on the map are on the same unit scale and in proportion to the amount of production within each category.

© Copyright by HAMMOND INCORPORATED, Maplewood, N.J.

- WHEAT
- OATS
- RYE

Corn, Rice and Barley Production

Circles on the map are on the same unit scale and in proportion to the amount of production within each category.

© Copyright by HAMMOND INCORPORATED, Maplewood, N.J.

- CORN
- RICE
- BARLEY

Sugar, Soybeans and Millet/Sorghum Production

Circles on the map are on the same unit scale and in proportion to the amount of production within each category.

© Copyright by HAMMOND INCORPORATED, Maplewood, N.J.

- SUGAR (BEET AND CANE)
- SOYBEANS
- MILLET/SORGHUM

Tea, Coffee and Cocoa Production

Circles on the map are on the same unit scale and in proportion to the amount of production within each category.

© Copyright by HAMMOND INCORPORATED, Maplewood, N.J.

- TEA
- COFFEE
- COCOA

Tobacco, Rubber and Potatoes Production

Circles on the map are on the same unit scale and in proportion to the amount of production within each category.

© Copyright by HAMMOND INCORPORATED, Maplewood, N.J.

- TOBACCO
- RUBBER
- POTATOES

Wool, Flax and Cotton Production

Circles on the map are on the same unit scale and in proportion to the amount of production within each category.

© Copyright by HAMMOND INCORPORATED, Maplewood, N.J.

- WOOL
- FLAX
- COTTON

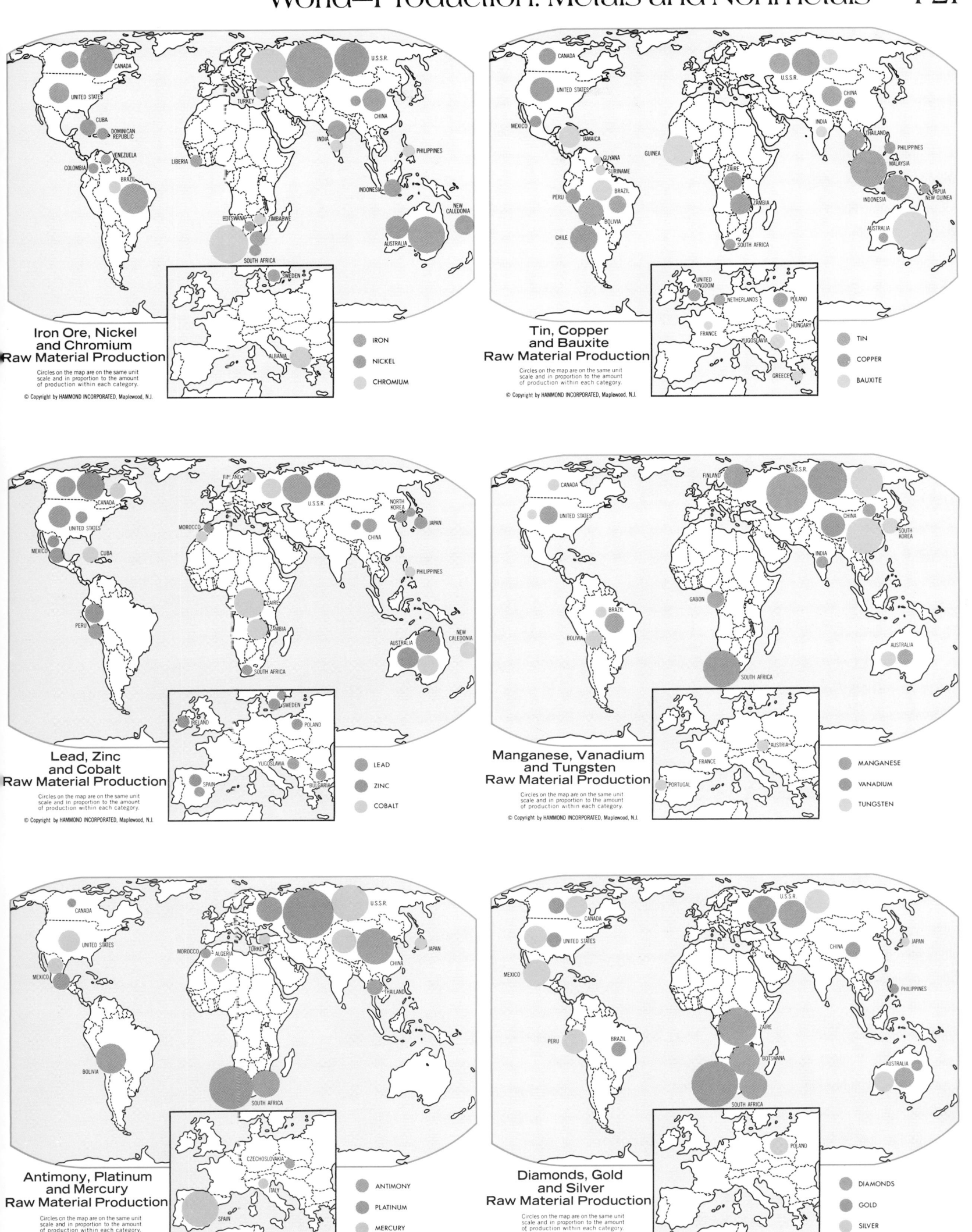

Iron Ore, Nickel and Chromium Raw Material Production

Circles on the map are on the same unit scale and in proportion to the amount of production within each category.

© Copyright by HAMMOND INCORPORATED, Maplewood, N.J.

- IRON
- NICKEL
- CHROMIUM

Tin, Copper and Bauxite Raw Material Production

Circles on the map are on the same unit scale and in proportion to the amount of production within each category.

© Copyright by HAMMOND INCORPORATED, Maplewood, N.J.

- TIN
- COPPER
- BAUXITE

Lead, Zinc and Cobalt Raw Material Production

Circles on the map are on the same unit scale and in proportion to the amount of production within each category.

© Copyright by HAMMOND INCORPORATED, Maplewood, N.J.

- LEAD
- ZINC
- COBALT

Manganese, Vanadium and Tungsten Raw Material Production

Circles on the map are on the same unit scale and in proportion to the amount of production within each category.

© Copyright by HAMMOND INCORPORATED, Maplewood, N.J.

- MANGANESE
- VANADIUM
- TUNGSTEN

Antimony, Platinum and Mercury Raw Material Production

Circles on the map are on the same unit scale and in proportion to the amount of production within each category.

© Copyright by HAMMOND INCORPORATED, Maplewood, N.J.

- ANTIMONY
- PLATINUM
- MERCURY

Diamonds, Gold and Silver Raw Material Production

Circles on the map are on the same unit scale and in proportion to the amount of production within each category.

© Copyright by HAMMOND INCORPORATED, Maplewood, N.J.

- DIAMONDS
- GOLD
- SILVER

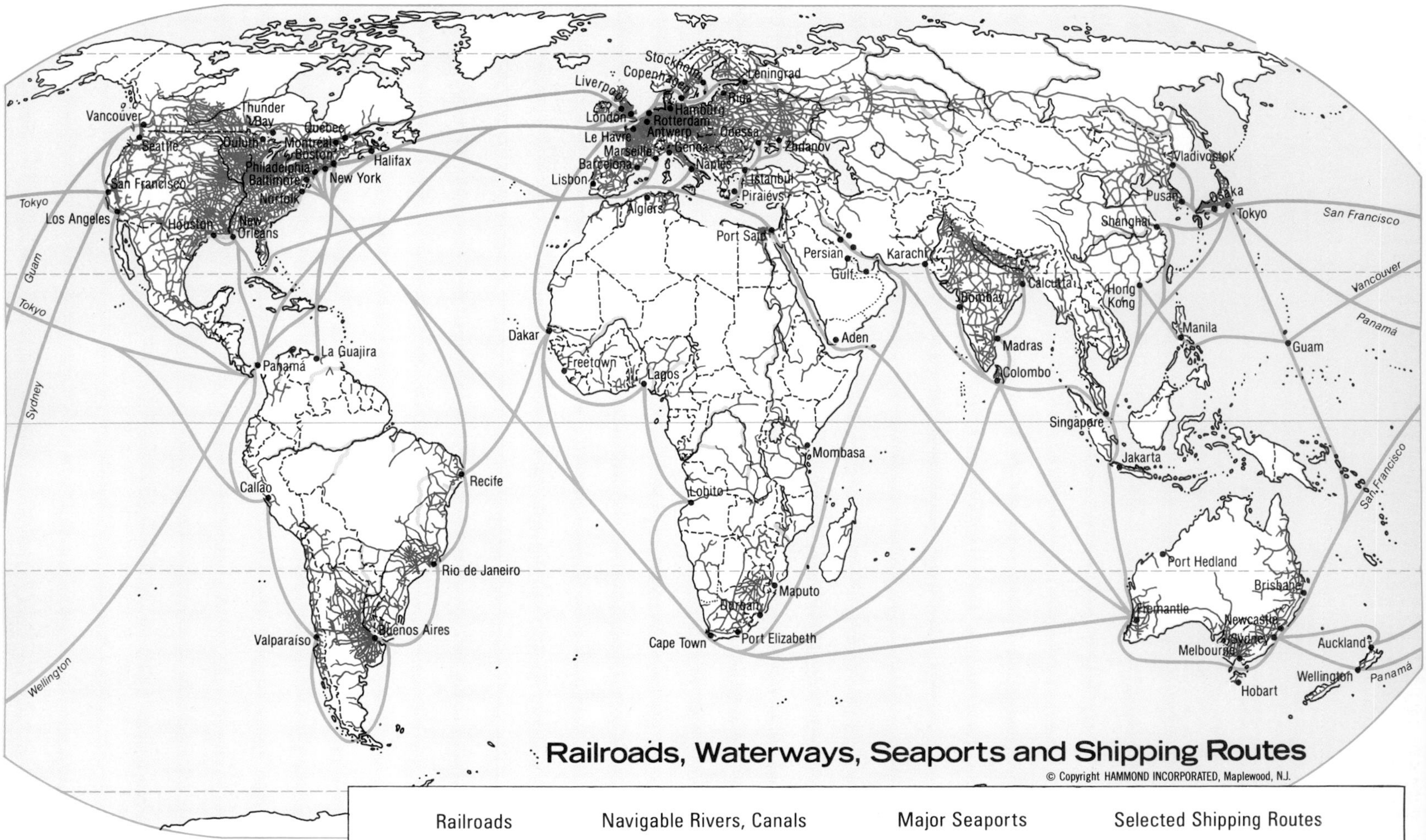

Railroads, Waterways, Seaports and Shipping Routes

© Copyright HAMMOND INCORPORATED, Maplewood, N.J.

Railroads	Navigable Rivers, Canals	Major Seaports	Selected Shipping Routes
		• New York	

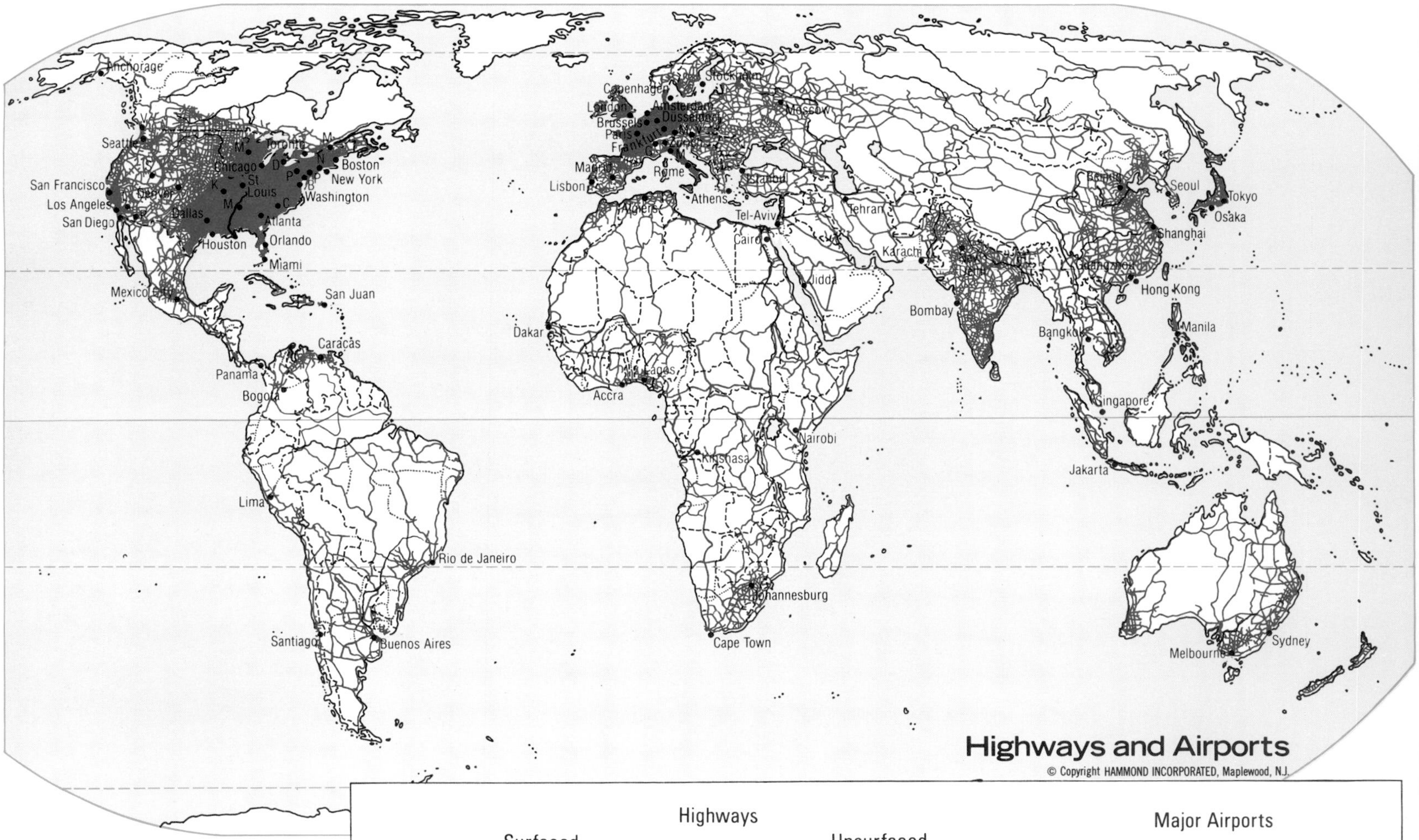

Labels (upper map): Vancouver, Thunder Bay, Quebec, Duluth, Montreal, Boston, Seattle, Halifax, San Francisco, Philadelphia, Baltimore, New York, Los Angeles, Norfolk, Houston, New Orleans, Tokyo, Guam, Tokyo, Sydney, Wellington, Panamá, La Guajira, Callao, Recife, Rio de Janeiro, Valparaíso, Buenos Aires, Lisbon, Dakar, Freetown, Lagos, Lobito, Mombasa, Maputo, Durban, Cape Town, Port Elizabeth, Liverpool, London, Le Havre, Marseille, Barcelona, Algiers, Genoa, Naples, Istanbul, Piraievs, Port Said, Stockholm, Copenhagen, Hamburg, Rotterdam, Antwerp, Riga, Leningrad, Odessa, Zhdanov, Persian Gulf, Aden, Karachi, Bombay, Calcutta, Madras, Colombo, Singapore, Jakarta, Vladivostok, Pusan, Shanghai, Hong Kong, Manila, Guam, Tokyo, Osaka, San Francisco, Vancouver, Panamá, San Francisco, Port Hedland, Brisbane, Fremantle, Newcastle, Sydney, Melbourne, Hobart, Auckland, Wellington, Panamá

Highways and Airports

© Copyright HAMMOND INCORPORATED, Maplewood, N.J.

Highways		Major Airports
Surfaced	Unsurfaced	• London

Labels (lower map): Anchorage, Seattle, San Francisco, Los Angeles, San Diego, Mexico City, Chicago, St Louis, Dallas, Houston, Detroit, Boston, New York, Washington, Atlanta, Orlando, Miami, San Juan, Caracas, Panama, Bogota, Lima, Santiago, Buenos Aires, Rio de Janeiro, Dakar, Accra, Kinshasa, Nairobi, Johannesburg, Cape Town, Lisbon, Madrid, Copenhagen, London, Brussels, Paris, Frankfurt, Düsseldorf, Rome, Stockholm, Moscow, Athens, Tel-Aviv, Cairo, Tehran, Jidda, Karachi, Bombay, Bangkok, Singapore, Jakarta, Seoul, Tokyo, Osaka, Shanghai, Hong Kong, Manila, Melbourne, Sydney

Air Distance (in miles) Between Major World Cities

	Anchorage	Beijing	Bombay	Buenos Aires	Cairo	Cape Town	Caracas	Chicago	Hong Kong	Honolulu	London	Los Angeles	Madrid	Melbourne	Mexico City	Montréal	Moscow	New Delhi	New York	Paris	Rio de Janeiro	Rome	San Francisco	Singapore	Tokyo
Amsterdam	4468	4890	4255	7112	2015	5997	4883	4118	5772	7254	222	5558	921	10,286	5735	3426	1337	3958	3654	271	5938	807	5465	6526	5788
Anchorage	—	3945	6300	8320	5116	10,478	5353	2858	5073	2778	4491	2340	5181	7729	3776	3133	4364	5709	3373	4697	8145	5263	2005	6678	3463
Athens	5500	4757	3207	7265	671	4957	5815	5447	5316	8353	1488	6900	1474	9297	7021	4737	1387	3120	4938	1305	6030	654	6792	5629	5924
Bangkok	6022	2027	1870	10,490	4521	6301	10,558	8569	1076	6610	5929	7637	6334	4579	9793	8337	4394	1812	8669	5877	9987	5493	7930	887	2865
Beijing	3997	—	2953	11,994	4687	8034	8978	6625	1195	5084	5089	6255	5759	5632	7772	6541	3627	2350	6867	5138	10,778	5076	5934	2754	1305
Bombay	6300	2953	—	9380	2698	5133	9034	8144	2679	8172	4526	8810	4689	6140	9818	7582	3132	722	7875	4367	8438	3846	8523	2425	4247
Buenos Aires	8320	11,994	9380	—	7360	4285	3155	5582	11,478	7554	6907	6148	6236	7219	4580	5597	8369	9823	5279	6857	1231	6925	6455	9940	11,411
Cairo	6116	4687	2698	7360	—	4510	6337	6116	5057	8818	2158	7675	2069	8700	7677	5403	1770	2752	5598	1973	6153	1305	7436	5152	5937
Cape Town	10,478	8034	5133	4285	4510	—	6361	8489	7377	11,534	5988	9981	5306	6428	8516	7920	6277	5769	7801	5782	3773	5231	10,248	6025	9155
Caracas	5353	8978	9034	3155	5337	6361	—	2480	10,171	6024	4662	3610	4351	9703	2234	2443	6176	8837	2124	4735	2805	5198	3908	11,408	8813
Chicago	2858	6625	8144	5582	5116	8489	2480	—	7797	4256	3960	1741	4192	9667	1688	746	4984	7486	714	4145	5288	4823	1860	9376	6313
Denver	2375	6385	8275	5935	5846	9331	3078	920	7476	3346	4701	828	5028	8755	1438	1639	5501	7730	1631	4900	5866	5887	953	9079	5815
Frankfurt	4656	4567	4076	7137	1730	5944	5290	4460	5403	7341	628	5783	1193	9882	6127	3787	961	3550	4028	589	6237	729	5709	6119	5533
Hong Kong	5073	1195	2679	11,478	5057	7377	10,171	7797	—	5557	5986	7217	6556	4605	8789	7736	4443	2339	8061	5992	11,002	5076	6904	1608	1792
Honolulu	2778	5084	8036	7554	3818	11,534	6024	4256	5557	—	7241	2565	7874	5501	3791	4919	7049	7413	4969	7452	8295	8040	2397	6728	3860
Houston	3256	7244	8875	5072	7005	8608	2262	942	8349	3902	4860	1373	5014	8979	961	1605	5925	8388	1419	5035	5015	5702	1648	9954	6685
Kinshasa	8875	7002	4200	5130	2618	2047	5752	7085	6904	11,178	3951	8850	3305	8112	7915	6378	4328	4692	6378	3742	4105	3186	8920	6132	8307
Lima	6385	10,356	10,389	1945	7725	6074	1699	3772	11,415	6316	4316	5907	8052	2635	3967	7855	10,430	3635	6367	2351	6748	4516	11,689	9628	
Lisbon	5110	6040	4975	5976	2352	5301	4040	4001	6862	7835	989	5600	317	11,049	5396	3255	2433	3377	3377	904	4777	1163	5679	7393	6943
London	4491	5089	4526	6919	2158	5988	4662	3960	5986	7241	—	5454	786	10,508	5558	3256	1556	4178	3473	215	5751	892	5369	6747	5956
Los Angeles	2340	6255	8810	6148	7675	9981	3610	1750	7217	2565	5454	—	5852	7928	1566	2468	6036	7015	2455	5661	6334	6336	349	8955	5476
Madrid	5181	5759	4689	6236	2069	5306	4351	4192	6556	7874	786	5852	—	10,766	5642	3449	2140	4528	3596	652	5045	849	5806	7079	6704
Melbourne	7729	5632	6101	7219	8700	6428	9703	9667	4605	5501	10,508	7928	10,766	—	8420	10,390	8965	6340	10,352	10,442	8218	9940	7850	3767	5070
Mexico City	3776	7772	9739	4580	7677	8516	2234	1688	8789	3791	5558	1566	5642	8420	—	2315	6671	9119	2086	5723	4769	6374	1889	10,331	7036
Montréal	3113	6541	7524	5597	5403	7920	2443	746	7736	4919	3256	2468	3449	10,390	2315	—	4397	7012	333	3432	5082	4102	2544	9207	6470
Moscow	4364	3627	3132	8369	770	6277	6176	4984	4443	7049	1556	6036	2140	8965	6671	4397	—	2703	4680	1550	7162	1477	5884	5236	4663
Nairobi	8287	5720	2811	6479	2217	2543	7179	8012	5447	10,740	4229	9600	3840	7159	9218	7267	3928	3371	7365	4020	5556	3340	9598	4636	6996
New Delhi	5709	2350	722	9823	2752	5769	8837	7486	2339	7413	4178	7015	4528	6340	9119	7012	2703	—	7319	4103	8747	3684	7691	2574	3638
New York	3373	6867	7811	5279	5598	7801	2124	714	8061	4969	3473	2455	3596	10,352	2086	333	4680	7319	—	3638	4805	4293	2574	9539	6757
Panama	5000	8939	9832	3319	7230	7090	867	2320	10,089	5254	5285	3025	5081	9027	1496	2542	6720	9422	2213	5388	3296	5916	3326	11,692	8441
Paris	4697	5138	4367	6857	1973	5782	4735	4145	5992	7452	215	5711	652	10,442	5723	3432	1550	4103	3638	—	5681	668	5579	6676	6054
Rio de Janeiro	8145	10,778	8334	1231	6153	3773	2805	5288	11,002	8295	5751	6334	5045	8218	4769	5082	7162	8747	4805	5681	—	5704	6621	9776	11,535
Rome	5263	5076	3845	6925	1305	5231	5198	4823	5773	8040	892	6336	849	9940	6374	4102	1477	3684	4293	668	5704	—	6259	6231	6140
San Francisco	2005	5934	8405	6455	7436	10,248	3908	1860	6904	2397	5369	349	5806	7850	1889	2544	5884	7691	2574	5579	6621	6259	—	8449	5148
Seattle	1442	5432	7830	6956	6809	10,205	4100	1737	6481	2681	4799	961	5303	8176	2340	2309	5217	7046	2409	5012	6890	5680	679	8074	4793
Singapore	6678	2754	2427	9870	5143	6007	11,408	9376	1608	6728	6747	8955	7079	3767	10,331	9207	5236	2574	9539	6676	9776	6231	8449	—	3304
Stockholm	4102	4197	3880	7799	2084	6422	5422	4288	5115	6873	892	5454	1613	9693	5965	3667	764	3466	3939	964	6638	1229	5372	5993	5091
Tehran	5654	3496	1743	8565	1220	5240	7322	6502	3844	8072	2739	7682	2974	7838	8182	5879	1534	1584	6141	2624	7386	2126	7362	4106	4775
Tokyo	3463	1305	4196	11,411	5937	9155	8813	6313	1792	3860	5956	5476	6704	5070	7036	6470	4663	3638	6757	6054	11,535	6140	5148	3304	—
Washington, D.C.	3300	6965	7900	5231	5800	7892	2051	594	8157	4839	3676	2295	3794	10,174	1883	490	4873	7500	203	3841	4783	4496	2444	9667	6792

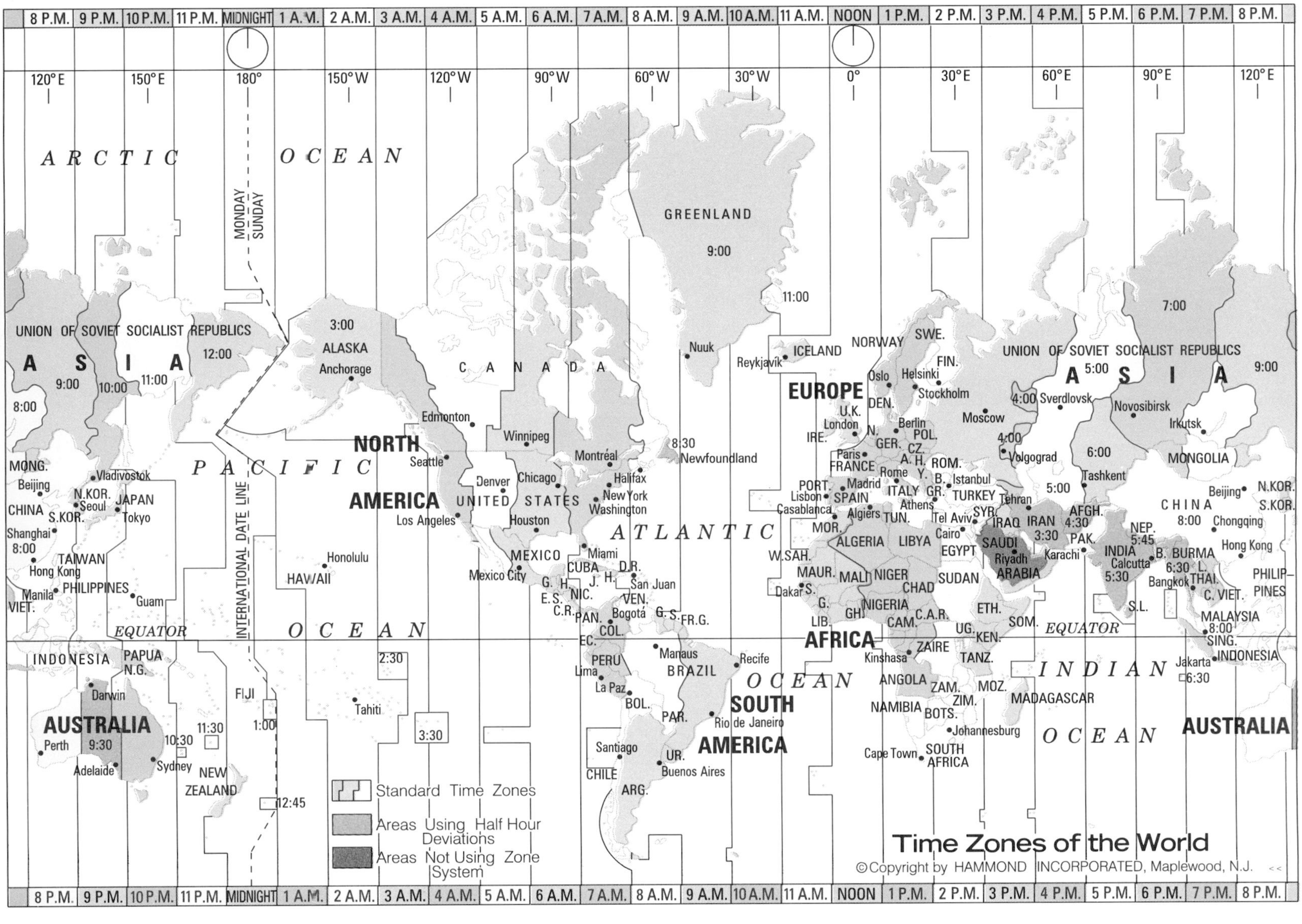

8 P.M.	9 P.M.	10 P.M.	11 P.M.	MIDNIGHT	1 A.M.	2 A.M.	3 A.M.	4 A.M.	5 A.M.	6 A.M.	7 A.M.	8 A.M.	9 A.M.	10 A.M.	11 A.M.	NOON	1 P.M.	2 P.M.	3 P.M.	4 P.M.	5 P.M.	6 P.M.	7 P.M.	8 P.M.

120°E 150°E 180° 150°W 120°W 90°W 60°W 30°W 0° 30°E 60°E 90°E 120°E

ARCTIC OCEAN

UNION OF SOVIET SOCIALIST REPUBLICS

ASIA

MONDAY / SUNDAY

GREENLAND 9:00

NORWAY SWE. FIN.

EUROPE

ALASKA Anchorage 3:00

CANADA

NORTH AMERICA

PACIFIC OCEAN

UNITED STATES

ATLANTIC

AFRICA

SOUTH AMERICA

INDIAN OCEAN

AUSTRALIA

Standard Time Zones
Areas Using Half Hour Deviations
Areas Not Using Zone System

Time Zones of the World

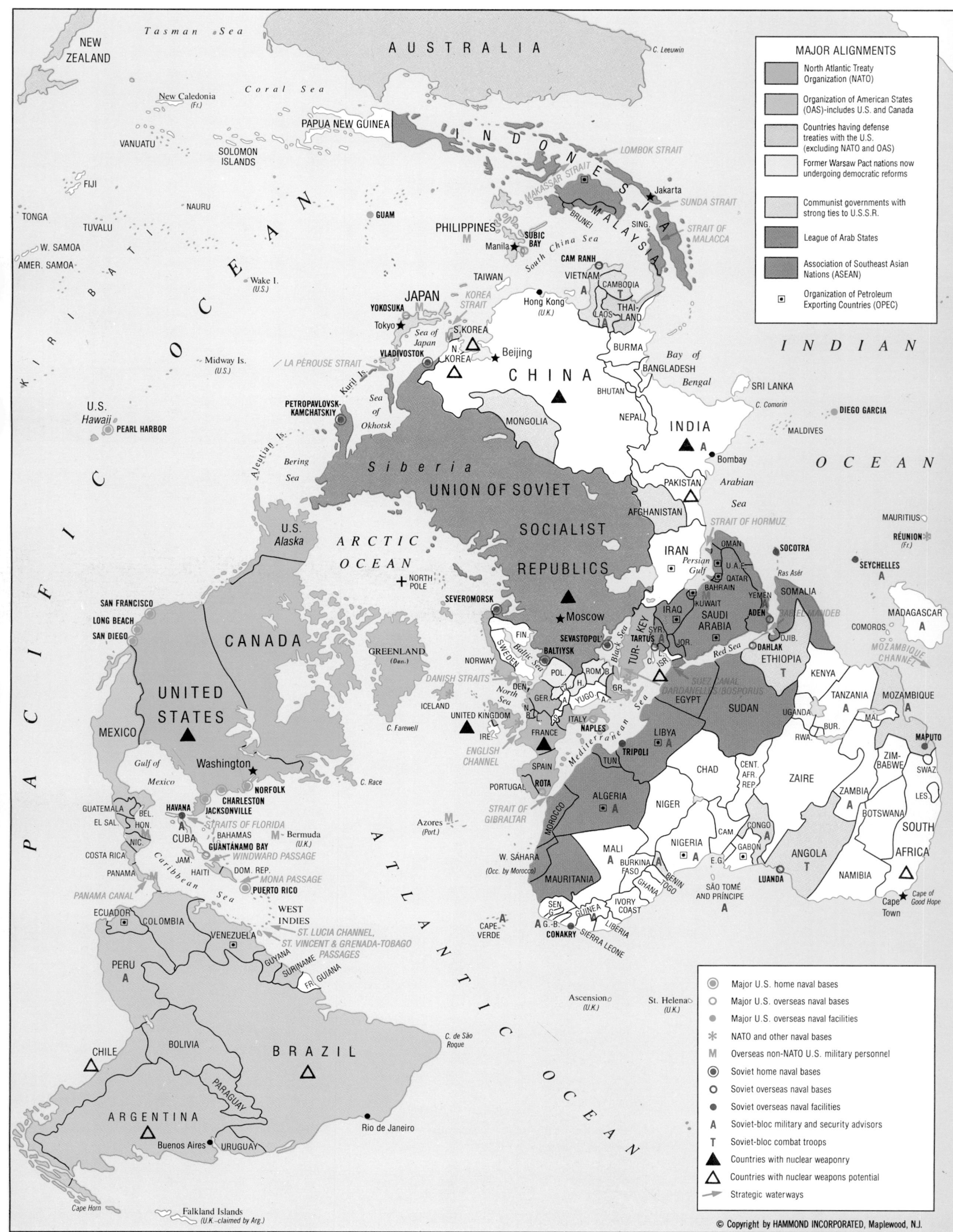

MAJOR ALIGNMENTS

North Atlantic Treaty Organization (NATO)

Organization of American States (OAS)-includes U.S. and Canada

Countries having defense treaties with the U.S. (excluding NATO and OAS)

Former Warsaw Pact nations now undergoing democratic reforms

Communist governments with strong ties to U.S.S.R.

League of Arab States

Association of Southeast Asian Nations (ASEAN)

Organization of Petroleum Exporting Countries (OPEC)

○ Major U.S. home naval bases
○ Major U.S. overseas naval bases
● Major U.S. overseas naval facilities
✳ NATO and other naval bases
M Overseas non-NATO U.S. military personnel
◉ Soviet home naval bases
○ Soviet overseas naval bases
● Soviet overseas naval facilities
A Soviet-bloc military and security advisors
T Soviet-bloc combat troops
▲ Countries with nuclear weaponry
△ Countries with nuclear weapons potential
→ Strategic waterways

© Copyright by HAMMOND INCORPORATED, Maplewood, N.J.

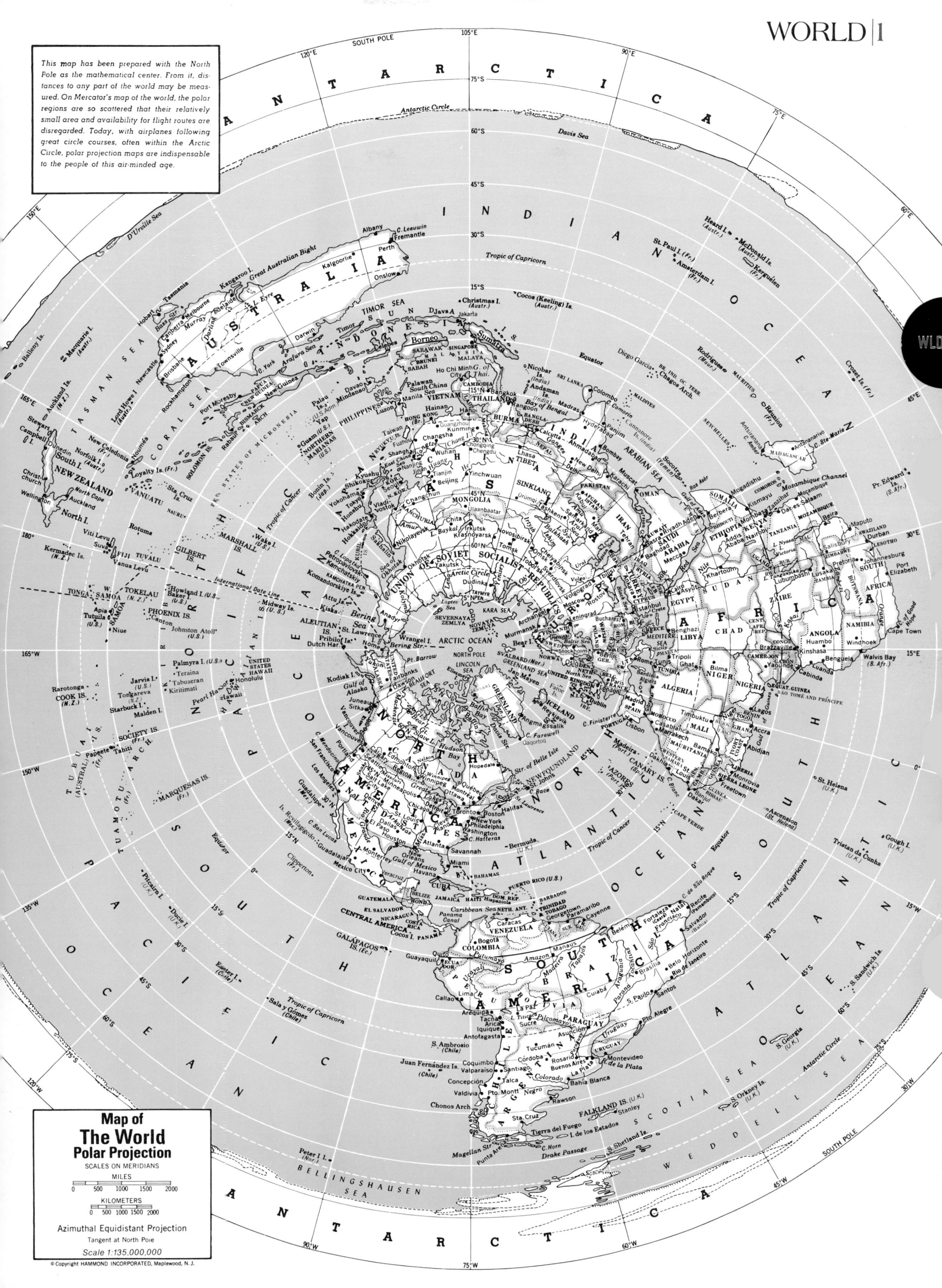

This map has been prepared with the North Pole as the mathematical center. From it, distances to any part of the world may be measured. On Mercator's map of the world, the polar regions are so scattered that their relatively small area and availability for flight routes are disregarded. Today, with airplanes following great circle courses, often within the Arctic Circle, polar projection maps are indispensable to the people of this air-minded age.

Map of
The World
Polar Projection

SCALES ON MERIDIANS

MILES
0   500   1000   1500   2000

KILOMETERS
0   500 1000 1500 2000

Azimuthal Equidistant Projection

Tangent at North Pole

Scale 1:135,000,000

The World

BRIESEMEISTER ELLIPTICAL EQUAL-AREA PROJECTION

Capitals of Countries .... ⊛
Other Capitals .... ⊛
International Boundaries ...... – – –

Scale 1:80,000,000

2

LAND AREA 57,970,000 sq. mi.
(150,142,300 sq. km.)
WATER AREA 139,781,000 sq. mi.
(362,032,790 sq. km.)
TOTAL SURFACE AREA 197,751,000 sq.mi.
(512,175,090 sq. km.)
POPULATION 5,292,000,000

NORTH PACIFIC OCEAN

MARSHALL IS.

SEA OF OKHOTSK

SOVIET SOCIALIST REPUBLICS

SIBERIA

MONGOLIA

CHINA

JAPAN

Tokyo

NORTHERN MARIANAS (U.S.)

Guam (U.S.)

FED. STATES OF MICRONESIA

KIRIBATI

NAURU

TUVALU

W. SAMOA

FIJI

TONGA

CORAL SEA

NEW CALEDONIA (Fr.)

VANUATU

TIBET

INDIA

BURMA

THAILAND

VIETNAM

PHILIPPINES

MALAYSIA

BRUNEI

INDONESIA

PAPUA NEW GUINEA

AUSTRALIA

Sydney

Canberra

TASMAN SEA

NEW ZEALAND

Wellington

Christchurch

Dunedin

Auckland

Norfolk I. (Austr.)

Lord Howe I. (Austr.)

Kermadec Is. (N.Z.)

ARABIAN SEA

INDIAN OCEAN

SRI LANKA

MALDIVES

Cocos (Keeling) Is. (Austr.)

Christmas I. (Austr.)

SEYCHELLES

Chagos Arch. (Br. Ind. Oc. Terr.)

Tropic of Capricorn

MAURITIUS

Réunion (Fr.)

Amsterdam I. (Fr.)

St. Paul I (Fr.)

MADAGASCAR

COMOROS

Kerguelen (Fr.)

McDonald Is. (Austr.)

Heard I. (Austr.)

Crozet Is. (Fr.)

Pr. Edward Is. (S. Afr.)

Antarctic Circle

Cape Adare

SOUTH AFRICA

Cape Town

Antarctica
AZIMUTHAL EQUIDISTANT PROJECTION
Scale 1:62,000,000

ATLANTIC OCEAN

Antarctic Circle

South Orkney Is. (U.K.)

Drake Passage

S. Shetland Is.

ANTARCTIC GRAHAM LAND PENINSULA

Larsen Ice Shelf

PALMER LAND

Bellingshausen Sea

9 Peter I I. (Nor.)

WEDDELL SEA

Berkner I.

Ronne Ice Shelf

10

COATS LAND

Filchner Ice Shelf

QUEEN MAUD LAND

Riiser-Larsen Pen.

ENDERBY LAND

Batterbee

AMERICAN HIGHLAND

Amery Ice Shelf

ANTARCTICA
11 + SOUTH POLE

INDIAN OCEAN

Shackleton Ice Shelf

WILKES LAND

MARIE BYRD LAND

Amundsen Sea

Ross Ice Shelf

Little America

Roosevelt I.

Ross I.

ROSS SEA

McMurdo So.

VICTORIA LAND

C. Adare

+ SOUTH MAGNETIC POLE

PACIFIC OCEAN

Scott I.

Antarctic Circle

Balleny Is.

Alaska (gulf), U.S.	D1	Beaufort (sea)	B1	Dvina, Northern (riv.),
Alaska (pen.), U.S.	D1	Belyy (isl.), U.S.S.R.	B6	U.S.S.R.	C7
Alaska (range), U.S.	C1	Bering (str.)	C1	East (Dezhnev) (cape),
Aleutian (isls.), U.S.	D1	Bol'shevik (isl.), U.S.S.R.	A4	U.S.S.R.	C1
Alexander (arch.), U.S.	D1	Boothia (gulf), Canada	B1	East Siberian (sea), U.S.S.R.	B1
Alexandra Land (isl.),		Boothia (pen.), Canada	B1	Echo Lake (Port Radium),
U.S.S.R.	A8	Borden (isl.), Canada	B1	Canada	C1
Amundsen (gulf), Canada	B1	Bristol (bay), U.S.	D1	Edge (isl.), Norway	B8
Anadyr', U.S.S.R.	C1	Brodeur (pen.), Canada	B1	Ellef Ringnes (isl.), Canada	B1
Anadyr' (riv.), U.S.S.R.	C1	Brooks (range), U.S.	C1	Ellesmere (isl.), Canada	C1
Anchorage, U.S.	D1	Canada	B1	Faddeyevskiy (isl.), U.S.S.R.	B2
Arctic Ocean	A1	Chelyuskin (cape), U.S.S.R.	B4	Farewell (cape), Greenl.	D1
Atlantic Ocean	D1	Chukchi (pen.), U.S.S.R.	C1	Finland	C8
Attu (isl.), U.S.	D1	Chukchi (sea)	C1	Franz Josef Land (isls.),
Axel Heiberg (isl.), Canada	A1	Columbia (cape), Canada	A1	U.S.S.R.	A7
Baffin (bay)	C1	Cook (inlet), U.S.	D1	Frederikshåb (Paamiut),
Baffin (isl.), Canada	C1	Cumberland (sound), Canada	C1	Greenl.	C1
Banks (isl.), Canada	B1	Davis (str.)	C1	George Land (isl.), U.S.S.R.	B7
Barents (sea)	B8	Denmark (str.)	C1	Godhavn (Qeqertarsuaq),
Barrow, U.S.	C1	Devon (isl.), Canada	C1	Greenl.	C1
Barrow (pt.), U.S.	B1	Dezhnev (cape), U.S.S.R.	C1	Godthåb (Nuuk) (cap.),
Bathurst (isl.), Canada	B1	Disko (isl.), Greenl.	C1	Greenl.	D1
Bear (isl.), Norway	B9	Dmitriya Lapteva (str.),		Graham Bell (isl.), U.S.S.R.	A6
Bear (isls.), U.S.S.R.	B1	U.S.S.R.	B2	Great Bear (lake), Canada	C1

Arctic Ice

Great Slave (lake), Canada	C1	Ob' (gulf), U.S.S.R.	
Greenland	B1	Ob' (riv.), U.S.S.R.	
Greenland (sea)	B1	October Revolution (isl.),
Hammerfest, Norway	B9	U.S.S.R.	
Hayes (isl.), Greenl.	B1	Omolon (riv.), U.S.S.R.	
Hekla (mt.), Ice.	C1	Paamiut, Greenl.	
Holman, Canada	B1	Pangnirtung, Canada	
Holsteinsborg (Sisimiut),		Peary Land (reg.), Greenl.	
Greenl.	C1	Pechora (riv.), U.S.S.R.	
Hope (isl.), Norway	B8	Pond Inlet, Canada	
Iceland	C1	Pribilof (isls.), U.S.	
Igloolik, Canada	C1	Prince Charles (isl.), Canada	
Indigirka (riv.), U.S.S.R.	C2	Prince of Wales (cape), U.S.	
Inuvik, Canada	C1	Prince of Wales (isl.), Canada	
Ittoqqortoormiit', Greenl.	B1	Prince Patrick (isl.), Canada	
Ivittuut, Greenl.	D1	Providentiya, U.S.S.R.	
Jan Mayen (isl.), Norway	C1	Qagortoq, Greenl.	
Julianehåb (Qagortoq),		Qeqertarsuaq, Greenl.	
Greenl.	D1	Queen Elizabeth (isls.),
Juneau, U.S.	D1	Canada	
Kalaallit Nunaat (Greenland)	B1	Repulse Bay, Canada	
Kanin (pen.), U.S.S.R.	C7	Resolute, Canada	
Kara (sea), U.S.S.R.	B6	Reykjavík (cap.), Ice.	
Karskiye Vorota (str.),		Rudolf (isl.), U.S.S.R.	
U.S.S.R.	B7	Sachs Harbour, Canada	
King Christian IX Land (reg.),		Saint Lawrence (isl.), U.S.	
Greenl.		Saint Matthew (isl.), U.S.	
King Christian X Land (reg.),		Scoresby (sound), Greenl.	
Greenl.		Scoresbysund
King Frederik VIII Land (reg.),		(Ittoqqortoormiit), Greenl.	
Greenl.	B1	Severnaya Zemlya (isls.),
Knud Rasmussen Land (reg.),		U.S.S.R.	
Greenl.	B1	Seward, U.S.	
Kola (pen.), U.S.S.R.	C8	Seward (pen.), U.S.	
Kolguyev (isl.), U.S.S.R.	B7	Shannon (isl.), Greenl.	
Kolyma (range), U.S.S.R.	C1	Siberia (reg.), U.S.S.R.	
Kolyma (riv.), U.S.S.R.	C1	Sisimiut, Greenl.	
Komsomolets (isl.), U.S.S.R.	A5	Sitka, U.S.	
Kotel'nyy (isl.), U.S.S.R.	B2	Somerset (isl.), Canada	
Kotuy (riv.), U.S.S.R.	B4	Søndre Strömfjord, Greenl.	
Kotzebue, U.S.	C1	Spitsbergen (isl.), Norway	
Kraulshavn (Nussaq), Greenl.	B1	Sukkertoppen (Maniitsoq),
Lancaster (sound), Canada	C1	Greenl.
Laptev (sea), U.S.S.R.	B3	Susuman, U.S.S.R.	
Lena (riv.), U.S.S.R.	C3	Svalbard (isls.), Norway	
Lincoln (sea)	A1	Sweden	
Lofoten (isls.), Norway	C9	Taymyr (lake), U.S.S.R.	
Longyearbyen, Norway	B1	Taymyr (pen.), U.S.S.R.	
Lyakhov (isls.), U.S.S.R.	B3	Taz (riv.), U.S.S.R.	
Mackenzie (bay), Canada	C1	Thule Air Base, Greenl.	
Mackenzie (mts.), Canada	C1	Tiksi, U.S.S.R.	
Mackenzie (riv.), Canada	C1	Timmiarmiut, Greenl.	
Mackenzie King (isl.), Canada	B1	Traill (isl.), Greenl.	
M'Clure (str.), Canada	B1	Tromsø, Norway	
Maniitsoq, Greenl.	C1	Tuktoyaktuk, Canada	
Melville (bay), Greenl.	B1	Uelen, U.S.S.R.	
Melville (isl.), Canada	B1	Umnak (isl.), U.S.	
Melville (pen.), Canada	C1	Unalaska (isl.), U.S.	
Mezen', U.S.S.R.	C7	Unimak (isl.), U.S.	
Morris Jesup (cape), Greenl.	A1	Union of Soviet
Mould Bay, Canada	B1	Socialist Republics	
Murmansk, U.S.S.R.	C8	United States of America	
Mys Shmidta, U.S.S.R.	C1	Upernavik, Greenl.	
Nanortalik, Greenl.	D1	Ural (mts.), U.S.S.R.	
Narsaq, Greenl.	C1	Ushakov (isl.), U.S.S.R.	
Narvik, Norway	C9	Ust'-Kuyga, U.S.S.R.	
Nar'yan-Mar, U.S.S.R.	C1	Vaygach (isl.), U.S.S.R.	
Navarin (cape), U.S.S.R.	C1	Verkhoyansk (range),
Nettilling (lake), Canada	C1	U.S.S.R.	
New Siberian (isls.), U.S.S.R.	B2	Victoria (isl.), Canada	
Nome, U.S.	C1	Vil'kitskogo (str.), U.S.S.R.	
Norman Wells, Canada	C1	Viscount Melville (sound),
North (cape), Norway	B8	Canada	
Northeast Foreland (pen.),		Wainwright, U.S.	
Greenl.	A1	Wandel (sea), Greenl.	
Northeast Land (isl.), Norway	B8	White (sea), U.S.S.R.	
North Magnetic Pole, Canada	B1	Whitehorse, Canada	
North Pole		Wiese (isl.), U.S.S.R.	
Norton (sound), U.S.	C1	Wilczek Land (isl.), U.S.S.R.	
Norway		Wrangel (isl.), U.S.S.R.	
Norwegian (sea)	C1	Yamal (pen.), U.S.S.R.	
Novaya Sibir' (isl.), U.S.S.R.	B2	Yana (riv.), U.S.S.R.	
Novaya Zemlya (isls.),		Yellowknife, Canada	
U.S.S.R.	B7	Yenisey (riv.), U.S.S.R.	
Nussaq, Greenl.	B1	York (cape), Greenl.	
Nuuk (cap.), Greenl.	C1	Yukon (riv.), N. Amer.	

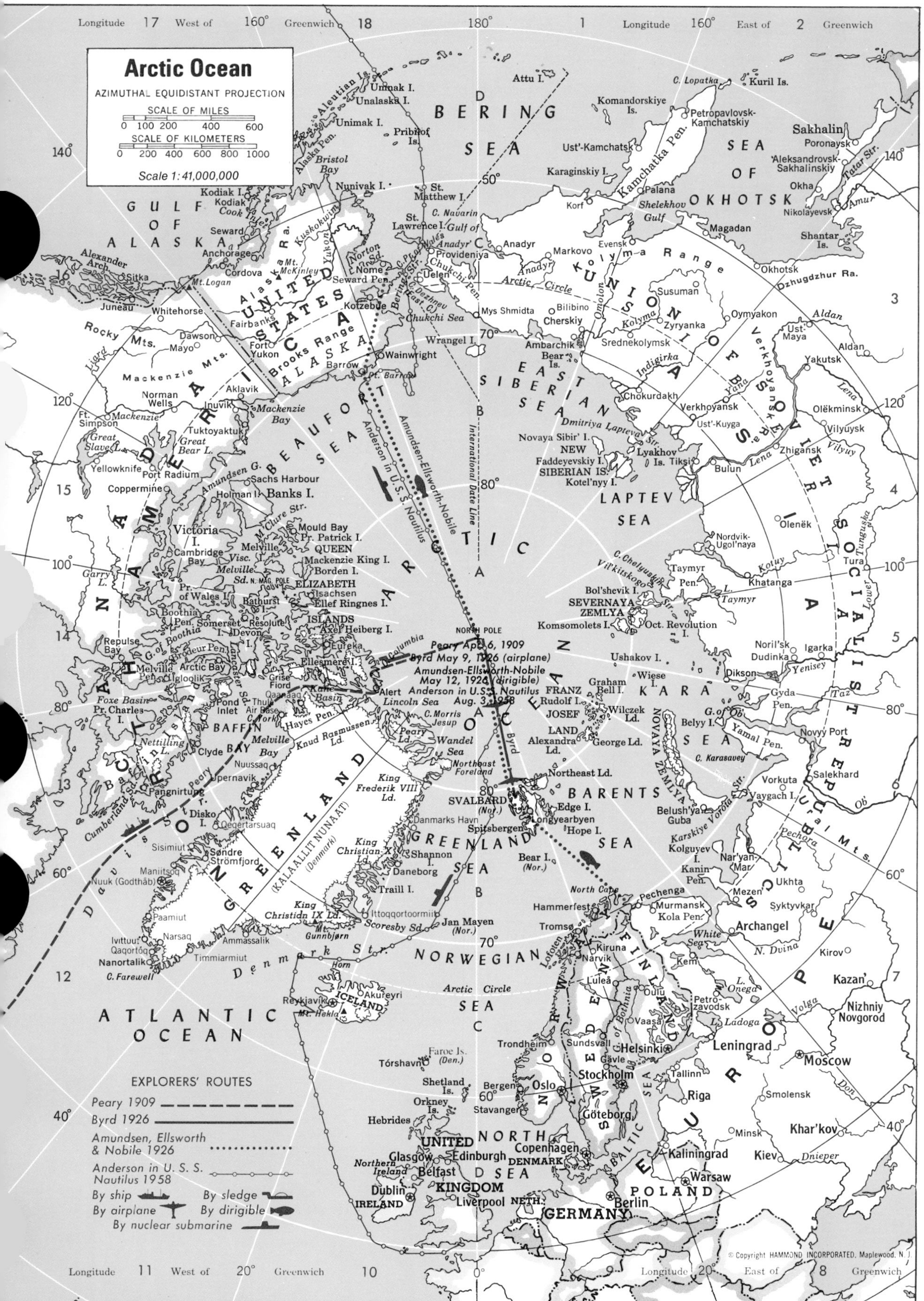

Arctic Ocean

AZIMUTHAL EQUIDISTANT PROJECTION

SCALE OF MILES
0 100 200 400 600

SCALE OF KILOMETERS
0 200 400 600 800 1000

Scale 1:41,000,000

EXPLORERS' ROUTES

Peary 1909

Byrd 1926

Amundsen, Ellsworth & Nobile 1926

Anderson in U.S.S. Nautilus 1958

By ship — By sledge
By airplane — By dirigible
By nuclear submarine

© Copyright HAMMOND INCORPORATED, Maplewood, N.J.

© C.S. Hammond & Co.

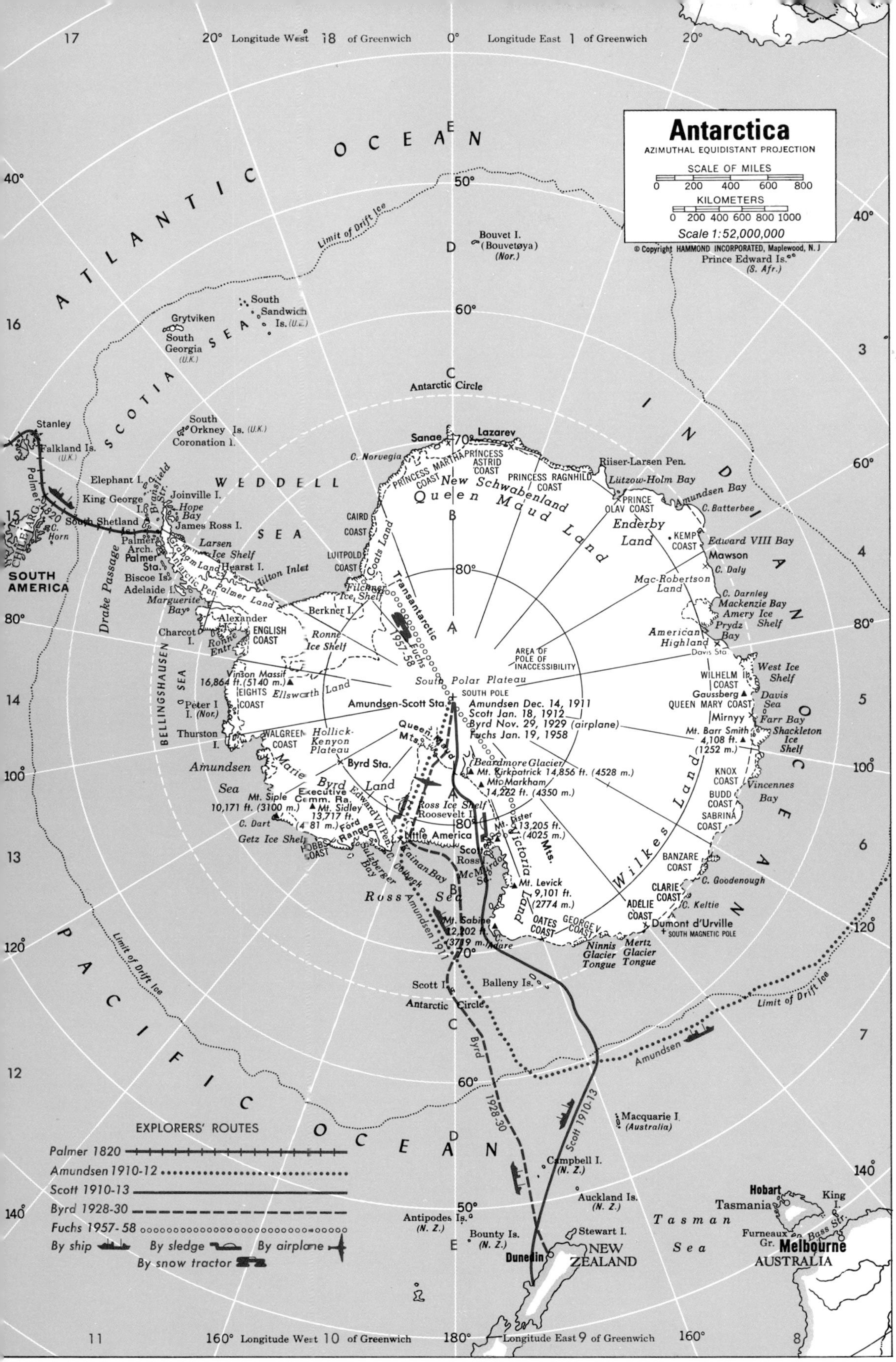

Antarctica

AZIMUTHAL EQUIDISTANT PROJECTION

SCALE OF MILES
0 200 400 600 800

KILOMETERS
0 200 400 600 800 1000

Scale 1:52,000,000

© Copyright HAMMOND INCORPORATED, Maplewood, N.J.

Adare (cape)	B9	Mackenzie (bay)	C4
Adelaide (isl.)	C15	Macquarie (isl.)	D8
Alexander (isl.)	B15	Mac-Robertson Land (reg.)	B4
Amery Ice Shelf	C4	Marguerite (bay)	C15
Amundsen (bay)	C3	Marie Byrd Land (reg.)	B13
Amundsen (sea)	B13	Markham (mt.)	A8
Amundsen-Scott Station	A14	Mawson Station	C4
Antarctic (pen.)	C15	McMurdo (sound)	B9
Balleny (isls.)	C9	Mertz Glacier Tongue	C8
Barr Smith (mt.)	C5	Mirnyy Station	C5
Beardmore (glac.)	A8	Ninnis Glacier Tongue	C8
Bellingshausen (sea)	C14	Norvegia (cape)	B18
Berkner (isl.)	B16	Oates Coast (reg.)	B8
Biscoe (isls.)	C15	Palmer (arch.)	C15
Bouvet (isl.)	D1	Palmer Land (reg.)	B15
Bransfield (str.)	C16	Palmer Station	C15
Byrd Station (site)	A12	Peter I (isl.)	B14
Caird Coast (reg.)	B17	Prince Edward (isls.)	E2
Campbell (isl.)	D9	Princess Astrid Coast (reg.)	B1
Charcot (isl.)	C15	Princess Martha Coast (reg.)	B18
Coats Land (reg.)	B17	Princess Ragnhild Coast
Colbeck (cape)	B10	(reg.)	B2
Coronation (isl.)	C16	Prydz (bay)	C4
Darnley (cape)	C4	Queen Mary Coast (reg.)	C5
Davis (sea)	C5	Queen Maud (mts.)	A12
Davis Station	C4	Queen Maud Land (reg.)	B1
Drake (passage)	C15	Riiser-Larsen (pen.)	C2
Dumont d'Urville Station	C7	Ronne Entrance (inlet)	B15
Edward VII (pen.)	B11	Ronne Ice Shelf	B15
Edward VIII (bay)	C4	Roosevelt (isl.)	A10
Elephant (isl.)	D16	Ross (isl.)	B9
Ellsworth Land (reg.)	B14	Ross (sea)	B10
Enderby Land (reg.)	B3	Ross Ice Shelf	A10
English Coast (reg.)	B15	Sabine (mt.)	B9
Executive Committee (range)	B12	Sanae Station	B18
Filchner Ice Shelf	B16	Scotia (sea)	D16
Ford Ranges (mts.)	B11	Scott (isl.)	C10
Gaussberg (mt.)	C5	Scott Station	B9
George V Coast (reg.)	C8	Shackleton Ice Shelf	C5
Getz Ice Shelf	B12	Sidley (mt.)	B12
Goodenough (cape)	C7	Siple (mt.)	B12
Graham Land (reg.)	C15	South Georgia (isl.)	D17
Grytviken, South Georgia Is.,		South Magnetic Pole	C7
Falkland. Is.	D17	South Orkney (isls.)	C16
Hearst (isl.)	B16	South Polar (plat.)	A1
Indian Ocean	C3	South Pole	A4
James Ross (isl.)	C16	South Sandwich (isls.)	D17
Joinville (isl.)	C16	South Shetland (isls.)	C15
King George (isl.)	C16	Sulzberger (bay)	B11
Kirkpatrick (mt.)	A8	Thurston (isl.)	C14
Knox Coast (reg.)	C6	Transantarctic (mts.)	B17
Larsen Ice Shelf	C16	Victoria Land (reg.)	B8
Lazarev Station	C1	Vincennes (bay)	C6
Levick (mt.)	B8	Vinson Massif (mt.)	B14
Lister (mt.)	B8	Walgreen Coast (reg.)	B13
Little America	B10	Weddell (sea)	C16
Luitpold Coast (reg.)	B17	West Ice Shelf	C5
Lützow-Holm (bay)	C3	Wilkes Land (reg.)	B7

EXPLORERS' ROUTES

Palmer 1820
Amundsen 1910-12
Scott 1910-13
Byrd 1928-30
Fuchs 1957-58
By ship   By sledge   By airplane
By snow tractor

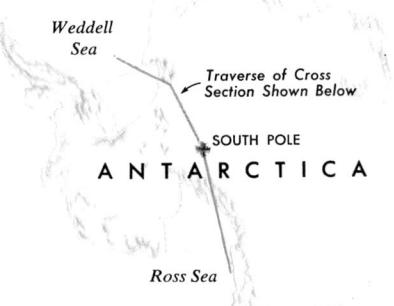

Weddell Sea

Traverse of Cross Section Shown Below

SOUTH POLE

ANTARCTICA

Ross Sea

Antarctic Cross Section: Weddell Sea to Ross Sea

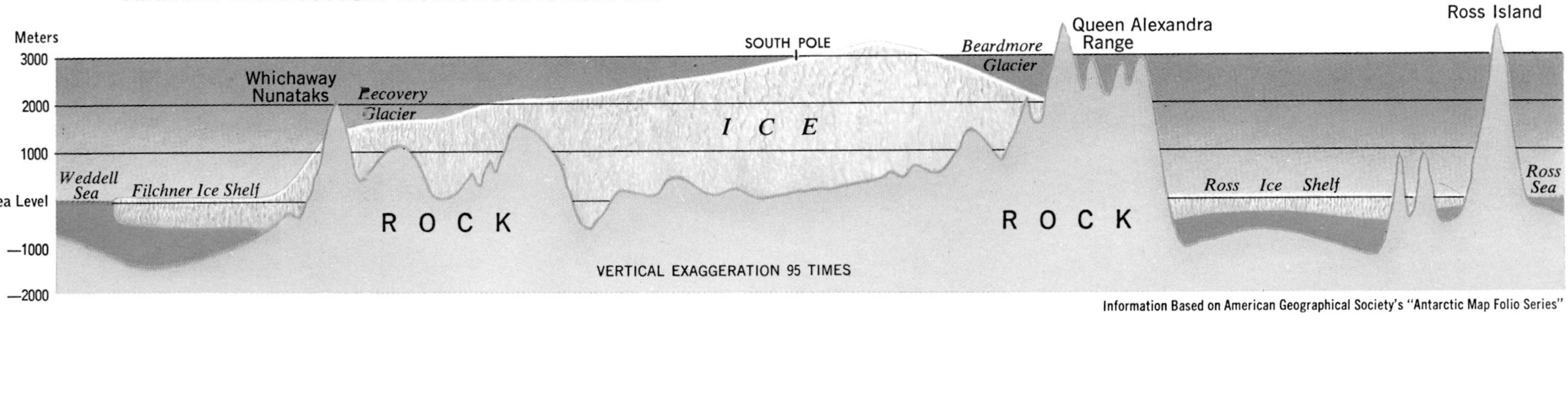

Meters
3000
2000
1000
Sea Level
-1000
-2000

SOUTH POLE

Beardmore Glacier

Queen Alexandra Range

Ross Island

Whichaway Nunataks

Recovery Glacier

ICE

Weddell Sea

Filchner Ice Shelf

ROCK

ROCK

Ross Ice Shelf

Ross Sea

VERTICAL EXAGGERATION 95 Times

Information Based on American Geographical Society's "Antarctic Map Folio Series"

Europe

POLYCONIC PROJECTION

SCALE OF MILES

0 100 200 300 400

KILOMETERS

0 100 200 300 400

Capitals of Countries..............⊛

Other Capitals......................⊚

International Boundaries ....–··–··–

Internal Boundaries ....–·–·–

Canals ....—·—·—

Scale 1:20,800,000

Aberdeen, Scotland D3
Adriatic (sea)......................F4
Aegean (sea).......................G5
Albania..............................G4
Ålborg, Denmark F3
Alps (mts.).........................E4
Andorra.............................E4
Antwerp, Belgium E3
Araks (riv.), U.S.S.R.............J5
Archangel, U.S.S.R...............J2
Århus, Denmark E3
Armenian S.S.R., U.S.S.R.......J4
Astrakhan', U.S.S.R...............J4
Athens (cap.), Greece G5
Austria..............................F4
Azerbaidzhan S.S.R., U.S.S.R...J4
Azov (sea), U.S.S.R...............H4
Baku, U.S.S.R......................J4
Balearic (isls.), Spain E5
Balkan (mts.).......................G4
Baltic (sea).........................F3
Barcelona, Spain E4
Barents (sea).......................J1
Basel, Switzerland.................E4
Belfast (cap.), N. Ireland........D3
Belgium..............................E3
Belgrade (cap.), Yugoslavia......G4
Belorussian S.S.R., U.S.S.R.....G3
Bergen, Norway E2
Berlin (cap.), Germany...........F3

Bern (cap.), Switzerland..........E4
Bilbao, Spain D4
Birmingham, England D3
Biscay (bay)........................B4
Black (sea)..........................H4
Bologna, Italy F4
Bonn, Germany E3
Bordeaux, France D4
Bornholm (isl.), Denmark F3
Bosporus (str.), Turkey G4
Bothnia (gulf)......................G2
Bratislava, Czech..................F4
Bremen, Germany E3
Bristol, England D3
British Isles.........................D3
Brussels (cap.), Belgium E3
Bucharest, Romania G4
Budapest (cap.), Hungary F4
Bulgaria..............................G4
Calais, France E3
Cardiff (cap.), Wales..............D3
Carpathian (mts.)..................G4
Cartagena, Spain D4
Caspian (sea), U.S.S.R...........J4
Caucasus (mts.), U.S.S.R........J4
Channel (isls.), U.K...............D3
Cologne, Germany E3
Copenhagen (cap.), Denmark....F3
Córdoba, Spain D5
Cork, Ireland D3

Corsica (isl.), France E4
Cracow, Poland F3
Crete (isl.), Greece................G5
Crimea (pen.), U.S.S.R...........H4
Czechoslovakia.....................F4
Danube (riv.).......................F4
Dardanelles (str.), Turkey G5
Denmark.............................E3
Dnieper (riv.), U.S.S.R...........H3
Dniester (riv.), U.S.S.R...........G4
Don (riv.), U.S.S.R................J4
Donets (riv.), U.S.S.R............J4
Douro (riv.), Portugal D4
Dover, England.....................E4
Dresden, Germany F3
Dublin (cap.), Ireland.............D3
Dvina, Northern (riv.),
   U.S.S.R...........................J2
Ebro (riv.), Spain..................D4
Edinburgh (cap.), Scotland D3
Elba (isl.), Italy F4
Elbe (riv.)...........................F3
El'brus (mt.), U.S.S.R............J4
England, U.K.......................D3
English (chan.).....................D3
Essen, Germany....................E3
Estonian S.S.R., U.S.S.R........G3
Etna (vol.), Italy...................F5
Faroe (isls.), Denmark D2
Finisterre (cape), Spain..........C4

Finland...............................G2
Finland (gulf), Finland G3
Florence, Italy F4
France................................E4
Frankfurt, Germany................E3
Gdańsk, Poland F3
Geneva, Switzerland E4
Genoa, Italy E4
Georgian S.S.R., U.S.S.R........J4
Germany.............................F3
Gibraltar.............................D5
Glasgow, Scotland D3
Göteborg, Sweden F3
Granada, Spain D5
Hague, The (cap.),
   Netherlands......................E3
Hamburg, Germany................F3
Helsinki (cap.), Finland G2
Hungary..............................F4
Iceland...............................C2
Ionian (sea).........................F5
Ireland...............................D3
Irish (sea)...........................D3
Istanbul, Turkey....................G4
Italy...................................F4
Jan Mayen (isl.), Norway.........F1
Jönköping, Sweden................F3
Kaliningrad, U.S.S.R...............G3
Karlsruhe, Germany...............E4
Katowice, Poland F3

Khar'kov, U.S.S.R.................H4
Kiev, U.S.S.R.......................H3
Kishinev, U.S.S.R..................G4
Kjölen (mts.)........................F2
Kola (pen.), U.S.S.R..............H2
Kursk, U.S.S.R.....................H3
Ladoga (lake), U.S.S.R...........H2
Land's End (prom.), England D3
Latvian S.S.R., U.S.S.R..........G3
Le Havre, France E4
Leeds, England D3
Leipzig, Germany F3
†Leningrad, U.S.S.R..............H3
León, Spain.........................D4
Liechtenstein........................F4
Liège, Belgium E3
Lille, France.........................E3
Limerick, Ireland D3
Limoges, France...................E4
Linz, Austria F4
Lisbon (cap.), Portugal D5
Lithuanian S.S.R., U.S.S.R......G3
Liverpool, England.................D3
Ljubljana, Yugoslavia F4
Łódź, Poland F3
Lofoten (isls.), Norway...........F2
Loire (riv.), France E4
London (cap.), England D3
Luxembourg.........................E3
Lyon, France........................E4

L'vov, U.S.S.R......................G4
Madrid (cap.), Spain..............D4
Majorca (isl.), Spain..............E5
Málaga, Spain D5
Malmö, Sweden F3
Malta.................................F5
Manchester, England D3
Marmara (sea), Turkey G4
Marseille, France...................E4
Mediterranean (sea)...............E5
Milan, Italy E4
Minsk, U.S.S.R.....................G3
Moldavian S.S.R., U.S.S.R. G4
Monaco..............................E4
Moscow (cap.), U.S.S.R..........H3
Munich, Germany F4
Murmansk, U.S.S.R................H2
Naples, Italy F4
Nice, France E4
Nizhniy Novgorod (Gor'kiy),
   U.S.S.R...........................J3
North (Nordkapp) (cape),
   Norway............................G1
North (sea)..........................E3
Northern Ireland....................D3
Norway...............................E2
Norwegian (sea)....................D2
Nürnberg (Nurnberg),
   Germany...........................F4
Odense, Denmark F3

Oder (riv.)...........................F3
Odessa, U.S.S.R....................H4
Onega (lake), U.S.S.R............H2
Orkney (isls.), Scotland D3
Orléans, France....................E4
Oslo (cap.), Norway F2
Palermo, Italy F5
Palma, Spain E5
Paris (cap.), France E4
Piraiévs, Greece....................G5
Plymouth, England D3
Po (riv.), Italy E4
Poland................................F3
Porto, Portugal D4
Portugal.............................D4
Poznań, Poland.....................F3
Prague (cap.), Czech. F3
Prut (riv.), U.S.S.R................G4
Pyrenees (mts.)....................D4
Reykjavík (cap.), Iceland B2
Rhine (riv.)..........................E4
Rhône (riv.), France E4
Riga, U.S.S.R.......................G3
Romania.............................G4
Rome (cap.), Italy..................F4
Rostov, U.S.S.R....................J4
Rotterdam, Netherlands E3
Russian S.F.S.R., U.S.S.R.......H3
Saarbrücken, Germany...........E4
Salzburg, Austria...................F4

AREA 4,057,000 sq. mi.
(10,507,630 sq. km.)
POPULATION 689,000,000
LARGEST CITY Paris
HIGHEST POINT El'brus 18,510 ft.
(5,642 m.)
LOWEST POINT Caspian Sea -92 ft.
(-28 m.)

Population Distribution

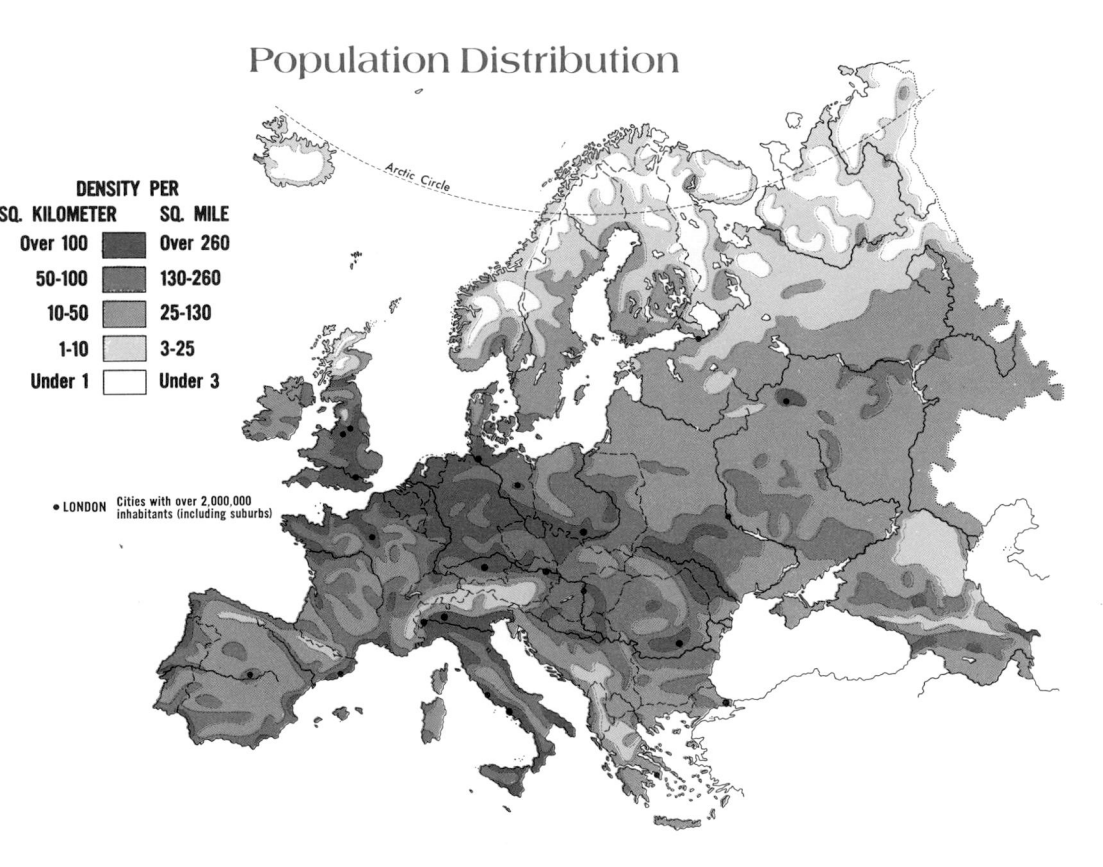

DENSITY PER

SQ. KILOMETER	SQ. MILE
Over 100	Over 260
50-100	130-260
10-50	25-130
1-10	3-25
Under 1	Under 3

● LONDON Cities with over 2,000,000
inhabitants (including suburbs)

Vegetation

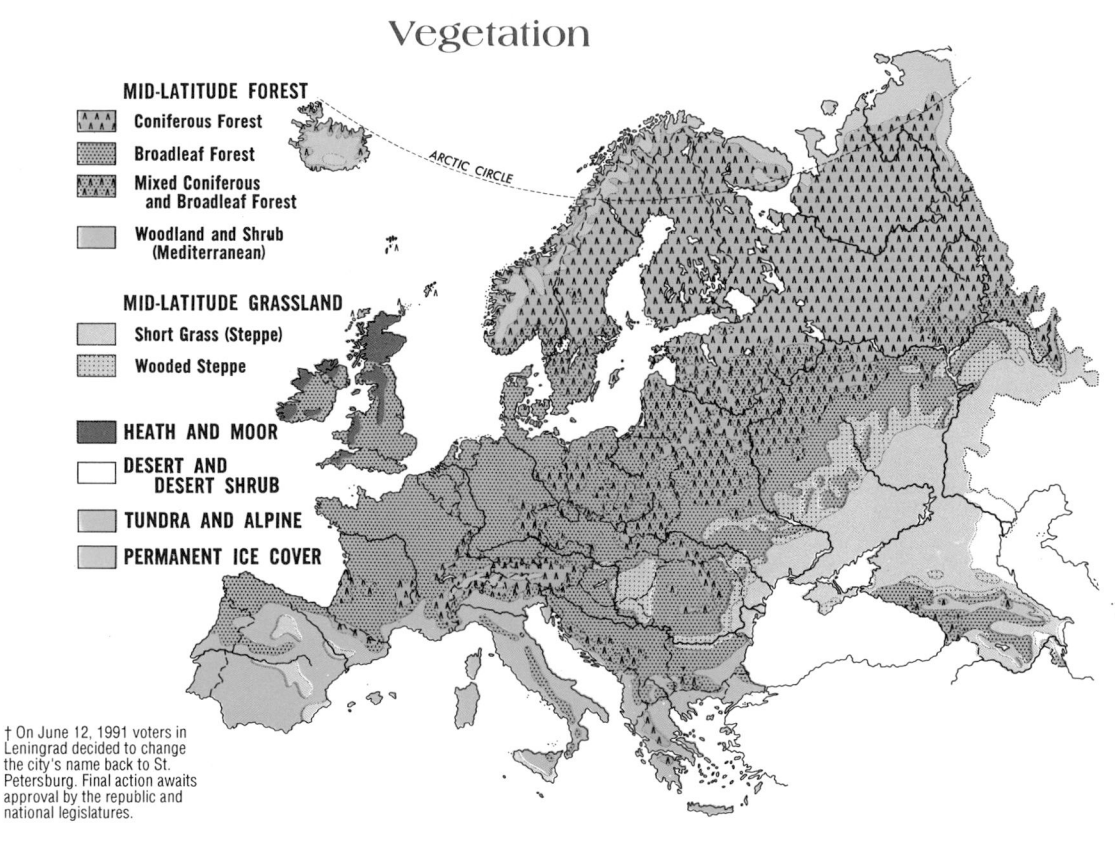

MID-LATITUDE FOREST

Coniferous Forest

Broadleaf Forest

Mixed Coniferous
and Broadleaf Forest

Woodland and Shrub
(Mediterranean)

MID-LATITUDE GRASSLAND

Short Grass (Steppe)

Wooded Steppe

HEATH AND MOOR

**DESERT AND
DESERT SHRUB**

TUNDRA AND ALPINE

PERMANENT ICE COVER

† On June 12, 1991 voters in
Leningrad decided to change
the city's name back to St.
Petersburg. Final action awaits
approval by the republic and
national legislatures.

© Copyright HAMMOND INCORPORATED, Maplewood, N.J.

Samara (Kuybyshev),
  U.S.S.R. K3
San Marino........................F4
San Sebastián, Spain.........D4
Saragossa, Spain...............D4
Sarajevo, Yugoslavia..........F4
Sardinia (isl.), Italy.............E4
Sava (riv.)..........................F4
Scotland...........................D3
Seine (riv.), France.............E4
Sevastopol', U.S.S.R...........H4
Seville, Spain....................D5
Sheffield, England..............D3
Shetland (isls.), Scotland....D2
Sicily (isl.), Italy.................F5
Skopje, Yugoslavia.............G4
Smolensk, U.S.S.R..............H3
Sofia (cap.), Bulgaria..........G4
Spain................................D4
Stockholm (cap.), Sweden...F3
Strasbourg, France............E4
Stuttgart, Germany.............E4
Sweden.............................F2
Switzerland E4
Tagus (riv.)........................D5
Tampere, Finland................G2
Taranto (gulf), Italy F5
Tbilisi, U.S.S.R...................J4
Tiranë (cap.), Albania..........F4
Trieste, Italy......................F4

Trondheim, Norway....... .....F2
Turin, Italy.........................E4
Turkey...............................H5
Tver', U.S.S.R....................H3
Tyrrhenian (sea).................F4
Ukrainian S.S.R., U.S.S.F....H3
Union of Soviet
  Socialist Republics...........H2
United Kingdom..................D3
Ural (mts.) U.S.S.R..............L2
Valencia, Spain..................D5
Valletta (cap.), Malta...........F5
Varna, Bulgaria..................G4
Vatican City.......................F4
Venice, Italy......................F4
Vienna (cap.), Austria.........F4
Vistula (riv.), Poland...........F3
Volga (riv.), U.S.S.R............J4
Volgograd, U.S.S.R.............J4
Wales...............................D3
Warsaw (cap.), Poland G3
Weser (riv.), Germany.........E3
White (sea), U.S.S.R............H2
Yalta, U.S.S.R....................H4
Yaroslavl', U.S.S.R..............H3
Yerevan, U.S.S.R................J4
Yugoslavia.........................F4
Zagreb, Yugoslavia.............F4
Zaporozh'ye, U.S.S.R...........H4
Zürich, Switzerland.............E4

Vegetation / Relief

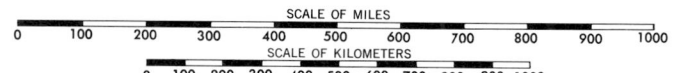

SCALE OF MILES

| 0 | 100 | 200 | 300 | 400 | 500 | 600 | 700 | 800 | 900 | 1000 |

SCALE OF KILOMETERS

| 0 | 100 | 200 | 300 | 400 | 500 | 600 | 700 | 800 | 900 | 1000 |

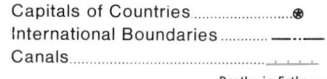

Capitals of Countries .... ⊛
International Boundaries .... —ᐧᐧ—
Canals ....

Depths in Fathoms

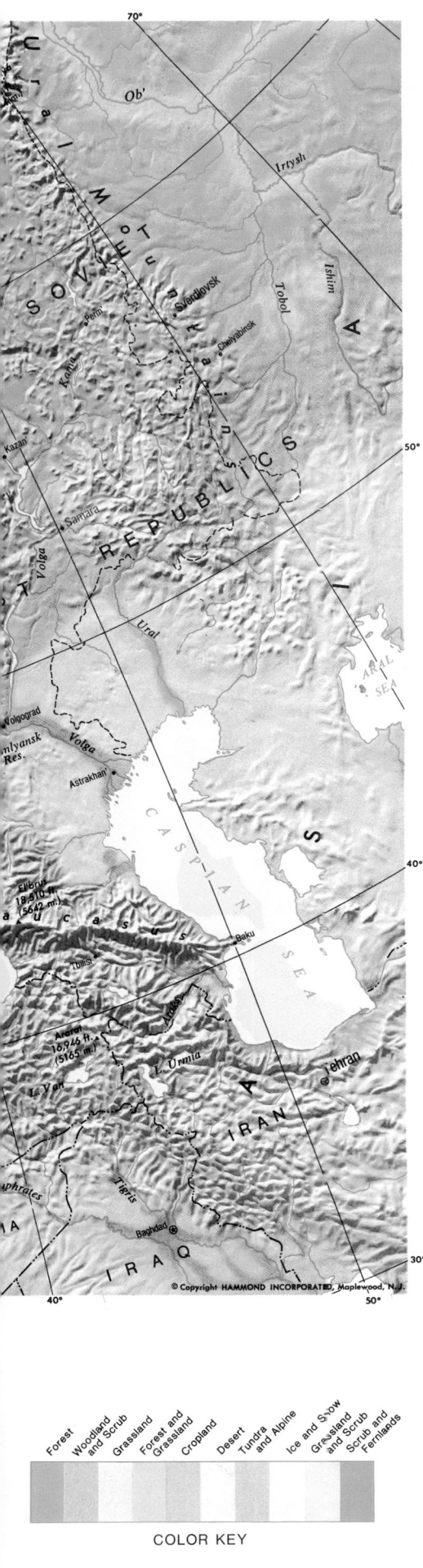

COLOR KEY

Forest | Woodland and Scrub | Grassland | Forest and Grassland | Cropland | Desert | Tundra and Alpine | Ice and Snow | Grassland and Scrub | Scrub and Ferrnlands

Rainfall

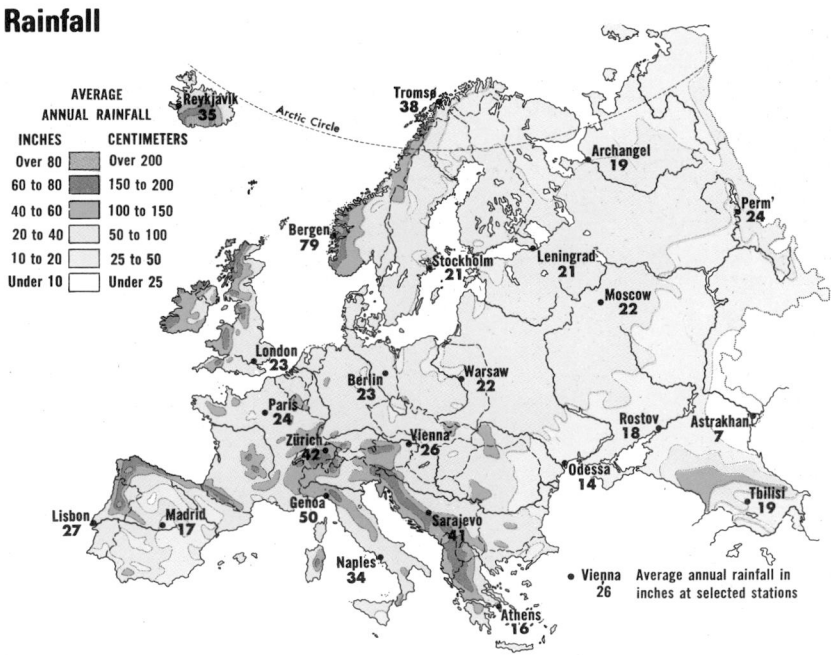

AVERAGE ANNUAL RAINFALL

INCHES | CENTIMETERS
Over 80 | Over 200
60 to 80 | 150 to 200
40 to 60 | 100 to 150
20 to 40 | 50 to 100
10 to 20 | 25 to 50
Under 10 | Under 25

Reykjavík 35
Tromsø 38
Archangel 19
Perm' 24
Bergen 79
Stockholm 21
Leningrad 21
Moscow 22
London 23
Berlin 23
Warsaw 22
Rostov 18
Astrakhan 7
Paris 24
Zürich 42
Vienna 26
Odessa 14
Tbilisi 19
Lisbon 27
Madrid 17
Genoa 50
Sarajevo 41
Naples 34
Athens 16

• Vienna 26 — Average annual rainfall in inches at selected stations

Average January Temperature

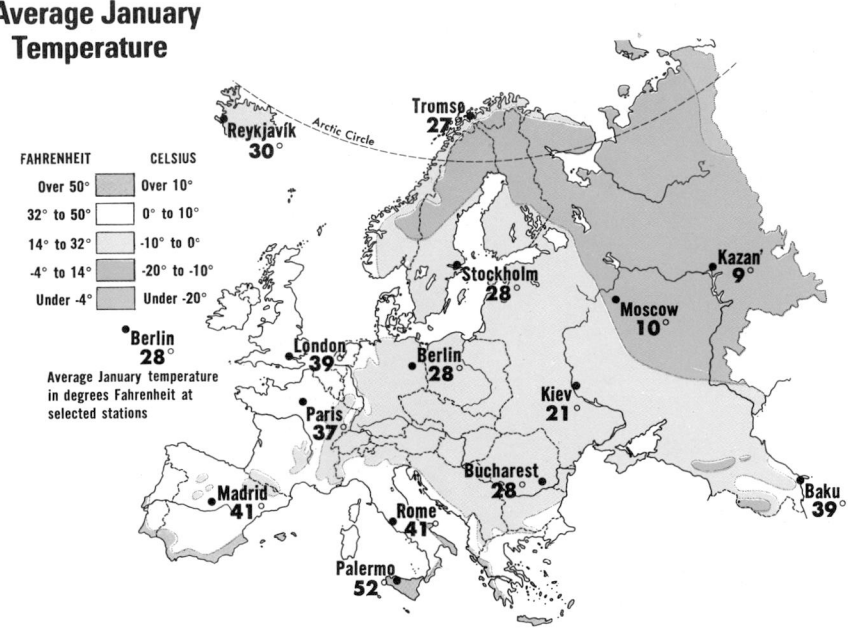

FAHRENHEIT | CELSIUS
Over 50° | Over 10°
32° to 50° | 0° to 10°
14° to 32° | -10° to 0°
-4° to 14° | -20° to -10°
Under -4° | Under -20°

Reykjavík 30°
Tromsø 27°
Stockholm 28°
Kazan' 9°
Moscow 10°
Berlin 28° — Average January temperature in degrees Fahrenheit at selected stations
London 39°
Berlin 28°
Kiev 21°
Paris 37°
Bucharest 28°
Baku 39°
Madrid 41°
Rome 41°
Palermo 52°

Average July Temperature

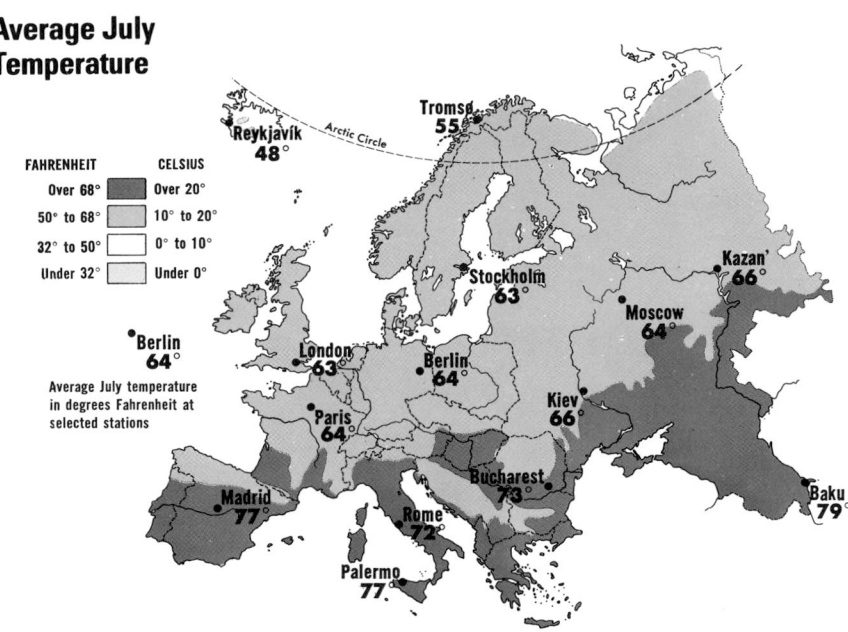

FAHRENHEIT | CELSIUS
Over 68° | Over 20°
50° to 68° | 10° to 20°
32° to 50° | 0° to 10°
Under 32° | Under 0°

Reykjavík 48°
Tromsø 55°
Stockholm 63°
Kazan' 66°
Moscow 64°
Berlin 64° — Average July temperature in degrees Fahrenheit at selected stations
London 63°
Berlin 64°
Kiev 66°
Paris 64°
Bucharest 73°
Baku 79°
Madrid 77°
Rome 72°
Palermo 77°

UNITED KINGDOM

AREA 94,399 sq. mi. (244,493 sq. km.)
POPULATION 57,236,000
CAPITAL London
LARGEST CITY London
HIGHEST POINT Ben Nevis 4,406 ft. (1,343 m.)
MONETARY UNIT pound sterling
MAJOR LANGUAGES English, Gaelic, Welsh
MAJOR RELIGIONS Protestantism, Roman Catholicism

IRELAND

AREA 27,136 sq. mi. (70,282 sq. km.)
POPULATION 3,540,643
CAPITAL Dublin
LARGEST CITY Dublin
HIGHEST POINT Carrantuohill 3,415 ft. (1,041 m.)
MONETARY UNIT Irish pound
MAJOR LANGUAGES English, Gaelic (Irish)
MAJOR RELIGION Roman Catholicism

UNITED KINGDOM

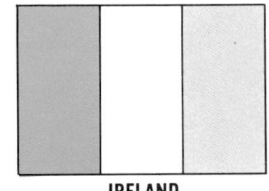

IRELAND

ENGLAND
(map on page 13)

COUNTIES

Avon 900,947	E6
Bedfordshire 502,164	G5
Berkshire 670,859	F6
Buckinghamshire 562,221	G6
Cambridgeshire 569,893	G5
Cheshire 921,623	E4
Cleveland 565,845	F3
Cornwall 418,631	C7
Cumbria 471,696	D3
Derbyshire 901,831	F5
Devon 930,112	D7
Dorset 578,993	E7
Durham 598,881	F3
East Sussex 641,016	H7
Essex 1,416,890	H6
Gloucestershire 493,166	E6
Hampshire 1,442,598	F6
Hereford and Worcester 624,393	E5
Hertfordshire 950,760	G6
Humberside 843,282	G4
Isle of Wight 114,879	F7
Isles of Scilly	A7
Kent 1,448,393	H6
Lancashire 1,362,801	E4
Leicestershire 835,647	F5
Lincolnshire 542,944	G4
London 6,608,598	H8
Manchester 2,575,407	H2

Merseyside 1,503,120	G2
Norfolk 685,232	H5
North Yorkshire 653,456	F3
Northamptonshire 524,967	G5
Northumberland 295,451	E2
Nottinghamshire 976,748	F4
Oxfordshire 507,230	F6
Shropshire 370,355	E5
Somerset 417,457	E6
South Yorkshire 1,292,029	F4
Staffordshire 1,005,64	E5
Suffolk 590,133	H5
Surrey 992,489	G6
Tyne and Wear 1,135,492	H3
Warwickshire 469,801	F5
West Midlands 2,628,419	F5
West Sussex 650,124	G7
West Yorkshire 2,021,707	J1
Wiltshire 512,635	E6
Yorkshire, North 653,456	F3
Yorkshire, South 1,292,029	F4
Yorkshire, West 2,021,707	J1

CITIES and TOWNS

Abingdon 29,130	F6
Accrington 36,459	H1
Adwick le Street 10,293	K2
Aldershot 53,665	G8
Aldridge 17,549	E5
Alfreton 21,284	F4
Alsager 12,944	E4
Alton 14,163	G6
Altrincham 39,528	H2

Amersham 21,326	G7
Andover 30,632	F6
Arnold 37,721	F4
Ashford 45,198	H6
Ashington 27,786	F2
Ashton-under-Lyne 43,605	H2
Aylesbury 51,999	G7
Aylesford 21,017	J8
Bacup 14,082	H1
Banbury 37,463	F5
Banstead 35,360	H8
Barking 149,132	H8
Barnet 289,277	H7
Barnoldswick 10,125	H1
Barnsley 76,783	J2
Barnstaple 24,490	D6
Barrow-in-Furness 50,174	D3
Basildon 94,800	J8
Basingstoke 73,027	F6
Bath 84,283	E6
Batley 45,582	J1
Beaconsfield 13,397	G8
Bebington 62,618	G2
Beccles 10,677	J5
Bedford 75,632	G5
Bedlington 15,074	F2
Bedworth 29,192	F5
Beeston and Stapleford 64,785	F5
Benfleet 50,783	J8
Bentley with Arksey 34,273	F4
Berkhamsted 16,874	G7
Berwick-upon-Tweed 12,772	F2
Beverley 19,368	G4

Bexhill 34,625	H7
Bexley 213,215	H8
Bicester 15,946	F6
Biddulph 16,697	H2
Bideford 13,826	C6
Biggleswade 10,905	G5
Birkenhead 99,075	G2
Birmingham 1,013,995	F5
Bishop Auckland 23,560	E3
Bishop's Stortford 22,535	H6
Blackburn 109,564	H1
Blackpool 146,297	G1
Blaydon 16,719	H3
Blyth 35,101	F2
Bodmin 11,992	C7
Bognor Regis 50,323	G7
Boldon 11,639	J3
Bolsover 11,497	J2
Bolton 143,960	H2
Bootle 70,860	G2
Boston 33,908	G5
Bournemouth 142,829	F7
Bracknell 52,257	G8
Bradford 293,336	J1
Braintree 30,975	H6
Brent 251,238	H8
Brentwood 51,212	J8
Bridgnorth 10,332	E5
Bridgwater 30,782	E6
Bridlington 28,426	G3
Bridport 10,615	E7
Brighouse 32,597	J1
Brighton 134,581	G7
Bristol 413,861	E6

Broadstairs 21,551	J6
Bromley 280,525	H8
Bromsgrove 24,576	E5
Brownhills 18,200	E5
Buckingham 6,439	G6
Burgess Hill 23,577	G7
Burnham-on-Sea 17,022	D6
Burnley 76,365	H1
Burntwood 28,938	F5
Burton upon Trent 59,040	F5
Bury 61,785	H2
Bury Saint Edmunds 30,563	H5
Bushey 15,759	H7
Buxton 19,502	J2
Calne 10,235	F6
Camborne-Redruth 34,262	B7
Cambridge 87,111	G5
Camden 161,098	H8
Cannock 54,503	E5
Canterbury 34,546	H6
Canvey Island 35,243	J8
Carlisle 72,206	D3
Carlton 46,053	F5
Carterton 10,876	F6
Caterham and Warlingham 30,331	H8
Charlton Kings 10,786	F6
Chatham 65,835	J8
Cheadle 10,470	E5
Cheadle and Gatley 59,478	H2
Chelmsford 91,109	J7
Cheltenham 87,188	E6
Chertsey 10,195	G8
Chesham 20,883	G7
Cheshunt 49,616	H7
Chester 80,154	G2
Chester-le-Street 34,776	J3
Chesterfield 73,352	J2
Chichester 26,050	G7
Chippenham 21,325	E6
Chorley 33,465	G2
Christchurch 32,854	F7
Cirencester 13,491	E6
Clacton 39,618	J6
Clay Cross 22,635	J2
Cleethorpes 33,238	H4
Clevedon 17,875	D6
Clitheroe 13,671	H1
Coalville 28,831	F5
Colchester 87,476	H6
Colne 19,094	H1
Congleton 23,482	H2
Consett 22,409	H3
Corby 48,704	G5
Corsham 11,259	E6
Coventry 318,718	F5
Cowes 16,134	F7
Cranleigh 10,334	G6
Crawley 80,113	G6
Crewe 59,097	E4
Crosby 54,103	G2
Crowborough 17,008	H6
Croydon 298,794	H8
Darlington 85,519	F3
Dartford 62,032	J8
Darton 13,743	J2
Darwen 30,883	H1
Daventry 16,096	F5
Deal 26,311	J6
Dearne 13,391	K2
Denton 37,784	H2
Derby 218,026	F5
Devizes 12,430	F6
Dewsbury 49,612	J1
Didcot 15,147	F6
Doncaster 74,727	F4
Dorchester 13,734	E7
Dorking 14,602	G8
Dover 33,461	J6
Droitwich 18,025	E5
Dronfield 22,641	J2
Dudley 186,513	E5
Dunstable 48,436	G6
Durham 38,105	J3
Ealing 278,677	H8
East Dereham 11,798	H5
East Grinstead 23,867	G6
East Retford 19,308	G4
Eastbourne 86,715	H7
Eastleigh 58,585	F7
Egham 21,810	G8
Ellesmere Port 65,829	G2

Enfield 257,154	H7
Epping 10,148	H7
Epsom and Ewell 65,830	G8
Esher 46,688	H8
Eston 37,694	F3
Eton	G8
Evesham 15,069	F5
Exeter 88,235	D7
Exmouth 28,037	D7
Falmouth 17,810	B7
Fareham 55,563	F7
Farnborough 48,063	G8
Farnham 34,541	G8
Farnworth 25,591	H2
Faversham 15,914	H6
Felixstowe 24,207	J6
Felling 36,377	J3
Fleet 27,406	G8
Fleetwood 27,899	D4
Folkestone 42,949	J6
Formby 26,852	G2
Frinton and Walton 12,689	J6
Frome 19,678	E6
Gainsborough 20,326	G4
Gateshead 91,421	J3
Gillingham 92,531	J8
Glastonbury 6,751	E6
Glossop 29,923	J2
Gloucester 106,526	E6
Godalming 18,758	G8
Golborne 20,633	G2
Goole 19,394	G4
Gosport 69,664	F7
Grantham 30,700	G5
Gravesend 53,450	J8
Great Grimsby 91,532	G4
Great Harwood 10,968	H1
Great Malvern (Malvern) 30,153	E5
Great Yarmouth 54,777	J5
Greenwich 211,013	H8
Guildford 61,509	G8
Guisborough 19,242	F3
Hackney 179,529	H8

Hailsham 16,367	H7
Hale 16,362	H2
Halesowen 57,533	E5
Halifax 76,675	J1
Hammersmith 144,616	H8
Haringey 202,650	H8
Harlow 79,150	H7
Harrogate 63,637	J1
Harrow 195,292	G8
Hartlepool 91,749	F3
Harwich 17,245	J6
Haslemere 10,544	G6
Haslingden 14,347	H1
Hastings 74,979	H7
Hatfield 33,174	H7
Havant 50,098	G7
Haverhill 16,970	H5
Havering 238,335	J8
Haxby 11,415	F3
Hazel Grove and Bramhall 40,819	H2
Heanor 21,863	F4
Hebburn 20,098	J3
Hemel Hempstead 80,110	G7
Henley-on-Thames 10,910	G8
Hereford 48,277	E5
Hertford 21,350	H7
Hetton 14,529	J3
Heywood 29,639	H2
High Wycombe 69,575	G8
Hillingdon 226,659	G8
Hinckley 35,510	F5
Hitchin 33,480	G6
Hoddesdon 37,960	H7
Holmfirth 21,138	J2
Horley 17,700	H8
Horsham 38,356	G6
Horwich 16,758	G2
Houghton-le-Spring 35,337	J3
Hounslow 198,938	G8
Hove 65,587	G7
Hoylake 24,815	G2
Hoyland Nether 15,845	J2
Hucknall 27,463	F4

(continued on following page)

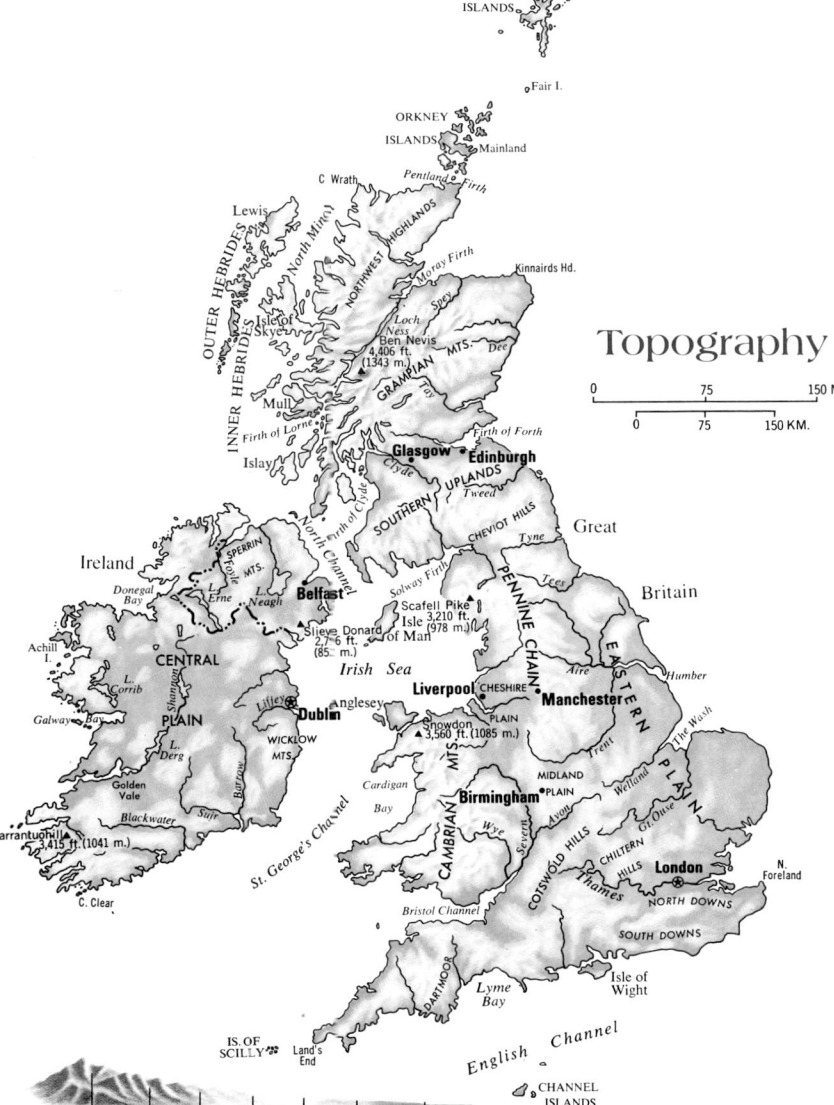

Topography

```
0        75              150 MI.
0        75              150 KM.
```

SHETLAND ISLANDS

Fair I.

ORKNEY ISLANDS Mainland

C. Wrath Pentland Firth

Lewis NORTHWEST HIGHLANDS Kinnairds Hd.
North Minch Moray Firth
OUTER HEBRIDES Spey
Isle of Skye Loch Ness Ben Nevis 4,406 ft. (1343 m.) Dee
INNER HEBRIDES GRAMPIAN MTS.
Firth of Lorne Firth of Forth
Mull Glasgow Edinburgh
Islay Clyde SOUTHERN UPLANDS Tweed
North Channel CHEVIOT HILLS Tyne Great

Ireland SPERRIN MTS. Solway Firth
Donegal Bay L. Erne L. Neagh Belfast PENNINE CHAIN Tees Britain
Achill I. Scafell Pike 3,210 ft. (978 m.) Isle of Man
L. Corrib CENTRAL Slieve Donard 2,796 ft. (852 m.) EASTERN
Galway Bay PLAIN Irish Sea Aire Humber
L. Derg Liverpool CHESHIRE Manchester PLAIN
Golden Vale Dublin Anglesey Snowdon 3,560 ft. (1085 m.) Trent The Wash
Carrantuohill 3,415 ft. (1041 m.) Blackwater WICKLOW MTS. CAMBRIAN MTS. MIDLAND PLAIN Wye Avon Birmingham
C. Clear Cardigan Bay St. George's Channel Severn COTSWOLD HILLS CHILTERN HILLS London N. Foreland
Bristol Channel NORTH DOWNS
IS. OF SCILLY Land's End DARTMOOR Lyme Bay Isle of Wight SOUTH DOWNS
English Channel CHANNEL ISLANDS
```

```
5,000 m.    2,000 m.    1,000 m.    500 m.    200 m.    100 m.    Sea    Below
16,404 ft.  6,562 ft.   3,281 ft.   1,640 ft. 656 ft.   328 ft.   Level
```

ENGLAND

AREA 50,516 sq. mi. (130,836 sq. km.)
POPULATION 46,220,955
CAPITAL London
LARGEST CITY London
HIGHEST POINT Scafell Pike 3,210 ft. (978 m.)

WALES

AREA 8,017 sq. mi. (20,764 sq. km.)
POPULATION 2,749,640
CAPITAL Cardiff
LARGEST CITY Cardiff
HIGHEST POINT Snowdon 3,560 ft. (1,085 m.)

SCOTLAND

AREA 30,414 sq. mi. (78,772 sq. km.)
POPULATION 5,130,735
CAPITAL Edinburgh
LARGEST CITY Glasgow
HIGHEST POINT Ben Nevis 4,406 ft. (1,343 m.)

NORTHERN IRELAND

AREA 5,452 sq. mi. (14,121 sq. km.)
POPULATION 1,543,000
CAPITAL Belfast
LARGEST CITY Belfast
HIGHEST POINT Slieve Donard 2,796 ft. (852 m.)
```

Huddersfield 147,825.........J2
Hugh Town.........A8
Hull 322,144.........G4
Huntingdon 14,395.........G5
Huyton-with-Roby 62,011.........G2
Hyde 30,461.........H2
Hythe 13,118.........H6
Ilkeston 34,683.........F5
Immingham 11,480.........G4
Ipswich 129,661.........J5
Islington 157,522.........H8
Jarrow 31,345.........J3
Kempston 15,454.........G5
Kendal 23,710.........E3
Kenilworth 18,782.........F5
Kensington and Chelsea 125,892.........G8
Kettering 44,758.........G5
Kidderminster 50,385.........E5
Kidsgrove 27,999.........E4
King's Lynn 37,323.........H5
Kingston upon Thames 130,829.........H8
Kingswood 54,736.........E6
Kirkby 52,825.........G2
Knaresborough 12,910.........F4
Knutsford 13,628.........H2
Lambeth 244,143.........H8
Lancaster 43,902.........E3
Leamington Spa 56,552.........F5
Leatherhead 42,399.........G8
Leeds 451,841.........J1
Leek 18,495.........H2
Leicester 324,394.........F5
Leigh 42,627.........H2
Letchworth 31,146.........G6
Lewes 14,499.........H7
Lewisham 230,488.........H8
Leyland 36,694.........G1
Lichfield 25,408.........F5
Lincoln 79,980.........G4
Litherland 21,939.........G2
Littlehampton 46,028.........G7
Liverpool 538,609.........G2
London (cap.) 7,566,620.........H8
Long Eaton 42,285.........F5
Longbenton 36,780.........J3
Loughborough 44,895.........F5
Louth 13,019.........H4
Lowestoft 59,430.........J5
Luton 163,209.........G6
Lymington 11,614.........F7
Lymm 10,036.........H2
Lytham Saint Anne's 39,559...G1
Macclesfield 47,525.........H2
Maidenhead 59,809.........G8
Maidstone 86,067.........J8
Maldon 14,638.........H6
Malvern 30,153.........E5
Manchester 448,604.........H2
Mangotsfield 28,664.........E6
Mansfield 71,325.........F4
Mansfield Woodhouse 17,564.F4
March 14,155.........H5
Margate 53,137.........J6
Market Harborough 15,852...G5
Marlow 18,584.........G8
Matlock 13,706.........J2
Melksham 13,248.........E6
Melton Mowbray 23,379.........G5
Merton 165,102.........H8
Middlesbrough 158,516.........F3
Middleton 51,373.........H2
Milton Keynes 93,305.........G5
Morpeth 14,301.........F2
Nantwich 11,867.........E4
Nelson 30,449.........H1
Neston 14,902.........G2
New Romney 6,559.........J7
Newark 33,143.........G4
Newbury 31,488.........F6
Newcastle upon Tyne 199,064.........H3
Newcastle-under-Lyme 73,208.........E4
Newham 209,128.........H8
Newhaven 10,697.........H7
Newmarket 15,861.........H5
Newport, Isle of Wight 19,758 F7
Newport, Shropshire 10,339...E5
Newport Pagnell 10,733.........G5
Newquay 13,905.........B7
Newton Abbot 20,567.........D7
Newton-le-Willows 19,466...H2
Northallerton 13,566.........F3
Northampton 154,172.........F5
Northfleet 21,400.........J8
Northwich 32,664.........H2
Norton-Radstock 17,668.........E6
Norwich 169,814.........J5
Nottingham 273,300.........F5
Nuneaton 60,337.........F5
Oadby 18,331.........F5
Oldham 107,095.........H2
Ormskirk 22,308.........G2
Oswaldtwistle 11,188.........H1
Oswestry 13,200.........E5
Oxford 113,847.........F6
Padiham 13,856.........H1
Penrith 12,086.........E3
Penzance 18,501.........B7
Peterborough 113,404.........G5
Peterlee 31,405.........F3
Petersfield 10,078.........F6
Plymouth 238,583.........C7
Ponteland 10,215.........H3
Poole 122,815.........E7
Portishead 13,684.........E6
Portslade 17,831.........G7
Portsmouth 174,218.........F7
Potters Bar 22,610.........H8
Poulton-le-Fylde 18,477.........G1
Preston 166,675.........G1
Prestwich 31,654.........H2
Prudhoe 11,140.........H3
Radcliffe 27,664.........H2
Ramsbottom 16,334.........H1
Ramsgate 36,678.........J6

Rawtenstall 21,247.........H1
Rayleigh 28,574.........J8
Reading 194,727.........G8
Redbridge 226,977.........H8
Redcar 35,373.........F3
Redditch 61,639.........E5
Reigate 48,241.........H8
Richmond upon Thames 157,304.........H8
Rickmansworth 15,960.........G8
Ringwood 10,941.........F7
Ripley 17,548.........F4
Ripon 13,036.........F3
Rochdale 97,292.........H2
Rochester 23,840.........J8
Romney (New Romney) 6,559.........J7
Romsey 14,818.........F6
Rotherham 122,374.........K2
Royal Leamington Spa 56,552.........F5
Royal Tunbridge Wells 57,699.........H6
Royston 12,904.........G5
Rugby 59,039.........F5
Rugeley 23,751.........E5
Runcorn 63,995.........G2
Rushden 22,394.........G5
Ryde 19,384.........F7
Ryton 15,138.........H3
Saffron Walden 11,879.........H5
Saint Albans 76,709.........H7
Saint Austell 20,267.........C7
Saint Helens 114,397.........G2
Saint Ives, Cambridgeshire 13,431.........G5
Saint Ives, Cornwall 9,439...B7
Saint Neots 12,468.........G5
Sale 57,872.........H2
Salford 96,525.........H2
Salisbury 36,890.........F6
Saltash 12,486.........C7
Sandbach 13,734.........H2
Sandhurst 13,539.........G8
Sandown-Shanklin 15,252...F7
Scarborough 36,665.........G3
Scunthorpe 79,043.........G4
Seaford 16,367.........H7
Seaham 21,807.........J3
Selby 12,224.........F4
Sevenoaks 24,493.........J8
Sheffield 470,685.........J2
Shepshed 10,479.........F5
Shildon 11,583.........F3
Shoreham 20,562.........G7
Shrewsbury 57,731.........E5
Sidmouth 10,808.........D7
Sittingbourne 35,893.........H6
Skegness 12,645.........H4
Skelmersdale 42,611.........G2
Skipton 13,009.........H1
Slough 106,341.........G8
Solihull 93,940.........F5
South Shields 86,488.........J3
Southampton 211,321.........F7
Southend-on-Sea 155,720...H6
Southport 88,596.........G1
Southwark 209,735.........H8
Southwick 11,364.........G7
Sowerby Bridge 11,280.........H1
Spalding 18,182.........G5
Spennymoor 18,563.........F3
Stafford 60,915.........E5
Staines 51,949.........G8
Stamford 16,127.........G5
Standish 11,504.........G2
Stanley 20,058.........H3
Staveley 24,457.........K2
Stevenage 74,757.........G6
Stockport 135,489.........H2
Stocksbridge 13,394.........J2
Stockton-on-Tees 86,699.....F3
Stoke-on-Trent 272,446...E4
Stone 12,119.........E5
Stourbridge 55,136.........E5
Stourport-on-Severn 17,880..E5
Stowmarket 10,913.........J5
Stratford-upon-Avon 20,941..F5
Stretford 47,522.........H2
Stroud 37,791.........E6
Sudbury 37,791.........H6
Sunbury 28,240.........G8
Sunderland 195,064.........J3
Sutton 165,323.........H8
Sutton in Ashfield 39,536...K2
Swadlincote 33,667.........F5
Swindon 127,348.........F6
Tadley 13,668.........F6
Tamworth 63,260.........F5
Taunton 47,793.........D6
Teignmouth 11,995.........D7
Telford 28,645.........E5
Tewkesbury 9,454.........E6
Thatcham 14,940.........F6
Thetford 19,529.........H5
Thornaby 26,319.........F3
Thornbury 11,948.........E6
Thorne 16,662.........F4
Thornton Cleveleys 26,697...G1
Tiverton 14,745.........D7
Todmorden 11,936.........H1
Tonbridge 34,407.........H8
Torbay 93,995.........D7
Tower Hamlets 139,996...H8
Tring 10,610.........G6
Trowbridge 27,299.........E6
Truro 17,852.........B7
Tynemouth 17,877.........J3
Uckfield 10,749.........H7
Ulverston 11,976.........D3
Urmston 43,706.........H2
Uttoxeter 10,008.........E5
Wakefield 74,764.........J2
Wallasey 62,465.........G2
Wallsend 44,542.........J3
Walsall 177,923.........E5
Waltham Forest 214,595...H8
Waltham Holy Cross 16,498...H7

Walton and Weybridge 50,031.........G8
Wandsworth 252,240.........H8
Ware 15,344.........H7
Warminster 14,826.........E6
Warrington 81,366.........G2
Warsop 10,294.........F4
Warwick 21,701.........F5
Washington 48,856.........J3
Waterloo 57,296.........G7
Watford 109,503.........H7
Wellingborough 38,598.........G5
Wellington 8,980.........D7
Welwyn 40,665.........H7
West Bridgford 27,463.........F5
West Bromwich 153,725.....F5
Westminster 163,892.........H8
Weston-super-Mare 60,821...D6
Weymouth 38,384.........E7
Whickham 17,882.........J3
Whitby 12,982.........G3
Whitehaven 27,512.........D3
Whitley Bay 36,040.........J3
Widnes 55,973.........G2
Wigan 88,725.........G2
Wigston 32,373.........F5
Wilmslow 28,827.........H2
Wilton 4,002.........F6
Wimborne Minster 14,193.....E7
Winchester 34,127.........F6
Windermere 6,835.........E3
Windsor 30,832.........G8
Winsford 26,548.........G2
Wisbech 22,932.........H5
Witham 21,875.........H6
Witney 14,215.........F6
Woking 92,667.........G8
Wokingham 30,344.........G8
Wolverhampton 263,501.....E5
Wombwell 17,143.........K2
Worcester 75,466.........E5
Workington 25,978.........D3
Worksop 34,551.........F4
Worsborough 10,821.........J2
Worthing 90,687.........G7
Yateley 14,121.........G8
Yeovil 36,114.........E7
York 123,126.........F4

CHANNEL ISLANDS

CITIES and TOWNS

Saint Helier (cap.), Jersey 27,549.........E8
Saint Peter Port (cap.), Guernsey 16,085.........E8
Saint Sampson's 7,475.........E8

OTHER FEATURES

Alderney (isl.) 2,130.........E8
Guernsey (isl.) 55,421.........E8
Herm (isl.) 59.........E8
Jersey (isl.) 82,809.........E8
Sark (isl.) 560.........E8

ISLE of MAN

CITIES and TOWNS

Castletown 2,788.........C3
Douglas (cap.) 19,897.........C3
Laxey 1,242.........C3
Onchan 6,395.........C3
Peel 3,295.........C3
Port Erin 2,356.........C3
Port Saint Mary 1,525.........C3
Ramsey 5,372.........C3

OTHER FEATURES

Ayre (pt.).........C3
Calf of Man (isl.).........C3
Langness (prom.).........C3
Snaefell (mt.).........C3

WALES

COUNTIES

Clwyd 385,581.........D4
Dyfed 323,040.........C6
Gwent 436,500.........D6
Gwynedd 222,291.........C4
Mid Glamorgan 533,770.....D6
Powys 108,121.........D5
South Glamorgan 376,718...A7
West Glamorgan 363,619...D6

CITIES and TOWNS

Abercarn 16,811.........B6
Aberdare 31,617.........A6
Abergavenny 13,880.........B6
Abergele 12,264.........D4
Abertillery and Brynmawr 28,239.........B6
Aberystwyth 10,290.........C5
Ammanford 10,735.........C6
Bangor 12,244.........C4
Barry 44,443.........B7
Bethesda 3,558.........D4
Brecknock (Brecon) 7,166...D6
Bridgend 31,008.........A7
Brynmawr and Abertillery 28,239.........B6
Buckley 16,693.........G2
Caernarfon 9,271.........C4
Caerphilly 28,681.........B6
Caldicot 12,310.........E6
Cardiff (cap.) 262,313.........B7
Cardigan 3,815.........C5
Carmarthen 13,860.........C6
Chepstow 9,039.........E6
Colwyn Bay 27,002.........D4
Connah's Quay 14,785.........G2
Cwmbran 44,592.........B6
Denbigh 7,710.........D4
Ebbw Vale 21,048.........B6
Ffestiniog 4,507.........D4
Flint 11,411.........G2
Gelligaer 16,812.........A6
Gwersyllt 13,374.........G2
Harlech 1,292.........C5
Haverfordwest 13,572.........B6
Hawarden 22,361.........G2
Holyhead 12,566.........C4
Holywell 11,101.........G2
Llandeilo 1,598.........C6
Llandovery 1,676.........D5
Llandrindod Wells 4,232...D5
Llandudno 13,202.........D4
Llanelli 45,336.........C6
Llanfairfechan 3,173.........D4
Llangollen 2,546.........D5
Llanidloes 2,392.........D5

Solway (firth).........D3
South Downs (hills).........G7
South Foreland (prom.).........J6
Spithead (chan.).........F7
Stonehenge (ruin).........F6
Stour (riv.).........H6
Stour (riv.).........E7
Stour (riv.).........J6
Swale (riv.).........F3
Tees (riv.).........F3
Thames (riv.).........H6
Tintagel (head).........C7
Trent (riv.).........G4
Tweed (riv.).........E2
Tyne (riv.).........F3
Ure (riv.).........F3
Walney, Isle of (isl.).........D3
Wash, The (bay).........H5
Weald, The (reg.).........H6
Wear (riv.).........F3
Welland (riv.).........G5
Wey (riv.).........G6
Wharfe (riv.).........E3
Wight (isl.) 114,879.........F7
Wirral (pen.).........G2
Wolds, The (hills).........G5
Wye (riv.).........D5
Yare (riv.).........J5
Yorkshire Dales National Park.E3

SCOTLAND
(map on page 15)

REGIONS

Borders 99,784.........E5
Central 273,391.........D4
Dumfries and Galloway 145,139.........E5
Fife 327,362.........E4
Grampian 471,942.........F3
Highland 200,150.........D3
Lothian 738,372.........E5
Orkney (islands area) 19,056..E1
Shetland (islands area) 27,277.....F2
Strathclyde 2,404,532.........C4
Tayside 391,846.........E4
Western Isles (islands area) 31,884.........A3

CITIES and TOWNS

Aberchirder 1,021.........F3
Aberdeen 190,465.........F3
Aberfeldy 1,613.........E4
Aberfoyle 793.........D4
Abernethy 776.........E4
Aboyne 1,529.........F3
Achiltibuie 1,564.........C3
Achnasheen 1,078.........C3
Airdrie 45,747.........C2
Alexandria 26,329.........A1
Alford 764.........F3
Alloa 26,428.........C1
Alness 6,289.........D3
Altnaharra 1,227.........D2
Alva 4,874.........C1
Alyth 2,289.........E4
Annan 8,314.........E6
Annbank Station 3,223.........D5
Arbroath 24,119.........F4
Ardrishaig 1,325.........C4
Ardrossan 11,421.........C5
Armadale 9,527.........C2
Auchinleck 4,463.........D5
Auchterarder 2,904.........E4
Auchtermuchty 1,646.........E4
Aviemore 1,224.........E3
Ayr 49,522.........D5
Baillieston 7,671.........B2

Llantrisant 8,317.........A7
Llantwit Major 13,375.........A7
Maesteg 21,821.........D6
Menai Bridge 2,942.........C4
Merthyr Tydfil 38,893.........A6
Milford Haven 13,883.........B6
Mold 8,487.........G2
Monmouth 7,379.........E6
Montgomery.........D5
Mountain Ash 23,520.........A6
Narberth.........C6
Neath 48,687.........D6
Nefyn 2,086.........C5
Newport 115,896.........B6
Newtown 8,906.........D5
Neyland 3,095.........B6
Ogmore 7,092.........A6
Pembroke 8,235.........C6
Penarth 22,467.........B7
Pontypool 36,064.........B6
Pontypridd 29,465.........A6
Port Talbot 40,078.........D6
Porthcawl 15,162.........D6
Prestatyn 16,246.........D4
Pwllheli 3,978.........C5
Rhondda 70,980.........A6
Rhosllanerchrugog 11,080...D4
Rhyl 23,130.........D4
Risca 16,627.........B6
Ruthin 4,417.........D4
Saint David's 1,428.........B6
Swansea 172,433.........C6
Tenby 5,226.........C6
Tredegar 16,188.........B6
Welshpool 4,869.........D5
Wrexham 39,929.........G2
Ystradgynlais 10,406.........D6

OTHER FEATURES

Anglesey (isl.).........C4
Bardsey (isl.).........C5
Brecon Beacons National Park.........D6
Bristol (chan.).........C6
Caldy (isl.).........C6
Cambrian (mts.).........D5
Cardigan (bay).........C5
Carmarthen (bay).........C6
Conwy (bay).........C4
Dee (riv.).........D4
Gower (pen.).........C6
Great Ormes (head).........C4
Holy (isl.).........C4
Irish (sea).........B4
Lleyn (pen.).........C5
Menai (strait).........C4
Milford Haven (inlet).........B6
Pembrokeshire Coast National Park.........C6
Radnor (for.).........D5
Saint Brides (bay).........B6
Saint George's (chan.).........B5
Severn (riv.).........E6
Snowdon (mt.).........C4
Snowdonia National Park.....D4
Taff (riv.).........C6
Teifi (riv.).........C5
Towy (riv.).........D6
Tremadoc (prom.).........C5
Usk (riv.).........D5
Wye (riv.).........D5
Ynys Môn (Anglesey) (isl.)...C4

 Population of parish.

Balerno 3,576.........D2
Balfron 1,127.........B1
Ballantrae 262.........C5
Ballater 1,218.........F3
Ballingry 7,021.........D1
Balloch 1,484.........B1
Banchory 4,890.........F3
Banff 3,938.........F3
Bankhead 1,492.........F3
Bannockburn 5,889.........C1
Barrhead 18,418.........B2
Bathgate 14,477.........C2
Bearsden 27,183.........B2
Beauly 1,148.........D3
Beith 5,742.........C5
Bellsbank 2,482.........D5
Bellshill 39,676.........C2
Berriedale 1,927.........E2
Bieldside 1,137.........F3
Biggar 1,938.........E5
Bishopbriggs 23,501.........B2
Bishopton 5,283.........B2
Blackburn 5,785.........C2
Blair Atholl 437.........E4
Blairgowrie and Rattray 7,184.E4
Blantyre 19,948.........B2
Bo'ness 14,641.........C2
Boddam 1,367.........G3
Bonhill 4,385.........B1
Bonnybridge 5,701.........C1
Bonnyrigg and Lasswade 14,399.........D2
Brechin 7,692.........F4
Bridge of Allan 4,694.........C1
Bridge of Don 4,086.........F3
Bridge of Weir 4,724.........A2
Brightons 3,106.........C1
Brora 1,736.........E2
Broxburn 12,032.........D1
Buckhaven and Methil 18,265.F4
Buckie 7,839.........E3
Bucksburn 6,567.........F3
Burghead 1,380.........E3
Burntisland 5,865.........D1
Callander 2,520.........D4
Cambuslang 14,607.........B2
Campbeltown 6,098.........C5
Caol 3,719.........C4
Cardenden 5,898.........D1
Carluke 11,674.........C5
Carnoustie 9,225.........F4
Carnwath 1,374.........C5
Carron 2,626.........C1
Castle Douglas 3,521.........C6
Catrine 2,790.........D5
Cawdor 111.........D3
Chirnside 1,263.........F5
Chryston 11,067.........C2
Clackmannan 3,258.........C1
Clarkston 8,404.........B2
Clydebank 51,854.........B2
Coalburn 1,241.........C5
Coatbridge 50,957.........C2
Cockenzie and Port Seton 3,760.........D1
Coldstream 1,645.........F5
Comrie 1,477.........D4
Cononbridge 2 187.........D3
Corpach 1,296.........C4
Coupar Angus 2,186.........E4
Cove and Kilcreggan 1,220...A1
Cove Bay 2,840.........F3
Cowdenbeath 12,272.........D1
Cowie 2,513.........C1
Crail 1,181.........F4
Creetown 769.........D6
Crieff 5,477.........E4
Crimond 1,002.........G3
Cromarty 492.........D3
Cruden Bay 1,453.........G3
Cullen 1,414.........F3
Culross 504.........C1
Cults 3,336.........F3
Cumbernauld 47,901.........C1
Cumnock and Holmhead 9,650.........D5
Cupar 6,637.........E4
Currie 6,764.........D2
Dailly 1,098.........D5
Dalbeattie 3,917.........E6
Dalkeith 11,255.........D2
Dalmellington 1,425.........D5
Dalry 5,856.........C5
Dalrymple 1,237.........D5
Darvel 3,461.........D5
Denny and Dunipace 23,158...C1
Dervaig 1,081.........B4
Dingwall 4,842.........D3
Dollar 2,466.........D1
Dornoch 880.........D3
Douglas 1,727.........E5
Doune 1,046.........D4
Drongan 3,129.........D5
Dufftown 1,643.........E3
Dumbarton 23,430.........B1
Dunbeattie 3,917.........D5
Dunbar 6,035.........F4
Dunblane 6,855.........D4
Dundee 174,345.........F4
Dunnet.........E5
Dunoon 9,369.........A2
Duns 2,253.........F5
Duntocher 3,532.........B2
Dyce 7,039.........F3
Eaglesham 3,166.........B2
Earlston 1,610.........F5
East Calder 5,112.........D2
East Kilbride 70,676.........B2
East Linton 1,206.........F5
Eastriggs 1,841.........E5
East Wemyss 1,782.........D1
Edinburgh (cap.) 420,169....D1
Elderslie 5,204.........B2
Elgin 18,908.........E3
Ellon 6,319.........F3
Errol 762.........E4
Eyemouth 3,398.........F5

Fairlie 1,326.........D5
Falkirk 36,880.........C1
Falkland 998.........E4
Fauldhouse 5,036.........C2
Findhorn 664.........E3
Findochty 1,019.........F3
Fochabers 1,483.........E3
Forfar 12,770.........F4
Forres 8,354.........E3
Forth 2,890.........C2
Fortrose 1,332.........D3
Fort William 11,061.........C4
Fraserburgh 12,512.........G3
Gairloch 125.........C3
Galashiels 12,244.........E5
Galston 3,515.........D5
Garelochhead 2,072.........A1
Gatehouse-of-Fleet 835.........D6
Giffnock 33,634.........B2
Girvan 7,795.........D5
Glamis 190.........F4
Glasgow 765,030.........B2
Glenbarr 691.........C5
Glencoe 195.........C4
Glenelg 1,468.........C3
Glenrothes 32,971.........E4
Golspie 1,491.........E3
Gorebridge 6,036.........D2
Gourock 11,203.........A1
Grangemouth 21,599.........C1
Grantown-on-Spey 2,034...E3
Greenock 59,016.........A2
Gretna 2,811.........E6
Gullane 2,232.........F4
Haddington 8,139.........F5
Halkirk 679.........E2
Hamilton 51,718.........C2
Hawick 16,364.........E5
Heathhall 1,365.........E5
Helensburgh 16,621.........A1
Helmsdale 727.........E2
Hillside 1,233.........F4
Hillswick 696.........G2
Hopeman 1,398.........E3
Huntly 3,952.........F3
Hurlford 4,294.........D5
Inchnadamph 833.........D2
Innerleithen 2,468.........E5
Insch 1,256.........F3
Inveraray 473.........C4
Inverbervie 1,799.........F4
Invercassley 1,067.........D3
Invergordon 4,067.........D3
Invergowrie 1,389.........E4
Inverie 1,468.........C3
Inverkeithing 5,770.........D1
Inverness 40,010.........D3
Inverurie 7,680.........F3
Irvine 32,968.........C5
Jedburgh 4,069.........F5
John O'Groats 195.........E2
Johnstone 42,669.........B2
Keith 4,407.........F3
Kelso 5,648.........F5
Kelty 5,623.........D1
Kemnay 3,034.........F3
Kilbarchan 2,669.........A2
Kilbirnie 8,710.........C5
Kilchoan 764.........B4
Kildonan 1,105.........E2
Killearn 1,771.........B1
Kilmacolm 3,676.........A2
Kilmarnock 52,083.........D5
Kilmaurs 2,738.........D5
Kilrenny and Anstruther 2,951 F4
Kilsyth 10,538.........C1
Kilwinning 16,266.........C5
Kinbrace 1,105.........E2
Kincardine 3,166.........C1
Kinghorn 2,698.........D1
Kingussie 1,229.........D3
Kinlochewe 1,794.........C3
Kinlochleven 1,047.........D4
Kinloss 2,813.........E3
Kinross 3,496.........E4
Kintore 1,644.........F3
Kirkcaldy 46,522.........D1
Kirkconnel 2,656.........E5
Kirkcudbright 3,427.........E6
Kirkintilloch 33,148.........B2
Kirkmuirhill 3,624.........C5
Kirkwall 5,995.........E1
Kirriemuir 5,326.........F4
Leslie 3,551.........E4
Lesmahagow 3,408.........C5
Letham 804.........F4
Leuchars 2,244.........F4
Leven 8,624.........E4
Lhanbryde 1,811.........E3
Limekilns 1,444.........D1
Linlithgow 9,582.........C1
Linwood 10,510.........B2
Livingston 38,954.........C2
Loanhead 6,159.........D2
Lochailort 673.........C4
Locharbriggs 4,282.........E5
Lochgelly 7,334.........D1
Lochgilphead 2,461.........C4
Lochinver 283.........C2
Lochmaben 1,713.........E5
Lochore 2,994.........D1
Lochwinnoch 2,273.........A2
Lockerbie 3,561.........E5

ENGLAND (OTHER FEATURES continued)

Aire (riv.).........F4
Avon (riv.).........F5
Barnstaple (bay).........C6
Beachy (head).........H7
Blackwater (riv.).........H6
Bristol (chan.).........C6
Cheviot (hills).........E2
Chiltern (hills).........G6
Cleveland (hills).........F3
Colne (riv.).........G8
Cotswold (hills).........E6
Cross Fell (mt.).........E3
Cumbrian (mts.).........D3
Dart (riv.).........D7
Dartmoor National Park.........C7
Dee (riv.).........G3
Derwent (riv.).........G3
Derwent (riv.).........H3
Don (riv.).........F4
Dove (riv.).........J2
Dover (strait).........J7
Dungeness (prom.).........J7
Eddystone (rocks).........C7
Eden (riv.).........E3
English (chan.).........D8
Esk (riv.).........D2
Exe (riv.).........D7
Exmoor National Park.........D6
Fens, The (reg.).........G5
Flamborough (head).........G3
Foulness Island (pen.).........J6
Great Ouse (riv.).........H5
Hartland (pt.).........C6
Holderness (pen.).........G4
Holy (isl.).........F2
Humber (riv.).........G4
Irish (sea).........B4
Kennet (riv.).........F6
Lake District National Park...D3
Land's End (prom.).........B7
Lea (riv.).........G6
Lincoln Wolds (hills).........G4
Lindisfarne (Holy) (isl.).........F2
Lizard (pt.).........B8
Lundy (isl.).........C6
Lyme (bay).........D7
Medway (riv.).........H6
Mendip (hills).........E6
Mersey (riv.).........G2
Morecambe (bay).........D3
Mounts (bay).........B7
Naze, The (prom.).........J6
Nene (riv.).........H5
New (for.).........F6
North (sea).........J4
North Downs (hills).........G6
North Foreland (prom.).........J6
Northumberland National Park.........E2
North York Moors National Park.........F3
Ouse (riv.).........G6
Ouse (riv.).........G4
Peak District National Park...F4
Peak, The (mt.).........J2
Pennine Chain (range).........E3
Portland, Bill of (pt.).........E7
Purbeck, Isle of (pen.).........F7
Ribble (riv.).........E4
Saint Bees (head).........D3
Saint Mary's (isl.).........A8
Scafell Pike (mt.).........D3
Scilly (isls.).........A7
Severn (riv.).........E6
Sheppey (isl.).........H6
Sherwood (for.).........F4
Solent (chan.).........F7

(continued)

England and Wales

CONIC PROJECTION

MILES

KILOMETERS

Capitals of Countries .... ☆
Other Capitals .... ⊛
Administrative Centers .... ◉
Canals ....

International Boundaries ....
County Boundaries ....
Other Boundaries ....

Scale 1:2,886,000

The administrative centers for MID GLAMORGAN, NORTHUMBERLAND and SURREY are Cardiff, Newcastle upon Tyne and Kingston upon Thames, respectively.

© Copyright HAMMOND INCORPORATED, Maplewood, N.J.

Longitude West of Greenwich   0°   Longitude East of Greenwich   1°

Lossiemouth and
 Branderburgh 6,847 ....E3
Macduff 3,887 ....F3
Mallaig 903 ....C4
Markinch 2,078 ....E4
Mauchline 3,663 ....D5
Maud 634 ....F3
Maybole 4,798 ....D5
Mayfield 1,333 ....D2
Melrose 2,345 ....F5
Melvaig 1,794 ....C3
Millport 1,472 ....A2
Milnathort 1,118 ....E4
Milngavie 12,067 ....B1
Mintlaw 2,299 ....F3
Moffat 2,051 ....E5
Monifieth 7,100 ....F4
Montrose 12,325 ....F4
Motherwell 30,676 ....C2
Muir of Ord 1,714 ....D3
Muirkirk 2,356 ....E5
Musselburgh 19,081 ....D1
Nairn 7,705 ....E3
Neilston 4,678 ....A2
Newarthill 7,003 ....C2
Newburgh 2,002 ....E4
Newcastleton 903 ....E5
New Cumnock 4,484 ....D5
New Galloway 337 ....D5
Newmains 6,847 ....C2
Newmilns and Greenholm
 3,339 ....D5
New Pitsligo 1,125 ....F3
Newport-on-Tay 3,652 ......F4
New Scone 4,173 ....E4
Newton Mearns 15,543 .....B2
Newton Stewart 3,246 ......D6
Newtown Saint Boswells
 1,095 ....F5
North Berwick 5,162 ....F4
Oakley 4,157 ....C1
Oban 8,111 ....C4
Old Kilpatrick 3,256 ....B2
Oldmeldrum 1,356 ....F3
Paisley 84,954 ....B2
Patna 2,490 ....D5
Peebles 6,692 ....E4
Penicuik 17,607 ....D2
Perth 43,010 ....E4
Peterculter 3,226 ....F3
Peterhead 17,085 ....G3
Pitlochry 12,621 ....E4
Pitmedden 1,103 ....F3
Pittenweem 1,544 ....F4
Poolewe 1,794 ....C3
Port Appin 2,172 ....C4
Port Askaig 1,795 ....B5
Port Bannatyne 1,414 ....A2
Port Ellen 1,020 ....B5
Port Glasgow 22,580 ....A2
Portknockie 1,239 ....F3
Portree 1,505 ....B3
Portsoy 1,784 ....F3

Prestonpans 7,621 ....D1
Prestwick 13,599 ....D5
Queensferry 7,540 ....D1
Renfrew 21,458 ....B2
Renton 3,443 ....A1
Rhu 1,540 ....A1
Rigside 1,066 ....E5
Rosehearty 1,243 ....F3
Rosneath 1,439 ....A1
Rothes 1,425 ....E3
Rothesay 5,455 ....A2
Rutherglen 24,091 ....B2
Saint Andrews 11,369 ......F4
Saint Monance 1,244 ....F4
Saline 1,192 ....C1
Saltcoats 12,834 ....D5
Sandbank 1,435 ....A1
Sanquhar 2,082 ....D5
Sauchie 6,082 ....C1
Selkirk 5,437 ....F5
Shotts 9,427 ....C2
Skelmorlie 1,689 ....A2
Slamannan 1,578 ....C2
Stanley 1,170 ....E4
Stenhousemuir 19,771 .....C1
Stevenston 11,337 ....D5
Stewarton 6,330 ....D5
Stirling 38,842 ....C1
Stonehaven 7,922 ....F4
Stonehouse 5,308 ....D5
Stornoway 8,638 ....B2
Stranraer 10,873 ....C6
Strathaven 6,152 ....C2
Stromeferry 1,724 ....C3
Stromness 1,832 ....E2
Sullam Voe G2
Tain 3,486 ....D3
Tarbert 1,403 ....C5
Tarbolton 2,012 ....D5
Tayport 3,029 ....F4
Thornhill, Central 443 ......D4
Thornhill, Dumfries and
 Galloway 1,473 ....E5
Thurso 8,896 ....E2
Tillicoultry 6,161 ....C1
Tobermory 652 ....B4
Tolob 2,033 ....G2
Tranent 8,079 ....F5
Troon 14,233 ....D5
Tullibody 6,082 ....C1
Turriff 3,683 ....F3
Tweedsmuir 105 ....E5
Tyndrum 1,153 ....D4
Uddingston 10,678 ....C2
Uig, Highland 103 ....B3
Uig, Western Isles 1,948 ...A2
Ullapool 1,146 ....C3
Uphall 3,035 ....C1
Viewpark 15,343 ....C2
Walkerburn 842 ....F5
Wemyss Bay 1,322 ....A2
West Calder 2,281 ....C2
West Kilbride 4,241 ....D5
West Linton 705 ....D2

Whitburn 12,610 ....C2
Whitehills 875 ....F3
Whithorn 990 ....D6
Wick 7,900 ....E2
Wigtown 1,015 ....D6
Winchburgh 2,398 ....D1
Wishaw 37,783 ....C2

OTHER FEATURES

A'Chralaig (mt.) C3
Annan (riv.) E5
Appin (dist.) 2,006 ....C4
Ardgour (dist.) 315 ....C4
Ardnamurchan (pt.) B4
Ardnamurchan (pen.) 764 ..B4
Argyll (dist.) 4,940 ....C4
Arisaig (sound) C4
Arkaig, Loch (lake) C4
Arran (isl.) 3,564 ....C5
Askival (mt.) B4
Assynt (dist.) 833 ....C2
Athol (dist.) 1,082 ....D4
Atlantic Ocean B2
Awe, Loch (lake) C4
Ayr (riv.) D5
Badenoch (dist.) 2,717 ....D4
Baleshare (isl.) 64 ....A3
Balmoral Castle (site) E3
Barra (head) A4
Barra (isl.) 1,005 ....A4
Barra Isles (isls.) 1,092 ....A4
Beauly (riv.) D3
Beinn a Ghlo (mt.) E4
Beinn Bheigeir (mt.) B5
Beinn Dearg (mt.) D3
Beinn Dhorain (mt.) E2
Beinn Eighe (mt.) C3
Ben Alder (mt.) D4
Ben Barvas (mt.) B2
Benbecula (isl.) 1,355 ......A3
Ben Cruachan (mt.) C4
Ben Hope (mt.) D2
Ben Kilbreck (mt.) D2
Ben Lawers (mt.) D4
Ben Lomond (mt.) D4
Ben Macdhui (mt.) E3
Ben Mhor (mt.) A3
Ben More (mt.) D4
Ben More Assynt (mt.) D2
Ben Nevis (mt.) D4
Bernera (isl.) 276 ....B2
Berneray (isl.) 131 ....A3
Berneray (isl.) 6 ....A4
Bidean nam Bian (mt.) D4
Black Isle (pen.) 7,209 .....D3
Blackwater (riv.) A1
Bracadale, Loch (inlet) B3
Braemar (dist.) 7,624 ......E3
Bran (riv.) D3
Breadalbane (dist.) 3,649 ..D4
Bressay (isl.) 248 ....G2
Broad (bay) B2
Broad Law (mt.) E5

Broom, Loch (inlet) C3
Brough Ness (prom.) F2
Buchan (dist.) 40,089 ......F3
Buchan Ness (prom.) G3
Burray (isl.) 209 ....F2
Burrow (head) D6
Bute (isl.) 8,423 ....C5
Butt of Lewis (prom.) B2
Cairn Gorm (mt.) E3
Cairngorm (mts.) E3
Cairnsmore (mt.) D5
Caledonian (canal) D3
Canna (isl.) 22 ....B3
Carn Eige (mt.) C3
Carrick (dist.) 21,425 ......D5
Carron (riv.) C1
Cheviot (hills) F5
Cheviot, The (mt.) F5
Clisham (mt.) B3
Clyde (firth) D5
Clyde (riv.) D5
Coll (isl.) 144 ....B4
Colonsay (isl.) 137 ....B4
Corserine (mt.) D5
Corsewall (pt.) C5
Cowal (dist.) 15,548 ....C4
Cromarty (firth) D3
Cuillin (hills) B3
Cuillin (sound) B3
Dee (riv.) E3
Dennis (head) F1
Deveron (riv.) F3
Don (riv.) F3
Doon (riv.) D5
Dornoch (firth) D3
Duirinish (dist.) 1,085 .....B3
Duncansby (head) E2
Dunnet (head) E2
Dunnet (bay) E2
Earn (riv.) E4
Earn, Loch (lake) D4
East Loch Tarbert (inlet) ..B3
Eday (isl.) 179 ....F1
Eddrachillis (bay) C2
Eigg (isl.) 69 ....B4
Eishort, Loch (inlet) B3
Enard (bay) C2
Eriboll, Loch (inlet) D2
Ericht, Loch (lake) D4
Eriskay (isl.) 219 ....A3
Erisort, Loch (inlet) B2
Esk (riv.) F5
Etive, Loch (inlet) C4
Ewe, Loch (inlet) C3
Eye (pen.) 850 ....B2
Eynhallow (sound) E1
Eynort, Loch (inlet) A3
Fair Isle (isl.) 65 ....F3
Fannich, Loch (lake) D3
Fetlar (isl.) 88 ....G2
Fife Ness (prom.) F4
Findhorn (riv.) E3
Fionn Loch (lake) C3
Flannan (isls.) 3 ....A2

Fleet, Loch (inlet) D3
Formartine (dist.) 10,768 ..F3
Forth (firth) F4
Forth (riv.) B1
Forth and Clyde (canal) ...B2
Foula (isl.) 33 ....F2
Fyne, Loch (inlet) C5
Gairloch, Loch (inlet) C3
Gallan (head) A2
Galloway (dist.) 54,972 ...D5
Galloway, Mull of (prom.) ..D6
Garioch (dist.) 6,863 ....F3
Garry, Loch (lake) D3
Gigha (isl.) 174 ....C5
Glen More (dist.) 55,035 ..D3
Goat Fell (mt.) C5
Grampian (mts.) E4
Great Cumbrae (isl.) 1,296 ..A2
Green Lowther (mt.) E5
Greenstone (pt.) C3
Gruinard (bay) C3
Harris (dist.) 2,175 ....B3
Heads of Ayr (cape) D5
Hebrides (sea) B3
Hebrides, Inner (isls.) 14,881 ..B4
Hebrides, Outer (isls.) 29,615 ..A3
Helmsdale (riv.) E2
Herma Ness (prom.) G2
Hope, Loch (lake) D2
Hourn, Loch (inlet) C3
Hoy (isl.) 419 ....E2
Indaal, Loch (inlet) B5
Inner (sound) B3
Inner Hebrides (isls.) 14,881 ..B4
Iona (isl.) 145 ....B4
Islay (isl.) 3,816 ....B5
Jura (isl.) 210 ....C5
Katrine, Loch (lake) D4
Kerrera (isl.) 27 ....C4
Kilbrannan (sound) C5
Kinnairds (head) G3
Kintyre (pen.) 10,077 ......C5
Kintyre, Mull of (prom.) ...C5
Knapdale (dist.) 4,082 .....C5
Kyle of Tongue (inlet) D2
Ladder (hills) E3
Lammermuir (hills) F5
Langavat (lake) B2
Laxford, Loch (inlet) C2
Lennox (hills) B1
Leven (lake) E4
Leven, Loch (inlet) D4
Lewis (dist.) 20,047 ....B2
Lewis, Butt of (prom.) B2
Liddel Water (riv.) F5
Linnhe, Loch (inlet) C4
Lismore (isl.) 166 ....C4
Little Minch (sound) B3
Lochaber (dist.) 13,813 ....C4
Lochnagar (mt.) E4
Lochy, Loch (lake) D3
Lomond, Loch (lake) D4
Long, Loch (inlet) D4
Lorne (dist.) 12,162 ....C4
Lorne (firth) C4
Loyal, Loch (lake) D2
Loyne, Loch (lake) C3
Luce (bay) D6
Luing (isl.) 151 ....C4
Machers, The (pen.) 6,192 ..D6
Maddy, Loch (inlet) A3
Mainland (isl.) 12,747 .....E1
Mainland (isl.) 12,944 .....G2
Mar (dist.) 23,931 ....F3
Maree, Loch (lake) C3
May, Isle of (isl.) 10 ....F4
Merrick (mt.) D5
Minginish (dist.) 772 ....B3
Mingulay (isl.) A4
Moidart (dist.) 155 ....C4

Monach (isls.) A3
Monadhliath (mts.) D3
Monar, Loch (lake) C3
Moorfoot (hills) E5
Morar, Loch (lake) C4
Moray (firth) E3
Morven (dist.) E2
Morven (dist.) 398 ....C4
Muck (isl.) 24 ....B4
Muckle Flugga (isl.) 3 .....G2
Mull (isl.) 2,024 ....C4
Mull (head) F2
Mullardoch, Loch (lake) ...C3
Mull of Galloway (prom.) ..D6
Mull of Kintyre (prom.) C5
Mull of Oa (prom.) B5
Nairn (riv.) D3
Naver (riv.) D2
Ness (riv.) D3
Ness, Loch (lake) D3
Nevis, Loch (inlet) C3
Nith (riv.) E5
North (chan.) C5
North (sea) G4
North (sound) F1
North Esk (riv.) F4
North Minch (sound) B3
North Ronaldsay (isl.) 134 ..F1
North Uist (isl.) 1,469 ......A3
Noss (isl.) F2
Noup (head) E1
Oa, Mull of (prom.) B5
Ochil (hills) E4
Oich, Loch (lake) D3
Orkney (isls.) 17,675 ......F1
Oronsay (isl.) 2 ....B4
Outer Hebrides (isls.) 29,615 ..A3
Oykel (riv.) D3
Pabbay (isl.) 4 ....A3
Papa Stour (isl.) 24 ....F2
Papa Westray (isl.) 106 ...F1
Paps of Jura (mt.) C5
Park (dist.) 210 ....B2
Peel Fell (mt.) F5
Pentland (firth) E2
Pentland (hills) D2
Quoich, Loch (lake) C3
Raasay (isl.) 163 ....C3
Rannoch (dist.) 1,177 .....D4
Rannoch, Loch (lake) D4
Renish (pt.) B3
Resort, Loch (inlet) A2
Rhinns (pt.) B5
Rhinns, The (pen.) 8,295 ..C6
Rhum (sound) B4
Riddon, Loch (inlet) C5
Roag, Loch (inlet) B2
Rona (isl.) 3 ....B3
Ronay (isl.) A3
Rora (head) E2
Ross of Mull (pen.) 585 ...B4
Rousay (isl.) 181 ....E1
Rudha Hunish (cape) B3
Rum (sound) B4
Rum (isl.) 40 ....B3
Ryan, Loch (inlet) C5
Saint Abbs (head) F5
Saint Kilda (isl.) 65 ....A2
Saint Magnus (bay) F2
Sanday (isl.) 592 ....F1
Sandray (isl.) A4
Scalpay (isl.) 483 ....B3
Scalpay (isl.) 5 ....C3
Scapa Flow (chan.) E2
Scarba (isl.) C4
Scarp (isl.) 12 ....A2
Scridain, Loch (inlet) B4
Seaforth, Loch (inlet) B3
Seil (isl.) 326 ....C4

Sgurr Alasdair (mt.) B3
Sgurr Mor (mt.) C3
Sgurr na Ciche (mt.) C3
Sgurr na Lapaich (mt.) C3
Shapinsay (isl.) 346 ....F1
Shetland (isls.) 18,494 ....G2
Shiant (isls.) B3
Shiel, Loch (lake) C4
Shin, Loch (lake) D2
Sidlaw (hills) E4
Sinclair's (bay) E2
Skye, Isle of (isl.) 7,183 ...B3
Sleat (dist.) 449 ....C3
Sleat (pt.) C3
Sleat (sound) C3
Small Isles (isls.) 171 ......B4
Snizort, Loch (inlet) B3
Soay (isl.) 5 ....B3
Solway (firth) E6
South Esk (riv.) F4
South Ronaldsay (isl.) 776 ..F2
South Uist (isl.) 2,281 .....A3
Spean (riv.) D4
Spey (riv.) E3
Staffa (isl.) B4
Start (pt.) F1
Stoer (pt.) C2
Storr, The (mt.) B3
Strathbogie (dist.) 7,959 ..F3
Strathmore (valley) E4
Strathspey (dist.) 6 668 ...E3
Striven Loch (inlet) A2
Stroma (isl.) 8 ....E2
Stronsay (isl.) 436 ....F1
Sumburgh (head) G2
Summer Isles (isls.) C2
Sunart Loch (inlet) C4
Taransay (isl.) 5 ....A3
Tarbat Ness (prom.) E3
Tarbert, East Loch (inlet) ..B3
Tarbert, Loch (inlet) B5
Tarbert, West Loch (inlet) ..A3
Tarbert, West Loch (inlet) ..C5
Tay (firth) F4
Tay (riv.) E4
Tay, Loch (lake) D4
Teith (riv.) D4
Teviot (riv.) F5
Thurso (riv.) E2
Tiree (isl.) 875 ....B4
Tiumpan (head) B2
Toe (head) A3
Tolsta (head) B2
Tor Ness (prom.) E2
Torridon, Loch (inlet) C3
Trossachs, The (valley) D4
Trotternish (dist.) 1,948 ...B3
Troup (head) F3
Tummel (lake) E4
Tweed (riv.) F5
Tyne (riv.) F5
Ulva (isl.) 23 ....B4
Unst (isl.) 1,124 ....G2
Vaternish (pt.) B3
Vaternish (dist.) 162 ....B3
Vatersay (isl.) 77 ....A4
Watten, Loch (lake) E2
West Loch Tarbert (inlet) ..C5
West Loch Tarbert (inlet) ..A3
Westray (isl.) 735 ....E1
Whalsay (isl.) 870 ....G2
White Coomb (mt.) E5
Wiay (isl.) A3
Wigtown (bay) D6
Wrath (cape) C2
Yarrow (riv.) E5
Yell (isl.) 1,143 ....G2
Yell (sound) G2

³ Population of parish.

Agriculture, Industry and Resources

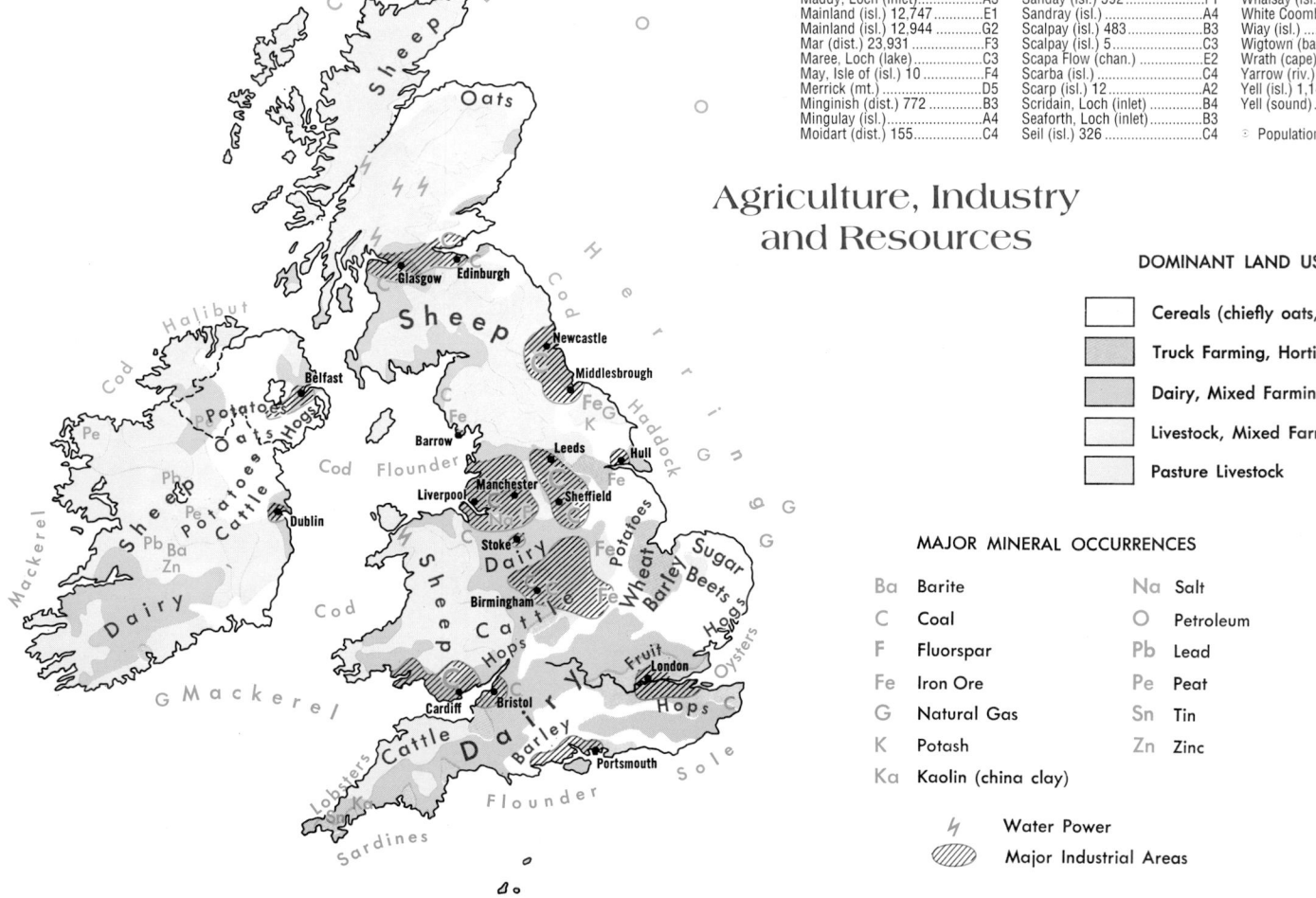

DOMINANT LAND USE

- Cereals (chiefly oats, barley)
- Truck Farming, Horticulture
- Dairy, Mixed Farming
- Livestock, Mixed Farming
- Pasture Livestock

MAJOR MINERAL OCCURRENCES

Ba	Barite	Na	Salt
C	Coal	O	Petroleum
F	Fluorspar	Pb	Lead
Fe	Iron Ore	Pe	Peat
G	Natural Gas	Sn	Tin
K	Potash	Zn	Zinc
Ka	Kaolin (china clay)		

⚡ Water Power

▨ Major Industrial Areas

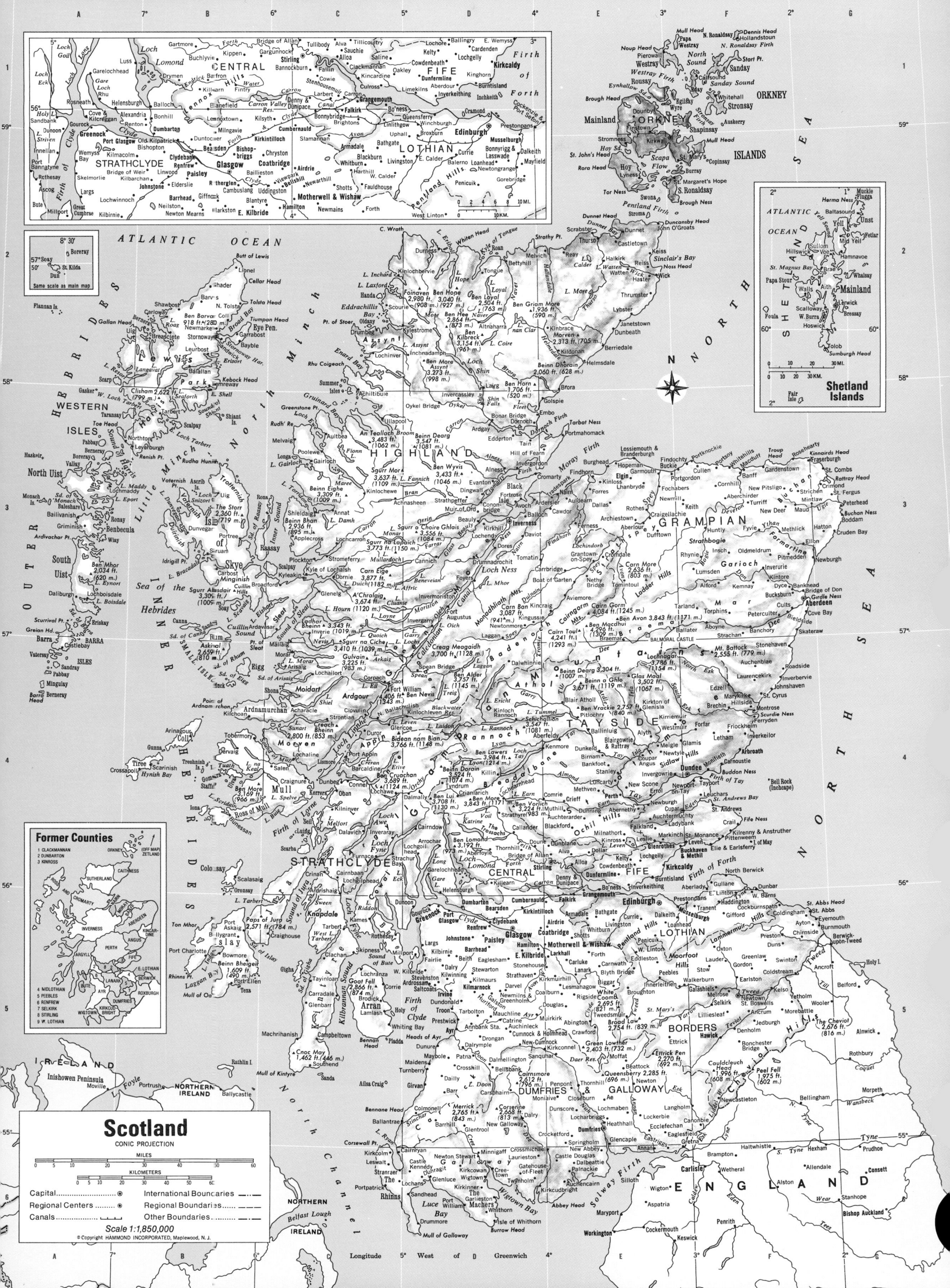

Scotland

CONIC PROJECTION

Capital............................⊛
Regional Centers..............●
Canals.............................

International Boundaries ____
Regional Boundaries _ _ _ _
Other Boundaries ....

Scale 1:1,850,000

© Copyright HAMMOND INCORPORATED, Maplewood, N.J.

Former Counties

1 CLACKMANNAN
2 DUNBARTON
3 KINROSS
4 MIDLOTHIAN
5 PEEBLES
6 RENFREW
7 SELKIRK
8 STIRLING
9 W. LOTHIAN

Shetland Islands

IRELAND

COUNTIES

Carlow 40,988 ...H6
Cavan 53,965 ...G4
Clare 91,344 ...D6
Cork 412,735 ...D7
Donegal 129,664 ...F2
Dublin 1,021,449 ...J5
Galway 178,552 ...D5
Kerry 124,159 ...B7
Kildare 116,247 ...H5
Kilkenny 73,186 ...G6
Laois 53,284 ...G6
Leitrim 27,035 ...E3
Leix (Laois) 53,284 ...G6
Limerick 164,569 ...D7
Longford 31,496 ...F4
Louth 91,810 ...J4
Mayo 115,184 ...C4
Meath 103,881 ...H4
Monaghan 52,379 ...H3
Offaly 59,835 ...F5
Roscommon 54,592 ...E4
Sligo 56,046 ...D3
Tipperary 136,619 ...F6
Waterford 91,151 ...F7
Westmeath 63,379 ...G5
Wexford 102,552 ...H7
Wicklow 94,542 ...J6

CITIES and TOWNS

Abbeyfeale 1,483 ...C7
Abbeyleix 1,468 ...G6
Adare 792 ...D6
Aghada-Farsid-Rostellan 818 ...E8
An Uaimh 3,660 ...H4
Ardee 3,253 ...H4
Ardfinnan 827 ...F7
Ardmore 343 ...F8
Arklow 8,388 ...J6
Ashford 782 ...J5
Askeaton 951 ...D6
Athboy 1,055 ...H4
Athenry 1,642 ...D5
Athlone 8,815 ...F5
Athy 4,734 ...H6
Aughrim 756 ...J6
Avoca 490 ...J6
Bagenalstown (Muinebeag) 2,653 ...H6
Baile Atha Cliath (Dublin) (cap.) 502,749 ...K5
Bailieborough 1,645 ...G4
Balbriggan 5,680 ...J4
Ballaghaderreen 1,366 ...E4
Ballina, Mayo 6,714 ...C3
Ballina, Tipperary 507 ...E6
Ballinamore 810 ...F3
Ballinasloe 6,125 ...E5
Ballincollig-Carrigrohane 7,231 ...D8
Ballineen 592 ...D8
Ballinrobe 1,270 ...C4
Ballybofey-Stranorlar 2,964 ...F2
Ballybunion 1,452 ...B7
Ballycastle 219 ...C3
Ballyconnell 466 ...F3
Ballygar 472 ...E4
Ballygeary 891 ...J7
Ballyhaunis 1,338 ...D4
Ballyheigue 660 ...B7
Ballyjamesduff 842 ...G4
Ballylanders 343 ...E7
Ballylongford 523 ...B6
Ballymahon 859 ...F4
Ballymore Eustace 575 ...J5
Ballymote 1,064 ...D3
Ballyragget 833 ...G6
Ballyshannon 2,573 ...E3
Baltinglass 1,089 ...H6
Banagher 1,465 ...F5
Bandon 1,943 ...D8
Bantry 2,811 ...C8
Belmullet 1,033 ...B3
Belturbet 1,228 ...G3
Bennettsbridge 601 ...G6
Birr 3,417 ...F5
Blanchardstown ...H5
Blarney 1,952 ...D8
Blessington 1,322 ...J5
Borrisokane 837 ...E6
Borrisoleigh 624 ...E6
Boyle 1,859 ...E4
Bray 24,686 ...K5
Bri Chualann (Bray) 24,686 ...K5
Bruff 819 ...D7
Bunbeg-Derrybeg 1,469 ...E1
Bunclody-Carrickduff 1,423 ...H6
Buncrana 3,106 ...G1
Bundoran 1,535 ...E3
Buttevant 1,133 ...D7
Cahir 2,118 ...F7
Cahirciveen 1,310 ...A8
Callan 1,266 ...G7
Cappamore 765 ...E6
Cappoquin 920 ...F7
Carlingford 635 ...J3
Carlow 11,509 ...H6
Carndonagh 1,600 ...G1
Carnew 723 ...H6
Carrickmacross 1,815 ...H4
Carrick-on-Shannon 1,984 ...F4
Carrick-on-Suir 5,353 ...F7
Carrigaline 5,893 ...E8
Carrigtwohill 1,272 ...E8
Cashel 2,458 ...F7
Castlebar 6,349 ...C4
Castlebellingham 848 ...J4
Castleblayney 2,157 ...H3
Castlebridge 655 ...H7
Castlecomer-Donaguile 1,490 ...G6
Castledermot 792 ...H6
Castlelfin 694 ...F2
Castleisland 2,281 ...B7
Castlemartyr 585 ...E8
Castlepollard 803 ...G4
Castlerea 1,840 ...D4
Castletown 303 ...F6
Castletownbere 905 ...B8
Castletownroche 474 ...D7
Cavan 3,381 ...G3
Ceanannus Mór 2,413 ...H4
Celbridge 7,135 ...H5
Charlestown-Bellahy 754 ...D4
Charleville (Rathluirc) 2,814 ...D7
Clara 2,736 ...F5
Claremorris 1,992 ...C4
Clifden 896 ...B5
Cloghan 496 ...F5
Clogh-Chatsworth 319 ...G6
Clogheen 502 ...F7
Clogherhead 765 ...J4
Clonakilty 2,567 ...D8
Clones 2,280 ...G3
Clonfert ...E5
Clonmel 11,759 ...F7
Cloughjordan 499 ...E6
Cloyne 721 ...E8
Coill Dubh 772 ...H5
Collooney 705 ...D3
Convoy 891 ...F2
Coolgreany 352 ...J6
Cootehill 1,487 ...G3
Cork 133,271 ...E8
Corofin 391 ...C6
Courtown Harbour 317 ...J6
Creeslough 340 ...F1
Croom 1,024 ...D6
Crosshaven 1,362 ...E8
Crossmolina 1,250 ...C3
Daingean 659 ...G5
Delvin 369 ...G4
Dingle 1,253 ...A7
Donabate 599 ...J5
Donegal 2,242 ...F2
Doneraile 846 ...D7
Dooagh-Keel 650 ...A4
Doon 308 ...E6
Drimoleague 381 ...C8
Drogheda 24,086 ...J4
Droichead Nua 5,983 ...H5
Dromahair 353 ...E3
Drumconrath 334 ...H4
Drumshanbo 622 ...E3
Dublin (cap.) 502,749 ...K5
Duleek 1,679 ...J4
Duncannon 388 ...H7
Dundalk 26,669 ...H3
Dunfanaghy 314 ...F1
Dungarvan 6,849 ...F7
Dungloe 940 ...E2
Dún Laoghaire 54,715 ...K5
Dunkineely 442 ...E2
Dunlavin 731 ...H5
Dunleer 1,184 ...J4
Dunmanway 1,382 ...C8
Dunmore 445 ...D4
Dunmore East 1,041 ...G7
Dunshaughlin 878 ...H5
Durrow 707 ...G6
Edenderry 3,539 ...G5
Elphin 513 ...E4
Emyvale 464 ...G3
Ennis 5,917 ...D6
Enniscorthy 4,483 ...J7
Enniskerry 1,229 ...J5
Ennistymon 1,039 ...C6
Eyrecourt 351 ...E5
Fahan 367 ...G1
Falcarragh 996 ...E1
Fenit 401 ...B7
Ferbane 1,374 ...F5
Fermoy 2,872 ...E7
Ferns 811 ...J6
Fethard 982 ...F7
Foxford 1,033 ...C4
Foynes 707 ...C6
Frankford (Kilcormac) 1,118 ...F5
Freshford 700 ...G6
Galbally 248 ...E7
Galway 47,104 ...C5
Geashill 339 ...G5
Glanworth 379 ...E7
Glenamaddy 369 ...D4
Glenties 914 ...E2
Glin 569 ...C6
Golden 295 ...F7
Gorey 2,445 ...J6
Gormanston 870 ...J4
Gort 1,021 ...D5
Gowran 517 ...G6
Graiguenamanagh-Tinnahinch 1,485 ...H6
Granard 1,338 ...F4
Greencastle 584 ...H1
Greystones 8,455 ...K5
Hacketstown 710 ...H6
Headford 675 ...C5
Holycross 274 ...F6
Hospital 751 ...E7
Inniscrone 633 ...C3
Johnstown 408 ...G6
Kanturk 1,870 ...D7
Keel-Dooagh 650 ...A4
Kells (Ceanannus Mór) 2,413 ...G4
Kenmare 1,130 ...B8
Kilbeggan 603 ...G5
Kilcar 345 ...D2
Kilcock 1,414 ...H5
Kilcoole 2,335 ...K5
Kilcormac 1,118 ...F5
Kilculen 1,693 ...H5
Kildare 4,268 ...H5
Kildysart 347 ...C6
Kilfinane 788 ...D7
Kilkee 1,448 ...B6
Kilkenny 8,969 ...G6
Killala 674 ...C3
Killaloe 1,033 ...D6
Killarney 7,837 ...C7
Killenaule 717 ...F6
Killeshandra 455 ...F3
Killorglin 1,304 ...B7
Killucan-Rathwire 353 ...G4
Killybegs 1,632 ...E2
Kilmacrennan 412 ...F1
Kilmacthomas 648 ...G7
Kilmallock 1,424 ...D7
Kilmihill 338 ...C6
Kilmore Quay 458 ...H7
Kilnaleck 321 ...G4
Kilronan 282 ...B5
Kilrush 2,961 ...C6
Kiltimagh 982 ...C4
Kilworth 411 ...E7
Kingscourt 1,242 ...H4
Kingstown (Dún Laoghaire) 54,715 ...K5
Kinnegad 433 ...G5
Kinnitty 261 ...F5
Kinsale 1,811 ...D8
Kinvara 425 ...D5
Knightstown 204 ...A8
Knock 332 ...D4
Knocklong 273 ...D7
Lahinch 511 ...C6
Lanesborough-Ballyleague 1,058 ...E4
Laytown-Bettystown-Mornington 3,321 ...J4
Leighlinbridge 540 ...H6
Leitrim ...F3
Leixlip 11,938 ...H5
Letterkenny 6,691 ...F2
Lifford 1,478 ...F2
Limerick 56,279 ...D6
Lisdoonvarna 648 ...C5
Lismore 703 ...F7
Listowel 3,494 ...C7
Littleton 566 ...F6
Longford 6,457 ...F4
Loughrea 3,360 ...D5
Louisburgh 209 ...B4
Louth 435 ...J4
Lucan 12,259 ...J5
Luimneach (Limerick) 56,279 ...D6
Lusk 1,831 ...J4
Macroom 2,449 ...C8
Malahide 9,940 ...J5
Mallow 6,488 ...D7
Manorhamilton 1,031 ...E3
Maryborough (Portlaoise) 3,773 ...G5
Maynooth 4,768 ...H5
Meathas Truim 806 ...G4
Midleton 3,111 ...E8
Milford 981 ...F1
Millstreet 1,330 ...D7
Milltown 347 ...A7
Miltownmalbay 719 ...C6
Mitchelstown 3,210 ...E7
Moate 1,659 ...F5
Mohill 930 ...F4
Monaghan 6,075 ...G3
Monasterevan 2,143 ...H5
Moneygall 346 ...F6
Mooncoin 868 ...G7
Mount Bellew 519 ...D5
Mountcharles 480 ...E2
Mountmellick 2,789 ...G5
Mountrath 1,402 ...F5
Moville 1,331 ...G1
Moycullen 366 ...C5
Muinebeag 2,653 ...H6
Mullagh 462 ...H4
Mullinahone 385 ...F7
Mullinavat 355 ...G7
Mullingar 8,077 ...G4
Naas 10,017 ...H5
Navan (An Uaimh) 3,660 ...H4
Nenagh 5,483 ...E6
Newbliss 293 ...G3
Newbridge (Droichead Nua) 5,983 ...H5
Newcastle 3,370 ...C7
Newmarket 1,022 ...C7
Newmarket-on-Fergus 1,678 ...D6
Newport, Mayo 492 ...C4
Newport, Tipperary 857 ...E6
New Ross 5,343 ...H7
Newtown Forbes 393 ...F4
Newtownmountkennedy 2,183 ...J5
Newtownsandes 357 ...C6
O'Briensbridge-Montpelier 385 ...D6
Oldcastle 869 ...G4
Oola 451 ...E6
Oranmore 1,064 ...D5
Oughterard 682 ...C5
Passage East 563 ...G7
Passage West 3,511 ...E8
Patrickswell 905 ...D6
Piltown 691 ...G7
Portarlington 3,295 ...G5
Portlaoise 3,773 ...G5
Portlaw 1,260 ...G7
Portmarnock 9,055 ...J5
Portumna 1,062 ...E5
Queenstown (Cóbh) 6,369 ...E8
Ramelton 989 ...F1
Raphoe 1,027 ...F2
Rathangan 1,270 ...G5
Rathcoole 2,991 ...J5
Rathdowney 1,095 ...F6
Rathdrum 1,307 ...J6
Rathkeale 1,815 ...D7
Rathluirc 2,814 ...D7
Rathmore 548 ...J5
Rathmullen 554 ...F1
Rathnew 1,389 ...J6
Rathvilly 512 ...H6
Ratoath 551 ...J5
Riverstown 1,416 ...D3
Roscommon 1,363 ...E4
Roscrea 4,378 ...F6
Rosscarbery 425 ...C8
Rosses Point 598 ...D3
Rosslare 704 ...J7
Rosslare Harbour (Ballygeary) 891 ...J7
Roundwood 371 ...J5
Rush 4,513 ...J4
Saint Johnston 468 ...F2
Scarriff 847 ...E6
Schull 509 ...B8
Shanagolden 402 ...C6
Shannon 8,005 ...D6
Shannon Bridge 310 ...F5
Shercock 406 ...G4
Shillelagh 334 ...J6
Shinrone 479 ...F5
Sixmilebridge 1,182 ...D6
Skerries 6,864 ...J4
Skibbereen 1,999 ...C8
Slane 689 ...H4
Sligo 17,259 ...E3
Sneem 309 ...B8
Stepaside 748 ...J5
Stradbally, Laois 1,046 ...G5
Stradbally, Waterford 255 ...F7
Strokestown 620 ...E4
Swinford 1,197 ...D4
Swords 15,312 ...J5
Taghmon 607 ...H7
Tallow 867 ...F7
Tarbert 683 ...C6
Templemore 2,258 ...F6
Templetuohy 242 ...F6
Termonfeckin 741 ...J4
Thomastown 1,465 ...G7
Thurles 7,049 ...F6
Timoleague 330 ...D8
Tinahely 594 ...H6
Tipperary 5,033 ...E7
Toomevara 428 ...F6
Tralee 17,109 ...B7
Tramore 5,999 ...G7
Trim 1,967 ...H4
Tuam 4,109 ...D4
Tubbercurry 1,250 ...D3
Tulla 403 ...D6
Tullamore 8,484 ...G5
Tullow 2,324 ...H6
Tyrrellspass 328 ...G5
Urlingford 676 ...F6
Virginia 699 ...G4
Waterford 39,529 ...G7
Waterville-Spunkane 475 ...A8
Westport 3,456 ...C4
Wexford 10,336 ...H7
Wicklow 5,304 ...K6
Woodford 242 ...E5
Youghal 5,706 ...F8

OTHER FEATURES

Achill (head) ...A4
Achill (isl.) ...A4
Allen (lake) ...E3
Allen, Bog of (marsh) ...H5
Annalee (riv.) ...G3
Aran (isls.) ...B5
Aran (isl.) ...D2
Arrow (lake) ...E3
Ballinskelligs (bay) ...A8
Ballyhoura (hills) ...E7
Ballyteige (bay) ...H7
Bandon (riv.) ...D8
Bantry (bay) ...B8
Barrow (riv.) ...H6
Baurtregaum (mt.) ...A7
Bear (isl.) ...B8
Ben Dash (hill) ...C6
Bertraghboy (bay) ...B5
Black (head) ...C5
Blacksod (bay) ...A3
Blackstairs (mt.) ...H6
Blackwater (riv.) ...H4
Blackwater (riv.) ...D7
Blasket (isls.) ...A7
Bloody Foreland (prom.) ...E1
Blue Stack (mts.) ...E2
Boderg (lake) ...F4
Boggeragh (mts.) ...D7
Bolus (head) ...A8
Boyne (riv.) ...J4
Brandon (bay) ...A7
Brandon (head) ...A7
Brandon (mt.) ...A7
Bray (head) ...A8
Bride (riv.) ...E7
Broad Haven (harb.) ...B3
Brosna (riv.) ...F5
Bull, The (isl.) ...A8
Caha (mts.) ...B8
Cahore (pt.) ...J6
Cark (mt.) ...F2
Carlingford (inlet) ...J3
Carnsore (pt.) ...J7
Carra (lake) ...C4
Carrantuohill (mt.) ...B7
Carrowmore (lake) ...B3
Clare (isls.) ...A4
Clare (riv.) ...D5
Clear (cape) ...B9
Clear (isl.) ...B9
Clew (bay) ...B4
Clonakilty (bay) ...D8
Comeragh (mts.) ...F7
Conn (lake) ...C3
Connacht (prov.) 431,409 ...C4
Connemara (dist.) ...B5
Cork (harb.) ...E8
Corrib (lake) ...C5
Croagh Patrick (mt.) ...C4
Cuilcagh (mt.) ...F3
Cullin (lake) ...C4
Curragh, The (plain) ...H5
Dash, Ben (hill) ...C6
Dee (riv.) ...H4
Deel (riv.) ...C7
Deel (riv.) ...C3
Deel (riv.) ...G4
Deele (riv.) ...F2
Derg (lake) ...F2
Derg (lake) ...E6
Derravaragh (lake) ...G4
Derryveagh (mts.) ...E2
Devilsbit (mt.) ...E6
Dingle (bay) ...A7
Donegal (bay) ...D3
Donegal (bay) ...B6
Doulus (head) ...A8
Downpatrick (head) ...C3
Drum (hills) ...F7
Dublin (bay) ...J5
Dunany (pt.) ...J4
Dundalk (bay) ...J4
Dungarvan (harb.) ...G7
Dunkellin (riv.) ...D5
Dunmanus (bay) ...B8
Dursey (isl.) ...A8
Eask (lake) ...E2
Ennell (lake) ...G5
Erne (riv.) ...E3
Errigal (mt.) ...E1
Erris (head) ...A3
Fanad (head) ...G1
Fastnet Rock (isl.) ...B9
Feale (riv.) ...C7
Feeagh (lake) ...B4
Fergus (riv.) ...D6
Finn (riv.) ...F2
Finn (riv.) ...G3
Foul (sound) ...B5
Foyle (inlet) ...G1
Foyle (riv.) ...G2
Galley (head) ...D9
Galtee (mts.) ...E7
Galtymore (mt.) ...E7
Galway (bay) ...C5
Gara (lake) ...D4
Garadice (lake) ...F3
Gill (lake) ...E3
Gola (isl.) ...E1
Golden Vale (plain) ...E7
Gorumna (isl.) ...B5
Gowna (lake) ...G4
Grand (canal) ...H5
Great Blasket (isl.) ...A7
Gregory's (head) ...B5
Gweebarra (bay) ...D2
Hags (head) ...B6
Hook (head) ...H7
Horn (head) ...E1
Iar Connacht (dist.) ...C5
Inishbofin (isl.) ...A4
Inisheer (isl.) ...B5
Inishmaan (isl.) ...B5
Inishmore (isl.) ...B5
Inishmurray (isl.) ...D3
Inishowen (head) ...H1
Inishowen (pen.) ...G1
Inishshark (isl.) ...A4
Inishtrahull (isl.) ...G1
Inishtrahull (sound) ...G1
Inishturk (isls.) ...A4
Inny (riv.) ...F4
Ireland's Eye (isl.) ...K5
Irish (sea) ...K4
Joyce's Country (dist.) ...B4
Keeper (mt.) ...E6
Kenmare (riv.) ...A8
Kerry (head) ...B7
Key (lake) ...E3
Kilkieran (bay) ...B5
Killala (bay) ...C3
Killary (harb.) ...A4
Kinsale (harb.) ...D8
Kinsale, Old Head of (head) ...E8
Kippure (mt.) ...J5
Knockanefune (mt.) ...C7
Knockboy (mt.) ...B8
Knockmealdown (mts.) ...F7
Lambay (hill) ...K4
Laune (riv.) ...B7
Leane (lake) ...B7
Lee (riv.) ...D8
Leinster (mt.) ...H6
Leinster (prov.) 1,852,649 ...G5
Lettermullan (isl.) ...B5
Liffey (riv.) ...H5
Liscannor (bay) ...B6
Loop (head) ...A6
Loughros More (bay) ...D2
Lugnaquillia (mt.) ...J6
Lung (riv.) ...D4
Macgillicuddy's Reeks (mts.) ...B7
Macnean (lake) ...F3
Maigue (riv.) ...D6
Malin (head) ...F1
Mangerton (mt.) ...C8
Mask (lake) ...C4
Maumakeogh (mt.) ...C3
Maumturk (mts.) ...B5
Melvin (lake) ...E3
Mine (head) ...F8
Mizen (head) ...B9
Mizen (head) ...K6
Moher (cliff) ...B6
Monavullagh (mts.) ...F7
Moy (riv.) ...C3
Mullaghareirk (mts.) ...C7
Mulroy (bay) ...F1
Munster (prov.) 1,020,577 ...D7
Mutton (isl.) ...B6
Mweelrea (mt.) ...B4
Nagles (mts.) ...E7
Nephin (mt.) ...C3
Nephin Beg (mt.) ...B3
Nore (riv.) ...G6
North (sound) ...B5
North Inishkea (isl.) ...A3
Oughter (lake) ...G3
Ovoca (riv.) ...J6
Owenmore (riv.) ...B3
Owenmore (riv.) ...C7
Paps, The (mt.) ...C7
Partry (mts.) ...C4
Pollaphuca (res.) ...J5
Puffin (isl.) ...A8
Punchestown ...H5
Ramor (lake) ...G4
Rathlin O'Birne (isl.) ...C2
Ree (lake) ...F5
Rinn (lake) ...F4
Roaringwater (bay) ...B9
Rosscarbery (bay) ...D9
Rosskeeragh (pt.) ...D3
Royal (canal) ...G4
Saint Finan's (bay) ...A8
Saint George's (chan.) ...K7
Saint John's (pt.) ...D2
Saltee (isls.) ...H7
Scarriff (isl.) ...A8
Seven Hogs, The (isls.) ...A7
Shannon (riv.) ...E6
Shannon, Mouth of the (delta) ...B6
Sheffry (hills) ...B4
Sheelin (lake) ...G4
Sheep Haven (harb.) ...F1
Sheeps (head) ...B8
Shehy (mts.) ...C8
Sherkin (isl.) ...C9
Silvermine (mts.) ...E6
Slaney (riv.) ...H6
Slieve Anierin (mt.) ...F3
Slieve Aughty (mts.) ...D5
Slieve Bernagh (mt.) ...D6
Slieve Bloom (mts.) ...F5
Slieve Callan (mt.) ...C6
Slieve Car (mt.) ...B3
Slieve Elva (mt.) ...C5
Slieve Gamph (Ox) (mts.) ...D3
Slievefelim (mts.) ...E6
Slievenaman (mt.) ...F7
Sligo (bay) ...D3
Slyne (head) ...A5
Smerwick (harb.) ...A7
South (sound) ...C5
Stacks (mts.) ...B7
Suck (riv.) ...E5
Sugarloaf (mt.) ...B8
Suir (riv.) ...F6
Swilly (inlet) ...F1
Tara (hill) ...H4
Toe (head) ...C9
Tory (isl.) ...E1
Tory (sound) ...E1
Tralee (bay) ...B7
Tramore (bay) ...G7
Truskmore (mt.) ...E3
Twelve Pins (mt.) ...B4
Ulster (part) 236,008 ...G2
Valencia (Valentia) (isl.) ...A8
Valentia (isl.) ...A8
Waterford (harb.) ...H7
Wexford (harb.) ...J7
Wexford (bay) ...J7
Wicklow (mts.) ...J6
Youghal (bay) ...F8

NORTHERN IRELAND

DISTRICTS

Antrim 44,384 ...J2
Ards 57,626 ...K2
Armagh 47,618 ...H3
Ballymena 54,426 ...J2
Ballymoney 22,873 ...J1
Banbridge 29,885 ...J3
Belfast 295,223 ...K2
Carrickfergus 28,458 ...K2
Castlereagh 60,757 ...K2
Coleraine 46,272 ...H1
Cookstown 26,624 ...H2
Craigavon 71,202 ...J3
Down 52,869 ...K3
Dungannon 41,073 ...H3
Fermanagh 51,008 ...F3
Larne 28,929 ...K2
Limavady 26,270 ...H1
Lisburn 82,091 ...J2
Londonderry 83,384 ...G2
Magherafelt 30,825 ...H2
Mourne (Newry and Mourne) 72,243 ...J3
Moyle 14,252 ...J1
Newtownabbey 71,631 ...J2
North Down 65,849 ...K2
Omagh 41,159 ...G2
Strabane 35,028 ...G2

CITIES and TOWNS

Annalong 1,823 ...K3
Antrim 22,342 ...J2
Armagh 12,700 ...H3
Augher 1,874 ...G3
Aughnacloy 1,659 ...H3
Ballycarry 1,652 ...K2
Ballycastle 3,284 ...J1
Ballyclare 6,159 ...J2
Ballygawley 2,099 ...G3
Ballymena 28,166 ...J2
Ballymoney 5,679 ...J1
Ballynahinch 3,721 ...J3
Banbridge 9,650 ...J3
Bangor 46,585 ...K2
Belfast (cap.) 295,223 ...K2
Bellaghy 1,854 ...H2
Belleek and Boa 2,469 ...E3
Beragh 2,028 ...G2
Bessbrook 2,756 ...J3
Brookeborough 2,250 ...G3
Broughshane 1,503 ...J2
Bushmills 1,381 ...J1
Caledon 1,633 ...H3
Carnlough 1,462 ...K2
Carrickfergus 17,633 ...K2
Carrowdore 3,019 ...K2
Carryduff 2,666 ...K2
Castledawson 1,460 ...H2
Castlederg 1,730 ...F2
Castlewellan 2,105 ...K3
Claudy 2,516 ...G2
Clogher 1,792 ...G3
Cloughmills 1,555 ...J2
Coalisland 3,324 ...H2
Coleraine 15,967 ...H1
Comber 7,600 ...K2
Cookstown 7,649 ...H2
Craigavon 10,195 ...J3
Crumlin 1,708 ...J2
Cullybackey 2,098 ...J2
Derrygonnelly 2,627 ...F3
Donaghadee 3,874 ...K2
Downpatrick 8,245 ...K3
Dromore, Banbridge 3,089 ...J3
Dromore, Omagh 2,286 ...G2
Drumquin 1,865 ...G2
Dundrum 2,295 ...
Dungannon 8,295 ...H3
Dungiven 2,249 ...H2
Dunloy 1,593 ...J2
Dunnamanagh 2,191 ...G2
Ederney, Kesh and Lark 2,607 ...
Enniskillen 10,429 ...F3
Feeny 1,402 ...
Fintona 1,353 ...
Fivemiletown 1,758 ...G3
Garvagh 2,222 ...
Gilford 1,512 ...
Glenarm 1,533 ...
Glenavy 2,402 ...
Glynn 1,689 ...
Gortin 1,877 ...
Greenisland 5,103 ...K2
Grey Abbey 2,945 ...
Groomsport 3,870 ...
Holywood 9,462 ...K2
Irvinestown 1,827 ...
Keady 2,561 ...
Kells 2,564 ...
Kesh, Ederney and Lark 2,607 ...
Kilkeel 6,036 ...
Killough 3,104 ...
Killyclogher 5,557 ...
Killyleagh 2,094 ...
Kilrea 1,320 ...
Lambeg ...
Larne 18,224 ...K2
Limavady 8,015 ...H1
Lisbellaw 2,395 ...
Lisburn 40,391 ...J2
Lisnaskea 1,568 ...
Londonderry (Derry) 62,692 ...G2
Loughbrickland 2,244 ...
Lurgan 20,991 ...
Macosquin 2,267 ...
Maghera 1,953 ...
Magherafelt 5,044 ...
Milisle 1,373 ...
Moy 2,163 ...
Newcastle 6,246 ...
Newry 19,426 ...
Newtownabbey 56,149 ...K2
Newtownards 20,531 ...
Newtownbutler 2,632 ...
Newtownhamilton 1,654 ...
Newtownstewart 1,425 ...
Omagh 14,627 ...G2
Pomeroy 1,638 ...
Portadown 21,333 ...H3
Portaferry 2,148 ...
Portglenone 2,017 ...
Portrush 5,114 ...
Portstewart 5,312 ...
Randalstown 3,591 ...
Rathfriland 2,243 ...
Richhill 1,728 ...
Rostrevor 1,852 ...
Sion Mills 1,771 ...
Sixmilecross 1,613 ...
Stewartstown 1,554 ...
Strabane 9,413 ...
Strangford 2,062 ...
Strathfoyle 2,050 ...
Tandragee 2,224 ...
Tempo 2,149 ...
Trillick 2,017 ...
Warrenpoint 4,798 ...
Whitehead 3,546 ...

OTHER FEATURES

Arney (riv.) ...
Bann (riv.) ...
Beg (lake) ...
Belfast (inlet) ...
Blackwater (riv.) ...
Bush (riv.) ...
Copeland (isl.) ...
Derg (riv.) ...
Divis (mt.) ...
Dundrum (bay) ...
Erne, Lough (lake) ...
Fair (head) ...
Foyle (riv.) ...
Foyle (inlet) ...
Garron (pt.) ...
Giant's Causeway ...
Lagan (riv.) ...
Larne (inlet) ...
Macnean (lake) ...
Magee, Island (pen.) ...
Main (riv.) ...
Mourne (riv.) ...
Mourne (mts.) ...
Neagh (lake) ...
North (chan.) ...
Owenkillew (riv.) ...
Rathlin (sound) ...
Rathlin (isl.) ...
Red (bay) ...
Roe (riv.) ...
Saint John's (pt.) ...
Slieve Beagh (mt.) ...
Slieve Donard (mt.) ...
Sperrin (mts.) ...
Strangford (inlet) ...
Trostan (mt.) ...
Ulster (part) (prov.) ...
Upper Lough Erne (lake) ...

Ireland

CONIC PROJECTION

SCALE OF MILES

SCALE OF KILOMETERS

Scale 1:1,660,000

Capitals.................★
County Towns &
District Capitals..........△
Canals.....................

Country Boundaries.....—··—··—
County & District
Boundaries.............—·—·—

Traditional Divisions

NORTHERN IRELAND is divided internally into
26 districts bearing the same names as their
respective capitals, except:

DISTRICTS	CAPITALS
ARDS	Newtownards
CASTLEREAGH ① *	Belfast
DOWN	Downpatrick
FERMANAGH	Enniskillen
MOURNE	Newry
MOYLE	Ballycastle
NEWTOWNABBEY ② *	Belfast
NORTH DOWN	Bangor

* Indicated by number on map
† Belfast also serves as capital of Belfast District

© Copyright HAMMOND INCORPORATED, Maplewood, N. J.

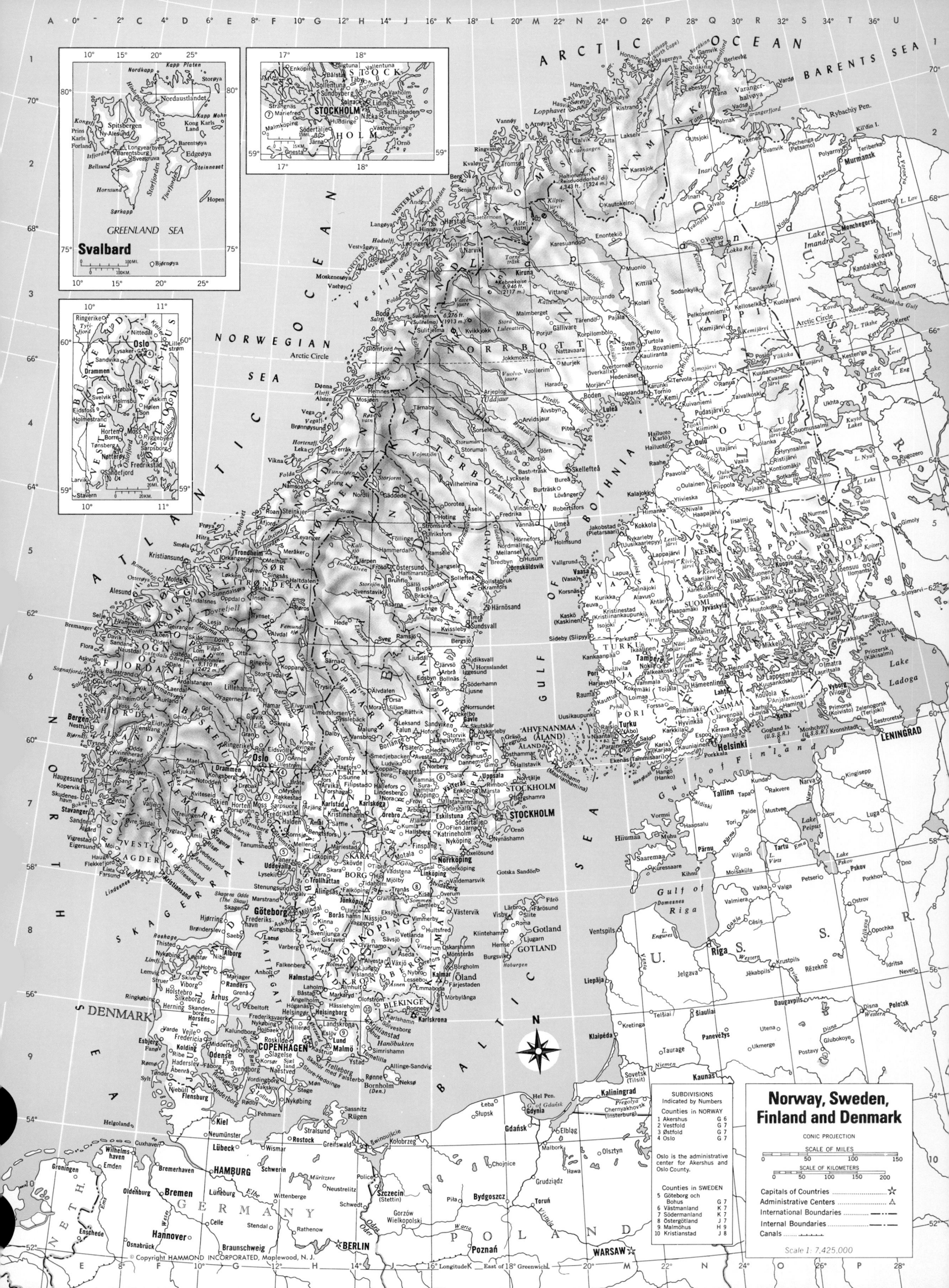

Norway, Sweden, Finland and Denmark

CONIC PROJECTION

SCALE OF MILES

SCALE OF KILOMETERS

Capitals of Countries ....★
Administrative Centers ....△
International Boundaries .... —·—·—
Internal Boundaries .... —··—··—
Canals ....

Scale 1: 7,425,000

SUBDIVISIONS
Indicated by Numbers

Counties in NORWAY
1 Akershus   G 6
2 Vestfold   G 7
3 Østfold   G 7
4 Oslo   G 7

Oslo is the administrative
center for Akershus and
Oslo County.

Counties in Sweden
5 Göteborg och
   Bohus   G 7
6 Västmanland   K 7
7 Södermanland   K 7
8 Östergötland   H 9
9 Malmöhus   H 8
10 Kristianstad   J 8

Svalbard

© Copyright HAMMOND INCORPORATED, Maplewood, N.J.

AREA 125,053 sq. mi.
(323,887 sq. km.)
POPULATION 4,242,000
CAPITAL Oslo
LARGEST CITY Oslo
HIGHEST POINT Glittertinden
8,110 ft. (2,472 m.)
MONETARY UNIT krone
MAJOR LANGUAGE Norwegian
MAJOR RELIGION Protestantism

AREA 173,665 sq. mi.
(449,792 sq. km.)
POPULATION 8,541,000
CAPITAL Stockholm
LARGEST CITY Stockholm
HIGHEST POINT Kebnekaise 6,946 ft.
(2,117 m.)
MONETARY UNIT krona
MAJOR LANGUAGE Swedish
MAJOR RELIGION Protestantism

AREA 130,128 sq. mi.
(337,032 sq. km.)
POPULATION 4,973,000
CAPITAL Helsinki
LARGEST CITY Helsinki
HIGHEST POINT Haltiatunturi
4,343 ft. (1,324 m.)
MONETARY UNIT markka
MAJOR LANGUAGES Finnish, Swedish
MAJOR RELIGION Protestantism

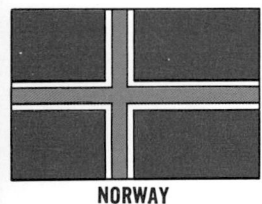

NORWAY

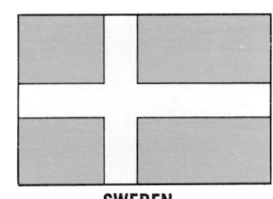

SWEDEN

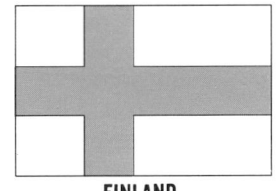

FINLAND

FINLAND

PROVINCES

Ahvenanmaa 23,591	L6
Åland (Ahvenanmaa) 23,591	L6
Häme 677,750	O6
Keski-Suomi 247,693	O5
Kuopio 256,036	P5
Kymi 340,665	Q6
Lappi 200,943	P3
Mikkeli 239,029	P6
Oulu 432,141	P4
Pohjois-Karjala 177,567	Q5
Turku ja Pori 713,050	N6
Uusimaa 1,187,851	O6
Vaasa 444,348	N5

CITIES and TOWNS

Abo (Turku) 161,398	N6
Alavus 10,701	N5
Äänekoski 11,447	O5
Anjalamkoski 19,703	P6
Borga 19,513	O6
Espoo 156,778	O6
Forssa 20,074	N6
Haapajärvi 8,454	O5
Hämeenlinna 42,382	O6
Hamina 10,313	P6
Hangö 12,071	N7
Hanko (Hangö) 12,071	N7
Harjavalta 8,955	M6
Heinola 16,112	P6
Helsinki (cap.) 485,795	O6
Hyvinkää 38,742	O6
Iisalmi 23,612	P5
Ikaalinen 9,184	N6
Imatra 35,085	Q6
Jakobstad 20,458	N5
Jämsä 12,498	O6
Järvenpää 27,220	O6
Joensuu 46,850	R5
Jyväskylä 65,282	O5
Kajaani 36,020	P4
Kankaanpää 13,652	M6
Karis (Karjaa)	N6
Karkkila 8,355	N6
Kauniainen 7,746	O6
Kemi 26,421	O4
Kemijärvi 12,762	P3
Kerava 26,207	O6
Kokemäki 9,741	N6
Kokkola 34,489	N5
Kotka 58,956	P6
Kouvola 31,829	P6
Kristiinankaupunki (Kristinestad) 9,081	N5
Kristinestad 9,081	N5
Kuopio 78,124	O5
Kurikka 11,512	M5
Kuusankoski 22,089	P6
Lahti 94,447	O6
Lappeenranta 54,102	P6
Lapua 14,644	N5
Lieksa 18,588	R5
Loimaa 7,053	N6
Lovisa 8,697	P6
Maarianhamina (Mariehamn) 9,829	M7
Mänttä 8,092	O6
Mariehamn 9,829	M7
Mikkeli 31,636	O6
Naantali 10,246	M6
Nokia 24,325	N6
Nurmes 11,419	Q5
Nykarleby 7,768	N5
Oulainen 8,225	O4
Oulu 97,297	O4
Outokumpu 9,678	Q5
Parainen 11,618	N6
Parkano 8,692	N6
Pieksämäki 14,372	P5
Pietarsaari (Jakobstad) 20,458	N5
Pori 78,376	M6
Pudasjärvi 11,453	P4
Raahe 18,932	O4
Raisio 19,671	M6
Rauma 30,921	M6
Riihimäki 24,366	O6
Rovaniemi 32,782	O3
Salo 20,495	N6
Savonlinna 28,667	Q6
Seinäjoki 26,257	N5
Suonenjoki 8,981	P5
Tampere 169,026	N6
Toijala 8,046	N6
Tornio 22,328	O4
Turku 161,398	N6
Utsjoki 1,548	P2
Uusikaarlepyy (Nykarleby) 7,768	N5
Uusikaupunki 14,026	M6
Vaasa 54,333	M5
Valkeakoski 22,582	N6
Vammala 16,024	N6
Vantaa 143,844	O6
Varkaus 24,856	Q5
Vasa (Vaasa) 54,333	M5
Virrat 9,391	N5
Ylivieska 12,559	O4

OTHER FEATURES

Åland (isls.)	L6
Baltic (sea)	K9
Bothnia (gulf)	M5
Finland (gulf)	P7
Hailuoto (isl.)	O4
Haltiatunturi (mt.)	M2
Haukivesi (lake)	Q5
Iijoki (riv.)	O4
Inari (lake)	P2
Ivalojoki (riv.)	P2
Kallavesi (lake)	P5
Karlö (Hailuoto) (isl.)	O4
Keitele (lake)	O5
Kemijärvi (lake)	Q3
Kemijoki (riv.)	O3
Lapland (reg.)	O3
Lappajärvi (lake)	N5
Lapuanjoki (riv.)	N5
Lokka (reg.)	Q3
Muojärvi (lake)	R4
Muonio (riv.)	M2
Näsijärvi (lake)	O6
Orihvesi (lake)	Q5
Oulujärvi (lake)	P4
Oulujoki (riv.)	O4
Ounasjoki (riv.)	O3
Päijänne (lake)	O6
Pielinen (lake)	Q5
Porkkala (pen.)	O7
Puruvesi (lake)	Q6
Saimaa (lake)	Q6
Tana (riv.)	P2
Tornionjoki (riv.)	O3
Ylikitka (lake)	Q3

NORWAY

COUNTIES

Akershus 399,797	G6
Aust-Agder 95,475	E7
Buskerud 221,384	F6
Finnmark 74,690	O2
Hedmark 186,305	G6
Hordaland 402,343	E6
Møre og Romsdal 237,489	E5
Nordland 241,048	J3
Nord-Trøndelag 126,648	H4
Oppland 181,620	F6
Oslo (city) 449,220	D3
Østfold 235,813	G7
Rogaland 326,611	D7
Sogn og Fjordane 105,466	E6
Sør-Trøndelag 247,354	G5
Telemark 162,595	F7
Troms 146,595	L2
Vest-Agder 141,284	D7
Vestfold 192,934	G7

CITIES and TOWNS

Ålesund 40,868	D5
Ålgård 2,322	D7
Alta 5,582	N2
Åndalsnes 2,574	F5
Årdalstangen 2,360	F6
Arendal 11,701	F7
Årnes 2,267	G6
Askim 8,413	E4
Bamble† 7,031	F7
Bergen 213,434	D6
Bodø 31,077	J3
Borge† 3,294	H2
Brate 2,107	G7
Brønnøysund 3,130	G4
Drammen 50,777	C4
Drøbak 4,538	D4
Eidsvoll 2,906	G6
Eigersund 11,379	D7
Elverum 7,391	G6
Farsund 8,908	D7
Flekkefjord 8,750	E7
Flora 8,822	D6
Fredrikstad 29,024	D4
Gjøvik 25,963	G6
Grimstad 13,091	F7
Halden 27,087	D4
Hamar 16,418	G6
Hammerfest 7,610	N1
Harstad 21,125	K2
Hauge 2,079	E7
Haugesund 27,386	D7
Holmestrand 8,246	C4
Honningsvag 3,780	O1
Horten 13,746	D4
Kirkenes 4,466	Q2
Kongsberg 19,854	F7
Kongsvinger 16,146	H6
Kopervik 4,221	D7
Kornsjø† 6,079	G7
Kragerø 5,249	F7
Kristiansand 59,488	F8
Kristiansund 18,847	E5
Kvinnherad† 2,898	E6
Larvik 9,097	C4
Lenvik† 11,098	L2
Levanger 5,066	G5
Lillehammer 21,248	F6
Lillesand 3,028	F7
Lillestrøm† 11,550	E3
Lodingen 1,840	J2
Longyearbyen	D2
Lysaker† 81,612	D3
Mandal 11,579	E7
Meråker† 2,907	G5
Mo 21,033	J3
Molde 20,334	E5
Mosjøen 9,341	H4
Moss 25,786	D4
Mysen 3,760	G7
Namsos 11,452	H4
Narvik 19,582	K2
Nesttun† 11,519	D6
Nittedal† 8,889	D3
Notodden 12,970	F7
Nøtterøy 11,944	D4
Odda 7,401	E6
Oppdal 2,173	F5
Orkanger 3,685	F5
Oslo (cap.) 462,732	D3
Oslo* 645,413	D3
Porsgrunn 31,709	G7
Rakkestad 2,392	G7
Ringerike 30,156	C3
Risør 6,560	F7
Rjukan 5,334	F7
Røros 3,041	G5
Saetermoen 2,114	L2
Sandefjord 33,350	C4
Sandnes 33,904	D7
Sandvika† 34,337	C3
Sarpsborg 12,889	D4
Seljet 3,386	D4
Ski 9,081	D4
Skien 47,105	F7
Skudeneshavn 2,206	D7
Stavanger 86,639	D7
Stavern 2,604	D4
Steinkjer 20,553	G4
Stor-Elvdal† 2,993	G6
Sunndalsøra 5,114	F5
Svelvik 2,256	D4
Svolvær 3,942	J2
Tana 1,893	Q1
Tønsberg 9,964	D4
Tromsø 43,830	L2
Trondheim 134,910	F5
Tvedestrand 1,689	F7
Ullensvang† 2,326	E6
Vadsø 6,019	Q1
Vanylven 1,966	E5
Vardø 3,875	R1
Vik 1,019	E6
Volda 3,511	E6
Voss 5,944	E6

OTHER FEATURES

Andøya (isl.)	J2
Barentsoya (isl.)	D2
Bjørnøya (isl.)	D3
Boknafjord (fjord)	D7
Dovrefjell (hills)	F5
Edgeøya (isl.)	E2
Femundsjø (lake)	G6
Folda (fjord)	G4
Folda (fjord)	J3
Frohavet (bay)	F5
Frøya (isl.)	F5
Glittertinden (mt.)	F6
Greenland (sea)	C3
Hadselfjorden (fjord)	J2
Haltiatunturi (mt.)	M2
Hardangerfjord (fjord)	D7
Hardangervidda (plat.)	E6
Hinlopenstreten (strait)	C1
Hinnøya (isl.)	K2
Hitra (isl.)	F5
Hortensfjord (fjord)	G4
Isfjorden (fjord)	C2
Kjølen (mts.)	K3
Kvaenangen (fjord)	N2
Kvaloy (isl.)	N1
Kvaløya (isl.)	O1
Laksefjorden (fjord)	P1
Langøya (isl.)	J2
Lapland (reg.)	J2
Lindesnes (cape)	E8
Lofoten (isls.)	H2
Lopphavet (bay)	M1
Magerøya (isl.)	P1
Moskenesøya (isl.)	H3
Namsen (riv.)	H4
Nordaustlandet (isl.)	D1
Nordfjord (fjord)	E6
Nordkapp (pt.)	C1
North Cape (Nordkapp) (cape)	P1
Norwegian (sea)	F3
Ofotfjorden (fjord)	K2
Oslofjord (fjord)	D4
Otra (riv.)	E7
Pasvikelv (riv.)	Q2
Porsangen (fjord)	O1
Prins Karls Forland (isl.)	B2
Rana (fjord)	H3
Rauma (riv.)	F5
Ringvassøy (isl.)	L2
Romsdalsfjorden (fjord)	E5
Saltfjorden (fjord)	J3
Seiland (isl.)	N1
Senja (isl.)	K2
Skagerrak (strait)	F8
Sognafjorden (fjord)	D6
Sørkapp (pt.)	C2
Sørøya (isl.)	N1
Spitsbergen (isl.)	C2
Steinneset (cape)	D2
Storfjorden (fjord)	D2
Sulitjelma (mt.)	J3
Svalbard (isls.)	C3
Tana (riv.)	P1
Tanafjord (fjord)	Q1
Trondheimsfjord (fjord)	G5
Tyrifjord (lake)	C3
Vannøy (isl.)	L1
Varangerfjord (fjord)	Q2
Varangerhalvøya (pen.)	Q1
Vegafjorden (fjord)	G4
Vesterålen (isls.)	J2
Vestfjord (fjord)	H3
Vestvågøya (isl.)	H3
Vikna (isls.)	G4

(continued on following page)

Nordkapp (North Cape)

Varangerfjord

VESTER-ÅLEN

LOFOTEN

Haltiatunturi 4,343 ft. (1324 m.)

Kebnekaise 6,946 ft. (2117 m.)

GULF OF BOTHNIA

Horn

Fontur

VATNA-JÖKULL

Faxaflói

Reykjavík

Hekla 4,891 ft. (1491 m.)

Hvannadalshnúkur 6,946 ft. (2117 m.)

Iceland

Oulujärvi

Saimaa

ÅLAND IS.

Helsinki

Stockholm

Gotland

Öland

Nordfjord

Sognafjorden

Bergen

Hardangerfjord

Lindesnes

Glittertinden 8,110 ft. (2472 m.)

Mjøsa

Oslo

Vänern

Vättern

Göta Kanal

Göteborg

Skagerrak

Kattegat

Yding Skovhøj 568 ft. (173 m.)

Fyn

Sjael land

Copenhagen

Lolland

Bornholm

Topography

0	100	200 MI.
0	100	200 KM.

Below Sea Level	100 m. 328 ft.	200 m. 656 ft.	500 m. 1,640 ft.	1,000 m. 3,281 ft.	2,000 m. 6,562 ft.	5,000 m. 16,404 ft.

SWEDEN

COUNTIES

Älvsborg 433,417 ....H7
Blekinge 149,544 ....J8
Gävleborg 287,004 ....K6
Göteborg och Bohus
  729,629 ....G7
Gotland 56,383 ....L8
Halland 247,417 ....H8
Jämtland 134,116 ....J5
Jönköping 304,021 ....H8
Kalmar 237,781 ....K8
Kopparberg 284,407 ....J6
Kristianstad 283,818 ....J8
Kronoberg 175,427 ....J8
Malmöhus 763,349 ....H9
Norrbotten 261,536 ....L3
Örebro 270,031 ....J7
Östergötland 396,919 ....J7
Skaraborg 272,126 ....H7
Södermanland 251,423 ....K7
Stockholm 1,617,038 ....L7
Uppsala 260,476 ....K7
Värmland 280,694 ....H7
Västerbotten 247,521 ....K4
Västernorrland 259,964 ....K5
Västmanland 254,847 ....K7

CITIES and TOWNS

Åhus 6,125 ....J9
Ålingsås 32,402 ....H7
Älmhult 15,645 ....H8
Alvkarleby 9,175 ....K6
Alvesta 19,579 ....J8
Älvsbyn 9,373 ....M4
Ängelholm 32,998 ....H8
Åmål 13,130 ....H7
Ånge 12,653 ....J5
Arboga 14,457 ....J7
Åre 9,787 ....H5
Årjäng 10,050 ....H7
Arvika 26,668 ....H7
Askim 17,609 ....G8
Atvidaberg 12,677 ....K7
Avesta 24,671 ....J6
Båstad 12,962 ....H8
Bengtsfors 11,836 ....H7
Boden 29,160 ....M4
Bollnäs 27,724 ....K6
Borås 100,795 ....H8
Borgholm 11,170 ....K8
Borlänge 46,343 ....J6
Danderyd 28,525 ....H1

Eksjö 17,857 ....J8
Emmaboda 10,694 ....J8
Enköping 33,700 ....G1
Eskilstuna 88,850 ....K7
Eslöv 27,097 ....H9
Fagersta 13,744 ....J6
Falkenberg 36,536 ....H8
Falköping 31,532 ....H7
Falun 52,448 ....J6
Filipstad 13,481 ....J6
Finspång 23,378 ....J7
Flen 17,016 ....K7
Forshaga 11,739 ....H7
Frösö 10,274 ....J5
Gällivare 22,717 ....M3
Gävle 87,747 ....K6
Göteborg 430,763 ....G8
Hagfors 16,346 ....H6
Hällefors 9,402 ....J7
Hallsberg 16,405 ....J7
Hallstahammar 16,637 ....K7
Halmstad 78,607 ....H8
Haparanda 10,159 ....N4
Härnösand 27,248 ....L5
Hässleholm 48,658 ....H8
Hedemora 16,644 ....K6
Helsingborg 107,443 ....H8
Hjo 8,952 ....J7
Hofors 12,204 ....K6
Höganäs 10,866 ....H8
Huddinge 71,921 ....H1
Hudiksvall 37,603 ....K6
Jönköping 109,890 ....H8
Kalix 19,160 ....N4
Kalmar 55,129 ....K8
Karlshamn 31,377 ....J8
Karlskoga 34,316 ....J7
Karlskrona 58,634 ....J8
Karlstad 75,412 ....H7
Katrineholm 32,254 ....K7
Kinna 13,676 ....H8
Kiruna 26,312 ....L3
Köping 26,253 ....J7
Kramfors 24,607 ....K5
Kristianstad 70,491 ....J8
Kristinehamn 26,006 ....H7
Kumla 17,884 ....J7
Kungälv 32,549 ....G8
Kungsbacka 52,027 ....G8
Laholm 21,881 ....H8
Landskrona 35,393 ....H9
Leksand 14,115 ....J6
Lessebo 8,769 ....J8

Linköping 119,167 ....K7
Ljungby 27,176 ....J8
Ljusdal 21,026 ....J6
Ludvika 29,283 ....J6
Luleå 67,443 ....N4
Lund 85,150 ....H9
Lycksele 14,020 ....L4
Malmberget 10,239 ....M3
Malmö 231,575 ....H9
Malung 11,611 ....H6
Mariestad 24,508 ....H7
Markaryd 11,044 ....H8
Märsta 17,066 ....H1
Mellerud 10,455 ....H7
Mjölby 25,952 ....J7
Mölndal 47,248 ....G8
Mönsterås 12,911 ....K8
Mora 20,078 ....J6
Mörbylanga 13,029 ....K8
Motala 41,502 ....J7
Nacka 61,931 ....H1
Nässjö 30,623 ....J8
Nora 10,200 ....J7
Norrköping 119,370 ....K7
Norrtälje 43,741 ....L7
Nybro 20,706 ....J8
Nyköping 64,739 ....K7
Nynäshamn 21,395 ....L7
Olofström 14,883 ....J8
Örebro 119,824 ....J7
Örnsköldsvik 58,967 ....L5
Oskarshamn 27,217 ....K8
Östersund 57,281 ....J5
Östhammar 21,338 ....L6
Oxelösund 12,923 ....K7
Piteå 39,079 ....M4
Rättvik 11,048 ....J6
Ronneby 28,868 ....J8
Säffle 17,935 ....H7
Sala 21,381 ....J6
Sandviken 39,740 ....K6
Säter 11,490 ....J6
Sävsjö 11,730 ....J8
Sigtuna 30,182 ....H1
Simrishamn 19,709 ....J9
Skara 18,402 ....H7
Skellefteå 74,127 ....M4
Skövde 46,712 ....H7
Smedjebacken 13,183 ....J6
Söderhamn 29,606 ....K6
Söderköping 12,838 ....K7
Södertälje 80,660 ....G1
Sollefteå 25,114 ....K5
Sollentuna 50,242 ....G1
Solna 50,964 ....H1
Sölvesborg 15,782 ....J9

Stenungsund 17,792 ....G7
Stockholm (cap.) 669,485 ....G1
Strängnäs 25,841 ....F1
Strömstad 10,457 ....G7
Strömsund 16,164 ....J5
Sundbyberg 31,095 ....G1
Sundsvall 92,983 ....K5
Sunne 13,245 ....H7
Surahammar 11,287 ....J7
Svenljunga 11,004 ....H8
Täby 56,339 ....H1
Tibro 11,044 ....J7
Tidaholm 13,048 ....H7
Tierp 19,620 ....K6
Timrå 18,392 ....K5
Tomelilla 12,241 ....J9
Torsby 15,030 ....H6
Tranås 17,675 ....J7
Trelleborg 34,465 ....H9
Trollhättan 50,296 ....H7
Uddevalla 46,489 ....G7
Ulricehamn 22,405 ....H8
Umeå 88,726 ....M5
Uppsala 161,820 ....K7
Vaggeryd 12,185 ....J8
Vallentuna 20,823 ....H1
Vänersborg 36,151 ....G7
Vara 16,787 ....H7
Varberg 47,566 ....G8
Värnamo 31,040 ....J8
Västeras 117,717 ....K7
Västerhaninge 14,125 ....H1
Västervik 39,522 ....K8
Växjö 68,499 ....J8
Vetlanda 27,833 ....J8
Vimmerby 15,688 ....J8
Visby 19,886 ....L8
Ystad 24,484 ....H9

OTHER FEATURES

Ångermanälven (riv.) K5
Baltic (sea) K9
Bothnia (gulf) N4
Dalälven (riv.) K6
Göta (canal) J7
Göta (riv.) H7
Gotland (isl.) L8
Hanöbukten (bay) J9
Hjälmaren (lake) J7
Hornslandet (pen.) K5
Indalsälven (riv.) J5
Kalixälv (riv.) N3
Kallsjö (lake) H5
Kalmarsund (sound) K8
Kattegat (strait) G8

Kebnekaise (mt.) L3
Klarälv (riv.) H6
Kölen (mts.) K3
Lapland (reg.) M2
Ljungan (riv.) K5
Ljusnan (riv.) H5
Luleälv (riv.) M4
Mälaren (lake) G1
Muonioälven (riv.) M2
Öland (isl.) K8
Öresund (sound) H9
Österdalälven (riv.) J6
Piteälv (riv.) M4
Siljan (lake) J6
Skagerrak (strait) F8
Skellefteälv (riv.) L4
Stora Lulevatten (lake) L3
Storsjön (lake) J6
Torneälv (riv.) M3
Torneträsk (lake) L2
Uddjaur (lake) L4
Umeälv (riv.) L4
Vänern (lake) H7
Västerdalälven (riv.) H6
Vättern (lake) J7

* City and suburbs.
† Population of commune.
‡ Population of parish.

DENMARK

COUNTIES

Århus 575,540 ....D5
Bornholm 47,499 ....F9
Copenhagen
  (commune) 493,771 ....F6
Faroe Islands 41,969 ....B2
Frederiksberg
  (commune) 88,167 ....F6
Frederiksborg 329,992 ....E5
Fyn 453,626 ....D7
København (Copenhagen)
  (commune) 493,771 ....F6
København 624,684 ....F6
Nordjylland 482,501 ....D4
Ribe 213,503 ....C6
Ringkøbing 263,519 ....B5
Roskilde 203,246 ....E6
Sønderjylland 250,872 ....C7
Storstrøm 260,160 ....E7
Vejle 326,559 ....C6
Vestsjaelland 278,592 ....E6
Viborg 231,758 ....C4

CITIES and TOWNS

Åbenrå 15,341 ....C7
Abybro 4,229 ....C3
Ålborg-Nørresundby 114,302 .C3
Ålestrup 2,288 ....C4
Århus 181,830 ....D5
Ars 5,972 ....C4
Asnaes 2,361 ....E6
Assens, Fyn 5,736 ....D7
Augustenborg 3,114 ....D8
Auning 2,293 ....D5
Avlum 2,719 ....B5
Ballerup 48,697 ....F6
Birkerød 13,513 ....F6
Bjerringbro 6,033 ....C5
Bogense 3,057 ....D6
Braedstrup 2,912 ....C6
Bramming 5,857 ....B7
Brande 5,693 ....B6
Broager 2,890 ....C8
Brønderslev 10,748 ....C4
Brørup 3,846 ....C7
Brovst 2,589 ....C3
Copenhagen
  (cap.) 1,381,882 ....F6
Dronninglund 2,715 ....D3
Ebeltoft 3,763 ....D5
Esbjerg 70,220 ....B7
Fåborg 6,795 ....D7
Fakse 3,350 ....F7
Fakse Ladeplads 2,111 ....F7
Farsø 2,954 ....C4
Farum 16,664 ....F6
Fredensborg 17,667 ....F6
Fredericia 29,350 ....C6
Frederikshavn 24,938 ....D3
Frederikshavn 88,167 ....F6
Frederikssund 13,584 ....E6
Frederiksvaerk 11,559 ....E6
Gentofte 66,782 ....F6
Gilleleje 3,976 ....F5
Give 3,522 ....C6
Glamsbjerg 2,853 ....D7
Glostrup 19,645 ....F6
Gørlev 2,113 ....E7
Graested 2,735 ....F5
Gram 2,462 ....C7
Gråsten 3,441 ....C8
Grenå 13,638 ....D5
Grindsted 8,742 ....B6
Haderslev 19,374 ....C7
Hadsten 5,563 ....C5
Hadsund 4,257 ....D4
Hammel 4,828 ....C5
Hammerum 2,984 ....C5
Hanstholm 2,490 ....B3
Hårby 2,240 ....D7
Haslev 9,146 ....E7
Havdrup 3,374 ....F6
Hedensted 3,397 ....C6
Hellebaek 4,123 ....F5
Helsinge 5,813 ....F6

CITIES and TOWNS

Helsingør 44,068 ....F6
Herning 29,522 ....B5
Hillerød 25,441 ....F6
Hinnerup 4,517 ....D5
Hirtshals 6,865 ....C3
Hjallerup 2,769 ....D3
Hjørring 23,697 ....C3
Hobro 8,889 ....C4
Holbaek 19,485 ....E6
Holstebro 28,270 ....B5
Høng 3,430 ....E7
Hornslet 3,296 ....D5
Horsens 46,855 ....C6
Hørsholm 21,572 ....F6
Hørve 2,055 ....E6
Hundested 5,443 ....E6
Hurup 2,747 ....B4
Hvide Sande 3,100 ....A5
Ikast 11,716 ....B5
Juelsminde 2,609 ....C6
Jyderup 3,441 ....E6
Kalundborg 15,413 ....D6
Karup 2,133 ....C5
Kastrup 10,550 ....F6
Kerteminde 4,984 ....D7
København (Copenhagen)
  (cap.) 1,381,882 ....F6
Køge 25,683 ....F7
Kolding 41,374 ....C7
Korsør 15,281 ....E7
Langå 2,498 ....C5
Lemvig 7,303 ....B4
Løgstør 4,160 ....C4
Løgumkloster 2,840 ....C7
Løsning 3,234 ....C6
Lunderskov 2,083 ....C7
Lyngby 51,703 ....F6
Malling 2,451 ....D5
Maribo 5,490 ....E8
Marstal 2,702 ....D8
Middelfart 12,064 ....C6
Naestved 38,455 ....E7
Nakskov 16,218 ....E8
Neksø 3,783 ....F9
Nibe 3,139 ....C4
Nordborg 8,403 ....C7
Nordby, Ribe 2,419 ....B7
Nørre Aby 2,541 ....C6
Nørre Alslev 2,024 ....E8
Nyborg 15,466 ....D7
Nykøbing, Storstrøm 19,038 .F7
Nykøbing,
  Vestsjaelland 5,062 ....E6
Nykøbing, Viborg 9,503 ......B4
Odder 8,198 ....D6
Odense 136,646 ....D7
Ølgod 3,470 ....B6
Otterup 3,976 ....D7
Padborg 4,332 ....C8
Pandrup 2,257 ....C3
Praesto 3,110 ....F7
Randers 56,672 ....C5
Ribe 7,646 ....B7

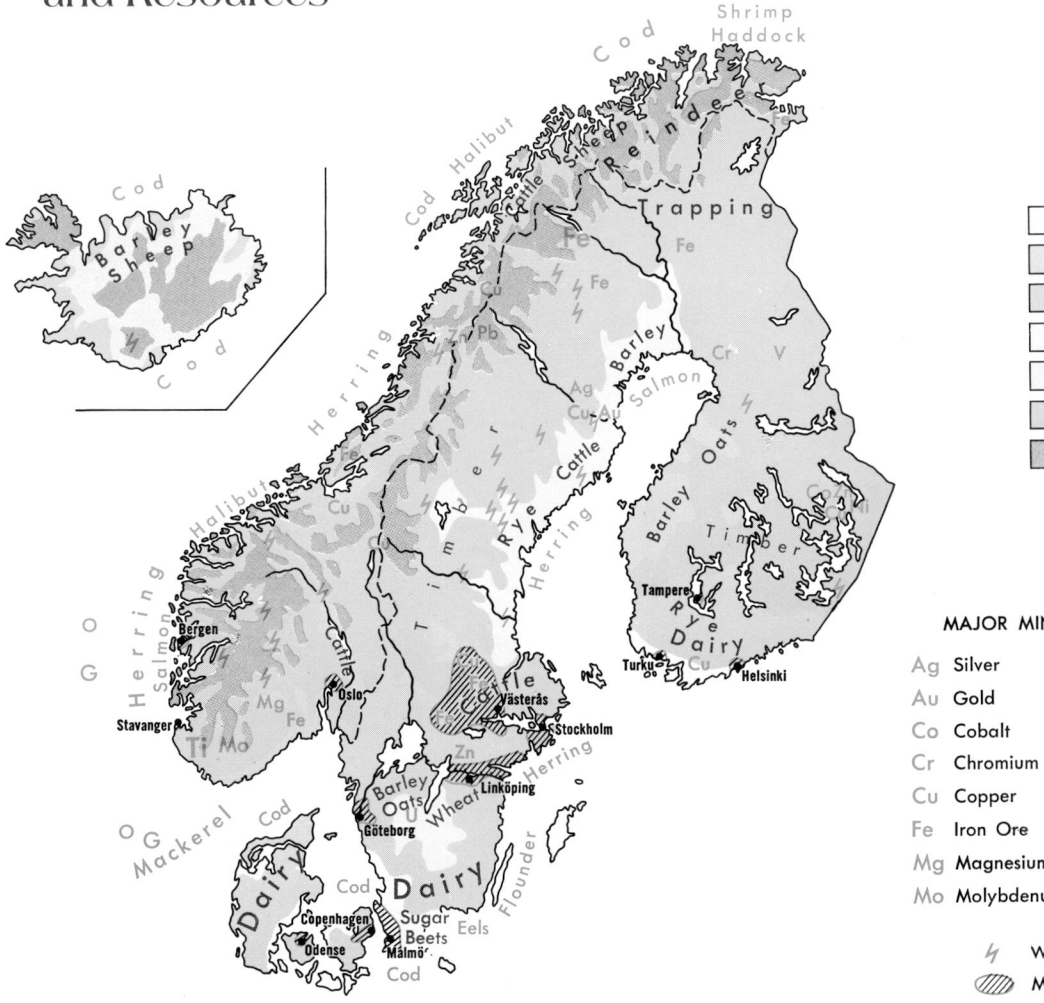

Agriculture, Industry and Resources

DOMINANT LAND USE

- Cash Cereals, Dairy
- Dairy, Cattle, Hogs
- Dairy, General Farming
- General Farming (chiefly cereals)
- Nomadic Sheep Herding
- Forests, Limited Mixed Farming
- Nonagricultural Land

MAJOR MINERAL OCCURRENCES

Ag	Silver	Ni	Nickel
Au	Gold	O	Petroleum
Co	Cobalt	Pb	Lead
Cr	Chromium	Ti	Titanium
Cu	Copper	U	Uranium
Fe	Iron Ore	V	Vanadium
Mg	Magnesium	Zn	Zinc
Mo	Molybdenum		

- Water Power
- Major Industrial Areas

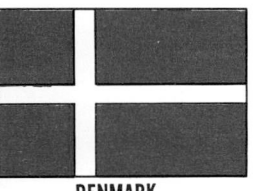

DENMARK

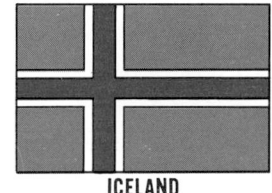

ICELAND

DENMARK

AREA 16,629 sq. mi. (43,069 sq. km.)
POPULATION 5,135,000
CAPITAL Copenhagen
LARGEST CITY Copenhagen
HIGHEST POINT Yding Skovhøj 568 ft. (173 m.)
MONETARY UNIT krone
MAJOR LANGUAGE Danish
MAJOR RELIGION Protestantism

ICELAND

AREA 39,768 sq. mi. (103,000 sq. km.)
POPULATION 250,000
CAPITAL Reykjavík
LARGEST CITY Reykjavík
HIGHEST POINT Hvannadalshnúkur 6,952 ft. (2,119 m.)
MONETARY UNIT króna
MAJOR LANGUAGE Icelandic
MAJOR RELIGION Protestantism

OTHER FEATURES

FAROE ISLANDS

CITIES and TOWNS

OTHER FEATURES

ICELAND

CITIES and TOWNS

OTHER FEATURES

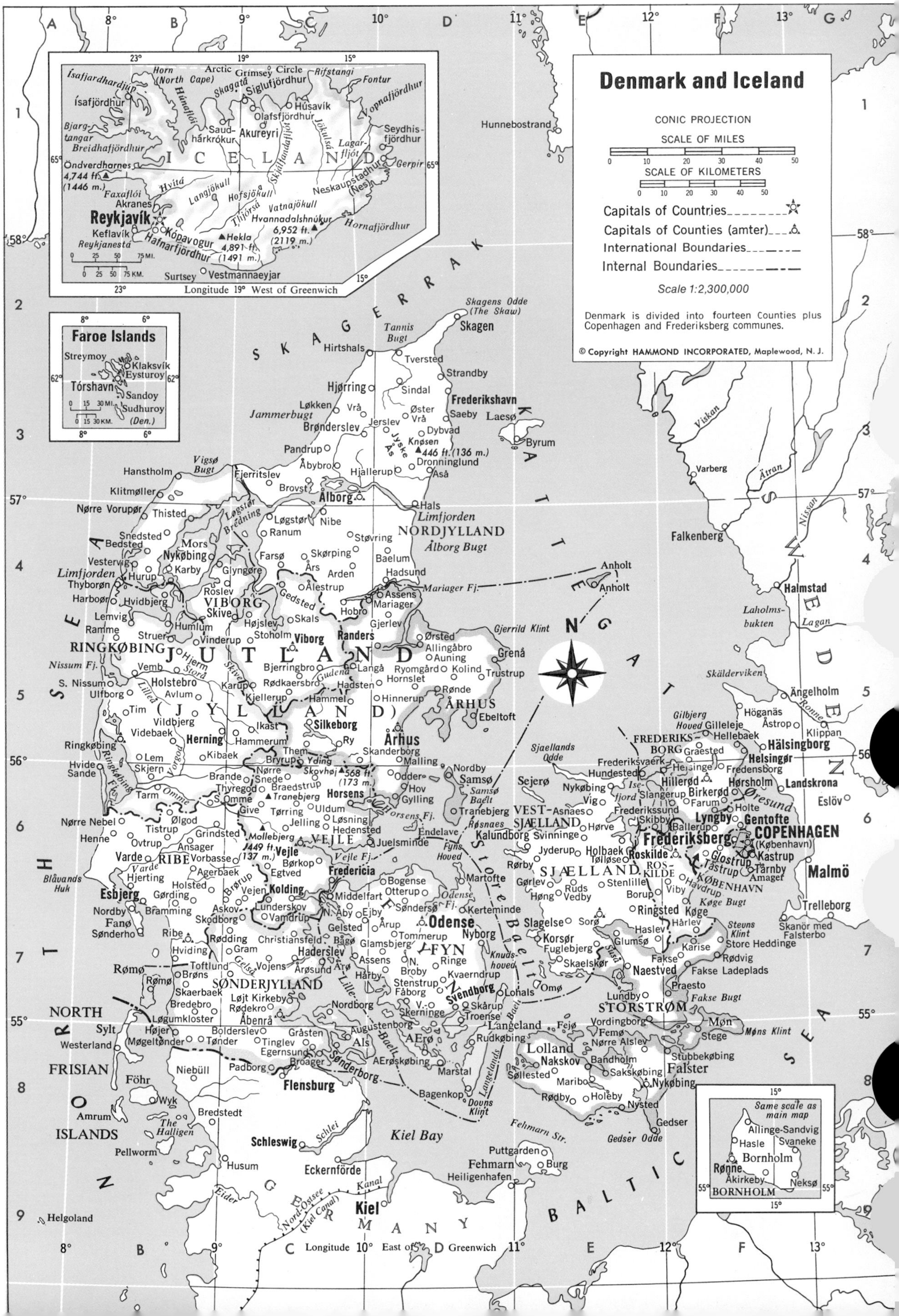

Germany

CONIC PROJECTION

SCALE OF MILES

SCALE OF KILOMETERS

Capitals of Countries .... ☆
State Capitals .... ◉
International Boundaries ....
State Boundaries ....
Canals ....

Scale 1:3,040,000

Berlin

© Copyright HAMMOND INCORPORATED, Maplewood, N.J.

AREA 137,753 sq. mi. (356,780 sq. km.)
POPULATION 78,890,000
CAPITAL Berlin
LARGEST CITY Berlin
HIGHEST POINT Zugspitze 9,718 ft. (2,962 m.)
MONETARY UNIT Deutsche mark
MAJOR LANGUAGE German
MAJOR RELIGIONS Protestantism, Roman Catholicism

GERMANY

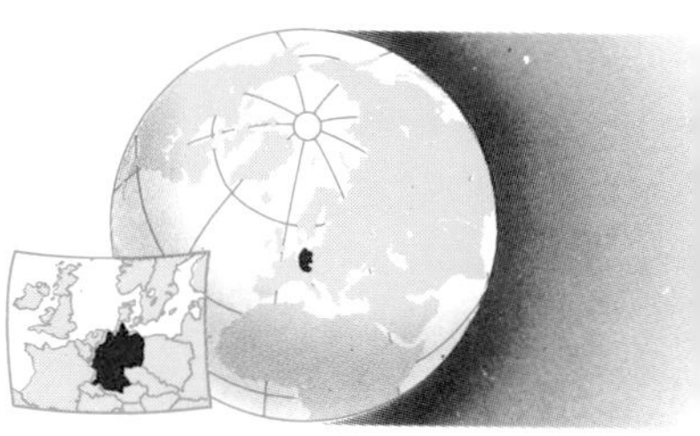

Topography

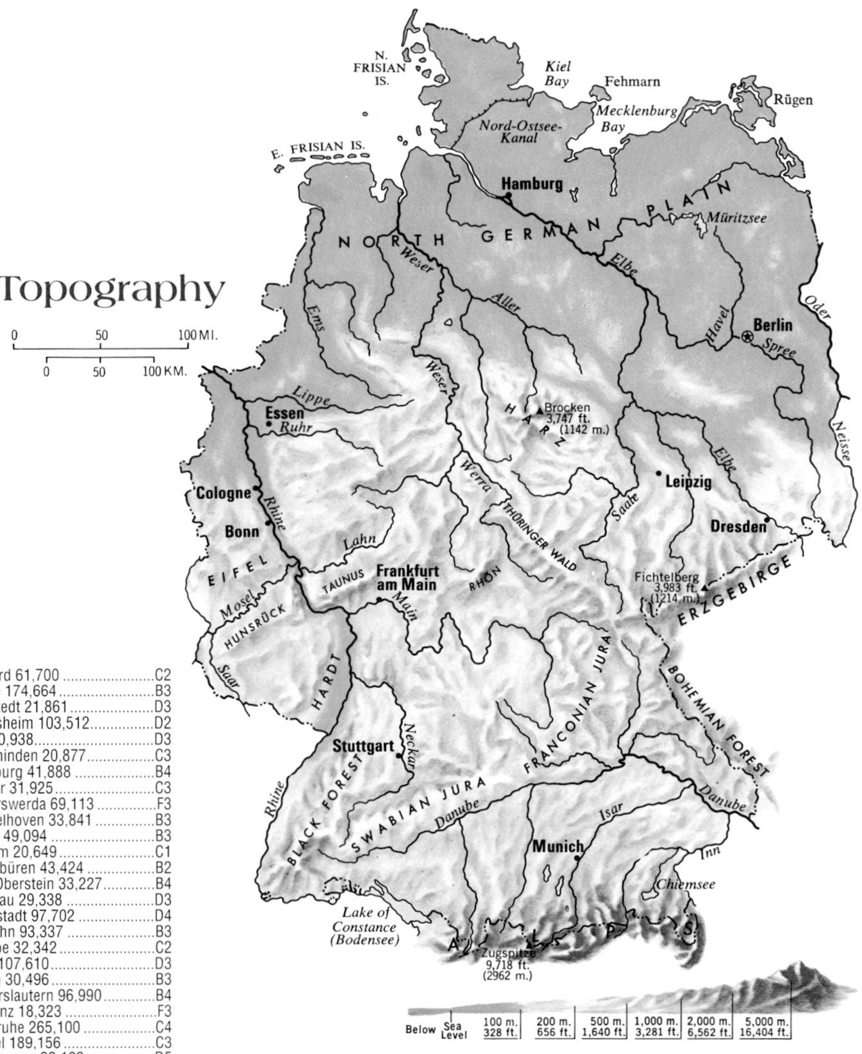
0 50 100 MI.
0 50 100 KM.
N. FRISIAN IS.
Kiel Bay
Fehmarn
Rügen
Mecklenburg Bay
Nord-Ostsee-Kanal
E. FRISIAN IS.
Hamburg
NORTH GERMAN PLAIN
Müritzsee
Weser
Aller
Elbe
Havel
Oder
Berlin
Spree
Ems
Lippe
Essen
Ruhr
Brocken 3,747 ft. (1142 m.)
HARZ
Neisse
Leipzig
Cologne
Rhine
Bonn
Werra
Saale
THÜRINGER WALD
Dresden
Lahn
EIFEL
TAUNUS
Frankfurt am Main
RHÖN
Fichtelberg 3,983 ft. (1214 m.)
ERZGEBIRGE
Mosel
HUNSRÜCK
Main
FRANCONIAN JURA
Saar
HARDT
BOHEMIAN FOREST
Stuttgart
Neckar
SWABIAN JURA
BLACK FOREST
Danube
Isar
Munich
Inn
Chiemsee
Lake of Constance (Bodensee)
ALPS
Zugspitze 9,718 ft. (2962 m.)
Below Sea Level
100 m. 328 ft.
200 m. 656 ft.
500 m. 1,640 ft.
1,000 m. 3,281 ft.
2,000 m. 6,562 ft.
5,000 m. 16,404 ft.

GERMANY

STATES

Baden-Württemberg 9,432,709 C4
Bavaria 11,049,263 D4
Berlin 3,304,561 E4
Brandenberg* E2
Bremen 661,992 C2
Hamburg 1,603,070 D2
Hesse 5,568,892 C3
Lower Saxony 7,184,943 C2
Mecklenburg-Western Pomerania* E2
North Rhine-Westphalia 16,874,059 B3
Rhineland-Palatinate 3,653,155 B4
Saarland 1,054,142 B4
Saxony* E3
Saxony-Anhalt* D3
Schleswig-Holstein 2,564,565 C1
Thuringia* D3

*East German States 15,611,488 D-E 2-3

CITIES and TOWNS

Aachen 233,255 B3
Aalen 62,812 D4
Ahaus 30,180 B2
Ahlen 52,836 B3
Ahrensburg 27,174 D2
Alfeld 21,986 C2
Alsdorf 46,328 B3
Alsfeld 16,686 C3
Altena 23,301 B3
Altenburg 53,602 E3
Amberg 42,246 D4
Andernach 27,171 B3
Anklam 19,946 E2
Annaberg-Buchholz 26,002 E3
Ansbach 36,912 D4
Apolda 28,230 D3
Arnsberg 73,912 C3
Arnstadt 30,207 D3
Aschaffenburg 62,048 C4
Aschersleben 34,166 D3
Aue 27,935 E3
Auerbach 22,324 E3
Augsburg 247,731 D4
Aurich 36,063 B2
Backnang 30,583 C4
Bad Berleburg 20,080 C3
Bad Driburg 16,698 C3
Bad Dürkheim 16,670 C4
Baden-Baden 50,761 C4
Bad Harzburg 23,079 D3
Bad Hersfeld 28,214 C3
Bad Homburg vor der Höhe 51,035 C3
Bad Honnef 21,812 B3
Bad Kissingen 20,237 D3
Bad Kreuznach 39,400 B4
Bad Langensalza 17,027 D3
Bad Mergentheim 19,801 C4
Bad Münstereifel 15,232 B3
Bad Nauheim 27,561 C3
Bad Neuenahr-Ahrweiler 24,610 B3
Bad Oldesloe 20,473 D2
Bad Pyrmont 20,437 C3
Bad Reichenhall 16,365 E5
Bad Salzuflen 50,875 C2
Bad Salzungen 21,387 C3
Bad Schwartau 19,960 D2
Bad Vilbel 24,567 C3
Bad Zwischenahn 23,348 B2
Balingen 30,615 C4
Bamberg 69,809 D4
Barsinghausen 37,792 C2
Bautzen 52 354 F3
Bayreuth 70,933 D4
Bensheim 34,241 C4
Berchtesgaden 7,644 E5
Bergen 16,713 E1
Bergisch Gladbach 101,983 B3
Berleburg (Bad Berleburg) 20,080 C3
Berlin (cap.) 3,304,561 E4
Bernau bei Berlin 19,919 E2
Bernburg 40,834 D3
Biberach an der Riss 2[illegible],319 C4
Bielefeld 311,946 C2
Bietigheim-Bissingen 37,573 C4
Bingen 23,141 B4
Bitburg 10,758 B4
Bitterfeld 20,869 E3
Blankenburg am Harz 19,279 D3
Böblingen 43,400 C4
Bocholt 67,565 B3
Bochum 389,087 B3
Bonn 282,190 B3
Borghorst 17,238 B2
Borken 34,710 B3
Borna 24,397 E3
Bornheim 34,536 B3
Bottrop 116,363 B3
Brake 16,069 C2
Bramsche 24,653 B2
Brandenburg 94,755 E2
Braunschweig 253,794 D2
Bremen 535,058 C2
Bremerhaven 126,934 C2
Bremervörde 17,629 C2
Bretten 23,894 C4
Brilon 24,341 C3
Bruchsal 36,831 C4
Brühl 40,710 B3
Buchholz in der Nordheide 30,523 C2
Bückeburg 19,758 C2
Büdingen 17,013 C3
Bühl 23,470 C4
Bünde 39,103 C2
Büren 17,720 C3
Burg bei Magdeburg 2[illegible],359 D2
Burghausen 16,761 E4
Burgsteinfurt 31,367 B2
Butzbach 21,095 C3
Buxtehude 31,132 C2
Castrop-Rauxel 77,660 B3
Celle 71,050 D2
Cham 16,641 E4
Chemnitz 313,799 E3
Clausthal-Zellerfeld 16,369 D3
Cloppenburg 22,536 B2
Coburg 43,233 D3
Coesfeld 31,979 B3
Cologne 937,482 B3
Coswig 27,590 E3
Cottbus 126,592 F3
Crailsheim 26,678 D4
Crimmitschau 24,440 E3
Cuxhaven 55,249 C2
Dachau 34,183 D4
Darmstadt 136,067 C4
Deggendorf 28,680 E4
Delitzsch 27,636 E3
Delmenhorst 72,901 C2
Demmin 16,992 E2
Dessau 103,538 E3
Detmold 66,809 C3
Dillenburg 23,672 C3
Dillingen 21,358 B4
Döbeln 27,706 E3
Donaueschingen 18,293 C5
Donauwörth 17,420 D4
Dorsten 75,518 B3
Dortmund 587,328 B3
Dresden 519,810 E3
Duderstadt 22,265 D3
Duisburg 527,447 B3
Dülmen 39,344 B3
Düren 83,120 B3
Düsseldorf 569,641 B3
Eberswalde-Finow 54,556 E2
Eckernförde 22,197 C1
Ehingen 22,580 C4
Eilenburg 21,931 E3
Einbeck 25,813 C3
Eisenach 49,534 D3
Eisenhüttenstadt 51,723 F2
Eisleben 26,484 D3
Ellwangen 21,857 D4
Elmshorn 42,784 C2
Emden 49,803 B2
Emmendingen 22,959 B4
Emmerich 27,906 B3
Emsdetten 31,063 B2
Erfurt 217,134 D3
Erkelenz 36,525 B3
Erlangen 100,583 D4
Eschwege 21,527 C3
Eschweiler 53,516 B3
Espelkamp 23,868 C2
Essen 620,594 B3
Esslingen am Neckar 90,537 C4
Ettlingen 37,269 C4
Euskirchen 47,756 B3
Eutin 16,567 D1
Falkensee 23,024 E3
Fellbach 39,612 C4
Finsterwalde 23,857 E3
Flensburg 85,830 C1
Forchheim 28,784 D4
Forst 26,501 F3
Frankenberg-Eder 16,283 C3
Frankenthal 45,408 C4
Frankfurt am Main 625,258 C3
Frankfurt an der Oder 86,441 F2
Frechen 42,516 B3
Freiberg 50,415 E3
Freiburg im Breisgau 183,979 B5
Freising 35,201 D4
Freital 43,092 E3
Freudenstadt 21,355 C4
Friedberg 24,279 C3
Friedrichshafen 52,295 C5
Fulda 54,320 C3
Fürstenfeldbruck 30,313 D4
Fürstenwalde 35,282 F2
Fürth 98,832 D4
Füssen 13,173 D5
Gaggenau 28,182 C4
Garbsen 59,225 C2
Garmisch-Partenkirchen 25,908 D5
Geesthacht 25,054 D2
Geislingen an der Steige 26,176 C4
Geldern 28,465 B3
Gelnhausen 18,866 C3
Gelsenkirchen 287,255 B3
Genthin 17,347 E2
Georgsmarienhütte 30,880 B2
Gera 132,319 E3
Geretsried 21,081 D5
Gifhorn 35,697 D2
Glauchau 28,309 E3
Goch 29,592 B3
Göppingen 52,873 C4
Görlitz 78,856 F3
Goslar 45,614 D3
Gotha 57,423 D3
Göttingen 118,073 D3
Greifswald 67,298 E1
Greiz 34,858 E3
Greven 29,671 B2
Grevenbroich 59,204 B3
Griesheim 20,531 C4
Grimma 17,812 E3
Gronau 39,397 B2
Guben 34,665 F3
Gummersbach 49,017 B3
Günzburg 18,303 D4
Güstrow 38,971 E2
Gütersloh 83,407 C3
Haar 16,553 D4
Hagen 210,640 B3
Halberstadt 47,017 D3
Haldensleben 20,369 D2
Halle 236,148 D3
Halle-Neustadt 93,477 D3
Haltern 33,093 B3
Hamburg 1,603,070 D2
Hameln 57,642 C2
Hamm 173,611 B3
Hanau 84,300 C3
Hannover 498,495 C2
Hassloch 18,646 C4
Heide 19,909 C1
Heidelberg 131,429 C4
Heidenau 19,133 E3
Heidenheim an der Brenz 48,497 D4
Heilbronn 112,279 C4
Helmstedt 26,554 D2
Hennef 30,516 B3
Hennigsdorf bei Berlin 26,574 E3
Herborn 20,409 C3
Herford 61,700 C2
Herne 174,664 B3
Hettstedt 21,861 D3
Hildesheim 103,512 D2
Hof 50,938 D3
Holzminden 20,877 C3
Homburg 41,888 B4
Höxter 31,925 C3
Hoyerswerda 69,113 F3
Hückelhoven 33,841 B3
Hürth 49,094 B3
Husum 20,649 C1
Ibbenbüren 43,424 B2
Idar-Oberstein 33,227 B4
Ilmenau 29,338 D3
Ingolstadt 97,702 D4
Iserlohn 93,337 B3
Itzehoe 32,342 C2
Jena 107,610 D3
Jülich 30,496 B3
Kaiserslautern 96,990 B4
Kamenz 18,323 F3
Karlsruhe 265,100 C4
Kassel 189,156 C3
Kaufbeuren 39,192 D5
Kehl 28,902 B4
Kempten 60,052 D5
Kevelaer 22,633 B3
Kiel 240,675 D1
Kirchheim unter Teck 34,534 C4
Kitzingen 19,085 C4
Koblenz 107,286 B3
Köln (Cologne) 937,482 B3
Königs Wusterhausen 19,085 E2
Königswinter 34,136 B3
Konstanz 72,862 C5
Köpenick 118,059 F4
Korbach 21,406 C3
Kornwestheim 28,519 C4
Köthen 34,617 E3
Krefeld 235,423 B3
Kreuztal 29,716 C3
Kronach 18,246 D3
Kulmbach 27,116 D3
Lage 32,612 C3
Lahnstein 17,972 B3
Lahr 33,369 B4
Lampertheim 30,263 C4
Landau in der Pfalz 36,297 C4
Landsberg am Lech 19,808 D4
Landshut 57,194 E4
Langen 31,206 C4
Langenhagen 46,298 C2
Lauchhammer 24,391 E3
Lauenburg an der Elbe 10,786 D2
Lauf an der Pegnitz 22,593 D4
Leer 31,292 B2
Lehrte 39,600 D2
Leipzig 550,641 E3
Lemgo 38,351 C2
Lengerich 20,235 B2
Leverkusen 157,358 B3
Lichtenberg 95,426 F4
Lichtenfels 20,252 D3
Limburg an der Lahn 29,196 C3
Limbach-Oberfrohna 22,059 E3
Lindau 23,699 C5
Lingen 47,837 B2
Lippstadt 60,396 C3
Löbau 18,492 F3
Löhne 36,882 C2
Lörrach 41,087 B5
Lübbenau 20,815 F3
Lübeck 210,681 D2
Luckenwalde 26,761 E2
Lüdenscheid 76,118 B3
Ludwigsburg 79,342 C4
Ludwigshafen am Rhein 158,478 C4
Lüneburg 60,053 D2
Lünen 85,584 B3
Magdeburg 288,975 D2
Mainz 174,828 C4
Mannheim 300,468 C4
Marburg 70,905 C3
Markkleeberg 19,240 E3
Marktredwitz 18,605 E4
Marl 89,601 B3
Mayen 18,427 B3
Mechernich 21,986 B3
Meerane 21,879 E3
Meiningen 25,823 D3
Meissen 37,757 E3
Melle 40,490 C2
Memmingen 37,942 D5
Meppen 29,900 B2
Merseburg 46,188 D3
Merzig 29,312 B4
Meschede 30,853 C3
Metzingen 19,895 C4
Minden 75,169 C2
Mittenwald 7,998 D5
Mittweida 18,469 E3
Mönchengladbach 252,910 B3
Mosbach 23,897 C4
Mülhausen 43,046 D3
Mülheim an der Ruhr 175,454 B3
München (Munich) 1,211,617 D4
Münden 24,794 C3
Munich 1,211,617 D4
Münster 248,919 B3
Nagold 20,405 C4
Naumburg 32,100 D3
Neckarsulm 21,765 C4
Neubrandenburg 87,235 E2
Neuburg an der Donau 24,502 D4
Neu-Isenburg 34,896 C3
Neumarkt in der Oberpfalz 33,603 D4
Neumünster 79,574 C1
Neunkirchen 50,784 B4
Neuruppin 26,934 E2
Neuss 143,976 B3
Neustadt an der Weinstrasse 50,453 B4
Neustadt bei Coburg 16,211 D3
Neustrelitz 27,300 E2
Neu-Ulm 45,116 D4
Neuwied 60,665 B3
Nienburg 29,545 C2
Norden 23,655 B2
Nordenham 28,393 C2
Norderstedt 66,747 D2
Nordhausen 47,681 D3
Nordhorn 48,556 B2
Nördlingen 18,278 D4
Northeim 30,349 C3
Nuremberg 480,078 D4
Nürnberg (Nuremberg) 480,078 D4
Nürtingen 36,807 C4
Oberammergau 4,980 D5
Oberhausen 221,017 B3
Oberursel 39,105 C3
Offenbach am Main 112,450 C3
Offenburg 51,730 B4
Oldenburg 140,785 C2
Oranienburg 28,667 E2
Oschatz 19,100 E3
Oschersleben 16,976 D2
Osnabrück 154,594 C2
Osterholz-Scharmbeck 24,205 C2
Osterode am Harz 26,631 D3
Paderborn 114,148 C3
Pankow 62,847 F3
Papenburg 29,237 B2
Parchim 23,454 D2
Passau 49,137 E4
Peenemünde E1
Peine 45,522 D2
Pfaffenhofen an der Ilm 18,335 D4
Pforzheim 108,887 C4
Pinneberg 36,583 C2
Pirmasens 47,102 B4
Pirna 46,991 E3
Plauen 77,514 E3
Plettenberg 28,113 C3
Pössneck 17,895 D3
Potsdam 141,231 E2
Prenzlau 23,642 E2
Quedlinburg 29,168 D3
Radeberg 15,702 E3
Radebeul 33,757 E3
Radolfzell 25,712 C5
Rastatt 40,909 C4
Rastede 18,191 C2
Rathenow 31,302 E2
Ratingen 89,880 B3
Ravensburg 44,146 C5
Recklinghausen 121,666 B3
Regensburg 119,078 E4

(continued on following page)

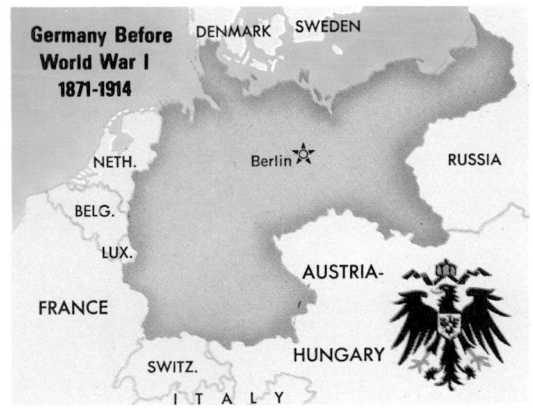

Germany Before World War I 1871-1914

DENMARK · SWEDEN · NETH. · BELG. · LUX. · FRANCE · SWITZ. · ITALY · RUSSIA · AUSTRIA-HUNGARY · Berlin ☆

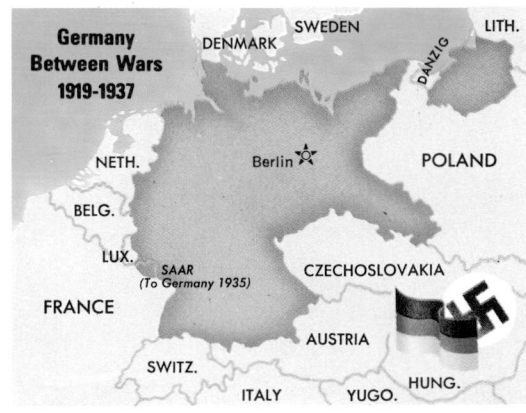

Germany Between Wars 1919-1937

DENMARK · SWEDEN · DANZIG · LITH. · NETH. · BELG. · LUX. · FRANCE · SWITZ. · ITALY · YUGO. · POLAND · CZECHOSLOVAKIA · AUSTRIA · HUNG. · Berlin ☆ · SAAR (To Germany 1935)

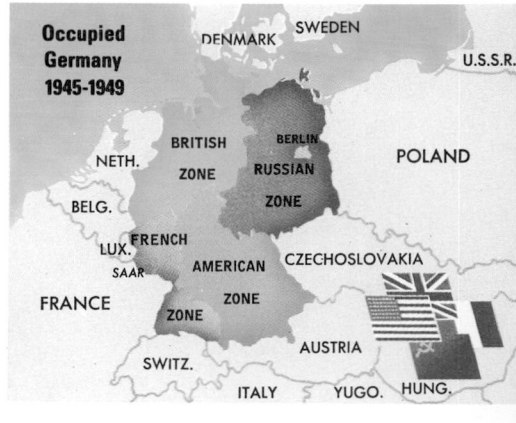

Occupied Germany 1945-1949

DENMARK · SWEDEN · U.S.S.R. · NETH. · BELG. · LUX. · FRANCE · SWITZ. · ITALY · YUGO. · HUNG. · AUSTRIA · POLAND · CZECHOSLOVAKIA · BRITISH ZONE · RUSSIAN ZONE · BERLIN · FRENCH ZONE · AMERICAN ZONE · SAAR

Reichenbach 24,749 ....E3
Remagen 14,375 ....B3
Remscheid 120,979 ....B3
Rendsburg 30,752 ....C1
Reutlingen 100,400 ....C4
Rheda-Wiedenbrück 36,990 ..C3
Rheine 69,324 ....B2
Rheinfelden 27,711 ....B5
Ribnitz-Damgarten 17,512 ...E1
Riesa 49,108 ....E3
Rietberg 23,058 ....C3
Rinteln 26,120 ....C2
Rosenheim 54,304 ....D5
Rostock 249,349 ....E1
Rotenburg 18,392 ....C2
Roth bei Nürnberg 20,288 ...D4
Rothenburg ob der Tauber
  11,071 ....D4
Rottenburg am Neckar
  33,907 ....C4
Rottweil 23,030 ....C4
Rudolstadt 32,264 ....D3
Rüsselsheim 58,426 ....C4
Saalfeld 33,453 ....D3
Saarbrücken 188,467 ....B4
Saarlouis 37,662 ....B4
Salzgitter 111,674 ....D2
Salzwedel 23,163 ....D2
Sangerhausen 33,604 ....D3
Sankt Ingbert 40,527 ....B4
Sankt Wende 26,649 ....B4
Saulgau 14,864 ....C5
Schleswig 26,648 ....C1
Schmalkalden 17,409 ....D3
Schneeberg 22,105 ....E3
Schönebeck 45,155 ....D2
Schramberg 18,208 ....C4
Schwabach 34,217 ....D4
Schwäbisch Gmünd 57,861 ..C4
Schwäbisch Hall 31,375 .....C4

Schwalmstadt 17,371 ....C3
Schwandorf im Bayern
  25,874 ....E4
Schwedt 51,753 ....F2
Schweinfurt 52,818 ....D3
Schwelm 29,564 ....B3
Schwerin 128,328 ....D2
Schwetzingen 18,029 ....C4
Seesen 21,604 ....D3
Selb 19,275 ....E3
Senftenberg 32,428 ....F3
Siegburg 34,402 ....B3
Siegen 106,160 ....C3
Sigmaringen 15,270 ....C4
Sindelfingen 57,524 ....C4
Singen 42,605 ....C5
Soest 40,775 ....C3
Solingen 160,824 ....B3
Soltau 19,115 ....C2
Sömmerda 23,398 ....D3
Sondershausen 24,178 ......D3
Sonneberg 28,512 ....D3
Sonthofen 20,037 ....D5
Spandau E3
Speyer 45,089 ....C4
Spremberg 24,815 ....F3
Springe 29,209 ....C2
Stade 41,223 ....C2
Stadthagen 22,218 ....C2
Starnberg 19,845 ....D4
Stassfurt 27,372 ....D3
Stendal 47,880 ....D2
Stolberg 56,182 ....B3
Stralsund 75,857 ....E1
Straubing 40,612 ....E4
Strausberg 27,527 ....F2
Stuttgart 562,658 ....C4
Suhl 55,295 ....D3
Sulzbach 19,753 ....B4
Sulzbach-Rosenberg 18,134 ..D4

Telgte 16,834 ....B3
Tempelhof F4
Thale 16,605 ....D3
Torgau 22,749 ....E3
Traunstein 17,145 ....E5
Treptow 58,938 ....F4
Treuchtlingen 12,314 ....D4
Triberg im Schwarzwald
  5,697 ....C4
Trier 95,692 ....B4
Troisdorf 62,011 ....B3
Tübingen 76,046 ....C4
Tuttlingen 31,752 ....C5
Ubach-Palenberg 23,005 ...B3
Überlingen 18,043 ....C5
Ueckermünde 12,304 ....F2
Uelzen 34,891 ....D2
Uetersen 17,218 ....C2
Ulm 106,508 ....C4
Varel 23,718 ....C2
Vechta 22,759 ....C2
Verden 23,770 ....C2
Viersen 76,163 ....B3
Villingen-Schwenningen
  76,258 ....C4
Völklingen 42,916 ....B4
Waldheim 10,316 ....E3
Waldkirch 18,893 ....B4
Waldkraiburg 23,177 ....E4
Waldshut-Tiengen 21,372 ...C5
Walsrode 22,232 ....C2
Waltershausen 14,127 ....D3
Wangen im Allgäu 23,822 ..C5
Warburg 21,802 ....C3
Waren 24,318 ....E2
Warendorf 33,891 ....B3
Wedel 30,158 ....C2
Weida 10,602 ....D3
Weiden in der Oberpfalz
  41,539 ....D4

Weilheim im Oberbayern
  17,602 ....D5
Weimar 63,910 ....D3
Weingarten 21,522 ....C5
Weinheim 41,876 ....C4
Weissenburg im Bayern
  17,318 ....D4
Weissenfels 38,763 ....D3
Weissensee 31,858 ....F3
Weisswasser 36,472 ....F3
Werdau 19,451 ....E3
Wernigerode 36,499 ....D3
Wertheim 20,457 ....C4
Wesel 57,986 ....B3
Westerstede 18,184 ....B2
Wiehl 21,897 ....C3
Wiesbaden 254,209 ....B3
Wiesmoor 10,827 ....B2
Wilhelmshaven 89,892 ......B2
Winsen 26,139 ....D2
Wismar 58,066 ....D2
Witten 103,637 ....B3
Wittenberg 53,670 ....D3
Wittenberge 30,389 ....D2
Wolfen 43,606 ....D3
Wolfenbüttel 50,960 ....D2
Wolfsburg 125,831 ....D2
Worms 74,809 ....C4
Wunstorf 37,115 ....C2
Wuppertal 371,283 ....B3
Würzburg 125,589 ....C4
Wurzen 19,330 ....E3
Xanten 16,097 ....B3
Zeitz 42,985 ....E3
Zerbst 18,717 ....E3
Zeulenroda 14,409 ....D3
Zirndorf 21,608 ....D4
Zittau 39,305 ....F3
Zweibrücken 33,377 ....B4
Zwickau 120,923 ....E3

OTHER FEATURES

Aller (riv.) C2
Allgäu (reg.) D5
Altmark (reg.) D2
Ammersee (lake) D4
Amrum (isl.) C1
Arkona (cape) E1
Baltic (sea) E1
Bavarian (forest) E4
Bavarian Alps (range) D5
Bayerischer Wald Nat'l Park ..E4
Black (forest) C4
Black Elster (riv.) E3
Bodensee (Constance) (lake) ..C5
Bohemian (forest) E4
Borkum (isl.) B2
Breisgau (reg.) B5
Brocken (mt.) D3
Chiemsee (lake) E5
Constance (lake) C5
Danube (riv.) C4
Donau (Danube) (riv.) C4
East Friesland (reg.) B2
Eder (riv.) C3
Elbe (riv.) D2
Elde (riv.) D2
Ems (riv.) B2
Erzgebirge (mts.) E3
Fehmarn (isl.) D1
Feldberg (mt.) C5
Fichtelberg (mt.) E3
Fichtelgebirge (range) D3
Föhr (isl.) C1
Franconian Jura (range) D4
Frisian, East (isls.) B2
Frisian, North (isls.) B1
Fulda (riv.) C3
Grosser Arber (mt.) E4
Harz (mts.) D3

Havel (riv.) E2
Hegau (reg.) C5
Helgoland (bay) C1
Helgoland (isl.) B1
Hunsrück (mts.) B4
Iller (riv.) D4
Ilmenau (riv.) D2
Inn (riv.) E4
Isar (riv.) E4
Jade (bay) B2
Juist (isl.) B2
Kaiserstuhl (mt.) B4
Kiel (bay) D1
Kiel (Nord-Ostsee) (canal) ..C1
Königssee (lake) E5
Lahn (riv.) C3
Langeoog (isl.) B2
Lech (riv.) D4
Leine (riv.) C2
Lippe (riv.) C3
Lusatia (reg.) F3
Main (riv.) C4
Mecklenburg (bay) D1
Mosel (riv.) B3
Mulde (riv.) E3
Müritzsee (lake) E2
Naab (riv.) E4
Neckar (riv.) C4
Neisse (riv.) F3
Norderney (isl.) B2
Nord-Ostsee (canal) C1
Nordstrand (isl.) C1
North (sea) C1
North Friesland (reg.) C1
Oder (riv.) F2
Oder-Haff (lag.) F2
Our (riv.) B3
Peene (riv.) E2

Pellworm (isl.) C
Plauersee (lake) ....D
Pomeranian (bay) ....E
Regnitz (riv.) ....D
Rhine (riv.) ....B
Rhön (mts.) C
Rügen (isl.) ....E
Ruhr (riv.) C
Saale (riv.) ....D
Saar (riv.) ....B
Salzach (riv.) ....E
Sauer (riv.) ....B
Sauerland (reg.) C
Schwarzwald (Black) (forest) ..C
Schwerinsee (lake) ....D
Spessart (range) C
Spiekeroog (isl.) ....B
Spree (riv.) ....F
Spreewald (forest) ....F
Starnbergsee (lake) ....D
Swabian Jura (range) C
Sylt (isl.) C
Taunus (range) C
Tegernsee (lake) ....D
Teutoburger Wald (forest) ..C
Thüringer Wald (forest) .....D
Unstrut (riv.) ....D
Usedom (isl.) ....F
Vechte (riv.) ....B
Vogelsberg (mts.) C
Walchensee (lake) ....D
Wasserkuppe (mt.) C
Watzmann (mt.) ....E
Werra (riv.) ....D
Weser (riv.) C
Westerwald (forest) C
White Elster (riv.) ....E
Würmsee (Starnbergersee)
  (lake) ....D
Zugspitze (mt.) ....D

Agriculture, Industry and Resources

DOMINANT LAND USE

- Wheat, Sugar Beets
- Cereals (chiefly rye, oats, barley)
- Potatoes, Rye
- Dairy, Livestock
- Mixed Cereals, Dairy
- Truck Farming
- Grapes, Fruit
- Forests

MAJOR MINERAL OCCURRENCES

Ag	Silver	K	Potash
Ba	Barite	Lg	Lignite
C	Coal	Na	Salt
Cu	Copper	O	Petroleum
Fe	Iron Ore	Pb	Lead
G	Natural Gas	U	Uranium
Gr	Graphite	Zn	Zinc

⚡ Water Power

▨ Major Industrial Areas

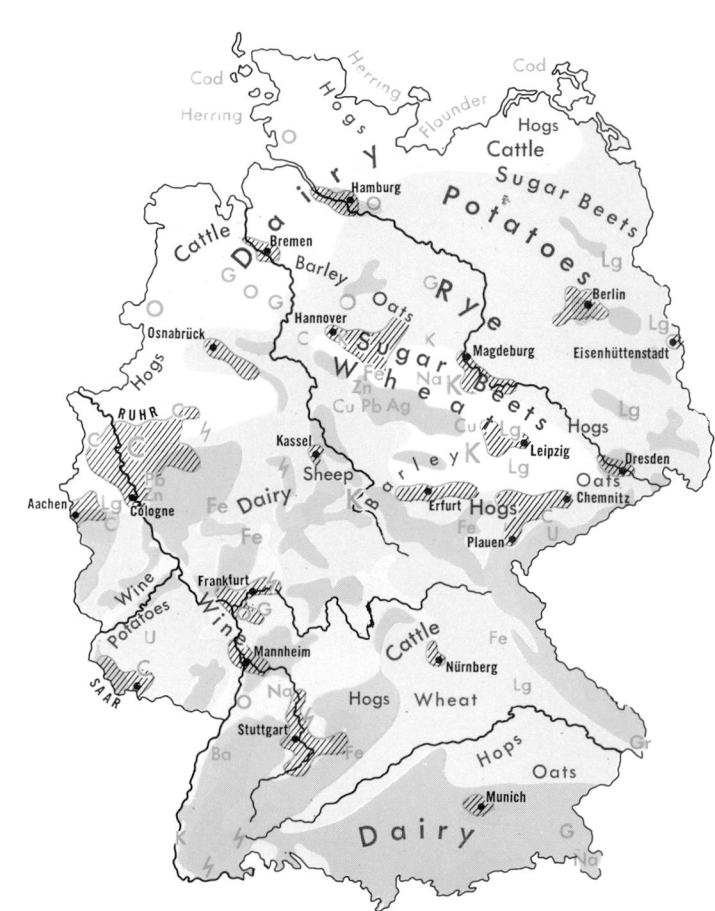

AREA 15,892 sq. mi. (41,160 sq. km.)
POPULATION 14,906,000
CAPITALS The Hague, Amsterdam
LARGEST CITY Amsterdam
HIGHEST POINT Vaalserberg 1,056 ft. (322 m.)
MONETARY UNIT guilder (florin)
MAJOR LANGUAGE Dutch
MAJOR RELIGIONS Protestantism, Roman Catholicism

AREA 11,781 sq. mi. (30,513 sq. km.)
POPULATION 9,883,000
CAPITAL Brussels
LARGEST CITY Brussels (greater)
HIGHEST POINT Botrange 2,277 ft. (694 m.)
MONETARY UNIT Belgian franc
MAJOR LANGUAGES French (Walloon), Flemish
MAJOR RELIGION Roman Catholicism

AREA 999 sq. mi. (2,587 sq. km.)
POPULATION 378,000
CAPITAL Luxembourg
LARGEST CITY Luxembourg
HIGHEST POINT Ardennes Plateau 1,825 ft. (556 m.)
MONETARY UNIT Luxembourg franc
MAJOR LANGUAGES Luxembourgeois (Letzeburgisch), French, German
MAJOR RELIGION Roman Catholicism

NETHERLANDS

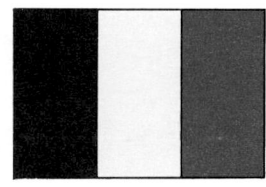

BELGIUM

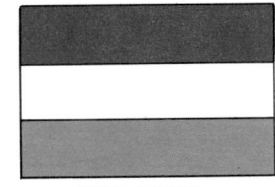

LUXEMBOURG

BELGIUM

PROVINCES

Antwerp 1,569,876 ..... F6
Brabant 2,221,222 ..... F7
East Flanders 1,331,192 ..... D7
Hainaut 1,301,477 ..... D7
Liège 999,413 ..... H7
Limburg 716,688 ..... G7
Luxembourg 221,926 ..... G9
Namur 407,400 ..... G8
West Flanders 1,079,253 ..... B7

CITIES and TOWNS

Aalst 78,938 ..... D7
Aalter 15,554 ..... C6
Aarlen (Arlon) 22,279 ..... H9
Aarschot 25,168 ..... F7
Aiken 9,563 ..... G7
Amay 12,725 ..... G7
Andenne 22,341 ..... H8
Anderlecht 94,764 ..... B9

Anderlues 11,700 ..... E8
Ans 26,016 ..... H7
Antoing 7,970 ..... C7
Antwerp 185,897 ..... E6
Antwerp* 918,144 ..... E6
Antwerpen (Antwerp) 185,897 ..... E6
Ardooie 9,458 ..... C7
Arendonk 10,561 ..... G6
Arlon 22,279 ..... H9
Asse 26,425 ..... E7
Assenede 13,353 ..... D6
Aubange 14,696 ..... H9
Audenarge (Oudenarde) 26,615 ..... D7
Auderghem 30,435 ..... C9
Aywaille 8,194 ..... H8
Baerle-Hertog 2,111 ..... F6
Balen 18,162 ..... G6
Bastenaken (Bastogne) 11,386 ..... H9
Bastogne 11,386 ..... H9
Beauraing 7,641 ..... F8
Beernem 13,526 ..... C6

Beloeil 13,553 ..... D7
Berchem 45,423 ..... F6
Berchem-Sainte-Agathe 18,719 ..... B9
Bergen (Mons) 94,417 ..... E8
Beringen 34,254 ..... G6
Bertrix 7,244 ..... G9
Beveren 40,857 ..... E6
Bilzen 25,683 ..... G7
Binche 33,651 ..... E8
Blankenberge 14,832 ..... C6
Bocholt 10,142 ..... H6
Boom 14,827 ..... E6
Borgerhout 43,521 ..... E6
Borgworm (Waremme) 11,907 ..... G7
Bourg-Léopold (Leopoldsburg) 9,593 ..... G6
Boussu 21,558 ..... D8
Braine-l'Alleud 30,028 ..... E7
Braine-le-Comte 16,475 ..... D7
Brecht 16,391 ..... F6
Bredene 10,538 ..... B6
Bree 13,345 ..... H6

Bruges 118,020 ..... C6
Brugge (Bruges) 118,020 ..... C6
Brussels (cap.)* 997,293 ..... C9
Bruxelles (Brussels) (cap.)* 997,293 ..... C9
Charleroi 222,343 ..... E8
Charleroi* 443,832 ..... E8
Châtelet 38,506 ..... F8
Chimay 9,273 ..... E8
Ciney 13,330 ..... G8
Comines 18,034 ..... B7
Courcelles 29,757 ..... E8
Courtrai (Kortrijk) 75,917 ..... C7
Couvin 12,909 ..... F8
Damme 9,881 ..... C6
De Haan 8,655 ..... C6
Deinze 24,871 ..... D7
Denderleeuw 16,497 ..... E7
Dendermonde 22,119 ..... E6
De Panne 9,507 ..... B6
Dessel 8,074 ..... G6
Destelbergen 15,741 ..... D6
Deurne 77,635 ..... F6
Diest 20,491 ..... F7

Diksmuide 15,347 ..... B6
Dilbeek 35,050 ..... B9
Dilsen 15,910 ..... H6
Dinant 12,105 ..... G8
Dison 14,225 ..... H7
Dixmude (Diksmuide) 15,347 ..... B6
Doornik (Tournai) 67,906 ..... C7
Dour 17,737 ..... D8
Duffel 14,684 ..... F6
Durbuy 7,729 ..... H8
Ecaussinnes 9,739 ..... E7
Edingen (Enghien) 10,095 ..... D7
Eeklo 19,637 ..... D6
Eghezée 10,683 ..... F7
Eigenbrakel (Braine-l'Alleud) 30,028 ..... E7
Ekeren 30,294 ..... E6
Enghien 10,095 ..... D7
Erquelinnes 10,029 ..... E8
Esneux 11,559 ..... H7
Essen 12,505 ..... F6
Estampuis 9,601 ..... C7
Etterbeek 44,218 ..... B9
Eupen 16,847 ..... J7

Evere 30,520 ..... C9
Evergem 28,974 ..... D6
Farciennes 12,205 ..... E8
Flémalle 28,217 ..... G7
Fleurus 22,574 ..... E8
Florennes 10,537 ..... F8
Forest 50,607 ..... B9
Fosses-La-Ville 7,678 ..... F8
Frameries 21,470 ..... D8
Frasnes-lez Anvaing 10,751 ..... D7
Furnes (Veurne) 11,253 ..... B6
Ganshoren 21,445 ..... B9
Geel 31,463 ..... G6
Geldenaken (Jodoigne) 8,983 ..... F7
Gembloux-sur-Orneau 17,636 ..... F7
Genk 61,502 ..... H7
Gent (Ghent) 239,256 ..... D6
Geraardsbergen 17,533 ..... D7
Gerpinnes 10,808 ..... F8
Ghent 239,256 ..... D6
Ghent* 485,565 ..... D6
Gistel 9,531 ..... B6
Grammont (Geraardsbergen) 17,533 ..... D7
Grez-Doiceau 8,795 ..... F7
Grimbergen 32,038 ..... E7
Haacht 11,285 ..... F7
Hal (Halle) 15,293 ..... E7
Halen 7,865 ..... G7
Halle 15,293 ..... E7
Hamme 22,790 ..... E6
Hamont-Achel 11,939 ..... H6
Hannuit (Hannut) 11,527 ..... G7
Hannut 11,527 ..... G7
Harelbeke 25,214 ..... C7
Hasselt 64,613 ..... G7
Heist-op-den-Berg 34,617 ..... F6
Hensies 6,806 ..... D8
Herentals 23,797 ..... F6
Herselt 11,340 ..... F6
Herstal 38,592 ..... H7
Herve 14,276 ..... H7
Heuvelland 8,540 ..... B7
Hoboken 34,563 ..... E6
Hoei (Huy) 17,331 ..... G8
Hoeselt 8,497 ..... G7
Hoogstraten 14,368 ..... F6
Huy 17,331 ..... G8
Ichtegem 12,259 ..... B6
Ieper 34,425 ..... B7
Ingelmunster 10,434 ..... C7
Ixelles 75,723 ..... C9
Izegem 26,410 ..... C7
Jabbeke 10,629 ..... C6
Jemappes 18,632 ..... D8
Jemeppe-sur-Sambre 17,120 ..... F8
Jette 40,109 ..... B9
Jodoigne 8,983 ..... F7
Kalmthout 14,960 ..... F6
Kapellen 14,536 ..... E6
Kasterlee 14,612 ..... F6
Kinrooi 10,138 ..... H6
Knokke-Heist 28,868 ..... C6
Koekelare 7,606 ..... B6
Koekelberg 16,643 ..... B9
Koksijde 13,679 ..... B6
Kontich 17,878 ..... E6
Kortemark 12,580 ..... C6
Kortrijk 75,917 ..... C7
Kraainem 11,780 ..... C9
La Louvière 77,326 ..... E8
Lanaken 20,272 ..... H7
Landen 14,081 ..... G7
Langemark-Poelkapelle 7,097 ..... B7
Lasne 10,919 ..... F7
Lede 17,249 ..... D7
Lens 3,726 ..... D7
Leopoldsburg 9,593 ..... G6
Le Roeulx 7,754 ..... E8
Lessen (Lessines) 16,553 ..... D7
Lessines 16,553 ..... D7
Leuven 85,076 ..... F7
Leuze-en-Hainaut 12,863 ..... D7
Libramont-Chevigny 7,859 ..... G9
Lichtervelde 7,459 ..... C6
Liedekerke 11,609 ..... D7
Liège 214,119 ..... H7
Liège* 605,123 ..... H7

Lier 31,261 ..... F6
Lierre (Lier) 31,261 ..... F6
Limbourg 5,350 ..... J7
Limburg (Limbourg) 5,350 ..... J7
Linter 6,568 ..... G7
Lochristi 16,125 ..... D6
Lokeren 33,369 ..... D6
Lommel 25,412 ..... G6
Louvain (Leuven) 85,076 ..... F7
Luik (Liège) 214,119 ..... H7
Lummen 11,793 ..... G7
Maaseik 20,056 ..... H6
Maasmechelen 33,618 ..... H7
Machelen 11,273 ..... C9
Maldegem 42,694 ..... C6
Malines (Mechelen) 77,269 ..... F6
Malmédy 10,036 ..... J8
Marche-en-Famenne 14,115 ..... G8
Mechelen 77,269 ..... F6
Meerhout 8,613 ..... G6
Meise 15,170 ..... E7
Menen 33,542 ..... C7
Menin (Menen) 33,542 ..... C7
Merchtem 12,972 ..... E7
Merelbeke 19,773 ..... D7
Merksem 41,600 ..... E6
Merksplas 6,136 ..... F6
Mettet 9,958 ..... F8
Meulebeke 10,471 ..... C7
Middelkerke 14,168 ..... B6
Moeskroen (Mouscron) 54,590 ..... C7
Mol 29,798 ..... G6
Molenbeek-Saint-Jean 70,850 ..... B9
Mons 94,417 ..... E8
Montigny-le-Tilleul 9,726 ..... E8
Moorslede 10,974 ..... B7
Mortsel 26,746 ..... E6
Mouscron 54,590 ..... C7
Namen (Namur) 102,321 ..... F8
Namur 102,321 ..... F8
Nazareth 9,248 ..... D7
Neerpelt 12,779 ..... G6
Neufchâteau 6,039 ..... G9
Nevele 10,471 ..... D6
Nieuport (Nieuwpoort) 8,195 ..... B6
Nieuwpoort 8,195 ..... B6
Nijvel (Nivelles) 21,580 ..... E7
Ninove 33,393 ..... D7
Nivelles 21,580 ..... E7
Oostende (Ostend) 68,915 ..... B6
Oostkamp 19,747 ..... C6
Opwijk 11,451 ..... E7
Ostend 68,915 ..... B6
Oudenaarde 26,615 ..... D7
Oudenburg 8,138 ..... B6
Oud-Turnhout 10,733 ..... F6
Oupeye 22,453 ..... H7
Overijse 21,428 ..... F7
Overpelt 11,233 ..... G6
Peer 12,099 ..... G6
Péruwelz 16,664 ..... D8
Philippeville 6,916 ..... F8
Poelkapelle-Langemark 7,097 ..... B7
Pont-à-Celles 15,444 ..... E8
Poperinge 19,886 ..... B7
Profondeville 8,724 ..... F8
Putte 14,017 ..... F6
Quaregnon 20,071 ..... D8
Quévy 7,391 ..... D8
Quiévrain 6,945 ..... D8
Raeren 8,046 ..... J7
Ravels 10,328 ..... F6
Rebecq 8,891 ..... E7
Renaix (Ronse) 25,056 ..... D7
Retie 8,359 ..... G6
Rochefort 4,357 ..... G8
Roeselare 51,984 ..... C7
Ronse (Renaix) 25,056 ..... D7
Roulers (Roeselare) 51,984 ..... C7
Saint-Gilles 46,076 ..... B9
Saint-Josse-ten-Noode 20,381 ..... C9
Saint-Nicolas 25,755 ..... D7
Saint-Trond (Sint-Truiden) 36,374 ..... G7
Saint-Vith (Sankt Vith) 8,434 ..... J8

(continued on following page)

Agriculture, Industry and Resources

DOMINANT LAND USE

- Dairy, Truck Farming
- Cash Crops, Livestock
- Mixed Cereals, Dairy
- Specialized Horticulture
- Grapes, Wine
- Forests
- Sand Dunes

MAJOR MINERAL OCCURRENCES

C Coal
Fe Iron Ore
G Natural Gas
Na Salt
O Petroleum

Major Industrial Areas

Sankt Vith 8,434 ..... J8
Schaerbeek 106,754 ..... C9
Schoten 31,128 ..... F6
Seraing 64,543 ..... G7
's-Gravenbrakel (Braine-le-Comte) 16,475 ... D7
Sint-Laureins 6,620 ..... D6
Sint-Niklaas 67,992 ..... E6
Sint-Pieters-Leeuw 27,968 ..... B9
Sint-Truiden 36,374 ..... G7
Soignies 23,352 ..... D7
Spa 9,619 ..... H8
Sprimont 9,660 ..... H8
Staden 11,135 ..... B7
Steenokkerzeel 9,638 ..... C9
Stekene 14,125 ..... E6
Tamise (Temse) 23,525 ..... E6
Temse 23,525 ..... E6
Termonde (Dendermonde) 22,119 ..... E6
Tessenderlo 13,800 ..... G6
Theux 9,167 ..... H8
Thuin 13,757 ..... E8
Tielt 19,103 ..... C7
Tielt-Winge 8,237 ..... F7
Tienen 32,620 ..... F7
Tirlemont 32,620 ..... F7
Tongeren 29,603 ..... G7
Tongres (Tongeren) 29,603 ... G7
Torhout 17,165 ..... C6
Tournai 67,906 ..... C7
Tubeke (Tubize) 19,827 ..... E7
Tubize 19,827 ..... E7
Turnhout 37,453 ..... F6
Uccle 76,004 ..... B9
Ukkel (Uccle) 76,004 ..... B9
Verviers 55,371 ..... H7
Veurne 11,253 ..... B6
Vielsalm 6,731 ..... H8
Vilvoorde 33,264 ..... F7
Vilvorde (Vilvoorde) 33,264 ..... F7
Viroinval 5,589 ..... F8
Virton 10,490 ..... H9
Visé 16,469 ..... H7
Vorst (Forest) 50,607 ..... B9
Waarschoot 7,574 ..... D6
Wachtebeke 6,951 ..... D6
Waimes (Weismes) 5,713 ..... J8
Walcourt 14,866 ..... F8
Waregem 32,810 ..... C7
Waremme 11,907 ..... G7
Waterloo 24,755 ..... E7
Watermael-Boitsfort 24,880 ..... C9
Watermael-Bosvoorde (Watermael-Boitsfort) 24,880 ..... C9
Waver (Wavre) 25,153 ..... F7
Wavre 25,153 ..... F7
Wemmel 13,547 ..... B9
Wervik 18,086 ..... B7
Westerlo 19,459 ..... F6
Wetteren 23,460 ..... D7
Wezembeek-Oppem 12,006 ..... D9
Wezet (Visé) 16,469 ..... H7
Willebroek 22,265 ..... E6
Wilrijk 42,328 ..... E6
Wingene 12,188 ..... C6
Woluwe-Saint-Lambert 48,801 ..... C9
Woluwe-Saint-Pierre 40,686 ..... C9
Ypres (Ieper) 34,425 ..... B7
Yvoir 6,527 ..... F8
Zaventem 25,393 ..... C9
Zedelgem 19,198 ..... C6
Zele 19,631 ..... E6
Zelzate 12,934 ..... D6
Zemst 17,167 ..... E7
Zinnik (Soignies) 23,352 ..... D7
Zonhoven 15,965 ..... G6
Zottegem 25,109 ..... D7

OTHER FEATURES

Albert (canal) F6
Ardennes (forest) F9
Botrange (mt.) J8
Dender (riv.) D7
Deûle (riv.) B7
Dyle (riv.) F7
Hohe Venn (plat.) H8
Lys (riv.) B7
Mark (riv.) F6
Meuse (riv.) F8
Nethe (riv.) F6
North (sea) D4
Ourthe (riv.) G8
Rupel (riv.) F7
Sambre (riv.) D8
Schelde (Scheldt) (riv.) C7
Scheldt (riv.) C7
Semois (riv.) G9
Senne (riv.) E7
Vaalserberg (mt.) J7
Vesdre (riv.) H7
Yser (riv.) B7

LUXEMBOURG

CITIES and TOWNS

Bascharage 4,870 ..... H9
Diekirch† 5,470 ..... J9
Differdange 15,940 ..... H9
Dudelange† 14,070 ..... J1
Echternach† 4,290 ..... J9
Esch-sur-Alzette† 23,800 ..... H9
Ettelbruck† 6,600 ..... J9
Grevenmacher† 2,940 ..... J9
Hesperange 9,470 ..... J9
Luxembourg (cap.) 75,540 ..... J9
Mamer 6,090 ..... H9
Mersch 5,560 ..... J9
Mertert 3,000 ..... J9
Pétange 11,800 ..... H9
Remich 2,430 ..... J9
Troisvierges 1,890 ..... J9
Vianden† 1,510 ..... J9
Wasserbillig 2,097 ..... J9
Wiltz 3,850 ..... H9

OTHER FEATURES

Alzette (riv.) J9
Clerf (riv.) J8
Mosel (riv.) J9
Our (riv.) J9
Sauer (riv.) J9

NETHERLANDS

PROVINCES

Drenthe 439,066 ..... K3
Flevoland 202,678 ..... G4
Friesland 599,190 ..... H2
Gelderland 1,794,678 ..... H4
Groningen 555,200 ..... K2
Limburg 1,099,622 ..... H6
North Brabant 2,172,604 ..... F5
North Holland 2,365,160 ..... F3
Overijssel 1,014,949 ..... J4
South Holland 3,200,408 ..... E5
Utrecht 1,004,632 ..... G4
Zeeland 355,585 ..... D6

CITIES and TOWNS

Aalsmeer 21,984 ..... F4
Aalten 18,202 ..... K5
Alkmaar 88,571 ..... F3
Almelo 62,008 ..... K4
Almere 63,785 ..... G4
Alphen aan de Rijn 59,586 ..... F4
Amersfoort 96,072 ..... G4
Amstelveen 69,505 ..... B5
Amsterdam (cap.) 694,680 ..... B4
Apeldoorn 147,270 ..... H4
Appingedam 12,668 ..... K2
Arnhem 128,946 ..... H4
Assen 49,398 ..... K3
Asten 14,965 ..... H6
Axel 12,219 ..... D6
Baarn 24,897 ..... G4
Barneveld 41,649 ..... H4
Beilen 14,057 ..... K3
Bemmel 15,842 ..... H5
Bergen 14,075 ..... F3
Bergen op Zoom 46,842 ..... E5
Berkel 15,690 ..... F5
Beverwijk 35,126 ..... F4
Bloemendaal 8,977 ..... E4
Bodegraven 17,720 ..... F4
Bolsward 9,799 ..... H2
Borculo 10,057 ..... J4
Borger 12,730 ..... K3
Borne 21,261 ..... K4
Boskoop 14,524 ..... F4
Boxmeer 14,363 ..... H5
Boxtel 24,951 ..... G5
Breda 121,362 ..... F5
Brielle 14,973 ..... E5
Brummen 20,802 ..... J4
Brunssum 29,799 ..... J7
Bussum 31,988 ..... G4
Capelle 57,423 ..... F5
Castricum 22,433 ..... F3
Coevorden 14,344 ..... K3
Culemborg 21,116 ..... G5
De Bilt 31,729 ..... G4
Delft 88,135 ..... E4
Delfzijl 23,472 ..... K2
Denekamp 12,206 ..... L4
Den Helder 62,094 ..... F3
Deurne 29,308 ..... H6
Deventer 66,398 ..... J4
Didam 16,036 ..... J5
Diemen 18,083 ..... C5
Dinxperlo 8,133 ..... K5
Dirksland 7,341 ..... E5
Doesburg 10,578 ..... J4
Doetinchem 41,260 ..... J5
Dongen 21,124 ..... F5
Doorn 10,419 ..... G4
Dordrecht 108,519 ..... F5
Driebergen 18,294 ..... G4
Dronten 24,281 ..... H3
Druten 14,630 ..... H5
Echt 16,927 ..... H6
Edam-Volendam 24,572 ..... G4
Ede 92,293 ..... H4
Egmond aan Zee 11,163 ..... E3
Eindhoven 190,736 ..... G6
Elst 17,654 ..... H5
Emmen 92,422 ..... K3
Enkhuizen 15,939 ..... G3
Enschede 145,223 ..... K4
Epe 33,872 ..... H4
Ermelo 25,644 ..... H4
Etten-Leur 32,010 ..... F5
Flushing 44,022 ..... C6
Geertruidenberg 6,645 ..... F5
Geldermalsen 22,017 ..... G5
Geldrop 25,817 ..... H6
Geleen 33,756 ..... H7
Gemert 17,613 ..... H5
Gendringen 20,186 ..... J5
Genemuiden 7,545 ..... H3
Gennep 16,264 ..... H5
Giessendam 16,722 ..... F5
Gilze 22,577 ..... F5
Goes 31,815 ..... D6
Goirle 18,852 ..... G5
Goor 11,804 ..... K4
Gorinchem 28,222 ..... G5
Gouda 63,232 ..... F4
Gramsbergen 6,080 ..... K3
Grave 10,447 ..... H5
Groenlo 8,895 ..... K4
Groesbeek 18,221 ..... H5
Groningen 167,788 ..... K2
Haaksbergen 22,690 ..... K4
Haarlem 149,198 ..... F4
Haarlemmermeer (Hoofddorp) 93,427 ..... F4
Hague, The (cap.) 443,845 ..... E4
Hardenberg 32,065 ..... J3
Harderwijk 34,600 ..... H4
Hardinxveld-Giessendam 16,722 ..... G5
Harlingen 15,727 ..... G2
Hasselt 6,871 ..... J3
Hattem 11,571 ..... H4
Heemskerk 32,910 ..... F3
Heemstede 26,308 ..... F4
Heerde 18,171 ..... H4
Heerenveen 37,700 ..... H3
Heerhugowaard 35,522 ..... F3
Heerlen 94,149 ..... J7
Heesch 11,309 ..... G5
Heiloo 20,467 ..... F3
Hellendoorn 34,287 ..... J4
Hellevoetsluis 34,276 ..... E5
Helmond 66,791 ..... H6
Hengelo 76,175 ..... J4
's Hertogenbosch 90,584 ..... G5
Heusden 5,761 ..... G5
Hillegom 20,001 ..... E4
Hilvarenbeek 9,975 ..... G6
Hilversum 84,983 ..... G4
Hoek van Holland (Hook of Holland) D4
Hoofddorp (Haarlemmermeer) 93,427 ..... F4
Hoogeveen 45,601 ..... J3
Hoogezand-Sappemeer 34,618 ..... K2
Hook of Holland D4
Hoorn 56,474 ..... G3
Horst 17,614 ..... H6
Huissen 15,544 ..... H5
Huizen 20,501 ..... G4
Hulst 18,575 ..... E6
IJsselstein 19,516 ..... F4
Kampen 32,769 ..... H3
Katwijk aan Zee 39,441 ..... E4
Kerkrade 52,994 ..... J7
Kesteren 9,389 ..... G5
Krimpen aan den IJssel 27,638 ..... F5
Landsmeer 9,121 ..... C4
Laren 11,643 ..... G4
Leek 17,743 ..... J2
Leerdam 19,015 ..... G5
Leeuwarden 85,296 ..... H2
Leiden 109,254 ..... E4
Lelystad 58,125 ..... H3
Lisse 20,826 ..... F4
Lith 6,115 ..... G5
Lochem 18,295 ..... J4
Loon op Zand 21,372 ..... G5
Losser 22,526 ..... L4
Maarssen 37,629 ..... F4
Maasbree 11,752 ..... H6
Maassluis 33,155 ..... E5
Maastricht 116,380 ..... H7
Margraten 13,365 ..... H7
Medemblik 6,876 ..... G3
Meerssen 20,462 ..... H7
Meppel 23,492 ..... J3
Middelburg 39,462 ..... C6
Middelharnis 15,480 ..... E5
Millingen aan den Rijn 5,287 ..... J5
Monnickendam 9,953 ..... C4
Montfoort 12,397 ..... G4
Muiden 6,772 ..... G4
Muntendam 5,022 ..... K2
Naaldwijk 27,683 ..... E4
Naarden 16,101 ..... G4
Neede 10,982 ..... K4
Nieuwegein 58,316 ..... G4
Nieuwkoop 10,723 ..... F4
Nijkerk 25,613 ..... H4
Nijmegen 145,405 ..... H5
Noordwijk 24,996 ..... E4
Norg 6,595 ..... J2
Nunspeet 24,573 ..... H4
Odoorn 12,225 ..... K3
Oisterwijk 18,177 ..... G5
Oldenzaal 29,680 ..... K4
Olst 9,039 ..... J4
Ommen 17,957 ..... J3
Oostburg 18,145 ..... C6
Oosterhout 48,157 ..... F5
Oostzaan 7,292 ..... C4
Oss 50,987 ..... H5
Oud-Beijerland 20,385 ..... E5
Oude-Pekela 8,028 ..... K2
Oudenbosch 12,576 ..... E5
Oudewater 9,410 ..... F4
Purmerend 56,233 ..... F4
Putten 20,898 ..... H4
Raalte 26,883 ..... J4
Renkum 33,841 ..... H5
Reusel 7,813 ..... G6
Rheden 46,088 ..... J4
Rhenen 16,613 ..... H5
Ridderkerk 46,163 ..... F5
Rijnsburg 13,412 ..... F4
Rijswijk 48,189 ..... E4
Roden 18,331 ..... J2
Roermond 38,486 ..... J6
Roosendaal 59,237 ..... E5
Rotterdam 576,232 ..... E5
Ruurlo 7,418 ..... J4
Sappemeer-Hoogezand 34,618 ..... K2
Schagen 16,759 ..... F3
Schiedam 69,438 ..... E5
Schijndel 21,397 ..... G5
Schoonebeek 7,740 ..... K3
Schoonhoven 11,231 ..... F5
's Gravendeel 8,424 ..... E5
's Gravenhage (The Hague) (cap.) 443,845 ..... E4
's Gravenzande 18,453 ..... E4
Simpelveld 11,882 ..... J7
Sittard 44,894 ..... H6
Sliedrecht 22,833 ..... F5
Slochteren 13,958 ..... K2
Sloten H3
Sluis 2,882 ..... C6
Smilde 9,212 ..... K3
Sneek 29,408 ..... H2
Soest 41,598 ..... G4
Stadskanaal 33,047 ..... L3
Staphorst 13,580 ..... J3
Staveren G3
Steenbergen 13,826 ..... E5
Steenwijk 20,907 ..... J3
Stiens H2
Tegelen 18,991 ..... J6
Ter Apel L3
Termunten 4,378 ..... K2
Terneuzen 35,043 ..... D6
The Hague (cap.) 443,845 ..... E4
Tholen 19,019 ..... E5
Tiel 31,394 ..... G5
Tilburg 155,110 ..... G5
Twello J4
Uden 35,057 ..... H5
Uithoorn 22,205 ..... F4
Uithuizen K2
Ulrum 3,657 ..... J2
Urk 12,728 ..... H3
Utrecht 230,634 ..... G4
Vaals 10,639 ..... H7
Valkenswaard 29,811 ..... H6
Veendam 28,234 ..... K2
Veenendaal 47,258 ..... G4
Veere 4,836 ..... D5
Veghel 25,701 ..... H5
Veldhoven 38,644 ..... G6
Velsen 57,608 ..... F4
Venlo 63,607 ..... J6
Venraij 34,172 ..... H6
Vianen 18,704 ..... G5
Vlaardingen 74,480 ..... E5
Vlagtwedde 16,181 ..... L3
Vlijmen 15,655 ..... G5
Vlissingen (Flushing) 44,022 ..... C6
Volendam-Edam 24,572 ..... G4
Voorburg 40,455 ..... E4
Voorst 23,678 ..... J4
Vorden 8,282 ..... J4
Vriezenveen 18,601 ..... K4
Vught 23,718 ..... G5
Waalre 15,126 ..... G6
Waalwijk 28,674 ..... G5
Wageningen 32,370 ..... H5
Warmenhuizen 4,765 ..... F3
Weert 40,068 ..... H6
Weesp 18,362 ..... C5
Westkapelle 2,666 ..... C5
Wierden 22,200 ..... K4
Wijhe 7,155 ..... J4
Wijk bij Duurstede 15,401 ..... G5
Willemstad 3,357 ..... F5
Winschoten 19,680 ..... L2
Winsum 6,583 ..... K2
Winterswijk 28,024 ..... K5
Woensdrecht 10,077 ..... E6
Woerden 34,166 ..... F4
Wolvega J3
Workum G3
Zaandam (Zaanstad) 129,653 ..... B4
Zaltbommel 9,534 ..... G5
Zandvoort 15,428 ..... E4
Zeewolde 5,930 ..... G4
Zeist 59,431 ..... G4
Zevenaar 26,848 ..... J5
Zevenbergen 15,562 ..... E5
Zierikzee 9,804 ..... D5
Zundert 13,385 ..... F6
Zutphen 31,144 ..... J4
Zwartsluis 4,465 ..... H3
Zwijndrecht 41,357 ..... E5
Zwolle 92,517 ..... J3

OTHER FEATURES

Alkmaardermeer (lake) F3
Ameland (isl.) H2
Beulaker Wijde (lake) H3
Borndiep (chan.) H2
De Fluessen (lake) G3
De Honte (bay) ..... D
De Peel (reg.) ..... H
De Twente (reg.) ..... K
De Zaan (riv.) ..... B
Dollard (bay) L
Dommel (riv.) ..... H
Duiveland (isl.) ..... D
Eems (riv.) ..... K
Eijerlandsche Gat (strait) ..... F
Flevoland Polders ..... G
Frisian, West (isls.) ..... G
Goeree (isl.) ..... D
Grevelingen (strait) ..... E
Griend (isl.) ..... G
Groninger Wad (sound) ..... J
Groote IJ Polder ..... B
Haarlemmermeer Polder ..... B
Haringvliet (strait) ..... E
Het IJ (est.) C
Hoek van Holland (cape) ..... D
Houtrak Polder ..... A
Hunse (riv.) ..... K
IJmeer (bay) C
IJssel (riv.) J4
IJsselmeer (lake) G3
Lauwers (chan.) ..... J
Lauwers Zee (bay) J2
Lek (riv.) F5
Lower Rhine (riv.) H5
Maas (riv.) G5
Marken (isl.) G4
Markerwaard Polder G3
Marsdiep (chan.) F3
North (sea) E3
North Beveland (isl.) D5
North East Polder H3
North Holland (canal) C4
North Sea (canal) F4
Old Rhine (riv.) E4
Oostzaan Polder B4
Orange (canal) K3
Overflakkee (isl.) E5
Rhine (riv.) J5
Roer (riv.) J6
Scheldt, Eastern (est.) D5
Scheldt, Western (De Honte) (bay) D6
Schiermonnikoog (isl.) J1
Schouwen (isl.) D5
Slotermeer (lake) H3
Sneekermeer (lake) H2
South Beveland (isl.) D6
Terschelling (isl.) G2
Texel (isl.) F2
Tjeukemeer (lake) H3
Vaalserberg (mt.) J7
Vecht (riv.) F4
Vechte (riv.) J3
Veersche Meer (lake) D5
Veluwe (reg.) H4
Vlieland (isl.) F2
Vliestroom (strait) G2
Voorne (isl.) D5
Waal (riv.) G5
Waddenzee (sound) G2
Walcheren (isl.) C5
West Frisian (isls.) F2
Wester Eems (chan.) K1
Western Scheldt (De Honte) (bay) D6
Wieringermeer Polder G3
Wilhelmina (canal) G6
Willems (canal) G5

* City and suburbs.
† Population of urban area.

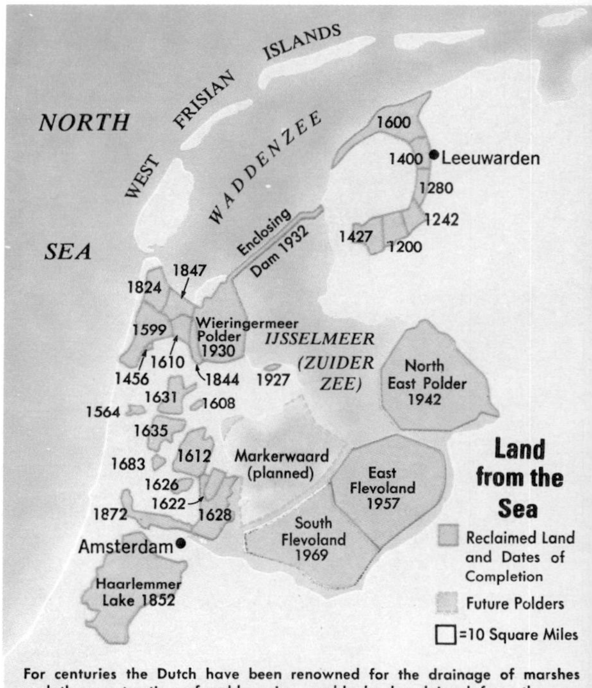

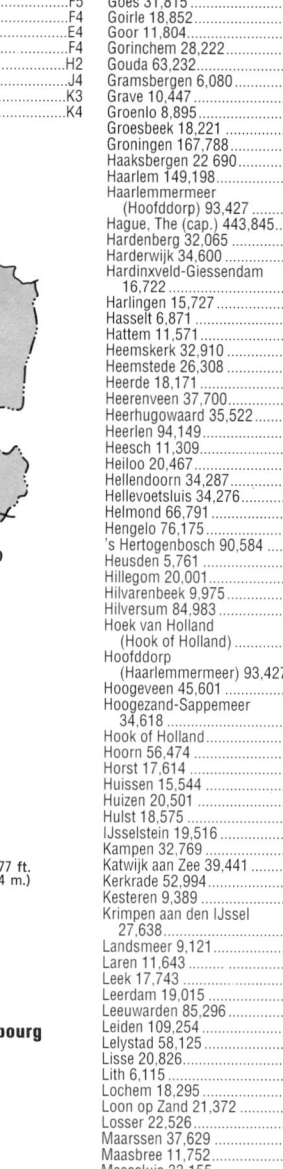

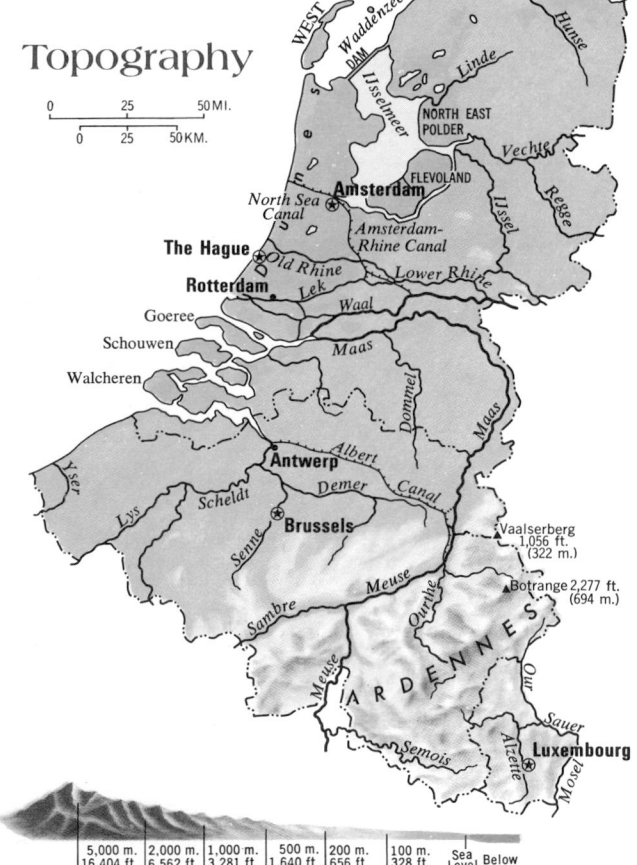

NORTH SEA
WEST FRISIAN ISLANDS
WADDENZEE
Enclosing Dam 1932
Leeuwarden
Wieringermeer Polder 1930
IJSSELMEER (ZUIDER ZEE)
North East Polder 1942
Markerwaard (planned)
East Flevoland 1957
South Flevoland 1969
Amsterdam
Haarlemmer Lake 1852
Land from the Sea
Reclaimed Land and Dates of Completion
Future Polders
=10 Square Miles

For centuries the Dutch have been renowned for the drainage of marshes and the construction of polders, i.e., arable land reclaimed from the sea. Future projects will convert much of the present IJsselmeer to agricultural land.

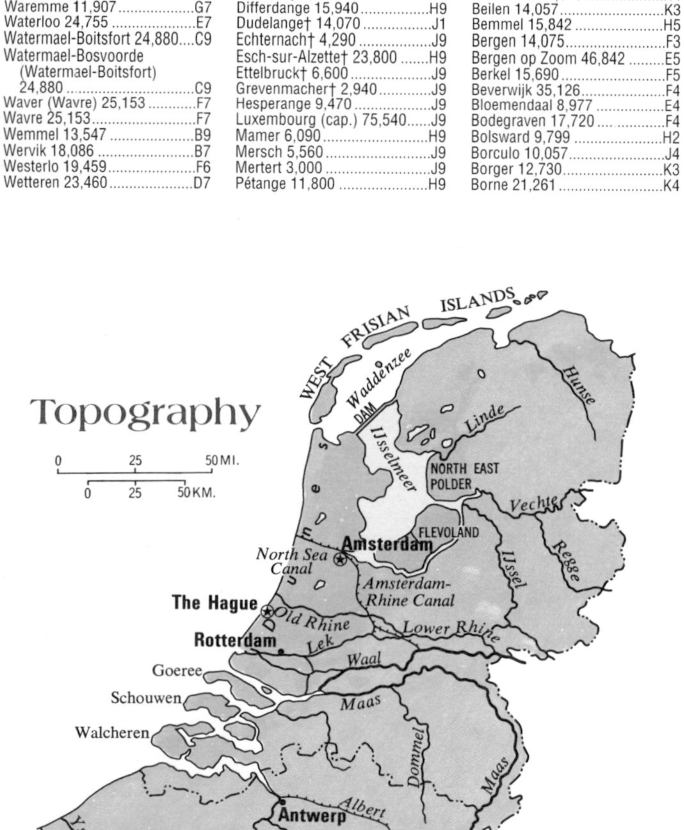

Topography
0 25 50 MI.
0 25 50 KM.
WEST FRISIAN ISLANDS
Waddenzee
IJsselmeer
NORTH EAST POLDER
FLEVOLAND
Amsterdam
North Sea Canal
Amsterdam-Rhine Canal
The Hague
Old Rhine
Lower Rhine
Rotterdam
Lek
Waal
Goeree
Schouwen
Walcheren
Maas
Dommel
Albert
Antwerp
Demer
Canal
Scheldt
Lys
Yser
Brussels
Senne
Vaalserberg 1,056 ft. (322 m.)
Botrange 2,277 ft. (694 m.)
Meuse
Sambre
Ourthe
ARDENNES
Our
Sauer
Semois
Alzette
Mosel
Luxembourg
Linde
Hunse
Vecht
Regge
IJssel
5,000 m. 16,404 ft.
2,000 m. 6,562 ft.
1,000 m. 3,281 ft.
500 m. 1,640 ft.
200 m. 656 ft.
100 m. 328 ft.
Sea Level
Below

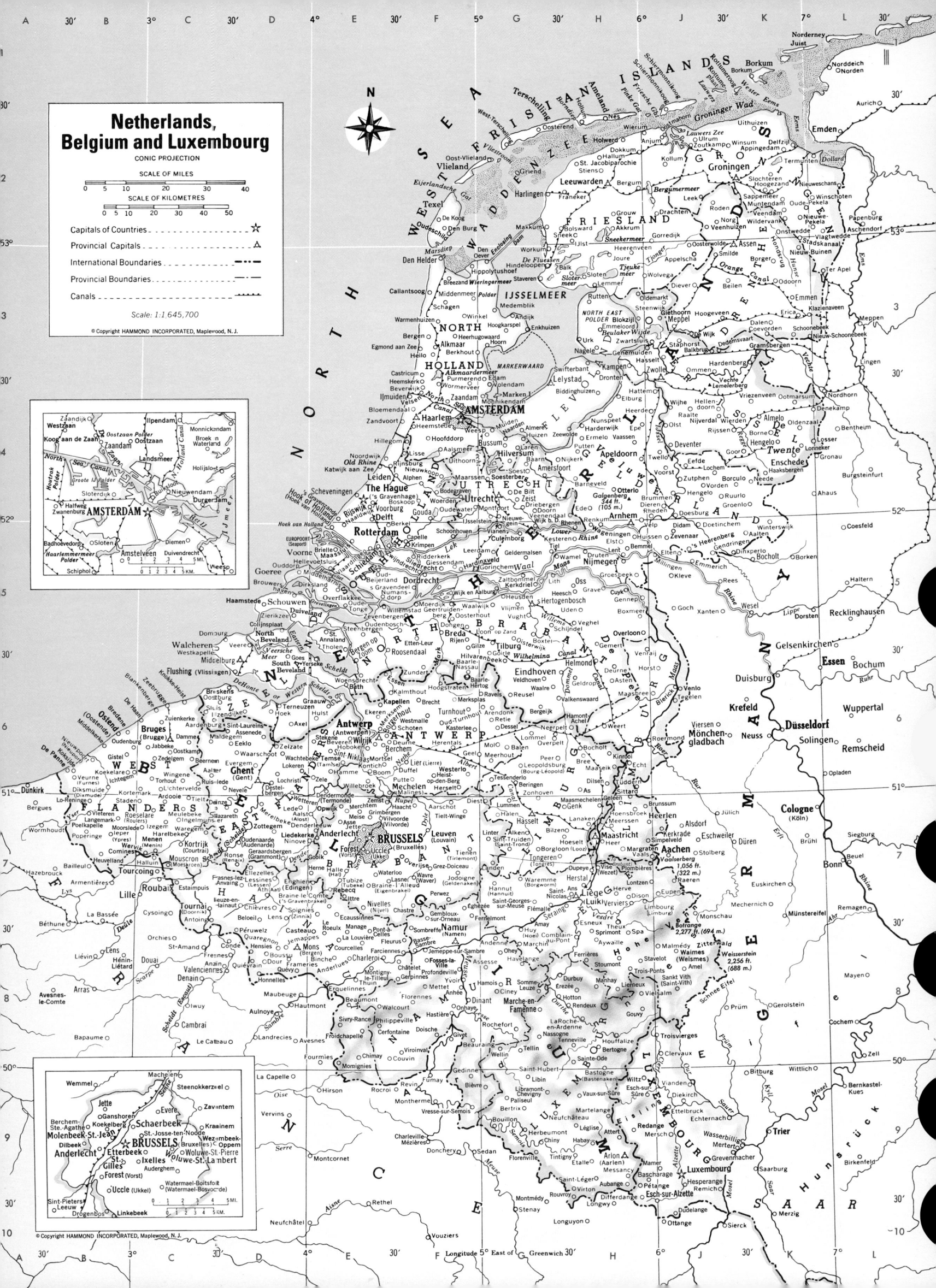

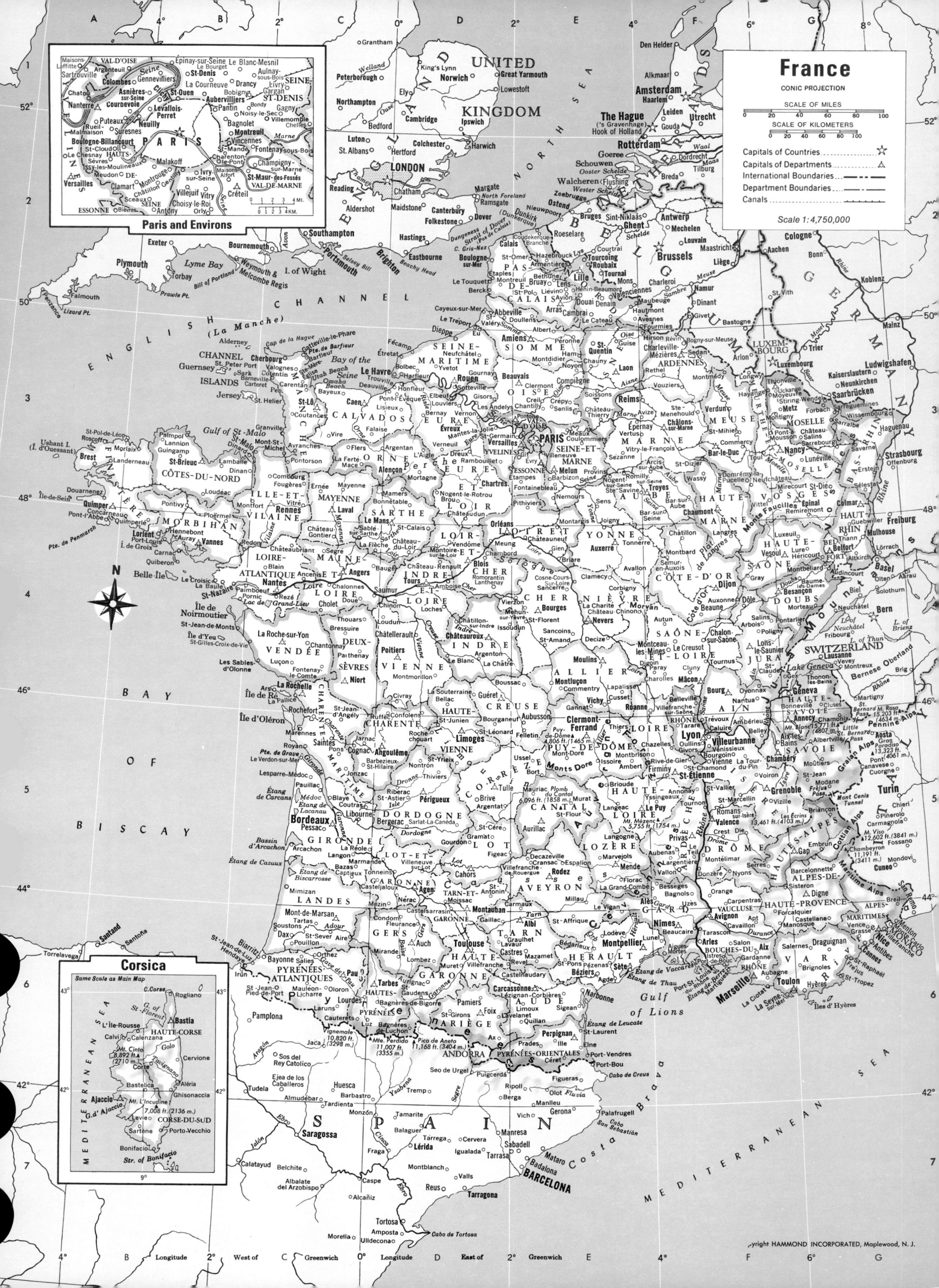

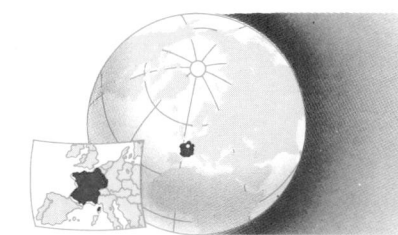

DEPARTMENTS

Ain 418,516...........F 4
Aisne 533,970..........E 3
Allier 369,580..........E 4
Alpes-de-Haute-
Provence 119,068.....G 5
Alpes-Maritimes
881,198..............G 6
Ardèche 267,970........F 5
Ardennes 302,338.......F 3
Ariège 135,725.........D 6
Aube 289,300..........E 3
Aude 280,686..........E 6
Aveyron 278,654........E 5
Bas-Rhin 915,676.......G 3
Belfort 131,999........G 4
Bouches-du-Rhône
1,724,199.............F 6
Calvados 589,559.......C 3
Cantal 162,838.........E 5
Charente 340,770.......D 5
Charente-Maritime
513,220..............C 5
Cher 320,174..........E 4
Corrèze 241,448........D 5
Corse du Sud
108,604..............B 6
Côte-d'Or 473,548......F 4
Côtes-du-Nord
538,869..............B 3
Creuse 139,968.........D 4
Deux-Sèvres
342,812..............C 4
Dordogne 377,356.......D 5
Doubs 477,163.........G 4
Drôme 389,781.........F 5
Essonne 988,000........E 3
Eure 462,323..........D 3
Eure-et-Loir 362,813....D 3
Finistère 828,364......A 3
Gard 530,478..........F 6
Gers 174,154..........D 6
Gironde 1,127,546......C 5
Haute-Corse
131,574..............B 6
Haute-Garonne
824,501..............D 6
Haute-Loire 205,895....E 5
Haute-Marne
210,670..............F 3
Hautes-Alpes
105,070..............G 5
Haute-Saône
231,962..............G 4
Haute-Savoie
494,505..............G 5
Hautes-Pyrénées
227,922..............D 6
Haute-Vienne
355,737..............D 5
Haut-Rhin 650,372......G 4
Hauts-de-Seine
1,387,039.............A 2
Hérault 706,499........E 6
Ille-et-Vilaine
749,764..............C 3
Indre 243,191.........D 4
Indre-et-Loire
506,097..............D 4
Isère 936,771.........F 5
Jura 242,925..........F 4
Landes 297,424........C 5

Loire 739,521..........F 5
Loire-Atlantique
995,498..............C 4
Loiret 535,669.........E 4
Loir-et-Cher 296,220....D 4
Lot 154,533..........D 5
Lot-et-Garonne
298,522..............D 5
Lozère 74,294.........E 5
Maine-et-Loire
675,321..............C 4
Manche 465,948........C 3
Marne 543,627.........F 3
Mayenne 271,784.......C 3
Meurthe-et-Moselle
716,846..............G 3
Meuse 200,101.........F 3
Morbihan 590,889.......B 4
Moselle 1,007,189......G 3
Nièvre 239,635.........E 4
Nord 2,520,526........E 2
Oise 661,781..........E 3
Orne 295,472..........C 3
Paris 2,188,918........B 2
Pas-de-Calais
1,412,413.............E 2
Puy-de-Dôme
594,365..............E 5
Pyrénées-Atlantiques
555,696..............C 6
Pyrénées-Orientales
334,557..............E 6
Rhône 1,445,208.......F 5
Saône-et-Loire
571,852..............F 4
Sarthe 504,768........D 3
Savoie 323,675........G 5
Seine-et-Marne
887,101..............E 3
Seine-Maritime
1,324,301............D 3
Seine-Saint-Denis
1,324,301............C 1
Somme 544,570.........E 3
Tarn 339,345..........E 6
Tarn-et-Garonne
190,485..............D 5
Val-de-Marne
1,193,655............C 1
Val-d'Oise 920,598.....E 3
Var 708,331..........G 6
Vaucluse 427,343......F 6
Vendée 483,027........C 4
Vienne 371,428........D 4
Vosges 395,769........G 3
Yonne 311,019.........E 4
Yvelines 1,196,111.....D 3

CITIES and TOWNS

Aigues-Mortes 4,106...F 6
Aix-en-Provence
100,221..............F 6
Aix-les-Bains 22,331...G 5
Ajaccio 48,324........B 7
Alençon 30,952........D 3
Amboise 10,823........D 4
Amiens 130,302........E 3
Angers 135,293........C 4
Angoulême 45,495......D 5
Annecy 49,753.........G 5
Antibes 62,427........G 6
Argenteuil 94,826.....A 1

Arles 37,554..........F 6
Armentières 22,849....E 2
Arras 41,376..........E 2
Asnières-sur-Seine
71,058...............A 1
Aubervilliers 67,684...B 1
Aubusson 5,326........E 4
Aulnay-sous-Bois
75,543...............B 1
Aurignac 772..........D 6
Avignon 75,178........F 6
Ax-les-Thermes
1,283................D 6
Bagnolet 32,556.......B 2
Barbizon 478..........E 3
Barcelonnette 2,674...G 5
Barfleur 617..........C 3
Bastia 43,502.........B 6
Bayeux 14,568.........C 3
Bayonne 40,088........C 6
Beaucaire 10,622......F 6
Beaune 19,110.........F 4
Beauvais 51,542.......E 3
Belfort 51,034........G 4
Bergerac 24,604.......D 5
Besançon 112,023......G 4
Bessèges 4,352........F 5
Béziers 74,114........E 6
Biarritz 26,579.......C 6
Blois 46,925..........D 4
Bobigny 42,630........B 1
Bonifacio 1,727.......B 7
Bordeaux 201,965......C 5
Boulogne-Billancourt
102,582..............A 2
Boulogne-sur-Mer
47,482...............D 2
Bourg-en-Bresse
37,582...............F 4
Bourges 74,622........E 4
Brest 154,110.........A 3
Brignoles 8,529.......G 6
Brive-la-Gaillarde
50,898...............D 5
Bruay-en-Artois
22,502...............E 2
Caen 112,332..........C 3
Calais 76,206.........D 2
Caluire-et-Cuire
41,864...............F 5
Cambrai 35,070........E 2
Cannes 71,888.........G 6
Carcassonne
38,379...............E 6
Castres 39,216........E 6
Chalons-sur-Marne
49,941...............F 3

AREA 210,038 sq. mi. (543,998 sq. km.)
POPULATION 56,160,000
CAPITAL Paris
LARGEST CITY Paris
HIGHEST POINT Mont Blanc 15,771 ft.
(4,807 m.)
MONETARY UNIT franc
MAJOR LANGUAGE French
MAJOR RELIGION Roman Catholicism

Topography

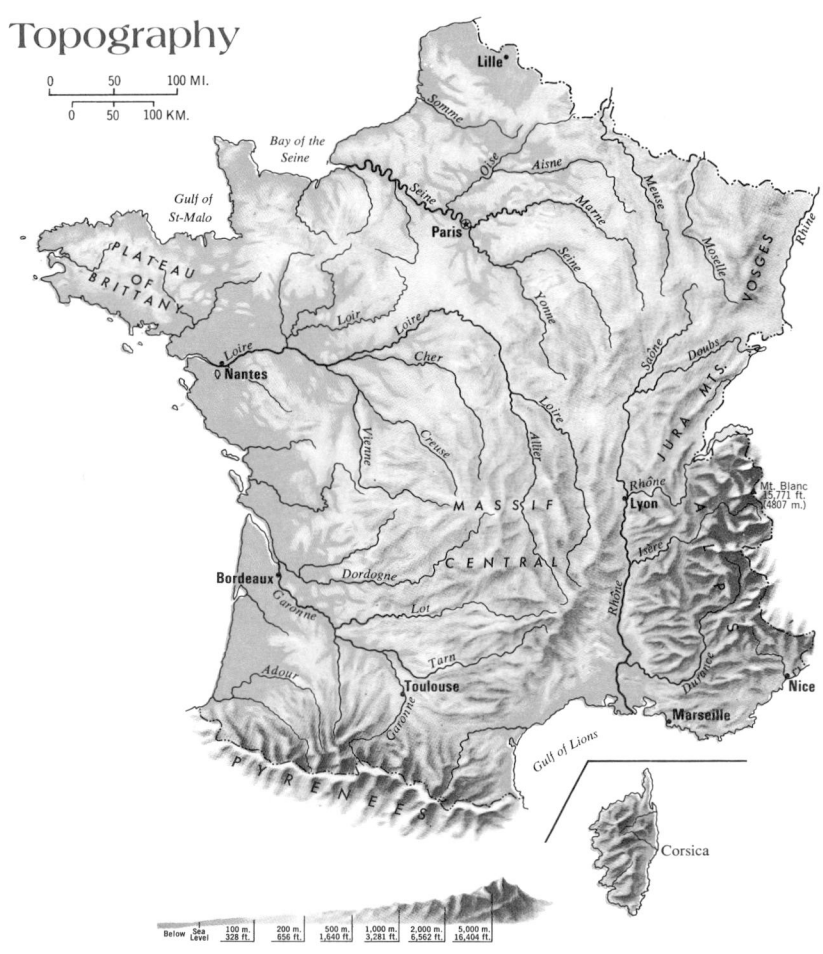

0   50   100 MI.
0   50   100 KM.

Below Sea Level | 100 m. 328 ft. | 200 m. 656 ft. | 500 m. 1,640 ft. | 1,000 m. 3,281 ft. | 2,000 m. 6,562 ft. | 5,000 m. 16,404 ft.

Historic Provinces

A resident of the city of Caen thinks of himself as a Norman rather than as a citizen of the modern department of Calvados. In spite of the passing of nearly two centuries, the historic provinces which existed before 1790 command the local patriotism of most Frenchmen.

Chalon-sur-Saône
53,893..............F 4
Chambéry 49,465.......F 5
Chambord 159..........D 4
Chamonix-Mont-Blanc
7,406................G 5
Champigny-sur-Marne
76,039...............C 2
Chantilly 10,065......E 3
Charleville-Mézières
7,814................F 3
Chartres 36,706.......D 3
Châteaudun 15,905.....D 3
Châteauneuf-sur-Loire
5,630................E 4
Châteauroux 51,744....D 4
Château-Thierry
14,427...............E 3
Chatou 28,435.........A 1
Cherbourg 28,324......C 3
Chinon 6,030..........D 4
Choisy-le-Roi 35,443...B 2
Cholet 51,620.........C 4
Clamart 48,210........A 2
Clermont-Ferrand
145,901..............E 5
Clichy 46,830.........B 1
Cluny 4,133...........F 4
Cognac 20,247.........D 5
Colmar 61,560.........G 3
Colombes 78,485.......A 1
Compiègne 39,909......E 3
Courbevoie 59,821.....A 1
Creil 34,332..........E 3
Créteil 71,559........B 2
Deauville 4,682.......C 3
Dieppe 35,659.........D 3
Digne 12,540..........G 5
Dijon 139,188.........F 4
Dinard 9,562..........B 3
Domrémy-la-Pucelle
162..................F 3
Douai 46,830..........E 2
Drancy 60,122.........B 1
Dunkirk 71,756........E 2

Ernée 5,253...........C 3
Évreux 45,215.........D 3
Falaise 8,424.........C 3
Fécamp 21,212.........D 3
Foix 9,212............D 6
Fontainebleau
14,687...............E 3
Fontenay-sous-Bois
52,397...............C 2
Gex 4,776............G 4
Grasse 24,257.........G 6
Grenoble 156,437......F 5
Guise 6,179...........E 3
Harfleur 9,470........D 3
Hazebrouck 19,266.....E 2
Hendaye 10,492........C 6
Héricourt 9,239.......G 4
Honfleur 8,125........D 3
Issy-les-Moulineaux
45,702...............A 2
Istres 21,286.........F 6
Ivry-sur-Seine
55,682...............B 2
La Baule-Escoublac
13,151...............B 4
La Courneuve
33,525...............B 1
Langres 9,718.........F 4
Lapalisse 3,173.......E 4
La Rochelle 74,728....C 4
La Roche-sur-Yon
42,026...............C 4
Laval 53,582..........C 3
Le Bourget 11,020.....B 1
Le Creusot 32,013.....F 4
Le Havre 198,700......C 3
Le Mans 145,976.......C 3
Le Puy 22,806.........F 5
Le Tréport 6,330......D 2
Levallois-Perret
53,485...............B 1
Lille 167,791.........E 2
Limoges 137,809.......D 5
Lisieux 24,454........D 3
Lorient 62,207........B 4

Lourdes 17,252........C 6
Lunéville 21,200......G 3
Lyon 410,455..........F 5
Mâcon 36,517..........F 4
Maisons-Alfort
51,041...............B 2
Maisons-Laffitte
22,565...............A 1
Mantes-la-Jolie
43,551...............D 3
Marmande 14,264.......C 5
Marseille 868,435.....F 6
Mayenne 12,156........C 3
Meaux 44,386..........E 3
Melun 34,379..........E 3
Mende 10,520..........E 5
Menton 22,234.........G 6
Metz 113,236..........G 3
Meudon 29,356.........A 2
Montauban 36,122......D 5
Montbéliard 31,174....G 4
Montceau-les-Mines
26,877...............F 4
Mont-de-Marsan
25,896...............C 6
Mont-Dore 2,091.......E 5
Montfort 4,029........C 3
Montluçon 49,737......E 4
Montmédy 1,880........F 3
Montpellier 190,423...E 6
Montreuil 96,441......B 2
Mont-Saint-Michel
65...................C 3
Mulhouse 111,742......G 4
Nancy 95,654..........G 3
Nanterre 88,567.......A 1
Nantes 237,789........C 4
Narbonne 38,222.......E 6
Nemours 12,413........E 3
Neufchâtel-en-Bray
5,452................D 3
Neuilly-sur-Seine
64,093...............A 1
Nice 331,165..........G 6

Nîmes 120,515.........F 6
Niort 56,256..........C 4
Nogent-le-Rotrou
11,963...............D 3
Noisy-le-Sec 36,821...B 1
Nontron 3,407.........D 5
Noyon 13,949..........E 3
Nyons 5,219...........F 5
Orléans 81,615........D 3
Orly 23,729...........B 2
Oyonnax 22,516........F 4
Paris (cap.)
2,165,892............B 2
Paris *10,073,059.....B 2
Pau 82,186............C 6
Périgueux 32,632......D 5
Perpignan 107,812.....E 6
Pessac 49,019.........C 5
Poitiers 76,793.......D 4
Pontoise 27,885.......E 3
Port-Vendres 4,871....E 6
Privas 9,253..........F 5
Quimper 52,335........A 4
Rambouillet 21,136....D 3
Redon 9,071...........C 4
Reims 176,419.........E 3
Rennes 190,861.......C 3
Roanne 48,574.........E 4
Rochefort 25,392......C 4
Roubaix 101,488.......E 2
Rouen 100,696.........D 3
Rueil-Malmaison
63,310...............A 2
Saint-Brieuc 48,259...B 3
Saint-Cloud 28,561....A 2
Saint-Denis 90,686....B 1
Saint-Dizier 34,074...F 3
Sainte-Mère-Eglise
1,205................C 3
Saint-Étienne
193,938..............F 5
Saint-Germain-en-Laye
36,585...............D 3
Saint-Jean-d'Angély
8,268................C 4

(continued on following page)

Monaco

CITIES and TOWNS

Wine Regions

Climate, soil and variety of grape planted determine the quality of wine. Long, hot and fairly dry summers with cool, humid nights constitute an ideal climate. The nature of the soil is such a determining influence that identical grapes planted in Bordeaux, Burgundy and Champagne, will yield wines of widely different types.

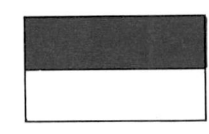

MONACO

AREA 368 acres (149 hectares)
POPULATION 27,063

Agriculture, Industry and Resources

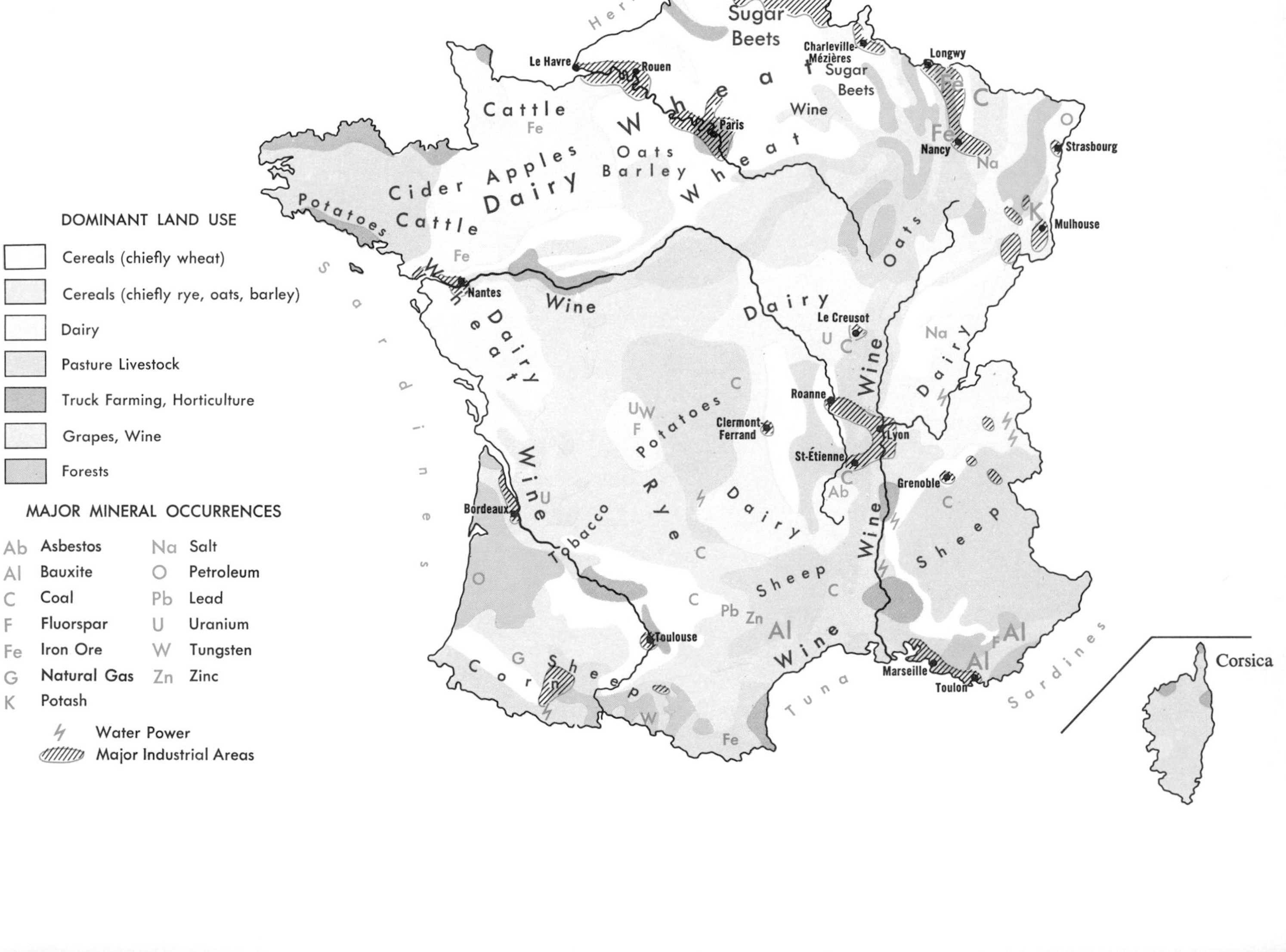

DOMINANT LAND USE

- Cereals (chiefly wheat)
- Cereals (chiefly rye, oats, barley)
- Dairy
- Pasture Livestock
- Truck Farming, Horticulture
- Grapes, Wine
- Forests

MAJOR MINERAL OCCURRENCES

Ab	Asbestos	Na	Salt
Al	Bauxite	O	Petroleum
C	Coal	Pb	Lead
F	Fluorspar	U	Uranium
Fe	Iron Ore	W	Tungsten
G	Natural Gas	Zn	Zinc
K	Potash		

⚡ Water Power
▨ Major Industrial Areas

ANDORRA

SPAIN

PORTUGAL

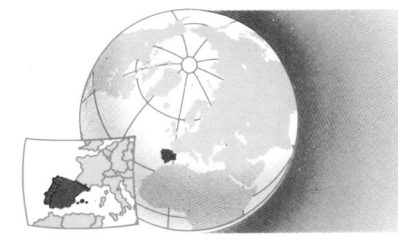

SPAIN

REGIONS

Andalusia 6,440,985..............D4
Aragón 1,196,952..................F2
Asturias 1,129,556.................C1
Balearic Islands 655,909.........H3
Basque Country 2,141,809......E1
Canary Islands 1,367,646.......F4
Cantabria 513,115..................D1
Castile and León 2,583,137....D2
Castile-La Mancha 1,648,584..E3
Catalonia 5,956,414...............G2
Extremadura 1,064,968..........C3
Galicia 2,811,912...................B1
La Rioja 254,349....................E1
Madrid 4,686,895...................E2
Murcia 955,487......................F4
Navarre 509,002....................F1
Valencia 3,646,778................F3

PROVINCES

Álava 257,850.......................E1
Albacete 339,373..................E3
Alicante 1,149,181................E3
Almería 410,831....................E4
Ávila 183,586........................D2
Badajoz 643,519...................C3
Baleares 655,509..................H3
Barcelona 4,623,204.............G2
Burgos 363,523.....................E1
Cáceres 421,449...................C3
Cádiz 988,388........................D4
Castellón 431,893.................G2
Ciudad Real 475,129.............D3
Córdoba 720,823...................D4
Cuenca 215,975.....................E3
Girona (Gerona) 467,000.......H1
Granada 758,618...................E4
Guadalajara 143,473.............E2
Guipúzcoa 694,681................E1
Huelva 418,584......................C4
Huesca 214,907....................F1
Jaén 639,821.........................E4
La Coruña 1,093,121.............B1
Las Palmas 708,762.............F4
Lérida 513,607.......................G1
Leida (Lérida) 353,160...........G2
Logroño 254,349...................E1
Lugo 405,365.........................C1
Madrid 4,686,895..................E2
Málaga 1,025,609.................D4
Murcia 955,487......................F4
Navarra 509,002....................F1
Orense 430,159.....................C1
Oviedo 1,129,556..................C1
Palencia 188,479...................D1
Pontevedra 883,267..............B1
Salamanca 364,305..............C2
Santa Cruz de Tenerife
  658,884...............................B5
Santander 513,115.................D1
Segovia 149,361....................D2
Sevilla 1,478.311...................D4
Soria 100,719........................E2
Tarragona 513,050................G2
Teruel 153,457.......................F2
Toledo 474,634......................D3
Valencia 2,065,704...............F3
Valladolid 481,786.................D2
Vizcaya 1,189,278.................E1
Zamora 227,771.....................D2
Zaragoza 828,588.................F2

CITIES and TOWNS

Adra 10,851..........................E4
Aguilar 12,893.......................D4
Aguilas 15,525......................F4
Albacete 82,607....................F3
Alburquerque 7,530...............C3
Alcalá de Guadaira 28,781.....D4
Alcalá de Henares 59,783......E2
Alcalá de los Gazules 5,262...D4
Alcalá la Real 9,849..............E4
Alcanar 5,961........................G2
Alcantarilla 19,895................F4
Alcaudete 8,557....................E4
Alcázar de San Juan 24,620...E3
Alcira 30,493.........................F3
Alcora 6,711..........................F2
Alcoy 61,371..........................F3
Alfaro 8,766...........................F1
Algeciras 74.754....................D4
Algemesi 21.158....................F3
Alhama de Granada 6,148......E4
Alhama de Murcia 9,274.........F4
Alicante 177,918....................F3
Almadén 10,713.....................D3
Almagro 9,056.......................E3
Almansa 16,965.....................F3
Almendralejo 21,929..............C3
Almería 104,008.....................E4
Almodóvar del Campo 7,310...D3
Almonte del Río 9,960............C4
Almuñécar 7,812....................E4
Alora 8,209............................D4
Altea 7,262............................G3
Amposta 11,767.....................F2
Andorra 6,485........................F2
Andújar 25,962.......................D3
Antequera 23,039...................D4
Aracena 5,390.......................C4
Aranda de Duero 18,183........E2
Aranjuez 28,559.....................E2
Archena 7,118.......................F3
Archidona 6,084....................D4
Arcos de la Frontera 16,217...D4
Arenys de Mar 8,325..............H2
Arganda 11,876.....................G4
Arnedo 9,809.........................E1
Arrecife 21,310......................G4
Arroyo de la Luz 8,130...........C3
Arucas 9,095.........................G4
Aspe 13,229..........................F3

Astorga 11.794......................C1
Ávila de los Caballeros
  30,958.................................D2
Avilés 67,136.........................C1
Ayamonte 9,897.....................C4
Azpeitia 7,635........................E1
Azuaga 10,719.......................D3
Badajoz 80.793......................C3
Badalona 162,888..................H2
Baena 16,496.........................D4
Baeza 12,607.........................E4
Bailén 13,207.........................E3
Balaguer 11,676.....................G2
Banyoles 9.807......................H1
Baracaldo 108,757.................E1
Barbastro 13,243...................F1
Barcarrota 5,012....................C3
Barcelona 1,741,144..............J1
Barcelona‡ 2,000,000...........H2
Baza 14,290...........................E4
Béjar 16,8C4..........................D2
Benavente 11,779..................D2
Benicarló 12,831....................G2
Berga 11,163..........................G1
Berja 7,081.............................E4
Bermeo 16,714.......................E1
Betanzos 7,283......................B1
Bilbao 393,179........................E1
Bilbao‡ 450,000......................E1
Binéfar 6,821.........................G2

Blanes 15,810........................H2
Bujalance 8,236.....................D4
Bullas 8,131...........................F3
Burgos 118,366......................E1
Burriana 21,298......................F3
Cabeza del Buey 8,704...........D4
Cabra 16,177.........................D4
Cáceres 53,108......................C3
Cádiz 135,743........................C4
Calahorra 16,315....................E1
Calasparra 7,238....................F3
Calatayud 16,524....................F2
Calella 9,696..........................H2
Callosa de Ensarriá 5,701......G3
Calzada de Calatrava 5,751....D3
Campanario 7,722...................D3
Campillos 7,014......................D4
Campo de Criptana 12,604.....E3
Candás 5,517.........................D1
Candeleda 5,153....................D2
Cangas de Narcea 4,826........C1
Caniles 5,099.........................E4
Caravaca de Cruz 10,411.......F3
Carballo 5,542........................B1
Carcagente 18,223.................F3
Carmona 22,832.....................D4
Cartagena 52,312...................F4
Caspe 8,766...........................G2
Castellón de la Plana 79,773..G2
Castro del Río 10,087............D4

Castro-Urdiales 8,369............E1
Castuera 8,060.......................D3
Caudete 7,332........................F3
Cazalla de la Sierra 5,382......D4
Cazorla 6,938.........................E4
Cehegín 9,661........................F3
Cervera 5,693.........................G2
Ceuta 65,264..........................D5
Chiclana de la Frontera
  22,986.................................C4
Cieza 22,929..........................F3
Ciudad Real 39,931...............D3
Ciudad-Rodrigo 11,694..........C2
Cocentaina 8,375...................F3
Coín 14,190............................D4
Colmenar Viejo 12,886...........E2
Constantina 10,227................D4
Consuegra 10,026..................E3
Córdoba 216,049....................D4
Corella 5,850.........................F1
Coria 8,083............................C3
Coria del Río 18,085...............C4
Corral de Almaguer 8,006.......E3
Crevillente 15,749..................F3
Cuéllar 6,118..........................D2
Cuenca 33,980.......................E2
Cullera 15,128........................F3
Denia 14,514..........................G3
Don Benito 21,351..................C3

Dos Hermanas 36,921...........D4
Durango 20,403......................E1
Écija 27,295...........................D4
Eibar 36,729...........................E1
Ejea de los Caballeros 9,766..F1
El Arahal 14,703.....................D4
Elche 101,271.........................F3
Elda 41,404............................F3
El Ferrol 75,464......................B1
Elizondo 2,516........................F1
El Puerto de Santa María
  36,451.................................D4
El Vendrell 7,951....................G2
Espejo 5,925..........................D4
Estella 10,371.........................E1
Estepa 9,376..........................D4
Estepona 18,560.....................D4
Felanitx 9,100.........................H3
Figueres 22,087......................H1
Fraga 9,665............................G2
Fregenal de la Sierra 6,826....C3
Fuengirola 20,597..................D4
Fuente de Cantos 5,967.........C3
Gandía 30,702........................F3
Gerona (Girona) 37,095..........H1
Getafe 68,680.........................G4
Gijón 159,806.........................D1
Girona 37,095........................H2
Granada 185,799....................E4
Granollers 30,066...................H2

Guadalajara 30,924................E2
Guadix 15,311.........................E4
Guareña 7,706........................C3
Guernica y Luno 12,046.........E1
Haro 8,393.............................E1
Hellín 15,934..........................F3
Herencia 8,212.......................E3
Hinojosa del Duque 9,873......D3
Hospitalet 241,978..................H1
Huelma 5,260.........................E4
Huelva 96,689........................C4
Huercal-Overa 5,158.............F4
Huesca 33,076.......................F1
Huéscar 6,384........................E4
Ibiza 16,943...........................G3
Igualada 27,941......................G2
Inca 16,930............................H3
Irún 38,014.............................F1
Iscar 5,192.............................D2
Isla Cristina 11.402.................C4
Jaca 9,936.............................F1
Jaén 71,145...........................E4
Jaraíz de la Vera 6,37G...........D2
Játiva 20,934..........................F3
Jávea 8,223...........................G3
Jerez de la Frontera 112,411...C4
Jerez de los Caballeros 8,607..C3
Jijona 8,117............................F3
Jódar 11,973...........................E4
Jumilla 16,407........................F3
La Bañeza 8,480....................D1
La Bisbal 6,374.......................H2
La Carolina 13,138.................E3
La Coruña 184,372.................B1
La Línea de la Concepción
  51,021.................................D4
La Orotava 8,246....................F5
La Palma del Condado 9,256..C4
La Puebla 9,923......................H3
La Puebla de Montalbán
  6,629..................................D3
La Rambla 6,525....................D4
Laredo 9,114..........................E1
La Roda 11,460......................E3
La Seu d'Urgell 6,604.............G1
La Solana 13,894...................E3
Las Palmas de Gran Canaria
  260,368...............................G5
Las Pedroñeras 5,846............E3
La Unión 9,998.......................F4
Lebrija 15,681.........................C4
Leganés 57,537......................G4
León 99,702............................D1
Lérida (Lleida) 73,148.............G2
Linares 45,330........................E3
Liria 11,323.............................F3
Lleida 73,148..........................G2
Llerena 5,728.........................C3

Llodio 15,587..........................E1
Lluchmayor 9,630...................H3
Logroño 83,117.......................E1
Loja 11,549............................D4
Lora del Río 15,741................D4
Lorca 25,208..........................F4
Los Santos de Maimona
  7,899..................................C3
Los Yébenes 5,477................D3
Lucena 21,527........................D4
Lugo 53,504...........................C1
Madrid (cap.) 3,146,071.........G4
Madrid‡ 3,500,000.................F4
Madridejos 9,948....................E3
Mahón 17,802.........................J3
Málaga 334,988......................D4
Malpartida de Cáceres 5,054..C3
Manacor 20,266......................H3
Mancha Real 7,547.................E4
Manlleu 13,169.......................H1
Manresa 52,355......................G2
Manzanares 15,024................E3
Marbella 19,648......................D4
Marchena 16,227....................D4
Marín 10,948..........................B1
Martos 16,395.........................E4
Mataró 73,129........................H2
Medina del Campo 16,345......D2
Medina-Sidonia 7,523............D4
Mérida 36,916........................C3
Miajadas 8,042.......................C3
Mieres 22,790........................C1
Miranda de Ebro 29,355.........E1
Moguer 7,629.........................C4
Mollerusa 6,685......................G2
Monesterio 5,923...................C3
Monforte 14,002.....................C1
Monóvar 9,071.......................F3
Montehermoso 5,952..............C2
Montijo 11,931........................C3
Montilla 18,670.......................D4
Montoro 9,295........................D3
Monzón 14,089.......................G2
Mora 10,523...........................E3
Moratalla 5,101.......................F3
Morón de la Frontera 25,662...D4
Mota del Cuervo 5,130............E3
Motril 25,121...........................E4
Mula 9,168.............................F3
Munera 5,003.........................E3
Murcia 102,242.......................F4
Navalmoral de la Mata 9,650...D3
Nerja 7,413.............................E4
Nerva 10,830..........................C4
Novelda 16,867......................F3
Nules 9,027............................F3
Ocaña 5,603..........................E3

(continued on following page)

SPAIN

AREA 194,881 sq. mi. (504,742 sq. km.)
POPULATION 39,328,000
CAPITAL Madrid
LARGEST CITY Madrid
HIGHEST POINT Pico de Teide 12,172 ft. (3,710 m.)
(Canary Is.); Mulhacén 11,411 ft. (3,478 m.)
(mainland)
MONETARY UNIT peseta
MAJOR LANGUAGES Spanish, Catalan, Basque,
Galician, Valencian
MAJOR RELIGION Roman Catholicism

ANDORRA

AREA 188 sq. mi. (487 sq. km.)
POPULATION 50,000
CAPITAL Andorra la Vella
MONETARY UNITS French franc, Spanish peseta
MAJOR LANGUAGE Catalan
MAJOR RELIGION Roman Catholicism

PORTUGAL

AREA 35,549 sq. mi. (92,072 sq. km.)
POPULATION 10,467,000
CAPITAL Lisbon
LARGEST CITY Lisbon
HIGHEST POINT Malhão da Estrela
6,532 ft. (1,991 m.)
MONETARY UNIT escudo
MAJOR LANGUAGE Portuguese
MAJOR RELIGION Roman Catholicism

GIBRALTAR

AREA 2.28 sq. mi. (5.91 sq. km.)
POPULATION 31,000
CAPITAL Gibraltar
MONETARY UNIT pound sterling
MAJOR LANGUAGES English, Spanish
MAJOR RELIGION Roman Catholicism

Agriculture, Industry and Resources

DOMINANT LAND USE

- Cereals (chiefly wheat)
- Livestock (chiefly sheep, goats)
- Mixed Cereals, Livestock
- Olives, Fruit
- Grapes, Fruit, Nuts, Mixed Cereals
- Forests
- Nonagricultural Land

MAJOR MINERAL OCCURRENCES

Ag	Silver	Na	Salt
C	Coal	O	Petroleum
Cu	Copper	Pb	Lead
Fe	Iron Ore	Py	Pyrites
G	Natural Gas	Sb	Antimony
Hg	Mercury	Sn	Tin
K	Potash	U	Uranium
Lg	Lignite	W	Tungsten
Mg	Magnesium	Zn	Zinc

⚡ Water Power
〰 Major Industrial Areas

(continued on following page)

Oliva 16,717	F3	
Oliva de la Frontera 8,560	C3	
Olivenza 7,616	C3	
Olot 18,062	H1	
Olvera 9,825	D4	
Onda 13,012	F3	
Onteniente 23,685	F3	
Orense 63,542	C1	
Orihuela 17,610	F3	
Osuna 17,384	D4	
Oviedo 130,021	D1	
Padul 6,377	E4	
Palafrugell 10,421	H2	
Palamós 7,679	H2	
Palencia 58,327	D2	
Palma 191,416	H3	
Palma del Río 15,075	D4	
Pamplona 142,686	E1	
Pego 8,861	F3	
Peñaranda de Bracamonte 6,094	D2	
Peñarroya-Pueblonuevo 15,649	D3	
Pinos-Puente 7,634	E4	
Plasencia 26,897	C3	
Pola de Lena 5,760	D1	
Pollensa 7,625	H3	
Ponferrada 22,838	C1	
Pontevedra 27,118	B1	
Porcuna 8,169	D4	
Portugalete 45,589	E1	
Posadas 7,245	D4	
Pozoblanco 13,280	D3	
Pozuelo de Alarcón 14,041	D4	
Priego de Córdoba 12,676	D4	
Puente-Genil 22,863	D4	
Puertollano 50,609	D3	
Puerto Real 13,993	C4	
Puigcerdá 4,418	G1	
Quesada 6,965	E4	
Quintana de la Serena 5,171	D3	
Quintanar de la Orden 7,764	E3	
Reinosa 10,863	D1	
Requena 9,836	F3	
Reus 47,240	G2	
Ripoll 9,283	H1	
Ronda 22,094	D4	
Roquetes 5,617	G2	
Roses 5,448	H1	
Rota 20,021	C4	
Rute 8,294	D4	
Sabadell 148,223	H2	
Sagunto 17,052	F3	
Salamanca 125,132	D2	
Sallent 7,118	H2	
Salobreña 5,961	E4	
Salt 5,572	H2	
San Clemente 6,016	E3	
San Fernando 59,309	C4	
San Lorenzo de El Escorial 8,098	E2	
San Roque 8,224	D4	
San Sebastián 159,557	E1	
Santa Cruz de la Palma 10,393	F4	
Santa Cruz de Mudela 6,354	E3	
Santa Cruz de Tenerife 74,910	F4	
Santa Eugenia de Ribeira 5,946	B1	
Santa Fé 8,990	D4	
Santander 130,019	E1	
Santiago 51,620	B1	
Santo Domingo de la Calzada 5,638	E1	
Santoña 9,546	E1	
San Vicente de Alcántara 7,006	C3	
Sanlúcar de Barrameda 29,483	C4	
Saragossa 449,319	F2	
Saragossa‡ 500,000	F2	
Segorbe 6,962	F3	
Segovia 41,880	D2	
Seville 511,447	D4	
Seville‡ 560,000	D4	
Sitges 8,906	G2	
Socuéllamos 12,610	E3	
Sóller 6,470	H3	
Solsona 5,346	G1	
Sonseca 6,594	E3	
Sotrondio 5,914	D1	
Sueca 20,019	F3	
Tabernes de Valldigna 13,962	F3	
Tafalla 8,858	F1	
Talavera de la Reina 39,889	D2	
Tarancón 8,238	E3	
Tarazona 11,067	F2	
Tarazona de la Mancha 5,952	F3	
Tarifa 9,201	D4	
Tarragona 53,548	G2	
Tárrega 9,036	G2	
Tauste 6,832	F2	
Telde 13,257	F5	
Terrassa 134,481	H1	
Teruel 20,614	F2	
Tobarra 5,887	F3	
Toledo 43,905	D3	
Tolosa 15,164	F1	
Tomelloso 26,041	E3	
Tordesillas 5,815	D2	
Toro 8,455	D2	
Torredonjimeno 12,507	D4	
Torrejón de Ardoz 21,081	G4	
Torrelavega 19,933	D1	
Torremolinos 20,484	D4	
Torrente 38,397	F3	
Torrevieja 9,431	F4	
Torrijos 6,362	D3	
Torrox 5,583	D4	
Tortosa 20,030	G2	
Totana 12,714	F4	
Trigueros 6,280	C4	
Trujillo 9,274	D3	
Tudela 20,942	F1	
Úbeda 28,306	E3	
Ubrique 13,166	D4	
Utiel 9,168	F3	
Utrera 28,287	D4	
Valdemoro 6,263	E2	
Valdepeñas 24,018	E3	
Valencia 626,675	F3	
Valencia‡ 700,000	F3	
Valencia de Alcántara 5,963	C3	
Valladolid 227,511	D2	
Vall de Uxó 23,976	F3	
Vallecas	G4	
Valls 14,189	G2	
Valverde del Camino 10,566	C4	
Vejer de la Frontera 6,184	C4	
Vélez-Málaga 20,794	D4	
Vergara 11,541	E1	
Vic 23,449	H2	
Vigo 114,526	B1	
Vilafranca del Penedés 16,875	G2	
Vilanova i la Geltrú 35,714	G2	
Villacañas 9,883	E3	
Villacarrillo 9,452	E3	
Villafranca de los Barros 12,610	C3	
Villagarcía 6,601	B1	
Villajoyosa 12,573	F3	
Villanueva de Córdoba 11,270	D3	
Villanueva del Arzobispo 8,076	E3	
Villanueva de la Serena 16,687	D3	
Villanueva de los Infantes 8,154	E3	
Villarreal de los Infantes 29,482	G3	
Villarrobledo 19,698	E3	
Villaverde	G4	
Villena 33,483	F3	
Vinaroz 13,727	G2	
Vitoria 124,791	E1	
Yecla 19,352	F3	
Zafra 11,583	C3	
Zalamea la Serena 6,017	D3	
Zamora 48,791	D2	
Zaragoza (Saragossa) 449,319	F2	

OTHER FEATURES

Adaja (riv.)	D2
Agueda (riv.)	C2
Alagón (riv.)	C2
Alarcón (res.)	E3
Albán (bay)	H3
Alborán (isl.)	E5
Alcántara (res.)	C3
Alcudia (bay)	H3
Almendra (res.)	C2
Almería (gulf)	E4
Almanzora (riv.)	F4
Aneto (peak)	G1
Aragón (riv.)	E1
Ardila (riv.)	C3
Arga (riv.)	E1
Arosa, Ría de (est.)	B1
Balearic (Baleares) (isls.)	H3
Biscay (bay)	D1
Cabrera (isl.)	H3
Cádiz (gulf)	C4
Calaburras (pt.)	D4
Canary (isls.)	F4
Cantabrian (range)	C1
Cijara (res.)	D3
Cinca (riv.)	G2
Columbretes (isls.)	G3
Cope (cape)	F4
Costa Brava (reg.)	H2
Costa de Sola (Costa del Sol) (reg.)	D4
Costa Verde (reg.)	C1
Cuenca, Sierra de (range)	F3
Demanda, Sierra de la (range)	E1
Duero (Douro) (riv.)	C2
Dragonera (isl.)	H3
Duratón (riv.)	E2
Ebro (riv.)	G2
Eresma (riv.)	D2
Esla (riv.)	D2
Estaca de Bares (pt.)	C1
Estats (peak)	G1
Finisterre (cape)	B1
Formentera (isl.)	G3
Formentor (cape)	H3
Fuerteventura (isl.)	G5
Gata (cape)	F4
Gata, Sierra de (mts.)	C2
Genil (riv.)	D4
Gibraltar (str.)	D5
Gomera (isl.)	F5
Graciosa (isl.)	G4
Gran Canaria (isl.)	F5
Gredos, Sierra de (range)	D2
Guadalimar (riv.)	E3
Guadalquivir (riv.)	D4
Guadarrama, Sierra de (range)	E2
Guadiana (riv.)	C4
Gúdar, Sierra de (range)	F2
Henares (riv.)	E2
Hierro (isl.)	F5
Huelva (riv.)	C4
Ibiza (isl.)	G3
Jalón (riv.)	E2
Jarama (riv.)	E2
Júcar (riv.)	F3
Lanzarote (isl.)	G4
La Palma (isl.)	F4
Llobregat (riv.)	G2
Mallorca (Majorca) (isl.)	H3
Mar Menor (lag.)	F4
Menorca (Minorca) (isl.)	H3
Mequinenza (res.)	F2
Miño (riv.)	B1
Moncayo (mt.)	E2
Moncayo, Sierra de (range)	F2
Morena, Sierra (range)	D3
Mulhacén (mt.)	E4
Nao (cape)	G3
Navia (riv.)	C1
Nevada, Sierra (mts.)	C4
Odiel (riv.)	C4
Órbigo (riv.)	D1
Ortegal (cape)	B1
Palma (bay)	H3
Palos (cape)	F4
Peñalara (mt.)	E2
Peñas (cape)	D1
Perdido (mt.)	F1
Prior (cape)	B1
Pyrenees (range)	F1
Ricobayo (res.)	D2
Rosas (gulf)	H1
Sacratif (gulf)	E4
Salinas (cape)	H3
San Jorge (gulf)	G2
San Pedro, Sierra de (range)	C3
Segre (riv.)	G1
Segura (riv.)	E3
Sil (riv.)	C1
Tagomago (isl.)	G3
Tagus (riv.)	D3
Tajo (Tagus) (riv.)	D3
Teide, Pico de (peak)	F5
Teleno (mt.)	C1
Tenerife (isl.)	B4
Ter (riv.)	H1
Toledo (mts.)	D3
Tortosa (cape)	G2
Trafalgar (cape)	C4
Turia (riv.)	F3
Ulla (riv.)	B1
Valdecañas (res.)	D3
Valencia (gulf)	G3

PORTUGAL

DISTRICTS

Aveiro 545,230	B2
Azores 275,900	B4
Beja 204,440	C3
Braga 609,415	B2
Bragança 180,395	C2
Castelo Branco 254,355	C3
Coimbra 399,380	B2
Évora 178,475	C3
Faro 268,040	B4
Guarda 210,720	C2
Leiria 376,940	B3
Lisbon 1,568,020	A1
Madeira 262,800	A2
Oporto (Porto) 1,309,560	B2
Portalegre 145,545	C3
Porto 1,309,560	B2
Santarém 427,995	B3
Sétubal 469,555	B3
Viano do Castelo 250,510	B2
Vila Real 265,605	C2
Viseu 410,795	C2

CITIES and TOWNS

Abrantes 11,775	B3
Águeda 9,343	B2
Alcácer do Sal 13,187	B3
Almada 38,990	A1
Almeirim 8,780	B3
Alportel 7,632	C4
Amadora 65,870	A1
Amora 10,330	A1
Angra do Heroísmo 13,795	A4
Aveiro 19,905	B2

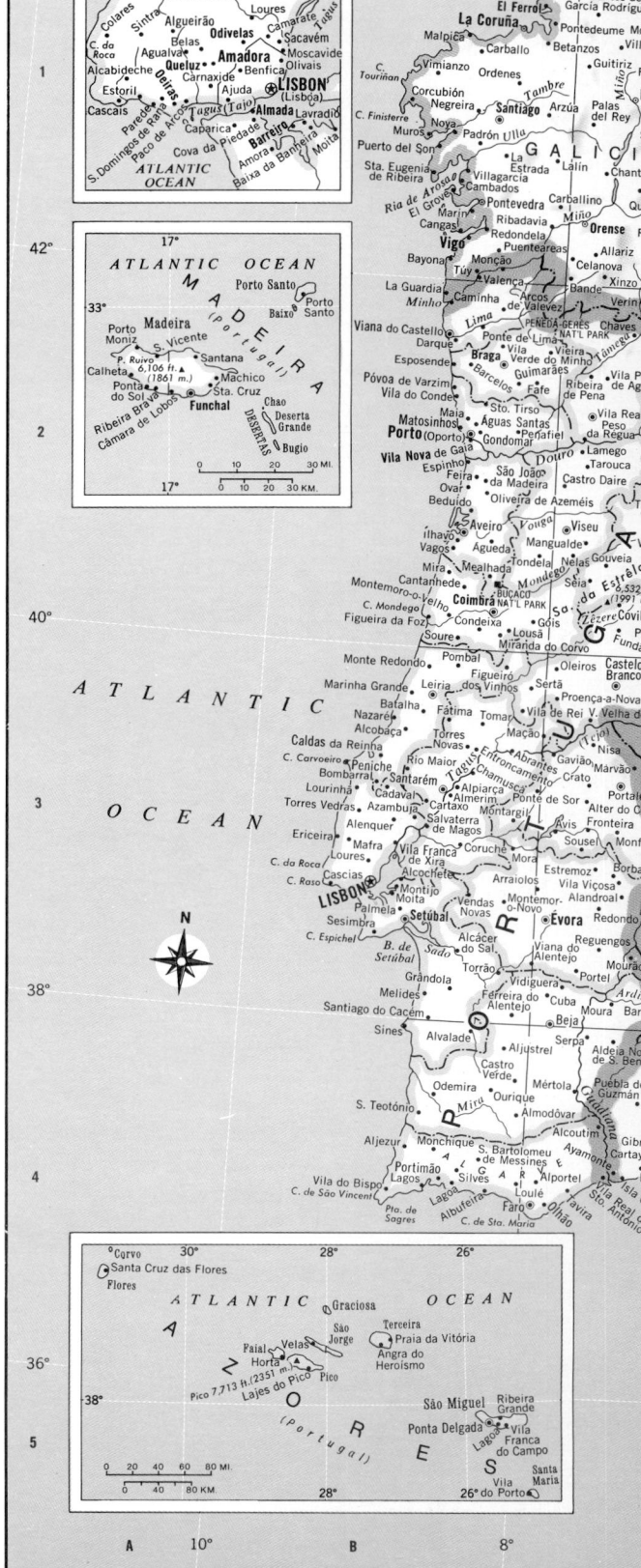

Topography

0 50 100 MI.

0 50 100 KM.

Below Sea Level	100 m. 328 ft.	200 m. 656 ft.	500 m. 1,640 ft.	1,000 m. 3,281 ft.	2,000 m. 6,562 ft.	5,000 m. 16,404 ft.

Baixa da Banheira 18,550 ......A1
Barreiro 53,690 ......A1
Beja 14,760 ......C3
Belas 12,001 ......A1
Benfica 39,459 ......A1
Braga 48,735 ......B2
Bragança 9,310 ......C2
Caldas da Rainha 13,070 ......A2
Câmara de Lobos 14,068 ......A2
Caparica 13,315 ......A1
Carnaxide 33,309 ......A1
Cascais 14,925 ......A1
Castelo Branco 18,740 ......C2
Chaves 11,465 ......C2
Coimbra 55,985 ......B2
Coruche 17,461 ......B3
Cova da Piedade 21,000 ......A1
Covilhã 26,530 ......C2
Elvas 10,305 ......C3
Espinho 11,745 ......B2
Estoril 15,740 ......A1

Évora 23,665 ......C3
Fafe 8,142 ......B2
Faro 20,470 ......B4
Figueira da Foz 10,485 ......B2
Funchal 38,340 ......A2
Gondomar 14,105 ......B2
Grândola 9,698 ......B3
Guarda 9,735 ......C2
Guimarães 24,280 ......B2
Ilhavo 11,083 ......B2
Lagos 10,359 ......B4
Lamego 10,350 ......C2
Lisbon (Lisboa) (cap.)
     769,410 ......A1
Lisbon‡ 1,100,000 ......A1
Loulé 12,777 ......B4
Machico 10,905 ......A2
Marinha Grande 18,548 ......B2
Matosinhos 22,505 ......B2
Mira 12,740 ......B2
Monchique 8,155 ......B4

Montemor-o-Novo 9,284 ......B3
Montijo 26,730 ......B3
Moscavide 21,765 ......A1
Moura 9,351 ......C3
Nazaré 8,553 ......B3
Odivelas 26,020 ......A1
Oeiras 14,880 ......A1
Olhão 11,155 ......C4
Olivais 55,138 ......A1
Oporto (Porto) 300,925 ......B2
Ovar 16,004 ......B2
Paço de Arcos 11,791 ......A1
Peniche 12,555 ......B3
Pombal 12,508 ......B3
Ponta Delgada 20,195 ......B5
Ponte de Sor 9,951 ......B3
Portalegre 10,970 ......C3
Portimão 10,300 ......B4
Porto 300,925 ......B2
Póvoa de Varzim 17,415 ......B2
Queluz 25,845 ......A1

Rio Maior 10,206 ......B3
Sacavém 12,625 ......A1
Santarém 16,850 ......B3
São Brás de Alportel (Alportel)
     7,632 ......C4
São João da Madeira 14,225 ......B2
Sesimbra 16,614 ......B3
Setúbal 49,670 ......B3
Silves 9,493 ......B4
Sintra 15,994 ......A1
Tavira 10,263 ......C4
Tomar 10,905 ......B3
Torres Novas 13,806 ......B3
Torres Vedras 14,833 ......B3
Vendas Novas 8,979 ......B3
Viana do Castelo 12,510 ......B2
Vila do Conde 16,485 ......B2
Vila do Porto 4,149 ......B5
Vila Franca de Xira 13,070 ......B3
Vila Nova de Foz Côa 2,439 ......C2
Vila Nova de Gaia 50,805 ......B2

Vila Real 10,050 ......C2
Vila Real de Santo António
     10,320 ......C4
Vila Velha de Ródão
     2,658 ......C3
Viseu 16,140 ......C2

OTHER FEATURES

Algarve (reg.) B4
Atlantic Ocean A3
Azores (isls.) B4
Baixo (cape) B2
Bugio (isl.) A1
Carvoeiro (cape) B3
Chao (isl.) A2
Corvo (isl.) A4
Deserta Grande (isl.) A2
Desertas (isls.) A2
Douro (riv.) B2
Espichel (cape) B3

Estrela, Serra da (mts.) C2
Faial (isl.) B4
Flores (isl.) A4
Graciosa (isl.) B4
Guadiana (riv.) C4
Lima (riv.) B2
Madeira (isl.) A2
Minho (riv.) B2
Mira (riv.) B4
Mondego (riv.) B2
Mondego (cape) B2
Pico (isl.) B4
Porto Santo (isl.) A2
Roca (cape) B3
Sado (riv.) B3
Santa Maria (cape) C4
Santa Maria (isl.) C5
São Jorge (isl.) B4
São Miguel (isl.) B5
São Vincent (cape) B4
Setúbal (bay) B3

Tagus (riv.) B3
Tâmega (riv.) C2
Terceira (isl.) B4

ANDORRA

CITIES and TOWNS

Andorra la Vella (cap.) 12,000 G1

GIBRALTAR

CITIES and TOWNS

Gibraltar 31,000 ......D4

OTHER FEATURES

Europa (pt.) D4

‡Population of metropolitan area

Italy

CONIC PROJECTION

SCALE OF MILES

SCALE OF KILOMETERS

Capitals of Countries _____ ☆
Regional Capitals _____ ⌖
Provincial Capitals _____ △
International Boundaries _____
Regional Boundaries _____

Scale 1:4,710,000

The regions are subdivided into provinces bearing the same names as their respective capitals, except:

PROVINCE	CAPITAL
MASSA-CARRARA	Massa
PESARO-URBINO	Pesaro

© Copyright HAMMOND INCORPORATED, Maplewood, N.J.

Vatican City

SCALE

Rome and Environs

VATICAN CITY

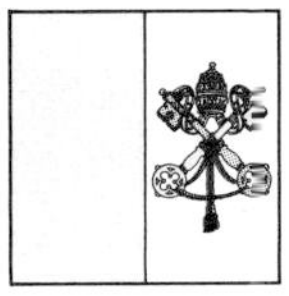

AREA 108.7 acres (44 hectares)
POPULATION 1,000

SAN MARINO

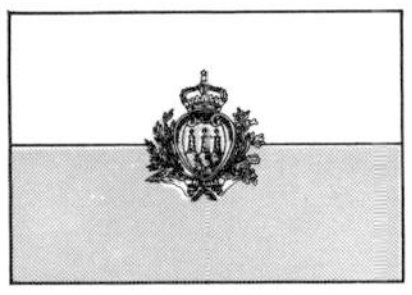

AREA 23.4 sq. mi. (60.6 sq. km.)
POPULATION 23,000

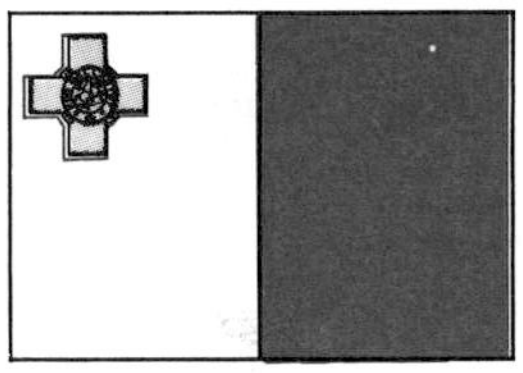

MALTA

AREA 122 sq. mi. (316 sq. km.)
POPULATION 353,000
CAPITAL Valletta
LARGEST CITY Sliema
HIGHEST POINT 787 ft. (240 m.)
MONETARY UNIT Maltese lira
MAJOR LANGUAGES Maltese, English
MAJOR RELIGION Roman Catholicism

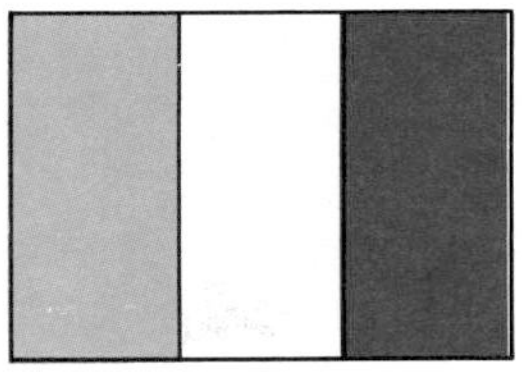

ITALY

AREA 116,303 sq. mi. (301,225 sq. km.)
POPULATION 57,574,000
CAPITAL Rome
LARGEST CITY Rome
HIGHEST POINT Dufourspitze (Mte. Rosa) 15,203 ft. (4,634 m.)
MONETARY UNIT lira
MAJOR LANGUAGE Italian
MAJOR RELIGION Roman Catholicism

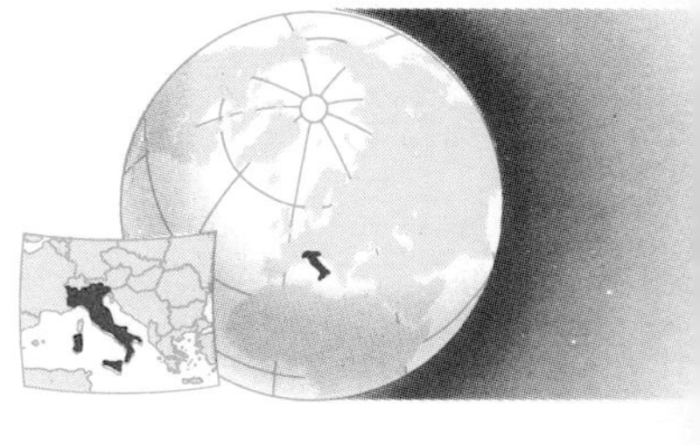

ITALY

REGIONS

Abruzzi 1,217,791 .... D3
Aosta 112,353 .... A2
Apulia (Puglia) 3,871,617 .... F4
Basilicata 610,186 .... F4
Calabria 2,061,182 .... F5
Campania 5,463,134 .... E4
Emilia-Romagna 3,957,513 .... C2
Friuli-Venezia Giulia 1,233,984 .... D1
Latium (Lazio) 5,001,684 .... D3
Liguria 1,807,893 .... B2
Lombardy 8,891,652 .... B2
Marche 1,412,404 .... D3
Molise 328,371 .... E4
Piedmont 4,479,031 .... A2
Sardinia 1,594,175 .... B4
Sicily 4,906,878 .... D6
Trentino-Alto Adige 873,413 .... C1
Tuscany 3,581,051 .... C3
Umbria 807,552 .... D3
Veneto 4,345,047 .... C2

PROVINCES

Agrigento 466,495 .... D6
Alessandria 466,102 .... B2
Ancona 433,417 .... D3
Arezzo 313,157 .... C3
Ascoli Piceno 352,567 .... D3
Asti 215,332 .... B2
Avellino 434,021 .... E4
Bari 1,464,627 .... F4
Belluno 220,335 .... D1
Benevento 289,143 .... E4
Bergamo 896,117 .... B2
Bologna 930,284 .... C2
Bolzano-Bozen 430,568 .... C1
Brescia 1,017,093 .... C2
Brindisi 391,064 .... G4
Cagliari 730,473 .... B5
Caltanissetta 285,829 .... D6
Campobasso 235,847 .... E4
Caserta 755,628 .... E4
Catania 1,005,577 .... E6
Catanzaro 744,834 .... F5
Chieti 370,534 .... E3
Como 755,979 .... B2
Cosenza 743,255 .... F5
Cremona 332,236 .... B2
Cuneo 548,452 .... A2
Enna 190,939 .... E6
Ferrara 381,118 .... C2
Florence 1,202,013 .... C3
Foggia 681,595 .... E4
Forlì 599,420 .... D2
Frosinone 460,395 .... D4
Genoa 1,045,109 .... B2
Gorizia 144,726 .... D2
Grosseto 220,905 .... C3
Imperia 223,738 .... B3
Isernia 92,524 .... E4
L'Aquila 291,742 .... D3
La Spezia 241,371 .... B2
Latina 434,086 .... D4
Lecce 762,017 .... G4
Livorno (Leghorn) 346,657 .... C3
Lucca 385,876 .... C3
Macerata 292,932 .... D3
Mantua 377,158 .... C2
Massa-Carrara 203,530 .... C2
Matera 203,570 .... F4
Messina 669,323 .... E5
Milan 4,018,108 .... B2
Modena 596,025 .... C2
Naples 2,970,563 .... E4
Novara 507,367 .... B2
Nuoro 274,817 .... B4
Padua 809,667 .... C2
Palermo 1,198,575 .... D5
Parma 400,192 .... C2
Pavia 512,895 .... B2
Perugia 580,988 .... D3
Pesaro e Urbino 333,488 .... D3
Pescara 286,240 .... E3
Piacenza 278,424 .... B2
Pisa 388,800 .... C3
Pistoia 264,995 .... C3
Pordenone 275,888 .... D2
Potenza 406,616 .... E4
Ragusa 274,583 .... E6
Ravenna 358,654 .... D2
Reggio di Calabria 573,093 .... E5
Reggio nell'Emilia 413,396 .... C2
Rieti 142,794 .... D3
Rome 3,695,961 .... F6
Rovigo 253,508 .... C2
Salerno 1,013,779 .... E4
Sassari 433,842 .... B4
Savona 297,675 .... B2
Siena 255,118 .... C3
Sondrio 174,009 .... B1
Syracuse 394,692 .... E6
Taranto 572,314 .... F4
Teramo 269,275 .... D3
Terni 807,552 .... D3
Trapani 420,865 .... D5
Trento 442,845 .... C1
Treviso 720,580 .... D2
Trieste 283,641 .... D2
Turin 2,345,771 .... A2
Udine 529,729 .... D1
Varese 788,057 .... B2
Venice 838,794 .... D2
Vercelli 395,957 .... B2
Verona 775,745 .... C2
Vicenza 726,418 .... C2
Viterbo 268,448 .... C3

CITIES and TOWNS

Acireale 46,711 .... E6
Acqui Terme 20,951 .... B2
Adrano 32,865 .... E6
Agrigento 38,681 .... D6
Alba 25,853 .... B2
Albano Laziale 27,796 .... F7
Alcamo 41,626 .... D6
Alessandria 79,552 .... B2
Alghero 32,519 .... B4
Altamura 50,539 .... F4
Amalfi 4,423 .... E4
Ancona 97,118 .... D3
Andria 84,070 .... F4
Anzio 25,932 .... D4
Aosta 36,649 .... A2
Aprilia 31,604 .... D4
Arezzo 74,477 .... C3
Ascoli Piceno 44,411 .... D3
Assisi 4,683 .... D3
Asti 65,483 .... B2
Augusta 37,162 .... E6
Avellino 50,894 .... E4
Aversa 55,788 .... E4
Avezzano 30,227 .... D3
Avola 30,360 .... E6
Bagheria 39,869 .... D5
Barcellona Pozzo di Gotto 33,404 .... E5
Bari 369,444 .... F4
Barletta 82,290 .... F4
Bassano del Grappa 33,724 .... C2
Belluno 28,468 .... D1
Benevento 51,831 .... E4
Bergamo 121,389 .... B2
Biancavilla 20,047 .... E6
Biella 52,587 .... B2
Bisceglie 46,209 .... F4
Bitonto 46,538 .... F4
Bologna 454,897 .... C2
Bolzano (Bolzen) 103,241 .... C1
Borgomanero 18,701 .... B2
Bra 21,304 .... A2
Brescia 202,539 .... C2
Brindisi 84,887 .... G4
Bronte 17,477 .... E6
Busto Arsizio 79,321 .... B2
Cagliari 219,423 .... B5
Caltagirone 32,860 .... E6
Caltanissetta 57,704 .... D6
Camaiore 24,284 .... C3
Campobasso 41,687 .... E4
Canicatti 31,726 .... D6
Canosa di Puglia 30,555 .... E4
Cantù 35,644 .... B2
Capannori 39,717 .... C3
Carbonia 25,140 .... B5
Carmagnola 19,581 .... A2
Carpi 49,370 .... C2
Carrara 61,709 .... C2
Casale Monferrato 37,157 .... B2
Cascina-Navacchio 32,570 .... C3
Caserta 59,185 .... E4
Cassino 22,406 .... D4
Castel Gandolfo 6,176 .... F7
Castelfranco Veneto 20,196 .... D2
Castellammare di Stabia 70,507 .... E4
Castelvetrano 29,503 .... D6
Castrovillari 18,648 .... F5
Catania 379,754 .... E6
Catanzaro 96,930 .... F5
Cava de'Tirreni 47,007 .... E4
Cecina 22,264 .... C3
Ceglie Messapico 17,915 .... F4
Cerignola 48,105 .... E4
Cesena 72,145 .... D2
Cesenatico 15,634 .... D2
Chiavari 29,171 .... B2
Chieri 28,296 .... A2
Chieti 49,267 .... E3
Chioggia 46,728 .... D2
Chivasso 22,230 .... A2
Ciampino 31,981 .... F7
Città di Castello 21,492 .... C3
Civitavecchia 46,465 .... C3
Comiso 25,469 .... E6
Como 94,167 .... B2
Conegliano 32,406 .... D2
Conversano 18,518 .... F4
Corato 41,078 .... F4
Cosenza 101,144 .... F5
Crema 33,901 .... B2
Cremona 74,341 .... B2
Crotone 51,204 .... F5
Cuneo 47,836 .... A2
Desenzano del Garda 17,296 .... C2
Domodossola 19,825 .... A1
Eboli 24,152 .... E4
Empoli 34,066 .... C3
Enna 26,760 .... E6
Fabriano 21,155 .... D3
Faenza 40,635 .... D2
Fano 42,440 .... D3
Fasano 22,918 .... F4
Favara 30,031 .... D6
Fermo 17,603 .... D3
Ferrara 117,590 .... C2
Fidenza 19,482 .... B2
Fiesole 3,711 .... C3
Firenze (Florence) 442,721 .... C3
Fiumicino 21,167 .... F7
Florence 442,721 .... C3
Floridia 17,790 .... E6
Foggia 150,480 .... E4
Foligno 41,696 .... D3
Fondi 19,580 .... D4
Forlì 91,366 .... D2
Formia 29,147 .... D4
Fossano 17,116 .... A2
Francavilla Fontana 31,371 .... F4
Frascati 18,356 .... F7
Frosinone 42,626 .... D4
Gaeta 23,190 .... D4
Galatina 22,611 .... G4
Gallarate 47,259 .... B2
Gela 74,077 .... E6
Genoa 755,389 .... B2
Genova (Genoa) 787,011 .... B2
Giarre 23,377 .... E6
Gioia del Colle 23,868 .... F4
Giovinazzo 18,832 .... F4
Giulianova 20,189 .... E3
Gorizia 40,679 .... D2
Gravina in Puglia 35,891 .... F4
Grosseto 55,569 .... C3
Grottaglie 27,140 .... F4
Iglesias 26,313 .... B5
Imola 47,365 .... C2
Imperia 39,151 .... B3
Isernia 16,919 .... E4
Ivrea 26,446 .... B2
Jesi 37,075 .... D3
L'Aquila 40,467 .... D3
La Spezia 110,632 .... B2
Lanciano 25,828 .... E3
Latina 64,529 .... D4
Lecce 80,127 .... G4
Lecco 51,160 .... B2
Leghorn (Livorno) 171,811 .... C3
Legnago 23,232 .... C2
Lentini 30,950 .... E6
Leonforte 15,745 .... E6
Licata 40,309 .... D6
Lido di Ostia 85,043 .... F7
Lido di Venezia 20,863 .... D2
Livorno 171,811 .... C3
Lodi 41,338 .... B2
Lucca 84,836 .... C3
Lucera 31,252 .... E4
Lugo 21,593 .... D2
Macerata 34,409 .... D3
Manduria 28,112 .... F4
Manfredonia 52,162 .... F4
Mantua 52,477 .... C2
Marino 30,261 .... F7
Marsala 76,843 .... D6
Martina Franca 34,911 .... F4
Massa 60,810 .... C2
Massafra 26,172 .... F4
Matera 48,226 .... F4
Mazara del Vallo 42,320 .... D6
Merano 31,854 .... C1
Mesagne 29,770 .... G4
Messina 240,121 .... E5
Mestre 197,952 .... D2
Milan 1,601,797 .... B2
Milazzo 29,868 .... E5
Minturno 15,795 .... D4
Mira Taglio 26,031 .... D2
Modena 164,529 .... C2
Modica 34,488 .... E6
Mola di Bari 25,744 .... F4
Molfetta 64,738 .... F4
Moncalieri 59,344 .... A2
Monfalcone 29,960 .... D2
Monopoli 33,928 .... F4
Monreale 18,168 .... D5
Monte Sant'Angelo 16,491 .... F4
Montebelluna 19,708 .... D2
Monterotondo 25,383 .... F6
Montevarchi 17,110 .... C3
Monza 122,541 .... B2
Naples 1,210,365 .... E4
Nardò 27,384 .... F4
Nettuno 27,929 .... D4
Nicastro-Sambiase 49,325 .... F5
Niscemi 25,677 .... E6
Nocera Inferiore 43,879 .... E4
Noto 20,609 .... E6
Novara 94,477 .... B2
Novi Ligure 28,756 .... B2
Nuoro 35,491 .... B4
Olbia 26,702 .... B4
Oristano 23,938 .... B5
Orvieto 7,509 .... D3
Ostia Antica 3,939 .... F7
Ostuni 27,948 .... F4
Otranto 4,334 .... G4
Pachino 20,631 .... E6
Padua 228,333 .... C2
Palermo 698,481 .... D5
Palma di Montechiaro 23,918 .... D6
Palmi 16,394 .... E5
Pantelleria 3,454 .... C6
Parma 160,374 .... C2
Partinico 27,479 .... D6
Paterno 42,916 .... E6
Pavia 82,629 .... B2
Perugia 103,542 .... D3
Pesaro 78,550 .... D3
Pescara 131,016 .... E3
Piacenza 103,584 .... B2
Piazza Armerina 20,119 .... E6
Pietrasanta 20,404 .... B3
Pinerolo 33,176 .... A2
Piombino 35,312 .... C3
Pisa 95,015 .... C3
Pistoia 78,105 .... C3
Poggibonsi 22,644 .... C3
Pomezia 19,453 .... F7
Pordenone 51,270 .... D2
Porto Empedocle 16,126 .... D6
Porto Torres 20,233 .... B4
Portocivitanova 28,155 .... D3
Portoferraio 8,108 .... C3
Portofino 615 .... B2
Potenza 55,175 .... E4
Pozzuoli 61,856 .... D4
Prato 156,894 .... C3
Putignano 22,361 .... F4
Quartu Sant'Elena 40,506 .... B5
Ragusa 60,871 .... E6
Rapallo 26,457 .... B2
Ravenna 87,582 .... D2
Reggio di Calabria 159,416 .... E5
Reggio nell'Emilia 107,484 .... C2
Rho 50,373 .... B2
Rieti 33,614 .... D3
Rimini 111,991 .... D2
Rome (cap.) 2,605,441 .... F6
Rovereto 31,286 .... C2
Rovigo 41,050 .... C2
Ruvo di Puglia 23,510 .... F4
Salerno 150,252 .... E4
Saluzzo 13,078 .... A2
San Benedetto del Tronto 43,189 .... E3
San Cataldo 20,694 .... D6
San Giovanni in Fiore 19,391 .... F5
Sannicandro Garganico 18,652 .... E4
San Remo 59,872 .... A3
San Severo 53,948 .... E4
Santa Maria Capua Vetere 32,129 .... E4
Santeramo in Colle 21,154 .... F4
San Vito dei Normanni 18,366 .... F4
Saronno 36,732 .... B2
Sassari 104,334 .... B4
Sassuolo 37,515 .... C2
Savona 65,040 .... B2
Schio 30,738 .... C2
Sciacca 35,063 .... D6
Scicli 18,419 .... E6
Senigallia 27,474 .... D3
Sesto Fiorentino 43,307 .... C3
Sestri Levante 19,672 .... B2
Siena 54,982 .... C3
Siracusa (Syracuse) 109,038 .... E6
Sondrio 19,955 .... B1
Sora 20,380 .... D4
Sorrento 15,747 .... E4
Spoleto 21,625 .... D3
Stresa 4,290 .... B2
Sulmona 21,504 .... D3
Syracuse 109,038 .... E6
Taranto 231,441 .... F4
Teramo 35,142 .... D3
Termini Imerese 24,252 .... D6

(continued on following page)

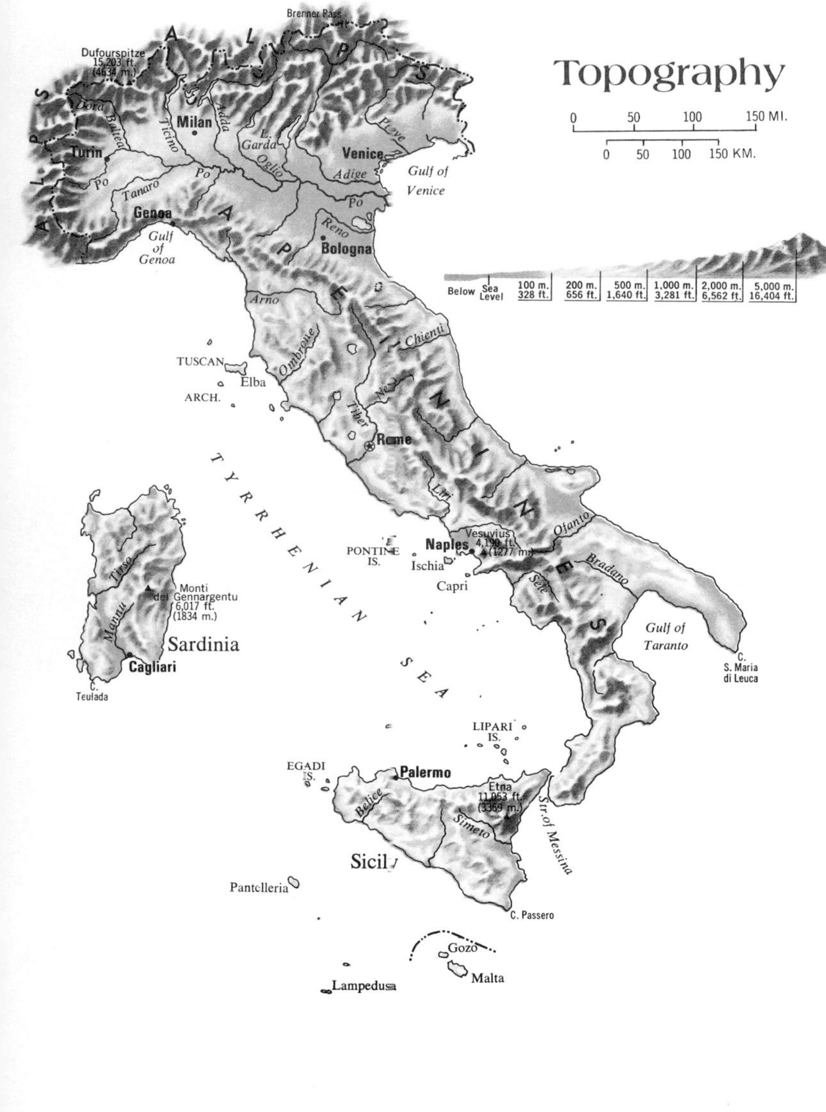
Topography
0 50 100 150 MI.
0 50 100 150 KM.
Below Sea Level
100 m. 328 ft.
200 m. 656 ft.
500 m. 1,640 ft.
1,000 m. 3,281 ft.
2,000 m. 6,562 ft.
5,000 m. 16,404 ft.
Brenner Pass
Dufourspitze 15,203 ft. (4634 m.)
Milan
Turin
Venice
Gulf of Venice
Genoa
Gulf of Genoa
Bologna
Po
Adige
Arno
Tiber
Rome
TUSCAN ARCH.
Elba
TYRRHENIAN SEA
Naples
Vesuvius
Ischia
Capri
PONTINE IS.
Sardinia
Cagliari
C. Teulada
Gulf of Taranto
C. S. Maria di Leuca
LIPARI IS.
EGADI
Palermo
Etna
Str. of Messina
Sicily
C. Passero
Pantelleria
Gozo
Malta
Lampedusa

Termoli 20,542 ....E3
Terni 94,772 ....D3
Terracina 27,384 ....D4
Tivoli 29,580 ....F6
Torino (Turin) 1,115,074 ....A2
Torre Annunziata 60,487 ....E4
Torre del Grecc 103,605 ....E4
Torremaggiore 16,946 ....E4
Tortona 24,618 ....B2
Trani 44,169 ....F4
Trapani 61,945 ....D5
Trento 80,490 ....C1
Treviglio 24,811 ....B2
Treviso 84,274 ....D2
Trieste 237,170 ....E2
Turin 1,115,074 ....A2
Udine 101,845 ....D2
Valdagno 23,655 ....C2
Valenza 20,427 ....B2
Varese 86,701 ....B2
Vasto 22,657 ....E3
Velletri 40,020 ....F7
Venezia (Venice) 92,400 ....D2
Venice 92,400 ....D2
Ventimiglia 23,773 ....A3
Verbania 31,054 ....B2
Vercelli 51,215 ....B2
Verona 238,553 ....C2
Viareggio 49,529 ....C3
Vibo Valentia 18,904 ....F5
Vicenza 110,928 ....C2
Vigevano 62,907 ....B2
Viterbo 46,513 ....C3
Vittoria 50,228 ....E6
Vittorio Veneto 26,028 ......D1
Voghera 40,053 ....B2

OTHER FEATURES

Adda (riv.) B2
Adige (riv.) C2
Adriatic (sea) E3
Albano (lake) F7
Alicudi (isl.) E5
Aniene (riv.) F6
Apennines, Central (range) D3
Apennines, Northern (range)..B2
Apennines, Southern (range) ..E4
Arno (riv.) C3
Asinara (gulf) B4
Asinara (isl.) B4
Belice (riv.) D6
Bernina (pass) C1
Bernina (peak) B1
Blanc (mt.) A2
Bolsena (lake) C3
Bonifacio (str.) B4
Bracciano (lake) D3
Brenner (pass) C1
Cagliari (gulf) B5
Capraia (isl.) B3
Capri (isl.) E4
Carbonara (cape) B5
Carnic Alps (range) D1
Castellammare (gulf) D5
Chambeyron (mt.) A2
Chienti (riv.) D3
Cimone (mt.) C2
Circeo (cape) D4
Coghinas (riv.) B4
Colonne (cape) F5
Como (lake) B1
Corno (mt.) D3
Costa Smeralda (region) B4
Costa Verde (region) B5
Cottian Alps (range) A2
Crati (riv.) F5
Dolomite Alps (range) C1
Dora Baltea (riv.) A2
Dora Riparia (riv.) A2
Egadi (isls.) C6
Elba (isl.) C3
Etna (vol.) E6
Falcone (cape) B4
Favignana (isl.) D6
Filicudi (isl.) E5
Fréjus (pass) A2
Gaeta (gulf) D4
Garda (lake) C2
Gennargentu, Monti del (mt.).B5
Genoa (gulf) B2
Giannutri (isl.) C3
Giglio (isl.) C3
Gorgona (isl.) B3
Graian Alps (range) A2
Gran Paradiso (mt.) A2
Great Saint Bernard (pass) ..A2
Ionian (sea) F6
Ischia (isl.) D4
Iseo (lake) C2
Julian Alps (range) D1
Lampedusa (isl.) D7
Lepontine Alps (range) B1
Lesina (lake) E3
Levanzo (isl.) D5
Licosa (cape) E4
Ligurian (sea) B3
Linosa (isl.) D7
Lipari (isl.) E5
Liri (riv.) D4
Maggiore (lake) B1
Malta (chan.) E6
Manfredonia (gulf) F4
Mannu (riv.) B5
Marettimo (isl.) C6
Maritime Alps (range) A2
Marmolada (mt.) C1
Mediterranean (sea) B6
Messina (str.) E6
Metauro (riv.) D3
Mincio (riv.) C2
Mont Cenis (tunnel) A2
Montecristo (isl.) C3
Nera (riv.) D3
Ofanto (riv.) E4
Oglio (riv.) C2
Ombrone (riv.) C3
Oristano (gulf) B5

Orosei (gulf) B4
Ortles (range) C1
Otranto (str.) G5
Ötztal Alps (range) C1
Palmarola (isl.) D4
Panarea (isl.) E5
Panaro (riv.) C2
Pantelleria (isl.) D6
Parma (riv.) C2
Passero (cape) E6
Pelagie (isls.) D7
Pennine Alps (range) A2
Pescara (riv.) D3
Piave (riv.) D2
Pianosa (isl.) C3
Po (riv.) C2
Policastro (gulf) E5
Pompeii (ruins) E4
Pontine (isls.) D4
Ponza (isl.) D4
Presanella (mt.) C1
Rosa (mt.) A1
Salerno (gulf) E4
Salina (isl.) E5
Salso (riv.) D6
Sangro (riv.) E4
San Pietro (isl.) B5
San Vito (cape) D5
Santa Maria di Leuca (cape) ..G5
Sant'Antioco (pen.) B5
Sant'Eufemia (gulf) F5
Sardinia (isl.) B4
Sele (riv.) E4
Sicily (isl.) E6
Sicily (str.) D6
Simeto (riv.) E6
Simplon (tunnel) A1
Spartivento (cape) F6
Spartivento (cape) B5
Splügen (pass) B1
Squillace (gulf) F5
Stromboli (isl.) E5
Stura (riv.) A2
Tagliamento (riv.) D1
Tanaro (riv.) A2
Taranto (gulf) F5
Testa (cape) B4
Testa del Gargano (cape) ...F4
Teulada (cape) B5
Tiber (riv.) D3
Tirso (riv.) B4
Trasimeno (lake) D3
Trebbia (riv.) B2
Tremiti (isls.) E3
Trieste (gulf) D2
Tuscan (arch.) B3
Tyrrhenian (sea) C4
Ustica (isl.) D5
Varano (lake) F3
Vaticano (cape) E5
Venice (gulf) D2
Ventotene (isl.) D4

Vesuvius (vol.) E4
Viso (mt.) A2
Volturno (riv.) E4
Vulcano (isl.) E5

MALTA

CITIES and TOWNS

Sliema 20,095 ....E7
Valletta (cap.) 14,042 ....E7
Victoria 5,249 ....E6

SAN MARINO

CITIES and TOWNS

San Marino (cap.) 4,238 ....D3

VATICAN CITY

CITIES and TOWNS

Vatican City 728 ....B6

Agriculture, Industry and Resources

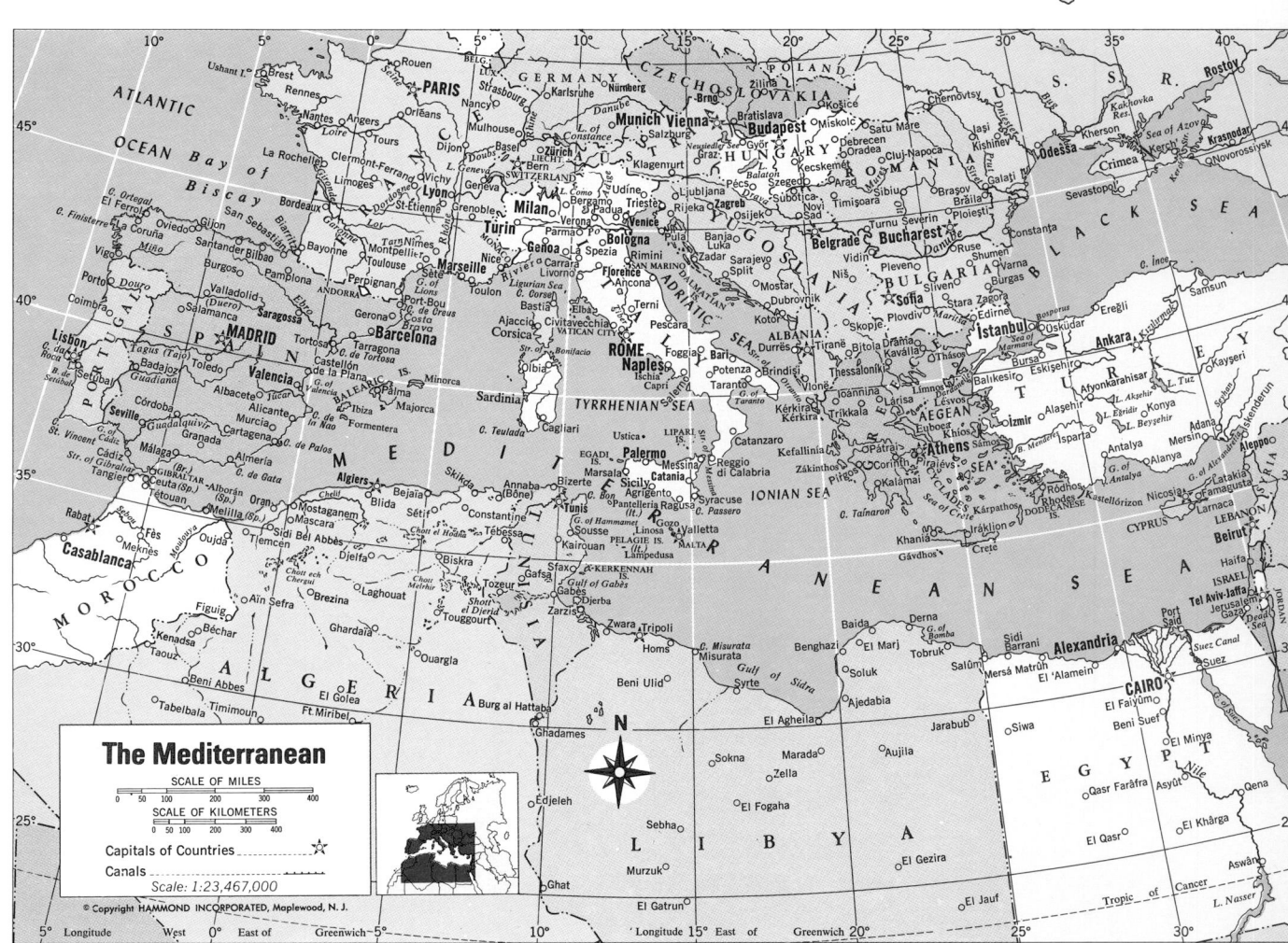

DOMINANT LAND USE

☐ Wheat, Rice, Dairy

☐ Pasture Livestock

☐ Cereals, Livestock

☐ Fruit, Truck and Mixed Farming

☐ Grapes, Wine

☐ Forests

☐ Nonagricultural Land

MAJOR MINERAL OCCURRENCES

Ab	Asbestos	K	Potash	Pb	Lead
Al	Bauxite	Lg	Lignite	Py	Pyrites
C	Coal	Mr	Marble	S	Sulfur
Fe	Iron Ore	Na	Salt	Sb	Antimony
G	Natural Gas	O	Petroleum	Zn	Zinc
Hg	Mercury				

⚡ Water Power

▨ Major Industrial Areas

The Mediterranean

SCALE OF MILES
0   50 100   200   300   400

SCALE OF KILOMETERS
0 50 100 200   300   400

Capitals of Countries ....☆

Canals

Scale: 1:23,467,000

© Copyright HAMMOND INCORPORATED, Maplewood, N.J.

SWITZERLAND

AREA 15,943 sq. mi. (41,292 sq. km.)
POPULATION 6,647,000
CAPITAL Bern
LARGEST CITY Zürich
HIGHEST POINT Dufourspitze
(Rosa) 15,203 ft. (4,634 m.)
MONETARY UNIT Swiss franc
MAJOR LANGUAGES German, French,
Italian, Romansch
MAJOR RELIGIONS Protestantism,
Roman Catholicism

LIECHTENSTEIN

AREA 61 sq. mi. (158 sq. km.)
POPULATION 28,000
CAPITAL Vaduz
LARGEST CITY Vaduz
HIGHEST POINT Grauspitze 8,527 ft.
(2,599 m.)
MONETARY UNIT Swiss franc
MAJOR LANGUAGE German
MAJOR RELIGION Roman Catholicism

SWITZERLAND

LIECHTENSTEIN

Languages

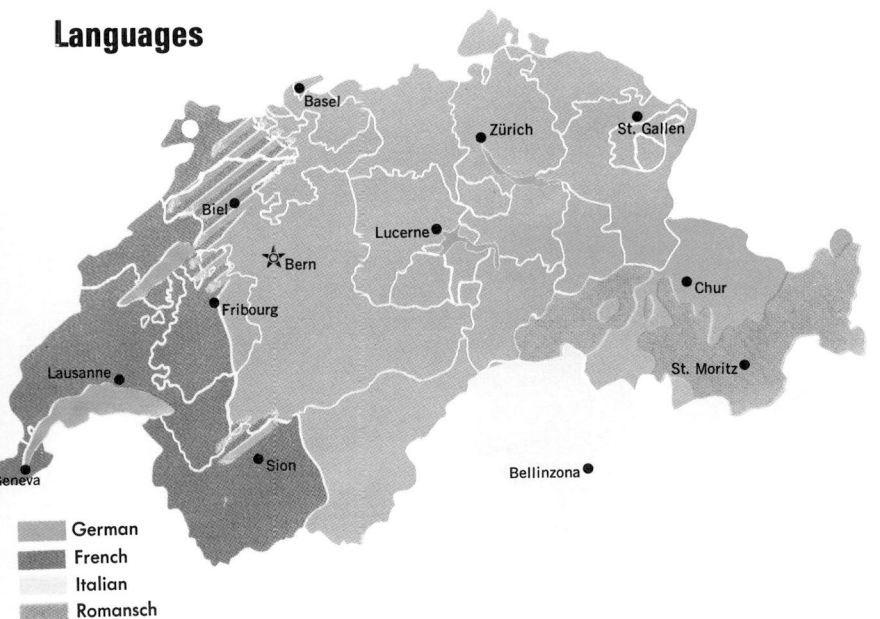

- German
- French
- Italian
- Romansch

Switzerland is a multilingual nation with four official languages. 70% of the people speak German, 19% French, 10% Italian and 1% Romansch.

Agriculture, Industry and Resources

DOMINANT LAND USE

- Cereals, Dairy
- Pasture Livestock
- General Farming, Livestock
- Fruit, Truck, Mixed Farming
- Forests
- Nonagricultural Land

⚡ Water Power
▨ Major Industrial Areas

SWITZERLAND

CANTONS

Aargau 453,442	F2
Appenzell, Ausser Rhoden 47,611	H2
Appenzell, Inner Rhoden 12,844	H2
Baselland 219,822	E2
Baselstadt 203,915	E1
Bern 912,022	D2
Fribourg 185,246	D3
Geneva (Genève) 349,040	B4
Glarus 36,718	H3
Graubünden (Grisons) 164,641	H3
Jura 64,986	D2
Lucerne (Luzern) 296,159	F2
Luzern 296,159	F2
Neuchâtel 158,368	C3
Nidwalden 28,617	F3
Obwalden 25,865	F3
Sankt Gallen 391,995	H2
Schaffhausen 69,413	G1
Schwyz 97,354	G2
Soleure (Solothurn) 218,102	E2
Solothurn 218,102	E2
Thurgau 183,795	H1
Ticino 265,899	G4
Uri 33,883	G3
Valais 218,707	D4
Vaud 528,747	B3

Zug 75,930	G2
Zürich 1,122,839	G2

CITIES and TOWNS

Aadorf 3,257	G2
Aarau 15,788	E2
Aarberg 3,212	D2
Aarburg 5,354	E2
Adelboden 3,276	E3
Adliswil 16,418	F2
Affoltern am Albis 8,064	F2
Aigle 6,233	C4
Allschwil 17,952	D1
Alpnach 3,556	F3
Altdorf 8,230	G3
Altstätten 9,260	J2
Amriswil 8,790	H1
Appenzell 4,781	H2
Arbedo-Castione 3,058	G4
Arbon 11,333	H1
Arosa 2,782	J3
Arth 7,795	F2
Ascona 4,722	G4
Au 5,434	J2
Avenches 2,177	D3
Baar 15,196	F2
Bad Ragaz 3,721	H2
Baden 13,870	F2
Balerna 3,455	G5
Balsthal 5,090	E2
Bäretswil 3,145	G2
Basel 182,143	E1

Basel 364,813	E1
Bassecourt 2,942	D2
Bauma 3,010	G2
Bellinzona 16,743	H4
Belp 7,578	D3
Bern (cap.) 145,254	D3
Bettlach 3,851	D2
Bex 4,843	D4
Biasca 5,447	H4
Biberist 7,519	D2
Biel 53,793	D2
Binningen 14,195	D1
Bischofszell 3,390	H1
Bolligen 32,312	E3
Boudry 4,488	C3
Breitenbach 2,518	E2
Bremgarten 4,815	F2
Brienz 2,759	F3
Brig 9,608	F4
Brittnau 2,822	E2
Brugg 8,911	F2
Bubikon 3,601	G2
Buchs 9,066	H2
Bülach 12,292	G1
Bulle 7,595	D3
Buochs 3,742	F3
Büren an der Aare 2,761	D2
Burgdorf 15,379	E2
Bürglen 3,456	G3
Bussigny-près-Lausanne 4,909	B3
Bütschwil 3,423	H2
Carouge 13,100	B4
Castagnola 4,430	G4
Cham 9,275	F2
Château-d'Oex 2,872	D4
Châtel-Saint-Denis 3,141	C3
Chêne-Bougeries 9,068	B4
Chiasso 8,583	G5
Chur 32,037	J3
Collombey-Muraz 2,982	C4
Collonge-Bellerive 4,531	B4
Conthey 4,828	D4
Courrendlin 2,435	D2
Couvet 2,627	C3
Davos 10,468	J3
Degersheim 3,269	H2
Delémont 11,682	D2
Derendingen 4,675	E2
Dielsdorf 3,767	F1
Diepoldsau 3,562	J2
Diessenhofen 2,535	G1
Dietikon 21,765	F2
Disentis-Mustér 2,320	G3
Domat-Ems 6,266	H3
Dornach 5,442	E2
Döttingen 3,264	F1
Dübendorf 20,683	G2
Düdingen 5,572	D3
Dürnten 4,927	G2
Ebnat-Kappel 4,950	H2
Echallens 2,163	C3
Ecublens 7,615	B3
Effretikon 14,788	G2
Egg 6,074	G2
Eggiwil 2,323	E3
Egnach 3,397	H1
Einsiedeln 9,629	G2
Elgg 3,041	G2
Emmen 22,392	F2
Engelberg 2,963	F3
Ennenda 2,512	H2
Entlebuch 3,238	F3
Erstfeld 4,158	G3
Eschenbach 3,661	G2
Escholzmatt 3,033	E3
Estavayer-le-Lac 3,662	C3
Feuerthalen 2,920	G1
Flawil 8,575	H2
Fleurier 3,573	C3
Flims 2,136	H3
Flums 4,228	H2
Frauenfeld 18,607	G1
Freienbach 9,912	G2
Fribourg 37,400	D3
Frick 3,116	E1
Frutigen 5,779	E3
Fully 3,926	D4
Gais 2,388	H2
Gelterkinden 4,954	E2

(continued on following page)

Topography

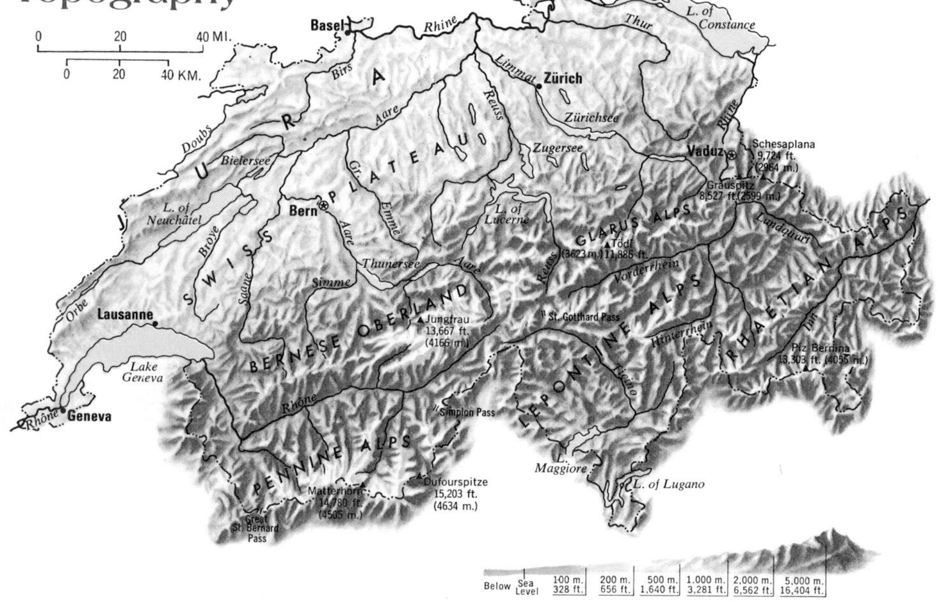

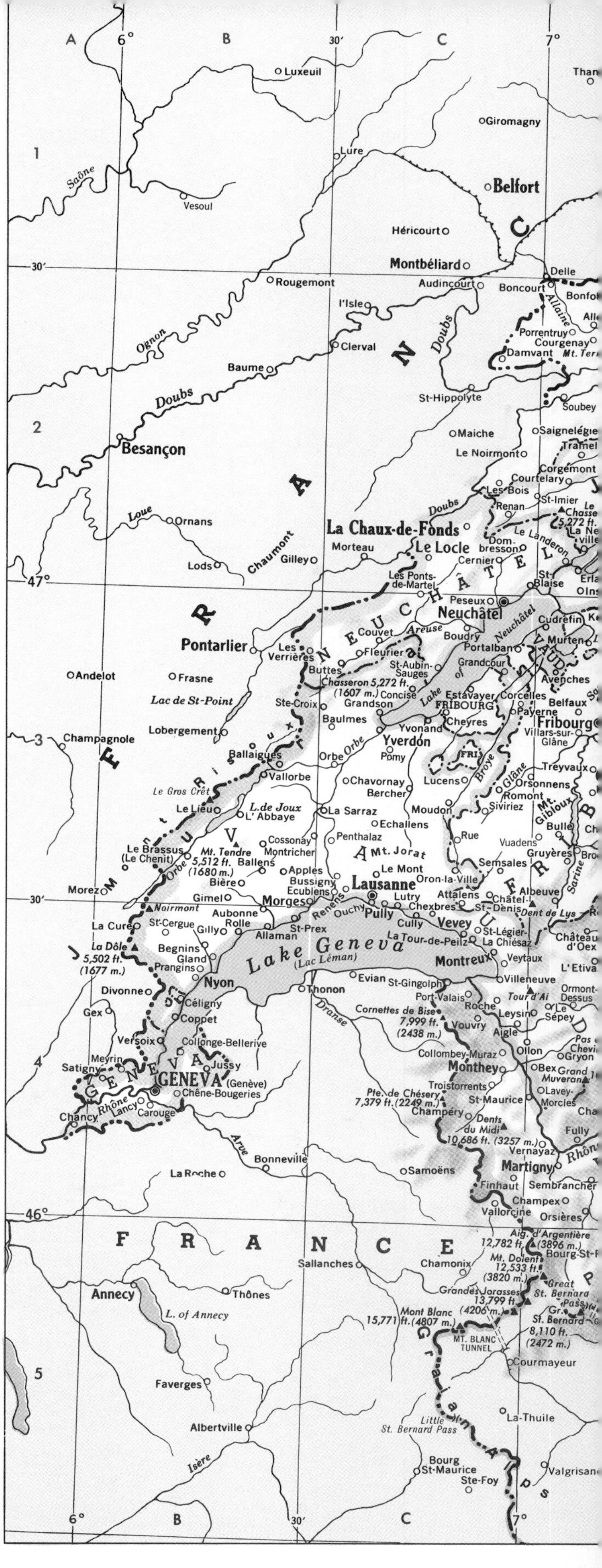

Geneva (Genève) 156,505 ... B4
Giswil 2,595 ... F3
Giubiasco 6,585 ... H4
Gland 4,906 ... B4
Glarus 5,969 ... H2
Glattfelden 2,753 ... F1
Glis 3,389 ... E4
Gordola 2,956 ... G4
Gossau 14,584 ... H2
Grabs 4,844 ... H2
Grenchen 16,800 ... D2
Grindelwald 3,555 ... E3
Grosswangen 2,235 ... F2
Gstaad ... D4
Heiden 3,620 ... H2
Heimberg 4,107 ... E3
Hergiswil 4,254 ... F3
Herisau 14,160 ... H2
Herzogenbuchsee 5,107 ... E2
Hilterfingen 3,600 ... E3
Hinwil 7,554 ... G2
Hochdorf 6,034 ... F2
Horgen 16,577 ... G2
Huttwil 4,612 ... E2
Igis 5,392 ... J3
Ingenbohl 6,232 ... G3
Ins 2,608 ... D2
Interlaken 4,852 ... E3
Jegenstorf 3,541 ... D2
Jona 12,156 ... G2
Kaltbrunn 2,735 ... H2
Kerns 4,200 ... F3
Kerzers 2,658 ... D3
Kirchberg, Bern 3,966 ... E2
Kirchberg, St. Gallen 6,398 ... G2
Klingnau 2,433 ... F1
Klosters-Serneus 3,487 ... J3
Kloten 15,845 ... G2
Kölliken 3,080 ... F2
Köniz 33,441 ... D3
Konolfingen 4,360 ... E3
Kreuzlingen 16,101 ... H1
Kriens 21,097 ... F2
Küsnacht 12,766 ... G2
Küssnacht am Rigi 8,091 ... F2
Küttigen 4,356 ... F2
La Chaux-de-Fonds 37,234 ... C2
Lachen 5,352 ... G2
Lancy 23,527 ... B4
La Neuveville 3,519 ... D2
Langenthal 13,408 ... E2
Langnau am Albis 6,694 ... G2
Langnau in Emmental 8,821 ... E3
La Tour-de-Peilz 9,411 ... C4
Laufen 4,444 ... D2
Laupen 2,261 ... D3
Lauperswil 2,482 ... E3
Lausanne 127,349 ... C3
Lauterbrunnen 3,077 ... E3
Le Brassus 4,359 ... B3
Le Châble 4,541 ... D4
Le Chenit (Le Brassus) 4,359 ... B3
Le Landeron 3,287 ... C2
Le Locle 12,039 ... C2
Le Mont-sur-Lausanne 3,664 ... C3
Lengnau 4,317 ... D2
Lenk 2,089 ... D4
Lens 2,412 ... D4
Lenzburg 7,585 ... F2
Leuk 2,983 ... E4
Leukerbad 1,070 ... E4
Liestal 12,158 ... E2
Liestal-Sissach 40,800 ... E2
Littau 14,996 ... F2
Locarno 14,103 ... G4
Lucerne 63,278 ... F2
Lugano 27,815 ... G4
Lutry 5,884 ... C3
Lützelflüh 3,770 ... E3
Luzern (Lucerne) 63,278 ... F2
Lyss 8,723 ... D2
Malters 4,900 ... F2
Männedorf 7,833 ... G2
Martigny 11,309 ... C4
Meilen 10,430 ... G2
Meiringen 4,072 ... F3
Mellingen 3,285 ... F2
Mels 6,235 ... H2
Mendrisio 6,590 ... G5
Menzingen 3,564 ... G2
Menznau 2,248 ... E2
Meyrin 18,808 ... B4
Minusio 5,602 ... G4
Möhlin 6,360 ... E1
Mollis 2,621 ... H2
Monthey 11,285 ... C4
Montreux 19,685 ... C4
Morges 13,057 ... B3
Moudon 3,805 ... C3
Moutier 7,959 ... D2
Mümliswil-Ramiswil 2,386 ... E2
Münchenbuchsee 8,395 ... E2
Münsingen 9,340 ... E3
Muotathal 2,896 ... G3
Muri 5,399 ... F2
Muri bei Bern 12,285 ... E3
Murten 4,558 ... D3
Muttenz 16,911 ... E1
Näfels 3,766 ... H2
Naters 6,662 ... E4
Nendaz 4,372 ... D4
Netstal 2,642 ... H2
Neuchâtel 34,428 ... C3
Neuenegg 3,727 ... D3
Neuhausen am Rheinfall 10,662 ... G1
Niederbipp 3,165 ... E2
Niederurnen 3,438 ... G2
Nyon 12,842 ... B4
Oberägeri 3,563 ... G2
Oberburg 2,869 ... E2
Oberdiessbach 2,319 ... E3
Oberriet 6,222 ... J2
Obersiggenthal 7,442 ... F1
Oberuzwil 4,616 ... H2
Oensingen 3,543 ... E2
Oftringen 9,006 ... E2
Ollon 4,429 ... D4
Olten 18,991 ... E2
Opfikon 11,444 ... G2
Orbe 3,985 ... C3
Orsières 2,357 ... D4
Paradiso 3,261 ... G5
Payerne 6,713 ... C3
Peseux 5,212 ... C3
Pfäffikon 8,306 ... G2
Pfaffnau 2,453 ... E2
Pieterlen 3,127 ... D2
Porrentruy 7,039 ... C2
Poschiavo 3,294 ... J4
Prangins 2,028 ... B4
Pratteln 15,751 ... E1
Pully 14,988 ... C4
Rafz 2,325 ... G1
Rapperswil 7,826 ... G2
Regensdorf 12,300 ... F2
Reichenbach im Kandertal 2,948 ... E3
Reiden 3,363 ... F2
Reinach in Aargau 5,696 ... F2
Reinach in Baselland 17,813 ... E2
Renens 16,977 ... C3
Rheineck 3,037 ... J2
Rheinfelden 9,456 ... E1
Richterswil 8,672 ... G2
Riehen 20,611 ... E1
Riggisberg 2,196 ... D3
Roggwil 3,333 ... E2
Rolle 3,409 ... B4
Romanshorn 7,893 ... H1
Romont 3,495 ... C3
Rorschach 9,878 ... H2
Rothrist 6,015 ... E2
Rüti, Zürich 9,331 ... G2
Rumlang 5,055 ... G2
Ruswil 4,870 ... F2
Saanen 5,522 ... D4
Sachseln 3,406 ... F3
Saint-Blaise 2,788 ... D2
Sainte-Croix 4,543 ... B3
Saint-Imier 5,430 ... D2
Saint-Légier-La Chiésaz 2,787 ... C4
Saint-Maurice 3,458 ... C4
Saint Moritz 5,900 ... J3
Saint Niklaus 2,036 ... E4
Saint-Prex 2,937 ... B4
Samedan 2,553 ... J3
Sankt Gallen 75,847 ... H2
Sankt Margrethen 4,935 ... J2
Sargans 4,267 ... H2
Sarnen 7,372 ... F3
Savièse 4,097 ... D4
Saxon 2,394 ... D4
Schänis 2,426 ... H2
Schaffhausen 34,250 ... G1
Schattdorf 4,516 ... G3
Schiers 2,253 ... J3
Schlieren 12,891 ... F2
Schönenwerd 4,746 ... E2
Schübelbach 4,720 ... G2
Schüpfheim 3,537 ... F3
Schwanden 2,519 ... H2
Schwyz 12,100 ... G2
Sempach 2,237 ... F2
Seon 3,826 ... F2
Seuzach 4,659 ... G1
Sevelen 2,839 ... H2
Sierre 13,050 ... D4
Signau 2,606 ... E3
Sigriswil 3,536 ... E3
Silenen 2,115 ... G3
Simplon 328 ... F4
Sins 2,625 ... F2
Sion 22,877 ... D4
Sirnach 4,170 ... G2
Sissach 4,564 ... E2
Solothurn (Soleure) 15,778 ... E2
Spiez 9,800 ... E3
Stäfa 10,558 ... G2
Stans 5,681 ... F3
Steckborn 3,232 ... G1
Steffisburg 12,539 ... E3
Stein am Rhein 2,507 ... G1
Suhr 7,366 ... F2
Sumiswald 5,070 ... E2
Sursee 7,645 ... F2
Tafers 2,263 ... D3
Tavannes 3,336 ... D2
Teufen 5,027 ... H2
Thal 4,725 ... J2
Thalwil 15,412 ... G2
Thayngen 3,751 ... G1
Therwil 7,311 ... E1
Thun 36,891 ... E3
Thunstetten 2,567 ... E2
Thusis 2,525 ... H3
Tramelan 4,733 ... D2
Turbenthal 2,975 ... G2
Uetendorf 4,538 ... E3
Unterägeri 5,371 ... G2
Unterkulm 2,558 ... F2
Unterseen 4,568 ... E3
Uster 23,702 ... G2
Utzenstorf 3,141 ... E2
Uznach 4,269 ... H2
Uzwil 9,614 ... H2
Vallorbe 3,375 ... B3
Vechigen 4,036 ... E3
Versoix 7,483 ... B4
Vevey 16,139 ... C4
Vevey-Montreux 60,558 ... C4
Villars-sur-Glâne 5,788 ... D3
Villeneuve 3,573 ... C4
Visp 6,383 ... E4
Wädenswil 18,485 ... G2
Wängi 2,909 ... G1
Wahlern 5,104 ... D3
Wald 7,447 ... G2
Waldkirch 2,622 ... H2
Walenstadt 3,605 ... H2
Wallisellen 10,887 ... G2
Wartau 3,692 ... H2
Wattwil 7,874 ... H2
Weinfelden 8,793 ... H1
Wettingen 18,377 ... F2
Wetzikon 15,859 ... G2
Wil 16,245 ... H2
Willisau 2,639 ... F2
Windisch 7,598 ... F1
Winterthur 86,758 ... G1
Wohlen 12,024 ... F2
Wohlen 15,746 ... F2
Wohlen bei Bern 7,666 ... D3
Wolhusen 3,670 ... F2
Worb 11,080 ... E3
Wünnewil 3,774 ... D3
Yverdon 20,802 ... C3
Zell 4,138 ... G2
Zermatt 3,548 ... E4
Zofingen 8,643 ... E2
Zollikofen 8,717 ... D3
Zollikon 12,134 ... G2
Zug 21,609 ... G2
Zürich 369,522 ... F2
Zurzach 3,068 ... F1
Zweisimmen 2,852 ... D3

OTHER FEATURES

Aa (riv.) ... F3
Aare (riv.) ... E3
Ägerisee (lake) ... G2
Aiguille d'Argentière (mt.) ... C5
Albristhorn (mt.) ... D4
Aletschhorn (mt.) ... F4
Allaine (riv.) ... D2
Areuse (riv.) ... C3
Aroser Rothorn (mt.) ... J3
Ault (peak) ... H3
Baldeggersee (lake) ... F2
Balmhorn (mt.) ... E4
Bärenhorn (mt.) ... H3
Basodino (peak) ... G4
Bernese Oberland (reg.) ... E3
Bernina (mts.) ... J4
Bernina (pass) ... K4
Bernina (peak) ... J4
Bernina (riv.) ... J4
Beverin (peak) ... H3
Bielersee (lake) ... D2
Bietschhorn (mt.) ... E4
Birs (riv.) ... D2
Blas (peak) ... G3
Blinnenhorn (mt.) ... F4
Blümlisalp (mt.) ... E3
Bodensee (Constance) (lake) ... H1
Borgne (riv.) ... D4
Breithor (mt.) ... E5
Breithorn (mt.) ... E4
Brienzer Rothorn (mt.) ... F3
Brienzersee (lake) ... F3
Broye (riv.) ... C3
Brule (mt.) ... D4
Buchegg (mts.) ... D2
Buin (peak) ... K3
Bürkelkopf (mt.) ... K3
Bütschelegg (mt.) ... D3
Calancasca (riv.) ... H4
Campo Tencia (peak) ... G4
Ceneri (mt.) ... G4
Chasseron (mt.) ... C3
Chésery, Pointe de (mt.) ... C4
Cheville (pass) ... D4
Churfirsten (mt.) ... H2
Clariden (mt.) ... G3
Collon (mt.) ... D5
Constance (Bodensee) (lake) ... H1
Cornettes de Bise (mts.) ... C4
Dammastock (mt.) ... F3
Davos (valley) ... J3
Dent Blanche (mt.) ... E5
Dent de Lys (mt.) ... D4
Dent de Ruth (mt.) ... D3
Dent d'Hérens (mt.) ... E5
Dents du Midi (mt.) ... C4
Diablerets (mt.) ... D4
Doldenhorn (mt.) ... E4
Dolent (mt.) ... C5
Dom (mt.) ... E4
Doubs (riv.) ... C2
Drance (riv.) ... D4
Dufourspitze (mt.) ... E5
Emmental (riv.) ... E3
Engadine (valley) ... K3
Err (peak) ... J3
Finsteraarhorn (mt.) ... F3
Finstermünz (pass) ... K3
Fletschhorn (mt.) ... F4
Fluchthorn (mt.) ... K3
Flüela (pass) ... J3
Fluhberg (mt.) ... G2
Fort (mt.) ... D4
Frienisberg (mt.) ... D2
Furka (pass) ... F3
Gelgia (riv.) ... J3
Generoso (mt.) ... H5
Geneva (lake) ... C4
Giacomo (pass) ... G4
Gibloux (mt.) ... D3
Glâne (riv.) ... C3
Glärnisch (mt.) ... H2
Glarus Alps (mts.) ... H3
Glatt (riv.) ... G2
Goms (valley) ... F4
Grand Combin (mt.) ... D5
Grand Muveran (mt.) ... D4
Grande Dixence (dam) ... D4
Grauehörner (mts.) ... H3
Great Saint Bernard (mt.) ... D5
Great Saint Bernard (pass) ... D5
Great Saint Bernard (tunnel) ... D5
Greifensee (lake) ... G2
Greina (pass) ... G3
Gridone (mt.) ... G4
Grimsel (pass) ... F3
Gross Emme (riv.) ... E2
Gross Litzner (mt.) ... K3
Hallwilersee (lake) ... F2
Hausstock (mt.) ... H3
Helsenhorn (mt.) ... F4
Hinterrhein (riv.) ... H3
Hochwang (mt.) ... J3
Hohenstollen (mt.) ... F3
Honegg (mt.) ... E3
Hörnli (mt.) ... G2
Ilfis (riv.) ... E3
Inn (riv.) ... K3
Joch (pass) ... F3
Jorat (mt.) ... C3
Joux (lake) ... B3
Jungfrau (mt.) ... E3
Jura (mts.) ... B3
Kaiseregg (mt.) ... D3
Kesch (peak) ... J3
Kisten (pass) ... H3
Klausen (pass) ... G3
Kleine Emme (riv.) ... F3
La Berra (mt.) ... D3
La Dôle (mt.) ... B4
Landquart (riv.) ... J3
Le Chasseral (mt.) ... D2
Le Gros Crêt (mt.) ... B3

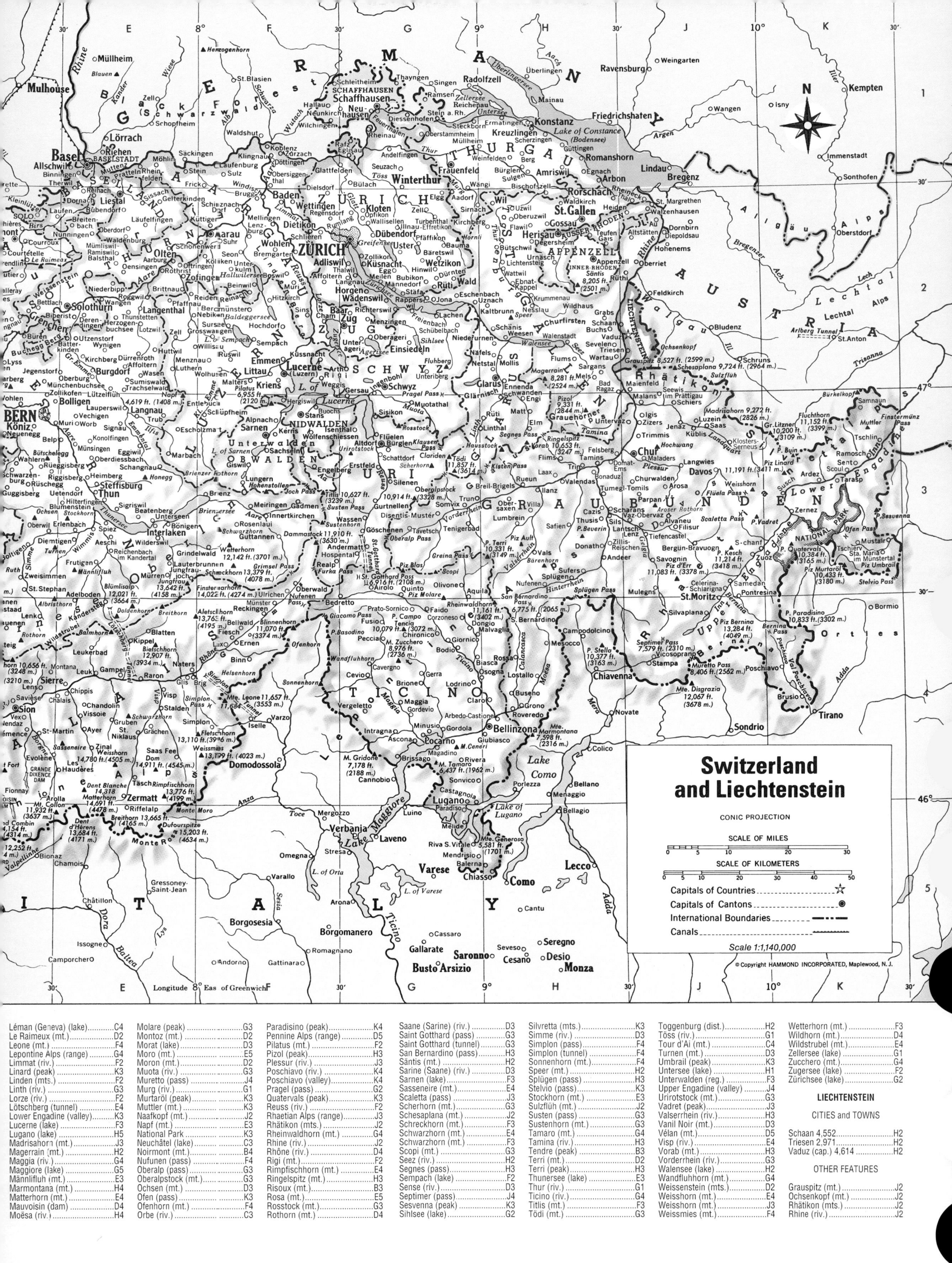

Switzerland and Liechtenstein

CONIC PROJECTION

SCALE OF MILES

SCALE OF KILOMETERS

Capitals of Countries .... ☆
Capitals of Cantons .... ◉
International Boundaries _____ ▬ ▬ ▬
Canals .... ∙∙∙∙∙∙∙∙∙∙∙∙

Scale 1:1,140,000

© Copyright HAMMOND INCORPORATED, Maplewood, N.J.

Léman (Geneva) (lake)....C4	Molare (peak)....G3	Paradisino (peak)....K4	Saane (Sarine) (riv.)....D3	Silvretta (mts.)....K3	Toggenburg (dist.)....H2	Wetterhorn (mt.)....F3
Le Raimeux (mt.)....D2	Montoz (mt.)....D2	Pennine Alps (range)....D5	Saint Gotthard (pass)....G3	Simme (riv.)....D3	Töss (riv.)....G1	Wildhorn (mt.)....D4
Leone (mt.)....F4	Morat (lake)....D3	Pilatus (mt.)....F2	Saint Gotthard (tunnel)....G3	Simplon (pass)....F4	Tour d'Ai (mt.)....C4	Wildstrubel (mt.)....E4
Lepontine Alps (range)....G4	Moro (mt.)....E5	Pizol (peak)....H3	San Bernardino (pass)....H3	Simplon (tunnel)....F4	Turnen (mt.)....D3	Zellersee (lake)....G1
Limmat (riv.)....F2	Moron (mt.)....D2	Plessur (riv.)....J3	Sarine (Saane) (riv.)....D3	Sonnenhorn (mt.)....F4	Umbrail (peak)....K3	Zucchero (mt.)....G4
Linard (peak)....K3	Murg (riv.)....G1	Poschiavo (riv.)....K4	Sarnen (lake)....F3	Speer (mt.)....H2	Untersee (lake)....H1	Zugersee (lake)....F2
Linden (mts.)....F2	Murtaröl (peak)....K3	Poschiavo (valley)....K4	Sassenaire (mt.)....E4	Spluga (pass)....H3	Unterwalden (reg.)....F3	Zürichsee (lake)....G2
Linth (riv.)....G3	Muota (riv.)....G3	Pragel (pass)....G2	Scaletta (pass)....J3	Stelvio (pass)....K3	Upper Engadine (valley)....J4	
Lorze (riv.)....F2	Muttler (mt.)....K3	Quatervals (peak)....K3	Scherhorn (mt.)....G3	Stockhorn (mt.)....E3	Urirotstock (mt.)....G3	**LIECHTENSTEIN**
Lötschberg (tunnel)....E4	Napf (mt.)....E3	Reuss (riv.)....F2	Schesaplana (mt.)....J2	Sulzflüh (mt.)....J2		
Lower Engadine (valley)....K3	National Park....K3	Rhaetian Alps (range)....J3	Schreckhorn (mt.)....F3	Susten (pass)....G3	Vadret (peak)....J3	CITIES and TOWNS
Lucerne (lake)....F3	Neuchâtel (lake)....C3	Rhätikon (mts.)....J2	Schwarzhorn (mt.)....E4	Sustenhorn (mt.)....G3	Valserrhein (mt.)....H3	
Lugano (lake)....H5	Noirmont (mt.)....B4	Rheinwaldhorn (mt.)....G4	Schwarzhorn (mt.)....F3		Vanil Noir (mt.)....D3	Schaan 4,552....H2
Madrisahorn (mt.)....J3	Nufenen (pass)....F4	Rhine (riv.)....J2	Scopi (mt.)....G3	Tamaro (mt.)....G4	Vélan (mt.)....D5	Triesen 2,971....H2
Magerrain (mt.)....H2	Oberalp (pass)....G3	Rhône (riv.)....D4	Seez (riv.)....H2	Tamina (riv.)....H3	Visp (riv.)....E4	Vaduz (cap.) 4,614....H2
Maggia (riv.)....G4	Oberalpstock (mt.)....G3	Rigi (mt.)....F2	Segnes (pass)....H3	Tendre (peak)....B3	Vorab (mt.)....H3	
Maggiore (lake)....G5	Ochsen (mt.)....D3	Rimpfischhorn (mt.)....E5	Sempach (lake)....F2	Terri (mt.)....D2	Vorderrhein (riv.)....G3	OTHER FEATURES
Männlifluh (mt.)....E3	Ofen (pass)....K3	Ringelspitz (mt.)....H3	Sense (riv.)....D3	Terri (mt.)....G3	Walensee (lake)....H2	
Marmontana (mt.)....H4	Ofenhorn (mt.)....F4	Risoux (mt.)....B3	Septimer (pass)....J4	Thunersee (lake)....E3	Wandfluhhorn (mt.)....G4	Grauspitz (mt.)....J2
Matterhorn (mt.)....E4	Orbe (riv.)....C3	Rosa (mt.)....E5	Sesvenna (peak)....K3	Thur (riv.)....G1	Weissenstein (mts.)....D2	Ochsenkopf (mt.)....J2
Mauvoisin (dam)....D4		Rosstock (mt.)....G3	Sihlsee (lake)....G2	Ticino (riv.)....G4	Weisshorn (mt.)....E4	Rhätikon (mts.)....J2
Moësa (riv.)....H4		Rothorn (mt.)....D4		Titlis (mt.)....F3	Weisshorn (mt.)....J3	Rhine (riv.)....J2
				Tödi (mt.)....G3	Weissmies (mt.)....F4	

AUSTRIA

PROVINCES

Burgenland 272,274 ....D3
Carinthia 536,727 ....B3
Lower Austria 1,439,137 ....C2
Salzburg 441,842 ....B3
Styria 1,187,512 ....B3
Tirol 586,139 ....A3
Upper Austria 1,270,426....B2
Vienna (city) 1,515,666 ....D2
Vorarlberg 305,615............A3

CITIES and TOWNS†

Altheim 4,702 ....B2
Althofen 4,274 ....B3
Amstetten 22,015 ....C2
Arnoldstein 6,641 ....B3
Attnang-Puchheim 8,058 ...B2
Bad Aussee 5,047 ....B3
Bad Goisern 6,500 ....B3
Bad Hofgastein 5,960 ......B3
Bad Ischl 13,027 ....B3
Bad Sankt-Leonhard im
  Lavanttal 5,008 ....C3
Baden 23,235 ....D2
Badgastein 5,600 ....B3
Berndorf 8,189 ....C3
Bischofshofen 9,520 ....B3
Bludenz 12,893 ....A3
Bramberg am Wildkogel
  3,410 ....B3
Braunau am Inn 16,192 ....B2
Bregenz 24,683 ....A3
Bruck an der Leitha 7,170..D2
Bruck an der Mur 15,086...C3
Deutsch Feistritz 3,719 ...C3
Deutschkreutz 3,563 ....D3
Deutsch Landsberg 7,623..C3

Hermagor-Preseggersee
  7,116 ....B3
Herzogenburg 7,313 ....C2
Hohenems 12,669 ....A3
Hollabrunn 10,254 ....D2
Hopfgarten in Nordtirol
  4,956 ....A3
Horn 6,319 ....C2
Imst 6,691 ....A3
Innsbruck 116,110 ....A3
Jenbach 5,725 ....A3
Jennersdorf 4,131 ....D3
Judenburg 11,199 ....C3
Kapfenberg 25,719 ....C3
Kaprun 2,764 ....B3
Kindberg 6,269 ....C3
Kirchdorf an der Krems
  3,708 ....B3
Kitzbühel 7,872 ....B3
Klagenfurt 86,303 ....C3
Klosterneuburg 23,307 ....D2
Knittelfeld 14,153 ....C3
Köflach 12,009 ....C3
Korneuburg 9,132 ....D2
Kötschach-Mauthen 3,633..B3
Krems an der Donau 23,123..C2
Kufstein 13,125 ....B3
Laa an der Thaya 6,485 ...D2
Laakirchen 7,670 ....B3
Landeck 7,325 ....A3
Landskron 10,429 ....B3
Langenlois 6,474 ....C2
Langenwang 4,187 ....C3
Lavamünd 3,824 ....C3
Leibnitz 6,659 ....C3
Lenzing 5,079 ....B3
Leoben 32,006 ....C3
Lienz 11,699 ....B3
Liezen 7,021 ....B3
Lilienfeld 3,030 ....C3
Linz 197,962 ....C2

Salzburg 138,213 ....B3
Sankt Johann in Tirol 6,495....B3
Sankt Michael im Lungau
  3,246 ....B3
Sankt Michael in
  Obersteiermark 3,604 ...C3
Sankt Paul im Lavanttal
  5,770 ....C3
Sankt Pölten 51,102 ....C2
Sankt Valentin 8,759 ......C2
Sankt Veit an der Glan 12,021..C3
Schärding 5,784 ....B2
Scheibbs 4,537 ....C2
Schladming 3,930 ....B3
Schrems 6,010 ....C2
Schwarzach im Pongau
  3,607 ....B3
Schwaz 10,936 ....A3
Schwechat 14,844 ....D2
Schwertberg 4,385 ....C2
Sierning 7,891 ....C2
Solbad Hall in Tirol 12,622....A3
Spittal an der Drau 14,769..B3
Steyr 38,967 ....C2
Stockerau 12,692 ....C2
Tamsweg 5,256 ....B3
Telfs 7,749 ....A3
Ternitz 16,154 ....C3
Traiskirchen 14,102 ....D2
Traun 21,524 ....C2
Trieben 4,471 ....C3
Trofaiach 8,959 ....C3
Tulln 11,287 ....C2
Velden am Wörthersee 7,458..C3
Vienna (cap.) 1,515,666 ...D2
Villach 52,744 ....B3
Vöcklabruck 11,039 ....B2
Voitsberg 110,951 ....C3
Völkermarkt 10,900 ....C3
Waidhofen an der Thaya
  5,401 ....C2

Waidhofen an der Ybbs
  11,339 ....C2
Weitensfeld-Flattnitz 5,158....C3
Weiz 8,418 ....C3
Wels 51,024 ....C2
Wien (Vienna) (cap.)
  1,515,666 ....D2
Wiener Neustadt 35,050...D2
Wilhelmsburg 6,339 ....C2
Wolfsberg 28,182 ....C3
Wörgl 8,644 ....A3
Ybbs an der Donau 5,983..C2
Zell am See 7,959 ....B3
Zeltweg 8,722 ....C3
Zistersdorf 5,814 ....D2
Zwettl-Niederösterreich
  11,579 ....C2

OTHER FEATURES

Allgäu Alps (mts.) A3
Atter See (lake) B3
Bavarian Alps (mts.) A3
Bodensee (Constance) (lake)..A3
Brenner (pass) A3
Carnic Alps (mts.) B3
Coglians (mt.) B3
Constance (lake) A3
Danube (riv.) C2
Donau (Danube) (riv.) D2
Drau (riv.) B3
Enns (riv.) C3
Greiner Wald (mts.) C2
Grosser Peilstein (mt.) ...C2
Grossglockner (mt.) B3
Hochgolling (mt.) B3
Hohe Tauern (range) B3
Hohe Warte (Coglians) (mt.)..B3
Inn (riv.) B2
Kamp (riv.) C2
Karawanken (range) C3

Lafnitz (riv.) D3
March (riv.) D2
Mühlviertel (reg.) C2
Mur (riv.) C3
Mürz (riv.) C3
Neusiedler See (lake) D3
Niedere Tauern (range) ...B3
Olsa (riv.) C3
Ötztal Alps (mts.) A3
Parseierspitze (mt.) A3
Raab (riv.) C3
Rhine (riv.) A3
Salzach (riv.) B2
Salzkammergut (reg.) B3
Semmering (pass) C3
Thaya (riv.) C2
Traun (riv.) B3
Traun See (lake) B3
Wildspitze (mt.) A3
Zugspitze (mt.) A3

CZECHOSLOVAKIA

REPUBLICS

Czech Rep. 10,291,927 ....B1
Slovak Rep. 4,991,168 ....E2

REGIONS

Bratislava (city) 380,259......D2
Jihočeský 689,229 ....C2
Jihomoravský 2,040,903 ...C2
Praha (city) 1,182,186 ....C1
Severočeský 1,167,231 ....C1
Severomoravský 1,932,722...D2
Středočeský 1,151,265 ....C2
Středoslovenský
  1,524,766 ....E2
Východočeský
  1,248,466 ....C1
Východoslovenský
  1,402,252 ....F2
Západočeský 879,925......C2
Západoslovenský 1,683,891..D2

CITIES and TOWNS

Aš 13,551 ....B1
Austerlitz (Slavkov) 6,316....D2
Bánovce nad Bebravou
  15,342 ....E2
Banská Bystrica 66,412....E2
Banská Štiavnica 9,180 ...E2
Bardejov 23,741 ....F2

Benešov 15,172 ....C2
Beroun 23,580 ....B2
Bílina 18,836 ....B1
Blansko 19,508 ....D2
Blatná 7,264 ....B2
Boskovice 12,025 ....D2
Brandýs nad Labem-Stará
  Boleslavv 15,071 ....C1
Bratislava 380,259 ....D2
Břeclav 23,978 ....D2
Brezno 17,872 ....E2
Brno 371,463 ....D2
Broumov 7,834 ....C1
Bruntál 17,062 ....D2
Bystřice nad Pernštejnem
  10,044 ....D2
Bystřice pod Hostýnem
  10,359 ....D2
Bytča 11,789 ....E2
Čadca 19,319 ....E2
Čalovo 8,063 ....D3
Čáslav 9,950 ....C2
Česká Kamenice 7,272 ....C1
Česká Lípa 24,924 ....C1
Česká Třebová 17,136 ....D2
České Budějovice 90,415..C2
Český Krumlov 13,776 ....C2

(continued)

Topography

Deutsch Wagram 5,111 ....D2
Dornbirn 38,663 ....A3
Ebensee 9,005 ....B3
Eggenburg 3,729 ....C2
Eisenerz 10,074 ....C3
Eisenkappel-Vellach 3,520...C3
Eisenstadt 10,150 ....D3
Enns 9,731 ....C2
Feldbach 4,073 ....C3
Feldkirch 23,876 ....A3
Feldkirchen in Kärnten
  12,181 ....B3
Ferlach 7,658 ....C3
Fieberbrunn 3,926 ....B3
Fohnsdorf 10,360 ....C3
Frankenmarkt 3,165 ....B3
Friesach 7,074 ....C3
Freistadt 6,289 ....C2
Frohnleiten 5,061 ....C3
Fürstenfeld 6,040 ....C3
Gaming 4,099 ....C3
Gänserndorf 4,948 ....D2
Gleisdorf 5,078 ....C3
Gloggnitz 6,290 ....C3
Gmünd 6,457 ....B3
Gmunden 12,720 ....B3
Golling an der Salzach 3,409..B3
Götzis 8,740 ....A3
Graz 243,405 ....C3
Grieskirchen 4,813 ....B2
Grosssiegharts 3,374 .....C2
Grünburg 3,630 ....C3
Güssing 3,630 ....D3
Haag 5,095 ....C2
Hainburg an der Donau
  5,749 ....D2
Hainfeld 3,735 ....C2
Hallein 15,404 ....B3
Hartberg 6,048 ....C3
Heidenreichstein 5,351 ...C2
Heiligenblut 1,334 ....B3

Lustenau 17,404 ....A3
Mannersdorf am
  Leithagebirge 3,878 .....D3
Marchegg 2,676 ....D2
Matrei in Osttirol 4,298 ..B3
Mattersburg 5,682 ....D3
Mattighofen 4,566 ....B2
Mauthausen 4,353 ....C2
Mauthen-Kötschach 3,633..B3
Mayrhofen 3,274 ....A3
Melk 5,074 ....C2
Mistelbach an der Zaya
  10,300 ....D2
Mittersill 5,033 ....B3
Mödling 19,333 ....D2
Mürzzuschlag 10,774 ......C3
Neumarkt am Wallersee
  3,703 ....B3
Neunkirchen 10,780 ....D3
Neusiedl am See 4,154 ....D3
Ober Grafendorf 4,475 ....C2
Oberndorf bei Salzburg 3,838..B3
Oberwart 5,973 ....C3
Oberwölz 9,510 ....C3
Paternion 5,914 ....B3
Perg 5,226 ....C2
Pinkafeld 4,802 ....C3
Pöchlarn 3,637 ....C2
Poysdorf 5,658 ....D2
Pregarten 3,823 ....C2
Raabs an der Thaya 3,839..C2
Radenthein 7,083 ....B3
Radstadt 3,994 ....B3
Rankweil 9,929 ....A3
Reichenau an der Rax 3,601..C3
Retz 4,373 ....C2
Reutte 5,145 ....A3
Ried im Innkreis 10,952...B2
Rottenmann 5,425 ....C3
Saalfelden am Steinernen
  Meer 11,436 ....B3

AREA 32,375 sq. mi. (83,85? sq. km.)
POPULATION 7,635,000
CAPITAL Vienna
LARGEST CITY Vienna
HIGHEST POINT Grossglockner
  12,457 ft. (3,797 m.)
MONETARY UNIT schilling
MAJOR LANGUAGE German
MAJOR RELIGION Roman Catholicism

AREA 49,373 sq. mi. (127,876 sq. km.)
POPULATION 15,679,000
CAPITAL Prague
LARGEST CITY Prague
HIGHEST POINT Gerlachovka 8,707 ft.
  (2,654 m.)
MONETARY UNIT koruna
MAJOR LANGUAGES Czech, Slovak
MAJOR RELIGIONS Roman Catholicism,
  Protestantism

AREA 35,919 sq. mi. (93,030 sq. km.)
POPULATION 10,553,000
CAPITAL Budapest
LARGEST CITY Budapest
HIGHEST POINT Kékes 3,330 ft.
  (1,015 m.)
MONETARY UNIT forint
MAJOR LANGUAGE Hungarian
MAJOR RELIGIONS Roman Catholicism,
  Protestantism

AUSTRIA

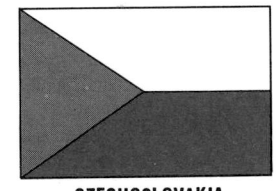

CZECHOSLOVAKIA

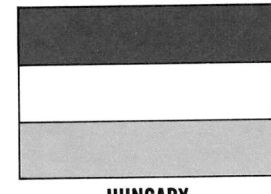

HUNGARY

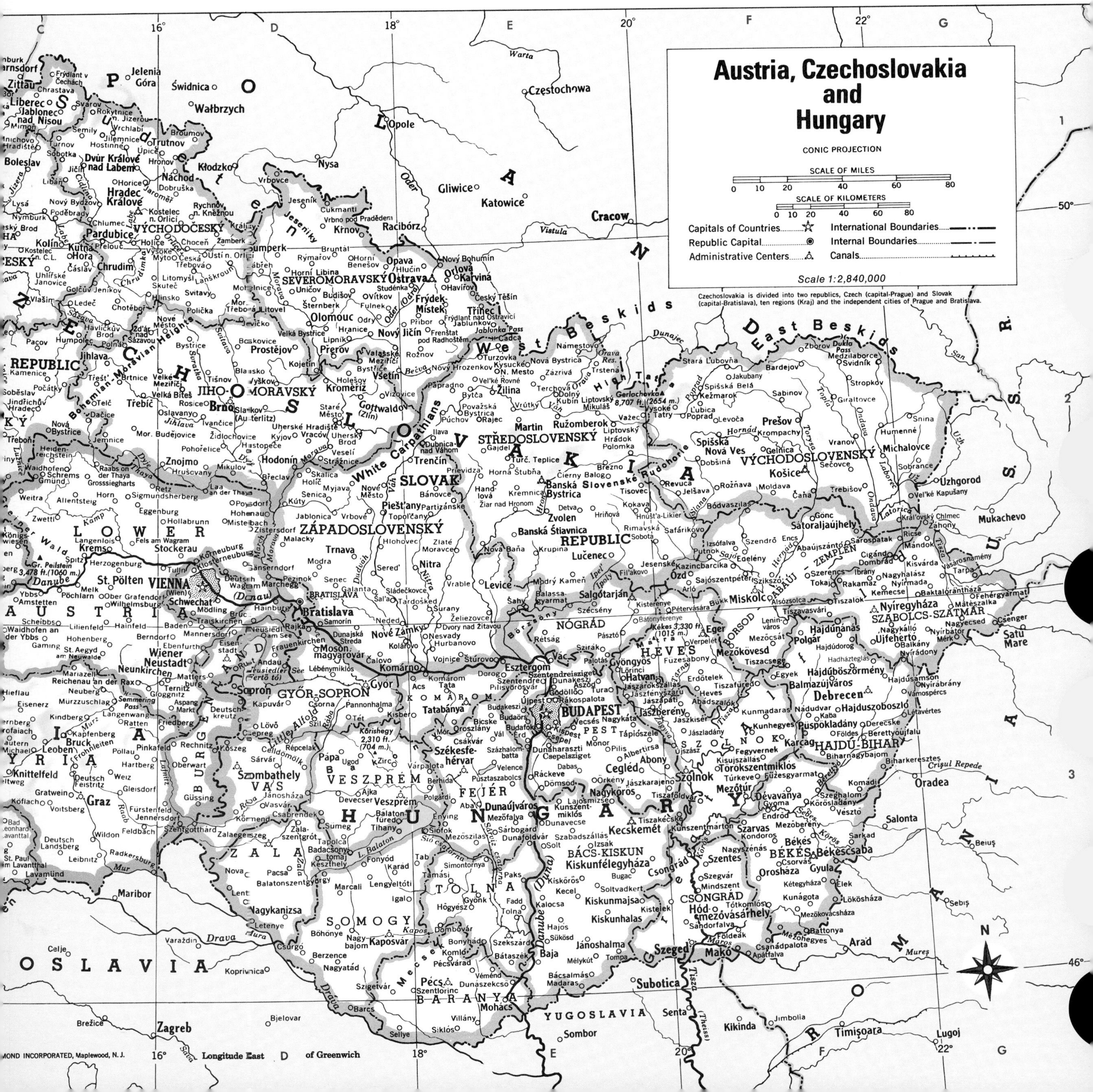

Austria, Czechoslovakia and Hungary

CONIC PROJECTION

SCALE OF MILES
0 10 20   40   60   80

SCALE OF KILOMETERS
0 10 20   40   60   80

Capitals of Countries............☆   International Boundaries.........
Republic Capital..................⊛   Internal Boundaries...............
Administrative Centers.........△   Canals.................................

Scale 1:2,840,000

Czechoslovakia is divided into two republics, Czech (capital-Prague) and Slovak
(capital-Bratislava), ten regions (Kraj) and the independent cities of Prague and Bratislava.

HAMMOND INCORPORATED, Maplewood, N.J.

Český Těšín 23,389 ....E2
Cheb 31,039 ....B1
Chodov 14,704 ....B1
Chomutov 51,769 ....B1
Chotěboř 8,744 ....C2
Chrastava 7,022 ....C1
Chrudim 20,517 ....C2
Dačice 7,443 ....C2
Děčín 49,682 ....C1
Detva 14,261 ....E2
Dobříš 7,466 ....C2
Dolný Kubín 13,971 ....E2
Domažlice 11,461 ....B2
Dubnica nad Váhom 15,580 ...E2
Duchcov 10,554 ....B1
Dunajská Streda 18,715 ....D3
Dvůr Králové nad Labem
   17,270 ....C1
Falknov (Sokolov) 28,523 ....B1
Fiľakovo 10,497 ....E2
Frenštát pod Radhoště
   10,434 ....E2
Frýdek-Místek 59,430 ....E2
Frýdlant nad
   Ostravicí 14,065 ....E2
Frýdlant v. Čechách 7,418 ....C1
Fulnek 8,214 ....D2
Galanta 15,477 ....D2
Gottwaldov 83,983 ....E2
Handlová 17,777 ....E2
Havířov 89,920 ....E2
Havlíčkův Brod 24,550 ....C2
Hlinsko 10,635 ....C2
Hlohovec 21,148 ....D2
Hlučín 22,581 ....D2
Hodonín 25,485 ....D2
Holešov 13,323 ....D2
Holíč 8,741 ....D2
Hořice v Podkrkonoší
   9,251 ....C1
Hradec Králové 95,588 ....C1
Hranice 18,099 ....D2
Hřínová 8,485 ....E2
Hronov 9,609 ....D1
Humenné 27,285 ....F2
Humpolec 10,042 ....C2
Hurbanovo 7,613 ....E3
Ivančice 9,746 ....D2
Jablonec nad Nisou 42,179 ...C1
Jablunkov 15,962 ....E2
Jaroměř 11,562 ....C1
Jeseník 14,314 ....D1
Jičín 16,440 ....C1
Jihlava 51,144 ....C2
Jindřichův Hradec 20,096 .....C2
Jiřkov 11,980 ....B1
Kadaň 18,420 ....B1
Karlovy Vary 60,950 ....B1
Karviná 78,334 ....E2
Kežmarok 17,570 ....F2
Kladno 71,141 ....B1
Klatovy 21,782 ....B2
Kojetín 8,881 ....D2
Kolárovo 11,295 ....D3
Kolín 30,921 ....C1
Komárno 32,520 ....D3
Košice 202,368 ....F2
Kralupy nad Vltavou 17,528 ...C1
Kraslice 7,371 ....B1
Kremnica 7,168 ....E2
Krnov 25,678 ....D1
Kroměříž 25,887 ....D2
Krupina 7,337 ....E2
Krupka 9,336 ....B1
Kutná Hora 20,927 ....C2
Kyjov 12,632 ....D2
Kysucké Nové Mesto 14,083 ...E2
Lanškroun 10,620 ....D2
Levice 26,132 ....E2
Levoča 11,025 ....F2

Liberec 97,474 ....C1
Lidice C1
Lipník nad Bečvou 9,961 ......D2
Liptovský Hrádok 9,197 ....E2
Liptovský Mikuláš 24,520 .....E2
Litoměřice 23,835 ....C1
Litomyšl 10,079 ....C2
Litovel 12,454 ....D2
Litvínov 22,624 ....B1
Louny 20,436 ....B1
Lovosice 11,456 ....C1
Lučenec 26,399 ....E2
Lysá nad Labem 9,113 ....C1
Malacky 15,218 ....D2
Mariánské Lázně 17,932 ......B2
Martin 56,208 ....E2
Mělník 18,941 ....C1
Michalovce 29,765 ....F2
Mikulov 8,472 ....D2
Milevsko 8,852 ....C2
Mimoň 7,437 ....C1
Mladá Boleslav 45,896 ....C1
Mnichovo Hradiště 7,340 ....C1
Modra 7,679 ....D2
Mohelnice 9,405 ....D2
Moravská Třebová 11,543 ...D2
Moravské Budějovice 8,943 ...C2
Most 60,119 ....B1
Myjava 11,668 ....D2
Náchod 19,892 ....D1
Nejdek 9,768 ....B1
Nitra 76,663 ....E2
Nová Baňa 8,321 ....E2
Nové Město na Moravě
   11,330 ....D2
Nové Město nad Váhom
   18,170 ....D2
Nové Zámky 34,147 ....D3
Nový Bohumín 16,700 ....E2
Nový Bor 10,493 ....C1
Nový Bydžov 9,317 ....C1
Nový Jičín 31,506 ....D2
Nymburk 14,033 ....C1
Odry 10,032 ....D2
Olomouc 102,112 ....D2
Opava 59,384 ....D2
Orlová 31,190 ....E2
Ostrava 322,073 ....E2
Ostrov 19,618 ....B1
Pardubice 91,855 ....C1
Partizánske 23,266 ....E2
Pezinok 17,116 ....D2
Piešťany 30,487 ....D2
Písek 28,104 ....C2
Plzeň 170,701 ....B2
Poděbrady 13,782 ....C1
Pohořelice 5,125 ....D2
Polička 8,972 ....C2
Poprad 38,077 ....F2
Považská Bystrica 30,444 ...E2
Prachatice 10,354 ....B2
Prague (Praha) (cap.)
   1,182,186 ....C1
Přelouč 8,561 ....C1
Přerov 50,265 ....D2
Prešov 71,500 ....F2
Příbor 12,711 ....E2
Příbram 37,854 ....C2
Prievidza 40,813 ....E2
Prostějov 49,599 ....D2
Púchov 17,554 ....E2
Rakovník 16,233 ....B1
Revúca 11,881 ....E2
Říčany u Prahy 10,703 ....C2
Rimavská Sobota 19,699 .....E2
Rokycany 15,041 ....B2
Roudnice nad Labem 13,956 ...C1
Rožňava 18,039 ....E2
Rožnov pod Radhoštěm
   15,468 ....E2

Rumburk 10,255 ....C1
Ružomberok 26,396 ....E2
Rychnov nad Kněžnou
   8,955 ....D1
Rýmařov 9,927 ....D2
Sabinov 7,008 ....F2
Šafárikovo 7,021 ....E2
Šahy 8,034 ....E2
Šaľa 19,167 ....D2
Samorín 9,677 ....D2
Sedlčany 7,453 ....C2
Semily 8,464 ....C1
Senec 10,772 ....D2
Senica 15,515 ....D2
Sereď 16,071 ....D2
Skalica 13,833 ....D2
Slaný 14,705 ....C1
Slavkov 6,316 ....D2
Snina 13,347 ....G2
Soběslav 8,406 ....C2
Sokolov 28,523 ....B1
Spišská Nová Ves 31,917 .....F2
Staré Město 6,293 ....D2
Šternberk 16,342 ....D2
Strakonice 22,611 ....B2
Stříbro 8,169 ....B2
Stropkov 7,405 ....F2
Studénka 12,497 ....E2
Šťúrovo 12,807 ....E3
Šumperk 31,873 ....D2
Šurany 11,320 ....E2
Sušice 11,400 ....B2
Svidník 7,538 ....F2
Svitavy 19,075 ....D2
Tábor 31,867 ....C2
Tachov 12,798 ....B2
Teplice 53,964 ....B1
Tišnov 12,179 ....D2
Topolčany 31,340 ....E2
Třebíč 30,246 ....C2
Trebišov 14,961 ....F2
Třeboň 8,878 ....C2
Trenčín 47,887 ....E2
Třinec 44,739 ....E2
Trnava 64,062 ....D2
Trutnov 27,648 ....C1
Turnov 13,906 ....C1
Turzovka 6,962 ....E2
Ústí nad Labem 87,909 ....C1
Ústí nad Orlicí 15,945 ....D2
Uherské Hradiště 36,756 .....D2
Uherský Brod 17,459 ....D2
Uničov 12,507 ....D2
Valašské Meziříčí
   26,531 ....D2
Varnsdorf 16,356 ....C1
Veľké Kapušany 8,459 ....G2
Velké Meziříčí 14,073 ....D2
Veselí nad Moravou 12,464 ...D2
Vimperk 7,257 ....B2
Vítkov 7,543 ....D2
Vlašim 13,284 ....C2
Vodňany 6,989 ....C2
Vráble 7,586 ....E2
Vranov nad Teplou 18,423 ...F2
Vrbno pod Pradědem
   6,912 ....D1
Vrchlabí 12,419 ....C1
Vsetín 29,927 ....D2
Vyškov 18,330 ....D2
Vysoké Mýto 10,887 ....D2
Zábřeh 15,184 ....D2
Žatec 19,529 ....B1
Žďár nad Sázavou 25,015 ....C2
Žiar nad Hronom 19,098 ......E2
Žilina 83,016 ....E2
Zlaté Moravce 14,119 ....E2
Zlín (Gottwaldov) 83,983 .....D2
Znojmo 39,271 ....D2
Zvolen 36,538 ....E2

OTHER FEATURES

Bečva (riv.) E2
Berounka (riv.) C2
Beskids, East (mts.) F1
Beskids, West (mts.) E2
Bohemian (for.) B2
Bohemian-Moravian Heights
   (hills) C2
Chrudimka (riv.) C2
Cidlina (riv.) C1
Danube (riv.) C2
Dudvá (riv.) D2
Dukla (pass) F2
Dunajec (riv.) F2
Dyje (riv.) C2
Erzgebirge (mts.) B1
Gerlachovka (mt.) F2
Hornád (riv.) F2
Hron (riv.) E2
Ipeľ (riv.) E2
Jablunka (pass) E2
Jeseníky (mts.) D1
Jihlava (riv.) C2
Jizera (riv.) C1
Krušné Hory (Erzgebirge)
   (mts.) B1
Labe (riv.) C1
Laborec (riv.) F2
Latorica (riv.) F2
Lipno (res.) B2
Lužnice (riv.) C2
Moldau (Vltava) (riv.) C2
Morava (riv.) D2
Mže (riv.) B2
Nitra (riv.) E2
Oder (Odra) (riv.) D2
Ohře (riv.) B1
Ondava (riv.) F2
Orava (riv.) E2
Orava (riv.) E2
Orlice (riv.) D1
Orlická (res.) C2
Otava (riv.) B2
Poprad (riv.) F2
Radbuza (riv.) B2
Sázava (riv.) C2
Slaná (riv.) E2
Slovenské Rudohorie (mts.) ...E2
Sudeten (mts.) C1
Svitava (riv.) D2
Svratka (riv.) D2
Tatra, High (riv.) F2
Topľa (riv.) F2
Torysa (riv.) F2
Úhlava (riv.) B2
Už (riv.) G2
Váh (riv.) D2
Vltava (riv.) C2
White Carpathians (mts.) ...E2

HUNGARY

COUNTIES

Bács-Kiskun 553,000 ....E3
Baranya 434,000 ....E4
Békés 416,000 ....F3
Borsod-Abaúj-Zemplén
   779,000 ....F2
Budapest (city) 2,104,000 ...E3
Csongrád 457,000 ....E3
Fejér 426,000 ....E3
Győr-Sopron 426,000 ....D3
Hajdú-Bihar 549,000 ....F3
Heves 338,000 ....E3
Komárom 320,000 ....D3
Nógrád 229,000 ....E3
Pest 988,000 ....E3

Szabolcs-Szatmár 570,000 ...G3
Szolnok 428,000 ....F3
Tolna 263,000 ....E3
Vas 277,000 ....D3
Veszprém 387,000 ....D3
Zala 311,000 ....D3

CITIES and TOWNS

Abádszalók 6,386 ....F3
Abaújszántó 4,209 ....F2
Abony 15,624 ....E3
Ács 8,423 ....D3
Ajka 34,000 ....D3
Albertirsa 11,252 ....E3
Alsózsolca 5,045 ....F2
Bácsalmás 8,000 ....E3
Baja 41,000 ....E3
Balassagyarmat 20,000 ......E2
Balatonfüred 15,000 ....D3
Balkány 7,667 ....F3
Balmazújváros 17,371 ....F3
Barcs 12,000 ....D4
Bátaszék 7,274 ....E3
Battonya 9,324 ....F3
Békés 22,000 ....F3
Békéscsaba 71,000 ....F3
Berettyóújfalu 18,000 ....F3
Bicske 13,000 ....E3
Bonyhád 15,000 ....E3
Budafok 40,623 ....E3
Budakeszi 10,429 ....E3
Budaörs 22,000 ....E3
Budapest (cap.) 2,104,000 ...E3
Cegléd 40,000 ....E3
Celldömölk 12,000 ....D3
Csepel 71,693 ....E3
Csongrád 21,000 ....E3
Csorna 13,000 ....D3
Dabas 13,075 ....E3
Debrecen 217,000 ....F3
Derecske 9,579 ....F3
Dévaványa 11,208 ....F3
Dombóvár 21,000 ....D3
Dorog 13,000 ....E3
Dunaföldvár 10,318 ....E3
Dunaharaszti 15,788 ....E3
Dunakeszi 29,000 ....E3
Dunaújváros 62,000 ....E3
Edelény 12,000 ....F2
Eger 67,000 ....E3
Egyek 7,956 ....F3
Endrőd 8,136 ....F3
Enying 7,518 ....E3
Érd 44,904 ....E3
Esztergom 30,476 ....E3
Fegyvernek 8,421 ....F3
Fehérgyarmat 9,000 ....G3
Füzesgyarmat 7,097 ....F3
Gödöllő 30,000 ....E3
Gyöngyös 36,000 ....E3
Gyoma 10,392 ....F3
Győr 131,000 ....D3
Gyula 36,000 ....F3
Hadháztéglás 13,626 ....F3
Hajdúboszormény 31,000 ...F3
Hajdúdorog 10,118 ....F3
Hajdúnánás 18,000 ....F3
Hajdúsámson 7,492 ....F3
Hajdúszoboszló 24,000 ....F3
Hatvan 25,000 ....E3
Heves 11,000 ....E3
Hódmezővásárhely 54,000 ...F3
Izsák 7,686 ....E3
Jánoshalma 12,534 ....E3
Jászapáti 10,424 ....F3
Jászárokszállás 10,139 ....E3
Jászberény 30,000 ....E3
Jászladány 7,823 ....F3
Kalocsa 20,000 ....E3

Kaposvár 74,000 ....D3
Kapuvár 11,000 ....D3
Karcag 25,000 ....F3
Kazincbarcika 39,000 ....F2
Kecel 10,493 ....E3
Kecskemét 105,000 ....E3
Keszthely 23,000 ....D3
Kisbér 8,000 ....D3
Kiskőrös 15,000 ....E3
Kiskunfélegyháza 35,000 ....E3
Kiskunhalas 32,000 ....E3
Kiskunmajsa 14,439 ....E3
Kispest 65,106 ....E3
Kistelek 8,544 ....E3
Kisújszállás 13,000 ....F3
Kisvárda 17,828 ....G2
Komádi 8,765 ....F3
Komárom 19,955 ....E3
Komló 30,301 ....E3
Kondoros 7,319 ....F3
Körmend 12,000 ....D3
Kőszeg 14,000 ....D3
Kunhegyes 10,116 ....F3
Kunmadaras 7,343 ....F3
Kunszentmárton 12,000 ......F3
Kunszentmiklós 7,952 ....E3
Lajosmizse 12,872 ....E3
Leninváros 19,000 ....F3
Lenti 9,000 ....D3
Létavértes 9,106 ....F3
Lőrinci 10,679 ....E3
Makó 29,000 ....F3
Marcali 13,000 ....D3
Mátészalka 20,000 ....G3
Mélykút 7,640 ....E3
Mezőberény 12,702 ....F3
Mezőhegyes 8,631 ....F3
Mezőkovácsháza 7,000 ....F3
Mezőkövesd 18,000 ....F3
Mezőtúr 21,000 ....F3
Mindszent 8,730 ....F3
Miskolc 210,000 ....F2
Mohács 21,000 ....E4
Monor 16,838 ....E3
Mór 12,066 ....E3
Mosonmagyaróvár 30,000 ...D3
Nádudvar 9,447 ....F3
Nagyatád 15,000 ....D3
Nagyecsed 8,225 ....G3
Nagykálló 11,282 ....F3
Nagykanizsa 55,000 ....D3
Nagykáta 11,922 ....E3
Nagykőrös 27,000 ....E3
Nagyszénás 7,124 ....F3
Nyíradony 7,146 ....F3
Nyírbátor 14,000 ....G3
Nyíregyháza 119,000 ....F3
Oroszlány 22,000 ....E3
Orosháza 36,000 ....F3
Ózd 45,000 ....F2
Paks 26,000 ....E3
Pápa 35,000 ....D3
Pásztó 12,000 ....E3
Pécs 182,000 ....E3
Pilis 9,055 ....E3
Pilisvörösvár 10,217 ....E3
Polgár 9,429 ....F3
Püspökladány 16,000 ....F3
Putnok 7,103 ....F2
Ráckeve 7,534 ....E3
Rákospalota 60,983 ....E3
Sajószentpéter 13,992 ....F2
Salgótarján 49,000 ....E2
Sárbogárd 13,000 ....E3
Sarkal 11,937 ....F3
Sárospatak 15,000 ....F2
Sárvár 16,000 ....D3
Sátoraljaújhely 20,000 ....F2
Siklós 11,000 ....E4
Siófok 24,000 ....E3

Soltvadkert 7,934 ....E3
Sopron 57,000 ....D3
Szabadszállás 8,223 ....E3
Szarvas 19,000 ....F3
Százhalombatta 18,000 ....E3
Szeged 188,000 ....E3
Szeghalom 10,000 ....F3
Székesfehérvár 113,000 ......E3
Szekszárd 39,000 ....E3
Szentendre 20,000 ....E3
Szentes 35,000 ....F3
Szentgotthárd 8,000 ....D3
Szerencs 10,000 ....F2
Szigetvár 13,000 ....D3
Szolnok 81,000 ....F3
Szombathely 87,000 ....D3
Tamási 10,000 ....E3
Tapolca 18,000 ....D3
Tata 26,000 ....E3
Tatabánya 76,000 ....E3
Tiszaföldvár 12,560 ....F3
Tiszafüred 14,000 ....F3
Tiszakécske 12,000 ....F3
Tiszavasvári 14,000 ....F3
Tolna 8,997 ....E3
Törökszentmiklós 24,000 ....F3
Tótkomlós 8,803 ....F3
Tura 8,235 ....E3
Túrkeve 11,000 ....F3
Újfehértó 14,412 ....F3
Újpest 80,384 ....E3
Vác 36,000 ....E3
Várpalota 28,000 ....E3
Vásárosnamény 9,000 ....G2
Vecsés 19,193 ....E3
Veszprém 66,000 ....D3
Vészto 9,815 ....F3
Zalaegerszeg 63,000 ....D3
Zalaszentgrót 8,000 ....D3
Zirc 11,000 ....D3

OTHER FEATURES

Bakony (mts.) D3
Balaton (lake) D3
Berettyó (riv.) F3
Börzsöny (mts.) E3
Bükk (mts.) F2
Csepelsziget (isl.) E3
Danube (riv.) E3
Dráva (riv.) D3
Duna (Danube) (riv.) E3
Fertő tó (Neusiedler See)
   (lake) D3
Great Alföld (plain) F3
Hernád (riv.) F2
Ipoly (riv.) E3
Kapos (riv.) D3
Kékes (mt.) E3
Korishegy (mt.) D3
Körös (riv.) F3
Little Alfold (plain) D3
Maros (riv.) F3
Mátra (mts.) E3
Mecsek (mts.) E3
Mura (riv.) D3
Rába (riv.) D3
Sajó (riv.) F2
Sárviz csatorna (canal) E3
Sebes Körös (riv.) F3
Sió csatorna (canal) E3
Szentendreisziget (isl.) E3
Tarna (riv.) E3
Tisza (riv.) F3
Zagyva (riv.) E3
Zala (riv.) D3

*City and suburbs.
†Population of Austrian cities
are communes.

Agriculture, Industry and Resources

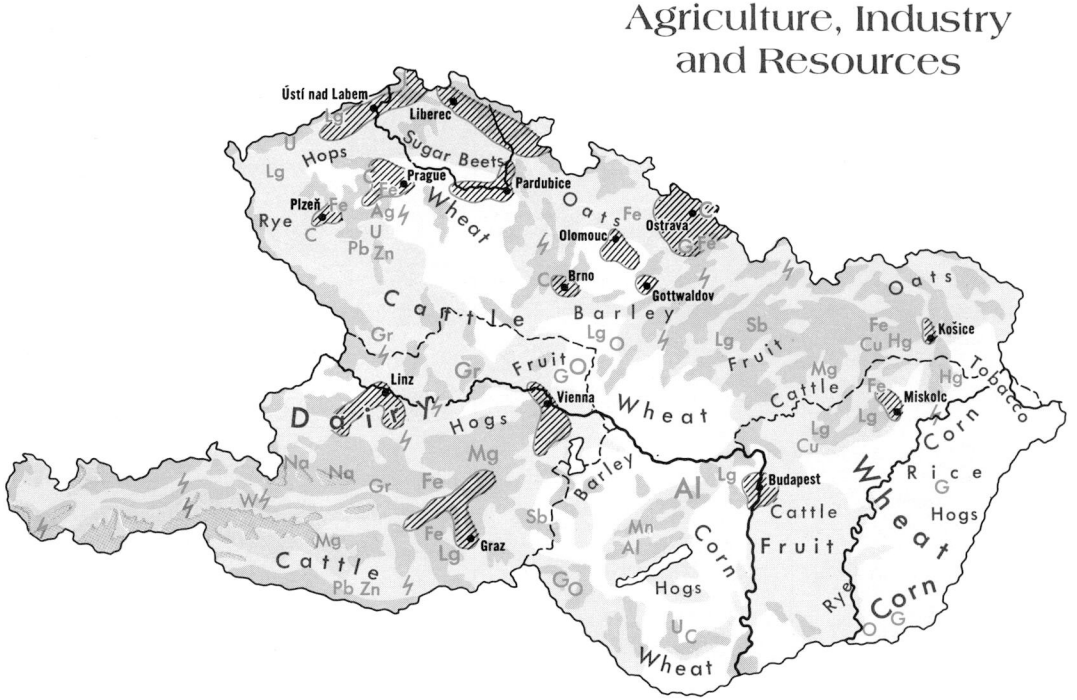

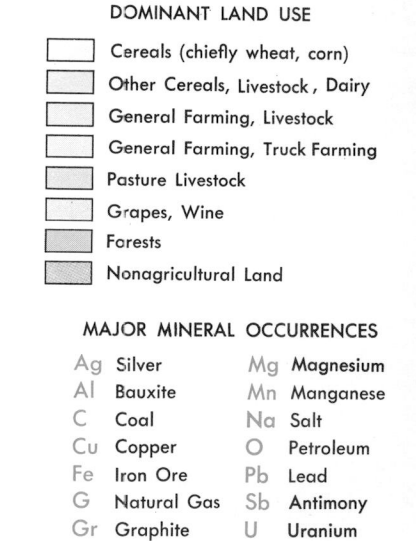

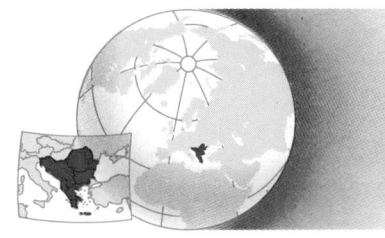

YUGOSLAVIA

AREA 98,766 sq. mi. (255,804 sq. km.)
POPULATION 23,798,000
CAPITAL Belgrade
LARGEST CITY Belgrade
HIGHEST POINT Triglav 9,393 ft. (2,863 m.)
MONETARY UNIT Yugoslav dinar
MAJOR LANGUAGES Serbo-Croation, Slovenian,
  Macedonian, Montenegrin, Albanian
MAJOR RELIGIONS Eastern Orthodoxy,
  Roman Catholicism, Islam

ALBANIA

AREA 11,100 sq. mi. (28,749 sq. km.)
POPULATION 3,199,000
CAPITAL Tiranë
LARGEST CITY Tiranë
HIGHEST POINT Korab 9,026 ft. (2,751 m.)
MONETARY UNIT lek
MAJOR LANGUAGE Albanian
MAJOR RELIGIONS Islam, Eastern Orthodoxy,
  Roman Catholicism

ROMANIA

AREA 91,699 sq. mi. (237,500 sq. km.)
POPULATION 23,249,000
CAPITAL Bucharest
LARGEST CITY Bucharest
HIGHEST POINT Moldoveanul 8,343 ft.
  (2,543 m.)
MONETARY UNIT leu
MAJOR LANGUAGES Romanian, Hungarian
MAJOR RELIGION Eastern Orthodoxy

BULGARIA

AREA 42,823 sq. mi. (110,912 sq. km.)
POPULATION 8,981,000
CAPITAL Sofia
LARGEST CITY Sofia
HIGHEST POINT Musala 9,597 ft. (2,925 m.)
MONETARY UNIT lev
MAJOR LANGUAGE Bulgarian
MAJOR RELIGION Eastern Orthodoxy

GREECE

AREA 50,944 sq. mi. (131,945 sq. km.)
POPULATION 9,983,000
CAPITAL Athens
LARGEST CITY Athens
HIGHEST POINT Olympus 9,570 ft. (2,917 m.)
MONETARY UNIT drachma
MAJOR LANGUAGE Greek
MAJOR RELIGION Eastern (Greek) Orthodoxy

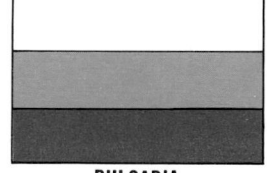

BULGARIA

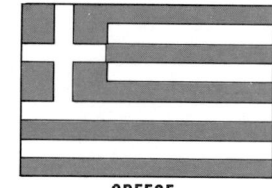

GREECE

YUGOSLAVIA

ALBANIA

ROMANIA

Agriculture, Industry and Resources

DOMINANT LAND USE

- Cereals (chiefly wheat, corn)
- Mixed Farming, Horticulture
- Pasture Livestock
- Tobacco, Cotton
- Grapes, Wine
- Forests
- Nonagricultural Land

MAJOR MINERAL OCCURRENCES

Ab	Asbestos	Mg	Magnesium
Ag	Silver	Mn	Manganese
Al	Bauxite	Mr	Marble
C	Coal	Na	Salt
Cr	Chromium	Ni	Nickel
Cu	Copper	O	Petroleum
Fe	Iron Ore	Pb	Lead
G	Natural Gas	Sb	Antimony
Hg	Mercury	U	Uranium
Lg	Lignite	Zn	Zinc

⚡ Water Power
▨ Major Industrial Areas

ALBANIA

CITIES and TOWNS

Berat 40,500 ....D5
Delvinë 6,000 ....D6
Durrës (Durazzo) 78,700 ...D5
Elbasan 78,300 ....E5
Fier 40,300 ....D5
Gjirokastër 23,800 ....E5
Kavajë 24,200 ....D5
Korçë 61,500 ....E5
Krujë 9,600 ....D5
Kuçovë (Stalin) 20,600 .....D5
Kukës 9,500 ....E4
Lezhë 6,900 ....D5
Lushnjë 26,900 ....D5
Peshkopi 7,600 ....E5
Pogradec 13,100 ....E5
Sarandë 10,800 ....D6
Shijak 6,200 ....D5
Shkodër 76,300 ....D4
Stalin 20,600 ....D5
Tiranë (Tirana)
  (cap.) 225,700 ....E5
Vlorë 67,700 ....D5

OTHER FEATURES

Adriatic (sea) B4
Drin (riv.) E4
Korab (mt.) E4
Ohrid (lake) E5
Otranto (str.) D5
Prespa (lake) E5
Sazan (isl.) D5
Scutari (lake) D4
Vijosë (riv.) D5

BULGARIA

CITIES and TOWNS

Akhtopol 1,108 ....H4
Ardino 5,498 ....G5
Asenovgrad 47,159 ....G5
Aytos 23,124 ....H4
Balchik 12,764 ....J4
Bansko 8,248 ....F5
Belogradchik 7,198 ....F4
Berkovitsa 16,340 ....F4
Blagoevgrad 65,481 ....F5
Botevgrad 22,659 ....G4
Burgas 182,856 ....H4
Byala 11,017 ....G4
Byala Slatina 16,034 ....G4
Chirpan 20,440 ....G4
Devin 7,985 ....G5
Dimitrovgrad 54,056 ....G4
Dobrich (Tolbukhin) 109,170 .H4
Dryanovo 10,306 ....G4
Elena 7,629 ....G4
Elin Pelin 6,955 ....F4
Elkhovo 13,655 ....H4
Gabrovo 81,629 ....G4
General-Toshevo 9,274 ....H4
Godech 5,438 ....F4
Gorna Oryakhovitsa 40,895 ..G4
Gotse Delchev 19,836 ......F5
Grudovo 10,736 ....H4
Ikhtiman 13,001 ....F4
Isperikh 11,235 ....H4
Karlovo 28,403 ....G4
Karnobat 22,536 ....H4
Kavarna 12,024 ....J4
Kazanlŭk 61,396 ....G4
Kharmanli 21,050 ....G5
Khaskovo 87,847 ....G5
Kotel 7,907 ....H4
Krumovgrad 6,597 ....G5
Kubrat 10,758 ....H4
Kula 5,163 ....F4
Kŭrdzhali 55,201 ....G5

Kyustendil 53,498 ....F4
Lom 32,307 ....F4
Lovech 48,992 ....G4
Lukovit 10,645 ....G4
Maritsa 8,742 ....H4
Mikhaylovgrad 51,714 ......F4
Momchilgrad 10,189 ....G5
Nesebŭr 8,130 ....H4
Nova Zagora 25,327 ....H4
Novi Pazar 16,314 ....H4
Omurtag 9,505 ....H4
Oryakhovo 14,012 ....F4
Panagyurishte 22,034 ......G4
Pazardzhik 77,603 ....G4
Pernik 94,460 ....F4
Peshtera 18,763 ....G4
Petrich 26,451 ....F5
Pirdop 8,248 ....G4
Pleven 129,863 ....G4
Plovdiv 343,064 ....G4
Pomorie 13,507 ....H4
Popovo 21,236 ....H4
Provadiya 15,762 ....H4
Radomir 16,733 ....F4
Razgrad 49,582 ....H4
Razlog 14,010 ....F5
Rositsa 185,485 ....H4
Ruse 185,485 ....H4
Samokov 27,485 ....F4
Sandanski 24,629 ....F5
Sevlievo 26,560 ....G4
Shumen 100,125 ....H4
Silistra 53,537 ....H3
Simeonovgrad
  (Maritsa) 8,742 ....H4
Sliven 9,037 ....H4
Smolyan 31,456 ....G5
Smyadovo 5,295 ....H4
Sofia (cap.) 1,121,763 .....F4
Stanke Dimitrov 41,897 ....F4
Stara Zagora 151,163 .....G4
Svilengrad 17,472 ....H5
Svishtov 30,555 ....G4
Teteven 12,784 ....G4
Tolbukhin 109,170 ....H4
Topolovgrad 7,437 ....H4
Troyan 26,179 ....G4
Tŭrgovishte 46,043 ....H4
Tutrakan 12,153 ....H4
Varna 302,816 ....H4
Veliko Tŭrnovo 69,173 ....G4
Vidin 62,541 ....F4
Vratsa 55,180 ....F4
Yambol 90,019 ....H4
Zlatograd 8,780 ....G5

OTHER FEATURES

Arda (riv.) G5
Balkan (mts.) G4
Black (sea) J4
Danube (riv.) H4
Dunav (Danube) (riv.) H4
Emine (cape) J4
Iskŭr (riv.) G4
Kaliakra (cape) J4
Maritsa (riv.) G4
Mesta (riv.) F5
Midzhur (mt.) F4
Musala (mt.) F4
Osŭm (riv.) G4
Rhodope (mts.) G5
Rujen (mt.) F5
Struma (riv.) F5
Timok (riv.) F3
Tundzha (riv.) G4
Vit (riv.) G4

GREECE

REGIONS

Aegean Islands 417,813 ...G6

Athens, Greater 3,027,331 ......F7
Áyion Óros (aut. dist.) 1,732 ..G5
Central Greece and
  Euboea 1,099,841 ....F6
Crete 502,165 ....G8
Epirus 324,541 ....E6
Ionian Islands 182,651 ....D6
Macedonia 2,121,953 ....F5
Pelopónnisos 1,012,528 ......F7
Thessaly 695,654 ....F6
Thrace 345,220 ....G5

CITIES and TOWNS

Agrínion 34,328 ....E6
Aíyina 6,333 ....F7
Aíyion 20,824 ....F6
Alexandroúpolis 34,535 ......G5
Almirós 6,143 ....F6
Amaliás 14,698 ....E7
Ámfissa 7,156 ....F6
Árgos 20,702 ....F7
Argostólion 6,788 ....E6
Arkhángelos 4,164 ....J7
Árta 18,283 ....E6
Atalándi 5,456 ....F6
Athens (cap.) 885,737 ....F7
Áyios Nikólaos 8,130 ....G8
Candia (Iráklion) 101,634 ...G8
Canea (Khaniá) 40,564 ....G8
Corinth 22,658 ....F7
Dhidhimótikhon 8,374 ....H5
Dráma 36,109 ....G5
Édhessa 16,054 ....F5
Elassón 6,527 ....F6
Ermoúpolis 13,876 ....G7
Fársala 7,094 ....F6
Filiatrá 4,931 ....E7
Flórina 12,562 ....E5
Gargaliánoi 5,371 ....E7
Grevená 7,433 ....E5
Ierápetra 8,575 ....G8
Igoumenítsa 5,879 ....E6
Ioánnina 44,829 ....E6
Iráklion 101,634 ....G8
Itháki 2,037 ....E6
Kalámai 41,911 ....E7
Kalampáka 5,692 ....E6
Kálimnos 10,118 ....H7
Kardhítsa 27,291 ....E6
Karpenísion 5,100 ....F6
Kastéllion (Kíssamos) 2,749 ...F8
Kastoría 17,133 ....E5
Kateríni 38,016 ....F5
Kaválla 56,375 ....G5
Kérkira 33,561 ....D6
Khalkís 44,867 ....F6
Khaniá 40,564 ....G8
Khíos 24,070 ....G6
Kiáton 7,392 ....F6
Kilkís 11,148 ....F5
Kíssamos 2,749 ....F8
Komotiní 34,051 ....G5
Koropí 11,214 ....G7
Kos 11,851 ....H7
Kozáni 30,994 ....F5
Lamía 41,667 ....F6
Langadhás 5,890 ....F5
Lárisa 102,048 ....F6
Lávrion 8,921 ....G7
Levádhia 16,864 ....F6
Levkás 6,818 ....E6
Litókhoron 6,109 ....F5
Marathón 2,052 ....G6
Megalópolis 4,735 ....F7
Mégara 17,719 ....F6
Mesolóngion 10,164 ....E6
Messíni 6,565 ....E7
Mirina 3,774 ....G6
Mitilíni 24,115 ....H6
Náousa 19,383 ....F5
Návpaktos 9,012 ....E6
Návplion 10,609 ....F7

(continued on following page)

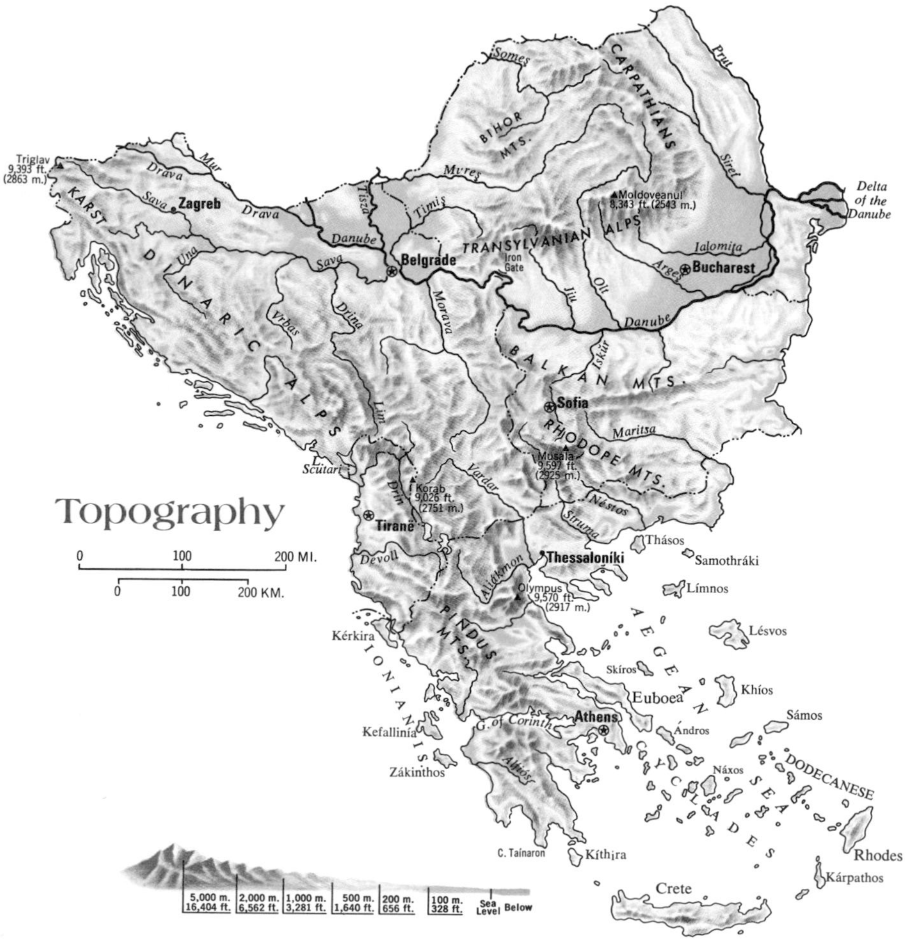
Triglav
9,393 ft.
(2863 m.)
Mur
Drava
Sava
Zagreb
KARST
DINARIC ALPS
Una
Vrbas
Drina
Lim
Scutari
Tiranë
Korab
9,026 ft.
(2751 m.)
Drin
Devoll
Belgrade
Danube
Tisza
Morava
Someş
Mureş
BIHOR MTS.
CARPATHIANS
Prut
Siret
Timiş
Moldoveanul
8,343 ft. (2543 m.)
TRANSYLVANIAN ALPS
Iron Gate
Jiu
Olt
Argeş
Ialomiţa
Bucharest
Delta
of the
Danube
BALKAN MTS.
Iskŭr
Sofia
Maritsa
RHODOPE MTS.
Musala
9,597 ft.
(2925 m.)
Vardar
Néstos
Struma
Thásos
Samothráki
Thessaloníki
Aliákmon
Olympus
9,570 ft.
(2917 m.)
Límnos
Lésvos
AEGEAN SEA
PINDUS MTS.
Kérkira
IONIAN SEA
Skíros
Euboea
Khíos
Sámos
Athens
G. of Corinth
Ándros
Kefallinía
Zákinthos
Náxos
DODECANESE
CYCLADES
Alfiós
C. Taínaron
Kíthira
Rhodes
Kárpathos
Crete
0 100 200 MI.
0 100 200 KM.
5,000 m. 16,404 ft.
2,000 m. 6,562 ft.
1,000 m. 3,281 ft.
500 m. 1,640 ft.
200 m. 656 ft.
100 m. 328 ft.
Sea Level
Below

Topography

Náxos 3,735 G7
Neméa 4,182 F7
Néon Karlóvasi 4,752 H7
Nigríta 6,531 F5
Orestías 12,685 H5
Pátrai 141,529 E6
Piraiévs (Piraeus) 196,389 F7
Pírgos 21,958 E7
Piryí 1,204 G6
Plomárion 3,503 H6
Políkastron 5,635 F5
Políkhnitos 3,342 G6
Políyiros 4,075 F5
Póros 3,605 F7
Préveza 12,662 E6
Psakhná 5,320 F6
Ptolemaís 22,109 E5
Réthimnon 17,736 G8
Rhodes (Ródhos) 40,392 J7
Salamís 20,437 F6
Salonika
(Thessaloníki) 406,413 F5
Sámos 5,575 H7
Samothráki 941 G5
Sápai 2,510 G5
Sérrai 45,213 F5
Sérvia 3,369 F5
Siátista 5,702 E5
Sidhirókastron 6,157 F5
Sitía 6,659 H8
Skíathos 3,838 F6
Skíros 2,217 G6
Skópelos 2,668 F6
Souflíon 5,043 H5
Sparta 11,911 F7
Spétsai 3,655 F7
Stilís 4,690 F6
Thásos 2,300 G5
Thessaloníki 406,413 F5
Thíra 1,573 G7
Thívai 18,712 F6
Timbákion 3,864 G8
Tínos 3,879 G7
Tirnávos 10,965 F6
Tríkkala 40,857 E6
Trípolis 21,311 F7
Vartholomión 3,236 E7
Velvendós 3,591 F5
Vérria 37,087 F5
Vólos 71,378 F6
Vónitsani 3,627 E6
Vrondádhes 3,979 G6
Xánthi 31,541 G5
Yiannitsá 21,082 F5
Yíthion 4,054 F7
Zante (Zákinthos) 9,764 E7

OTHER FEATURES

Aegean (sea) G6
Akrí (cape) E7
Aktí (pen.) G5
Amorgós (isl.) G7
Anáfi (isl.) G7
Andikíthira (isl.) F8
Ándros (isl.) G7
Árda (riv.) G5
Argolís (gulf) F7
Astipálaia (isl.) H7
Áthos (mt.) G5
Áyios Evstrátios (isl.) G6
Áyios Yeóryios (cape) G5
Cephalonia (Kefallinía) (isl.) E6
Corfu (Kérkira) (isl.) D6
Corinth (gulf) F6
Crete (isl.) G8
Crete (sea) G8
Cyclades (isls.) G7
Día (isl.) G8
Dodecanese (isls.) H8
Euboea (Évvoia) (isl.) G6
Évros (riv.) H5
Gávdhos (isl.) G8
Ídhi (mt.) G8
Ikaría (isl.) G7
Ionian (sea) D7
Íos (isl.) G7
Itháki (Ithaca) (isl.) E6
Kafirévs (cape) G6
Kálimnos (isl.) H7
Kárpathos (isl.) H8
Kásos (isl.) H8
Kassándra (pen.) F6
Kéa (isl.) G7
Kefallinía (isl.) E6
Kérkira (isl.) D6
Khálki (isl.) H7
Khaniá (gulf) G8
Khíos (isl.) G6
Kímilos (isl.) G7
Kiparissía (gulf) E7
Kíthira (isl.) F7
Kíthnos (isl.) G7
Kos (isl.) H7
Kriós (cape) F8
Kriti (Crete) (isl.) G8
Lakonía (gulf) F7
Léros (isl.) H7
Lésvos (isl.) G6
Levítha (isl.) H7
Levkás (isl.) E6
Límnos (isl.) G6
Maléa (cape) F7
Matapan (Taínaron) (cape) F7
Merabéllou (gulf) H8
Mesará (gulf) G8
Messíni (gulf) E7
Míkinos (isl.) G7
Mílos (isl.) G7
Mirtóön (sea) F7
Náxos (isl.) G7
Néstos (riv.) G5
Nísiros (isl.) H7
Northern Sporades (isls.) F6
Olympia (isls.) E7
Olympus (mt.) F5
Parnassus (mt.) F6
Páros (isl.) G7
Pátmos (isl.) H7
Paxoí (isl.) D6
Pindus (mts.) E6
Pinió (riv.) E6
Prespa (lake) E5
Psará (isl.) G6
Psevdhókavos (cape) G6
Rhodes (isl.) H7
Rhodope (mts.) G5
Salonika (Thermaic) (gulf) F6
Sámos (isl.) H7
Samothráki (isl.) G5
Saría (isl.) H8
Saronic (gulf) F7
Sérifos (isl.) G7
Sídheros (cape) H8
Sífnos (isl.) G7
Sími (isl.) H7
Síros (isl.) G7
Sithoniá (pen.) F5
Skíros (isl.) G6
Spátha (cape) F8
Strimón (gulf) G5
Strofádhes (isls.) E7
Taínaron (cape) F7
Thásos (isl.) G5
Thermaic (gulf) F5
Thíra (isl.) G7
Tílos (isl.) H7
Tínos (isl.) G7
Toronaic (gulf) F5
Vardar (riv.) E5
Vólvi (lake) F5
Voïviis (lake) F6
Voúxa (cape) F8
Zákinthos (Zante) (isl.) E7

ROMANIA

CITIES and TOWNS

Aiud 27,600 F2
Alba Iulia 53,000 F2
Alexandria 43,700 G3
Anina 11,300 E3
Arad 182,000 E2
Babadag 9,000 J3
Bacău 156,200 H2
Baia Mare 123,300 F2
Băileşti 21,500 F3
Balş 17,300 G3
Beiuş 10,100 F2
Bicaz 9,300 G2
Bîrlad 63,800 H2
Bistrita 59,800 G2
Blaj 22,200 F2
Borşa 25,287 F2
Botoşani 84,900 H2
Brad 18,600 F2
Brăila 219,200 H3
Braşov 320,200 G3
Bucharest (Bucureşti)
(cap.) 1,929,400 G3
Buhuşi 20,300 H2
Buzău 116,300 H3
Buziaş 8,700 E3
Calafat 17,100 F3
Călăraşi 58,000 H3
Caracal 33,600 G3
Caransebeş 28,800 F3
Carei 25,500 F2
Cernavodă 15,000 J3
Chişineu Criş 9,600 E2
Cîmpia Turzii 25,300 F2
Cîmpina 35,300 G3
Cîmpulung 37,400 G3
Cîmpulung Moldovenesc
20,500 G2
Cisnădie 21,100 G3
Cluj-Napoca 289,800 F2
Comăneşti 18,500 H2
Constanta 293,900 J3
Corabia 20,300 G4
Costeşti 10,900 G3
Craiova 239,700 F3
Curtea de Argeş 26,900 G3
Darabani 11,500 H1
Dej 36,500 F2
Deva 73,300 F3
Dorohoi 25,700 H2
Drăgăneşti Olt 11,800 G3
Drăgăşani 17,300 G3
Drobeta-Turnu Severin
86,600 F3
Făgăraş 37,200 G3
Fălticeni 24,000 H2
Făurei 3,800 H3
Feteşti 29,600 H3
Focşani 70,700 H3
Găeşti 14,000 G3
Galati 268,000 H3
Gheorghe Gheorghiu-Dej
46,100 H2
Gheorghieni 21,800 G2
Gherla 20,700 G2
Giurgiu 57,000 G4
Hateg 10,200 F3
Hîrlău 8,900 H2
Hîrşova 9,000 J3
Huedin 8,700 F2
Hunedoara 85,700 F3
Huşi 26,000 J2
Iaşi 279,800 H2
Ineu 10,800 E2
Isaccea 5,400 J3
Jimbolia 14,600 E3
Lipova 12,900 E2
Luduş 16,000 G2
Lugoj 50,000 E3
Lupeni 29,100 F3
Mangalia 31,100 J4
Medgidia 45,300 J3
Mediaş 69,000 G2
Miercurea Ciuc 40,400 G2
Mizil 15,200 H3
Moineşti 21,200 H2
Moldova Nouă 17,800 E3
Moreni 18,900 G3
Nădlac 8,500 E2
Năsăud 9,500 G2
Negreşti 7,700 H2
Ocna Mureş 16,200 G2
Odobeşti 8,600 H3
Odorheiu Secuiesc 36,200 G2
Oltenita 26,800 H3
Oradea 192,600 E2
Orăştie 19,900 F3
Oravita 114,300 E3
Orşova 115,800 F3
Panciu 77,900 H3
Paşcani 229,500 H2
Petrila 25,900 F3
Petroşeni 45,600 F3
Piatra Neamt 93,300 H2
Piteşti 143,600 G3
Ploieşti 219,900 H3
Pucioasa 14,100 G3
Rădăuti 26,000 G2
Reghin 33,600 G2
Reşita 96,800 E3
Rîmnicu Sărat 32,400 H3
Rîmnicu Vîlcea 78,900 G3
Roman 62,700 H2
Roşiori de Vede 31,700 G3
Săcele 33,900 G3
Salonta 20,400 E2
Satu Mare 115,600 F2
Sebeş 29,500 F3
Sebiş 6,700 F2
Segarcea 8,700 F3
Sfîntu Gheorghe 57,900 G3
Sfîntu Gheorghe J3
Sibiu 164,200 G3
Sighetu Marmaţiei 40,500 F2
Sighişoara 33,000 G2
Şimleul Silvaniei 15,100 F2
Sinaia 14,700 G3
Sînnicolaul Mare 13,600 E2
Slănic 8,100 G3
Slatina 62,800 G3
Slobozia 39,400 H3
Solca 4,500 G2
Sovata 11,200 G2
Strehaia 11,800 F3
Suceava 76,500 H2
Sulina 5,400 J3
Tăşnad 10,400 F2
Techirghiol 11,800 J3
Tecuci 40,300 H3
Timişoara 288,200 E3
Tîrgovişte 77,500 G3
Tîrgu Frumos 6,900 H2
Tîrgu Jiu 75,200 F3
Tîrgu Mureş 141,300 G2
Tîrgu Neamt 16,600 H2
Tîrgu Ocna 12,800 H2
Tîrgu Secuiesc 19,800 H2
Tîrnăveni 27,900 G2
Toplita 15,200 G2
Tulcea 73,600 J3
Turda 58,700 F2
Turnu Măgurele 33,000 G4
Urlata 11,200 H3
Urziceni 14,300 H3
Vaslui 50,100 H2
Vatra Dornei 17,800 G2
Videle 11,500 G3
Vişeu de Sus 20,800 G2
Zalău 43,300 F2
Zărneşti 25,000 G3
Zimnicea 16,400 G4

OTHER FEATURES

Argeş (riv.) G3
Bîrlad (riv.) H2
Black (sea) J4
Brăila (marshes) H3
Buzău (riv.) H3
Carpathian (mts.) G2
Crişul Alb (riv.) F2
Crişul Repede (riv.) F2
Danube (delta) J3
Danube (riv.) H4
Ialomiţa (marshes) J3
Ialomiţa (riv.) H3
Jijia (riv.) H2
Jiu (riv.) F3
Moldoveanul (mt.) G3
Mureş (riv.) E2
Olt (riv.) G3
Peleaga (mt.) F3
Pietrosul (mt.) G2
Prut (riv.) J2
Siret (riv.) H2
Someş (riv.) F2
Timiş (riv.) E3
Tîrnava Mare (riv.) G2
Transylvanian Alps (mts.) G3

YUGOSLAVIA

INTERNAL DIVISIONS

Bosnia and Hercegovina
(rep.) 3,710,965 C3
Croatia (rep.) 4,396,397 C3
Kosovo (aut. reg.) 1,240,919 E4
Macedonia (rep.) 1,623,598 E5
Montenegro (rep.) 527,207 [illegible]
Serbia (rep.) 8,401,673 E[illegible]
Slovenia (rep.) 1,697,068 B2
Vojvodina
(aut. prov.) 1,953,980 D3

CITIES and TOWNS

Aleksinac 11,943 E4
Apatin 17,501 D3
Arendjelovac 15,659 E3
Bačka Topola 16,028 D3
Banja Luka 85,786 C3
Bar 3,594 D4
Bečej 26,616 E3
Bela Crkva 11,137 E3
Belgrade (cap.) 727,945 E3
Beli Manastir 7,325 D3
Beograde (Belgrade)
(cap.) 727,945 E3
Bihać 24,155 B3
Bijeljina 24,888 D3
Bijelo Polje 9,298 D4
Biograd 3,595 B4
Bitola 64,467 E5
Bjelovar 21,019 C3
Bled 4,710 A2
Bor 27,520 E3
Bosanska Dubica 9,191 C3
Bosanska Gradiška 9,742 C3
Bosanska Krupa 8,947 C3
Bosanski Brod 10,113 D3
Bosanski Novi 9,861 C3
Bosanski Šamac 4,949 D3
Brčko 25,575 D3
Bugojno 9,079 C3
Čačak 38,890 E4
Čakovec 11,766 C2
Caribrod (Dimitrovgrad)
5,449 F4
Celje 30,827 B2
Cetinje 12,089 D4
Ćuprija 17,691 E4
Daruvar 8,478 C3
Debar 8,597 E5
Derventa 11,887 C3
Dimitrovgrad 5,449 F4
Djakovica 29,499 E4
Djakovo 15,833 D3
Doboj 18,073 C3
Drvar 6,237 C3
Dubrovnik 31,213 D4
Fiume (Rijeka) 128,883 B3
Foča 9,370 D4
Gevgelija 9,319 F5
Gnjilane 21,359 E4
Gornji Milanovac 1[illegible],114 E3
Gospić 8,238 B3
Gostivar 18,805 E5
Gračanica 9,302 D3
Gradačac 7,571 D3
Herceg Novi 6,645 D4
Ivangrad 11,373 D4
Jajce 9,221 C3
Jesenice 16,163 A2
Kanjiža 11,348 D2
Karlovac 47,046 B3
Kavadarci 17,974 E5
Kičevo 14,189 E5
Kikinda 37,392 E3
Knin 7,279 C3
Knjaževac 11,734 F4
Kočani 16,611 F5
Kočevje 7,277 B3
Konjic 9,161 C4
Koper 16,683 A3
Koprivnica 16,398 C2
Kosovska Mitrovica 42,526 E4
Kotor 5,728 D4
Kragujevac 72,080 E3
Kraljevo 28,065 E4
Kranj 26,341 B2
Križevci 8,501 C2
Krško 4,451 B3
Kruševac 29,902 E4
Kumanovo 44,791 E4
Kutina 10,892 C3
Leskovac 46,050 E4
Livno 7,223 C4
Ljubljana 169,064 B3
Loznica 13,513 D3
Makarska 6,589 C4
Maribor 94,976 B2
Modriča 7,406 D3
Mostar 47,821 C4
Murska Sobota 9,665 C2
Negotin 11,325 F3
Nevesinje 3,077 D4
Nikšić 28,940 D4
Niš 128,231 E4
Nova Gradiška 11,735 C3
Novi Pazar 28,696 E4
Novi Sad 143,591 D3
Novo Mesto 9,553 B3
Ogulin 9,975 B3
Ohrid 26,352 E5
Omiš 3,515 C4
Opatija 9,238 B3
Osijek 94,989 D3
Pag 2,318 B3
Pančevo 53,979 E3
Paraćin 21,555 E4
Peć 41,783 E4
Petrinja 12,236 C3
Piran 5,485 A3
Pirot 29,658 F4
Pljevlja 14,459 D4
Pola (Pula) 47,117 A3
Poreč 4,512 A3
Postojna 6,085 B3
Požarevac 33,336 E3
Preševo 7,634 E4
Priboj 12,556 D4
Prijedor 22,379 C3
Prijepolje 7,960 D4
Prilep 48,045 E5
Priština 71,264 E4
Prizren 41,875 E4
Prokuplje 20,617 E4
Ptuj 9,245 B2
Pula 47,117 A3
Radoviš 9,373 F5
Ragusa (Dubrovnik) 31,213 C4
Ravne na Koroškem 6,529 B2
Rijeka 128,883 B3
Rovinj 8,998 A3
Ruma 24,180 D3
Šabac 43,539 D3
Samobor 7,821 B3
Sanski Most 8,718 C3
Sarajevo 245,058 D4
Senj 4,927 B3
Senta 24,694 D3
Šibenik 29,619 C4
Šid 11,867 D3
Sinj 4,705 C4
Sisak 37,215 C3
Sjenica 9,118 E4
Škofja Loka 4,971 B2
Skopje 308,117 E5
Slavonska Požega 18,160 C3
Slavonski Brod 38,829 D3
Smederevo 39,200 E3
Smederevska Palanka 18,837 E3
Sombor 44,210 D3
Split 150,739 C4
Srebrenica 3,101 D3
Sremska Mitrovica 32,569 D3
Štip 27,218 F5
Struga 11,369 E5
Strumica 22,770 F5
Subotica 89,476 D2
Surdulica 7,048 F4
Svetozarevo 27,812 E4
Svilajnac 7,848 E3
Tetovo 35,293 E5
Titograd 54,639 D4
Titovo Užice 35,465 D4
Titov Veles 35,583 E5
Travnik 12,745 C3
Trbovlje 16,393 B2
Trebinje 3,553 D4
Trogir 6,162 C4
Trstenik 7,167 E4
Tržič 4,435 B2
Tuzla 53,836 D3
Ub 3,785 E3
Ulcinj 7,472 D5
Uroševac 22,763 E4
Valjevo 26,655 D3
Varaždin 34,662 C2
Vareš 7,632 D3
Velenje 11,225 B2
Velika Plana 12,664 E3
Veliki Bečkerek
(Zrenjanin) 60,201 E3
Vinkovci 29,257 D3
Virovitica 16,389 C3
Visoko 9,365 D4
Vranje 25,909 E4
Vrbas 22,502 D3
Vršac 33,573 E3
Vučitrn 11,701 E4
Vukovar 29,500 D3
Zadar 43,588 B3
Zagreb 561,773 C3
Zaječar 27,724 F4
Zara (Zadar) 43,588 B3
Zenica 49,522 C3
Zrenjanin 60,201 E3
Zvornik 8,498 D3

OTHER FEATURES

Adriatic (sea) B4
Bobotov Kuk (mt.) D4
Bosna (riv.) D3
Brač (isl.) C4
Cazma (riv.) C3
Cres (isl.) B3
Čvrsnica (mt.) C4
Dalmatia (reg.) C4
Danube (riv.) E3
Dinaric Alps (mts.) B3
Drava (riv.) C3
Drina (riv.) D3
Dugi Otok (isl.) B3
Hvar (isl.) C4
Ibar (riv.) E4
Istria (pen.) A3
Kamenjak (cape) A3
Korab (mt.) E5
Korčula (isl.) C4
Kornat (isl.) B4
Krk (isl.) B3
Kupa (riv.) B3
Kvarner (gulf) B3
Lastovo (Lagosta) (isl.) C4
Lim (riv.) D4
Lošinj (isl.) B3
Midzhur (mt.) F4
Mljet (isl.) C4
Morava (riv.) E3
Mur (riv.) B2
Neretva (riv.) C4
Ohrid (lake) E5
Pag (isl.) B3
Palagruža (Pelagosa) (isl.) C4
Prespa (lake) E5
Rab (isl.) B3
Rujen (mt.) F4
Sava (riv.) D3
Scutari (lake) D4
Slavonia (reg.) C3
Šolta (isl.) C4
Tara (riv.) D4
Timok (riv.) F3
Tisa (riv.) E3
Triglav (mt.) A2
Una (riv.) C3
Vardar (riv.) E5
Vis (isl.) C4
Vrbas (riv.) C3
Žirje (riv.) B4

The Balkan States

CONIC PROJECTION

SCALE OF MILES

0 25 50 75 100 125 150 175

SCALE OF KILOMETERS

0 25 50 75 100 125 150 175

Capitals of Countries _____ ☆
Administrative Centers _____ ⌐
International Boundaries _____ ▬▬▬
Major Internal Boundaries _____ ▬ ▬
Minor Internal Boundaries _____ ⋯⋯
Canals _____ ⊢⊣

Scale 1:6,150,000

BULGARIA and GREECE are divided into regions and departments, respectively. Because of the scale no attempt has been made to delimit and name these sub-divisions; their administrative centers have, however, been designated.

The larger divisions named in Greece are well-known geographical regions, without administrative function.

ROMANIA consists of thirty-nine counties and three cities of regional status, Bucharest, Constanţa and Petroşeni. Scale does not permit delimiting these counties.

ALBANIA is divided into twenty-seven districts. Scale does not permit the delimitation of these divisions.

YUGOSLAVIA is a federation of six republics. The Serbian republic includes an autonomous province (Vojvodina), and an autonomous region (Kosovo).

© Copyright HAMMOND INCORPORATED, Maplewood, N.J.

Topography

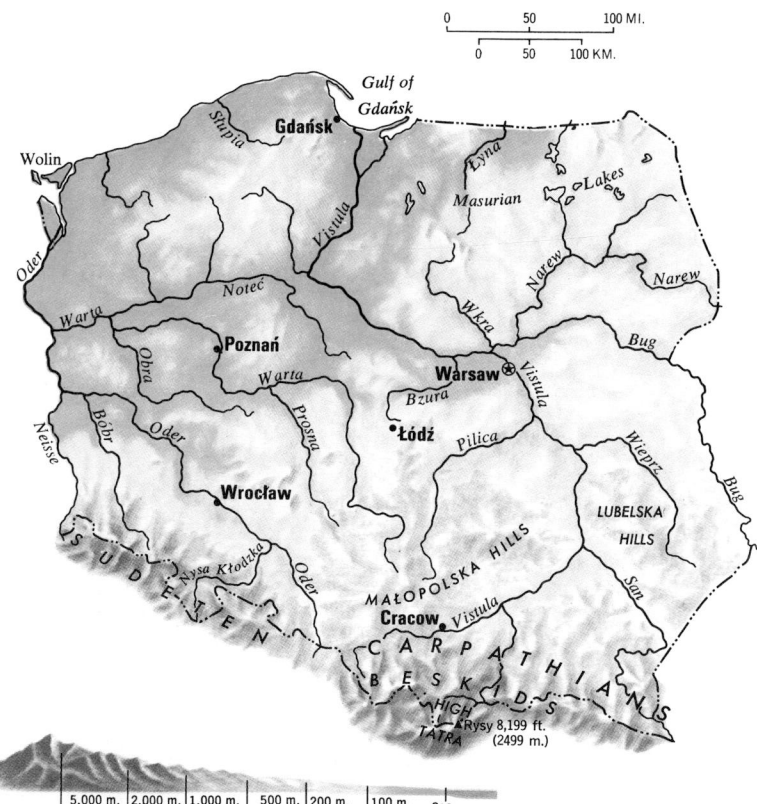

0   50   100 MI.
0   50   100 KM.

5,000 m. | 2,000 m. | 1,000 m. | 500 m. | 200 m. | 100 m. | Sea
16,404 ft. | 6,562 ft. | 3,281 ft. | 1,640 ft. | 656 ft. | 328 ft. | Level Below

Agriculture, Industry and Resources

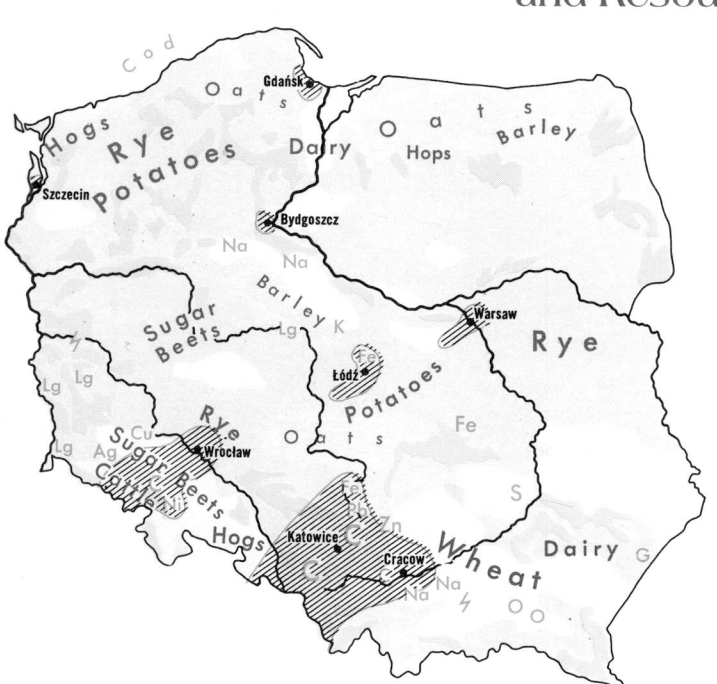

MAJOR MINERAL OCCURRENCES

Ag Silver
C   Coal
Cu Copper
Fe Iron Ore
G   Natural Gas
K   Potash
Lg Lignite

Na Salt
Ni Nickel
O   Petroleum
Pb Lead
S   Sulfur
Zn Zinc

⚡ Water Power
▨ Major Industrial Areas

DOMINANT LAND USE

☐ Cereals (chiefly wheat)
☐ Rye, Oats, Barley, Potatoes
☐ General Farming, Livestock
▨ Forests

PROVINCES

Biała Podlaska 304,028 ....F3
Białystok 687,806 ....F2
Bielsko 895,357 ....D4
Bydgoszcz 1,104,048.............C2
Chełm 245,484 ....F3
Ciechanów 425,608 ....E2
Cracow (Kraków) 1,223,137 ...E3
Cracow (city) 651,300.............E3
Częstochowa 773,365...........D3
Elbląg 475,862 ....D1
Gdańsk 1,417,801 ....D1
Gorzów 497,342 ....B2
Jelenia Góra 514,947............B3
Kalisz 706,514 ....D3
Katowice 3,953,769..............D3
Kielce 1,123,691 ....E3
Konin 465,928 ....D2
Koszalin 502,750 ....C1
Krosno 491,471 ....E4
Legnica 510,000 ....C3
Leszno 383,315 ....C3
Łódź 777,800 ....D3
Łódź (city) 1,139,379............D3
Łomża 344,518 ....F2
Lublin 1,010,641 ....F3
Nowy Sącz 690,737.............E4
Olsztyn 746,185 ....E2
Opole 1,010,416 ....C3
Ostrołęka 393,427................E2
Piła 475,953 ....C2

Piotrków 638,948 ....D3
Płock 512,626.......................D2
Poznań 1,323,368 ....C2
Przemyśl 404,200 ....F4
Radom 745,374 ....E3
Rzeszów 716,317 ....F4
Siedlce 648,111 ....F2
Sieradz 408,082...................D3
Skierniewice 416,690............E3
Słupsk 410,049 ....C1
Suwałki 467,048..................F1
Szczecin 964,298.................C2
Tarnobrzeg 594,255.............E3
Tarnów 664,953...................E4
Toruń 656,421......................D2
Wałbrzych 738,092...............C3
Warsaw 2,415,950...............E2
Warsaw (city) 1,377,100........E2
Włocławek 427,418..............D2
Wrocław 1,122,806...............C3
Zamość 488,193 ....F3
Zielona Góra 655,146............B3

CITIES and TOWNS

Aleksandrów Lódzki 19,711....D3
Allenstein (Olsztyn) 160,956...E2
Andrychów 22,387................D4
Augustów 28,307 ....F2
Auschwitz (Oświęcim)
    45,402.............................D3
Bartoszyce 25,195 ....E1

Bedzin 76,883 ....B3
Belchatów 55,632.................B3
Beuthen (Bytom) 229,991.......A3
Biala Podlaska 52,119...........F3
Bialogard 23,973 ....C1
Bialystok 267,670.................F2
Bielawa 34,224 ....C3
Bielsk Podlaski 26,145 ....F2
Bielsko-Biala 181,072............D4
Bilgoraj 25,542.....................F3
Bochnia 28,846.....................E4
Bogatynia 18,616..................B3
Boguszów-Gorce 19,452........B3
Bolesławiec 43,076...............B3
Braniewo 17,594 ....D1
Breslau (Wrocław) 640,557....C3
Brieg (Brzeg) 38,504.............C3
Brodnica 26,056...................D2
Brzeg 38,504........................C3
Busko Zdrój 17,675...............E3
Bydgoszcz 380,426...............C2
Bytom 229,991 ....A3
Bytów 16,720 ....C1
Chelm 64,683.......................F3
Chelmno 21,506 ....D2
Chodziez 19,831 ....C2
Chojnice 37,733....................C2
Chorzów 131,850..................B4
Chrzanów 42,195..................B4
Ciechanów 43,068................E2
Cieszyn 36,682.....................D4
Cracow 745,568....................E3

Poland 1938

0   50   100 MILES

Poland 1945

0   50   100 MILES

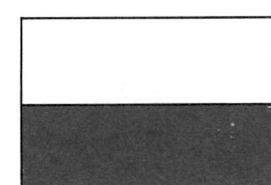

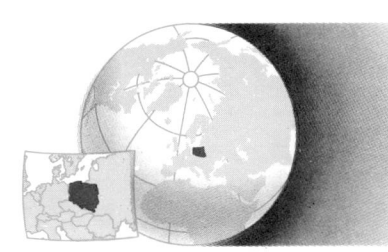

AREA 120,725 sq. mi. (312,678 sq. km.)
POPULATION 37,931,000
CAPITAL Warsaw
LARGEST CITY Warsaw
HIGHEST POINT Rysy 8,199 ft. (2,499 m.)
MONETARY UNIT zloty
MAJOR LANGUAGE Polish
MAJOR RELIGION Roman Catholicism

Czechowice-Dziedzice 35,194 ... D4
Czeladź 37,569 ... B4
Czestochowa 256,578 ... D3
Dabrowa Górnicza 134,934 ... B3
Danzig (Gdańsk) 462,076 ... D1
Debica 44,966 ... E3
Deblin 18,763 ... E3
Dzialdowo 19,295 ... E2
Dzierzoniów 37,908 ... C3
Elbing (Elblag) 125,778 ... D1
Elblag 125,778 ... D1
Elk 51,274 ... F2
Gdańsk 462,076 ... D1
Gdynia 251,303 ... D1
Gizycko 28,918 ... E1
Gleiwitz (Gliwice) 212,481 ... A4
Gliwice 212,481 ... A4
Głogów (Glogau) 71,854 ... C3
Gniezno 69,646 ... C2
Goleniów 21,756 ... B2
Gorlice 29,019 ... E4
Gorzów Wielkopolski 123,222 ... B2
Gostyń 19,344 ... C3
Gostynin 18,738 ... D2
Grajewo 20,635 ... F2
Grodzisk Mazowiecki 24,648 ... E2
Grudziadz 101,571 ... D2
Grünberg (Zielona Góra) 113,108 ... B3
Gryfice 17,294 ... B2
Gryfino 20,783 ... B2
Guben (Gubin) 17,779 ... B3
Hajnowka 23,390 ... F2
Hindenburg (Zabrze) 202,824 ... A4
Hirschberg (Jelenia Góra) 93,205 ... B3
Iława 31,312 ... D2
Inowrocław 76,497 ... D2
Jarocin 24,692 ... C3
Jaroslaw 41,267 ... F4
Jaslo 37,046 ... E4
Jastrzebie Zdroj 102,312 ... D3
Jawor 24,079 ... C3
Jaworzno 98,480 ... B4
Jedrzejów 18,109 ... E3
Jelenia Góra 93,205 ... B3
Kamienna Góra 21,000 ... B3
Katowice 366,077 ... B4
Kedzierzyn-Koźle 71,012 ... D3
Ketrzyn 29,987 ... E1
Kety 18,731 ... D4
Kielce 213,012 ... E3
Klodzko 30,261 ... C3
Kluczbork 25,988 ... D3
Knurów 44,468 ... A4
Kolberg (Kołobrzeg) 44,426 ... B1
Kolo 22,807 ... D2
Kołobrzeg 44,426 ... B1
Konin 79,315 ... D2
Końskie 21,548 ... E3
Kościan 23,554 ... C2
Kościerzyna 22,287 ... C1
Köslin (Koszalin) 107,592 ... C1
Koszalin 107,592 ... C1
Kozienice 20,557 ... E3
Kraków (Cracow) 745,568 ... E3
Krapkowice 19,452 ... D3
Kraśnik Fabryczny 36,202 ... F3
Krasnystaw 19,832 ... F3
Krosno 49,094 ... E4
Krotoszyn 27,807 ... C3
Kutno 49,753 ... D2
Kwidzin 36,409 ... D2
Landsberg (Gorzów Wielkopolski) 123,222 ... B2
Lask 19,569 ... D3
Laziska Górne 19,569 ... A4
Lebork 33,981 ... C1
Leczyca 16,491 ... D2
Legionowo 50,577 ... E2
Legnica 103,949 ... C3
Leszcyny 29,746 ... A4
Leszno 57,673 ... C3
Liegnitz (Legnica) 103,949 ... C3
Lódź 849,204 ... D3
Lomza 57,976 ... F2
Lowicz 30,322 ... D2
Lubań 23,708 ... B3
Lubartów 22,117 ... F3
Lubin 80,757 ... C3
Lublin 348,881 ... F3
Lubliniec 33,084 ... D3
Luboń 20,255 ... C2
Luków 30,356 ... F3
Malbork (Marienburg) 39,018 ... D1
Miedzyrzecz 19,805 ... B2
Mielec 60,187 ... E3
Mikolow 37,022 ... B4
Mińsk Mazowiecki 33,913 ... E2
Mlawa 28,743 ... E2
Mragowo 21,674 ... E2
Myslowice 92,009 ... B4
Myszków 33,084 ... D3
Naklo nad Notecia 20,056 ... C2
Neissa (Nysa) 46,686 ... C3
Nowa Ruda 27,507 ... C3
Nowa Sól 43,053 ... B3
Nowy Dwór Mazowiecki 26,842 ... E2
Nowy Sacz 76,658 ... E4
Nowy Targ 32,143 ... E4
Nysa 46,686 ... C3
Olawa 31,188 ... C3
Oleśnica 37,767 ... C3
Olkusz 40,571 ... D3
Olsztyn 160,956 ... E2
Opoczno 20,670 ... E3
Opole (Oppeln) 126,962 ... C3
Orzesze 18,100 ... A4
Ostróda 33,641 ... E2
Ostroleka 49,032 ... E2
Ostrów Mazowiecka 20,367 ... E2
Ostrów Wielkopolski 72,085 ... C3
Ostrowiec Świetokrzyski 77,466 ... E3
Oświecim 45,402 ... D3
Otwock 44,488 ... E2
Ozorków 21,676 ... D3
Pabianice 74,755 ... D3
Piaseczno 24,359 ... D2
Piekary Ślaskie 68,274 ... B4
Pila 71,109 ... C2
Pionki 20,701 ... E3
Piotrków Trybunalski 80,598 ... D3
Pisz 18,286 ... E2
Pleszew 17,712 ... C3
Plock 120,933 ... D2
Płońsk 20,956 ... E2
Police 33,478 ... B2
Polkowice 20,823 ... C3
Poznań 586,908 ... C2
Prudnik 24,598 ... C3
Pruszcz Gdanski 20,575 ... D1
Pruszków 53,889 ... E2
Przemyśl 68,121 ... F4
Pulawy 52,624 ... F3
Pultusk 17,619 ... E2
Racibórz 62,733 ... D3
Radom 226,025 ... E3
Radomsko 50,059 ... D3
Ratibor (Racibórz) 62,733 ... D3
Rawa Mazowiecka 17,428 ... E3
Rawicz 20,548 ... C3
Ruda Ślaska 169,017 ... B4
Rumia 36,762 ... D1
Rybnik 142,059 ... D3
Rzeszów 150,702 ... F4
Sandomierz 23,815 ... E3
Sanok 39,163 ... F4
Schneidemühl (Piła) 71,109 ... C2
Schweidnitz (Świdnica) 62,424 ... C3
Siedlce 70,529 ... F2
Siemianowice Ślaskie 80,412 ... B4
Sieradz 42,041 ... D3
Sierpc 18,956 ... D2
Skarzysko-Kamienna 50,455 ... E3
Skawina 23,487 ... D4
Skierniewice 43,963 ... E3
Słupsk 100,127 ... C1
Sochaczew 38,170 ... E2
Sokólka 19,059 ... F2
Sopot 46,874 ... D1
Sosnowiec 259,318 ... B4
Śrem 27,719 ... C2
Środa Wielkopolska 20,053 ... C2
Stalowa Wola 68,856 ... F3
Starachowice 55,996 ... E3
Stargard Szczeciński 69,852 ... B2
Starogard Gdański 47,142 ... D2
Stettin (Szczecin) 411,275 ... B2
Stolp (Słupsk) 100,127 ... C1
Strzegom 17,185 ... C3
Strzelce Opolskie 21,238 ... D3
Suwalki 59,684 ... F1
Swarzedz 22,022 ... C2
Świdnica 62,424 ... C3
Świdnik 39,651 ... F3
Świebodzice 24,392 ... C3
Świebodzin 21,617 ... B2
Świecie 25,415 ... D2
Świetochlowice 58,770 ... A4
Świnoujście (Swinemünde) 42,932 ... B1
Szamotuly 17,970 ... C2
Szczecin 411,275 ... B2
Szczecinek 40,428 ... C2
Szczytno 26,878 ... E2
Tarnobrzeg 45,702 ... E3
Tarnów 120,639 ... E4
Tarnowskie Góry 73,460 ... A3
Tczew 58,887 ... D1
Tomaszów Lubelski 20,011 ... F3
Tomaszów Mazowiecki 69,579 ... E3
Toruń 200,860 ... D2
Trzebinia-Siersza 20,376 ... C4
Turek 28,559 ... D2
Tychy 189,816 ... B4
Wadowice 18,691 ... D4
Wagrowiec 22,736 ... C2
Wałbrzych 141,504 ... C3
Walcz 26,367 ... C2
Waldenburg (Wałbrzych) 141,504 ... C3
Warsaw (Warszawa) (cap.) 1,651,225 ... E2
Wejherowo 46,465 ... D1
Wieliczka 17,775 ... E3
Wieluń 24,061 ... D3
Włocławek 120,680 ... D2
Wodzislaw Ślaski 111,099 ... D4
Wolomin 36,762 ... E2
Wrocław 640,557 ... C3
Września 27,449 ... C2
Wyszków 23,411 ... E2
Zabrze 202,824 ... A4
Zagań 27,333 ... B3
Zakopane 28,417 ... D4
Zambrów 22,175 ... F2
Zamość 60,565 ... F3
Zary 39,172 ... B3
Zawiercie 56,017 ... D3
Zduńska Wola 44,686 ... D3
Zgierz 58,836 ... D3
Zgorzelec 36,008 ... B3
Zielona Góra 113,108 ... B3
Zlotów 17,533 ... C2
Zyrardów 33,196 ... E2
Zywiec 30,572 ... D4

OTHER FEATURES

Baltic (sea) ... B1
Beskids (range) ... D4
Biebrza (riv.) ... F2
Bobr (riv.) ... B3
Brda (riv.) ... C2
Brynica (riv.) ... B4
Bug (riv.) ... F2
Danzig (Gdańsk) (gulf) ... D1
Dukla (pass) ... E4
Dunajec (riv.) ... E4
Frisches Haff (lag.) ... D1
Gwda (riv.) ... C2
Hel (pen.) ... D1
High Tatra (range) ... D4
Jezioro Śniardwy (lake) ... E2
Kłodnica (riv.) ... A4
Łyna (riv.) ... E1
Mamry, Jezioro (lake) ... E1
Masurian (lakes) ... E2
Narew (riv.) ... E2
Neisse (riv.) ... B3
Noteć (riv.) ... B2
Nysa Łuzycka (Neisse) (riv.) ... B3
Nysa Kłodzka (riv.) ... C3
Oder (riv.) ... B2
Oder-Haff (lag.) ... B2
Orava (res.) ... D4
Pilica (riv.) ... D3
Plonia (riv.) ... B2
Pomeranian (bay) ... B1
Prosna (riv.) ... C3
Przemsza (riv.) ... B4
Rega (riv.) ... B2
Rysy (mt.) ... D4
San (riv.) ... F3
Słupia (riv.) ... C1
Sudeten (range) ... B3
Uznam (Usedom) (isl.) ... B1
Vistula (riv.) ... D2
Vistula (spit) ... D1
Warmia (reg.) ... D1
Warta (riv.) ... B2
Wieprz (riv.) ... F3
Wisła (Vistula) (riv.) ... D2
Wkra (riv.) ... E2
Włocławskie (lake) ... D2
Wolin (Wollin) (isl.) ... B2
Zegrzýnskie (lake) ... E2

Poland
CONIC PROJECTION
SCALE OF MILES
SCALE OF KILOMETERS
Capitals of Countries
Other Capitals
International Boundaries
Internal Boundaries
Canals
Scale 1:4,500,000
Poland is divided into 49 provinces (bearing the same name as their capitals) and the autonomous cities of Warsaw, Łódź and Cracow.
BALTIC SEA
Gulf of Gdańsk
Pomeranian Bay
DENMARK
GERMANY
U.S.S.R.
CZECHOSLOVAKIA
Warsaw
Berlin
Gdańsk
Szczecin
Poznań
Wrocław
Cracow
Łódź
Katowice
Lublin
Rysy 8,199 ft. (2499 m.)
Gerlachovka 8,707 ft. (2654 m.)
Longitude East of Greenwich
© Copyright HAMMOND INCORPORATED, Maplewood, N.J.

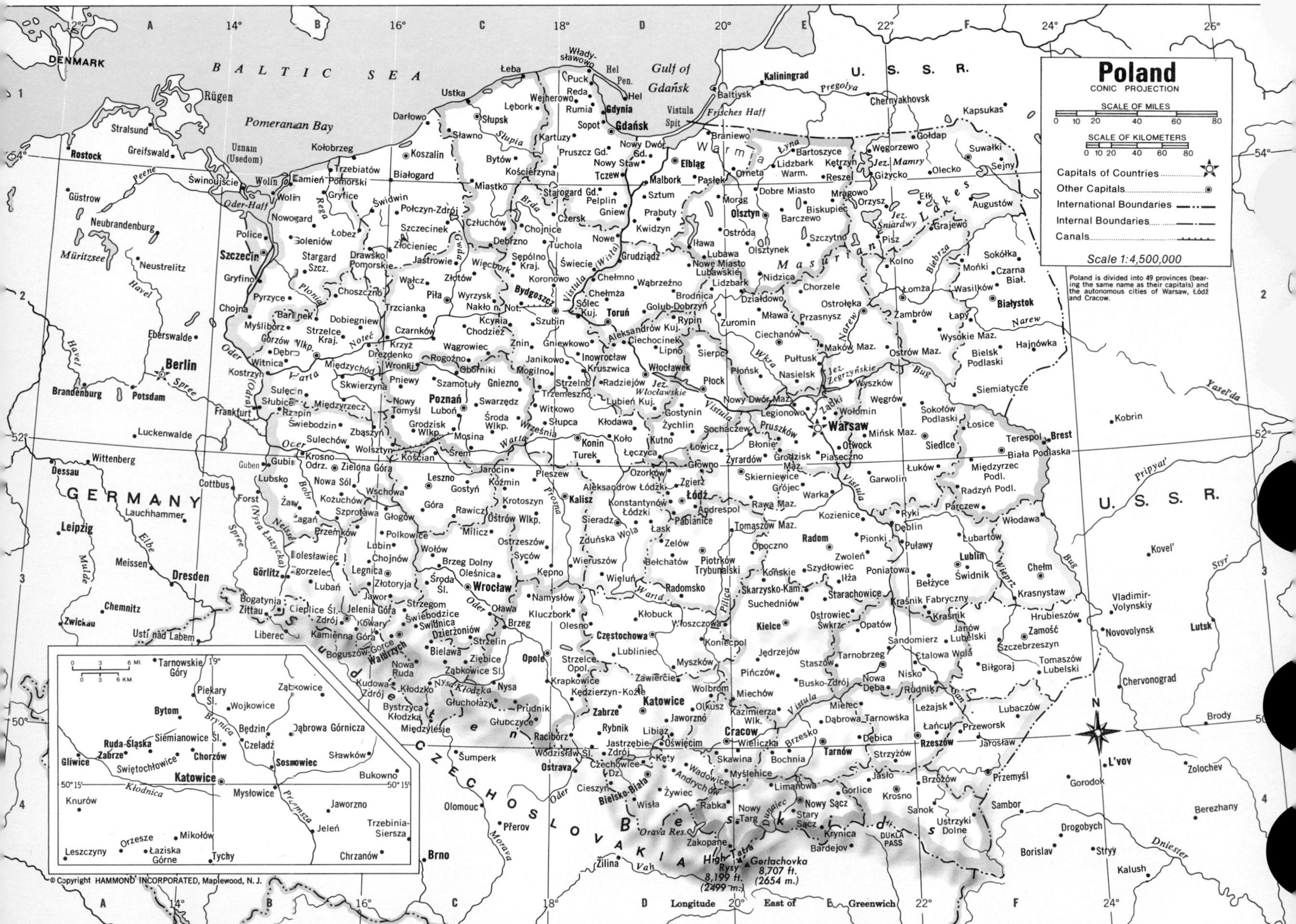

UNION REPUBLICS

Armenian S.S.R. 3,283,000....E6
Azerbaidzhan S.S.R. 7,029,000....E5
Belorussian S.S.R. 10,200,000....C4
Estonian S.S.R. 1,573,000....C4
Georgian S.S.R. 5,449,000....D5
Kazakh S.S.R. 16,538,000....G5
Kirgiz S.S.R. 4,291,000....H5
Latvian S.S.R. 2,681,000....C4
Lithuanian S.S.R. 3,690,000....C4
Moldavian S.S.R. 4,341,000....C5
Russian S.F.S.R. 147,386,000....D4
Tadzhik S.S.R. 5,112,000....H6
Turkmen S.S.R. 3,534,000....F6
Ukrainian S.S.R. 51,704,000....C5
Uzbek S.S.R. 19,906,000....G5

INTERNAL DIVISIONS

Abkhaz A.S.S.R. 537,000....E5
Adygey Aut. Obl. 432,000....D5
Adzhar A.S.S.R. 393,000....E5
Aginsk Buryat Aut. Okr. 77,000....M4
Bashkir A.S.S.R. 3,952,000....F4

Buryat A.S.S.R. 1,042,000.....M4
Chechen-Ingush A.S.S.R. 1,277,000.....E5
Chukchi Aut. Okr. 158,000....R3
Chuvash A.S.S.R. 1,336,000....E4
Dagestan A.S.S.R. 1,792,000....E5
Evenki Aut. Okr. 24,000....K3
Gorno-Altay Aut. Obl. 192,000 J4
Gorno-Badakhshan Aut. Obl. 161,000....H6
Kabardin-Balkar A.S.S.R. 760,000....E5
Kalmuck A.S.S.R. 322,000....E5
Karachay-Cherkess Aut. Obl. 418,000....E5
Karakalpak A.S.S.R. 1,214,000....G5
Karelian A.S.S.R. 792,000....D3
Khakass Aut. Obl. 569,000....J4
Khanty-Mansi Aut. Okr. 1,269,000....G3
Komi A.S.S.R. 1,263,000....F3
Komi-Permyak Aut. Okr. 294,000....F4
Koryak Aut. Okr. 39,000....R3
Mari A.S.S.R. 750,000....E4
Mordvinian A.S.S.R. 964,000....E4
Nagorno-Karabakh Aut. Obl. 188,000....E5

Nakhichevan' A.S.S.R. 295,000....E6
Nenets Aut. Okr. 55,000....F3
North Ossetian A.S.S.R. 634,000....E5
South Ossetian Aut. Obl. 99,000....E5
Tatar A.S.S.R. 3,640,000....F4
Taymyr Aut. Okr. 55,000....K2
Tuvinian A.S.S.R. 309,000....K4
Udmurt A.S.S.R. 1,609,000....F4
Ust'-Ordynskiy Buryat Aut. Okr. 136,000....L4
Yakut A.S.S.R. 1,081,000....N3
Yamal-Nenets Aut. Okr. 487,000....H3
Yevrey Aut. Obl. 216,000....O5

CITIES and TOWNS

Abakan 154,000....K4
Abay 34,245....H5
Achinsk 122,000....K4
Akmolinsk (Tselinograd) 277,000....H4
Aktyubinsk 253,000....F4
Aldan 17,689....N4

Aleksandrovsk-Sakhalinskiy 20,342....P4
Aleysk 32,487....J4
Alga 12,000....F5
Alma-Ata 1,128,000....H5
Anadyr' 7,703....S3
Andizhan 293,000....H5
Andropov 252,000....D4
Angarsk 266,000....L4
Angren 131,000....H5
Anzhero-Sudzhensk 108,000....J4
Aral'sk 37,722....G5
Archangel (Arkhangel'sk) 416,000....E3
Armavir 161,000....E5
Arsen'yev 60,000....O5
Artem 69,000....O5
Arys' 26,414....H5
Arzamas 109,000....E4
Asbest 79,000....G4
Asino 89,000....J4
Ashkhabad 398,000....F6
Astrakhan' 509,000....E5
Atbasar 37,228....G4
Ayaguz 35,827....J5
Baku 1,150,000....F5
Balakovo 198,000....E4
Balashov 93,000....E4
Baley 27,215....M4

Balkhash 78,000....H5
Barabinsk 37,274....H4
Baranovichi 159,000....C4
Barnaul 602,000....J4
Batumi 136,000....E5
Baykonyr
Bayram-Ali 31,987....G6
Belgorod 300,000....D4
Belogorsk 63,000....N4
Belomorsk 16,595....D3
Belovo 112,000....J4
Berdichev 80,000....C5
Berdsk 67,000....J4
Berezniki 201,000....F4
Berezovo 6,000....G3
Beruni
Birobidzhan 69,000....O5
Biysk 233,000....J4
Blagoveshchensk 206,000....N4
Bobruysk 223,000....C4
Bodaybo 19,000....M4
Borisoglebsk 68,000....E4
Borzya 27,815....M4
Bratsk 255,000....L4
Brest 258,000....C4
Bryansk 452,000....D4
Bugul'ma 80,000....F4
Bukhara 224,000....G5

Buzuluk 76,000....F4
Chapayevsk 85,000....F4
Chardzhou 161,000....G6
Cheboksary 420,000....E4
Chelyabinsk 1,143,000....G4
Cheremkhovo 77,000....L4
Cherepovets 310,000....D4
Cherkessk 113,000....E5
Chernenko 54,000....K4
Chernigov 296,000....D4
Chernogorsk 71,000....K4
Chernovtsy 257,000....C5
Chimkent 393,000....H5
Chirchik 156,000....H5
Chita 366,000....M4
Dal'negorsk 33,506....O5
Dal'nerechensk 28,224....O5
Daugavpils 127,000....C4
Dimitrovgrad 124,000....F4
Dneprodzerzhinsk 206,000....D5
Dnepropetrovsk 1,179,000....D5
Donetsk 1,110,000....D5
Drogobych 66,000....C5
Dudinka 19,701....J3
Dushanbe 595,000....G6
Dzhalal-Abad 55,000....H5
Dzhambul 307,000....H5
Dzhetygara 32,169....G4
Dzhezkazgan 109,000....G5

Ekibastuz 135,000....H4
Elista 70,000....E5
Engel's 182,000....E4
Fergana 200,000....H5
Fort-Shevchenko 12,000....E5
Frolovo 33,398....E5
Frunze 616,000....H5
Gomel' 500,000....D4
Gorno-Altaysk 34,413....J4
Grodno 270,000....C4
Groznyy 401,000....E5
Gubakha 33,243....F4
Gulistan 30,879....H5
Gur'yev 149,000....F5
Gusinoozersk 10,000....L4
Gyandzhe 278,000....E5
Igarka 15,624....J3
Inta 51,000....G3
Irkutsk 626,000....L4
Ishim 63,000....H4
Isil'kul' 25,958....H4
Ivano-Frankovsk 214,000....C5
Ivanovo 481,000....D4
Izhevsk 635,000....F4
Izmail 83,000....C5
Kagan 34,117....G6
Kalinin (Tver') 451,000....D4
Kaliningrad 401,000....B4
Kaluga 312,000....D4

Union of Soviet Socialist Republics
CONIC PROJECTION
SCALE OF MILES
0   100 200 300 400 500 600
SCALE OF KILOMETERS
0 100 200 300 400 500 600

Capitals   Boundaries
National
Union Republic
A.S.S.R.
Autonomous Oblast
Autonomous Okrug
Scale 1:30,400,000

ADMINISTRATIVE DIVISIONS NOT NAMED ON MAP

Division	Ref.	Division	Ref.
1. Abkhaz A.S.S.R.	E5	13. Khakass Aut. Oblast	J4
2. Adygey Aut. Oblast	D5	14. Komi-Permyak Aut. Okrug	F4
3. Adzhar A.S.S.R.	E5	15. Mari A.S.S.R.	E4
4. Aginsk Buryat Autonomous Okrug	M4	16. Mordvinian A.S.S.R.	E4
5. Chechen-Ingush A.S.S.R.	E5	17. Nagorno-Karabakh Aut. Oblast	E5
6. Chuvash A.S.S.R.	E4	18. Nakhichevan' A.S.S.R.	E6
7. Gorno-Altay Aut. Oblast	J4	19. North Ossetian A.S.S.R.	E5
8. Gorno-Badakhshan Aut. Oblast	H6	20. South Ossetian Aut. Oblast	E5
9. Jewish Aut. Oblast	O5	21. Tatar A.S.S.R.	F4
10. Kabardin-Balkar A.S.S.R.	E5	22. Tuvinian A.S.S.R.	K4
11. Karachay-Cherkess Aut. Oblast	E5	23. Udmurt A.S.S.R.	F4
12. Karakalpak A.S.S.R.	G5	24. Ust-Ordynskiy Buryat Autonomous Okrug	L4

AREA 8,649,490 sq. mi. (22,402,179 sq. km.)
POPULATION 286,730,817
CAPITAL Moscow
LARGEST CITY Moscow
HIGHEST POINT Communism Peak 24,599 ft. (7,498 m.)
MONETARY UNIT ruble
MAJOR LANGUAGES Russian, Ukrainian, White Russian, Uzbek,
Azerbaidzhani, Tatar, Georgian, Lithuanian, Armenian, Yiddish,
Latvian, Mordvinian, Kirgiz, Tadzhik, Estonian, Kazakh, Moldavian
(Romanian), German, Chuvash, Turkmenian, Bashkir
MAJOR RELIGIONS Eastern (Russian) Orthodoxy, Islam, Judaism,
Protestantism (Baltic States)

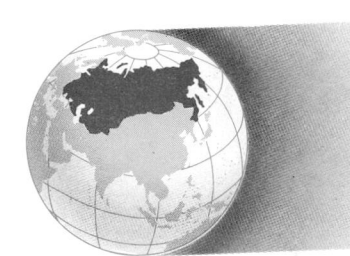

Kamen'-na-Obi 35,604	H4	Kemerovo 520,000	J4
Kamenskoye	R3	Kentau 52,000	G5
Kamensk-Ural'skiy 209,000	G4	Khabarovsk 601,000	O5
Kamyshin 122,000	E4	Khanty-Mansiysk 24,754	H3
Kandalaksha 42,656	C3	Khar'kov 1,611,000	D4
ansk 110,000	K4	Kherson 355,000	D5
Karaganda 614,000	H5	Khiva 24,139	F5
aratau 26,962	H5	Khodzheyli 36,435	F5
arshi 156,000	G6	Kholmsk 37,412	P5
artaly 42,801	G4	Khorog 12,295	H6
aunas 423,000	C4	Kiev 2,587,000	D4
azan' 1,094,000	F4	Kirov 441,000	E4
em' 21,025	D3	Kirovabad (Gyandzhe) 278,000	E5

UNION REPUBLICS

	AREA (sq. mi.)	AREA (sq. km.)	POPULATION	CAPITAL and LARGEST CITY
RUSSIAN S.F.S.R.	6,592,812	17,075,400	147,386,000	Moscow 8,769,000
KAZAKH S.S.R.	1,048,300	2,715,100	16,538,000	Alma-Ata 1,128,000
UKRAINIAN S.S.R.	233,089	603,700	51,704,000	Kiev 2,587,000
TURKMEN S.S.R.	188,455	488,100	3,534,000	Ashkhabad 398,000
UZBEK S.S.R.	173,591	449,600	19,906,000	Tashkent 2,073,000
BELORUSSIAN S.S.R.	80,154	207,600	10,200,000	Minsk 1,589,000
KIRGIZ S.S.R.	76,641	198,500	4,291,000	Frunze 616,000
TADZHIK S.S.R.	55,251	143,100	5,112,000	Dushanbe 595,000
AZERBAIDZHAN S.S.R.	33,436	86,600	7,029,000	Baku 1,150,000
GEORGIAN S.S.R.	26,911	69,700	5,449,000	Tbilisi 1,260,000
LITHUANIAN S.S.R.	25,174	65,200	3,690,000	Vilnius 582,000
LATVIAN S.S.R.	24,595	63,700	2,681,000	Riga 915,000
ESTONIAN S.S.R.	17,413	45,100	1,573,000	Tallinn 482,000
MOLDAVIAN S.S.R.	13,012	33,700	4,341,000	Kishinev 665,000
ARMENIAN S.S.R.	11,506	29,800	3,283,000	Yerevan 1,199,000

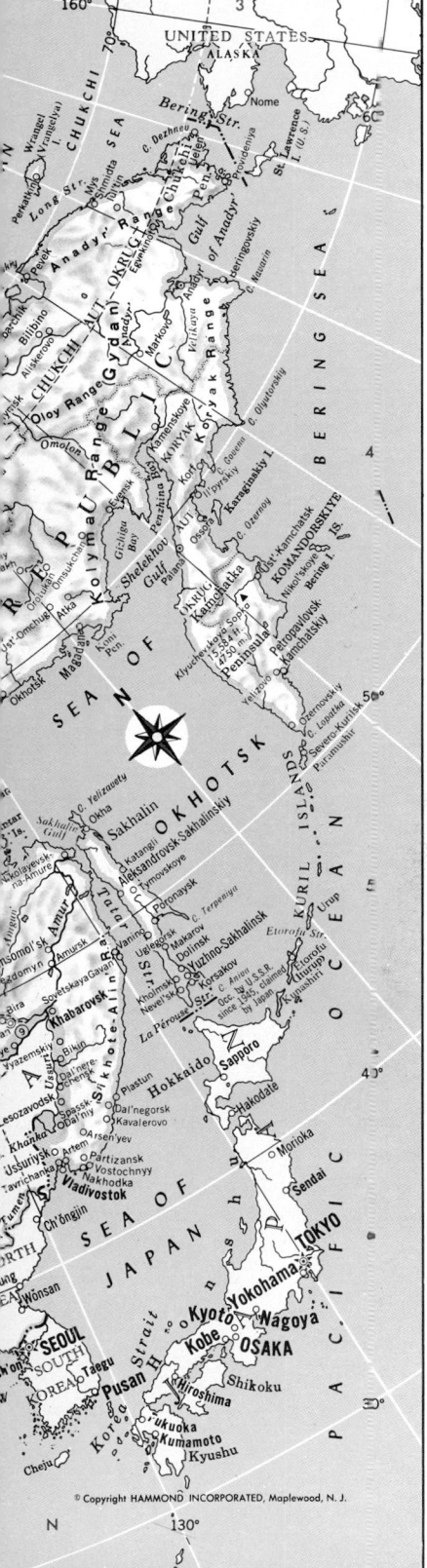

Kirovograd 269,000	D5	Krasnoyarsk 912,000	K4	Lenkoran' 35,505	E6	Monchegorsk 51,000	C3	Nizhniy Tagil 440,000	G4
Kiselevsk 128,000	J4	Kremenchug 236,000	D5	Lesozavodsk 34,957	O5	Moscow (cap.) 8,769,000	D4	Nordvik-Ugol'naya	M2
Kishinev 665,000	C5	Krivoy Rog 713,000	D5	Liepāja 114,000	B4	Motygino 10,000	K4	Noril'sk 174,000	J3
Kizel 46,264	F4	Kudymkar 26,350	F4	Lipetsk 450,000	E4	Mozyr' 101,000	C4	Novgorod 229,000	D4
Kizyl-Arvat 21,671	F6	Kul'sary 16,427	F5	Luga 31,965	D4	Murmansk 468,000	D3	Novokazalinsk 34,815	G5
Klaipeda 204,000	B4	Kulyab 55,000	H6	Lugansk 497,000	E5	Muynak 12,000	F5	Novokuznetsk 600,000	J4
Kokand 182,000	H5	Kungur 80,000	F4	Lutsk 198,000	C4	Mys Shmidta	T3	Novomoskovsk 146,000	E4
Kokchetav 137,000	H4	Kurgan 356,000	G4	L'vov 790,000	C4	Nakhichevan' 33,279	E6	Novorossiysk 186,000	D5
Kolomna 162,000	D4	Kurgan-Tyube 34,620	G6	Lys'va 75,000	F4	Nakhodka 165,000	O5	Novosibirsk 1,436,000	J4
Komsomol'sk-na-Amure 315,000	O4	Kursk 424,000	D4	Magadan 152,000	P4	Nal'chik 235,000	E5	Novozybkov 34,433	D4
Kondopoga 27,908	D3	Kustanay 224,000	G4	Magnitogorsk 440,000	G4	Namangan 308,000	H5	Novyy Port	G3
Kopeysk 146,000	G4	Kutaisi 235,000	D5	Makhachkala 315,000	E5	Nar'yan-Mar 16,864	F3	Novyy Urengoy	H3
Korsakov 38,210	P5	Kuybyshev 40,166	H4	Mariupol 517,000	D5	Naryn 21,098	H5	Nukus 169,000	G5
Kostroma 278,000	E4	Kuybyshev (Samara) 1,257,000	F4	Mary (Merv) 74,000	G6	Navoi 107,000	G5	Odessa 1,115,000	D5
Kotlas 61,000	E3	Kyakhta 15,316	L4	Maykop 149,000	D5	Nebit-Dag 71,000	F6	Okha 30,890	P4
Kovel' 33,351	C4	Kyzyl 66,000	K4	Mednogorsk 38,024	F4	Nefteyugansk 52,000	H3	Okhotsk	P4
Kovrov 160,000	E4	Kyzyl-Orda 153,000	G5	Mezen'	E3	Nikol'skiy 32,862	G5	Omsk 1,148,000	H4
Krasnodar 620,000	D5	Leninabad 160,000	G5	Miass 168,000	G4	Nikolayev 503,000	D5	Omutninsk 28,777	F4
Krasnokamensk 51,000	M4	Leninakan 120,000	E5	Michurinsk 109,000	E4	Nikolayevsk-na-Amure 30,082	P4	Onega 25,047	D3
Krasnokamsk 56,000	F4	Leningrad 4,456,000	D4	Millerovo 34,627	E5	Nizhneudinsk 39,743	K4	Ordzhonikidze 300,000	E5
Krasnotur'insk 61,000	G3	Leninogorsk 68,000	J4	Minsk 1,589,000	C4	Nizhnevartovsk 242,000	H3	Orel 337,000	D4
Krasnoural'sk 39,743	G4	Leninsk	E4	Minusinsk 56,000	K4	Nizhniy Novgorod (Gor'kiy) 1,438,000	E4	Orenburg 547,000	F4
Krasnovodsk 53,000	F5	Leninsk-Kuznetskiy 165,000	J4	Mogilev 356,000	D4			Orsk 271,000	F4
				Molodechno 73,000	C4			Osh 213,000	H5

(continued on following page)

† On June 12, 1991 voters in Leningrad decided to change the city's name back to St. Petersburg. Final action awaits approval by the republic and national legislatures.

Topography

© Copyright HAMMOND INCORPORATED, Maplewood, N.J.

Ostrogozhsk 29,921 .....D4
Pärnu 51,000 .....C4
Partizansk 48,345 .....O5
Pavlodar 331,000 .....H4
Pechenga D2
Pechora 56,000 .....F3
Penza 483,000 .....E4
Perm' 1,091,000 .....F4
Pervoural'sk 142,000 .....F4
Petropavlovsk 241,000 .....G4
Petropavlovsk-Kamchatskiy 269,000 .....R4
Petrovsk-Zabaykal'skiy 28,313 .....L4
Petrozavodsk 270,000 .....D3
Pinsk 119,000 .....C4
Podol'sk 210,000 .....D4
Poltava 315,000 .....D5
Polyarnyy 15,321 .....D3
Poronaysk 23,610 .....P5
Prikumsk 35,768 .....E5
Prokop'yevsk 274,000 .....J4
Przheval'sk 51,000 .....H5
Pskov 204,000 .....C4
Pushkin 90,000 .....C4
Raychikhinsk 25,157 .....N5
Riga 915,000 .....C4
Rostov 1,020,000 .....E5
Rovno 228,000 .....C4
Rubtsovsk 172,000 .....J4
Rudnyy 124,000 .....G4
Ryazan' 515,000 .....E4
Rybinsk 252,000 .....D4
Rzhev 69,000 .....D4
Salekhard 21,929 .....G3
Sal'sk 57,000 .....E5
Samara 1,257,000 .....F4
Samarkand 366,000 .....G6
Saran' 55,000 .....H5
Saransk 312,000 .....E4
Sarapul 111,000 .....F4
Saratov 905,000 .....E4
Segezha 28,810 .....D3
Semipalatinsk 334,000 .....H4
Serov 104,000 .....G4
Serpukhov 144,000 .....D4
Sevastopol' 356,000 .....D5
Severodvinsk 249,000 .....E3
Severo-Kuril'sk 8,000 .....Q4
Severoural'sk 29,880 .....G3
Severo-Yeniseyskiy K3
Shadrinsk 82,000 .....G4
Shakhtinsk 50,000 .....H5
Shakhty 224,000 .....E5
Shar'ya 25,788 .....E4
Shchuchinsk 40,432 .....H4
Shevchenko 159,000 .....F5
Shushenskoye 10,000 .....K4
Šiauliai 145,000 .....C4
Simferopol' 344,000 .....D5
Skovorodino 10,000 .....N4
Slavgorod 32,908 .....H4
Slobodskoy 34,374 .....E4
Smolensk 341,000 .....D4
Sochi 337,000 .....D5
Sokol 48,243 .....E4
Solikamsk 110,000 .....F3
Sortavala 22,188 .....C3
Sovetskaya Gavan' 28,455 .....O5
Spassk-Dal'niy 53,000 .....O5
Sretensk 16,000 .....M4
Stalingrad (Volgograd) 999,000 .....E5
Stavropol' 318,000 .....E5
Stepanakert 30,293 .....E6
Sterlitamak 248,000 .....F4
Sukhumi 121,000 .....E5
Sumy 291,000 .....D4
Surgut 248,000 .....H3
Susuman 12,000 .....P3
Sverdlovsk 1,367,000 .....F4
Svobodnyy 75,000 .....N4
Syktyvkar 233,000 .....F3
Syzran' 174,000 .....E4
Taganrog 291,000 .....D5
Taldy-Kurgan 119,000 .....H5
Talgar 31,273 .....H5
Tallinn 482,000 .....C4
Tambov 305,000 .....E4
Tartu 114,000 .....C4
Tashauz 112,000 .....F5
Tashkent 2,073,000 .....G5
Tatarsk 29,589 .....H4
Tayshet 34,232 .....K4
Tbilisi 1,260,000 .....E5
Tedzhen 25,708 .....F6
Tekeli 29,846 .....H5
Temirtau 212,000 .....H4
Termez 57,000 .....G6
Ternopol' 205,000 .....C5
Tobol'sk 62,000 .....G4
Togliatti (Tol'yatti) 630,000 .....F4
Tommot 8,000 .....N4
Tomsk 502,000 .....J4
Troitsk 88,000 .....G4
Tselinograd 277,000 .....H4
Tskhinvali 30,311 .....E5
Tula 540,000 .....D4
Tulun 52,000 .....L4
Tura 3,528 .....L3
Turkestan 67,000 .....G5
Tyumen' 477,000 .....G4
Uelen T3
Ufa 1,083,000 .....F4
Ukhta 111,000 .....F3
Ulan-Ude 353,000 .....L4
Ul'yanovsk 625,000 .....E4
Ural'sk 200,000 .....F4
Urgench 128,000 .....G5
Usol'ye-Sibirskoye 107,000 .....L4
Ussuriysk 162,000 .....O5
Ust'-Ilimsk 109,000 .....L4
Ust'-Kamchatsk 10,000 .....R4
Ust'-Kamenogorsk 324,000 .....J5
Ust'-Kut 50,000 .....L4
Ust'-Olenëk M2
Ust'-Ordynskiy 10,693 .....L4

Vanino 15,401 .....P5
Velikiye Luki 114,000 .....D4
Velikiy Ustyug 36,737 .....E3
Ventspils 40,467 .....B4
Verkhoyansk 2,000 .....N3
Vilnius (Vilna) 582,000 .....C4
Vinnitsa 374,000 .....C5
Vitebsk 350,000 .....D4
Vladimir 350,000 .....D4
Vladivostok 648,000 .....O5
Volgograd 999,000 .....E5
Vologda 283,000 .....E4
Vorkuta 116,000 .....G3
Voronezh 887,000 .....E4
Voroshilovgrad (Lugansk) 497,000 .....E5
Votkinsk 103,000 .....F4
Vyborg 76,000 .....C3
Vyshniy Volochek 72,000 .....D4
Yakutsk 187,000 .....N3
Yalutorovsk 25,426 .....G4
Yaroslavl' 633,000 .....D4
Yartsevo 36,662 .....J4
Yelets 120,000 .....D4
Yeniseysk 19,880 .....K4
Yerevan 1,199,000 .....E6
Yermak 28,133 .....H4
Yoshkar-Ola 242,000 .....E4
Yurga 78,000 .....J4
Yuzhno-Sakhalinsk 157,000 .....P5
Zaozernyy 27,216 .....K4
Zaporozh'ye 884,000 .....D5
Zhigansk N3
Zhitomir 292,000 .....C4
Zima 41,567 .....L4
Zlatoust 208,000 .....F4
Zyryanovsk 51,000 .....J5

OTHER FEATURES

Alakol' (lake) J5
Alazeya (riv.) Q3
Aldan (plat.) N4
Aldan (riv.) O3
Alexandra Land (isl.) E1
Altai (mts.) J5
Amga (riv.) O3
Amgun' (riv.) O4
Amudar'ya (riv.) G5
Amur (riv.) O4
Anabar (riv.) M2
Anadyr' (gulf) T3
Anadyr' (range) S3
Anadyr' (riv.) S3
Angara (riv.) K4
Aniva (cape) P5
Aral (sea) F5
Arctic Ocean K1
Argun (riv.) M4
Arkticheskiy Institut (isls.) H2
Atrek (riv.) F6
Ayon (isl.) R2
Azov (sea) D5
Balkhash (lake) H5
Baltic (sea) B4
Barents (sea) D2
Baykal (lake) L4
Baykal (mts.) L4
Beloye (lake) D3
Belyy (isl.) G2
Bering (isl.) R4
Bering (sea) S4
Bering (strait) U3
Bet-Pak-Dala (des.) H5
Black (sea) D5
Bol'shevik (isl.) K2
Bol'shoy Lyakhovskiy (isl.) P2
Bolvanskiy Nos (cape) G2
Bratsk (res.) L4
Caucasus (mts.) E5
Chelyuskin (cape) L2
Cherskiy (range) P3
Chu (riv.) H5
Chukchi (pen.) T3
Chukchi (sea) T2
Chulym (riv.) J4
Chuna (riv.) K4
Chunya (riv.) K3
Communism (peak) H6
Crimea (pen.) D5
Dezhnev (cape) T3
Dmitriya Lapteva (strait) O2
Dnieper (riv.) D5
Dniester (riv.) C5
Don (riv.) E5
Donets (riv.) D5
Dulgalakh (riv.) O3
Dvina, Northern (riv.) E3
Dvina, Western (riv.) C4
Dzhugdzhur (range) O4
East Siberian (sea) S2
Emba (riv.) F5
Etorofu (Iturup) (isl.) P5
Etorofu (str.) P5
Faddeyevskiy (isl.) P2
Finland (gulf) C4
Franz Josef Land (isls.) F1
George Land (isl.) G1
Gizhiga (bay) Q3
Govena (cape) R4
Graham Bell (isl.) G1
Gyda (pen.) H2
Gydan (Kolyma) (range) Q3
Hiiumaa (isl.) C4
Ili (riv.) H5
Imandra (lake) D3
Indigirka (riv.) P3
Irtysh (riv.) H4
Ishim (riv.) G4
Issyk-Kul' (lake) H5
Japan (sea) O6
Kakhovka (res.) D5
Kamchatka (pen.) Q4
Kanin (pen.) E3
Kanin Nos (cape) E3
Kara (sea) G2
Kara-Bogaz-Gol (gulf) F5
Karaginskiy (isl.) R4

Kara-Kum (canal) F6
Kara-Kum (des.) F5
Karskiye Vorota (strait) F2
Khanka (lake) O5
Kharasavey (cape) G2
Kheta (riv.) K2
Klyuchevskaya Sopka (vol.) Q4
Kola (pen.) D3
Kolguyev (isl.) E3
Kolyma (range) Q3
Kolyma (riv.) Q3
Komandorskiye (isls.) R4
Komsomolets (isl.) L1
Koni (pen.) Q4
Koryak (range) S3
Kotel'nyy (isl.) O2
Kotuy (riv.) L3
Kuma (riv.) E5
Kunashiri (isl.) P5
Kura (riv.) E6
Kuril (isls.) P5
Kuybyshev (res.) F4
Kyzyl-Kum (des.) G5
Ladoga (lake) D3
La Pérouse (strait) P5
Laptev (sea) N2

Lena (riv.) N3
Little Yenisey (riv.) K4
Long (strait) S2
Lopatka (cape) Q4
Lower Tunguska (riv.) K3
Lyakhovskiye (isls.) O2
Mangyshlak (pen.) F5
Markha (riv.) M3
Matochkin Shar (strait) F2
Maya (riv.) O4
Mezen' (riv.) E3
Murgab (riv.) G6
Nadym (riv.) H3
Narodnaya (mt.) G3
Navarin (cape) T3
New Siberian (isls.) P2
Northern Dvina (riv.) E3
Novaya Sibir' (isl.) P2
Novaya Zemlya (isls.) F2
Ob' (gulf) H3
Ob' (riv.) G3
October Revolution (isl.) L2
Oka (riv.) L4
Okhotsk (sea) P4
Olëkma (riv.) N4
Olënek (bay) N2

Olënek (riv.) M3
Oloy (range) R3
Olyutorskiy (cape) S4
Omolon (riv.) Q3
Omoloy (riv.) O3
Onega (lake) D3
Onega (riv.) D3
Ozernoy (cape) R4
Paramushir (isl.) Q4
Pechora (riv.) F3
Peipus (lake) C4
Penzhina (bay) R3
Pioner (isl.) J2
Pobeda (peak) J5
Pobeda (mt.) H3
Pur (riv.) H3
Pyasina (riv.) J2
Riga (gulf) C4
Rybachiy (pen.) D3
Rybinsk (res.) D4
Saaremaa (isl.) B4
Sakhalin (isl.) P4
Sakhalin (gulf) P4
Sannikova (strait) O2
Sarysu (riv.) H5
Sayan (mts.) K4
Selemdzha (riv.) O4

Sergeya Kirova (isls.) J2
Severnaya Zemlya (isls.) L1
Shantar (isls.) O4
Shelagskiy (cape) R2
Shelekhov (gulf) Q4
Siberia (reg.) M3
Sikhote-Alin' (range) O5
Stanovoy (range) N4
Stony Tunguska (riv.) K3
Syrdar'ya (riv.) G5
Tannu-Ola (range) K4
Tatar (strait) P4
Taymyr (lake) L2
Taymyr (pen.) L2
Taymyr (riv.) K2
Taz (riv.) J3
Tengiz (lake) G4
Terpeniye (cape) P5
Tobol (riv.) G4
Tsimlyansk (res.) E5
Tym (riv.) J3
Tyung (riv.) M3
Uda (riv.) O4
Ural (mts.) F4
Ural (riv.) F5
Urup (isl.) Q5

Ussuri (riv.) O5
Ust'-Urt (plat.) F5
Vakh (riv.) J3
Velikaya (riv.) S3
Verkhoyansk (range) N3
Vil'kitskogo (strait) L2
Vilyuy (range) M3
Vilyuy (res.) M3
Vilyuy (riv.) L3
Vitim (riv.) M4
Volga (riv.) E5
Western Dvina (riv.) C4
White (sea) D3
Wiese (isl.) H2
Wilczek Land (isl.) G1
Wrangel (isl.) T2
Yablonovyy (range) M4
Yamal (pen.) O3
Yana (riv.) O3
Yelizavety (cape) P4
Yenisey (riv.) J3
Zaysan (lake) J5
Zeya (riv.) N4
Zhelaniye (cape) H2

*City and suburbs.

Agriculture, Industry and Resources

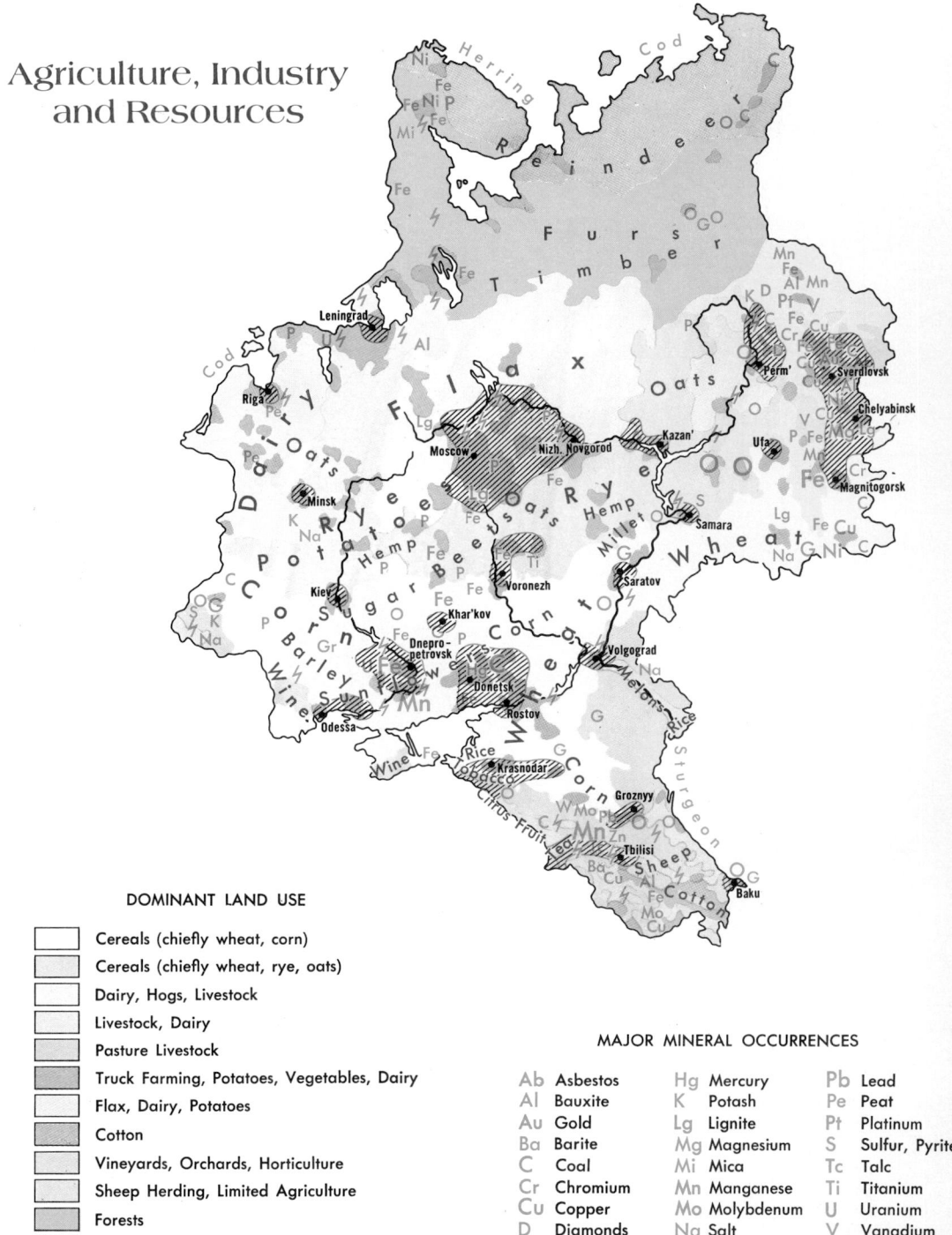

DOMINANT LAND USE

- Cereals (chiefly wheat, corn)
- Cereals (chiefly wheat, rye, oats)
- Dairy, Hogs, Livestock
- Livestock, Dairy
- Pasture Livestock
- Truck Farming, Potatoes, Vegetables, Dairy
- Flax, Dairy, Potatoes
- Cotton
- Vineyards, Orchards, Horticulture
- Sheep Herding, Limited Agriculture
- Forests
- Nonagricultural Land

MAJOR MINERAL OCCURRENCES

Ab	Asbestos	Hg	Mercury	Pb	Lead
Al	Bauxite	K	Potash	Pe	Peat
Au	Gold	Lg	Lignite	Pt	Platinum
Ba	Barite	Mg	Magnesium	S	Sulfur, Pyrites
C	Coal	Mi	Mica	Tc	Talc
Cr	Chromium	Mn	Manganese	Ti	Titanium
Cu	Copper	Mo	Molybdenum	U	Uranium
D	Diamonds	Na	Salt	V	Vanadium
Fe	Iron Ore	Ni	Nickel	W	Tungsten
G	Natural Gas	O	Petroleum	Zn	Zinc
Gr	Graphite	P	Phosphates		

⚡ Water Power ▨ Major Industrial Areas

Agriculture, Industry and Resources

DOMINANT LAND USE

- Cereals (chiefly wheat, corn)
- Livestock, Dairy
- Truck Farming, Potatoes, Vegetables, Dairy
- Cotton
- Sheep Herding, Limited Agriculture
- Forests
- Nonagricultural Land

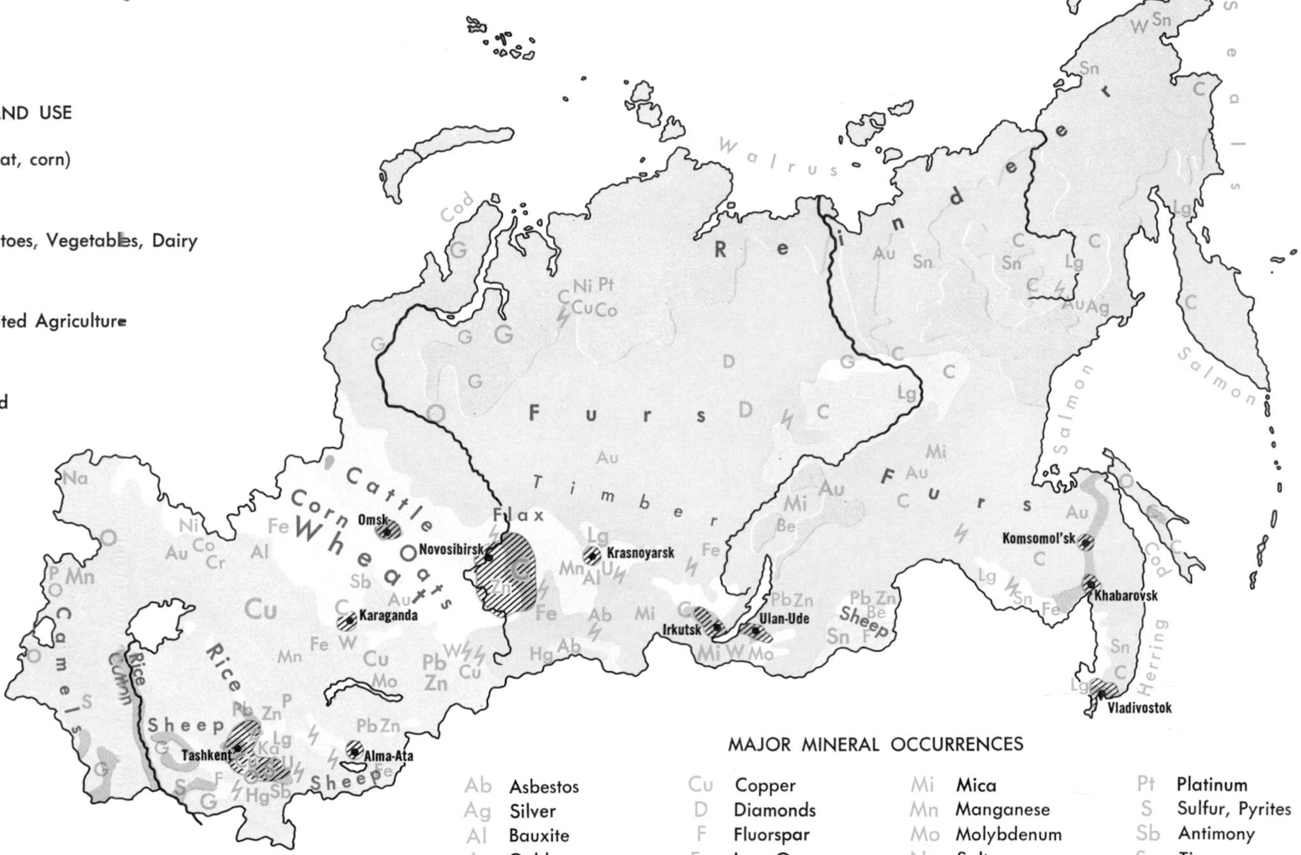

MAJOR MINERAL OCCURRENCES

Ab	Asbestos	Cu	Copper	Mi	Mica	Pt	Platinum
Ag	Silver	D	Diamonds	Mn	Manganese	S	Sulfur, Pyrites
Al	Bauxite	F	Fluorspar	Mo	Molybdenum	Sb	Antimony
Au	Gold	Fe	Iron Ore	Na	Salt	Sn	Tin
Be	Beryl	G	Natural Gas	Ni	Nickel	U	Uranium
C	Coal	Hg	Mercury	O	Petroleum	W	Tungsten
Co	Cobalt	Ka	Kaolin	P	Phosphates	Zn	Zinc
Cr	Chromium	Lg	Lignite	Pb	Lead		

⚡ Water Power   ▨ Major Industrial Areas

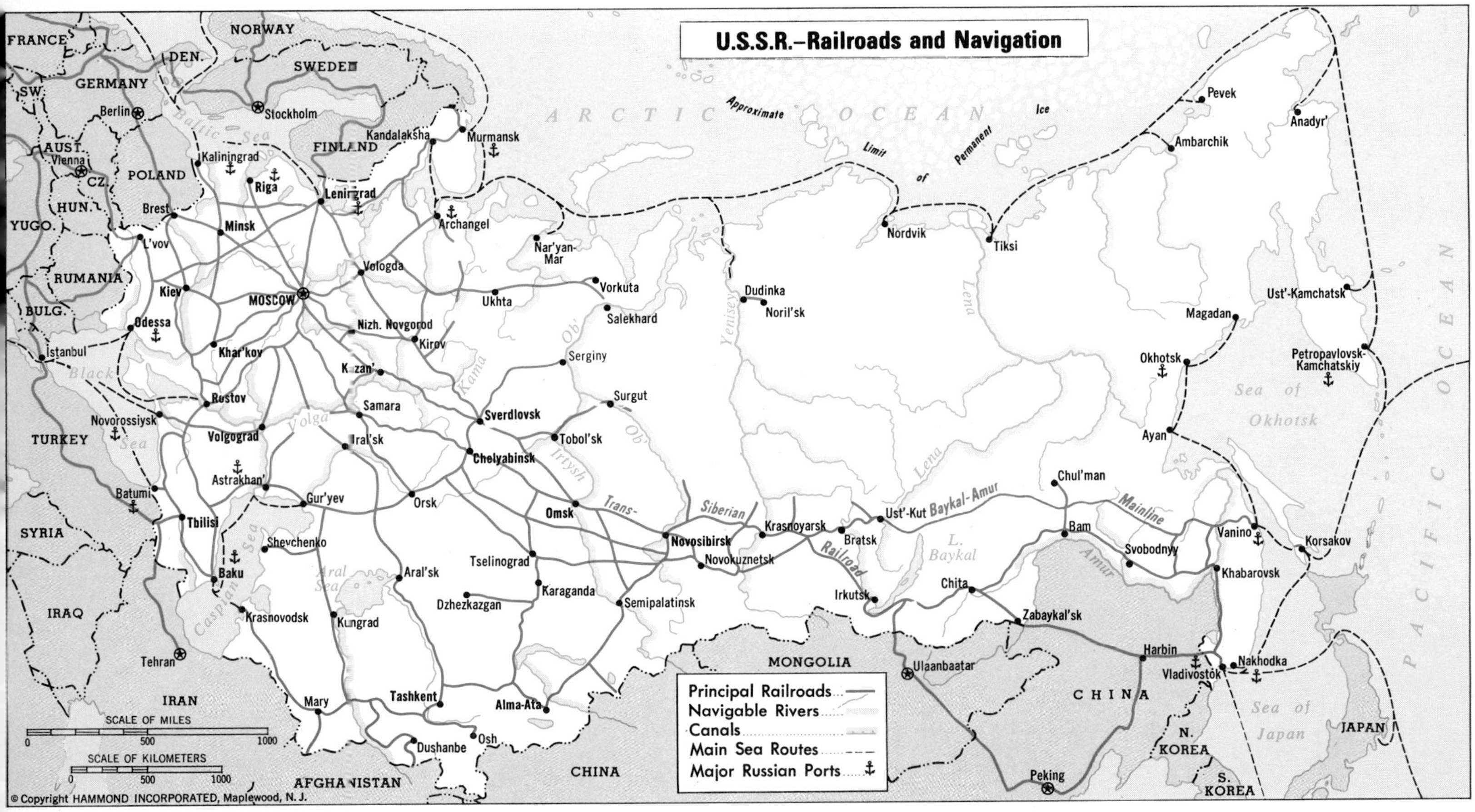

U.S.S.R.–Railroads and Navigation

Principal Railroads
Navigable Rivers
Canals
Main Sea Routes
Major Russian Ports ⚓

SCALE OF MILES
0   500   1000

SCALE OF KILOMETERS
0   500   1000

© Copyright HAMMOND INCORPORATED, Maplewood, N.J.

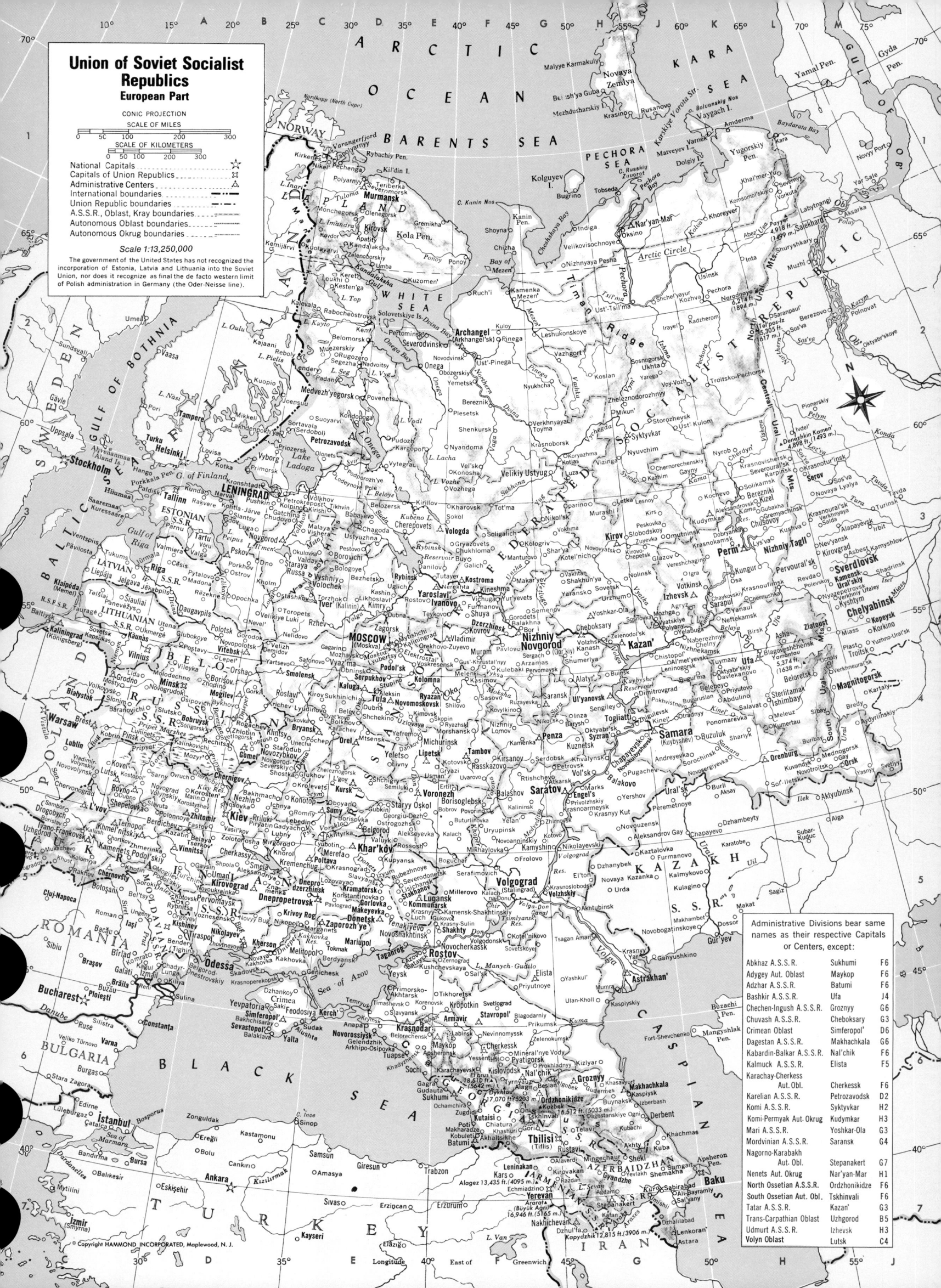

Union of Soviet Socialist Republics

European Part

CONIC PROJECTION

SCALE OF MILES

SCALE OF KILOMETERS

Scale 1:13,250,000

National Capitals
Capitals of Union Republics
Administrative Centers
International boundaries
Union Republic boundaries
A.S.S.R., Oblast, Kray boundaries
Autonomous Oblast boundaries
Autonomous Okrug boundaries

The government of the United States has not recognized the incorporation of Estonia, Latvia and Lithuania into the Soviet Union, nor does it recognize as final the de facto western limit of Polish administration in Germany (the Oder-Neisse line).

Administrative Divisions bear same names as their respective Capitals or Centers, except:

Abkhaz A.S.S.R.	Sukhumi	F6
Adygey Aut. Oblast	Maykop	F6
Adzhar A.S.S.R.	Batumi	F6
Bashkir A.S.S.R.	Ufa	J4
Chechen-Ingush A.S.S.R.	Groznyy	G6
Chuvash A.S.S.R.	Cheboksary	G3
Crimean Oblast	Simferopol'	D6
Dagestan A.S.S.R.	Makhachkala	G6
Kabardin-Balkar A.S.S.R.	Nal'chik	F6
Kalmuck A.S.S.R.	Elista	F5
Karachay-Cherkess Aut. Obl.	Cherkessk	F6
Karelian A.S.S.R.	Petrozavodsk	D2
Komi A.S.S.R.	Syktyvkar	H2
Komi-Permyak Aut. Okrug	Kudymkar	H3
Mari A.S.S.R.	Yoshkar-Ola	G3
Mordvinian A.S.S.R.	Saransk	G4
Nagorno-Karabakh Aut. Obl.	Stepanakert	G7
Nenets Aut. Okrug	Nar'yan-Mar	H1
North Ossetian A.S.S.R.	Ordzhonikidze	F6
South Ossetian Aut. Obl.	Tskhinvali	F6
Tatar A.S.S.R.	Kazan'	G3
Trans-Carpathian Oblast	Uzhgorod	B5
Udmurt A.S.S.R.	Izhevsk	H3
Volyn Oblast	Lutsk	C4

© Copyright HAMMOND INCORPORATED, Maplewood, N.J.

U.S.S.R. - EUROPEAN

UNION REPUBLICS

rmenian S.S.R. 3,283,000.....F6
ze-baidzhan S.S.R.
7,029,000.....G6
elorussian S.S.R.
10,200,000.....C4
stonian S.S.R. 1,573,000......C3
ecrgian S.S.F. 5,449,000......F6
atvian S.S.R. 2,681,000........B3
ithuanian S.S.R. 3,690,000...B3
loldavian S.S.R. 4,341,000...C5
ussian S.F.S.R. 147,386,000 F3
krainian S.S.R. 51,704,000..D5

INTERNAL DIVISIONS

bkhaz A.S.S.R. 537,000........F6
dygey Aut. Obl. 432,000........F6
dzhar A.S.S.R. 393,000.........F6
ashkir A.S.S.R. 3,952,000.....J4
hechen-Ingush A.S.S.R.
1,277,000.....G6
huvash A.S.S.R. 1,336,000..G3
rimean Oblast 2,456,000......D6
agestan A.S.S.R. 1,792,000 .G6
abardin-Balkar A.S.S.R.
760,000.....F6
almuck A.S.S.R. 322,000......F5
arachay-Cherkess Aut. Obl.
418,000.....F6
arelian A.S.S.R. 792,000......D2
omi A.S.S.R. 1,263,000........H2
omi-Permyak Aut. Okr.
159,000.....H3
ari A.S.S.R. 750,000............G3
ordvinian A.S.S.R. 964,000 .G4
agorno-Karabakh Aut. Obl.
188,000.....G7
akhichevan' A.S.S.R.
295,000.....F7
enets Aut. Okr. 55,000.........H1
orth Ossetian A.S.S.R.
634,000.....F6
outh Ossetian Aut. Obl.
99,000.....F6
atar A.S.S.R. 3,640,000........G3
rans-Carpathian Oblast
1,252,000.....B5
dmurt A.S.S.R. 1,609,000....H3
olyn Oblast 1,062,000..........C4

CITIES and TOWNS

khtubinsk 51,000.....G5
khty.....G6
khtyrka 41,354.....E4
kkerman (Belgorod
Dnestrovskiy) 51,000.....D5
latyr' 43,499.....G4
leksandriya 103,000.....D5
leksin 70,000.....E4
l'met'yevsk 129,000.....H3
lushta 22,016.....D6
mderma.....K1
napa 29,900.....E6
patity 74,000.....D1
rchangel (Arkhangel'sk)
416,000.....F2
rmavir 161,000.....F5
rzamas 109,000.....F3
strakhan' 509,000.....G5
zov 79,000.....E5
akhchisaray 15,912.....D6
aku 1,150,000.....H6
alaklava.....D6
alakovo 198,000.....G4
alashov 97,000.....F4
altiysk 20,300.....A4
aranovichi 159,000.....C4
ataysk 95,000.....E5
atumi 136,000.....F6
elaya Tserkov' 197,000.....C5
elgorod 300 000.....E4
elgorod-Dnestrovskiy
51,000.....D5
elomorsk 16,595.....D2
eloretsk 74,000.....J4
elozersk.....E3
el'tsy 159,000.....C5
elush'ya Guba.....H1
endery 130,000.....C5
erdichev 85,000.....C5
erdyansk 132,000.....E5
erezniki 201,000.....J3
obruysk 223,000.....C4
or 64,000.....F3
orisoglebsk 63,000.....F4
orisov 144,000.....C4
orovichi 63,000.....D3
rest 258,000.....B4
ryansk 452,000.....D4
ugul'ma 85,000.....H4
uguruslan 53,000.....H4
uzuluk 76,000.....H4
hapayevsk 86,000.....G4
haykovskiy 76,000.....H3
heboksary 420,000.....G3
herepovets 310,000.....E3
herkassy 290,000.....D5
herkessk 113,000.....F6
hernigov 296,000.....D4
hernovtsy 257,000.....C5
hervonograd 64,000.....B4
histopol' 65,000.....H3
husovoy 58,000.....J3
augavpils 127,000.....C3
erbent 78,000.....G6
mitrovgrad 124,000.....G4
neprodzerzhinsk 282,000.....D5
nepropetrovsk 1,179,000.....D5
onetsk 1,110,000.....E5
rogobych 73,000.....B5
ubna 60,000.....E3
vinsk (Daugavpils) 127,000..C3
zerzhinsk 235,000.....F3

Dzhankoy 50,000.....D5
Elektrostal' 153,000.....E3
Elista 80,000.....F5
Engel's 182,000.....G4
Fastov 54,000.....C4
Feodosiya 81,000.....D5
Furmanov 40,155.....F3
Gagra 23,025.....E6
Gatchina 78,000.....D3
Gdov.....C3
Genichesk 20,031.....E5
Georgiu-Dezh 52,000.....E4
Glazov 104,000.....H3
Glubokoye.....C3
Gomel' 500,000.....D4
Gori 60,000.....F6
Gorlovka 337,000.....E5
Gremikha.....E1
Grodno 270,000.....B4
Groznyy 401,000.....G6
Gryazi 41,292.....F4
Gubkin 70,000.....E4
Gukovo 71,000.....F5
Gus'-Khrustal'nyy 74,000.....F3
Gyandzhe 278,000.....G6
Inta 55,000.....K1
Ishimbay 63,000.....J4
Ivano-Frankovsk 214,000.....B5
Ivanovo 481,000.....E3
Izhevsk (Ustinov) 635,000.....H3
Izmail 87,000.....C5
Izyum 62,000.....E5
Jēkabpils 22,440.....C3
Jelgava 70,000.....B3
Jūrmala 63,000.....B3
Kadiyeuka (Stakhanov)
112,000.....E5
Kalach-na-Donu 20,795.....F5
Kalinin (Tver') 451,000.....E3
Kaliningrad, Kaliningrad
401,000.....B4
Kaliningrad, Moscow Oblast
160,000.....E3
Kaluga 312,000.....E4
Kalush 64,000.....B5
Kamenets-Podol'skiy
102,000.....C5
Kamensk-Shakhtinskiy
75,000.....F5
Kamyshin 122,000.....F4
Kanash 40,682.....G3
Kandalaksha 42,656.....D1
Karachayevsk.....F6
Karachev 15,972.....E4
Kashin 17,678.....E3
Kaspiysk 57,000.....G6
Kaunas 423,000.....B4
Kazan' 1,094,000.....G3
Kem' 21,025.....D2
Kerch' 174,000.....E5
Khar'kov 1,611,000.....E5
Khasavyurt 72,000.....G6
Kherson 355,000.....D5
Khmel'nitskiy 237,000.....C5
Khvalynsk 16,249.....G4
Kiev 2,587,000.....D4
Kimovsk 44,490.....E4
Kimry 60,000.....E3
Kineshma 105,000.....F3
Kirov 441,000.....G3
Kirovabad (Gyandzhe)
278,000.....G6
Kirovakan 162,000.....F6
Kirovo-Chepetsk 83,000.....H3
Kirovograd 269,000.....D5
Kishinev 665,000.....C5
Kislovodsk 114,000.....F6
Kizel 46,264.....J3
Klaipeda 204,000.....B3
Klintsy 71,000.....D4
Kobuleti 18,051.....F6
Kohtla-Järve 77,000.....C3
Kolomna 162,000.....E4
Kolomyya 59,000.....B5
Kolpino 142,000.....D3
Kommunarsk 126,000.....E5
Königsberg (Kaliningrad)
410,000.....B4
Konotop 82,000.....D4
Konstantinovka 108,000.....E5
Korosten' 69,000.....C4
Kostroma 278,000.....F3
Kotlas 66,000.....G2
Kovel' 61,000.....C4
Kovrov 160,000.....F3
Kramatorsk 198,000.....E5
Krasnoarmeysk 60,000.....G4
Krasnodar 620,000.....E6
Krasnokamsk 57,000.....H3
Krasnovishersk.....J2
Krasnyy Kut 17,087.....G4
Krasnyy Luch 113,000.....E5
Krasnyy Sulin 41,684.....F5
Kremenchug 236,000.....D5
Krivoy Rog 713,000.....D5
Kronshtadt 39,477.....C3
Kropotkin 73,000.....F5
Krymsk 49,000.....E5
Kulebaki 46,252.....F3
Kumertau 58,000.....J4
Kunda.....C3
Kungur 82,000.....J3
Kuressaare 12,140.....B3
Kursk 424,000.....E4
Kutaisi 235,000.....F6
Kuybyshev (Samara)
1,257,000.....H4
Kuznetsk 97,000.....G4
Kuzomen'.....E1
Labinsk 57,000.....F6
Lakhdenpokh'ya.....C2
Leninakan 120,000.....F6
Leningrad 4,456,000.....C3
Leninogorsk 69,000.....H4
Lida 73,000.....C4
Liepāja 114,000.....B3
Lipetsk 450,000.....E4
Lisichansk 127,000.....E5

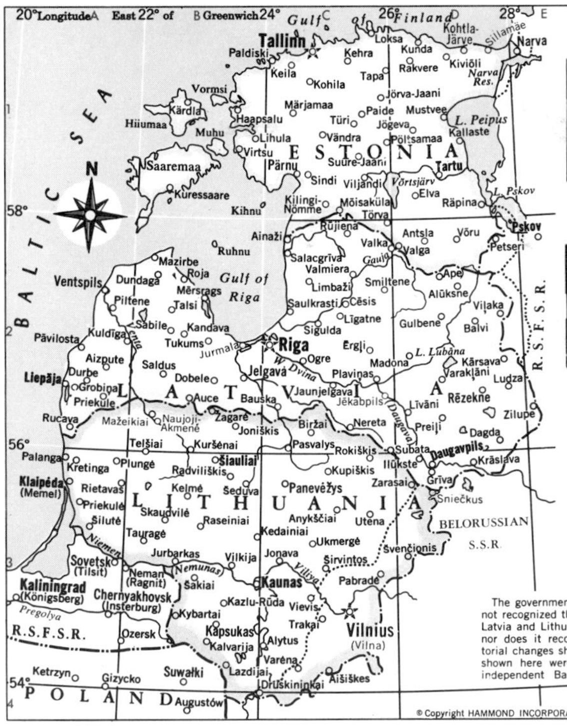

The government of the United States has not recognized the incorporation of Estonia, Latvia and Lithuania into the Soviet Union, nor does it recognize other post-war territorial changes shown on this map. The flags shown here were the official flags of the independent Baltic States prior to 1939.

© Copyright HAMMOND INCORPORATED, Maplewood, N. J.

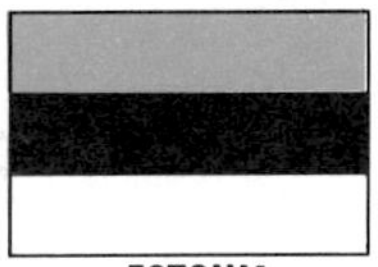

ESTONIA

LATVIA

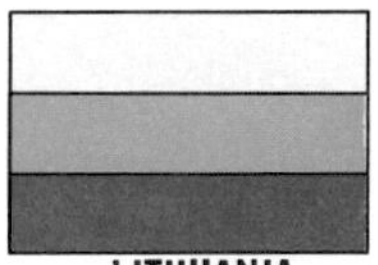

LITHUANIA

The Baltic States

SCALE OF MILES
0 25 50 75 100
SCALE OF KILOMETERS
0 30 60 90 120 150 180

Capitals.....☆
International Boundaries.....—·—
Union Republic Boundaries.....—·—
Prewar boundaries of the Baltic States where divergent from present boundaries.....·········

Scale 1:7,200,000

BALTIC STATES

Alytus 55.000	C 3
Biržai 11.400	C 2
Cēsis 17.696	C 2
Daugava (Western Dvina) (riv.)	D 2
Daugavpils 127.000	D 3
Dobele 10.100	B 2
Druskininkai 11.200	C 3
Dvina, Western (riv.)	C 2
Finland (gulf)	D 1
Gauja (riv.)	C 2
Haapsalu 11.483	B 1
Hiiumaa (isl.)	B 1
Jēkabpils 22.440	C 2
Jelgava 68.000	B 2
Jonava 14.400	C 3
Jūrmala 61.000	B 2
Kapsukas 28.763	B 3
Kaunas 423.000	C 3
Kedainiai 19.677	C 3
Kihnu (isl.)	B 1
Kingisepp (Kuressaare) 12.140	B 1
Kiviõli 11.153	D 1
Klaipeda 204.000	A 3
Kohtla-Järve 73.000	D 1
Kretinga 13.000	A 3
Kuldīga 12.300	A 2
Kuressaare 12.140	B 1
Kuršenai 11.500	B 2
Liepāja 114.000	A 2
Lubāna (lake)	D 2
Mažeikiai 13.400	A 2
Memel (Klaipeda) 204.000	A 3
Muhu (isl.)	B 1
Narva 73.000	E 1
Naujoji-Akmene 10.200	B 2
Niemen (riv.)	A 3
Ogre 15.708	C 2
Panevežys 126.000	C 3
Pärnu 51.000	C 1
Peipus (lake)	D 1
Plunge 13.600	B 3
Radviliškis 16.841	B 3
Rakvere 17.891	D 1
Rēzekne 30.803	D 2
Riga (cap.), Latvia 915.000	C 2
Riga (gulf)	B 2
Saaremaa (isl.)	B 1
Saldus 10.000	B 2
Šiauliai 145.000	B 3
Sillamäe 13.505	D 1
Šilute 12.400	A 3
Tallinn (cap.), Estonia 482.000	C 1
Tapa 10.037	C 1
Tartu 114.000	D 1
Taurage 19.461	B 3
Telšiai 20.220	B 2
Tukums 14.800	B 2
Ukmerge 21.663	C 3
Utena 13.300	C 3
Valga 16.795	D 2
Valmiera 20.331	C 2
Venta (riv.)	B 2
Ventspils 40.467	A 2
Viliya (riv.)	C 3
Viljandi 20.814	C 1
Vilnius (Vilna) (cap.), Lithuania 582.000	C 3
Vormsi (isl.)	B 1
Võrtsjärv (lake)	D 1
Võru 15.398	D 2
Western Dvina (riv.)	C 2

Lodeynoye Pole 19,632.....D2
Lozovaya 62,000.....E5
Lubny 57,000.....D4
Lugansk 497,000.....E5
Lutsk 198,000.....B4
L'vov (Lwów) 790,000.....B5
Lys'va 76,000.....J3
Lyubertsy 165,000.....E3
Makeyevka 430,000.....E5
Makhachkala 315,000.....G6
Makharadze 21,679.....F6
Malaya Vishera 15,381.....D3
Malgobek 20,548.....F6
Marganets 53,000.....D5
Mariupol' 517,000.....E5
Marks 17,132.....G4
Maykop 149,000.....F6
Melitopol' 174,000.....D5
Memel (Klaipeda) 204,000.....B3
Mezen'.....F1
Michurinsk 109,000.....F4
Mikhaylovka 58,000.....F4
Mineral'nye Vody 72,000.....F6
Mingechaur 60,000.....G6
Minsk 1,589,000.....C4
Mogilev 356,000.....C4
Molodechno 82,000.....C4
Molotov (Perm') 1,091,000.....J3
Monchegorsk 60,000.....D1
Morshansk 44,245.....F4
Moscow (Moskva)
(cap.) 8,769,000.....E3
Mozhga 38,930.....H3
Mozyr' 101,000.....C4
Mukachevo 82,000.....B5
Murmansk 468,000.....D1
Murom 124,000.....F3
Mytishchi 154,000.....E3
Naberezhnye Chelny 501,000 .H3
Nal'chik 235,000.....F6
Narva 79,000.....C3
Nar'yan-Mar 16,864.....H1
Neftekamsk 107,000.....H3
Nevinnomyssk 121,000.....F6
Nezhin 70,000.....D4
Nikel' 21,299.....C1
Nikolayev 503,000.....D5
Nikopol' 158,000.....D5
Nizhnekamsk 191,000.....H3
Nizhniy Novgorod
(Gor'kiy) 1,438,000.....F3
Novaya Kakhovka 50,000.....D5
Novgorod 229,000.....D3
Novgorod-Severskiy.....D4
Novocherkassk 187,000.....F5
Novograd-Volynskiy 51,000....C4
Novokuybyshevsk 113,000.....G4
Novomoskovsk 146,000.....E4
Novopolotsk 67,000.....C3
Novorossiysk 186,000.....E6
Novoshakhtinsk 106,000.....E5
Novotroitsk 106,000.....J4
Novouzensk.....G4
Novovolynsk 41,187.....B4
Obninsk 100,000.....E3
Ochamchira 18,718.....F6
Odessa 1,115,000.....D5
Oktyabr'skiy 105,000.....H4
Olonets.....D2
Ordzhonikidze 300,000.....F6
Orekhovo-Zuyevo 137,000.....D3
Orel 337,000.....E4
Orenburg 547,000.....J4
Orsha 123,000.....D4
Orsk 271,000.....J4
Osa 15,038.....J3
Osipenko (Berdyansk)
132,000.....E5
Ostashkov 23,419.....D3
Otradnyy 44,426.....H4

Panevežys 126,000.....B3
Pärnu 53,000.....C3
Pavlograd 131,000.....E5
Pavlovo 70,000.....F3
Pechenga.....D1
Pechora 61,000.....J1
Perm' 1,091,000.....J3
Pervomaysk 76,000.....D5
Petrokrepost'.....D3
Petrozavodsk 270,000.....D2
Petsamo (Pechenga).....D1
Pinsk 119,000.....C4
Podol'sk 210,000.....E3
Polotsk 71,000.....C3
Poltava 315,000.....D5
Polyarnyy 15,321.....D1
Poti 45,979.....F6
Povenets.....E2
Priluki 70,000.....D4
Primorsk.....C2
Priozersk 16,652.....D2
Prokhladnyy 51,000.....F6
Pskov 204,000.....C3
Pushkin 91,000.....C3
Pyatigorsk 129,000.....F6
Rasskazovo 40,038.....F4
Rechitsa 67,000.....C4
Revel (Tallinn) 482,000.....B3
Riga 915,000.....B3
Romny 52,000.....D4
Roslavl' 60,000.....D4
Rossosh' 51,000.....E4
Rostov 1,020,000.....F5
Rovno 228,000.....C4
Rtishchevo 37,146.....F4
Rubezhnoye 68,000.....E5
Rustavi 159,000.....G6
Ruzayevka 41,084.....F4
Ryazan' 515,000.....E4
Rybinsk 252,000.....E3
Rzhev 70,000.....D3
Safonovo 55,000.....D3
Saki 24,208.....D5
Salavat 150,000.....H4
Sal'sk 61,000.....F5
Samara 1,257,000.....H4
Saransk 312,000.....G4
Sarapul 111,000.....H3
Saratov 905,000.....G4
Serdobol (Sortavala) 22,188...D2
Serpukhov 144,000.....E4
Sevastopol' 356,000.....D6
Severodonetsk 131,000.....E5
Severodvinsk 249,000.....E2
Severomorsk 54,000.....D1
Shakhty 224,000.....F5
Shchekino 70,000.....E4
Shchigry 17,133.....E4
Sheki 52,000.....G6
Shemakha 17,986.....G6
Shepetovka 38,707.....C4
Shostka 82,000.....D4
Shuya 72,000.....F3
Šiauliai 145,000.....B3
Simferopol' 344,000.....D6
Skopin 24,429.....F4
Slantsy 41,146.....C3
Slavyansk 135,000.....E5
Slavyansk-na-Kubani 56,000..E5
Slutsk 51,000.....C4
Smela 70,000.....D5
Smolensk 341,000.....D4
Sochi 337,000.....E6
Sokol 48,243.....F3
Soligorsk 82,000.....C4
Solikamsk 110,000.....J3
Sol'Iletsk 22,227.....J4
Soroki 21,924.....C5
Sortavala 22,188.....D2
Stakhanov 112,000.....E5

Stalingrad (Volgograd)
999,000.....F5
Staryy Oskol 174,000.....E4
Stavropol' 318,000.....F5
Sterlitamak 248,000.....J4
Storozhevsk.....H2
Stupino 72,000.....E4
Sukhumi 121,000.....F6
Sumgait 231,000.....G6
Sumy 291,000.....E4
Svetlogorsk 55,000.....C4
Svetlograd 40,265.....F5
Syktyvkar 233,000.....H2
Syzran' 174,000.....G4
Taganrog 291,000.....E5
Tallinn 482,000.....B3
Tambov 305,000.....F4
Tartu 114,000.....C3
Tbilisi 1,260,000.....F6
Telavi 21,179.....G6
Temryuk 23,172.....E5
Ternopol' 205,000.....C5
Teykovo 41,607.....E3
Tiflis (Tbilisi) 1,260,000.....F6
Tighina (Bendery) 130,000.....C5
Tikhoretsk 66,000.....F5
Tikhvin 66,000.....D3
Tiraspol' 182,000.....D5
Togliatti (Tol'yatti) 630,000....G4
Toropets 16,863.....D3
Torzhok 45,443.....D3
Troitsko-Pechorsk.....J2
Tskhinvali 30,311.....F6
Tuapse 63,000.....E6
Tukums 14,800.....B3
Tula 540,000.....E4
Tver' 451,000.....E3
Tyrnyauz 18,253.....F6
Ufa 1,083,000.....J4
Ukhta 111,000.....H2
Ukmerge 21,663.....C3
Ul'yanovsk 625,000.....G4
Uman' 85,000.....D5
Usinsk.....J1
Uzhgorod 117,000.....B5
Uzlovaya 64,000.....E4
Valga 16,795.....C3
Valmiera 20,331.....C3
Velikiye Luki 114,000.....D3
Ventspils 51,000.....B3
Vichuga 51,000.....F3
Viipuri (Vyborg) 79,000.....C2
Vileyka.....C4
Vilnius (Vilna) 582,000.....C4
Vinnitsa 374,000.....C5
Vitebsk 350,000.....C3
Vladimir 350,000.....F3
Volgodonsk 176,000.....F5
Volgograd 999,000.....F5
Volkhov 50,000.....D3
Vologda 283,000.....F3
Vol'sk 66,000.....G4
Volzhsk 57,000.....G3
Volzhskiy 269,000.....G5
Vorkuta 116,000.....K1
Voronezh 887,000.....E4
Voroshilovgrad (Lugansk)
497,000.....E5
Voskresensk 79,000.....E3
Votkinsk 103,000.....H3
Vyaz'ma 55,000.....D3
Vyborg 79,000.....C2
Vyksa 58,000.....F3
Vyshniy Volochek 71,000.....D3
Yalta 85,000.....D6
Yaroslavl' 633,000.....E3
Yefremov 55,000.....E4
Yelets 120,000.....E4
Yenakiyevo 121,000.....E5
Yerevan 1,199,000.....F6

Yessentuki 82,000.....F6
Yevpatoriya 108,000.....D5
Yeysk 75,000.....E5
Yoshkar-Ola 242,000.....G3
Yur'yevets 20,144.....F3
Zagorsk 115,000.....E3
Zaporozh'ye 884,000.....E5
Zelenodol'sk 88,000.....G3
Zheleznodorozhnyy 76,000.....H2
Zheleznogorsk 74,000.....E4
Zhigulevsk 52,130.....G4
Zhitomir 292,000.....C4
Znamenka 27,393.....D5

OTHER FEATURES

Alagez (mt.).....F6
Apsheron (pen.).....H6
Araks (riv.).....G7
Azov (sea).....E5
Baltic (sea).....B3
Barents (sea).....E1
Baydarata (bay).....L1
Belaya (riv.).....H3
Beloye (lake).....E2
Berezina (riv.).....C4
Black (sea).....D6
Bolvanskiy Nos (cape).....K1
Bug (riv.).....B4
Caucasus (mts.).....F6
Central Ural (mts.).....J2
Cheshskaya (bay).....G1
Chir (riv.).....F5
Crimea (pen.).....D5
Denezhkin Kamen' (mt.).....J2
Desna (riv.).....D4
Dnieper (riv.).....D5
Dniester (riv.).....C5
Dolgiy (isl.).....J1
Don (riv.).....F5
Donets (riv.).....E5
Dvina (bay).....E2
Dvina (riv.).....F2
Dvina, Northern (riv.).....F2
Western Dvina (riv.).....C3
Dykhtau (mt.).....F6
El'brus (mt.).....F6
Finland (gulf).....C3
Goryn' (riv.).....C4
Hiiumaa (isl.).....B3
Il'men' (lake).....D3
Ilek (riv.).....J4
Imandra (lake).....D1
Izhma (riv.).....H2
Kakhovka (res.).....D5
Kama (riv.).....H2
Kama (res.).....J3
Kandalaksha (gulf).....D1
Kanin (pen.).....G1
Kanin Nos (cape).....F1
Kapydzhik (mt.).....G7
Kara (sea).....K1
Karskiye Vorota (str.).....J1
Kazbek (mt.).....F6
Khoper (riv.).....F4
Kiev (res.).....C4
Kil'din (isl.).....D1
Kinel' (riv.).....H4
Kola (pen.).....E1
Kolguyev (isl.).....G1
Kolva (riv.).....J1
Kuban' (riv.).....E5
Kubeno (lake).....E3
Kuma (riv.).....G5
Kura (riv.).....G6
Kuybyshev (res.).....G4
Kuyto (lake).....D2
Lacha (lake).....E2
Ladoga (lake).....D2
Lapland (reg.).....D1

Lovat' (riv.).....D3
Mansel'ka (mts.).....C1
Manych-Gudilo (lake).....F5
Matveyev (isl.).....J1
Medveditsa (riv.).....F4
Mezen' (bay).....F1
Mezen' (riv.).....G1
Mezhdusharskiy (isl.).....H1
Moksha (riv.).....F4
Moskva (riv.).....E3
Msta (riv.).....D3
Narodnaya (mt.).....J1
Niemen (riv.).....B4
North Ural (mts.).....K1
Novaya Zemlya (isls.).....H1
Oka (riv.).....F4
Onega (bay).....E2
Onega (lake).....E2
Onega (riv.).....E2
Payyer (mt.).....K1
Pechora (bay).....H1
Pechora (riv.).....H1
Pechora (sea).....H1
Peipus (lake).....C3
Pinega (riv.).....G2
Ponoy (riv.).....E1
Pripet (marshes).....C4
Pripyat' (riv.).....C4
Prut (riv.).....C5
Psel (riv.).....D4
Riga (gulf).....B3
Russkiy Zavorot (cape).....H1
Rybachiy (pen.).....D1
Rybinsk (res.).....E3
Saaremaa (isl.).....B3
Samara (riv.).....H4
Seg (lake).....D2
Sevan (lake).....G6
Seym (riv.).....D4
Solovetskiye (isls.).....E1
South Ural (mts.).....J4
Suda (riv.).....E3
Sukhona (riv.).....F2
Sura (riv.).....G4
Svir' (riv.).....D2
Sysola (riv.).....H2
Tel'pos-Iz (mt.).....K2
Timan (ridge).....G1
Top (lake).....D1
Tsil'ma (riv.).....H1
Tsimlyansk (res.).....F5
Tuloma (riv.).....D1
Ufa (riv.).....J3
Unzha (riv.).....F3
Ural (mts.).....J2
Ural (riv.).....J4
Usa (riv.).....K1
Vaga (riv.).....F2
Valday (hills).....D3
Vashka (riv.).....G2
Vaygach (isl.).....K1
Velikaya (riv.).....C3
Vetluga (riv.).....G3
Vishera (riv.).....J2
Vodl (lake).....E2
Volga (riv.).....G5
Volga-Don (canal).....F5
Volgograd (res.).....G5
Volkhov (riv.).....D3
Vorona (riv.).....F4
Vorskla (riv.).....E4
Vozhe (lake).....F2
Vyatka (riv.).....H3
Vychegda (riv.).....G2
Vyg (lake).....E2
Vym' (riv.).....H2
White (sea).....E1
Yamantau (mt.).....J4
Yug (riv.).....G2
Yugorskiy (pen.).....K1

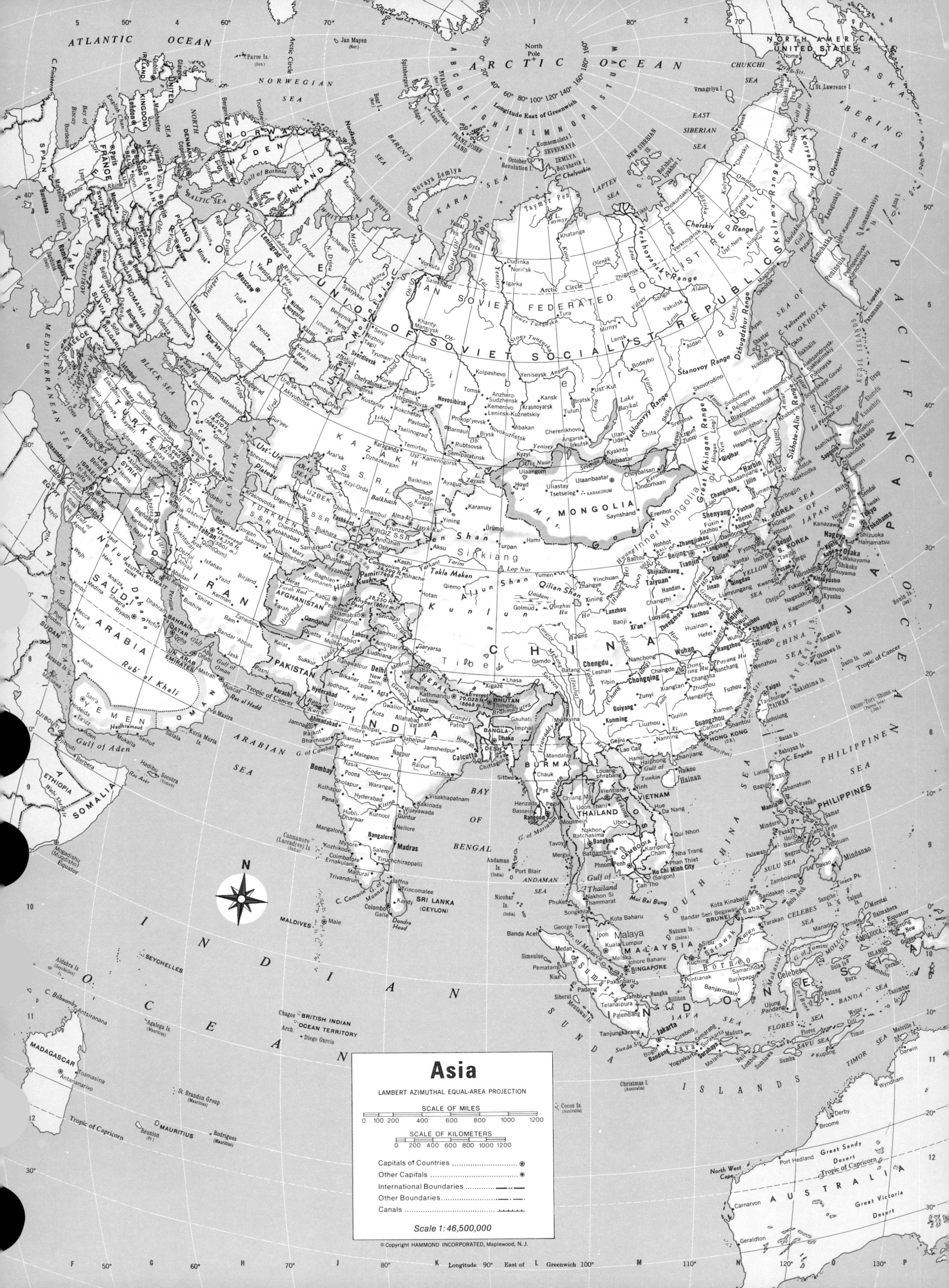

Asia

LAMBERT AZIMUTHAL EQUAL-AREA PROJECTION

SCALE OF MILES

0 100 200   400   600   800   1000   1200

SCALE OF KILOMETERS

0   200 400 600 800 1000 1200

Capitals of Countries .... ⊛
Other Capitals .... ⊛
International Boundaries .... ▬▬▬▬
Other Boundaries .... ▬ ▪ ▬ ▪ ▬
Canals .... ┼┼┼┼┼

Scale 1:46,500,000

© Copyright HAMMOND INCORPORATED, Maplewood, N.J.

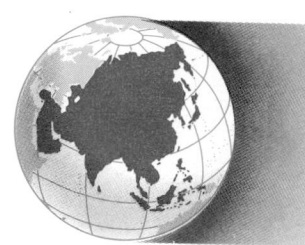

Population Distribution

AREA 17,128,500 sq. mi.
(44,362,815 sq. km.)
POPULATION 3,176,000,000
LARGEST CITY Tokyo
HIGHEST POINT Mt. Everest 29,028 ft.
(8,848 m.)
LOWEST POINT Dead Sea -1,296 ft.
(-395 m.)

Vegetation

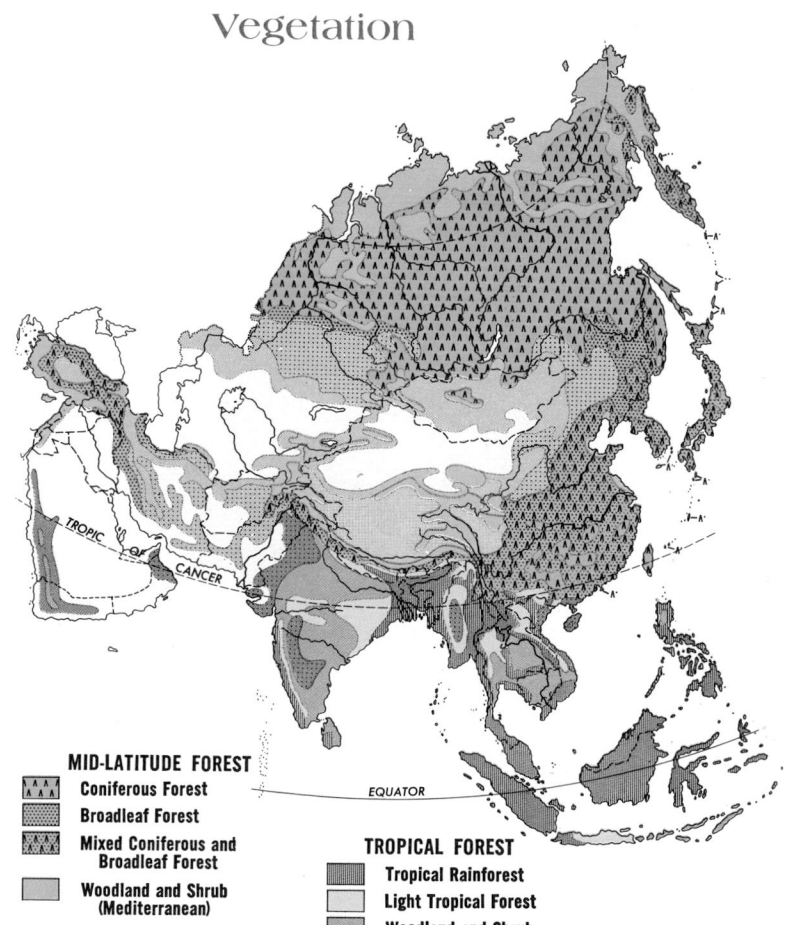

DENSITY PER

SQ. KILOMETER	SQ. MILE
Over 100	Over 260
50-100	130-260
10-50	25-130
1-10	3-25
Under 1	Under 3

• Cities with over 3,000,000 inhabitants (including suburbs)

EQUATOR

MID-LATITUDE FOREST

- Coniferous Forest
- Broadleaf Forest
- Mixed Coniferous and Broadleaf Forest
- Woodland and Shrub (Mediterranean)

MID-LATITUDE GRASSLAND

- Short Grass (Steppe)
- Wooded Steppe

DESERT AND DESERT SHRUB

TROPICAL FOREST

- Tropical Rainforest
- Light Tropical Forest
- Woodland and Shrub

TROPICAL GRASSLAND

- Grass and Shrub (Savanna)
- Wooded Savanna

- TUNDRA AND ALPINE
- UNCLASSIFIED HIGHLANDS

EQUATOR

ASIA

Abadan, Iran . . . . F 6
Abu Dhabi (cap.), U.A.E. . . . G 7
Adana, Turkey . . . . E 6
Aden, Yemen . . . . F 8
Aden (gulf) . . . . F 8
Afghanistan . . . . H 6
Agra, India . . . . J 7
Ahmadabad, India . . . . J 7
Aleppo, Syria . . . . E 6
Al Kuwait (cap.), Kuwait . . . F 7
Alma-Ata, U.S.S.R. . . . . . . J 5
Altai (mts.) . . . . K 5
Altun Shan (range), China . . K 6
Amman (cap.), Jordan . . . . . E 6
Amudar'ya (riv.), U.S.S.R. . . H 5
Amur (riv.) . . . . P 5
Andaman (isls.), India . . . . . L 8
Ankara (cap.), Turkey . . . . . E 5
Aqaba (gulf) . . . . E 7
Arabian (sea) . . . . H 8
Araks (riv.) . . . . F 6
Ararat (mt.), Turkey . . . . . . F 6
Arctic (ocean) . . . . C 1
Asahikawa, Japan . . . . P 5
Ashkhabad, U.S.S.R. . . . . . G 6
Baghdad (cap.), Iraq . . . . . . F 6
Bahrain . . . . G 7
Bahawalpur, Pakistan . . . . . J 7
Bakhash (lake), U.S.S.R. . . . J 5
Balkhash (lake), U.S.S.R. . . . J 5
Bandar Seri Begawan (cap.),
Brunei . . . . N 9
Bandung, Indonesia M10
Bangalore, India . . . . J 8
Bangkok (cap.), Thailand . . . M 8
Bangladesh . . . . L 7
Basra, Iraq . . . . F 6
Baykal (lake), U.S.S.R. . . . . N 4
Beijing (Peking) (cap.), China . N 5
Beirut (cap.), Lebanon . . . . . E 6
Bengal (bay) . . . . K 8
Bering (sea) . . . . V 4
Bering (strait) . . . . W 3
Bhutan . . . . L 7
Black (sea) . . . . E 5
Blagoveshchensk, U.S.S.R. . . O 4
Bombay, India . . . . J 8
Bonin (isls.), Japan . . . . . . E 7
Borneo (isl.) . . . . N 9
Brahmaputra (riv.) . . . . L 7
British Indian Ocean
Territory J10
Brunei . . . . N 9
Bukhara, U.S.S.R. . . . . H 5
Burma . . . . L 7

Calcutta, India . . . . K 7
Cambodia . . . . M 8
Cannanore (isls.),
India . . . . H 8
Caspian (sea) . . . . G 5
Celebes (isl.), Indonesia . . . N10
Chang Jiang (Yangtze)
(riv.), China . . . . N 6
Chelyabinsk, U.S.S.R. . . . . H 4
Chengdu, China . . . . M 6
China . . . . L 6
Chittagong, Bangladesh . . . . L 7
Chongqing, China . . . . M 7
Christmas (isl.), Australia . . . M11
Chukchi (pen.), U.S.S.R. . . . V 3
Cocos (isls.), Australia L11
Colombo (cap.),
Sri Lanka . . . . J 9
Comorin (cape), India . . . . . J 9
Cyprus . . . . E 6
Dalian, China . . . . O 6
Damascus (cap.), Syria . . . . E 6
Da Nang, Vietnam . . . . M 8
Delhi, India . . . . J 7
Dhahran, Saudi Arabia . . . . F 7
Dhaka (cap.), Bangladesh . . . L 7
Diego Garcia (isl.),
Br. Ind. Ocean Terr. J10
Doha (cap.), Qatar . . . . G 7
Dushanbe, U.S.S.R. . . . . . . H 6
East China (sea) . . . . O 7
Euphrates (riv.) . . . . F 6
Everest (mt.) . . . . K 7
Frunze, U.S.S.R. . . . . J 5
Fukuoka, Japan . . . . O 6
Ganges (riv.) . . . . K 7
George Town, Malaysia . . . . M 9
Gobi (des.) . . . . M 5
Great Khingan (range),
China . . . . O 5
Great Wall (ruins), China . . . N 5
Guangzhou (Canton),
China . . . . N 7
Hadhramaut (reg.),
Yemen . . . . F 8
Hainan (isl.), China . . . . . . N 8
Haiphong, Vietnam . . . . M 7
Hakodate, Japan . . . . R 5
Halmahera (isl.),
Indonesia . . . . O 9
Hangzhou, China . . . . N 6
Hanoi (cap.), Vietnam . . . . . M 7
Harbin, China . . . . O 5
Herat, Afghanistan . . . . H 6
Himalaya (mts.) . . . . L 7
Hindu Kush (mts.) . . . . J 6

Hiroshima, Japan . . . . P 6
Ho Chi Minh City, Vietnam . . M 8
Hokkaido (isl.), Japan . . . . . R 5
Hong Kong . . . . N 7
Honshu (isl.), Japan . . . . . . P 6
Huang He (Hwang Ho)
(riv.), China . . . . N 6
Hue, Vietnam . . . . M 8
Hyderabad, India . . . . J 8
Hyderabad, Pakistan . . . . . . H 7
Inch'ŏn, S. Korea . . . . O 6
India . . . . J 7
Indian (ocean) H10
Indonesia M10
Indus (riv.) . . . . H 7
Inner Mongolia (reg.), China . N 5
Iran . . . . G 7
Iraq . . . . F 6
Irkutsk, U.S.S.R. . . . . M 4
Irrawaddy (riv.), Burma . . . . L 7
Irtysh (riv.), U.S.S.R. . . . . . J 4
Isfahan, Iran . . . . G 6
Islamabad (cap.), Pakistan . . J 6
Israel . . . . E 6
Izmir, Turkey . . . . D 6
Jakarta (cap.), Indonesia . . . M10
Japan . . . . R 6
Japan (sea) . . . . P 6
Java (isl.), Indonesia M10
Jerusalem (cap.), Israel . . . . E 6
Jidda, Saudi Arabia . . . . . . E 7
Jordan . . . . E 6
Kabul (cap.), Afghanistan . . . H 6
Kamchatka (pen.), U.S.S.R. . . S 4
Kanpur, India . . . . K 7
Kara (sea), U.S.S.R. . . . . . H 2
Karachi, Pakistan . . . . H 7
Karakorum (ruins), Mongolia . M 5
Kathmandu (cap.), Nepal . . . K 7
Kazakh, S.S.R., U.S.S.R. . . . H 5
Kerman, Iran . . . . G 6
Khabarovsk, U.S.S.R. . . . . . P 5
Khyber (pass) . . . . J 6
Kirgiz S.S.R., U.S.S.R. . . . . J 5
Kistna (riv.), India . . . . J 8
Kitakyushu, Japan . . . . P 6
Kobe, Japan . . . . P 6
Kolyma (range), U.S.S.R. . . . S 3
Krasnoyarsk, U.S.S.R. . . . . L 4
Kuala Lumpur (cap.),
Malaysia . . . . M 9
Kunlun (range), China . . . . . K 6
Kunming, China . . . . M 7
Kuril (isls.), U.S.S.R. . . . . . R 5
Kuwait . . . . F 7

Kyoto, Japan . . . . P 6
Kyushu (isl.), Japan . . . . . . P 6
Lahore, Pakistan . . . . J 6
Lanzhou, China . . . . M 6
Laos . . . . M 8
Laptev (sea), U.S.S.R. . . . . O 2
Latakia, Syria . . . . E 6
Lebanon . . . . E 6
Lena (riv.), U.S.S.R. . . . . . O 3
Leyte (isl.), Philippines . . . . O 8
Lhasa, China . . . . L 7
Lucknow, India . . . . K 7
Luzon (isl.), Philippines . . . . O 8
Macau . . . . N 7
Madras, India . . . . K 8
Magnitogorsk, U.S.S.R. . . . . H 4
Makassar (str.), Indonesia . . N10
Malacca (str.) . . . . M 9
Malaya (reg.), Malaysia . . . . M 9
Malaysia . . . . M 9
Maldives . . . . J 9
Male (cap.), Maldives . . . . . J 9
Mandalay, Burma . . . . L 7
Manila (cap.), Philippines . . . N 8
Mecca (cap.), Saudi Arabia . . F 7
Medan, Indonesia . . . . L 9
Medina, Saudi Arabia . . . . . F 7
Mekong (riv.) . . . . M 8
Mindanao (isl.),
Philippines . . . . O 9
Molucca (isls.), Indonesia . . O10
Mongolia . . . . M 5
Mosul, Iraq . . . . F 6
Muscat (cap.), Oman . . . . . G 7
Mysore, India . . . . J 8
Nagasaki, Japan . . . . O 6
Nagoya, Japan . . . . P 6
Naha, Japan . . . . O 7

Nanjing, China . . . . N 6
Nepal . . . . K 7
New Delhi, India . . . . J 7
New Guinea (isl.) P10
Nicosia (cap.), Cyprus . . . . E 6
North Korea . . . . O 5
Novosibirsk, U.S.S.R. . . . . . J 4
Ob' (riv.), U.S.S.R. . . . . . . H 3
Okhotsk (sea), U.S.S.R. . . . R 4
Okinawa (isls.), Japan . . . . O 7
Oman . . . . G 8
Omsk, U.S.S.R. . . . . J 4
Osaka, Japan . . . . P 6
Pacific (ocean) . . . . T 5
Pakistan . . . . H 7
Pamir (plat.) . . . . J 6
Peking (cap.), China . . . . . . N 5
Persian (gulf) . . . . G 7
Philippines . . . . O 8
Phnom Penh (cap.),
Cambodia . . . . M 8
Poona, India . . . . J 8
Pusan, S. Korea . . . . O 6
P'yongyang (cap.),
N. Korea . . . . O 6
Qatar . . . . G 7
Rangoon (cap.), Burma . . . . L 8
Rawalpindi, Pakistan . . . . . J 6
Red (sea) . . . . E 7
Riyadh (cap.),
Saudi Arabia . . . . F 7
Russian Soviet Federated
Socialist Republic,
U.S.S.R. . . . . L 3
Ryukyu (isls.), Japan . . . . . O 7
Sabah (reg.), Malaysia . . . . N 9
Saigon (Ho Chi Minh City),
Vietnam . . . . M 8

Sakhalin (isl.), U.S.S.R. . . . R 4
Salween (riv.) . . . . L 8
Samarkand, U.S.S.R. . . . . . H 6
San'a (cap.), Yemen . . . . . . F 8
Sapporo, Japan . . . . P 5
Sarawak (reg.), Malaysia . . . N 9
Saudi Arabia . . . . F 7
Seoul (cap.), S. Korea . . . . O 8
Severnaya Zemlya (isls.),
U.S.S.R. . . . . M 1
Shanghai, China . . . . O 6
Shikoku, Japan . . . . P 6
Siberia (reg.), U.S.S.R. . . . . M 4
Singapore . . . . M 9
Sinkiang (reg.), China . . . . . K 5
Socotra (isl.), Yemen . . . . . G 8
South China (sea) . . . . N 8
South Korea . . . . O 6
Sri Lanka . . . . K 9
Sulu (sea), Philippines . . . . N 9
Sumatra (isl.), Indonesia . . . L 9
Sunda (str.), Indonesia . . . . M 10
Surabaya, Indonesia . . . . . N 10
Sverdlovsk, U.S.S.R. . . . . . H 4
Syrdar'ya (riv.), U.S.S.R. . . . H 5
Syria . . . . E 6
Tabriz, Iran . . . . F 6
Tadzhik S.S.R.,
U.S.S.R. . . . . H 6
Taipei (cap.), Taiwan . . . . . O 7
Taiwan (isl.) . . . . N 7
Ta'izz, Yemen . . . . F 8
Takla Makan (des.),
China . . . . K 6
Tashkent, U.S.S.R. . . . . . . H 5
Taymyr (pen.), U.S.S.R. . . . L 2
Tehran (cap.), Iran . . . . G 6
Tel Aviv-Jaffa, Israel . . . . . E 6

Thailand . . . . M 8
Tianjin, China . . . . N 6
Tibet (reg.), China . . . . K 6
Tien Shan (range) . . . . K 5
Tigris (riv.) . . . . F 6
Timor (isl.), Indonesia . . . . . O 10
Tokyo (cap.), Japan . . . . . . R 6
Tonkin (gulf) . . . . M 8
Turkey . . . . E 6
Turkmen S.S.R.,
U.S.S.R. . . . . G 6
Ulaanbaatar (cap.),
Mongolia . . . . M 5
Union of Soviet Socialist
Republics . . . . L 3
United Arab Emirates . . . . . G 7
Ural (mts.), U.S.S.R. . . . . . G 4
Urmia (lake), Iran . . . . F 6
Ürümqi, China . . . . K 5
Uzbek S.S.R., U.S.S.R. . . . . H 5
Varanasi, India . . . . K 7
Verkhoyansk, U.S.S.R. . . . . P 3
Vientiane (cap.), Laos . . . . . M 8
Vietnam . . . . M 8
Vladivostok, U.S.S.R. . . . . . P 5
Wŏnsan, N. Korea . . . . O 6
Wuhan, China . . . . N 6
Xi'an, China . . . . M 6
Yakutsk, U.S.S.R. . . . . O 3
Yalu (riv.) . . . . O 5
Yangtze (riv.), China . . . . . N 6
Yellow (sea) . . . . O 6
Yemen . . . . F 8
Yenisey (riv.), U.S.S.R. . . . . K 3
Yogyakarta,
Indonesia . . . . M 10
Yokohama, Japan . . . . R 6
Zhengzhou, China . . . . S 3

Average January Temperature

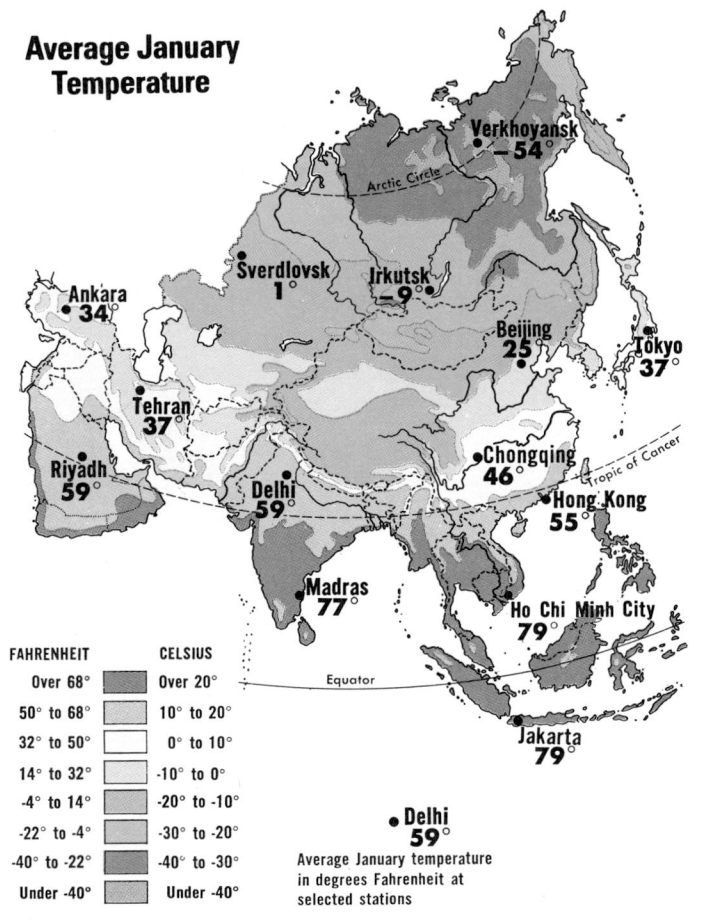

Verkhoyansk −54°

Sverdlovsk 1°   Irkutsk −9°

Ankara 34°   Beijing 25°   Tokyo 37°

Tehran 37°

Riyadh 59°   Delhi 59°   Chongqing 46°

Hong Kong 55°

Madras 77°

Ho Chi Minh City 79°

Jakarta 79°

Equator

FAHRENHEIT	CELSIUS
Over 68°	Over 20°
50° to 68°	10° to 20°
32° to 50°	0° to 10°
14° to 32°	−10° to 0°
−4° to 14°	−20° to −10°
−22° to −4°	−30° to −20°
−40° to −22°	−40° to −30°
Under −40°	Under −40°

Delhi 59°
Average January temperature in degrees Fahrenheit at selected stations

Average July Temperature

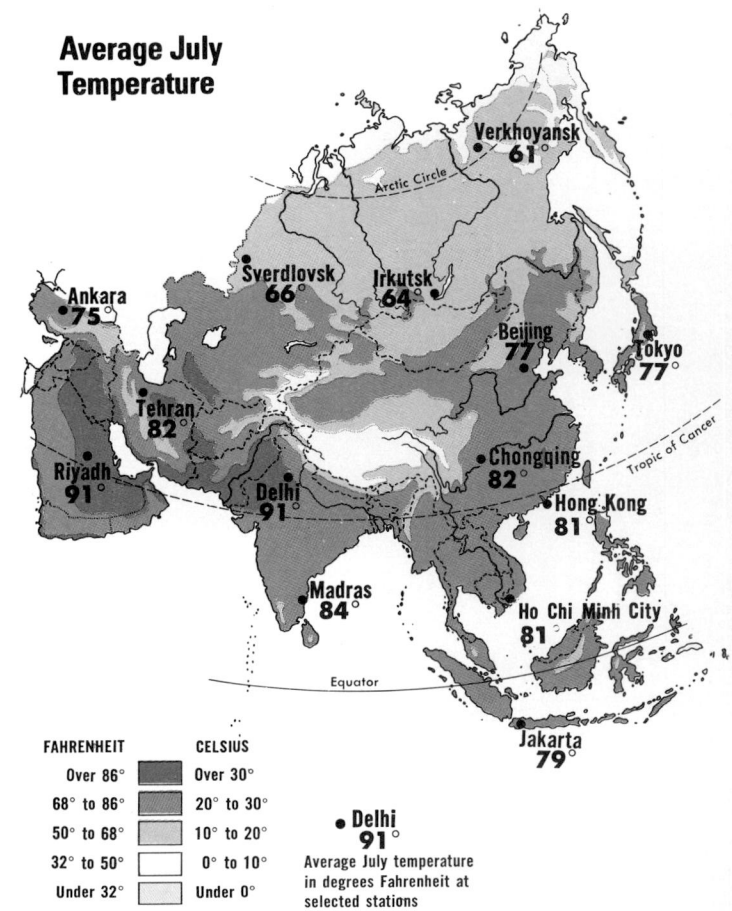

Verkhoyansk 61°

Ankara 75°   Sverdlovsk 66°   Irkutsk 64°

Beijing 77°   Tokyo 77°

Tehran 82°

Riyadh 91°   Delhi 91°   Chongqing 82°

Hong Kong 81°

Madras 84°

Ho Chi Minh City 81°

Equator

Jakarta 79°

FAHRENHEIT	CELSIUS
Over 86°	Over 30°
68° to 86°	20° to 30°
50° to 68°	10° to 20°
32° to 50°	0° to 10°
Under 32°	Under 0°

Delhi 91°
Average July temperature in degrees Fahrenheit at selected stations

Rainfall

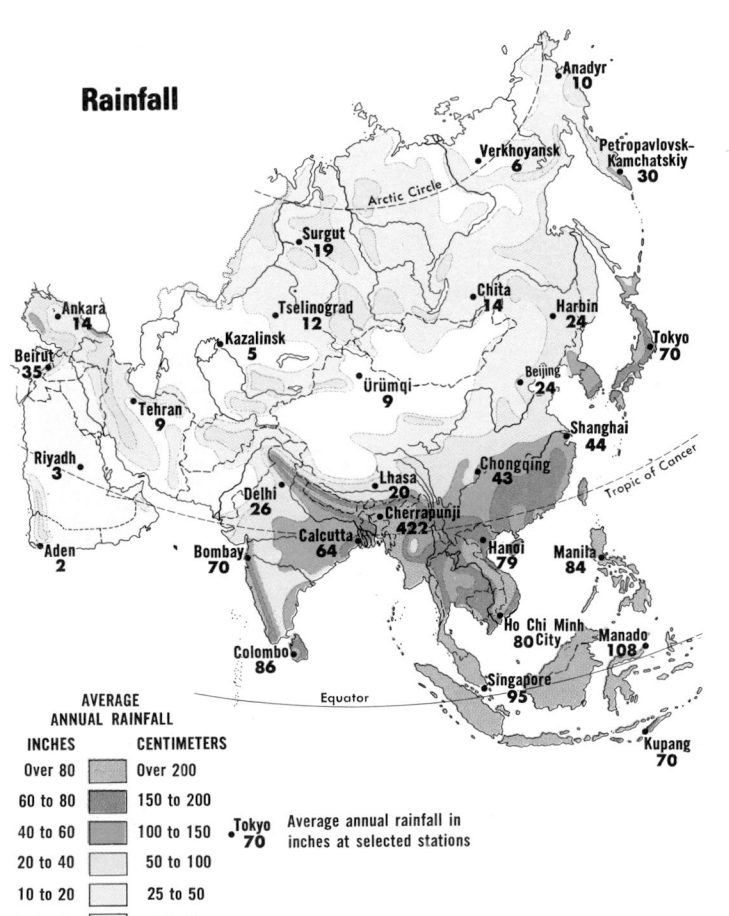

Anadyr 10°

Verkhoyansk 6°   Petropavlovsk-Kamchatskiy 30

Surgut 19

Ankara 14   Chita 14   Harbin 24

Tselinograd 12   Tokyo 70

Beirut 35   Kazalinsk 5

Tehran 9   Ürümqi 9   Beijing 24

Riyadh 3   Shanghai 44

Lhasa 20   Chongqing 43

Delhi 26   Cherrapunji 422

Calcutta 64   Hanoi 79   Manila 84

Aden 2   Bombay 70

Ho Chi Minh 80 City   Manado 108

Colombo 86

Singapore 95   Equator

Kupang 70

AVERAGE ANNUAL RAINFALL

INCHES	CENTIMETERS
Over 80	Over 200
60 to 80	150 to 200
40 to 60	100 to 150
20 to 40	50 to 100
10 to 20	25 to 50
Under 10	Under 25

Tokyo 70
Average annual rainfall in inches at selected stations

Vegetation / Relief

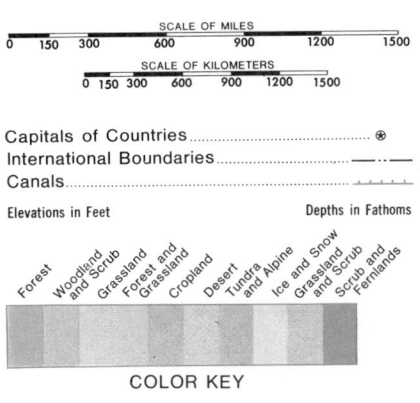

SCALE OF MILES
0 150 300   600   900   1200   1500

SCALE OF KILOMETERS
0 150 300   600   900   1200   1500

Capitals of Countries .... ⊗
International Boundaries ....
Canals ....

Elevations in Feet   Depths in Fathoms

Forest   Woodland and Scrub   Grassland   Forest and Grassland   Cropland   Desert   Tundra and Alpine   Ice and Snow   Grassland and Scrub   Fernlands

COLOR KEY

SAUDI ARABIA

KUWAIT

YEMEN

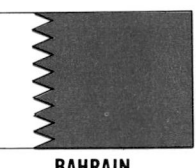
BAHRAIN

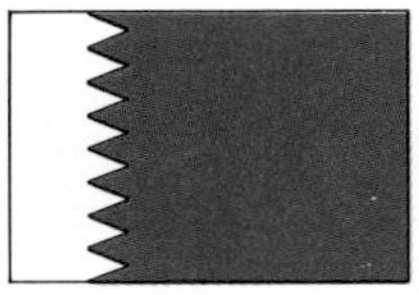

QATAR

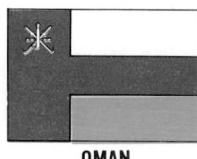
OMAN

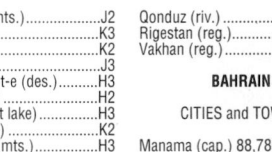

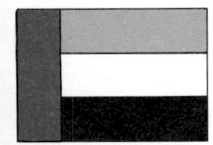

UNITED ARAB EMIRATES

Muharraq 37,732 ....F4	**IRAN**	Anarak 2,038 ....F3	Bam 22,000 ....G4
		Arak 114,507 ....E3	Bandar 'Abbas 89,103 ......G4
GAZA STRIP	CITIES and TOWNS	Ardabil 147,404 ....E2	Bandar-e Anzali (Enzeli)
		Ardestan 5,868 ....F3	55,978 ....E2
CITIES and TOWNS	Abadan 296,081 ....E3	Asterabad (Gorgan) 88,348....F2	Bandar-e Bushehr 57,681 ......F4
	Abadeh 16,000 ....F3	Babol 67,790 ....F2	Bandar-e Khomeyni 6,000......E3
Gaza*	Abarqu 8,000 ....F3	Bafq 5,000 ....G3	Bandar-e Lengeh 4,920 ....G4
118,272 ....B3	Ahvaz 329,006 ....E3	Baft 6,000 ....G4	Bandar-e Rig 1,889 ....F4
	Amol 68,782 ....F2	Bakhtaran 290,861 ....E3	Bandar-e Torkeman 13,000......F2

Bejestan 3,823 ....G3			
Birjand 25,854 ....G3			
Bojnurd 31,248 ....G2			
Borazjan 20,000 ....F4			
Borujerd 100,103 ....E3			
Chalus 15,000 ....F2			
Damghan 13,000 ....F2			
Darab 13,000 ....G4			
Dezful 110,287 ....E3			

(continued on following page)

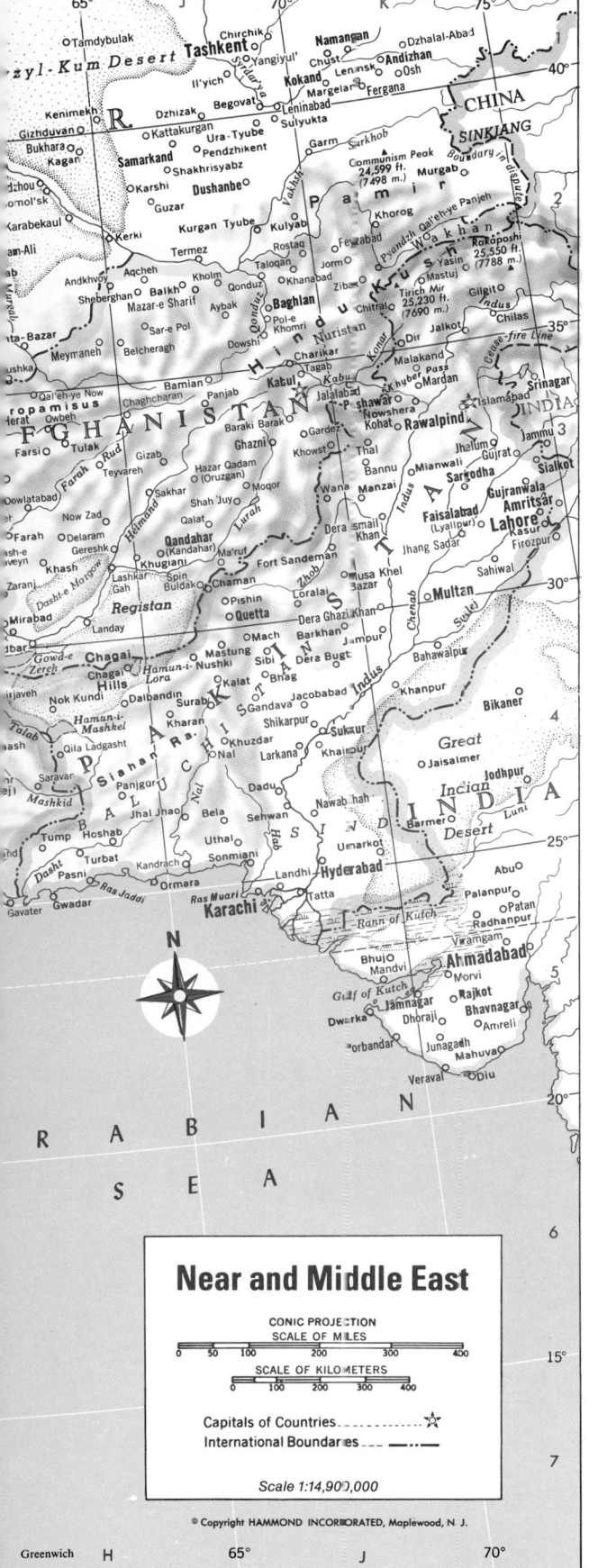

SAUDI ARABIA

AREA 829,995 sq. mi.
(2,149,687 sq. km.)
POPULATION 14,435,000
CAPITAL Riyadh
MONETARY UNIT Saudi riyal
MAJOR LANGUAGE Arabic
MAJOR RELIGION Islam

KUWAIT

AREA 6,532 sq mi. (16,918 sq. km.)
POPULATION 2,048,000
CAPITAL Al Kuwait
MONETARY UNIT Kuwaiti dinar
MAJOR LANGUAGE Arabic
MAJOR RELIGION Islam

YEMEN

AREA 188,321 sq. mi. (487,792 sq. km.)
POPULATION 10,183,000
CAPITAL San'a
MONETARY UNIT Yemeni rial
MAJOR LANGUAGE Arabic
MAJOR RELIGION Islam

BAHRAIN

AREA 240 sq. mi. (622 sq. km.)
POPULATION 489,000
CAPITAL Manama
MONETARY UNIT Bahraini dinar
MAJOR LANGUAGE Arabic
MAJOR RELIGION Islam

QATAR

AREA 4,247 sq. mi. (11,000 sq. km.)
POPULATION 422,000
CAPITAL Doha
MONETARY UNIT Qatari riyal
MAJOR LANGUAGE Arabic
MAJOR RELIGION Islam

OMAN

AREA 120,000 sq. mi. (310,800 sq. km.)
POPULATION 2,000,000
CAPITAL Muscat
MONETARY UNIT Omani rial
MAJOR LANGUAGE Arabic
MAJOR RELIGION Islam

UNITED ARAB EMIRATES

AREA 32,278 sq. mi. (83,600 sq. km.)
POPULATION 1,206,000
CAPITAL Abu Dhabi
MONETARY UNIT dirham
MAJOR LANGUAGE Arabic
MAJOR RELIGION Islam

Near and Middle East

CONIC PROJECTION
SCALE OF MILES
0 50 100 200 300 400
SCALE OF KILOMETERS
0 100 200 300 400

Capitals of Countries..............☆
International Boundaries ___ _ ___

Scale 1:14,900,000

© Copyright HAMMOND INCORPORATED, Maplewood, N. J.

Topography

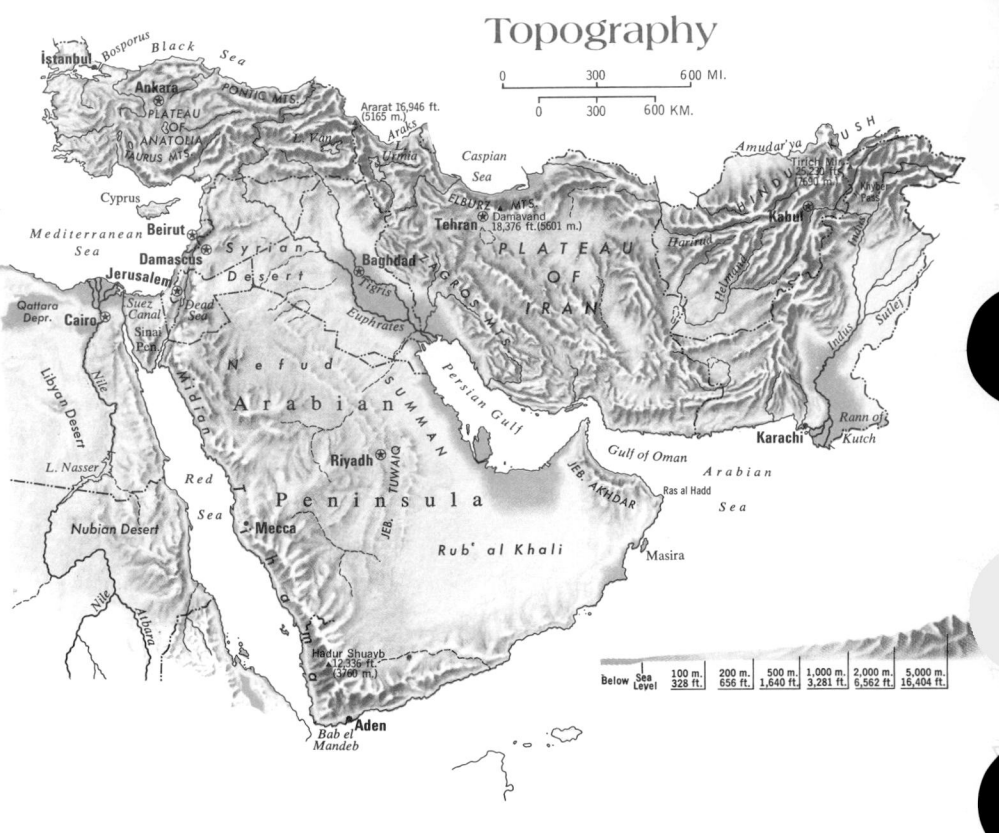

0 300 600 MI.
0 300 600 KM.

Below Sea Level	Sea Level	100 m. 328 ft.	200 m. 656 ft.	500 m. 1,640 ft.	1,000 m. 3,281 ft.	2,000 m. 6,562 ft.	5,000 m. 16,404 ft.

Dezh Shahpur 1,384 .....E2
Enzeli 55,978 .....E2
Estahbanat 18,187 .....F4
Fahrej (Iranshahr) 5,000 .....H4
Fasa 19,000 .....F4
Ferdows 11,000 .....G3
Garmsar 4,723 .....F2
Goḷpayegan 20,515 .....F3
Gonabad 8,000 .....G3
Gorgan 88,348 .....F2
Hamadan 155,846 .....E3
Iranshahr 5,000 .....H4
Isfahan 671,825 .....F3
Jahrom 38,236 .....F4
Jask 1,078 .....G4
Kangan 2,682 .....F4
Kangavar 9,414 .....E3
Kashan 84,545 .....F3
Kashmar 17,000 .....G2
Kazerun 51,309 .....F4
Kerman 140,309 .....G3
Khash 7,439 .....H4
Khorramabad 104,928 .....E3
Khorramshahr 146,709 .....E3
Khvaf 5,000 .....G3
Khvor 2,912 .....G3
Khvoy 70,040 .....E2
Lar 22,000 .....F4
Mahabad 28,610 .....E2
Maragheh 60,820 .....E2
Marand 24,000 .....E2
Meshed 670,180 .....H2
Mianeh 28,447 .....E2
Minab 4,228 .....G4
Mirjaveh 11,000 .....H4
Nahavand 24,000 .....E3
Na'in 5,925 .....F3
Najafabad 76,236 .....F3
Nasratabad (Zabol) 20,000 .....H3
Natanz 4,370 .....F3
Nehbandan 2,130 .....G3
Neyshabur 59,101 .....G2
Nikshahr 1,879 .....H4
Qasr-e Qand 1,879 .....H4
Qayen 6,000 .....G3
Qazvin 138,527 .....E2
Qom 246,831 .....F3
Qum 246,831 .....F3
Rafsanjan 21,000 .....G3
Rasht 187,203 .....E2
Ravar 5,074 .....G3
Rey 102,825 .....F2
Reza'iyeh (Urmia) 163,991 .....D2
Sabzevar 69,174 .....G2
Sabzvaran 7,000 .....G4
Sa'idabad 20,000 .....G4
Sanandaj 95,834 .....E2
Saqqez 17,000 .....E2
Saravan 4,012 .....H4
Sari 70,936 .....F2
Saveh 17,565 .....F2
Semnan 31,058 .....F2
Shahdad 2,777 .....G3
Shahreza 34,220 .....F3
Shahrud 30,767 .....G2

Shiraz 416,408 .....F4
Shirvan 11,000 .....G2
Shushtar 24,000 .....E3
Sirjan (Sa'idabad) 20,000 .....G4
Susangerd 21,000 .....E3
Tabas 10,000 .....G3
Tabriz 598,576 .....E2
Tehran (cap.) 4,496,159 .....F2
Tonekabon 12,000 .....F2
Torbat-e Heydariyeh 30,106 .....G2
Torbat-e Jam 13,000 .....H2
Torud 721 .....F2
Urmia 163,991 .....D2
Yazd 135,978 .....F3
Zabol 20,000 .....H3
Zahedan 92,628 .....H4
Zanjan 99,967 .....E2
Zarand 5,000 .....G3

OTHER FEATURES

'Aliabad, Kuh-e (mt.) F3
Aras (riv.) E2
Bazman, Kuh-e (mt.) H4
Damavand (mt.) F2
Dez (riv.) E3
Elburz (mts.) F2
Euphrates (riv.) E3
Gavkhuni (lake) F3
Gorgan (riv.) F2
Halil (riv.) G4
Hormuz (str.) G4
Jaz Murian, Hamun-e (marsh) G4
Karun (riv.) E3
Kavir, Dasht-e (salt des.) G3
Kavir-e Namak (salt des.) G3
Khark (isl.) E3
Kukalar, Kuh-e (mt.) F3
Laleh Zar, Kuh-e (mt.) G4
Lut, Dasht-e (salt des.) G3
Madvar, Kuh-e (mt.) F3
Maidani, Ras (cape) G4
Mand Rud (riv.) F4
Mashkid (riv.) H4
Mehran (riv.) F4
Namak, Daryacheh-ye (salt lake) F3
Namakzar-e Shahdad (salt lake) G3
Oman (gulf) G4
Persian (gulf) F4
Qeshm (isl.) G4
Qeys (isl.) F4
Qezel Owzan (riv.) E2
Safidar, Kuh-e (mt.) F4
Shaikh Shu'aib (isl.) F4
Shatt-al-'Arab (riv.) E3
Shir Kuh (mt.) F3
Taftan, Kuh-e (mt.) H4
Talab (riv.) H4
Tashk (lake) F4
Tigris (riv.) E3
Urmia (lake) E2
Varzarin, Kuh-e (mt.) E3
Zagros (mts.) E3

IRAQ

CITIES and TOWNS

Al 'Aziziya 7,450 .....E3
Al Falluja 38,072 .....D3
Al Fatha 15,329 .....D2
Al Musaiyib 15,955 .....D3
Al Qurna 5,638 .....E3
'Amara 64,847 .....E3
'Ana 15,729 .....D3
An Najaf 128,096 .....D3
An Nasiriya 60,405 .....E3
Arbela (Erbil) 90,320 .....D2
Ar Rahhaliya 1,579 .....D3
As Salman 1,789 .....D3
Baghdad (cap.) 502,503 .....E3
Baghdad* 1,745,328 .....E3
Baq'uba 34,575 .....D3
Basra 313,327 .....E3
Erbil 90,320 .....D2
Habbaniya 14,405 .....D3
Haditha 6,870 .....D3
Hai 16,988 .....E3
Hilla 84,717 .....D3
Hit 9,131 .....D3
Karbal'a 83,301 .....D3
Khanaqin 23,522 .....E2
Kirkuk 167,413 .....D2
Kirkuk* 176,794 .....D2
Kut 42,116 .....E3
Mosul 315,157 .....D2
Qal'a Sharqat 2,434 .....D2
Ramadi 28,723 .....D3
Rutba 5,091 .....D3
Samarra 24,746 .....D3
Samawa 33,473 .....D3
Shithatha 2,326 .....D3
Sulaimaniya 86,822 .....E2
Tikrit 9,921 .....D3

OTHER FEATURES

'Ar'ar, Wadi (dry riv.) D3
'Aneiza, Jebel (mt.) C3
Batin, Wadi al (dry riv.) E4
Euphrates (riv.) D3
Hauran, Wadi (dry riv.) D3
Mesopotamia (reg.) E3
Persian (gulf) F4
Shatt-al-'Arab (riv.) E4
Syrian (El Hamad)(des.) D3
Tigris (riv.) E3

KUWAIT

CITIES and TOWNS

Al Kuwait (cap.) 181,774 .....E4
Mina al Ahmadi E4
Mina Sa'ud E4

OTHER FEATURES

Bubiyan (isl.) E4
Persian (gulf) F4

OMAN

CITIES and TOWNS

'Ibri G5
Matrah 15,000 .....G5
Muscat (cap.) 7,500 .....G5
Quryat G5
Raysut (Risut) F6
Salala 4,000 .....F6
Sohar G5
Suwaiq G5

OTHER FEATURES

Akhdar, Jebel (range) G5
Batina (reg.) G5
Dhofar (reg.) F6
Hadd, Ras al (cape) G5
Hallaniya (isl.) G6
Hormuz (str.) G4
Jibsh, Ras (cape) G5
Kuria Muria (isls.) G6
Madraka, Ras (cape) G6
Masira (gulf) G5
Masira (isl.) G5
Musandam, Ras (cape) G4
Nus, Ras (cape) G6
Oman (gulf) G5
Oman (reg.) G5
Ruus al Jibal (dist.) G4
Sauqira (bay) G6
Sauqira, Ras (cape) G6
Sham, Jebel (mt.) G5
Sharbatat, Ras (cape) G6

QATAR

CITIES and TOWNS

Doha (cap.) 150,000 .....F4
Dukhan F4
Umm Sa'id F5

OTHER FEATURES

Persian (gulf) F4
Rakan, Ras (cape) F4

SAUDI ARABIA

CITIES and TOWNS

Aba as Sa'ud 47,501 .....D6
Abha 30,150 .....D6
Abu 'Arish D6
Abu Hadriya E4
'Ain al Mubarrak C5
Al 'Ain C4
Al Birk D6
Al Hilla E5
Al Lidam D6
Al Muadhdham C4
'Anaiza D4
Artawiya E4
Ayun D4
Badr C5
Bisha D5
Buraida 69,940 .....D4
Dammam 127,844 .....F4
Dhaba C4
Dhahran E4
Dilam E5
El Haql C4
Er Raṣ D4
Hadiya C4
Hafar al Batin D4
Hail 40,502 .....D4
Hofuf 101,271 .....E4
Jauf C4
Jidda 561,104 .....C5
Jizan (Qizan) 32,812 .....D6
Jubail E4
Jubba D4
Kaf C3
Khaibar, Hejaz C4
Khamis Mushait 49,581 .....D6
Mastaba C5
Mastura C5
Mecca 366,801 .....C5
Medina 198,186 .....D5
Mubarraz 54,325 .....E4
Najran (Aba as Sa'ud) 47,501 .....D6
Nisab D4
'Oqair E5
Qadhima C5
Qatif E4
Qizan 32,812 .....D6
Ra's al Khafji E4
Ras Tanura E4
Riyadh (cap.) 666,840 .....E5
Rumah E5
Sakaka D4
Shaqra D5
Sufeina D5
Taif 204,857 .....D5
Tebuk (Tabuk) 74,825 .....C4
Turaba D5
Umm Lajj C4
Wejh C4
Yenbo C5
Zahran D6
Zalim D5

OTHER FEATURES

Abu-Mad, Ras (cape) C5
'Aneiza, Jebel (mt.) C3
Aqaba (gulf) C4
Arafat, Jebel (mt.) D5
'Ar'ar, Wadi (dry riv.) D4
Arma (plat.) E4
'Asir (reg.) D6
Aswad, Ras al (cape) C5
Bab el Mandeb (str.) D7
Bahr es Safi (des.) E6
Barida, Ras (cape) C5
Batin, Wadi al (dry riv.) E4
Bisha, Wadi (dry riv.) D5
Dahana (des.) E5
Dawasir, Hadhb (range) D5
Dawasir, Wadi (dry riv.) D5
Farasan (isls.) D6
Hatiba, Ras (cape) C5
Hejaz (reg.) C4
Jafura (des.) F5
Mashabi (isl.) C4
Midian (dist.) C4
Misha'ab, Ras (cape) E4
Nefud (des.) D4
Nefud Dahi (des.) D5
Nejd (reg.) D4
Persian (gulf) E5
Ranya, Wadi (dry riv.) D5
Red (sea) C4
Rima, Wadi (dry riv.) D4
Rimal, Ar (des.) F5
Rub al Khali (des.) E6
Safaniya, Ras (cape) E4
Salma, Jebel (mts.) D4
Shaibara (isl.) C4
Shammar, Jebel (plat.) D4
Sirhan, Wadi (dry riv.) C3
Subh, Jebel (mt.) C4
Summan (plat.) E4
Tihama (reg.) C5
Tiran (isl.) C4
Tiran (str.) C4
Tuwaiq, Jebel (range) E5

UNITED ARAB EMIRATES

CITIES and TOWNS

Abu Dhabi (cap.) 347,000 .....F5
'Ajman G4
Buraimi G5
Dubai F4
Fujairah G4
Jebel Dhanna F5
Ras al Khaimah G4
Ruwais F5
Sharjah F4
Umm al Qaiwain G4

OTHER FEATURES

Das (isl.) F4
Oman (gulf) G5
Yas (isl.) F5
Zirko (isl.) F5

WEST BANK

CITIES and TOWNS

Hebron 38,309 .....C3

OTHER FEATURES

Dead (sea) C3

YEMEN

CITIES and TOWNS

Aden 240,370 .....E7
Al Hawtah E6
'Amran D6
Bait al Faqih D7
Balhaf E7
Bir 'Ali E7
Damqut D7
Dhamar 19,467 .....D7
El Beida 5,975 .....D7
Hadibu F7
Hajja 5,814 .....D6
Hodeida 80,314 .....D7
Hureidha E6
Ibb 19,066 .....D7
Lodar E7
Luhaiya D6
Madinat ash Sha'b E6
Marib 292 .....E6
Meifa E7
Mocha D7
Mukalla 45,000 .....E7
Nisab E7
Qabr Hud F6
Qishn F6
Riyan F6
Sa'ada 4,252 .....D6
Saihut F6
San'a (cap.) 134,588 .....D6
Sana D6
Seiyun 20,000 .....E6
Shabwa E6
Sheikh Sa'id D7
Shibam E6
Shihr F6
Shuqra E7
Ta'izz 78,642 .....D7
Tarim E6
Yarim D7
Yeshbum E7
Zabid D7

OTHER FEATURES

Bab el Mandeb (str.) D7
Fartak, Ras (cape) F6
Hadhramaut (dist.) E7
Hadhramaut, Wadi (dry riv.) F7
Hanish (isls.) D7
Jebel Manar (mt.) D7
Jebel Sabir (mt.) D7
Kamaran (isl.) D7
Manar, Jebel (mt.) D7
Mandeb, Bab el (str.) D7
Maqatin (ruins) E7
Perim (isl.) D7
Qamr (bay) F6
Ras Fartak (cape) F6
Red (sea) C5
Sabir, Jebel (mt.) D7
Socotra (isl.) F7
Tihama (reg.) C5
Wadi Hadhramaut (dry riv.) F7
Zuqar (isl.) D7

† Population of commune.
* City and suburbs.

Agriculture, Industry and Resources

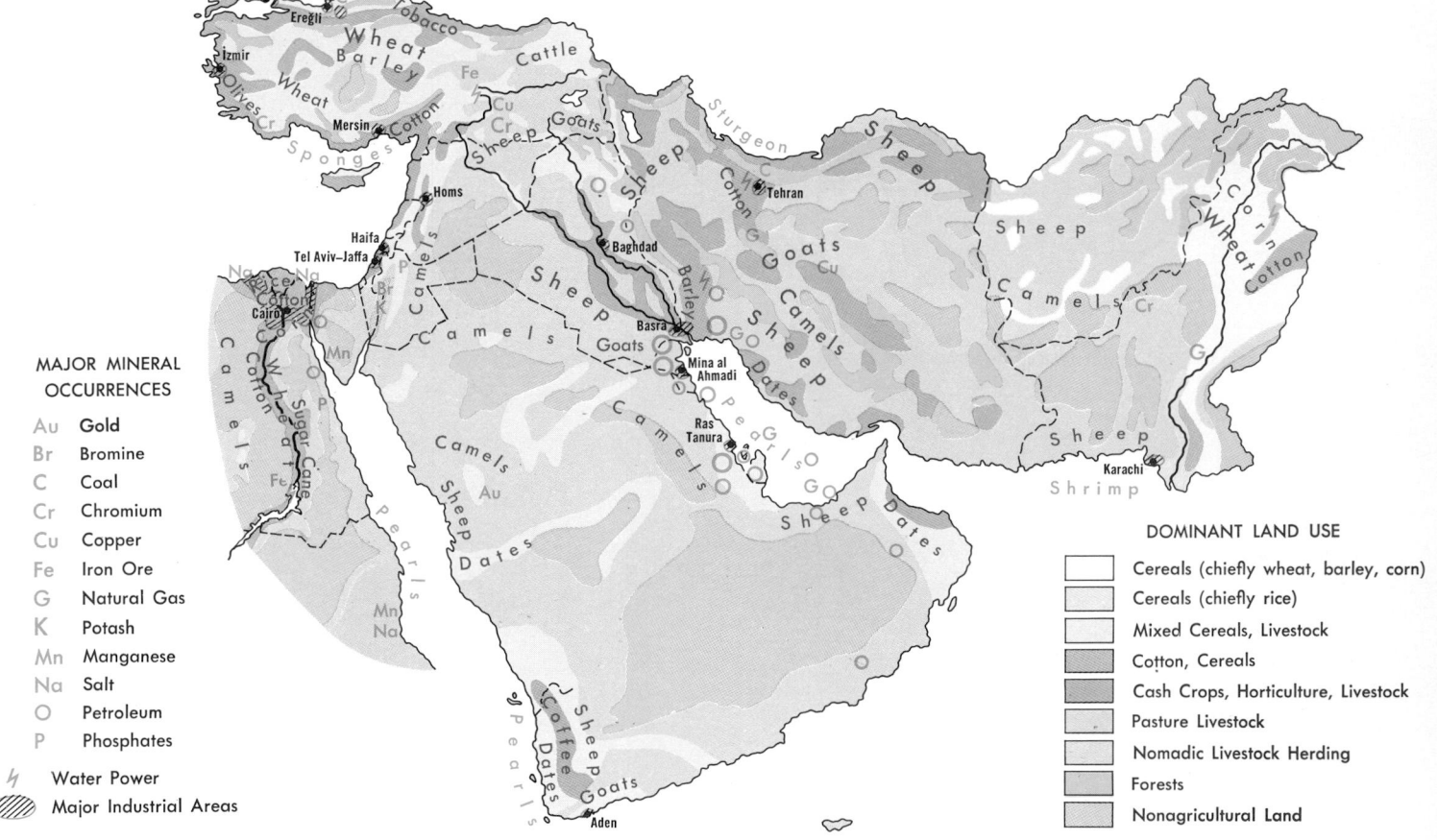

MAJOR MINERAL OCCURRENCES

- Au Gold
- Br Bromine
- C   Coal
- Cr Chromium
- Cu Copper
- Fe Iron Ore
- G   Natural Gas
- K   Potash
- Mn Manganese
- Na Salt
- O   Petroleum
- P   Phosphates
- ⚡ Water Power
- Major Industrial Areas

DOMINANT LAND USE

- Cereals (chiefly wheat, barley, corn)
- Cereals (chiefly rice)
- Mixed Cereals, Livestock
- Cotton, Cereals
- Cash Crops, Horticulture, Livestock
- Pasture Livestock
- Nomadic Livestock Herding
- Forests
- Nonagricultural Land

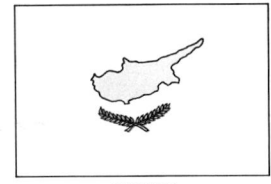
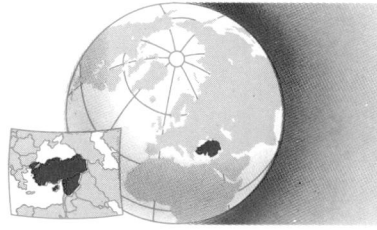

TURKEY

SYRIA

LEBANON

CYPRUS

AREA 300,946 sq. mi.
(779,450 sq. km.)
POPULATION 56,741,000
CAPITAL Ankara
LARGEST CITY Istanbul
HIGHEST POINT Ararat 16,946 ft.
(5,165 m.)
MONETARY UNIT Turkish lira
MAJOR LANGUAGE Turkish
MAJOR RELIGION Islam

AREA 71,498 sq. mi. (185,180 sq. km.)
POPULATION 11,719,000
CAPITAL Damascus
LARGEST CITY Damascus
HIGHEST POINT Hermon 9,232 ft.
(2,814 m.)
MONETARY UNIT Syrian pound
MAJOR LANGUAGES Arabic, French,
Kurdish, Armenian
MAJOR RELIGIONS Islam, Christianity

AREA 4.015 sq. mi. (10,399 sq. km.)
POPULATION 2,897,000
CAPITAL Beirut
LARGEST CITY Beirut
HIGHEST POINT Qurnet es Sauda
10,131 ft. (3,088 m.)
MONETARY UNIT Lebanese pound
MAJOR LANGUAGES Arabic, French
MAJOR RELIGIONS Christianity, Islam

AREA 3,473 sq. mi. (8,995 sq. km.)
POPULATION 699,000
CAPITAL Nicosia
LARGEST CITY Nicosia
HIGHEST POINT Troödos 6,406 ft. (1,953 m.)
MONETARY UNIT Cypriot pound
MAJOR LANGUAGES Greek, Turkish, English
MAJOR RELIGIONS Eastern (Greek) Orthodoxy,

CYPRUS

CITIES and TOWNS

Famagusta 38,960	F5
Kyrenia 3,892	E5
Kythrea 3,400	E5
Lapithos 3,600	E5
Larnaca 19,608	E5
Lefka 3,650	E5
Limassol 79,641	E5
Morphou 9,040	E5
Nicosia (cap.) 115,718	E5
Paphos 8,984	E5
Polis 2,200	E5
Rizokarpasso 3,600	F5
Yialousa 2,750	E5

OTHER FEATURES

Andreas (cape)	F5
Arnauti (cape)	E5
Famagusta (bay)	E5
Gata (cape)	E5
Greco (cape)	F5
Klides (isls.)	F5
Kormakiti (cape)	E5
Larnaca (bay)	E5
Morphou (bay)	E5
Pomos (pt.)	E5
Troodos (mt.)	E5

LEBANON

CITIES and TOWNS

'Aleih 18,630	F6
Amyun 7,926	F5
Ba'albek 15,560	G4
Beirut (cap.) 474,870	F6
Beirut* 938 940	F6
Merj 'Uyun 9,318	F6
Rasheiya 6,731	F6
Saida 32,200	F6

Sidon (Saida) 32,200	F6
Sur 16,483	F6
Tarabulus 127,611	F5
Tripoli (Tarabulus) 127,611	F5
Tyre (Sur) 16,483	F6
Zahle 53,121	F6
Zegharta 18,210	G5

OTHER FEATURES

Lebanon (mts.)	F6
Leontes (Litani) (riv.)	F6
Litani (riv.)	F6
Sauda, Qurnet es (mt.)	G5

SYRIA

PROVINCES

Aleppo 1,316,872	G4
Damascus 1,457,934	G6
Deir ez Zor 292,780	H5
Der'a 230,481	G6
El Quneitra 16,490	F6
Es Suweida 139,650	G6
Hama 514,748	G5
Haseke 468,506	J4
Homs 546,176	G5
Idlib 383,695	G5
Latakia 389,552	G5
Rashid 243,736	H5
Tartus 302,065	G5

CITIES and TOWNS

Abu Kemal 6,907	J5
'Ain el 'Arab 4,529	H4
Aleppo 639,428	G4
Azaz 13,923	G4
Baniyas 8,537	F5
Damascus (cap.) 836,668	G6
Damascus* 923,253	G6
Deir ez Zor 66,164	H5
Der'a 27,651	G6

Dimashq (Damascus) (cap.) 836,668	G6
Duma 30,050	G6
El Bab 27,366	G4
El Haseke 32,746	J4
El Ladhiqya (Latakia) 125,716	F5
El Qaryatein	G5
El Quneitra 17,752	F6
El Rashid 37,151	H5
En Nebk 16,334	G5
Es Suweida 29,524	G6
Et Tell el Abyad	H4
Haffe 4,656	G5
Haleb (Aleppo) 639,428	G4
Hama 137,421	G5
Harim 6,837	G4
Homs 215,423	G5
Idlib 34,515	G5
Izra 3,226	G6
Jeble 15,715	F5
Jerablus 8,610	G4
Jisr esh Shughur 13,131	G5
Khan Sheikhun	G5
Latakia 125,716	F5
Masyaf 7,058	G5
Membij 13,796	G4
Meskene	G4
Meyadin 12,515	J5
Qal'at es Salihiye	J5
Qamishliye 31,448	J4
Quteife 4,993	G6
Raqqa (El Rashid) 37,151	H5
Safita 9,650	G5
Selemiya 21,677	G5
Tadmur 10,670	H5
Tartus 29,842	F5
Telkalakh 6,242	F5
Zebdani 10,010	G6

OTHER FEATURES

Abdul 'Aziz, Jebel (mts.)	J4
'Amrit (ruins)	F5
Arwad (Ruad) (isl.)	F5
'Asi (Orontes) (riv.)	G5
Bahrat Assad (lake)	H4
Druz, Jebel ed (mts.)	G6
El Furat (riv.)	H4
Euphrates (El Furat) (riv.)	H4
Hermon (mt.)	F6
Khabur (riv.)	J5
Orontes (riv.)	G5
Palmyra (Tadmor) (ruins)	H5
Tigris (riv.)	K4

TURKEY

PROVINCES

Adana 1,485,743	F4
Adıyaman 367,595	H4
Afyonkarahisar 597,516	D3
Ağrı 368,009	K3
Amasya 341,287	F2
Ankara 2,854,689	E3
Antalya 748,706	D4
Artvin 228,997	J2
Aydın 652,488	B4
Balıkesir 853,177	B3
Bilecik 147,001	D2
Bingöl 228,702	J3
Bitlis 257,908	J3
Bolu 471,751	D2
Burdur 235,009	D4
Bursa 1,148,492	C2
Çanakkale 338,091	B2
Çankırı 258,436	E2
Çorum 571,831	F2
Denizli 603,338	C4
Diyarbakır 778,150	H4
Edirne 363,286	B2
Elâzığ 440,808	H3
Erzincan 282,022	H3
Erzurum 801,809	J3
Eskişehir 543,802	D3
Gaziantep 808,697	G4
Giresun 480,083	H2
Gümüşhane 275,191	H2

CITIES and TOWNS

Adalia (Antalya) 176,446	D4
Adana 842,845	F4
Adapazarı 131,400	D2

Hakkâri 155,463	K4
Hatay 856,271	G4
İçel 842,817	F4
Isparta 301,166	D4
İstanbul 3,264,393	C2
İzmir 1,976,763	B3
Kahramanmaraş 738,032	G4
Kars 700,238	K2
Kastamonu 450,946	E2
Kayseri 778,383	F3
Kırklareli 283,408	B2
Kırşehir 240,497	F3
Kocaeli 596,899	C2
Konya 1,562,139	E4
Kütahya 497,089	C3
Malatya 669,962	H3
Manisa 941,941	B3
Mardin 564,967	J4
Muğla 438,145	C4
Muş 302,406	J3
Nevşehir 256,933	F3
Niğde 512,071	F4
Ordu 713,535	G2
Rize 361,258	J2
Samsun 1,008,113	F2
Siirt 445,483	J4
Sinop 276,242	F2
Sivas 750,144	G3
Tekirdağ 360,742	B2
Tokat 624,508	G2
Trabzon 731,045	H2
Tunceli 157,974	H3
Urfa 602,736	H4
Uşak 247,224	C3
Van 468,646	K3
Yozgat 504,433	F3
Zonguldak 972,856	D2

CITIES and TOWNS

Adalia (Antalya) 176,446	D4
Adana 842,845	F4
Aybastı 13,517	G2
Aydın 37,696	B4

Adilcevaz 10,342	K3
Adıyaman 116,986	H4
Afşin 20,084	G3
Afyonkarahisar 597,516	D3
Ağrı (Karaköse) 41,103	K3
Ahlat 10,422	K3
Akçaabat 13,384	H2
Akçadağ 8,015	G3
Akçakale 11,184	H4
Akçakoca 9,639	D2
Akdağmadeni 10,192	F3
Akhisar 61,491	B3
Aksaray 62,927	F3
Akşehir 40,312	D3
Akseki 6,815	D4
Akyazı 14,795	D2
Alaca 15,649	F3
Alaçam 11,402	F2
Alaşehir 25,611	C3
Alexandretta (İskenderun) 120,985	G4
Alibeyköyü 33,387	D6
Altındağ 608,689	E2
Altınova 6,980	B3
Alucra 8,795	H2
Amasya 48,010	F2
Anamur 23,025	E4
Andırın 6,045	G4
Ankara (cap.) 2,203,729	E3
Antakya 99,551	F4
Antalya 176,446	D4
Antioch (Antakya) 99,551	F4
Arapkir 8,816	H3
Ardahan 14,912	K2
Ardeşen 9,582	J2
Arhavi 6,801	J2
Arsin 6,892	H2
Artvin 14,203	J2
Aşkale 12,045	J3
Avanos 8,927	F3
Ayancık 8,257	F1
Aybastı 13,517	G2
Aydın 37,696	B4

Aydıncık 19,371	E4
Ayvalık 19,371	B3
Babaeski 18,145	B2
Bafra 50,213	F2
Bahçe 12,366	G4
Bakırköy 234,226	D6
Balıkesir 124,122	B3
Banaz 8,356	C3
Bandırma 53,497	B2
Bartın 20,728	E2
Başkale 5,366	K3
Batman 86,172	J4
Bayat 5,366	F2
Bayburt 22,578	J2
Bayındır 12,440	B3
Bayramiç 7,854	B3
Bergama 34,716	B3
Beşiktaş 188,117	D6
Besni 15,833	G4
Beykoz 94,101	D5
Beyoğlu 223,360	D6
Beypazarı 16,971	D2
Beyşehir 15,845	D4
Biga 16,359	B2
Bigadiç 8,955	C3
Bilecik 15,108	D2
Bingöl (Çapakçur) 27,904	J3
Birecik 20,412	H4
Bismil 19,059	J4
Bitlis 27,114	J3
Bodrum 32,517	B4
Boğazlıyan 10,827	F3
Bolu 38,400	D2
Bolvadin 30,599	D3
Bor 45,480	F4
Bornova 60,397	B3
Boyabat 14,397	F2
Bozdoğan 7,682	C4
Bozova 5,510	H4
Bozüyük 18,052	C3
Bucak 18,852	D4
Bulancak 16,089	H2
Bulanık 9,140	K3
Buldan 10,939	C3

(continued on following page)

Agriculture, Industry and Resources

DOMINANT LAND USE

- Cereals (chiefly wheat, barley , Livestock
- Cash Crops, Horticulture, Livestock
- Pasture Livestock
- Nomadic Livestock Herding
- Forests
- Nonagricultural Land

MAJOR MINERAL OCCURRENCES

Ab	Asbestos	Na	Salt
Al	Bauxite	O	Petroleum
C	Coal	P	Phosphates
Cr	Chromium	Pb	Lead
Cu	Copper	Py	Pyrites
Fe	Iron Ore	Sb	Antimony
Hg	Mercury	Zn	Zinc
Mg	Magnesium		

⚡ Water Power

▨ Major Industrial Areas

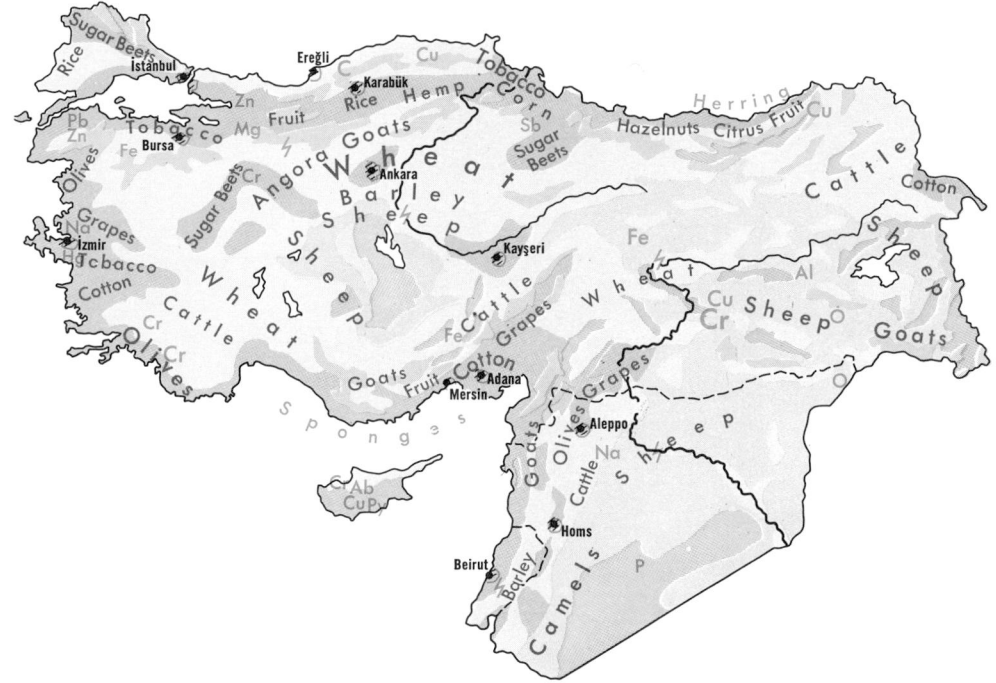

Bünyan 12,930	G3	Cide 9,809	E2	Diyarbakır 233,289	H4	Ergani 23,870	H3	Gemlik 26,757	C2	Güney 7,077	C3	Ilıca 8,947	J3

The map index (alphabetical gazetteer):

Bünyan 12,930 ....G3
Burdur 44,750 ....D4
Burhaniye 15,522 ....B3
Bursa 466,178 ....C2
Çan 15,137 ....B2
Çanakkale 39,943 ....B6
Çandır 6,986 ....F3
Çankaya 921,882 ....E3
Çankırı 35,040 ....E2
Çapakçur 27,904 ....J3
Çarşamba 28,422 ....G2
Çatalca 7,988 ....C2
Çay 11,166 ....D3
Çaycuma 9,688 ....E2
Çayeli 14,926 ....J2
Çayıralan 6,047 ....F3
Çekerek 5,517 ....F2
Çerkezköy 12,908 ....C2
Çermik 9,798 ....H3
Çeşme 6,451 ....A3
Ceyhan 57,307 ....F4
Ceylânpınar 20,171 ....H4

Cide 9,809 ....E2
Çifteler 10,669 ....D3
Çine 13,186 ....B4
Çivril 9,343 ....C3
Cizre 20,003 ....K4
Çölemerik 18,514 ....K4
Çorlu 47,086 ....B2
Çorum 76,020 ....F2
Çumra 20,919 ....E4
Darende 9,144 ....G3
Demirci 14,538 ....C3
Denizli 134,673 ....C4
Derik 15,288 ....J4
Derinkuyu 6,591 ....F3
Develi 22,491 ....F3
Devrek 12,265 ....D2
Dicle 5,729 ....J3
Dikili 7,637 ....B3
Dinar 20,937 ....D3
Divriği 14,679 ....H3
Diyadin 6,011 ....K3

Diyarbakır 233,289 ....H4
Doğanhisar 7,618 ....D3
Doğanşehir 10,172 ....G3
Doğubeyazıt 23,513 ....K3
Dörtyol 25,905 ....G4
Düzce 37,858 ....D2
Dursunbey 10,293 ....C3
Edirne 71,927 ....B2
Edremit 27,145 ....B3
Eğridir 12,415 ....D4
Elâzığ 142,787 ....H3
Elbistan 35,437 ....G3
Eleşkirt 10,294 ....K3
Elmalı 11,531 ....C4
Emet 8,285 ....C3
Emirdağ 15,010 ....D3
Erciş 27,514 ....K3
Erdek 10,140 ....B2
Ereğli, Konya 61,100 ....F4
Ereğli, Zonguldak 50,096 ....D2

Ergani 23,870 ....H3
Ermenak 12,535 ....E4
Erzin 15,314 ....G4
Erzincan 73,335 ....H3
Erzurum 190,121 ....J3
Eşme 8,982 ....C3
Eskimalatya 10,182 ....H3
Eskişehir 309,335 ....D3
Espiye 9,172 ....H2
Eynesil 6,455 ....H2
Eyüp 101,764 ....D6
Ezine 9,526 ....B3
Fatih 485,165 ....D6
Fatsa 21,983 ....G2
Fethiye 14,308 ....C4
Foça 6,150 ....B3
Gallipoli 14,554 ....C5
Gaziantep 371,000 ....G4
Gazipaşa 8,010 ....E4
Gebze 58,212 ....C2
Gediz 13,788 ....C3
Gelibolu (Gallipoli) 14,554 ....C5

Gemlik 26,757 ....C2
Genç 7,516 ....J3
Gerede 9,823 ....E2
Germencik 9,569 ....B4
Gerze 6,327 ....F2
Gevaş 7,406 ....K3
Geyve 8,943 ....D2
Giresun 46,068 ....H2
Göksun 12,784 ....G3
Gölbaşı 20,432 ....H3
Gölcük 45,006 ....C2
Göle 7,952 ....K2
Gölhisar 8,314 ....C4
Gölköy 12,125 ....H2
Gölmarmara 11,982 ....C3
Gönen 19,037 ....B2
Gördes 8,575 ....C3
Gülnar 6,817 ....E4
Gülşehir 5,087 ....F3
Gümüşhacıköy 13,159 ....F2
Gümüşhane 12,755 ....H2

Güney 7,077 ....C3
Gürün 9,581 ....G3
Hacılar 15,622 ....F3
Hadım 11,050 ....E4
Hafik 8,447 ....G3
Hakkari (Çölemerik) 18,514 ....K4
Hani 8,118 ....J3
Haruniye 12,837 ....G4
Hassa 6,230 ....G4
Havran 8,144 ....B3
Havza 15,468 ....F2
Hayrabolu 14,090 ....B2
Hekimhan 11,096 ....G3
Hendek 17,172 ....D2
Hınıs 11,182 ....J3
Hopa 10,136 ....J2
Horasan 10,193 ....K2
İdil 6,142 ....J4
Iğdır 24,395 ....K3
Ilgın 16,522 ....D3

Ilıca 8,947 ....J3
İmranli 6,331 ....H2
İncesu 7,003 ....F3
İnebolu 7,115 ....E2
İpsala 10,551 ....B2
İskenderun 120,985 ....G4
İskilip 16,936 ....F2
İslâhiye 22,589 ....G4
İsparta 91,544 ....D4
İspir 7,312 ....J2
İstanbul 2,853,539 ....C2
İzmir 753,749 ....B3
İzmit 19,140 ....C2
İznik 13,507 ....C2
Kadıköy 478,609 ....D6
Kadınhanı 13,611 ....D3
Kadirli 38,125 ....F4
Kağıthane 164,448 ....D6
Kağızman 13,383 ....K2
Kâhta 16,631 ....H3
Kalan 12,859 ....H3

Map legend box:

Turkey is divided into provinces bearing the same names as their capital towns, except:

Province	Capital	
AĞRI	Karaköse	K 3
BİNGÖL	Çapakçur	J 3
HAKKÂRI	Çölemerik	K 4
HATAY	Antakya	G 4
İÇEL	Mersin	F 4
KOCAELİ	İzmit	C 2
SAKARYA	Adapazarı	D 2
TUNCELİ	Kalan	H 3

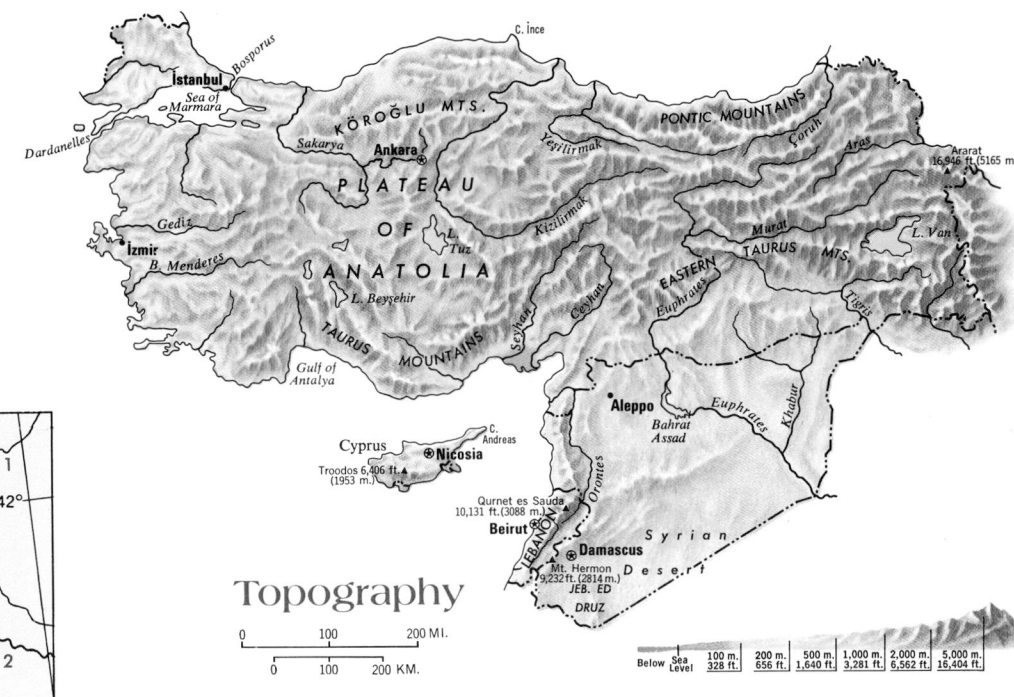

Topography

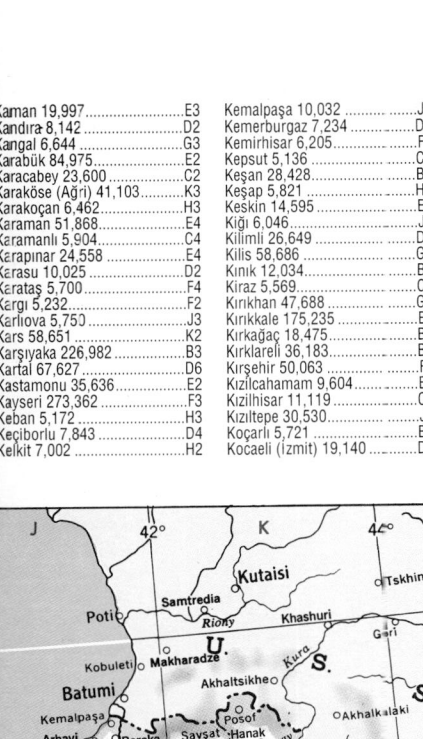

Kaman 19,997	E3	Kemalpaşa 10,032	J2	
Kandıra 8,142	D2	Kemerburgaz 7,234	D5	
Kangal 6,644	G3	Kemirhisar 6,205	F4	
Karabük 84,975	E2	Kepsut 5,136	C3	
Karacabey 23,600	C2	Keşan 28,428	B2	
Karaköse (Ağrı) 41,103	K3	Keşap 5,821	H2	
Karaçoban 6,462	H3	Keskin 14,595	E3	
Karaman 51,868	E4	Kiği 6,046	J3	
Karamanlı 5,904	C4	Kilimli 26,649	D2	
Karapınar 24,558	E4	Kilis 58,686	G4	
Karasu 10,025	D2	Kınık 12,034	B3	
Karataş 5,700	F4	Kiraz 5,569	C3	
Kergi 5,232	F2	Kırıkhan 47,688	G4	
Karlıova 5,750	J3	Kırıkkale 175,235	E3	
Kars 58,651	K2	Kırşehir 50,063	F3	
Karşıyaka 226,982	B3	Kızılcahamam 9,604	E2	
Kartal 67,627	D6	Kızılhisar 11,119	C4	
Kastamonu 35,636	E2	Kızıltepe 30,530	J4	
Kayseri 273,362	F3	Koçarlı 5,721	B4	
Keban 5,172	H3	Kocaeli (İzmit) 19,140	D2	
Keçiborlu 7,843	D4			
Kelkit 7,002	H2			

Konya 325,850	E4	Safranbolu 19,155	E2	Turgutlu 55,575	B3	
Korkuteli 10,774	D4	Sakarya (Adapazarı) 131,400	D2	Turhal 47,364	F2	
Köyceğiz 5,347	C4	Salihli 51,638	C3	Tuzluca 6,716	K3	
Kozaklı 6,764	F3	Samandağı 25,349	G4	Tuzlukçu 6,716	D3	
Kozan 42,410	F4	Samsun 198,266	F2	Ula 5,119	C4	
Kozlu 27,322	D2	Sandıklı 15,966	D3	Uluborlu 6,002	D3	
Kozluk 10,215	J3	Sapanca 10,228	D2	Uludere 4,989	K4	
Küçükköy 56,411	C6	Sarayköy 11,009	C4	Ulukışla 7,841	F4	
Kula 12,763	C3	Sarayönü 8,643	E3	Ünye 27,946	G2	
Kulp 5,577	J3	Sarıgöl 7,880	C3	Urfa 148,434	H4	
Kulu 12,183	E4	Sarıkamış 23,331	K2	Ürla 14,347	B3	
Kumluca 7,977	D4	Sarıkaya 7,297	F3	Ürgüp 6,955	F3	
Kurşunlu 6,678	E2	Sarıköy 4,695	B3	Üsküdar 255,899	D6	
Kurtalan 9,748	J3	Sarıyer 110,555	D5	Uzunköprü 27,706	B2	
Kuşadası 14,299	B4	Şarkikaraağaç 5,905	D3	Vakfıkebir 13,814	H2	
Kuyucak 6,532	C4	Şarköy 6,755	B2	Van 93,823	K3	
Lâdik 7,200	F2	Savaştepe 7,110	B3	Varto 7,360	J3	
Lice 8,486	J3	Savur 6,170	J4	Vezirköprü 13,547	F2	
Lüleburgaz 35,643	B2	Şebinkarahisar 12,550	H2	Viranşehir 41,934	H4	
Mağara 5,037	G3	Şefaatli 7,513	F3	Vize 9,528	B2	
Mahmudiye 5,352	D3	Şeferihisar 6,506	B3	Yahyalı 15,585	F4	
Malatya 184,390	H3	Selçuk 12,819	B3	Yalova 41,869	C2	
Malazgirt 14,150	K3	Selendi 5,012	C3	Yalvaç 19,986	D3	
Malkara 15,570	B2	Şemdinli 19,677	L4	Yatağan 7,350	C4	
Maltepe 66,343	D6	Şenirkent 8,382	D3	Yayladağı 5,300	F5	
Manavgat 14,392	D4	Şereflikoçhisar 22,208	E3	Yenice, Çanakkale 4,016	B3	
Manisa 93,970	B3	Şerik 15,662	D4	Yenice, İçel 4,106	F4	
Maraş (Kahramanmaraş) 177,919	G4	Seydişehir 30,394	E4	Yenice, Zonguldak 5,791	D2	
Mardin 37,750	H4	Siirt 42,692	J4	Yeniceoba 5,740	E3	
Marmaris 7,710	C4	Şile 4,870	C3	Yenimahalle 265,752	E3	
Mazıdağı 7,941	J4	Şilifke 22,045	E4	Yenişehir 17,013	C2	
Mecitözü 5,874	F2	Silivri 13,922	C2	Yerköy 20,623	F3	
Menemen 22,080	B3	Silopi 6,832	K4	Yeşilhisar 11,132	F3	
Mersin 215,300	E4	Silvan 44,412	J3	Yeşilova, Burdur 4,393	C4	
Merzifon 32,031	F2	Simav 10,775	C3	Yeşilova, Niğde 5,237	E3	
Mesudiye 5,013	G2	Sındırgı 8,992	C3	Yeşilyurt 7,040	H3	
Midyat 20,112	J4	Sinop 18,381	F2	Yıldızeli 11,124	G2	
Milâs 20,333	B4	Şiran 6,088	H2	Yozgat 36,220	F3	
Mucur 9,386	F3	Şırnak 10,947	K4	Yüksekova 11,867	L4	
Mudanya 10,556	C2	Sivas 173,831	G3	Yunak 7,144	D3	
Mudurnu 5,307	D2	Sivaslı 4,627	C3	Zara 10,196	G2	
Muğla 27,162	C4	Siverek 30,000	H4	Zeytinburnu 126,899	D6	
Muradiye 10,036	K3	Sivrihisar 9,608	D3	Zile 30,066	G2	
Muş 40,297	J3	Smyrna (İzmir) 753,749	B3	Zonguldak 108,661	D2	
Mustafakemalpaşa 30,099	C3	Söğüt 6,353	D2			
Mut 14,029	E4	Söke 37,362	B4	**OTHER FEATURES**		
Nallıhan 9,791	D2	Solhan 7,170	J3			
Nazilli 64,015	C4	Soma 30,219	B3	Abydos (ruins)	B6	
Nevşehir 37,106	F3	Sorgun 19,623	F3	Acı (lake)	C4	
Niğde 39,972	F4	Şuhut 8,154	D3	Adalar (isl.)	D6	
Niksar 23,570	G2	Sulakyurt 4,712	E2	Aegean (sea)	A3	
Nizip 39,267	G4	Sultandağı 5,115	D3	Ağrı, Büyük (Ararat) (mt.)	L3	
Nurhak 5,330	G4	Sultanhanı 5,112	E3	Akbaba Tepesi (mt.)	H3	
Nusaybin 32,620	J4	Suluova 25,682	F2	Akşehir (lake)	D3	
Ödemiş 40,652	C3	Sungurlu 24,170	F2	Aksu (riv.)	D4	
Oğuzeli 7,826	G4	Sürmene 10,152	J2	Alexandretta (gulf)	F4	
Oltu 12,288	J2	Sürüç 19,000	H4	Amanos (mts.)	G4	
Ordu 52,080	G2	Suşehri 11,442	H2	Anatolia (reg.)	D3	
Orhangazi 18,537	C2	Susurluk 16,113	C3	Ankara (riv.)	D3	
Ortaca 8,604	C4	Tarsus 120,270	F4	Anti-Taurus (mts.)	G3	
Ortaköy 8,848	F3	Taşkent 7,098	E4	Araks (riv.)	K2	
Osmancık 15,304	F2	Taşköprü 8,659	F2	Ararat (mt.)	L3	
Osmaneli 6,664	D2	Taşova 6,208	G2	Arpa (riv.)	K2	
Osmaniye 84,338	G4	Tatvan 40,324	K3	Baba (cape)	A3	
Palu 6,842	H3	Tavas 10,335	C4	Bafra (cape)	G2	
Pasinler 20,039	J3	Tavşanlı 23,325	C3	Banaz (riv.)	C3	
Patnos 18,040	K3	Tekirdağ 51,327	B2	Batı Fırat (riv.)	H3	
Pazarcık 19,821	G4	Tercan 5,506	J3	Bey (riv.)	D4	
Pazaryeri 6,005	C3	Terme 15,530	G2	Beyşehir (lake)	D4	
Pera (Beyoğlu) 94,101	D5	Tire 32,242	B3	Bingöl Dağları (mts.)	J3	
Perşembe 7,190	G2	Tirebolu 9,274	H2	Black (sea)	E1	
Pervari 5,021	K4	Tokat 60,369	G2	Bosporus (strait)	D2	
Pınarbaşı 10,578	G3	Tomarza 7,733	F3	Burgaz (isl.)	D6	
Pınarhisar 10,649	B2	Tonya 11,010	H2	Büyük Ağrı (Ararat) (mt.)	L3	
Polatlı 43,514	E3	Tortum 4,280	J2	Büyük Hasan Dağı (mt.)	E3	
Pozantı 6,297	F4	Torbalı 15,504	B3	Büyük Kemikli (cape)	B6	
Refahiye 7,505	H3	Tosya 18,544	F2	Çanakkale Boğazı (Dardanelles) (str.)	B6	
Reşadiye 5,588	G2	Trebizond (Trabzon) 107,412	H2	Çandarlı (gulf)	B3	
Reyhanlı 30,843	G4	Tunceli (Kalan) 12,859	H3	Çekerek (riv.)	F3	
Rize 41,740	J2	Türkoğlu 8,528	G4			

Ceyhan (riv.)	F4
Çıldır (lake)	K2
Çilo Dağı (mt.)	K4
Çoruh (riv.)	J2
Çorum (riv.)	F2
Dalaman (riv.)	C4
Dardanelles (strait)	B6
Delice (riv.)	E2
Devrez (riv.)	E2
Dicle (riv.)	J4
Eastern Taurus (mts.)	J3
Edremit (gulf)	B3
Eğridir (lake)	D4
Emir Dağı (mt.)	D3
Ephesus (ruins)	B3
Erciyas-Dağı (mt.)	F3
Ergene (riv.)	B2
Euphrates (Fırat) (riv.)	G4
Filyos (riv.)	D2
Fırat (riv.)	G4
Gediz (riv.)	C3
Gelidonya (cape)	D4
Gökçeada (isl.)	A2
Gökırmak (riv.)	F2
Göksu (riv.)	E4
Hakkâri (mts.)	K4
Helles (cape)	B6
Heybeli (isl.)	D6
Hoyran (lake)	D3
Ilgaz (mts.)	E2
Ilium (ruins)	B6
İmroz (Gökçeada) (isl.)	A2
İnce (cape)	F1
İstranca (mts.)	B2
İzmir (gulf)	B3
İznik (lake)	C2
Kaçkar Dağı (mt.)	J2
Karacadağ (mt.)	H4
Karadeniz Boğazı (Bosporus) (str.)	C2
Karasu-Aras (riv.)	J3
Karataş (cape)	F4
Kelkit (riv.)	G2
Kerme (gulf)	B4
Keşiş Tepesi (mt.)	H3
Kırmasti (riv.)	C3
Kızılırmak (riv.)	F2
Köroğlu (mts.)	E2
Küre (mts.)	E2
Kuş (mts.)	B2
Kuşada (gulf)	B4
Mandalya (gulf)	B4
Marmara (gulf)	B2
Marmara (sea)	C2
Medetsiz Tepe (mt.)	F4
Menderes, Büyük (riv.)	C4
Meriç (riv.)	B2
Murat (riv.)	H3
Murat Dağı (mt.)	C3
Pontic (mts.)	H2
Porsuk (riv.)	D3
Prinkipo (Adalar) (isl.)	D6
Sakarya (riv.)	D2
Saros (gulf)	B2
Seyhan (riv.)	F4
Simav (riv.)	C3
Sinop (cape)	F1
Süphan Dağı (mt.)	K3
Taşucu (gulf)	D4
Taurus (mts.)	D4
Tecer (mts.)	G3
Tigris (Dicle) (riv.)	J4
Troy (Ilium) (ruins)	B6
Türkmen Dağı (mt.)	D3
Tuz (lake)	E3
Ulubat (lake)	C2
Uludağ (mt.)	C2
Van (lake)	K3
Yaralıgöz Dağı (mt.)	F2
Yeşilırmak (riv.)	G2

*City and suburbs

Turkey, Syria, Lebanon and Cyprus

© Copyright HAMMOND INCORPORATED, Maplewood, N.J.

SCALE OF MILES
0 25 50 75 100 125 150

SCALE OF KILOMETERS
0 25 50 75 100 125 150

Capitals of Countries ★
Capitals of Provinces △
Provincial Boundaries

Scale 1:5,440,000

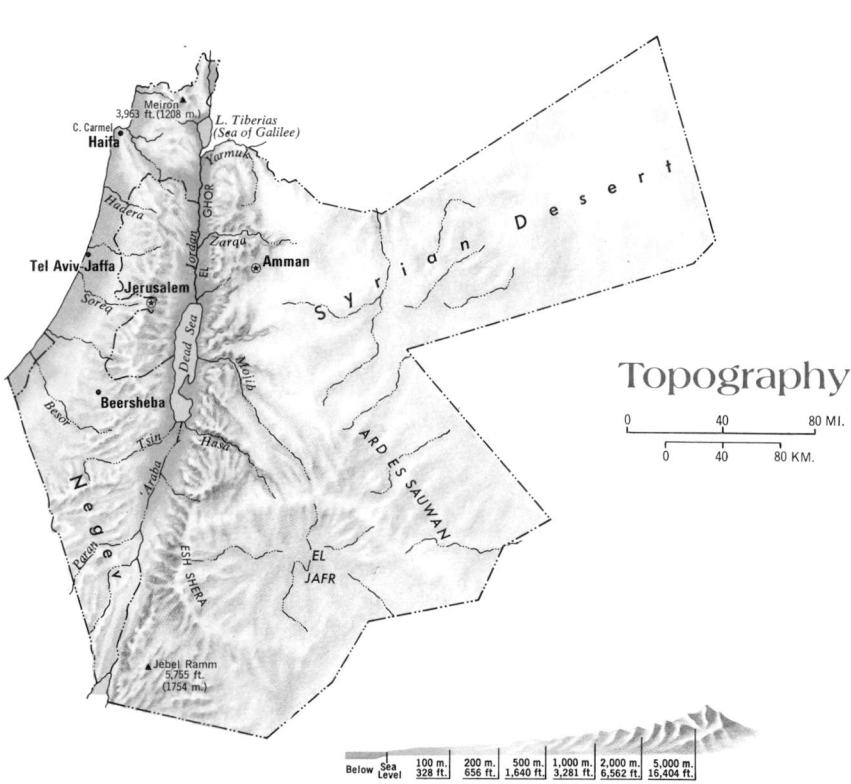

Topography

0   40   80 MI.
0   40   80 KM.

Below Sea Level	100 m. 328 ft.	200 m. 656 ft.	500 m. 1,640 ft.	1,000 m. 3,281 ft.	2,000 m. 6,562 ft.	5,000 m. 16,404 ft.

ISRAEL

DISTRICTS

Central 572,300 ....B3
Haifa 480,800 ....C2
Jerusalem 338,600 ....B4
Northern 473,700 ....C2
Southern 351,300 ....B5
Tel Aviv 905,100 ....B3

CITIES and TOWNS

Acre 34,400 ....C2
Afiqim 1,243 ....D2
'Afula 17,400 ....C2
Akko (Acre) 34,400 ....C2
Arad 5,400 ....C5
'Arrabe 6,000 ....C2
Ashdod 40,500 ....B4
Ashdot Ya'aqov 1,197 ....D2
Ashqelon 43,100 ....B4
Atlit 1,516 ....B2
Bat Yam 124,100 ....B3
Be'eri 390 ....A5
Beersheba
  (Beer Sheva) 101,000 ....B5
Bene Beraq 74,100 ....B3
Bet She'an 11,300 ....D3
Bet Shemesh 10,100 ....B4
Binyamina 2,701 ....B2
Carmiel C2
Dalyat al-Karmel 6,200 ....B2
Dan 498 ....D1
Dimona 23,700 ....D4
Dor 195 ....B2
'Ein Harod 1,372 ....C2
Elat 12,800 ....D6
Elath (Elat) 12,800 ....D6
Even Yehuda 3,464 ....B3
Gat 430 ....B4
Gedera 5,400 ....B4
Ginnosar 473 ....D2
Giv'atayim 48,500 ....B3
Giv'at Brenner 1,505 ....B4
Giv'at Hayyim 1,360 ....B3
Hadera 31,900 ....B2
Haifa 227,800 ....B2
Haifa* 367,400 ....B2
Helez 466 ....B4
Herzeliyya 41,200 ....B3
Hod Hasharon 13,500 ....B3
Hodiyya 400 ....B4
Holon 121,200 ....B3
Iksal 2,156 ....C2
Jerusalem (cap.) 376,000 ....C4
Jish 1,498 ....C1
Kafar Kanna 5,200 ....C2
Kafr Yasif 2,975 ....C2

Karkur-Pardes Hanna 13,600 ..C3
Kefar Blum 565 ....D1
Kefar Gil'adi 701 ....C1
Kefar Ruppin 306 ....D3
Kefar Sava 26,500 ....B3
Kefar Vitkin 808 ....B3
Kefar Zekhariya 420 ....B4
Kinneret 909 ....D2
Lod (Lydda) 30,500 ....B4
Lydda 30,500 ....B4
Magen 149 ....A5
Mash 'Abbe Sade 238 ....B6
Mavqi'im 177 ....B4
Megiddo C2
Metula 261 ....D1
Migdal 688 ....C2
Mikhmoret 608 ....B3
Mishmar Hanegev 336 ....B5
Mishmar Hayarden D1
Mivtahim 398 ....A5
Mizpe Ramon 331 ....D5
Moza Illit 219 ....C4
Mughar 4,010 ....C2
Muqeible 459 ....C2
Nahariyya 24,000 ....C1
Nazareth 33,300 ....C2
Negba 453 ....B4
Nesher 9,400 ....C2
Nes Ziyyona 11,700 ....B4
Netanya 70,700 ....B3
Nevatim 436 ....B5
Newe Yam 211 ....B2
Nizzanim 479 ....B4
Pardes Hanna-Karkur 13,600...B2
Peduyim 361 ....B5
Petah Tiqwa 112,000 ....B3
Qadima 2,937 ....B3
Qedma 157 ....B4
Qiryat Bialik 18,000 ....C2
Qiryat Gat 19,200 ....B4
Qiryat Mal'akhi B4
Qiryat Motzkin 17,600 ....C2
Qiryat Shemona 15,200 ....C1
Qiryat Tiv'on 9,800 ....C2
Qiryat Yam 19,800 ....C2
Ra'anana 14,900 ....B3
Ramat Gan 120,900 ....B3
Ramat Hasharon 20,100 ....B3
Rame 2,986 ....C2
Ramla 34,100 ....B4
Rehovot 39,200 ....B4
Re'im 155 ....A5
Revadim 175 ....B4
Revivim 258 ....D5
Rishon Le Ziyyon 51,900 ....B4
Rosh Pinna 700 ....D2
Ruhama 497 ....B4
Sa'ad 418 ....B5
Safad (Zefat) 13,600 ....C2

Sakhnin 8,400 ....C2
Sedot Yam 511 ....B3
Shave Ziyyon 269 ....C2
Shefar'am 11,800 ....C2
Shefayim 614 ....C2
Shoval 393 ....B5
Tayibe 11,700 ....C2
Tel Aviv-Jaffa 343,300 ....B3
Tel Aviv-Jaffa* 1,219,000 ....B3
Tiberias 23,800 ....C2
Tirat Hakarmel 14,400 ....B2
Tirat Zevi 353 ....D3
Tur'an 2,304 ....C2
Umm el Fahm 13,300 ....C2
Uzza 487 ....B4
Yad Mordekhai 416 ....A4
Yagur 1,266 ....C2
Yavne 10,100 ....B4
Yavne'el 1,580 ....D2
Yehud 40,500 ....B3
Yeroham 5,800 ....D5
Yesud Hama'ala 428 ....D1
Yirka 2,715 ....C2
Zavdi'el 396 ....B4
Zefat 13,600 ....C2
Zikhron Ya'aqov 6,500 ....B2

OTHER FEATURES

Aqaba (gulf) D6
'Araba, Wadi (valley) D5
Beer Sheva (dry riv.) B5
Besor (riv.) B4
Carmel (cape) B2
Carmel (mt.) C2
Dead (sea) C4
Dimona (mt.) C5
Galilee, Sea of
  (Tiberias) (lake) C2
Galilee (reg.) C2
Gerar (dry riv.) B5
Haifa (bay) C1
Haniqra, Rosh (cape) C1
Hatira (mt.) C5
Jordan (riv.) C2
Judaea (reg.) C4
Lakhish (dry riv.) B4
Meiron (mt.) C1
Negev (reg.) C5
Qarn (riv.) C1
Qishon (riv.) C2
Ramon (riv.) D5
Rubin (dry riv.) B4
Shiqma (riv.) B4
Tabor (mt.) C2
Tiberias (lake) C2
Yarmuk (riv.) C2
Yarqon (riv.) B3

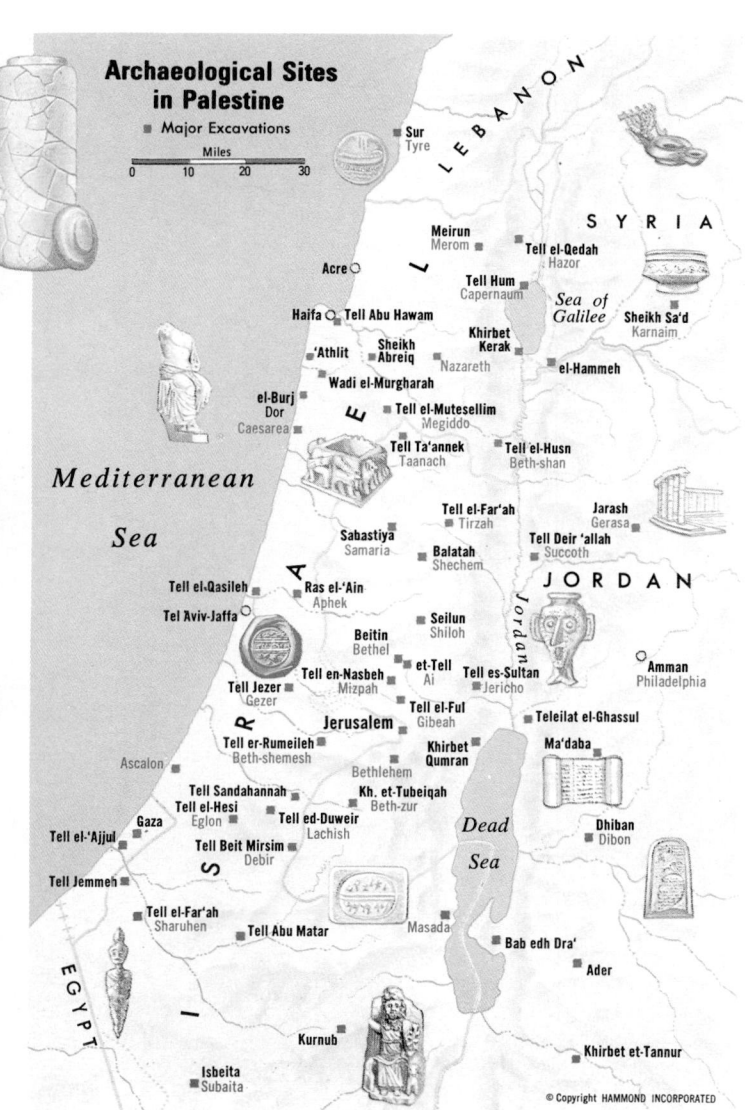

Archaeological Sites in Palestine

■ Major Excavations

Miles
0   10   20   30

LEBANON
SYRIA
JORDAN
EGYPT
ISRAEL

Sur / Tyre
Meirun / Merom
Tell el-Qedah / Hazor
Acre
Tell Hum / Capernaum
Sheikh Sa'd
Sea of Galilee
Haifa
Tell Abu Hawam
Khirbet Kerak / Karnaim
'Athlit
Sheikh Abreiq
Nazareth
el-Hammeh
el-Burj / Dor
Wadi el-Murgharah
Caesarea
Tell el-Mutesellim / Megiddo
Jarash / Gerasa
Tell Ta'annek / Taanach
Tell el-Husn / Beth-shan
Sabastiya / Samaria
Tell Deir 'allah / Succoth
Tell el-Qasileh
Balatah / Shechem
Ras el-'Ain / Aphek
Tel Aviv-Jaffa
Seilun / Shiloh
Beitin / Bethel
et-Tell / Ai
Tell es-Sultan / Jericho
Amman / Philadelphia
Tell en-Nasbeh / Mizpah
Tell Jezer / Gezer
Tell el-Ful / Gibeah
Jerusalem
Teleilat el-Ghassul
Tell er-Rumeileh / Beth-shemesh
Khirbet Qumran
Ma'daba
Ascalon
Bethlehem
Tell Sandahannah
Kh. et-Tubeiqah / Beth-zur
Tell el-Hesi / Eglon
Tell ed-Duweir / Lachish
Gaza
Dhiban / Dibon
Tell el-'Ajjul
Tell Beit Mirsim / Debir
Dead Sea
Tell Jemmeh
Tell el-Far'ah / Sharuhen
Tell Abu Matar
Masada
Bab edh Dra'
Ader
Kurnub
Khirbet et-Tannur
Isbeita / Subaita

Mediterranean Sea

© Copyright HAMMOND INCORPORATED

Agriculture, Industry and Resources

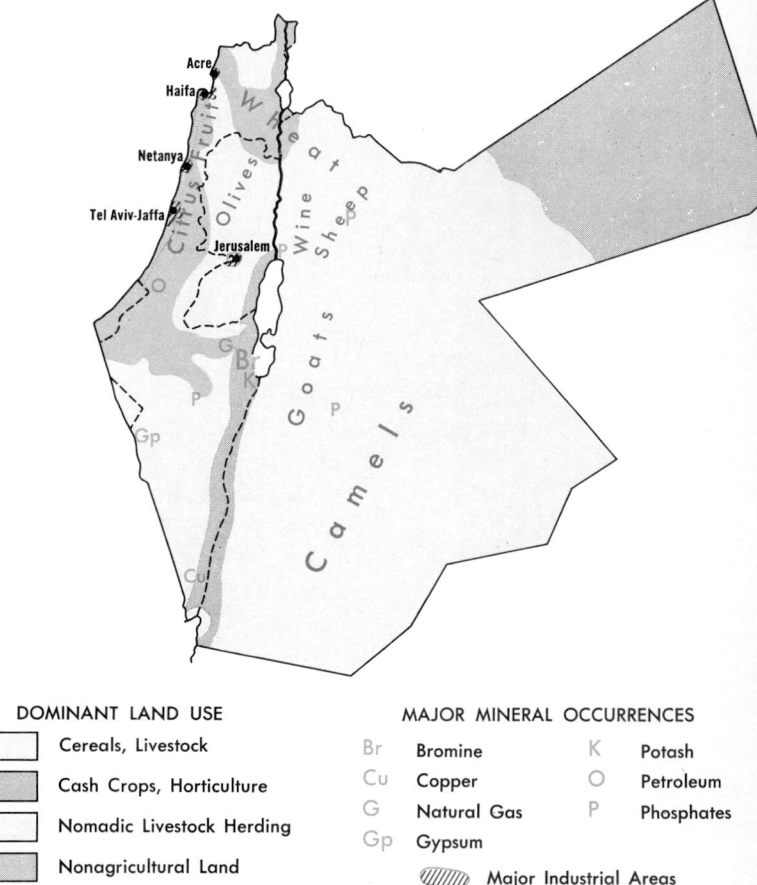

Acre
Haifa
Netanya
Tel Aviv-Jaffa
Jerusalem
Citrus Fruit
Olives
Wheat
Wine
Sheep
Goats
Camels

DOMINANT LAND USE

☐ Cereals, Livestock
▨ Cash Crops, Horticulture
☐ Nomadic Livestock Herding
▨ Nonagricultural Land

MAJOR MINERAL OCCURRENCES

Br   Bromine   K   Potash
Cu   Copper   O   Petroleum
G   Natural Gas   P   Phosphates
Gp   Gypsum

▨▨▨ Major Industrial Areas

ISRAEL

JORDAN

ISRAEL

AREA 7,847 sq. mi. (20,324 sq. km.)
POPULATION 4,625,000
CAPITAL Jerusalem
LARGEST CITY Tel Aviv-Jaffa
HIGHEST POINT Meiran 3,963 ft. (1,208 m.)
MONETARY UNIT shekel
MAJOR LANGUAGES Hebrew, Arabic
MAJOR RELIGIONS Judaism, Islam, Christianity

JORDAN

AREA 35,000 sq. mi. (90,650 sq. km.)
POPULATION 2,779,000
CAPITAL Amman
LARGEST CITY Amman
HIGHEST POINT Jeb. Ramm 5,755 ft. (1,754 m.)
MONETARY UNIT Jordanian dinar
MAJOR LANGUAGE Arabic
MAJOR RELIGION Islam

GAZA STRIP

CITIES and TOWNS

Abasan 1,481 ....A5
Bani Suheila 7,561 ....A5
Beit Hanun 4,756 ....A4
Deir el Balah 10,854 ....A5
Deir el Balah* 18,118 ....A5
Gaza 87,793 ....A5
Gaza* 118,272 ....A5
Jabaliya 10,508 ....A4
Jabaliya* 43,604 ....A4
Khan Yunis 29,522 ....A5
Khan Yunis* 52,997 ....A5
Rafah 10,812 ....A5
Rafah* 49,812 ....A5

WEST BANK

CITIES and TOWNS

Ajja 1,322 ....C3
Anabta 3,426 ....C3
Anin 914 ....C2
Anza 807 ....C3
'Aqqaba 1,127 ....C3
Aqraba 2,501 ....C3
Ariha (Jericho) 5,312 ....C4
'Arraba 4,231 ....C3
Arura 849 ....C3
'Attil 3,808 ....C3
Beit Fajjar 2,474 ....C4
Beit Hanina 1,177 ....C4
Beit Jala 6,041 ....C4
Beit Lahm
  (Bethlehem) 14,439 ....C4
Beit Sahur 5,380 ....C4
Bethlehem 14,439 ....C4
Biddu 1,259 ....C4
Birqin 2,036 ....C3
Bir Zeit 2,311 ....C3
Burqa 2,477 ....C3
Deir Ballut 1,058 ....C3
Deir Sharaf 973 ....C3
Dhahiriya 4,875 ....B5
Dura 4,954 ....C4
El Bira 9,674 ....C4
El Bira* 13,037 ....C4
Er Rihiya 679 ....C5
Ez Zababida 1,474 ....C3
Halhul 6,041 ....C4
Hebron 38,309 ....C4
Idna 3,713 ....B4
Jaba 2,817 ....C3
Jalama 784 ....C3
Jalbun 914 ....C3
Jenin 8,346 ....C3
Jenin* 13,365 ....C3
Jericho 5,312 ....C4
Jericho* 6,931 ....C4
Jifna 655 ....C4
Kharas 1,364 ....C4
Nablus (Nabulus) 41,799 ....C3
Nahhalin 1,109 ....C4
Ni'lin 1,227 ....C4
Qabalan 1,970 ....C3
Qabatiya 6,005 ....C3
Qaffin 2,480 ....C3
Qalqiliya 8,926 ....C3
Qibya 926 ....C4
Rafidiya 1,123 ....C3
Ramallah 12,134 ....C4
Rammun 1,198 ....C4
Rantis 897 ....C3
Salfit 3,201 ....C3
Samu 3,784 ....C5
Shu'fat 14,000 ....C4
Shuweika 2,332 ....C3
Silat Dhahr 2,104 ....C3
Sinjil 1,823 ....C3
Siris 1,285 ....C3
Tammun 2,952 ....C3
Tarqumiya 2,412 ....C4
Tubas 5,262 ....C3
Tulkarm 10,255 ....C3
Tulkarm* 15,275 ....C3
Tur 12,200 ....C4
Ya'bad 4,857 ....C3
Yamun 4,384 ....C3
Yatta 7,281 ....C5

OTHER FEATURES

Ebal (mt.) C3
Golan Heights (reg.) D1
Judaea (reg.) C4
Khirhet Qumran (site) C4
Mashash, Wadi (riv.) C4
Samaria (reg.) C3
Tell 'Asur (mt.) C4
West Bank (reg.) C3

JORDAN

GOVERNORATES

Amman 1,000,000 ....D4
El Balqa 113,000 ....D4
El Karak 93,000 ....E5
Irbid 506,000 ....D3
Ma'an 62,000 ....D5

CITIES and TOWNS

'Ajlun 42,000 ....D3
Amman (cap.) 711,850 ....D4
'Anjara 3,163 ....D3
'Aqaba 15,000 ....D6
Bal'ama 769 ....E3
Baqura 3,042 ....D2
Damiya 483 ....D3
Dana 844 ....E5
Deir Abu Sa'id 1,927 ....D3
El 'Al 492 ....D4
El Husn 3,728 ....D3
El Karak 10,000 ....E4
El Kitta 987 ....D3
El Mafraq 15,500 ....E3
Er Rafid 787 ....D2
Er Ramtha 19,000 ....E2
Er Ruseifa 6,200 ....E4
Es Sahab 2,580 ....E4
Es Salt 24,000 ....D4
Es Sukhna 649 ....E4
Esh Shaubak 4,634 ....D5
Et Tafila 17,000 ....E5
Et Taiyiba 2,606 ....D3
Ez Zarqa' 263,400 ....E3
Harima 635 ....D2
Hawara 2,342 ....D3
Hisban 718 ....D4
'Ibbin 1,364 ....D3
Irbid 136,770 ....D3
Jarash 29,000 ....D3
Kitim 1,026 ....D3
Kufrinja 3,922 ....D3
Ma'ad 125 ....D2
Ma'an 9,500 ....D5
Ma'daba 22,600 ....D4
Ma'in 1,271 ....D4
Mazra' D5
Na'ur 2,382 ....D4
Qumeim 955 ....D2
Ra's en Naqb 225 ....E5
Safi E5
Safut 4,210 ....D3
Samar 716 ....D4
Sarih 3,298 ....D2
Subeihi 514 ....D4
Suweilih 3,457 ....D3
Suweima 315 ....D4
Um Jauza 582 ....D4
Wadi es Sir 4,455 ....D4
Wadi Musa 654 ....E5
Waqqas 2,321 ....D2

OTHER FEATURES

'Ajlun, Jebel (range) D3
Aqaba (gulf) D6
'Araba, Wadi (valley) D5
Dead (sea) D4
Hasa, Wadi el (dry riv.) E5
Jordan (riv.) D3
Nebo (mt.) D4
Petra (ruins) D5
Ramm, Jebel (mt.) D5
Shallala, Wadi esh (dry riv.) D2
Shu'eib, Wadi (dry riv.) D4
Zarqa' (riv.) D3

*City and suburbs
Ⓢ Population of subdivision.

IRAN

INTERNAL DIVISIONS

Azerbaijan, East (prov.)
3,194,543 ....E1
Azerbaijan, West (prov.)
1,404,875 ....D1
Bakhtaran (prov.) 1,016,199...E3
Bakhtaran (governorate)
394,300 ....F4
Bushehr (prov.) 345,427 ....G6
Central (Markazi) (prov.)
6,921,283 ....G3
Esfahan (Isfahan) (prov.)
1,974,938 ....H4
Fars (prov.) 2,020,947.......H6
Gilan (prov.) 1,577,800 ......F2
Hamadan (governorate)
1,086,512 ....F3
Hormozgan (prov.) 463,419...J7
Ilam (governorate) 244,222...E4
Isfahan (prov.) 1,974,938.....H4
Kerman (prov.) 1,088,045.....K6
Khorasan (prov.) 3,266,650...K3
Khuzestan (prov.) 2,176,612...F5
Kohkiluyeh and Boyer
Ahmediyeh (governorate)
244,750 ....G5
Kordestan (Kurdistan) (prov.)
781,889 ....E3

Lorestan (Luristan)
(governorate) 924,848 ......F4
Mazandaran (prov.)
2,384,226 ....H2
Semnan (governorate)
485,875 ....J3
Yazd (governorate) 356,218...J5
Zanjan (governorate) 579,000.F2

CITIES and TOWNS

Abadan 296,081 ....F5
Abadeh 16,000 ....H5
Abhar 24,000 ....F2
Agha Jari 24,195 ....F5
Ahar 24,000 ....E1
Ahvaz (Ahwaz) 329,006....F5
Amol 68,782 ....H2
Andimeshk 16,000 ....F4
Arak 114,507 ....F3
Ardabil 147,404 ....F1
Asterabad (Gorgan) 88,348...J2
Babol 67,790 ....H2
Bakhtaran (Kermanshah)
290,861 ....E3
Bam 22,000 ....L6
Bandar 'Abbas 89,103 .....J7
Bandar Behesti (Bahar)
1,800 ....M8

Bandar-e Anzali (Enzeli)
55,978 ....F2
Bandar-e Bushehr (Bushire)
57,681 ....G6
Bandar-e Khomeyni 6,000...F5
Bandar-e Lingeh 4,920 ....J7
Bandar-e Ma'shur 17,000...F5
Bandar-e Torkeman 13,000...H2
Behbehan 39,874 ....G5
Behshahr 26,032 ....H2
Birjand 25,854 ....L4
Bojnurd 31,248 ....K2
Borazjan 20,000 ....G6
Borujerd 100,103 ....F4
Bostan 4,619 ....F5
Chalus 15,000 ....G2
Damghan 13,000 ....J2
Dasht-e Azadegan
(Susangerd) 21,000 ......F5
Dizful (Dezful) 110,287...F4
Duzdab (Zahedan) 92,628...M6
Emamshahr (Shahrud)
30,767 ....J2
Enzeli 55,978 ....F2
Esfahan (Isfahan) 671,825...G4
Eslamabad 12,000 ....E3
Estahbanat 18,187 ....J6
Fahraj (Iranshahr) 5,000...M7
Fasa 19,000 ....H6
Ganaveh 9,000 ....G6
Garmsar 4,723 ....H3

Ghaemshahr 63,289 ....H2
Golpayegan 20,515 ....G4
Golshan (Tabas) 10,000...K4
Gonbad-e Kavus 59,868....J2
Gorgan (Gurgan) 88,348...J2
Hamadan 155,846 ....F3
Hormoz 2,569 ....J7
Iranshahr 16,000 ....M7
Isfahan 671,825 ....G4
Jahrom 38,236 ....H6
Karaj 138,774 ....G3
Kashan 84,545 ....G3
Kashmar 17,000 ....L3
Kazerun 51,309 ....H6
Kazvin (Qazvin) 138,527...F2
Kerman 140,309 ....K5
Khomeinishahr 46,836 ....G4
Khorramabad 104,928 .....F4
Khorramshahr 146,709 ....F5
Khvoy (Khoi) 70,040......D1
Lahijan 25,725 ....G2
Lar 22,000 ....J7
Mahabad 28,610 ....D1
Malayer 28,434 ....F3
Maragheh 60,820 ....E2
Marand 24,000 ....D1
Marv Dasht 25,498 ....H6
Masjed Soleyman 77,161...F5
Mashhad (Meshed) 670,180...L2
Miandowab 19,000 ....E2
Mianeh 28,447 ....E2

Nahavand 24,000 ....F3
Nasrabad (Zabol) 20,000...M5
Neyriz 16,114 ....H6
Nishapur (Neyshabur) 59,101.L2
Nosratabad 20,000 ....L6
Orumiyeh (Urmia) 163,991...D2
Pahlevi (Enzeli) 55,978...F2
Qayen 6,000 ....L4
Qazvin 138,527 ....F2
Quchan 29,133 ....L2
Qum (Qom) 246,831 ......G3
Rafsanjan 21,000 ....K5
Resht (Rasht) 187,203....F2
Reza'iyeh (Urmia) D2
Sa'idabad 20,000 ....J6
Sakht-Sar 12,000 ....G2
Salmas 13,161 ....D1
Sanandaj 95,834 ....E3
Saqqez 17,000 ....E2
Sari 70,936 ....H2
Savanat (Estabanat) 18,187...J6
Saveh 17,565 ....G3
Semnan 31,058 ....H3
Shahr Kord 24,000 ....G4
Shahreza 34,220 ....H4
Shahrud 30,767 ....J2
Shiraz 416,408 ....H6
Shushtar 24,000 ....F4

Sinneh (Sanandaj) 95,834...E3
Sirjan (Sai'dabad) 20,000...J6
Sultanabad (Kashmar)
17,000 ....L3
Susangerd 21,000 ....L3
Tabas 10,000 ....K4
Tabriz 598,576 ....D2
Tajrish 157,486 ....G3
Tehran (cap.) 4,496,159...G3
Torbat-e Heydariyeh 30,106...L3
Urmia 163,991 ....D2
Yazd (Yezd) 135,978 .....J5
Zabol 20,000 ....M5
Zahedan 92,628 ....M6
Zenjan (Zanjan) 99,967...F2

OTHER FEATURES

'Arabi (isl.) G7
Araks (Aras) (riv.) E1
Atrak (Atrek) (riv.) J2
Azerbaijan (reg.) D1
Bakhtegan (lake) J6
Baluchistan (reg.) M7
Bampur (riv.) M7
Behistun (ruins) E3
Caspian Sea (sea) G1
Damavand (Demavend)
(mt.) H2
Daryacheh-ye Namak
(salt lake) G3

Daryacheh-ye Sistan
(salt lake) M5
Dasht-e Kavir (salt des.)...J3
Dasht-e Lut (des.) L5
Dez (riv.) F4
Elburz (mts.) H2
Farsi (isl.) G7
Gabrik (riv.) M8
Gamas Ab (riv.) E3
Gavkhuni (marsh) H4
Gorgan (riv.) J2
Hamadan (reg.) F3
Hamun-e Saberi (lake) M3
Harirud (riv.) M3
Hormoz (isl.) J7
Hormuz (str.) J7
Jaba Kuh (mts.) E4
Joveyn (riv.) L2
Kabir Kuh (mts.) E4
Karkheh (riv.) F4
Karun (riv.) F5
Khark (Kharg) (isl.)......G6
Khusf Rud (riv.) L4
Khvojeh Lak, Kuh-e (mt.)...E3
Kor (riv.) H6
Laristan (reg.) J7
Makran (reg.) M8
Mand (riv.) H6
Mand (riv.) G6
Mashkid (riv.) N7
Mehran (riv.) N7
Nahang (riv.) N7

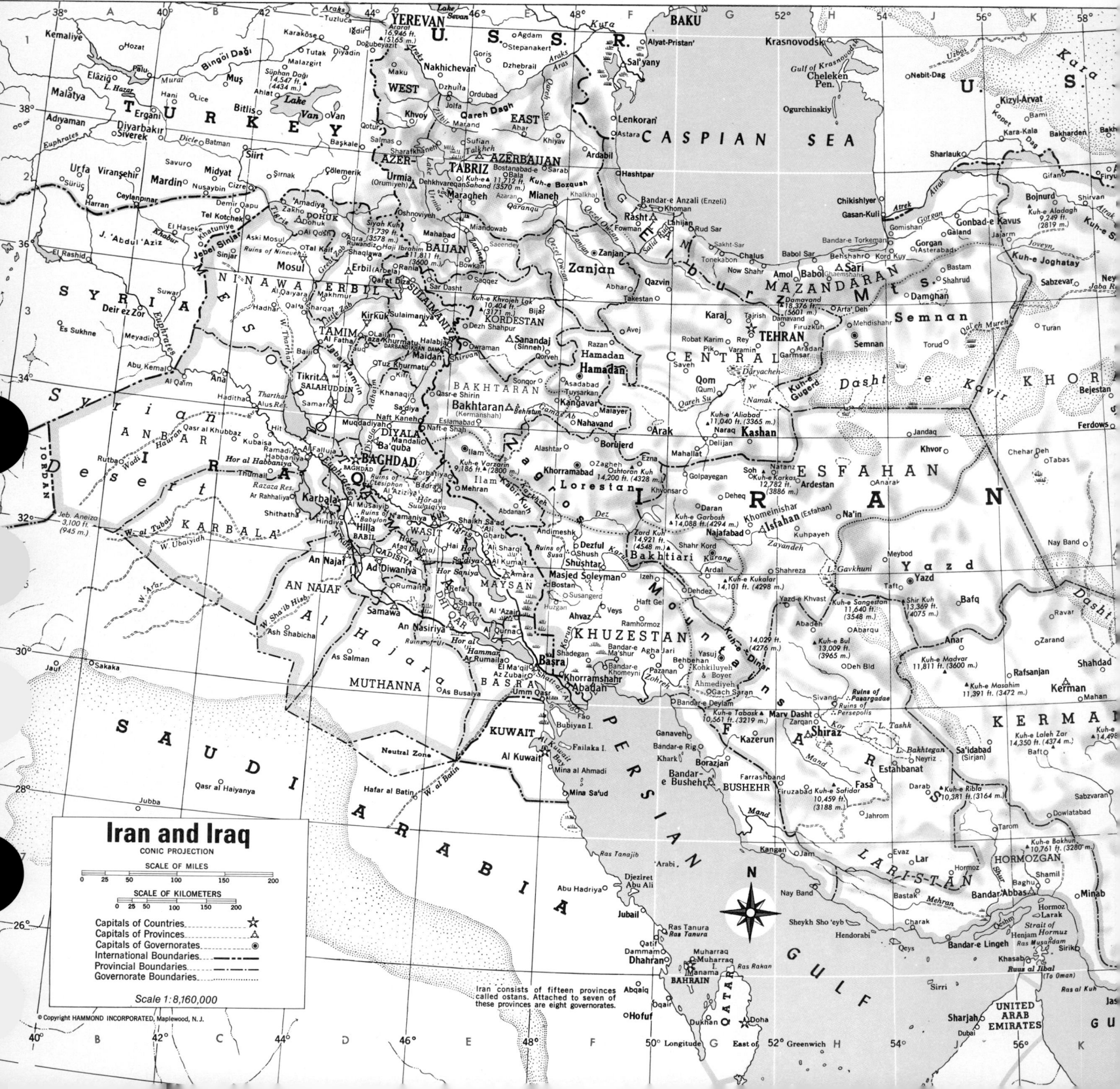

Iran and Iraq

CONIC PROJECTION

SCALE OF MILES
0 25 50   100   150   200

SCALE OF KILOMETERS
0 25 50   100   150   200

Capitals of Countries ....☆
Capitals of Provinces ....△
Capitals of Governorates ....◉
International Boundaries ....
Provincial Boundaries ....
Governorate Boundaries ....

Scale 1:8,160,000

© Copyright HAMMOND INCORPORATED, Maplewood, N.J.

Iran consists of fifteen provinces
called ostans. Attached to seven of
these provinces are eight governorates.

Namaksar (lake) M4
Namakzar-e Shahdad
  (salt lake) L5
Oman (gulf) M8
Pasargadae (ruins) H5
Persepolis (ruins) H6
Persian (gulf) F6
Qaranqu (riv.) E2
Qareh Dagh (mts.) E1
Qareh Su (riv.) E1
Qeshm (isl.) J7
Qezel Owzam (riv.) F2
Ras al Kuh (cape) K8
Ras-e Meydani (cape) L8
Safid Rud (riv.) F2
Seistan (reg.) M5
Shatt-al-'Arab (riv.) F5
Shelagh (riv.) M5
Shirvan (riv.) E3
Shur (riv.) J7
Sirri (isl.) J8
Susa (ruins) F4
Talab (riv.) N6
Talkheh (riv.) E1
Tashk (lake) J6
Urmia (lake) D2
Zagros (mts.) E4
Zarineh (riv.) E2
Zayandeh (riv.) H4
Zilbir (riv.) D1
Zohreh (riv.) F5

IRAQ

GOVERNORATES

Anbar 535,627 ....B4
An Najaf 438,971 ....C5
Babil 680,700 ....D4
Baghdad 4,038,430 ....D4
Basra 1,184,500 ....E5
Dhi Qar 683,537 ....E5
Diyala 650,211 ....D4
Dohuk 296,339 ....C2
Erbil 657,294 ....C3
Karbala' 305,627 ....B4
Maysan 395,666 ....E5
Muthanna 239,044 ....D5
Ninawa 1,258,001 ....B3
Qadisiya 475,676 ....D4
Salahuddin 411,734 ....C3
Sulaimaniya 816,406 ....D3
Tamin 587,079 ....C3
Wasit 455,853 ....D4

CITIES and TOWNS

Ad Diwaniya 60,553 ....D5
'Afaq 5,390 ....D4
Al 'Aziziya 7,450 ....D4
Al Falluja 38,072 ....C4
Al Fatha† 15,329 ....C3
'Ali Gharbi 15,456 ....E4

'Ali Sharqi 8,398 ....E4
Al Kufa 30,862 ....D4
Al Musaiyib 15,955 ....D4
'Amara 64,847 ....E5
'Ana 15,729 ....B3
An Najaf 128,096 ....D5
An Nasiriya 60,405 ....D5
Arbela (Erbil) 90,320 ....D2
Ar Rumaila 1,439 ....E5
'Aqra 8,659 ....D2
Az Zubair 41,408 ....E5
Baghdad (cap.) 502,503 ....D4
Ba'quba 34,575 ....D4
Basra 313,327 ....E5
Dohuk 16,998 ....C2
Erbil 90,320 ....D2
Fao 15,399 ....F6
Habbaniya 14,405 ....C4
Hai 16,988 ....E4
Halabja 11,206 ....D3
Hilla 84,717 ....D4
Hindiya 16,436 ....C4
Hit 9,131 ....C4
Karbal'a 83,301 ....C4
Khanaqin 23,522 ....D3
Kifri 8,500 ....D3
Kirkuk 167,413 ....D3
Kut 42,116 ....D4
Mandali 11,262 ....D4
Mosul 315,157 ....C2
Muqdadiyah 12,181 ....D4
N'amaniya 11,943 ....D4
Qal'at Diza 6,250 ....D2
Ramadi 28,723 ....C4
Rumaitha 10,222 ....D5
Samarra 24,746 ....C3
Samawa 33,473 ....D5
Shatra 18,822 ....E5
Sinjar 7,942 ....B2
Sulaimaniya 86,822 ....D3
Tal Kaif 7,482 ....C2
Taza Khurmatu 2,681 ....D3
Tikrit 9,921 ....C3
Tuz Khurmatu 13,860 ....D3
Zakho 14,790 ....C2

OTHER FEATURES

Adhaim (riv.) D3
Al Hajara (plain) D5
'Aneiza, Jebel (mt.) A4
'Ar'ar, Wadi (dry riv.) B5
Babylon (ruins) D4
Batin, Wadi al (dry riv.) E6
Ctesiphon (ruins) D4
Dalmaj, Hor (lake) D4
Darbandikhan (dam) D3
Diyala (riv.) D4
Euphrates (riv.) D4
Great Zab (riv.) C2
Habbaniya, Hor al (lake) C4
Haji Ibrahim (mt.) D2
Hammar, Hor al (lake) E5
Hamrin, Jabal (mts.) D3
Hauran, Wadi (dry riv.) B4
Little Zab (riv.) C3
Mesopotamia (reg.) B3
Nineveh (ruins) C2
Razaza (res.) C4
Sa'diya, Hor (lake) E4
Saniya, Hor (lake) D4
Sha'ib Hisb, Wadi (dry riv.) .C5
Shatt-al-'Arab (riv.) F5
Sinjar, Jebel (mts.) B2
Siyah Kuh (mt.) D2
Suwaiqiya, Hor as (lake) ...D4
Tharthar (res.) C3
Tharthar, Wadi (dry riv.) C3
Tigris (riv.) E4
Tubal, Wadi al (dry riv.) B4
Ubaiyidh, Wadi (dry riv.) ...B5
Ur (ruins) E5

† Population of commune.

IRAN

IRAQ

AREA   636,293 sq. mi. (1,648,000 sq. km.)
POPULATION   55,208,000
CAPITAL   Tehran
LARGEST CITY   Tehran
HIGHEST POINT   Damavand 18,376 ft. (5,601 m.)
MONETARY UNIT   Iranian rial
MAJOR LANGUAGES   Persian, Azerbaijani, Kurdish
MAJOR RELIGION   Islam

AREA   172,476 sq. mi. (446,713 sq. km.)
POPULATION   16,335,000
CAPITAL   Baghdad
LARGEST CITY   Baghdad
HIGHEST POINT   Haji Ibrahim 11,811 ft.
  (3.600 m.)
MONETARY UNIT   Iraqi dinar
MAJOR LANGUAGES   Arabic, Kurdish
MAJOR RELIGION   Islam

Topography

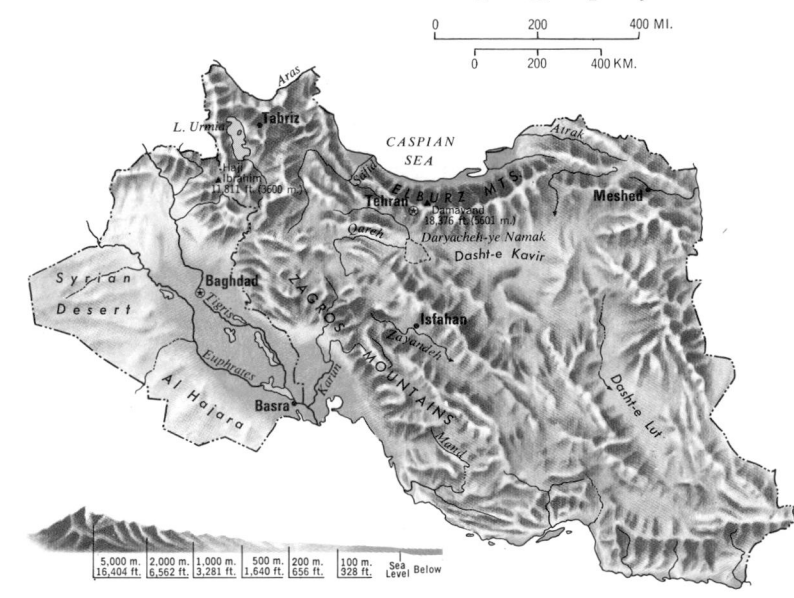

Agriculture, Industry and Resources

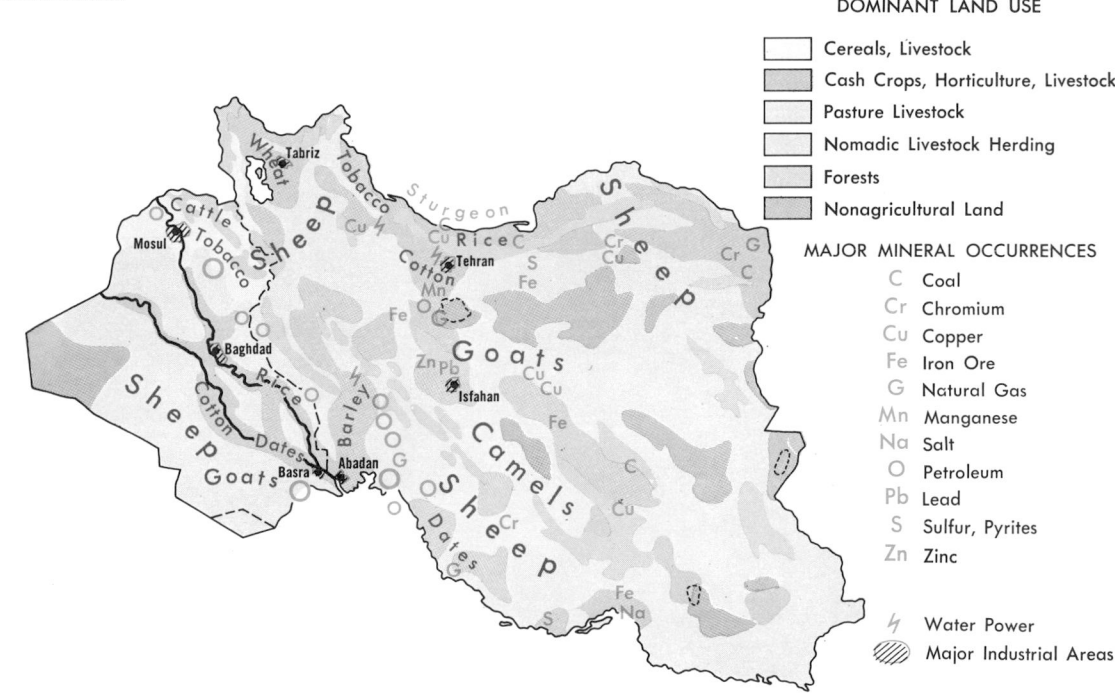

DOMINANT LAND USE

Cereals, Livestock
Cash Crops, Horticulture, Livestock
Pasture Livestock
Nomadic Livestock Herding
Forests
Nonagricultural Land

MAJOR MINERAL OCCURRENCES

C   Coal
Cr   Chromium
Cu   Copper
Fe   Iron Ore
G   Natural Gas
Mn   Manganese
Na   Salt
O   Petroleum
Pb   Lead
S   Sulfur, Pyrites
Zn   Zinc

⚡ Water Power
      Major Industrial Areas

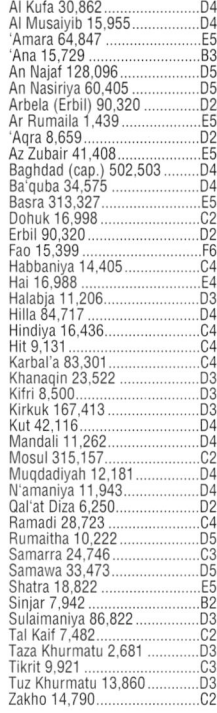

Indian Subcontinent and Afghanistan

CONIC PROJECTION

SCALE OF MILES

KILOMETERS

Capitals of Countries .... ☆
Provincial and State Capitals .... ◉
International Boundaries .... — ·· — ··
Provincial and State Boundaries — · — ·
Canals ....

Scale 1:14,500,000

© Copyright HAMMOND INCORPORATED, Maplewood, N.J.

BOMBAY

CALCUTTA

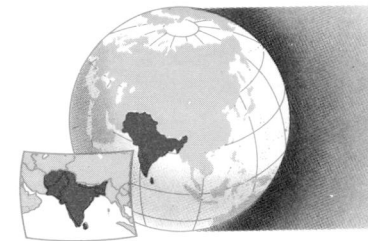

INDIA

AREA 1,269,339 sq. mi. (3,287,588 sq. km.)
POPULATION 843,130,861
CAPITAL New Delhi
LARGEST CITY Calcutta (greater)
HIGHEST POINT Nanda Devi 25,645 ft. (7,817 m.)
MONETARY UNIT Indian rupee
MAJOR LANGUAGES Hindi, English, Bengali,
Telugu, Marathi, Tamil, Urdu, Gujarati,
Malayalam, Kannada, Oriya, Punjabi,
Assamese, Kashmiri, Sindhi
MAJOR RELIGIONS Hinduism, Islam, Christianity,
Sikhism, Buddhism, Jainism, Zoroastrianism, Animism

PAKISTAN

AREA 310,403 sq. mi. (803,944 sq. km.)
POPULATION 112,050,000
CAPITAL Islamabad
LARGEST CITY Karachi
HIGHEST POINT K2 (Godwin Austen)
28,250 ft. (8,611 m.)
MONETARY UNIT Pakistani rupee
MAJOR LANGUAGES Urdu, English, Punjabi,
Pushtu, Sindhi, Baluchi, Brahui
MAJOR RELIGIONS Islam, Hinduism, Sikhism,
Christianity, Buddhism

SRI LANKA (CEYLON)

AREA 25,332 sq. mi.
(65,610 sq. km.)
POPULATION 16,806,000
CAPITAL Colombo
LARGEST CITY Colombo
HIGHEST POINT Pidurutalagala
8,281 ft. (2,524 m.)
MONETARY UNIT Sri Lanka rupee
MAJOR LANGUAGES Sinhala, Tamil,
English
MAJOR RELIGIONS Buddhism,
Hinduism, Christianity, Islam

AFGHANISTAN

AREA 250,775 sq. mi.
(649,507 sq. km.)
POPULATION 15,814,000
CAPITAL Kabul
LARGEST CITY Kabul
HIGHEST POINT Nowshak
24,557 ft. (7,485 m.)
MONETARY UNIT afghani
MAJOR LANGUAGES Pushtu, Dari,
Uzbek
MAJOR RELIGION Islam

NEPAL

AREA 54,663 sq. mi.
(141,577 sq. km.)
POPULATION 18,442,000
CAPITAL Kathmandu
LARGEST CITY Kathmandu
HIGHEST POINT Mt. Everest
29,028 ft. (8,848 m.)
MONETARY UNIT Nepalese rupee
MAJOR LANGUAGES Nepali,
Maithili, Tamang, Newari, Tharu
MAJOR RELIGIONS Hinduism,
Buddhism

MALDIVES

AREA 115 sq. mi. (298 sq. km.)
POPULATION 206,000
CAPITAL Male
LARGEST CITY Male
HIGHEST POINT 20 ft. (6 m.)
MONETARY UNIT Maldivian rufiyaa
MAJOR LANGUAGE Divehi
MAJOR RELIGION Islam

BHUTAN

AREA 18,147 sq. mi.
(47,000 sq. km.)
POPULATION 1,483,000
CAPITAL Thimphu
LARGEST CITY Thimphu
HIGHEST POINT Kula Kangri
24,784 ft. (7,554 m.)
MONETARY UNIT ngultrum
MAJOR LANGUAGES Dzongka,
Nepali
MAJOR RELIGIONS Buddhism,
Hinduism

BANGLADESH

AREA 55,126 sq. mi.
(142,776 sq. km.)
POPULATION 106,507,000
CAPITAL Dhaka
LARGEST CITY Dhaka
HIGHEST POINT Keokradong
4,034 ft. (1,230 m.)
MONETARY UNIT taka
MAJOR LANGUAGES Bengali,
English
MAJOR RELIGIONS Islam,
Hinduism Christianity

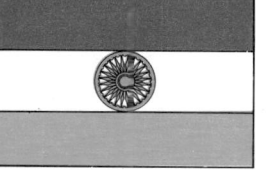

INDIA

PAKISTAN

SRI LANKA (CEYLON)

BHUTAN

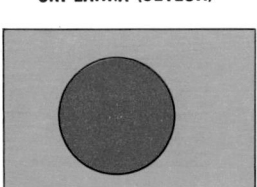

AFGHANISTAN

MALDIVES

BANGLADESH

NEPAL

AFGHANISTAN

CITIES and TOWNS

Andkhvoy 13,137 .... A1
Aybak 33,016 .... B1
Baghlan 75,130 .... B1
Bamian 7,355 .... B2
Chaghcharan 2,974 .... B2
Charikar 25,093 .... B1
Farah 18,797 .... A2
Feyzabad 10,142 .... C1
Gardez 11,415 .... B2
Gereshk A2
Ghazni 30,425 .... B2
Ghurian 12,404 .... A2
Hazar Qadam B2
Herat 163,960 .... A2
Jalalabad 56,384 .... B2
Kabul (cap.) 905,108 .... B2
Kalat (Qalat) 5,946 .... B2
Kandahar (Qandahar)
178,409 .... B2
Khanabad 26,803 .... B1
Khash A2
Kholm 28,078 .... B1
Khowst B2
Konduz 107,191 .... B1
Kuhestan A2
Lashkar Gah 26,646 .... A2
Mazar-e Sharif 122,56" B1
Meymaneh 54,954 .... A1
Mirabad A2
Oruzgan (Hazar Qadam) B2
Panjab B2
Pol-e Khomri 31,101 .... B2
Qalat 5,946 .... B2
Qal'eh-ye Now 5,340 .... A1
Qandahar 178,409 .... B2
Qonduz (Konduz) 107,191 .... B1
Sakhar B2
Sar-e Pol 15,699 .... B1
Sheberghan 54,870 .... B1
Shindand A2
Tagab B2
Taloqan 46,202 .... B1
Zaranj 6,477 .... A2

OTHER FEATURES

Baroghil (pass) C1
Chagai (hills) A3
Margow, Dasht-e (des.) A2
Farah Rud (riv.) A2
Gowd-e Zereh (depr.) A3
Harirud (riv.) A1
Helmand (riv.) B2
Hindu Kush (mts.) B1
Kabul (riv.) C2
Konar (riv.) C1
Konduz (riv.) B1
Lurah (riv.) B2
Namaksar (salt lake) A2
Nuristan (reg.) C1

Panj (riv.) C1
Paropamisus (range) A2
Qonduz (Konduz) (riv.) B1
Registan (reg.) A2
Tarnak (riv.) B2

BANGLADESH

CITIES and TOWNS

Barisal 159,298 .... G4
Bogra 68,237 .... F4
Chalna Port 14,590 .... F4
Chittagong 1,388,476 .... G4
Comilla 126,130 .... G4
Cox's Bazar G4
Dhaka (cap.) 3,458,602 .... G4
Dinajpur 96,348 .... F3
Faridpur 66,911 .... F4
Habiganj 16,281 .... G4
Jamalpur 89,847 .... F4
Jessore 149,426 .... F4
Khulna 623,184 .... F4
Kishorganj 52,081 .... G4
Madaripur 58,645 .... G4
Maheshkhali 29,530 .... G4
Mymensingh (Nasirabad)
107,863 .... G4
Narayanganj 196,139 .... G4
Nasirabad 107,863 .... G4
Nawabganj 65,286 .... F4
Noakhali 32,490 .... G4
Pabna 101,080 .... F4
Rajshahi 171,600 .... F4
Rangamati 36,490 .... G4
Rangpur 72,829 .... F3
Sirajganj 74,457 .... F4
Sylhet 59,546 .... G4

OTHER FEATURES

Bengal, Bay of (bay) F5
Brahmaputra (riv.) G3
Ganges (riv.) F3
Ganges, Mouths of the (delta) .F3
Mowdok Mual (mt.) G4
Sundarbans (reg.) F4

BHUTAN

CITIES and TOWNS

Bumthang 10,000 .... G3
Paro 35,000 .... F3
Punakha 12,000 .... G3
Taga Dzong 18,000 .... G3
Thimphu (cap.) 50,000 .... G3
Tongsa Dzong 2,500 .... G3

OTHER FEATURES

Chomo Lhari (mt.) F3
Himalaya (mts.) E2
Kula Kangri (mt.) G3

(continued on following page)

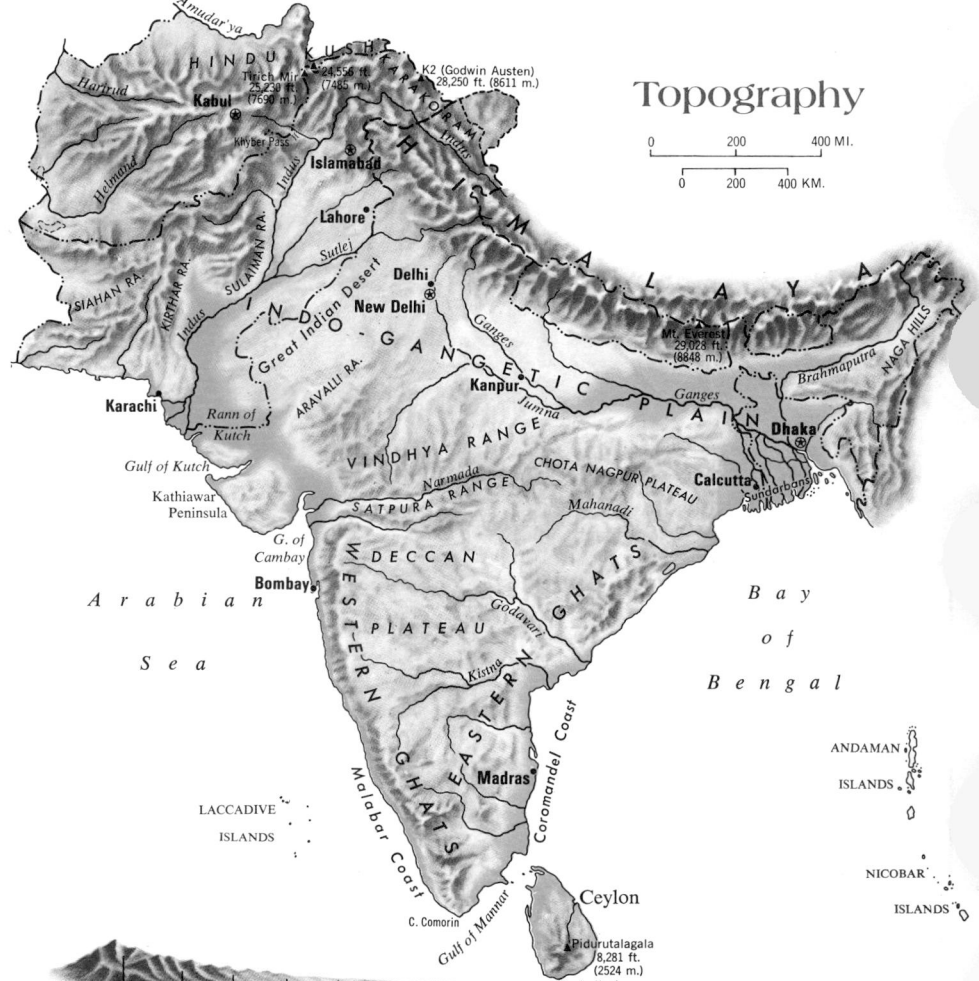

Topography

| 0 | 200 | 400 MI. |
| 0 | 200 | 400 KM. |

5,000 m. / 16,404 ft. — 2,000 m. / 6,562 ft. — 1,000 m. / 3,281 ft. — 500 m. / 1,640 ft. — 200 m. / 656 ft. — 100 m. / 328 ft. — Sea Level — Below

INDIA

INTERNAL DIVISIONS

Andaman and Nicobar Isls. (terr.) 188,741...........G6
Andhra Pradesh (state) 53,549,673...........D5
Arunachal Pradesh (state) 631,839...........G3
Assam (state) 19,902,826...........G3
Bihar (state) 69,914,734...........F4
Chandigarh (terr.) 451,610...........D2
Dādra and Nagar Haveli (terr.) 103,676...........C4
Daman and Diu (state)...........C4
Delhi (terr.) 6,220,406...........D3
Goa (state)...........C4
Gujarat (state) 34,085,799...........C4
Haryana (state) 12,922,618...........D3
Himachal Pradesh (state) 4,280,818...........D2
Jammu and Kashmir (state) 5,987,389...........D2
Karnataka (state) 37,135,714...........D6
Kerala (state) 25,453,680...........D6
Lakshadweep (terr.) 40,249...........C6
Madhya Pradesh (state) 52,178,844...........D4
Mahārāshtra (state) 62,784,171...........C5
Manipur (state) 1,420,953...........G4
Meghalaya (state) 1,335,819...........G3
Mizoram (state) 493,757...........G4
Nagaland (state) 774,930...........G3
Orissa (state) 26,370,271...........E5
Pondicherry (terr.) 604,471...........E6
Punjab (state) 16,788,915...........D2
Rajasthan (state) 34,261,862...........C3
Sikkim (state) 316,385...........F3
Tamil Nadu (state) 48,408,077...........D6
Tripura (state) 2,053,058...........G4
Uttar Pradesh (state) 110,862,013...........D3
West Bengal (state) 54,580,647...........F4

CITIES and TOWNS

Abu 9,840...........C4
Achalpur 42,326...........D4
Adoni 108,905...........D5
Agartala 131,513...........G4
Agra 770,352...........D3
Ahmadabad 2,515,195...........C4
Ahmadnagar 181,239...........C5
Ajmer 374,350...........C3
Akola 225,402...........D4
Alibag 11,913...........C5
Aligarh 319,981...........D3
Allahabad 642,420...........E3
Alleppey-Cochin 160,166...........D7
Almora 19,671...........D3
Alwar 139,973...........C3
Amalner 55,544...........C4
Ambala 121,135...........D2
Ambikapur 23,087...........E4
Amravati 261,387...........D4
Amreli 39,520...........C4
Amritsar 589,229...........C2
Anakapalle 57,273...........D6
Anantapur 119,536...........D6
Arrah 124,614...........E3
Aruppukkottai 62,223...........D7
Asansol 366,371...........F4
Azamgarh 40,963...........E3
Badagara 53,938...........D6
Bagalkot 51,746...........D5
Bahraich 102,580...........E3
Baidyabati 54,130...........F1
Balasore 46,239...........F4
Ballia 47,101...........E3
Balurghat 67,088...........F3
Banda 50,575...........D3
Bandar (Machilipatnam) 138,525...........E5
Bandra...........B7
Bangalore 4,100,000...........D6
Bankura 79,129...........F4
Bansberia 61,748...........F1
Baranagar 136,842...........F1
Barasat 42,642...........F1
Bareilly 437,801...........D3
Barmer 38,630...........C3
Baroda (Vadodara) 744,043...........C4
Barrackpore 96,889...........F1
Barsi 62,374...........D5
Barwani 22,099...........D4
Basirhat 63,816...........F4
Batala 100,790...........D2
Beawar 66,114...........C3
Belgaum 300,290...........C5
Bellary 201,014...........D5
Benares (Varanasi) 793,542...........E3
Berhampore 100,150...........F4
Berhampur 162,407...........F5
Bettiah 51,018...........E3
Bhadrak 40,487...........F4
Bhadravati 130,459...........D6
Bhadreswar 45,586...........F1
Bhagalpur 221,276...........F3
Bhandara 39,423...........E4
Bharatpur 105,239...........D3
Bharuch 91,589...........C4
Bhatinda 127,450...........C2
Bhatpara 204,750...........F1
Bhavnagar 308,194...........C4
Bhawanipatna 22,808...........E5
Bhilainagar 157,173...........E4
Bhilwara 122,338...........C3
Bhimavaram 101,940...........E5
Bhind 42,371...........D3
Bhir (Bir) 49,965...........D5
Bhiwandi 115,256...........C5
Bhiwani 101,263...........D3
Bhopal 672,329...........D4
Bhubaneswar 219,419...........F4
Bhuj 102,177...........B4
Bhusawal 132,142...........D4
Bidar 50,670...........D5
Bihar 151,308...........F3
Bijapur 146,808...........D5
Bijnor 43,290...........D3
Bikaner 280,356...........C3
Bilaspur 186,885...........E4
Bir 49,965...........D5
Bodhan 37,589...........D5
Bodinayakkanur 54,176...........D6
Bolangir 35,748...........E4
Bombay (Greater)* 8,227,332...........B7
Broach (Bharuch) 91,589...........C4
Budaun 72,204...........D3
Budge-Budge 51,039...........F2
Bundi 34,279...........D3
Burdwan 143,318...........F4
Burhanpur 141,142...........D4
Calcutta 10,860,000...........F2
Calicut (Kozhikode) 333,979...........D6
Cambay 62,097...........C4
Cannanore 157,777...........C6
Cawnpore (Kanpur) 1,688,242...........E3
Chaibasa 35,386...........F4
Chamba 11,814...........D2
Champdani 58,596...........F1
Chanderi 10,294...........D4
Chandernagore 75,238...........F1
Chandrapur 115,352...........D5
Chandigarh 421,256...........D2
Chapra 111,461...........E3
Chhatarpur 32,271...........D4
Chhindwara 53,492...........D4
Chidambaram 48,811...........E6
Chikmagalur 41,639...........D6
Chinglept 38,419...........E6
Chirala 54,487...........E5
Chitradurga 50,254...........D6
Chittoor 63,035...........D6
Churachandpur 8,706...........G4
Churu 52,502...........C3
Cocanada (Kakinada) 226,642...........E5
Cochin-Alleppey 439,066...........D6
Coimbatore 917,155...........D6
Colachel 18,819...........D7
Cooch Behar 53,684...........F3
Cuddalore 127,569...........E6
Cuddapah 103,146...........D6
Cuttack 326,468...........F4
Dabhoi 37,892...........C4
Damoh 59,489...........D4
Darbhanga 175,879...........F3
Darjeeling 42,873...........F3
Datia 36,439...........D3
Davangere 196,481...........D6
Dehra Dun 293,628...........D2
Delhi 8,380,000...........D3
Deoghar 40,356...........F4
Deolali 55,436...........C5
Deoria 38,161...........E3
Dewas 51,545...........D4
Dhanbad 676,736...........F4
Dhar 36,172...........D4
Dharmsala 10,939...........D2
Dharwar-Hubli 379,166...........C5
Dhoraji 59,773...........C4
Dhubri 36,503...........G3
Dhulia 210,927...........C4
Dibrugarh 80,348...........G3
Dindigul 170,196...........D6
Diphu 10,200...........G3
Diu 6,214...........C4
Dungarpur 19,773...........C4
Durg 67,892...........E4
Durg-Bhilainagar 490,158...........E4
Durgapur 305,838...........F4
Dwarka 17,801...........B4
Eluru 168,148...........E5
English Bazar 61,335...........F3
Erode 275,103...........D6
Etawah 112,426...........D3
Faizabad-cum-Ayodhya 102,835...........E3
Faridabad 326,968...........D3
Farrukhabad-cum-Fatehgarh 160,927...........D3
Firozabad 202,837...........D3
Firozpur 49,545...........C2
Gadag 116,596...........D5
Ganganagar 121,516...........C3
Gangtok 12,000...........F3
Garden Reach 154,913...........F1
Garulia 44,271...........F1
Gauhati 123,783...........G3
Gaya 246,778...........F4
Ghaziabad 291,995...........D3
Ghazipur 45,635...........E3
Godhra 66,403...........C4
Gonda 52,662...........E3
Gondal 54,928...........C4
Gondia 100,342...........E4
Gorakhpur 306,399...........E3
Gulbarga 218,621...........D5
Guna 40,000...........D4
Guntakal 66,320...........D5
Guntur 367,219...........E5
Gwalior 38,472...........D3
Haflong 5,197...........G3
Hanumangarh 30,017...........C3
Hardoi 46,639...........E3
Hardwar 146,186...........D2
Hassan 51,325...........D6
Hathras 74,349...........D3
Hazaribagh 54,818...........F4
Hindupur 42,959...........D6
Hinganghat 44,349...........D4
Hissar 137,254...........D3
Honavar 12,444...........C5
Hooghly-Chinsura 105,241...........F1
Hospet 114,711...........D5
Howrah 737,877...........F2
Hubli-Dharwar 526,493...........C5
Hyderabad 4,270,000...........D5
Ichchapuram 15,850...........F5
Imphal 155,639...........G4
Indore 827,021...........D4
Itanagar▲ 18,787...........G3
Itarsi 44,191...........D4
Jabalpur 757,726...........D4
Jaipur 1,004,669...........D3
Jaisalmer 16,578...........C3
Jajpur 16,707...........F4
Jalgaon 145,254...........D4
Jalna 122,246...........D4
Jalor 15,478...........C3
Jalpaiguri 55,159...........F3
Jamalpur 61,731...........F3
Jammu 155,338...........D2
Jamnagar 317,037...........B4
Jamshedpur 669,984...........F4
Jaora 37,235...........D4
Jaunpur 104,994...........E3
Jhansi 231,332...........D3
Jind 38,161...........D3
Jodhpur 493,604...........C3
Jubbulpore (Jabalpur) 757,726...........D4
Jullundur 296,106...........D2
Junagadh 120,072...........B4
Kadayanallur 50,295...........D7
Kakinada 226,642...........E5
Kalyan 99,547...........C5
Kamarhati 169,404...........F1
Kamptee 51,843...........D4
Kanchipuram 145,329...........E6
Kanchrapara 78,768...........F1
Kandla 17,995...........C4
Kanker 9,278...........E4
Kanpur 1,688,242...........E3
Karad 42,329...........C5
Karaikudi 100,187...........D7
Kargil 2,390...........D2
Karnal 132,067...........D3
Kasganj 46,467...........D3
Katni (Murwara) 125,096...........E4
Katihar 121,693...........F3
Kavaratti 4,420...........C6
Kendrapara 20,079...........F4
Khamgaon 53,692...........D4
Khamman 56,919...........D5
Khandwa 114,463...........D4
Kharagpur 234,931...........F4
Kirkee 65,497...........C5
Kishangarh 37,405...........C3
Kishtwar 5,276...........D2
Kohima 21,545...........G3
Kolar 43,418...........D6
Kolar Gold Fields 144,406...........D6
Kolhapur 351,073...........C5
Koraput 21,505...........E5
Korba 30,963...........E4
Kota 346,928...........D3
Kottaguden 75,542...........E5
Kottayam 59,714...........D7
Kozhikode 333,979...........D6
Krishnanagar 85,923...........F4
Kumbakonam 141,639...........D6
Kumta 19,112...........C6
Kurnool 206,661...........D5
Latur 111,961...........D5
Leh 5,519...........D2
Lucknow 1,006,538...........E3
Ludhiana 606,250...........D2
Machilipatnam 138,525...........E5
Madras 5,360,000...........E6
Madugula 8,376...........E5
Madurai 904,362...........D7
Mahabaleshwar 7,318...........C5
Mahbubnagar 51,756...........D5
Mahe 8,972...........D6
Mahuva 39,497...........C4
Malegaon 245,769...........C4
Maler Kotla 48,536...........D2
Malkapur 35,476...........D4
Malvan 17,579...........C5
Mandi 16,849...........D2
Mandla 24,406...........E4
Mandsaur 52,347...........C4
Mangalore 3,055,113...........C6
Mannargudi 42,783...........E6
Margao 41,655...........C5
Marmagoa 44,065...........C5
Mathura 160,995...........D3
Mau 64,058...........E3
Mayuram 60,195...........D6
Meerut 538,461...........D3
Mehsana 51,598...........C4
Mercara 19,357...........D6
Mhow 59,037...........D4
Midnapore 71,326...........F4
Miraj 77,606...........D5
Mirzapur-cum-Vindhyachal 128,179...........E4
Monghyr 102,474...........F3
Moradabad 347,983...........D3
Morena 44,901...........D3
Morvi 60,976...........C4
Murwara 125,096...........D4
Muzaffarnagar 172,435...........D3
Muzaffarpur 189,765...........E3
Mysore 476,446...........D6
Nadiad 142,279...........C4
Nagappattinam 68,026...........E6
Nagaur 36,448...........C3
Nagercoil 171,641...........D7
Nagina 37,066...........D3
Nagpur 1,297,977...........D4
Nahan 16,017...........D2
Naihati 82,080...........F1
Naini Tal 23,986...........D3
Nander 190,819...........D5
Nandurbar 54,070...........C4
Nandyal 63,193...........D5
Nasik 428,778...........C5
Navsari 129,122...........C4
Nellore 236,225...........E6
New Delhi (cap.) 301,801...........D3
Nimach 47,113...........C4
Nipani 35,116...........C5
Nizamabad 183,135...........D5
Nova Goa (Panaji) 34,953...........C5
Nowgong 56,537...........G3
Okha Port 10,687...........B4
Ongole 53,330...........E5
Ootacamund 63,310...........D6
Orai 42,513...........D3
Pachmarhi 1,212...........D4
Palanpur 42,114...........C4
Palayankottai 70,070...........D7
Palghat 117,961...........D6
Pali 49,834...........C3
Palni 49,575...........D6
Panaji 34,953...........C5
Panchur 59,021...........F1
Pandharpur 53,638...........D5
Panihati 148,046...........F1
Panipat 137,953...........D3
Panna 22,316...........E4
Parbhani 109,328...........D5
Pasighat 5,116...........G3
Patan 105,191...........C4
Pathankot 108,777...........D2
Patiala 205,849...........D2
Patna 916,102...........F3
Pilibhit 68,273...........D3
Pondicherry 251,471...........E6
Ponnani 35,723...........D6
Poona (Pune) 1,135,034...........C5
Porbandar 133,545...........B4
Port Blair 26,218...........G6
Porto Novo 17,412...........E6
Proddatur 107,068...........D6
Puducheri (Pondicherry) 251,471...........E6
Pudukkottai 66,384...........D6
Pune 1,135,034...........C5
Puri 101,089...........F5
Purli 31,078...........D5
Purnea 109,649...........F3
Purulia 57,708...........F4
Quilon 167,583...........D7
Raichur 124,620...........D5
Raigarh 46,745...........E4
Raipur 338,973...........E4
Rajahmundry 267,749...........E5
Rajapalaiyam 101,633...........D7
Rajapur 9,017...........C5
Rajkot 444,156...........C4
Rajnandgaon 41,183...........E4
Rajpur 34,393...........F2
Rameswaram 16,755...........D7
Ranchi 500,593...........F4
Ratlam 156,490...........C4
Ratnagiri 37,551...........C5
Raurkela 321,326...........F4
Raxaul 12,064...........F3
Rewa 100,519...........E3
Rishra 63,486...........F1
Rohtak 166,631...........D3
Sadiya▲ 64,252...........H3
Sagar 207,401...........D4
Saharanpur 294,391...........D3
Salem 515,021...........D6
Sambalpur 162,190...........E4
Sambhal 108,379...........D3
Sangli 268,962...........C5
Santipur 61,166...........F1
Sardarshahr 37,703...........C3
Sasaram 48,282...........E3
Satara 66,433...........C5
Satna 57,531...........E4
Sehore 35,657...........D4
Seoni 38,396...........E4
Serampore 102,023...........F1
Seringapatam 14,100...........D6
Shahjahanpur 205,325...........E3
Shillong 173,064...........G3
Shimoga 151,562...........D6
Shivpuri 42,120...........D3
Sholapur 514,461...........D5
Sidhi 8,341...........E4
Sidhpur 40,521...........C4
Sikar 102,946...........D3
Silchar 52,596...........G4
Siliguri 153,825...........F3
Simla 55,368...........D2
Sirohi 18,774...........C4
Sirsa 48,808...........D3
Sitapur 66,715...........E3
South Dum Dum 174,538...........F1
South Suburban 272,600...........F2
Srikakulam 45,179...........E5
Srinagar 403,413...........D2
Sundargarh 17,244...........F4
Surat 912,568...........C4
Surendranagar 66,667...........C4
Tanda 41,611...........E3
Tellicherry 68,759...........C6
Tenali 119,216...........E5
Tezpur 39,870...........G3
Thana 388,577...........B6
Thanjavur 183,464...........D6
Tinsukia 54,911...........H3
Tiruchchirappalli 607,815...........D6
Tiruchendur 18,126...........D7
Tirunelveli 324,034...........D7
Tirupati 115,244...........D6
Tiruppattur 40,357...........D6
Tiruppur 215,743...........D6
Tiruvannamalai 61,370...........D6
Titagarh 88,218...........F1
Tonk 55,866...........C3
Tranquebar 17,318...........E6
Trichur 170,093...........D6
Trivandrum 519,766...........D7
Tumkur 109,231...........D6
Tura 15,489...........G3
Tuticorin 250,673...........D7
Udaipur 229,762...........C4
Udhampur 16,392...........D2
Ujjain 231,878...........D4
Ulhasnagar 648,149...........C5
Unnao 38,195...........E3
Uttarpara-Kotrung 67,568...........F1
Vadodara 744,043...........C4
Valsad 43,254...........C4
Vaniyambadi 51,810...........D6
Varanasi 793,542...........E3
Vellore 246,937...........D6
Vengurla 11,805...........C5
Veraval 58,771...........B4

British India

Map labels:

U.S.S.R. — GILGIT AGENCY — AFGHANISTAN — KASHMIR & JAMMU — N.W. FRONTIER PROV. — PUNJAB — PUNJAB STATES — IRAN — BALUCHISTAN — BAHAWALPUR (PUNJ. ST.) — DELHI — RAMPUR — Gwadar (Oman) — PUNJ. ST. — RAJPUTANA — AJMER-MERWARA — SIND — UNITED PROVINCES — TIBET — NEPAL — CHINA — SIKKIM — BHUTAN — E. ST. — KHASI HILLS — ASSAM — GWALIOR — CENTRAL INDIA — BENARES — BIHAR — BENGAL — TRIPURA (E. ST.) — MANIPUR — WESTERN INDIA — Diu (Port.) — Damão (Port.) — CENTRAL PROVINCES — BERAR — EASTERN STATES — ORISSA — Chandernagore (Fr.) — BURMA — Arabian Sea — BOMBAY — DECCAN STATES — HYDERABAD — Yanaon (Fr.) — Bay of Bengal — Gôa (Port.) — MYSORE — COORG — Bangalore (Br.) — MADRAS — Mahé (Fr.) — Pondichéry (Fr.) — Karikal (Fr.) — M. ST. — Laccadive Islands (Madras) — Cochin (Br.) — MADRAS STATES — Andaman Islands (Br.) — Nicobar Islands (Br.) — CEYLON

Legend:

British India. The provinces of British India were directly administered by Britain. A few areas were leased from the Indian princes.

Indian States. The Indian States, sometimes referred to as the "Native" or "Princely States," were under the nominal control of maharajas or other hereditary princes.

Possessions of Other Countries in India

State or Provincial Boundaries

Other Internal Boundaries

INDIAN SUBCONTINENT and AFGHANISTAN | 71

Vidisha 43,212 ... D4
Vijayawada 344,958 ... D5
Villupuram 60,242 ... D6
Viramgam 43 790 ... C4
Visakhapatnam 594,259 ... E5
Visnagar 34,863 ... C4
Vizagapatam (Visakhapatnam) 594,259 ... E5
Vizianagaram 115,209 ... E5
Warangal 336,018 ... D5
Wardha 69,037 ... D4
Yadgir 32,756 ... D5
Yanam 8,291 ... E5
Yeola 24,533 ... C4

OTHER FEATURES

Abor (hills) ... G3
Adam's Bridge (sound) ... D7
Agatti (isl.) ... C6
Amindiri (isl.) ... C6
Amindivi (isls.) ... C6
Amini (Amindiri) (isl.) ... C6
Anai Mudi (mt.) ... D6
Andaman (isls.) ... G6
Andaman (sea) ... G6
Androth (isl.) ... C6
Anjidiv (Angedeva) (isl.) ... C6
Arabian (sea) ... B5
Back (bay) ... B7
Banas (riv.) ... D3
Baratang (isl.) ... G6
Barren (isl.) ... G6
Batti Malv (isl.) ... G7
Bengal, Bay of (bay) ... F5
Berar (reg.) ... D4
Betwa (riv.) ... D4
Bhima (riv.) ... D5
Bidyadhari (riv.) ... F2
Bombay (harbor) ... B7
Brahmaputra (riv.) ... G3
Butcher (isl.) ... B7
Cambay (gulf) ... C4
Camorta (isl.) ... G7
Cannanore (isls.) ... C6
Chambal (riv.) ... D3
Chenab (riv.) ... C2
Cherial (riv.) ... F2
Chetlat (isl.) ... C6
Chilka (lake) ... F5
Coco (chan.) ... G6
Colaba (pt.) ... B7
Colair (lake) ... E5
Comorin (cape) ... D7
Coromandel Coast (reg.) ... E6
Daman (dist.) ... C4
Damodar (riv.) ... F4
Deccan (plat.) ... D6
Diu (dist.) ... C4
Duncan (passage) ... G6
Eastern Ghats (mts.) ... D6
Eight Degree (chan.) ... C7
Elephanta (isl.) ... B7
False Divi (pt.) ... E5
Ganga (Ganges) (riv.) ... F3
Ganges, Mouths of the (delta) ... F4
Ganges (riv.) ... F3
Ghaghra (riv.) ... E3
Ghea (riv.) ... F1
Goa (dist.) ... C5
Godavari (riv.) ... D5
Golconda (ruins) ... D5
Great (chan.) ... G7
Great Indian (des.) ... C3
Great Nicobar (isl.) ... G7
Hagari (riv.) ... D6
Himalaya (mts.) ... D2
Hindu Kush (mts.) ... C1
Hooghly (riv.) ... F2
Indira (Pygmalion) (pt.) ... G7
Indravati (riv.) ... E5
Indus (riv.) ... B3
Interview (isl.) ... G6
Jhelum (riv.) ... C2
Jumna (riv.) ... E3
Kachchh (gulf) ... B4
Kachchh (reg.) ... B4
Kachchh, Rann of (salt marsh) ... B4
Kadmat (isl.) ... C6
Kalpeni (isl.) ... C7
Kamet (mt.) ... D2
Kanchenjunga (mt.) ... F3
Karakoram (mts.) ... D1
Katchall (isl.) ... G7
Kathiawar (pen.) ... B4
Kaveri (riv.) ... D6
Khasi (hills) ... G3
Kiltan (isl.) ... C6
Kistna (Krishna) (riv.) ... D5
Kunlun (range) ... D1
Kutch (Kachchh) (reg.) ... B4
Kutch (Kachchh), Rann of (salt marsh) ... B4
Laccadive (Cannanore) (isls.) ... C6
Ladakh (reg.) ... D2
Lakshadweep (sea) ... C6
Landfall (isl.) ... G6
Little Andaman (isl.) ... G6
Little Nicobar (isl.) ... G7
Luni (riv.) ... C3
Mahanadi (riv.) ... E4
Mahim (bay) ... B7
Malabar (hill) ... B7
Malabar (pt.) ... B7
Malabar Coast (reg.) ... C6
Malad (creek) ... B7
Mannar (gulf) ... D7
Manori (creek) ... B7
Middle Andaman (isl.) ... G6
Minicoy (isl.) ... C7
Miri (hills) ... G3
Mishmi (hills) ... H3
Mizo (hill) ... G4
Nancowry (isl.) ... G7
Nanda Devi (mt.) ... D2
Narcondam (isl.) ... G6
Narmada (riv.) ... D4
Nicobar (isls.) ... G7
Nine Degree (chan.) ... C7
North Andaman (isl.) ... G6
North Sentinel (isl.) ... G6
Palk (str.) ... D6
Palmyras (pt.) ... F4
Pangong Tso (lake) ... D2
Penganga (riv.) ... D5
Penner (riv.) ... D6
Periyar (lake) ... D7
Pitti (isl.) ... C6
Pulicat (lake) ... E6
Pygmalion (pt.) ... G7
Ritchies (arch.) ... G6
Rutland (isl.) ... G6
Salsette (isl.) ... B7
Sambhar (lake) ... C3
Saraswati (riv.) ... F1
Sarsati (riv.) ... F1
Satpura (range) ... D4
Shipki (pass) ... D2
Soda (plains) ... D1
Sombrero (chan.) ... G7
Son (riv.) ... E3
South Andaman (isl.) ... G6
Suheli Par (atoll) ... C6
Sundarbans (reg.) ... F4
Sutlej (riv.) ... C3
Tapti (riv.) ... D4
Tel (riv.) ... E4
Ten Degree (chan.) ... G7
Teressa (isl.) ... G7
Thana (creek) ... B7
Tillanchong (isl.) ... G7
Tolly's Nullah (riv.) ... F2
Towers of Silence ... B7
Travancore (reg.) ... D7
Tulsi (lake) ... B6
Tungabhadra (riv.) ... D5
Vehar (lake) ... B7
Vindhya (range) ... D4
Wardha (riv.) ... D4
Western Ghats (mts.) ... C5
Zaskar (mts.) ... D2

MALDIVES

Maldives 143,046 ... C7

NEPAL

CITIES and TOWNS

Baitadi 128,696 ... E3
Bhaktapur 40,112 ... F3
Bhaktapur▲ 110,157 ... F3
Bhojpur 194,506 ... F3
Biratnagar 45,100 ... F3
Dailekh 156,072 ... E3
Dhankuta 107,649 ... F3
Doti 166,070 ... E3
Janakpur 14,294 ... F3
Jumla▲ 122,753 ... E3
Kathmandu (cap.) 150,402 ... E3
Kathmandu▲ 353,752 ... E3
Lalitpur 59,049 ... E3
Lalitpur▲ 154,998 ... E3
Mustang▲ 26,944 ... E3
Nepalganj 23,523 ... E3
Palpa 212,633 ... E3
Pokhara 20,611 ... E3
Pyuthan▲ 137,338 ... E3
Ramechhap 157,349 ... F3
Sallyan▲ 141,457 ... E3

OTHER FEATURES

Annapurna (mt.) ... E3
Bheri (riv.) ... E3
Dhaulagiri (mt.) ... E3
Everest (mt.) ... F3
Himalaya (mts.) ... D2
Kanchenjunga (mt.) ... F3

PAKISTAN

PROVINCES

Azad Kashmir ... C2
Balochistan 4,332,376 ... B3
Federal Administrated Tribal Areas 2,198,547 ... C2
Islamabad District 340,286 ... C2
Northern Areas ... D1
North-West Frontier 11,061,328 ... C2
Punjab 47,292,441 ... C2
Sindh 19,028,666 ... B3

CITIES and TOWNS

Abbottabad 66,000 ... C2
Ahmadpur East 57,000 ... C3
Attock 40,000 ... C2
Badin 23,000 ... B4
Bahawalnagar 74,000 ... C2
Bahawalpur 178,000 ... C3
Baltit ... C1
Bannu 43,000 ... C2
Bela 11,000 ... B3
Bhera 29,000 ... C2
Bunji ... C1
Campbellpore 19,041 ... C2
Chagai▲ 41,263 ... A3
Chaman 30,000 ... B2
Chiniot 106,000 ... C2
Chitral ... C1
Dadu 39,000 ... B3
Dera Ghazi Khan 103,000 ... C3
Dera Ismail Khan 68,000 ... C2
Diplo 7,000 ... B4
Faisalabad 1,092,000 ... C2
Fort Sandeman 8,058 ... B2
Gujranwala 654,000 ... C2
Gujrat 154,000 ... C2
Gwadar 17,000 ... A4
Hunza (Baltit) ... C1
Hyderabad 795,000 ... B3
Islamabad (cap.) 201,000 ... C2
Jacobabad 80,000 ... B3
Jhang Sadar 195,000 ... C2
Jhelum 106,000 ... C2
Kalat 11,000 ... B3
Karachi 4,979,000 ... B4
Kasur 155,000 ... C2
Khairpur 62,000 ... B3
Khanewal 89,000 ... C2
Khanpur 71,000 ... C3
Kharan Kalat 10,000 ... A3
Khushab 56,000 ... C2
Kohat 78,000 ... C2
Kotri 38,000 ... B3
Lahore 3,922,000 ... C2
Larkana 123,000 ... B3
Leiah 52,000 ... C2
Loralai 14,000 ... B2
Lyallpur (Faisalabad) 1,092,000 ... C2
Mach 8,000 ... B3
Malakand ... C2
Mardan 148,000 ... C2
Mastung 17,000 ... B3
Mianwali 59,000 ... C2
Mirpur Khas 124,000 ... B3
Multan 730,000 ... C2
Muzaffarabad ... C2
Nagar ... D1
Nawabshah 102,000 ... B3
Nok Kundi 861 ... A3
Nowshera 75,000 ... C2
Nushki 11,000 ... B3
Pasni 18,000 ... A3
Peshawar 555,000 ... C2
Pindi Gheb 20,000 ... C2
Quetta 285,000 ... B2
Rahimyar Khan 119,000 ... C3
Rawalpindi 806,000 ... C2
Risalpur Cantonment 20,000 ... C2
Rohri 32,000 ... B3
Sahiwal 152,000 ... C2
Saidu 15,920 ... C2
Sargodha 294,000 ... C2
Shikarpur 88,000 ... B3
Sialkot 296,000 ... C2
Sibi 23,000 ... B3
Skardu ... D1
Sonmiani ... B3
Sukkur 193,000 ... B3
Tando Adam 63,000 ... B3
Tando Allahyar 31,000 ... B3
Tatta 12,786 ... B4
Turbat 52,000 ... A3
Uch 5,483 ... B3
Wah 122,000 ... C2
Wana ... C2
Yasin ... C1

OTHER FEATURES

Aksai Chin (reg.) ... D2
Arabian (sea) ... B5
Baltistan (reg.) ... D1
Baroghil (pass) ... C1
Bejhi (riv.) ... B3
Bolan (pass) ... B3
Chagai (hills) ... A3
Chenab (riv.) ... C2
Dasht (riv.) ... A3
Gilgit (dist.) ... C1
Hab (riv.) ... B3
Hamun-i-Lora (swamp) ... B3
Hamun-i-Mashkel (swamp) ... A3
Hindu Kush (mts.) ... B1
Indus (riv.) ... B3
Indus, Mouths of the (delta) ... B4
Jaddi, Ras (pt.) ... A4
Jhelum (riv.) ... C2
K2 (mt.) ... D1
Kabul (riv.) ... C2
Kachchh, Rann of (salt marsh) ... B4
Karakoram (mts.) ... D1
Khyber (pass) ... C2
Konar (riv.) ... C1
Kutch (Kachchh), Rann of (salt marsh) ... B4
Mashkid (riv.) ... A3
Mohenjo Daro (ruins) ... B3
Muari, Ras (cape) ... B4
Nal (riv.) ... B3
Nanga Parbat (mt.) ... D1
Rakaposhi (mt.) ... C1
Ravi (riv.) ... C2
Siahan (range) ... A3
Sulaiman (range) ... C3
Sutlej (riv.) ... C3
Talab (riv.) ... A3
Taxila (ruins) ... C2
Thar (des.) ... C3
Tirich Mir (mt.) ... C1
Zhob (riv.) ... B2

SRI LANKA (CEYLON)

CITIES and TOWNS

Anuradhapura 34,836 ... E7
Badulla 34,658 ... E7
Batticaloa 36,761 ... E7
Colombo (cap.) 618,000 ... D7
Colombo* 852,098 ... D7
Dehiwala-Mt. Lavinia 54,785 ... D7
Galle 72,720 ... D7
Hambantota 6,908 ... E7
Jaffna 112,000 ... E7
Kalmunai 19,176 ... E7
Kalutara 28,748 ... D7
Kandy 93,602 ... E7
Kurunegala 25,189 ... E7
Mannar 11,157 ... E7
Matara 36,641 ... E7
Moratuwa 96,489 ... D7
Mullaittivu 4,930 ... E7
Negombo 57,115 ... D7
Nuwara Eliya 16,347 ... E7
Polonnaruwa 9,551 ... E7
Puttalam 17,982 ... D7
Ratnapura 29,116 ... D7
Sigiriya 1,446 ... E7
Tangalla 8,748 ... E7
Trincomalee 41,780 ... E7
Vavuniya 15,639 ... E7

OTHER FEATURES

Adam's (peak) ... E7
Adam's Bridge (shoals) ... D7
Dondra (head) ... E7
Kirigalpota (mt.) ... E7
Mannar (gulf) ... D7
Palk (str.) ... D7
Pedro (pt.) ... E6
Pidurutalagala (mt.) ... E7

* City and suburbs.
▲ Population of district.

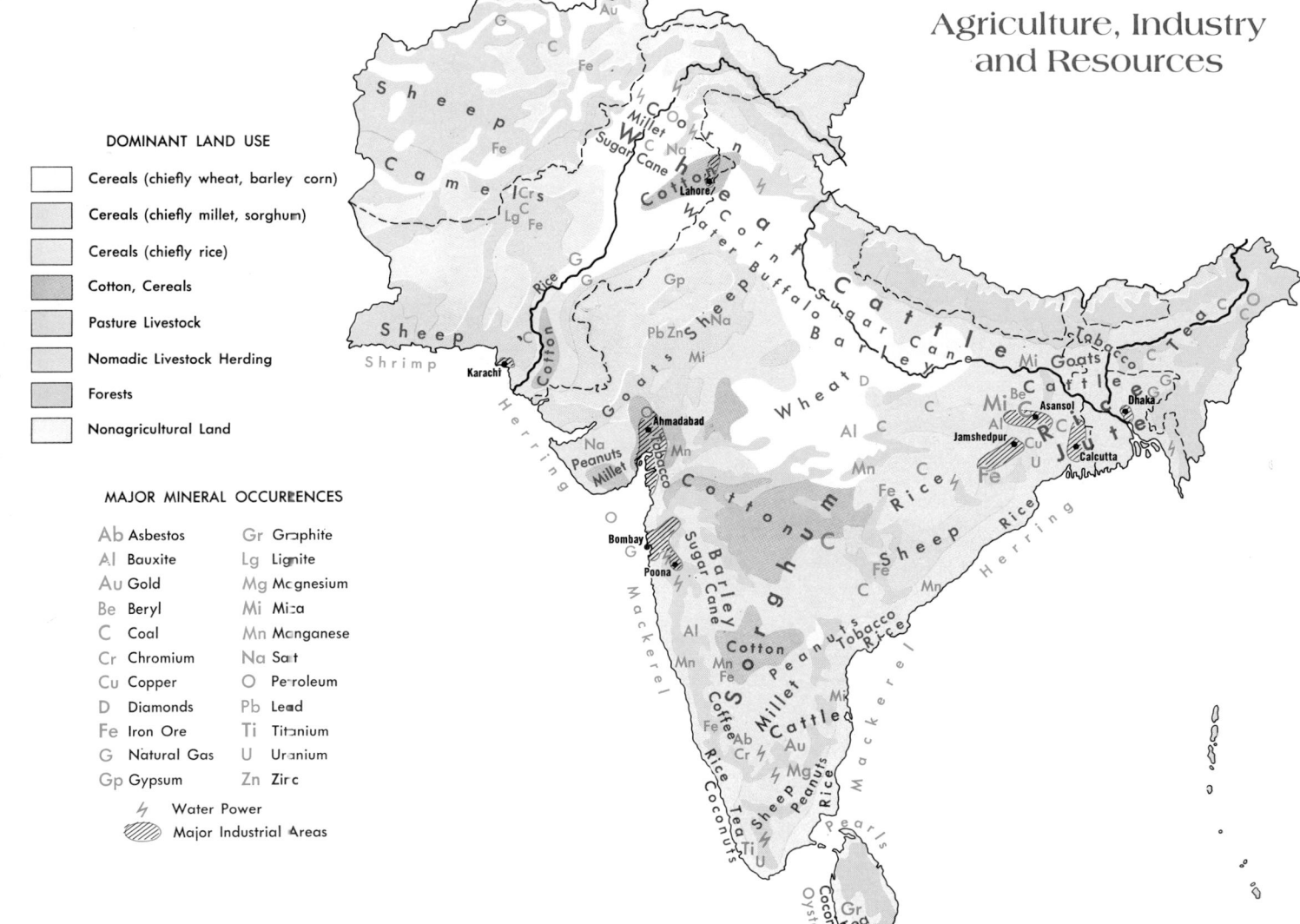

Agriculture, Industry and Resources

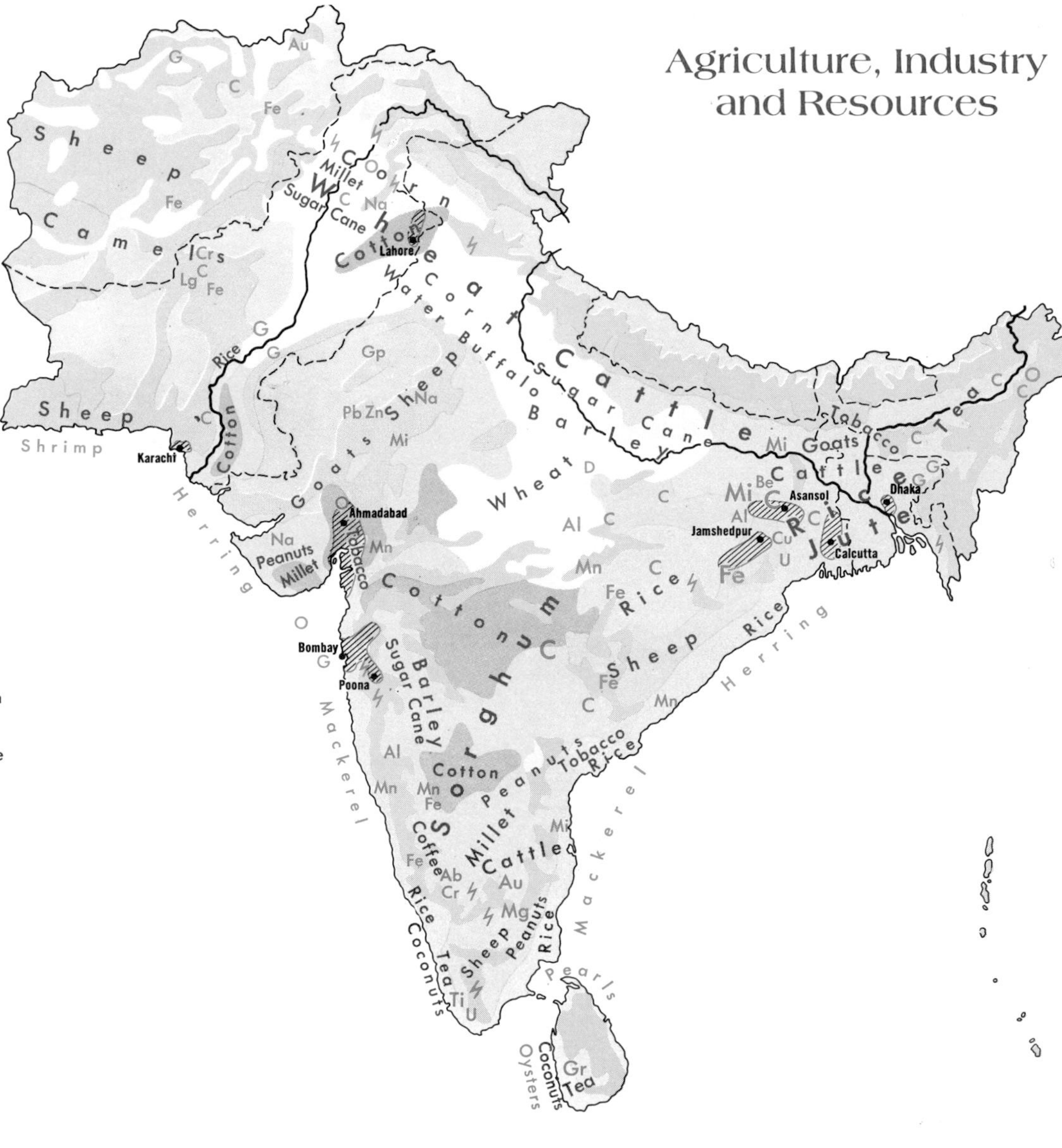

DOMINANT LAND USE

- Cereals (chiefly wheat, barley corn)
- Cereals (chiefly millet, sorghum)
- Cereals (chiefly rice)
- Cotton, Cereals
- Pasture Livestock
- Nomadic Livestock Herding
- Forests
- Nonagricultural Land

MAJOR MINERAL OCCURRENCES

Ab	Asbestos	Gr	Graphite
Al	Bauxite	Lg	Lignite
Au	Gold	Mg	Magnesium
Be	Beryl	Mi	Mica
C	Coal	Mn	Manganese
Cr	Chromium	Na	Salt
Cu	Copper	O	Petroleum
D	Diamonds	Pb	Lead
Fe	Iron Ore	Ti	Titanium
G	Natural Gas	U	Uranium
Gp	Gypsum	Zn	Zinc

ϟ Water Power
Major Industrial Areas

Burma, Thailand, Indochina and Malaya

CONIC PROJECTION

SCALE OF MILES

SCALE OF KILOMETERS

International Boundaries _____
Division and State Boundaries _____
Capitals of Countries _____ ☆
Division and State Capitals _____ ◉

Scale 1:10,000,000

© Copyright HAMMOND INCORPORATED, Maplewood, N.J.

Longitude East 96° of Greenwich

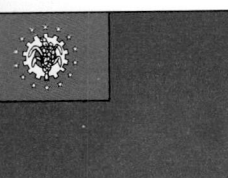

BURMA

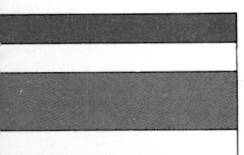

THAILAND

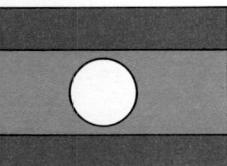

LAOS

CAMBODIA

VIETNAM

MALAYSIA

SINGAPORE

BURMA

AREA 261,789 sq. mi. (678,034 sq. km.)
POPULATION 38,541,000
CAPITAL Rangoon
LARGEST CITY Rangoon
HIGHEST POINT Hkakabo Razi 19,296 ft.
   (5,881 m.)
MONETARY UNIT kyat
MAJOR LANGUAGES Burmese, Karen, Shan,
   Kachin, Chin, Kayah, English
MAJOR RELIGIONS Buddhism, tribal religions

THAILAND

AREA 198,455 sq. mi. (513,998 sq. km.)
POPULATION 55,448,000
CAPITAL Bangkok
LARGEST CITY Bangkok
HIGHEST POINT Doi Inthanon 8,452 ft.
   (2,576 m.)
MONETARY UNIT baht
MAJOR LANGUAGES Thai, Lao, Chinese,
   Khmer, Malay
MAJOR RELIGIONS Buddhism, tribal religions

LAOS

AREA 91,428 sq. mi. (236,800 sq. km.)
POPULATION 3,721,000
CAPITAL Vientiane
LARGEST CITY Vientiane
HIGHEST POINT Phou Bia 9,252 ft. (2,820 m.)
MONETARY UNIT kip
MAJOR LANGUAGE Lao
MAJOR RELIGIONS Buddhism, tribal religions

CAMBODIA

AREA 69,898 sq. mi. (181,036 sq. km.)
POPULATION 8,055,000
CAPITAL Phnom Penh
LARGEST CITY Phnom Penh
HIGHEST POINT 5,948 ft. (1,813 m.)
MONETARY UNIT riel
MAJOR LANGUAGE Khmer (Cambodian)
MAJOR RELIGION Buddhism

VIETNAM

AREA 128,405 sq. mi. (332,569 sq. km.)
POPULATION 64,412,000
CAPITAL Hanoi
LARGEST CITY Ho Chi Minh City (Saigon)
HIGHEST POINT Fan Si Pan 10,308 ft.
   (3,142 m.)
MONETARY UNIT dong
MAJOR LANGUAGES Vietnamese, Thai,
   Muong, Meo, Yao, Khmer, French,
   Chinese, Cham
MAJOR RELIGIONS Buddhism, Taoism,
   Confucianism, Roman Catholicism,
   Cao-Dai

MALAYSIA

AREA 128,308 sq. mi. (332,318 sq. km.)
POPULATION 17,377,000
CAPITAL Kuala Lumpur
LARGEST CITY Kuala Lumpur
HIGHEST POINT Mt. Kinabalu 13,455 ft.
   (4,101 m.)
MONETARY UNIT ringgit
MAJOR LANGUAGES Malay, Chinese, English,
   Tamil, Dayak, Kadazan
MAJOR RELIGIONS Islam, Confucianism,
   Buddhism, tribal religions, Hinduism,
   Taoism, Christianity, Sikhism

SINGAPORE

AREA 226 sq. mi. (585 sq. km.)
POPULATION 2,704,000
CAPITAL Singapore
LARGEST CITY Singapore
HIGHEST POINT Bukit Timah 581 ft. (177 m.)
MONETARY UNIT Singapore dollar
MAJOR LANGUAGES Chinese, Malay, Tamil,
   English, Hindi
MAJOR RELIGIONS Confucianism, Buddhism,
   Taoism, Hinduism, Islam, Christianity

Topography

0   200   400 MI.
0   200   400 KM.

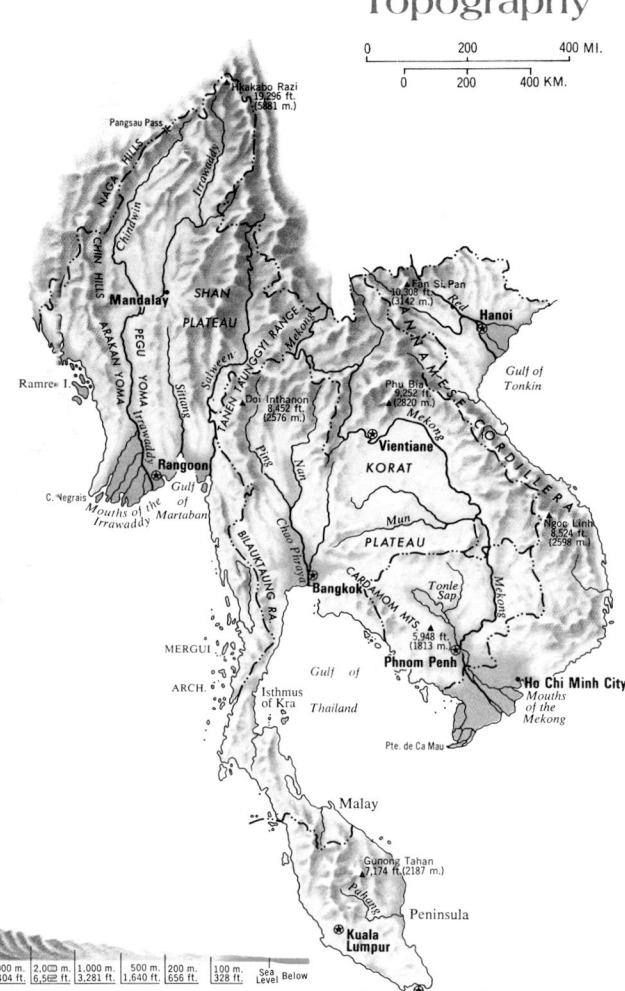

5,000 m. | 2,000 m. | 1,000 m. | 500 m. | 200 m. | 100 m. | Sea Level | Below
16,404 ft. | 6,562 ft. | 3,281 ft. | 1,640 ft. | 656 ft. | 328 ft. | |

BURMA

INTERNAL DIVISIONS

Chin (state) 368,985 ....B2
Irrawaddy (div.) 4,991,057 ...B3
Kachin (state) 903,982 ....C1
Karen (state) 1,057,505 ....C3
Kayah (state) 168,355 ....C3
Magwe (div.) 3,241,103 ....B2
Mandalay (div.) 4,580,923 .....B2
Mon (state) 1,682,041 ....C4
Pegu (div.) 3,800,240 ....C3
Rakhine (state) 1,710,913 .....B3
Rangoon (div.) 3,973,782 ......C3
Sagaing (div.) 3,855,991 ....B1
Shan (state) 3,718,706 ....C2
Tenasserim (div.) 917,628 .....C4

CITIES and TOWNS

Akyab (Sittwe) 107,607 ....B2
Allanmyo 15,580 ....B3
Amarapura 11,268 ....B2
Amherst 6,000 ....C3
Bassein 144,092 ....B3
Bhamo 9,821 ....C1
Chauk 24,466 ....B2
Gyobingauk 9,922 ....C3
Henzada 82,531 ....B3
Hmawbi 23,032 ....C3
Insein 143,625 ....C3
Kanbalu 3,281 ....B2
Katha 7,648 ....C1
Kawthaung 1,520 ....C5
Kyaikto 13,154 ....C3
Kyangin 6,073 ....B3
Kyaukpadaung 5,480 ....B2
Kyaukpyu 7,335 ....B2
Kyaukse 8,659 ....C2
Labutta 12,982 ....B3
Lashio 69,567 ....C2
Letpadan 15,896 ....B3
Madauk 4,618 ....C3
Magwe 13,270 ....B2
Mandalay 532,895 ....C2
Martaban 5,661 ....C3
Ma-ubin 23,362 ....B3
Maungdaw 3,772 ....B2
Mawlaik 2,993 ....B2
Maymyo 58,059 ....C2
Meiktila 73,210 ....C2
Mergui 67,351 ....C4
Minbu 9,096 ....B2
Minhla 6,470 ....B3
Mogaung 2,920 ....C1
Mogok 8,334 ....C2
Monywa 106,873 ....B2
Moulmein 219,991 ....C3
Mudon 20,136 ....C3
Myanaung 11,155 ....B3
Myaungmya 24,532 ....B3
Myingyan 70,162 ....B2
Myitkyina 12,382 ....C1
Myohaung 6,534 ....B2
Okkan 14,443 ....B3
Pakokku 58,132 ....B2
Palaw 5,596 ....C4

Paungde 17,286 ....B3
Pegu 150,447 ....C3
Prome (Pye) 36,997 ....B3
Pyapon 19,174 ....B3
Pye 36,997 ....B3
Pyinmana 22,025 ....C3
Pyu 10,443 ....C3
Rangoon (cap.) 2,458,712 ....C3
Rathedaung 2,969 ....B2
Sagaing 15,382 ....B2
Sandoway 5,172 ....B3
Shwebo 17,827 ....B2
Singu 4,027 ....C2
Sittwe 107,607 ....B2
Syriam 15,296 ....C3
Taungdwingyi 16,233 ....B2
Taunggyi 107,907 ....C2
Tavoy 60,435 ....C4
Tharrawaddy 8,977 ....C3
Thaton 51,025 ....C3
Thayetmyo 11,649 ....B3
Thazi 7,531 ....C2
Thongwa 10,829 ....C3
Toungoo 31,589 ....C3
Wakema 20,716 ....B3
Yamethin 11,167 ....C2
Yandoon 15,245 ....B3
Ye 12,852 ....C4
Yenangyaung 57,652 ....B2
Ye-u 5,307 ....B2
Zalun 899 ....B3

OTHER FEATURES

Amya (pass) C4
Andaman (sea) B4
Arakan Yoma (mts.) B3
Ataran (riv.) C4
Bengal, Bay of (bay) B3
Bentinck (isl.) C5
Bilauktaung (range) C4
Chaukan (pass) C1
Cheduba (isl.) B3
Chin (hills) B2
Chindwin (riv.) B2
Coco (chan.) B4
Combermere (bay) B3
Daung Kyun (isl.) C4
Dawna (range) C3
Great Coco (isl.) B4
Great Tenasserim (riv.) C4
Heinze Chaung (bay) C4
Heywood (chan.) B3
Hkakabo Razi (mt.) C1
Hka, Nam (riv.) C2
Indawgyi (lake) C1
Inle (lake) C2
Irrawaddy (riv.) B3
Irrawaddy, Mouths of the
  (delta) B4
Kadan Kyun (isl.) C4
Kaladan (riv.) B2
Kalegauk (isl.) C4
Khao Luang (mt.) C5
Lanbi Kyun (isl.) C5
Launglon Bok (isls.) C4
Letsôk-aw Kyun (isl.) C5
Little Coco (isl.) B4

(continued on following page)

Loi Leng (mt.)........................C2
Mali (riv.)...........................C1
Mali Kyun (isl.)......................C4
Manipur (riv.)........................B2
Martaban (gulf).......................C4
Mekong (riv.).........................C5
Mergui (arch.)........................C5
Mon (riv.)............................B2
Mu (riv.).............................B2
Myitnge (riv.)........................C2
Negrais (cape)........................B3
Nmai (riv.)...........................C1
Pakchan (riv.)........................C5
Pangsau (pass)........................C1
Pawn, Nam (riv.)......................B3
Pegu Yoma (mts.)......................B3
Popa Hill (mt.).......................B2
Preparis (isl.).......................B4
Preparis North (chan.)................B4
Preparis South (chan.)................B4
Ramree (isl.).........................B3
Salween (riv.)........................C3
Shan (plat.)..........................C2
Shweli (riv.).........................C2
Sittang (riv.)........................C3
Taping (riv.).........................C1
Taungthonton (mt.)....................B1
Tavoy (pt.)...........................C4
Tenasserim (isl.).....................C4
Teng, Nam (riv.)......................C2
Thayawthadangyi Kyun (isl.)...........C4
Three Pagodas (pass)..................C4
Victoria (mt.)........................B2
Zadetkyi Kyun (isl.)..................C5

CAMBODIA (KAMPUCHEA)

CITIES and TOWNS

Batdambang (Battambang).....D4
Kampong Cham................E4
Kampong Chhnang.............D4
Kampong Saom................D5
Kampong Spoe................E5
Kampong Thum................E4
Kampot......................E5
Kracheh.....................E4
Krong Kaoh Kong.............D5
Krong Keb...................E5
Lumphat.....................E4
Paoy Pet....................D4
Phnom Penh (cap.) 300,000...E5
Phnum Tbeng Meanchey........E4
Phumi Samraong..............D4
Pouthisat...................E5
Prey Veng...................E5
Pursat (Pouthisat)..........E4
Senmonoron..................E4
Siemreab....................D4
Stoeng Treng................E4
Svay Rieng..................E5

OTHER FEATURES

Angkor Wat (ruins)..........D4
Chrouy Samit (pt.)..........D5
Dangrek (mts.)..............E4
Drang, la (riv.)............E4
Joncs (plain)...............E5
Kong, Kaoh (isl.)...........E5
Khong, Se (riv.)............E4
Mekong (riv.)...............E4
Rung, Kaoh (isl.)...........D5
San, Se (riv.)..............E4
Sen, Stoeng (riv.)..........E4
Srepok (riv.)...............E4
Tang, Kaoh (isl.)...........D5
Tonle Sap (lake)............D4
Wai, Poulo (isls.)..........D5

LAOS

CITIES and TOWNS

Attapu 2,750................E4
Ban Kèngkok 2,000...........E3
Boun Nua 2,500..............D2
Champasak 3,500.............E4
Khamkeut▲ 31,206............E3
Louang Namtha 1,459.........D2
Louangphrabang 7,596........D3
Mahaxai 2,000...............E3
Muang Hinboun 1,750.........E3
Muang Khammouan 5,500.......E3
Muang Khôngxédôn 2,000......E4
Muang Ou Tai................D2
Muang Pak-Lay 2,000.........D3
Muang Pakxan 2,500..........D3
Muang Xaignabouri
  (Sayaboury) 2,500.........D3
Muang Xay 2,000.............D2
Pakxé 8,000.................E4
Phiafai▲ 17,216.............E4
Phôngsali 2,500.............D2
San Nua (Sam Neua) 3,000....D2
Saravan 2,350...............E4
Savannakhét 8,500...........E3
Sayaboury (Muang Xaignabouri)
  2,500.....................D3
Thakhek (Muang Khammouan)
  5,500.....................E3
Viangchan (Vientiane)
  132,253...................D3
Vientiane (cap.) 132,253....D3
Xiangkhoang 3,500...........D3

OTHER FEATURES

Bolovens (plat.)............E4
Jars (plain)................D3
Mekong (riv.)...............D3
Ou, Nam (riv.)..............D2
Phou Bia (mt.)..............D3

Phou Cô Pi (mt.)............E3
Phou Loi (mt.)..............D2
Phou San (mt.)..............D3
Rao Co (mt.)................E3
Se Khong (riv.).............E4
Tha, Nam (riv.).............D2
Xiangkhoang (plat.).........D3

MALAYA, MALAYSIA
(See Southeast Asia, p. 85 for
other part of Malaysia.)

STATES

Federal Territory 937,875......D7
Johor (Johore) 1,601,504......D7
Kedah 1,102,200..............D6
Kelantan 877,575.............D6
Melaka 453,153...............D7
Negeri Sembilan 563,955......D7
Pahang 770,644...............D7
Penang (Pinang) 911,586......D6
Perak 1,762,288..............D6
Perlis 147,726...............D6
Pinang (Penang) 911,586......D6
Selangor 1,467,441...........D7
Terengganu 542,280...........D6

CITIES and TOWNS

Alor Gajah 2,222.............D7
Alor Setar 66,260............D6
Bandar Maharani (Muar)
  61,218.....................D7
Bandar Penggaram
  (Batu Pahat) 53,291........D7
Batu Gajah 10,692............D7
Batu Pahat 53,291............D7
Bentong 22,683...............D7
Butterworth 61,187...........D6
Chukai 12,514................D6
Gemas 5,214..................D7
George Town (Pinang)
  269,603....................C6
Ipoh 247,953.................D6
Johor Baharu (Johore Bharu)
  136,234....................F5
Kampar 26,591................D7
Kampong Kuala Besut 3,524....D6
Kangar 8,758.................D6
Kelang 113,611...............D7
Keluang 43,272...............D7
Kota Baharu 55,124...........D6
Kota Tinggi 8,725............F5
Kuala Dungun 17,560..........D6
Kuala Lipis 9,270............D6
Kuala Lumpur (cap.) 451,977..D7
Kuala Pilah 12,508...........D7
Kuala Rompin 1,384...........D7
Kuala Selangor 3,132.........D7
Kuala Terengganu 53,320......D6
Kuantan 43,358...............D7
Kulai 11,841.................F5
Lumut 3,255..................D7
Malacca (Melaka) 87,160......D7
Mersing 18,246...............E7
Muar 61,218..................D7
Pekan 4,682..................D7
Pinang (George Town)
  269,603....................C6
Pontian Kechil 8,349.........E5
Port Dickson 10,300..........D7
Port Weld 3,233..............D6
Raub 18,433..................D7
Segamat 17,796...............D7
Seremban 80,921..............D7
Sungai Petani 35,959.........D6
Taiping 54,645...............D6
Tanah Merah 7,012............D6
Teluk Intan 44,524...........D6
Tumpat 10,673................D6

OTHER FEATURES

Aur, Pulau (isl.)............E7
Belumut, Gunong (mt.).......D7
Benom, Gunong (mt.)..........D7
Gelang, Tanjong (pt.)........D7
Johore (str.)................E6
Johor, Sungai (riv.).........F5
Kelantan, Sungai (riv.)......D6
Langkawi, Pulau (isl.).......C6
Ledang, Gunong (mt.).........D7
Lima, Pulau (isl.)...........F6
Malacca (str.)...............D7
Malay (pen.).................D6
Malaya (West Malaysia)
  (reg.).....................D6
Pahang, Sungai (riv.)........D7
Pangkor, Pulau (isl.)........D6
Perak, Gunong (mt.).........D6
Perhentian, Kepulauan (isls.)..D6
Piai, Tanjong (pt.)..........E6
Pinang, Pulau (isl.).........C6
Pulai, Sungai (riv.).........E5
Ramunia, Tanjong (pt.).......F5
Redang, Pulau (isl.).........D6
Sedili Kechil, Tanjong (pt.)..F5
Singapore (str.).............F6
Tahan, Gunong (mt.)..........D6
Temiang, Bukit (mt.).........D6
Tenggol, Pulau (isl.)........D6
Tinggi, Pulau (isl.).........E7
Tioman, Pulau (isl.).........E7

SINGAPORE

CITIES and TOWNS

Jurong 50,974................E6
Nee Soon 37,641..............F6
Paya Lebar 21,636............F6
Serangoon 89,558.............F6
Singapore (cap.) 2,413,945...F6

OTHER FEATURES

Keppel (harb.)..............F6
Main (str.).................F6
Singapore (str.)............F6
Tekong Besar, Pulau (isl.)..F6

THAILAND (SIAM)

CITIES and TOWNS

Ang Thong 7,267.............C4
Ayutthaya (Phra Nakhon Si
  Ayutthaya) 37,213.........D4
Ban Aranyaprathet 12,276....D4
Bangkok (cap.) 1,867,297....D4
Ban Pak Phanang 13,590......D5
Buriram 16,431..............D4
Chachoengsao 22,106.........D4
Chainat 9,944...............D4
Chaiyaphum 12,540...........D4
Chanthaburi 15,479..........D4
Chiang Mai 101,594..........C3
Chiang Rai 13,927...........C3
Chon Buri 115,350...........D4
Chumphon 11,643.............C5
Hat Yai 47,953..............C6
Hua Hin 21,426..............C4
Kalasin 14,960..............D3
Kamphaeng Phet 12,378.......C3
Kanchanaburi 16,397.........C4
Khon Kaen 29,431............D3
Khorat (Nakhon Ratchasima)
  66,071....................D4
Krabi 8,764.................C5
Krung Thep (Bangkok) (cap.)
  1,867,297.................D4
Lampang 40,100..............C3
Lamphun 11,309..............C3
Lang Suan 4,020.............C5
Loei 10,137.................D3
Lom Sak 10,597..............D3
Lop Buri 23,112.............D4
Mae Hong Son 3,981..........C3
Maha Sarakham 19,707........D3
Nakhon Nayok 8,185..........D4
Nakhon Pathom 34,300........C4
Nakhon Phanom 20,385........D3
Nakhon Ratchasima 66,071....D4
Nakhon Sawan 46,853.........D4
Nakhon Si Thammarat
  102,123...................D5
Nan 17,738..................D3
Narathiwat 21,256...........D6
Nong Khai 21,150............D3
Pattani 21,938..............D6
Phanat Nikhom 10,514........D4
Phangnga 5,738..............C5
Phatthalung 13,336..........D6
Phayao 20,346...............C3
Phet Buri 27,755............C4
Phetchabun 6,240............D3
Phichit 10,814..............D3
Phitsanulok 33,883..........D3
Phrae 17,555................C3
Phra Nakhon Si Ayutthaya
  37,213....................D4
Phuket 34,362...............C6
Prachin Buri 14,167.........D4
Prachuap Khiri Khan 9,075...D5
Rahaeng (Tak) 16,317........C3
Ranong 10,301...............C5
Rat Buri 32,271.............C4
Rayong 14,846...............D4
Roi Et 20,242...............D4
Sakon Nakhon 18,943.........E3
Samut Prakan 46,632.........D4
Samut Sakhon 33,619.........C4
Samut Songkhram 23,574......C4
Sara Buri 25,025............D4
Satun 7,315.................C6
Sawankhalok 8,387...........C3
Sing Buri 9,050.............D4
Singora (Songkhla) 172,604..D6
Sisaket 13,662..............E4
Songkhla 172,604............D6
Sukhothai 15,488............D3
Suphan Buri 18,768..........C4
Surat Thani 24,923..........C5
Surin 16,342................D4
Tak 16,317..................C3
Takua Pa 7,825..............C5
Thon Buri 628,015...........D4
Trang 32,985................C6
Trat 7,917..................D4
Ubon 40,650.................E4
Udon Thani 56,218...........D3
Uthai Thani 10,525..........C4
Uttaradit 12,022............D3
Warin Chamrap 21,520........E4
Yala 30,051.................D6
Yasothon 12,079.............D4

OTHER FEATURES

Amya (pass).................C4
Bilauktaung (range).........C4
Chang, Ko (isl.)............D5
Chan, Ko (isl.).............C5
Chao Phraya, Mae Nam (riv.).D4
Chi, Mae Nam (riv.).........D3
Dangrek (Dong Rak) (mts.)...D4
Doi Inthanon (mt.)..........C3
Doi Pha Hom Pok (mt.).......C2
Doi Pia Fai (mt.)...........C3
Khao Luang (mt.)............C5
Kao Prawa (mt.).............C3
Khwae Noi, Mae Nam (riv.)...C4
Kra (isth.).................C5
Kut, Ko (isl.)..............D5
Laem Chong Phra (cape)......C4
Laem Pho (cape).............D6
Laem Talumphuk (cape).......D5
Lanta, Ko (isl.)............C6

Libong, Ko (isl.)...........C6
Luang (mt.).................C5
Mae Klong, Mae Nam (riv.)...C4
Malay (pen.)................D6
Mekong (riv.)...............E3
Mun, Mae Nam (riv.).........D4
Nan, Mae Nam (riv.).........D3
Nong Lahan (lake)...........D3
Pakchan (riv.)..............C5
Pa Sak, Mae Nam (riv.)......D4
Phangan, Ko (isl.)..........C5
Phuket, Ko (isl.)...........C6
Ping, Mae Nam (riv.)........C3
Rawi, Ko (isl.).............C6
Salween (riv.)..............C3
Samui (str.)................D5
Samui, Ko (isl.)............C5
Tao, Ko (isl.)..............C5
Tapi, Mae Nam (riv.)........C5
Terutao, Ko (isl.)..........C6
Tha Chin, Mae Nam (riv.)....C4
Thale Luang (lag.)..........D6
Thalu, Ko (isls.)...........C4
Three Pagodas (pass)........C4
Wang, Mae Nam (riv.)........C3

VIETNAM

CITIES and TOWNS

An Loc (Binh Long) 15,276...E5
An Tuc (An Khe).............F4
Bac Giang...................E2
Bac Lieu 53,841.............E5
Bac Ninh 22,560.............E5
Ban Me Thuot 68,771.........F4
Bien Hoa 87,135.............E5
Binh Long (An Loc) 15,276...E5
Cam Ranh 118,111............F5
Can Tho 182,424.............E5

Cao Bang 565,967............E2
Cao Lanh 16,482.............E5
Chau Phu 37,175.............E5
Chu Lai.....................F4
Da Lat 105,072..............F5
Da Nang 492,194.............F4
Dien Bien Phu...............D2
Dong Hoi....................E3
Go Cong 33,191..............E5
Ha Giang....................E2
Haiphong* 1,447,614.........E2
Hanoi (cap.) 3,056,549......E2
Ha Tinh.....................E3
Ho Chi Minh City (Saigon)*
  3,934,326.................E5
Hoa Binh....................E2
Hoi An 45,059...............F4
Hon Gai 100,000.............E2
Hue 209,043.................E3
Khanh Hung 59,015...........E5
Khe Sanh....................E3
Kon Tum 33,554..............E4
Lac Giao (Ban Me Thuot)
  68,771....................F4
Lai Chau 437,983............D2
Lang Son 610,501............E2
Lao Cai.....................E2
Loc Ninh....................E5
Long Xuyen 72,658...........E5
My Tho 119,892..............E5
Nam Dinh 125,000............E2
Nha Trang 216,227...........F4
Ninh Binh...................E2
Phan Rang 53,841............F5
Phan Thiet 80,122...........F5
Phu Cuong 28,267............E5
Phu Ly......................E2
Phu Tho 10,888..............E2
Phu Vinh 48,485.............E5
Pleiku 23,720...............F4

Quang Ngai 14,119...........F4
Quang Tri 15,874............E3
Quan Long 59,331............E5
Qui Nhon 213,757............F4
Rach Gia 104,161............E5
Sa Dec 51,867...............E5
Saigon (Ho Chi Minh City)*
  3,934,326.................E5
Son La 682,385..............D2
Son Tay 19,213..............E2
Song Cau....................F4
Tam Ky 38,532...............F4
Tam Quan....................F4
Tan An 38,082...............E5
Tay Ninh 791,762............E5
Thai Binh 1,632,525.........E2
Thai Nguyen 110,000.........E2
Thanh Hoa 2,991,317.........E3
Tra Vinh (Phu Vinh) 48,485..E5
Truc Giang 68,629...........E5
Tuy Hoa 63,552..............F4
Vinh 43,954.................E3
Vinh Long 30,667............E5
Vinh Yen....................E2
Vung Tau 136,225............E5
Yen Bai.....................E2

OTHER FEATURES

Bach Long Vi, Dao (isl.).....F2
Ba Den, Nui (mt.)...........E5
Bai Bung, Mui (Ca Mau) (pt.)..E5
Ba Lang An, Mui (cape)......F4
Ben Goi (bay)...............F4
Black (riv.)................D2
Ca Mau (Mui Bai Bung) (pt.)..E5
Cam Ranh, Vinh (bay)........F5
Cao Nguyen Dac Lac (plat.)..F4
Cat Ba, Dao (isl.)..........E2
Chon May, Vung (bay)........F3

Con Son (isls.)............
Cu Lao, Hon (isls.)........
Da Nang, Mui (Ca Mau) (pt.)..
Deux Frères, Les (isls.)...
Dinh, Mui (cape)...........
Fan Si Pan (mt.)...........
Gio, Hon (isl.)............
Hon Tho Chau (isl.)........
Ia Drang (riv.)............
Indochina (reg.)...........
Joncs (plain)..............
Khoai, Hon (isl.)..........
Kontum (plat.).............
Lang Bian, Nui (mts.)......
Lay, Mui (cape)............
Mekong, Mouths of the
  (delta).................
Nam Tram, Mui (cape).......
Ngoc Linh (mt.)............
Nightingale (Bach Long Vi)
  (isl.)...................
Panjang, Hon (Hon Tho Chau)
  (isl.)...................
Phu Quoc, Dao (isl.).......
Quan Son Mun Du (isls.)....
Rao Co (mt.)...............
Red (riv.).................
Ron, Mui (cape)............
Se San (riv.)..............
Sip Song Chau Thai (mts.)..
Song Ba (riv.).............
Song Cai (riv.)............
South China (sea.).........
Tonkin (gulf)..............
Varella, Mui (cape)........
Yang Sin, Chu (mt.)........

*City and suburbs.
▲Population of district.

Agriculture, Industry and Resources

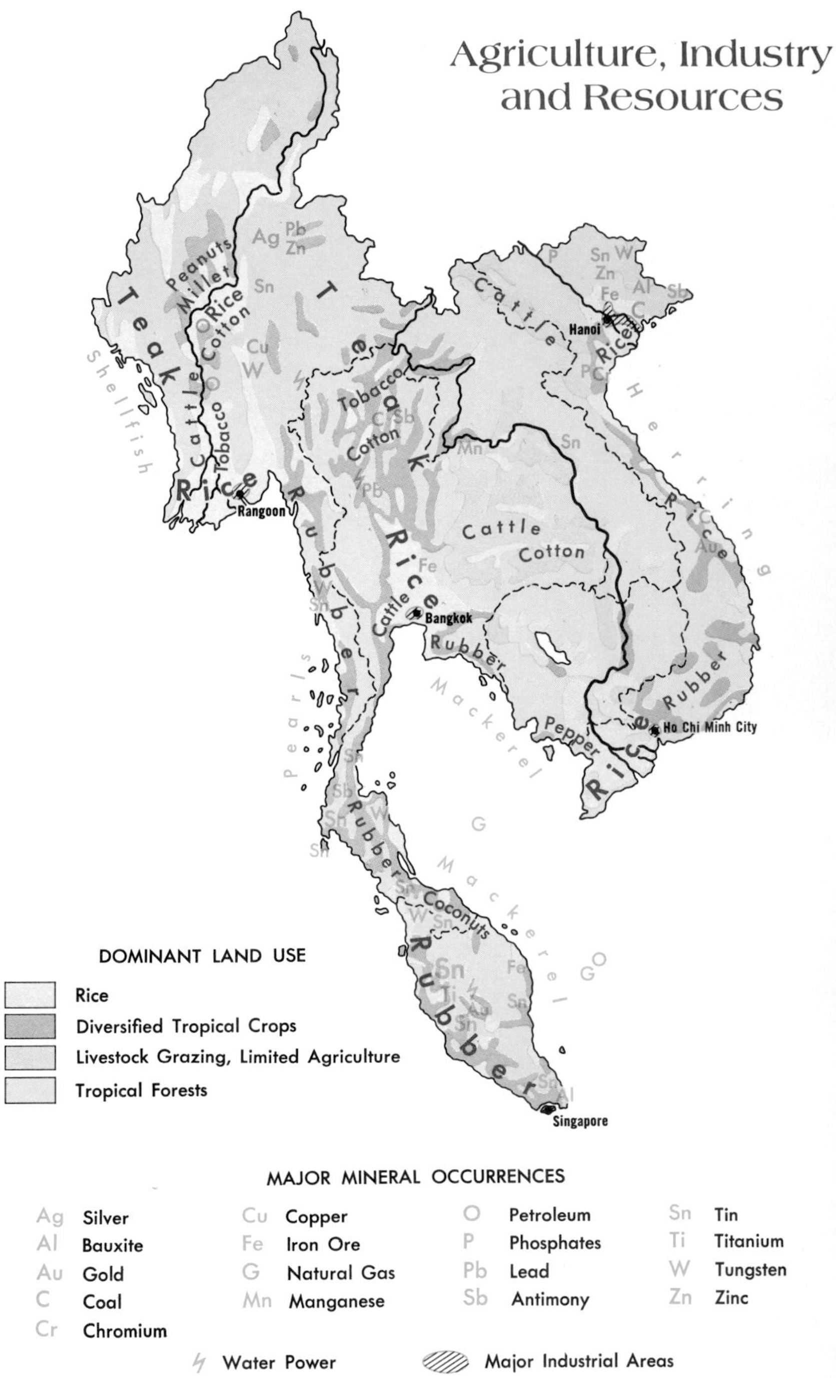

DOMINANT LAND USE

Rice

Diversified Tropical Crops

Livestock Grazing, Limited Agriculture

Tropical Forests

MAJOR MINERAL OCCURRENCES

Ag Silver	Cu Copper	O Petroleum	Sn Tin
Al Bauxite	Fe Iron Ore	P Phosphates	Ti Titanium
Au Gold	G Natural Gas	Pb Lead	W Tungsten
C Coal	Mn Manganese	Sb Antimony	Zn Zinc
Cr Chromium			

Water Power   Major Industrial Areas

CHINA (MAINLAND)

AREA 3,691,000 sq. mi. (9,559,690 sq. km.)
POPULATION 1,133,682,501
CAPITAL Beijing
LARGEST CITY Shanghai
HIGHEST POINT Mt. Everest 29,028 ft.
(8,848 m.)
MONETARY UNIT yuan
MAJOR LANGUAGES Chinese, Chuang, Uigur,
Yi, Tibetan, Miao, Mongol, Kazakh
MAJOR RELIGIONS Confucianism, Buddhism,
Taoism, Islam

CHINA (TAIWAN)

AREA 13,971 sq. mi. (36,185 sq. km.)
POPULATION 20,204,880
CAPITAL Taipei
LARGEST CITY Taipei
HIGHEST POINT Yü Shan 13,113 ft. (3,997 m.)
MONETARY UNIT new Taiwan yüan (dollar)
MAJOR LANGUAGES Chinese, Formosan
MAJOR RELIGIONS Confucianism, Buddhism,
Taoism, Christianity, tribal religions

MONGOLIA

AREA 606,163 sq. mi. (1,569,962 sq. km.)
POPULATION 2,070,000
CAPITAL Ulaanbaatar
LARGEST CITY Ulaanbaatar
HIGHEST POINT Tabun Bogdo 14,288 ft.
(4,355 m.)
MONETARY UNIT tughrik
MAJOR LANGUAGES Khalkha Mongolian,
Kazakh (Turkic)
MAJOR RELIGION Buddhism

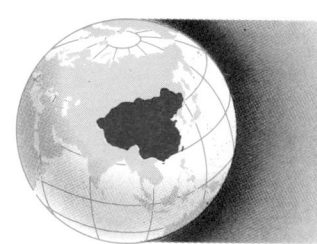

HONG KONG

AREA 403 sq. mi. (1,044 sq. km.)
POPULATION 5,761,000
CAPITAL Victoria
MONETARY UNIT Hong Kong dollar
MAJOR LANGUAGES Chinese, English
MAJOR RELIGIONS Confucianism, Buddhism,
Christianity

MACAU

AREA 6 sq. mi. (16 sq. km.)
POPULATION 448,000
CAPITAL Macau
MONETARY UNIT pataca
MAJOR LANGUAGES Chinese, Portuguese
MAJOR RELIGIONS Confucianism, Buddhism,
Taoism, Christianity

CHINA (MAINLAND)

CHINA (TAIWAN)

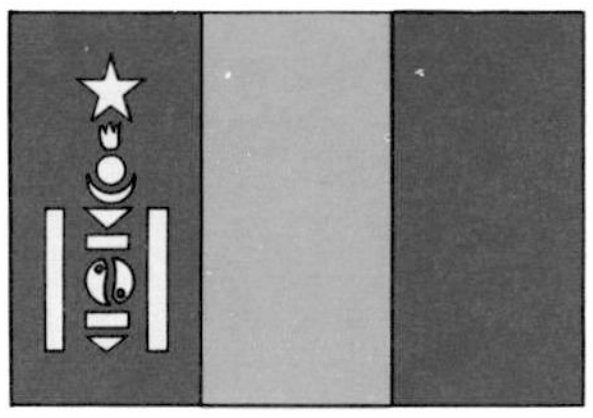

MONGOLIA

CHINA

PROVINCES

Anhui (Anhwei) 49,665,724 ....J5
Chekiang (Zhejiang)
38,884,603 ....K6
Fujian (Fukien) 25,931,106....J6
Gansu (Kansu) 19,569,261 ....E3
Guangdong (Kwangtung)
59,299,220 ....H7
Guangxi Zhuangzu
(Kwangsi Chuang Aut. Reg.)
36,420,960 ....G7
Guizhou (Kweiichow)
28,552,997 ....G6
Hainan H8
Hebei (Hopei) 53,005,875 ....J4
Heilongjiang (Heilungkiang)
32,665,546 ....K2
Henan (Honan) 74,422,739 ...H5
Hubei (Hupei) 47,804,150 ....H5
Hunan 54,008,851 ....H6
Inner Mongolian Aut. Reg.
(Nei Monggol) 19,274,279 .H3
Jiangsu (Kiangsu)
60,521,114 ....K5
Jiangxi (Kiangsi) 33,184,827 ..J6
Jilin (Kirin) 22,560,053 ....L3
Kansu (Gansu) 19,569,261 ....E3
Kiangsi (Jiangxi) 33,184,827 ..J6
Kiangsu (Jiangsu)
60,521,114 ....K5
Kirin (Jilin) 22,560,053 ....L3
Kwangsi Chuang Aut. Reg.
(Guangxi Zhuang)
36,420,960 ....G7

Kwangtung (Guangdong)
59,209,220 ....H7
Kweiichow (Guizhou)
28,552,997 ....G6
Liaoning 35,721,693 ....K3
Nei Monggol
(Inner Mongolian Aut. Reg.)
19,274,279 ....H3
Ningxia Huizu
(Ningsia Hui Aut. Reg.)
3,895,578 ....F3
Qinghai (Tsinghai) 3,895,706 .E4
Shaanxi (Shensi) 28,904,423 .G5
Shandong (Shantung)
74,419,054 ....J4
Shanxi (Shansi) 25,291,389 ...H4
Sichuan (Szechwan)
99,713,310 ....F5
Sinkiang-Uigur Aut. Reg.
(Xinjiang Uygur) 13,081,631 ..B3
Taiwan 16,609,961 ....K7
Tibet Aut. Reg. (Xizang)
1,892,393 ....B5
Tsinghai (Qinghai) 3,895,706 .E4
Xinjian Uygur
(Sinkiang-Uigur Aut. Reg.)
13,081,631 ....B3
Xizang (Tibet Aut. Reg.)
1,892,393 ....B5
Yunnan 32,553,817 ....F7
Zhejiang (Chekiang)
38,884,603 ....K6

CITIES and TOWNS

Aihui (Aigun) (Heihe) 73,660 ..L1
Amoy (Xiamen) 507,390 ....J7
Anqing (Anking) 449,310 .....J5
Anshan 1,195,580 ....K3
Anshun 200,680 ....G6
Anyang 501,390 ....H4
Baicheng, Jilin 276,420 ......K2
Baoding (Paoting) 495,140 ...J4
Baoji (Paoki) 341,240 ....G5
Baotou (Paotow) 1,075,920 ...G3
Beihai (Pakhoi) 173,740 ....G7
Beijing• (Peking) (cap.)
5,531,460 ....J3
Bengbu (Pengpu) 550,360 ....J5
Canton (Guangzhou,
Kwangchow) 3,181,510 .....H7
Changchih (Changzhi)
450,320 ....H4
Changchow (Changzhou)
533,940 ....J5
Changchow (Zhangzhou)
283,490 ....J7
Changchun 1,747,410 ....K3
Changde (Changteh) 213,890 .H6
Changhua 185,816 ....K7
Changsha 1,066,030 ....H6
Changteh (Changde) 213,890 .H6
Changzhi (Changchih)
450,320 ....H4
Changzhou (Changchow)
533,940 ....K5
Chankiang (Zhanjiang)
853,970 ....H7
Chaotung (Zhaotung)
133,080 ....F6
Chaoyang, Liaoning 206,700 ..J3
Chefoo (Yantai) 385,180 ....K4
Chengchow (Zhengzhou)
1,404,050 ....H5
Chengde (Chengteh) 326,910 .J3
Chengdu (Chengtu)
2,499,000 ....F5
Chiai 251,840 ....K7
Chifeng 293,460 ....J3
Chinchow (Jinzhou) 599,490 ..K3
Chinkiang (Zhenjiang)
345,560 ....J5
Chinwangtao (Qinhuangdao)
374,210 ....K4
Chongqing (Chungking)
2,673,170 ....G6
Chüanchow (Quanzhou)
403,180 ....J7
Chuchow (Zhuzhou) 382,950 .H6
Chumatien (Zhumadian)
150,440 ....H5
Chungking (Chongqing)
2,673,170 ....G6
Chungshan (Zhongshan)
135,000 ....H7
Conghua 280,250 ....H7
Dafang 962,470 ....G6
Dalian 1,480,240 ....K4
Dandong (Tantung) 545,180 ..K3
Daqing 758,430 ....L2
Datong (Tatung), Shanxi
962,470 ....H3
Da Xian 193,490 ....G5
Dezhou (Tehchow) 258,860 ...J4
Dukou 497,330 ....F6
Fatshan (Foshan) 273,840 ....H7
Fengcheng 995,900 ....K3
Foochow (Fuzhou) 1,111,550 .J6

(continued on following page)

China and Mongolia Transportation

Railroads	———
Under Construction	– – –
Connecting Roads	———
Navigable Rivers	———
Canals	———
Major Seaports	⚓

© Copyright HAMMOND INCORPORATED, Maplewood, N.J.

Foshan (Fatshan) 273,840......H7
Fowyang (Fuyang) 177,850...J5
Fushun 1,184,940.................K3
Fuxin (Fusin) 646,580...........K3
Fuyang (Fowyang) 177,850...J5
Fuzhou (Foochow), Fujian
1,111,550..........................J6
Fuzhou, Jiangxi 158,300.......J6
Ganzhou (Kanchow) 362,880 .H6
Gejiu (Kokiu) 352,980.........F7
Guangzhou (Canton)
3,181,510..........................H7
Guilin (Kweilin) 432,410.......G6
Guiyang (Kweiyang), Guizhou
1,350,190..........................G6
Gulja (Yining) 257,280.........B3
Haikou (Hoihow) 263,280.....H7
Hailar 157,490....................J2
Hanchung (Hanzhong)
374,270..............................G5
Handan (Hantan) 929,530....H4
Hangzhou (Hangchow)
1,171,550..........................J5
Hanton (Handan) 929,530....H4
Hanzhong (Hanchung)
374,270..............................G5
Harbin 2,519,120................L2
Hebi 336,430......................H4
Hefei (Hofei) 795,420..........J5
Hegang (Hokang) 592,470....L2
Heihe (Aigun, Aihui) 73,660...L1
Hengshui 101,260................H4
Hengyang 531,730...............H6
Hofei (Hefei) 795,420..........J5
Hohhot (Huhehcht) 754,120...H3
Hoihow (Haikou) 263,280.....H7
Hokang (Hegang) 592,470....L2
Horqin Youyi Qianqi
(Ulanhot) 174,050............K2
Houma 144,460....................H4
Hsüchang (Xuchang)
218,960..............................H5
Huaibei 444,820..................J5
Huaian 1,029,220................J5
Huangshi 375,640................J5
Huhehot (Hohhot) 754,120...H3
Huize 158,380......................F6
Hunjiang 694,160................L3
Huzhou (Wuxing) 925,900....K5
Hwainan (Huainan) 1,029,220.J5
Hwangshi (Huangshi)
375,640..............................J5
Ichang (Yichang) 365,000....H5
Ichun (Yichun) 755,830.......L2
Ipin (Yibin) 245,240.............F6
Jiamusi (Kiamusze) 540,190 .M2

Ji'an (Kian) 167,550.............J6
Jiangmen (Kongmoon)
212,450..............................H7
Jiaozuo (Tsiaotso) 484,370 ...H4
Jiaxing (Kashing) 656,130...K5
Jilin (Kirin) 1,808,420.........L3
Jinan (Tsinan) 1,359,130.....J4
Jingdezhen (Kingtehchen)
611,030..............................J6
Jinhua (Kinhwa) 869,490.....J6
Jining (Tsining), Nei Monggol
158,570..............................H3
Jining (Tsining), Shandong
190,420..............................J4
Jinzhou (Chinchow) 599,490..K3
Jiujiang (Kiukiang) 350,910 ...J6
Jixi (Kisi) 781,800...............M2
Kaifeng 602,230..................H5
Kaiyuan, Yunnan 223,420....F7
Kalgan (Zhangjiakou)
617,130..............................J3
Kanchow (Ganzhou) 362,880.H6
Kaohsiung 1,227,454...........J7
Karamay 156,970................B2
Kashi 256,890......................A4
Kashing (Jiaxing) 656,130...K5
Keelung 347,828..................J6
Kiamusze (Jiamusi) 540,190.M2
Kian (Ji'an) 167,550............J6
Kingtehchen (Jingdezhen)
611,030..............................J6
Kinhwa (Jinhua) 869,490.....J6
Kirin (Jilin) 1,808,420.........L3
Kisi (Jixi) 781,800...............M2
Kiukiang (Jiujiang) 350,910 ...J6
Kokiu (Gejiu) 352,980.........F7
Kongmoon (Jiangmen)
212,450..............................H7
Korla 117,690.....................C3
Kuldja (Yining) 257,280.......B3
Kunming 1,418,640.............F7
Kuytun 239,870..................C3
Kwangchow (Canton)
3,181,510..........................H7
Kweilin (Guilin) 432,410......G6
Kweisui (Hohhot) 754,120...H3
Kweiyang (Guiyang)
1,350,190..........................G6
Lanzhou (Lanchow)
1,364,480..........................F4
Lengshuijiang 254,590........H6
Leshan (Loshan) 958,360....F6
Lianyungang (Lienyünkang)
397,090..............................J5
Liaoyang 646,580................K3

Liaoyuan 771,510................K3
Linfen 208,210....................H4
Liuzhou (Liuchow) 581,940...G7
Loho (Luohe) 157,670.........H5
Longyan 346,700.................J6
Loshan (Leshan) 958,360....F6
Loyang (Luoyang) 951,610...H5
Lu'an 145,880.....................J5
Luchow (Luzhou) 305,220....G6
Lüde (Dalian) 1,480,240.....K4
Luohe 157,670....................H5
Luoyang (Loyang) 951,610...H5
Luzhou (Luchow) 305,220....G6
Ma'anshan 351,880.............J5
Manchouli (Manzhouli)
104,220..............................J2
Maoming (Mowming)
412,540..............................H7
Mianyang, Sichuan 768,500...G5
Mowming (Maoming)
412,540..............................H7
Mudanjiang (Mutankiang)
581,300..............................M3
Mukden (Shenyang)
3,944,240..........................K3
Nanchang 1,075,710...........J6
Nanchong (Nanchung)
228,340..............................G5
Nanjing (Nanking) 2,091,400 ..J5
Nanning 889,790................G7
Nanping 407,810................J6
Nantong 402,990................J5
Nanyang 288,300................H5
Neijiang (Neikiang) 270,950...G6
Ningbo (Ningpo) 478,940.....K6
Ningpo (Ningbo) 478,940.....K6
Ningsia (Yinchuan,
Yinchuan) 354,100...........G4
Paicheng (Baicheng) 276,420.K2
Pakhoi (Beihai) 173,740.......G7
Paoki (Baoji) 341,240.........H5
Paoting (Baoding) 495,140....J4
Paotow (Baotou) 1,075,920...G3
Peking• (Beijing) (cap.)
5,531,460..........................J4
Pengpu (Bengbu) 550,360....J5
Pingtung 189,347................K7
Pingxiang, Guangxi
Zhuangzu 1,189,030........G7
Pingxiang, Jiangxi 76,260...H6
Qingdao (Tsingtao)
1,172,370..........................K4
Qingjiang 234,750..............J5
Qinhuangdao (Chinwangtao)
374,210..............................K4
Qinzhou 981,280................G7

Qiqihar (Tsitsihar) 1,209,180..K2
Qitaihe 283,420..................M2
Quanzhou (Chüanchow)
403,180..............................J7
Sanmenxia 147,050............H5
Sanming 199,230................J6
Shanghai• 6,292,960..........J5
Shangqiu (Shangkiu) 186,760.J5
Shangrao (Shangiao)
135,160..............................J6
Shantou (Swatow) 717,620...J7
Shaoguan (Shiukwan)
370,550..............................H7
Shaoxing (Shaohing)
1,091,170..........................K5
Shaoyang 396,600..............H6
Shashi 238,960..................H5
Shenyang (Mukden)
3,944,240..........................K3
Shenzhen 98,060................H7
Shihezi (Shihhotzu) 563,740...C3
Shijiazhuang (Shihkiachwang)
1,068,720..........................J4
Shiukwan (Shaoyuan)
370,550..............................H7
Shiyan 306,830..................H5
Shuangyashan 400,050.......M2
Siakwan (Xiaguan) 117,190...E6
Sian (Xi'an) 2,185,040.........G5
Siangfan (Xiangfan) 323,000..H5
Siangtan (Xiangtan) 493,040..H6
Sienyang (Xianyang) 501,810.G5
Sinchu 208,038..................K7
Singtai (Xingtai) 334,210.....H4
Sining (Xining) 566,650.......F4
Sinsiang (Xinxiang) 525,280 ..H4
Sinyang (Xinyang) 240,000...H5
Soochow (Suzhou) 191,710...K5
Süchow (Xuzhou) 776,770...J5
Suizhong 669,940...............K3
Suzhou (Soochow) 191,710...K5
Swatow (Shantou) 717,620...J7
Szeping (Siping) 333,850.....K3
Tai'an 1,274,770................J4
Taichow (Taizhou) 161,200...K5
Taichung 565,255...............K7
Tainan 541,390..................J7
Taipeh 2,108,193...............K7
Taiyuan 1,745,820.............H4
Taizhou (Taichow) 161,200...K5
Tangshan 1,407,840...........J4
Tantung (Dandong) 545,180...K3
Tatung (Datong) 962,470....H3
Tehchow (Dezhou) 258,860 ...J4

Tianjin• (Tientsin) 5,142,565...J4
Tianshui 185,230................F5
Tieling 220,850..................K3
Tientsin• (Tianjin) 5,142,565...J4
Tienshui (Tianshui) 185,230 ...F5
Tongchuan (Tungchwan)
353,520..............................G5
Tongliao 213,470................K3
Tongling 184,060................J5
Tsiaotso (Jiaozuo) 484,370...H4
Tsinan (Jinan) 1,359,130.....J4
Tsingkiang (Qingjiang)
234,750..............................J5
Tsingtao (Qingdao)
1,172,370..........................K4
Tsining (Jining), Nei Monggol
158,570..............................H3
Tsining (Jining), Shandong
190,420..............................J4
Tsinyi (Zunyi) 250,670.........G6
Tsitsihar (Qiqihar) 1,209,180..K2
Tsunyi (Zunyi) 250,670.......G6
Tungchwan (Tongchuan)
353,520..............................G5

Tunghwa (Tonghua) 359,960..L3
Tungliao (Tongliao) 213,470...K3
Tunxi (Tunki) 103,560.........J6
Tzekung (Zigong) 866,020....F6
Tzepo (Zibo) 2,197,668.......J4
Ulanhot (Horqin Youyi
Qianqi) 174,050...............K2
Ürümqi (Urumchi)
961,240..............................C3
Wanxian (Wanhsien) 267,000.G5
Weifang 393,410................J4
Weihai (Weihaiwei) 205,010...K4
Wenchow (Wenzhou)
515,650..............................J6
Wenzhou 515,650..............J6
Wuchow (Wuzhou) 245,250...H7
Wuchung (Wuzhong)
245,250..............................G4
Wuhan 3,287,720..............H5
Wuhu 449,070....................J5
Wusih (Wuxi) 798,310.........K5
Wuxi (Wusih) 798,310.........K5
Wuxing 925,900.................K5

Wuzhong (Wuchung)
245,250..............................G4
Wuzhou (Wuchow) 245,250...H7
Xiaguan (Siakwan) 117,190...E6
Xiamen (Amoy) 507,390......J7
Xi'an (Sian) 2,185,040.........G5
Xiangfan (Siangfan) 323,000..H5
Xiangtan (Siangtan) 493,040..H6
Xianyang (Sienyang) 501,810.G5
Xingtai (Singtai) 334,210.....H4
Xining (Sining) 566,650.......F4
Xinxiang (Sinsiang) 525,280 ..H4
Xinyang (Sinyang) 240,000...H5
Xuchang (Hsüchang) 218,960.H5
Xuzhou (Süchow) 776,770...J5
Ya'an 254,420....................F6
Yangchow (Yangzhou)
302,090..............................J5
Yangchüan (Yangquan)
477,570..............................H4
Yangquan (Yangchüan)
477,570..............................H4
Yangzhou (Yangchow)

Topography

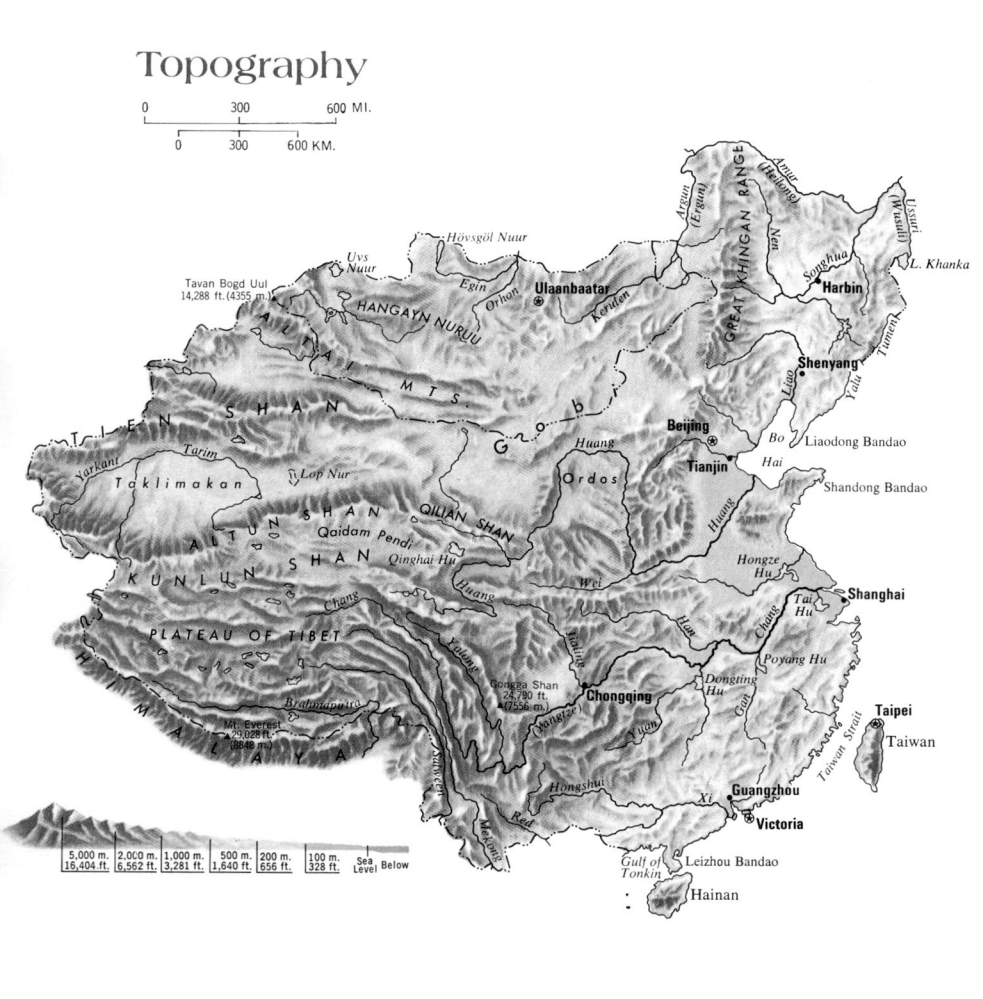

0   300   600 MI.
0   300   600 KM.

5,000 m. | 2,000 m. | 1,000 m. | 500 m. | 200 m. | 100 m. | Sea
16,404 ft. | 6,562 ft. | 3,281 ft. | 1,640 ft. | 656 ft. | 328 ft. | Level Below

On this map Chinese place-names have been rendered according to the Pinyin spelling system within the area controlled by the People's Republic of China. Alphabetically listed below are selected Chinese place-names spelled in the traditional manner, followed by the equivalent Pinyin form.

Amoy (Hsiamen)	Xiamen	Kirin	Jilin	Sian	Xi'an
Anhwei	Anhui	Kiukiang	Jiujiang	Siangtan	Xiangtan
Canton		Kwangsi	Guangxi	Sining	Xining
(Kwangchow)	Guangzhou	Kwangtung	Guangdong	Sinkiang-	
Chefoo (Yentai)	Yantai	Chuang	Zhuangzu	Uighur	Xinjiang Uygur
Chekiang	Zhejiang	Kweichow	Guizhou	Soochow	Suzhou
Chengchow	Zhengzhou	Kweilin	Guilin	Süchow	Xuzhou
Chengtu	Chengdu	Kweiyang	Guiyang	Swatow	Shantou
Chinchow	Jinzhou	Lanchow	Lanzhou	Szechwan	Sichuan
Chungking	Chongqing	Liuchow	Liuzhou	Tachai	Dazhai
Foochow	Fuzhou	Loyang	Luoyang	Tatung	Datong
Fukien	Fujian	Lüta	Dalian	Tibet	Xizang
Hangchow	Hangzhou	Mutankiang	Mudanjiang	Tientsin	Tianjin
Heilungkiang	Heilongjiang	Nanking	Nanjing	Tsinan	Jinan
Hofei	Hefei	Ningpo	Ningbo	Tsinghai	Qinghai
Honan	Henan	Ningsia Hui	Ningxia Huizu	Tsingtao	Qingdao
Hopei	Hebei	Paoting	Baoding	Tsining	Jining
Huhehot	Hohhot	Paotow	Baotou	Tsitsihar	Qiqihar
Hupeh	Hubei	Penki	Benxi	Tsunyi	Zunyi
Hwainan	Huainan	Peking	Beijing	Tungchwan	Tongchuan
Inner Mongolia	Nei Monggol	Pengpu	Bengbu	Tzepo	Zibo
Kansu	Gansu	Shansi	Shanxi	Urumchi	Urumqi
Kiangsi	Jiangxi	Shantung	Shandong	Wusih	Wuxi
Kiangsu	Jiangsu	Shensi	Shaanxi	Yenan	Yan'an
Kingtehchen	Jingdezhen	Shihkiachwang	Shijiazhuang	Yinchuan	Yinchuan

302,090	J5
Yanji (Yenki) 176,000	L3
Yantai (Chefoo) 385,180	K4
Yenki (Yanji) 176,000	L3
Yibin (Ipin) 245,240	F6
Yichang (Ichang) 365,000	H5
Yichun, Heilongjiang 755,830	L2
Yichun, Jiangxi 171,720	H6
Yinchuan Ningsia 354,100	C4
Yingkou 422,590	K3
Yining 257,280	B3
Yiyang 165,040	H6
Yuci (Yütze) 270,890	H4
Yueyang 971,790	H6
Yumen 195,290	E4
Yungkia (Wenzhou) 515,650	J6
Yütze (Yuci) 270,890	H4
Zaozhuang 1,244,020	J5
Zhangjiakou (Kalgan)	
617,120	J3
Zhangzhou (Changchow)	
283,490	J7
Zhanjiang (Chankiang)	

853,970	H7
Zhaoqing 172,080	H7
Zhaotong (Chaotung)	
133,080	F6
Zhengzhou (Chengchow)	
1,404,050	H5
Zhenjiang (Chinkiang)	
345,560	J5
Zhongshan (Chungshan)	
135,000	H7
Zhumadian (Chumatien)	
150,440	H5
Zhuzhou (Chuchow) 332,950	H6
Zibo (Tzepo) 2,197,663	J4
Zigong (Tzekung) 866,020	F6
Zunyi (Tsunyi) 350,670	G6

OTHER FEATURES

Altun Shan (range)	C4
Alxa Shamo (des.)	F4
Amur (Heilong Jiang) riv.)	L2
A'nyêmaqên Shan (mts.)	E5

Aqqikkol Hu (lake)	C4
Argun' (Ergun He) (riv.)	K1
Ayakkum Hu (lake)	C4
Bagrax (Bosten Hu) (lake)	C3
Bangong Co (lake)	A5
Bashi (chan.)	K7
Bayan Har Shan (range)	E5
Bo Hai (gulf)	J4
Bosten Hu (Bagrax) (lake)	C3
Chang Jiang (Yangtze) (riv.)	K5
Daba Shan (range)	G5
Da Hinggan Ling (range)	J3
Dian Chi (lake)	F7
Dogai Coring (lake)	C5
Dongsha (isl.)	J7
Dongting Hu (lake)	H6
East China (sea)	L6
Ebinur Hu (lake)	B2
Ergun He (Argun') (riv.)	K1
Er Hai (lake)	F6
Everest (mt.)	C6
Fen He (riv.)	H4
Formosa (Taiwan) (isl.)	K7

Formosa (Taiwan) (str.)	J7
Gangdisê Shan (range)	B5
Gan He (riv.)	K2
Gaoyou Hu (lake)	J5
Ghenghis Khan Wall (ruin)	H2
Gobi (des.)	G3
Gongga Shan (mt.)	F6
Grand (canal)	J4
Great Wall (ruins)	G4
Gurla Mandhada (mt.)	B5
Gyaring Co (lake)	C5
Gyaring Hu (lake)	E4
Hailar He (riv.)	K2
Hainan (isl.)	H8
Hangzhou Wan (bay)	K5
Han Shui (riv.)	H5
Har Hu (lake)	E4
Heilong Jiang (Amur) (riv.)	L2
Hengduan Shan (range)	E6
Himalaya (range)	C6
Hoh Xil Shan (mts.)	C4
Hongshui He (riv.)	G7
Hongze Hu (lake)	J5

Hotan He (riv.)	B4
Huang He (Yellow) (riv.)	F5
Hulun Nur (lake)	J2
Huma He (riv.)	K1
Inner Mongolia (reg.)	H3
Jinmen (Quemoy) (isl.)	J7
Jinsha Jiang (Yangtze) (riv.)	E5
Junggar Pendi (desert basin)	C2
Kangrinboqê Feng (mt.)	B5
Karakax He (riv.)	A4
Karakhoto (ruins)	F3
Karamiran Shankou (pass)	C4
Keriya He (riv.)	B4
Keriya Shankou (pass)	B4
Khanka (lake)	M3
Kongur Shan (mt.)	A4
Konqi He (riv.)	C3
Künes He (riv.)	B3
Kunlun Shan (range)	B4
Kuruktag Shan (range)	C3
Lancang Jiang (riv.)	F7
Laoha He (riv.)	J3
Leizhou Bandao (pen.)	G7

Liao He (riv.)	K3
Liaodong Bandao (pen.)	K3
Lop Nor (Lop Nur) (lake)	D3
Lumajangdong Co (lake)	B5
Manas He (riv.)	C3
Manas Hu (lake)	C2
Margai Caka (lake)	C4
Mazu (Matsu) (isl.)	K6
Mekong (Lancang Jiang) (riv.)	F7
Min Jiang (riv.)	J6
Moron Us He (riv.)	D5
Mudan Jiang (riv.)	L3
Mu Us Shamo (des.)	G4
Muztag (mt.)	B4
Muztagata (mt.)	A4
Nam Co (lake)	C5
Namzha Parwa (mt.)	E6
Nan Ling (mts.)	H6
Nanpan Jiang (riv.)	F7
Nen Jiang (riv.)	K2
Ngangla Ringco (lake)	B5
Ngangzê Co (lake)	C5
Ngom Qu (riv.)	E5

Ngoring Hu (lake)	E5
Nu Jiang (riv.)	E6
Nyainqêntanglha Shan	
(range)	D5
Ordos (reg.)	G4
Penghu (Pescadores) (isls.)	J7
Pingtan (isl.)	K6
Pobeda (peak)	A3
Poyang Hu (lake)	J6
Pratas (Dongsha) (isl.)	J7
Qaidam Pendi (basin)	D4
Qarqan He (riv.)	C4
Qilian Shan (range)	E4
Qinghai Hu (lake)	E4
Qumar He (riv.)	D4
Rola Co (lake)	C4
Salween (Nu Jiang) (riv.)	E6
Siling Co (lake)	C5
Songhua Hu (lake)	L3
Songhua Jiang (Sungari)	
(riv.)	M2
Tai Hu (lake)	J5
Taiwan (Formosa) (isl.)	K7

(continued on following page)

China and Mongolia

SCALE OF MILES
0 100 200 300 400 500

SCALE OF KILOMETERS
0 100 200 300 400 500

Capitals of Countries......⊛   International Boundaries......
Provincial Capitals......●   Provincial Boundaries......
Canals......   Walls......

Scale 1:19,100,000

© Copyright HAMMOND INCORPORATED, Maplewood, N.J.

Taiwan (Formosa) (str.) J7
Taizhou (Tachen) (isls.) K6
Takla Makan (Taklimakan
  Shamo) (des.) B4
Tanggula Shan (range) D5
Tangra Yumco (lake) C5
Tarim He (riv.) B3
Tarim Pendi (basin) B4
Tian Shan (range) C3
Tibet (reg.) B5
Tongtian He (Zhi Qu) (riv.) E5
Tonkin (gulf) G7
Toson Hu (lake) E4
Tumen (riv.) L3
Tuotuo He (riv.) D5
Ulu Muztag (mt.) C4
Ulungur He (riv.) C2
Ulungur Hu (lake) C2
Ussuri (Wusuli Jiang) (riv.).....M2
Wei He (riv.) G5
Wu Jiang (riv.) G6
Wusuli Jiang (Ussuri) (riv.)....M2
Wuyi Shan (range) J6
Xar Moron He (riv.) J3
Xiang Jiang (riv.) H6
Xi Jiang (riv.) H7
Xinyi (riv.) J5
Yagradagzê Shan (mt.) D4
Yalong Jiang (riv.) F6
Yalu (riv.) L3
Yamzho Yumco (lake) C6
Yangtze (Chang Jiang) (riv.)...K5
Yarkant He (riv.) A4
Yellow (Huang He) (riv.).....F5
Yellow (sea) K4
Yibug Caka (lake) C5
Yin Shan (mts.) G3
Yuan Jiang (riv.) H6
Yuhuan (isl.) K6
Yurungkax He (riv.) A4
Yü Shan (mt.) K7
Yushan (isls.) K6

Za Qu (riv.) E5
Zhari Namco (lake) C5
Zhaxi Co (lake) C5
Zhoushan (arch.) K5

HONG KONG

CITIES and TOWNS

Kowloon* 2,450,187 ....H7
Victoria (cap.) 1,183,621........H7

**MACAU
(MACAO)**

CITIES and TOWNS

Macau (Macao) (cap.)
  238,413 ....H7

MONGOLIA

PROVINCES

Arhangay 90,500 ....F2
Bayamhongor 64,900 ....E2
Bayan-Olgiy 73,300 ....C2
Bulgan 45,700 ....F2
Dornod 51,100 ....H2
Dornogov‍ĭ 36,400 ....G3
Dundgov‍ĭ 37,800 ....G2
Dzavhan 87,600 ....E2
Gov‍ĭ-Altay 59,200 ....E3
Hentiy 49,900 ....H2
Hövsgöl 89,600 ....E1
Hovd 68,300 ....D2
Ömnögov‍ĭ 32,200 ....F3
Övörhangay 84,100 ....F2
Selenge 53,700 ....G2
Sühbaatar 44,100 ....H2
Töv 74,900 ....G2
Uvs 76,300 ....D2

CITIES and TOWNS

Altay 10,000 ....E2
Arvayheer 9,100 ....F2
Baatsagaan 800 ....E2
Baruun-Urt 8,200 ....H2
Bayandalay 500 ....F3
Bayangov‍ĭ 400 ....F3
Bayanhongor 11,300 ....E2
Bayan-Öndör 300 ....E3
Bayan-Uul 1,200 ....E2
Beger 800 ....E2
Bulgan, Bulgan 9,800 ....F2
Bulgan, Hovd 700 ....F3
Bulgan, Omnögov‍ĭ 3,100 ....D2
Bürentsogt 3,000 ....H2
Chandman‍ĭ 700 ....E2
Choybalsan 31,000 ....J2
Dalandzadgad 6,600 ....G3
Darhan (Darkhan) 56,400 ....G2
Dashbalbar 1,100 ....H2
Dashinchilen 600 ....F2
Dzam‍ĭn Üüd 1,500 ....H3
Dzüünharaa 8,100 ....G2
Dzuunmod 38,700 ....G2
Erdenetsagaan 1,500 ....J2
Hanh 500 ....F1
Hatgal 5,000 ....E1
Hovd (Kobdo Jirgalanta)
  12,400 ....D2
Hyargas 1,600 ....D2
Jibhalanta (Uliastay) 13,000 ....E2
Kobdo (Hovd) 12,400 ....D2
Mandalgov‍ĭ 7,000 ....G2
Mörön (Muren) 10,700 ....F2
Nalayh (Nalaikha) 14,000 ....G2
Ölgiy (Ulegei) 11,700 ....C2
Ondörhaan (Undur Khan)
  7,900 ....G2
Onon 2,600 ....H2
Saynshand 10,000 ....H3
Selenge 1,300 ....F2

Sühbaatar (Sukhe Bator)
  35,000 ....G1
Tsagaan-Ovoo 900 ....H2
Tsagaannuur 2,000 ....C2
Tsagaan-Uul 1,700 ....E2
Tsetseg 700 ....D2
Tsetserleg 12,400 ....F2
Ulaanbaatar (Ulan Bator)
  (cap.) 435,400 ....G2
Ulaangom (Ulangom) 14,000 ....D2
Ulegei (Olgiy) 11,700 ....C2
Uliastay (Jibhalanta) 13,000 ....E2
Urga (Ülaanbaatar) (cap.)
  435,400 ....G2

OTHER FEATURES

Altai (mts.) D2
Dörgön Nuur (lake) D2
Dzavhan Gol (riv.) E2
Ghenghis Khan Wall (ruins) G3
Gobi (des.) G3
Hangayn Nuruu (mts.) E2
Har Us Nuur (lake) D2
Herlen Gol (Kerulen) (riv.) H2
Hovd Gol (riv.) D2
Hövsgöl Nuur (lake) F1
Hyargas Nuur (lake) D2
Ider Gol (riv.) F2
Karakorum (ruins) F2
Kerulen (riv.) H2
Munku-Sardyk (mt.) F1
Orhon Gol (riv.) F2
Selenge Mörön (riv.) F2
Tannu-Ola (range) D1
Tavan Bogd Uul (mt.) C2
Uvs Nuur (lake) D1

• Population of municipality.
*City and suburbs.

† Populations of mainland cities, excluding Peking (Beijing), Shanghai and Tianjin (Tientsin), courtesy of Kingsley Davis.
Office of Int'l Pop. and Research, Inst. of Int'l Studies Univ. of California.

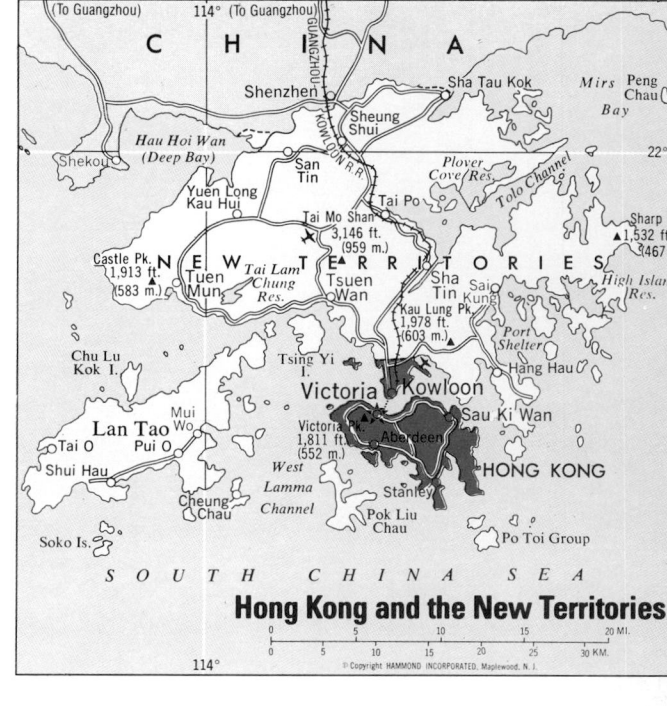

Hong Kong and the New Territories

Agriculture, Industry and Resources

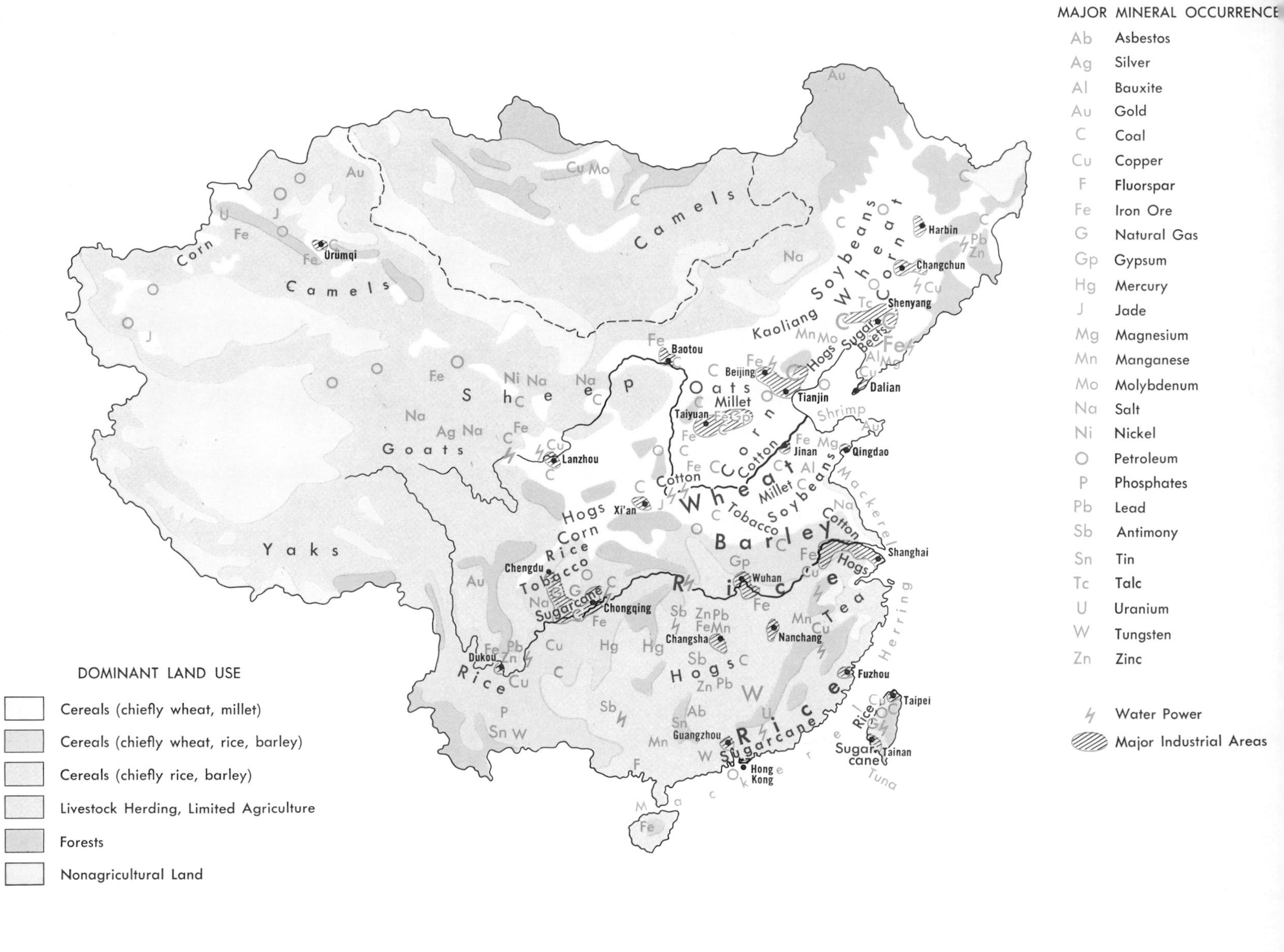

DOMINANT LAND USE

Cereals (chiefly wheat, millet)
Cereals (chiefly wheat, rice, barley)
Cereals (chiefly rice, barley)
Livestock Herding, Limited Agriculture
Forests
Nonagricultural Land

MAJOR MINERAL OCCURRENCE

Ab	Asbestos
Ag	Silver
Al	Bauxite
Au	Gold
C	Coal
Cu	Copper
F	Fluorspar
Fe	Iron Ore
G	Natural Gas
Gp	Gypsum
Hg	Mercury
J	Jade
Mg	Magnesium
Mn	Manganese
Mo	Molybdenum
Na	Salt
Ni	Nickel
O	Petroleum
P	Phosphates
Pb	Lead
Sb	Antimony
Sn	Tin
Tc	Talc
U	Uranium
W	Tungsten
Zn	Zinc

⚡ Water Power
▨ Major Industrial Areas

AREA 145,730 sq. mi. (377,441 sq. km.)
POPULATION 123,116,000
CAPITAL Tokyo
LARGEST CITY Tokyo
HIGHEST POINT Fuji 12,389 ft. (3,776 m.)
MONETARY UNIT yen
MAJOR LANGUAGE Japanese
MAJOR RELIGIONS Buddhism, Shintoism

AREA 46,540 sq. mi. (120,539 sq. km.)
POPULATION 22,419,000
CAPITAL P'yŏngyang
LARGEST CITY P'yŏngyang
HIGHEST POINT Paektu 9,003 ft. (2,744 m.)
MONETARY UNIT won
MAJOR LANGUAGE Korean
MAJOR RELIGIONS Confucianism, Buddhism, Ch'ondogyo

AREA 38,175 sq. mi. (98,873 sq. km.)
POPULATION 42,793,000
CAPITAL Seoul
LARGEST CITY Seoul
HIGHEST POINT Halla 6,398 ft. (1,950 m.)
MONETARY UNIT won
MAJOR LANGUAGE Korean
MAJOR RELIGIONS Confucianism, Buddhism, Ch'ondogyo, Christianity

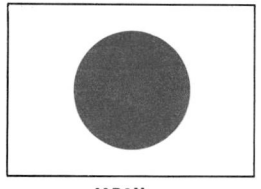
JAPAN

NORTH KOREA

SOUTH KOREA

JAPAN

PREFECTURES

chi 6,221,638 ....H6
kita 1,256,745 ....J4
omori 1,523,907 ....K3
iba 4,735,424 ....P2
hime 1,506,637 ....F7
ukui 794,354 ....G5
ukushima 2,035,272 ....K5
fu 1,960,107 ....H6
umma 1,846,562 ....J5
roshima 2,739,161 ....G6
okkaido 5,575,989 ....K2
yogo 5,144,892 ....H7
baraki 2,558,007 ....J5
hikawa 1,119,304 ....H5
wate 1,421,927 ....K4
açawa 999,864 ....G6
ar agawa 6,924,348 ....O2
ochi 831,275 ....F7
umamoto 1,790,327 ....E7
yoto 2,527,330 ....J7
ie 1,686,936 ....H6
iyagi 2,082,320 ....K4
iyazaki 1,151,587 ....E8
agano 2,083,934 ....J5
Nagasaki 1,590,564 ....D7
Nara 1,209,365 ....J8
Niigata 2,451,357 ....J5
Oita 1,228,913 ....E7
Okayama 1,871,023 ....F6
Okinawa 1,106,559 ....N6
Osaka 8,473,446 ....J8
Saga 865,574 ....E7
Saitama 5,420,480 ....O2
Shiga 1,079,898 ....J7
Shimane 784,795 ....F6
Shizuoka 3,446,804 ....H6
Tochigi 1,792,201 ....K5
Tokushima 825,261 ....G7
Tokyo 11,618,281 ....O2
Tottori 604,221 ....G6
Toyama 1,103,459 ....H5
Wakayama 1,087,012 ....G6
Yamagata 1,251,917 ....K4
Yamaguchi 1,587,079 ....E6
Yamanashi 804,256 ....J6

CITIES and TOWNS

Abashiri 44,777 ....M1
Ageo 166,243 ....O2
Aizuwakamatsu 114,528 ....J5
Akashi 254,869 ....H8
Akita 284,863 ....J4
Amagasaki 523,650 ....H8
Amagi 42,863 ....E7
Anan 61,253 ....G7
Aomori 287,594 ....K3
Asahi 35,721 ....K6
Asahikawa 352,619 ....L2
Ashikaga 165,756 ....J5
Ashiya 81,745 ....H8
Atami 50,082 ....J6
Atsugi 145,392 ....O2
Ayabe 42,552 ....G6
Beppu 136,485 ....E7
Chiba 746,430 ....P2
Chichibu 61,285 ....O3
Chigasaki 171,016 ....O3
Chitose 66,788 ....K2
Chofu 180,548 ....O2
Choshi 89,416 ....K6
Daito 116,635 ....J8
Ebetsu 86,349 ....K2
Eniwa 42,911 ....K2
Fuchu, Hiroshima 49,026 ....F6
Fuchu, Tokyo 192,198 ....O2
Fuji 205,751 ....J6
Fujieda 103,225 ....J6
Fujisawa 300,248 ....O3
Fukagawa 35,376 ....L2
Fukuchiyama 63,788 ....G6
Fukue 32,135 ....D7
Fukui 240,962 ....G5
Fukuoka 1,088,588 ....D7
Fukushima 262,837 ....K5
Fukuyama 346,030 ....F6
Funabashi 479,439 ....P2
Furukawa 57,060 ....K4
Gifu 410,357 ....H6
Goshogawara 50,632 ....K3
Habikino 103,181 ....J8
Hachinohe 238,179 ....K3
Hachioji 387,178 ....O2
Hadano 123,133 ....J6
Hagi 53,693 ....E6
Hakodate 320,154 ....K3
Hamada 50,799 ....E6
Hamamatsu 490,824 ....H6
Hanamaki 68,873 ....K4
Hanno 61,179 ....O2
Haramachi 46,052 ....K5
Higashiosaka 521,558 ....J8
Hikone 89,701 ....H6
Himeji 446,256 ....G6
Himi 62,413 ....H5
Hino 145,448 ....O2
Hirakata 353,358 ....J7
Hiratsuka 214,293 ....O3
Hirosaki 175,330 ....K3
Hiroshima 899,399 ....F6
Hitachi 204,596 ....K5
Hitoyoshi 42,236 ....E7
Hofu 111,468 ....E6
Hondo 42,460 ....E7
Honjo 42,962 ....J4
Hyuga 58,347 ....E7
Ibaraki 234,062 ....J7
Ichihara 216,394 ....P3
Ichikawa 364,244 ....P2
Ichinomiya 253,139 ....H6
Ichinoseki 60,214 ....K4
Iida 78,515 ....H6
Iizuka 80,288 ....E7
Ikeda 101,121 ....H7
Ikoma 70,461 ....J8
Imabari 123,234 ....F6
Imari 61,243 ....D7
Ina 56,086 ....H6
Isahaya 83,723 ....D7
Ise 105,621 ....H6
Ishinomaki 120,699 ....K4
Ishioka 47,829 ....K5
Itami 178,228 ....H7
Ito 69,638 ....J6
Itoman 42,239 ....N6
Iwaki 342,074 ....K5
Iwakuni 112,525 ....E6
Iwamizawa 78,311 ....L2
Iwata 75,810 ....H6
Iwatsuki 94,696 ....O2
Izumi 124,323 ....J8
Izumiotsu 67,474 ....J8
Izumisano 90,684 ....G6
Izumo 77,303 ....F6
Joetsu 127,842 ....H5
Joyo 74,350 ....J7
Kadoma 138,902 ....J7
Kaga 65,282 ....H5
Kagoshima 505,360 ....E8
Kaizuka 81,162 ....H8
Kakogawa 212,233 ....G6
Kamaishi 65,250 ....L4
Kamakura 172,629 ....O3
Kameoka 69,410 ....J7
Kanazawa 417,684 ....H5
Kanonji 44,927 ....F6
Kanoya 73,242 ....E8
Kanuma 85,159 ....J5
Karatsu 77,710 ....D7
Kaseda 25,392 ....D8
Kashihara 107,316 ....J8
Kashiwa 239,198 ....P2
Kashiwara 69,836 ....J8
Kashiwazaki 83,499 ....J5
Kasugai 244,119 ....H6
Kasukabe 155,555 ....O2
Katsuta 92,621 ....K5
Kawachinagano 78,572 ....J8
Kawagoe 259,314 ....O2
Kawaguchi 379,360 ....J6
Kawanishi 129,834 ....H7
Kawasaki 1,040,802 ....O2
Kesennuma 68,551 ....K4
Kimitsu 77,286 ....P3
Kiryu 132,889 ....J5
Kisarazu 110,711 ....P3
Kishiwada 180,317 ....J8
Kitaibaraki 47,670 ....K5
Kitakami 53,647 ....K4
Kitakyushu 1,065,078 ....E6
Kitami 102,915 ....L2
Kobayashi 40,033 ....E8
Kobe 1,367,390 ....H7
Kochi 300,822 ....F7
Kodaira 154,610 ....O2
Kofu 199,262 ....J6
Koga 56,657 ....J5
Koganei 102,456 ....O2
Komatsu 104,329 ....H5
Koriyama 286,451 ....K5
Koshigaya 223,241 ....P2
Kuki 54,410 ....O2
Kumagaya 136,806 ....J5
Kumamoto 525,662 ....E7
Kurashiki 403,785 ....F6
Kurayoshi 52,270 ....F6
Kure 234,549 ....F6
Kuroiso 46,574 ....K5
Kurume 216,972 ....E7
Kushiro 214,694 ....M2
Kyoto 1,473,065 ....J7
Machida 295,405 ....O2
Maebashi 265,169 ....J5
Maizuru 97,578 ....G6
Masuda 52,756 ....E6
Matsubara 135,849 ....H8
Matsudo 400,863 ....P2
Matsue 135,568 ....F6
Matsumoto 192,085 ....H5
Matsusaka 113,481 ....H6
Matsuto 43,766 ....H5
Matsuyama 401,703 ....F7
Mihara 84,450 ....F6
Miki 70,201 ....H7
Minoo 104,112 ....J7
Mitaka 164,526 ....O2
Mito 215,566 ....K5
Mitsukaido 40,435 ....P2
Miura 48,687 ....O3
Miyako 62,478 ....L4
Miyakonojo 129,009 ....E8
Miyazaki 264,855 ....E8
Mizusawa 55,226 ....K4
Mobara 71,521 ....K6
Mooka 52,764 ....K5
Moriguchi 165,630 ....J7
Morioka 229,114 ....K4
Muko 50,604 ....J7
Muroran 150,199 ....K2
Musashino 136,910 ....O2
Mutsu 47,610 ....K3
Nagahama 54,935 ....H6
Nagano 324,360 ....J5
Nagaoka 180,259 ....J5
Nagaokakyo 71,445 ....J7
Nagasaki 447,091 ....D7
Nago 45,991 ....N6
Nagoya 2,087,902 ....H6
Naha 295,778 ....N6
Nakatsu 63,941 ....E7
Nanao 50,394 ....H5
Nankoku 44,866 ....F7
Nara 297,953 ....J8
Narashino 125,155 ....P2
Naze 49,021 ....O5
Nemuro 42,880 ....M2
Neyagawa 255,859 ....J7
Nichinan 52,949 ....E8
Niigata 457,785 ....J5
Niihama 132,339 ....F6
Niitsu 62,282 ....J5
Nishinomiya 410,329 ....H8
Nobeoka 136,598 ....E7
Noboribetsu 56,503 ....K2
Noda 93,958 ....P2
Nogata 62,595 ....E7
Noshiro 60,674 ....J3
Noto 15,480 ....H5
Numata 47,150 ....J5
Numazu 203,695 ....J6
Obihiro 153,861 ....L2
Oda 38,026 ....F6

(continued on following page)

Agriculture, Industry and Resources

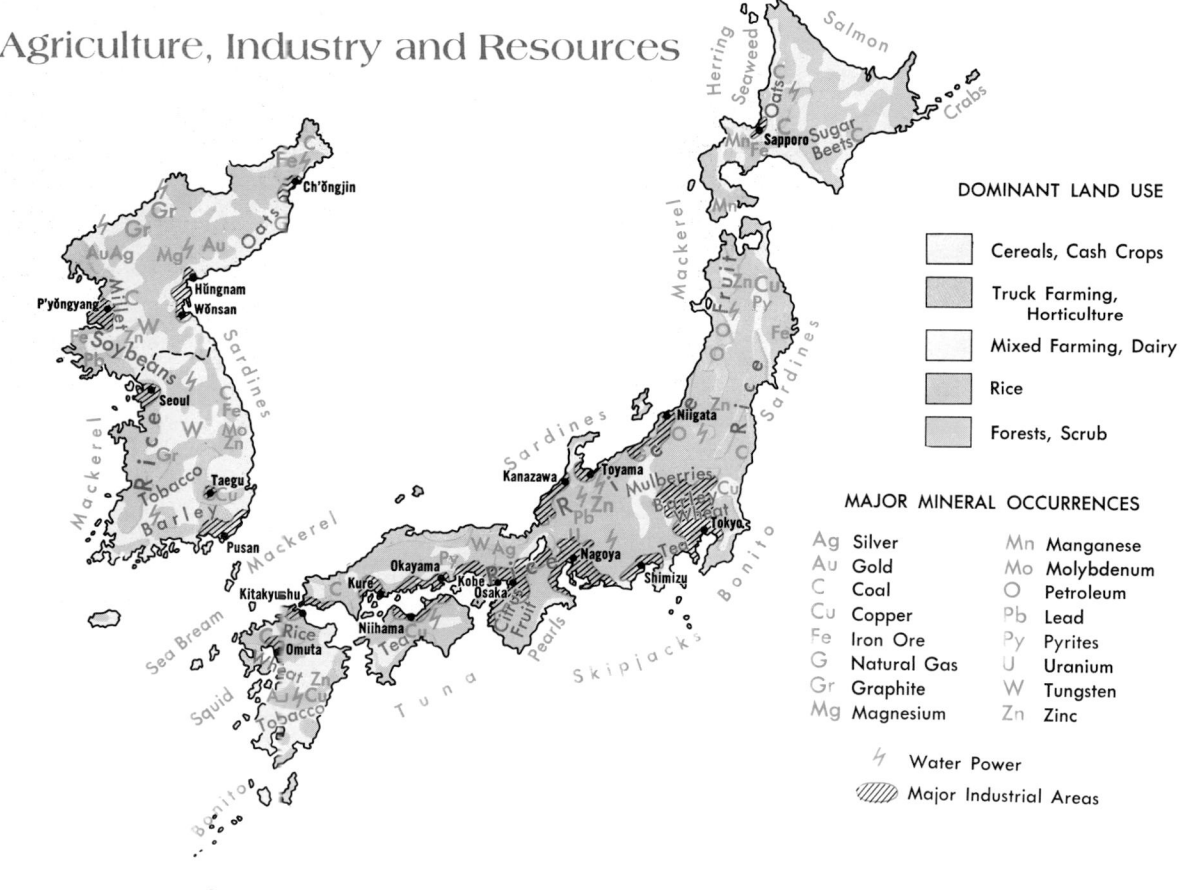

DOMINANT LAND USE

- Cereals, Cash Crops
- Truck Farming, Horticulture
- Mixed Farming, Dairy
- Rice
- Forests, Scrub

MAJOR MINERAL OCCURRENCES

Ag	Silver	Mn	Manganese
Au	Gold	Mo	Molybdenum
C	Coal	O	Petroleum
Cu	Copper	Pb	Lead
Fe	Iron Ore	Py	Pyrites
G	Natural Gas	U	Uranium
Gr	Graphite	W	Tungsten
Mg	Magnesium	Zn	Zinc

⚡ Water Power

▨ Major Industrial Areas

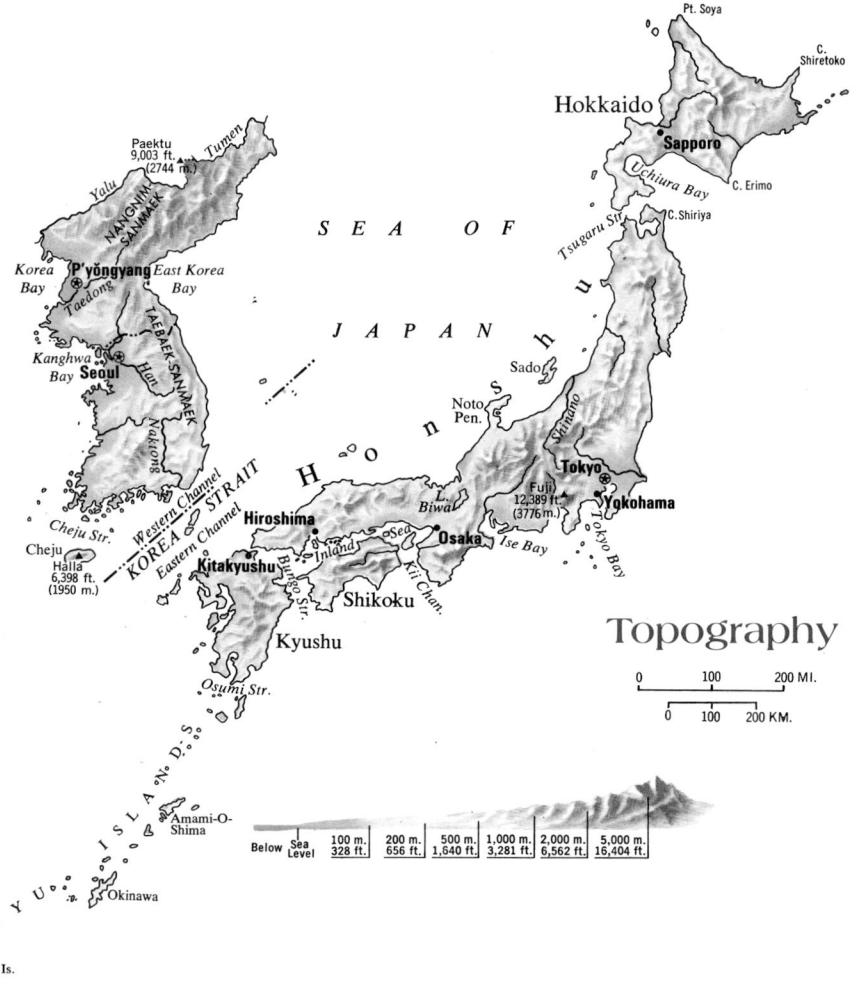

Topography

Sata (cape).....E8
Shikoku (isl.).....F7
Shikotan (isl.).....N2
Shikotsu (lake).....K2
Shimane (pen.).....F6
Shimokita (pen.).....K3
Shinano (riv.).....J5
Shiono (cape).....H7
Shiragami (cape).....J3
Shirane (mt.).....H6
Shiretoko (cape).....M1
Shiriya (cape).....K3
Soya (pt.).....L1
Suo (sea).....E7
Suruga (bay).....J6
Suzu (pt.).....H5
Takeshima (isls.).....F5
Tanega (isl.).....E8
Tappi (cape).....K3
Teshio (riv.).....L1

Tokachi (riv.).....L2
Tokachi (mt.).....L2
Tokara (isls.).....O5
Tokuno (isl.).....O5
Tokyo (bay).....O2
Tone (riv.).....K6
Tosa (bay).....F7
Towada (lake).....K3
Toya (lake).....K2
Toyama (bay).....H5
Tsu (isls.).....D6
Tsugaru (strait).....K3
Tsurugi (mt.).....G7
Uchiura (bay).....L2
Volcano (isls.).....M4
Wakasa (bay).....G6
Western Channel (strait).....D6
Yaeyama (isls.).....K7
Yaku (isl.).....E8
Yonaguni (isl.).....K7

Odate 72,478 .....K3
Odawara 177,467 .....J6
Ofunato 40,023 .....K4
Oga 38,940 .....J4
Ogaki 143,151 .....H6
Oita 360,478 .....E7
Ojiya 44,963 .....J5
Okawa 49,537 .....E7
Okaya 62,210 .....H5
Okayama 545,765 .....F6
Okazaki 262,372 .....H6
Omagari 41,764 .....K4
Omiya 354,084 .....O2
Omura 65,638 .....E7
Omuta 163,000 .....E7
Onagawa 16,105 .....K4
Ono 41,901 .....H6
Onoda 44,803 .....E6
Onomichi 102,056 .....F6
Osaka 2,648,180 .....J8
Ota 123,115 .....J5
Otaru 180,728 .....K2
Otawara 46,662 .....K5
Otofuke 31,134 .....L2
Oyabe 36,497 .....H5
Oyama 127,226 .....J5
Ozu 38,719 .....F7
Rumoi 36,626 .....K2
Ryugasaki 43,132 .....P2
Sabae 59,579 .....H5
Saga 163,765 .....E7
Sagamihara 439,300 .....O2
Saiki 54,306 .....E7
Saito 37,836 .....E7
Sakado 77,335 .....O2
Sakai 810,106 .....J8
Sakaide 66,290 .....G6
Sakaiminato 37,278 .....F6
Sakata 102,600 .....J4
Saku 57,361 .....J5
Sakurai 56,439 .....J8
Sanda 36,529 .....H7
Sanjo 85,275 .....J5
Sapporo 1,401,757 .....K2
Sasebo 251,187 .....D7
Satte 49,704 .....O1
Sawara 49,200 .....K6
Sayama 124,029 .....O2
Sendai, Kagoshima 65,645 .....E8
Sendai, Miyagi 664,868 .....K4
Shibata 76,209 .....J5
Shimabara 46,637 .....E7
Shimizu 241,576 .....J6
Shimonoseki 268,957 .....H7
Shingu 39,993 .....H7
Shinjo 42,911 .....K4
Shiogama 61,040 .....K4
Shirakawa 43,187 .....K5
Shiroishi 41,275 .....K4
Shizuoka 458,341 .....H6
Soka 186,618 .....O2
Suita 332,418 .....J7
Sukagawa 57,110 .....K5
Sumoto 44,131 .....G6

Suwa 50,558 .....H6
Suzuka 156,250 .....H6
Tachikawa 142,675 .....O2
Tagawa 60,077 .....E7
Tajimi 74,311 .....H6
Takaishi 66,815 .....H8
Takamatsu 316,661 .....F6
Takaoka 175,055 .....H5
Takarazuka 183,628 .....H7
Takasaki 221,429 .....J5
Takatsuki 340,720 .....J7
Takayama 63,813 .....H5
Takefu 67,104 .....G6
Takikawa 51,192 .....K2
Tanabe, Kyoto 39,198 .....J7
Tanabe, Wakayama 69,575 .....G7
Tateyama 56,257 .....K6
Tendo 52,597 .....K4
Tenri 64,894 .....J8
Teshio 6,281 .....K1
Togane 35,603 .....K6
Tokamachi 49,555 .....J5
Tokorozawa 236,476 .....O2
Tokushima 249,343 .....G7
Tokuyama 111,469 .....F6
Tokyo (cap.) 8,351,893 .....O2
Tokyo* 11,618,281 .....O2
Tomakomai 151,967 .....K2
Tondabayashi 97,495 .....J8
Tosu 54,254 .....E7
Tottori 131,060 .....G6
Towada 58,886 .....K3
Toyama 305,055 .....H5
Toyohashi 304,273 .....H6
Toyonaka 403,174 .....J7
Toyooka 47,458 .....G6
Toyota 281,608 .....H6
Tsu 144,991 .....H6
Tsubame 44,236 .....J5
Tsuchiura 112,517 .....J5
Tsuruga 61,844 .....G6
Tsuruoka 99,751 .....J4
Tsuyama 83,136 .....F6
Ube 168,958 .....E6
Ueda 111,540 .....J5
Uji 152,692 .....J7
Uozu 49,512 .....H5
Urawa 358,185 .....O2
Utsunomiya 377,746 .....K5
Uwajima 71,586 .....F7
Wajima 32,662 .....H5
Wakayama 400,802 .....G7
Wakkanai 53,471 .....K1
Warabi 70,876 .....O2
Yaizu 104,363 .....J6
Yamagata 237,041 .....K4
Yamaguchi 114,744 .....E6
Yamato 167,935 .....O2
Yamatokoriyama 81,266 .....J8
Yamatotakada 61,711 .....J8
Yao 272,706 .....J8
Yatsushiro 108,194 .....E7
Yawata 64,882 .....J7
Yawatahama 43,823 .....F7

Yokkaichi 255,442 .....H6
Yokohama 2,773,674 .....O3
Yokosuka 421,107 .....O3
Yokote 43,773 .....K4
Yonago 127,374 .....F6
Yonezawa 92,823 .....K5
Yono 72,326 .....O2
Yubari 41,715 .....L2
Yukuhashi 61,838 .....E7
Yuzawa 37,800 .....K4
Zushi 58,479 .....O3

OTHER FEATURES

Agano (riv.) J4
Akan National Park M2
Amakusa (isls.) D7
Amami (isls.) N5
Amami-O-Shima (isl.) N5
Asahi (mt.) J4
Asama (mt.) J5
Ashizuri (cape) F7
Aso (mt.) E7
Atsumi (bay) H6
Awaji (isl.) H8
Bandai (mt.) K5
Biwa (lake) H6
Bonin (isls.) M3
Boso (pen.) K6
Bungo (strait) F7
Chichi (isl.) M3
Daio (cape) H6
Daisetsu (mt.) L2
Dogo (isl.) F5
Dozen (isls.) F5
East China (sea) D8
Eastern Channel (strait) D7
Erimo (cape) L3
Etorofu (isl.) N1
Fuji (mt.) J6
Fuji (riv.) J6
Fuji-Hakone-Izu Nat'l Park H6
Gassan (mt.) J4
Goto (isls.) D7
Habomai (isls.) N2
Hachijo (mts.) J3
Haha (isl.) M3
Hakken (isl.) J6
Haku (mt.) H5
Harima (sea) G6
Hida (riv.) H6
Hodaka (mt.) H5
Hokkaido (isl.) L2
Honshu (isl.) J5
Ie (isl.) N6
Iki (isl.) D7
Inawashiro (lake) K5
Inubo (cape) K6
Iriomote (isl.) K7
Iro (cape) J6
Ise (bay) H6
Ishigaki (isl.) L7
Ishikari (riv.) L2
Ishikari (bay) K2

Iwaki (mt.) K3
Iwate (mt.) K4
Iwo (Iwo Jima) (isl.) M4
Iwo Jima (isl.) M4
Iyo (sea) E7
Izu (isls.) J6
Izu (pen.) J6
Japan (sea) G4
Kagoshima (bay) E8
Kamui (cape) K2
Kasumiga (lagoon) K5
Kazan-retto (Volcano) (isls.) M4
Kii (chan.) G7
Kikai (isl.) O5
Kita Iwo (isl.) M4
Kitakami (riv.) K4
Komaga (mt.) K2
Kuju (mt.) E7
Kume (isl.) M6
Kunashiri (isl.) M1
Kutcharo (lake) M2
Kyushu (isl.) E7
Meakan (mt.) L2
Minami Iwo (isl.) M5
Miyako (isl.) L7
Mogami (riv.) K4
Muko (isl.) M3
Muroto (pt.) G7
Mutsu (bay) K3
Nampo-Shoto (isls.) M3
Nansei Shoto (Ryukyu) (isls.) .L7
Nantai (mt.) J5
Nasu (mt.) J5
Nemuro (strait) M1
Nii (isl.) J6
Nikko National Park J5
Nojima (cape) K6
Noto (pen.) H5
Nyudo (cape) J4
Oga (pen.) J4
Ogasawara-gunto (Bonin) (isls.) M3
Okhotsk (sea) M1
Oki (isls.) F5
Okinawa (isls.) N6
Okinawa (isl.) N6
Okinoerabu (isl.) N5
Okushiri (isl.) J2
Oma (cape) K3
Omono (riv.) J4
Ono (riv.) E7
Ontake (mt.) H6
Osaka (bay) H8
O-Shima (isl.) J6
Osumi (isls.) E8
Osumi (strait) E8
Otakine (mt.) K5
Rebun (isl.) K1
Rishiri (isl.) K1
Ryukyu (isls.) L7
Sado (isl.) J4
Sagami (bay) O3
Sagami (sea) J6
Sakishima (isls.) K7

JAPAN is divided into prefectures bearing the same names as their capitals except:

Prefecture	Capital	Ref.
AICHI	NAGOYA	H 6
EHIME	MATSUYAMA	F 7
GUMMA	MAEBASHI	J 5
HOKKAIDO	SAPPORO	K 2
HYOGO	KOBE	H 7
IBARAKI	MITO	K 5
ISHIKAWA	KANAZAWA	H 5
IWATE	MORIOKA	K 4
KAGAWA	TAKAMATSU	F 6
KANAGAWA	YOKOHAMA	O 3
MIE	TSU	H 6
MIYAGI	SENDAI	K 4
OKINAWA	NAHA	N 6
SAITAMA	URAWA	O 2
SHIGA	OTSU	J 7
SHIMANE	MATSUE	F 6
TOCHIGI	UTSUNOMIYA	K 5
YAMANASHI	KOFU	J 6

Yoshino (riv.).................G6

KOREA (NORTH)

CITIES and TOWNS

Anju.................................B4
Ch'ŏngjin 306,000............E3
Kapsan..............................C3
Changyŏn...........................B4
Chasŏng............................C3
Chŏngju.............................B4
Haeju 40,000......................C4
Hamhŭng 484,000.............C4
Heiju (P'yŏngyang) (cap.)
        1,250,000................C4
Hongwŏn............................C3
Hŭich'ŏn............................C3
Hŭngnam...........................C4
Hyesan..............................D3

Kaesŏng 175,000..............C4
Kapsan...............................C3
Kimch'aek 100,000.............D3
Koksan...............................C4
Kosŏng...............................D4
Kusŏng...............................B4
Manp'o................................C3
Musan.................................D2
Najin...................................E2
Namp'o 140,000.................B4
Nanam................................D3
Ongjin.................................B5
Onsŏng...............................E2
P'ungsan.............................D3
P'yŏngyang (cap.)
        1,250,000................C4
Pukch'ŏng...........................D3
Sariwŏn...............................B4
Sinp'o.................................D4

Sinŭiju 300,000..................B3
Sŏhŭng...............................C4
Sŏnch'ŏn............................B4
Songnim.............................C4
Sunch'ŏn............................B4
Tanch'ŏn.............................D3
T'ongch'ŏn...........................D4
Ŭiju....................................B3
Unggi..................................E2
Unsan.................................C3
Wŏnsan 275,000................C4
Yangdŏk.............................C4
Yŏnghŭng...........................C4
Yongamp'o..........................B4

OTHER FEATURES

Baktu (Paektu) (mt.)............C3
Changbaek-sanmaek (mts.)..D2
Changjin (res.)....................C3

KOREA (SOUTH)

CITIES and TOWNS

Andong 102,024................D5
Chech'ŏn 74,239................D5

East Korea (bay)................D4
Japan (sea).......................G4
Kanghwa (bay)..................B5
Korea (bay)........................B4
Kwanmo (mt.)....................D3
Nangnim-sanmaek (range)..C3
Paektu (mt.).......................C3
Puksubaek (mt.).................C3
Supung (res.).....................B3
Taedong (riv.).....................C4
Tumen (riv.).......................D2
Yalu (riv.)...........................C3
Yellow (sea).......................B6

Cheju 167,546...................C7
Chinhae 112,098...............D6
Chinju 202,753..................D6
Ch'ŏnan 120,618...............C5
Ch'ŏngju 252,985..............C5
Chŏngŭp 54,864................C6
Chŏnju 366,997.................C6
Ch'unch'ŏn 155,247...........D5
Ch'ungju 113,138...............C5
Inch'ŏn 1,084,730.............C5
Iri 145,358........................C6
Kangnŭng 116,903............D5
Kimch'ŏn 72,229...............C5
Kimhae 203,428................D6
Kimje 221,414....................C6
Koĥŭng 217,446................D6
Kongju 39,756...................C5
Kunsan 165,318................C6
Kwangju 727,627...............C6
Kyŏngju 122,038...............D6

Masan 386,773..................D6
Miryang 42,951..................D6
Mokp'o 221,856.................C6
Namwŏn 50,857................C6
Nonsan 226,429................C5
P'anmunjŏm.......................C5
P'ohang 201,355................D5
Pusan 3,160,276................D6
Samch'ŏk 42,526..............D5
Sangju 52,839...................D6
Seoul (cap.) 8,366,756......C5
Sŏ'chŏn 65,798.................D4
Sŏsan 38,081.....................C5
Sunch'ŏn 114,223..............C6
Suwŏn 310,757..................C5
Taegu 1,607,458................D6
Taejŏn 651,642..................C5
Ulsan 418,415....................D6
Wŏnju 136,961...................D5
Yanggu 277,986................C4

Yŏngch'ŏn 50,765..............D6
Yŏngju 77,890...................D5
Yŏsu 161,009.....................C6

OTHER FEATURES

Cheju (isl.).........................C7
Dagelet (Ullŭng) (isl.).........E5
East China (sea).................C8
Halla (mt.)..........................C7
Han (riv.)............................C5
Japan (sea)........................G4
Kanghwa (bay)..................B5
Kŏje (isl.)...........................D6
Korea (strait)......................D6
Naktong (riv.).....................D6
Quelpart (Cheju) (isl.).........C7
Ullŭng (isl.)........................E5
Yellow (sea).......................B6

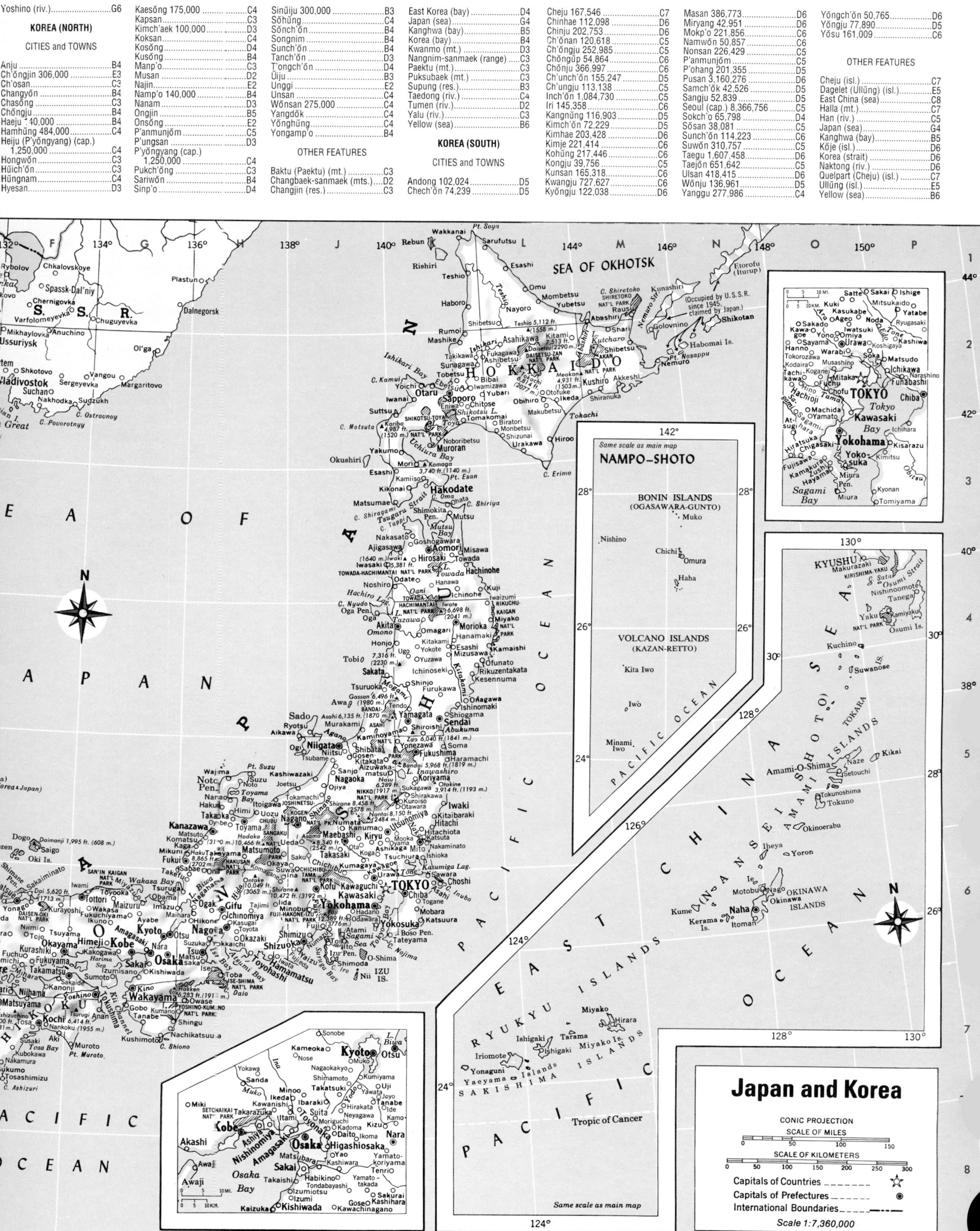

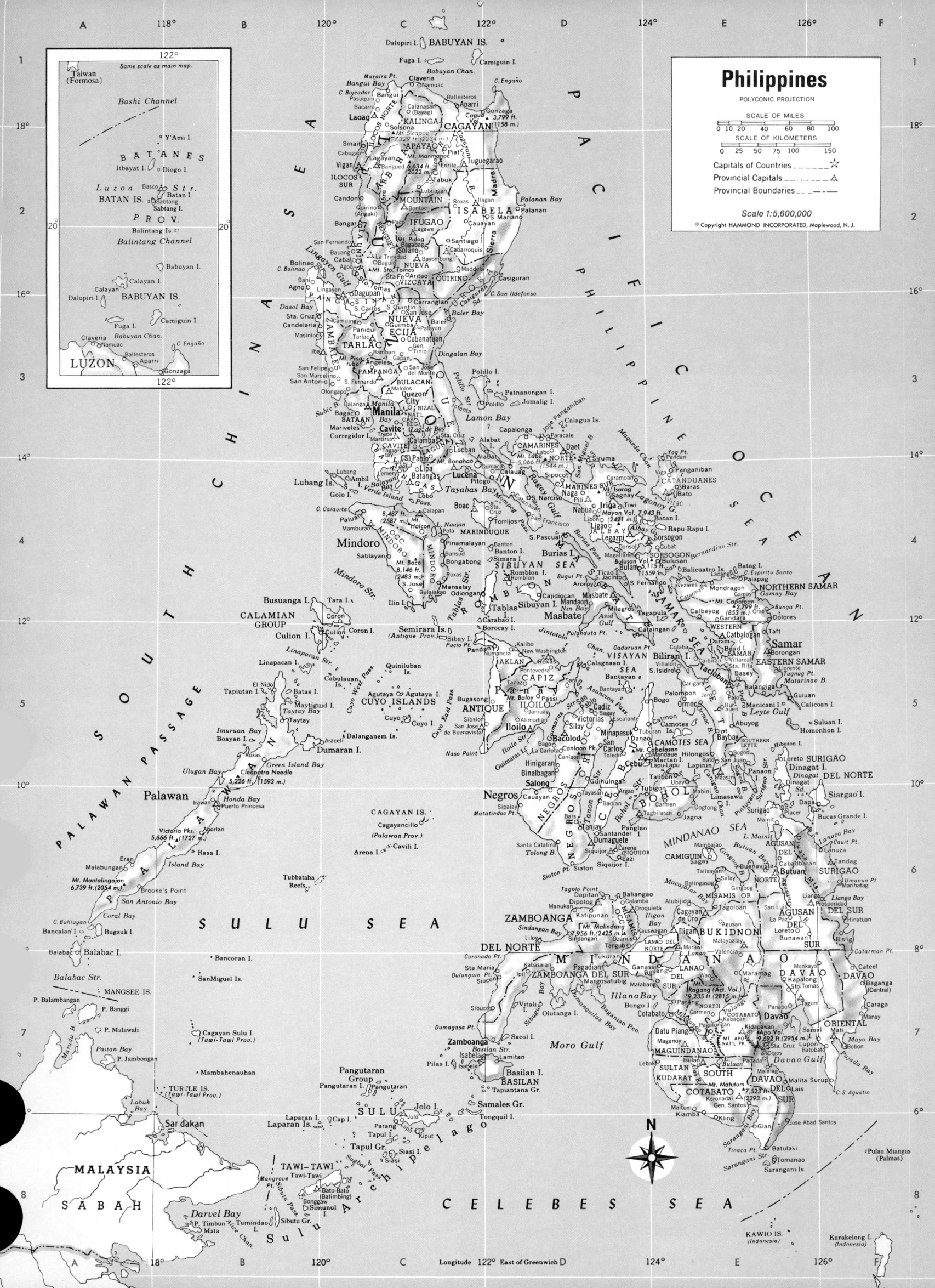

Philippines

POLYCONIC PROJECTION

SCALE OF MILES

0 10 20 40 60 80 100

SCALE OF KILOMETERS

0 25 50 75 100 150

Capitals of Countries _____ ☆
Provincial Capitals _____ △
Provincial Boundaries _____

Scale 1:5,600,000

© Copyright HAMMOND INCORPORATED, Maplewood, N.J.

LUZON

Taiwan (Formosa)

Bashi Channel

BATANES

Luzon Str.

BATAN IS. PROV.

Balintang Channel

BABUYAN IS.

SOUTH CHINA SEA

PALAWAN PASSAGE

PALAWAN

SULU SEA

MALAYSIA

SABAH

Sulu Archipelago

CELEBES SEA

PACIFIC OCEAN

PHILIPPINE SEA

Longitude 122° East of Greenwich

PHILIPPINES | 83

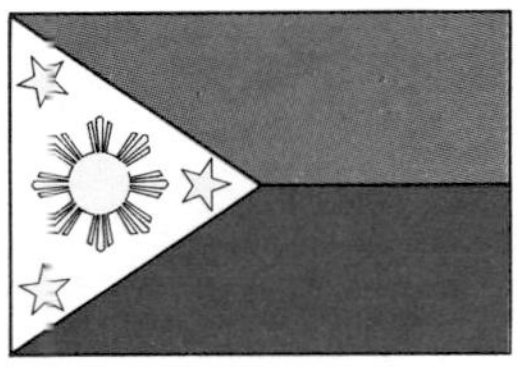

AREA 115,707 sq. mi. (299,681 sq. km.)
POPULATION 60,097,000
CAPITAL Manila
LARGEST CITY Manila
HIGHEST POINT Apo 9,692 ft. (2,954 m.)
MONETARY UNIT peso
MAJOR LANGUAGES Pilipino (Tagalog), English, Spanish, Bisayan, Ilocano, Bikol
MAJOR RELIGIONS Roman Catholicism, Islam, Protestantism, tribal religions

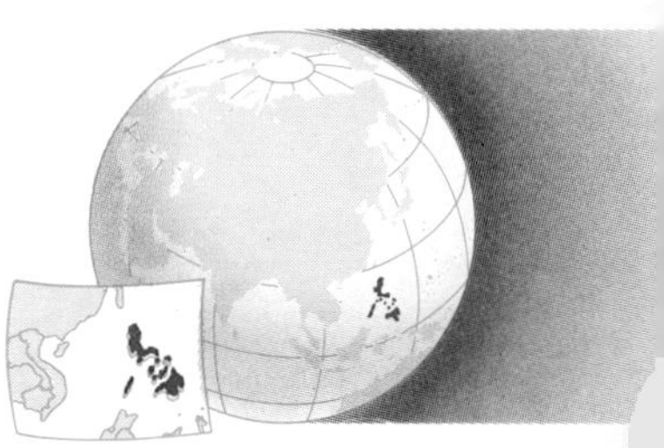

PROVINCES

Abra 160,198 .... C2
Agusan del Norte 365,421 .. E6
Agusan del Sur 631,634 .... E6
Aklan 324,563 .... D5
Albay 809,177 .... D4
Antique 344,879 .... D5
Aurora 107,145 .... C3
Basilan 201,407 .... D7
Bataan 323,254 .... C3
Batanes 12,091 .... A2
Batangas 1,174,201 .... C4
Benguet 354,751 .... C2
Bohol 806,031 .... E6
Bukidnon 631,634 .... E6
Bulacan 1,098,046 .... C3
Cagayan 711,476 .... C1
Camarines Norte 368,007... D3
Camarines Sur 1,099,346 .. D4
Camiguin 57,126 .... E6
Capiz 492,231 .... D5
Catanduanes 175,247 ...... E4
Cavite 771,320 .... C3
Cebu 2,091,602 .... D5
Davao 725,153 .... E7
Davao del Sur 1,133,599 ... E7
Davao Oriental 339,931..... F7
Eastern Samar 320,637 .... E5
Ifugao 111,368 .... C2
Ilocos Norte 390,666 ...... C1
Ilocos Sur 443,591 .... C2
Iloilo 1,433,641 .... D5
Isabela 870,604 .... C2
Kalinga-Apayao 185,063.... C1
Laguna 973,104 .... C3
Lanao del Norte 461,049 ... E6
Lanao del Sur 404,971 ..... E7
La Union 452,578......... C2
Leyte 1,302,648 .... E5
Maguindanao 536,546 ..... E7
Manila 5,925,884 .... C3
Marinduque 173,715 ...... C4
Masbate 584,526 .... D4
Misamis Occidental 386,328 D6
Misamis Oriental 690,032... E6
Mountain 103,052 .... C2
National Capital Region (Manila) 5,925,884...... C3
Negros Occidental 1,930,301.............. D6
Negros Oriental 819,399 ... D6
North Cotabato 564,599 .... E7
Northern Samar 378,516 ... E4
Nueva Ecija 1,069,409 ..... C3
Nueva Vizcaya 241,690..... C2
Occidental Mindoro 222,431 C4
Oriental Mindoro 448,938... C4
Palawan 371,782 .... B6
Pampanga 1,181,590 ...... C3
Pangasinan 1,636,057 ..... C3
Quezon 1,129,277 .... C3
Quirino 83,230 .... C2
Rizal 555,533 .... C3
Romblon 193,174 .... D4
Siquijor 70,300.......... D6
Sorsogon 500,685 .... E4
South Cotabato 770,473.... E7
Southern Leyte 298,294 .... E5
Sultan Kudarat 303,784 .... E7
Sulu 360,588 .... C7
Surigao del Norte 363,414 .. F5
Surigao del Sur 377,647 ... F6
Tarlac 638,457 .... C3
Tawi-Tawi 194,651 .... B8
Western Samar 501,439.... E5
Zambales 444,037 .... C3
Zamboanga del Norte 588,015 .... D6
Zamboanga del Sur 1,183,845............. D7

CITIES and TOWNS

Angeles 188,834.......... C3
Aparri 45,070 .... C1
Bacolod 262,415 .... D5
Bagac 13,109 .... C3
Bago 99,631........... D5
Baguio 119,009 .... C2
Balanga 39,132.......... C3
Baler 18,349........... C3
Balimbing (Bato-Bato) 22,189 .... C8
Bamban 26,072 .... C3
Basco 4,341 .... A2
Batangas 143,570........ C4
Bato-Bato 22,189 .... C8
Baybay 74,640 .... E5
Bislig 81,615........... F6
Boac 37,005 .... C4
Bontoc 17,091 .... C2
Burauen 48,058 .... E5
Butuan 172,489 .... E6
Cabanatuan 138,298...... C3
Cabarroquis 17,450 ...... C2
Cadiz 129,632 .... D5
Cagayan de Oro 227,312 ... E6
Calamba 121,175 .... C3
Calbayog 106,719........ E4
Carigara 34,377 .... E5
Cauayan 70,017 .... D6
Cavite 87,666 .... C3
Cebu 490,281........... D5
Cotabato 83,871......... D7
Dagupan 98,344 .... C2
Davao 610,375 .... E7
Digos 70,065 .... E7
Escalante 71,293 .... D5
General Santos 149,396 ... E7
Gingoog 79,937 .... E6
Guihulngan 84,156........ D5
Guimba 58,847.......... C3
Iba 22,791 .... B3
Ilagan 79,336 .... C2
Iligan 167,358.......... E6
Iloilo 244,827.............D5
Infanta 27,914.............C3
Jaro 29,739...............E5
Jolo 52,429 ....C8
Koronadal 80,566 ....E7
Lagawe 15,075 ....C2
Lapu-Lapu 98,723...........E5
Legazpi 99,766 ....D4
Ligao 69,860 ....D4
Lingayen 65,187 ....C2
Lipa 121,166 ....C4
Lucena 107,880.............C4
Maganoy 45,845............E7
Mainit 18,078 ....E6
Malabang 18,955 ....D7
Malolos 95,699.............C3
Mandaue 110,590 ....E5
Manila (cap.) 1,630,485 .....C3
Mariveles 48,594 ....C3
Mati 78,178 ....F7
Naga 90,712 ....D4
Olongapo 156,430 ....C3
Ormoc 104,978 ....E5
Ozamis 77,832 ....D6
Pagadian 80,861............D7
Palo 31,124 ....E5
Palompon 40,242 ....E5
Panabo 71,098 ....E7
Prosperidad 33,824 ....F6
Puerto Princesa 60,234.....B6
Quezon City 1,165,865 ......C3
Romblon 24,251............D4
Roxas 81,183 ....D5
Sagay 99,118..............D5
San Antonio 42,969 ....B3
San Carlos, Negros Occ. 91,627.................D5
San Carlos Pangasinan 101,243 ....C3
San Fernando, La Union 68,410.................C2
San Fernando, Pampanga 110,891 ....C3
San Jose 64,254 ....C3
San Jose del Monte 90,732 ..C3
San Pablo 131,655 ....C3
Santa Fe 6,338 ....C2
Santiago 69,877 ....C2
Silay 111,131 ....D5
Siquijor 17,533 ....D6
Surigao 79,745 ....E6
Tacloban 102,523 ....E5
Tagaytay 16,322 ....C3
Tagum 86,201 ....E7
Tarlac 175,691 ....C3
Toledo 91,668 .... D5
Tuguegarao 73,507........ C2
Zamboanga 343,722....... C7

OTHER FEATURES

Agusan (riv.)............. E6
Alabat (isl.).............. D3
Apo (vol.) E7
Babuyan (isl.) B2
Balabac (isl.)............. A7
Balayan (bay) C4
Balintang (chan.) A2
Baloy (mt.) D5
Bantayan (isl.) D5
Banton (isl.) D4
Bashi (chan.) A1
Basilan (isl.) D7
Batan, Albay (isl.)......... E4
Batan, Batanes (isl.) B2
Batan (isls.) A2
Bay, Laguna de (lake)...... C3
Biliran (isl.) E5
Bohol (isl.) E6
Bojeador (cape) C1
Borocay (isl.) D5
Bucas Grande (isl.) F6
Bugsuk (isl.) A6
Buliluyan (cape) A6
Bunga (pt.) E4
Burias (isl.).............. D4
Busuanga (isl.) B4
Cabalasan (mt.) E5
Cabulauan (isls.).......... C5
Cagayan (isls.) C6
Cagayan (riv.) C2
Cagayan Sulu (isl.) B7
Cagua (vol.) D1
Calagua (isls.) D3
Calarnian Group (isls.) B4
Calayan (isl.)............. A2
Calicoan (isl.) E5
Camiguin, Cagayan (isl.) ... B3
Camiguin, Camiguin (isl.)... E6
Camotes (isls.) E5
Camotes (sea)............ E5
Canigao (chan.) E5
Canlaon (peak) D5
Capotoan (mt.) E4
Carabao (isl.) D4
Catanduanes (isl.)......... E4
Cebu (isl.)............... D5
Celebes (sea) D8
Cleopatra Needle (mt.) B5
Coron (isl.) C5

Topography

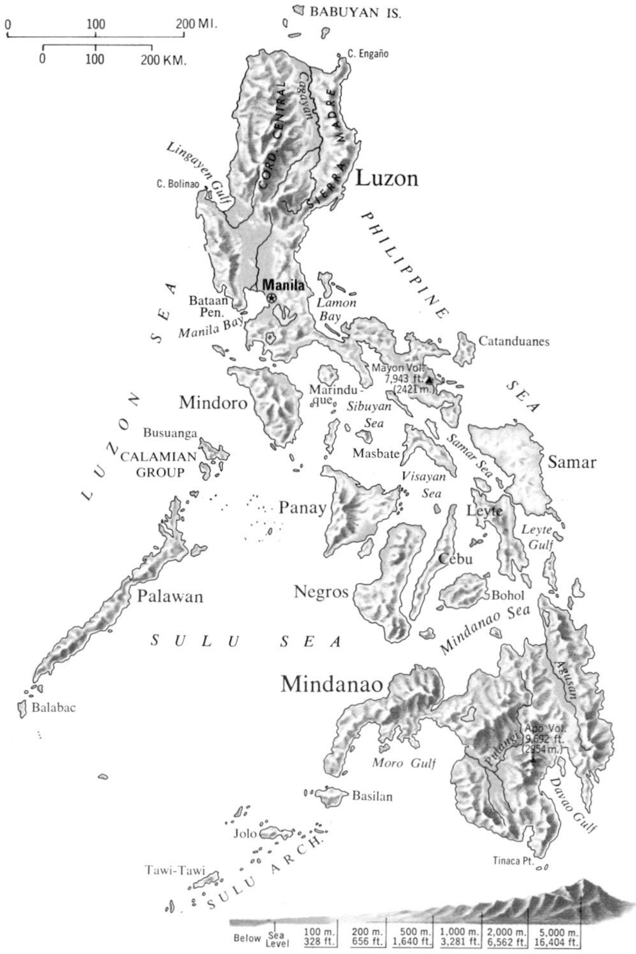

0 100 200 MI.
0 100 200 KM.
BABUYAN IS.
C. Engaño
CORD. CENTRAL
SIERRA MADRE
Cagayan
Lingayen Gulf
C. Bolinao
Luzon
PHILIPPINE
Manila
Bataan Pen.
Manila Bay
Lamon Bay
Catanduanes
Mayon Vol. 7,943 ft. (2421 m.)
Marinduque
Sibuyan Sea
Mindoro
Busuanga
CALAMIAN GROUP
Masbate
Samar Sea
Samar
Visayan Sea
LUZON
SEA
Panay
Leyte
Leyte Gulf
Cebu
Palawan
Negros
Bohol
Mindanao Sea
SULU SEA
Mindanao
Balabac
Agusan
Apo Vol. 9,692 ft. (2954 m.)
Moro Gulf
Davao Gulf
Basilan
Jolo
Tinaca Pt.
Tawi-Tawi
SULU ARCH.
Below Sea Level
100 m. 328 ft.
200 m. 656 ft.
500 m. 1,640 ft.
1,000 m. 3,281 ft.
2,000 m. 6,562 ft.
5,000 m. 16,404 ft.

Agriculture, Industry and Resources

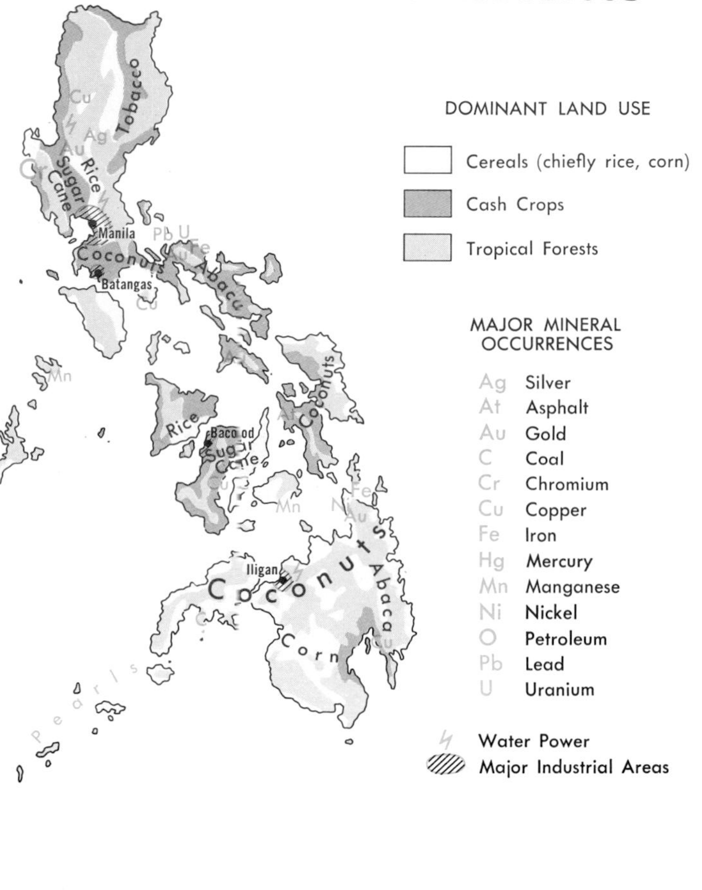

Tobacco
Cu
Ag
Au
Rice
Sugar Cane
Manila
Pb
U
Coconuts
Abaca
Batangas
Mn
O
Hg
Rice
Bacolod
Sugar Cane
Fe
Au
Iligan
Coconuts
Abaca
Corn
Pearls
DOMINANT LAND USE
Cereals (chiefly rice, corn)
Cash Crops
Tropical Forests
MAJOR MINERAL OCCURRENCES
Ag Silver
At Asphalt
Au Gold
C Coal
Cr Chromium
Cu Copper
Fe Iron
Hg Mercury
Mn Manganese
Ni Nickel
O Petroleum
Pb Lead
U Uranium
Water Power
Major Industrial Areas

Corregidor (isl.) C3
Culion (isl.)............... B5
Cuyo (isl.)................ C5
Cuyo (isls.)............... C5
Daram (isl.)............... E5
Davao (gulf) E7
Dinagat (isl.).............. E5
Diuata (mts.).............. E6
Dumanquilas (bay) D7
Dumaran (isl.) C5
Engaño (cape) D1
Espiritu Santo (cape)....... E4
Fuga (isl.) A3
Guimaras (isl.) D5
Halcon (mt.) C4
Hibuson (isl.) E5
Homonhon (isl.) E5
Honda (bay) B6
Iligan (bay) E6
Ilin (isl.) C4
Illana (bay) D7
Imuruan (bay).............. B5
Island (bay)............... B6
Itbayat (isl.) A2
Jintotolo (chan.)........... D5
Jolo (isl.) C7
Jomalig (isl.) D3
Lagonoy (gulf)............. E4
Lamon (bay) C3
Lanao (lake) E7
Laparan (isls.) B8
Lapinin (isl.) E5
Leyte (gulf) E5
Leyte (isl.)................ E5
Limasawa (isl.) E6
Linapacan (isl.)............ B5
Lingayen (gulf) C2
Lubang (isls.)............. B4
Luzon (isl.)............... C3
Luzon (str.)............... A2
Macajalar (bay) E6
Malindang (mt.) D6
Mangsee (isls.)............ A7
Manila (bay) C3
Mantalingajan (mt.) A6
Maqueda (chan.) D3
Maraira (pt.) C1
Marinduque (isl.) C4
Masbate (isl.) D4
Mayon (vol.) D4
Maytiguid (isl.) B5
Mindanao (isl.) D7
Mindanao (riv.) E7
Mindoro (isl.) C4
Mindoro (str.) C4
Mompog (passg.)........... D4
Moro (gulf) D7
Mount Apo National Park ... E7
Naso (pt.) C5
Negros (isl.) D6
Olutanga (isl.)............. D7
Pacsan (mt.)............... C2
Palawan (isl.) B6
Palawan (passg.) A6
Panaon (isl.) E5
Panay (isl.)............... D5
Panglao (isl.) D6
Pangutaran (isl.)........... C7
Pangutaran Group (isls.) ... C7
Patnanongan (isl.) D3
Philippine (sea)............ D3
Pilas (isl.) C7
Pinatubo (mt.) C3
Polillo (isl.)............... C3
Pujada (bay) F7
Pulangi (riv.) E7
Ragang (vol.) E7
Ragay (gulf) D4
Rapu-Rapu (isl.)........... E4
Romblon (isl.) D4
Sabtang (isl.) B2
Sacol (isl.) D7
Samal (isl.)............... E7
Samales Group (isls.)...... D7
Samar (isl.)............... E5
Samar (sea) E4
San Agustin (cape) F7
San Bernardino (str.) E4
San Miguel (bay) D3
San Pedro (bay) E5
Santo Tomas (mt.) C2
Semirara (isls.)........... C5
Siargao (isl.) F6
Sibay (isl.) C5
Sibuguey (bay)............ D7
Sibutu Group (isls.) B8
Sibuyan (isl.) D4
Sibuyan (sea) D4
Sierra Madre (mt.) D2
Simunul (isl.) B8
Siquijor (isl.) D6
South China (sea).......... B3
Subic (bay)............... C3
Sulu (arch.) B8
Sulu (sea)................ B6
Suluan (isl.) F5
Surigao (str.) E6
Taal (lake)................ C4
Tablas (isl.)............... D4
Tablas (str.) C4
Tagapula (isl.)............. E4
Tagolo (pt.)............... D6
Tanon (str.)............... D6
Tapul (isl.) C8
Tapul Group (isls.) C8
Tara (isl.) C4
Tawi-Tawi (isl.) B8
Tayabas (bay) C4
Ticao (isl.) D4
Tinaca (pt.)............... E8
Tongquil (isl.)............. D8
Tumindao (isl.) B8
Turtle (isls.) B7
Verde Island (passg.) C4
Victoria (peaks)........... B6
Visayan (sea) D5

BRUNEI

CITIES and TOWNS

- Bandar Seri Begawan 63,868 E4
- Seria 23,511 E5

INDONESIA

CITIES and TOWNS

- Adaut J7
- Agats K7
- Ambon (Amboina) 208,898 H6
- Amuntai F6
- Amurang G5
- Atambua G7
- Aubá H7
- Baa G8
- Bagansiapiapi C5
- Balikpapan 280,675 F6
- Banda Aceh 72,090 A4
- Bandanaira H6
- Bandung 1,462,637 H2
- Banggai G6
- Banjarmasin 381,286 E6
- Banyumas J2
- Batang J2
- Batavia (Jakarta) (cap.) 6,503,449 H1
- Baukau H7
- Bekasi H2
- Belawan B5
- Bengkulu 64,783 C6
- Beo H5
- Biak K6
- Binjai 76,464 B5
- Bintuhan C6
- Blitar 78,503 K2
- Bogor 247,409 H2
- Bojonegoro J2
- Bukittinggi 70,771 B6
- Bula H6
- Bulukumba G7
- Buntok F6
- Cianjur H2
- Cimahi H2
- Cirebon 223,776 H2
- Demta L6
- Denpasar E7
- Dili H7
- Djambi (Jambi) 230,373 C6
- Djokjakarta (Yogyakarta) 398,727 J2
- Dobo J7
- Donggala F6
- Enaratoli K6
- Ende G7
- Fakfak J6
- Garut H2
- Gorontalo 97,628 G5
- Hollandia (Jayapura) K6
- Indramayu H2
- Jailolo H5
- Jakarta (cap.) 6,503,449 H1
- Jambi 230,373 C6
- Jayapura (Hollandia) K6
- Jogjakarta (Yogyakarta) 398,727 J2
- Jombang K2
- Kaimana J6
- Kampung Baru (Tolitoli) G5
- Kediri 221,820 K2
- Kendari G6
- Kepi K7
- Ketapang E6
- Kokonau K6
- Kolonodale G6
- Kotabaharu E6
- Kotabaru F6
- Kotawaringin E6
- Kragen K2
- Kupang G8
- Kutaraja (Banda Aceh) 72,090 A4
- Labuha H6
- Labuhan G2
- Laiwui H6
- Larantuka G7
- Lekitobi G6
- Longiram F5
- Madiun 150,562 K2
- Magelang 123,484 J2
- Majalengka H2
- Makassar (Ujung Pandang) 709,038 F7
- Malang 511,780 K2
- Malili G6
- Manado 217,159 G5
- Manokwari J6
- Maumere G7
- Medan 1,378,955 B5
- Menggala D6
- Merauke K7
- Mindiptana L7
- Mojokerto 68,849 K2
- Muarasiberut B6
- Nangatayap E6
- Pacitan J2
- Padang 480,922 B6
- Padangpanjang 34,517 B6
- Padangsidempuan B5
- Pakanbaru 186,262 C5
- Palangkaraya 60,447 E6
- Palembang 787,187 D6
- Pangkalanbuun E6
- Pangkalpinang 90,096 D6
- Parepare 86,450 F6
- Pasangkayu F6
- Pasuruan 95,864 K2
- Payakumbuh 78,836 C6
- Pekalongan 132,558 J2
- Pemalang J2
- Pematangsiantar 150,376 B5
- Pinrang F6
- Plaju D6
- Pontianak 304,778 D6
- Probolinggo 100,296 K2
- Purbolinggo J2
- Raha G6
- Rantauprapat C5
- Rembang K2
- Sabang, Celebes F5
- Sabang, Weh 23,821 B4
- Salatiga 85,849 J2
- Samarinda 264,718 F6
- Sampit E6
- Sarmi K6
- Sawahlunto 13,561 C6
- Seba G8
- Semarang 1,026,671 J2
- Semitau E5
- Serui K6
- Sibolga 59,897 B5
- Sigli B4
- Sinabang B5
- Singaraja F7
- Solo (Surakarta) 469,888 J2
- Solok 31,724 C6
- Sorong J6
- Sragen J2
- Subang H2
- Sukabumi 109,994 H2
- Sumbawa Besar F7
- Sumedang H2
- Surabaya 2,027,913 K2
- Surakarta 469,888 J2
- Tanahmerah K7
- Tanjungbalai 41,894 C5
- Tanjungkarang 284,275 D7
- Tanjungpinang C5
- Tanjungselor F5
- Tarakan F5
- Tebingtinggi 92,087 B5
- Tegal 131,728 J2
- Telukbayur C6
- Tepa H7
- Terempa D5
- Tjilatjap (Cilicap) H2
- Tjirebon (Cirebon) 223,776 H2
- Tolitoli G5
- Tuban K2
- Ujung Pandang 709,038 F7
- Vikeke H7
- Wahai H6
- Waigama H6
- Wajabula H5
- Waren K6
- Weda H5
- Wonreli H7
- Yogyakarta 398,727 J2

OTHER FEATURES

- Anambas (isls.) 29,572 D5
- Arafura (sea) J8
- Aru (isls.) 34,195 K7
- Babar (isl.) H7
- Bali (isl.) 2,074,438 F7
- Banda (sea) H7
- Banggai (arch.) 169,025 G6
- Bangka (isl.) 298,017 D6
- Banyak (isls.) 1,980 B5
- Barisan (mts.) C6
- Barito (riv.) E6
- Batu (isls.) 16,390 B6
- Bawean (isl.) 64,551 K1
- Belitung (Billiton) (isl.) 128,694 D6
- Berau (bay) J6
- Biak (isl.) K6
- Billiton (isl.) 128,694 D6
- Binongko (isl.) 11,549 G7
- Bone (gulf) G7
- Borneo (isl.) E5
- Bosch, van den (cape) J6
- Bunguran (Great Natuna) (isl.) D5
- Buru (isl.) 23,034 H6
- Butung (isl.) 188,173 G6
- Celebes (Sulawesi) (isl.) 7,732,383 G5
- Celebes (sea) G5
- Cenderawasih (bay) K6
- Dampier (str.) J6
- Digul (riv.) K7
- Doberai (pen.) J6
- Enggano (isl.) 1,082 C7
- Ewab (Kai) (isls.) 108,328 J7
- Flores (isl.) 860,328 G7
- Flores (sea) F7
- Frederik Hendrik (Kolepom) (isl.) K7
- Geelvink (Cenderawasih) (bay) K6
- Great Kai (isl.) 38,748 J7
- Halmahera (isl.) 122,521 H5
- Irian Jaya (reg.) 923,440 J6
- Jambuair (cape) B4
- Jamursba (cape) J5
- Java (head) C7
- Java (isl.) 73,712,411 J2
- Java (sea) D6
- Jaya, Puncak (mt.) K6
- Jayawijaya (range) K6
- Jemaja (isl.) 5,628 D5
- Kabaena (isl.) G7
- Kai (isls.) 108,328 J7
- Kalao (isl.) G7
- Kalaotoa (isl.) G5
- Kalimantan (reg.) 4,956,865 E5
- Kangean (isl.) F7
- Kapuas (riv.) D6
- Karakelong (isl.) H5
- Karimata (arch.) 9,398 D6
- Karimunjawa (isls.) 5,025 J1
- Kerinci (mt.) C6
- Kisar (isl.) H7
- Komodo (isl.) 30,407 F7
- Krakatau (Rakata) (isl.) C7
- Laut (isl.) 55,711 F6
- Leuser (mt.) B5
- Lingga (arch.) 46,658 D5
- Lingga (isl.) 18,027 D6
- Lombok (isl.) 1,581,193 F7
- Madura (isl.) 1,509,774 K2
- Mahakam (riv.) F6
- Makassar (str.) F6
- Malacca (str.) C5
- Mamberamo (riv.) K6
- Maoke (mts.) K6
- Mapia (isls.) J5
- Mentawai (isls.) 30,107 B6
- Misool (isl.) J6
- Molucca (sea) H6
- Moluccas (isls.) 944,240 H6
- Morotai (isl.) 27,333 H5
- Muli (str.) K7
- Müller (mts.) E5
- Muna (isl.) 156,186 G7
- Musi (riv.) C6
- Natuna (isls.) 23,893 D5
- Ngunju (cape) F8
- Nias (isl.) 356,093 B5
- Numfoor (isl.) J6
- Obi (isls.) 12,437 H6
- Ombai (str.) H7
- Pantar (isl.) 28,259 G7
- Perkam (cape) K6
- Puting, Borneo (cape) E6
- Puting, Sumatra (cape) C7
- Raja Ampat Group (isls.) H6
- Rakata (isl.) C7
- Rantekombola (mt.) F6
- Raya (mt.) E6
- Riau (arch.) 483,230 C5
- Rokan (riv.) C5
- Roti (isl.) 76,270 G8
- Salawati (isl.) J6
- Sangihe (isl.) H5
- Sangihe (isls.) 183,000 G5
- Sawu (isls.) 51,002 G8
- Sawu (sea) G7
- Schouten (isls.) 110,148 K6
- Schwaner (mts.) E6
- Sebuku (bay) F5
- Selatan (cape) E6
- Selayar (isl.) 92,342 G7
- Semeru (mt.) K2
- Siau (isl.) 46,801 H5
- Siberut (str.) B6
- Simeulue (isl.) 29,147 A5
- Singkep (isl.) 28,631 D6
- Sipura (isl.) 6,051 B6
- Slamet (mt.) J2
- Sorikmerapi (mt.) B5
- South Natuna (isls.) D5
- Sudirman (range) K6
- Sula (isls.) 36,922 H6
- Sulawesi (isl.) 7,732,383 G6
- Sumatra (isl.) 19,360,400 B5
- Sumba (isl.) 291,190 F7
- Sumba (str.) F7
- Sumbawa (isl.) 621,140 F7
- Sunda (str.) C7
- Tahulandang (isl.) 21,493 H5
- Talaud (isls.) 46,395 H5
- Taliabu (isl.) 18,303 G6
- Tambelan (isls.) 4,032 D5
- Tanimbar (isls.) 55,405 J7
- Tariku (riv.) K6
- Tidore (isl.) 28,655 H5
- Timor (reg.) 1,435,527 H7
- Timor (sea) H7
- Toba (lake) B5
- Tolo (gulf) G6
- Tomini (gulf) G6
- Tukangbesi (isls.) 73,106 G7
- Vals (cape) K7
- Vogelkop (Doberai) (pen.) J6
- Waigeo (isl.) J5
- Wakde (isl.) K6
- Wangiwangi (isl.) 28,469 G7
- We (isl.) B4
- Wetar (isl.) H7
- Yapen (isl.) 50,888 K6

MALAYSIA

STATES

- North Borneo (Sabah) 1,002,608 F3
- Sarawak 1,294,753 E5

CITIES and TOWNS

- Beaufort 2,709 F4
- Bintulu 4,424 E5
- Kabong E5
- Kampong Sibuti E5
- Kapit 1,929 E5
- Keningau 2,037 F4
- Kota Kinabalu 40,939 F4
- Kuching 63,535 E5
- Kudat 5,089 F4
- Labuan 7,216 E4
- Lahad Datu 5,169 F5
- Lamag F4
- Marudi 4,700 E5
- Miri 35,702 E5
- Mukah 1,717 E5

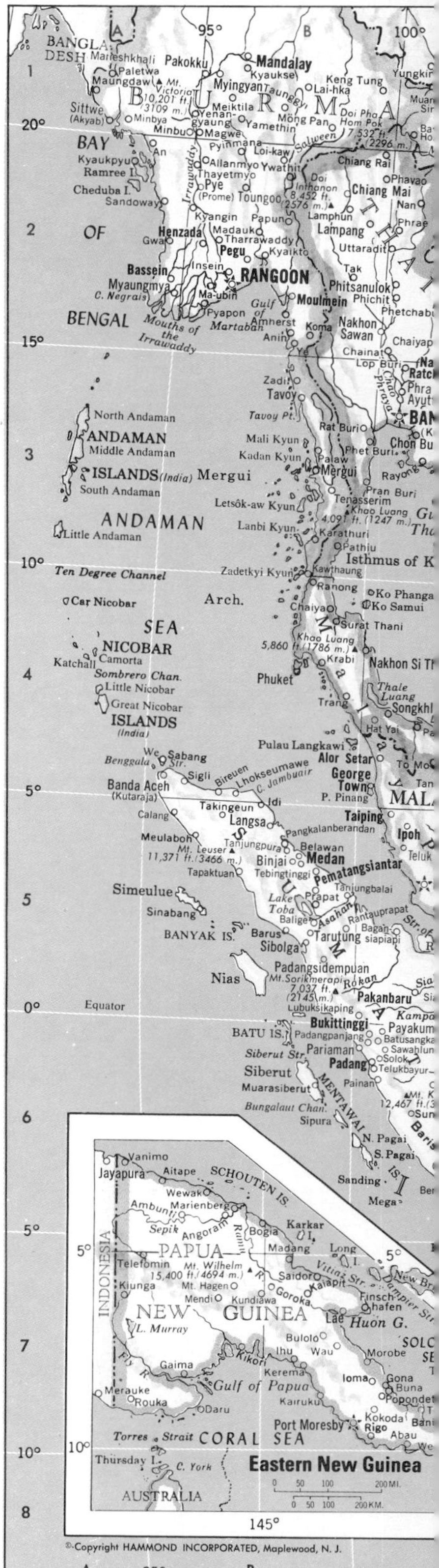

Topography

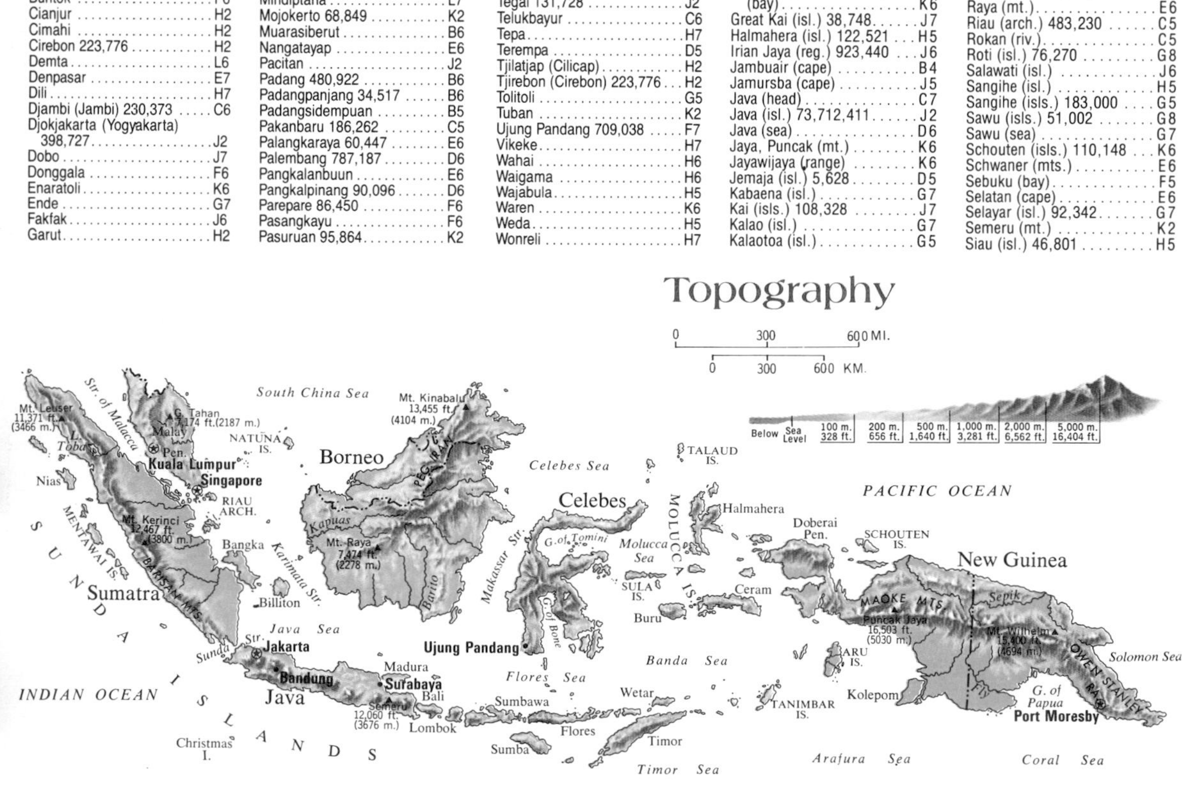

Agriculture, Industry and Resources

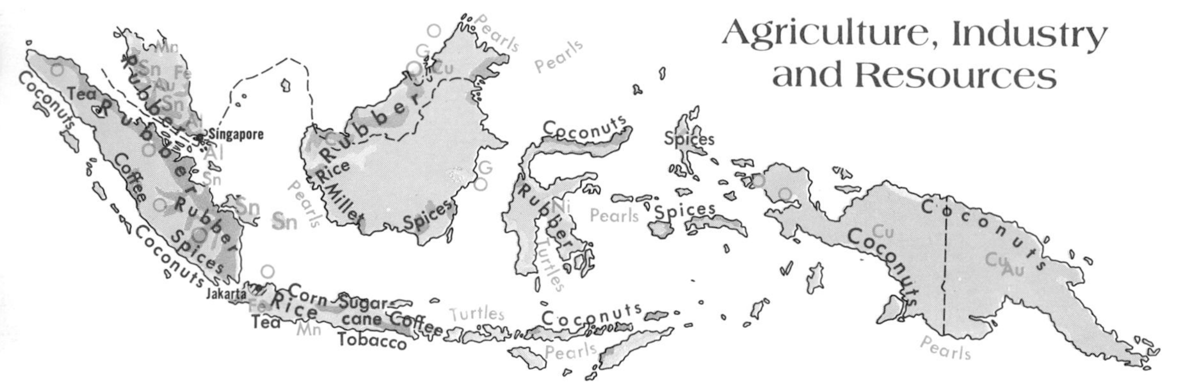

DOMINANT LAND USE

- Cereals (chiefly rice, corn)
- Diversified Tropical Crops
- Forests

MAJOR MINERAL OCCURRENCES

Al	Bauxite	Cu	Copper	Mn	Manganese	O	Petroleum
Au	Gold	Fe	Iron Ore	Ni	Nickel	Sn	Tin
C	Coal	G	Natural Gas				

Major Industrial Areas

par 1,855 ....F4
nau 2,024 ....F4
ncakan 42,413 ......F4
matan D5
mporna 3,371 ....F5
rian 2,209 ....E5
u 50,635 ....E5
manggang 8,445 ....E5
ai E5
wau 24,247 ....F5
 ....F4

OTHER FEATURES

lambangan (isl.) F4
nggi (isl.) E5
an (mts.) E5
ırebalu (mt.) F4
bʋk (isl.) 17,189 ...E4
ubʋk (bay) F4
ajang (riv.) E5
rik (cape) E5

PAPUA NEW GUINEA

CITIES and TOWNS

bau C7
tape 3,368 ....B6
mounti 1,035 ....B6
ngcoram 1,846 ......B6

Baniara C7
Bogia 755 ....B6
Bulolo 6,730 ....B7
Buna C7
Daru 7,127 ....B7
Finschhaffen 756. ..B7
Gaima B7
Gehua C8
Gona C7
Goroka 18,511 ......C7
Ihu 541 ....C7
Ioma C7
Kaiapit 515 ....C7
Kerema 3,389 ....C7
Kikori 763 ....B7
Kiunga 1,407 ....B7
Kokoda B7
Kundiawa 4,299 ....B7
Lae 61,617 ....B7
Madang 21,335 ......B7
Marienberg B6
Mendi 4,130 ....C7
Morobe C7
Mount Hagen 13,441 ..B7
Popondetta 6,429 ...C7
Port Moresby
  (cap.) 123,624 ...B7
Rouka B7
Saidor 500 ....B7
Samarai 864 ....C8

Telefomin B7
Vanimo 3,071 ....B6
Wau 2,349 ....B7
Wedau C7
Wewak 19,890 ....B6

OTHER FEATURES

Dampier (str.) C7
D'Entrecasteaux (isls.) ..C7
Fly (riv.) A7
Huon (gulf) C7
Karkar (isl.) B6
Kiriwina (isl.) C7
Long (isl.) B7
Louisiade (arch.) ...D8
Milne (bay) C8
Misima (isl.) C8
New Britain (isl.) 148,773 ..C7
Ramu (riv.) B7
Rossel (isl.) D8
Schouten (isls.) B6
Sepik (riv.) B6
Solomon (sea) C7
Tagula (isl.) C8
Torres (str.) A7
Trobriand (isls.) C7
Vitiaz (str.) B7
Woodlark (isl.) C7

★See page 74 for other
  Malaysian entries.

INDONESIA

AREA 788,430 sq. mi. (2,042,034 sq. km.)
POPULATION 179,136,000
CAPITAL Jakarta
LARGEST CITY Jakarta
HIGHEST POINT Puncak Jaya 16,503 ft.
  (5,030 m.)
MONETARY UNIT rupiah
MAJOR LANGUAGES Bahasa Indonesia,
  Indonesian and Papuan languages,
  English
MAJOR RELIGIONS Islam, tribal religions,
  Christianity, Hinduism

PAPUA NEW GUINEA

AREA 183,540 sq. mi. (475,369 sq. km.)
POPULATION 3,593,000
CAPITAL Port Moresby
LARGEST CITY Port Moresby
HIGHEST POINT Mt. Wilhelm 15,400 ft.
  (4,694 m.)
MONETARY UNIT kina
MAJOR LANGUAGES pidgin English,
  Hiri Motu, English
MAJOR RELIGIONS Tribal religions,
  Christianity

BRUNEI

AREA 2,226 sq. mi. (5,765 sq. km.)
POPULATION 249,000
CAPITAL Bandar Seri Begawan
LARGEST CITY Bandar Seri Begawan
HIGHEST POINT Pagon 6,070 ft.
  (1,850 m.)
MONETARY UNIT Brunei Dollar
MAJOR LANGUAGES Malay, English,
  Chinese
MAJOR RELIGIONS Islam, Buddhism,
  Christianity, tribal religions

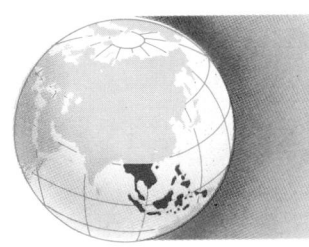

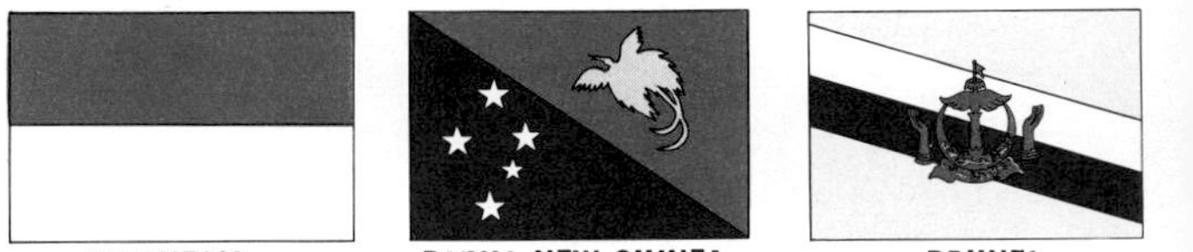

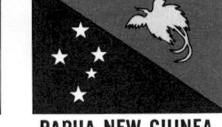

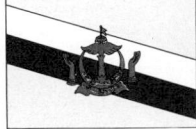

INDONESIA   PAPUA NEW GUINEA   BRUNEI

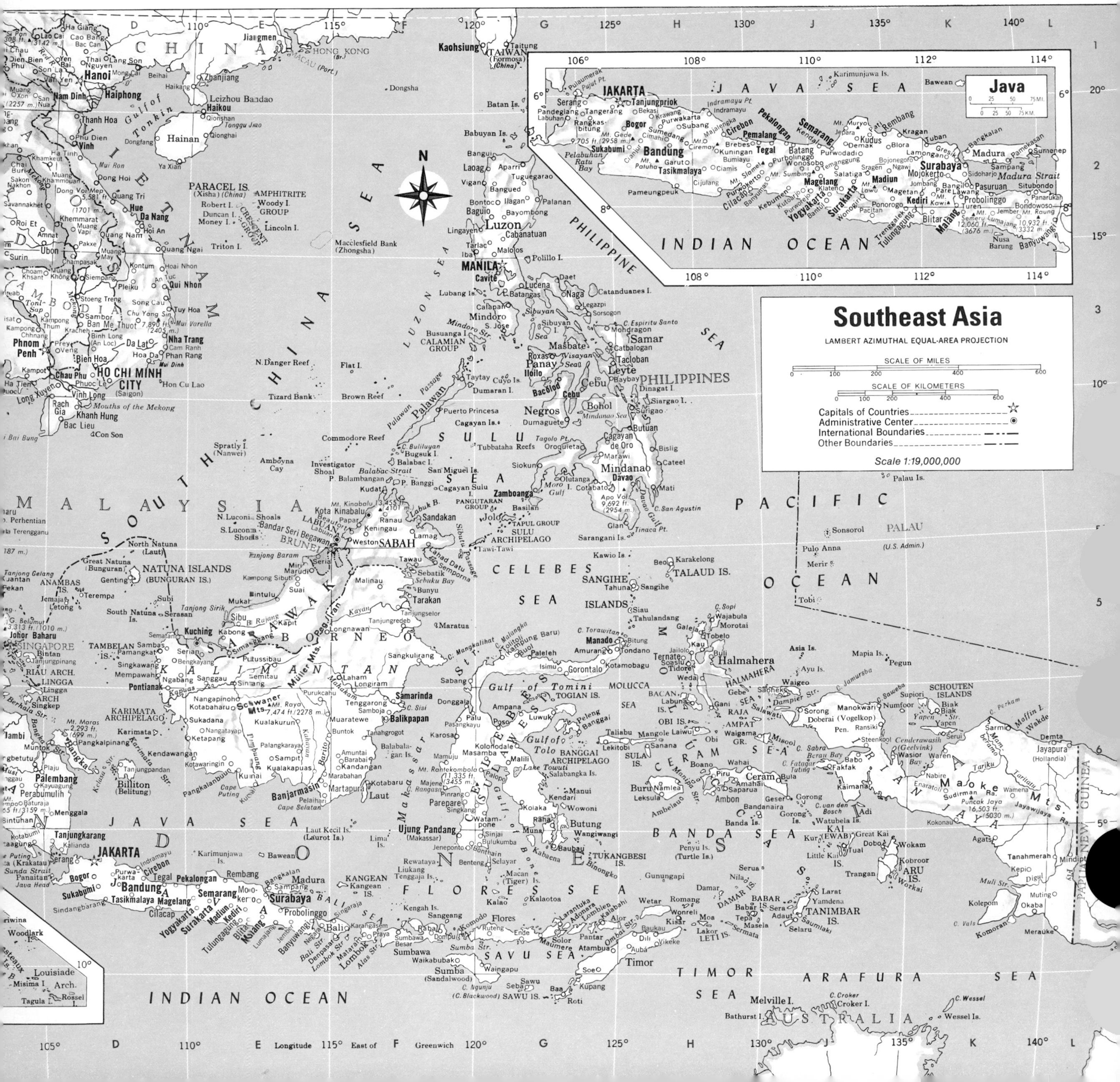

FIJI

AREA 7,055 sq. mi. (18,272 sq. km.)
POPULATION 727,000
CAPITAL Suva
LARGEST CITY Suva
HIGHEST POINT Tomaniivi 4,341 ft.
(1,323 m.)
MONETARY UNIT Fijian dollar
MAJOR LANGUAGES Fijian, Hindi, English
MAJOR RELIGIONS Protestantism, Hinduism

KIRIBATI

AREA 291 sq. mi. (754 sq. km.)
POPULATION 64,000
CAPITAL Bairiki (Tarawa)
HIGHEST POINT (on Banaba I.) 285 ft. (87 m.)
MONETARY UNIT Australian dollar
MAJOR LANGUAGES I-Kiribati, English
MAJOR RELIGIONS Protestantism, Roman
Catholicism

NAURU

AREA 7.7 sq. mi. (20 sq. km.)
POPULATION 9,000
CAPITAL Yaren (district)
MONETARY UNIT Australian dollar
MAJOR LANGUAGES Nauruan, English
MAJOR RELIGION Protestantism

SOLOMON ISLANDS

AREA 11,500 sq. mi. (29,785 sq. km.)
POPULATION 299,000
CAPITAL Honiara
HIGHEST POINT Mount Popomanatseu
7,647 ft. (2,331 m.)
MONETARY UNIT Solomon Islands dollar
MAJOR LANGUAGES English, pidgin English,
Melanesian dialects
MAJOR RELIGIONS Tribal religions,
Protestantism, Roman Catholicism

TONGA

AREA 270 sq. mi. (699 sq. km.)
POPULATION 95,000
CAPITAL Nuku'alofa
LARGEST CITY Nuku'alofa
HIGHEST POINT 3,389 ft. (1,033 m.)
MONETARY UNIT pa'anga
MAJOR LANGUAGES Tongan, English
MAJOR RELIGION Protestantism

TUVALU

AREA 9.78 sq. mi. (25.33 sq. km.)
POPULATION 9,000
CAPITAL Fongafale (Funafuti)
HIGHEST POINT 15 ft. (4.6 m.)
MONETARY UNIT Australian dollar
MAJOR LANGUAGES English, Tuvaluan
MAJOR RELIGION Protestantism

Abaiang (atoll) 3,296 . . . . H 5
Abemama (atoll) 2,300 . . . . H 5
Adamstown (cap.), Pitcairn Is.
54 . . . . N 8
Admiralty (isls.) . . . . E 6
Agaña (cap.), Guam 896 . . . . . E 4
Agrihan (isl.) . . . . E 4
Ailinglapalap (atoll) 1,385 . . . . G 5
Ailuk (atoll) 413 . . . . H 4
Aitutaki (atoll) 2,348 . . . . K 7
Alofi (cap.), Niue 960 . . . . K 7
Alotau 4,310 . . . . E 7
Ambrym (isl.) 6,324 . . . . G 7
American Samoa 32,297 . . . . . J 7
Anaa (atoll) . . . . M 7
Angaur (isl.) 243 . . . . D 5
Apataki (atoll) . . . . M 7
Apia (cap.), W.
Samoa 33,100 . . . . J 7
Arno (atoll) 1,487 . . . . H 5
Arorae (atoll) 1,626 . . . . H 6
Atafu (atoll) 577 . . . . J 6
Atiu (isl.) 1,225 . . . . L 8
Austral (isls.) 5,208 . . . . L 8
Avarua (cap.), Cook Is. . . . . . . L 8
Avarua (cap.), Cook Is.
Babelthuap (isl.) 10,391 . . . . . D 5
Bairiki (cap.), Kiribati 1,777 . . . H 5
Baker (isl.) . . . . J 5
Banaba (isl.) 2,314 . . . . G 6
Banks (isls.) 3,158 . . . . G 7
Belep (isls.) 624 . . . . G 7
Bellona (reefs) . . . . G 8
Beru (atoll) 2,318 . . . . H 6
Bikini (atoll) . . . . G 4
Bismarck (arch.) 218,339 . . . . . E 6
Bonin (isls.) 1,879 . . . . E 3
Bora-Bora (isl.) 2,572 . . . . L 7
Bougainville (isl.) 71,761 . . . . . F 6
Bounty (isls.) . . . . H 10
Bourail 3,149 . . . . G 8
Butaritari (atoll) 2,971 . . . . . . H 5
Capitol Hill (cap.), No.
Marianas 592 . . . . E 4
Caroline (isl.) . . . . M 7
Caroline (isls.) . . . . E 5
Chichi (isl.) 1,879 . . . . E 3
Choiseul (isl.) 10,349 . . . . F 6
Christmas (Kiritimati) (isl.) 674 L 5
Cook (isls.) 17,695 . . . . K 7
Coral (sea) . . . . F 7
Danger (Pukapuka) (atoll)
797 . . . . K 7
Daru 7,127 . . . . E 6
Disappointment (isls.) 373 . . . . N 7
Ducie (isl.) . . . . O 8
Easter (isl.) 1,598 . . . . Q 8
Ebon (atoll) 887 . . . . G 5
Efate (isl.) 18,038 . . . . G 7
Enderbury (isl.) . . . . J 6
Enewetak (Eniwetok) (atoll)
542 . . . . G 4
Erromanga (isl.) 945 . . . . H 7
Espiritu Santo (isl.) 16,220 . . . G 7
Fais (isl.) 207 . . . . E 5
Fakaofo (atoll) 654 . . . . J 6
Fanning (Tabuaeran) (atoll) 340 L 5
Faraulep (atoll) 132 . . . . E 5
Fatuhiva (isl.) 386 . . . . N 7
Fiji 588,068 . . . . H 8
Flint (isl.) . . . . L 7
Fly (riv.) . . . . E 6
Fongafale (cap.), Tuvalu . . . . . H 6
Futuna (Hoorn) (isls.) 3,173 . . . J 7
Funafuti (atoll) 2,120 . . . . H 6
Gambier (isls.) 556 . . . . N 8
Gardner (Nukumaroro) (isl.) . . . J 6
Gilbert (isls.) 47,711 . . . . H 6
Greenwich (Kapingamarangi)
(atoll) 508 . . . . F 5
Guadalcanal (isl.) 46,619 . . . . . F 7
Guam (isl.) 105,979 . . . . E 4
Hall (isls.) 647 . . . . F 5
Hawaiian (isls.) 964,691 . . . . . J 3
Henderson (isl.) . . . . O 8
Hivaoa (isl.) 1,159 . . . . N 6
Honiara (cap.), Solomon Is.
14,942 . . . . F 6
Hoorn (isls.) 3,173 . . . . J 7
Howland (isl.) . . . . J 5
Huahine (isl.) 3,140 . . . . L 7
Hull (Orona) (isl.) . . . . J 6
Huon (gulf) . . . . E 6
Ifalik (atoll) 389 . . . . E 5
Iwo (isl.) . . . . E 3
Jaluit (atoll) 1,450 . . . . G 5
Jarvis (isl.) . . . . K 6
Johnston (atoll) 327 . . . . K 4
Kadavu (Kandavu) (isl.) 8,699 . . H 7
Kanton (isl.) . . . . J 6
Kapingamarangi (atoll) 508 . . . . F 5
Kavieng 4,633 . . . . E 6
Kermadec (isls.) 5 . . . . J 9
Kieta 3,491 . . . . F 6
Kimbe 4,662 . . . . F 6
Kingman (reef) . . . . K 5
Kiribati 57,500 . . . . J 6
Kiritimati (isl.) 674 . . . . L 5
Kolonia (cap.), Micronesia
5,549 . . . . F 5
Koror (cap.), Belau 6,222 . . . . . D 5
Kosrae (isl.) 5,491 . . . . G 5
Kwajalein (atoll) 6,624 . . . . . . G 5
Lae 61,617 . . . . E 6
Lau Group (isls.) 14,452 . . . . . J 7
Lavongai (isl.) . . . . F 6
Lifu (isl.) 7,585 . . . . G 8
Line (isls.) . . . . K 5
Little Makin (atoll) 1,445 . . . . . H 5
Lord Howe (Ontong Java) (isl.)
1,082 . . . . G 6
Lord Howe (isl.) 287 . . . . G 9
Lorengau 3,986 . . . . E 6
Louisiade (arch.) . . . . F 7
Loyalty (isls.) 14,518 . . . . G 8
Luganville 4,935 . . . . G 7
Madang 21,335 . . . . E 6

Majuro (atoll) (cap.), Marshall
Is. 8,583 . . . . H 5
Makin (Butaritari) (atoll) 2,971 . H 5
Malaita (isl.) 50,912 . . . . G 6
Malden (isl.) . . . . L 6
Malekula (isl.) 15,931 . . . . G 7
Maloelap (atoll) 763 . . . . H 5
Mangaia (isl.) 1,364 . . . . L 8
Mangareva (isl.) 556 . . . . N 8
Manihiki (atoll) 405 . . . . K 7
Manua (isls.) 1,459 . . . . K 7
Manus (isl.) 25,844 . . . . E 6
Marcus (isl.) . . . . F 3
Maré (isl.) 4,156 . . . . G 8
Marianas, Northern 16,780 . . . . E 4
Mariana Trench . . . . E 4
Marquesas (isls.) 5,419 . . . . . . N 6
Marshall Islands 30,873 . . . . . G 4
Marutea (atoll) . . . . N 8
Mata Utu (cap.), Wallis and
Futuna 558 . . . . J 7
Mauke (isl.) 684 . . . . L 8
Melanesia (reg.) . . . . E 5
Micronesia (reg.) . . . . E 4
Micronesia, Federated States
of 73,160 . . . . F 5
Midway (isls.) 453 . . . . J 3
Mili (atoll) 763 . . . . H 5
Moen (isl.) 10,351 . . . . F 5
Moorea (isl.) 5,788 . . . . L 7

Mururoa (isl.) . . . . M 8
Nadi 6,938 . . . . H 7
Namonuito (atoll) 783 . . . . E 5
Namorik (atoll) 617 . . . . G 5
Nanumea (atoll) 844 . . . . H 6
Nauru 7,254 . . . . G 6
Ndeni (isl.) 4,854 . . . . G 7
New Britain (isl.) 148,773 . . . . F 6
New Caledonia 133,233 . . . . . G 8
New Caledonia (isl.)
118,715 . . . . G 8
New Georgia (isl.) 16,472 . . . . F 6
New Guinea (isl.) . . . . D 6
New Ireland (isl.) 65,657 . . . . . F 6
Ngatik (atoll) 560 . . . . F 5
Ngulu (atoll) 21 . . . . D 5
Niuatoputapu (isl.) 1,650 . . . . . J 7
Niue (isl.) 3,578 . . . . K 7
Niutao (atoll) 866 . . . . H 6
Nomoi (isls.) 1,879 . . . . F 5
Nonouti (atoll) 2,223 . . . . H 6
Norfolk Island (terr.) 2,175 . . . J 8
Northern Marianas 116,780 . . . E 4
Nouméa (cap.), New Caled. . . . G 8
Nouméa *74,335 . . . . G 8
Nui (atoll) 603 . . . . H 6
Nuku'alofa (cap.), Tonga
18,356 . . . . J 8
Nukuhiva (isl.) 1,484 . . . . M 6

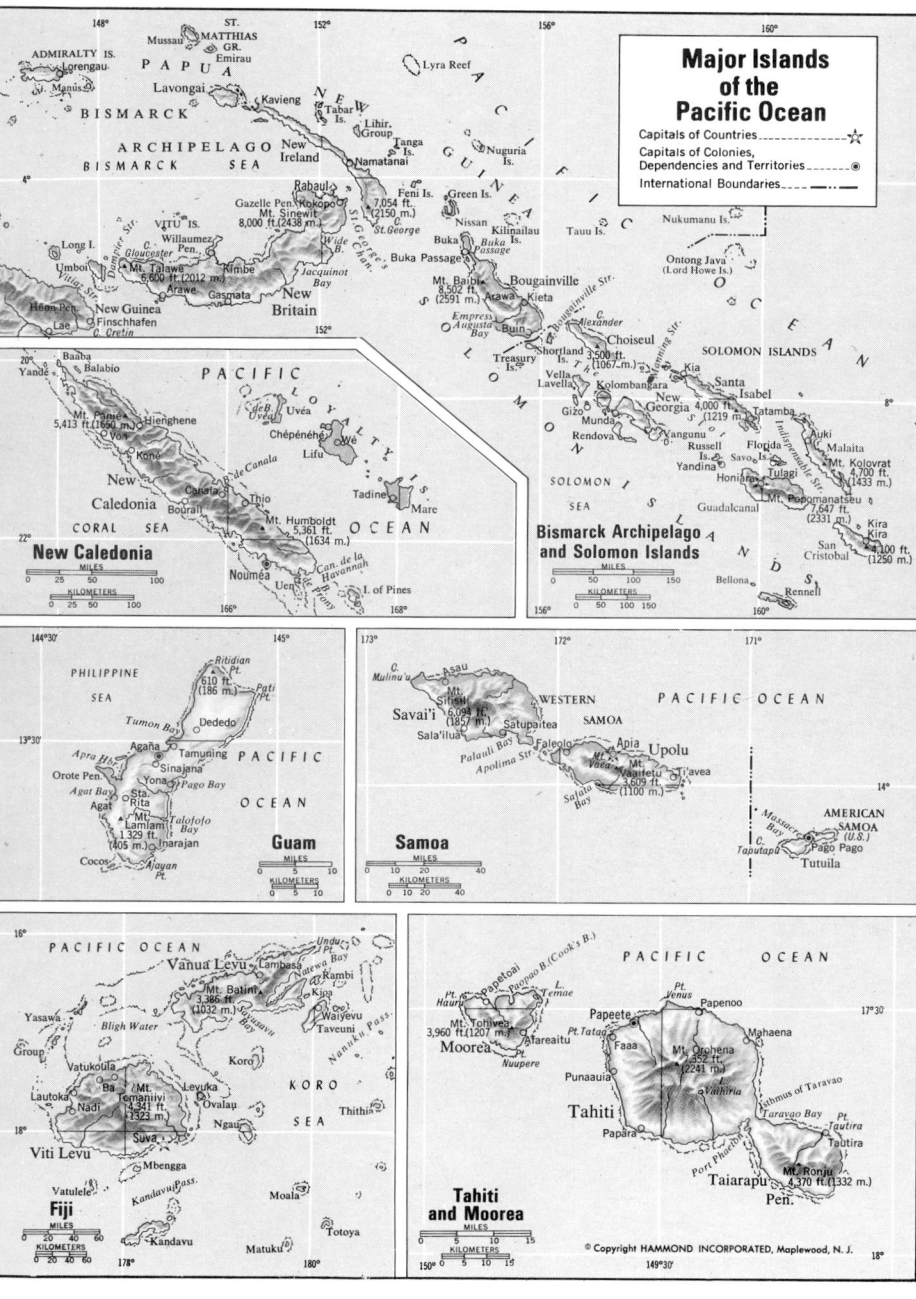

**Major Islands
of the
Pacific Ocean**

Capitals of Countries . . . . ☆
Capitals of Colonies,
Dependencies and Territories . . . . ◉
International Boundaries . . . .

New Caledonia

**Bismarck Archipelago
and Solomon Islands**

Guam

Samoa

Fiji

**Tahiti
and Moorea**

© Copyright HAMMOND INCORPORATED, Maplewood, N.J.

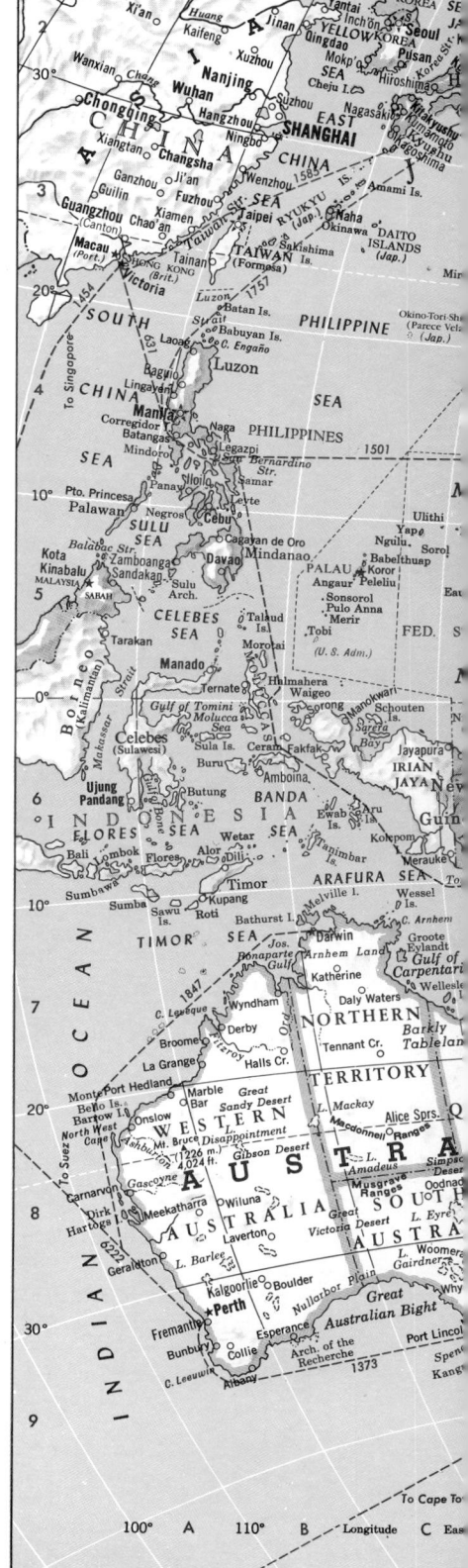

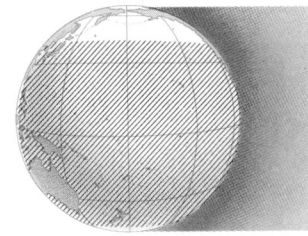

Ocean (Banaba) (isl.) 2,314	G 6	
Oeno (isl.)	O 8	
Onotoa (atoll) 1,997	H 6	
Ontong Java (isl.) 1,082	G 6	
Pagan (isl.)	E 4	
Pago Pago (cap.), Amer.		
Samoa 3,075	D 5	
Palau 12,116	D 5	
Palmyra (atoll)	K 5	
Papeete (cap.), Fr. Poly.		
22,967	M 7	
Papeete ●51,987	M 7	
Papua (gulf)	E 6	
Papua New Guinea		
3,010,727	E 6	
Peleliu (reg.) 609	D 5	
Penrhyn (Tongareva) (atoll)		
608	L 6	
Phoenix (isls.)	J 6	
Pines (isl.) 1,095	G 8	
Pitcairn (isl.) 54	O 8	
Pohnpei (isl.) 19,935	F 5	
Polynesia (reg.)	K 7	
Popondetta 6,429	E 6	
Port Moresby (cap.), Papua		
N.G. 123,624	E 6	
Pukapuka (atoll) 797	K 7	
Pulap (atoll) 427	E 5	
Puluwat (atoll) 441	E 5	
Rabaul 14,954	F 6	
Raiatea (isl.) 2,517	L 7	
Raivavae (isl.) 1,023	M 8	
Rakahanga (atoll) 269	K 7	
Ralik Chain (isls.)	G 5	
Rangiroa (atoll)	M 7	
Rapa (isl.) 398	M 8	
Rarotonga (isl.) 9,477	K 8	
Ratak Chain (isls.)	G 5	
Reao (atoll) 424	N 7	
Rennell (isl.) 1,132	F 7	
Rikitea	N 8	
Rimatara (isl.) 813	L 8	
Rongelap (atoll) 235	G 4	
Rota (isl.) 1,261	E 4	
Rotuma (isl.) 2,805	H 7	
Rurutu (isl.) 1,555	L 8	
Saipan (isl.) 14,549	E 4	
Sala y Gómez (isl.)	P 8	
Samarai 869	E 7	
Samoa (isls.)	J 7	
San Cristobal (isl.) 11,212	G 7	
Santa Cruz (isls.) 5,421	G 6	
Santa Isabel (isl.) 10,420	G 6	
Savai'i (isl.) 43,150	J 7	
Senyavin (isls.) 20,035	F 5	
Society (isls.) 117,703	L 7	
Solomon (isls.)	F 6	
Solomon (sea)	F 6	
Solomon Islands 221,000	G 6	
Starbuck (isl.)	L 6	
Suva (cap.), Fiji 63,628	H 7	
Suva *117,827	H 7	
Swains (isl.) 27	K 7	
Sydney (isl.)	K 6	
Tabiteuea (atoll) 3,942	H 6	
Tabuaeran (isl.) 340	L 5	
Tahaa (isl.) 3,513	L 7	
Tahiti (isl.) 95,604	L 7	
Takaroa (atoll) 337	N 7	
Tanna (isl.) 15,715	H 7	
Tarawa (atoll) 17,129	H 5	
Tasman (sea)	G 9	
Teraina (isl.) 458	L 5	
Tinian (isl.) 866	E 4	
Tokelau (isls.) 1,575	J 6	
Tonga 90,128	J 8	
Tongareva (atoll) 608	L 6	
Tongatapu (isls.) 57,130	J 8	
Torres (isls.) 325	G 7	
Torres (strait)	E 6	
Trobriand (isls.)	F 6	
Truk (isls.) 37,488	F 5	
Tuamotu (arch.) 9,052	M 7	
Tubuai (Austral) (isls.) 5,208	M 8	
Tubuai (isl.) 1,419	M 8	
Tutuila (isl.) 30,538	J 7	
Tuvalu 7,349	H 6	
Uapou (isl.) 1,563	M 6	
Ujelang (atoll) 309	F 5	
Ulithi (atoll) 710	D 4	

VANUATU

AREA 5,700 sq. mi. (14,763 sq. km.)
POPULATION 155,000
CAPITAL Vila
HIGHEST POINT Mt. Tabwemasana
6,165 ft. (1,879 m.)
MONETARY UNIT vatu
MAJOR LANGUAGES Bislama, English,
French
MAJOR RELIGIONS Christian, animist

WESTERN SAMOA

AREA 1,133 sq. mi. (2,934 sq. km.)
POPULATION 163,000
CAPITAL Apia
LARGEST CITY Apia
HIGHEST POINT Mt. Silisili 6,094 ft.
(1,857 m.)
MONETARY UNIT tala
MAJOR LANGUAGES Samoan, English
MAJOR RELIGIONS Protestantism,
Roman Catholicism

Upolu (isl.) 114,620	J 7	Vila *14,797	G 7	Wau 2,349	E 6
Uturoa 2,517	L 7	Viti Levu (isl.) 445,422	H 7	Western Samoa 158,130	J 7
Uvéa (isl.) 2,777	G 7	Volcano (isls.)	E 3	Wewak 19,890	E 6
Vaitupu (atoll) 1,273	H 6	Vostok (isl.)	L 7	Woleai (isl.) 638	E 5
Vanikoro (isl.) 267	G 7	Wake (isl.) 302	G 4	Wotje (atoll) 535	H 5
Vanimo 3,071	E 6	Wallis (isls.) 6,019	J 7	Yap (isl.) 6,670	D 5
Vanua Levu (isl.) 103,122	H 7	Wallis and Futuna 9,192	J 7		
Vanuatu 112,596	G 7	Washington (Teraina) (isl.)		*City and suburbs.	
Vila (cap.), Vanuatu 4,729	G 7	458	L 5	●Population of urban area.	

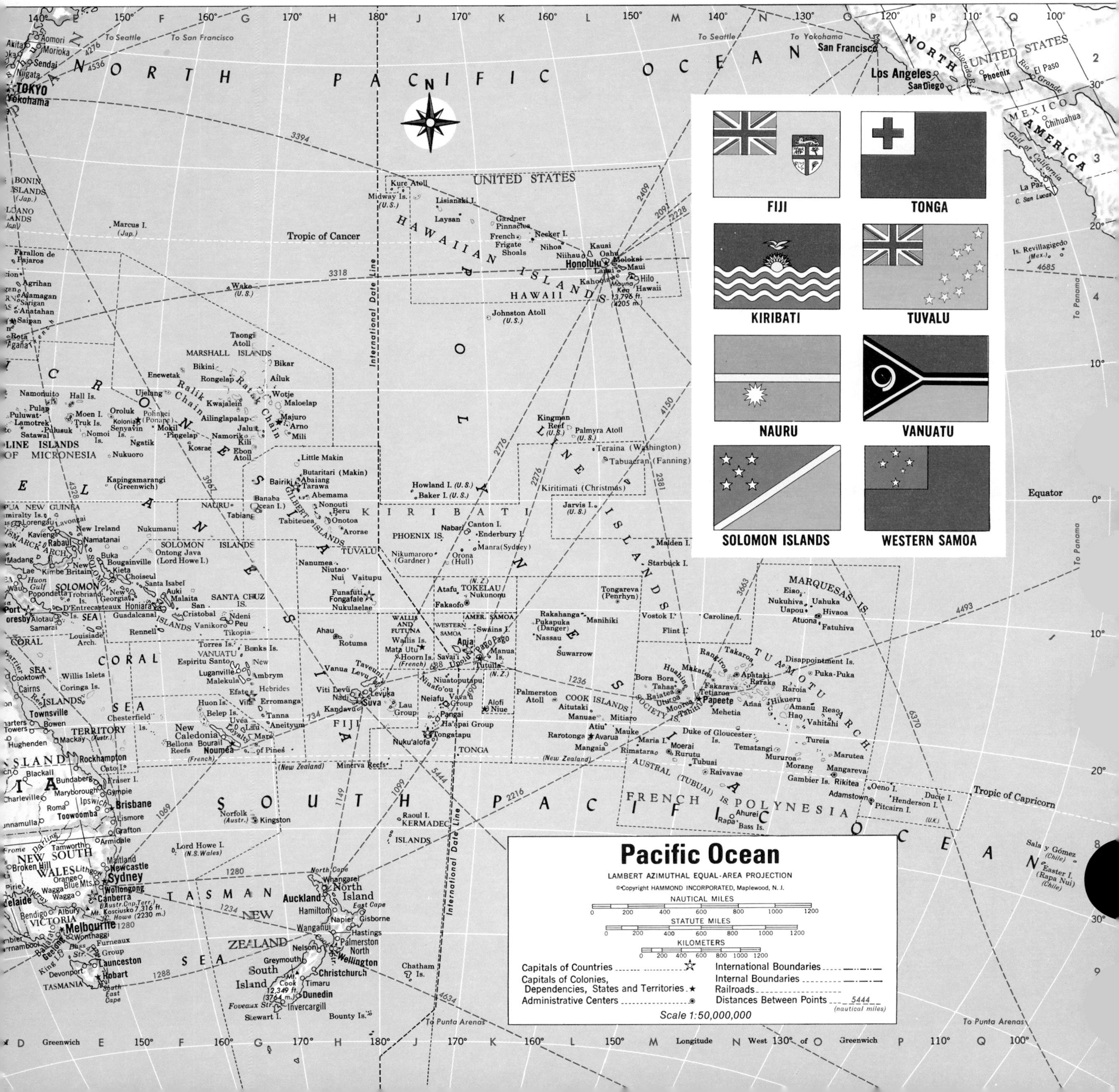

(Map of the Pacific Ocean with flags of FIJI, TONGA, KIRIBATI, TUVALU, NAURU, VANUATU, SOLOMON ISLANDS, WESTERN SAMOA)

Pacific Ocean

LAMBERT AZIMUTHAL EQUAL-AREA PROJECTION

©Copyright HAMMOND INCORPORATED, Maplewood, N.J.

NAUTICAL MILES
0 200 400 600 800 1000 1200

STATUTE MILES
0 200 400 600 800 1000 1200

KILOMETERS
0 200 400 600 800 1000 1200

Capitals of Countries .... ☆
Capitals of Colonies,
Dependencies, States and Territories ... ★
Administrative Centers .... ●

International Boundaries ---------------
Internal Boundaries -------------
Railroads ----------------
Distances Between Points ----- 5444
(nautical miles)

Scale 1:50,000,000

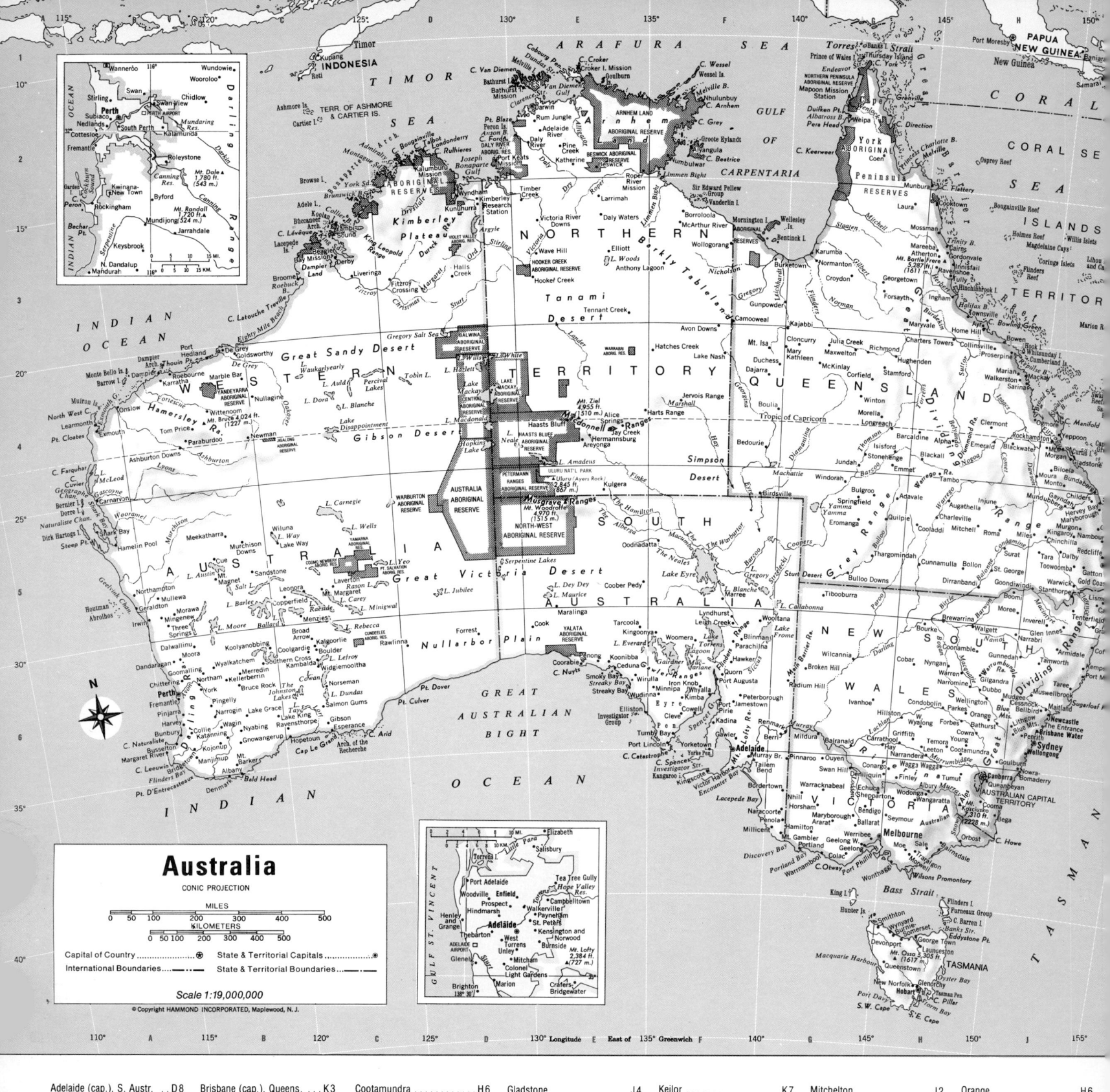

Australia

CONIC PROJECTION

MILES
0 50 100 200 300 400 500

KILOMETERS
0 50 100 200 300 400 500

Capital of Country .... ⊛   State & Territorial Capitals .... ⊛
International Boundaries.........   State & Territorial Boundaries.... _ . _ . _

Scale 1:19,000,000

© Copyright HAMMOND INCORPORATED, Maplewood, N.J.

Adelaide (cap.), S. Austr. . . D8	Brisbane (cap.), Queens. . . . K3	Cootamundra H6	Gladstone J4
Albany B6	Brisbane Water J6	Coral Sea Is. Terr. J3	Glenelg D8
Albury H7	Broadmeadows L6	Corinda K3	Glen Innes J3
Alice Springs E4	Broken Hill G6	Cowra H6	Glenorchy H8
Altona K7	Brunswick K7	Crafters-Bridgewater E8	Gold Coast J5
Ararat G7	Bunbury B6	Cranbourne M8	Goulburn J6
Armidale J6	Bundaberg J4	Croydon M7	Graceville K3
Ashfield K4	Burnie H8	Dalby J5	Grafton J5
Ashgrove K2	Burnside E8	Dandenong M7	Greenslopes K3
Ashmore and Cartier Is.,	Burwood K4	Darwin (cap.), North. Terr. . E2	Griffith H6
Terr. of C2	Busselton A6	Deniliquin H6	Gunnedah J6
Aspley K2	Cairns H3	Devonport H8	Gympie J5
Auburn K4	Caloundra J5	Doncaster and Templestowe . L7	Hamilton G7
Australian Capital Territory . H7	Camberwell L7	Drummoyne K4	Hawthorn L7
Ayr H3	Campbelltown E8	Dubbo H6	Heidelberg L7
Bairnsdale H7	Camp Hill K3	Echuca H7	Hervey Bay J4
Ballarat G7	Canberra (cap.), Australia . . H7	Elizabeth E7	Hindmarsh D8
Bankstown K4	Canterbury K4	Eltham L6	Hobart (cap.), Tasmania . . . H8
Banyo K2	Carina K3	Enfield D7	Holyroyd K3
Bathurst H6	Casino J5	Enoggera K2	Hornsby K3
Baulkham Hills K4	Caulfield L7	Esperance C6	Horsham G7
Beenleigh J5	Cessnock-Bellbird J6	Essendon K7	Hunters Hill K4
Bendigo G7	Charters Towers H4	Fairfield K4	Hurstville K4
Blacktown K4	Chelsea L8	Fitzroy L7	Inala K3
Blue Mountains J6	Chermside K2	Footscray K7	Indooroopilly K3
Botany L4	Coburg K7	Forbes H6	Innisfail H3
Boulder-Kalgoorlie C6	Coffs Harbour J5	Fremantle B6	Inverell J5
Bowen H3	Colac G7	Gawler F6	Ipswich J3
Box Hill L7	Collingwood K7	Geelong L7	Kalgoorlie C6
Brighton D8	Concord K4	Geelong West G7	Kalgoorlie-Boulder C6
Brighton L7	Cooma H7	Geraldton A5	Karratha B4

Keilor K7	Mitchelton J2	Orange H6
Kempsey J6	Moe H7	Parkes H6
Kenmore J3	Moorabbin L7	Parramatta K4
Kensington and Norwood . . E8	Mooroka K3	Payneham E8
Kew L7	Mordialloc L7	Penrith K4
Knox M7	Moree H5	Perth (cap.), W. Austr. B2
Kogarah K4	Morningside K2	Port Adelaide D7
Ku-ring-gai K4	Morwell H7	Port Augusta F6
Kwinana-New Town B2	Mosman L4	Port Hedland B3
Lane Cove L4	Mount Gambier G7	Portland G7
Launceston H8	Mount Isa F4	Port Lincoln E6
Leeton H6	Mudgee H6	Port Macquarie K6
Leichhardt L4	Murray Bridge F7	Port Melbourne K7
Lismore J5	Murwillumbah J5	Port Pirie F6
Lithgow J6	Muswellbrook J6	Prahan L7
Liverpool K4	Narrabri H6	Preston L7
Mackay H3	Narrandera H6	Prospect H7
Maitland J6	Nedlands B2	Queanbeyan H7
Malvern L7	Newcastle J6	Queensland G4
Mandurah B3	Newman C4	Randwick L4
Manly L4	New Norfolk H8	Red Cliffe J5
Mareeba G3	New South Wales H6	Richmond L7
Marion D8	Norfolk Island 2,180	Ringwood M7
Maroochydore-Mooloolaba . J5	Northam B6	Rockdale K4
Marrickville L4	Northcote L7	Rockhampton J4
Maryborough J5	Northern Territory E3	Rockingham B2
Maryborough G7	North Sydney L4	Roma H5
Melbourne (cap.),	Nowra-Bomaderry J6	Ryde K4
Victoria H7	Nunawading L7	Saint Kilda L7
Mildura G6	Nundah K2	Saint Lucia K3
Mitcham D8	Oakleigh L7	Sale H7

AREA 2,966,136 sq. mi. (7,682,300 sq. km.)
POPULATION 15,602,156
CAPITAL Canberra
LARGEST CITY Sydney
HIGHEST POINT Mt. Kosciusko 7,310 ft.
(2,228 m.)
LOWEST POINT Lake Eyre -39 ft. (-12 m.)
MONETARY UNIT Australian dollar
MAJOR LANGUAGE English
MAJOR RELIGIONS Protestantism,
Roman Catholicism

Population Distribution

• Cities with over
  500,000 inhabitants
  (including suburbs)

TROPIC OF CAPRICORN

DENSITY PER

SQ. KILOMETER	SQ. MILE
Over 50	Over 130
10-50	25-130
1-10	3-25
Under 1	Under 3

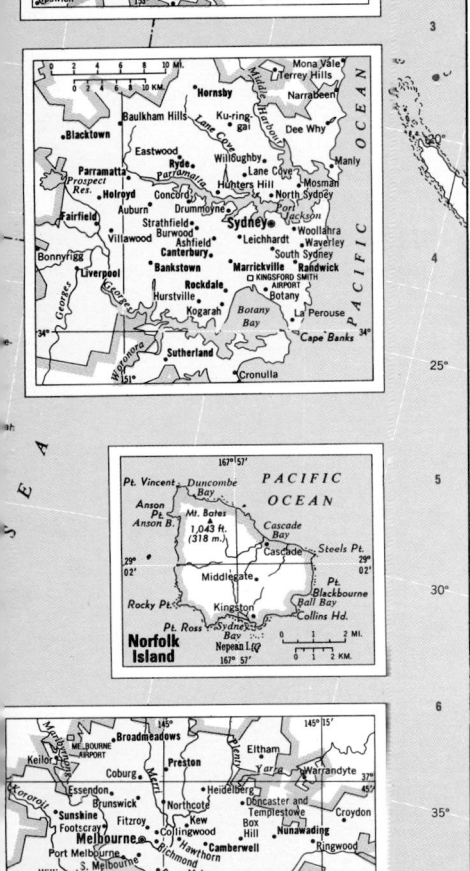

Vegetation

TROPIC OF CAPRICORN

TROPICAL FOREST
Tropical Rainforest
Light Tropical Forest
Woodland and Shrub

TROPICAL GRASSLAND
Grass and Shrub (Savanna)
Wooded Savanna

MID-LATITUDE FOREST
Mixed Coniferous and Broadleaf Forest
Mixed Woodland
Woodland and Shrub (Mediterranean)

MID-LATITUDE GRASSLAND

SCRUB AND FERNLANDS

DESERT AND DESERT SHRUB

ALPINE

AUST

Salisbury	E7	Traralgon	H7
Sandgate	K2	Tumut	H7
Sandringham	L7	Unley	D8
Seymour	H7	Victoria	G7
Shepparton (Shepparton-Mooroopna)	G7	Wagga Wagga	H7
		Wangaratta	H7
South Australia	F6	Wanneroo	B2
South Melbourne	K7	Warrnambool	G7
South Perth	B2	Warwick	J5
South Sydney	L4	Waverley	L4
Springvale	L7	Waverley	L7
Stafford (Stafford-Stafford Heights)	K2	Werribee	G7
		Western Australia	B5
Stirling	B2	West Torrens	D8
Strathfield	K4	Whyalla	F6
Subiaco	B2	Williamstown	K7
Sunshine	K7	Willoughby	K3
Sutherland	K5	Windsor	K2
Swan Hill	G7	Wodonga	H7
Sydney (cap.), N. S. Wales	L4	Wollongong	J6
Tamworth	J6	Woodville	D7
Taree	J6	Woollahra	L4
Tasmania	H8	Wynnum	L2
Tea Tree Gully	E7	Yeppoon	J4
Temora	H6	Young	H6
Thebarton	D8		
The Entrance (The Entrance-Terrigal)	J6		
The Gap	J2		
Toowoomba	J5		
Townsville	H3		

*City and suburbs.
†Population of met. area.
‡Population of urban area.

Average January Temperature

Darwin 83°
Derby 88°
Onslow 85°
Alice Springs 82°
Cairns 81°
Brisbane 77°
Kalgoorlie 78°
Broken Hill 79°
Perth 74°
Adelaide 72°
Sydney 70°
Albany 63°
Melbourne 67°
Hobart 62°
Auckland 66°
Dunedin 60°

Tropic of Capricorn

FAHRENHEIT | CELSIUS
Over 86° | Over 30°
68° to 86° | 20° to 30°
50° to 68° | 10° to 20°
32° to 50° | 0° to 10°
Under 32° | Under 0°

• Sydney 70° Average January temperature in degrees Fahrenheit at selected stations

Average July Temperature

Darwin 76°
Derby 72°
Onslow 63°
Alice Springs 52°
Cairns 70°
Brisbane 59°
Kalgoorlie 52°
Broken Hill 51°
Perth 55°
Adelaide 52°
Sydney 54°
Albany 53°
Melbourne 49°
Hobart 46°
Auckland 52°
Dunedin 43°

Tropic of Capricorn

FAHRENHEIT | CELSIUS
Over 68° | 20° to 30°
50° to 68° | 10° to 20°
32° to 50° | 0° to 10°
Under 32° | Under 0°

• Sydney 54° Average July temperature in degrees Fahrenheit at selected stations

Rainfall

Darwin 60
Thursday Island 66
Derby 23
Tennant Creek 15
Cloncurry 19
Cairns 86
Onslow 12
Mackay 63
Alice Springs 12
William Creek 5
Brisbane 45
Geraldton 19
Kalgoorlie 9
Broken Hill 9
Perth 36
Adelaide 20
Albury 28
Sydney 47
Albany 37
Melbourne 26
Auckland 48
Hokitika 116
Wellington 48
Hobart 25
Dunedin 36

South Tropic Line (Tropic of Capricorn)

AVERAGE ANNUAL RAINFALL
INCHES | CENTIMETERS
Over 80 | Over 200
60 to 80 | 150 to 200
40 to 60 | 100 to 150
20 to 40 | 50 to 100
10 to 20 | 25 to 50
Under 10 | Under 25

• Sydney 47 Average annual rainfall in inches at selected stations

DOMINANT LAND USE

- Cereals (chiefly wheat), Livestock
- Dairy, Truck Farming
- Cash Crops, Horticulture, Fruit
- Pasture Livestock
- Range Livestock
- Forests
- Nonagricultural Land

MAJOR MINERAL OCCURRENCES

Ab Asbestos
Ag Silver
Al Bauxite
Au Gold
C   Coal
Cu Copper
D   Diamonds
Fe Iron Ore
G   Natural Gas
Gp Gypsum
Lg Lignite
Ls Limestone
Mg Magnesium
Mi Mica
Mn Manganese

Na Salt
Ni Nickel
O   Petroleum
Op Opals
P   Phosphates
Pb Lead
S   Sulfur, Pyrites
Sb Antimony
Sn Tin
Ti Titanium
U   Uranium
W   Tungsten
Zn Zinc
Zr Zirconium

⚡ Water Power
▨ Major Industrial Areas

Agriculture, Industry and Resources

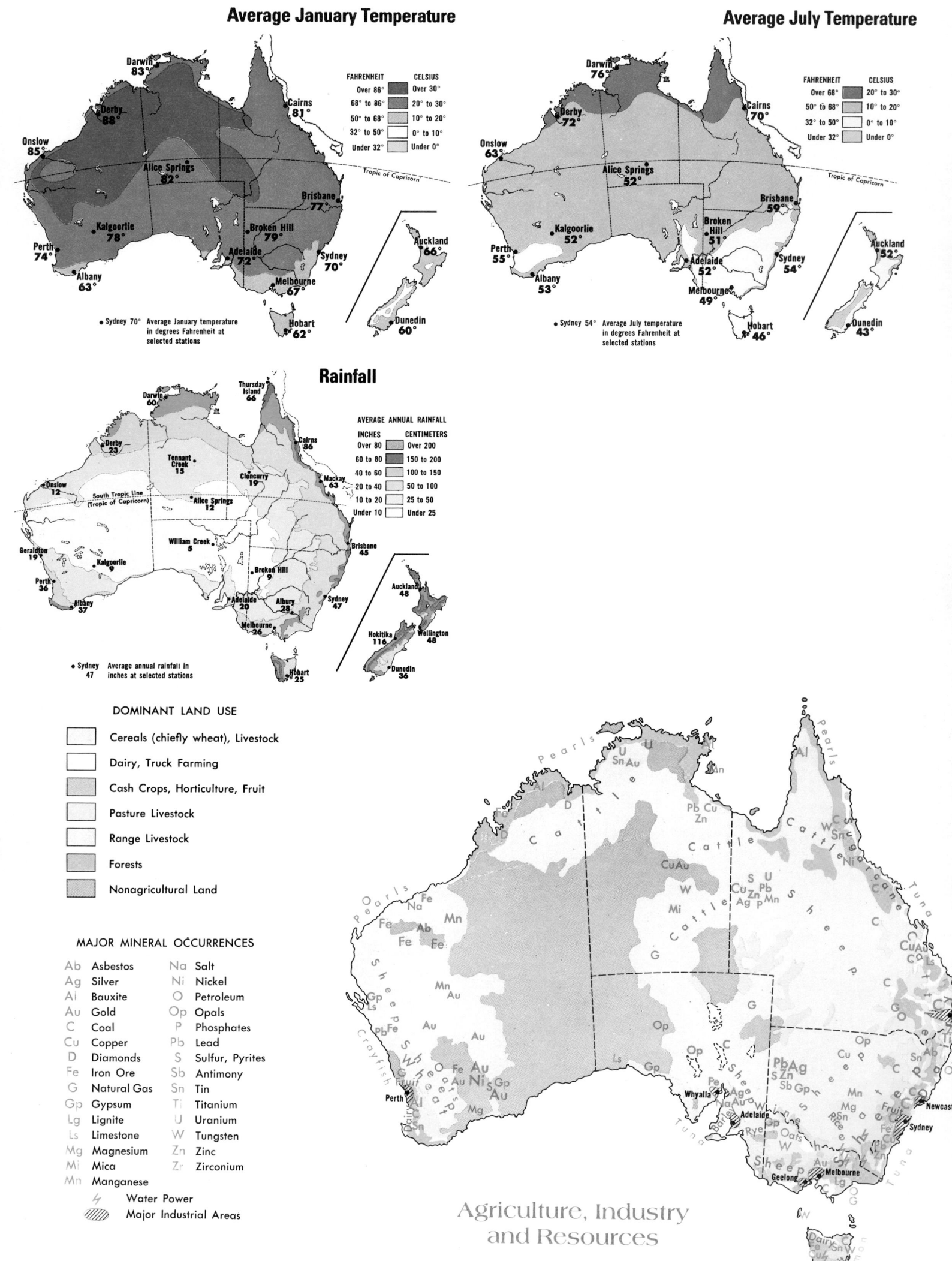

Vegetation / Relief

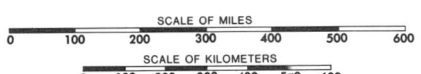

SCALE OF MILES
0   100   200   300   400   500   600

SCALE OF KILOMETERS
0   100   200   300   400   500   600

Capital of Country...⊛
State and Territorial Capitals.........................◉
International Boundaries..............................——·——
State and Territorial Boundaries..............——·——

Elevations in Feet   Depths in Fathoms

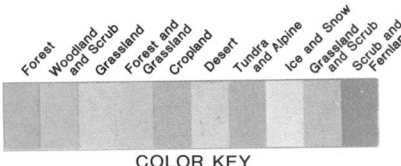

Forest | Woodland and Scrub | Grassland | Forest and Grassland | Cropland | Desert | Tundra and Alpine | Ice and Snow | Grassland and Scrub | Scrub and Fernlands

COLOR KEY

© Copyright HAMMOND INCORPORATED, Maplewood, N. J.

AREA 975,096 sq. mi.
(2,525,500 sq. km.)
POPULATION 1,406,929
CAPITAL Perth
LARGEST CITY Perth
HIGHEST POINT Mt. Bruce 4,024 ft.
(1,227 m.)

Topography

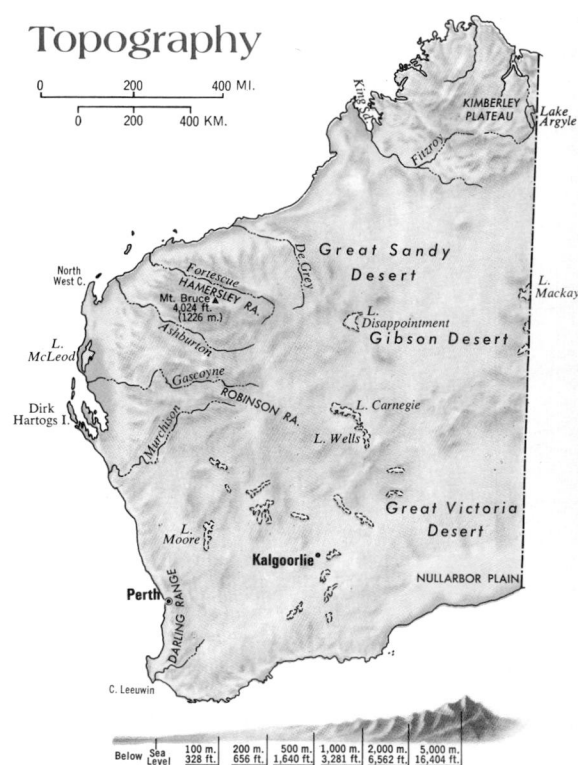

Below Sea Level | 100 m. 328 ft. | 200 m. 656 ft. | 500 m. 1,640 ft. | 1,000 m. 3,281 ft. | 2,000 m. 6,562 ft. | 5,000 m. 16,404 ft.

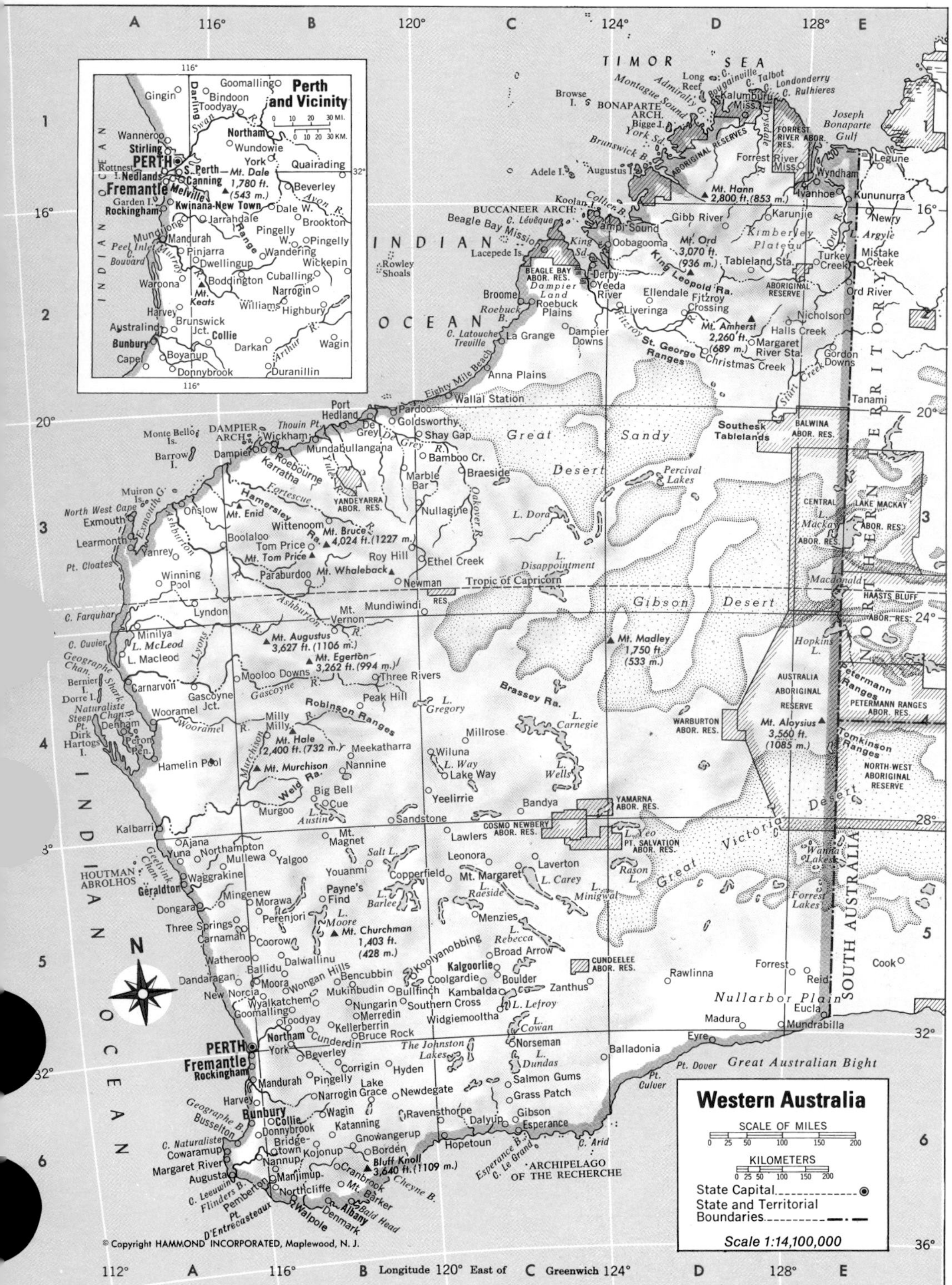

CITIES and TOWNS

Albany 15,222 .... B6
Augusta 588 .... A6
Australind 1,681 .... A2
Balladonia D6
Beverley 756 .... B1
Boddington 367 .... B2
Boulder-Kalgoorlie 19,848 .. C5
Boyanup 365 .... A2
Bridgetown 1,521 .... B6
Brookton 595 .... B2
Broome 3,666 .... C2
Bruce Rock 565 .... B5
Brunswick Junction 889 .. A2
Bunbury 21,749 .... A2
Busselton 6,463 .... A6
Canning 52,816 .... A1
Capel 680 .... A2
Carnamah 422 .... A5
Carnarvon 5,053 .... A4
Collie 7,667 .... B2
Coolgardie 891 .... C5

Coorow 226 .... B5
Corrigin 841 .... B6
Cranbrook 316 .... B6
Cuballing ○647 .... B2
Cue 320 .... A4
Cunderdin 731 .... B5
Dalwallinu 639 .... B5
Dampier 2,471 .... B3
Dandaragan ○1,748 .... A5
Darkan 242 .... B2
Denham 402 .... A4
Denmark 985 .... B6
Derby 2,933 .... C2
Dongara-Port Denison 1,155 A5
Donnybrook 1,197 .... A2
Dwellingup 453 .... B2
Esperance 6,375 .... C6
Eucla E5
Exmouth 2,583 .... A3
Fitzroy Crossing D2
Fremantle 22,484 .... A1
Geraldton 20,895 .... A5
Gingin 382 .... A1
Gnowangerup 872 .... B6

Goldsworthy 923 .... B3
Goomalling 600 .... B1
Halls Creek 966 .... D2
Harvey 2,479 .... A2
Hopetoun C6
Hyden B6
Jarrahdale 315 .... B2
Kalbarri 820 .... A4
Kalgoorlie 9,145 .... C5
Kalgoorlie-Boulder 19,848 .. C5
Kambalda 4,463 .... C5
Karratha 8,341 .... B3
Katanning 4,413 .... B6
Kellerberrin 1,091 .... B5
Kojonup 544 .... B6
Koolyanobbing 277 .... B5
Kununurra 2,081 .... E2
Kwinana New Town 12,355.. A1
Lake Grace 575 .... B6
Laverton 872 .... C5
Learmonth A3
Leonora 524 .... C5
Madura D5
Mandurah 10,978 .... A2

Manjimup 4,150 .... B6
Marble Bar 357 .... C3
Margaret River 798 .... A6
Meekatharra 989 .... B4
Melville 61,211 .... A1
Menzies 232 .... C5
Merredin 3,520 .... B5
Mingenew 368 .... A5
Moora 1,677 .... B5
Morawa 694 .... B5
Mount Barker 1,519 .... B6
Mount Magnet 618 .... B5
Mukinbudin 370 .... B5
Mullewa 918 .... A5
Mundijong 356 .... A2
Nannup 552 .... B6
Narrogin 4,969 .... B2
Nedlands 20,257 .... A1
Newman 5,466 .... B3
New Norcia A5
Norseman 1,895 .... C6
Northam 6,791 .... B1
Northampton 750 .... A5
Northcliffe B6
Nungarin ○332 .... B5
Onslow 594 .... A3
Pannawonica 1,170 .... B3
Paraburdoo 2,357 .... B3
Pardoo B3
Pemberton 871 .... A6
Perenjori 257 .... B5
Perth (cap.) 809,035 .... A1
Perth *898,918 .... A1
Pingelly 937 .... B2
Pinjarra 1,336 .... A2
Port Denison-Dongara 1,155 A5
Port Hedland 12,948 .... B3
Quairading 741 .... B5
Ravensthorpe 327 .... C5
Rockingham 24,932 .... A2
Roebourne 1,688 .... B3

Sandstone ○133 .... B4
Shay Gap 853 .... C3
Southern Cross 798 .... B5
South Perth 31,524 .... A1
Stirling 161,858 .... A1
Three Springs 638 .... A5
Tom Price 3,540 .... B3
Toodyay 560 .... B1
Turkey Creek 212 .... E2
Wagin 1,488 .... B2
Walpole 291 .... B6
Wandering ○470 .... B2
Wanneroo 6,745 .... A1
Waroona 1,462 .... A2
Wickepin 267 .... B2
Wickham 2,387 .... B3
Williams 453 .... B2
Wiluna 221 .... C4
Wittenoom 247 .... B3
Wongan Hills 947 .... B5
Wundowie 720 .... B5
Wyalkatchem 453 .... B5
Wyndham 1,509 .... E1
Yalgoo ○315 .... B5
Yampi Sound C2
York 1,136 .... B1

OTHER FEATURES

Adele (isl.) C1
Admiralty (gulf) D1
Aloysius (mt.) E4
Argyle (lake) E2
Arid (cape) C6
Ashburton (riv.) A3
Augustus (mt.) B4
Austin (lake) B4
Australia Aboriginal Res. .. E4
Bald (head) B6
Balwina Aboriginal Res. .. E3
Barlee (lake) B5
Barrow (isl.) A3
Beaglebay Aboriginal Res. .. C2
Bluff Knoll (mt.) B6
Bonaparte (arch.) D1
Bougainville (cape) D1
Brassey (range) C4
Bruce (mt.) B3
Brunswick (bay) D1
Buccaneer (arch.) C2
Carey (lake) C5
Carnegie (lake) C4
Central Aboriginal Res. .. E3
Churchman (mt.) B5
Collier (bay) C1
Cosmo Newbery Aboriginal
Res. C5
Cowan (lake) C5
Cundeelee Aboriginal Res. .. C5
Dale (mt.) B1
Dampier (arch.) B3
Dampier Land (reg.) C2
De Grey (riv.) B3
D'Entrecasteaux (pt.) A6
Dirk Hartogs (isl.) A4
Disappointment (lake) C3
Drysdale (riv.) D1
Dundas (lake) C6
Egerton (mt.) B4
Eighty Mile (beach) C2
Enid (mt.) B3
Esperance (bay) C6

Exmouth (gulf) A3
Fitzroy (riv.) D2
Flinders (bay) A6
Forrest River Aboriginal Res. D1
Fortescue (riv.) B3
Garden (isl) A1
Gascoyne (riv.) B4
Geelvink (chan.) A5
Geographe (bay) A6
Geographe (chan.) A4
Gibson (des.) D3
Great Australian (bight) E6
Great Sandy (des.) C3
Great Victoria (des.) D5
Hamersley (range) B3
Hann (mt.) D1
Hopkins (lake) E4
Houtman Abrolhos (isls.) .. A5
Indian Ocean A4
Johnston, The (lakes) C6
Joseph Bonaparte (gulf) .. E1
Kimberley (plat.) D1
King (sound) C2
King Leopold (range) D1
Koolan (isl.) C1
Leeuwin (cape) A6
Le Grand (cape) C6
Lévêque (cape) C2
Londonderry (cape) D1
Lyons (riv.) A4
Macdonald (lake) E3
Mackay (lake) E3
McLeod (lake) A4
Minigwal (lake) C5
Monte Bello (isls.) A3
Moore (lake) B5
Murchison (riv.) A4
Murray (riv.) A2
Naturaliste (cape) A6
Naturaliste (chan.) A4
North West (cape) A3
North-West Aboriginal Res. E4
Nullarbor (plain) D6
Oakover (riv.) C3
Ord (mt.) D1
Ord (lake) E2
Ord (riv.) E2
Percival (lakes) D3
Peron (pen.) A4
Petermann (ranges) E4
Rason (lake) D5
Rebecca (lake) C5
Recherche (arch.) C6
Robinson (ranges) B4
Roebuck (bay) C2
Rottnest (isl.) A1
Saint George (ranges) D2
Shark (bay) A4
Southesk Tablelands D3
Sturt (creek) D2
Swan (riv.) A1
Timor (sea) D1
Tomkinson (ranges) E4
Wanna (lakes) D5
Warburton Aboriginal Res. .. D4
Way (lake) C4
Weld (range) B4
Wells (lake) C4
Whaleback (mt.) B3
Wooramel (riv.) A4
York (sound) D1

○ Population of district.
*Population of met. area.

Western Australia

SCALE OF MILES

KILOMETERS

State Capital .... ◉
State and Territorial
Boundaries ....

Scale 1:14,100,000

© Copyright HAMMOND INCORPORATED, Maplewood, N.J.

Perth and Vicinity

CITIES and TOWNS

delaide River B2
ileron C7
lice Springs 18,395 . . . . D7
yangula 1,181 . . . . E2
ncurugu 597 . . . . E3
nthony Lagoon D4
reyonga C8
rltunga D7
ven Downs E5
arnyili-Beswick 685 . . . . . . C3
arka Banka C5
arrow Creek D6
atchelor B2
athurst Island 1,032 . . . . . . B1
irdum C3
irrimbah C3
irrindudu A5
orroloola 420 . . . . E4
undooma D8
urramurra E6
harlotte Waters D8
laravale B3
oniston C7
oolibah B3
reswell Downs E4
rcker Island Mission C1
aly River B2
aly Waters C4
arwin (cap.) 56,482 . . . . . . B2
ocker River 217 . . . . A8
lliott C4
penarra D6
rldunda C8
va Downs D5

Ewaninga D7
Goulburn Island 277 . . . . . . C1
Gove (Nhulunbuy) 3,879 . . . E2
Harts Range D7
Hatches Creek D6
Helen Springs C5
Henbury C8
Hermannsburg 541 . . . . . . C7
Hooker Creek 671 . . . . . . B5
Humpty Doo B2
Katherine 3,737 . . . . B3
Kildurk A4
Koolpinyah B2
Kulgera C8
Kurundi D6
Lake Nash E6
Larrimah C3
Legune A3
Limbunya B4
Lucy Creek D7
Mainoru C3
Maningrida 702 . . . . C2
Mataranka C3
Milingimbi 564 . . . . D2
Mistake Creek A4
Montejinnie C4
Mount Cavenagh C8
Mount Doreen B7
Murray Downs D6
Napperby C7
Newcastle Waters C4
Nhulunbuy 3,879 . . . . E2
Numbulwar 422 . . . . D3
Oenpelli 452 . . . . C2
O. T. Downs D4
Papunya 635 . . . . B7
Pine Creek 214 . . . . C2

Plenty River Mine D7
Port Keats 819 . . . . A3
Powell Creek C5
Rankine Store E5
Robinson River E4
Rockhampton Downs D5
Rodinga D8
Rum Jungle B2
Santa Teresa 479 . . . . D8
Soudan E6
Stirling Station C6
Tanami A5
Tarlton Downs E7
Tea Tree Well C7
Tempe Downs C8
Tennant Creek 3,118 . . . . . C5
The Granites B6
Top Springs C4
Ucharonidge D4
Umbakumba 247 . . . . E2
Umbeara C8
Urapunga D3
Utopia D7
Victoria River Downs B4
Warrabri 459 . . . . D6
Warrego 991 . . . . C5
Wave Hill B4
White Quartz Hill D7
Willeroo B3
Willowra C6
Wollogorang F4
Yambah C7
Yirrkala 543 . . . . E2
Yuendumu 687 . . . . B7

OTHER FEATURES

Amadeus (lake) B8

Arafura (sea) D1
Arnhem (cape) E2
Arnhem Land (reg.) D2
Arnhem Land Aboriginal
Res. C2
Arnold (riv.) D3
Barkly Tableland D4
Bathurst (isl.) A1
Beagle (gulf) A2
Beatrice (cape) E3
Bennett (lake) B7
Beswick Aboriginal Res. . . . C3
Bickerton (Isl.) E2
Blaze (pt.) A2
Carpentaria (gulf) E3
Central Wedge (mt.) C7
Clarence (str.) B2
Cobourg (pen.) C1
Conner (mt.) B8
Croker (cape) E6
Daly (riv.) B2
Daly River Aboriginal Res. . . A2
Davenport (mt.) B7
Dundas (str.) B1
East Alligator (riv.) C2
Ehrenberg (range) B7
Elcho (isl.) D1
Finke (riv.) C8
Fitzmaurice (riv.) B3
Ford (cape) A2
Georgina (riv.) E6
Goulburn (isls.) C1
Goyder (riv.) D2
Groote Eylandt (isl.) 2,230 . . E3
Haasts Bluff Aboriginal
Res. B7
Hale (riv.) D8

Hanson (riv.) C6
Hay (dry riv.) E7
Hogarth (mt.) E6
Hopkins (lake) A8
Joseph Bonaparte (gulf) . . . A3
Kata Tjuta
(Olga) (mt.) B8
Katherine (riv.) C3
Lake MacKay Aboriginal
Res. A6
Lander (riv.) C6
Leisler (mt.) A7
Limmen Bight (riv.) D4
Macdonald (lake) B7
Macdonnell (ranges) C7
MacKay (lake) A7
Mann (riv.) D2
Marshall (riv.) D7
Melville (bay) E2
Melville (isl.) B1

Murchison (range) D6
Napier (mt.) A4
Neale (lake) A8
Newcastle (creek) C4
Nicholson (riv.) E5
Peron (isls.) A2
Petermann (ranges) A8
Petermann Ranges
Aboriginal Res. A8
Port Darwin (inlet) B2
Ranken (riv.) E6
Robinson (riv.) E4
Roper (riv.) C3
Sandover (riv.) D6
Simpson (des.) E8
Singleton (mt.) B6
Sir Edward Pellew Group
(isls.) E3
South Alligator (riv.) C2
Stanley (mt.) B7

Stewart (cape) D1
Stirling (creek) A4
Sturt (plain) C4
Tanami (des.) C5
Timor (sea) A2
Todd (riv.) D8
Uluru Nat'l Park B8
Vanderlin (isl.) E3
Van Diemen (cape) A1
Van Diemen (gulf) B1
Victoria (riv.) B3
Wagait Aboriginal Res B2
Warwick (chan.) E3
Wessel (cape) E1
Wessel (isls.) E1
West Baines (riv.) A4
White (lake) A6
Woods (lake) C4
Young (mt.) D3
Ziel (mt.) C7

AREA   519,768 sq. mi.
(1,346.200 sq. km.)
POPULATION   154,848
CAPITAL   Darwin
LARGEST CITY   Darwin
HIGHEST POINT   Mt. Ziel 4,955 ft.
(1,510 m.)

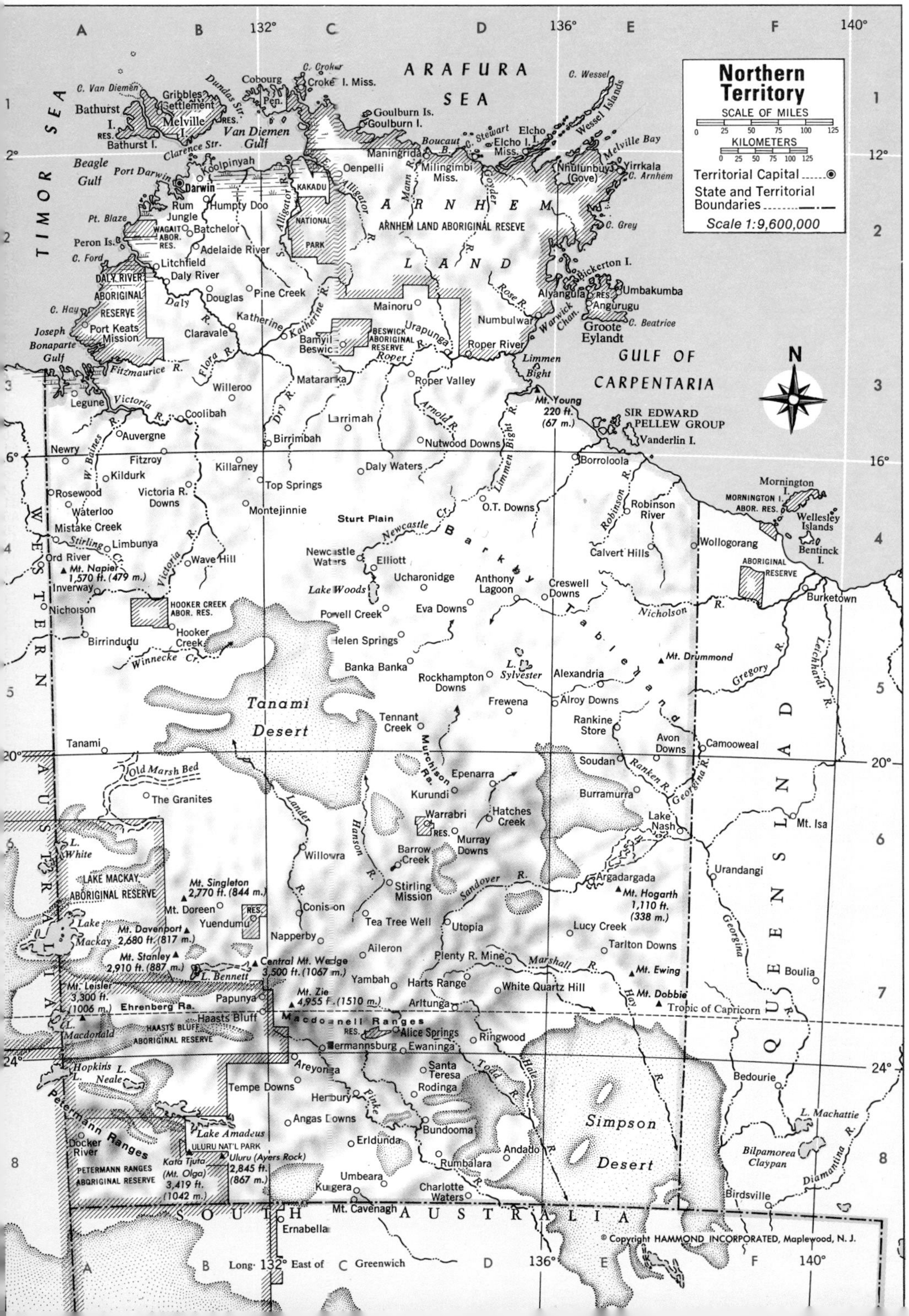

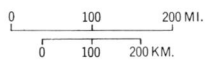

Topography

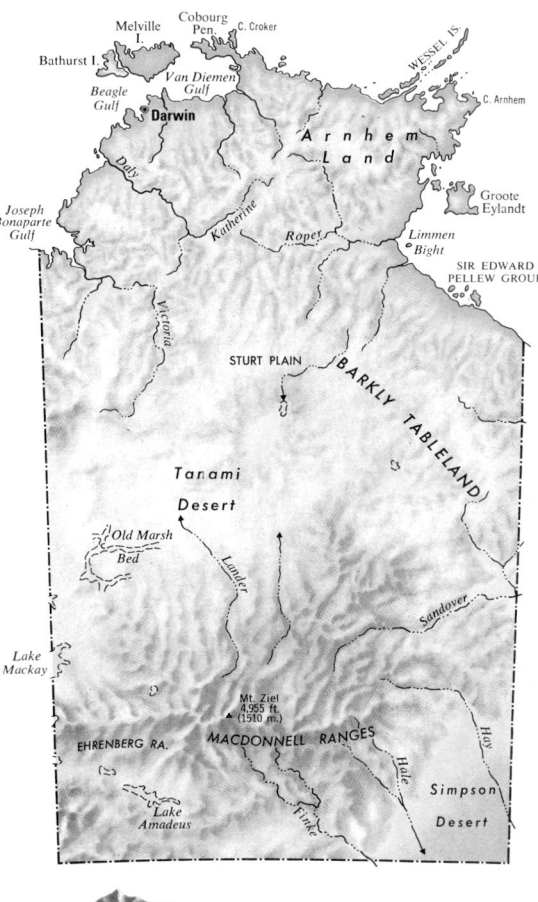

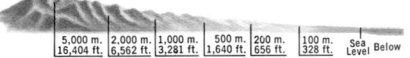

| 5,000 m. | 2,000 m. | 1,000 m. | 500 m. | 200 m. | 100 m. | Sea |
| 16,404 ft. | 6,562 ft. | 3,281 ft. | 1,640 ft. | 656 ft. | 328 ft. | Level Below |

AREA 379,922 sq. mi. (984,000 sq. km.)
POPULATION 1,345,945
CAPITAL Adelaide
LARGEST CITY Adelaide
HIGHEST POINT Mt. Woodroffe 4,970 ft.
(1,515 m.)

CITIES and TOWNS

Adelaide (cap.) 882,520 . . . . B6
Adelaide *931,886 . . . . B6
Andamooka 402 . . . . E4
Angaston 1,753 . . . . F6
Balaklava 1,306 . . . . F6
Barmera 2,014 . . . . G6
Beachport 357 . . . . F7
Berri 3,419 . . . . G6
Birdwood 397 . . . . C7
Blinman F4
Bordertown 2,138 . . . . G7
Brighton 19,441 . . . . A8
Burnside 37,593 . . . . B8
Burra 1,222 . . . . F5
Campbelltown 43,084 . . . . . B7
Ceduna 2,794 . . . . D5
Clare 2,381 . . . . F5
Cleve 827 . . . . E5
Coober Pedy 2,078 . . . . . . D3
Cowell 626 . . . . E5
Crafters-Bridgewater 9,764 . . B8
Crystal Brook 1,240 . . . . . E5
Cummins 767 . . . . D6
Edithburgh 359 . . . . E6
Elizabeth 32,608 . . . . B7
Elliston ○1,345 . . . . D5
Enfield 66,797 . . . . B7
Gawler 9,433 . . . . B6
Gladstone 680 . . . . F5
Glenelg 13,306 . . . . A8
Gumeracha 387 . . . . C7
Hahndorf 1,274 . . . . C8
Hawker 351 . . . . F4
Hindmarsh 7,593 . . . . A7
Iron Knob 398 . . . . E5
Jamestown 1,384 . . . . F5
Kadina 2,943 . . . . E5
Kapunda 1,340 . . . . F6
Keith 1,147 . . . . G7
Kensington and Norwood
8,950 . . . . B8
Kimba 862 . . . . E5
Kingscote 1,236 . . . . E6
Kingston 1,325 . . . . G7
Lameroo 599 . . . . G6
Laura 504 . . . . F5
Leigh Creek 1,635 . . . . . . F4
Lobethal 1,522 . . . . C7
Lock 213 . . . . D5
Loxton 3,100 . . . . G6
Lyndoch 539 . . . . C6
Maitland 1,085 . . . . E6
Mannum 1,984 . . . . F6
Marion 66,580 . . . . A8
Marree E3
Meadows 388 . . . . B8
Meningie 807 . . . . F6
Millicent 5,255 . . . . F7
Minlaton 865 . . . . E6
Mitcham 60,309 . . . . B8
Moonta 1,751 . . . . E5
Mount Barker 4,190 . . . . . C8
Mount Gambier 18,193 . . . . G7
Murray Bridge 8,664 . . . . . F6
Nairne 706 . . . . C8
Nangwarry 758 . . . . G7

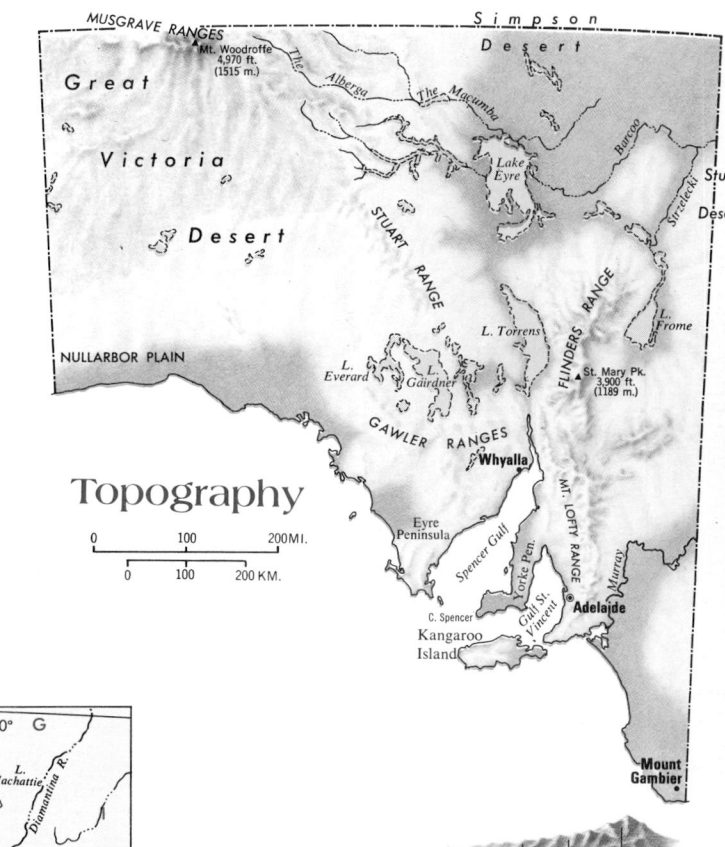

Topography

0	100	200 MI.
0	100	200 KM.

Below Sea Level	100 m. 328 ft.	200 m. 656 ft.	500 m. 1,640 ft.	1,000 m. 3,281 ft.	2,000 m. 6,562 ft.	5,000 m. 16,404 ft.

Naracoorte 4,758 . . . . G7
Noarlunga 60,928 . . . . A8
Nuriootpa 2,851 . . . . F6
Oodnadatta D2
Orroroo 604 . . . . F5
Payneham 16,502 . . . . B7
Penola 1,205 . . . . G7
Peterborough 2,575 . . . . . . F5
Pinnaroo 731 . . . . G6
Port Adelaide 35,407 . . . . . A7
Port Augusta 15,566 . . . . . E5
Port Broughton 587 . . . . . . F5
Port Lincoln 9,846 . . . . . . E6
Port Pirie 14,695 . . . . E5
Prospect 18,591 . . . . B7
Quorn 1,049 . . . . F5
Renmark 3,475 . . . . G5
Robe 590 . . . . F7
Salisbury 86,451 . . . . B7
Snowtown 492 . . . . E5
Strathalbyn 1,756 . . . . . . F6
Streaky Bay 985 . . . . D5
Tailem Bend 1,677 . . . . . . F6
Tanunda 2,621 . . . . C6
Tea Tree Gully 67,237 . . . . B7
Thebarton 9,208 . . . . A7
Tumby Bay 933 . . . . E6
Unley 35,844 . . . . B8
Uraidla 303 . . . . B8
Victor Harbor 4,522 . . . . . F6
Virginia 353 . . . . B7
Waikerie 1,629 . . . . F6
Wallaroo 2,043 . . . . E5
West Torrens 45,099 . . . . . A8
Whyalla 30,518 . . . . E5
Williamstown 495 . . . . C7
Willunga 667 . . . . F6
Wilmington 227 . . . . F5
Woodside 724 . . . . C8
Woodville 77,634 . . . . A7
Woomera 1,658 . . . . E4
Wudinna 572 . . . . D5
Yorketown 713 . . . . E6

OTHER FEATURES

Acraman (lake) D5
Alberga, The (riv.) D2
Alexandrina (lake) F6
Anxious (bay) D5
Arckaringa (creek) D2
Barcoo (creek) F3
Birksgate (range) A2
Blanche (lake) F3
Brady (mt.) D3
Cadibarrawirracanna (lake) . . D3
Callabonna (lake) F3
Catastrophe (cape) D6
Coffin (bay) D6
Coffin Bay (pen.) D6
Coopers (Barcoo) (creek) . . . F3
Coorong, The (lag.) F6
Dey Dey (lake) B3
Encounter (bay) F6
Everard (lake) D4
Everard (ranges) C2
Eyre (pen.) D5
Eyre North (lake) E3
Eyre South (lake) E3
Finke (riv.) C1

Flinders (range) . . . . F
Frome (lake) . . . . G
Gairdner (lake) . . . . E
Gawler (ranges) . . . . D
Gawler (riv.) . . . . B
Gilles (lake) . . . . E
Goyders (lag.) . . . . F
Great Australian (bight) . . . A
Great Victoria (des.) . . . . . B
Gregory (lake) . . . . F
Hack (mt.) . . . . F
Hamilton, The (riv.) D2
Harris (lake) . . . . D
Head of Bight (bay) C5
Indian Ocean . . . . A
Investigator (str.) . . . . . . E
Investigator Group (isls.) . . D6
Island (lag.) E4
Jaffa (cape) G7
Kangaroo (isl.) 3,515 . . . . E6
Lacepede (bay) F7
Lofty (mt.) B8
Macfarlane (lake) E5
Macumba, The (riv.) D2
Maurice (lake) A3
Meramangye (lake) B2
Morris (mt.) A2
Murray (res.) F6
Musgrave (ranges) A2
Neales, The (riv.) D2
Northumberland (cape) F7
Nukey Bluff (mt.) D5
Nullarbor (plain) B4
Nuyts (arch.) C5
Nuyts (cape) C5
Peera Peera Poolanna (lake) . . F2
Saint Mary (peak) F4
Saint Vincent (gulf) E6
Serpentine (lakes) A3
Simpson (des.) E1
Sir Joseph Banks Group
(isls.) E6
Spencer (cape) E6
Spencer (gulf) E6
Stevenson, The (riv.) D2
Streaky (bay) C5
Strzelecki (creek) G3
Stuart (range) D3
Sturt (des.) F2
The Alberga (riv.) D2
The Coorong (lag.) F6
The Hamilton (riv.) D2
The Macumba (riv.) D2
The Neales (riv.) D2
The Stevenson (riv.) D2
The Warburton (riv.) E2
Thistle (isl.) E6
Torrens (lake) E4
Torrens (riv.) B8
Warburton, The (riv.) E2
Wilkinson (lakes) B3
Woodroffe (mt.) A2
Yalata Aboriginal Res. B4
Yarle (lakes) B4
Yorke (pen.) E6

○ Population of district.
*Population of met. area.

Adelaide and Vicinity

South Australia

SCALE OF MILES
0 25 50 100 150

KILOMETERS
0 25 50 100 150

State Capital
State and Territorial Boundaries
Scale 1:9,790,000

© Copyright HAMMOND INCORPORATED, Maplewood, N.J.

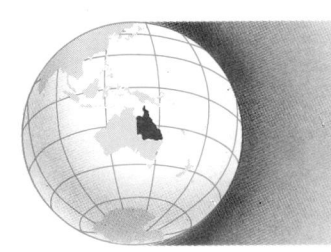

CITIES and TOWNS

Aramac 428 .... C4
Archerfield 785 .... D3
Ascot 4,298 .... E2
Atherton 4,196 .... C3
Ayr 8,787 .... C3
Balmoral 2,915 .... E2
Barcaldine 1,432 .... C4
Beaudesert 3,780 .... E6
Biloela 4,643 .... D5
Birdsville 210 .... A3
Blackall 1,609 .... C5
Blackwater 5,434 .... D4
Boulia 292 .... A4
Bowen 7,663 .... D3
Brisbane (cap.) 689,378 .... D2
Bucasia 1,356 .... D4
Bundaberg 32,560 .... D5
Burketown 210 .... A3
Cairns 48,557 .... C3
Caloundra 16,758 .... E5
Camooweal 251 .... A3
Camp Hill 8,999 .... E3
Capella 660 .... D4
Cardwell 1,249 .... C3
Charleville 3,523 .... C5
Charters Towers 6,823 .... C4
Cherbourg 963 .... D5
Chermside 6,892 .... D2
Clermont 1,659 .... C4
Cloncurry 1,941 .... B4
Collinsville 2,756 .... C4
Cooktown 913 .... C2
Coopers Plains 4,492 .... D3
Corinda 4,894 .... D3
Croydon ○255 .... B3
Cunnamulla 1,627 .... C5
Dalby 8,784 .... D5
Dirranbandi 480 .... D6
East Brisbane 4,853 .... E3
Eidsvold 613 .... D5
Emerald 4,628 .... C4
Esk 676 .... E5
Gatton 4,190 .... E5
Gayndah 1,708 .... D5
Geebung 4,850 .... E2
Georgetown 319 .... B3
Gladstone 22,083 .... D4
Gold Coast 135,437 .... E6
Goondiwindi 3,576 .... D6
Gordonvale 2,375 .... C3
Greenslopes 7,219 .... E3
Gympie 10,768 .... E5

Hervey Bay 13,569 .... E5
Holland Park 7,363 .... E3
Home Hill 3,138 .... C3
Hughenden 1,657 .... B4
Inala 17,383 .... D3
Indooroopilly 7,959 .... D3
Ingham 5,598 .... C3
Injune 407 .... D5
Innisfail 7,933 .... C3
Ipswich 68,297 .... E5
Isisford ○605 .... C5
Jandowae 781 .... D5
Jericho ○1,177 .... C4
Julia Creek 602 .... B4
Karumba 670 .... B3
Kilcoy 1,257 .... E5
Kingaroy 5,134 .... D5
Longreach 2,971 .... B4
Mackay 35,361 .... D4
Mareeba 6,309 .... C3
Marian 796 .... D4
Maroochydore-Mooloolab.
17,460 .... E5
Maryborough 20,111 .... E5
Mary Kathleen 830 .... A4
McKinlay ○1,477 .... B4
Millmerran 1,107 .... D5
Mitchell 1,171 .... C5
Mitchelton 5,810 .... D2
Monto 1,397 .... D5
Moorooka 8,740 .... D3
Moranbah 4,362 .... C9
Mossman 1,614 .... C3
Mount Isa 23,679 .... A4
Moura 2,871 .... D5
Murgon 2,327 .... D5
Nambour 7,965 .... E5
Newmarket 3,520 .... D2
Normanton 926 .... B3
Nundah 7,358 .... E2
Proserpine 3,058 .... D4
Quilpie 694 .... C5
Ravenshoe 915 .... C3
Redcliffe 42,223 .... E5
Richmond 784 .... B4
Rockhampton 50,146 .... D4
Roma 5,706 .... D5
Saint George 2,204 .... D5
Saint Lucia 6,075 .... D3
Sandgate 6,776 .... D2
Sarina 2,815 .... D4
Springsure 774 .... D5
Stafford (Stafford Heights)
13,731 .... D2
Stanthorpe 3,966 .... D6
Tara 864 .... D5

Taroom 688 .... D5
Tewantin-Noosa 9,965 .... E5
Theodore 643 .... D5
Thursday Island 2,283 .... B1
Toowoomba 63,401 .... D5
Townsville 86,112 .... C3
Tully 2,728 .... C3
Walkerston 1,277 .... D4
Warwick 8,853 .... D6
Weipa 2,433 .... B2
Windsor 6,119 .... D2
Winton 1,259 .... B4
Wynnum 10,794 .... E5
Yeppoon 6,447 .... D4
Yeronga 4,579 .... D3

OTHER FEATURES

Albatross (bay) B2
Archer (riv.) B2
Balonne (riv.) D6
Banks (isl.) B1
Barcoo (creek) B5
Barkly Tableland A4
Bartle Frere (mt.) C3
Beal (range) B5

AREA 666,872 sq. mi. (1,727,200 sq. km.)
POPULATION 2,587,315
CAPITAL Brisbane
LARGEST CITY Brisbane
HIGHEST POINT Mt. Bartle Frere 5,287 ft.
(1,611 m.)

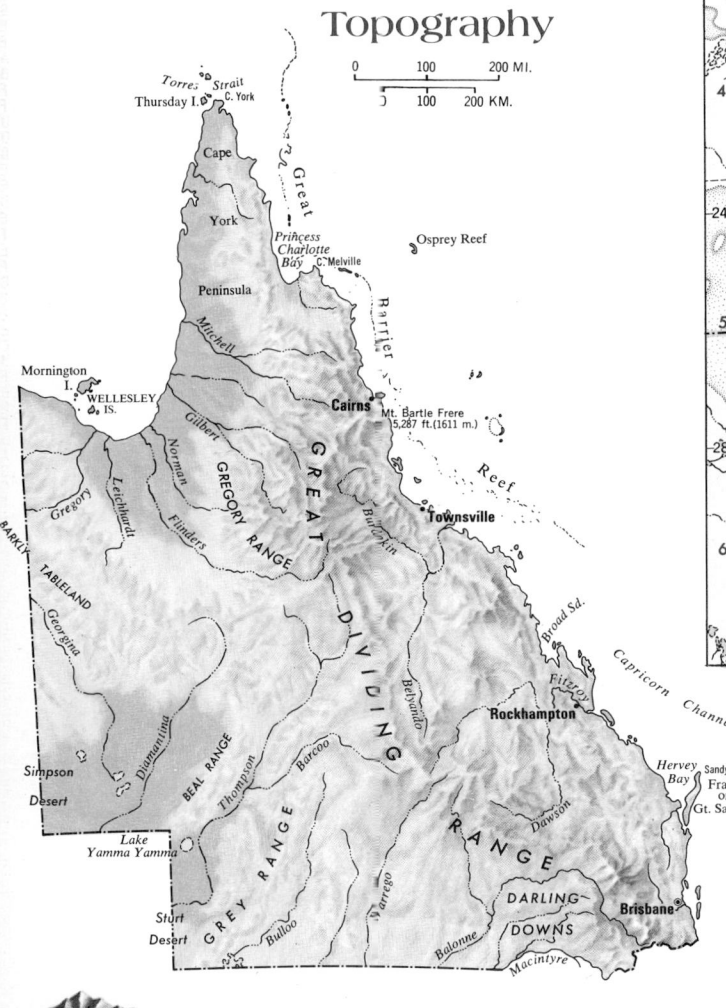

Topography

© Copyright HAMMOND INCORPORATED, Maplewood, N.J.

Belyando (riv.) C4
Broad (sound) D4
Bulloo (lake) B6
Bulloo (riv.) B6
Bunker Group (isls.) E4
Burdekin (riv.) C3
Cape York (pen.) B2
Capricorn (chan.) D4
Capricorn Group (isls.) E4
Carnarvon (range) D5
Carpentaria (gulf) A2
Cloncurry (riv.) B4
Coopers (Barcoo) (creek) B5
Coral (sea) C1
Culgoa (riv.) C6
Cumberland (isls.) D4
Curtis (isl.) D4
Darling Downs D5
Dawson (riv.) D5
Diamantina (riv.) B4
Drummond (range) C5
Duifken (pt.) B2
Endeavour (str.) B1

Fitzroy (riv.) D4
Flinders (riv.) B3
Fraser (isl.) E5
Georgina (riv.) A4
Gilbert (riv.) B3
Great Dividing (range) C4
Gregory (range) B3
Gregory (riv.) A3
Grey (range) B5
Hamilton (riv.) B4
Hervey (bay) E5
Hinchinbrook (isl.) C3
Hook (isl.) D4
Leichhardt (riv.) A3
Machattie (lake) A4
Macintyre (riv.) D6
Maranoa (riv.) C5
Mary (riv.) E5
Melville (cape) C2
Mitchell (riv.) B4
Moreton (bay) E5
Moreton (isl.) E5
Mornington (isl.) A3

Norman (riv.) B3
Northern Peninsula
Aboriginal Res. B1
Prince of Wales (isl.) B1
Princess Charlotte (bay) C2
Sandy (cape) E5
Selwyn (range) B4
Simpson (des.) A5
Sturt (des.) B3
Suttor (riv.) C4
Swain (reefs) E4
Thompson (riv.) B5
Torres (str.) B1
Warrego (range) C5
Warrego (riv.) C5
Wellesley (isls.) A3
Whitsunday (isl.) D4
Willies (range) C6
Yamma Yamma (lake) B5
York (cape) B1

○ Population of district.
*Population of met. area.

AUSTRALIAN CAPITAL TERRITORY

CITIES and TOWNS

Canberra (cap.), Australia
220,423 ....E4
Canberra †220,822 ....E4
Jervis Bay 787 ....F4

NEW SOUTH WALES

CITIES and TOWNS

Aberdeen 1,410 ....F3
Adaminaby 378 ....E5

Adelong 806 ....D4
Albury 35,072 ....D5
Alstonville 2,936 ....G1
Ardlethan 602 ....D4
Ariah Park 301 ....D4
Armidale 18,922 ....F2
Ashfield 41,253 ....J3
Ashford 594 ....F1
Attunga 282 ....F2
Auburn 46,622 ....J3
Avondale 2,265 ....F3
Ballina 9,738 ....G1
Balranald 1,442 ....B4
Bangalow 614 ....G1
Bankstown 152,636 ......J3
Baradine 723 ....E2

Barellan 380 ....D4
Bargo 868 ....F4
Barham-Koondrook 1,039 ..C4
Barmedman 223 ....D4
Barooga 556 ....C4
Barraba 1,679 ....F2
Barringun C1
Batemans Bay 4,924 ......F4
Bathurst 19,640 ....E3
Batlow 1,354 ....E4
Baulkham Hills 93,084 ....H3
Bega 4,388 ....E5
Bellbird-Cessnock 16,916 ..F3
Bellbird-Cessnock *38,724 ..F3
Bellingen 1,593 ....G2

Bendemeer 231 ....F2
Bermagui 827 ....F5
Berridale 695 ....E5
Berrigan 960 ....C4
Berry 1,220 ....E4
Binalong 212 ....E4
Bingara 1,257 ....F1
Blacktown 181,139 ....H3
Blayney 2,694 ....E3
Blue Mountains 55,877 ....F3
Bodalla 224 ....F5
Bogan Gate D3
Boggabilla 528 ....F1
Boggabri 1,023 ....F2
Bomaderry-Nowra 17,887 ..F4

Bombala 1,504 ....E5
Bonalbo 466 ....G1
Booligal C3
Boorooban C4
Boorowa 1,183 ....E4
Botany 34,703 ....J4
Bourke 3,326 ....D2
Bowral 6,862 ....F4
Bowraville 848 ....G2
Braidwood 944 ....E4
Branxton-Greta 2,849 ....F3
Bredbo E4
Brewarrina 1,236 ....D1
Bribbaree D4
Brisbane Water 71,984 ....F3
Broken Hill 26,913 ......A3

Browning E4
Brunswick Heads 1,877 ...G1
Budgewoi Lake 25,474 ....F3
Bugaldie E2
Bulahdelah 972 ....G3
Bundanoon 1,018 ....F4
Bundarra 377 ....F2
Bungendore 683 ....E4
Burcher D3
Burns A3
Burraboi C4
Burwood 28,896 ....J3
Byrock D2
Byron Bay 3,187 ....G1

Campbelltown 91,525 .....F4
Candelo 255 ....E5
Canowindra 1,720 ....E3
Canterbury 126,741 ......J3
Captains Flat 309 ....E4
Caragabal D3
Carcoar 277 ....E3
Carinda D2
Carrathool ○1,210 ......C3
Carroll F2
Casino 9,743 ....G1
Cassilis E3
Cessnock-Bellbird 16,916 ..F3
Cessnock-Bellbird *38,724 ..F3
Cobar 3,583 ....D3
Cobargo 285 ....E5

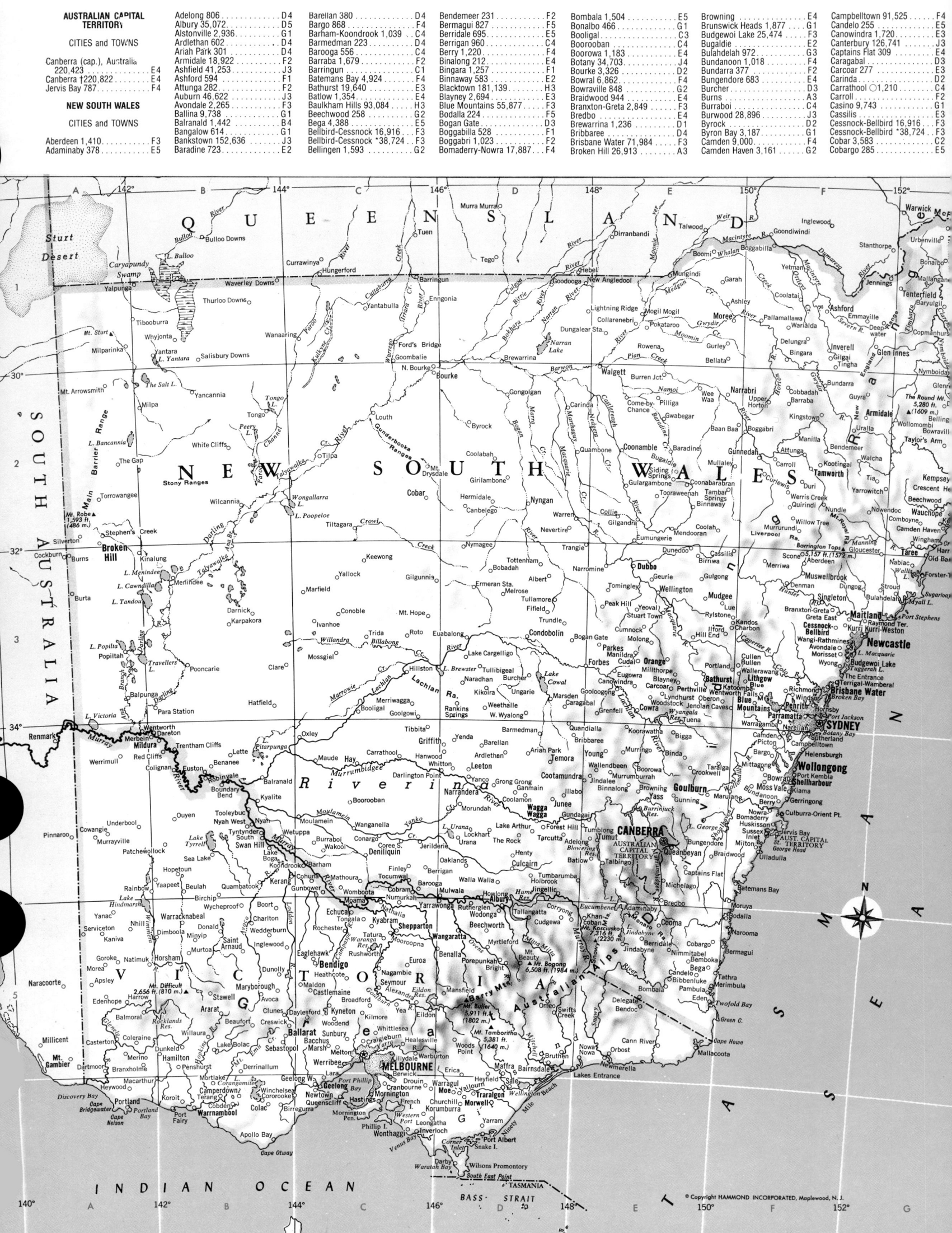

Cobbadah F2	Coraki 895 . . . . G1	Dee Why K3
Coffs Harbour 16,020 . . . . G2	Coramba 202 . . . . G1	Delegate 347 . . . . E5
Collarenebri 602 . . . . E1	Corowa-Wahgunyah 3,390 . . D4	Delungra 332 . . . . F1
Collie E2	Cowra 7,900 . . . . E3	Deniliquin 7,354 . . . . C4
Comboyne G2	Crescent Head 944 . . . . . . G2	Denman 1,122 . . . . F3
Concord 23,926 . . . . J3	Cronulla J4	Dorrigo 1,192 . . . . G2
Condobolin 3,355 . . . . D3	Crookwell 2,063 . . . . E4	Drummoyne 30,961 . . . . . . J3
Conoble C3	Cudal 400 . . . . E3	Dubbo 23,986 . . . . E3
Coogee K3	Cullburra-Orient Point 2,068 . F4	Dunedoo 836 . . . . E3
Coolah 878 . . . . E2	Culcairn 1,027 . . . . D4	Dungalear Station D1
Coolamon 1,088 . . . . D4	Cullen Bullen 231 . . . . . . F3	Dungog 2,126 . . . . F3
Cooma 7,978 . . . . E5	Cumnock 252 . . . . E3	Eden 3,107 . . . . E5
Coonabarabran 3,001 . . . . E2	Curlewis 487 . . . . F2	Emmaville 503 . . . . F1
Coonamble 3,090 . . . . E2	Dareton 612 . . . . B4	Ermeran Station D3
Cootamundra 6,540 . . . . . D4	Darlington Point 599 . . . . . C4	Eugowra 577 . . . . E3
Copmanhurst ○2,857 . . . . G1	Deepwater 260 . . . . F1	Evans Head 1,802 . . . . . . G1

NEW SOUTH WALES
AREA 309,498 sq. mi.
(801,600 sq. km.)
POPULATION 5,401,881
CAPITAL Sydney
LARGEST CITY Sydney
HIGHEST POINT Mt. Kosciusko
7,310 ft. (2,228 m.)

VICTORIA
AREA 87,876 sq. mi.
(227,600 sq. km.)
POPULATION 4,019,478
CAPITAL Melbourne
LARGEST CITY Melbourne
HIGHEST POINT Mt. Bogong
6,508 ft. (1,984 m.)

Topography

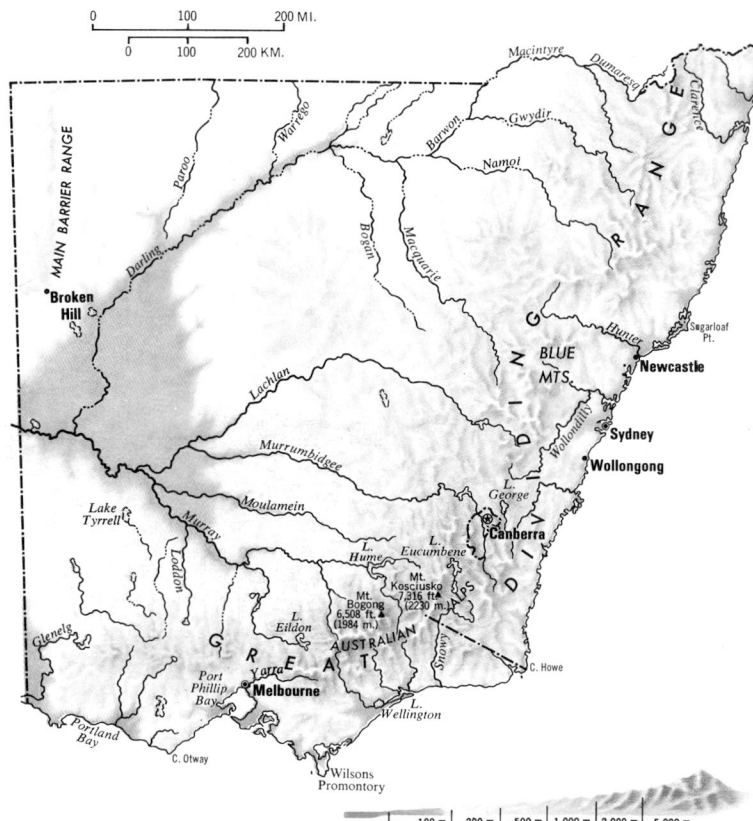

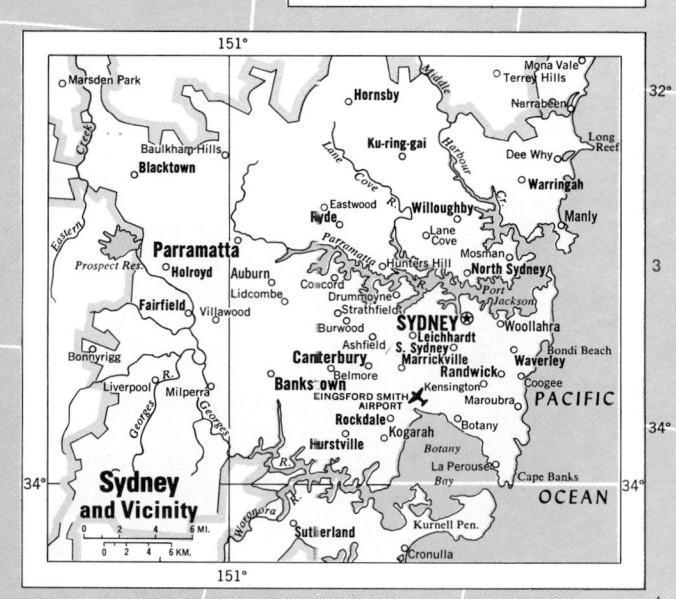

Fairfield 129,557 . . . . H3	Keewong C3	Moss Vale 4,415 . . . . F4
Finley 2,193 . . . . C4	Kempsey 9,037 . . . . G2	Mossgiel C4
Forbes 8,029 . . . . E3	Kendall 522 . . . . G2	Moulamein 396 . . . . C4
Forest Hill 1,977 . . . . D4	Khancoban 515 . . . . E5	Mount Arrowsmith A2
Forster-Tuncurry 9,261 . . . . G3	Kiama 7,717 . . . . F4	Mount Drysdale C2
Frederickton 616 . . . . G2	Kinalung B3	Mount Hope C3
Ganmain 650 . . . . D4	Kogarah 46,322 . . . . J4	Mudgee 6,015 . . . . E3
Gerringong 1,775 . . . . F4	Koorawatha 262 . . . . E4	Mullumbimby 2,234 . . . . . G1
Geurie 290 . . . . E3	Kootingal 731 . . . . F2	Mungindi 707 . . . . E1
Gilgai 257 . . . . F1	Ku-ring-gai 101,501 . . . . . J3	Murrumburrah 2,070 . . . . . E4
Gilgandra 2,700 . . . . E2	Kurri Kurri-Weston 12,795 . . F3	Murrurundi 861 . . . . F2
Gilgunnia C3	Kyogle 3,070 . . . . G1	Murwillumbah 7,807 . . . . . G1
Glen Innes 6,052 . . . . F1	Lake Cargelligo 1,240 . . . . D3	Muswellbrook 8,548 . . . . . F3
Glenreagh 233 . . . . G2	Lane Cove 29,113 . . . . . . J3	Nabiac 363 . . . . G3
Gloucester 2,488 . . . . F2	Leeton 6,498 . . . . D4	Nambucca Heads 4,053 . . . G2
Goodooga 248 . . . . D1	Leichhardt 57,332 . . . . . . J3	Narellan 2,104 . . . . F3
Goolgowi 245 . . . . C3	Lette B4	Narooma 2,758 . . . . F5
Gooloogong 221 . . . . E3	Lidcombe J3	Narrabeen K3
Goombalie C1	Lightning Ridge 1,112 . . . . E1	Narrabri 7,296 . . . . E2
Goulburn 21,755 . . . . E4	Lismore 24,033 . . . . G1	Narrandera 5,013 . . . . D4
Grafton 17,005 . . . . G1	Lithgow 12,793 . . . . F3	Narromine 2,994 . . . . E3
Grenfell 2,070 . . . . E3	Liverpool 92,715 . . . . H4	New Angledool E1
Greta-Branxton 2,849 . . . . F3	Lockhart 923 . . . . D4	Newcastle 135,207 . . . . . . F3
Greta East 398 . . . . F3	Macksville 2,352 . . . . G2	Newcastle †389,237 . . . . . F3
Griffith 13,187 . . . . C4	Maclean 2,593 . . . . G1	Nimmitabel 257 . . . . E5
Gulargambone 457 . . . . . . E2	Maitland 38,865 . . . . F3	North Sydney 48,500 . . . . . J3
Gulgong 1,740 . . . . E3	Manildra 520 . . . . E3	Nowra-Bomaderry 17,887 . . F4
Gundagai 2,308 . . . . D4	Manilla 1,884 . . . . F2	Nundle 235 . . . . F2
Gunnedah 8,909 . . . . F2	Manly 37,080 . . . . K3	Nymboida ○2,044 . . . . . . G1
Gunning 438 . . . . E4	Maroubra K3	Nyngan 2,485 . . . . D2
Guyra 1,840 . . . . F2	Marrickville 83,448 . . . . . . J3	Oaklands 283 . . . . D4
Hanwood 306 . . . . C4	Marsden D3	Oberon 1,937 . . . . E3
Harrington 1,183 . . . . G2	Marsden Park 518 . . . . . . H3	Old Bar 970 . . . . G2
Hay 2,958 . . . . C4	Marulan 330 . . . . E4	Orange 27,626 . . . . E3
Henty 883 . . . . D4	Mathoura 582 . . . . C4	Pallamallawa 340 . . . . F1
Hillston 999 . . . . C3	Melrose D3	Pambula 604 . . . . E5
Holbrook 1,276 . . . . D4	Mendooran 325 . . . . E2	Parkes 9,047 . . . . E3
Holroyd 80,116 . . . . H3	Menindee 455 . . . . B3	Parramatta 130,943 . . . . . H3
Hornsby 111,081 . . . . J3	Merimbula 2,899 . . . . F5	Peak Hill 1,037 . . . . E3
Howlong 1,072 . . . . D4	Merriwa 943 . . . . F3	Penrith 108,720 . . . . F3
Hunters Hill 12,537 . . . . . J3	Millthorpe 607 . . . . E3	Perthville 639 . . . . E3
Hurstville 64,910 . . . . J4	Milpa B2	Picton 1,817 . . . . F4
Huskisson 2,296 . . . . F4	Milperra H4	Piliga 206 . . . . E2
Iluka 1,362 . . . . G1	Milton 740 . . . . F4	Popiltah A3
Inverell 9,734 . . . . F1	Mittagong 4,266 . . . . F4	Portland 1,980 . . . . E3
Ivanhoe 517 . . . . C3	Moama C5	Port Kembla F4
Jerilderie 1,075 . . . . C4	Mogil Mogil E1	Port Macquarie 19,581 . . . . G2
Jindabyne 1,602 . . . . E5	Molong 1,374 . . . . E3	Queanbeyan 19,383 . . . . . E4
Junee 3,993 . . . . D4	Mona Vale K2	Quirindi 2,851 . . . . F2
Kandos 1,626 . . . . E3	Moree 10,459 . . . . E1	Randwick 116,202 . . . . . . J3
Karpakora B3	Morisset 1,593 . . . . F3	Raymond Terrace 7,548 . . . F3
Katoomba-Wentworth Falls	Morpeth ...	Richmond-Windsor 15,491 . . F3
13,942 . . . . F3	Moruya 2,003 . . . . F5	Rockdale 83,719 . . . . J4
	Mosman 26,200 . . . . J3	

(continued on following page)

Ryde 88,948 . . . . J3
Rylstone 651 . . . . E3
Salisbury Downs B1
Sawtell 5,970 . . . . G2
Scone 3,949 . . . . F3
Shellharbour 41,790 . . . . . F4
Singleton 9,572 . . . . F3
Smithtown-Gladstone 953 . . G2
South Sydney 30,776 . . . . J3
South West Rocks 1,314 . . G2
Stephen's Creek A2
Strathfield 25,882 . . . . . . J3
Stroud 522 . . . . G3
Sussex Inlet 1,293 . . . . . . F4
Sutherland 165,336 . . . . . J4
Sydney (cap.) 2,876,508 . . J3
Sydney †3,204,696 . . . . . J3
Talbingo 481 . . . . E4
Tamworth 29,657 . . . . . . F2
Taralga 272 . . . . E4
Tarcutta 263 . . . . D4
Taree 14,697 . . . . G2
Tathra 1,077 . . . . F5
Temora 4,350 . . . . D4
Tenterfield 3,402 . . . . G1
Terrigal-The Entrance 37,891 F3
The Rock 693 . . . . D4
Thurloo Downs B1
Tibbita C4
Tibooburra B1
Tiltagara C2
Tingha 886 . . . . F1
Tocumwal 1,174 . . . . C4
Tongo B2
Torrowangee A2
Tottenham 366 . . . . D3
Trangie 977 . . . . D3
Trundle 515 . . . . D3
Tullamore 324 . . . . D3
Tumbarumba 1,536 . . . . . D4
Tumut 5,816 . . . . E4
Tweed Heads G1
Ulladulla 6,018 . . . . F4
Ulmarra 395 . . . . G1
Ungarie 428 . . . . D3
Uralla 2,090 . . . . F2
Urana 419 . . . . D4
Urbenville 282 . . . . G1
Urunga 2,045 . . . . G2
Villawood H3
Wagga Wagga 36,837 . . . D4
Wakool 278 . . . . C4
Walcha 1,674 . . . . F2
Walgett 2,157 . . . . E2
Walla Walla 593 . . . . D4

Wallerawang 1,855 . . . . . F3
Wangi-Rathmines 5,106 . . . F3
Warialda 1,340 . . . . F1
Warragamba 1,406 . . . . . F3
Warren 2,153 . . . . D2
Warringah ○172,653 . . . . K3
Wauchope 3,645 . . . . G2
Waverley 61,575 . . . . K3
Waverley Downs B1
Wee Waa 1,904 . . . . E2
Wellington 5,280 . . . . E3
Wentworth 1,180 . . . . B4
Werris Creek 1,924 . . . . . F2
West Wyalong 3,778 . . . . D3
Wetuppa B4
White Cliffs B2
Whitton 344 . . . . D4
Whyjonta B1
Wilcannia 982 . . . . B2
Willoughby 52,120 . . . . . . J3
Willow Tree 258. . . . . F2
Wingham 3,937 . . . . G2
Wollongong 169,381 . . . . F4
Wollongong †222,539 . . . . F4
Woodburn 647 . . . . G1
Woodenbong 409 . . . . . . G1
Woodstock 266 . . . . E3
Woolgoolga 2,081 . . . . . . G2
Wooli 457 . . . . G1
Woollahra 51,659 . . . . . . K3
Wyong 3,902 . . . . F3
Yallock C3
Yalpunga A1
Yamba 2,528 . . . . G1
Yancannia B2
Yanco 415. . . . . D4
Yantara B1
Yass 4,283 . . . . E4
Yenda 697 . . . . D4
Yeoval 288. . . . . E3
Young 6,906 . . . . E4

OTHER FEATURES

Ana Branch, Darling (riv.) . . A3
Australian Alps (mts.) D5
Barrington Tops (mt.) F2
Barwon (riv.) D2
Blue (mts.) F3
Bogan (riv.) D2
Bondi (beach) K3
Botany (bay) J4
Broken (bay) F3
Burrinjuck (res.) E4
Byron (cape) G1

Caryapundy (swamp) B1
Castlereagh (riv.) E2
Cawndilla (lake) A3
Clarence (riv.) G1
Colo (riv.) F3
Cowal (lake) D3
Culgoa (riv.) D1
Cuttaburra (creek) C1
Darling (riv.) B3
Dumaresq (riv.) F1
Eucumbene (lake) E5
George (lake) E4
Georges (riv.) H4
Gower (mt.) J2
Great Dividing (range) E3
Green (cape) F5
Gunderbooka (ranges) . . . C2
Gwydir (riv.) E1
Howe (cape) F5
Hume (res.) D4
Hunter (riv.) F3
Kosciusko (mt.) E5
Kurnell (pen.) J4
Lachlan (range) C3
Lachlan (riv.) C3
Liverpool (range) F2
Lord Howe (isl.) 287 . . . . . J2
Macintyre (riv.) E1
Macquarie (lake) F3
Macquarie (riv.) D2
Main Barrier (range) A2
Manning (riv.) F2
Marthaguy (creek) D2
McPherson (range) G1
Menindee (lake) B3
Monaro (range) E5
Moonie (riv.) E1
Moulamein (creek) C4
Mount Royal (range) F2
Murray (riv.) A4
Murrumbidgee (riv.) C4
Myall (lake) G3
Namoi (riv.) E2
Narran (riv.) D1
New England (range) F1
Paroo (riv.) C1
Parramatta (riv.) J3
Poopeloe (lake) C2
Port Jackson (inlet) J3
Port Stephens (inlet) G3
Richmond (range) G1
Richmond (riv.) G1
Riverina (reg.) C4
Robe (mt.) A2
Round, The (mt.) G2

Salt, The (lake) B2
Shoalhaven (riv.) E4
Smoky (cape) G2
Snowy (mts.) E5
Snowy (riv.) E5
Stony (ranges) B2
Sturt (mt.) A1
Sugarloaf (pt.) G3
Talyawalka (creek) B2
Tandou (lake) A3
Tasman (sea) H4
The Round (mts.) G2
The Salt (lake) B2
Timbarra (riv.) G1
Tuggerah (lake) F3
Victoria (lake) A3
Warrego (riv.) C1
Willandra Billabong (creek) . . C3
Wollondilly (riv.) F4

VICTORIA

CITIES and TOWNS

Alexandra 1,756 . . . . C5
Altona 30,909 . . . . H5
Apollo Bay 921 . . . . B6
Ararat 8,336 . . . . B5
Avoca 1,032 . . . . B5
Bacchus Marsh 6,224 . . . . C5
Bairnsdale 9,459 . . . . D5
Ballarat 35,681 . . . . C5
Ballarat †71,930 . . . . C5
Balmoral 257 . . . . A5
Beaufort 1,214 . . . . B5
Beechworth 3,154 . . . . . . D5
Belgrave Heights J5
Belgrave South K5
Benalla 8,151 . . . . D5
Bendigo 31,841 . . . . C5
Bendigo †58,818 . . . . C5
Berwick 36,181 . . . . K6
Beulah 290 . . . . B4
Birchip 895 . . . . B4
Birregurra 416. . . . . B6
Boort 863 . . . . B5
Box Hill 47,579 . . . . J5
Bright 1,545. . . . . D5
Brighton 33,697 . . . . J5
Broadford 1,580 . . . . C5
Broadmeadows 103,540 . . . H4
Brunswick 44,464 . . . . . . H5
Bruthen 449 . . . . D5
Bundoora J4
Camberwell 85,883 . . . . . J5

Camperdown 3,545 . . . . . C6
Cann River 345 . . . . E5
Casterton 1,945 . . . . A5
Castlemaine 7,583 . . . . . . C5
Caulfield 69,922 . . . . J5
Charlton 1,377 . . . . B5
Chelsea 26,034 . . . . J6
Churchill 4,796 . . . . D6
Clunes 761 . . . . B5
Cobden 1,453 . . . . B6
Cobram 3,817 . . . . C4
Coburg 55,035 . . . . H5
Cohuna 2,178 . . . . C4
Colac 10,587 . . . . B6
Coldstream 1,395 . . . . . . K4
Coleraine 1,232 . . . . A5
Collingwood 15,089 . . . . . J5
Corryong 1,320 . . . . D5
Craigieburn 4,296 . . . . . . C5
Cranbourne 9,400 . . . . . . C5
Creswick 2,036 . . . . B5
Croydon 36,210 . . . . K5
Dandenong 54,962 . . . . . K5
Darby D6
Dartmoor 349 . . . . A5
Daylesford 2,883 . . . . C5
Derrinallum 287 . . . . B5
Dimboola 1,675 . . . . B5
Donald 1,609 . . . . B5
Doncaster and Templestowe
90,660 . . . . J5
Drouin 3,492 . . . . C6
Dunkeld 402 . . . . A5
Dunolly 621 . . . . B5
Eaglehawk 7,355 . . . . C5
Echuca 7,943 . . . . C5
Edenhope 827 . . . . A5
Eildon 737 . . . . C5
Eltham 34,648 . . . . J4
Erica 236 . . . . D5
Essendon 56,380 . . . . H5
Euroa 2,640 . . . . C5
Fitzroy 19,112 . . . . H5
Footscray 49,756 . . . . H5
Geelong 14,471 . . . . C6
Geelong †137,173 . . . . . . C6
Geelong West 14,823 . . . . C6
Goroke 370 . . . . A5
Gunbower 259 . . . . C4
Hamilton 9,751 . . . . B5
Hawthorn 30,689 . . . . J5
Healesville 4,526 . . . . C5
Heathcote 1,213 . . . . C5
Heidelberg 64,757 . . . . . . J5
Heyfield 1,635 . . . . D6

Heywood 1,266 . . . . A6
Hopetoun 1,832 . . . . B4
Horsham 12,034 . . . . B5
Inglewood 674 . . . . B5
Inverloch 1,523 . . . . C6
Kaniva 956 . . . . A5
Keilor 81,762 . . . . H5
Kerang 4,049 . . . . B4
Kew 28,870 . . . . J5
Kilmore 1,728 . . . . C5
Knox 25,891 . . . . K5
Koroit 1,988 . . . . B6
Korumburra 2,798 . . . . . . D6
Kyabram 5,414 . . . . C5
Kyneton 3,185 . . . . C5
Lake Boga 502 . . . . B4
Lake Bolac 211 . . . . B5
Lakes Entrance 3,414 . . . . E5
Lara 4,231 . . . . C6
Leongatha 3,736 . . . . C6
Lillydale 62,077 . . . . J4
Macarthur 322 . . . . A6
Maffra 3,822 . . . . D5
Maldon 1,009 . . . . C5
Mallacoota 726 . . . . E5
Malvern 43,211 . . . . J5
Mansfield 1,920 . . . . D5
Maryborough 7,858 . . . . . B5
Melbourne (cap.)
2,578,759 . . . . H5
Melbourne †2,722,817 . . . . H5
Melton 20,599 . . . . C5
Merbein 1,735 . . . . A4
Merino 298 . . . . A5
Mildura 15,763 . . . . A4
Minyip 567 . . . . B5
Moe 16,649 . . . . D6
Montmorency J4
Montrose K5
Moorabbin 97,810 . . . . . . J5
Mooroopna C5
Mordialloc 27,869 . . . . . . J6
Morea A5
Mornington 23,512 . . . . . . C6
Mortlake 1,056 . . . . B6
Morwell 16,491 . . . . D5
Mount Beauty 1,509 . . . . . D5
Murrayville 313 . . . . A4
Murtoa 946 . . . . B5
Myrtleford 2,815 . . . . D5
Nagambie 1,102 . . . . C5
Narre Warren North 761 . . . K5
Nathalia 1,222 . . . . C4
Natimuk 482 . . . . A5
Newtown 10,210 . . . . C6

Nhill 1,567 . . . . A5
Northcote 51,235 . . . . J5
Numurkah 2,713 . . . . C4
Nunawading 97,052 . . . . . J5
Nyah 351 . . . . B4
Nyah West 535 . . . . B4
Oakleigh 55,612 . . . . J5
Omeo 272. . . . . D5
Orbost 2,586 . . . . E5
Ouyen 1,527 . . . . A4
Penshurst 558. . . . . B5
Porepunkah 268 . . . . D5
Port Albert 267 . . . . D6
Port Fairy 2,276 . . . . B6
Portland 9,353 . . . . A6
Port Melbourne 8,585 . . . . H5
Prahran 45,018 . . . . J5
Preston 84,519 . . . . J4
Quambatook 359 . . . . B4
Queenscliff 3,420 . . . . . . C6
Rainbow 700. . . . . A4
Red Cliffs 2,409 . . . . B4
Richmond 24,506 . . . . . . J5
Ringwood 38,665 . . . . K5
Robinvale 1,751 . . . . B4
Rochester 2,399 . . . . C5
Rushworth 994 . . . . C5
Rutherglen 1,454 . . . . D5
Saint Arnaud 2,721 . . . . . B5
Saint Kilda 49,366 . . . . . . J5
Sale 12,968 . . . . D6
Sandringham 31,175 . . . . . J5
Sea Lake 943 . . . . B4
Sebastopol 6,462 . . . . . . C5
Seymour 6,494 . . . . C5
Shepparton-Mooroopna
‡28,373 . . . . C5
South Barwon 35,307 . . . . C6
South Melbourne 19,955 . . . J5
Springvale 80,186 . . . . . . J5
Stawell 6,160 . . . . B5
Sunbury 11,085 . . . . C5
Sunshine 94,419 . . . . H5
Swan Hill 8,398 . . . . B4
Swifts Creek 288 . . . . D5
Tallangatta 950 . . . . D5
Tatura 2,697 . . . . C5
Templestowe and Doncaster
90,660 . . . . J5
Terang 2,111 . . . . B6
Tongala 994 . . . . C5
Traralgon 18,057 . . . . D6
Underbool 274 . . . . A4
Wangaratta 16,202 . . . . . . D5
Warburton 2,009 . . . . C5
Warracknabeal 2,735 . . . . B5
Warragul 7,712 . . . . D6
Warrnambool 21,414 . . . . . B6
Waverley 122,471 . . . . . . J5
Wedderburn 868 . . . . B5
Werrimull A4
Whittlesea 65,657 . . . . . . C5
Willaura 377 . . . . B5
Williamstown 25,554 . . . . . H5
Winchelsea 825 . . . . B6
Wodonga 19,208 . . . . D5
Wonthaggi 4,797 . . . . C6
Woodend 1,785 . . . . C5
Wycheproof 938 . . . . B5
Yallourn 26 . . . . D6
Yarram 2,085 . . . . D6
Yarrawonga 3,442 . . . . . . C4
Yea 996 . . . . C5

OTHER FEATURES

Australian Alps (mts.) D5
Avoca (riv.) B5
Barry (mts.) D5
Bogong (mt.) D5
Bridgewater (cape) A6
Buller (mt.) D5
Campaspe (riv.) C5
Corangamite (lake) B6
Corner (inlet) D6
Dandenong (mt.) K5
Difficult (mt.) B5
Discovery (bay) A6
Eildon (lake) C5
French (isl.) 123 . . . . C6
Gippsland (reg.) D6
Glenelg (riv.) A5
Goulburn (riv.) C5
Hindmarsh (lake) A5
Hobsons (bay) H5
Hopkins (riv.) B5
Hume (lake) D4
Indian Ocean B6
Loddon (riv.) B5
Mitchell (riv.) D5
Mitta Mitta (riv.) D5
Mornington (pen.) C6
Mount Emu (creek) B5
Murray (riv.) A4
Nelson (cape) A6
Ninety Mile (beach) D6
Otway (cape) B6
Ovens (riv.) D5
Phillip (isl.) 2,832 . . . . . . C6
Portland (bay) A6
Port Phillip (bay) C6
Rocklands (res.) B5
Snowy (riv.) E5
South East (pt.) D6
Tasman (sea) F5
Tyrrell (lake) B4
Waratah (bay) C6
Wellington (lake) D6
Western Port (inlet) C6
Wilsons (prom.) D6
Wimmera (riv.) A5
Yarra (riv.) A5

*City and suburbs.
○ Population of district.
†Population of met. area.
‡Population of urban area.

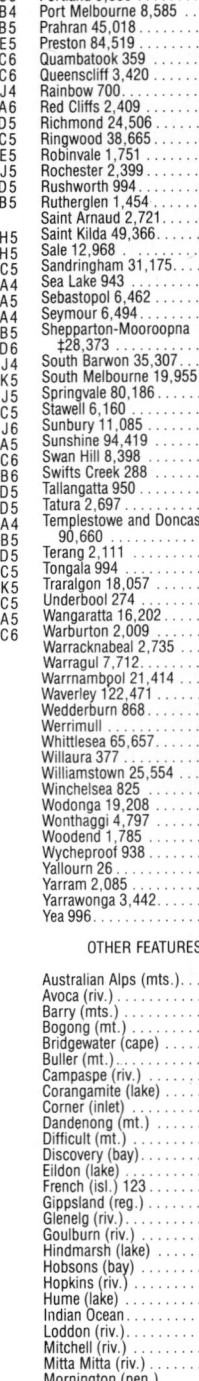

Irrigation Areas and Artesian Basins in Australia

Darwin

TANAMI DESERT

GREAT SANDY DESERT

GREAT VICTORIA DESERT

GREAT ARTESIAN BASIN

SOMERSET

Brisbane

L. Eyre

L. Torrens

L. Gairdner

Darling

MENINDEE

BURRENDONG

Perth

WARRAGAMBA

Adelaide L. ALEXANDRINA

BURRINJUCK

Sydney

Murray

HUME

Canberra

ADAMINABY

BIG EILDON

Snowy

Melbourne

Hobart

Permanent Rivers

Non-Permanent Rivers

Flowing Water Bores

Major Dams

Major Irrigation and Other Water Supply Areas

Basins Where Artesian Water Is Generally Available

Prepared from Atlas of Australian Resources.

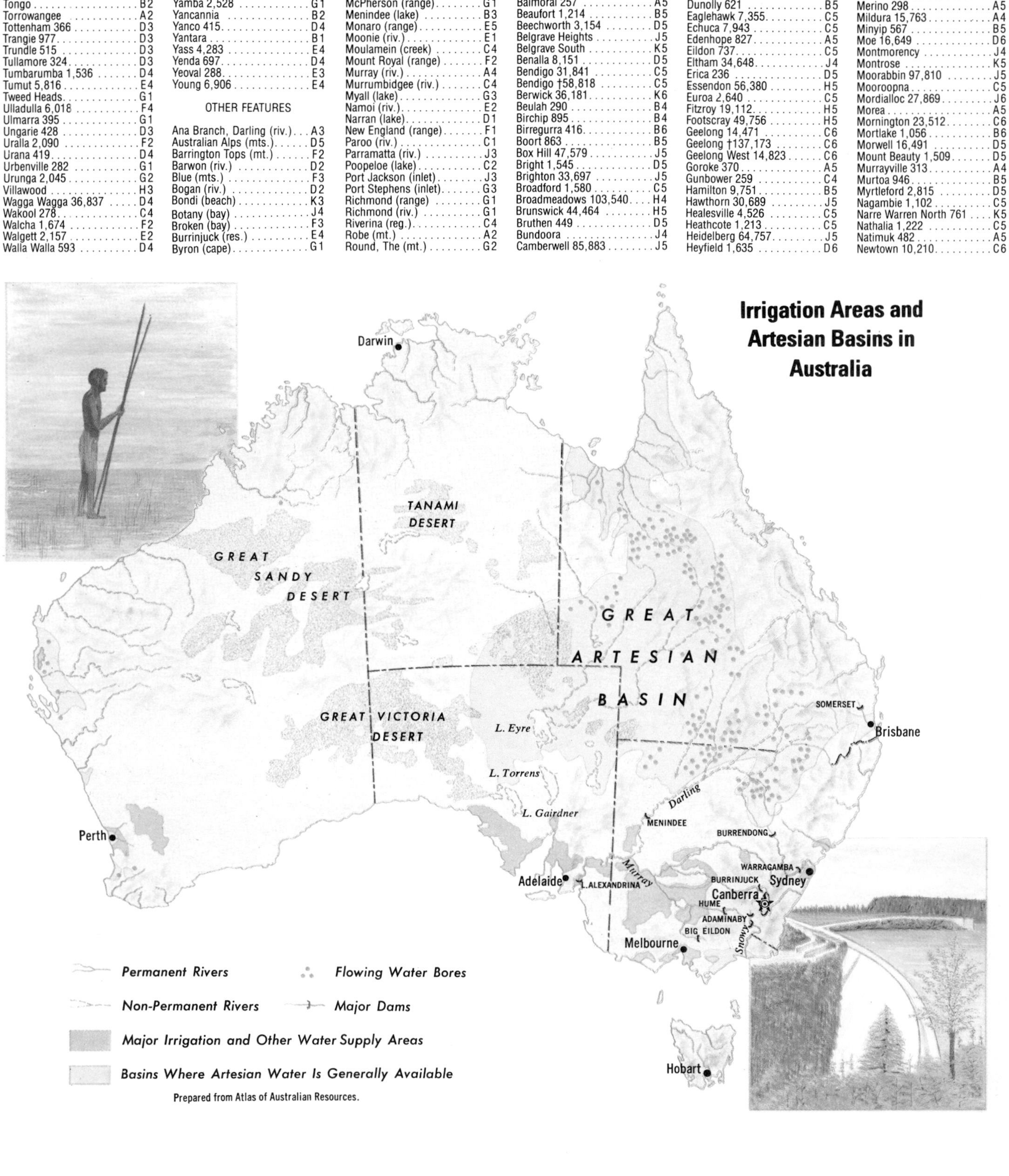

Topography

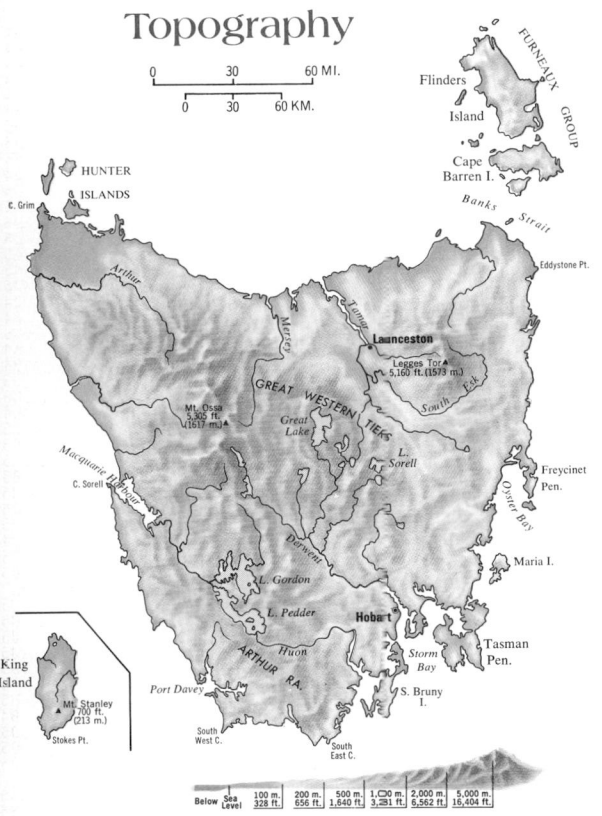

0   30   60 MI.
0   30   60 KM.

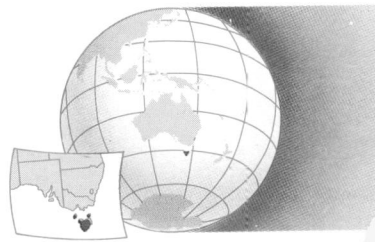

TASMANIA

AREA 26,178 sq. mi. (67,800 sq. km.)
POPULATION 436,353
CAPITAL Hobart
LARGEST CITY Hobart
HIGHEST POINT Mt. Ossa 5,305 ft.
(1,617 m.)

Below Sea Level | 100 m. 328 ft. | 200 m. 656 ft. | 500 m. 1,640 ft. | 1,000 m. 3,281 ft. | 2,000 m. 6,562 ft. | 5,000 m. 16,404 ft.

Forth (riv.)	C3
Frankland (cape)	D1
Frankland (range)	B4
Franklin (riv.)	B4
Frenchmans Cap (mt.)	B4
Freycinet (pen.)	E4
Furneaux Group (isls.) 1,039	E1
Gordon (lake)	C4
Gordon (riv.)	B4
Great (lake)	C3
Great Western Tiers (mts.)	C3
Grim (cape)	A2
Hartz (mt.)	C5
Hibbs (pt.)	B4
Hogan Group (isl.)	D1
Hummock (isl.)	D2
Hunter (isl.)	A2
Hunter (isl.)	B2
Huon (riv.)	C5
Indian Ocean	
Kent Group (isls.)	D1
King (isl.) 2,592	A1

King (riv.)	B4
King William (lake)	C4
Lake (isl.)	D3
Legges Tor (mt.)	D3
Leven (riv.)	C3
Lofty (range)	B3
Low Rocky (pt.)	B4
Lyell (mt.)	B4
Maatsuyker (isl.)	C5
Macquarie (harb.)	B4
Macquarie (riv.)	D3
Maria (isl.)	E4
Marion (bay)	E4
Mersey (riv.)	C3
Munro (mt.)	E2
Naturaliste (cape)	E2
Nive (riv.)	C4
Norfolk (bay)	D4
North (pt.)	E1
North Bruny (isl.)	D5
North Esk (riv.)	D3
Ossa (mt.)	C3

Ouse (riv.)	C4
Oyster (bay)	E4
Pedder (riv.)	B4
Phoques (bay)	A1
Picton (mt.)	C5
Pieman (riv.)	B3
Pillar (cape)	E5
Port Davey (inlet)	B5
Portland (cape)	D2
Ramsey (mt.)	B3
Raoul (cape)	D5
Reid (rapid)	B1
Ringarooma (bay)	D2
Robbins (isl.)	A2
Saint Clair (lake)	C4
Saint Helens (pt.)	E3
Saint Vincent (cape)	B5
Savage (riv.)	B3
Schouten (isl.)	E4
Sorell (cape)	B4
Sorell (lake)	D4
South (cape)	C5

South Bruny (isl.)	D5
South East (cape)	C5
South Esk (riv.)	D3
South West (cape)	B5
Stanley (mt.)	A1
Stokes (pt.)	A1
Storm (bay)	D5
Strzelecki (mt.)	D2
Tamar (riv.)	D3
Tasman (head)	D5
Tasman (pen.)	E5
Tasman (sea)	E4
Three Hummock (isl.)	B2
Vansittart (isl.)	E2
West (pt.)	A2
West Sister (isl.)	D1
Wickham (cape)	A1

○ Population of district.
*Population of met. area.

CITIES and TOWNS

Adventure Bay	D5
Avoca	D3
Bagdad	D4
Beaconsfield 898	C3
Beauty Point 998	C3
Bell Bay	C3
Bicheno 674	E3
Boat Harbour	B2
Bothwell 356	C4
Bracknell 347	C3
Branxholm 273	D3
Bridgewater 6,880	D4
Bridport 885	D3
Brighton 9,441	D4
Burnie 19,994	B3
Campbell Town 879	D3
Chudleigh	C3
Colebrook	D4
Cressy 640	C3
Currie 859	A1
Cygnet 715	C5
Deloraine 1,923	C3
Derwent Bridge	C4
Devonport 21,424	C3
Dover 570	C5
Dunalley 203	D4
Evandale 614	D3
Exeter 353	C3
Fingal 424	E3
Forth 273	C3
Franklin 479	C5
Geeveston 860	C5
George Town 5,592	C3
Glenorchy 41,019	D4
Gormanston 126	B4
Gowrie Park	C3
Grassy 780	B1
Gravelly Beach 535	C3
Hadspen 908	D3
Hagley 232	C3
Hamilton 2,488	C4
Heybridge 395	C3
Hobart (cap.) 128,603	D4
Hobart *168,359	D4
Huonville-Ranelagh 1,347	C5
Kettering 288	D5
Kingston 8,556	D4
Latrobe 2,401	C3
Lauderdale 2,117	D4
Launceston 31,273	C3
Launceston *64,555	C3
Legana 964	C3
Lilydale 308	D3
Longford 2,027	C3
Luina 522	B3
Margate 476	D4
Maydena 461	C4
Meander	C3
Mole Creek 303	C3
New Norfolk 6,243	C4
Nubeena 225	D5
Oatlands 545	D4
Orford 378	D4
Penguin 2,616	C3
Perth 1,229	D3
Poatina	C3
Port Sorell 859	C3
Queenstown 3,714	B4
Railton 857	C3
Richmond 587	D4
Ridgley 452	B3

Ringarooma 223	D3
Rosebery 2,675	B3
Ross 289	D4
Rossarden 365	D3
Saint Helens 1,005	E3
Saint Marys 653	E3
Sassafras	C3
Savage River 1,141	B3
Scottsdale 2,002	D3
Sheffield 945	C3
Smithton 3,378	A2
Snug 684	D5
Sorell-Midway Point 2,544	D4
Stanley 603	B2
Storeys Creek	D3
Strahan 402	B4
Strathgordon	C4
Sulphur Creek 367	C3
Swansea 428	D4
Tarraleah 498	C4
Temma	A3
Triabunna 924	D4
Tullah 1,894	B3
Ulverstone 9,413	C3
Waratah 342	B3
Wesley Vale	C3
Westbury 1,161	C3
Whitemark	D2
Woodbridge 259	D5
Wynyard 4,582	B3
Zeehan 1,750	B3

OTHER FEATURES

Anderson (bay)	D2
Anne (mt.)	C4
Anser Group (isls.)	C1
Arthur (lake)	D4
Arthur (range)	C5
Arthur (riv.)	B3
Babel (isl.)	E1
Banks (str.)	D2
Barn Bluff (mt.)	B3
Barren (cape)	E2
Bass (str.)	C1
Bathurst (gulf)	C5
Cape Barren (isl.)	E2
Chappell (isls.)	D2
Circular (gulf)	B2
Clarke (isl.)	E2
Clyde (riv.)	D4
Cox (bight)	C5
Cradle (mt.)	B3
Cradle Mt.-Lake St. Clair Nat'l Park	B3
Crescent (lake)	D4
Curtis Group (isls.)	C1
D'Aguilar (range)	B4
Davey (riv.)	B4
Deal (isl.)	D1
Dee (riv.)	C4
Denison (range)	C4
D'Entrecasteaux (chan.)	D5
Derwent (riv.)	C4
East Sister (isl.)	E1
Echo (lake)	C4
Eddystone (pt.)	E2
Elliott (isl.)	B5
Fires (bay)	E3
Flinders (isl.) 2,150	D1
Florence (riv.)	C4
Forestier (chan.)	E4
Forestier (pen.)	E4

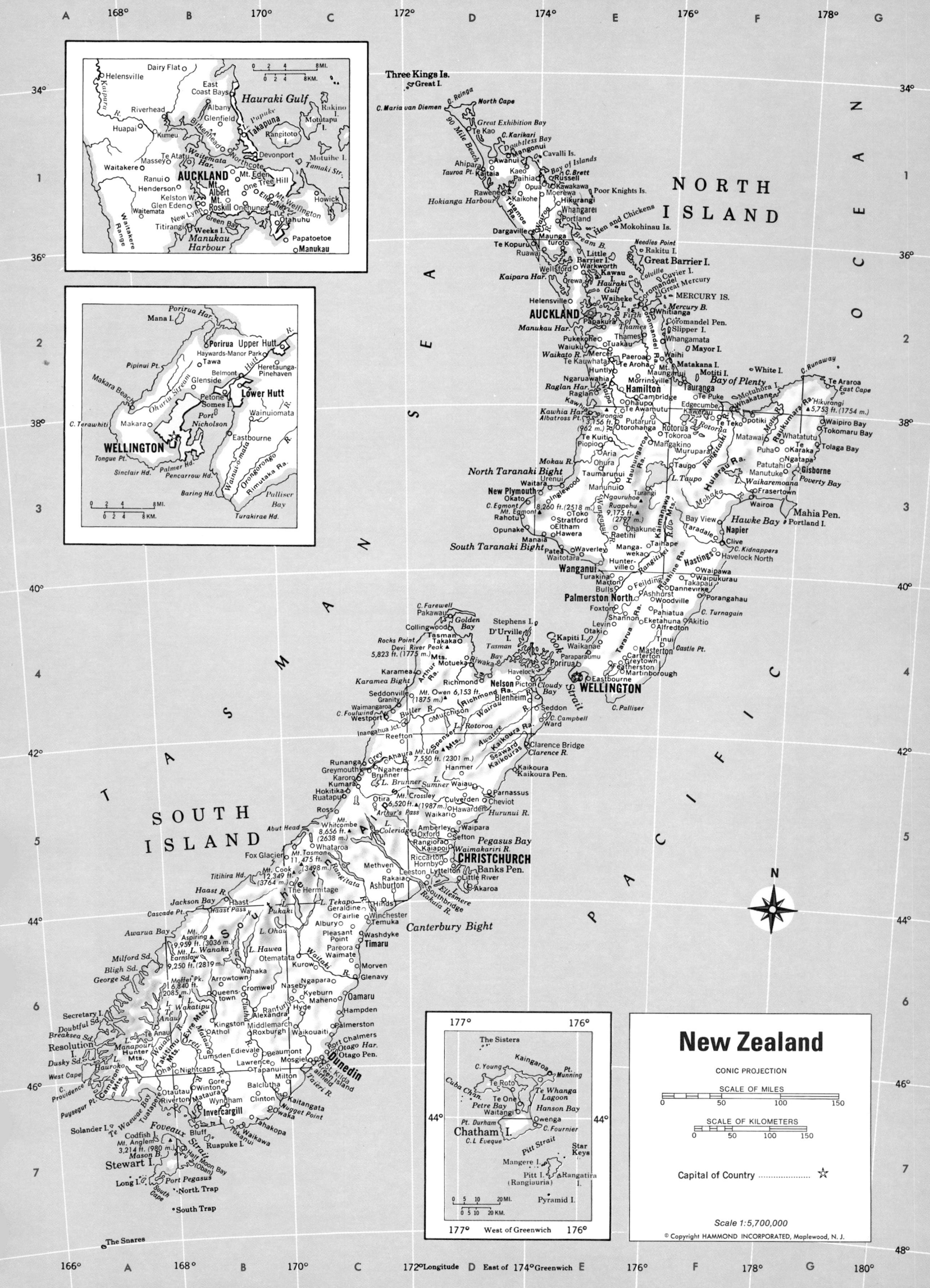

New Zealand

CONIC PROJECTION

SCALE OF MILES

SCALE OF KILOMETERS

Capital of Country .... ☆

Scale 1:5,700,000

© Copyright HAMMOND INCORPORATED, Maplewood, N.J.

Topography

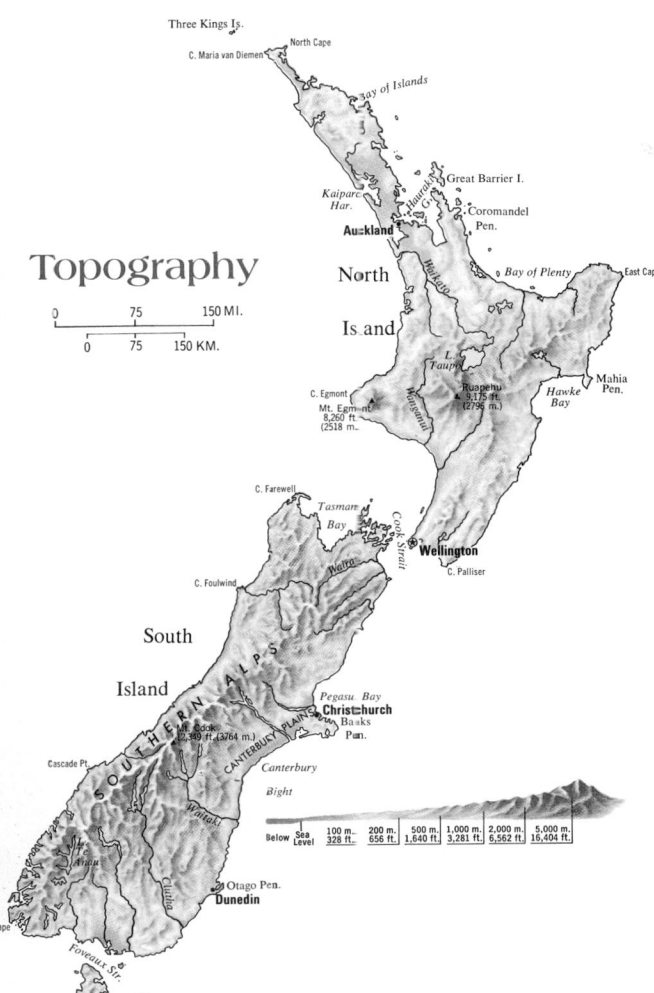

0 75 150 MI.
0 75 150 KM.

North Island

South Island

Below Sea Level | 100 m. 328 ft. | 200 m. 656 ft. | 500 m. 1,640 ft. | 1,000 m. 3,281 ft. | 2,000 m. 6,562 ft. | 5,000 m. 16,404 ft.

Three Kings Is., C. Maria van Diemen, North Cape, Bay of Islands, Kaipara Har., Great Barrier I., Coromandel Pen., Auckland, Bay of Plenty, East Cape, C. Egmont, Mt. Egmont 8,260 ft. (2518 m.), Ruapehu 9,175 ft. (2796 m.), L. Taupo, Mahia Pen., Hawke Bay, C. Farewell, Tasman Bay, Cook Strait, Wellington, C. Palliser, C. Foulwind, SOUTHERN ALPS, Mt. Cook 12,349 ft. (3764 m.), Pegasus Bay, Christchurch, Banks Pen., Canterbury Bight, Cascade Pt., Otago Pen., Dunedin, West Cape, Foveaux Str., Stewart I.

AREA 103,736 sq. mi. (268,676 sq. km.)
POPULATION 3,389,000
CAPITAL Wellington
LARGEST CITY Auckland
HIGHEST POINT Mt. Cook 12,349 ft. (3,764 m.)
MONETARY UNIT New Zealand dollar
MAJOR LANGUAGES English, Maori
MAJOR RELIGIONS Protestantism, Roman Catholicism

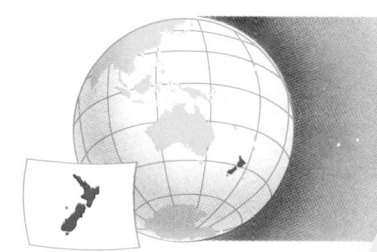

CITIES and TOWNS

Albany 2,001 .... B1
Alexandra 4,348 .... B6
Ashburton 14,151 .... C5
Ashhurst 1,906 .... E4
Auckland 144,963 .... B1
Auckland †769,558 .... B1
Balclutha 4,495 .... B7
Belmont 2,402 .... B2
Birkenhead 21,324 .... B1
Blenheim 17,849 .... D4
Bluff 2,720 .... B7
Bulls 1,839 .... E4
Cambridge 8,514 .... E2
Carterton 3,971 .... E4
Christchurch 164,680 .... D5
Christchurch †289,959 .... D5
Cromwell 2,364 .... B6
Dannevirke 5,663 .... F4
Dargaville 4,747 .... D1
Devonport 10,410 .... C1
Dunedin 77,176 .... C6
Dunedin †107,445 .... C6
Eastbourne 4,561 .... B3
East Coast Bays 28,866 .... B1
Edgecumbe 1,929 .... F2
Ellerslie 5,404 .... C1
Eltham 2,411 .... E3
Fairfield 1,849 .... C6
Featherston 2,458 .... E4
Feilding 11,522 .... E4
Foxton 2,719 .... E4
Geraldine 2,128 .... C6
Gisborne 29,986 .... G3
Gisborne †32,062 .... G3
Glen Eden 9,406 .... B1
Glenfield 3,691 .... B1
Gore 9,185 .... B7
Green Bay 3,035 .... B1
Green Island 6,899 .... C7
Greymouth 8,103 .... C5
Greytown 1,797 .... E4
Half Moon Bay (Oban) 2,448 .... B7
Hamilton 91,109 .... E2
Hamilton †97,907 .... E2
Hastings 36,083 .... F3
Hastings †52,563 .... F3
Havelock North 8,507 .... F3
Hawera 8,400 .... E3
Helensville 1,360 .... B1
Henderson 6,645 .... B1
Heretaunga-Pinehaven 6,171 .... C2
Hokitika 3,414 .... C5
Hornby 8,215 .... D5
Howick 13,866 .... C1
Huntly 6,534 .... E2
Hutt (Upper and Lower) †131,257 .... B2
Inglewood 2,839 .... E3

Invercargill 49,446 .... B7
Invercargill †53,868 .... B7
Kaiapoi 4,894 .... D5
Kaikohe 3,663 .... D1
Kaikoura 2,180 .... D5
Kaitaia 4,737 .... D1
Kawerau 8,593 .... F3
Kumeu 3,414 .... B1
Levin 14,652 .... E4
Lower Hutt 63,245 .... B2
Lyttelton 3,184 .... D5
Manukau 159,362 .... C1
Marton 4,858 .... E4
Masterton 18,785 .... E4
Mataura 2,345 .... B7
Milton 2,193 .... B7
Morrinsville 5,080 .... E2
Mosgiel 9,264 .... C6
Motueka 4,693 .... D4
Mount Albert 26,462 .... B1
Mount Eden 18,305 .... B1
Mount Maunganui 11,391 .... E2
Mount Roskill 33,577 .... B1
Mount Wellington 19,528 .... C1
Murupara 2,964 .... F3
Napier 48,314 .... F3
Napier †51,330 .... F3
Nelson 33,304 .... D4
Nelson †43,121 .... D4
New Lynn 10,445 .... B1
New Plymouth 36,043 .... D3
New Plymouth †44,035 .... D3
Ngaruawahia 4,435 .... E2
Northcote 10,061 .... B1
Oamaru 13,043 .... C6
Oban (Half Moon Bay) 2,448 .... B7
Onehunga 15,386 .... B1
One Tree Hill 11,078 .... B1
Opotiki 3,388 .... F3
Orewa 5,552 .... E2
Otahuhu 10,298 .... C1
Otaki 4,301 .... E4
Otorohanga 2,574 .... E3
Paeroa 3,702 .... E2
Pahiatua 2,599 .... F4
Paihia 1,740 .... D1
Palmerston North 60,105 .... E4
Palmerston North †66,691 .... E4
Papakura 22,473 .... E2
Papatoetoe 21,700 .... C1
Patea 1,938 .... E3
Petone 8,113 .... B2
Picton 3,220 .... D4
Pinehaven (Heretaunga-Pinehaven) 6,171 .... C2
Porirua 41,104 .... B2
Port Chalmers 2,917 .... C6
Pukekohe 9,070 .... E2
Putaruru 4,222 .... E3
Queenstown 3,367 .... B6

Raetihi 1,247 .... E3
Raglan 1,414 .... E2
Rangiora 6,385 .... D5
Reefton 1,200 .... C5
Riccarton 6,709 .... D5
Richmond 6,847 .... D4
Riverton 1,479 .... B7
Rotorua 38,157 .... F3
Rotorua †48,314 .... F3
Runanga 1,264 .... C5
Russell 932 .... E1
Saint Kilda 6,147 .... C7
Shannon 1,465 .... E4
Stratford 5,518 .... E3
Taihape 2,586 .... E3
Takapuna 64,844 .... B1
Tapanui 1,042 .... B6
Taradale 4,681 .... F3
Taumarunui 6,541 .... E3
Taupo 13,651 .... F3
Tauranga 37,099 .... F2
Tauranga †53,097 .... F2
Tawa 12,216 .... B2
Te Anau 2,610 .... A6
Te Atatu 14,713 .... B1
Te Awamutu 7,922 .... E3
Te Kauwhata 842 .... E2
Te Kuiti 4,795 .... E3
Temuka 3,771 .... C6
Te Puke 4,577 .... F2
Thames 6,456 .... E2
The Hermitage C5
Timaru 28,412 .... C6
Timaru †29,225 .... C6
Titirangi 8,426 .... B1
Tokoroa 18,713 .... F3
Tuakau 1,982 .... E2
Tuatapere 884 .... A7
Turangi 5,517 .... E3
Upper Hutt 31,405 .... B2
Waihi 3,538 .... E2
Waikanae 4,818 .... E4
Waikouaiti 858 .... C6
Waimate 3,393 .... C6
Wainuiomata 19,192 .... B3
Waipawa 1,732 .... F3
Waipukurau 3,648 .... F4
Wairoa 5,439 .... F3
Waitangi D7
Waitara 6,012 .... E3
Waitemata 87,452 .... B1
Waiuku 3,654 .... E2
Waaanaka 1,155 .... B6
Wanganui 37,012 .... E3
Wanganui †39,595 .... E3
Warkworth 1,734 .... E2
Washdyke 949 .... C6
Waverley 1,239 .... E3
Wellington (cap.) 135,688 .... A3

Wellington †321,004 .... A3
Wellsford 1,621 .... E2
Westport 4,686 .... C4
Whakatane 12,286 .... F2
Whangamata 1,566 .... F2
Whangarei 36,550 .... E1
Whangarei †40,212 .... E1
Whitianga 1,960 .... E2
Winton 2,035 .... B7
Woodville 1,647 .... F4

OTHER FEATURES

Arthur's (pass) C5
Aspiring (mt.) B6
Banks (pen.) D5
Bream (bay) E1
Brett (cape) E1
Buller (riv.) D4
Campbell (cape) E4
Canterbury (bight) D6
Cascade (pt.) B6
Chatham (isls.) 751 .... D7
Cloudy (bay) E4
Clutha (riv.) B6
Coleridge (lake) C5
Colville (cape) E2
Cook (mt.) C5
Cook (str.) E4
Coromandel (pen.) F2
Devil River (peak) D4
D'Urville (isl.) D4
Dusky (sound) A6
East (cape) G2
Egmont (cape) D3
Egmont (mt.) D3
Ellesmere (lake) D5
Farewell (cape) D4
Foulwind (cape) C4
Fournier (cape) E7
Foveaaux (str.) A7
Golden (bay) D4
Great Barrier (isl.) 572 .... E2
Haast (pass) B6
Hauraki (gulf) C1
Hawke (bay) F3
Hikurangi (mt.) G2
Hokianga (harb.) D1
Huiarau (range) F3
Hutt (riv.) C2
Islands (bay) E1
Jackson (bay) B5
Kaikoura (range) D5
Kaimanawa (range) E3
Kaipara (harb.) D2
Karamea (bight) C4
Kawhia (harb.) E3
Kidnappers (cape) F3
Mahia (pen.) G3
Manapouri (lake) A6
Manukau (harb.) B1
Maria van Diemen (cape) D1
Mataura (riv.) B6
Mercury (isls.) F2
Milford (sound) A6
Needles (pt.) E2
Nicholson, Port (inlet) B3
Ninety Mile (beach) D1
North (cape) D1
North (isl.) 2,322,989 .... F1
North Taranaki (bight) D3
Otago (pen.) C6
Owen (mt.) D4
Palliser (cape) E4
Pegasus (bay) D5
Pitt (isl.) E7
Plenty (bay) F2
Port Nicholson (inlet) B3
Port Pegasus (inlet) B7
Pukaki (lake) B6
Puysegur (pt.) A7
Rakaia (riv.) C5
Rangitata (riv.) C5
Rangitikei (riv.) E3
Raukumara (range) F3
Reinga (cape) D1
Resolution (isl.) A6
Richmond (range) D4
Rocks (pt.) C4
Rotorua (lake) F3
Ruahine (range) F4
Ruapehu (mt.) E3
Ruapuke (isl.) B7
South (cape) A7
Southern Alps (range) C5
South (isl.) 852,748 .... B5
South Taranaki (bight) D3
Spenser (mts.) D5
Stewart (isl.) 600 .... A7
Tararua (range) E4
Tasman (bay) D4
Tasman (mt.) C5
Tasman (mts.) D4
Tasman (sea) B4
Taupo (lake) F3
Tauroa (pt.) D1

Te Anau (lake) A6
Tekapo (lake) C5
Terawhiti (cape) A3
Thames (firth) E2
Three Kings (isls.) D1
Turakirae (head) B3
Una (mt.) D5
Waiheke (isl.) 3,223 .... E2
Waikato (riv.) E2
Waimakariri (riv.) D5
Waipa (riv.) E2
Wairau (riv.) D4
Waitaki (riv.) C6
Waitemata (harb.) B1
Wakatipu (lake) B6
Wanaka (lake) B6
Wanganui (riv.) E3
West (cape) A6
Whitcombe (mt.) C5

†Population of urban area.

Agriculture, Industry and Resources

Snapper, Kauri, Fruit, Auckland, Dairy, Sheep, Snapper, Sheep, Dairy, G, Wellington, Cu, Sheep, Wheat, Christchurch, Crayfish, Sheep, Wheat, Soles, Sheep, Lg, Lg, Dunedin, Oysters, Crayfish

DOMINANT LAND USE

Mixed Farming, Livestock
Dairy
Truck Farming, Horticulture
Pasture Livestock (chiefly sheep)
Livestock Herding
Forests
Nonagricultural Land

MAJOR MINERAL OCCURRENCES

C Coal
G Natural Gas
J Jade
Ka Kaolin
Lg Lignite
O Petroleum
U Uranium

Water Power
Major Industrial Areas

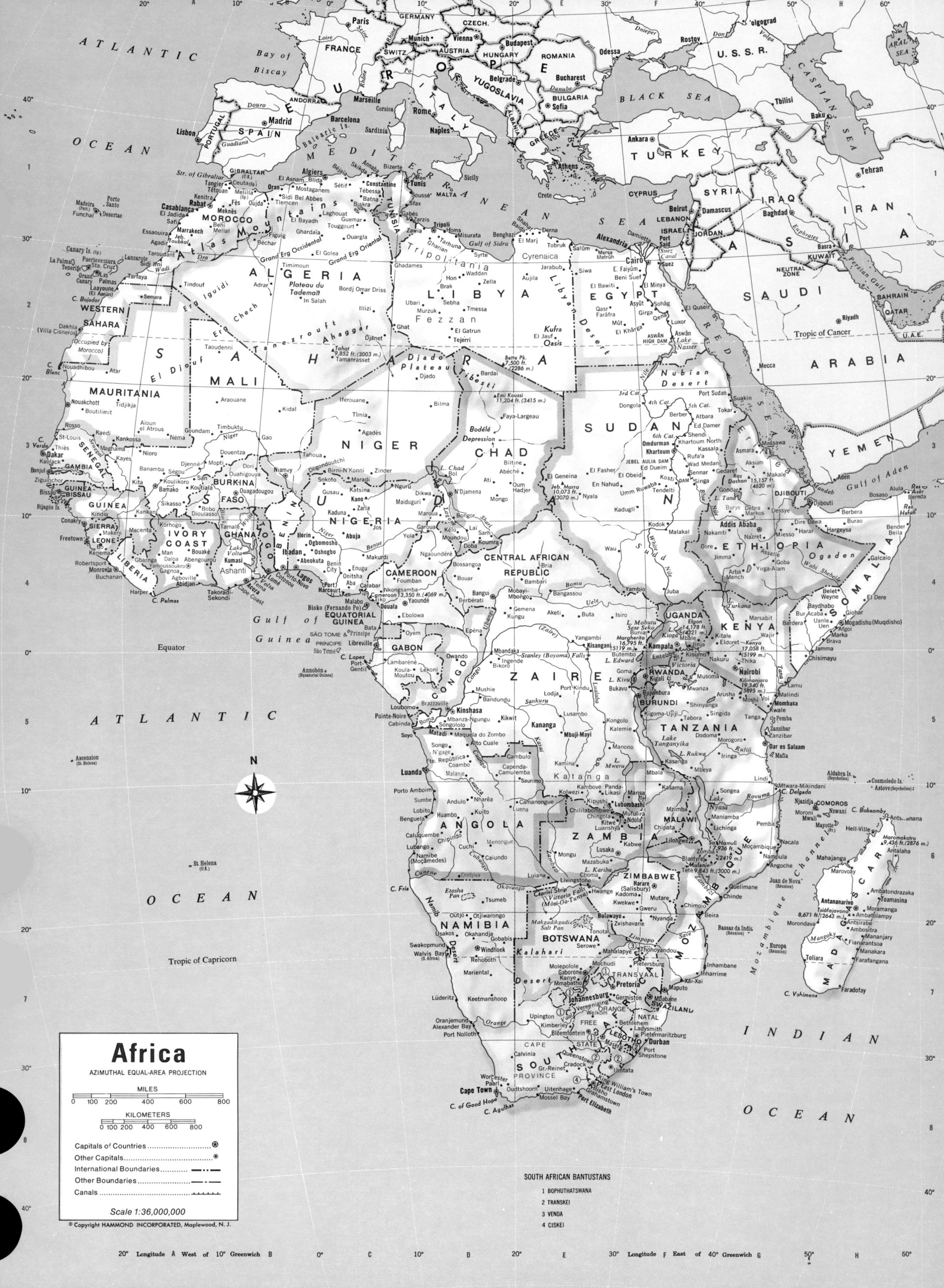

Africa

AZIMUTHAL EQUAL-AREA PROJECTION

MILES
0 100 200 400 600 800

KILOMETERS
0 100 200 400 600 800

Capitals of Countries ....⊛
Other Capitals ....◉
International Boundaries ....─·─·─
Other Boundaries ....─·─·─
Canals ....─·─·─

Scale 1:36,000,000

© Copyright HAMMOND INCORPORATED, Maplewood, N.J.

SOUTH AFRICAN BANTUSTANS

1 BOPHUTHATSWANA

2 TRANSKEI

3 VENDA

4 CISKEI

Population Distribution

AREA 11,707,000 sq. mi. (30,321,130 sq. km.)
POPULATION 648,000,000
LARGEST CITY Cairo
HIGHEST POINT Kilimanjaro 19,340 ft.
(5,895 m.)
LOWEST POINT Lake Assal, Djibouti -512 ft.
(-156 m.)

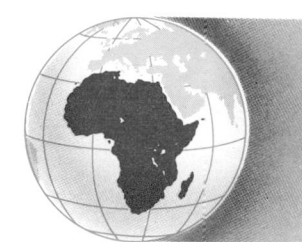

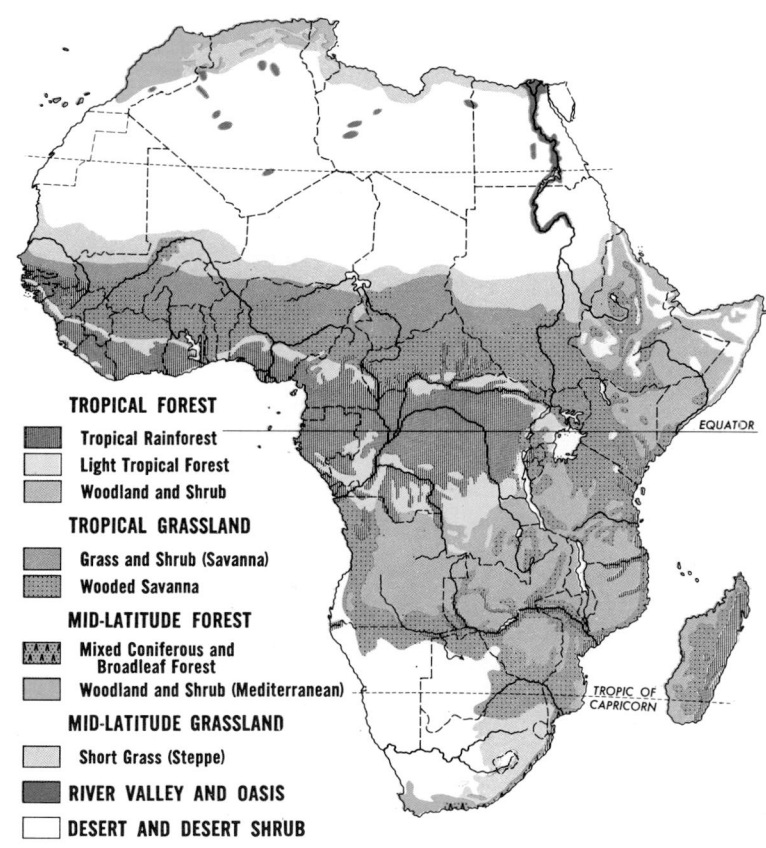

Vegetation

DENSITY PER

SQ. KILOMETER	SQ. MILE
Over 100	Over 260
50-100	130-260
10-50	25-130
1-10	3-25
Under 1	Under 3

• Cities with over 1,000,000
inhabitants (including suburbs)

TROPICAL FOREST
- Tropical Rainforest
- Light Tropical Forest
- Woodland and Shrub

TROPICAL GRASSLAND
- Grass and Shrub (Savanna)
- Wooded Savanna

MID-LATITUDE FOREST
- Mixed Coniferous and Broadleaf Forest
- Woodland and Shrub (Mediterranean)

MID-LATITUDE GRASSLAND
- Short Grass (Steppe)

RIVER VALLEY AND OASIS

DESERT AND DESERT SHRUB

UNCLASSIFIED HIGHLANDS

Abéché, Chad D3
Abidjan, Ivory Coast B4
Accra (cap.), Ghana B4
Addis Ababa (cap.),
 Ethiopia F4
Aden (gulf) G3
Agulhas (cape), S. Africa . . . D8
Ahaggar (range), Algeria . . . C2
Alexandria, Egypt E1
Algeria C2
Algiers (cap.), Algeria C1
Angola D6
Annaba, Algeria C1
Annobon (isl.), Equat.
 Guinea C5
Antananarivo (cap.),
 Madagascar G6
Arusha, Tanzania F5
Ascension (isl.),
 St. Helena A5
Asmara, Ethiopia F3
Aswân, Egypt F2
Asyût, Egypt F2
Atbara, Sudan F3
Atlas (mts.) B1
Bab el Mandeb (str.) G3
Bamako (cap.), Mali B3
Bangui (cap.), Cent.
 Afr. Rep. D4
Banjul (cap.), Gambia A3
Béchar, Algeria B1
Beira, Mozambique F7
Benghazi, Libya D1
Benguela, Angola D6
Benin C4
Bioko (isl.), Equat. Guinea . . C4
Biskra, Algeria C1
Bissau (cap.), Guinea-Biss. . A3
Bizerte, Tunisia C1
Blanc (cape), Mauritania . . . A2
Blantyre, Malawi F6
Bloemfontein, S. Africa E7
Blue Nile (riv.) F3
Bobaomby (cape),
 Madagascar G6
Bobo Dioulasso,
 Burkina Faso B3
Bon (cape), Tunisia D1
Bophuthatswana, S. Africa . . E7
Botswana E7
Bouaké, Ivory Coast B4
Boyoma (Stanley) (falls),
 Zaire E5
Brazzaville (cap.), Congo . . . D5
Buchanan, Liberia A4
Bujumbura (cap.), Burundi . . F5
Bukavu, Zaire E5
Bulawayo, Zimbabwe E7
Burkina Faso B3

Burundi F5
Cabinda, Angola D5
Cairo (cap.), Egypt F2
Cameroon D4
Canary (isls.), Spain A2
Cape (prov.), S. Africa E8
Cape Town (cap.), S. Africa . D8
Casablanca, Morocco B1
Central African Republic . . . D4
Ceuta, Spain B1
Chad D3
Chad (lake) D3
Comoros G6
Conakry (cap.), Guinea A4
Congo D5
Congo (riv.) D5
Constantine, Algeria C1
Cotonou, Benin C4
Cyrenaica (reg.), Libya E1
Dakar (cap.), Senegal A3
Damietta, Egypt F1
Dar es Salaam (cap.),
 Tanzania F5
Djibouti G3
Djibouti (cap.), Djibouti G3
Dodoma, Tanzania F5
Douala, Cameroon D4
Durban, S. Africa F7
East London, S. Africa E8
Edward (lake) E5
Egypt E2
El Bayadh, Algeria C1
El Faiyûm, Egypt E2
El Fasher, Sudan E3
El Minya, Egypt E2
El Obeid, Sudan E3
Elgon (mt.) F4
Emi Koussi (mt.), Chad D3
Entebbe, Uganda F5
Equatorial Guinea C4
Eritrea (reg.), Ethiopia F3
Ethiopia F3
Etosha Salt Pan, Namibia . . D6
Fernando Po (Bioko) (isl.),
 Equat. Guinea C4
Fès, Morocco B1
Fezzan (reg.), Libya D2
Fianarantsoa, Madagascar . . G7
Freetown (cap.), S. Leone . . A4
Funchal (cap.), Madeira,
 Portugal A1
Gabon D4
Gaborone (cap.), Botswana . . E7
Gambia A3
Garoua, Cameroon D4
Germiston, S. Africa E7
Ghana B4
Gharian, Libya D1

Gibraltar (str.) B1
Good Hope (cape), S. Africa D8
Grand Erg Occidental (des.),
 Algeria C1
Grand Erg Oriental (des.),
 Algeria C1
Guinea A3
Guinea (gulf) C4
Guinea-Bissau A3
Gweru, Zimbabwe F6
Harar, Ethiopia G4
Harare (cap.), Zimbabwe . . . E6
Hargeysa, Somalia G4
Huambo, Angola D6
Ibadan, Nigeria C4
Iguidi Erg (des.) B2
Ilorin, Nigeria C4
Ivory Coast B4
Johannesburg, S. Africa . . . E7
Jinja, Uganda F4
Kalahari (des.) E7
Kampala (cap.), Uganda . . . F4
Kananga, Zaire E5
Kankan, Guinea B3
Kano, Nigeria C3
Kaolack, Senegal A3
Kariba (lake) E6
Kasai (riv.) E5
Kassala, Sudan F3
Katanga (reg.), Zaire E5
Kayes, Mali A3
Kenitra, Morocco B4
Kenya F4
Kenya (mt.), Kenya F4
Khartoum (cap.), Sudan . . . F3
Kigali (cap.), Rwanda F5
Kilimanjaro (mt.), Tanzania . . F5
Kimberley, S. Africa E7
Kinshasa (cap.), Zaire D5
Kisangani, Zaire E4
Kisumu, Kenya F5
Kitwe, Zambia E6
Kumasi, Ghana B4
Laayoune, W. Sahara A2
Lagos (cap.), Nigeria C4
Las Palmas (cap.),
 Canary Is., Spain A2
Lesotho E7
Liberia B4
Libreville (cap.), Gabon . . . C4
Libya D2
Libyan (des.) E2
Limpopo (riv.) E7
Lobito, Angola D6
Lomé (cap.), Togo C4
Luanda (cap.), Angola D5
Luanshya, Zambia E6

Lubumbashi, Zaire E6
Lusaka (cap.), Zambia E6
Luxor, Egypt F2
Madagascar G7
Madeira (isls.), Portugal . . . A1
Malabo (cap.), Equat.
 Guinea C4
Malawi F6
Mali B2
Maputo (cap.), Mozambique . F7
Marrakech, Morocco B1
Maseru (cap.), Lesotho E8
Massawa, Ethiopia F3
Matadi, Zaire D5
Mauritania A2
Mayotte (isl.), France G6
Mbabane (cap.), Swaziland . . F7
Mbuji-Mayi, Zaire E5
Mekeès, Morocco B1
Melilla, Spain B1
Misurata, Libya D1
Mmabatho (cap.),
 Bophuthatswana,
 S. Africa E7
Mobuto SeSe Seko (lake) . . . F4
Moçambique, Mozambique . . F6
Mogadishu (cap.), Somalia . . G4
Mombasa, Kenya G5
Monrovia (cap.), Liberia . . . A4
Morocco B1
Moroni (cap.), Comoros . . . G6
Mosi-Oa-Tunya (Victoria)
 (falls) E6
Mostaganem, Algeria C1
Mozambique F6
Mozambique (chan.) G6
Muqdisho (Mogadishu)
 (cap.), Somalia G4
Nairobi (cap.), Kenya F5
Nakuru, Kenya F5
Namibia D7
Nasser (lake), Egypt F2
Natal (prov.), S. Africa F7

N'Djamena (cap.), Chad . . . D3
Ndola, Zambia E6
Niamey (cap.), Niger C3
Niger C3
Niger (riv.) C4
Nigeria C4
Nile (riv.) F2
Nouadhibou, Mauritania . . . A2
Nouakchott (cap.),
 Mauritania A3
Nubian (des.), Sudan F2
Nyasa (lake) F6
Ogaden (reg.), Ethiopia . . . G4
Ogbomosho, Nigeria C4
Okavango (riv.) D6
Omdurman, Sudan F3
Oran, Algeria B1
Orange (riv.) D7
Orange Fee State (prov.),
 S. Africa E7
Oshogbo, Nigeria C4
Ouagadougou (cap.),
 Burkina Faso B3
Oujda, Morocco B1
Palmas (cape) B4
Pemba (isl.), Tanzania G5
Pietermaritzburg (cap.),
 Natal, S. Africa F7
Pointe-Noire, Congo D5
Port Elizabeth, S. Africa . . . E8
Port Harcourt, Nigeria C4
Porto-Novo (cap.), Benin . . . C4
Port Said, Egypt F1
Port Sudan, Sudan F3
Pretoria (cap.), S. Africa . . . E7
Rabat (cap.), Morocco B1
Ras Asèr (cape), Somalia . . H3
Red (sea) F2
Rufiji (riv.), Tanzania F5
Rwanda F5
Sahara (des.) C2
Saint Helena (isl.), U.K. . . . B6
Saint-Louis, Senegal A3

Salisbury (Harare) (cap.),
 Zimbabwe E6
Santa Cruz (cap.),
 Canary Is., Spain A2
São Tomé and Principe C4
Ségou, Mali B3
Senegal A3
Sétif, Algeria C1
Sfax, Tunisia D1
Sidi Bel Abbes, Algeria C1
Sidi Ifni, Morocco A2
Sierra Leone A4
Skikda, Algeria C1
Sohâg, Egypt F2
Somalia G4
Sousse, Tunisia D1
South Africa E7
Stanley (falls), Zaire E5
Sudan E3
Sudan (reg.) D3
Suez, Egypt F2
Suez (canal), Egypt F1
Swaziland F7
Takoradi-Sekondi,
 Ghana B4
Tamale, Ghana B4
Tana (lake), Ethiopia F3
Tanezrouft (des.), Algeria . . C2
Tanga, Tanzania F5
Tanganyika (lake) E5
Tangier, Morocco B1
Tanzania F5
Tenerife (isl.), Spain A2
Thiès, Senegal A3
Thohoyandou (cap.),
 Venda, S. Africa F7
Tibesti (mts.) D2
Tidjikja, Mauritania A3
Timbuktu, Mali B3
Tlemcen, Algeria B1
Toamasina, Madagascar . . . G6
Tobruk, Libya E1
Togo C4

Toubkal, Jebel (mt.),
 Morocco B1
Touggourt, Algeria C1
Transkei, S. Africa E8
Transvaal (prov.), S. Africa . E7
Tripoli (cap.), Libya D1
Tripolitania (reg.), Libya . . . D1
Tunis (cap.), Tunisia D1
Tunisia C1
Turkana (lake), Kenya F4
Ubangi (riv.) D4
Uganda F4
Uitenhage, S. Africa E8
Umtata (cap.), Transkei,
 S. Africa E8
Upper Volta (Burkina
 Faso) B3
Vaal (riv.), S. Africa E7
Venda, S. Africa F7
Verde (cape), Senegal A3
Victoria (lake) F5
Victoria (falls) E6
Vohimena (cape),
 Madagascar G7
Volta (lake), Ghana B4
Volta (riv.), Ghana C4
Wabi Shebelle (riv.) G4
Wad Medani, Sudan F3
Walvis Bay, S. Africa D7
Western Sahara A2
White Nile (riv.) F4
Windhoek (cap.), Namibia . . D7
Yamoussoukro (cap.), Ivory
 Coast B4
Yaoundé (cap.), Cameroon . . D4
Zaire E5
Zaire (Congo) (riv.) E4
Zambezi (riv.) F6
Zambia E6
Zanzibar, Tanzania F5
Zanzibar (isl.), Tanzania . . . F5
Zimbabwe E6
Zomba, Malawi F6

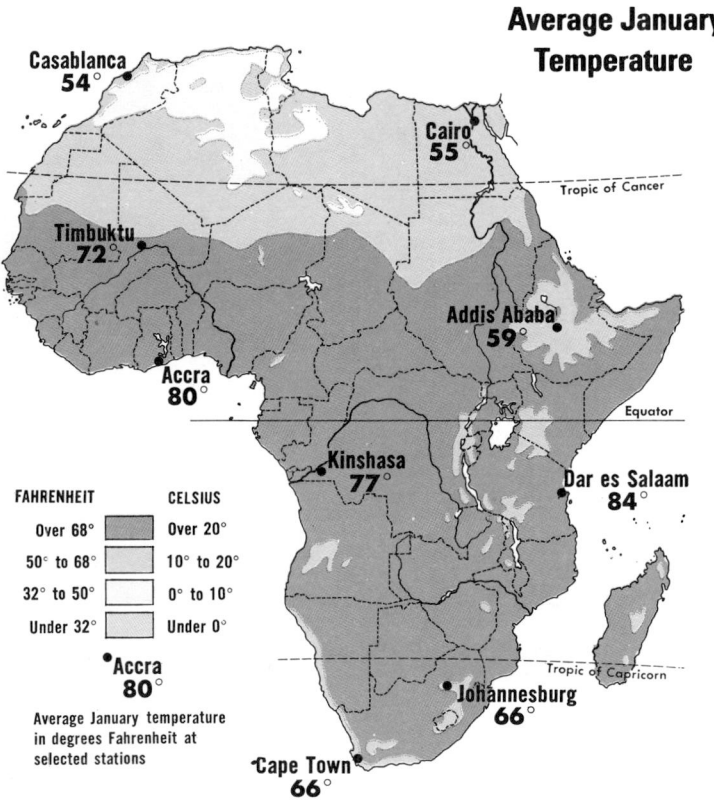

Average January Temperature

Casablanca 54°
Cairo 55°
Timbuktu 72°
Addis Ababa 59°
Accra 80°
Kinshasa 77°
Dar es Salaam 84°
Johannesburg 66°
Cape Town 66°

Tropic of Cancer
Equator
Tropic of Capricorn

FAHRENHEIT   CELSIUS
Over 68°   Over 20°
50° to 68°   10° to 20°
32° to 50°   0° to 10°
Under 32°   Under 0°

• Accra 80°
Average January temperature in degrees Fahrenheit at selected stations

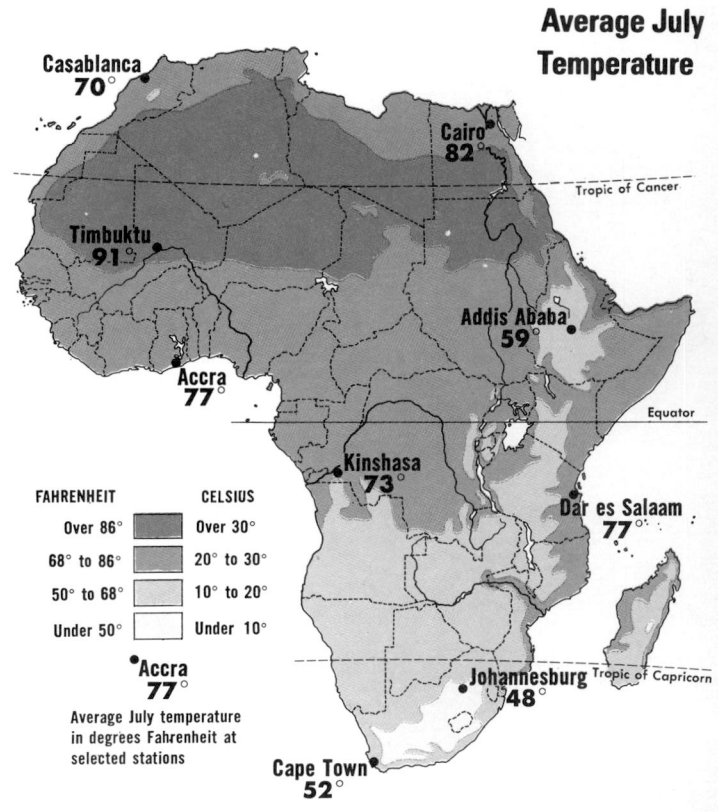

Average July Temperature

Casablanca 70°
Cairo 82°
Timbuktu 91°
Addis Ababa 59°
Accra 77°
Kinshasa 73°
Dar es Salaam 77°
Johannesburg 48°
Cape Town 52°

Tropic of Cancer
Equator
Tropic of Capricorn

FAHRENHEIT   CELSIUS
Over 86°   Over 30°
68° to 86°   20° to 30°
50° to 68°   10° to 20°
Under 50°   Under 10°

• Accra 77°
Average July temperature in degrees Fahrenheit at selected stations

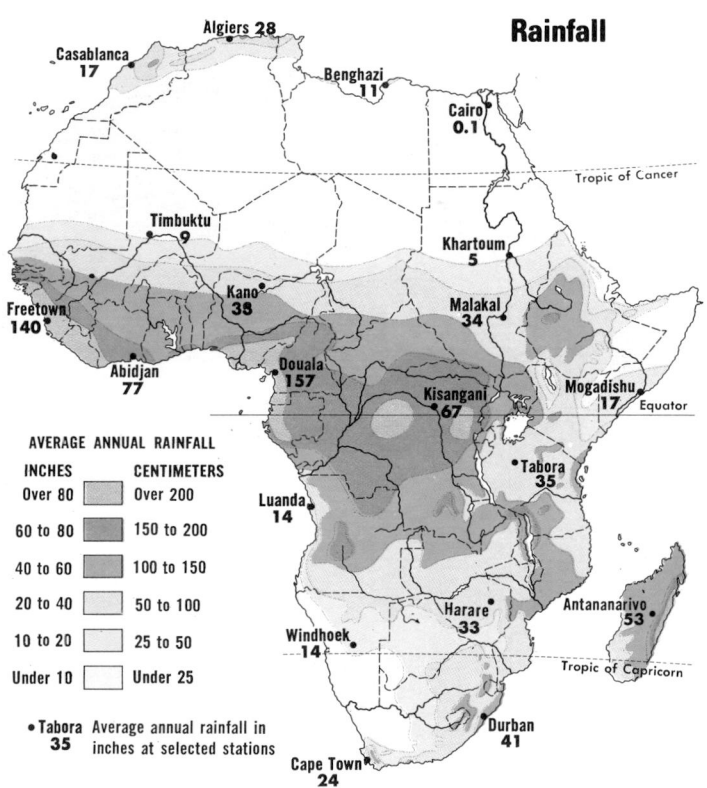

Rainfall

Algiers 28
Casablanca 17
Benghazi 11
Cairo 0.1
Timbuktu 9
Khartoum 5
Kano 35
Malakal 34
Freetown 140
Abidjan 77
Douala 157
Kisangani 67
Mogadishu 17
Tabora 35
Luanda 14
Harare 33
Antananarivo 53
Windhoek 14
Durban 41
Cape Town 24

Tropic of Cancer
Equator
Tropic of Capricorn

AVERAGE ANNUAL RAINFALL
INCHES   CENTIMETERS
Over 80   Over 200
60 to 80   150 to 200
40 to 60   100 to 150
20 to 40   50 to 100
10 to 20   25 to 50
Under 10   Under 25

• Tabora 35   Average annual rainfall in inches at selected stations

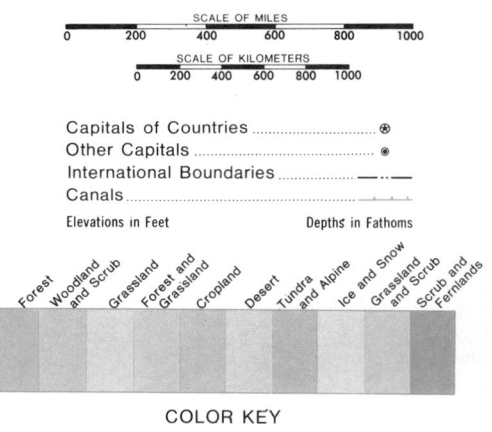

Vegetation / Relief

SCALE OF MILES
0   200   400   600   800   1000

SCALE OF KILOMETERS
0   200   400   600   800   1000

Capitals of Countries .... ⊛
Other Capitals .... ⊛
International Boundaries ....
Canals ....

Elevations in Feet   Depths in Fathoms

Forest
Woodland and Scrub
Grassland
Forest and Grassland
Cropland
Desert
Tundra and Alpine
Ice and Snow
Grassland and Scrub
Scrub and Fernlands

COLOR KEY

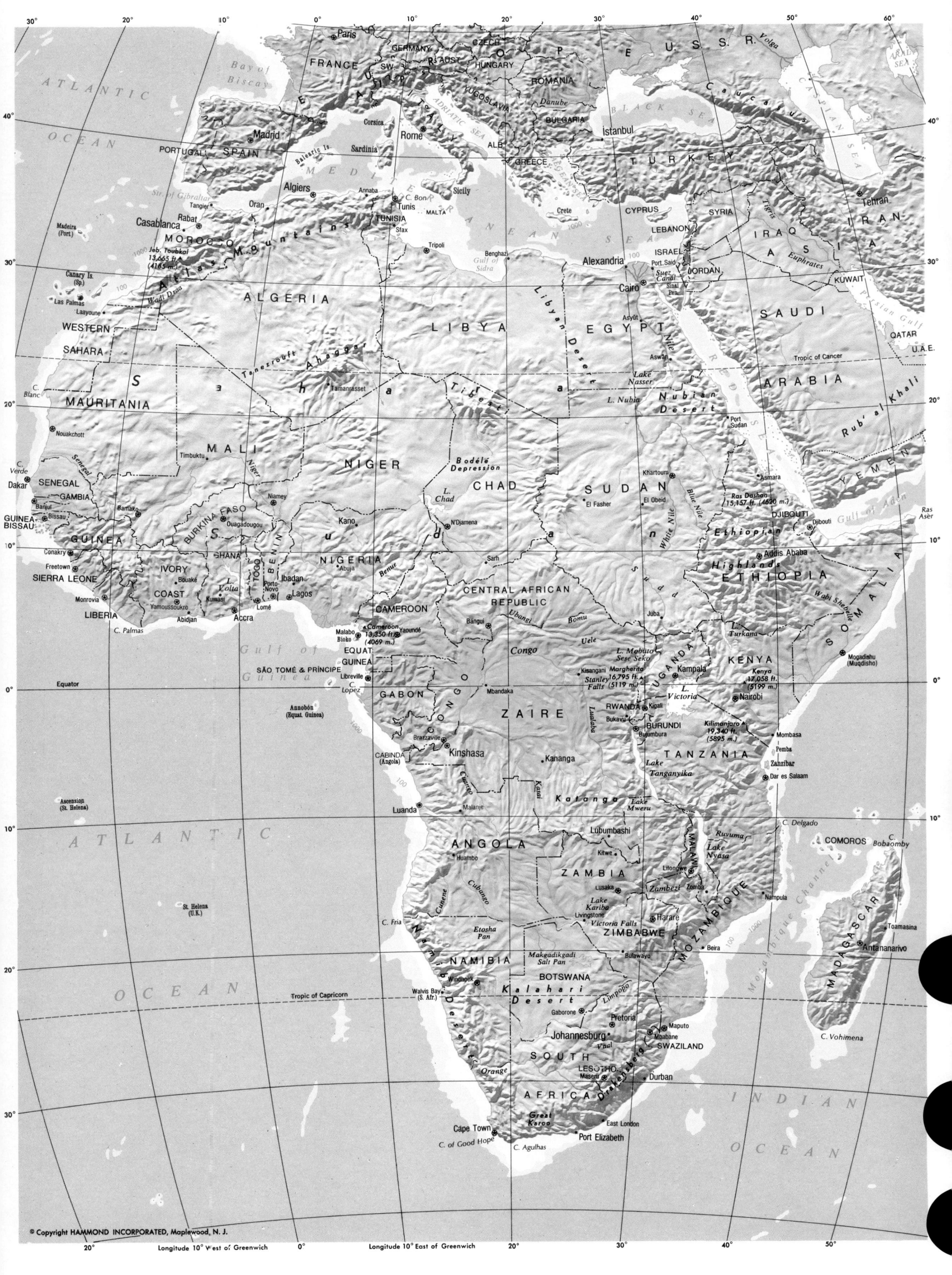

Longitude 10° West of Greenwich 0° Longitude 10° East of Greenwich

Western Africa

CONIC EQUAL-AREA PROJECTION

SCALE OF MILES

0 100 200 400

SCALE OF KILOMETERS

0 100 200 400

Capitals of Countries .... ☆
Other Capitals _____ ◉
International Boundaries _ _ _ _ _
Internal Boundaries _ . _ . _ . _

Scale 1:15,200,000

© Copyright HAMMOND INCORPORATED, Maplewood, N. J.

Cape Verde

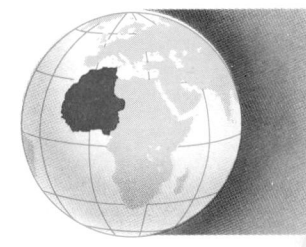

ALGERIA

AREA 919,591 sq. mi. (2,381,740 sq. km.)
POPULATION 22,971,000
CAPITAL Algiers
LARGEST CITY Algiers
HIGHEST POINT Tahat 9,852 ft. (3,003 m.)
MONETARY UNIT Algerian dinar
MAJOR LANGUAGES Arabic, Berber,
  French
MAJOR RELIGION Islam

BENIN

AREA 43,483 sq. mi. (112,620 sq. km.)
POPULATION 4,591,000
CAPITAL Porto-Novo
LARGEST CITY Cotonou
HIGHEST POINT Atakora Mts. 2,083 ft.
  (635 m.)
MONETARY UNIT CFA franc
MAJOR LANGUAGES Fon, Somba, Yoruba,
  Bariba, French, Mina, Dendi
MAJOR RELIGIONS Tribal religions, Islam,
  Roman Catholicism

CAPE VERDE

AREA 1,557 sq. mi. (4,033 sq. km.)
POPULATION 347,000
CAPITAL Praia
LARGEST CITY Praia
HIGHEST POINT 9,281 ft. (2,829 m.)
MONETARY UNIT Cape Verde escudo
MAJOR LANGUAGE Portuguese
MAJOR RELIGION Roman Catholicism

GAMBIA

AREA 4,127 sq. mi. (10,689 sq. km.)
POPULATION 688,000
CAPITAL Banjul
LARGEST CITY Banjul
HIGHEST POINT 100 ft. (30 m.)
MONETARY UNIT dalasi
MAJOR LANGUAGES Mandingo, Fulani,
  Wolof, English, Malinke
MAJOR RELIGIONS Islam, tribal religions,
  Christianity

GHANA

AREA 92,099 sq. mi. (238,536 sq. km.)
POPULATION 13,391,000
CAPITAL Accra
LARGEST CITY Accra
HIGHEST POINT Togo Hills 2,900 ft.
  (884 m.)
MONETARY UNIT cedi
MAJOR LANGUAGES Twi, Fante, Dagbani,
  Ewe, Ga, English, Hausa, Akan
MAJOR RELIGIONS Tribal religions,
  Christianity, Islam

GUINEA

AREA 94,925 sq. mi. (245,856 sq. km.)
POPULATION 6,706,000
CAPITAL Conakry
LARGEST CITY Conakry
HIGHEST POINT Nimba Mts. 6,070 ft.
  (1,850 m.)
MONETARY UNIT syli
MAJOR LANGUAGES Fulani, Mandingo,
  Susu, French
MAJOR RELIGIONS Islam, tribal religions

GUINEA-BISSAU

AREA 13,948 sq. mi. (36,125 sq. km.)
POPULATION 943,000
CAPITAL Bissau
LARGEST CITY Bissau
HIGHEST POINT 689 ft. (210 m.)
MONETARY UNIT Guinea-Bissau peso
MAJOR LANGUAGES Balante, Fulani,
  Crioulo, Mandingo, Portuguese
MAJOR RELIGIONS Islam, tribal religions,
  Roman Catholicism

IVORY COAST
(CÔTE-D'IVOIRE)

AREA 124,504 sq. mi. (322,465 sq. km.)
POPULATION 9,300,000
CAPITAL Yamoussoukro
LARGEST CITY Abidjan
HIGHEST POINT 5,745 ft. (1,751 m.)
MONETARY UNIT CFA franc
MAJOR LANGUAGES Bale, Bete, Senufu,
  French, Dioula
MAJOR RELIGIONS Tribal religions, Islam

LIBERIA

AREA 43,000 sq. mi. (111,370 sq. km.)
POPULATION 2,508,000
CAPITAL Monrovia
LARGEST CITY Monrovia
HIGHEST POINT Wutivi 5,584 ft.
  (1,702 m.)
MONETARY UNIT Liberian dollar
MAJOR LANGUAGES Kru, Kpelle, Bassa,
  Vai, English
MAJOR RELIGIONS Christianity, tribal
  religions, Islam

MALI

AREA 464,873 sq. mi. (1,204,021 sq. km.)
POPULATION 7,960,000
CAPITAL Bamako
LARGEST CITY Bamako
HIGHEST POINT Hombori Mts. 3,789 ft.
  (1,155 m.)
MONETARY UNIT CFA franc
MAJOR LANGUAGES Bambara, Senufu,
  Fulani, Soninke, French
MAJOR RELIGIONS Islam, tribal religions

MAURITANIA

AREA 419,229 sq. mi. (1,085,803 sq. km.)
POPULATION 1,970,000
CAPITAL Nouakchott
LARGEST CITY Nouakchott
HIGHEST POINT 2,972 ft. (906 m.)
MONETARY UNIT ouguiya
MAJOR LANGUAGES Arabic, Wolof,
  Tukolor, French
MAJOR RELIGION Islam

MOROCCO

AREA 172,414 sq. mi. (446,550 sq. km.)
POPULATION 24,522,000
CAPITAL Rabat
LARGEST CITY Casablanca
HIGHEST POINT Jeb. Toubkal 13,665 ft.
  (4,165 m.)
MONETARY UNIT dirham
MAJOR LANGUAGES Arabic, Berber, French
MAJOR RELIGIONS Islam, Judaism,
  Christianity

NIGER

AREA 489,189 sq. mi. (1,267,000 sq. km.)
POPULATION 7,250,000
CAPITAL Niamey
LARGEST CITY Niamey
HIGHEST POINT Banguezane 6,234 ft.
  (1,900 m.)
MONETARY UNIT CFA franc
MAJOR LANGUAGES Hausa, Songhai, Fulani,
  French, Tamashek, Djerma
MAJOR RELIGIONS Islam, tribal religions

NIGERIA

AREA 357,000 sq. mi. (924,630 sq. km.)
POPULATION 104,957,000
CAPITAL Lagos
LARGEST CITY Lagos
HIGHEST POINT Dimlang 6,700 ft. (2,042 m.)
MONETARY UNIT naira
MAJOR LANGUAGES Hausa, Yoruba, Ibo, Ijaw,
  Fulani, Tiv, Kanuri, Ibibio, English, Edo
MAJOR RELIGIONS Islam, Christianity,
  tribal religions

SÃO TOMÉ AND PRÍNCIPE

AREA 372 sq. mi. (963 sq. km.)
POPULATION 116,000
CAPITAL São Tomé
LARGEST CITY São Tomé
HIGHEST POINT Pico 6,640 ft. (2,024 m.)
MONETARY UNIT dobra
MAJOR LANGUAGES Bantu languages,
  Portuguese
MAJOR RELIGIONS Tribal religions,
  Roman Catholicism

SENEGAL

AREA 75,954 sq. mi. (196,720 sq. km.)
POPULATION 7,113,000
CAPITAL Dakar
LARGEST CITY Dakar
HIGHEST POINT Futa Jallon 1,640 ft. (500 m.)
MONETARY UNIT CFA franc
MAJOR LANGUAGES Wolof, Peul (Fulani),
  French, Mende, Mandingo, Dida
MAJOR RELIGIONS Islam, triba religions,
  Roman Catholicism

SIERRA LEONE

AREA 27,925 sq. mi. (72,325 sq. km.)
POPULATION 4,047,000
CAPITAL Freetown
LARGEST CITY Freetown
HIGHEST POINT Loma Mts. 6,390 ft.
  (1,947 m.)
MONETARY UNIT leone
MAJOR LANGUAGES Mende, Temne, Vai,
  English, Krio (pidgin)
MAJOR RELIGIONS Tribal religions, Islam,
  Christianity

TOGO

AREA 21,622 sq. mi. (56,000 sq. km.)
POPULATION 3,296,000
CAPITAL Lomé
LARGEST CITY Lomé
HIGHEST POINT Agou 3,445 ft. (1,050 m.)
MONETARY UNIT CFA franc
MAJOR LANGUAGES Ewe, French, Twi,
  Hausa
MAJOR RELIGIONS Tribal religions,
  Roman Catholicism, Islam

TUNISIA

AREA 63,378 sq. mi. (164,149 sq. km.)
POPULATION 7,465,000
CAPITAL Tunis
LARGEST CITY Tunis
HIGHEST POINT Jeb. Chambi 5,066 ft.
  (1,544 m.)
MONETARY UNIT Tunisian dinar
MAJOR LANGUAGES Arabic, French
MAJOR RELIGION Islam

BURKINA FASO

AREA 105,869 sq. mi. (274,200 sq. km.)
POPULATION 9,001,000
CAPITAL Ouagadougou
LARGEST CITY Ouagadougou
HIGHEST POINT 2,352 ft. (717 m.)
MONETARY UNIT CFA franc
MAJOR LANGUAGES Mossi, Lobi, French,
  Samo, Gourounsi
MAJOR RELIGIONS Islam, tribal religions,
  Roman Catholicism

WESTERN SAHARA

AREA 102,703 sq. mi.
  (266,000 sq. km.)
POPULATION 174,000
HIGHEST POINT 2,700 ft. (823 m.)
MAJOR LANGUAGE Arabic
MAJOR RELIGION Islam

Topography

0   200   400   600 MI.

0   200   400   600 KM.

5,000 m. 2,000 m. 1,000 m. 500 m. 200 m. 100 m. Sea Below
16,404 ft. 6,562 ft. 3,281 ft. 1,640 ft. 656 ft. 328 ft. Level

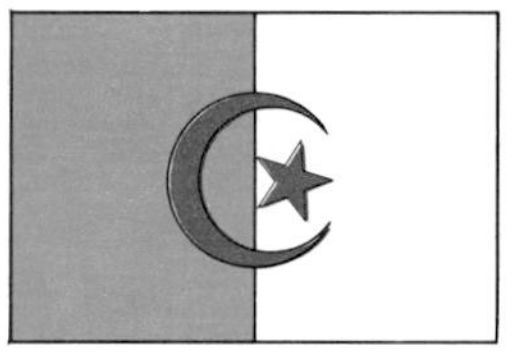
ALGERIA

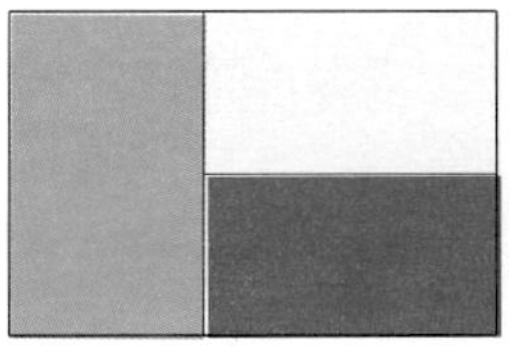
BENIN

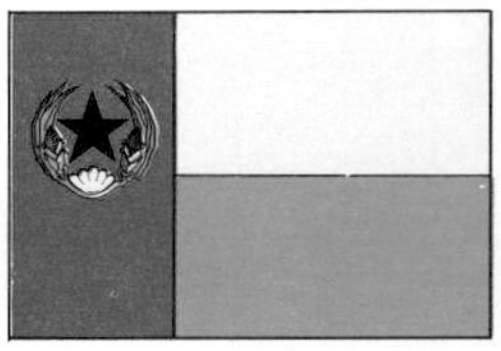
CAPE VERDE

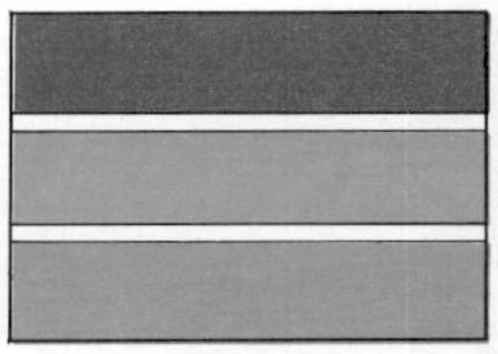
GAMBIA

GHANA

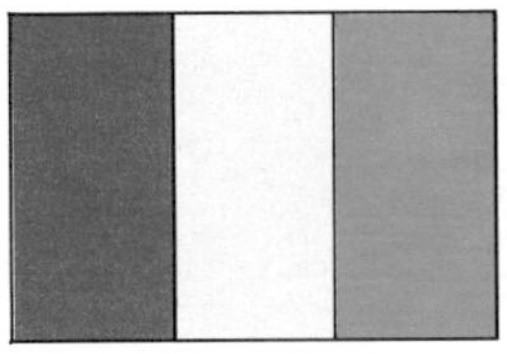
GUINEA

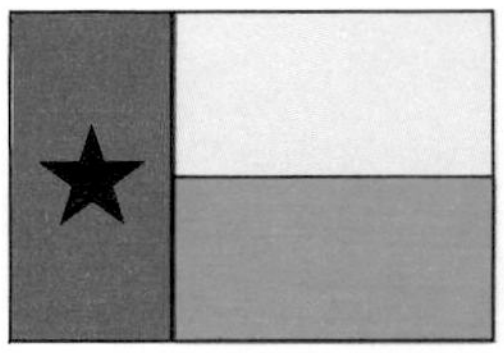
GUINEA-BISSAU

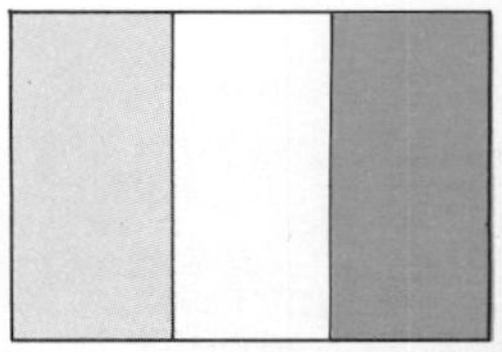
IVORY COAST

LIBERIA

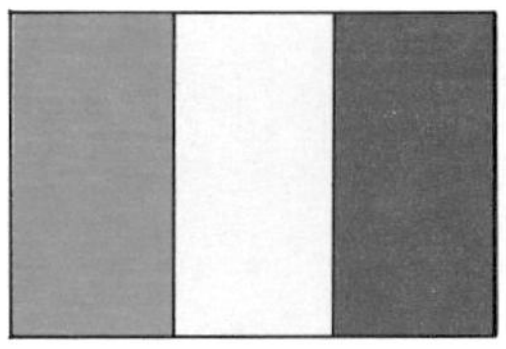
MALI

MAURITANIA

MOROCCO

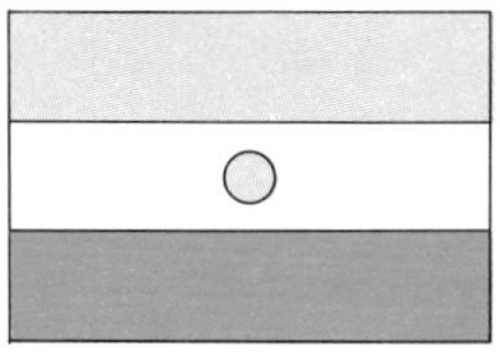
NIGER

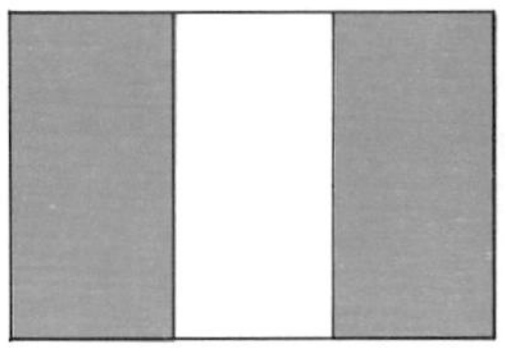
NIGERIA

SÃO TOMÉ AND PRINCIPE

SENEGAL

SIERRA LEONE

TOGO

TUNISIA

BURKINA FASO

ALGERIA

CITIES and TOWNS

Adrar 28,495 .... D3
Aïn Beïda 67,281 .... F1
Aïn Sefra 22,400 .... D2
Aïn Temouchent 48,935 .... D1
Algiers (cap.) 1,687,579 .... E1
Annaba 227,795 .... F1
Aoulef 10,259 .... E3
Batna 184,833 .... F1
Béchar 107,042 .... D2
Bejaïa 118,233 .... F1
Beni Abbès 7,370 .... D2
Beni Saf 30,700 .... D1
Biskra 129,611 .... F2
Blida 131,615 .... E1
Bone (Annaba) 227,795 .... F1
Bordj Bou Arreridj 86,997 .... E1
Bordj Omar Driss 1,900 .... F3
Boufarik 54,023 .... E1
Bougie (Bejaïa) 118,233 .... F1
Bou Saâda 50,000 .... E1
Brezina 10,000 .... E2
Cherchell 32,572 .... E1
Constantine 449,602 .... F1
Dellys 29,700 .... E1
Djelfa 88,929 .... E2
Djemaa 34,600 .... F2
El Abiod Sidi Cheikh 15,300 .... E2
El Asnam 103,998 .... E1
El Bayadh 44,925 .... E2
El Djezair (Algiers) (cap.) 1,687,579 .... E1
El Goléa 24,400 .... E2
El Oued 73,093 .... F2
Ghardaïa 62,518 .... E2
Ghazaouet 29,795 .... D2
Guelma 84,826 .... F1
Guerara 22,300 .... E2
Hassi Messaoud F2
Hassi R'Mel 10,545 .... E2
In Guezzam 10,304 .... F5
In Salah 20,733 .... E3
Jijel 69,274 .... F1
Khemis Miliana 57,101 .... E1
Ksar el Boukhari 41,200 .... E1
Laghouat 71,808 .... E2
Mascara 70,885 .... D1
Mecheria 40,251 .... D2
Médéa 84,062 .... E1
Metlili Chaamba 21,300 .... E2
Miliana 36,400 .... E1
Mohammadia 58,967 .... D1
Mostaganem 115,302 .... D1
M'Sila 82,877 .... E1
Oran 598,525 .... D1
Orléansville (El Asnam) 103,998 .... E1
Ouargla 76,270 .... F2
Ouled Djellal 33,278 .... F2
Philippeville (Skikda) 128,503 .... F1
Reggane 10,061 .... D3
Relizane 83,864 .... E1
Saïda 84,371 .... E2
Sétif 185,786 .... F1
Sidi Bel-Abbes 154,745 .... D1
Skikda 128,503 .... F1
Souk Ahras 85,873 .... F1
Tamanrasset 38,146 .... F4
Tébessa 111,688 .... F1
Ténès 26,510 .... E1
Tiaret 105,562 .... E1
Timimoun 21,556 .... E3
Tindouf 6,500 .... C3
Tizi Ouzou 93,025 .... E1
Tlemcen 108,145 .... D2
Touggourt 75,600 .... F2
Zaouiet Kounta 10,707 .... D3

OTHER FEATURES

Adrar des Iforas (plat.) E5
Ahaggar (range) F4
Anaï (well) G4
Aouinet Bel Egrâ (well) C3
Atlas (mts.) E2
Aurès (lag.) F1
Azzel Mati, Sebkha (lake) E3
Bougaroun (cape) F1
Chech, Erg (des.) D3
Chelia (mt.) F1
Chelif (riv.) E1
Chergui, Chott Ech (salt lake) E2
Dra, Wadi (dry river) C3
Dra Hamada (plat.) C3
Gourara (oasis) E3
Grand Erg Occidental (des.) E2
Grand Erg Oriental (des.) F2
Guir Hamada (des.) D2
High Plateaus (ranges) D2
Iguidi, Erg (des.) C3
In Ezzane (well) G4
Irharhar, Wadi (dry river) F3
Kabylia (reg.) E1
Mediterranean (sea) E1
Medjerda (riv.) F1
Mekerrhane, Sebkha (salt lake) E3
Melrhir, Chott (salt lake) F2
Mouydir (mts.) E3
Mya, Wadi (dry river) E2
M'zab (oasis) E2
Raoui, Erg er (des.) D3
Rhir, Wadi (dry river) F2
Sahara (des.) E4
Saharan Atlas (ranges) E2
Saoura, Wadi (dry river) D3
Souf (oasis) F2
Tademaït, Plateau du (plat.) E3
Tafassasset, Wadi (dry river) F4
Tahat (mt.) F4
Tamanrasset, Wadi (dry river) E4
Tanezrouft (des.) E4
Tassili N'Ahagger (plat.) E4
Tassili N'Ajjer (plat.) F3
Tidikelt (oasis) E3
Timmissao (well) E4
Tindouf, Sebkha de (salt lake) C3
Tinrhert, Hamada de (des.) F3
Tni Haïa (well) D4
Touat (oasis) E3
Touila (well) C3

BENIN

CITIES and TOWNS

Abomey 38,000 .... E7
Cotonou 178,000 .... E7
Grand-Popo E7
Kandi E6
Natitingou 49,000 .... E6
Ouidah E7
Parakou 21,000 .... E7
Porto-Novo (cap.) 104,000 .... E7

OTHER FEATURES

Atakora (mts.) E6
Benin (bight) E8
Guinea (gulf) E8
Mono (riv.) E7
Niger (riv.) E6
Ouémé (riv.) E7
Slave Coast (reg.) E7
Sudan (reg.) E6

BURKINA FASO

CITIES and TOWNS

Banfora 12,358 .... D6
Bobo Dioulasso 115,063 .... D6
Bogandé E6
Dédougou D6
Diébougou D6
Djibo D6
Dori D6
Fada-N'Gourma 12,000 .... E6
Gaoua D6
Kaya 18,000 .... D6
Koudougou 36,838 .... D6
Koupela D6
Léo D6
Ouagadougou (cap.) 172,661 .... D6
Ouahigouya 25,690 .... D6
Po D6
Tenkodogo E6
Tougan D6
Yako D6
Zabré D6

OTHER FEATURES

Black Volta (Mouhoun) (riv.) D6
Comoé (riv.) D7
Mouhoun (riv.) D6
Nakanbe (riv.) D6
Nazinan (riv.) D6
Oti (riv.) E7
Red Volta (Nazinan) (riv.) D6
Sudan (reg.) D6
White Volta (Nakanbe) (riv.) D6

CAPE VERDE

CITIES and TOWNS

Mindelo 28,797 .... A7
Praia (cap.) 21,494 .... B8
Ribeira Grande 1,892 .... B7
Sal Rei 1,296 .... B8

OTHER FEATURES

Boa Vista (isl.) B8
Brava (isl.) B8
Fogo (isl.) B8
Maio (isl.) B8
Sal (isl.) B7
Santa Luzia (isl.) B8
Santo Antão (isl.) A7
São Nicolau (isl.) B8
São Tiago (isl.) B8
São Vicente (isl.) B7

GAMBIA

CITIES and TOWNS

Banjul (cap.) 39,476 .... A6
Basse Santa Su 2,899 .... B6
Brikama 9,483 .... A6
Georgetown 2,510 .... A6

GHANA

CITIES and TOWNS

Accra (cap.) 859,600 .... D7
Attebubu 9,800 .... D7
Axim 13,100 .... D8
Bawku 33,900 .... D6
Bekwai 11,800 .... D7
Berekum 21,900 .... D7
Bolgatanga 31,500 .... D6
Cape Coast 57,700 .... D7
Damongo 12,600 .... D7
Dunkwa 16,900 .... D7
Elmina 15,600 .... D8
Ho 37,200 .... E7
Keta 12,700 .... E7
Kintampo 14,100 .... D7
Koforidua 54,400 .... D7
Kpandu 15,800 .... D7
Kumasi 348,900 .... D7
Mampong 19,800 .... D7
Nsawam 31,900 .... D7
Obuasi 60,100 .... D7
Oda 20,957 .... D7
Prestea 16,300 .... D7
Salaga 10,600 .... D7
Sekondi 32,400 .... D8
Sunyani 36,100 .... D7
Takoradi 61,500 .... D8
Tamale 136,800 .... D7
Tarkwa 22,000 .... D7
Tema 99,600 .... E7
Wa 36,000 .... D6
Wenchi 18,400 .... D7
Winneba 26,200 .... D7
Yendi 30,700 .... D7

OTHER FEATURES

Ashanti (reg.) D7
Benin (bight) E8
Black Volta (riv.) D7
Gold Coast (reg.) D8
Guinea (gulf) E8
Oti (riv.) E7
Red Volta (riv.) D6
Saint Paul (cape) E7
Three Points (cape) D8
Volta (lake) D7
Volta (riv.) E7
White Volta (riv.) D7

GUINEA

CITIES and TOWNS

Boffa B6
Conakry (cap.) 525,671 .... B7
Dabola B6
Dubréka B7
Fria B6
Kankan 85,310 .... C6
Kérouané C7
Kindia 79,861 .... B6
Kissidougou B7
Koundara 6,000 .... B6
Kouroussa C6
Labé 79,670 .... B6
Mali B6
N'Zérékoré 23,000 .... C7
Siguiri C6
Télimélé 12,000 .... B6
Tougué B6

OTHER FEATURES

Bafing (riv.) B6
Bakoy (riv.) B6
Futa Jallon (lag.) B6
Los (isls.) B7
Milo (riv.) C7
Moa (riv.) B7
Niger (riv.) C6
Nimba (lag.) C7
Verga (cape) B6

GUINEA-BISSAU

CITIES and TOWNS

Bissau (cap.) 109,486 .... A6
Bolama ○ 9,133 .... A6
Bubaque ○ 8,441 .... A6
Cacheu ○ 15,194 .... A6

OTHER FEATURES

Bijagós (isls.) A6

IVORY COAST

CITIES and TOWNS

Abengourou 31,239 .... D7
Abidjan 6 85,828 .... D7
Aboisso 14,272 .... D7
Agboville 27,192 .... D7
Bingerville 18,218 .... D7
Bondoukou 19,111 .... D7
Bouaflé 15,917 .... C7
Bouaké 1 73,248 .... D7
Dabou 23,870 .... D7
Daloa 60,958 .... C7
Danané 19,872 .... C7
Dimbokro 30,986 .... D7
Divo 37,896 .... C7
Ferkessédougou 25,307 .... D7
Gagnoa 42,362 .... C7
Grand-Bassam 25,808 .... D7
Grand-Lahou 4,070 .... C8
Guiglo 10,441 .... C7
Issia 11,143 .... C7
Katiola 21,559 .... C7
Korhogo 47,657 .... C7
Man 50,315 .... C7
Odienné 13,864 .... C7
Port-Bouet 72,616 .... D7
San Pedro 27,616 .... C8
Séguéla 12,587 .... C7
Sinfra 16,399 .... C7
Tabou 7,255 .... C8
Toumodi 12,983 .... D7
Yamoussoukro (cap.) 35,585 .... C7

OTHER FEATURES

Aby (lag.) D8
Bagoé (riv.) C6
Bandama (riv.) C7
Baoulé (riv.) C6
Black Volta (riv.) D6
Cavally (riv.) C7
Comoé (riv.) D7
Ebrié (lag.) D8
Guinea (gulf) E8
Ivory Coast (reg.) C8
Kossou, Lac de (lake) C7
Nimba (lag.) C7
Sassandra (riv.) C7

LIBERIA

CITIES and TOWNS

Buchanan 23,999 .... B7
Gbarnga 6,896 .... C7
Greenville 8,462 .... C8
Harbel 11,445 .... B7
Harper 10,627 .... C8
Monrovia (cap.) 166,507 .... B7
River Cess 2,041 .... C7
Robertsport 2,562 .... B7
Tapeta 3,927 .... C7
Tubmanburg 14,089 .... B7
Zwedru 6,094 .... C7

OTHER FEATURES

Bong (range) B7
Cavalla (riv.) C7
Cestos (riv.) C7
Grain Coast (reg.) B8
Kru Coast (reg.) C8
Mano (riv.) B7
Mount (cape) B7
Nimba (lag.) C7
Palmas (cape) C8
Roberts Field Int'l Airport C7

MALI

CITIES and TOWNS

Ansongo 3,485 .... E5
Bafoulabé 2,163 .... B6
Bamako (cap.) 404,022 .... C6
Banamba 6,776 .... C6
Bandiagara 8,920 .... D6
Bankass 3,229 .... D6
Bougouni 17,246 .... C6
Bourem 4,538 .... E5
Dioila 4,953 .... C6
Dire 8,941 .... D5
Djenné 10,251 .... D6
Douentza 6,746 .... D6
Gao 30,714 .... E5
Goundam 10,262 .... D5
Gourma-Rharous 4,671 .... D5
Kéniéba 4,510 .... B6
Kadiolo 3,991 .... C6
Kangaba 3,184 .... C6
Kati 24,991 .... C6
Kayes 44,736 .... B6
Ké-Macina 5,426 .... C6
Kidal 3,308 .... E5
Kita 17,538 .... C6
Kolokani 8,923 .... C6
Kolondiéba 5,882 .... C6
Koulikoro 16,376 .... C6
Koutiala 27,497 .... C6
Ménaka 3,693 .... E5
Mopti 53,885 .... D6
Nara 6,091 .... C5
Niafunké 6,399 .... D5
Niono 12,290 .... C6
Nioro 11,617 .... C5
San 22,962 .... D6
Ségou 64,890 .... C6
Sikasso 47,030 .... C6
Ténenkou 4,708 .... C6
Timbuktu (Tombouctou) 20,483 .... D5
Yanfolila 3,809 .... C6
Yelimané 1,481 .... B5
Yorosso 2,390 .... C6

OTHER FEATURES

Achourat (well) D4
Adrar des Iforas (plat.) E5
Agueraktem (well) C4
Asselar (well) D5
Azaouad (reg.) D5
Azaouak (dry riv.) E5
Bafing (riv.) B6
Bagoé (riv.) C6
Bakoy (riv.) B6
Bani (riv.) C6
Baoulé (dry riv.) C6
Baoulé (riv.) C6
Bir Ksaib Ounane (well) C4
Bir Ounane (well) D4
Chech, Erg (des.) D4
Debo (lake) D5
El Mraiti (well) D5
Faguibine (lake) D5
Falémé (riv.) B6
Haricha Hamada (des.) D4
Hombori (mts.) D5
In Dagouber (well) D4
Macina (depr.) D6
Niger (riv.) D5
Oum el Asel (well) D4
Sahara (des.) D4
Sekkane, Erg (des.) D4
Senegal (riv.) B5
Sudan (reg.) D6
Tadjnout Hagguerete (well) D4
Terhazza (ruins) C4
Tilemsi (valley) E5
Toufourine (well) C4

MAURITANIA

CITIES and TOWNS

Aïoun el Atrous C5
Akjoujt 8,044 .... B5
Aleg 6,415 .... B5
Atar 16,326 .... B4
Bassikounou C5
Boutilimit 7,261 .... B5
Fdérik (Fort Gouraud) 2,160 .... B4
Káedi 20,248 .... B5
Kiffa 10,629 .... B5
M'Bout B5
Néma 8,232 .... C5
Nouadhibou 21,961 .... A4
Nouakchott (cap.) 134,986 .... A5
Oualata C5
Rosso 16,466 .... A5
Sélibaby 5,994 .... B5
Tidjikja 7,870 .... B5
Timbédra 5,317 .... C5
Zouïrât 17,474 .... B4

OTHER FEATURES

Adafer (reg.) B5
Adrar (reg.) B4
Affolé (reg.) B5
Agueraktem (well) C4
Aïn ben Tili (well) C3
Arguin (bay) A4
Assaba (reg.) B5
Atoui, Wadi (dry riv.) B4
Ben Guerdane (well) B3
Bir el Khzaim (well) C4
Blanc (cape) A4
Brakna (reg.) B5
Chegga (well) C3
Djouf, El (des.) C4
El Mrayer (well) C4
El Mreïti (well) C4
Gorgol (reg.) B5
Hodh (reg.) C5
Iguidi, Erg (des.) C3
Inchiri (reg.) A5
Koumbi Saleh (ruins) C5

ėvrier (bay) A4
akteïr (des.) B4
eraia (reg.) C5
irik (Timiris) (cape) A5
uarane (reg.) B4
ahara (des.) C4
enegal (riv.) B5
agant (reg.) B5
dra (isl.) A5
miris (cape) A5
ouila (well) C3
rarza (reg.) A5

MOROCCO

CITIES and TOWNS

gadir 61,192 .... C2
l Hoceima 18,686 .... D1
zemmour 17,182 .... C2
zrou 20,756 .... C2
eni Mellal 53,826 .... C2
oujad 18,838 .... C2
asablanca 1,506,373 .... C2
ar-el-Beida (Casablanca) 1,506,373 .... C2
Jadida 55,501 .... C2
Kelaa des Srarhna 17,163 ... C2
r Rachidia 16,775 .... D2
ssaouira 30,061 .... C2
ès (Fez) 325,327 .... D2
erada 30,633 .... D2
enitra 139,206 .... C2
henifra 25,526 .... C2
houribga 73,667 .... C2
sar el Kebir 48,262 .... C2
arache 45,710 .... C1
larrakech 332,741 .... C2
lazagan (El Jadida) 55,501 .... C2
leknès 248,369 .... C2
lcgador (Essaouira) 30,061 .. B2
lchammedia 70,392 .... C2
ador 32,490 .... D1
ued Zem 33,323 .... C2
uezzane 33,267 .... C2
ujda 175,532 .... D2
ort-Lyautey (Kénitra) 139,206 .... C2
abat (cap.) 367,620 .... C2
ai 129,113 .... C2
adia D2
a é 155,557 .... C2
efrou 28,607 .... D2
ettat 42,325 .... C2
idi Ifni 13,650 .... B3
idi Kacem 26,831 .... C2
angier (Tanger) 187,894 .... C1
afaya 1,104 .... B3
aroudannt 22,272 .... C2
aza 55,157 .... D2
étouan 139,105 .... C1
oussoufia 22,435 .... C2

OTHER FEATURES

nti-Atlas (ranges) C3
tlas (mts.) C2
ani, Jebel (mts.) C3
eddouza, Ras (cape) C2
ra, Wadi (dry riv.) C3
ibraltar (str.) C1
igh Atlas (ranges) C2
uby (cape) B3
lediterranean (sea) D1
liddle Atlas (ranges) C2
loulouya (riv.) D2
heris, Wadi (dry riv.) D2
hir (cape) B2
if, Er (range) D2
arhro, Jebel (mts.) C2
ebou (riv.) C2
im (cape) B2
oubkal, Jebel (mt.) C2
iz, Wadi (dry riv.) D2

NIGER

CITIES and TOWNS

gadès 11,000 .... F5
rhli (Arlit) F5
ilma G5
irni-N'Konni 10,000 .... E6
osso G6
akoro F6
ffa G6
osso E6
ilingué 10,000 .... E6
aya 5,000 .... E6
ouré G6
férouane F5
r-Gall F5
Vagaria F6
Vainé-Soro G6
Varadi 45,852 .... F6
N'Guigmi G6
Niamey (cap.) 225,314 .... E6
Say E6
Tahoua 31,265 .... F6
Tanout F6
Tillabéry E6
Zinder 58,436 .... F6

OTHER FEATURES

Achégour (well) G5
Agadem (well) G5
Air (mts.) F5
Anaye (well) G5
Assakarai (dry riv.) F5
Azaoua (reg.) E5
Azbine (Air) (mts.) F5
Eagam (well) F5
Eanguezane (mt.) F5
Eedouaram (well) G5
Chad (lake) G6
Dallol Bosso (dry riv.) E6
Dillia (dry riv.) G5
Djado (plat.) G4
El War (well) G4
In Azaoua (well) F4
Komadugu Yobe (riv.) G6
Mantas (well) E5
Niger (riv.) E6
Rima (riv.) F6
Sahara (des.) F4
Sudan (reg.) F6
Tafassasset, Wadi (dry riv.) F4
Talak (reg.) E5
Ténéré (des.) G5
Timboulaga (well) F5
Tummo (El War) (well) G4
Zoo Baba (well) G5

NIGERIA

STATES

Abuja Capital Territory F7
Anambra 2,300,000 .... F7
Bauchi 2,496,329 .... F6
Bendel 2,336,000 .... F7
Benue 2,641,496 .... F7
Borno 2,853,553 .... G6
Cross River 3,633,582 .... F7
Gongola 1,585,200 .... G7
Imo 5,000,000 .... F7
Kaduna 4,098,303 .... F6
Kano 5,775,000 .... F6
Kwara 5,240,600 .... E7
Lagos 1,100,000 .... E7
Niger 2,900,000 .... F7
Ogun 1,448,966 .... E7
Ondo 2,727,676 .... F7
Oyo 5,208,884 .... E7
Plateau 1,367,450 .... F7
Rivers 1,544,314 .... F8
Sokoto 1,367,450 .... F6

CITIES and TOWNS

Abeokuta 253,000 .... E7
Abuja F7
Ado 213,000 .... E7
Aku F7
Akure F7
Baga G6
Bama G6
Baro F7
Bauchi F6
Benin City 136,000 .... F7
Biu G6
Bonny F8
Calabar 103,000 .... F7
Degema F8
Dikwa G6
Ede 182,000 .... E7
Enugu 187,000 .... F7
Geidam G6
Gumel F6
Gummi F6
Gusau F6
Ibadan 847,000 .... E7
Ibi F7
Ife 176,000 .... E7
Ijebu-Ode E7
Ilesha 224,000 .... E7
Ilorin 282,000 .... E7
Iseyin 115,083 .... E7
Iwo 214,000 .... E7
Jega E6
Jos F7
Kaduna 202,000 .... F6
Kano 399,000 .... F6
Katsina 109,424 .... F6
Katsina Ala F7
Kontagora F6
Kumo G7
Kuta F7
Lagos (cap.) 1,060,848 .... E7
Maiduguri 189,000 .... G6
Maigatari F6
Makurdi F7
Minna F7
Nnewi F7
Nsukka F7
Ogbomosho 432,000 .... E7
Ondo E7
Onitsha 220,000 .... F7
Oshogbo 282,000 .... F7
Owerri F7
Owo F7
Oyo 152,000 .... E7
Panyam F7
Port Harcourt 242,000 .... F8
Shaki E7
Shendam F7
Sokoto F6
Toungo G7
Wamba F7
Wukari F7
Yan G7
Yelwa F6
Yola G7
Zaria 224,000 .... F6

OTHER FEATURES

Adamawa (reg.) G7
Benin (bight) E8
Benue (riv.) F7
Biafra (bight) F8
Biu (plat.) G6
Bonny (bight) F8
Chad (lake) G6
Cross (riv.) F7
Dimlang (mt.) G7
Donga (riv.) G7
Gongola (riv.) G6
Guinea (gulf) E8
Hadejia (riv.) F6
Jos (plat.) F7
Kaduna (riv.) F7
Kainji (res.) E6
Komadugu Yobe (riv.) G6
Niger (delta) F8
Niger (riv.) F7
Osse (riv.) F7
Rima (riv.) F6
Slave Coast (reg.) E7
Sokoto (riv.) F6
Sudan (reg.) F6

PORTUGAL-Madeira

CITIES and TOWNS

Funchal (cap.) 38,340 .... A2

OTHER FEATURES

Desertas (isls.) A2
Madeira (isl.) A2
Pôrto Santo (isl.) A2

SÃO TOMÉ AND PRINCIPE

CITIES and TOWNS

São Tomé (cap.) 7,681 .... F8
Santo António 1,618 .... F8

OTHER FEATURES

Guinea (gulf) E8
Príncipe (isl.) F8
São Tomé (isl.) F8

SENEGAL

CITIES and TOWNS

Bignona 14,537 .... A6
Dagana 10,506 .... A5
Dakar (cap.) 798,792 .... A6
Diourbel 50,618 .... A6
Kaffrine 11,211 .... A6
Kaolack 106,899 .... A6
Kolda 19,302 .... B6
Louga 35,063 .... A5
Matam 10,002 .... B5
M'Bour 37,663 .... A6
Nioro-du-Rip 7,824 .... A6
Podor 6,914 .... B5
Rufisque A6
Saint-Louis 88,404 .... A5
Tambacounda 25,147 .... B6
Thiès 117,333 .... A5
Tivaouane 17,351 .... A5
Ziguinchor 72,726 .... A6

OTHER FEATURES

Casamance (riv.) A6
Falémé (riv.) B6
Ferlo (reg.) B6
Gambia (riv.) B6
Senegal (riv.) B5
Verde (cape) A6

SIERRA LEONE

CITIES and TOWNS

Bo 42,216 .... B7
Bonthe 6,230 .... B7
Freetown (cap.) 274,000 .... B7
Kabala 4,610 .... B7
Kenema 33,880 .... B7
Makeni 28,684 .... B7
Moyamba 4,564 .... B7
Pendembu 2,696 .... B7
Port Loko 5,809 .... B7
Pujehun 2,034 .... B7

OTHER FEATURES

Loma, Mansa (lag.) B7
Mano (riv.) B7
Moa (riv.) B7
Sherbro (isl.) B7
Yawri (bay) B7

SPAIN-Canary Islands, Ceuta and Melilla

CITIES and TOWNS

Arrecife 21,310 .... B3
Ceuta 60,639 .... C1
Las Palmas de Gran Canaria 260,368 .... B3
Melilla 64,942 .... D1
Santa Cruz de la Palma 10,393 .... A3
Santa Cruz de Tenerife 74,910 .... A3

OTHER FEATURES

Canary (isls.) A3
Fuerteventura (isl.) B3
Gomera (isl.) A3
Grand Canary (isl.) A3
Hierro (isl.) A3
Lanzarote (isl.) B3
La Palma (isl.) A3
Tenerife (isl.) A3

TOGO

CITIES and TOWNS

Aného (Anécho) 10,889 .... E7
Atakpamé 17,440 .... E7
Dapaong 10,100 .... E6
Kpalimé 19,801 .... E7
Lama-Kara 9,400 .... E7
Lomé (cap.) 148,443 .... E7
Mango 9,600 .... E6
Sokodé 29,623 .... E7

OTHER FEATURES

Benin (bight) E8
Guinea (gulf) E8
Mono (riv.) E7
Oti (riv.) E7
Slave Coast (reg.) E7

TUNISIA

CITIES and TOWNS

Béja 39,226 .... F1
Ben Gardane 6,593 .... G2
Bizerte 62,856 .... F1
El Djem 10,666 .... G1
El Kef 27,939 .... F1
Gabès 40,585 .... F2
Gafsa 42,225 .... F2
Halq el Oued 41,912 .... G1
Jendouba 18,127 .... F1
Kairouan 54,546 .... F1
Kalaa-Kebia 23,508 .... F1
Kasserine 22,594 .... F1
La Goulette (Halq el Oued) 41,912 .... G1
La Skhirra 4,565 .... G2
Mahdia 25,711 .... G1
Mareth 2,185 .... F2
Mateur 19,645 .... F1
Médenine 15,826 .... G2
Menzel Bourguiba 42,111 .... F1
Menzel Temime 18,857 .... G1
Moknine 26,035 .... G1
Monastir 26,759 .... G1
Msaken 33,559 .... G1
Nabeul 30,476 .... G1
Nefta 12,476 .... F2
Sfax 171,297 .... G2
Sousse 69,530 .... G1
Tatahouine 10,399 .... G2
Tozeur 16,772 .... F2
Tunis (cap.) 550,404 .... G1
Zarzis 14,420 .... G2

OTHER FEATURES

Abiad, Ras el (Blanc) (cape) ... G1
Blanc (cape) G1
Bon (cape) G1
Chambi, Jebel (mt.) F2
Djerba (isl.) G2
Djerid, Shott el (salt lake) F2
Gabès (gulf) G2
Grand Erg Oriental (des.) F2
Hammamet (gulf) G1
Jefara (reg.) G2
Kerkennah (isls.) G2
Mediterranean (sea) F1
Medjerda (riv.) F1
Tib, Ras el (Bon) (cape) G1
Tunis (gulf) G1

WESTERN SAHARA

CITIES and TOWNS

Dakhla 6,554 .... A4
El Aaiún (Laayoune) 24,519 .... B3
Villa Cisneros (Dakhla) 6,554 .. A4

OTHER FEATURES

Ausert (well) B4
Barbas (cape) A4
Bir Ganduz (well) A4
Bir Nzaran (well) B4
Blanc (cape) A4
Bojador (cape) B3
Durnford (pt.) A4
Guelta de Zemmur (well) B3
Saguia el Hamra (dry riv.) B3
Tichlá (well) B4
Atoui, Wadi (dry riv.) B4

○ Population of sub-district or division.

Agriculture, Industry and Resources

DOMINANT LAND USE

- Cereals, Horticulture, Livestock
- Market Gardening, Diversified Tropical Crops
- Plantation Agriculture
- Oases
- Pasture Livestock
- Nomadic Livestock Herding
- Forests
- Nonagricultural Land

MAJOR MINERAL OCCURRENCES

Al	Bauxite	Hg	Mercury
Au	Gold	Mn	Manganese
C	Coal	Na	Salt
Co	Cobalt	O	Petroleum
Cr	Chromium	P	Phosphates
Cu	Copper	Pb	Lead
D	Diamonds	Sb	Antimony
Fe	Iron Ore	Sn	Tin
G	Natural Gas	Ti	Titanium
Gn	Granite	U	Uranium
Gp	Gypsum	Zn	Zinc

Water Power

Major Industrial Areas

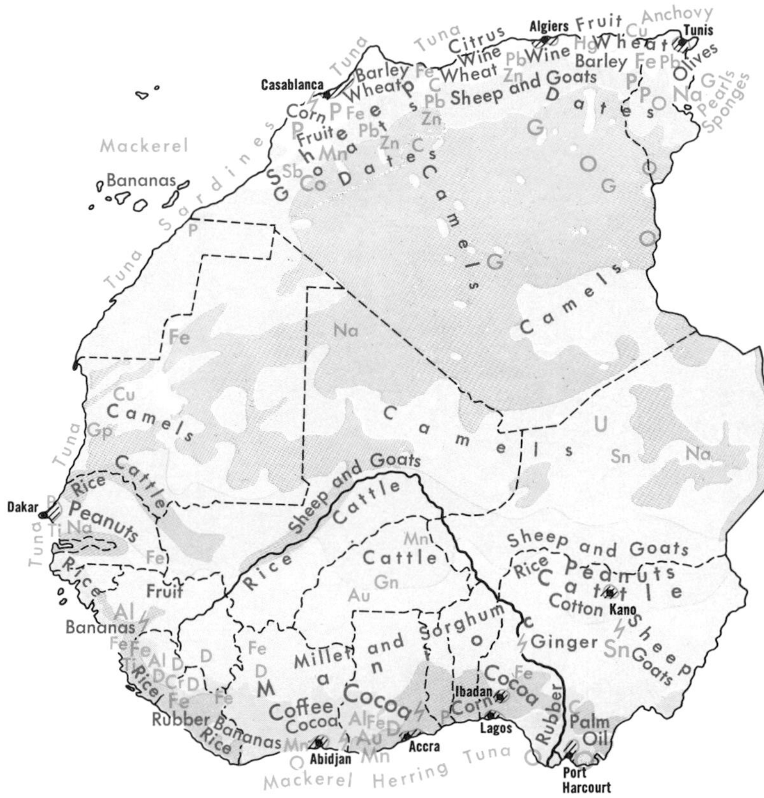

LIBYA

EGYPT

CHAD

SUDAN

ETHIOPIA

DJIBOUTI

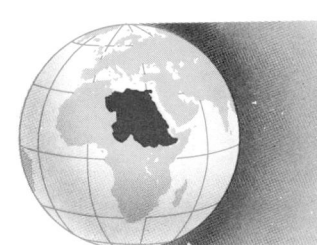

LIBYA

AREA   679,358 sq. mi. (1,759,537 sq. km.)
POPULATION   3,773,000
CAPITAL   Tripoli
LARGEST CITY   Tripoli
HIGHEST POINT   Bette Pk. 7,500 ft. (2,286 m.)
MONETARY UNIT   Libyan dinar
MAJOR LANGUAGES   Arabic, Berber
MAJOR RELIGION   Islam

EGYPT

AREA   386,659 sq. mi. (1,001,447 sq. km.)
POPULATION   53,080,000
CAPITAL   Cairo
LARGEST CITY   Cairo
HIGHEST POINT   Jeb. Katherina 8,651 ft.
   (2,637 m.)
MONETARY UNIT   Egyptian pound
MAJOR LANGUAGE   Arabic
MAJOR RELIGIONS   Islam, Coptic Christianity

CHAD

AREA   495,752 sq. mi. (1,283,998 sq. km.)
POPULATION   5,538,000
CAPITAL   N'Djamena
LARGEST CITY   N'Djamena
HIGHEST POINT   Emi Koussi 11,204 ft.
   (3,415 m.)
MONETARY UNIT   CFA franc
MAJOR LANGUAGES   Arabic, Bagirmi, French,
   Sara, Massa, Moudang
MAJOR RELIGIONS   Islam, tribal religions

SUDAN

AREA   967,494 sq. mi. (2,505,809 sq. km.)
POPULATION   24,485,000
CAPITAL   Khartoum
LARGEST CITY   Khartoum
HIGHEST POINT   Jeb. Marra 10,073 ft.
   (3,070 m.)
MONETARY UNIT   Sudanese pound
MAJOR LANGUAGES   Arabic, Dinka, Nubian,
   Beja, Nuer
MAJOR RELIGIONS   Islam, tribal religions

ETHIOPIA

AREA   471,776 sq. mi. (1,221,900 sq. km.)
POPULATION   50,774,000
CAPITAL   Addis Ababa
LARGEST CITY   Addis Ababa
HIGHEST POINT   Ras Dashan 15,157 ft.
   (4,620 m.)
MONETARY UNIT   birr
MAJOR LANGUAGES   Amharic, Gallinya,
   Tigrinya, Somali, Sidamo, Arabic, Ge'ez
MAJOR RELIGIONS   Coptic Christianity, Islam

DJIBOUTI

AREA   8,880 sq. mi. (23,000 sq. km.)
POPULATION   456,000
CAPITAL   Djibouti
LARGEST CITY   Djibouti
HIGHEST POINT   Moussa Ali 6,768 ft.
   (2,063 m.)
MONETARY UNIT   Djibouti franc
MAJOR LANGUAGES   Arabic, Somali,
   Afar, French
MAJOR RELIGIONS   Islam,
   Roman Catholicism

Northeastern Africa

CONIC EQUAL AREA PROJECTION

SCALE OF MILES
0   50   100   200   300

SCALE OF KILOMETERS
0   50   100   200   300

Capitals of Countries _ _ _ _ _ _ _ _ _ ☆
Other Capitals _ _ _ _ _ _ _ _ _ _ ◉
International Boundaries _ _ _ _ _ _ _ _
Internal Boundaries _ _ _ _ _ _ _ _

Scale 1:14,300,000

© Copyright HAMMOND INCORPORATED, Maplewood, N.J.

CHAD

CITIES and TOWNS

Abéché 28,100	D5
Abou Deïa	C5
Adré	D5
Am-Timan 4,200	D5
Arada	D4
Ati 7,500	C5
Baibokoum 5,500	C6
Biltine 3,900	D5
Bitkine 5,000	C5
Bokoro 6,500	C5
Bol 2,500	B5
Bongor 14,300	C5
Bousso 4,500	C5
Doba 13,300	C6
Fada	D4
Faya-Largeau 6,800	C4
Fianga 10,000	C6
Goré	C6
Goz Beïda	D5
Guéréda	D4
Iriba	D4
Kélo 16,800	C6
Koumra 17,000	C6
Kouno	C6
Kyabé 5,000	C6
Laï 10,400	C6
Léré	B6
Mangueigne	D5
Mao 4,900	C5
Massakory	C5
Massénya	C5
Melfi	C5
Mogororo	D5
Moïssala 5,100	C6
Mongo 8,300	C5
Moundou 39,600	C6
Moussoro 7,700	C5
N'Djamena (cap.) 179,000	C5
Oum Hadjer 5,600	C5
Ounianga-Kébir	D4
Pala 13,200	B6
Sarh 43,700	C6
Wour	C3
Zouar	C3

OTHER FEATURES

Aouk, Bahr (riv.)	D5
Azoum, Bahr (riv.)	D5
Baguirmi (reg.)	C5
Bahr el Ghazal (dry riv.)	C4
Batha (riv.)	C5
Bodélé (depr.)	C4
Borku (reg.)	C4
Chad (lake)	C5
Emi Koussi (mt.)	C4
Ennedi (plat.)	D4
Fittri (lake)	C5
Kanem (reg.)	C5
Logone (reg.)	C5
Maro (riv.)	C4
Mbéré (dry riv.)	C6
Mourdi (riv.)	D4
Ouham (depr.)	C6
Pendé (riv.)	C6
Sahara (reg.)	C3
Salamat, Bahr (des.)	C6
Shari (riv.)	C5
Sudan (riv.)	C5
Tibesti (mts.)	C3
Wadai (reg.)	D5

DJIBOUTI

CITIES and TOWNS

Ali Sabieh	H5
Dikhil	H5
Djibouti (cap.) 96,000	H5
Obock	H5
Tadjoura	H5

OTHER FEATURES

Abbe (lake)	H5
Aden (gulf)	J5
Bab el Mandeb (strait)	H5

EGYPT

CITIES and TOWNS

Abnûb 39,343	J4
Akhmim 53,234	F2
Alexandria 2,318,655	J2
Aswân 144,377	F3
Asyût 213,983	J4
Benha 88,992	J3
Beni Mazar 39,373	J4
Beni Suef 118,148	J3
Biba 33,074	J4
Bur Sa'id
(Port Said) 262,620	K2
Cairo (cap.) 5,084,463	J3
Dairût 31,624	J4
Damanhur 188,927	J3
Damietta 93,546	J3
Disûq 58,650	J3

(continued on following page)

Topography

0   200   400   600 MI.

0   200   400   600 KM.

5,000 m. | 2,000 m. | 1,000 m. | 500 m. | 200 m. | 100 m. | Sea Level | Below
16,404 ft. | 6,562 ft. | 3,281 ft. | 1,640 ft. | 656 ft. | 328 ft.

(continued on following page)

Dumyât (Damietta) 93,546.....J3
El 'Alamein.....E1
El 'Arish.....F1
El Faiyûm 167,081.....J3
El Fashn 33,506.....J4
El Iskandarîya
(Alexandria) 2,318,655.....J2
El Karnak.....F2
El Khârga 26,375.....F3
El Mahalla el Kubra 292,853.....J3
El Mansûra 257,866.....J3
El Minya 146,423.....J4
El Qâhira (Cairo)
(cap.) 5,084,463.....J3
El Qantara 919.....K3
El Quseir 12,297.....F3
El Wasta 17,659.....J3
Girga 51,110.....J3
Giza 1,246,713.....J3
Heliopolis'.....J3
Helwân.....J3
Idfu 34,858.....F3
Ismailia 145,978.....K3
Isna 34,186.....F2
Karnak (El Karnak).....F2
Kôm Ombo 44,531.....F3
Luxor 92,748.....F2
Maghâgha 40,802.....J4
Mallawi 74,256.....J4
Manfalût 41,126.....J4
Mersá Matrûh 27,857.....E1
Minûf 55,131.....J3
Mût 8,032.....E2
Port Fuad.....K3
Port Safâga.....F2
Port Said 262,620.....K2
Port Taufiq.....K3
Qalyub 62,739.....J3
Qena 94,013.....F2
Rashid (Rosetta) 42,962.....J2
Rudeis.....F2
Salûm 4,161.....E1
Samalût 48,146.....J4
Shibin el Kom 102,844.....J3
Sidi Barrani 1,574.....E1
Sinnûris 42,022.....J3
Sohâg 101,758.....J3
Suez 194,001.....K3
Tahta 45,242.....J3
Tanta 284,636.....J3
Zagazig 202,637.....J3
Zifta 50,410.....J3

OTHER FEATURES

Abu Qir (bay).....J2
Abydos (ruins).....F2
Aqaba (gulf).....G2
Arabian (des.).....F2
Aswân (dam).....F3
Aswân High (dam).....F3
Bahariya (oasis).....E2
Bânâs, Ras (cape).....G3
Berenice (ruins).....F3

Birket Qârûn (lake).....J3
Bitter (lakes).....K3
Dakhla (oasis).....E2
Eastern (Arabian) (des.).....F2
Farâfra (oasis).....E2
Foul (bay).....G3
Gilf Kebir (plat.).....E3
Great Sand Sea (des.).....D2
Katherina, Jebel (mt.).....F2
Khârga (oasis).....F2
Libyan (des.).....E3
Libyan (plat.).....E1
Mediterranean (sea).....E1
Memphis (ruins).....J3
Muhammad, Ras (cape).....F2
Nasser (lake).....F3
Nile (riv.).....J3
Pyramids (ruins).....J3
Qattara (depr.).....E2
Sahara (des.).....E3
Sinai (mt.).....F2
Sinai (pen.).....F2
Siwa (oasis).....E2
Suez (canal).....K3
Suez (gulf).....F2
Tiran (strait).....F2
'Uweinat, Jebel (mt.).....E3

ETHIOPIA

PROVINCES

Arusi 852,900.....G6
Bale 707,800.....H6
Eritrea 1,947,600.....G4
Gamu-Gofa 698,800.....G6
Gojjam 1,750,100.....G5
Gondar 1,355,800.....G5
Harar 3,359,200.....H6
Ilubabor 688,800.....F6
Kaffa 1,693,000.....G6
Shoa 5,369,500.....G6
Sidamo 2,479,800.....G7
Tigre 1,828,900.....H5
Wallaga 1,269,100.....F6
Wallo 2,459,900.....H5

CITIES and TOWNS

Addis Ababa (cap.)
1,196,300.....G6
Addis Alam 5,500.....G6
Adigrat 9,400.....G5
Adi Ugri 12,800.....G4
Adwa 16,400.....G5
Aksum 12,800.....G5
Ankober.....H6
Arba Mench 7,660.....G6
Asmara 393,800.....G4
Assab 16,000.....H5
Asselle 19,390.....G6
Awareh.....H6
Axum (Aksum) 12,800.....G5
Bahir Dar 25,100.....G5

Dagabur.....H6
Dangila.....G5
Debra Birhan 16,700.....G6
Debra Markos 30,260.....G5
Debra Tabor 8,700.....G5
Dembidollo 7,600.....F6
Dessye 49,750.....H5
Dilla 13,800.....G6
Dire Dawa 63,700.....H6
El Carre.....H6
Gabredarre.....H6
Galadi.....J6
Gambela.....F6
Gardula 5,800.....G6
Gerlogubi.....H6
Ghimbi 8,300.....G6
Ginir.....H6
Goba 13,500.....H6
Gondar 38,600.....G5
Gore 8,500.....F6
Gorrahei.....H6
Harar 48,440.....H6
Hosseina 8,500.....G6
Jijiga 8,000.....H6
Jimma 47,360.....G6
Jiran.....G6
Karkabat.....G4
Keren.....G4
Kibre Mengist 8,300.....G6
Lalibela.....G5
Magdala.....G5
Maji.....G6
Makale 30,780.....G5
Massawa 19,800.....G4
Mersa Fatma.....H5
Metamma.....G5
Metu 6,860.....G6
Miesso.....H6
Mizan Teferi.....G6
Moyale.....G7
Murle.....H6
Mustahil.....H6
Nakamti 18,310.....G6
Nakfa.....G4
Nazret 42,900.....G6
Negelli 8,800.....G6
Nejo.....G6
Saio (Dembidollo) 7,600.....F6
Soddu 11,900.....G6
Sokota.....G5
Tessenei.....G4
Thio.....H5
Tori.....F6
Umm Hajar.....G4
Waka.....G6
Waldia 9,600.....G5
Wardere.....J6
Wolta.....G5
Yaballo.....G7
Zula.....G4

OTHER FEATURES

Abay (riv.).....G5

Abaya (lake).....G6
Abbe (lake).....H5
Akobo (riv.).....F6
Assal (lake).....H5
Assale (lake).....H5
Atbara (riv.).....G4
Awash (riv.).....H5
Bale (mt.).....G6
Baraka (riv.).....G4
Blue Nile (Abay) (riv.).....G5
Buri (pen.).....H4
Chamo (lake).....G6
Dahlak (arch.).....H4
Dahlak (isl.).....H4
Danakil (reg.).....H5
Dawa (riv.).....G7
Dinder (riv.).....F5
Fafan (riv.).....H6
Ganale Dorya (riv.).....H6
Gughe (mt.).....G6
Haud (reg.).....J6
Kasar, Ras (cape).....G4
Ogaden (reg.).....H6
Omo (riv.).....G6
Ras Dashan (mt.).....G5
Red (sea).....H4
Rudolf (Turkana) (lake).....G7
Simen (mts.).....G5
Takkaze (riv.).....G5
Tana (lake).....G5
Tisisat (fall).....G5
Turkana (lake).....G7
Zwai (lake).....G6

LIBYA

CITIES and TOWNS

Ajedabia○ 53,170.....D1
Aujila○ 6,695.....D2
Baida○ 59,765.....D1
Barce (El Marj)○ 55,444.....D1
Benghazi 286,943.....C1
Beni Ulid○ 19,113.....B1
Brak○ 16,307.....B2
Cyrene (Shahat)○ 17,157.....D1
Derj○ 2,152.....B1
Derna○ 44,145.....D1
El Abiar○ 17,685.....D1
El Agheila 3.....C1
El Azizia○ 34,077.....B1
El Bardi○ 4,330.....D1
El Barkat○ 2,139.....B3
El Gatrun.....B3
El Jauf○ 6,481.....D3
El Marj○ 55,444.....D1
Es Sidr○ 706.....C1
Ez Zuetina○ 7,256.....D1
Ghadames○ 6,172.....A2
Gharian○ 65,224.....B1
Ghat○ 6,924.....B3
Ghemines○ 4,313.....C1
Homs○ 66,890.....B1

Hon○ 2,766.....C2
Jaghbub (Jarabub)○ 1,436.....D2
Jarabub○ 1,436.....D2
Marada○ 3,201.....C2
Marsa el Brega○ 2,618.....D1
Marsa el Hariga○ 5,043.....D1
Misurata○ 102,439.....C1
Mizda○ 11,472.....B1
Murzuk○ 22,185.....B2
Nalut○ 23,535.....B1
Ras Lanuf○ 1,990.....C1
Sabrathaa○ 30,836.....B1
Sebha○ 35,879.....B2
Shahat○ 17,157.....D1
Sinawen○ 1,549.....B1
Sokna○ 3,757.....C2
Soluk○ 6,501.....D1
Syrte○ 22,797.....C1
Tarhuna○ 52,657.....B1
Tobruk○ 58,384.....D1
Tokra○ 10,714.....D1
Tripoli (cap.)○ 550,438.....B1
Ubari○ 19,132.....B2
Waddan○ 5,347.....C2
Wau el Kebir.....C2
Zawia○ 72,092.....B1
Zella○ 72,092.....C2
Zliten○ 58,981.....B1
Zwara○ 15,078.....B1

OTHER FEATURES

Akhdar, Jebel (mts.).....D1
Barqa (Cyrenaica) (reg.).....D1
Ben Ghnema, Jebel (mts.).....C2
Bette (peak).....C3
Bey el Kebir, Wadi (dry riv.).....B1
Bir Hakeim (ruins).....D1
Bomba (gulf).....D1
Buzeima (well).....D3
Calansho Sand Sea (des.).....D2
Calansho, Serir (des.).....D2
Cyrenaica (reg.).....D1
Fezzan (reg.).....B2
Great Sand Sea (des.).....D2
Harug el Asued, El (mts.).....C2
Homra, Hamada el (des.).....B2
Idehan Murzuk (des.).....B2
Idehan Ubari (des.).....B2
Jalo (oasis).....D1
Jefara (reg.).....B1
Jef Jef es Seghin (plat.).....D3
Jofra (oasis).....C2
Kufra (oasis).....D3
Leptis Magna (ruins).....B1
Libyan (des.).....D2
Libyan (plat.).....D1
Mediterranean (sea).....C1
Nefusa, Jebel (mts.).....B1
Rebiana (oasis).....D3
Rebiana Sand Sea (des.).....D3
Sahara (des.).....C3
Shati, Wadi esh (dry riv.).....B2

Sidra (gulf).....C1
Soda, Jebel es (mts.).....C2
Tazerbo (oasis).....D2
Tibesti, Serir (des.).....C3
Tinghert Hamada
(Tinrhert) (des.).....B2
Tripolitania (reg.).....B1
'Uweinat, Jebel (mt.).....E3
Zelten, Jebel (mts.).....D2

SUDAN

PROVINCES

Central.....F5
Darfur.....D5
Eastern.....G4
Khartoum.....F4
Kordofan.....E5
Northern.....E4
Southern.....E6

CITIES and TOWNS

'Abri.....F3
Abu Hamed.....F4
Adok.....F6
Akobo.....F6
Amadi.....F6
Argo.....F4
Aroma.....G4
Atbara 66,000.....F4
Babanusa.....E5
Bara.....F5
Bentiu.....E6
Berber.....F4
Bor.....F6
Buram.....E5
Damazin
(Ed Damazin) 12,000.....F5
Deim Zubeir.....E6
Dongola 6,000.....F4
Dungunab.....G3
Ed Damazin 12,000.....F5
Ed Damer 17,000.....F4
Ed Dueim 27,000.....F5
El Fasher 52,000.....D5
El Geneina 33,000.....D5
El Obeid 90,000.....E5
El Odaiya.....E5
En Nahud 23,000.....E5
Er Roseires.....F5
Fashoda (Kodok).....F6
Gedaref 92,000.....G5
Gogrial.....E6
Goz Regeb.....G4
Haiya Junction.....G4
Halaib.....G3
Jonglei.....F6
Juba 50,000.....F7
Kadugli 18,000.....E5
Kaka.....F5
Karima.....F4

Kerma.....F4
Khartoum (cap.) 334,000.....F4
Khartoum North 151,000.....F4
Khashm el Girba.....G4
Kodok.....F6
Kosti 57,000.....F5
Kurmuk.....F5
Kutum.....D5
Malakal 35,000.....F6
Maridi.....F6
Melut.....F5
Merowe.....F4
Meshra er Req.....F6
Mongalla.....F6
Muglad.....E5
Muhammad Qol.....G3
Nagishot.....F7
Nasir.....F6
Nyala 60,000.....D5
Nyamlell.....E6
Nyerol.....F6
Omdurman 299,000.....F4
Opari.....F6
Pibor Post.....F6
Port Sudan 133,000.....G4
Qala'en Nahl.....F5
Raga.....E6
Rashad.....F5
Rejaf.....F7
Renk.....F5
Rufa'a.....F5
Rumbek 17,000.....E6
Sennar.....F5
Shambe.....F6
Shendi.....F4
Shereik.....F4
Showak.....G5
Singa.....F5
Sinkat.....G4
Sodiri.....E5
Suakin.....G4
Suki.....F5
Tali Post.....F6
Talodi.....F5
Tambura.....E6
Tendelti.....F5
Tokar.....G4
Tombe.....F6
Tonga.....F6
Tonj.....E6
Torit.....F7
Trinkitat.....G4
Umm Keddada.....E5
Umm Ruwaba.....F5
Wadi Halfa.....F3
Wad Medani 107,000.....F5
Wankai.....E6
Wau 53,000.....E6
Yambio 7,000.....E6
Yei.....F6
Yirol.....F6
Zalingei.....D5

OTHER FEATURES

Abu Habl, Wadi (dry riv.).....F5
Abu Shagara, Ras (cape).....G3
Adda (riv.).....D6
Atbara (riv.).....G4
Bahr Azoum (riv.).....D5
Bahr el 'Arab (riv.).....E6
Bahr ez Zeraf (riv.).....F6
Blue Nile (riv.).....F5
Dar Hamid (reg.).....F5
Dar Masalit (reg.).....D5
Dinder (riv.).....F5
El 'Atrun (oasis).....E4
Fifth Cataract (falls).....F4
Fourth Cataract (falls).....F4
Gabgaba, Wadi (dry riv.).....F3
Ghalla, Wadi el (dry riv.).....E5
Hadarba, Ras (cape).....G3
Howar, Wadi (dry riv.).....E4
Ibra, Wadi (dry riv.).....D5
Jebel Aulia (dam).....F5
Jonglei (canal).....F6
Jur (riv.).....E6
Kinyeti (mt.).....F7
Libyan (des.).....E3
Lol (dry riv.).....E6
Lotagipi Swamp (plain).....F7
Marra, Jebel (mt.).....D5
Meroe (ruins).....F4
Milk, Wadi el (dry riv.).....E4
Muqaddam, Wadi (dry riv.).....E4
Napata (ruins).....F4
Naqa (ruins).....F4
Nile (riv.).....F4
Nuba (mts.).....E5
Nubia (lake).....F3
Nubian (des.).....F3
Nukheila (oasis).....E4
Nuri (ruins).....F4
Oda, Jebel (mt.).....G3
Pibor (riv.).....F6
Red (sea).....G3
Red Sea (hills).....G3
Sahara (des.).....E3
Selima (oasis).....E3
Sennar (dam).....F5
Setit (riv.).....G5
Sixth Cataract (falls).....F4
Sobat (riv.).....F6
Suakin (arch.).....G4
Sudan (reg.).....E5
Sudd (swamp).....E6
Sue (riv.).....E6
Third Cataract (falls).....F4
'Uweinat, Jebel (mt.).....E3
White Nile (riv.).....F5

○ Population of sub-district or
division

Agriculture, Industry and Resources

DOMINANT LAND USE

Cereals, Horticulture, Livestock

Cash Crops, Mixed Cereals

Cotton, Cereals

Market Gardening, Diversified
Tropical Crops

Plantation Agriculture

Oases

Pasture Livestock

Nomadic Livestock Herding

Forests

Nonagricultural Land

MAJOR MINERAL OCCURRENCES

Ab Asbestos   Mn Manganese
Au Gold   Na Salt
Cr Chromium   O Petroleum
Fe Iron Ore   P Phosphates
G Natural Gas   Pt Platinum
K Potash

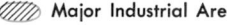 Water Power

Major Industrial Areas

ANGOLA

AREA 481,351 sq. mi. (1,246,700 sq. km.)
POPULATION 9,747,000
CAPITAL Luanda
LARGEST CITY Luanda
HIGHEST POINT Mt. Moco 8,593 ft. (2,620 m.)
MONETARY UNIT kwanza
MAJOR LANGUAGES Mbundu, Kongo, Lunda,
 Portuguese
MAJOR RELIGIONS Tribal religions, Roman
 Catholicism

BURUNDI

AREA 10,747 sq. mi. (27,835 sq. km.)
POPULATION 5,302,000
CAPITAL Bujumbura
LARGEST CITY Bujumbura
HIGHEST POINT 8,858 ft. (2,700 m.)
MONETARY UNIT Burundi franc
MAJOR LANGUAGES Kirundi, French, Swahili
MAJOR RELIGIONS Tribal religions, Roman
 Catholicism, Islam

CAMEROON

AREA 183,568 sq. mi.
 (475,441 sq. km.)
POPULATION 11,540,000
CAPITAL Yaoundé
LARGEST CITY Douala
HIGHEST POINT Cameroon 13,350 ft. (4,069 m.)
MONETARY UNIT CFA tranc
MAJOR LANGUAGFS Fang, Bamileke, Fulani,
 Duala, French, English
MAJOR RELIGIONS Tribal religions, Christianity, Islam

CENTRAL AFRICAN REP.

AREA 242,000 sq. mi. (626,780 sq. km.)
POPULATION 2,740,000
CAPITAL Bangui
LARGEST CITY Bangui
HIGHEST POINT Gao 4,659 ft. (1,420 m.)
MONETARY UNIT CFA franc
MAJOR LANGUAGES Banda, Gbaya, Sangho,
 French
MAJOR RELIGIONS Tribal religions,
 Christianity, Islam

CONGO

AREA 132,046 sq. mi. (342,000 sq. km.)
POPULATION 1,843,000
CAPITAL Brazzaville
LARGEST CITY Brazzaville
HIGHEST POINT Leketi Mts. 3,412 ft.
 (1,040 m.)
MONETARY UNIT CFA franc
MAJOR LANGUAGES Kikongo, Bateke,
 Lingala, French
MAJOR RELIGIONS Christianity, tribal
 religions, Islam

EQUATORIAL GUINEA

AREA 10,831 sq. mi. (28,052 sq. km.)
POPULATION 341,000
CAPITAL Malabo
LARGEST CITY Malabo
HIGHEST POINT 9,868 ft. (3,008 m.)
MONETARY UNIT CFA franc
MAJOR LANGUAGES Fang, Bubi, Spanish
MAJOR RELIGIONS Tribal religions,
 Christianity

GABON

AREA 103,346 sq. mi. (267,666 sq. km.)
POPULATION 1,206,000
CAPITAL Libreville
LARGEST CITY Libreville
HIGHEST POINT Ibounzi 5,165 ft. (1,574 m.)
MONETARY UNIT CFA franc
MAJOR LANGUAGES Fang and other Bantu
 languages, French
MAJOR RELIGIONS Tribal religions,
 Christianity, Islam

KENYA

AREA 224,960 sq. mi. (582,646 sq. km.)
POPULATION 24,872,000
CAPITAL Nairobi
LARGEST CITY Nairobi
HIGHEST POINT Kenya 17,058 ft. (5,199 m.)
MONETARY UNIT Kenya shilling
MAJOR LANGUAGES Kikuyu, Luo, Kavirondo,
 Kamba, Swahili, English
MAJOR RELIGIONS Tribal religions,
 Christianity, Hinduism, Islam

MALAWI

AREA 45,747 sq. mi. (118,485 sq. km.)
POPULATION 8,022,000
CAPITAL Lilongwe
LARGEST CITY Blantyre
HIGHEST POINT Mulanje 9,843 ft. (3,000 m.)
MONETARY UNIT Malawi kwacha
MAJOR LANGUAGES Chichewa, Yao,
 English, Nyanja, Tumbuka, Tonga,
 Ngoni
MAJOR RELIGIONS Tribal religions, Islam,
 Christianity

RWANDA

AREA 10,169 sq. mi. (26,337 sq. km.)
POPULATION 6,274,000
CAPITAL Kigali
LARGEST CITY Kigali
HIGHEST POINT Karisimbi 14,780 ft.
 (4,505 m.)
MONETARY UNIT Rwanda franc
MAJOR LANGUAGES Kinyarwanda, French,
 Swahili
MAJOR RELIGIONS Tribal religions,
 Roman Catholicism, Islam

SOMALIA

AREA 246,200 sq. mi. (637,658 sq. km.)
POPULATION 7,339,000
CAPITAL Mogadishu
LARGEST CITY Mogadishu
HIGHEST POINT Surud Ad 7,900 ft.
 (2,408 m.)
MONETARY UNIT Somali shilling
MAJOR LANGUAGES Somali, Arabic,
 Italian, English
MAJOR RELIGION Islam

TANZANIA

AREA 363,708 sq. mi. (942,003 sq. km.)
POPULATION 24,802,000
CAPITAL Dar es Salaam
LARGEST CITY Dar es Salaam
HIGHEST POINT Kilimanjaro 19,340 ft.
 (5,895 m.)
MONETARY UNIT Tanzanian shilling
MAJOR LANGUAGES Nyamwezi-Sukuma,
 Swahili, English
MAJOR RELIGIONS Tribal religions,
 Christianity, Islam

UGANDA

AREA 91,076 sq. mi. (235,887 sq. km.)
POPULATION 17,804,000
CAPITAL Kampala
LARGEST CITY Kampala
HIGHEST POINT Margherita 16,795 ft.
 (5,119 m.)
MONETARY UNIT Ugandan shilling
MAJOR LANGUAGES Luganda, Acholi, Teso,
 Nyoro, Soga, Nkole, English, Swahili
MAJOR RELIGIONS Tribal religions,
 Christianity, Islam

ZAIRE

AREA 905,063 sq. mi. (2,344,113 sq. km.)
POPULATION 34,491,000
CAPITAL Kinshasa
LARGEST CITY Kinshasa
HIGHEST POINT Margherita 16,795 ft.
 (5,119 m.)
MONETARY UNIT zaire
MAJOR LANGUAGES Tshiluba, Mongo, Kikongo,
 Kingwana, Zande, Lingala, Swahili,
 French
MAJOR RELIGIONS Tribal religions,
 Christianity

ZAMBIA

AREA 290,586 sq. mi. (752,618 sq. km.)
POPULATION 8,073,000
CAPITAL Lusaka
LARGEST CITY Lusaka
HIGHEST POINT Sunzu 6,782 ft.
 (2,067 m.)
MONETARY UNIT Zambian kwacha
MAJOR LANGUAGES Bemba, Tonga,
 Lozi, Luvale, Nyanja, English
MAJOR RELIGIONS Tribal religions

ANGOLA

PROVINCES

rgo 68,885 ....B5
rguela 474,897 ....B6
e 650,337 ....C6
binda 80,857 ....B5
ando Cubango 112,073 ....C7
lanza-Norte 298,062 ....B5
lanza-Sul 458,592 ....C6
nene 147,394 ....C7
uambo 837,627 ....C6
ila 497,470 ....B7
landa 491,704 ....B5
nda Norte 210,000 ....C5
nda Sul 98,000 ....D5
alanje 558,630 ....C6
oxico 213,119 ....D6
amibe 53,058 ....B7
ge 386,037 ....B5
ire 41,766 ....B5

CITIES and TOWNS

mbriz B5
aia dos Tigres B7
aia Farta B6
embe B6
enguela 40,996 ....B6
aála 8,894 ....B5
abinda 21,124 ....B5
aconda C7
eiundo C7
amacupa 5,740 ....D6
amanongue D6
ambundi-Catembo C5
apelongo C7
assinga C7
atumbela C6
axito C6
hinguar C6
hitato D5
ango C6
uito-Cuanavale C7
ondo B5
orte República C5
oz do Cunene B7
abela 6,930 ....B6
anda 2,538 ....C6
olungo Alto B5
Huambo 61,885 ....C6
Katchiungo C6
Kuito 18,941 ....C6
Kuvango C6
obito 59,528 ....B6
onga C6

Lóvua D5
Luacano D6
Luanda (cap.)
 475,328 ....B5
Luau D6
Lubango 31,674 ....B6
Lucapa D5
Luena 2,539 ....C6
Luiana D7
Malanje 31,599 ....C6
Maquela do Zombo C5
Massango
 (Forte República) ...C5
Mbanza Congo 4,002 ...B5
Menongue 3,023 ......C6

Moçâmedes (Namibe)
 12,076 ....B7
Namibe 12,076 ....B7
N'dalatando 7,342 ....B5
N'gage 2,548 ....B5
Ngunza (Sumbe) 7,911 .B6
N'zeto B5
Ondjiva B7
Porto Amboim B6
Saurimo 12,901 ......C6
Soyo B5
Sumbe 7,911 ....B6
Tombua 8,235 ....B7
Uíge 11,972 ....C5
Waku Kungo 2,784 ...C6

OTHER FEATURES

Bero (riv.) B7
Chicapa (riv.) D5
Chiumbe (riv.) D5
Congo (riv.) C4
Coporolo (riv.) B6
Cuando (riv.) C7
Cuango (riv.) C6
Cuanza (riv.) C5
Cubango (riv.) C7
Cuito (riv.) C7
Cunene (dam) B7
Cunene (riv.) B7

Cuvo (riv.) B6
Kasai (riv.) D5
Kwilu (riv.) C5
Loange (riv.) C5
Loge (riv.) B5
Lungwebungu
 (riv.) D6
Matala (dam) B6
M'Bridge (riv.) B5
Moco (mt.) C6
Negro (cape) B7
Palmeirinhas (pt.) ...B5
Ruacana Falls (dam) .B7
Santa Maria (cape) ..B6
Zambezi (riv.) D6

BURUNDI

CITIES and TOWNS

Bujumbura (cap.)
 141,040 ....E4
Bururi 7,800 ....E4
Gitega 19,500 ....F4

OTHER FEATURES

Ruzizi (riv.) E4
Tanganyika (lake) E5

CAMEROON

CITIES and TOWNS

Bafia 17,855 ....B3
Bafoussam 62,239 ......B2
Bamenda 48,111 ....B2
Banyo 10,293 ....B2
Bertoua 13,985 ....B3
Bétaré-Oya B2
Bonabéri A3
Buea 24,584 ....A3
Djoum B3
Douala 458,426 .....A3
Dschang 16,629 .....A2

(continued on following page)

ANGOLA

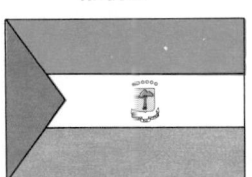

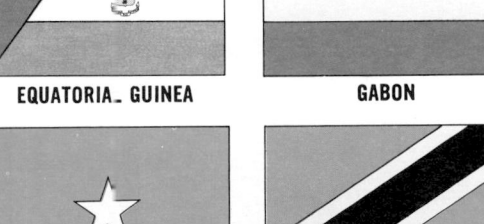

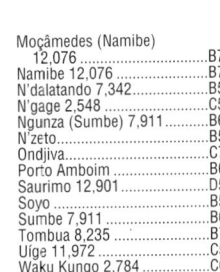

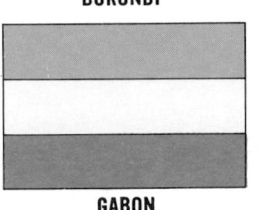

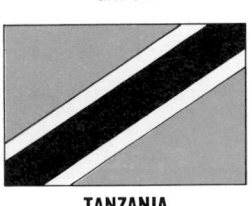

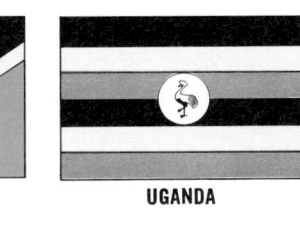

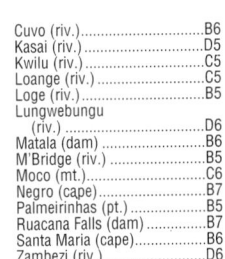

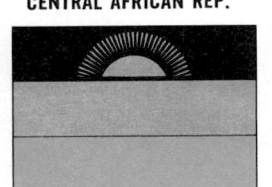

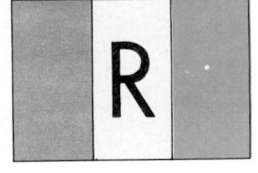

ANGOLA BURUNDI CAMEROON CENTRAL AFRICAN REP. CONGO

EQUATORIAL GUINEA GABON KENYA MALAWI RWANDA

SOMALIA TANZANIA UGANDA ZAIRE ZAMBIA

Ebolowa 24,000 ....B3	Maroua 67,187 ....B1	Tignére...........B2	Cameroon (mt.) A3	**CENTRAL AFRICAN REPUBLIC**		Berberati 27,285 ....C3	Grimari 7,308 ....C2
Fort Foureau (Kousseri)	Mbalmayo 22,106 ....B3	Tiko 13,824 ....A3	Cross (riv.) A2	CITIES and TOWNS		Birao 3,317 ....D1	Ippy 10,816 ....D2
11,627 ....B1	Meiganga 15,906 ....B2	Wum 15,149 ....A2	Dja (riv.) B3			Bocaranga 6,202 ....C2	Kaga Bandoro 11,876 ....C2
Fouman 33,944 ....B2	Moloundou C3	Yagoua 13,541 ....B1	Donga (riv.) A2	Alindao 12,295 ....D2		Boda 8,771 ....C3	Kembe 5,051 ....D3
Garoua 63,900 ....B2	Monatélé B3	Yaoundé (cap.) 313,706 ....B3	Ivindo (riv.) B3	Baboua 3,999 ....C2		Bossangoa 25,150 ....C2	Mbaïki 12,346 ....C3
Guidder 16,053 ....B2	Nanga-Eboko B3	Yoko B2	Kadei (riv.) C2	Bambari 31,285 ....D2		Bossembele 5,091 ....C2	Mobaye 4,220 ....D3
Kousseri 11,627 ....B1	Ngaoundéré 38,992 ....B2		Logone (riv.) B2	Bangassou 21,773 ....D3		Bouar 29,528 ....C2	Ndele 5,858 ....D2
Kumba 44,175 ....A3	Nkongsamba 71,298 ....B3	OTHER FEATURES	Lom (riv.) B2	Bangui (cap.)		Bouca 8,874 ....C2	Nola 6,703 ....C3
Kumbo 11,699 ....B2	Poli B2		Mbakou (res.) B2	279,792 ....C3		Bozoum 13,573 ....C2	Obo 3,978 ....E2
Limbe 27,016 ....A3	Sangmélima 13,776 ....B3	Adamawa (reg.) B2	Mbéré (riv.) B2	Bania C3		Bria 14,786 ....D2	Ouadda 3,009 ....D2
Lomié B3	Tchollíré B2	Benué (riv.) A2	Sanaga (riv.) B3	Batangafo 12,543 ....C2		Carnot 17,863 ....C3	Paoua 7,052 ....C2
Makari B1	Tibati B2	Biafra (bight) A3	Sanga (riv.) B3			Dekoa 7,663 ....C2	Zemio 3,259 ....D2

OTHER FEATURES

Bamingui (riv.) C2
Bomu (riv.) D3
Dar Rounga (reg.) D2
Gao (mt.) D2
Kadei (riv.) C3
Kotto (riv.) D2
Lobaye (riv.) C2
Mbéré (riv.) B2
Ouham (riv.) C2
Pendé (riv.) C2

Sangha (riv.) C3
Shari (riv.) C2
Shinko (riv.) D2
Ubangi (riv.) D2

CONGO

CITIES and TOWNS

Abala C4
Boundji C4
Brazzaville (cap.) 298,967 ....C4

Djambala B4
Impfondo C3
Kinkala B4
Loubomo 29,600 ....B4
Makoua C3
Mbinda B4
Mossaka B4
Mossendjo B4
Nkayi 30,600 ....B4
Ouesso C3
Owando C4
Pointe-Noire 141,700 ....B4

OTHER FEATURES

Alima (riv.) B4
Congo (riv.) C4
Crystal (mts.) B4
Dja (riv.) B3
Ivindo (riv.) B3
Kadei (riv.) B3
Kouilou (riv.) B4
Likouala (riv.) C3
N'Gounié (riv.) B4
Niari (riv.) B4

OGOOUÉ

Ogooué (riv.) A4
Sangha (riv.) C3
Ubangi (riv.) C3

EQUATORIAL GUINEA

TERRITORIES

Bioko 78,000 ....A3
Río Muni 203,000 ....B3

CITIES and TOWNS

Bata 270,241 ....A3
Luba 19,933 ....A3
Malabo (cap.) 37,237 ....A3
Mbini 14,503 ....A3

OTHER FEATURES

Biafra (bight) A3
Corisco (isl.) A3
Elobey (isls.) A3
Fernando Po (Bioko) (isl.) A3

GABON

CITIES and TOWNS

Bitam 5,936 ....B3
Cocobeach A3
Fougamou B4
Franceville 9,345 ....B4
Kango B3
Koula-Moutou 8,032 ....B4
Lambaréné 17,770 ....B4
Lastoursville B4
Libreville (cap.) 105,080 ....A3
Makokou 5,005 ....B4
Mayumba B4
M'Bigou B4
Médouneu B3
Mekambo B3
Mimongo B4
Minvoul B3
Moanda 10,709 ....B4
Mouila 15,016 ....B4
Mounana 4,000 ....B4
N'Dendé B4
N'Djolé B4
Okondja B4
Omboué A4
Owendo A3
Oyem 12,455 ....B3
Port-Gentil 48,190 ....A4
Tchibanga 14,001 ....B4

OTHER FEATURES

Crystal (mts.) B4
Ibounzi (mt.) B4
Ivindo (riv.) B3
Lopez (cape) A4
N'Dogo (lag.) B4
N'Gounié (riv.) B4
N'Komi (lag.) A4
Ogooué (riv.) B4
Pongara (pt.) A3

KENYA

PROVINCES

Central 1,675,647 ....G4
Coast 944,082 ....G4
Eastern 1,907,301 ....G4
Nairobi 509,286 ....G4
North-Eastern 245,757 ....G4
Nyanza 2,122,045 ....F4
Rift Valley 2,210,289 ....G3
Western 1,328,298 ....G3

Baragoi 2,383 ....G3
Bunyala F3
Eldoret 18,196 ....G3
Embu 3,928 ....G4
Fort Hall 4,750 ....G4
Galole 3,609 ....G4
Garissa G4
Gilgil 4,178 ....G4
Isiolo 8,201 ....G4
Kajiado 1,755 ....G4
Kakamega 6,244 ....F3
Kaningo 2,450 ....G4
Kapenguria 1,790 ....G3
Kericho 10,144 ....F4
Kiambu 2,776 ....G4
Kilifi 2,662 ....G4
Kisii 6,080 ....G4
Kisumu 32,431 ....F3
Kitale 11,573 ....G3
Kitui 3,071 ....G4
Kwale 1,092 ....G4
Lamu 7,403 ....H4
Lokitaung 4,090 ....G3
Machakos 6,312 ....G4
Mado Gashi 1,003 ....G3
Malindi 10,757 ....H4
Maralal 3,878 ....G3
Marsabit 6,635 ....G3
Migori 2,066 ....F4
Mombasa 247,073 ....G4
Nairobi (cap.) 509,286 ....G4
Naivasha 6,920 ....G4
Nakuru 47,151 ....G4
Nanyuki 11,624 ....G4
Narok 2,608 ....G4
Ngong 1,583 ....G4
Nyeri 2,436 ....G4
Rumuruti 1,484 ....G3
Thika 18,387 ....G4
Thomson's Falls 7,602 ....G3
Vanga G4
Voi 5,313 ....G4
Wajir H3
Wamba 2,650 ....G3

OTHER FEATURES

Daua (riv.) H3
Elgon (mt.) F3
Formosa (bay) G4
Galana (riv.) G4
Gedi (ruins) G4
Kenya (riv.) G4
Lak Dera (dry riv.) H3
Lorian (swamp) G3
Natron (lake) G3
Nyiru (mt.) G3
Patta (isl.) H4
Rudolf (Turkana) (lake) G3
Tana (riv.) G4
Tsavo Nat'l Park G4
Turkana (lake) G3
Victoria (lake) F4
Winam (bay) G4

MALAWI

CITIES and TOWNS

Blantyre 222,153 ....F7
Chitipa 3,079 ....F5
Dedza 5,448 ....F6
Dowa 2,067 ....F6
Karonga 11,873 ....F5
Lilongwe (cap.) 102,924 ....F6
Mangochi 3,341 ....G6
Mchinji 1,962 ....F6
Mwanza 2,271 ....F7
Mzimba 4,962 ....F6

Ncheu 1,326 ....F6
Nkhata Bay 4,024 ....F6
Nkhotakota 10,312 ....F6
Nsanje 6,091 ....G7
Rumphi 3,998 ....F6
Salima 4,646 ....F6
Thyolo 4,186 ....F7
Zomba 21,000 ....G7

OTHER FEATURES

Chilrua (lake) G7
Malawi (Nyasa) (lake) F6
Mulanje (mt.) G7
Nyasa (lake) F6
Shire (riv.) G7

RWANDA

CITIES and TOWNS

Butare 21,691 ....E4
Cyangugu 7,042 ....E4
Gisenyi 12,436 ....E4
Kigali (cap.) 117,749 ....F4
Nyabisindu 8,587 ....F4

OTHER FEATURES

Kagera Nat'l Park F4
Karisimbi (mt.) E4
Kivu (lake) E4
Ruzizi (riv.) E4
Virunga (range) E4

SOMALIA

PROVINCES

Bakool 100,000 ....H3
Bari 155,000 ....J1
Bay 302,000 ....H3
Galguduud 182,000 ....J2
Gedo 202,800 ....H3
Hiiraan 147,000 ....J3
Jubbada Hoose 246,000 ....H3
Mogadiscio 371,000 ....J3
Mudug 215,000 ....J2
Nugaal 85,000 ....J2
Sanaag 369,000 ....J1
Shabeellaha Dhexe 237,000 ....J3
Shabeellaha Hoose 398,000 ....H3
Togdheer 258,000 ....J2
Woqooyi Galbeed 440,000 ....H1

CITIES and TOWNS

Afgoi J3
Afmadu 2,580 ....H3
Alula K1
Ankhor J1
Balad 1,233 ....J3
Barawa (Brava) 6,167 ....H3
Baydhabo 14,962 ....H3
Belet Weyne 11,426 ....J3
Bender Cassim J1
Berbera 12,219 ....J2
Borama 3,244 ....H1
Bosaso J1
Brava 6,167 ....H3
Bulo Burti 5,247 ....J3
Bur Acaba H3
Burao 12,617 ....J2
Candala J1
Chisimayu 17,872 ....H4
Coriole 4,341 ....H3
Dante (Hafun) K1
Dusa Mareb J2
Eil J2
El Athale (Itala) J3
Erigabo 4,279 ....J1

(continued on following page)

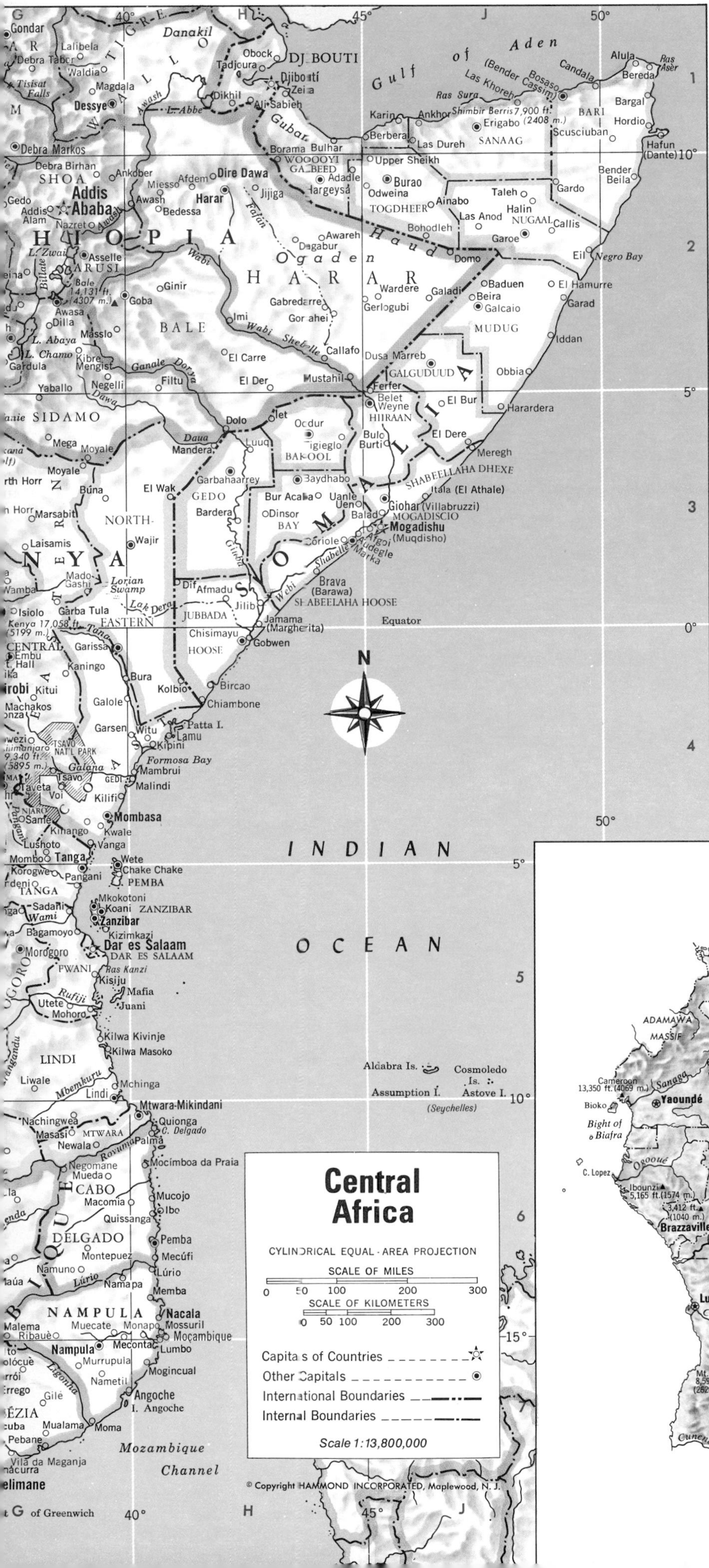

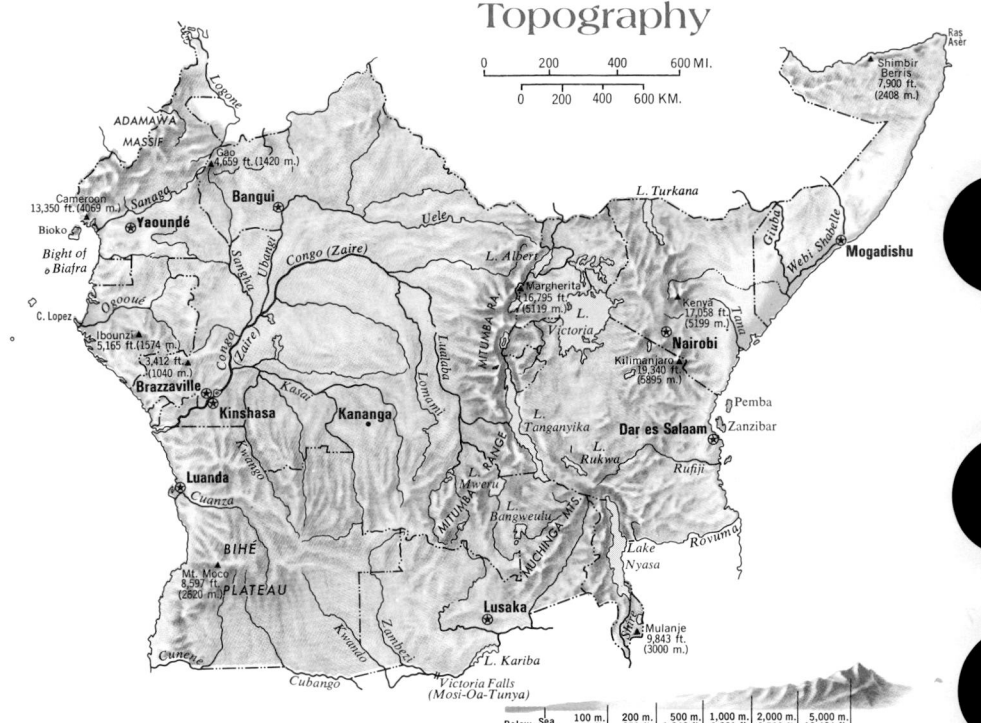

Topography

Galcaio J2
Garbahaarrey H3
Garoe J2
Giohar 13,156 ....J3
Hafun K1
Hargeysa 40,254 ....H2
Itala J3
Jamama 5,408 ....H3
Jilib 3,232 ....H3
Kismayu (Chisimayu) 17,872 .H4
Las Anod 2,441 ....J2
Las Khoreh 2,245 ....J1
Luuq H3
Margherita (Jamama) H3
Marka (Merka) 17,708 ....H3
Mogadishu (cap.) 371,000 ...J3
Muqdisho (Mogadishu)
   (cap.) 371,000 ....J3
Oddur H3
Odweina 1,422 ....J2
Uanle Uen H3
Villabruzzi (Johar) J3
Zeila 1,226 ....H1

OTHER FEATURES

Aden (gulf) J1
Asèr, Ras (cape) K1
Giuba (riv.) H3
Guban (reg.) H1
Haud (plat.) J2
Lak Dera (dry riv.) H3
Negro (bay) J2
Shimbir Berris (mt.) J1
Sura, Ras (cape) J1
Webi Shabelle (riv.) H3

TANZANIA

PROVINCES

Arusha 928,478 ....G4
Dar es Salaam G5
Dodoma 971,921 ....G5
Iringa 922,801 ....G5
Kagera 1,009,379 ....F4
Kigoma 648,950 ....F4
Kilimanjaro 902,394 ....G4
Lindi 527,902 ....G5
Mara 723,295 ....F4
Mbeya 1,080,241 ....F5
Morogoro 939,190 ....G5
Mtwara 771,726 ....G5
Mwanza 1,443,418 ....F4
Pemba 205,870 ....H5
Pwani (Coast) 516,949 ......G5
Rukwa 451,897 ....F5
Ruvuma 564,113 ....G6
Shinyanga 1,323,482 ....F4
Singida 614,030 ....F5
Tabora 818,049 ....F5
Tanga 1,088,592 ....G5
Zanzibar Mjini 143,616 ......G5

Zanzibar Shambani North
   77,424 ....G5
Zanzibar Shambani South
   52,325 ....G5

CITIES and TOWNS

Arusha 55,281 ....G4
Bagamoyo 5,112 ....G5
Biharamulo 1,011 ....F4
Bukene 2,288 ....F4
Bukoba 20,430 ....F4
Chake Chake 4,862 ....H5
Chunya 2,398 ....F5
Dar es Salaam (cap.) 757,346 G5
Dodoma 45,703 ....F4
Geita 3,066 ....F4
Iringa 57,182 ....G5
Kahama 3,211 ....F4
Kasulu F4
Kibondo F4
Kigoma-Ujiji 50,044 ....E4
Kilosa 4,458 ....G5
Kilwa Kivinje 2,790 ....G5
Kilwa Masoko G5
Koani 1,102 ....H5
Kondoa 4,514 ....G4
Kongwa G5
Korogwe 6,675 ....G5
Lindi 27,308 ....G5
Lushoto 1,803 ....G4
Mahenge G5
Manyoni G5
Masasi G6
Mbeya 76,606 ....F5
Mbulu G4
Mchinga G5
Mkokotoni 2,220 ....G5
Morogoro 61,890 ....G5
Moshi 52,223 ....G4
Mpanda F5
Mpwapwa 2,429 ....G5
Mtwara-Mikindani 48,510 ....H6
Musoma 32,658 ....F4
Mwadui 7,383 ....F4
Mwanza 110,611 ....F4
Nachingwea 3,751 ....G6
Newala G6
Ngara F4
Njombe F5
Nzega 2,386 ....F4
Pangani 2,955 ....G5
Shinyanga 21,703 ....F4
Singida 29,252 ....F4
Songea 17,954 ....G6
Sumbawanga 28,586 ....F5
Tabora 67,392 ....F5
Tanga 103,409 ....G4
Tukuyu 4,089 ....F5
Tunduru G6
Utete G5
Wete 8,469 ....G4
Zanzibar 110,669 ....G5

OTHER FEATURES

Eyasi (lake) F4
Great Ruaha (riv.) G5
Juani (isl.) G5
Kagera Nat'l Park F4
Kalambo (falls) F5
Kilimanjaro (mt.) G4
Kilombero (riv.) G5
Mafia (isl.) H5
Manyara (lake) G4
Masai (steppe) G4
Mbarangandu (riv.) G5
Mbemkuru (riv.) G5
Meru (mt.) G4
Mikumi Nat'l Park G5
Natron (lake) G4
Ngorongoro (crater) F4
Njombe (riv.) F5
Nyasa (lake) F6
Olduvai Gorge (canyon) G4
Pangani (riv.) G4
Pemba (isl.) H5
Ras Kanzi (cape) G5
Rovuma (riv.) G6
Ruaha Nat'l Park F5
Rufiji (riv.) G5
Rukwa (lake) F5
Rungwa (riv.) F5
Rungwa (riv.) F5
Serengeti Nat'l Park F4
Tanganyika (lake) E5
Tarangire Nat'l Park G4
Victoria (lake) F4
Wami (riv.) G5
Wembere (riv.) F4
Zanzibar (isl.) G5

UGANDA

CITIES and TOWNS

Arua 10,837 ....F3
Butiaba 261 ....F3
Entebbe 21,096 ....F4
Fort Portal 7,947 ....F3
Gulu 18,170 ....F3
Hoima 2,339 ....F3
Jinja 52,509 ....F3
Kabale 8,234 ....E4
Kampala (cap.) 478,895 .....F3
Kasese 7,213 ....F3
Kitgum 3,242 ....F3
Lira 7,340 ....F3
Masaka 12,987 ....F4
Masindi 2,100 ....F3
Mbale 23,544 ....F3
Mbarara 16,078 ....F4
Moroto 5,488 ....F3
Moyo 266 ....F3
Mubende 6,004 ....F3
Rhino Camp 198 ....F3
Soroti 8,130 ....F3

Tororo 15,977 ....F3

OTHER FEATURES

Albert (Mobuto Sese Seko)
   (lake) F3
Edward (lake) E4
Elgon (mt.) F3
George (lake) F4
Kabalega (falls) F3
Kagalega Nat'l Park F3
Kidepo Nat'l Park F3
Kioga (lake) F3
Margherita (mt.) F3
Mobuto Sese Seko (lake) F3
Owen Falls (dam) F3
Ruwenzori (range) E3
Sese (isls.) F4
Victoria (lake) F4
Virunga (range) E4
Virunga Nat'l Park F4

ZAIRE

PROVINCES

Bandundu 2,600,556 ....C4
Bas-Zaïre 1,504,361 ....B5
Equateur 2,431,812 ....D3
Haut-Zaïre 3,356,419 ....D3
Kasai-Occidental 2,433,861 ...D4
Kasai-Oriental 1,872,231 ....D5
Kinshasa 1,323,039 ....C4
Kivu 3,361,883 ....E4
Shaba 2,753,714 ....E5

CITIES and TOWNS

Aba 7,600 ....F3
Aketi 17,200 ....D3
Bambesa E3
Banalia E3
Banana B5
Bandundu 74,467 ....C4
Basankusu C3
Basoko 9,100 ....D3
Befale D3
Beni 22,800 ....E3
Bikoro C4
Boende 12,800 ....D4
Bokungu D4
Bolobo 10,300 ....C4
Bolomba 7,200 ....C3
Boma 61,100 ....B5
Bomongo C3
Bondo 10,000 ....D3
Bongandanga 12,900 ....D3
Bosobolo 11,100 ....D3
Budjala C3
Bukama E5
Bukavu 134,861 ....E4
Bulungu 16,300 ....C4
Bumba 34,700 ....D3

Bunia 28,800 ....E3
Bunkeya 5,100 ....E6
Businga 11,000 ....D3
Busu-Djanoa D3
Buta 19,800 ....D3
Butembo 27,800 ....E3
Dekese D4
Demba 22,000 ....D5
Dibaya 11,400 ....D5
Dibaya-Lubue 7,900 ....C4
Dilolo 14,000 ....D6
Dimbelenge D5
Djolu D3
Djugu F3
Dungu 9,100 ....E3
Faradje 10,400 ....E3
Feshi C5
Fizi E4
Gandájika 60,100 ....D5
Gemena 37,300 ....C3
Goma 48,600 ....E4
Gungu C5
Idiofa C4
Ikela D4
Ilebo 32,200 ....D4
Ingende C4
Inongo 14,800 ....C4
Irumu 9,300 ....E3
Isangi D3
Isiro 49,300 ....E3
Kabalo 22,600 ....E5
Kabambare E4
Kabare 12,600 ....E4
Kabinda 60,500 ....D5
Kabongo 6,500 ....E5
Kahemba C5
Kalehe E4
Kalemie 60,300 ....E5
Kalima 27,500 ....E4
Kama 69,100 ....E4
Kambove 18,900 ....E6
Kamina 56,300 ....D5
Kampene 14,600 ....E4
Kananga 428,960 ....D5
Kaniama D5
Kapanga D5
Kasangulu 11,900 ....C4
Kasenga E6
Kasese E4
Kasongo 37,800 ....E4
Kasongo-Lunda C5
Katako-Kombe D4
Kazumba D5
Kenge 17,500 ....C4
Kibombo E4
Kikwit 111,960 ....C5
Kinshasa (cap.) 1,323,039 ....C4
Kipushi 32,900 ....E6
Kisangani 229,596 ....E3
Kolwezi 81,600 ....E6
Kongolo 14,800 ....E5
Kutu 10,000 ....C4
Libenge 13,000 ....C3

Lisala D3
Lodja 20,300 ....D4
Lomela D4
Lubefu D4
Lubudi 6,000 ....E5
Lubumbashi 318,000 ....E6
Lubutu E4
Luebo 21,800 ....D5
Lukula 9,400 ....B5
Luozi 7,000 ....B5
Lusambo 13,100 ....D4
Mambasa 7,400 ....E3
Mangai 41,200 ....C4
Manono 44,500 ....E5
Masi-Manimba 6,300 ....C4
Masisi E4
Matadi 110,436 ....B5
Mbandaka 107,910 ....C3
Mbanza-Ngungu 55,800 ....C5
Mbuji-Mayi 256,154 ....D5
Mitwaba E5
Monkoto C4
Muanda 6,400 ....B5
Mungbere E3
Mushie 13,700 ....C4
Muyumba E5
Mweka 24,900 ....D4
Mwene-Ditu 71,200 ....D5
Mwenga E4
Niangara 9,200 ....E3
Nyunzu 11,300 ....E5
Opala D4
Oshwe C4
Panda-Likasi 146,394 ....E6
Pangi E4
Poko E3
Popokabaka C5
Port Kindu 42,800 ....E4
Punia E4
Rutshuru E4
Sakania E6
Sandoa D5
Sentery 24,300 ....E5
Shabunda 6,900 ....E4
Songolola 4,600 ....B5
Tshela 10,700 ....B5
Tshikapa 38,900 ....D5
Ubundu 630 ....E4
Uvira 15,900 ....E4
Virunga 21,900 ....E3
Wamba 11,500 ....E3
Watsa 21,250 ....E3
Yangambi 22,600 ....D3

OTHER FEATURES

Albert (Mobuto Sese Seko)
   (lake) F3
Aruwimi (riv.) E3
Bomu (riv.) D3
Boyoma (Stanley) (falls) D3
Chicapa (riv.) D5
Congo (riv.) C4

Edward (lake) E4
Elila (riv.) E4
Fimi (riv.) C4
Garamba Nat'l Park E3
Giri (riv.) C3
Itimbiri (riv.) D3
Ituri (for.) E3
Karisimbi (mt.) E4
Kasai (riv.) C4
Kivu (lake) E4
Kwa (riv.) C4
Kwango (riv.) C5
Kwilu (riv.) C4
Lindi (riv.) E3
Livingstone (falls) B5
Loange (riv.) C5
Lokoro (riv.) C4
Lomami (riv.) D4
Lomela (riv.) D4
Lowa (riv.) E4
Lua (riv.) C3
Lualaba (riv.) E4
Luapula (riv.) E6
Lubilash (riv.) D5
Lufira (riv.) E5
Luilaka (riv.) C4
Lukenie (riv.) C4
Lukuga (riv.) E5
Lulua (riv.) D5
Luvua (riv.) E5
Mai-Ndombe (lake) C4
Malebo (Stanley Pool) (lake) ..C4
Margherita (mt.) E4
Marungu (mts.) E5
Mobuto Sese Seko (lake) E3
Mweru (lake) E5
Ruwenzori (range) E4
Ruzizi (riv.) E4
Salonga Nat'l Park D4
Sankuru (riv.) D5
Stanley (falls) D3
Stanley Pool (lake) C4
Tanganyika (lake) E5
Tshuapa (riv.) D4
Tumba (lake) C4
Ubangi (riv.) C3
Uele (riv.) D3
Ulindi (riv.) E4
Upemba (lake) E5
Upemba Nat'l Park E5
Virunga (range) E4
Virunga Nat'l Park E4
Zaire (Congo) (riv.) C4

ZAMBIA

CITIES and TOWNS

Abercorn (Mbala) 11,179 ....E5
Bancroft (Chililabombwe)
   61,928 ....E6
Broken Hill (Kabwe) 143,635 ..E6
Chilanga 12,503 ....
Chililabombwe 61,928 ......
Chingola 145,869 ....
Chipata 32,291 ....
Choma 17,943 ....
Fort Rosebery (Mansa)
   34,801 ....
Isoka 6,832 ....
Kabompo 5,357 ....
Kabwe 143,635 ....
Kafue 29,794 ....
Kalabo 7,398 ....
Kalomo 5,878 ....
Kaoma 6,731 ....
Kapiri Mposhi 13,677 ....
Kasama 38,093 ....
Kawambwa 7,235 ....
Kitwe 314,794 ....
Livingstone 71,987 ....
Luanshya 132,164 ....
Lusaka (cap.) 538,469 ......
Mansa 34,801 ....
Mazabuka 29,602 ....
Mbala 11,179 ....
Mongu 24,919 ....
Monze 13,141 ....
Mpika 25,880 ....
Mporokoso 6,008 ....
Mpulungu 6,354 ....
Mufulira 149,778 ....
Mumbwa 7,570 ....
Ndola 282,439 ....
Petauke 7,531 ....
Senanga 7,204 ....
Serenje 6,008 ....
Solwezi 15,032 ....
Zambezi 8,166 ....

OTHER FEATURES

Bangweulu (lake) ....
Barotseland (reg.) ....
Chambeshi (riv.) ....
Cuando (riv.) ....
Dongwe (riv.) ....
Kabompo (riv.) ....
Kafue (riv.) ....
Kafue Nat'l Park ....
Kalambo (falls) ....
Kariba (dam) ....
Kariba (lake) ....
Luangwa (riv.) ....
Luapula (riv.) ....
Lungwebungu (riv.) ....
Mosi-Oa-Tunya (Victoria)
   (falls) ....
Mulungushi (dam) ....
Mweru (lake) ....
Sunzu (mt.) ....
Tanganyika (lake) ....
Victoria (falls) ....
Zambezi (riv.) ....

Agriculture, Industry and Resources

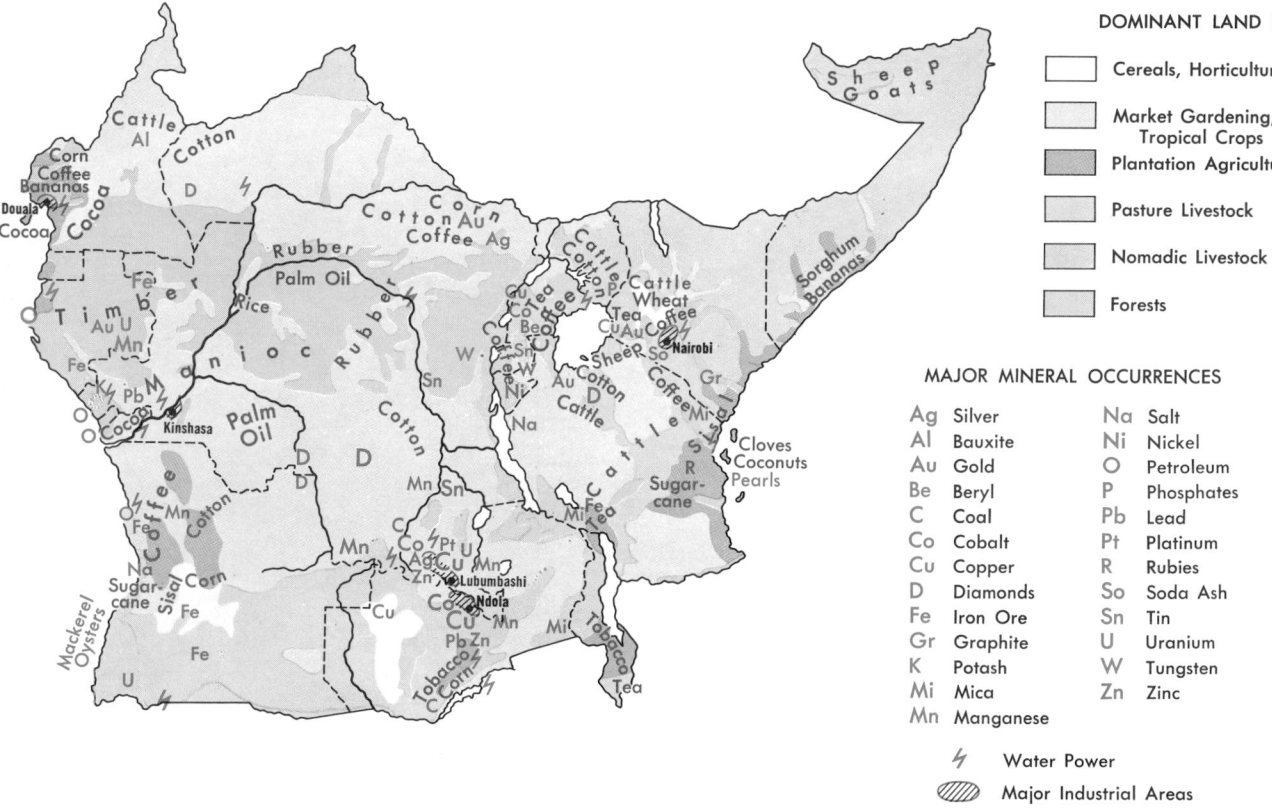

DOMINANT LAND USE

- Cereals, Horticulture, Livestock
- Market Gardening, Diversified Tropical Crops
- Plantation Agriculture
- Pasture Livestock
- Nomadic Livestock Herding
- Forests

MAJOR MINERAL OCCURRENCES

Ag	Silver	Na	Salt
Al	Bauxite	Ni	Nickel
Au	Gold	O	Petroleum
Be	Beryl	P	Phosphates
C	Coal	Pb	Lead
Co	Cobalt	Pt	Platinum
Cu	Copper	R	Rubies
D	Diamonds	So	Soda Ash
Fe	Iron Ore	Sn	Tin
Gr	Graphite	U	Uranium
K	Potash	W	Tungsten
Mi	Mica	Zn	Zinc
Mn	Manganese		

⚡ Water Power

〰 Major Industrial Areas

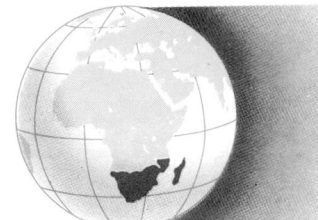

NAMIBIA

AREA 317,827 sq. mi. (823,172 sq. km.)
POPULATION 1,818,000
CAPITAL Windhoek
LARGEST CITY Windhoek
HIGHEST POINT Brandberg 8,550 ft.
(2,606 m.)
MONETARY UNIT rand
MAJOR LANGUAGES Ovambo, Hottentot,
Herero, Afrikaans, English
MAJOR RELIGIONS Tribal religions,
Protestantism

BOTSWANA

AREA 224,764 sq. mi. (582,139 sq. km.)
POPULATION 1,256,000
CAPITAL Gaborone
LARGEST CITY Francistown
HIGHEST POINT Tsodilo Hill 5,922 ft.
(1,805 m.)
MONETARY UNIT pula
MAJOR LANGUAGES Setswana, Shona,
Bushman, English, Afrikaans
MAJOR RELIGIONS Tribal religions,
Protestantism

ZIMBABWE

AREA 150,803 sq. mi. (390,580 sq. km.)
POPULATION 9,122,000
CAPITAL Harare
LARGEST CITY Harare
HIGHEST POINT Mt. Inyangani 8,517 ft.
(2,596 m.)
MONETARY UNIT Zimbabwe dollar
MAJOR LANGUAGES English, Shona,
Ndebele
MAJOR RELIGIONS Tribal religions,
Protestantism

SOUTH AFRICA

AREA 455,318 sq. mi. (1,179,274 sq. km.)
POPULATION 34,492,000
CAPITALS Cape Town, Pretoria
LARGEST CITY Johannesburg
HIGHEST POINT Injasuti 11,182 ft. (3,408 m.)
MONETARY UNIT rand
MAJOR LANGUAGES Afrikaans, English,
Xhosa, Zulu, Sesotho
MAJOR RELIGIONS Protestantism,
Roman Catholicism, Islam, Hinduism,
tribal religions

MOZAMBIQUE

AREA 303,769 sq. mi. (786,762 sq. km.)
POPULATION 15,326,000
CAPITAL Maputo
LARGEST CITY Maputo
HIGHEST POINT Mt. Binga 7,992 ft.
(2,436 m.)
MONETARY UNIT metical
MAJOR LANGUAGES Makua, Thonga,
Shona, Portuguese
MAJOR RELIGIONS Tribal religions,
Roman Catholicism, Islam

MADAGASCAR

AREA 226,657 sq. mi. (587,041 sq. km.)
POPULATION 9,985,000
CAPITAL Antananarivo
LARGEST CITY Antananarivo
HIGHEST POINT Maromokotro 9,436 ft.
(2,876 m.)
MONETARY UNIT Madagascar franc
MAJOR LANGUAGES Malagasy, French
MAJOR RELIGIONS Tribal religions,
Roman Catholicism, Protestantism

MAURITIUS

AREA 790 sq. mi. (2,046 sq. km.)
POPULATION 1,068,000
CAPITAL Port Louis
LARGEST CITY Port Louis
HIGHEST POINT 2,711 ft. (826 m.)
MONETARY UNIT Mauritian rupee
MAJOR LANGUAGES English, French,
French Creole, Hindi, Urdu
MAJOR RELIGIONS Hinduism, Christianity,
Islam

LESOTHO

AREA 11,720 sq. mi. (30,355 sq. km.)
POPULATION 1,700,000
CAPITAL Maseru
LARGEST CITY Maseru
HIGHEST POINT 11,425 ft. (3,482 m.)
MONETARY UNIT loti
MAJOR LANGUAGES Sesotho, English
MAJOR RELIGIONS Tribal religions,
Christianity

SWAZILAND

AREA 6,705 sq. mi. (17,366 sq. km.)
POPULATION 681,000
CAPITAL Mbabane
LARGEST CITY Manzini
HIGHEST POINT Emlembe 6,109 ft.
(1,862 m.)
MONETARY UNIT lilangeni
MAJOR LANGUAGES siSwati, English
MAJOR RELIGIONS Tribal religions,
Christianity

COMOROS

AREA 719 sq. mi. (1,862 sq. km.)
POPULATION 484,000
CAPITAL Moroni
LARGEST CITY Moroni
HIGHEST POINT Karthala 7,746 ft.
(2,361 m.)
MONETARY UNIT CFA franc
MAJOR LANGUAGES Arabic, French,
Swahili
MAJOR RELIGION Islam

SEYCHELLES

AREA 145 sq. mi. (375 sq. km.)
POPULATION 67,000
CAPITAL Victoria
LARGEST CITY Victoria
HIGHEST POINT Morne Seychellois
2,993 ft. (912 m.)
MONETARY UNIT Seychellois rupee
MAJOR LANGUAGES English, French,
Creole
MAJOR RELIGION Roman Catholicism

REUNION

AREA 969 sq. mi. (2,510 sq. km.)
POPULATION 570,000
CAPITAL St-Denis

MAYOTTE

AREA 144 sq. mi. (373 sq. km.)
POPULATION 47,300
CAPITAL Dzaoudzi

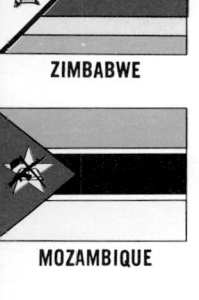

ZIMBABWE **BOTSWANA** **SOUTH AFRICA** **LESOTHO** **SWAZILAND**

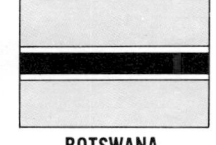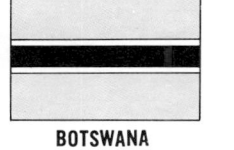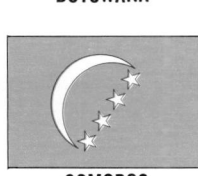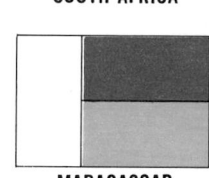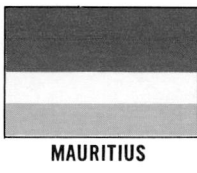

MOZAMBIQUE **COMOROS** **MADAGASCAR** **MAURITIUS** **SEYCHELLES**

NAMIBIA

Agriculture, Industry and Resources

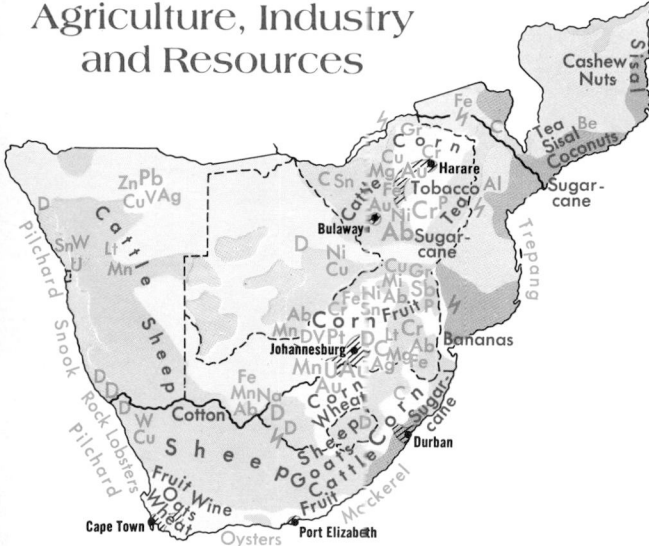

DOMINANT LAND USE

☐	Cereals, Horticulture, Livestock
☐	Market Gardening, Diversified Tropical Crops
☐	Plantation Agriculture
☐	Pasture Livestock
☐	Nomadic Livestock Herding
☐	Forests
☐	Nonagricultural Land

⚡ Water Power
▨ Major Industrial Areas

MAJOR MINERAL OCCURRENCES

Ab	Asbestos	Cu	Copper	Mn	Manganese
Ag	Silver	D	Diamonds	Na	Salt
Al	Bauxite	Fe	Iron Ore	Ni	Nickel
Au	Gold	Gr	Graphite	P	Phosphates
Be	Beryl	Lt	Lithium	Pb	Lead
C	Coal	Mg	Magnesium	Pt	Platinum
Cr	Chromium	Mi	Mica		
Sb	Antimony
Sn	Tin
U	Uranium
V	Vanadium
W	Tungsten
Zn	Zinc

BOTSWANA

CITIES and TOWNS

Dinokwe 560 .... D4
Francistown 22,000 .... D4
Gaborone (cap.) 21,000 ..... D4
Ghanzi 1,198 .... C4
Kanye 10,664 .... D5
Kasane 1,476 .... D3
Lobatse 11,936 .... D5
Mahalapye 12,056 .... D4
Maun 9,614 .... C4
Mochudi 6,945 .... D4
Molepolole 9,448 .... D4
Palapye 5,217 .... D4
Ramotswa 7,991 .... D4
Selebi-Pikwe 20,572 ...... D4
Serowe 15,723 .... D4

OTHER FEATURES

Chobe (riv.) C3
Chobe Nat'l Park D3
Dau (lake) C4
Kalahari (des.) C4
Kaukauveld (mts.) C3
Limpopo (riv.) D4
Mababe (depr.) C3
Makgadikgadi (salt pan) .. D3
Molopo (riv.) C5
Ngami (lake) C4
Ngamiland (reg.) C3
Nossob (riv.) B4
Okovango (riv.) C3
Okovango (swamps) C3
Orange (riv.) B5
Shashe (riv.) D4
Tati (riv.) D4
Tsodilo Hill (mt.) C3
Xau (Dau) (lake) C4

COMOROS

CITIES and TOWNS

Fomboni 3,229 .... G2
Mitsamiouli 3,196 .... G2
Moroni (cap.) 12,000 ...... G2
Mutsamudu 7,652 .... G2

OTHER FEATURES

Mwali (Mohéli) (isl.) G2
Njazidja (Grand Comoro) (isl.) G2
Nzwani (Anjouan) (isl.) G2

LESOTHO

CITIES and TOWNS

Leribe 5,200 .... D5

Mafeteng 4,600 .... D5
Maseru (cap.) 71,500 ...... D5
Mohaleshoek 3,600 .... D6

MADAGASCAR

PROVINCES

Antananarivo 2,167,973 .... H3
Antsiranana 597,982 .... H2
Fianarantsoa 1,804,365 .... H4
Mahajanga 819,750 .... H3
Toamasina 1,179,660 .... H3
Toliara 1,034,114 .... G4

CITIES and TOWNS

Ambalavao 6,988 .... H4
Ambanja 12,258 .... H2
Ambatolampy 11,539 ...... H3
Ambatondrazaka 18,044 .. H3
Ambilobe 9,415 .... H2
Ambodifototra 1,112 .... J3
Ambositra 16,780 .... H4
Andapa 6,275 .... H2
Antalaha 17,541 .... J2
Antananarivo (cap.)
451,808 .... H3
Antsirabe 32,979 .... H3
Antsiranana 40,443 .... H2
Antsohihy 8,721 .... H2
Arivonimamo 8,497 .... H3
Belo-Tsiribihina 4,403 .... G3
Brickaville (Vohibinany)
1,741 .... H3
Diégo-Suarez (Antsiranana)
40,443 .... H2
Faradofay 19,605 .... H5
Farafangana 10,817 .... H4
Fenoarivo, Toamasina 7,696 ... H3
Fianarantsoa 68,054 .... H4
Fort-Dauphin (Faradofay)
19,605 .... H5
Foulpointe H3
Hell-Ville 6,183 .... H2
Ihosy 4,521 .... H4
Maevatanana 7,197 .... H3
Maintirano 6,375 .... G3
Majunga 65,864 .... H3
Manakara 19,768 .... H4
Mananjary 14,638 .... H4
Mandritsara 6,826 .... H3
Maroantsetra 6,645 .... J3
Marovoay 20,253 .... H3
Moramanga 10,806 .... H3
Morombe 6,967 .... G4
Morondava 19,061 .... G4
Port-Bergé 4,734 .... H2
Sambava 6,215 .... J2
Sosumav 10,946 .... H2
Tamatave (Toamasina)
77,395 .... H3
(continued on following page)

Topography

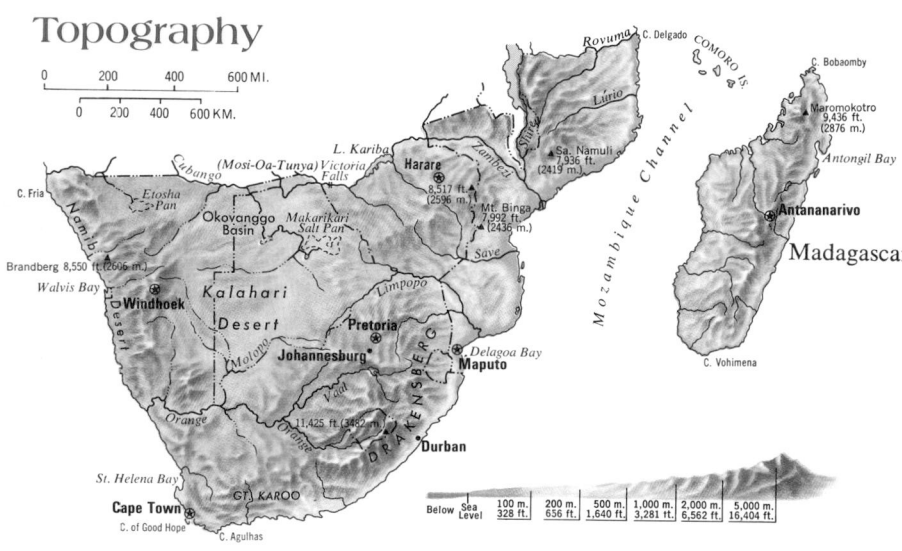

0 200 400 600 MI.
0 200 400 600 KM.

Below Sea Level | 100 m. 328 ft. | 200 m. 656 ft. | 500 m. 1,640 ft. | 1,000 m. 3,281 ft. | 2,000 m. 6,562 ft. | 5,000 m. 16,404 ft.

Tananarive (Antananarivo) 451,808 ....H3
Tanganinony 6,952 ....H4
Toamasina 77 395 ....H3
Toliara (Tuléar) 45,676 ....G4
Tsiroanomandidy 11,444 ....H3
Vangaindrano 3,249 ....H4
Vohibinany 1,741 ....H3
Vohimarina (Vohémar) 4,289 ..J2
Vohipeno 2,736 ....H4

OTHER FEATURES

Alaotra (lake) H3
Amber (Bobaomby) (cape) H2
Antongil (bay) J3
Barren (isls.) G3
Betsiboka (riv.) H3
Bobaomby (Amber) (cape) H2
Boby, Pic (mt.) H4
Chesterfield (isl.) G3
Ikopa (riv.) H3
Itasy (lake) H3
Mahajamba (bay) H2
Mananara (riv.) H4
Mananbao (riv.) G3
Mangoky (riv.) G4
Mangoro (riv.) H3
Maromokotro (mt.) H2
Masoala (pen.) J3
Menarandra (riv.) H4
Mozambique (chan.) G3
Nosy Be (isl.) H2
Nosy Boraha (isl.) J3
Onilahy (riv.) G4
Pangalanes (canal) H4
Radama (isls.) H2
Saint-André (cape) G3
Saint-Marie (Nosy Boraha) (isl.) J3
Saint-Marie (Vohimena) (cape) G5
Saint-Sébastien (cape) H2
Sofia (riv.) H3
Tsiafajavona (mt.) H3
Tsiribihina (riv.) G3
Vohimena (cape) G5

MAURITIUS

CITIES and TOWNS

Curepipe 52,709 ....G5
Mahébourg 15,463 ....G5
Port Louis (cap.) 141,022 ......G5
Quatre Bornes 51,638 ....G5
Souillac 3,361 ....G5

OTHER FFATURES

Mascarene (isls.) F5

MAYOTTE

CITIES and TOWNS

Dzaoudzi (cap.) 196 ....H2

MOZAMBIQUE

PROVINCES

Cabo Delgado 940,000 ....F2
Gaza 999,900 ....E4
Inhambane 977,000 ....E4
Manica 541,200 ....E4
Maputo 491,800 ....E5
Maputo (city) 755,300 ....E5
Nampula 2,402,700 ....F2
Niassa 514,100 ....F2
Sofala 1,055,200 ....E3
Tete 831,000 ....E3
Zambézia 2,500,000 ....F3

CITIES and TOWNS

Angoche 1,714 ....G3
Bartolomeu Dias ○ 6,102 ....F4
Beira 46,293 ....F3
Beira* 130,398 ....F3
Chibuto 23,763 ....E4
Chicualacuala 2,050 ....E4
Chimoio 4,507 ....E3
Chinde 742 ....F3
Dona Ana (Mutarara) 686 .....F3
Dondo 2,112 ....F3
Funhalouro ○ 42,366 ....E4
Ibo 1,015 ....G2
Inhambane 4,975 ....F4
Inhaminga 1,607 ....F3
Inharrime 856 ....F4
Lichinga 3,011 ....F2
Lumbo ○ 11,080 ....G3
Lúrio ○ 13,417 ....G2
Mabalane ○ 13,158 ....E4
Mabote ○ 28,900 ....E4
Machanga ○ 15,754 ....F4
Machaze ○ 42,496 ....E4
Mandié ○ 24,382 ....E3
Mandimba ○ 7,634 ....F2
Manhiça 1,680 ....E5
Maniamba ○ 2,045 ....F2
Maputo (cap.) 755,300 ....E5
Massangena ○ 3,301 ....E4
Massinga 517 ....F4
Moçambique 1,730 ....G3
Mocímboa da Praia 935 ....G2
Mocuba 2,293 ....F3
Montepuez 2,837 ....F2
Mualama ○ 34,992 ....F3
Mucojo ○ 15,867 ....G2
Mueda 1,583 ....F2
Mutarara (Dona Ana) 686 .....F3
Nacala 4,601 ....G2
Nampula 23,072 ....F3
Pafúri ○ 2,599 ....E4
Pemba 3,629 ....G2
Quelimane 10,522 ....F3
Quionga ○ 3,181 ....G2
Quissico 2,615 ....E4
Songo 2,230 ....E3
Tete 4,549 ....E3
Vila de Sena ○ 21,074 ....E3
Xai-Xai 5,234 ....E5

OTHER FEATURES

Angoche (isl.) G3
Bazaruto, Ilha do (isl.) F4
Binga (mt.) E3
Cabora Bassa (dam) E3
Changane (riv.) E4
Chirua (lake) F3
Delagoa (bay) E5
Delgado (cape) G2
Gorongosa Nat'l Park E3
Ligonha (riv.) F3
Limpopo (riv.) E4
Lugenda (riv.) F2
Lúrio (riv.) F2
Mazoe (riv.) E3
Mozambique (chan.) G3
Namuli, Serra (mt.) F3
Nyasa (lake) E2
Olifants (riv.) D4
Rovuma (riv.) F2
São Sebastião (pt.) F4
Save (riv.) E4
Shire (riv.) E3
Zambezi (riv.) E3

NAMIBIA

CITIES and TOWNS

Aroab 783 ....B5
Aus 767 ....B5
Berseba B5
Bethanie 1,207 ....B5
Gibeon B5
Gobabis 4,428 ....B4
Grootfontein 4,627 ....B3
Kalkfeld 587 ....B4
Kamanjab 713 ....A3
Karasburg 2,693 ....B5
Karibib 1,653 ....B4
Keetmanshoop 10,297 ....B5
Koes 514 ....B5
Lüderitz 6,642 ....A5
Maltahöhe 1,313 ....B4
Mariental 4,629 ....B4
Okahandja 1,688 ....B4
Omaruru 2,783 ....B4
Ondangwa B3
Opuno A3
Oranjemund 2,594 ....B5
Oshakati B3
Otavi 1,814 ....B3
Otjiwarongo 8,018 ....B4
Outjo 2,545 ....B4
Rehoboth 5,363 ....B4
Rundu 521 ....B3
Stampriet 271 ....B4
Swakopmund 5,681 ....A4
Tsumeb 12,338 ....B3
Usakos 2,334 ....B4
Warmbad 810 ....B5
Windhoek (cap.) 61,369 ....B4
Witvlei 303 ....B4

OTHER FEATURES

Brandberg (mt.) A4
Caprivi Strip (reg.) C3
Chobe (riv.) C3
Cross (cape) A4
Cubango (riv.) B3
Cunene (riv.) A3
Damaraland (reg.) B4
Diamond Coast (reg.) A5
Elephant (riv.) B5
Etosha Pan (salt pan) B3
Fish (riv.) B5
Fria (cape) A3
Great Namaland (reg.) B4
Hollam's Bird (isl.) A4
Hottentot (bay) A5
Kalahari (des.) C4
Kaokoveld (reg.) A3
Kaukauveld (mts.) C3
Kuiseb (riv.) B4
Lüderitz (bay) A5
Namib (des.) A3
Nossob (riv.) B4
Okovango (riv.) C3
Omatako (riv.) B3
Ovamboland (reg.) B3
Ruacana Falls (falls) A3
Skeleton Coast (reg.) A3
Swakop (riv.) B4
Ugab (riv.) A4
Zambezi (riv.) C3

REUNION

CITIES and TOWNS

Le Port 21,564 ....F5
Saint-Benoît 7,778 ....G5
Saint-Denis (cap.) 80,075 ......F5
Saint-Denis* 104,603 ....F5
Saint-Joseph 8,928 ....G6
Saint-Louis 10,252 ....F5
Saint-Pierre 21,817 ....F5

OTHER FEATURES

Bassas da India (isl.) F4
Europa (isl.) G4
Glorioso (isls.) H2

Juan de Nova (isl.) G3
Mascarene (isls.) F5
Piton des Neiges (mt.) G5

SEYCHELLES

CITIES and TOWNS

Anse Boileau† 3,420 ....H5
Anse Royale† 3,182 ....H5
Cascade† 2,600 ....H5
Victoria (cap.) 15,559 ....H5
Victoria* 23,012 ....H5

OTHER FEATURES

Aldabra (isls.) H1
Assumption (isl.) H1
Astove (isl.) H2
Cerf (isl.) H5
Cosmoledo (isls.) H1
Curieuse (isl.) H5
Félicité (isl.) J5
Frigate (isl.) J5
La Digue (isl.) J5
Mahé (isl.) H5
Morne Seychellois (mt.) H5
North (isl.) H5
Praslin (isl.) H5
Sainte Anne (isl.) H5
Silhouette (isl.) H5

SOUTH AFRICA

PROVINCES

Cape Province 5,543,506 ....C6
Natal 5,722,215 ....E5
Orange Free State 1,833,216 ..D5
Transvaal 10,673,033 ....D4

AUTONOMOUS REPUBLICS

Bophuthatswana 1,200,000 ....D5
Ciskei D6
Transkei 2,000,000 ....D6
Venda 450,000 ....E4

CITIES and TOWNS

Alberton 23,988 ....H6
Alexandra 57,040 ....H6
Aliwal North 12,311 ....D6
Barberton 12,382 ....E5
Beaufort West 17,862 ....C6
Bellville 49,026 ....F6
Benoni 151,294 ....J6
Bethlehem 29,918 ....D5
Bisho D6
Bloemfontein 149,836 ....D5
Boksburg 106,126 ....J6
Brakpan 73,210 ....J6
Brits 12,182 ....D5
Butterworth (Gcuwa) 2,769 ...D6
Cape Town (cap.) 697,514 ......E6
Carltonville 40,641 ....G7
Cradock 20,822 ....C6
De Aar 18,057 ....C6
Dundee 17,162 ....E5
Durban 736,852 ....E5
East London 119,727 ....D6
Edendale 41,194 ....D5
Edenvale 25,126 ....H6
Elsiesrivier 63,706 ....F6
Ermelo 19,036 ....E5
Eshowe 4,552 ....E5
Estcourt 10,922 ....D5
Fort Beaufort 11,640 ....D6
Gcuwa 2,769 ....D6
George 24,625 ....C6
Germiston 221,972 ....H6
Glencoe 10,513 ....E5
Goodwood 31,592 ....F6

Graaff-Reinet 22,392 ....C6
Grahamstown 41,302 ....D6
Grassy Park 32,709 ....E6
Griquatown 2,996 ....C5
Harrismith 16,082 ....D5
Heidelberg 12,521 ....J7
Hermanus 4,956 ....G7
Howick 12,429 ....E5
Johannesburg 654,232 ....H6
Kempton Park 37,205 ....J6
Kimberley 105,258 ....C5
King William's Town 15,798 ...D6
Klerksdorp 63,558 ....D5
Knysna 13,479 ....C6
Kokstad 10,227 ....D6
Kraaifontein 10,286 ....F6
Kroonstad 51,988 ....D5
Krugersdorp 92,725 ....H6
Ladybrand 8,757 ....D5
Ladysmith 28,920 ....D5
Lambert's Bay 3,247 ....B6
Mafikeng (Mafeking) 6,515 ...D5

Matatiele 3,853 ....D6
Messina 21,121 ....D4
Middelburg, Cape Prov. 12,121 ....D6
Middelburg, Transvaal 26,942 ....D5
Milnerton 10,893 ....F6
Mmabatho D5
Mossel Bay 17,574 ....C6
Nelspruit 25,092 ....E5
Newcastle 14,407 ....E5
Nigel 41,179 ....J7
Nyanga 15,655 ....E6
Odendaalsrus 15,603 ....D5
Oudtshoorn 26,907 ....C6
Paarl 49,244 ....F6
Parow 60,768 ....F6
Parys 17,447 ....D5
Pietermaritzburg 114,822 ......E5
Pietersburg 27,174 ....D4
Piet Retief 10,056 ....D5
Pinelands 11,769 ....F6

Pinetown 22,721 ....E6
Port Elizabeth 392,231 ....D6
Port Nolloth 2,893 ....B5
Port Saint Johns (Umzimbuvu) 1,817 ....D6
Potchefstroom 57,443 ....D5
Pretoria (cap.) 545,450 ....D5
Queenstown 39,304 ....D6
Randburg 43,257 ....H6
Randfontein 50,481 ....H6
Richards Bay 3,598 ....E5
Robertson 10,237 ....C6
Roodeport 115,366 ....H6
Rustenburg 22,303 ....D5
Saldanha 4,994 ....B6
Simonstown 12,137 ....E7
Sishen 2,692 ....C5
Somerset East 10,383 ....D6
Somerset West 11,828 ....F6
Soweto 602,043 ....H6
Springs 142,812 ....H6
Standerton 21,038 ....D5

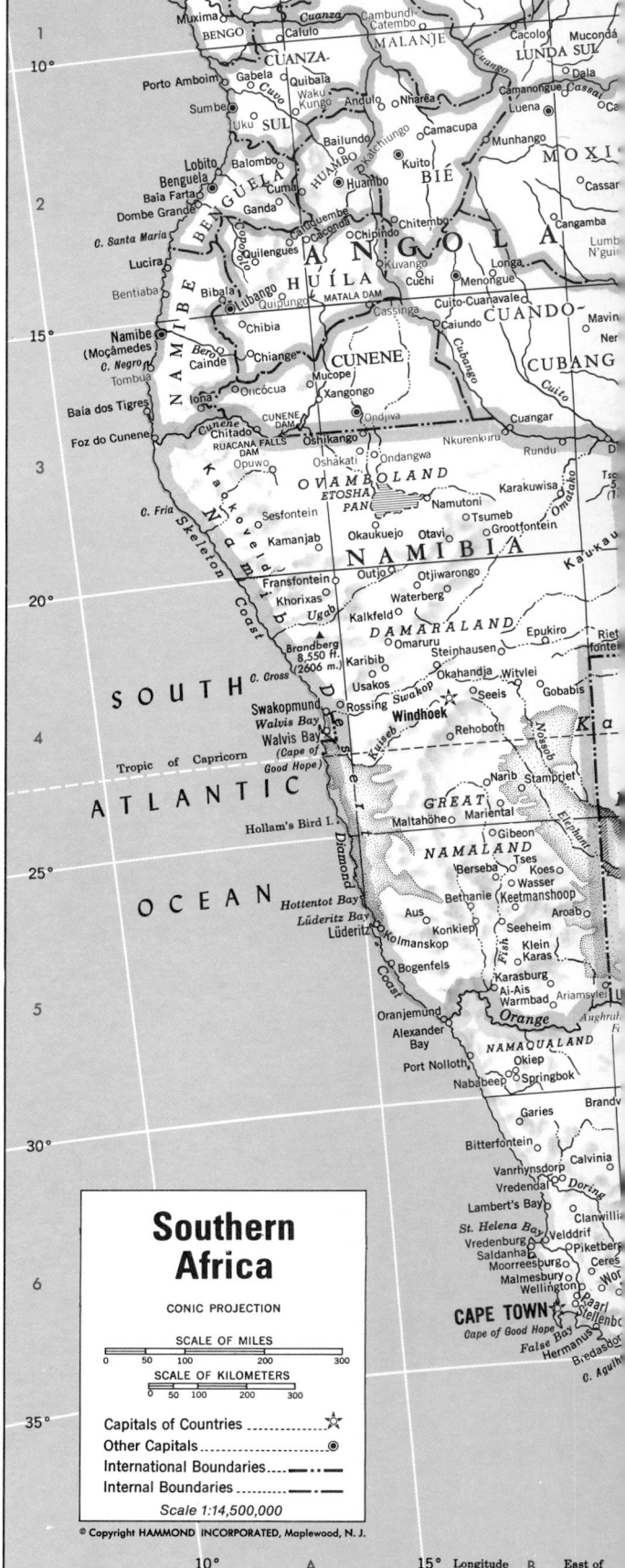

Southern Africa

CONIC PROJECTION

SCALE OF MILES
0 50 100 200 300

SCALE OF KILOMETERS
0 50 100 200 300

Capitals of Countries ....☆
Other Capitals ....◎
International Boundaries ....▬ ▪ ▬
Internal Boundaries ....▬▬

Scale 1:14,500,000

® Copyright HAMMOND INCORPORATED, Maplewood, N. J.

Stanger 11,064 .....E5
Stellenbosch 29,955 .....F6
Strand 24,503 .....F7
Stutterheim 12,077 .....D6
Taung 1,316 .....C5
Tembisa 81,821 .....H6
Thabazimbi 6,711 .....D4
Thohoyandou E4
Uitenhage 70,517 .....D6
Ulundi E5
Umtata 25,216 .....D6
Umzimkulu 1,817 .....D6
Upington 28,632 .....C5
Vanderbijl Park 78,754 .....D5
Ventersdorp G6
Vereeniging 172,549 .....D5
Volksrust 10,238 .....D5
Vryburg 16,916 .....C5
Vryheid 16,992 .....E5
Walvis Bay 21,725 .....A4
Warmbad 8,343 .....D5
Welkom 67,472 .....D5

Wellington 17,092 .....B6
Westonaria 36,253 .....H7
Witbank 37,456 .....E5
Worcester 41,198 .....B6
Zeerust 6,972 .....D5

OTHER FEATURES
Addo Nat'l Park D6
Agulhas (cape) B6
Algoa (bay) D6
Aughrabies (falls) B5
Blesbok (riv.) J7
Bot (riv.) G7
Bredasdorp Nat'l Park C7
Cape (pen.) E7
Cape (pt.) F7
Crocodile (riv.) H6
Diep (riv.) F6
Doring (riv.) B6
Drakensberg (range) D5
Duiker (pt.) E6

False (bay) F7
Good Hope (cape) E7
Great Fish (riv.) D6
Great Karoo (reg.) C6
Great Kei (riv.) D6
Griqualand West (reg.) C5
Groote (riv.) C6
Hangklip (cape) F7
Hartbees (riv.) C5
Hout (riv.) E6
Jukskei (riv.) H6
Kalahari Gemsbok Nat'l Park C5
King George's (falls) B5
Klip (riv.) H6
Kruger Nat'l Park E4
Kruis (riv.) F7
Limpopo (riv.) D4
Maclear (cape) F7
Molopo (riv.) C5
Mountain Zebra Nat'l Park C6
Namaqualand (reg.) B5
Nieuweld (range) C6

Olifants (riv.) D4
Orange (riv.) B5
Palmiet (riv.) F7
Plettenberg (bay) C6
Pondoland (reg.) D6
Robben (isl.) E6
Royal Natal Nat'l Park D5
Saint Francis (bay) D6
Saint Helena (bay) B6
Saint Lucia (cape) E5
Saint Lucia (lake) E5
Sak (riv.) C6
Sandown (bay) E7
Seal (isl.) F7
Slangkop (pt.) F6
Sneeuwkop (mt.) F6
Stettyn (mt.) G6
Table (bay) E6
Table (mt.) E6
Vaal (riv.) D5
Verwoerd (dam) D6

Walvis (bay) A4
Witwatersberg (range) G6
Witwatersrand (reg.) H7
Zonderend (riv.) G6
Zululand (reg.) E5
Zwart (riv.) G7

SWAZILAND

CITIES and TOWNS

Manzini 28,837 .....E5
Mbabane (cap.) 23,109 .....E5
Siteki 1,362 .....E5

ZIMBABWE

CITIES and TOWNS

Bindura 17,000 .....E3
Bulawayo 359,000 .....D3
Chegutu 12,000 .....E3

Chinhoyi 25,000 .....D3
Gweru 68,000 .....D3
Harare (cap.) 601,000 .....E3
Hwange 33,000 .....D3
Kadoma 32,000 .....D3
Kwekwe 54,000 .....D3
Marondera 23,000 .....E3
Masvingo 22,000 .....E4
Matopos* 11,330 .....D4
Mutare 61,000 .....E3
Mwenezi* 7,830 .....E4
Rusape 5,286 .....E3
Salisbury (Harare) (cap.)
  601,000 .....E3
Shurugwi 8,387 .....E3
Tuli* 340 .....D4
Zvishavane 20,000 .....E4

OTHER FEATURES

Inyanga Nat'l Park E3
Kariba (dam) D3

Kariba (lake) D3
Lundi (riv.) E4
Mashonaland (reg.) E3
Matabeleland (reg.) D3
Mazowe (riv.) D3
Mushandike Nat'l Park D4
Sabi (riv.) E3
Sanyati (riv.) D3
Shangani (riv.) D3
Shashe (riv.) D3
Victoria (falls) C3
Zambezi (riv.) D3
Zimbabwe Nat'l Park E4

*City and suburbs.
†Population of parish.
‡Population of subdivision.

Population Distribution

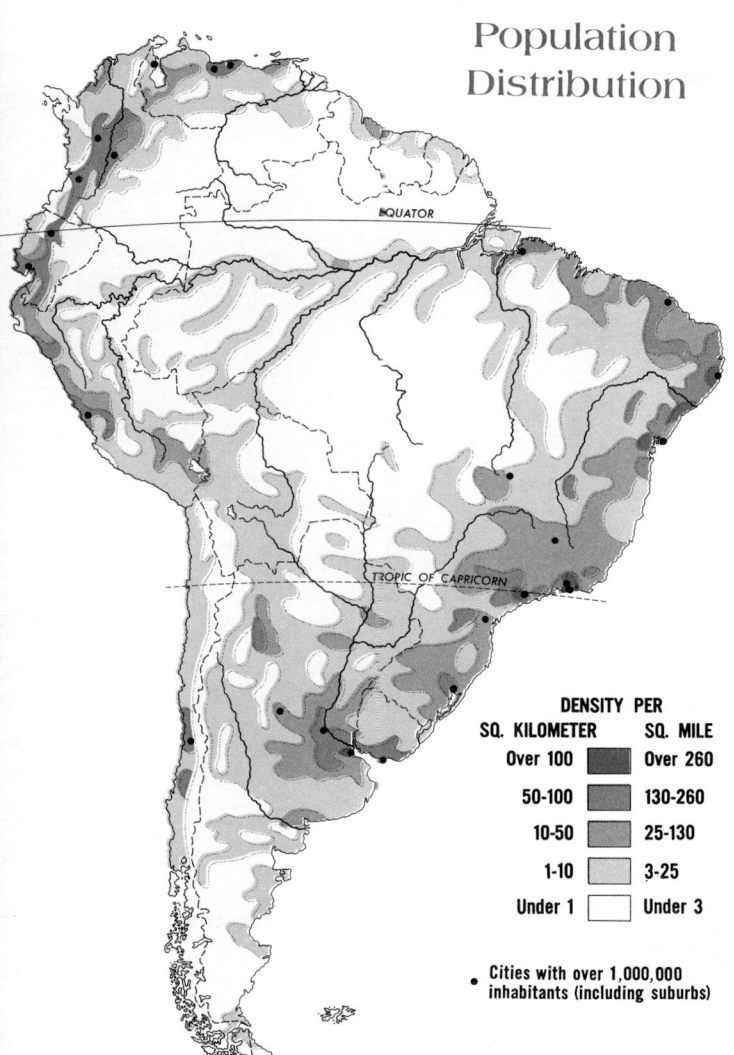

AREA   6,875,000 sq. mi. (17,806,250 sq. km.)
POPULATION   297,000,000
LARGEST CITY   São Paulo
HIGHEST POINT   Cerro Aconcagua 22,831 ft.
     (6,959 m.)
LOWEST POINT   Salina Grande -131 ft. (-40 m.)

DENSITY PER

SQ. KILOMETER	SQ. MILE
Over 100	Over 260
50-100	130-260
10-50	25-130
1-10	3-25
Under 1	Under 3

• Cities with over 1,000,000 inhabitants (including suburbs)

Vegetation

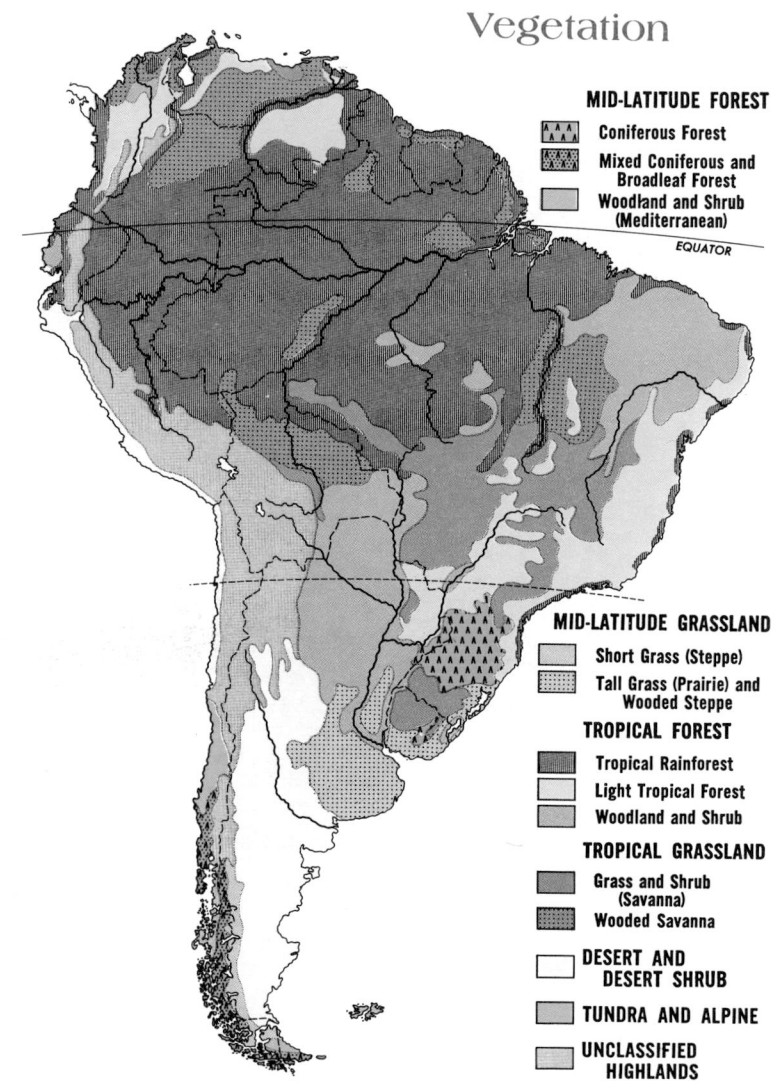

MID-LATITUDE FOREST
- Coniferous Forest
- Mixed Coniferous and Broadleaf Forest
- Woodland and Shrub (Mediterranean)

EQUATOR

MID-LATITUDE GRASSLAND
- Short Grass (Steppe)
- Tall Grass (Prairie) and Wooded Steppe

TROPICAL FOREST
- Tropical Rainforest
- Light Tropical Forest
- Woodland and Shrub

TROPICAL GRASSLAND
- Grass and Shrub (Savanna)
- Wooded Savanna

DESERT AND DESERT SHRUB

TUNDRA AND ALPINE

UNCLASSIFIED HIGHLANDS

Aconcagua (mt.) ...C6
Aguja (pt.), Peru ...A3
Alagoinhas, Brazil ...F4
Alto Ritacuva (mt.),
     Colombia ...B2
Amazon (riv.), Brazil ...D3
Anápolis, Brazil ...E4
Ancohuma (mt.), Bolivia ...C4
Andes (range) ...B3
Antofagasta, Chile ...B5
Aracaju, Brazil ...F4
Araguaia (riv.), Brazil ...E3
Arequipa, Peru ...B4
Argentina ...C6
Arica, Chile ...B4
Aripuanã (riv.), Brazil ...D3
Asunción (cap.), Paraguay ...D5
Atacama (des.), Chile ...C5
Ayacucho, Peru ...B4
Bahía Blanca, Argentina ...C6
Bananal (isl.), Brazil ...E4
Barcelona, Venezuela ...C2
Barquisimeto, Venezuela ...C1
Barranquilla, Colombia ...B1
Belém, Brazil ...E3
Belo Horizonte, Brazil ...E4
Boa Vista, Brazil ...C2
Bogotá (cap.), Colombia ...B2
Bolivia ...C4
Borba, Brazil ...D3
Bragança, Brazil ...E3
Brasília (cap.), Brazil ...E4
Brazil ...C3
Bucaramanga, Colombia ...B2
Buenaventura, Colombia ...B2
Buenos Aires (cap.),
     Argentina ...C6
Caatingas (for.), Brazil ...E3
Cajamarca, Peru ...B3
Caldera, Chile ...C5
Cali, Colombia ...B2
Callao, Peru ...B4
Campana (isl.), Chile ...B7
Campinas, Brazil ...E5
Campo Grande, Brazil ...D5
Campos, Brazil ...E5
Caquetá (riv.), Colombia ...B2
Caracas (cap.), Venezuela ...C2
Caroní (riv.), Venezuela ...C2
Cartagena, Colombia ...B1
Catamarca, Argentina ...C5
Cauca (riv.), Colombia ...B2
Caviana (isl.), Brazil ...E2
Caxias do Sul, Brazil ...D5
Cayenne (cap.), Fr. Guiana ...D2
Cerro de Pasco, Peru ...B4
Chiclayo, Peru ...B3
Chile ...B5

Chillán, Chile ...B6
Chiloé (isl.), Chile ...B7
Chimborazo (mt.), Ecuador ...B3
Chimbote, Peru ...B3
Chivilcoy, Argentina ...C6
Chonos (arch.), Chile ...B7
Chubut (riv.), Argentina ...C7
Ciénaga, Colombia ...B1
Ciudad Bolívar, Venezuela ...C2
Cochabamba, Bolivia ...C4
Colombia ...B2
Colorado (riv.), Argentina ...C6
Comodoro Rivadavia,
     Argentina ...C7
Concepción, Chile ...B6
Concepción, Paraguay ...D5
Concordia, Argentina ...D6
Copiapó, Chile ...B5
Coquimbo, Chile ...B6
Corcovado (gulf), Chile ...B7
Córdoba, Argentina ...C6
Coro, Venezuela ...C1
Corrientes, Argentina ...D5
Corrientes (cape), Colombia ...B2
Cúcuta, Colombia ...B2
Cuenca, Ecuador ...B3
Cuiabá, Brazil ...D4
Cumaná, Venezuela ...C2
Cusco, Peru ...B4
Deseado (riv.), Argentina ...C7
Devil's (isl.), Fr. Guiana ...D2
Ecuador ...B3
Encarnación, Paraguay ...D5
Esmeraldas, Ecuador ...A2
Essequibo (riv.), Guyana ...D2
Falkland Islands ...D8
Florianópolis, Brazil ...E5
Formosa, Argentina ...D5
Fortaleza, Brazil ...F3
French Guiana ...D2
Frio (cape), Brazil ...E5
Georgetown (cap.), Guyana ...D2
Goiânia, Brazil ...E4
Gran Chaco (reg.), Brazil ...C5
Grande (riv.), Brazil ...D4
Guaviare (riv.), Colombia ...C2
Guayaquil, Ecuador ...A3
Gurí (res.), Venezuela ...C2
Guyana ...D2
Horn (cape), Chile ...C8
Hoste (isl.), Chile ...B8
Huacho, Peru ...B4
Huaráz, Peru ...B3
Huascarán (mt.), Peru ...B3
Huila (mt.), Colombia ...B2
Humaitá, Brazil ...C3
Ibagué, Colombia ...B2
Ibarra, Ecuador ...B2

Ica, Peru ...B4
Iguazú (falls) ...D5
Ilhéus, Brazil ...F4
Iquique, Chile ...B5
Iquitos, Peru ...B3
Itaipu (dam), Paraguay ...D5
Japurá (riv.), Argentina ...C3
Jequié, Brazil ...E4
João Pessoa, Brazil ...F3
Joinville, Brazil ...E5
Juan Fernández (isls.), Chile ...B6
Juazeiro, Brazil ...E3
Juazeiro do Norte, Brazil ...F3
Juiz de Fora, Brazil ...E5
Jujuy, Argentina ...C5
Juliaca, Peru ...B4
Junín, Argentina ...C6
Juruá (riv.), Brazil ...C3
Juruena (riv.), Brazil ...D4
La Guaira, Venezuela ...C1
La Oroya, Peru ...B4
La Paz (cap.), Bolivia ...C4
La Plata, Argentina ...D6
La Rioja, Argentina ...C5
La Serena, Chile ...B5
Leticia, Colombia ...B3
Lima (cap.), Peru ...B4
Llanos (plain) ...B2
Llullaillaco (mt.) ...C5
Loja, Ecuador ...B3
Londrina, Brazil ...D5
Macapá, Brazil ...D2
Maceió, Brazil ...F3
Madeira (riv.), Brazil ...C3
Madre de Dios (isl.), Chile ...B8
Magdalena (riv.), Colombia ...B2
Magellan (str.) ...C8
Malpelo (isl.), Colombia ...A2
Mamoré (riv.), Bolivia ...C4
Manaus, Brazil ...D3
Manicoré, Brazil ...C3
Manizales, Colombia ...B2
Manta, Ecuador ...A3
Maracaibo, Venezuela ...B1
Maracaibo (lake), Venezuela ...B2
Marajó (isl.), Brazil ...E3
Marañón (riv.), Peru ...B3
Mar del Plata, Argentina ...D6
Margarita (isl.), Venezuela ...C1
Mato Grosso (plat.), Brazil ...D4
Medellín, Colombia ...B2
Melo, Uruguay ...D6
Mendoza, Argentina ...C6
Mercedes, Argentina ...C6
Mercedes, Uruguay ...D6
Mérida, Venezuela ...B2
Misti, El (mt.), Peru ...B4
Mollendo, Peru ...B4

Montes Claros, Brazil ...E4
Montevideo (cap.), Uruguay ...D6
Moquegua, Peru ...B4
Morawhanna, Guyana ...D2
Nahuel Huapi (lake),
     Argentina ...B7
Nassau (bay), Chile ...C8
Natal, Brazil ...F3
Negro (riv.), Argentina ...C6
Negro (riv.), Brazil ...C3
Neiva, Colombia ...B2
Netherlands Antilles ...C1
New Amsterdam, Guyana ...D2
Niterói, Brazil ...E5
Ojos del Salado (mt.) ...C5
Orinoco (delta), Venezuela ...C2
Oruro, Bolivia ...C4
Ovalle, Chile ...B6
Pampas (plain), Argentina ...C6
Paraguai (riv.) ...D4
Paraguay ...D5
Paramaribo (cap.), Suriname ...D2
Paraná (riv.) ...D5
Paraná, Argentina ...C6
Parnaíba, Brazil ...E3
Parnaíba (riv.), Brazil ...E3
Passo Fundo, Brazil ...D5
Pasto, Colombia ...B2
Patagonia (reg.), Argentina ...C7
Paysandú, Uruguay ...D6
Pelotas, Brazil ...D6
Pergamino, Argentina ...C6
Peru ...B3
Pisco, Peru ...B4
Piura, Peru ...A3
Poopó (lake), Bolivia ...C4
Popayán, Colombia ...B2
Porto Alegre, Brazil ...D6
Posadas, Argentina ...D5
Potosí, Bolivia ...C4

Puerto Cabello, Venezuela ...C1
Puerto Madryn, Argentina ...C7
Puerto Montt, Chile ...B7
Puno, Peru ...B4
Punta Arenas, Chile ...B8
Purus (riv.), Brazil ...C3
Putumayo (riv.) ...B3
Quito (cap.), Ecuador ...B2
Rancagua, Chile ...B6
Recife, Brazil ...F3
Resistencia, Argentina ...D5
Ribeirão Preto, Brazil ...E5
Riobamba, Ecuador ...B3
Rio de Janeiro, Brazil ...E5
Rio Grande, Brazil ...D6
Rivera, Uruguay ...D6
Roraima (mt.) ...C2
Rosario, Argentina ...C6
Salado (riv.), Argentina ...C6
Salta, Argentina ...C5
Salto, Uruguay ...D6
Salto Grande (falls),
     Colombia ...B3
Salvador, Brazil ...F4
San Ambrosio (isl.), Chile ...B5
San Antonio (cape),
     Argentina ...D6
San Carlos de Bariloche,
     Argentina ...B7
San Fernando, Venezuela ...C2
San Jorge (gulf), Argentina ...C7
San Juan, Argentina ...C6
San Julián, Argentina ...C7
San Luis, Argentina ...C6
San Miguel de Tucumán,
     Argentina ...C5
San Rafael, Argentina ...C6
Santa Catarina (isl.), Brazil ...E5
Santa Cruz, Argentina ...C8
Santa Cruz, Bolivia ...C4

Santa Fe, Argentina ...C6
Santa Marta, Colombia ...B1
Santarém, Brazil ...D3
Santiago (cap.), Chile ...B6
Santiago del Estero,
     Argentina ...C5
Santos, Brazil ...E5
São Francisco (riv.), Brazil ...E4
São Luís, Brazil ...E3
São Paulo, Brazil ...E5
São Roque (cape), Brazil ...F3
Sarmiento, Argentina ...C7
Selvas (for.), Brazil ...C3
Senhor do Bonfim, Brazil ...F4
Serrinha, Brazil ...F4
Sete Lagoas, Brazil ...E4
Sobradinho (res.), Brazil ...E3
Sobral, Brazil ...E3
Sorocaba, Brazil ...E5
Stanley (cap.), Falkland Is. ...D8
Sucre (cap.), Bolivia ...C4
Sullana, Peru ...A3
Suriname ...D2
Tacna, Peru ...B4
Taguatinga, Brazil ...E4
Taitao (pen.), Chile ...B7
Talara, Argentina ...A3
Talca, Chile ...B6
Talcahuano, Chile ...B6
Taltal, Chile ...B5
Tandil, Argentina ...D6
Tapajós (riv.), Brazil ...D3
Tarapoto, Peru ...B3
Tarija, Bolivia ...C5
Temuco, Chile ...B6
Teófilo Otoni, Brazil ...E4
Teresina, Brazil ...E3
Tierra del Fuego (isl.) ...C8
Titicaca (lake) ...C4
Tocantins (riv.), Brazil ...E4

Tolima (vol.), Colombia ...B2
Trinidad, Bolivia ...C4
Trujillo, Peru ...B3
Trujillo, Venezuela ...C2
Tubarão, Brazil ...E5
Tucuruí (res.), Brazil ...E3
Tumaco, Colombia ...B2
Tumbes, Peru ...A3
Tunjá, Colombia ...B2
Uberaba, Brazil ...E4
Uberlândia, Brazil ...E4
Ucayali (riv.), Peru ...B3
Uruguaiana, Brazil ...D5
Uruguay ...D6
Uruguay (riv.) ...D5
Ushuaia, Argentina ...C8
Uyuni, Bolivia ...C5
Valdés (pen.), Argentina ...C7
Valdivia, Chile ...B6
Valença, Brazil ...F4
Valencia, Venezuela ...C2
Valera, Venezuela ...B2
Valledupar, Colombia ...B1
Vallegrande, Bolivia ...C4
Valparaíso, Chile ...B6
Vaupés (riv.), Colombia ...B2
Venezuela ...C2
Venezuela (gulf), Venezuela ...B1
Viacha, Bolivia ...C4
Viedma, Argentina ...C7
Viedma (lake), Argentina ...B7
Villa María, Argentina ...C6
Villavicencio, Colombia ...B2
Villazón, Bolivia ...C5
Viña del Mar, Chile ...B6
Vitória, Brazil ...F5
Vitória da Conquista, Brazil ...E4
Volta Redonda, Brazil ...E5
Xingu (riv.), Brazil ...D3
Zapala, Argentina ...B6

SO AM

Average January Temperature

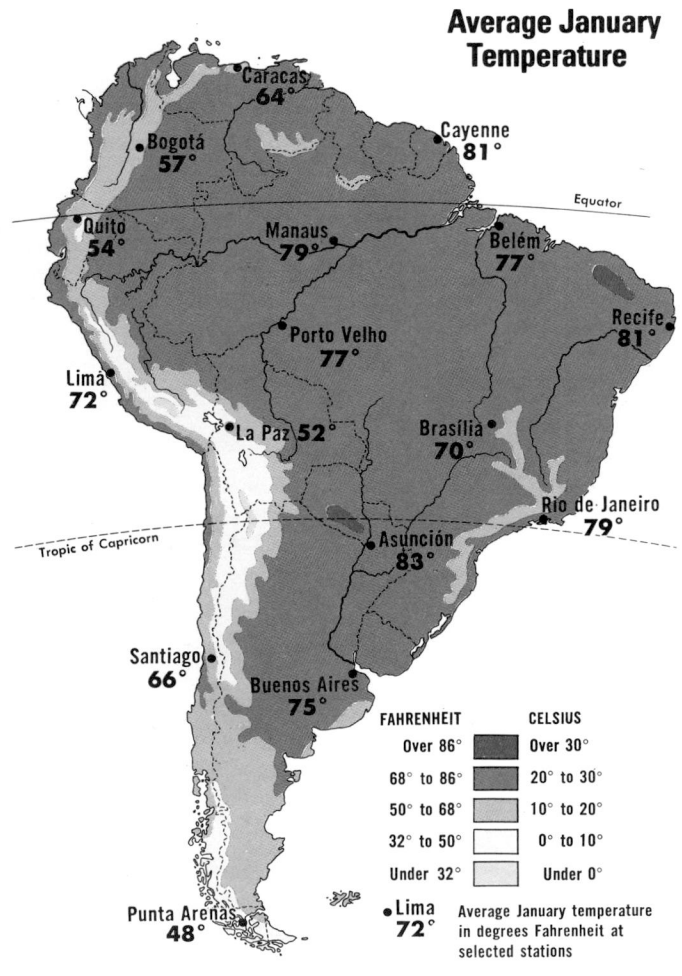

Caracas 64°
Bogotá 57°
Cayenne 81°
Equator
Quito 54°
Manaus 79°
Belém 77°
Lima 72°
Porto Velho 77°
Recife 81°
La Paz 52°
Brasília 70°
Rio de Janeiro 79°
Tropic of Capricorn
Asunción 83°
Santiago 66°
Buenos Aires 75°
Punta Arenas 48°

FAHRENHEIT	CELSIUS
Over 86°	Over 30°
68° to 86°	20° to 30°
50° to 68°	10° to 20°
32° to 50°	0° to 10°
Under 32°	Under 0°

• Lima 72° Average January temperature in degrees Fahrenheit at selected stations

Average July Temperature

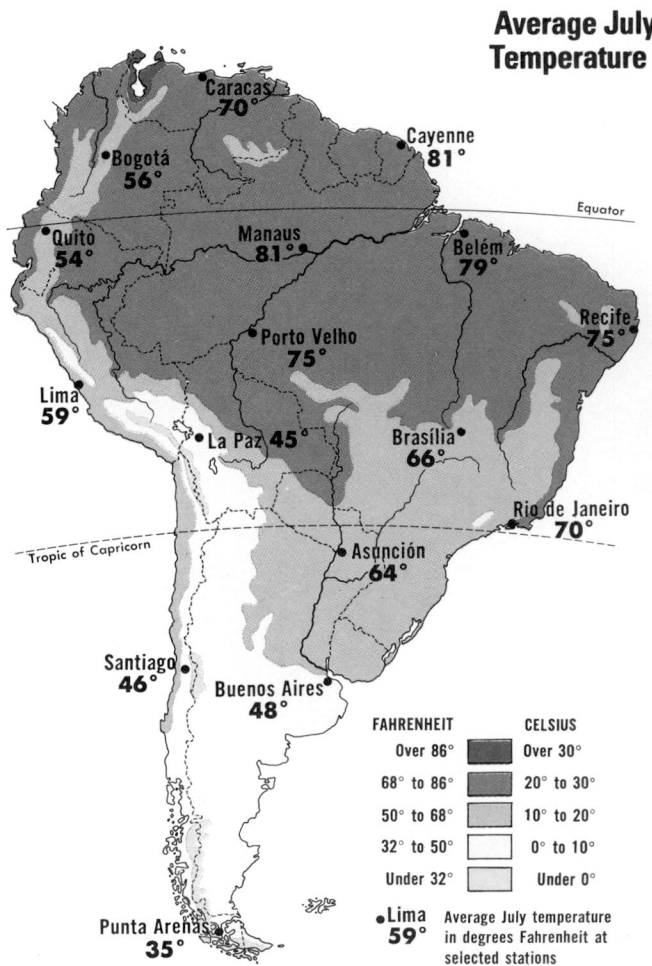

Caracas 70°
Bogotá 56°
Cayenne 81°
Equator
Quito 54°
Manaus 81°
Belém 79°
Lima 59°
Porto Velho 75°
Recife 75°
La Paz 45°
Brasília 66°
Rio de Janeiro 70°
Tropic of Capricorn
Asunción 64°
Santiago 46°
Buenos Aires 48°
Punta Arenas 35°

FAHRENHEIT	CELSIUS
Over 86°	Over 30°
68° to 86°	20° to 30°
50° to 68°	10° to 20°
32° to 50°	0° to 10°
Under 32°	Under 0°

• Lima 59° Average July temperature in degrees Fahrenheit at selected stations

Rainfall

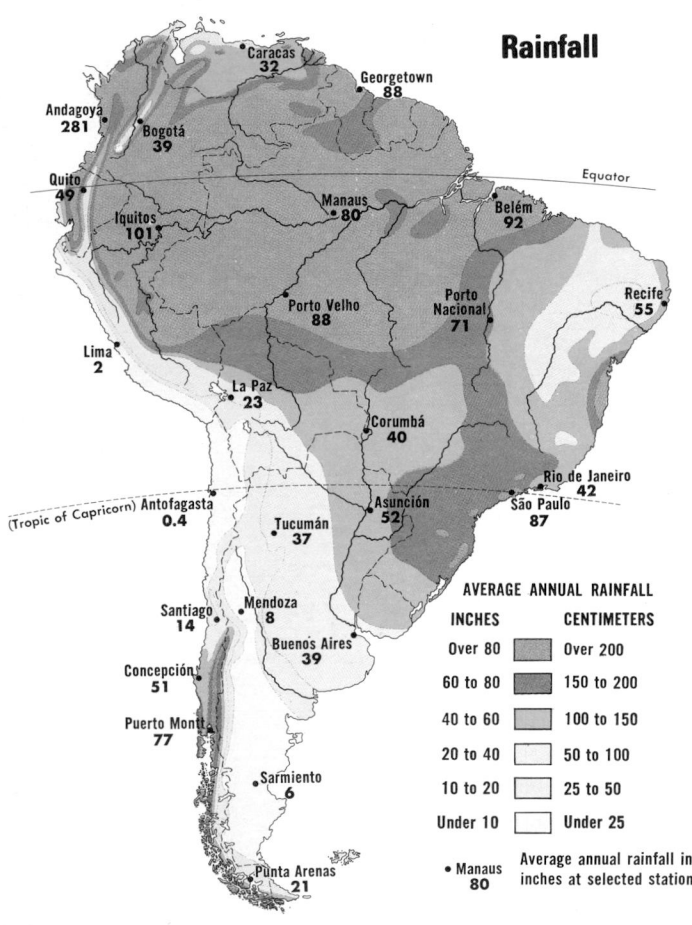

Caracas 32
Georgetown 88
Andagoya 281
Bogotá 39
Quito 49
Equator
Iquitos 101
Manaus 80
Belém 92
Lima 2
Porto Velho 88
Porto Nacional 71
Recife 55
La Paz 23
Corumbá 40
Rio de Janeiro 42
(Tropic of Capricorn) Antofagasta 0.4
Tucumán 37
Asunción 52
São Paulo 87
Santiago 14
Mendoza 8
Buenos Aires 39
Concepción 51
Puerto Montt 77
Sarmiento 6
Punta Arenas 21

AVERAGE ANNUAL RAINFALL

INCHES	CENTIMETERS
Over 80	Over 200
60 to 80	150 to 200
40 to 60	100 to 150
20 to 40	50 to 100
10 to 20	25 to 50
Under 10	Under 25

• Manaus 80 Average annual rainfall in inches at selected stations

Vegetation / Relief

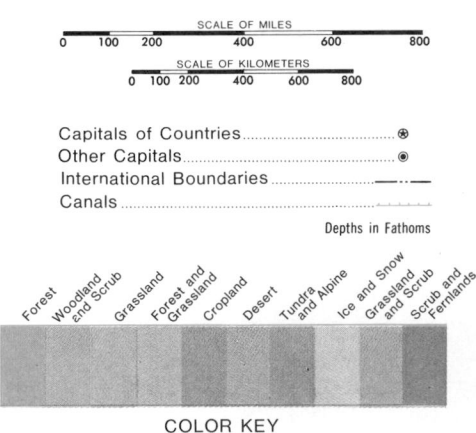

SCALE OF MILES
0 100 200 400 600 800

SCALE OF KILOMETERS
0 100 200 400 600 800

Capitals of Countries.................... ⊛
Other Capitals.................... ⊙
International Boundaries..................
Canals....................

Depths in Fathoms

Forest
Woodland and Scrub
Grassland
Forest and Grassland
Cropland
Desert
Tundra and Alpine
Ice and Snow
Grassland and Scrub
Scrub and Fernlands

COLOR KEY

30° Longitude West of Greenwich 20°

STATES

Amazonas (terr.) 21,696 ....E5
Anzoátegui 683,717 ....F3
Apure 188,717 ....D4
Aragua 891,623 ....E3
Barinas 326,166 ....D3
Bolívar 668,340 ....F4
Carabobo 1,062,268 ....D2
Cojedes 133,991 ....D3
Delta Amacuro (terr.) 48,139..H3
Dependencias Federales
  (terr.) 463 ....E2
Distrito Federal 1,860,637 .....E2
Falcón 503,896 ....D2
Guárico 393,467 ....E3
Lara 945,064 ....D2
Mérida 459,361 ....C3
Miranda 1,421,442 ....E2
Monagas 388,536 ....G3
Nueva Esparta 197,198 ....G2
Portuguesa 424,984 ....D3
Sucre 585,698 ....G2
Táchira 660,234 ....C4
Trujillo 433,735 ....C3

Yaracuy 300,597 ....D2
Zulia 1,674,252 ....B2

CITIES and TOWNS

Acarigua 56,743 ....D3
Achaguas 4,633 ....D4
Aguada Grande 2,901 ....D2
Agua Fría E5
Agua Linda E5
Altagracia 11,116 ....C2
Altagracia de Orituco 18,717..E3
Amuay C2
Anaco 29,487 ....F3
Aparurén G5
Apurito 740 ....D4
Arabopó H5
Aragua de Barcelona 9,107 ..F3
Aragua de Maturín 4,051 ......G3
Aroa 22,466 ....D3
Aroa 5,418 ....D2
Bachaquero C2
Barbacoas 2,513 ....E3
Barcelona 78,201 ....F2
Barinas 56,329 ....C3

Barinitas 9,644 ....C3
Barquisimeto 330,815 ....D2
Barrancas, Barinas 4,489 .....C3
Barrancas, Monagas 5,738 ...G3
Betijoque 5,851 ....C3
Biruaca 2,266 ....E4
Biscucuy 6,114 ....D3
Bobures 2,468 ....C3
Boca de Aroa 2,756 ....D2
Boca del Mangle D2
Boconó 15,915 ....C3
Borbón F4
Buena Vista, Anzoátegui F3
Buena Vista, Apure D4
Cabimas 118,037 ....C2
Cabruta 1,927 ....E4
Cabudare 14,593 ....D3
Cachipo G3
Cacuri F5
Cagua 29,601 ....E2
Caicara 6,092 ....E3
Caicara de Orinoco 6,867 .....E4
Calabozo 37,282 ....E3
Camaguán 4,143 ....E4
Camatagua 3,335 ....E3

Candelaria F4
Cantaura 15,839 ....F3
Capatárida 1,375 ....D2
Carabobo, Bolívar H4
Carabobo, Carabobo D2
Caracas (cap.) 1,035,499 .....E2
Carache 3,966 ....C3
Cariaco 6,549 ....G2
Caribén E4
Caripe 4,729 ....G2
Caripito 19,053 ....G2
Carirubana 15,701 ....C2
Carmelo 2,556 ....C2
Carora 36,115 ....C2
Carrasquero 2,193 ....B2
Casanay 4,985 ....G2
Casigua 3,665 ....B3
Cáua 9,953 ....E2
Caucagua 6,218 ....E2
Chaguaramas 2,748 ....E3
Chichiriviche 3,236 ....D2
Chivacoa 19,210 ....D2
Churuguara 6,636 ....C3
Ciudad Bolívar 103,728 ....G3
Ciudad Bolivia 4,864 ....C3

Ciudad Guayana 143,540 .....G3
Ciudad Ojeda 83,083 ....C2
Ciudad Piar 3,965 ....G4
Clarines 2,099 ....F3
Cojoro C2
Colón E6
Comunidad E6
Coporito H3
Coro 68,701 ....D2
Corozo Pando D4
Cuchivero F4
Cumanacoa 9,179 ....H3
Curiapo H3
Dabajuro 4,516 ....C2
Democracia E6
Ejido 11,170 ....C3
El Almacén G4
El Amparo de Apure 2,015 ....C4
El Callao 4,270 ....G4
El Chaparro 3,768 ....F3
El Cristo D4
Elorza 3,184 ....D4
El Palmar 2,758 ....G4
El Pao 1,259 ....G3
El Perú H4

El Pilar 3,278 ....G2
El Roque E2
El Socorro F3
El Sombrero 8,373 ....E3
El Tigre 49,801 ....F3
El Tocuyo 19,351 ....C3
El Toro H3
El Vigía 20,970 ....C3
El Vínculo G3
Encontrados 5,607 ....B3
Esperanza E6
Garcitas C3
Guacara 35,111 ....D2
Guaina G5
Guana G5
Guanare 34,148 ....D3
Guanarito 3,150 ....D3
Guanoco G3
Guanta 9,017 ....F2
Guarero B2
Guarico 3,259 ....D3
Guasdualito 7,793 ....C4
Guasimal 582 ....D4
Guayabal E6

Güiria 13,905 ....G2
Guri G4
Guzmán Blanco E6
Higuerote 5,008 ....F2
Icabarú H5
Independencia 4,897 ....B4
Irapa 4,470 ....G2
Juangriego 6,062 ....G2
Jusepín G3
Judibana D1
Kavanayen H5
La Aduana G3
La Canoa F3
La Ceiba C2
La Concepcion C2
La Concepción 13,885 ....B2
La Esmeralda F5
La Esperanza H3
La Fría 8,134 ....B3
La Grita 9,954 ....C3
La Guaira 20,344 ....E2
Lagunas C2
Lagunillas C2
La Horqueta G3
La Inglesa G3

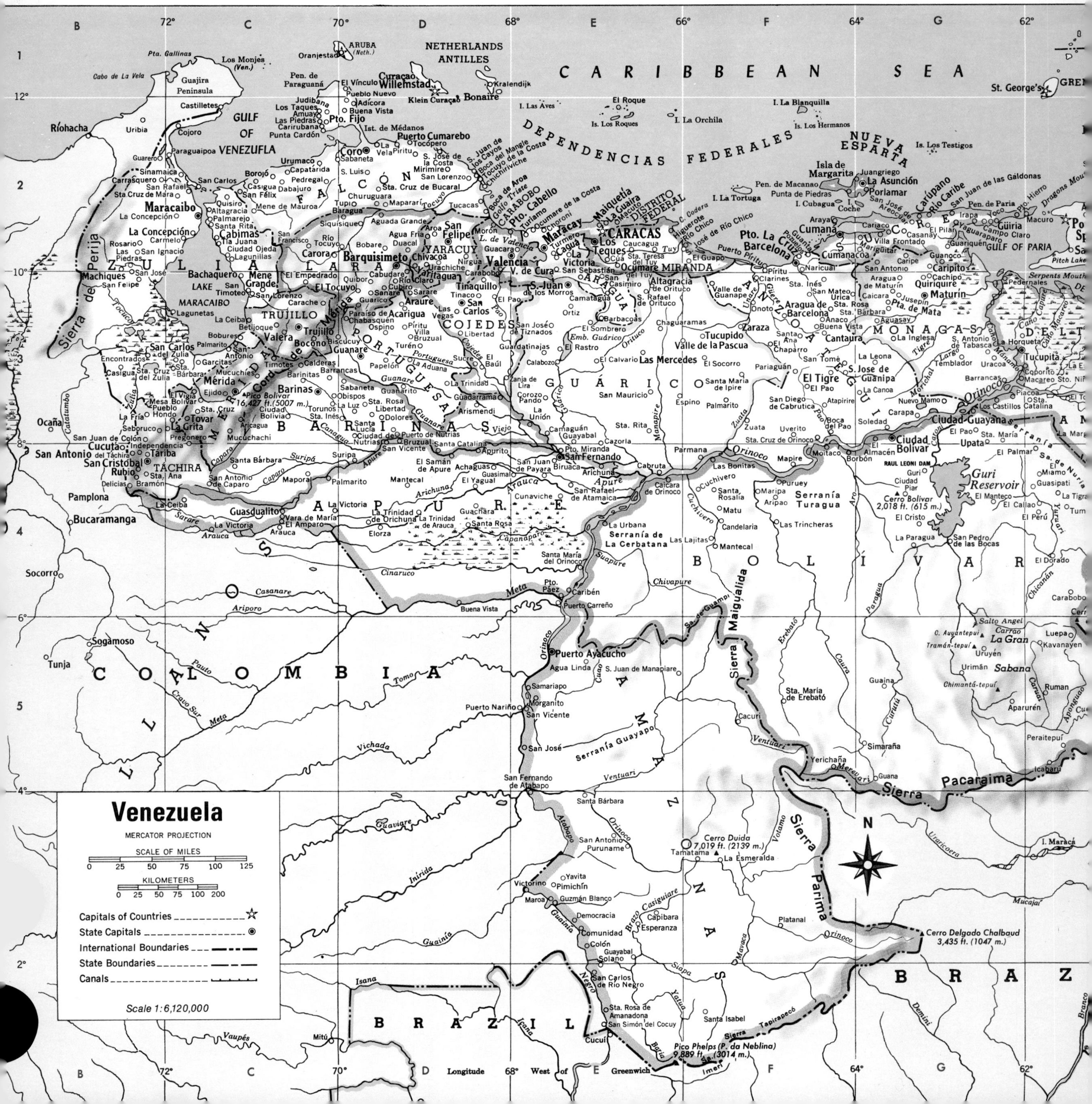

Venezuela

MERCATOR PROJECTION

SCALE OF MILES

0 25 50 75 100 125

KILOMETERS

0 25 50 75 100 200

Capitals of Countries .... ☆
State Capitals _____ ◉
International Boundaries _._._._
State Boundaries _.._.._..
Canals _____

Scale 1:6,120,000

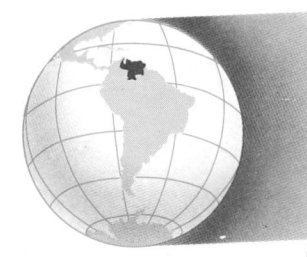

La Leona	G3	Mene de Mauroa 4,336	C2	
La Margarita	H3	Mene Grande 11,498	C3	
Las Lajitas	F4	Mesa Bolívar 956	C3	
Las Mercedes 6,739	E3	Mirimire 3,424	D2	
Las Piedras, Falcón	C2	Morganito	E5	
Las Piedras, Zulia 4,583	B2	Morón 19,451	D2	
Las Trincheras	F4	Naricual 1,047	F2	
Las Vegas 3,212	D3	Nirgua 11,918	D2	
La Tigra	H4	Nuevo Mamo	G3	
La Trinidad de Arauca	D4	Ocumare de la Costa 2,840	E2	
La Vela de Coro 7,172	D2	Ocumare del Tuy 24,229	E2	
La Victoria, Apure	C4	Ospino 3,544	D3	
La Victoria, Aragua 40,731	E2	Palmarejo	D3	
Libertad 2,072	D3	Palmarito, Apure 926	D4	
Los Castillos	G3	Palmarito, Guárico	D3	
Los Teques 63,106	E2	Paraguaipoa 3,850	C2	
Macareo Santo Niño	H3	Paraíso de Chabasquén		
Machiques 18,898	B3	2,094	D3	
Macuro 1,122	H2	Pariaguán 8,173	F3	
Macuto 11,704	E2	Parmana	F4	
Maiquetía 59,238	E2	Pedernales	G3	
Mantecal	F4	Peraitepuí	H5	San Juan de Colón	B3
Maracaibo 651,574	C2	Piacoa	H3	San Juan de los Morros	
Maracay 255,134	E2	Pimichín	E6	38,265	E3
Marigüitar 5,645	G2	Piritu, Anzoátegui 2,479	F2	San Juan de Manapiare	E5
		Piritu, Portuguesa 8,128	D3	San Juan de Payara 1,018	E4
		Platanal	F6	San Lorenzo	C3
		Porlamar 31,985	G2	San Mateo 2,424	F3
		Pozuelos 45,391	F2	San Mauricio	E3
		Pregonero 3,598	C3	San Pedro de las Bocas	G4
		Pueblo Hondo	B3	San Rafael 10,910	C2
		Pueblo Nuevo 3,426	D1	San Sebastián 5,582	E2
		Puerto Ayacucho 10,417	E5	San Simón del Cocuy	E3
		Puerto Cabello 72,103	E2	Santa Ana, Anzoátegui 3,558	F3
		Puerto Cumarebo 10,054	D2	Santa Ana, Táchira 5,116	B4
		Puerto Hierro	H2	Santa Bárbara, Amazonas	E6
		Puerto La Cruz 63,276	F2	Santa Bárbara, Barinas 6,155	C4
		Puerto Miranda	E4	Santa Bárbara, Monagas	
		Puerto Píritu 3,495	F2	2,034	G3
		Punta Cardón 18,182	C2	Santa Bárbara, Zulia	C3
		Punta de Mata 7,777	G3	Santa Cruz	C3
		Punta de Piedras 2,826	F2	Santa Cruz de Bucaral 2,904	D2
		Punto Fijo 5,548	D2	Santa Cruz de Mara 5,773	C2
		Puruey	F4	Santa Cruz del Zulia 4,221	B3
		Puruname	E6	Santa Elena 608	H5
		Quibor 12,216	D3	Santa Isabel	F7
		Quiriquire 7,304	G3	Santa María, Bolívar	G3
		Río Claro 2,460	D3	Santa María de Erebató	F5
		Rosario	B2	Santa María de Ipire 3,307	F3
		Rubio 19,156	B4	Santa María del Orinoco	E4
		Sabaneta 4,680	D3	Santa Rita, Guárico	E3
		Samariapo	E5	Santa Rita, Zulia 15,668	C2
		San Antonio, Amazonas	E6	Santa Rosa	D4
		San Antonio, Monagas		Santa Rosa de Amanadona	E7
		4,235	G2	Santa Teresa 10,220	E2
		San Antonio, Zulia	C3	Santa Timoteo 3,635	C3
		San Antonio del Táchira		San Tomé	F3
		20,342	B4	San Vicente	E5
		San Antonio de Tabasca	G3	Sarare 4,236	D3
		Sanare 6,717	D3	Seboruco 2,616	B3
		San Carlos 21,029	D3	Simaraña	G5
		San Carlos del Zulia 20,762	C3	Sinamaica	B2
		San Casimiro 4,843	E3	Siquisique 3,821	D2
		San Felipe, Yaracuy 43,801	D2	Solano	E6
		San Felipe, Zulia	B3	Soledad 7,108	G3
		San Félix 379	C2	Suripa	D4
		San Fernando 38,960	E4	Tamatama	F6
		San Ignacio	B2	Táriba 15,683	B4
		San José, Amazonas	E5	Temblador 5,380	G3
		San José, Zulia 4,498	B3	Tia Juana	C2
		San José de Amacuro	E5	Timotes 3,229	C3
		San José de Guanipa 22,530	G3	Tinaco 7,263	D3
		San José de la Costa	D2	Tinaquillo 12,015	D3
		San José de Río Chico 3,600	F2	Tocuyo de la Costa 4,023	D2

Tovar 12,814	C3	Uverito 468	F3	**OTHER FEATURES**		
Trujillo 25,921	C3	Valencia 367,171	E2			
Tucacas 4,780	D2	Valera 76,740	C3	Amacuro (riv.)	H4	
Tucupido 9,522	F3	Valle de Guanape 3,468	F3	Angel (fall)	G5	
Tucupita 21,417	H3	Valle de la Pascua 36,809	F3	Aponguao (riv.)	H5	
Tumeremo 5,036	H4	Villa Bruzual 14,003	D3	Apure (riv.)	E4	
Turén	D3	Villa de Cura 27,832	E2	Arauca (riv.)	E4	
Turiamo	E2	Yaguaraparo 3,931	G2	Arichuna (riv.)	D4	
Turmero 43,832	E2	Yaritagua 21,363	D2	Aro (riv.)	F4	
Upata 22,793	G3	Yavita	E6	Atabapo (riv.)	E6	
Urachiche 4,759	D2	Yerichaña	F5	Auyantepui (mt.)	G5	
Urica 1,881	F3	Yoco 2,196	G2	Baria (riv.)	E7	
Urimán	G5	Zanja de Lira	E3	Boca Grande (gulf)	H3	
Uruyén	G5	Zaraza 15,480	F3	Bolívar, Pico (peak)	C3	
				Canagua (riv.)	C3	
				Caño Capure (riv.)	H3	
				Caño Macareo (riv.)	H3	
				Caño Mánamo (riv.)	G3	
				Capanaparo (riv.)	E4	
				Caparo (riv.)	C4	
				Carrao (riv.)	G5	
				Caruai (riv.)	H5	
				Casiquiare, Brazo (riv.)	E6	
				Catatumbo (riv.)	B3	
				Caura (riv.)	F5	
				Chicanán (riv.)	H4	
				Chimantá-tepuí (mt.)	G5	
				Chivapure (riv.)	E4	
				Cinaruco (riv.)	D4	
				Coche (isl.)	F2	
				Codera (cape)	F2	
				Cojedes (riv.)	D3	
				Cuao (riv.)	E5	
				Cubagua (isl.)	F2	
				Cuchivero (riv.)	F4	
				Cuquenán (riv.)	H5	
				Curutú (riv.)	G5	
				Cuyuni (riv.)	H4	
				Delgado Chalbaud, Cerro		
				(mt.)	E7	
				Dragons Mouth (str.)	H2	
				Duida, Cerro (mt.)	F6	
				Erebato (riv.)	F5	
				Guainía (riv.)	E6	
				Guampí, Sierra de (mts.)	F4	
				Guanare (riv.)	D3	
				Guanare Viejo (riv.)	D3	
				Guárico (res.)	E3	
				Guárico (riv.)	E3	
				Guayapo, Serranía (mts.)	E5	
				Güere (riv.)	F3	
				Guri (res.)	G4	
				Imataca, Serranía (mts.)	H4	
				Imeri, Sierra (mts.)	F7	
				La Blanquilla (isl.)	F2	
				La Cerbatana, Serranía de		
				(mts.)	E4	
				La Gran Sabana (plain)	G5	
				La Orchila (isl.)	F2	

Las Aves (isls.)	E2	
La Tortuga (isl.)	F2	
Los Hermanos (isls.)	F2	
Los Monjes (isls.)	C1	
Los Roques (isls.)	E2	
Los Testigos (isls.)	G2	
Macanao (pen.)	F2	
Maigualida, Sierra (range)	F4	
Manapire (riv.)	E3	
Maracaibo (lake)	C3	
Margarita (isl.)	F2	
Mavaca (riv.)	F6	
Médanos (isth.)	D2	
Merevari (riv.)	F5	
Mérida, Cordillera de (range)	C3	
Meta (riv.)	E4	
Morichal Largo (riv.)	G3	
Neblina (Phelps) (peak)	E7	
Negro (riv.)	E7	
Nuria, Sierra de (mts.)	H4	
Orinoco (delta)	H3	
Orinoco (riv.)	G3	
Orituco (riv.)	E3	
Pacaraima, Sierra (mts.)	G5	
Pao (riv.)	D3	
Paragua (riv.)	G4	
Paria (gulf)	H2	
Paria (pen.)	G2	
Parima, Sierra (mts.)	F6	
Perijá, Sierra de (mts.)	B2	
Phelps (peak)	E7	
Portuguesa (riv.)	D3	
Raul Leoni (dam)	G4	
Roraima (mt.)	H5	
Salto Angel (fall)	G5	
Sarare (riv.)	C4	
Serpents Mouth (passage)	H3	
Siapa (riv.)	E7	
Supure (riv.)	E4	
Suripá (riv.)	C4	
Tapirapecó, Sierra (mts.)	F7	
Tigre (riv.)	G3	
Tocuco (riv.)	B3	
Tocuyo (riv.)	D2	
Tramán-tepuí (mt.)	G5	
Triste (gulf)	D2	
Turagua, Serranía (mts.)	F4	
Tuy (riv.)	E2	
Unare (riv.)	F3	
Valencia (lake)	E2	
Venamo (riv.)	H4	
Venamo, Cerro (mt.)	H4	
Venezuela (gulf)	C2	
Ventuari (riv.)	E5	
Votamo (riv.)	F6	
Yatua (riv.)	E7	
Yuruari (riv.)	H4	
Zuata (riv.)	F3	
Zulia (riv.)	B3	

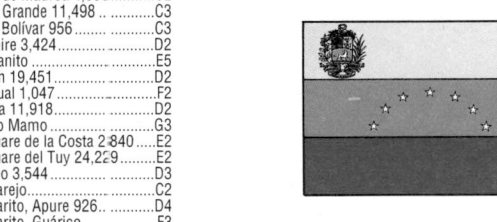

AREA 352,143 sq. mi. (912,050 sq. km.)
POPULATION 19,246,000
CAPITAL Caracas
LARGEST CITY Caracas
HIGHEST POINT Pico Bolívar 16,427 ft.
(5,007 m.)
MONETARY UNIT Bolívar
MAJOR LANGUAGE Spanish
MAJOR RELIGION Roman Catholicism

Topography

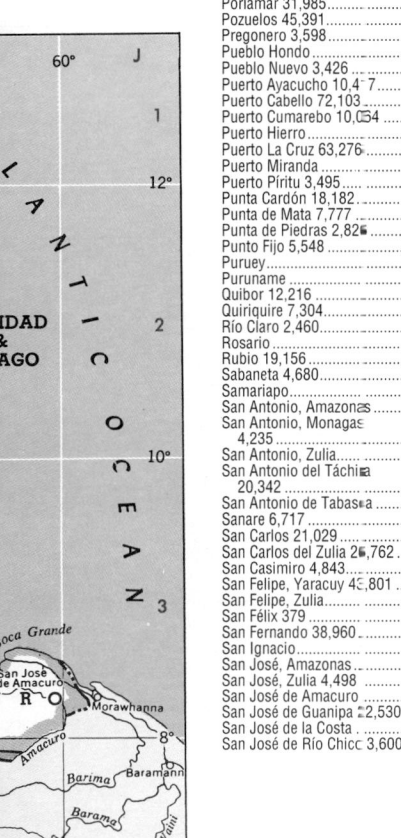

0	100	200 MI.
0	100	200 KM.

5,000 m. 16,404 ft.	2,000 m. 6,562 ft.	1,000 m. 3,281 ft.	500 m. 1,640 ft.	200 m. 656 ft.	100 m. 328 ft.	Sea Level	Below

MAJOR MINERAL OCCURRENCES

Al	Bauxite
Au	Gold
C	Coal
D	Diamonds
Fe	Iron Ore
G	Natural Gas
Mn	Manganese
Na	Salt
O	Petroleum

⚡ Water Power
▨ Major Industrial Areas

Agriculture, Industry and Resources

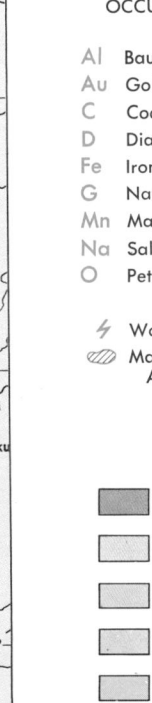

DOMINANT LAND USE

- Diversified Tropical Crops (chiefly plantation agriculture)
- Upland Cultivated Areas
- Upland Livestock Grazing, Limited Agriculture
- Extensive Livestock Ranching
- Forests

HAMMOND INCORPORATED, Maplewood, N.J.

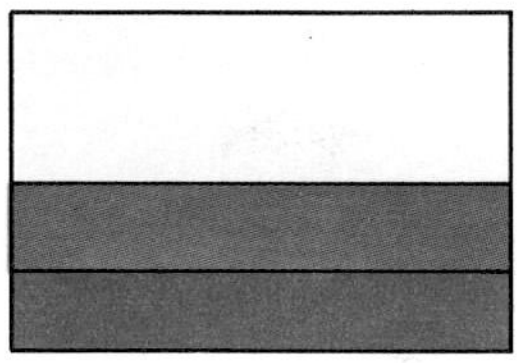

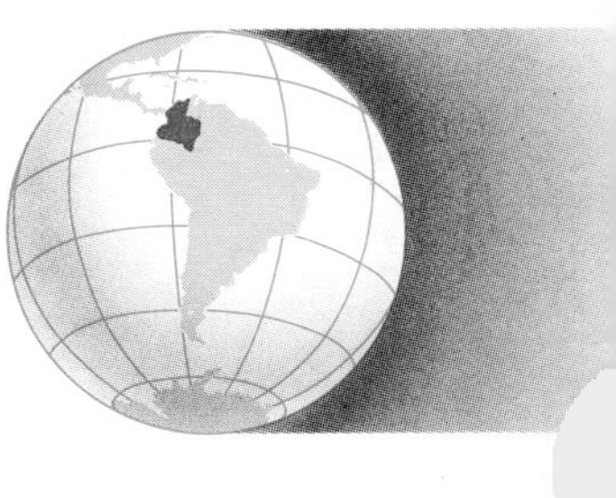

AREA 439,513 sq. mi. (1,138,339 sq. km.)
POPULATION 30,241,000
CAPITAL Bogotá
LARGEST CITY Bogotá
HIGHEST POINT Pico Cristóbal Colón 19,029 ft. (5,800 m.)
MONETARY UNIT Colombian peso
MAJOR LANGUAGE Spanish
MAJOR RELIGION Roman Catholicism

INTERNAL DIVISIONS

Amazonas (comm.) 6,825 ... D8
Antioquia (dept.) 3,888,067 ... B4
Arauca (inten.) 19,884 ... E4
Atlántico (dept.) 958,560 ... C2
Bolívar (dept.) 802,407 ... C3
Boyacá (dept.) 1,084,766 ... D5
Caldas (dept.) 700,954 ... C5
Caquetá (inten.) 57,103 ... C7
Casanare (inten.) ... E5
Cauca (dept.) 603,894 ... B6
Cesar (dept.) 339,843 ... D3
Chocó (dept.) 201,915 ... B4
Córdoba (dept.) 645,478 ... C3
Cundinamarca
(dept.) 1,106,626 ... C5
Distrito Especial 2,855,065 ... C5
Guainía (comm.) 1,792 ... F6
Huila (dept.) 469,834 ... C6
La Guajira (dept.) 180,520 ... D2
Magdalena (dept.) 536,122 ... C3
Meta (dept.) 245,176 ... D6
Nariño (dept.) 807,112 ... B7
Norte de Santander
(dept.) 693,298 ... D3
Putumayo (inten.) 22,916 ... C7
Quindío (dept.) 321,677 ... C5
Risaralda (dept.) 452,626 ... B5
San Andrés y Providencia
(inten.) 22,719 ... B1
Santander (dept.) 1,130,977 ... D4
Sucre (dept.) 354,412 ... C3
Tolima (dept.) 903,520 ... C5
Valle del Cauca
(dept.) 2,204,722 ... B6
Vaupés (comm.) 6,923 ... E7
Vichada (comm.) 2,172 ... F5

CITIES and TOWNS

Acacías 9,238 ... D6
Acandí 2,358 ... B3
Agrado 2,771 ... C6
Aguachica 16,771 ... D3
Aguadas 9,995 ... C5
Agua de Dios 9,689 ... C5
Agustín Codazzi 28,194 ... D3
Aipe 3,794 ... C6
Algeciras 5,022 ... C6
Amalfi 6,494 ... C4
Andes 14,957 ... C5
Anserma 15,559 ... B5
Antioquia 6,841 ... B4
Aracataca 7,511 ... D2
Arauca 7,613 ... E4
Arjona 29,465 ... C2
Armenia 180,221 ... B5
Armero 19,567 ... C5
Ayapel 7,475 ... C3
Baranoa 27,394 ... C2
Baraya 2,581 ... C6
Barbacoas 4,653 ... A7
Barbosa 7,960 ... D5
Barichara 2,548 ... D4
Barrancabermeja 137,406 ... C4
Barrancas 2,979 ... D2
Barranco de Loba 2,215 ... C3
Barranquilla 896,649 ... C2
Belén de los Andaquíes 2,190 ... C7
Bello 206,297 ... C4
Bogotá (cap.) 3,974,813 ... D5
Bolívar 13,259 ... C5
Bucaramanga 341,513 ... D4
Buenaventura 160,342 ... B6
Buesaco 2,763 ... B7
Buga 82,992 ... B6
Cáceres 7,154 ... C4
Caicedonia 21,959 ... C5
Calamar 5,867 ... C2
Calarcá 29,349 ... C5
Cali 1,323,944 ... B6
Campo de la Cruz 13,137 ... C2
Campoalegre 11,799 ... C6
Cañasgordas 3,900 ... B4
Cartagena 491,368 ... C2
Cartago 92,524 ... B5
Caucasia 24,138 ... C4
Cereté 25,890 ... C3
Cerro de San Antonio 3,394 ... C2
Chaparral 14,546 ... C6
Chimichaqua 6,382 ... D3
Chinácota 4,478 ... D4
Chinchiná 33,441 ... C5
Chinú 10,023 ... C3
Chiquinquirá 21,727 ... C5
Chiriguaná 6,611 ... D3
Ciénaga 56,860 ... C2
Ciénaga de Oro 10,607 ... C3
Cisneros 7,226 ... C4
Colombia 2,903 ... C6
Condoto 4,798 ... B5
Contratación 3,057 ... D4
Convención 7,545 ... D3
Corinto 6,933 ... B6
Corozal 29,471 ... C3
Cúcuta 357,026 ... D4
Cumbal 2,891 ... B7
Dabeiba 7,600 ... B4
Dagua 5,392 ... B6
Duitama 56,390 ... D5
El Banco 20,756 ... D3
El Carmen 2,362 ... D3
El Carmen de Bolívar 30,778 ... C3
El Cerrito 23,575 ... B6
El Cocuy 2,740 ... D4
El Tambo 2,179 ... B6
Envigado 85,539 ... C4
Espinal 37,563 ... C5
Facatativá 44,331 ... C5
Florencia 66,430 ... C7
Fonseca 9,988 ... D2
Fontibón ... C5
Fresno 8,141 ... C5
Fundación 29,002 ... C2
Fusagasugá 41,033 ... C5
Gamarra 5,071 ... D3
Garzón 13,783 ... C6
Gigante 4,880 ... C6
Girardot 66,385 ... C5
Gramalote 2,880 ... D4
Guamal, Meta 2,854 ... D6
Guamal, Magdalena 4,986 ... C3
Guapí 5,005 ... B6
Guateque 6,032 ... D5
Honda 25,040 ... C5
Ibagué 269,495 ... C5
Ipiales 45,419 ... B7
Istmina 5,575 ... B5
Itagüí 135,797 ... C4
Ituango 5,561 ... C4
La Cruz 4,353 ... B7
La Dorada 48,572 ... C5
La Gloria 2,632 ... D3
La Palma 5,430 ... C5
La Plata 8,047 ... C6
La Unión 5,392 ... B7
Líbano 23,703 ... C5
Lorica 24,264 ... C3
Magangué 49,160 ... C3
Maicao 46,033 ... D2
Majagual 2,329 ... C3
Málaga 10,645 ... D4
Manizales 275,067 ... C5
Medellín 1,418,554 ... C4
Mercaderes 3,877 ... B7
Miraflores 3,584 ... D5
Miranda 6,439 ... B6
Mitú 1,637 ... E7
Mocoa 6,221 ... B7
Mompós 14,076 ... C3
Moniquirá 5,711 ... D5
Montería 157,466 ... B3
Natagaima 7,772 ... C6
Neiva 178,130 ... C6
Ocaña 51,443 ... D3
Ortega 5,150 ... C6
Pacho 6,786 ... C5
Páez 2,098 ... C6
Paipa 4,260 ... D5
Palmira 175,186 ... B6
Pamplona 34,213 ... D4
Pasto 197,407 ... B7
Patía 5,306 ... B6
Paz de Ariporo 2,584 ... E5
Paz de Río 3,464 ... D4
Pereira 233,271 ... C5
Piedecuesta 34,646 ... D4
Piendamó 5,046 ... B6
Pitalito 27,104 ... B7
Pivijay 10,172 ... C2
Planeta Rica 24,238 ... C3

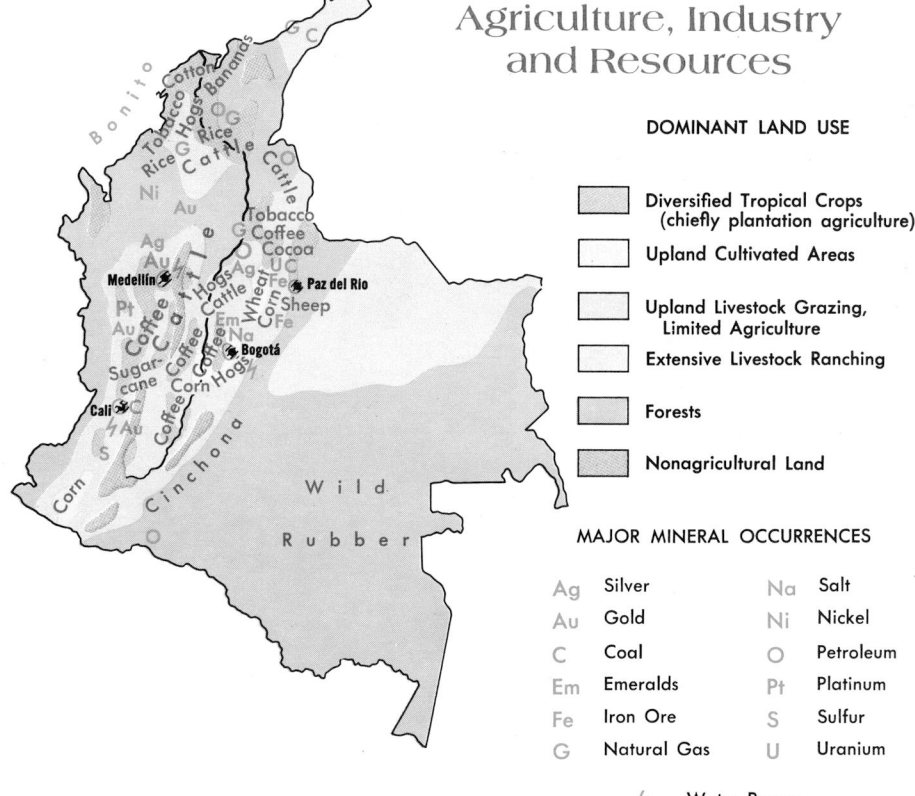

Agriculture, Industry and Resources

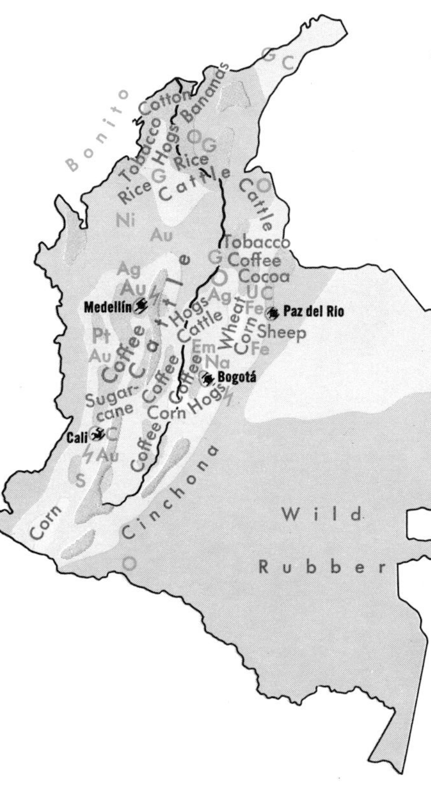
Bonito
Cotton
Tobacco
Hogs
Bananas
Rice
Cattle
Ni
Au
Ag
Medellín
Paz del Rio
Bogotá
Cali
Coffee
Tobacco
Cocoa
Wheat
Corn
Sheep
Sugar-cane
Cinchona
Wild
Rubber

DOMINANT LAND USE

- Diversified Tropical Crops (chiefly plantation agriculture)
- Upland Cultivated Areas
- Upland Livestock Grazing, Limited Agriculture
- Extensive Livestock Ranching
- Forests
- Nonagricultural Land

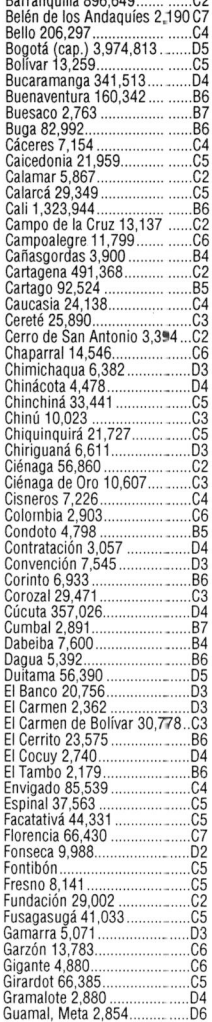

MAJOR MINERAL OCCURRENCES

Ag	Silver	Na	Salt
Au	Gold	Ni	Nickel
C	Coal	O	Petroleum
Em	Emeralds	Pt	Platinum
Fe	Iron Ore	S	Sulfur
G	Natural Gas	U	Uranium

Water Power
Major Industrial Areas

Topography

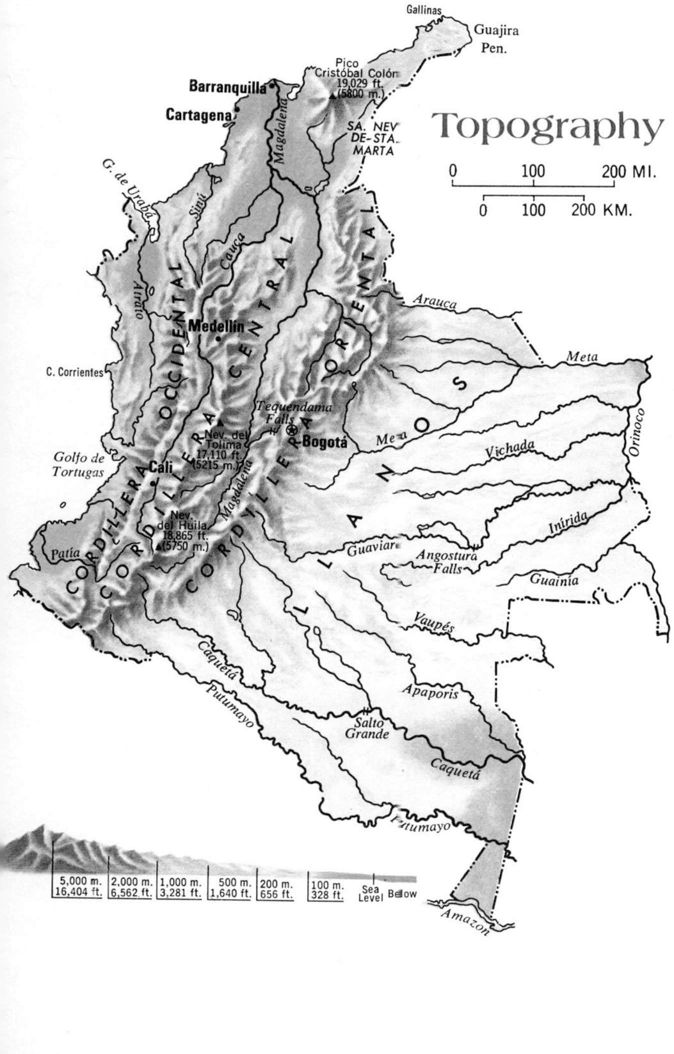
Gallinas
Guajira Pen.
Pico Cristóbal Colón 19,029 ft. (5800 m.)
Barranquilla
Cartagena
SA. NEV. DE STA. MARTA
G. de Urabá
Magdalena
Sinú
Cauca
Atrato
Medellín
C. Corrientes
Arauca
Meta
Tequendama Falls
Bogotá
Nev. del Tolima 17,110 ft. (5215 m.)
Cali
Golfo de Tortugas
Nev. del Huila 18,865 ft. (5750 m.)
Patía
CORDILLERA OCCIDENTAL
CORDILLERA CENTRAL
CORDILLERA ORIENTAL
LLANOS
Vichada
Orinoco
Guaviare
Angostura Falls
Inírida
Guainía
Vaupés
Apaporis
Caquetá
Salto Grande
Putumayo
Amazon
0 100 200 MI.
0 100 200 KM.
5,000 m. 16,404 ft.
2,000 m. 6,562 ft.
1,000 m. 3,281 ft.
500 m. 1,640 ft.
200 m. 656 ft.
100 m. 328 ft.
Sea Level
Below

Plato 24,895 ... C3
Popayán 141,964 ... B6
Pradera 27,152 ... B6
Puente Nacional 4,317 ... D5
Puerto Asís 6,364 ... B7
Puerto Berrío 21,414 ... C4
Puerto Carreño 2,172 ... G4
Puerto Colombia 9,255 ... C2
Puerto Escondido 1,368 ... B3
Puerto Inírida 1,792 ... F6
Puerto Leguízamo 3,179 ... C8
Puerto López 4,948 ... D5
Puerto Rico 4,853 ... C7
Puerto Rondón 1,010 ... E4
Puerto Salgar 6,396 ... C5
Puerto Tejada 26,573 ... B6
Puerto Wilches 5,282 ... D4
Pupiales 2,723 ... B7
Purificación 8,164 ... C6
Quibdó 47,950 ... B5
Remedios 4,681 ... C4
Remolino 3,408 ... C2
Restrepo 2,704 ... D5
Río de Oro 2,985 ... D3
Riohacha 46,667 ... D2
Rionegro, Antioquia 22,654 ... C4
Rionegro, Santander 3,491 ... D4
Riosucio, Caldas 11,619 ... C5
Riosucio, Chocó 2,184 ... B4
Robles 5,422 ... D2
Rovira 5,105 ... C5
Sabanalarga 35,786 ... C2
Sahagún 28,686 ... C3
Salamina 12,136 ... C5
Salazar 2,791 ... D4
Samaniego 4,790 ... B7
San Agustín 4,532 ... B7
San Andrés, Antioquia 2,003 ... C4
San Andrés,San Andrés y
Providencia 23,325 ... A9
San Antero 7,129 ... C3
Sandoná 7,222 ... B7
San Gil 24,599 ... D4
San Jacinto 13,459 ... C3
San José del Guaviare 4,138 ... D6
San Juan del César 9,468 ... D2
San Marcos 26,542 ... C3
San Martín 8,281 ... D6
San Onofre 7,899 ... C3
San Pablo 3,662 ... B7
San Roque 4,972 ... C4
San Vicente del Caguán 3,182 C6
Santa Bárbara 11,848 ... C5
Santa Marta 177,922 ... D2
Santa Rosa de Cabal 37,112 ... C5
Santa Rosa de Osos 8,593 ... C4
Santander 22,644 ... B6
Sardinata 3,726 ... D3
Segovia 10,000 ... C4
Sevilla 31,309 ... C5
Sibundoy-Las Casas 2,853 ... B7
Silvia 3,045 ... B6
Simití 3,062 ... C4
Sincé 11,909 ... C3
Sincelejo 120,537 ... C3
Sitionuevo 5,919 ... C2
Soatá 4,294 ... D4
Socorro 15,596 ... D4
Sogamoso 64,437 ... D5
Soledad 164,494 ... C2
Sonsón 15,990 ... C5
Sopetrán 5,223 ... C4
Tadó 3,102 ... B5
Tame 4,811 ... E4
Tibaná 1,100 ... D5
Tierralta 7,950 ... C3
Timaná 4,262 ... C7
Timbío 4,755 ... B6
Timbiquí 1,048 ... B6
Toledo 2,942 ... D4
Tolú 9,118 ... C3
Trinidad 729 ... E5
Tuluá 99,721 ... B5
Tumaco 45,456 ... A7
Tunjá 87,851 ... D5
Túquerres 12,058 ... B7
Turbaco 28,161 ... C2
Turbo 25,992 ... B3
Ubaté 7,716 ... D5
Uribia 2,193 ... D2
Urrao 8,577 ... B4
Valdivia 4,318 ... C4
Valledupar 142,771 ... D2
Vélez 8,241 ... D4
Venadillo 8,383 ... C5
Villa Rosario 8,668 ... D4
Villanueva 9,836 ... D2
Villavicencio 82,869 ... D5
Villeta 6,507 ... C5
Yarumal 21,333 ... C4
Yopal 5,851 ... D5
Yumbo 43,508 ... B6
Zapatoca 6,258 ... D4
Zaragoza 9,660 ... C4
Zarzal 22,014 ... B5
Zipaquirá 45,676 ... D5

OTHER FEATURES

Aguarico (riv.) ... B7
Aguja, La (cape) ... C2
Alto Ritacuva (mt.) ... D4
Amazon (riv.) ... E9
Ancón de Sardinas (bay) ... A7
Angostura (falls) ... E6
Apaporis (riv.) ... F8
Arauca (riv.) ... E4
Ariari (riv.) ... D6
Ariguaní (riv.) ... D3
Ariporo (riv.) ... E4
Atabapo (riv.) ... G6
Atrato (riv.) ... B4
Baudó, Serranía de (mts.) ... B5
Caguán (riv.) ... C7
Cahuinari (riv.) ... E8
Caquetá (riv.) ... E8
Caraparaná (riv.) ... D8
Casanare (riv.) ... E4
Catatumbo (riv.) ... D3
Cauca (riv.) ... B3
Cazueleja, Cerro (mt.) ... C6
César (riv.) ... D2
Central, Cordillera (range) ... C5
Charambirá (pt.) ... B5
Chicamocha (riv.) ... D4
Chocó (bay) ... B6
Corrientes (cape) ... B5
Cristóbal Colón, Pico (peak) ... D2
Cuemaní (riv.) ... D7
Cupica (gulf) ... B4
Cusachón (isl.) ... D1
Espada (pt.) ... E1
Gallinas (pt.) ... E1
Grande (isl.) ... B4
Grande, Salto (falls) ... D8
Guainía (riv.) ... F6
Guajira (pen.) ... E1
Guaviare (riv.) ... F6
Guayabero (riv.) ... D6
Huila, Nevado del (mt.) ... C6
Igara-Paraná (riv.) ... D8
Inírida (riv.) ... F6
Isana (riv.) ... F7
La Aguja (cape) ... C2
La Macarena, Serranía de
(mts.) ... D6
Llanos (plain) ... D5
Macarena, Serranía de la
(mts.) ... D6
Magdalena (riv.) ... C3
Manacacías (riv.) ... D6
Meta (riv.) ... E5
Metica (riv.) ... D6
Mira (riv.) ... A7
Miritiparaná (riv.) ... D8
Morrosquillo (gulf) ... C3
Nechí (riv.) ... C4
Negro (riv.) ... G7
Occidental, Cordillera (range) ... B5
Oriental, Cordillera (range) ... D5
Orinoco (riv.) ... G5
Orteguaza (riv.) ... C7
Papurí (riv.) ... F7
Patía (riv.) ... B6
Pauto (riv.) ... E5
Perijá, Serranía de (mts.) ... D2
Providencia (isl.) ... B9
Puracé (vol.) ... B6
Putumayo (riv.) ... E9
Quitasueño (bank) ... A8
Roncador (cays) ... B9
Saldaña (riv.) ... C6
Salto Grande (falls) ... D8
San Andrés (isl.) ... A10
San Jorge (riv.) ... C3
San Juan (riv.) ... B5
Santa Marta, Sierra Nevada de
(range) ... D2
Serrana (bank) ... B9
Serranilla (bank) ... B8
Sinú (riv.) ... B3
Sogamoso (riv.) ... D4
Suárez (riv.) ... D4
Tarairá (riv.) ... F8
Tequendama (falls) ... C5
Tibugá (gulf) ... B5
Tolima (vol.) ... C5
Tomo (riv.) ... F5
Tortugas (gulf) ... B6
Tunahí, Sierra (mts.) ... E7
Urabá (gulf) ... B3
Uva (riv.) ... E6
Vaupés (riv.) ... E7
Vela, La (cape) ... D1
Vichada (riv.) ... F5
Yarí (riv.) ... D8
Zapatosa, Ciénaga de
(swamp) ... D3

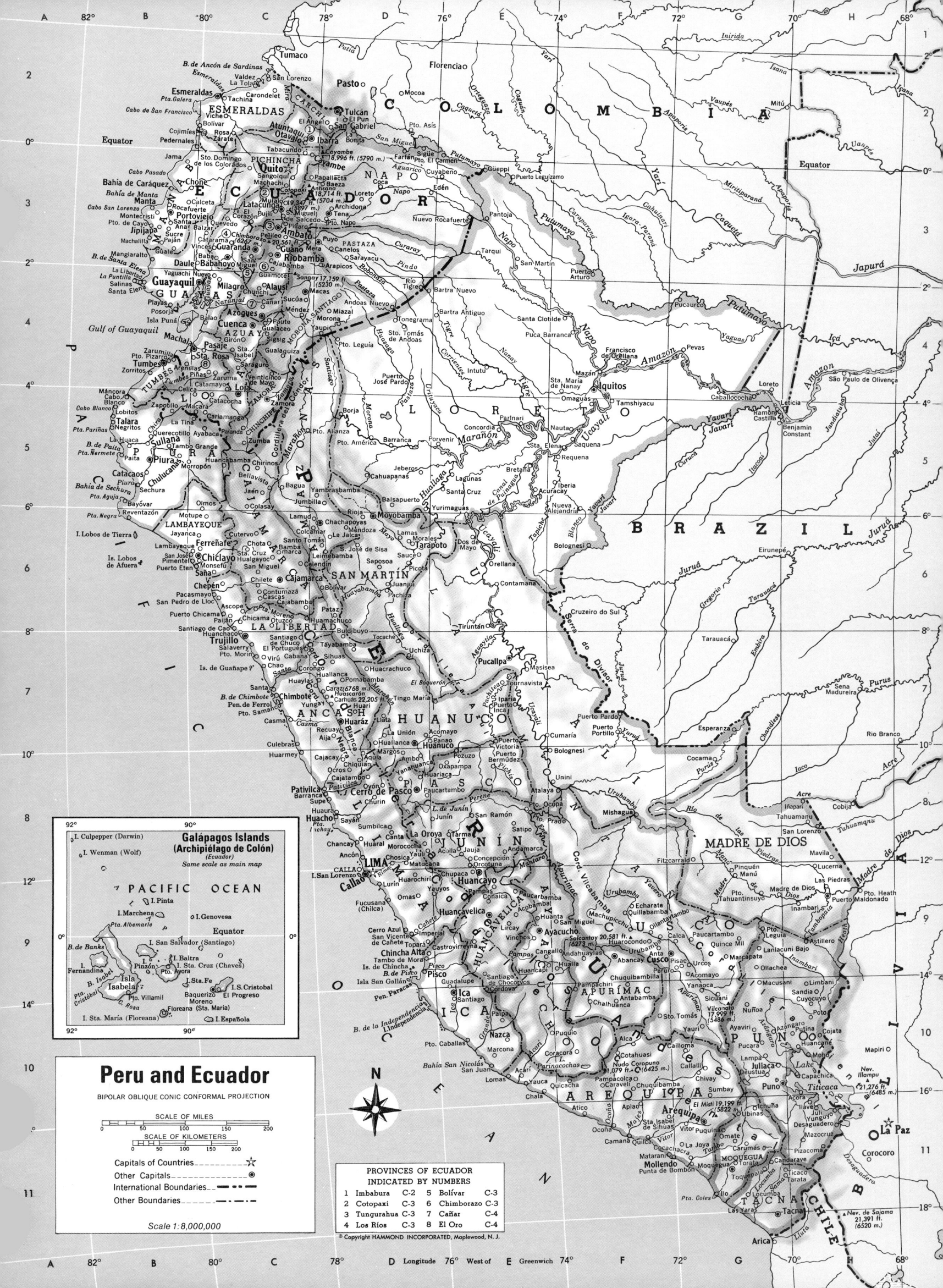

Peru and Ecuador

BIPOLAR OBLIQUE CONIC CONFORMAL PROJECTION

Galápagos Islands
(Archipiélago de Colón)
(Ecuador)
Same scale as main map

PACIFIC OCEAN

SCALE OF MILES
0 50 100 150 200

SCALE OF KILOMETERS
0 50 100 150 200

Capitals of Countries ....★
Other Capitals ....◉
International Boundaries ___·___·___
Other Boundaries ___·___·___

Scale 1:8,000,000

© Copyright HAMMOND INCORPORATED, Maplewood, N.J.

PROVINCES OF ECUADOR
INDICATED BY NUMBERS

1 Imbabura	C-2	5 Bolívar	C-3
2 Cotopaxi	C-3	6 Chimborazo	C-3
3 Tungurahua	C-3	7 Cañar	C-4
4 Los Ríos	C-3	8 El Oro	C-4

PERU

ECUADOR

PERU

AREA 496,222 sq. mi. (1,285,215 sq. km.)
POPULATION 22,332,000
CAPITAL Lima
LARGEST CITY Lima
HIGHEST POINT Huascarán 22,205 ft. (6,768 m.)
MONETARY UNIT inti
MAJOR LANGUAGES Spanish, Quechua, Aymara
MAJOR RELIGION Roman Catholicism

ECUADOR

AREA 109,483 sq. mi. (283,561 sq. km.)
POPULATION 10,490,000
CAPITAL Quito
LARGEST CITY Guayaquil
HIGHEST POINT Chimborazo 20,561 ft. (6,267 m.)
MONETARY UNIT sucre
MAJOR LANGUAGES Spanish, Quechua
MAJOR RELIGION Roman Catholicism

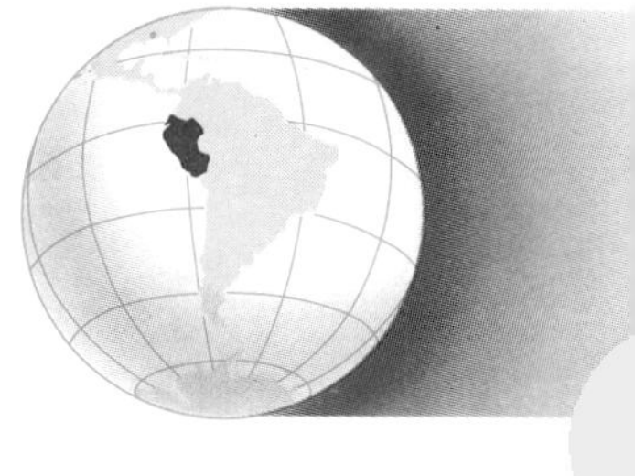

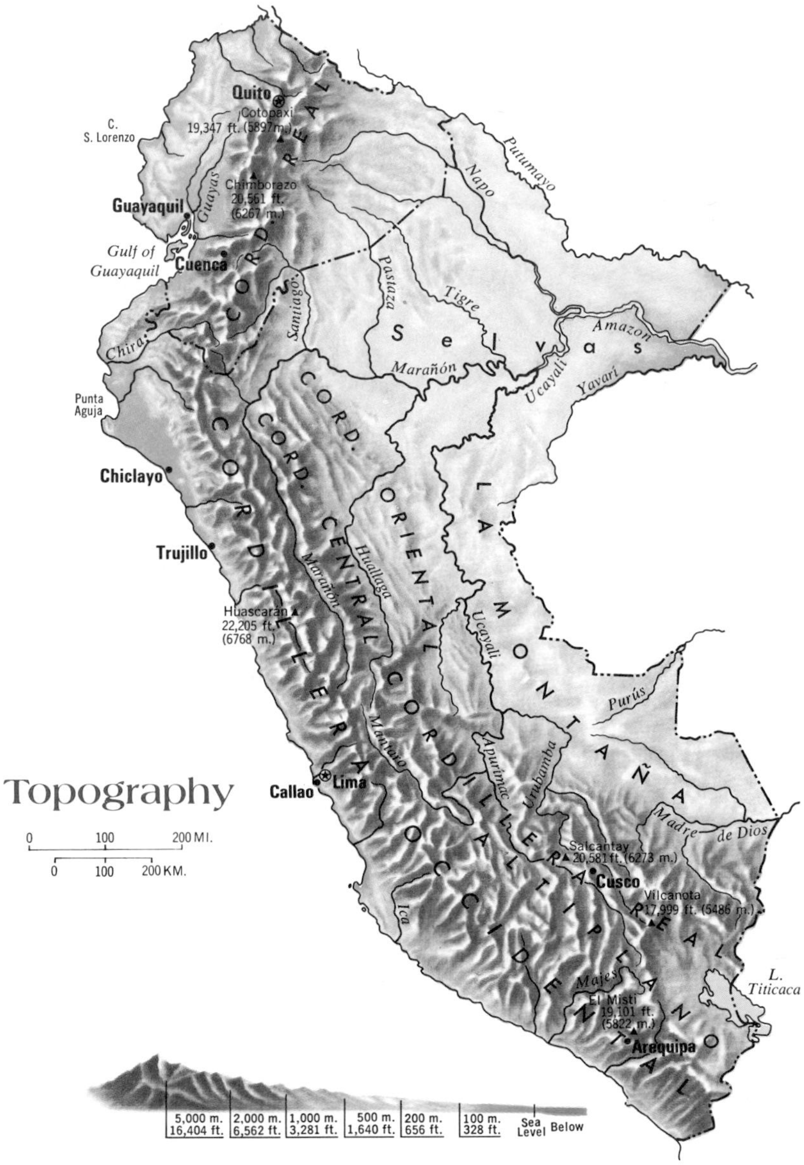

PERU

DEPARTMENTS

Amazonas 256,460 ... C5
Ancash 815,646 ... D7
Apurímac 321,936 ... F10
Arequipa 702,308 ... F10
Ayacucho 500,732 ... E9
Cajamarca 1,044,689 ... C6
Callao (prov.) 446,730 ... D9
Cusco 829,294 ... F9
Huánuco 481,924 ... D7
Huancavelica 346,460 ... E9
Ica 431,442 ... E10
Junín 848,993 ... E8
La Libertad 960,537 ... C6
Lambayeque 683,425 ... B6
Lima 4,738,266 ... D8
Loreto 446,316 ... E5
Madre de Dios 36,555 ... G8
Moquegua 99,287 ... G11
Pasco 221,219 ... E8
Piura 1,168,442 ... B5
Puno 893,586 ... G10
San Martín 319,670 ... D6
Tacna 133,240 ... G11
Tumbes 103,979 ... B4
Ucayali 200,085 ... E6

CITIES and TOWNS

Abancay 19,807 ... F9
Acarí 4,907 ... E10
Acobamba 2,156 ... E9
Acolla 5,717 ... E8
Acomayo, Cusco 1,419 ... G9
Acomayo, Huánuco 2,883 ... E7
Acora 1,910 ... H11
Acuracay 1,282 ... F5
Aija 1,843 ... D7
Alca 755 ... F10
Ambo 3,060 ... D8
Ananea 668 ... H10
Ancón 8,610 ... D8
Andahuaylas 7,654 ... F9
Anta 3,703 ... F9
Antabamba 2,223 ... F10
Aplao 1,941 ... F11
Aquia 970 ... D8
Arequipa 107,858 ... G11
Arequipa* 447,431 ... G11
Ascope 12,070 ... C6
Atalaya 2,132 ... E8
Atico 2,316 ... F11
Ayabaca 4,543 ... C5
Ayacucho 68,535 ... F9
Ayaviri 11,067 ... G10
Azángaro 7,658 ... H10
Bagua 9,735 ... C5
Bambamarca 6,867 ... C6
Barranca, Lima 21,312 ... C8
Barranca, Loreto 1,351 ... D5
Bellavista 4,906 ... C5
Bolívar 1,106 ... D6
Bretaña 1,035 ... E5
Buldibuyo 582 ... D7
Cabana 1,804 ... C7
Cailloma 1,187 ... G10
Cajabamba 7,282 ... C6
Cajamarca 60,280 ... C6
Cajatambo 1,721 ... D8
Calca 6,112 ... G9
Callalli 819 ... G10
Callao 260,581 ... D9
Callao* 441,374 ... D9
Camaná 11,386 ... F11
Candarave 1,207 ... G11
Cangallo 1,584 ... E9
Canta 3,431 ... D8
Capachica 307 ... H10
Caravelí 1,827 ... F10
Caraz 6,376 ... D7
Carhuás 3,147 ... D7
Carumás 1,031 ... G11
Cascas 2,638 ... C6
Casma 12,725 ... C7
Castrovirreyna 1,749 ... E9
Catacaos 30,927 ... B5
Celendín 8,538 ... D6
Cerro Azul 2,314 ... D9
Cerro de Pasco 71,558 ... D8
Chachapoyas 11,919 ... D6
Chala 1,646 ... E10
Chalhuanca 3,071 ... F10
Chancay 18,993 ... D8
Chepén 29,919 ... C6
Chicama 11,160 ... C6
Chiclayo 280,244 ... C6
Chilca (Pucusana) 3,329 ... D9
Chilete 2,537 ... C6
Chimbote 216,406 ... C7
Chincha Alta 37,475 ... D9
Chiquián 3,521 ... D8
Chirinos 1,061 ... C5
Chivay 3,296 ... G10
Chota 8,299 ... C6
Chulucanas 34,977 ... B5
Chupaca 5,422 ... E9
Chuquibamba 2,630 ... F10
Chuquibambilla 2,147 ... F9
Churín 1,801 ... D8
Cocachacra 5,985 ... G11
Cojata 888 ... H10
Colasay 721 ... C5
Colcamar 1,216 ... D6
Conaica 1,154 ... E9
Concepción 7,129 ... E8
Concordia 1,372 ... E5
Contamana 5,718 ... E6
Contumazá 2,491 ... C6
Coracora 4,598 ... F10
Córdova 453 ... E10
Corongo 1,762 ... D7
Cotahuasi 1,301 ... F10
Cusco (Cuzco) 85,044 ... F9
Cusco* 171,604 ... F9
Cutervo 6,890 ... C6
Cuyocuyo 1,101 ... H10
Desaguadero 2,682 ... H11
Deustua 544 ... G10
Dos de Mayo 574 ... E6
Echarate 1,071 ... F9
El Portugués ... C7
Esperanza 375 ... G7
Espinar 6,381 ... G10
Ferreñafe 22,200 ... C6
Fitzcarrald ... G8
Francisco de Orellana 445 ... F4
Guadalupe 7,613 ... E9
Huacho 43,402 ... D8
Huacrachuco 1,210 ... D7
Hualgayoc 1,691 ... C6
Hualla 4,042 ... F9
Huallanca, Ancash 930 ... D7
Huallanca, Huánuco 4,8[illegible]6 ... D7
Huamachuco 8,273 ... D6
Huancabamba 4,393 ... C5
Huancané 5,227 ... H10
Huancapi 2,539 ... E9
Huancavelica 20,889 ... E9
Huancayo 165,132 ... E9
Huanchaco 6,005 ... C7
Huanta 11,213 ... E9
Huánuco 52,628 ... E7
Huaral 34,235 ... D8
Huaráz 45,116 ... D7
Huari 2,344 ... D7
Huariaca 2,671 ... E8
Huarmey 11,094 ... C8
Huarochirí 1,828 ... D9
Huarocondo 2,498 ... F9
Huaura 9,338 ... D8
Huaylas 1,344 ... C7
Iberia 2,307 ... F5
Ica 111,087 ... E10
Ichuña 277 ... G11
Ilave 9,891 ... H11
Ilo 31,549 ... G11
Imperial 20,894 ... D9
Inambari ... H9
Iñapari 188 ... H8
Intutu 746 ... E4
Iparia 278 ... E7
Iquitos 173,629 ... F4
Jaén 24,356 ... C5
Jauja 14,630 ... E8
Jayanca 6,401 ... B6
Jeberos 1,493 ... D5
Juanjuí 9,324 ... D6
Juli 5,575 ... H11
Juliaca 77,976 ... G10
Jumbilla 1,035 ... C5
Junín 8,988 ... E8
Lagunas 4,601 ... E5
La Huaca 5,161 ... B5
La Jalca 1,769 ... D6
La Joya 5,000 ... G11
Lamas 8,937 ... D6
Lambayeque 23,746 ... B6
Lampa 4,319 ... G10
Lamud 2,405 ... C6
Lanlacuni Bajo 405 ... G9
La Oroya 33,305 ... D8
Las Piedras ... H9
Las Yaras 759 ... G11
La Tina ... B5
La Unión 2,828 ... D7
Leimebamba 1,957 ... D6
Lima (cap.) 375,957 ... D8
Lima* 3,968,972 ... D8
Limbani 728 ... H10
Lircay 5,213 ... E9
Llata 2,922 ... D7
Lobitos 2,975 ... B5
Lurín 14,405 ... D9
Machupicchu 544 ... F9
Macusani 3,389 ... G10
Madre de Dios 660 ... G9
Manú 234 ... G9
Máncora 5,358 ... B5
Marcapata 369 ... G9
Marcona 25,962 ... E10
Margos 1,622 ... D8
Masisea 1,586 ... E7
Matarani ... F11
Matucana 4,196 ... D8
Mazocruz 1,580 ... H11
Mendoza 1,902 ... D6
Moho 2,560 ... H10
Mollendo 21,206 ... F11
Monsefú 17,186 ... C6
Moquegua 21,488 ... G11
Morales 4,370 ... D6
Morococha 11,234 ... D8
Morropón 7,611 ... C5
Motupe 3,411 ... C6
Moyobamba 14,319 ... D6
Nauta 4,083 ... F5
Nazca 22,756 ... E10
Negritos 12,476 ... B5
Nuñoa 3,613 ... G10
Ocoña 1,062 ... F11
Ocros 1,037 ... D8
Ollachea 1,308 ... G9
Ollantaytambo 1,500 ... F9
Olmos 7,946 ... C5
Omate 1,131 ... G11
Orcotuna 3,359 ... E8
Orellana 1,550 ... E6
Otuzco 5,765 ... C6
Oxapampa 5,233 ... E8
Oyón 6,279 ... D8
Pacasmayo 17,588 ... C6
Pachiza 889 ... D6
Paiján 12,699 ... C6
Paita 18,749 ... B5
Palpa 3,393 ... E10
Pampacolca 2,010 ... F10
Pampas 3,850 ... E9
Panao 1,363 ... E7
Paruro 1,727 ... F9
Paucarbama 534 ... E9
Paucartambo, Cusco 1,620 ... G9
Paucartambo, Pasco 3,497 ... E8
Pevas 1,347 ... G4
Picota 2,288 ... D6
Pimentel 9,129 ... B6
Pisac 1,566 ... G9
Pisco 53,414 ... D9
Piura 186,354 ... B5
Pomabamba 2,489 ... D7
Pucallpa 91,953 ... E7
Pucará 2,268 ... G10
Pucaurco 628 ... G4
Pucusana 3,329 ... D9
Puerto Bermúdez 1,133 ... E8
Puerto Chicama 3,630 ... C6
Puerto Eten 2,575 ... B6
Puerto Inca 1,286 ... E7
Puerto Maldonado 12,609 ... H9
Puerto Ocopa 1,088 ... E8
Puerto Samanco 1,435 ... C7
Puno 66,477 ... G10
Punta de Bombón 4,647 ... F11
Puquina 1,026 ... G11
Putina 5,414 ... H10
Querecotillo 10,637 ... B5
Quillabamba 16,837 ... F9
Ramón Castilla 1,811 ... G5
Recuay 2,764 ... D7
Requena 8,270 ... F5
Rioja 9,876 ... D6
Salaverry 5,539 ... C7
Saña 40,144 ... C6
Sandia 1,682 ... H10
San José 4,070 ... B6
San José de Sisa 3,782 ... D6
San Miguel, Ayacucho 1,440 ... F9
San Miguel, Cajamarca 1,798 ... C6
San Pedro de Lloc 11,463 ... C6
San Ramón 7,145 ... E8
Santa 20,490 ... C7
Santa Clotilde 1,068 ... E4
Santa Cruz, Cajamarca 2,739 ... C6
Santa Cruz, Loreto 449 ... E5
Santiago 5,092 ... E10
Santiago de Cao 22,119 ... C6
Santiago de Chuco 5,189 ... C7
Santo Tomás, Amazonas 1,093 ... C6
Santo Tomás, Cusco 2,755 ... G10
San Vicente de Cañete 15,277 ... D9
Saposoa 4,541 ... D6
Saquena 2,755 ... F5
Satipo 9,208 ... E8
Sauce 2,263 ... D6
Sayán 5,129 ... D8
Sechura 11,724 ... B5
Sicuani 21,176 ... G10
Sihuas 2,178 ... D7
Sullana 80,947 ... B5
Sumbilca 1,155 ... D8
Supe 10,061 ... D8
Tacna 92,862 ... G11
Tahuamanu 2,619 ... H8
Talara 55,722 ... B5
Tambo de Mora 2,790 ... D9
Tambo Grande 10,087 ... B5
Tamshiyacu 2,040 ... F5
Tarapoto 33,429 ... D6
Tarata 2,624 ... H11
Tarma 34,369 ... E8
Tayabamba 1,649 ... D7
Tingo María 25,030 ... D7
Tocache 5,940 ... D7
Torata 6,320 ... G11
Trujillo 354,557 ... C7
Tumbes 48,187 ... B4
Uchiza 2,471 ... D7
Urcos 4,155 ... G9
Urubamba 4,686 ... F9
Virú 6,587 ... C7
Yambrasbamba 277 ... D5
Yanahuanca 5,109 ... D8
Yanaoca 1,152 ... G10
Yauca 1,805 ... E10
Yauli 1,020 ... D8
Yauri (Espinar) 6,381 ... G10
Yauyos 1,296 ... E9
Yunguyo 7,253 ... H11
Yurimaguas 22,858 ... E5
Zarumilla 9,713 ... B4
Zorritos 4,497 ... B4

OTHER FEATURES

Acarí (riv.) ... E10
Aguaytía (riv.) ... E7
Aguja (pt.) ... B5
Amazon (riv.) ... F4
Andes, Cordillera de los (mts.) ... F10
Apurímac (riv.) ... F9
Azángaro (riv.) ... G10
Azul, Cordillera (range) ... E7
Blanca, Cordillera (range) ... D7
Blanco (cape) ... B5
Boquerón, El (pass) ... E7
Cañete (riv.) ... D9
Chimbote (bay) ... C7
Chincha (isls.) ... D9
Chira (riv.) ... B5
Cóndor, Cordillera del (range) ... C5
Coropuna, Nudo (mt.) ... F10
Corrientes (riv.) ... E4
Ene (riv.) ... E8
Ferrol (pt.) ... C7
Grande (riv.) ... E10
Guañape (isls.) ... C7
Heath (riv.) ... H9
Huallaga (riv.) ... D5
Huasaga (riv.) ... D4
Huascarán (mt.) ... D7
Huayabamba (riv.) ... D6
Ica (riv.) ... E10
Inambari (riv.) ... H9
Independencia (bay) ... D10
Independencia (isl.) ... D10
Junín (lake) ... E8
Juruá (riv.) ... F7
Lobos de Afuera (isls.) ... B6
Lobos de Tierra (isl.) ... B6
Locumba (riv.) ... G11
Madre de Dios (riv.) ... G9
Majes (riv.) ... F1
Mantaro (riv.) ... E8
Manú (riv.) ... G8
Marañón (riv.) ... E5
Mayo (riv.) ... D6
Misti, El (mt.) ... G11
Montaña, La (reg.) ... F8
Morona (riv.) ... D5
Nanay (riv.) ... E4
Napo (riv.) ... F4
Negra, Cordillera (range) ... D7
Negra (pt.) ... B6
Ñermete (pt.) ... B5
Occidental, Cordillera (range) ... F10
Ocoña (riv.) ... F11
Oriental, Cordillera (range) ... H10
Pachitea (riv.) ... E7
Paita (bay) ... B5
Pampas (riv.) ... E9
Paracas (pt.) ... D9
Pariñas (pt.) ... B5
Parinacochas (lake) ... F10
Pastaza (riv.) ... D5
Pativilca (riv.) ... D8
Perené (riv.) ... E8
Piedras, Las (riv.) ... G8
Pisco (bay) ... D9
Pisco (riv.) ... D9
Piura (riv.) ... B5
Purús (riv.) ... G8
Putumayo (riv.) ... G4
Rímac (riv.) ... D9
Salcantay (mt.) ... F9
Sama (riv.) ... G11
San Gallán (isl.) ... D9
San Lorenzo (isl.) ... D9
San Nicolás (bay) ... E10
Santa (riv.) ... C7
Santiago (riv.) ... D4
Sechura (bay) ... B5
Tambo (riv.) ... G11
Tapiche (riv.) ... E6
Tigre (riv.) ... E4
Titicaca (lake) ... H10
Tumbes (riv.) ... B4
Ucayali (riv.) ... F5
Urubamba (riv.) ... F8

(continued on following page)

Vilcabamba, Cordillera
  (range) F9
Vilcanota (mt.) G10
Vitor (riv.) F11
Yaguas (riv.) G4
Yavarí (riv.) G5
Yavero (riv.) F9
Yuruá (riv.) F7

ECUADOR

PROVINCES

Azuay 367,324 ....C4

Bolívar 144,593 ....C3
Cañar 146,570 ....C4
Carchi 120,857 ....C2
Chimborazo 304,316 ....C3
Colón, Archipiélago de
  (terr.) 4,037 ....C8
Cotopaxi 236,313 ....C3
El Oro 262,564 ....C4
Esmeraldas 203,151 ....C2
Guayas 1,512,333 ....B4
Imbabura 216,027 ....C2
La Bonita 184 ....D2
Loja 342,339 ....C4
Los Ríos 383,432 ....C3

Manabí 817,966 ....B3
Mera 631 ....C3
Morona-Santiago 53,325 ...C4
Napo 65,186 ....D3
Pastaza 23,465 ....D3
Pichincha 988,306 ....C3
Tungurahua 279,920 ....C3
Zamora-Chinchipe 34,493 ..C5

CITIES and TOWNS

Alausí 7,137 ....C4
Ambato 77,955 ....C3
Arenillas 5,862 ....B4

Atuntaqui 9,907 ....C2
Azogues 10,953 ....C4
Baba 953 ....C3
Babahoyo 28,914 ....C3
Baeza 253 ....D3
Bahía de Caráquez 11,258 .B3
Balzar 10,924 ....C3
Baquerizo Moreno 1,311 ...C9
Bolívar C2
Cajabamba 2,318 ....C3
Calceta 7,152 ....C3
Cañar 6,727 ....C4
Cariamanga 6,682 ....C5
Catacocha 3,280 ....C5

Catarama 2,868 ....C3
Cayambe 11,199 ....D3
Celica 3,081 ....B4
Chone 23,627 ....B3
Chunchi 2,802 ....C4
Coca 1,211 ....D3
Cuenca 104,470 ....C4
Dayle 13,170 ....B3
El Ángel 3,660 ....C2
El Corazón 1,073 ....C3
El Pun D2
Esmeraldas 60,364 ....B2
Girón 2,361 ....C4
Gualaceo 4,575 ....C4

Gualaquiza 1,679 ....C4
Guamote 2,438 ....C4
Guano 5,389 ....C3
Guaranda 11,364 ....C3
Guayaquil 823,219 ....B4
Ibarra 41,335 ....D2
Jipijapa 19,996 ....B3
La Bonita 184 ....D2
La Libertad 26,078 ....B4
Latacunga 21,921 ....C3
Loja 47,697 ....C4
Loreto D3
Macará 8,063 ....C5
Macas 1,934 ....D4
Machachi 4,745 ....C3
Machala 69,170 ....B4
Machalilla B3
Manglaralto B3
Manta 64,519 ....B3
Méndez 1,043 ....C4
Mera 631 ....C3
Milagro 53,106 ....C4
Montecristi 6,386 ....B3
Nuevo Rocafuerte 198 .....E3
Otavalo 13,605 ....C2
Paján 2,610 ....B3
Pasaje 20,790 ....C4
Paute 1,998 ....C4
Pelileo 3,754 ....C3
Pillaro 4,052 ....C3
Piñas 5,770 ....C4
Portoviejo 59,550 ....B3
Puerto Ayora 900 ....B9
Puerto El Carmen 308 .....E3
Pujilí 2,510 ....C3
Puyo 4,730 ....D3
Quevedo 43,101 ....C3
Quito (cap.) 599,828 .....C3
Riobamba 58,087 ....C3
Rocafuerte 5,519 ....B3
Rosa Zárate 4,847 ....C2
Salinas 12,409 ....B4
San Gabriel 10,036 ....D2
Sangolquí 10,554 ....C3
San Lorenzo C2
San Miguel 2,743 ....C4
San Miguel de Salcedo 4,159 .C3
Santa Ana 5,004 ....B3
Santa Elena 7,687 ....B4
Santa Isabel 2,068 ....C4
Santa Rosa 19,696 ....C4
Santo Domingo de los
  Colorados 30,523 ......C3
Saraguro 1,739 ....C4
Sarayacu D3
Sigsig 2,021 ....C4
Sucre 2,929 ....B3
Sucúa 9,694 ....C4
Tabacundo 1,942 ....C2
Tachina C2
Tulcán 24,398 ....D2
Valdez 3,837 ....C2
Venticinco de Mayo 266 ...C4
Vinces 10,126 ....C3
Yaguachi Nuevo 3,816 .....B4
Zamora 2,667 ....C5
Zumba 905 ....C5

OTHER FEATURES

Aguarico (riv.) D3
Albemarle (pt.) B9
Ancón de Sardinas (bay) ..C2
Antisana (mt.) D3
Baltra (isl.) B9
Banks (bay) B9
Bobonaza (riv.) D3
Cayambe (mt.) D2
Chaves (Santa Cruz) (isl.) .C9
Chimborazo (mt.) C3
Chira (riv.) B5
Cóndor, Cordillera del
  (range) C5
Cotopaxi (mt.) C3
Cristóbal (pt.) B9
Culpepper (isl.) B8
Curaray (riv.) D3
Darwin (Culpepper) (isl.) .B8
Esmeraldas (riv.) C2
Española (isl.) C10
Fernandina (isl.) B9
Floreana (Santa María)
  (isl.) B10
Galápagos (isls.) C8
Genovesa (isl.) C9
Guayaquil (gulf) B4
Guayas (riv.) C4
Isabela (isl.) B9
La Puntilla (cape) B4
Manta (bay) B3
Marchena (isl.) B9
Mira (riv.) C2
Napo (riv.) D3
Naranjal (riv.) C4
Pastaza (riv.) D4
Pinta (isl.) B9
Pinzón (isl.) B9
Puná (isl.) B4
Putumayo (riv.) E2
Rosa (cape) B10
San Cristóbal (isl.) C9
San Francisco (cape) B3
Sangay (mt.) C4
San Lorenzo (cape) B3
San Miguel (riv.) D2
San Salvador (isl.) B9
Santa Cruz (isl.) C9
Santa Fe (isl.) C9
Santa María (isl.) B10
Santiago (San Salvador)
  (isl.) B9
Tumbes (riv.) B4
Wenman (isl.) B8
Wolf (Wenman) (isl.) B8
Zamora (riv.) C4

FRENCH GUIANA

DISTRICTS

Cayenne 61,587 ....E3
Saint-Laurent du Maroni
  11,435 ....E4

CITIES and TOWNS

Camopi 228 ....E4
Cayenne (cap.) 37,097 ....E3
Grand Santi 305 ....E3
Guisanbourg E3
Inini E3
Iracoubo 483 ....E3
Kourou 6,465 ....E3
Macouria 94 ....E3
Malmanoury E3
Mana 623 ....E3
Maripasoula 556 ....D4
Matoury 586 ....E3
Montsinéry 94 ....E3
Ouanary 61 ....F3
Paul Isnard D3
Régina 258 ....E3
Rémire 5,921 ....E3
Roura 160 ....E3
Saint-Élie 57 ....E3
Saint-Georges 921 ....F4
Saint-Laurent du Maroni
  5,042 ....E3
Saül 60 ....E3
Saut-Tigre E3
Sinnamary 1,669 ....E3

OTHER FEATURES

Approuague (riv.) E4
Béhague (mts.) F3
Camopi (riv.) E4
Devil's (isl.) E4
Inini (riv.) E4
Lawa (riv.) D4
Litani (riv.) D4
Mana (riv.) E3
Maroni (riv.) D3
Marouini (riv.) D4
Oyapock (riv.) E4
Rémire (isls.) F3
Salut (isls.) E3
Sinnamary (riv.) E3
Tampoc (riv.) E4
Tumuc-Humac (mts.) D3

GUYANA

DISTRICTS

East Berbice-Courantyne ..C3
East Demerara-West
  Coast Berbice C2
Mazaruni-Potaro A2
North West A2
Rupununi B4
West Demerara-Essequibo
  Coast B2

CITIES and TOWNS

Adventure° 645 ....B2
Annai° 569 ....B4
Anna Regina 1,124 ....B2
Apoteri° 74 ....B3
Baramanni° 231 ....B2
Bartica° 4,087 ....B2
Biloku° 290 ....B4
Charity° 1,175 ....B2
Corriverton 10,502 ....C2
Danielstown 861 ....B2
Epira° 230 ....C3
Georgetown (cap.) 63,184 .C2
Georgetown° * 164,039 ....C2
Imbaimadai° 270 ....A3
Issano° 207 ....B3
Issineru° 124 ....A3
Kamakusa° 211 ....A3
Kamarang° 308 ....A3
Kurupukari° 284 ....B3
Lethem° 645 ....B4
Linden 23,956 ....B2
Mabaruma° 391 ....B1
Mahaica° 6,967 ....C2
Mahaicony Village° 4,665 .C2
Mahdia° 147 ....B3
Mara° 203 ....C3
Morawhanna° 292 ....B1
Mount Everard° 369 ....B2
New Amsterdam 17,782 .....C2
Orealla° 674 ....C3
Parika° 1,101 ....B2
Pickersgill° 508 ....B2
Queenstown° 1,211 ....B2
Rockstone° 728 ....B2
Rosignol° 2,001 ....C2
Suddie° 705 ....B2
Tumatumari° 353 ....B3
Tumereng° 238 ....B3
Vreed-en-Hoop° 3,054 .....B2
Wichabai° 290 ....B4

OTHER FEATURES

Acarai (mts.) B5
Amakura (riv.) A2
Amuku (mts.) B4
Barama (riv.) B2
Barima (riv.) B2
Berbice (riv.) B3
Burro-Burro (riv.) B3
Courantyne (riv.) B3
Cuyuni (riv.) A2
Demerara (riv.) B3
Essequibo (riv.) B3
Great (fall) B3
Ireng (riv.) B3
Kaieteur (fall) B3

*City and suburbs

Agriculture, Industry and Resources

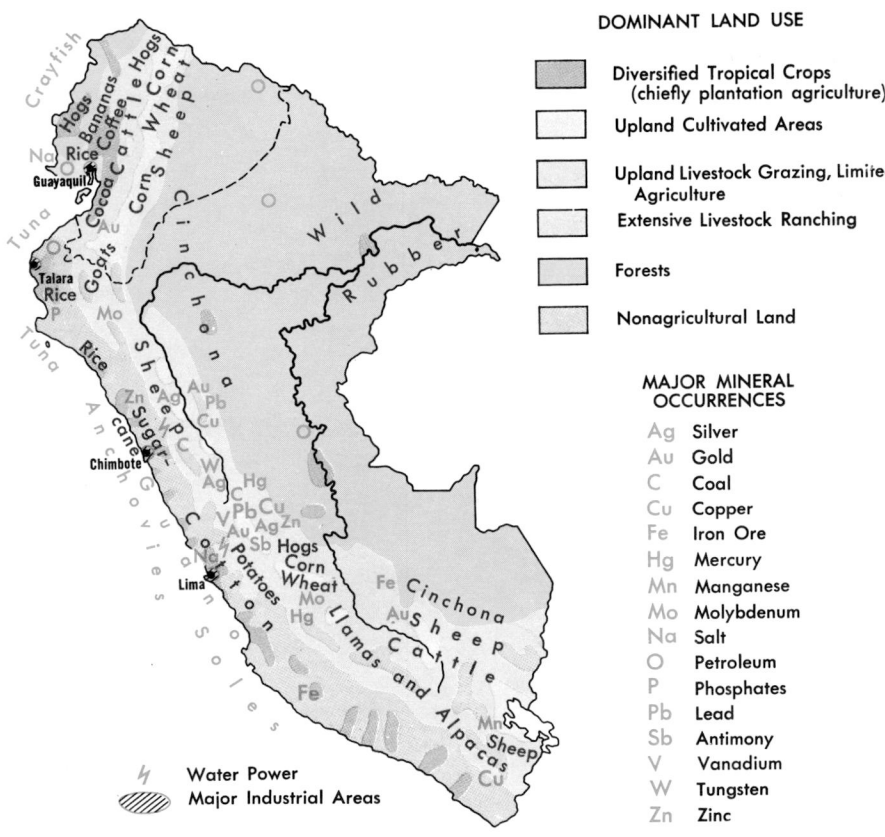

DOMINANT LAND USE

- Diversified Tropical Crops (chiefly plantation agriculture)
- Upland Cultivated Areas
- Upland Livestock Grazing, Limited Agriculture
- Extensive Livestock Ranching
- Forests
- Nonagricultural Land

MAJOR MINERAL OCCURRENCES

- Ag   Silver
- Au   Gold
- C   Coal
- Cu   Copper
- Fe   Iron Ore
- Hg   Mercury
- Mn   Manganese
- Mo   Molybdenum
- Na   Salt
- O   Petroleum
- P   Phosphates
- Pb   Lead
- Sb   Antimony
- V   Vanadium
- W   Tungsten
- Zn   Zinc

⚡ Water Power
▨ Major Industrial Areas

Agriculture, Industry and Resources

DOMINANT LAND USE

- Diversified Tropical Crops (chiefly plantation agriculture)
- Extensive Livestock Ranching
- Forests

MAJOR MINERAL OCCURRENCES

- Al   Bauxite
- Au   Gold
- D   Diamonds
- Mn   Manganese

⚡ Water Power

GUYANA

AREA 83,000 sq. mi. (214,970 sq. km.)
POPULATION 1,024,000
CAPITAL Georgetown
LARGEST CITY Georgetown
HIGHEST POINT Mt. Roraima 9,094 ft.
(2,772 m.)
MONETARY UNIT Guyana dollar
MAJOR LANGUAGES English, Hindi
MAJOR RELIGIONS Christianity, Hinduism,
Islam

SURINAME

AREA 55,144 sq. mi. (142,823 sq. km.)
POPULATION 400,000
CAPITAL Paramaribo
LARGEST CITY Paramaribo
HIGHEST POINT Julianatop 4,200 ft. (1,280 m.)
MONETARY UNIT Suriname guilder
MAJOR LANGUAGES Dutch, Hindi, Indonesian
MAJOR RELIGIONS Christianity, Islam,
Hinduism

FRENCH GUIANA

AREA 35,135 sq. mi. (91,000 sq. km.)
POPULATION 90,000
CAPITAL Cayenne
LARGEST CITY Cayenne
HIGHEST POINT 2,723 ft. (830 m.)
MONETARY UNIT French franc
MAJOR LANGUAGE French
MAJOR RELIGIONS Roman Catholicism,
Protestantism

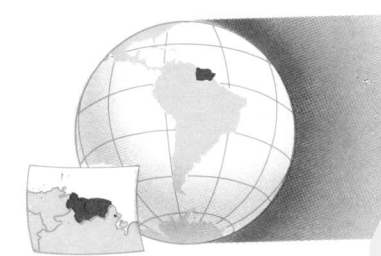

Kamaria (falls) B2	Lelydorp 300 ....D3
Kuyuwini (riv.) B4	Mariënburg 3,500 ....D2
Kwitaro (riv.) B4	Moengo 2,100 ....D3
Leguan (isl.) B2	Nieuw-Amsterdam 1,400 ....D2
Mazaruni (riv.) A2	Nieuw-Nickerie 34,480 ....C2
Moruka (riv.) B2	Paramaribo (cap.) 67,905 ....D2
New (riv.) C4	Paranam D3
Pakaraima (mts.) A3	Totness 1,300 ....C3
Pomeroon (riv.) B2	Uitkijk D3
Potaro (riv.) B3	Wageningen 800 ....C3
Puruni (riv.) B2	Zanderij D3
Roraima (mt.) A3	
Rupununi (riv.) B4	OTHER FEATURES
Takutu (riv.) B4	
Venamo (mt.) A3	Bakhuys (mts.) C3
Waini (riv.) B2	Coeroeni (riv.) C4
Wenamu (riv.) A2	Commewijne (riv.) D3
	Coppename (riv.) C3
SURINAME	Corantijn (riv.) C3
	Cottica (riv.) D3
DISTRICTS	Eilerts de Haan (mts.) C4
	Frederik Willem IV (falls) C4
Brokopondo 17,763 ....D4	Julianatop (mt.) C4
Commewijne 18,740 ....D3	Kutari (riv.) C4
Coronie 3,251 ....C3	Lely (mts.) D3
Marowijne 25,911 ....D4	Litani (riv.) D4
Nickerie 35,178 ....C3	Marowijne (riv.) D3
Para 16,635 ....D3	Nickerie (riv.) C3
Paramaribo 102,297 ....D2	Orange (mts.) D4
Saramacca 13,554 ....C3	Saramacca (riv.) D3
Suriname 151,585 ....D3	Sipaliwini (riv.) C4
	Suriname (riv.) D3
CITIES and TOWNS	Tapanahoni (riv.) D4
Albina 1,000 ....D3	
Brokopondo D3	
Calcutta 1,100 ....C3	
Domburg 1,200 ....D3	
Groningen 500 ....D2	

*City and suburbs.
° Population of sub-district or division.
□ Population of district.

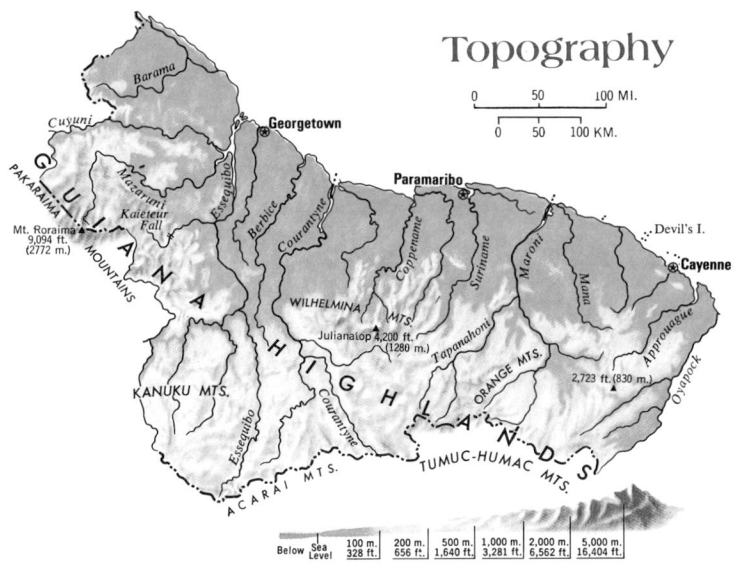

Topography

0   50   100 MI.
0   50   100 KM.

Below Sea Level	100 m. 328 ft.	200 m. 656 ft.	500 m. 1,640 ft.	1,000 m. 3,281 ft.	2,000 m. 6,562 ft.	5,000 m. 16,404 ft.

GUYANA

SURINAME

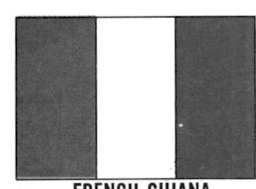

FRENCH GUIANA

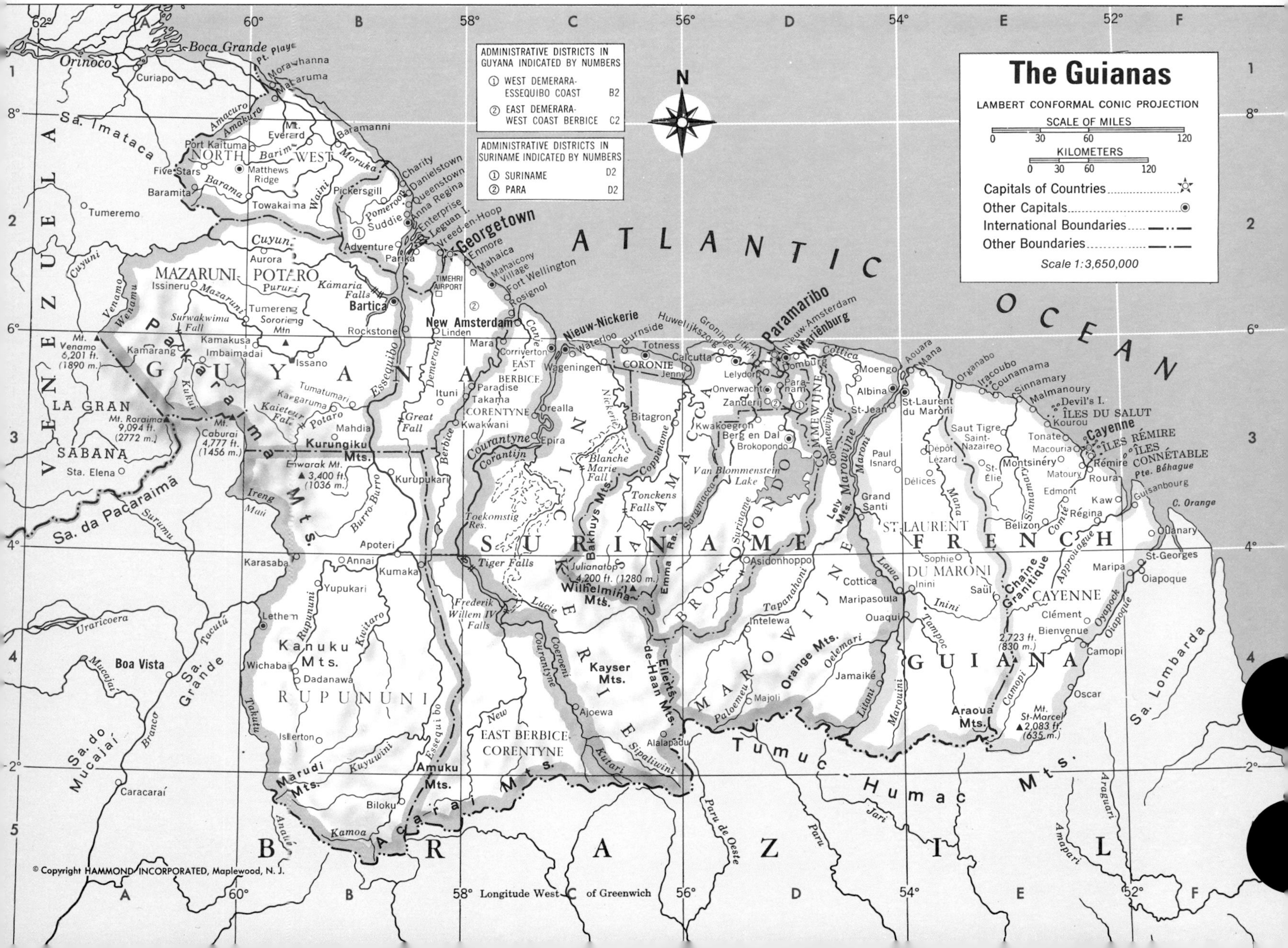

The Guianas

LAMBERT CONFORMAL CONIC PROJECTION

SCALE OF MILES
0   30   60   120

KILOMETERS
0   30   60   120

Capitals of Countries ....☆
Other Capitals ....◉
International Boundaries ....
Other Boundaries ....

Scale 1:3,650,000

ADMINISTRATIVE DISTRICTS IN GUYANA INDICATED BY NUMBERS
① WEST DEMERARA-ESSEQUIBO COAST B2
② EAST DEMERARA-WEST COAST BERBICE C2

ADMINISTRATIVE DISTRICTS IN SURINAME INDICATED BY NUMBERS
① SURINAME D2
② PARA D2

© Copyright HAMMOND INCORPORATED, Maplewood, N.J.

Longitude West of Greenwich

Brazil

BIPOLAR OBLIQUE CONIC CONFORMAL PROJECTION

SCALE OF MILES

SCALE OF KILOMETERS

Capitals of Countries .... ⊛
State Capitals .... ◉
International Boundaries .... — · —
State Boundaries .... — · · —

Scale 1:14,700,000

© Copyright HAMMOND INCORPORATED, Maplewood, N.J.

BRAZIL
WESTERN PART

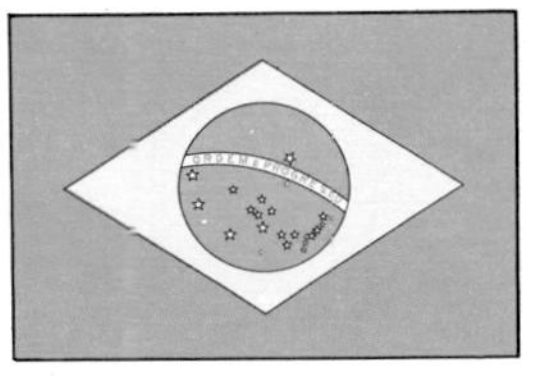

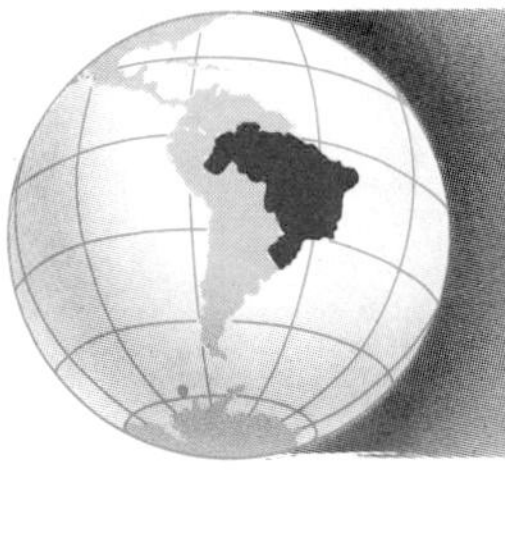

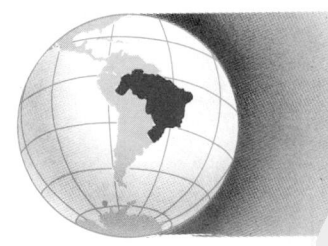

AREA 3,284,426 sq. mi. (8,506,663 sq. km.)
POPULATION 150,368,000
CAPITAL Brasília
LARGEST CITY São Paulo (greater)
HIGHEST POINT Pico da Neblina 9,889 ft. (3,014 m.)
MONETARY UNIT cruzado
MAJOR LANGUAGE Portuguese
MAJOR RELIGION Roman Catholicism

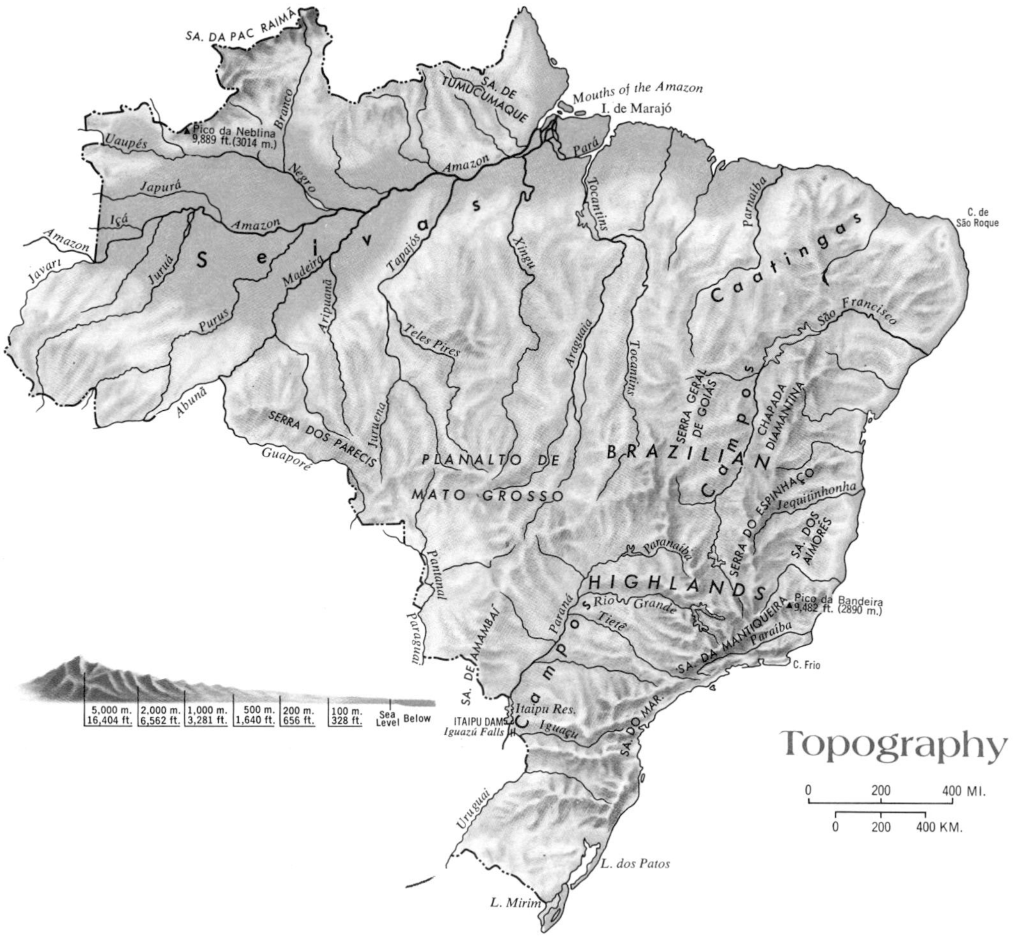
SA. DA PAC RAIMÃ
SA. DE TUMUCUMAQUE
Mouths of the Amazon
I. de Marajó
Pico da Neblina 9,889 ft. (3014 m.)
Branco
Uaupés
Negro
Amazon
Pará
Japurá
Içá
Tocantins
Parnaíba
C. de São Roque
Javari
Juruá
S e l v a s
Tapajós
Xingu
C a a t i n g a s
Madeira
Purus
Aripuanã
São Francisco
Teles Pires
Araguaia
Abunã
SERRA DOS PARECIS
Juruena
SERRA GERAL DE GOIÁS
CHAPADA DIAMANTINA
Guaporé
PLANALTO DE MATO GROSSO
BRAZILIAN HIGHLANDS
Campos
SERRA DO ESPINHAÇO
Jequitinhonha
SA. DOS AIMORÉS
Paranaíba
Pantanal
Rio Grande
Pico da Bandeira 9,482 ft. (2890 m.)
Paraná
Tietê
SA. DE AMAMBAÍ
Paraguai
SA. DA MANTIQUEIRA
Paraíba
C. Frio
Itaipu Res.
ITAIPU DAMS
Iguaçu Falls
Iguaçu
SA. DO MAR
Uruguai
L. dos Patos
L. Mirim
5,000 m. 16,404 ft.
2,000 m. 6,562 ft.
1,000 m. 3,281 ft.
500 m. 1,640 ft.
200 m. 656 ft.
100 m. 328 ft.
Sea Level
Below
0 200 400 MI.
0 200 400 KM.

Topography

STATES and TERRITORIES

Acre 301,605 .... G10
Alagoas 1,987,581 .... G5
Amapá (terr.) 175,634 .... D2
Amazonas 1,432,066 .... G9
Bahia 9,474,263 .... F6
Ceará 5,294,876 .... G4
Espirito Santo 2,023,821 .... F7
Federal District 1,177,393 .... E6
Goiás 3,865,482 .... D6
Maranhão 4,002,599 .... E4
Mato Grosso 1,141,661 .... B6
Mato Grosso do Sul 1,370,333 .... C7
Minas Gerais 13,390,805 .... E7
Pará 3,411,868 .... C4
Paralba 2,772,600 .... G4
Paraná 7,630,466 .... D9
Pernambuco 6,147,102 .... G5
Piaul 2,140,066 .... F4
Rio de Janeiro 11,297,327 .... F8
Rio Grande do Norte 1,899,720 .... G4
Rio Grande do Sul 7,777,212 .... C10
Rondônia 492,810 .... H10
Roraima (terr.) 79,153 .... H8
Santa Catarina 3,628,751 .... D9
São Paulo 25,040,698 .... D8
Sergipe 1,141,834 .... G5
Tocantins D5

CITIES and TOWNS

Abaeté 12,861 .... E7
Abaetetuba 33,031 .... D3
Acaraú 7,144 .... F3
Acopiara 10,747 .... G4
Açu 20,544 .... G4
Agudos 18,790 .... *B3
Alagoa Grande 14,204 .... H4
Alagoinhas 76,377 .... G6
Alcobaça 3,430 .... G7
Alegre 9,441 .... *F2
Alegrete 54,786 .... B10
Além Paralba 23,028 .... *E2
Alenquer 16,477 .... C3
Alfenas 31,815 .... *D2
Altamira 24,846 .... C3
Altos 13,621 .... F4
Amambal 12,507 .... C8
Amapá 2,676 .... D2
Amarante 6,848 .... F4
Amargosa 11,118 .... F6
Americana 121,794 .... *C3
Amparo 26,970 .... *C3
Anápolis 160,520 .... D7
Anchieta 5,741 .... F8
Andaral 2,476 .... F6
Andradina 42,036 .... D8
Andrelândia 8,737 .... *D2
Angra dos Reis 24,894 .... *D3
Antonina 11,950 .... *B4
Aparecida 27,265 .... *D3
Apiai 7,809 .... *B4
Aquidauana 21,514 .... C8
Aracaju 288,106 .... G5
Aracati 20,282 .... G4
Araçatuba 113,486 .... *A2
Araçuaí 12,292 .... F7
Araquari 73,302 .... D7
Araranquá 22,468 .... D10
Araraquara 77,202 .... *B2
Araras 54,323 .... *C3
Araxá 51,339 .... E7
Arcoverde 40,646 .... G5
Areia Branca 12,979 .... G4
Assis 57,217 .... *A3
Avaré 40,716 .... *B3
Bacabai 43,229 .... E4
Bagé 66,743 .... C10
Bahia (Salvador) 1,496,276 .... G6
Baixo Guandu 13,714 .... F7
Balsas 13,566 .... E4
Bambui 14,172 .... *C2
Barão de Cocais 11,950 .... *E1
Barbacena 69,675 .... *E2
Bariri 15,372 .... *B3
Barra 10,809 .... F5
Barra do Corda 19,280 .... E4
Barra do Piraí 51,214 .... *E3
Barra Mansa 123,421 .... *D3
Barras 8,904 .... F4
Barreiras 30,355 .... E6
Barreiros 19,419 .... H5
Barretos 65,294 .... *B2
Batatais 30,478 .... *C2
Baturité 12,388 .... G4
Bauru 178,861 .... *B3
Bebedouro 39,070 .... *B2
Bela Vista 11,936 .... C8
Belém 758,117 .... E3
Belém †1,000,349 .... E3
Belo Horizonte 1,442,483 .... *D1
Belo Horizonte †2,541,788 .... *D1
Benjamin Constant 6,563 .... G9
Bento Gonçalves 40,323 .... C10
Betim 71,599 .... *D2
Bicas 8,611 .... *E2
Birigui 45,348 .... *A2
Blumenau 144,819 .... D9
Boa Esperanca 17,394 .... *D2
Boa Vista 43,131 .... H8
Bocaiúva 16,616 .... E7
Bom Conselho 13,196 .... G5
Bom Despacho 22,941 .... *D1
Bom Jesus da Lapa 19,978 .... F6
Bom Sucesso 10,331 .... *D2
Borba 5,366 .... H9
Bragança Paulista 61,021 .... *C3
Brasiléia 4,835 .... G10
Brasília (cap.) 411,305 .... E6
Brasilia de Minas 10,171 .... F7
Brejo 5,859 .... F3
Breves 31,452 .... D3
Brumado 24,663 .... F6
Brusque 37,898 .... D9
Cabedolo 18,581 .... H4
Cabo Frio 40,668 .... *F3
Caçador 25,287 .... D9
Caçapava 45,258 .... *D3
Caçapava do Sul 15,180 .... C10
Cáceres 33,472 .... B7
Cachoeira 11,520 .... G6
Cachoeira do Sul 59,967 .... C10
Cachoeiro de Itapemirim 84,994 .... G8
Caeté 23,331 .... *E1
Caetité 8,823 .... F6
Caiaponia 9,358 .... C7
Caicó 30,777 .... G4
Cajazeiras 30,834 .... G4
Cajuru 9,670 .... *C2
Camaquá 28,078 .... C10
Cambará 13,218 .... *A3
Cambui 8,552 .... *C3
Cametá 15,539 .... D3
Camocim 19,921 .... F3
Campina Grande 222,229 .... G4
Campinas 566,517 .... *C3
Campo Belo 30,392 .... *D2
Campo Formoso 10,324 .... F5
Campo Grand 282,844 .... C8
Campo Largo 34,506 .... *B4
Campo Major 24,009 .... F4
Campos 174,218 .... *F2
Cananéia 5,581 .... *C4
Canavieiras 14,076 .... G6
Canindé 18,573 .... G4
Canoas 214,115 .... D10
Canoinhas 25,880 .... D9
Capanema 28,272 .... E3
Capão Bonito 24,081 .... *B4
Caraguatatuba 22,932 .... *D3
Carangola 15,621 .... *E2
Caratinga 39,621 .... *E1
Caravelas 3,704 .... G7
Carazinho 41,913 .... C10
Carolina 10,136 .... E4
Caruaru 137,636 .... G5
Casa Banca 13,739 .... *C2
Cascavel 16,238 .... G4
Cássia 10,701 .... *C2
Castanhal 51,797 .... E3
Castelo 9,162 .... F8
Castro 21,079 .... *B4
Castro Alves 11,286 .... G6
Cataguases 40,659 .... *E2
Catalão 30,516 .... E7
Catanduva 64,813 .... *B2
Catolé do Rocha 12,165 .... G4
Caxambu 16,221 .... *D2
Caxias 56,755 .... F4
Caxias do Sul 198,824 .... D10
Ceará (Fortaleza) 648,815 .... G3
Ceará-Mirim 17,097 .... H4
Ceres 13,671 .... D6
Chapecó 53,198 .... C9
Coari 14,841 .... H9
Codajás 4,923 .... H9
Codó 11,593 .... E4
Colatina 61,057 .... F7
Conceição do Araguaia 18,143 .... D5
Concórdia 17,973 .... D9
Conselheiro Lafaiete 66,262 .... E2
Corinto 17,056 .... E7
Cornélio Procópio 31,201 .... D8
Coroatá 16,070 .... F3
coromandel 11,604 .... F7
Corumbá 66,014 .... B7
Coxim 14,876 .... C7
Crateús 29,905 .... F4
Crato 49,244 .... G4
Criciúma 74,003 .... D10
Cristalina 10,521 .... E7
Cruz Alta 53,315 .... C10
Cruzeiro 55,175 .... *D3
Cruzeiro do Sul 11,189 .... G10
Cubatão 78,327 .... *C3
Cuiabá 167,894 .... C6
Curitiba 843,733 .... *B4
Curitiba †1,441,743 .... *B4
Currais Novos 25,663 .... G4
Cururupu 10,358 .... E3
Curvelo 37,734 .... E7
Diamantina 20,197 .... F7
Divinópolis 108,344 .... *D2
Dois Córregos 11,811 .... *B3
Dom Pedrito 25,773 .... C10
Dores do Indaiá 13,058 .... E7
Dourados 76,838 .... C8
Duque de Caxias 306,057 .... *E3
Erexim 46,927 .... C9
Esperanca 12,964 .... G4
Esplanada 9,822 .... G5
Estancia 28,250 .... G5
Feira de Santana 225,0[illegible]3 .... G5
Fernandópolis 39,737 .... *A2
Floriano 35,761 .... F4
Florianópolis 153,547 .... E9
Fonte Boa 3,278 .... G9
Formiga 36,681 .... *D2
Formosa 29,304 .... E6
Fortaleza 648,815 .... G3
Fortaleza †1,581,588 .... G3
Foz do Iguacu 93,619 .... C9
Franca 143,630 .... *C2
Frutal 22,955 .... *B2
Garanhuns 64,854 .... G5
Garca 26,527 .... *B3
Goiana 30,108 .... H4
Goiânia 703,263 .... D7
Goiás 15,768 .... D6
Governador Valadares 173,699 .... F7
Grajaú 11,147 .... E4
Guacul 12,715 .... *F2
Guajará-Mirim 19,992 .... H10
Guarapuava 17,189 .... C9
Guarantiguetá 68,370 .... *D3
Guarujá 67,730 .... *C4
Guarulhos 395,117 .... *C3
Guaxupé 23,637 .... *C2
Guirantinga 8,981 .... C7
Gurupi 27,39 .... D5
Humaitá 10,004 .... H10
Ibaiti 11,352 .... *A3
Ibiá 11,161 .... E7
Ibicaraí 18,202 .... G6
Ibitinga 23,359 .... *B2
Icó 13,007 .... G4
Igarapava 15,342 .... C2
Igarapé-Miri 12,172 .... D3
Iguape 16,827 .... *C4
Iguatu 39,611 .... G4
Ijui 51,925 .... C10
Ilhéus 71,240 .... G6
Imbituba 9,998 .... D10
Imperatiz 111,818 .... E4
Inhumas 23,455 .... D7
Ipameri 14,163 .... E7
Ipu 12,787 .... F4
Irati 21,956 .... *A4
Itabaiana, Paralba 17,843 .... H4
Itabaiana, Sergipe 26,055 .... G5
Itaberaba 27,590 .... F6
Itabira 57,691 .... F7
Itabirito 22,978 .... *E2
Itabuna 129,938 .... G6
Itacoatiara 26,737 .... B3
Itaituba 19,644 .... C4
Itajai 78,867 .... D9
Itajubá 53,506 .... *D3
Itanhaem 26,181 .... C4
Itapecerica 10,234 .... *D2
Itapecuru-Mirim 12,216 .... F3
Itapemirim 16,829 .... F8
Itaperuna 34,644 .... *F2
Itapetinga 36,897 .... G6
Itapetininga 61,344 .... *B3
Itapeva 36,551 .... *B3
Itapipoca 19,463 .... G3
Itapira 36,308 .... *C3
Itápolis 13,750 .... *B2
Itaporanga 8,988 .... G4
Itaqui 23,136 .... B10
Itararé 24,368 .... *B4
Itatiba 35,537 .... *C3
Itaúna 49,372 .... *D2
Itu 62,211 .... *C3
Ituacu 1,749 .... F6
Ituiutaba 65,178 .... D7
Itumbiara 56,602 .... D7
Iturama 12,363 .... *A1
Ituverava 21,323 .... *C2
Jaboatao 67,129 .... H5
Jaboticabal 40,276 .... *B2
Jacarel 103,652 .... *D3
Jacarezinho 23,684 .... *A3
Jacobina 26,723 .... F5
Jacupiranga 7,044 .... B4
Jaguaquara 11,336 .... F6
Jaguarao 18,165 .... C11
Jaguariaiva 8,566 .... *B4
Januária 20,484 .... E6
Jatai 40,957 .... D7
Jaú 59,522 .... *B3
Jequié 84,792 .... F6
Jequitinhonha 10,900 .... F7
Ji-Paraná 31,724 .... H10
Joacaba 16,195 .... D9
Joao Pessoa 290,424 .... H4
Joao Pinheiro 17,013 .... E7
Joinvile 217,074 .... D9
Juazeiro 60,940 .... G5
Juazeiro do Norte 125,248 .... F4
Juiz de Fora 299,728 .... *E2
Jundiai 210,015 .... *C3
Lages 108,768 .... D9
Laguna 27,743 .... D10
Lambari 9,722 .... *D2
Lapa 13,314 .... D9
Laranjeiras do Sul 19,329 .... C9
Lavras 35,345 .... *D2
Leme 40,155 .... *C3
Leopoldina 28,554 .... *E2
Limeira 137,812 .... *C3
Limoeiro 36,088 .... H4
Limoeiro do Norte 13,112 .... G4
Linhares 51,575 .... F7
Lins 44,633 .... *B2
Londrina 258,054 .... D8
Lorena 51,276 .... *D3
Luis Correia 3,576 .... F3
Luz 10,068 .... *D1
Luziania 67,284 .... E7
Macaé 39,644 .... *F3
Macalba 17,036 .... H4
Macapá 89,081 .... D2
Macau 17,543 .... G4
Maceio 376,479 .... H5
Machado 16,164 .... *C2
Mafra 26,226 .... D9
Magé 37,597 .... *E3
Mamanguape 16,321 .... H4
Manacapuru 17,016 .... H9
Manaus 613,068 .... H9
Manhuacu 22,678 .... *E2
Manhumirim 11,085 .... *E2
Manicoré 9,532 .... H9
Marabá 41,564 .... D4
Maracaju 9,699 .... C8
Maragogipe 13,512 .... G6
Maranguape 20,098 .... G3
Marechal Deodoro 9,400 .... H5
Mariana 11,785 .... *E2
Marilla 103,904 .... *A3
Maringá 158,047 .... D8
Mata de São João 23,741 .... G6
Mato Grosso (Vila Bela da Santissima Trindade) 1,401 .... B6
Maués 10,846 .... B3
Mineiros 16,844 .... C7
Miracema 15,545 .... *E2
Miracema do Norte D5
Mirassol 25,173 .... *B2
Mococa 33,682 .... *C2
Mogi das Cruzes 122,265 .... *C3
Mogi-Mirim 41,827 .... *C3
Monte Alegre 10,646 .... C3
Monte Aprazivel 9,767 .... *A2
Monteiro 11,051 .... G4
Montenegro 27,246 .... D10
Montes Claros 151,881 .... E7
Morrinhos 20,154 .... D7
Mossoró 118,007 .... G4
Muriaé 50,040 .... *E2
Muzambinho 8,803 .... *C2
Nanuque 34,445 .... F7
Natal 376,552 .... H4
Nazaré 18,068 .... G6
Niquelandia 8,828 .... D6
Niterói 386,185 .... *E3
Nova Cruz 12,824 .... H4
Nova Era 11,126 .... *E1
Nova Friburgo 88,943 .... *E3
Nova Iguaçu 491,802 .... *E3
Nova Lima 35,035 .... *E2
Nova Russas 10,021 .... F4
Novo Hamburgo 132,066 .... D10
Novo Horizonte 18,439 .... *B2
Óbidos 17,143 .... C3
Oeiras 12,406 .... F4
Olimpia 24,376 .... *B2
Olinda 266.392 .... H4
Oliveira 22,642 .... *D2
Oriximiná 12,078 .... C3
Orlândia 22,924 .... *C2
Osasco 376,689 .... *C3
Ourinhos 52,698 .... *B3
Ouro Preto 27,821 .... *E2
Palmares 40,624 .... H5
Palmas 15,823 .... C9
Palmeira 11,521 .... *B4
Palmeira das Missões 23,943 .... C9
Pará (Belém) 758,117 .... E3
Paracatu 29,911 .... E7
Pará de Minas 37,127 .... *D1
Paraguaçu Paulista 17,399 .... D8
Paralba do Sul 13,510 .... *E3
Paranalba 21,305 .... D7
Paranaguá 68,366 .... *B4
Parati 8,684 .... *D3
Parintins 29,369 .... B3
Parnalba 78,718 .... F3
Passo Fundo 103,121 .... D10
Passos 56,998 .... *C2
Patos 58,735 .... G4
Patos de Minas 59,896 .... E7
Patrocínio 29,520 .... E7
Pau dos Ferros 12,985 .... G4
Paulo Afonso 62,066 .... G5
Pederneiras 18,864 .... *B3
Pedra Azul 13,615 .... F6
Pedreiras 30,843 .... E4
Pedro Segundo 9,693 .... F4
Pelotas 197,092 .... C10
Penápolis 32,168 .... *A2
Penedo 27,064 .... G5
Pernambuco (Recife) 1,184,215 .... H5
Petrolina 73,436 .... G5
Petrópolis 149,427 .... *E3
Picos 33,098 .... F4
Piedade 13,054 .... *C3
Pilar 14,778 .... H5
Pindamonhangaba 51,174 .... *D3

(continued on following page)

Pinhal (Espírito Santo do
  Pinhal) 23,235 . . . . *C3
Pinheiro 19,556 . . . . .E3
Piquete 10,316 . . . . *D3
Piracanjuba 11,151 . . . . .D7
Piracicaba 179,395 . . . . *C3
Piracuruca 9,419 . . . . .F3
Piral do Sul 13,709 . . . . *B4
Piraju 16,288 . . . . *B3
Pirapora 31,533 . . . . .E7
Pirassununga 32,510 . . . . . . *C2
Pires do Rio 16,659 . . . . .D7
Piripiri 29,497 . . . . .F4
Pitangui 12,116 . . . . *D1
Piúí 17,327 . . . . *D2
Poções 16,036 . . . . F6
Poconé 12,960 . . . . .B7
Poços de Caldas 81,448 . . . . *C2
Pombal 14,831 . . . . .G4
Pompéia 11,282 . . . . *A3
Ponta Grossa 171,111 . . . . . *B4
Ponta Porã 25,807 . . . . C8
Ponte Nova 34,807 . . . . *E2
Porangatu 21,192 . . . . .D6
Porto Alegre 1,108,883 . . . . .D10
Porto Alegre †2,232,370 . . . .D10
Porto Feliz 19,680 . . . . *C3
Porto Nacional 19,052 . . . . . .E5
Porto Seguro 5,007 . . . . .G7
Porto União 19,426 . . . . .D9
Porto Velho 101,644 . . . . . . .H10
Pouso Alegre 50,517 . . . . . . *D3
Presidente Dutra 14,506 . . . . .E4
Presidente Prudente
  127,623 . . . . D8
Presidente Venceslau 26,720 . D8
Propriá 19,034 . . . . .G5
Promissão 15,333 . . . . *B2
Prudentópolis 8,645 . . . . D9
Quaraí 15,091 . . . . .C10
Quixadá 25,149 . . . . G4
Quixeramobim 14,387 . . . . . . F4
Raposos 11,078 . . . . *E2
Raul Soares 10,055 . . . . *E2
Recife 1,184,215 . . . . H5
Recife †2,348,362 . . . . H5
Registro 28,702 . . . . *C4
Remanso 13,067 . . . . F5
Resende 36,633 . . . . *D3
Ribamar (São José de
  Ribamar) 17,560 . . . . F3
Ribeirão Preto 300,704 . . . . *C2
Rio Bonito 20,561 . . . . *E3
Rio Branco 87,462 . . . . G10
Rio Claro 103,174 . . . . *C3
Rio de Janeiro 5,093,237 . . . *E3
Rio de Janeiro †9,018,637 . . *E3
Rio do Sul 33,408 . . . . D9
Rio Grande 124,706 . . . . . . .D11
Rio Negro 15,851 . . . . .D9
Rio Pardo 18,370 . . . . .C10
Rio Pomba 9,319 . . . . *E2
Rio Tinto 12,511 . . . . .H4
Rio Verde 47,639 . . . . .D7
Rio Verde de Mato Grosso
  10,001 . . . . .C7
Rosário 11,669 . . . . F3
Rosário do Sul 30,753 . . . . . .C10
Russas 16,259 . . . . .G4
Sabará 22,883 . . . . *E1
Sacramento 10,524 . . . . *C1
Salgueiro 25,915 . . . . G5
Salinas 12,613 . . . . .F7
Salinópolis 10,395 . . . . E3
Salto 42,351 . . . . *C3
Salvador 1,496,276 . . . . G6
Salvador †1,772,018 . . . . . . G6
Santa Cruz 13,172 . . . . G4
Santa Cruz do Rio Pardo
  20,507 . . . . *B3
Santa Cruz do Sul 52,050 . . . C10
Santa Helena de Goiás
  20,067 . . . . .D7
Santa Leopoldina 1,217 . . . . .G7
Santa Maria 151,202 . . . . . .C10
Santa Maria da Vitória
  16,294 . . . . .F6
Santana do Ipanema 15,311 .G5
Santana do Livramento
  58,165 . . . . C10
Santarém 101,534 . . . . *C3
Santa Rita do Sapucaí
  15,005 . . . . *D3
Santa Vitória do Palmar
  14,758 . . . . .C11
Santiago 30,406 . . . . .C10
Santo Amaro 29,627 . . . . . . .G6
Santo Ângelo 50,161 . . . . . . C10
Santo André 549,278 . . . . . *C3
Santo Antônio da Platina
  21,284 . . . . *A3
Santos 411,023 . . . . *C3
Santos Dumont 31,053 . . . . *E2
São Bento 9,607 . . . . E3
São Bernardo do Campo
  381,261 . . . . *C3
São Borja 41,598 . . . . .C10
São Carlos 109,231 . . . . . . *C3
São Cristóvão 11,720 . . . . . .G5
São Fidélis 11,713 . . . . *F2
São Francisco 12,011 . . . . . .E6
São Francisco do Sul
  13,914 . . . . E9
São Gabriel 40,497 . . . . . . .C10
São Gonçalo 221,278 . . . . . .F8
São João da Boa Vista
  45,712 . . . . *C2
São João del Rei 53,401 . . *D2
São João dos Patos 12,848 . .F4
São João Nepomuceno
  12,752 . . . . *E2
São Joaquim da Barra
  26,273 . . . . *C2

São José 37,562 . . . . .D9
São José do Rio Pardo
  21,914 . . . . *C2
São José do Rio Preto
  171,982 . . . . *B2
São José dos Campos
  268,073 . . . . *D3
São José dos Pinhais
  53,422 . . . . D9
São Leopoldo 94,864 . . . . . .D10
São Lourenço 23,047 . . . . . *D3
São Lourenço do Sul
  13,251 . . . . .C10
São Luís 182,466 . . . . F3
São Luís Gonzaga 29,188 . .C10
São Manuel 17,028 . . . . . . *B3
São Mateus 22,522 . . . . E3
São Miguel do Guamá 9,929 E3
São Miguel dos Campos
  18,495 . . . . G5
São Paulo 7,033,529 . . . . . *C3
São Paulo †12,588,439 . . . *C3
São Paulo de Olivença 3,102 G9
São Raimundo Nonato 8,574 F5
São Roque 26,118 . . . . *C3
São Sebastião 11,065 . . . . . *D3
São Sebastião do Paraíso
  28,482 . . . . *C2
São Vicente 192,770 . . . . . *C4
Senador Pompeu 10,109 . . .G4
Sena Madureira 6,668 . . . .G10
Senhor do Bonfim 33,811 . . .F5
Serra do Navio 415 . . . . . . .C2
Serra Talhada 28,912 . . . . . .G4
Serrinha 23,920 . . . . G5
Sertânia 11,410 . . . . G5
Sete Lagoas 94,502 . . . . . . E7
Sobral 69,072 . . . . .G3
Socorro 12,111 . . . . *C3
Sorocaba 254,718 . . . . *C3
Soure 11,306 . . . . D3
Taguatinga 480,109 . . . . . . .D6
Taquaritinga 28,018 . . . . . . *B2
Tarauacá 6,889 . . . . .G10
Tatuí 44,816 . . . . *C3
Taubaté 155,371 . . . . E8
Tefé 14,670 . . . . .G9
Teófilo Otoni 83,108 . . . . . . F7
Teresina 339,264 . . . . F4
Teresópolis 78,782 . . . . . . *E3
Tijucas 8,979 . . . . .D9
Timon 55,318 . . . . .F4
Tocantinópolis 8,427 . . . . . .D4
Touros H4

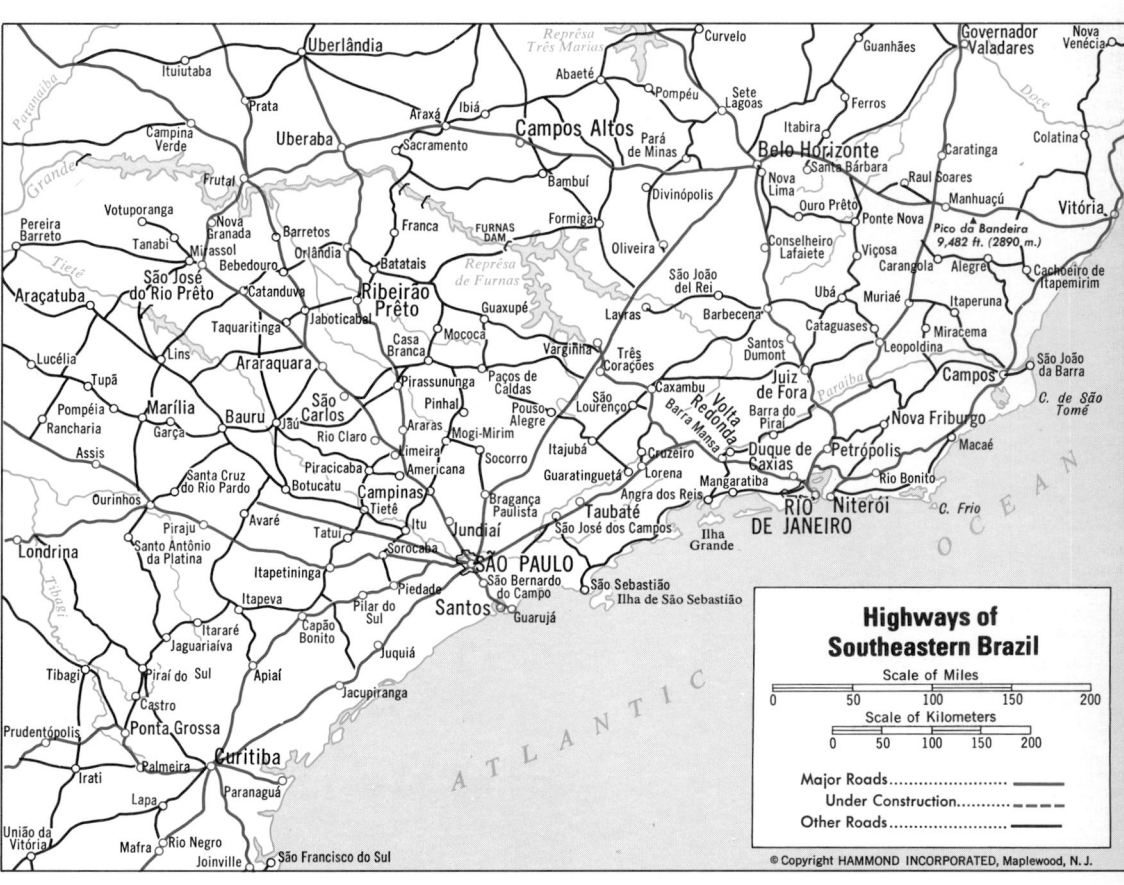

Highways of Southeastern Brazil

Scale of Miles
0   50   100   150   200

Scale of Kilometers
0   50   100   150   200

Major Roads ....
Under Construction ....
Other Roads ....

© Copyright HAMMOND INCORPORATED, Maplewood, N.J.

Agriculture, Industry and Resources

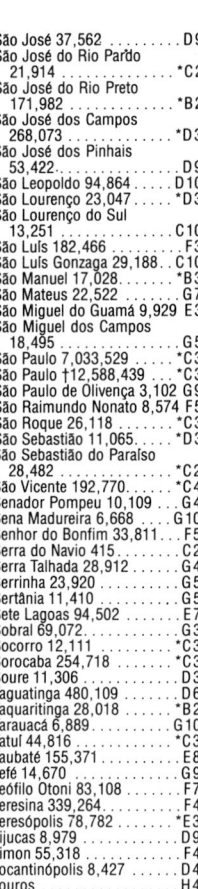

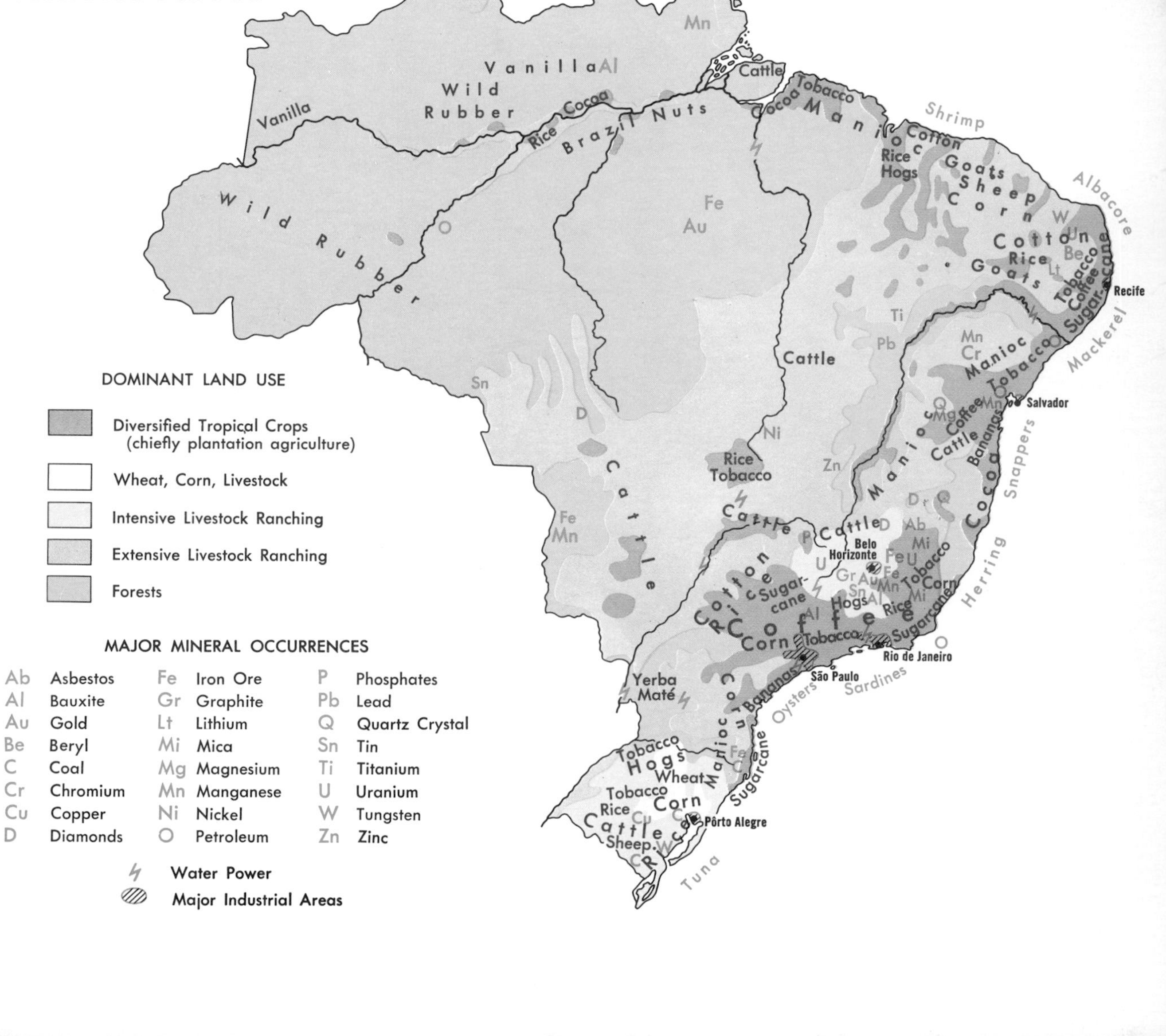

DOMINANT LAND USE

Diversified Tropical Crops
(chiefly plantation agriculture)

Wheat, Corn, Livestock

Intensive Livestock Ranching

Extensive Livestock Ranching

Forests

MAJOR MINERAL OCCURRENCES

Ab	Asbestos	Fe	Iron Ore	P	Phosphates
Al	Bauxite	Gr	Graphite	Pb	Lead
Au	Gold	Lt	Lithium	Q	Quartz Crystal
Be	Beryl	Mi	Mica	Sn	Tin
C	Coal	Mg	Magnesium	Ti	Titanium
Cr	Chromium	Mn	Manganese	U	Uranium
Cu	Copper	Ni	Nickel	W	Tungsten
D	Diamonds	O	Petroleum	Zn	Zinc

Water Power

Major Industrial Areas

rês Corações 36,179 ..... *D2
res Lagoas 45,171 ..... C8
res Pontas 24,225 ..... *D2
rês Rios 47,497 ..... *E3
rindade 22,321 ..... D7
ubarão 64,585 ..... D10
ucurul 27,209 ..... D3
upã 44,450 ..... *A2
upanciretã 13,103 ..... C10
utóia 4,766 ..... F3
bá 43,080 ..... *E2
baitaba 9,413 ..... G6
batuba 23,078 ..... *D3
beraba 180,296 ..... *C1
berlândia 230,400 ..... E7
nal 28,148 ..... E7
nião 9,396 ..... H8
nião da Vitória 22,682 ..... D9
nião dos Palmares 20,876 ..... H5
ruaçu 19,607 ..... D6
ruçul 6,047 ..... E4
ruguaiana 79,059 ..... B10
acaria 37,370 ..... D10
alença 34,231 ..... *E3
arginha 57,448 ..... *D2
iana 9,753 ..... E3
içosa 9,843 ..... G5
içosa 29,198 ..... *E2
ila Velha Argolas 74,166 ..... F8
igia 14,749 ..... E3
ilhena 12,565 ..... H10
iscondé dos Rio Branco
17,295 ..... *E2
itória 144,143 ..... G8
itória da Conquista 125,717 F6
itória de Santo Antão
62,890 ..... G4
olta Redonda 177,772 ..... *D3
otuporanga 44,169 ..... *B2
apuri 3,122 ..... G10
ique-Xique 17,625 ..... F5

OTHER FEATURES

bacaxis (riv.) B4
buná (riv.) G10
caral, Serra do (range) B2
cre (riv.) G10
iama (lake) H9
mambaí, Serra de (range) C7
mapari (riv.) C2
mazon (riv.) C3

Anauá (riv.) B2
Aporé (riv.) D7
Araguaia (riv.) D4
Araguari (riv.) D4
Aripuanã (riv.) A4
Arinos (riv.) B5
Aripuanã (riv.) A4
Armando Laydner (res.) *B3
Bailique (isl.) D2
Balsas (riv.) E5
Bananal (isl.) D5
Bandeira, Pico da (mt.) *E2, F8
Braço Maior do Araguaia
(riv.) D5
Braço Menor do Araguaia
(riv.) D6
Branco (riv.) H8
Buzios (cape) *F3
Canumã (riv.) B4
Capim (riv.) D3
Carajás, Serra dos (range) D4
Cardoso (isl.) *C4
Cassiporé (cape) D2
Caviana (isl.) D2
Chavantes, Serra dos
(range) D5
Claro (riv.) D7
Comprida (isl.) *C4
Cuiabá (riv.) B7
Culuene (riv.) C6
Curuá (riv.) C4
Doce (riv.) *E2, F7
Dois Irmãos, Serra (range) F5
Espigão Mestre (Geral
de Goiás) (range) E6
Espinhaço, Serra do (range) F7
Estrondo, Serra do (range) D4
Feia (lake) *F3
Feio (riv.) *B2
Formosa, Serra (range) C5
Frio (cape) *F3
Furnas (dam) *C2
Geral de Goiás, Serra E6
Gi-Paraná (riv.) H10
Gradaús, Serra dos (range) D4
Grajaú (riv.) E4
Grande (isl.) *F3
Grande (riv.) *D2, E8
Guanabara (bay) *E3
Guaporé (riv.) H10

Gurguéia (riv.) E5
Gurupi, Serra do (range) E4
Gurupi (riv.) E3
Ibicuí (riv.) C10
Içá (riv.) G9
Iguaçu (riv.) C9
Iguazú (falls) C9
Ilha Grande (bay) *D3
Iriri (riv.) C4
Itaipu (dam) C9
Itaipu (riv.) D5
Itapecuru (riv.) F4
Itapi (riv.) B3
Itapicuru (riv.) G5
Itararé (riv.) *B3
Ival (riv.) C8
Jaculpe (riv.) G4
Jaguaribe (riv.) G4
Jamanxim (riv.) C4
Japurá (riv.) G9
Jari (riv.) C3
Jauari, Serra (mts.) C3
Javari (riv.) F9
Jequitinhonha (riv.) F7
Juruá (riv.) G10
Juruena (riv.) B5
Jutaí (riv.) G9
Lombarda, Serra (mts.) C3
Madeira (riv.) A4
Mangueira (lag.) D11
Manso (riv.) C6
Mantiqueira (range) *D3
Mapuera (riv.) B3
Mar, Serra do (range) *C4, E9
Maracá (isl.) D2
Marajó (bay) E2
Marajó (isl.) 147,895 ..... D3
Mato Grosso, Planalto de
(plat.) B6
Maués-Açu (riv.) B3
Mearim (riv.) E4
Mexiana (isl.) D2
Miranda (riv.) B8
Mirim (lag.) C11
Mogi Guaçu (riv.) *C2
Mortes (Manso) (riv.) D6
Neblina, Pico da (peak) G8
Negro (riv.) G7
Nhamundá (riv.) B3
Norte, Serra do (range) B5
Oiapoque (Oyapock) (riv.) C2

Orange (cape) D1
Órgãos (range) *E3
Oyapock (riv.) C2
Pacajá Grande (riv.) D4
Pacaraima, Serra da (mts.) H8
Papagaio (riv.) B6
Pará (riv.) D3
Paracatu (riv.) F6
Paraguaçu (riv.) F6
Paraguai (riv.) B8
Paraíba (riv.) *E2
Paraná (riv.) C8
Paraná (riv.) E6
Paranapanema (riv.) *B3, C8
Paranapiacaba (range) *B4
Paranatinga (riv.) C6
Pardo (riv.) *B2, D8
Pardo (riv.) D3
Pardo (riv.) F6
Parecis, Serra dos (range) B6
Parnaíba (riv.) F3
Paru (riv.) C3
Patos (lag.) D10
Penitente, Serra do (range) E5
Piauí, Serra do (range) F5
Piauí (riv.) F5
Purus (riv.) *H9
Ribeira (riv.) *B4
Roncador, Serra do (range) C5
Ronuro (riv.) C6
Roosevelt (riv.) A5
Salto Grande (res.) B10
Santa Catarina (isl.) 138,556 E9
São Lourenço (riv.) C7
São Marcos (bay) F3
São Roque (cape) H4
São Francisco (riv.) *D2, G5
São Sebastião (isl.) 5,724 ..... *D3, E8
São Tomé (cape) F8
Sapucaí (riv.) *D2
Sepetiba (bay) *D3
Sete Quedas (Grande) (isl.) C8
Sobradinho (res.) F5
Sono (chan.) E5
Sul (chan.) D1
Tacutu (riv.) B2
Tapajós (riv.) B4
Taquari (riv.) C7
Tefé (riv.) G9
Teles Pires (riv.) B5

Tibagi (riv.) *A4
Tietê (riv.) *B2, D8
Tiracambu, Serra (range) E3
Tocantins (riv.) D3
Tombador, Serra do (range) B6
Trombetas (riv.) B3
Tucuruí (res.) D4
Tumucumaque, Serra de
(range) C2

Turvo (riv.) *B2
Uaupés (riv.) G9
Uraricoera (riv.) H8
Urubu (riv.) A3
Urubupungá (dam) C8
Urucún, Morro do (mt.) B7
Uruguai (riv.) C9
Vasa Barris (riv.) G5
Velhas (riv.) E7

Verde (riv.) C7
Verdinho (riv.) D7
Xavantes (res.) *B3
Xingu (riv.) C3

†Population of met. area.
*preceding reference indicates
that the name will be found on
S.E. Brazil map, page 135

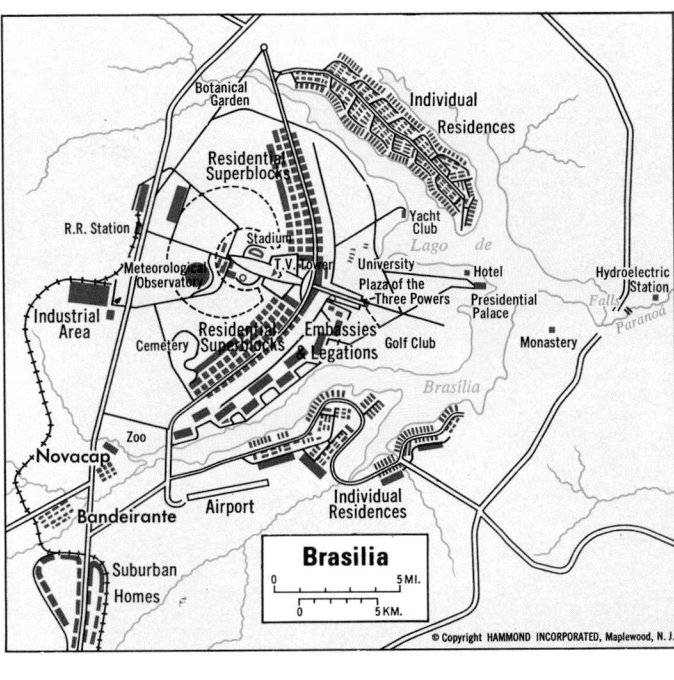

Brasilia

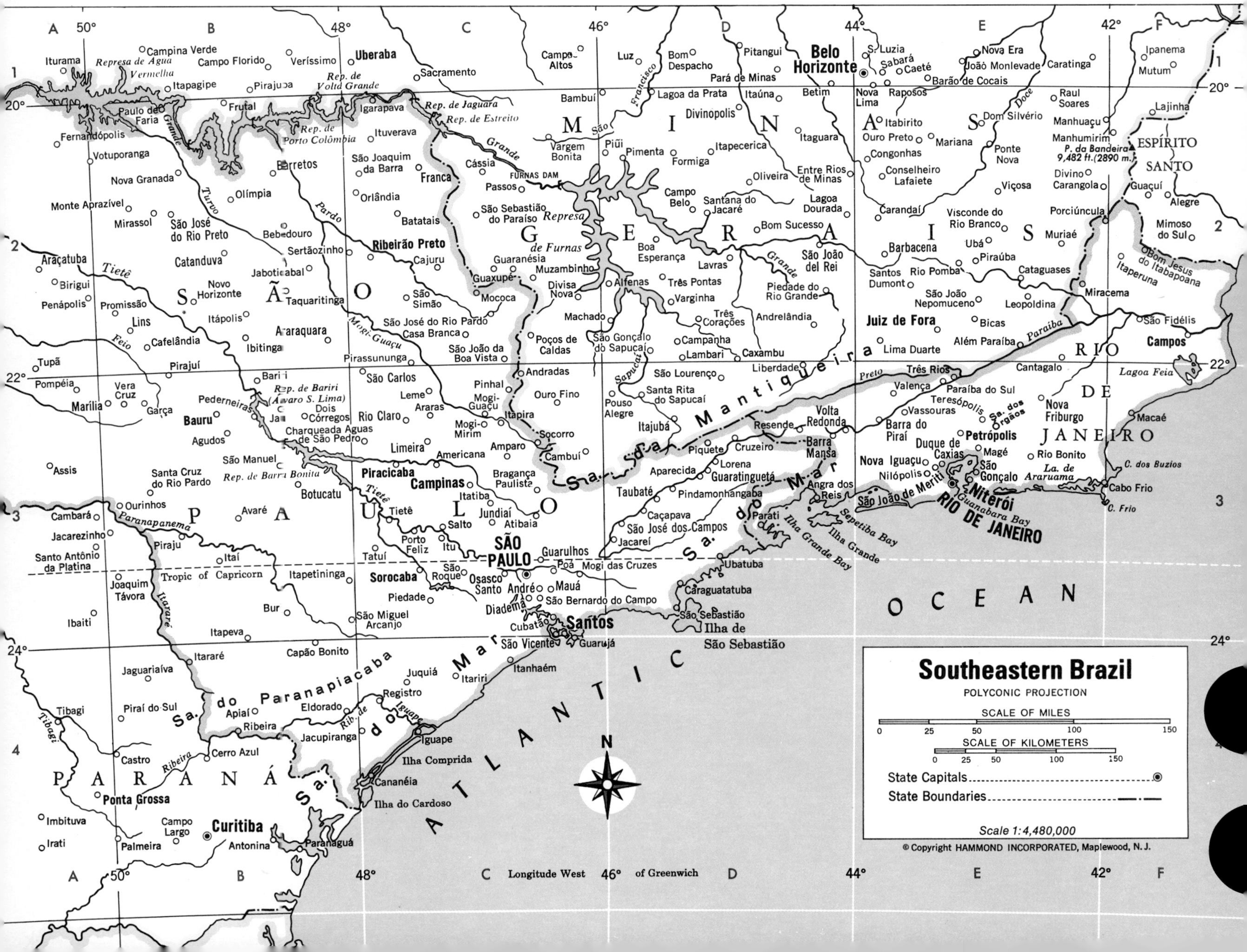

DEPARTMENTS	CITIES and TOWNS				
Beni, El 168,367 ....C3	Achacachi 3,621 ....A5	Arampampa 829 ....B5	Boyuibe 537 ....D7	Caracollo 909 ....B5	Choquecuta‡ 1,976 ....A6	Colquiri 806 ....B
Chuquisaca 358,516 ......C6	Aiquile 3,465 ....C6	Arcopongo‡ 2,223 ......B5	Cachuela Esperanza 1,073 ..C2	Caranavi‡ 525 ....B4	Chulumani 2,362 ....B5	Comarapa 1,096 C
Cochabamba 720,952 ......C5	Alto Seco 3,414 ....C6	Aroma‡ 873 ....B6	Caiza 838 ....C7	Carandaiti 1,403 ....D7	Chuma 931 ....A4	Concepción 1,056 ....B
La Paz 1,465,078 ....A4	Amarete 992 ....A4	Arque 1,254 ....C6	Calamarca 802 ....A5	Carmen‡ 845 ....B2	Chuquichambi 1,094 ......C5	Condo‡ 5,525 ....B
Oruro 310,409 ....A6	Ancoraimes 769 ....A4	Ascención (Añez) 2,097 ....D4	Callapa 636 ....A5	Cataricahua 3,240 ....B6	Chuquichuqui‡ 1,892 ......C6	Conquista‡ 1,162 C
Pando 34,493 ....B2	Añez (Ascención) D4	Atocha‡ 3,964 ....B7	Camacho‡ 875 ....C7	Cavinas‡ 1,011 ....B2	Cliza 3,121 ....C5	Copacabana 1,981 ....A
Potosí 657,743 ....B7	Andamarca‡ 5,187 ....B6	Ayacucho 729 ....D5	Camargo 1,609 ....C7	Chaguaya 643 ....C7	Cobija 3,650 ....A2	Coripata 1,647 ....B
Santa Cruz 710,724 ......E5	Anzaldo 1,056 ....C5	Azurduy 1,234 ....C6	Camatindi‡ 297 ....D7	Challana‡ 1,206 ....A4	Cocani‡ 658 ....B7	Corocoro 4,431 ....A
Tarija 187,204 ....D7	Apolo 1,043 ....A4	Baures 592 ....D3	Camiri 4,969 ....D7	Challapata 2,529 ....B6	Cocapata‡ 2,855 ....B5	Coroico 2,235 ....B
	Araca‡ 3,537 ....B5	Berenguela‡ 2,412 ......A5	Capinota 1,734 ....B5	Charagua 1,185 ....D6	Cochabamba 204,684 ......C5	Cotagaita 1,353 C
		Betanzos 1,097 ....C6	Caquiaviri 760 ....A5	Charaña 794 ....A5	Cohoni 890 ....B5	Cotoca 915 ....E
			Carabuco 626 ....A4	Chayanta 1,272 ....B6	Colquechaca 1,070 ......B6	Cuevo 902 C

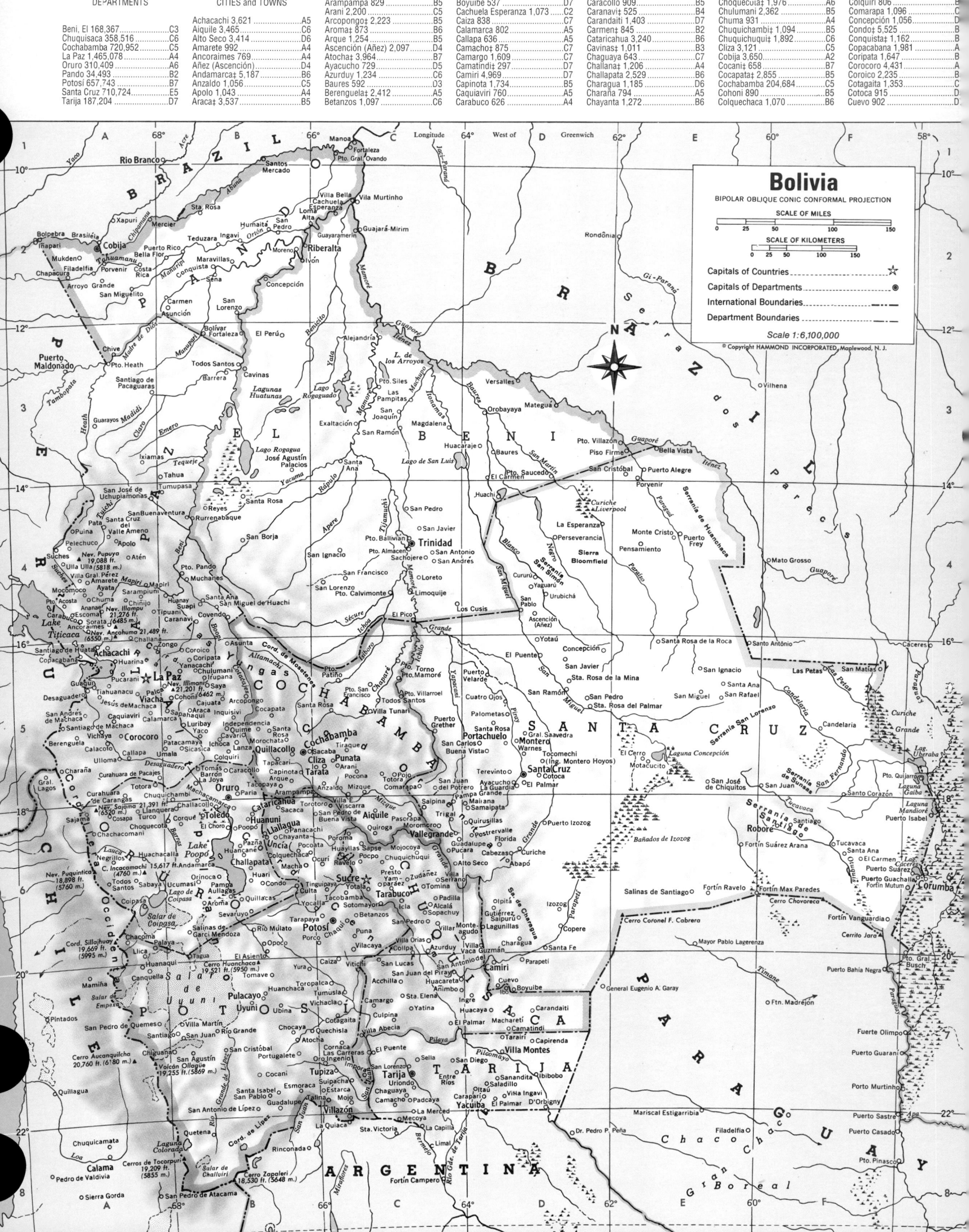

AREA 424,163 sq. mi. (1,098,582 sq. km.)
POPULATION 7,193,000
CAPITALS La Paz, Sucre
LARGEST CITY La Paz
HIGHEST POINT Nevada Ancohuma 21,489 ft. (6,550 m.)
MONETARY UNIT Bolivian peso
MAJOR LANGUAGES Spanish, Quechua, Aymara
MAJOR RELIGION Roman Catholicism

Culpina 981 ....C7
Culta‡ 4,412 ....B6
Curahuara de Pacajes 510 ......A5
El Palmar, Chuquisaca‡ 772 ...D7
El Palmar, Tarija 832 ....D7
El Puente, Santa Cruz‡
  1,185 ....D5
El Puente, Tarija‡ 1,310 ....C7
Entre Ríos 1,011 ....C7
Esmoraca‡ 1,137 ....B7
Estarca‡ 2,331 ....C7
Filadelfia‡ 942 ....A2
Fortaleza‡ 765 ....B3
Fortín Mutum F6
General Saavedra 1,006 ....D5
Guadalupe 2,355 ....C6
Guaqui 2,266 ....A5
Guayaramerín 1,470 ....C2
Huacaraje 673 ....D3
Huachacalla 801 ....A6
Huanay 574 ....B4
Huanchaca ....
Huanuni 5,696 ....B6
Huari 1,070 ....B6
Huarina 1,151 ....A5
Ichoca 591 ....A6
Independencia 1,742 ....B5
Ingeniero Montero Hoyos
  (Tocomechi) 575 ....D5
Inquisivi 530 ....B5
Irupana 1,937 ....B5
Ivón‡ 772 ....C2
Izozog‡ 2,759 ....D6
Jesús de Machaca 529 ....A5
José Agustín Palacios‡
  2,273 ....B3
La Capilla‡ 1,870 ....C8
Lagunillas 840 ....D6
La Merced‡ 688 ....B5
Lanza 526 ....B5
La Paz (cap.) 635,283 ....B5
Limal‡ 524 ....C8
Llallagua 6,719 ....B6
Llanquera 613 ....B5
Llica 560 ....A6
Loreto 589 ....C6
Macha 1,050 ....B6
Machacamarca 1,746 ....B5
Macharetí‡ 1,164 ....D7
Magdalena 1,724 ....C3
Mairana 503 ....D6
Mecoya‡ 585 ....C8
Mizque 870 ....C5
Mocomoco 977 ....A4
Mojo 469 ....C7
Mojocoya 498 ....C6
Monteagudo 971 ....C6
Montero 2,713 ....D5
Morochata 461 ....B5
Moromoro 556 ....C6
Motacucito‡ 585 ....E5
Ocurí 1,531 ....C6
Orinoca‡ 2,380 ....B6
Orobayaya‡ 1,132 ....D3
Oro Ingenio‡ 945 ....C7
Oruro 124,213 ....B5
Padcaya 524 ....C7
Padilla 2,462 ....C6
Palaya 300 ....A6
Palca 887 ....A5
Palometas‡ 3,453 ....D5
Pampa Aullagas‡ 1,834 ....B6
Pampa Grande 727 ....D6
Panacachi 952 ....B6
Paria 335 ....B5
Pasorapa 1,016 ....C6
Pata 122 ....A4
Patacamaya 1,278 ....B5
Pazña 671 ....B6
Pelechuco 873 ....A4
Pocoata 859 ....B6
Pocona 518 ....C5

Pocpo‡ 2,791 ....C6
Pojo 1,047 ....C5
Poopó 736 ....B6
Porco 817 ....B6
Poroma 171 ....C6
Portachuelo 2,456 ....D5
Portugalete‡ 1,590 ....B7
Porvenir‡ 846 ....A2
Postrervalle 750 ....D6
Potosí 77,397 ....C6
Presto 725 ....C6
Pucara 762 ....C6
Pucarani 1,041 ....A5
Puerto Acosta 1,302 ....A4
Puerto Almacen 358 ....C4
Puerto General Ovando ‡58 ....C1
Puerto Heath‡ 570 ....A3
Puerto Rico‡ 539 ....B2
Puerto Siles 357 ....C3
Puerto Suárez 1,159 ....F6
Pulacayo 7,984 ....B7
Puna 852 ....C6
Punata 5,014 ....C5
Quechisla 171 ....C7
Queteña 183 ....B8
Quillacas 1,170 ....B6
Quillacollo 9,123 ....B5
Quime 1,256 ....B5
Quiroga‡ 3,467 ....C6
Quirusillas 433 ....C6
Ravelo 907 ....C6
Reyes 1,404 ....B4
Riberalta 6,549 ....C2
Río Grande 281 ....B7
Río Mulato 381 ....B6
Roboré 3,715 ....F6
Rurrenabaque 1,225 ....B4
Sabaya 649 ....A6
Sacaba 2,752 ....C5
Sacaca 1,778 ....B6
Sachojere 401 ....C4
Saipina 573 ....C6
Sajama 231 ....A6
Saladillo‡ 1,315 ....D7
Salinas de Garci Mendoza
  335 ....B6
Samaipata 1,656 ....D6
San Agustín‡ 810 ....B7
Sanandita 379 ....D7
San Andrés 399 ....C4
San Andrés de Machaca 101 ..A5
San Antonio, El Beni 435 ....C3
San Antonio de López‡ 77 .....B7
San Antonio del Parapetí
  497 ....D7
San Borja 708 ....B4
San Buenaventura 307 ....A4
San Carlos 570 ....D5
San Cristóbal‡ 1,200 ....B7
San Diego‡ 773 ....D7
San Francisco 185 ....C4
San Ignacio, El Beni 1,757 .....C3
San Ignacio, Santa Cruz
  1,819 ....E5
San Javier, El Beni 233 ....C4
San Javier, Santa Cruz 364 ....D5
San Joaquín 1,959 ....C3
San José de Chiquitos 1,933 ..E5
San José de Uchupiamonas
  277 ....A4
San Juan, Potosí 131 ....B7
San Juan, Santa Cruz‡ 482 ....F5
San Juan del Piray 541 ....C7
San Juan del Potrero 243 ....C5
San Lorenzo, El Beni 496 ....C2
San Lorenzo, Pando‡ 317 ....B2
San Lorenzo, Tarija 785 ....C7
San Lucas 925 ....C7
San Matías 887 ....F5
San Miguel 502 ....E5
San Miguel de Huachi 25 ....B4
San Pablo 11 ....B7

San Pedro, Chuquisaca 182 ....C6
San Pedro, El Beni 262 ....C4
San Pedro, Pando‡ 312 ....B2
San Pedro, Santa Cruz 80 ......D5
San Pedro de Buena Vista
  1,094 ....C6
San Pedro de Quemes‡ 290 ...A7
San Rafael‡ 1,282 ....E5
San Ramón, El Beni 1,161 ......C3
San Ramón, Santa Cruz 379 ...D5
Santa Ana, El Beni 2,225 ....C3
Santa Ana, La Paz 171 ....B4
Santa Ana, Santa Cruz 275 ....C5
Santa Ana, Santa Cruz 2,225 ..F6
Santa Cruz 254,682 ....D5
Santa Cruz del Valle Ameno
  442 ....A4
Santa Elena‡ 4,474 ....C7
Santa Isabel‡ 323 ....B7
Santa Rosa, Cochabamba‡
  942 ....B5
Santa Rosa, Cochabamba‡
  276 ....C5
Santa Rosa, El Beni 765 ....B4
Santa Rosa, Pando‡ 105 ....B2
Santa Rosa, Santa Cruz 995 ...B5
Santa Rosa de la Mina 99 ....D5
Santa Rosa de la Roca 101 .....E5
Santa Rosa del Palmar 441 .....E5
Santiago, Potosí 172 ....A7
Santiago, Santa Cruz 765 ....F6
Santiago de Huata 948 ....A5
Santiago de Machaca 218 ......A5
Santo Corazón‡ 963 ....F5
Sapahaqui 55 ....B5
Sapsé‡ 89 ....C6
Sarampiuni 138 ....A4
Saya 339 ....B5
Sená‡ 660 ....B2
Sevaruyo 475 ....B6
Sicasica 1,486 ....B5
Scpachuy 713 ....C6
Scrata 2,087 ....A4
Sctomayor 510 ....C6
Staipi‡ 1,750 ....B4
Stiches‡ 231 ....C4
Sucre (cap.) 63,625 ....C6
Suipacha‡ 2,701 ....C6
Tacobamba‡ 6,933 ....C6
Tacopaya 795 ....B5
Talina 122 ....B7
Tapacarí 980 ....B5
Tarabuco 2,833 ....C6
Tarairí‡ 394 ....D7
Tarapaya 357 ....C6
Tarata 3,016 ....C5
Tarija 38,916 ....C7
Teduzara‡ 271 ....B2
Terevinto‡ 3,790 ....D5
Tiahuanacu 1,227 ....A5

Tinguipaya 766 ....C6
Tipuani‡ 1,216 ....B4
Tiraque 1,390 ....C5
Tocomechi 575 ....D5
Todos Santos, Cochabamba
  408 ....C5
Todos Santos, Oruro 68 ....A6
Toledo 3,273 ....B6
Tomás Barrón 1,852 ....B5
Tomave 201 ....B7
Tomina 708 ....C6
Toropalca‡ 199 ....B7
Torotoro 1,233 ....C6
Totora C5
Trigal 749 ....C6
Trinidad 14,505 ....C4
Tumupasa 349 ....B4
Tumusla‡ 526 ....C7
Tupiza 8,248 ....C7
Turco 131 ....A6
Ubina‡ 462 ....B6
Ucumasi‡ 1,040 ....B6
Ulla Ulla 52 ....A4
Ulloma 116 ....A5
Umala 481 ....B5
Uncía 4,507 ....B6
Uriondo 860 ....C7
Urubichá 1,369 ....D4
Uyuni 6,968 ....B7
Vallegrande 5,094 ....C6
Versalles 83 ....D3
Viacha 6,607 ....A5
Vichacla 317 ....A5
Vichaya 422 ....A5
Vilacaya 200 ....C6
Villa Abecia 539 ....C7
Villa Bella 88 ....C2
Villa E. Viscarra 658 ....C6
Villa General Pérez 802 ....A4
Villa Ingavi 122 ....D7
Villa Martín 543 ....B7
Villa Montes 3,105 ....D7
Villa Orías 404 ....C6
Villar 322 ....C6
Villa Serrano 1,570 ....C6
Villa Tunari 510 ....C5
Villa Vaca Guzmán 699 ....D6
Villazón 6,261 ....C7
Vitichi 1,515 ....C7
Warnes 1,571 ....D5
Yaco 835 ....B5
Yacuiba 5,027 ....D7
Yamparaéz 725 ....C6
Yanacachi‡ 1,964 ....B5
Yatina‡ 1,850 ....C6
Yocalla‡ 1,814 ....B6
Yotala 1,554 ....C6
Yura 136 ....B7
Zongo 141 ....B5
Zudáñez 1,868 ....C6

OTHER FEATURES

Abuná (riv.) B2
Altamachi (riv.) B5
Ancohuma, Nevada (mt.) A4
Apere (riv.) C4
Arroyos, Los (lake) C3
Barras (riv.) B6
Baures (riv.) D3
Beni (riv.) B4
Benicito (riv.) C3
Bermejo (riv.) C8
Blanco (riv.) D4

Bloomfield, Sierra (mts.) D4
Boopi (riv.) B4
Cáceres (lag.) G6
Candelaria (riv.) F5
Capitán Ustarés, Cerro (mt.) ..E6
Central, Cordillera (range) C6
Challviri (salt dep.) B8
Chaparé (riv.) C5
Charagua, Sierra de (mts.) D6
Chipamanu (riv.) A2
Chovoreca, Cerro (mt.) F6
Claro (riv.) A3
Coipasa (lag.) B6
Coipasa (salt dep.) A6
Colorada (lag.) A8
Concepción (lag.) E5
Coronel F. Gabrera E6
Cotacajes (riv.) B5
Desaguadero (riv.) B5
Emero (riv.) B3
Empexa (salt dep.) A7
Gaiba (lag.) F5
Grande (marsh) F5
Grande (riv.) C4
Grande (riv.) C6
Grande de López (riv.) B7
Guaporé (riv.) C3
Heath (riv.) A3
Huanchaca, Cerro (mt.) B7
Huanchaca, Serranía de
  (mts.) E4
Huatunas (lag.) B3
Ichilo (riv.) C5
Ichoa (riv.) C4
Illampu, Nevada (mt.) A4
Illimani, Nevada (mt.) B5
Incacamachi, Cerro (mt.) A6
Isiboro (riv.) C3
Iténez (Guaporé) (riv.) C3
Itonamas (riv.) C3
Izozog (swamp) E6
Jara, Cerrito (mt.) F6
Lauca (riv.) A5
Lípez, Cordillera de (range) B8
Liverpool (swamp) D4
Machupo (riv.) C3
Madidi (riv.) A3
Madre de Diós (riv.) A3
Mamoré (riv.) C3
Mandioré (lag.) F6
Manupari (riv.) B3
Manuripi (riv.) B2
Mapiri (riv.) A4
Mizque (riv.) C6

Mosetenes, Cordillera de
  (range) B5
Negro (riv.) D4
Occidental, Cordillera (range) .A6
Ollagüe (vol.) B7
Oriental, Cordillera (range) C5
Ortón (riv.) B2
Otuquis (riv.) F6
Paraguá (riv.) E4
Paraguay (riv.) F7
Paraíso (riv.) E4
Parapetí (riv.) D6
Petas, Las (riv.) F5
Pilaya (riv.) C7
Pilcomayo (riv.) D7
Piray (riv.) D5
Poopó (lake) B6
Pupuya, Nevada (mt.) A4
Puquíntica, Nevado (mt.) A6
Rápulo (riv.) C4
Real, Cordillera (range) A5
Rogagua (lake) B3
Rogaguado (lake) C3
Sajama, Nevada (mt.) A6
San Fernando (riv.) F5
San Juan (riv.) C7
San Lorenzo, Serranía
  (mts.) E5
San Luis (lake) C3
San Martín (riv.) D3
San Miguel (riv.) D4
San Simón, Serranía (mts.) D4
Santiago, Serranía de (mts.) ...F6
Sécure (riv.) C4
Sillajhuay, Cordillera (mt.) A6
Suches (riv.) A4
Sunsas, Serranía de (mts.) F5
Tahuamanu (riv.) B2
Tarija, Río Grande de (riv.) C8
Tequeje (riv.) B3
Tijamuchi (riv.) C4
Titicaca (lake) A4
Tocorpuri, Cerros de (mt.) A8
Tucavaca (riv.) F6
Tuichi (riv.) A4
Uberaba (lag.) G5
Uyuni (salt dep.) B7
Yacuma (riv.) B3
Yapacani (riv.) C5
Yata (riv.) C3
Yungas, Las (reg.) B5
Zapaleri, Cerro (mt.) B8

‡Population of canton.

Topography

0   100   200 MI.
0   100   200 KM.

| Below Sea Level | 100 m. 328 ft. | 200 m. 656 ft. | 500 m. 1,640 ft. | 1,000 m. 3,281 ft. | 2,000 m. 6,562 ft. | 5,000 m. 16,404 ft. |

Agriculture, Industry and Resources

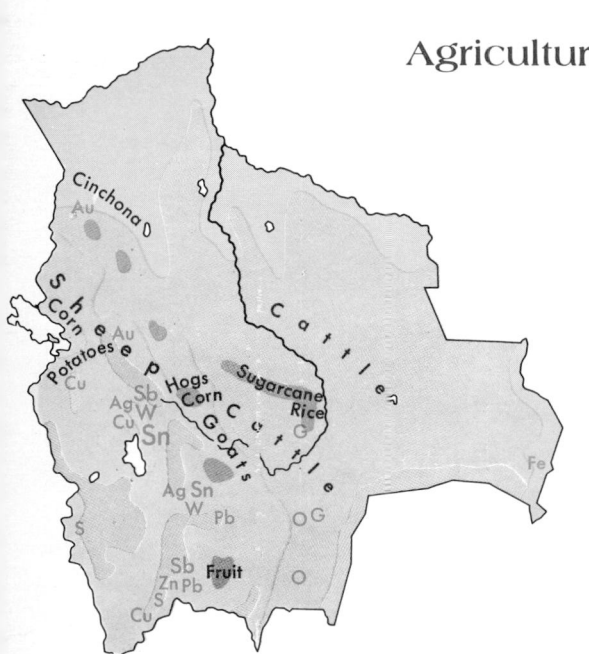

DOMINANT LAND USE

- Diversified Tropical Crops (chiefly plantation agriculture)
- Upland Cultivated Areas
- Upland Livestock Grazing, Limited Agriculture
- Extensive Livestock Ranching
- Forests
- Nonagricultural Land

MAJOR MINERAL OCCURRENCES

Ag	Silver	G	Natural Gas	Sb	Antimony
Au	Gold	O	Petroleum	Sn	Tin
Cu	Copper	Pb	Lead	W	Tungsten
Fe	Iron Ore	S	Sulfur	Zn	Zinc

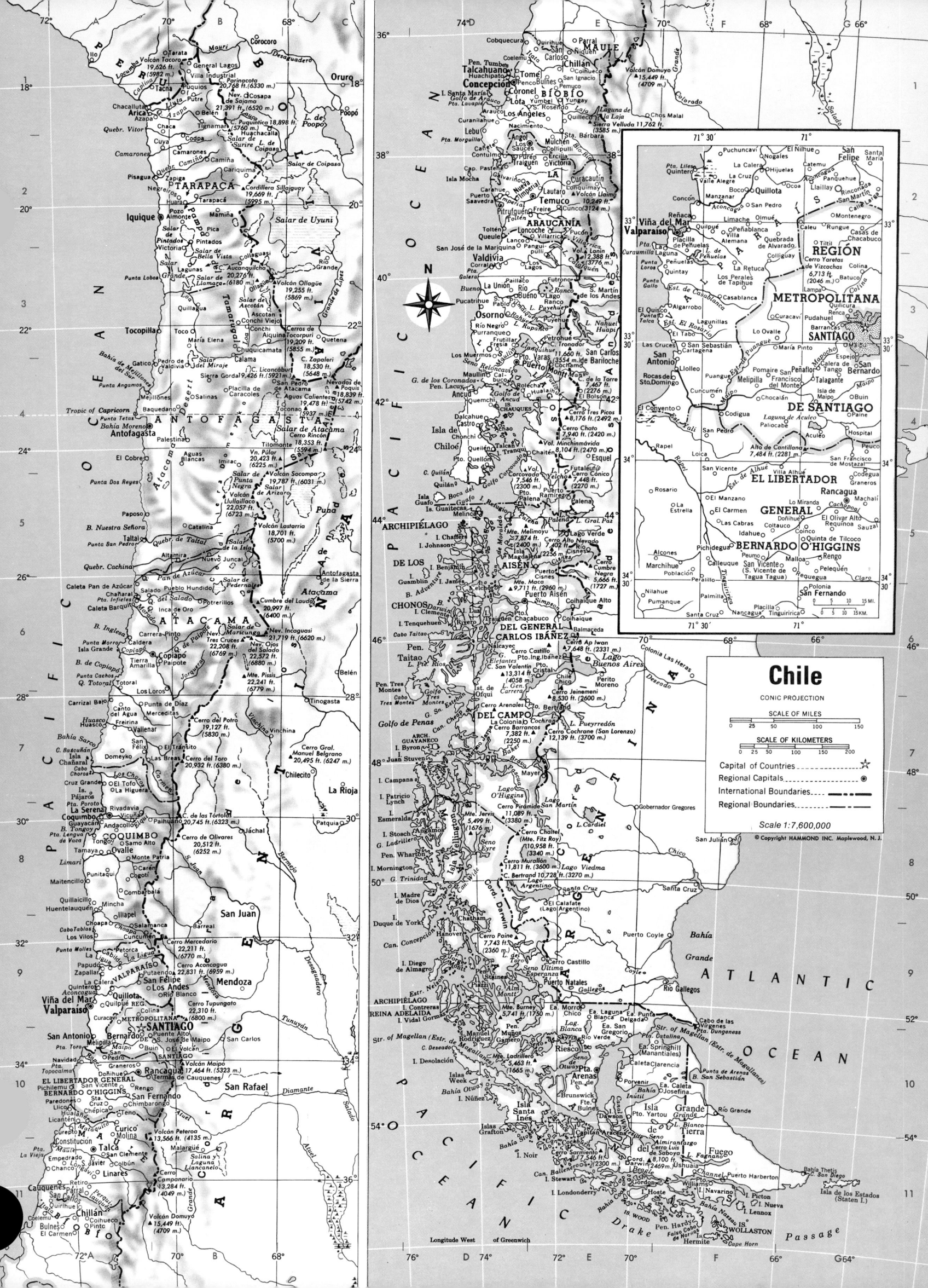

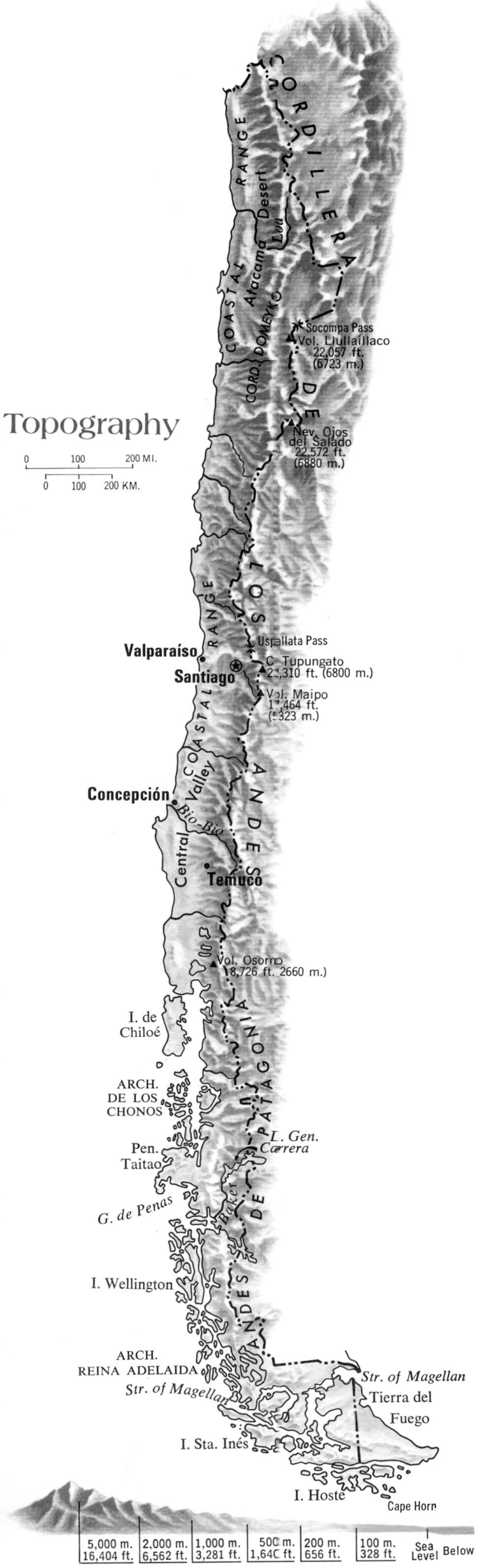
Topography
0 100 200 MI.
0 100 200 KM.
CORDILLERA
DE LOS ANDES
COASTAL RANGE
Atacama Desert
Loa
CORD. DOMEYKO
Socompa Pass
Vol. Llullaillaco 22,057 ft. (6723 m.)
Nev. Ojos del Salado 22,572 ft. (6880 m.)
Valparaíso
Santiago
Uspallata Pass
C. Tupungato 22,310 ft. (6800 m.)
Vol. Maipo 17,464 ft. (5323 m.)
Central Valley
Concepción
Bío Bío
Temuco
Vol. Osorno 8,726 ft. 2660 m.)
I. de Chiloé
ARCH. DE LOS CHONOS
Pen. Taitao
I. Gen. Carrera
ANDES DE PATAGONIA
G. de Penas
Baker
I. Wellington
ARCH. REINA ADELAIDA
Str. of Magellan
Str. of Magellan
Tierra del Fuego
I. Sta. Inés
I. Hoste
Cape Horn
5,000 m. 16,404 ft.
2,000 m. 6,562 ft.
1,000 m. 3,281 ft.
500 m. 1,640 ft.
200 m. 656 ft.
100 m. 328 ft.
Sea Level
Below

AREA 292,257 sq. mi. (756,946 sq. km.)
POPULATION 12,961,000
CAPITAL Santiago
LARGEST CITY Santiago
HIGHEST POINT Ojos del Salado 22,572 ft. (6,880 m.)
MONETARY UNIT Chilean peso
MAJOR LANGUAGE Spanish
MAJOR RELIGION Roman Catholicism

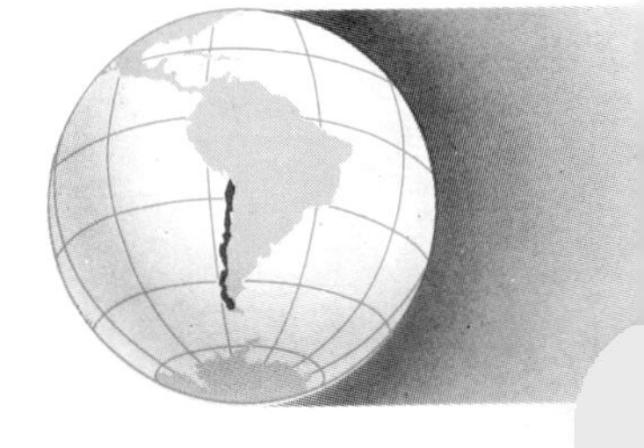

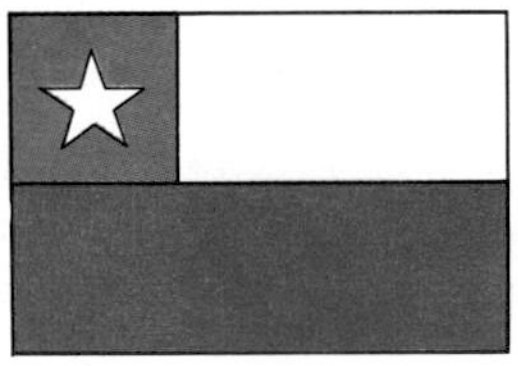

REGIONS

Aisén del General Carlos Ibáñez del Campo 65,478 . . . . . E6
Antofagasta 341,203 . . . . . B4
Atacama 183,071 . . . . . B6
Bíobío 1,516,552 . . . . . E1
Coquimbo 419,178 . . . . . A8
El Libertador General Bernardo O'Higgins 584,989 . . . . . A10
La Araucanía 692,924 . . . . . E2
Los Lagos 843,430 . . . . . D3
Magallanes 132,333 . . . . . E10
Maule 723,224 . . . . . A11
Santiago, Región Metropolitana de (Santiago Metropolitan Region) 4,294,938 . . . . . A9
Tarapacá 273,427 . . . . . B2
Valparaíso 1,204,693 . . . . . A9

CITIES and TOWNS

Achao ○11,501 . . . . . D4
Aguas Blancas ○203 . . . . . B4
Algarrobo ○3,941 . . . . . F3
Ancud 11,900 . . . . . D4
Andacollo 6,000 . . . . . A8
Angol 42,670 . . . . . D1
Antofagasta 125,100 . . . . . A4
Arauco 5,400 . . . . . D1
Arica 87,700 . . . . . A1
Ascotán B3
Barrancas ○184,241 . . . . . G3
Belén ○925 . . . . . B1
Buin 11,800 . . . . . G4
Bulnes 6,900 . . . . . E1
Cabildo 5,800 . . . . . A9
Calama 45,900 . . . . . B3
Calbuco ○21,673 . . . . . D4
Caldera ○3,268 . . . . . A6
Calera de Tango ○6,198 . . . G4
Calle Larga ○7,172 . . . . . G2
Cañete 7,900 . . . . . D2
Carahue ○12,733 . . . . . D2
Cartagena ○7,124 . . . . . F3
Casablanca 5,500 . . . . . F3
Casas de Chacabuco G2
Castro 11,200 . . . . . D4
Catalina ○1,637 . . . . . B5
Catemu ○8,728 . . . . . G2
Cauquenes 20,200 . . . . . A11
Cerro Castillo ○537 . . . . . E9
Cerro Manantiales F10
Chaitén ○4,067 . . . . . E4
Chañaral ○36,949 . . . . . A6
Chanco ○12,433 . . . . . A11
Chépica ○11,199 . . . . . A10
Chillán 128,515 . . . . . A11
Chimbarongo 5,300 . . . . . A10
Chonchi ○8,911 . . . . . D4
Chuquicamata 22,100 . . . . . B3
Cobquecura ○6,298 . . . . . D1
Cochamó ○5,042 . . . . . E3
Codegua ○6,757 . . . . . G4
Codpa ○950 . . . . . B1
Coelemu 5,400 . . . . . D1
Coihaique 32,129 . . . . . E6
Coihueco ○17,276 . . . . . A11
Coinco ○4,942 . . . . . G5
Colbún ○12,924 . . . . . A11
Colina 7,400 . . . . . G3
Collipulli 7,200 . . . . . E2
Coltauco ○11,857 . . . . . F5
Combarbalá ○17,332 . . . . . A8
Concepción 206,226 . . . . . D1
Constitución 11,500 . . . . . A11
Contulmo ○13,987 . . . . . D2
Copiapó 45,200 . . . . . B6
Coquimbo 73,953 . . . . . A8
Coronel 37,300 . . . . . D1
Corral ○5,533 . . . . . D3
Cunco ○18,836 . . . . . E2
Curacautín 9,800 . . . . . E2
Curacaví 5,800 . . . . . G3
Curanilahue 13,200 . . . . . D1
Curepto ○13,020 . . . . . A10
Curicó 41,300 . . . . . A10
Dalcahue ○7,084 . . . . . D4
Domeiko A7
Doñihue ○8,837 . . . . . G5
El Carmen ○13,226 . . . . . A11
El Monte 7,000 . . . . . G4
El Quisco ○2,152 . . . . . E3
El Tabo ○2,180 . . . . . F3
El Tofo A7
Empedrado ○7,887 . . . . . A11
Ercilla ○8,061 . . . . . E2
Estancia Caleta Josefina ○1,042 . . . . . F10
Estancia Morro Chico ○785 . E9
Estancia San Gregorio ○1,156 . . . . . E9
Estancia Springhill (Cerro Manantiales) F10
Freire ○23,313 . . . . . E2
Freirina ○5,523 . . . . . A7
Fresia ○15,359 . . . . . D3
Frutillar ○12,721 . . . . . D3
Futaleufú ○2,366 . . . . . E4
Futrono ○7,109 . . . . . E3
Galvarino ○9,495 . . . . . D2
General Lagos ○810 . . . . . B1
Graneros 8,900 . . . . . G5
Guayacán A8
Hijuelas ○7,128 . . . . . F2
Hualañé ○6,912 . . . . . A10
Huara ○1,934 . . . . . B2
Huasco ○4,971 . . . . . A7
Illapel 12,200 . . . . . A8
Inca de Oro 1,406 . . . . . B6
Iquique 64,500 . . . . . A2
Isla de Maipo ○12,903 . . . . G4
La Calera 24,600 . . . . . F2
La Cruz ○8,907 . . . . . F2
La Estrella ○3,707 . . . . . F5
Lago Ranco ○12,767 . . . . . E3
Lagunas ○5,653 . . . . . B3
La Higuera ○6,991 . . . . . A7
La Ligua 7,500 . . . . . A9
Lampa ○10,220 . . . . . G3
Lanco 5,200 . . . . . D2
Las Cabras ○12,119 . . . . . F5
La Serena 99,908 . . . . . A8
La Unión 15,200 . . . . . D3
Lautaro 11,900 . . . . . E2
Lebu 12,500 . . . . . D1
Licantén ○6,354 . . . . . A10
Limache 15,200 . . . . . F2
Linares 37,900 . . . . . A11
Llay-Llay 9,700 . . . . . G2
Loica F4
Loncoche ○17,539 . . . . . D2
Longaví ○15,909 . . . . . A11
Lonquimay ○9,524 . . . . . E2
Los Andes 23,500 . . . . . B9
Los Ángeles 49,500 . . . . . D1
Los Lagos ○14,934 . . . . . D3
Los Muermos ○9,296 . . . . . D3
Los Sauces ○7,613 . . . . . D2
Los Vilos ○10,453 . . . . . A9
Lota 48,100 . . . . . D1
Machalí 5,800 . . . . . G5
Maipú ○117,872 . . . . . G3
Malloa ○9,742 . . . . . G5
Marchigüe ○4,451 . . . . . F5
María Elena 5,900 . . . . . B3
María Pinto ○5,980 . . . . . G3
Maullín ○14,544 . . . . . D4
Mejillones ○3,333 . . . . . A4
Melipilla 23,900 . . . . . F4
Mincha ○11,329 . . . . . A8
Molina 9,400 . . . . . A10
Monte Patria ○18,927 . . . . . A8
Mulchén 13,700 . . . . . E1
Nacimiento ○17,651 . . . . . D1
Nancagua ○11,076 . . . . . F6
Navidad ○6,618 . . . . . A10
Negreiros ○1,144 . . . . . B2
Ñiquén ○13,640 . . . . . E1
Nogales ○18,529 . . . . . F2
Nueva Imperial 8,000 . . . . . D2
Olivar Alto ○5,414 . . . . . G5
Ollagüe B3
Olmué ○8,804 . . . . . F2
Osorno 68,800 . . . . . D3
Ovalle 31,700 . . . . . A8
Paihuano ○6,048 . . . . . B8
Paillaco 5,200 . . . . . D3
Paine ○21,876 . . . . . G4
Palena ○2,508 . . . . . E5
Palmilla ○7,965 . . . . . F6
Panguipulli 5,700 . . . . . E2
Panquehue ○4,230 . . . . . G2
Papudo ○2,594 . . . . . A9
Paredones ○7,404 . . . . . A10
Parral 17,000 . . . . . A11
Pedro de Valdivia 6,200 . . . . B4
Pemuco ○7,577 . . . . . E1
Peñaflor 15,500 . . . . . G4
Penco ○33,962 . . . . . D1
Peñuelas F3
Petorca ○8,343 . . . . . A9
Petrohué E3
Peumo ○11,308 . . . . . F5
Pica ○1,487 . . . . . B2
Pichidegua ○13,550 . . . . . F5
Pichilemu ○8,042 . . . . . A10
Pinto ○8,687 . . . . . A11
Pisagua ○1,880 . . . . . A2
Pitrufquén 7,800 . . . . . D2
Placilla ○6,441 . . . . . F6
Porvenir ○4,000 . . . . . E10
Potrerillos 5,800 . . . . . B6
Pozo Almonte ○1,798 . . . . . B2
Puchuncaví ○7,542 . . . . . F2
Pucón 18,000 . . . . . E2
Pudahuel G3
Pueblo Hundido 6,200 . . . . . B6
Puente Alto 65,100 . . . . . B10
Puerto Aisén 17,848 . . . . . E6
Puerto Cisnes ○2,800 . . . . . E5
Puerto Ingeniero Ibáñez ○1,900 . . . . . E6
Puerto Montt 119,059 . . . . . E4
Puerto Natales 17,280 . . . . . E9
Puerto Quellón ○7,734 . . . . D4
Puerto Varas 10,900 . . . . . E3
Puerto Williams ○949 . . . . F11
Pumanque ○3,137 . . . . . F6
Punitaqui ○16,167 . . . . . A8
Punta Arenas 2,140 . . . . . E10
Purén ○11,604 . . . . . D2
Purranque 5,900 . . . . . D3
Putaendo ○12,806 . . . . . A9
Putre ○855 . . . . . B1
Puyehue E3
Queilén ○6,055 . . . . . D4
Quemchi ○6,707 . . . . . D4
Quilicura 8,100 . . . . . G3
Quillagua B3
Quilleco ○16,043 . . . . . E1
Quillota 36,500 . . . . . F2
Quilpué 40,600 . . . . . F2
Quinta de Tilcoco ○6,513 . . G5
Quintero 9,900 . . . . . F2
Quirihue ○11,178 . . . . . E1
Rancagua 140,589 . . . . . G5
Renca ○67,168 . . . . . G3
Rengo 12,400 . . . . . G5
Requínoa ○10,730 . . . . . G5
Retiro ○15,146 . . . . . A11
Rinconada San Martín ○4,118 . . . . . G2
Río Blanco B9
Río Bueno 9,600 . . . . . D3
Río Negro 5,100 . . . . . D3
Río Verde ○554 . . . . . E10
Rocas de Santo Domingo ○4,114 . . . . . F4
Rosario ○3,383 . . . . . F5
Salamanca ○18,741 . . . . . A9
Samo Alto ○5,689 . . . . . A8
San Antonio 46,700 . . . . . F3
San Bernardo ○117,766 . . . G4
San Carlos 17,000 . . . . . E1
San Clemente ○23,273 . . . A11
San Felipe 26,100 . . . . . G2
San Fernando 23,600 . . . . . G6
San Francisco de Mostazal ○11,439 . . . . . G4
San Ignacio ○13,523 . . . . . E1
San Javier 10,800 . . . . . A11
San José de Maipo ○9,601 . . . . . B10
San Pablo ○7,978 . . . . . D3
San Pedro ○8,255 . . . . . F4
San Pedro de Atacama C4
San Rosendo ○14,337 . . . . . E1
Santa Bárbara ○14,345 . . . . E1
Santa Cruz 8,600 . . . . . F6
Santa María ○8,162 . . . . . G2
Santiago (cap.) 3,614,947 . . G3
Santiago *3,672,374 . . . . . G3
San Vicente F4
San Vicente (San Vicente de Tagua Tagua) ○28,333 F5
Sierra Gorda ○8,805 . . . . . B4
Talagante 16,500 . . . . . G4
Talca 133,160 . . . . . A11
Talcahuano 148,300 . . . . . D1
Taltal 6,400 . . . . . A5
Tamaya A8
Tarapacá B2
Temuco 197,232 . . . . . E2
Teno ○17,675 . . . . . A10
Termas de Cauquenes B10
Tierra Amarilla ○7,899 . . . . . A6
Tiltil ○9,198 . . . . . G2
Toco ○8,734 . . . . . B3
Toconao C4
Tocopilla 22,000 . . . . . A3
Toltén ○16,265 . . . . . D2
Tomé 29,600 . . . . . D1
Traiguén 11,400 . . . . . D2
Valdivia 115,536 . . . . . D3
Vallenar 26,800 . . . . . A7
Valparaíso 271,580 . . . . . E2
Victoria 16,500 . . . . . D2
Vicuña 5,100 . . . . . A8
Villa Alemana 29,600 . . . . . F2
Villa Alhué ○5,078 . . . . . G4
Villarrica 25,091 . . . . . E2
Viña del Mar 281,361 . . . . . F2
Yumbel ○21,858 . . . . . E1
Yungay ○10,725 . . . . . E1
Zapallar ○2,894 . . . . . A9
Zapiga B2

OTHER FEATURES

Aconcagua (riv.) F2
Aculeo (lag.) G4
Adventure (bay) D5
Aguas Calientes, Cerro (mt.) C4
Almirantazgo (bay) F11
Almirante Montt (gulf) D9
Ancud (gulf) D4
Angamos (isl.) D8
Angamos (pt.) A4
Ap Iwan, Cerro (mt.) E6
Arauco (gulf) D1
Arenales, Cerro (mt.) D7
Atacama (des.) B4
Atacama, Salar de (salt dep.) C4
Aucanquilcha, Cerro (mt.) . . B3
Azapa, Quebrada (riv.) B1
Baker (riv.) D7
Ballenero (chan.) E11
Bascuñán (cape) A7
Beagle (chan.) E11
Bella Vista, Salar de (salt dep.) B3
Benjamín (isl.) D5
Bío-Bío (riv.) E2
Blanca (lag.) E10
Blanco (lake) F10
Bravo (riv.) D7
Brunswick (pen.) E10
Bueno (riv.) D3
Buenos Aires (lake) E6
Byron (isl.) D7
Cachapoal (riv.) G5
Cachina, Quebrada (riv.) A5
Cachos (pt.) A6
Calafquén (lake) E3
Camarones (riv.) A2
Camiña, Quebrada (riv.) B2
Campana (isl.) D7
Campanario, Cerro (mt.) . . A10
Capitán Aracena (isl.) E10
Carmen (riv.) B7
Castillo, Cerro (mt.) E6
Catalina (pt.) F10
Chaffers (isl.) D5
Chaltel, Cerro (mt.) E8
Chañaral (isl.) A7
Chatham (isl.) D9
Chauques (isls.) D4
Cheap (chan.) D7
Chiloé (isl.) 119,286 . . . . . D4
Choapa (riv.) A9
Chonos (arch.) D6
Choros (cape) A7
Cisnes (riv.) E5
Clarence (isl.) E10
Clemente (isl.) D6
Cochrane (lake) E7
Cochrane, Cerro (mt.) E7
Cockburn (chan.) E11
Concepción (chan.) D9
Cónico, Cerro (mt.) E4
Contreras (isl.) D9
Cook (bay) E11
Copiapó (bay) A6
Copiapó (riv.) A6
Corcovado (gulf) D4
Corcovado (vol.) D5
Coronados (gulf) D4
Curaumilla (pt.) E2
Darwin (bay) D6
Darwin, Cordillera (mts.) . . . D8
Darwin, Cordillera (mts.) . . E11

(continued on following page)

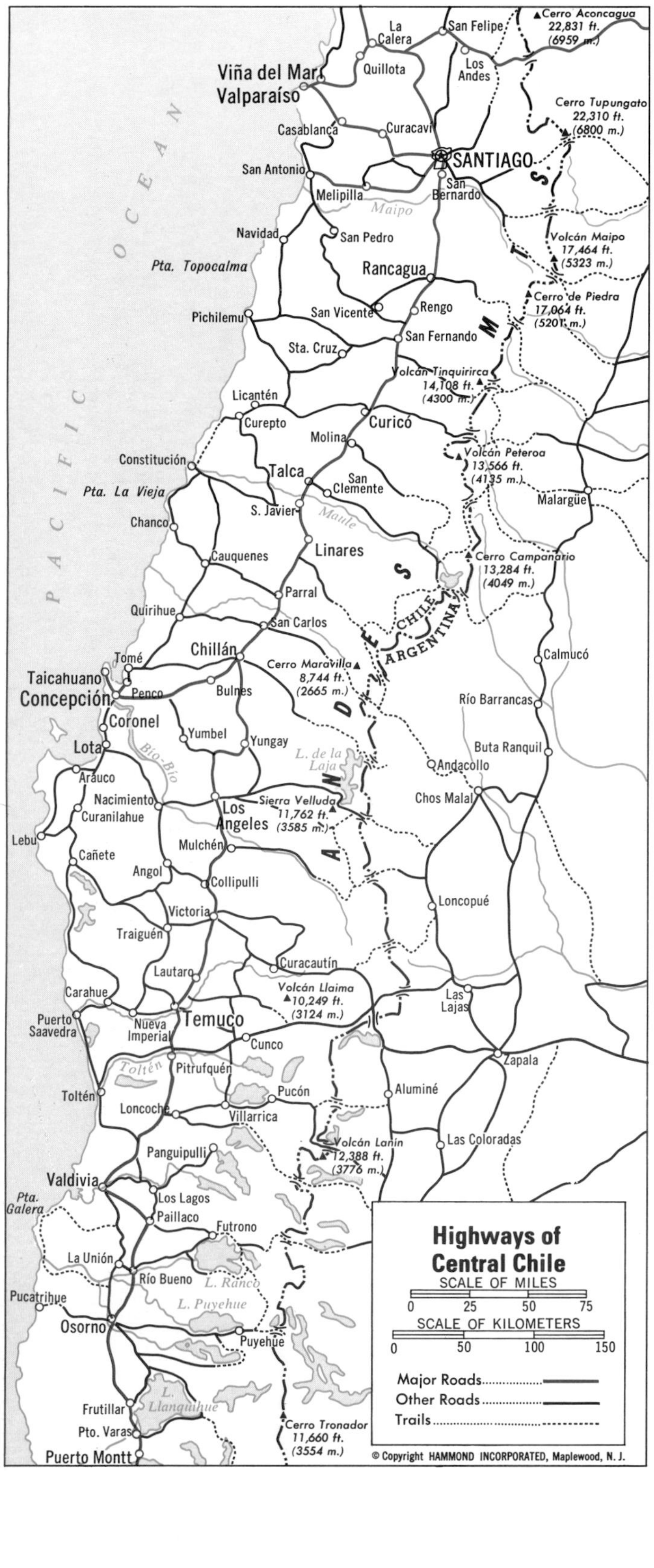

Agriculture, Industry and Resources

DOMINANT LAND USE

- Cereals, Livestock
- Mediterranean Agriculture (cereals, fruit, livestock)
- Pasture Livestock
- Extensive Livestock Ranching
- Limited Seasonal Grazing
- Forests
- Nonagricultural Land

MAJOR MINERAL OCCURRENCES

Ag	Silver	Hg	Mercury
Au	Gold	Id	Iodine
C	Coal	Mn	Manganese
Cu	Copper	Mo	Molybdenum
Fe	Iron Ore	N	Nitrates
G	Natural Gas	Na	Salt
Gp	Gypsum	O	Petroleum
		S	Sulfur

⚡ Water Power   ▨ Major Industrial Areas

Highways of Central Chile

SCALE OF MILES

0   25   50   75

SCALE OF KILOMETERS

0   50   100   150

Major Roads . . . .
Other Roads . . . .
Trails . . . .

© Copyright HAMMOND INCORPORATED, Maplewood, N.J.

PROVINCES

Buenos Aires 10,796,036...D4
Catamarca 206,204.......C2
Chaco 692,410.......D2
Chubut 262,196.......C5
Córdoba 2,407,135.......D3
Corrientes 657,716.......E2
Distrito Federal 2,908,001...H7
Entre Ríos 902,241.......E3
Formosa 292,479.......D1
Jujuy 408,514.......C1
La Pampa 207,132.......C4
La Rioja 163,342.......C2
Mendoza 1,187,305.......C3
Misiones 579,579.......F2
Neuquén 241,904.......C4
Río Negro 383,896.......C5
Salta 662,369.......D1
San Juan 469,973.......C3
San Luis 212,837.......C3
Santa Cruz 114,479.......C6
Santa Fe 2,457,188.......D3
Santiago del Estero 652,318 D2
Tierra del Fuego, Antártida, e Islas del Atlántico Sur 29,451.......C7
Tucumán 968,066.......C2

CITIES and TOWNS

Abra Pampa 2,929.......C1
Adolfo Alsina 7,707.......D4
Aguaray 4,802.......D1
Aguilares 20,286.......C2
Aimogasta 4,640.......C2
Alberti 6,440.......G7
Alcorta 5,818.......F6
Algarrobo del Águila.......C4
Allen 14,041.......C5
Alpachiri 1,657.......D4
Alta Gracia 30,628.......D3
Aluminé 1,560.......B4
Alvear 5,419.......C4
Ameghino 2,775.......D3
Añatuya 15,025.......D2
Andalgalá 6,853.......C2
Antofagasta de la Sierra.......C2
Apóstoles 11,252.......F2
Arrecifes 17,719.......F7
Arroyo Seco 12,886.......F6
Ascensión 3,031.......F7
Avellaneda 330,654.......H7
Ayacucho 12,363.......E4
Azul 43,582.......E4
Bahía Blanca 220,765.......D4
Bahía Bustamante.......C6
Bahía Thetis.......E4
Balcarce 28,985.......E4
Balnearia 4,531.......D3
Baradero 20,103.......F6
Barrancas 3,602.......F6
Barranqueras.......E2
Barreal 2,739.......C3
Basavilbaso 7,657.......G6
Belén 7,411.......C2

Bella Vista, Corrientes 14,229.......E2
Bella Vista, Tucumán 9,177. D2
Bell Ville 26,559.......D3
Bolívar 16,382.......F6
Bovril 4,735.......G5
Bragado 27,101.......F6
Buenos Aires (cap.) 2,908,001.......H7
Buenos Aires *9,927,404...H7
Cafayate 5,048.......C2
Calafate.......B7
Calchaquí 5,958.......F5
Caleta Olivia 20,141.......C6
Camarones.......C6
Campana 51,498.......G6
Cañada de Gómez 24,706. F6
Canals 6,627.......D3
Cañuelas 14,831.......G7
Carcarañá 11,121.......F6
Carlos Casares 13,286.......F7
Carlos Tejedor 4,421.......D4
Carmen de Areco 7,882....F7
Carmen de Patagones 13,981.......D5
Carmen del Uruguay 46,065.......G6
Casilda 23,492.......F6
Castelli 4,507.......H7
Catamarca 88,432.......C2
Caucete 14,512.......C3
Ceres 10,743.......D2
Chabás 5,156.......F6
Chacabuco 26,492.......F7
Chajarí 15,242.......G5

Chamical 6,333.......C3
Charadai 1,078.......D2
Charata 13,070.......D2
Chascomús 21,864.......H7
Chepes 4,775.......C3
Chicoana 1,844.......C2
Chilecito 14,010.......C2
Chivilcoy 43,779.......F7
Choele-Choel 6,191.......C4
Chos-Malal 4,823.......C4
Cinco Saltos 15,094.......C4
Cipolletti 40,123.......C4
Clorinda 21,008.......E2
Colón, Buenos Aires 16,070. F6
Colón, Entre Ríos 11,648...G6
Colonia Las Heras 3,176....C6
Comandante Fontana 4,468..C2
Comandante Luis Piedrabuena 2,492.......C6
Comodoro Rivadavia 96,865. C6
Concepción 29,359.......C2
Concepción de la Sierra 2,778.......E2
Concepción del Uruguay 46,065.......G6
Concordia 93,618.......G5
Constanza 1,313.......G6
Córdoba 982,018.......D3
Coronda 11,554.......F6
Coronel Brandsen 10,484...H7
Coronel Dorrego 10,661...D4
Coronel Pringles 16,592...D4
Coronel Suárez 16,359...D4

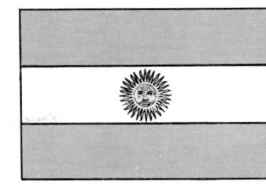

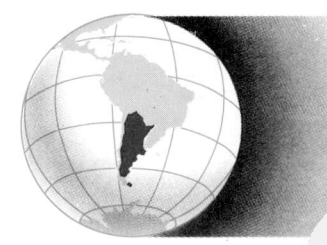

AREA 1,072,070 sq. mi. (2,776,661 sq. km.)
POPULATION 31,929,000
CAPITAL Buenos Aires
LARGEST CITY Buenos Aires
HIGHEST POINT Cerro Aconcagua 22,831 ft. (6,959 m.)
MONETARY UNIT austral
MAJOR LANGUAGE Spanish
MAJOR RELIGION Roman Catholicism

Agriculture, Industry and Resources

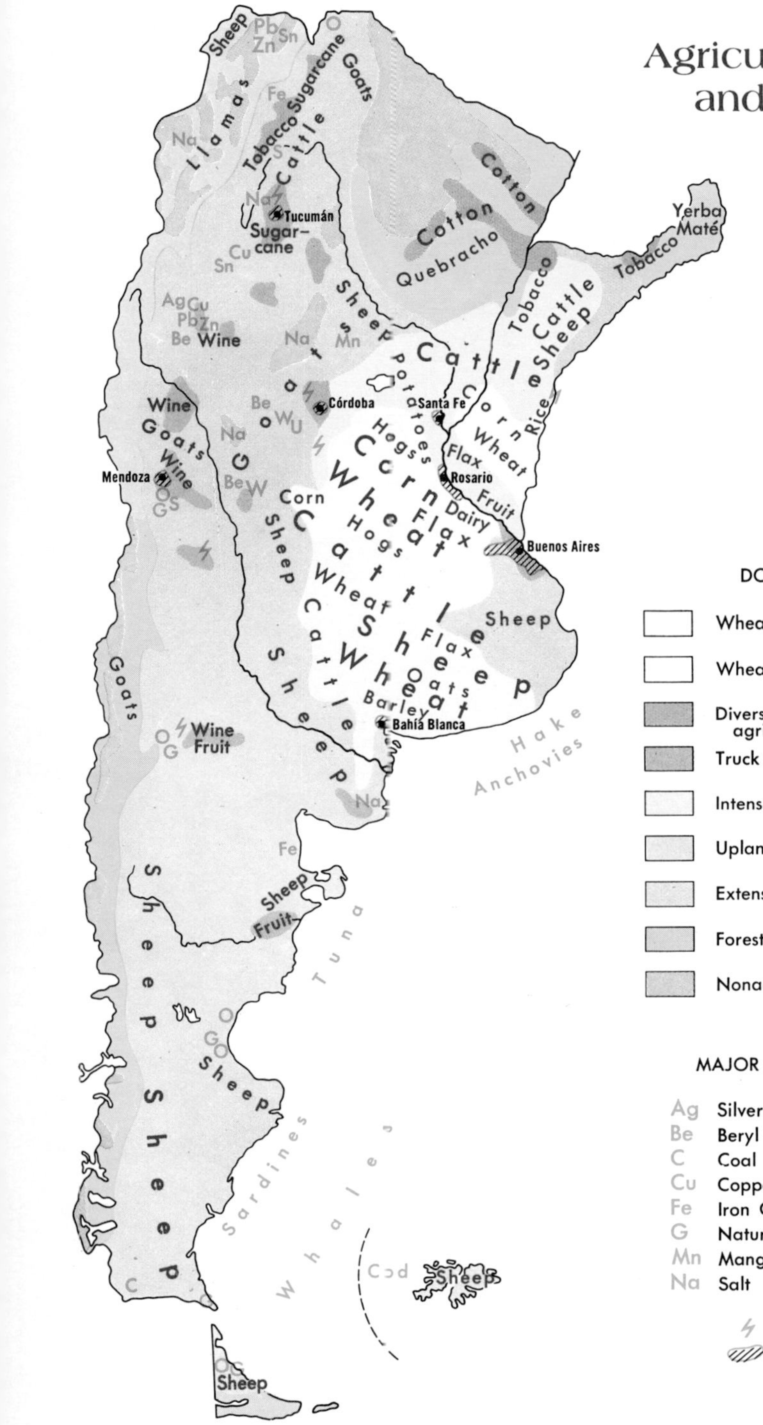

DOMINANT LAND USE

Wheat, Livestock

Wheat, Corn, Livestock

Diversified Tropical Crops (chiefly plantation agriculture)

Truck Farming, Horticulture, Special Crops

Intensive Livestock Ranching

Upland Livestock Grazing, Limited Agriculture

Extensive Livestock Ranching

Forests

Nonagricultural Land

MAJOR MINERAL OCCURRENCES

Ag Silver
Be Beryl
C Coal
Cu Copper
Fe Iron Ore
G Natural Gas
Mn Manganese
Na Salt

O Petroleum
Pb Lead
S Sulfur
Sn Tin
U Uranium
W Tungsten
Zn Zinc

⚡ Water Power
▨ Major Industrial Areas

Coronel Vidal 4,774.......E4
Corral de Bustos 8,613....D3
Corrientes 179,590.......E2
Cosquín 13,929.......D3
Crespo 10,668.......F6
Cruz del Eje 23,473.......C3
Curuzú Cuatiá 24,955.......G5
Cutral-Có 25,870.......C4
Daireaux 8,150.......D4
Deán Funes 16,306.......D3
Diamante 13,464.......F6
Dolavon 1,778.......C5
Dolores 19,307.......E4
Eduardo Castex 5,397.......D4
El Bolsón 5,001.......B5
Eldorado 22,821.......F2
El Maitén 2,350.......B5
Elortondo 4,939.......F6
El Quebrachal 2,202.......D2
Embarcación 9,016.......D1
Empedrado 4,732.......E2
Escobar 70,829.......G7
Esperanza 22,838.......F5
Esquel 17,228.......B5
Esquina 10,380.......G5
Famatina 1,237.......C2
Federación 7,259.......G5
Felipe Yofré 1,140.......G4
Fernández 6,062.......D2
Fiambalá 1,201.......C2
Firmat 13,588.......F6
Formosa 95,067.......E2
Fortín Olmos 1,101.......F4
Gaiman 2,651.......C5
Gálvez 14,711.......F6
General Acha 7,647.......C4
General Alvear, Buenos Aires 5,481.......F7
General Alvear, Mendoza 21,250.......C3
General Arenales 3,332....F7
General Belgrano 10,909...C5
General Conesa 3,566.......C5
General Galarza 3,057.......G6
General Güemes 15,534...D1
General José de San Martín 16,296.......E2
General Juan Madariaga 13,409.......E4
General La Madrid 5,154...D4
General Las Heras 6,005...G7
General Paz 5,127.......H7
General Pico 30,180.......D4
General Ramírez 5,393.......F6
General Roca 38,296.......C4
General San Martín, Buenos Aires 384,306.......G7
General San Martín, La Pampa 2,168.......D4
General Viamonte 10,112..F7
General Villegas 11,307....D4
Gobernador Crespo 2,972..F5
Godoy Cruz 141,553.......C3
Goya 47,357.......G4
Gualeguay 24,883.......G6
Gualeguaychú 51,057.......G6
Guandacol 1,351.......C2
Hasenkamp 2,804.......F5
Helvecia 3,927.......F5
Hernandarias 3,002.......F5
Hernando 8,619.......D3
Huinca Renancó 7,187.......D3
Humahuaca 3,963.......C1
Humberto (Humberto Primo) 4,163.......F5
Ibarreta 5,262.......D2
Ibicuy 3,082.......G6
Ingeniero Huergo 3,385...C4
Ingeniero Jacobacci 4,045..C5
Ingeniero Luiggi 3,002.......D4
Intendente Alvear 3,640...D4
Itatí 3,269.......E2

Ituzaingó 8,687.......E2
Jáchal 8,832.......C3
Jesús María 17,594.......D3
Joaquín V. González 6,054..D2
Juárez 11,798.......E4
Jujuy 124,487.......C1
Junín 62,080.......F7
Junín de los Andes 5,638...B4
La Banda 46,994.......D2
Laboulaye 16,883.......D3
La Carlota 8,614.......D3
La Cruz 4,132.......E2
La Cumbre 6,110.......D3
La Falda 12,502.......D3
Laguna Paiva 11,129.......F5
Lanús 465,891.......H7
La Paz, Entre Ríos 14,920..G5
La Paz, Mendoza 4,604...C3
La Plata 560,341.......H7
Laprida 6,495.......D4
La Quiaca 8,289.......C1
La Rioja 66,826.......C2
Larroque 3,147.......F5
Las Flores 18,287.......E4
Las Lomitas 4,047.......D1
Las Palmas 5,061.......E2
Las Parejas 7,430.......F6
Las Rosas 9,725.......F6
Las Varillas 10,605.......D3
La Toma 4,325.......C3
Lincoln 19,009.......F7
Loberfa 8,898.......E4
Lobos 20,798.......G7
Lomas de Zamora 508,620..G7
Lucas González 3,015.......G6
Luján 38,919.......G7
Lules 11,391.......C2
Maciel 4,066.......F6
Magdalena 7,135.......H7
Maipú 7,289.......E4
Malabrigo 3,294.......F4
Malargüe 9,496.......C4
Maquinchao 1,299.......C5
Marcos Juárez 19,827.......D3
Mar del Plata 407,024.......E4
Máximo Paz 3,216.......F6
Mburucuyá 3,044.......E2
Médanos 4,511.......D4
Mendoza 596,796.......C3
Mercedes, Buenos Aires 46,581.......G7
Mercedes, Corrientes 20,603.......G4
Mercedes, San Luis 50,856..C3
Merlo 293,059.......G7
Metán 18,928.......D2
Miramar 15,473.......E4
Monte Caseros 18,247.......G5
Monte Quemado 4,707.......D2
Monteros 15,832.......C2
Morón 596,769.......G7
Morteros 11,456.......D3
Navarro 7,176.......G7
Necochea 50,939.......E4
Neuquén 90,037.......C4
Nogoyá 15,862.......F6
Norquincó.......B5
Nueve de Julio 26,608.......F7
Oberá 27,311.......F2
Olavarría 63,686.......D4
Oliva 9,231.......D3
Palo Santo 3,088.......E2
Paraná 159,581.......F5
Paso de Los Libres 24,112..E2
Pedro Luro 3,142.......D4
Pehuajó 25,613.......D4
Pellegrini 3,940.......D4
Pergamino 68,989.......F6
Pico Truncado 9,626.......C6
Pigüé 10,793.......D4
Pilar 3,805.......F5
Pirané 9,039.......E2
Plaza Huincul 7,988.......B4

(continued on following page)

Posadas 139,941 .... E2
Presidencia de
la Plaza 4,904 .... D2
Presidencia Roque
Sáenz Peña 49,261 ...... D2
Puán 4,148 .... D4
Puerto Deseado 4,017 .... D6
Puerto Harberton C7
Puerto Iguazú 10,250 .... F2
Puerto Madryn 20,709 .... C5
Puerto Rico 8,195 .... D1
Punta Alta 54,375 ...... D4
Quequén 11,737 .... E4
Quimili 8,972 .... D2
Quines 3,352 .... C3
Quitilipi 9,937 .... D2
Rafaela 53,132 .... F5
Ramallo 8,248 .... F6
Rauch 8,348 .... E4
Rawson 12,981 .... D5
Reconquista 32,442 ..... E2
Recreo 3,502 .... C2
Resistencia 218,438 ..... D2
Rinconada C1
Río Colorado 7,361 ..... D4
Río Cuarto 110,148 ..... D3
Río Gallegos 43,479 .... C7
Río Grande 13,271 ..... C7
Río Segundo 12,839 .... D3
Río Tercero 34,735 ..... D3
Rivadavia 10,953 ...... C3
Rojas 14,247 .... F7
Romang 4,017 .... F4
Roque Pérez 5,434 ..... G7
Rosario 954,606 .... F6
Rosario de la
Frontera 13,531 ...... D2
Rosario de Lerma 9,540 .. C1
Rosario del Tala 9,552 .. G6
Rufino 15,306 .... D3
Saladas 7,345 .... E2
Saladillo 14,806 ...... G7
Salliqueló 5,479 ...... D4
Salta 260,323 .... C1
Salto 18,462 .... F7
San Antonio de
Areco 12,932 .... G7
San Antonio de
los Cobres 2,357 ..... C1
San Antonio Oeste 8,690 . C5
San Carlos 7,613 ...... F6
San Carlos de
Bariloche 48,222 ..... B5
San Cayetano 5,960 .... E4

San Cristóbal 13,345 .... F5
San Fernando 128,939 ... G7
San Francisco, Córdoba
58,616 .... D3
San Francisco, San Luis
2,448 .... F6
San Genaro 2,977 ...... F6
San Ignacio 3,437 ...... E2
San Jaime de la
Frontera 2,811 ...... G5
San Javier 7,557 ...... F5
San José de Feliciano 4,986 . G5
San Juan 290,479 ...... C3
San Julián 4,278 ...... C6
San Justo 14,135 ...... F5
San Luis 70,632 .... C3
San Martín 29,746 ..... C3
San Martín de
los Andes 9,507 ..... C5
San Miguel del Monte 8,414 G7
San Miguel de
Tucumán 496,914 .... D2
San Nicolás 96,313 ..... F6
San Pedro, Buenos Aires
27,058 .... F6
San Pedro, Jujuy 36,907 . D1
San Rafael 70,477 ..... C3
San Ramón de la
Nva. Orán 32,955 .... D1
San Salvador 4,342 .... G5
San Sebastián C7
Santa Cruz 2,353 ...... C7
Santa Elena 14,655 .... F5
Santa Fe 287,240 ...... F5
Santa Lucía 4,452 ..... E2
Santa María 5,380 ..... C2
Santa Rosa, Córdoba 4,306 . D3
Santa Rosa, La Pampa
51,689 .... D4
Santa Rosa, San Luis 2,878 . C3
Santa Victoria D1
Santiago del Estero 148,357 D2
Santo Tomé, Corrientes
14,352 .... E2
Santo Tomé, Santa Fe
35,363 .... F5
Sarmiento 6,313 .... B6
Sauce 4,677 .... G5
Sierra Grande 9,585 .... C5
Suipacha 4,505 .... G7
Sunchales 12,493 ..... F5
Suncho Corral 3,837 ... D2
Tafí Viejo 26,625 ..... C2
Tandil 78,821 .... E4

Tapalqué 5,356 .... E4
Tartagal 31,367 ...... D1
Tigre 199,366 .... G7
Tinogasta 7,829 ...... C2
Toay 3,617 .... C4
Tornquist 4,696 ...... D4
Tostado 10,492 ...... D2
Trelew 52,073 .... C5
Trenque Lauquen 22,504 . D4
Tres Arroyos 42,118 ... E4
Trevelín 2,935 .... B5
Tunuyán 14,665 ...... C3
Urdinarrain 5,472 ..... G6
Ushuaia 10,988 ...... C7
Valcheta 2,994 ...... C5
Vedia 6,273 .... F7
Veinticinco de Mayo 18,936 . F7
Venado Tuerto 46,775 .. F6
Vera 13,555 .... F5
Verónica 5,657 ...... H7
Viale 5,635 .... G6
Vicente López 289,815 .. G7
Victoria 18,883 ...... F6
Victorica 3,895 ...... C4
Vicuña Mackenna 5,665 . D3
Viedma 24,338 ...... D5
Villa Ángela 25,586 ... D2
Villa Atuel 2,935 ..... C3
Villa Cañas 7,303 .... F6
Villa Constitución 36,157 . F6
Villa del Rosario 10,133 . F5
Villa Dolores 21,508 .. C3
Villa Elisa 4,106 ..... G6
Villa Federal 9,222 ... G5
Villaguay 18,699 ..... G6
Villa Guillermina 2,971 . D2
Villa Huidobro 4,154 .. D3
Villa María 67,490 .... E3
Villa María Grande 4,517 . F5
Villa Nueva 4,604 .... C3
Villa Ocampo 9,162 ... D2
Villa Regina 14,017 ... C4
Villa San José 6,800 .. G6
Villa San Martín 6,237 . D2
Vinchina 1,070 ...... C2
Zapala 18,293 .... B4
Zárate 65,504 .... G6
Zavalla 3,800 .... F6

OTHER FEATURES

Aconcagua, Cerro (mt.) ... C3
Andes, Cordillera
de los (mts.) C2

Argentino (lake) B7
Arizaro, Salar de (salt dep.) . C2
Arrecifes (riv.) G6
Atacama, Puna de (reg.) .. C2
Atuel (riv.) C4
Bermejo (riv.) D4
Blanca (bay) D4
Brazo Sur, Pilcomayo (riv.) . E1
Buenos Aires (lake) B6
Campanario, Cerro (mt.) .. C4
Chaco Austral (reg.) D2
Chaco Central (reg.) D1
Chico (riv.) C5
Chico (riv.) C6
Chico (riv.) C5
Chubut (riv.) C5
Colhué Huapi (lake) C6
Colorado (riv.) D4
Cónico, Cerro (mt.) B5
Corrientes (riv.) E2
Coyle (riv.) B7
Delgada (pt.) D5
Desaguadero (riv.) C3
Deseado (riv.) C6
Diamante (riv.) C3
Domuyo (vol.) B4
Dos Bahías (cape)) D5
Dulce (riv.) D2
Dungeness (pt.) C7
El Chocón (res.) C4
Estados, Los (isl.) D7
Fagnano (lake) C7
Famatina, Sierra de (mts.) . C2
Feliciano (riv.) G5
Gallegos (riv.) B7
General Manuel Belgrano,
Cerro (mt.) C2
Gran Chaco (reg.) D1
Grande (bay) C7
Grande (riv.) E3
Grande (falls) C7
Grande de Tierra del
Fuego (isl.) C7
Gualeguay (riv.) G5
Guayaquilaró (riv.) G5
Iguazú (falls) F2
Iguazú Nat'l Park E2
Lanín (vol.) B4
Lanín Nat'l Park B4
Lechiguanas (isls.) G6
Lennox (isl.) C8
Limay (riv.) C4
Llancanelo, Salina y
Laguna (salt lake) C4
Llullaillaco (vol.) C1

Maipo (vol.) C3
Mar Chiquita (lake) D3
Mendoza (riv.) C3
Mercedario, Cerro (mt.) .. B3
Mogotes (pt.) E4
Montemayor (plat.) C5
Nahuel Huapi (lake) B5
Nahuel Huapi Nat'l Park .. B5
Negro (riv.) D4
Neuquén (riv.) C4
Ninfas (pt.) D5
Norte (pt.) D5
Nuevo (gulf) D5
Ojos del Salado, Cerro (mt.) . C2
Pampa de las Tres
Hermanas (plain) C6
Pampas (plain) D4
Paraná (riv.) E2
Patagonia (reg.) C6
Peteroa (vol.) B4
Pilcomayo (riv.) E1
Pissis (mt.) C2
Plata, Río de la (est.) .. E4
Pueyrredón (lake) B6
Puna de Atacama (reg.) . C2
Quinto (riv.) D3
Rincón, Cerro (mt.) ... C1
Saladillo (riv.) D2
Salado (riv.) C3
Salado (riv.) H7
Salado del Norte (riv.) . D2
Salí (riv.) C2
Salto (riv.) F7
Samborombón (bay) ... E4
San Antonio (cape) ... E4
San Diego (cape) C7
San Jorge (gulf) C6
San Juan (riv.) C3
San Lorenzo, Cerro (mt.) . B6
San Martín (lake) B6
San Matías (gulf) D5
Santa Cruz (riv.) B7

Senguerr (riv.) B6
Staten (Los Estados) (isl.) . D7
Tarija (riv.) D1
Tercero (riv.) D3
Teuco (riv.) C2
Tierra del Fuego,
Grande de (isl.) C7
Toro, Cerro del (mt.) .. B2
Tres Puntas (cape) ... C6
Trinidad (isl.) D4
Tronador (mt.) B5
Tunuyán (riv.) C3
Tupungato, Cerro (mt.) . B3
Uruguay (riv.) E3
Valdés (pen.) D5
Viedma (lake) B6
Zapaleri, Cerro (mt.) . C1

FALKLAND ISLANDS

CITIES and TOWNS

Stanley (cap.) 1,050 ..... E7

OTHER FEATURES

Adventure (sound) E7
Choiseul (sound) E7
East Falkland (isl.) 1,491 ... E7
Falkland (isls.) D7
Falkland (sound) D7
George (isl.) D7
Jason (isls.) D7
Lively (isl.) E7
Malvinas (Falkland) (isls.) .. D7
Pebble (isl.) D7
Saunders (isl.) D7
Weddel (isl.) D7
West Falkland (isl.) 322 ... D7

*City and suburbs.

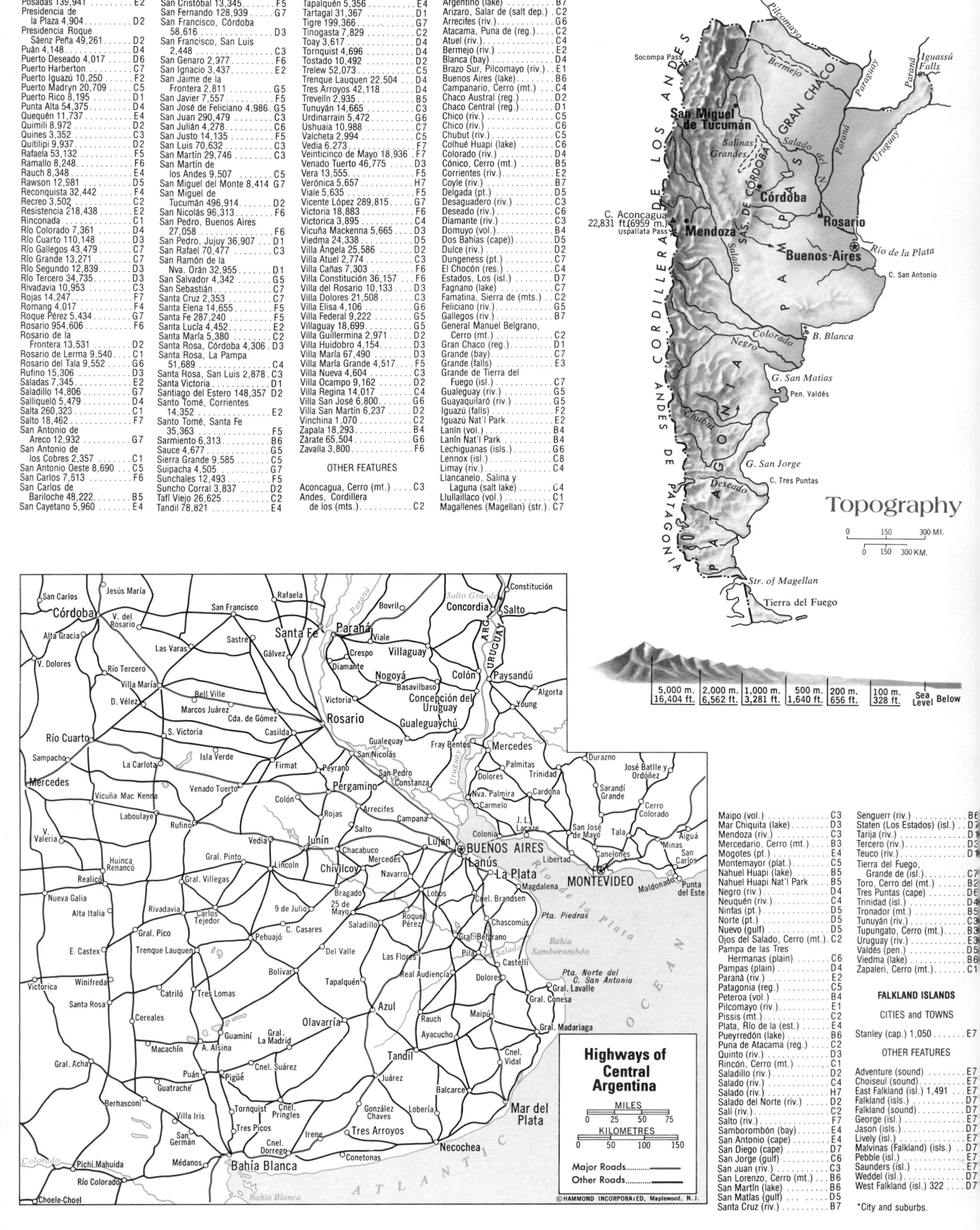

Topography

Highways of Central Argentina

© HAMMOND INCORPORATED, Maplewood, N.J.

Argentina

CONIC PROJECTION

SCALE OF MILES

SCALE OF KILOMETERS

Capitals of Countries	☆
Capitals of Provinces	◉
International Boundaries	
Boundaries of Provinces	

Scale 1:13,000,000

© Copyright HAMMOND INCORPORATED, Maplewood, N.J.

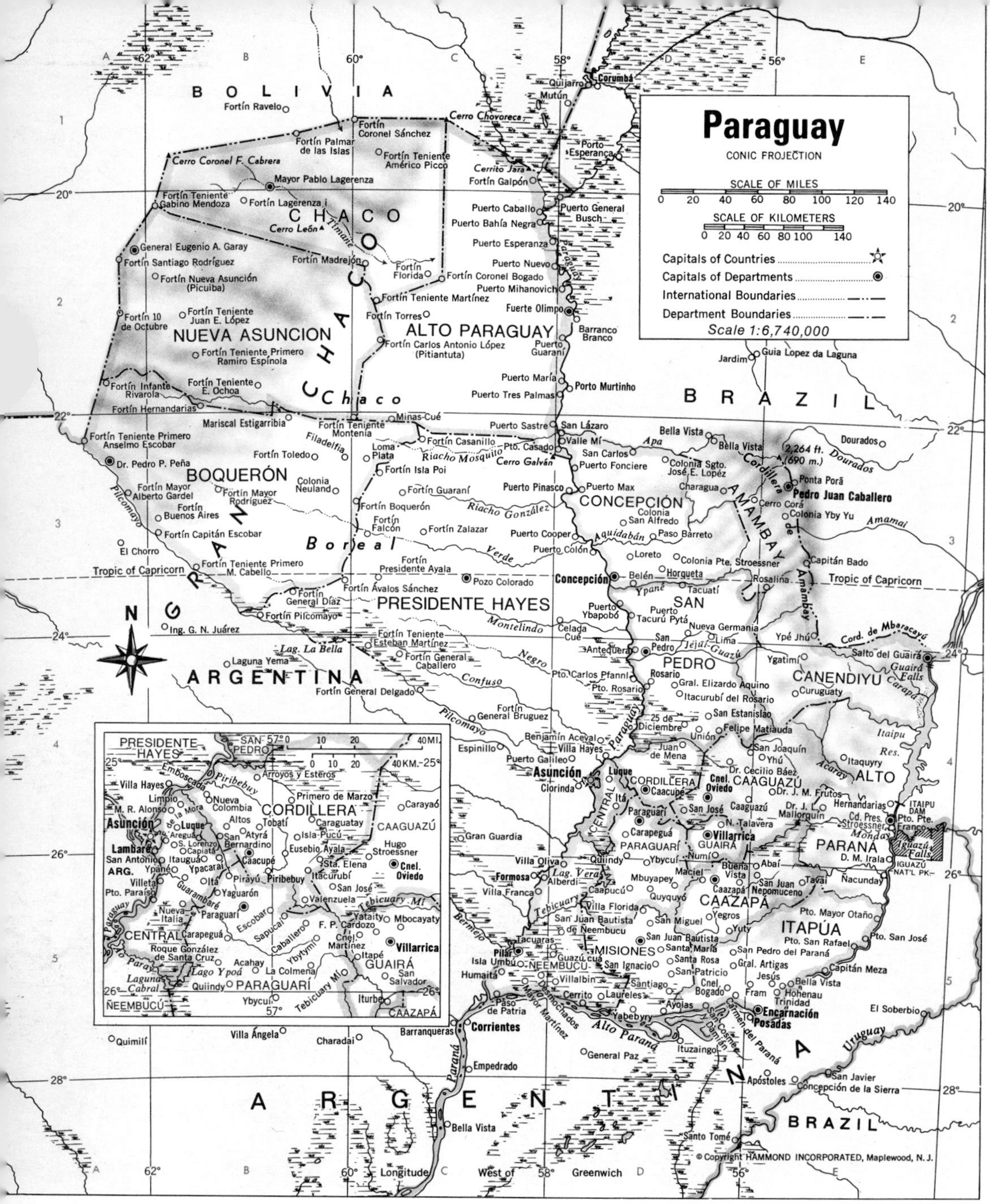

Paraguay

CONIC PROJECTION

SCALE OF MILES
0 20 40 60 80 100 120 140

SCALE OF KILOMETERS
0 20 40 60 80 100 140

Capitals of Countries .... ★
Capitals of Departments .... ◉
International Boundaries .... —··—
Department Boundaries .... —·—·
Scale 1:6,740,000

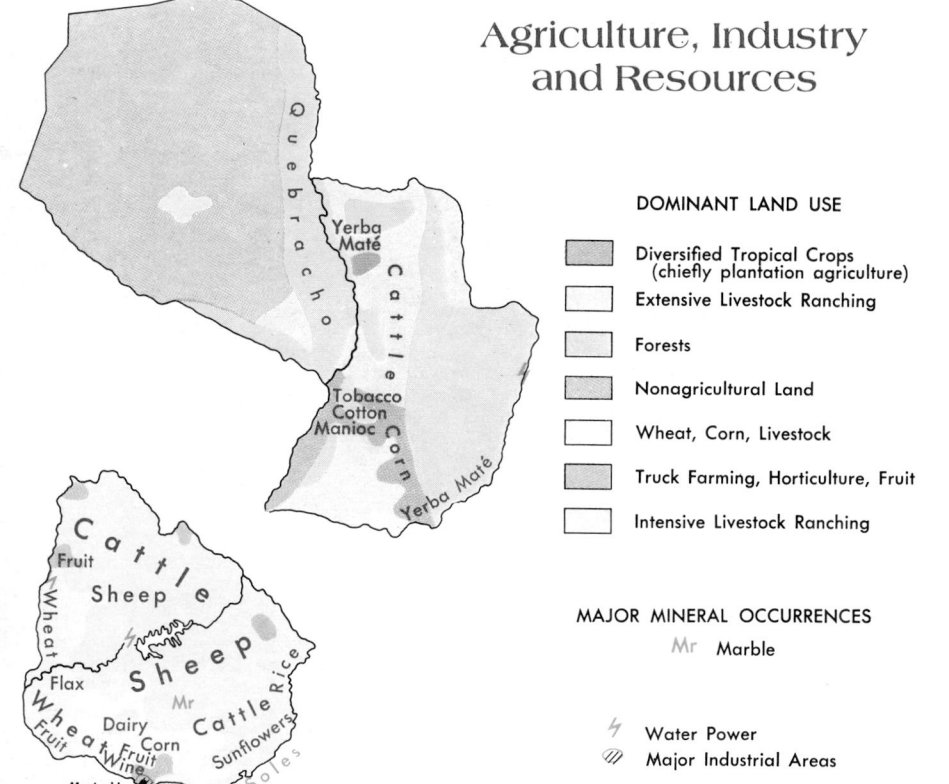

Agriculture, Industry and Resources

DOMINANT LAND USE

Diversified Tropical Crops (chiefly plantation agriculture)

Extensive Livestock Ranching

Forests

Nonagricultural Land

Wheat, Corn, Livestock

Truck Farming, Horticulture, Fruit

Intensive Livestock Ranching

MAJOR MINERAL OCCURRENCES

Mr Marble

⚡ Water Power

▨ Major Industrial Areas

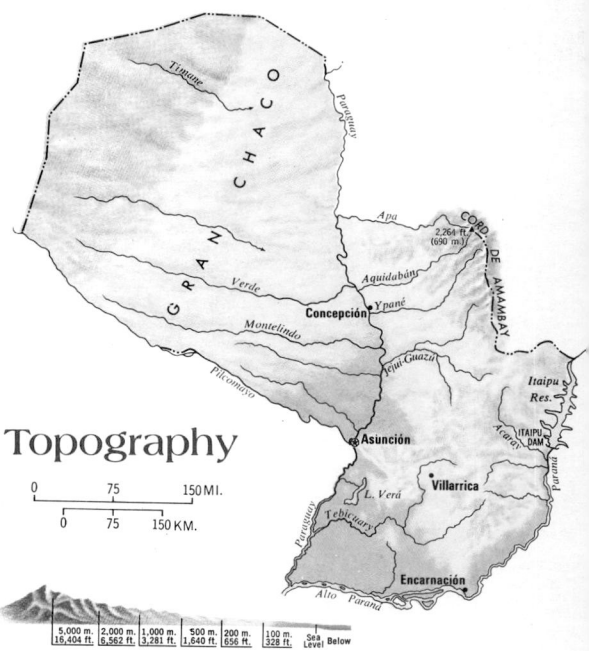

Topography

0   75   150 MI.
0   75   150 KM.

5,000 m. | 2,000 m. | 1,000 m. | 500 m. | 200 m. | 100 m. | Sea
16,404 ft. | 6,562 ft. | 3,281 ft. | 1,640 ft. | 656 ft. | 328 ft. | Level Below

PARAGUAY

DEPARTMENTS

Alto Paraguay C2
Alto Paraná E4
Amambay D3
Asunción A4
Boquerón B3
Caaguazú D-E4
Caazapá D-E5
Canendiyu E4
Central D4
Chaco B-C2
Concepción D3
Cordillera D4
Guairá D4
Itapúa E5
Misiones D5
Ñeembucú C-D5
Nueva Asunción B2
Paraguarí ....D 4-5
Presidente Hayes C3
San Pedro ....D 4-5

CITIES and TOWNS

Abaí 1,507 ....E4
Acahay 1,937 ....B5
Alberdi 2,346 ....D5
Altos 1,441 ....B4
Antequera 1,281 ....D4
Areguá 3,941 ....B4
Arroyos y Esteros 1,253 ....B4
Asunción (cap.) 387,676 ....A4
Atyrá 1,427 ....B4
Belén 1,219 ....D3
Bella Vista 3,101 ....D3
Bella Vista 1,421 ....E4
Benjamín Aceval 2,877 ....C4
Buena Vista 1,353 ....D5
Caacupé 7,278 ....B5
Caaguazú 7,950 ....D4
Caapucú 1,400 ....D5
Caazapá 3,132 ....D5
Capiatá 2,827 ....B4
Carapeguá 3,416 ....B5
Carmen del Paraná 1,980 ....D5
Ciudad Presidente
  Stroessner 7,085 ....E4
Concepción 19,392 ....D3
Coronel Bogado 3,973 ....D5
Coronel Martínez 1,598 ....B5
Coronel Oviedo 13,786 ....C5
Doctor Cecilio Báez 1,300 ....D4
Doctor Juan L. Mallorquín
  1,913 ....E4
Doctor Juan Manuel Frutos
  1,494 ....E4
Encarnación 23,343 ....E5
Eusebio Ayala 4,328 ....B4
Fernando de la Mora 36,834 ....B4
Filadelfia 1,438 ....B3
Fuerte Olimpo 3,063 ....C2
General Artigas 3,542 ....D5
General Elizardo Aquino
  1,304 ....D4
Guarambaré 3,640 ....B5
Hernandarias 3,898 ....E4
Horqueta 4,328 ....D3
Isla Pucú 1,766 ....B4
Itá 7,041 ....B5
Itacurubí 1,997 ....B5
Itacurubí del Rosario 2,467 .....D4
Itapé 1,376 ....C5
Itauguá 3,767 ....B5
Iturbe 3,413 ....C5
Jesús 1,495 ....E5
La Colmena 1,804 ....B5
Lambaré 31,656 ....A4
Limpio 2,219 ....B4
Loreto 1,258 ....D3
Luque 13,921 ....B4
Mariano Roque Alonso 1,492 ...A4
Mariscal Estigarribia 3,150 .....B3
Mbuyapey 1,560 ....D5

Natalicio Talavera 1,228 ....D
Nueva Italia 1,517 ....B
Paraguari 5,036 ....D
Pedro Juan Caballero 21,033 ...E
Pilar 12,506 ....E
Pirayú 2,698 ....B
Piribebuy 4,497 ....B
Primero de Marzo 696 ....B
Puerto Casado 4,078 C
Puerto Guaraní 302 C
Puerto Pinasco 5,477 C
Puerto Presidente
  Franco 4,152 ....E
Quiindy 2,664 ....B
Roque González de
  Santa Cruz 1,375 ....B
Rosario 4,165 ....D
San Antonio 4,906 ....A
San Estanislao 4,753 ....D
San Ignacio 6,116 ....D
San José 3,102 ....B
San Juan Bautista 6,457 ....D
San Juan Nepomuceno 2,974 .E
San Lázaro 1,767 C
San Lorenzo 11,616 ....B
San Pedro 3,186 ....D
San Pedro del Paraná 2,723 ....D
Santa Elena 1,439 ....B
Santa Rosa 3,736 ....D
Santiago 1,265 ....D
Sapucai 1,864 ....B
Tobatí 4,983 ....B
Unión 1,286 C
Valenzuela 1,108 ....B
Valle Mí 1,318 C
Villa Florida 1,261 ....D
Villa Hayes 4,749 ....A
Villarrica 17,687 C
Villeta 3,156 ....A
Yaguarón 3,368 ....B
Ybycuí 1,736 ....B
Ypacaraí 5,195 ....B
Ypané 1,474 ....B
Yuty 2,392 ....D

OTHER FEATURES

Acaray (riv.) E4
Alto Paraná (riv.) D5
Amambay, Cordillera de
  (mts.) D3
Ao Paray (riv.) D3
Apa (riv.) D3
Aquidabán (riv.) D3
Cabral (lake) D5
Carapa (riv.) E4
Chaco Boreal (reg.) C3
Chovoreca (mt.) C2
Confuso (riv.) C4
Coronel F. Cabrera (mt.) B2
Galván (mt.) C3
González, Riacho (riv.) C3
Gran Chaco (reg.) B4
Itaipú (dam) E4
Itaipú (res.) ....E
Jara (hill) B2
Jejuí-Guazú (riv.) D4
La Bella (lag.) B4
León (mt.) B4
Mbaracayú, Cordillera de
  (mts.) E4
Monday (riv.) E4
Montelindo (riv.) C3
Mosquito, Riacho (riv.) C3
Negro (riv.) C4
Paraguay (riv.) D4
Pilcomayo (riv.) C4
Piribebuy (riv.) B4
Tebicuary (riv.) C5
Tebicuary Mí (riv.) C5
Tímane (riv.) B2
Vera (lag.) D5
Verde (riv.) C3
Ypané (riv.) D3
Ypoá (lake) B5

© Copyright HAMMOND INCORPORATED, Maplewood, N.J.

URUGUAY

DEPARTMENTS

Artigas 52,843 ....B1
Canelones 258,195 ....D5
Cerro Largo 71,023 ....E3
Colonia 105,350 ....B5
Durazno 53,635 ....C4
Flores 23,530 ....C4
Florida 63,987 ....D4
Lavalleja 65,823 ....D5
Maldonado 61,259 ....E5
Montevideo 1,202,757 ......B7
Paysandú 88,029 ....B3
Río Negro 46,861 ....B3
Rivera 77,086 ....D2
Rocha 55,097 ....E4
Salto 92,183 ....B2
San José 79,563 ....C5
Soriano 77,906 ....B4
Tacuarembó 76,964 ....C2
Treinta y Tres 43,419 ....E4

CITIES and TOWNS

Aceguá 930 ....E2
Achar 606 ....C3
Agraciada 638 ....B5
Aguas Corrientes 992 ....A6
Aiguá 2,470 ....E5
Algorta 1,372 ....B3
Artigas 29,256 ....C1
Atlántida 2,268 ....B6
Balneario Solís 288 ....D5
Baltasar Brum 1,753 ....B1
Belén 2,129 ....B1
Bella Unión 7,778 ....B1
Bernabé Rivera 540 ....B1
Blanquillo 1,053 ....D3
Cañada Nieto 503 ....B4
Canelones 15,938 ....B6
Cardal 847 ....C5
Cardona 4,126 ....B4
Carlos Reyles 961 ....C4
Carmelo 13,631 ....A4
Carmen 2,318 ....D4
Casupá 2,265 ....D5
Cebollatí 1,233 ....F4
Cerrillos 1,690 ....A6
Cerro Chato,
  Treinta y Tres 1,850 ....D4
Chamizo 486 ....D5
Chuy 4,472 ....F4
Colón, Lavalleja 367 ....E4
Colonia 16,895 ....B5
Colonia Valdense 2,113 .....B5
Conchillas 748 ....B5
Constitución 3,217 ....A2
Costa Azul 453 ....E5
Cufré 430 ....B5
Curtina 723 ....D3
Diez y Nueve (19) de Abril
  308 ....E5
Diez y Ocho (18) de Julio
  742 ....F5
Dolores 12,771 ....A4
Durazno 25,811 ....C4
Egaña 667 ....B4
Empalme Olmos 2,084 ......B6
Estación Atlántida 1,845 ....B6
Estación Migues 241 ....C6
Florida 25,030 ....C5
Fraile Muerto 2,468 ....E3
Fray Bentos 19,569 ....A4
Fray Marcos 1,573 ....D5
Garzón 258 ....E5
General Enrique Martínez 973 .F4
Goñi 284 ....C4
Grecco 447 ....B3
Guichón 4,720 ....B3
Ituzaingó 717 ....A6
Javier de Viana 286 ....C1
Joanico 692 ....B6
Joaquín Suárez,
  Canelones 3,517 ....B6
José Batlle y Ordóñez 2,044 .D4
José Enrique Rodó 1,334 ....B4
José Pedro Varela 3,541 .....E4
Juan L. Lacaze 11,133 ....B5
La Coronilla 571 ....F4
La Cruz 633 ....C4

La Paloma 1,558 ....F5
La Paz, Canelones 14,402 ..B6
Lascano 6,043 ....E4
Las Flores 403 ....D5
Las Piedras 53,983 ....B6
Las Toscas 893 ....E3
Libertad 6,071 ....C5
Lorenzo Geyres 474 ....B3
Mal Abrigo 209 ....C5
Maldonado 22,159 ....D6
Mariscala 1,393 ....E5
Melo 38,260 ....E3
Mercedes 34,667 ....B4
Merinos 403 ....C3
Miguelete 533 ....B5
Migues 2,183 ....C6
Minas 35,433 ....D5
Minas de Corrales 2,518 ....D2
Montes 2,217 ....D5
Montevideo (cap.) 1,173,254 ..B7
Nueva Helvecia 8,508 ....B5
Nueva Palmira 6,934 ....A4
Nuevo Berlín 1,970 ....B3
Ombúes de Lavalle 1,689 ...B4
Palmitas 1,332 ....B4
Pan de Azúcar 4,862 ....D5
Pando 16,184 ....B6
Paso del Cerro 317 ....C2
Paso de los Toros 13,178 ...C3
Paysandú 62,412 ....A3
Piedras Coloradas 487 ......B3
Piedra Sola 233 ....C3
Piñera 261 ....C3
Piraraja 774 ....E4
Piriápolis 5,221 ....D5
Porvenir 705 ....B3
Progreso 8,257 ....B6
Punta del Este 6,914 ....E6
Quebracho 1,514 ....B2
Reboledo 373 ....C5
Río Branco 5,697 ....F3
Rivera 49,013 ....D1
Rocha 21,612 ....E5
Rodríguez 1,575 ....C5
Rosario 8,302 ....B5
Salto 72,948 ....B2
San Antonio, Canelones
  1,122 ....B6
San Bautista 1,472 ....C6
San Carlos 16,883 ....E5
San Gregorio,
  Tacuarembó 2,892 ....D3
San Jacinto 2,292 ....C6
San Javier 1,583 ....A3
San José de Mayo 28,427 ..C5
San Ramón 6,570 ....C5
Santa Catalina 885 ....B4
Santa Clara de Olimar 2,857 .D3
Santa Lucía 14,101 ....B6
Santa Rosa 2,736 ....B6
Santiago Vázquez 1,323 ....A7
Sarandí del Yi 6,326 ....D4
Sarandí de Navarro 259 .....C3
Sarandí Grande 5,598 ....C4
Solís 356 ....D5
Solís de Mataojo 1,763 ......D5
Soriano 1,125 ....A4
Tacuarembó 34,152 ....D2
Tala 3,611 ....D5
Tambores 1,534 ....C2
Toledo 3,127 ....B6
Tomás Gomensoro 2,105 ...B1
Tranqueras 3,922 ....D2
Treinta y Tres 25,757 ....E4
Trinidad 17,598 ....C4
Tupambaé 1,039 ....E3
Valentines 153 ....E4
Veinticinco (25) de Agosto
  1,891 ....A6
Veinticinco (25) de Mayo
  1,744 ....C5
Velázquez 1,042 ....E5
Vergara 2,822 ....E3
Vichadero 1,989 ....E2
Villa Darwin 507 ....B4
Young 11,080 ....B4
Zapicán 764 ....E4
Zapucay D2

OTHER FEATURES

Arapey Grande (riv.) B2

PARAGUAY

AREA 157,047 sq. mi. (406,752 sq. km.)
POPULATION 4,157,000
CAPITAL Asunción
LARGEST CITY Asunción
HIGHEST POINT Amambay Range
  2,264 ft. (690 m.)
MONETARY UNIT guaraní
MAJOR LANGUAGES Spanish, Guaraní
MAJOR RELIGION Roman Catholicism

URUGUAY

AREA 72,172 sq. mi. (186,925 sq. km.)
POPULATION 3,077,000
CAPITAL Montevideo
LARGEST CITY Montevideo
HIGHEST POINT Mirador Nacional 1,644 ft.
  (501 m.)
MONETARY UNIT Uruguayan peso
MAJOR LANGUAGE Spanish
MAJOR RELIGION Roman Catholicism

Bonete (dam) C3
Brava (pt.) B7
Cañas (range) C2
Caraguatá (riv.) D3
Castillos (lag.) F5
Cebollatí (riv.) F4
Cordobés (riv.) D3
Cuareim (riv.) B1
Cuñapirú, Arroyo (riv.) D2
Daymán (riv.) B2
Durazno, Grande del
  (range) D4
Este (pt.) D6
Grar de (range) D5
Haedo (range) C2
India Muerta (riv.) E4
Lobos (isl.) E6
Merín (lag.) F4
Mirador Nacional (mt.) D5
Negra (lag.) F5

Negro (riv.) B4
Negro, Arroyo (riv.) B3
Olimar Grande (riv.) E4
Plata, La (riv.) B5
Polonio (cape) F5
Quequay Grande (riv.) B3
Río Negro (res.) D3
Rocha (lag.) E5
Salto Grande (falls) A2
San José (riv.) C4
San Miguel (swamp) F4
San Salvador (riv.) B4
Santa Ana (range) D2
Santa Lucía (riv.) D5
Santa María (cape) F5
Tacuarembó (riv.) D2
Tacuarí (riv.) E3
Uruguay (riv.) A3
Yaguarón (riv.) F3
Yi (riv.) B4

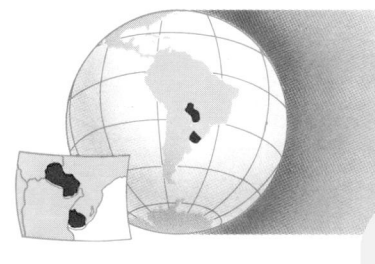

PARAGUAY

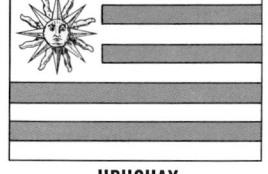

URUGUAY

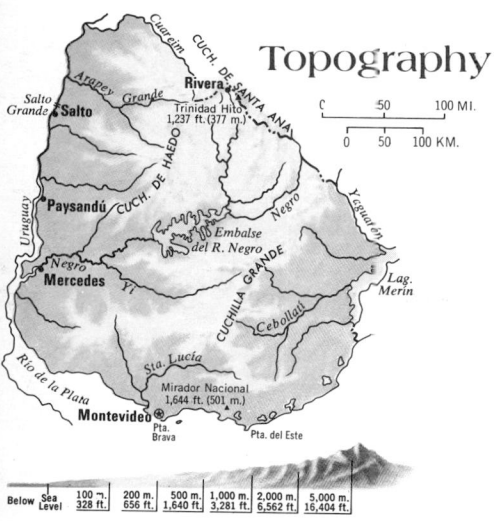

Topography

Below Sea Level · 100 m. 328 ft. · 200 m. 656 ft. · 500 m. 1,640 ft. · 1,000 m. 3,281 ft. · 2,000 m. 6,562 ft. · 5,000 m. 16,404 ft.

Uruguay

CONIC PROJECTION

SCALE OF MILES
0   20   40   60

SCALE OF KILOMETERS
0   20   40   60

Capitals of Countries ....☆
Department Capitals ....◉
International Boundaries ......–··–··–
Department Boundaries ....––·––·––

Scale 1:3,800,000

© Copyright HAMMOND INCORPORATED, Maplewood, N.J.

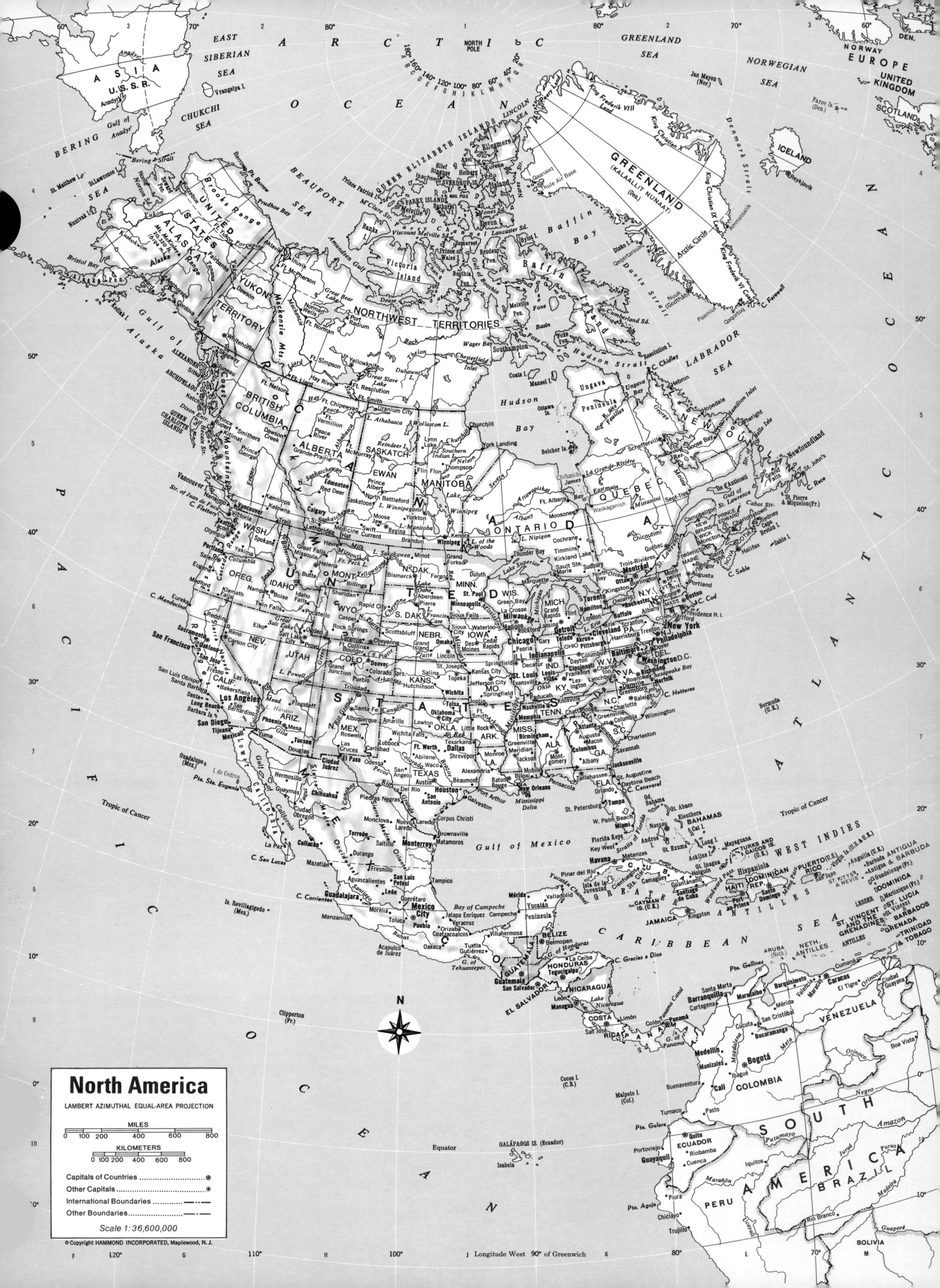

North America

LAMBERT AZIMUTHAL EQUAL-AREA PROJECTION

MILES
0 100 200   400   600   800

KILOMETERS
0 100 200   400   600   800

Capitals of Countries .... ⊛
Other Capitals .... ⊛
International Boundaries .... —·—·—
Other Boundaries .... —··—··—

Scale 1:36,600,000

© Copyright HAMMOND INCORPORATED, Maplewood, N.J.

Population Distribution

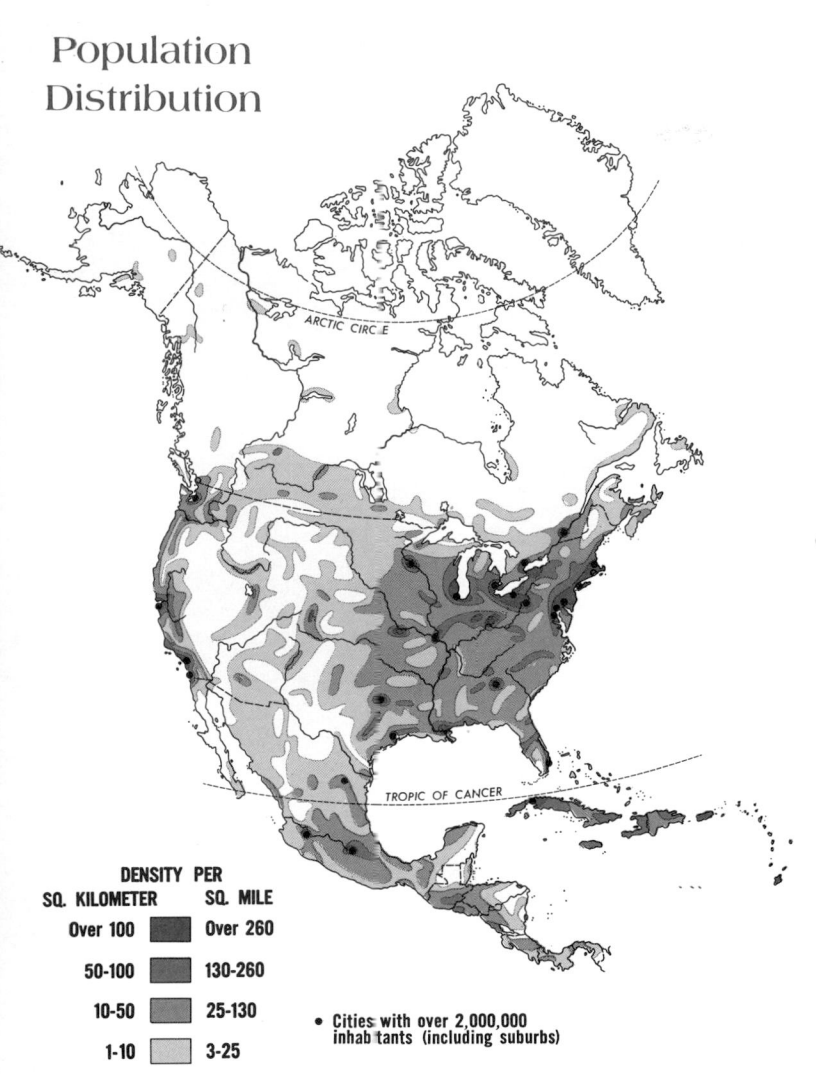

AREA 9,363,000 sq. mi.
(24,250,170 sq. km.)
POPULATION 427,000,000
LARGEST CITY New York
HIGHEST POINT Mt. McKinley 20,320 ft.
(6,194 m.)
LOWEST POINT Death Valley -282 ft.
(-86 m.)

DENSITY PER

SQ. KILOMETER	SQ. MILE
Over 100	Over 260
50-100	130-260
10-50	25-130
1-10	3-25
Under 1	Under 3

• Cities with over 2,000,000 inhabitants (including suburbs)

Vegetation

MID-LATITUDE FOREST
- Coniferous Forest
- Broadleaf Forest
- Mixed Coniferous and Broadleaf Forest
- Woodland and Shrub (Mediterranean)

MID-LATITUDE GRASSLAND
- Short Grass (Steppe)
- Tall Grass (Prairie)

TROPICAL FOREST
- Tropical Rainforest
- Light Tropical Forest

TROPICAL GRASSLAND
- Wooded Savanna

DESERT AND DESERT SHRUB

- TUNDRA AND ALPINE
- PERMANENT ICE

Acapulco de Juárez, Mex. H8
Akron, Ohio. K5
Alabama (state), U.S. K6
Alaska (gulf)........................D4
Alaska (pen.), Alaska C4
Alaska (state), U.S. C3
Alberta (prov.), Canada.........G4
Albuquerque, N. Mex. H6
Amarillo, Texas....................H6
Anchorage, Alaska................D3
Antigua (isl.)........................M8
Appalachian (mts.). K6
Arizona (state), U.S. G6
Arkansas (state), U.S. J6
Aruba (isl.)..........................M8
Athabasca (lake), Can..........H4
Atlanta (cap.), Ga. K6
Austin (cap.), Texas J6
Baffin (bay).........................M2
Baffin (isl.), N.W.T. L2
Bahamas............................L7
Baltimore, Md......................L6
Barbados............................N8
Barrow (pt.), Alaska C2
Baton Rouge (cap.), La. J6
Beaufort (sea).....................D2
Belize.................................K8
Bering (sea).........................A3
Bermuda (isls.)....................M6
Birmingham, Ala...................K6
Boise (cap.), Idaho G5
Boston (cap.), Mass..............L5
British Columbia (prov.),
  Canada..............................F4
Buffalo, N.Y.........................L5
Calgary, Alta.......................G4
California (gulf), Mex.............G7
California (state), U.S. F6
Canada................................G4
Canaveral (cape), Fla............L7
Caribbean (sea)....................K8
Cascade (range), U.S. F5
Cayman Islands....................K8
Charleston, S.C....................K6
Charlotte, N.C......................K6
Chattanooga, Tenn...............K6
Chesapeake (bay), U.S..........L6
Chicago, Ill.........................K5
Chihuahua, Mex...................H7
Cincinnati, Ohio...................K5
Ciudad Juárez, Mex..............H6
Cleveland, Ohio....................K5
Clipperton (isl.)....................E8
Coast (ranges), U.S..............F5
Cod (cape), Mass. L5
Colorado (riv.), U.S...............G6
Colorado (state), U.S. H6
Columbia (riv.), U.S. F5

Columbus (cap.), Ohio..........K6
Connecticut (state), U.S. L5
Costa Rica...........................K8
Cuba...................................L7
Dallas, Texas.......................J6
Davis (strait)........................N3
Dayton, Ohio.......................K6
Delaware (state), U.S............L6
Denver (cap.), Colo...............H6
Des Moines (cap.), Iowa........J5
Detroit, Mich........................K5
Devon (isl.), N.W.T. K2
Dominica.............................M8
Dominican Republic..............L8
Duluth, Minn........................J5
Edmonton (cap.), Alta...........G4
Ellesmere (isl.), N.W.T. K1
El Paso, Texas.....................H6
El Salvador..........................J8
Erie (lake)...........................K5
Fairbanks, Alaska.................D3
Farewell (cape), Greenl. P4
Florida (state), U.S. K7
Fort Worth, Texas.................J6
Foxe (basin), N.W.T. L3
Fraser (riv.), Br. Col..............F4
Fresno, Calif........................G6
Georgia (state), U.S..............K6
Grand Rapids, Mich..............K5
Great Bear (lake), N.W.T F3
Great Salt (lake), Utah...........G5
Great Slave (lake), N.W.T. H3
Greenland............................P2
Greenland (sea)....................T2
Grenada...............................M8
Guadalajara, Mex..................H7
Guadeloupe (isl.)..................M8
Guatemala............................J8
Guatemala (cap.), Guat..........J8
Haiti....................................L8
Halifax (cap.), N.S.................M5
Hamilton, Ont.......................K5
Harrisburg (cap.), Pa. L5
Hartford (cap.), Conn. L5
Hatteras (cape), N.C..............L6
Havana (cap.), Cuba..............K7
Honduras.............................K8
Honduras (gulf)....................K8
Houston, Texas.....................J7
Hudson (bay), Can................K4
Hudson (strait), Can..............L3
Huron (lake).........................K5
Idaho (state), U.S..................G5
Illinois (state), U.S. K5
Indiana (state), U.S. K6
Indianapolis (cap.), Ind..........K5
Inuvik, N.W.T. E3

Iowa (state), U.S...................J5
Jackson (cap.), Miss..............K6
Jacksonville, Fla....................K6
Jamaica...............................L8
James (bay), Can..................K4
Juan de Fuca (str.) F5
Juneau (cap.), Alaska............E4
Kalaallit Nunaat (Greenland) ...P2
Kansas (state), U.S. J6
Kansas City, Mo....................J6
Kentucky (state), U.S.............K6
Kingston (cap.), Jamaica L8
Knoxville, Tenn.....................K6
Kodiak (isl.), Alaska..............C4
Labrador (reg.), Newf.............M4
Lansing (cap.), Mich. K5
Las Vegas, Nev.....................G6
León, Mex............................H7
Lesser Antilles (isls.) M8
Lethbridge, Alta....................G5
Lexington, Ky........................K6
Lincoln (cap.), Nebr. J5
Little Rock (cap.), Ark. J6
London, Ont.........................K5
Los Angeles, Calif.................G6
Louisiana (state), U.S. J6
Louisville, Ky........................K6
Lower California (pen.), Mex. ..G7
Lubbock, Texas.....................H6
Mackenzie (riv.), N.W.T. F3
Maine (state), U.S. M5
Managua (cap.), Nic..............K8
Manitoba (prov.), Canada.......J4
Martinique (isl.).....................M8
Maryland (state), U.S............L6
Massachusetts (state), U.S. ...L5
Matanzas, Cuba....................K7
Mazatlán, Mex......................H7
McKinley (mt.), Alaska...........C3
Melville (isl.), Canada............G2
Memphis, Tenn.....................K6
Mérida, Mex.........................J7
Mexicali, Mex.......................G6
Mexico.................................H7
Mexico (gulf)........................K7
Mexico City (cap.), Mex.........J7
Miami, Fla............................K7
Michigan (lake), U.S..............K5
Michigan (state), U.S.............K5
Milwaukee, Wis.....................K5
Minneapolis, Minn.................J5
Minnesota (state), U.S...........J5
Mississippi (riv.), U.S.............J6
Mississippi (state), U.S..........K6
Missouri (riv.), U.S................J5
Missouri (state), U.S..............J6
Mobile, Ala...........................K6
Montana (state), U.S.............H5

Monterrey, Mex.....................J7
Montréal, Qué. L5
Nashville (cap.), Tenn. K6
Nassau (cap.), Bahamas L7
Nebraska (state), U.S. J5
Nelson (riv.), Man. J4
Netherlands Antilles M8
Nevada (state), U.S. G6
New Brunswick (prov.),
  Canada..............................M5
Newfoundland (isl.), Can. N5
Newfoundland (prov.),
  Canada..............................M4
New Jersey (state), U.S. L5
New Mexico (state), U.S. H6
New Orleans, La....................K7
New York, N.Y.......................L5
New York (state), U.S. L5
Nicaragua.............................K8
Nicaragua (lake), Nic.............K8
Nome, Alaska.......................B3
Norfolk, Va...........................L6
North Carolina (state), U.S. K6
North Dakota (state), U.S. H5
Northwest Territories (terr.),
  Canada..............................G3
Nova Scotia (prov.), Canada ..M5
Nuevo Laredo, Mex...............H7
Nuuk (Godthåb) (cap.),
  Greenl.................................N3
Oakland, Calif.......................F6
Ohio (riv.), U.S.....................K6
Ohio (state), U.S...................K5
Oklahoma (state), U.S. J6
Oklahoma City (cap.), Okla....J6
Omaha, Nebr........................J5
Ontario (lake).......................O5
Ontario (prov.), Canada K4
Oregon (state), U.S. F5
Ottawa (cap.), Can................L5

Panama................................K9
Panamá (canal), Pan..............L8
Panamá (cap.), Pan...............L9
Peace (riv.), Can...................G4
Pennsylvania (state), U.S. L5
Philadelphia, Pa....................L6
Phoenix (cap.), Ariz...............G6
Pittsburgh, Pa.......................L5
Platte (riv.), U.S....................J5
Port-au-Prince (cap.), Haiti L8
Portland, Maine.....................M5
Portland, Oreg......................F5
Prince Edward Island (prov.),
  Canada..............................M5
Prince of Wales (isl.), Can......J2
Providence (cap.), R.I. L5
Puebla de Zaragoza, Mex.......J8
Puerto Rico...........................M8
Québec (cap.), Qué...............L5
Québec (prov.), Canada L4
Queen Charlotte (isls.),
  Br. Col...............................E4
Race (cape), Can..................N5
Raleigh (cap.), N.C................K6
Red (riv.), U.S......................J6
Red River of the North
  (riv.), U.S...........................J5
Regina (cap.), Sask...............H4
Rhode Island (state), U.S. L5
Richmond (cap.), Va..............L6
Rochester, N.Y......................F4
Rocky (mts.).........................G4
Sacramento (cap.), Calif........F6
Saint Kitts and Nevis.............M8
Saint John, N. Bruns..............M5
Saint John's (cap.), Newf. N5
Saint Lawrence (cap.), Mex....M5
Saint Lawrence (riv.).............L5
Saint Louis, Mo.....................K6
Saint Lucia...........................M8

Saint Paul (cap.), Minn..........J5
Saint Pierre and Miquelon
  (isls.)..................................N5
Saint Vincent and
  The Grenadines....................M8
Salt Lake City (cap.), Utah G5
Saltillo, Mex.........................H7
San Antonio, Texas J7
San Diego, Calif....................G6
San Francisco, Calif..............F6
San José, C. Rica..................K9
San José (cap.), C. Rica.........K9
San Juan (cap.), P. Rico.........M8
San Lucas (cape), Mex..........G7
San Luis Potosí, Mex.............H7
San Salvador (cap.), El Salv....J8
Santiago de Cuba, Cuba.........L8
Santo Domingo (cap.),
  Dom. Rep............................L8
Saskatchewan (prov.),
  Canada..............................H4
Saskatoon, Sask...................H4
Seattle, Wash.......................F5
Shreveport, La.......................J6
Sierra Nevada (range), Calif. ..F6
South Carolina (state), U.S. K6
South Dakota (state), U.S. H5
Southampton (cape), Can.......K3
Spokane, Wash.....................G5
Springfield (cap.), Ill. J6
Sudbury, Ont.........................K5
Superior (lake)......................K5
Tacoma, Wash......................F5
Tallahassee (cap.), Fla...........K6
Tampa, Fla...........................K7
Tampico, Mex.......................J7
Tegucigalpa (cap.), Hond.......K8
Tehuantepec, Mex.................J8
Tennessee (state), U.S. K6
Texas (state), U.S. J6

Thule Air Base, Greenl...........M2
Thunder Bay, Ont..................K5
Tijuana, Mex.........................G6
Toledo, Ohio K5
Toronto (cap.), Ont................K5
Torreón, Mex.........................H7
Trenton (cap.), N.J................L5
Trinidad and Tobago..............N8
Tucson, Ariz.........................G6
Tulsa, Okla...........................J6
Turks and Caicos Islands L7
Ungava (pen.), Qué. L3
United States of America H5
Utah (state), U.S...................G6
Vancouver, Br. Col.................F4
Vancouver (isl.), Br. Col. F5
Veracruz, Mex.......................J8
Vermont (state), U.S..............F5
Victoria (cap.), Br. Col............F5
Victoria (isl.), N.W.T...............G2
Virginia (state), U.S. L6
Virgin Islands (isls.)...............M8
Washington (state), U.S..........F5
Washington, D.C. (cap.), U.S. ..L6
West Indies (isls.)..................M7
West Palm Beach, Fla............K7
West Virginia (state), U.S. K6
Whitehorse (cap.), Yukon E3
Wichita, Kansas....................J6
Wilmington, Del.....................L6
Winnipeg (cap.), Man.............J5
Winnipeg (lake), Man.............J4
Winnipegosis (lake), Man.......H4
Wisconsin (state), U.S...........K5
Wyoming (state), U.S. H5
Yellowknife (cap.), N.W.T.......G3
Yucatán (pen.), Mex...............K7
Yukon (riv.)..........................C3
Yukon Territory (terr.),
  Canada..............................E3

NO AM

Average January Temperature

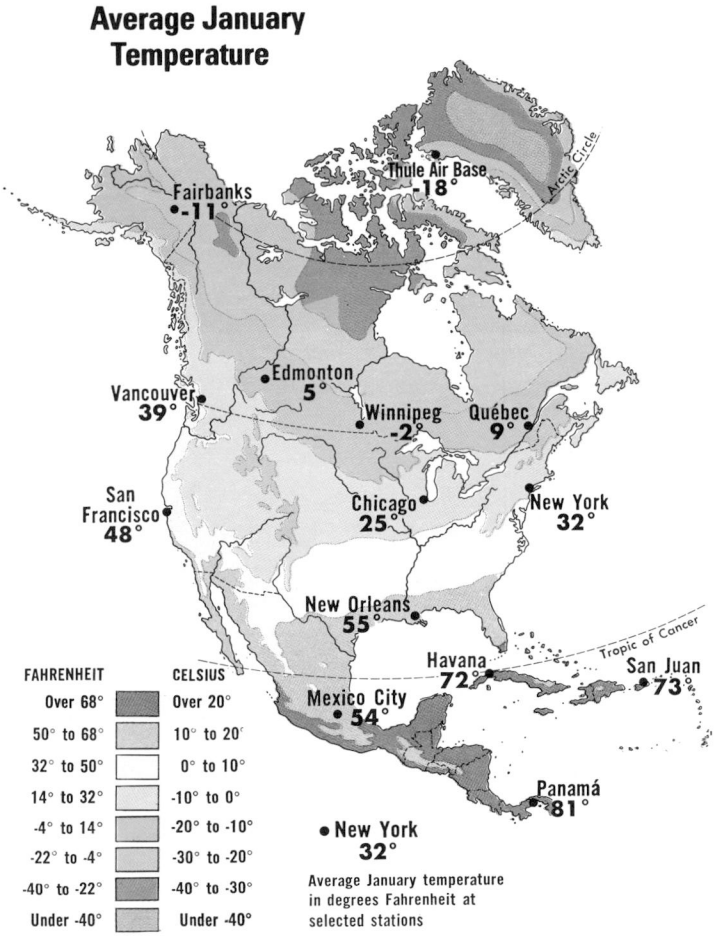

Fairbanks -11°
Thule Air Base -18°
Edmonton 5°
Vancouver 39°
Winnipeg -2°
Québec 9°
San Francisco 48°
Chicago 25°
New York 32°
New Orleans 55°
Havana 72°
San Juan 73°
Mexico City 54°
Panamá 81°

FAHRENHEIT	CELSIUS
Over 68°	Over 20°
50° to 68°	10° to 20°
32° to 50°	0° to 10°
14° to 32°	-10° to 0°
-4° to 14°	-20° to -10°
-22° to -4°	-30° to -20°
-40° to -22°	-40° to -30°
Under -40°	Under -40°

● New York 32°

Average January temperature in degrees Fahrenheit at selected stations

Average July Temperature

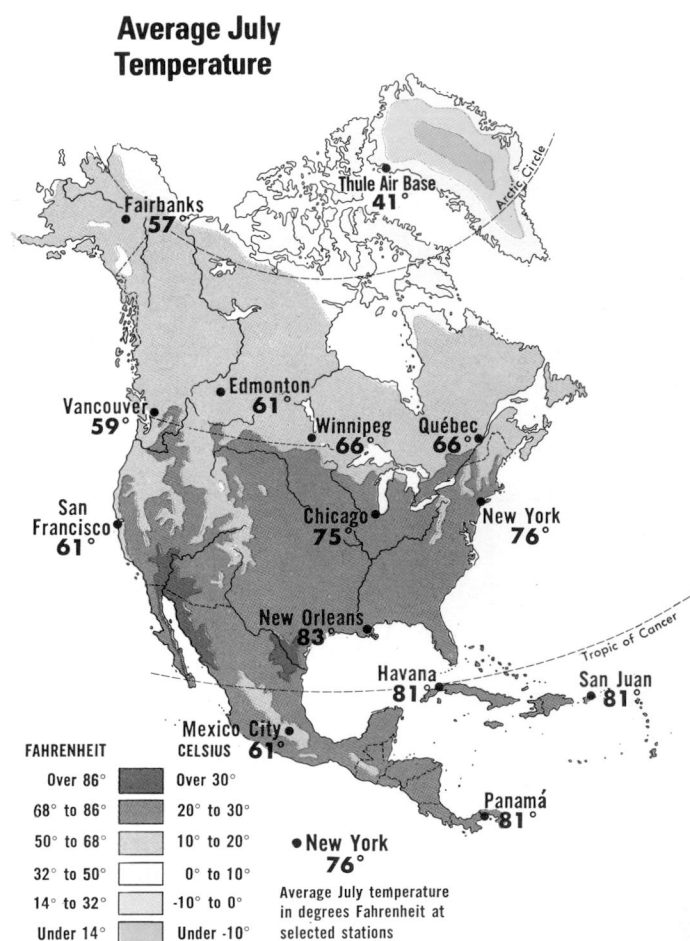

Fairbanks 57°
Thule Air Base 41°
Edmonton 61°
Vancouver 59°
Winnipeg 66°
Québec 66°
San Francisco 61°
Chicago 75°
New York 76°
New Orleans 83°
Havana 81°
San Juan 81°
Mexico City 61°
Panamá 81°

FAHRENHEIT	CELSIUS
Over 86°	Over 30°
68° to 86°	20° to 30°
50° to 68°	10° to 20°
32° to 50°	0° to 10°
14° to 32°	-10° to 0°
Under 14°	Under -10°

● New York 76°

Average July temperature in degrees Fahrenheit at selected stations

Rainfall

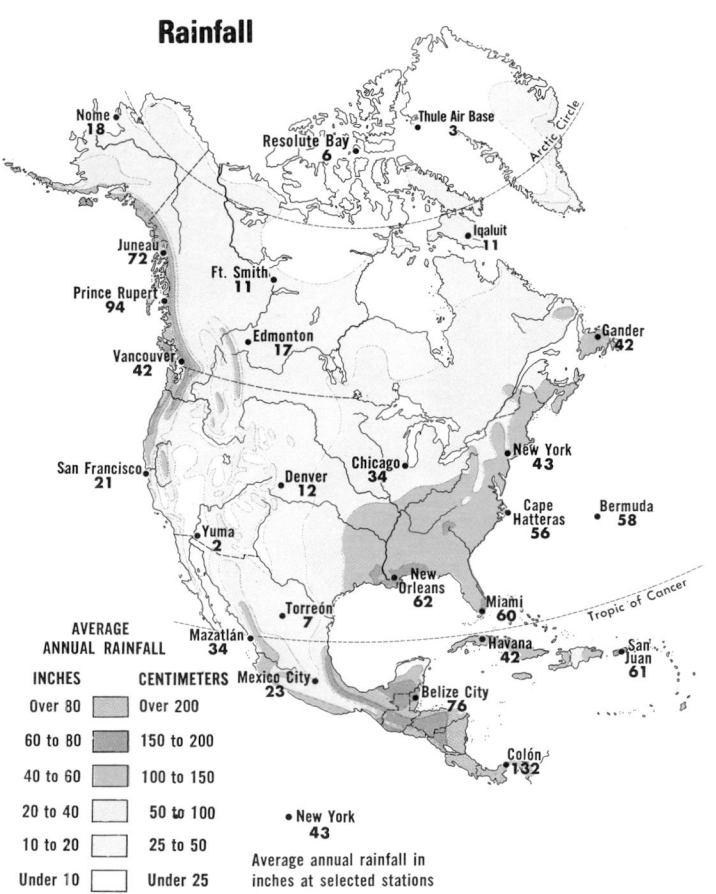

Nome 18
Resolute Bay 6
Thule Air Base 3
Iqaluit 11
Juneau 72
Ft. Smith 11
Prince Rupert 94
Gander 42
Vancouver 42
Edmonton 17
San Francisco 21
Chicago 34
New York 43
Denver 12
Cape Hatteras 56
Bermuda 58
Yuma 2
New Orleans 62
Miami 60
Torreón 7
Mazatlán 34
Havana 42
San Juan 61
Mexico City 23
Belize City 76
Colón 132

AVERAGE ANNUAL RAINFALL

INCHES	CENTIMETERS
Over 80	Over 200
60 to 80	150 to 200
40 to 60	100 to 150
20 to 40	50 to 100
10 to 20	25 to 50
Under 10	Under 25

● New York 43

Average annual rainfall in inches at selected stations

Vegetation / Relief

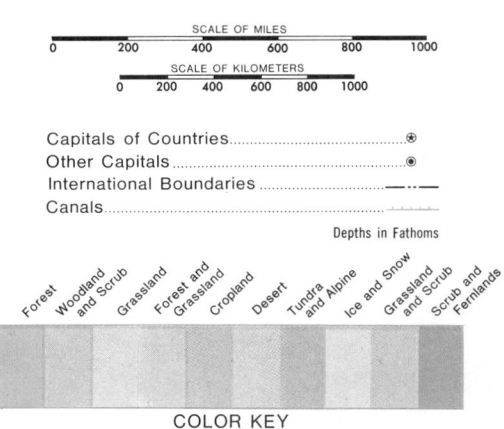

SCALE OF MILES
0   200   400   600   800   1000

SCALE OF KILOMETERS
0   200   400   600   800   1000

Capitals of Countries...................................⊛
Other Capitals...◉
International Boundaries ....――――
Canals...

Depths in Fathoms

Forest Woodland and Scrub Grassland Forest and Grassland Cropland Desert Tundra and Alpine Ice and Snow Grassland and Scrub Scrub and Fernlands

COLOR KEY

Longitude 90° West of Greenwich

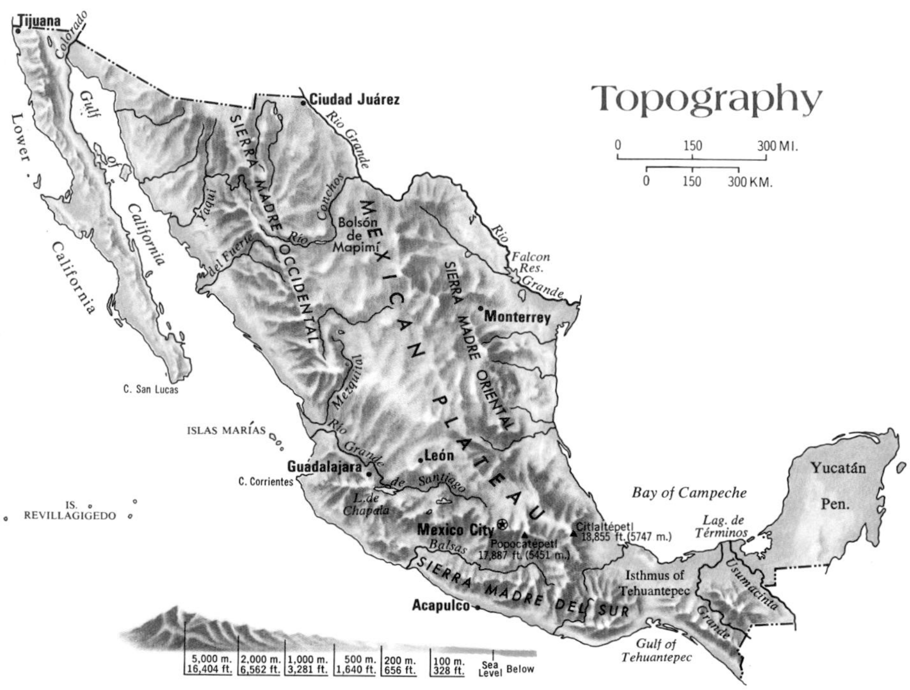
Topography
0 150 300 MI.
0 150 300 KM.
Tijuana
Colorado
Ciudad Juárez
Lower California
Gulf of California
SIERRA MADRE OCCIDENTAL
Río Grande
Conchos
Bolsón de Mapimí
MEXICAN PLATEAU
SIERRA MADRE ORIENTAL
Falcon Res.
Monterrey
C. San Lucas
ISLAS MARÍAS
IS. REVILLAGIGEDO
Guadalajara
C. Corrientes
L. de Chapala
León
Mexico City
Citlaltépetl 18,855 ft. (5747 m.)
Popocatépetl 17,887 ft. (5451 m.)
Balsas
SIERRA MADRE DEL SUR
Acapulco
Bay of Campeche
Lag. de Términos
Yucatán Pen.
Isthmus of Tehuantepec
Usumacinta
Gulf of Tehuantepec
5,000 m. 16,404 ft.
2,000 m. 6,562 ft.
1,000 m. 3,281 ft.
500 m. 1,640 ft.
200 m. 656 ft.
100 m. 328 ft.
Sea Level
Below

STATES

Aguascalientes 504,300..........H6
Baja California 1,227,400........B1
Baja California Sur 221,000....C3
Campeche 371,800.................O7
Chiapas 2,097,500..................N8
Chihuahua 1,935,100..............F2
Coahuila 1,561,000.................H3
Colima 339,400......................G7
Distrito Federal 9,377,300.......L1
Durango 1,160,300.................G4
Guanajuato 3,045,600.............J6
Guerrero 2,174,200.................J8
Hidalgo 1,518,200..................K6
Jalisco 4,296,500...................H6
México 7,542,300...................K7
Michoacán 3,049,400.............H7
Morelos 931,400....................K7
Nayarit 729,500......................G6
Nuevo León 2,463,500............K4
Oaxaca 2,517,500...................L8
Puebla 3,285,300....................L7
Querétaro 730,900..................J6
Quintana Roo 209,900............P7
San Luis Potosí 1,669,900......J5
Sinaloa 1,882,200...................F4
Sonora 1,498,100....................D2
Tabasco 1,150,000..................N7
Tamaulipas 1,924,900............K4
Tlaxcala 548,500....................N1
Veracruz 5,263,800.................L7
Yucatán 1,034,300..................P6
Zacatecas 1,144,700...............H5

CITIES and TOWNS

Acala 11,483...........................N8
Acámbaro 32,257....................J7
Acaponeta 11,844...................G5
Acapulco de Juárez 309,254...K8
Acatlán de Osorio 7,624..........K7
Acatzingo de Hidalgo 6,905....N2
Acayucan 21,173...................M8
Actopan 11,037......................K6
Agua Dulce 21,060.................M7
Agua Prieta 20,754.................E1
Aguascalientes 181,277..........H6
Aguililla 5,715.........................H7
Ahuacatitlán 6,436..................L1
Ahuacatlán 5,350....................G6
Ahumada 6,466.......................F1
Ajalpan 8,238..........................L7
Alamo 9,954............................L6
Aldama 6,047.........................G2
Allende, Coahuila 11,076.........J2
Allende, Nuevo León 9,914.....J4
Altamira 6,053........................L5
Altepexi 6,661.........................L7
Altotonga 6,754.......................P1
Alvarado 15,792.....................M7
Ameca 21,018........................H6
Amecameca de Juárez
16,276...................................L1
Amozoc de Mota 9,203...........N2
Anáhuac, Chihuahua 10,886....F2
Anáhuac, Nuevo León 8,168...J3
Apan 13,705..........................M1
Apatzingán de la Constitución
44,849...................................H7
Apizaco 21,189.......................N1
Arandas 18,934......................H6
Arcelia 10,024.........................J7
Ario de Rosales 8,774.............J7
Armería 10,616.......................G7
Arriaga 13,193........................N8
Arteaga 5,324.........................H7
Atlixco 41,967........................M2
Atotonilco el Alto 16,271........H6
Atoyac de Álvarez 8,874..........J8
Autlán de Navarro 20,398.......G7
Axochiapan 8,283..................M2
Azcapotzalco 534,554.............L1
Bamoa 5,866..........................E4
Benjamín Hill 5,366................D1
Bernardino de Sahagún
12,327..................................M1
Cabo San Lucas 1,534............E5
Cacahoatán 5,079...................N9
Cadereyta Jiménez 13,586......K4
Calkiní 6,870...........................O6
Calpulálpan 8,659..................M1
Calvillo 6,453..........................H6
Campeche 69,506...................O7
Cananea 17,518......................D1
Canatlán 5,983........................G4
Cancún 326............................Q6
Cañitas de Felipe Pescador
4,885....................................H5
Capulhuac de Mirafuentes
8,289....................................K1
Cárdenas, San Luis Potosí
12,020..................................K6
Cárdenas, Tabasco 15,643.....N8
Castaños 8,996.......................J3
Catemaco 11,786...................M7
Celaya 79,977.........................J6
Cerritos 10,421.......................J5
Cerro Azul 20,259...................L6
Chahuites 5,218.....................M8
Chalco de Díaz Covarrubias
12,172..................................M1
Champotón 6,606...................O7
Charcas 10,491.......................J5
Chetumal 23,685....................Q7
Chiapa de Corzo 8,571...........N8
Chiautempan 12,327...............N1
Chietla 4,602.........................M2
Chihuahua 327,313.................F2
Chilapa de Álvarez 9,204.........K8
Chilpancingo de los Bravos
36,193..................................K8
China, Nuevo León 4,958........K4
Chocomán 5,114.....................P2
Cholula de Rivadavia 15,399..M1
Cihuatlán 9,451......................G7
Cintalapa de Figueroa 12,036.N8
Ciudad Acuña (Villa Acuña)
30,276..................................J2
Ciudad Altamirano 8,694.........J7
Ciudad Camargo, Chihuahua
24,030..................................G3
Ciudad Camargo, Tamaulipas
5,953....................................K3
Ciudad de Río Grande 11,651.H5
Ciudad del Carmen 34,656.....N7
Ciudad del Maíz 5,241............K5
Ciudad Delicias 52,446...........G2
Ciudad Guzmán 48,166..........H7
Ciudad Hidalgo, Chiapas
4,105....................................N9
Ciudad Hidalgo, Michoacán
24,692..................................J7
Ciudad Juárez 424,135............F1
Ciudad Lerdo 19,803..............H4
Ciudad Madero 115,302..........L5
Ciudad Mante 51,247..............K5
Ciudad Mendoza 18,696.........O2
Ciudad Miguel Alemán
11,259..................................K3
Ciudad Obregón 144,795........E3
Ciudad Río Bravo 39,018........K4
Ciudad Satélite 35,083............L1
Ciudad Serdán 9,581..............O2
Ciudad Valles 47,587..............K5
Ciudad Victoria 83,897...........K5
Coalcomán de Matamoros
4,875....................................H7
Coatepec 21,542.....................P1
Coatetelco 5,268.....................L2
Coatzacoalcos 69,753............M7
Cocorit 4,478..........................E3
Colima 58,450........................H7
Colotlán 6,135........................H5
Comala 5,592..........................H7
Comalcalco 14,963.................N7
Comitán de Domínguez
21,249..................................O8
Compostela 9,801..................G6
Concepción del Oro 8,144.......J4
Contla 7,517...........................N1
Coquimatlán 6,212..................G7
Córdoba 78,495......................P2
Cosamaloapan de Carpio
19,766..................................M7
Coscomatepec de Bravo
6,023....................................P2
Costa Rica 11,795...................F4
Cotija de la Paz 9,178.............H7
Coyoacán 339,446..................L1
Coyotepec 8,888.....................L1
Coyuca de Benítez 6,328.........J8
Cozumel 5,858.......................Q6
Cuatrociénagas de Carranza
5,523....................................H3
Cuauhtémoc 26,598................F2
Cuautepec de Hinojosa 5,501.K6
Cuautitlán de Romero Rubio
11,439..................................L1
Cuautla Morelos 13,946..........L2
Cuernavaca 239,813...............L2
Cuitlahuac 4,813.....................P2
Culiacán 228,001....................F4
Dolores Hidalgo de la
Independencia Naci 16,849.J6
Durango 182,633....................G4
Dzidzantún 7,064....................P6
Dzitbalché 4,393.....................P6
Ebano 17,489.........................K5
Ecatepec de Morelos 11,899...L1
Ejutla de Crespo 5,263............L8
Eldorado 8,115........................E4
El Fuerte 7,179.......................E3
El Salto 7,818.........................G5
Empalme 24,927.....................D2
Encarnación de Díaz 10,474...H6
Ensenada 77,687....................A1
Escarcega 7,248.....................O7
Escuinapa de Hidalgo 16,442.G5
Escuintla 4,111.......................N9
Esperanza, Sonora 11,762......E3
Espita 5,394...........................Q6
Fortín de las Flores 9,358.......P2
Francisco I. Madero 12,613....H4
Fresnillo de González
Echeverría 44,475..................H5
Frontera 10,066......................N7
General Terán 5,354...............K4
Gómez Palacio 79,650............G4
González 6,440.......................K5
Guadalajara 1,478,383............H6
Guadalupe, Nuevo León
51,899..................................K4
Guadalupe, Zacatecas 13,246.H5
Guadalupe Victoria, Durango
7,931....................................H4
Guamúchil 17,151...................E4
Guanajuato 36,809..................J6
Guasave 26,080......................E4
Guaymas 57,492.....................D3
Gustavo Díaz Ordaz 10,154.....K3
Gutiérrez Zamora 9,099..........L6
Halachó 4,804........................O6
Hermosillo 232,691.................D2
Heroica Caborca 20,771..........C1
Heroica Nogales 52,108..........D1
Hidalgo del Parral (Parral)
57,619..................................G3
Huachinango 16,826...............K7
Huajuapan de León 13,822.....L8
Huamantla 15,565...................N1
Huatabampo 18,506...............D3
Huatusco de Chicuellar 9,501.P2
Huauchinango 16,826.............L6
Huautla de Jiménez 6,132.......L7
Huejotzingo 8,552..................M1
Huejutla 6,854........................K6
Huetamo 9,333........................J7
Huimanguillo 7,075................N8
Huitzuco de los Figueroa
9,406....................................K7
Huixtepec 5,927......................L8
Huixtla 15,737........................N9
Hunucmá 8,020......................O6
Iguala de la Independencia
45,355..................................K7
Irapuato 135,596.....................J6
Isla, Veracruz 8,075...............M7
Isla Mujeres 2,663..................Q6
Ixmiquilpan 6,048...................K6
Ixtapa......................................J8
Ixtapalapa 522,095..................L1
Ixtenco 5,035..........................N1
Ixtepec 14,025.......................M8
Ixtlán del Río 10,986...............G6
Izamal 9,749...........................P6
Izúcar de Matamoros 21,164.M2
Jala 4,535...............................G6
Jalapa Enríquez 161,352.........P1
Jalpa 9,904.............................H6
Jalpa de Méndez 4,785...........N7
Jáltipan de Morelos 15,170....M8
Jerez de García Salinas
20,325..................................H5
Jico 7,269...............................P1
Jiménez, Chihuahua 18,095....G3
Jojutla de Juárez 14,438..........L2
José Cardel 5,396...................Q1
Juan Aldama 9,667.................H4
Juchipila 6,328........................H6
Juchitán de Zaragoza 30,218.M8
La Barca 18,055.....................H6
Lagos de Moreno 33,782.........J6
La Paz 46,011.........................D5
La Piedad Cavadas 34,963......H6
Las Choapas 20,166...............M7
Las Rosas 7,658.....................N8
León 468,887..........................J6
Lerdo de Tejada 11,628.........M8
Libres 4,830...........................O1
Linares 24,456........................K4
Loma Bonita 15,804...............M7
Loreto 7,132...........................J5
Los Mochis 67,953..................E4
Los Reyes de Salgado
19,452..................................H7
Macuspana 12,293..................N8
Madera 9,759..........................F2
Magdalena de Kino 10,281.....D1
Maltrata 5,457........................O2
Manzanillo 20,777..................G7
Mapastepec 5,907..................N9
Martínez de la Torre 17,203....L6
Mascota 5,674........................G6
Matamoros, Coahuila 15,125..H4
Matamoros, Tamaulipas
165,124................................L4
Matehuala 28,799....................J5
Matías Romero 13,200...........M8
Maxcanú 6,505.......................O6
Mazatlán 147,010....................F5
Melchor Múzquiz 18,868.........H3
Melchor Ocampo del Balsas
4,766....................................H8
Meoquí 12,308.......................G2
Mérida 233,912......................P6
Metepec 4,625.......................M2
Mexicali 317,228....................B1
Mexico City (cap.) 9,377,300..L1
Miahuatlán de Porfirio Díaz
5,714....................................L8
Mier 5,636..............................K3
Miguel Auza 9,303.................H4
Minatitlán 68,397...................M8
Mineral del Monte 8,887.........K6
Misantla 8,799........................P1
Monclova 78,134.....................J3
Montemorelos 18,642............K4
Monterrey 1,006,221...............J4
Morelia 199,099.......................J7
Moroleón 25,620.....................J6
Motozintla de Mendoza 4,682.N9
Motul de Felipe Carrillo
Puerto 12,949........................P6
Muna 5,491.............................P6
Naica 7,190............................G2
Namiquipa 4,875.....................F2
Nanacamilpa 6,356................M1
Naranjos 14,732......................L6
Naucalpan de Juárez 9,425.....L1
Navojoa 43,817.......................E3
Navolato 12,799......................E4
Netzahualcóyotl 580,436.........L1
Nochistlán 8,780.....................H6
Nogales 14,254.......................P2
Nueva Casas Grandes 20,023..F1
Nueva Italia de Ruiz 14,718.....J7
Nueva Rosita 34,706...............J2
Nuevo Ideal 5,252...................G4
Nuevo Laredo 184,622.............J3
Oaxaca de Juárez 114,948......L8
Ocampo 4,801.........................K5
Ocotlán 35,361.......................H6
Ocotlán de Morelos 5,882.......L8
Ojinaga 12,757.......................G2
Ojocaliente 7,582....................H5
Ometepec 7,342......................K8
Oriental 6,009.........................O1
Orizaba 105,150......................P2
Oxkutzcab 8,182.....................P6
Ozumba de Alzate 6,876........M1
Pachuca de Soto 83,892.........K6
Padilla 4,581...........................K5
Palenque 2,595.......................O8
Pánuco 14,277........................K6
Papantla de Olarte 26,773.......L6
Paraíso 7,561..........................N7
Parral 57,619..........................G3
Parras de la Fuente 18,207.....H4
Paso de Ovejas 4,371............Q2
Pátzcuaro 17,299....................J7
Pedro Montoya 4,563.............K6
Pénjamo 9,245........................J6
Pericos 4,445..........................F4
Perote 12,742.........................O1
Petatlán 9,419.........................J8
Peto 8,362..............................P6
Pichucalco 4,615....................N8
Piedras Negras, Coahuila
41,033..................................J2
Piedras Negras, Veracruz
4,099....................................Q2
Pijijiapan 5,053.......................N9
Poza Rica de Hidalgo
152,276................................L6
Profesor Rafael Ramírez
5,338....................................O1
Progreso 17,518.....................P6

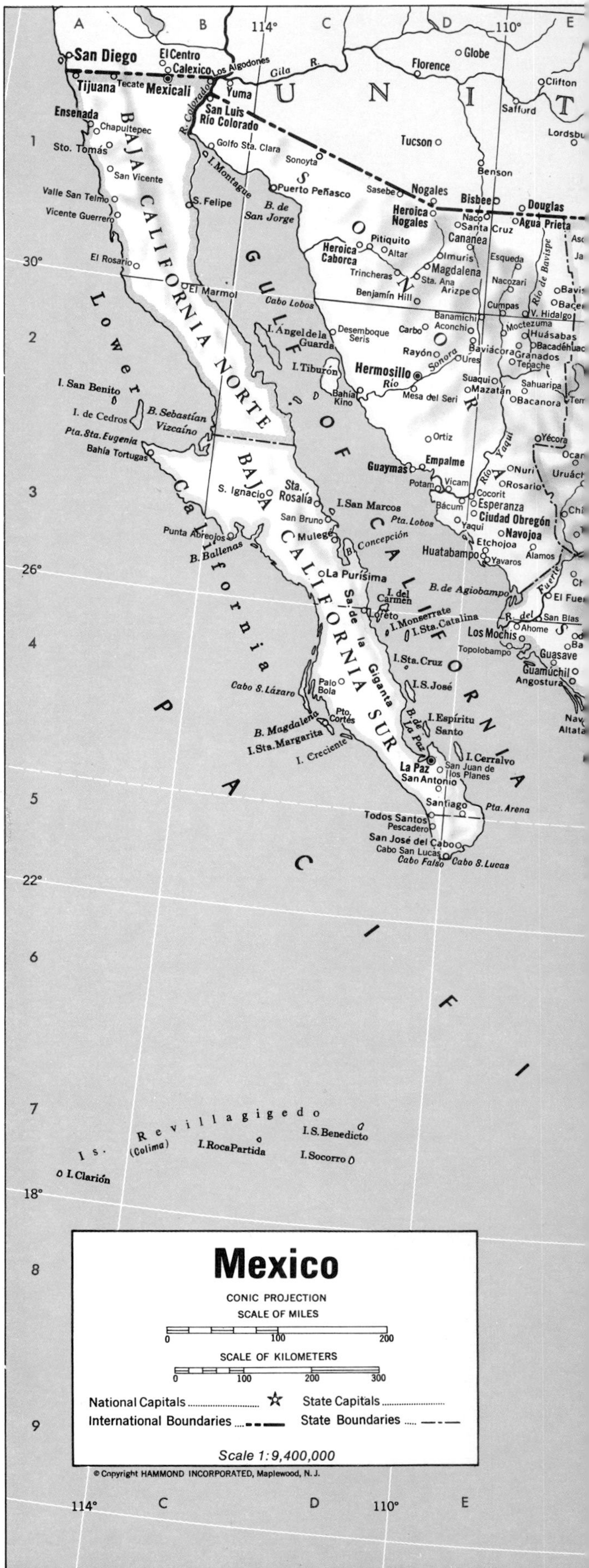
Mexico
CONIC PROJECTION
SCALE OF MILES
0 100 200
SCALE OF KILOMETERS
0 100 200 300
National Capitals
State Capitals
International Boundaries
State Boundaries
Scale 1: 9,400,000
© Copyright HAMMOND INCORPORATED, Maplewood, N. J.
San Diego
El Centro
Calexico
Tijuana
Mexicali
Ensenada
Yuma
San Luis Río Colorado
BAJA CALIFORNIA NORTE
BAJA CALIFORNIA SUR
GULF OF CALIFORNIA
Lower California
PACIFIC
Hermosillo
Guaymas
Ciudad Obregón
Navojoa
Huatabampo
Los Mochis
La Paz
Santa Rosalía
Loreto
San José del Cabo
Cabo San Lucas
Heroica Nogales
Heroica Caborca
Cananea
Agua Prieta
Douglas
Bisbee
Tucson
Nogales
Is. Revillagigedo
I. Socorro
I. Clarión
I. Roca Partida
I. S. Benedicto

(continued on following page)

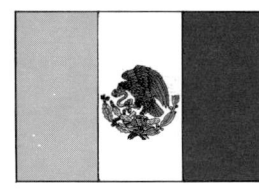

AREA 761,601 sq. mi. (1,972,546 sq. km.)
POPULATION 86,154,000
CAPITAL Mexico City
LARGEST CITY Mexico City
HIGHEST POINT Citlaltépetl 18,855 ft. (5,747 m.)
MONETARY UNIT Mexican peso
MAJOR LANGUAGE Spanish
MAJOR RELIGION Roman Catholicism

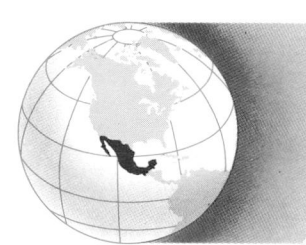

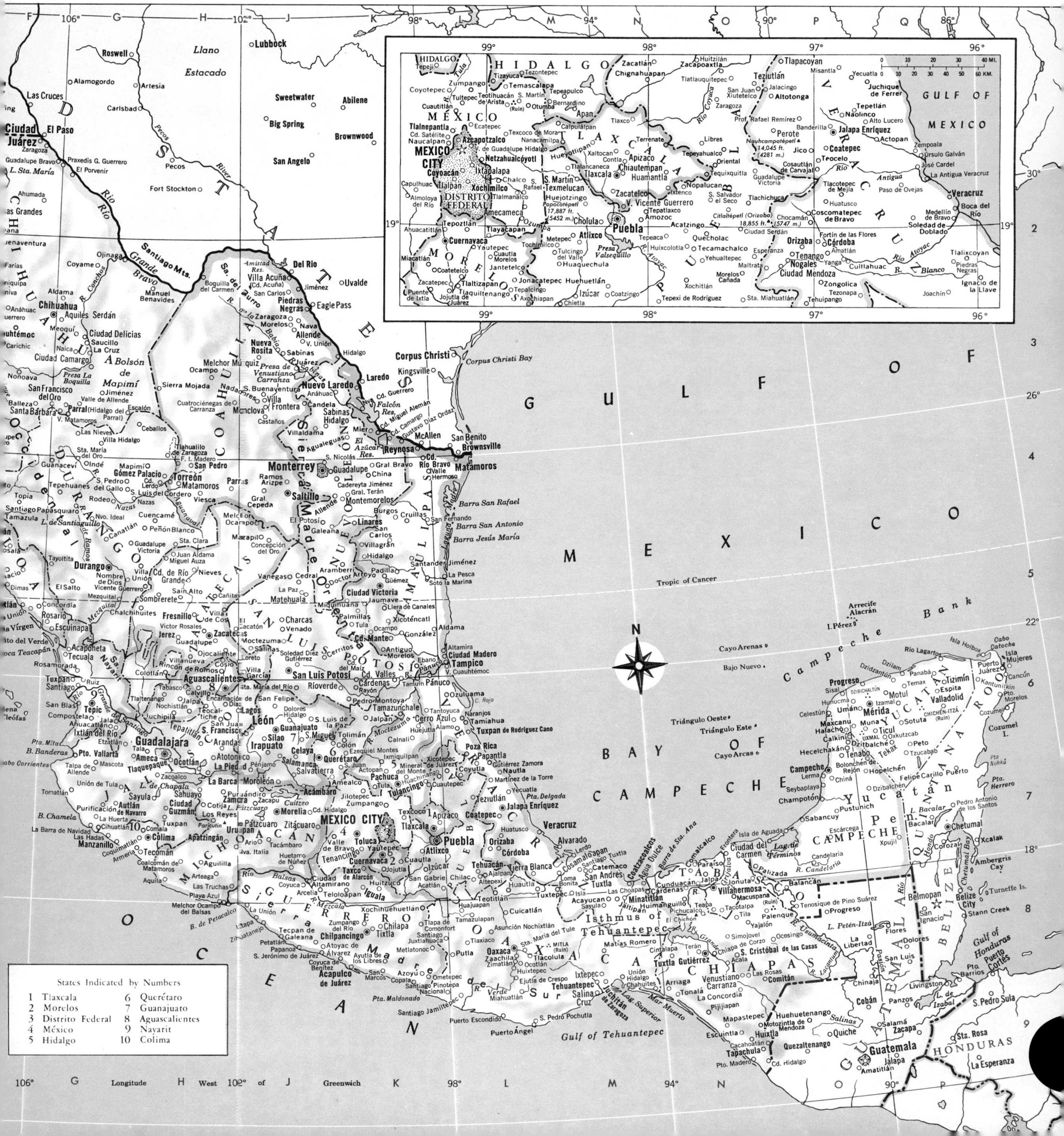
GULF OF MEXICO
BAY OF CAMPECHE
OCEAN
MEXICO CITY
DISTRITO FEDERAL
Tropic of Cancer
Longitude West of Greenwich
States Indicated by Numbers
1 Tlaxcala
2 Morelos
3 Distrito Federal
4 México
5 Hidalgo
6 Querétaro
7 Guanajuato
8 Aguascalientes
9 Nayarit
10 Colima

152 | MEXICO

San Luis de la Paz 12,654 ....J6
San Luis Potosí 271,123 ....J5
San Luis Río Colorado 49,990 ....B1
San Marcos 5,861..................K8
San Martín de las Pirámides 4,575 ....M1
San Martín Texmelucan 23,355 ....M1
San Miguel de Allende 24,286.J6
San Nicolás de los Garza 28,803.................J3
San Pedro de las Colonias 26,882 ....H4
San Rafael 8,974..................M1
San Salvador el Seco 7,729....O1
Santa Ana 7,020 ....D1
Santa Ana Chiautempan (Chiautempan) 12,327........N1
Santa Bárbara 16,978.............F3
Santa María del Río 4,972.......J6
Santa Rosalía 7,356...............C3
Santiago Ixcuintla 17,321 ....G6
Santiago Jamiltepec 5,280......K8
Santiago Miahuatlán 4,917.....O2
Santiago Papasquiaro 6,636 ...F4
Santiago Pinotepa Nacional 9,382 ....K8
Santiago Tuxtla 9,426 ....M7
Saucillo 8,467.........................G2
Sayula 14,339.........................H7
Sayula de Alemán 4,896 ....M8
Silao 31,825...........................J6
Soledad de Doblado 6,612......Q2
Soledad Díez Gutiérrez 9,622 ..J5
Sombrerete 11,077................H5
Tacámbaro de Codallos 9,695.J7
Tala 15,744............................H6
Tamazunchale 12,302.............K6
Tamiahua 6,264 ....L6
Tampico 212,188....................L5
Tamuín 7,251..........................K6
Tantoyuca 11,902 ....L6
Tapachula 60,620 ....N9
Taxco de Alarcón 27,089 ....K7
Teapa 6,534............................N8
Tecate 14,738 ....A1
Tecomán 31,625......................H7
Tecpan de Galeana 8,095 ....J8
Tecuala 12,461 ....G5
Tehuacán 47,497 ....L7
Tehuantepec 16,179 ....M8
Tekax de Álvaro Obregón 10,326 ....P6
Teloloapan 10,335..................J7
Temax 4,915...........................P6
Tenancingo de Degollado 12,807 ....K7
Tenango de Río Blanco 12,302 ....O2
Tenosique de Pino Suárez 11,393 ....O8
Teocaltiche 13,745 ....H6
Teocelo 4,572 ....P1
Teotihuacán de Arista 2,238....L1
Tepalcingo 5,968 ....M2
Tepatitlán de Morelos 29,292 .H6
Tepatlaxco de Hidalgo 8,833 ..N1
Tepeaca 7,466 ....N2
Tepeapulco 7,027 ....M1
Tepeji del Río 10,365 ....L1
Tepic 108,924.........................G6
Tepoztlán 6,851 ....L1
Tequixquitla 4,825 ....O1
Terán 5,215 ....N8
Texcoco de Mora 18,044 ....M1
Teziutlán 23,948 ....O1
Ticul 14,341............................P6
Tierra Blanca 22,727 ....L7
Tijuana 363,154 ....A1
Tixtla de Guerrero 10,334 ....K8
Tizayuca 6,262 ....L1
Tizimín 18,343........................Q6
Tlacolula de Matamoros 8,300...............L8
Tlahualilo de Zaragoza 8,951 ..H3
Tlalancaneca 5,090 ....M1
Tlalmanalco de Velásquez 5,744...............L1
Tlalnepantla de Comonfort 45,575...............L1
Tlalpan 130,719 ....L1
Tlaltenango de Sánchez Román 7,698.....................H6
Tlaltizapan 6,384 ....L2
Tlapacoyan 13,172..................P1
Tlapa de Comonfort 6,676 ......K8
Tlaquepaque 59,760 ....G6
Tlaquiltenango 8,625 ....L2
Tlaxcala de Xicotencatl 9,972.M1
Tlaxco 4,969..........................N1
Toluca de Lerdo 136,092........K7
Tonalá 15,611.........................N8
Topolobampo 4,685................E4
Torreón 244,309......................H4
Tula, Tamaulipas 5,407...........K5
Tula de Allende 10,720 ....K6
Tulancingo 35,799..................K7
Tultepec 8,321 ....L1
Tuxpan, Nayarit 20,322 ....G6
Tuxpan, Jalisco 14,693...........H7
Tuxpan de Rodríguez Cano 33,901...............L6
Tuxtepec 17,701 ....L7
Tuxtla Gutiérrez 66,851 ....N8
Tzucabab 4,876 ....P7
Umán 8,371 ....P6
Unión de Tula 6,399 ....G7
Unión Hidalgo 8,658 ....M8
Uruapan del Progreso 108,124...............H7
Valladolid 14,663 ....P6
Valle de Allende 4,973 ....G3
Valle de Bravo 7,628 ....J7
Valle Hermoso 19,278.............L4
Venustiano Carranza 23,624...N8
Veracruz 255,646 ....Q1
Vicente Guerrero, Durango 8,451 ....G5
Victor Rosales 7,629 ....H5
Villa Acuña 30,276 ....J2
Villa Cuauhtémoc 6,611 ....L5
Villa de Guadelupe Hidalgo 88,537...............L1
Villa Frontera 25,761 ....J3
Villahermosa 133,181.............N8
Villanueva 5,895 ....H5
Villa Unión, Sinaloa 6,789 ....F5
Villa Vicente Guerrero 18,280.N1
Xicoténcatl 6,374 ....K5
Xicotepec de Juárez 12,656 ....L6
Xochimilco 116,493................L1
Yaqui 8,061 ....D3
Yautepec 13,952 ....L2
Zaachila 7,270.........................L8
Zacapoaxtla 4,527 ....O1
Zacapu 31,989 ....J7
Zacatecas 50,251....................H5
Zacatelco 14,117 ....N1
Zacatepec 16,839....................L2
Zacatlán 7,909 ....N1
Zacoalco de Torres 11,343 .....H6
Zamora de Hidalgo 5,775 ....H7
Zaragoza, Coahuila 6,797 ....J2
Zaragoza, Puebla 4,754 ....O1
Zempoala 5,064.......................Q1
Zihuatanejo 4,879....................J8
Zimatlán de Álvarez 5,746.......L8
Zitácuaro 36,911 ....J7
Zumpango de Ocampo 12,923...............L1
Zumpango del Río 8,162.........J8

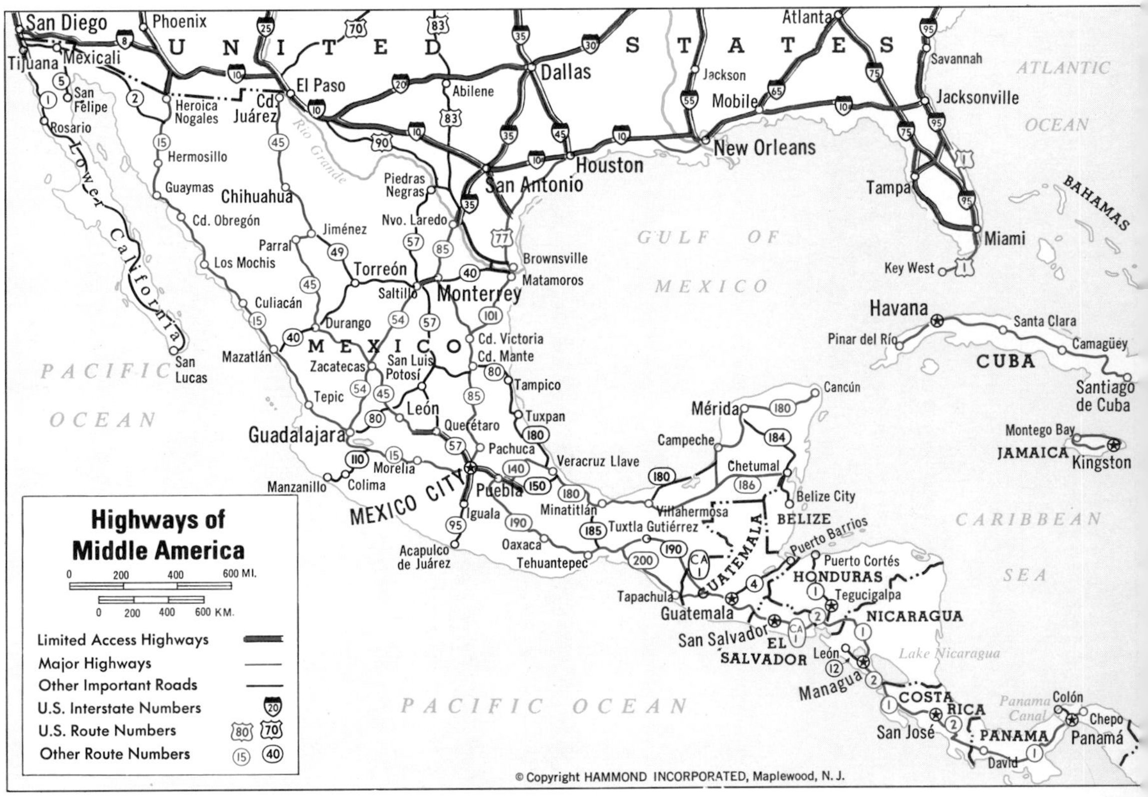
Highways of Middle America
0 200 400 600 MI.
0 200 400 600 KM.
Limited Access Highways
Major Highways
Other Important Roads
U.S. Interstate Numbers
U.S. Route Numbers
Other Route Numbers
San Diego
Phoenix
Tijuana
Mexicali
El Paso
Cd. Juárez
Dallas
Abilene
Atlanta
Jackson
Mobile
Savannah
Jacksonville
New Orleans
Houston
San Antonio
Tampa
Miami
Key West
Hermosillo
Guaymas
Chihuahua
Cd. Obregón
Los Mochis
Culiacán
Mazatlán
San Lucas
Durango
Torreón
Saltillo
Monterrey
Nvo. Laredo
Piedras Negras
Brownsville
Matamoros
Cd. Victoria
Cd. Mante
Tampico
Zacatecas
San Luis Potosí
Tepic
León
Querétaro
Guadalajara
Pachuca
Tuxpan
Veracruz Llave
Manzanillo
Colima
Morelia
MEXICO CITY
Puebla
Iguala
Minatitlán
Oaxaca
Acapulco de Juárez
Tehuantepec
Tuxtla Gutiérrez
Villahermosa
Mérida
Campeche
Cancún
Chetumal
Belize City
BELIZE
GUATEMALA
Tapachula
Guatemala
San Salvador
EL SALVADOR
HONDURAS
Tegucigalpa
Puerto Cortés
Puerto Barrios
NICARAGUA
León
Managua
COSTA RICA
San José
PANAMA
Panamá
Colón
Chepo
David
Havana
Pinar del Río
Santa Clara
Camagüey
CUBA
Santiago de Cuba
Montego Bay
JAMAICA
Kingston
BAHAMAS
UNITED STATES
GULF OF MEXICO
PACIFIC OCEAN
ATLANTIC OCEAN
CARIBBEAN SEA
MEXICO
Lower California
Rio Grande
© Copyright HAMMOND INCORPORATED, Maplewood, N. J.

OTHER FEATURES

Agiobampo (bay) E3
Aguanaval (riv.) H4
Alacrán (reef).........................P5
Amistad (res.) J2
Ángel de la Guarda (isl.) C2
Antigua (riv.) Q1
Arcas (cay) N6
Arena (pt.).............................E5
Arenas (cay) O5
Atoyac (riv.)...........................N2
Atoyac (riv.)...........................Q2
Babia (riv.) J2
Bacalar (lake).........................P7
Ballenas (bay).........................C3
Balsas (riv.)............................J7
Banderas (bay) G6
Bavispe, Río de (riv.)..............E1
Blanco (riv.)...........................Q2
Bravo (Grande) (riv.) G2
Burro (mts.) J2
California (gulf)......................D3
Campeche (bank) O6
Campeche (bay) N7
Candelaria (riv.) O8
Carmen (isl.)..........................D3
Carranza, Venustiano (res.).....J3
Casas Grandes (riv.)................F1
Catoche (cape) Q6
Cedros (isl.) B2
Cerralvo (isl.) E4
Chamela (bay) G7
Chapala (lake).........................H6
Chetumal (bay) P8
Chichén-Itzá (ruin)..................P6
Citlaltépetl (mt.).....................O2
Clarión (isl.) B7
Colorado (riv.) B1
Concepción (bay) D3
Conchos (riv.).........................G2
Corrientes (cape).....................F6
Coyuca (riv.)...........................O1
Cozumel (isl.) Q6
Creciente (isl.) D5
Cuitzeo (lake) J7
Delgada (pt.) L7
Dzibichaltún (ruin) P6
El Azúcar (res.) K3
El Chichón (vol.) N8
Espíritu Santo (isl.).................D4
Falcón (res.)...........................K3
Falso (cape)............................D5
Fuerte (riv.) E3
Giganta, Sierra de la (mts.).....D4
Grande (Bravo) (riv.) G2
Grande de Santiago (riv.)........G6
Grijalva (riv.)..........................N7
Guzmán (lake) F1
Herrero (pt.) Q7
Hondo (riv.) P7
Jesús María (reef)...................L4
La Boquilla (res.) G3
Lacantum (riv.).......................O8
La Paz (bay)...........................D4
Lobos (cape)...........................C2
Lobos (pt.).............................D3
Lower California (pen.) C3
Madre (lag.) L4
Madre del Sur, Sierra (mts.)...K8
Madre Occidental, Sierra (mts.) F3
Madre Oriental, Sierra (mts.) J4
Magdalena (bay) C4
Maldonado (pt.) K8
Mapimí (depr.)........................G3
María Cleófas (isl.) F6
María Madre (isl.)....................F6
María Magdalena (isl.).............F6
Marías, Islas (isls.)..................F6
Mar Muerto (lag.) N9
Mexico (gulf) N4
Mezcala (riv.) J8
Mezquital (riv.) G5
Mita (pt.) G6
Mitla (ruin)............................M8
Moctezuma (riv.) K6
Monserrate (isl.)......................D4
Montague (isl.) B1
Muerto, Mar (lag.) N9
Nauhcampatépetl (mt.)...........O1
Nayarit, Sierra (mts.) G5
Nazas (riv.) G4
Nohkú (pt.) Q7
Nuevo, Bajo (reef)...................O6
Orizaba (Citlaltépetl) (mt.) O2
Palenque (ruin).......................O8
Palmito de la Vírgen (isl.)........F5
Palmito del Verde (isl.)............F5
Pánuco (riv.)...........................K5
Paricutín (vol.)........................H7
Pátzcuaro (lake) J7
Pérez (isl.) P5
Petacalco (bay)........................H8
Popocatépetl (mt.) M1
Ramos (riv.) G4
Revillagigedo (isls.) C7
Roca Partida (isl.)...................C7
Rojo (cape) L6
Sabinas (riv.)...........................J3
San Antonio (reef)...................L4
San Benedicto (isl.) D7
San Benito (isl.) B2
San Jorge (bay) C1
San José (isl.).........................D4
San Lázaro (cape)...................C4
San Lucas (cape) E5
San Marcos (isl.) D3
San Rafael (reef) L4
Santa Ana (reef)......................N7
Santa Catalina (isl.).................D4
Santa Cruz (isl.)......................D4
Santa Eugenia (pt.) B3
Santa Margarita (isl.)..............C4
Santa María (lake) F1
Santa María (riv.) F1
Santiaguillo (lake)...................G4
Sebastián Vizcaíno (bay).........B2
Socorro (isl.) D7
Sonora (riv.) D2
Superior (lag.)........................M9
Teacapán (inlet).......................F5
Tehuantepec (isth.)................M8
Tehuantepec (gulf)..................M9
Teotihuacán (ruin) M1
Términos (lag.).......................O7
Tiburón (isl.)..........................C2
Triángulo Este (isl.) N6
Triángulo Oeste (isl.) N6
Tula (riv.) L1
Urique (riv.)...........................F3
Usumacinta (riv.)....................O8
Uxmal (ruins)..........................P6
Valsequillo (res.) N2
Venustiano Carranza (res.)......J3
Verde (riv.).............................F3
Verde (riv.).............................L8
Yaqui (riv.).............................E2
Yucatán (pen.) P7

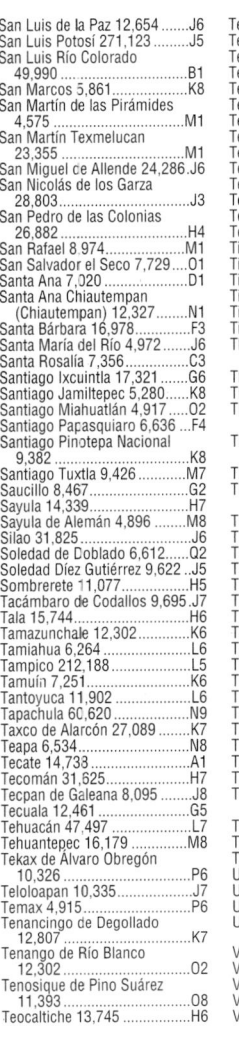

Agriculture, Industry and Resources

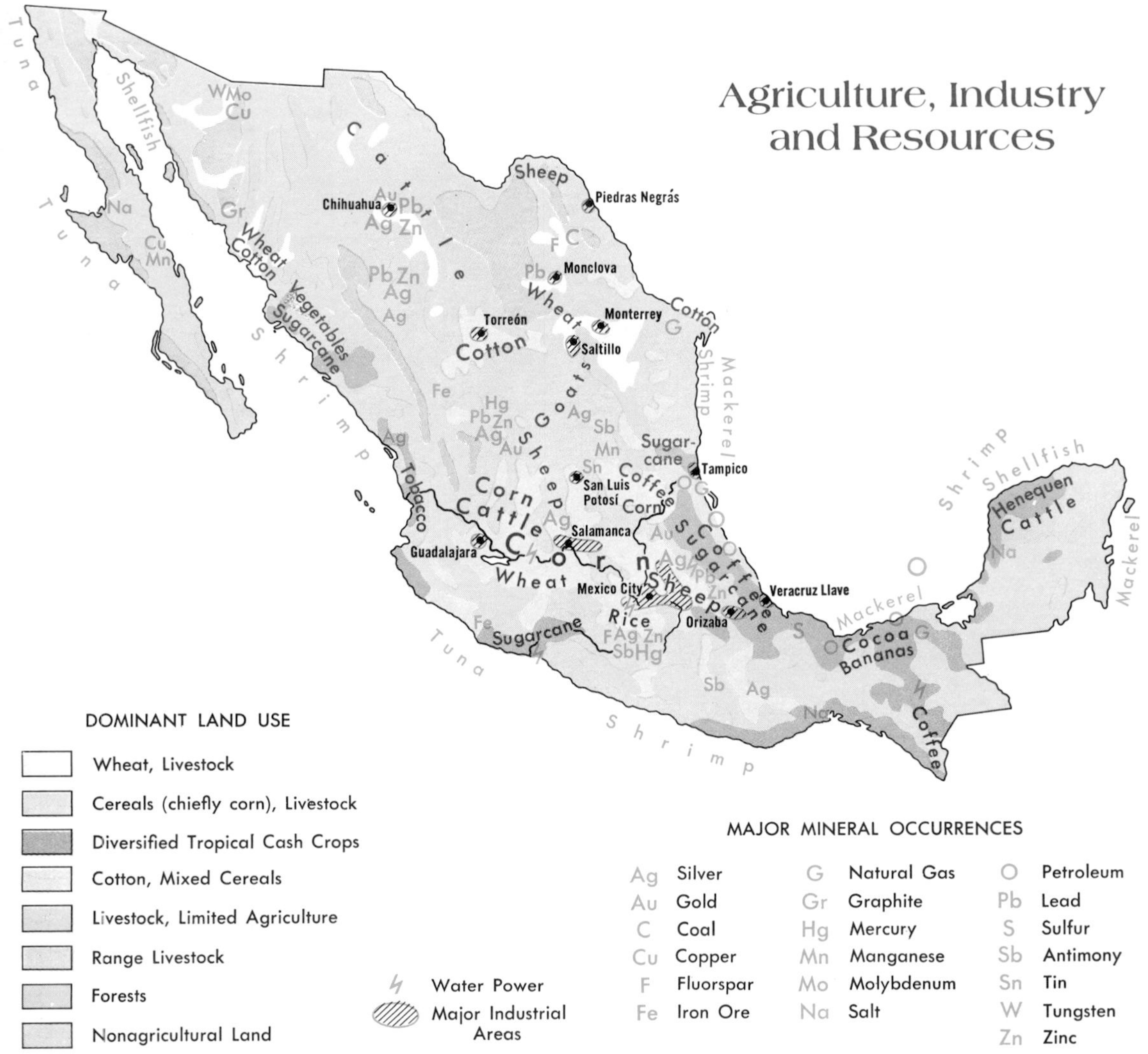
Chihuahua
Piedras Negras
Monclova
Torreón
Monterrey
Saltillo
Tampico
San Luis Potosí
Salamanca
Guadalajara
Mexico City
Veracruz Llave
Orizaba
Cattle
Sheep
Wheat
Cotton
Goats
Vegetables
Sugarcane
Tobacco
Corn
Coffee
Rice
Henequen
Cocoa
Bananas
Tuna
Shrimp
Shellfish
Mackerel
DOMINANT LAND USE
Wheat, Livestock
Cereals (chiefly corn), Livestock
Diversified Tropical Cash Crops
Cotton, Mixed Cereals
Livestock, Limited Agriculture
Range Livestock
Forests
Nonagricultural Land
Water Power
Major Industrial Areas
MAJOR MINERAL OCCURRENCES
Ag Silver
Au Gold
C Coal
Cu Copper
F Fluorspar
Fe Iron Ore
G Natural Gas
Gr Graphite
Hg Mercury
Mn Manganese
Mo Molybdenum
Na Salt
O Petroleum
Pb Lead
S Sulfur
Sb Antimony
Sn Tin
W Tungsten
Zn Zinc

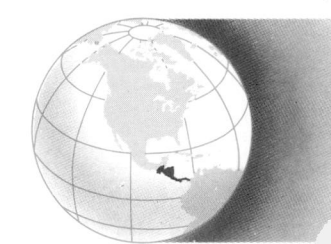

GUATEMALA

AREA 42,042 sq. mi. (108,889 sq. km.)
POPULATION 9,197,000
CAPITAL Guatemala
LARGEST CITY Guatemala
HIGHEST POINT Tajumulco 13,845 ft.
(4,220 m.)
MONETARY UNIT quetzal
MAJOR LANGUAGES Spanish, Quiché
MAJOR RELIGION Roman Catholicism

BELIZE

AREA 8,867 sq. mi. (22,966 sq. km.)
POPULATION 180,000
CAPITAL Belmopan
LARGEST CITY Belize City
HIGHEST POINT Victoria Peak 3,681 ft. (1,122 m.)
MONETARY UNIT Belize dollar
MAJOR LANGUAGES English, Spanish, Mayan
MAJOR RELIGIONS Roman Catholicism, Protestantism

EL SALVADOR

AREA 8,260 sq. mi. (21,393 sq. km.)
POPULATION 5,207,000
CAPITAL San Salvador
LARGEST CITY San Salvador
HIGHEST POINT Santa Ana 7,825 ft.
(2,385 m.)
MONETARY UNIT colón
MAJOR LANGUAGE Spanish
MAJOR RELIGION Roman Catholicism

HONDURAS

AREA 43,277 sq. mi. (112,087 sq. km.)
POPULATION 4,951,000
CAPITAL Tegucigalpa
LARGEST CITY Tegucigalpa
HIGHEST POINT Las Minas 9,347 ft.
(2,849 m.)
MONETARY UNIT lempira
MAJOR LANGUAGE Spanish
MAJOR RELIGION Roman Catholicism

NICARAGUA

AREA 45,698 sq. mi. (118,358 sq. km.)
POPULATION 3,384,000
CAPITAL Managua
LARGEST CITY Managua
HIGHEST POINT Cerro Mocotón 6,913 ft.
(2,107 m.)
MONETARY UNIT córdoba
MAJOR LANGUAGE Spanish
MAJOR RELIGION Roman Catholicism

COSTA RICA

AREA 19,575 sq. mi. (50,700 sq. km.)
POPULATION 2,959,000
CAPITAL San José
LARGEST CITY San José
HIGHEST POINT Chirripó Grande
12,530 ft. (3,819 m.)
MONETARY UNIT colón
MAJOR LANGUAGE Spanish
MAJOR RELIGION Roman Catholicism

PANAMA

AREA 29,761 sq. mi. (77,082 sq. km.)
POPULATION 2,418,000
CAPITAL Panamá
LARGEST CITY Panamá
HIGHEST POINT Vol. Baru 11,401 ft.
(3,475 m.)
MONETARY UNIT balboa
MAJOR LANGUAGE Spanish
MAJOR RELIGION Roman Catholicism

Agriculture, Industry and Resources

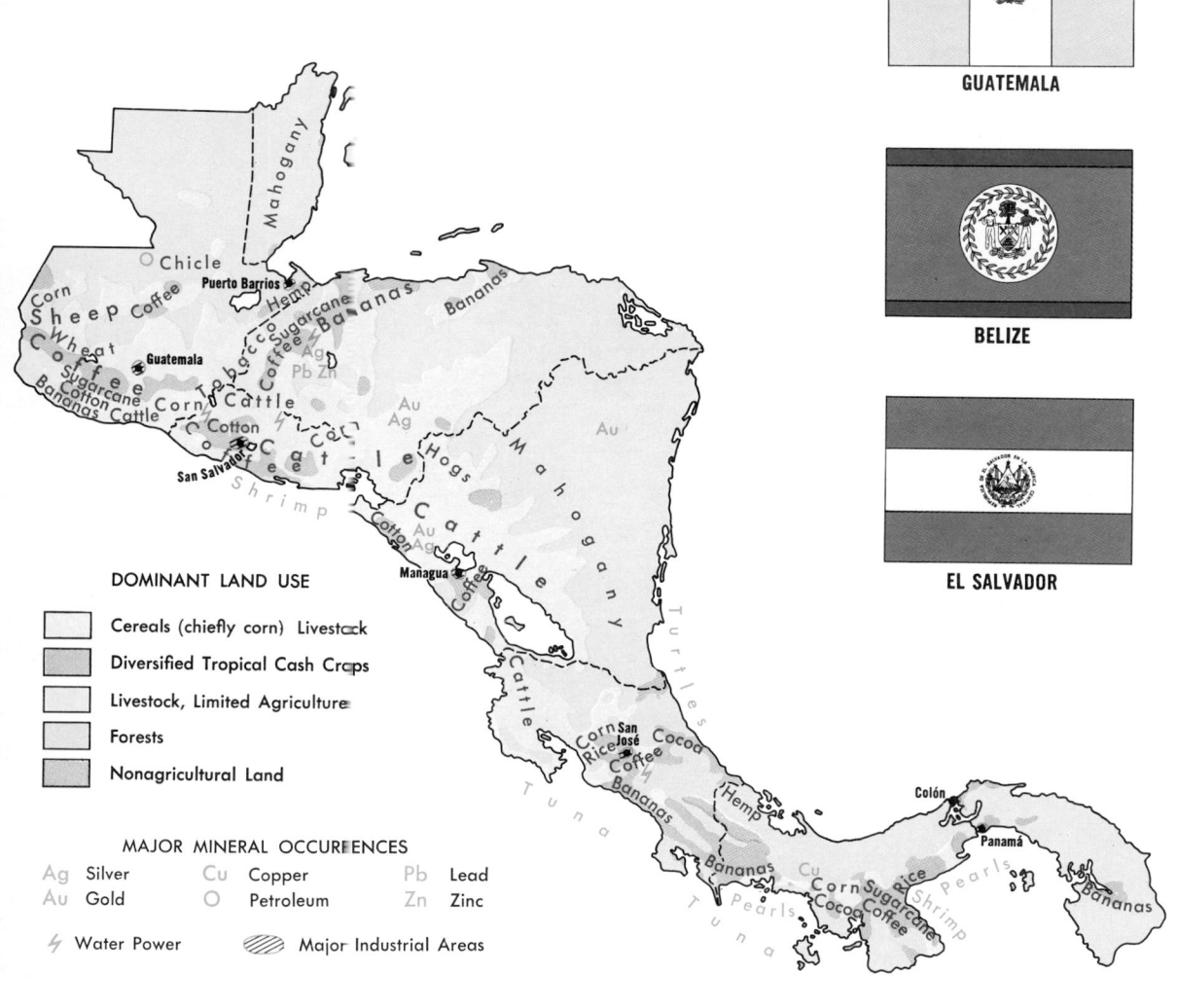

DOMINANT LAND USE

- Cereals (chiefly corn) Livestock
- Diversified Tropical Cash Crops
- Livestock, Limited Agriculture
- Forests
- Nonagricultural Land

MAJOR MINERAL OCCURRENCES

Ag Silver   Cu Copper   Pb Lead
Au Gold   O Petroleum   Zn Zinc

⚡ Water Power   ▨ Major Industrial Areas

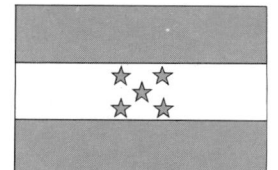

GUATEMALA

HONDURAS

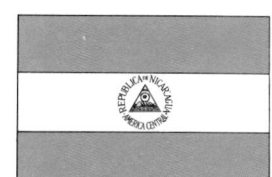

BELIZE

NICARAGUA

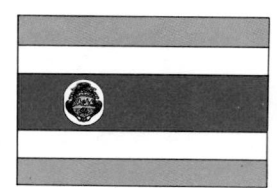

EL SALVADOR

COSTA RICA

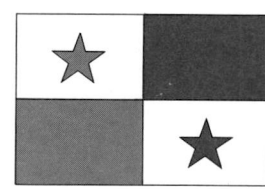

PANAMA

BELIZE

CITIES and TOWNS

Belize City 39,887 ....C2
Belmopan (cap.) 2,932 ....C2
Corozal Town 6,862 ....C1
Hattieville 904 ....C2
Independence 225 ....C2
Libertad 856 ....C1

Orange Walk Town 8,411 ....C1
Punta Gorda 2,219 ....C2
San Ignacio 5,606 ....C2
San José 420 ....C2
San Pedro 213 ....D2
Stann Creek Town 6,627 ....C2

OTHER FEATURES

Ambergris (cay) D1

Belize (riv.) C2
Glover (reef) D2
Half Moon (cay) D2
Hondo (riv.) C1
Honduras (gulf) D2
Mauger (cay) D2
Mya (mts.) C2
New (riv.) C2
Saint Georges (cay) D2
Sarstún (riv.) C3
Turneffe (isls.) D2

COSTA RICA

CITIES and TOWNS

Alajuela 33,122 ....E6
Atenas 1,728 ....E6
Bagaces 2,129 ....E5
Boruca 1,892 ....F6

Buenos Aires 302 ....F6
Cañas 6,053 ....E5
Cartago 21,753 ....F6
Ciudad Quesada 9,754 ....E5
Esparta 4,699 ....E5
Filadelfia 2,958 ....E5
Golfito 6,962 ....F6
Grecia 8,355 ....E5
Guácimo 1,168 ....F5
Guápiles 3,524 ....F5

Heredia 22,700 ....E5
Las Juntas 1,129 ....E5
Liberia 10,802 ....E5
Limón 29,621 ....F6
Miramar 1,673 ....E5
Nicoya 7,474 ....E5
Orotina 3,170 ....E5
Palmares 3,083 ....F6
Paquera F6
Paraíso 8,446 ....F6

Playa Bonita E6
Puerto Cortés 2,070 ....F6
Puntarenas 26,331 ....E6
Quepos 2,155 ....E6
San Ignacio 446 ....E6
San José (cap.) 215,441 ....F5
San Marcos 917 ....F5
San Ramón 9,245 ....E5
Santa Cruz 5,777 ....E5
Santa Rosa E5

continued on following page

Central America

CONIC PROJECTION

SCALE OF MILES
0 25 50   100   150

SCALE OF KILOMETERS
0 25 50   100   150

Capitals of Countries .... ☆
International Boundaries .... — ·· —
Canals .... ·····

Scale 1:5,780,000

© Copyright HAMMOND INCORPORATED, Maplewood, N.J.

San Pedro (riv.) B2
Sarstún (riv.) C3
Tacaná (vol.) A3
Tajumulco (vol.) B3
Tres Puntas (cape) C3
Usumacinta (riv.) B2

HONDURAS

CITIES and TOWNS

Amapala 2,274.....................D4
Brus Laguna 933..................E3
Catacamas 9,134..................E3
Cedros 917...........................D3
Choloma 961.........................C3
Choluteca 26,152..................D4
Comayagua 15,941................C3
Concepción de María 579........D4
Concordia 646.......................D3

Corquín 2,629....................C3
Danlí 10,825.....................D3
El Dulce Nombre 1,297........E3
El Paraíso 6,709................D4
El Paraíso 2,164................C3
El Porvenir 1,076...............D3
El Progreso 28,105.............D3
El Triunfo 2,925.................D4
Goascorán 996..................D4
Gracias 2,299....................C3
Guaimaca 3,953.................D3
Guanaja 1,947...................E2
Guarita 419.......................C3
Guayape 804.....................D3
Jacaleapa 1,609.................D3
Jesús de Otoro 2,976..........C3
Jutiapa 1,126.....................D3
Juticalpa 10,075................D3
La Ceiba 38,788................D3
La Esperanza 2,146...........C3

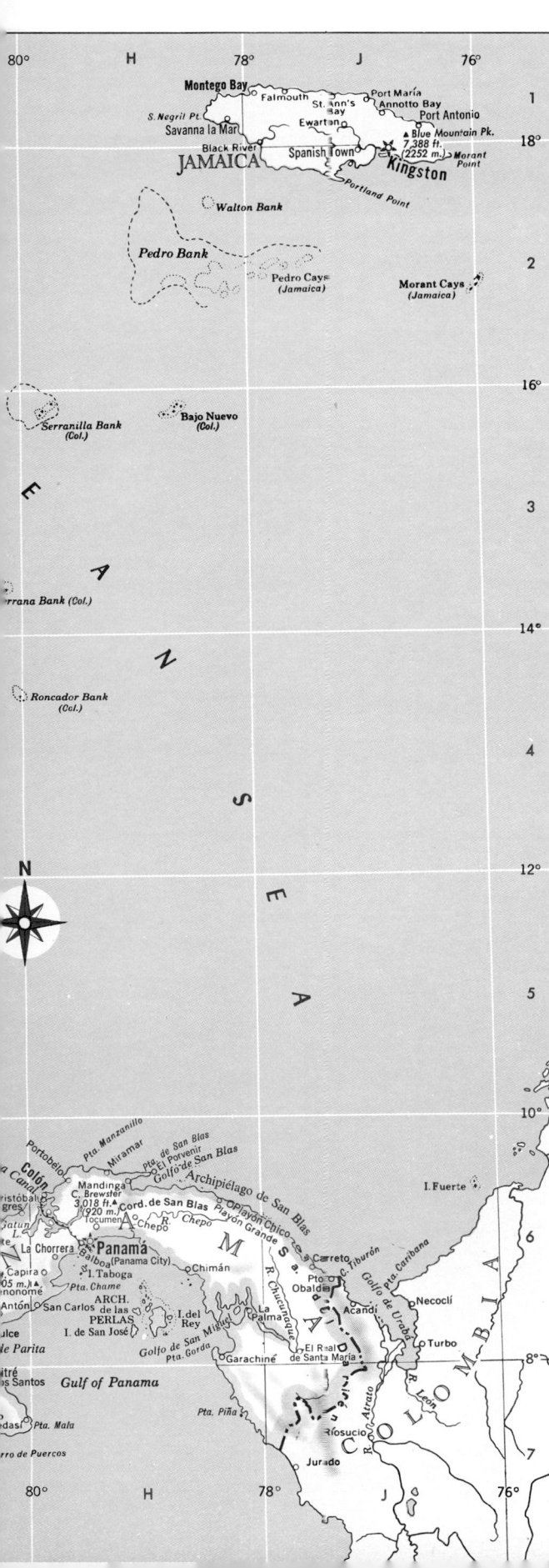

La Paz 6,811.........................D3
Limón 1,704..........................E3
Marcala 3,183.......................C3
Morazán 4,367......................D3
Morocelí 1,442......................D3
Nacaome 6,159......................D4
Namasigüe 816......................D4
Naranjito 2,770......................C3
Nueva Armenia 670................D4
Nueva Ocotepeque 4,724........C3
Olanchito 7,411.....................D3
Omoa 9,161..........................C3
Pespire 1,895........................D4
Puerto Cortés 25,817.............D2
Puerto Lempira 727................F3
Roatán 1,943.........................D2
Sabanagrande 1,446..............D4
San Esteban 610....................D3
San Francisco 1,557...............D3
San Francisco de la Paz 2,291 D3
San Juan de Flores 1,184........C3
San Luis 2,237.......................C3
San Marcos 2,499..................C3
San Pedro Sula 150,991.........C3
San Pedro Zacapa 648............D3
Santa Bárbara 5,883..............C3
Santa Cruz de Yojoa 1,848......D3
Santa Rita 5,298....................C3
Santa Rosa de Aguán 1,622....E2
Santa Rosa de Copán 12,413...C3
Siguatepeque 12,456..............C3
Sinuapa 831..........................C3
Sonaguera 2,264...................D3
Sulaco 1,121.........................D3
Tegucigalpa (cap.) 273,894.....D3
Tela 19,055...........................D3
Teupasenti 2,003...................D3
Tocoa 2,803..........................E3
Trinidad 1,598.......................C3
Trujillo 3,961.........................E3
Utila 1,177............................D2
Villa de San Antonio 2,359......D3
Yoro 4,449............................D3
Yuscarán 1,835.....................D4

OTHER FEATURES

Aguán (riv.) D3
Bahía (isls.) D2
Brus (lag.) E2
Camarón (cape) E2
Caratasca (lag.) F3
Choluteca (riv.) D4
Coco (riv.) E3
Colón (mts.) E3
Esperanza (mts.) D3
Fonseca (gulf) D4
Gorda (bank) F3
Guanaja (isl.) E2
Honduras (cape) E2
Honduras (gulf) D2
Patuca (pt.) E3
Patuca (riv.) E3
Paulaya (riv.) E3
Pija, Sierra de (mts.) D3
Roatán (isl.) D2
San Pablo, Sierra (mts.) E3
Santanilla (Swan) (isls.) F2
Sico (riv.) E3
Sulaco (riv.) D3
Ulúa (riv.) D3
Utila (isl.) D2
Vivorillo (cays) F3
Yojoa (lake) D3

NICARAGUA

CITIES and TOWNS

Acoyapa 2,588 ....E5
Barra de Río Grande.............F4
Bilwaskarma.........................F3
Bluefields 14,252..................F4
Boaco 6,372.........................E4
Bonanza...............................E4
Bragmans Bluff
 (Puerto Cabezas) 5,457......F3
Cabo Gracias a Dios 3,846.....F3
Camoapa 4,385....................E4
Chichigalpa 14,498...............D4
Chinandega 30,441...............D4
Ciudad Darío 5,304...............D4
Comalapa 508......................E4
Condega 3,414.....................D4
Corinto 13,404......................D4
Diriamba 10,085...................D5
El Jícaro 1,669......................E4
El Jicaral 428........................D4
El Limón...............................E4
El Realejo 2,229....................D4
El Sauce 3,202......................D4
El Viejo 8,507........................D4
Esquipulas 2,232..................E4
Estelí 20,222.........................D4
Granada 34,976....................E5
Greytown
 (San Juan del Norte) 294 ...F5
Jalapa 3,633.........................E4
Jinotega 9,506......................E4
Jinotepe 12,473....................D5
Juigalpa 8,497......................E4
La Conquista 458..................D5
La Cruz 150..........................E4
La Libertad 1,286..................E4
La Paz Central 6,175.............D4
La Paz de Oriente 957...........E5
La Trinidad 3,548..................D4
León 55,625..........................D4
Managua (cap.) 398,514.........D4
Masatepe 6,307....................D5
Masaya 30,753......................D5
Matagalpa 21,385.................E4
Mateare 1,405.......................D4
Morrito 368...........................E5
Moyogalpa 1,551..................E5
Muy Muy 1,373.....................E4
Nagarote 7,185.....................D4
Nandaime 5,631....................E5
Ocotal 8,215.........................E4
Palsagua..............................E4
Poneloya..............................D4
Prinzapolka 8,979.................F4
Puerto Cabezas 5,457...........F3
Quilalí 1,245.........................E4
Rama 1,341..........................E5
Rivas 10,125.........................E5
San Carlos 2,022..................E5
San Jorge 2,874....................E5
San Juan del Norte 294..........F5
San Juan del Sur 2,393..........D5
San Miguelito 1,312...............E5
San Rafael del Norte 1,938.....E4
San Rafael del Sur 2,914........D4
Santo Domingo 1,949............E4
Santo Tomás 2,309...............E5
Siuna....................................E4
Somotillo 1,864.....................D4
Somoto 5,847........................D4

Telpaneca 991......................D4
Terrabona 904.......................E4
Teustepe 1,060......................E4
Tipitapa 5,758........................E4
Waspán 1,246........................E3
Yablis....................................F4

OTHER FEATURES

Coco (riv.) E3
Coseguina (pt.) D4
Dariense, Cordillera (range) ...E4
Dipilto, Cordillera (range) D4
Escondido (riv.) F4
Fonseca (gulf) D4
Gracias a Dios (cape) F3
Grande (riv.) E4
Great Corn (isl.) F4
Isabelia, Cordillera (range).....E4
Kukalaya (riv.) F4
Little Corn (isl.) F4
Managua (lake) E4
Miskitos (cays) F3
Monkey (pt.) F5
Mosquitos, Costa de (reg.) E4
Nicaragua (lake) E5
Ometepe (isl.) E5
Perlas (lag.) F4
Perlas (pt.) F4
Prinzapolka (riv.) F4
Salinas (bay) D5
San Juan (riv.) E5
San Juan del Norte (bay) F5
Segovia (riv.) E3
Tuma (riv.) E4
Tyra (cays) F4
Waspuk (riv.) E3
Wawa (riv.) F4
Zapatera (isl.) E5

PANAMA

CITIES and TOWNS

Aguadulce 10,659.................G6
Alanje 866............................F6
Almirante 4,664....................F6
Antón 4,259..........................G6
Bajo Boquete 2,831...............G6
Balboa 1,952........................H6
Bocas del Toro 2,515.............F6
Calobre 609..........................G6
Cañazas 1,526......................G6
Capira 1,749.........................G6
Changuinola 9,528................F6
Chepo 4,529.........................H6
Chiriquí Grande.....................F6
Chitré 17,156........................G6
Coclé del Norte.....................G6
Colón 59,832........................G6
Cristóbal 7,959......................G6
David 50,621.........................F6
Dolega 1,019........................F6
El Porvenir............................H6
El Real de Santa María 912 ....J6
Garachiné 1,116....................H6
Gualaca 1,510.......................F6
Hato del Volcán.....................F6
Horconcitos 1,090.................F6
La Chorrera 36,971................H6
La Concepción 10,460...........F6
La Palma 164........................H6
La Pintada 1,100...................G6
Las Palmas 738.....................G6

Las Tablas 5,230...................G7
Los Santos 4,644...................G7
Mandinga 81.........................H6
Montijo 1,152........................G6
Natá 5,603............................G6
Ocú 2,353.............................G7
Panamá (cap.) 388,638..........H6
Panamá* 498,624..................H6
Parita 1,616..........................G6
Pedasí 934............................G7
Penonomé 7,389...................G6
Playón Chico 1,395...............H6
Portobelo 551.......................H6
Puerto Armuelles 12,488........F6
San Carlos 562.....................H6
San Félix 617........................G6
San Francisco 990.................G6
Santa Fe 490........................G6
Santiago 21,809....................G6
Soná 4,471...........................G6
Tocumen⁼ 21,745..................H6
Tolé 1,052............................G6
Tonosí 891............................G7

OTHER FEATURES

Azuero (pen.) G7
Barú (vol.) F6
Bastimentos (isl.) G6
Brewster, Cerro (mt.) H6
Burica, Punta (cape) F6
Cébaco (isl.) G7
Chame (pt.) H6
Chepo (riv.) H6
Chiriquí (lag.) G6
Chiriquí (gulf) F7
Chucunaque (riv.) J6
Coiba, Isla de (isl.) F7
Colón, Isla de (isl.) G6
Contreras (isls.) F7
Darién (mts.) J6
Escudo de Veraguas (isl.) G6
Gatun (lake) G6
Gorda (pt.) H6
Jicarón (isl.) F7
Mala, Punta (cape) H6
Mariato, Punta (cape) G7
Montijo (gulf) G7
Mosquitos, Golfo de los
 (gulf) G6
Panama (canal) G6
Panama (gulf) H7
Pando, Cerro (mt.) F6
Parida (isl.) F6
Parita (bay) G6
Perlas (arch.) H6
Rey (isl.) H6
San Blas, Archipiélago de
 (arch.) J7
San Blas, Cordillera de
 (mts.) H6
San Blas, Golfo de (bay) H6
San Blas, Pta. de (pt.) H6
San José (isl.) H6
San Miguel, Golfo de (bay) ...H6
Santiago, Cerro (mt.) G7
Secas (isls.) G7
Tabasará (mts.) G6
Taboga (isl.) H6
Tiburón (isl.) F6
Valiente (pen.) G6

* City and suburbs
⁼ Population of district

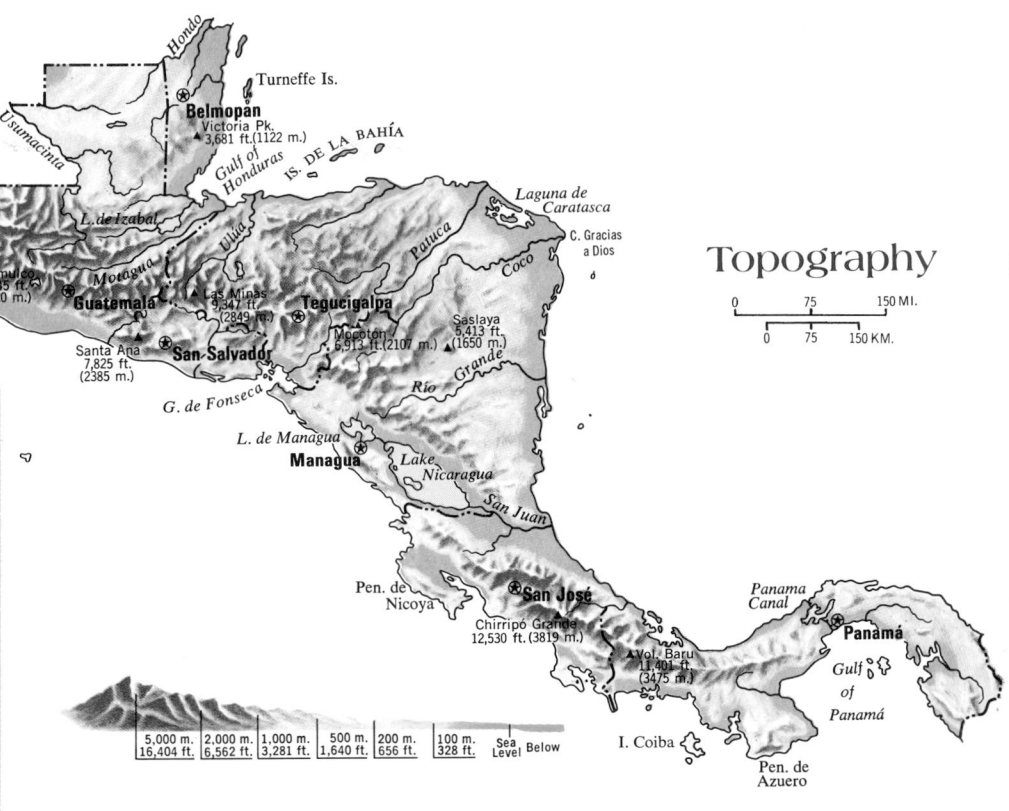

Topography

5,000 m. / 16,404 ft. — 2,000 m. / 6,562 ft. — 1,000 m. / 3,281 ft. — 500 m. / 1,640 ft. — 200 m. / 656 ft. — 100 m. / 328 ft. — Sea Level — Below

CUBA

HAITI

DOMINICAN REPUBLIC

JAMAICA

TRINIDAD AND TOBAGO

BARBADOS

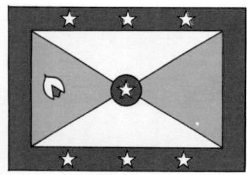
GRENADA

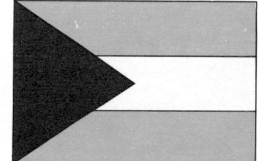
BAHAMAS

DOMINICA

ST. LUCIA

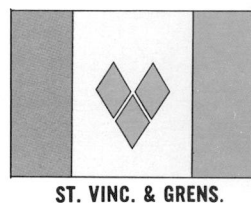
ST. VINC. & GRENS.

ANTIGUA AND BARBUDA

CUBA
AREA 44,206 sq. mi. (114,494 sq. km.)
POPULATION 10,617,000
CAPITAL Havana
LARGEST CITY Havana
HIGHEST POINT Pico Turquino
   6,561 ft. (2,000 m.)
MONETARY UNIT Cuban peso
MAJOR LANGUAGE Spanish
MAJOR RELIGION Roman Catholicism

HAITI
AREA 10,694 sq. mi. (27,697 sq. km.)
POPULATION 5,609,000
CAPITAL Port-au-Prince
LARGEST CITY Port-au-Prince
HIGHEST POINT Pic La Selle 8,793 ft. (2,680 m.)
MONETARY UNIT gourde
MAJOR LANGUAGES Creole French, French
MAJOR RELIGION Roman Catholicism

DOMINICAN REPUBLIC
AREA 18,704 sq. mi. (48,443 sq. km.)
POPULATION 6,867,000
CAPITAL Santo Domingo
LARGEST CITY Santo Domingo
HIGHEST POINT Pico Duarte
   10,417 ft. (3,175 m.)
MONETARY UNIT Dominican peso
MAJOR LANGUAGE Spanish
MAJOR RELIGION Roman Catholicism

JAMAICA
AREA 4,411 sq. mi. (11,424 sq. km.)
POPULATION 2,392,000
CAPITAL Kingston
LARGEST CITY Kingston
HIGHEST POINT Blue Mountain Peak
   7,402 ft. (2,256 m.)
MONETARY UNIT Jamaican dollar
MAJOR LANGUAGE English
MAJOR RELIGIONS Protestantism,
   Roman Catholicism

PUERTO RICO
AREA 3,515 sq. mi. (9,104 sq. km.)
POPULATION 3,522,037
CAPITAL San Juan
MONETARY UNIT U.S. dollar
MAJOR LANGUAGES Spanish, English
MAJOR RELIGION Roman Catholicism

NETHERLANDS ANTILLES
AREA 390 sq. mi. (1,010 sq. km.)
POPULATION 246,000
CAPITAL Willemstad
MONETARY UNIT Antilles guilder
MAJOR LANGUAGES Dutch, Papiamento, English
MAJOR RELIGIONS Roman Catholicism,
   Protestantism

BERMUDA
AREA 21 sq. mi. (54 sq. km.)
POPULATION 67,761
CAPITAL Hamilton
MONETARY UNIT Bermuda dollar
MAJOR LANGUAGE English
MAJOR RELIGION Protestantism

ARUBA
AREA 75 sq. mi (193 sq. km.)
POPULATION 66,790
CAPITAL Oranjestad
MONETARY UNIT Aruba guilder
MAJOR LANGUAGES Dutch, Papiamento
MAJOR RELIGION Roman Catholic

ANGUILLA

Anguilla (isl.) 6,519 . . . . F3

ANTIGUA and BARBUDA

Antigua (isl.) 76,213 . . . . G3
Barbuda (isl.) 1,071 . . . . G3
Caribbean (sea) B4
Codrington 1,071 . . . . G3
Falmouth 1,134 . . . . F3
Redonda (isl.) F3
Saint John's (cap.) 21,814 . . . . . . G3

ARUBA

Aruba (isl.) 66,790 . . . . E4

BAHAMAS

Acklins (isl.) 616 . . . . C2
Andros (isl.) 8,397 . . . . B1
Atwood (Samana) (cay) D2
Berry (isls.) 509 . . . . B1
Biminis, The (isls.) 1,432 . . . . . . B1
Caicos (passg.) D2
Cat (isl.) 2,143 . . . . C1
Cay Sal (bank) B2
Crooked (isl.) 517 . . . . D2
Eleuthera (isl.) 8,326 . . . . C1
Exuma (cays) C1
Flamingo (cay) C2
Freeport 22,301 . . . . B1
Grand Bahama (isl.) 33,102 . . . . . B1
Great Abaco (isl.) 7,324 . . . . C1
Great Bahama (bank) B1
Great Exuma (isl.) C2
Great Inagua (isl.) 939 . . . . D2
Great Isaac (isl.) B1

Gun (cay) B1
Harbour (isl.) C1
Little Inagua (isl.) D2
Long (cay) 33 . . . . C2
Long (isl.) 3,353 . . . . C2
Mayaguana (isl.) 476 . . . . D2
Mira Por Vos (cays) C2
Nassau (cap.) 135,437 . . . . C1
New Providence (isl.) 135,437 . . . C1
Old Bahama (chan.) B2
Plana (cays) D2
Ragged (isl.) 146 . . . . C2
Rum (cay) C2
Samana (cay) D2
San Salvador (isl.) D1
Santarén (chan.) B1
Tongue of the Ocean (chan.) C1
Verde (cay) C2
Watling (San Salvador) (isl.) C1

BARBADOS

Bridgetown (cap.) 7,552 . . . . G4
Speightstown G4

BERMUDA

Bermuda (isl.) H3
Castle (harb.) H2
Great (sound) G3
Hamilton (cap.) 1,617 . . . . G3
Harrington (sound) H3
Ireland (isl.) G3
North (rapid) H2
Saint Davids (isl.) H2
Saint George 1,647 . . . . H2
Saint George's (isl.) H2
Somerset (isl.) G3

CAYMAN ISLANDS

Bartlett Deep B3
Cayman Brac (isl.) 1,603 . . . . B3
George Town (cap.) 7,617 . . . . . . B3
Grand Cayman (isl.) 15,000 . . . . . B3
Little Cayman (isl.) 74 . . . . B3
Misteriosa (bank) A3

CUBA

Bayamo 109,201 . . . . C2
Camagüey 245,235 . . . . B2
Cienfuegos 107,396 . . . . B2
Florida (str.) B1
Guanabacoa 89,741 . . . . B2
Guantánamo 178,129 . . . . C2
Havana (cap.) 1,924,886 . . . . A2
Holguín 190,155 . . . . C2
Juventud (Pines) (isl.) 57,879 . . . A2
Manzanillo 95,420 . . . . C2
Marianao ○127,563 . . . . A2
Matanzas 103,302 . . . . B2
Pinar del Río 104,598 . . . . A2
San Felipe (cays) A2
Santa Clara 175,113 . . . . B2
Santiago de Cuba 362,432 . . . . . C3
Windward (passg.) C3

DOMINICA

Portsmouth 2,329 . . . . G4
Roseau (cap.) 9,968 . . . . G4

DOMINICAN REPUBLIC

'La Romana 91,571 . . . . E3
San Francisco de Macorís 64,906 . E3
San Pedro de Macorís 78,562 . . . E3
Santiago 278,638 . . . . E3
Santo Domingo (cap.) 1,313,172 . . E3

GRENADA

Carriacou (isl.) 6,052 . . . . G4
Gouyave 2,498 . . . . F4
Grenadines (isls.) G4
Saint George's (cap.) 6,463 . . . . . F5

GUADELOUPE

Basse-Terre (cap.) 13,397 . . . . . . F4
Saint-Barthélemy (isl.) 3,059 . . . . F3
Saint Martin (isl.) 8,072 . . . . F3

HAITI

Cap-Haïtien 64,406 . . . . D3
Gonaïves 34,209 . . . . D3
Port-au-Prince (cap.) 449,831 . . . . D3
Gonâve (isl.) D3
Jamaica (chan.) C3
Tortuga (isl.) D2

JAMAICA

Blue Mountain (peak) C3
Jamaica (chan.) C3
Kingston (cap.) 106,791 . . . . C3
Montego Bay 43,521 . . . . B3
Pedro (cays) C3
Savanna-la-Mar 11,759 . . . . B3

MARTINIQUE

Fort-de-France (cap.) 96,649 . . . . G4
Saint-Pierre 4,923 . . . . G4
Pelée (vol.) G4

MONTSERRAT

Plymouth (cap.) 1,623 . . . . F3

NETHERLANDS ANTILLES

Bonaire (isl.) E4
Curaçao (isl.) E4
Oranjestad 10,100 . . . . D4
Saba (isl.) F3
Saint Eustatius (isl.) F3
Saint Martin (Sint Maarten) (isl.) . F3
Willemstad (cap.) 95,000 . . . . . . E4

PUERTO RICO

Bayamón 185,087 . . . . G1
Caguas 87,214 . . . . G1
Culebra (isl.) 1,265 . . . . G1
Mayagüez 82,968 . . . . F1
Mona (passg.) E3
Ponce 161,739 . . . . F1

San Juan (cap.) 424,600 . . . . G1
Vieques (isl.) 7,662 . . . . G1

SAINT KITTS and NEVIS

Basseterre (cap.) 14,725 . . . . F3
Nevis (isl.) 9,300 . . . . F3
Saint Christopher (isl.) 35,104 . . . F3

SAINT LUCIA

Castries (cap.) ●42,770 . . . . G4
Vieux Fort ●10,675 . . . . G4

SAINT VINCENT and THE GRENADINES

Bequia (isl.) G4
Georgetown 1,100 . . . . G4
Grenadines (isls.) 8,371 . . . . G4
Kingstown (cap.) 17,117 . . . . G4

TRINIDAD and TOBAGO

Port-of-Spain (cap.) 67,978 . . . . . G5
Scarborough 6,057 . . . . G5
Tobago (isl.) 39,695 . . . . G5
Trinidad (isl.) 1,020,130 . . . . G5

TURKS and CAICOS ISLANDS

Caicos (isls.) 4,008 . . . . D2
Cockburn Harbour D2
Grand Caicos (isl.) 371 . . . . D2
Grand Turk (isl.) 3,146 . . . . D2
Providenciales (isl.) 979 . . . . D2
Turks (isls.) 3,348 . . . . D2

VIRGIN ISLANDS (British)

Anegada (isl.) 89 . . . . H1
Jost Van Dyke (isl.) 135 . . . . G1
Road Town (cap.) 2,200 . . . . H1
Tortola (isl.) 9,257 . . . . H1
Virgin Gorda (isl.) 1,443 . . . . H1

VIRGIN ISLANDS (U.S.)

Charlotte Amalie (cap.) 11,842 . . . H1
Christiansted 2,914 . . . . H1
Fredriksted 1,046 . . . . G2
Saint Croix (isl.) 49,725 . . . . H2
Saint John (isl.) 2,472 . . . . H1
Saint Thomas (isl.) 44,372 . . . . . G1

WEST INDIES

Antilles, Greater (isls.) B2
Antilles, Lesser (isls.) E4
Aves (Bird) (isl.) F4
Hispaniola (isl.) D2
Leeward (isls.) F3
Navassa (isl.) C3
Windward (isls.) G4

● Population of district.
○ Population of municipality.

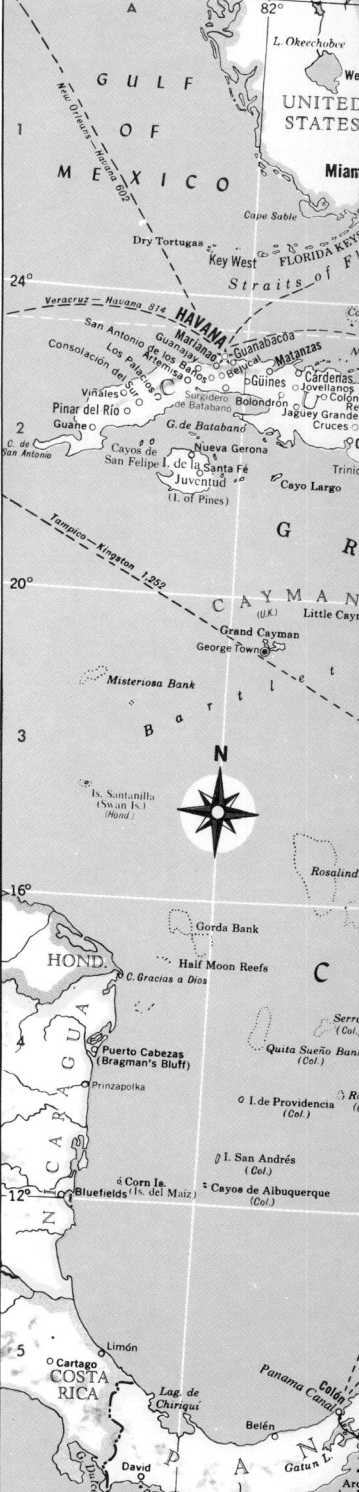

Topography

TRINIDAD AND TOBAGO

AREA 1,980 sq. mi. (5,128 sq. km.)
POPULATION 1,212,000
CAPITAL Port of Spain
LARGEST CITY Port of Spain
HIGHEST POINT Mt. Aripo 3,084 ft. (940 m.)
MONETARY UNIT Trinidad and Tobago dollar
MAJOR LANGUAGES English, Hindi
MAJOR RELIGIONS Roman Catholicism,
Protestantism, Hinduism, Islam

SAINT KITTS AND NEVIS

SAINT LUCIA

AREA 238 sq. mi. (616 sq. km.)
POPULATION 148,000
CAPITAL Castries
HIGHEST POINT Mt. Gimie 3,117 ft. (950 m.)
MONETARY UNIT East Caribbean dollar
MAJOR LANGUAGES English, French patois
MAJOR RELIGIONS Roman Catholicism,
Protestantism

BARBADOS

AREA 166 sq. mi. (430 sq. km.)
POPULATION 256,000
CAPITAL Bridgetown
LARGEST CITY Bridgetown
HIGHEST POINT Mt. Hillaby 1,104 ft.
(336 m.)
MONETARY UNIT Barbadian dollar
MAJOR LANGUAGE English
MAJOR RELIGION Protestantism

BAHAMAS

AREA 5,382 sq. mi. (13,939 sq. km.)
POPULATION 253,000
CAPITAL Nassau
LARGEST CITY Nassau
HIGHEST POINT Mt. Alvernia 206 ft. (63 m.)
MONETARY UNIT Bahamian dollar
MAJOR LANGUAGE English
MAJOR RELIGIONS Roman Catholicism,
Protestantism

SAINT VINCENT AND THE GRENADINES

AREA 150 sq. mi. (388 sq. km.)
POPULATION 124,000
CAPITAL Kingstown
HIGHEST POINT Soufrière 4,000 ft. (1,219 m.)
MONETARY UNIT East Caribbean dollar
MAJOR LANGUAGE English
MAJOR RELIGIONS Protestantism,
Roman Catholicism

GRENADA

AREA 133 sq. mi. (344 sq. km.)
POPULATION 103,103
CAPITAL St. George's
LARGEST CITY St. George's
HIGHEST POINT Mt. St. Catherine
2,757 ft. (840 m.)
MONETARY UNIT East Caribbean dollar
MAJOR LANGUAGES English, French patois
MAJOR RELIGIONS Roman Catholicism,
Protestantism

DOMINICA

AREA 290 sq. mi. (751 sq. km.)
POPULATION 81,000
CAPITAL Roseau
HIGHEST POINT Morne Diablotin
4,747 ft. (1,447 m.)
MONETARY UNIT Dominican dollar
MAJOR LANGUAGES English, French patois
MAJOR RELIGIONS Roman Catholicism,
Protestantism

ANTIGUA AND BARBUDA

AREA 171 sq. mi. (443 sq. km.)
POPULATION 76,000
CAPITAL St. John's
HIGHEST POINT Boggy Peak 1,319 ft. (402 m.)
MONETARY UNIT East Caribbean dollar
MAJOR LANGUAGE English
MAJOR RELIGION Protestantism

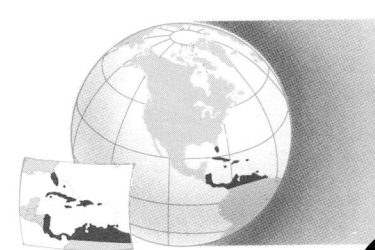

SAINT KITTS & NEVIS

AREA 104 sq. mi. (269 sq. km.)
POPULATION 44,404
CAPITAL Basseterre
HIGHEST POINT Mt. Misery 4,314 ft.
(1,315 m.)
MONETARY UNIT East Caribbean dollar
MAJOR LANGUAGE English
MAJOR RELIGIONS Protestantism,
Roman Catholicism

The West Indies

CONIC PROJECTION

SCALE OF MILES

0   50   100   150   200

SCALE OF KILOMETERS

0   50   100   200   300

Capitals of Countries _____ ☆
Other Capitals _____ ◉

Scale 1:11,200,000

Distances are given in Nautical Miles

Puerto Rico

Bermuda Islands

© Copyright HAMMOND INCORPORATED, Maplewood, N.J.

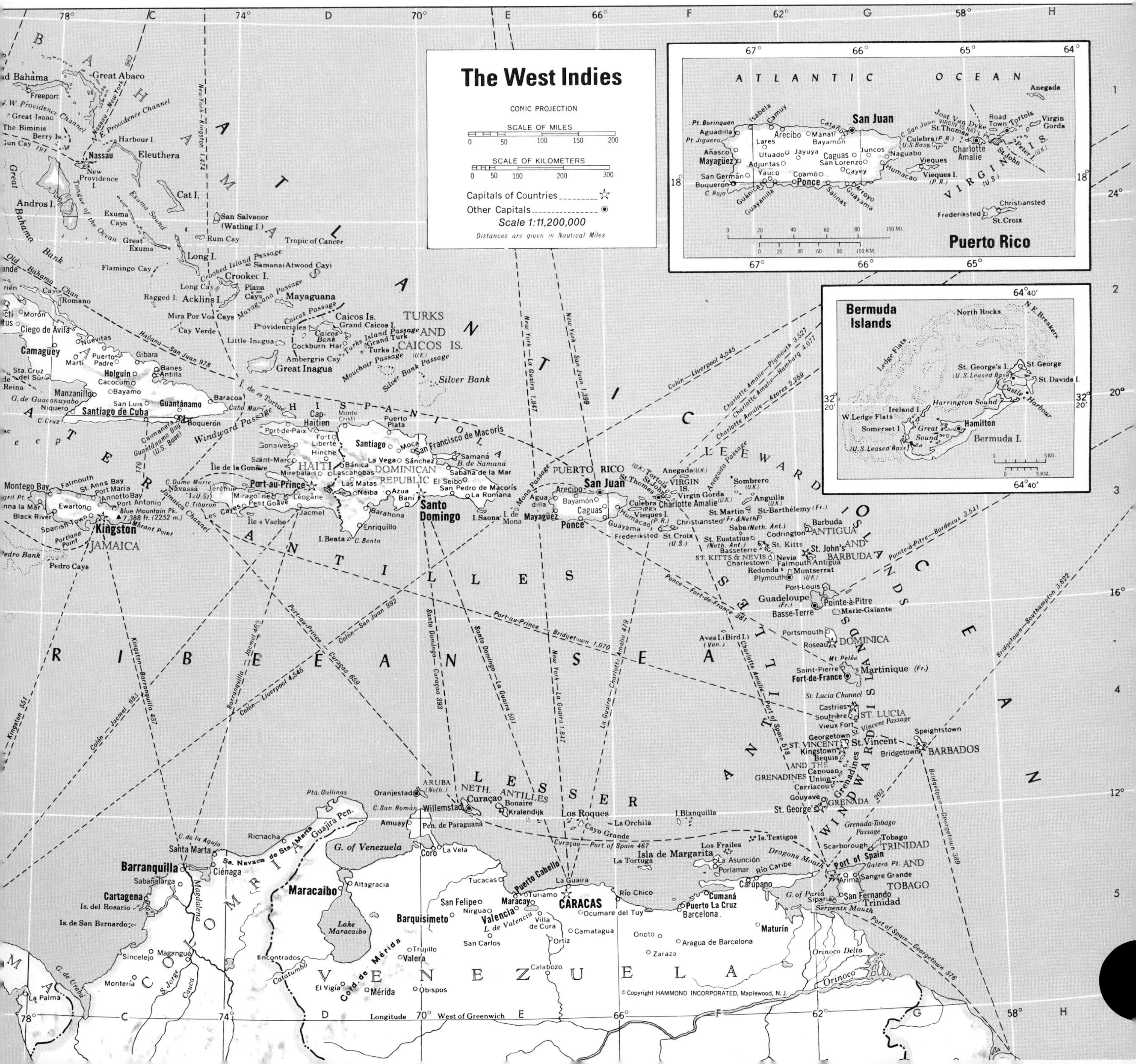

CUBA

PROVINCES

Camagüey, 664,566 ....G2
Ciego de Ávila 320,961 ...F2
Cienfuegos 326,412 ....E2
Granma 739,335 ....H4
Guantánamo 466,609 ......K4
Holguín 911,034 ....J3
Juventud (municipio
  especial) 57,879 ....C2
La Habana, Ciudad de
  Habana 1,924,886 ....C1
La Habana (Havana) 586,029 C1
Las Tunas 436,341 ....H3
Matanzas 557,628 ....D1
Pinar del Río 640,740 .....A2
Sancti Spíritus 399,700 ...F2
Santiago de Cuba 909,506 .H4
Villa Clara 764,743 ....E1

CITIES and TOWNS

Abreus 14,267 ....D2
Agramonte 4,603 ....G3
Aguada de Pasajeros 20,219 D2
Alacranes 4,959 ....D1
Alonso Rojas 1,427 ....B2
Alquízar 12,691 ....C1
Altagracia 1,722 ....G3
Alto Songo-La Maya 25,188 .J4

Amarillas 2,767 ....D2
Amazonas 1,066 ....F2
Antilla 10,052 ....J3
Arroyo Blanco 1,431 ....F2
Artemisa 45,689 ....B1
Báez 4,178 ....E2
Báguanos 12,678 ....J3
Bahía Honda 16,901 ....B1
Baire 4,879 ....H4
Banao 803 ....F2
Banes 38,905 ....J3
Baracoa 36,702 ....K4
Baraguá 12,633 ....G2
Bauta 26,826 ....C1
Bayamo 109,201 ....H4
Bejucal 15,649 ....C1
Bolondrón 5,840 ....D1
Buenaventura 4,711 ......H3
Buenavista 1,303 ....F2
Buey Arriba 8,017 ....H4
Cabaiguán 36,544 ....F2
Cabañas 4,897 ....B1
Cabezas 5,262 ....C1
Cacocum 14,145 ....H3
Caibarién 32,094 ....F2
Caimanera 6,664 ....K4
Calabazar de Sagua 9,023 .E1
Calimete 19,925 ....D1
Camagüey 245,235 ....G2
Campechuela 20,743 ......G4
Canasí 1,637 ....C1

Candelaria 10,810 ....B1
Cárdenas 65,585 ....D1
Cartagena 2,166 ....D2
Cascajal 3,530 ....E1
Cauto del Embarcadero 949 .H4
Cauto el Cristo 1,626 ....J3
Central Amancio Rodríguez
  22,506 ....G3
Central Bolivia 6,301 ....J4
Central Brasil 4,904 .....G2
Central Cándido González
  3,414 ....G3
Central Colombia 16,799 ..G2
Central Frank País 9,066 ..K3
Central Guatemala 5,584 ..J3
Central Haití 3,609 ......J3
Central Los Reynaldos 3,997 .J4
Central Loynaz Echeverría
  3,245 ....J3
Central Manuel Tames 7,864 K4
Céspedes 6,634 ....G2
Chambas 19,877 ....F2
Chaparra 8,428 ....H3
Cidra 3,567 ....D1
Ciego de Ávila 80,010 ....F2
Cienfuegos 107,396 ......E2
Colón 47,010 ....D1
Condado 33,115 ....F2
Consolación del Norte 4,681 B1
Consolación del Sur 34,334 .B2
Contramaestre 44,991 ....J4
Corralillo 15,822 ....D1

Cruces 20,324 ....E2
Cueto 23,183 ....J3
Cumanayagua 25,338 .....E2
Daiquirí J4
Delicias 10,562 ....H3
Dos Caminos 3,772 ......J4
Dos Ríos 1,786 ....J4
El Caney 3,921 ....J4
El Cobre 3,952 ....J4
El Santo 2,473 ....E1
Encrucijada 23,029 ......E1
Esmeralda 17,205 ....G1
Esperanza 9,241 ....E2
Florencia 6,979 ....F2
Florida 43,881 ....G2
Fomento 17,310 ....E2
Gaspar 2,682 ....F2
Gibara 23,137 ....J3
Guáimaro 29,712 ....G3
Guanabacoa 89,741 ......C1
Guanajay 21,042 ....B1
Guane 14,126 ....A2
Guantánamo 178,129 .....K4
Guaro 3,086 ....J3
Guasimal 3,057 ....E2
Guayabal 3,703 ....G3
Guayos 6,753 ....F2
Güines 51,691 ....C1
Güira de Melena 19,851 ..C1
Guisa 5,182 ....H4
Havana (cap.) 1,924,886 ..C1
Herradura 3,762 ....B1

Holguín 190,155 ....J3
Ignacio Agramonte 1,487 .G3
Imías 4,491 ....K4
Isabela de Sagua 3,721 ...E1
Jagüey Grande 30,205 ....D2
Jamaica 5,128 ....K4
Jaruco 16,844 ....C1
Jatibonico 17,047 ....F2
Jíbaro 1,263 ....F2
Jiguaní 25,069 ....H4
Jobabo 14,899 ....H3
Jovellanos 35,043 ......D1
La Coloma 3,462 ....B2
La Maya-Alto Songo 25,188 .J4
Las Martinas 4,511 ......A2
Limonar 9,629 ....D1
Los Arabos 10,664 ......E1
Los Palacios 21,884 .....B1
Lugareño 4,396 ....G3
Mabay 6,176 ....H4
Maceo 2,652 ....J4
Majagua 9,110 ....F2
Manacas 5,914 ....E1
Manatí 11,054 ....H3
Manguito 2,739 ....D1
Manicaragua 33,900 ......E2
Mantua 9,165 ....A2
Mapos (Amazonas) 1,066 ..F2
Manzanillo 95,420 ....G4
Mariano ○127,563 ....C1
Mariel 24,115 ....B1
Martí 11,474 ....D1

Matanzas 103,302 ....C1
Máximo Gómez, Ciego
  de Ávila 5,116 ....F2
Máximo Gómez, Matanzas
  4,970 ....D1
Mayajigua 4,425 ....E2
Mayarí 54,699 ....J3
Mayarí Arriba 2,302 .....J4
Media Luna 13,794 ......G4
Mendoza 2,914 ....A2
Meneses 4,768 ....F2
Minas 17,675 ....G2
Minas de Matahambre
  14,976 ....A1
Moa 28,696 ....K3
Morón 40,396 ....F2
Nicaro 9,056 ....J3
Niquero 15,544 ....G4
Nueva Gerona 17,175 ....B2
Nuevitas 35,103 ....G2
Orozco 4,256 ....B1
Palma Soriano 66,222 ....J4
Palmira 19,680 ....E2
Pedro Betancourt 22,915 ..C1
Perico 20,633 ....D1
Pilón 10,194 ....H4
Pinar del Río 104,598 ....B2
Placetas 46,038 ....E2
Primero Enero 14,807 ....F2
Puerto Esperanza 3,499 ..A1
Puerto Padre 46,806 .....H3
Quemado de Güines 11,208 E1

Rancho Veloz 3,966 ......D1
Ranchuelo 34,255 ....E2
Regla 38,491 ....C1
Remedios 27,722 ....E1
República Dominicana
  2,540 ....E2
Río Cauto 19,550 ....H4
Rodas 16,350 ....E2
Sagua de Tánamo 15,327 ..K3
Sagua la Grande 52,315 ...E1
San Andrés 2,127 ....H3
San Antonio de los Baños
  28,137 ....C1
San Cristóbal 30,769 ....B1
San Diego de los Baños
  1,430 ....B2
San Germán 12,362 ......J3
San José de las Lajas
  37,149 ....C1
San José de los Ramos
  1,726 ....D1
San Juan y Martínez 13,227 .B2
San Luis, Pinar del Río
  5,677 ....B2
San Luis, Santiago de Cuba
  32,826 ....J4
San Nicolás 12,368 ......C1
San Ramón 2,676 ....H4
Santa Clara 175,113 .....E2
Santa Cruz del Norte
  15,239 ....C1

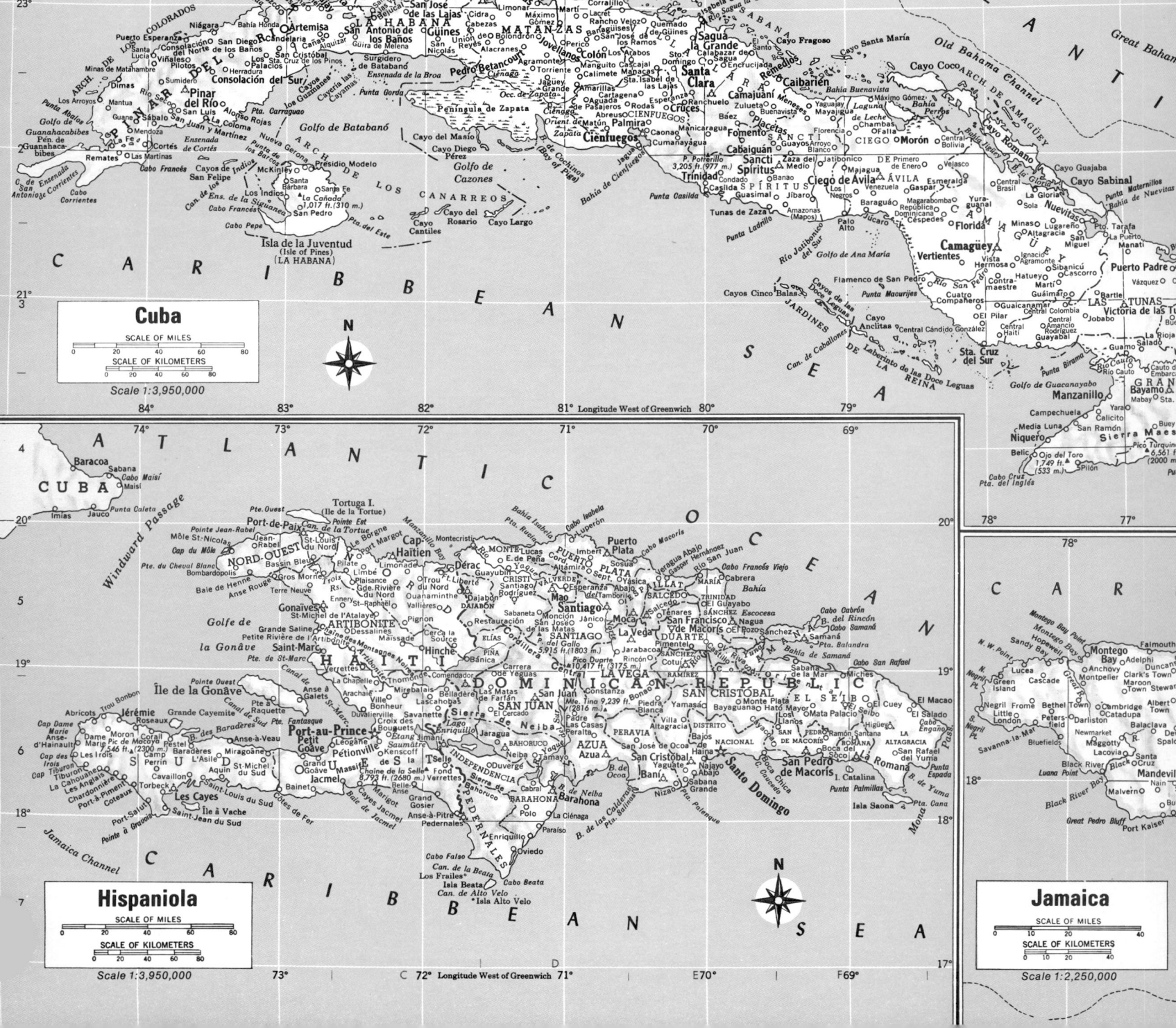

Cuba
SCALE OF MILES
0 20 40 60 80
SCALE OF KILOMETERS
0 20 40 60 80
Scale 1:3,950,000

Hispaniola
SCALE OF MILES
0 20 40 60 80
SCALE OF KILOMETERS
0 20 40 60 80
Scale 1:3,950,000

Jamaica
SCALE OF MILES
0 10 20 30 40
SCALE OF KILOMETERS
0 10 20 30 40
Scale 1:2,250,000

Santa Cruz de los Pinos
3,545 .... B1
Santa Cruz del Sur 27,142 . G3
Santa Fe 3,925 .... B2
Santa Isabel de las Lajas
7,279 .... E2
Santa Lucía 3,734 .... J3
Santa Rita 6,358 .... H4
Santiago de Cuba 362,432 . J4
Santiago de las Vegas
29,325 .... C1
Santo Domingo 32,950 .... E1
Sibanicú 14,252 .... G3
Sola 2,436 .... G2
Sumidero 980 .... A2
Surgidero de Batabanó
11,533 .... C1
Tacajó 4,469 .... J3
Torriente 1,759 .... D11
Trinidad 42,080 .... E2
Unión de Reyes 28,422 .... C1
Varadero 14,737 .... D1
Vázquez 3,851 .... H3
Velasco 5,618 .... H3
Venezuela 13,744 .... F2
Vertientes 25,178 .... G3
Victoria de las Tunas 87,522 H3
Viñales 2,049 .... A1
Yaguajay 30,720 .... F2
Yara 238,879 .... H4
Zaza del Medio 7,495 ..... F2
Zulueta 5,425 .... E2

OTHER FEATURES

Abalos (pt.) A2
Ana María (gulf) F3
Anclitas (cay) F3
Batabanó (gulf) C2
Birama (pt.) G4
Broa (inlet) C1
Buenavista (bay) F2
Caballones (chan.) F3
Camagüey (arch.) G2
Cantiles (cay) C3
Cárdenas (bay) D1
Carraguao (pt.) B2
Casilda (pt.) E2
Cauto (riv.) H3
Cayamas (cays) C2
Cayos (cays) C2
Cazones (gulf) C2
Cienfuegos (bay) D2
Cinco Balas (cays) E3
Cochinos (bay) D2
Coco (cay) G1
Corrientes (cape) A2
Corrientes (inlet) A2
Cortés (inlet) B2
Cristal, Sierra del (mts.) . J3
Cruz (cape) G4
Diego Pérez (cay) C2
Doce Leguas (cays) F3
Este (pt.) C3
Fragoso (cay) F1
Francés (cape) A2

Gorda (pt.) C2
Gran Piedra (mt.) J4
Guacanayabo (gulf) G4
Guajaba (cay) G2
Guanahacabibes (gulf) A2
Guanahacabibes (pen.) A2
Guantánamo (bay) J4
Guantánamo Bay U.S. Nav.
Reserve K4
Guárico (pt.) K3
Guzmanes (cays) B2
Hicacos (pen.) D1
Hicacos (pt.) D1
Honda (bay) B1
Indios (chan.) B2
Inglés (pt.) G4
Jardines de la Reina (arch.) F3
Jatibonico del Sur (riv.) .. F3
Jigüey (bay) G2
Juventud, Isla de la (Pines)
(isl.) 57,879 .... B3
Laberinto de las Doce
Leguas (cays) F3
Ladrillo (pt.) E3
Largo (cay) D2
Leche (lag.) F2
Los Barcos (cays) B2
Los Canarreos (arch.) C2
Los Colorados (arch.) A1
Lucrecia (cape) J3
Macurijes (pt.) F3
Maestra, Sierra (mts.) H4
Maisí (cape) K4
Mangle (pt.) J3
Maslo (cay) C2
Matanzas (bay) D1
Nicholas (chan.) E1
Nipe (bay) J3
Nuevitas (bay) H2
Ojo del Toro (mt.) G4
Old Bahama (chan.) G1
Pepe (cape) B3
Perros (bay) G2
Pigs (Cochinos) (bay) D2
Pines (Isla de la Juventud)
(isl.) 57,879 .... B3
Potrerillo (peak) E2
Quemado (cay) K4
Romano (cay) G2
Rosario (cay) C2
Sabana (arch.) E1
Sabinal (cay) H2
Sagua la Grande (riv.) ... E1
San Antonio (cape) A2
San Felipe (cays) B2
San Pedro (riv.) G3
Santa Clara (bay) D1
Santa María (cay) F1
Siguanea (bay) B2
Tabacal (pt.) H4
Toa, Cuchillas de (mts.) . K4
Tortuguilla (pt.) K4
Turquino (peak) H4
Zapata (pen.) C2
Zapata Occidental (swamp) . D2
Zapata Oriental (swamp) .. D2

DOMINICAN REPUBLIC
PROVINCES

Azua 142,770 .... D6

Bahoruco 78,636 .... D6
Barahona 137,160 .... D6
Dajabón 57,709 .... D5
Distrito Nacional 1,550,739 . E6
Duarte 235,544 .... E5
El Seibo 157,866 .... F6
Ellas Piña 65,384 .... C5
Espaillat 164,017 .... E5
Independencia 38,768 ... D6
La Altagracia 100,112 ... F6
La Romana 109,769 ..... F6
La Vega 385,043 .... D6
María Trinidad Sánchez
112,629 .... E5
Monte Cristi 83,407 ..... D5
Pedernales 17,006 ...... D7
Peravia 168,123 .... E6
Puerto Plata 206,757 .... E5
Salcedo 99,191 .... E5
Samaná 65,699 .... F5
Sánchez Ramírez 126,567 . E5
San Cristóbal 446,132 ... E6
San Juan 239,957 .... D6
San Pedro de Macorís
152,890 .... F6
Santiago 550,372 .... D5
Santiago Rodríguez 55,411 . D5
Valverde 100,319 .... D5

CITIES and TOWNS

Altamira 2,759 .... D5
Azua 31,481 .... D6
Bajos de Haina 33,135 ... E6
Baní 36,705 .... E6
Barahona 49,334 .... D6
Bonao 44,486 .... E6
Cabrera 2,542 .... E5
Comendador 5,962 ..... C6
Constanza 15,141 ...... D6
Cotuí 16,688 .... E5
Dajabón 8,808 .... D5
El Seibo 13,511 .... F6
Hato Mayor 17,859 .... F6
Higüey 33,501 .... F6
Imbert 5,931 .... D5
Jarabacoa 13,416 ..... E5
Jimaní 3,327 .... D6
La Romana 91,571 .... F6
La Vega 52,432 .... E5
Luperón 2,500 .... D5
Mao 33,527 .... D5
Moca 31,176 .... D5
Monción 3,344 ...... D5
Nagua 20,912 .... E5
Puerto Plata 45,348 .. D5
Sabana de la Mar 9,983 . F5
Sabaneta 9,170 ...... D5
Samaná 5,023 .... F5
Sánchez 7,919 ...... E5
San Cristóbal 58,520 . E6
San Francisco de Macorís
64,906 .... E5
San Juan 49,764 .... D6
San Pedro de Macorís
78,562 .... F6
Santiago 278,638 ... D5
Santo Domingo (cap.)
1,313,172 .... E6
Tenares 4,065 .... E5
Villa Altagracia 20,890 . E6

OTHER FEATURES

Alto Velo (chan.) C7
Alto Velo (isl.) D7
Balandra (pt.) F5
Beata (cape) D7
Beata (chan.) C7
Beata (isl.) C7
Cabrón (cape) F5
Calderas (bay) D6
Caña (pt.) F6
Catalina (isl.) F6
Caucedo (capee) E6
Central, Cordillera (range) . D5
Duarte (peak) D5
Engaño (cape) F6
Enriquillo (lake) ... D6
Escocesa (bay) E5
Espada (pt.) F5
Falso (cape) C7
Francés Viejo (cape) . E5
Gallo (mt.) D5
Isabela (bay) D5
Isabela (pt.) D5
Los Frailes (isl.) . C7
Macorís (cape) ... E5
Manzanillo (bay) . C5
Mona (passg.) ... F6
Neiba (bay) D6
Neiba, Sierra de (mts.) . D6
Ocoa (bay) E6
Oriental, Cordillera (range) . F6
Palenque (pt.) ... E6
Palmillas (pt.) .. F5
Rincón (bay) F5
Rucia (pt.) D5
Salinas (pt.) E6
Samaná (bay) ... F5
Samaná (cape) .. F5
San Rafael (cape) . F5
Saona (isl.) F6
Septentrional, Cordillera
(range) D5
Tina (mt.) D6
Yaque del Norte (riv.) . D5
Yaque del Sur (riv.) .. D6
Yuma (bay) F6
Yuna (riv.) E5

HAITI

DEPARTMENTS

Artibonite C5
Nord C5
Nord-Ouest B5
Ouest C6
Sud A6

CITIES and TOWNS

Anse-à-Galets 3,623 ... B6
Anse-d'Hainault 5,220 . A6
Aquin 3,820 .... B6
Cap-Haïtien 64,406 .. C5
Croix des Bouquets 4,365 . C6
Dame Marie 4,320 .. A6
Dérac 1,300 .... C5

Dessalines 7,984 ...... C5
Fort Liberté 5,012 ..... C5
Gonaïves 34,209 ..... B5
Grande Rivière du Nord
6,007 .... C5
Gros Morne 4,739 ... B5
Hinche 10,070 ...... C5
Jacmel 13,730 ..... C6
Jérémie 18,493 .... A6
Kenscoff 2,605 .... C6
Lascahobas 3,805 . C6
Léogâne 5,782 .... C6
Les Cayes 34,090 . B6
Limbé 10,476 .... C5
Miragoâne 4,327 . B6
Mirebalais 6,069 . C6
Ouanaminthe 7,276 . C5
Pétionville 35,333 . C6
Petite Rivière de l'Artibonite
10,099 .... B5
Petit Goâve 7,310 . B6
Pignon 4,576 .... C5
Port-au-Prince (cap.)
449,831 .... C6
Port-de-Paix 15,540 . B5
Saint-Louis du Nord 7,203 . B5
Saint-Marc 24,165 ... B5
Saint-Michel de l'Atalaye
7,559 .... C5
Saint-Raaphaël 3,889 . C5
Trou du Nord 7,637 . C5
Verrettes 3,670 .... C5

OTHER FEATURES

Artibonite (riv.) C5
Baradères (bay) B6
Cheval Blanc (pt.) ... B5
Dame Marie (cape) .. A6
Est (pt.) C4
Fantasque (pt.) B5
Gonâve (gulf) B5
Gonâve (isl.) B6
Grande Cayemite (isl.) . B6
Gravois (pt.) A7
Irois (cape) A6
Jean-Rabel (pt.) ... B5
Macaya (mt.) A6
Manzanillo (bay) .. C5
Môle (cape) B5
Noires (mts.) C5
Ouest (pt.) B4
Ouest (pt.) B6
Saint-Marc (chan.) . B6
Saint-Marc (pt.) .. B5
Saumâtre (lake) .. C6
Selle (peak) C6
Sud (chan.) B6
Tortue (chan.) ... C5
Tortue (Tortuga) (isl.) . C4
Tortuga (isl.) C4
Trois-Rivières (riv.) . B5
Vache (pt.) B6
Windward (passg.) . A5

JAMAICA

CITIES and TOWNS

Alley J7

Alligator Pond H6
Anchovy 2,558 ...... H5
Annotto Bay K6
Bamboo 2,971 ..... J6
Bath K6
Black River 2,701 .. H6
Bog Walk J6
Bowden K6
Browns Town 5,479 . J6
Bull Savanna-Junction
5,110 .... H6
Cambridge 2,449 ... H6
Catadupa H6
Christiana H6
Discovery Bay 1,814 . J5
Falmouth 3,937 ... H5
Green Island G6
Hope Bay K6
Kingston (cap.) 106,791 . K6
Kingston *516,865 . J7
Linstead J6
Lucea 3,635 ...... G5
Mandeville 14,421 . H6
Maroon Town 2,717 . H6
May Pen 26,074 ... J6
Montego Bay 43,521 . H5
Montpelier H6
Morant Bay 7,465 . K7
Negril G6
Ocho Rios 5,851 .. J6
Oracabessa J5
Port Antonio 10,538 . K6
Port Kaiser H7
Port Maria 5,259 .. J6
Port Morant K6
Saint Ann's Bay 7,101 . J5
Saint Margaret's Bay . K6
Savanna-la-Mar 11,759 . G6
Spanish Town 40,731 . J6
Williamsfield H6

OTHER FEATURES

Black (riv.) H6
Black River (bay) ... G6
Blue (mts.) J6
Blue Mountain (peak) . K6
Galina (pt.) J6
Grande (riv.) K6
Great (riv.) H5
Great Pedro Bluff (prom.) . H6
Long (bay) H7
Luana (pt.) G6
Minho (riv.) J6
Montego (bay) ... G5
Montego Bay (pt.) . G5
North East (pt.) . K6
North Negril (pt.) . G6
North West (pt.) . G5
Old Harbour (bay) . J6
Portland (pt.) J7
Sir John's (peak) . K6
South East (pt.) . K6
South Negril (pt.) . G6

*City and Suburbs.
○ Population of municipality.

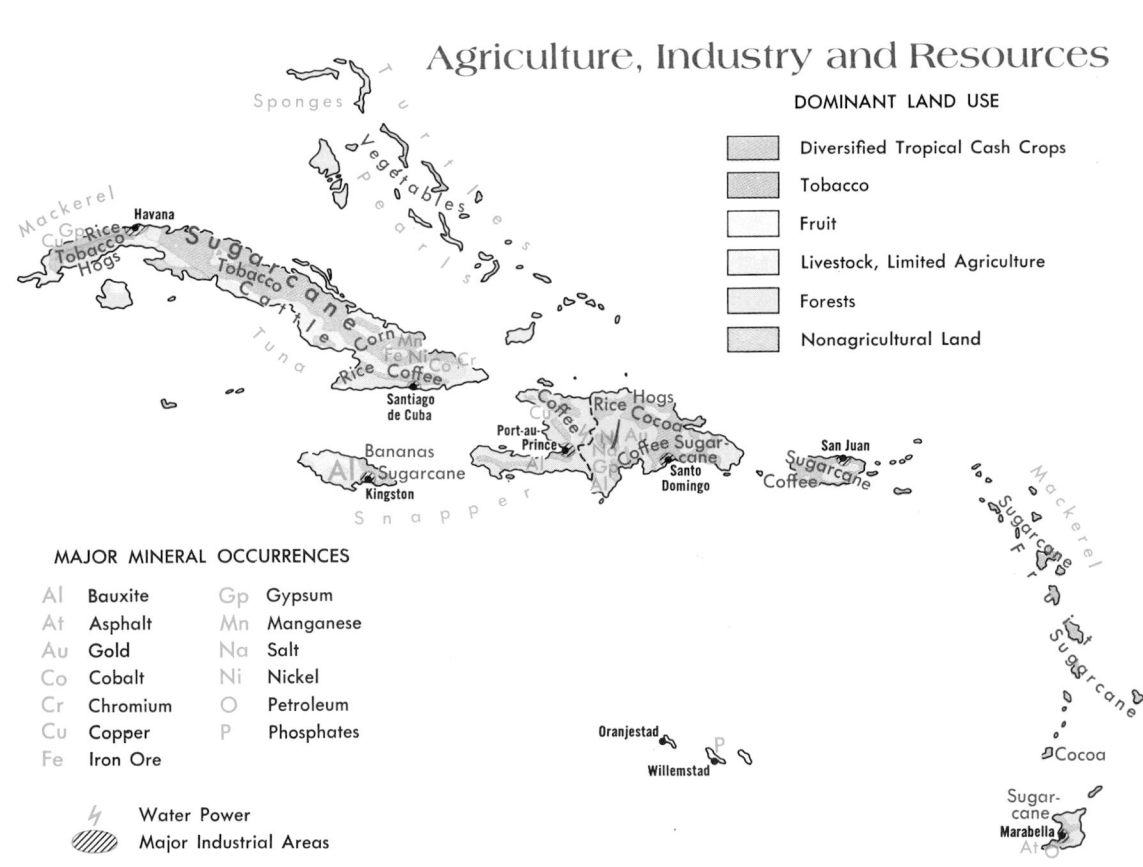

Agriculture, Industry and Resources

DOMINANT LAND USE

Diversified Tropical Cash Crops
Tobacco
Fruit
Livestock, Limited Agriculture
Forests
Nonagricultural Land

MAJOR MINERAL OCCURRENCES

Al Bauxite
At Asphalt
Au Gold
Co Cobalt
Cr Chromium
Cu Copper
Fe Iron Ore
Gp Gypsum
Mn Manganese
Na Salt
Ni Nickel
O Petroleum
P Phosphates

⚡ Water Power
▨ Major Industrial Areas

PUERTO RICO

DISTRICTS

Aguadilla ... A1
Arecibo ... C1
Bayamón ... D1
Guayama ... D2
Humacao ... E2
Mayagüez ... B2
Ponce ... C2
San Juan ... D1

CITIES and TOWNS

Adjuntas 5,239 ... B2
Aguada 5,025 ... A1
Aguadilla 22,039 ... A1
Aguas Buenas 3,766 ... E2
Aibonito 9,331 ... D2
Añasco 5,646 ... A1
Ángeles ○2,817 ... B2
Arecibo 48,779 ... B1
Arroyo 8,435 ... E3
Bahomamey ... A1
Bajadero 3,678 ... C1
Barceloneta 4,502 ... C1
Barranquitas 3,618 ... D2
Bayamón 185,087 ... D1
Boquerón ○3,675 ... A3
Cabo Rojo 10,292 ... A2
Caguas 87,214 ... E2
Caguas †156,819 ... E2
Camuy 3,834 ... B1
Carolina 147,835 ... E1
Cataño 26,243 ... D1
Cayey 23,305 ... D2
Ceiba 4,973 ... F2
Central Aguirre 1,049 ... D3
Ciales 3,582 ... C1
Cidra 6,069 ... D2
Coamo 12,851 ... D2
Comerío 5,736 ... D2
Coquí 3,018 ... D3
Corozal 5,889 ... D1
Coto Laurel ○5,192 ... C2
Culebra (Dewey) 938 ... G1
Dorado 10,203 ... D1
Ensenada ... B3
Esperanza 1,130 ... G2
Fajardo 26,928 ... F1
Florida 3,641 ... C1
Guánica 9,628 ... B3
Guayama 21,097 ... E3
Guayanilla 6,163 ... B3
Guaynabo 65,075 ... D1
Gurabo 7,645 ... E2
Hatillo 5,019 ... B1
Hato Rey ... E1
Hormigueros 12,031 ... A2
Humacao 19,147 ... E2
Isabela 12,087 ... A1
Isabel Segunda 2,330 ... G2
Jayuya 3,588 ... C2
Jobos 4,194 ... D3
Juana Díaz 10,469 ... C2
Juncos 7,851 ... E2
Lajas 4,275 ... A2
Lares 5,224 ... B2
Las Piedras 4,857 ... E2
Levittown 31,613 ... D1
Loíza 3,932 ... E1
Loíza Aldea ... E1
Luquillo 4,531 ... F1
Manatí 17,347 ... C1
Maricao 1,390 ... B2
Mayagüez 82,968 ... A2
Mayagüez †98,155 ... A2
Moca 3,960 ... A1
Naguabo 4,135 ... F2
Naranjito 2,849 ... D1
Palmer 1,566 ... F1
Palo Seco 1,172 ... D1
Parguera ... A3
Patillas 3,172 ... E2
Peñuelas 4,235 ... B2
Playa de Fajardo ... F1
Playa de Humacao ○5,573 ... F2
Ponce 161,739 ... C3
Ponce †168,272 ... C3
Puerto Nuevo ... D1
Puerto Real 2,390 ... A2
Puerto Real (Playa de Fajardo) ... F1
Punta Santiago (Playa de Humacao) ○5,573 ... F2
Quebradillas 3,770 ... B1
Río Blanco 1,433 ... F2
Río Grande 12,047 ... E1
Río Piedras ... E1
Rosario ... A2
Sábana Grande 7,435 ... B2
Sabana Seca 11,431 ... D1
Salinas 6,220 ... D3
San Antonio 2,681 ... A1
San Germán 13,054 ... A2
San Juan (cap.) 424,600 ... E1
San Lorenzo 8,880 ... E2
San Sebastián 10,619 ... B1
Santa Isabel 6,948 ... C3
Santurce ... E1
Tallaboa 1,059 ... B3
Toa Alta 4,427 ... D1
Toa Baja 1,992 ... D1
Trujillo Alto 41,141 ... E1
Utuado 11,113 ... B2
Vega Alta 10,582 ... D1
Vega Baja 18,233 ... D1
Vieques (Isabel Segunda) 2,330 ... G2
Villalba 3,469 ... C2
Yabucoa 6,797 ... E2
Yauco 14,594 ... B2

OTHER FEATURES

Aguadilla (bay) ... A1
Algarrobo (pt.) ... A2
Añasco (bay) ... A1
Arenas (pt.) ... F2
Bauta (riv.) ... C2
Bayamón (riv.) ... D1
Boquerón (bay) ... A3
Borinquen (pt.) ... A1
Cabullones (pt.) ... C3
Caja de Muertos (isl.) ... C3
Camuy (riv.) ... B1
Canovanas (riv.) ... E1
Caonillas (lake) ... C2
Carite (lake) ... E2
Carraízo (lake) ... E1
Cayey, Sierra de (mts.) ... D2
Central, Cordillera (range) ... C2
Cerro Gordo (pt.) ... D1
Coamo (res.) ... D3
Coamo (riv.) ... D3
Culebra (isl.) 1,265 ... G1
Culebrinas (riv.) ... A1
Culebrita (isl.) ... G2
El Toro (mt.) ... F2
El Yunque (mt.) ... F1
Este (pt.) ... G2
Fajardo (riv.) ... F1
Figuras (pt.) ... E3
Fosforescente (bay) ... A3
Grande de Añasco (riv.) ... B2
Grande de Arecibo (riv.) ... C1
Grande de Loíza (riv.) ... E1
Grande de Manatí (riv.) ... C1
Guajataca (lake) ... B1
Guanajibo (pt.) ... A2
Guanajibo (riv.) ... A2
Guánica (lake) ... B3
Guaniquilla (pt.) ... A2
Guayabal (lake) ... C2
Guayanés (pt.) ... F2
Guayanés (riv.) ... E2
Guayanilla (bay) ... B3
Guayo (lake) ... B2
Guilarte (mt.) ... B2
Honda (bay) ... F2
Jacaguas (riv.) ... C2
Jaicoa, Cordillera (mts.) ... B1
Jiguero (pt.) ... A1
Jobos (bay) ... D3
Lima (pt.) ... F2
Luquillo, Sierra de (mts.) ... F1
Manglillo (pt.) ... B3
Mayagüez (bay) ... A2
Miquillo (pt.) ... F1
Molinos (pt.) ... G1
Mona (passg.) ... A2
Negra (pt.) ... G2
Nigua (riv.) ... D2
Ola Grande (pt.) ... D3
Palmas Altas (pt.) ... C1
Patillas (lake) ... E2
Petrona (pt.) ... D3
Pirata (mt.) ... F2
Plata (riv.) ... D2
Puerca (pt.) ... F2
Puerto Medio Mundo (bay) ... F2
Punta, Cerro de (mt.) ... C2
Ramey A.F.B. ... A1
Rincón (bay) ... D3
Rojo (cape) ... A3
Roosevelt Road Naval Res. ... F2
Salinas (pt.) ... D1
San José (lag.) ... E1
San Juan, Cabezas de (prom.) ... F1
San Juan Nat'l Hist. Site ... D1
Soldado (pt.) ... G2
Sucia (bay) ... A3
Tanamá (riv.) ... B1
Toro, El (mt.) ... F2
Torrecilla (lag.) ... E1
Tortuguero (lag.) ... D1
Tuna (pt.) ... E3
Vacía Talega (pt.) ... E1
Vieques (isl.) 7,662 ... G2
Vieques (passg.) ... F2
Vieques (sound) ... G2
Yagüez (riv.) ... A2
Yauco (lake) ... B2
Yeguas (pt.) ... F3

ANTIGUA

CITIES and TOWNS

All Saints 1,796 ... E11
Cedar Grove 1,460 ... E11
Falmouth 1,134 ... E11
Freetown 1,250 ... E11
Jennings 1,370 ... D11
Liberta 2,394 ... E11
Old Road 1,244 ... D11
Parham 1,570 ... E11
Saint John's (cap.) 21,814 ... E11
Willikies 1,843 ... E11

OTHER FEATURES

Antigua (isl.) 76,213 ... E11
Boggy (peak) ... D11
Boon (pt.) ... E11
Green (isl.) ... E11
Guiana (isl.) ... E11
Long (isl.) ... E11
Saint John's (harb.) ... C11
Standfast (pt.) ... E11
Willoughby (bay) ... E11

ARUBA

CITIES and TOWNS

Aresji ... D9
Balashi ... E10
Bubali ... D10
Bushiribana ... E10
Druif ... D1
Oranjestad (cap.) Aruba 10,100 ... D10
Sint Nicolaas ... E10
Westpunt ... D10

OTHER FEATURES

Aruba (isl.) 66,790 ... E9
Basora (pt.) ... E10
Jamanota (mt.) ... E10
Paarden (bay) ... D10
Palm (beach) ... D10

BARBADOS

CITIES and TOWNS

Bathsheba ... B8
Belleplaine ... B8
Bridgetown (cap.) 7,552 ... B9
Carlton ... B8
Cave Hill ... B9
Checker Hall ... B8
Codrington ... B8
Crab Hill ... B8
Crane ... C9
Drax Hall ... B8
Ellerton ... B8
Greenland ... B8
Holetown ... B8
Kendal ... B8
Lodge Hill ... B8
Marchfield ... B9
Mount Standfast ... B8
Oistins ... B9
Rose Hill ... B8
Rouen ... B8
Saint Lawrence ... C9
Saint Martins ... B9
Scarboro ... B9
Seawell ... B9
Six Mens ... B8
Speightstown ... B8
Spring Hall ... B8
Welchman Hall ... B8

OTHER FEATURES

Carlisle (bay) ... B9
Hillaby (mt.) ... B8
Long (bay) ... B9
North (pt.) ... B8
Oistins (bay) ... B9
Pelican (isl.) ... B9
Ragged (pt.) ... C8
Sam Lord's Castle ... C9
South (pt.) ... B9

DOMINICA

CITIES and TOWNS

Barroui 1,480 ... E6
Castle Bruce 1,975 ... F6
Coulihaut 1,735 ... E6
Delice ... F7
Grand Bay 3,152 ... F7
Hampstead ... E5
La Plaine ... F6
Mahout 2,095 ... E6
Marigot 3,183 ... F6
Petit Soufrière ... F6
Portsmouth 2,329 ... E5
Rosalie ... F6
Roseau (cap.) 9,968 ... E7
Roseau *16,035 ... E7
Saint Joseph 2,643 ... E6
Salybia ... F6
Soufrière ... E7
Vieille Case ... E5
Wesley 2,002 ... F5

OTHER FEATURES

Capuchin (cape) ... E5
Carib Reserve ... F6
Clyde (riv.) ... F6
Crumpton (pt.) ... F5
Diablotin, Morne (mt.) ... E6
Dominica (passg.) ... E5
Douglas (bay) ... E5
Grand (bay) ... F7
Jaquet (pt.) ... F7
Layou (riv.) ... E6
Martinique (passg.) ... E7
Micotrin (mt.) ... F6
Pagoua (bay) ... F6
Prince Rupert (bay) ... E5
Scotts (head) ... E7
Soufrière (bay) ... E7
Trois Pitons, Morne (mt.) ... E6

GRENADA

CITIES and TOWNS

Gouyave 2,498 ... C8
Grand Roy ... C8
Grenville 1,723 ... D8
Hermitage ... D8
La Taste ... D8
Marquis ... D8
Mount Tivoli ... D8
Saint George's (cap.) 6,463 ... C9
Saint George's *34,624 ... C9
Sauteurs 605 ... D8
Victoria 1,673 ... D8
Woodford ... C8

OTHER FEATURES

Bedford (pt.) ... D8
David (pt.) ... D8
Great Bacolet (pt.) ... D8
Green (isl.) ... D8
Grenville (bay) ... D8
Gros (pt.) ... C8
Halifax (harb.) ... C8
Irvin's (bay) ... D8
Les Tantes (isls.) ... D7

Sint Nicolaas ... E10
Westpunt ... D10

Molinière (pt.) ... C8
Prickly (pt.) ... C9
Ronde (isl.) ... D7
Saint Catherine (mt.) ... D8
Saline (pt.) ... C9
Sinai (mt.) ... D8
Telescope (pt.) ... D8

GUADELOUPE

Total Population 329,017

CITIES and TOWNS

Anse-Bertrand 1,921 ... A5
Baie-Mahault 5,874 ... A6
Baillif 3,844 ... A7
Bananier ... A7
Basse-Terre (cap.) 13,397 ... A7
Bouillante 1,821 ... A6
Bourg-des-Saintes 907 ... A7
Capesterre 7,541 ... A7
Ferry ... A6
Gosier 13,741 ... B6
Gourbeyre 5,637 ... A7
Goyave 1,709 ... A6
Grand-Bourg 3,249 ... B7
Lamentin 2,319 ... A6
Les Abymes 51,837 ... A6
Morne-à-l'Eau 9,457 ... A6
Moule 9,800 ... A6
Petit-Bourg 5,097 ... A6
Petit-Canal 1,581 ... A6
Pigeon ... A6
Pointe-à-Pitre 25,151 ... B6
Pointe-Noire 2,180 ... A6
Port-Louis 4,517 ... B5
Saint-Claude 6,755 ... A7
Sainte-Anne 11,527 ... B6
Sainte-Marguerite ... A6
Sainte-Marie ... A6
Sainte-Rose 4,805 ... A6
Saint-François 3,141 ... B6
Trois-Rivières 7,881 ... A7
Vieux-Fort 1,073 ... B7
Vieux-Habitants 4,065 ... A7

OTHER FEATURES

Allègre (pt.) ... A6
Antigues (pt.) ... A7
Basse-Terre (isl.) 138,777 ... A6
Châteaux (pt.) ... B6
Constant, Morne (hill) ... B7
Désirade, La (isl.) 1,602 ... B6
Fajou (isl.) ... A6
Grand Cul-de-Sac Marin (bay) ... A6
Grande-Terre (isl.) ... B6
Grande Vigie (pt.) ... B5
Grand-Îlet ... A7
Guadeloupe (isl.) 167,896 ... A6
Guadeloupe (passg.) ... A5
Guadeloupe Nat'l Park ... A4
Kahouanne (isl.) ... A6
Marie-Galante (isl.) 13,757 ... B7
Nord (pt.) ... B7
Nord-Est (bay) ... A6
Petit Cul-de-Sac Marin (bay) ... A6
Petite-Terre (isls.) ... B6
Saintes (chan.) ... A7
Saintes (isls.) 2,901 ... A7
Salée (riv.) ... A6
Sans Toucher (mt.) ... A6
Soufrière (mt.) ... A7
Terre-de-Bas (isl.) 1,427 ... A7
Terre-de-Haut (isl.) 1,453 ... A7
Vieux-Fort (pt.) ... A7

MARTINIQUE

Total Population 330,220

CITIES and TOWNS

Ajoupa-Bouillon 1,569 ... C5
Basse-Pointe 2,163 ... C5
Bellefontaine 818 ... C6
Case-Pilote 1,776 ... C6
Ducos 4,429 ... D6
Fond-Saint-Denis 962 ... C6
Fort-de-France (cap.) 96,649 ... C6
Grand' Rivière 1,053 ... C5
Gros-Morne 1,976 ... D6
La Trinité 3,380 ... D6
Le Carbet 2,321 ... C6
Le François 2,940 ... D6
Le Lamentin 6,872 ... C6
Le Lorrain 2,024 ... D6
Le Marin 2,651 ... D7
Le Morne-Rouge 2,650 ... C5
Le Prêcheur 1,350 ... C5
Le Robert 3,610 ... D6
Le Saint-Esprit 3,947 ... D6
Les Trois-Îlets 1,484 ... C6
Le Vauclin 3,054 ... D6
Macouba 1,142 ... C5
Marigot 1,765 ... D6
Rivière-Pilote 1,587 ... D7
Rivière-Salée 1,859 ... C7
Sainte-Luce 1,502 ... D7
Sainte-Marie 3,966 ... D5
Saint-Joseph 2,052 ... C6
Saint-Pierre 4,923 ... C6
Schoelcher 16,412 ... C6

OTHER FEATURES

Cabet, Pitons du (mt.) ... C6
Cabrits (isl.) ... D7
Cul-de-Sac du Marin (bay) ... D7
Diable (pt.) ... D5
Ferré (cape) ... E7
Fort-de-France (bay) ... C6
Galion (bay) ... D6
Lézarde (riv.) ... D6
Long (isl.) ... D6
Lorrain (riv.) ... D5

Martinique (passg.) ... C5
Pelée (vol.) ... C5
Pilote (riv.) ... D7
Ramiers (isl.) ... C6
Ramville (isl.) ... D6
Robert (harb.) ... D6
Rose (pt.) ... D6
Saint-Martin (cape) ... C5
Saint-Pierre (bay) ... C6
Salines (pt.) ... D7
Salomon (pt.) ... C7
Vauclin (mt.) ... D6

NETHERLANDS ANTILLES

CITIES and TOWNS

Ascension ... F8
Bacuna ... E8
Boven Bolivia ... F8
Dokterstuin ... F8
Emmastad ... F9
Entrejo ... E8
Fontein ... E8
Groot Sint Joris ... G9
Hato ... G8
Kralendijk (cap.), Bonaire 2,500 ... E8
Lagoen ... F8
Montanja di Reij ... G9
New Port ... G9
Noord di Salinja ... E8
Onima ... E8
Otrabanda ... F9
Patrick ... F8
Rincon ... E8
Rooi ... E8
Santa Barbara ... G9
Santa Catharina ... G9
Savonet ... F8
Sint Kruis ... F9
Sint Martha ... F9
Sint Michiel ... F9
Sint Willebrordus ... F9
Terra Corra ... E8
Westpunt ... F8
Willemstad (cap.) 95,000 ... F9
Willemstad *130,000 ... F9

OTHER FEATURES

Bonaire (isl.) 8,087 ... E9
Bullen (bay) ... F8
Caracas (bay) ... G9
Curaçao (isl.) 145,430 ... G7
Goto (lake) ... D8
Kanon (pt.) ... G9
Klein Bonaire (isl.) ... E8
Kudarebe (pt.) ... D9
Lac (bay) ... D9
Lacre (pt.) ... E9
Malmok (pt.) ... E8
Noord (pt.) ... D8
Noord (pt.) ... D8
Pekelmeer (lake) ... E9
Piscadera (bay) ... F9
Schottegat (bay) ... G9
Sint Anna (bay) ... F9
Sint Christoffel (mt.) ... F8
Sint Joris (bay) ... G9
Slag (bay) ... D8
Vierkant (pt.) ... E8

SAINT KITTS and NEVIS

CITIES and TOWNS

Basseterre (cap.) 14,725 ... C10
Cayon ... C10
Charlestown 1,326 ... C11
Cotton Ground 471 ... C11
Dieppe Bay ... C10
Frigate Bay ... C10
Gingerland ... D11
Golden Rock ... C10
Newcastle ... D11
Old Road Town ... C10
Sadlers Village ... C10
Sandy Point 862 ... C10
Tabernacle ... C10
Zion Hill ... D11

OTHER FEATURES

Brimstone (hill) ... C10
Dogwood (pt.) ... D11
Fort (pt.) ... C11
Great Salt (pond) ... D10
Heldens (pt.) ... C10
Horse Shoe (pt.) ... C11
Misery (mt.) ... C10
Monkey (hill) ... C10
Narrows, The (str.) ... D11
Nevis (isl.) 9,300 ... D11
Nevis (peak) ... D11
North Friars (bay) ... D10
Pinney's (beach) ... D11
Saint Christopher (Saint Kitts) (isl.) 35,104 ... D10
South Friars (bay) ... C10

SAINT LUCIA

CITIES and TOWNS

Anse la Raye ●5,007 ... F6
Canaries ●2,075 ... G6
Castries (cap.) ●42,770 ... G6
Choc ... G5
Choiseul ●6,382 ... F7
Dauphin ... G5
Dennery ●9,654 ... G6
Gros Islet ●10,329 ... G5
Laborie ●6,944 ... G7

Marigot ... G6
Marquis ... G6
Micoud ●12,264 ... G6
Preslin ... G6
Soufrière ●7,456 ... F6
Vieux Fort ●10,675 ... G7

OTHER FEATURES

Beaumont (pt.) ... F6
Canaries, Piton (mt.) ... G6
Cannelles (pt.) ... G7
Cannelles (riv.) ... G6
Cap (pt.) ... G5
Choc (bay) ... G5
Fond d'Or (bay) ... G6
Gimie (mt.) ... G6
Grand Caille (pt.) ... F6
Grand Cul de Sac (riv.) ... G6
Gros Islet (bay) ... G5
Gros Piton (mt.) ... F6
La Sorcière (mt.) ... G6
Maria (isls.) ... G7
Ministre (pt.) ... G7
Moule-à-Chique (cape) ... G7
Petit Piton (mt.) ... F6
Pigeon (isl.) ... G5
Port Castries (harb.) ... G6
Port Praslin (bay) ... G6
Roseau (riv.) ... G6
Saint Lucia (chan.) ... G5
Saint Vincent (chan.) ... G7
Savannes (bay) ... G7
Sorcière, La (mt.) ... G6
Soufrière (bay) ... F6
Vierge (pt.) ... G6

SAINT VINCENT and THE GRENADINES

CITIES and TOWNS

Barrouallie 1,298 ... A9
Calliaqua 627 ... A9
Camden Park ... A9
Colonarie ... A9
Georgetown 1,100 ... A8
Kingstown (cap.) 17,117 ... A9
Kingstown *23,330 ... A9
Layou 1,147 ... A9
Wallibu ... A8

OTHER FEATURES

Colonarie (pt.) ... A9
Cumberland (bay) ... A8
Dark (head) ... A8
De Volet (pt.) ... A8
Espagnol (pt.) ... A9
Greathead (bay) ... A9
Kingstown (bay) ... A9
Owia (bay) ... A8
Porter (pt.) ... A8
Richmond (peak) ... A8
Saint Andrew (mt.) ... A8
Saint Vincent (isl.) ... A8
Saint Vincent (passg.) ... A8
Soufrière (mt.) ... A8
Yambou (head) ... A9

TRINIDAD and TOBAGO

CITIES and TOWNS

Arima 11,390 ... B10
Arouca ... B10
Basse Terre ... B11
Biche ... B10
Blanchisseuse ... B10
California ... A11
Carapichaima ... B10
Caroni ... B10
Cedros ... A11
Chaguanas 6,122 ... B10
Chaguaramas ... A10
Couva 3,635 ... B10
Cunapo ... B10
Flanagin Town ... A11
Fullarton ... A11
Fyzabad 1,564 ... A11
Grande Rivière ... B10
Guaico ... B10
Guayaguayare ... B11
La Brea 1,487 ... A11
Marabella 18,158 ... A11
Matelot ... B10
Matura ... B10
Mayaro 2,638 ... B11
Moruga ... B11
Mucurapo ... A10
Palo Seco ... A11
Peñal 3,606 ... B11
Point Fortin 6,538 ... A11
Port-of-Spain (cap.) 67,978 ... A10
Princes Town 8,288 ... B11
Redhead ... B10
Rio Claro 2,423 ... B11
Saint Joseph 4,132 ... B10
Saint Joseph ... A11
San Fernando 33,490 ... A11
San Francique ... A11
Sangre Grande 8,948 ... B1
San Juan ... A10
Sans Souci ... B10
Siparia 5,773 ... B11
Tabaquite 2,309 ... B11
Talparo ... B10
Toco 1,287 ... B10
Tunapuna 10,251 ... A10
Upper Manzanilla ... B1
Valencia ... B10
Waterloo ... A10

OTHER FEATURES

Aripo, El Cerro del (mt.) ... B10
Boca Grande (passg.) ... A10
Chacachacare (isl.) ... A10

Chupara (pt.) ... B10
Cocos (pt.) ... B10
Dragons Mouth (str.) ... A10
El Tucuche (mt.) ... B10
Erin (pt.) ... A11
Galeota (pt.) ... B11
Galera (pt.) ... C10
Guapo (bay) ... A11
Guataro (pt.) ... B11
Icacos (pt.) ... A11
Maracas (bay) ... C10
Pitch (lake) ... A11

VIRGIN ISLANDS (Br.)

CITIES and TOWNS

Road Town (cap.) 2,200 ... D3
West End ... C4

OTHER FEATURES

Flanagan (passg.) ... D4
Frenchman (cay) ... C4
Great Thatch (isl.) ... B3
Great Tobago (isl.) ... B3
Jost Van Dyke (isl.) 135 ... C3
Little Tobago (isl.) ... B3
Narrows, The (str.) ... C4
Norman (isl.) ... D4
Peter (isl.) ... D4
Road (bay) ... D3
Sage (mt.) ... D4
Sir Francis Drake (chan.) ... D4
Tortola (isl.) 9,257 ... D3

VIRGIN ISLANDS (U.S.)

CITIES and TOWNS

Bethlehem ... E4
Canebay ... E3
Charlotte Amalie (cap.) 11,842 ... B4
Christiansted 2,914 ... F4
Cruz Bay 1,928 ... C4
Diamond ... D4
Eastend ... F4
Emmaus ... C4
Fredensdal ... F4
Frederiksted 1,046 ... E4
Grove Place 3,599 ... E4
Kingshill ... F4
Longford ... F4
Negro Bay ... E4

OTHER FEATURES

Altona (lag.) ... F4
Annaly (bay) ... E3
Baron Bluff (prom.) ... F3
Bordeaux (mt.) ... B4
Brass (isls.) ... A4
Buck (isl.) ... G3
Buck Island (mt.) ... F3
Buck Island Reef Nat'l Mon. ... G3
Butler (bay) ... E4
Caneel (bay) ... B4
Capella (isls.) ... B5
Christiansted Nat'l Hist. Site ... F4
Coral (bay) ... C4
Crown (mt.) ... A4
Dutch Cap (cay) ... A4
Eagle (pt.) ... E4
East (pt.) ... G4
Flanagan (passg.) ... D4
Flat (cays) ... A4
Grass (pt.) ... E4
Great (pond) ... G4
Great Pond (bay) ... G4
Green (cay) ... G4
Hams Bluff (prom.) ... E3
Hans Lollik (isls.) ... B4
Hassel (isl.) ... B4
Jersey (bay) ... B4
Krause Lagoon (chan.) ... F4
Leeward (passg.) ... B4
Long (pt.) ... D4
Long (pt.) ... A4
Lovango (cay) ... B4
Magens (bay) ... B4
Maho (bay) ... C4
Narrows, The (str.) ... B4
Nulliberg (mt.) ... B4
Perseverance (bay) ... A4
Picara (pt.) ... B4
Pillsbury (sound) ... B4
Privateer (pt.) ... C4
Pull (pt.) ... F3
Ram (head) ... C4
Red (pt.) ... D4
Reef (bay) ... C4
Saba (isl.) ... A4
Saint Croix (isl.) 49,725 ... F4
Saint James (isls.) ... B4
Saint John (isl.) 2,472 ... C4
Saint Thomas (harb.) ... B4
Saint Thomas (isl.) 44,372 ... A4
Salt (cay) ... A4
Salt (riv.) ... F4
Salt River (bay) ... F4
Sandy (pt.) ... D4
Savana (isl.) ... A4
Southwest (cape) ... E4
Tague (bay) ... G4
Thatch (cay) ... B4
Turner Hole (bay) ... G4
U.S. Nav. Air Sta. ... F4
Virgin (str.) ... C4
Virgin Isls. Nat'l Park ... C4
Water (isl.) ... A4
Westend Saltpond (lag.) ... E4

*City and suburbs.
● Population of district.
†Population of met. area.
○ Population of municipality.

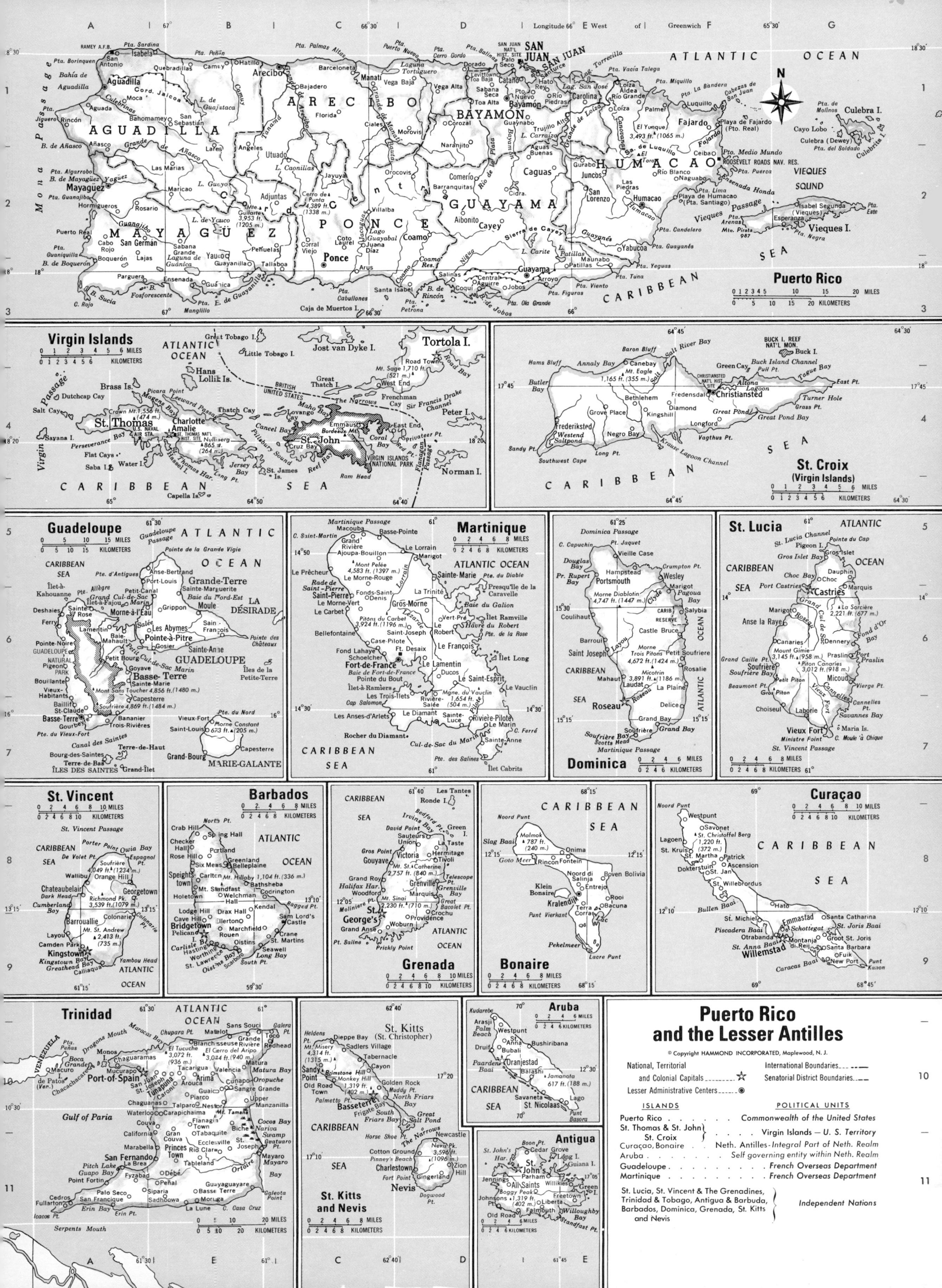

Puerto Rico and the Lesser Antilles

© Copyright HAMMOND INCORPORATED, Maplewood, N.J.

National, Territorial and Colonial Capitals ⭐	International Boundaries
Lesser Administrative Centers ◉	Senatorial District Boundaries

ISLANDS — POLITICAL UNITS

ISLANDS	POLITICAL UNITS
Puerto Rico	Commonwealth of the United States
St. Thomas & St. John	Virgin Islands — U. S. Territory
St. Croix	
Curaçao, Bonaire	Neth. Antilles - Integral Part of Neth. Realm
Aruba	Self governing entity within Neth. Realm
Guadeloupe	French Overseas Department
Martinique	French Overseas Department
St. Lucia, St. Vincent & The Grenadines, Trinidad & Tobago, Antigua & Barbuda, Barbados, Dominica, Grenada, St. Kitts and Nevis	Independent Nations

Canada

CONIC PROJECTION

SCALE OF MILES

0   50   100   200   300

SCALE OF KILOMETERS

0 50 100   200   300   400   500

Capitals of Countries .... ☆
Provincial & Territorial Capitals .... △
Administrative Centers .... ◉
International Boundaries ....
Provincial Boundaries ....
Regional Boundaries ....

Scale 1:19,600,000

© Copyright HAMMOND INCORPORATED, Maplewood, N.J.

Abitibi (lake), Ont. H6
Aklavik, N.W.T. 721 . . . . . . C2
Albany (riv.), Ont. H5
Alberta (prov.) 2,365,825 . . . . E5
Amherst, N.S. 9,684 . . . . . K6
Amos, Que. 9,421 . . . . K6
Anticosti (isl.) Que. K6
Athabasca (lake) F4
Athabasca (riv.), Alta. E4
Axel Heiburg (isl.), N.W.T. . . N3
Baffin (reg.), N.W.T. 8,300 . . G1
Baffin (bay), N.W.T. J1
Baffin (isl.), N.W.T. J1
Baker Lake, N.W.T. 954 . . . . G3
Banff Nat'l Park, Alta. E5
Banks (isl.), N.W.T. D1
Bathurst, N. Br. 15,705 . . . . K6
Belle Isle (str.), Newf. L5
Bonavista, Newf. 4,460 . . . . L6
Boothia (pen.), N.W.T. G1
Brandon, Man. 36,242 . . . . F6
British Columbia (prov.)
      2,883,367 . . . . D4
Cabot (str.) K6
Calgary, Alta. 592,743 . . . . E5
Cambridge Bay, N.W.T. 815 . . F2
Campbellton, N.Br. 9,818 . . . K6
Camrose, Alta. 12,570 . . . . E5
Cape Breton (isl.) N.S. K6
Cartwright, Newf. 658 . . . . . L5
Channel-Port aux Basques,
      Newf. 5,988 . . . . L6
Charlottetown (cap.), P.E.I.
      15,282 . . . . K6
Chatham, N. Br. 6,779 . . . . K6

Chesterfield Inlet, N.W.T. 249 G3
Chibougamau, Que. 10,732 . . J6
Chicoutimi, Que. 60,064 . . . J6
Chidley (cape), Newf. K3
Chilliwack, Br.Col. ◉40,642 . . D6
Chisasibi, Que. 2,222 . . . . . J5
Churchill, Man. 1,186 . . . . . G4
Coast (mts.) C4
Coppermine, N.W.T. 809 . . . E2
Corner Brook, Newf. 24,339 . . K6
Cornwall, Ont. 46,144 . . . . . J7
Cranbrook, Br. Col. 15,915 . . E6
Cree (lake), Sask. F4
Dartmouth, N.S. 62,277 . . . . K7
Dauphin, Man. 8,971 . . . . . F5
Davis (str.), N.W.T. K1
Dawson, Yukon 697 . . . . . . C3
Devon (isl.), N.W.T. M3
Drumheller, Alta. 6,508 . . . . E5
Echo Bay (Port Radium),
      N.W.T. 56 . . . . E2
Edmonton (cap.), Alta.
      532,246 . . . . E5
Edmundston, N. Br. 12,044 . . K6
Ellesmere (isl.), N.W.T. N3
Eskimo Point, N.W.T. 1,022 . . G3
Estevan, Sask. 9,174 . . . . . F6
Finlay (riv.) Br. Col. D4
Flin Flon, Man.-Sask. 8,261 . . F4
Fogo (isl.), Newf. L5
Fort Frances, Ont. 8,906 . . . G6
Fort Franklin, N.W.T. 521 . . . D3
Fort McMurray, Alta. 31,000 . . E4
Fort McPherson, N.W.T. 632 . . C2
Fort Nelson, Br. Col. 3,724 . . D4

Fort Providence, N.W.T. 605 . . E3
Fort Saskatchewan, Alta.
      12,169 . . . . E5
Fort Simpson, N.W.T. 980 . . . D3
Fort Smith, (reg.), N.W.T.
      22,384 . . . . E3
Fort Smith, N.W.T. 2,298 . . . E3
Foxe (basin), N.W.T. J2
Fraser (riv.), Br. Col. D5
Fredericton, N. Br. 43,723 . . K6
Fundy (bay) K7
Gander, Newf. 10,404 . . . . . L6
Gaspé, Que. 17,261 . . . . . . K6
Georgian (bay), Ont. H6
Geraldton, Ont. 2,956 . . . . . H6
Glace Bay, N.S. 21,466 . . . . L6
Goose Bay, Newf. 7,103 . . . . K4
Gouin (riv.), Que. J6
Grand Falls, Newf. 8,765 . . . L6
Grande Prairie, Alta. 24,263 . . E4
Great Bear (lake), N.W.T. . . . D2
Great Slave (lake), N.W.T. . . . E3
Guelph, Ont. 71,207 . . . . . . H7
Halifax (cap.), N.S. 114,594 . . K7
Hamilton, Ont. 306,434 . . . . H7
Harbour Grace, Newf. 2,988 . . L6
Havre-St-Pierre, Que. 3,200 . . K5
Hay River, N.W.T. 2,863 . . . . E3
Hearst, Ont. 5,533 . . . . H6
Hecate (str.), Br. Col. C5
Hull, Que. 56,225 . . . . J6
Inuvik (reg.), N.W.T. 7,485 . . D2
Inuvik, N.W.T. 3,147 . . . . . C2
Iqaluit, N.W.T. 2,333 . . . . . K3
Iroquois Falls, Ont. 6,339 . . . H6

Jasper Nat'l Park, Alta E5
Jonquière Que. 60,354 . . . . J6
Juan de Fuca (str.), Br. Col. . . D6
Kamloops, Br. Col. 64,048 . . D5
Kane (basin), N.W.T. N3
Kapuskasing, Ont. 12,014 . . . H6
Keewatin (reg.), N.W.T. 4,327 G2
Kelowna, Br. Col. 59,196 . . . D6
Kenora, Ont. 9,817 . . . . . . G5
Kingston, Ont. 52,616 . . . . . J7
Kirkland Lake, Ont. 12,219 . . H6
Kitikmeot (reg.), N.W.T. 3,245 F1
Kitimat, Br. Col. 12,462 . . . . D5
Kluane (lake), Yukon C3
Kootenay (lake), Br. Col. . . . E5
Kuujjuac, Que. K4
Kuujjuarapik, Que. 435 . . . . J4
Labrador (reg.), Newf. K4
Lacombe, Alta. 5,591 . . . . . E5
Lake Harbour, N.W.T. 252 . . J3
Lancaster (sound), N.W.T. . . . H1
Leduc, Alta. 12,471 . . . . . . E5
Lesser Slave (lake), Alta. . . . E4
Lethbridge, Alta. 54,072 . . . E6
Liard (riv.), Br. Col. D3
Lloydminster, Alta.-Sask.
      15,031 . . . . E5
Logan (mt.), Yukon B3
London, Ont. 254,280 . . . . . H7
Mackenzie (dist.), N.W.T. . . . E3
Mackenzie (riv.), N.W.T. . . . C2
Magdalen (isls.), Que. K6
Manicouagan (riv.), Que. . . . K5
Manitoba (lake), Man. G5
Manitoba (prov.), 1,063,016 . . G5

Manitoulin (isl.), Ont. H6
Maple Creek, Sask. 2,470 . . F6
Marathon, Ont. 2,271 . . . . . H6
Mayo, Yukon 398 . . . . C3
M'Clintock (chan.), N.W.T. . . F1
Medicine Hat, Alta. 40,380 . . E5
Melville, Sask. 5,092 . . . . . F5
Melville (isl.), N.W.T. E1
Merritt, Br. Col. 6,110 . . . . . D5
Minto (lake), Que. J4
Mistassibi (riv.), Que. J5
Mistassini (lake), Que. J5
Moncton, N. Br. 54,743 . . . . K6
Mont-Joli, Que. 6,359 . . . . . K6
Mont-Laurier, Que. 8,405 . . . J6
Montréal, Que. 980,354 . . . . J7
Moose Jaw, Sask. 33,941 . . . F6
Moosomin, Sask. 2,579 . . . . F5
Moosonee, Ont. 1,433 . . . . . H5
Morden, Man. 4,579 . . . . . . G6
Nain, Newf. 938 . . . . K4
Nanaimo, Br. Col. 47,069 . . . D6
Nares (str.), N.W.T. N3
Nelson, Br. Col. 9,143 . . . . . E6
Nelson (riv.), Man. G4
New Brunswick (prov.)
      709,442 . . . . K6
Newfoundland (isl.) L6
Nefoundland (prov.) 568,349 L5
New Westminster, Br. Col.
      38,550 . . . . D6
Niagara Falls, Ont. 70,960 . . J7
Norman Wells, N.W.T. 420 . . D2
North Battleford, Sask.
      14,030 . . . . F5

North Bay, Ont. 51,268 . . . . J6
North Magnetic Pole F1
North Saskatchewan (riv.) . . . E5
N. Vancouver, Br. Col. 33,952 . D6
Northwest Territories
      52,238 . . . . E2
Nova Scotia (prov.)
      873,176 . . . . K7
Okanagan (lake), Br. Co. . . . D6
Ontario (prov.) 9,101,694 . . . H5
Ottawa (cap.), Canada
      295,163 . . . . J6
Ottawa (riv.) J6
Owen Sound, Ont. 19,883 . . . H7
Pangnirtung, N.W.T. 839 . . . K2
Parry (chan.), N.W.T. E-H1
Parry Sound, Ont. 6,124 . . . J6
Peace (riv.), Alta. E4
Peel (riv.) C2
Pelly (riv.), Yukon C3
Pembroke, Ont. 14,026 . . . . J6
Péribonca (riv.), Que. J5
Peterborough, Ont.
      60,620 . . . . J7
Pincher Creek, Alta. 3,757 . . E6
Pond Inlet, N.W.T. 705 . . . . J1
Portage la Prairie, Man.
      13,086 . . . . G5
Povungnituk, Que. J3
Prince Albert, Sask. 31,380 . . F5
Prince Edward Island (prov.)
      126,646 . . . . K6
Prince George, Br. Col.
      67,559 . . . . D5

Prince Patrick (isl.), N.W.T. . . M3
Prince Rupert, Br. Col. 16,197 . C5
Québec (prov.) 6,532,461 . . . J5
Québec (cap.), Que. 166,474 . J6
Queen Charlotte (isls.), Br.
      Col. C5
Queen Elizabeth (isls.),
      N.W.T. M3
Quesnel, Br. Col. 8,240 . . . . D5
Race (cape), Newf. L6
Rainy (lake), Ont. G6
Rainy River, Ont. 1,061 . . . . G6
Rankin Inlet, N.W.T. 1,109 . . G3
Ray (cape), Newf. L6
Red Deer, Alta. 46,393 . . . . E5
Regina (cap.), Sask. 162,613 F6
Reindeer (lake) F4
Revelstoke, Br. Col. 5,544 . . E5
Riding Mountain Nat'l Park,
      Man. F5
Rimouski, Que. 29,120 . . . . K6
Rivière-du-Loup, Que. 13,459 K6
Roberval, Que. 11,429 . . . . J6
Robson (mt.), Br. Col. D5
Rocky (mts.) D4
Rocky Mountain House, Alta.
      4,698 . . . . E5
Rouyn, Que. 17,224 . . . . . . J6
Sable (cape), N.S. K7
Sable (isl.), N.S. L7
Saint Elias (mt.), Yukon B3
Saint John, N. Br. 80,521 . . . K6
St. John's (cap.), Newf.
      83,770 . . . . L6
Saint Lawrence (riv.) K6

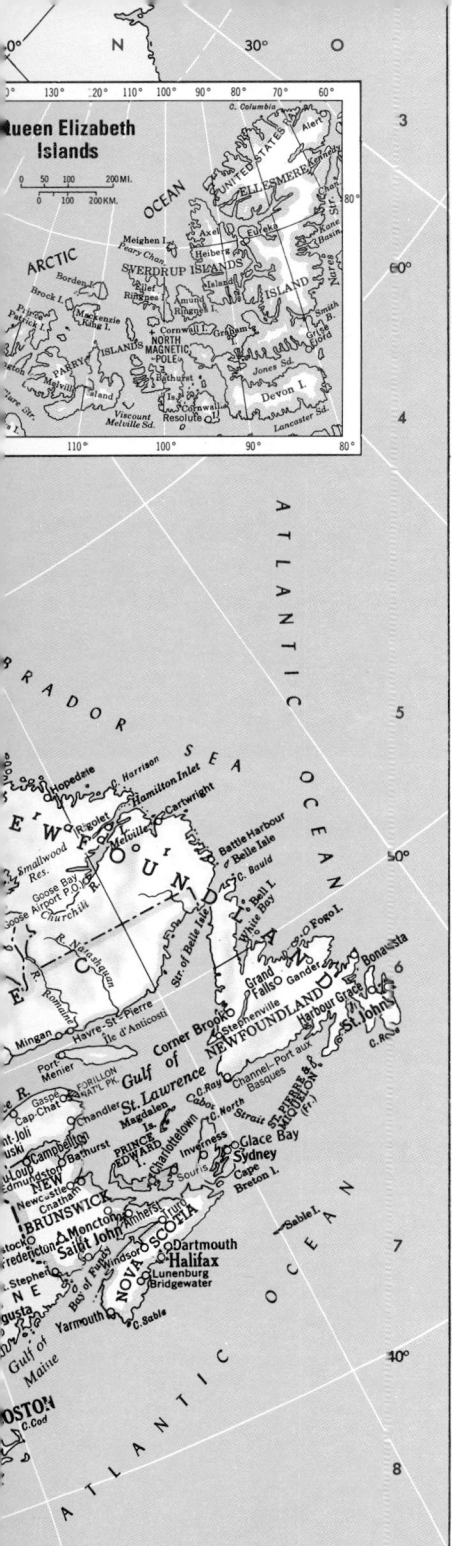

AREA 3,851,787 sq. mi. (9,976,139 sq. km.)
POPULATION 25,309,331
CAPITAL Ottawa
LARGEST CITY Montréal
HIGHEST POINT Mt. Logan 19,524 ft. (5,951 m.)
MONETARY UNIT Canadian dollar
MAJOR LANGUAGES English, French
MAJOR RELIGIONS Protestantism, Roman Catholicism

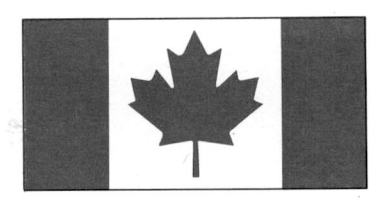

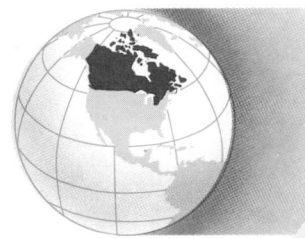

Population Distribution

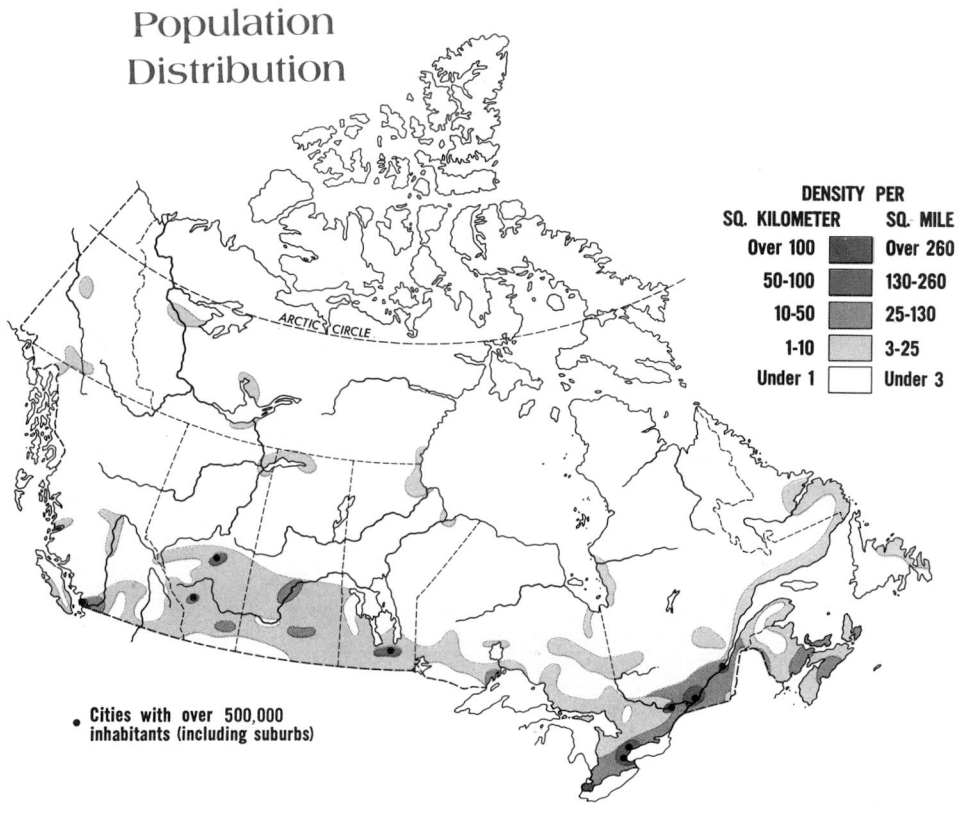

DENSITY PER

SQ. KILOMETER	SQ. MILE
Over 100	Over 260
50-100	130-260
10-50	25-130
1-10	3-25
Under 1	Under 3

● Cities with over 500,000 inhabitants (including suburbs)

Vegetation

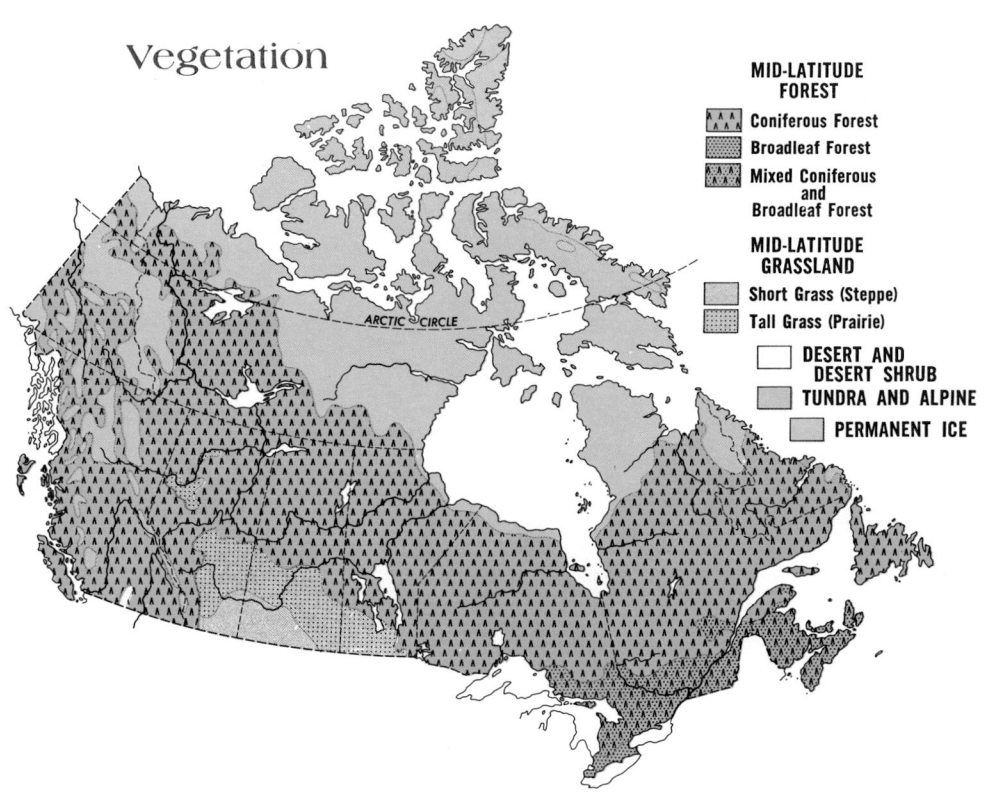

MID-LATITUDE FOREST
Coniferous Forest
Broadleaf Forest
Mixed Coniferous and Broadleaf Forest

MID-LATITUDE GRASSLAND
Short Grass (Steppe)
Tall Grass (Prairie)

DESERT AND DESERT SHRUB
TUNDRA AND ALPINE
PERMANENT ICE

Saint Pierre & Miquelon (isls.)
6 041 . . . . L6
Sarnia, Ont. 50,892 . . . . H7
Saskatchewan (prov.) 1,009,613 F5
Saskatchewan (riv.) F5
Saskatoon, Sask. 154,210 . . . F5
Sault Sainte Marie, Ont.
82,697 . . . . H6
Schefferville, Que. 1,997 . . . . K5
Selkirk, Man. 10,037 . . . . . . G5
Sept-Iles, Que. 29,262 . . . . . K5
Shawinigan, Que. 23,011 . . . . J6
Sherbrooke, Que. 74,075 . . . . J7
Sioux Lookout, Ont. 3,074 . . . G5
Skeena (riv.), Br. Col. D5
Slave (riv.) E3
Smallwood (res.), Newf. K5
Southampton (isl.), N.W.T. . . H2
Stettler, Alta. 5,136 . . . . E5
Stewart (riv.), Yukon C3
Stikine (riv.), Br. Col. C4
Sudbury, Ont. 91,829 . . . . . . H6
Swift Current, Sask. 14,747 . . F5
Sydney, N.S. 29,444 . . . . K6
Terrace, Br. Col. ○10,914 . . . D5
The Pas, Man. 6,390 . . . . F5
Thompson, Man. 14,288 . . . . G4
Thunder Bay, Ont. 112,486 . . H6
Timmins Ont. 46,114 . . . . . . H6
Toronto (cap.), Ont.
599,217 . . . . H7
Trail, Br. Col. 9,599 . . . . E6
Trois-Rivières, Que. 50,466 . . J6
Truro, N.S. 12,552 . . . . K6
Tuktoyaktuk, N.W.T. 772 . . . . C2

Val-d'Or, Que. 21,371 . . . . . . J6
Vancouver, Br. Col. 414,281 . . D6
Vancouver (isl.), Br. Col. D6
Vanderhoof, Br. Col. 2,323 . . D5
Vegreville, Alta. 5,25 . . . . . . E5
Vernon, Br. Col. 19,987 . . . . E5
Victoria (cap.), Br. Col. 64,379 . . D6
Victoria (isl.), N.W.T. E1
Wabush, Newf. 3,155 . . . . . . K5
Waterton-Glacier International
Peace Park, Alta. E6
Wetaskiwin, Alta. 9,597 . . . . E5
Weyburn, Sask. 9,523 . . . . . . F6
Whitehorse (cap.), Yukon
14,814 . . . . C3
Williams Lake, Br. Col. 8,362 . . D5
Williston (lake), Br. Col. D4
Windsor, N.S. 3,646 . . . . K7
Windsor, Ont. 192,083 . . . . . H7
Winnipeg (cap.), Man.
564,473 . . . . G6
Winnipeg (lake), Man. G5
Winnipegosis (lake), Man. . . . F5
Wood Buffalo Nat'l Park, Alta. E4
Woods (lake) G6
Wrigley, N.W.T. 137 . . . . D3
Yarmouth, N.S. 7,475 . . . . . . K7
Yellowknife (cap.), N.W.T.
9,483 . . . . E3
Yoho Nat'l Park, Br. Col. E5
York Factory, Man. G4
Yorkton, Sask. 15,339 . . . . . . F5
Yukon Territory 23,504 . . . . . C3

○Population of municipality

Average January Temperature

FAHRENHEIT	CELSIUS
Over 32°	Over 0°
14° to 32°	-10° to 0°
-4° to 14°	-20° to -10°
-22° to -4°	-30° to -20°
Under -22°	Under -30°

Resolute -26°

Dawson -18°

Baker Lake -27°

Iqaluit -16°

Winnipeg -2°

Average January temperature in degrees Fahrenheit at selected stations

Inukjuak -13°

Edmonton 5°

Gander 21°

Vancouver 39°

Kamloops 21°

Winnipeg -2°

Thunder Bay 7°

Québec 9°

Montréal 16°

Toronto 25°

Average July Temperature

FAHRENHEIT	CELSIUS
Over 68°	Over 20°
50° to 68°	10° to 20°
Under 50°	Under 10°

Resolute 40°

Dawson 60°

Winnipeg 66°

Average July temperature in degrees Fahrenheit at selected stations

Baker Lake 51°

Iqaluit 46°

Inukjuak 48°

Edmonton 61°

Gander 62°

Vancouver 59°

Kamloops 70°

Winnipeg 66°

Thunder Bay 64°

Québec 66°

Montréal 71°

Toronto 72°

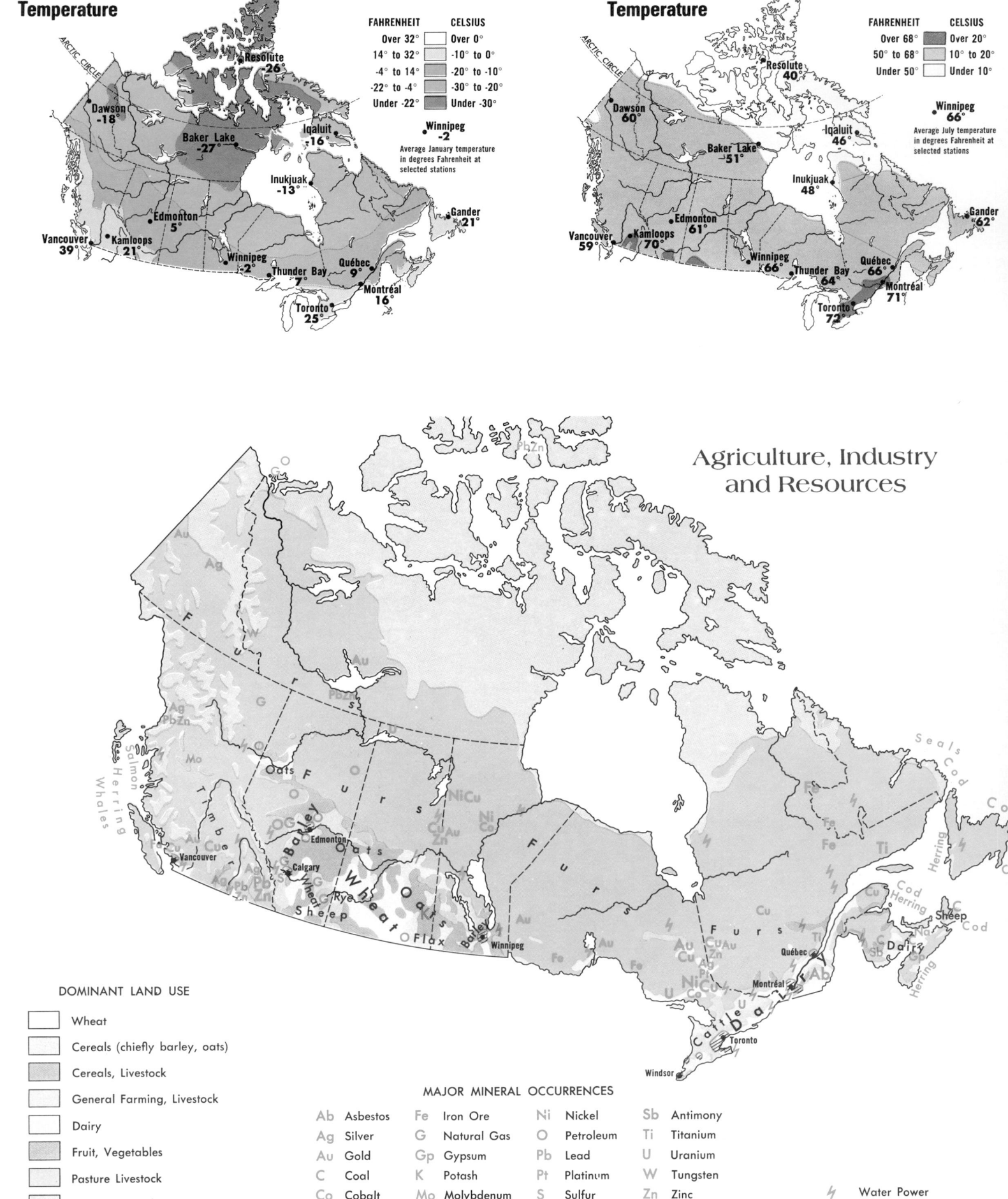

Agriculture, Industry and Resources

DOMINANT LAND USE

- Wheat
- Cereals (chiefly barley, oats)
- Cereals, Livestock
- General Farming, Livestock
- Dairy
- Fruit, Vegetables
- Pasture Livestock
- Range Livestock
- Forests
- Nonagricultural Land

MAJOR MINERAL OCCURRENCES

Ab	Asbestos	Fe	Iron Ore	Ni	Nickel	Sb	Antimony
Ag	Silver	G	Natural Gas	O	Petroleum	Ti	Titanium
Au	Gold	Gp	Gypsum	Pb	Lead	U	Uranium
C	Coal	K	Potash	Pt	Platinum	W	Tungsten
Co	Cobalt	Mo	Molybdenum	S	Sulfur	Zn	Zinc
Cu	Copper	Na	Salt				

⚡ Water Power

▨ Major Industrial Areas

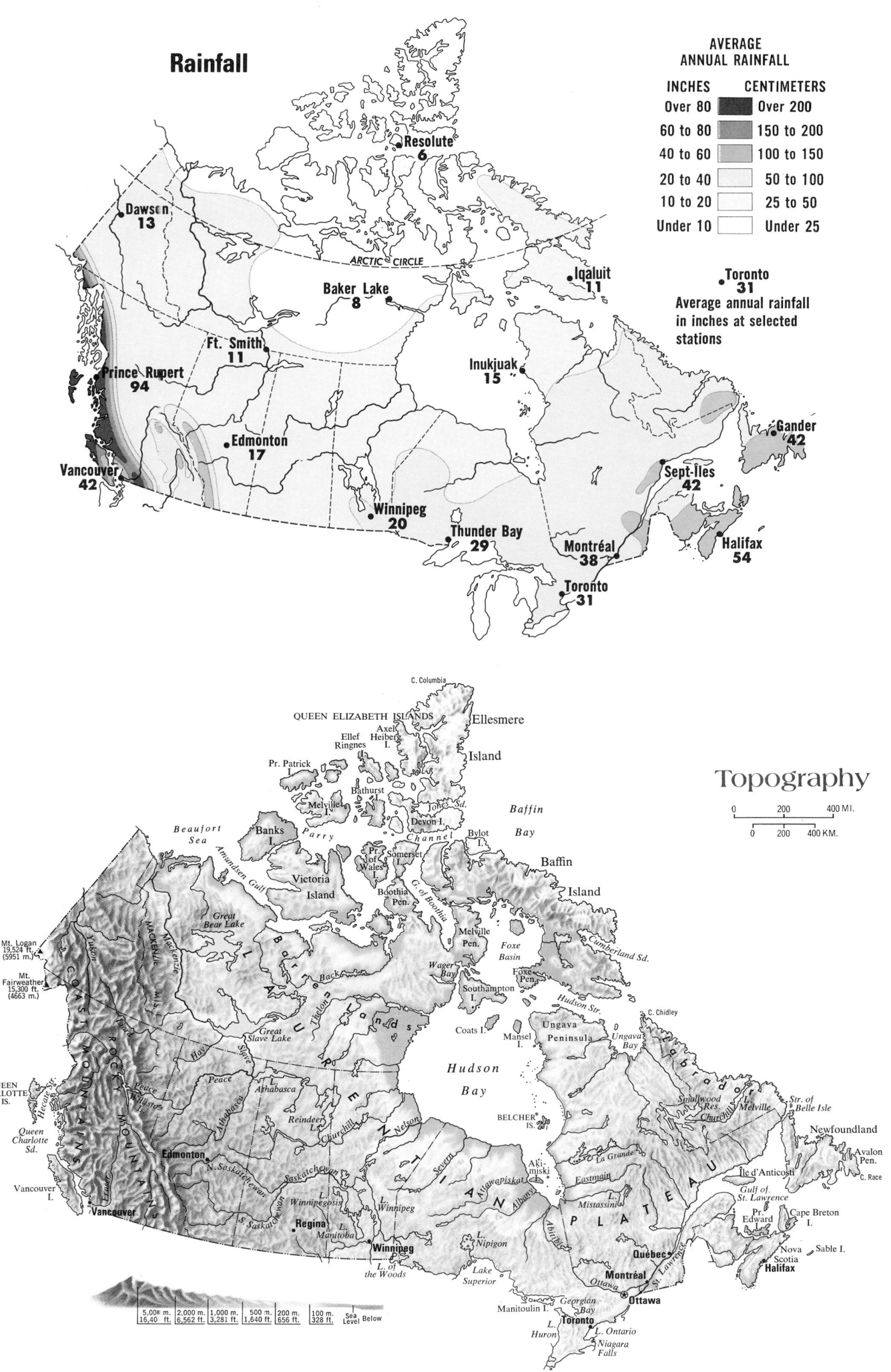

Rainfall

AVERAGE ANNUAL RAINFALL

INCHES	CENTIMETERS
Over 80	Over 200
60 to 80	150 to 200
40 to 60	100 to 150
20 to 40	50 to 100
10 to 20	25 to 50
Under 10	Under 25

Toronto
31
Average annual rainfall
in inches at selected
stations

Resolute
6

Dawson
13

ARCTIC CIRCLE

Baker Lake
8

Iqaluit
11

Ft. Smith
11

Inukjuak
15

Prince Rupert
94

Gander
42

Edmonton
17

Sept-Îles
42

Vancouver
42

Winnipeg
20

Thunder Bay
29

Montréal
38

Halifax
54

Toronto
31

Topography

0   200   400 MI.
0   200   400 KM.

C. Columbia

QUEEN ELIZABETH ISLANDS   Ellesmere

Axel
Heiberg
Ellef   I.
Ringnes
I.   Island

Pr. Patrick
I.

Bathurst
I.   Jones Sd.   Baffin

Melville I.   Devon I.   Bay

Beaufort   Banks   Parry   Bylot
Sea   I.   Channel   I.   Baffin

Amundsen Gulf   Pr.
of   Island
Wales   Somerset
I.
Victoria   Boothia
Island   Pen.

Great
Bear Lake   G. of Boothia   Cumberland Sd.

Mt. Logan
19,524 ft.   Melville
(5951 m.)   Pen.   Foxe
Mt.   Basin
Fairweather   Back   Wager
15,300 ft.   Bay   Foxe
(4663 m.)   Pen.

Great   Southampton
Slave Lake   I.   Hudson Str.

C. Chidley

Coats I.   Ungava
Mansel   Peninsula   Ungava
Bay

QUEEN   Hudson
CHARLOTTE
IS.   Bay   Smallwood   L.
Res.   Melville   Str. of
Churchill   Belle Isle
Queen   Reindeer
Charlotte   L.   Churchill   Newfoundland
Sd.   BELCHER
IS.   Avalon
Edmonton   Pen.
Vancouver   Île d'Anticosti   C. Race
I.   N. Saskatchewan   Akimiski   La Grande
Gulf of
Eastmain   St. Lawrence
Vancouver   L.   Cape Breton
Winnipegosis   L.   Mistassini   Pr.   I.
Winnipeg   Edward
Regina   Nova   Sable I.
L.   Québec   Scotia
Manitoba   Halifax
Winnipeg   Montréal
Ottawa
L. of   Lake   Toronto   L. Ontario
the Woods   Superior   Niagara
Falls

5,000 m. 2,000 m. 1,000 m. 500 m. 200 m. 100 m. Sea
16,400 ft. 6,562 ft. 3,281 ft. 1,640 ft. 656 ft. 328 ft. Level Below

NEWFOUNDLAND

CITIES and TOWNS

dmiral's Beach 362 D2
dmiral's Cove 99 D2
nchor Point 368 C3
quaforte 200 D2
rgentia 93 C2
rnold's Cove 1,124 C2
vondale 890 D2
adger 1,090 C4
adger's Quay-Valleyfield-Pool's Island 1,566 D4
aie Verte 2,491 C4
attle Harbour C3
auline 423 D2
ay Bulls 1,081 D2
ay de Verde 786 D2
ay L'Argent 483 D4
ay Roberts 4,512 D2
ellburns 147 C3
elleoram 565 C4
ellevue 286 D2
ide Arm 339 C3
ig Pond 167 D2
irchy Bay 707 D4
ird Cove 400 C3
ishop's Falls 4,395 C4
lack Tickle 194 C3
lackhead Road 1,855 D2
laketown 617 D2
loomfield 715 D2
onavista 4,460 D2
otwood 4,074 C4
ranch 462 D2
rigus 898 D2
road Cove 198 D2
rooklyn 197 D2
rownsdale 199 D2
uchans 1,655 C4
unyan's Cove 590 C2
urgeo 2,504 C4
urin 2,904 C4
urnt Islands 991 C4
urnt Point 260 D2
alvert 482 D2
ampbellton 703 D4
ape Broyle 698 D2
ape Ray 484 C4
aplin Cove 150 D2
arbonear 5,335 D2
armanville 966 D4
artwright 658 C3
atalina 1,162 D2
avendish 343 D2
hampney's West 141 D2
hance Cove 498 D2
hange Islands 580 D4
hannel-Port aux Basques 5,988 C4
hapel Arm 689 D2
harlottetown 330 D2
harlottetown 250 C3
hurchill Falls 936 B3
larenville 2,878 C2
larke's Beach 1,009 D2
odroy 346 C4
olinet 318 D2
olliers 819 D2
ome By Chance 337 C2
onception Harbour 917 D2
onche 464 C3
ook's Harbour 388 C3
orner Brook 24,339 C4
Cow Head 695 C4
Cox's Cove 980 C4
Cupids 706 D2
Daniell's Harbour 614 C3
Dark Cove 1,344 D4
Davis Inlet 240 B2
Deep Bight 243 C2
Deer Lake 4,348 C4
Dildo 877 D2
Dunville 1,817 D2
Durrell 1,145 D4
Eastport 597 D1
Elliston 527 D2
Embree 846 C4
Englee 998 C3
English Harbour 118 D2
English Harbour West 327 C4
Fermeuse 584 D2
Ferryland 795 D2
Flat Bay 322 C4
Flat Rock 808 D2
Fleur de Lys 616 C3
Flowers Cove 459 C3
Fogo 1,105 D4
Forteau 520 C3
Fortune 2,473 C4
Fox Harbour 280 C3
Fox Harbour 538 D2
François 219 C4
Freshwater 1,276 C2
Freshwater 209 D2
Gambo 2,932 D4
Gander 10,404 D4
Garnish 761 C4
Gaskiers-Point la Haye 505 D2
Gaultois 558 C4
Georges Brook 356 D2
Glenwood 1,129 D4
Glovertown 2,165 C1
Goobies 185 D2
Goose Bay-Happy Valley 7,103 B3
Gooseberry Cove 195 C2
Goose Cove 134 C2
Goose Cove 368 C3
Goulds 4,242 D2
Grand Bank 3,901 C4
Grand Falls 8,765 C4
Grates Cove 275 D2
Green Island Cove 222 C3
Green's Harbour 785 D2
Greenspond 423 D2
Grey River 234 C4
Gull Island 362 D2
Hampden 838 C4
Hant's Harbour 542 D2
Happy Adventure 352 D2
Happy Valley-Goose Bay 7,103 B3
Harbour Breton 2,464 C4
Harbour Deep 278 C4
Harbour Grace 2,988 D2
Harbour Main-Chapel Cove-Lakeview 1,303 D2
Hare Bay 1,520 D4
Hawke's Bay 553 C3
Head of Bay d'Espoir 586 C4
Heart's Content 625 D2
Heart's Delight-Islington 899 D2
Heart's Desire 416 D2
Heatherton 328 C4
Hermitage 863 C4
Hickman's Harbour 479 D2
Hillview 295 D2
Hodge's Cove 438 D2
Holyrood 1,789 D2
Hopedale 425 B2
Howley 456 C4
Isle aux Morts 1,238 C4
Jackson's Arm 623 C4
Jeffrey's 276 C4
Jerseyside 641 B3
Job's Cove 201 D2
Joe Batt's Arm-Barr'd Islands 1,155 D4
Keels 129 D1
Kelligrews (Foxtrap-Greeleytown-Peachtown-Kelligrews) 2,292 D2
Kilbride 5,014 D2
King's Cove 253 D1
King's Point 825 C4
Kippens 1,219 C4
Labrador City 11,538 A3
Lamaline 548 C4
L'Anse-au-Clair 267 C3
L'Anse-au-Loup 589 C3
L'Anse au Meadow 66 C3
La Poile 186 C4
Lark Harbour 783 C4
La Scie 1,422 C4
Lawn 999 C4
Lethbridge 686 D2
Lewisporte 3,963 C4
Little Bay Islands 407 C4
Little Catalina 750 D2
Little Heart's Ease 467 D2
Lodge Bay 124 C3
Long Harbour-Mount Arlington Heights 660 D2
Lourdes 932 C4
Lower Island Cove 415 D2
Lumsden 645 D4
Main Brook 514 C3
Makkovik 347 C2
Markland 344 D2
Mary's Harbour 408 C3
Marystown 6,299 C4
McCallum 243 C4
Melrose 416 D2
Middle Arm, Green Bay 575 C4
Millertown 228 C4
Milltown-Head of Bay d Espoir 1,376 C4
Milton 258 D2
Mobile 171 D2
Mount Carmel-Mitchell's Brook-St. Catherine's 699 D2
Mount Pearl 11,543 D2
Musgrave Harbour 1,554 D4
Musgravetown 635 C2
Nain 938 B2
New Bonaventure 106 D2
New Chelsea 144 D2
New Harbour 777 D2
Newmans Cove 231 D2
New Perlican 350 D2
Newtown 511 D4
Nippers Harbour 259 C4
Norman's Cove-Long Cove 1,152 D2
Norris Arm 1,216 C4
Norris Point 1,033 C4
North Harbour 151 D2
North River 245 D2
North West Brook 279 C2
North West River 515 B3
O'Donnells 280 D2
Old Bonaventure 111 D2
Old Perlican 709 D2
Paradise 2,861 D2
Parkers Cove 424 D4
Parson's Pond 605 C3
Pasadena 2,685 C4
Patrick's Cove 155 C2
Perry's Cove 141 D2
Peterview 1,119 C4
Petites 108 C4
Petley 147 D2
Petty Harbour-Maddox Cove 853 D2
Picadilly 524 C4
Pinware River 201 C3
Placentia 2,204 C2
Plate Cove 474 D2
Point La Haye 195 D2
Point Lance 141 C2
Point Leamington 848 C4
Point Verde 296 C2
Pollards Point 502 C4
Port au Bras 366 D4
Port au Choix 1,311 C3
Port au Port 603 C4
Port Blandford 702 C2
Port Hope Simpson 581 C3
Port Kirwan 164 D2
Port Rexton 489 D2
Port Saunders 769 C3
Portugal Cove 2,361 D2
Portugal Cove South 371 D2
Port Union 671 D2
Postville 223 B3
Pouch Cove 1,522 D2
Princeton 204 D2
Raleigh 373 C3
Ramea 1,386 C4
Red Bay 316 C3
Red Head Cove 225 D2
Rencontre East 230 C4
Renews-Cappahayden 578 D2
Rigolet 271 C3
Riverhead 431 D2
River of Ponds 304 C3
Robert's Arm 1,005 C4
Rocky Harbour 1,273 C4
Roddickton 1,142 C3
Rose Blanche-Harbour le Cou 975 C4
Rushoon 520 D4
Saint Alban's 1,968 C4
Saint Andrew's 262 C4
Saint Anthony 3,107 C3
Saint Brendan's 468 D4
Saint Bride's 599 C2
Saint George's 1,756 C4
St. John's (cap.) 83,770 D2
Saint Joseph's 262 D2
Saint Lawrence 2,012 C4
Saint Lunaire-Griquet 1,010 C3
Saint Mary's 701 D2
Saint Paul's 454 C4
Saint Phillips 1,365 D2
Saint Shotts 239 D2
Saint Vincent's-Saint Stephens-Peter's River 796 D2
Sally's Cove 100 C4
Salmon Cove 786 D2
Seal Cove 751 C3
Seal Cove-White Bay 498 C4
Seldom-Little Seldom 560 D4
Ship Harbour 265 D2
Shoal Cove 223 C3
Shoal Harbour 1,000 C2
South Branch 264 C4
South Brook, Hall's Bay Dist. 786 C4
South Brook, Humber Dist. 477 C4
Southern Harbour 772 C2
South River 645 D2
Spaniard's Bay 2,125 D2
Springdale 3,501 C4
Stephenville 8,876 C4
Stephenville Crossing 2,172 C4
Summerford 1,198 C4
Summerville 346 D2
Sunnyside 703 D2
Sweet Bay 204 D2
Swift Current 329 C2
Terrenceville 796 D4
Tilting 427 D4
Torbay 3,394 D2
Tors Cove 355 D2
Traytown 383 D1
Trepassey 1,473 D2
Trinity 522 D2
Trinity 375 D4
Trout River 759 C4
Twillingate 1,506 C4
Upper Island Cove 2,025 D2
Victoria 1,870 D2
Wabana 4,254 D2
Wabush 3,155 A3
Wesleyville 1,125 D4
Western Bay 463 D2
West Saint Modeste 273 C3
Whitbourne 1,233 D2
Wild Cove 152 C3
Windsor 5,747 C4
Winterton 753 D2
Witless Bay 907 D2

OTHER FEATURES

Alexis (riv.) C3
Anguille (cape) C4
Annieopscotch (mts.) C4
Ashuanipi (lake) A3
Ashuanipi (riv.) A3
Atikonak (lake) B3
Attikamagen (lake) A3
Avalon (pen.) D2
Barachois Pond Prov. Park C4
Bauld (cape) C3
Bell (isl.) C3
Bell (isl.) D2
Belle Isle (isl.) C3
Belle Isle (str.) C3
Blackhead (bay) D2
Bonavista (bay) D1
Bonavista (cape) D1
Bonne (bay) C4
Branch (riv.) C2
Broyle (cape) D2
Bull Arm (inlet) D2
Burin (pen.) C4
Butter Pot Prov. Park D2
Cabot (str.) B4
Canada (bay) C3
Chidley (cape) B1
Churchill (falls) B3
Churchill (riv.) B3
Cirque (mt.) B2
Clode (sound) D2
Conception (bay) D2
Deep (inlet) B2
Double Mer (lake) C3
Dyke (lake) A3
Eagle (riv.) C3
Espoir (bay) C4
Exploits (riv.) C4
Fogo (isl.) D4
Fortune (bay) C4
Freels (cape) D3
Gander (lake) D4
Gander (riv.) D4
Glover (isl.) C4
Goose (riv.) B3
Grand (lake) B3
Grand (lake) C4
Grates (pt.) D2
Great Colinet (isl.) D2
Grey (isls.) C3
Groais (isl.) C3
Gros Morne (mt.) C4
Gros Morne Nat'l Park C4
Groswater (bay) C3
Hamilton (inlet) C3
Hamilton (sound) D4
Hare (bay) C3
Hawke (hills) D2
Hebron (fjord) B2
Hermitage (bay) C4
Holyrood (bay) D2
Horse (isls.) C3
Horse Chops (head) D2
Humber (riv.) C4
Ingornachoix (bay) C3
Ireland's Eye (isl.) D2
Islands (bay) C4
Kaipokok (bay) B3
Kanairiktok (riv.) B3
Kaumajet (mts.) B2
Kingurutik (mesa) B2
Labrador (reg.) B2
Labrador (sea) C2
La Manche Valley Prov. Park D2
La Poile (bay) C4
Little Mecatina (riv.) B3
Long (isl.) C2
Long (lake) A3
Long (pt.) C4
Long Range (mts.) C4
Main Topsail (mt.) C4
Makkovik (cape) C2
McLelan (str.) B1
Mealy (lake) C3
Meelpaeg (lake) C4
Melville (lake) C3
Menihek (lakes) A3
Merasheen (isl.) C2
Mistaken (pt.) D2
Mistastin (lake) B2
Nachvak (fjord) B2
Naskaupi (riv.) B3
Newfoundland (isl.) C4
Newman (sound) D2
New World (isl.) C4
Norman (cape) C3
North Aulatsivik (isl.) B2
Notre Dame (bay) C4
Okak (bay) B2
Ossokmanuan (res.) B3
Petitsikapau (lake) A3
Pine (cape) D2
Pinware (riv.) C3
Pistolet (bay) C3
Placentia (bay) C2
Ponds (isl.) C3
Port au Port (bay) C4
Port au Port (pen.) C4
Port Manvers (harb.) B2
Race (cape) D2
Ramah (bay) B2
Ramea (isls.) C4
Random (isl.) D2
Random (sound) D2
Ray (cape) C4
Red (isl.) C2
Red Indian (lake) C4
Red Wine (riv.) B3
Rocky (riv.) D2
Round (pond) C4
Saglek (bay) B2
Saint Francis (cape) D2
Saint George (cape) C4
Saint George's (bay) C4
Saint John (bay) C3
Saint John (cape) C3
Saint Lawrence (gulf) B4
Saint Lewis (cape) C3
Saint Mary's (bay) C2
Saint Mary's (cape) C2
Saint Michaels (bay) C3
Salmonier (riv.) D2
Sandwich (bay) C3
Shabogamo (lake) A3
Shoal (bay) D2
Smallwood (res.) B3
Smith (sound) D2
South Aulatsivik (isl.) B2
Spear (cape) D2
Squires Mem. Park C4
Swale (isl.) D1
Terra Nova (riv.) C2
Terra Nova Nat'l Park C2
Territok (cape) B2
Thoresby (mt.) B2
Torbay (pt.) D2
Torngat (mts.) B2
Trespassey (bay) D2
Trinity (bay) D2
Tunungayualok (isl.) B2
Ukasiksalik (isl.) B2
Victoria (lake) C4
White (bay) C3
White Bear (lake) C4
White Handkerchief (cape) B2

SAINT PIERRE and MIQUELON

CITIES and TOWNS

Saint-Pierre (cap.) 5,415 C4

OTHER FEATURES

Miquelon (isl.) 626 C4
Saint Pierre (isl.) 5,415 C4

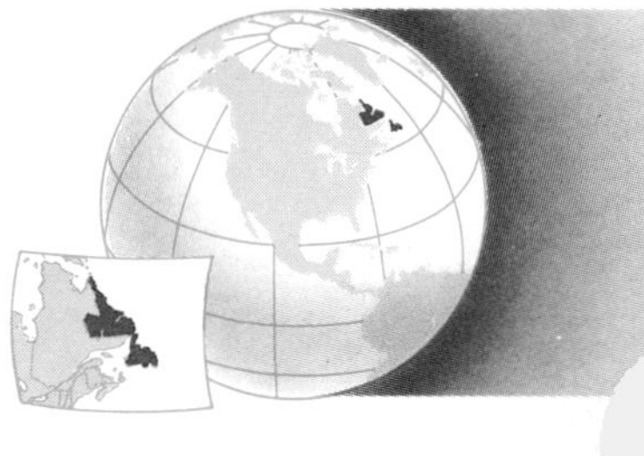

AREA 156,184 sq. mi. (404,517 sq. km.)
POPULATION 568,349
CAPITAL St. John's
LARGEST CITY St. John's
HIGHEST POINT in Torngat Mountains 5,420 ft. (1,652 m.)
SETTLED IN 1610
ADMITTED TO CONFEDERATION 1949
PROVINCIAL FLOWER Pitcher Plant

Agriculture, Industry and Resources

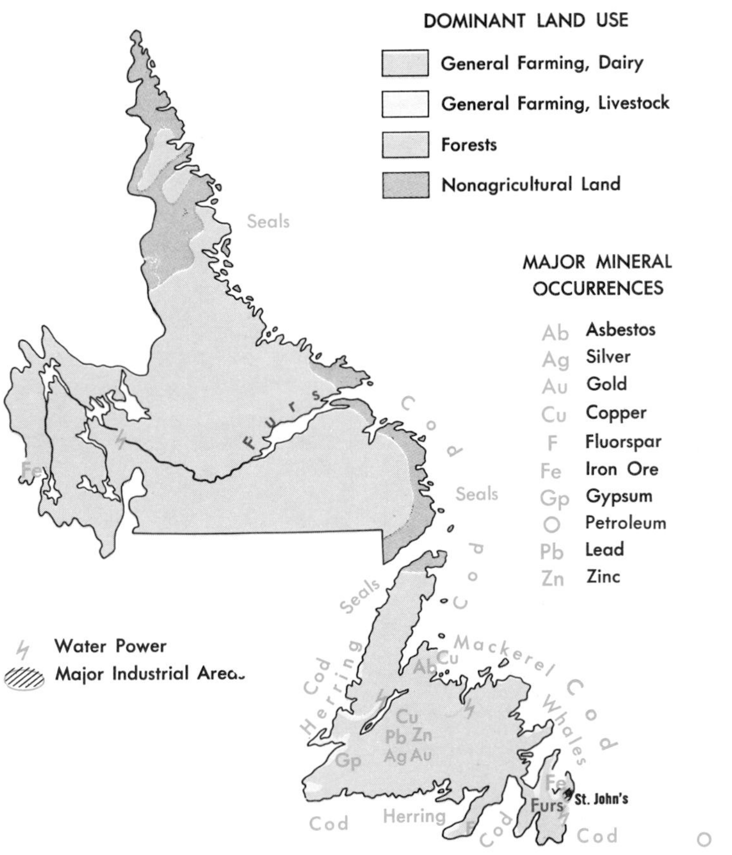

DOMINANT LAND USE
General Farming, Dairy
General Farming, Livestock
Forests
Nonagricultural Land
MAJOR MINERAL OCCURRENCES
Ab Asbestos
Ag Silver
Au Gold
Cu Copper
F Fluorspar
Fe Iron Ore
Gp Gypsum
O Petroleum
Pb Lead
Zn Zinc
Water Power
Major Industrial Area
Seals
Furs
Cod
Herring
Mackerel
Whales
St. John's

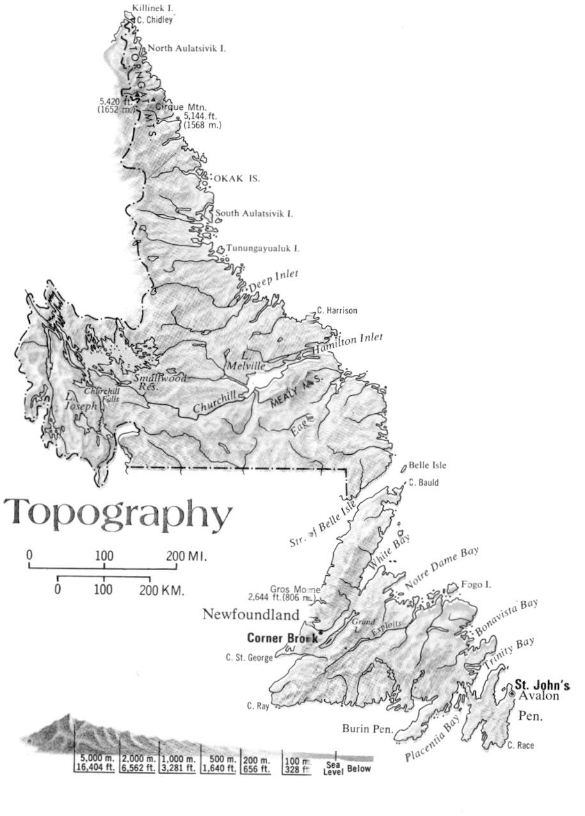

Killinek I.
C. Chidley
North Aulatsivik I.
Cirque Mtn.
OKAK IS.
South Aulatsivik I.
Tunungayualuk I.
Deep Inlet
C. Harrison
Hamilton Inlet
Melville
Smallwood Res.
Churchill
MEALY MTS.
Belle Isle
C. Bauld
Str. of Belle Isle
White Bay
Notre Dame Bay
Fogo I.
Gros Morne
Newfoundland
Corner Brook
C. St. George
Bonavista Bay
Trinity Bay
St. John's
Avalon Pen.
C. Ray
Burin Pen.
Placentia Bay
C. Race

Topography

0 100 200 MI.
0 100 200 KM.

NOVA SCOTIA

CITIES and TOWNS

COUNTIES

Annapolis 22,522	C 4
Antigonish 18,110	F 3
Cape Breton 127,035	H 3
Colchester 43,224	E 3
Cumberland 35,231	D 3
Digby 21,689	C 4
Guysborough 12,752	F 3
Halifax 288,126	E 4
Hants 33,121	D 4
Inverness 22,337	G 2
Kings 49,739	D 4
Lunenburg 45,746	D 4
Pictou 50,350	F 3
Queens 13,126	D 4
Richmond 12,284	H 3
Shelburne 17,328	C 5
Victoria 8,432	H 2
Yarmouth 26,290	C 5

Alder Point 651	H 2
Aldershot	D 3
Amherst⊛ 9,684	D 3
Annapolis Royal⊛ 631	C 4
Antigonish⊛ 5,205	F 3
Arichat 824	H 3
Aylesford 744	D 4
Baddeck⊛ 972	H 2
Barrington Passage 722	C 5
Bear River-Sissiboo 854	C 4
Beaverbank 1,322	E 4
Berwick 1,699	D 4
Bridgetown 1,047	C 4
Bridgewater 6,669	D 4
Brookfield 619	E 3
Brooklyn 1,269	D 4
Cambridge Station 799	D 3
Canning 763	D 3
Canso 1,255	H 3
Centreville 765	D 3
Chéticamp 1,022	G 2

Chester 1,131	D 4
Chester Basin 639	D 4
Church Point 318	B 4
Clark's Harbour 1,059	C 5
Coldbrook Station 617	D 3
Cow Bay 670	E 4
Dartmouth 62,277	E 4
Debert 618	E 3
Digby⊛ 2,558	C 4
Dominion 2,856	J 2
Donkin 873	J 2
Ellershouse-Hartville 662	D 4
Elmsdale 1,172	E 4
Enfield 1,510	E 4
Fall River 1,897	E 4
Falmouth 1,110	D 3
Glace Bay 21,466	J 2
Guysborough⊛ 496.	G 3
Halifax (cap.)⊛ 114,594	E 4
Halifax *277,727	E 4
Hantsport 1,395	D 3
Herring Cove 1,323.	E 4
Hilden 1,262	E 3

Ingonish 471	H 2
Inverness 2,013.	G 2
Judique 925	G 3
Kentville⊛ 4,974	D 3
Kingston 1,612	D 4
Lakeside 936	E 4
Lantz 1,172	E 4
Liverpool⊛ 3,304	D 4
Lockeport 724	C 5
Louisbourg 1,410	J 3
Louisdale 979	G 3
Lower West Pubnico 790	C 5
Lunenburg⊛ 3,014	D 4
Mahone Bay 1,228	D 4
Meteghan 890	B 4
Middleton 1,834	C 4
Milford Station 748	E 3
Milton 1,678	D 4
Mount Uniacke 1,145	D 4
Mulgrave 903	G 3
Musquodoboit Harbour 936.	E 4
New Glasgow 10,464	F 3
New Victoria 1,374	H 2

New Waterford 8,808	J 2
North Sydney 7,820	H 2
Oxford 1,470	E 3
Parrsboro 1,799	D 3
Pictou⊛ 4,628	F 3
Porters Lake 893	E 4
Port Hastings 312	G 3
Port Hawkesbury 3,850	G 3
Port Hood 701.	G 2
Port Morien 717.	J 2
Port Williams 1,227.	D 3
Prospect 693	E 4
Pugwash 648	E 3
Reserve Mines 2,472	H 2
River Hébert 835.	D 3
Saint Peters 669	H 3
Sandy Point 691	C 5
Scotchtown 2,037.	H 2
Sheet Harbour 819.	F 4
Shelburne⊛ 2,303.	C 5
Shubenacadie 984	E 3
Springhill 4,896	E 3
Stellarton 5,435.	F 3

Stewiacke 1,174	E 3
Sydney 29,444	H 2
Sydney Mines 8,501.	H 2
Terence Bay 960	E 4
Thorburn 1,014.	F 3
Three Mile Plains 1,355	D 4
Timberlea 1,159	E 4
Trenton 3,154.	F 3
Truro⊛ 12,552.	E 3
Waterville 687	D 3
Waverley 1,699	E 4
Wedgeport 827	C 5
Western Shore 1,712	D 4
Westmount 3,097	H 2
Westville 4,522	F 3
Wileville 746.	D 4
Windsor⊛ 3,235	D 3
Wolfville 3,235.	D 3
Yarmouth⊛ 7,475	B 5

OTHER FEATURES

Advocate (bay)	D 3

Ainslie (lake)	G 2
Amet (sound)	E 3
Andrew (isl.)	H 2
Annapolis (basin)	C 4
Annapolis (riv.)	C 4
Antigonish (harb.)	G 3
Argos (cape)	H 2
Aspy (bay)	H 1
Baccaro (pt.)	C 5
Baddeck (riv.)	H 2
Barachois (pt.).	G 3
Barren (isl.)	H 3
Barrington (bay)	C 5
Bedford (basin)	E 4
Berry (head).	D 3
Boularderie (isl.)	H 2
Bras d'Or (lake)	H 2
Breton (cape)	J 3
Brier (isl.)	B 4
Canso (cape)	H 3
Canso (str.)	H 3
Cap d'Or (cape)	D 3

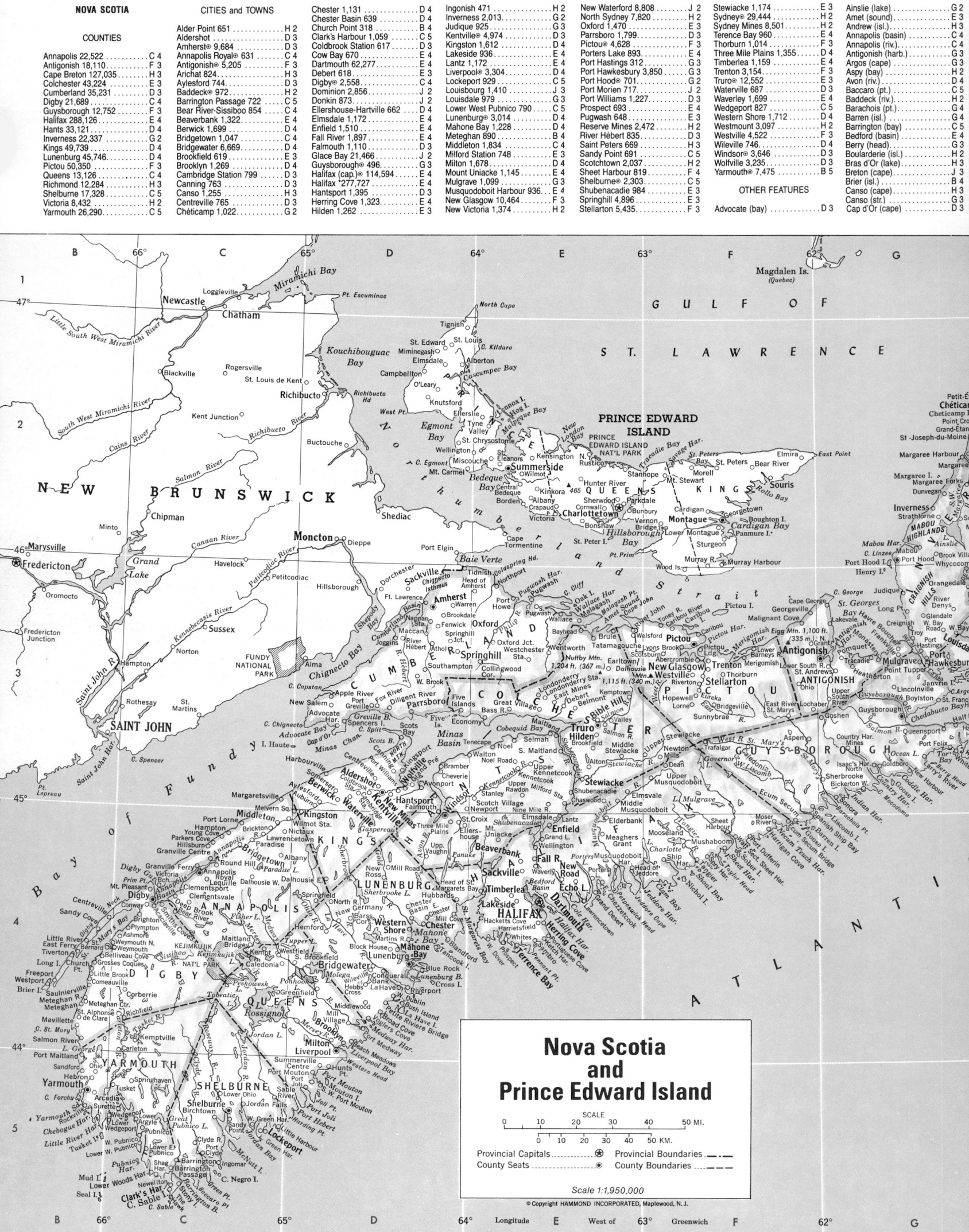

Nova Scotia and Prince Edward Island

SCALE
0   10   20   30   40   50 MI.
0   10   20   30   40   50 KM.

Provincial Capitals .... ⊛
County Seats .... ⊛
Provincial Boundaries ____ . ____
County Boundaries ____ ____

Scale 1:1,950,000

© Copyright HAMMOND INCORPORATED, Maplewood, N.J.

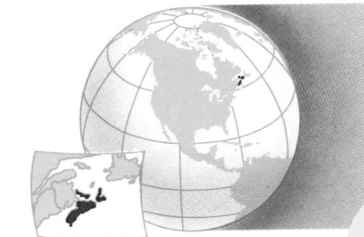

Cape Breton (isl.)	J 2
Cape Breton Highlands Nat'l Park	H 2
Cape Negro (isl.)	C 5
Cape Sable (isl.)	C 5
Capstan (cape)	D 3
Caribou (isl.)	F 3
Carleton (riv.)	C 4
Charlotte (lake)	F 4
Chebogue (harb.)	B 5
Chedabucto (bay)	G 3
Chéticamp (isl.)	G 2
Chignecto (bay)	D 3
Chignecto (cape)	C 3
Chignecto (isth.)	C 3
Clam (bay)	F 4
Cliff (cape)	E 3
Clyde (riv.)	C 5
Cobequid (bay)	E 3
Coddle (harb.)	G 3
Coldspring (head)	E 3
Cole (harb.)	E 4
Country (harb.)	G 3

Craignish (hills)	G 3
Cross (isl.)	D 4
Cumberland (basin)	D 3
Dalhousie (mt.)	E 3
Dauphin (cape)	H 2
Digby Gut (chan.)	C 4
Digby Neck (pen.)	B 4
East (bay)	H 3
East (riv.)	F 3
East Bay (hills)	H 3
Egmont (cape)	H 2
Eigg (mt.)	F 3
Fisher (lake)	C 4
Five (isls.)	D 3
Forchu (bay)	B 5
Forchu (cape)	B 5
Framboise Cove (bay)	H 3
Fundy (bay)	C 3
Gabarus (bay)	H 3
Gabarus (cape)	J 3
George (cape)	G 3
George (lake)	B 5

Gold (riv.)	D 4
Goose (isl.)	F 4
Goose (isl.)	G 3
Governor (lake)	F 3
Great Bras d'Or (chan.)	H 2
Great Pubnico (lake)	C 5
Green (pt.)	C 5
Greville (bay)	D 3
Guysborough (riv.)	G 3
Halifax (harb.)	E 4
Harding (pt.)	D 5
Haute (isl.)	C 3
Hébert (riv.)	D 3
Henry (isl.)	G 3
Indian (harb.)	G 3
Ingonish North (bay)	H 2
Janvrin (isl.)	G 3
Jeddore (harb.)	F 4
John (cape)	E 3
Joli (pt.)	D 5
Jordan (bay)	C 5
Jordan (lake)	C 4
Jordan (riv.)	C 5
Kejimkujik (lake)	C 4
Kejimkujik Nat'l Park	C 4
Kennetcook (riv.)	E 3
La Have (isl.)	D 4
La Have (riv.)	D 4
Linzee (cape)	G 2
Liscomb (isl.)	G 4
Little River (harb.)	B 5
Liverpool (bay)	D 5
Lomond, Loch (lake)	H 3
Long (isl.)	B 4
Louisbourg Nat'l Hist. Park	J 3
Lunenburg (bay)	D 4
Mabou (harb.)	G 2
Mabou Highlands (hills)	G 2
Madame (isl.)	H 3
Mahone (bay)	D 4
Malagash (pt.)	E 3
Margaree (riv.)	F 4
McNutt (isl.)	C 5
Medway (harb.)	D 4
Medway (riv.)	C 4
Merigomish (harb.)	F 3
Mersey (riv.)	C 4
Michaud (pt.)	H 3
Minas (basin)	D 3
Minas (chan.)	D 3
Mira (bay)	J 2
Mira (riv.)	H 3
Mocodome (cape)	G 3
Molega (lake)	D 4
Morien (cape)	J 2
Mouton (isl.)	D 5
Mud (isl.)	B 5
Mulgrave (lake)	F 3
Musquodoboit (riv.)	E 4
Necum Teuch (harb.)	F 4
Nichol (isl.)	F 4
North (cape)	H 1
North (isl.)	D 3
North Aspy (riv.)	H 2
North Bay Ingonish (bay)	H 2
North East Margaree (riv.)	H 2
Northumberland (str.)	E 2
Nuttby (mt.)	E 3
Oak (isl.)	E 3
Ocean (lake)	G 3
Ohio (riv.)	D 4
Panuke (lake)	D 4
Paradise (lake)	C 4
Pennant (pt.)	E 4
Percé (cape)	J 2
Peskowesk (lake)	C 4
Petit-de-Grat (isl.)	H 3
Petpeswick (head)	E 4
Philip (riv.)	E 3
Pictou (harb.)	F 3
Pictou (isl.)	F 2
Pleasant (bay)	H 2
Ponhook (lake)	D 4
Porters (lake)	E 4
Port Hebert (harb.)	D 5
Port Hood (isl.)	G 2
Port Joli (harb.)	D 5
Port Mouton (harb.)	D 5
Poulet Cove (bay)	H 2
Prim (cape)	C 4
Pubnico (harb.)	C 5
Pugwash (harb.)	E 3
Roseway (riv.)	C 4
Rossignol (lake)	C 4
Sable (cape)	C 5
Sable (isl.)	H 5
Saint Andrews (chan.)	H 2
Saint Anns (bay)	H 2
Saint Georges (bay)	G 3
Saint Lawrence (bay)	H 1
Saint Lawrence (cape)	H 1
Saint Margarets (bay)	E 4
Saint Mary (cape)	B 4
Saint Marys (bay)	B 4
Saint Mary's (riv.)	F 3
Saint Patrick (chan.)	G 3
Saint Paul (isl.)	H 1
Saint Peters (bay)	H 3

Salmon (riv.)	E 3
Salmon (riv.)	G 3
Scatarie (isl.)	J 2
Scots (bay)	D 3
Seall (isl.)	B 5
Sheet (harb.)	F 4
Sherbrooke (lake)	D 4
Sherbrooke (riv.)	D 4
Shoal (bay)	C 4
Shubenacadie (lake)	E 4
Shubenacadie (riv.)	E 3
Sissiboo (riv.)	C 4
Smoky (cape)	H 2
Sober (isl.)	F 4
South West Margaree (riv.)	G 2
Split (cape)	D 3
Spry (harb.)	F 4
Stewiacke (riv.)	E 3
Sydney (harb.)	H 2
Tangier (riv.)	F 4
Taylor (head)	F 4
Tobeatic (lake)	C 4
Tor (bay)	G 3
Tupper (lake)	D 4
Tusket (isl.)	B 5

Tusket (riv.)	C 4
Verte (bay)	D 2
Wallace (harb.)	E 3
West (bay)	G 3
West (pt.)	H 5
West (riv.)	F 3
Western (head)	D 5
West Liscomb (riv.)	F 3
West Saint Mary's (riv.)	F 3
Whitehaven (harb.)	G 3
Yarmouth (sound)	B 5

PRINCE EDWARD ISLAND

COUNTIES

Kings 19,215	F 2
Prince 42,821	D 2
Queens 60,470	E 2

CITIES and TOWNS

Alberton 1,020	E 2
Bunbury 1,024	F 2
Charlottetown (cap.)⊚ 15,282	E 2

Cornwall 1,838	E 2
Georgetown⊚ 737	F 2
Kensington 1,143	E 2
Miscouche 752	D 2
Montague 1,957	F 2
Murray Harbour 443	F 2
North Rustico 688	E 2
O'Leary 736	D 2
Parkdale 2,018	E 2
Saint Edward 650	D 2
Saint Eleanors 2,716	E 2
Sherwood 5,681	E 2
Souris 1,413	F 2
Summerside⊚ 7,828	E 2
Tignish 982	D 2
Wilmot 1,563	E 2

OTHER FEATURES

Bedeque (bay)	E 2
Boughton (isl.)	F 2
Cardigan (bay)	F 2
Cascumpeque (bay)	E 2
East (pt.)	G 2
Egmont (bay)	D 2

Egmont (cape)	D 2
Hillsborough (bay)	E 2
Hog (isl.)	E 2
Kildare (cape)	E 2
Lennox (isl.)	E 2
Malpeque (bay)	E 2
New London (bay)	E 2
North (pt.)	E 1
Northumberland (str.)	F 2
Panmure (isl.)	F 2
Prim (pt.)	F 2
Prince Edward Island Nat'l Park	E 2
Rollo (bay)	F 2
Saint Lawrence (gulf)	F 2
Saint Peters (bay)	F 2
Saint Peters (isl.)	E 2
Savage (harb.)	F 2
Tracadie (bay)	F 2
West (pt.)	D 2
Wood (isls.)	F 3

⊚ County seat.
*Population of metropolitan area.

PRINCE EDWARD ISLAND

AREA 2,184 sq. mi. (5,657 sq. km.)
POPULATION 126,646
CAPITAL Charlottetown
LARGEST CITY Charlottetown
HIGHEST POINT 465 ft. (142 m.)
SETTLED IN 1720
ADMITTED TO CONFEDERATION 1873
PROVINCIAL FLOWER Lady's Slipper

NOVA SCOTIA

AREA 21,425 sq. mi. (55,491 sq. km.)
POPULATION 873,176
CAPITAL Halifax
LARGEST CITY Halifax
HIGHEST POINT Cape Breton Highlands 1,747 ft. (532 m.)
SETTLED IN 1605
ADMITTED TO CONFEDERATION 1867
PROVINCIAL FLOWER Trailing Arbutus or Mayflower

Topography

0   30   60 MI.
0   30   60 KM.

Below Sea Level	100 m. 328 ft.	200 m. 656 ft.	500 m. 1,640 ft.	1,000 m. 3,281 ft.	2,000 m. 6,562 ft.	5,000 m. 16,404 ft.

Agriculture, Industry and Resources

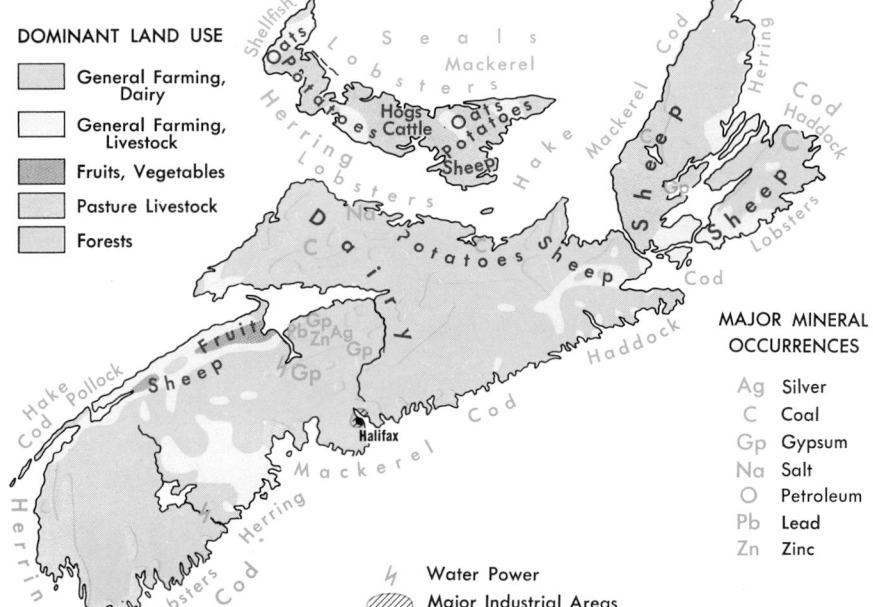

DOMINANT LAND USE

- General Farming, Dairy
- General Farming, Livestock
- Fruits, Vegetables
- Pasture Livestock
- Forests

MAJOR MINERAL OCCURRENCES

- Ag Silver
- C   Coal
- Gp Gypsum
- Na Salt
- O   Petroleum
- Pb Lead
- Zn Zinc

Water Power
Major Industrial Areas

COUNTIES

Albert 23,632 .... F 3
Carleton 24,659 .... C 2
Charlotte 26,571 .... C 3
Gloucester 86,156 .... E 1
Kent 30,799 .... E 2
King's 51,114 .... E 3
Madawaska 34,892 .... B 1
Northumberland 54,134 .... D 2
Queen's 12,485 .... D 3
Restigouche 40,593 .... C 1
Saint John 86,148 .... E 3
Sunbury 21,012 .... D 3
Victoria 20,815 .... C 1
Westmorland 107,640 .... F 2
York 74,213 .... C 3

CITIES and TOWNS

Acadie Siding 64 .... E 2
Acadieville 176 .... E 2
Adamsville 94 .... E 2
Albert Mines 120 .... F 3
Alcida 174 .... E 1
Aldouane 82 .... E 2
Allardville 478 .... E 1
Alma 329 .... F 3
Anagance 114 .... E 3
Anse-Bleue 562 .... E 1

Apohaqui 341 .... E 3
Argyle 63 .... C 2
Armstrong Brook 191 .... E 1
Aroostook 403 .... C 2
Arthurette 178 .... C 2
Astle 201 .... D 2
Atholville 1,694 .... D 1
Aulac 113 .... F 3
Back Bay 455 .... D 3
Baie-Sainte-Anne 709 .... F 1
Baie-Verte 175 .... F 2
Bairdsville 81 .... C 2
Baker Brook 527 .... B 1
Balmoral 1,823 .... D 1
Barachois 686 .... F 2
Barnaby River 38 .... E 2
Barnettville 117 .... D 2
Bartibog Bridge 122 .... E 1
Bas-Caraquet 1,859 .... F 1
Bass River 112 .... E 2
Bath 794 .... C 2
Bathurst⊙ 15,705 .... E 1
Bayfield 81 .... G 2
Bayside .... C 3
Beaubois 211 .... E 1
Beaver Brook Station 95 .... D 1
Beaver Harbour 316 .... D 3
Beechwood 111 .... C 2
Beersville 52 .... E 2
Belledune 690 .... E 1

Bellefleur 83 .... C 1
Bellefond 243 .... E 1
Belleisle Creek 145 .... E 3
Benjamin River 171 .... D 1
Ben Lomond .... E 3
Benton 101 .... C 3
Beresford 3,652 .... E 1
Berry Mills 238 .... E 2
Bertrand 1,268 .... E 1
Berwick 129 .... E 3
Black Point 131 .... D 1
Black River 150 .... E 3
Blacks Harbour 1,356 .... D 3
Blackville 892 .... E 2
Blissfield 119 .... D 2
Bloomfield Ridge 153 .... D 2
Bloomfield Station 62 .... E 3
Bocabec 34 .... C 3
Boiestown 299 .... D 2
Bonny River 153 .... D 3
Bossé 193 .... B 1
Bourgeois 215 .... F 2
Brantville 1,066 .... E 1
Breau-Village 293 .... F 2
Brest 94 .... E 2
Brewers Mills 199 .... C 2
Briggs Corner 89 .... E 2
Bristol 824 .... C 2
Brockway (Lower Brockway-Brockway) 97 .... C 3

Browns Flat 295 .... D 3
Burnsville 156 .... E 1
Burton⊙ 291 .... D 3
Burtts Corner 484 .... D 2
Cambridge-Narrows 433 .... E 3
Campbellton 9,818 .... D 1
Canaan 115 .... E 2
Canaan Forks 78 .... E 2
Canaan Road 86 .... E 2
Canterbury 474 .... C 3
Cap-Bateau 417 .... F 1
Cape Tormentine 229 .... G 2
Cap Lumière 262 .... F 2
Cap-Pelé 2,199 .... F 2
Caraquet 4,315 .... E 1
Carlingford 229 .... C 2
Carlisle 75 .... C 2
Caron Brook 171 .... B 1
Carrolls Crossing 119 .... D 2
Castalia 145 .... D 4
Central Blissville 155 .... D 3
Centre-Saint-Simon (St. Simon) 991 .... E 1
Centreville 577 .... C 2
Chance Harbour 63 .... D 3
Charlo 1,603 .... D 1
Chatham 6,779 .... E 1
Chatham Head .... E 1
Chipman 1,829 .... E 2

Clair 915 .... B 1
Clarendon 80 .... D 3
Cliffordvale (Limestone-Cliffordvale) 69 .... C 2
Clifton 194 .... E 1
Coal Branch 90 .... E 2
Coal Creek 61 .... E 2
Cocagne Cape 278 .... F 2
Cocagne-Cocagne Sud 600 .... F 2
Codys 125 .... E 3
Coldstream 217 .... C 2
Coles Island 160 .... E 3
College Bridge 536 .... F 3
Collette 198 .... E 2
Connell 58 .... C 2
Connors 96 .... B 1
Cork 54 .... E 3
Cornhill 111 .... E 3
Coughlan 181 .... E 2
Cross Creek 192 .... D 2
Cumberland Bay 231 .... E 2
Dalhousie⊙ 4,958 .... D 1
Dalhousie Junction 105 .... D 1
Darlington 749 .... D 1
Daulnay 398 .... E 1
Dawsonville 278 .... C 1
Debec 200 .... C 2
Dieppe 8,511 .... F 2
Dipper Harbour 166 .... D 3
Doaktown 1,009 .... D 2

Dorchester⊙ 1,101 .... F 3
Dorchester Crossing 605 .... F 2
Douglastown 1,091 .... E 1
Drummond 849 .... C 1
Duguayville 337 .... E 1
Dupuis Corner 303 .... F 2
Durham Bridge 255 .... D 2
East Riverside-Kingshurst 989 .... E 3
Edmundston⊙ 12,044 .... B 1
Eel River Bridge 377 .... D 1
Eel River Crossing 1,431 .... D 1
Elgin 301 .... E 3
Enniskillen 63 .... D 3
Escuminac 194 .... F 1
Evandale 58 .... E 3
Evangeline 356 .... F 1
Everett 48 .... C 1
Fairfield 250 .... E 3
Fairhaven 142 .... C 4
Fairisle 415 .... E 1
Fairvale 3,960 .... E 3
Ferry Road 325 .... C 1
Fielding 197 .... C 2
Five Fingers 189 .... C 1
Flatlands 249 .... D 1
Florenceville 709 .... C 2
Forest City 25 .... C 3
Fosterville 58 .... C 3

Four Falls 69 .... C 2
Fredericton (cap.)⊙ 43,723 .... D 3
Fredericton Junction 711 .... D 3
Gagetown⊙ 849 .... D 3
Gardner Creek 56 .... D 3
Geary 654 .... D 3
Germantown 62 .... C 2
Gillespie 96 .... C 2
Glassville 147 .... C 2
Glencoe 147 .... D 1
Glenlivet 284 .... D 1
Gloucester Junction 36 .... E 1
Gondola Point 3,076 .... E 3
Grafton 385 .... C 2
Grand Bay 3,173 .... D 3
Grande-Anse 817 .... E 1
Grand Falls 6,203 .... C 1
Grand Falls Hill 152 .... C 1
Grand Harbour 614 .... D 4
Gray Rapids 266 .... E 2
Hammondvale 72 .... E 3
Hampstead 87 .... D 3
Hampton⊙ 3,141 .... E 3
Harcourt 127 .... E 2
Hardwicke 114 .... E 1
Hardwood Ridge 191 .... D 2
Hartland 846 .... C 2
Harvey, Albert 58 .... F 3
Harvey, York 356 .... D 3
Hatfield Point 176 .... E 3

New Brunswick

SCALE
0 5 10 20 30 40 MI.
0 5 10 20 30 40 KM.

Provincial Capitals ⊛
County Seats ⊙
International Boundaries
Provincial Boundaries
County Boundaries

Scale 1:1,900,000

© Copyright HAMMOND INCORPORATED, Maplewood, N.J.

Havelock 439 . . . . E 3
Hayesville 107 . . . . D 2
Hazeldean 108 . . . . C 2
Head of Millstream 61 . . . . E 3
Hillman 69 . . . . C 2
Hillsborough 1,239 . . . . F 3
Holmesville 146 . . . . C 2
Holtville 222 . . . . D 2
Honeydale 77 . . . . C 3
Hopewell Cape® 144 . . . . . F 3
Hopewell Hill 172 . . . . F 3
Howard 77 . . . . F 3
Howland Ridge 55 . . . . C 2
Hoyt 114 . . . . D 3
Inkerman 396 . . . . F 1
Irishtown 605 . . . . F 2
Island View 240 . . . . D 3
Jacksonville 363 . . . . C 2
Jacquet River 778 . . . . E 1
Janeville 204 . . . . F 1
Jeanne Mance 89 . . . . E 1
Jemseg 228 . . . . D 3
Jolicure 96 . . . . F 3
Juniper 525 . . . . C 2
Kedgwick 1,222 . . . . C 1
Keenan Siding 86 . . . . E 2
Kent Junction 112 . . . . E 2
Kent Lake 57 . . . . E 2
Keswick 260 . . . . D 3
Kilburn 134 . . . . C 2
Killam 60 . . . . E 2
Kingsclear 250 . . . . D 3
Kingsley 145 . . . . D 2
Kirkland 69 . . . . C 3
Knowlesville 82 . . . . C 2
Kouchibouguac 213 . . . . . . F 2
Lac Baker 292 . . . . B 1
Lagacéville 227 . . . . E 1
Lake George 170 . . . . C 3
Laketon 81 . . . . E 2
Lakeville 201 . . . . C 2
Lambertville 109 . . . . C 3
Lamèque 1,571 . . . . F 1
Landry 281 . . . . E 1
Laplante 197 . . . . E 1
Lavillette 576 . . . . E 1
Lawrence Station 229 . . . . . C 3
Leech 584 . . . . E 1
Léger Brook . . . . F 2
Légerville 184 . . . . F 2
Le Goulet 1,173 . . . . F 1
Leonardville 158 . . . . C 4
Lepreau 208 . . . . D 3
Levesque 77 . . . . C 1
Little Cape 513 . . . . F 2
Little Shippegan 131 . . . . . F 1
Loggieville 781 . . . . E 1
Lorne 937 . . . . D 1

Lower Coverdale 616 . . . . . . F 2
Lower Derby 206 . . . . F 2
Lower Durham 52 . . . . D 2
Lower Hainesville 66 . . . . . C 2
Lower Kars 30 . . . . D 3
Lower Millstream 184 . . . . . E 3
Lower Sapin . . . . F 2
Lower Southampton . . . . . . C 2
Ludlow 100 . . . . D 2
Maces Bay 182 . . . . D 3
Madran 247 . . . . E 1
Magaguadavic 126 . . . . C 3
Maisonnette 757 . . . . E 1
Malden 93 . . . . G 2
Manners Sutton 159 . . . . . . D 3
Manuels 332 . . . . F 1
Mapleview 65 . . . . C 2
Marcelville 61 . . . . E 1
Martin 104 . . . . C 1
Maugerville 249 . . . . D 3
Maxwell 64 . . . . C 3
McAdam 1,837 . . . . C 3
McGivney 156 . . . . D 2
McKendrick 608 . . . . D 1
McNamee 147 . . . . D 2
Meductic 234 . . . . C 3
Melrose 121 . . . . F 2
Memramcook 276 . . . . F 2
Mennewal 110 . . . . C 1
Midgic Station 208 . . . . F 3
Mill Cove 253 . . . . D 3
Millerton 130 . . . . E 2
Millville 309 . . . . D 2
Minto 3,399 . . . . D 3
Miscou Centre 554 . . . . F 1
Miscou Harbour 106 . . . . . . F 1
Mispec 180 . . . . E 3
Moncton 54,743 . . . . F 2
Moores Mills 117 . . . . C 3
Morrisdale 202 . . . . D 3
Moulin-Morneault 459 . . . . . B 1
Murray Corner 233 . . . . G 2
Nackawic 1,357 . . . . C 2
Napadogan 103 . . . . D 2
Nash Creek 235 . . . . D 1
Nashwaak Bridge 142 . . . . . D 2
Nashwaak Village 258 . . . . . D 2
Nauwigewauk 139 . . . . E 3
Neguac 1,755 . . . . E 1
Nelson-Miramichi 1,452 . . . . E 2
Newcastle® 6,284 . . . . E 2
Newcastle Creek 210 . . . . . D 2
New Denmark 112 . . . . C 1
New Jersey 65 . . . . E 1
New Market 143 . . . . D 3
New Maryland 485 . . . . D 3
New River Beach 33 . . . . . . D 3
Newtown 154 . . . . E 3

New Zion 171 . . . . D 2
Nicholas Denys 170 . . . . . . D 1
Nictau 30 . . . . C 1
Nigadoo 1,075 . . . . E 1
Noinville 50 . . . . E 2
Nordin 393 . . . . E 1
North Head 661 . . . . D 4
Norton 1,372 . . . . E 3
Notre-Dame 344 . . . . F 2
Oak Bay 183 . . . . C 3
Oak Point 83 . . . . D 3
Oromocto 9,064 . . . . D 3
Paquetville 626 . . . . E 1
Peel 117 . . . . C 2
Pelletier Mills 88 . . . . B 1
Pennfield . . . . D 3
Penniac 179 . . . . D 2
Penobsquis 259 . . . . E 3
Perth-Andover® 1,872 . . . . . C 2
Petitcodiac 1,401 . . . . E 3
Petite-Rivière-de-l'Île 549 . . F 1
Petit Rocher 1,860 . . . . E 1
Petit Rocher Sud . . . . E 1
Pigeon Hill 595 . . . . F 1
Plaster Rock 1,222 . . . . C 2
Pocologan 150 . . . . D 3
Point de Bute 155 . . . . F 3
Pointe-du-Chêne 482 . . . . . F 2
Pointe-Sapin 331 . . . . F 2
Pointe-Verte 1,335 . . . . E 1
Pollett River 73 . . . . E 3
Pontgrave 229 . . . . F 1
Pont-Lafrance 875 . . . . E 1
Pont-Landry 444 . . . . F 1
Port Elgin 504 . . . . F 2
Prime 89 . . . . B 1
Prince of Wales 138 . . . . . . D 3
Prince William 225 . . . . C 3
Quarryville 205 . . . . E 2
Queenstown 112 . . . . D 3
Quispamsis 6,022 . . . . E 3
Red Bank 141 . . . . E 2
Renforth 1,490 . . . . E 3
Renous 192 . . . . E 2
Rexton 928 . . . . F 2
Richardsville . . . . D 1
Richibucto® 1,722 . . . . F 2
Richibucto Village 442 . . . . . F 2
Richmond Corner 84 . . . . . . C 2
Riley Brook 126 . . . . C 1
Ripples 233 . . . . D 3
River de Chute 22 . . . . C 2
River Glade 268 . . . . E 3
Riverside-Albert 478 . . . . . . F 3
Riverview 14,907 . . . . F 2
Rivière-du-Portage 661 . . . . F 1
Rivière Verte 1,054 . . . . B 1
Robertville 733 . . . . E 1

Robichaud 485 . . . . F 2
Robinsonville 206 . . . . C 1
Rogersville 1,237 . . . . E 2
Rollingdam 65 . . . . C 3
Rcsaireville 86 . . . . E 2
Rothesay 1,764 . . . . E 3
Rowena 73 . . . . F 2
Roy 173 . . . . F 2
Royal Road 41 . . . . D 2
Rusagonis 231 . . . . D 3
Sackville 5,654 . . . . F 3
Saint Almo 17 . . . . C 2
Saint-André 385 . . . . C 1
Saint Andrews® 1,760 . . . . . C 3
Saint-Antoine 1,217 . . . . . . F 2
Saint Arthur 369 . . . . D 1
Saint-Basile 3,214 . . . . B 1
Saint-Charles 355 . . . . F 2
Saint Croix 86 . . . . C 3
Sainte-Anne 329 . . . . B 1
Sainte-Anne-de-Kent 337 . . . F 2
Sainte-Anne-de-Madawaska
  1,332 . . . . B 1
Saint-Édouard-de-Kent 157 . . F 2
Sainte-Marie-de-Kent 283 . . F 2
Sainte-Marie-sur-Mer 539 . . F 1
Sainte-Rose-Gloucester 410 . F 1
Saint-François-de-Madawaska
  753 . . . . B 1
Saint George 1,163 . . . . D 3
Saint Hilaire 244 . . . . B 1
Saint-Ignace 96 . . . . F 2
Saint-Isidore 794 . . . . E 1
Saint-Jacques 2,297 . . . . . . B 1
Saint-Jean-Baptiste-de-
  Restigouche 228 . . . . C 1
Saint John® 80,521 . . . . E 3
Saint-Joseph 630 . . . . F 3
Saint-Joseph-de-Madawaska
  173 . . . . B 1
Saint-Léolin 799 . . . . E 1
Saint Leonard 1,566 . . . . . . C 1
Saint-Louis-de-Kent 1,166 . . F 2
Saint Margarets 63 . . . . C 2
Saint Martin de Restigouche
  124 . . . . C 1
Saint Martins 530 . . . . E 3
Saint-Paul 365 . . . . E 2
Saint Quentin 2,334 . . . . . . C 1
Saint-Raphaël-sur-Mer 562 . . F 1
Saint Sauveur 252 . . . . E 1
Saint Stephen 5,120 . . . . . . C 3
Saint Wilfred . . . . E 1
Salisbury 1,672 . . . . E 2
Salmon Beach 277 . . . . E 1
Salmon Creek 38 . . . . E 2
Saumarez 690 . . . . E 1
Scoudouc 207 . . . . F 2
Seal Cove 548 . . . . D 4
Shannon 39 . . . . E 3
Shediac 4,285 . . . . F 2
Shediac Bridge 441 . . . . F 2
Sheffield 112 . . . . D 3
Sheila 1,172 . . . . F 1
Shemogue 199 . . . . F 2
Shepody 86 . . . . F 3
Shippegan 2,471 . . . . F 1
Siegas 227 . . . . C 1
Sillikers 292 . . . . E 2
Simonds 221 . . . . C 2
Sisson Ridge 170 . . . . C 2
Six Roads 239 . . . . F 1
Smiths Creek 163 . . . . E 3
Somerville 326 . . . . C 2
South Branch 86 . . . . F 2
Springfield, King's 116 . . . . . E 3
Springfield, York 130 . . . . . . C 2
Stanley 432 . . . . D 2
Stickney 232 . . . . C 2
Storeytown 140 . . . . D 2
Sunny Corner 405 . . . . E 2
Sunnyside 87 . . . . D 1
Sussex 3,972 . . . . E 3
Sussex Corner 1,023 . . . . . . E 3
Tabusintac 231 . . . . E 1

Taxis River 118 . . . . D 2
Tay Creek 161 . . . . D 2
Taymouth 301 . . . . D 2
Temperance Vale 357 . . . . . C 2
The Range 58 . . . . E 2
Thibault 306 . . . . C 1
Tide Head 952 . . . . D 1
Tilley 95 . . . . C 2
Tobique Narrows 140 . . . . . . C 2
Tracadie 2,452 . . . . F 1
Tracy 636 . . . . D 3
Turtle Creek 81 . . . . F 3
Tweedside 87 . . . . C 3
Upham 107 . . . . E 3
Upper Blackville 60 . . . . E 2
Upper Buctouche 158 . . . . . F 2
Upper Gagetown 236 . . . . . D 3
Upper Hainesville 189 . . . . . C 2
Upper Kent 203 . . . . C 2
Upper Maugerville 543 . . . . . D 3
Upper Mills 153 . . . . C 3
Upper Rockport 18 . . . . F 3
Upper Sheila 706 . . . . E 1
Upper Woodstock 257 . . . . . C 2
Upsalquitch 112 . . . . D 1
Val-Comeau 534 . . . . F 1
Val d'Amour 462 . . . . D 1
Val Doucet 505 . . . . E 1
Verret 637 . . . . B 1
Village-Saint-Laurent 187 . . . E 1
Waasis 264 . . . . D 3
Wapske 195 . . . . C 2
Waterford 120 . . . . E 3
Waterville 181 . . . . C 2
Waweig . . . . C 3
Wayerton 188 . . . . E 1
Weaver 86 . . . . E 2
Weldon 227 . . . . F 3
Welsford 230 . . . . D 3
Welshpool 260 . . . . D 4
Westfield 1,100 . . . . D 3
West Quaco 48 . . . . E 3
White Head 185 . . . . D 4
White Rapids 238 . . . . E 2
Whitney 216 . . . . E 2
Wickham 72 . . . . D 3
Wicklow 143 . . . . C 2
Williamsburg 258 . . . . D 2
Williamstown 156 . . . . C 2
Willow Grove 509 . . . . E 3
Wilmot 57 . . . . C 3
Wilson Point 45 . . . . C 2
Wilsons Beach 844 . . . . D 4
Windsor 43 . . . . C 3
Wirral 110 . . . . D 3

Woodstock® 4,649 . . . . C 2
Woodwards Cove 146 . . . . . D 4
Youngs Cove 65 . . . . E 3
Zealand 458 . . . . D 2

OTHER FEATURES

Bald (mt.) . . . . C 1
Bartibog (riv.) . . . . E 1
Bay du Vin (riv.) . . . . E 2
Big Tracadie (riv.) . . . . E 1
Buctouche (harb.) . . . . F 2
Buctouche (riv.) . . . . F 2
Campobello (isl.) . . . . D 4
Canaan (riv.) . . . . E 2
Carleton (mt.) . . . . D 1
Chaleur (bay) . . . . E 1
Chignecto (bay) . . . . F 3
Chiputneticook (lakes) . . . . . C 3
Cocagne (isl.) . . . . F 2
Cumberland (basin) . . . . F 3
Deer (isl.) . . . . D 4
Digdeguash (riv.) . . . . C 3
Escuminac (bay) . . . . D 1
Escuminac (pt.) . . . . F 1
Fundy (bay) . . . . E 3
Fundy Nat'l Park . . . . E 3
Gaspereau (riv.) . . . . D 2
Grand (bay) . . . . D 3
Grand (lake) . . . . C 3
Grand (lake) . . . . D 3
Grand Manan (chan.) . . . . . . C 4
Grand Manan (isl.) . . . . D 4
Grande (riv.) . . . . C 1
Green (riv.) . . . . B 1
Hammond (riv.) . . . . E 3
Harvey (lake) . . . . C 3
Heron (isl.) . . . . D 1
Kedgwick (riv.) . . . . C 1
Kennebecasis (riv.) . . . . E 3
Keswick (riv.) . . . . C 2
Kouchibouguac (bay) . . . . . . F 2
Kouchibouguacis (riv.) . . . . . F 2
Kouchibouguac Nat'l Park . . . F 2
Lamèque (isl.) . . . . F 1
Lepreau (riv.) . . . . D 3
Little (riv.) . . . . D 3
Long (isl.) . . . . D 3
Long Reach (inlet) . . . . D 3
Maces (bay) . . . . D 3
Mactaquac (lake) . . . . C 2
Madawaska (riv.) . . . . B 1
Magaguadavic (lake) . . . . . . C 3
Magaguadavic (riv.) . . . . C 3
Miramichi (bay) . . . . E 1

Miscou (isl.) . . . . F 1
Miscou (pt.) . . . . F 1
Mount Carleton Prov. Park . . . D 1
Musquash (harb.) . . . . D 3
Nashwaak (riv.) . . . . D 2
Nepisiguit (bay) . . . . E 1
Nepisiguit (riv.) . . . . D 1
Nerepis (riv.) . . . . D 3
Northern (head) . . . . D 4
North Sevogle (riv.) . . . . D 1
Northumberland (str.) . . . . . . F 2
Northwest Miramichi (riv.) . . . D 1
Oromocto (lake) . . . . C 3
Oromocto (riv.) . . . . D 3
Passamaquoddy (bay) . . . . . C 3
Patapédia (riv.) . . . . C 1
Petitcodiac (riv.) . . . . F 3
Pokemouche (riv.) . . . . E 1
Pokesudie (isl.) . . . . F 1
Pollett (riv.) . . . . E 3
Quaco (head) . . . . E 3
Renous (riv.) . . . . D 2
Restigouche (riv.) . . . . C 1
Richibucto (harb.) . . . . F 2
Richibucto (riv.) . . . . E 2
Roosevelt Campobello Int'l
  Park . . . . D 4
Saint Croix (riv.) . . . . C 3
Saint Francis (riv.) . . . . A 1
Saint John (harb.) . . . . E 3
Saint John (riv.) . . . . D 3
Saint Lawrence (gulf) . . . . . . F 1
Salisbury (bay) . . . . F 3
Salmon (riv.) . . . . C 1
Salmon (riv.) . . . . E 2
Shediac (isl.) . . . . F 2
Shepody (bay) . . . . F 3
Shippegan (bay) . . . . E 1
Shippegan Gully (str.) . . . . . . F 1
South Sevogle (riv.) . . . . D 1
Southwest (head) . . . . D 4
Southwest Miramichi (riv.) . . . D 2
Spear (cape) . . . . G 2
Spednik (lake) . . . . C 3
Spencer (cape) . . . . E 3
Tabusintac (riv.) . . . . E 1
Tabusintac Gully (str.) . . . . . F 1
Tetagouche (riv.) . . . . D 1
Tobique (riv.) . . . . C 2
Upsalquitch (riv.) . . . . D 1
Utopia (lake) . . . . C 3
Verte (bay) . . . . G 2
Washademoak (lake) . . . . . . E 3
West (isls.) . . . . D 4
White Head (isl.) . . . . D 4

®County seat.

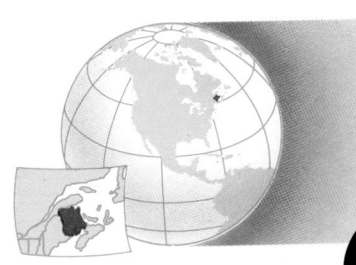

AREA 28,354 sq. mi. (73,437 sq. km.)
POPULATION 709,442
CAPITAL Fredericton
LARGEST CITY Saint John
HIGHEST POINT Mt. Carleton 2,690 ft.
  (820 m.)
SETTLED IN 1611
ADMITTED TO CONFEDERATION 1867
PROVINCIAL FLOWER Purple Violet

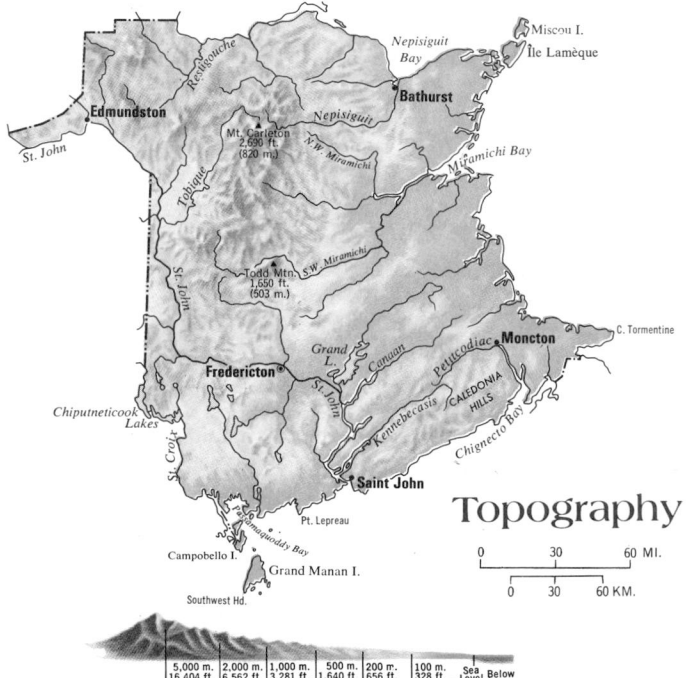

Topography

0   30   60 MI.

0   30   60 KM.

| 5,000 m. 16,404 ft. | 2,000 m. 6,562 ft. | 1,000 m. 3,281 ft. | 500 m. 1,640 ft. | 200 m. 656 ft. | 100 m. 328 ft. | Sea Level | Below |

Agriculture, Industry and Resources

DOMINANT LAND USE

- Cereals, Livestock
- Dairy
- Potatoes
- General Farming, Livestock
- Pasture Livestock
- Forests

MAJOR MINERAL OCCURRENCES

Ag Silver   Pb Lead
C   Coal   Sb Antimony
Cu Copper   Zn Zinc

⚡ Water Power
▨ Major Industrial Areas

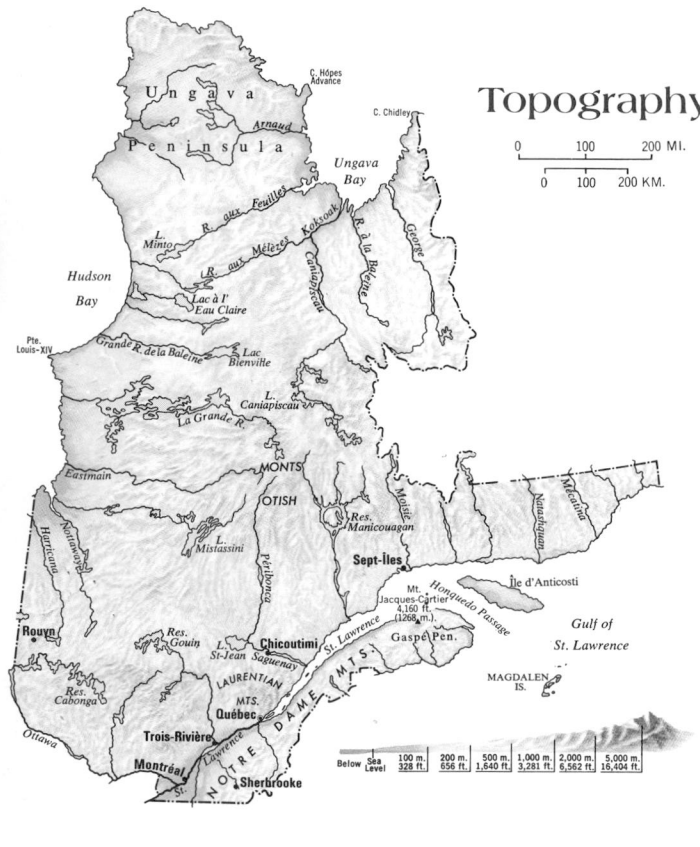

Topography

0   100   200 MI.

0   100   200 KM.

Below Sea Level | 100 m. 328 ft. | 200 m. 656 ft. | 500 m. 1,640 ft. | 1,000 m. 3,281 ft. | 2,000 m. 6,562 ft. | 5,000 m. 16,404 ft.

COUNTIES

Argenteuil 32,454 .... C 4
Arthabaska 59,277 .... E 4
Bagot 26,840 .... E 4
Beauce 73,427 .... G 3
Beauharnois 54,034 .... C 4
Bellechasse 23,559 .... G 3
Berthier 31,096 .... C 3
Bonaventure 40,487 .... C 2
Brome 17,436 .... E 4
Chambly 307,090 .... J 4
Champlain 119,595 .... E 2
Charlevoix-Est 17,448 .... G 2
Charlevoix-Ouest 14,172 .... G 2
Châteauguay 59,968 .... D 4
Chicoutimi 174,441 .... G 1
Compton 20,536 .... F 4
Deux-Montagnes 71,252 .... C 4
Dorchester 33,949 .... G 3
Drummond 69,770 .... E 4
Frontenac 26,814 .... G 4

Gaspé-Est 41,173 .... D 1
Gaspé-Ouest 18,943 .... C 1
Gatineau 54,229 .... B 3
Hull 131,213 .... B 4
Huntingdon 16,953 .... C 4
Iberville 23,180 .... D 4
Île-de-Montréal 1,760,122 .... H 4
Île-Jésus 268,335 .... H 4
Joliette 60,384 .... C 3
Kamouraska 28,642 .... H 2
Labelle 34,395 .... B 3
Lac-Saint-Jean-Est 47,891 .... F 1
Lac-Saint-Jean-Ouest 62,952. E 1
Laprairie 105,962 .... H 4
L'Assomption 109,705 .... D 4
Lévis 94,104 .... J 3
L'Islet 22,062 .... G 2
Lotbinière 29,653 .... F 3
Maskinongé 20,763 .... D 3
Matane 29,955 .... B 1
Matapédia 23,715 .... B 2
Mégantic 57,892 .... F 3

Missisquoi 36,161 .... D 4
Montcalm 27,557 .... C 3
Montmagny 25,622 .... G 3
Montmorency No. 1 23,048. F 2
Montmorency No. 2 6,436. G 3
Napierville 13,562 .... D 4
Nicolet 33,513 .... E 3
Papineau 37,975 .... C 4
Pontiac 20,283 .... A 3
Portneuf 58,843 .... E 3
Québec 458,980 .... F 3
Richelieu 53,058 .... D 4
Richmond 40,871 .... E 4
Rimouski 69,099 .... J 1
Rivière-du-Loup 41,250 .... H 1
Rouville 42,391 .... D 4
Saguenay 115,881 .... H 1
Saint-Hyacinthe 55,888 .... D 4
Saint-Jean 55,576 .... D 4
Saint-Maurice 107,703 .... D 3
Shefford 70,733 .... E 4
Sherbrooke 115,983 .... E 4

CITIES and TOWNS

Acton Vale 4,371 .... E 4
Albanel 992 .... E 1
Alma⊚ 26,322 .... F 1
Amqui⊚ 4,048 .... B 2
Ancienne-Lorette 12,935 .... H 3
Angers .... B 4
Anjou 37,346 .... H 4
Annaville 712 .... E 3
Armagh 878 .... G 3
Arthabaska⊚ 6,827 .... F 3
Arvida .... F 1
Asbestos 7,967 .... F 4
Ascot Corner 847 .... F 4
Audet 760 .... G 4
Ayer's Cliff⊚ 810 .... F 4
Aylmer 26,695 .... B 4
Baie-Comeau 12,866 .... A 1
Baie-d'Urfé 3,674 .... G 4
Baie-Saint-Paul⊚ 3,961 .... G 2
Baie-Trinité 749 .... B 1
Beaconsfield 19,613 .... H 4
Beauceville 4,302 .... G 3
Beauharnois⊚ 7,025 .... D 4
Beaumont 791 .... F 3
Beauport 60,447 .... J 3
Beaupre 2,740 .... F 3
Bécancour⊚ 10,247 .... E 3
Bedford⊚ 2,832 .... E 4
Beebe Plain 1,072 .... E 4
Bélair (Val-Bélair) 12,695 .... H 3
Beloeil 17,540 .... D 4
Bernierville 2,120 .... F 3
Berthier-en-Bas 562 .... G 3
Berthierville⊚ 4,049 .... D 3
Bic 2,994 .... J 1
Biencourt 824 .... J 2
Black Lake 5,148 .... F 4
Blainville 14,682 .... H 4
Boischatel 3,345 .... J 3
Bois-des-Filion 4,943 .... H 4
Bolduc 1,565 .... G 4
Bonaventure 1,371 .... C 2
Boucherville 29,704 .... J 4
Bromont 2,831 .... E 4
Bromptonville 3,035 .... F 4
Brossard 52,232 .... H 4
Brownsburg 2,875 .... C 4
Buckingham 7,992 .... B 4
Cabano 3,291 .... J 2
Cacouna 1,160 .... H 2
Calumet 729 .... C 4
Candiac 8,502 .... J 4
Cap-à-l'Aigle 819 .... G 2
Cap-Chat 3,464 .... B 1
Cap-de-la-Madeleine 32,626. E 3
Caplan-Rivière Caplan 1,139. C 2
Cap-Saint-Ignace 1,485 .... G 2
Cap-Santé⊚ 671 .... F 3
Carignan 4,544 .... J 4
Carleton 2,710 .... C 2
Causapscal 2,501 .... B 2
Chambly 12,190 .... J 4
Chambord 961 .... E 1

Chandler 3,946 .... D 2
Charlemagne 4,827 .... H 4
Charlesbourg 68,326 .... J 3
Charny 8,240 .... J 3
Châteauguay 36,928 .... H 4
Château-Richer⊚ 3,628 .... F 3
Chénéville 633 .... B 4
Chicoutimi⊚ 60,064 .... G 1
Chicoutimi-Jonquière
  *135,172 .... G 1
Chute-aux-Outardes 2,280 .... A 1
Clermont 3,621 .... G 2
Coaticook 6,271 .... F 4
Coleraine 1,660 .... F 4
Compton 728 .... F 4
Contrecoeur 5,449 .... D 4
Cookshire⊚ 1,480 .... F 4
Coteau-du-Lac 1,247 .... C 4
Coteau-Landing⊚ 1,386 .... C 4
Côte-Saint-Luc 27,531 .... H 4
Courcelles 608 .... G 4
Courville .... J 3
Cowansville 12,240 .... E 4
Crabtree 1,950 .... D 4
Danville 2,200 .... E 4
Daveluyville 1,257 .... E 3
Deauville 942 .... E 4
Dégelis 3,477 .... J 2
Delisle 4,011 .... F 1
Delson 4,935 .... H 4
Desbiens 1,541 .... F 1
Deschaillons-sur-Saint-
  Laurent 990 .... E 3
Deschambault 977 .... E 3
Deschênes .... B 4
Deux-Montagnes 9,944 .... H 4
Didyme 667 .... E 1
Disraëli 3,181 .... F 4
Dolbeau 8,766 .... E 1
Dollard-des-Ormeaux 39,940. H 4
Donnacona 5,731 .... F 3
Dorion 5,749 .... C 4
Dorval 17,727 .... H 4
Dosquet 703 .... F 3
Douville .... D 4
Drummondville 27,347 .... E 4
Drummondville-Sud 9,220 .... E 4
Dunham 2,887 .... E 4
Durham-Sud 1,045 .... E 4
East Angus 4,016 .... F 4
East Broughton 1,397 .... F 3
East Broughton Station 1,302. F 3
Eastman 612 .... E 4
Entrelacs 1,735 .... C 3
Farnham 6,498 .... D 4
Ferme-Neuve 2,266 .... B 3
Forestville 4,271 .... H 1
Frampton 684 .... G 3
Francoeur 1,422 .... E 3
Gaspé 17,261 .... D 1
Gatineau 74,988 .... B 4
Giffard .... J 3
Girardville 1,128 .... E 1
Gracefield 869 .... A 3
Granby 38,069 .... E 4
Grand'Mère 15,442 .... E 3
Grande-Rivière 4,420 .... D 2
Grandes-Bergeronnes 748 .... H 1
Grande-Vallée 700 .... D 1
Greenfield Park 18,527 .... J 4
Grenville 1,417 .... C 4
Gros-Morne 612 .... C 1
Hampstead 7,598 .... H 4
Ham-Sud⊚ 62 .... F 4
Hauterive 13,995 .... A 1
Hébertville 2,515 .... F 1
Hébertville-Station 1,442 .... F 1
Hemmingford 737 .... D 4
Henryville 595 .... D 4
Howick 639 .... D 4
Hudson 4,414 .... C 4
Hull⊚ 56,225 .... B 4
Huntingdon⊚ 3,018 .... C 4
Île-Perrot 5,945 .... G 4
Iberville⊚ 8,587 .... D 4
Inverness⊚ 329 .... F 3
Joliette⊚ 16,987 .... D 3
Jonquière 60,354 .... F 1
Jonquière-Chicoutimi
  *135,172 .... F 1
Kingsey Falls 818 .... E 4
Kirkland 10,476 .... H 4
Knowlton (Lac-Brome)⊚
  4,316 .... E 4
La Baie 20,935 .... G 1
Labelle 1,534 .... C 3
Lac-à-la-Croix 1,017 .... F 1
Lac-Alouette-Lac-Brière 1,356 D 4
Lac-au-Saumon 1,332 .... B 2
Lac-aux-Sables 838 .... E 3
Lac-Beaufort .... F 3
Lac-Bouchette 1,703 .... E 1
Lac-Carré 717 .... C 3
Lac-des-Écorces 766 .... B 3
Lac-Drolet 1,120 .... G 4
Lac-Etchemin 2,729 .... G 3
Lachenaie 8,631 .... D 4
Lachine 37,521 .... H 4
Lachute⊚ 11,729 .... C 4
Lac-Mégantic⊚ 6,119 .... G 4
Lacolle 1,319 .... D 4
Lac-Saint-Charles 5,837 .... H 3
Lafontaine 4,799 .... C 4
La Guadeloupe 1,692 .... G 4
Lambton 1,559 .... F 4
L'Annonciation 2,384 .... C 3
Lanoraie (Lanoraie-d'Autry)
  1,613 .... D 4
La Pêche 4,977 .... B 4
La Pérade 1,039 .... E 3
La Pocatière 4,560 .... H 2

Soulanges 15,429 .... C 4
Stanstead 38,186 .... F 4
Témiscouata 52,570 .... J 2
Terrebonne 193,865 .... H 4
Vaudreuil 50,043 .... C 4
Verchères 63,353 .... J 4
Wolfe 15,635 .... F 4
Yamaska 14,797 .... E 3

La Prairie⊚ 10,627 .... J 4
La Providence 4,827 .... E 4
Larouche 662 .... F 1
La Salle 76,299 .... H 4
L'Ascension 1,287 .... F 1
L'Assomption⊚ 4,844 .... D 4
La Station-du-Coteau 892 .... C 4
Laterrière 788 .... F 1
La Tuque 11,556 .... E 2
Laurentides 1,947 .... D 4
Laurier-Station 1,123 .... F 3
Laurierville 939 .... F 3
Lauzon 13,362 .... J 3
Laval 268,335 .... H 4
Lavaltrie 2,053 .... D 4
L'Avenir 1,116 .... E 4
Lawrenceville 562 .... E 4
Le Moyne 6,137 .... H 4
L'Épiphanie 2,971 .... D 4
Les Méchins 803 .... B 1
Lévis 17,895 .... J 4
Lennoxville 3,922 .... F 4
Léry 2,239 .... H 4
Linière 1,168 .... G 3
L'Islet 1,070 .... G 2
L'Islet-sur-Mer 774 .... G 2
L'Isle-Verte 1,142 .... G 1
Longueuil 124,320 .... J 4
Loretteville 15,060 .... H 3
Lorraine 6,881 .... H 4
Louiseville 3,735 .... E 3
Luceville 1,524 .... J 1
Lyster 830 .... F 3
Magog 13,604 .... E 4

Maniwaki⊚ 5,424 .... B 3
Manseau 626 .... E 3
Maple Grove 2,009 .... H 4
Maria 1,178 .... C 2
Marieville⊚ 4,877 .... D 4
Mascouche 20,345 .... H 4
Maskinongé 1,005 .... E 3
Masson 4,264 .... B 4
Massueville 671 .... D 4
Matane⊚ 13,612 .... B 1
Matapédia 586 .... B 2
Melocheville 1,892 .... C 4
Mercier 6,352 .... H 4
Metabetchouan 3,406 .... F 1
Mirabel⊚ 14,080 .... H 4
Mistassini 6,682 .... E 1
Montauban 557 .... E 3
Mont-Carmel 807 .... J 4
Montcerf 570 .... A 3
Montebello 1,229 .... B 4
Mont-Joli 6,359 .... J 1
Mont-Laurier⊚ 8,405 .... B 3
Mont-Louis 756 .... C 1
Montmagny⊚ 12,405 .... G 3
Montréal⊚ 980,354 .... H 4
Montréal *2,828,349 .... H 4
Montréal-Est 3,778 .... H 4
Montréal-Nord 94,914 .... H 4
Mont-Rolland 1,517 .... C 4
Mont-Royal 19,247 .... H 4
Mont-Saint-Hilaire 10,066 .... D 4
Morin Heights 592 .... C 4
Murdochville 3,396 .... C 1
Nantes 1,167 .... F 4

Agriculture, Industry and Resources

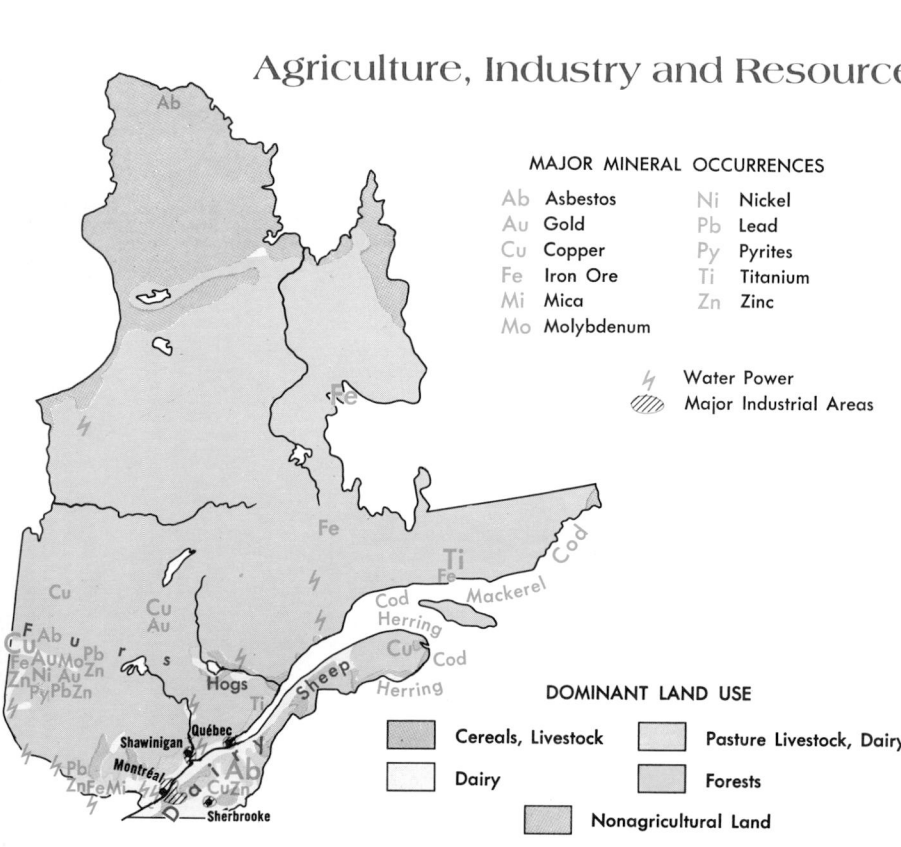

MAJOR MINERAL OCCURRENCES

Ab   Asbestos
Au   Gold
Cu   Copper
Fe   Iron Ore
Mi   Mica
Mo   Molybdenum

Ni   Nickel
Pb   Lead
Py   Pyrites
Ti   Titanium
Zn   Zinc

⚡ Water Power
▨ Major Industrial Areas

DOMINANT LAND USE

▨ Cereals, Livestock   ▨ Pasture Livestock, Dairy
☐ Dairy   ▨ Forests
▨ Nonagricultural Land

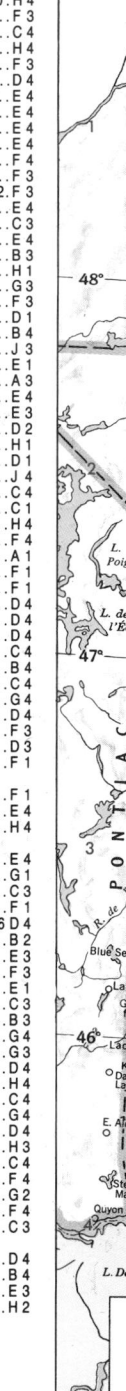

Québec
Southern Part

SCALE
0 5 10   20   30   40 MI.
0 5 10   20   30   40 KM.

National Capital ⊛
Provincial Capital ⊛
County Seats ⊚
International Boundaries

Provincial & State
  Boundaries
County Boundaries

Scale 1:2,250,000

apierville 2,343 ....D 4
euville 996 ....F 3
New Carlisle 1,292 ....D 2
New Richmond 4,257 ....E 3
icolet 4,880 ....E 3
ominique 881 ....B 3
ormandin 4,041 ......E 1
orth Hatley 689 ......E 1
otre-Dame-de-la-Doré 1,064 E 1
otre-Dame-des-Laurentides H 3
otre-Dame-des-Prairies
  6,150 ....D 3
otre-Dame-du-Bon-Conseil
  1,089 ....E 4
otre-Dame-du-Lac 2,258 ...J 2
ouvelle 669 ....D 1
ka 1,538 ....C 4
merville 1,398 ....E 4
rmstown 1,659 ......D 4
rsainville ....H 3
tis 673 ....G 1
tterburn Park 4,268 ......H 4
utremont 24,338 ......H 4
abos 1,295 ....D 2
abos-Mills 1,565 ......D 2
apineauville 1,481 ......C 4
aspébiac 1,914 ....D 1
ercé 4,839 ....D 1
etit-Cap 1,023 ....D 1
etite-Matane 1,065 ......J 1
etit-Saguenay (Saint-
  François-d'Assise) 804 ...G 1
ierreville 38,390 ....H 4
ierreville 1,212 ....E 3

Pincourt 8,750 ....D 4
Pintendre 1,849 ......J 3
Plaisance 748 ....B 4
Plessisville 7,249 ......F 3
Pohénégamooke 3,702 ...H 2
Pointe-à-la-Croix 1,481 ...C 2
Pointe-au-Père 796 ......J 1
Pointe-au-Pic 1,054 ......G 2
Pointe-aux-Outardes 1,056 ..A 1
Pointe-aux-Trembles 36,270 ..J 4
Pointe-Calumet 2,935 ....G 4
Pointe-Claire 24,571 ....H 4
Pointe-du-Lac 5,359 ......E 3
Pointe-Gatineau ....B 4
Pointe-Lebel 1,573 ......A 1
Pont-Rouge 3,580 ......F 3
Port-Alfred 8,621 ....G 1
Portneuf 1,333 ....F 3
Portneuf-sur-Mer (Rivière-
  Portneuf-sur-Mer) 1,255 ..H 1
Price 2,273 ....A 1
Princeville 4,023 ......F 3
Proulxville 588 ....E 3
Québec (cap.) 166,474 ....H 3
Québec *576,075 ......H 3
Quyon 744 ....A 4
Rawdon 2,958 ....D 3
Repentigny 34,419 ......J 4
Richelieu 1,832 ....D 4
Richmond 3,568 ......E 4
Rigaud 2,268 ....C 4
Rimouski 29,120 ....J 1
Rimouski-Est 2,506 ......J 1
Ripon 620 ....B 4

Rivière-à-Pierre 615 ....E 3
Rivière-au-Renard 2,211 ....D 1
Rivière-Bleue 1,690 ....J 2
Rivière-Bois-Clair 604 ......F 3
Rivière-du-Loup 13,459 ....H 2
Rivière-du-Moulin
  2,475 ....
Rivière-Éternité 659 ....G 1
Rivière-Portneuf-Portneuf-sur-
  Mer 1,255 ....H 1
Robertsonville 1,987 ....F 3
Roberval 11,429 ....E 1
Rock Island 1,179 ....E 4
Rosemère 7,778 ....H 4
Rougemont 972 ....D 4
Roxboro 6,292 ....H 4
Roxton Falls 1,245 ....E 4
Sacré-Coeur-de-Saguenay
  1,678 ....H 1
Saint-Adelme 618 ....B 1
Saint-Adelphe 1,159 ....E 3
Saint-Adolphe-d'Howard
  1,686 ....C 4
Saint-Adrien 597 ....E 3
Saint-Agapitville 2,954 ......F 3
Saint-Aimé-des-Lacs 861 ....G 2
Saint-Alban 673 ....E 3
Saint-Alexandre-de-
  Kamouraska 1,048 ......H 2
Saint-Alexis-des-Monts 1,984 .D 3
Saint-Amable 2,424 ....J 4
Saint-Ambroise 3,606 ......F 1
Saint-Anaclet 1,377 ....J 1
Saint-André-Avellin 1,312 ....B 4
Saint-André-Est 1,293 ......C 4

Saint-Anselme 1,808 ....F 3
Saint-Antoine 7,012 ....H 4
Saint-Antonin 941 ....H 2
Saint-Aubert 884 ....G 2
Saint-Augustin-de-Québec
  2,475 ....
Saint-Basile-Sud 1,719 ......F 3
Saint-Basile-le-Grand 7,658 ..J 4
Saint-Benjamin 1,027 ....G 3
Saint-Bernard 585 ....F 3
Saint-Bernard-sur-Mer 711 ..G 2
Saint-Boniface-de-Shawinigan
  3,164 ....E 3
Saint-Bruno 2,580 ....F 1
Saint-Bruno-de-Montarville
  22,880 ....J 4
Saint-Camille-de-Bellechasse
  1,744 ....G 3
Saint-Casimir 1,133 ....E 3
Saint-Césaire 2,935 ....D 4
Saint-Charles 1,019 ....G 3
Saint-Charles-de-Mandeville
  1,392 ....D 3
Saint-Chrysostome 1,018 ....D 4
Saint-Côme 660 ....D 3
Saint-Constant 9,938 ....H 4
Saint-Cyprien 860 ....J 2
Saint-Cyrille 1,041 ....E 4
Saint-Damien-de-Buckland
  1,522 ....G 3
Saint-David 5,380 ....J 3
Saint-David-de-Falardeau
  1,876 ....F 1
Saint-Denis 861 ....D 4

Sainte-Catherine 1,474 ......F 3
Saint-Donat-de-Montcalm
  1,521 ....C 3
Sainte-Adèle 4,675 ....C 3
Sainte-Agathe 709 ....F 3
Sainte-Agathe-des-Monts
  5,641 ....C 3
Sainte-Anne-de-Beaupré
  3,292 ....F 2
Sainte-Anne-de-Bellevue
  3,981 ....H 4
Sainte-Anne-des-Monts
  6,062 ....C 1
Sainte-Anne-des-Plaines
  4,258 ....H 4
Sainte-Anne-du-Lac 686 ....B 3
Sainte-Aurélie 1,045 ....G 3
Sainte-Blandine 849 ....J 1

Sainte-Claire 1,566 ....G 3
Sainte-Croix 1,814 ....F 3
Sainte-Félicité 711 ....B 1
Sainte-Foy 68,883 ....H 3
Sainte-Geneviève 2,573 ....H 4
Sainte-Geneviève-de-
  Batiscan 356 ....E 3
Sainte-Hélène-de-Bagot
  1,328 ....E 4
Sainte-Hénédine 639 ....F 3
Sainte-Julie-de-Verchères
  14,243 ....J 4
Sainte-Julienne 750 ....D 4
Sainte-Justine 1,080 ....G 3
Saint-Élie 743 ....E 3
Saint-Elzéar 743 ....G 3
Sainte-Marie 8,937 ....G 3

Sainte-Martine 2,196 ....D 4
Saint-Émile 5,216 ....H 3
Sainte-Monique 705 ....F 1
Sainte-Pétronille 982 ....J 3
Sainte-Perpétue-de-L'Islet
  1,232 ....H 2
Saint-Éphrem-de-Tring 973 ..G 3
Saint-Épiphane 647 ....H 2
Sainte-Pudentienne 866 ....E 4
Sainte-Rosalie 2,862 ....E 4
Saint-Esprit 1,068 ....D 4
Sainte-Thérèse 18,750 ......H 4
Sainte-Thérèse-Ouest
  (Boisbriand) 13,471 ......H 4
Sainte-Thècle 1,703 ....E 3
Saint-Étienne-de-Grès 845 ..E 3
Saint-Étienne-de-Lauzon
  1,218 ....J 3

AREA 594,857 sq. mi. (1,540,680 sq. km.)
POPULATION 6,532,461
CAPITAL Québec
LARGEST CITY Montréal
HIGHEST POINT Mont D'Iberville 5,420 ft.
  (1,652 m.)
SETTLED IN 1608
ADMITTED TO CONFEDERATION 1867
PROVINCIAL FLOWER White Garden Lily

COUNTIES
indicated by numbers:

1 Iberville ....D 4
2 Napierville ....D 4
3 Rouville ....D 4
4 St-Hyacinthe ....D 4
5 Île-de-Montréal ....C 4
6 Deux-Montagnes ....C 4
7 Laval ....C 4
8 Soulanges ....C 4
9 Beauharnois ....C 4
10 Hull ....C 4
11 Richelieu ....D 4
12 Vaudreuil ....C 4

Gaspé Peninsula

Internal divisions represent Municipal Counties

© Copyright HAMMOND INCORPORATED, Maplewood, N.J.

Saint-Eustache 29,716. . . . . . H 4
Saint-Fabien 1,361 . . . . J 1
Saint-Félicien 9,058 . . . . E 1
Saint-Félix-de-Valois 1,462 . . . D 3
Saint-Ferréol-les-Neiges
1,758. . . . . G 2
Saint-Flavien 734 . . . . F 3
Saint-François-de-Sales 831 . . E 1
Saint-François-du-Lac 942 . . . E 3
Saint-Fulgence 950 . . . . G 1
Saint-Gabriel 3,161 . . . . D 3
Saint-Gabriel-de-Rimouski
779 . . . . J 1
Saint-Gédéon, Frontenac
1,569. . . . . G 4
Saint-Gédéon, Lac-St-Jean-E.
1,000 . . . . F 1
Saint-Georges, Beauce
10,342 . . . . G 3
Saint-Georges, Champlain
3,344 . . . . E 3
Saint-Georges-Ouest 6,378 . . . G 3
Saint-Germain-de-Grantham
1,373 . . . . E 4
Saint-Gervais 973 . . . . G 3
Saint-Gilles 912 . . . . F 3
Saint-Grégoire (Mont-St-
Grégoire) 740 . . . . D 4
Saint-Henri 1,970 . . . . J 3
Saint-Honoré, Beauce 1,116 . . G 3
Saint-Honoré, Chicoutimi
1,790 . . . . F 1
Saint-Hubert 60,573 . . . . J 4
Saint-Hubert-de-Témiscouata
871 . . . . J 2
Saint-Hyacinthe® 38,246. . . . . D 4
Saint-Isidore 811 . . . . D 4
Saint-Isidore-de-Laprairie 769 . D 4
Saint-Jacques 2,152 . . . . D 4
Saint-Jacques-le-Mineur
1,203 . . . . H 4
Saint-Jean-Chrysostome
6,930 . . . . J 3
Saint-Jean-de-Dieu 1,377 . . . . J 1
Saint-Jean-de-Matha 931 . . . . D 3
Saint-Jean-Port-Joli 1,813 . . . G 2
Saint-Jean-sur-Richelieu
35,640 . . . . D 4
Saint-Jérôme 25,123 . . . . H 4
Saint-Joachim 1,139 . . . . G 2
Saint-Joseph-de-Beauce
3,216 . . . . G 3
Saint-Jovite 3,841 . . . . C 3
Saint-Joseph-de-Sorel 2,545 . D 3
Saint-Lambert 20,557 . . . . . . J 4
Saint-Laurent 65,900 . . . . . . H 4

Saint-Lazare 731 . . . . G 3
Saint-Léonard 79,429 . . . . H 4
Saint-Léonard-d'Aston 992 . . . E 3
Saint-Léon-de-Chicoutimi 749 F 1
Saint-Léon-de-Standon 816 . . G 3
Saint-Léon-le-Grand 722 . . . . B 2
Saint-Liboire® 746 . . . . E 4
Saint-Louis-de-Gonzague
615 . . . . D 4
Saint-Louis-de-Terrebonne
14,172 . . . . H 4
Saint-Louis-du-Ha! Ha! 809 . . H 2
Saint-Luc 8,815 . . . . D 4
Saint-Luc-de-Matane 598 . . . . B 1
Saint-Marc-des-Carrières
2,822 . . . . E 3
Saint-Méthode-de-Frontenac
925 . . . . F 3
Saint-Michel-de-Bellechasse
963 . . . . G 3
Saint-Michel-des-Saints
1,584. . . . . D 3
Saint-Nazaire-de-Chicoutimi
962 . . . . F 1
Saint-Nérée 970 . . . . G 3
Saint-Nicolas 5,074 . . . . H 3
Saint-Noël 666 . . . . B 1
Saint-Odilon 580 . . . . G 3
Saint-Omer 718 . . . . C 2
Saint-Ours 625 . . . . D 4
Saint-Pacôme 1,996 . . . . H 2
Saint-Pamphile 3,428 . . . . . . H 3
Saint-Pascal® 2,763 . . . . H 2
Saint-Paul-de-Montminy 602 . G 3
Saint-Paulin 663 . . . . D 3
Saint-Paul-l'Ermite (Le
Gardeur) 8,312 . . . . J 4
Saint-Philippe-de-Néri 715 . . . H 2
Saint-Pie 1,725 . . . . E 4
Saint-Pierre 5,305 . . . . H 4
Saint-Pierre-d'Orléans 880 . . . G 3
Saint-Polycarpe 602 . . . . C 4
Saint-Prime 2,522 . . . . E 1
Saint-Prosper-de-Dorchester
2,150 . . . . G 3
Saint-Raphaël® 4,463 . . . . . . G 3
Saint-Raymond 3,605 . . . . . . F 3
Saint-Rédempteur 4,463 . . . . J 3
Saint-Régis 1,370 . . . . C 4
Saint-Rémi 687 . . . . B 1
Saint-Roch-de-l'Achigan
1,160. . . . . D 4
Saint-Roch-de-Richelieu
1,650 . . . . D 4
Saint-Romuald-d'Etchemin®
9,849 . . . . J 3

Saint-Sauveur-des-Monts
2,348 . . . . C 4
Saint-Siméon 1,152 . . . . G 2
Saint-Simon 602 . . . . H 1
Saint-Stanislas 1,443 . . . . . . E 3
Saint-Sylvère 1,006 . . . . E 3
Saint-Timothée 2,113 . . . . . . D 4
Saint-Tite 3,031 . . . . E 3
Saint-Tite-des-Caps 626 . . . . G 2
Saint-Ubald 1,605 . . . . E 3
Saint-Ulric 792 . . . . B 1
Saint-Urbain-de-Charlevoix
1,079 . . . . G 2
Saint-Victor 1,104 . . . . G 3
Saint-Zacharie 1,284 . . . . . . G 3
Saint-Zotique 1,774 . . . . C 4
Sault-au-Mouton 828 . . . . . . H 1
Sawyerville 939 . . . . F 4
Sayabec 1,721. . . . . B 2
Scotstown 762 . . . . F 4
Senneville 1,221. . . . . G 4
Shannon 3,488 . . . . F 3
Shawbridge 942 . . . . C 4
Shawinigan 23,011 . . . . E 3
Shawinigan-Sud 11,325 . . . . . E 3
Shawville 1,608 . . . . A 4
Sherbrooke® 74,075 . . . . E 4
Sherrington 614 . . . . D 4
Sillery 12,825 . . . . J 3
Sorel® 20,347 . . . . D 4
Squatec 1,000 . . . . J 2
Stanstead Plain 1,093 . . . . . . E 4
Sutton 1,599 . . . . E 4
Tadoussac® 900 . . . . H 1
Templeton . . . . B 4
Terrebonne 11,769 . . . . H 4
Thetford Mines 19,965 . . . . . . F 3
Thurso 2,780 . . . . B 4
Tourelle (Tourelle-Grand-
Tourelle) 942 . . . . C 1
Tourville 659 . . . . H 2
Tracy 12,843 . . . . D 3
Tring-Jonction 1,315. . . . . . . F 3
Trois-Pistoles 4,445 . . . . H 1
Trois-Rivières 50,466 . . . . . . E 3
Trois-Rivières *111,453 . . . . . E 3
Trois-Rivières-Ouest 13,107 . E 3
Upton 926. . . . . E 4
Val-Barrette 609 . . . . B 3
Val-Brillant 687 . . . . B 1
Valcourt 2,601 . . . . E 4
Val-David 2,336 . . . . C 3
Vallée-Jonction 1,200 . . . . . . G 3
Valleyfield (Salaberry-de-
Valleyfield) 29,574 . . . . C 4
Vanier 10,725 . . . . J 3

Varennes 8,764 . . . . J 4
Vaudreuil 7,608. . . . . C 4
Verchères® 4,473 . . . . J 4
Verdun 61,287 . . . . H 4
Victoriaville 21,838 . . . . F 3
Villeneuve . . . . J 3
Warwick 2,847 . . . . E 4
Waterloo® 4,664 . . . . E 4
Waterville 1,397 . . . . F 4
Weedon-Centre 1,263 . . . . . . F 4
Westmount 20,480 . . . . H 4
Wickham 2,043 . . . . E 4
Windsor 5,233 . . . . F 4
Wottonville 673 . . . . F 4
Yamachiche® 1,258 . . . . E 3

OTHER FEATURES

Alma (isl.) . . . . F 1
Aylmer (lake) . . . . A 4
Baskatong (res.) . . . . B 3
Batiscan (riv.) . . . . E 2
Bécancour (riv.) . . . . F 3
Bonaventure (isl.) . . . . D 1
Bonaventure (riv.) . . . . C 1
Brome (lake) . . . . E 4
Brompton (lake) . . . . E 4
Cascapédia (riv.) . . . . C 1
Chaleur (bay) . . . . C 2
Champlain (lake) . . . . D 4
Chaudière (riv.) . . . . G 4
Chic-Chocs (mts.) . . . . C 1
Chicoutimi (riv.) . . . . F 2
Coudres (isl.) . . . . G 2
Deschênes (lake) . . . . A 4
Deux Montagnes (lake) . . . . . C 4
Ditton (riv.) . . . . F 4
Forillon Nat'l Park . . . . D 1
Fort Chambly Nat'l Hist. Park . J 4
Gaspé (bay) . . . . D 1
Gaspé (cape) . . . . D 1
Gaspé (pen.) . . . . D 2
Gaspésie Prov. Park . . . . C 1
Gatineau (riv.) . . . . B 3
Îles (lake) . . . . B 3
Jacques-Cartier (mt.) . . . . . . C 1
Jacques-Cartier (riv.) . . . . . . F 2
Kénogami (lake) . . . . F 1
Kiamika (lake) . . . . B 3
La Vérendrye Nat'l Park . . . . D 3
Laurentides Prov. Park . . . . . F 2
Lièvres (riv.) . . . . B 3
Lièvres (isl.) . . . . H 2
Maskinongé (riv.) . . . . D 3
Matane (riv.) . . . . B 1
Matane Prov. Park . . . . B 1

Matapédia (riv.) . . . . B 2
Mégantic (lake) . . . . G 4
Memphremagog (lake) . . . . . . E 4
Mercier (dam) . . . . B 3
Métabetchouane (riv.) . . . . . . F 1
Mille Îles (riv.) . . . . H 4
Montmorency (riv.) . . . . F 2
Mont-Tremblant Prov. Park . . . C 3
Nicolet (riv.) . . . . E 3
Nominingue (lake) . . . . B 3
Nord (riv.) . . . . C 4
Orléans (isl.) . . . . F 3
Ottawa (riv.) . . . . B 4
Ouareau (riv.) . . . . D 3
Ouelle (riv.) . . . . H 2
Patapédia (riv.) . . . . B 2
Péribonca (riv.) . . . . F 1
Petite Nation (riv.) . . . . B 4
Prairies (riv.) . . . . H 4
Rimouski (riv.) . . . . J 1
Ristigouche (riv.) . . . . B 2
Saguenay (riv.) . . . . G 1
Sainte-Anne (riv.) . . . . F 3
Sainte-Anne (riv.) . . . . F 2
Saint-François (lake) . . . . . . F 4
Saint-François (riv.) . . . . E 3
Saint-Jean (lake) . . . . E 1
Saint Lawrence (gulf) . . . . . . D 2
Saint Lawrence (riv.) . . . . . . H 1
Saint-Louis (lake) . . . . H 4
Saint-Maurice (riv.) . . . . E 2
Saint-Pierre (lake) . . . . E 3
Shawinigan (lake) . . . . E 3
Shipshaw (riv.) . . . . F 1
Soeurs (isl.) . . . . H 4
Témiscouata (lake) . . . . H 2
Tremblant (lake) . . . . C 3
Trente et un Milles (lake) . . . . B 3
Verte (isl.) . . . . H 1
Yamaska (riv.) . . . . E 4
York (riv.) . . . . D 1

® County seat.
*Population of metropolitan area.

QUÉBEC, NORTHERN

INTERNAL DIVISIONS

Abitibi (county) 93,529. . . . . . B 2
Abitibi (terr.) . . . . B 2
Berthier (county) 31,096 . . . . B 3
Bonaventure (county) 40,487 . D 3
Champlain (county) 119,595. . C 3
Charlevoix-Est (co.) 17,448. . . C 3

Charlevoix-Ouest (county)
14,172 . . . . C 3
Chicoutimi (county) 174,441. . C 2
Gaspé-Est (county) 41,173. . . E 3
Gaspé-Ouest (county) 18,943 D 3
Gatineau (county) 54,229 . . . B 3
Joliette (county) 60,384 . . . . B 3
Lac-Saint-Jean-Est (county)
47,891 . . . . C 3
Lac-Saint-Jean-Ouest
(county) 62,952 . . . . C 3
Maskinongé (county) 20,763 . C 3
Matane (county) 29,955. . . . . C 3
Matapédia (county) 23,715 . . C 3
Mistassini (terr.) . . . . C 2
Montcalm (county) 27,557. . . B 3
Montmorency No.1 (county)
23,048 . . . . C 3
Nouveau-Québec (terr.) . . . . . E 1
Pontiac (county) 20,283. . . . . C 3
Portneuf (county) 58,843. . . . C 3
Québec (county) 458,980 . . . C 3
Rimouski (county) 69,099 . . . D 2
Saguenay (county) 115,881 . . C 2
Saint-Maurice (co.) 107,703 . C 3
Témiscamingue (co.) 52,570. . B 3

CITIES and TOWNS

Alma® 26,322 . . . . C 3
Amos® 9,421 . . . . B 3
Baie-Comeau 12,866. . . . . . . D 3
Baie-du-Poste 1,690 . . . . C 2
Chicoutimi® 60,064 . . . . C 3
Gaspé 17,261 . . . . E 3
Hauterive 13,995 . . . . D 3
Jonquière 60,354 . . . . C 3
Lévis 17,895 . . . . D 3
La Tuque 11,556 . . . . C 3
Manicouagan . . . . D 2
Maniwaki® 5,424 . . . . B 3
Matane® 13,612 . . . . D 3
Mistassini (Baie-du-Poste)
1,690 . . . . C 2
Mont-Laurier® 8,405 . . . . B 3
Montmagny® 12,405 . . . . C 3
New Carlisle® 781 . . . . E 3
Percé® 4,839 . . . . E 3
Port-Cartier-Ouest . . . . D 3
Port-Menier® . . . . D 2
Povungnituk 745 . . . . E 1
Québec (cap.)® 166,474 . . . . C 3
Rimouski® 29,120 . . . . D 3
Rivière-au-Tonnerre 480 . . . . D 2
Rivière-du-Loup 13,459 . . . . D 3
Rouyn 17,224 . . . . B 3

Sept-Îles 29,262 . . . . D 2
Shawinigan 23,011 . . . . C 3
Tadoussac 900 . . . . C 3
Val-d'Or 21,371 . . . . B 3
Ville-Marie 2,651 . . . . B 3
Wemindji . . . . B 2

OTHER FEATURES

Allard (lake) . . . . E 2
Anticosti (isl.) . . . . E 3
Baleine, Grand Rivière de la
(riv.) . . . . A 1
Bell (riv.) . . . . F 1
Bienville (lake) . . . . C 1
Broadback (riv.) . . . . B 2
Caniapiscau (lake) . . . . D 1
Cabonga (res.) . . . . B 3
Caniapiscau (riv.) . . . . D 1
Eastmain (riv.) . . . . B 2
Eau Claire (lake) . . . . C 1
Feuilles (riv.) . . . . C 1
Gaspésie Prov. Park . . . . D 3
George (riv.) . . . . F 2
Gouin (res.) . . . . C 3
Grande Rivière, La (riv.) . . . . B 2
Honguedo (passage) . . . . . . E 3
Hudson (bay) . . . . A 1
Hudson (str.) . . . . F 1
Jacques-Cartier (passage) . . E 3
James (bay) . . . . A 2
Koksoak (riv.) . . . . D 1
Laurentides Prov. Park . . . . . C 3
Louis-XIV (pt.) . . . . B 2
Manicouagan (res.) . . . . D 2
Minto (lake) . . . . E 2
Mistassini (riv.) . . . . C 3
Mistassini (lake) . . . . C 3
Moisie (riv.) . . . . D 2
Natashquan (riv.) . . . . E 2
Nottaway (riv.) . . . . A 2
Nouveau-Québec (crater) . . . F 1
Otish (mts.) . . . . C 2
Ottawa (riv.) . . . . B 3
Péribonca (riv.) . . . . C 2
Plétipi (lake) . . . . C 2
Saguenay (riv.) . . . . C 3
Saint-Jean (lake) . . . . C 3
Saint Lawrence (gulf) . . . . . . E 3
Saint Lawrence (riv.) . . . . . . D 3
Ungava (pen.) . . . . E 1

® County seat.
*Population of metropolitan area.

Northern Québec

SCALE
0 50 100 150 200 MI.
0 50 100 150 200 KM.

Provincial Capital — Provincial Boundaries
County Seats — County Boundaries
International Boundaries — Territorial Boundaries

Scale 1:8,400,000

© Copyright HAMMOND INCORPORATED, Maplewood, N.J.

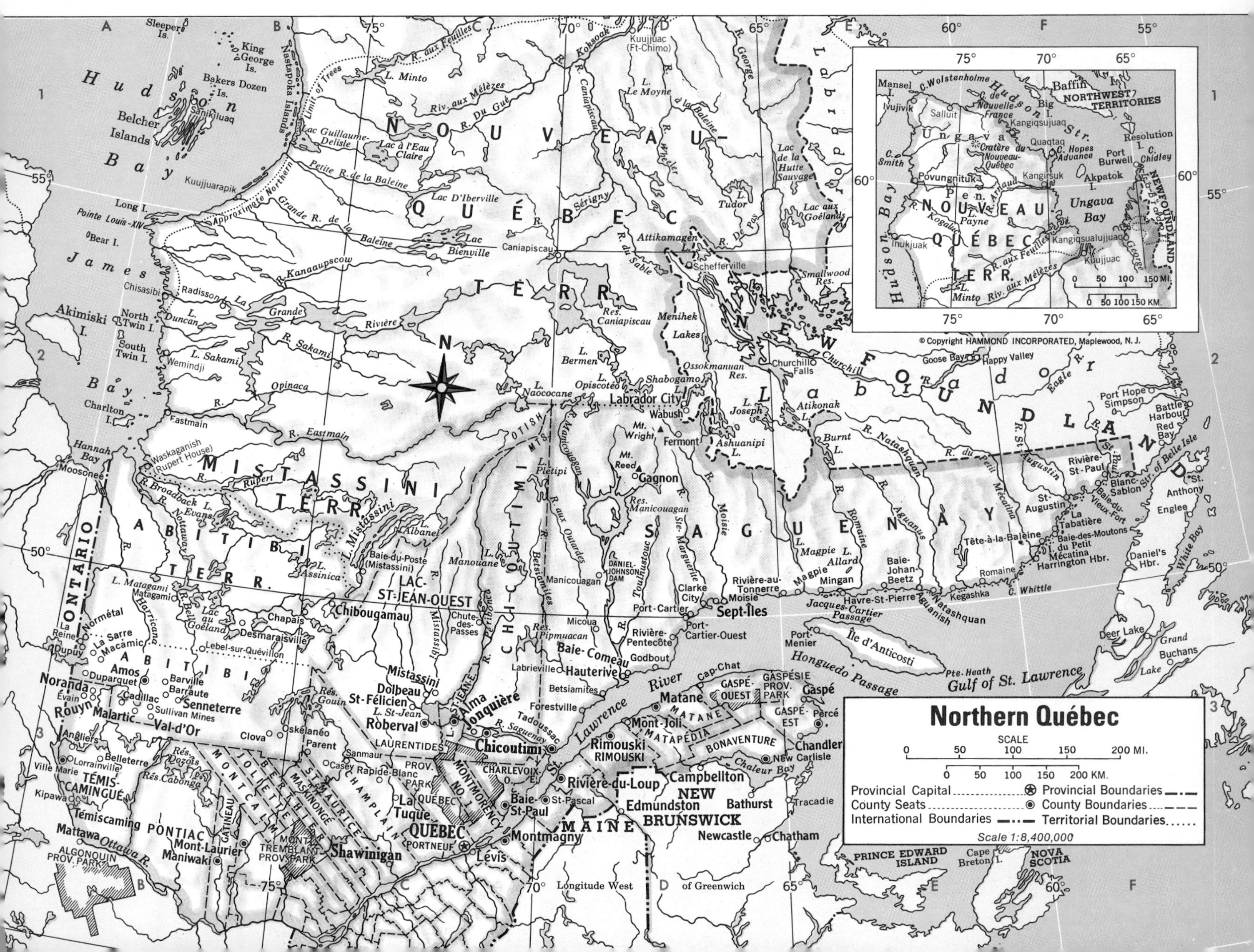

ONTARIO, NORTHERN

INTERNAL DIVISIONS

Algoma (terr. dist.) 133,553 ... D 3
Cochrane (terr. dist.) 96,875 .. D 2
Kenora (terr. dist.) 59,421 .... C 2
Manitoulin (terr. dist.) 11,001 . D 3
Nipissing (terr. dist.) 80,268 .. E 3
Parry Sound (terr. dist.) 33,528 ... E 3
Rainy River (terr. dist.) 22,798 B 3
Renfrew (county) 87,484 ..... E 3
Sudbury (reg. munic.) 159,779 ... D 3
Sudbury (terr. dist.) 27,068 ... D 3
Thunder Bay (terr. dist.) 153,997 ... C 3
Timiskaming (terr. dist.) 41,288 ... D 3

CITIES and TOWNS

Chalk River 1,010 ... E 3
Elliot Lake 16,723 ... D 3
Fort Albany 482 ... D 2
Fort Frances⊙ 8,906 ... B 3
Kapuskasing 12,014 ... D 3
Kenora⊙ 9,817 ... B 3
Kirkland Lake 12,219 ... D 3
Moose Factory 1,452 ... D 2
Moosonee 1,433 ... D 2
Nickel Centre 12,318 ... D 3
North Bay⊙ 51,268 ... E 3
Pembroke⊙ 14,026 ... E 3
Sault Sainte Marie⊙ 82,697 .. D 3
Sudbury 91,829 ... D 3
Thunder Bay⊙ 112,486 ... C 3
Timmins 46,114 ... D 3
Valley East 20,433 ... D 3

OTHER FEATURES

Abitibi (lake) ... E 3
Abitibi (riv.) ... D 2
Albany (riv.) ... C 2
Algonquin Prov. Park ... E 3
Asheweig (riv.) ... C 2
Attawapiskat (lake) ... C 2
Attawapiskat (riv.) ... C 2
Basswood (lake) ... B 3
Berens (riv.) ... A 2
Big Trout (lake) ... B 2
Black Duck (riv.) ... C 1
Bloodvein (riv.) ... A 2
Caribou (isl.) ... C 3
Cobham (riv.) ... A 2
Eabamet (lake) ... C 2
Ekwan (riv.) ... C 2
English (riv.) ... B 2
Fawn (riv.) ... C 2
Finger (lake) ... B 2
Georgian (bay) ... D 3
Hannah (bay) ... D 2
Henrietta Maria (cape) ... D 1
Hudson (bay) ... D 1
Huron (lake) ... D 3
James (bay) ... D 2
Kapiskau (riv.) ... D 2
Kapuskasing (riv.) ... D 3
Kenogami (riv.) ... C 2
Kesagami (riv.) ... E 2
Lake of the Woods (lake) ... B 3
Lake Superior Prov. Park ... D 3
Little Current (riv.) ... C 2
Long (lake) ... C 3
Manitoulin (isl.) ... D 3
Mattagami (riv.) ... D 3
Michipicoten (isl.) ... C 3
Mille Lacs (lake) ... B 3
Missinaibi (lake) ... D 3
Missinaibi (riv.) ... D 2
Missisa (lake) ... D 2
Nipigon (lake) ... C 3
Nipissing (lake) ... E 3
North (chan.) ... D 3
North Caribou (lake) ... B 2
Nungesser (lake) ... B 2
Ogidaki (mt.) ... D 3
Ogoki (riv.) ... C 2
Opazatika (riv.) ... D 3
Opinnagau (riv.) ... D 2
Otoskwin (riv.) ... B 2
Ottawa (riv.) ... E 3
Pipestone (riv.) ... B 2
Polar Bear Prov. Park ... D 2
Pukaskwa Prov. Park ... C 3
Quetico Prov. Park ... B 3
Rainy (lake) ... B 3
Red (lake) ... B 2
Sachigo (riv.) ... B 2
Saganaga (lake) ... B 3
Saint Ignace (isl.) ... C 3
Saint Joseph (lake) ... B 2
Sandy (lake) ... B 2
Savant (lake) ... B 2
Seine (riv.) ... B 3
Seul (lake) ... B 2
Severn (lake) ... B 2
Severn (riv.) ... B 2
Shamattawa (riv.) ... C 2
Shibogama (lake) ... C 2
Sibley Prov. Park ... C 3
Slate (isls.) ... C 3
Stout (lake) ... B 2
Superior (lake) ... C 3
Sutton (lake) ... D 2
Sutton (riv.) ... D 2
Temigami (lake) ... D 3
Timiskaming (lake) ... E 3
Trout (lake) ... B 2
Wabuk (pt.) ... D 1
Winisk (lake) ... C 2
Winisk (riv.) ... C 2
Winnipeg (riv.) ... A 2
Woods (lake) ... B 3

ONTARIO

INTERNAL DIVISIONS

Algoma (terr. dist.) 133,553 ... J 5
Brant (county) 104,427 ... D 4
Bruce (county) 60,020 ... C 3
Cochrane (terr. dist.) 96,875 .. J 4
Dufferin (county) 31,145 ... D 3
Dundas (county) 18,946 ... J 2
Durham (reg. munic.) 283,639 F 3
Elgin (county) 69,707 ... C 5
Essex (county) 312,467 ... B 5
Frontenac (county) 108,133 .. H 3
Glengarry (county) 20,254 ... K 2
Grenville (county) 27,176 ... J 3
Grey (county) 73,824 ... D 3
Haldimand-Norfolk (reg. munic.) 89,456 ... E 5
Haliburton (county) 11,361 ... F 2
Halton (reg. munic.) 253,883 . E 4
Hamilton-Wentworth (reg. munic.) 411,445 ... D 4
Hastings (county) 106,883 ... G 3
Huron (county) 56,127 ... C 4
Kenora (terr. dist.) 59,421 ... G 5
Kent (county) 107,022 ... B 5
Lambton (county) 123,445 ... B 5
Lanark (county) 45,676 ... H 3
Leeds (county) 53,765 ... H 3
Lennox and Addington (county) 33,040 ... G 3
Manitoulin (terr. dist.) 11,001 . B 2
Middlesex (county) 318,184 .. C 4
Muskoka (dist. munic.) 38,370 ... E 3
Niagara (reg. munic.) 368,288 E 4
Nipissing (terr. dist.) 80,268 .. F 2
Northumberland (county) 64,966 ... G 3
Ottawa-Carleton (reg. munic.) 546,849 ... J 2
Oxford (county) 85,920 ... D 4
Parry Sound (terr. dist.) 33,528 ... D 2
Peel (reg. munic.) 490,731 ... E 4
Perth (county) 66,096 ... C 4
Peterborough (county) 102,452 ... F 3
Prescott (county) 30,365 ... K 2
Prince Edward (county) 22,336 ... G 3
Rainy River (terr. dist.) 22,798 G 5
Renfrew (county) 87,484 ... G 2
Russell (county) 22,412 ... J 2
Simcoe (county) 225,071 ... E 3
Stormont (county) 61,927 ... K 2
Sudbury (reg. munic.) 159,779 ... K 6
Sudbury (terr. dist.) 27,068 ... J 5
Thunder Bay (terr. dist.) 153,997 ... H 5
Timiskaming (terr. dist.) 41,288 ... K 5
Toronto (metro. munic.) 2,137,395 ... K 4
Victoria (county) 47,854 ... F 3
Waterloo (reg. munic.) 305,496 ... D 4
Wellington (county) 129,432 .. D 4
York (reg. munic.) 252,053 ... E 4

CITIES and TOWNS

Ailsa Craig 765 ... C 4
Ajax 25,475 ... E 4
Alban 342 ... D 1
Alexandria 3,271 ... K 2
Alfred 1,057 ... K 2
Alliston 4,712 ... E 3
Almonte 3,855 ... H 2
Alvinston 736 ... B 5
Amherstburg 5,685 ... A 5
Amherst View 6,110 ... H 3
Ancaster 14,428 ... D 4
Angus 3,085 ... E 3
Apsley 264 ... F 3
Arkona 473 ... C 4
Armstrong 378 ... H 4
Arnprior 5,828 ... H 2
Aroland 291 ... H 4
Arthur 1,700 ... D 4
Astorville 340 ... E 1
Athens 948 ... J 3
Atherley 366 ... E 3
Atikokan 4,452 ... G 5

AREA 412,580 sq. mi. (1,068,582 sq. km.)
POPULATION 9,101,694
CAPITAL Toronto
LARGEST CITY Toronto
HIGHEST POINT in Timiskaming Dist. 2,275 ft. (693 m.)
SETTLED IN 1749
ADMITTED TO CONFEDERATION 1867
PROVINCIAL FLOWER White Trillium

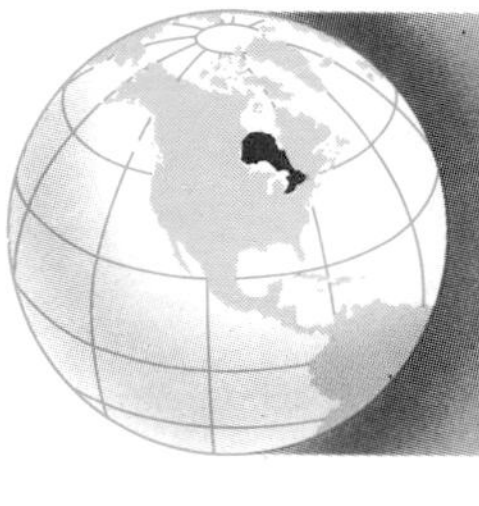

Atwood 723 ... D 4
Aurora 16,267 ... J 3
Avonmore 273 ... K 2
Aylmer 5,254 ... C 5
Ayr 1,295 ... D 4
Ayton 424 ... D 3
Baden 945 ... D 4
Bala 577 ... E 2
Bancroft 2,329 ... G 2
Barrie⊙ 38,423 ... E 3
Barry's Bay 1,216 ... G 2
Batawa 430 ... G 3
Bath 1,071 ... H 3
Bayfield 649 ... C 4
Beachburg 682 ... H 2
Beachville 917 ... D 4
Beardmore 583 ... H 5
Beaverton 1,952 ... E 3
Beeton 1,989 ... E 3
Belle River 3,568 ... B 5
Belleville⊙ 34,881 ... G 3
Belmont 831 ... C 5
Bethany 365 ... F 3
Bewdley 508 ... F 3
Binbrook 306 ... E 4
Blackstock 720 ... F 3
Blenheim 4,044 ... C 5
Blind River 3,444 ... J 5
Bloomfield 718 ... G 4
Blyth 926 ... C 4
Bobcaygeon 1,625 ... F 3
Bonfield 540 ... E 1
Bothwell 915 ... C 5
Bourget 1,057 ... J 2
Bracebridge⊙ 9,063 ... E 2
Bradford 7,370 ... E 3
Braeside 492 ... H 2
Brampton⊙ 149,030 ... J 4
Brantford⊙ 74,315 ... D 4
Bridgenorth 1,633 ... F 3
Brigden 635 ... B 5
Brighton 3,147 ... G 3
Britt 419 ... D 2
Brockville⊙ 19,896 ... J 3
Bruce Mines 635 ... J 5
Brussels 962 ... C 4
Burford 1,461 ... D 4
Burgessville 302 ... D 4
Burk's Falls 922 ... E 2
Burlington 114,853 ... E 4
Cache Bay 665 ... D 1
Caesarea 551 ... F 3
Calabogie 256 ... H 2
Caledon 26,645 ... E 4
Callander 1,158 ... E 1
Cambridge 77,183 ... D 4
Campbellford 3,409 ... G 3
Cannington 1,623 ... E 3
Capreol 3,845 ... K 5
Caramat 265 ... H 5
Cardinal 1,753 ... J 3
Carleton Place 5,626 ... H 2
Carlisle 781 ... D 4
Carlsbad Springs 616 ... J 2
Carp 707 ... H 2
Cartier 590 ... J 5
Casselman 1,675 ... J 2
Castleton 346 ... F 3
Chalk River 1,010 ... G 1
Chapleau 3,243 ... J 5
Charing Cross 443 ... B 5
Chatham⊙ 40,952 ... B 5
Chatsworth 383 ... D 3
Cherry Valley 289 ... G 4
Chesley 1,840 ... C 3
Chesterville 1,430 ... J 2
Chute-à-Blondeau 365 ... K 2
City View ... J 2
Clarence Creek 796 ... J 2
Clarksburg 508 ... D 3
Clifford 645 ... D 4
Clinton 3,081 ... C 4
Cobalt 1,759 ... K 5
Cobden 997 ... H 2
Coboconk 426 ... F 3
Cobourg⊙ 11,385 ... F 4
Cochrane⊙ 4,848 ... K 5
Colborne 1,796 ... G 4
Colchester 711 ... B 6
Coldwater 964 ... E 3
Collingwood 12,064 ... D 3
Comber 667 ... B 5
Consecon 295 ... G 3
Cookstown 918 ... E 3
Cornwall⊙ 46,144 ... K 2
Cottam 404 ... B 5
Courtland 647 ... D 5
Courtright 1,024 ... B 5
Crediton 370 ... C 4
Creemore 1,182 ... D 3
Crysler 540 ... J 2
Cumberland 518 ... J 2
Cumberland Beach-Bramshot-Buena Vista 679 ... E 3
Dashwood 426 ... C 4
Deep River 5,095 ... G 1
Delaware 481 ... C 5
Delhi 4,043 ... D 5
Delta 360 ... H 3
Deseronto 1,740 ... G 3
Douglas 303 ... H 2
Drayton 809 ... D 4
Dresden 2,550 ... B 5
Drumbo 476 ... D 4
Dryden 6,640 ... G 4
Dublin 295 ... C 4
Dubreuilville △988 ... J 5
Dundalk 1,250 ... D 3
Dundas 19,586 ... D 4
Dungannon 284 ... C 4
Dunnville 11,353 ... E 5
Durham 2,458 ... D 3
Dutton 1,115 ... C 5
Earlton 1,028 ... K 5
East York 101,974 ... J 4
Echo Bay 786 ... J 5
Eden Mills 318 ... D 4
Eganville 1,245 ... G 2
Egmondville 465 ... C 4
Elgin 327 ... H 3
Elk Lake 526 ... K 5
Elliot Lake 16,723 ... B 1
Elmira 7,063 ... D 4
Elmvale 1,183 ... E 3
Elmwood 364 ... C 3
Elora 2,666 ... D 4
Embro 727 ... C 4
Embrun 1,883 ... J 2
Emeryville-Puce 1,611 ... B 5
Emo 762 ... F 5
Englehart 1,689 ... K 5
Enterprise 357 ... H 3
Erieau 430 ... C 5
Erin 2,313 ... D 4
Espanola 5,836 ... J 5
Essex 6,295 ... B 5
Etobicoke 298,713 ... J 4
Everett 570 ... E 3
Exeter 3,732 ... C 4
Fauquier 561 ... J 5
Fenelon Falls 1,701 ... F 3
Fergus 6,064 ... D 4
Field 462 ... E 1
Finch 353 ... J 2
Fingal 380 ... C 5
Fitzroy Harbour 446 ... H 2
Flesherton 565 ... D 3
Foleyet 484 ... J 5
Fordwich 365 ... C 4
Forest 2,671 ... C 4
Formosa 393 ... C 3
Fort Erie 24,096 ... E 5
Fort Frances⊙ 8,906 ... F 5
Foxboro 597 ... G 3
Frankford 1,919 ... G 3
Fraserdale 303 ... J 5
Freelton 307 ... D 4
Gananoque 4,863 ... H 3
Garden Village 270 ... E 1
Geraldton 2,956 ... H 5
Glencoe 1,694 ... C 5
Glen Miller 639 ... G 3
Glen Robertson 378 ... K 2
Glen Walter 710 ... K 2
Goderich⊙ 7,322 ... C 4
Gogama 652 ... J 5
Goodwood 335 ... E 3
Gore Bay⊙ 777 ... B 2
Gorrie 468 ... C 4
Grafton 409 ... G 4
Grand Bend 680 ... C 4
Grand Valley 1,226 ... D 4
Granton 315 ... C 4
Gravenhurst 8,532 ... E 3
Greely 567 ... J 2
Green Valley 459 ... K 2
Grimsby 15,797 ... E 4
Guelph⊙ 71,207 ... D 4

(continued on following page)

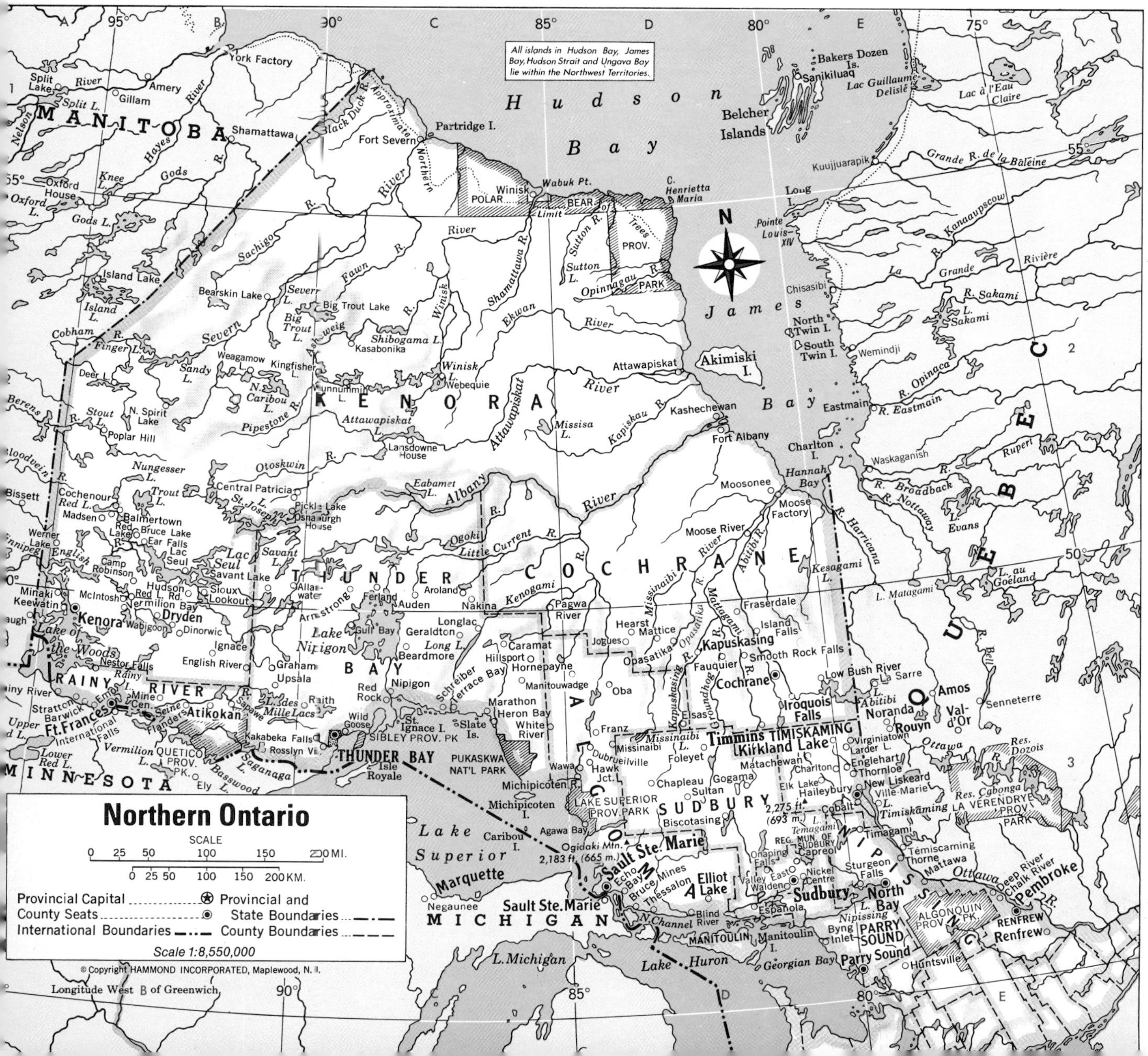
All islands in Hudson Bay, James Bay, Hudson Strait and Ungava Bay lie within the Northwest Territories.
Hudson Bay
James Bay
MANITOBA
KENORA
THUNDER BAY
COCHRANE
ALGOMA
SUDBURY
NIPISSING
TIMISKAMING
RAINY RIVER
QUEBEC
MINNESOTA
MICHIGAN
Lake Superior
Lake Huron
L. Michigan
Georgian Bay
Northern Ontario
SCALE
0 25 50 100 150 200 MI.
0 25 50 100 150 200 KM.
Provincial Capital ⊛ Provincial and State Boundaries
County Seats ⊙
International Boundaries
County Boundaries
Scale 1:8,550,000
© Copyright HAMMOND INCORPORATED, Maplewood, N. J.
Longitude West of Greenwich

Haileybury⊙ 4,925 . . . . K 5
Haldimand 16,866 . . . . E 5
Haliburton 1,443 . . . . F 2
Halton Hills 35,190 . . . . . . E 4
Hamilton⊙ 306,434 . . . . . . E 4
Hamilton *542,095 . . . . . . E 4
Hanover 6,316 . . . . C 3
Harriston 1,954 . . . . D 4
Harrow 2,274 . . . . B 5
Harrowsmith 599 . . . . H 3
Harwood 332 . . . . F 3
Hastings 975 . . . . G 3
Havelock 1,385 . . . . G 3
Hawkesbury 9,877 . . . . . . K 2
Hawkestone 275 . . . . E 3
Hawk Junction 349 . . . . . . J 5
Hearst 5,533 . . . . H 5
Hensall 973 . . . . C 4
Hepworth 393 . . . . C 3
Hickson 263 . . . . D 4
Highgate 435 . . . . C 5
Hillsburgh 1,065 . . . . D 4
Hillsdale 370 . . . . E 3
Holland Landing 2,771 . . . . E 3
Honey Harbour 505 . . . . . . E 3
Hornepayne 1,848 . . . . . . J 5
Hudson 515 . . . . G 4
Huntsville 11,467 . . . . . . E 3
Huron Park 1,104 . . . . . . C 4
Ignace 2,499 . . . . G 5
Ilderton 301 . . . . C 4
Ingersoll 8,494 . . . . D 4
Ingleside 1,400 . . . . J 2
Innerkip 715 . . . . D 4
Inverhuron 438 . . . . C 3
Iron Bridge 821 . . . . A 1

Iroquois 1,211 . . . . J 3
Iroquois Falls 6,339 . . . . . J 5
Johnstown 789 . . . . J 3
Kakabeka Falls 300 . . . . . . G 5
Kanata 19,728 . . . . J 2
Kapuskasing 12,014 . . . . . J 5
Kars 449 . . . . J 2
Kearney 538 . . . . E 2
Keene 353 . . . . F 3
Keewatin 1,863 . . . . F 5
Kemptville 2,362 . . . . . . J 2
Kenora⊙ 9,817 . . . . F 4
Killaloe Station 634 . . . . . G 2
Killarney 433 . . . . C 2
Kincardine 5,778 . . . . . . C 3
Kingsville 5,134 . . . . B 6
Kingston⊙ 52,616 . . . . . . H 3
Kinmount 262 . . . . F 3
Kirkland Lake 12,219 . . . . . K 5
Kitchener⊙ 139,734 . . . . . D 4
Kitchener *287,801 . . . . . D 4
Komoka 1,152 . . . . C 4
Lakefield 2,374 . . . . F 3
Lanark 753 . . . . H 2
Lancaster 637 . . . . K 2
Langton 348 . . . . D 5
Lansdowne 540 . . . . J 3
Larder Lake 1,084 . . . . . . K 5
Latchford 397 . . . . K 5
Leamington 12,528 . . . . . B 6
Limoges 930 . . . . J 2
Lincoln 14,196 . . . . E 4
Linden Beach 579 . . . . . . B 6
Lindsay 13,596 . . . . F 3
Linwood 450 . . . . D 4
Lion's Head 467 . . . . C 2

Lisle 265 . . . . E 3
Listowel 5,026 . . . . D 4
Little Britain 265 . . . . . . F 3
Little Current 1,507 . . . . . B 2
London⊙ 254,280 . . . . . . C 4
London *283,668 . . . . . . C 4
Longlac 2,431 . . . . H 5
Long Sault 1,227 . . . . . . K 2
L'Orignal 1,819 . . . . K 2
Lucan 1,616 . . . . C 4
Lucknow 1,088 . . . . C 4
Lyn 518 . . . . J 3
Lynden 451 . . . . D 4
Lynhurst 685 . . . . C 5
MacGregor's Bay 861 . . . . . G 2
MacTier 647 . . . . E 2
Madawaska 264 . . . . F 2
Madoc 1,249 . . . . G 3
Maitland 667 . . . . J 3
Mallorytown 368 . . . . . . J 3
Manitouwadge 3,155 . . . . . H 5
Manitowaning 518 . . . . . . C 2
Manotick-Hillside Gardens
  2,694 . . . . J 2
Marathon 2,271 . . . . H 5
Markdale 1,289 . . . . D 3
Markham 77,037 . . . . . . K 4
Markstay 444 . . . . D 1
Marmora 1,304 . . . . G 3
Martintown 388 . . . . K 2
Massey 1,274 . . . . C 1
Matachewan 443 . . . . . . J 5
Matheson 966 . . . . K 5
Mattawa 2,652 . . . . F 1
Mattice 803 . . . . J 5
Maxville 836 . . . . K 2

Maynooth 277 . . . . G 2
McGregor 1,145 . . . . B 5
McKerrow 260 . . . . C 1
Meaford 4,367 . . . . D 3
Melbourne 346 . . . . C 4
Merlin 745 . . . . B 5
Merrickville 984 . . . . . . J 3
Metcalfe 687 . . . . J 2
Midhurst 1,457 . . . . E 3
Midland 12,132 . . . . D 3
Mildmay 928 . . . . C 3
Milford Bay 401 . . . . E 2
Millbank 337 . . . . D 4
Millbrook 927 . . . . F 3
Milton 28,067 . . . . E 4
Milverton 1,463 . . . . D 4
Minaki 397 . . . . F 4
Mindemoya 376 . . . . B 2
Minden⊙ 838 . . . . F 2
Mississauga 315,056 . . . . . J 4
Mitchell 2,777 . . . . C 4
Monkton 520 . . . . C 4
Moonbeam 438 . . . . J 5
Moorefield 308 . . . . D 4
Mooretown 344 . . . . B 5
Moose Creek 393 . . . . . . K 2
Morewood 264 . . . . J 2
Morpeth 284 . . . . C 5
Morrisburg 2,308 . . . . . . J 3
Mount Albert 1,165 . . . . . E 3
Mount Brydges 1,557 . . . . C 4
Mount Forest 3,474 . . . . . D 4
Mount Hope 557 . . . . E 4
Munster 1,531 . . . . J 2

Napanee 4,803 . . . . G 3
Navan 419 . . . . J 2
Neustadt 511 . . . . D 3
Newboro 260 . . . . H 3
Newburgh 617 . . . . H 3
Newbury 441 . . . . C 4
Newcastle 32,229 . . . . . . F 4
New Hamburg 3,923 . . . . . D 4
New Liskeard 5,551 . . . . . K 5
Newmarket⊙ 29,753 . . . . E 3
Niagara Falls 70,960 . . . . . E 4
Niagara-on-the-Lake 12,186 . E 4
Nickel Centre 12,318 . . . . D 1
Nipigon 2,377 . . . . H 5
Nobel 386 . . . . D 2
Nobleton 1,861 . . . . E 4
Noelville 702 . . . . D 1
North Bay 51,268 . . . . . . E 1
North Gower 811 . . . . . . J 2
Norwich 2,117 . . . . D 5
Norwood 1,278 . . . . F 3
Nottawa 360 . . . . D 3
Oakville 75,773 . . . . E 4
Oakwood 404 . . . . F 3
Odessa 849 . . . . H 3
Oil City 266 . . . . B 5
Oil Springs 627 . . . . B 5
Omemee 819 . . . . F 3
Onaping Falls 6,198 . . . . . J 5
Opasatika 413 . . . . J 5
Orangeville⊙ 13,740 . . . . D 4
Orillia 23,955 . . . . E 3
Osgoode 1,138 . . . . J 2
Oshawa 117,519 . . . . . . F 4
Oshawa *154,217 . . . . . . F 4

Ottawa⊙ (cap.), Canada
  295,163 . . . . J 2
Ottawa-Hull *717,978 . . . . J 2
Otterville 760 . . . . D 5
Owen Sound⊙ 19,883 . . . . D 3
Paincourt 414 . . . . B 5
Paisley 1,039 . . . . C 3
Pakenham 837 . . . . H 2
Palmerston 1,989 . . . . . . D 4
Paris 7,485 . . . . D 4
Parkhill 1,358 . . . . C 4
Parry Sound⊙ 6,124 . . . . E 2
Pefferlaw 857 . . . . E 3
Pelham 11,104 . . . . E 4
Pembroke 14,026 . . . . . . G 2
Penetanguishene 5,315 . . . . D 3
Perth 5,655 . . . . H 3
Petawawa 5,520 . . . . G 2
Peterborough⊙ 60,620 . . . . F 3
Petrolia 4,234 . . . . B 5
Pickering 37,754 . . . . . . K 4
Picton 4,361 . . . . G 3
Plantagenet 870 . . . . K 2
Plattsville 495 . . . . D 4
Point Edward 2,383 . . . . . B 4
Pontypool 759 . . . . F 3
Port Burwell 655 . . . . . . D 5
Port Carling 629 . . . . . . E 2
Port Colborne 19,225 . . . . E 5
Port Elgin 6,131 . . . . . . C 3
Port Franks 547 . . . . C 4
Port Hope 9,992 . . . . . . F 4
Port Lambton 921 . . . . . . B 5
Portland 271 . . . . H 3
Port McNicoll 1,883 . . . . . E 3
Port Perry 4,712 . . . . . . E 3

Port Rowan 811 . . . . D 5
Port Stanley 1,891 . . . . . . C 5
Pottageville 286 . . . . J 3
Powassan 1,169 . . . . E 1
Prescott 4,670 . . . . J 3
Princeton 462 . . . . D 4
Puce-Emeryville 1,611 . . . . B 5
Rainy River 1,061 . . . . . . F 5
Ramore 382 . . . . K 5
Rayside-Balfour 15,017 . . . . K 5
Red Rock 1,260 . . . . H 5
Renfrew 8,283 . . . . H 2
Richards Landing 405 . . . . A 1
Richmond 2,880 . . . . J 2
Richmond Hill 37,778 . . . . K 4
Ridgetown 3,062 . . . . . . C 5
Ripley 591 . . . . C 3
River Valley 275 . . . . D 1
Rockcliffe Park 1,869 . . . . J 2
Rockland 3,961 . . . . J 2
Rockwood 1,068 . . . . D 4
Rodney 1,007 . . . . C 5
Rosslyn Village 362 . . . . . G 5
Round Lake Centre 255 . . . . G 2
Russell 1,099 . . . . J 2
Ruthven 649 . . . . B 6
Saint Albert 254 . . . . J 2
Saint Catharines⊙ 124,018 . . E 4
Saint Catharines-Niagara
  *304,353 . . . . E 4
Saint Charles 382 . . . . . . D 1
Saint Clair Beach 2,845 . . . B 5
Saint Clements 890 . . . . . D 4
Saint-Eugène 470 . . . . . . K 2
Saint George 865 . . . . . . D 4
Saint Isidore de Prescott 746 . K 2

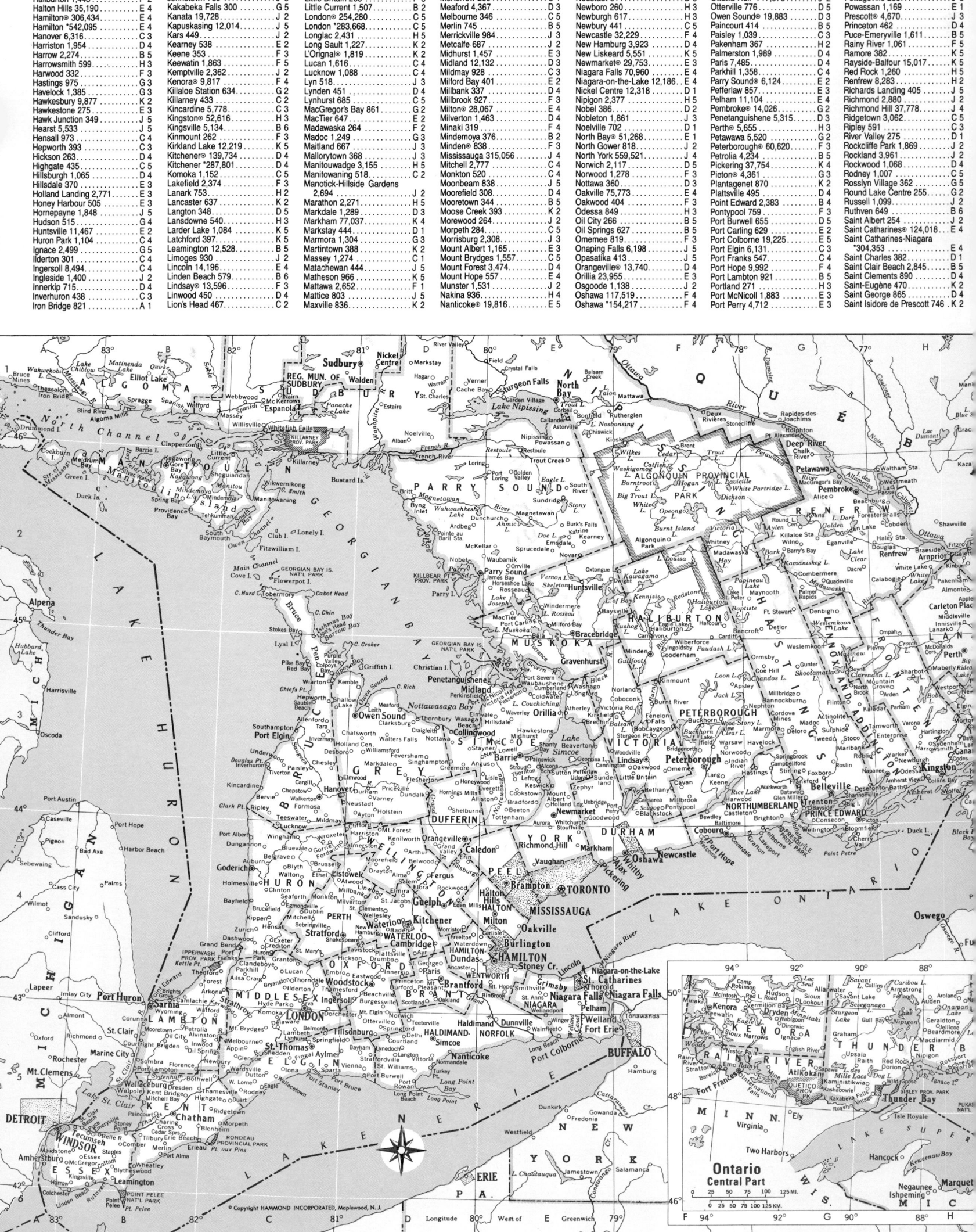

Index (place names)

Name	Ref
Saint Jacobs 1,189	D 4
Saint Mary's 4,883	C 4
Saint Thomas 28,165	C 5
Saint Williams 442	D 5
Salem 825	D 4
Sarnia◉ 50,892	B 5
Sauble Beach 729	C 3
Sault Sainte Marie◉ 82,697	J 5
Scarborough 443,353	K 4
Schomberg 923	J 3
Schreiber 1,968	H 5
Scotland 600	C 4
Seaforth 2,114	C 4
Searchmont 384	J 5
Sebringville 579	C 4
Seeleys Bay 503	H 3
Shakespeare 602	D 4
Shallow Lake 418	C 3
Shannonville 314	G 3
Shanty Bay 358	E 3
Sharbot Lake 495	H 3
Shedden 292	C 5
Shelburne 2,862	D 3
Simcoe◉ 14,326	D 5
Sioux Lookout 3,074	G 4
Sioux Narrows 394	F 5
Smithfield 349	G 3
Smiths Falls 8,831	H 3
Smithville 1,936	E 5
Smooth Rock Falls 2,352	J 5
Sombra 420	B 5
Southampton 2,830	C 3
South Mountain 285	J 3
South River 1,109	E 2
Spanish 1,063	J 5
Sparta 283	C 5
Spencerville 438	J 3
Springfield 555	C 5
Springford 309	D 5
Stayner 2,530	E 3
Stirling 1,638	G 3
Stittsville 2,652	J 2
Stoney Creek 36,762	E 4
Stoney Point 1,090	B 5
Straffordville 752	D 5
Stratford◉ 26,262	C 4
Strathroy 8,748	C 5
Sturgeon Falls 6,045	E 1
Sudbury◉ 91,829	K 5
Sudbury *149,923	K 5
Sunderland 703	E 3
Sundridge 734	E 2
Sydenham 595	H 3
Tamworth 402	H 3
Tara 687	C 3
Tavistock 1,885	D 4
Tecumseh 6,364	B 5
Teeswater 1,026	C 3
Terrace Bay 2,639	H 5
Thamesford 1,920	C 4
Thamesville 961	C 5
Thedford 694	C 4
Thessalon 1,620	J 5
Thornbury 1,435	D 3
Thorndale 581	C 4
Thornton 414	E 3
Thorold 15,412	E 4
Thunder Bay◉ 112,486	H 5
Thunder Bay *121,379	H 5
Tilbury 4,298	B 5
Tillsonburg 10,487	D 5
Timmins 46,114	J 5
Tiverton 806	C 3
Tobermory 282	C 2
Toronto (cap.)◉ 599,217	K 4
Toronto *2,998,947	K 4
Tottenham 3,022	E 3
Trenton 15,085	G 3
Trout Creek 652	E 2
Turkey Point 407	D 5
Tweed 1,574	G 3
Udora 375	E 3
Union 485	C 5
Uxbridge 4,209	E 3
Valley East 20,433	J 5
Vanier 18,792	J 2
Vankleek Hill 1,774	K 2
Vars 527	J 2
Vaughan 29,674	J 4
Vermilion Bay 505	G 4
Verner 1,076	D 1
Vernon 303	J 2
Verona 754	H 3
Victoria Harbour 1,125	E 3
Vienna 369	D 5
Virginiatown 1,010	K 5
Vittoria 420	D 5
Wabigoon 268	G 5
Walden 10,139	J 5
Walkerton◉ 4,682	C 3
Wallaceburg 11,506	B 5
Wardsville 450	C 5
Warkworth 618	G 3
Warren 579	D 1
Warsaw 314	F 3
Wasaga Beach 4,705	D 3
Washago 569	E 3
Waterloo 49,428	D 4
Watford 1,402	C 5
Waubaushene 878	E 3
Wawa 4,206	J 5
Webbwood 519	C 1
Welcome 293	F 4
Welland 454,448	E 5
Wellesley 997	D 4
Wellington 1,082	G 4
Wendover 326	J 2
West Lorne 1,258	C 5
Westmeath 262	H 2
Westport 621	H 3
Wheatley 1,638	B 5
Whitby◉ 36,698	F 4
Whitchurch-Stouffville 13,557	J 3
White River △1,006	J 5
Whitney 766	F 2
Wiarton 2,074	C 3
Wikwemikong 1,030	C 2
Williamsburg 407	J 3
Williamsford 256	D 3
Williamstown 328	K 2
Winchester 2,001	J 2
Windsor◉ 192,083	B 5
Windsor *246,110	B 5
Wingham 2,897	C 4
Wolfe Island 271	H 3
Woodstock◉ 26,603	D 4
Woodville 575	F 3
Wroxeter 350	C 4
Wyoming 1,682	B 5
Yarker 319	H 3
York 134,617	J 4
Zephyr 330	E 3
Zurich 795	C 4

OTHER FEATURES

Name	Ref
Abitibi (riv.)	J 5
Algonquin Prov. Park	F 2
Amherst (isl.)	H 3
Balsam (lake)	F 3
Barrie (isl.)	B 1
Bays (pen.)	F 2
Big Rideau (lake)	H 3
Black (riv.)	E 3
Bruce (pen.)	C 2
Buckhorn (lake)	F 3
Cabot (head)	C 2
Charleston (lake)	J 3
Christian (isl.)	D 3
Clear (lake)	F 3
Cockburn (isl.)	A 2
Couchiching (lake)	E 3
Croker (cape)	D 3
Don (riv.)	J 4
Doré (lake)	G 2
Douglas (pt.)	C 3
Erie (lake)	E 5
Flowerpot (isl.)	C 2
French (riv.)	D 1
Georgian (bay)	D 2
Georgian Bay Is. Nat'l Park	C 2, D 3
Georgina (isl.)	E 3
Grand (riv.)	D 4
Humber (riv.)	J 3
Hurd (cape)	C 2
Huron (lake)	B 3
Ipperwash Prov. Park	C 4
Joseph (lake)	E 2
Killarney Prov. Park	C 1
Killbear Point Prov. Park	D 2
Lake of the Woods (lake)	F 5
Lake Superior Prov. Park	J 5
Lonely (isl.)	C 2
Long (pt.)	D 5
Long Point (bay)	D 5
Madawaska (riv.)	G 2
Magnetawan (riv.)	D 2
Main (chan.)	C 2
Manitou (lake)	C 2
Manitoulin (isl.)	B 2
Mattagami (riv.)	J 5
Michipicoten (isl.)	H 5
Missinaibi (riv.)	J 5
Mississagi (riv.)	A 1
Mississippi (lake)	H 2
Muskoka (lake)	E 2
Niagara (riv.)	E 4
Nipigon (lake)	H 5
Nipissing (lake)	E 1
North (chan.)	A 1
Nottawasaga (bay)	D 3
Ogidaki (mt.)	J 5
Ontario (lake)	G 4
Opeongo (lake)	F 2
Ottawa (riv.)	H 2
Owen (sound)	D 3
Panache (lake)	C 1
Parry (isl.)	D 2
Parry (sound)	D 2
Pelee (pt.)	B 6
Petre (pt.)	G 4
Point Pelee Nat'l Park	B 5
Presqu'ile Prov. Park	G 4
Pukaskwa Prov. Park	H 5
Quetico Prov. Park	G 5
Rainy (lake)	G 5
Rice (lake)	F 3
Rideau (lake)	H 3
Rondeau Prov. Park	C 5
Rosseau (lake)	E 2
Saint Clair (lake)	B 5
Saint Clair (riv.)	B 5
Saint Lawrence (lake)	K 3
Saint Lawrence (riv.)	J 3
Saint Lawrence Is. Nat'l Park	J 3
Saugeen (riv.)	C 3
Scugog (lake)	F 3
Seul (lake)	G 4
Severn (riv.)	E 3
Sibley Prov. Park	H 5
Simcoe (lake)	E 3
South (bay)	C 2
Spanish (riv.)	C 1
Stony (lake)	G 3
Superior (lake)	H 5
Sydenham (riv.)	B 5
Temagami (lake)	K 5
Thames (riv.)	B 5
Theano (pt.)	J 5
Thousand (isls.)	H 3
Trout (lake)	E 1
Vernon (lake)	E 2
Walpole (isl.)	B 5
Welland (canal)	E 5
Woods (lake)	E 5

◉County seat.
*Population of metropolitan area.
△Population of town or township.

Ontario — Southern Part

SCALE
0 10 20 30 40 50 MI.
0 10 20 30 40 50 KM.

◉ National Capital
◉ Provincial Capital
◉ County Seats
International Boundaries
Provincial & State Boundaries
County Boundaries
Canals

Scale 1:2,620,000

Topography

0 100 200 MI.
0 100 200 KM.

Below Sea Level | 100 m. 328 ft. | 200 m. 656 ft. | 500 m. 1,640 ft. | 1,000 m. 3,281 ft. | 2,000 m. 6,562 ft. | 5,000 m. 16,404 ft.

Agriculture, Industry and Resources

DOMINANT LAND USE

- Cereals, Cash Crops, Livestock
- Dairy
- General Farming, Livestock
- Fruits, Vegetables
- Pasture Livestock
- Forests
- Nonagricultural Land

MAJOR MINERAL OCCURRENCES

Ab	Asbestos	Mg	Magnesium
Ag	Silver	Mr	Marble
Au	Gold	Na	Salt
Co	Cobalt	Ni	Nickel
Cu	Copper	Pb	Lead
Fe	Iron Ore	Pt	Platinum
G	Natural Gas	U	Uranium
Gr	Graphite	Zn	Zinc

⚡ Water Power
▨ Major Industrial Areas

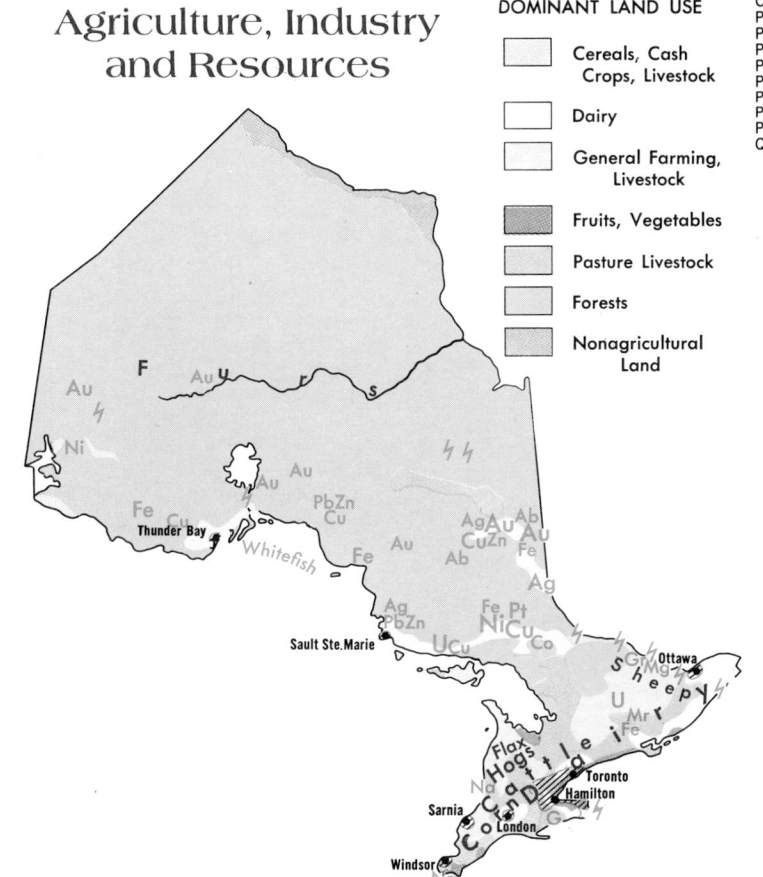

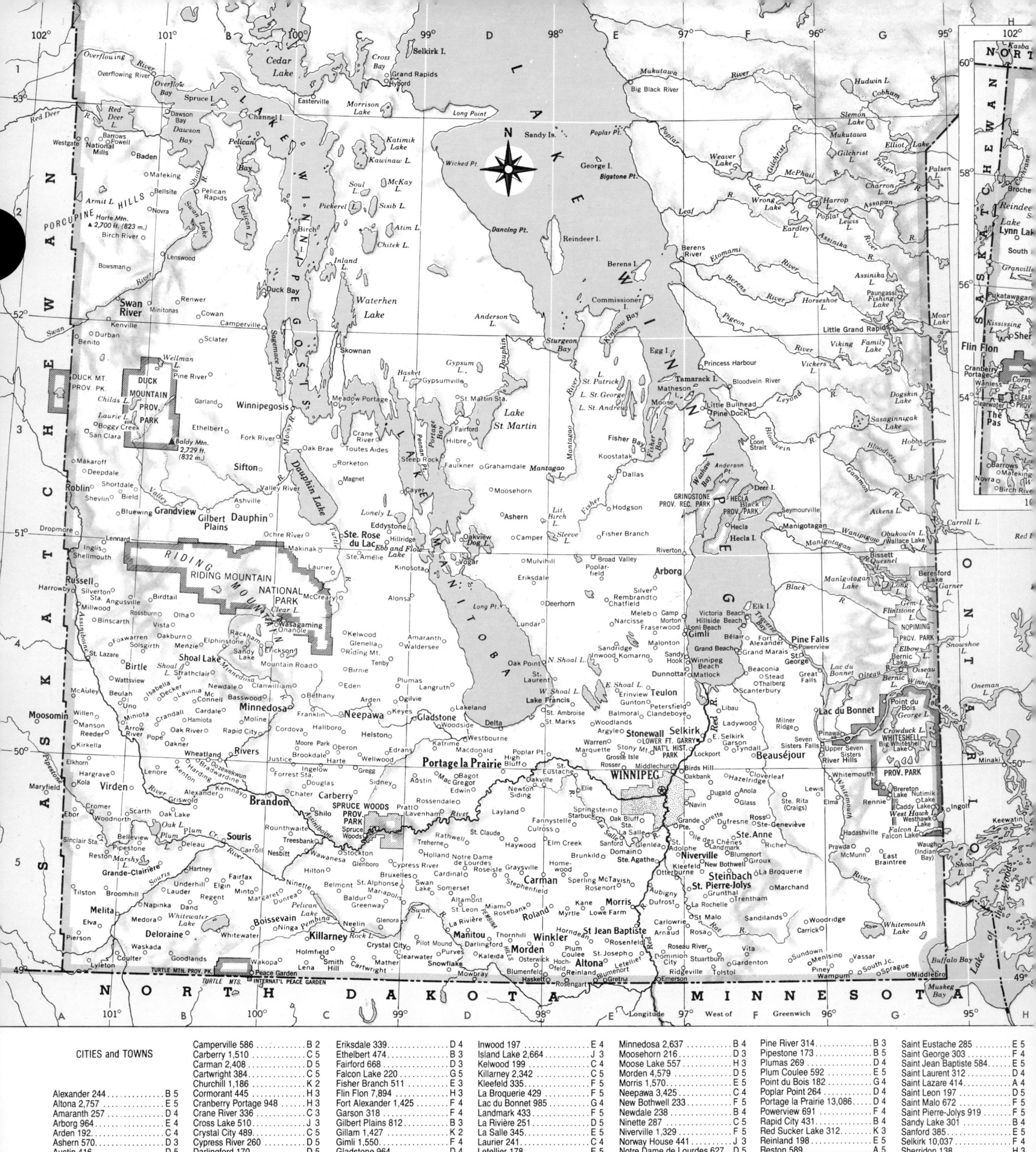

CITIES and TOWNS

Alexander 244 .... B 5	Camperville 586 .... B 2	Eriksdale 339 .... D 4	Inwood 197 .... E 4
Altona 2,757 .... E 5	Carberry 1,510 .... C 5	Ethelbert 474 .... B 3	Island Lake 2,664 .... J 3
Amaranth 257 .... D 4	Carman 2,408 .... D 5	Fairford 668 .... D 3	Kelwood 199 .... C 4
Arborg 964 .... E 4	Cartwright 384 .... C 5	Falcon Lake 220 .... G 5	Killarney 2,342 .... C 5
Arden 192 .... C 4	Churchill 1,186 .... K 2	Fisher Branch 511 .... E 3	Kleefeld 335 .... F 5
Ashern 570 .... D 3	Cormorant 445 .... H 3	Flin Flon 7,894 .... H 3	Lac du Bonnet 985 .... G 4
Austin 416 .... D 5	Cranberry Portage 948 .... H 3	Fort Alexander 1,425 .... F 4	Landmark 433 .... F 5
Baldur 344 .... C 5	Crane River 336 .... C 3	Garson 318 .... F 5	La Broquerie 429 .... F 5
Barrows 199 .... A 2	Cross Lake 510 .... J 3	Gilbert Plains 812 .... B 3	La Rivière 251 .... D 5
Beauséjour 2,462 .... F 4	Crystal City 489 .... C 5	Gillam 1,427 .... K 2	La Salle 345 .... E 5
Belmont 314 .... C 5	Cypress River 260 .... D 5	Gimli 1,550 .... E 4	Laurier 241 .... C 4
Benito 441 .... A 3	Darlingford 170 .... D 5	Gladstone 964 .... D 4	Letellier 138 .... E 5
Berens River 681 .... F 2	Dauphin 8,971 .... B 3	Glenboro 741 .... C 5	Little Grand Rapids 559 .... G 2
Binscarth 472 .... A 4	Deloraine 1,136 .... B 5	Grand Marais 207 .... F 4	Lockport 212 .... F 4
Birch River 597 .... A 2	Dominion City 437 .... E 5	Grand Rapids 567 .... C 1	Lorette 1,092 .... F 5
Birds Hill 711 .... F 5	Douglas 170 .... C 5	Grandview 1,013 .... B 3	Lowe Farm 241 .... E 5
Birtle 887 .... B 4	Duck Bay 594 .... B 2	Great Falls 272 .... F 4	Lundar 634 .... D 4
Bloodvein River 413 .... F 3	Dugald 410 .... F 5	Gretna 545 .... E 5	Lynn Lake 2,087 .... H 2
Blumenort 533 .... F 5	Dunnottar 287 .... E 4	Grosse Isle 171 .... E 4	MacGregor 795 .... D 5
Boissevain 1,660 .... B 5	Easterville 589 .... C 1	Grunthal 572 .... F 5	Mafeking 266 .... B 2
Bowsman 454 .... A 2	East Selkirk 985 .... F 4	Hamiota 728 .... B 4	Manigotagan 216 .... F 3
Brandon 36,242 .... C 5	Elgin 172 .... B 5	Hartney 490 .... B 5	Manitou 861 .... D 5
Brochet 215 .... H 2	Elie 450 .... E 5	Haywood 240 .... D 5	McCreary 618 .... C 4
	Elkhorn 509 .... A 5	Hillridge 201 .... C 3	Melita 1,156 .... A 5
	Elm Creek 293 .... E 4	Hochfeld 187 .... E 5	Miami 401 .... D 5
	Elphinstone 201 .... B 4	Holland 418 .... D 5	Middlechurch 342 .... F 5
	Emerson 762 .... E 5	Île des Chênes 814 .... F 5	Miniota 247 .... B 4
	Erickson 540 .... C 4	Inglis 209 .... A 4	Minitonas 628 .... B 2

Minnedosa 2,637 .... B 4	Pine River 314 .... B 3	Saint Eustache 285 .... E 5
Moosehorn 216 .... D 3	Pipestone 173 .... B 5	Saint George 303 .... F 4
Moose Lake 557 .... H 3	Plumas 269 .... D 4	Saint Jean Baptiste 584 .... E 5
Morden 4,579 .... D 5	Plum Coulee 592 .... E 5	Saint Laurent 312 .... D 4
Morris 1,570 .... E 5	Point du Bois 182 .... G 4	Saint Lazare 414 .... A 4
Neepawa 3,425 .... C 4	Poplar Point 264 .... D 4	Saint Leon 197 .... D 5
New Bothwell 233 .... F 5	Portage la Prairie 13,086 .... D 4	Saint Malo 672 .... F 5
Newdale 238 .... B 4	Powerview 691 .... F 4	Saint Pierre-Jolys 919 .... F 5
Ninette 287 .... C 5	Rapid City 431 .... B 4	Sandy Lake 301 .... B 4
Niverville 1,329 .... F 5	Red Sucker Lake 312 .... K 3	Sanford 385 .... E 5
Norway House 441 .... J 3	Reinland 198 .... E 5	Selkirk 10,037 .... F 4
Oakbank 1,277 .... F 5	Reston 589 .... A 5	Sherridon 138 .... H 3
Oakburn 255 .... B 4	Richer 288 .... F 5	Shoal Lake 835 .... B 4
Oak Lake 369 .... B 5	Riding Mountain 168 .... C 4	Sifton 210 .... B 3
Oak River 179 .... B 4	Rivers 1,107 .... B 4	Snow Lake 1,853 .... H 3
Oakville 383 .... D 4	Riverton 657 .... E 3	Somerset 596 .... D 5
Ochre River 284 .... C 3	Roblin 1,953 .... A 3	South Indian Lake 770 .... H 2
Onanole 386 .... C 4	Roland 301 .... D 5	Split Lake 985 .... J 2
Oozewekwun 453 .... B 5	Rorketon 229 .... C 3	Sprague 199 .... F 5
Paungassi 296 .... G 2	Rosenfeld 263 .... E 5	Starbuck 224 .... E 5
Pelican Rapids 178 .... B 2	Rossburn 696 .... B 4	Steinbach 6,676 .... F 5
Petersfield 170 .... E 4	Russell 1,660 .... A 4	Stonewall 2,210 .... E 4
Pierson 238 .... A 5	Saint Adolphe 928 .... E 5	Stony Mountain 1,313 .... E 4
Pikwitonei 175 .... J 3	Saint Ambroise 263 .... E 4	Strathclair 390 .... B 4
Pilot Mound 838 .... D 5	Saint Claude 592 .... D 5	Swan Lake 367 .... D 5
Pinawa 2,006 .... G 4	Sainte Agathe 326 .... E 5	Swan River 3,782 .... A 2
Pine Falls 885 .... F 4	Sainte Anne 1,338 .... F 5	Teulon 925 .... E 4
	Sainte Rose du Lac 1,090 .... C 3	

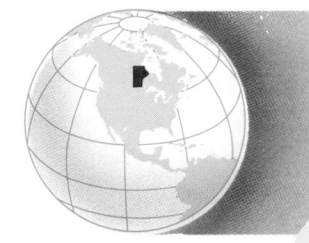

Manitoba — Northern Part

Scale 0 40 80 120 MI.
0 40 80 120 KM.

Manitoba — Southern Part

SCALE
0 5 10 20 40 60 MI.
0 5 10 20 40 60 KM.

Provincial Capital ... ⊛
International Boundaries ... ___ ___
Provincial Boundaries ... ___ ___

Scale 1:2,340,000

© Copyright HAMMOND INCORPORATED, Maplewood, N.J.

The Pas 6,390 .... H 3
Thicket Portage 195 .... J 3
Thompson 14,288 .... J 2
Treherne 743 .... D 5
Tyndall 421 .... F 4
Virden 2,940 .... A 5
Vita 364 .... F 5
Wabowden 655 .... J 3
Wallace Lake ●2,044 .... G 3
Wanless 193 .... H 3
Warren 459 .... E 4
Waskada 239 .... B 5
Wawanesa 492 .... C 5
Whitemouth 320 .... G 5
Whitewater ●856 .... B 5
Winkler 5,046 .... E 5
Winnipeg (cap.) 564,473 ..... E 5
Winnipeg *584,842 .... E 5
Winnipeg Beach 565 .... F 4
Winnipegosis 855 .... B 3
Woodlands 185 .... E 4
Wooodridge 170 .... G 5
York Landing 229 .... J 2

AREA 250,999 sq. mi. (650,087 sq. km.)
POPULATION 1,063,016
CAPITAL Winnipeg
LARGEST CITY Winnipeg
HIGHEST POINT Baldy Mtn. 2,729 ft.
(832 m.)
SETTLED IN 1812
ADMITTED TO CONFEDERATION 1870
PROVINCIAL FLOWER Prairie Crocus

OTHER FEATURES

Aikens (lake) .... G 3
Anderson (lake) .... D 2
Anderson (pt.) .... F 3
Armit (lake) .... A 2
Assapan (riv.) .... G 2
Assiniboine (riv.) .... C 5
Assinika (lake) .... G 2
Assinika (riv.) .... G 2
Atim (lake) .... C 2
Baldy (mt.) .... B 3
Basket (lake) .... C 3
Beaverhill (lake) .... J 3
Berens (isl.) .... E 2
Berens (riv.) .... F 2
Bernic (lake) .... G 4
Big Sand (lake) .... H 2
Bigstone (lake) .... J 3
Bigstone (pt.) .... E 2
Bigstone (riv.) .... J 3
Birch (isl.) .... C 2
Black (isl.) .... F 3
Black (lake) .... F 4
Bloodvein (riv.) .... F 3
Bonnet (lake) .... G 4
Buffalo (bay) .... G 5
Burntwood (riv.) .... J 2
Caribou (riv.) .... J 1
Carroll (lake) .... G 3
Cedar (lake) .... B 1
Channel (isl.) .... B 2
Charron (lake) .... G 2
Childs (lake) .... A 3
Chitek (lake) .... C 2
Churchill (cape) .... K 2
Churchill (riv.) .... J 2
Clear (lake) .... C 4
Clearwater Lake Prov. Park .. H 3
Cobham (riv.) .... G 1
Cochrane (riv.) .... H 2
Commissioner (isl.) .... E 2
Cormorant (lake) .... H 3
Cross (bay) .... C 1
Cross (lake) .... J 3
Crowduck (lake) .... G 4
Dancing (pt.) .... D 2
Dauphin (lake) .... C 3
Dauphin (riv.) .... D 3
Dawson (bay) .... B 2
Dog (lake) .... D 3
Dogskin (lake) .... G 3
Duck Mountain Prov. Park ... B 3
Eardley (lake) .... F 2

East Shoal (lake) .... E 4
Ebb and Flow (lake) .... C 3
Egg (isl.) .... E 3
Elbow (lake) .... G 4
Elk (isl.) .... F 4
Elliot (lake) .... G 2
Etawney (lake) .... J 2
Etomami (riv.) .... F 2
Falcon (lake) .... G 5
Family (lake) .... G 3
Fisher (bay) .... E 3
Fisher (riv.) .... E 3
Fishing (lake) .... G 2
Flintstone (lake) .... G 4
Fox (riv.) .... K 2
Gammon (riv.) .... G 3
Garner (lake) .... G 4
Gem (lake) .... G 4
George (isl.) .... E 2
George (lake) .... G 4
Gilchrist (creek) .... F 2
Gilchrist (lake) .... G 2
Gods (lake) .... K 3
Gods (riv.) .... K 3
Granville (lake) .... H 2
Grass (riv.) .... J 3
Grass River Prov. Park ...... H 3
Grindstone Prov. Rec. Park .. F 4
Gunisao (lake) .... J 3
Gypsum (lake) .... D 3
Harrop (lake) .... G 2
Harte (lake) .... A 2
Hayes (riv.) .... K 3
Hecla (isl.) .... F 3
Hecla Prov. Park .... F 3
Hobbs (lake) .... G 3
Horseshoe (lake) .... G 2
Hubbart (pt.) .... K 2
Hudson (bay) .... K 2
Hudwin (lake) .... G 1
Inland (lake) .... G 4
International Peace Garden .. B 5
Island (lake) .... K 3
Katimik (lake) .... C 2
Kawinaw (lake) .... C 2
Kinwow (bay) .... E 2
Kississing (lake) .... H 2
Knee (lake) .... J 3
Lake of the Woods (lake) .... H 5
La Salle (riv.) .... E 5
Laurie (lake) .... A 3
Leaf (riv.) .... F 2
Lewis (lake) .... G 2
Leyond (lake) .... F 3
Little Birch (lake) .... E 3
Lonely (lake) .... C 3
Long (lake) .... G 4
Long (pt.) .... D 1
Long (pt.) .... D 4
Manigotagan (lake) .... G 4

Manigotagan (riv.) .... G 3
Manitoba (lake) .... D 4
Mantagao (riv.) .... E 3
Marshy (lake) .... B 5
McKay (lake) .... C 2
McPhail (riv.) .... F 2
Minnedosa (riv.) .... B 4
Moar (lake) .... G 2
Molson (lake) .... J 3
Moose (lake) .... E 3
Morrison (lake) .... C 1
Mossy (riv.) .... C 3
Mukutawa (lake) .... G 2
Mukutawa (riv.) .... E 1
Muskeg (bay) .... G 6
Nejanilini (lake) .... J 1
Nelson (riv.) .... J 2
Nopiming Prov. Park .... G 4
Northern Indian (lake) ...... J 2
North Knife (lake) .... J 2
North Seal (riv.) .... H 2
North Shoal (lake) .... E 4
Nueltin (lake) .... H 1
Oak (lake) .... B 5
Obukowin (lake) .... G 3
Oiseau (lake) .... G 4
Oiseau (riv.) .... G 4
Overflow (bay) .... A 1
Overflowing (riv.) .... A 1
Owl (riv.) .... K 2
Oxford (lake) .... J 3
Paint (lake) .... J 2
Palsen (riv.) .... G 2
Pelican (bay) .... B 2
Pelican (lake) .... B 2
Pelican (lake) .... C 5
Pembina (hills) .... D 5
Pembina (riv.) .... C 5
Peonan (pt.) .... D 3
Pickerel (lake) .... C 2
Pigeon (riv.) .... F 2
Pipestone (creek) .... A 5
Plum (creek) .... B 5
Plum (lake) .... B 5
Poplar (riv.) .... E 2
Porcupine (hills) .... A 2
Portage (bay) .... D 3
Punk (isl.) .... F 3
Quesnel (lake) .... G 4
Rat (riv.) .... F 5
Red (riv.) .... F 4
Red Deer (lake) .... A 2
Red Deer (riv.) .... A 2
Reindeer (isl.) .... E 2
Reindeer (lake) .... H 2
Riding (mt.) .... B 4
Riding Mountain Nat'l Park .. B 4
Rock (lake) .... C 5
Ross (isl.) .... J 3
Sagemace (bay) .... B 3

Saint Andrew (lake) .... E 3
Saint George (lake) .... E 3
Saint Martin (lake) .... D 3
Saint Patrick (lake) .... E 3
Sale (riv.) .... E 5
Sandy (isls.) .... D 2
Sasaginnigak (lake) .... G 3
Seal (riv.) .... J 2
Selkirk (isl.) .... C 1
Setting (lake) .... H 3
Shoal (lake) .... G 5
Shoal (riv.) .... B 2
Sipiwesk (lake) .... J 3
Sisib (lake) .... C 2
Sleeve (lake) .... E 3
Slemon (lake) .... G 1
Snowshoe (lake) .... G 4
Soul (lake) .... C 2
Souris (riv.) .... B 5
Southern Indian (lake) ...... H 2
South Knife (riv.) .... J 2
South Seal (riv.) .... J 2
Split (lake) .... J 2
Spruce (isl.) .... B 1
Spruce Woods Prov. Park .... C 5
Stevenson (lake) .... J 3
Sturgeon (bay) .... E 3
Swan (lake) .... B 2
Swan (lake) .... D 5
Swan (riv.) .... A 3
Tadoule (lake) .... J 2
Tamarack (isl.) .... F 3
Tatnam (cape) .... K 2
Traverse (bay) .... F 4
Turtle (mts.) .... B 5
Turtle (riv.) .... C 3
Turtle Mountain Prov. Park .. B 5
Valley (riv.) .... B 3
Vickers (lake) .... F 3
Viking (lake) .... G 3
Wanipigow (riv.) .... G 3
Washow (bay) .... F 3
Waterhen (lake) .... C 2
Weaver (lake) .... F 2
Wellman (lake) .... A 3
West Hawk (lake) .... G 5
West Shoal (lake) .... E 4
Whitemouth (lake) .... G 5
Whitemouth (riv.) .... G 5
Whiteshell Prov. Park .... G 4
Whitewater (lake) .... B 5
Wicked (pt.) .... D 2
Winnipeg (lake) .... E 2
Winnipeg (lake) .... G 4
Winnipegosis (lake) .... C 2
Woods (lake) .... H 5
Wrong (lake) .... F 2

*Population of metropolitan area.
●Population of rural municipality.

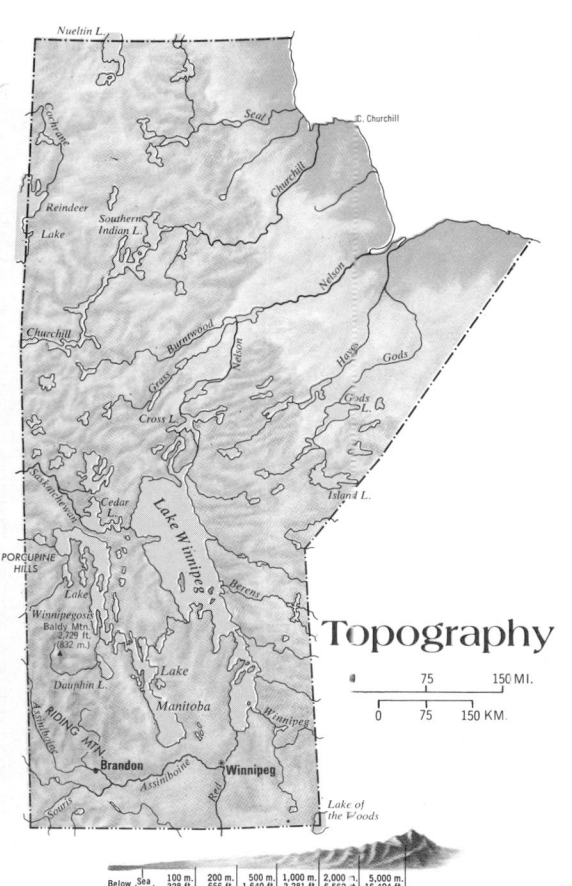

Topography

Below Sea Level | 100 m. 328 ft. | 200 m. 656 ft. | 500 m. 1,640 ft. | 1,000 m. 3,281 ft. | 2,000 m. 6,562 ft. | 5,000 m. 16,404 ft.

0 75 150 MI.
0 75 150 KM.

Agriculture, Industry and Resources

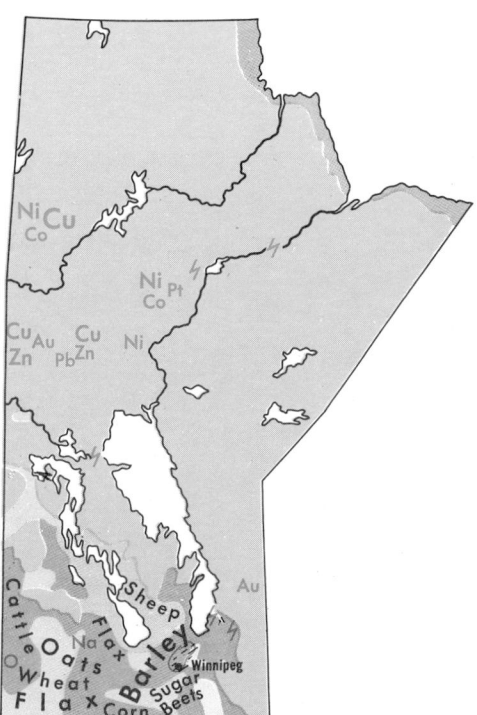

DOMINANT LAND USE

Cereals (chiefly barley, oats)
Cereals, Livestock
Dairy
Livestock
Forests
Nonagricultural Land

MAJOR MINERAL OCCURRENCES

Au Gold
Co Cobalt
Cu Copper
Na Salt

Ni Nickel
O Petroleum
Pb Lead
Pt Platinum
Zn Zinc

⚡ Water Power
Major Industrial Areas

Topography

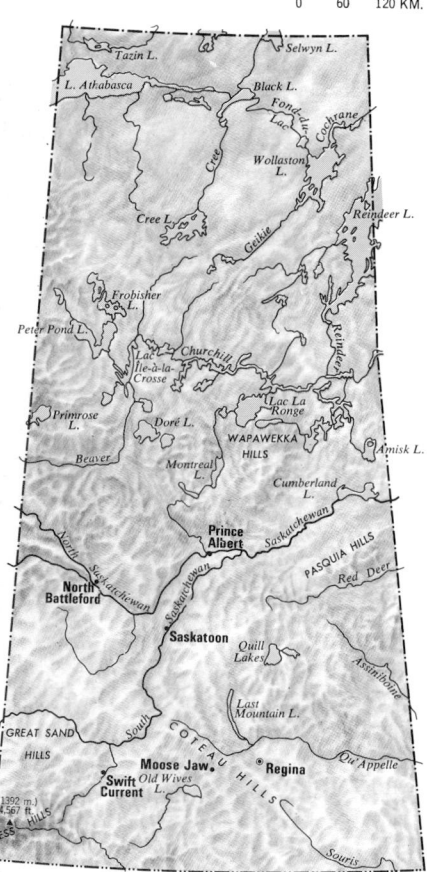

0   60   120 MI.
0   60   120 KM.

5,000 m. 2,000 m. 1,000 m. 500 m. 200 m. 100 m. Sea Level Below
16,404 ft. 6,562 ft. 3,281 ft. 1,640 ft. 656 ft. 328 ft.

CITIES and TOWNS

Abbey 218 .... C 5
Aberdeen 496 .... E 3
Abernethy 300 .... H 5
Air Ronge 557 .... M 3
Alameda 318 .... J 6
Alida 169 .... K 6
Allan 871 .... E 4
Alsask 652 .... B 4
Annaheim 209 .... G 3
Antelope ●231 .... C 5
Arborfield 439 .... H 2
Archerwill 286 .... H 3
Arcola 493 .... J 6
Arlington Beach ●432 ... F 4
Asquith 507 .... D 3
Assiniboia 2,924 .... E 6
Avonlea 442 .... G 5
Baildon ●799 .... F 5
Balcarres 739 .... H 5
Balgonie 777 .... G 5
Batoche .... E 3
Battleford 3,565 .... C 3
Beauval 606 .... L 3
Beechy 279 .... D 5
Bengough 536 .... F 6
Bethune 369 .... F 5
Bienfait 835 .... J 6
Big River 819 .... D 2
Birch Hills 957 .... F 3
Bjorkdale 269 .... H 3
Blaine Lake 653 .... D 3
Borden 197 .... D 3
Brabant Lake 245 .... M 3
Bradwell 168 .... E 4
Bredenbury 467 .... K 5
Briercrest 151 .... F 5
Broadview 840 .... J 5
Brock 184 .... C 4
Browning ●687 .... J 6
Bruno 772 .... F 3
Buchanan 392 .... J 4
Buffalo Gap ●598 .... F 6
Buffalo Narrows 1,088 .. L 1
Burstall 550 .... B 5
Cabri 632 .... C 5
Cadillac 173 .... D 6
Calder 164 .... K 4
Candle Lake 219 .... F 2
Cando 163 .... C 3
Canoe Lake 182 .... L 3
Canora 2,667 .... J 4
Canwood 340 .... E 2
Carievale 246 .... K 6
Carlyle 1,074 .... J 6
Carnduff 1,043 .... K 6
Carrot River 1,169 .... H 2

Central Butte 548 ...... E 5
Ceylon 184 .... G 6
Chaplin 389 .... E 5
Chitek Lake 170 .... D 2
Choiceland 543 .... G 2
Christopher Lake 227 ... F 2
Churchbridge 972 .... J 5
Clavet 234 .... E 4
Climax 293 .... C 6
Cochin 221 .... C 2
Codette 236 .... H 2
Coleville 383 .... B 4
Colonsay 594 .... F 4
Connaught Heights ●982 . G 3
Conquest 256 .... D 4
Consul 153 .... B 6
Coronach 1,032 .... F 6
Craik 565 .... F 4
Craven 206 .... G 5
Creelman 184 .... H 6
Creighton 1,636 .... N 4
Cudworth 947 .... F 3
Cumberland House 831 .. J 2
Cupar 669 .... G 5
Cut Knife 624 .... B 3
Dalmeny 1,064 .... E 3
Davidson 1,166 .... E 4
Debden 403 .... E 2
Delisle 980 .... D 4
Denare Beach 592 ...... M 4
Denzil 199 .... B 3
Deschambault Lake 386 . M 3
Dinsmore 398 .... D 4
Dodsland 272 .... C 4
Domremy 209 .... F 3
Drake 211 .... E 4
Duck Lake 699 .... E 3
Dundurn 531 .... E 4
Dysart 275 .... H 5
Earl Grey 303 .... G 5
Eastend 723 .... C 6
Eatonia 528 .... B 4
Ebenezer 164 .... J 4
Edam 384 .... C 2
Edenwold 143 .... G 5
Elbow 313 .... E 4
Eldorado 229 .... L 2
Elfros 199 .... H 4
Elrose 624 .... D 4
Elstow 143 .... E 4
Endeavour 199 .... J 3
Englefeld 271 .... F 3
Erwood 149 .... J 3
Esterhazy 3,065 .... K 5
Eston 1,413 .... C 4
Estevan 9,174 .... J 6
Eyebrow 168 .... E 5
Fillmore 396 .... H 6
Fleming 141 .... K 5
Flin Flon 367 .... N 4

Foam Lake 1,452 .... H 4
Fond du Lac 494 .... L 2
Fort Qu'Appelle 1,827 . H 5
Francis 182 .... H 5
Frobisher 166 .... J 6
Frontier 619 .... C 6
Gainsborough 308 ...... K 6
Gerald 197 .... K 5
Glaslyn 430 .... C 2
Glenavon 284 .... J 5
Glen Ewen 168 .... K 6
Goodsoil 263 .... L 4
Govan 394 .... G 4
Grand Coulee 208 ...... G 5
Gravelbourg 1,338 ..... E 6
Grayson 264 .... J 5
Green Acres 139 .... F 2
Green Lake 634 .... L 4
Grenfell 1,307 .... J 5
Guernsey 198 .... F 4
Gull Lake 1,095 .... C 5
Hafford 557 .... D 3
Hague 625 .... E 3
Hanley 484 .... E 4
Harris 259 .... D 4
Hawarden 137 .... E 4
Hearts Hill ●552 ...... B 3
Hepburn 411 .... E 3
Herbert 1,019 .... D 5
Hodgeville 329 .... E 5
Holdfast 297 .... F 5
Hudson Bay 2,361 ...... J 3
Humboldt 4,705 .... F 3
Hyas 165 .... J 4
Île-à-la-Crosse 1,035 . L 3
Imperial 501 .... F 4
Indian Head 1,889 ..... H 5
Invermay 353 .... J 4
Ituna 870 .... H 4
Jansen 223 .... G 4
Jasmin ●14 .... H 4
Kamsack 2,688 .... K 4
Kelliher 397 .... H 4
Kelvington 1,054 ...... H 3
Kenaston 345 .... E 4
Kennedy 275 .... J 5
Kerrobert 1,141 .... C 4
Kincaid 256 .... D 6
Kindersley 3,969 ...... B 4
Kinistino 783 .... F 3
Kipling 1,016 .... J 5
Kisbey 228 .... J 6
Kronau 154 .... G 5
Kyle 516 .... C 5
Lac Pelletier ●586 .... C 5
Lafleche 583 .... E 6
Laird 233 .... E 3
Lake Lenore 361 .... F 3
Lampman 651 .... J 6
Lancer 156 .... C 5
Landis 277 .... C 3
Lang 219 .... G 6
Langenburg 1,324 ...... K 5
Langham 1,151 .... E 3
Lanigan 1,732 .... F 4
La Ronge 2,579 .... L 3
Lashburn 813 .... B 2
Leader 1,108 .... B 5
Leask 478 .... E 3
Lebret 274 .... H 5
Lemberg 414 .... H 5
Leoville 393 .... D 2
Leroy 504 .... G 4
Lestock 402 .... G 4
Limerick 164 .... E 6
Lintlaw 234 .... H 3

Lipton 364 .... H 5
Lloydminster 6,034 .... A 2
Loon Lake 369 .... B 1
Loreburn 201 .... E 4
Lucky Lake 333 .... D 5
Lumsden 1,303 .... G 5
Luseland 704 .... B 3
Macdowall 171 .... E 2
Macklin 976 .... A 3
Macoun 190 .... H 6
Maidstone 1,001 .... B 2
Mankota 375 .... D 6
Manor 368 .... K 6
Maple Creek 2,470 ..... B 6
Marcelin 238 .... E 3
Margo 153 .... H 4
Marriott ●627 .... D 4
Marsden 229 .... B 3
Marshall 453 .... B 2
Martensville 1,966 .... E 3
Maryfield 431 .... K 6
Maymont 212 .... D 3
McLean 189 .... G 5
Meacham 178 .... F 3
Meadow Lake 3,857 ..... C 1
Meath Park 262 .... F 2
Medstead 163 .... C 2
Melfort 6,010 .... G 3
Melville 5,092 .... J 5
Meota 235 .... C 2
Mervin 155 .... C 2
Midale 564 .... H 6
Middle Lake 275 .... F 3
Milden 251 .... D 4
Milestone 602 .... G 5
Montmartre 544 .... H 5
Montreal Lake 448 ..... F 1
Moose Jaw 33,941 ...... F 5
Moose Range ●679 ...... H 2
Moosomin 2,579 .... K 5
Morse 416 .... D 5
Mortlach 293 .... E 5
Mossbank 464 .... E 6
Muenster 385 .... F 3
Naicam 886 .... G 3
Neilburg 354 .... B 3
Neuanlage 144 .... E 3
Neudorf 425 .... J 5
Neuhorst 146 .... E 3
Nipawin 4,376 .... H 2
Nokomis 524 .... F 4
Norquay 552 .... J 4
North Battleford 14,030 C 3
North Portal 164 ...... J 6
Odessa 232 .... H 5
Ogema 441 .... G 6
Osler 587 .... E 3
Outlook 1,976 .... E 4
Oxbow 1,191 .... J 6
Paddockwood 211 .... F 2
Pangman 227 .... G 5
Paradise Hill 421 ..... B 2
Patuanak 173 .... L 3
Paynton 210 .... B 2
Pelican Narrows 331 ... N 3
Pelly 391 .... K 4
Pennant 202 .... C 5
Pense 472 .... G 5
Perdue 407 .... D 4
Pierceland 425 .... K 4
Pilger 150 .... F 3
Pilot Butte 1,255 ..... G 5
Pine House 612 .... M 3
Plenty 175 .... C 4
Plunkett 150 .... F 4
Ponteix 769 .... D 6
Porcupine Plain 937 ... H 3
Preeceville 1,243 ..... J 4

Prelate 317 .... B 5
Prince Albert 31,380 .. F 2
Prud'homme 222 .... F 3
Punnichy 394 .... G 4
Qu'Appelle 653 .... H 5
Quill Lake 514 .... G 3
Quinton 169 .... G 4
Rabbit Lake 159 .... D 2
Radisson 439 .... D 3
Radville 1,012 .... G 6
Rama 133 .... H 4
Raymore 635 .... G 4
Redvers 859 .... K 6
Regina (cap.) 162,613 . G 5
Regina *164,313 .... G 5
Regina Beach 603 ...... F 5
Rhein 271 .... J 4
Richmound 188 .... B 5
Riverhurst 193 .... E 5
Rocanville 934 .... K 5
Roche Percé 142 .... J 6
Rockglen 511 .... F 6
Rosetown 2,664 .... D 4
Rose Valley 538 .... H 3
Rosthern 1,609 .... E 3
Rouleau 443 .... G 5
Saint Benedict 157 .... F 3
Saint Brieux 401 ...... G 3
Saint Louis 448 .... F 3
Saint Philips ●538 .... K 4
Saint Walburg 802 ..... B 2
Saltcoats 549 .... J 4
Sandy Bay 756 .... N 3
Saskatoon 154,210 ..... E 3
Saskatoon *154,210 .... E 3
Sceptre 169 .... B 5
Scott 203 .... C 3
Sedley 373 .... H 5
Semans 344 .... G 4
Shaunavon 2,112 .... C 6
Sheho 285 .... H 4
Shell Lake 220 .... D 2
Shellbrook 1,228 ...... E 2
Simpson 237 .... F 4
Sintaluta 215 .... H 5
Smeaton 246 .... G 2
Southey 697 .... G 5
Spalding 337 .... G 3
Spiritwood 926 .... D 2
Spy Hill 354 .... K 5
Springside 533 .... J 4
Star City 527 .... G 3
Stenen 391 .... J 4
Stockholm 391 .... J 5
Stonehenge ●701 .... F 6
Storthoaks 142 .... K 6
Stoughton 716 .... J 6
Strasbourg 842 .... G 4
Sturgis 789 .... J 4
Swift Current 14,747 .. D 5
Tantallon 196 .... K 5
Theodore 473 .... J 4
Timber Bay 152 .... F 1
Tisdale 3,107 .... H 3
Togo 181 .... K 4
Tompkins 275 .... C 5
Torch River ●2,440 .... G 2
Torquay 311 .... H 6
Tramping Lake 178 ..... B 3
Tugaske 175 .... E 5
Turnor Lake 166 .... L 3
Turtleford 505 .... B 2
Unity 2,408 .... B 3
Uranium City 2,507 .... L 2
Val Marie 236 .... D 6
Vanguard 292 .... D 6
Vanscoy 298 .... D 4
Vibank 369 .... H 5

Viscount 386 .... F 4
Vonda 313 .... F 3
Wadena 1,495 .... H 4
Wakaw 1,030 .... F 3
Waldeck 292 .... D 5
Waldheim 758 .... E 3
Walpole ●711 .... K 6
Wapella 487 .... K 5
Warman 2,076 .... E 3
Waseca 169 .... B 2
Waskesiu Lake 176 ..... E 2
Watrous 1,830 .... F 4
Watson 901 .... G 3
Wawota 622 .... J 6
Weldon 279 .... F 3
Welwyn 170 .... K 5
Weyburn 9,523 .... H 6
White City 602 .... G 5
White Fox 394 .... H 2
Whitewood 1,003 .... J 5
Wilcox 202 .... G 5
Wilkie 1,501 .... C 3
Willow Bunch 494 ...... F 6
Willow Creek ●1,218 ... B 6
Windthorst 254 .... J 5
Wiseton 195 .... D 4
Wishart 212 .... H 4
Wolseley 904 .... H 5
Wymark 162 .... D 5
Wynyard 2,147 .... G 4
Yarbo 158 .... K 5

Yellow Grass 477 ...... H 6
Yorkton 15,339 .... J 4
Young 456 .... F 4
Zenon Park 273 .... H 2

OTHER FEATURES

Allan (lake) .... E 4
Amisk (lake) .... M 4
Antelope (lake) .... C 5
Antler (riv.) .... K 6
Arm (riv.) .... F 5
Assiniboine (riv.) .... J 3
Athabasca (lake) .... L 1
Bad (hills) .... D 4
Bad (hills) .... E 5
Batoche Nat'l Hist. Site . E 3
Battle (creek) .... B 6
Battle (riv.) .... B 3
Bear (hills) .... C 4
Beaver (lake) .... L 2
Beaver (riv.) .... L 4
Beaverlodge (lake) .... L 2
Big Muddy (lake) .... G 6
Bigstick (lake) .... B 5
Birch (lake) .... C 3
Bitter (lake) .... C 4
Black (lake) .... M 2
Boundary (plat.) .... B 6
Brightsand (lake) .... C 2
Bronson (lake) .... B 2

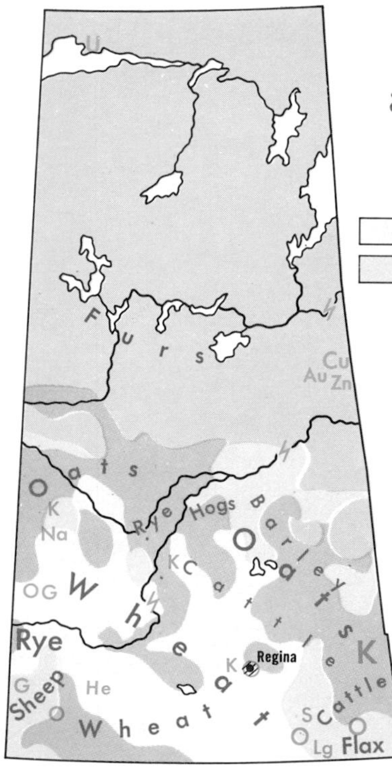

Agriculture, Industry and Resources

DOMINANT LAND USE

☐ Wheat
☐ Cereals (chiefly barley, oats)
▨ Cereals, Livestock
▨ Livestock
▨ Forests

MAJOR MINERAL OCCURRENCES

Au Gold
Cu Copper
G Natural Gas
He Helium
K Potash

Na Salt
O Petroleum
S Sulfur
U Uranium
Zn Zinc
Lg Lignite

⚡ Water Power
▨ Major Industrial Areas

Buffalo Pound Prov. Park .... F 5
Cabri (lake) .... B 4
Cactus (hills) .... F 5
Candle (lake) .... F 2
Cannington Manon Hist. Park J 6
Canoe (lake) .... L 3
Carrot (river) .... J 2
Chaplin (lake) .... E 5
Chipman (riv.) .... M 2
Chitek (lake) .... D 2
Churchill (riv.) .... M 3
Clearwater (riv.) .... L 3
Cochrane (riv.) .... N 2
Coteau (hills) .... D 4
Cowan (lake) .... D 2
Crane (lake) .... B 5
Crean (lake) .... E 1
Cree (lake) .... L 3
Cree (lake) .... M 2
Cumberland (lake) .... J 1
Cypress (hills) .... B 6
Cypress (lake) .... B 6
Cypress Hills Prov. Park .... B 6
Danielson Prov. Park .... E 4
Delaronde (lake) .... E 1
Diefenbaker (lake) .... E 4
Doré (lake) .... L 3
Douglas Prov. Park .... E 4
Duck Lake Hist. Park .... E 3
Duck Mountain Prov. Park .... K 4
Eagle (hills) .... C 3
Eaglehill (creek) .... D 4

Ear (lake) .... B 3
Echo Valley Prov. Park .... G 5
Etomami (riv.) .... J 3
Eyebrow (lake) .... E 5
Eyehill (creek) .... B 3
Fife (lake) .... E 6
File (hills) .... H 5
Fir (riv.) .... J 2
Fond du Lac (riv.) .... M 2
Forrest (lake) .... L 3
Fort Battleford Nat'l Hist. Park C 3
Fort Carlton Hist. Park .... E 3
Fort Pitt Hist. Park .... B 2
Fort Walsh Nat'l Hist. Park ...... A 6
Foster (riv.) .... M 3
Frenchman (river) .... C 6
Frobisher (lake) .... L 3
Gap (creek) .... B 6
Gardiner (dam) .... D 4
Geikie (riv.) .... M 3
Good Spirit (lake) .... J 4
Goodspirit Lake Prov. Park .... J 4
Great Sand (hills) .... B 5
Green (lake) .... D 1
Greenwater Lake Prov. Park .... H 3
Haultain (riv.) .... L 3
Île-à-la-Crosse (lake) .... L 3
Ironspring (creek) .... G 3
Jackfish (lake) .... C 2
Katepwa Prov. Park .... H 5
Kingsmere (lake) .... E 1
Kiyiu (lake) .... C 4

Lac La Ronge Prov. Park .... M 3
Lanigan (creek) .... F 4
Last Mountain (lake) .... F 4
Leaf (lake) .... J 2
Leech (lake) .... J 4
Lenore (lake) .... G 3
Little Manitou (lake) .... F 4
Lodge (creek) .... B 6
Long (creek) .... H 6
Loon (creek) .... G 4
Makwa (lake) .... B 1
Makwa (riv.) .... B 1
Manito (lake) .... B 3
Maple (lake) .... B 5
McFarlane (riv.) .... L 2
Meadow (lake) .... C 1
Meadow Lake Prov. Park .... K 4
Meeting (lake) .... D 2
Midnight (lake) .... C 2
Ministikwan (lake) .... B 1
Missouri Coteau (hills) .... F 5
Montreal (lake) .... F 1
Moose (mt.) .... J 6
Moose Jaw (riv.) .... G 5
Moose Mountain (creek) .... J 6
Moose Mountain Prov. Park .... J 6
Mossy (riv.) .... H 1
Muddy (lake) .... B 3
Mudjatik (riv.) .... L 3
Nipawin (riv.) .... G 1
North Saskatchewan (riv.) .... D 3
Notukeu (creek) .... D 6

Oldman (riv.) .... L 2
Old Wives (lake) .... E 5
Opuntia (lake) .... C 4
Overflowing (riv.) .... K 2
Pasquia (hills) .... J 2
Pasquia (riv.) .... K 2
Pelican (lake) .... E 5
Peter Pond (lake) .... L 3
Pheasant (hills) .... J 5
Pine Lake Prov. Park .... E 4
Pinto (creek) .... D 6
Pipestone (creek) .... J 6
Pipestone (riv.) .... L 2
Ponass (lakes) .... H 3
Poplar (riv.) .... E 6
Porcupine (hills) .... K 3
Primrose (lake) .... L 3
Primrose Lake Air Weapons
  Range .... L 3
Prince Albert Nat'l Park .... E 1
Qu'Appelle (riv.) .... J 5
Quill (lakes) .... G 4
Red Deer (lake) .... A 5
Red Deer (riv.) .... K 3
Reindeer (lake) .... N 3
Reindeer (riv.) .... M 3
Riou (lake) .... M 2
Rivers (lake) .... F 6
Ronge, La (lake) .... M 3
Rowans Ravine Prov. Park .... F 4
St. Victor Petroglyphs Hist.
  Park .... E 6

Saskatchewan (riv.) .... H 2
Saskatchewan Landing Prov.
  Park .... C 5
Saskeram (riv.) .... K 2
Scott (lake) .... M 2
Selwyn (lake) .... M 2
Souris (riv.) .... H 6
South Saskatchewan (riv.) .... C 5
Steele Narrows Hist. Park .... B 2
Stripe (lake) .... C 4
Sturgeon (riv.) .... E 2
Swan (lake) .... J 3
Swift Current (creek) .... D 5
Tazin (riv.) .... L 2
The Battlefords Prov. Park .... C 2

Thickwood (hills) .... D 2
Thunder (hills) .... L 4
Tobin (lake) .... H 2
Torch (riv.) .... H 2
Touchwood (hills) .... G 4
Tramping (lake) .... C 3
Trout (lake) .... L 2
Turtle (lake) .... C 2
Twelvemile (lake) .... E 6
Vermilion (riv.) .... E 5
Wapawekka (hills) .... M 4
Waskana (creek) .... G 5
Waskesiu (lake) .... E 2
Watham (riv.) .... M 3
Weed (hills) .... J 5

White Fox (riv.) .... G 2
White Gull (creek) .... G 2
Whiteshore (lake) .... C 3
Whiteswan (lakes) .... F 1
William (riv.) .... L 2
Willow Bunch (lake) .... F 6
Witchekan (lake) .... D 2
Wollaston (lake) .... N 2
Wood (mt.) .... E 6
Wood (riv.) .... E 6
Wood Mountain Hist. Park .... E 6

*Population of metropolitan area.
●Population of rural municipality.

AREA 251,699 sq. mi. (651,900 sq. km.)
POPULATION 1,009,613
CAPITAL Regina
LARGEST CITY Regina
HIGHEST POINT Cypress Hills 4,567 ft.
   (1,392 m.)
SETTLED IN 1774
ADMITTED TO CONFEDERATION 1905
PROVINCIAL FLOWER Prairie Lily

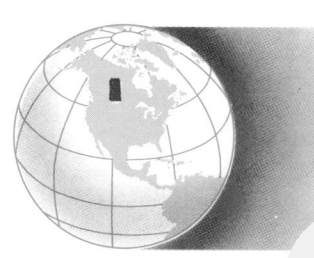

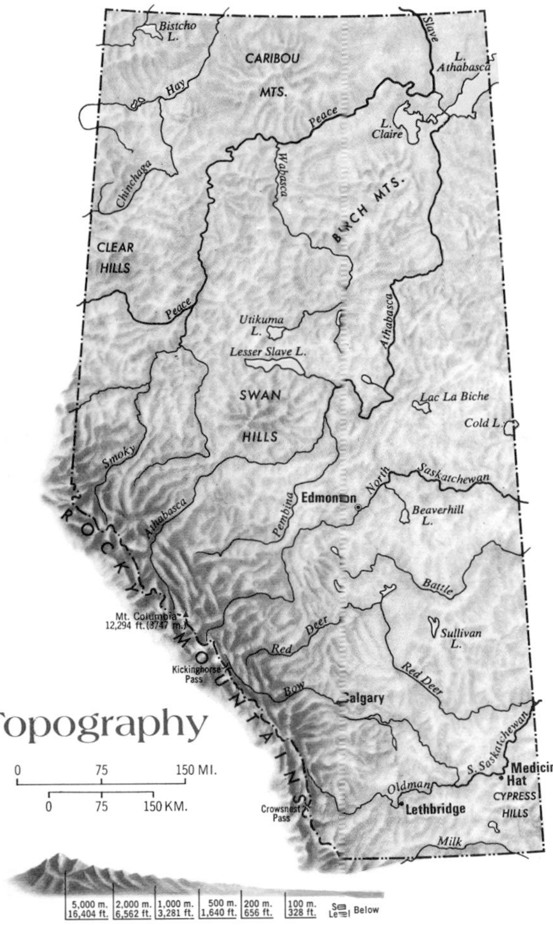
Bistcho L.
CARIBOU MTS.
L. Athabasca
Slave
Hay
Peace
L. Claire
Chinchaga
Wabasca
BIRCH MTS.
CLEAR HILLS
Utikuma L.
Lesser Slave L.
Athabasca
SWAN HILLS
Lac La Biche
Cold L.
Smoky
North Saskatchewan
Pembina
Edmonton
Beaverhill L.
Battle
Sullivan L.
Mt. Columbia 12,294 ft. (3747 m.)
Kickinghorse Pass
ROCKY MOUNTAINS
Red Deer
Bow
Calgary
S. Saskatchewan
Medicine Hat
Oldman
Lethbridge
CYPRESS HILLS
Crowsnest Pass
Milk
0 75 150 MI.
0 75 150 KM.
5,000 m. 16,404 ft.
2,000 m. 6,562 ft.
1,000 m. 3,281 ft.
500 m. 1,640 ft.
200 m. 656 ft.
100 m. 328 ft.
Sea Level
Below

Topography

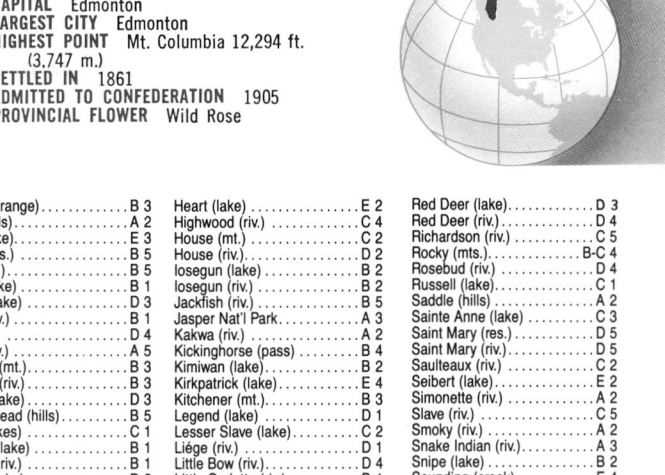

AREA 255,285 sq. mi. (661,185 sq. km.)
POPULATION 2,365,825
CAPITAL Edmonton
LARGEST CITY Edmonton
HIGHEST POINT Mt. Columbia 12,294 ft. (3,747 m.)
SETTLED IN 1861
ADMITTED TO CONFEDERATION 1905
PROVINCIAL FLOWER Wild Rose

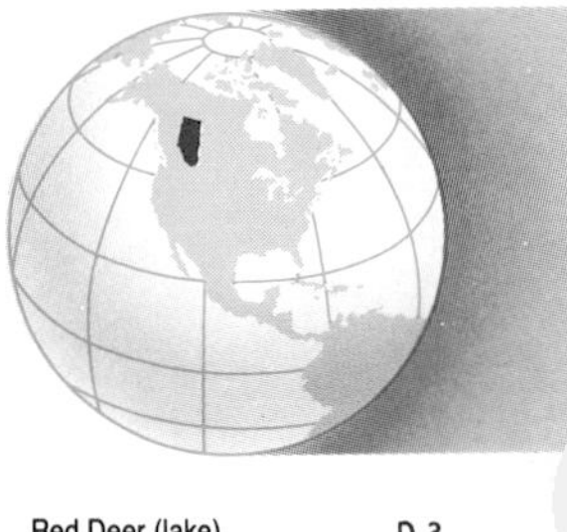

CITIES and TOWNS

Acme 457	D 4
Airdrie 8,414	C 4
Alberta Beach 485	C 3
Alix 837	D 3
Andrew 548	D 3
Antler Lake 334	D 3
Ardmore 224	E 2
Arrowwood 156	D 4
Athabasca 1,731	D 2
Banff 4,208	C 4
Barnwell 359	D 5
Barons 315	D 4
Barrhead 3,736	C 2
Bashaw 875	D 3
Bassano 1,200	D 4
Bawlf 350	D 3
Beaumont 2,638	D 3
Beaverlodge 1,937	A 2
Beiseker 580	D 4
Bentley 823	C 3
Berwyn 557	B 1
Big Valley 360	D 3
Black Diamond 1,444	C 4
Blackfalds 1,488	D 3
Blackfoot 220	E 3
Blackie 298	D 4
Bon Accord 1,376	D 3
Bonnyville 4,454	E 2
Bowden 989	C 4
Bow Island 1,491	E 5
Boyle 638	D 2
Bragg Creek 505	C 4
Breton 552	C 3
Brooks 9,421	E 4
Bruce 88	E 3
Bruderheim 1,136	D 3
Burdett 220	E 5
Calgary 592,743	C 4
Calgary *592,743	C 4
Calmar 1,003	D 3
Camrose 12,570	D 3
Canmore 3,484	C 4
Carbon 434	D 4
Cardston 3,267	D 5
Carmangay 266	D 4
Caroline 436	C 3
Carseland 484	D 4
Carstairs 1,587	D 4
Castor 1,123	D 3
Cereal 249	E 4
Champion 339	D 4
Chauvin 298	E 3
Chipman 266	D 3
Clairmont 469	A 2
Claresholm 3,493	D 4
Clive 364	D 3
Clyde 364	D 2
Coaldale 4,579	D 5
Coalhurst 882	D 5
Cochrane 3,544	C 4
Cold Lake 2,110	E 2
College Heights 267	D 3
Consort 632	E 3
Cooking Lake 218	D 3
Coronation 1,309	E 3
Coutts 400	D 5
Cowley 304	D 5
Cremona 382	C 4
Crossfield 1,217	C 4
Daysland 679	D 3
Delburne 574	D 3
Desmarais 260	D 2
Devon 3,885	D 3
Didsbury 3,095	C 4
Donalda 280	D 3
Donnelly 336	B 2
Drayton Valley 5,042	C 3
Drumheller 6,508	D 4
Duchess 429	E 4
East Coulee 218	D 4
Eckville 870	C 3
Edgerton 387	E 3
Edmonton (cap.) 532,246	D 3
Edmonton *657,057	D 3
Edmonton Beach 280	C 3
Edson 5,835	B 3
Elk Point 1,022	E 3
Elnora 249	D 3
Entwistle 462	C 3
Erskine 259	D 3
Evansburg 779	C 3
Exshaw 353	C 4
Fairview 2,869	A 1
Falher 1,102	B 2
Faust 399	C 2
Foremost 568	E 5
Forestburg 924	E 3
Fort Assiniboine 207	C 2
Fort Chipewyan 944	C 5
Fort Macleod 3,139	D 5
Fort McKay 267	E 1
Fort McMurray 31,000	E 1
Fort Saskatchewan 12,169	D 3
Fort Vermilion 752	B 5
Fox Creek 1,978	B 2
Fox Lake 634	B 5
Gibbons 2,276	D 3
Gift Lake 428	C 2
Girouxville 325	B 2
Gleichen 381	D 4
Glendon 430	E 2
Glenwood 259	D 5
Grand Centre 3,146	E 2
Grande Cache 4,523	A 3
Grande Prairie 24,263	A 2
Granum 399	D 5
Grimshaw 2,316	B 1
Grouard Mission 221	C 2
Hanna 2,806	E 4
Hardisty 641	E 3
Hay Lakes 302	D 3
Heisler 212	D 3
High Level 2,194	A 5
High Prairie 2,506	B 2
High River 4,792	D 4
Hines Creek 575	A 1
Hinton 8,342	B 3
Holden 430	D 3
Hughenden 267	E 3
Hythe 639	A 2
Innisfail 5,247	D 3
Innisfree 255	E 3
Irma 474	E 3
Irricana 558	D 4
Irvine 360	E 5
Jasper 3,269	B 3
John d'Or Prairie 437	B 5
Joussard 330	B 2
Killam 1,005	E 3
Kinuso 285	C 2
Kitscoty 497	E 3
Lac La Biche 2,007	E 2
Lacombe 5,591	D 3
La Crete 479	B 5
Lake Louise 355	B 4
Lamont 1,563	D 3
Leduc 12,471	D 3
Legal 1,022	D 3
Lethbridge 54,072	D 5
Linden 407	D 4
Little Buffalo Lake 253	B 1
Lloydminster 8,997	E 3
Longview 301	C 4
Lougheed 226	E 3
Lundbreck 244	C 5
Magrath 1,576	D 5
Manning 1,173	B 1
Mannville 788	E 3
Marlboro 211	B 3
Marwayne 500	E 3
Mayerthorpe 1,475	C 3
McLennan 1,125	B 2
Medicine Hat 40,380	E 4
Milk River 894	D 5
Millet 1,120	D 3
Mirror 507	D 3
Monarch 212	D 5
Morinville 4,657	D 3
Morrin 244	D 4
Mundare 604	D 3
Myrnam 397	E 3
Nacmine 369	D 4
Nampa 334	B 1
Nanton 1,641	D 4
New Norway 291	D 3
New Sarepta 417	D 3
Nobleford 534	D 5
North Calling Lake 234	D 2
Okotoks 3,847	C 4
Olds 4,813	D 4
Onoway 621	C 3
Oyen 975	E 4
Peace River 5,907	B 1
Penhold 1,531	D 3
Picture Butte 1,404	D 5
Pincher Creek 3,757	D 5
Plamondon 259	D 2
Pollockville 19	E 4
Ponoka 5,221	D 3
Provost 1,645	E 3
Rainbow Lake 504	A 5
Ralston 357	E 4
Raymond 2,837	D 5
Redcliff 3,876	E 4
Red Deer 46,393	D 3
Redwater 1,932	D 3
Rimbey 1,685	C 3
Robb 230	B 3
Rockyford 329	D 4
Rocky Mountain House 4,698	C 3
Rosemary 328	E 4
Rycroft 649	A 2
Ryley 483	D 3
Saint Albert 31,996	D 3
Saint Paul 4,884	E 3
Sangudo 398	C 3
Sedgewick 879	E 3
Sexsmith 1,180	A 2
Shaughnessy 270	D 5
Sherwood Park 29,285	D 3
Slave Lake 4,506	C 2
Smith 216	D 2
Smoky Lake 1,074	D 2
Spirit River 1,104	A 2
Spruce Grove 10,326	D 3
Standard 379	D 4
Stavely 504	D 4
Stettler 5,136	D 3
Stirling 688	D 5
Stony Plain 4,839	C 3
Strathmore 2,986	D 4
Strome 281	E 3
Sundre 1,742	C 4
Swan Hills 2,497	C 2
Sylvan Lake 3,779	C 3
Taber 5,988	E 5
Thorhild 576	D 2
Thorsby 737	C 3
Three Hills 1,787	D 4
Tilley 345	E 4
Tofield 1,504	D 3
Trochu 880	D 4
Turner Valley 1,311	C 4
Two Hills 1,193	E 3
Valleyview 2,061	B 2
Vauxhall 1,049	D 4
Vegreville 5,251	E 3
Vermilion 3,766	E 3
Veteran 314	E 3
Viking 1,232	E 3
Vilna 345	E 2
Vulcan 1,489	D 4
Wabamun 662	C 3
Wabasca 701	D 2
Wainwright 4,266	E 3
Warburg 501	C 3
Warner 477	D 5
Waskatenau 290	D 2
Wembley 1,169	A 2
Westlock 4,424	C 2
Wetaskiwin 9,597	D 3
Whitecourt 5,585	C 2
Wildwood 441	C 3
Willingdon 366	E 3
Youngstown 297	E 4

OTHER FEATURES

Abraham (lake)	B 3
Alberta (mt.)	B 3
Assiniboine (mt.)	C 4
Athabasca (lake)	C 5
Athabasca (riv.)	D 1
Banff Nat'l Park	B 4
Battle (riv.)	D 3
Bear (lake)	A 2
Beaver (riv.)	E 2
Beaverhill (lake)	D 3
Behan (lake)	E 2
Belly (riv.)	D 5
Berland (riv.)	A 3
Berry (creek)	E 4
Biche (lake)	E 2
Big (isl.)	B 5
Big Horn (dam)	B 3
Bighorn (range)	B 3
Birch (hills)	A 2
Birch (lake)	E 3
Birch (mts.)	B 5
Birch (riv.)	B 5
Bison (lake)	B 1
Bittern (lake)	D 3
Botha (riv.)	B 1
Bow (riv.)	D 4
Boyer (riv.)	A 5
Brazeau (mt.)	B 3
Brazeau (riv.)	B 3
Buffalo (lake)	D 3
Buffalo Head (hills)	B 5
Burnt (lakes)	C 1
Cadotte (lake)	B 1
Cadotte (riv.)	B 1
Calling (lake)	D 2
Canal (creek)	E 5
Cardinal (lake)	B 1
Caribou (mts.)	B 5
Chinchaga (riv.)	A 5
Chip (lake)	C 3
Chipewyan (lake)	D 1
Chipewyan (riv.)	D 1
Christina (lake)	E 2
Christina (riv.)	E 1
Claire (lake)	B 5
Clear (hills)	A 1
Clearwater (riv.)	C 4
Clearwater (riv.)	E 1
Clyde (lake)	E 2
Cold (lake)	E 2
Columbia (mt.)	B 3
Crowsnest (pass)	C 5
Cypress (hills)	E 5
Cypress Hills Prov. Park	E 5
Dillon (riv.)	E 2
Dowling (lake)	D 4
Dunkirk (riv.)	D 1
Eisenhower (mt.)	C 4
Elbow (riv.)	C 4
Elk Island Nat'l Park	D 3
Ells (riv.)	D 1
Etzikom Coulee (riv.)	E 5
Eva (lake)	B 5
Farrell (lake)	D 4
Firebag (riv.)	E 1
Forbes (mt.)	B 4
Freeman (riv.)	C 2
Frog (lake)	E 3
Garson (lake)	E 1
Gipsy (lake)	E 1
Gordon (lake)	E 1
Gough (lake)	D 3
Graham (lake)	C 1
Gull (lake)	C 3
Haig (lake)	B 1
Hawk (hills)	B 1
Hay (lake)	A 5
Hay (riv.)	A 5
Heart (lake)	E 2
Highwood (riv.)	C 4
House (mt.)	C 2
House (riv.)	D 2
Iosegun (lake)	B 2
Iosegun (riv.)	B 2
Jackfish (riv.)	B 5
Jasper Nat'l Park	A 3
Kakwa (riv.)	A 2
Kickinghorse (pass)	B 4
Kimiwan (lake)	B 2
Kirkpatrick (lake)	E 4
Kitchener (mt.)	B 3
Legend (lake)	D 1
Lesser Slave (lake)	C 2
Liége (riv.)	D 1
Little Bow (riv.)	D 4
Little Cadotte (riv.)	B 1
Little Smoky (riv.)	B 2
Livingstone (range)	C 4
Logan (lake)	E 2
Loon (lake)	C 1
Loon (riv.)	C 1
Lubicon (lake)	C 1
Lyell (mt.)	B 4
MacKay (riv.)	D 1
Maligne (lake)	B 3
Margaret (lake)	B 5
Marie (lake)	E 2
Marion (lake)	D 3
Marten (mt.)	C 2
McClelland (lake)	E 1
McGregor (lake)	D 4
McLeod (riv.)	B 3
Meikle (riv.)	A 1
Mikkwa (riv.)	B 5
Milk (riv.)	D 5
Mistehae (lake)	C 2
Muriel (lake)	E 2
Muskwa (lake)	C 1
Muskwa (riv.)	C 1
Namur (lake)	D 1
Newell (lake)	E 4
Nordegg (riv.)	C 3
North Saskatchewan (riv.)	E 3
North Wabasca (lake)	D 1
Notikewin (riv.)	A 1
Oldman (riv.)	D 5
Otter (lakes)	B 1
Pakowki (lake)	E 5
Panny (riv.)	C 1
Peace (riv.)	B 1
Peerless (lake)	C 1
Pelican (lake)	D 2
Pelican (mts.)	D 2
Pembina (riv.)	C 3
Pigeon (lake)	D 3
Pinehurst (lake)	E 2
Porcupine (hills)	C 4
Primrose (lake)	E 2
Rainbow (lake)	A 5
Red Deer (lake)	D 3
Red Deer (riv.)	D 4
Richardson (riv.)	C 5
Rocky (mts.)	B-C 4
Rosebud (riv.)	D 4
Russell (lake)	C 1
Saddle (hills)	A 2
Sainte Anne (lake)	C 3
Saint Mary (res.)	D 5
Saint Mary (riv.)	D 5
Saulteaux (riv.)	C 2
Seibert (lake)	E 2
Simonette (riv.)	A 2
Slave (riv.)	C 5
Smoky (riv.)	A 2
Snake Indian (riv.)	A 3
Snipe (lake)	B 2
Sounding (creek)	E 4
South Saskatchewan (riv.)	E 4
South Wabasca (lake)	D 2
Spencer (lake)	E 2
Spray (mts.)	C 4
Sturgeon (lake)	B 2
Sullivan (lake)	D 3
Swan (hills)	C 2
Swan (riv.)	C 2
Temple (mt.)	B 4
The Twins (mt.)	B 3
Thickwood (hills)	D 1
Touchwood (lake)	E 2
Travers (res.)	D 4
Trout (mt.)	C 1
Trout (riv.)	C 1
Utikuma (lake)	C 2
Utikuma (riv.)	C 1
Utikumasis (lake)	C 2
Vermilion (riv.)	E 3
Wabasca (riv.)	C 1
Wallace (mt.)	C 2
Wapiti (riv.)	A 2
Wappau (lake)	E 2
Watchusk (lake)	E 1
Waterton-Glacier Int'l Peace Park	C 5
Waterton Lakes Nat'l Park	C 5
Whitemud (riv.)	A 1
Wildhay (riv.)	B 3
Willmore Wilderness Prov. Park	A 3
Winagami (lake)	B 2
Winefred (lake)	E 2
Winefred (riv.)	E 2
Wolf (lake)	E 2
Wolverine (riv.)	B 1
Wood Buffalo Nat'l Park	B 5
Yellowhead (pass)	A 3
Zama (lake)	A 5

*Population of metropolitan area.

Agriculture, Industry and Resources

DOMINANT LAND USE

- Wheat
- Cereals (chiefly barley, oats)
- Cereals, Livestock
- Dairy
- Pasture Livestock
- Range Livestock
- Forests
- Nonagricultural Land

MAJOR MINERAL OCCURRENCES

- C Coal
- O Petroleum
- G Natural Gas
- S Sulfur
- Na Salt
- Water Power
- Major Industrial Areas

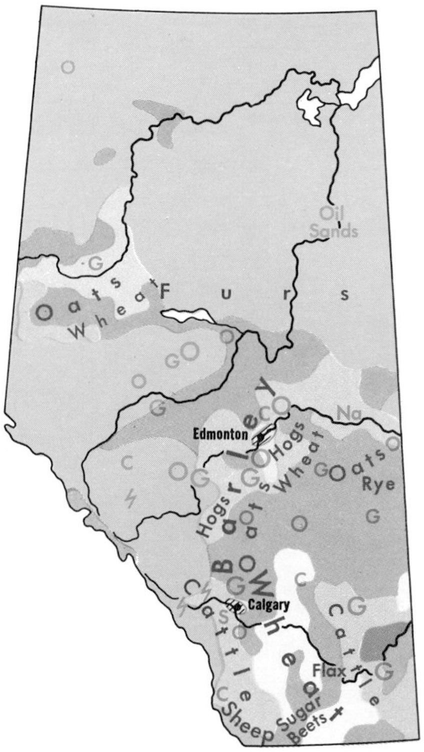
Oil Sands
Furs
Oats
Wheat
Edmonton
Barley
Hogs
Wheat
Oats
Rye
Calgary
Cattle
Sheep
Sugar Beets
Flax
Na

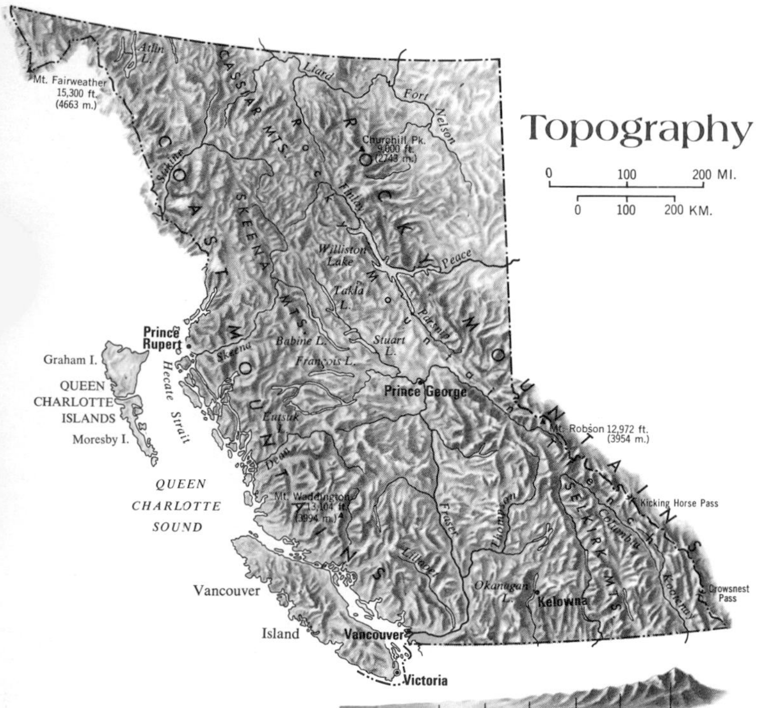
Topography
0 100 200 MI.
0 100 200 KM.
Mt. Fairweather 15,300 ft. (4663 m.)
Prince Rupert
Prince George
Graham I.
QUEEN CHARLOTTE ISLANDS
Moresby I.
Hecate Strait
QUEEN CHARLOTTE SOUND
Mt. Robson 12,972 ft. (3954 m.)
Kicking Horse Pass
Crowsnest Pass
Kelowna
Vancouver
Island
Victoria
Below Sea Level
100 m. 328 ft.
200 m. 656 ft.
500 m. 1,640 ft.
1,000 m. 3,281 ft.
2,000 m. 6,562 ft.
5,000 m. 16,404 ft.

CITIES and TOWNS

Abbotsford 12,745 .... L 3
Alert Bay 626 .... D 5
Armstrong 2,683 .... H 5
Ashcroft 2,156 .... G 5
Ashton Creek 452 .... H 5
Balfour 472 .... J 5
Barlow 441 .... F 3
Barrière 1,370 .... H 4
Blueberry Creek 635 .... J 5
Blue River 384 .... H 4
Boston Bar 498 .... G 5
Bowen Island 1,125 .... K 3
Brackendale 1,719 .... F 5
Burnaby ○136,494 .... K 3
Burns Lake 1,777 .... D 3
Cache Creek 1,308 .... G 5
Campbell River 15,370 .... E 5
Canal Flats 919 .... K 5
Canyon 698 .... J 5
Cassiar 1,045 .... K 2
Castlegar 6,902 .... J 5
Cawston 785 .... H 5
Central Saanich ○9,890 .... K 3
Chase 1,777 .... H 5
Chemainus 2,069 .... J 3
Cherry Creek 450 .... G 5
Chetwynd 2,553 .... G 2
Chilliwack ○40,642 .... M 3
Clearwater 1,461 .... G 4
Clinton 804 .... G 4
Coldstream ○6,450 .... H 5
Comox 6,607 .... H 2
Coquitlam ○61,077 .... K 3
Courtenay 8,992 .... E 5
Cranbrook 15,915 .... K 5
Creston 4,190 .... J 5
Crofton 1,303 .... J 3
Cultus Lake 481 .... M 3
Cumberland 1,947 .... E 5
Dawson Creek 11,373 .... G 2
Delta ○74,692 .... K 3
Duncan 4,228 .... J 3
Elkford 3,126 .... K 5
Enderby 1,816 .... H 5
Erickson 972 .... J 5
Errington 609 .... J 3
Esquimalt ○15,870 .... K 4
Falkland 478 .... H 5
Fernie 5,444 .... K 5
Forest Grove 444 .... G 4
Fort Fraser 574 .... E 3
Fort Langley 2,326 .... L 3
Fort Nelson 3,724 .... M 2
Fort Saint James 2,284 .... E 3
Fort Saint John 13,891 .... G 2
Fraser Lake 1,543 .... E 3
Fruitvale 1,904 .... J 5
Gabriola 1,627 .... J 3
Galiano 669 .... K 3
Ganges 1,118 .... K 3
Gibsons 2,594 .... K 3
Gold River 2,225 .... D 5
Golden 3,476 .... J 4
Grand Forks 3,486 .... H 6
Granisle 1,430 .... D 3
Greenwood 856 .... H 5
Hagensborg 350 .... D 4
Harrison Hot Springs 569 .... M 3
Hatzic 1,055 .... L 3
Hazelton 393 .... D 2
Hedley 426 .... G 5
Holberg 444 .... C 5
Honeymoon Bay 474 .... J 3
Hope 3,205 .... M 3
Hornby Island 474 .... H 2
Horsefly 430 .... G 4
Houston 1,714 .... D 3
Hudson Hope 984 .... F 2
Invermere 1,969 .... J 5
Kaleden 998 .... H 5
Kamloops 64,048 .... G 5
Kaslo 854 .... J 5
Kelowna 59,196 .... H 5
Kent ○3,394 .... M 3
Keremeos 830 .... G 5
Kimberley 7,375 .... K 5
Kitimat 12,462 .... C 3
Kitsault 554 .... C 2
Kitwanga 369 .... D 2
Lac La Hache 647 .... G 4
Ladysmith 4,558 .... J 3
Lake Cowichan 2,391 .... J 3
Langley 15,124 .... L 3
Lantzville 969 .... J 3
Likely 425 .... G 4
Lillooet 1,725 .... G 5
Lion's Bay 1,078 .... K 3
Logan Lake 2,637 .... G 5
Lumby 1,266 .... H 5
Lytton 428 .... G 5
Mackenzie 5,797 .... F 2
Mackenzie ○5,890 .... F 2
Malakwa 392 .... H 5
Maple Bay 393 .... K 3
Maple Ridge ○32,232 .... L 3
Masset 1,569 .... B 3
Matsqui ○42,001 .... L 3
Mayne 546 .... K 3
McBride 641 .... G 3
Merritt 6,110 .... G 5
Midway 633 .... H 6
Mill Bay 583 .... K 3
Mission ○20,056 .... L 3
Mission City 9,948 .... L 3
Montrose 1,229 .... J 5
Nakusp 1,495 .... J 5
Nanaimo 47,069 .... J 3
Naramata 876 .... H 5
Nelson 9,143 .... J 5
New Denver 642 .... J 5
New Hazelton 792 .... D 2
New Westminster 38,550 .... K 3
Nicomen Island 360 .... L 3
Nootka .... D 5
North Cowichan ○18,210 .... J 3
North Pender Island 906 .... K 3
North Saanich ○6,117 .... K 3
North Vancouver 33,952 .... K 3
North Vancouver ○65,367 .... K 3
Oak Bay ○16,990 .... K 4
Okanagan Falls 1,030 .... H 5
Okanagan Landing 834 .... H 5
Okanagan Mission .... H 5
Old Barkerville 11 .... G 3
Oliver 1,893 .... H 5
One Hundred Mile House 1,925 .... G 4
Osoyoos 2,738 .... H 5
Oyama 430 .... H 5
Parksville 5,216 .... J 3
Peachland ○2,865 .... G 5
Penticton 23,181 .... H 5
Pitt Meadows ○6,209 .... L 3
Port Alberni 19,892 .... H 3
Port Alice 1,668 .... D 5
Port Clements 380 .... B 3
Port Coquitlam 27,535 .... L 3
Port Edward 989 .... B 3
Port Hardy ○3,778 .... D 5
Port McNeill 2,474 .... D 5
Port Moody 14,917 .... L 3
Pouce-Coupé 821 .... G 2
Powell River ○13,423 .... E 5
Prince George 67,559 .... F 3
Prince Rupert 16,197 .... B 3
Princeton 3,051 .... G 5
Qualicum Beach 2,844 .... J 3
Queen Charlotte 1,070 .... A 3
Quesnel 8,240 .... F 4
Radium Hot Springs 419 .... J 5
Revelstoke 5,544 .... J 5
Richmond ○96,154 .... K 3
Roberts Creek 926 .... J 3
Robson 1,008 .... J 5
Rossland 3,967 .... H 6
Royston 754 .... H 2
Saanich ○78,710 .... K 3
Salmo 1,169 .... J 5
Salmon Arm 1,946 .... H 5
Salmon Arm ○10,780 .... H 5
Saltair 1,356 .... J 3
Sandspit 794 .... B 3
Sayward 482 .... D 5
Sechelt 1,096 .... J 2
Shawnigan Lake 419 .... J 3
Shoreacres 555 .... J 5
Sicamous 1,057 .... H 5
Sidney 7,946 .... K 3
Slocan 351 .... J 5
Slocan Park 414 .... J 5
Smithers 4,570 .... D 3
Sointula 567 .... D 5
Sooke 852 .... J 4
Sorrento 659 .... H 5
South Hazelton 500 .... D 2
South Wellington 620 .... J 3
Spallumcheen 4,213 .... H 5
Sparwood 3,267 .... K 5
Sproat Lake 440 .... H 3
Squamish 1,590 .... F 5
Stewart ○1,456 .... C 2
Summerland ○7,473 .... G 5
Surrey ○147,138 .... K 3
Tahsis 1,739 .... D 5
Taylor 966 .... G 2
Telkwa 840 .... D 3
Terrace 8,893 .... C 3
Terrace ○10,914 .... C 3
Thornhill 4,281 .... C 3
Thrums 360 .... J 5
Tofino 705 .... E 5
Trail 9,599 .... J 6
Ucluelet 1,593 .... E 6
Union Bay 601 .... H 2
Valemount 1,130 .... H 4
Vancouver 414,281 .... K 3
Vancouver (Greater) *1,169,831 .... K 3
Vanderhoof 2,323 .... E 3
Vavenby 479 .... H 4
Vernon 19,987 .... H 5
Victoria (cap.) 64,379 .... K 4
Victoria *233,481 .... K 4
Warfield 1,969 .... J 5
Wasa 345 .... K 5
Wells 417 .... G 3
Westbank 1,271 .... H 5
West Vancouver ○35,728 .... K 3
Westwold 409 .... G 5
Whistler ○1,365 .... F 5
White Rock 13,550 .... K 3
Williams Lake 8,362 .... F 4
Wilson Creek 611 .... J 2
Windermere 611 .... K 5
Winlaw 435 .... J 5
Woss Lake 395 .... D 5
Wynndel 566 .... J 5
Yarrow 1,201 .... M 3
Youbou 965 .... J 3

OTHER FEATURES

Adams (lake) .... H 4
Adams (riv.) .... H 4
Alberni (inlet) .... H 3
Alsek (riv.) .... H 1
Aristazabal (isl.) .... C 4
Assiniboine (mt.) .... K 5
Atlin (lake) .... J 1
Azure (lake) .... G 4
Babine (lake) .... E 3
Babine (riv.) .... D 2
Banks (isl.) .... B 3
Barkley (sound) .... E 6
Beale (cape) .... E 6
Beatton (riv.) .... G 1
Bella Coola (riv.) .... D 4
Bennett, W.A.C. (dam) .... F 2
Birkenhead Lake Prov. Park F 5
Bowron Lake Prov. Park .... G 3
Bowser (lake) .... C 2
Brooks (pen.) .... D 5
Browning Entrance (str.) .... B 3
Bryce (mt.) .... J 4
Bugaboo Glacier Prov. Park J 5
Bulkley (riv.) .... D 2
Burke (chan.) .... D 4
Burnaby (isl.) .... B 4
Bute (inlet) .... E 5
Caamaño (sound) .... C 4
Calvert (isl.) .... C 4
Canim (lake) .... G 4
Canoe Reach (riv.) .... H 4
Cariboo (mts.) .... G 3
Carpenter (lake) .... F 5
Carp Lake Prov. Park .... F 3
Cassiar (mts.) .... K 2
Castle (mt.) .... A 2
Cathedral Prov. Park .... H 5
Charlotte (lake) .... E 4
Chatham (sound) .... B 3
Chehalis (lake) .... L 3
Chilcotin (riv.) .... E 4
Chilko (lake) .... F 4
Chilko (riv.) .... E 4
Chilkoot (pass) .... J 1
Chuchi (lake) .... E 2
Churchill (peak) .... L 2
Clayoquot (sound) .... D 5
Clearwater (lake) .... G 4
Clearwater (riv.) .... G 4
Coast (mts.) .... D 3
Columbia (lake) .... K 5
Columbia (mt.) .... J 4
Columbia (riv.) .... H 4
Columbia Reach (riv.) .... H 4
Cook (cape) .... C 5
Cowichan (lake) .... J 3
Crowsnest (pass) .... K 5
Cypress Prov. Park .... K 3
Dean (chan.) .... D 4
Dean (riv.) .... D 4
Dease (lake) .... K 2
Dease (riv.) .... K 2
Devils Thumb (mt.) .... A 1
Dixon Entrance (chan.) .... A 3
Douglas (chan.) .... C 3
Duncan (riv.) .... J 5
Dundas (isl.) .... B 3
Elk (riv.) .... K 5
Elk Lakes Prov. Park .... K 5
Eutsuk (lake) .... D 3
Fairweather (mt.) .... H 1
Finlay (riv.) .... E 1
Fitzhugh (sound) .... D 4
Flathead (riv.) .... K 6
Flores (isl.) .... D 5
Fontas (riv.) .... M 2
Forbes (mt.) .... J 4
Fort Nelson (riv.) .... M 2
François (lake) .... D 3
Fraser (lake) .... E 3
Fraser (riv.) .... F 4
Fraser Reach (chan.) .... C 3
Galiano (isl.) .... K 3
Gardner (canal) .... C 3
Garibaldi Prov. Park .... F 5
Georgia (str.) .... J 3
Germansen (lake) .... E 2
Gil (isl.) .... C 3
Glacier Nat'l Park .... J 4
Golden Ears Prov. Park .... L 2
Gordon (riv.) .... H 3
Graham (isl.) .... A 3
Graham Reach (chan.) .... C 3
Grenville (chan.) .... C 3
Halfway (riv.) .... F 2
Hamber Prov. Park .... H 4
Harrison (lake) .... M 2
Hawkesbury (isl.) .... C 3
Hazelton (mts.) .... C 2
Hecate (str.) .... B 3
Hobson (lake) .... H 4
Homathko (riv.) .... E 4
Horsefly (lake) .... G 4
Howe (sound) .... K 2
Hunter (isl.) .... C 4

Agriculture, Industry and Resources

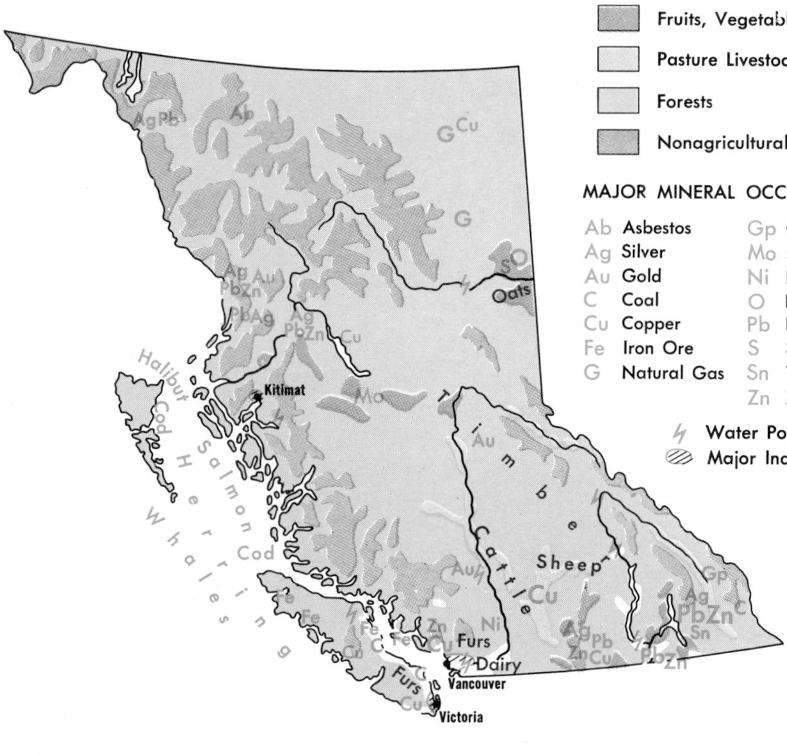
Kitimat
Vancouver
Victoria
Timber
Cattle
Sheep
Furs
Dairy
Oats
Cod
Salmon
Halibut
Herring
Whales

DOMINANT LAND USE

- Cereals, Livestock
- Dairy
- Fruits, Vegetables
- Pasture Livestock
- Forests
- Nonagricultural Land

MAJOR MINERAL OCCURRENCES

- Ab Asbestos
- Ag Silver
- Au Gold
- C Coal
- Cu Copper
- Fe Iron Ore
- G Natural Gas
- Gp Gypsum
- Mo Molybdenum
- Ni Nickel
- O Petroleum
- Pb Lead
- S Sulfur
- Sn Tin
- Zn Zinc

Water Power
Major Industrial Areas

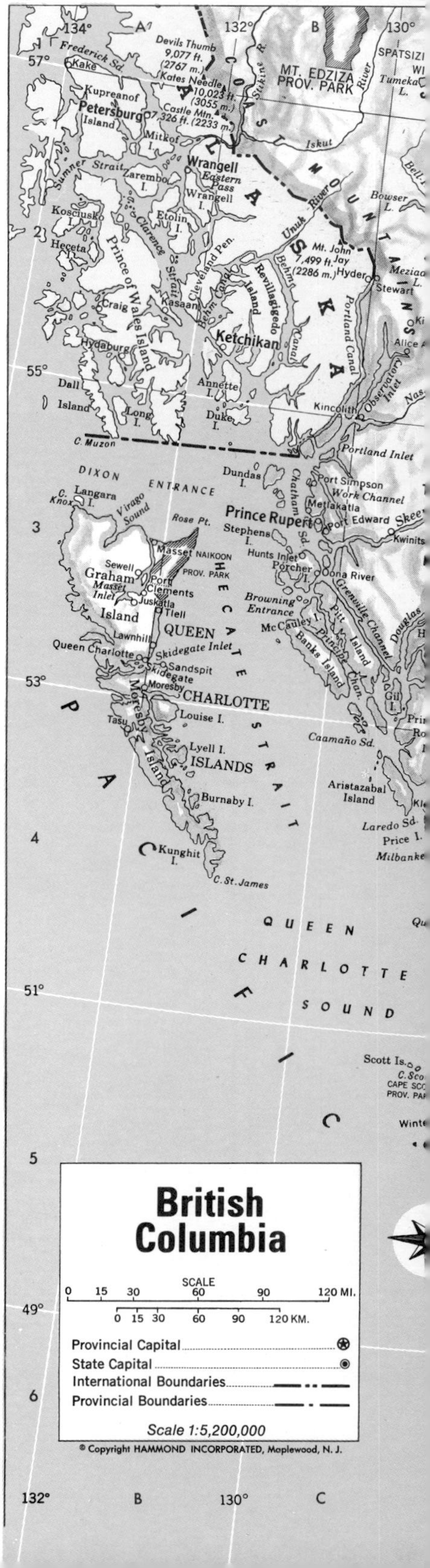
British Columbia
SCALE
0 15 30 60 90 120 MI.
0 15 30 60 90 120 KM.
Provincial Capital
State Capital
International Boundaries
Provincial Boundaries
Scale 1:5,200,000
Prince Rupert
Ketchikan
Wrangell
Petersburg
QUEEN CHARLOTTE ISLANDS
HECATE STRAIT
DIXON ENTRANCE
QUEEN CHARLOTTE SOUND
MT. EDZIZA PROV. PARK

© Copyright HAMMOND INCORPORATED, Maplewood, N. J.

Inzana (lake) .... E 3
Isaac (lake) .... G 3
Iskut (riv.) .... B 2
Jervis (inlet) .... E 5
John Jay (mt.) .... B 2
Johnstone (str.) .... D 5
Juan de Fuca (str.) .... J 4
Kates Needle (mt.) .... A 1
Kechika (riv.) .... L 2
Kenney (dam) .... D 3
Kettle (riv.) .... H 5
Kicking Horse (pass) .... J 4
Kinbasket (lake) .... H 4
King (isl.) .... D 4
Klinaklini (riv.) .... E 4
Kloch (lake) .... E 2
Knight (inlet) .... D 4
Knox (cape) .... A 3
Kokanee Glacier Prov. Park .... J 6
Kootenay (lake) .... J 5
Kootenay (riv.) .... K 5
Kootenay Nat'l Park .... J 4
Kotcho (lake) .... M 2
Kotcho (riv.) .... M 2
Kunghit (isl.) .... B 4
Kyuquot (sound) .... D 5
Langara (isl.) .... A 3
Laredo (sound) .... C 4
Liard (riv.) .... L 2
Lillooet (riv.) .... F 5
Louise (isl.) .... B 4
Lower Arrow (lake) .... H 5

Lyell (isl.) .... B 4
Lyell (mt.) .... J 4
Mabel (lake) .... H 5
Mahood (lake) .... G 4
Malaspina (str.) .... J 2
Manning Prov. Park .... G 5
Masset (inlet) .... A 3
McCauley (isl.) .... B 3
McGregor (riv.) .... G 3
Meziadin (lake) .... C 2
Mica (dam) .... H 4
Milbanke (sound) .... C 4
Moberly (riv.) .... F 2
Monashee (mts.) .... H 4
Moresby (isl.) .... B 3
Morice (lake) .... D 3
Morice (riv.) .... D 3
Mount Assiniboine Prov. Park K 5
Mount Edziza Prov. Park and
  Rec. Area. .... B 1
Mount Revelstoke Nat'l Park H 4
Mount Robson Prov. Park .... H 4
Muncho Lake Prov. Park .... L 2
Murray (riv.) .... G 3
Murtle (lake) .... H 4
Muskwa (isl.) .... M 2
Nanika (dam) .... D 3
Nass (riv.) .... C 2
Nation (riv.) .... F 2
Nechako (riv.) .... E 3
Nitinat (lake) .... H 3
Nootka (isl.) .... D 5
Nootka (sound) .... D 5

Nootka (sound) .... D 5
North Thompson (riv.) .... G 4
Observatory (inlet) .... C 2
Okanagan (lake) .... H 5
Okanagan Mtn. Prov. Park .... G 5
Okanogan (riv.) .... H 6
Omineca (mts.) .... E 2
Omineca (riv.) .... E 2
Ootsa (lake) .... D 3
Owikeno (lake) .... D 4
Pacific Rim Nat'l Park .... E 6
Parsnip (riv.) .... F 3
Peace (riv.) .... F 2
Pend Oreille (riv.) .... J 6
Petitot (riv.) .... M 2
Pinchi (lake) .... E 3
Pine (riv.) .... G 2
Pitt (isl.) .... C 3
Pitt (lake) .... L 2
Porcher (isl.) .... B 3
Portland (canal) .... B 2
Portland (inlet) .... C 3
Price (isl.) .... C 4
Princess Royal (isl.) .... C 3
Principe (chan.) .... B 3
Prophet (riv.) .... J 2
Purcell (mts.) .... J 5
Quatsino (sound) .... C 5
Queen Charlotte (isls.) .... B 3
Queen Charlotte (sound) .... C 4
Queen Charlotte (str.) .... D 5
Queens (sound) .... C 4
Quesnel (lake) .... G 4

Quesnel (riv.) .... F 4
Rivers (inlet) .... D 4
Robson (mt.) .... H 3
Rocky (mts.) .... F 2
Roderick (isl.) .... C 4
Rose (pt.) .... B 3
Saint James (cape) .... B 4
Salmon (riv.) .... F 3
Salmon Arm (inlet) .... J 2
San Juan (riv.) .... J 3
Schoen Lake Prov. Park .... E 5
Scott (cape) .... C 5
Scott (isls.) .... C 5
Seechelt (inlet) .... J 2
Seechelt (pen.) .... J 2
Selkirk (mts.) .... J 4
Seymour (inlet) .... D 4
Sheslay (riv.) .... J 2
Sikanni Chief (riv.) .... F 1
Silver Star Prov. Park .... H 5
Sir Sandford (mt.) .... J 4
Skagit (riv.) .... G 6
Skeena (mts.) .... C 2
Skeena (riv.) .... C 3
Skidegate (inlet) .... B 3
Slocan (lake) .... J 5
Smith (sound) .... D 4
South Bentinck Arm (inlet) .... D 4
Stave (lake) .... L 3
Stephens (isl.) .... B 3
Stikine (riv.) .... B 1
Stone Mountain Prov. Park .... L 2

Strathcona Prov. Park. .... E 5
Stuart (lake) .... E 3
Sustut (riv.) .... D 2
Tahtsa (lake) .... D 3
Tagish (lake) .... J 1
Takla (lake) .... D 3
Taku (riv.) .... J 2
Tatlatui (lake) .... E 4
Tatlayoko (lake) .... E 4
Tchentlo (lake) .... E 2
Teslin (lake) .... K 1
Tetachuck (lake) .... E 3
Texada (isl.) .... J 2
Tezzeron (lake) .... E 3
Thompson (riv.) .... G 5

Three Guardsmen (mt.) .... H 1
Thutade (lake) .... D 2
Tiedemann (mt.) .... E 4
Toad (riv.) .... L 2
Toba (inlet) .... E 5
Tochcha (lake) .... D 3
Top Of The World Prov. Park .... K 5
Trembleur (lake) .... E 3
Troitsa (lake) .... D 3
Tumeka (lake) .... C 1
Turnagain (riv.) .... K 2
Tuya (riv.) .... K 2
Tweedsmuir Prov. Park. .... D 3
Upper Arrow (lake) .... H 5
Valdes (isl.) .... K 3

Vancouver (isl.) .... D 5
Virago (sound) .... A 3
Waddington (mt.). .... E 4
Wapiti (riv.) .... H 3
Wells Gray Prov. Park. .... H 4
West Road (riv.) .... E 3
Whitesail (lake) .... D 3
Williston (lake) .... F 2
Work (chan.) .... C 3
Yellowhead (pass) .... H 4
Yoho Nat'l Park .... J 4

*Population of metropolitan area.
○Population of municipality.

AREA 366,253 sq. mi. (948,596 sq. km.)
POPULATION 2,883,367
CAPITAL Victoria
LARGEST CITY Vancouver
HIGHEST POINT Mt. Fairweather 15,300 ft.
  (4,663 m.)
SETTLED IN 1806
ADMITTED TO CONFEDERATION 1871
PROVINCIAL FLOWER Dogwood

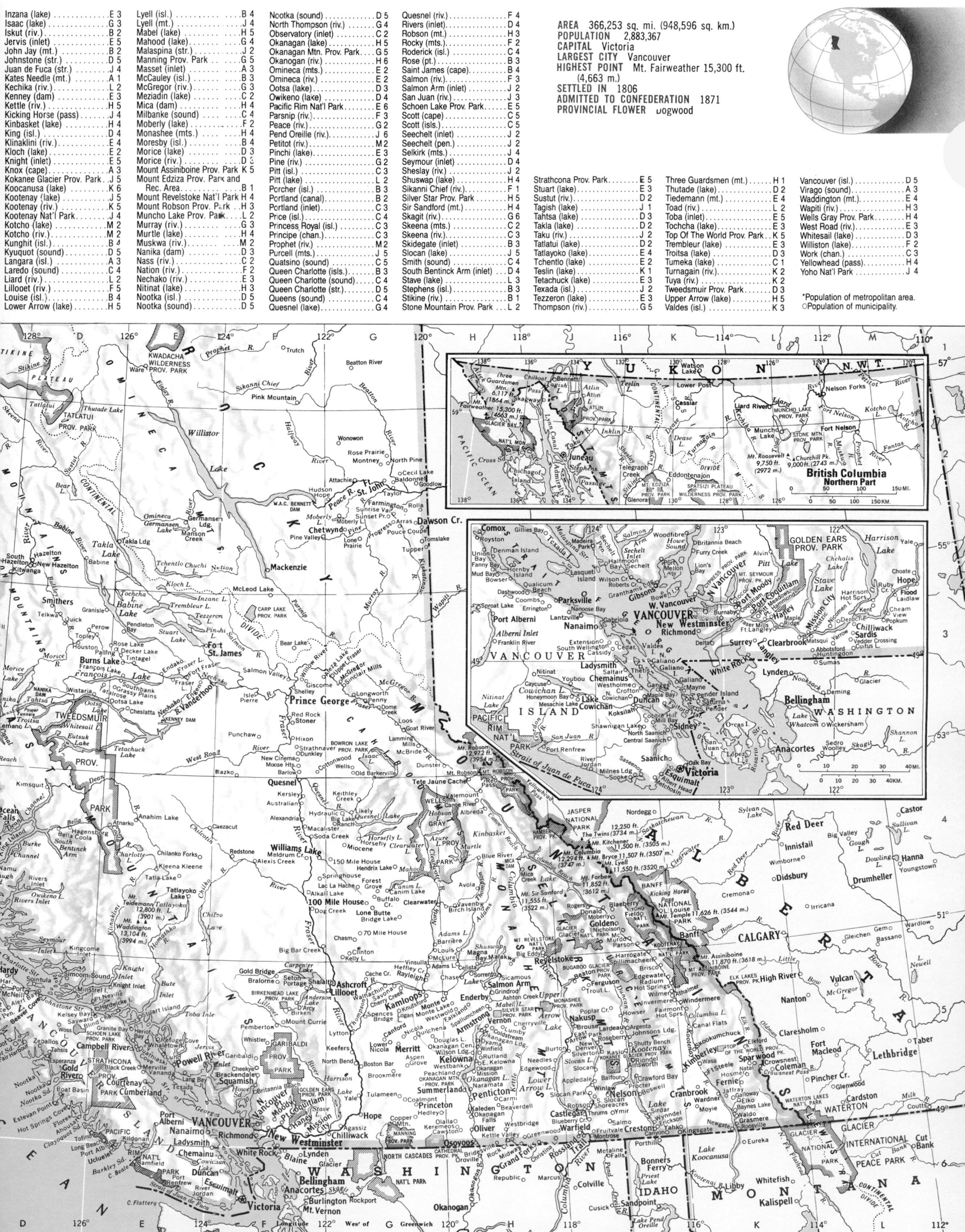

NORTHWEST TERRITORIES

REGIONS

Baffin 8,300 . . . . .J2
Fort Smith 22,384 . . . . .G3
Inuvik 7,485 . . . . .F3
Keewatin 4,327 . . . . .J3
Kitikmeot 3,245 . . . . .G2

CITIES and TOWNS

Aklavik 721 . . . . .E3
Alert M1
Amadjuak L3
Arctic Bay 375 . . . . .K2
Arctic Red River 120. . . . . . .E3
Baker Lake 954 . . . . .J3
Bathurst Inlet 20 . . . . .H3
Bell Rock G3
Broughton Island 378 . . . . . .M3
Buffalo River Junction G3
Cambridge Bay 815 . . . . . . .H3
Cape Dorset 784 . . . . .K3
Cape Dyer M3
Cape Smith L3
Chesterfield Inlet 249 . . . . . .K3
Clyde River 443 . . . . .M2
Colville Lake 57 . . . . .F3
Coppermine 809. . . . . .G3
Coral Harbour 429 . . . . .K3
Detah 143 . . . . .G3
Dory Point G3
Echo Bay (Port Radium) 56 . .G3
Enterprise 46 . . . . .G3
Eskimo Point 1,022 . . . . .J3
Eureka K2
Fort Franklin 521 . . . . .F3
Fort Good Hope 463 . . . . . . .F3
Fort Liard 405. . . . . .F3
Fort McPherson 632. . . . . . . .E3
Fort Norman 286 . . . . .F3
Fort Providence 605. . . . . . . .G3
Fort Resolution 480. . . . . . . .G3
Fort Simpson 980. . . . . .F3
Fort Smith 2,298 . . . . .G4
Gjoa Haven 523. . . . . .J3
Grise Fiord 106 . . . . .K2
Hall Beach 349 . . . . .K3
Hay River 2,863 . . . . .G3
Holman 300 . . . . .G2
Igloolik 746 . . . . .K3
Inuvik 3,147. . . . . .E3
Iqaluit 2,333 . . . . .M3
Isachsen H2
Jean-Marie River 69 . . . . . . .F3
Kakisa 36 . . . . .G3
Kipisa 43 . . . . .M3
Lac la Martre 268. . . . . .G3
Lake Harbour 252. . . . . .L3
Mould Bay F2
Nahanni Butte 85 . . . . .F3
Nanisivik 261 . . . . .K2
Norman Wells 420 . . . . .F3
Pangnirtung 839 . . . . .M3
Paulatuk 174 . . . . .F3
Pelly Bay 257 . . . . .K3
Pine Point 1,861 . . . . .G3
Pond Inlet 705 . . . . .L2
Port Burwell M3
Rae-Edzo 1,378 . . . . .G3
Rae Lakes 200 . . . . .G3
Rankin Inlet 1,109 . . . . .G3
Reliance 15 . . . . .H3
Repulse Bay 352. . . . . .K3
Resolute 168 . . . . .J2
Resolution Island. M3

Rocher River G3
Sachs Harbour 161 . . . . . . .F2
Salt River G3
Sawmill Bay G3
Snare Lake 69 . . . . .G3
Snowdrift 253 . . . . .H3
Spence Bay 431 . . . . .J3
Trout Lake 59 . . . . .F3
Tuktoyaktuk 772 . . . . .E3
Tungsten 320 . . . . .F3
Umingmaktok 60 . . . . .H3
Whale Cove 188. . . . . .J3
Wrigley 137 . . . . .F3
Yellowknife (cap.) 9,483. . . . .G3

OTHER FEATURES

Adelaide (pen.) J3
Admiralty (inlet) K2
Air Force (isl.) L3
Akpatok (isl.) M3
Amadjuak (lake) L3
Amund Ringnes (isl.) J2
Amundsen (gulf) F2
Anderson (riv.) F3
Arctic Red (riv.) E3
Artillery (lake) H3
Auyuittug Nat'l Park M3
Axel Heiberg (isl.) J2
Aylmer (lake) H3
Back (riv.) J3
Baffin (bay) M2
Baffin (isl.) L2
Baker (lake) J3
Banks (isl.) F2
Barbeau (peak) L1
Barrow (str.) J2
Bathurst (cape) F2
Bathurst (inlet) H3
Bathurst (isl.) H2
Beaufort (sea) D2
Bellot (str.) J2
Boothia (gulf) K3
Boothia (pen.) J2
Borden (isl.) G2
Borden (pen.) K2
British Empire (range) L1
Brodeur (pen.) K2
Bruce (mts.) L2
Buchan (gulf) L2
Burnside (riv.) G3
Byam Martin (chan.) H2
Byam Martin (isl.) H2
Bylot (isl.) L2
Camsell (riv.) G3
Chantrey (inlet) J3
Chesterfield (inlet) J3
Chidley (cape) M3
Clinton-Colden (lake) H3
Clyde (inlet) M2
Coats (isl.) K3
Coburg (isl.) L2
Columbia (cape) M1
Colville (lake) F3
Committee (bay) K3
Contwoyto (lake) G3
Coppermine (riv.). G3
Cornwall (isl.) J2
Cornwallis (isl.) J2
Coronation (gulf) G3
Croker (bay) K2
Crown Prince Frederik (isl.) . .J3
Cumberland (pen.) M3
Cumberland (sound) M3
Dalhousie (cape) E2
Davis (str.) M3
Dease (str.) H3

Denmark (bay) H2
Devon (isl.). K2
Dolphin and Union (str.) G3
Dubawnt (lake) H3
Dubawnt (riv.) H3
Dundas (pen.) G2
Dyer (cape) M3
Eclipse (sound) L2
Eglinton (isl.) F2
Ellef Ringnes (isl.) H2
Ellesmere (isl.) K2
Ellesmere Is.
  Nat'l Park Res. L1
Ennadai (lake) H3
Eskimo (lakes) E3
Eureka (sound) K2
Evans (str.) K3
Exeter (sound) M3
Fisher (str.) K3
Fosheim (pen.) K1
Foxe (basin) L3
Foxe (chan.) K3
Foxe (pen.) L3
Franklin (bay) F2
Franklin (mts.) F3
Franklin (str.) J2
Frobisher (bay) M3
Frozen (str.) K3
Fury and Hecla (str.) K3
Gabriel (str.) M3
Garry (lake) H3
Gods Mercy (bay) K3
Great Bear (lake) F3
Great Bear (riv.) F3
Great Slave (lake) G3
Greely (fjord) K1
Grinnell (pen.) J2
Hadley (bay) H2
Hall (basin) M1
Hall (pen.) M3
Hayes (riv.) J3
Hazen (lake) L1
Hazen (str.) G2
Henik (lakes) J3
Henry Kater (cape) M3
Home (bay) M3
Hood (riv.) G3

Horn (mts.) G3
Hornaday (riv.) F3
Horton (riv.) F3
Hottah (lake) G3
Hudson (bay) K3
Hudson (str.) L3
Isachsen (cape) H2
James Ross (str.) J3
Jenny Lind (isl.) H3
Jens Munk (isl.) K3
Jones (sound) K2
Kaminuriak (lake) J3
Kane (basin) L2
Kasba (lake) H3
Kazan (riv.) H3
Keele (riv.) F3
Keith Arm (inlet) F3
Kellett (cape) F2
Kellett (str.) G2
Kennedy (chan.) M1
Kent (pen.) H3
King Christian (isl.) H2
King William (isl.) J3
Lady Ann (str.) K2
La Martre (lake) G3
Lancaster (sound) K2
Lands End (cape) F2
Larsen (sound) J2
Liard (riv.) F4
Lincoln (sea) M1
Liverpool (bay) E2

Lockhart (riv.) H3
Lougheed (isl.) H2
Lyon (inlet) K3
MacKay (lake) G3
Mackenzie (bay) E3
Mackenzie (mts.) E3
Mackenzie (riv.) F3
Mackenzie King (isl.) G2
Macmillan (pass) F3
Maguse (lake) J3
Makinson (inlet) L2
Mansel (isl.) K3
Marian (lake) G3
Markham (inlet) L1
McLeod (bay) G3
M'Clintock (chan.) H2
M'Clure (str.) G2
McTavish Arm (inlet) G3
Melghen (isl.) H1
Melville (isl.) G2
Melville (pen.) K3
Mercy (cape) M3
Mills (lake) G3
Minto (inlet) G2
Mistake (bay) J3
Nahanni Nat'l Park F3
Nansen (sound) J1
Nares (str.) L2
Navy Board (inlet) K2
Nelson Head (prom.) F2

Nettilling (lake) L3
Nonacho (lake) H3
North Arm (inlet) G3
North Magnetic Pole H2
Norwegian (bay) J2
Nottingham (isl.) L3
Nueltin (lake) H3
Ommanney (bay) H2
Padloping (isl.) M3
Parry (bay) K3
Parry (chan.) G2
Parry (isls.) G2
Parry (pen.) F2
Peary (chan.) H2
Peel (sound) J2
Pelly (bay) J3
Penny (str.) J2
Point (lake) G3
Pond (inlet) L2
Prince Albert (pen.) G2
Prince Albert (sound) G2
Prince Charles (isl.) L3
Prince Gustav Adolf (sea) H2
Prince of Wales (isl.) J2
Prince of Wales (str.) G2
Prince Patrick (isl.) F2
Prince Regent (inlet) J2
Queen Elizabeth (isls.) H1
Queen Maud (gulf) H3
Queens (chan.) J2

Topography

QUEEN ELIZABETH
ISLANDS

Barbeau Peak
8,584 ft.
(2616 m.)

Axel Heiberg I.   Ellesmere
                        Island

Pr. Patrick I.

Melville I.   Devon I.
Banks I.   Somer-
            Parry   set
                        Channel
            Pr. of   Baffin
            Wales I.   Boothia   Island
Amundsen Gulf   Pen.
            Victoria I.   Melville
Peel   Pen.
Stewart   Foxe
Mt. Logan   Basin
19,524 ft.   Great Bear
(5951 m.)   Lake   Barren
                          Grounds
Whitehorse   Mt. SirJames MacBrien
              9,062 ft.
              (2762 m.)   Southampton I.
              Great
              Slave
              Lake
Yellowknife

Hudson
Bay

0   200   400 MI.
0   200   400 KM.

| 5,000 m. 16,404 ft. | 2,000 m. 6,562 ft. | 1,000 m. 3,281 ft. | 500 m. 1,640 ft. | 200 m. 656 ft. | 100 m. 328 ft. | Sea Level | Below |

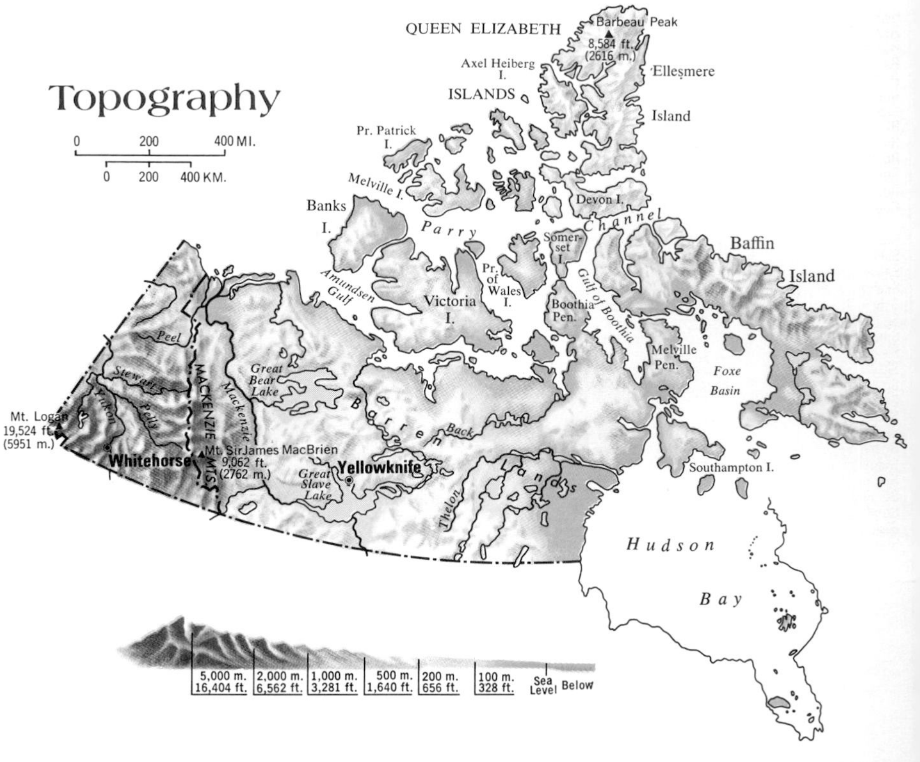

Agriculture, Industry and Resources

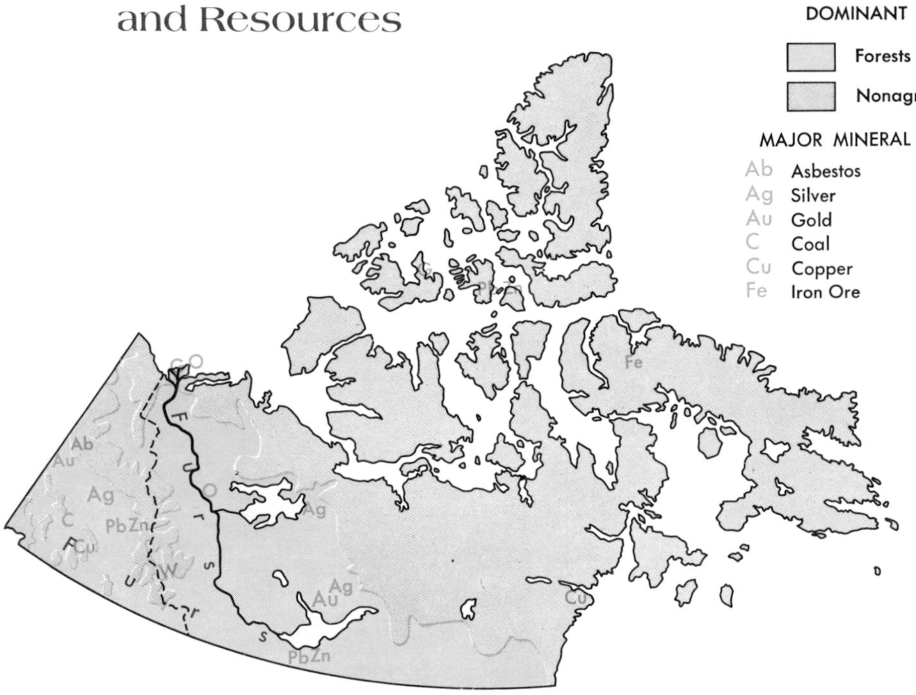

DOMINANT LAND USE

- Forests
- Nonagricultural Land

MAJOR MINERAL OCCURRENCES

Ab	Asbestos	G	Natural Gas
Ag	Silver	O	Petroleum
Au	Gold	Pb	Lead
C	Coal	W	Tungsten
Cu	Copper	Zn	Zinc
Fe	Iron Ore		

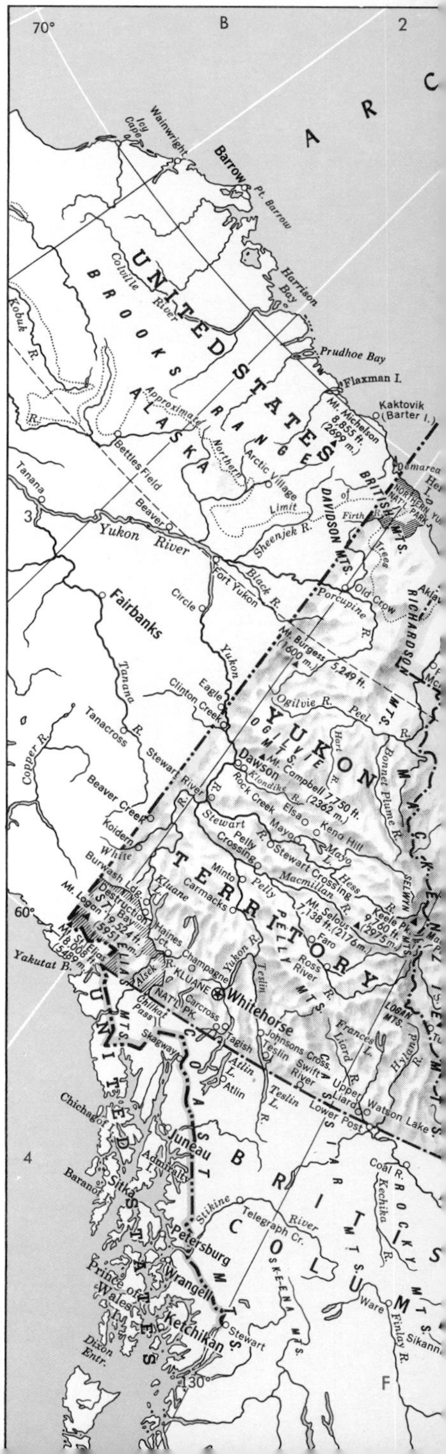

Raanes (pen.) K2
Rae (isth.) K3
Rae (riv.) G3
Rae (str.) J3
Ramparts (riv.) E3
Resolution (isl.) M3
Richard Collinson (inlet) . . .G2
Richards (isl.) E3
Richardson (mts.) E3
Robeson (chan.) M1
Roes Welcome (sound) K3
Rowley (isl.) K3
Royal Geographical
  Society (isls.) J3
Russell (isl.) J2
Sabine (pen.) H2
Salisbury (isl.) L3
Seahorse (pt.) L3
Selwyn (lake) H4
Sherman (inlet) J3
Simpson (pen.) K3
Sir James MacBrien (mt.) . .F3
Slave (riv.) G3
Smith (bay) L2
Smith (cape) L3
Smith (sound) L2
Snare (riv.) G3
Snowbird (lake) H3
Somerset (isl.) J2
South (bay) K3
Southampton (isl.) K3
South Nahanni (riv.) F3
Stallworthy (cape) J1
Steensby (inlet) L2

Stefansson (isl.) H2
Sverdrup (chan.) J1
Sverdrup (isls.) J2
Takijug (lake) G3
Talbot (inlet) L2
Taltson (riv.) G3
Tathlina (lake) G3
Tha-anne (riv.) J3
Thelon (riv.) H3
Thlewiaza (riv.) J3
Trout (lake) F3
Ungava (bay) M4
Vansittart (isl.) K3
Victoria (isl.) G2
Victoria (str.) H3
Viscount Melville (sound) . .G2
Wager (bay) K3
Wales (isl.) K3
Walsingham (cape) M3
Wellington (chan.) J2
Wholdaia (lake) H3
Winter (harb.) H2
Wollaston (pen.) G3
Wood Buffalo Nat'l Park G3
Wynniatt (bay) G2
Yathkyed (lake) J3
Yellowknife (riv.) G3

YUKON TERRITORY
CITIES and TOWNS

Beaver Creek 90 . . . . .D3
Burwash Landing 73 . . . . . .D3
Carcross 216 . . . . .E3

YUKON TERRITORY

AREA 207,075 sq. mi.
  (536,324 sq. km.)
POPULATION 23,504
CAPITAL Whitehorse
LARGEST CITY Whitehorse
HIGHEST POINT Mt. Logan 19,524 ft.
  (5,951 m.)
SETTLED IN 1897
ADMITTED TO CONFEDERATION 1898
PROVINCIAL FLOWER Fireweed

NORTHWEST TERRITORIES

AREA 1,304,896 sq. mi. (3,379,683 sq. km.)
POPULATION 52,238
CAPITAL Yellowknife
LARGEST CITY Yellowknife
HIGHEST POINT Mt. Sir James MacBrien
  9,062 ft. (2,762 m.)
SETTLED IN 1800
ADMITTED TO CONFEDERATION 1870
PROVINCIAL FLOWER Mountain Avens

Carmacks •256 . . . . .E3
Champagne E3
Clinton Creek D3
Cowley E3
Dawson 697 . . . . .D3
Destruction Bay 45 . . . . . . .E3
Elsa 336 . . . . .E3
Faro 1,652 . . . . .E3
Haines Junction •366 . . . . . .E3
Johnson's Crossing 13 . . . . .E3
Keno Hill 88 . . . . .E3
Koidern D3
Mayo 398 . . . . .E3

Minto E3
Old Crow 243 . . . . .E3
Pelly Crossing 182 . . . . .E3
Rock Creek 59 . . . . .E3
Ross River 294 . . . . .E3
Stewart Crossing 20 . . . . . . .E3
Stewart River D3
Swift River 24 . . . . .E3
Tagish 89 . . . . .E3
Teslin •310 . . . . .E3
Upper Liard 130 . . . . .F3
Watson Lake •748 . . . . .F3
Whitehorse (cap.) 14,814 . . .E3

OTHER FEATURES

Alsek (riv.) E3
Bonnet Plume (riv.) E3
British (mts.) D3
Campbell (mt.) E3
Cassiar (mts.) E3
Frances (lake) E3
Herschel (isl.) E3
Hess (riv.) E3
Hyland (riv.) F3
Keele (peak) E3
Klondike (riv.) E3
Kluane (lake) E3

Kluane Nat'l Park E3
Liard (riv.) E3
Logan (mt.) D3
Logan (mts.) F3
Mackenzie (mts.) E3
Macmillan (riv.) E3
Mayo (lake) E3
Northern Yukon Nat'l Pk. . . .E3
Ogilvie (mts.) E3
Ogilvie (riv.) E3
Peel (riv.) E3
Pelly (mts.) E3
Pelly (riv.) E3

Porcupine (riv.) E3
Richardson (mts.) E3
Rocky (mts.) F4
Saint Elias (mt.) D3
Saint Elias (mts.) D3
Selous (mt.) E3
Selwyn (mts.) E3
Stewart (riv.) E3
Teslin (lake) E4
Teslin (riv.) E3
White (riv.) D3
Yukon (riv.) E3

• Population of district.

Yukon and Northwest Territories

SCALE
0   50 100   200   300 MI.
0 50 100   200   300 KM.

Territorial Capitals . . . . ⊛
Regional Capitals . . . . ⊙
International Boundaries . . . . —··—
Provincial & Territorial Boundaries . . . . —·—
Regional Boundaries . . . . — —

Scale 1:14,000,000

All islands in Hudson Bay, James Bay, Hudson Strait and Ungava Bay lie within the Northwest Territories.

© Copyright HAMMOND INCORPORATED, Maplewood, N.J.

Longitude West K of Greenwich

United States

POLYCONIC PROJECTION

SCALE OF MILES

SCALE OF KILOMETERS

Capitals of Countries ....★
State Capitals ....△
International Boundaries ....———

Scale 1:17,400,000

© Copyright HAMMOND INCORPORATED, Maplewood, N. J.

Alabama (state) 4,062,608......J4
Alaska (state) 551,947......C5
Alaska (gulf), Alaska......D6
Albany (cap.), N.Y.‡ 101,082..M2
Albuquerque, N. Mex.‡
   384,736......E3
Aleutian (isls.), Alaska......D6
Amarillo, Texas‡ 157,615......F3
Anchorage, Alaska‡ 226,338..D6
Annapolis (cap.), Md.‡
   33,187......L3
Appalachian (mts.)......K3
Arizona (state) 3,677,985......D4
Arkansas (state) 2,362,239...H3
Arkansas (riv.)......H3
Atlanta (cap.), Ga.‡ 394,017...K4
Attu (isl.), Alaska......D6
Augusta (cap.), Maine‡
   21,325......N2
Aurora Colo. ‡222,103......F3
Austin (cap.), Texas‡
   465,622......G4
Baltimore, Md.‡ 736,014......L3
Baton Rouge (cap.), La.‡
   219,531......H4
Bering (sea), Alaska......C6
Bering (str.), Alaska......C5
Bighorn (riv.)......E2
Bismarck (cap.), N. Dak.‡
   49,256......F2
Black Hills (mts.)......F2
Boise (cap.), Idaho‡ 125,738..C2
Borah (peak), Idaho......•D2

Boston (cap.), Mass.‡
   574,283......M2
Brazos (riv.), Texas......G4
Brooks (range), Alaska......C5
Buffalo, N .Y.‡ 328,123......L2
California (state) 29,839,250...B3
Canadian (riv.)......F3
Canaveral (Kennedy) (cape),
   Fla.......L5
Cape Fear (riv.), N.C.......L4
Carson City (cap.), Nev.
   40,443......C3
Cascade (range)......B1
Champlain (lake)......M2
Charleston (cap.), W. Va.‡
   57,287......K3
Charlotte, N.C.‡ 395,934......L3
Chattahoochee (riv.)......K4
Chesapeake (bay)......L3
Cheyenne (cap.), Wyo.‡
   50,008......E2
Chicago, Ill.‡ 2,783,726......J2
Cimarron (riv.)......G3
Cincinnati, Ohio‡ 364,040......K3
Cleveland, Ohio‡ 505,616......K2
Coast (ranges)......B2
Cod (cape), Mass.......N2
Colorado (state) 3,307,912......E3
Colorado (riv.)......D4
Colorado (riv.), Texas......G4
Columbia (cap.), S.C.‡
   98,052......K4
Columbia (riv.)......B1

Columbus (cap.), Ohio‡
   632,910......K3
Concord (cap.), N.H. 36,006..M2
Connecticut (state)
   3,295,669......M2
Corpus Christi, Texas‡
   257,453......G5
Cumberland (riv.)......J3
Dallas, Texas‡ 1,006,877......G4
Death Valley (depr.), Calif....C3
Delaware (bay)......M3
Delaware (state) 668,696......L3
Denver (cap.), Colo.‡
   467,610......F3
Des Moines (cap.), Iowa‡
   193,187......H2
Detroit, Mich.‡ 1,027,974......K2
District of Columbia 609,909...L3
Dover (cap.), Del. 27,630......L3
El Paso, Texas‡ 515,342......E4
Erie (lake)......K2
Everglades, The (swamp), Fla. K5
Florida (state) 13,003,362......K5
Florida (keys), Fla.......K6
Fort Worth, Texas 447,619...G4
Frankfort (cap.), Ky. 25,968...K3
Fresno, Calif.‡ 354,202......C3
Georgia (state) 6,508,419......K4
Gila (riv.)......D4
Glacier Nat'l Park, Mont......D1
Golden Gate (chan.), Calif....B3
Grand Canyon Nat'l Park, Ariz.D3
Great Salt (lake), Utah......D2

Harrisburg (cap.), Pa.‡......L2
   52,376......
Hatteras (cape), N.C.......M3
Havasu (lake)......D4
Hawaii (state) 1,115,274......F5
Hawaii (isl.), Hawaii......F6
Helena (cap.), Mont. 24,569...D1
Honolulu (cap.), Hawaii‡
   365,272......
Houston, Texas‡ 1,630,553...G5
Huron (lake)......K2
Idaho (state) 1,011,986......D2
Illinois (state) 11,466,682......J3
Indiana (state) 5,564,228......J3
Indianapolis (cap.), Ind.
   741,952......J3
Iowa (state) 2,787,424......H2
Jackson (cap.), Miss.‡
   196,637......J4
Jacksonville, Fla.‡ 672,971...K4
Jefferson City
   (cap.), Mo. 35,481......H3
Juneau (cap.), Alaska 26,751..E6
Kansas (state) 2,485,600......G3
Kansas City, Kans.-Mo.‡
   435,146......H3
Kentucky (state) 3,698,969......J3
Lansing (cap.), Mich.‡
   127,321......K2
Las Vegas, Nev.‡ 258,295......C3
Lexington, Ky.‡ 225,366......K3
Lincoln (cap.), Nebr.‡
   191,972......

Little Missouri (riv.)......F1
Little Rock (cap.), Ark.‡
   175,795......H4
Long (isl.), N.Y.......M2
Long Beach, Calif. 429,433.....C4
Los Angeles, Calif.‡
   3,485,398......C4
Louisiana (state) 4,238,216...H4
Madison (cap.), Wis.‡
   191,206......H2
Maine (state) 1,233,223......N1
Maryland (state) 4,798,622......L3
Massachusetts (state)
   6,029,051......M2
Maui (isl.), Hawaii......F5
Mauna Kea (mt.), Hawaii......G6
Mauna Loa (mt.), Hawaii......G6
May (cape), N.J.......M3
McKinley (mt.), Alaska......D6
Memphis, Tenn.‡ 610,337......J3
Mendocino (cape), Calif.......A2
Mexico (gulf)......J5
Miami, Fla.‡ 358,548......K5
Michigan (state) 9,328,784......J1
Michigan (lake)......J2
Milwaukee, Wis.‡ 628,088......J2
Minneapolis, Minn.‡
   368,383......H1
Minnesota (state) 4,387,029...H1
Mississippi (state) 2,586,443..J4
Mississippi (riv.)......H4
Missouri (state) 5,137,804......H3
Missouri (riv.)......H3

Mobile, Ala.‡ 196,278......J4
Montana (state) 803,655......E1
Montgomery (cap.), Ala.‡
   187,106......J4
Montpelier (cap.), Ver. 8,241..M2
Nantucket (isl.), Mass.......N2
Nashville (cap.), Tenn.‡
   510,784......J3
Nebraska (state) 1,584,617...F2
Nevada (state) 1,206,152......C3
Newark, N.J.‡ 275,221......L2
New Hampshire (state)
   1,113,915......M2
New Jersey (state)
   7,748,634......M3
New Mexico (state)
   1,521,779......E3
New Orleans, La.‡ 496,938...H5
New York (state) 18,044,505..L2
New York, N.Y.‡ 7,322,564....M2
Norfolk, Va.‡ 261,229......L3
North Carolina (state)
   6,657,630......K3
North Dakota (state) 641,364..F1
Oahu (isl.), Hawaii......F5
Oakland, Calif.‡ 372,242......B3
Ohio (state) 10,887,325......K2
Ohio (riv.)......J3
Oklahoma (state) 3,157,604...G3
Oklahoma City (cap.), Okla.‡
   444,719......G3
Olympia (cap.), Wash.‡
   33,840......B1

Omaha, Nebr.‡ 335,795......G2
Ontario (lake), N.Y.......L2
Oregon (state) 2,853,733......B2
Ozark (mts.)......H3
Pennsylvania (state)
   11,924,710......L2
Philadelphia, Pa.‡
   1,585,577......M2
Phoenix (cap.), Ariz.‡
   983,403......D4
Pierre (cap.), S. Dak. 12,906..F2
Pikes (peak), Colo.......F3
Pittsburgh, Pa.‡ 369,879......L2
Platte (riv.), Nebr.......G2
Pontchartrain (lake), La.......J5
Portland, Maine‡ 437,319......N2
Potomac (riv.)......L3
Providence (cap.), R.I.‡
   160,728......M2
Rainier (mt.), Wash.......B1
Raleigh (cap.), N.C.‡
   207,951......L3
Red (riv.)......H4
Red River of the North (riv.)..G1
Rhode Island (state)
   1,005,984......M2
Richmond (cap.), Va.‡
   203,056......L3
Rio Grande (riv.)......F5
Rochester, N.Y.‡ 231,636......L2
Rocky (mts.)......D2
Sacramento (cap.), Calif.‡
   369,365......B3

AREA 3,623,420 sq. mi.
(9,384,658 sq. km.)
POPULATION 249,632,692
CAPITAL Washington
LARGEST CITY New York
HIGHEST POINT Mt. McKinley 20,320 ft.
(6,194 m.)
MONETARY UNIT U.S. dollar
MAJOR LANGUAGE English
MAJOR RELIGIONS Protestantism,
Roman Catholicism, Judaism

Population Distribution

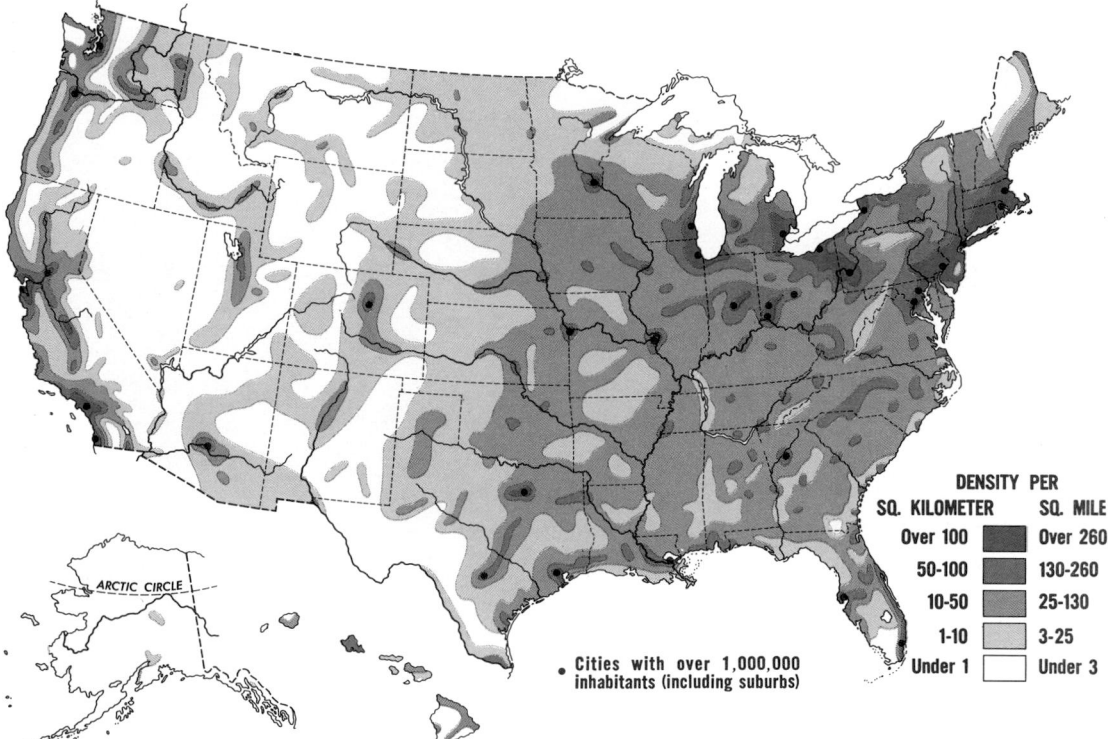

DENSITY PER

SQ. KILOMETER	SQ. MILE
Over 100	Over 260
50-100	130-260
10-50	25-130
1-10	3-25
Under 1	Under 3

• Cities with over 1,000,000
inhabitants (including suburbs)

Vegetation

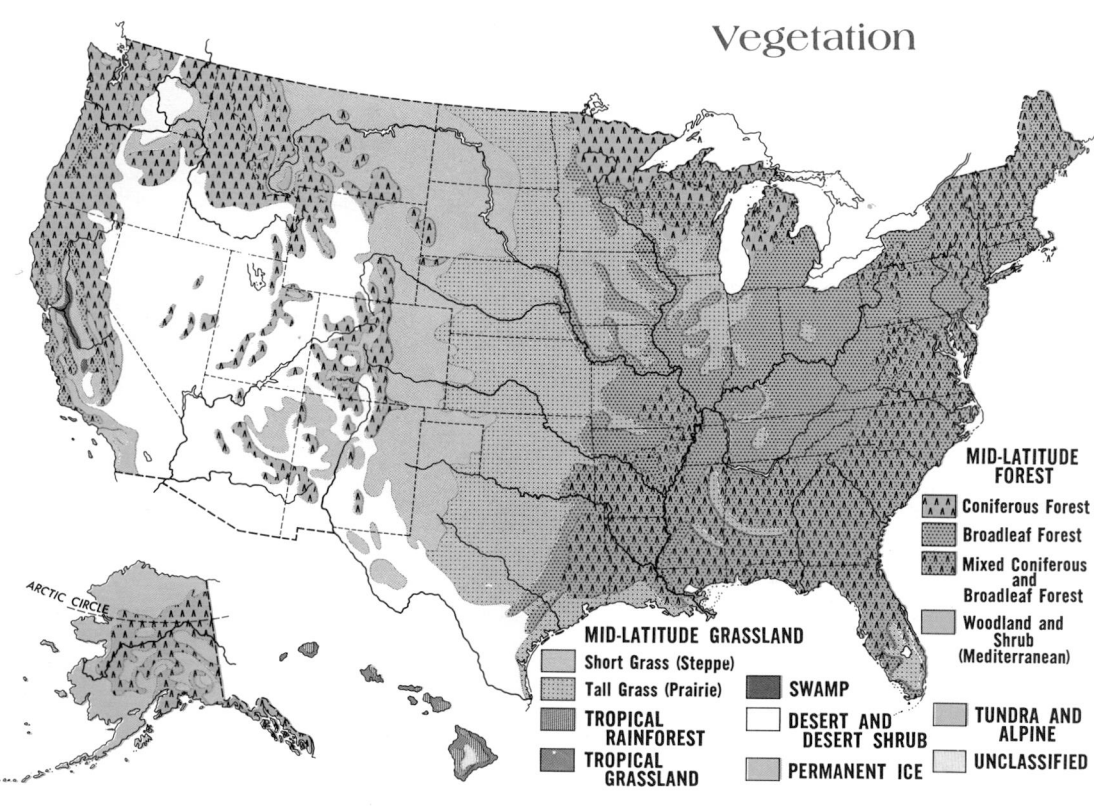

MID-LATITUDE FOREST

Coniferous Forest
Broadleaf Forest
Mixed Coniferous and Broadleaf Forest
Woodland and Shrub (Mediterranean)

MID-LATITUDE GRASSLAND

Short Grass (Steppe)
Tall Grass (Prairie)

TROPICAL RAINFOREST
TROPICAL GRASSLAND

SWAMP
DESERT AND DESERT SHRUB
PERMANENT ICE

TUNDRA AND ALPINE
UNCLASSIFIED

Saint Lawrence (riv.), N.Y.......N1
Saint Louis, Mo.‡ 396,685 .....H3
Saint Paul (cap.), Minn.
  272,235 ....H1
Sakakawea (lake), N. Dak. F1
Salem (cap.), Oreg.‡
  107,786 ....B1
Salt Lake City (cap.), Utah‡
  159,936 ....D2
Salton Sea (lake), Calif..........C4
San Antonio, Texas‡
  935,933 ....G5
San Diego, Calif.‡ 1,110,549 ..C4
San Francisco, Calif.‡
  723,959 ....B3
San Joaquin (riv.), Calif..........C3
San Jose, Calif.‡ 782,248 ....B3
Santa Ana, Calif.‡ 293,742......C4
Santa Fe (cap.), N. Mex.
  55,859............................E3
Seattle, Wash.‡ 516,259.........B1
Shasta (mt.), Calif..................B2
Shreveport, La.‡ 198,525........H4
Sierra Nevada (mts.)...............B3
Snake (riv.).............................C1
South Carolina (state)
  3,505,707 ....K4
South Dakota (state) 699,999 .F2
Spokane, Wash. 177,196.........C1
Springfield (cap.), Ill.‡
  105,227 ....H3
Stockton, Calif.‡ 210,943 ......B3
Superior (lake)........................H1

Tacoma, Wash.‡ 176,664 ....B1
Tahoe (lake).............................C3
Tallahassee (cap.), Fla.‡
  124,773 ....K4
Tampa, Fla.‡ 280,015 ....K5
Tennessee (state) 4,896,641 ...J3
Texas (state) 17,059,805 ....G4
Toledo, Ohio‡ 332,943 ....K2
Topeka (cap.), Kans.‡
  119,883 ....G3
Trenton (cap.), N.J.‡ 88,675...M2
Tucson, Ariz.‡ 405,390...........D4
Tulsa, Okla.‡ 367,302.............G3
Utah (state) 1,727,784............D3
Vermont (state) 564,964..........M2
Virginia (state) 6,216,568 ....L3
Virginia Beach, Va. 393,069 ....L3
Wabash (riv.)...........................J3
Washington (state) 4,887,941.B1
Washington, D.C. (cap.), U.S.‡
  606,909...........................L3
West Virginia (state)
  1,801,625 ....K3
Whitney (mt.), Calif.................C3
Wichita, Kans.‡ 304,01 ....G3
Wisconsin (state) 4,906,745 ...J2
Wyoming (state) 455,975 ....E2
Yellowstone Nat'l Park, Wyo....E2
Yosemite Nat'l Park, Calif.......C3
Yukon (riv.), Alaska.................C5

‡ Population of metropolitan
area.

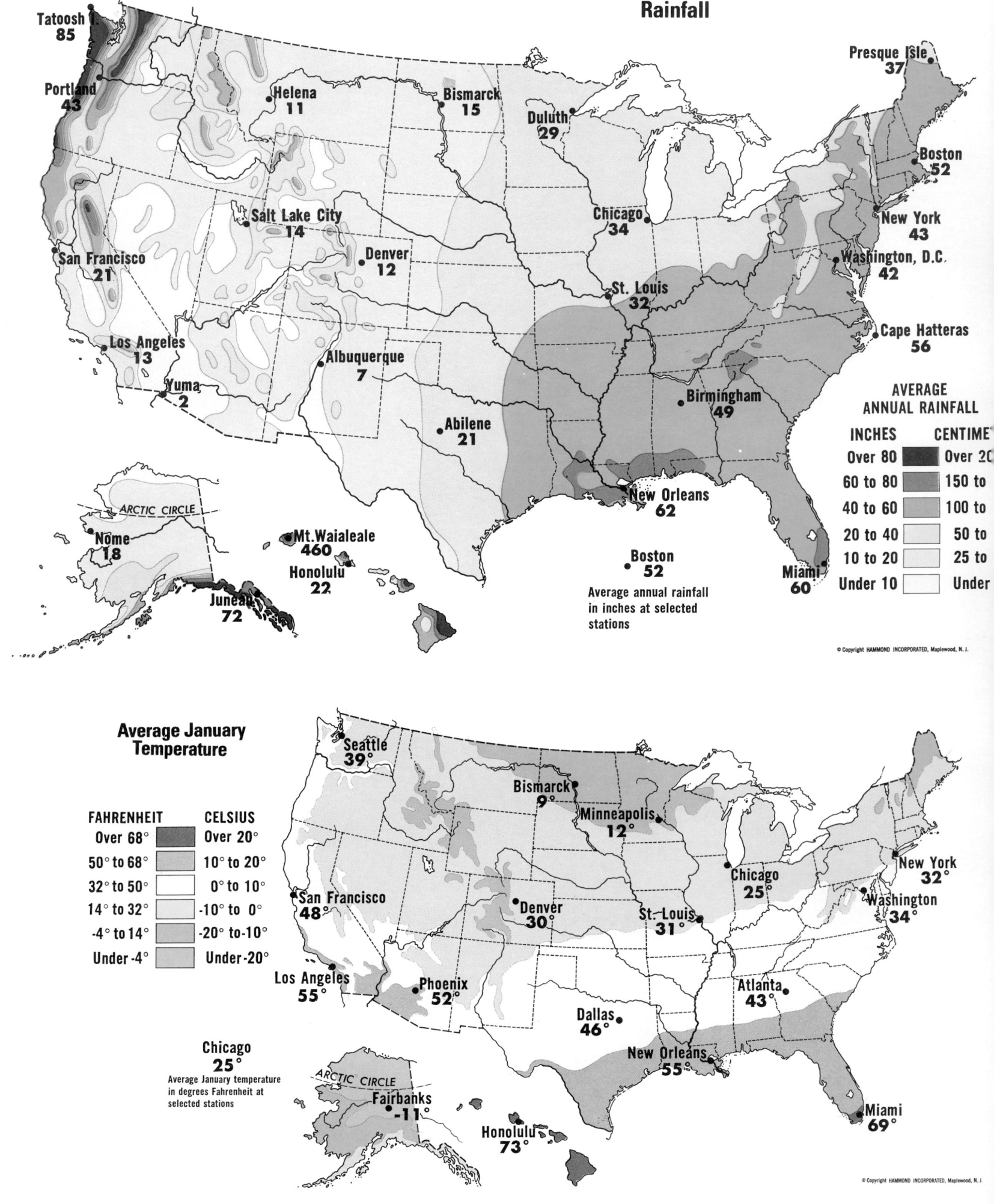

Rainfall

Tatoosh I.
85

Portland
43

Helena
11

Bismarck
15

Duluth
29

Presque Isle
37

Boston
52

Chicago
34

New York
43

Salt Lake City
14

Washington, D.C.
42

San Francisco
21

Denver
12

St. Louis
32

Los Angeles
13

Albuquerque
7

Cape Hatteras
56

Yuma
2

Abilene
21

Birmingham
49

New Orleans
62

ARCTIC CIRCLE

Nome
18

Mt. Waialeale
460

Miami
60

Honolulu
22

Boston
52

Average annual rainfall
in inches at selected
stations

Juneau
72

AVERAGE ANNUAL RAINFALL

INCHES	CENTIME
Over 80	Over 20
60 to 80	150 to
40 to 60	100 to
20 to 40	50 to
10 to 20	25 to
Under 10	Under

© Copyright HAMMOND INCORPORATED, Maplewood, N.J.

Average January Temperature

FAHRENHEIT	CELSIUS
Over 68°	Over 20°
50° to 68°	10° to 20°
32° to 50°	0° to 10°
14° to 32°	-10° to 0°
-4° to 14°	-20° to -10°
Under -4°	Under -20°

Seattle
39°

Bismarck
9°

Minneapolis
12°

Chicago
25°

New York
32°

Washington
34°

San Francisco
48°

Denver
30°

St. Louis
31°

Los Angeles
55°

Phoenix
52°

Dallas
46°

Atlanta
43°

New Orleans
55°

Chicago
25°

Average January temperature
in degrees Fahrenheit at
selected stations

ARCTIC CIRCLE

Fairbanks
-11°

Honolulu
73°

Miami
69°

© Copyright HAMMOND INCORPORATED, Maplewood, N.J.

Topography

C. Flattery
Seattle
Mt. Rainier 14,410 ft. (4392 m.)
Mt. St. Helens 8,364 ft. (2549 m.)
COAST RANGES
CASCADE RANGE
DITTERROOT RANGE
ROCKY
COLUMBIA PLATEAU
Columbia
Snake
Yellowstone
Missouri
GREAT
Fort Peck Lake
Lake Sakakawea
Rainy
Lake Superior
Keweenaw Pen.
St. Lawrence
Gulf of Maine
Great Basin
SIERRA NEVADA
Central Valley
Great Salt Lake
COLORADO
MOUNTAINS
Denver
Mt. Elbert 14,431 ft. (4399 m.)
Red
Lake Oahe
James
Missouri
Minneapolis
Wisconsin
Milwaukee
Lake Michigan
Lake Huron
Detroit
Lake Erie
Cleveland
Lake Ontario
Niagara Falls
L. Champlain
Boston
C. Cod
Long Island
New York
Philadelphia
San Francisco
PACIFIC
OCEAN
Mt. Whitney 14,494 ft. (4418 m.)
Lake Powell
Colorado
Arkansas
N. Platte
Platte
Des Moines
Illinois
Chicago
Kansas City
Missouri
St. Louis
Indianapolis
Ohio
Wabash
Washington
ATLANTIC
Pt. Conception
SANTA BARBARA IS.
Los Angeles
Mead
Grand Canyon
PLATEAU
Mojave Desert
Colorado
Gila
San Diego
Phoenix
Rio Grande
LLANO ESTACADO
PLAINS
Red
Dallas
Canadian
Red
Arkansas
OZARK PLATEAU
Memphis
Tennessee
Wheeler
Mt. Mitchell 6,684 ft. (2037 m.)
APPALACHIAN MOUNTAINS
ALLEGHENY MTS.
PIEDMONT
Atlanta
Savannah
Chattahoochee
Chesapeake Bay
C. Hatteras
OCEAN
C. Fear
EDWARDS PLATEAU
Pecos
Brazos
Colorado
Houston
Mississippi
New Orleans
Mississippi Delta
COASTAL PLAIN
Jacksonville
C. Canaveral
Gulf of Mexico
L. Okeechobee
The Everglades
Miami
FLORIDA KEYS

0   200   400 MI.
0   200   400 KM.

ARCTIC OCEAN
BROOKS RA.
Bering Str.
St. Lawrence I.
Yukon
Tanana
Mt. McKinley 20,320 ft. (6194 m.)
Alaska Ra.
Anchorage
Gulf of Alaska
BERING SEA
Kodiak I.
ALEXANDER ARCHIPELAGO
Aleutian Islands
Alaska Pen.

0   200   400 MI.
0   200   400 KM.

Kauai
Oahu
Molokai
HAWAIIAN ISLANDS
Honolulu
Maui
PACIFIC OCEAN
Mauna Kea 13,796 ft. (4205 m.)
Hawaii

0   50   100 MI.
0   50   100 KM.

5,000 m. 16,404 ft. | 2,000 m. 6,562 ft. | 1,000 m. 3,281 ft. | 500 m. 1,640 ft. | 200 m. 656 ft. | 100 m. 328 ft. | Sea Level | Below

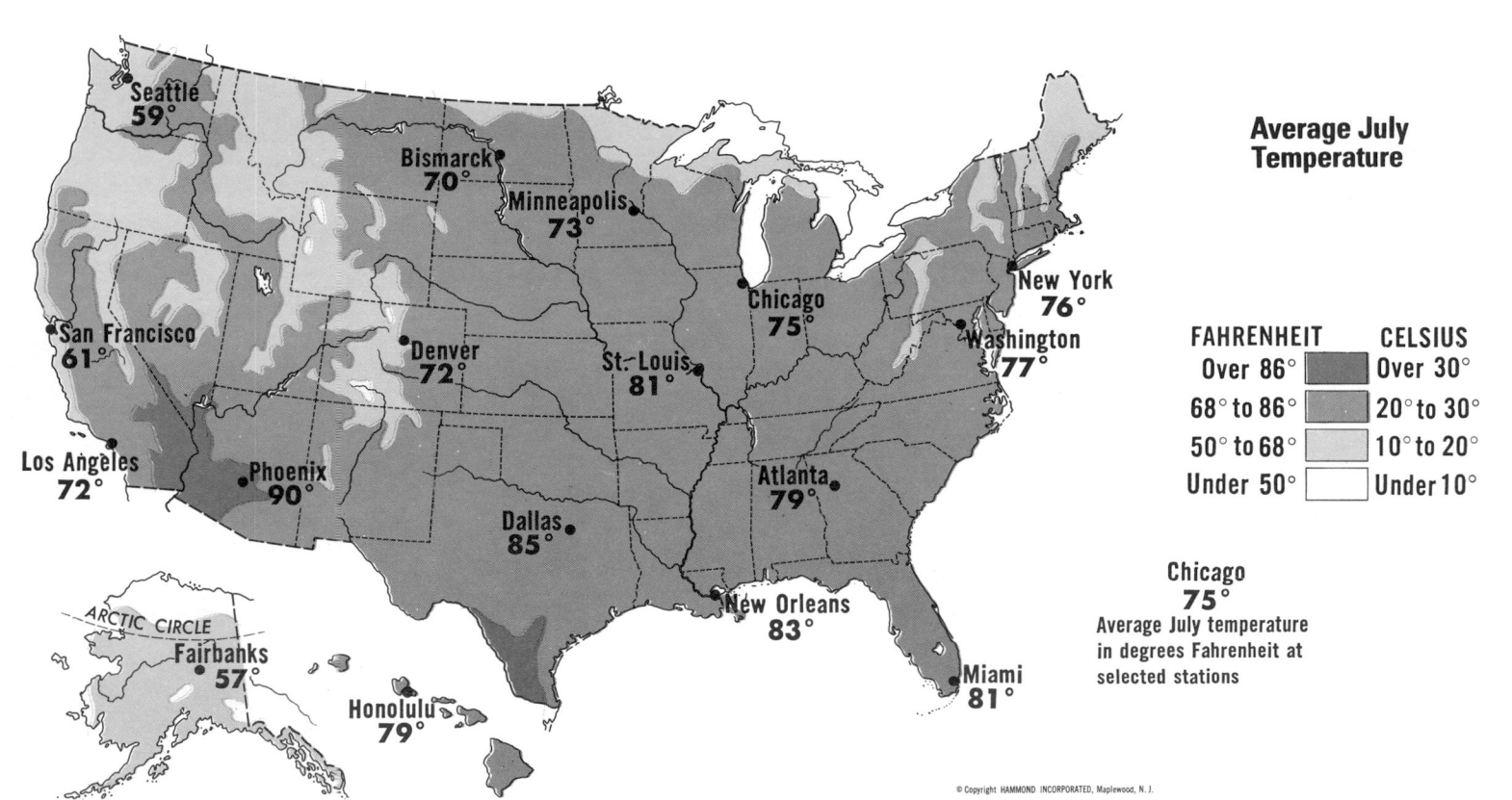

Average July Temperature

Seattle 59°
Bismarck 70°
Minneapolis 73°
Chicago 75°
New York 76°
Washington 77°
San Francisco 61°
Denver 72°
St. Louis 81°
Los Angeles 72°
Phoenix 90°
Atlanta 79°
Dallas 85°
New Orleans 83°
Miami 81°
Fairbanks 57°
Honolulu 79°
ARCTIC CIRCLE

FAHRENHEIT	CELSIUS
Over 86°	Over 30°
68° to 86°	20° to 30°
50° to 68°	10° to 20°
Under 50°	Under 10°

Chicago 75°
Average July temperature in degrees Fahrenheit at selected stations

United States Standard Time Zones

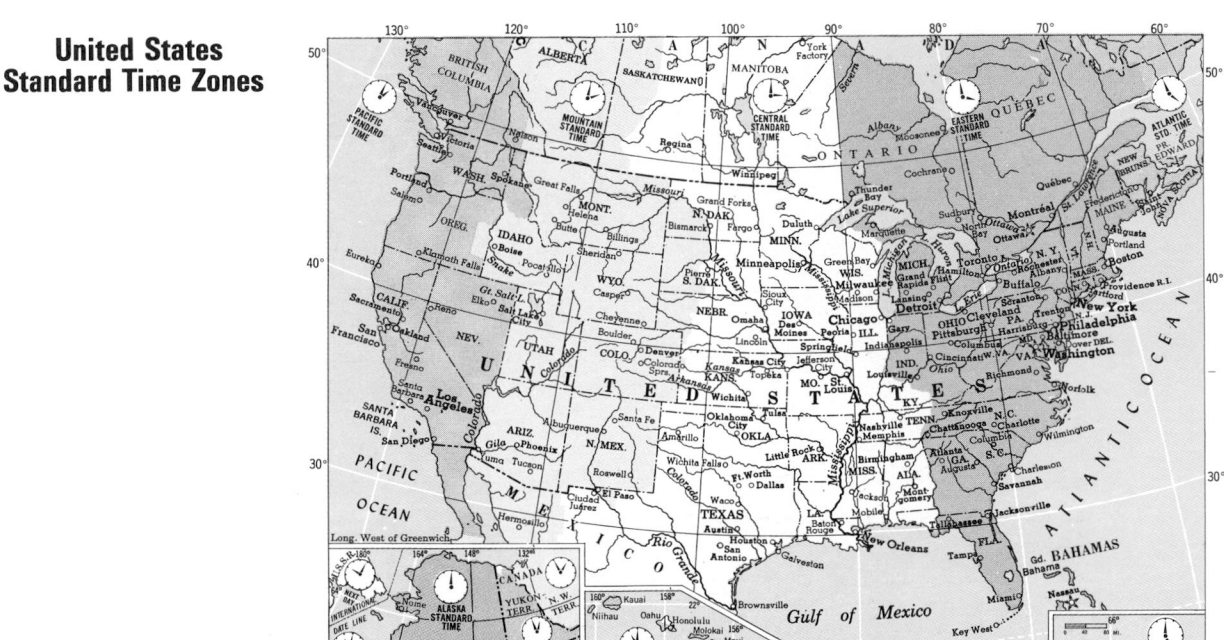

U. S. STANDARD TIME ZONES
Established by the Uniform Time Act

SCALE OF MILES

Agriculture, Industry and Resources

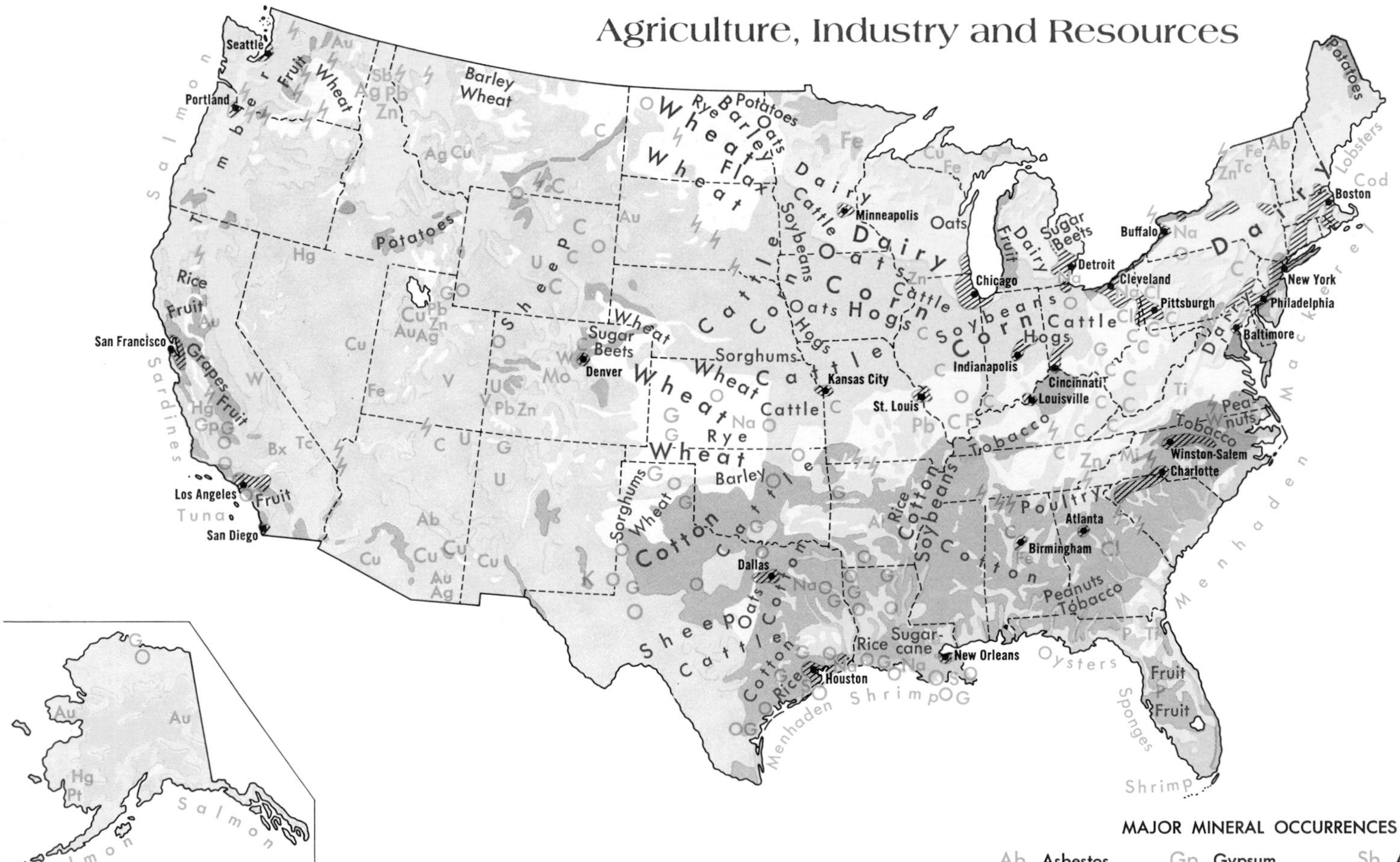

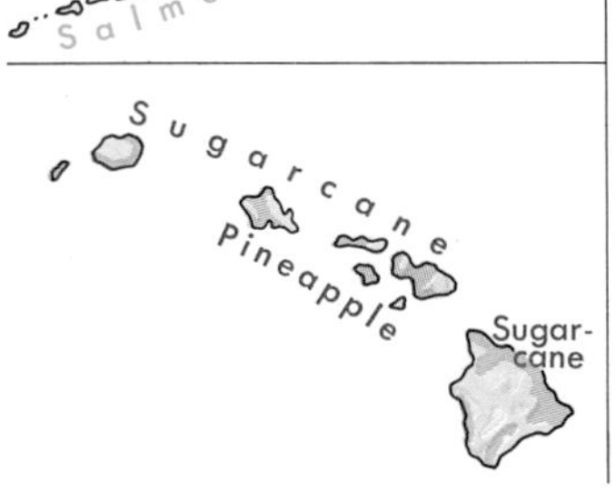

DOMINANT LAND USE

- Wheat and Small Grains
- Feed Grains and Livestock
- Dairy
- General Farming
- Cotton
- Fruit, Truck and Mixed Farming
- Tobacco and General Farming
- Special Crops and General Farming
- Range Livestock
- Forests
- Swampland
- Nonagricultural Land

MAJOR MINERAL OCCURRENCES

Ab	Asbestos	Gp	Gypsum	Sb	Antimony
Ag	Silver	Hg	Mercury	Tc	Talc
Al	Bauxite	K	Potash	Ti	Titanium
Au	Gold	Mi	Mica	U	Uranium
Bx	Borax	Mo	Molybdenum	V	Vanadium
C	Coal	Na	Salt	W	Tungsten
Cl	Clay	O	Petroleum	Zn	Zinc
Cu	Copper	P	Phosphates		
F	Fluorspar	Pb	Lead	⚡	Water Power
Fe	Iron Ore	Pt	Platinum	▨	Major Industrial Areas
G	Natural Gas	S	Sulfur		

AREA 51,705 sq. mi. (133,916 sq. km.)
POPULATION 4,062,608
CAPITAL Montgomery
LARGEST CITY Birmingham
HIGHEST POINT Cheaha Mtn. 2,407 ft. (734 m.)
SETTLED IN 1702
ADMITTED TO UNION December 14, 1819
POPULAR NAME Heart of Dixie; Cotton State; Yellowhammer State
STATE FLOWER Camellia
STATE BIRD Yellowhammer

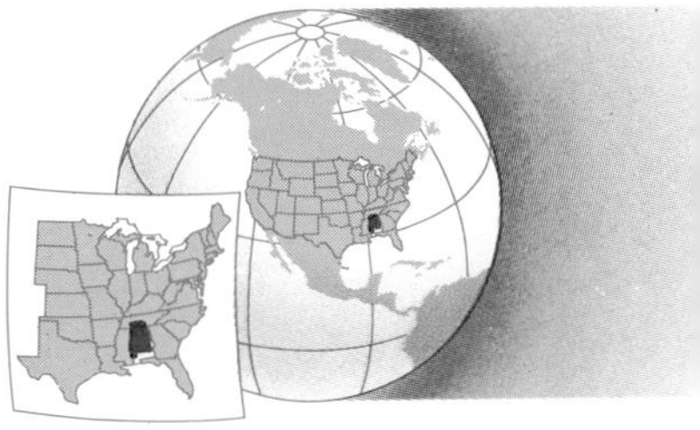

COUNTIES

Autauga 34,222 E5
Baldwin 98,280 C9
Barbour 25,417 H7
Bibb 16,576 D5
Blount 39,248 E2
Bullock 11,042 G6
Butler 21,892 E7
Calhoun 116,034 G3
Chambers 36,876 H5
Cherokee 19,543 G2
Chilton 32,458 E5
Choctaw 16,018 B6
Clarke 27,240 C7
Clay 13,252 G4
Cleburne 12,730 G3
Coffee 40,240 G8
Colbert 51,666 C1
Conecuh 14,054 E8
Coosa 11,063 F5
Covington 36,478 F8
Crenshaw 13,635 F7
Cullman 67,613 E2
Dale 49,633 G8
Dallas 48,130 D6
De Kalb 53,658 G2
Elmore 49,210 F5
Escambia 35,518 D8
Etowah 99,840 F2
Fayette 17,962 C3
Franklin 27,814 C2
Geneva 23,647 G8
Greene 10,153 C5
Hale 15,498 C5
Henry 15,374 H7
Houston 81,331 H8
Jackson 47,796 F1
Jefferson 651,525 E3
Lamar 15,715 B3
Lauderdale 79,661 C1
Lawrence 31,513 D1
Lee 87,146 H5
Limestone 54,135 E1
Lowndes 12,658 E6
Macon 24,928 G6
Madison 238,912 E1
Marengo 23,084 C6
Marion 29,830 C2
Marshall 70,832 F2
Mobile 378,643 B9
Monroe 23,968 D7
Montgomery 209,085 F6
Morgan 100,043 E2
Perry 12,759 D5
Pickens 20,699 B4
Pike 27,595 G7
Randolph 19,881 H4
Russell 46,860 H6
Saint Clair 41,205 F3
Shelby 99,358 E4
Sumter 16,174 B5
Talladega 74,107 F4
Tallapoosa 38,826 G5
Tuscaloosa 150,522 C4
Walker 67,670 D3
Washington 16,694 B8
Wilcox 13,568 D7
Winston 22,053 D2

CITIES and TOWNS

Abbeville▲ 3,173 H7
Abernant 405 D4
Adamsville 4,161 D3
Addison 626 D2
Adger 400 D4
Akron 468 C5
Alabaster 14,732 E4
Albertville 14,507 F2
Aldrich 500 E4
Alexander City 14,917 G5
Alexandria 600 G3
Aliceville 3,009 B4
Allgood 464 F3
Allsboro 300 B1
Alma 500 C8
Altoona 960 F2
Andalusia▲ 9,269 E8
Anderson 339 D1
Anniston▲ 26,623 G3
Arab 6,321 E2
Ardmore 1,090 E1
Argo 930 E3
Ariton 743 G7
Arley 338 D2
Ashby 500 E4
Ashford 1,926 H8
Ashland▲ 2,034 G4
Ashville▲ 1,494 F3
Athens▲ 16,901 E1
Atmore 8,046 C8
Attalla 6,859 F2
Auburn 33,830 H5
Autaugaville 681 E6
Avon 462 H8
Axis 500 B9
Babbie 576 F8
Baileyton 352 E2
Baker Hill 300 H7
Banks 195 G7
Barnwell 700 C10
Bay Minette▲ 7,168 C9
Bayou La Batre 2,456 B10
Bear Creek 913 C2
Beatrice 454 D7
Beaverton 319 B3
Belgreen 500 C2
Belk 255 C3
Bellamy 700 B6
Belle Mina 675 E1
Bellwood 400 G8
Benton 48 E6
Berry 1,218 C3
Bessemer 33,497 D4
Beulah 500 H5
Billingsley 150 E5
Birmingham▲ 265,968 D3
Black 174 G8
Blountsville 1,527 E2
Blue Mountain 221 G3
Blue Springs 108 G7
Boaz 6,928 F2
Boligee 268 C5
Bon Air 91 F4
Bon Secour 850 C10
Branchville 370 F3
Brantley 1,015 F7
Brent 2,776 D5
Brewton▲ 5,885 D8
Bridgeport 2,936 G1
Brighton 4,518 D4
Brilliant 751 C2
Brookside 1,365 E3
Brookwood 658 D4
Browns 375 D6
Brownville 2,386 C4
Brundidge 2,472 G7
Butler▲ 1,872 B6
Cahaba 4,778 D6
Calera 2,136 E4
Calhoun 950 F6
Calvert 600 B8
Camden▲ 2,414 D7
Camp Hill 1,415 G5
Canoe 560 D8
Carbon Hill 2,115 D3
Cardiff 72 E3
Carolina 201 E8
Carrollton▲ 1,170 B4
Carrville 820 G5
Carson 400 C8
Castleberry 669 D8
Cedar Bluff 1,174 G2
Centre▲ 2,893 G2
Centreville▲ 2,508 D5
Chatom▲ 1,094 B8
Chelsea 1,329 E4
Cherokee 1,479 C1
Chickasaw 6,649 B9
Childersburg 4,579 F4
Choccolocco 500 G3
Choctaw 600 B6
Chrysler 400 C8
Chunchula 700 B9
Citronelle 3,671 B8
Clanton▲ 7,669 E5
Clayhatchee 411 G8
Clayton▲ 1,564 G7
Cleveland 739 E3
Clio 1,365 G7
Coaling 400 D4
Coden 600 B10
Coffee Springs 294 G8
Coffeeville 431 B7
Coker 800 C4
Collinsville 1,429 G2
Columbia 922 H8
Columbiana▲ 2,968 E4
Coosada 912 F5
Cordova 2,623 D3
Cottondale 500 D4
Cottonton 324 H6
Cottonwood 1,385 H8
County Line 124 F8
County Line 199 E3
Courtland 803 D1
Cowarts 1,400 H8
Coy 950 D7
Crane Hill 355 D2
Creola 1,896 B9
Cromwell 650 B6
Crossville 1,350 G2
Cuba 390 B6
Cullman▲ 13,367 E2
Cullomburg 325 B7
Cusseta 650 H5
Dadeville▲ 3,276 G5
Daleville 5,117 G8
Daphne 11,290 C9
Dauphin Island 824 B10
Daviston 261 G4
Dayton 77 C6
De Armanville 350 G3
Decatur▲ 48,761 D1
Demopolis 7,512 C6
Detroit 291 B2
Dolomite D4
Dora 2,214 D3
Dothan▲ 53,589 H8
Double Springs▲ 1,138 D2
Douglas 474 F2
Dozier 483 F7
Dutton 243 G1
East Brewton 2,579 E8
Eclectic 1,087 F5
Edwardsville 118 H3
Elba▲ 4,011 F8
Elberta 458 C10
Eldridge 225 C3
Elkmont 389 E1
Elmore 600 F5
Elrod 746 C4
Emelle 44 B5
Empire 600 D3
Enterprise 20,123 G8
Epes 267 B5
Ethelsville 52 B4
Eufaula 13,220 H7
Eunola 199 G8
Eutaw▲ 2,281 C5
Eva 438 E2
Evergreen▲ 3,911 E8
Excel 571 D8
Fairfield 12,200 E4
Fairhope 8,485 C10
Fairview 383 E2
Falkville 1,337 E2
Faunsdale 96 C6
Fayette▲ 4,909 C3
Five Points 200 H4
Flat Rock 750 G1
Flint City 1,033 D1
Flomaton 1,811 D8
Florala 2,075 F8
Florence▲ 36,426 C1
Foley 4,937 C10
Forestdale 10,395 E3
Forkland 667 C5
Fort Davis 500 G6
Fort Deposit 1,240 E7
Fort Mitchell 900 H6
Fort Payne▲ 11,838 G2
Fosters 400 C4
Franklin 133 G6
Franklin 152 D7
Frisco City 1,581 D8
Fruitdale 500 B8
Fruithurst 177 G3
Fulton 384 C7
Fultondale 6,400 E3
Fyffe 1,094 G2
Gadsden▲ 42,523 G2
Gainesville 449 B5
Gallant 475 F2
Gantt 265 E8
Gantt's Quarry F4
Garden City 578 E2
Gardendale 9,251 E3
Gaylesville 149 G2
Geiger 270 B5
Geneva▲ 4,681 G8
Georgiana 1,933 E7
Geraldine 801 G2
Gilbertown 235 B7
Glen Allen 350 C3
Glencoe 4,670 G3
Glenwood 208 F7
Goldville 61 G4
Good Hope 1,700 E2
Goodsprings 360 D3
Goodwater 1,840 F4
Gordo 1,918 C4
Gordon 493 H8
Gorgas 500 D3
Goshen 302 F7
Gosport 500 C7
Grand Bay 3,383 B10
Grant 638 F1
Graysville 2,241 D3
Green Pond 750 D4
Greensboro▲ 3,047 C5
Greenville▲ 7,492 E7
Grimes 443 H8
Grove Hill▲ 1,551 C7
Gu-Win 243 C3
Guin 2,464 C3
Gulf Shores 3,261 C10
Guntersville▲ 7,038 F2
Gurley 1,007 F1
Hackleburg 1,161 C2
Haleburg 97 H8
Haleyville 4,452 C2
Hamilton▲ 5,787 C2
Hammondville 420 G1
Hanceville 2,246 E2
Hardaway 600 G6
Harpersville 772 F4
Hartford 2,448 G8
Hartselle 10,795 E2
Harvest 1,922 E1
Hatchechubbee 840 H6
Hatton 950 D1
Hayden 385 E3
Hayneville▲ 969 E6
Hazel Green 2,208 E1
Headland 3,266 H8
Heath 182 F8
Heflin▲ 2,906 G3
Heiberger 310 D5
Helena 3,918 E4
Henagar 1,934 G1
Higdon 925 G1
Highland Lake 304 F3
Hillsboro 587 D1
Hobson City 794 G3
Hodges 272 C2
Hokes Bluff 3,739 G3
Hollins 500 F4
Holly Pond 602 E2
Hollywood 916 G1
Holt 4,125 D4
Holy Trinity 400 H6
Homewood 22,922 E4
Hoover 39,788 E4
Hope Hull 975 F6
Horn Hill 186 F8
Hueytown 15,280 D4
Huntsville▲ 159,789 E1
Hurtsboro 707 H6
Hytop 350 F1
Ider 671 G1
Inverness 2,528 G6
Irondale 9,454 E3
Jack 5,819 F7
Jackson 789 C8
Jacksons Gap 800 G5
Jacksonville 10,283 G3
Jasper▲ 13,553 D3
Jemison 1,898 E5
Kansas 230 C3
Kellyton 375 F5
Kennedy 523 B3
Key 400 G2
Killen 1,047 D1
Kimberly 1,096 E3
Kinsey 1,679 H8
Kinston 595 F8
Laceys Spring 400 E1
Lafayette▲ 3,151 H5
Lakeview 166 G2
Lanett 8,985 H5
Langdale 2,034 H5
Langston 207 G1
Larkinsville 425 F1
Lavaca 500 B6
Leeds 9,946 E3
Leesburg 218 G2
Leighton 988 D1
Leroy 699 B8
Lester 89 D1
Level Plains 1,473 G8
Lexington 821 D1
Libertyville 133 F8
Lillian 350 D10
Lincoln 2,941 F3
Linden▲ 2,548 C6
Lineville 2,394 G4
Lipscomb 2,892 E4
Lisman 481 B6
Little River 400 C8
Little Shawmut 2,793 H5
Littleville 925 C1
Livingston▲ 3,530 B5
Loachapoka 259 G5
Lockhart 484 F8
Locust Fork 342 E3
Longview 475 E4
Louisville 728 G7
Lower Peach Tree 926 C7
Lowndesboro 139 E6
Loxley 1,161 C9
Luverne▲ 2,555 F7
Lynn 611 C2
Madison 14,904 E1
Madrid 211 H8
Magnolia Springs 800 C10
Malvern 570 G8
Manchester 400 D3
Maplesville 725 E5
Margaret 616 F3
Marion Junction 400 D6
Marion▲ 4,211 D5
Maylene 500 E4
McCalla 657 E4
McCullough 500 D8
McIntosh 250 B8
McKenzie 464 E7
McWilliams 305 D7
Memphis 54 B4
Mentone 474 G1
Meridianville 2,852 F1
Midfield 5,559 E4
Midland City 1,819 H8
Midway 455 H6
Mignon 1,548 F4
Millbrook 6,050 F6
Millerville 345 G4
Millport 1,203 B3
Millry 781 B7
Minter 450 D6
Mobile▲ 196,278 B9
Monroeville▲ 6,993 D7
Monrovia 500 E1
Montevallo 4,239 E4
Montgomery (cap.)▲ 187,106 F6
Montrose 750 C9
Moody 4,921 F3
Mooresville 54 E1
Morris 1,136 E3
Morvin 355 C7
Moulton▲ 3,248 D2
Moundville 1,348 C5
Mount Vernon 902 B8
Mountain Brook 19,810 E4
Mountainboro 261 F2
Munford 700 G3
Muscle Shoals 9,611 C1
Myrtlewood 197 C6
Nanafalia 500 B6
Napier Field 462 H8
Nauvoo 240 D3
Nectar 238 E3
Needham 99 B7
New Brockton 1,184 G8
New Hope 2,248 F1
New Market 1,094 F1
New Site 669 G4
Newbern 222 C5
Newton 1,580 G8
Newville 531 H8
North Johns 177 D4
Northport 17,366 C4
Notasulga 979 G5
Oak Grove 436 B9
Oak Grove 638 F4
Oak Hill 28 D7
Oakman 846 D3
Odenville 796 F3
Ohatchee 1,042 G3
Oneonta▲ 4,844 E3
Onycha 150 F8
Opelika▲ 22,122 H5
Opp 6,985 F8
Orange Beach 2,253 C10
Orrville 234 D6
Owens Cross Roads 695 E1
Oxford 9,362 G3
Ozark▲ 12,922 G8
Paint Rock 214 F1
Parrish 1,433 D3
Pelham 9,765 E4
Pell City▲ 8,118 F3
Pennington 302 B6
Perdido 500 C8
Peterman 600 D7
Peterson D4
Petrey 80 F7
Phenix City▲ 25,312 H6
Phil Campbell 1,317 C2
Pickensville 169 B4
Piedmont 5,288 G3
Pinckard 618 G8
Pine Apple 365 E7
Pine Hill 481 C7
Pinson 10,987 E3
Pisgah 652 G1
Plantersville 650 E5
Pleasant Grove 8,458 D4
Point Clear 2,125 C10
Pollard 100 D8
Powell's Crossroads 636 G1
Prattville▲ 19,587 E6
Priceville 1,323 E1
Prichard 34,311 B9
Providence 307 C6
Ragland 1,807 F3
Rainbow City 7,673 F3
Rainsville 3,875 G2
Ramer 680 F6
Ranburne 447 H3
Red Bay 3,451 B2
Red Level 588 E8
Reece City 657 G2
Reform 2,105 C4
Remlap 800 E3
Renfroe 400 F4
Repton 293 D8
Republic 500 E3
River Falls 710 E8

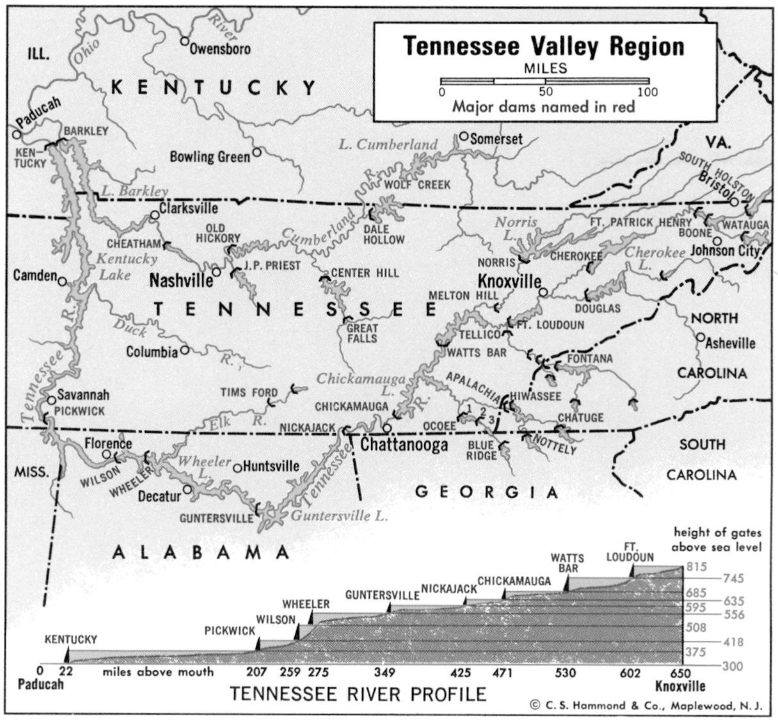
Tennessee Valley Region
MILES
0 50 100
Major dams named in red
ILL.
KENTUCKY
Owensboro
Paducah
KENTUCKY
BARKLEY
Bowling Green
L. Cumberland
Somerset
WOLF CREEK
VA.
SOUTH HOLSTON
Bristol
L. Barkley
Clarksville
DALE HOLLOW
OLD HICKORY
CHEATHAM
Kentucky Lake
J.P. PRIEST
Nashville
CENTER HILL
Norris L.
FT. PATRICK HENRY
BOONE
WATAUGA
NORRIS
CHEROKEE
Cherokee L.
Johnson City
Camden
Knoxville
MELTON HILL
TENNESSEE
FT. LOUDOUN
DOUGLAS
NORTH
GREAT FALLS
TELLICO
Asheville
Columbia
WATTS BAR
FONTANA
CAROLINA
Chickamauga L.
APALACHIA
Savannah
PICKWICK
TIMS FORD
CHICKAMAUGA
HIWASSEE
CHATUGE
Elk R.
NICKAJACK
OCOEE
BLUE RIDGE
NOTTELY
Florence
Chattanooga
SOUTH
MISS.
WILSON
WHEELER
Wheeler L.
Huntsville
CAROLINA
Decatur
GEORGIA
GUNTERSVILLE
Guntersville L.
ALABAMA
height of gates above sea level
KENTUCKY
PICKWICK
WILSON
WHEELER
GUNTERSVILLE
NICKAJACK
CHICKAMAUGA
WATTS BAR
FT. LOUDOUN
815
745
685
635
595
556
508
418
375
300
0 22 miles above mouth 207 259 275 349 425 471 530 602 650
Paducah
Knoxville
TENNESSEE RIVER PROFILE

(continued on following page)

Agriculture, Industry and Resources

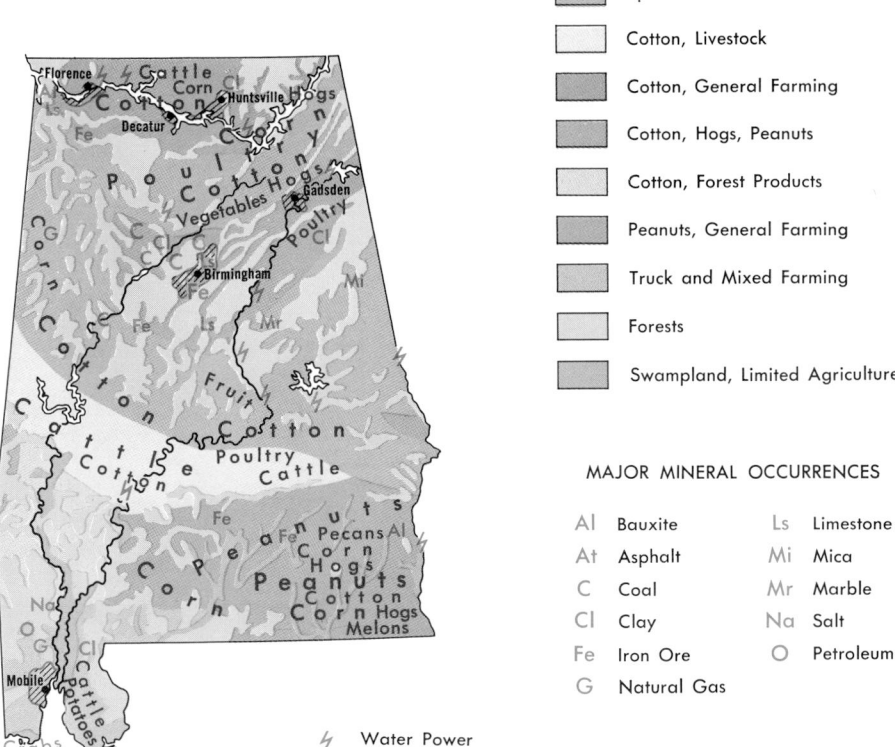

DOMINANT LAND USE

- Specialized Cotton
- Cotton, Livestock
- Cotton, General Farming
- Cotton, Hogs, Peanuts
- Cotton, Forest Products
- Peanuts, General Farming
- Truck and Mixed Farming
- Forests
- Swampland, Limited Agriculture

MAJOR MINERAL OCCURRENCES

Al	Bauxite	Ls	Limestone
At	Asphalt	Mi	Mica
C	Coal	Mr	Marble
Cl	Clay	Na	Salt
Fe	Iron Ore	O	Petroleum
G	Natural Gas		

Water Power

Major Industrial Areas

Topography

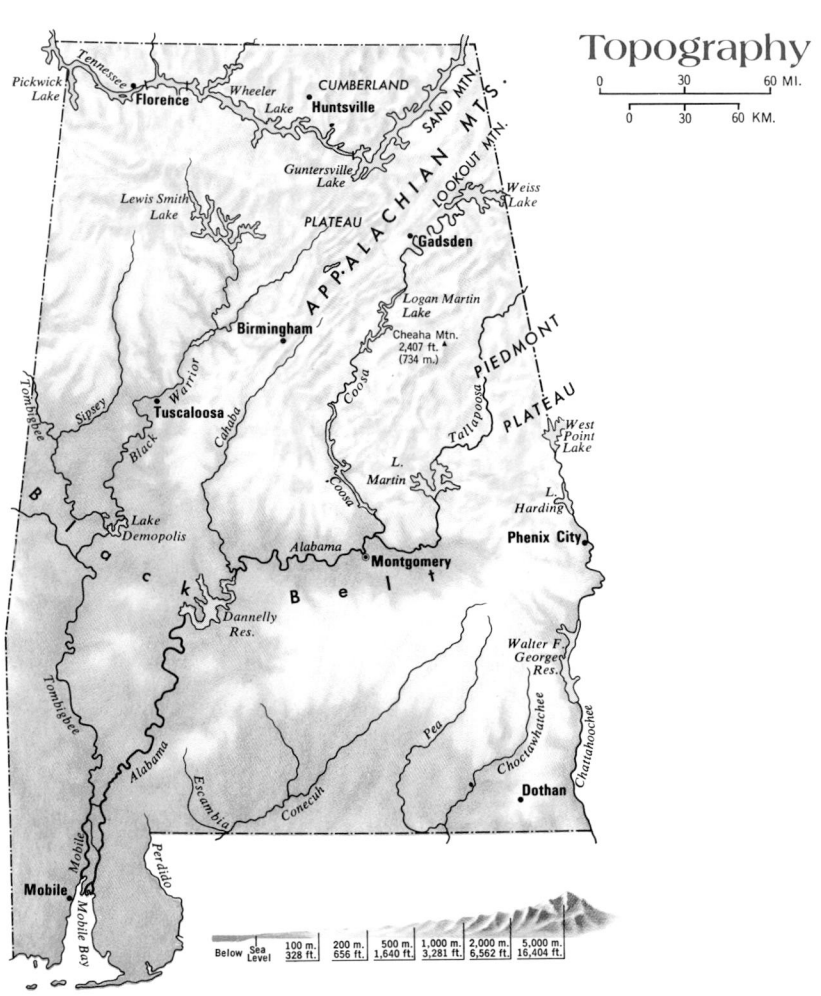

0   30   60 MI.
0   30   60 KM.

Cheaha Mtn.
2,407 ft.
(734 m.)

Below Sea Level	100 m. 328 ft.	200 m. 656 ft.	500 m. 1,640 ft.	1,000 m. 3,281 ft.	2,000 m. 6,562 ft.	5,000 m. 16,404 ft.

River View 1,314 ....H5
Riverside 1,004 ....F3
Riverview 90 ....D8
Roanoke 6,362 ....H4
Robertsdale 2,401 ....C9
Rock Mills 600 ....H4
Rockford▲ 461 ....F5
Rogersville 1,125 ....D1
Roosevelt City 3,352 ....E4
Rosa 139 ....E3
Rural C7
Russellville▲ 7,812 ....C2
Rutledge 473 ....F7
Saginaw 475 ....E4
Saint Elmo 700 ....B10
Saint Florian 388 ....C1
Saint Stephens 700 ....B7
Salem 350 ....H5
Salitpa 550 ....C7
Samantha 400 ....C4
Samson 2,190 ....F8
Sanford 282 ....F8
Saraland 11,751 ....B9
Sardis 1,301 ....E6
Sardis 883 ....F2
Satsuma 5,194 ....B9
Sayre 700 ....E3
Scottsboro▲ 13,786 ....F1
Seale 350 ....H6
Section 777 ....G1
Selma▲ 23,755 ....E6
Selmont 3,823 ....E6
Shady Grove F7
Shawmut 2,284 ....H5
Sheffield 10,380 ....C1
Shelby 500 ....E4
Shiloh 252 ....C6
Shiloh 297 ....G2
Shorter 461 ....G6
Shorterville 400 ....H7
Silas 245 ....B7
Silverhill 556 ....C9
Sipsey 568 ....D3
Slocomb 1,906 ....G8
Smiths 3,456 ....H5
Snead 632 ....F2
Somerville 211 ....E2
South 543 ....E8
Southside 5,580 ....F3
Spanish Fort 3,732 ....C9
Spring Valley 600 ....C1
Springville 1,910 ....E3
Stapleton 975 ....C9
Steele 1,046 ....F3
Sterrett 350 ....F4
Stevenson 2,046 ....G1
Stewart 450 ....C5
Stockton 500 ....C9
Suggsville 400 ....C7
Sulligent 1,886 ....B3
Sumiton 2,604 ....D3
Summerdale 559 ....C10
Sunny South 350 ....C7
Sweet Water 243 ....C6
Sycamore 800 ....F4
Sylacauga 12,520 ....F4
Sylvania 932 ....G1
Talladega Springs 148 ......F4
Talladega▲ 18,175 ....F4
Tallassee 5,112 ....G5
Tanner 600 ....E1
Tarrant 8,046 ....E3
Taylor 1,352 ....H8
Theodore 6,509 ....B9
Thomaston 497 ....C6
Thomasville 4,301 ....C7
Thorsby 1,465 ....E5
Tibbie 675 ....B8
Town Creek 1,379 ....D1
Townley 500 ....D3
Toxey 211 ....B7
Trafford 739 ....E3
Triana 499 ....E1
Trinity 1,380 ....D1
Troy▲ 13,051 ....G7
Trussville 8,266 ....E3
Tuscaloosa▲ 77,759 ....C4
Tuscumbia▲ 8,413 ....C1
Tuskegee Institute G6
Tuskegee▲ 12,257 ....G6
Union 321 ....C5
Union Grove 119 ....E2
Union Springs▲ 3,975 ......G6
Uniontown 1,730 ....D6
Uriah 450 ....D8
Valhermoso Springs 500 ...E2
Valley 8,173 ....H5
Valley Head 577 ....G1
Vance 248 ....D4
Vandiver 700 ....F4
Verbena 500 ....E5
Vernon▲ 2,247 ....B3
Vestavia Hills 19,749 ....E4
Vina 356 ....B2
Vincent 1,767 ....F4
Vinemont E2
Vredenburgh 313 ....D7
Wadley 517 ....G4
Wadsworth 500 ....E5
Wagarville 550 ....B8
Waldo 309 ....F4
Walker Springs 500 ....C7
Walnut Grove 717 ....F2
Warrior 3,280 ....E3
Waterloo 250 ....B1
Wattsville 550 ....F3
Waverly 152 ....G5
Weaver 2,715 ....G3
Webb 1,039 ....H8
Wedowee▲ 796 ....H4
Wegra D3
Weogufka 500 ....F4
West Blocton 1,468 ....D4
West Jefferson 388 ....D3
West Point 257 ....D2
West Selmont 5,255 ....E6
Weston 384 ....B2

Westover 500 ....E
Wetumpka▲ 4,670 ....F
Whatley 800 C
White Hall 814 ....E
White Plains 350 ....G
Whites Chapel 336 ....G
Wicksburg 400 ....G
Wilmer 494 ....B
Wilsonville 1,185 ....E
Wilton 602 ....E
Winfield 3,689 C
Woodland 189 ....G
Woodstock 340 ....D
Woodville 687 ....G
Yantley 500 ....B
Yellow Bluff 245 C
Yellow Pine 350 ....B
York 3,160 ....B

OTHER FEATURES

Alabama (riv.) C
Aliceville (dam) ....B
Anniston Army Depot ....G
Bankhead (lake) ....D
Bartletts Ferry (dam) ....H
Big Canoe (creek) ....E
Big Creek (lake) ....D
Black Warrior (riv.) C
Bon Secour (bay) C1
Brookley Air Force Base ...B
Buttahatchee (riv.) ....B
Cahaba (riv.) ....D
Cedar (pt.) B1
Chattahoochee (riv.) ....H
Chattooga (riv.) ....H
Cheaha (mt.) ....G
Choctawhatchee (riv.) ......H
Coffeeville (dam) ....B
Conecuh (riv.) ....E
Coosa (riv.) ....F
Cowikee, North Fork (creek) ...H
Cumberland (plat.) ....F
Dannelly (res.) ....D
Demopolis (dam) C
Elk (riv.) ....D
Escambia (creek) ....D
Escambia (riv.) ....D
Escatawpa (riv.) ....B
Fort Gaines B1
Fort McClellan
    Military Reservation 4,128..G
Fort Morgan C
Fort Rucker 7,593 ....G
Gainesville (dam) ....B
Goat Rock (dam) ....H
Goat Rock (lake) ....H
Grants Pass (chan.) B1
Gunter Air Force Base ......F
Guntersville (dam) ....G
Guntersville (lake) ....G
Harding (lake) ....H
Herbes (isl.) ....B
Holt (dam) ....D
Horseshoe Bend
    Nat'l Mil. Park ....G
Inland (lake) ....E
Jordan (dam) ....F
Jordan (lake) ....F
Lay (dam) ....E
Lewis Smith (dam) ....D
Lewis Smith (lake) ....D
Little (riv.) ....H
Little (riv.) ....G
Locust Fork (riv.) ....E
Logan Martin (lake) ....F
Lookout (mt.) ....G
Martin (dam) ....G
Martin (lake) ....G
Maxwell Air Force Base ....E
Mexico (gulf) ....B
Mississippi (sound) B1
Mitchell (lake) ....F
Mobile (bay) B1
Mobile (pt.) ....B
Mobile (riv.) ....B
Mulberry (creek) ....D
Mulberry Fork (riv.) ....D
Neely Henry (lake) ....F
Oakmulgee (creek) ....D
Oliver (dam) ....H
Paint Rock (riv.) ....E
Patsaliga (creek) ....F
Pea (riv.) ....G
Perdido (bay) D1
Perdido (riv.) ....E
Pickwick (lake) ....B
Pigeon (creek) ....E
Redstone Arsenal ....E
Russell Cave Nat'l Mon. ...B1
Sand (mt.) ....G
Sandy (creek) ....H
Sepulga (riv.) ....E
Sipsey (riv.) C
Sipsey Fork (riv.) ....D
Tallapoosa (riv.) ....G
Tennessee (riv.) ....D
Tennessee-Tombigbee
    Waterway ....B
Tensaw (riv.) C
Thurlow (dam) ....G
Tombigbee (riv.) ....B
Town (creek) ....F
Tuscaloosa (lake) C
Tuskegee Institute
    Nat'l Hist. Site ....G
Walter F. George (dam) ....H
Walter F. George (res.) .....H
Warrior (dam) ....D
Weiss (lake) ....G
West Point (lake) ....H
Wheeler (dam) ....D
Wheeler (lake) ....D
Wilson (dam) ....D
Yates (dam) ....G

▲County seat.

Alabama

SCALE
0 5 10 20 30 40 MI.

0 5 10 20 30 40 KM.

State Capitals ⊛
County Seats ⊙
Major Limited Access Hwys. ▬▬▬

Scale 1:1,930,000

© Copyright HAMMOND INCORPORATED, Maplewood, N.J.

GULF OF MEXICO

CITIES and TOWNS

Akiachak 481 ....F2
Akolmiut (Kasigluk) F2
Akutan 589 ....E4
Alakanuk 544 ....E2
Anchor Point 866 ....B2
Anchorage 226,338 ....B1
Anderson 628 ....H2
Angoon 638 ....M1
Aniak 540 ....G2
Barrow 3,469 ....G1
Bethel 4,674 ....F2
Big Lake 1,477 ....B1
Butte 2,039 ....C1
Chevak 598 ....E2
Clear 504 ....J2
Clover Pass 451 ....N2
Cohoe 508 ....B1
College 11,249 ....J1
Copper Center 449 ....J2
Cordova 2,110 ....D1
Craig 1,260 ....M2
Delta Junction 652 ....J2
Dillingham 2,017 ....G3
Emanguk (Emmonak) 567 ......E2
Fairbanks 30,843 ....J2
Fort Yukon 580 ....J1
Fritz Creek 1,426 ....B2
Galena 833 ....G2
Gambell 525 ....D2
Glennallen 451 ....D1
Haines 1,238 ....M1
Healy 487 ....J2

Homer 3,660 ....B2
Hoonah 795 ....M1
Hooper Bay 845 ....E2
Houston 697 ....B1
Hydaburg 384 ....M2
Juneau (cap.) 26,751 ....N1
Kachemak City 365 ....B2
Kake 700 ....M1
Kasigluk 425 ....F2
Kasilof 383 ....B1
Kenai 6,327 ....B1
Ketchikan 8,263 ....N2
Kiana 385 ....F1
King Cove 451 ....F4
King Salmon 696 ....G3
Kipnuk 470 ....F2
Klawock (Klawak) 722 ....M2
Kodiak 6,365 ....H3
Kotlik 461 ....F2
Kotzebue 2,751 ....F1
Kwethluk 558 ....F2
Manokotak 385 ....G3
McGrath 528 ....H2
Metlakatla 1,407 ....N2
Mountain Point 396 ....N2
Mountain Village 674 ....E2
Naknek 575 ....G3
Nenana 393 ....J2
New Stuyahok 391 ....G3
Ninilchik 456 ....B1
Nome 3,500 ....E2
Noorvik 531 ....F1
North Pole 1,456 ....J2
Nulato 359 ....G2

Nunapitchuk 378 ....F2
Palmer 2,866 ....C1
Petersburg 3,207 ....N2
Pilot Station 463 ....F2
Point Hope 639 ....E1
Quinhagak 501 ....F3
Saint Marys (Andreafski) 441 ..F2
Saint Paul Island 763 ....D3
Sand Point 878 ....G3
Savoonga 519 ....E2
Saxman 369 ....N2
Selawik 596 ....F1
Seward 2,699 ....C1
Shishmaref 456 ....E1
Sitka 8,588 ....M1
Skagway 692 ....M1
Soldotna 3,482 ....B1
Stebbins 400 ....F2
Sterling 3,802 ....B1
Thorne Bay 569 ....M2
Togiak 613 ....F3
Tok 935 ....K2
Toksook Bay 420 ....F2
Unalakleet 714 ....G2
Unalaska 3,089 ....E4
Valdez 4,068 ....D1
Wainwright 492 ....F1
Wasilla 4,028 ....B1
Wrangell 2,479 ....N2
Yakutat 534 ....L3

OTHER FEATURES

Adak (isl.) L4

Admiralty (isl.) M1
Afognak (isl.) H3
Agattu (isl.) J3
Akutan (isl.) E4
Alaska (gulf) K3
Alaska (range) H2
Aleutian (isls.) J4
Aleutian (range) G3
Alexander (arch.) L1
Amchitka (isl.) K4
Amlia (passage) L4
Amukta (isl.) D4
Andreanof (isls.) L4
Atka (isl.) L4
Attu (isl.) J3
Baird (mts.) F1
Baranof (isl.) M1
Barrow (pt.) G1
Bear (mt.) K2
Beaufort (sea) K1
Becharof (lake) G3
Bering (glac.) K2
Bering (sea) D2
Bering (str.) E1
Blackburn (mt.) K2
Bona (mt.) K2
Bristol (bay) F3
British (mts.) K1
Brooks (range) G1
Chandalar (riv.) J1
Chatham (str.) M1
Chichagof (isl.) M1
Chignik (bay) G3
Chilkoot (pass) M1

Chirikof (isl.) G3
Chitina (riv.) K2
Christian (sound) M2
Chugash (mts.) C1
Chukchi (sea) E1
Clarence (str.) N2
Clark (lake) H2
Clear (cape) D1
Coast (mts.) N1
Columbia (glac.) C1
Colville (riv.) G1
Constantine (cape) G3
Cook (inlet) B1
Cook (mt.) K2
Copper (riv.) J2
Cordova (bay) M2
Coronation (isl.) M2
Cross (sound) L1
Dease (inlet) H1
Decision (cape) M2
Denali Nat'l Park H2
Devils Paw (mt.) N1
Dixon Entrance (chan.) M2
Douglas (mt.) H3
Dry (bay) L3
Eielson A.F.B. 5,251 ....J2
Elmendorf A.F.B. B1
Endicott (mts.) H1
Etolin (isl.) N2
Fairweather (cape) L1
Fairweather (mt.) L1
Firth (riv.) K1
Foraker (mt.) H2
Fort Davis E2

Fort Greely 1,147 ....J2
Fort Richardson C1
Fort Wainwright J1
Four Mountains (isls.) E4
Fox (isls.) E4
Frederick (sound) N1
Gates of the Arctic Nat'l Park ..H1
Glacier (bay) M1
Glacier Bay Nat'l Park M1
Goodhope (bay) F1
Great Sitkin (isl.) L4
Guyot (glac.) K2
Hagemeister (isl.) F3
Halkett (cape) H1
Hall (isl.) D2
Harding Icefield C2
Harrison (bay) H1
Hayes (mt.) J2
Hazen (bay) E2
Hinchinbrook (isl.) D1
Hoonah (sound) M1
Hope (pt.) E1
Howard (pass) G1
Icy (bay) K3
Icy (cape) K3
Icy (pt.) L1
Icy (str.) M1
Iliamna (lake) G3
Iliamna (vol.) H3
Innoko (riv.) G2
Kachemak (bay) B2
Kanaga (isl.) L4
Kates Needle (mt.) N1
Katmai (vol.) H3

Katmai Nat'l Park H3
Kayak (isl.) K3
Kenai (lake) C1
Kenai (mts.) C2
Kenai (pen.) C2
Kenai Fjords Nat'l Park C3
Kennedy Entrance (str.) H3
King (isl.) M1
Kiska (isl.) J4
Kiska (vol.) J4
Klondike Gold Rush Nat'l
  Hist. Park N1
Knight (isl.) C1
Knik Arm (inlet) C1
Kobuk (riv.) F1
Kobuk Valley Nat'l Park F1
Kodiak (isl.) H3
Kotzebue (sound) E1
Koyukuk (riv.) G2
Krusenstern (cape) F1
Kuiu (isl.) M2
Kuk (riv.) G1
Kuskokwim (bay) F3
Kuskokwim (mts.) G2
Kuskokwim (riv.) G2
Kvichak (bay) G3
Lake Clark Nat'l Park H2
Lisburne (cape) E1
Little Diomede (isl.) E1
Little Sitkin (isl.) K4
Lynn Canal (inlet) M1
Makushin (vol.) E4
Malaspina (glac.) K3
Marcus Baker (mt.) C1

Agriculture, Industry and Resources

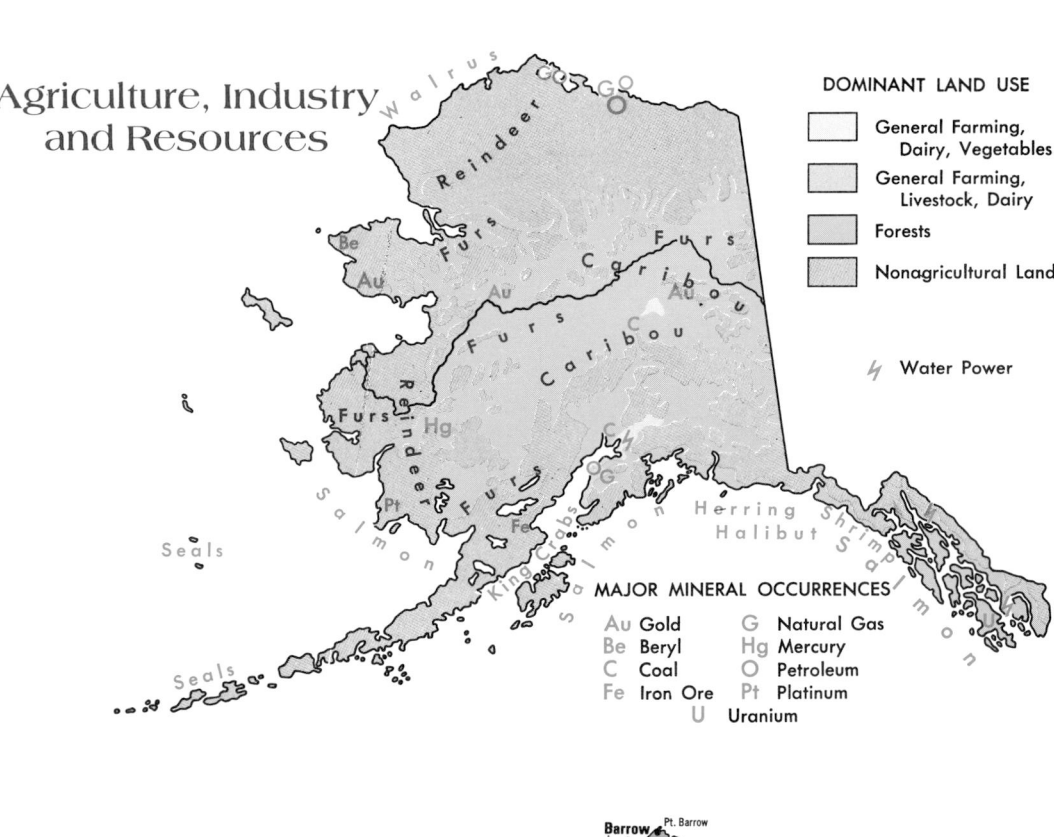

DOMINANT LAND USE

- General Farming, Dairy, Vegetables
- General Farming, Livestock, Dairy
- Forests
- Nonagricultural Land

⚡ Water Power

MAJOR MINERAL OCCURRENCES

Au Gold   G Natural Gas
Be Beryl   Hg Mercury
C Coal   O Petroleum
Fe Iron Ore   Pt Platinum
U Uranium

Topography

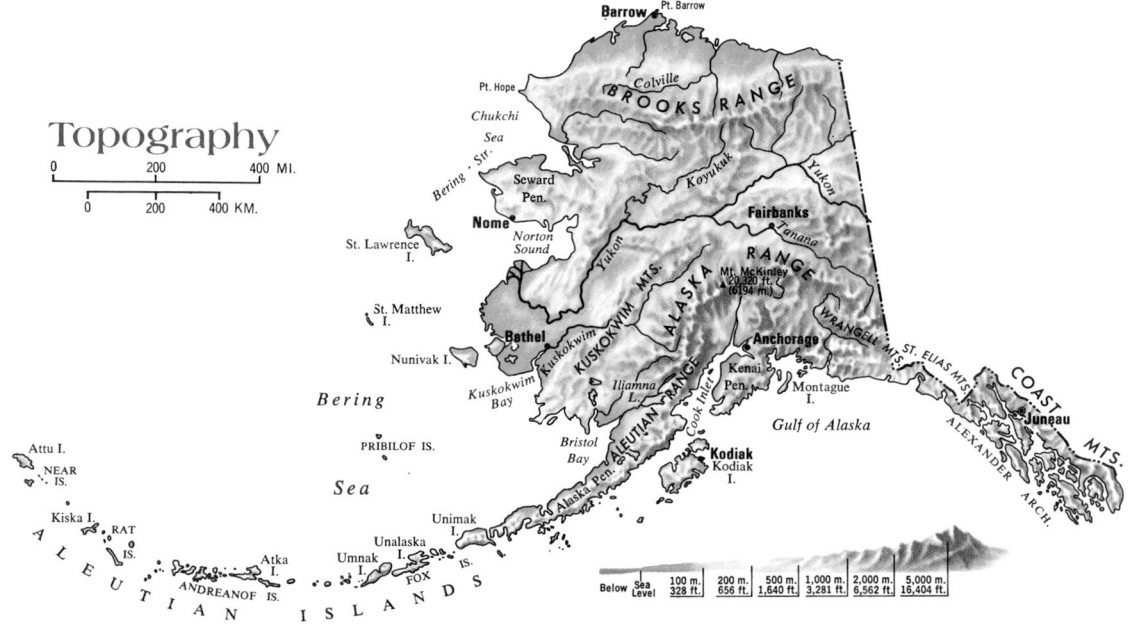

Alaska

POLYCONIC PROJECTION
SCALE
0 50 100 150 200 MI.
0 50 100 150 200 KM.

State and Territorial Capitals .... ⊛
International Boundaries .... — — —
Major Highways

Scale 1:10,500,000

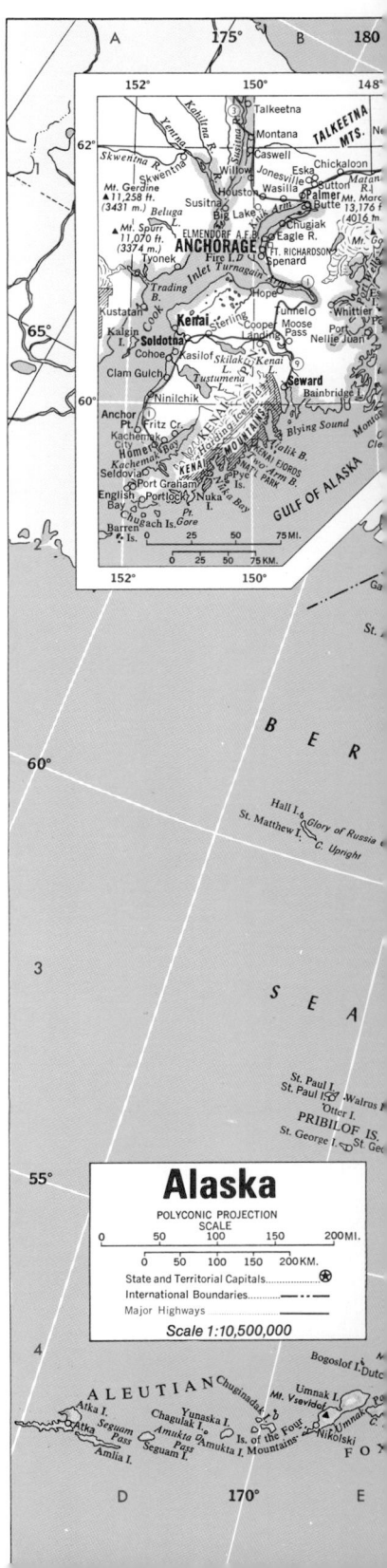

Marmot (isl.) H3	Port Clarence (inlet) E1
Matanuska (riv.) C1	Port Heiden (inlet) G1
McKinley (mt.) H2	Portland Canal (inlet) N2
Meade (riv.) G1	Port Moller (inlet) F3
Mendenhall (cape) E3	Port Wells (inlet) C1
Mentasta (pass) K2	Pribilof (isls.) D3
Merrill (pass) H2	Prince of Wales (cape) N2
Michelson (pass) K1	Prince of Wales (isl.) N2
Middleton (isl.) J3	Prince William (sound) D1
Misty Fjords Nat'l Mon. N2	Prudhoe (bay) H1
Mitkof (isl.) M1	Rat (isls.) K4
Montague (isl.) D1	Redoubt (vol.) H2
Muir (glac.) M1	Revillagigedo (chan.) N2
Mulchatna (riv.) G2	Revillagigedo (isl.) N2
Muzon (cape) M2	Romanzof (cape) E2
Naknek (lake) G3	Saint Elias (cape) K3
Near (isls.) H3	Saint Elias (mt.) K2
Nelson (isl.) E2	Saint George (isl.) D3
Newenham (cape) F3	Saint Lawrence (isl.) B1
Noatak (riv.) F1	Saint Matthew (isl.) B1
Norton (bay) F2	Saint Paul (isl.) D3
Norton (sound) E2	Salisbury (sound) M1
Nowitna (riv.) H2	Sanak (isl.) F4
Nuka (bay) C2	Sanford (mt.) K2
Nunivak (isl.) E3	Schwatka (mts.) G1
Nushagak (riv.) G2	Seguam (isl.) D4
Nuyakuk (lake) G2	Selawik (lake) F1
Ommaney (cape) M2	Semichi (isls.) J3
Otter (isl.) D3	Semidi (isls.) G3
Pastol (bay) F2	Semisopochnoi (isl.) K4
Pavlof (bay) F3	Seward (pen.) E1
Pavlof (vol.) F3	Sheenjek (riv.) K1
Philip Smith (mts.) J1	Shelikof (str.) H3
Porcupine (riv.) K1	

Shemya (isl.) J3	Tugidak (isl.) G3
Shishaldin (vol.) E4	Turnagain Arm (inlet) B1
Shumagin (isls.) G4	Tustumena (lake) C1
Shuyak (isl.) H3	Two Arm (bay) C2
Sitka (sound) M1	Ugashik (lakes) G3
Sitka Nat'l Hist. Park M1	Umnak (isl.) E4
Sitk nak (str.) H3	Umnak (passage) E4
Skilak (lake) C1	Unalaska (isl.) E4
Skwentna (riv.) A1	Unga (isl.) F3
Smith (bay) H1	Unimak (isl.) E4
Spencer (cape) L1	Unimak (passage) F4
Stephens (passage) N1	Utukok (riv.) F1
Stevenson Entrance (str.) H3	Valley of Ten
Stikine (riv.) N2	Thousand Smokes G3
Stikine (str.) N2	Vancouver (mt.) L2
Stony (riv.) G2	Veniaminof (crater) F3
Stuart (isl.) F2	Vsevidof (mt.) E4
Suemez (isl.) M2	Walrus (isl.) E3
Sumner (str.) M2	Walrus (isls.) E3
Susitna (riv.) B1	Waring (mts.) G1
Sutwik (isl.) G3	West Point (mt.) K2
Taku (glac.) N1	White (pass) N1
Taku (riv.) N1	White (riv.) K2
Talkeetna (mts.) J2	White Mountains Nat'l
Tanaga (isl.) K4	Rec .Area J1
Tanaga (vol.) K4	Witherspoon (mt.) C1
Tanana (riv.) J2	Wrangell (cape) H3
Tay or (mts.) J2	Wrangell (isl.) N2
Tazlina (lake) D1	Wrangell (mts.) N2
Tazlina (riv.) D1	Wrangell-St. Elias Nat'l Park ...K2
Teshekpuk (lake) H1	Yakobi (isl.) M1
Tikchik (lakes) G2	Yakutat (bay) K3
Tigalda (isl.) F4	Yentna (riv.) A1
Togiak (bay) F3	Yukon (riv.) F2

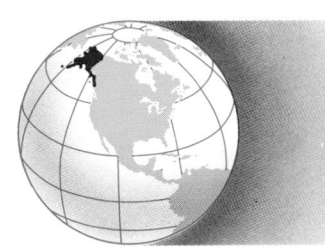

AREA 591,004 sq. mi. (1,530,700 sq. km.)
POPULATION 551,947
CAPITAL Juneau
LARGEST CITY Anchorage
HIGHEST POINT Mt. McKinley 20,320 ft. (6194 m.)
SETTLED IN 1801
ADMITTED TO UNION January 3, 1959
POPULAR NAME Great Land; Last Frontier
STATE FLOWER Forget-me-not
STATE BIRD Willow Ptarmigan

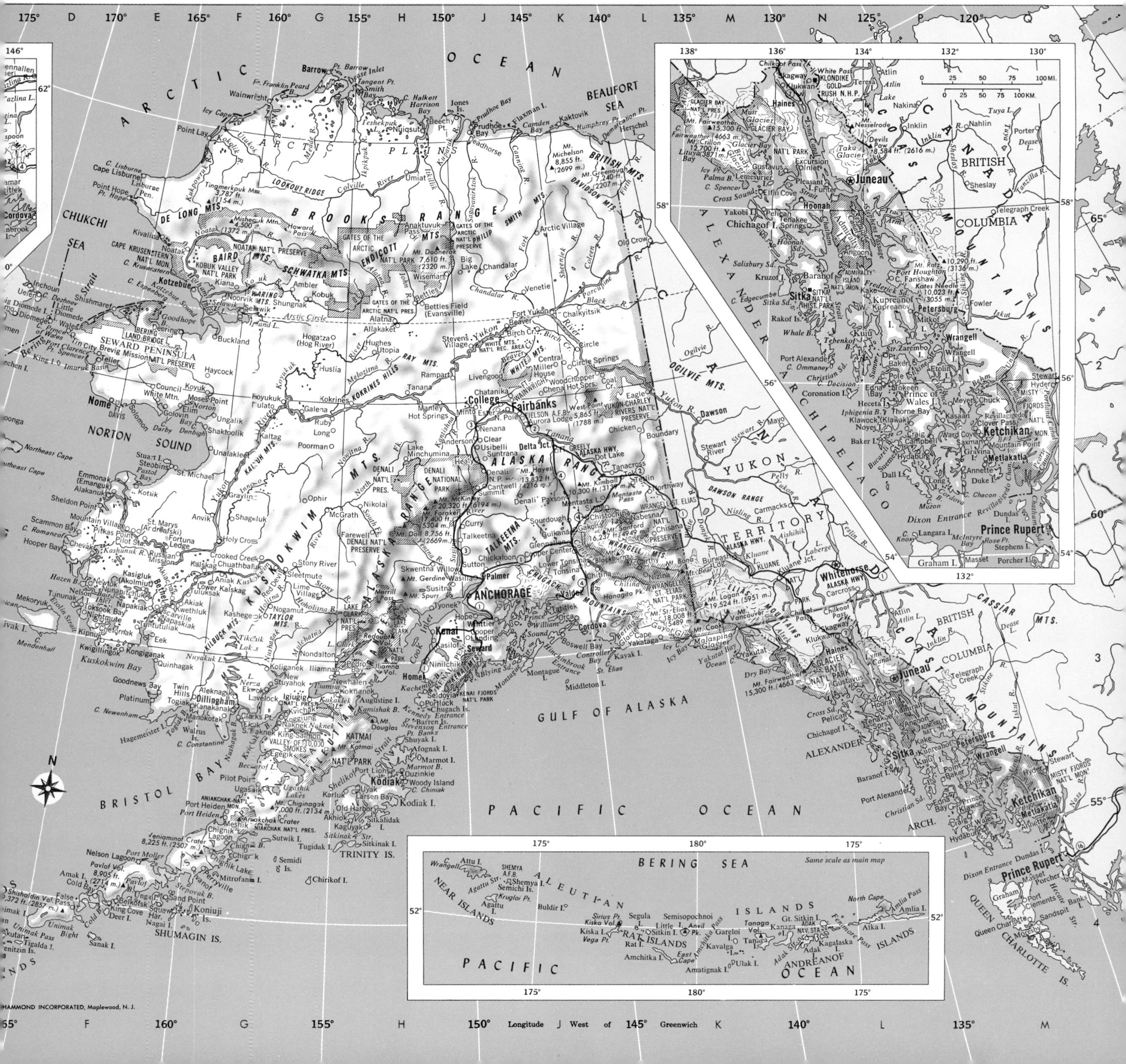

HAMMOND INCORPORATED, Maplewood, N.J.

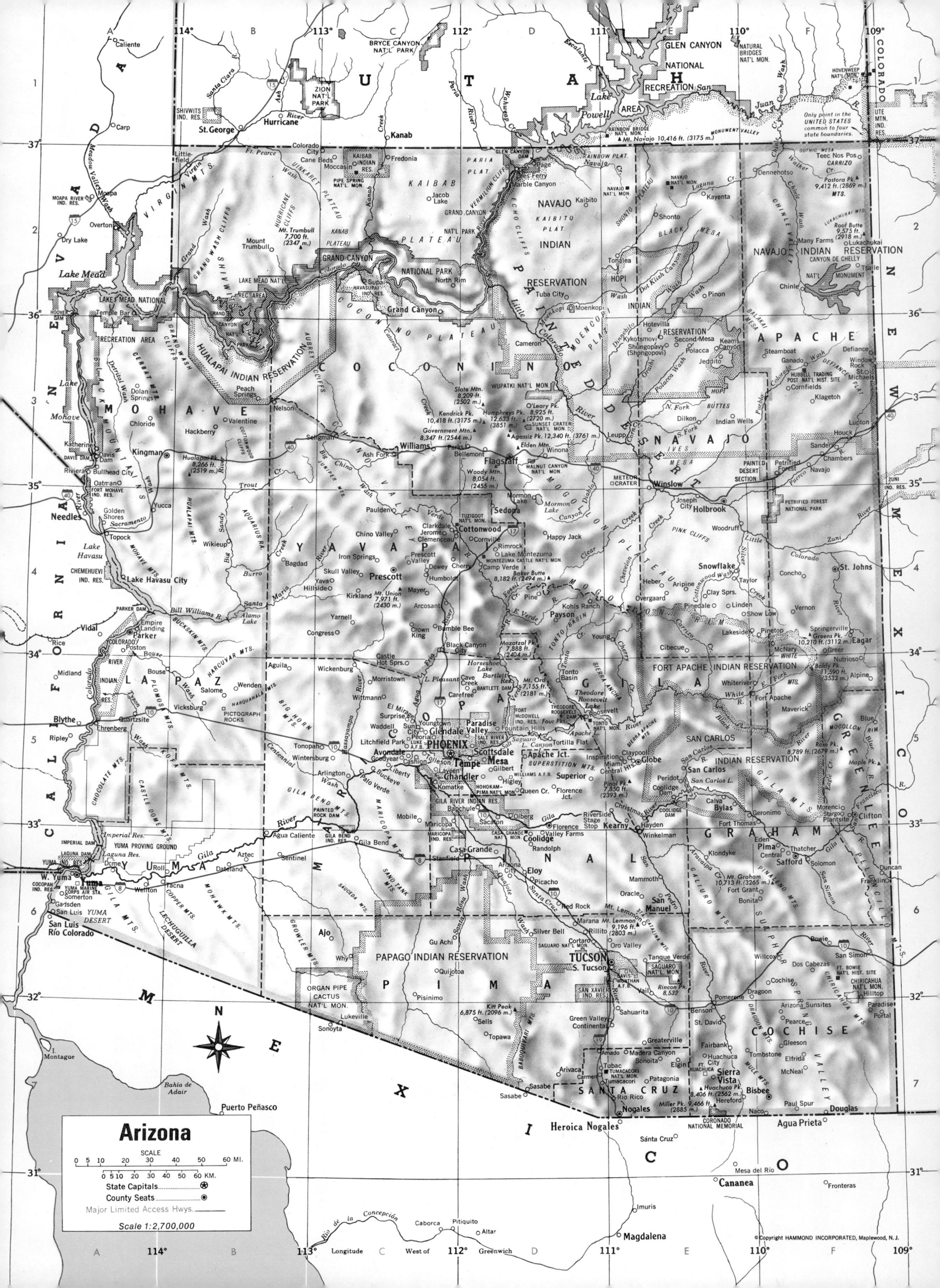

Arizona

SCALE

0 5 10 20 30 40 50 60 MI.

0 5 10 20 30 40 50 60 KM.

State Capitals............⊗

County Seats.............○

Major Limited Access Hwys._____

Scale 1:2,700,000

© Copyright HAMMOND INCORPORATED, Maplewood, N.J.

AREA 114,000 sq. mi. (295,260 sq. km.)
POPULATION 3,677,985
CAPITAL Phoenix
LARGEST CITY Phoenix
HIGHEST POINT Humphreys Pk. 12,633 ft.
(3851 m.)
SETTLED IN 1752
ADMITTED TO UNION February 14, 1912
POPULAR NAME Grand Canyon State
STATE FLOWER Saguaro Cactus Blossom
STATE BIRD Cactus Wren

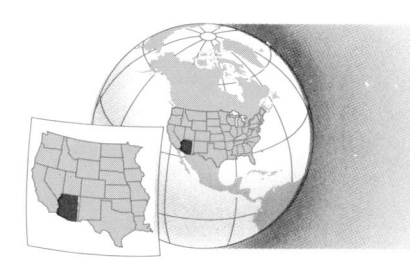

Agriculture, Industry and Resources

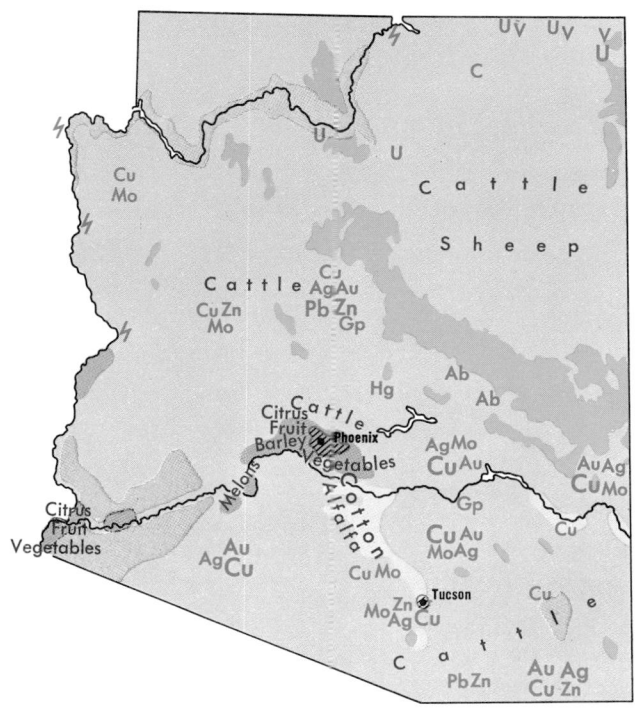

MAJOR MINERAL OCCURRENCES

Ab	Asbestos	Cu	Copper	Pb	Lead
Ag	Silver	Gp	Gypsum	U	Uranium
Au	Gold	Hg	Mercury	V	Vanadium
C	Coal	Mo	Molybdenum	Zn	Zinc

DOMINANT LAND USE

Fruit, Truck and Mixed Farming

Cotton and Alfalfa

General Farming, Livestock, Special Crops

Range Livestock

Forests

Nonagricultural Land

⚡ Water Power

▨ Major Industrial Areas

COUNTIES

Apache 61,591 ....F3
Cochise 97,624 ....F7
Coconino 96,591 ....C3
Gila 40,216........................E5
Graham 26,554 ....E6
Greenlee 8,008...................F5
La Paz 13,844 ....A5
Maricopa 2,122,101............C5
Mohave 93,497 ....A3
Navajo 77,658 ....E3
Pima 666,880.....................D6
Pinal 116,379.....................D6
Santa Cruz 29,676...............E7
Yavapai 107,714.................C4
Yuma 106,895 ....A5

CITIES and TOWNS

Agua Caliente 60 ....B6
Aguila 900..........................B5
Ajo 2,919............................C6
Alpine 450..........................F5
Amado 75............................D7
Apache Junction 18,100......D5
Arcosanti C4
Aripine 25 ....E4
Arivaca 400.........................D7
Arizona City 1,940 ....D6
Arizona Sunsites 825 ....F7
Arlington 950......................C5
Ash Fork 800 ....C3
Avondale 16,169.................C5
Aztec 20 ....B6
Bagdad 1,858......................B4
Bapchule 400......................D5

Bellemont 210 ....D3
Benson 3,824......................E7
Bisbee▲ 6,288.....................F7
Black Canyon City 1,811 ......C4
Blue 50................................F5
Bonita 20.............................E6
Bouse 500...........................A5
Bowie 600 ....F6
Buckeye 5,038.....................C5
Bullhead City
(Bullhead City-Riviera)
21,951 ....A3
Bumble Bee 15.....................C4
Bylas 1,219..........................E6
Calva 10 ....E5
Cameron 493.......................D3
Camp Verde 6,243...............D4
Cane Beds 30.......................B2
Carefree 1,666.....................C5
Carmen 200.........................D7
Casa Grande 19,082............D6
Cashion 3,014......................C5
Castle Hot Springs 50...........D5
Cave Creek 2,925.................D5
Central 300..........................F6
Central Heights
(Central Heights-
Midland City) 2,791..........E5
Chambers 500......................F3
Chandler 90,533..................D5
Cherry 20 ....C4
Chinle 5,059........................F2
Chino Valley 4,837...............C4
Chloride 225........................A3
Christmas 201......................E5
Cibecue 1,254 ....E4
Clarkdale 2,144....................C4

Clay Springs 500..................E4
Claypool 1,942....................E5
Clemenceau 300..................C4
Clifton▲ 2,840.....................F5
Cochise 150.........................F6
Colorado City 2,426.............B2
Concho 100..........................F4
Congress 800.......................C4
Continental 250...................D7
Coolidge 6,927.....................D6
Coolidge Dam 42.................E5
Cornfields 200......................F3
Cornville 2,089.....................D4
Cortaro 375..........................D6
Cottonwood 5,918................C4
Crown King 100....................C4
Dateland 100........................B6
Davis Dam 125.....................A3
Dennehotso 616...................F2
Dewey 100...........................C4
Dilkon 90.............................E3
Dolan Springs 1,090.............A3
Dome 48..............................A6
Dos Cabezas 30....................F6
Douglas 12,822....................F7
Dragoon 150........................F6
Duncan 662.........................F6
Eagar 4,025..........................F4
Eden 89...............................F6
Ehrenberg 1,226...................A5
El Mirage 5,001....................C5
Elfrida 700...........................F7
Elgin 525.............................E7
Eloy 7,211...........................D6
Empire Landing.....................A4
Fairbank 100........................E7
Flagstaff▲ 45,857.................D3

(continued on following page)

Topography

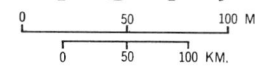

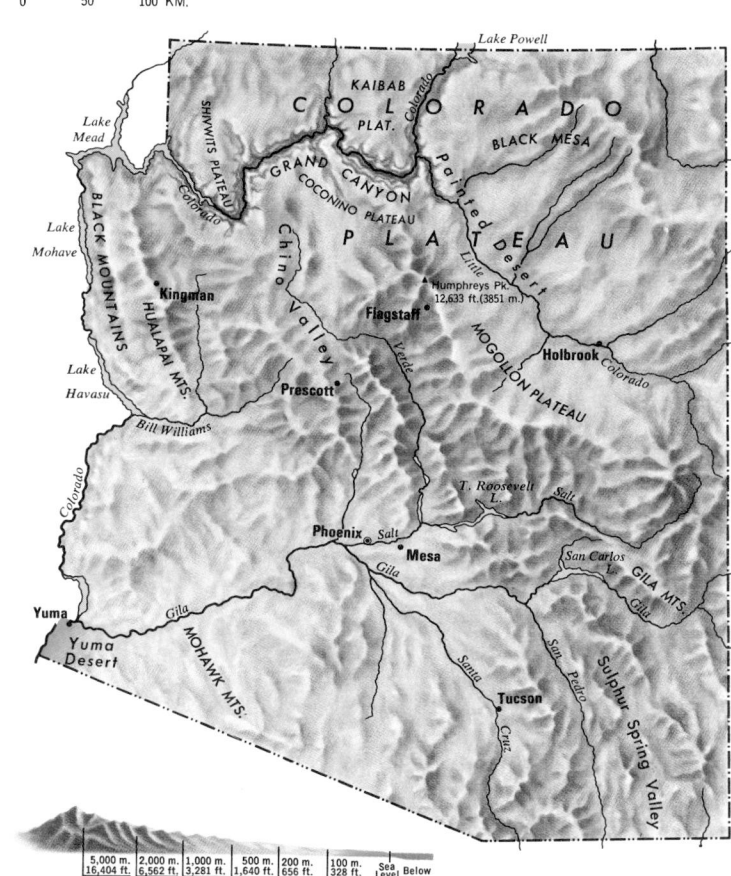

Florence▲ 7,510 ....D5
Florence Junction 35 ....D5
Fort Apache 500 ....F5
Fort Defiance 4,489 ....F3
Fort Grant 240 ....E6
Fort Thomas 450 ....E5
Fountain Hills 10,030 ....D5
Franklin 300 ....F6
Fredonia 1,207 ....C2
Gadsden 250 ....A6
Ganado 1,257 ....F3
Geronimo 25 ....F5
Gila Bend 1,747 ....C6
Gilbert 29,188 ....D5
Gleeson 15 ....F7
Glendale 148,134 ....C5
Globe▲ 6,062 ....E5
Golden Shores A4
Goodyear 6,258 ....C5
Grand Canyon 1,348 ....C2
Greaterville 15 ....E7
Green Valley 13,231 ....D7
Greer 385 ....F4
Gu Achi 339 ....C6
Hackberry 250 ....B3
Happy Jack 50 ....D4
Hayden 909 ....E5
Heber 1,581 ....E4
Hereford 10 ....E7
Higley 500 ....D5
Hillside 100 ....B4
Hilltop 9 ....F6
Holbrook▲ 4,686 ....E4
Hotevilla 869 ....E3
Houck 900 ....F3
Huachuca City 1,782 ....E7
Humboldt 787 ....C4
Indian Wells 150 ....E3
Inspiration 500 ....D5
Iron Springs 175 ....C4
Jacob Lake 16 ....C2
Jeddito 20 ....E3
Jerome 403 ....C4
Joseph City 650 ....E4
Kaibito 641 ....D2
Katherine 102 ....A3
Kayenta 4,372 ....E2
Keams Canyon 393 ....E3
Kearny 2,262 ....E5
Kingman▲ 12,722 ....A3
Kirkland 100 ....C4
Klagetoh 200 ....F3
Klondyke 86 ....E6
Kohls Ranch 100 ....D4
Komatke 1,116 ....C5
Lake Havasu City 24,363 ....A4
Lake Montezuma 1,841 ....D4
Lakeside 1,333 ....E4
Laveen 800 ....C5
Lees Ferry 10 ....D2
Leupp 857 ....E3
Liberty 150 ....C5
Linden 50 ....E4
Litchfield Park 3,303 ....C5
Littlefield 40 ....B2
Lukachukai 113 ....F2
Lukeville 50 ....C7
Lupton 250 ....F3
Madera Canyon 75 ....E7
Mammoth 1,845 ....E6
Many Farms 1,294 ....F2
Marana 2,187 ....D6
Marble Canyon 6 ....D2
Maricopa 750 ....C5
Maverick 50 ....F5
Mayer 810 ....C4
McNary 355 ....F4

McNeal 100 ....F7
Mesa 288,091 ....D5
Miami 2,018 ....E5
Mobile 100 ....C5
Moccasin 150 ....C2
Moenkopi 924 ....D2
Morenci 1,799 ....F5
Mormon Lake 20 ....D4
Morristown 400 ....C5
Mount Lemmon 400 ....E6
Mount Trumbull 14 ....B2
Naco 750 ....E7
Navajo 100 ....F3
Nelson 39 ....B3
Nogales▲ 19,489 ....E7
North Rim 50 ....C2
Nutrioso 500 ....F5
Oatman 175 ....A3
Olberg 65 ....D5
Oracle 3,043 ....E6
Oraibi 600 ....E3
Oro Valley 6,670 ....E6
Overgaard 750 ....E4
Page 6,598 ....D2
Palo Verde 500 ....C5
Paradise 15 ....F7
Paradise Valley 11,671 ....D5
Parker 2,897 ....A4
Parks 175 ....C3
Patagonia 888 ....E7
Paul Spur 34 ....F7
Paulden 350 ....C4
Payson 8,377 ....D4
Peach Springs 787 ....B3
Pearce 700 ....F7
Peoria 50,618 ....C5
Peridot 957 ....E5
Petrified Forest 80 ....F3
Phoenix (cap.)▲
    983,403 ....C5
Picacho 850 ....D6
Pima 1,725 ....F6
Pine 800 ....D4
Pinedale 400 ....E4
Pinetop 1,527 ....F4
Pinon 468 ....E2
Pisinimo 187 ....C6
Plantsite F5
Polacca 1,108 ....E3
Pomerene 365 ....E6
Portal 72 ....F7
Poston 480 ....A4
Prescott▲ 26,455 ....C4
Prescott Valley 8,858 ....C4
Quartzsite 1,876 ....A5
Queen Creek 2,667 ....D5
Quijotoa 200 ....C6
Randolph 350 ....D6
Red Rock 250 ....D6
Rillito 400 ....D6
Rimrock 217 ....D4
Rio Rico 1,407 ....E7
Riverside Stage Stop 418 ....D5
Riviera (Riviera-
    Bullhead City) A3
Roll 700 ....A6
Roosevelt 125 ....D5
Sacaton 1,452 ....D5
Safford▲ 7,359 ....F6
Sahuarita 200 ....E7
Saint David 1,468 ....E7
Saint Johns▲ 3,294 ....F4
Saint Michaels 1,119 ....F3
Salome 800 ....B5
San Carlos 2,918 ....E5
San Luis 4,212 ....A6
San Manuel 4,009 ....E6

San Simon 400 ....F6
Sanders 900 ....F3
Sasabe 50 ....D7
Scottsdale 130,069 ....D5
Second Mesa 929 ....E3
Sedona 7,720 ....D4
Seligman 510 ....B3
Sells 2,750 ....D7
Sentinel 40 ....B6
Shonto 710 ....E2
Show Low 5,019 ....F4
Shungopavy
    (Shongopovi) 570 ....E3
Sierra Vista 32,983 ....E7
Silver Bell 900 ....D6
Skull Valley 250 ....C4
Snowflake 3,510 ....E4
Solomon 700 ....F6
Somerton 5,282 ....A6
Sonoita 220 ....E7
South Tucson 5,093 ....D6
Springerville 1,802 ....F4
Stanfield 150 ....C6
Stargo 1,038 ....F5
Steamboat 100 ....F3
Sun City 38,126 ....C5
Supai 423 ....C2
Superior 3,468 ....D5
Surprise 7,122 ....C5
Tacna 950 ....B6
Tanque Verde 850 ....E6
Taylor 2,418 ....E4
Teec Nos Pos 317 ....F2
Tempe 141,865 ....D5
Temple Bar 84 ....A2
Thatcher 3,763 ....F6
Tolleson 4,434 ....C5
Tombstone 1,220 ....F7
Tonalea 125 ....E2
Tonopah 54 ....B5
Tonto Basin 250 ....D5
Topawa 500 ....D7
Topock 325 ....A4
Tortilla Flat 37 ....D5
Tsaile 1,043 ....F2
Tuba City 7,323 ....D2
Tubac 140 ....E7
Tucson▲ 405,390 ....D6
Tumacacori 100 ....E7
Vail 175 ....E6
Valentine 100 ....B3
Valley Farms 240 ....D6
Vernon 75 ....F4
Vicksburg 16 ....B5
Waddell 100 ....C5
Wellton 1,066 ....A6
Wenden 400 ....B5
West Yuma A6
Whiteriver 3,775 ....E5
Why 65 ....C6
Wickenburg 4,515 ....C5
Wikieup 150 ....B4
Willcox 3,122 ....F6
Williams 2,532 ....C3
Window Rock 3,306 ....F3
Winkelman 676 ....E6
Winona 25 ....D3
Winslow 8,190 ....E3
Wintersburg 400 ....B5
Wittmann 600 ....C5
Woodruff 280 ....E4
Yarnell 800 ....C4
Yava 40 ....C4
Young 500 ....D4
Youngtown 2,542 ....C5
Yucca 250 ....A4
Yuma▲ 54,923 ....A6

OTHER FEATURES

Agassiz (peak) D3
Agua Fria (riv.) C5
Alamo (lake) B4
Apache (lake) D5
Aquarius (range) B4
Aravaipa (creek) E6
Aubrey (cliffs) B3
Baboquivari (mts.) D7
Baker Butte (mt.) D4
Balakai (mesa) F3
Baldy (peak) F4
Bartlett (dam) D5
Bartlett (res.) D5
Big Chino Wash (dry riv.) C3
Big Horn (mts.) B5
Big Sandy (riv.) B4
Bill Williams (riv.) B4
Black (mesa) E2
Black (riv.) A3
Black (riv.) F5
Blue (riv.) F5
Bouse Wash (dry riv.) A4
Buckskin (mts.) B4
Burro (creek) B4
Canyon (lake) D5
Canyon de Chelly Nat'l Mon. ..F2
Carrizo (creek) F2
Carrizo (mts.) F2
Casa Grande Ruins Nat'l Mon. D6
Castle Dome (mts.) A5
Cataract (creek) C3
Centennial Wash (dry riv.) B5
Cerbat (mts.) A3
Cherry (creek) E4
Chevelon (creek) E4
Chinle (creek) F2
Chinle (valley) F2
Chinle Wash (dry riv.) F2
Chino (valley) C3
Chiricahua (mts.) F6
Chiricahua Nat'l Mon. F6
Chocolate (mts.) A5
Clear (creek) D4
Coconino (plat.) C3
Cocopah Ind. Res. A6
Colorado (riv.) A5
Colorado River Ind. Res. A5
Coolidge (dam) E5
Copper (mts.) B6
Corn (creek) E3
Coronado Nat'l Memorial E7
Cottonwood (cliffs) B3
Cottonwood Wash (dry riv.) E4
Davis (dam) A3
Defiance (plat.) F3
Detrital Wash (dry riv.) A3
Diablo (canyon) D4
Dinnebito Wash (dry riv.) E3
Dot Klish (canyon) E2
Dragoon (mts.) F7
Eagle (creek) F5
East Verde (riv.) D4
Echo (cliffs) D2
Elden (mt.) D3
Fort Apache Ind. Res. E5
Fort Bowie Nat'l Hist. Site F6
Fort Huachuca E7
Fort McDowell Ind. Res. D5
Fort Mohave Ind. Res. A4
Fort Pearce Wash (dry riv.) B2
Fossil (creek) D4
Four Peaks (mt.) D5
Galiuro (mts.) E6
Gila (mts.) A6
Gila (mts.) F5

Gila (riv.) B6
Gila Bend (mts.) B5
Gila Bend Ind. Res. C6
Gila River Ind. Res. D5
Glen Canyon (dam) D2
Glen Canyon Nat'l Rec. Area ..E1
Gothic (mesa) F2
Government (mt.) C3
Graham (mt.) F6
Grand Canyon Nat'l Park C2
Grand Wash (butte) B5
Grand Wash (riv.) B2
Greens (peak) F4
Growler (mts.) B6
Harcuvar (mts.) B5
Harquahala (mts.) B5
Hassayampa (riv.) C5
Havasu (lake) A4
Havasupai Ind. Res. C2
Hohokam-Pima Nat'l Mon. D5
Hoover (dam) A2
Hopi (buttes) E3
Hopi Ind. Res. E2
Horseshoe (lake) D5
Huachuca (peak) E7
Hualapai (mts.) B4
Hualapai (peak) B3
Hualapai Ind. Res. B3
Hubbell Trading Post
    Nat'l Hist. Site F3
Humphreys (peak) D3
Hurricane (cliffs) B2
Imperial (res.) A6
Ives Mesa B4
Juniper (mts.) B4
Kaibab (plat.) C2
Kaibab Ind. Res. C2
Kaibito (plat.) D2
Kanab (creek) C2
Kanab (plat.) C2
Kendrick (peak) D3
Kitt (peak) D6
Kofa (mts.) B5
Laguna (creek) F2
Laguna (res.) A6
Lake Mead Nat'l Rec. Area ..A2
Lechuguilla (des.) A6
Lemmon (mt.) E6
Little Colorado (riv.) D3
Lukachukai (mts.) F2
Luke A.F.B. C5
Maple (peak) F5
Marble Canyon Nat'l Mon. D2
Maricopa (mts.) C6
Maricopa Ind. Res. C6
Mazatzal (peak) D4
Mead (lake) A2
Meteor (crater) E3
Miller (peak) E7
Moencopi (plat.) D3
Moenkopi Wash (dry riv.) D2
Mogollon (plat.) D4
Mogollon Rim (cliffs) D4
Mohave (lake) A3
Mohave (mts.) A4
Mohawk (mts.) B6
Montezuma Castle Nat'l Mon. ..D4
Mormon (lake) D4
Mule (mts.) E7
Navajo (creek) D2
Navajo Ind. Res. D2
Navajo Nat'l Mon. E2
Navajo Ord. Depot D3
O'Leary (peak) D3
Oraibi Wash (dry riv.) D3
Ord (mt.) D5
Organ Pipe Cactus Nat'l Mon. ..C6

Painted (des.) D2
Painted Desert Section
    (Petrified Forest) F3
Painted Rock C5
Papago Ind. Res. C6
Paria (plat.) D2
Paria (riv.) D1
Parker (dam) A4
Pastora (peak) F2
Peloncillo (mts.) F6
Petrified Forest Nat'l Park F3
Pinal (peak) E5
Pinaleno (mts.) F6
Pink (cliffs) C2
Pipe Spring Nat'l Mon. C2
Pleasant (lake) C5
Plomosa (mts.) A5
Polacca Wash (dry riv.) E3
Powell (lake) D1
Pueblo Colorado Wash
    (dry riv.) F3
Puerco (riv.) F3
Quajote Wash (dry riv.) D6
Rainbow (plat.) D2
Rincon (peak) E6
Roof Butte (mt.) F2
Rose (peak) F5
Sacramento Wash (dry riv.) A4
Saguaro (lake) D5
Saguaro Nat'l Mon. E6
Salt (riv.) D5
Salt River Ind. Res. D5
San Carlos (lake) E5
San Carlos (riv.) E5
San Carlos Ind. Res. E5
Sand Tank (mt.) C6
San Francisco (riv.) F5
San Pedro (riv.) E6
San Simon (riv.) F6
Santa Catalina (mts.) D6
Santa Cruz (riv.) D6
Santa Maria (riv.) B4
Santa Rosa Wash (dry riv.) D6
San Xavier Ind. Res. D6
Sauceda (mts.) C6
Shivwits (plat.) B2
Shonto (plat.) E2
Sierra Ancha (mts.) D5
Sierra Apache (mts.) E5
Silver (creek) E4
Slate (mt.) D3
Sulphur Spring (valley) F6
Sunset Crater Nat'l Mon. D3
Superstition (mts.) D5
Theodore Roosevelt (lake) D5
Tonto (creek) D4
Tonto Nat'l Mon. D5
Trout (creek) B3
Trumbull (mt.) B2
Tumacacori Nat'l Mon. E7
Tuzigoot Nat'l Mon. D4
Tyson Wash (dry riv.) A5
Uinkaret (plat.) B2
Union (mt.) C4
Verde (riv.) D5
Virgin (riv.) B2
Walker (creek) F2
Walnut Canyon Nat'l Mon. D3
White (riv.) E5
Williams A.F.B. D5
Woody (mt.) D3
Wupatki Nat'l Mon. D3
Yuma (des.) A6
Yuma Proving Ground A6
Zuni (riv.) F4

▲County seat.

Grand Canyon Cross Section

FORMATION	THICKNESS IN FEET	GEOLOGIC PERIOD
Kaibab Limestone	325	PERMIAN
Toroweap Formation	285	PERMIAN
Coconino Sandstone	350	PERMIAN
Hermit Shale	225	PERMIAN
Supai Formation (Sandstone and Shale)	825	PENNSYLVANIAN
Redwall Limestone	450 to 500	MISSISSIPPIAN
Temple Butte Limestone	0 to 30	DEVONIAN
Muav Limestone	100	CAMBRIAN
Bright Angel Shale	450 to 640	CAMBRIAN
Tapeats Sandstone	225	CAMBRIAN
		PRE-CAMBRIAN

Characteristic fossil remains indicated in red type

Information based on National Park Service diagram

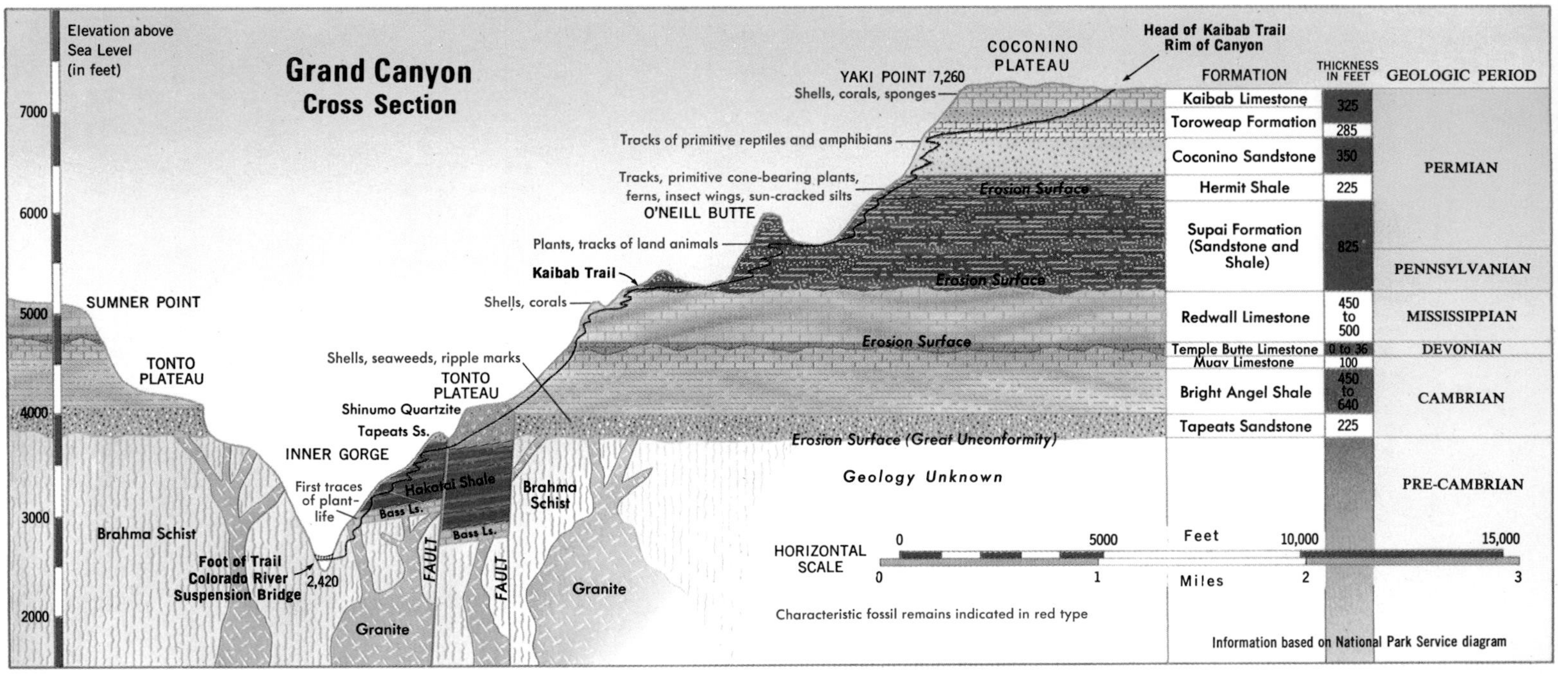

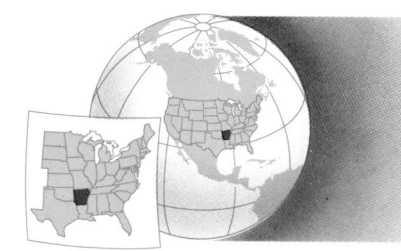

AREA 53,187 sq. mi. (137,754 sq. km.)
POPULATION 2,362,239
CAPITAL Little Rock
LARGEST CITY Little Rock
HIGHEST POINT Magazine Mtn. 2,753 ft. (839 m.)
SETTLED IN 1685
ADMITTED TO UNION June 15, 1836
POPULAR NAME Land of Opportunity
STATE FLOWER Apple Blossom
STATE BIRD Mockingbird

Agriculture, Industry and Resources

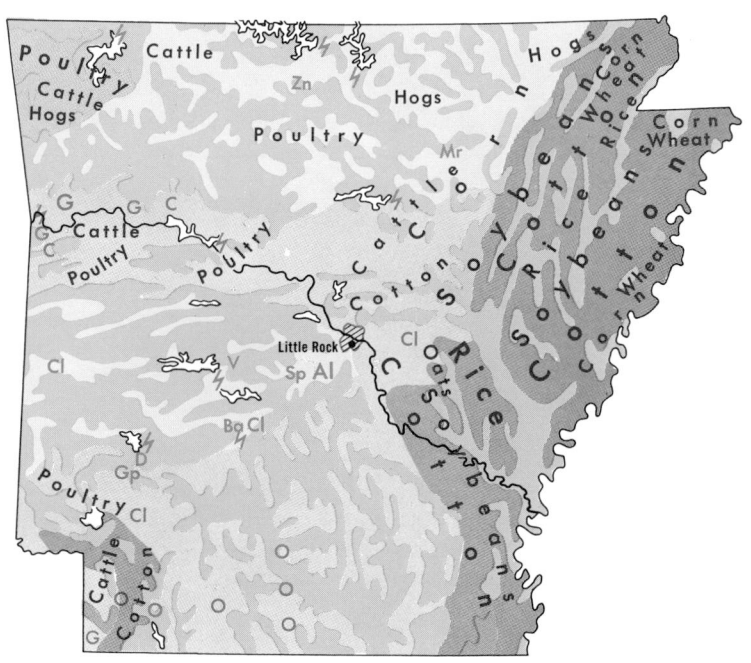

DOMINANT LAND USE

- Fruit and Mixed Farming
- Specialized Cotton
- Cotton, General Farming
- Rice, General Farming
- General Farming, Livestock, Truck Farming, Cotton
- Forests
- Swampland, Limited Agriculture

MAJOR MINERAL OCCURRENCES

Al	Bauxite	Gp	Gypsum
Ba	Barite	Mr	Marble
C	Coal	O	Petroleum
Cl	Clay	Sp	Soapstone
D	Diamonds	V	Vanadium
G	Natural Gas	Zn	Zinc

 Water Power   ///// Major Industrial Areas

COUNTIES

Arkansas 21,653 ... H5
Ashley 24,319 ... G7
Baxter 31,186 ... F1
Benton 97,499 ... B1
Boone 28,297 ... D1
Bradley 11,793 ... F7
Calhoun 5,826 ... E6
Carroll 18,654 ... C1
Chicot 15,713 ... H7
Clark 21,437 ... D5
Clay 18,107 ... K1
Cleburne 19,411 ... F2
Cleveland 7,781 ... F6
Columbia 25,691 ... D7
Conway 19,151 ... E3
Craighead 68,956 ... J2
Crawford 42,493 ... B2
Crittenden 49,939 ... K3
Cross 19,225 ... J3
Dallas 9,614 ... E6
Desha 16,798 ... H6
Drew 17,369 ... G6
Faulkner 60,006 ... F3
Franklin 14,897 ... C2
Fulton 10,037 ... G1
Garland 73,397 ... D4
Grant 13,948 ... F5
Greene 31,804 ... J1
Hempstead 21,621 ... C6
Hot Spring 26,115 ... E5
Howard 13,569 ... C5
Independence 31,192 ... G2
Izard 11,364 ... G1
Jackson 18,944 ... H2
Jefferson 85,487 ... G5
Johnson 18,221 ... C2
Lafayette 9,643 ... C7
Lawrence 17,457 ... H1
Lee 13,053 ... J4
Lincoln 13,690 ... G6
Little River 13,966 ... B6
Logan 20,557 ... C3
Lonoke 39,268 ... G4
Madison 11,618 ... C1
Marion 12,001 ... E1
Miller 38,457 ... C7
Mississippi 57,525 ... K2
Monroe 11,333 ... H4
Montgomery 7,841 ... C4
Nevada 10,101 ... D6
Newton 7,666 ... D2
Ouachita 30,574 ... E6
Perry 7,969 ... E4
Phillips 28,838 ... J5
Pike 10,085 ... C5
Poinsett 24,664 ... J2
Polk 17,347 ... B5
Pope 45,883 ... D3
Prairie 9,518 ... G4
Pulaski 349,660 ... F4
Randolph 16,558 ... H1
Saint Francis 30,858 ... J3
Saline 64,183 ... E4
Scott 10,205 ... B4
Searcy 7,841 ... E2
Sebastian 99,590 ... B3
Sevier 13,637 ... B6
Sharp 14,109 ... G1
Stone 9,775 ... F2
Union 46,719 ... E7
Van Buren 14,008 ... E2
Washington 113,409 ... B2
White 54,676 ... G3
Woodruff 9,520 ... H3
Yell 17,759 ... D3

CITIES and TOWNS

Adona 146 ... E3
Alco 200 ... F2
Alexander 201 ... F4
Alicia 157 ... H2
Alix 225 ... C3
Alleene 200 ... B6
Allport 188 ... G4
Alma 2,959 ... B3
Almyra 311 ... H5
Alpena 319 ... D1
Altheimer 972 ... G5
Altus 433 ... C3
Amagon 108 ... H2
Amity 526 ... D5
Antoine 160 ... D5
Arkadelphia▲ 10,014 ... D5
Arkansas City▲ 523 ... H6
Armorel 500 ... L2
Ash Flat▲ 667 ... G1
Ashdown▲ 5,150 ... B6
Athens ... C5
Atkins 2,834 ... E3
Aubrey 204 ... J4
Augusta▲ 2,759 ... H3
Austin 235 ... G4
Avoca 269 ... B1
Bald Knob 2,653 ... G3
Banks 88 ... F6

Barling 4,078 ... B3
Bassett 199 ... K2
Bates 9,187 ... B4
Batesville▲ 8,263 ... G2
Bauxite 412 ... F4
Bay 1,660 ... J2
Bearden 1,021 ... E6
Beaver 57 ... C1
Beebe 4,455 ... G3
Beedville 183 ... H3
Bella Vista 9,083 ... B1
Bellefonte 361 ... D1
Belleville 390 ... D3
Ben Lomond 157 ... B6
Benton▲ 18,177 ... E4
Bentonville▲ 11,257 ... B1
Bergman 324 ... E1
Berryville▲ 3,212 ... C1
Bethel Heights 281 ... B1
Bethesda 285 ... G2
Big Flat 93 ... F1
Bigelow 340 ... E3
Biggers 337 ... J1
Birdsong 104 ... K3
Birta ... D3
Biscoe 486 ... H4
Black Oak 277 ... K2
Black Rock 736 ... H1
Black Springs 97 ... C5
Blevins 253 ... C6
Blue Eye 38 ... D1
Blue Mountain 146 ... C3
Bluff City 227 ... D6
Blytheville▲ 22,906 ... L2
Bodcaw 161 ... D6
Bonanza 520 ... B3
Bono 1,220 ... J2
Booneville▲ 3,804 ... C3
Bradford 874 ... G3
Bradley 585 ... C7
Branch 299 ... C3
Brickeys ... J4
Brinkley 4,234 ... H4
Brookland 919 ... J2
Bryant 5,269 ... F4
Buckner 325 ... D7
Bull Shoals 1,534 ... E1
Burdette 148 ... L2
Cabot 8,319 ... F4
Caddo Valley 389 ... D5
Caldwell 334 ... J3
Cale 70 ... D6
Calico Rock 938 ... F1
Calion 558 ... E7
Camden▲ 14,380 ... E6
Cammack Village 828 ... E4
Campbell Station 247 ... H2
Canfield 365 ... C7
Caraway 1,178 ... K2
Carlisle 2,253 ... G4
Carthage 452 ... E5
Casa 200 ... D3
Cash 214 ... J2
Cass 225 ... C2
Casscoe 297 ... H4
Caulksville 224 ... C3
Cave City 1,503 ... G2
Cave Springs 465 ... B1
Cedarville 375 ... B2
Center Point ... C5
Centerton 491 ... B1
Centerville 300 ... D3
Central City 419 ... B3
Charleston▲ 2,128 ... B3
Cherokee Village (Cherokee Village-Hidden Valley) 4,416 ... G1
Cherry Hill 250 ... B4
Cherry Valley 659 ... J3
Chester 125 ... B2
Chidester 489 ... D6
Clarendon▲ 2,072 ... H4
Clarkedale 300 ... K3
Clarksville▲ 5,833 ... D3
Cleveland ... E3
Clinton▲ 2,213 ... F2
Coal Hill 912 ... C3
College City 339 ... J1
Collins ... G6
Colt 334 ... J3
Columbus 265 ... C6
Concord 262 ... G2
Conway▲ 26,481 ... F3
Cord 250 ... H2
Corinth 63 ... C3
Corning▲ 3,323 ... J1
Cotter 867 ... E1
Cotton Plant 1,150 ... H3
Cove 346 ... B5
Coy 142 ... G4
Crawfordsville 617 ... K3
Crossett 6,282 ... G7
Crystal Springs 215 ... D5
Curtis 300 ... D6
Cushman 428 ... G2
Daisy 122 ... C5
Dalark ... E5
Damascus 246 ... F3

Danville▲ 1,585 ... D3
Dardanelle▲ 3,722 ... D3
Datto 120 ... J1
De Queen▲ 4,633 ... B5
De Valls Bluff▲ 702 ... H4
De Witt▲ 3,553 ... H5
Decatur 918 ... A1
Delaplaine 146 ... J1
Delight 311 ... C5
Dell 258 ... K2
Denning 206 ... C3
Dermott 4,715 ... H7
Des Arc▲ 2,001 ... G4
Diamond City 601 ... E1
Diaz 1,363 ... H2
Dierks 1,263 ... B5
Donaldson 300 ... E5
Dover 1,055 ... D3
Dryden ... J2
Dumas 5,520 ... H6
Dyer 502 ... B3
Dyess 466 ... K2
Earle 3,393 ... K3
East Camden 783 ... E6
Edmondson 286 ... K3
El Dorado▲ 23,146 ... E7
Elaine 846 ... J5
Elkins 692 ... C1
Elm Springs 893 ... B1
Emerson 317 ... D7
Emmet 486 ... D6
England 3,351 ... G4
Enola 179 ... F3
Eudora 3,155 ... H7
Eureka Springs▲ 1,900 ... C1
Evening Shade 328 ... G1
Everton 150 ... E1
Fargo 140 ... H4
Farmington 1,322 ... B1
Fayetteville▲ 42,099 ... B1
Felsenthal 95 ... F7
Fifty-Six 156 ... F2
Fisher 245 ... J2
Flippin 1,006 ... E1
Fordyce▲ 4,729 ... F6
Foreman 1,267 ... B6
Formosa 224 ... E3
Forrest City▲ 13,364 ... J3
Fort Smith▲ 72,798 ... B3
Fouke 634 ... C7
Fountain Hill 195 ... G7
Franklin 205 ... G1
Fredonia (Biscoe) 484 ... H4
Friendship 160 ... E5
Fulton 269 ... C6
Garfield 308 ... C1
Garland City 415 ... C7
Garner 191 ... G3
Gassville 1,167 ... F1
Gateway 65 ... C1
Genoa 350 ... C7
Gentry 1,726 ... A1
Georgetown 126 ... G3
Gillett 883 ... H5
Gillham 210 ... B5
Gilmore 331 ... K3
Glenwood 1,354 ... C5
Goodwin 225 ... J4
Goshen 589 ... C1
Gosnell 3,783 ... K2
Gould 1,470 ... G6
Grady 586 ... G5
Grannis 507 ... B5
Gravelly 300 ... C4
Gravette 1,412 ... B1
Green Forest 2,050 ... D1
Greenbrier 2,130 ... F3
Greenland 757 ... B1
Greenway 212 ... K1
Greenwood▲ 3,984 ... B3
Greers Ferry 724 ... F2
Griffithville 237 ... G3
Grubbs 528 ... H2
Gum Springs 157 ... D5
Gurdon 2,199 ... D6
Guy 241 ... F3
Hackett 490 ... B3
Halley ... H6
Hamburg▲ 3,098 ... G7
Hampton▲ 1,562 ... F6
Hardy 538 ... H1
Harrell 258 ... F7
Harrisburg▲ 1,943 ... J2
Harrison▲ 9,922 ... D1
Hartford 721 ... B3
Hartman 498 ... C3
Haskell 1,342 ... E4
Havana 358 ... D3
Haynes 268 ... J4
Hazen 1,668 ... G4
Heber Springs▲ 5,628 ... G2
Hector 478 ... E3
Helena▲ 7,491 ... J4
Hensley 500 ... F4
Hermitage 639 ... F7
Hickory Ridge 436 ... J3

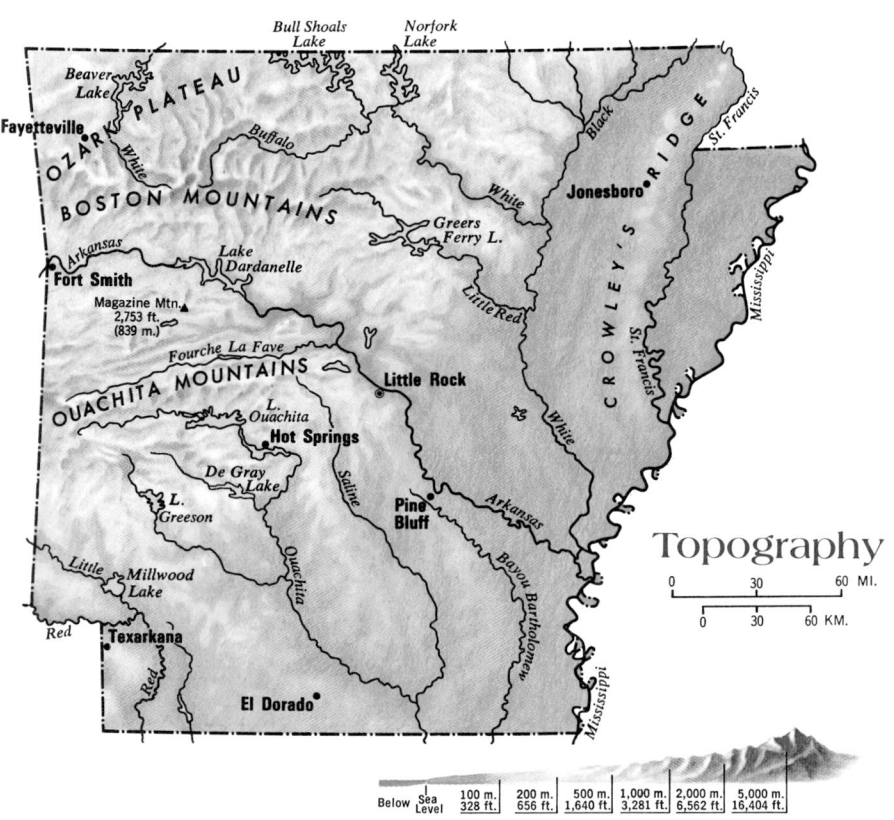

Topography

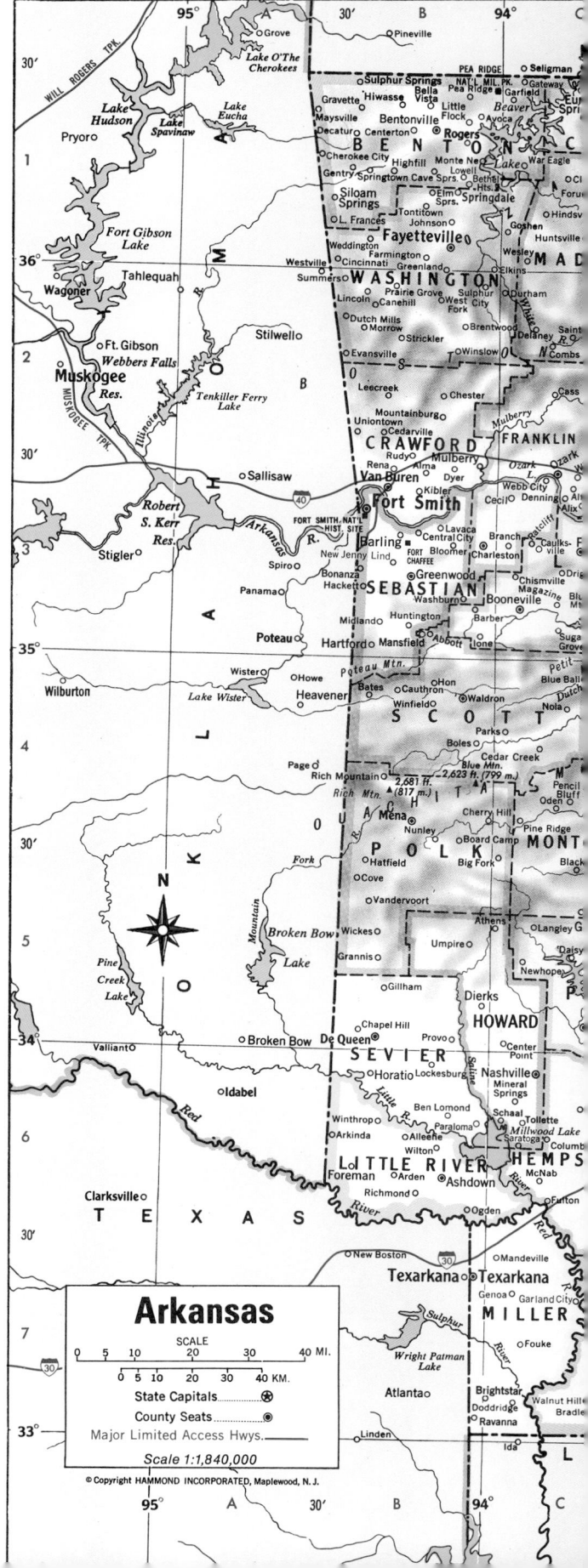

Arkansas

SCALE

0 5 10 20 30 40 MI.
0 5 10 20 30 40 KM.

State Capitals ⊛
County Seats ◉
Major Limited Access Hwys.

Scale 1:1,840,000

© Copyright HAMMOND INCORPORATED, Maplewood, N.J.

Saint Charles 169	H5	Smale	H4	Summit 480	E1
Saint Francis 201	K1	Smithville 86	H1	Sunset 571	K3
Saint Paul 88	C2	Snow Lake	H5	Swan Lake	G5
Salado 250	G2	Snyder 700	G7	Sweet Home 350	F4
Salem▲ 1,474	G1	South Lead Hill 96	D1	Swifton 830	H2
Salesville 374	F1	Sparkman 553	E6	Taylor 621	D7
Saratoga	C6	Springdale 29,941	B1	Texarkana▲ 22,631	C7
Scottsville 241	D3	Springtown	B1	Thornton 502	F6
Scranton 218	C3	Stamps 2,478	C7	Tichnor 350	H5
Searcy▲ 15,180	G3	Star City▲ 2,138	G6	Tillar 221	H6
Sedgwick 86	J2	Stephens 1,137	E7	Tinsman 69	E6
Shannon Hills 1,755	F4	Steprock 600	G3	Tollette 316	C6
Sheridan▲ 3,098	F5	Strawberry 273	H2	Tontitown 460	B1
Sherrill 55	F5	Strong 624	F7	Traskwood 488	E5
Sherwood 18,893	F4	Stuttgart▲ 10,420	H4	Trumann 6,304	J2
Shirley 363	F2	Subiaco 538	C3	Tucker 2,020	F5
Sidney 271	G1	Success 170	J1	Tuckerman 2,078	H2
Siloam Springs 8,151	B1	Sulphur Rock 356	H2	Tull 313	E5
Smackover 2,232	E7	Sulphur Springs 523	B1	Tupelo 208	H3

Higden 92	F2	Lundell 250	H5	Oak Grove 231	C1
Higginson 255	G3	Luxora 1,338	K2	Oden 126	C4
Highfill 84	B1	Lynn 299	H2	Ogden 264	B6
Hindsville 69	C1	Mabelvale 350	F4	Oil Trough 208	G2
Holly Grove 675	H4	Madison 1,263	J4	Okolona 113	D5
Hon 250	B4	Magazine 799	C3	Ola 1,090	D3
Hope▲ 9,643	C6	Magness 158	H2	Omaha 207	D1
Hopper	C5	Magnet Cove 230	E5	Oppelo 643	E3
Horatio 793	B6	Magnolia▲ 11,151	D7	Osceola▲ 8,930	K2
Horseshoe Bend 2,239	G1	Malvern▲ 9,256	E5	Oxford 562	G1
Hot Springs National Park▲ 32,462	D4	Mammoth Spring 1,097	G1	Ozan 69	C6
Houston 149	E3	Manila 2,635	K2	Ozark▲ 3,330	C3
Hoxie 2,676	H1	Mansfield 1,018	B3	Palestine 711	J4
Hughes 1,810	J4	Marianna▲ 5,910	J4	Pangburn 630	G3
Humnoke 311	G4	Marie 129	K2	Paragould▲ 18,540	J1
Humphrey 743	G5	Marion▲ 4,391	K3	Paraloma	B6
Hunter 137	H3	Marked Tree 3,100	K2	Paris▲ 3,674	C3
Huntington 715	B3	Marmaduke 1,164	K1	Parkdale 393	H7
Huntsville▲ 1,605	C1	Marshall▲ 1,318	E2	Parkin 1,847	J3
Huttig 831	F7	Marvell 1,545	J4	Parks 600	B4
Imboden 616	H1	Mayflower 1,415	F4	Patterson 445	H3
Jacksonport 264	H2	Maynard 354	J1	Pea Ridge 1,620	B1
Jacksonville 29,101	F4	McCaskill 75	C6	Peach Orchard 197	J1
Jamestown	G2	McCrory 1,971	H3	Pearcy 400	D5
Jasper▲ 332	D1	McDougal 208	K1	Perla 145	E5
Jefferson 250	F5	McGehee 4,997	H6	Perry 228	E3
Jericho 210	K3	McNab 95	C6	Perrytown 248	C6
Jerusalem 300	E3	McNeil 686	D7	Perryville▲ 1,141	E3
Jessieville 350	D4	McRae 669	G3	Piggott▲ 3,777	K1
Johnson 599	B1	Melbourne▲ 1,562	G1	Pindall 135	E1
Joiner 645	K3	Mellwood 250	H5	Pine Bluff▲ 57,140	F5
Jones Mills 210	E5	Mena▲ 5,475	B4	Pineville 220	F1
Jonesboro▲ 46,535	J2	Menifee 355	E3	Piney 2,500	D3
Judsonia 1,915	G3	Midland 220	B3	Plainview 685	D4
Junction City 674	E7	Mineral Springs 1,004	C6	Pleasant Plains 256	G2
Keiser 805	K2	Minturn 124	H2	Plumerville 832	E3
Kelso	H6	Mitchell 513	G1	Pocahontas▲ 6,151	H1
Kensett 1,741	G3	Mitchellville 618	H6	Pollard 229	K1
Keo 154	G4	Monette 1,115	K2	Poplar Grove 300	J4
Kibler 931	B3	Monroe 154	H4	Portia 521	H1
Kingsland 395	F6	Monticello▲ 8,116	G6	Portland 560	H7
Kirby 800	C5	Montrose 528	H7	Pottsville 984	D3
Knobel 317	J1	Moorefield 160	G2	Powhatan 51	H1
Knoxville 239	D3	Moro 287	H4	Poyen 303	E5
Ladelle	G7	Morrilton▲ 6,551	E3	Prairie Grove 1,761	B2
Lafe 315	J1	Morrison Bluff 84	C3	Prattsville 251	F5
Lake City▲ 1,833	K2	Moscow 325	G5	Prescott▲ 3,673	D6
Lake Frances	B1	Mount Holly 250	E7	Princeton	E6
Lake View 526	J5	Mount Ida▲ 775	C4	Pruitt	D1
Lake Village▲ 2,791	H7	Mount Pleasant 422	G2	Pyatt 185	E1
Lakeview 485	E1	Mount Vernon 192	F3	Quitman 632	F3
Lamar 768	D3	Mountain Home▲ 9,027	F1	Ratcliff 180	C3
Lavaca 1,253	B3	Mountain Pine 866	D4	Ratio 250	J5
Lawson 250	E7	Mountain View▲ 2,439	F2	Ravenden 330	H1
Leachville 1,743	K2	Mountainburg 488	B2	Ravenden Springs 131	H1
Lead Hill 283	D1	Mulberry 1,448	B2	Reader 56	D6
Leola 476	E5	Murfreesboro▲ 1,542	C5	Readland 225	H7
Lepanto 2,033	K2	Nashville▲ 4,639	C6	Rector 2,268	K1
Leslie 446	E2	Newark 1,159	H2	Redfield 1,082	F5
Letona 218	G3	New Jenny Lind 250	B3	Reed 355	H6
Lewisville▲ 1,424	C7	Newhope 300	C5	Rena	B3
Lexa 295	J4	Newport▲ 7,459	H2	Reyno 467	J1
Lincoln 1,460	B2	Nimmons 96	K1	Rison▲ 1,258	F6
Little Flock 944	B1	Noble Lake 250	G5	Rivervale 225	K2
Little Rock (cap.)▲ 175,795	F4	Norfork 394	F1	Rockport 388	E5
Lockesburg 608	B6	Norman 423	C5	Roe 135	H4
London 825	D3	Norphlet 706	E7	Rogers 24,692	B1
Lonoke▲ 4,022	G4	Norristown 625	D3	Rondo 283	J4
Lonsdale 127	E4	North Crossett 3,358	G7	Rose Bud 156	F3
Louann 158	E7	North Little Rock 61,741	F4	Rosston 262	D6
Lowell 1,224	B1	Norvell	K3	Russell 180	G3
		O'Kean 291	J1	Russellville▲ 21,260	D3

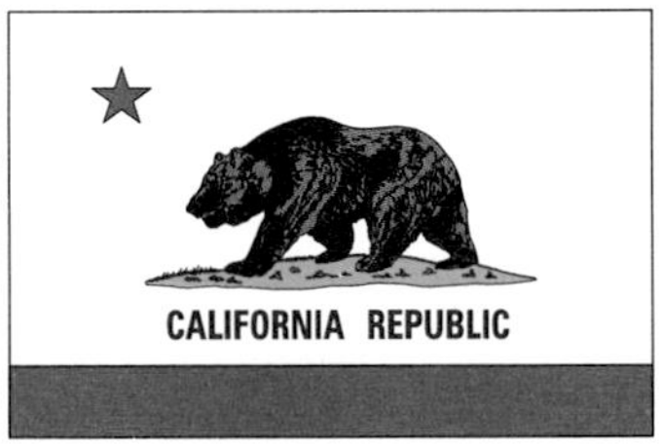
CALIFORNIA REPUBLIC

AREA 158,706 sq. mi. (411,049 sq. km.)
POPULATION 29,839,250
CAPITAL Sacramento
LARGEST CITY Los Angeles
HIGHEST POINT Mt. Whitney 14,494 ft. (4418 m.)
SETTLED IN 1769
ADMITTED TO UNION September 9, 1850
POPULAR NAME Golden State
STATE FLOWER Golden Poppy
STATE BIRD California Valley Quail

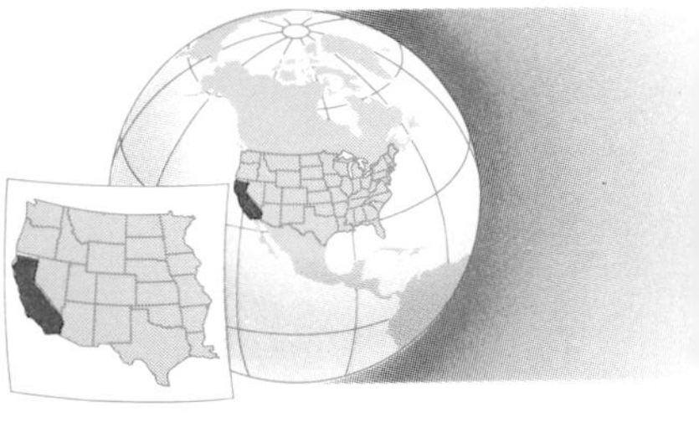

COUNTIES

Alameda 1,279,182 ....D6
Alpine 1,113 ....F5
Amador 30,039 ....E5
Butte 182,120 ....D4
Calaveras 31,998 ....E5
Colusa 16,275 ....C4
Contra Costa 803,732 ....D6
Del Norte 23,460 ....B2
El Dorado 125,995 ....E5
Fresno 667,490 ....E7
Glenn 24,798 ....C4
Humboldt 119,118 ....B3
Imperial 109,303 ....K1
Inyo 18,281 ....H7
Kern 543,477 ....G8
Kings 101,469 ....E8
Lake 50,631 ....C4
Lassen 27,598 ....E3
Los Angeles 8,863,164 ....G9
Madera 88,090 ....F6
Marin 230,096 ....C5
Mariposa 14,302 ....E6
Mendocino 80,345 ....B4
Merced 178,403 ....E6
Modoc 9,678 ....E2
Mono 9,956 ....F5
Monterey 355,660 ....D7
Napa 110,765 ....C5
Nevada 78,510 ....E4
Orange 2,410,556 ....H1
Placer 172,796 ....E4
Plumas 19,739 ....E4
Riverside 1,170,413 ....J1
Sacramento 1,041,219 ....D5
San Benito 36,697 ....D7
San Bernardino 1,418,380 ....J9
San Diego 2,498,016 ....J1
San Francisco 723,959 ....J2
San Joaquin 480,628 ....D5
San Luis Obispo 217,162 ....E8
San Mateo 649,623 ....J3
Santa Barbara 369,608 ....E9
Santa Clara 1,497,577 ....D6
Santa Cruz 229,734 ....C6
Shasta 147,036 ....C3
Sierra 3,318 ....E4
Siskiyou 43,531 ....C2
Solano 340,421 ....D5
Sonoma 388,222 ....C5
Stanislaus 370,522 ....D6
Sutter 64,415 ....D4
Tehama 49,625 ....C3
Trinity 13,063 ....B3
Tulare 311,921 ....G7
Tuolumne 48,456 ....F5
Ventura 669,016 ....F9
Yolo 141,092 ....D5
Yuba 58,228 ....D4

CITIES and TOWNS

Adelanto 8,517 ....H9
Alameda 76,459 ....J2
Alamo 12,277 ....K2
Albany 16,327 ....J2
Alhambra 82,106 ....C10
Alpine 9,695 ....J11
Alta Loma E10
Altadena 42,658 ....C10
Alturas▲ 3,231 ....E2
Amador City 196 ....C9
Anaheim 266,406 ....D11
Anderson 8,299 ....C3
Angels Camp 2,302 ....E5
Angwin 3,503 ....C5
Antioch 62,195 ....L1
Apple Valley 46,079 ....H9
Aptos 9,061 ....K4
Arbuckle 1,912 ....C4
Arcadia 48,290 ....C10
Arcata 15,197 ....A3
Arden-Arcade 92,040 ....B8
Armona 3,122 ....F7
Arnold 3,788 ....E5
Aromas 2,275 ....D7
Arroyo Grande 14,378 ....E8
Artesia 15,464 ....C11
Arvin 9,286 ....G8
Ashland 16,590 ....K2
Asti 75 ....C5
Atascadero 23,138 ....E8
Atherton 7,163 ....K3
Atwater 22,282 ....E6
Auberry 1,866 ....F6
Auburn▲ 10,592 ....C8
Avalon 2,918 ....G10
Avenal 9,770 ....E8
Azusa 41,333 ....D10
Baker 174 820 ....J8
Bakersfield▲ 105,611 ....G8
Baldwin Park 69,330 ....D10
Banning 23,570 ....J10
Barstow 21,472 ....H9
Bayview 1,318 ....A3
Baywood Park (Baywood Park-Los Osos) 10,933 ....E8
Beaumont 9,685 ....J10
Bell 34,365 ....C11
Bell Gardens 42,355 ....C11
Bellflower 61,815 ....C11
Belmont 24,127 ....J3
Belvedere 2,147 ....H2
Ben Lomond 7,884 ....K4
Benicia 24,437 ....K1
Berkeley 102,724 ....J2
Bethel Island 2,115 ....L1
Beverly Hills 31,971 ....B10
Big Bear City (Sugarloa Post Office) 4,920 ....J9
Big Bear Lake 5,351 ....J9
Big Pine 1,158 ....G6
Biggs 1,581 ....D4
Bishop 3,475 ....G6
Bloomington 15,116 ....E10
Blue Lake 1,235 ....B3
Blythe 8,428 ....L10
Bodfish 1,283 ....G8
Bolinas 1,098 ....H1
Boron 2,101 ....H8
Borrego Springs 2,244 ....J10
Boulder Creek 6,725 ....J4
Bowman C7
Brawley 18,923 ....K11
Brea 32,873 ....D11
Brentwood 7,563 ....L2
Bridgeport▲ 525 ....F5
Brisbane 2,952 ....J2
Broderick (Broderick-Bryte) 10,194 ....B8
Bryte (Bryte-Broderick) 10,194 ....B8
Buellton 3,506 ....E9
Buena Park 68,784 ....D11
Burbank 93,643 ....C10
Burlingame 26,801 ....J2
Burney 3,423 ....D3
Buttonwillow 1,301 ....F8
Cabazon 1,588 ....J10
Calexico 18,633 ....K11
California City 5,955 ....H8
Calipatria 2,690 ....K10
Calistoga 4,468 ....C5
Calwa 6,640 ....F7
Camarillo 52,303 ....G9
Cambria 5,382 ....D8
Campbell 36,048 ....K3
Canoga Park B10
Canyon 7,938 ....K2
Capistrano Beach 6,168 ....H10
Capitola 10,171 ....K4
Cardiff-by-the-Sea 10,054 ....H10
Carlsbad 63,126 ....H10
Carmel 4,407 ....D7
Carmel Valley 4,013 ....D7
Carmichael 48,702 ....C8
Carpinteria 13,747 ....F9
Carson 83,995 ....C11
Caruthers 1,603 ....E7
Casitas Springs 1,038 ....F9
Castro Valley 48,619 ....K2
Castroville 5,272 ....D7
Cathedral City 30,085 ....J10
Cayucos 2,960 ....E8
Central Valley 4,340 ....C3
Ceres 26,314 ....D6
Cerritos 53,240 ....C11
Chatsworth B10
Chemeketa Park (Chemeketa Park-Redwood Estates) 1,847 ....K4
Cherryland 11,088 ....K2
Chester 2,082 ....D3
Chico 40,079 ....D4
China Lake 4,275 ....H8
Chinese Camp 150 ....E6
Chino 59,682 ....D10
Chowchilla 5,930 ....E6
Chula Vista 135,163 ....J11
Citrus Heights 107,439 ....C8
Claremont 32,503 ....D10
Clay 7,317 ....C9
Clayton 4,325 ....K2
Clearlake 11,804 ....C5
Clearlake Oaks 2,419 ....C4
Cloverdale 4,924 ....B5
Clovis 50,323 ....F7
Coachella 16,896 ....J10
Coalinga 8,212 ....E7
Colfax 1,306 ....E4
Colton 40,213 ....E10
Columbia 1,799 ....E5
Colusa▲ 4,934 ....C4
Commerce 12,135 ....C10
Compton 90,454 ....C11
Concord 111,348 ....K1
Corcoran 13,364 ....F7
Corning 5,870 ....C4
Corona 76,095 ....E11
Coronado 26,540 ....H11
Corralitos 2,513 ....L4
Corte Madera 8,272 ....J2
Costa Mesa 96,357 ....D11
Cotati 5,714 ....C5
Cottonwood 1,747 ....C3
Covina 43,207 ....D10
Crescent City▲ 4,380 ....A2
Crestline 8,594 ....H9
Crockett 3,228 ....J1
Crowley Lake G6
Cudahy 22,817 ....C11
Culver City 38,793 ....B10
Cupertino 40,263 ....K3
Cutler 4,450 ....F7
Cutten 1,516 ....A3
Cypress 42,655 ....D11
Daly City 92,311 ....H2
Dana Point 31,896 ....H10
Danville 31,306 ....K2
Davis 46,209 ....B8
Death Valley Junction J7
Deer Park 1,825 ....C5
Del Mar 4,860 ....H11
Del Rey Oaks 1,661 ....D7
Del Rosa F10
Delano 22,762 ....F8
Delhi 3,280 ....E6
Desert Hot Springs 11,668 ....J9
Desert View Highlands 2,154 ....G9
Diamond Springs 2,872 ....D8
Dinuba 12,743 ....F7
Dixon 10,401 ....B9
Dorris 892 ....D2
Dos Palos 4,196 ....E6
Downey 91,444 ....C11
Downieville▲ 500 ....E4
Duarte 20,688 ....D10
Dublin 23,229 ....K2
Dunsmuir 2,129 ....C2
Durham 4,784 ....D4
Earlimart 5,881 ....F8
East Blythe 1,511 ....L10
East Los Angeles 126,379 ....C10
Easton 1,877 ....F7
Edgemont E11
Edison G8
El Cajon 88,693 ....J11
El Centro▲ 31,384 ....K11
El Cerrito 4,490 ....J2
El Dorado 6,395 ....C8
El Dorado Hills 3,453 ....C8
El Granada 4,426 ....H3
El Monte 106,209 ....D10
El Rio 6,419 ....F9
El Segundo 15,223 ....B11
El Toro 62,685 ....E11
Elk 17,483 ....B4
Elk Grove 10,959 ....B9
Emeryville 5,740 ....J2
Empire D6
Encinitas 55,386 ....H10
Encino B10
Enterprise C3
Escalon 4,437 ....E6
Escondido 108,635 ....J10
Esparto 1,487 ....C5
Eureka▲ 27,025 ....A3
Exeter 7,276 ....F7
Fair Oaks 26,867 ....C8
Fairfax 6,931 ....H1
Fairfield▲ 77,211 ....K1
Fallbrook 22,095 ....H10
Farmersville 6,235 ....F7
Felton 5,350 ....K4
Ferndale 1,331 ....A3
Fillmore 11,992 ....G9
Firebaugh 4,429 ....E7
Florin 24,330 ....B8
Folsom 29,802 ....C8
Fontana 87,535 ....E10
Ford City 3,781 ....F8
Forest Knolls (Forest Knolls-Lagunitas) H1
Foresthill 1,409 ....E4
Fort Bragg 6,078 ....B4
Fortuna 8,788 ....A3
Foster City 28,176 ....J2
Fountain Valley 53,691 ....D11
Fowler 3,208 ....F7
Frazier Park 2,201 ....F9
Freedom 8,361 ....L4
Fremont 173,339 ....K3
Fresno▲ 354,202 ....F7
Fullerton 114,144 ....D11
Galt 8,889 ....C9
Garden Grove 143,050 ....D11
Gardena 49,847 ....C11
Gilroy 31,487 ....D6
Glen Avon Heights 8,444 ....E10
Glendale 180,038 ....C10
Glendora 47,828 ....D10
Goleta F9
Gonzales 4,660 ....D7
Goshen 1,809 ....F7
Granada Hills B10
Grand Terrace 10,946 ....E10
Grass Valley 9,048 ....D4
Graton 1,409 ....C5
Greenacres 7,379 ....F8
Greenfield 7,464 ....D7
Greenville 1,396 ....E3
Gridley 4,631 ....D4
Groveland 2,753 ....E6
Grover City 11,656 ....E8
Guadalupe 5,479 ....E9
Guerneville 1,966 ....B5
Gustine 3,931 ....D6
Half Moon Bay 8,886 ....H3
Hamilton City 1,811 ....C4
Hanford▲ 30,897 ....F7
Harbor City C11
Hawthorne 71,349 ....C11
Hayfork 2,605 ....B3
Hayward 111,498 ....K2
Healdsburg 9,469 ....B5
Heber 2,566 ....K11
Hemet 36,094 ....H10
Hercules 16,829 ....J1
Herlong 1,188 ....E3
Hermosa Beach 18,219 ....B11
Hesperia 50,418 ....H9
Hidden Hills 1,729 ....B10
Highgrove 3,175 ....E10
Highland 34,439 ....H9
Hillsborough 10,667 ....J2
Hilmar (Hilmar-Irwin) 3,392 ....E6
Hollister▲ 19,212 ....D7
Hollywood C10
Holt 4,820 ....D6
Holtville 4,399 ....K11
Home Gardens 7,780 ....E11
Homeland 3,312 ....H10
Hughson 3,259 ....E6
Huntington Beach 181,519 ....C11
Huntington Park 56,065 ....C11
Huron 4,766 ....E7
Idyllwild (Idyllwild-Pine Cove) 2,853 ....J10
Imperial 4,113 ....K11
Imperial Beach 26,512 ....H11
Independence▲ 748 ....H7
Indian Wells 2,647 ....J10
Indio 36,793 ....J10
Inglewood 109,602 ....B11
Inverness 1,422 ....B5
Ione 6,516 ....C9
Irvine 110,330 ....D11
Isla Vista 20,395 ....E9
Ivanhoe 3,293 ....F7
Jackson▲ 3,545 ....C9
Jamestown 2,178 ....E6
Joshua Tree 3,898 ....J9
Julian 1,284 ....J10
Kelseyville 2,861 ....C5
Kensington 4,974 ....J2
Kerman 5,448 ....E7
Kernville 1,656 ....G8
Kettleman City 1,411 ....E7
Keyes 2,878 ....E6
King City 7,634 ....D7
Kings Beach 2,796 ....F4
Kingsburg 7,205 ....F7
La Canada Flintridge 19,378 ....C10
La Crescenta (La Crescenta-Montrose) 16,968 ....C10
La Habra 51,266 ....D11
La Mesa 52,931 ....H11
La Mirada 40,452 ....D11
La Puente 36,955 ....D10
La Selva Beach 1,603 ....K4
La Verne 30,897 ....D10
Lafayette 23,501 ....K2
Laguna Beach 23,170 ....G10
Laguna Hills 46,731 ....D11
Laguna Niguel 44,400 ....H10
Lagunitas (Lagunitas-Forest Knolls) 1,821 ....H1
Lake Arrowhead 6,539 ....H9
Lake Elsinore 18,285 ....F11
Lake Isabella 3,323 ....G8
Lakeland Village 5,159 ....E11
Lakeport▲ 4,390 ....C4
Lakewood 73,557 ....C11
Lamont 11,517 ....G8
Lancaster 97,291 ....G9
Larkspur 11,070 ....H1
Lathrop 6,841 ....D6
Laton 1,415 ....F7
Lawndale 27,331 ....B11
Le Grand 1,205 ....E6
Lemon Grove 23,984 ....J11
Lemoore 13,622 ....F7
Lenwood 3,190 ....H9
Leucadia 9,478 ....H10
Lewiston 1,187 ....C3
Lincoln 7,248 ....B8
Linda 13,033 ....D4
Linden 1,339 ....D5
Lindsay 8,338 ....F7
Live Oak 11,482 ....K4
Live Oak 3,103 ....D4
Live Oak 4,320 ....K4
Livermore 56,741 ....L2
Livingston 7,317 ....E6
Locke 2,722 ....B9
Lockeford 1,852 ....C9
Lodi 51,874 ....C9
Loma Linda 17,400 ....F10
Lomita 19,382 ....C11
Lompoc 37,649 ....E9
Lone Pine 1,818 ....H7
Long Beach 429,433 ....C11
Loomis 5,705 ....C8
Los Alamitos 11,676 ....D11
Los Altos 26,303 ....K3
Los Altos Hills 7,514 ....J3
Los Angeles▲ 3,485,398 ....C10
Los Banos 14,519 ....E6
Los Gatos 27,357 ....K4
Los Molinos 1,709 ....D3
Los Osos (Los Osos-Baywood Park) 10,933 ....E8
Lost Hills 1,212 ....F8
Lower Lake 1,217 ....C5
Lucerne 2,011 ....C4
Lynwood 61,945 ....C11
Madera▲ 29,281 ....E7
Magalia 8,987 ....D4
Mammoth Lakes 4,785 ....G6
Manhattan Beach 32,063 ....B11
Manteca 40,773 ....D6
Maricopa 1,193 ....F8
Marina 26,436 ....D7
Mariposa▲ 1,152 ....F6
Markleeville▲ 500 ....F5
Martinez▲ 31,808 ....K1
Marysville▲ 12,324 ....D4
Maywood 27,850 ....C10
McCloud 1,555 ....C2
McFarland 7,005 ....F8
McKinleyville 10,749 ....A3
Mecca 1,966 ....K10
Meiners Oaks (Meiners Oaks-Mira Monte) 3,329 ....F9
Mendota 6,821 ....E7
Menlo Park 28,040 ....J3
Mentone 5,675 ....H9
Merced▲ 56,216 ....E6
Mill Valley 13,038 ....H2
Millbrae 20,412 ....J2
Milpitas 50,686 ....L3
Mira Loma 15,786 ....E10
Mission Viejo 72,820 ....D11
Modesto▲ 164,730 ....D6
Mojave 3,763 ....G8
Monrovia 35,761 ....D10
Montague 1,415 ....C2
Montara 2,552 ....H3
Montclair 28,434 ....D10
Monte Sereno 3,287 ....K4
Montebello 59,564 ....C10
Monterey 31,954 ....D7
Monterey Park 60,738 ....C10
Montrose (Montrose-La Crescenta) C10
Moorpark 25,494 ....G9
Moraga 15,852 ....K2
Moreno Valley 118,779 ....H10
Morgan Hill 23,928 ....L4
Morro Bay 9,664 ....D8
Moss Beach 3,002 ....H3
Mount Shasta 3,460 ....C2
Mountain View 67,460 ....K3
Mulberry 1,946 ....D4
Murphys 1,517 ....E5
Murrieta 1,628 ....H10
Muscoy 7,541 ....E10
Napa▲ 61,842 ....C5
National City 54,249 ....J11
Needles 5,191 ....L9
Nevada City▲ 2,855 ....D4
Newark 37,861 ....K3
Newhall 12,029 ....G9
Newman 4,151 ....D6
Newport Beach 66,643 ....D11
Nipomo 7,109 ....E8
Norco 23,302 ....E11
North Edwards 1,259 ....H8
North Highlands 42,105 ....B8
Norwalk 94,279 ....C11
Novato 47,585 ....H1
Oak View 3,606 ....F9
Oakdale 11,961 ....E6
Oakhurst 2,602 ....F6
Oakland▲ 372,242 ....J2
Oakley 18,374 ....L1
Oceano 6,169 ....E8
Oceanside 128,398 ....H10
Oildale 26,553 ....F8
Ojai 7,613 ....F9
Ontario 133,179 ....D10
Opal Cliffs 5,940 ....K4
Orange 110,658 ....D11
Orange Cove 5,604 ....F7
Orinda 16,642 ....J2
Orland 5,052 ....C4
Orosi 5,486 ....F7
Oroville▲ 11,960 ....D4
Oxnard 142,216 ....F9
Pacheco (Pacheco-Vine Hill) 3,325 ....K1
Pacific Grove 16,117 ....C7
Pacifica 37,670 ....H2
Pajaro 3,332 ....D7
Palermo 5,260 ....D4
Palm Desert 23,252 ....J10
Palm Springs 40,181 ....J10
Palmdale 68,842 ....G9
Palo Alto 55,900 ....K3
Palos Verdes Estates 13,512 ....B11
Paradise 25,408 ....D4
Paramount 47,669 ....C11
Parlier 7,938 ....F7
Pasadena 131,591 ....C10
Paso Robles 18,583 ....E8
Patterson 8,626 ....D6
Pebble Beach C7
Pedley 8,869 ....E10
Perris 21,460 ....F11
Petaluma 43,184 ....H1
Pico Rivera 59,177 ....C10
Piedmont 10,602 ....J2
Pine Valley 1,297 ....J11
Pinole 17,460 ....J1
Piru 1,157 ....G9
Pismo Beach 7,669 ....E8
Pittsburg 47,564 ....L1
Pixley 2,457 ....F8
Placentia 41,259 ....D11
Placerville▲ 8,355 ....C8
Planada 3,531 ....E6
Pleasant Hill 31,585 ....K2
Pleasanton 50,553 ....L2
Pollock Pines 4,291 ....E5
Pomona 131,723 ....D10
Poplar (Poplar-Cotton Center) 1,901 ....F7

(continued on following page)

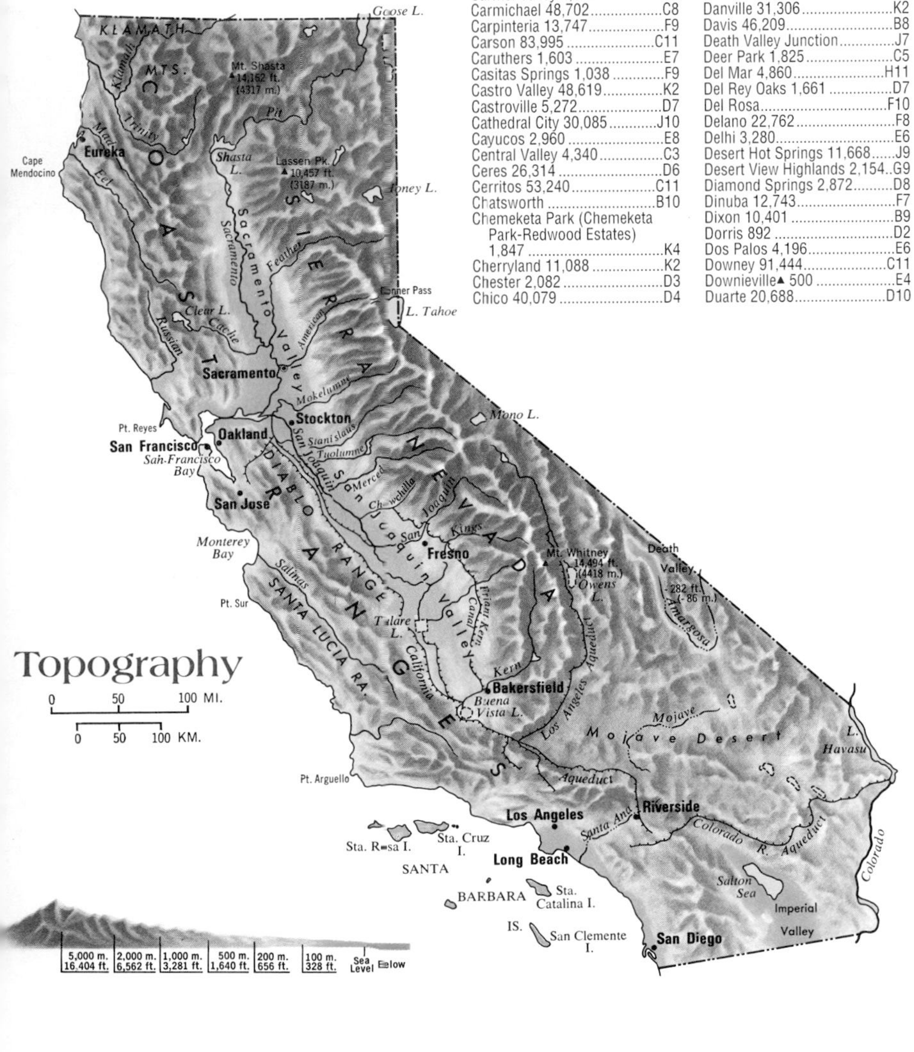
Topography
0 50 100 MI.
0 50 100 KM.
5,000 m. 16,404 ft.
2,000 m. 6,562 ft.
1,000 m. 3,281 ft.
500 m. 1,640 ft.
200 m. 656 ft.
100 m. 328 ft.
Sea Level
Below
Goose L.
KLAMATH MTS.
Mt. Shasta 14,162 ft. (4317 m.)
Eureka
Cape Mendocino
Shasta L.
Lassen Pk. 10,457 ft. (3187 m.)
Sacramento
Feather
Donner Pass
L. Tahoe
Clear L.
Russian
Sacramento
Pt. Reyes
San Francisco
San Francisco Bay
Oakland
Stockton
Mono L.
San Jose
Monterey Bay
Fresno
Mt. Whitney 14,494 ft. (4418 m.)
Death Valley
-282 ft. (-86 m.)
Owens L.
Pt. Sur
Tulare L.
Bakersfield
Buena Vista L.
Mojave Desert
Pt. Arguello
Aqueduct
Los Angeles
Riverside
Colorado R. Aqueduct
L. Havasu
Colorado
Sta. Cruz I.
Sta. Rosa I.
SANTA BARBARA IS.
Long Beach
Sta. Catalina I.
San Clemente I.
San Diego
Salton Sea
Imperial Valley

Port Hueneme 20,319 ....F9
Porterville 29,563 ....G7
Portola 2,193 ....E4
Portola Valley 4,194 ....J3
Poway 43,516 ....J11
Project City 1,657 ....C3
Quartz Hill 9,626 ....G9
Quincy▲ (Quincy-East Quincy)
4,271..........E4
Ramona 13,040 ....J10
Rancho Cordova 48,731 ....C8
Rancho Cucamonga
(Cucamonga) 101,409 ....E10
Rancho Mirage 9,778 ....J10
Rancho Palos Verdes
41,659 ....B11
Rancho Santa Fe 4,014..........H10
Red Bluff▲ 12,363 ....C3
Redding▲ 66,462 ....C3
Redlands 60,394 ....H9
Redondo Beach 60,167..........B11
Redway 1,212..........B3
Redwood City▲ 66,072..........J3
Redwood Estates (Redwood
Estates-Chemeketa Park)
1,847..........K4
Reedley 15,791 ....F7
Rialto 72,388 ....E10
Richgrove 1,899..........F8
Richmond 87,425..........J1
Ridgecrest 27,725 ....H8
Rio Dell 3,012..........A3
Rio Linda 9,481 ....C8
Rio Vista 3,316 ....L1
Ripon 7,455..........D6
Riverbank 8,547..........E6
Riverdale 1,980 ....E7
Riverside▲ 226,505..........E11
Rocklin 19,033..........B8
Rodeo 7,589..........J1
Rohnert Park 36,326..........C5
Rolling Hills 1,871 ....B11
Rolling Hills Estates 7,789..........B11
Rosamond 7,430 ....G9
Rosemead 51,638..........C10
Roseville 44,685..........B8
Ross 2,123..........H1
Rubidoux 24,367 ....E10
Sacramento (cap.)▲ 369,365..B8
Saint Helena 4,990..........C5
Salinas▲ 108,777 ....D7
San Andreas▲ 2,115 ....E5
San Anselmo 11,743 ....H1
San Bernardino▲ 164,164..........E10
San Bruno 38,961 ....J2
San Carlos 26,167 ....J3
San Clemente 41,100 ....H10
San Diego▲ 1,110,549..........H11
San Dimas 32,397 ....D10
San Fernando 22,580..........C10
San Francisco▲ 723,959..........H2
San Gabriel 37,120 ....C10
San Jacinto 16,210..........H10
San Joaquin 2,311 ....E7
San Jose▲ 782,248..........L3
San Juan Bautista 1,570..........D7
San Juan Capistrano 26,183..H10
San Leandro 68,223..........J2
San Lorenzo 19,987..........K2
San Luis Obispo▲ 41,958 ....E8
San Marcos 38,974 ....H10
San Marino 12,959 ....C10
San Martin 1,713..........L4
San Mateo 85,486..........J3
San Pablo 25,158..........J1
San Rafael▲ 48,404..........J1
San Ramon 35,303 ....K2
Sanger 16,839..........F7
Santa Ana▲ 293,742..........D11
Santa Barbara▲ 85,571 ....F9
Santa Clara 93,613..........K3
Santa Clarita 110,642 ....G9
Santa Cruz▲ 49,040..........K4
Santa Fe Springs 15,520..........C11
Santa Maria 61,284..........F9
Santa Monica 86,905..........B10
Santa Paula 25,062 ....F9
Santa Rosa▲ 113,313..........C5
Santa Venetia 3,362 ....J1
Santee 52,902 ....J11
Saratoga 28,061 ....K4
Sausalito 7,152..........H2
Scotts Valley 8,615..........K4
Seal Beach 25,098..........C11
Seaside 38,901 ....D7
Sebastopol 7,004..........C5
Seeley 1,228..........K11
Selma 14,757 ....F7
Shafter 8,409 ....F8
Shingle Springs 2,049..........C8
Sierra Madre 10,762..........D10
Signal Hill 8,371 ....C11
Simi Valley 100,217..........G9
Solana Beach 12,962..........H11
Soledad 7,146..........D7
Solvang 4,741..........E9
Sonoma 8,121..........C5
Sonora▲ 4,153..........E6
Soquel 9,188..........K4
South Dos Palos 1,214 ....E7
South El Monte 20,850 ....C10
South Gate 86,284..........C11
South Lake Tahoe 21,586..........F5
South Oroville 7,463..........D4
South Pasadena 23,936..........C10
South San Francisco 54,312..J2
South Taft 1,728..........F8
Stanford 18,097..........J3
Stanton 30,491 ....D11
Stockton▲ 210,943..........D6
Strathmore 2,353..........F7
Suisun City 22,686 ....K1
Summit City 1,136..........C3
Sun City 14,930..........F11
Sunnyvale 117,229..........K3
Susanville▲ 7,279 ....E3
Sutter 2,606..........D4

Sutter Creek 1,835..........C9
Taft 5,902..........F8
Tehachapi 5,791..........G8
Temecula 27,099..........H10
Temple City 31,100..........D10
Templeton 2,887 ....E8
Terra Bella 2,740 ....G8
Thermal 5,646..........J10
Thermalito 4,961..........D4
Thousand Oaks 104,352..........G9
Thousand Palms 4,122..........J10
Tiburon 7,532..........J2
Tipton 1,383..........F7
Torrance 133,107 ....C11
Tracy 33,558..........D6
Truckee 3,484..........E4
Tulare 33,249..........F7
Tulelake 1,010..........D2
Tuolumne 1,686..........E6
Turlock 42,198..........E6
Tustin 50,689..........D11
Twain 2,170..........D4
Twain Harte 1,369..........E6
Twentynine Palms 11,821..........K9
Twin Lakes 5,379..........K4
Ukiah▲ 14,599 ....B4
Union City 53,762..........K2
Upland 63,374..........E10
Vacaville 71,479 ....D5
Valencia 12,163 ....G9
Vallejo 109,199 ....J1
Ventura▲ 92,575 ....F9
Victor 40,674 ....C9
Victorville 14,220..........H9
Villa Park 6,299 ....D11
Visalia▲ 75,636 ....F7
Vista 71,872 ....H10
Walnut 29,105..........D10
Walnut Creek 60,569 ....K2
Wasco 12,412 ....F8
Waterford 4,771..........E6
Watsonville 31,099..........D7
Weaverville▲ 3,370..........B3
Weed 3,062..........C2
West Covina 96,086..........D10
West Hollywood 36,118..........B10
West Pittsburg 17,453..........K1
West Sacramento 28,898..........B8
Westminster 78,118..........D11
Westmont 31,044..........C11
Westmorland 1,380..........K10
Westwood 2,017..........D3
Wheatland 1,631 ....D4
Whittier 77,671..........D11
Wildomar 10,411..........H10
Williams 2,297..........C4
Willits 5,027..........B4
Willow Creek 1,576..........B3
Willows▲ 5,988..........C4
Wilton 3,858..........C9
Windsor 13,371 ....C5
Winters 4,639..........D5
Winton 7,559..........E6
Woodbridge 3,456..........B9
Woodcrest 7,796..........E11
Woodlake 5,678..........G7
Woodland▲ 39,802..........B8
Woodside 5,035..........J3
Wrightwood 3,308..........D10
Yorba Linda 52,422..........D11
Yountville 3,259..........C5
Yreka▲ 6,948..........C2
Yuba City▲ 27,437..........D4
Yucaipa 32,824..........J9
Yucca Valley 13,701..........J9

OTHER FEATURES

Agua Caliente Ind. Res. J10
Alameda (creek)..........K3
Alamo (riv.) K10
Alcatraz (isl.)..........J2
Alkali (lakes) E2
All American (canal)..........K11
Almanor (lake) D3
Amargosa (range) J7
Amargosa (riv.) J7
American (riv.) C8
Anacapa (isl.) F10
Angel (isl.)..........J2
Ano Nuevo (pt.)..........J4
Arena (pt.)..........B5
Arguello (pt.)..........E9
Argus (range) H7
Arroyo del Valle (dry riv.)..........L3
Arroyo Hondo (dry riv.)..........L3
Arroyo Mocho (dry riv.)..........L2
Arroyo Seco (dry riv.)..........K10
Beale A.F.B. D4
Berryessa (lake) D5
Bethany (res.)..........L2
Big Sage (res.)..........E2
Black Butte (lake)..........C4
Bodega (bay) B5
Bonita (pt.) H2
Bristol (lake) K9
Buchon (pt.)..........D8
Buena Vista (lake) F8
Cabrillo Nat'l Mon...........H11
Cachuma (lake)..........F9
Cadiz (lake)..........K9
Cahuilla Ind. Res...........J10
Calaveras (res.)..........L3
California Aqueduct..........E7
Camanche (res.) D6
Camp Pendleton 21,672..........H10
Campo Ind. Res...........J11
Capitan Grande Ind. Res...........J11
Cascade (range)..........D1
Castle A.F.B...........E6
Channel Islands Nat'l Park..........E10
Chemehuevi Valley Ind. Res...L9
China Lake Naval Weapons
Center..........H8
Chocolate (mts.)..........K10
Clair Engle (lake)..........C3
Clear (lake)..........C4

Clear Lake (res.) D2
Coachella (canal) K10
Coast (ranges) D7
Colorado (riv.) L8
Colorado River Aqueduct....K10
Colorado River Ind. Res...........L10
Conception (pt.) E9
Cooper (pt.)..........D7
Copco (lake) C2
Cosumnes (riv.) C9
Cottonwood (creek)..........C3
Coyote (res.)..........L4
Crowley (lake)..........G6
Crystal Springs (res.)..........J3
Cuyama (riv.)..........E8
Cuyamaca Ind. Res...........J11
Danby (lake) K9
Death (valley)..........H7
Death Valley Nat'l Mon...........H7
Delgada (pt.)..........A3
Del Valle (res.) L3
Devils Postpile Nat'l Mon...........F6
Donner (pass)..........E4
Dume (pt.)..........G10
Duxbury (pt.)..........H2
Eagle (lake) E3
Eagle (peak)..........E2
Eagle Crags (mt.)..........J8
Edison (lake) F6
Edwards A.F.B. H9
Eel (riv.)..........B4
Elsinore (lake) E11
El Toro Marine Air Station ...D11
Estero (pt.)..........D8
Estrella (riv.)..........E8
Eugene O'Neill Nat'l Hist. Site..K2
Farallon (isls.)..........B6
Farallons, The (gulf)..........H2
Feather (riv.)..........D4
Florence (lake) G6
Folsom (lake)..........C8
Fort Bidwell Ind. Res...........E2
Fort Hunter Liggett D7
Fort Independence Ind. Res...G7
Fort MacArthur..........C11
Fort Mohave Ind. Res...........L9
Fort Ord..........D7
Fort Point Nat'l Hist. Site..........J2
Freel (peak)..........F5
Fremont (peak)..........H8
Fresno (riv.)..........E7
Friant-Kern (canal)..........F7
General Grant Grove Section
(King's Canyon)..........G7
George A.F.B...........H9
Golden Gate (chan.)..........H2
Golden Gate Nat'l Rec. Area..H2
Goose (lake)..........E1
Grapevine (mts.)..........H7
Grizzly (bay)..........K1
Guadalupe (pt.)..........K3
Haiwee (res.)..........H7
Hamilton (mt.)..........H1
Hat (peak)..........E2
Havasu (lake)..........L9
Hay Fork, Trinity (riv.)..........B3
Hetch Hetchy (res.)..........F6
Hoffman (mt.)..........D2

Honey (lake) E3
Hoopa Valley Ind. Res..........A2
Humboldt (bay)..........A3
Imperial (res.)..........L10
Imperial (valley)..........K10
Ingalls (mt.)..........E3
Inyo (mts.)..........G6
Iron Gate (res.)..........C2
Isabella (lake)..........G8
John Muir Nat'l Hist. Site..........K1
Joshua Tree Nat'l Mon...........J10
Kern (riv.)..........G8
Kings (riv.)..........F7
Kings Canyon Nat'l Park..........G7
Klamath (riv.)..........B2
Laguna (res.)..........L11
La Jolla Ind. Res..........J10
Lassen (peak)..........D3
Lassen Volcanic Nat'l Park..........D3
Lava Beds Nat'l Mon...........D2
Lemoore N.A.S...........F7
Leroy Anderson (res.)..........L4
Lopez (pt.)..........D7
Los Angeles Aqueduct..........G8
Los Coyotes Ind. Res...........J10
Lost (riv.)..........D1
Lower Alkali (lake)..........E2
Lower Klamath (lake)..........D1
Mad (riv.)..........B3
Manzanita Ind. Res...........J11
March A.F.B...........E11
Mare Island Navy Yard..........J1
Mather A.F.B...........C8
Mathews (lake)..........E11
McClellan A.F.B...........B8
McClure (lake)..........E6
Mendocino (cape)..........A3
Merced (riv.)..........E6
Middle Alkali (lake)..........E2
Mill (creek)..........D3
Millerton (lake)..........F6
Moffett N.A.S...........K3
Mojave (des.)..........H9
Mojave (riv.)..........J9

Mokelumne (riv.)..........C9
Mono (lake)..........G5
Monterey (bay)..........K4
Moon (lake)..........E2
Morongo Ind. Res...........J10
Mountain Meadows (res.)..........E3
Muir Woods Nat'l Mon...........H2
Nacimiento (riv.)..........D8
Navarro (riv.)..........B4
Nevada, Sierra (mts.)..........E4
New (riv.)..........K11
Norton A.F.B...........F10
Noyo (riv.)..........B4
Oakland Army Base..........J2
Old (riv.)..........L1
Oroville (lake)..........D4
Owens (lake)..........H7
Owens (peak)..........H8
Owens (riv.)..........G6
Oxnard A.F.B...........F9
Pala Ind. Res...........H10
Palomar (mt.)..........J10
Panamint (range)..........H7
Panamint (valley)..........H7
Pescadero (pt.)..........J3
Piedras Blancas (pt.)..........D8
Pillar (pt.)..........H3
Pillsbury (lake)..........C4
Pine (creek)..........D3
Pine Flat (lake)..........F7
Pinnacles Nat'l Mon...........D7
Pit (riv.)..........D2
Point Mugu Pacific Missile
Test Center..........F9
Point Reyes Nat'l Seashore..H1
Presidio..........J2
Providence (mts.)..........K8
Punta Gorda (pt.)..........A3
Quartz (lake)..........L11
Railroad Canyon (res.)..........E11
Redwood Nat'l Park..........A2
Reyes (pt.)..........B6
Rogers (lake)..........H9
Rosamond (lake)..........G9

Round Valley Ind. Res...........B4
Russian (riv.)..........B4
Sacramento (riv.)..........D5
Sacramento Army Depot...........B8
Salinas (riv.)..........D7
Salmon (riv.)..........B2
Salton Sea (lake)..........K10
San Andreas (lake)..........H2
San Antonio (lake)..........E8
San Benito (riv.)..........D7
San Bernardino (mts.)..........J10
San Clemente (isl.)..........G11
San Diego (bay)..........H11
San Francisco (bay)..........J2
San Gabriel (res.)..........D10
San Joaquin (riv.)..........E6
San Joaquin (valley)..........D6
San Lorenzo (riv.)..........K4
San Luis (res.)..........E7
San Martin (cape)..........D8
San Miguel (isl.)..........E9
San Nicolas (isl.)..........F10
San Pablo (bay)..........J1
San Pedro (bay)..........C11
Santa Ana (riv.)..........E11
Santa Barbara (chan.)..........E9
Santa Barbara (isl.)..........G10
Santa Barbara (isls.)..........F10
Santa Catalina (gulf)..........G11
Santa Catalina (isl.)..........G10
Santa Cruz (chan.)..........F10
Santa Cruz (isl.)..........F10
Santa Maria (riv.)..........E9
Santa Rosa (isl.)..........E10
Santa Rosa Ind. Res...........J10
Santa Ynez (riv.)..........E9
Santa Ysabel Ind. Res...........J10
Searles (lake)..........H8
Sequoia Nat'l Park..........G7
Sharpe Army Depot..........D6
Shasta (lake)..........C3
Shasta (mt.)..........C2

Shasta (riv.)..........C2
Sierra Army Depot..........E3
Sierra Nevada (mts.)..........E4
Siskiyou (mts.)..........B2
Smith (riv.)..........A2
Soda (lake)..........K8
South Bay Aqueduct..........L2
South Cow (creek)..........C3
Stony Gorge (res.)..........C4
Suisun (bay)..........K1
Sur (pt.)..........D7
Susan (riv.)..........D3
Tahoe (lake)..........F4
Tamalpais (mt.)..........H1
Tehachapi (mts.)..........H7
Telescope (peak)..........H7
Tomales (pt.)..........B5
Torres Martinez Ind. Res...........J10
Travis A.F.B...........L1
Trinidad (head)..........A2
Trinity (riv.)..........B3
Truckee (riv.)..........E4
Tulare (lake)..........F7
Tule (lake)..........D1
Tule River Ind. Res...........G7
Twentynine Palms
Marine Base..........J9
Twitchell (res.)..........E9
Upper Alkali (lake)..........E2
Vandenberg A.F.B...........E9
Vizcaino (cape)..........A3
Walnut (creek)..........K1
Wheeler (peak)..........H7
Whipple (mts.)..........L9
Whiskeytown-Shasta-Trinity
Nat'l Rec. Area..........C3
Whitney (mt.)..........G7
Willow (creek)..........E3
Wilson (mt.)..........D10
Yosemite Nat'l Park..........F6
Yuba (riv.)..........D4
Yuma Ind. Res...........L11

▲County seat

Agriculture, Industry and Resources

DOMINANT LAND USE

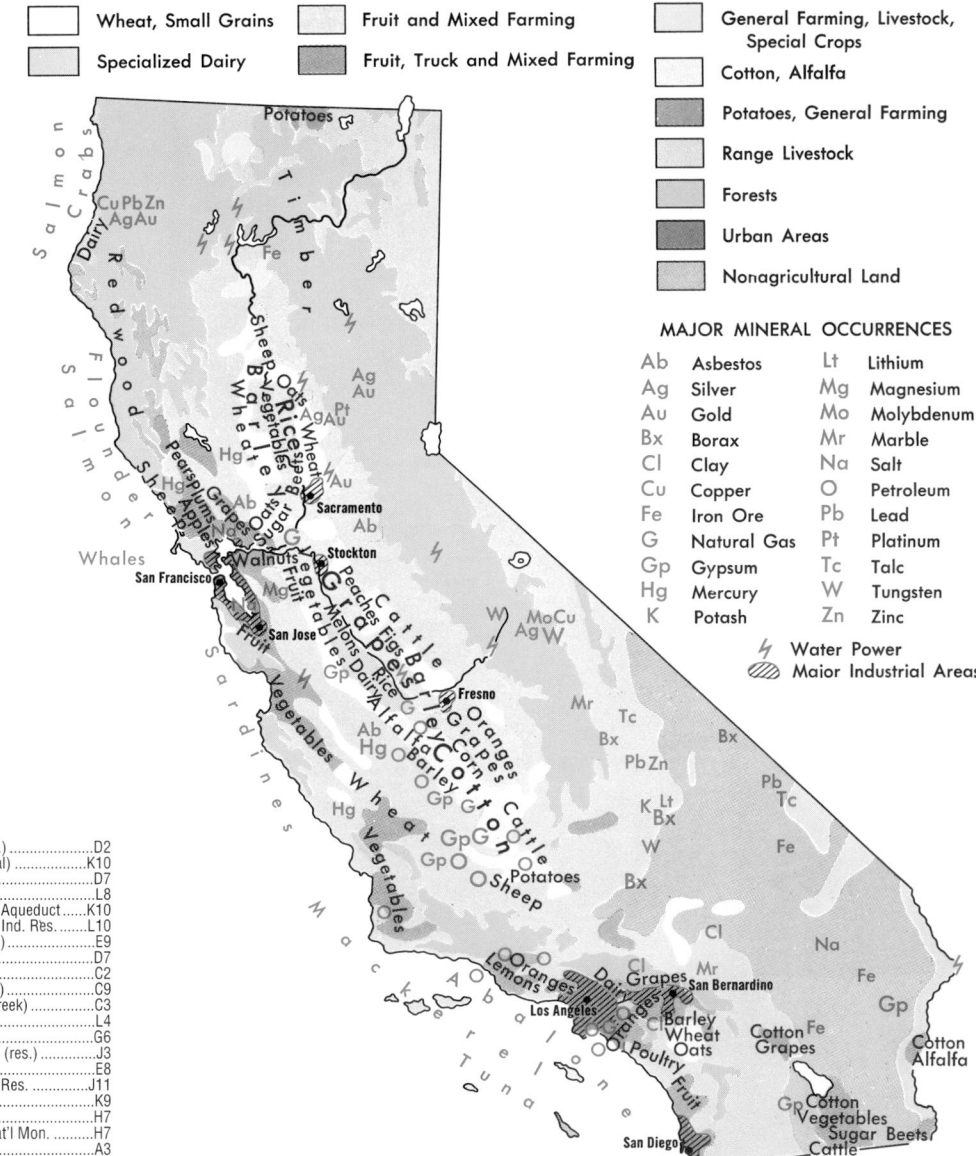

- Wheat, Small Grains
- Specialized Dairy
- Fruit and Mixed Farming
- Fruit, Truck and Mixed Farming
- General Farming, Livestock, Special Crops
- Cotton, Alfalfa
- Potatoes, General Farming
- Range Livestock
- Forests
- Urban Areas
- Nonagricultural Land

MAJOR MINERAL OCCURRENCES

Ab	Asbestos	Lt	Lithium
Ag	Silver	Mg	Magnesium
Au	Gold	Mo	Molybdenum
Bx	Borax	Mr	Marble
Cl	Clay	Na	Salt
Cu	Copper	O	Petroleum
Fe	Iron Ore	Pb	Lead
G	Natural Gas	Pt	Platinum
Gp	Gypsum	Tc	Talc
Hg	Mercury	W	Tungsten
K	Potash	Zn	Zinc

⚡ Water Power

Major Industrial Areas

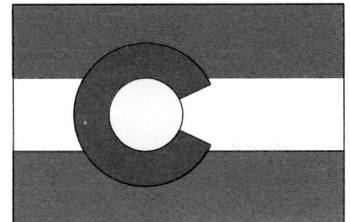

AREA 104.091 sq. mi. (269,596 sq. km.)
POPULATION 3,307,912
CAPITAL Denver
LARGEST CITY Denver
HIGHEST POINT Mt. Elbert 14,433 ft. (4399 m.)
SETTLED IN 1858
ADMITTED TO UNION August 1, 1876
POPULAR NAME Centennial State
STATE FLOWER Rocky Mountain Columbine
STATE BIRD Lark Bunting

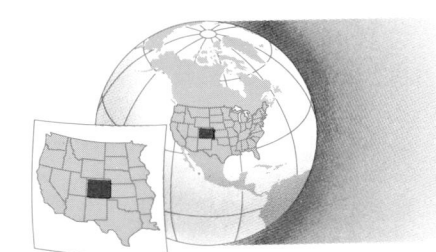

COUNTIES

Adams 265,038 ....L3
Alamosa 13,617 ....H7
Arapahoe 391,511 ....L3
Archuleta 5,345 ....E8
Baca 4,556 ....O8
Bent 5,048 ....N7
Boulder 225,339 ....J2
Chaffee 12,684 ....G5
Cheyenne 2,397 ....O5
Clear Creek 7,619 ....H3
Conejos 7,453 ....G8
Costilla 3,190 ....J8
Crowley 3,946 ....M6
Custer 1,926 ....J6
Delta 20,980 ....D5
Denver 467,610 ....K3
Dolores 1,504 ....C7
Douglas 60,391 ....K4
Eagle 21,928 ....F3
El Paso 397,014 ....K5
Elbert 9,646 ....L4
Fremont 32,273 ....J5
Garfield 29,974 ....C3
Gilpin 3,070 ....H3
Grand 7,966 ....G2
Gunnison 10,273 ....E5
Hinsdale 467 ....E7
Huerfano 6,009 ....K7
Jackson 1,605 ....G1
Jefferson 438,430 ....J3
Kiowa 1,688 ....O6
Kit Carson 7,140 ....O4
La Plata 32,284 ....D8
Lake 6,007 ....G4
Larimer 186,136 ....H1
Las Animas 13,765 ....L8
Lincoln 4,529 ....M5
Logan 17,567 ....N1
Mesa 93,145 ....B5
Mineral 558 ....F7
Moffat 11,357 ....C1
Montezuma 18,672 ....B8
Montrose 24,423 ....C6
Morgan 21,939 ....M2
Otero 20,185 ....M7
Ouray 2,295 ....D6
Park 7,174 ....H4
Phillips 4,189 ....P1
Pitkin 12,661 ....F4
Prowers 13,347 ....P7
Pueblo 123,051 ....K6
Rio Blanco 5,972 ....C3
Rio Grande 10,770 ....G7
Routt 14,088 ....E1
Saguache 4,619 ....G6
San Juan 745 ....D7
San Miguel 3,653 ....C6
Sedgwick 2,690 ....P1
Summit 12,881 ....G3
Teller 12,468 ....J5
Washington 4,812 ....N3
Weld 131,821 ....L1
Yuma 8,954 ....P2

CITIES and TOWNS

Agate 90 ....M4
Aguilar 520 ....K8
Akron▲ 1,599 ....N2
Alamosa▲ 7,579 ....H8
Allenspark 200 ....J2
Alma 148 ....G4
Almont 135 ....F5
Amherst 35 ....P1
Anton 875 ....N3
Antonito 1,103 ....H8
Arapahoe 300 ....P5
Arlington 37 ....N6
Arriba 220 ....N4
Arriola 5,372 ....B8
Arvada 89,235 ....J3
Aspen▲ 5,049 ....F4
Atwood 100 ....N1
Ault 1,107 ....K1
Aurora 222,103 ....K3
Austin D5
Avon 1,798 ....F3
Avondale 750 ....L6
Bailey 150 ....H4
Barnesville 20 ....L2
Basalt 1,128 ....E4
Bayfield 1,090 ....D8
Bedrock 45 ....B6
Beecher Island 5 ....P3
Bellvue 250 ....J1
Bennett 1,757 ....L3
Berthoud 2,990 ....J2
Berthoud Pass 40 ....H3
Bethune 173 ....P4
Beulah 650 ....K6
Black Forest 8,143 ....K4
Black Hawk 227 ....J3
Blanca 272 ....H8
Blue River 440 ....G4
Bonanza 16 ....G6
Boncarbo 200 ....K8
Bond 65 ....F3
Boone 341 ....L6
Boulder▲ 83,312 ....J2
Bowie 18 ....D5
Boyero 12 ....N5
Brandon 30 ....P6
Branson 58 ....M8
Breckenridge▲ 1,285 ....G4
Briggsdale 85 ....L1
Brighton▲ 14,203 ....K3
Bristol 200 ....P6
Brookside 183 ....J6
Broomfield 24,638 ....J3
Brush 4,165 ....M2
Buckingham 5 ....L1
Buena Vista 1,752 ....G5
Buffalo Creek 150 ....J4
Burlington▲ 2,941 ....P4
Burns 100 ....F3
Byers 1,065 ....L3
Cahone 200 ....B7
Calhan 562 ....L4
Campo 121 ....O8
Canon City▲ 12,687 ....J6
Capulin 600 ....G8
Carbondale 3,004 ....E4
Carr 49 ....K1
Cascade 1,479 ....K5
Castle Rock▲ 8,708 ....K4
Cedaredge 1,380 ....D5
Center 1,963 ....G7
Central City▲ 335 ....J3
Chama 239 ....J8
Cheraw 265 ....N6
Cheyenne Wells▲ 1,128 ....P5
Chimney Rock 76 ....E8
Chivington 20 ....O6
Chromo 115 ....F8
Cimarron 50 ....D6
Clark 20 ....F1
Clifton 12,671 ....C4
Climax 350 ....G4
Coal Creek 157 ....J6
Coaldale 153 ....H6
Coalmont 50 ....F1
Cokedale 116 ....K8
Collbran 228 ....C4
Colona 54 ....D6
Colorado City 1,149 ....K6
Colorado Springs▲ 281,140 ...K5
Columbine 23,969 ....E1
Commerce City 16,466 ....K3
Como 30 ....H4
Conejos▲ 200 ....G8
Cope 110 ....O3
Cornish 15 ....L2
Cortez▲ 7,284 ....B8
Cotopaxi 250 ....H6
Cowdrey 80 ....G1
Craig▲ 8,091 ....D2
Crawford 221 ....D5
Creede▲ 362 ....E7
Crested Butte 878 ....E5
Crestone 39 ....H7
Cripple Creek▲ 584 ....J5
Crook 148 ....O1
Crowley 225 ....M6
Cuchara 43 ....J8
Dacono 2,228 ....K2
Dailey 20 ....O1
De Beque 257 ....C4
Deckers 4 ....J4
Deer Trail 476 ....M3
Del Norte▲ 1,674 ....G7
Delhi 10 ....M7
Delta▲ 3,789 ....D5
Denver (cap.)▲ 467,610 ....K3
Deora 2 ....O7
Dillon 553 ....H3
Dinosaur 324 ....B2
Divide 700 ....J5
Dolores 866 ....C8
Dove Creek▲ 643 ....A7
Doyleville 75 ....F6
Drake 300 ....J2
Durango▲ 12,430 ....D8
Eads▲ 780 ....O6
Eagle▲ 1,580 ....F3
Eaton 1,959 ....K1
Eckley 211 ....P2
Edgewater 4,613 ....J3
Edwards 250 ....F3
Egnar 50 ....B7
Elbert 200 ....L4
Eldora 100 ....H3
Elizabeth 818 ....K4
Elk Springs 18 ....C2
Empire 401 ....H3
Englewood 29,387 ....K3
Erie 1,258 ....K2
Estes Park 3,184 ....J2
Eureka 25 ....D7
Evans 5,877 ....K2
Evergreen 7,582 ....J3
Fairplay▲ 387 ....H4
Farisita 116 ....J7
Federal Heights 9,342 ....J3
Firestone 1,358 ....K2
Firstview 6 ....O5
Flagler 564 ....N4
Fleming 344 ....O1
Florence 2,987 ....J6
Florissant 130 ....J5
Fort Collins▲ 87,758 ....J1
Fort Garland 700 ....J8
Fort Lupton 5,159 ....K2
Fort Lyon 500 ....N6
Fort Morgan▲ 9,068 ....M2
Fountain 9,984 ....K5
Fowler 1,154 ....L6
Foxton 12 ....J4
Franktown 200 ....K4
Fraser 575 ....H3
Frederick 988 ....K2
Freshwater (Guffey) 24 ....H5
Frisco 1,601 ....G3
Fruita 4,045 ....B4
Galeton 200 ....K1
Garcia 75 ....J8
Gardner 100 ....J7
Garfield 30 ....G5
Gateway 7,510 ....B5
Genoa 167 ....N4
Georgetown▲ 891 ....H3
Gilcrest 1,084 ....K2
Gill 250 ....L2
Gilman 160 ....G3
Glade Park 100 ....B5
Glen Haven 110 ....H2
Glendevey 50 ....H1
Glenwood Springs▲ 6,561 ......E4
Golden▲ 13,116 ....J3
Goodrich 85 ....M2
Gould 12 ....G2
Granada 513 ....P6
Granby 966 ....H2
Grand Junction▲ 29,034 ....B4
Grand Lake 259 ....G2
Granite 47 ....G4
Grant 50 ....H4
Greeley▲ 60,536 ....K2
Green Mountain Falls 663 ......K5
Greenland 21 ....K4
Greystone 2 ....B1
Grover 135 ....L1
Guffey 24 ....H5
Gulnare 6 ....K8
Gunnison▲ 4,636 ....E5
Gypsum 1,750 ....F3
Hale 4 ....P3
Hamilton 100 ....D2
Hartman 108 ....P6
Hartsel 69 ....H4
Hasty 150 ....O6
Haswell 62 ....N6
Haxtun 952 ....O1
Hayden 1,444 ....E2
Hereford 50 ....L1
Hesperus 250 ....C8
Hillrose 169 ....N2
Hillside 79 ....H6
Hoehne 400 ....L8
Holly 877 ....P6
Holyoke▲ 1,931 ....P1
Hooper 112 ....H7
Hot Sulphur Springs▲ 347 ......H2
Hotchkiss 744 ....D5
Howard 200 ....H6
Hoyt 60 ....L2
Hudson 918 ....K2
Hugo▲ 660 ....N4
Hygiene 450 ....J2
Idaho Springs 1,834 ....H3
Idalia 125 ....P3
Ignacio 720 ....D8
Iliff 174 ....N1
Jamestown 251 ....J2
Jansen 267 ....K8
Jaroso 50 ....H8
Jefferson 50 ....H4
Joes 100 ....O3
Johnstown 1,579 ....K2
Julesburg▲ 1,295 ....P1
Karval 51 ....N5
Keenesburg 570 ....L2
Keota 5 ....L1
Kersey 980 ....L2
Kim 76 ....N8
Kiowa▲ 275 ....L4
Kirk 30 ....P3
Kit Carson 305 ....O5
Kremmling 1,166 ....G2
Kutch 2 ....M5
La Garita 10 ....G7
La Jara 725 ....H8
La Junta▲ 7,637 ....M7
La Salle 1,783 ....K2
La Veta 726 ....J8
Lafayette 14,548 ....K3
Laird 105 ....P2
Lake City▲ 223 ....E6
Lake George 500 ....J5
Lakewood 126,481 ....J3
Lamar▲ 8,343 ....O6
Laporte 950 ....J1
Larkspur 232 ....K4
Las Animas▲ 2,481 ....N6
Lasauces 150 ....H8
Lavalley 237 ....J8
Lawson 108 ....H3
Lay 40 ....D2
Lazear 60 ....D5
Leadville▲ 2,629 ....G4
Lebanon 50 ....B8
Lewis 150 ....B8
Limon 1,831 ....M4
Lincoln Park 3,728 ....J6
Lindon 60 ....N3
Littleton▲ 33,685 ....K3
Livermore 150 ....J1
Lochbuie 1,168 ....K2
Log Lane Village 667 ....M2
Loma 265 ....B4
Longmont 42,942 ....J2
Longview 10 ....J4
Louisville 12,361 ....J3
Louviers 300 ....K4
Loveland 37,352 ....J2
Lucerne 135 ....K2
Lycan 4 ....P7
Lyons 1,227 ....J2
Mack 380 ....B4
Maher 75 ....D5
Malta 200 ....G4
Manassa 988 ....H8
Mancos 842 ....C8
Manitou Springs 4,535 ....J5
Manzanola 437 ....M6
Marble 64 ....E4
Marvel 176 ....C8
Masonville 200 ....J2
Masters 50 ....L2

(continued on following page)

Agriculture, Industry and Resources

DOMINANT LAND USE

Specialized Wheat

Wheat, Range Livestock

Wheat, Grain Sorghums, Range Livestock

Dry Beans, General Farming

Sugar Beets, Dry Beans, Livestock, General Farming

Fruit, Mixed Farming

General Farming, Livestock, Special Crops

Range Livestock

Forests

Urban Areas

Nonagricultural Land

MAJOR MINERAL OCCURRENCES

Ag Silver
Au Gold
Be Beryl
C Coal
Cl Clay
Cu Copper
F Fluorspar
Fe Iron Ore
G Natural Gas

Mi Mica
Mo Molybdenum
Mr Marble
O Petroleum
Pb Lead
U Uranium
V Vanadium
W Tungsten
Zn Zinc

⚡ Water Power
▨ Major Industrial Areas

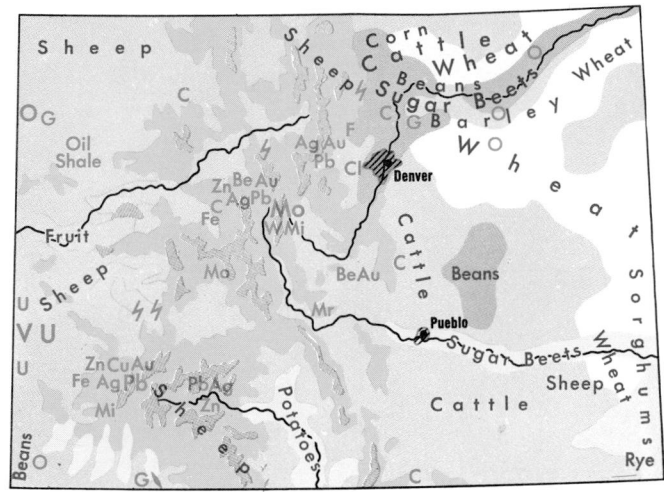

Topography

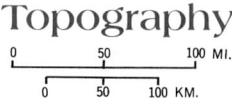

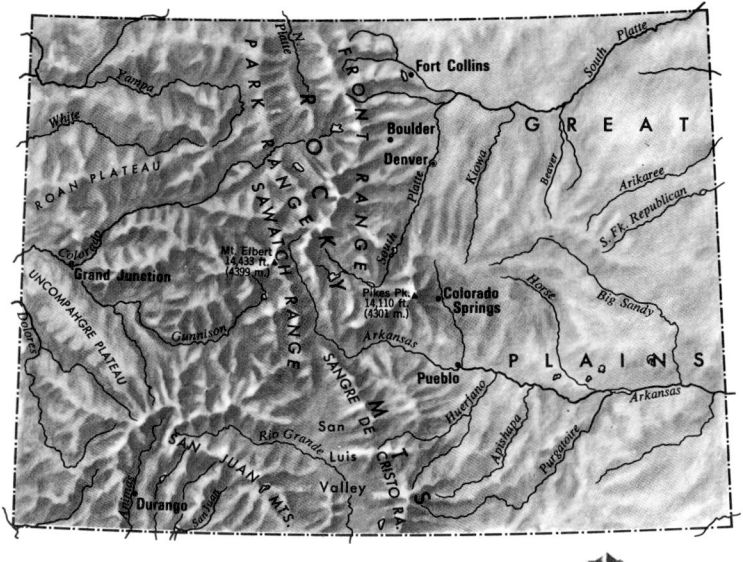

0   50   100 MI.
0   50   100 KM.

Below Sea Level | 100 m. 328 ft. | 200 m. 656 ft. | 500 m. 1,640 ft. | 1,000 m. 3,281 ft. | 2,000 m. 6,562 ft. | 5,000 m. 16,404 ft.

Matheson 120 ...M4
Maybell 130 ...C2
McClave 125 ...O6
McCoy 62 ...F3
Mead 456 ...K2
Meeker▲ 2,098 ...D2
Meredith 47 ...F4
Merino 238 ...N2
Mesa 120 ...C4
Mesa Verde National Park 45 ..C8
Mesita 70 ...H8
Milliken 1,605 ...K2
Milner 196 ...F2
Minturn 1,066 ...G3
Model 200 ...L8
Moffat 99 ...H6
Molina 200 ...D4
Monte Vista 4,324 ...G7
Montezuma 6 ...H3
Montrose▲ 8,854 ...D6
Monument 1,020 ...K4
Morrison 465 ...J3
Mosca 100 ...H7
Nathrop 150 ...H5
Naturita 434 ...B6
Nederland 1,099 ...H3
New Castle 679 ...E3
New Raymer 80 ...M1
Ninaview 7 ...N7
Niwot 2,666 ...J2
North Avondale 110 ...L6
North La Junta 1,076 ...N7
Northglenn 27,195 ...K3
Norwood 429 ...C6
Nucla 656 ...B6
Nunn 324 ...K1
Oak Creek 673 ...F2
Ohio 100 ...F5
Olathe 1,263 ...D5
Olney Springs 340 ...M6
Ophir 69 ...D7
Orchard 2,218 ...L2
Orchard Mesa 5,977 ...C4
Ordway▲ 1,025 ...M6
Ortiz 163 ...H8
Otis 451 ...O2
Ouray▲ 644 ...D6
Ovid 349 ...P1
Padroni 100 ...N1
Pagosa Junction 15 ...E8
Pagosa Springs▲ 1,207 ...E8
Palisade 1,871 ...C4
Palmer Lake 1,480 ...J4
Paoli 29 ...P1
Paonia 1,403 ...D5
Parachute 658 ...C4
Paradox 250 ...B6
Parkdale 21 ...H6
Parker 5,450 ...K4
Parlin 100 ...F6
Parshall 80 ...G2
Peetz 179 ...N1
Penrose 2,235 ...K6
Peyton 250 ...K4
Phippsburg 300 ...F2
Pierce 823 ...K1

Pine 100 ...J4
Pinecliffe 375 ...J3
Pinon 50 ...K6
Pitkin 53 ...F5
Placerville 50 ...D6
Plateau City 35 ...D4
Platner 30 ...N2
Platteville 1,515 ...K2
Pleasant View 300 ...B7
Poncha Springs 244 ...G6
Portland ...D6
Portland 17 ...K6
Powderhorn 100 ...E6
Pritchett 153 ...O8
Proctor 25 ...N1
Pryor 50 ...K8
Pueblo▲ 98,640 ...K6
Radium 22 ...G3
Ramah 94 ...L4
Rand 50 ...G2
Rangely 2,278 ...B2
Raymer (New Raymer) ...M1
Red Cliff 297 ...G4
Red Feather Lakes 150 ...H1
Red Mesa 100 ...C8
Red Wing 200 ...J7
Redstone 115 ...E4
Redvale 300 ...B6
Rico 92 ...C7
Ridgway 423 ...D6
Rifle 4,636 ...D3
Rio Blanco 4 ...C3
Rockvale 321 ...J6
Rocky Ford 4,162 ...M6
Roggen 100 ...L2
Romeo 341 ...G8
Rush 40 ...L5
Rye 168 ...K7
Saguache▲ 584 ...G6
Saint Elmo 75 ...G5
Salida▲ 4,737 ...H6
San Acacio 50 ...J8
San Isabel 8 ...K7
San Luis▲ 800 ...J8
San Pablo 150 ...J8
Sanford 750 ...H8
Sargents 31 ...F6
Sawpit 36 ...D7
Security (Security-Widefield) 18,768 ...K5
Sedalia 200 ...K4
Sedgwick 183 ...O1
Segundo 200 ...K8
Seibert 181 ...O4
Severance 106 ...K1
Shawnee 100 ...H4
Sheridan 4,976 ...J3
Sheridan Lake 95 ...P6
Silt 1,095 ...D4
Silver Cliff 322 ...J6
Silver Plume 134 ...H3
Silverthorne 1,768 ...G3
Silverton▲ 716 ...D7
Simla 481 ...M4
Slater 10 ...E1
Snowmass 1,449 ...E4

Snyder 200 ...M2
Somerset 200 ...E5
South Fork 500 ...F7
Springfield▲ 1,475 ...O8
Starkville 104 ...L8
Steamboat Springs▲ 6,695 ...F2
Sterling▲ 10,362 ...N1
Stoneham 35 ...M1
Stonington 27 ...P8
Strasburg 1,005 ...L3
Stratton 649 ...O4
Sugar City 252 ...M6
Sunbeam 19 ...C1
Superior 255 ...J3
Swink 584 ...M7
Tabernash 250 ...H3
Telluride▲ 1,309 ...D7
Tennessee Pass 5 ...G4
Texas Creek 80 ...H6
Thatcher 50 ...L7
Thornton 55,031 ...K3
Tiffany 24 ...D8
Timnath 190 ...J2
Timpas 25 ...M7
Tincup 8 ...F5
Toponas 55 ...F2
Towaoc 700 ...B8
Towner 61 ...P6
Trinchera 30 ...M8
Trinidad▲ 8,580 ...L8
Truckton 10 ...L5
Twin Lakes 40 ...G4
Two Buttes 63 ...P7
Tyrone 9 ...L8
Uravan 500 ...B6
Utleyville 2 ...O8
Vail 3,659 ...G3
Valdez 12 ...K8
Vernon 50 ...P3
Victor 258 ...J5
Vilas 105 ...P8
Villa Grove 37 ...G6
Villegreen 6 ...M8
Vineland 100 ...K6
Virginia Dale 2 ...J1
Vona 104 ...O4
Wagon Wheel Gap 20 ...F7
Walden▲ 890 ...G1
Walsenburg▲ 3,300 ...K7
Walsh 692 ...P8
Ward 159 ...H2
Weldona 200 ...M2
Wellington 1,340 ...K1
Westcliffe▲ 312 ...H6
Westcreek 2 ...J4
Westminster 74,625 ...J3
Weston 150 ...K8
Wetmore 150 ...J6
Wheat Ridge 29,419 ...J3
Whitewater 300 ...C5
Wiggins 499 ...L2
Wild Horse 13 ...N5
Wiley 406 ...O6
Williamsburg 253 ...J6
Windsor 5,062 ...J2
Winter Park 528 ...H3

Wolcott 30 ...F3
Woodland Park 4,610 ...J4
Woodrow 24 ...M3
Woody Creek 400 ...F4
Wray▲ 1,998 ...P2
Yampa 317 ...F2
Yellow Jacket 115 ...B7
Yoder 25 ...L5
Yuma 2,719 ...O2

OTHER FEATURES

Adams (mt.) ...H6
Adobe Creek (res.) ...N6
Air Force Academy 9,062 ...K5
Alamosa (creek) ...G8
Alva B. Adams (tunnel) ...H2
Animas (riv.) ...D8
Antero (mt.) ...G5
Antero (res.) ...H5
Antora (peak) ...G6
Apishapa (riv.) ...L8
Arapaho Nat'l Rec. Area. ...G2
Arapahoe (peak) ...H2
Arikaree (riv.) ...O3
Arkansas (riv.) ...P6
Arkansas Divide (mts.) ...L4
Baker (mt.) ...H2
Bald (mt.) ...H4
Bear (creek) ...P8
Beaver (creek) ...M3
Bennett (peak) ...G7
Bent's Old Fort Nat'l Hist. Site ...M6
Big Grizzly (creek) ...G1
Big Sandy (creek) ...N4
Big Thompson (riv.) ...H2
Bijou (creek) ...L3
Black Canyon of the Gunnison Nat'l Mon. ...D5
Black Squirrel (creek) ...L5
Blanca (peak) ...H7
Blue (mt.) ...B2
Blue (riv.) ...G3
Blue Mesa (res.) ...E5
Bonny (res.) ...P3
Box Elder (creek) ...K4
Cache la Poudre (riv.) ...H1
Cameron (peak) ...H1
Carbon (peak) ...E5
Castle (peak) ...F5
Cebolla (creek) ...E6
Cedar (creek) ...M1
Chacuaco (creek) ...M8
Cheesman (lake) ...J4
Clay (peak) ...O7
Cochetopa (creek) ...F6
Colorado (riv.) ...A5
Colorado Nat'l Mon. ...B4
Conejos (creek) ...G8
Conejos (riv.) ...G8
Crestone (peak) ...H7
Crow (creek) ...L1
Culebra (creek) ...H8
Culebra (peak) ...J8
Curecanti Nat'l Rec. Area ...F6

Del Norte (peak) ...F7
De Weese (plat.) ...J6
Dinosaur Nat'l Mon. ...B2
Disappointment (creek) ...B7
Dolores (riv.) ...B5
Douglas (creek) ...B3
Eagle (riv.) ...E3
Elbert (mt.) ...G4
El Diente (peak) ...C7
Eleven Mile Canyon (res.) ...H5
Elk (riv.) ...F1
Empire (res.) ...L2
Ent A.F.B. ...K5
Ethel (mt.) ...F1
Evans (mt.) ...H3
Florissant Fossil Beds Nat'l Mon. ...J5
Fort Carson 11,309 ...K5
Fountain (creek) ...K5
Frenchman (creek) ...P1

Frenchman, North Fork (creek) ...O1
Frenchman, South Fork (creek) ...O1
Front (range) ...H1
Gore (range) ...G3
Graham (peak) ...E8
Granby (lake) ...G4
Great Sand Dunes Nat'l Mon. ...H7
Green (riv.) ...A2
Green Mountain (res.) ...G3
Gunnison (riv.) ...C5
Gunnison (tunnel) ...D6
Gunnison, North Fork (riv.) ...D5
Handies (peak) ...E7
Harvard (mt.) ...G5
Hermosa (peak) ...D7
Hesperus (mt.) ...C8
Holy Cross (mt.) ...F4
Horse (creek) ...M5

Horse Creek (res.) ...N6
Horsetooth (res.) ...J1
Hovenweep Nat'l Mon. ...A8
Huerfano (riv.) ...L7
Illinois (riv.) ...G1
Jackson Lake (res.) ...M2
James (peak) ...H3
John Martin (res.) ...N6
Juniper (mt.) ...C2
Kiowa (creek) ...L2
Kit Carson (mt.) ...H7
La Garita (mts.) ...F7
La Plata (peak) ...G5
La Plata (riv.) ...C8
Lake Fork, Gunnison (riv.) ...D6
Landsman (creek) ...P4
Laramie (mts.) ...H1
Laramie (riv.) ...H1
Lincoln (mt.) ...G4
Lone Cone (mt.) ...C7

Colorado

SCALE
0 5 10 20 30 40MI.
0 5 10 20 30 40KM.

State Capitals ... ⊛   County Seats ... ◉
Major Limited Access Hwys. ———

Scale 1:2,200,000

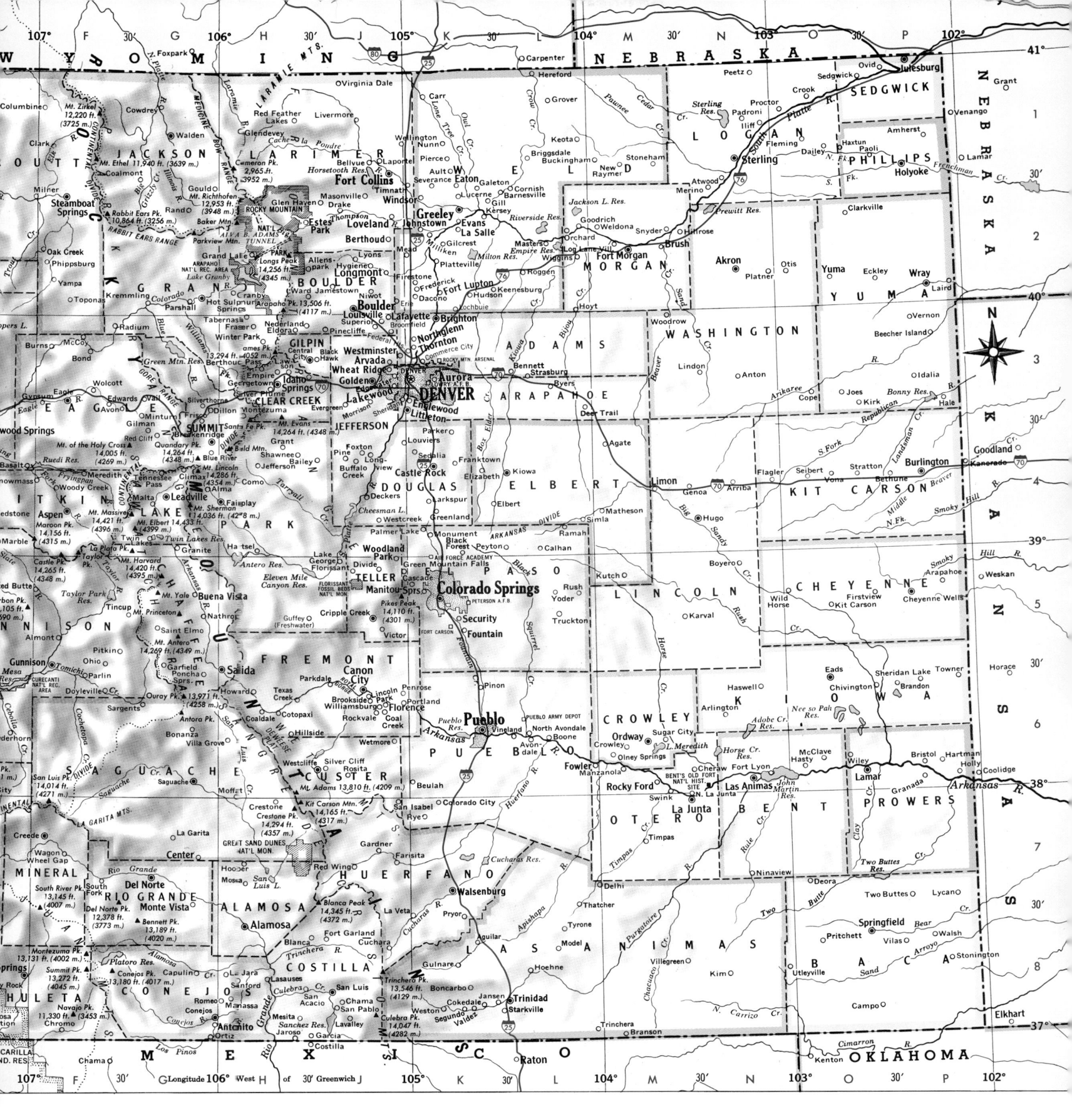

Lone Tree (creek)..........K1	North Platte (riv.)..........G1	Quandary (peak)..........G4	Rush (creek)..........N5	South Platte (riv.)..........N1	Uncompahgre (riv.)..........D5
Longs (peak)..........H2	Ouray (peak)..........G6	Rabbit Ears (peak)..........G2	Saguache (creek)..........F6	South River (peak)..........F7	Ute Mountain Ind. Res...........B8
Los Pinos (riv.)..........G8	Ow (creek)..........K1	Rabbit Ears (range)..........F2	Sanchez (res.)..........H8	Southern Ute Ind. Res...........D8	Vallecito (res.)..........D8
Lowry A.F.B...........K3	Pagoda (peak)..........E2	Redcloud (peak)..........E6	Sand Arroyo (dry riv.)..........O8	Sterling (res.)..........N1	Wet (mts.)..........J6
Mancos (riv.)..........B8	Park (range)..........F1	Republican (riv.)..........P3	Sangre de Cristo (mts.)..........H6	Summit (peak)..........F8	Wetterhorn (peak)..........D6
Maroon (peak)..........F4	Parkview (mt.)..........G2	Richthofen (mt.)..........G2	San Juan (riv.)..........E8	Tarryall (creek)..........H4	White (riv.)..........B2
Massive (mt.)..........F4	Pawnee (creek)..........M1	Rifle (creek)..........D3	San Luis (creek)..........H6	Taylor (peak)..........F5	Williams Fork, Colorado (riv.).G3
McElmo (creek)..........B8	Peterson A.F.B...........K5	Rio Grande (res.)..........E7	San Luis (lake)..........H7	Taylor (riv.)..........F5	Williams Fork, Yampa (riv.)..........B2
Medicine Bow (range)..........G1	Picance (creek)..........C3	Rio Grande (riv.)..........H8	San Miguel (mts.)..........C7	Taylor Park (res.)..........F5	Wilson (peak)..........C7
Meredith (lake)..........M6	Piedra (creek)..........E8	Rio Grande Pyramid (mt.)..........E7	San Miguel (riv.)..........B6	Timpas (creek)..........M7	Windom (peak)..........D7
Mesa Verde Nat'l Park..........C8	Pikes (peak)..........J5	Riverside (res.)..........L2	Santa Fe (peak)..........H4	Tomichi (creek)..........F5	Yale (mt.)..........G5
Middle Beaver (creek)..........P4	Piros (riv.)..........D8	Roan (creek)..........C4	Sawatch (range)..........G4	Trappers (lake)..........E3	Yampa (riv.)..........B2
Milton (res.)..........K2	Plateau (creek)..........C4	Roan (plat.)..........B3	Sheep (mts.)..........E6	Trinchera (peak)..........J8	Yellow (creek)..........C3
Montezuma (peak)..........F8	Plateoro (res.)..........F8	Roaring Fork, Colorado (riv.)..........E4	Sherman (mt.)..........G4	Trinchera (riv.)..........H8	Yucca House Nat'l Mon...........B8
Morrow Point (res.)..........E6	Po (mts.)..........A1	Rocky (mts.)..........F1	Slate (riv.)..........E5	Trout (creek)..........E2	Zenobia (res.)..........B1
Muddy (creek)..........E4	Prewitt (res.)..........N2	Rocky Mountain Arsenal..........K3	Smoky Hill (riv.)..........P5	Twin Lakes (res.)..........G4	Zirkel (mt.)..........F1
Navajo (peak)..........F8	Princeton (mt.)..........G5	Rocky Mountain Nat'l Park..........H2	Smoky Hill, North Fork (riv.)..........P4	Two Butte (creek)..........N7	
Navajo (res.)..........E8	Pueblo (res.)..........K6	Royal Gorge (canyon)..........J6	Sneffels (mt.)..........D7	Two Buttes (res.)..........O7	
Nee so Pah (res.)..........D6	Pueblo Army Depot..........L6	Ruedi (res.)..........F4		Uncompahgre (peak)..........E6	▲County seat
North Carrizo (creek)..........N8	Purgatoire (riv.)..........M8	Rule (creek)..........N7		Uncompahgre (plat.)..........B5	

Connecticut

SCALE

0 — 5 — 10 — 15 MI.

0 — 5 — 10 — 15 KM.

⊛ State Capitals

Major Limited Access Hwys. ———

Scale 1:610,000

Topography

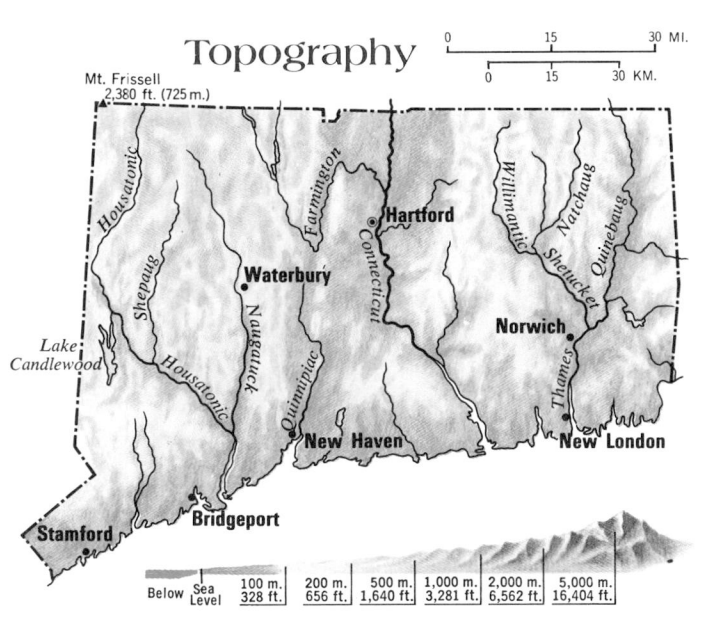

Mt. Frissell
2,380 ft. (725 m.)

Below Sea Level	100 m. 328 ft.	200 m. 656 ft.	500 m. 1,640 ft.	1,000 m. 3,281 ft.	2,000 m. 6,562 ft.	5,000 m. 16,404 ft.

0 — 15 — 30 MI.

0 — 15 — 30 KM.

COUNTIES

Fairfield 827,645	B3
Hartford 851,783	D1
Litchfield 174,092	B1
Middlesex 143,196	E3
New Haven 804,219	D3
New London 254,957	G2
Tolland 128,699	F1
Windham 102,525	H1

CITIES and TOWNS

Abington 600	G1
Addison 700	E2
Allingtown	D3
Amston 900	F2
Andover ● 2,540	F2
Ansonia 18,403	C3
Ashford P.O. (Warrenville) 500	G1
Ashford ● 3,765	G1
Avon 1,434	D1
Avon ● 13,937	D1
Bakersville 750	C1
Ballouville 800	H1
Baltic	G2
Bantam 757	B2
Barkhamsted ● 3,369	D1
Beacon Falls ● 5,083	C3
Berkshire 500	B3
Berlin ● 16,787	E2

Bethany ● 4,608	C3
Bethel 8,835	B3
Bethel ● 17,541	B3
Bethlehem 1,762	C2
Bethlehem ● 3,071	C2
Bloomfield ● 19,483	E1
Blue Hills 3,206	E1
Bolton ● 4,575	F1
Branchville 600	B3
Branford 5,688	D3
Branford ● 27,603	D3
Bridgeport 141,686	C4
Bridgewater ● 1,654	B2
Bristol 60,640	D2
Broad Brook 3,585	E1
Brookfield ● 14,113	B3
Brookfield Center	B3
Brooklyn ● 6,681	H1
Buckingham 800	E2
Burlington ● 7,026	D1
Burnside	E1
Byram	A4
Canaan 1,057	B1
Canaan ● 1,194	B1
Canterbury ● 4,467	H2
Canton 1,680	D1
Canton ● 8,268	D1
Center Groton 600	G3
Centerbrook 800	F3
Central Village 950	H2
Chaplin ● 2,048	G1
Cheshire 5,759	D2

Cheshire ● 25,684	D2
Chester 1,563	F3
Chester ● 3,417	F3
Clinton 3,439	E3
Clinton ● 12,767	E3
Clintonville	D3
Cobalt 700	E2
Colchester 3,212	F2
Colchester ● 10,980	F2
Colebrook 1,365	C1
Collinsville 2,591	D1
Columbia ● 4,510	F2
Cornwall ● 1,414	B1
Cos Cob	A4
Coventry 3,769	F1
Coventry ● 10,063	F1
Cranbury 700	B4
Cromwell 12,286	E2
Crystal Lake 1,175	F1
Danbury 65,585	B3
Danielson 4,441	H1
Darien ● 18,196	B4
Dayville	H1
Deep River 2,520	F3
Deep River ● 4,332	F3
Derby 12,199	C3
Devon	C4
Durham 2,650	E3
Durham ● 5,732	E3
Durham Center 500	E3
East Berlin 950	E2
East Brooklyn 1,481	H1

East Canaan 800	B1
East Granby ● 4,302	E1
East Haddam ● 6,676	F3
East Hampton 2,167	E2
East Hampton ● 10,428	E2
East Hartford ● 50,452	E1
East Hartland 900	D1
East Haven ● 26,144	D3
East Killingly 900	H1
East Lyme ● 15,340	G3
East Morris 800	C2
East Norwalk	B4
East Putnam 500	H1
East River 500	E3
East Windsor ● 10,081	E1
East Windsor Hill 500	E1
Eastford ● 1,314	G1
Easton ● 6,303	B4
Ellington ● 11,197	F1
Elmwood	E1
Enfield 8,151	E1
Enfield ● 45,532	E1
Essex 2,500	F3
Essex ● 5,904	F3
Fabyan 600	H1
Fairfield ● 53,418	B4
Falls Village 600	B1
Farmington ● 20,608	D1
Fenwick 89	F3
Forestville	D2
Foxon	D3
Franklin ● 1,810	F2

AREA 5,018 sq. mi. (12,997 sq. km.)
POPULATION 3,295,669
CAPITAL Hartford
LARGEST CITY Bridgeport
HIGHEST POINT Mt. Frissell (S. Slope) 2,380 ft.
 (725 m.)
SETTLED IN 1635
ADMITTED TO UNION January 9, 1788
POPULAR NAME Constitution State; Nutmeg State
STATE FLOWER Mountain Laurel
STATE BIRD Robin

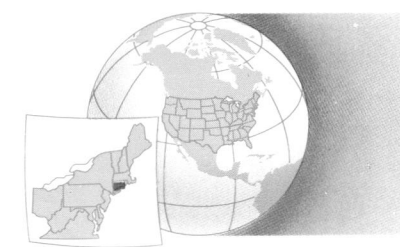

Milldale 975	D2	Poquonock Bridge 2,770	G3
Milton 600	C1	Portland 5,645	E2
Mohegan 700	G3	Portland • 8,418	E2
Monroe • 16,896	C3	Preston 5,006	H2
Monroe P.O. (Stepney)	B3	Prospect • 7,775	D2
Montowese	D3	Putnam 6,835	H1
Montville 1,711	G3	Putnam • 9,031	H1
Montville • 16,673	G3	Putnam Heights 500	H1
Moodus 1,170	F2	Quaker Hill 2,052	G3
Moosup 3,289	H2	Quinebaug 1,031	H1
Morningside Park	G3	Quinnipiac	D3
Morris • 2,039	C2	Redding • 7,927	B3
Mystic 2,618	H3	Redding Ridge 550	B3
Naugatuck 30,625	C2	Ridgefield 6,363	B3
New Canaan • 17,864	B4	Ridgefield • 20,919	B3
New Fairfield • 12,911	B3	Riverside	A4
New Hartford 1,269	C1	Rockfall 900	E2
New Hartford • 5,769	C1	Rockville	F1
New Haven 130,474	D3	Rocky Hill • 16,554	E2
New London 28,540	G3	Rogers 650	H1
New Milford 5,775	B2	Round Hill 900	A4
New Milford • 23,629	B2	Rowayton	B4
New Preston 1,217	B2	Roxbury • 1,825	B2
Newington • 29,208	E2	Salem • 3,310	F3
Newtown 1,800	B3	Salisbury • 4,090	B1
Newtown • 20,779	B3	Sandy Hook	B3
Niantic 3,048	G3	Saugatuck	B4
Nichols	C4	Saybrook Point 700	F3
Noank 1,406	H3	Scantic 500	E1
Norfolk • 2,060	C1	Scotland • 1,215	G2
Noroton	B4	Seymour • 14,288	C3
Noroton Heights	B4	Sharon • 2,928	B1
North Bloomfield 500	E1	Shelton 35,418	C3
North Branford • 12,996	E3	Sherman • 2,809	B2
North Franklin 500	G2	Short Beach	D3
North Granby 1,455	D1	Simsbury 5,577	D1
North Grosvenor Dale 1,705	H1	Simsbury • 22,023	D1
North Guilford	E3	Somers 1,643	F1
North Haven • 22,249	D3	Somers • 9,108	F1
North Lyme	F3	Somersville 750	F1
North Stonington • 4,884	H3	South Coventry (Coventry)	
North Wilton 900	B4	1,257	F1
North Woodbury 900	C2	South Glastonbury	E2
Northfield 600	C2	South Killingly 500	H1
Northford	D3	South Norwalk	B4
Northville 700	B2	South Wilton	B4
Norwalk 78,331	B4	South Windham 1,644	G2
Norwich 37,391	G2	South Windsor • 22,090	E1
Norwichtown	G2	South Woodstock 1,112	G1
Oakdale 608	G3	Southbury • 15,818	C3
Oakville 8,741	C2	Southington • 38,518	D2
Occum	F1	Southport	C4
Old Greenwich	A4	Stafford • 11,091	F1
Old Lyme • 6,535	F3	Stafford Springs 4,100	F1
Old Mystic 600	H3	Staffordville 500	G1
Old Saybrook 1,820	F3	Stamford 108,056	A4
Old Saybrook • 9,552	F3	Stepney	B3
Oneco 550	H2	Sterling • 2,357	H2
Orange • 12,830	C3	Stonington 1,100	H3
Oxford • 8,685	C3	Stonington • 16,919	H3
Pawcatuck 5,289	H3	Stony Creek	E3
Pequabuck 642	D2	Storrs 12,198	F1
Plainfield 2,856	H2	Stratford • 49,389	C4
Plainfield • 14,363	H2	Suffield 1,353	E1
Plainville • 17,392	D2	Suffield • 11,427	E1
Plantsville	D2	Taftville	G2
Pleasure Beach 1,356	G3	Talcottville 875	F1
Plymouth • 11,822	C2	Tariffville 1,477	D1
Pomfret • 3,102	H1	Terryville 5,426	C2
Poquonock	E1	Thamesville	G2
		Thomaston • 6,947	C2

Thompson • 8,668	H1	Colebrook River (lake)	C1
Thompsonville 8,458	E1	Congamond (lakes)	E1
Tolland 11,001	F1	Connecticut (riv.)	E2
Torringford	C1	Dennis (hill)	C1
Torrington 33,687	C1	Easton (res.)	B3
Totoket 950	D3	Eight Mile (riv.)	F3
Trumbull • 32,016	C4	Farmington (riv.)	D1
Uncasville 1,597	G3	French (riv.)	H1
Union • 612	G1	Frissell (mt.)	B1
Union City	D1	Gaillard (lake)	D3
Unionville	D1	Gardner (lake)	G2
Vernon Center	F1	Hammonasset (pt.)	E3
Vernon • 29,841	F1	Hammonasset (res.)	E3
Versailles 540	G2	Haystack (mt.)	C1
Voluntown • 2,113	H2	Highland (lake)	C1
Wallingford 17,827	D3	Hockanum (riv.)	E1
Wallingford • 40,822	D3	Hop (riv.)	F1
Warehouse Point	E1	Housatonic (riv.)	C3
Warren • 1,226	C1	Lillinonah (lake)	B3
Washington • 3,905	B2	Little (riv.)	G2
Washington Depot 900	B2	Long Island (sound)	C4
Waterbury 108,961	C2	Mad (riv.)	C1
Waterford 2,736	G3	Mashapaug (lake)	G1
Waterford • 17,930	G3	Mason (isl.)	H3
Watertown 20,456	C2	Mattabesset (riv.)	E2
Wauregan 1,079	H2	Mianus (riv.)	A4
Weatogue 2,521	D1	Mohawk (mt.)	B1
West Avon	D1	Moosup (riv.)	H2
West Granby 567	D1	Mount Hope (riv.)	G1
West Hartford • 60,110	D1	Mudge (pond)	B1
West Haven 54,021	D3	Mystic (riv.)	H3
West Mystic 3,595	H3	Natchaug (riv.)	G1
West Norwalk 950	B4	Naugatuck (riv.)	C3
West Simsbury 2,149	D1	Nepaug (res.)	D1
West Suffield	E1	Niantic (riv.)	G3
Westbrook 2,060	F3	Norwalk (riv.)	B4
Westbrook • 5,414	F3	Pachaug (pond)	H2
Westfield	E2	Pawcatuck (riv.)	H3
Weston • 8,648	B4	Pequabuck (riv.)	D2
Westport • 24,410	B4	Pequonnock (riv.)	C3
Wethersfield • 25,651	E2	Pocotopaug (lake)	E2
Whitneyville	D3	Quaddick (res.)	H1
Willimantic 14,746	G2	Quinebaug (riv.)	H2
Willington • 5,979	F1	Quinnipiac (riv.)	D3
Wilton 15,989	B4	Rippowam (riv.)	A4
Winchester• 11,524	C1	Sachem (head)	E4
Windham • 22,039	G2	Salmon (brook)	D1
Windsor 17,517	E1	Salmon (riv.)	F2
Windsor • 27,817	E1	Saugatuck (res.)	B3
Windsor Locks • 12,358	E1	Scantic (riv.)	E1
Winnipauk 650	B4	Shenipsit (lake)	F1
Winsted 8,254	C1	Shepaug (riv.)	B2
Winthrop 750	F3	Shetucket (riv.)	G2
Wolcott • 13,700	D2	Silvermine (riv.)	B4
Woodbridge • 7,924	D3	Spectacle (lakes)	B2
Woodbury 1,212	C2	Still (riv.)	B3
Woodbury • 8,131	C2	Still (riv.)	C1
Woodmont 1,770	D4	Talcott (range)	D1
Woodstock • 6,008	G1	Thames (riv.)	G3
Yalesville	D3	Thomaston (res.)	C2
Yantic	G2	Titicus (riv.)	A3
		Trap Falls (res.)	C3
OTHER FEATURES		Twin (lakes)	B1
		Wamgumbaug (lake)	F1
Aspetuck (res.)	B4	Waramaug (lake)	B2
Bantam (lake)	C2	West Rock Ridge (hills)	D3
Barkhamsted (res.)	D1	Willimantic (riv.)	F1
Bear (mt.)	B1	Wononskopomuc (lake)	B1
Byram (riv.)	A4	Yantic (riv.)	G2
Candlewood (lake)	A2	
Coast Guard Academy	G3	• Population of town or township

Gales Ferry 1,191	G3	Ivoryton	F3
Gaylordsville 960	A2	Jewett City 3,349	H2
Georgetown 1,694	B4	Kensington 8,306	D2
Glastonbury 7,082	E2	Kent • 2,918	B2
Glastonbury • 27,901	E2	Killingly • 15,889	H1
Glenville	A4	Killingworth • 4,814	E3
Goshen • 2,329	C1	Lake Pocotopaug 3,02C	F2
Granby 1,912	D1	Lakeville	B1
Granby • 9,369	D1	Lebanon • 6,041	G2
Greenfield Hill	B4	Ledyard • 14,913	G3
Greenwich • 58,441	A4	Leetes Island 500	E3
Grosvenor Dale 700	H1	Lisbon • 3,790	G2
Groton 9,837	G3	Litchfield 1,378	C2
Groton • 45,144	G3	Litchfield • 8,365	C2
Guilford 2,588	E3	Long Hill	C3
Guilford • 19,848	E3	Lords Point 500	H3
Haddam • 6,769	E3	Lyons Plain 700	B4
Hamden • 52,434	D3	Madison 2,139	E3
Hampton • 1,578	G1	Madison • 15,485	E3
Hanover 500	G2	Manchester 31,058	E1
Hartford (cap.) 139,739	E1	Manchester • 51,618	E1
Hartland • 1,866	D1	Mansfield • 21,103	F1
Harwinton 3,293	C1	Mansfield Center 1,043	G1
Harwinton • 5,228	C1	Marion 900	D2
Hawleyville 600	B3	Marlborough 1,039	F2
Hazardville 5,179	E1	Marlborough • 5,535	F2
Hebron • 7,079	F2	Meriden 59,479	D2
Higganum 1,692	E2	Middlebury • 6,145	C2
Highland Park 500	F1	Middlefield • 3,925	E2
Hockanum	E2	Middletown 42,762	E2
Huntington	C3	Milford 48,168	C4
Indian Neck	D3	Mill Plain 750	A3

Agriculture, Industry and Resources

DOMINANT LAND USE

Specialized Dairy

Dairy, Poultry, Mixed Farming

Forests

Urban Areas

MAJOR MINERAL OCCURRENCES

Cl Clay Mi Mica

Major Industrial Areas

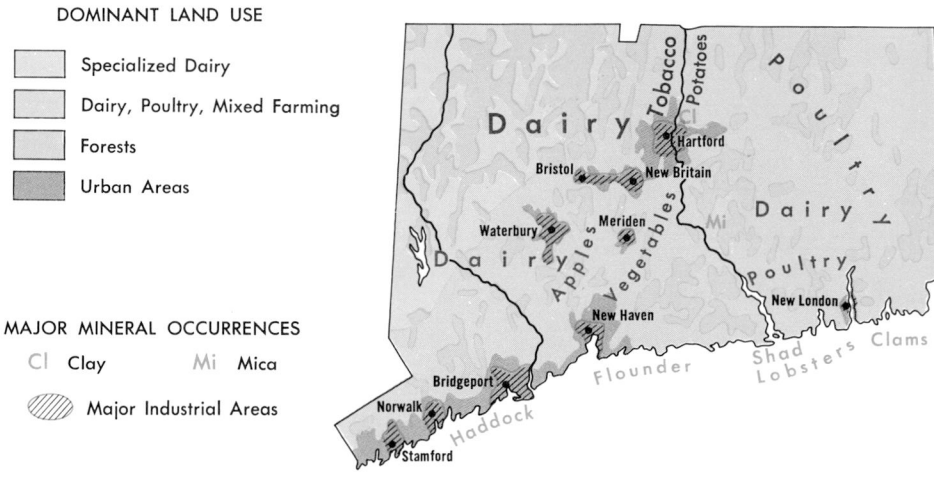

AREA 58,664 sq. mi. (151,940 sq. km.)
POPULATION 13,003,362
CAPITAL Tallahassee
LARGEST CITY Jacksonville
HIGHEST POINT (Walton County) 345 ft. (105 m.)
SETTLED IN 1565
ADMITTED TO UNION March 3, 1845
POPULAR NAME Sunshine State; Peninsula State
STATE FLOWER Orange Blossom
STATE BIRD Mockingbird

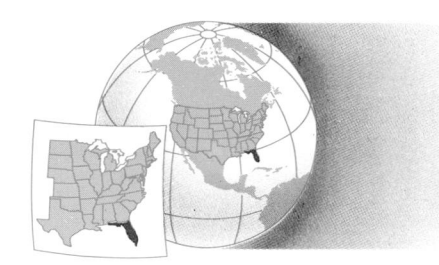

Topography

Daytona Beach 2,335	F2
Daytona Beach Shores 1,324	F2
De Bary 7,176	E3
De Funiak Springs▲ 5,120	C6
De Land▲ 16,491	E2
De Leon Springs 1,481	E2
Deer Park 250	F3
Deerfield Beach 46,325	F5
Delray Beach 47,181	F5
Deltona 50,828	E3
Destin 8,080	C6
Doctors Inlet 800	E1
Dover 2,606	D4
Dowling Park 250	C1
Dundee 2,335	E3
Dunedin 34,012	B2
Dunnellon 1,624	D2
Eagle Lake 1,758	E4
Earleton 350	D2
East Lake-Orient Park 6,171	C2
East Naples 22,951	E5
East Palatka 1,989	E2
Eastpoint 1,577	B2
Eatonville 2,170	E3
Ebro 255	C6
Edgewater 15,337	F3
Edgewood 1,062	E3
Egypt Lake 14,580	C2
El Portal 2,457	B4
Elfers 12,356	D3
Elkton 240	E2
Englewood 15,025	D5
Ensley 16,362	B6
Espanola 300	E2
Estero 3,177	E5
Esto 253	C5
Eustis 12,967	E3
Everglades City 524	E6
Fairbanks 300	D2
Fairfield 450	D2
Fanning Springs 493	C2
Felda 500	E5
Fellsmere 2,179	F4
Fernandina Beach▲ 8,765	E1
Five Points 1,136	D1
Flagler Beach 3,820	E2
Florahome 400	E2
Floral City 2,609	D3
Florida City 5,806	F6
Florida Ridge 12,218	F4
Foley 525	C1
Fort Denaud 600	E5
Fort Green 300	E4
Fort Lauderdale▲ 149,377	C4
Fort McCoy 600	E2
Fort Meade 4,976	E4
Fort Myers Beach 9,284	E5
Fort Myers▲ 45,206	E5
Fort Ogden 900	E4
Fort Pierce▲ 36,830	F4
Fort Walton Beach 21,471	C6
Fort White 268	D2
Fountain 900	D6
Freeport 843	C6
Frink 275	D6
Frostproof 2,808	E4
Fruitland Park 2,754	D3
Fruitville 9,808	D4
Gainesville▲ 84,770	D2
Geneva 1,120	E3
Georgetown 687	E2
Gibsonton 7,706	C3
Gifford 6,278	F4
Glen Saint Mary 462	D1
Glenwood 400	E2
Golden Beach 774	C4
Golden Gate 14,148	E5
Golf 234	F5
Gomez 400	F4
Gonzalez 7,669	B6
Goodland 600	E6
Goulding 4,159	B6
Goulds 7,284	F6
Graceville 2,675	D5
Graham 225	D2
Grand Ridge 536	A1
Grandin 250	E2
Grant 500	F3
Green Cove Springs▲ 4,497	E2
Greenacres City 18,683	F5
Greensboro 586	B1
Greenville 950	C1
Greenwood 474	A1
Gretna 1,981	B1
Grove City 2,374	D5
Groveland 2,300	E3
Gulf Breeze 5,530	B6
Gulf Hammock 325	D2
Gulf Harbors	D3
Gulf Stream 690	F5
Gulfport 11,727	B3
Haines City 11,683	E3
Hallandale 30,996	B4
Hampton 296	D2
Harlem 2,826	F5
Harold 500	B6

Hastings 595	E2
Havana 1,654	B1
Hawthorne 1,305	D2
Hernando 2,103	D3
Hialeah 188,004	B4
Hialeah Gardens 7,713	B4
High Point 2,288	B3
High Springs 3,144	D2
Highland Beach 3,209	F5
Highland City 1,919	E4
Highland Park 155	E4
Hiland Park 3,865	C6
Hillcrest Heights 221	E4
Hilliard 1,751	E1
Hillsboro Beach 1,748	F5
Hinson 250	B1
Hobe Sound 11,507	F4
Holder 350	D3
Hollister 980	E2
Holly Hill 11,141	E2
Hollywood 121,697	B4
Holmes Beach 4,810	D4
Holt 850	C6
Homestead 26,866	F6
Homosassa 2,113	D3
Homosassa Springs 6,271	D3
Horseshoe Beach 252	C2
Hosford 750	B1
Howey In The Hills 724	E3
Hudson 7,344	D3
Hurlburt	B6
Hypoluxo 830	F5
Immokalee 14,120	E5
Indialantic 2,844	F3
Indian Creek 44	B4
Indian Harbour Beach 6,933	F3
Indian River Shores 2,278	F4
Indian Rocks Beach 3,963	B3
Indian Shores 1,405	B3
Indiantown 4,794	F4
Inglis 1,241	D2
Intercession City 600	E3
Interlachen 1,160	E2
Inverness▲ 5,797	D3
Islamorada 1,220	F7
Islandia 13	F6
Jacksonville▲ 672,971	E1
Jacksonville Beach 17,839	E1
Jasmine Estates 17,136	D3
Jasper▲ 2,099	D1
Jay 666	B5
Jennings 712	C1
Jensen Beach 9,884	F4
June Park 4,080	F3
Juno Beach 2,121	F5
Jupiter 24,986	F5
Jupiter Island 549	F4
Kathleen 2,743	D3
Kenansville 650	F4
Kendall 87,271	B5
Kenneth City 4,462	B3
Key Biscayne 8,854	B5
Key Colony Beach 977	F7
Key Largo 11,336	F6
Key West▲ 24,832	E7
Keystone Heights 1,315	E2
Kinard 295	D6
Kissimmee▲ 30,050	E3
La Belle▲ 2,703	E5
La Crosse 122	D2
Lacoochee 2,072	D3
Lady Lake 8,071	E3
Lake Alfred 3,622	E3
Lake Buena Vista 1,776	E3
Lake Butler▲ 2,116	D1
Lake Carroll 13,012	C2
Lake City▲ 10,005	D1
Lake Como 340	E2
Lake Forest	B4
Lake Harbor 600	F5
Lake Helen 2,344	E3
Lake Jem 314	E3
Lake Magdalene 15,973	D3
Lake Mary 5,929	E3
Lake Monroe 500	E3
Lake Park 6,704	F5
Lake Placid 1,158	E4
Lake Wales 9,670	E4
Lake Worth 28,564	G5
Lakeland 70,576	D3
Lakeport 311	C5
Lakewood 7,211	C5
Land O'Lakes 7,892	D3
Lantana 8,392	F5
Largo 65,674	B3
Lauderdale Lakes 27,341	B3
Lauderdale-by-the-Sea 2,990	C3
Lauderhill 49,708	B3
Laurel 8,245	D4
Laurel Hill 543	C5
Lawtey 676	D1
Layton 183	F7
Lazy Lake 33	B3
Lecanto 1,243	D3
Lee 306	C1
Leesburg 14,903	E3

(continued on following page)

COUNTIES

Alachua 181,596	D2
Baker 18,486	D1
Bay 126,994	C6
Bradford 22,515	D2
Brevard 398,978	F3
Broward 1,255,488	F5
Calhoun 11,011	D6
Charlotte 110,975	E5
Citrus 93,515	D3
Clay 105,986	E2
Collier 152,099	E5
Columbia 42,613	D1
Dade 1,937,094	F6
De Soto 19,039	E4
Dixie 10,585	C2
Duval 672,971	E1
Escambia 262,798	B6
Flagler 28,701	E2
Franklin 8,967	C2
Gadsden 41,105	B1
Gilchrist 9,667	D2
Glades 7,591	E5
Gulf 11,504	D7
Hamilton 10,930	D1
Hardee 19,499	E4
Hendry 25,773	E5
Hernando 101,115	D3
Highlands 68,432	E4
Hillsborough 834,054	D4
Holmes 15,778	C5
Indian River 90,208	F4
Jackson 41,375	D5
Jefferson 11,296	C1
Lafayette 5,578	C2
Lake 152,104	E3
Lee 335,113	E5
Leon 192,493	B1
Levy 25,923	D2
Liberty 5,569	B1
Madison 16,569	C1

Manatee 211,707	D4
Marion 194,833	D2
Martin 100,900	F4
Monroe 78,024	E7
Nassau 43,941	E1
Okaloosa 143,776	C6
Okeechobee 29,627	F4
Orange 677,491	E3
Osceola 107,728	E3
Palm Beach 863,518	F5
Pasco 281,131	D3
Pinellas 851,659	D4
Polk 405,382	E4
Putnam 65,070	E2
Saint Johns 51,303	E2
Saint Lucie 87,182	F4
Santa Rosa 81,608	B6
Sarasota 277,776	D4
Seminole 287,529	E3
Sumter 31,577	D3
Suwannee 26,780	C1
Taylor 17,111	C1
Union 10,252	D1
Volusia 370,712	E2
Wakulla 14,202	B1
Walton 27,760	C6
Washington 16,919	C6

CITIES and TOWNS

Alachua 4,529	D2
Alford 472	D6
Altamonte Springs 34,879	E3
Altha 497	A1
Altoona 800	E3
Alturas 900	E4
Alva 1,036	E5
Anna Maria 1,744	D4
Anthony 500	D2
Apalachicola▲ 2,602	A2
Apollo Beach 6,025	C3
Apopka 13,512	E3

Arcadia▲ 6,488	E4
Archer 1,372	D2
Aripeka 450	D3
Astatula 981	E3
Astor 1,273	E2
Atlantic Beach 11,636	E1
Auburndale 8,858	E3
Avon Park 8,042	E4
Azalea Park 8,926	E3
Babson Park 1,125	E4
Bagdad 1,457	B6
Baker 500	C6
Bal Harbour 3,045	C4
Baldwin 1,450	E1
Barberville 500	E2
Bartow▲ 14,716	E4
Bascom 90	A1
Basinger 300	F4
Bay Harbor Islands 4,703	A4
Bay Lake	E3
Bay Pines 4,171	B3
Bayshore 17,062	E5
Bayshore Gardens 14,945	D4
Bee Ridge 6,406	D4
Bell 267	D2
Belle Glade 16,177	F5
Belle Glade Camp 1,616	F5
Belle Isle 5,272	E3
Belleair 3,968	B2
Belleair Beach 2,070	B2
Belleair Bluffs 2,128	B3
Belleair Shore 80	B3
Belleview 2,666	D2
Beverly Beach 312	E2
Biscayne Park 3,068	B4
Bithlo 4,834	E3
Blountstown▲ 2,404	A1
Boca Grande 900	D5
Boca Raton 61,492	F5
Bokeelia 750	D5
Bonifay▲ 2,612	C5
Bonita Sings 5,435	E5

Bostwick 500	E2
Boulogne	E1
Bowling Green 1,836	E4
Boynton Beach 46,194	F5
Bradenton Beach 1,657	D4
Bradenton▲ 43,779	D4
Bradley 1,108	D4
Brandon 57,985	D4
Branford 670	D2
Briny Breezes 400	G5
Bristol▲ 937	B1
Broadview Park-Rock Hill 6,022	B4
Bronson▲ 875	D2
Brooker 312	D2
Brooksville▲ 7,440	D3
Browardale 6,257	B4
Browns Village	B5
Bruce 250	C6
Bunche Park 4,388	B4
Bunnell▲ 1,873	E2
Bushnell▲ 1,998	D3
Callahan 946	E1
Callaway 12,253	D6
Campbellton 202	D5
Canal Point 900	F5
Candler 275	E2
Cantonment	B6
Cape Canaveral 8,014	F3
Cape Coral 74,991	E5
Carol City 53,331	B4
Carrabelle 1,200	B2
Caryville 631	C6
Cassadaga 325	E3
Casselberry 18,911	E3
Cedar Grove 1,479	D6
Cedar Key 668	C2
Center Hill 735	D3
Century 1,859	B5
Charlotte Harbor 3,327	E5
Chattahoochee 4,382	B1
Cherry Lake Farms 400	C1

Chiefland 1,917	D2
Chipley▲ 3,866	D6
Chokoloskee 600	E6
Christmas 800	E3
Cinco Bayou 322	B6
Citra 350	D2
Clarksville 350	D6
Clearwater▲ 98,784	B2
Clermont 6,910	E3
Cleveland 2,896	E5
Clewiston 6,085	E5
Cocoa 17,722	F3
Cocoa Beach 12,123	F3
Coconut Creek 27,485	F5
Coleman 857	D3
Compass Lake 296	D6
Concord 300	B1
Cooper City 20,791	B4
Copeland 350	E6
Coral Cove 2,042	D4
Coral Gables 40,091	B5
Coral Springs 79,443	F5
Cornwell 700	E4
Cortez 4,509	D4
Cottage Hill 500	B6
Cottondale 900	D6
Crawfordville▲ 1,110	B1
Crescent City 1,859	E2
Crestview▲ 9,886	C6
Cross City▲ 2,041	C2
Crystal Lake 5,300	D6
Crystal River 4,044	D3
Crystal Springs 800	D3
Cutler Ridge 21,268	F6
Cypress 9,188	A1
Cypress Gardens 8,043	E3
Cypress Quarters 1,343	F4
Dade City▲ 5,633	D3
Dania 13,024	B4
Davenport 1,529	E3
Davie 47,217	B4
Day 61,921	C1

Lehigh Acres 13,611 ......E5
Leisure City 19,379 ......F6
Leonia 350 ......C5
Leto 9,003 ......C2
Lighthouse Point 10,378 ......F5
Live Oak▲ 6,332 ......D1
Lloyd 500 ......C1
Lochloosa 400 ......E2
Longboat Key 5,937 ......D4
Longwood 13,316 ......E3
Lorida 950 ......E4
Loughman 1,214 ......E3
Lowell 250 ......D2
Loxahatchee 950 ......F5
Lutz 10,552 ......D3
Lynn Haven 9,298 ......C6
Macclenny▲ 3,966 ......D1
Madeira Beach 4,225 ......B3
Madison▲ 3,345 ......C1
Maitland 9,110 ......E3
Malabar 1,977 ......F3
Malone 765 ......A1
Mango 8,700 ......D4
Marathon 8,857 ......E7
Marco (Marco Island) 9,493 ...E6
Margate 42,985 ......F5
Marianna▲ 6,292 ......A1
Marineland 21 ......E2
Mary Esther 4,139 ......B6
Masaryktown 389 ......D3
Mascotte 1,761 ......E3
Mayo▲ 917 ......C1
McDavid 500 ......B5
McIntosh 411 ......D2
Medley 663 ......B4
Melbourne 59,646 ......F3
Melbourne Beach 3,021 ......F3
Melrose 6,477 ......D2
Melrose Park 5,672 ......B4
Memphis 6,760 ......B4
Merritt Island 32,886 ......F3
Mexico Beach 992 ......D6
Miami Beach 92,639 ......C5
Miami Lakes 12,750 ......B4
Miami Shores 10,084 ......B4
Miami Springs 13,268 ......B5
Miami▲ 358,548 ......B5
Micanopy 612 ......D2
Micco 8,757 ......F4
Miccosukee 300 ......B1
Middleburg 6,223 ......E1
Midway 852 ......B1
Milligan 950 ......C6
Milton▲ 7,216 ......B6
Mims 9,412 ......F3
Minneola 1,515 ......E3
Miramar 40,663 ......B4
Molino 1,207 ......B6

Montbrook 250 ......D2
Monticello▲ 2,573 ......C1
Montverde 890 ......E3
Moore Haven▲ 1,432 ......E5
Mossy Head 280 ......C6
Mount Dora 7,196 ......E3
Mulberry 2,988 ......E4
Murdock 272 ......D4
Myakka City 672 ......D4
Myrtle Grove 17,402 ......B6
Naples Park 8,002 ......E5
Naples▲ 19,505 ......E5
Naranja 5,790 ......F6
Neptune Beach 6,816 ......E1
New Port Richey 14,044 ......D3
New Smyrna Beach 16,543 ....F2
Newberry 1,644 ......D2
Niceville 10,507 ......C6
Nichols 300 ......E4
Nocatee 950 ......E4
Nokomis 3,448 ......D4
Noma 207 ......C5
Norland 22,109 ......B4
North Bay Village 5,383 ......B4
North Fort Myers 30,027 ......E5
North Lauderdale 26,506 ......B3
North Miami 49,998 ......B4
North Miami Beach 35,359 ....C4
North Naples 13,422 ......E5
North Palm Beach 11,343 ......F5
North Port 11,973 ......D4
North Redington Beach 1,135.B3
Oak Hill 917 ......F3
Oakland 700 ......E3
Oakland Park 1,743 ......B3
Ocala▲ 42,045 ......D2
Ocean Breeze Park 519 ......F4
Ocean Ridge 1,570 ......F5
Ochopee 750 ......E6
Ocoee 12,778 ......E3
Odessa 500 ......D3
Ojus 15,519 ......B4
Okahumpka 900 ......D3
Okeechobee▲ 4,943 ......F4
Oklawaha 700 ......E2
Old Town 850 ......C2
Oldsmar 8,361 ......B2
Olustee 400 ......D1
Ona E4
Oneco 6,417 ......D4
Opa Locka 14,460 ......B4
Orange 5,347 ......B1
Orange City 2,795 ......E3
Orange Lake 900 ......D2
Orange Park 9,488 ......E1
Orange Springs 500 ......E2
Orchid 10 ......F4
Orlando▲ 164,693 ......E3

Ormond Beach 29,721 ......E2
Ormond-by-the-Sea 7,665 ....E2
Osprey 2,597 ......D4
Osteen 875 ......E3
Otter Creek 136 ......D2
Oviedo 11,114 ......E3
Oxford D3
Ozona 900 ......B3
Pace 6,277 ......B6
Pahokee 6,822 ......F5
Palatka▲ 10,201 ......E2
Palm Bay 62,632 ......F3
Palm Beach 9,814 ......G5
Palm Beach Gardens 22,965 ...F5
Palm Beach Shores 1,040 ....G5
Palm City 3,925 ......F4
Palm Coast 14,287 ......E2
Palm Harbor 50,256 ......D3
Palm River-Clair Mel 14,447..C3
Palm Shores 210 ......F3
Palm Springs 9,763 ......G5
Palmetto 9,268 ......D4
Panacea 950 ......B1
Panama City Beach 4,051 ......C6
Panama City▲ 34,378 ......C6
Parker 4,598 ......C6
Parkland 3,558 ......F5
Parrish 950 ......D4
Paxton 600 ......C5
Pembroke Park 4,933 ......B4
Pembroke Pines 65,452 ......B4
Penney Farms 609 ......E2
Pennsuco 15 ......B4
Pensacola▲ 58,165 ......B6
Perrine 15,576 ......F6
Perry▲ 7,151 ......C1
Pierce 500 ......E4
Pierson 2,988 ......E2
Pine Hills 35,322 ......E3
Pineland 900 ......D5
Pinellas Park 43,426 ......B3
Placida 250 ......D5
Plant City 22,754 ......D3
Plantation 1,885 ......B4
Plymouth 950 ......E3
Polk City 1,439 ......E3
Pomona Park 663 ......E2
Pompano Beach 72,411 ......F5
Ponce Inlet 1,704 ......F2
Ponce de Leon 406 ......C6
Ponte Vedra Beach E1
Port Charlotte 41,535 ......D5
Port Mayaca 400 ......F5
Port Orange 35,317 ......F2
Port Richey 2,523 ......D3
Port Saint Joe 4,044 ......D6
Port Saint Lucie 55,866 ......F4
Port Salerno 7,786 ......F4

Portland 300 ......C6
Princeton 7,073 ......F6
Progress Village C3
Punta Gorda▲ 10,747 ......E5
Quincy▲ 7,444 ......B1
Raiford 198 ......D1
Raleigh 275 ......D2
Red Bay 300 ......C6
Reddick 554 ......D2
Redington Beach 1,626 ......B3
Redington Shores 2,366 ......B3
Richland 250 ......D3
Richmond Heights 8,583 ......F6
Riverland 5,919 ......B4
Riverview 6,478 ......D4
Riviera Beach 27,639 ......G5
Rockledge 16,023 ......F3
Roseland 1,379 ......F4
Round Lake 275 ......D6
Ruskin 6,046 ......C3
Safety Harbor 15,124 ......B3
Saint Augustine Beach 3,657 .E2
Saint Augustine▲ 11,692 ......E2
Saint Catherine 486 ......D3
Saint Cloud 12,453 ......E3
Saint James City 1,904 ......D5
Saint Leo 1,009 ......D3
Saint Lucie 584 ......F4
Saint Marks 307 ......B1
Saint Petersburg 238,629 ......B3
Saint Petersburg Beach 9,200 B3
Samoset 3,119 ......D4
Samsula (Samsula-Spruce
  Creek) 3,404 ......F2
San Antonio 776 ......D3
San Mateo 975 ......E2
Sanderson 800 ......D1
Sanford▲ 32,387 ......E3
Sanibel 5,468 ......D5
Sarasota Springs 16,088 ......D4
Sarasota▲ 50,961 ......D4
Satellite Beach 9,889 ......F3
Satsuma 610 ......E2
Scottsmoor 900 ......F3
Sea Ranch Lakes 619 ......C3
Sebastian 10,205 ......F4
Sebring▲ 8,900 ......E4
Seffner 5,371 ......D4
Seminole 9,251 ......B3
Seville 500 ......E2
Sewalls Point 1,187 ......F4
Shalimar 341 ......C6
Sharpes 3,348 ......F3
Siesta Key 7,772 ......D4
Silver Springs 6,421 ......D2
Sneads 1,746 ......B1
Sopchoppy 367 ......B1
Sorrento 500 ......E3

South Bay 3,558 ......F5
South Daytona 12,482 ......F2
South Miami 10,404 ......B5
South Miami Heights 30,030..F6
South Pasadena 5,644 ......B3
South Patrick Shores 10,249 .F3
South Venice 11,951 ......D4
Southport 1,992 ......C6
Sparr 902 ......D2
Springfield 8,715 ......C6
Starke▲ 5,226 ......D2
Steinhatchee 800 ......C2
Stuart▲ 11,936 ......F4
Summerfield 780 ......D2
Summerland Key 350 ......E7
Sun City Center 5,605 ......C4
Sunny Isles 11,772 ......C4
Sunnyside 1,008 ......C6
Sunrise 64,407 ......B4
Surfside 4,108 ......C4
Suwannee 365 ......C2
Sweetwater 13,909 ......B5
Switzerland 3,906 ......E1
Taft 900 ......E3
Tallahassee (cap.)▲ 124,773..B1
Tamarac 44,822 ......B3
Tampa▲ 280,015 ......D4
Tarpon Springs 17,906 ......D3
Tavares▲ 7,383 ......E3
Tavernier 2,433 ......F6
Telogia 400 ......B1
Temple Terrace 16,444 ......C2
Tequesta 4,499 ......F5
Terra Ceia 450 ......D4
Thonotosassa 900 ......D3
Tice 3,971 ......E5
Titusville▲ 39,394 ......F3
Town'n Country 60,946 ......B3
Treasure Island 7,266 ......B3
Trenton▲ 1,287 ......D2
Trilby 930 ......D3
Umatilla 2,350 ......E3
University 23,760 ......C2
Valparaiso 4,672 ......C6
Venice 16,922 ......D4
Venus 500 ......E4
Vernon 778 ......C6
Vero Beach▲ 17,350 ......F4
Villa Tasso 365 ......C6
Virginia Gardens 2,212 ......B5
Wabasso 1,145 ......F4
Wacissa 350 ......B1
Waldo 1,017 ......D2
Walnut Hill 500 ......B5
Ward Ridge 104 ......D7

Watertown 3,340 ......D1
Wauchula▲ 3,253 ......E4
Wausau 313 ......D6
Waverly 2,071 ......E4
Webster 746 ......D3
Weeki Wachee 53 ......D3
Weirsdale 995 ......E2
Welaka 533 ......E2
Wellborn 300 ......D1
West Bay 500 ......C6
West Eau Gallie 2,591 ......F3
West Melbourne 8,399 ......F3
West Miami 5,727 ......B5
West Palm Beach▲ 67,643 ....F5
West Pensacola 22,107 ......B6
Westville 257 ......C6
Westwood Lakes 11,522 ......B5
Wewahitchka▲ 1,779 ......D6
White City 4,645 ......F4
White Springs 704 ......D1
Wildwood 3,421 ......D3
Williston 2,179 ......D2
Wilton Manors 11,804 ......B3
Wimauma 2,932 ......D4
Windermere 1,371 ......E3
Winter Beach 350 ......F4
Winter Garden 9,745 ......E3
Winter Haven 24,725 ......E3
Winter Park 22,242 ......E3
Winter Springs 22,151 ......E3
Woodville 2,760 ......B1
Worthington Springs 178 ......D2
Yalaha 1,168 ......E3
Yankeetown 635 ......D2
Youngstown 900 ......D6
Yulee 6,915 ......E1
Zellwood 1,760 ......E3
Zephyrhills 8,220 ......D3
Zolfo Springs 1,219 ......E4

OTHER FEATURES

Alapaha (riv.) C1
Alligator (lake) E3
Amelia (isl.) E1
Anastasia (isl.) E2
Anclote (keys) D3
Apalachee (bay) B2
Apalachicola (bay) B2
Apalachicola (riv.) A1
Apopka (lake) E3
Arbuckle (lake) E4
Aucilla (riv.) C1
Banana (riv.) F3
Beresford (lake) E3
Big Cypress (swamp) E5
Big Cypress Nat'l Preserve..E5
Biscayne (bay) F6
Biscayne (key) B5
Biscayne Nat'l Park F6
Blackwater (riv.) B6
Blue Cypress (lake) F4
Boca Chica (key) E7
Boca Ciega (bay) B3
Boca Grande (key) D7
Bryant (lake) E2
Caloosahatchee (riv.) E5
Canaveral (cape) F3
Captiva (isl.) D5
Casey (key) D4
Castillo de San Marcos
  Nat'l Mon. E2
Cecil Field Naval Air Sta. E1
Charlotte (harb.) D5
Chattahoochee (riv.) B1
Chipola (riv.) D6
Choctawhatchee (riv.) C6
Crescent (lake) E2
Cumberland Island
  Nat'l Seashore E1
Cypress (lake) E3
De Soto Nat'l Mem. D4
Dead (lake) D6
Dexter (lake) E2
Dog (isl.) B2
Dorr (lake) E2
Dry Tortugas (keys) D7
Dumfoundling (bay) C4
East (pt.) E6
Eglin A.F.B 8,347 ......C6
Egmont (key) D4
Elliott (key) F6
Escambia (riv.) B6
Estero (isl.) E5
Eureka (res.) E2
Everglades, The (swamp) F6
Everglades Nat'l Park F6
Fenholloway (riv.) C1
Florida (bay) F6
Florida (cape) F6
Florida (keys) E7
Florida (strs.) F7
Fort Caroline Nat'l Mem. E1
Fort Jefferson Nat'l Mon. C7
Fort Matanzas Nat'l Mon. E2
Gasparilla (isl.) D5
George (lake) E2
Grassy (key) F7
Gulf Islands Nat'l Seashore..B6
Harney (lake) F3
Hart (lake) E3
Hillsborough (bay) C3
Hillsborough (canal) F5
Hillsborough (riv.) C2
Homestead A.F.B 5,153 ......F6
Homosassa (isls.) D3
Iamonia (lake) B1
Indian (riv.) F4
Iron (mt.) E4
Istokpoga (lake) E4
Jackson (lake) B1
Jackson (lake) D6
Jacksonville Naval Air Sta. ..E1
John F. Kennedy
  Space Center F3
June in Winter (lake) E4
Kerr (lake) E2

Key Largo (key) ......F
Key Vaca (key) ......
Key West Naval Air Sta. ......
Kissimmee (lake) ......E
Kissimmee (lake) ......
Largo (key) ......
Levy (lake) ......
Lochloosa (lake) ......
Long (key) ......
Long (key) ......
Longboat (key) ......
Lower Matecumbe (key) ......
Lowery (lake) ......
MacDill A.F.B. ......
Marco (isl.) ......
Marian (lake) ......
Marquesas (keys) ......
Matanzas (inlet) ......
Mayport Naval Air Sta. ......
McCoy A.F.B. ......
Merritt (isl.) ......
Mexico (gulf) ......
Miami (canal) ......
Miami (riv.) ......
Miccosukee (lake) ......
Monroe (lake) ......
Mosquito (lag.) ......
Mullet (key) ......
Myakka (riv.) ......
Nassau (riv.) ......
Nassau (sound) ......
New (riv.) ......
New (riv.) ......
Newnans (lake) ......
North Merritt (isl.) ......
North New River (canal) ......
Ochlockonee (riv.) ......
Okaloacoochee Slough
  (swamp) ......
Okeechobee (lake) ......
Okefenokee (swamp) ......
Oklawaha (riv.) ......
Old Rhodes (key) ......
Old Tampa (bay) ......
Olustee (riv.) ......
Orange (lake) ......
Patrick A.F.B. ......
Peace (riv.) ......
Pensacola (bay) ......
Pensacola Naval Air Sta. ......
Perdido (riv.) ......
Pine (isl.) ......
Pine Island (sound) ......
Pinellas (pt.) ......
Piney (pt.) ......
Piney (pt.) ......
Placid (lake) ......
Plantation (key) ......
Poinsett (lake) ......
Ponce de Leon (bay) ......
Port Everglades (harb.) ......
Poet Tampa (harb.) ......
Raccoon (pt.) ......
Reedy (lake) ......
Romano (cape) ......
Sable (cape) ......
Saint Andrew (pt.) ......
Saint George (cape) ......
Saint George (isl.) ......
Saint George (sound) ......
Saint Johns (riv.) ......
Saint Joseph (bay) ......
Saint Joseph (pt.) ......
Saint Lucie (canal) ......
Saint Lucie (inlet) ......
Saint Marys (riv.) ......
Saint Marys Entrance (inlet)..
Saint Vincent (isl.) ......
San Blas (cape) ......
Sand (key) ......
Sands (key) ......
Sanibel (isl.) ......
Santa Fe (lake) ......
Santa Fe (riv.) ......
Santa Rosa (isl.) ......
Santa Rosa (sound) ......
Sarasota (pt.) ......
Seminole (lake) ......
Seminole Ind. Res. ......
Seminole Ind. Res. ......
Shark (pt.) ......
Shoal (riv.) ......
Snake Creek (canal) ......
South New River (canal) ......
Stafford (lake) ......
Sugarloaf (key) ......
Suwannee (riv.) ......
Suwannee (sound) ......
Talbot (isl.) ......
Talquin (lake) ......
Tamiami (canal) ......
Tampa (bay) ......
Ten Thousand (isls.) ......
Torch (key) ......
Treasure (isl.) ......
Tsala Apopka (lake) ......
Tyndall A.F.B. ......
Upper Matecumbe (key) ......
Vaca (key) ......
Virginia (key) ......
Waccasassa (bay) ......
Waccasassa (riv.) ......
Washington (lake) ......
Weir (lake) ......
Weohyakapka (lake) ......
West Palm Beach (canal) ......
Whitewater (bay) ......
Whiting Field Naval Air Sta. ..
Wimico (lake) ......
Winder (lake) ......
Withlacoochee (lake) ......
Withlacoochee (riv.) ......
Yale (lake) ......
Yellow (riv.) ......

▲County seat

Agriculture, Industry and Resources

DOMINANT LAND USE

- Fruit, Truck & Mixed Farming
- Truck & Mixed Farming
- Truck Farming
- Cotton, Tobacco, Hogs, Peanuts
- Peanuts, General Farming
- General Farming, Forest Products, Truck Farming, Cotton
- Livestock Grazing
- Forests
- Swampland, Limited Agriculture
- Urban Areas
- Nonagricultural Land

MAJOR MINERAL OCCURRENCES

Cl Clay
Ls Limestone
O Petroleum
P Phosphates
Pe Peat
Ti Titanium
Zr Zirconium

⚡ Water Power   ▨ Major Industrial Areas

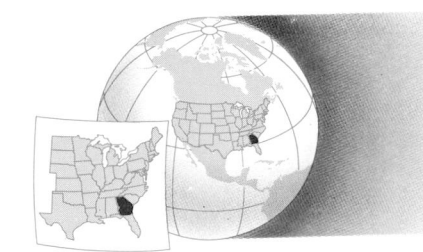

AREA 58,910 sq. mi. (152,577 sq. km.)
POPULATION 6,508,419
CAPITAL Atlanta
LARGEST CITY Atlanta
HIGHEST POINT Brasstown Bald 4,784 ft.
(1458 m.)
SETTLED IN 1733
ADMITTED TO UNION January 2, 1788
POPULAR NAME Empire State of the South;
Peach State
STATE FLOWER Cherokee Rose
STATE BIRD Brown Thrasher

COUNTIES

Appling 15,744	H7
Atkinson 6,213	G8
Bacon 9,566	G7
Baker 3,615	D8
Baldwin 39,530	F4
Banks 10,308	E2
Barrow 29,721	E2
Bartow 55,911	C2
Ben Hill 16,245	F7
Berrien 14,153	F8
Bibb 149,967	E5
Bleckley 10,430	F6
Brantley 11,077	J8
Brooks 15,398	E9
Bryan 15,438	K6
Bulloch 43,125	J6
Burke 20,579	J4
Butts 15,326	E3
Calhoun 5,013	C7
Camden 30,167	J9
Candler 7,744	H6
Carroll 71,422	B3
Catoosa 42,464	B1
Charlton 8,496	H9
Chatham 215,935	K6
Chattahoochee 16,934	C6
Chattooga 22,242	B1
Cherokee 90,204	D2
Clarke 87,594	E2
Clay 3,364	B7
Clayton 182,052	D3
Clinch 6,160	G9
Cobb 447,745	C3
Coffee 29,592	G8
Colquitt 36,645	E8
Columbia 66,031	H3
Cook 13,456	F8
Coweta 53,853	C4
Crawford 8,991	E5
Crisp 20,011	E7
Dade 13,147	A1
Dawson 9,429	D2
De Kalb 483,024	D3
Decatur 25,511	C9
Dodge 17,607	F6
Dooly 9,901	E6
Dougherty 96,311	D7
Douglas 71,120	C3
Early 11,854	C8
Echols 2,334	G9
Effingham 25,687	K6
Elbert 18,949	G2
Emanuel 20,546	H5
Evans 8,724	J6
Fannin 15,992	D1
Fayette 62,415	C4
Floyd 81,251	B2
Forsyth 44,083	D2
Franklin 16,650	F2
Fulton 648,951	D3
Gilmer 13,368	D1
Glascock 2,357	H4
Glynn 62,496	J8
Gordon 35,072	C2
Grady 20,279	D9
Greene 11,793	F3
Gwinnett 352,910	D2
Habersham 27,621	E1
Hall 95,428	E2
Hancock 8,908	G4
Haralson 21,966	B3
Harris 17,788	C5
Hart 19,712	G2
Heard 8,628	B4
Henry 58,741	D4
Houston 89,208	E6
Irwin 8,649	F7
Jackson 30,005	E2
Jasper 8,453	E4
Jeff Davis 12,032	G7
Jefferson 17,408	H4
Jenkins 8,247	J5
Johnson 8,329	G5
Jones 20,739	E5
Lamar 13,038	D4
Lanier 5,531	F8
Laurens 39,988	G6
Lee 16,250	D7
Liberty 52,745	J7
Lincoln 7,442	H3
Long 6,202	J7
Lowndes 75,981	F9
Lumpkin 14,573	D1
Macon 13,114	D6
Madison 21,050	F2
Marion 5,590	C6
McDuffie 20,119	H4
McIntosh 8,634	K7
Meriwether 22,411	C4
Miller 6,280	C8
Mitchell 20,275	D8
Monroe 17,113	E4
Montgomery 7,163	G6
Morgan 12,883	F3
Murray 26,147	C1
Muscogee 179,278	C6
Newton 41,808	E3
Oconee 17,618	F3
Oglethorpe 8,929	F3
Paulding 41,611	C3
Peach 21,189	E5
Pickens 14,432	D2
Pierce 13,328	H8
Pike 10,224	D4
Polk 33,815	B3
Pulaski 8,108	E6
Putnam 14,137	F4
Quitman 2,209	B7
Rabun 11,648	F1
Randolph 8,023	C7
Richmond 189,719	H4
Rockdale 54,091	D3
Schley 3,588	D6
Screven 13,842	J5
Seminole 9,010	C9
Spalding 54,457	D4
Stephens 23,257	F1
Stewart 5,654	C6
Sumter 30,228	D6
Talbot 6,524	C5
Taliaferro 1,915	G3
Tattnall 17,722	H6
Taylor 7,642	D5
Telfair 11,000	G7
Terrell 10,653	D7
Thomas 38,986	E9
Tift 34,998	E7
Toombs 24,072	H6
Towns 6,754	E1
Treutlen 5,994	G6
Troup 55,536	B4
Turner 8,703	E7
Twiggs 9,806	F5
Union 11,993	E1
Upson 26,300	D5
Walker 58,340	B1
Walton 38,586	E3
Ware 35,471	H8
Warren 6,078	G4
Washington 19,112	G4
Wayne 22,356	J7
Webster 2,263	C6
Wheeler 4,903	G6
White 13,006	E1
Whitfield 72,462	B1
Wilcox 7,008	F7
Wilkes 10,597	G3
Wilkinson 10,228	F5
Worth 19,745	E8

CITIES and TOWNS

Abbeville 907	F7
Acworth 4,519	C2
Adairsville 2,131	C2
Adel 5,093	F8
Adrian 615	G5
Ailey 579	G6
Alamo▲ 855	G6
Alapaha 812	F8
Albany▲ 78,122	D7
Aldora 127	D4
Allenhurst 594	J7
Allentown 273	F5
Alma▲ 3,663	G7
Alpharetta 13,002	D2
Alston 160	H6
Alto 651	E2
Alvaton 91	C4
Ambrose 288	G7
Americus▲ 16,512	D6
Andersonville 277	D6
Appling▲ 150	H3
Arabi 433	E7
Aragon 902	B2
Arcade 697	E2
Arco 6,189	J8
Argyle 206	G8
Arlington 1,513	C8
Armuchee 600	B2
Arnoldsville 275	F3
Ashburn▲ 4,827	E7
Athens▲ 45,734	F2
Atlanta (cap.)▲ 394,017	K1
Attapulgus 380	D9
Auburn 3,139	E2
Augusta▲ 44,639	J4
Austell 4,173	J1
Avalon 159	F1
Avera 215	G4
Avondale Estates 2,209	L1
Baconton 623	D7
Bainbridge▲ 10,712	C9
Baldwin 1,439	E2
Ball Ground 905	D2
Barnesville▲ 4,747	D5
Barney 146	E8
Bartow 292	G5
Barwick 385	E9
Baxley▲ 3,841	H7
Bellville 192	H6
Belvedere 18,089	L1
Benevolence 138	C7
Berkeley Lake 791	D3
Berlin 480	E8
Bethlehem 348	E3
Between 82	E3
Bibb City 597	B5
Bishop 158	F3
Blackshear▲ 3,263	H8
Blairsville▲ 564	E1
Blakely▲ 5,595	C8
Bloomingdale 2,271	K6
Blue Ridge▲ 1,336	D1
Bluffton 138	C7
Blythe 300	H4
Bogart 1,018	E3
Boston 1,395	E9
Bostwick 307	E3
Bowdon 1,981	B3
Bowersville 311	F2
Bowman 791	G2
Box Springs 518	C5
Braselton 418	E2
Braswell 247	C3
Bremen 4,356	B3
Brinson 238	C9
Bronwood 513	D7
Brookfield 600	F8
Brookhaven	K1
Brooklet 1,013	J6
Brooks 328	D4
Broxton 1,211	G7
Brunswick▲ 16,433	K8
Buchanan▲ 1,009	B3
Buckhead 176	F3
Buena Vista▲ 1,472	D6
Buford 8,771	D2
Butler▲ 1,673	D5
Byromville 452	E6
Byron 2,276	E5
Cadwell 458	G6
Cairo▲ 9,035	D9
Calhoun▲ 7,135	C2
Calvary 500	D9
Camak 220	G4
Camilla▲ 5,008	D8
Campton	E3
Canon 737	F2
Canton▲ 4,817	C2
Carl 263	E3
Carlton 282	F2
Carnesville▲ 514	F2
Carrollton▲ 16,029	C3
Carters 12,035	C1
Cartersville▲ 9,247	C2
Cataula 500	C5
Cave Spring 950	B2
Cecil 376	F8
Cedar Grove	A1
Cedartown▲ 7,978	B2
Center 3,251	F2
Centerville 2,622	E5
Centralhatchee 301	B4
Chalybeate Springs 265	C5
Chamblee 7,668	K1
Charles	H6
Chatsworth▲ 2,865	C1
Chauncey 312	F6
Chester 1,072	F6
Chickamauga 2,149	B1
Chula 500	E8
Clarkesville▲ 1,151	F1
Clarkston 5,385	L1
Claxton▲ 2,464	J6
Clayton▲ 1,613	F1
Clermont 402	E2
Cleveland▲ 1,653	E1
Climax 226	D9
Clyattville 500	F9
Cobb 338	E7
Cobbtown 494	H6
Cochran▲ 4,390	F6
Cohutta 529	C1
Colbert 443	F2
Coleman 137	C7
Colemans Lake	H5
College Park 20,457	K2
Collins 528	H6
Colquitt▲ 1,991	C8
Columbus▲ 179,278	C6
Comer 939	F2
Commerce 4,108	E2
Concord 211	D4
Conley 5,528	K2
Constitution	K2
Conyers▲ 7,380	D3
Coolidge 610	E8
Coosa 600	B2
Cordele▲ 10,321	E7
Corinth 136	B4
Cornelia 3,219	E1
Cotton 122	D8
Covington▲ 10,026	E3
Crandall	C1
Crawford 694	F3
Crawfordville▲ 577	G3
Crosland	E8
Crystal Springs 500	B2
Culloden 242	D5
Cumming▲ 2,828	D2
Cusseta▲ 1,107	C6
Cuthbert▲ 3,730	C7
Dacula 2,217	E3
Dahlonega▲ 3,086	D1
Daisy 138	J6
Dallas▲ 2,810	C3
Dalton▲ 21,761	C1
Damascus 290	C8
Danielsville▲ 318	F2
Danville 480	F5
Darien▲ 1,783	K8
Dasher 659	F9
Davisboro 407	G5
Dawson▲ 5,295	D7
Dawsonville▲ 467	D2
De Soto 258	D7
Dearing 547	H4
Decatur▲ 17,336	K1
Deenwood 2,055	H8
Deepstep 111	G4
Demorest 1,088	F1
Denton 335	G7
Dexter 475	G6
Dickey	C7
Dillard 199	F1
Dixie 259	E9
Dock Junction (Arco)	J8
Doerun 899	E8
Donalsonville▲ 2,761	C8
Dooling 28	E6
Doraville 7,626	K1
Douglas▲ 10,464	G7
Douglasville▲ 11,635	C3
Dry Branch 700	F5
Du Pont 177	G9
Dublin▲ 16,312	G5
Ducktown	D2
Dudley 430	F5
Duluth 9,029	D2
Dunwoody 26,302	K1
Durand 206	C5
East Dublin 2,524	G5
East Ellijay 303	C1
East Juliette	E4
East Newnan 1,173	C4
East Point 34,402	K2
Eastman▲ 5,153	F6
Eastville	E3
Eatonton▲ 4,737	F4
Eden 990	K6
Edge Hill 22	G4
Edison 1,182	C7
Elberta 1,559	E5
Elberton▲ 5,682	G2
Elizabeth 950	J1
Ellabell 500	K6
Ellaville▲ 1,724	D6
Ellenton 227	E8
Ellenwood	L2
Ellerslie 700	C5
Ellijay▲ 1,178	C1
Emerson 1,201	C2
Enigma 611	F8
Ephesus 324	B4

(continued on following page)

Agriculture, Industry and Resources

DOMINANT LAND USE

- Specialized Cotton
- Cotton, General Farming
- Cotton, Tobacco, Hogs, Peanuts
- Peanuts, General Farming
- General Farming, Livestock, Fruit, Tobacco
- General Farming, Forest Products, Cotton, Truck Farming
- Forests
- Swampland, Limited Agriculture
- Urban Areas

MAJOR MINERAL OCCURRENCES

Al	Bauxite
Ba	Barite
C	Coal
Cl	Clay
Fe	Iron Ore
Gn	Granite
Mi	Mica
Mn	Manganese
Mr	Marble
Sl	Slate
Tc	Talc
Ti	Titanium

Water Power ⚡   ▨ Major Industrial Areas

Eton 315 ....C1
Euharlee 850 ....C2
Evans 13,713 ....H3
Experiment 3,762 ....D4
Fair Oaks 6,996 ....J1
Fairburn 4,013 ....J2
Fairmount 657 ....C2
Fargo 800 ....G9
Farmington F3
Farrar E4
Fayetteville▲ 5,827 ....C4
Felton 500 ....B3
Finleyson 101 ....F6
Fitzgerald▲ 8,612 ....F7
Fleming 279 ....K7
Flemington 440 ....K7
Flippen 600 ....D3
Flovilla 602 ....E4
Flowery Branch 1,251 ....E2
Floyd J1
Folkston▲ 2,285 ....H9
Forest Park 16,925 ....K2
Forsyth▲ 4,268 ....E4
Fort Gaines▲ 1,248 ....C7
Fort Oglethorpe 5,880 ....B1
Fort Valley▲ 8,198 ....D5
Franklin Springs 475 ....F2
Franklin▲ 876 ....C4
Funston 248 ....E8
Gainesville▲ 17,885 ....E2
Garden City 7,410 ....K6
Garfield 255 ....H5
Gay 133 ....C4
Geneva 182 ....C5
Georgetown▲ 913 ....B7
Gibson▲ 679 ....G4
Gillsville 113 ....E2
Gilmore J1
Girard 195 ....J4
Glenn 3,676 ....B4
Glennville 4,144 ....J7
Glenwood 824 ....G6
Glenwood 881 ....L1
Glynco J8
Good Hope 181 ....E3
Gordon 2,468 ....F5
Grantville 1,180 ....C4
Gray▲ 2,189 ....F4
Grayson 529 ....E3
Graysville 193 ....B1
Greensboro▲ 2,860 ....F3
Greenville 1,167 ....C4
Griffin▲ 21,347 ....D4
Grovetown 3,596 ....H4
Gumbranch 291 ....J7
Guyton 740 ....K6
Haddock 800 ....F4
Hagan 787 ....J6
Hahira 1,353 ....F9
Hamilton▲ 454 ....C5

Hampton 2,694 ....D4
Hapeville 5,483 ....K2
Hardwick (Midway-
  Hardwick) 8,977 ....F4
Harlem 2,199 ....H4
Harrison 414 ....G5
Hartwell▲ 4,555 ....G2
Hawkinsville▲ 3,527 ....E6
Hazlehurst▲ 4,202 ....G7
Helen 300 ....E1
Helena 1,256 ....G6
Hephzibah 2,466 ....H4
Hiawassee▲ 547 ....E1
Higgston 274 ....F6
Hilltonia 402 ....J5
Hinesville▲ 21,603 ....J7
Hiram 1,389 ....C3
Hoboken 440 ....H8
Hogansville 2,976 ....C4
Holly Springs 2,406 ....D2
Homeland 981 ....H9
Homer▲ 742 ....F2
Homerville▲ 2,560 ....G8
Hoschton 642 ....E2
Howell J1
Hull 156 ....F2
Ideal 554 ....D6
Ila 297 ....F2
Indian Springs 1,273 ....E4
Industrial City 1,054 ....C1
Inman 500 ....D4
Iron City 503 ....C8
Irwinton▲ 641 ....F5
Isle of Hope 975 ....K7
Ivey 1,053 ....F5
Jackson▲ 4,076 ....E4
Jacksonville 128 ....G7
Jakin 137 ....C8
Jasper▲ 1,772 ....D2
Jefferson▲ 2,763 ....F2
Jeffersonville▲ 1,545 ....F5
Jenkinsburg 213 ....E4
Jersey 149 ....E3
Jesup▲ 8,958 ....J7
Jonesboro▲ 3,635 ....D4
Juliette 600 ....E4
Junction City 182 ....C5
Juno 522 ....D2
Kennesaw 8,936 ....C2
Keysville 284 ....H4
Kingsland 4,699 ....J9
Kingston 616 ....C2
Kite 297 ....G5
Knoxville▲ 75 ....D5
La Fayette▲ 6,313 ....B1
La Grange▲ 25,597 ....C4
Lake City 2,733 ....K2
Lake Park 500 ....F9
Lakeland▲ 2,467 ....F8

Lavonia 1,840 ....F2
Lawrenceville▲ 16,848 ....D3
Leary 701 ....C8
Lebanon 800 ....D2
Leesburg▲ 1,452 ....D7
Leland J1
Lenox 783 ....F8
Leslie 445 ....D7
Lexington▲ 230 ....F3
Lilburn 9,301 ....D3
Lilly 138 ....E6
Lincoln Park 1,755 ....D5
Lincolnton▲ 1,476 ....G3
Lindale 4,187 ....B2
Linwood 342 ....B1
Lithia Springs 11,403 ....C3
Lithonia 2,448 ....D3
Lizella 975 ....E5
Locust Grove 1,681 ....D4
Loganville 3,180 ....E3
Lollie G6
Lone Oak 161 ....C4
Lookout Mountain 1,636 ....B1
Louisville▲ 2,429 ....H4
Lovejoy 754 ....D4
Lovett G5
Ludowici▲ 1,291 ....J7
Lula 1,018 ....E2
Lumber City 1,429 ....G7
Lumpkin▲ 1,250 ....C6
Luthersville 741 ....C4
Lyerly 493 ....B2
Lyons▲ 4,502 ....G6
Mableton 25,725 ....J1
Macon▲ 106,612 ....E5
Madison▲ 3,483 ....F3
Manassas 123 ....H6
Manchester 4,104 ....C5
Mansfield 341 ....E4
Marietta▲ 44,129 ....J1
Marlow 500 ....K6
Marshallville 1,457 ....D6
Martin 243 ....F2
Martinez 33,731 ....H3
Matthews H4
Maxeys 180 ....F3
Maysville 728 ....E2
McCaysville 1,065 ....D1
McDonough▲ 2,929 ....D4
McIntosh 500 ....K7
McIntyre 552 ....F5
McRae▲ 3,007 ....G6
Meansville 250 ....D4
Mechanicsville L1
Meigs 1,120 ....D8
Meldrim 510 ....K6
Menlo 538 ....B1
Merrillville E9
Metcalf E9
Metter▲ 3,707 ....H6

Middleton G2
Midville 620 ....H5
Midway 863 ....K7
Milan 1,056 ....G6
Milledgeville▲ 17,727 ....F4
Millen▲ 3,808 ....J5
Milner 321 ....D4
Milstead D3
Mineral Bluff 153 ....D1
Mitchell 181 ....G4
Modoc H5
Molena 439 ....D4
Monroe▲ 9,759 ....E3
Montezuma 4,506 ....E6
Monticello▲ 2,289 ....E4
Montrose 117 ....F5
Moreland 366 ....C4
Morgan▲ 252 ....C7
Morganton 295 ....D1
Morrow 5,168 ....K2
Morven 536 ....F9
Moultrie▲ 14,865 ....E8
Mount Airy 543 ....F1
Mount Berry B2
Mount Bethel K1
Mount Vernon▲ 1,914 ....G6
Mount Zion 511 ....B3
Mountain City 784 ....D1
Mountain Park 554 ....D2
Mountain View K2
Mountville 168 ....C4
Murrayville 550 ....E2
Nahunta▲ 1,049 ....H8
Nashville▲ 4,782 ....F8
Naylor 111 ....G7
Nelson 486 ....D2
New Holland 950 ....E2
Newborn 404 ....E3
Newington 319 ....J5
Newnan▲ 12,497 ....C4
Newton▲ 703 ....D8
Nicholls 1,003 ....G7
Nicholson 555 ....F2
Norcross 5,947 ....D3
Norman Park 711 ....E8
Normantown G6
North Canton 955 ....C2
North High Shoals 268 ....E3
Norwood 238 ....G4
Nunez 135 ....H6
Oak Park 269 ....H6
Oakfield 113 ....E7
Oakman 150 ....C1
Ochlocknee 588 ....E8
Ocilla▲ 3,182 ....F7
Oconee 234 ....F4
Odessadale 142 ....C5
Odum 388 ....H7
Oglethorpe▲ 1,302 ....D6

Ohoopee H6
Oliver 242 ....J5
Omaha 116 ....C6
Omega 912 ....E8
Orchard Hill 239 ....D4
Oxford 1,945 ....D3
Palmetto 2,612 ....C3
Pantherville 9,874 ....L1
Parrott 140 ....C7
Patterson 626 ....H8
Pavo 774 ....E9
Payne 192 ....D4
Peachtree City 19,027 ....C4
Pearson▲ 1,714 ....G8
Pelham 3,869 ....D8
Pembroke▲ 1,503 ....J6
Pendergrass 298 ....E2
Penfield F3
Perry▲ 9,452 ....E6
Phillipsburg 1,044 ....E8
Piedmont D3
Pine Lake 810 ....D3
Pine Mountain 875 ....C5
Pine Park D9
Pinehurst 388 ....E6
Pineora 387 ....K6
Pineview 594 ....F6
Pitts 214 ....E6
Pittsburg L1
Plainfield 128 ....F6
Plains 716 ....D6
Plainville 231 ....C2
Pocotalago F2
Pooler 4,453 ....K6
Port Wentworth 4,012 ....K6
Portal 522 ....J5
Porterdale 1,278 ....D3
Poulan 962 ....E8
Powder Springs 6,893 ....C3
Preston▲ 388 ....C6
Primrose 30 ....L1
Pulaski 264 ....J6
Putney 3,108 ....D8
Quitman▲ 5,292 ....F9
Raleigh C5
Ranger 153 ....C2
Ray City 603 ....F8
Rayle 107 ....F3
Rebecca 148 ....E7
Red Oak 950 ....C3
Register 195 ....J6
Reidsville▲ 2,469 ....H6
Remerton 463 ....F9
Reno D9
Rentz 364 ....F5
Resaca 604 ....C1
Rest Haven 176 ....E2
Reynolds 1,166 ....D5
Rhine 466 ....F6
Riceboro 745 ....K7

Richland 1,668 ....C6
Richmond Hill 2,934 ....K7
Riddleville 79 ....G5
Rincon 2,697 ....K6
Ringgold▲ 1,675 ....B1
Riverdale 9,359 ....K2
Riverside 74 ....B2
Riverside 99 ....E8
Roberta 939 ....D5
Rochelle 1,510 ....F7
Rockmart 3,356 ....B2
Rocky Face 500 ....C1
Rocky Ford 197 ....J5
Rocky Mount 56 ....C4
Rome▲ 30,326 ....B2
Roopville 248 ....B4
Rossville 3,601 ....B1
Roswell 47,923 ....D2
Royston 2,758 ....F2
Ruckersville F3
Russell 871 ....E3
Rutledge 659 ....E3
Saint George 600 ....H9
Saint Marks 36 ....C4
Saint Marys 8,187 ....J9
Saint Simons Island 12,026 ...K8
Sale City 324 ....D8
Sandersville▲ 6,290 ....G5
Sandy Springs 67,842 ....K1
Santa Claus 154 ....H6
Sardis 1,116 ....J5
Sargent 800 ....C4
Sasser 335 ....D7
Savannah▲ 137,560 ....L6
Scotland 244 ....G6
Scott 8,636 ....G5
Scottdale 8,770 ....L1
Screven 819 ....H7
Sea Island 600 ....K8
Senoia 956 ....C4
Seville 209 ....E7
Shady Dale 180 ....E4
Shannon 1,703 ....B2
Sharon 94 ....G3
Sharpsburg 224 ....C4
Shellman 1,162 ....C7
Shiloh 329 ....C5
Siloam 329 ....F3
Silver Creek 500 ....B2
Six Flags Over Georgia J1
Sky Valley 187 ....F1
Smithonia F2
Smithville 804 ....D7
Smyrna 30,981 ....K1
Snellville 12,084 ....D3
Social Circle 2,755 ....E3
Soperton▲ 2,797 ....G6
Sparks 1,205 ....F8
Sparta▲ 1,710 ....G4
Spring Place 246 ....C1
Springfield▲ 1,415 ....K6
Stapleton 330 ....H4
Statenville▲ 700 ....G9
Statesboro▲ 15,854 ....J6
Statham 1,360 ....E3
Stillmore 615 ....H6
Stockbridge 3,359 ....D3
Stockton 532 ....G9
Stone Mountain 6,494 ....D3
Stonewall 950 ....J2
Sugar Hill 4,557 ....E2
Sugar Valley C1
Summertown 153 ....H5
Summerville▲ 5,025 ....B2
Sumner 209 ....E7
Sunny Side 215 ....D4
Surrency 253 ....H7
Suwanee 2,412 ....D2
Swainsboro▲ 7,361 ....H5
Sycamore 417 ....E7
Sylvania▲ 2,871 ....J5
Sylvester▲ 5,702 ....E7
Talbotton▲ 1,046 ....C5
Talking Rock 62 ....D1
Tallapoosa 2,805 ....B3
Tallulah Falls 147 ....F1
Talmo 189 ....E2
Tarrytown 130 ....H6
Tate 950 ....D2
Taylorsville 269 ....C2
Tazewell D6
Tell J2
Temple 1,870 ....B3
Tennille 1,552 ....G5
The Rock 88 ....D5
Thomaston▲ 9,127 ....D5
Thomasville▲ 17,457 ....E9
Thomson▲ 6,862 ....H4
Thunderbolt 2,786 ....K6
Tifton▲ 14,215 ....F8
Tiger 301 ....E1
Tignall 711 ....G3
Toccoa▲ 8,266 ....F1
Toco Hills K1
Toomsboro 617 ....F5
Towns G7
Trenton▲ 1,994 ....A1
Trion 1,661 ....B1
Tunnel Hill 970 ....C1
Turin 189 ....C4
Twin City 1,466 ....H5
Ty Ty 579 ....E8
Tybee Island 2,842 ....L6
Tyrone 2,724 ....C4
Unadilla 1,620 ....E6
Union City 8,375 ....J2
Union Point 1,753 ....F3
Unionville 2,710 ....F8
Uvalda 561 ....H6
Valdosta▲ 39,806 ....F9
Van Wert 303 ....B3
Vanna F2
Varnell 358 ....C1
Vernonburg 74 ....K7
Vidalia 11,078 ....H6
Vidette H4

Vienna▲ 2,708 ....
Villa Rica 6,542 ....
Vinings 7,417 ....
Waco 461 ....
Wadley 2,473 ....
Waleska 700 ....
Walnut Grove 458 ....
Walthourville 2,024 ....
Waresboro 582 ....
Warm Springs 407 ....
Warner Robins 43,726 ....
Warrenton▲ 2,056 ....
Warwick 501 ....
Watkinsville▲ 1,600 ....
Waverly 769 ....
Waverly Hall 913 ....
Waycross▲ 16,410 ....
Waynesboro▲ 5,701 ....
Welcome All ....
Wesley ....
West Point 3,571 ....
Weston 42 ....
Whigham 605 ....
White 542 ....
White Plains 286 ....
White Sulphur Springs 118 C
Whitesburg 643 ....
Willacoochee 1,205 ....
Williamson 295 ....
Wilmington Island 11,230 .....
Winder▲ 7,373 ....
Winterville 876 ....
Woodbine▲ 1,212 ....
Woodbury 1,429 ....
Woodland 552 ....
Woodstock 4,361 ....
Woodville 415 ....
Woolsey 120 ....
Wrens 2,414 ....
Wrightsville▲ 2,331 ....
Yatesville 409 ....
Young Harris 604 ....
Zebulon▲ 1,035 ....

OTHER FEATURES

Alapaha (riv.) ....F
Allatoona (lake) C
Altamaha (riv.) ....H
Andersonville Nat'l Hist. Site ..D
Atlanta Naval Air Sta. ....
Banks (lake) ....
Bartletts Ferry (dam) ....
Blackshear (lake) ....
Blue Ridge (mts.) ....
Brasstown Bald (mt.) ....
Burton (lake) ....
Carters (lake) ....
Chattahoochee (lake) ....
Chattahoochee River
  Nat'l Rec. Area ....
Chattooga (riv.) ....
Chattooga (riv.) ....
Chatuge (lake) ....
Chickamauga and Chattanooga
  Nat'l Mil. Park ....
Coosa (riv.) ....
Coosawattee (riv.) ....
Cumberland (isl.) ....
Cumberland Island
  Nat'l Seashore. ....K
Dobbins A.F.B. ....
Doboy (sound) ....
Etowah (riv.) ....
Flint (riv.) ....
Fort Benning ....
Fort Frederica Nat'l Mon. ....
Fort Gordon 9,140 ....
Fort McPherson ....
Fort Pulaski Nat'l Mon. ......
Fort Stewart 13,774 ....
Goat Rock (lake) ....
Harding (lake) ....
Hartwell (lake) ....
Jekyll (isl.) ....
Jimmy Carter Nat'l Hist. Site ..D
Kennesaw Mtn. Nat'l
  Battlefield Park ....
Martin Luther King, Jr.,
  Nat'l Hist. Site. ....
Moody A.F.B.1,288. ....
Morgan Falls (dam) ....
Nottely (lake) ....
Ochlockonee (riv.) ....
Ocmulgee (riv.) ....
Ocmulgee Nat'l Mon. ....
Oconee (riv.) ....
Ogeechee (riv.) ....
Okefenokee (swamp) ....
Oliver (lake) ....
Oostanaula (riv.) ....
Ossabaw (sound) ....
Rabun (lake) ....
Robins A.F.B. 3,092 ....
Saint Andrew (sound) ....
Saint Catherines (isl.) ......
Saint Mary's (riv.) ....
Saint Simons (isl.) ....
Sapelo (isl.) ....
Satilla (riv.) ....
Savannah (riv.) ....
Sea (isls.) ....
Seminole (lake) ....
Sidney Lanier (lake) ....
Sinclair (lake) ....
Skidaway (isl.) ....
Springer (mt.) L
Strom Thurmond (lakes) ....
Suwannee (riv.) ..... G ....F
Walter F. George (res.) ......
Wassaw (sound) ....
Weiss (lake) ....
West Point (lake) ....

▲County seat

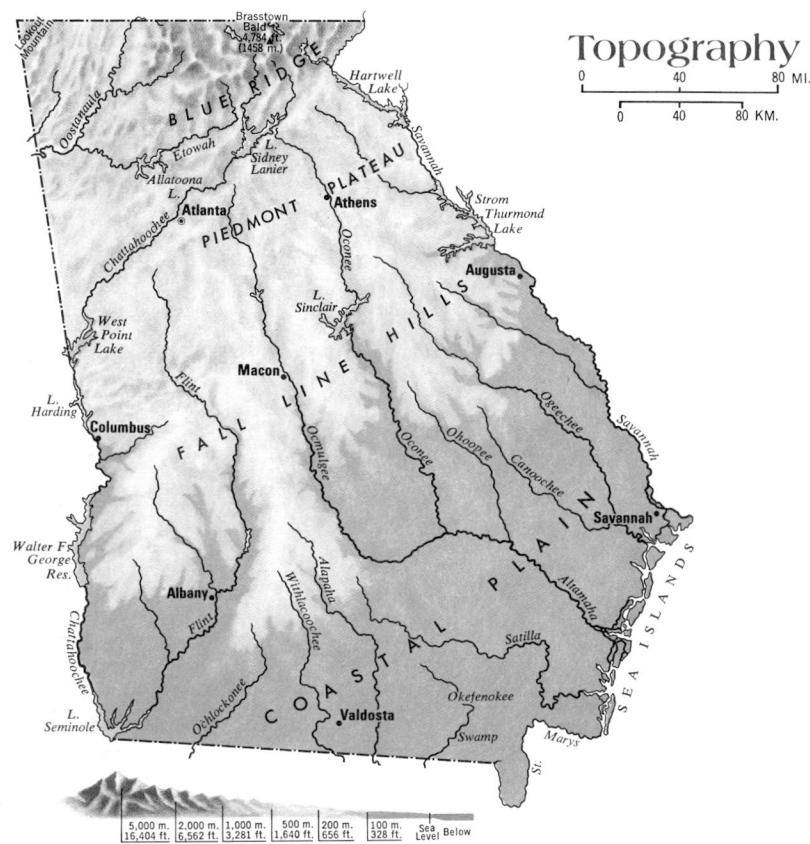

Topography

0   40   80 MI.

0   40   80 KM.

Brasstown Bald
4,784 ft.
(1458 m.)

BLUE RIDGE
Lookout Mountain
Oostanaula
Etowah
L. Allatoona
L. Sidney Lanier
Atlanta
PIEDMONT
Chattahoochee
PLATEAU
Athens
Hartwell Lake
Savannah
Strom Thurmond Lake
Augusta
West Point Lake
L. Sinclair
FALL LINE HILLS
Macon
Flint
L. Harding
Columbus
Oconee
Ocmulgee
Ohoopee
Oconee
Ogeechee
Canoochee
Savannah
Savannah
Walter F. George Res.
Alapaha
Withlacoochee
Alapaha
Flint
COASTAL PLAIN
Albany
Chattahoochee
Ochlockonee
Okefenokee
Satilla
Altamaha
SEA ISLANDS
Valdosta
Swamp
Marys
S

5,000 m. | 2,000 m. | 1,000 m. | 500 m. | 200 m. | 100 m. | Sea
16,404 ft. | 6,562 ft. | 3,281 ft. | 1,640 ft. | 656 ft. | 328 ft. | Level | Below

Georgia

SCALE
0 5 10   20   30   40 MI.
0 5 10   20   30   40 KM.

State Capitals .... ⊛
County Seats .... ⊙
Major Limited Access Hwys. _____

Scale 1:2,210,000

© Copyright HAMMOND INCORPORATED, Maplewood, N.J.

COUNTIES

Hawaii 120,317 ....K7
Honolulu 836,231 ....D3
Kalawao 130 ....G1
Kauai 51,177 ....A1
Maui 100,374 ....J1

CITIES and TOWNS

Aiea 8,906 ....B3
Aina Haina F2
Ala Moana C4
Anahola 1,181 ....C1
Barbers Point 2,218 ....E2
Captain Cook 2,595 ....G5
Eleele 1,489 ....C2
Ewa 14,315 ....A4
Ewa Beach 14,369 ....A4
Haena 200 ....C1
Haiku 4,509 ....J2
Haina 333 ....H3
Hakalau J4
Halawa Heights B3
Halawa, Hawaii 50 ....G3
Haleiwa 2,442 ....E1
Halfway House 150 ....H6
Haliimaile 841 ....J2
Hana 683 ....K2
Hanalei 461 ....C1

Hanamaulu 3,611 ....C1
Hanapepe 1,395 ....C2
Hauula 3,479 ....E1
Hawaii Kai F2
Hawaii National Park 250 ...J6
Hawi 924 ....G3
Hickam Housing 6,553 ....B4
Hilo▲ 37,808 ....J5
Holualoa 3,834 ....G5
Honaunau 2,373 ....G6
Honohina 125 ....J4
Honokaa 2,186 ....H4
Honokahua 309 ....H1
Honokohau 200 ....G5
Honokohau 309 ....H1
Honolulu (cap.)▲ 365,272 ...C4
Honomu 532 ....J4
Honouliuli 600 ....A3
Hoolehua G1
Huehue 100 ....G5
Huumula 50 ....H5
Hulopoe Bay H2
Huumula 125 ....H4
Iroquois Point 4,188 ....A4
Iwilei C4
Kaaawa 1,138 ....F1
Kaanapali 579 ....H2
Kahakuloa 75 ....J1
Kahala D5
Kahaluu 3,068 ....E2
Kahuku 2,063 ....E1

Kahului 16,889 ....J2
Kailua (Kailua Kona),
  Hawaii 9,126 ....F5
Kailua Kona F5
Kailua, Oahu 36,818 ....F2
Kaimuki D4
Kainaliu 512 ....G5
Kalae 150 ....G1
Kalaheo 3,592 ....C2
Kalaoa 4,490 ....G5
Kalapana 75 ....J6
Kalaupapa▲ 170 ....G1
Kalihi 435 ....C4
Kamalo 60 ....H1
Kamuela 1,179 ....G4
Kaneohe 35,448 ....F2
Kapaa 8,149 ....D1
Kapaahu 850 ....J6
Kapaau 1,083 ....G3
Kapalama C4
Kapoho 300 ....K5
Kapulena 125 ....H4
Kaumakani 803 ....C2
Kaumalapau Harbor G2
Kaunakakai 2,658 ....G1
Kaupakulua 600 ....K2
Kaupo 65 ....K2
Kawaihae 50 ....G4
Kawailoa 200 ....E1
Keaau 1,584 ....J5

Kealakekua 1,453 ....G5
Kealia 550 ....G6
Kealia, Kauai 300 ....D1
Keanae 280 ....K2
Keauhou F5
Kekaha 3,506 ....C2
Keokea 500 ....G6
Keokea 750 ....J2
Kihei 11,107 ....J2
Kilauea 1,685 ....C1
Kipahulu 75 ....K2
Koali 60 ....K2
Kohala (Kapaau) G3
Kokomo 500 ....K2
Koloa 1,791 ....C2
Koloa Landing C2
Kualapuu 1,661 ....G1
Kukaiau 75 ....H4
Kukuihaele 316 ....H3
Kula 800 ....J2
Kunia 550 ....E2
Kurtistown 910 ....J5
Lahaina 9,073 ....H2
Laie 5,577 ....E1
Lanai City 2,400 ....H2
Laupahoehoe 508 ....J4
Lawai 1,787 ....C2
Lihue▲ 5,536 ....C2
Lower Paia 1,500 ....J1
Maalaea 443 ....J2

Maili 6,059 ....D2
Makaha 7,990 ....D2
Makaiwa H2
Makakilo 9,828 ....E2
Makapala G3
Makawao 5,405 ....K2
Makaweli 500 ....B2
Makena 100 ....J2
Makiki C4
Mana B2
Manele Bay H2
Maunaloa 405 ....G1
Maunawili 4,847 ....F2
Mililani Town 29,359 ....E2
Mililii 120 ....G6
Moiliili C4
Mokapu 11,615 ....F2
Mokuleia 1,776 ....D1
Mountain View 3,075 ....J5
Naalehu 1,027 ....H7
Nanakuli 9,575 ....D2
Napili-Honokowai 4,332 ...H1
Ninole 75 ....J4
Olowalu 750 ....H2
Ookala 401 ....J4
Opihikao 125 ....K6
Paauhau 350 ....H4
Paauilo 620 ....H4
Pacific Heights 5,305 ....C4
Pacific Palisades E2

Pahala 1,520 ....H6
Pahoa 1,027 ....J5
Paia 2,091 ....J2
Papa 1,634 ....G6
Papaaloa J4
Papaikou 1,567 ....J5
Paukaa 495 ....J5
Pauwela 468 ....K2
Peahi 308 ....K2
Pearl City 30,993 ....B3
Pepeekeo 1,813 ....J4
Poipu 975 ....C2
Princeville 1,244 ....C1
Puako 397 ....G4
Puhi 1,210 ....C2
Pukalani 5,879 ....J2
Punaluu 672 ....H7
Puuanahulu 56 ....G4
Puuiki 75 ....K2
Puunene 572 ....J2
Puunui C4
Puuwai 200 ....A2
Schofield Barracks 19,597 ..E2
Spreckelsville 350 ....J1
Sunset Beach E1
Ulumalu 201 ....K2
Ulupalakua 75 ....J2
Volcano 1,516 ....J6
Wahiawa 17,386 ....E2
Waiakoa J2

Waialae D4
Waialua, Oahu 3,943 ....E1
Waianae 8,758 ....D2
Waihee 4,004 ....J2
Waikane 717 ....F2
Waikapu 729 ....J2
Waikiki 50 ....H4
Wailea, Hawaii 150 ....J4
Wailea-Makena, Maui 3,799 ..J2
Wailuku▲ 10,688 ....J2
Waimalu 29,967 ....B3
Waimanalo 3,508 ....F2
Waimanalo Beach 4,185 ...F2
Waimea (Kamuela), Hawaii
  1,840 ....G4
Waimea 200 ....C1
Waimea, Kauai 5,972 ....B2
Wainaku 1,243 ....J5
Wainiha 175 ....C1
Waiohinu 200 ....G7
Waipahu 31,435 ....A3
Waipio 11,812 ....H3
Waipio Acres 5,304 ....E2
Whitmore Village 3,373 .....E1

OTHER FEATURES

Alalakeiki (chan.) J3

Topography

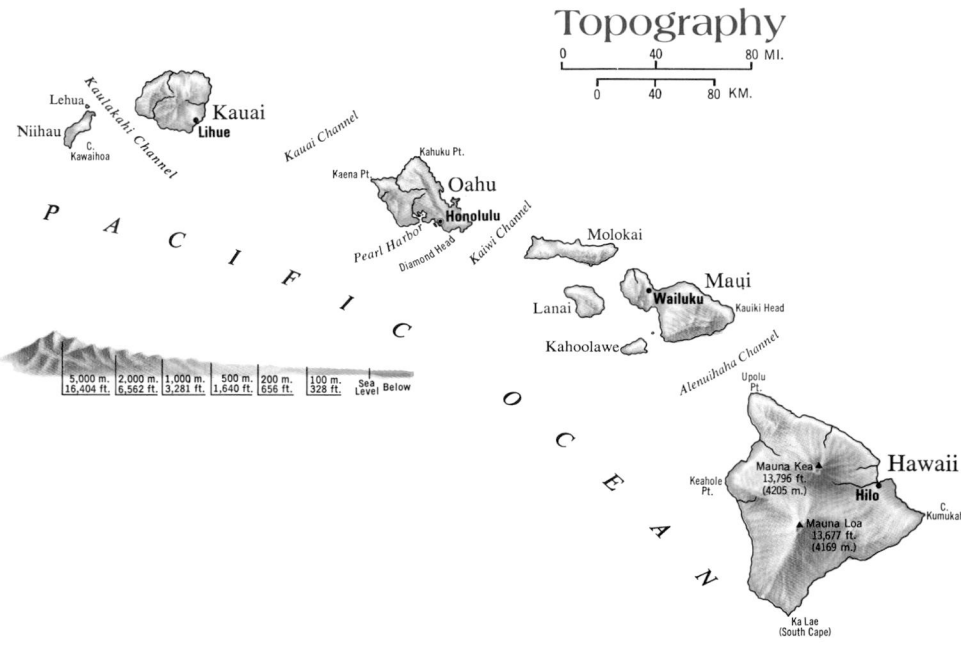

Agriculture, Industry and Resources

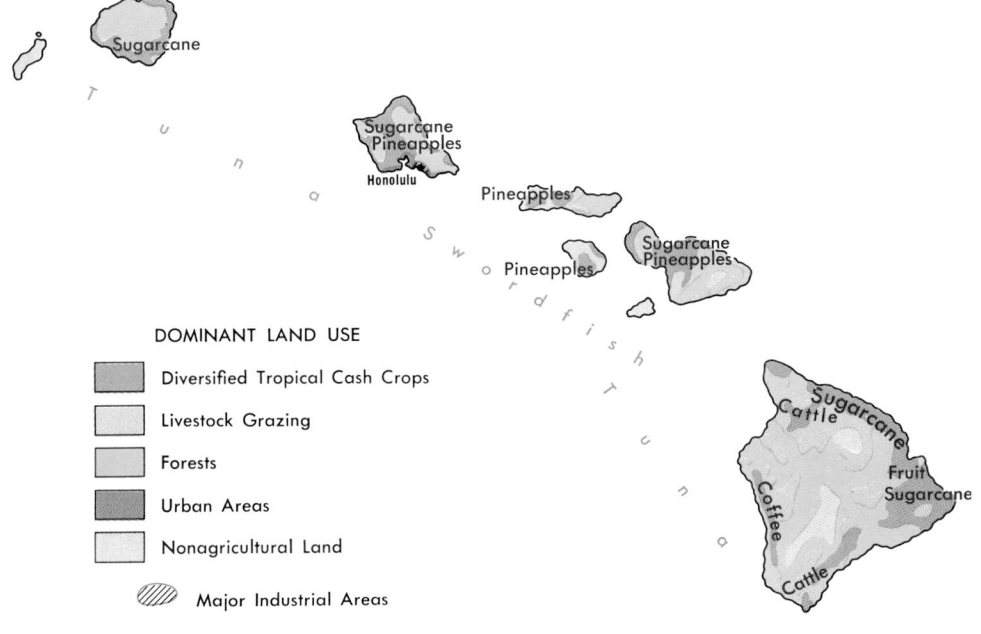

DOMINANT LAND USE

Diversified Tropical Cash Crops

Livestock Grazing

Forests

Urban Areas

Nonagricultural Land

Major Industrial Areas

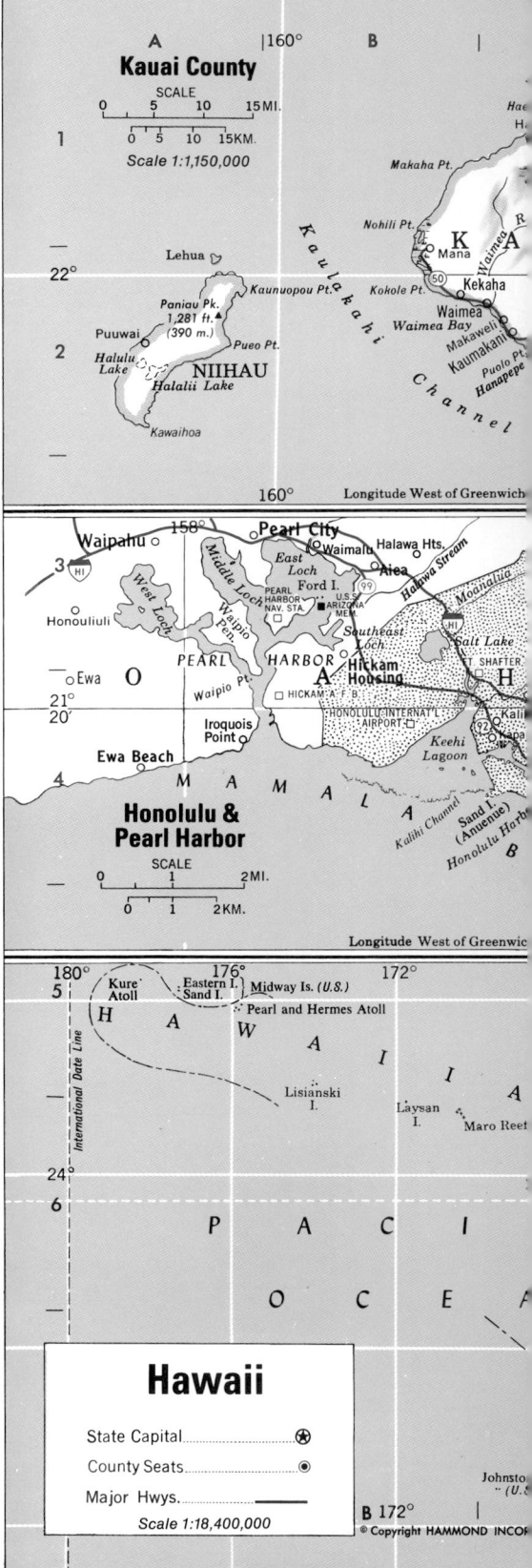

Kauai County

SCALE
Scale 1:1,150,000

Honolulu & Pearl Harbor

SCALE

Hawaii

State Capital ....⊛
County Seats ....⊙
Major Hwys. ....━━━

Scale 1:18,400,000

© Copyright HAMMOND INCOR

Alenuihaha (chan.) E7	Kamakou (peak) H1	Lisianski (isl.) B5
Anuenue (Sand) (isl.) C4	Kanapou (bay) J3	Lua Makika (mt.) J3
Auau (chan.) H2	Kaneohe Bay U.S.M.C.	Maalaea (bay) J2
Barbers Point Naval Air Sta....E2	Air Station F2	Makaha (pt.) B1
Diamond (head) C5	Kau (des.) J6	Makahuena (pt.) C2
East Loch (inlet) B3	Kauai (chan.) E6	Makapuu (pt.) F2
Ford (isl.) B3	Kauai (isl.) C1	Mamala (bay) B4
Fort Shafter 2,952 ....C3	Kauiki (head) K2	Manana (isl.) F2
French Frigate (shoals) C6	Kaulakahi (chan.) B2	Maro (reef) C6
Gardner Pinnacles (isls.)....C6	Kawaihae (bay) G4	Maui (isl.) J2
Halalii (lake) A2	Kawaihoa (cape) A2	Mauna Kea (mt.) H4
Halawa (bay) H1	Kawaikini (peak) C1	Mauna Loa (mt.) G6
Haleakala (crater) K2	Keahi (pt.) A4	Middle Loch (inlet) A3
Haleakala Nat'l Park K2	Kealaikahiki (chan.) H3	Moanalua (stream) B3
Hawaii (isl.) H5	Kealakekua (bay) G5	Mokapu (pen.) F2
Hawaii Volcanoes Nat'l Park ..H6	Kealakekua (bay) F6	Mokolii (isl.) F2
Hickam A.F.B. B4	Keanapapa (pt.) G2	Mokolii (isl.) F2
Hilo (bay) J5	Keehi (lag.) B4	Mokuaweoweo (crater) H6
Honolulu (harb.) C4	Kiholo (bay) F4	Molokai (isl.) G1
Honolulu Int'l Airport B4	Kilauea (crater) H6	Molokini (isl.) J2
Ilio (pt.) G1	Kohala (mts.) G4	Nawiliwili (bay) D2
Kaala (mt.) D1	Koko (head) F2	Necker (isl.) D6
Kahala (pt.) D1	Konahuanui (peak) D3	Nihoa (isl.) D6
Kahana (bay) F1	Koolau (range) E2	Niihau (isl.) A2
Kaiwi (chan.) E6	Kumukahi (cape) K5	Oahu (isl.) E1
Ka Lae (cape) G7	Kure (atoll) A5	Pailolo (chan.) H1
Kalaupapa Nat'l Hist. Park H1	Laau (pt.) G1	Palolo (stream) D4
Kalohi (chan.) G1	Laanihale (mt.) H2	Paniau (peak) A2
Kaloko-Honokohau	Lanai (isl.) H2	Pearl (harb.) A3
Nat'l Hist. Park F5	Laysan (isl.) B6	Pearl and Hermes (atoll) ...B5
		Pearl Harbor Naval Sta. B3
		Punchbowl (hill) C4

Puolo (pt.) C2	
Puuhonua O Honaunau	
Nat'l Hist. Park F6	
Puu Keahiakahoe (mt.) D3	
Puukohola Heiau	
Nat'l Hist. Park G4	
Puu Kukui (mt.) J2	
Red Hill (mt.) K2	
Roundtop (mt.) C4	
Salt (lake) B3	
Sand (isl.) B4	
South (Ka Lae) (cape) G7	
Southeast Loch (inlet) B3	
Sugarloaf (hill) C4	
Tantalus (mt.) D4	
Upolu (pt.) G3	
U.S.S. Arizona Memorial B3	
Waialeale (mt.) C1	
Waikiki (beach) C4	
Wailuku (riv.) J5	
Waimea (bay) B2	
Waimea (riv.) C2	
Wainiha (riv.) C1	
Waipio (bay) H3	
Waipio (pen.) A3	
Waipio (pt.) A4	
West Loch (inlet) A3	
Wheeler A.F.B. 2,600 ....E1	

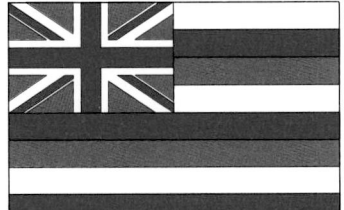

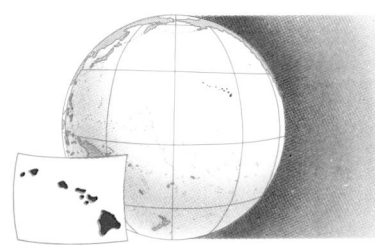

AREA 6,471 sq. mi. (16,760 sq. km.)
POPULATION 1,115,274
CAPITAL Honolulu
LARGEST CITY Honolulu
HIGHEST POINT Mauna Kea 13,796 ft. (4205 m.)
SETTLED IN —
ADMITTED TO UNION August 21, 1959
POPULAR NAME Aloha State
STATE FLOWER Hibiscus
STATE BIRD Nene (Hawaiian Goose)

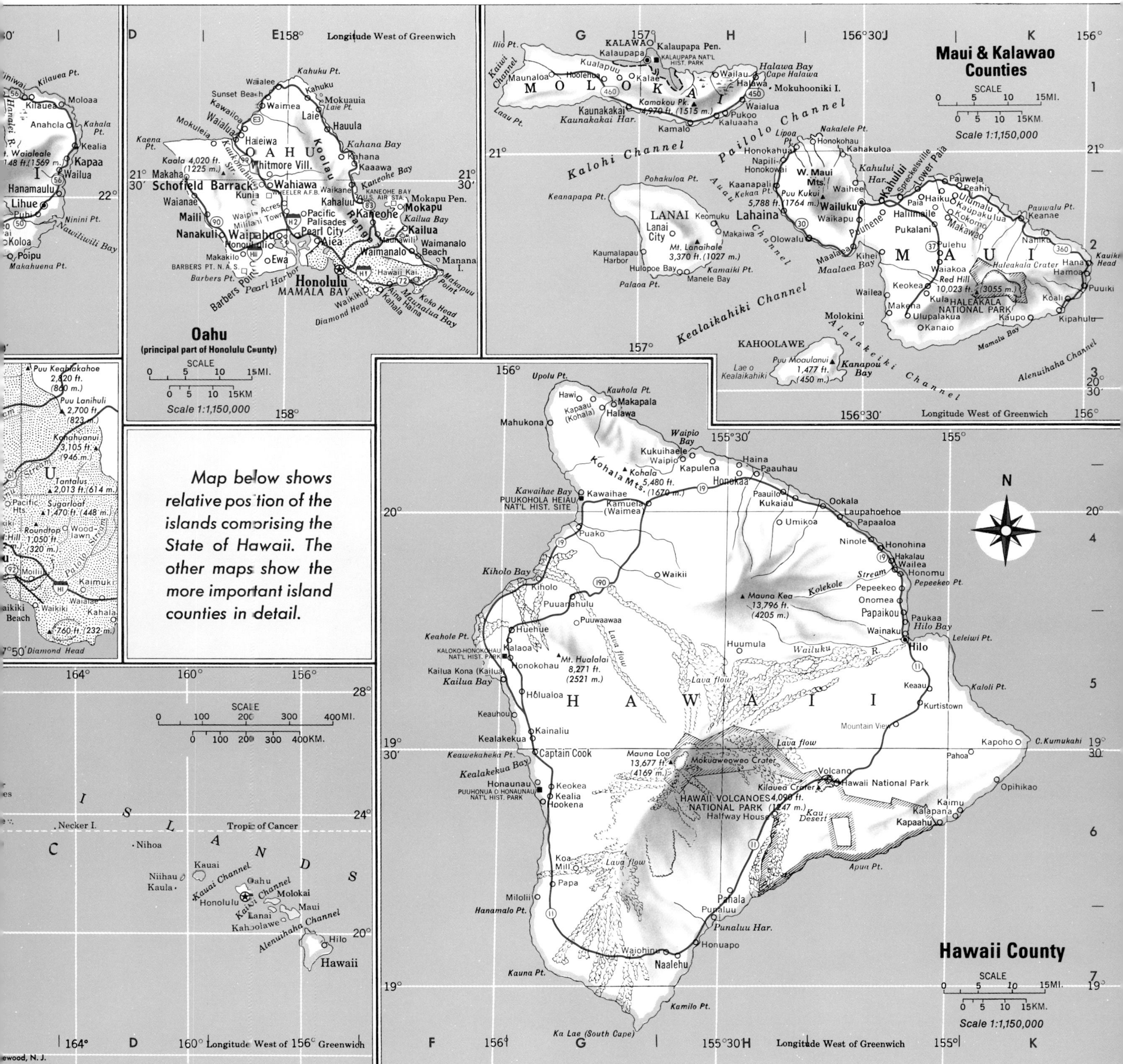

Map below shows relative position of the islands comprising the State of Hawaii. The other maps show the more important island counties in detail.

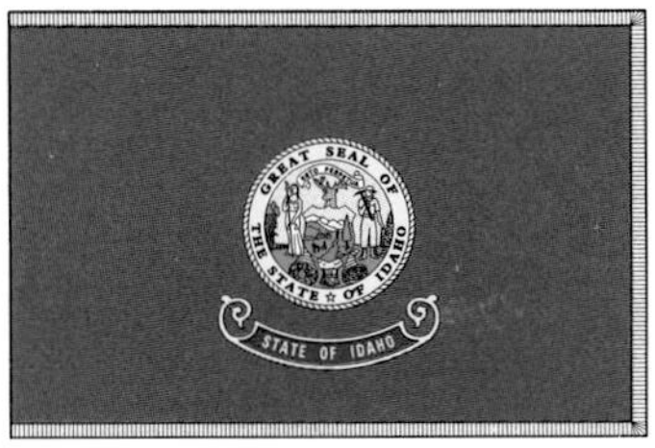
GREAT SEAL OF THE STATE OF IDAHO
STATE OF IDAHO

AREA 83,564 sq. mi. (216,431 sq. km.)
POPULATION 1,011,986
CAPITAL Boise
LARGEST CITY Boise
HIGHEST POINT Borah Pk. 12,662 ft. (3859 m.)
SETTLED IN 1842
ADMITTED TO UNION July 3, 1890
POPULAR NAME Gem State
STATE FLOWER Syringa
STATE BIRD Mountain Bluebird

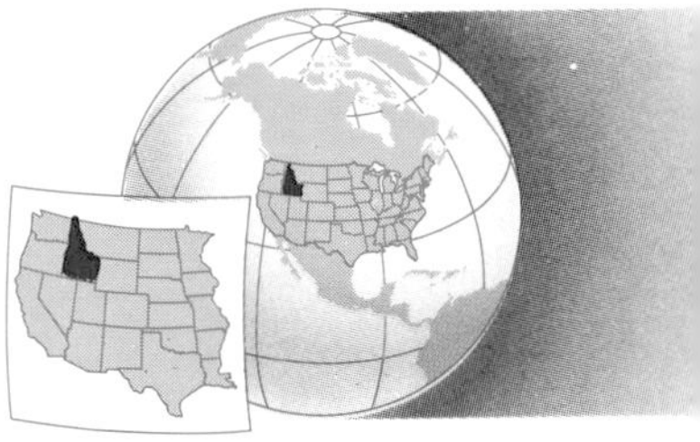

COUNTIES

Ada 205,775 B6
Adams 3,254 B5
Bannock 66,026 F7
Bear Lake 6,084 G7
Benewah 7,937 B2
Bingham 37,583 F6
Blaine 13,552 D6
Boise 3,509 C6
Bonner 26,622 B1
Bonneville 72,207 G6
Boundary 8,332 B1
Butte 2,918 E6
Camas 727 D6
Canyon 90,076 B6
Caribou 6,963 G7
Cassia 19,532 E7
Clark 762 F5
Clearwater 8,505 C3
Custer 4,133 D5
Elmore 21,205 C6
Franklin 9,232 G7
Fremont 10,937 G5
Gem 11,844 B6
Gooding 11,633 D6
Idaho 13,783 C4
Jefferson 16,543 F6
Jerome 15,138 D7
Kootenai 69,795 B2
Latah 30,617 B3
Lemhi 6,899 D4
Lewis 3,516 B3
Lincoln 3,308 D6
Madison 23,674 G6
Minidoka 19,361 E7
Nez Perce 33,754 B3
Oneida 3,492 F7
Owyhee 8,392 B7
Payette 16,434 B5
Power 7,086 F7
Shoshone 13,931 B2
Teton 3,439 G6
Twin Falls 53,580 D7
Valley 6,109 C5
Washington 8,550 B5

CITIES and TOWNS

Aberdeen 1,406 F7
Acequia 106 E7
Ahsahka 160 B3
Albion 305 E7
American Falls▲ 3,757 E7
Ammon 5,002 G6
Arco▲ 1,016 E6
Arimo 311 F7
Ashton 1,114 G5
Athol 346 B2
Atomic City 25 F6
Bancroft 393 G7
Basalt 407 F6
Bayview 350 B2
Bellevue 1,275 D6
Bern 154 G7
Blackfoot▲ 9,646 F6
Bliss 185 D7
Bloomington 197 G7
Boise (cap.)▲ 102,160 B6
Bonners Ferry▲ 2,193 B1
Bovill 256 B3
Bruneau 160 C7
Buhl 3,516 D7
Burgdorf B4
Burke 150 C2
Burley▲ 8,702 E7
Butte City 59 E6
Calder 200 B2
Caldwell▲ 18,400 B6
Cambridge 374 B5
Carey 800 E6
Cascade▲ 877 C5
Castleford 179 C7
Cataldo 150 B2
Challis▲ 1,073 D5
Chatcolet 72 B2
Chester 300 G5
Chilly E5
Chubbuck 7,791 F7
Clark Fork 448 B1
Clarkia 175 B2
Clayton 26 D5
Clifton 228 F7
Coeur d'Alene▲ 24,563 B2
Colburn 250 B1
Conda 200 G7
Coolin 150 B1
Cottonwood 822 B3
Council▲ 831 B5
Craigmont 542 B3
Crouch 75 B5
Culdesac 280 B3
Dalton Gardens 1,951 B2
Dayton 357 F7
Deary 529 B3
Declo 279 E7
Dietrich 127 D7
Dingle 300 G7
Donnelly 135 B5
Dover 294 B1
Downey 626 F7
Driggs▲ 846 G6
Drummond 37 G5
Dubois▲ 420 F5
Eagle 3,327 B6
East Hope 215 B1
Eden 314 D7
Elk City 500 C4
Elk River 149 B3
Emida 175 B2
Emmett▲ 4,601 B6
Fairfield▲ 371 D6
Ferdinand 135 B3
Fernan Lake 178 B2
Fernwood 608 B2
Filer 1,511 D7
Firth 429 F6
Fort Hall 2,681 F6
Franklin 478 G7
Fruitland 2,400 B6
Fruitvale 200 B5
Garden City 6,369 B6
Garden Valley 250 C5
Genesee 725 B3
Geneva 220 G7
Georgetown 558 G7
Gilmore E5
Glenns Ferry 1,304 C7
Gooding▲ 2,820 D7
Grace 973 G7
Grand View 330 B7
Grangeville▲ 3,226 B4
Greenleaf 648 B6
Grimes Pass C5
Hagerman 600 D7
Hailey▲ 3,687 D6
Hamer 79 F6
Hammett 180 C7
Hansen 848 D7
Harrison 226 B2
Hauser 380 A2
Hayden 3,744 B2
Hayden Lake 338 B2
Hazelton 394 E7
Headquarters 165 C3
Heise 84 G6
Heyburn 2,714 E7
Hollister 144 D7
Homedale 1,963 A6
Hope 99 B1
Horseshoe Bend 643 B6
Huetter 82 B2
Idaho City▲ 322 C6
Idaho Falls▲ 43,929 F6
Inkom 769 F7
Iona 1,049 G6
Irwin 108 G6
Island Park 159 G5
Jerome▲ 6,529 D7
Juliaetta 488 B3
Kamiah 1,157 B3
Kellogg 2,591 B2
Kendrick 325 B3
Ketchum 2,523 D6
Kimberly 2,367 D7
Kooskia 692 C3
Kootenai 327 B1
Kuna 1,955 B6
Laclede 400 B1
Lake Fork 250 B5
Lapwai 932 B3
Lava Hot Springs 420 F7
Leadore 74 E5
Lewiston▲ 28,082 A3
Lewisville 471 F6
Lost River (Grouse) 29 E6
Lowman 180 C5
Mackay 574 E6
Macks Inn 200 G5
Malad City▲ 1,946 F7
Malta 171 E7
Marsing 798 B6
McCall 2,005 C5
McCammon 722 F7
Meadows 250 B5
Melba 252 B6
Menan 601 F6
Meridian 9,596 B6
Middleton 1,851 B6
Midvale 110 B5
Minidoka 67 E7
Monteview 200 F6
Montpelier 2,656 G7
Moore 190 E6
Moreland 600 F6
Moscow▲ 18,519 B3
Mountain Home▲ 7,9[illegible]3 C6
Moyie Springs 415 B1
Mud Lake 179 F6
Mullan 821 C2
Murphy▲ 200 B6
Murtaugh 114 D7
Nampa 28,365 B6
Naples 250 B1
New Meadows 534 B4
New Plymouth 1,313 B6
Newdale 377 G6
Nezperce▲ 453 B3
Nordman 300 B1
North Fork 250 D4
Notus 380 B6
Oakley 635 D7
Ola 175 B5
Oldtown 151 A1
Onaway 203 B3
Orofino▲ 2,868 B3
Osburn 1,579 B2
Oxford 44 F7
Paris▲ 581 G7
Parker 288 G6
Parma 1,597 B6
Patterson 4 E5
Paul 901 E7
Payette▲ 5,592 B5
Pearl 8 B6
Peck 160 B3
Pierce 746 C3
Pinehurst 1,722 B2
Placerville 14 C6
Plummer 804 B2
Pocatello▲ 46,080 F7
Ponderay 449 B1
Post Falls 7,349 A2
Potlatch 790 A3
Preston▲ 3,710 G7
Priest River 1,560 A1
Rathdrum 2,000 A2
Reubens 46 B3
Rexburg▲ 14,302 G6
Richfield 383 D6
Rigby▲ 2,681 F6
Riggins 443 B4
Ririe 596 G6
Roberts 557 F6
Rockland 264 F7
Rupert▲ 5,455 E7
Sagle 600 B1
Saint Anthony▲ 3,010 G6
Saint Charles 211 G7
Saint Maries▲ 2,442 B2
Salmon▲ 2,941 D4
Samuels 467 B1
Sandpoint▲ 5,203 B1
Shelley 3,536 F6
Shoshone▲ 1,249 D7
Silver City 1 B6
Smelterville 464 B2
Soda Springs▲ 3,111 G7
Spencer 11 F5
Spirit Lake 790 A2
Stanley 71 D5
Star 500 B6
State Line 26 A2
Stites 204 C3
Sugar City 1,275 G6
Sun Valley 938 D6
Swan Valley 141 G6
Sweet 290 B6
Tendoy 155 E5
Tensed 90 B2
Terreton 400 F6
Teton 570 G6
Tetonia 132 G6
Thatcher 300 G7
Thornton 177 G6
Troy 699 B3
Twin Falls▲ 27,591 D7
Ucon 895 F6
Victor 292 G6
Wallace▲ 1,010 C2
Wardner 246 B2
Warm Lake 200 C5
Warm River 9 G5
Wayan 175 G7
Weippe 532 C3
Weiser▲ 4,571 B5
Wendell 1,963 D7
Weston 390 F7
White Bird 108 B4
Wilder 1,232 A6
Winchester 262 B3
Worley 182 B2

OTHER FEATURES

Albeni Falls (dam) B1
Albion (mts.) E7
Allan (mt.) D4
American Falls (res.) F6
Anderson Ranch (res.) C6
Antelope (creek) E6
Arrowrock (res.) C6
Auger (falls) D7
Badger (peak) E7
Bald (mt.) D5
Bannock (creek) F7
Bannock (peak) F7
Bannock (range) F7
Bargamin (creek) C4
Battle (creek) B7
Bear (lake) G7
Bear (riv.) G7
Bear River (range) G7
Beaver (creek) F5
Beaverhead (mts.) E4
Big (creek) C4
Big Boulder (creek) B7
Big Elk (peak) G6
Big Hole (mts.) G6
Big Lost (riv.) E6
Big Southern (butte) E6
Big Wood (riv.) D6
Birch (creek) F5
Birch Creek (valley) E5
Bitterroot (range) D3
Blackfoot (res.) G7
Black Pine (mts.) E7
Blue Nose (mt.) D4
Boise (mts.) B6
Boise (riv.) B6
Borah (peak) E5
Boulder (mts.) D6
Brownlee (dam) B5
Bruneau (riv.) C7
Camas (creek) D5
Camas (creek) D6
Camas (creek) F5
Canyon (creek) C6
Cape Horn (mt.) C5
Caribou (mt.) G6
Caribou (range) G6
Cascade (res.) C5
Castle (creek) B7
Castle (peak) D5
Cedar Creek (peak) E7
Cedar Creek (res.) D7
Centennial (mts.) F5
Chesterfield (res) F7
Clearwater (mts.) C3
Clearwater (riv.) B3
Coeur d'Alene (lake) B2
Coeur d'Alene (mts.) C2
Coeur d'Alene (riv.) B2
Cottonwood (butte) C4
Craig (mts.) B4
Crane Creek (res.) B5
Craters of the Moon
Nat'l Mon. E6
Deadwood (res.) C5
Deep (creek) B7
Deep (creek) F7
Deep Creek (mts.) F7
Diamond (peak) E5
Duck Valley Ind. Res. B7
Dworshak (res.) C3
East Sister (peak) C2
Eighteen Mile (peak) E5
Fish Creek (res.) E6
Fort Hall Ind. Res. F6
Goldstone (mt.) E4
Goose (creek) E7
Goose Creek (mts.) E7
Grand Canyon of the Snake
River (canyon) B4
Grays (lake) G6
Grays Lake Outlet (creek) G6
Greylock (mt.) C6
Hayden (lake) B2
Hells (canyon) B4
Hells Canyon
Nat'l Rec. Area B4
Henrys (lake) G5
Henrys Fork, Snake (riv.) G5
Hunter (peak) D3
Hyndman (peak) D6
Indian (creek) C5
Island Park (res.) G5
Jarbidge (riv.) C7
Johnson (creek) C5
Jordan (creek) A7
Kootenai (riv.) C1
Lemhi (pass) E5
Lemhi (range) E5
Lemhi (riv.) E5
Little Lost (riv.) E5
Little Owyhee (riv.) B7
Little Salmon (riv.) B4
Little Weiser (riv.) B5
Little Wood (riv.) D6
Lochsa (riv.) C3
Lolo (creek) C3
Lolo (pass) D3
Lone Pine (peak) D5
Lookout (mt.) D5
Lookout (mt.) F5
Lost River (range) E5
Lost Trail (pass) D4
Lowell (lake) B6
Lower Goose Creek (res.) D7
Lower Granite (lake) A3
Lucky Peak (lake) B6
Mackay (res.) E6
Magic (res.) D6
Malad (riv.) F7
Marsh (creek) F7
McGuire (mt.) D4
Meade (peak) G7
Meadow (creek) C4
Medicine Lodge (creek) F5
Middle Fork (peak) D5
Monument (peak) B4
Moose (creek) D3
Mores (creek) C6
Mormon (mt.) C4
Mountain Home (res.) C6
Mountain Home A.F.B. 5,936 C6
Moyie (riv.) B1
Mud (lake) F6
National Reactor Testing Sta. F6
Nez Perce Nat'l Hist. Park C3
Norton (peak) D6
Orofino (creek) C3
Owyhee (mts.) B6
Owyhee, East Fork (riv.) B7
Oxbow (dam) B5
Pack (riv.) B1
Pahsimeroi (riv.) E5
Palisades (res.) G6
Palouse (riv.) B3
Panther (creek) D4
Payette (lake) C4
Payette (mts.) B5
Payette (riv.) B6
Peale (mts.) G7
Pend Oreille (lake) B1
Pend Oreille (mt.) B1
Pend Oreille (riv.) A1
Pilot (peak) C4
Pilot (peak) C6
Pilot Knob (mt.) C4
Pinyon (peak) C5
Pioneer (mts.) D6
Pot (mt.) C3
Potlatch (riv.) B3
Priest (lake) B1
Priest (riv.) B1
Purcell (mts.) B1
Pyramid (peak) E4
Raft (riv.) E7
Rainbow (mt.) C5
Ranger (peak) D3
Rays (lake) F6
Red (riv.) C4
Redfish (lake) D5
Reynolds (creek) B6
Rhodes (peak) D3
Rock (creek) F7
Rocky (mts.) D1
Rocky Ridge (mt.) C3
Ryan (peak) D6
Saddle (mt.) D3
Saddle (mt.) F6
Sailor (creek) C7
Saint Joe (riv.) B2
Saint Maries (riv.) B2
Salmon (falls) C7
Salmon (riv.) B4
Salmon Falls (creek) D7
Salmon Falls Creek (res.) D7
Salmon River (mts.) C5
Sawtooth (range) C6
Sawtooth Nat'l Rec. Area D5
Secesh (riv.) C4
Selkirk (mts.) B1
Selway (riv.) C3
Seven Devils (mts.) B4
Shoshone (falls) D7
Sleeping Deer (mt.) D5
Smith (creek) B1
Smoky (mts.) D6
Snake (riv.) A3
Snake River (plain) D7
Snake River (range) G6
Spirit (lake) B2
Squaw (creek) B5
Squaw (peak) D4
Steamboat (mt.) C4
Steel (mt.) C6
Strike, C.J. (res.) C7
Sublett (mts.) E7
Sunset (peak) E6
Taylor (mt.) D5
Teton (riv.) G6
Thompson (peak) C5
Trinity (mt.) C6
Trout (creek) B1
Twin (falls) D7
Twin Peaks (mt.) D5
Walcott (lake) E7
Waugh (mt.) D4
Weiser (riv.) B5
White Knob (mts.) E6
Wickahoney (creek) C7
Willow (creek) G6
Wilson Lake (res.) D7
Yankee Fork, Salmon (riv.) D5
Yellowstone Nat'l Park H5

▲County seat

Agriculture, Industry and Resources

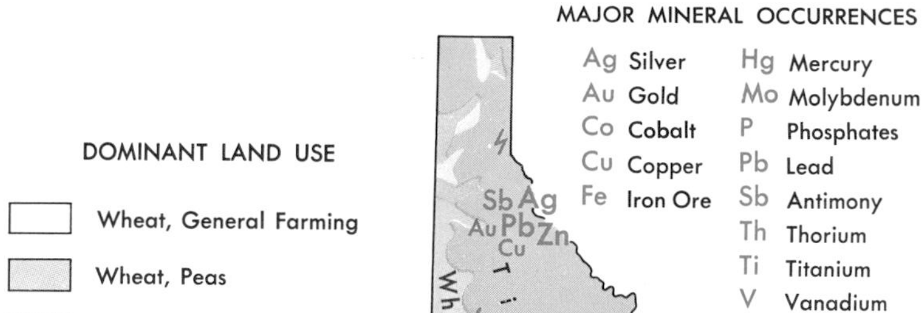
MAJOR MINERAL OCCURRENCES
Ag Silver
Au Gold
Co Cobalt
Cu Copper
Fe Iron Ore
Hg Mercury
Mo Molybdenum
P Phosphates
Pb Lead
Sb Antimony
Th Thorium
Ti Titanium
V Vanadium
W Tungsten
Zn Zinc
Water Power
DOMINANT LAND USE
Wheat, General Farming
Wheat, Peas
Specialized Dairy
Potatoes, Beans, Sugar Beets, Livestock, General Farming
General Farming, Dairy, Hay, Sugar Beets
General Farming, Livestock, Special Crops
General Farming, Dairy, Range Livestock
Range Livestock
Forests
Wheat
Timber
Dairy
Cattle
Sheep
Potatoes
Beans
Sugar Beets
Wheat
Barley

ILLINOIS | 223

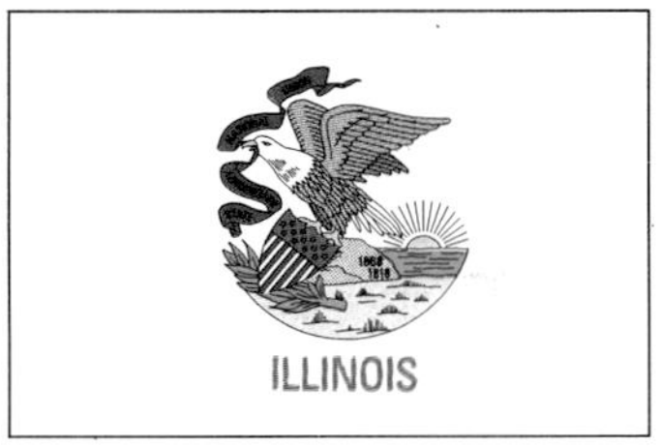
ILLINOIS

AREA 56,345 sq. mi. (145,934 sq. km.)
POPULATION 11,466,682
CAPITAL Springfield
LARGEST CITY Chicago
HIGHEST POINT Charles Mound 1,235 ft. (376 m.)
SETTLED IN 1720
ADMITTED TO UNION December 3, 1818
POPULAR NAME Prairie State; Land of Lincoln
STATE FLOWER Native Violet
STATE BIRD Cardinal

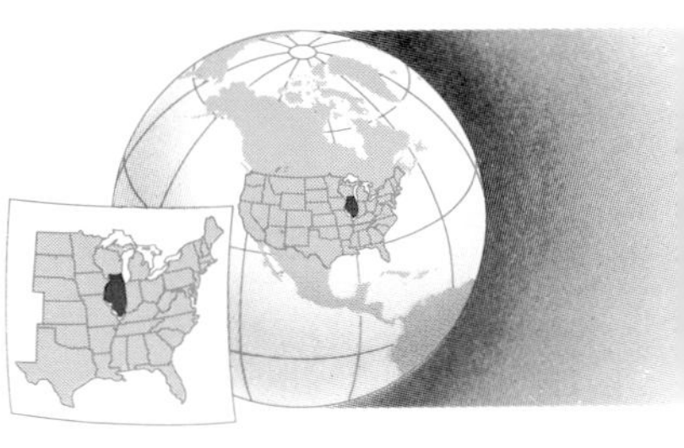

COUNTIES

Adams 66,090 B4
Alexander 10,626 D6
Bond 14,991 D5
Boone 30,806 E1
Brown 5,836 C4
Bureau 35,688 D2
Calhoun 5,322 C4
Carroll 16,805 D1
Cass 13,437 C4
Champaign 173,025 E3
Christian 34,418 D4
Clark 15,921 F4
Clay 14,460 E5
Clinton 33,944 D5
Coles 51,644 E4
Cook 5,105,067 F2
Crawford 19,464 F4
Cumberland 10,670 E4
De Kalb 74,624 E2
De Witt 16,516 E3
Douglas 19,464 E4
Du Page 658,858 E2
Edgar 19,595 F4
Edwards 7,440 E5
Effingham 31,704 E4
Fayette 20,893 D4
Ford 14,275 E3
Franklin 40,319 E5
Fulton 38,080 C3
Gallatin 6,909 E6
Greene 15,317 C4
Grundy 32,337 E2
Hamilton 8,499 E5
Hancock 21,373 B3
Hardin 5,189 E6
Henderson 8,096 C3
Henry 51,159 C2
Iroquois 30,787 F3
Jackson 61,067 D6
Jasper 10,609 E4
Jefferson 37,020 E5
Jersey 20,539 C4
Jo Daviess 21,821 C1
Johnson 11,347 E6
Kane 317,471 E2
Kankakee 96,255 F2
Kendall 39,413 E2
Knox 56,393 C3
La Salle 106,913 E2
Lake 516,418 E1
Lawrence 15,972 F5
Lee 34,392 D2
Livingston 39,301 E3
Logan 30,798 D3
Macon 117,206 E4
Macoupin 47,679 D4
Madison 249,238 D5
Marion 41,561 E5
Marshall 12,846 D2
Mason 16,269 D3
Massac 14,752 E6
McDonough 35,244 C3
McHenry 183,241 E1
McLean 129,180 E3
Menard 11,164 D3
Mercer 17,290 C2
Monroe 22,422 C5
Montgomery 30,728 D4
Morgan 36,397 C4
Moultrie 13,930 E4
Ogle 45,957 D1
Peoria 182,827 D3
Perry 21,412 D5
Piatt 15,548 E4
Pike 17,577 C4
Pope 4,373 E6
Pulaski 7,523 D6
Putnam 5,730 D2
Randolph 34,583 D5
Richland 16,545 E5
Rock Island 148,723 C2
Saint Clair 267,531 C5
Saline 26,551 E6
Sangamon 178,386 D4
Schuyler 7,498 C3
Scott 5,644 C4
Shelby 22,261 E4
Stark 6,534 D2
Stephenson 48,052 D1
Tazewell 123,692 D3
Union 17,619 D6
Vermilion 88,257 F3
Wabash 13,111 F5
Warren 19,181 C3
Washington 14,965 D5
Wayne 17,241 E5
White 16,522 E5
Whiteside 60,186 D2
Will 357,313 F2
Williamson 57,733 E6
Winnebago 252,913 D1
Woodford 32,653 D3

CITIES and TOWNS

Abingdon 3,597 C3
Addison 32,058 B5
Albany 835 C2
Albers 700 D5
Albion▲ 2,116 E5
Aledo▲ 3,681 C2
Alexis 908 C2
Algonquin 11,663 E1
Alhambra 709 D5
Allendale 476 F5
Alorton 2,960 B2
Alpha 753 C2
Alsip 18,227 B6
Altamont 2,296 E4
Alton 32,905 A2
Altona 559 C2
Amboy 2,377 D2
Andalusia 1,052 C2
Andover 579 C2
Anna 4,805 D6
Annawan 802 C2
Antioch 6,105 E1
Arcola 2,678 E4
Arenzville 432 C4
Argenta 940 E4
Arlington Heights 75,460 B5
Aroma Park 690 F2
Arthur 2,112 E4
Ashkum 650 E3
Ashland 1,257 C4
Ashley 583 D5
Ashmore 800 F4
Ashton 1,042 D2
Assumption 1,244 E4
Astoria 1,205 C3
Athens 1,404 D4
Atkinson 950 C2
Atlanta 1,616 D3
Atwood 1,253 E4
Auburn 3,724 D4
Augusta 614 C3
Aurora 99,581 E2
Ava 674 D6
Aviston 924 D5
Avon 957 C3
Baldwin 426 D5
Bannockburn 1,388 B5
Barrington 9,504 A5
Barrington Hills 4,202 A5
Barry 1,391 B4
Bartlett 19,373 A5
Bartonville 5,643 D3
Batavia 17,076 E2
Beardstown 5,270 C3
Beckemeyer 1,070 D5
Bedford Park 566 B6
Beecher 2,032 F2
Beecher City 437 E4
Belgium 511 F3
Belleville▲ 42,785 B3
Bellwood 20,241 B5
Belvidere▲ 15,958 E1
Bement 1,668 E4
Benld 1,604 D4
Bensenville 17,767 B5
Benton▲ 7,216 E6
Berkeley 5,137 B5
Berwyn 45,426 B6
Bethalto 9,507 B2
Bethany 1,369 E4
Blandinsville 762 C3
Bloomingdale 16,614 A5
Bloomington▲ 51,972 D3
Blue Island 21,203 B6
Blue Mound 1,161 D4
Bluffs 774 C4
Bluford 747 E5
Bolingbrook 40,843 A6
Bourbon 13,934 E4
Bourbonnais 13,280 F2
Bowen 462 B3
Braceville 587 E2
Bradford 678 D2
Bradley 10,792 F2
Braidwood 3,584 E2
Breese 3,567 D5
Bridgeport 2,118 F5
Bridgeview 14,402 B6
Brighton 2,270 C4
Brimfield 797 D3
Broadview 8,713 B6
Brookfield 18,876 B6
Brooklyn (Lovejoy) 1,144 A2
Brookport 1,070 E6
Brownstown 668 E5
Buckley 557 F3
Buckner 478 E6
Buda 563 D2
Buffalo 503 D4
Buffalo Grove 36,427 B5
Bunker Hill 1,722 D4
Burbank 27,600 B6
Burnham 3,916 C6
Burr Ridge 7,669 B6
Bushnell 3,288 C3
Byron 2,284 D1
Cahokia 17,550 A3
Cairo▲ 4,846 D6
Calumet City 37,840 C6
Calumet Park 8,418 C6
Cambria 1,230 D6
Cambridge▲ 2,124 C2
Camp Point 1,230 B3
Canton 13,922 C3
Capron 682 E1
Carbon Cliff 1,492 C2
Carbondale 27,033 D6
Carlinville▲ 5,416 D4
Carlyle▲ 3,474 D5
Carmi▲ 5,564 E5
Carol Stream 31,716 A5
Carpentersville 23,049 E1
Carrier Mills 2,268 E6
Carrollton▲ 2,507 C4
Carterville 3,630 D6
Carthage▲ 2,657 B3
Cary 10,043 E1
Casey 2,914 F4
Caseyville 4,419 B2
Catlin 2,173 F3
Cave in Rock 381 E6
Cedarville 751 D1
Central City 1,390 D5
Centralia 14,274 D5
Centreville 7,489 B3
Cerro Gordo 1,436 E4
Chadwick 557 D1
Champaign 63,502 E3
Chandlerville 689 C3
Channahon 4,266 E2
Chapin 632 C4
Charleston▲ 20,398 E4
Chatham 6,074 D4
Chatsworth 1,186 E3
Chebanse 1,082 F3
Chenoa 1,732 E3
Cherry 487 D2
Cherry Valley 1,615 D1
Chester▲ 8,194 D6
Chicago Heights 33,072 C6
Chicago Ridge 13,643 B6
Chicago▲ 2,783,726 C5
Chillicothe 5,959 D3
Chrisman 1,136 F4
Christopher 2,774 D6
Cicero 67,436 B5
Cisne 645 E5
Cissna Park 805 F3
Clarendon Hills 6,994 B6
Clay City 929 E5
Clayton 726 B3
Clifton 1,347 F3
Clinton▲ 7,437 E3
Coal City 3,907 E2
Coal Valley 2,683 C2
Cobden 1,090 D6
Coffeen 736 D4
Colchester 1,645 C3
Colfax 854 E3
Collinsville 22,446 B2
Colona 2,237 C2
Columbia 5,524 C5
Cordova 638 C2
Cornell 556 E3
Cortland 963 E2
Coulterville 984 D5
Country Club Hills 15,431 B6
Countryside 5,716 B6
Cowden 599 E4
Creal Springs 791 E6
Crescent City 541 F3
Crest Hill 10,643 E2
Creston 535 D2
Crestwood 10,823 B6
Crete 6,773 F2
Creve Coeur 5,938 D3
Crossville 805 F5
Crystal Lake 24,512 E1
Cuba 1,440 C3
Cullom 568 E3
Cutler 523 D5
Dahlgren 512 E5
Dakota 549 D1
Dallas City 1,037 B3
Dalton City 573 E4
Dalzell 587 D2
Danforth 457 E3
Danvers 981 D3
Danville▲ 33,828 F3
Darien 18,341 B6
Davis 541 D1
Dawson 536 D4
De Kalb 34,925 E2
De Land 458 E3
De Soto 1,500 D6
Decatur▲ 83,885 E4
Deer Creek 630 D3
Deer Park 2,887 A5
Deerfield 17,327 B5
Delavan 1,642 D3
Depue 1,729 D2
Des Plaines 53,223 B5
Dieterich 568 E4
Divernon 1,178 D4
Dix 456 E5
Dixmoor 3,647 C6
Dixon▲ 15,144 D2
Dolton 23,930 C6
Dongola 728 D6
Dow 465 C4
Dowell 480 D6
Downers Grove 46,858 A6
Downs 620 E3
Du Quoin 6,697 D5
Dundee (East and West Dundee) 6,169 E1
Dunlap 851 D3
Dupo 3,164 A3
Durand 1,100 D1
Dwight 4,230 E2
Earlville 1,435 E2
East Alton 7,063 A2
East Cape Girardeau 451 D6
East Carondelet 630 A3
East Dubuque 1,914 C1
East Dundee (Dundee) 2,721 E1
East Galesburg 813 C3
East Hazelcrest 1,570 C6
East Moline 20,147 C2
East Peoria 21,378 D3
East Saint Louis 40,944 A2
Edgewood 502 E5
Edinburg 982 D4
Edwards 14,579 D3
Edwardsville▲ 12,480 B2
Effingham▲ 11,851 E4
El Paso 2,499 D3
Elburn 1,275 E2
Eldorado 4,536 E6
Elgin 77,010 E1
Elizabeth 641 C1
Elizabethtown▲ 427 E6
Elk Grove Village 33,429 B5
Elkhart 475 D3
Elkville 958 D6
Elmhurst 42,029 B5
Elmwood 1,841 D3
Elmwood Park 23,206 B5
Elsah 851 C5
Elwood 951 E2
Emden 459 D3
Energy 1,106 E6
Enfield 683 E5
Equality 748 E6
Erie 1,572 C2
Essex 482 E2
Eureka▲ 4,435 D3
Evanston 73,233 B5
Evansville 844 D5
Evergreen Park 20,874 B6
Fairbury 3,643 E3
Fairfield▲ 5,439 E5
Fairmont 2,894 A2
Fairmont City 2,140 B2
Fairmount 678 F3
Fairview 510 C3
Fairview Heights 14,351 B3
Farina 575 E5
Farmer City 2,114 E3
Farmersville 698 D4
Farmington 2,535 C3
Findlay 787 E4
Fisher 1,526 E3
Fithian 512 F3
Flanagan 987 E3
Flat Rock 421 F5
Flora 5,054 E5
Flossmoor 8,651 B6
Ford Heights 4,259 C6
Forest Homes 1,701 B2
Forest Park 14,918 B5
Forest View 743 B6
Forrest 1,124 E3
Forreston 1,361 D1
Forsyth 1,275 D4
Fox Lake 7,478 A4
Fox River Grove 3,551 A5
Frankfort 7,180 B6
Franklin 634 C4
Franklin Grove 968 D2
Franklin Park 18,485 B5
Freeburg 3,115 D5
Freeport▲ 25,840 D1
Fulton 3,698 C2
Galatia 983 E6
Gale 3,647 D6
Galena▲ 3,876 C1
Galesburg▲ 33,530 C3
Galva 2,742 D2
Gardner 1,237 E2
Geneseo 5,990 C2
Geneva▲ 12,617 E2
Genoa 3,083 E1
Georgetown 3,678 F4
German Valley 480 D1
Germantown 1,167 D5
Gibson City 3,498 E3
Gifford 845 E3
Gilberts 987 E1
Gillespie 3,645 D4
Gilman 1,816 E3
Glasford 1,115 D3
Glen Carbon 7,731 B2
Glen Ellyn 24,944 A5
Glencoe 8,499 B5
Glendale Heights 27,973 A5
Glenview 37,093 B5
Glenwood 9,289 C6
Godfrey 5,436 A2
Golconda▲ 823 E6
Golden 565 B3
Golf 454 B5
Goodfield 454 D3
Goreville 872 E6
Grafton 918 C5
Grand Ridge 560 E2
Grand Tower 775 D6
Grandview 1,647 D4
Granite City 32,862 A2
Grant Park 1,024 F2
Granville 1,407 D2
Grayslake 7,388 B4
Grayville 2,043 E5
Green Oaks 2,101 B4
Green Rock 2,615 C2
Green Valley 745 D3
Greenfield 1,162 C4
Greenup 1,616 E4
Greenview 848 D3
Greenville▲ 4,806 D5
Gridley 1,304 E3
Griggsville 1,218 C4
Gurnee 13,701 B4
Hamel 530 B2
Hamilton 3,281 B3
Hammond 527 E4
Hampshire 1,843 E1
Hampton 1,601 C2
Hanna City 1,205 D3
Hanover 908 C1
Hanover Park 32,895 A5
Hardin▲ 1,071 C4
Harrisburg▲ 9,289 E6
Harristown 1,319 D4
Hartford 1,676 A2
Harvard 5,975 E1
Harvey 29,771 B6
Harwood Heights 7,680 B5
Havana▲ 3,610 D3
Hawthorn Woods 4,423 B5
Hazel Crest 13,334 B6
Hebron 809 E1
Hecker 534 D5
Hegeler 1,853 F3
Hennepin▲ 669 D2
Henry 2,591 D2
Herrick 466 D4
Herrin 10,857 E6
Herscher 1,278 E2
Heyworth 1,627 E3
Hickory Hills 13,021 B6
Highland 7,525 D5
Highland Park 30,575 B5
Highwood 5,331 B5
Hillcrest 828 D2
Hillsboro▲ 4,400 D4
Hillsdale 489 C2
Hillside 7,672 B5
Hinckley 1,682 E2
Hinsdale 16,029 B6
Hodgkins 1,963 B6
Hoffman 492 D5
Hoffman Estates 46,561 A5
Holiday Hills 807 A4
Homer 1,264 F3
Hometown 4,769 B6
Homewood 19,278 B6
Hoopeston 5,871 F3
Hopedale 805 D3
Hopkins Park 601 F2
Hoyleton 508 D5
Hudson 1,006 E3
Hull 514 B4
Humboldt 470 E4
Hunt 2,453 E4
Huntley 1,646 E1
Hurst 842 D6
Hutsonville 622 F4
Illiopolis 934 D4
Ina 489 E5
Industry 571 C3
Inverness 6,503 A5
Ipava 483 C3
Irving 516 D4
Irvington 827 D5
Island Lake 4,449 A4
Itasca 6,947 B5
Jacksonville▲ 19,324 C4
Jerome 1,206 D4
Jerseyville▲ 7,382 C4
Johnston City 3,706 E6
Joliet▲ 76,836 E2
Jonesboro▲ 1,728 D6
Joppa 492 E6
Joy 452 C2
Junction City 539 D5
Justice 11,137 B6

(continued on following page)

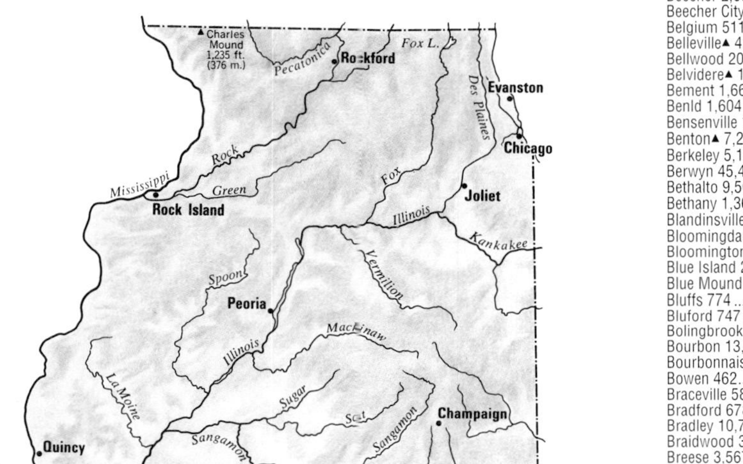
Charles Mound 1,235 ft. (376 m.)
Pecatonica
Rockford
Fox L.
Evanston
Des Plaines
Chicago
Rock
Mississippi
Green
Rock Island
Fox
Joliet
Illinois
Kankakee
Spoon
Vermilion
Peoria
Mackinaw
Illinois
La Moine
Sugar
Salt
Sangamon
Champaign
Quincy
Sangamon
Springfield
Decatur
Mississippi
Illinois
Macoupin
Kaskaskia
Embarrass
Silver
Shoal
Carlyle L.
Little Wabash
East St. Louis
Kaskaskia
Skillet Fk.
Wabash
Rend L.
Mississippi
Big Muddy
Saline
Ohio
5,000 m. 16,404 ft.
2,000 m. 6,562 ft.
1,000 m. 3,281 ft.
500 m. 1,640 ft.
200 m. 656 ft.
100 m. 328 ft.
Sea Level
Below
0
40
80 MI.
0
40
80 KM.

Topography

Agriculture, Industry and Resources

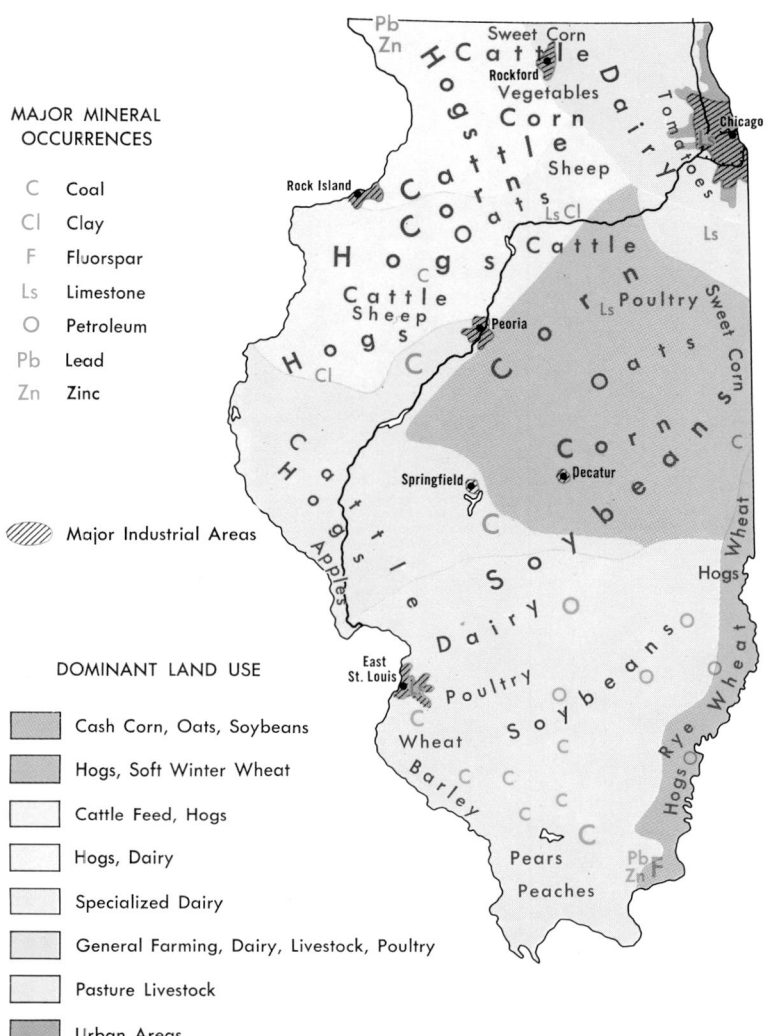

MAJOR MINERAL OCCURRENCES

C   Coal
Cl   Clay
F   Fluorspar
Ls   Limestone
O   Petroleum
Pb   Lead
Zn   Zinc

Major Industrial Areas

DOMINANT LAND USE

Cash Corn, Oats, Soybeans
Hogs, Soft Winter Wheat
Cattle Feed, Hogs
Hogs, Dairy
Specialized Dairy
General Farming, Dairy, Livestock, Poultry
Pasture Livestock
Urban Areas

Kane 456 .... C4
Kankakee▲ 27,575 .... F2
Kansas 887 .... F4
Karnak 581 .... E6
Kaskaskia 32 .... C6
Keithsburg 747 .... B2
Kenilworth 2,402 .... B5
Kewanee 12,969 .... C2
Keyesport 440 .... D5
Kildeer 2,257 .... A5
Kincaid 1,353 .... D4
Kingston 562 .... E1
Kinmundy 879 .... E5
Kirkland 1,011 .... E1
Kirkwood 884 .... C3
Knoxville 3,243 .... C3
La Grange 15,362 .... B6
La Grange Park 12,861 .. B5
La Harpe 1,407 .... B3
La Moille 654 .... D2
La Salle 9,717 .... E2
Lacon▲ 1,986 .... D2
Ladd 1,283 .... D2
Lake Barrington 3,855 ... A5
Lake Bluff 5,513 .... B4
Lake Catherine 1,515 .... E1
Lake Forest 17,836 .... B4
Lake Villa 2,857 .... A4
Lake Zurich 14,947 .... A5
Lake in the Hills 5,866 ... E1
Lakemoor 1,322 .... A4
Lakewood 1,609 .... A5
Lanark 1,382 .... D1
Lansing 28,086 .... D4
Latham 482 .... D4
Lawrenceville▲ 4,897 .... F5
Le Roy 2,777 .... E3
Leaf River 546 .... D1
Lebanon 3,688 .... D5
Leland 862 .... E2
Lemont 7,343 .... B6
Lena 2,605 .... D1
Lenzburg 510 .... D5
Lewistown▲ 2,572 .... C3
Lexington 1,809 .... E3
Liberty 541 .... B4
Libertyville 19,174 .... B4
Lincoln▲ 15,418 .... D3

Lincolnshire 4,931 .... B5
Lincolnwood 11,365 ..... B5
Lindenhurst 8,038 .... B4
Lisle 19,512 .... A6
Litchfield 6,883 .... D4
Livingston 928 .... D5
Loami 802 .... C3
Lockport 9,401 .... B6
Lomax 473 .... B3
Lombard 39,408 .... A5
London Mills 485 .... C3
Long Grove 4,740 .... A5
Lostant 510 .... D2
Louisville▲ 1,098 .... E5
Lovejoy 1,233 .... A2
Lovington 1,143 .... E4
Loves Park 15,462 .... E1
Lyndon 615 .... C2
Lynwood 6,535 .... C6
Lyons 9,828 .... B6
Machesney Park 19,033 .. D1
Mackinaw 1,331 .... D3
Macomb▲ 19,952 .... C3
Macon 1,282 .... E4
Madison 4,629 .... A2
Mahomet 3,103 .... E3
Malta 865 .... E2
Manhattan 2,059 .... F2
Manito 1,711 .... D3
Mansfield 929 .... E3
Manteno 3,488 .... F2
Maple Park 641 .... E1
Marengo 4,768 .... E1
Marine 972 .... D5
Marion▲ 14,545 .... E6
Marissa 2,375 .... D5
Markham 13,136 .... B6
Maroa 1,602 .... E3
Marquette Heights 3,077 .. D3
Marseilles 4,811 .... E2
Marshall▲ 3,555 .... F4
Martinsville 1,161 .... F4
Maryville 2,576 .... A2
Mascoutah 5,511 .... D5
Mason City 2,323 .... D3
Matherville 708 .... C2
Matteson 11,378 .... B6
Mattoon 18,441 .... E4

Maywood 27,139 .... B5
Mazon 764 .... E2
McCullom Lake 1,033 ... E1
McHenry 16,177 .... E1
McLean 797 .... D3
McLeansboro▲ 2,677 ... E5
Meadowbrook 1,082 .... B2
Mechanicsburg 538 ..... D4
Medora 473 .... C4
Melrose Park 20,859 ... B5
Melvin 466 .... E3
Mendon 854 .... B3
Mendota 7,018 .... D2
Meredosia 1,134 .... C4
Merrionette Park 2,065 .. B6
Metamora 2,520 .... D3
Metropolis▲ 6,734 ...... E6
Middletown 436 .... D3
Midlothian 14,372 ...... B6
Milan 5,831 .... C2
Milford 1,512 .... F3
Milledgeville 1,076 ...... D1
Millington 470 .... E2
Millstadt 2,566 .... B3
Minier 1,155 .... D3
Minonk 1,982 .... D3
Minooka 2,561 .... E2
Mokena 6,128 .... B6
Nokomis 2,534 .... D4
Moline 43,202 .... C2
Momence 2,968 .... F2
Monee 1,044 .... F2
Monmouth▲ 9,489 ..... C3
Montgomery 4,267 ..... E2
Monticello▲ 4,549 ...... E3
Morris▲ 10,270 .... E2
Morrison▲ 4,363 .... C2
Morrisonville 1,113 ..... D4
Morton 13,799 .... D3
Morton Grove 22,408 .. B5
Mound City▲ 765 .... D6
Mounds 1,407 .... D6
Mount Auburn 544 ..... D4
Mount Carmel▲ 8,287 .. F5
Mount Carroll▲ 1,726 .. D1
Mount Morris 2,919 .... D1
Mount Olive 2,126 ..... D4
Mount Prospect 53,170 .. B5
Mount Pulaski 1,610 .... D3

Mount Sterling▲ 1,922 .. C4
Mount Vernon▲ 16,988 .. E5
Mount Zion 4,522 .... E4
Moweaqua 1,785 .... E4
Mulberry Grove 660 .... D5
Mundelein 21,215 ...... A4
Murphysboro▲ 9,176 ... D6
Murrayville 673 .... C4
Naperville 85,351 .... A6
Naplate 609 .... E2
Nashville▲ 3,202 .... D5
Nauvoo 1,108 .... B3
Neoga 1,678 .... E4
Neponset 529 .... D2
New Athens 2,010 ..... D5
New Baden 2,602 ...... D5
New Berlin 797 .... D4
New Boston 620 .... B2
New Haven 459 .... E6
New Lenox 9,627 .... B6
New Millford 463 .... D1
New Windsor 840 .... C2
Newark 840 .... E2
Newman 960 .... F4
Newton▲ 3,154 .... E5
Niantic 647 .... D4
Niles 28,284 .... B5
Noble 756 .... E5
Nokomis City 1,341 ..... E5
Normal 40,023 .... E3
Norridge 14,459 .... B5
Norris City 1,341 .... E6
North Aurora 5,940 .... E2
North Barrington 1,787 .. A5
North Chicago 34,978 .. B4
North Pekin 1,556 ...... D3
North Riverside 6,005 .. B5
North Utica (Utica) 848 .. E2
Northbrook 32,308 ..... A5
Northfield 4,635 .... B5
Northlake 12,505 .... B5
O'Fallon 16,073 .... B2
Oak Brook 9,178 .... A6
Oak Forest 26,203 ..... B6
Oak Grove 626 .... C2
Oak Lawn 56,182 ...... B6
Oak Park 53,648 .... B5
Oakbrook Terrace 1,907 .. B5

Oakland 996 .... F4
Oakwood 1,533 .... F3
Oakwood Hills 1,498 ... E1
Oblong 1,616 .... F5
Odell 1,030 .... E2
Odin 1,150 .... D5
Ogden 671 .... F3
Oglesby 3,619 .... D2
Ohio 426 .... D2
Okawville 1,274 .... D5
Olney▲ 8,664 .... E5
Olympia Fields 4,248 ... B6
Onarga 1,281 .... F3
Oneida 723 .... C2
Oquawka▲ 1,442 ...... B3
Orangeville 451 .... D1
Oreana 847 .... E4
Oregon▲ 3,891 .... D1
Orient 428 .... E6
Orion 1,821 .... C2
Orland Hills 5,510 ...... B6
Orland Park 35,720 .... B6
Oswego 3,876 .... E2
Ottawa▲ 17,451 .... E2
Palatine 39,253 .... B5
Palestine 1,619 .... F4
Palmyra 722 .... C4
Palos Heights 11,478 .. B6
Palos Hills 17,803 ...... B6
Palos Park 4,199 .... B6
Pana 5,796 .... D4
Paris▲ 8,987 .... F4
Park City 4,677 .... B4
Park Forest 24,656 .... B6
Park Forest South 6,245 .. F2
Park Ridge 36,175 ..... B5
Patoka 656 .... D5
Pawnee 2,384 .... D4
Pawpaw 761 .... E2
Paxton▲ 4,289 .... E3
Payson 1,114 .... B4
Pearl City 670 .... D1
Pecatonica 1,760 ...... D1
Pekin▲ 32,254 .... D3
Peoria Heights 6,930 .. D3
Peoria▲ 113,504 ...... D3
Peotone 2,947 .... F2
Percy 925 .... D5
Perry 491 .... C4
Peru 9,302 .... D2
Pesotum 558 .... E4
Petersburg▲ 2,261 .... D4
Philo 1,028 .... E3
Phoenix 2,217 .... C6
Pierron 554 .... D5
Pinckneyville▲ 3,372 .. D5
Piper City 760 .... E3
Pittsburg 602 .... E6
Pittsfield▲ 4,231 ...... C4
Plainfield 4,557 .... A6
Plano 5,104 .... E2
Pleasant Hill 1,030 .... C4
Pleasant Plains 701 ... D4
Plymouth 521 .... C3
Pocahontas 837 ...... D5
Poio 2,514 .... D1
Pontiac▲ 11,428 ..... E3
Pontoon Beach 4,013 .. A2
Poplar Grove 743 .... E1
Port Byron 1,002 ..... C2
Posen 4,226 .... B6
Potomac 753 .... F3
Prairie City 497 .... C3
Prairie Grove 654 ..... E1
Prairie du Rocher 540 .. C5
Preston 2,750 .... D5
Princeton▲ 7,197 .... D2
Princeville 1,421 ..... D3
Prophetstown 1,749 .. D2
Prospect Heights 15,239 .. B5
Quincy▲ 39,681 ...... B4
Ramsey 963 .... D4
Rankin 619 .... F3
Ransom 438 .... E2
Rantoul 17,212 ...... E3
Rapids City 932 ..... C2
Ray 820 .... C3
Raymond 957 .... D4
Red Bud 2,918 ...... D5
Reynolds 583 .... C2
Richmond 1,016 .... E1
Richton Park 10,523 .. B6
Ridge Farm 939 ..... F4
Ridgway 1,103 ...... E6
River Forest 11,669 .. B5
River Grove 9,961 ... B5
Riverdale 13,671 .... C6
Riverside 8,774 ..... B6
Riverton 2,638 ...... D4
Riverwoods 2,868 .. A5
Roanoke 1,910 ..... D3
Robbins 7,498 ...... B6
Robinson▲ 6,740 .... F5
Rochelle 8,769 ...... D2
Rochester 2,676 .... D4
Rock Falls 9,654 .... D2
Rock Island▲ 40,552 .. C2
Rockdale 1,709 ..... A6
Rockford▲ 139,426 .. D1
Rockton 2,928 ...... E1
Rolling Meadows 22,591 .. B5
Rome 1,902 .... D3
Romeoville 14,074 .. B6
Roodhouse 2,139 ... C4
Roscoe 2,079 .... D1
Roselle 20,819 ...... A5
Rosemont 3,995 .... B5
Roseville 1,151 ...... C3
Rosewood Heights 4,821 .. B2
Rosiclare 1,378 ...... E6
Rossville 1,334 ...... F3
Round Lake 3,550 .... A4
Round Lake Beach 16,434 .. A4
Round Lake Park 4,045 .. A4
Roxana 1,562 .... B2
Royalton 1,191 ...... D6
Rushville▲ 3,229 .... C3

Sadorus 469 .... E4
Saint Anne 1,153 .... F2
Saint Charles 22,501 .. E2
Saint David 603 ...... C3
Saint Elmo 1,473 .... E4
Saint Francisville 851 .. F5
Saint Jacob 752 ..... D5
Saint Joseph 2,052 .. E3
Saint Libory 525 .... D5
Salem▲ 7,470 .... E5
San Jose 519 .... D3
Sandoval 1,535 ..... D5
Sandwich 5,567 .... E2
Sauk Village 9,926 .. C6
Savanna 3,819 ...... C1
Savoy 2,674 .... E3
Saybrook 767 .... E3
Schaumburg 68,586 .. A5
Schiller Park 11,189 .. B5
Schram City 692 .... D4
Seneca 1,878 .... E2
Sesser 2,087 .... D5
Shabbona 897 ...... E2
Shannon 887 .... D1
Shawneetown▲ 1,575 .. E6
Sheffield 951 .... C2
Shelbyville▲ 4,943 .. E4
Sheldon 1,109 ...... F3
Sheridan 1,288 ..... E2
Sherman 2,080 ..... D4
Sherrard 697 .... C2
Shiloh 2,655 .... B3
Shipman 624 .... C4
Shorewood 6,264 .. E2
Sidell 584 .... F4
Sidney 1,027 .... E3
Silvis 6,926 .... C2
Skokie 59,432 ...... B5
Sleepy Hollow 3,241 .. E1
Smithton 1,587 .... C5
Somonauk 1,263 ... E2
Sorento 596 .... D4
South Barrington 2,937 .. A5
South Beloit 4,072 .. E1
South Chicago Heights 3,597 .. C6
South Elgin 7,474 .. E2
South Holland 22,105 .. C6
South Jacksonville 3,187 .. C4
South Pekin 1,184 .. D3
South Roxana 1,961 .. B2
South Wilmington 698 .. E2
Sparta 4,853 .... D5
Spaulding 440 ..... D4
Spring Bay 439 .... D3
Spring Grove 1,066 .. E1
Spring Valley 5,246 .. D2
Springfield (cap.)▲ 105,227 .. D4
Stanford 620 .... D3
Stanton 4,806 ..... D5
Steeleville 2,059 ... D5
Steger 8,584 .... F2
Sterling 15,132 .... D2
Stewardson 660 ... E4
Stickney 5,678 ..... B6
Stillman Valley 848 .. D1
Stockton 1,871 .... C1
Stone Park 4,383 .. B5
Stonington 1,006 .. D4
Strasburg 473 ..... E4
Streamwood 30,987 .. A5
Streator 14,121 .... E2
Stronghurst 799 ... B3
Sugar Grove 2,005 .. E2
Sullivan▲ 4,354 .... E4
Summerfield 509 .. D5
Summit-Argo 10,110 .. B6
Sumner 1,083 ..... F5
Sunnyside 1,529 .. A4
Swansea 8,201 ... B3
Sycamore▲ 9,708 .. E2
Tallula 598 .... D4
Tamaroa 780 ..... D5
Tamms 748 .... D6
Tampico 833 ...... C2
Taylor Springs 670 .. D4
Taylorville▲ 11,133 .. D4
Teutopolis 1,417 .. E4
Thayer 730 .... D4
Thebes 461 .... D6
Third Lake 1,248 .. B4
Thomasboro 1,250 .. E3
Thompsonville 602 .. E6
Thomson 538 ..... C2
Thornton 2,778 ... C6
Tilden 919 .... D5
Tilton 2,729 .... F3
Tinley Park 37,121 .. B6
Tiskilwa 830 ...... D2
Toledo▲ 1,199 ... E4
Tolono 2,605 ..... E3
Toluca 1,315 ..... D2
Tonica 715 .... E2
Toulon▲ 1,328 ... D2
Tovey 533 .... D4
Towanda 856 .... E3
Tower Hill 601 ... E4
Tower Lakes 1,333 .. A4
Tremont 2,088 ... D3
Trenton 2,481 ... D5
Troy 6,046 .... B2
Tuscola▲ 4,155 .. E4
Union 542 .... E1
Urbana▲ 36,344 .. E3
Ursa 506 .... B3
Utica E2
Valier 708 .... D5
Valmeyer 897 ... C5
Vandalia▲ 6,114 .. D5
Venice 3,571 ... A2
Vermont 806 ... C3
Vernon Hills 15,319 .. B4
Versailles 480 .. C4
Vienna▲ 1,446 .. E6
Villa Grove 2,734 .. E4
Villa Park 22,253 .. B5
Viola 964 .... C2
Virden 3,635 .... D4

Virginia▲ 1,767 ..... C4
Wadsworth 1,826 ... B4
Walnut 1,463 .... D2
Wamac 1,501 ...... D5
Wapella 608 .... D3
Warren 1,550 ...... C1
Warrensburg 1,274 .. D3
Warrenville 11,333 .. A6
Warsaw 1,882 ..... B3
Washburn 1,075 ... D3
Washington 10,099 .. D3
Washington Park 7,431 .. A2
Wataga 879 .... C2
Waterloo▲ 5,072 ... C5
Waterman 1,074 ... E2
Watseka▲ 5,424 .. F3
Watson 646 .... E4
Wauconda 6,294 .. A4
Waukegan▲ 69,392 .. B4
Waverly 1,402 .... D4
Wayne 1,541 ..... A5
Wayne City 1,099 .. E5
Waynesville 440 .. D3
Wenona 950 ..... D2
West Chicago 14,796 .. A5
West City 747 .... E6
West Dundee (Dundee) 3,728 .. E1
West Frankfort 8,526 .. E6
West Salem 1,042 .. F5
Westchester 17,301 .. B5
Western Springs 11,984 .. B6
Westfield 676 .... F4
Westmont 21,228 .. A6
Westville 3,387 ... F3
Wheaton▲ 51,464 .. A5
Wheeling 29,911 .. B5
White Hall 2,814 .. C4
Williamsfield 571 .. C3
Williamsville 1,140 .. D4
Willisville 577 .... D6
Willow Springs 4,509 .. B6
Willowbrook 1,808 .. A6
Wilmette 26,690 .. B5
Wilsonville 609 ... D4
Winchester▲ 1,769 .. C4
Windsor (New Windsor) 774 .. C2
Windsor 1,228 ... E4
Winfield 7,096 ... A5
Winnebago 1,840 .. D1
Winnetka 12,174 .. B5
Winthrop Harbor 6,240 .. B4
Witt 866 .... D4
Wonder Lake 1,024 .. E1
Wood Dale 12,425 .. A5
Wood River 11,490 .. B2
Woodhull 808 ... C2
Woodlawn 582 ... D5
Woodridge 26,256 .. A6
Woodson 472 ... C4
Woodstock▲ 14,353 .. A4
Worden 896 .... D5
Worth 11,208 ... B6
Wyanet 1,017 ... D2
Wyoming 1,462 .. D2
Yates City 760 .. C3
Yorkville▲ 3,925 .. E2
Zeigler 1,746 ... D6
Zion 19,775 .... B4

OTHER FEATURES

Apple (creek) C
Apple (riv.) C
Argonne Nat'l Laboratory .. B
Big Bureau (riv.) .... D
Big Muddy (riv.) .... D
Bonpas (creek) .... E
Cache (riv.) C
Calumet (lake) C
Carlyle (lake) .... D
Chanute A.F.B. .... E
Charles Mound (hill) C
Chicago Portage
   Nat'l Hist. Site ...... B
Crab Orchard (lake) .... D
Des Plaines (riv.) ...... A
Du Page (riv.) .... A
Edwards (riv.) C
Embarras (riv.) .... E
Fort Sheridan .... B
Fox (lake) .... A
Fox (riv.) .... E
Fox (riv.) .... E
Glenview Naval Air Sta. .. B
Granite City Army Depot .. A
Great Lakes Naval Trng. Ctr. .. B
Green (riv.) C
Henderson (riv.) ...... B
Illinois (riv.) C
Illinois-Mississippi (canal) .. C
Iroquois (riv.) .... F
Kankakee (riv.) .... F
Kaskaskia (riv.) ...... D
La Moine (riv.) C
Little Wabash (riv.) ... E
Mackinaw (riv.) ..... D
Macoupin (riv.) C
Michigan (lake) C
Mississippi (riv.) C
O'Hare International Airport .. B
Ohio (riv.) .... E
Plum (riv.) C
Pope (creek) C
Rend (lake) .... D
Rock (creek) .... D
Rock (riv.) C
Saline (riv.) .... E
Salt (creek) .... D
Sangamon (riv.) ... C
Savanna Army Depot .. C
Scott A.F.B. 7,245 .. D
Shelbyville (lake) ... E
Shoal (creek) ...... D
Spoon (riv.) C
Wabash (riv.) ...... F

▲County seat

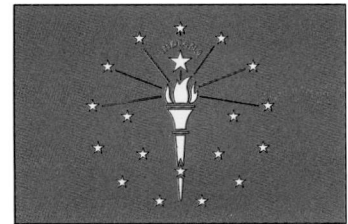

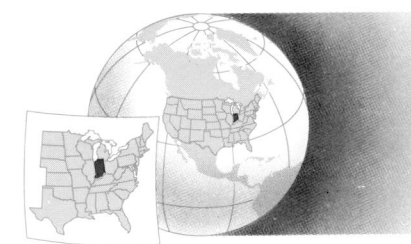

AREA 36,185 sq. mi. (93,719 sq. km.)
POPULATION 5,564,228
CAPITAL Indianapolis
LARGEST CITY Indianapolis
HIGHEST POINT 1,257 ft. (383 m.) (Wayne County)
SETTLED IN 1730
ADMITTED TO UNION December 11, 1816
POPULAR NAME Hoosier State
STATE FLOWER Peony
STATE BIRD Cardinal

COUNTIES

Adams 31,095 ....H3
Allen 300,836 ....G2
Bartholomew 63,657 ....F6
Benton 9,441 ....C3
Blackford 14,067 ....G4
Boone 38,147 ....E4
Brown 14,080 ....E6
Carroll 18,809 ....D3
Cass 38,413 ....E3
Clark 87,777 ....F8
Clay 24,705 ....C6
Clinton 30,974 ....E4
Crawford 9,914 ....E8
Daviess 27,533 ....C7
De Kalb 35,324 ....H2
Dearborn 38,835 ....H6
Decatur 23,645 ....G6
Delaware 119 659 ....G4
Dubois 36,616 ....D8
Elkhart 156,198 ....F1
Fayette 26,015 ....G5
Floyd 64,404 ....F8
Fountain 17,808 ....C4
Franklin 19,580 ....G6
Fulton 18,840 ....E2
Gibson 31,913 ....B8
Grant 74,169 ....F3
Greene 30,410 ....D6
Hamilton 108,936 ....E4
Hancock 45,527 ....F5
Harrison 29,890 ....E8
Hendricks 75 717 ....D5
Henry 48,139 ....G5
Howard 80,827 ....E4
Huntington 35,427 ....G3
Jackson 37,730 ....E7
Jasper 24,960 ....C2
Jay 21,512 ....G4
Jefferson 29,797 ....G7
Jennings 23,661 ....F7
Johnson 88,109 ....E6
Knox 39,884 ....C7
Kosciusko 65,294 ....F2
LaPorte 108,632 ....D1
Lagrange 29,477 ....G1
Lake 475,594 ....C2
Lawrence 42 836 ....E7
Madison 130,669 ....F4
Marion 797,159 ....E5
Marshall 42,182 ....E2
Martin 10,369 ....D7
Miami 36,897 ....E3
Monroe 108,978 ....D6
Montgomery 34,436 ....D4
Morgan 55,920 ....E6
Newton 13,551 ....C3
Noble 37,877 ....G2
Ohio 5,315 ....H7
Orange 18,409 ....E7
Owen 17,281 ....D6
Parke 15,410 ....C5
Perry 19,107 ....D8
Pike 12,509 ....C8
Porter 128,932 ....C1
Posey 25,968 ....B8
Pulaski 12,643 ....D2
Putnam 30,315 ....D5
Randolph 27,148 ....G4
Ripley 24,616 ....G6
Rush 18,129 ....G5
Saint Joseph 241,617 ....E1
Scott 20,991 ....F7
Shelby 40,307 ....F5
Spencer 19,490 ....C9
Starke 22,747 ....D2
Steuben 27,446 ....G1
Sullivan 18,993 ....C6
Switzerland 7,738 ....G7
Tippecanoe 130,598 ....D4
Tipton 16,119 ....E3
Union 6,976 ....H5
Vanderburgh 165,058 ....B8
Vermillion 16,773 ....C5
Vigo 106,107 ....C6
Wabash 35,069 ....F3
Warren 8,176 ....C4
Warrick 44,920 ....C8
Washington 23,717 ....E7
Wayne 71,951 ....G5
Wells 25,948 ....G3
White 23,265 ....D3
Whitley 27,651 ....F2

CITIES and TOWNS

Abington 200 ....H5
Adams 250 ....F6
Adamsboro 325 ....E3
Advance 520 ....D5
Akron 1,001 ....E2
Alamo 112 ....D5
Albany 2,357 ....G4
Albion▲ 1,823 ....G2
Alexandria 5,709 ....F4
Altona 156 ....G2

Ambia 249 ....C4
Amboy 370 ....F3
Americus 150 ....D3
Amity 200 ....E6
Amo 380 ....D5
Anderson▲ 59,459 ....F4
Andersonville 225 ....G5
Andrews 1,118 ....F3
Angola▲ 5,824 ....G1
Anthony 130 ....G4
Arcadia 1,468 ....E4
Arcola 300 ....G2
Ardmore 800 ....E1
Argos 1,642 ....E2
Arlington 500 ....F5
Ashley 767 ....G1
Athens 145 ....E2
Atlanta 703 ....E4
Attica 3,457 ....C4
Atwood 300 ....F2
Auburn▲ 9,379 ....G2
Aurora 3,825 ....H6
Austin 4,310 ....F7
Avilla 1,366 ....G2
Avoca 400 ....D7
Azalia 194 ....F6
Bainbridge 682 ....D5
Bargersville 1,681 ....E5
Batesville 4,720 ....G6
Battle Ground 806 ....D3
Bear Branch 150 ....G7
Bedford▲ 13,817 ....E7
Beech Grove 13,383 ....E5
Bellmore 160 ....C5
Bennetts Switch 138 ....E3
Benton 220 ....F2
Berne 3,559 ....H3
Bethany 90 ....E5
Beverly Shores 622 ....D1
Bicknell 3,357 ....C7
Bippus 300 ....F3
Birdseye 472 ....D8
Black Oak C1
Blanford 500 ....B5
Blocher 400 ....F7
Bloomfield▲ 2,592 ....D6
Blooming Grove 300 ....G5
Bloomingdale 341 ....C5
Bloomington▲ 60,633 ....D6
Blountsville 155 ....G4
Blue Ridge 219 ....F5
Bluffton▲ 9,020 ....G3
Boggstown 200 ....F5
Boone Grove 220 ....C2
Boonville▲ 6,724 ....C8
Borden F8
Boston 159 ....H5
Boswell 767 ....C3
Bourbon 1,672 ....E2
Bowling Green 200 ....D6
Bradford 350 ....E8
Brazil▲ 7,640 ....C5
Bremen 4,725 ....E2
Bridgeton 250 ....C5
Bright 3,945 ....H6
Brimfield 292 ....G2
Bringhurst 275 ....E3
Bristol 1,133 ....F1
Brook 899 ....C3
Brooklyn 1,162 ....E6
Brooksburg 79 ....G7
Brookston 1,804 ....D3
Brookville▲ 2,529 ....G6
Brownsburg 7,628 ....E5
Brownstown▲ 2,872 ....F7
Brownsville 250 ....H5
Bruceville 471 ....C7
Bryant 273 ....G3
Buck Creek 225 ....D4
Buckskin 200 ....C8
Buffalo 500 ....D3
Bunker Hill 1,010 ....E3
Burket 200 ....F2
Burlington 568 ....E4
Burnettsville 401 ....D3
Burney 300 ....F6
Burns City 140 ....D7
Burns Harbor 788 ....C1
Burrows 250 ....E3
Butler 2,601 ....H2
Butlerville 300 ....F6
Byron 200 ....E5
Cadiz 202 ....G5
Cambridge City 2,091 ....G5
Camden 607 ....D3
Cammack 250 ....G4
Campbellsburg 606 ....E7
Cannelburg 97 ....C7
Cannelton▲ 1,786 ....D9
Carbon 350 ....C5
Carefree 26 ....E8
Carlisle 613 ....C7
Carmel 25,380 ....E5
Cartersburg 300 ....E5
Carthage 887 ....F5
Cassville 159 ....C4
Cates 125 ....C4

Cayuga 1,083 ....C5
Cedar Grove 246 ....H6
Cedar Lake 8,885 ....C2
Celestine 150 ....D8
Centenary 150 ....B5
Center 278 ....E4
Centerpoint 242 ....C6
Centerton 250 ....E5
Centerville 2,398 ....H5
Chalmers 525 ....D3
Chandler 3,099 ....C8
Chapel Hill 175 ....E6
Charlestown 5,889 ....F8
Charlottesville 300 ....F5
Chelsea 200 ....F7
Chester 2,730 ....H5
Chesterfield 2,701 ....F4
Chesterton 9,124 ....D1
Chili 280 ....F3
Chrisney 511 ....C8
Churubusco 1,781 ....G2
Cicero 3,268 ....E4
Clarks Hill 716 ....D4
Clarksburg 300 ....G6
Clarksville 19,833 ....F8
Clay City 929 ....C6
Claypool 411 ....F2
Clayton 610 ....D5
Clear Creek 200 ....E6
Clear Lake 272 ....H1
Clifford 308 ....F6
Clinton 5,040 ....C5
Cloverdale 1,681 ....D5
Cloverland 175 ....C6
Clymers 150 ....E3
Coal City 225 ....D6
Coalmont 450 ....C6
Coatesville 469 ....D5

Coesse 150 ....G2
Colburn 300 ....D3
Colfax 727 ....D4
Collegeville 993 ....C3
Columbia City▲ 5,706 ....G2
Columbus▲ 31,802 ....E6
Commiskey 150 ....F7
Connersville▲ 15,550 ....G5
Converse 1,144 ....F3
Correct 131 ....G7
Cortland 175 ....F7
Corunna 241 ....G2
Cory 2,661 ....C6
Corydon▲ 2,724 ....E8
Covington▲ 2,747 ....C4
Cowan 428 ....G4
Craigville 130 ....G3
Crandall 147 ....E8
Crane 216 ....D7
Crawfordsville▲ 13,584 ....D4
Cromwell 520 ....F2
Cross Plains 254 ....G7
Crothersville 1,687 ....F7
Crown Point▲ 17,728 ....C1
Crumstown 175 ....E1
Culver 1,404 ....E2
Cumberland 1,624 ....F5
Cutler 140 ....D4
Cynthiana 669 ....B8
Dale 1,553 ....D8
Daleville 1,681 ....F4
Dana 612 ....C5
Danville▲ 4,345 ....D5
Darlington 740 ....D4
Darmstadt 1,346 ....B8
Dayton 996 ....D4
Decatur▲ 8,644 ....H3
Decker 281 ....B7

Deer Creek 250 ....E3
Deerfield 300 ....H4
Delaware 135 ....G6
Delong 156 ....E2
Delphi▲ 2,531 ....D3
Demotte 2,482 ....C2
Denham 140 ....D2
Denver 504 ....F3
Depauw 150 ....E8
Deputy 200 ....F7
Desoto 385 ....G4
Dillsboro 1,200 ....G6
Donaldson 320 ....E2
Doolittle Mills 200 ....D8
Dublin 805 ....G5
Dubois 550 ....D8
Dugger 936 ....C6
Dundee 160 ....F4
Dune Acres 263 ....C1
Dunkirk 2,739 ....G4
Dunlap 5,705 ....F1
Dunreith 205 ....F5
Dupont 391 ....G7
Dyer 10,923 ....C1
Eagletown 306 ....E4
Earl Park 443 ....C3
East Chicago 33,892 ....C1
East Enterprise 250 ....H7
East Germantown
  (Pershing) 372 ....G5
Eaton 1,614 ....G4
Economy 151 ....G5
Edgewood 2,057 ....F4
Edinburg 4,536 ....E6
Edwardsport 380 ....C7
Edwardsville 700 ....F8
Elberfeld 635 ....C8

Elizabethtown 495 ....F6
Elkhart 43,627 ....F1
Ellettsville 3,275 ....D6
Elnora 679 ....C7
Elrod 200 ....G6
Elston 500 ....D4
Elwood 9,494 ....F4
Eminence 200 ....D6
English▲ 614 ....E8
Etna 578 ....F2
Etna Green 522 ....F2
Eugene 400 ....B5
Evansville▲ 126,272 ....C9
Everton 500 ....G5
Fair Oaks 175 ....C2
Fairbanks 165 ....B6
Fairland 1,348 ....F5
Fairmount 3,130 ....F4
Fairview 1,446 ....F2
Fairview Park 1,545 ....C5
Farmersburg 1,159 ....C6
Farmland 1,412 ....G4
Fayetteville 180 ....D7
Ferdinand 2,318 ....D8
Fillmore 497 ....D5
Finly 400 ....F5
Fishers 7,508 ....E5
Flat Rock 323 ....F6
Flora 2,179 ....E3
Florence 155 ....H7
Floyds Knobs 500 ....F8
Fontanet 325 ....C5
Forest 400 ....E4
Fort Branch 2,447 ....B8
Fort Wayne▲ 173,072 ....G2
Fortville 2,690 ....F5
Fountain 766 ....C4
Fountain City 839 ....H5

Fountaintown 225 ....F5
Fowler▲ 2,333 ....C3
Fowlerton 306 ....F4
Francesville 969 ....D3
Francisco 560 ....B8
Frankfort▲ 14,754 ....E4
Franklin▲ 12,907 ....E6
Frankton 1,736 ....F4
Fredericksburg 155 ....E8
Freelandville 600 ....C7
Freetown 600 ....E7
Fremont 1,407 ....H1
French Lick 2,087 ....D7
Fulton 371 ....E3
Galena 1,231 ....F8
Galveston 1,609 ....E3
Garrett 5,349 ....G2
Gary 116,646 ....C1
Gas City 6,296 ....F4
Gaston 979 ....G4
Geneva 1,280 ....H3
Gentryville 277 ....C8
Georgetown 2,092 ....F8
Gessie 144 ....C4
Glenwood 285 ....G5
Glezen 300 ....C8
Goldsmith 235 ....E4
Goodland 1,033 ....C3
Goshen▲ 23,797 ....F1
Gosport 764 ....D6
Grabill 751 ....H2
Grandview 761 ....C9
Granger 20,241 ....E1
Grantsburg 189 ....E8
Gravelton 150 ....F2
Greencastle▲ 8,984 ....D5
Greendale 3,881 ....H6
Greenfield▲ 11,657 ....F5

(continued on following page)

Agriculture, Industry and Resources

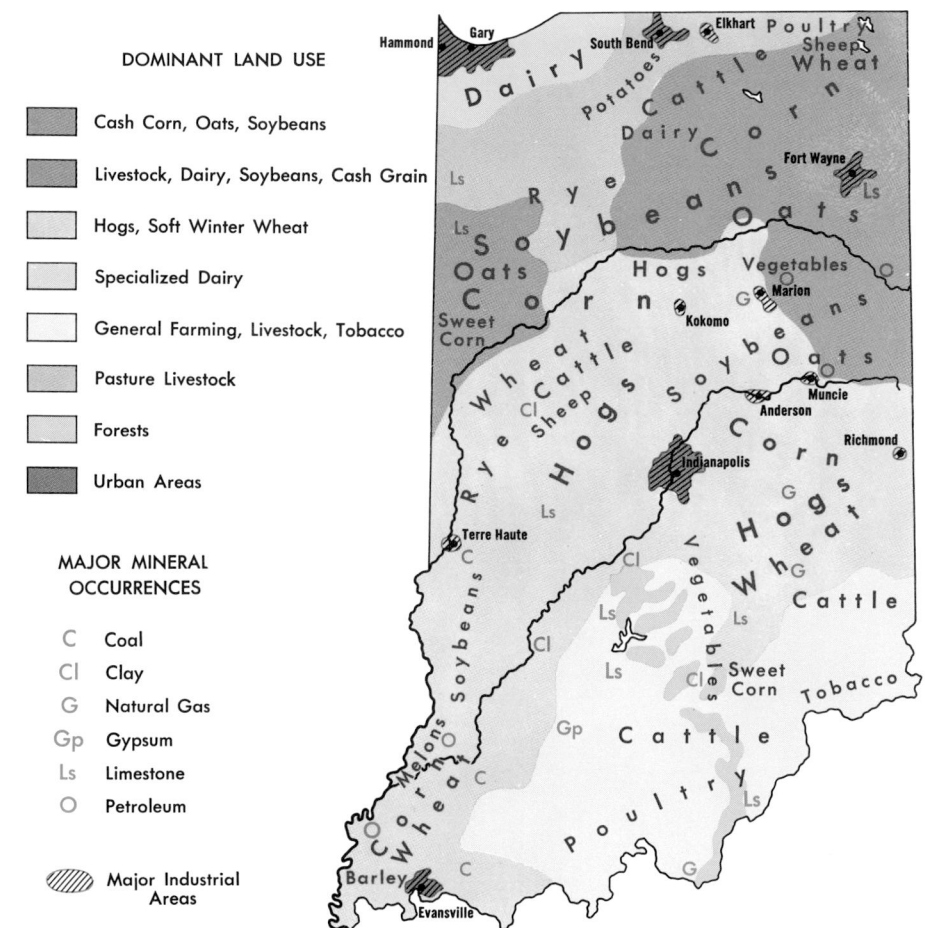

DOMINANT LAND USE

- Cash Corn, Oats, Soybeans
- Livestock, Dairy, Soybeans, Cash Grain
- Hogs, Soft Winter Wheat
- Specialized Dairy
- General Farming, Livestock, Tobacco
- Pasture Livestock
- Forests
- Urban Areas

MAJOR MINERAL OCCURRENCES

- C Coal
- Cl Clay
- G Natural Gas
- Gp Gypsum
- Ls Limestone
- O Petroleum

/// Major Industrial Areas

Greens Fork 416 ....H5
Greensboro 204 ....G5
Greensburg▲ 9,286 ....G6
Greentown 2,172 ....E4
Greenville 508 ....F8
Greenwood 26,265 ....E5
Griffin 171 ....B8
Griffith 17,916 ....C1
Grovertown 150 ....D2
Gwynneville 250 ....F5
Hagerstown 1,835 ....G5
Hamilton 684 ....H1
Hamlet 789 ....D2
Hammond 84,236 ....B1
Hanna 550 ....D2
Hanover 3,610 ....F7
Hardinsburg 322 ....E8
Harlan 840 ....H2
Harmony 645 ....C5
Harrodsburg 400 ....D6
Hartford City▲ 6,960 ....G4
Hartsville 391 ....F6
Hatfield 800 ....C9
Haubstadt 1,455 ....B8
Hayden 300 ....F7
Haysville 600 ....D8
Hazelwood 650 ....D5
Hazleton 357 ....B8
Hebron 3,183 ....C2
Helmsburg 150 ....E6
Heltonville 400 ....E7
Hemlock 300 ....F4
Henryville 1,132 ....F7
Hibbard 150 ....E2
Highland 23,696 ....B1
Hillisburg 180 ....E4
Hillsboro 499 ....C4
Hillsdale 500 ....C5
Hoagland 600 ....H3
Hobart 21,822 ....C1
Hobbs 200 ....F4
Holland 675 ....C8
Hollandsburg 150 ....C5
Holton 451 ....G6
Homer 235 ....F5
Hope 2,171 ....F6
Hortonville 240 ....E4
Houston 200 ....E6
Howe 800 ....G1
Hudson 438 ....G1
Hudson Lake 1,347 ....D1
Huntertown 1,330 ....G2
Huntingburg 5,242 ....D8
Huntington▲ 16,389 ....G3
Huntsville 1,200 ....G4
Huron 250 ....D7
Hymera 771 ....C6
Idaville 655 ....D3
Independence 150 ....C4
Indian Village 142 ....E1
Indianapolis (cap.)▲ 741,952 ....E5
Ingalls 889 ....F5
Inglefield 378 ....B8
Inwood 150 ....E2
Ireland 600 ....C8
Jamestown 764 ....D5
Jasonville 2,220 ....C6
Jasper▲ 10,030 ....C8
Jefferson 21,841 ....D4
Jeffersonville▲ 21,220 ....F8
Jolietville 300 ....E4
Jonesboro 2,073 ....F4
Jonesville 221 ....F6
Kempton 362 ....E4
Kendallville 7,773 ....G2
Kennard 382 ....G5
Kent 1,798 ....F7
Kentland▲ 1,936 ....C3
Kewanna 542 ....E2
Keystone 204 ....G3
Kimmell 250 ....F2
Kingman 561 ....C5
Kingsbury 258 ....D1
Kingsford Heights 1,486 ....D2
Kirklin 707 ....E4
Knightstown 2,048 ....F5
Knightsville 740 ....C5
Knox▲ 3,705 ....D2
Kokomo▲ 44,962 ....E4
Koontz Lake 1,615 ....D2
Kouts 1,603 ....C2
La Crosse 677 ....D2
La Fontaine 909 ....F3
Ladoga 1,124 ....D5
Lafayette▲ 43,764 ....D4
Lagrange▲ 2,382 ....F1
Lagro 496 ....F3
Lake Bruce 160 ....E2
Lake James 400 ....H1
Lake Station 13,899 ....C1
Lake Village 900 ....C2
Laketon 500 ....F3
Lakeville 655 ....E1
Lancaster 275 ....F7
Landess 150 ....F3
Lanesville 512 ....E8
Laotto 361 ....G2
Lapaz 562 ....E2
Lapel 1,742 ....F4
LaPorte▲ 21,507 ....D1
Laconia 75 ....E8
Larwill 219 ....F2
Laurel 544 ....G6
Lawrence 26,763 ....E5
Lawrenceburg▲ 4,375 ....H6
Leavenworth 320 ....E8
Lebanon▲ 12,059 ....D4
Lee 584 ....D3
Leesburg 629 ....F2
Leesville 164 ....E7
Leiters Ford 280 ....E2
Leo 500 ....G2
Leopold 175 ....D8
Leroy 400 ....C2
Letts 247 ....F6
Lewis 437 ....C6
Lewisville 577 ....G5

Lexington F7
Liberty Center 275 ....G3
Liberty Mills 200 ....F2
Liberty▲ 2,051 ....H5
Ligonier 3,443 ....F2
Lincoln City 160 ....C8
Lincolnville 150 ....F3
Linden 718 ....D4
Linn Grove 175 ....H3
Linton 5,814 ....C6
Linwood 157 ....F4
Lisbon 200 ....G2
Little York 155 ....F7
Livonia 136 ....E7
Lizton 410 ....D5
Logan 16,812 ....H6
Logansport▲ 17,731 ....E3
Long Beach 2,044 ....D1
Loogootee 2,884 ....D7
Losantville 253 ....G4
Lowell 6,430 ....C2
Lucerne 135 ....E3
Lydick E1
Lyford 400 ....C5
Lynn 1,183 ....H4
Lynnville 640 ....C8
Lyons 753 ....C7
Mackey 89 ....C8
Macy 218 ....E3
Madison▲ 12,006 ....G7
Majenica 150 ....G3
Manchester 250 ....H6
Manilla 350 ....F5
Mansfield 200 ....C5
Marco 150 ....C7
Marengo 856 ....E8
Mariah Hill 300 ....D8
Marietta 234 ....F6
Marion▲ 32,618 ....F3
Markle 1,208 ....G3
Markleville 412 ....F5
Marshall 379 ....C5
Martinsburg 200 ....E8
Martinsville▲ 11,677 ....D6
Matthews 571 ....F4
Mauckport 95 ....E8
Maxinkuckee 150 ....E2
Maxwell 300 ....F5
Mays 156 ....G5
McCordsville 684 ....F5
Mecca 331 ....C5
Mechanicsburg 150 ....G5
Medaryville 689 ....D2
Medora 805 ....E7
Mellott 222 ....C4
Memphis 300 ....F8
Mentone 912 ....E2
Merom 257 ....B6
Merrillville 27,257 ....C1
Metamora 350 ....G6
Metz 200 ....H1
Mexico 1,003 ....E3
Miami 350 ....E3
Michiana Shores 378 ....D1
Michigan City 33,822 ....C1
Michigantown 472 ....E4
Middlebury 2,004 ....F1
Middletown 2,333 ....F4
Midland 250 ....C6
Milan 1,529 ....G6
Milford 126 ....F2
Milford 177 ....H4
Mill Creek 208 ....D1
Millersburg 854 ....F1
Millhousen 151 ....G6
Milltown 917 ....E8
Millville 275 ....G5
Milroy 750 ....G6
Milton 634 ....G5
Mishawaka 42,608 ....E1
Mitchell 4,669 ....D7
Modoc 218 ....G4
Mongo 225 ....G1
Monon 1,585 ....D3
Monroe 788 ....H3
Monroe City 538 ....C7
Monroeville 1,232 ....H3
Monrovia 800 ....E5
Monterey 230 ....D2
Montezuma 1,134 ....C5
Montgomery 351 ....C7
Monticello▲ 5,237 ....D3
Montmorenci 300 ....D4
Montpelier 1,880 ....G3
Mooreland 465 ....G5
Moores Hill 649 ....G6
Mooresville 5,541 ....E5
Morgantown 978 ....E6
Morocco 1,044 ....C3
Morris 980 ....G6
Morristown 989 ....F5
Mount Auburn 138 ....G5
Mount Ayr 151 ....C3
Mount Carmel 108 ....H6
Mount Etna 111 ....F3
Mount Summit 238 ....G4
Mount Vernon▲ 7,217 ....B9
Mulberry 1,262 ....D4
Muncie▲ 71,035 ....G4
Munster 19,949 ....B1
Murray 136 ....G3
Nabb 150 ....F8
Napoleon 238 ....G6
Nappanee 5,510 ....F2
Nashville▲ 873 ....E6
Needmore 200 ....E7
New Albany▲ 36,322 ....E8
New Amsterdam 30 ....E8
New Carlisle 1,446 ....E1
New Castle▲ 17,753 ....G5
New Chicago 2,066 ....C1
New Goshen 500 ....B5
New Harmony 846 ....B8
New Haven 9,320 ....H2
New Lebanon 150 ....C6
New Lisbon 300 ....G5
New London 200 ....E4

New Marion 200 ....G6
New Market 614 ....D5
New Middletown 82 ....E8
New Palestine 671 ....F5
New Paris 1,007 ....F2
New Pekin 1,095 ....F7
New Point 296 ....G6
New Providence (Borden)
270 ....F8
New Richmond 312 ....D4
New Ross 331 ....D5
New Salem 200 ....G5
New Salisbury 350 ....E8
New Trenton 200 ....H6
New Washington 800 ....F7
New Waverly 162 ....E3
New Whiteland 4,097 ....E5
New Winchester 180 ....D5
Newbern 150 ....F6
Newberry 207 ....C7
Newburgh 2,880 ....C9
Newport▲ 627 ....C5
Newtonville 136 ....D8
Newtown 243 ....C4
Newville 150 ....H2
Noblesville▲ 17,655 ....F4
North Grove 91 ....F3
North Judson 1,582 ....D2
North Liberty 1,366 ....E1
North Manchester 6,383 ......F3
North Salem 499 ....D5
North Terre Haute 4,331 ......C5
North Vernon 5,311 ....F6
North Webster 881 ....F2
Norway 300 ....D3
Notre Dame E1
Nulltown 235 ....G6
Oakford 325 ....E4
Oakland City 2,810 ....C8
Oaktown 655 ....C7
Oakville 220 ....G4
Odon 1,475 ....C7
Ogden Dunes 1,499 ....C1
Oldenburg 715 ....G6
Onward 63 ....E3
Oolitic 1,424 ....E7
Ora 200 ....D2
Orange 200 ....G5
Orestes 458 ....F4
Orland 361 ....G1
Orleans 2,083 ....D7
Osceola 1,999 ....E1
Osgood 1,688 ....G6
Ossian 2,428 ....G3
Oswego 150 ....F2
Otis 250 ....D1
Otisco 450 ....F7
Otterbein 1,291 ....C4
Otwell 600 ....C7
Owensburg 785 ....D7
Owensville 1,053 ....B8
Oxford 1,273 ....C3
Packertown 150 ....F2
Palestine 800 ....F5
Palmyra 621 ....E8
Paoli▲ 3,542 ....E7
Paragon 515 ....D6
Parker City 1,323 ....G4
Patoka 704 ....B8
Patricksburg 250 ....D6
Patriot 190 ....H7
Paxton 200 ....C7
Pekin 950 ....E7
Pendleton 2,309 ....F5
Pennville 637 ....G3
Perkinsville 175 ....F4
Perrysville 443 ....C4
Pershing 425 ....E2
Pershing G5
Peru▲ 12,843 ....E3
Petersburg 2,449 ....C7
Petroleum 212 ....G3
Pierceton 1,030 ....F2
Pilot Knob 150 ....C6
Pimento 150 ....C6
Pine Lake 1,676 ....D1
Pine Village 134 ....C4
Pittsboro 815 ....D5
Pittsburg 175 ....D3
Plainfield 10,433 ....E5
Plainville 444 ....C7
Pleasant Lake 800 ....H1
Pleasant Mills 175 ....H3
Plymouth▲ 8,303 ....E2
Poe 162 ....G3
Poland 230 ....C6
Poneto 236 ....G3
Portage 29,060 ....C1
Porter 3,118 ....C1
Portland▲ 6,483 ....H4
Poseyville 1,089 ....B8
Pottawattomie Park 281 ....C1
Prairie Creek 275 ....C6
Prairieton 200 ....B6
Preble 150 ....H3
Princes Lakes 1,055 ....E6
Princeton▲ 8,127 ....B8
Providence 250 ....E6
Putnamville 250 ....D5
Quincy 250 ....D5
Ragsdale 135 ....C7
Ramsey 550 ....E8
Ray 200 ....H1
Rays Crossing 157 ....F5
Reddington 400 ....F6
Redkey 1,383 ....G4
Reelsville 210 ....D5
Remington 1,247 ....C3
Rensselaer▲ 5,045 ....C3
Reynolds 528 ....D3
Richland 965 ....C7
Richmond▲ 38,705 ....H5
Ridgeville 808 ....G4
Rigdon 150 ....F4
Riley 232 ....C6
Rising Sun▲ 2,311 ....H7
Roachdale 902 ....D5

Roann 447 ....F3
Roanoke 1,018 ....G3
Rochester▲ 5,969 ....E2
Rockfield 300 ....D3
Rockport▲ 2,315 ....C9
Rockville▲ 2,706 ....C5
Rolling Prairie 550 ....D1
Rome 1,138 ....D9
Rome City 1,319 ....G1
Romney 250 ....D4
Rosedale 783 ....C5
Roseland 706 ....E1
Roselawn 200 ....C2
Rossville 1,175 ....D4
Royal Center 859 ....E3
Royerton 300 ....G4
Rushville▲ 5,533 ....G5
Russellville 336 ....D5
Russiaville 988 ....E4
Saint Anthony 470 ....D8
Saint Bernice 500 ....C5
Saint Henry 560 ....D8
Saint Joe 452 ....H2
Saint John 4,921 ....C2
Saint Leon 493 ....H6
Saint Louis Crossing 150 ......F6
Saint Mary-of-the-Woods
920 ....B6
Saint Marys E1
Saint Meinrad 910 ....D8
Saint Paul 1,032 ....F6
Saint Peter 175 ....H6
Saint Philip 400 ....B9
Saint Wendel 250 ....B8
Salamonia 138 ....H4
Salem 5,619 ....H3
Salem▲ 5,290 ....E7
Saltillo 117 ....E7
San Pierre 325 ....D2
Sandborn 455 ....C7
Santa Claus 927 ....D8
Saratoga 266 ....H4
Sardinia 133 ....F6
Schererville 19,926 ....C2
Schneider 310 ....C2
Schnellville 250 ....D8
Scipio 200 ....F6
Scott 5,334 ....F1
Scottsburg▲ 5,068 ....F7
Sedalia 160 ....E4
Seelyville 1,090 ....C6
Sellersburg 5,745 ....F8
Selma 800 ....G4
Servia 212 ....F3
Seymour 15,576 ....F7
Shadeland 1,674 ....C4
Shamrock Lakes 207 ....G4
Sharpsville 769 ....E4
Shelburn 1,147 ....C6
Shelby 15,336 ....C2
Shelbyville▲ 14,989 ....F6
Shepardsville 325 ....B5
Sheridan 2,046 ....E4
Shideler 275 ....G4
Shipshewana 524 ....F1
Shirley 817 ....F5
Shirley City (Woodburn)
..................................H2
Shoals▲ 853 ....D7
Sidney 167 ....F2
Silver Lake 528 ....F2
Sims 250 ....E5
Smith Valley E5
Smithville 500 ....D6
Solsberry 200 ....D6
Somerset 350 ....F3
Somerville 223 ....C8
South Bend▲ 105,511 ....E1
South Milford 270 ....G1
South Whitley 1,482 ....F2
Southport 1,969 ....E5
Spartanburg 201 ....H4
Speed 13,092 ....F8
Speedway 12,641 ....E5
Spelterville 200 ....C5
Spencer▲ 2,609 ....D6
Spencerville 400 ....G2
Spiceland 757 ....F5
Spring Grove 420 ....H5
Spring Lake 216 ....F5
Springport 194 ....G4
Springville 279 ....D7
Spurgeon 149 ....C8
Stanford 200 ....D6
Star City 351 ....D3
State Line 182 ....C4
Staunton 592 ....C6
Stendal 175 ....C8
Stewartsville 225 ....B8
Stilesville 298 ....D5
Stillwell 225 ....D1
Stinesville 204 ....D6
Stockwell 310 ....D4
Straughn 318 ....G5
Stroh 350 ....G1
Sullivan▲ 4,663 ....C6
Sulphur 257 ....E8
Sulphur Springs 345 ....G4
Sumava Resorts 300 ....C2
Summitville 1,010 ....F4
Sunman 623 ....G6
Swayzee 1,059 ....F4
Sweetser 924 ....F3
Switz City 257 ....C7
Syracuse 2,729 ....F2
Talma 170 ....E2
Taylorsville 1,044 ....F6
Tell City 8,088 ....D9
Tennyson 267 ....C8
Terhune 150 ....E4
Terre Haute▲ 57,483 ....C5
Thayer 350 ....C2
Thorntown 1,506 ....D4
Tippecanoe 320 ....E2
Tipton▲ 4,751 ....E4
Tocsin 160 ....G3
Topeka 912 ....F1

Town of Pines 789 ....D1
Trafalgar 531 ....E6
Trail Creek 2,463 ....D1
Tri Lakes 3,299 ....G2
Troy 465 ....D9
Tunnelton 150 ....E7
Twelve Mile 240 ....E3
Tyner 245 ....E2
Underwood 550 ....F7
Union 3,612 ....C8
Union City 3,908 ....H4
Union Mills 650 ....D2
Uniondale 289 ....G3
Unionville 225 ....E6
Universal 392 ....C5
Upland 3,295 ....F4
Urbana 400 ....F3
Utica 411 ....F8
Valeene 150 ....E8
Vallonia 550 ....E7
Valparaiso▲ 24,414 ....C2
Van Buren 934 ....F3
Veedersburg 2,192 ....C4
Velpen 375 ....C8
Vera Cruz 83 ....G3
Vernon▲ 370 ....F7
Versailles▲ 1,791 ....G6
Vevay▲ 1,393 ....G7
Vicksburg 175 ....D6
Vienna 175 ....F7
Vincennes▲ 19,859 ....C7
Wabash▲ 12,127 ....F3
Wadesville 450 ....B8
Wakarusa 1,667 ....F1
Waldron 850 ....F5
Walesboro 214 ....F6
Walkerton 2,061 ....E2
Wallace 89 ....C4
Wallen 945 ....G2
Walton 1,053 ....E3
Wanatah 852 ....D2
Warren 1,185 ....G3
Warrington 200 ....F5
Warsaw▲ 10,968 ....F2
Washington▲ 10,838 ....C7
Waterloo 2,040 ....G2
Watson 200 ....F8
Waveland 474 ....D5
Wawaka 320 ....F2
Wawasee 600 ....F2
Wawpecong 175 ....F3
Waynetown 911 ....C4
Webster 350 ....H5
West Baden Springs 675 .....D7
West College Corner 686 .....H5
West Harrison 318 ....H6
West Lafayette 25,907 ....D4
West Lebanon 760 ....C4
West Middleton 327 ....E4
West Terre Haute 2,495 ......B6
Westfield 3,304 ....E4
Westphalia 300 ....C7
Westpoint 375 ....C4
Westport 1,478 ....F6
Westville 5,255 ....D1
Wheatfield 621 ....C2

Wheatland 439 ....C7
Wheeler 540 ....C1
Wheeling 180 ....G4
Wheeling 500 ....C8
Whiteland 2,446 ....E5
Whitestown 476 ....E5
Whitewater 111 ....H5
Whiting 5,155 ....C1
Wilkinson 446 ....F5
Williams 425 ....D7
Williamsport▲ 1,798 ....C4
Willow Branch 145 ....F5
Wilmington 600 ....H6
Winamac▲ 2,262 ....D2
Winchester▲ 5,095 ....G4
Windfall 779 ....F4
Windsor 150 ....G4
Wingate 275 ....C4
Winona Lake 4,053 ....F2
Winslow 875 ....C8
Wirt 150 ....G7
Wolcott 886 ....C3
Wolcottville 879 ....G1
Wolflake 230 ....F2
Woodburn 1,321 ....H2
Woodland 400 ....E1
Woodlawn Heights 109 ......F4
Worthington 1,473 ....C6
Wyandotte 26 ....E8
Wyatt 250 ....E1
Yankeetown 250 ....C9
Yeoman 131 ....D3
Yoder 250 ....H3
Yorktown 4,106 ....G4
Young America 259 ....E3
Youngstown 350 ....C6
Zanesville 575 ....G3
Zenas 225 ....G6
Zionsville 5,281 ....E5

OTHER FEATURES

Anderson (riv.) D8
Bass (lake) D2
Beanblossom (creek) D6
Big (creek) B8
Big Blue (riv.) F5
Big Pine (creek) C3
Big Raccoon (creek) C5
Big Walnut (creek) D5
Blue (riv.) E8
Brookville (lake) G6
Buck (creek) F5
Busseron (creek) C7
Camp (creek) E6
Cedar (creek) G2
Clifty (creek) F6
Coal (coal) F5
Crooked (creek) D2
Cypress (pond) B8
Deer (creek) E3
Deer (creek) D4
Eagle (creek) E4
Eel (riv.) C6
Eel (riv.) F3
Elkhart (riv.) F1

Fawn (riv.) G1
Flatrock (creek) F5
Fort Benjamin Harrison E5
Freeman (lake) D3
Geist (res.) F5
George Rogers Clark
Nat'l Hist. Park B7
Graham (creek) F7
Grissom A.F.B. 4,271 ....E3
Huntington (lake) F3
Indian (creek) D6
Indian (creek) E8
Indiana Dunes Nat'l
Lakeshore C1
Iroquois (riv.) B3
Jefferson Proving Ground G7
Kankakee (riv.) C2
Lemon (lake) E6
Lincoln Boyhood Nat'l Mem. .C8
Little (riv.) G3
Little Elkhart (riv.) F1
Little Pigeon (creek) C9
Little Vermilion (riv.) B5
Lost (riv.) D7
Maria (creek) C7
Maumee (riv.) H2
Maxinkuckee (lake) E2
Michigan (lake) C1
Mill (creek) E6
Mississinewa (lake) E4
Mississinewa (riv.) F3
Monroe (lake) E6
Morse (res.) E4
Muscatatuck (riv.) E7
Ohio (riv.) B9
Patoka (riv.) C8
Pigeon (creek) C8
Pigeon (riv.) F1
Pipe (creek) F4
Prairie (creek) C7
Richland (creek) D6
Saint Joseph (riv.) E1
Saint Joseph (riv.) H2
Saint Marys (lake) H3
Saint Marys (riv.) H3
Salamonie (lake) F3
Salamonie (riv.) F4
Salt (creek) E6
Sand (creek) F6
Shafer (lake) D3
Silver (creek) F8
Sugar (creek) B3
Sugar (creek) C5
Sugar (creek) F5
Tippecanoe (riv.) E2
Vermilion (riv.) B4
Vernon Fork (creek) F6
Wabash (riv.) C7
Wawasee (lake) F2
White (riv.) B8
White, East Fork (riv.) C7
White, West Fork (riv.) C7
Whitewater (riv.) H6
Wildcat (creek) E4

▲County seat

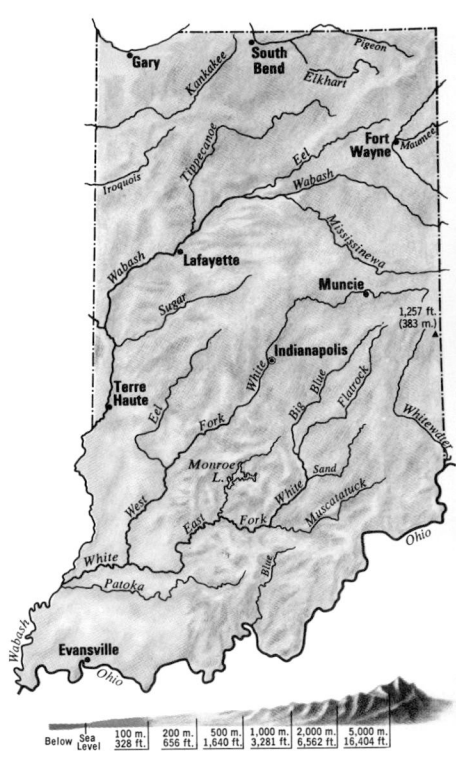

Topography

0   40   80 MI.

0   40   80 KM.

Gary   South Bend   Elkhart
Kankakee   Pigeon
Iroquois   Tippecanoe   Eel   Fort Wayne
Wabash   Maumee
Lafayette   Wabash
Muncie
Mississinewa
1,257 ft.
(383 m.)
Terre Haute   Indianapolis
White   Blue   Flatrock
Eel   Fork   Big   Whitewater
Monroe L.   White   Sand
West   Fork   East   Blue   Muscatatuck
White   Ohio
Patoka
Wabash
Evansville
Ohio

Below Sea Level | 100 m. 328 ft. | 200 m. 656 ft. | 500 m. 1,640 ft. | 1,000 m. 3,281 ft. | 2,000 m. 6,562 ft. | 5,000 m. 16,404 ft.

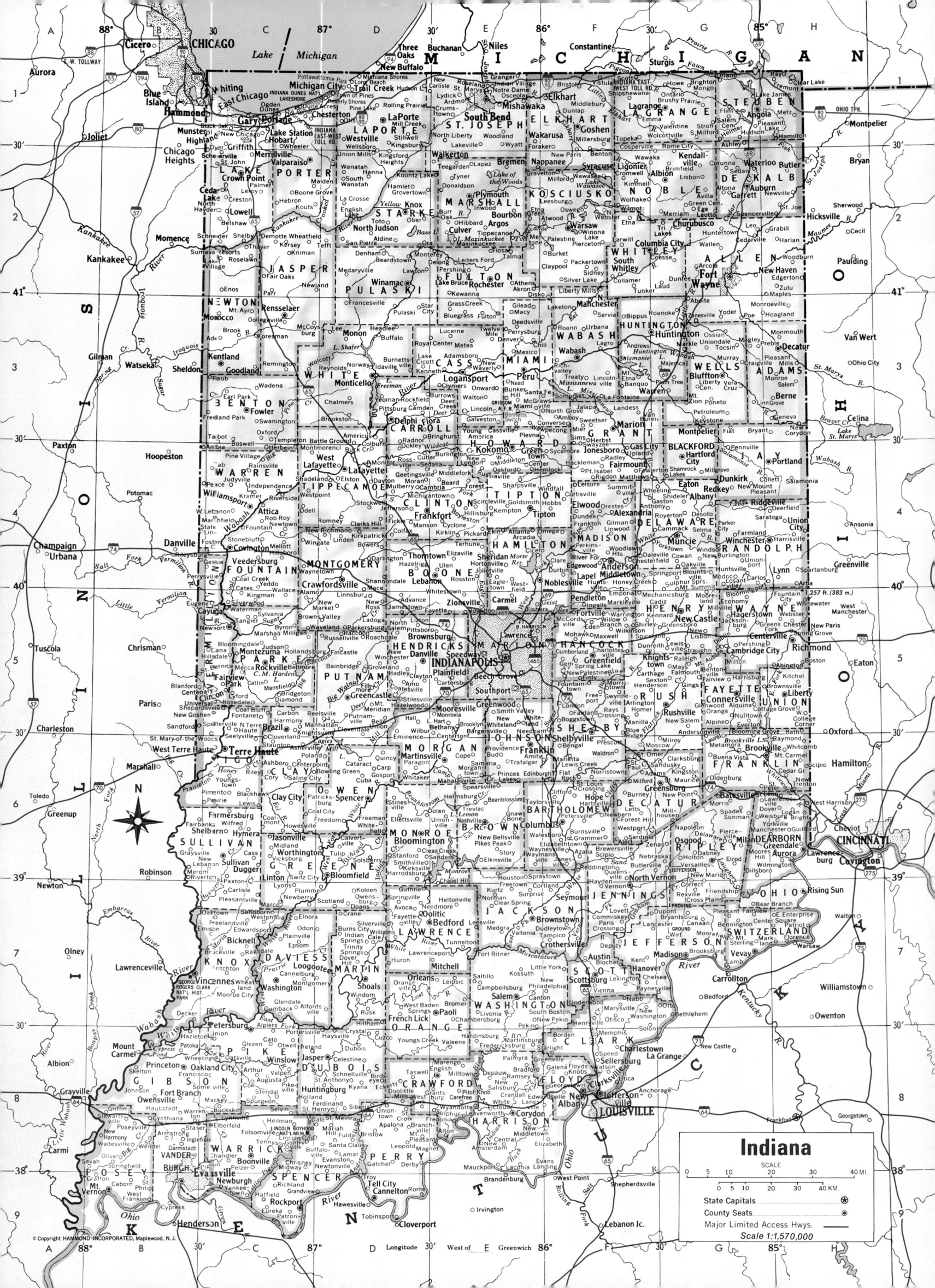

Indiana

SCALE
0 5 10   20   30   40 MI.
0 5 10   20   30   40 KM.
State Capitals ⊛
County Seats ◉
Major Limited Access Hwys. ━━━
Scale 1:1,570,000

COUNTIES

Adair 8,409	E6
Adams 4,866	D6
Allamakee 13,855	L2
Appanoose 13,743	H7
Audubon 7,334	D5
Benton 22,429	J4
Black Hawk 123,798	J4
Boone 25,186	F5
Bremer 22,813	J3
Buchanan 20,844	K4
Buena Vista 19,965	C3
Butler 15,731	H3
Calhoun 11,508	D4
Carroll 21,423	D4
Cass 15,128	D6
Cedar 17,381	L5
Cerro Gordo 46,733	G2
Cherokee 14,098	B3
Chickasaw 13,295	J2
Clarke 8,287	F6
Clay 17,585	C2
Clayton 19,054	L3
Clinton 51,040	M5
Crawford 16,775	C4
Dallas 29,755	E5
Davis 8,312	J7
Decatur 8,338	F7
Delaware 18,035	L4
Des Moines 42,614	L7
Dickinson 14,909	C2
Dubuque 86,403	M4
Emmet 11,569	D2
Fayette 21,843	K3
Floyd 17,058	H2
Franklin 11,364	G3
Fremont 8,226	B7
Greene 10,045	E5
Grundy 12,029	H4
Guthrie 10,935	D5
Hamilton 16,071	F4
Hardin 19,094	G4
Harrison 14,730	B5
Henry 19,226	K6
Howard 9,809	H2
Humboldt 10,756	E3
Ida 8,365	C4
Iowa 14,630	J5
Iowa 2,913,808	J5
Jackson 19,950	M4
Jasper 34,795	G5
Jefferson 16,310	K6
Johnson 96,119	K5
Jones 19,444	L4
Keokuk 11,624	J6
Kossuth 18,591	E2
Lee 38,687	L7
Linn 168,767	K4
Louisa 11,592	L6
Lucas 9,070	G6
Lyon 11,952	A2
Madison 12,483	E6
Mahaska 21,522	H6
Marion 30,001	G6
Marshall 38,276	G4
Mills 13,202	B6
Mitchell 10,928	H2
Monona 10,034	B4
Monroe 8,114	H7
Montgomery 12,076	C6
Muscatine 39,907	L5
O'Brien 16,972	B2
Osceola 7,267	B2
Page 16,870	C7
Palo Alto 10,669	D2
Plymouth 23,388	A3
Pocahontas 9,525	D3
Polk 327,140	F5
Pottawattamie 82,628	B6
Poweshiek 19,033	H5
Ringgold 5,420	E7
Sac 12,324	C4
Scott 150,979	M5
Shelby 13,230	C5
Sioux 29,903	A2
Story 74,252	G4
Tama 17,419	H4
Taylor 7,114	D7
Union 12,750	E7
Van Buren 7,676	K7
Wapello 35,687	J6
Warren 36,033	F6
Washington 19,612	K6
Wayne 7,067	G7
Webster 40,342	E4
Winnebago 12,122	F2
Winneshiek 20,847	K2
Woodbury 98,276	B4
Worth 7,991	G2
Wright 14,269	F3

CITIES and TOWNS

Ackley 1,696	G3
Adair 894	D6
Adel▲ 3,304	E6
Afton 953	E6
Agency 616	J7
Ainsworth 506	K6
Akron 1,450	A3
Albert City 779	C3
Albia▲ 3,870	H6
Albion 588	H4
Alburnett 456	K4
Alden 585	G4
Alexander 170	G3
Algona▲ 6,015	E2
Alleman 340	F5
Allerton 599	G7
Allison▲ 1,000	H3
Alta 1,820	C3
Alta Vista 246	J2
Alton 1,063	A3
Altoona 7,191	G5
Alvord 204	A2
Amana 300	K5
Ames 47,198	F4
Anamosa▲ 5,100	L4
Andrew 319	M4
Anita 1,068	D6
Ankeny 18,482	F5
Anthon 638	B4
Aplington 1,034	H3
Arcadia 485	C4
Arion 148	C5
Arlington 465	K3
Armstrong 1,025	D2
Arnolds Park 953	C2
Arthur 272	C4
Asbury 2,013	M4
Ashton 462	B2
Atalissa 357	L5
Atkins 637	K4
Atlantic▲ 7,432	D6
Auburn 283	D4
Audubon▲ 2,524	D5
Aurelia 1,034	C3
Aurora 196	K3
Avoca 1,497	C6
Ayrshire 195	D2
Badger 569	E3
Bagley 303	E5
Baldwin 137	M4
Bancroft 857	E2
Barnes City 221	H6
Barnum 174	E4
Batavia 520	J6
Battle Creek 818	C4
Baxter 938	G5
Bayard 511	D5
Beacon 509	H6
Beaman 183	H4
Bedford▲ 1,528	D7
Belle Plaine 2,834	J5
Bellevue 2,239	M4
Belmond 2,500	F3
Bennett 395	L5

Bertram 201	K5	Bristow 197	H3
Bettendorf 28,132	N5	Britt 2,133	F2
Birmingham 386	K7	Bronson 209	A4
Blairsburg 269	F4	Brooklyn 1,439	J5
Blairstown 672	J5	Brunsville 137	A3
Blakburg 404	H7	Buffalo 1,260	M6
Blencoe 250	A5	Buffalo Center 1,081	F2
Blockton 213	D7	Burlington▲ 27,208	L7
Bloomfield▲ 2,580	J7	Burt 575	E2
Blue Grass 1,214	M5	Bussey 494	H6
Bode 335	E3	Calamus 379	M5
Bonaparte 465	K7	Callender 384	E4
Bondurant 1,584	G5	Calmar 1,026	K2
Boone▲ 12,392	F4	Calumet 160	B3
Bouton 149	E5	Camanche 4,436	N5
Boxholm 214	E4	Cambridge 714	G5
Boyden 651	B2	Cantril 262	J7
Braddyville 219	D7	Carlisle 3,241	G6
Bradgate 124	E3	Carroll▲ 9,579	D4
Brandon 320	K4	Carson 705	C6
Brayton 148	D5	Carter Lake 3,200	B6
Breda 467	C4	Cascade 1,812	L4
Bridgewater 209	D6	Casey 441	D5
Brighton 684	K6	Castalia 177	K2

IOWA

AREA 56,275 sq. mi. (145,752 sq. km.)
POPULATION 2,787,424
CAPITAL Des Moines
LARGEST CITY Des Moines
HIGHEST POINT (Osceola Co.) 1670 ft. (509 m.)
SETTLED IN 1788
ADMITTED TO UNION December 28, 1846
POPULAR NAME Hawkeye State
STATE FLOWER Wild Rose
STATE BIRD Eastern Goldfinch

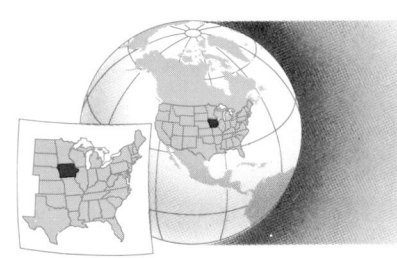

Iowa

SCALE
0 5 10 20 30 40 MI.
0 5 10 20 30 40 KM.

State Capitals ... ✪
County Seats ... ⊙
Major Limited Access Hwys.
Scale 1:1,700,000

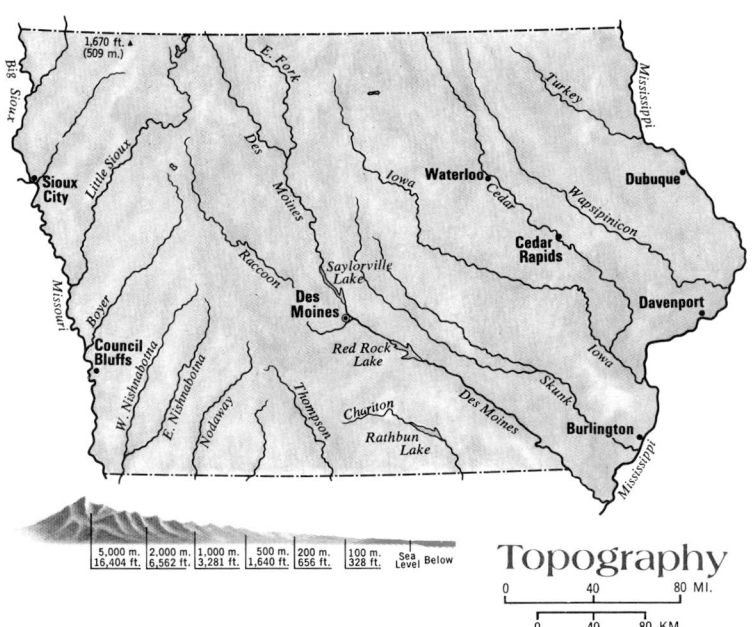

Topography

5,000 m. / 16,404 ft. — 2,000 m. / 6,562 ft. — 1,000 m. / 3,281 ft. — 500 m. / 1,640 ft. — 200 m. / 656 ft. — 100 m. / 328 ft. — Sea Level — Below

0 40 80 MI.
0 40 80 KM.

Castana 159	B4	Dayton 818	E4	Exira 955	D5
Cedar 34,298	H6	De Soto 1,033	E5	Exline 187	H7
Cedar Falls 36,322	H3	De Witt 4,514	N5	Fairbank 1,018	K3
Cedar Rapids▲ 108,751	K5	Decatur 177	F7	Fairfax 780	K5
Center Junction 166	L4	Decorah▲ 8,063	K2	Fairfield▲ 9,768	J6
Center Point 1,693	K4	Dedham 264	D5	Farley 1,354	L3
Centerville▲ 5,936	H7	Deep River 345	J5	Farmersburg 291	L3
Central City 1,063	K4	Defiance 312	C5	Farmington 655	K7
Chariton▲ 4,616	G6	Delaware 176	L4	Farnhamville 414	D4
Charles City▲ 7,878	H2	Delhi 485	L4	Farragut 498	C7
Charlotte 359	M5	Delmar 517	M4	Fayette 1,317	K3
Charter Oak 497	C4	Deloit 296	C4	Fenton 346	E2
Chelsea 336	J5	Delta 409	J6	Ferguson 166	H5
Cherokee▲ 6,026	B3	Denison▲ 6,604	C4	Fertile 382	G2
Chester 158	J2	Denver 1,600	J3	Floris 172	J7
Churdan 423	D4	Derby 135	G7	Floyd 359	H2
Cincinnati 363	G7	Des Moines (cap.)▲ 193,187	F5	Fonda 731	D3
Clare 161	E3	Dexter 628	E5	Fontanelle 712	E6
Clarence 936	M5	Diagonal 298	E7	Forest City▲ 4,430	F2
Clarinda▲ 5,104	C7	Dickens 214	C2	Fort Atkinson 367	J2
Clarion▲ 2,703	F3	Dike 875	H4	Fort Dodge▲ 25,894	E3
Clarksville 1,382	H3	Dixon 202	M5	Fort Madison▲ 11,618	L7
Clear Lake 8,183	G2	Donahue 316	M5	Fostoria 205	C2
Clearfield 417	D7	Donnellson 940	L7	Franklin 152	L7
Cleghorn 275	B3	Doon 476	A2	Fredericksburg 1,011	J3
Clemons 173	G4	Dow City 439	B5	Frederika 188	J3
Clermont 523	K3	Dows 660	F3	Fredonia 201	L6
Clinton▲ 29,201	N5	Drakesville 172	J7	Fremont 701	H6
Clive 7,462	F5	Dubuque▲ 57,546	M3	Fruitland 511	L6
Clutier 219	J4	Dumont 705	H3	Galva 398	C3
Coggon 645	L4	Duncombe 488	E4	Garden Grove 229	F7
Coin 278	C7	Dundee 174	L4	Garnavillo 727	L3
Colesburg 439	L3	Dunkerton 746	J3	Garner▲ 2,916	F2
Colfax 2,462	G5	Dunlap 1,251	B5	Garrison 320	J4
College Springs 230	C7	Durant 1,549	M5	Garwin 533	H4
Collins 455	G5	Dyersville 3,703	L3	Geneva 169	G3
Colo 771	G4	Dysart 1,230	J4	George 1,066	B2
Columbus City 328	L6	Eagle Grove 3,671	F3	Gilbert 796	F4
Columbus Junction 1,616	L6	Earlham 1,157	E6	Gilbertville 748	J4
Conesville 334	L6	Earling 466	C5	Gilman 586	H5
Conrad 964	H4	Earlville 822	L4	Gilmore City 560	D3
Coon Rapids 1,266	D5	Early 649	C4	Gladbrook 881	H4
Coralville 10,347	K5	Eddyville 1,010	H6	Glenwood▲ 4,571	B6
Corning▲ 1,806	D7	Edgewood 776	K3	Glidden 1,099	D4
Correctionville 897	B4	Elberon 203	J4	Goldfield 710	F3
Corwith 354	F3	Eldon 1,070	J7	Goodell 201	F3
Corydon▲ 1,675	G7	Eldora▲ 3,038	G4	Goose Lake 221	N5
Coulter 252	G3	Eldridge 3,378	M5	Gowrie 1,028	E4
Council Bluffs▲ 54,315	B6	Elgin 637	K3	Graettinger 813	D2
Crawfordsville 265	K6	Elk Horn 672	C5	Grafton 282	G2
Cresco▲ 3,669	J2	Elk Run Heights 1,088	J4	Grand Junction 808	E4
Creston▲ 7,911	E6	Elkader▲ 1,510	L3	Grand Mound 619	M5
Crystal Lake 266	F2	Elkhart 388	G5	Grand River 171	F7
Cumberland 295	D6	Elliott 399	C6	Grandview 514	L6
Cumming 132	F6	Ellsworth 451	G3	Granger 624	F5
Cushing 220	B4	Elma 653	J2	Granville 298	B3
Dakota City▲ 1,024	E3	Ely 517	K5	Gravity 218	D7
Dallas 1,454	G6	Emerson 476	C6	Greeley 263	L3
Dallas Center 1,360	F5	Emmetsburg▲ 3,940	D2	Greene 1,142	H3
Danbury 430	B4	Epworth 1,297	M4	Greenfield▲ 2,074	D6
Danville 926	L7	Essex 916	C7	Grimes 2,653	F5
Davenport▲ 95,333	M5	Estherville▲ 6,720	D2	Grinnell 8,902	H5
Davis City 257	F7	Evansdale 4,638	J4	Griswold 1,049	C6
Dawson 174	E5	Everly 706	C2	Grundy Center▲ 2,491	H4

(continued on following page)

© Copyright HAMMOND INCORPORATED, Maplewood, N.J.

Agriculture, Industry and Resources

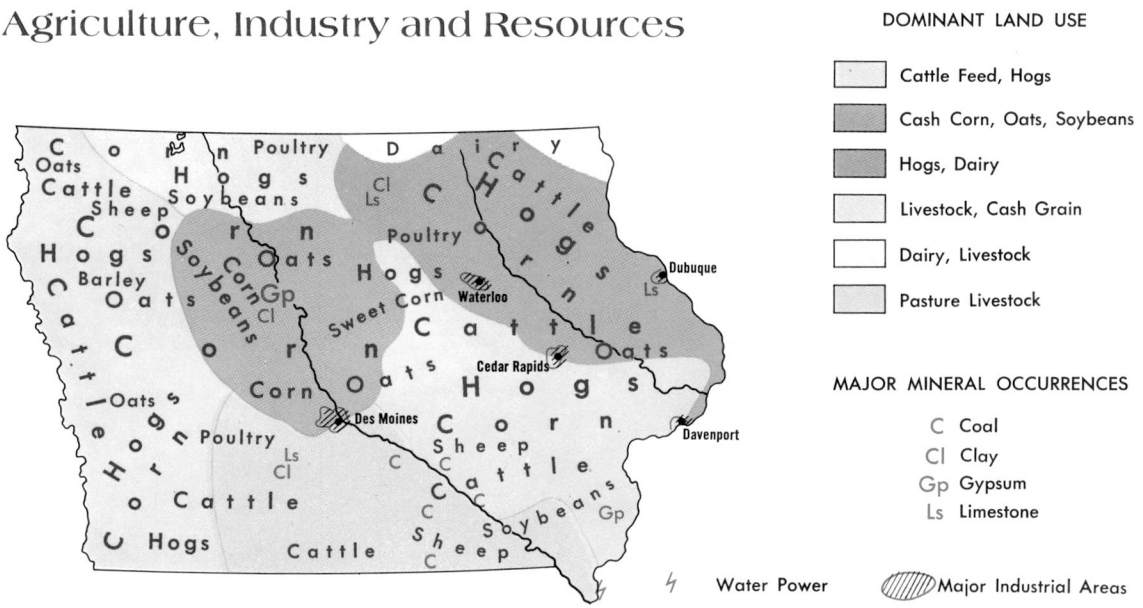

DOMINANT LAND USE

Cattle Feed, Hogs

Cash Corn, Oats, Soybeans

Hogs, Dairy

Livestock, Cash Grain

Dairy, Livestock

Pasture Livestock

MAJOR MINERAL OCCURRENCES

C Coal
Cl Clay
Gp Gypsum
Ls Limestone

⚡ Water Power   Major Industrial Areas

Guthrie Center▲ 1,614 ....D5
Guttenberg 2,257 ....L3
Halbur 215............D4
Hamburg 1,248............B7
Hampton▲ 4,133 ....G3
Hancock 201............C6
Hanlontown 193............G2
Harcourt 306............E4
Harlan▲ 5,148............C5
Harper 147............J6
Harpers Ferry 284 ....L2
Harris 170............C2
Hartford 768............G6
Hartley 1,632............C2
Harvey 235............H6
Hastings 187............C6
Havelock 217............D3
Haverhill 144............H5
Hawarden 2,439............A2
Hawkeye 460............J3
Hazleton 733............K3
Hedrick 810............J6
Henderson 205............B6
Hiawatha 4,986............K4
Hills 662............K5
Hillsboro 151............K7
Hinton 697............A3
Holland 215............H4
Holstein 1,449............B4
Holy Cross 304............L3
Hopkinton 695............L4
Hornick 222............A4
Hospers 643............B2
Hubbard 814............G4
Hudson 2,037............H4
Hull 1,724............A2
Humboldt 4,438............E3
Humeston 553............G7
Huxley 2,047............F5
Ida Grove▲ 2,357............B4
Independence▲ 5,972............K4
Indianola▲ 11,340............F6
Inwood 824............A2
Ionia 304............J2
Iowa City▲ 59,738............L5
Iowa Falls 5,424............G3
Ireton 597............A3
Irwin 394............C5
Jamaica 232............E5
Janesville 822............J3
Jefferson▲ 4,292............E4
Jesup 2,121............J4
Jewell 1,106............F4
Johnston 4,702............F5
Joice 245............G2
Kalo 1,942............E4
Kalona 1,862............K6
Kamrar 203............F4
Kanawha 763............F3
Kellerton 314............E7
Kelley 246............F5
Kellogg 626............H5
Kensett 298............G2
Keokuk▲ 12,451............L8
Keosauqua▲ 1,020............J7
Keota 1,000............K6
Keswick 284............J6
Keystone 568............J5
Kimballton 289............D5
Kingsley 1,129............A3
Kiron 301............C4
Kirkville 177............H6
Klemme 587............F3
Knoxville▲ 8,232............G6
La Motte 219............M4
La Porte City 2,128............J4
Lacona 357............G6
Ladora 308............J5
Lake City 1,841............D4
Lake Mills 2,143............F2

Lake Park 996............C2
Lake View 1,303............C4
Lakeside 522............C3
Lakota 281............E2
Lambs Grove 212............G5
Lamoni 2,319............E7
Lamont 471............K3
Lanesboro 182............D4
Lansing 1,007............L2
Larchwood 739............A2
Larrabee 175............B3
Latimer 430............G3
Laurel 271............H5
Laurens 1,550............D3
Lawler 517............J2
Lawton 482............A4
Le Claire 2,734............N5
Le Grand 854............H5
Le Mars▲ 8,454............A3
Ledyard 164............E2
Lehigh 536............E4
Leighton 142............H6
Leland 311............F2
Lenox 1,303............D7
Leon▲ 2,047............F7
Lester 257............A2
Letts 390............L6
Lewis 433............C6
Libertyville 264............K7
Lidderdale 202............D4
Lime Springs 438............J2
Lincoln 173............H4
Linden 201............E5
Lineville 289............G7
Linn Grove 194............C3
Lisbon 1,452............L5
Liscomb 258............H4
Little Rock 493............B2
Little Sioux 205............B5
Livermore 436............E3
Lockridge 270............K7
Logan▲ 1,401............B5
Lohrville 453............D4
Lone Rock 185............E2
Lone Tree 979............L6
Long Grove 605............M5
Lorimor 377............E6
Lost Nation 467............M5
Lovilia 581............H6
Low Moor 280............N5
Lowden 726............M5
Lu Verne 328............E3
Luana 190............K2
Lucas 224............G6
Luther 154............F5
Luxemburg 257............L3
Lynnville 393............H5
Lytton 320............D4
Macedonia 262............C6
Madrid 2,395............F5
Magnolia 204............B5
Malcom 447............H5
Mallard 360............D3
Malvern 1,210............B7
Manchester▲ 5,137............L3
Manilla 898............C5
Manly 1,349............G2
Manning 1,484............C5
Manson 1,844............D3
Mapleton 1,294............B4
Maquoketa▲ 6,111............M4
Marathon 320............C3
Marble Rock 361............H3
Marcus 1,171............B3
Marengo▲ 2,270............J5
Marion 20,403............K4
Marne 149............C6
Marquette 479............L2
Marshalltown▲ 25,178............G4
Martelle 290............L4

Martensdale 491............F6
Martinsburg 157............J6
Mason City▲ 29,040............G2
Masonville 129............K4
Massena 372............D6
Maurice 243............A3
Maxwell 788............G5
Maynard 513............K3
Maysville 170............M5
McCallsburg 292............G4
McCausland 308............M5
McClelland 139............B6
McGregor 797............L2
McIntire 147............H2
Mechanicsville 1,012............L5
Mediapolis 1,637............L6
Melbourne 669............G5
Melcher 1,302............G6
Melrose 150............G7
Melvin 250............B2
Menlo 356............E5
Meriden 193............B3
Merrill 729............A3
Meservey 292............G3
Middle 386............K5
Middletown 487............L7
Miles 409............N4
Milford 2,170............C2
Miller 188............F2
Millersburg 184............J5
Milo 864............G6
Milton 506............J7
Minburn 346............E5
Minden 498............C6
Mingo 252............G5
Missouri Valley 2,888............B5
Mitchell 170............H2
Mitchellville 1,670............G5
Modale 289............B5
Mondamin 403............B5
Monmouth 169............M4
Monona 1,520............L2
Monroe 1,739............G5
Montezuma▲ 1,651............H5
Monticello 3,522............L4
Montour 312............H5
Montrose 957............L7
Moorhead 259............B5
Moorland 209............E4
Moravia 679............H7
Morning Sun 841............L6
Moulton 613............H7
Mount Auburn 134............J4
Mount Ayr▲ 1,796............E7
Mount Pleasant▲ 8,027............L7
Mount Union 140............L6
Mount Vernon 3,657............K5
Moville 1,306............A4
Murray 731............F6
Muscatine▲ 22,881............L6
Mystic 545............H7
Nashua 1,476............J3
Neola 894............B6
Nevada▲ 6,009............G5
New Albin 534............L2
New Hampton▲ 3,660............J2
New Hartford 683............H3
New Liberty 139............M5
New London 1,922............L7
New Market 481............D7
New Providence 240............G4
New Sharon 1,136............H6
New Vienna 376............L3
New Virginia 433............F6
Newell 1,089............D3
Newhall 854............J5
Newton▲ 14,789............H5
Nichols 366............L6
Nodaway 153............D7
Nora Springs 1,505............H2

North Buena Vista 145 ....L3
North English 944 ....J5
North Liberty 2,926............K5
Northwood▲ 1,940............G2
Norwalk 5,726............F6
Norway 583............K5
Numa 151............G7
Oakland 1,496............C6
Oakland Acres 152............H5
Oakville 442............L6
Ocheyedan 539............B2
Odebolt 1,158............C4
Ogden 1,909............E4
Okoboji 775............C2
Olds 205............K6
Olin 663............L5
Ollie 207............J6
Onawa▲ 2,936............A4
Onslow 216............L4
Oran 4,940............J3
Orange City▲ 4,588............A2
Orient 376............E6
Orleans 560............C2
Osage▲ 3,439............H2
Osceola▲ 4,164............F6
Oskaloosa▲ 10,632............H6
Ossian 810............K2
Otho 529............E4
Ottumwa▲ 24,488............J6
Oxford 663............K5
Oxford Junction 581............M4
Pacific Junction 548............B6
Packwood 208............J6
Palmer 230............D3
Palo 514............K4
Panama 201............B5
Panora 1,100............E5
Parkersburg 1,804............H3
Parnell 209............J5
Paton 255............E4
Patterson 128............F6
Paullina 1,134............B3
Pella 9,270............H6
Peosta 128............M4
Perry 6,652............E5
Persia 312............B5
Peterson 390............C3
Pierson 341............B3
Pilot Mound 199............F4
Pisgah 268............B5
Plainfield 455............J3
Pleasant Hill 3,671............G5
Pleasant Plain 128............K6
Pleasantville 1,536............G6
Plymouth 453............G2
Pocahontas▲ 2,085............D3
Polk City 1,908............F5
Pomeroy 762............D3
Portsmouth 209............C5
Postville 1,472............K2
Prairie City 1,360............G5
Prairieburg 213............L4
Prescott 287............D6
Preston 1,025............N4
Primghar▲ 950............B2
Princeton 806............N5
Protivin 305............J2
Pulaski 221............J7
Quasqueton 579............K4
Quimby 334............B3
Radcliffe 574............G4
Rake 238............F2
Randall 161............F4
Randolph 243............B7
Raymond 619............J4
Readlyn 773............J3
Reasnor 191............G5
Red Oak▲ 6,264............C7
Redfield 883............E5

Reinbeck 1,605............H4
Rembrandt 229............C3
Remsen 1,513............B3
Renwick 287............E3
Rhodes 272............G5
Riceville 827............H2
Richland 522............K6
Rickardsville 171............M3
Ridgeway 295............K2
Ringsted 481............D2
Rippey 275............E5
Riverdale 433............N5
Riverside 824............K6
Riverton 333............B7
Robins 875............K4
Rock Falls 130............G2
Rock Rapids▲ 2,601............A2
Rock Valley 2,540............A2
Rockford 863............H2
Rockwell 1,008............G3
Rockwell City▲ 1,981............D4
Roland 1,035............F4
Rolfe 721............D3
Rose Hill 171............J6
Rowan 189............F3
Rowley 272............K4
Royal 466............C2
Rudd 429............H2
Runnells 306............G5
Russell 531............G7
Ruthven 707............D2
Rutland 149............E3
Ryan 382............K4
Sabula 710............N4
Sac City▲ 2,492............C4
Sageville 288............M3
Saint Ansgar 1,063............H2
Saint Anthony 112............G4
Saint Charles 537............F6
Saint Donatus 145............M4
Saint Lucas 174............K2
Saint Olaf 111............L3
Saint Paul 120............L7
Salem 453............K7
Salix 367............A4
Sanborn 1,345............B2
Schaller 768............C4
Schleswig 851............B4
Scranton 583............D4
Searsboro 164............H5
Sergeant Bluff 2,772............A4
Seymour 869............G7
Shambaugh 190............D7
Sheffield 1,174............G3
Shelby 637............C5
Sheldahl 315............F5
Sheldon 4,937............B2
Shell Rock 1,385............H3
Shellsburg 765............K4
Shenandoah 5,572............C7
Sherrill 148............M3
Shueyville 223............K5
Sibley▲ 2,815............B2
Sidney▲ 1,253............B7
Sigourney▲ 2,111............J6
Silver City 252............B6
Sioux Center 5,074............A2
Sioux City▲ 80,505............A3
Sioux Rapids 761............C3
Slater 1,268............F5
Sloan 938............A4
Smithland 235............B4
Soldier 205............B5
Solon 1,050............L5
Somers 161............E4
South English 224............J6
Spencer▲ 11,066............C2
Spillville 387............J2
Spirit Lake▲ 3,871............C2
Springville 1,068............L4

Stacyville 481............H2
Stanhope 447............F4
Stanton 692............C7
Stanwood 646............L5
State Center 1,248............G5
Steamboat Rock 335............G4
Stockport 260............K7
Stockton 187............M5
Storm Lake▲ 8,769............C3
Story City 2,959............F4
Stout 192............H3
Stratford 715............F4
Strawberry Point 1,357............K3
Stuart 1,522............E6
Sully 841............H5
Sumner 2,078............J3
Superior 128............D2
Sutherland 714............B3
Swaledale 190............G3
Swea City 634............E2
Swisher 645............K5
Tabor 957............B7
Tama 2,697............H5
Templeton 321............D5
Terril 383............C2
Thompson 498............F2
Thor 205............E3
Thornton 431............G3
Thurman 239............B7
Tiffin 460............K5
Tingley 179............E7
Tipton▲ 2,998............L5
Titonka 612............E2
Toledo▲ 2,380............H4
Traer 1,552............J4
Treynor 897............B6
Tripoli 1,188............J3
Truesdale 132............C3
Truro 391............F6
Underwood 515............B6
Union 448............G4
Unionville 133............H7
University Heights 1,042............K5
University Park 604............H6
Urbana 595............K4
Urbandale 23,500............F5
Ute 395............B4
Vail 388............C4
Van Horne 695............J4
Van Meter 751............E5
Van Wert 249............F7
Ventura 590............F2
Victor 966............J5
Villisca 1,332............C7
Vincent 185............E3
Vinton▲ 5,103............J4
Volga 306............L3
Wadena 236............K3
Wahpeton 484............C2
Walcott 1,356............M5
Walford 303............K5
Walker 673............K4
Wall Lake 875............C4
Wallingford 196............D2
Walnut 857............C6
Wapello▲ 2,013............L6
Washington▲ 7,074............K6
Washta 284............B3
Waterloo▲ 66,467............J4
Waterville 140............L2
Waucoma 277............J2
Waukee 2,512............F5
Waukon▲ 4,019............L2
Waverly▲ 8,539............J3
Wayland 838............K6
Webb 167............D3
Webster City▲ 7,894............F4
Weldon 151............F7
Wellman 1,085............K6
Wellsburg 682............H3

Welton 177 ....M5
Wesley 444............E2
West 862............J5
West Bend 941............D3
West Branch 1,908............L5
West Burlington 3,083............L7
West Chester 178............K6
West Des Moines 31,702............F5
West Liberty 2,935............L5
West Okoboji 263............C2
West Point 1,079............L7
West Union▲ 2,490............K3
Westfield 160............A2
Westgate 207............K3
Westphalia 144............C5
Westside 348............C4
What Cheer 762............J6
Wheatland 723............M5
Whiting 683............A4
Whittemore 535............E2
Whitten 137............H4
Williams 368............F3
Williamsburg 2,174............J5
Williamson 166............G6
Wilton 2,577............M5
Windsor Heights 5,190............F5
Winfield 1,051............L6
Winterset▲ 4,196............E6
Winthrop 742............K4
Wiota 160............D6
Woden 259............F2
Woodbine 1,500............B5
Woodburn 240............F7
Woodward 1,197............E5
Woolstock 212............F3
Worthington 439............L4
Wyoming 659............L4
Yale 220............E5
Zearing 614............G4

OTHER FEATURES

Big Sioux (riv.) A3
Boyer (riv.)............B5
Cedar (riv.)............K4
Chariton (riv.)............G7
Clear (lake)............G2
Des Moines (riv.)............J7
Eagle (lake)............F2
East Nishnabotna (riv.)............C6
Effigy Mounds Nat'l Mon.............L2
Five Island (lake)............D2
Floyd (riv.)............A3
Herbert Hoover Nat'l
  Hist. Site............L5
Iowa (riv.)............H4
Little Sioux (riv.)............B3
Lost Island (lake)............D2
Mississippi (riv.)............L7
Missouri (riv.)............A4
Nodaway (riv.)............C7
Palo Alto (lake)............D4
Platte (riv.)............D8
Raccoon (riv.)............D4
Rathbun (lake)............G7
Red Rock (lake)............G6
Rock (riv.)............A2
Sac and Fox Ind. Res.............H6
Skunk (riv.)............K6
Spirit (lake)............C2
Storm (lake)............C3
Summit (lake)............G6
Thompson (riv.)............E7
Trumbull (lake)............D2
Turkey (riv.)............K3
Upper Iowa (riv.)............H4
Wapsipinicon (riv.)............L4
West Nishnabotna (riv.)............C6

▲County seat

KANSAS

AREA 82,277 sq. mi. (213,097 sq. km.)
POPULATION 2,485,600
CAPITAL Topeka
LARGEST CITY Wichita
HIGHEST POINT Mt. Sunflower 4,039 ft. (1231 m.)
SETTLED IN 1831
ADMITTED TO UNION January 29, 1861
POPULAR NAME Sunflower State
STATE FLOWER Sunflower
STATE BIRD Western Meadowlark

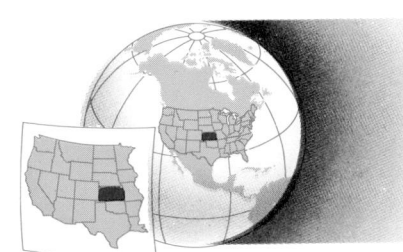

Agriculture, Industry and Resources

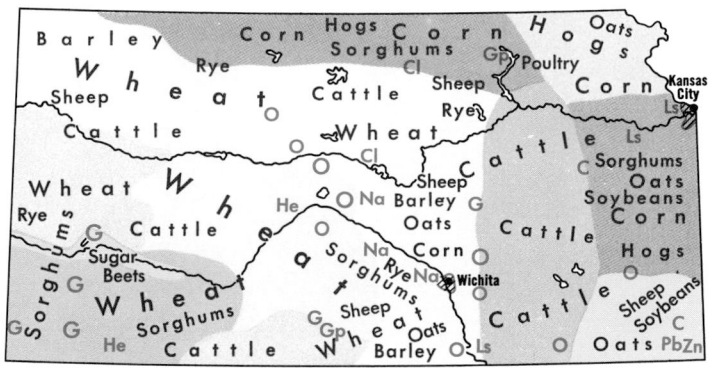

DOMINANT LAND USE

- Specialized Wheat
- Wheat, General Farming
- Wheat, Range Livestock
- Wheat, Grain Sorghums, Range Livestock
- Cattle Feed, Hogs
- Livestock, Cash Grain
- Livestock, Cash Grain, Dairy
- General Farming, Livestock, Cash Grain
- General Farming, Livestock, Special Crops
- Range Livestock

MAJOR MINERAL OCCURRENCES

C	Coal	Ls	Limestone
Cl	Clay	Na	Salt
G	Natural Gas	O	Petroleum
Gp	Gypsum	Pb	Lead
He	Helium	Zn	Zinc

Major Industrial Areas

COUNTIES

llen 15,654 ....G4
nderson 7,803 ....G3
tchison 16,932 ....G2
arber 5,874 ....D4
arton 29,382 ....D3
ourbon 14,966 ....H4
rown 11,128 ....G2
utler 50,580 ....E4
hase 3,021 ....F3
hautauqua 4,407 ....F4
herokee 21,374 ....H4
heyenne 3,243 ....A2
lark 2,418 ....C4
lay 9,158 ....E2
oud 11,023 ....E2
offey 8,404 ....G3
omanche 2,313 ....C4
owley 36,915 ....F4
rawford 35,568 ....H4
ecatur 4,021 ....B2
ickinson 18,958 ....E3
oniphan 8,134 ....G2
ouglas 81,798 ....G3
dwards 3,787 ....C4
lk 3,327 ....F4
llis 26,004 ....C3
llsworth 6,586 ....D3
inney 33,070 ....B3
ord 27,463 ....C4
ranklin 21,994 ....G3
eary 30,453 ....F3
ove 3,231 ....B3
rant 7,159 ....A4
ray 5,396 ....B4
reeley 1,774 ....A3
reenwood 7,847 ....F4
amilton 2,388 ....A3
arper 7,124 ....D4
arvey 31,028 ....E3
askell 3,886 ....B4
odgeman 2,177 ....C3
ackson 11,525 ....G2
efferson 15,905 ....G2
ohnson 355,054 ....H3
earny 4,027 ....A3
ingman 8,292 ....D4
owa 3,660 ....C4
abette 23,693 ....G4
ane 2,375 ....B3
eavenworth 64,371 ....G2
incoln 3,653 ....D2
nn 8,254 ....H3
ogan 3,081 ....A3
yon 34,732 ....F3
arion 12,888 ....E3
arshall 11,705 ....F2
cPherson 27,268 ....E3
eade 4,247 ....B4
iami 23,466 ....H3
itchell 7,203 ....D2
ontgomery 38,816 ....G4
orris 6,198 ....F3
orton 3,480 ....A4
emaha 10,446 ....F2
eosho 17,035 ....G4
ess 4,033 ....C3
orton 5,947 ....C2
sage 15,248 ....G3
sborne 4,867 ....D2
ttawa 5,634 ....E2
awnee 7,555 ....C3
hillips 6,590 ....C2
ottawatomie 16,128 ....F2
ratt 9,702 ....D4
awlins 3,404 ....A2
eno 62,389 ....D4
epublic 6,482 ....E2
ice 10,610 ....D3
ley 67,139 ....F2
ooks 6,039 ....C2
ush 3,842 ....C3
ussell 7,835 ....D3
aline 49,301 ....E3
cott 5,289 ....B3
edgwick 403,662 ....E4
eward 18,743 ....B4
hawnee 160,976 ....G2
heridan 3,043 ....B2
herman 6,926 ....A2
mith 5,078 ....C2
tafford 5,365 ....D3
tanton 2,333 ....A4
tevens 5,048 ....A4
umner 25,841 ....E4
homas 8,258 ....A2
rego 3,694 ....C3
abaunsee 6,603 ....F3
allace 1,821 ....A3
ashington 7,073 ....E2
ichita 2,758 ....A3
ilson 10,289 ....G4
oodson 4,116 ....G4
yandotte 161,993 ....H2

CITIES and TOWNS

bbyville 123 ....D4
bilene▲ 6,242 ....E3
da 120 ....E2
dmire 147 ....F3
genda 81 ....E2
gra 322 ....C2
amota 50 ....B3
lbert 229 ....C3
lden 182 ....D3
lexander 85 ....C3
liceville 60 ....G3
llen 191 ....F3
lma▲ 871 ....F2
lmena 423 ....C2
lta Vista 477 ....F3
ltamont 1,048 ....G4
lton 115 ....D2

Altoona 456 ....G4
Americus 891 ....F3
Ames 65 ....E2
Andale 566 ....E4
Andover 4,047 ....E4
Angola 55 ....G4
Anthony▲ 2,516 ....D4
Arcadia 338 ....H4
Argonia 529 ....E4
Arkansas City 12,762 ....E4
Arlington 457 ....D4
Arma 1,542 ....H4
Ash Valley 50 ....C3
Ashland▲ 1,032 ....C4
Assaria 387 ....E3
Atchison▲ 10,656 ....G2
Athol 86 ....D2
Atlanta 232 ....F4
Attica 716 ....D4
Atwood▲ 1,388 ....B2
Auburn 908 ....G3
Augusta 7,876 ....F4
Aurora 101 ....E2
Axtell 432 ....F2
Baileyville 130 ....F2
Baldwin City 2,961 ....G3
Barnard 129 ....D2
Barnes 167 ....F2
Bartlett 107 ....G4
Basehor 1,591 ....G2
Bassett 20 ....G4
Bavaria 100 ....E3
Baxter Springs 4,351 ....H4
Bazine 373 ....C3
Beagle 88 ....G3
Beattie 221 ....F2
Beaumont 112 ....F4
Beaver 57 ....D3
Beeler 80 ....B3
Belle Plaine 1,649 ....E4
Belleville▲ 2,517 ....E2
Beloit▲ 4,066 ....D2
Belpre 116 ....C4
Belvue 207 ....F2
Bendena 125 ....G2
Benedict 16 ....G4
Bennington 568 ....E2
Bentley 360 ....E4
Benton 669 ....E4
Bern 190 ....F2
Berryton 150 ....G3
Beverly 131 ....E2
Big Bow 55 ....A4
Bird City 467 ....A2
Bison 252 ....C3
Blaine 50 ....F2
Bloom 65 ....C4
Blue Mound 251 ....H3
Blue Rapids 1,131 ....F2
Bluff City 69 ....E4
Bogue 150 ....C2
Bonner Springs 6,413 ....H2
Brazilton 91 ....H4
Bremen 60 ....F2
Brewster 296 ....A2
Bridgeport 95 ....E3
Bronson 343 ....H4
Brookville 226 ....E3
Brownell 44 ....C3
Bucklin 710 ....C4
Bucyrus 135 ....H3
Buffalo 293 ....G4
Buhler 1,277 ....E3
Bunker Hill 111 ....D3
Burden 518 ....F4
Burdett 248 ....C3
Burdick 100 ....E3
Burlingame 1,074 ....G3
Burlington▲ 2,735 ....G3
Burns 226 ....E4
Burr Oak 278 ....D2
Burrton 866 ....E3
Bushong 57 ....F3
Bushton 341 ....D3
Byers 46 ....D4
Caldwell 1,351 ....E4
Cambridge 74 ....F4
Caney 2,062 ....G4
Canton 794 ....E3
Carbondale 1,526 ....G3
Carlton 39 ....E3
Carlyle 75 ....G4
Cassoday 95 ....F3
Catharine 121 ....C3
Cawker City 588 ....D2
Cedar 25 ....D2
Cedar Point 39 ....F3
Cedar Vale 760 ....F4
Centerville 104 ....H3
Centralia 452 ....F2
Chanute 9,488 ....G4
Chapman 1,264 ....E3
Chase 577 ....D3
Chautauqua 132 ....F4
Cheney 1,560 ....E4
Cherokee 651 ....H4
Cherryvale 2,464 ....G4
Chetopa 1,357 ....G4
Chicopee 300 ....H4
Cimarron▲ 1,626 ....B4
Circleville 153 ....G2
Claflin 678 ....D3
Clay Center▲ 4,613 ....E2
Clayton 91 ....B2
Clearview City G3
Clearwater 1,875 ....E4
Clifton 561 ....E2
Climax 57 ....F4
Clyde 793 ....E2
Coats 127 ....D4
Codell 90 ....C2
Coffeyville 12,917 ....G4
Colby▲ 5,396 ....A2
Coldwater▲ 939 ....C4
Collyer 144 ....B2
Colony 447 ....G3
Columbus▲ 3,268 ....H4

Colwich 1,091 ....E4
Concordia▲ 6,167 ....E2
Conway 1,384 ....E3
Conway Springs 1,313 ......E4
Coolidge 90 ....A3
Copeland 290 ....B4
Corning 142 ....F2
Cottonwood Falls▲ 889 .....F3
Council Grove▲ 2,228 ....F3
Courtland 343 ....E2
Coyville 78 ....G4
Crestline 85 ....H4
Cuba 242 ....E2
Cullison 120 ....D4
Culver 162 ....E3
Cummings 150 ....G2
Cunningham 535 ....D4
Damar 112 ....C2
Danville 56 ....E4
De Soto 2,291 ....H3
Dearing 428 ....G4
Deerfield 677 ....A4
Delia 172 ....G2
Delphos 494 ....E2
Denison 225 ....G2
Dennis 96 ....G4

Denton 166 ....G2
Derby 14,699 ....E4
Detroit 90 ....E3
Devon 108 ....H4
Dexter 320 ....F4
Dighton▲ 1,361 ....B3
Dodge City▲ 21,129 ....B4
Dorrance 195 ....D3
Douglass 1,722 ....F4
Dover 192 ....G3
Downs 1,119 ....D2
Dresden 79 ....B2
Dunlap 65 ....F3
Durham 119 ....E3
Dwight 365 ....F3
Earlton 69 ....G4
Eastborough 896 ....E4
Easton 405 ....G2
Edgerton 1,244 ....H3
Edmond 37 ....C2
Edna 438 ....G4
Edson 55 ....A2
Edwardsville 3,979 ....H2
Effingham 540 ....G2
El Dorado▲ 11,504 ....F4
Elbing 184 ....E3

Elgin 118 ....F4
Elk City 334 ....G4
Elk Falls 122 ....F4
Elkhart▲ 2,318 ....A4
Ellinwood 2,329 ....D3
Ellis 1,814 ....C3
Ellsworth▲ 2,294 ....D3
Elmdale 83 ....F3
Elmont 112 ....G2
Elsmore 91 ....G4
Elwood 1,079 ....H2
Elyria 100 ....E3
Emmett 165 ....F2
Emporia▲ 25,512 ....F3
Englewood 96 ....B4
Ensign 192 ....B4
Enterprise 865 ....E3
Erie▲ 1,276 ....G4
Esbon 167 ....D2
Eskridge 518 ....G3
Eudora 3,006 ....G3
Eureka▲ 2,974 ....F4
Everest 310 ....G2
Fairview 306 ....G2
Fairway 4,173 ....H2
Fall River 113 ....G4

Falun 89 ....E3
Farlington 80 ....H4
Florence 636 ....E3
Fontana 131 ....H3
Ford 247 ....C4
Formoso 128 ....D2
Fort Dodge 400 ....C4
Fort Leavenworth H2
Fort Scott▲ 8,362 ....H4
Fowler 571 ....B4
Frankfort 927 ....F2
Franklin 400 ....H4
Frederick 18 ....D3
Fredonia▲ 2,599 ....G4
Freeport 8 ....E4
Frontenac 2,588 ....H4
Fulton 191 ....H4
Galatia 47 ....D3
Galena 3,308 ....H4
Galesburg 160 ....G4
Galva 651 ....E3
Garden City▲ 24,097 ....B4
Garden Plain 731 ....E4
Gardner 3,191 ....H3
Garfield 236 ....C3
Garland 112 ....H4

Garnett▲ 3,210 ....G3
Gas 505 ....G4
Gaylord 173 ....D2
Gem 104 ....B2
Geneseo 382 ....D3
Geuda Springs 219 ....E4
Girard▲ 2,794 ....H4
Glade 101 ....C2
Glasco 556 ....E2
Glen Elder 448 ....D2
Goddard 1,804 ....E4
Goessel 506 ....E3
Goff 156 ....G2
Goodland▲ 4,983 ....A2
Gorham 284 ....D3
Gove▲ 103 ....B3
Grainfield 357 ....B2
Grandview Plaza 1,233 ......F2
Grantville 220 ....G2
Great Bend▲ 15,427 ....D3
Greeley 339 ....G3
Green 150 ....E2
Greenleaf 353 ....E2
Greensburg▲ 1,792 ....C4
Grenola 256 ....F4
Gridley 356 ....G3

(continued on following page)

Grinnell 348 ....B2	Herington 2,685 ....E3	Hudson 159 ....D3	Kanorado 276 ....A2	Lansing 7,120 ....H2	Liberty 140 ....G4	Mahaska 98 ....E2
Gypsum 365 ....E3	Herkimer 80 ....F2	Hugoton▲ 3,179 ....A4	Kansas City▲ 149,767 ....H2	Larned▲ 4,490 ....C3	Liebenthal 112 ....C3	Maize 1,520 ....E4
Haddam 195 ....E2	Herndon 170 ....B2	Humboldt 2,178 ....G4	Keats 150 ....F2	Latham 160 ....F4	Lincoln▲ 1,381 ....D2	Manchester 80 ....E2
Hallowell 100 ....H4	Hesston 3,012 ....E3	Hunnewell 87 ....E4	Kechi 517 ....E4	Latimer 20 ....F3	Lincolnville 197 ....E3	Manhattan▲ 37,712 ....F2
Halstead 2,015 ....E4	Hiattville 60 ....H4	Hunter 116 ....D2	Kendall 50 ....A4	Lawrence▲ 65,608 ....G3	Lindsborg 3,076 ....E3	Mankato▲ 1,037 ....D2
Hamilton 301 ....F4	Hiawatha▲ 3,603 ....G2	Huron 75 ....G2	Kensington 553 ....C2	Lawton 65 ....H4	Linn 472 ....E2	Manter 186 ....A4
Hamlin 50 ....G2	Hickok 68 ....A4	Hutchinson 39,308 ....D3	Kincaid 170 ....G3	Le Loup 61 ....G3	Linwood 409 ....H2	Maple Hill 406 ....F2
Hanover 696 ....F2	Highland 942 ....G2	Idana 96 ....E2	Kingman▲ 3,196 ....D4	Le Roy 568 ....G3	Little River 496 ....E3	Mapleton 96 ....H3
Hanston 326 ....C3	Hill City▲ 1,835 ....C2	Independence▲ 9,942 ....G4	Kingsdown 130 ....C4	Leavenworth▲ 38,495 ....H2	Logan 633 ....C2	Marienthal 100 ....A3
Hardtner 198 ....D4	Hillsboro 2,704 ....E3	Industry 60 ....E2	Kinsley▲ 1,875 ....C4	Leawood 19,693 ....H3	Lone Elm 32 ....G3	Marion▲ 1,906 ....E3
Harlan 62 ....D2	Hillsdale 210 ....H3	Ingalls 301 ....B4	Kiowa 1,160 ....D4	Lebanon 364 ....D2	Long Island 170 ....C2	Marquette 593 ....E3
Harper 1,735 ....D4	Hoisington 3,182 ....D3	Inman 1,035 ....E3	Kipp 77 ....E3	Lebo 835 ....F3	Longford 68 ....E2	Marysville▲ 3,359 ....F2
Harris 39 ....G4	Holcomb 1,400 ....B3	Iola▲ 6,351 ....G4	Kirwin 269 ....C2	Lecompton 619 ....G2	Longton 389 ....F4	Matfield Green 33 ....F3
Hartford 541 ....F3	Hollenberg 28 ....F2	Ionia 90 ....D2	Kismet 421 ....B4	Lehigh 180 ....E3	Lorraine 147 ....D3	Mayetta 267 ....G2
Harveyville 267 ....F3	Holton▲ 3,196 ....G2	Isabel 104 ....D4	La Crosse▲ 1,427 ....C3	Lenexa 34,034 ....H3	Lost Springs 106 ....E3	Mayfield 110 ....E4
Havana 121 ....G4	Holyrood 492 ....D3	Iuka 197 ....D4	La Cygne 1,066 ....H3	Lenora 329 ....C2	Louisburg 1,964 ....H3	McCracken 231 ....C3
Haven 1,198 ....E4	Home 145 ....F2	Jamestown 325 ....E2	La Harpe 650 ....G4	Leon 707 ....F4	Louisville 207 ....F2	McCune 462 ....G4
Havensville 135 ....F2	Homewood 75 ....G3	Jarbalo 73 ....H2	Labette 74 ....G4	Leona 39 ....G2	Lucas 452 ....D2	McDonald 184 ....A2
Haviland 624 ....C4	Hope 404 ....E3	Jennings 188 ....B2	Lafontaine 115 ....G4	Leonardville 374 ....F2	Ludell 90 ....B2	McFarland 224 ....F2
Hays▲ 17,767 ....C3	Horace 168 ....A3	Jetmore▲ 850 ....B3	Lake City 76 ....D4	Leoti▲ 1,738 ....A3	Luray 261 ....D2	McLouth 719 ....G2
Haysville 8,364 ....E4	Horton 1,885 ....G2	Jewell 529 ....D2	Lakin▲ 2,060 ....A4	Leoville 57 ....B2	Lyndon▲ 1,981 ....G3	McPherson▲ 12,422 ....E3
Hazelton 128 ....D4	Howard▲ 815 ....F4	Johnson▲ 1,348 ....A4	Lancaster 299 ....G2	Levant 85 ....A2	Lyons▲ 3,688 ....D3	Meade▲ 1,526 ....B4
Healy 275 ....B3	Hoxie▲ 1,342 ....B2	Junction City▲ 20,604 ....E2	Lane 247 ....G3	Lewis 451 ....C4		Medicine Lodge▲ 2,453 ....D4
Hepler 150 ....H4	Hoy 489 ....G2	Kanopolis 605 ....D3	Langdon 62 ....D4	Liberal▲ 16,573 ....B4	Madison 845 ....F3	Medora 62 ....E3

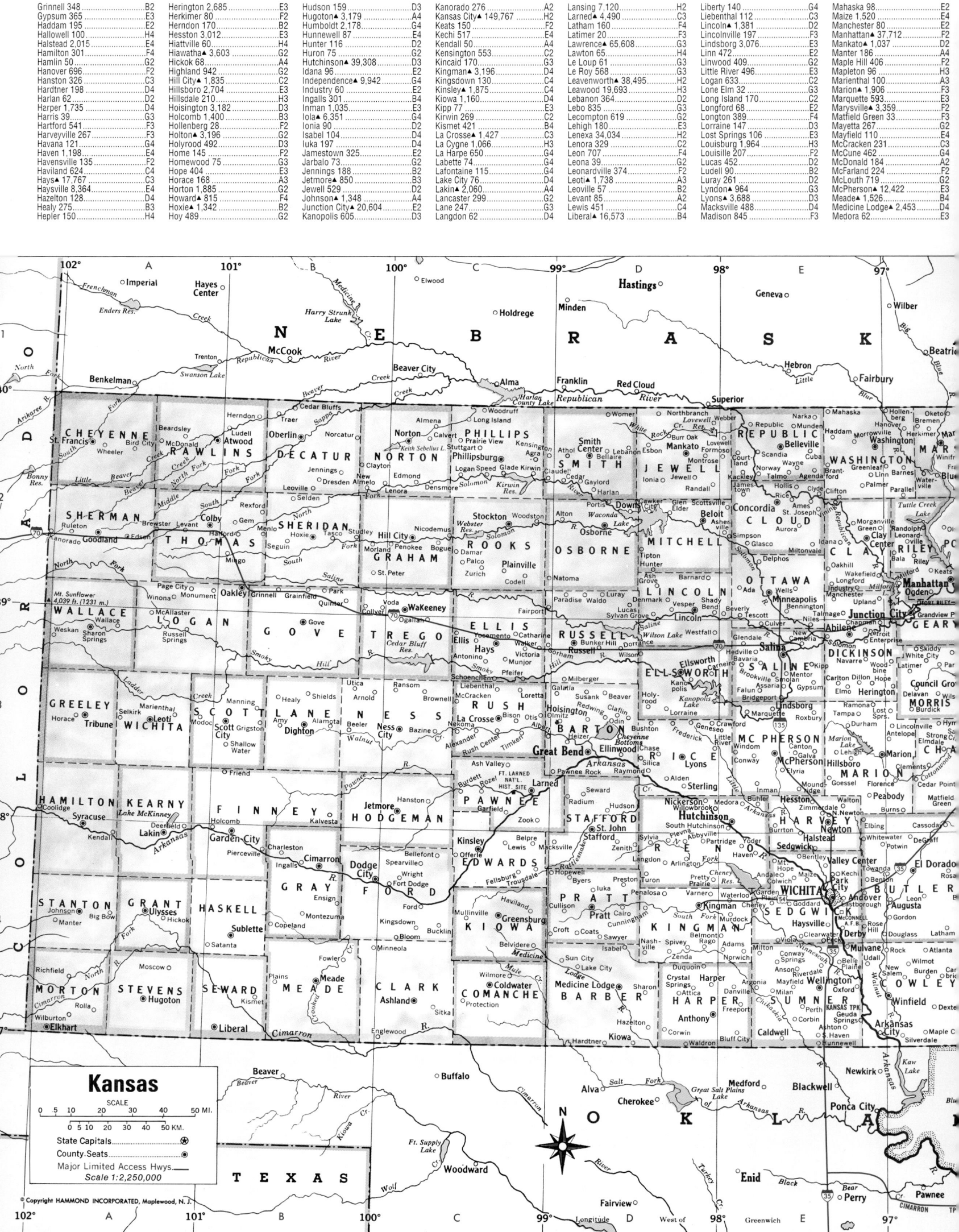

Kansas

SCALE

0 5 10 20 30 40 50 MI.

0 5 10 20 30 40 50 KM.

State Capitals ....⍟

County Seats ....◉

Major Limited Access Hwys.

Scale 1:2,250,000

© Copyright HAMMOND INCORPORATED, Maplewood, N.J.

Melvern 423 ....G3	Moscow 252 ....A4
Menlo 50 ....B2	Mound City▲ 789 ....H3
Mentor 100 ....E3	Mound Valley 405 ......G4
Mercier 85 ....G2	Moundridge 1,531 ......E3
Meriden 622 ....G2	Mount Hope 805 ....E4
Merriam 11,821 ....H3	Mulberry 555 ....H4
Michigan Valley 65 ....G3	Mullinville 289 ....C4
Milan 109 ....E4	Mulvane 4,674 ....E4
Mildred 46 ....G3	Munden 143 ....E2
Milford 384 ....F2	Munjor 200 ....C3
Milton 484 ....E4	Murdock 75 ....D4
Miltonvale 588 ....E2	Muscotah 194 ....G2
Minneapolis▲ 1,983 ...E2	Narka 113 ....E2
Minneola 705 ....C4	Nashville 118 ....D4
Mission 9,504 ....H2	Natoma 392 ....D2
Moline 473 ....F4	Navarre 66 ....E3
Montezuma 838 ....B4	Neal 72 ....G4
Monument 85 ....A2	Neodesha 2,837 ....G4
Moran 551 ....G4	Neosho Falls 157 ......G3
Morehead 65 ....G4	Neosho Rapids 235 ....F3
Morganville 181 ....E2	Ness City▲ 1,724 ....C3
Morland 234 ....B2	Netawaka 167 ....G2
Morrill 299 ....G2	New Albany 60 ....G4
Morrowville 173 ....E2	New Almelo 80 ....B2

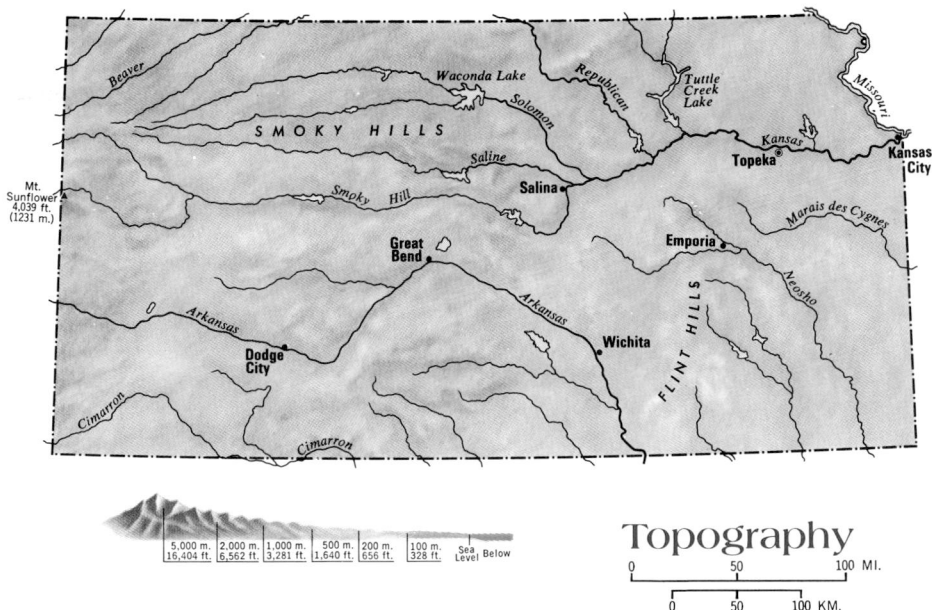

Topography

5,000 m. 2,000 m. 1,000 m. 500 m. 200 m. 100 m. Sea Level Below
16,404 ft. 6,562 ft. 3,281 ft. 1,640 ft. 656 ft. 328 ft.

0   50   100 MI.

0   50   100 KM.

New Cambria 152 ....E3	Preston 177 ....D4	Stafford 1,344 ....D4	Wichita▲ 304,011 ....E4
New Lancaster 52 ....H3	Pretty Prairie 601 ....D4	Stanley 450 ....H3	Willard 110 ....G2
New Salem 100 ....F4	Princeton 275 ....G3	Stark 79 ....G4	Williamsburg 261 ....G3
New Strawn (Strawn) 428 .....G3	Protection 625 ....C4	Sterling 2,115 ....D3	Williamstown 89 ....G2
Newton▲ 16,700 ....E3	Quenemo 369 ....G3	Stilwell 350 ....H3	Willis 86 ....D3
Nickerson 1,137 ....D3	Quinter 945 ....B2	Stockton▲ 1,507 ....C2	Willowbrook 95 ....D3
Niles 75 ....E2	Radium 47 ....D3	Strawn G3	Wilmore 78 ....C4
Niotaze 99 ....F4	Ramona 106 ....E3	Strong City 617 ....F3	Wilsey 149 ....F3
North Newton 1,262 ....E3	Randall 96 ....D2	Studley 60 ....B2	Wilson 834 ....D3
Norcatur 198 ....B2	Randolph 129 ....F2	Stuttgart 70 ....C2	Winchester 613 ....G2
Norton▲ 3,017 ....C2	Ransom 386 ....C3	Sublette▲ 1,378 ....B4	Windom 136 ....E3
Nortonville 643 ....G2	Rantoul 200 ....G3	Summerfield 169 ....F2	Winfield▲ 11,931 ....F4
Norway 60 ....E2	Raymond 125 ....D3	Sun City 88 ....D4	Winifred 80 ....F2
Norwich 455 ....E4	Reading 264 ....F3	Susank 61 ....D3	Winona 194 ....A2
Oakhill 13 ....E2	Redfield 143 ....H4	Sycamore 150 ....G4	Woodbine 186 ....E3
Oakley▲ 2,045 ....B2	Reece 60 ....F4	Sylvan Grove 321 ......D2	Woodston 121 ....C2
Oberlin▲ 2,197 ....B2	Republic 177 ....E2	Sylvia 308 ....D4	Wright 300 ....C4
Odin 105 ....D3	Reserve 108 ....G2	Syracuse▲ 1,606 ....A3	Yates Center▲ 1,815 ...G4
Offerle 228 ....C4	Rexford 161 ....B2	Talmage 130 ....E2	Yoder 160 ....E4
Ogallah 75 ....C3	Richfield 50 ....A4	Tampa 113 ....E3	Zenda 96 ....D4
Ogden 1,494 ....F2	Richland 100 ....G3	Tecumseh 300 ....G2	Zurich 151 ....C2
Oketo 116 ....F2	Richmond 528 ....G3	Tescott 317 ....E2	
Olathe▲ 63,352 ....H3	Riley 804 ....F2	Thayer 435 ....G4	OTHER FEATURES
Olivet 59 ....G3	Riverton 650 ....H4	Timken 87 ....C3	
Olmitz 130 ....D3	Robinson 268 ....G2	Tipton 267 ....D2	Arkansas (riv.) D3
Olpe 431 ....F3	Rock 250 ....F4	Tonganoxie 2,347 .....G2	Beaver (creek) A2
Olsburg 192 ....F2	Rock Creek 93 ....G2	Topeka (cap.)▲ 119,883 ...G2	Big Blue (riv.) F1
Onaga 761 ....F2	Roeland Park 7,706 ....H2	Toronto 317 ....G4	Cedar Bluff (res.) C3
Oneida 79 ....G2	Rolla 387 ....A4	Towanda 1,289 ....E4	Cheney (res.) E4
Opolis 165 ....H4	Rosalia 125 ....F4	Treece 172 ....H4	Cheyenne Bottoms (lake) D3
Osage City 2,689 ......G3	Rose Hill 2,399 ....E4	Tribune▲ 918 ....A3	Chikaskia (riv.) D4
Osawatomie 4,590 .....H3	Roseland 98 ....H4	Trousdale 54 ....C4	Cimarron (riv.) B4
Osborne▲ 1,778 ....D2	Rossville 1,052 ....G2	Troy▲ 1,073 ....G2	Cottonwood (riv.) F3
Oskaloosa▲ 1,074 ......G2	Roxbury 115 ....E3	Turon 393 ....D4	Council Grove (lake) ...F3
Oswego▲ 1,870 ....G4	Rozel 187 ....C3	Tyro 243 ....G4	Crooked (creek) B4
Otis 385 ....C3	Rush Center 177 ....C3	Udall 824 ....E4	Elk (riv.) F4
Ottawa▲ 10,667 ....G3	Russell Springs 29 .....A3	Ulysses▲ 5,474 ....A4	Fall (riv.) G4
Overbrook 920 ....G3	Russell▲ 4,781 ....D3	Uniontown 290 ....G4	Fall River (lake) F4
Overland Park 111,790 ...H3	Sabetha 2,341 ....G2	Utica 208 ....B3	Fort Larned Nat'l Hist. Site C3
Oxford 1,143 ....E4	Saint Benedict 55 ......F2	Valley Center 3,624 ...E4	Fort Riley-Camp Whiteside ...F2
Ozawkie 403 ....G2	Saint Francis▲ 1,495 ...A2	Valley Falls 1,253 ......G2	Fort Scott Nat'l Hist. Site ...H4
Page City 60 ....A2	Saint George 397 ....F2	Vassar 90 ....G3	Hulah (lake) F5
Palco 295 ....C2	Saint John▲ 1,357 ......D3	Vermillion 113 ....F2	John Redmond (res.) ...G3
Palmer 121 ....E2	Saint Marys 1,791 ......G2	Victoria 1,157 ....C3	Kanopolis (lake) D3
Paola▲ 4,698 ....H3	Saint Paul 687 ....G4	Vining 55 ....F2	Kansas (riv.) G2
Paradise 66 ....D2	Salina▲ 42,303 ....E3	Vinland 102 ....G3	Keith Sebelius (lake) ...C2
Park 150 ....C3	Satanta 1,073 ....B4	Viola 185 ....D4	Kickapoo Ind. Res. G2
Park City 5,050 ....E4	Savonburg 93 ....G4	Virgil 91 ....F4	Kirwin (res.) C2
Parker 256 ....H3	Sawyer 183 ....D4	Vliets 56 ....F2	Little Arkansas (riv.) ...E3
Parkerville 28 ....F3	Scammon 466 ....H4	WaKeeney▲ 2,161 .....C2	Little Blue (riv.) E1
Parsons 11,924 ....G4	Scandia 421 ....E2	Wabaunsee 75 ....F2	Lovewell (res.) D2
Partridge 213 ....D4	Schoenchen 128 ....C3	Wakarusa 171 ....G3	Marion (lake) E3
Pauline 250 ....G3	Scott City▲ 3,785 ....B3	Wakefield 900 ....E2	McConnell A.F.B. E4
Pawnee Rock 367 ....D3	Scottsville 26 ....D2	Waldo 57 ....D2	McKinney (lake) A3
Paxico 174 ....F2	Scranton 674 ....G3	Waldron 19 ....D4	Medicine Lodge (riv.) ..D4
Peabody 1,349 ....E3	Sedan▲ 1,306 ....F4	Walker 104 ....C3	Milford (lake) F2
Peck 250 ....E4	Sedgwick 1,438 ....E4	Wallace 75 ....A3	Missouri (riv.) G1
Penalosa 21 ....D4	Selden 248 ....B2	Walnut 214 ....G4	Nemaha (riv.) G1
Penokee 73 ....C2	Seneca▲ 2,027 ....G2	Walton 226 ....E3	Neosho (riv.) G4
Perry 881 ....G2	Severance 98 ....G2	Wamego 3,706 ....F2	Ninnescah (riv.) E4
Peru 206 ....F4	Severy 357 ....F4	Washington▲ 1,304 ....F2	Pawnee (riv.) B3
Petrolia 69 ....G4	Seward 71 ....D3	Waterville 601 ....F2	Perry (lake) G2
Pfeifer 80 ....C3	Shallow Water 100 .....B3	Wathena 1,160 ....G2	Pomona (lake) G3
Phillipsburg▲ 2,828 ....C2	Sharon 256 ....D4	Waverly 618 ....G3	Potawatomi Ind. Res. ..G2
Piedmont 96 ....F4	Sharon Springs▲ 872 ...A3	Wayside 85 ....G4	Rattlesnake (creek) D4
Pierceville 135 ....B4	Shaw 37,993 ....G4	Webber 39 ....E2	Republican (riv.) E2
Piper City H2	Shawnee 29,653 ....H2	Weir 730 ....H4	Sac-Fox-Iowa Ind. Res. G2
Piqua 103 ....F4	Shields 110 ....B3	Welda 150 ....G3	Saline (riv.) C2
Pittsburg 17,775 ....H4	Silver Lake 1,390 ......G2	Wellington▲ 8,411 ......E4	Sappa (creek) B2
Plains 957 ....B4	Simpson 107 ....E2	Wells 1,563 ....G3	Smoky Hill (riv.) C3
Plainville 2,173 ....C2	Skiddy 55 ....F3	Wellsville 1,612 ....G3	Solomon (riv.) D2
Pleasanton 1,231 ......H3	Smith Center▲ 2,016 ...C2	Weskan 200 ....A2	Sunflower (mt.) A2
Plevna 117 ....D4	Smolan 195 ....E3	West Mineral 226 ......H4	Toronto (lake) F4
Pomona 835 ....G3	Soldier 135 ....G2	West Plains (Plains) B4	Tuttle Creek (lake) F2
Portis 129 ....D2	Solomon 939 ....E3	Westmoreland▲ 541 ...F2	Verdigris (riv.) G5
Potter 175 ....G2	South Haven 420 ....E4	Westphalia 152 ....G3	Walnut (riv.) E4
Potwin 448 ....F4	South Hutchinson 2,444 ...D3	Wetmore 284 ....G2	Webster (res.) C2
Powhattan 111 ....G2	Sparks 71 ....G2	Wheaton 106 ....F2	White Rock (creek) D2
Prairie View 111 ....C2	Spearville 716 ....C4	White City 533 ....F3	Wilson (lake) D3
Prairie Village 23,186 ..H3	Speed 64 ....C2	White Cloud 255 ....G2	
Pratt▲ 6,687 ....D4	Spivey 88 ....D4	Whitewater 683 ....E4	▲County seat
Prescott 301 ....H3	Spring Hill 2,191 ....H3	Whiting 213 ....G2	

KENTUCKY

COUNTIES

Adair 15,360 ....L6
Allen 14,628 ....J7
Anderson 14,571 ....M5
Ballard 7,902 ....C6
Barren 34,001 ....K7
Bath 9,692 ....O4
Bell 31,506 ....O7
Boone 57,589 ....M3
Bourbon 19,236 ....N4
Boyd 51,150 ....R4
Boyle 25,641 ....M5
Bracken 7,766 ....N3
Breathitt 15,703 ....P5
Breckinridge 16,312 ....J5
Bullitt 47,567 ....K5
Butler 11,245 ....H6
Caldwell 13,232 ....F6
Calloway 30,735 ....E7
Campbell 83,866 ....N3
Carlisle 5,238 ....C7
Carroll 9,292 ....L3
Carter 24,340 ....P4
Casey 14,211 ....M6
Christian 68,941 ....F7
Clark 29,496 ....N4
Clay 21,746 ....O6
Clinton 9,135 ....L7
Crittenden 9,196 ....E6
Cumberland 6,784 ......L7
Daviess 87,189 ....G5
Edmonson 10,357 ....J6
Elliott 6,455 ....P4
Estill 14,614 ....O5
Fayette 225,366 ....M5
Fleming 12,292 ....O4
Floyd 43,586 ....R5
Franklin 43,781 ....M4
Fulton 8,271 ....C7
Gallatin 5,393 ....M3
Garrard 11,579 ....M5
Grant 15,737 ....M3
Graves 33,550 ....D7
Grayson 21,050 ....J5
Green 10,371 ....K6
Greenup 36,742 ....R3
Hancock 7,864 ....H5
Hardin 89,240 ....K5
Harlan 36,574 ....P7
Harrison 16,248 ....N4
Hart 14,890 ....K6
Henderson 43,044 ......F5
Henry 12,823 ....L4
Hickman 5,566 ....C7
Jackson 11,955 ....N6
Jefferson 664,937 .....K4
Jessamine 30,508 ......M5
Johnson 23,248 ....R5
Kenton 142,031 ....M3
Knott 17,906 ....R6
Knox 29,676 ....O7
Larue 11,679 ....K5
Laurel 43,438 ....N6
Lawrence 13,998 ....R4
Lee 7,422 ....O5
Leslie 13,642 ....P6
Letcher 27,000 ....R6
Lewis 13,029 ....P3
Lincoln 20,045 ....M6
Livingston 9,062 ......E6
Logan 24,416 ....H7
Lyon 6,624 ....E7

Madison 57,508 ....N5
Magoffin 13,077 ....P5
Marion 16,499 ....L5
Marshall 27,205 ....E7
Martin 12,526 ....R5
Mason 16,666 ....O3
McCracken 62,879 ......D6
McCreary 15,603 ....N7
McLean 9,628 ....G5
Meade 24,170 ....J5
Menifee 5,092 ....O5
Mercer 19,148 ....M5
Metcalfe 8,963 ....K7
Monroe 11,401 ....K7
Montgomery 19,561 .....O4
Morgan 11,648 ....P5
Muhlenberg 31,318 .....G6
Nelson 29,710 ....K5
Nicholas 6,725 ....N4
Ohio 21,105 ....H6
Oldham 33,263 ....L4
Owen 9,035 ....M3
Owsley 5,036 ....O6
Pendleton 12,036 ......N3
Perry 30,283 ....P6
Pike 72,583 ....R6
Powell 11,686 ....O5
Pulaski 49,489 ....M6
Robertson 2,124 ....N3
Rockcastle 14,803 .....N6
Rowan 20,353 ....P4
Russell 14,716 ....L6
Scott 23,867 ....M4
Shelby 24,824 ....L4
Simpson 15,145 ....H7
Spencer 6,801 ....L4
Taylor 21,146 ....L6
Todd 10,940 ....G7
Trigg 10,361 ....F7
Trimble 6,090 ....L3
Union 16,557 ....F5
Warren 76,673 ....H6
Washington 10,441 .....L5
Wayne 17,468 ....M7
Webster 13,955 ....F5
Whitley 33,326 ....N7
Wolfe 6,503 ....O5
Woodford 19,955 ....M4

CITIES and TOWNS

Adairville 906 ....H7
Ages 500 ....P7
Albany▲ 2,062 ....L7
Alexandria▲ 5,592 .....N3
Allen 229 ....R5
Allensville 218 ....G7
Amburgey 500 ....R6
Anchorage 2,082 ....L2
Annville 470 ....O6
Arjay 975 ....O7
Arlington 449 ....D7
Ashland 23,622 ....R4
Auburn 1,273 ....H7
Audubon Park 1,520 ....J2
Augusta 1,336 ....N3
Austin 500 ....K7
Auxier 900 ....R5
Bancroft 582 ....K1
Banner 900 ....R5
Barbourmeade 1,402 ....K1
Barbourville▲ 3,658 ...O7
Bardstown▲ 6,801 ......L5
Bardwell▲ 819 ....D7
Barlow 706 ....D6

Baskett 550 ....F5
Beattyville▲ 1,131 ....O5
Beauty 800 ....S5
Beaver Dam 2,904 ......H6
Bedford▲ 761 ....L3
Bee Spring 500 ....J6
Beechwood Village 1,263..K2
Belcher 500 ....S5
Belfry 800 ....S5
Bellemeade 927 ....K1
Bellevue 6,997 ....S1
Benham 717 ....R7
Benton▲ 3,899 ....E7
Berea 9,126 ....N5
Berry 240 ....N3
Betsy Layne 975 ....R5
Big Creek 700 ....O6
Blaine 271 ....R4
Blandville 95 ....D7
Bloomfield 845 ....L5
Blue Ridge Manor 565 ..L2
Boldman 510 ....R5
Bonnieville 300 ....K6
Bonnyman 800 ....P6
Boone 232 ....N5
Booneville▲ 191 ....O6
Bowling Green▲ 40,641..H6
Bradford 199 ....N3
Bradfordsville 331 ....L6
Brandenburg▲ 1,857 ....J4
Bremen 267 ....G6
Briensburg E7
Broadfields 273 ....K2
Brodhead 1,140 ....N6
Bromley 1,137 ....S2
Brooks 2,464 ....K4
Brooksville▲ 670 ......N3
Brownsboro Farm 670 ...L1
Brownsville 897 ....J6
Buechel 7,081 ....K2
Buffalo K6
Bulan 800 ....P6
Burgin 1,009 ....M5
Burkesville▲ 1,815 ....L7
Burlington▲ 6,070 .....R2
Burnside 695 ....M6
Butler 625 ....N3
Cadiz▲ 2,148 ....F7
Calhoun▲ 854 ....G5
California 130 ....N3
Calvert City 2,531 ....E6
Camargo 1,022 ....O4
Campbellsburg 604 .....L3
Campbellsville▲ 9,577..L6
Campton▲ 484 ....O5
Caney 549 ....P5
Caneyville 642 ....J6
Cannel City 600 ....P5
Carlisle▲ 1,639 ....N4
Carrollton▲ 3,715 .....L3
Carter P4
Catlettsburg▲ 2,231 ...R4
Cave City 1,953 ....K6
Cawood 800 ....P7
Center 383 ....K6
Centertown 462 ....G6
Centerville S6
Central City 4,979 ....G6
Cerulean F7
Clarkson 611 ....J6
Clay 1,173 ....F6
Clay City 1,258 ....O5
Clearfield 1,250 ......P4
Clinton▲ 1,547 ....D7
Clover Bottom 600 .....N5

Cloverport 1,207 ......H5
Coal Run 262 ....R5
Cold Spring 2,880 .....T2
Columbia▲ 3,845 ....L6
Columbus 252 ....C7
Combs 900 ....P6
Corbin 7,419 ....N7
Corinth 137 ....M3
Corydon 790 ....F5
Covington 43,264 ......S2
Crab Orchard 825 ......M6
Crescent Springs 2,179.R2
Crestview 356 ....S2
Crestview Hills 2,546..R2
Crittenden 731 ....M3
Crofton 699 ....F6
Crestwood 1,435 ....L4
Cumberland 3,112 ......R6
Cynthiana▲ 6,497 ......N4
Danville▲ 12,420 ......M5
Dawson Springs 3,129..F6
Dayton 6,576 ....T1
Devondale 1,164 ....K2
Dexter F5
Dixon▲ 552 ....F5
Dorton 750 ....R6
Douglass Hills 5,549..L2
Dover 297 ....O3
Drakesboro 565 ....G6
Dry Ridge 1,601 ....M3
Earlington 1,833 ......F6
East Bernstadt 550 ....N6
Echols 576 ....H6
Eddyville▲ 1,889 ......E6
Edgewood 8,143 ....S2
Edmonton▲ 1,477 ....K7
Elizabethtown▲ 18,167.K5
Elkhorn City 813 ......S5
Elkton▲ 1,789 ....G7
Elsmere 6,847 ....R2
Eminence 2,055 ....L4
Eolia 875 ....R6
Erlanger 15,979 ....R2
Essie 650 ....P6
Eubank 354 ....M6
Evarts 1,063 ....P7
Ewing 268 ....O4
Fairdale 6,563 ....K4
Fairfield 142 ....L5
Fairview 119 ....G7
Fairview 198 ....S2
Fallsburg R4
Falmouth▲ 2,378 ....N3
Fancy Farm 800 ....D7
Farmington 600 ....D7
Fedscreek 950 ....S6
Ferguson 934 ....M6
Fincastle 838 ....L1
Flat 7,799 ....O5
Flat Lick 600 ....O7
Flatwoods 8,354 ....R4
Fleming (Fleming-Neon) 759..R6
Flemingsburg▲ 3,071 ...O4
Florence 18,624 ....R2
Ford 522 ....N5
Fordsville 561 ....H5
Forest Hills 454 ......L2
Fort Knox 21,495 ......K5
Fort Mitchell 7,438 ...S2
Fort Thomas 16,032 ....S2
Fort Wright 6,570 .....S2
Fountain Run 729 ......K7
Frankfort (cap.)▲ 25,968..M4
Franklin▲ 7,607 ....J7
Fredonia 490 ....E6

Frenchburg▲ 625 ....O5
Fullerton 950 ....P3
Fulton 3,078 ....D7
Gamaliel 462 ....K7
Garrison 700 ....P3
Georgetown▲ 11,414 ....M4
Germantown 213 ....O3
Ghent 365 ....L3
Gilbertsville E7
Glasgow▲ 12,351 ....J7
Glencoe 257 ....M3
Glenview 653 ....K1
Goose Creek 321 ....L1
Goshen 2,447 ....K4
Gramoor 1,167 ....K1
Grand Rivers 351 ......E7
Gray 2,911 ....O7
Grayson▲ 3,510 ....R4
Greensburg▲ 1,990 .....K6
Greenup▲ 1,158 ....R3
Greenville▲ 4,689 .....G6
Guthrie 1,504 ....G7
Hammond 510 ....O7
Hanson 450 ....F6
Hardin 595 ....E7
Hardinsburg▲ 1,906 ....H5
Hardy 900 ....S5
Harlan▲ 2,686 ....P7
Harold 520 ....R5
Harrodsburg▲ 7,335 ....M5
Hartford▲ 2,532 ....H6
Hatfield 700 ....S5
Hawesville▲ 998 ....H5
Hazard▲ 5,416 ....P6
Hazel 460 ....E7
Hebron 930 ....R2
Helton 600 ....P7
Henderson▲ 25,945 .....F5
Hickman▲ 2,689 ....C7
Hickory 152 ....D7
Highland Heights 4,223.T2
Hima 600 ....O6
Himyar 545 ....O7
Hindman▲ 798 ....R6
Hiseville 220 ....K6
Hitchins 750 ....R4
Hodgenville▲ 2,721 ....K5
Hollow Creek 991 ......L2
Hopkinsville▲ 29,809 ..F7
Horse Cave 2,284 ......K6
Houston Acres 496 .....K2
Hustonville 313 ....M6
Hyden▲ 375 ....P6
Independence▲ 10,444 ..M3
Indian Hills 1,074 ....K1
Inez▲ 511 ....S5
Irvine▲ 2,836 ....O5
Irvington 1,180 ....J5
Island 446 ....G6
Ivel 850 ....R5
Jackson▲ 2,466 ....P5
Jamestown▲ 1,641 ......L7
Jeff 23,221 ....P6
Jeffersontown 15,795 ..L2
Jeffersonville 1,854 ..O5
Jenkins 2,751 ....R6
Junction City 1,983 ...M5
Keavy 900 ....N6
Keene 393 ....M5
Kenton 358 ....N3
Kenton Vale 145 ....S2
Kenvir 800 ....P7
Kevil 337 ....D6
King 399 ....O7
Kingsley 464 ....K2

Kitts 800 ....P7
Kuttawa 535 ....E6
La Center 1,040 ....C6
La Fayette 106 ....F7
La Grange▲ 3,853 ......L4
Lackey R6
Lake 3,131 ....O6
Lakeside Park 3,062 ...R2
Lancaster▲ 3,421 ......M5
Lawrenceburg▲ 5,911 ...M4
Leatherwood 800 ....P6
Lebanon▲ 5,695 ....L5
Lebanon Junction 1,741.K5
Leitchfield▲ 4,965 ....J6
Lejunior 597 ....P7
Lewisburg 772 ....G6
Lewisport 1,778 ....H5
Lexington▲ 204,165 ....M5
Liberty▲ 1,937 ....M6
Littcarr 645 ....R6
Livermore 1,534 ....G5
Livingston 241 ....N6
Lockport 84 ....M4
London▲ 5,757 ....N6
Lone Oak 465 ....D6
Lookout 600 ....S6
Lookout Heights S2
Loretto 820 ....L5
Lothair 600 ....P6
Louisa▲ 1,990 ....R4
Louisville▲ 269,063 ...J2
Loyall 1,100 ....P7
Ludlow 4,736 ....S2
Lynch 1,166 ....R7
Mackville 200 ....L5
Madisonville▲ 16,200 ..F6
Majestic 600 ....S5
Manchester▲ 1,634 .....O6
Marion▲ 3,320 ....E6
Marshes Siding 800 ....M7
Martha 650 ....R4
Martin 694 ....R5
Mary 177 ....O5
Mason 1,119 ....M3
Mayfield▲ 9,935 ....D7
Maysville▲ 7,169 ......O3
McAndrews 975 ....S5
McCarr 592 ....S5
McHenry 414 ....H6
McKee▲ 870 ....O6
McRoberts 1,101 ....R6
McVeigh 650 ....S5
Meadow Vale 798 ....L1
Meally 550 ....R5
Melbourne 660 ....T2
Mentor 169 ....N3
Meta 600 ....R5
Middlesboro 11,328 ....O7
Middletown 5,016 ......L2
Midway 1,290 ....M4
Millersburg 937 ....N4
Millstone 550 ....R6
Milton 563 ....L3
Minor Lane Heights 1,675.K4
Monterey 164 ....M4
Monticello▲ 5,357 .....M7
Moorland 467 ....L2
Morehead▲ 8,357 ....P4
Morgan 3,776 ....N3
Morganfield▲ 3,781 ....E5
Morgantown▲ 2,284 .....H6
Mortons Gap 987 ....F6
Mount Olivet▲ 384 .....N3
Mount Sterling▲ 5,362..N4
Mount Vernon▲ 2,654 ...N6

Mount Washington 5,226..K4
Mouthcard 900 ....S6
Muldraugh 1,376 ....K4
Munfordville▲ 1,556 ...K6
Murray▲ 14,439 ....E7
Nebo 227 ....F6
Neon (Neon-Fleming) ...R6
New Castle▲ 893 ....L4
New Concord 800 ....E7
New Haven 796 ....L5
New Hope L5
Newport 18,871 ....S1
Nicholasville▲ 13,603..M5
North Middletown 602 ..N4
Northfield 898 ....L1
Nortonville 1,209 .....G6
Oak Grove 2,863 ....F7
Oakland 202 ....H6
Oil Springs 900 ....R4
Okolona 18,902 ....K4
Oldtown 500 ....R4
Olive Hill 1,809 ......P4
Owensboro▲ 53,549 .....G5
Owenton▲ 1,306 ....M3
Owingsville▲ 1,491 ....O4
Paducah▲ 27,256 ....D6
Paintsville▲ 4,354 ....R5
Paris▲ 8,730 ....N4
Park City 549 ....K6
Park Hills 3,321 ......S2
Parksville 560 ....M5
Parkway Village 707 ...K2
Pembroke 640 ....G7
Perryville 815 ....M5
Petersburg R2
Pewee Valley 1,283 ....L2
Phelps 1,298 ....S6
Philpot 700 ....G5
Pikeville▲ 6,324 ......S6
Pine Knot 1,549 ....N7
Pineville▲ 2,198 ......O7
Pittsburg N6
Plantation 830 ....K1
Pleasure Ridge Park 25,131.J4
Pleasureville 761 .....L4
Plum Springs 361 ......H6
Powderly 748 ....G6
Premium 729 ....R6
Preston 3,558 ....O4
Prestonsburg▲ 4,011 ...R5
Prestonville 205 ......L3
Princeton▲ 6,940 ......F6
Prospect 2,788 ....K4
Providence 4,123 ......F6
Raceland 2,256 ....R4
Radcliff 19,772 ....K5
Ravenna 804 ....O5
Raywick 157 ....L5
Richmond▲ 21,155 ......N5
Riverwood 506 ....K2
Robards 701 ....F5
Rochester 191 ....H6
Rockford 385 ....H6
Rockholds 775 ....N7
Rolling Fields 593 ....K2
Rolling Hills 1,135 ...L1
Russell 4,014 ....R3
Russell Springs 2,363.L6
Russellville▲ 7,454 ...H7
Ryland Heights 279 ....M3
Sacramento 563 ....G6
Sadieville 255 ....M4
Saint Charles 316 .....F6
Saint Matthews 15,800..K2

Agriculture, Industry and Resources

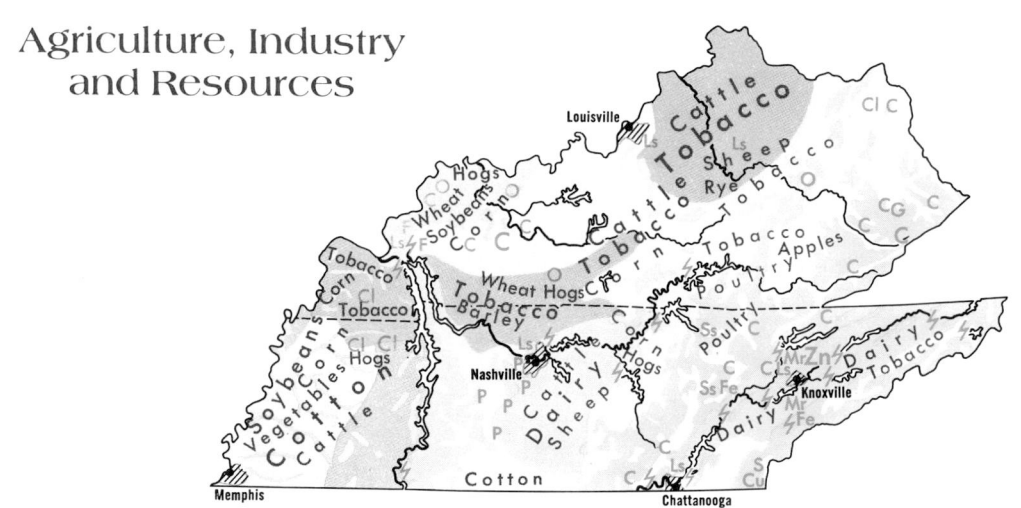

DOMINANT LAND USE

- ☐ Hogs, Soft Winter Wheat
- ▨ Tobacco, General Farming
- ☐ General Farming, Livestock, Tobacco
- ☐ General Farming, Livestock, Dairy
- ☐ General Farming, Livestock, Fruit, Tobacco
- ▨ Specialized Cotton
- ☐ Cotton, General Farming
- ☐ Cotton, Livestock
- ▨ Forests
- ▨ Swampland, Limited Agriculture

MAJOR MINERAL OCCURRENCES

C	Coal	G	Natural Gas	P	Phosphates
Cl	Clay	Ls	Limestone	S	Pyrites
Cu	Copper	Mr	Marble	Ss	Sandstone
F	Fluorspar	O	Petroleum	Zn	Zinc
Fe	Iron Ore				

⚡ Water Power   ▨ Major Industrial Areas

KENTUCKY

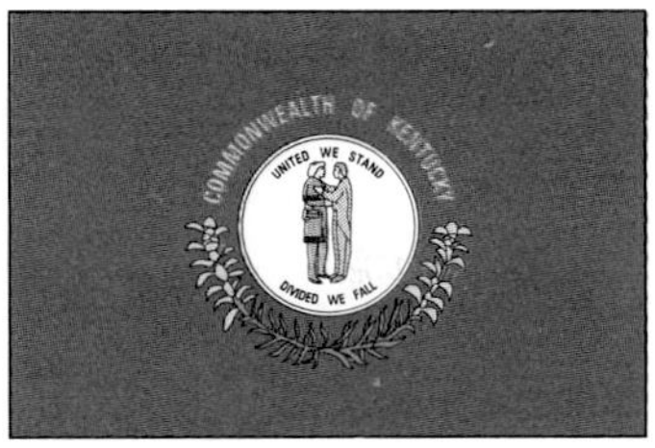

AREA 40,409 sq. mi. (104,659 sq. km.)
POPULATION 3,698,969
CAPITAL Frankfort
LARGEST CITY Louisville
HIGHEST POINT Black Mtn. 4,145 ft. (1263 m.)
SETTLED IN 1774
ADMITTED TO UNION June 1, 1792
POPULAR NAME Bluegrass State
STATE FLOWER Goldenrod
STATE BIRD Cardinal

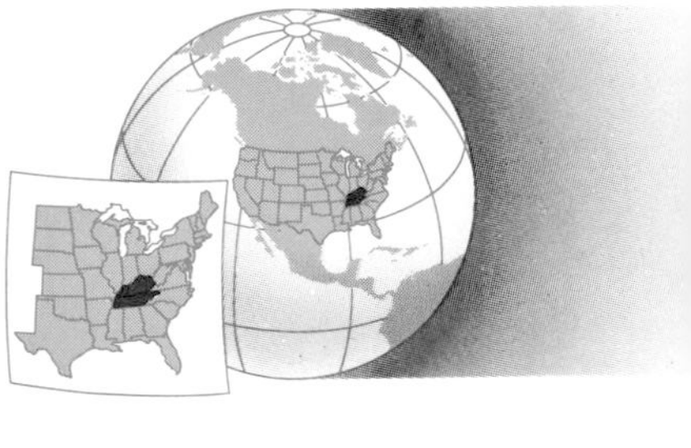

TENNESSEE

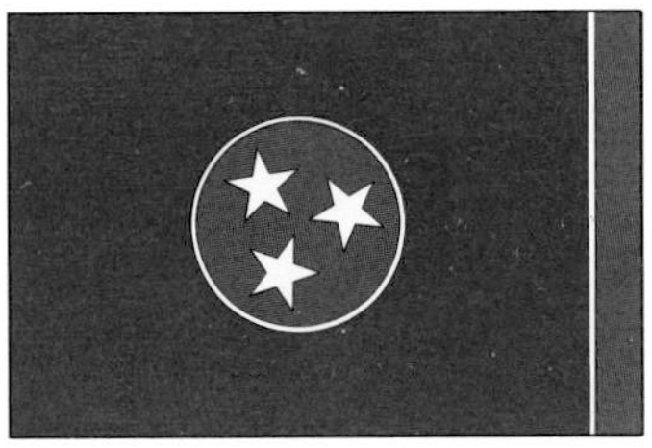

AREA 42,144 sq. mi. (109,153 sq. km.)
POPULATION 4,896,641
CAPITAL Nashville
LARGEST CITY Memphis
HIGHEST POINT Clingmans Dome 6,643 ft. (2025 m.)
SETTLED IN 1757
ADMITTED TO UNION June 1, 1796
POPULAR NAME Volunteer State
STATE FLOWER Iris
STATE BIRD Mockingbird

aint Regis Park 1,756 ... K2
alem 770 ... E6
alt Lick 342 ... O4
alyersville▲ 1,917 ... P5
anders 231 ... M3
andy Hook▲ 548 ... P4
ardis 171 ... O3
cience Hill 628 ... M6
cottsville▲ 4,278 ... J7
ebree 1,510 ... F5
eco ... R6
edalia ... D7
eneca Gardens 684 ... K2
extons Creek 975 ... O6
harpsburg 315 ... O4
helbyville▲ 6,238 ... L4
hepherdsville▲ 4,805 ... K4
hively 15,535 ... K4
ilver Grove 1,102 ... T2
impson 907 ... P5
impsonville 642 ... L4
laughters 235 ... F6
milax 987 ... P6
mithfield 115 ... L4
mithland▲ 384 ... E6
miths Grove 703 ... J6
omerset▲ 10,733 ... M6
onora 295 ... K5
outh 202 ... J6
outh Carrollton 262 ... G6
outh Portsmouth 900 ... P3
outh Shore 1,318 ... R3
outh Williamson 1,016 ... S5
outhgate 3,266 ... T2
parta 133 ... M3
pottsville 914 ... G5
pringfield▲ 2,875 ... L5
pringlee 451 ... K2
taffordsville 700 ... R5
tamping Ground 698 ... M4
tanford▲ 2,636 ... M5
tanton▲ 2,795 ... O5
tearns 1,550 ... N7
tone 900 ... S5
trathmoor Village 361 ... K2
turgis 2,184 ... F5
ateville 680 ... M7
aylor Mill 5,530 ... S2
aylorsville▲ 774 ... L4
healka 600 ... R5
hornhill 146 ... K1
ollesboro 808 ... O3
ompkinsville▲ 2,861 ... K7
renton 378 ... G7
yner 590 ... O6
nion 1,001 ... M3
niontown 1,008 ... F5
pton 719 ... K6
alley Station 22,840 ... K4
an 1,050 ... R6
an Lear 2,035 ... R5
anceburg▲ 1,713 ... P3
erda 1,133 ... P7
ersailles▲ 7,269 ... M4
icco 244 ... P6
illa Hills 7,739 ... R2
ine Grove 3,586 ... K5
irgie 600 ... R6
isalia 190 ... N3
Vallins Creek 261 ... O7
Valton 2,034 ... M3
Varfield 364 ... S5
Varsaw▲ 1,202 ... M3
Vashington 795 ... O3
Vater Valley 321 ... D7
Vaverly 345 ... F5
Vayland 359 ... R6
Veeksbury 850 ... R6
Vellington 593 ... O5
Vellington 653 ... K2
Vest Buechel 1,587 ... K2
Vest Liberty▲ 1,887 ... P5
Vest Point 1,216 ... K4
Vest Somerset 850 ... M6
Vestwood 734 ... R4
Vestwood 826 ... L1
Vheatcroft 206 ... F5
Vheelwright 721 ... R6
Vhite Plains 598 ... G6
Vhitesburg▲ 1,636 ... R6
Vhitesville 682 ... H5
Vhitley City▲ 1,133 ... N7
Vickliffe▲ 851 ... C7
Vilders 633 ... S2
Villard ... R4
Villiamsburg▲ 5,493 ... N7
Villiamstown▲ 3,023 ... M3
Villisburg 223 ... L5
Vilmore 4,215 ... M5
Vinchester▲ 15,799 ... N5
Vindy Hills 2,452 ... K1
Vingo 568 ... D7
Vinston Park ... S2
Volf Creek 600 ... J4
Voodbine 900 ... N7
Voodburn 343 ... J7
Voodbury 117 ... H6
Voodland Hills 714 ... L2
Voodlawn (Oakdale) 308 ... D6
Voodlawn 331 ... T2
Voodlawn Park 1,099 ... K2
Vooton 750 ... P6
Vorthington 1,751 ... R3
Vorthville 191 ... L3
Vurtland 1,221 ... R3
ebulon 750 ... S5

OTHER FEATURES

Abraham Lincoln Birthplace Nat'l Hist. Site ... K5
Barkley (dam) ... E6
Barkley (lake) ... F7
Barren (riv.) ... H6
Barren River (lake) ... J7
Beech Fork (riv.) ... L5
Big Sandy (riv.) ... R4
Black (mt.) ... R7
Buckhorn (lake) ... O6
Chaplin (riv.) ... L5
Clarks, East Fork (riv.) ... E7
Cove Run (lake) ... P4
Cumberland (lake) ... M7
Cumberland (mt.) ... P7
Cumberland (riv.) ... K8
Cumberland Gap Nat'l Hist. ... P7
Dale Hollow (lake) ... L7
Dewey (lake) ... R5
Dix (riv.) ... M5
Drakes (creek) ... J7
Dry (creek) ... R2
Eagle (creek) ... M3
Fishtrap (lake) ... S6
Fort Campbell ... G7
Grayson (lake) ... P4
Green (riv.) ... G6
Green River (lake) ... L6
Herrington (lake) ... M5
Hinkston (creek) ... N4
Kentucky (dam) ... E7
Kentucky (lake) ... E8
Kentucky (riv.) ... M3
Land Between The Lakes Rec. Area ... E7
Laurel River (lake) ... N6
Lexington Blue Grass Army Depot ... N4
Licking (riv.) ... N3
Mammoth Cave Nat'l Park ... J6
Mayfield (creek) ... C7
Mississippi (riv.) ... 10
Mud (riv.) ... H7
Nolin (lake) ... K6
Nolin (riv.) ... J6
Obion (creek) ... C7
Ohio (riv.) ... F5
Paint Lick (riv.) ... M5
Panther (creek) ... G5
Pine (mt.) ... O7
Pond (riv.) ... G6
Red (riv.) ... G7
Red (riv.) ... O5
Rockcastle (riv.) ... N6
Rolling Fork (riv.) ... K5
Rough (riv.) ... H5
Rough River (lake) ... J5
Salt (riv.) ... K5
Tennessee (riv.) ... D6
Tradewater (riv.) ... F6
Tug Fork (riv.) ... S5

TENNESSEE

COUNTIES

Anderson 68,250 ... N8
Bedford 30,411 ... J9
Benton 14,524 ... E8
Bledsoe 9,669 ... L9
Blount 85,969 ... O9
Bradley 73,712 ... M1
Campbell 35,079 ... N8
Cannon 10,467 ... J9
Carroll 27,514 ... E9
Carter 51,505 ... S8
Cheatham 27,140 ... G8
Chester 12,819 ... D1
Claiborne 26,137 ... O8
Clay 7,238 ... K7
Cocke 29,141 ... P9
Coffee 40,339 ... J9
Crockett 13,378 ... C9
Cumberland 34,736 ... L9
Davidson 510,784 ... H8
De Kalb 13,589 ... K9
Decatur 10,472 ... E9
Dickson 35,061 ... G8
Dyer 34,854 ... C8
Fayette 25,559 ... C1
Fentress 14,669 ... M8
Franklin 34,725 ... J1
Gibson 46,315 ... D9
Giles 25,741 ... G1
Grainger 17,095 ... O8
Greene 55,853 ... R8
Grundy 13,362 ... K1
Hamblen 50,480 ... P8
Hamilton 285,536 ... L1
Hancock 6,739 ... P7
Hardeman 23,377 ... C1
Hardin 22,633 ... E1
Hawkins 44,565 ... P8
Haywood 19,437 ... C9
Henderson 21,844 ... E9
Henry 27,888 ... E8
Hickman 16,754 ... G9
Houston 7,018 ... F8
Humphreys 15,795 ... F8
Jackson 9,297 ... K8
Jefferson 33,016 ... P8
Johnson 13,766 ... T7
Knox 335,749 ... O9
Lake 7,129 ... B8
Lauderdale 23,491 ... B9
Lawrence 35,303 ... G1
Lewis 9,247 ... F9
Lincoln 28,157 ... H1
Loudon 31,255 ... N9
Macon 15,906 ... J7
Madison 77,982 ... D9
Marion 24,860 ... K1
Marshall 21,539 ... H1
Maury 54,812 ... G9
McMinn 42,383 ... M1
McNairy 22,422 ... D1
Meigs 8,033 ... M9
Monroe 30,541 ... N1
Montgomery 100,498 ... G8
Moore 4,721 ... J1
Morgan 17,300 ... M8
Obion 31,717 ... C8
Overton 17,636 ... L8
Perry 6,612 ... F9
Pickett 4,548 ... M7
Polk 13,643 ... N1
Putnam 51,373 ... K8
Rhea 24,344 ... M9
Roane 47,227 ... M9
Robertson 41,494 ... H7
Rutherford 118,570 ... J9
Scott 18,358 ... M8
Sequatchie 8,863 ... L1
Sevier 51,043 ... O9
Shelby 826,330 ... B1
Smith 14,143 ... J8
Stewart 9,479 ... F7
Sullivan 143,596 ... S7
Sumner 103,281 ... J8
Tipton 37,568 ... B9
Trousdale 5,920 ... J8
Unicoi 16,549 ... S8
Union 13,694 ... O8
Van Buren 4,846 ... L9
Warren 32,992 ... K9
Washington 92,315 ... R8
Wayne 13,935 ... F1
Weakley 31,972 ... D8
White 20,090 ... L9
Williamson 81,021 ... H9
Wilson 67,675 ... J8

CITIES and TOWNS

Adams 587 ... G7
Adamsville 1,745 ... E10
Afton 800 ... R8
Alamo▲ 2,426 ... C9
Alcoa 6,400 ... N9
Alexandria 730 ... J8
Algood 2,399 ... K8
Allardt 609 ... M8
Allons 600 ... L8
Altamont▲ 679 ... K10
Apison 750 ... L10
Ardmore 866 ... H10
Arlington 1,541 ... B10
Armathwaite 700 ... M8
Arthur 500 ... O7
Ashland City▲ 2,552 ... G8
Athens▲ 12,054 ... M10
Atoka 659 ... B10
Atwood 1,066 ... D9
Auburntown 240 ... J9
Baileyton 309 ... R8
Banner Hill 1,717 ... R8
Bartlett 26,989 ... B10
Bath Springs 800 ... E10
Baxter 1,289 ... K8
Bean Station 500 ... P8
Beechgrove 550 ... J9
Beersheba Springs 596 ... K10
Bell Buckle 326 ... J9
Belle Meade 2,839 ... H8
Bells 1,643 ... C9
Benton▲ 992 ... M10
Berry Hill 802 ... H8
Berry's Chapel 2,703 ... H9
Bethel Springs 755 ... D10
Big Sandy 505 ... E8
Birchwood 550 ... M10
Blaine 1,326 ... O8
Bloomingdale 10,953 ... R7
Bloomington Springs 800 ... K8
Blountville▲ 2,605 ... S7
Bluff City 1,390 ... S8
Bolivar▲ 5,969 ... C10
Braden 354 ... B10
Bradford 1,154 ... D8
Braemar ... S8
Brentwood 16,392 ... H8
Briceville 850 ... N8
Brighton 717 ... B10
Bristol 23,421 ... S7
Brownsville▲ 10,019 ... C9
Bruceton 1,586 ... E8
Buena Vista 500 ... E9
Bulls Gap 659 ... P8
Burlison 394 ... B9
Burns 1,127 ... G8
Butler 500 ... T8
Byrdstown▲ 998 ... L7
Calhoun 552 ... M10
Camden▲ 3,643 ... E8
Carthage▲ 2,386 ... K8
Caryville 1,751 ... N8
Castalian Springs 650 ... J8
Cedar Hill 347 ... H7
Celina▲ 1,493 ... K7
Centertown 332 ... K9
Centerville▲ 3,616 ... G9
Chapel Hill 833 ... H9
Charleston 653 ... M10
Charlotte▲ 854 ... G8
Chattanooga▲ 152,466 ... K10
Chuckey 500 ... R8
Church Hill 4,834 ... R7
Clairfield 650 ... O7
Clarksburg 321 ... E9
Clarksville▲ 75,494 ... G7
Cleveland▲ 30,354 ... M10
Clifton 620 ... F10
Clinton▲ 8,972 ... N8
Coalfield 712 ... N8
Coalmont 813 ... K10
Cokercreek 500 ... N10
College Grove 580 ... H9
Collegedale 5,048 ... M10
Collierville 14,427 ... B10
Collinwood 1,014 ... F10
Colonial Heights 6,716 ... R8
Columbia▲ 28,583 ... G9
Concord 8,569 ... N9
Cookeville▲ 21,744 ... L8
Copperhill 362 ... N10
Cordova 600 ... B10
Cornersville 683 ... H10
Corryton 500 ... O8
Counce 975 ... E10
Covington▲ 7,487 ... B9
Cowan 1,738 ... K10
Crab Orchard 876 ... M9
Crockett Mills 500 ... C9
Cross Plains 1,025 ... H7
Crossville▲ 6,930 ... L9
Crump 2,028 ... E10
Cumberland City 319 ... F8
Cumberland Gap 210 ... O8
Cypress Inn 500 ... F10
Dandridge▲ 1,540 ... O8
Dayton▲ 5,671 ... L9
Decatur▲ 1,361 ... M9
Decaturville▲ 879 ... E9
Decherd 2,196 ... J10
Dickson 8,791 ... G8
Dover▲ 1,341 ... F8
Dowelltown 308 ... K8
Doyle 345 ... K9
Dresden▲ 2,488 ... D8
Drummonds 800 ... A10
Duck River 750 ... G9
Ducktown 421 ... N10
Dunlap▲ 3,731 ... L10
Dyer 2,204 ... D8
Dyersburg▲ 16,317 ... C8
Eads 550 ... B10
Eagleton Village 5,169 ... O9
Eagleville 462 ... H9
East Ridge 21,101 ... L11
Eastview 563 ... D10
Elgin 700 ... M8
Elizabethton▲ 11,931 ... S8
Elk Valley 750 ... N7
Elkton 448 ... H10
Ellendale 850 ... B10
Embreeville Junction ... R8
Emory Gap 500 ... M9
Englewood 1,611 ... M10
Enville 211 ... E10
Erin▲ 1,586 ... F8
Erwin▲ 5,015 ... S8
Estill Springs 1,408 ... J10
Ethridge 565 ... G10
Etowah 3,815 ... M10
Eva 500 ... E8
Fairfield 2,209 ... J9
Fairview 4,210 ... G9
Fall Branch 1,203 ... R8
Farner 750 ... N10
Fayetteville▲ 6,921 ... H10
Finger 279 ... D10
Finley 1,014 ... B8
Flintville 500 ... H10
Forest Hills 4,231 ... H8
Fort Pillow 700 ... B9
Fowlkes 700 ... C9
Franklin▲ 20,098 ... H9
Friendship 467 ... C9
Friendsville 792 ... N9
Gadsden 561 ... D9
Gainesboro▲ 1,002 ... K8
Gallatin▲ 18,794 ... H8
Gallaway 762 ... B10
Garland 194 ... B9
Gates 608 ... C9
Gatlinburg 3,417 ... O9
Germantown 32,893 ... B10
Gibson 281 ... D9
Gilt Edge 447 ... B9
Gleason 1,402 ... D8
Goodlettsville 8,177 ... H8
Gordonsville 891 ... K8
Grand Junction 365 ... C10
Grandview ... M9
Graysville 1,301 ... L10
Greenback 611 ... N9
Greenbrier 2,873 ... H8
Greeneville▲ 13,532 ... R8
Greenfield 2,105 ... D8
Grimsley 650 ... L8
Gruetli 1,810 ... K10
Guys 497 ... D10
Habersham 750 ... N8
Halls 2,431 ... C9
Halls Crossroads ... O8
Hampshire 788 ... G9
Hampton 2,236 ... S8
Harriman 7,119 ... M9
Harris 7,191 ... C8
Harrison 6,206 ... L10
Harrogate (Shawanee) 2,657 ... O8
Hartsville▲ 2,188 ... J8
Helenwood 675 ... M8
Henderson▲ 4,760 ... D10
Hendersonville 32,188 ... H8
Henning 802 ... B9
Henry 317 ... E8
Hickory Valley 159 ... C10
Hixson ... L10
Hohenwald▲ 3,760 ... F9
Hollow Rock 902 ... E8
Hornbeak 445 ... C8
Hornsby 313 ... D10
Humboldt 9,651 ... D9
Huntingdon▲ 4,180 ... E8
Huntland 885 ... J10
Huntsville▲ 660 ... N8
Hurricane Mills 850 ... F9
Iron City 402 ... F10
Jacksboro▲ 1,568 ... N8
Jackson▲ 48,949 ... D9
Jamestown▲ 1,862 ... M8
Jasper▲ 2,780 ... K10
Jefferson City 5,494 ... P8
Jellico 2,447 ... N7
Johnson City 49,381 ... S8
Jones 3,091 ... C9
Jonesborough▲ 2,829 ... R8
Karns 1,458 ... N9
Kenton 1,366 ... C8
Kimball 1,243 ... K10
Kimberlin Heights 500 ... O9
Kingsport 36,365 ... R7
Kingston Springs 1,529 ... G8
Kingston▲ 4,552 ... N9
Knoxville▲ 165,121 ... O9
Kodak 700 ... O9
La Follette 7,192 ... N8
La Grange 167 ... C10
La Vergne 7,499 ... H9
Laager 675 ... K10
Lafayette▲ 3,641 ... J7
Lake City 2,166 ... N8
Lakeland 1,204 ... B10
Lakesite 732 ... L10
Lakewood 2,009 ... H8
Lawrenceburg▲ 10,412 ... G10
Lebanon▲ 15,208 ... J8
Lenoir City 6,147 ... N9
Leoma 600 ... G10
Lewisburg▲ 9,879 ... H10
Lexington▲ 5,810 ... E9
Liberty 391 ... K8
Linden▲ 1,099 ... F9
Livingston▲ 3,809 ... L8
Lobelville 830 ... F9
Long Island ... S7
Lookout Mountain 1,901 ... L11
Loretto 1,515 ... G10
Loudon▲ 4,026 ... N9
Louisville 500 ... N9
Luttrell 812 ... O8
Lutts 740 ... F10
Lyles 500 ... G9
Lynchburg▲ 668 ... J10
Lynnville 344 ... G10
Madisonville▲ 3,033 ... N9
Malesus 600 ... D9
Manchester▲ 7,709 ... J10
Martel 500 ... N9
Martin 8,600 ... D8
Maryville▲ 19,208 ... O9
Mascot 2,138 ... O8
Mason 337 ... B10
Maury City 782 ... C9
Maynardville▲ 1,298 ... O8
McDonald 500 ... M10
McEwen 1,442 ... F8
McKenzie 5,168 ... E8
McLemoresville 280 ... D9
McMinnville▲ 11,194 ... K9
Medina 658 ... D9
Medon 137 ... D10
Memphis▲ 610,337 ... B10
Michie 677 ... E10
Middleton 536 ... D10
Midway 2,953 ... P8
Milan 7,512 ... D9
Milledgeville 279 ... E10
Milligan College 600 ... S8
Millington 17,866 ... B10
Minor Hill 372 ... G10
Mitchellville 193 ... J7
Monteagle 1,138 ... K10
Monterey 2,559 ... L8
Morley 600 ... N7
Morrison 570 ... K9
Morrison City 2,032 ... R7
Morristown▲ 21,385 ... P8
Moscow 384 ... C10
Mosheim 1,451 ... R8
Mount Carmel 4,082 ... R8
Mount Juliet 5,389 ... H8
Mount Pleasant 4,278 ... G9
Mountain City▲ 2,169 ... T8
Munford 2,326 ... B10
Murfreesboro▲ 44,922 ... J9
Murray Lake Hills ... L10
Nashville (cap.)▲ 488,374 ... H8
Neubert 800 ... O9
New Hope 854 ... K11
New Johnsonville 1,643 ... E8
New Market 1,086 ... O8
New Tazewell 1,864 ... O8
Newbern 2,515 ... C8
Newport▲ 7,123 ... P9
Niota 745 ... M9
Norma 118 ... N8
Normandy 118 ... J10
Norris 1,303 ... N8
Oak Hill 4,301 ... H8
Oak Ridge 27,310 ... N8
Oakdale 268 ... M9
Oakland 392 ... B10
Obion 1,241 ... C8
Oliver Springs 3,433 ... N8
Oneida 3,502 ... N7
Ooltewah 4,903 ... M10
Orebank 1,284 ... R7
Orlinda 469 ... H7
Orme 150 ... K10
Pall Mall 750 ... M7
Palmer 769 ... K10
Paris▲ 9,332 ... E8
Parrotsville 121 ... P8
Parsons 2,033 ... E9
Pegram 1,371 ... G8
Petersburg 514 ... H10
Petros 1,286 ... M8
Philadelphia 463 ... M9
Pickwick Dam 650 ... E10
Pigeon Forge 3,027 ... O9
Pikeville▲ 1,771 ... L9
Piperton 612 ... B10
Pittman Center 478 ... P9
Pleasant Hill 494 ... L9
Pleasant View 625 ... G8
Portland 5,165 ... H7
Powder Springs 600 ... O8
Powell 7,534 ... N8
Powells Crossroads 1,098 ... L10
Primm Springs 750 ... G9
Pulaski▲ 7,895 ... G10
Puryear 592 ... E8
Ramer 337 ... D10
Red Bank 12,322 ... L10
Red Boiling Springs 905 ... K7
Rheatown ... R8
Ridgely 1,775 ... B8
Ridgeside 400 ... L10
Ripley▲ 6,188 ... B9
Rives 344 ... C8
Roan Mountain 1,220 ... S8
Rockford 646 ... O9
Rockwood 5,348 ... M9
Rogersville▲ 4,149 ... P8
Rosemark 950 ... B10
Rossville 291 ... B10
Russellville 1,069 ... P8
Rutherford 1,303 ... C8
Rutledge▲ 903 ... P8
Saint Joseph 789 ... G10
Sale Creek 900 ... L10
Saltillo 383 ... E10
Samburg 374 ... C8
Sardis 305 ... E10
Saulsbury 106 ... C10
Saundersville ... H8
Savannah▲ 6,547 ... E10
Scotts Hill 594 ... E10
Selmer▲ 3,838 ... D10
Sequatchie 800 ... K10
Sevierville▲ 7,178 ... P9
Sewanee 2,128 ... K10
Seymour 7,026 ... O9
Sharon 1,047 ... D8
Shelbyville▲ 14,049 ... H10
Sherwood 900 ... K10
Signal Mountain 7,034 ... L10
Smithville▲ 3,791 ... K9
Smyrna 13,647 ... H9
Sneedville▲ 1,446 ... P7
Soddy-Daisy (Daisy-Soddy) 8,240 ... L10
Somerville▲ 2,047 ... C10
South Carthage 851 ... K8
South Cleveland 5,372 ... M10
South Clinton 1,671 ... N8
South Fulton 2,688 ... D8
South Pittsburg 3,295 ... K10
Southside 800 ... G8
Sparta▲ 4,681 ... K9
Spencer▲ 1,125 ... L9
Spring City 2,199 ... M9
Spring Hill 1,464 ... H9
Springfield▲ 11,227 ... H8
Stanton 487 ... C10
Stantonville 264 ... E10
Strawberry Plains 680 ... O8
Sullivan Gardens 2,513 ... R8
Summertown 850 ... G10
Surgoinsville 1,499 ... R8
Sweetwater 5,066 ... N9
Talbott 975 ... P8
Tazewell▲ 2,150 ... O8
Tellico Plains 657 ... N10
Ten Mile 700 ... M9
Tennessee Ridge 1,271 ... F8
Tiftona ... L11
Tipton 2,149 ... B10
Tiptonville▲ 2,438 ... B8
Toone 279 ... D10
Townsend 329 ... O9
Tracy City 1,556 ... K10
Treadway 712 ... P8
Trenton▲ 4,836 ... D9
Trezevant 874 ... D9
Trimble 694 ... C8
Troy 1,047 ... C8
Tullahoma 16,761 ... J10
Tusculum 1,918 ... R8
Union City▲ 10,513 ... C8
Vanleer 369 ... G8
Victoria 800 ... K10
Viola 125 ... K9
Vonore 605 ... N9
Walden 1,523 ... L10
Walterhill 1,043 ... J9
Wartburg▲ 932 ... M8
Wartrace 494 ... J9

(continued on following page)

Watauga 389.....................S8
Watertown 1,250.................J8
Waverly▲ 3,925.................F8
Waynesboro▲ 1,824.............F10
Western Institute 850..........C10
Westmoreland 1,726.............J7
White Bluff 1,988..............G8
White House 2,987..............H8
White Pine 1,771...............P8
Whiteville 1,050...............C10
Whitwell 1,622.................K10
Williston 427..................C10
Winchester▲ 6,305..............J10
Winfield 564...................M7
Woodbury▲ 2,287................J9
Woodland Mills 398.............C8
Yorkville 347..................C8

OTHER FEATURES

Andrew Johnson
  Nat'l Hist. Site.............R8
Appalachian (mts.)............M10
Bald (mts.)....................R9
Barkley (lake).................F7
Big Sandy (riv.)...............E9
Boone (lake)...................S8
Buffalo (riv.).................F9
Caney Fork (riv.)..............L9
Center Hill (lake).............K9
Cheatham (dam).................G8
Cheatham (dam).................H8
Cherokee (dam).................P8
Cherokee (lake)................P8
Chickamauga (dam).............L10
Chickamauga (lake)............L10
Chilhowee (mt.)................O9
Clinch (riv.)..................N9
Clingmans Dome (mt.)..........P10
Collins (riv.).................K9
Conasauga (riv.)..............M11
Cordell Hull (res.)............K8
Cumberland (plat.).............L9
Cumberland (riv.)..............K8
Cumberland Gap
  Nat'l Hist. Park.............O7
Dale Hollow (lake).............L7
Douglas (lake).................P9
Duck (riv.)....................F9
Elk (riv.)....................H10
Emory (riv.)...................M8
Forked Deer (riv.).............C9
Fort Campbell..................G7
Fort Donelson Nat'l Mil. Park..F8
Fort Loudoun (lake)............N9
French Broad (riv.)............R9
Great Falls (dam)..............K9
Great Smoky (mts.).............P9
Great Smoky Mountains
  Nat'l Park...................P9
Green (riv.)..................F10
Guyot (mt.)....................P9
Harpeth (riv.).................G8
Hatchie (riv.).................B9
Hiwassee (riv.)...............O10
Holston (riv.).................O8
Iron (mts.)....................S8
Kentucky (lake)................E7
Land Between The Lakes
  Rec. Area....................E7
Lick (creek)...................R8
Little Tennessee (riv.).......N10
Loosahatchie (riv.)...........B10
Melton Hill (lake).............N9
Memphis Naval Air Sta.........B10
Meriwether Lewis Park,
  Natchez Trace Pkwy..........G10
Mississippi (riv.)............A10
Nolichucky (riv.)..............R8
Norris (dam)...................N8
Norris (lake)..................O8
Obed (riv.)....................M8
Obion (riv.)...................C8
Ocoee (riv.)..................M10
Old Hickory (dam)..............H8
Old Hickory (lake).............J8
Pickwick (lake)...............E11
Powell (riv.)..................P8
Priest, J. Percy (lake)........J8
Red (riv.).....................G7
Reelfoot (lake)................C8
Richland (creek)..............G10
Rutherford Fork, Obion (riv.)..D8
Sewart A.F.B...................J8
Shiloh Nat'l Mil. Park........E10
Shoal (creek).................F10
South Holston (lake)...........S7
Stone (mts.)...................T8
Stones (riv.)..................J9
Stones River Nat'l Battlefield.J9
Sulphur Fork, Red (riv.).......H8
Tellico (riv.)................N10
Tennessee (riv.)..............E10
Tims Ford (lake)..............J10
Unaka (mts.)...................S8
Unicoi (mts.)................N10
Watauga (lake).................T8
Watts Bar (dam)................M9
Watts Bar (lake)...............M9
Whiteoak (creek)...............F8
Wolf (riv.)...................B10
Woods (lake)..................J10
Yellow (creek).................F8

▲ County seat.

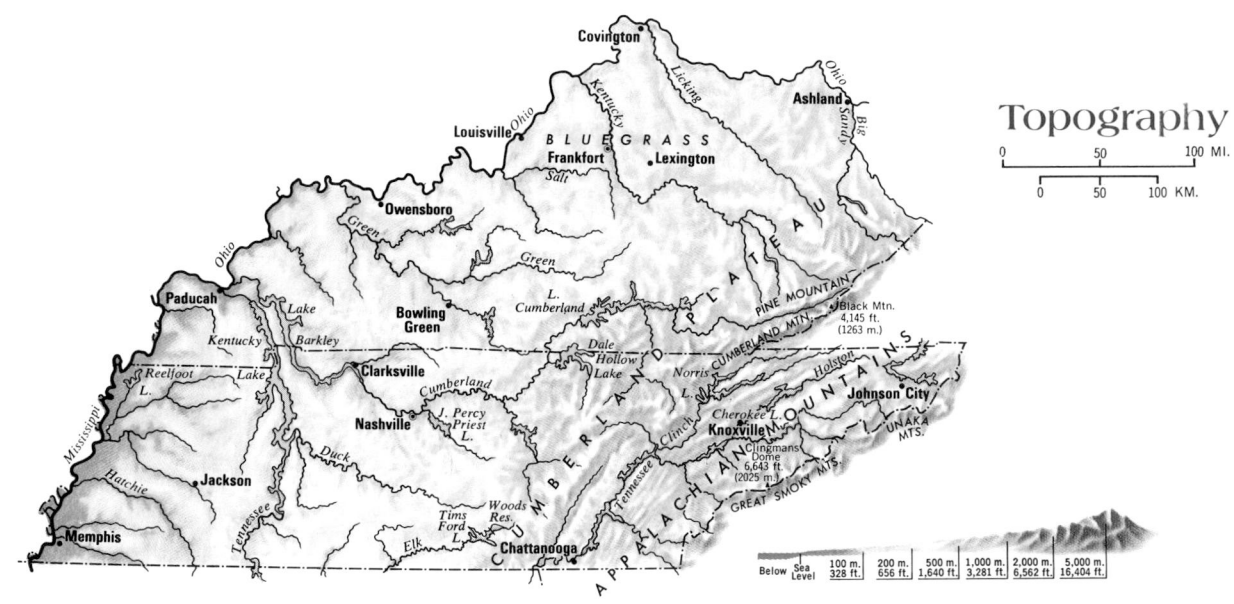

Topography

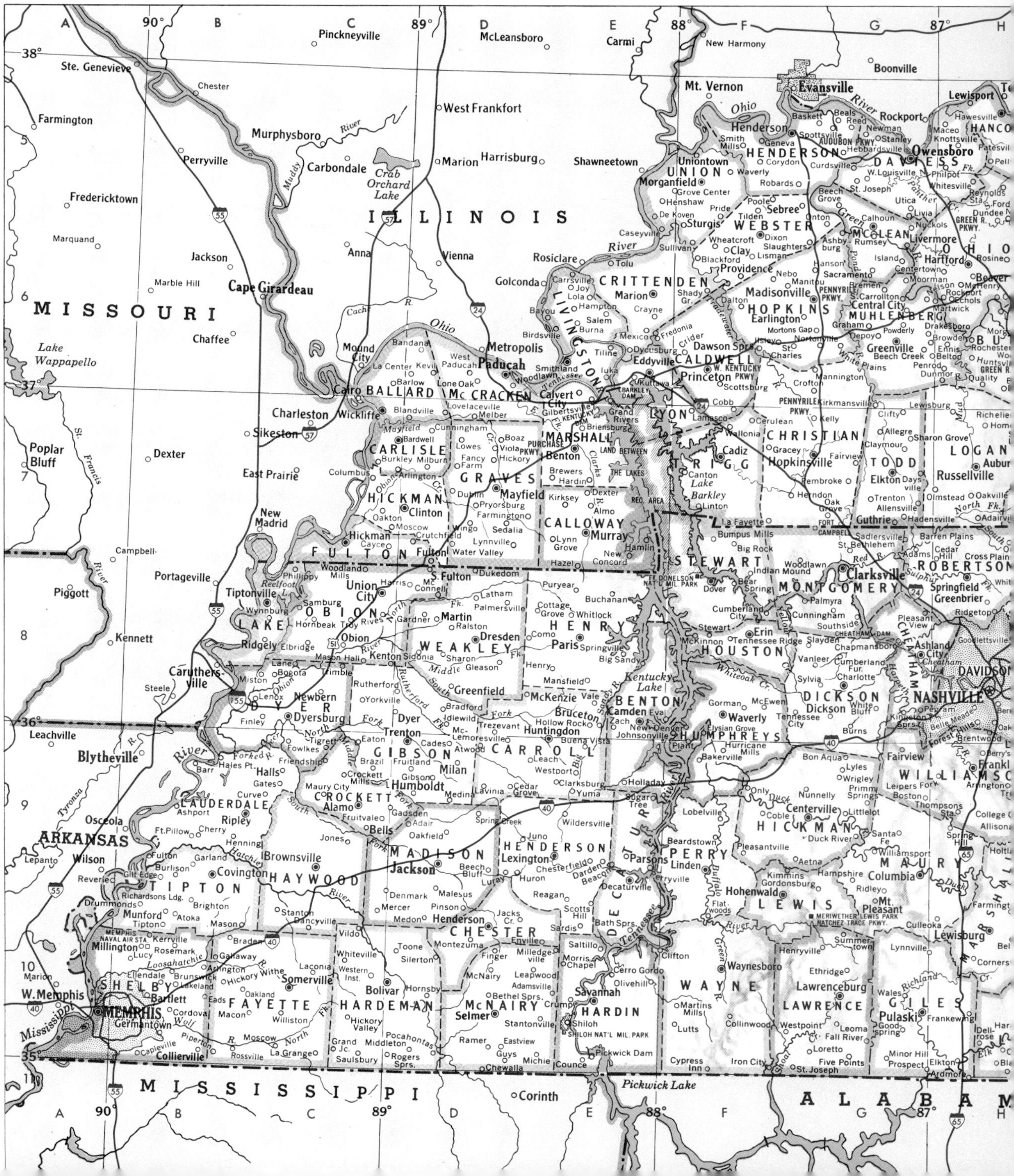

Kentucky
and Tennessee

SCALE
0 5 10   20   30   40MI
0 5 10   20   30   40 KM.

State Capitals .... ⊛
County Seats .... ⊙
Major Limited Access Hwys. ....

Scale 1:1,970,000

© Copyright HAMMOND INCORPORATED, Maplewood, N.J.

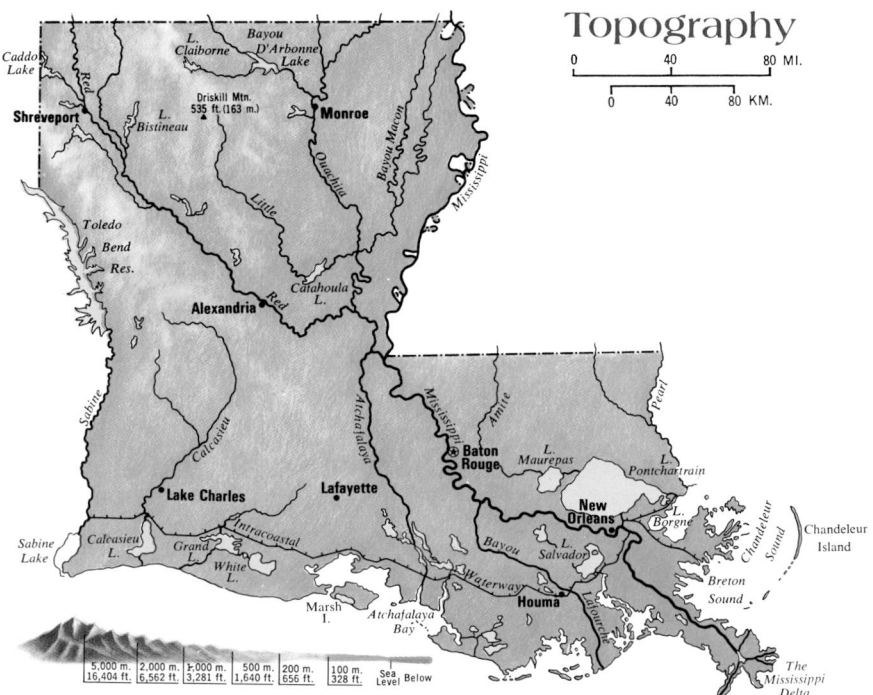

Topography

0 40 80 MI.

0 40 80 KM.

5,000 m. | 2,000 m. | 1,000 m. | 500 m. | 200 m. | 100 m. | Sea Level
16,404 ft. | 6,562 ft. | 3,281 ft. | 1,640 ft. | 656 ft. | 328 ft. | Below

The Mississippi Delta

PARISHES

Acadia 56,427	F6
Allen 21,390	E5
Ascension 50,068	L3
Assumption 22,084	H7
Avoyelles 41,393	G4
Beauregard 29,692	D5
Bienville 16,387	D2
Bossier 80,721	C1
Caddo 252,437	C1
Calcasieu 167,223	D6
Caldwell 10,761	F2
Cameron 9,336	D7
Catahoula 12,287	G3
Claiborne 17,095	D1
Concordia 22,981	G4
De Soto 25,727	C2
East Baton Rouge 366,191	K1
East Carroll 11,772	H1
East Feliciana 19,015	H5
Evangeline 33,343	F5
Franklin 24,141	G2
Grant 16,703	E3
Iberia 63,752	G7
Iberville 32,159	H6
Jackson 17,321	E2
Jefferson 454,592	K7
Jefferson Davis 32,168	E6
La Salle 17,004	F3
Lafayette 150,017	F6
Lafourche 82,483	K7
Lincoln 39,763	E1
Livingston 58,806	L2
Madison 15,682	H2
Morehouse 34,803	G1
Natchitoches 39,863	D3
Orleans 557,927	L6
Ouachita 139,241	F2
Plaquemines 26,049	L8
Pointe Coupee 24,045	G5
Rapides 135,282	E4
Red River 10,433	D2
Richland 22,187	G2
Sabine 25,280	C3
Saint Bernard 64,097	L7
Saint Charles 37,259	K7
Saint Helena 9,827	J5
Saint James 21,495	L3
Saint John the Baptist 31,924	M3
Saint Landry 84,128	F5
Saint Martin 40,214	G6
Saint Mary 64,253	H7
Saint Tammany 110,869	L6
Tangipahoa 80,698	K5
Tensas 8,525	H2
Terrebonne 94,393	J8
Union 21,167	F1
Vermilion 48,458	F7
Vernon 53,475	D4
Washington 44,207	K5
Webster 43,631	D1
West Baton Rouge 19,086	H6
West Carroll 12,922	H1
West Feliciana 12,186	H5
Winn 17,253	E3

CITIES and TOWNS

Abbeville▲ 11,187	F7
Abita Springs 1,296	L6
Acme 235	G4
Acy 570	L3
Addis 1,222	J2
Adeline 200	G7

Akers 150	N2
Albany 645	M1
Alberta 150	D2
Alexandria▲ 49,188	E4
Allen 175	D3
Alto 132	G2
Alton 500	L6
Amelia 2,447	H7
Amite▲ 4,301	K5
Anacoco 823	D4
Anandale	F4
Andrew 100	F6
Angie 235	L5
Angola 600	G5
Ansley 100	E2
Arabi 8,787	P4
Arbroth 250	H5
Arcadia▲ 3,079	E1
Archibald 425	G2
Archie 280	G3
Arcola 245	K5
Arnaudville 1,444	G6
Ashland 289	D2
Athens 278	E1
Atlanta 118	E3
Avery Island 500	G7
Bains 400	H5
Baker 13,233	K1
Baldwin 2,379	G7
Ball 3,305	F4
Bancroft 114	C5
Baptist 150	M1
Barataria 1,160	K7
Basile 1,808	E5
Baskin 243	G2
Bastrop▲ 13,916	G1
Batchelor 500	G5
Baton Rouge (cap.)▲ 219,531	K2
Bayou Barbary 200	M2
Bayou Cane 15,876	J7
Bayou Goula 850	J3
Bayou Vista 4,733	H7
Baywood 100	K1
Beaver 350	E5
Beekman 150	G1
Bel 150	D6
Belcher 249	C1
Bell City 400	D6
Belle Alliance	H6
Belle Chasse 8,512	O4
Belle D'Eau 120	F4
Belle Rose 900	K3
Bellwood 150	D3
Belmont 350	C3
Benson 200	C3
Bentley 120	E3
Benton▲ 2,047	C1
Bernice 1,543	E1
Bertrandville 175	L7
Bethany 300	B2
Bienville 316	D2
Blanchard 1,175	C1
Bogalusa 14,280	L5
Bolinger 200	N4
Bonita 500	G1
Boothville 300	M8
Bordelonville 350	G4
Bosco 480	F2
Bossier City 52,721	C1
Boudreaux 275	J8
Bourg 2,073	J7
Boutte 2,702	N4
Boyce 1,361	E4
Braithwaite 350	P4
Branch 200	F6

Breaux Bridge 6,515	G6
Brittany 475	L3
Broussard 3,213	G6
Brusly 1,824	J2
Bryceland 103	E2
Buckeye 280	F4
Bunkie 5,044	F5
Buras (Buras-Triumph) 4,137	L8
Burnside 500	L3
Bush 275	L5
Cade 175	G6
Calcasieu 400	E4
Calhoun 350	F2
Calumet 100	H7
Calvin 207	E3
Cameron▲ 2,041	D7
Campti 929	D3
Cankton 323	F6
Carencro 5,429	G6
Carlisle 975	L7
Carville 1,108	K3
Castor 196	D2
Cecelia 550	G6
Center Point 850	F4
Centerville 600	H7
Central 546	L3
Chacahoula 150	J7
Chalmette▲ 31,860	P4
Charenton 1,584	H7
Chase 200	G2
Chataignier 281	F5
Chatham 617	F2
Chauvin 3,375	J8
Cheneyville 1,005	F4
Chopin 175	E4
Choudrant 557	F1
Church Point 4,677	F6
Clarence 577	E3
Clarks 650	F2
Clay 400	E2
Clayton 917	H3
Clear Lake 100	E3
Clinton▲ 1,904	J5
Clio 125	M2
Cloutierville 100	E3
Colfax▲ 1,696	E3
Collinston 375	G1
Columbia▲ 386	F2
Convent▲ 400	L3
Converse 436	C3
Corey 110	F2
Cotton Valley 1,130	D1
Cottonport 2,600	F5
Couchwood 150	D1
Coushatta▲ 1,845	D2
Covington▲ 7,691	L6
Cow Island 200	F7
Cravens 200	D7
Creole 175	D7
Crescent 300	J2
Creston 135	E3
Crowley▲ 13,983	F6
Crowville 400	G2
Cullen 1,642	D1
Curtis 110	C3
Cut Off 5,325	K7
Dalcour 275	P4
Danville 100	E2
Darrow 500	K3
Davant 175	L7
De Quincy 3,474	D6
De Ridder▲ 9,868	D5
Deerford 100	K1
Delcambre 1,978	G7
Delhi 3,169	H2
Delta 234	J2

Denham Springs 8,381	L2
Des Allemands 2,504	N4
Destrehan 8,031	N4
Deville 1,113	F4
Diamond 370	L7
Dixie 330	C1
Dixie Inn 347	D1
Dodson 350	E2
Donaldsonville▲ 7,949	K3
Donner 500	J7
Downsville 101	F1
Doyline 884	D1
Dry Creek 300	D5
Dry Prong 380	E3
Dubach 843	E1
Dubberly 253	D1
Dulac 3,273	J8
Dunn 225	G2
Duplessis 500	K2
Duson 1,465	F6
East Hodge 421	E2
East Point 100	D2
Easton 365	F5
Echo 525	F4
Edgard▲ 2,753	M3
Edgefield 207	D2
Edgerly 250	C6
Effie 300	F4
Elizabeth 414	E5
Elm Grove 100	C2
Elm Park 200	H5
Elmer 200	E4
Elton 1,277	E6
Empire 2,654	L8
Enterprise 375	G3
Epps 541	G1
Erath 2,428	F7
Eros 177	F2
Erwinville 790	H5
Esther 745	F7
Estherwood 745	F6
Ethel 250	H5
Eunice 11,162	F6
Eva 100	G4
Evangeline 400	F6
Evans 500	D5
Evergreen 283	F5
Extension 500	G3
Fairbanks 300	F1
Farmerville▲ 3,334	F1
Fenton 265	E6
Ferriday 4,111	G3
Fields 125	C5
Fisher 277	D4
Flatwoods 360	E4
Flora 300	D3
Florien 626	D4
Fluker 400	K5
Folsom 469	K5
Forbing 100	C2
Fordoche 869	G5
Forest 263	H1
Forest Hill 408	E4
Fort Jesup 150	D4
Fort Necessity 150	G2
Franklin▲ 9,004	G7
Franklinton▲ 4,007	K5
French Settlement 829	L2
Frierson 700	C2
Frost 500	L2
Fryeburg 150	D2
Fullerton 120	D4
Galbraith 4,294	K8
Galvez 200	L2
Garden City 225	H7
Garyville 3,181	M3

(continued)

Louisiana

SCALE
0 5 10 20 30 40 MI.
0 5 10 20 30 40 KM.

State Capitals ⊛
Parish Seats ⊚
Canals
Major Limited Access Hwys.

Scale 1:2,000,000

AREA 47,752 sq. mi. (123,678 sq. km.)
POPULATION 4,238,216
CAPITAL Baton Rouge
LARGEST CITY New Orleans
HIGHEST POINT Driskill Mtn. 535 ft. (163 m.)
SETTLED IN 1699
ADMITTED TO UNION April 30, 1812
POPULAR NAME Pelican State
STATE FLOWER Magnolia
STATE BIRD Eastern Brown Pelican

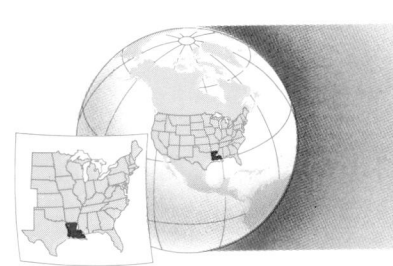

New Orleans, Baton Rouge and Vicinity

© Copyright HAMMOND INCORPORATED, Maplewood, N.J.

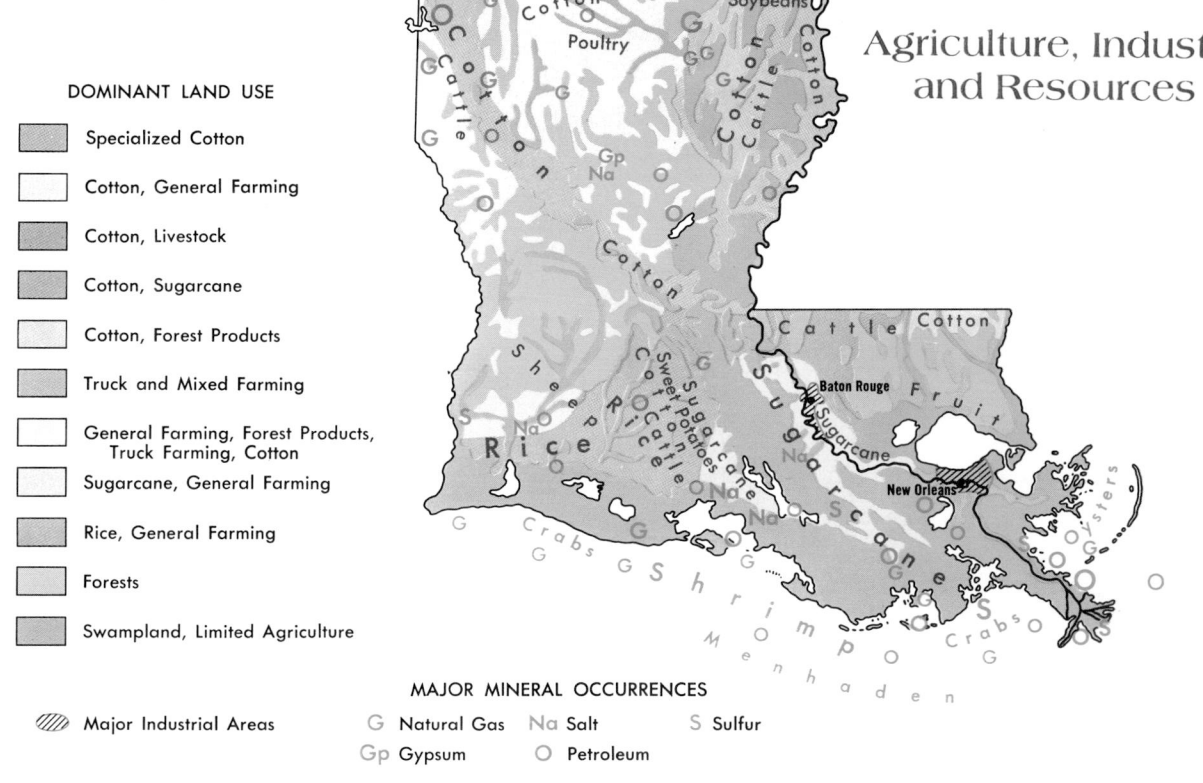

Agriculture, Industry and Resources

DOMINANT LAND USE

- Specialized Cotton
- Cotton, General Farming
- Cotton, Livestock
- Cotton, Sugarcane
- Cotton, Forest Products
- Truck and Mixed Farming
- General Farming, Forest Products, Truck Farming, Cotton
- Sugarcane, General Farming
- Rice, General Farming
- Forests
- Swampland, Limited Agriculture

Major Industrial Areas

MAJOR MINERAL OCCURRENCES

G Natural Gas   Na Salt   S Sulfur
Gp Gypsum   O Petroleum

Geismar 300 .... K3
Georgetown 273 .... F3
Gheens 350 .... K7
Gibsland 1,354 .... E1
Gibson 950 .... J7
Gilbert 704 .... G2
Gilleyville G2
Gilliam 202 .... C1
Girard 150 .... G2
Glencoe 200 .... G7
Glenmora 1,686 .... E5
Gloster 780 .... C2
Glynn 700 .... H5
Golden Meadow 2,049 ... K8
Goldonna 417 .... D2
Gonzales 7,003 .... L2
Good Hope 500 .... N4
Good Pine (Good Pine-Trout) 1,033 .... F3
Gorum 150 .... E4
Grambling 5,484 .... E1
Gramercy 2,412 .... M3
Grand Cane 233 .... C2
Grand Chenier 710 ...... E7
Grand Coteau 1,118 ..... G6
Grand Isle 1,455 .... L8
Grand Lake 400 .... D6
Grant 225 .... E5
Gray 4,260 .... J7
Grayson 529 .... F2
Greensburg▲ 583 .... J5
Greenwell Springs 350 ... K1
Greenwood 2,092 .... B2
Gretna▲ 17,208 .... O4
Grosse Tete 541 .... G6
Gueydan 1,611 .... E6
Gurley 150 .... H5
Hackberry 1,664 .... D7
Hahnville▲ 2,599 .... N4
Haile 300 .... F1
Hall Summit 227 .... D2
Hammond 15,871 .... N1
Hanna 138 .... D3
Happy Jack 800 .... L7
Harahan 9,927 .... O4
Harrisonburg▲ 453 ...... G3
Harvey 21,222 .... O4
Haughton 1,664 .... C1
Hawthorn 400 .... D4
Hayes 600 .... E6
Haynesville 2,854 .... D1
Head of Island 420 ...... L2
Hebert 150 .... G2
Heflin 253 .... D2
Henderson 1,543 .... G6
Hessmer 578 .... F4
Hester 250 .... L3
Hicks 379 .... E4
Hico 120 .... E1
Hineston 400 .... E4
Hodge 562 .... E2
Hohen Solms 125 .... K3
Holden 400 .... M1
Holly Ridge 100 .... G2
Hollywood D6
Home Place 600 .... L8
Homer▲ 4,152 .... D1
Hornbeck 427 .... D4
Hosston 417 .... C1
Houma▲ 30,495 .... J7
Humphreys 900 .... J7
Iberville 367 .... K2
Ida 250 .... C1
Independence 1,632 .... M1
Indian Village 100 ...... H6
Innis 1,410 .... G5
Iota 1,256 .... E6
Iowa 2,588 .... D6
Isabel 550 .... K5
Ivan 125 .... C1
Jackson 3,891 .... H5
Jamestown 148 .... D2
Jean Lafitte 1,469 ...... K7
Jeanerette 6,205 .... G7
Jefferson 14,521 .... O4
Jena▲ 2,626 .... F3
Jennings▲ 11,305 ...... E6
Jesuit Bend 100 .... K7
Jigger 300 .... G2
Johnsons Bayou 300 .... C7
Jones 4,305 .... G1
Jonesboro▲ 4,305 ...... E2
Jonesville 2,720 .... G3
Joyce 700 .... E3
Junction City 749 .... E1
Kaplan 4,535 .... F6
Keatchie 342 .... C2
Keithville 500 .... C2
Kelly 325 .... F3
Kenner 72,033 .... N4
Kentwood 2,468 .... J5
Kilbourne 409 .... H1
Killian 721 .... M2
Killona 950 .... M4
Kinder 2,246 .... E6
Kisatchie 150 .... D4
Klotzville 248 .... K3
Kraemer 350 .... M4
Krotz Springs 1,285 ..... G5
La Place 24,194 .... N3
Labadieville 1,821 ...... K4
Lacamp 150 .... E4
Lacassine 400 .... E6
Lacombe 6,523 .... L6
Lafayette▲ 94,440 ...... F6
Lafitte 1,507 .... K7
Lafourche 200 .... J7
Lagan L7
Lake Arthur 3,194 ...... E6
Lake Charles▲ 70,580 ... D6
Lake Providence▲ 5,380 ... H1
Lakeland 800 .... H5
Larose 5,772 .... K7
Larto 500 .... G4
Lawtell 1,014 .... F5
Le Blanc 400 .... E5
Leander 145 .... E4

Lebeau 200 .... F5
Lecompte 1,661 .... F4
Leesville▲ 7,638 .... D4
Lena 300 .... E4
Leonville 825 .... G6
Leton 125 .... D1
Lettsworth 200 .... G5
Lewisburg 265 .... F6
Libuse 500 .... F4
Lillie 145 .... E1
Linville 150 .... F1
Lisbon 160 .... E1
Lismore 380 .... G3
Little Farms N4
Livingston▲ 999 .... L1
Livonia 970 .... G5
Lobdell 200 .... J1
Lockport 2,503 .... K7
Logansport 1,390 .... C3
Lonepine 850 .... F5
Longstreet 189 .... B2
Longville 800 .... D5
Loranger 250 .... N1
Loreauville 860 .... G6
Lottie 400 .... G5
Lucky 342 .... E2
Lucy 825 .... M3
Luling 2,803 .... N4
Lunita 100 .... C6
Lutcher 3,907 .... L3
Madisonville 659 .... K6
Mamou 3,483 .... F5
Mandeville 7,083 .... L6
Mangham 598 .... G2
Mansfield▲ 5,389 .... C2
Mansura 1,601 .... G4
Many▲ 3,112 .... C3
Maplewood D6
Maringouin 1,149 .... G6
Marion 775 .... F1
Marksville▲ 5,526 ...... G4
Marrero 36,671 .... O4
Marthaville 150 .... D3
Martin 545 .... D2
Mathews 3,009 .... J7
Maurepas 200 .... M2
Maurice 432 .... F6
Mayna 122 .... G4
McCall 150 .... K3
McNary 248 .... E5
Melder 500 .... E4
Melrose 500 .... E3
Melville 1,562 .... G5
Mer Rouge 586 .... G1
Mermentau 760 .... E6
Merryville 1,235 .... D5
Metairie 149,428 .... O4
Midland 560 .... F6
Milton 450 .... F6
Mimosa Park 4,516 ..... N4
Minden▲ 13,661 .... D1
Mira 354 .... C1
Mitchell 155 .... C3
Mix 150 .... G5
Modeste 225 .... K3
Monroe▲ 54,909 .... F1
Montegut 1,784 .... J8
Monterey 800 .... G4
Montgomery 645 .... E3
Montpelier 247 .... M1
Montz 200 .... M3

Mooringsport 873 .... B1
Mora 427 .... E4
Moreauville 919 .... G4
Morgan City 14,531 .... H7
Morganza 759 .... G5
Morrow 600 .... F5
Morse 782 .... F6
Mound 16 .... H2
Mount Airy 700 .... M3
Mount Hermon 170 .... K5
Mount Lebanon 102 ... D2
Myrtle Grove 100 ...... K7
Nairn 500 .... L8
Napoleonville▲ 802 ... K4
Natalbany 1,289 .... N1
Natchez 434 .... D3
Nebo 200 .... F3
Negreet 400 .... C4
New Era 200 .... G4
New Iberia▲ 31,828 ... G6
New Orleans▲ 496,938 ... O4
New Roads▲ 5,303 .... G5
New Sarpy 2,946 ...... N4
Newellton 1,576 .... H2
Newllano 2,660 .... D4
Noble 225 .... C3
Norco 3,385 .... N3
North Hodge 477 ...... E2
Norwood 317 .... H5
Oak Grove▲ 2,126 .... H1
Oak Ridge 174 .... G1
Oakdale 6,832 .... E5
Oberlin▲ 1,808 .... E5
Odenburg 175 .... G5
Oil City 1,282 .... C1
Olivier 300 .... G7
Olla 1,410 .... F3
Opelousas▲ 18,151 ... G5
Oretta 110 .... D5
Oscar 650 .... H5
Otis 400 .... E4
Oxford 125 .... C3
Paincourtville 1,550 ... K3
Palmetto 229 .... G5
Paradis 750 .... M4
Parhams 100 .... G4
Parks 400 .... G6
Patoutville 230 .... G7
Patterson 4,736 .... H7
Paulina 500 .... L3
Pearl River 1,507 ..... L6
Peason 120 .... D4
Pecan Island 480 ..... F7
Pelican 250 .... C3
Perry 230 .... F7
Perryville 100 .... G1
Phoenix 525 .... L7
Pilottown 175 .... M8
Pine Grove 570 .... J5
Pine Prairie 713 ...... E5
Pineville 12,251 ...... F4
Pioneer 116 .... H1
Pitkin 600 .... E5
Plain Dealing 1,074 ... C1
Plaquemine▲ 7,186 ... J2
Plattenville 205 .... K4
Plaucheville 187 ...... G5
Pleasant Hill 824 ..... C3
Pointe a la Hache▲ 750 ... L7
Pollock 330 .... F3

Ponchatoula 5,425 ..... N2
Port Allen▲ 6,277 ..... J2
Port Barre 2,144 .... G5
Port Hudson 200 ...... J1
Port Sulphur 3,523 .... L8
Port Vincent 446 ...... L2
Powhatan 147 .... D3
Prairieville 500 .... K2
Pride 100 .... K1
Princeton 350 .... C1
Provencal 538 .... D3
Quitman 162 .... E2
Raceland 5,564 .... J7
Rayne 8,502 .... F6
Rayville▲ 4,411 ...... G2
Reddell 500 .... F5
Reeves 188 .... D5
Reggio 400 .... L7
Remy 850 .... L3
Reserve 8,847 .... M3
Richmond 447 .... H2
Richwood 1,253 ..... F2
Ridgecrest 804 ...... G3
Ringgold 1,655 ...... D2
Rio 100 .... L5
Roanoke 800 .... E6
Robeline 149 .... D3
Robert 600 .... N1
Rocky Mount 150 ... C1
Rodessa 294 .... B1
Rogers 150 .... F3
Romeville 133 ...... L3
Rosa 300 .... G5
Rosedale 807 ...... G6
Roseland 1,093 .... J5
Rosepine 1,135 .... D5
Ruby 400 .... F4
Ruston▲ 20,027 ... E1
Saint Amant 900 .. L2
Saint Benedict 190 . K5
Saint Bernard 750 . L7
Saint Francisville▲ 1,700 ... H5
Saint Gabriel 975 . K2
Saint James 600 .. L3
Saint Joseph▲ 1,517 ... H3
Saint Landry 550 . F5
Saint Martinville▲ 7,137 ... G6
Saint Maurice 560 . E3
Saint Rose 6,259 .. N4
Saint Tammany 150 . L6
Saline 272 .... F4
Samtown F4
Sarepta 886 ...... D1
Schriever 4,958 .. J7
Scotlandville 15,113 ... J1
Scott 4,912 ...... F6
Seymourville 2,891 ... J2
Shongaloo 161 .. D1
Shreveport▲ 198,525 ... C2
Sibley 997 ...... D1
Sicily Island 421 ... G3
Sieper 226 ...... E4
Sikes 120 ...... F2
Simmesport 2,092 ... G5
Simpson 536 ... D4
Simsboro 634 .. E1
Singer 250 .... D5
Slagle 650 .... D4
Slaughter 827 . H5
Slidell 24,124 . L6
Smoke Bend 300 ... K3

Sondheimer 225 ...... H1
Sorrento 1,119 .... L3
South Mansfield 407 . C3
Spearsville 132 ...... E1
Springfield 439 ..... M2
Springhill 5,668 .... D1
Standard 190 ...... F3
Stanley 131 .... C3
Starks 750 ...... C6
Start 200 .... G2
Sterlington 1,140 . F1
Stonewall 1,266 .. C2
Sugartown 375 ... D5
Sulphur 20,125 .. D6
Summerfield 170 . E1
Sun 429 .... L5
Sunset 2,201 ... F6
Sunshine 900 .. K2
Supreme 1,020 . K4
Swartz 3,698 .. G1
Sweet Lake 300 . D7
Talisheek 315 .. L5
Tallulah▲ 8,526 . H2
Tangipahoa 569 . J5
Taylor 500 .... D1
Taylortown 150 . C2
Temple 250 ... E4
Tendal 200 ... H2
Terry Town 23,548 . O4
Theriot 450 .. J8
Thibodaux▲ 14,035 . J7
Tickfaw 565 . M1
Tioga 457 ... F4
Toro 100 ... C4
Transylvania 400 . H1
Trees 327 . B1
Triumph (Triumph-Buras) 4,137 ... L8
Trout (Trout-Good Pine) 1,033 . F3
Tullos 427 ... E2
Tunica 500 .. G5
Turkey Creek 283 . F5
Union 665 . L3
Urania 782 . F3
Vacherie 2,169 . L3
Valverda 200 . G5
Varnado 236 . L5
Venice 900 . M8
Vernon 150 . E2
Vick 500 . F4
Vidalia▲ 4,953 . G3
Vienna 404 . E1
Ville Platte▲ 9,037 . F5
Vinton 3,154 . C6
Violet 8,574 . P4
Vivian 4,156 . B1
Wadesboro 400 . H2
Wakefield 400 . H5
Walker 3,727 . L1
Wallace 200 . M3
Walters 500 . G3
Warden 130 . H1
Wardville . F4
Washington 1,253 . G5
Waterproof 1,080 . H3
Watson 800 . L1
Waverly 350 . H2
Weeks 400 . G7
Welcome 450 . L3
Welsh 3,299 . E6
West Monroe 14,096 . F1

West Pointe a la Hache 250 ... L7
Westlake 5,007 .... D6
Westwego 11,218 ..... O4
Weyanoke 500 .... H5
White Castle 2,102 .. J3
Whitehall 380 ...... M2
Whiteville 150 ..... F5
Wildsville 800 .... G3
Wills Point 150 .. L7
Wilson 707 ...... H5
Winnfield▲ 6,138 . E3
Winnsboro▲ 5,755 . G2
Wisner 1,153 .... G3
Woodhaven M1
Woodlawn 150 .. E6
Woodworth 754 . E4
Youngsville 1,195 . G6
Zachary 9,036 ... K1
Zwolle 1,779 ... C3

OTHER FEATURES

Allemands (lake) M4
Alligator (pt.) L6
Amite (riv.) L2
Anacoco (lake) D4
Atchafalaya (bay) ... H8
Atchafalaya (riv.) ... G6
Barataria (bay) L8
Barataria (passage) . L8
Barksdale A.F.B. ... C2
Bayou D'Arbonne (lake) . E1
Bird (isl.) M8
Bistineau (lake) ... D2
Black (lake) D3
Black Lake (bayou) . D1
Boeuf (lake) J7
Boeuf (riv.) G1
Bonnet Carré Spillway and Floodway ... N3
Borgne (lake) ... L7
Boudreau (bay) . M7
Boudreaux (lake) . J8
Breton (isl.) M8
Breton (sound) . M7
Bundick (lake) . D5
Caddo (lake) . B1
Caillou (bay) . J8
Calcasieu (lake) . D7
Calcasieu (passage) . D7
Calcasieu (riv.) . D6
Catahoula (lake) . F4
Cataouatche (lake) . N4
Cat Island (chan.) . M6
Cat Island (passage) . J8
Chandeleur (isls.) . N7
Chandeleur (sound) . M7
Chenier (lake) . F2
Chicot (pt.) . M7
Claiborne (lake) . E1
Clear (lake) . D3
Cocodrie (lake) . E5
Cotile (lake) . E4
Cross (lake) . C2
Curlew (lake) . M7
Dernieres (isls.) . J8
Door (pt.) . M6
Driskill (mt.) . E2
Drum (bay) . M7
East (bay) . M8
East Cote Blanche (bay) . G7

Edwards (lake) C2
Eloi (bay) M7
England A.F.B. E4
Fields (lake) J7
Fort Polk 14,730 ... D4
Free Mason (isls.) .. M7
Garden Island (bay) . M8
Grand (lake) E7
Grand (lake) H7
Grand Terre (isls.) . L8
Iatt (lake) E3
Jean Lafitte Nat'l Hist. Park . P4
Lafourche (bayou) . K8
Little (riv.) F3
Louisiana (pt.) .. C7
Macon (bayou) . G1
Main (passage) . M8
Manchac (passage) . N2
Marsh (isl.) G7
Maurepas (lake) . M2
Mermentau (riv.) . E7
Mexico (gulf) .. F8
Mississippi (delta) . M8
Mississippi (riv.) . H3
Mississippi (sound) . M6
Mississippi River Gulf Outlet (canal) ... L7
Mozambique (pt.) . M7
Mud (lake) ... D7
Naval Air Sta. ... O4
North (isls.) ... M7
North (pass) ... N8
North (pt.) ... M8
Northeast (pass) . M8
Ouachita (riv.) . F1
Palourde (lake) . H7
Pearl (riv.) . L5
Point au Fer (isl.) . H8
Point au Fer (pt.) . H8
Pontchartrain (lake) . O3
Pontchartrain Causeway . L6
Poverty Pt. Nat'l Mon. . H1
Raccoon (pt.) ... H8
Red (riv.) G4
Sabine (lake) .. C7
Sabine (passage) . C5
Sabine (riv.) ... C5
Saline (lake) ... E4
Salvador (lake) . K7
Smithport (lake) . C3
South (pass) ... M8
South (pt.) ... M8
Southeast (pass) . M8
Southwest (pass) . L8
Tangipahoa (riv.) . N1
Tensas (riv.) ... G3
Terrebonne (bay) . J8
Tickfaw (riv.) .. M1
Timbalier (bay) . K8
Timbalier (isl.) . K8
Toledo Bend (res.) . C3
Turkey Creek (lake) . G3
Vermilion (bay) . F7
Vernon (lake) . D4
Verret (lake) . H7
Wallace (lake) . C2
West (bay) . M8
West Cote Blanche (bay) . G7
White (lake) . E7

▲ Parish seat

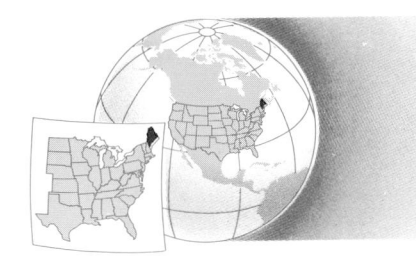

AREA 33,265 sq. mi. (86,156 sq. km.)
POPULATION 1,233,223
CAPITAL Augusta
LARGEST CITY Portland
HIGHEST POINT Katahdin 5,268 ft. (1606 m.)
SETTLED IN 1624
ADMITTED TO UNION March 15, 1820
POPULAR NAME Pine Tree State
STATE FLOWER White Pine Cone & Tassel
STATE BIRD Chickadee

COUNTIES

Androscoggin 105,259 ....C7
Aroostook 86,936 ....F2
Cumberland 243,135 ....C8
Franklin 29,008 ....B5
Hancock 46,948 ....G6
Kennebec 115,904 ....D7
Knox 36,310 ....F5
Lincoln 30,357 ....D7
Oxford 52,602 ....B7
Penobscot 146,601 ....F5
Piscataquis 18,653 ....E4
Sagadahoc 33,535 ....C7
Somerset 49,767 ....C4
Waldo 33,018 ....E6
Washington 35,308 ....H6
York 164,587 ....B9

CITIES and TOWNS

Abbot Village • 576 ....D5
Acton 850 ....B8
Acton • 1,727 ....B8
Addison 350 ....H6
Addison • 1,114 ....H6
Albion • 1,736 ....E6
Alexander • 478 ....H5
Alfred 1,890 ....B9
Alfred • 2,238 ....B9
Allagash • 359 ....F1
Alna • 571 ....D7
Alton • 771 ....F5
Amherst • 226 ....G6
Andover 350 ....B6
Andover • 953 ....B6
Anson 950 ....D6
Anson • 2,382 ....D6
Appleton • 1,069 ....F5
Argyle 202 ....F5
Ashland 750 ....G2
Ashland • 1,542 ....G2
Athens 300 ....D6
Athens • 897 ....D6
Atkinson • 332 ....E5
Auburn▲ 24,309 ....C7
Augusta (cap.)▲ 21,325 ....D7
Aurora • 82 ....G6
Bailey Island 500 ....D8
Bancroft H4
Bancroft • 66 ....H4
Bangor▲ 33,181 ....F6
Bar Harbor 2,685 ....G7
Bar Harbor • 2,768 ....G7
Bar Mills 800 ....C8
Baring 235 ....J5
Baring • 275 ....J5
Bass Harbor 450 ....G7
Bath▲ 9,799 ....D8
Bayside F7
Beals • 667 ....H7
Beddington • 43 ....H6
Belfast▲ 6,355 ....F7
Belgrade 950 ....D7
Belgrade • 2,375 ....D7
Belgrade Lakes 700 ....D6
Belmont • 652 ....E7
Benedicta • 225 ....G4
Benton • 2,312 ....D6
Berwick 2,378 ....B9
Berwick • 5,995 ....B9
Bethel 750 ....B7
Bethel • 2,329 ....B7
Biddeford 20,710 ....B9
Biddeford Pool 500 ....C9
Bingham 1,074 ....D5
Bingham • 1,071 ....D5
Birch Harbor 300 ....H7
Blaine-Mars Hill 1,921 ....H2
Blaine • 784 ....H2
Blanchard 78 ....D5
Blue Hill 850 ....F7
Blue Hill • 1,941 ....F7
Bolsters Mills 150 ....B7
Boothbay 200 ....D8
Boothbay • 2,648 ....D8
Boothbay Harbor 1,267 ....D8
Bowdoinham • 2,192 ....D7
Bowerbank • 72 ....E5
Bradford 150 ....F5
Bradford • 1,103 ....F5
Bradley • 1,136 ....F6
Brewer 9,021 ....F6
Bridgewater • 647 ....H3
Bridgton 1,639 ....B7
Bridgton • 2,195 ....B7
Brighton • 94 ....D5
Bristol 450 ....D8
Bristol • 2,326 ....D8
Brooklin • 735 ....F7
Brooks 900 ....E6
Brooksville • 760 ....F7
Brookton 175 ....H4
Brownfield 300 ....B8
Brownfield • 1,034 ....B8
Brownville 600 ....E5

Brownville • 1,506 ....E5
Brownville Junction 950 ....E5
Brunswick 10,990 ....C8
Brunswick • 14,683 ....C8
Bryant Pond 600 ....B7
Buckfield • 1,566 ....C7
Bucks Harbor 300 ....J6
Bucksport 2,853 ....F6
Bucksport • 2,989 ....F6
Burlington • 360 ....G5
Burnham • 961 ....E6
Buxton • 6,494 ....C8
Byron • 111 ....B6
Calais 3,963 ....J5
Cambridge • 490 ....E6
Camden 3,743 ....F7
Camden • 4,022 ....F7
Canaan • 1,636 ....D6
Canton • 951 ....C7
Cape Neddick 2,193 ....B9
Cape Porpoise 500 ....C9
Caratunk 98 ....C5
Cardville 223 ....F5
Caribou 9,415 ....G2
Carmel • 1,906 ....E6
Carrabassett Valley • 325 ....C5
Carroll • 185 ....G5
Carthage • 458 ....C6
Cary • 235 ....H4
Casco 400 ....B7
Casco • 3,018 ....B7
Castine • 1,161 ....F7
Centerville • 30 ....H6
Chapman • 422 ....G2
Charleston • 1,187 ....F5
Charlotte • 271 ....J5
Chebeague Island 900 ....C8
Chelsea • 2,497 ....D7
Cherryfield • 1,183 ....H6
Chester • 442 ....F5
Chesterville • 1,012 ....C6
China 2,918 ....E7
China • 3,713 ....E7
Chisholm 1,653 ....C7
Clifton • 607 ....G6
Clinton 1,305 ....D6
Clinton • 1,485 ....D6
Columbia • 437 ....H6
Columbia Falls • 552 ....H6
Cooper • 124 ....H6
Coopers Mills 200 ....E7
Corea 375 ....H7
Corinna • 2,196 ....E6
Cornish • 1,178 ....B8
Cornville • 1,008 ....D6
Costigan 200 ....F5
Cranberry Isles • 189 ....G7
Crawford • 89 ....H5
Crescent Lake 325 ....C7
Criehaven F8
Crouseville 450 ....G2
Crystal • 303 ....G4
Cumberland Center 2,015 ....C8
Cumberland Center • 1,890 ....C8
Cundys Harbor 150 ....D8
Cushing • 988 ....E7
Cutler 400 ....J6
Cutler • 779 ....J6
Damariscotta • 1,811 ....E7
Damariscotta-Newcastle
1,567 ....E7
Danforth 650 ....H4
Danforth • 710 ....H4
Deblois • 73 ....H6
Dedham • 1,229 ....F6
Deer Isle 600 ....F7
Deer Isle • 1,829 ....F7
Denmark • 855 ....B8
Dennysville • 355 ....J6
Derby 300 ....E5
Detroit • 751 ....E6
Dexter 3,118 ....E5
Dexter • 2,650 ....E5
Dixfield 1,725 ....C6
Dixfield • 1,300 ....C6
Dixmont • 1,007 ....E6
Dover-Foxcroft▲ 2,974 ....E5
Dover-Foxcroft • 3,077 ....E5
Dresden • 1,332 ....D7
Dry Mills 700 ....C8
Dryden 675 ....C6
Dyer Brook • 243 ....G3
Eagle Lake 675 ....F1
Eagle Lake • 942 ....F1
East Andover 250 ....B6
East Baldwin 175 ....B8
East Blue Hill 150 ....G7
East Boothbay 800 ....D8
East Corinth 525 ....F5
East Dixfield 250 ....C6
East Eddington 200 ....F6
East Hiram 198 ....B8
East Holden 600 ....F6
East Lebanon 950 ....B9
East Limington 200 ....B8
East Livermore 500 ....C7

East Machias 850 ....J6
East Machias • 1,218 ....J6
East Madison 400 ....D6
East Millinocket 2,361 ....F4
East Millinocket • 2,075 ....F4
East Parsonfield 400 ....B8
East Peru 200 ....C7
East Poland 200 ....C7
East Stoneham 300 ....B7
East Sullivan 496 ....G6
East Vassalboro 300 ....D7
East Waterboro 365 ....B8
East Wilton 650 ....C6
Easton • 1,291 ....H2
Eastport 1,965 ....K6
Eddington 250 ....F6
Eddington • 1,947 ....F6
Edgecomb • 993 ....D8
Edmunds 430 ....J6
Eliot • 5,329 ....B9
Ellsworth▲ 5,975 ....F6
Enfield 150 ....F5
Enfield • 1,476 ....F5
Etna • 977 ....E6
Eustis • 616 ....B5
Exeter • 937 ....E6
Fairbanks 400 ....C6
Fairfield 3,169 ....D6
Fairfield Center 975 ....D6
Falmouth 1,655 ....C8
Falmouth • 7,610 ....C8
Farmingdale 2,014 ....D7
Farmingdale • 2,070 ....D7
Farmington▲ 3,583 ....C6
Farmington • 4,197 ....C6
Farmington Falls 500 ....C6
Fayette • 855 ....C7
Five Islands 225 ....D8
Fort Fairfield 2,282 ....H2

Fort Fairfield • 1,729 ....H2
Fort Kent 2,375 ....F1
Fort Kent • 2,123 ....F1
Fort Kent Mills 200 ....F1
Foxcroft 2,974 ....E5
Frankfort • 1,020 ....F6
Franklin 350 ....G6
Franklin • 1,141 ....G6
Freedom • 593 ....E6
Freeport 1,906 ....C8
Freeport • 1,829 ....C8
Frenchboro • 44 ....G7
Frenchville 980 ....G1
Frenchville • 1,338 ....G1
Friendship 700 ....E7
Friendship • 1,099 ....E7
Fryeburg 1,644 ....A7
Fryeburg • 1,580 ....A7
Gardiner • 6,746 ....D7
Garland 300 ....E5
Garland • 1,064 ....E5
Georgetown 190 ....D8
Georgetown • 914 ....D8
Gilead • 204 ....B7
Glen Cove 250 ....E7
Glenburn • 3,198 ....F6
Goodwins Mills 340 ....B8
Goose Rocks Beach 200 ....C9
Gorham 4,052 ....C8
Gorham • 3,618 ....C8
Gouldsboro 498 ....H7
Gouldsboro • 1,986 ....H7
Grand Isle 600 ....G1
Grand Isle • 558 ....G1
Grand Lake Stream • 174 ....H5
Gray 525 ....C8
Gray • 5,904 ....C8
Great Pond • 59 ....G6
Greene • 3,661 ....C7
Greenville • 1,839 ....D5

Greenville 1,601 ....D5
Greenville Junction 650 ....D5
Guilford 1,235 ....E5
Guilford • 1,082 ....E5
Hallowell 2,534 ....D7
Hamlin • 204 ....H1
Hampden 3,538 ....F6
Hampden • 3,895 ....F6
Hampden Highlands 950 ....F6
Hancock • 1,757 ....G6
Hanover • 272 ....B7
Harmony 450 ....D6
Harmony • 838 ....D6
Harpswell • 5,012 ....D8
Harrington • 893 ....H6
Harrison • 1,951 ....B7
Hartford • 722 ....C7
Hartland 1,041 ....D6
Hartland • 1,038 ....D6
Haynesville • 243 ....G4
Hebron • 878 ....C7
Hermon • 3,755 ....F6
Highland Lake 600 ....B8
Hiram 175 ....B8
Hiram • 1,260 ....B8
Hodgdon • 1,257 ....H3
Hollis Center • 2,892 ....B8
Hope 175 ....E7
Hope • 1,017 ....E7
Houlton▲ 5,730 ....H3
Houlton • 5,627 ....H3
Howland 1,502 ....F5
Howland • 1,304 ....F5
Hudson • 1,048 ....F5
Hulls Cove 200 ....G7
Island Falls • 897 ....G3
Isle Au Haut • 57 ....F7
Islesboro 200 ....F7
Islesboro • 579 ....F7
Jackman 700 ....C4

Jackman • 920 ....C4
Jacksonville 200 ....J6
Jay 850 ....C7
Jay • 5,080 ....C7
Jefferson • 2,111 ....D7
Jonesboro • 585 ....J6
Jonesport 1,050 ....H6
Jonesport • 1,525 ....H6
Keegan 450 ....G1
Kenduskeag • 1,234 ....E6
Kennebunk 3,294 ....B9
Kennebunk • 4,206 ....B9
Kennebunkport 1,685 ....C9
Kennebunkport • 1,100 ....C9
Kennebunk Beach 200 ....C9
Kents Hill 300 ....D7
Kezar Falls 680 ....B8
Kingfield • 1,114 ....C6
Kingman 246 ....G4
Kingsbury • 13 ....D5
Kittery 5,465 ....B9
Kittery • 5,151 ....B9
Kittery Point 1,093 ....B9
Knox • 681 ....E6
Lagrange 250 ....F5
Lagrange • 509 ....F5
Lake View • 23 ....F5
Lamoine • 1,311 ....G6
Lee • 832 ....G5
Leeds • 1,669 ....C7
Levant • 1,627 ....F6
Lewiston 39,757 ....C7
Liberty 200 ....E7
Liberty • 790 ....E7
Lille 300 ....G1
Limerick • 1,688 ....B8
Limestone 1,334 ....H2
Limestone • 1,245 ....H2
Limington • 2,796 ....B8
Lincoln 3,524 ....G5

Lincoln • 3,399 ....G5
Lincoln Center 325 ....G5
Lincolnville 800 ....E7
Lincolnville • 1,809 ....E7
Lincolnville Center 200 ....E7
Linneus • 810 ....H3
Lisbon • 9,457 ....C7
Lisbon Falls 4,674 ....C7
Lisbon-Lisbon Center 1,865 ....C7
Litchfield • 2,650 ....D7
Little Deer Isle 475 ....F7
Little Falls-South Windham
1,715 ....C8
Littleton • 956 ....H3
Livermore 280 ....C7
Livermore • 1,950 ....C7
Livermore Falls 2,441 ....C7
Livermore Falls • 1,935 ....C7
Locke Mills 600 ....B7
Lovell 180 ....B7
Lovell • 888 ....B7
Lowell • 267 ....F5
Lubec 900 ....K6
Lubec • 1,853 ....K6
Ludlow • 430 ....G3
Machias • 1,277 ....J6
Machias • 1,773 ....J6
Machiasport 374 ....H6
Machiasport • 1,166 ....H6
Macwahoc • 114 ....G4
Madawaska 4,165 ....G1
Madawaska • 3,653 ....G1
Madison 2,788 ....D6
Madison • 2,956 ....D6
Madrid • 178 ....B6
Manchester • 2,099 ....D7
Mapleton • 1,853 ....G2
Mars Hill • 1,760 ....H2
Mars Hill-Blaine 1,717 ....H2
Masardis • 305 ....G3

(continued on following page)

Agriculture, Industry and Resources

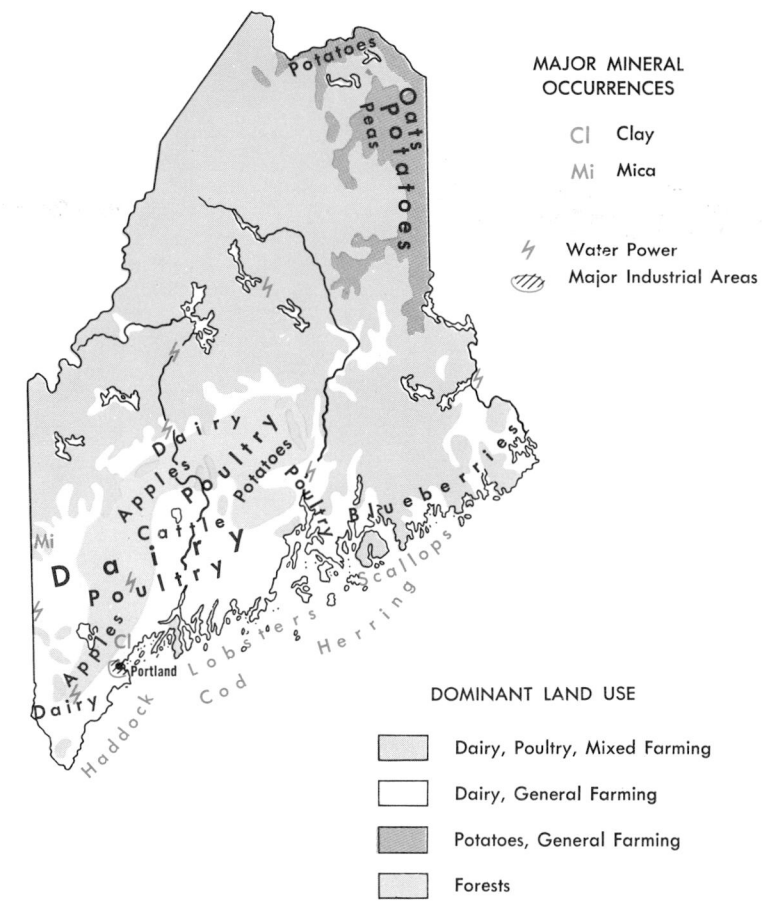

MAJOR MINERAL OCCURRENCES

Cl Clay

Mi Mica

⚡ Water Power
Major Industrial Areas

DOMINANT LAND USE

Dairy, Poultry, Mixed Farming

Dairy, General Farming

Potatoes, General Farming

Forests

Matinicus 66 ....F8
Mattawamkeag• 830....G5
Mechanic Falls 2,198....C7
Mechanic Falls• 2,388....C7
Meddybemps• 133....J5
Medford 194....F5
Medway• 1,922....G4
Mercer• 593....D6
Mexico 3,207....B6
Mexico• 2,302....B6
Milbridge• 1,305....H6
Milford 1,688....F6
Milford• 2,228....F6
Millinocket• 6,922....F4
Milo 2,255....F5
Milo• 2,129....F5
Minot 250....C7
Minot• 1,664....C7
Minturn 150....G7
Monhegan• 88....E8
Monmouth 500....D7
Monmouth• 3,353....C7
Monroe• 802....E6
Monson• 744....E5
Monticello• 872....H3
Montville• 877....E7
Moody 500....B9
Moose River• 233....C4
Morrill• 644....E7
Mount Desert 150....G7
Mount Desert• 1,899....G7
Mount Vernon• 1,362....D7
Naples• 2,860....B8
New Gloucester 400....C8
New Gloucester• 3,916....C8
New Harbor 850....E8
New Limerick• 524....G3
New Portland 300....C6
New Portland• 789....C6
New Sharon• 1,175....C6
New Sweden 175....G2
New Sweden• 715....G2
New Vineyard• 661....C6
Newburgh• 1,317....F6
Newcastle• 1,538....D7
Newcastle-Damariscotta 1,411....E7
Newfield 200....B8
Newfield• 1,042....B8
Newport 1,748....E6
Newport• 1,843....E6
Newry• 316....B6
Nobleboro• 1,455....D7
Norridgewock 1,318....D6
Norridgewock• 1,496....D6
North Anson 950....D6
North Belgrade 300....D7
North Berwick 1,436....B9
North Berwick• 1,568....B9
North Bridgton 300....B7
North Cutler 153....J6
North Fryeburg 250....B7
North Haven 400....F7
North Haven• 332....F7
North Jay 800....C6
North Limington 400....B8
North Livermore 250....C7
North Lubec 250....J6
North New Portland 500....C6
North Penobscot 403....F7
North Raymond 225....C8
North Turner 350....C7
North Vassalboro 950....D7
North Waldoboro 250....E7
North Waterboro 200....B8
North Waterford 390....B7
North Wayne 175....C7
North Whitefield 300....D7
North Windham 4,077....C8
North Yarmouth 500....C8
North Yarmouth• 2,429....C8
Northeast Harbor 800....G7
Northfield• 99....H6
Northport• 1,201....E7
Norway 2,653....B7
Norway• 3,023....B7
Oakfield• 846....G3
Oakland 3,387....D6
Oakland• 3,510....D6
Ocean Park 200....C9
Ogunquit 974....B9
Olamon 150....F5
Old Orchard Beach 6,023....C9
Old Orchard Beach• 7,789....C9
Old Town 8,317....F6
Oquossoc 150....B6
Orient• 157....H4
Orland 200....F6
Orland• 1,805....F6
Orono 9,891....F6
Orono• 9,789....F6
Orrington 250....F6
Orrington• 3,309....F6
Orrs Island 600....D8
Otisfield• 1,136....B7
Otter Creek 260....G7
Owls Head• 1,574....F7
Oxbow• 69....G3
Oxford 550....B7
Oxford• 1,284....B7
Palermo• 1,021....E7
Palmyra• 1,867....E6
Paris• 4,492....B7
Parkman• 790....D5
Passadumkeag• 428....F5
Patten 1,057....F4
Patten• 1,256....F4
Pejepscot 200....D8
Pemaquid 200....E8
Pembroke 300....J6
Pembroke• 852....J6
Penobscot 150....F7
Penobscot• 1,131....F7
Perham• 395....G2
Perry• 758....J6
Peru• 1,541....C6
Phillips• 1,148....C6

Phippsburg 1,527....D8
Phippsburg• 1,815....D8
Pine Point 650....C8
Pittsfield 3,117....E6
Pittsfield• 3,222....E6
Pittston• 2,444....D7
Plymouth• 1,152....E6
Poland 500....C7
Poland• 4,342....C7
Port Clyde 400....E8
Portage• 562....G2
Porter 225....B8
Porter• 1,301....B8
Portland▲ 64,358....C8
Pownal• 1,262....C8
Prentiss• 245....G5
Presque Isle 10,550....H2
Princeton• 973....H5
Prospect• 542....F6
Prospect Harbor 445....H7
Randolph• 1,949....D7
Rangeley 900....B6
Rangeley• 103....B6
Raymond 550....B8
Raymond• 3,311....B8
Readfield 300....D7
Readfield• 2,033....D7
Red Beach 210....J5
Richmond 1,578....D7
Richmond• 1,775....D7
Richmond Corner 200....D7
Ripley• 445....E5
Robbinston 200....J5
Robbinston• 495....J5
Robinsons 160....H3
Rockland▲ 7,972....E7
Rockport 875....E7
Rockport• 2,854....E7
Rockville 250....E7
Rockwood 265....D4
Rome• 758....D6
Roque Bluffs• 234....H6
Round Pond 400....E8
Roxbury• 437....B6
Rumford 6,256....B6
Rumford• 5,419....B6
Rumford Center 325....B7
Rumford Point 320....B6
Sabattus 1,234....C7
Sabattus• 3,696....C7
Saco 15,181....C8
Saint Agatha• 1,035....G1
Saint Albans• 1,400....E6
Saint David 915....G1
Saint Francis• 839....E1
Saint George 700....E7
Saint George• 1,948....E7
Saint John• 322....F1
Sandy Point 350....F7
Sanford 10,268....B9
Sanford• 10,296....B9
Sangerville• 1,398....E5
Scarborough 2,280....C8
Scarborough• 2,586....C8
Seal Cove 215....G7
Seal Harbor 500....G7
Searsmont 400....E7
Searsmont• 938....E7
Searsport 1,348....F7
Searsport• 1,151....F7
Sebago Lake 800....B8
Sebec• 554....E5
Seboeis• 40....F5
Sedgwick• 905....F7
Shapleigh• 1,911....B8
Shawmut 500....D6
Sheepscott 150....D7
Sheridan 300....F2
Sherman 1,021....G4
Sherman• 1,027....G4
Sherman Mills 600....G4
Sherman Station 650....F4
Shirley Mills 242....D5
Shirley Mills• 208....D5
Sidney• 2,593....D7
Sinclair• 264....G1
Skowhegan▲ 6,517....D6
Skowhegan• 6,990....D6
Smithfield• 665....D6
Smyrna Mills• 354....G3
Soldier Pond 500....F1
Solon• 916....D6
Somerville• 458....D7
Somesville (Mount Desert) 150....D7
Sorrento• 295....G7
South Berwick 2,120....B9
South Berwick• 5,877....B9
South Bridgton 373....B8
South Bristol• 825....D8
South Casco 750....B8
South China 225....D7
South Eliot 3,112....B9
South Harpswell 650....C8
South Hiram 350....B8
South Hope 200....E7
South La Grange 150....F5
South Lebanon 200....A9
South Lincoln 150....F5
South Monmouth 400....D7
South Orrington 400....F6
South Paris▲ 2,320....C7
South Penobscot 150....F7
South Portland 23,163....C8
South Sanford 3,929....B9
South Thomaston• 1,227....E7
South Waldoboro 300....E7
South Waterford 300....B7
South Windham (Little Falls-South Windham)....C8
Southport 400....D8
Southport• 645....D8
Southwest Harbor 1,052....G7
Southwest Harbor• 1,952....G7
Springfield• 406....G5
Springvale 3,542....B9
Stacyville 155....F4

Stacyville• 480....F4
Standish 700....B8
Standish• 7,678....B8
Starks• 508....D6
Steep Falls 500....B8
Stetson• 847....E6
Steuben 190....H6
Steuben• 1,084....H6
Stillwater 700....F6
Stockholm• 286....G1
Stockton Springs 500....F7
Stockton Springs• 1,383....F7
Stonington• 1,252....F7
Stow• 283....A7
Stratton 600....B5
Strong• 1,217....C6
Sullivan• 1,118....G6
Sumner• 761....C7
Sunset 165....F7
Surry• 1,004....F7
Swans Island• 348....G7
Swanville• 1,130....E6
Sweden• 222....B7
Temple• 560....C6
Tenants Harbor 900....E8
Thomaston 2,348....E7
Thomaston• 2,445....E7
Thorndike• 702....E6
Topsfield• 235....H5
Topsham 4,657....D8
Topsham• 6,147....D8
Tremont 175....G7
Tremont• 1,324....G7
Trenton• 1,060....G7
Trevett 400....D8
Troy• 802....E6
Turner 400....C7
Turner• 4,315....C7
Union 300....E7
Union• 1,989....E7
Unity• 36....E6
Upper Frenchville 405....G1
Upton• 70....B6
Van Buren 3,282....G1
Van Buren• 2,759....G1
Vanceboro• 201....J4
Vassalboro• 3,679....D7
Veazie• 1,633....F6
Vienna• 417....D6
Vinalhaven• 1,072....F7
Waite• 119....H5
Waldo• 626....E7
Waldoboro 1,195....E7
Waldoboro• 1,420....E7
Walnut Hill 400....C8
Waltham• 276....G6
Warren 770....E7
Warren• 3,192....E7
Washburn 1,221....G2
Washburn• 1,880....G2
Washington• 1,185....E7
Waterboro 700....B8
Waterboro• 4,510....B8
Waterford• 1,299....B7
Waterville 17,173....D6
Wayne 175....D7
Wayne• 1,029....D7

Weeks Mills 235....E7
Weld• 430....C6
Wellington• 270....D5
Wells 950....B9
Wells• 7,778....B9
Wells Beach 600....B9
Wesley• 146....H6
West Baldwin 198....B8
West Bath• 1,716....D8
West Bethel 160....B7
West Brooksville 156....F7
West Buxton 185....B8
West Enfield 609....F5
West Farmington 700....C6
West Forks• 63....D5
West Franklin 350....G6
West Gouldsboro 225....G7
West Jonesport 400....H6
West Kennebunk 750....B9
West Lubec 275....J6
West Minot 400....C7
West Newfield 300....B8
West Paris• 1,514....B7
West Peru 700....C7
West Poland 250....C7
West Rockport 350....E7
West Scarborough 500....C8
West Tremont 250....G7
Westbrook 16,121....C8
Westfield• 589....G2
Weston• 207....H4
Whitefield 550....D7
Whitefield• 1,931....D7
Whiting• 407....J6
Whitneyville• 241....H6
Willimantic• 170....E5
Wilton 4,382....C6
Wilton• 2,453....C6
Windsor• 1,895....D7
Winn 250....G5
Winn• 479....G5
Winslow 5,903....D6
Winslow• 5,436....D6
Winter Harbor• 1,157....G7
Winterport 1,126....F6
Winterport• 1,274....F6
Winterville• 217....F2
Winthrop 3,264....C7
Winthrop• 2,819....C7
Wiscasset 975....D7
Wiscasset• 1,233....D7
Woodland• 1,287....H5
Woolwich• 2,570....D8
Wyman Dam 300....D5
Yarmouth 2,981....C8
Yarmouth• 3,338....C8
York 4,530....B9
York Beach 900....B9
York Harbor 2,555....B9
York• 9,818....B9

OTHER FEATURES

Abraham (mt.)....C5
Acadia Nat'l Park....G7
Allagash (lake)....D3
Allagash (riv.)....E2
Androscoggin (riv.)....C7
Aroostook (riv.)....G2
Attean (pond)....C4
Baker (lake)....D3
Baskahegan (lake)....H5
Bear (riv.)....B6
Big (brook)....E2
Big (lake)....H5
Big Black (riv.)....D2
Bigelow (bight)....C9
Big Spencer (mt.)....E4
Black (pond)....D3
Blue (mt.)....C6
Blue Hill (bay)....G7
Bog (lake)....H6
Brassua (lake)....D4
Casco (bay)....C8
Cathance (lake)....J6
Caucomgomoc (lake)....D3
Center (pond)....E5
Chamberlain (lake)....E3
Chemquasabamticook (lake)....D3
Chesuncook (lake)....E3
Chiputneticook (lakes)....H4
Clayton (lake)....D2
Clifford (lake)....H5
Cold Stream (pond)....G5
Crawford (lake)....H5
Cross (isl.)....J6
Cross (lake)....G1
Cupsuptic (riv.)....B5
Dead (riv.)....C5
Deer (isl.)....F7
Duck (isls.)....G7
Eagle (lake)....E3
Eagle (lake)....F1
East Machias (riv.)....H6
East Musquash (lake)....H5
Elizabeth (cape)....C8
Ellis (pond)....B6
Ellis (riv.)....B6
Embden (pond)....D6
Endless (lake)....F5
Englishman (bay)....J6
Eskutassis (pond)....G5
Fifth (lake)....H5
Fish (riv.)....F2
Fish River (lake)....F2
Flagstaff (lake)....C5
Fourth (lake)....H5
Frenchman (bay)....G7
Gardner (lake)....J6
Georges (isls.)....E8
Graham (lake)....G6
Grand (lake)....H4
Grand Falls (lake)....H5
Grand Lake Seboeis (lake)....F3
Grand Manan (chan.)....K6
Great Moose (lake)....D6
Great Wass (isl.)....J7
Green (isl.)....F8
Harrington (lake)....E4
Haut (isl.)....G7
Indian (pond)....D4
Islesboro (isl.)....F7
Jo-Mary (lakes)....E4
Katahdin (mt.)....F4

Kennebec (riv.)....D7
Kezar (lake)....B7
Kezar (pond)....B7
Kingsbury (pond)....D5
Little Black (riv.)....E1
Little Madawaska (riv.)....G2
Lobster (lake)....E4
Long (lake)....B7
Long (lake)....E2
Long (lake)....G1
Long (pond)....C4
Long (pond)....D6
Long (pond)....E5
Long Falls (dam)....C5
Longfellow (mts.)....B6
Loon (lake)....D3
Loring A.F.B. 7,829....H2
Lower Roach (pond)....E4
Lower Sysladobsis (lake)....G5
Machias (bay)....J6
Machias (riv.)....F2
Machias (riv.)....H6
Machias Seal (isl.)....J7
Madagascal (pond)....G5
Marshall (isl.)....G7
Matinicus Rock (isl.)....F8
Mattamiscontis (lake)....F4
Mattawamkeag (lake)....G4
Mattawamkeag (riv.)....G4
Meddybemps (lake)....J5
Metinic (isl.)....E8
Millinocket (lake)....F3
Millinocket (lake)....F4
Molunkus (lake)....G4
Monhegan (isl.)....E8
Moose (pond)....B7
Moose (riv.)....D4
Moosehead (lake)....D4
Mooseleuk (stream)....F2
Mooselookmeguntic (lake)....B6
Mopang (lake)....H6
Mount Desert (isl.)....G7
Mount Desert Rock (isl.)....G8
Moxie (lake)....D5
Munsungan (lake)....E3
Muscongus (bay)....E8
Musquacook (lakes)....E2
Nahmakanta (lake)....E4
Nicatous (lake)....G5
Nollesemic (lake)....F4
Old (stream)....H6
Onawa (lake)....E5
Parlin (pond)....C4
Parmachenee (lake)....B5
Passamaquoddy (bay)....J5
Passamaquoddy Ind. Res....J6
Pemadumcook (lake)....E4
Penobscot (bay)....F7
Penobscot (lake)....C4
Penobscot (riv.)....F5
Penobscot Ind. Res....F6
Pierce (pond)....C5
Piscataquis (riv.)....B9
Piscataquis (riv.)....E5
Pleasant (lake)....E3
Pleasant (lake)....G3
Pleasant (lake)....H5

Pleasant (riv.)....H6
Pocomoonshine (lake)....H5
Portage (lake)....F2
Presque Isle A.F.B....G2
Priestly (lake)....E2
Pushaw (lake)....F6
Ragged (isl.)....F8
Ragged (lake)....E4
Rainbow (lake)....E4
Rangeley (lake)....B6
Richardson (lakes)....B6
Rocky (lake)....J6
Round (pond)....E2
Rowe (lake)....F2
Saco (riv.)....B8
Saint Croix (riv.)....J5
Saint Croix Island Nat'l Mon....J5
Saint Francis (riv.)....E
Saint Froid (lake)....F2
Saint John (pond)....D3
Saint John (riv.)....G
Salmon Falls (riv.)....B9
Sandy (riv.)....C6
Schoodic (lake)....F5
Scraggly (lake)....F3
Scraggly (lake)....H5
Seal (isl.)....F8
Sebago (lake)....B8
Sebasticook (lake)....E6
Seboeis (lake)....F5
Seboeis (riv.)....F3
Seboomook (lake)....D4
Shallow (lake)....E3
Small (cape)....D8
Sourdnahunk (lake)....F3
Spencer (pond)....D4
Spencer (stream)....C
Spider (lake)....E
Squa Pan (lake)....G
Square (lake)....G
Sunday (riv.)....B
Swift (riv.)....B
Sysladobsis, Lower (lake)....G
Third (lake)....H
Twin (lakes)....F
Umbagog (lake)....A
Umcalcus (lake)....G
Umsaskis (lake)....E
Union, West Branch (riv.)....G
Vinalhaven (isl.)....F
Wassataquoik (stream)....F
Webb (lake)....C
Webster (brook)....E
West Grand (lake)....H
West Musquash (lake)....H
West Quoddy (head)....K
Wilson (ponds)....E
Winnecook (lake)....E
Wooden Ball (isl.)....F
Wyman (lake)....C
Wytopitlock (lake)....G

▲County seat.
•Population of town or township.

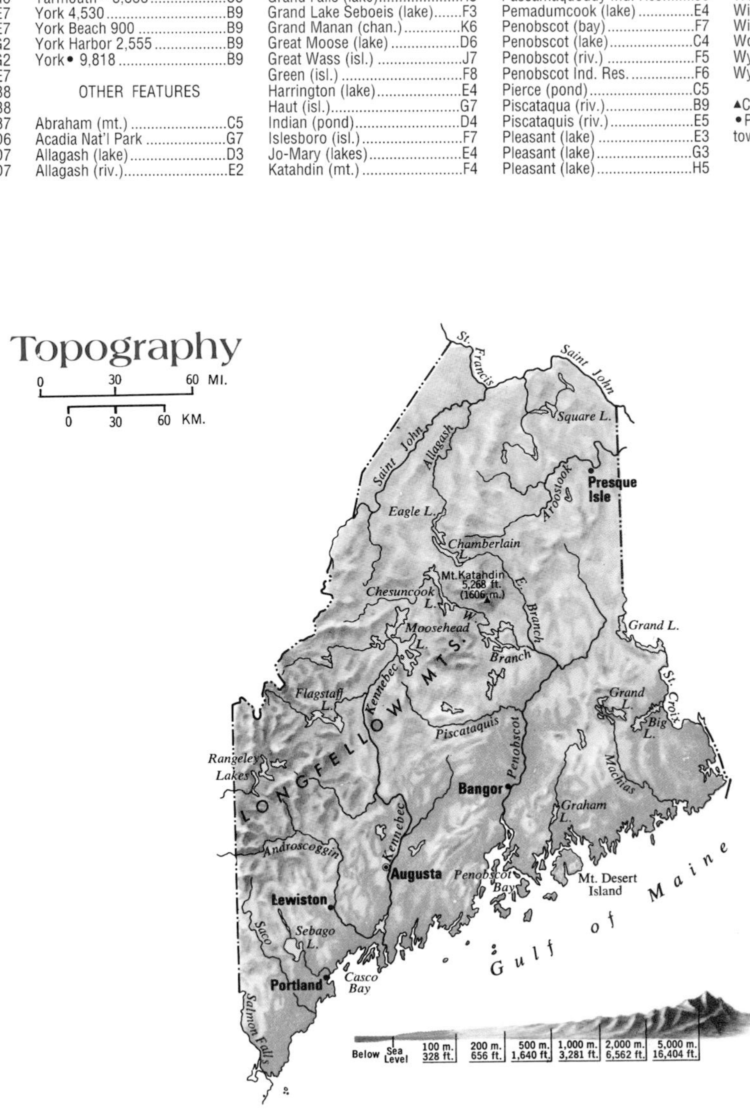
Topography
0 30 60 MI.
0 30 60 KM.
St. Francis
Saint John
Square L.
Presque Isle
Allagash
Saint John
Aroostook
Eagle L.
Chamberlain
Mt. Katahdin 5,268 ft. (1606 m.)
Chesuncook L.
E. Branch
W. Branch
Moosehead L.
Grand L.
Flagstaff
Kennebec
LONGFELLOW MTS.
Piscataquis
Penobscot
Grand L.
St. Croix
Big L.
Rangeley Lakes
Machias
Bangor
Graham L.
Kennebec
Androscoggin
Augusta
Penobscot Bay
Mt. Desert Island
Gulf of Maine
Lewiston
Saco
Sebago L.
Portland
Casco Bay
Salmon Falls
Below Sea Level
100 m. 328 ft.
200 m. 656 ft.
500 m. 1,640 ft.
1,000 m. 3,281 ft.
2,000 m. 6,562 ft.
5,000 m. 16,404 ft.

Maine

SCALE
0 5 10   20   30   40 MI.

0 5 10   20   30   40 KM.

State Capitals .... ⊛
County Seats .... ◉
Major Limited Access Hwys. _____

Scale 1:1,680,000

© Copyright HAMMOND INCORPORATED, Maplewood, N.J.

MARYLAND

COUNTIES

Allegany 74,946 ....C2
Anne Arundel 427,239 .....M4
Baltimore 692,134 ....M3
Baltimore (city county)
736,775 ....M3
Calvert 51,372 ....M6
Caroline 27,035 ....P5
Carroll 123,372 ....K2
Cecil 71,347 ....P2
Charles 101,154 ....K6
Dorchester 30,236 ....O7
Fredrick 114,792 ....J3
Garrett 28,138 ....A2
Harford 182,132 ....N2
Howard 187,323 ....L4
Kent 17,842 ....O3
Montgomery 757,027 ....J4
Prince Georges 665,071 .....L5
Queen Annes 25,508 ....P4
Saint Marys 59,895 ....M7
Somerset 23,440 ....R8
Talbot 30,549 ....O5
Washington 121,393 ....G2
Wicomico 74,339 ....R7
Worcester 35,028 ....S8

CITIES and TOWNS

Aberdeen 13,087 ....O2
Abingdon 500 ....N3
Accident 349 ....A2
Accokeek 4,477 ....L6
Adamstown 300 ....H3
Allen 250 ....R7
Annapolis (cap.) 33,187 ......M5
Annapolis Junction 775 ......M4
Aquasco 950 ....L6
Arbutus 19,750 ....M3
Ardmore 500 ....G4
Aspen Hill 45,494 ....K4
Baltimore 736,014 ....M3
Barclay 170 ....P4
Barnesville 170 ....J4
Barstow 500 ....M6
Barton 530 ....B2
Bayview 200 ....P2
Beaver Creek 290 ....H2
Bel Air▲ 8,860 ....N2
Bel Alton 800 ....L7
Bellevue 300 ....O6
Beltsville 14,476 ....G3
Benedict 850 ....M6
Berlin 2,616 ....T7
Berwyn Heights 2,952 ....G4
Bethesda 62,936 ....E4
Bethlehem 500 ....P6
Betterton 360 ....O3
Bishops Head 250 ....O7
Bishopville 300 ....T7
Bivalve 175 ....P7
Bladensburg 8,064 ....G4
Bloomington 486 ....B3
Boonsboro 2,445 ....H2
Borden Shaft 200 ....B2
Boring 290 ....L2
Boulevard Heights 500 ....F5
Bowens 250 ....M6
Bowie 37,589 ....L4
Boyds 300 ....J4
Bozman 700 ....N5
Brandywine 1,406 ....L6
Brentwood 3,005 ....F4
Brooklyn Park 10,987 ....M4
Brownsville 190 ....H3
Brunswick 5,117 ....H3
Buckeystown 400 ....J3
Burkittsville 194 ....H3
Bushwood 750 ....L7
Butler 200 ....M2
Cabin John (Cabin John-
Brookmont) 5,341 ....D4
California 7,626 ....M7
Calvert 1,728 ....O2
Calverton 12,046 ....L4
Cambridge▲ 11,514 ....O6
Camp Springs 16,392 ....G6
Cape Saint Claire 7,878 ......N4
Capitol Heights 3,633 ....G5
Cardiff 475 ....N2
Carmody Hills (Carmody Hills-
Pepper Mill Village) 4,815 ..G5
Cascade (Cascade-Highfield)
1,096 ....J2
Castleton 750 ....N2
Catoctin Furnace 516 ....J2
Catonsville 35,233 ....M3
Cavetown 1,533 ....H2
Cecilton 489 ....P3
Cedar Grove 300 ....K4
Cedar Heights G5
Cedarville 200 ....L6
Centreville▲ 2,097 ....O4
Chance 600 ....P8
Chaptico 300 ....M7
Charlestown 578 ....P2
Charlotte Hall 1,992 ....M7
Chase 300 ....N3
Cheltenham 950 ....L6
Cherry Hill 250 ....P2
Chesapeake Beach 2,403 .....N6
Chesapeake City 735 ....P2
Chester 4,005 ....N5
Chestertown▲ 3,300 ....O4
Cheverly 6,023 ....G4
Chevy Chase 2,675 ....E4
Chevy Chase Section Four
2,903 ....E4
Chewsville 300 ....H2
Chillum 31,309 ....F4
Church Hill 481 ....O4
Churchville 500 ....N2
Claiborne 225 ....N5
Clarksburg 400 ....J4

Clarksville 500 ....L4
Clear Spring 415 ....G2
Clements 800 ....L7
Cockeysville 18,668 ....M3
College Park 21,927 ....G4
Colesville 18,819 ....K4
Colmar Manor 1,249 ....F4
Coltons Point 600 ....M8
Columbia 75,883 ....L4
Compton 500 ....M7
Cooksville 497 ....K3
Coral Hills 11,032 ....G5
Cordova 365 ....O5
Corriganville 1,020 ....C2
Cottage City 1,236 ....F4
Cox Station (Bel Alton) 800 ...L7
Creagerstown 240 ....J2
Crellin 275 ....A3
Cresaptown 4,586 ....C2
Crisfield 2,880 ....P9
Crofton 12,781 ....M4
Crownsville 1,514 ....M4
Crumpton 350 ....P4

Cumberland▲ 23,706 ....D2
Damascus 9,817 ....K3
Dameron 759 ....N8
Dames Quarter 250 ....P8
Dargan 352 ....H3
Darlington 850 ....N2
Darnestown 950 ....J4
Davidsonville 250 ....M5
Deal Island 800 ....P8
Deale 4,151 ....M5
Defense Heights G4
Delmar 1,430 ....R7
Denton▲ 2,977 ....P5
Derwood 413 ....K4
Dickerson 530 ....J4
District Heights 6,704 ....G5
Doubs 200 ....J3
Downsville 255 ....G2
Drayden 400 ....N8
Dublin 366 ....N2
Dundalk 65,800 ....N3
Eagle Harbor 38 ....M6
East New Market 153 ....P6

Easton▲ 9,372 ....O5
Eden 800 ....R7
Edgemere 9,226 ....N4
Edgewood 23,903 ....N3
Edmonston 851 ....F4
Eldersburg 9,720 ....L3
Elk Mills 550 ....P2
Elk Neck 700 ....P2
Elkridge 12,953 ....M4
Elkton▲ 9,073 ....P2
Ellerslie 950 ....A2
Ellicott City▲ 41,396 ....L3
Emmitsburg 1,688 ....J2
Essex 40,872 ....N3
Ewell 595 ....O9
Fair Hill 250 ....P2
Fairlee 300 ....O4
Fairmount 1,238 ....P8
Fairmount Heights 1,616 .....G5
Fallston 5,730 ....N2
Federalsburg 2,365 ....P6
Ferndale 16,355 ....M4
Finksburg 950 ....L3

Fishing Creek 595 ....N7
Flintstone 400 ....D2
Forest Heights 2,859 ....F5
Forest Hill 450 ....N2
Forestville 16,731 ....G5
Fort Foote 700 ....F6
Fort Howard 1,745 ....G2
Foxville 175 ....H2
Frederick▲ 40,148 ....J3
Freeland 500 ....N2
Friendship 600 ....M6
Friendsville 577 ....A2
Frizzellburg 300 ....K2
Frostburg 8,075 ....C2
Fruitland 3,511 ....R7
Funkstown 1,136 ....H2
Gaithersburg 39,542 ....K4
Galena 324 ....P3
Galesfown 123 ....P6
Galesville 600 ....M5
Gamber 500 ....L3
Gambrills 460 ....M4
Garrett Park 884 ....E3

Garrison 5,045 ....L3
Germantown 41,145 ....J4
Girdletree 350 ....S8
Glen Arm 350 ....N3
Glen Burnie 37,305 ....M4
Glen Echo 234 ....E4
Glenarden 5,025 ....G4
Glenelg 400 ....L3
Glyndon L3
Goldsboro 185 ....P4
Good Luck G4
Graceham 300 ....J2
Granite 950 ....L3
Grantsville 505 ....B2
Grasonville 2,439 ....O5
Green Haven 14,416 ....N4
Greenbelt 21,096 ....G4
Greenmount 325 ....J2
Greensboro 1,441 ....P5
Hagerstown▲ 35,445 ....G2
Halfway 8,873 ....G2
Hampstead 2,608 ....L2
Hancock 1,926 ....D2
Hanover 500 ....M4

Harmans 400 ....M4
Harney 270 ....K2
Havre de Grace 8,952 ....N2
Hebron 665 ....R7
Helen 300 ....L3
Henryton 300 ....L3
Hereford 680 ....M2
Hillandale 10,318 ....F4
Hillcrest Heights 17,136 ......F5
Hillsboro 164 ....P5
Hollywood 500 ....M7
Hoopersville 180 ....L6
Huntingtown 450 ....M6
Hurlock 1,706 ....P6
Hyattsville 13,864 ....F4
Indian Head▲3,543 ....K6
Island Creek 400 ....M4
Issue 250 ....L7
Jacksonville 172 ....M2
Jarrettsville 2,148 ....M2
Jefferson 300 ....J3
Jennings 172 ....B2
Johnsville 200 ....K2

(continued)

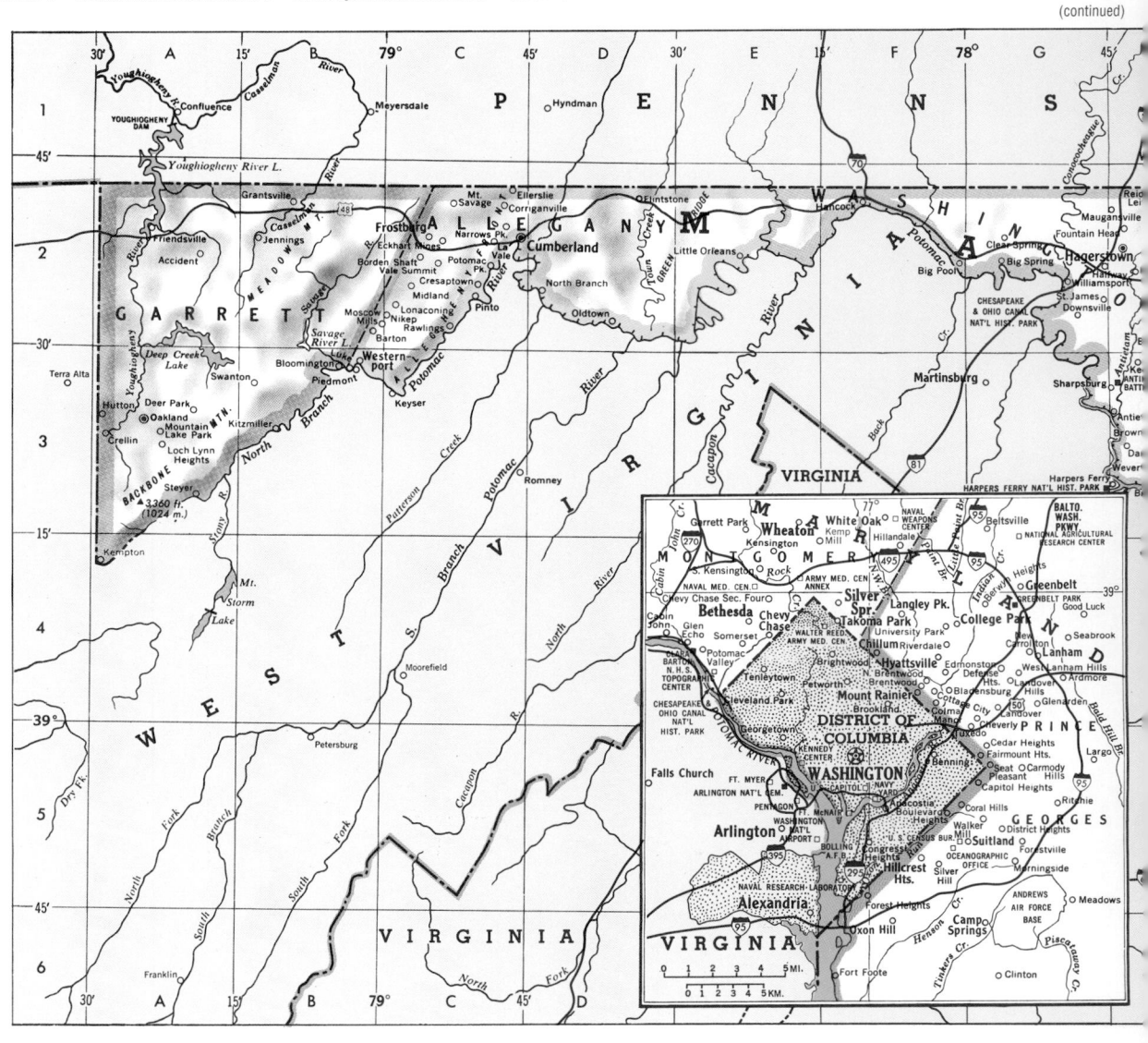

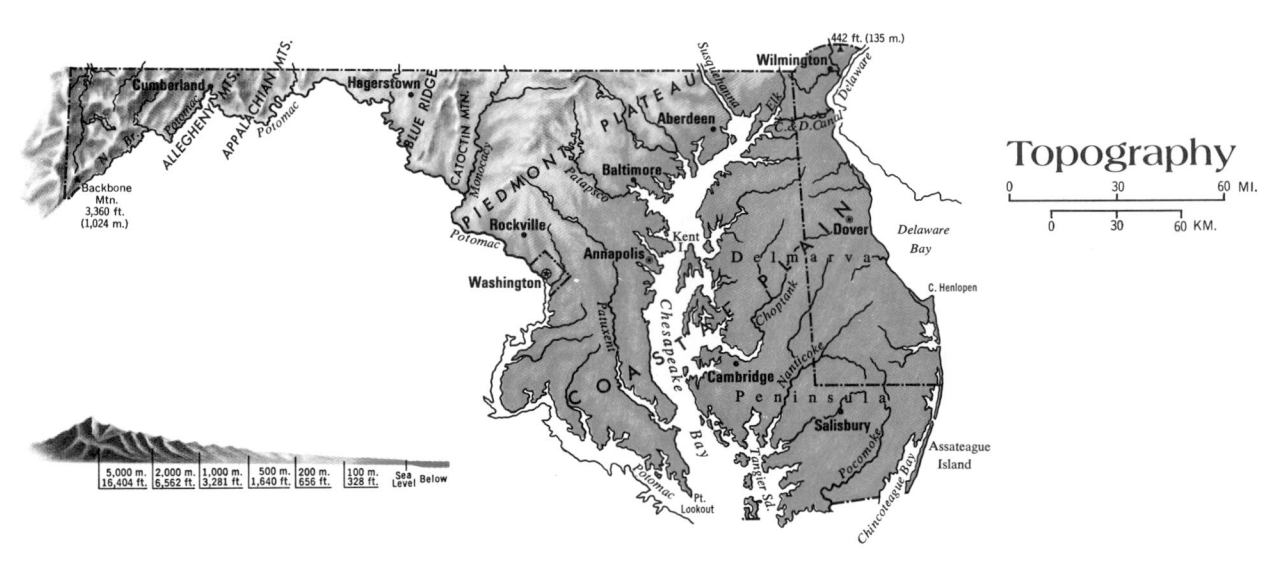

Topography

MARYLAND

AREA 10,460 sq. mi. (27,091 sq. km.)
POPULATION 4,798,622
CAPITAL Annapolis
LARGEST CITY Baltimore
HIGHEST POINT Backbone Mtn. 3,360 ft. (1024 m.)
SETTLED IN 1634
ADMITTED TO UNION April 28, 1788
POPULAR NAME Old Line State; Free State
STATE FLOWER Black-eyed Susan
STATE BIRD Baltimore Oriole

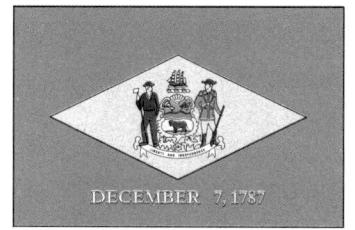

DECEMBER 7, 1787

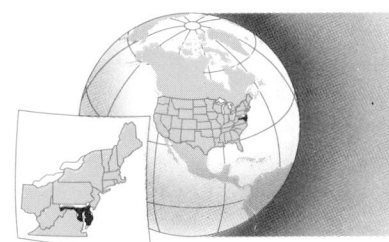

DELAWARE

AREA 2,044 sq. mi. (5,294 sq. km.)
POPULATION 668,696
CAPITAL Dover
LARGEST CITY Wilmington
HIGHEST POINT Ebright Road 442 ft. (135 m.)

SETTLED IN 1627
ADMITTED TO UNION December 7, 1787
POPULAR NAME First State; Diamond State
STATE FLOWER Peach Blossom
STATE BIRD Blue Hen Chicken

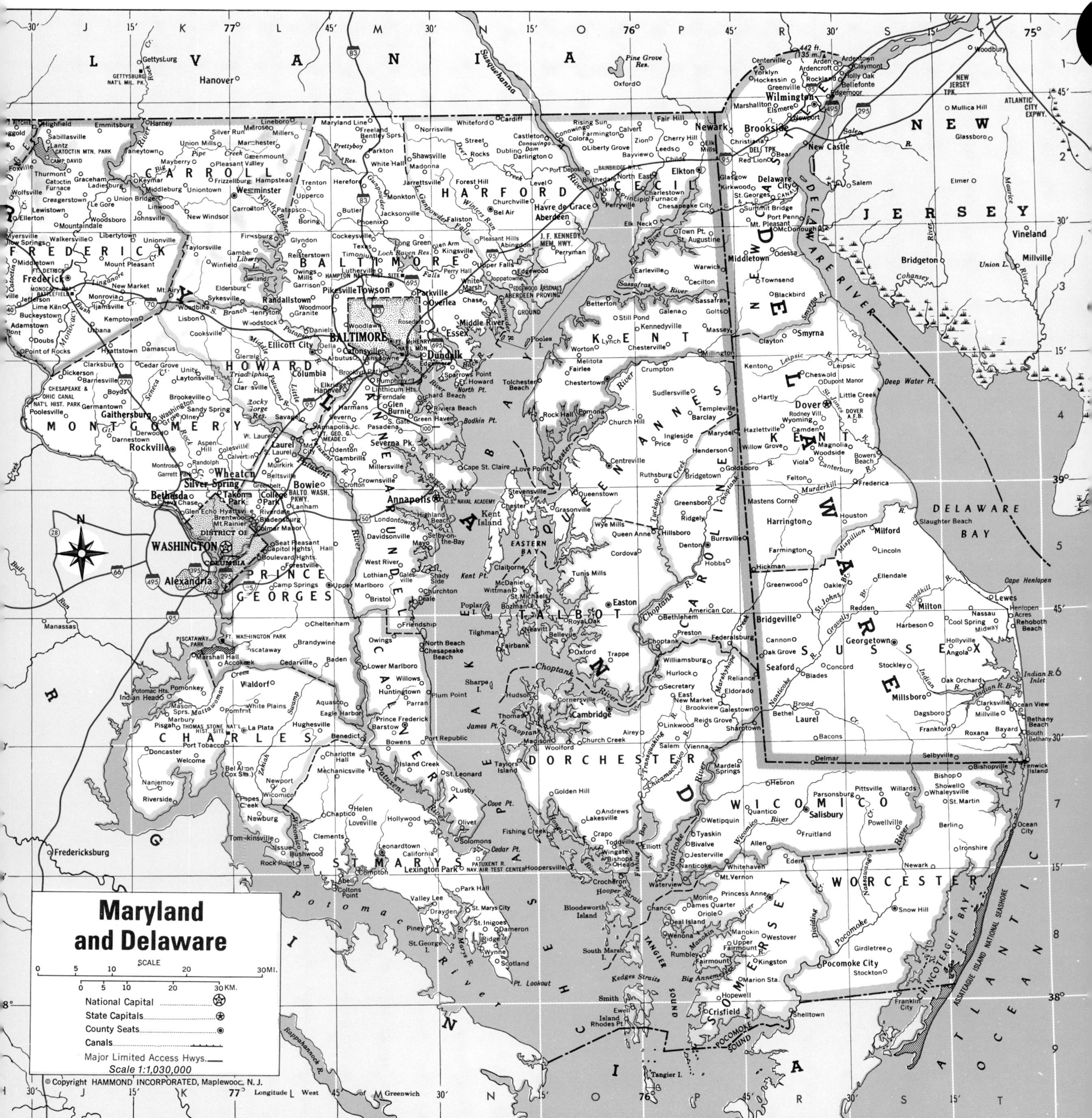

Maryland and Delaware

SCALE
0 5 10   20   30 MI.
0 5 10 20   30 KM.

National Capital .... ⊛
State Capitals .... ⊛
County Seats .... ◉
Canals ....

Major Limited Access Hwys. _____
Scale 1:1,030,000

© Copyright HAMMOND INCORPORATED, Maplewood, N.J.

Joppatowne 11,084 ... N3
Keedysville 464 ... H3
Kemp Mill ... F3
Kemptown 250 ... J3
Kennedyville 225 ... P3
Kensington 1,713 ... E4
Keymar 200 ... K2
Kingsville 3,550 ... N3
Kitzmiller 275 ... B3
Knoxville 500 ... H3
La Plata▲ 5,841 ... L6
La Vale (La Vale-Narrows Park) 4,694 ... C2
Landover 5,052 ... G4
Landover Hills 2,074 ... G4
Langley Park 17,474 ... F4
Lanham (Lanham-Seabrook) 16,792 ... G4
Lansdowne (Lansdowne-Baltimore Highlands) 15,509 ... M3
Largo 9,475 ... G5
Laurel 19,438 ... L4
Laytonsville 248 ... K4
Le Gore 500 ... J2
Leeds 177 ... P2
Leitersburg 350 ... H2
Leonardtown▲ 1,475 ... M7
Level 250 ... O2
Lewistown 600 ... J2
Lexington Park 9,943 ... M7
Libertytown 400 ... J3
Lime Kiln 230 ... J3
Lineboro 300 ... L2
Linkwood 250 ... P6
Linthicum Heights 7,547 ... M4
Little Orleans 600 ... E2
Loch Lynn Heights 461 ... A3
Lonaconing 1,122 ... C2
Londontowne 6,992 ... M5
Long Green 1,626 ... M3
Loveville 600 ... M7
Luke 184 ... B3
Lutherville (Lutherville-Timonium) 16,442 ... M3
Madison 350 ... O6
Manchester 2,810 ... L2
Manokin 270 ... P8
Mapleville 200 ... H2
Marbury 1,244 ... K6
Mardela Springs 360 ... P7
Marion Station 400 ... R8
Marshall Hall 325 ... K6
Marydel 143 ... P4
Maryland City 6,813 ... L4
Maryland Line 281 ... M2
Massey 280 ... P3
Maugansville 1,707 ... H2
Mayo 2,537 ... M5
McDaniel 275 ... N5
Meadows 200 ... G5
Mechanicsville 784 ... M7
Middle River 24,616 ... N3
Middleburg 200 ... K2
Middletown 1,834 ... J3
Midland 574 ... C2
Millersville 380 ... M4
Millington 409 ... P3
Monkton 307 ... M2
Montrose ... K4
Morningside 930 ... G5
Moscow Mills 260 ... B2
Mount Airy 3,730 ... K3
Mount Pleasant 400 ... J3
Mount Rainier 7,954 ... F4
Mount Savage 1,640 ... C2
Mount Vernon 900 ... P8
Mountain Lake Park 1,938 ... A3
Mountaindale 400 ... J2
Muirkirk 950 ... L4
Myersville 464 ... H3
Nanjemoy 238 ... K7
Nanticoke 450 ... P7
Narrows Park (Narrows Park-La Vale) ... C2
Neavitt 300 ... N6
New Carrollton 12,002 ... G4
New Market 328 ... J3
New Windsor 757 ... K2
Newark 900 ... S7
Newburg 550 ... L7
Nikep 200 ... C2
North Beach 1,173 ... N6
North Brentwood 512 ... F4
North East 1,913 ... P2
North Potomac 18,456 ... K4
Oakland 2,242 ... L3
Oakland▲ 1,741 ... A3
Ocean City 5,146 ... T7
Odenton 12,833 ... M4
Oella 600 ... L3
Oldtown 200 ... D2
Olivet 200 ... N7
Olney 23,019 ... K4
Orchard Beach 200 ... M4
Overlea 12,137 ... N3
Owings 9,474 ... M6
Owings Mills 9,526 ... L3
Oxford 699 ... O6
Oxon Hill 35,794 ... F6
Park Hall 775 ... N8
Parkton 290 ... M2
Parkville 31,617 ... M3
Parran 200 ... M6
Parsonsburg 200 ... R7
Pasadena 10,012 ... M4
Perry Hall 22,723 ... N3
Perryman 2,160 ... O3
Perryville 2,456 ... O2
Petersville 320 ... H3
Phoenix 165 ... M2
Pikesville 24,815 ... M3
Piney Point 950 ... M8
Pinto 175 ... C2
Piscataway 500 ... L6
Pisgah 650 ... K6
Pittsville 602 ... S7
Pleasant Hills 2,591 ... N3
Pleasant Valley 200 ... L2
Plum Point 200 ... N6
Pocomoke City 3,922 ... R8
Point of Rocks 210 ... J3
Pomfret 600 ... L6
Pomonkey 410 ... K6
Poolesville 3,796 ... J4
Port Deposit 685 ... O2
Potomac Heights 1,524 ... K6
Potomac Park (Potomac Park-Bowling Green) 2,275 ... C2
Potomac Valley ... E4
Powellville 400 ... S7
Preston 437 ... P6
Prince Frederick▲ 1,885 ... M6
Princess Anne▲ 1,666 ... P8
Pumphrey 5,483 ... M4
Quantico 200 ... R7
Queen Anne 250 ... O5
Queenstown 453 ... O5
Randallstown 26,277 ... L3
Randolph ... K4
Rawlings 500 ... C2
Reid 320 ... H2
Reisterstown 19,314 ... L3
Ridge 1,034 ... N8
Ridgely 933 ... P5
Ringgold 200 ... H2
Rising Sun 1,263 ... O2
Ritchie 950 ... G5
Riverdale 5,185 ... F4
Riviera Beach 11,376 ... N4
Rock Hall 1,584 ... O4
Rocks 450 ... N2
Rockville▲ 44,835 ... K4
Rohrersville 525 ... H3
Rosedale 18,703 ... M3
Rosemont 256 ... H3
Royal Oak 600 ... O6
Rumbley 200 ... P8
Sabillasville 450 ... J2
Saint Inigoes 750 ... N8
Saint Leonard 244 ... N7
Saint Marys City ... N8
Saint Michaels 1,301 ... N5
Salisbury▲ 20,592 ... R7
Sandy Spring (Sandy Spring-Ashton) 2,659 ... K4
Savage (Savage-Guilford) 9,669 ... L4
Scotland 475 ... N8
Seabrook (Seabrook-Lanham) ... G4
Seat Pleasant 5,359 ... G5
Secretary 528 ... P6
Selby-on-the-Bay 3,101 ... N5
Severn 24,499 ... M4
Severna Park 25,879 ... M4
Shady Side 4,107 ... M5
Sharpsburg 659 ... G3
Sharptown 609 ... R6
Silver Run 350 ... K2
Silver Spring 76,046 ... F4
Smithsburg 1,221 ... H2
Snow Hill▲ 2,217 ... S8
Solomons 250 ... N7
Somerset 993 ... E4
South Gate 27,564 ... M4
South Kensington 8,777 ... E4
South Laurel 18,591 ... L4
Sparrows Point ... N4
Stevensville 1,862 ... N5
Still Pond 350 ... O3
Stockton 400 ... S8
Street 200 ... N2
Sudlersville 428 ... P4
Suitland (Suitland-Silver Hill) 35,111 ... F5
Swanton 223 ... A3
Sykesville 2,303 ... K3
Takoma Park 16,700 ... F4
Taneytown 3,695 ... K2
Taylors Island 400 ... N7
Texas 300 ... M3
Thurmont 3,398 ... J2
Tilghman 979 ... N6
Timonium (Timonium-Lutherville) ... M3
Toddville 500 ... O7
Tompkinsville 200 ... L7
Towson▲ 49,445 ... M3
Trappe 974 ... O6
Tuxedo 500 ... G5
Union Bridge 910 ... K2
Union Mills 225 ... K2
Uniontown 250 ... K2
Unionville 200 ... K3
University Park 2,243 ... F4
Upper Fairmount 500 ... P8
Upper Falls 550 ... N3
Upper Marlboro▲ 745 ... M5
Upperco 500 ... L2
Vale Summit 175 ... C2
Valley Lee 600 ... M8
Vienna 264 ... P7
Waldorf 15,058 ... L6
Walker Mill 10,920 ... F5
Walkersville 4,145 ... J3
Warwick 550 ... P3
Washington Grove 434 ... K4
Welcome 438 ... K7
Wenona 270 ... P8
West Lanham Hills 350 ... G4
West Laurel 4,151 ... L4
West River 300 ... M5
Westernport 2,454 ... B3
Westminster▲ 13,068 ... L2
Westover 450 ... R8
Wheaton (Wheaton-Glenmont) 53,720 ... E3
White Hall 360 ... M2
White Marsh 8,183 ... N3
White Oak 18,671 ... F3
White Plains 3,560 ... L6
Whiteford 500 ... N2
Wicomico 210 ... L7
Willards 708 ... S7
Williamsport 2,103 ... G2
Willows 250 ... M6
Winfield 200 ... K3
Wingate 225 ... O7
Wittman 544 ... N5
Woodbine 872 ... K3
Woodlawn 5,329 ... M3
Woodmoor ... L3
Woodsboro 513 ... J2
Woolford 330 ... O7
Worton 200 ... O3
Wye Mills 315 ... O5
Wynne 450 ... N8
Yellow Springs 940 ... H3
Zion 225 ... P2

OTHER FEATURES

Aberdeen Proving Ground 5,267 ... N3
Allegheny Front (mts.) ... C2
Andrews A.F.B. 10,228 ... G5
Antietam (creek) ... H2
Antietam Nat'l Battlefield ... H3
Back (riv.) ... N4
Backbone (mt.) ... A3
Bainbridge N.T.C. ... O2
Bald Hill Branch (riv.) ... G4
Big Annemessex (riv.) ... P8
Big Pipe (creek) ... K2
Bloodsworth (isl.) ... O8
Blue Ridge (mts.) ... H3
Bodkin (pt.) ... N4
Bush (creek) ... J3
Cabin John (creek) ... D4
Camp David ... J2
Casselman (riv.) ... B2
Catoctin (creek) ... H3
Catoctin Mt. Park ... J2
Cedar (pt.) ... N7
Census Bureau ... F5
Chesapeake (bay) ... N7
Chesapeake and Delaware (canal) ... R2
Chesapeake and Ohio Canal Nat'l Hist. Park ... J4
Chester (riv.) ... O4
Chicamacomico (riv.) ... P7
Chincoteague (bay) ... S8
Choptank (riv.) ... O6
Clara Barton Nat'l Hist. Site ... E4
Conococheague (bay) ... G1
Conowingo (dam) ... O2
Cove (pt.) ... N7
Deep Creek (lake) ... A3
Deer (creek) ... N2
Dividing (creek) ... R8
Eastern (bay) ... N5
Elk (riv.) ... P3
Fishing (bay) ... O7
Fort Detrick ... J3
Fort George G. Meade 12,509 ... L4
Fort McHenry Nat'l Mon. ... M3
Fort Ritchie 1,249 ... H2
Fort Washington Park ... L6
Great Seneca (creek) ... J4
Greenbelt Park ... G4
Green Ridge (mts.) ... E2
Gunpowder (riv.) ... N3
Gunpowder Falls (creek) ... M2
Hampton Nat'l Hist. Site ... M3
Harpers Ferry Nat'l Hist. Park ... G3
Henson (creek) ... F6
Honga (riv.) ... O7
Hooper (str.) ... O8
Indian (creek) ... G4
James (pt.) ... N6
Kedges (strs) ... O8
Kent (isl.) ... N5
Kent (pt.) ... N5
Liberty (lake) ... L3
Linganore (creek) ... J3
Little Choptank (riv.) ... N6
Little Gunpowder Falls (creek) ... M2
Little Paint Branch (riv.) ... F4
Little Patuxent (riv.) ... L4
Loch Raven (res.) ... M3
Lookout (pt.) ... N8
Manokin (riv.) ... P8
Marshyhope (creek) ... P6
Mattawoman (creek) ... K6
Meadow (mt.) ... B2
Middle Patuxent (riv.) ... L3
Monocacy (riv.) ... J3
Monocacy Nat'l Battlefield ... J3
Nanticoke (riv.) ... P7
Nassawango (creek) ... S8
National Agricultural Research Center ... G3
Naval Academy, U.S. 5,420 ... N5
Naval Medical Center ... E4
Naval Weapons Center ... F3
North (pt.) ... N4
Oceanographic Office ... F5
Oxon Run (riv.) ... F5
Paint Branch (riv.) ... F4
Patapsco (riv.) ... M4
Patuxent (riv.) ... M7
Patuxent River Nav. Air Test Ctr. ... N7
Piscataway (creek) ... G6
Piscataway Park ... K6
Pocomoke (riv.) ... S8
Pocomoke (sound) ... P9
Pooles (isl.) ... O3
Poplar (isl.) ... N5
Potomac (riv.) ... M8
Prettyboy (res.) ... M2
Rock (creek) ... K4
Rocky Gorge (res.) ... L4
Saint George (isl.) ... M8
Saint Marys (riv.) ... N8
Sassafras (riv.) ... P3
Savage (riv.) ... B2
Savage River (lake) ... B2
Severn (riv.) ... N4
Sharps (isl.) ... N6
Smith (isl.) ... O8
South Marsh (isl.) ... O8
Susquehanna (riv.) ... N1
Tangier (sound) ... P8
Thomas Stone Nat'l Hist. Site ... K6
Tinkers (creek) ... F5
Topographic Center ... E4
Town (creek) ... D2
Transquaking (riv.) ... P7
Triadelphia (lake) ... L4
Tuckahoe (creek) ... P5
Walter Reed Army Medical Center Annex ... E4
Wicomico (riv.) ... L7
Wicomico (riv.) ... R7
Winters Run (creek) ... N2
Youghiogheny (riv.) ... A3
Youghiogheny River (lake) ... A2
Zekiah Swamp (riv.) ... L7

DELAWARE

COUNTIES

Kent 110,993 ... R4
New Castle 441,946 ... R2
Sussex 113,229 ... S6

CITIES and TOWNS

Arden 477 ... R1
Ardencroft 282 ... R1
Ardentown 325 ... S1
Bear 200 ... R2
Bellefonte 1,243 ... S1
Bethany Beach 326 ... T6
Bethel 178 ... R6
Blades 834 ... R6
Bowers Beach 198 ... S4
Bridgeville 1,210 ... R6
Brookside 15,307 ... R2
Camden 1,899 ... R4
Centerville 800 ... R1
Cheswold 321 ... R4
Christiana 500 ... R2
Clarksville 350 ... T6
Claymont 9,800 ... S1
Clayton 1,163 ... R3
Concord 200 ... R6
Cool Spring 200 ... T6
Dagsboro 398 ... S6
Delaware City 1,682 ... R2
Delmar 962 ... R7
Dover (cap.)▲ 27,630 ... R4
Dupont Manor 1,059 ... R4
Edgemoor 5,853 ... S1
Ellendale 313 ... S5
Elsmere 5,935 ... R2
Farmington 122 ... R5
Felton 683 ... R4
Fenwick Island 186 ... T7
Frankford 591 ... S6
Frederica 761 ... S4
Georgetown▲ 3,732 ... S6
Glasgow 350 ... R2
Greenville 230 ... R1
Greenwood 578 ... R5
Harbeson 300 ... S6
Harrington 2,311 ... R5
Hockessin 950 ... R1
Houston 487 ... S5
Kenton 232 ... R4
Kirkwood 350 ... R2
Laurel 3,226 ... R6
Leipsic 236 ... S4
Lewes 2,295 ... T5
Lincoln 757 ... S5
Little Creek 167 ... S4
Magnolia 211 ... R4
Middletown 3,834 ... R3
Midway 250 ... T6
Milford 6,040 ... S5
Millsboro 1,643 ... S6
Millville 206 ... T6
Milton 1,417 ... S5
New Castle 4,837 ... R2
Newark 25,098 ... R2
Newport 1,240 ... R2
Oak Orchard 350 ... T6
Ocean View 606 ... T6
Odessa 303 ... R3
Port Penn 300 ... R2
Rehoboth Beach 1,234 ... T6
Rodney Village 1,745 ... R4
Roxana 250 ... T6
Saint Georges 450 ... R2
Seaford 5,689 ... R6
Selbyville 1,335 ... S7
Smyrna 5,231 ... R3
South Bethany 148 ... T6
Townsend 322 ... R3
Viola 153 ... R4
Wilmington▲ 71,529 ... R2
Woodside 140 ... R4
Wyoming 977 ... R4

OTHER FEATURES

Broad (creek) ... R6
Broadkill (riv.) ... S5
Chesapeake and Delaware (canal) ... R2
Choptank (riv.) ... P5
Deep Water (pt.) ... S4
Delaware (bay) ... T5
Delaware (riv.) ... R3
Dover A.F.B. ... S4
Henlopen (cape) ... T5
Indian (riv.) ... S6
Indian River (bay) ... T6
Indian River (inlet) ... T6
Leipsic (riv.) ... R4
Mispillion (riv.) ... S5
Murderkill (riv.) ... R5
Nanticoke (riv.) ... R6
Saint Jones (riv.) ... R4
Smyrna (res.) ... R3

DISTRICT OF COLOMBIA

CITIES and TOWNS

Georgetown ... E5
Washington D.C. (cap), U.S. 609,909 ... F5

OTHER FEATURES

Anacostia (riv.) ... F5
Bolling A.F.B. ... F5
Fort Lesley J. McNair ... E5
Kennedy Center ... A5
Naval Yard ... F5
U.S. Capitol ... F5
Walter Reed Army Med. Ctr. ... E4

▲County seat.

Agriculture, Industry and Resources

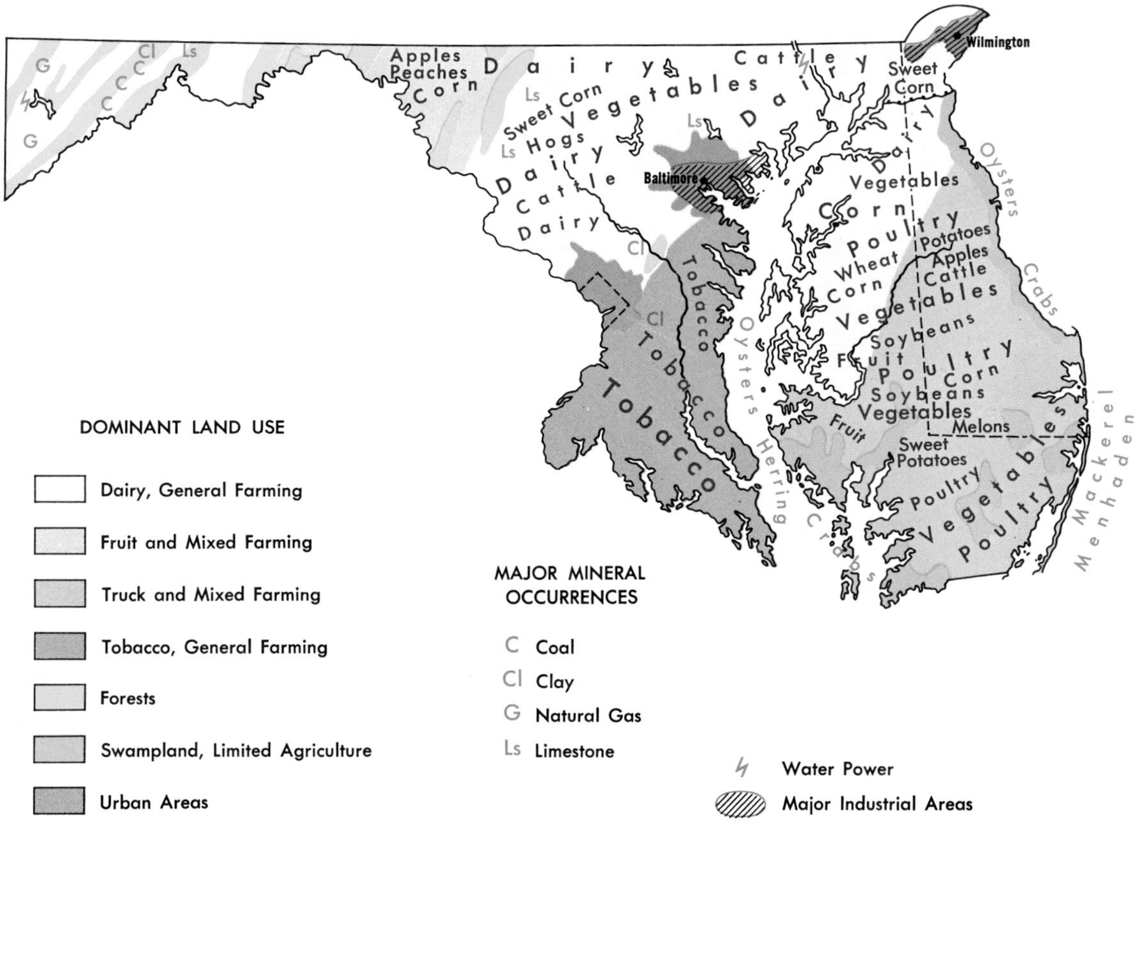

Apples
Peaches
Corn
Dairy
Cattle
Vegetables
Sweet Corn
Hogs
Wilmington
Baltimore
Tobacco
Poultry
Wheat
Potatoes
Soybeans
Fruit
Melons
Sweet Potatoes
Oysters
Crabs
Herring
Mackerel
Menhaden
DOMINANT LAND USE
Dairy, General Farming
Fruit and Mixed Farming
Truck and Mixed Farming
Tobacco, General Farming
Forests
Swampland, Limited Agriculture
Urban Areas
MAJOR MINERAL OCCURRENCES
C Coal
Cl Clay
G Natural Gas
Ls Limestone
Water Power
Major Industrial Areas

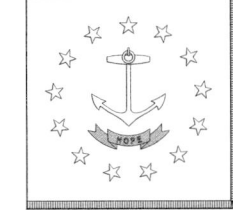

MASSACHUSETTS
AREA 8,284 sq. mi. (21,456 sq. km.)
POPULATION 6,029,051
CAPITAL Boston
LARGEST CITY Boston
HIGHEST POINT Mt. Greylock 3,491 ft. (1064 m.)
SETTLED IN 1620
ADMITTED TO UNION February 6, 1788
POPULAR NAME Bay State; Old Colony
STATE FLOWER Mayflower
STATE BIRD Chickadee

RHODE ISLAND
AREA 1,212 sq. mi. (3,139 sq. km.)
POPULATION 1,005,984
CAPITAL Providence
LARGEST CITY Providence
HIGHEST POINT Jerimoth Hill 812 ft. (247 m.)
SETTLED IN 1636
ADMITTED TO UNION May 29, 1790
POPULAR NAME Little Rhody; Ocean State
STATE FLOWER Violet
STATE BIRD Rhode Island Red

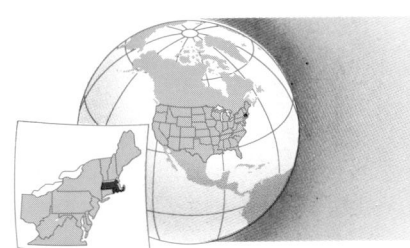

Agriculture, Industry and Resources

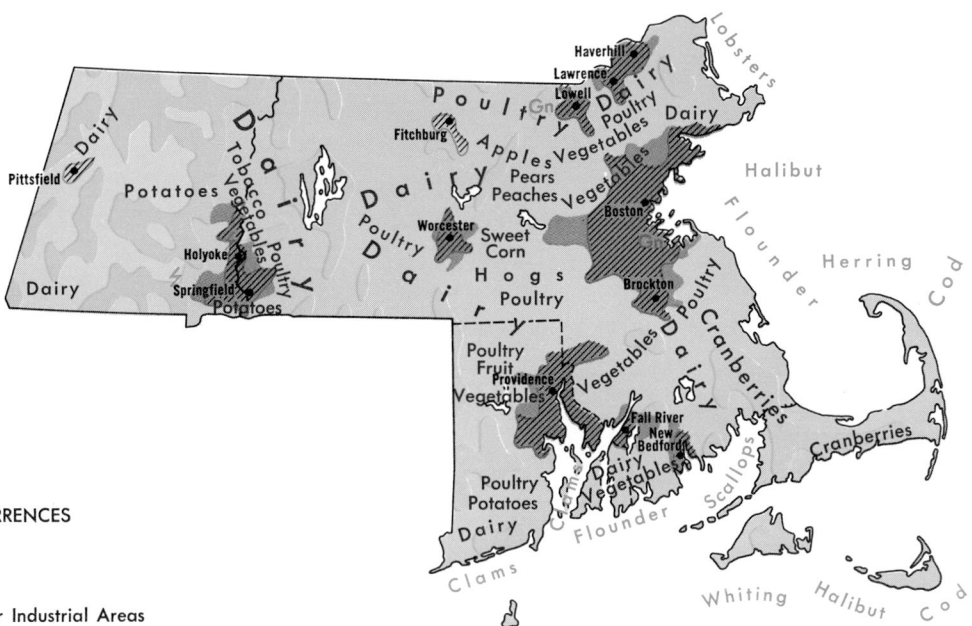

DOMINANT LAND USE

- Specialized Dairy
- Dairy, Poultry, Mixed Farming
- Forests
- Urban Areas

MAJOR MINERAL OCCURRENCES

Gn Granite

⚡ Water Power   Major Industrial Areas

MASSACHUSETTS

COUNTIES

Barnstable 186,605 ....N6
Berkshire 139,352 ....B3
Bristol 506,325 ....K5
Dukes 11,639 ....M7
Essex 670,080 ....L2
Franklin 70,092 ....D2
Hampden 456,310 ....D4
Hampshire 146,568 ....D3
Middlesex 1,398,468 ....J3
Nantucket 6,012 ....O7
Norfolk 616,087 ....K4
Plymouth 435,276 ....L5
Suffolk 663,906 ....K3
Worcester 709,705 ....G3

CITIES and TOWNS

Abington • 13,817 ....L4
Acton • 17,872 ....J3
Acushnet • 9,554 ....L6
Adams 6,356 ....B2
Adams • 9,445 ....B2
Agawam • 27,323 ....D4
Alford • 418 ....A4
Allerton 900 ....E7
Amesbury 12,109 ....L1
Amesbury • 14,997 ....L1
Amherst 17,824 ....E3
Amherst • 35,228 ....E3
Andover 8,242 ....K2
Andover • 29,151 ....K2
Arlington • 44,630 ....C6
Ashburnham 900 ....G2
Ashburnham • 5,433 ....G2
Ashby • 2,717 ....G2
Ashfield • 1,715 ....C2
Ashland • 12,066 ....J3
Ashley Falls 600 ....A4
Assinippi 950 ....E8
Assonet 950 ....K5
Athol 8,732 ....F2
Athol • 11,451 ....F2
Attleboro 38,383 ....J5
Attleboro Falls J5
Auburn • 15,005 ....G4
Auburndale B7
Avon • 4,558 ....K4
Ayer 2,889 ....H2
Ayer • 6,871 ....H2
Baldwinville 1,795 ....F2
Ballardvale K2
Barnstable▲ 2,790 ....N6
Barnstable • 30,898 ....N6
Barre 1,094 ....F3
Barre • 4,546 ....F3
Barrowsville 600 ....K5
Becket • 1,481 ....B3
Bedford • 12,996 ....B6

Belchertown 2,339 ....E3
Belchertown • 10,579 ....E3
Bellingham 4,535 ....J4
Bellingham • 14,877 ....J4
Belmont • 24,720 ....C6
Berkley • 4,237 ....K5
Berlin • 2,293 ....H3
Bernardston • 2,048 ....D2
Beverly 38,195 ....E5
Billerica • 37,609 ....J2
Blackstone 8,023 ....H4
Blandford • 1,187 ....C4
Bolton • 3,134 ....H3
Bondsville 1,992 ....E4
Boxford 2,072 ....L2
Boxford • 6,266 ....L2
Boylston • 3,517 ....H3
Braintree • 33,836 ....D8
Brant Rock-Ocean Bluff M4
Brewster 1,818 ....O5
Brewster • 8,440 ....O5
Bridgewater 7,242 ....K5
Bridgewater • 21,249 ....K5
Brimfield • 3,001 ....F4
Brockton 92,788 ....K4
Brookfield 2,968 ....F4
Brookfield • 2,397 ....F4
Brookline • 54,718 ....C7
Brookville D8
Buckland • 1,928 ....C2
Burlington • 23,302 ....C5
Buzzards Bay 3,250 ....M5
Byfield 950 ....L1
Cambridge▲ 95,802 ....C7
Canton • 18,530 ....C8
Carlisle • 4,333 ....J2
Carver • 10,590 ....M5
Cataumet 650 ....M6
Centerville 9,190 ....N6
Central Village 800 ....K6
Charlemont • 1,249 ....C2
Charlton • 9,576 ....F4
Charlton City 950 ....F4
Chartley 950 ....K5
Chatham 1,916 ....P6
Chatham • 6,579 ....P6
Chelmsford • 32,388 ....J2
Chelsea 28,710 ....D6
Cherry Valley G3
Cheshire • 3,479 ....B2
Chester • 1,280 ....C3
Chesterfield • 1,048 ....C3
Chicopee 56,632 ....D4
Chilmark • 650 ....M7
Chiltonville 600 ....M5
City Mills 500 ....J4
Clicquot-Millis A8

Clinton • 7,943 ....H3
Cochituate 6,046 ....A7
Cohasset • 7,075 ....F7
Collinsville J2
Colrain • 1,757 ....D2
Concord • 17,076 ....B6
Conway • 1,529 ....D2
Cordaville 1,530 ....H3
Cotuit 2,364 ....N6
Cummington • 785 ....C3
Dalton • 7,155 ....B3
Danvers • 24,174 ....D5
Danversport E5
Dartmouth • 27,244 ....K6
Dedham▲ 23,782 ....C7
Deerfield • 5,018 ....D2
Dennis • 2,633 ....O5
Dennis Port 2,775 ....O6
Dighton • 5,631 ....K5
Dorchester D7
Douglas • 5,438 ....H4
Dover 2,163 ....B7
Dover • 4,915 ....B7
Dracut • 25,594 ....J2
Dudley • 9,540 ....G4
Dunstable • 2,236 ....J2
Duxbury 1,637 ....M4
Duxbury • 13,895 ....M4
East Braintree D8
East Brewster 900 ....O5
East Bridgewater • 11,104 ....L4
East Brookfield 1,396 ....G4
East Brookfield • 2,033 ....G4
East Dedham C8
East Dennis 2,584 ....O5
East Douglas 1,945 ....G4
East Falmouth (Teaticket) 5,577 ....M6
East Foxboro 750 ....K4
East Freetown 600 ....L5
East Harwich 3,828 ....O6
East Longmeadow • 13,367 ....E4
East Milton D7
East Norton 750 ....K5
East Orleans 600 ....P5
East Otis 600 ....B4
East Pembroke 582 ....M4
East Pepperell 2,296 ....H2
East Sandwich 3,171 ....N6
East Templeton 950 ....F2
East Walpole C8
East Wareham 950 ....M5
East Weymouth E8
East Whately 650 ....D3
Eastham • 4,462 ....O5
Easthampton 15,537 ....D3
Easton 19,807 ....K4
Edgartown 600 ....K4
Edgartown • 3,062 ....M7
Edgartown • 2,204 ....M7
Erving • 1,372 ....E2
Essex 1,507 ....L2

Essex • 3,260 ....L2
Cochituate 6,046 ....D6
Fairhaven • 16,132 ....L6
Fall River 92,703 ....K6
Falmouth • 23,640 ....M6
Falmouth • 27,960 ....M6
Fayville 975 ....H3
Feeding Hills D4
Fisherville H4
Fiskdale 2,189 ....F4
Fitchburg▲ 41,194 ....G2
Florida • 742 ....B2
Forge Village 925 ....H2
Foxboro 5,706 ....J4
Foxboro • 14,148 ....J4
Framingham 64,994 ....A7
Framingham Center 16,000 ....J3
Franklin 9,965 ....J4
Franklin • 22,095 ....J4
Gardner 20,125 ....G2
Gay Head • 201 ....L7
Georgetown • 6,384 ....L2
Gilbertville 1,029 ....F3
Gill • 1,583 ....D2
Gloucester 28,716 ....M2
Goshen • 830 ....C3
Grafton • 13,035 ....H4
Granby 1,327 ....E3
Granby • 5,565 ....E3
Graniteville 970 ....J2
Granville • 1,403 ....C4
Great Barrington 2,810 ....A4
Great Barrington • 7,725 ....A4
Green Harbor 2,002 ....M4
Greenbush 950 ....F8
Greenfield▲ 14,016 ....D2
Greenfield • 18,666 ....D2
Greenwood D6
Groton 1,044 ....H2
Groton • 7,511 ....H2
Groveland • 5,214 ....L1
Hadley • 4,231 ....D3
Halifax • 6,526 ....L4
Hamilton • 7,280 ....L2
Hampden • 4,709 ....E4
Hancock • 628 ....A2
Hanover • 11,912 ....L4
Hanson 2,188 ....L4
Hanson • 9,028 ....L4
Hardwick • 2,385 ....F3
Harvard • 12,329 ....H2
Harwich 10,275 ....O6
Harwich • 1,668 ....O6
Harwich Port 1,742 ....O6
Hatfield 1,234 ....D3
Hatfield • 3,184 ....D3
Haverhill 51,418 ....K1
Haydenville 900 ....D3
Heath • 716 ....C2
Hingham 5,685 ....E8
Hingham • 19,821 ....E8
Hinsdale • 1,959 ....B3

Holbrook • 11,041 ....D8
Holden • 14,628 ....G3
Holland • 1,331 ....F4
Holliston • 12,926 ....A8
Holyoke 43,704 ....D4
Hopedale 3,961 ....H4
Hopedale • 5,666 ....H4
Hopkinton 2,305 ....J4
Hopkinton • 9,191 ....J4
Housatonic 1,184 ....A3
Hubbardston • 2,797 ....F3
Hudson 14,267 ....H3
Hudson • 17,233 ....H3
Hull • 10,466 ....E7
Huntington • 1,987 ....C4
Hyannis 14,120 ....N6
Hyannis Port 750 ....N6
Hyde Park C7
Interlaken 700 ....A3
Ipswich 4,132 ....L2
Ipswich • 11,873 ....L2
Islington C8
Jamaica Plain C7
Jefferson G3
Kingston 4,774 ....M5
Kingston • 9,045 ....M5
Lakeville 7,785 ....L5
Lakeville • 5,931 ....L5
Lancaster • 6,661 ....H3
Lanesboro • 3,131 ....A2
Lawrence▲ 70,207 ....K2
Lee 2,020 ....B3
Lee • 5,849 ....B3
Leicester • 10,191 ....G4
Lenox 1,687 ....A3
Lenox • 5,069 ....A3
Lenox Dale 600 ....B3
Leominster 38,145 ....G2
Leverett • 1,785 ....E3
Lexington 28,974 ....B6
Leyden • 662 ....D2
Lincoln • 7,666 ....B6
Lincoln Center 945 ....B6
Linwood 995 ....H4
Littleton Common 2,867 ....J2
Littleton • 7,051 ....H2
Longmeadow • 15,467 ....D4
Lowell▲ 103,439 ....J2
Ludlow • 18,820 ....E4
Ludlow Center 750 ....E4
Lunds Corner L6
Lunenburg 1,694 ....H2
Lunenburg • 9,117 ....H2
Lynn 81,245 ....D6
Lynnfield • 11,274 ....C5
Malden 53,884 ....D6
Manchaug 975 ....G4
Manchester-by-the-Sea • 5,286 ....F5
Manomet 950 ....M5
Mansfield 7,170 ....J4
Mansfield • 13,453 ....J4

Marblehead • 19,971 ....E7
Marion 1,426 ....L6
Marion • 3,932 ....L6
Marlborough 31,813 ....H3
Marshfield 4,002 ....M4
Marshfield • 21,531 ....M4
Marshfield Hills 2,201 ....M4
Marstons Mills 8,017 ....N6
Mashpee • 7,884 ....M6
Mattapan C7
Mattapoisett 2,949 ....L6
Mattapoisett • 5,597 ....L6
Maynard • 10,325 ....J3
Medfield 5,985 ....B8
Medfield • 10,531 ....B8
Medford 57,407 ....C6
Medway • 9,931 ....J4
Melrose 28,150 ....D6
Mendon • 4,010 ....H4
Merino Village G4
Merrimac 5,166 ....L1
Methuen • 39,990 ....K2
Middleboro 6,837 ....L5
Middleboro • 16,404 ....L5
Middlefield • 392 ....B3
Middleton • 4,921 ....K2
Milford 23,339 ....H4
Milford • 25,355 ....H4
Millbury • 12,228 ....H4
Millers Falls 1,084 ....E2
Millis-Clicquot 4,081 ....A8
Millis • 7,613 ....J4
Millville • 2,236 ....H4
Milton • 25,725 ....D7
Monson 2,101 ....E4
Monson • 7,315 ....E4
Montague • 8,316 ....E2
Monterey • 805 ....B4
Monument Beach 1,842 ....M6
Moores Corner E2
Mount Washington • 135 ....A4
Nabnasset 975 ....J2
Nahant • 3,828 ....E6
Nantasket Beach E7
Nantucket▲ 3,069 ....O7
Nantucket • 6,012 ....O7
Natick • 30,510 ....J3
Needham Heights B7
Needham • 27,557 ....B7
Neponset D7
New Bedford▲ 99,922 ....K6
New Braintree • 881 ....F3
New Marlborough • 1,240 ....B4
New Salem • 802 ....E2
Newbury • 5,623 ....L1
Newburyport▲ 16,317 ....L1
Newton 82,585 ....C7
Newton Center C7
Newton Highlands C7
Newton Lower Falls 950 ....B7
Newton Upper Falls C7
Newtonville C7

Norfolk • 9,270 ....J4
North Abington L4
North Adams 16,797 ....B2
North Amherst 6,239 ....E3
North Andover • 22,792 ....K2
North Attleboro • 16,178 ....J5
North Billerica J2
North Brookfield 2,635 ....F3
North Brookfield • 4,708 ....F3
North Chelmsford J2
North Dartmouth K6
North Dighton 1,174 ....K5
North Eastham 1,570 ....O5
North Easton K4
North Falmouth 2,625 ....M6
North Grafton H4
North Hadley 600 ....D3
North Hanover 950 ....L4
North Oxford G4
North Pembroke 2,485 ....M4
North Plymouth 3,450 ....L5
North Reading • 12,002 ....C5
North Scituate 4,891 ....F8
North Truro 675 ....O4
North Uxbridge H4
North Waltham B6
North Weymouth D8
North Wilbraham E4
Northampton▲ 29,289 ....D3
Northborough 5,761 ....H3
Northborough • 11,929 ....H3
Northbridge • 13,371 ....H4
Northfield 1,322 ....E2
Northfield • 2,838 ....E2
Norton 1,899 ....K5
Norton • 12,690 ....K5
Norwell • 9,279 ....F8
Norwood • 28,700 ....B8
Nutting Lake B5
Oak Bluffs 2,804 ....M7
Oak Bluffs • 1,984 ....M7
Oakdale 850 ....G3
Oakham • 1,503 ....F3
Ocean Bluff-Brant Rock 4,541 ....M4
Ocean Grove 3,169 ....K6
Old Sturbridge Village 500 ....F4
Onset 1,461 ....M6
Orange 3,791 ....E2
Orange • 7,312 ....E2
Orleans 1,699 ....O5
Orleans • 5,838 ....O5
Osterville 2,911 ....N6
Otis • 1,073 ....B4
Otter River 700 ....F2
Oxford 5,969 ....G4
Oxford • 12,588 ....G4
Palmer 4,069 ....E4
Palmer • 12,054 ....E4
Paxton • 4,047 ....G3
Peabody 47,039 ....E5
Pelham • 1,373 ....E3

(continued on following page)

Pembroke • 14,544...........L4
Pepperell 2,350...........H2
Pepperell • 10,098...........H2
Petersham • 1,131...........F3
Phillipston • 1,485...........F2
Pigeon Cove...........M2
Pinehurst 6,614...........B5
Pittsfield 48,622...........A3
Plainfield • 571...........C2
Plainville • 6,871...........J4
Pleasant Lake 525...........O6
Plymouth▲ 7,258...........M5
Plymouth • 45,608...........M5
Plympton • 2,384...........L5
Pocasset 2,756...........M6
Princeton • 3,189...........G3
Provincetown 3,374...........O4
Provincetown • 3,561...........O4
Quincy 84,985...........D7
Randolph • 30,093...........D8

Raynham Center 3,709...........K5
Raynham • 9,867...........K5
Reading • 22,539...........C5
Readville...........C8
Rehoboth • 8,656...........K5
Revere 42,786...........D6
Richmond • 1,677...........A3
Rochdale 1,105...........G4
Rochester • 3,921...........L6
Rockland • 16,123...........L4
Rockport • 5,448...........M2
Rowe • 378...........C2
Rowley 1,144...........L2
Rowley • 4,452...........L2
Roxbury...........C7
Royalston • 1,147...........F2
Russell • 1,594...........C4
Rutland 2,145...........G3
Rutland • 4,936...........G3
Sagamore 2,589...........M5

Salem▲ 38,091...........E5
Salisbury 3,729...........L1
Salisbury • 6,882...........L1
Salisbury Beach 950...........L1
Sand Hills...........M4
Sandisfield • 667...........B4
Sandwich 2,998...........N5
Sandwich • 15,489...........N5
Saugus • 25,549...........D6
Saundersville 975...........G4
Savoy • 634...........B2
Saxonville...........A7
Scituate 5,180...........F8
Scituate • 16,786...........F8
Seekonk • 13,046...........J5
Sharon 5,893...........K4
Sharon • 15,517...........K4
Shawsheen Village...........K2
Sheffield • 2,910...........A4
Shelburne Falls 1,996...........D2

Sherborn • 3,989...........A8
Shirley 1,559...........H2
Shirley • 6,118...........H2
Shore Acres...........F8
Shrewsbury 24,146...........H3
Shutesbury • 1,561...........E3
Somerset • 17,655...........K5
Somerville 76,210...........C6
South Acton 950...........J3
South Amherst • 5,053...........E3
South Ashburnham 1,110...........G2
South Barre 900...........F3
South Braintree...........D8
South Carver 750...........M5
South Chatham 725...........O6
South Dartmouth...........L6
South Deerfield 1,906...........D3
South Dennis 3,559...........O6
South Duxbury 3,017...........M4
South Easton...........K4

South Egremont 700...........A4
South Grafton (Fisherville)...........H4
South Groveland 950...........L2
South Hadley Falls...........D4
South Hadley • 16,685...........D4
South Hanover...........L4
South Harwich 875...........O6
South Lancaster 1,772...........H3
South Lee 600...........A3
South Lynnfield...........D5
South Middleboro 600...........L5
South Natick...........A7
South Orleans 800...........O5
South Sudbury...........J3
South Walpole...........K4
South Wellfleet 583...........P5
South Weymouth...........E8
South Yarmouth 10,358...........O6
Southampton • 4,478...........C4
Southborough • 6,628...........H3

Southbridge 13,631...........G4
Southbridge • 17,816...........G4
Southville 600...........H3
Southwick • 7,667...........C4
Spencer 6,306...........F3
Spencer • 11,645...........F3
Springfield▲ 156,983...........D4
Sterling • 6,481...........G3
Stockbridge 2,408...........A3
Stockbridge • 2,328...........A3
Stoneham • 22,203...........C6
Stoughton • 26,777...........K4
Stow • 5,328...........H3
Sturbridge 2,093...........F4
Sturbridge • 7,775...........F4
Sudbury • 14,358...........A6
Sunderland • 3,399...........D3
Sutton 6,824...........H4
Swampscott • 13,650...........E6
Swansea • 15,411...........K5

Swansea Center 950...........K5
Taunton▲ 49,832...........K5
Teaticket 1,856...........M6
Templeton • 6,438...........F2
Tewksbury 27,266...........K2
Thorndike 900...........E4
Three Rivers 3,006...........E4
Tolland • 289...........B4
Topsfield 2,711...........L2
Topsfield • 5,754...........L2
Townsend 1,164...........H2
Townsend • 8,496...........H2
Townsend Harbor 600...........H2
Truro • 1,573...........O5
Turners Falls 4,731...........D3
Tyngsboro • 5,683...........J2
Tyringham • 369...........A4
Upton-West Upton 2,347...........H4
Upton • 4,677...........H4
Uxbridge • 10,415...........H4

Vineyard Haven 1,762............M7
Waban.........................B7
Wakefield • 24,825.............C5
Wales • 1,566.................F4
Walpole 5,495.................B8
Walpole • 20,212..............B8
Waltham 57,878................B6
Ware 6,533....................E3
Ware • 9,308..................E3
Wareham 19,232................L5
Wareham • 18,457..............L5
Wareham Center 2,607..........L5
Warren 1,516..................F4
Warren • 4,437................F4
Warwick • 740.................E2
Washington • 615..............B3
Watertown • 33,284............C6
Waverley......................B6
Wayland • 11,874..............A7
Webster 11,849................G4

Webster • 16,196..............G4
Wellesley • 26,615............B7
Wellesley Hills...............B7
Wellfleet • 2,493.............O5
Wendell • 899.................E2
Wenham • 4,212................L2
West Acton 975................H3
West Barnstable 1,503.........N6
West Boxford 950..............K2
West Boylston • 6,61..........G3
West Bridgewater • 6,389......K4
West Brookfield 1,419.........F4
West Brookfield • 3,532.......F4
West Chatham 1,504............O6
West Chelmsford...............J2
West Concord 5,761............A6
West Dennis 2,307.............O6
West Falmouth 1,752...........M6
West Groton 950...............H2
West Hanover..................L4

West Harwich 883..............O6
West Mansfield 950............K5
West Medway...................J4
West Newbury • 3,421..........L1
West Newton...................B7
West Springfield • 27,537.....D4
West Stockbridge • 1,483......A3
West Tisbury • 1,704..........M7
West Townsend 950.............H2
West Upton-Upton..............H4
West Wareham 2,059............L5
West Warren...................F4
West Yarmouth 5,409...........N6
Westborough 3,917.............H3
Westborough • 14,133..........H3
Westfield • 38,372............D4
Westford • 16,392.............J2
Westhampton • 1,327...........C3
Westminster • 6,191...........G2
Weston • 10,200...............B6

Westport 13,852...............K6
Westport • 13,763.............K6
Westwood • 12,557.............B8
Weymouth 54,063...............D8
Whately • 1,375...............D3
Whitinsville 5,639............H4
Whitman • 13,240..............L4
Wilbraham 3,352...............E4
Wilbraham • 12,635............E4
Williamsburg • 2,515..........C3
Williamstown 4,791............B2
Williamstown • 8,220..........B2
Wilmington • 17,654...........C5
Winchendon 4,316..............F2
Winchendon • 8,805............F2
Winchester • 20,267...........C6
Windsor • 770.................B2
Winthrop 18,127...............D6
Woburn 35,943.................C6
Woods Hole 1,080..............M6
Worcester▲ 169,759............H3
Worthington • 1,156...........C3
Wrentham • 9,006..............J4
Yarmouth Port 4,271...........N6
Yarmouth • 21,174.............O6

OTHER FEATURES

Adams Nat'l Hist. Site........D7
Agawam (riv.).................M5
Allerton (pt.)................E7
Ann (cape)....................M2
Ashmere (lake)................B3
Assabet (riv.)................H3
Assawompset (pond)............L5
Batchelor (brook).............D3
Berkshire (hills).............B4
Big (pond)....................B4
Bigelow (bight)...............M1
Blackstone (riv.).............G3
Blue (hills)..................C8
Boston (bay)..................E6
Boston (harb.)................D7
Boston Nat'l Hist. Park.......D6
Brewster (isls.)..............E7
Buel (pond)...................A4
Buzzards (bay)................L7
Cambridge (res.)..............B6
Cape Cod (bay)................N5
Cape Cod (canal)..............N5
Cape Cod Nat'l Seashore.......P5
Chappaquiddick (isl.).........N7
Charles (riv.)................C7
Chicopee (riv.)...............D4
Cobble Mountain (res.)........C4
Cochituate (lake).............A7
Cod (cape)....................O4
Concord (riv.)................J2
Congamond (lakes).............D4
Connecticut (riv.)............D2
Cuttyhunk (isl.)..............L7
Deer (isl.)...................E7
Deerfield (riv.)..............C2
East (pt.)....................E6
East Chop (pt.)...............M7
Eastern (pt.).................M2
Elizabeth (isls.).............L7
Everett (mt.).................A4
Falls (riv.)..................D2
Fort Devens 8,973.............H2
Fresh (pond)..................C6
Gammon (pt.)..................N6

Gay Head (prom.)..............L7
Grace (mt.)...................E2
Great (pt.)...................O7
Green (riv.)..................B2
Greylock (mt.)................B2
Gurnet (pt.)..................M4
Hingham (bay).................E7
Holyoke (range)...............D3
Hoosac (mts.).................B2
Hoosic (riv.).................A1
Housatonic (riv.).............A4
Ipswich (riv.)................L2
John F. Kennedy
   Nat'l Hist. Site...........C7
Knightville (res.)............C3
Laurence G. Hanscom Field.....B6
Little (riv.).................C4
Logan Int'l Airport...........D7
Long (isl.)...................E7
Long (pt.)....................O4
Long (pond)...................L5
Longfellow Nat'l Hist. Site...C6
Lowell Nat'l Hist. Park.......J2
Maine (gulf)..................M2
Manhan (riv.).................D4
Manomet (pt.).................N5
Marblehead (neck).............F6
Martha's Vineyard (isl.)......M7
Massachusetts (bay)...........M4
Merrimack (riv.)..............K1
Mill (riv.)...................C3
Mill (riv.)...................D3
Millers (riv.)................E2
Minute Man Nat'l Park.........B6
Mishaum (pt.).................L6
Monomonac (lake)..............G2
Monomoy (isl.)................O6
Monomoy (pt.).................O6
Mount Hope (bay)..............K6
Muskeget (chan.)..............N7
Muskeget (isl.)...............N7
Mystic (lake).................C6
Mystic (riv.).................C6
Nahant (pt.)..................E6
Nantucket (isl.)..............O8
Nantucket (sound).............N6
Nashawena (isl.)..............L7
Nashua (riv.).................H3
Naushon (isl.)................L7
Neponset (riv.)...............C8
Nomans Land (isl.)............L7
Nonamesset (isl.).............M6
North (riv.)..................D2
North (riv.)..................L4
Onota (lake)..................A3
Otis (res.)...................B4
Otis A.F.B....................M6
Pasque (isl.).................L7
Plum (isl.)...................L2
Plymouth (bay)................M5
Poge (cape)...................N7
Pontoosuc (lake)..............A3
Quabbin (res.)................E3
Quaboag (riv.)................F4
Quincy (bay)..................D7
Quinebaug (riv.)..............F4
Race (pt.)....................N4
Salem Maritime
   Nat'l Hist. Site...........E5
Saugus Iron Works
   Nat'l Hist. Site...........D6
Shawshine (riv.)..............K2

Silver (lake).................L4
South (riv.)..................D2
South Weymouth
   Nav. Air Sta...............E8
Springfield Armory
   Nat'l Hist. Site...........D4
Squibnocket (pt.).............M7
Stillwater (riv.).............G3
Sudbury (res.)................H3
Sudbury (riv.)................A6
Swift (riv.)..................E4
Taconic (mts.)................A2
Taunton (riv.)................K5
Thompson (isl.)...............D7
Toby (mt.)....................E3
Tom (mt.).....................D4
Tuckernuck (isl.).............N7
Vineyard (sound)..............L7
Wachusett (lake)..............G3
Wachusett (res.)..............G3
Walden (pond).................A6
Ware (riv.)...................F3
Watuppa (pond)................K6
Webster (lake)................G4
Wellfleet (harb.).............O5
West (riv.)...................H4
West Chop (pt.)...............M7
Westfield (riv.)..............C3
Westover A.F.B................D4
Weweantic (riv.)..............L5
Whitman (riv.)................G2
Winter I. Coast Guard Air Sta..E5

RHODE ISLAND

COUNTIES

Bristol 48,859................J6
Kent 161,135..................H6
Newport 87,194................K6
Providence 596,270............H5
Washington 110,006............H7

CITIES and TOWNS

Anthony.......................H6
Apponaug......................J6
Arctic........................J6
Arnold Mills..................J5
Ashaway 1,584.................G7
Ashton........................J5
Barrington • 15,849...........J6
Block Island •................H8
Bradford 1,604................H7
Bristol▲• 21,625..............J6
Centerdale....................H5
Central Falls 17,637..........J5
Charlestown 6,478.............H7
Conimicut.....................J6
Coventry (Washington)
   31,083.....................H6
Coventry Center...............H6
Cranston 76,060...............J5
East Greenwich▲ • 11,865......J6
East Providence 50,380........J5
Esmond........................H5
Exeter • 5,461................H6
Georgiaville..................H5
Greenville 8,303..............H5
Harrisville 1,654.............H5
Hillsgrove....................J6
Hope Valley 1,446.............H6

Hopkinton • 6,873.............H7
Island Park...................J6
Jamestown 4,999...............J6
Jamestown • 4,040.............J6
Kingston 6,504................J7
La Fayette....................H6
Little Compton • 3,339........K6
Lonsdale......................J5
Manville......................H5
Middletown • 19,460...........J6
Narragansett 14,985...........J7
Narragansett • 12,088.........J7
Natick........................H6
New Shoreham
   (Block Island) • 836.......H8
Newport▲ 28,227...............J7
North Kingstown • 23,786......J6
North Providence • 32,090.....H5
North Tiverton................K6
Norwood.......................J6
Oakland Beach.................J6
Pascoag 5,011.................H5
Pawtucket 72,644..............J5
Peace Dale-Wakefield 7,134....J7
Pontiac.......................J6
Portsmouth • 16,857...........J6
Providence (cap.)▲ 160,728....H5
Riverside.....................J5
Rumford.......................J5
Tiverton 7,259................K6
Tiverton • 14,312.............K6
Valley Falls 11,175...........J5
Wakefield-Peace Dale 7,134....J7
Warren • 11,385...............J6
Warwick 85,427................J6
Watch Hill 300................G7
West Kingston 950.............H7
West Warwick 29,268...........H6
Westerly▲ 16,477..............G7
Westerly • 21,605.............G7
Woonsocket▲ 43,877............J4

OTHER FEATURES

Black Rock (pt.)..............H8
Block (isl.)..................H8
Block Island (sound)..........H8
Brenton (pt.).................J7
Conanicut (isl.)..............J6
Dickens (pt.).................H8
Durfee (hill).................G5
Grace (pt.)...................H8
Jerimoth (hill)...............G5
Judith (pt.)..................J7
Mount Hope (bay)..............K6
Narragansett (bay)............J6
Noyes (pt.)...................H7
Pawcatuck (riv.)..............G7
Prudence (isl.)...............J6
Rhode Island (isl.)...........J6
Rhode (sound).................J7
Roger Williams Nat'l Mem......J5
Sakonnet (pt.)................K7
Sakonnet (riv.)...............K7
Sandy (pt.)...................H8
Scituate (res.)...............H5
Touro Synagogue
   Nat'l Hist. Site...........J7
Watch Hill (pt.)..............G7

▲County seat or Shire town
• Population of town or township

Massachusetts and Rhode Island

SCALE

0 5 10 15 20 MI.

0 5 10 15 20 KM.

State Capitals.............✪
County Seats (Shire Towns).◉
Canals.....................
Major Limited Access Hwys..

Scale 1:670,000

© Copyright HAMMOND INCORPORATED, Maplewood, N. J.

Topography

0 20 40 MI.

0 20 40 KM.

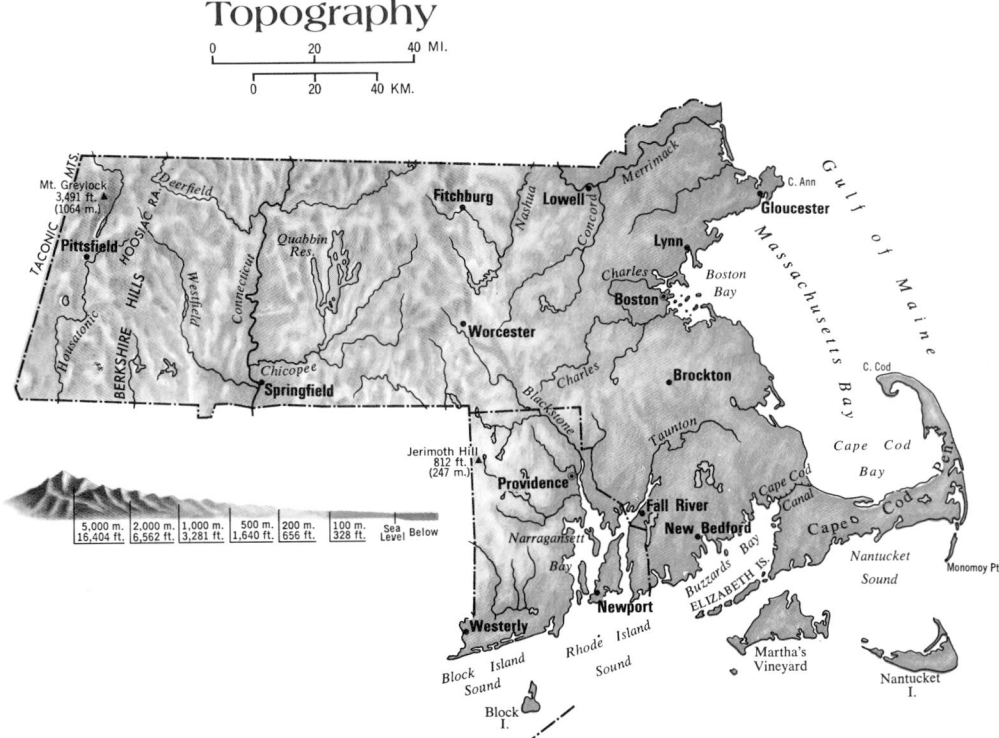

| 5,000 m. | 2,000 m. | 1,000 m. | 500 m. | 200 m. | 100 m. | Sea | Below |
| 16,404 ft. | 6,562 ft. | 3,281 ft. | 1,640 ft. | 656 ft. | 328 ft. | Level | |

Michigan

SCALE
0 5 10   20   30   40   50 MI.
0 5 10   20   30   40   50 KM.

State Capitals .... ⊛
County Seats .... ⊙
Canals ....
Major Limited Access Hwys. ——

Scale 1:2,360,000

© Copyright HAMMOND INCORPORATED, Maplewood, N.J.

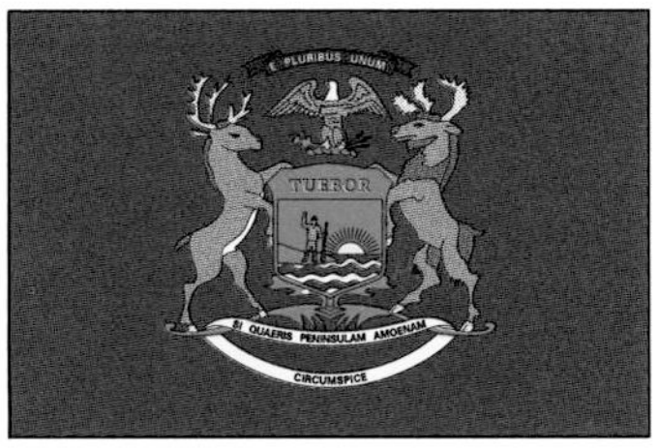
E PLURIBUS UNUM
TUEBOR
SI QUAERIS PENINSULAM AMOENAM
CIRCUMSPICE

AREA 58,527 sq. mi. (151,585 sq. km.)
POPULATION 9,328,784
CAPITAL Lansing
LARGEST CITY Detroit
HIGHEST POINT Mt. Curwood 1,980 ft. (604 m.)
SETTLED IN 1650
ADMITTED TO UNION January 26, 1837
POPULAR NAME Wolverine State
STATE FLOWER Apple Blossom
STATE BIRD Robin

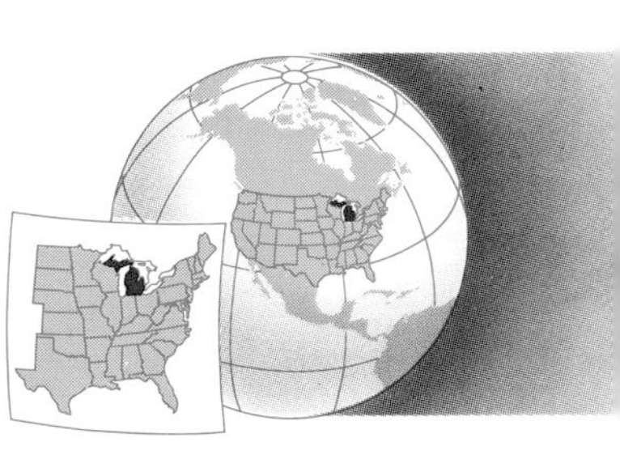

Topography

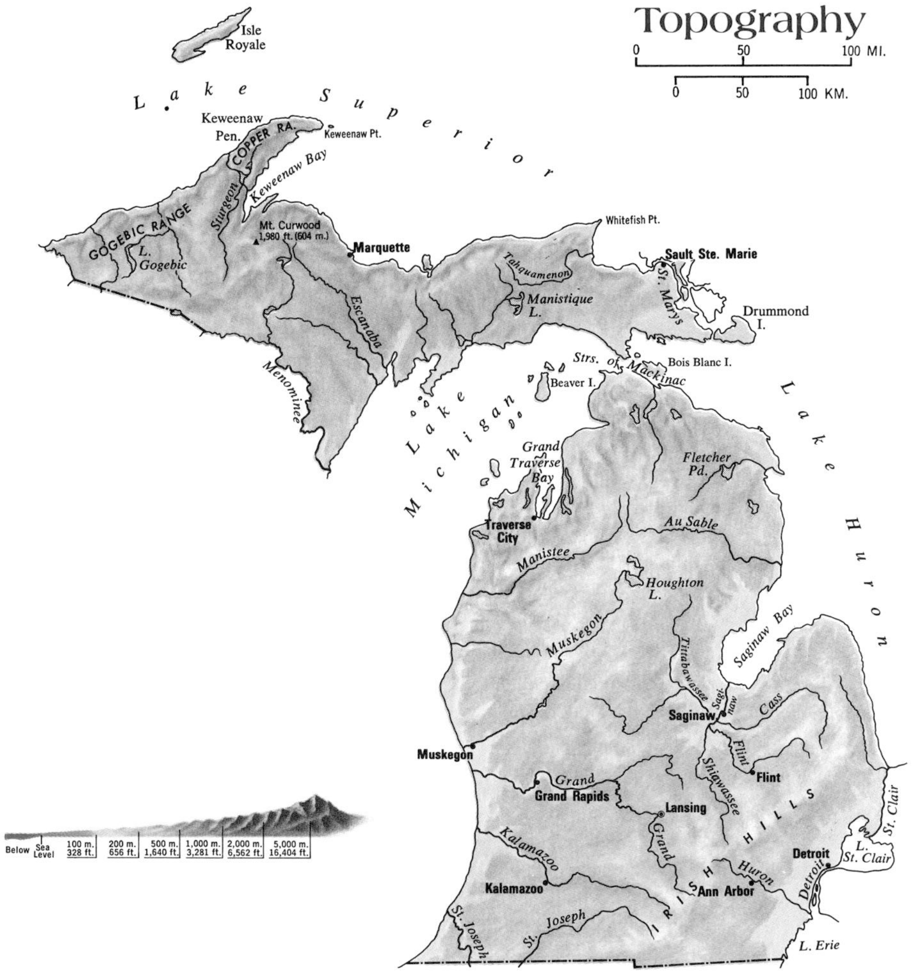
0 50 100 MI.
0 50 100 KM.
Isle Royale
Lake Superior
Keweenaw Pen.
COPPER RA.
Keweenaw Pt.
Keweenaw Bay
Sturgeon
GOGEBIC RANGE
L. Gogebic
Mt. Curwood 1,980 ft. (604 m.)
Marquette
Whitefish Pt.
Tahquamenon
Manistique L.
Sault Ste. Marie
St. Marys
Drummond I.
Escanaba
Menominee
Strs. of Mackinac
Bois Blanc I.
Beaver I.
Lake Michigan
Lake Huron
Grand Traverse Bay
Fletcher Pd.
Traverse City
Au Sable
Manistee
Houghton L.
Muskegon
Tittabawassee
Saginaw Bay
Saginaw
Cass
Flint
Muskegon
Grand
Grand Rapids
Lansing
Shiawassee
HILLS
St. Clair
L. St. Clair
Detroit
Kalamazoo
Kalamazoo
IRISH HILLS
Huron
Ann Arbor
St. Joseph
Joseph
L. Erie
Below Sea Level
100 m. 328 ft.
200 m. 656 ft.
500 m. 1,640 ft.
1,000 m. 3,281 ft.
2,000 m. 6,562 ft.
5,000 m. 16,404 ft.

COUNTIES

Alcona 10,145 ..... F4
Alger 8,972 ..... C2
Allegan 90,509 ..... D6
Alpena 30,605 ..... F4
Antrim 18,185 ..... D3
Arenac 14,931 ..... F4
Baraga 7,954 ..... A2
Barry 50,057 ..... D6
Bay 111,723 ..... E5
Benzie 12,200 ..... C4
Berrien 161,378 ..... C7
Branch 41,502 ..... D7
Calhoun 135,982 ..... D6
Cass 49,477 ..... C7
Charlevoix 21,468 ..... D3
Cheboygan 21,398 ..... E3
Chippewa 34,604 ..... E2
Clare 24,952 ..... E5
Clinton 57,883 ..... E6
Crawford 12,260 ..... E4
Delta 37,780 ..... C2
Dickinson 26,831 ..... B2
Eaton 92,879 ..... E6
Emmet 25,040 ..... E3
Genesee 430,459 ..... F5
Gladwin 21,896 ..... E4
Gogebic 18,052 ..... F2
Grand Traverse 64,273 ..... D4
Gratiot 38,982 ..... E5
Hillsdale 43,431 ..... E7
Houghton 35,446 ..... G1
Huron 34,951 ..... F5
Ingham 281,912 ..... E6
Ionia 57,024 ..... D6
Iosco 30,209 ..... F4
Iron 13,175 ..... G2
Isabella 54,624 ..... E5
Jackson 149,756 ..... E6
Kalamazoo 223,411 ..... D6
Kalkaska 13,497 ..... D4
Kent 500,631 ..... D5
Keweenaw 1,701 ..... A1
Lake 8,583 ..... D5
Lapeer 74,768 ..... F5
Leelanau 16,527 ..... D4
Lenawee 91,476 ..... E7
Livingston 115,645 ..... F6
Luce 5,763 ..... D2
Mackinac 10,674 ..... D2
Macomb 717,400 ..... G6
Manistee 21,265 ..... C4
Marquette 70,887 ..... B2
Mason 25,537 ..... C4
Mecosta 37,308 ..... D5
Menominee 24,920 ..... B3
Midland 75,651 ..... E5
Missaukee 12,147 ..... D4
Monroe 133,600 ..... F7
Montcalm 53,059 ..... D5
Montmorency 8,936 ..... E3
Muskegon 158,983 ..... C5
Newaygo 38,202 ..... D5
Oakland 1,083,592 ..... F6
Oceana 22,454 ..... C5
Ogemaw 18,681 ..... E4
Ontonagon 8,854 ..... F1
Osceola 20,146 ..... D5
Oscoda 7,842 ..... E4
Otsego 17,957 ..... E3
Ottawa 187,768 ..... C6
Presque Isle 13,743 ..... F3
Roscommon 19,776 ..... E4
Saginaw 211,946 ..... E5
Saint Clair 138,802 ..... G6
Saint Joseph 56,083 ..... D7
Sanilac 39,928 ..... G5
Schoolcraft 8,302 ..... C2
Shiawassee 69,770 ..... E6
Tuscola 55,498 ..... F5
Van Buren 66,814 ..... C6
Washtenaw 282,937 ..... F6
Wayne 2,111,687 ..... F6
Wexford 26,360 ..... D4

CITIES and TOWNS

Addison 632 ..... E7
Adrian▲ 22,097 ..... F7
Akron 421 ..... F5
Alabaster 46 ..... F4
Alanson 677 ..... E3
Albion 10,066 ..... E6
Algonac 4,551 ..... G6
Allegan▲ 4,547 ..... D6
Allen 201 ..... E7
Allen Park 31,092 ..... B7
Alma 9,034 ..... E5
Almont 2,354 ..... F6
Alpena▲ 11,354 ..... F3
Alpha 219 ..... A2
Anchorville 3,202 ..... G6
Ann Arbor▲ 109,592 ..... F6
Applegate 297 ..... G5
Arcadia 780 ..... C4
Armada 1,548 ..... G6
Ashley 518 ..... E5
Athens 990 ..... D6
Atlanta▲ 475 ..... E3
Atlantic Mine 809 ..... G1
Au Gres 838 ..... F4
Au Sable 1,542 ..... F4
Auburn 1,855 ..... F5
Auburn Heights 7,500 ..... F6
Augusta 927 ..... D6
Averill 800 ..... E5
Bad Axe▲ 3,484 ..... G5
Baldwin▲ 821 ..... D5
Bancroft 599 ..... E6
Bangor 1,922 ..... C6
Baraga 1,231 ..... G1
Bark River 800 ..... B3
Baroda 657 ..... C7
Barryton 393 ..... D5
Barton Hills 320 ..... F6
Battle Creek 53,540 ..... D6
Bay City▲ 38,936 ..... F5
Bay Port 750 ..... F5
Beal City 345 ..... D5
Bear Lake 339 ..... C4
Beaverton 1,150 ..... E5
Beechwood 2,676 ..... C6
Belding 5,969 ..... D5
Bellaire▲ 1,104 ..... D4
Belleville 3,270 ..... F6
Bellevue 1,401 ..... E6
Benton Harbor 12,818 ..... C6
Benton Heights 5,465 ..... C6
Benzonia 449 ..... D4
Berkley 16,960 ..... B6
Berrien Springs 1,927 ..... C7
Bessemer▲ 2,272 ..... F2
Beulah▲ 421 ..... C4
Beverly Hills 10,610 ..... B6
Big Rapids▲ 12,603 ..... D5
Birch Run 992 ..... F5
Birmingham 19,997 ..... B6
Bitely 750 ..... D5
Blissfield 3,172 ..... F7
Bloomfield Hills 4,288 ..... B6
Bloomingdale 503 ..... C6
Boyne City 3,478 ..... E3
Boyne Falls 369 ..... E3
Breckenridge 1,301 ..... E5
Breedsville 213 ..... C6
Bridgeport 8,569 ..... F5
Bridgman 2,140 ..... C7
Brighton 5,686 ..... F6
Britton 694 ..... F6
Bronson 2,342 ..... D7
Brooklyn 1,027 ..... E6
Brown City 1,244 ..... G5
Buchanan 4,992 ..... C7
Buckley 402 ..... D4
Burlington 294 ..... D6
Burr Oak 882 ..... D7
Burt 1,169 ..... F5
Burton 27,617 ..... F6
Byron 573 ..... E6
Byron Center 900 ..... D6
Cadillac▲ 10,104 ..... D4
Caledonia 885 ..... D6
Calumet 818 ..... A1
Camden 482 ..... E7
Capac 1,583 ..... G5
Carleton 2,770 ..... F6
Carney 197 ..... B3
Caro▲ 4,054 ..... F5
Carrollton 6,521 ..... E5
Carson City 1,158 ..... E5
Carsonville 583 ..... G5
Caseville 857 ..... F5
Casnovia 376 ..... D5
Caspian 1,031 ..... G2
Cass City 2,276 ..... F5
Cassopolis▲ 1,822 ..... C7
Cedar Springs 2,600 ..... D5
Cement City 493 ..... E6
Center Line 9,026 ..... B6
Central Lake 954 ..... D3
Centreville▲ 1,516 ..... D7
Charlevoix▲ 3,116 ..... D3
Charlotte▲ 8,083 ..... E6
Chatham 268 ..... B2
Cheboygan▲ 4,999 ..... E3
Chelsea 3,772 ..... E6
Chesaning 2,567 ..... E5
Clare 3,021 ..... E5
Clarkston 1,005 ..... F6
Clarksville 360 ..... D6
Clawson 13,874 ..... B6
Clayton 384 ..... E7
Clifford 354 ..... F5
Climax 677 ..... D6
Clinton 2,475 ..... F6
Clio 2,629 ..... F5
Coldwater▲ 9,607 ..... D7
Coleman 1,237 ..... E5
Coloma 1,679 ..... C6
Colon 1,224 ..... D7
Columbiaville 934 ..... F5
Comstock• 11,162 ..... D6
Concord 944 ..... E6
Constantine 2,032 ..... D7
Coopersville 3,421 ..... C5
Copemish 222 ..... D4
Copper City 198 ..... A1
Corunna▲ 3,091 ..... E6
Croswell 2,174 ..... G5
Crystal 800 ..... E5
Crystal Falls▲ 1,922 ..... A2
Curtis 800 ..... D2
Custer 312 ..... C5
Cutlerville 11,228 ..... D6
Daggett 260 ..... B3
Dansville 437 ..... E6
Davison 5,693 ..... F5
De Tour Village 407 ..... E3
De Witt 3,964 ..... E6
Dearborn 89,286 ..... B7
Dearborn Heights 60,838 ..... B7
Decatur 1,760 ..... C6
Deckerville 1,015 ..... G5
Deerfield 922 ..... F7
Detroit Beach 2,113 ..... F7
Detroit▲ 1,027,974 ..... B7
Dexter 1,497 ..... F6
Dimondale 1,247 ..... E6
Dollar Bay 950 ..... G1
Douglas 1,040 ..... C6
Dowagiac 6,409 ..... D6
Drayton Plains F6
Drummond Island• 746 ..... F3
Dryden 628 ..... F6
Dundee 2,664 ..... F7
Durand 4,283 ..... E6
Eagle River▲ 20 ..... A1
East Detroit 35,283 ..... B6
East Grand Rapids 10,807 ..... D6
East Jordan 2,240 ..... D3
East Kingsford A3
East Lansing 50,677 ..... E6
East Tawas 2,887 ..... F4
Eastlake 473 ..... C4
Eastwood 6,340 ..... D6
Eaton Rapids 4,695 ..... E6
Eau Claire 494 ..... C6
Ecorse 12,180 ..... B7
Edmore 1,126 ..... E5
Edwardsburg 1,142 ..... C7
Elberta 478 ..... C4
Elk Rapids 1,626 ..... D4
Elkton 958 ..... F5
Ellsworth 418 ..... D3
Elsie 957 ..... E5
Emmett 297 ..... G6
Empire 355 ..... C4
Erie 750 ..... F7
Escanaba▲ 13,659 ..... C3
Essexville 4,088 ..... F5
Estral Beach 430 ..... F7
Evart 1,744 ..... D5
Ewen 821 ..... F2
Fair Haven 1,505 ..... G6
Fair Plain 8,051 ..... C6
Fairgrove 592 ..... F5
Farmington 10,132 ..... F6
Farmington Hills 74,652 ..... F6
Farwell 851 ..... E5
Fennville 1,023 ..... C6
Fenton 8,444 ..... F6
Ferndale 25,084 ..... B6
Ferrysburg 2,919 ..... C5
Fife Lake 394 ..... D4
Flat Rock 7,290 ..... F6
Flint▲ 140,761 ..... F5
Flushing 8,542 ..... F5
Fountain 165 ..... C4
Fowler 912 ..... E5
Fowlerville 2,648 ..... F6
Frankenmuth 4,408 ..... F5
Frankfort 1,546 ..... C4
Franklin 2,626 ..... B6
Fraser 13,899 ..... B6
Freeland 1,421 ..... E5
Freeport 458 ..... D6
Fremont 3,875 ..... D5
Fruitport 1,090 ..... C5
Gaastra 376 ..... G2
Gagetown 337 ..... F5
Gaines 427 ..... F6
Galesburg 1,863 ..... D6
Galien 596 ..... C7
Garden 268 ..... C3
Garden City 31,846 ..... F6
Gaylord▲ 3,256 ..... E3
Gibraltar 4,297 ..... F6
Gladstone 4,565 ..... C3
Gladwin▲ 2,682 ..... E5
Gobles 769 ..... D6
Goodrich 916 ..... F6
Grand Blanc 7,760 ..... F6
Grand Haven▲ 11,951 ..... C5
Grand Ledge 7,579 ..... E6
Grand Rapids▲ 189,126 ..... D5
Grandville 15,624 ..... D6
Grant 764 ..... D5
Grass Lake 903 ..... E6
Grayling▲ 1,944 ..... E4
Greenville 8,101 ..... D5
Grosse Ile 9,781 ..... B7
Grosse Pointe 5,681 ..... B7
Grosse Pointe Farms 10,092 ..... B6
Grosse Pointe Park 12,857 ..... B7
Grosse Pointe Shores 2,955 ..... B6
Grosse Pointe Woods 17,715 ..... B6
Gulliver 962 ..... D2
Gwinn 2,370 ..... B2
Hamilton 950 ..... C6
Hamtramck 18,372 ..... B6
Hancock 4,547 ..... G1
Hanover 481 ..... E6
Harbor Beach 2,089 ..... G5
Harbor Springs 1,540 ..... D3
Harper Woods 14,903 ..... B6
Harrison▲ 1,835 ..... E4
Harrisville▲ 470 ..... F4
Hart▲ 1,942 ..... C5
Hartford 2,341 ..... C6
Haslett 10,230 ..... E6
Hastings▲ 6,549 ..... D6
Hazel Park 20,051 ..... B6
Hemlock 1,601 ..... E5
Hermansville 950 ..... B3
Hersey 354 ..... D5
Hesperia 846 ..... D5
Highland Park 20,121 ..... B6
Hillman 643 ..... F3
Hillsdale▲ 8,170 ..... E7
Holland 30,745 ..... C6
Holly 5,595 ..... F6
Holt 11,744 ..... E6
Homer 1,758 ..... E6
Honor 292 ..... D4
Hopkins 546 ..... D6
Houghton Lake 3,353 ..... E4
Houghton Lake Heights E4
Houghton▲ 7,498 ..... G1
Howard City 1,351 ..... D5
Howell▲ 8,184 ..... E6
Hubbardston 404 ..... E5
Hubbell 1,174 ..... A1
Hudson 2,580 ..... E7
Hudsonville 6,170 ..... D6
Huntington Woods 6,419 ..... B6
Ida 970 ..... F7
Imlay City 2,921 ..... F5
Indian River 950 ..... E3
Inkster 30,772 ..... B7
Interlochen 600 ..... D4
Ionia▲ 5,935 ..... D6
Iron Mountain▲ 8,525 ..... B3
Iron River 2,095 ..... G2
Ironwood 6,849 ..... F2
Ishpeming 7,200 ..... B2
Isle Royale National Park E1
Ithaca▲ 3,009 ..... E5
Jackson▲ 37,446 ..... E6
Jenison 17,882 ..... D6
Jonesville 2,283 ..... E6
Kalamazoo▲ 80,277 ..... D6
Kaleva 484 ..... C4
Kalkaska▲ 1,952 ..... D4
Keego Harbor 2,932 ..... F6
Kent City 899 ..... D5
Kentwood 37,826 ..... D6
Kinde 473 ..... G5
Kingsford 5,480 ..... A3
Kingsley 738 ..... D4
Kingston 439 ..... F5
L'Anse▲ 2,151 ..... G1
Laingsburg 1,148 ..... E6
Lake Ann 217 ..... D4
Lake City▲ 858 ..... D4
Lake George 950 ..... E5
Lake Linden 1,203 ..... A1
Lake Michigan Beach 1,694 ..... C6
Lake Odessa 2,256 ..... D6
Lake Orion 3,057 ..... F6
Lakeview 1,108 ..... D5
Lakewood Club 659 ..... C5

(continued on following page)

Lambertville 7,860 ....F7
Lansing (cap.) 127,321 ....E6
Lapeer▲ 7,759 ....F5
Laurium 2,268 ....A1
Lawrence 915 ....C6
Lawton 1,685 ....D6
Le Roy 251 ....D4
Leland▲ 776 ....D3
Lennon 534 ....E5
Leonard 357 ....F6
Leslie 1,872 ....E6
Levering 967 ....E3
Lexington 779 ....G5
Lincoln 337 ....F4
Lincoln Park 41,832 ....B7
Linden 2,415 ....F6
Litchfield 1,317 ....E6
Little Lake 975 ....B2
Livonia 100,850 ....F6
Lowell 3,983 ....D6
Ludington▲ 8,507 ....C5
Luna Pier 1,507 ....F7
Luther 343 ....D4
Lyons 824 ....E6
Mackinac Island 469 ....E3
Mackinaw City 875 ....D3
Madison Heights 32,196 ....B6
Mancelona 1,370 ....D4
Manchester 1,753 ....E6
Manistee▲ 6,734 ....C4
Manistique▲ 3,456 ....C2
Manton 1,161 ....D4
Maple Rapids 680 ....E5
Marcellus 1,193 ....D6
Marine City 4,556 ....G6
Marion 807 ....D4
Marlette 1,924 ....G5
Marquette▲ 21,977 ....B2
Marshall▲ 6,891 ....E6
Martin 462 ....D6
Marysville 8,515 ....G6
Mason▲ 6,768 ....E6
Mass City 850 ....G1
Mattawan 2,456 ....D6
Maybee 500 ....F6
Mayville 1,010 ....F5
McBain 692 ....D4
McBrides 252 ....D5
Mecosta 393 ....D5
Melvindale 11,216 ....B7
Memphis 1,221 ....G6
Mendon 920 ....D6
Menominee▲ 9,398 ....B3
Merrill 755 ....E5
Mesick 406 ....D4
Metamora 447 ....F6
Michiana 164 ....C7
Michigan Center 4,863 ....E6
Middleville 1,966 ....D6
Midland▲ 38,053 ....E5
Milan 4,040 ....F6
Milford 5,511 ....F6
Millersburg 250 ....F3

Millington 1,114 ....F5
Minden City 233 ....G5
Mineral Hills 200 ....G2
Mio▲ 1,886 ....E4
Mohawk 800 ....A1
Monroe▲ 22,902 ....F7
Montague 2,276 ....C5
Montgomery 388 ....E7
Montrose 1,811 ....F5
Morenci 2,342 ....E7
Morley 528 ....D5
Morrice 630 ....E6
Mount Clemens▲ 18,405 ....F6
Mount Morris 3,292 ....F5
Mount Pleasant▲ 23,285 ....E5
Muir 667 ....D5
Mulliken 590 ....E6
Munising▲ 2,783 ....C2
Muskegon▲ 40,283 ....C5
Muskegon Heights 13,176 ....C5
Napoleon 1,332 ....E6
Nashville 1,654 ....E6
Naubinway 850 ....D2
Negaunee 4,741 ....B2
New Baltimore 5,798 ....G6
New Boston 1,200 ....F6
New Buffalo 2,317 ....C7
New Era 520 ....C5
New Haven 2,331 ....G6
New Lothrop 596 ....F5
Newaygo 1,336 ....D5
Newberry▲ 1,873 ....D2
Niles 12,458 ....C7
North Adams 512 ....E7
North Branch 1,023 ....F5
North Muskegon 3,919 ....C5
Northport 605 ....D3
Northville 6,226 ....F6
Norton Shores 21,755 ....C5
Norway 2,910 ....B3
Novi 32,998 ....F6
Oak Park 30,462 ....B7
Oakley 362 ....E5
Okemos 20,216 ....E6
Olivet 1,604 ....E6
Omer 385 ....E4
Onaway 1,039 ....E3
Onekama 515 ....C4
Onsted 801 ....E6
Ontonagon▲ 2,040 ....F1
Orchard Lake 1,798 ....F6
Ortonville 1,252 ....F6
Oscoda 1,061 ....E4
Ossineke 1,091 ....F4
Otisville 724 ....F5
Otsego 3,937 ....D6
Otter Lake 474 ....F5
Ovid 1,442 ....E5
Owendale 285 ....F5
Owosso 16,322 ....E5
Oxford 2,929 ....F6
Parchment 1,958 ....D6
Parma 809 ....E6

Paw Paw Lake 3,782 ....C6
Paw Paw▲ 3,169 ....D6
Pearl Beach 3,394 ....G6
Peck 558 ....G5
Pellston 583 ....E3
Pentwater 1,050 ....C5
Perrinton 393 ....E5
Perry 2,163 ....E6
Petersburg 1,201 ....F7
Petoskey▲ 6,056 ....E3
Pewamo 520 ....E6
Pierson 207 ....D5
Pigeon 1,207 ....F5
Pinckney 1,603 ....F6
Pinconning 1,291 ....E5
Plainwell 4,057 ....D6
Pleasant Ridge 2,775 ....F6
Plymouth 9,560 ....F6
Pontiac▲ 71,166 ....F6
Port Austin 815 ....F4
Port Hope 313 ....G4
Port Huron▲ 33,694 ....G6
Port Sanilac 656 ....G5
Portage 41,042 ....D6
Portland 3,889 ....E6
Posen 263 ....F4
Potterville 1,523 ....E6
Powers 271 ....B3
Prescott 314 ....E4
Prudenville 1,513 ....E4
Quincy 1,680 ....E7
Quinnesec 1,254 ....A3
Ramsay F2
Rapid River 950 ....C3
Ravenna 919 ....D5
Reading 1,127 ....E7
Reed City▲ 2,379 ....D5
Reese 1,414 ....F5
Republic 900 ....B2
Richland 465 ....D6
Richmond 4,141 ....G6
River Rouge 11,314 ....B7
Riverview 13,894 ....B7
Rochester 7,130 ....F6
Rockford 3,750 ....D5
Rockwood 3,141 ....F6
Rogers City▲ 3,642 ....F3
Romeo 3,520 ....F6
Romulus 22,897 ....F6
Roosevelt Park 3,885 ....C5
Roscommon▲ 858 ....E4
Rose City 686 ....E4
Rosebush 333 ....E5
Roseville 51,412 ....B6
Rothbury 407 ....C5
Royal Oak 65,410 ....B6
Rudyard 950 ....E2
Saginaw▲ 69,512 ....F5
Saint Charles 2,144 ....E5
Saint Clair 5,116 ....G6
Saint Clair Shores 68,107 .....B6
Saint Ignace▲ 2,568 ....E3
Saint James • 240 ....D3

Saint Johns▲ 7,284 ....E6
Saint Joseph▲ 9,214 ....C6
Saint Louis 3,828 ....E5
Saline 6,660 ....E6
Sand Lake 456 ....D5
Sandusky▲ 2,403 ....G5
Sanford 889 ....E5
Saranac 1,461 ....D6
Saugatuck 954 ....C6
Sault Sainte Marie▲ 14,689 ....E2
Schoolcraft 1,517 ....D6
Scottville 1,287 ....C5
Sebewaing 1,923 ....F5
Shelby 1,871 ....C5
Shepherd 1,413 ....E5
Sheridan 730 ....D5
Sherwood 320 ....D6
Shoreham 737 ....C6
Shorewood 1,735 ....C7
South Haven 5,563 ....C6
South Lyon 5,857 ....F6
South Monroe 5,266 ....F7
South Range 745 ....G1
South Rockwood 1,221 ....F7
Southfield 75,728 ....F6
Southgate 30,771 ....F6
Sparlingville 1,974 ....G6
Sparta 3,968 ....D5
Spring Arbor 2,010 ....E6
Spring Lake 2,537 ....C5
Springfield 5,582 ....D6
Springport 707 ....E6
Stambaugh 1,281 ....G2
Standish▲ 1,377 ....F5
Stanton▲ 1,504 ....D5
Stanwood 174 ....D5
Stephenson 904 ....B3
Sterling 520 ....E4
Sterling Heights 117,810 ......B6
Stevensville 1,230 ....C6
Stockbridge 1,202 ....E6
Sturgis 10,130 ....D7
Sunfield 610 ....D6
Suttons Bay 561 ....D3
Swartz Creek 4,851 ....F6
Sylvan Lake 1,884 ....F6
Tawas City▲ 2,009 ....F4
Taylor 70,811 ....B7
Tecumseh 7,462 ....E7
Tekonsha 722 ....E6
Temperance 6,542 ....F7
Thompsonville 416 ....C4
Three Oaks 1,786 ....C7
Three Rivers 7,413 ....D7
Traverse City▲ 15,155 ....D4
Trenton 20,586 ....B7
Troy 72,884 ....F6
Tustin 236 ....D4
Twin Lake 1,328 ....C5
Twining 169 ....E4
Ubly 821 ....G5
Union City 1,767 ....D6
Union Pier 1,039 ....C7

Unionville 590 ....F5
Utica 5,081 ....F6
Vandalia 357 ....D7
Vanderbilt 605 ....E3
Vassar 2,559 ....F5
Vermontville 776 ....E6
Vernon 913 ....F6
Vicksburg 2,320 ....D6
Wakefield 2,318 ....G2
Waldron 581 ....E7
Walker 17,279 ....D6
Walkerville 262 ....C5
Walled Lake 6,278 ....F6
Warren 144,864 ....B6
Watersmeet 850 ....G2
Watervliet 1,867 ....C6
Wayland 2,751 ....D6
Wayne 19,899 ....F6
Webberville 1,698 ....E6
Weidman 696 ....D5
Wells B3
West Branch▲ 1,914 ....E4
Westland 84,724 ....F6
Westphalia 780 ....E6
White Cloud▲ 1,147 ....D5
White Pigeon 1,458 ....D7
White Pine 1,142 ....F1
Whitehall 3,027 ....C5
Whitmore Lake 3,251 ....F6
Whittemore 463 ....F4
Williamston 2,922 ....E6
Wixom 8,550 ....F6
Wolf Lake 4,110 ....D6
Wolverine 364 ....E3
Wolverine Lake 4,727 ....F6
Woodhaven 11,631 ....F6
Woodland 466 ....D6
Wyandotte 30,938 ....B7
Wyoming 63,891 ....D6
Yale 1,977 ....G5
Ypsilanti 24,846 ....F6
Zeeland 5,417 ....C6
Zilwaukee 1,850 ....F5

OTHER FEATURES

Abbaye (pt.) B2
Au Sable (pt.) C2
Au Sable (pt.) F4
Au Sable (riv.) E4
Au Train (bay) C2
Bad (riv.) E5
Barques (pt.) G4
Beaver (lake) D3
Beaver (isl.) D3
Belle (riv.) G6
Bete Grise (bay) B1
Big Bay (pt.) B2
Big Bay de Noc (bay) C3
Big Iron (riv.) F1
Big Sable (pt.) C4
Big Sable (riv.) C4
Big Star (lake) C5

Black (lake) E3
Black (riv.) E3
Black (riv.) G5
Blake (pt.) E1
Boardman (riv.) D4
Bois Blanc (isl.) E3
Bond Falls (res.) G2
Brevoort (lake) D3
Brule (riv.) A3
Burt (lake) E3
Cass (riv.) F5
Cedar (lake) F4
Charlevoix (lake) D2
Chippewa (riv.) E5
Crisp (pt.) D2
Crystal (lake) C4
Curwood (mt.) E5
Dead (riv.) B2
Deer (riv.) A2
De Tour (passage) E3
Detour (pt.) C3
Detroit (riv.) B7
Drummond (isl.) F2
Duck (lake) C5
Elk (lake) D4
Erie (lake) F7
Escanaba (riv.) B2
False Detour (chan.) F3
Father Marquette Nat'l Mem. ...E3
Fawn (riv.) D7
Fence (riv.) A2
Firesteel (riv.) G1
Flint (riv.) F5
Fletcher (pond) F4
Ford (riv.) B2
Forty Mile (pt.) F3
Fourteen Mile (pt.) F1
Garden (isl.) D3
Garden (pen.) C3
Glen (lake) D4
Gogebic (lake) F2
Good Harbor (bay) D4
Government (peak) F1
Grand (isl.) C2
Grand (lake) F3
Grand (riv.) D6
Grand Traverse (bay) D3
Granite (pt.) B2
Green (bay) B4
Gun (lake) D6
Hamlin (lake) C4
Higgins (lake) E4
High (isl.) D3
Hog (isl.) D3
Houghton (lake) E4
Hubbard (lake) F4
Huron (bay) B2
Huron (isl.) B2
Huron (lake) G4
Huron (riv.) F6
Huron River (pt.) B2
Independence (lake) B2
Indian (lake) C2
Isle Royale (isl.) D1

Isle Royale Nat'l Park E1
Kalamazoo (riv.) C6
Keweenaw (bay) A1
Keweenaw (pt.) B1
K.I. Sawyer A.F.B. 6,577 ......B2
L'Anse Ind. Res. B2
Laughing Fish (pt.) B2
Leelanau (lake) D4
Light House (pt.) D3
Little Bay de Noc (bay) B3
Little Girl (pt.) E1
Little Sable (pt.) C5
Little Summer (isl.) C3
Little Traverse (bay) D3
Long (lake) E4
Lookingglass (riv.) E6
Mackinac (isl.) E3
Mackinac (str.) E3
Manistee (riv.) C4
Manistique (lake) D2
Manistique (riv.) D2
Manitou (isl.) B1
Maple (riv.) E5
Margrethe (lake) E4
Marquette (isl.) E3
Maumee (bay) F7
Menominee (riv.) B2
Michigamme (lake) A2
Michigamme (res.) B2
Michigamme (riv.) B2
Michigan (lake) E5
Mill (creek) F5
Millecoquins (lake) D2
Misery (bay) G1
Misery (riv.) G1
Montreal (riv.) F1
Mullett (lake) E3
Munuscong (lake) E2
Muskegon (riv.) C5
Neebish (isl.) E2
Net (riv.) G2
Ninemile (pt.) G2
North (chan.) F2
North (pt.) G4
North Fox (isl.) D3
North Manitou (isl.) D3
Oak (pt.) G5
Ontonagon (riv.) F1
Ontonagon Ind. Res. F1
Otsego (lake) E4
Paint (riv.) A2
Paradise (lake) E3
Passage (isl.) E1
Patterson (pt.) D3
Paw Paw (riv.) C6
Peninsula (pt.) C3
Perch (lake) G2
Perch (riv.) G2
Pere Marquette (riv.) C5
Pictured Rocks (cliff) C2
Pictured Rocks
   Nat'l Lakeshore C2
Pigeon (riv.) D7
Pigeon (riv.) E3
Pine (riv.) D4
Pine (riv.) E5
Platte (lake) C4
Porcupine (mts.) F1
Potagannissing (bay) F2
Poverty (isl.) C3
Prairie (riv.) C7
Presque Isle (riv.) F1
Rabbit (riv.) C6
Raisin (riv.) F7
Rapid (riv.) E2
Reedsburg (res.) E4
Rifle (riv.) E4
Royale (isl.) E1
Saginaw (bay) F5
Saginaw (riv.) F5
Saint Clair (lake) G6
Saint Clair (riv.) G6
Saint Joseph (riv.) C7
Saint Martin (bay) E3
Saint Martin (isl.) C3
Saint Marys (riv.) E2
Salt (pt.) E2
Sand (pt.) F5
Seul Choi (pt.) D3
Shelldrake (riv) D2
Shiawassee (riv.) E5
Siskiwit (bay) E1
Sleeping Bear Dunes
   Nat'l Lakeshore C4
South (bay) C2
South (pt.) F4
South (chan.) E3
South Fox (isl.) D3
South Manitou (isl.) C3
Sturgeon (riv.) C2
Sugar (isl.) E2
Summer (isl.) C3
Superior (lake) C2
Tahquamenon (falls) D2
Tahquamenon (riv.) D2
Tawas (lake) F4
Tawas (pt.) F4
Thunder (bay) F4
Thunder Bay (riv.) F3
Tittabawassee (riv.) E5
Torch (lake) D3
Traverse (lake) A1
Traverse (pt.) A1
Turtle (lake) F4
Two Hearted (riv.) D2
Vieux Desert (lake) E3
Walloon (lake) E3
White (lake) C5
Whitefish (bay) E2
Whitefish (pt.) E2
Whitefish (pt.) C2
Wood (isl.) C2
Wurtsmith A.F.B. 5,080 ....F4
Yellow Dog (riv.) B2

▲County Seat
• Population of town or township

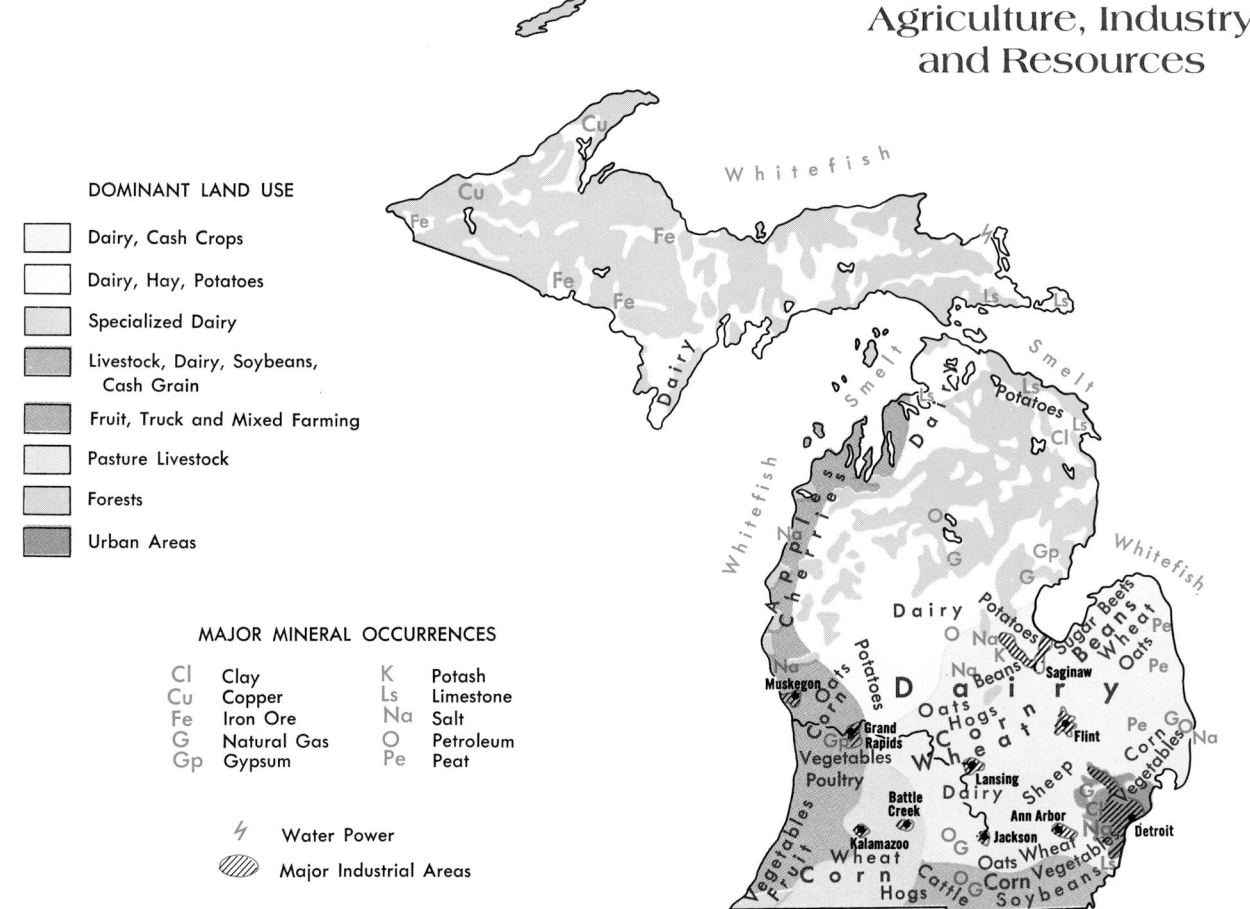

Agriculture, Industry and Resources

DOMINANT LAND USE

- Dairy, Cash Crops
- Dairy, Hay, Potatoes
- Specialized Dairy
- Livestock, Dairy, Soybeans, Cash Grain
- Fruit, Truck and Mixed Farming
- Pasture Livestock
- Forests
- Urban Areas

MAJOR MINERAL OCCURRENCES

Cl	Clay	K	Potash
Cu	Copper	Ls	Limestone
Fe	Iron Ore	Na	Salt
G	Natural Gas	O	Petroleum
Gp	Gypsum	Pe	Peat

⚡ Water Power

▨ Major Industrial Areas

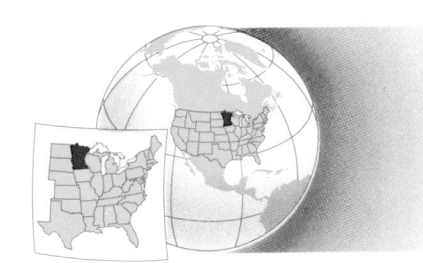

AREA 84,402 sq. mi. (218,601 sq. km.)
POPULATION 4,387,029
CAPITAL St. Paul
LARGEST CITY Minneapolis
HIGHEST POINT Eagle Mtn. 2,301 ft. (701 m.)
SETTLED IN 1805
ADMITTED TO UNION May 11, 1858
POPULAR NAME North Star State; Gopher State
STATE FLOWER Pink & White Lady's-Slipper
STATE BIRD Common Loon

COUNTIES

itkin 12,425	E4
noka 243,641	E5
ecker 27,881	C4
eltrami 34,384	C2
enton 30,185	D5
g Stone 6,285	B5
ue Earth 54,044	D6
rown 26,984	D6
arlton 29,259	F4
arver 47,915	E6
ass 21,791	D4
hippewa 13,228	C5
hisago 30,521	F5
ay 50,422	B4
earwater 8,309	C3
ook 3,868	H3
ottonwood 12,694	C6
row Wing 44,249	D4
akota 275,227	E6
odge 15,731	F7
ouglas 28,674	C5
aribault 16,937	D7
llmore 20,777	F7
reeborn 33,060	E7
oodhue 40,690	F6
rant 6,246	B5
ennepin 1,032,431	E5
ouston 18,497	G7
ubbard 14,939	D3
anti 25,921	E5
asca 40,863	E3
ackson 11,677	C7
anabec 12,802	E5
andiyohi 38,761	C5
ittson 5,767	B2
oochiching 16,299	E2
ac qui Parle 8,924	B6
ake 10,415	G3
ake of the Woods 4,076	D2
e Sueur 23,239	E6
Lincoln 6,890	B6
Lyon 24,789	C6
Mahnomen 5,044	C3
Marshall 10,993	B2
Martin 22,914	D7
McLeod 32,030	D6
Meeker 20,846	D5
Mille Lacs 18,670	E5
Morrison 29,604	D4
Mower 37,385	F7
Murray 9,660	C6
Nicollet 28,076	D6
Nobles 20,098	C7
Norman 7,975	B3
Olmsted 106,470	F7
Otter Tail 50,714	C4
Pennington 13,306	B2
Pine 21,264	F4
Pipestone 10,491	B6
Polk 32,498	B3
Pope 10,745	C5
Ramsey 485,765	E5
Red Lake 4,525	B3
Redwood 17,254	C6
Renville 17,673	C6
Rice 49,183	E6
Rock 9,806	B7
Roseau 15,026	C2
Saint Louis 222,229	F3
Scott 57,846	E6
Sherburne 41,945	E5
Sibley 14,366	D6
Stearns 118,791	D5
Steele 30,729	E7
Stevens 10,634	B5
Swift 10,724	C5
Todd 23,363	D4
Traverse 4,463	B5
Wabasha 19,744	F6
Wadena 13,154	D4
Waseca 18,079	E6
Washington 145,896	F5
Watonwan 11,682	D7
Wilkin 7,516	B4
Winona 47,828	G6
Wright 68,710	D5
Yellow Medicine 11,684	B6

CITIES and TOWNS

Ada▲ 1,708	B3
Adams 756	F7
Adrian 1,141	C7
Afton 2,645	F6
Aitkin▲ 1,698	E4
Akeley 393	D3
Albany 1,548	D5
Albert Lea▲ 18,310	E7
Alberta 136	B5
Albertville 1,251	E5
Alborn 500	F4
Alden 623	E7
Aldrich 70	C4
Alexandria▲ 7,838	C5
Alpha 105	D7
Altura 349	G6
Alvarado 356	B2
Amboy 517	D7
Andover 15,216	E5
Annandale 2,054	D5
Anoka▲ 17,192	E5
Apple Valley 34,598	G6
Appleton 1,552	C5
Arco 104	B6
Argyle 636	B2
Arlington 1,886	D6
Arnold 2,891	F4
Ashby 469	C4
Askov 343	F4
Atwater 1,053	D5
Audubon 411	C4
Aurora 1,965	F3
Austin▲ 21,907	E7
Avoca 150	C7
Avon 970	D5
Babbitt 1,562	G3
Backus 240	D4
Badger 381	B2
Bagley▲ 1,388	C3
Balaton 737	C6
Barnesville 2,066	B4
Barnum 482	F4
Barrett 350	B5
Barry 40	B5
Battle Lake 698	C4
Baudette▲ 1,146	D2
Baxter 3,695	D4
Bayport 3,200	F5
Beardsley 297	B5
Beaver Bay 147	G3
Beaver Creek 249	B7
Becker 902	E5
Bejou 110	B3
Belgrade 700	C5
Belle Plaine 3,149	E6
Bellechester 110	F6
Bellingham 247	B5
Beltrami 137	B3
Belview 383	C6
Bemidji▲ 11,245	D3
Bena 147	D3
Benson▲ 3,235	C5
Bertha 507	C4
Bethel 394	E5
Big Falls 341	E2
Big Lake 3,113	E5
Bigelow 232	C7
Bigfork 384	E3
Bingham Lake 155	C7
Bird Island 1,326	D6
Biscay 113	D6
Biwabik 1,097	F3
Blackduck 718	D3
Blaine 38,975	G5
Blomkest 183	D6
Blooming Prairie 2,043	E7
Bloomington 86,335	G6
Blue Earth▲ 3,745	D7
Bluffton 187	C4
Bock 115	E5
Borup 119	B3
Bovey 662	E3
Bowlus 260	D5
Boy River 43	D3
Boyd 251	C6
Braham 1,139	E5
Brainerd▲ 12,353	D4
Branch 2,400	F5
Brandon 441	C5
Breckenridge▲ 3,708	B4
Breezy Point 432	D4
Brewster 532	C7
Bricelyn 426	E7
Brook Park 125	F5
Brooklyn Center 28,887	G5
Brooklyn Park 56,381	G5
Brooks 158	B3
Brookston 107	F4
Brooten 589	C5
Browerville 782	D4
Browns Valley 804	B5
Brownsdale 695	F7
Brownsville 415	G7
Brownton 781	D6
Bruno 89	F4
Buckman 201	D5
Buffalo Lake 734	D6
Buffalo▲ 6,856	E5
Buhl 915	F3
Burnsville 51,288	E6
Burtrum 172	D5
Butterfield 509	D7
Byron 2,441	F6
Caledonia▲ 2,846	G7
Callaway 212	C3
Calumet 382	E3
Cambridge▲ 5,094	E5
Campbell 233	B4
Canby 1,826	B6
Cannon Falls 3,232	F6
Canton 362	F7
Carlos 361	C5
Carlton▲ 923	F4
Carver 744	E6
Cass Lake 923	D3
Cedar Mills 80	D6
Center City▲ 451	F5
Centerville 1,633	E5
Ceylon 461	D7
Champlin 16,849	G5
Chandler 316	C7
Chanhassen 11,732	F6
Chaska▲ 11,339	F6
Chatfield 2,226	F7
Chickamaw Beach 132	D4
Chisago City 2,009	E5
Chisholm 5,290	E3
Chokio 521	B5
Circle Pines 4,704	G5
Clara City 1,307	C6
Claremont 530	E6
Clarissa 637	C4
Clarkfield 924	C6
Clarks Grove 675	E7
Clear Lake 315	E5
Clearbrook 560	C3
Clearwater 597	D5
Clements 191	D6
Cleveland 699	E6
Climax 264	B3
Clinton 574	B5
Clitherall 109	C4
Clontarf 172	C5
Cloquet 10,885	F4
Coates 186	E6
Cobden 62	D6
Cohasset 2,073	E3
Cokato 2,180	D5
Cold Spring 2,459	D5
Coleraine 1,041	E3
Cologne 563	E6
Columbia Heights 18,910	G5
Comfrey 433	D6
Comstock 123	B4
Conger 143	E7
Cook 680	F3
Coon Rapids 52,978	G5
Corcoran 5,199	F5
Correll 60	B5
Cosmos 610	D6
Cottage Grove 22,935	F6
Cotton 982	F3
Cottonwood 924	C6
Courtland 412	D6
Cromwell 221	F4
Crookston▲ 8,119	B3
Crosby 2,073	D4
Crosslake 1,132	E4
Crystal 23,788	G5
Currie 303	C6
Cuyuna 172	E4
Cyrus 328	C5
Dakota 360	G7
Dalton 204	C4
Danube 562	C6
Danvers 98	C5
Darfur 128	D6
Darwin 252	D5
Dassel 1,082	D5
Dawson 1,626	B6
Day 4,443	E5
De Graff 149	C5
Deephaven 3,653	G5
Deer Creek 303	C4
Deer River 838	E3
Deerwood 524	E4
Delano 2,709	E5
Delavan 245	D7
Delhi 69	C6
Dellwood 887	F5
Denham 36	F4
Dennison 152	E6
Dent 177	C4
Detroit Lakes▲ 6,635	C4
Dexter 303	F7
Dilworth 2,562	B4
Dodge Center 1,954	F6
Donaldson 57	B2
Donnelly 221	B5
Doran 78	B4
Dover 416	F7
Dovray 60	C6
Duluth▲ 85,493	F4
Dumont 126	B5
Dundas 473	E6
Dundee 107	C7
Dunnell 187	D7
Eagan 47,409	G6
Eagle Bend 524	D4
Eagle Lake 1,703	E6
East Bethel 8,050	E5
East Grand Forks 8,658	B3
East Gull Lake 687	D4
Easton 229	E7
Echo 304	C6
Eden Prairie 39,311	G6
Eden Valley 732	D5
Edgerton 1,106	B7
Edina 46,070	G5
Effie 130	E3
Eitzen 221	G7
Elba 220	F6
Elbow Lake▲ 1,186	B5
Elgin 733	F6
Elizabeth 152	B4
Elk River▲ 11,143	E5
Elko 223	E6
Elkton 142	F7
Ellendale 549	E7
Ellsworth 580	C7
Elmdale 130	D5
Elmore 709	D7
Elrosa 205	C5
Ely 3,968	G3
Elysian 445	E6
Emily 613	E4
Emmons 439	E7
Erhard 181	B4
Erskine 422	B3
Esko 500	F4
Evan 83	D6
Evansville 566	C4
Eveleth 4,064	F3
Excelsior 2,367	E6
Eyota 1,448	F7
Fairfax 1,276	D6
Fairmont▲ 11,265	D7
Falcon Heights 5,380	G5
Faribault▲ 17,085	E6
Farmington 5,940	E6
Farwell 74	C5
Federal Dam 118	D3
Felton 211	B3
Fergus Falls▲ 12,362	B4
Fertile 853	B3
Fifty Lakes 299	D4
Finlayson 242	F4
Fisher 413	B3
Flensburg 213	D5
Floodwood 574	E4
Florence 53	B6
Florenton 635	F3
Foley▲ 1,854	D5
Forada 171	C5
Forest Lake 5,833	F5
Foreston 354	E5
Fort Ripley 92	D4
Fosston 1,529	C3
Fountain 327	F7
Foxhome 160	B4
Franklin 512	D6
Frazee 1,176	C4
Freeborn 301	E7
Freeport 556	D5
Fridley 28,335	G5
Frost 236	D7
Fulda 1,212	C7
Garfield 203	C5
Garrison 138	E4
Garvin 149	C6
Gary 200	B3
Gaylord▲ 1,935	D6
Geneva 444	E7
Genola 85	D5
Georgetown 107	B3
Ghent 316	C6
Gibbon 712	D6
Gilbert 1,934	F3
Gilman 192	E5
Glen 4,648	E4
Glencoe▲ 4,396	D6
Glenville 778	E7
Glenwood▲ 2,573	C5
Glyndon 862	B4
Golden Valley 20,971	G5
Gonvick 302	C3
Good Thunder 561	D6
Goodhue 533	F6
Goodridge 115	C2
Goodview 2,878	G6
Graceville 671	B5
Granada 374	D7
Grand Marais▲ 1,171	G2
Grand Meadow 967	F7
Grand Rapids▲ 7,976	E3
Granite Falls▲ 3,083	C6
Grasston 119	E5
Green Isle 239	E6
Greenbush 800	B2
Greenfield 1,450	F5
Greenwald 209	D5
Grey Eagle 353	D5
Grove City 547	D5
Grygla 220	C2
Gully 128	C3
Hackensack 245	D4
Hadley 94	C7
Hallock▲ 1,304	A2
Halma 73	B2
Halstad 611	B3
Ham Lake 8,924	E5
Hamburg 492	D6
Hamel	F5
Hammond 205	F6
Hampton 363	E6
Hancock 723	C5
Hanley Falls 246	C6
Hanover 787	E5
Hanska 443	D6
Harding 76	E4
Hardwick 234	B7
Harmony 1,081	F7
Harris 843	F5
Hartland 270	E7
Hastings▲ 15,445	F6
Hatfield 66	B7
Hawley 1,655	B4
Hayfield 1,283	F7
Hayward 246	E7
Hazel Run 81	C6
Hector 1,145	D6
Heidelberg 73	E6
Henderson 746	E6
Hendricks 684	B6
Hendrum 309	B3
Henning 738	C4
Henriette 78	E5
Herman 485	B5
Hermantown 6,761	F4
Heron Lake 730	C7
Hewitt 269	C4
Hibbing 18,046	F3

(continued on following page)

Agriculture, Industry and Resources

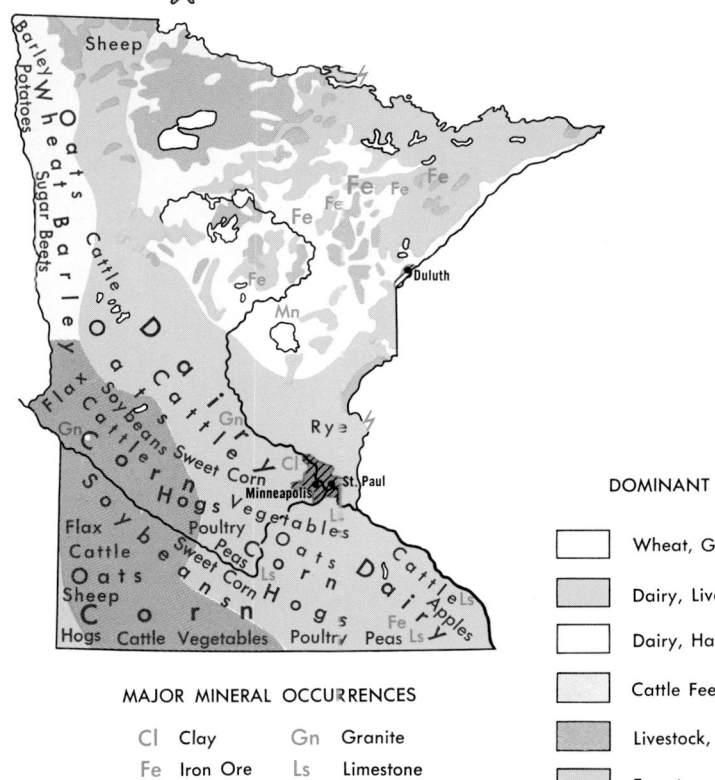

DOMINANT LAND USE

- Wheat, General Farming
- Dairy, Livestock
- Dairy, Hay, Potatoes
- Cattle Feed, Hogs
- Livestock, Cash Grain
- Forests
- Swampland, Limited Agriculture
- Urban Areas

MAJOR MINERAL OCCURRENCES

- Cl Clay
- Fe Iron Ore
- Gn Granite
- Ls Limestone
- Mn Manganese

⚡ Water Power

▨ Major Industrial Areas

Hill City 469 ....E4
Hillman 45 ....E4
Hills 607 ....B7
Hinckley 946 ....E4
Hitterdal 242 ....B4
Hoffman 576 ....C5
Hokah 687 ....G7
Holdingford 561 ....D5
Holland 216 ....B6
Hollandale 289 ....E7
Holloway 123 ....C5
Holt 88 ....B2
Hopkins 16,534 ....G5
Houston 1,013 ....G7
Howard Lake 1,343 ....D5
Hoyt Lakes 2,348 ....E4
Hugo 4,417 ....E5
Humboldt 74 ....A2
Hutchinson 11,523 ....D6
Ihlen 101 ....B7
Independence 2,822 ....F5
Indus E2
International Falls▲ 8,325 ....E2
Inver Grove Heights 22,477 ....E6
Iona 158 ....C7
Iron 133 ....F3
Ironton 553 ....D4
Isanti 1,228 ....E5
Island View 150 ....E2
Isle 566 ....E4
Ivanhoe▲ 751 ....B6
Jackson▲ 3,559 ....C7
Janesville 1,969 ....E6
Jasper 599 ....B7
Jeffers 443 ....C6
Jenkins 262 ....D4
Johnson 46 ....B5
Jordan 2,909 ....E6
Kandiyohi 506 ....D5
Karlstad 881 ....B2
Kasota 655 ....D6
Kasson 3,514 ....F6
Keewatin 1,118 ....E3
Kelliher 348 ....D3
Kellogg 423 ....G6
Kelly Lake 900 ....F3
Kennedy 337 ....B2
Kenneth 81 ....B7
Kensington 295 ....C5
Kent 131 ....B4
Kenyon 1,552 ....E6
Kerkhoven 732 ....C5
Kerrick 56 ....F4
Kettle River 190 ....F4
Kiester 606 ....E7
Kilkenny 167 ....E6
Kimball 690 ....D5
Kingston 131 ....D5
Kinney 257 ....F3
La Crescent 4,311 ....G7
La Prairie 438 ....E3
La Salle 98 ....D6
Lafayette 462 ....D6
Lake Benton 693 ....B6
Lake Bronson 272 ....B2
Lake City 4,391 ....F6
Lake Crystal 2,084 ....D6
Lake Elmo 5,903 ....F6
Lake Henry 90 ....D5
Lake Lillian 229 ....C6
Lake Park 638 ....B4
Lake Saint Croix Beach 1,078 ....F6

Lake Shore 693 ....D4
Lake Wilson 319 ....B7
Lakefield 1,679 ....C7
Lakeland 2,000 ....F6
Lakeville 24,854 ....E6
Lamberton 972 ....C6
Lancaster 342 ....B2
Lanesboro 858 ....G7
Laporte 101 ....D3
Lastrup 112 ....D4
Lauderdale 2,700 ....G5
Le Center▲ 2,006 ....E6
Le Roy 904 ....F7
Le Sueur 3,714 ....E6
Lengby 112 ....C3
Leonard 26 ....C3
Leonidas 70 ....F3
Lester Prairie 1,180 ....D6
Lewiston 1,298 ....G6
Lewisville 255 ....D7
Lexington 2,279 ....G5
Lilydale 506 ....G5
Lindstrom 2,461 ....E5
Lino Lakes 8,807 ....G5
Lismore 248 ....B7
Litchfield▲ 6,041 ....D5
Little Falls▲ 7,232 ....D5
Little Rock 714 ....D5
Littlefork 838 ....E2
Long Beach 204 ....C5
Long Lake 1,984 ....F5
Long Prairie▲ 2,786 ....D5
Longville 224 ....D4
Lonsdale 1,252 ....E6
Loretto 404 ....F5
Louisburg 42 ....B5
Lowry 233 ....C5
Lucan 235 ....C6
Luverne▲ 4,382 ....B7
Lyle 504 ....F7
Lynd 287 ....B6
Mabel 745 ....G7
Madelia 2,237 ....D6
Madison Lake 643 ....E6
Madison▲ 1,951 ....B5
Magnolia 155 ....B7
Mahnomen▲ 1,154 ....C3
Mahtomedi 5,569 ....F5
Manchester 69 ....E7
Manhattan Beach 61 ....E4
Mankato▲ 31,477 ....E6
Mantorville▲ 874 ....F6
Maple Grove 38,736 ....G5
Maple Lake 1,394 ....D5
Maple Plain 2,005 ....F5
Mapleton 1,526 ....E6
Mapleview 206 ....E7
Maplewood 30,954 ....G5
Marble 618 ....E3
Marietta 211 ....B5
Marine on Saint Croix 602 ....F5
Marshall▲ 12,023 ....C6
Mayer 471 ....D6
Maynard 419 ....C5
Mazeppa 722 ....F6
McGrath 62 ....E4
McGregor 376 ....E4
McIntosh 665 ....C3
McKinley 116 ....F3
Meadowlands 92 ....F3
Medford 733 ....E6
Medicine Lake 385 ....G5

Medina (Hamel) 3,096 ....F5
Meire Grove 124 ....C5
Melrose 2,561 ....D5
Menahga 1,076 ....C4
Mendota 164 ....G5
Mendota Heights 9,431 ....G6
Mentor 94 ....B3
Middle River 285 ....B2
Miesville 135 ....F6
Milaca▲ 2,182 ....D5
Milan 353 ....C5
Millerville 104 ....C4
Millville 163 ....F6
Milroy 297 ....C6
Miltona 181 ....C4
Minneapolis▲ 368,383 ....G5
Minneiska 127 ....G6
Minneota 1,417 ....C6
Minnesota City 258 ....G6
Minnesota Lake 681 ....E7
Minnetonka 48,370 ....G5
Minnetrista 3,439 ....F5
Mizpah 100 ....D3
Montevideo▲ 5,499 ....C6
Montgomery 2,399 ....E6
Monticello 4,941 ....E5
Montrose 1,008 ....E5
Moorhead▲ 32,295 ....B4
Moose Lake 1,206 ....F4
Mora▲ 2,905 ....E5
Morgan 965 ....D6
Morris▲ 5,613 ....C5
Morristown 784 ....E6
Morton 448 ....C6
Motley 441 ....D4
Mound 9,634 ....F5
Mounds View 12,541 ....G5
Mountain Iron 3,362 ....F3
Mountain Lake 1,906 ....D7
Murdock 282 ....C5
Myrtle 72 ....E7
Nashua 63 ....B4
Nashwauk 1,026 ....E3
Nassau 83 ....B5
Naytahwaush 378 ....C3
Nelson 177 ....C5
Nerstrand 210 ....E6
Nevis 375 ....D4
New Auburn 363 ....D6
New Brighton 22,207 ....G5
New Germany 353 ....E6
New Hope 21,853 ....G5
New London 971 ....C5
New Market 227 ....E6
New Munich 314 ....D5
New Prague 3,569 ....E6
New Richland 1,237 ....E7
New Trier 96 ....F6
New Ulm▲ 13,132 ....D6
New York Mills 940 ....C4
Newfolden 345 ....B2
Newport 3,720 ....F6
Nicollet 795 ....D6
Nielsville 100 ....B3
Nimrod 65 ....D4
Nisswa 1,391 ....D4
Norcross 86 ....B5
North Branch 1,867 ....F5
North Mankato 10,164 ....D6
North Oaks 3,386 ....G5
North Redwood 203 ....D6
North Saint Paul 12,376 ....G5

Northfield 14,684 ....E6
Northome 283 ....D3
Northrop 276 ....D7
Norwood 1,351 ....E6
Oak Park 3,486 ....E5
Oakdale 18,374 ....E5
Odessa 155 ....B5
Odin 102 ....D7
Ogema 164 ....C3
Ogilvie 510 ....E5
Okabena 223 ....C7
Oklee 441 ....C3
Olivia▲ 2,623 ....C6
Onamia 676 ....D4
Ormsby 159 ....D7
Oronoco 727 ....F6
Orr 265 ....F2
Ortonville▲ 2,205 ....B5
Osakis 1,256 ....C5
Oslo 362 ....A2
Osseo 2,704 ....G5
Ostrander 276 ....F7
Ottertail 313 ....C4
Owatonna▲ 19,386 ....E6
Palisade 144 ....E4
Park Rapids▲ 2,863 ....D4
Parkers Prairie 956 ....C4
Payne 2,275 ....F3
Paynesville 2,140 ....D5
Pease 178 ....E5
Pelican Lakes (Breezy Point) D4
Pelican Rapids 1,886 ....B4
Pemberton 228 ....E6
Pengilly 625 ....E3
Pennock 476 ....C5
Pequot Lakes 843 ....D4
Perham 2,075 ....C4
Perley 132 ....B4
Peterson 259 ....G7
Pierz 1,014 ....D5
Pillager 306 ....D4
Pine City▲ 2,613 ....E5
Pine Island 2,125 ....F6
Pine River 871 ....D4
Pipestone▲ 4,554 ....B7
Plainview 2,768 ....F6
Plato 355 ....D6
Pleasant Lake 79 ....D5
Plummer 277 ....B3
Plymouth 50,889 ....G5
Ponemah 704 ....D2
Porter 210 ....B6
Preston▲ 1,530 ....F7
Princeton 3,719 ....E5
Prinsburg 502 ....C6
Prior Lake 11,482 ....E6
Proctor 2,974 ....F4
Quamba 124 ....E5
Racine 288 ....F7
Ramsey 12,408 ....E5
Randall 571 ....D4
Randolph 331 ....E6
Ranier 199 ....E2
Ray 668 ....E2
Raymond 723 ....C5
Red Lake Falls▲ 1,481 ....B3
Red Wing▲ 15,134 ....F6
Redby 787 ....D3
Redwood Falls▲ 4,859 ....C6
Regal 51 ....D5
Remer 342 ....D3

Renville 1,315 ....C6
Revere 117 ....C6
Rice 610 ....D5
Richfield 35,710 ....G6
Richmond 965 ....D5
Richville 121 ....C4
Riverton 122 ....D4
Robbinsdale 14,396 ....G5
Rochester▲ 70,745 ....F6
Rock Creek 1,040 ....F5
Rockford 2,665 ....F5
Rockville 579 ....D5
Rogers 698 ....F5
Rollingstone 697 ....G6
Ronneby 58 ....E5
Roosevelt 180 ....C2
Roscoe 141 ....D5
Rose Creek 363 ....F7
Roseau▲ 2,396 ....C2
Rosemount 8,622 ....E6
Roseville 33,485 ....G5
Rothsay 443 ....B4
Round Lake 463 ....C7
Royalton 802 ....D5
Rush City 1,497 ....E5
Rushford 1,485 ....G7
Rushmore 381 ....C7
Russell 394 ....C6
Ruthton 328 ....B6
Rutledge 152 ....E4
Sabin 495 ....B4
Sacred Heart 603 ....C6
Saint Anthony 7,727 ....G5
Saint Anthony 81 ....D5
Saint Bonifacius 1,180 ....F5
Saint Charles 2,642 ....F7
Saint Clair 633 ....E6
Saint Cloud▲ 48,812 ....D5
Saint Francis 2,538 ....E5
Saint Hilaire 298 ....B2
Saint James▲ 4,364 ....D7
Saint Joseph 3,294 ....D5
Saint Leo 111 ....C6
Saint Louis Park 43,787 ....G5
Saint Martin 274 ....D5
Saint Michael 2,506 ....E5
Saint Paul (cap.)▲ 272,235 ....G6
Saint Paul Park 4,965 ....G6
Saint Peter▲ 9,421 ....E6
Saint Rosa 75 ....D5
Saint Stephen 607 ....D5
Saint Vincent 116 ....A2
Sanborn 459 ....C6
Sandstone 2,057 ....F4
Sargeant 78 ....F7
Sartell 5,393 ....D5
Sauk Centre 3,581 ....C5
Sauk Rapids 7,825 ....D5
Savage 9,906 ....G6
Scanlon 878 ....F4
Seaforth 87 ....C6
Sebeka 662 ....C4
Sedan 63 ....C5
Shafer 368 ....F5
Shakopee▲ 11,739 ....G6
Shelly 225 ....B3
Sherburn 1,105 ....D7
Shevlin 157 ....C3
Shoreview 24,587 ....G5
Shorewood 5,917 ....F5
Silver Bay 1,894 ....G3
Silver Lake 764 ....D6
Skyline 272 ....D6
Slayton▲ 2,147 ....C7
Sleepy Eye 3,694 ....D6
Sobieski 199 ....D5
Solway 74 ....C3
Soudan 900 ....F3
South Haven 193 ....D5
South International Falls 2,806 ....E2
South Saint Paul 20,197 ....G6
Spicer 1,020 ....C5
Spring Grove 1,153 ....G7
Spring Hill 77 ....D5
Spring Lake 6,532 ....E5
Spring Lake Park 6,477 ....G5
Spring Park 1,571 ....F5
Spring Valley 2,461 ....F7
Springfield 2,173 ....C6
Squaw Lake 139 ....D3
Stacy 1,081 ....E5
Staples 2,754 ....D4
Starbuck 1,143 ....C5
Steen 176 ....B7
Stephen 707 ....A2
Stewart 566 ....D6
Stewartville 4,520 ....F7
Stillwater▲ 13,882 ....F5
Stockton 529 ....G6
Storden 283 ....C6
Strandquist 98 ....B2
Strathcona 40 ....B2
Sturgeon Lake 230 ....F4
Sunburg 117 ....C5
Sunfish Lake 413 ....E6
Swanville 324 ....D5
Taconite 310 ....E3
Tamarack 53 ....E4
Taopi 83 ....F7
Taunton 175 ....B6
Taylors Falls 694 ....F5
Tenstrike 184 ....D3
Thief River Falls▲ 8,010 ....B2
Thomson 132 ....F4
Tintah 74 ....B5
Tonka Bay 1,472 ....F5
Tower 502 ....F3
Tracy 2,059 ....C6
Trail 67 ....C3
Trimont 745 ....D7
Trommald 80 ....D4
Trosky 120 ....B7
Truman 1,292 ....D7
Turtle River 62 ....D3
Twin Lakes 154 ....E7
Twin Valley 821 ....B3

Two Harbors▲ 3,651 ....G3
Tyler 1,257 ....B6
Ulen 547 ....B3
Underwood 284 ....C4
Upsala 371 ....D5
Urbank 73 ....C4
Utica 220 ....D4
Vadnais Heights 11,041 ....G5
Vergas 287 ....C4
Vermillion 510 ....F6
Verndale 560 ....D4
Vernon Center 339 ....D7
Vesta 302 ....C6
Victoria 2,354 ....F5
Viking 103 ....B2
Villard 247 ....C5
Vining 84 ....C4
Virginia 9,410 ....F3
Wabasha▲ 2,384 ....G6
Wabasso 684 ....C6
Waconia 3,498 ....E6
Wadena▲ 4,131 ....C4
Wahkon 197 ....E4
Waite Park 5,020 ....D5
Waldorf 243 ....E7
Walker▲ 950 ....D3
Walnut Grove 625 ....C6
Walters 86 ....E7
Waltham 170 ....F7
Wanamingo 847 ....F6
Wanda 103 ....C6
Warba 137 ....E3
Warren▲ 1,813 ....B2
Warroad 1,679 ....C2
Waseca▲ 8,385 ....E6
Watertown 2,408 ....E6
Waterville 1,771 ....E6
Watkins 849 ....D5
Watson 211 ....C5
Waubun 330 ....C3
Waverly 600 ....E5
Wayzata 3,806 ....G5
Welcome 790 ....D7
Wells 2,465 ....E7
Wendell 159 ....B4
West Concord 871 ....F6
West Saint Paul 19,248 ....G5
West Union 54 ....C4
Westbrook 853 ....C6
Westport 47 ....C5
Whalan 94 ....G7
Wheaton▲ 1,615 ....B5
White Bear Lake 24,704 ....G5
White Earth 319 ....C3
Wilder 83 ....C7
Willernie 584 ....F5
Williams 212 ....D2
Willmar▲ 17,531 ....C5
Willow River 284 ....F4
Wilmont 351 ....C7
Wilton 171 ....C3
Windom▲ 4,283 ....C7
Winger 167 ....B3
Winnebago 1,565 ....D7
Winona▲ 25,399 ....G6
Winsted 1,581 ....D6
Winthrop 1,279 ....D6
Winton 169 ....G3
Wolf Lake 35 ....C4
Wolverton 158 ....B4
Wood Lake 406 ....C6
Woodbury 20,075 ....F6
Woodstock 159 ....B7
Worthington▲ 9,977 ....C7
Wrenshall 296 ....F4
Wright 144 ....E4
Wykoff 493 ....F7
Wyoming 2,142 ....F5
Young America 1,354 ....E6
Zemple 63 ....E3
Zim 1,350 ....F3
Zumbro Falls 237 ....F6
Zumbrota 2,312 ....F6

OTHER FEATURES

Ash (riv.) F2
Bald Eagle (lake) G3
Basswood (lake) G2
Battle (riv.) D3
Baudette (riv.) D2
Bear (riv.) E3
Bemidji (lake) D3
Benton (lake) B6
Big Fork (riv.) E2
Big Sandy (lake) E4
Big Stone (lake) B5
Birch (lake) G3
Black (riv.) D2
Blue Earth (riv.) D7
Bois de Sioux (riv.) B4
Bowstring (lake) E3
Buffalo (riv.) B4
Burntside (lake) F3
Cass (lake) D3
Cedar (riv.) E7
Chippewa (riv.) C5
Christina (lake) C4
Clearwater (riv.) C3
Cloquet (riv.) F4
Cobb (riv.) E7
Cottonwood (riv.) C6
Crooked (creek) F7
Crooked (lake) G2
Crow (riv.) F5
Crow Wing (riv.) D4
Cuyuna (range) D4
Dead (lake) C4
Deer (lake) E3
Des Moines (riv.) C7
Eagle (mt.) G2
East Swan (riv.) F3
Elbow (lake) C3
Emily (lake) D4
Fond du Lac Ind. Res. F4
Grand Portage Ind. Res. G2
Grand Portage Nat'l Mon. G2

Green (lake) ....D
Greenwood (lake) ....D
Gull (lake) ....D
Heron (lake) C
Hill (riv.) C
Independence (lake) ....F
Isabella (lake) ....G
Itasca (lake) ....D
Kabetogama (lake) C
Kanaranzi (creek) ....B
Kettle (riv.) ....F
Knife (lake) ....G
La Croix (lake) ....F
Lac qui Parle (lake) ....B
Lac qui Parle (riv.) ....B
Lake of the Woods ....D
Leaf (riv.) C
Leech (lake) ....D
Leech Lake Ind. Res. ....D
Lida (lake) C
Little Fork (riv.) ....E
Little Rock (creek) ....D
Long (lake) C
Long (lake) ....D
Long Prairie (riv.) ....D
Lost (riv.) C
Lower Red (lake) ....D
Maple (lake) ....B
Maple (lake) ....D
Marsh (lake) ....B
Mary (lake) C
Mesabi (range) ....E
Middle (riv.) ....B
Mille Lacs Ind. Res. ....E
Mille Lacs (lake) ....E
Miltona (lake) C
Minneapolis-Saint Paul Airport ....G
Minnesota (riv.) ....E
Minnetonka (lake) ....G
Minnewaska (lake) C
Misquah (hills) ....G
Mississippi (riv.) ....D
Moose (riv.) C
Mud (lake) C
Mud (riv.) ....B
Muskeg (bay) C
Mustinka (riv.) ....B
Nemadji (riv.) ....F
Nett (lake) ....F
Nett Lake Ind. Res. ....F
North (lake) ....F
Otter Tail (lake) C
Otter Tail (riv.) ....B
Partridge (riv.) ....F
Pelican (lake) C
Pelican (lake) C
Pelican (lake) C
Pelican (lake) ....D
Pelican (lake) ....F
Pepin (lake) ....F
Pigeon (riv.) ....G
Pike (riv.) ....F
Pipestone Nat'l Mon. ....B
Pokegama (lake) ....E
Pomme de Terre (riv.) C
Poplar (riv.) ....G
Prairie (riv.) ....E
Rainy (lake) ....E
Rainy (riv.) ....D
Rapid (riv.) C
Redeye (riv.) ....D
Red Lake (riv.) C
Red Lake Ind. Res. C
Red River of the North (riv.) ....A
Redeye (riv.) ....D
Redwood (riv.) C
Reno (riv.) ....D
Rice (lake) ....F
Rock (riv.) ....B
Root (riv.) ....G
Roseau (riv.) ....B
Rum (riv.) ....E
Saganaga (lake) ....H
Saint Croix (riv.) ....F
Saint Louis (riv.) ....F
Sand (creek) ....F
Sand Hill (riv.) C
Sarah (lake) C
Schoolcraft C
Shakopee (creek) C
Shell (riv.) C
Shetek (lake) C
Sleepy Eye (creek) ....D
Snake (riv.) ....E
Snake (riv.) ....A
Snake (riv.) ....E
South Fowl (lake) ....G
Star (lake) C
Sturgeon (riv.) ....F
Superior (lake) ....G
Swan (lake) ....D
Tamarac (riv.) ....A
Tamarack (riv.) ....D
Thief (lake) ....B
Thief (riv.) ....B
Traverse (lake) ....B
Trout (lake) ....G
Two Rivers (riv.) ....A
Upper Red (lake) ....D
Vermilion (lake) ....F
Vermilion (range) ....F
Vermilion (riv.) ....F
Voyageurs Nat'l Park ....F
Wabatawangang (lake) ....G
West Swan (riv.) ....F
White Earth Ind. Res. C
Whiteface (riv.) ....F
Whitefish (lake) ....D
White Iron (lake) ....G
Wild Rice (lake) ....F
Wild Rice (riv.) ....B
Willow (riv.) ....F
Winnibigoshish (lake) ....D
Woods (lake) C
Zumbro (riv.) ....F

▲County seat

Topography

0   50   100 MI.

0   50   100 KM.

Below Sea Level | 100 m. 328 ft. | 200 m. 656 ft. | 500 m. 1,640 ft. | 1,000 m. 3,281 ft. | 2,000 m. 6,562 ft. | 5,000 m. 16,404 ft.

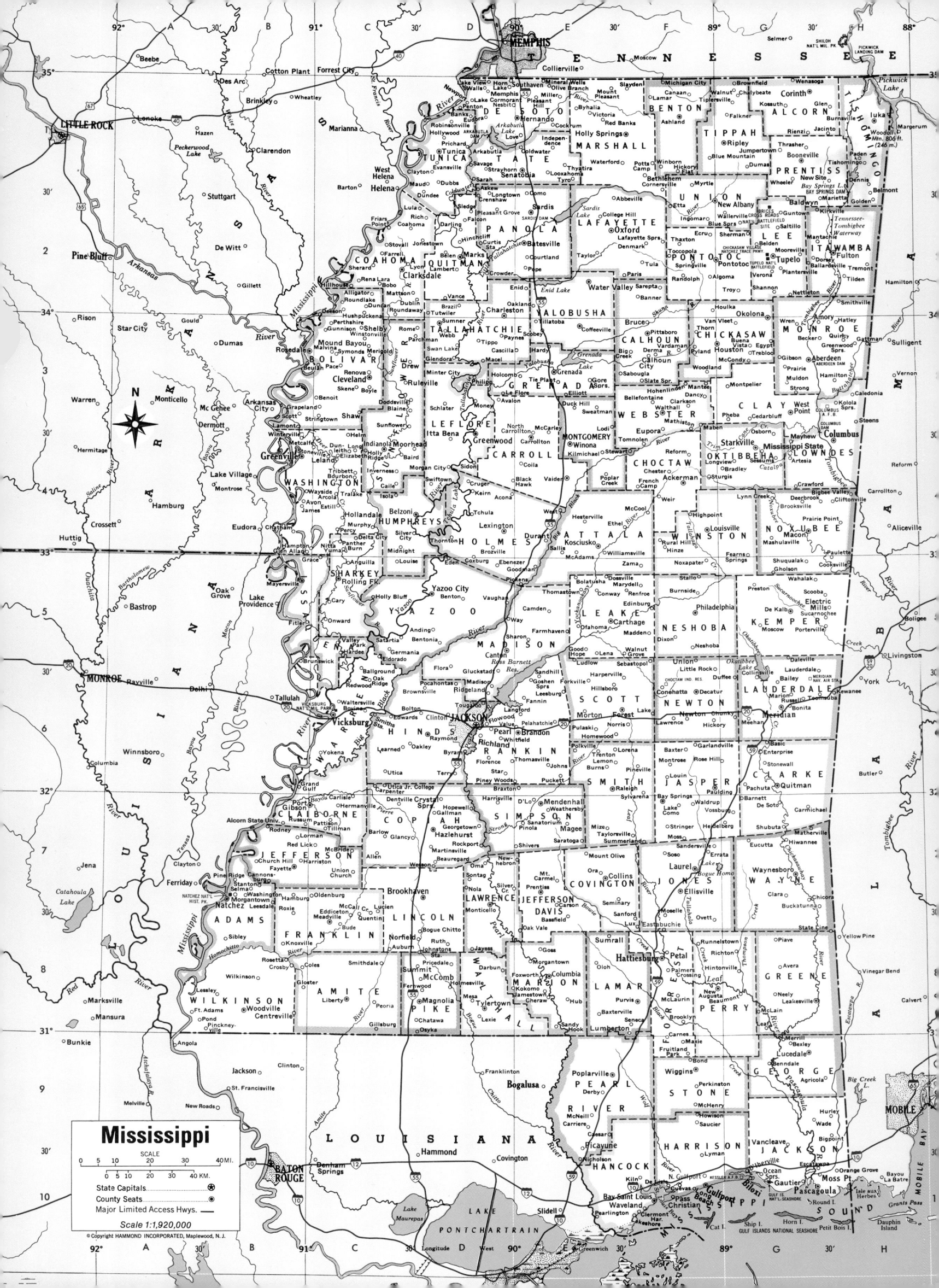

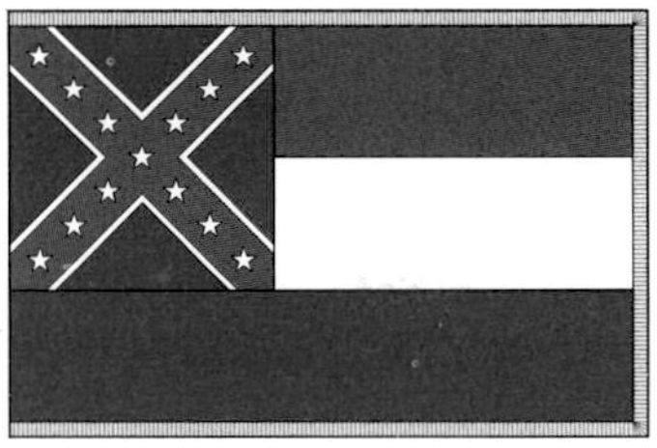

AREA 47,689 sq. mi. (123,515 sq. km.)
POPULATION 2,586,443
CAPITAL Jackson
LARGEST CITY Jackson
HIGHEST POINT Woodall Mtn. 806 ft. (246 m.)
SETTLED IN 1716
ADMITTED TO UNION December 10, 1817
POPULAR NAME Magnolia State
STATE FLOWER Magnolia
STATE BIRD Mockingbird

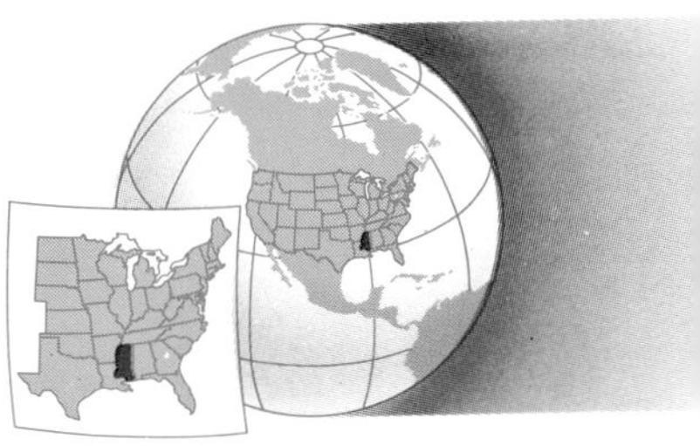

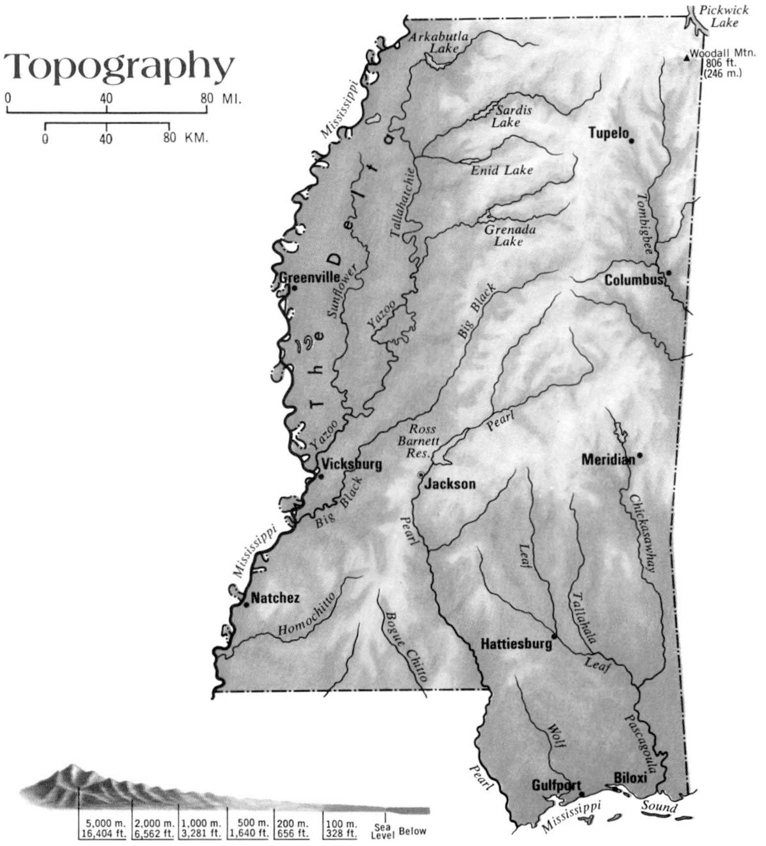

COUNTIES

Adams 35,356 B8
Alcorn 31,722 G1
Amite 13,328 C8
Attala 18,481 E4
Benton 8,046 F1
Bolivar 41,875 C3
Calhoun 14,908 F3
Carroll 9,237 E4
Chickasaw 18,085 G3
Choctaw 9,071 F4
Claiborne 11,370 C7
Clarke 17,313 G6
Clay 21,120 G3
Coahoma 31,665 C2
Copiah 27,592 D7
Covington 16,527 E7
De Soto 53,930 E1
Forrest 68,314 F8
Franklin 8,377 C8
George 16,673 G9
Greene 10,220 G8
Grenada 21,555 E3
Hancock 31,760 E10
Harrison 165,365 F10
Hinds 254,441 D6
Holmes 21,604 D4
Humphreys 12,134 C4
Issaquena 1,909 B5
Itawamba 20,017 H2
Jackson 115,243 G9
Jasper 17,114 F6
Jefferson 8,653 B7
Jefferson Davis 14,051 E7
Jones 62,031 F7
Kemper 10,356 G5
Lafayette 31,826 E2
Lamar 30,424 E8
Lauderdale 75,555 G6
Lawrence 12,458 D7
Leake 18,436 E5
Lee 65,581 G2
Leflore 37,341 D3
Lincoln 30,278 D8
Lowndes 59,308 H4
Madison 53,794 D5
Marion 25,544 E8
Marshall 30,361 E1
Monroe 36,582 H3
Montgomery 12,388 E4
Neshoba 24,800 F5
Newton 20,291 F6
Noxubee 12,604 G4
Oktibbeha 38,375 G4
Panola 29,996 E2
Pearl River 38,714 E9
Perry 10,865 G8
Pike 36,882 D8
Pontotoc 22,237 F2
Prentiss 23,278 G1
Quitman 10,490 D2
Rankin 87,161 E6
Scott 24,137 E6
Sharkey 7,066 C5
Simpson 23,953 E7
Smith 14,798 E6
Stone 10,750 F9
Sunflower 32,867 C3
Tallahatchie 15,210 D3
Tate 21,432 E1
Tippah 19,523 G1
Tishomingo 17,683 H1
Tunica 8,164 D1
Union 22,085 F2
Walthall 14,352 E8
Warren 47,880 C6
Washington 67,935 C4
Wayne 19,517 G7
Webster 10,222 F3
Wilkinson 9,678 B8
Winston 19,433 F4
Yalobusha 12,033 E2
Yazoo 25,506 D5

CITIES and TOWNS

Abbeville 399 F2
Aberdeen▲ 6,837 H3
Ackerman▲ 1,573 F4
Acona 200 D4
Agricola 200 G9
Alcorn State University C7
Algoma 420 G2
Alligator 187 C2
Amory 7,093 H3
Anguilla 883 C5
Arcola 564 C4
Arkabutla 400 D1
Artesia 484 G4
Ashland▲ 490 F1
Askew 300 D1
Auburn 500 C8
Avalon 100 D3
Avera 150 G8
Avon 400 B4
Bailey 320 G6
Baird 150 C4
Baldwyn 3,204 G2
Ballardsville 105 H2
Banks 100 D1
Banner 120 F2
Bassfield 249 E8
Batesville▲ 6,403 E2
Baxterville 100 E8
Bay Saint Louis▲ 8,063 F10
Bay Springs▲ 1,729 F7
Beaumont 1,054 G8
Beauregard 206 D7
Becker 350 G3
Belden 241 G2
Belen 400 D2
Bellefontaine 400 F3
Belmont 1,554 H1
Belzoni▲ 2,536 C4
Benndale 500 G9
Benoit 641 C3
Benton 390 D5
Bentonia 518 D5
Bethlehem 210 F1
Beulah 460 B3
Bexley 130 G9
Big Creek 123 F3
Bigbee Valley 370 H4
Bigpoint 350 H9
Biloxi 46,319 G10
Blue Mountain 667 G1
Blue Springs 140 G2
Bobo 200 C2
Bogue Chitto 689 D8
Bolatusha 87 E5
Bolton 637 D6
Bond 350 F9
Bonita 300 G6
Booneville▲ 7,955 G1
Bourbon 200 C4
Boyle 651 C3
Brandon▲ 11,077 E6
Braxton 141 D6
Brazil 229 D2
Brookhaven▲ 10,243 C7
Brooklyn 450 F8
Brooksville 1,098 G4
Brownfield 125 G1
Brownsville 200 D6
Brozville 150 D4
Bruce 2,127 F3
Brunswick 90 C5
Buckatunna 500 G7
Bude 969 C8
Burns 949 E6
Burnsville 889 H1
Byhalia 955 E1
Byram 250 D6
Caesar 80 E9
Caledonia 821 H3
Calhoun City 1,838 F3
Camden 150 E5
Canaan 200 F1
Cannonsburg 240 B7
Canton▲ 10,062 D5
Carlisle 425 C7
Carpenter 200 C6
Carriere 900 E9
Carrollton▲ 221 E4
Carson 400 E7
Carthage▲ 3,819 E5
Cary 392 C5
Cascilla 230 D3
Cedarbluff 175 G3
Centreville 1,771 B8
Chalybeate 350 G1
Charleston▲ 2,328 D2
Chatawa 300 D8
Chatham 150 B4
Cheraw 100 E8
Chunky 292 G6
Church Hill 350 B7
Clara 275 G7
Clarksdale▲ 19,717 D2
Clarkson 100 F3
Clermont Harbor 550 F10
Cleveland▲ 15,384 C3
Cliftonville 280 H4
Clinton 21,847 D6
Coahoma 254 C2
Cockrum 150 E1
Coffeeville▲ 825 E3
Coldwater 1,502 E1
Coles 150 C8
College Hill 150 E2
Collins▲ 2,541 E7
Collinsville 1,364 G6
Columbia▲ 6,815 E8
Columbus▲ 23,799 H3
Como 1,387 E1
Conehatta 925 F6
Corinth▲ 11,820 G1
Courtland 329 E2
Coxburg 300 D5
Crawford 668 G4
Crenshaw 978 D2
Crosby 465 B8
Crowder 758 D2
Cruger 548 D4
Crystal Springs 5,643 D7
Cuevas 200 F10
Curtis Station 350 D2
D'Iberville 6,566 G10
D'Lo 421 E7
Daleville 210 G5
Dancy 116 F3
Darbun 100 D8
Darling 275 D2
De Kalb▲ 1,073 G5
De Lisle 450 F10
De Soto 150 G7
Decatur▲ 1,248 F6
Delta City 310 C4
Dennis 150 H1
Dentville 175 C7
Derby 298 E9
Derma 959 F3
Dixon 125 F5
Doddsville 149 C3
Dorsey 100 H2
Drew 2,349 C3
Dublin 100 C2
Duck Hill 586 E3
Duffee 175 G6
Dumas 407 G1
Duncan 416 C2
Dundee 600 D1
Dunleith 140 C4
Durant 2,838 E4
Eastabuchie 200 F8
Ebenezer 200 D5
Ecru 696 F2
Eden 88 D5
Edinburg 200 F5
Edwards 1,279 C6
Egypt 100 G3
Electric Mills 100 G5
Elizabeth 500 C4
Elliott 200 E3
Ellisville▲ 3,634 F7
Enid E2
Enterprise 477 G6
Errata 85 F7
Escatawpa 3,902 G10
Estill 100 C4
Ethel 454 F4
Eudora 200 D1
Eupora 2,145 F3
Falcon 167 D2
Falkner 232 G1
Fannin 250 E6
Farrell 300 C2
Fayette▲ 1,853 B7
Fernwood 500 D8
Fitler 175 B5
Flora 1,482 D5
Florence 1,831 D6
Flowood 2,860 D6
Forest▲ 5,060 F6
Forkville 185 E6
Foxworth 800 E8
French Camp 320 F4
Friars Point 1,334 C2
Fulton▲ 3,387 H2
Gallman D7
Garlandville 150 F6
Gattman 120 H3
Gautier 10,088 G10
Georgetown 332 D7
Glen 165 H1
Glen Allan 650 B4
Glendora 220 D3
Gloster 1,323 B8
Gluckstadt 150 D5
Golden 202 H2
Good Hope 125 E5
Goodman 1,256 E5
Gore Springs 125 E3
Goshen Springs 100 E6
Goss 100 E8
Grace 325 C5
Grapeland 200 B3
Greenville▲ 45,226 B4
Greenwood Springs 170 H3
Greenwood▲ 18,906 D4
Grenada▲ 10,864 E3
Gulfport▲ 40,775 F10
Gunnison 611 C3
Guntown 692 G2
Hamburg 150 B7
Hamilton 500 H3
Hampton 200 B4
Hardee 100 C5
Harperville 200 E6
Harriston 500 C7
Harrisville 500 D7
Hatley 529 H3
Hattiesburg▲ 41,882 F8
Hazlehurst▲ 4,221 D7
Heidelberg 981 F7
Helm 80 C4
Hermanville 750 C7
Hernando▲ 3,125 E1
Hickory 493 F6
Hickory Flat 535 F1
Hillsboro 800 E6
Hintonville 300 F8
Hiwannee 250 G7
Hohenlinden 96 F3
Hollandale 3,576 C4
Holly Bluff 700 C5
Holly Ridge 350 C4
Holly Springs▲ 7,261 E1
Hollywood 80 D1
Hopewell 250 D7
Horn Lake 9,069 D1
Houlka G2
Houston▲ 3,903 G3
Howison 300 F9
Hub 80 E8
Hurley 500 H9
Independence 150 E1
Indianola▲ 11,809 C4
Ingomar 150 F2
Inverness 1,174 C4
Isola 732 C4
Itta Bena 2,377 D4
Iuka▲ 3,122 H1
Jackson (cap.)▲ 196,637 D6
James 100 B4
Jayess 200 D8
Johns 90 E6
Jonestown 1,467 D2
Jumpertown 438 G1
Kewanee 250 H6
Kilmichael 826 E4
Kiln 1,262 F10
Kirkville 200 H2
Kokomo 250 E8
Kolola Springs 100 H3
Kosciusko▲ 6,986 E4
Kossuth 245 G1
Lafayette Springs 80 F2
Lake 369 F6
Lake Como 150 F7
Lake Cormorant 300 D1
Lake View 125 D1
Lakeshore 550 F10
Lamar 200 F1
Lambert 1,131 D2
Lamont 400 B3
Langford 100 E6
Lauderdale 600 G5
Laurel▲ 18,827 F7
Lawrence 250 F6
Le Flore 99 D3
Leaf 250 G8
Leakesville▲ 1,129 G8
Learned 111 C6
Leland 6,366 C4
Lemon 90 E6
Lena 175 E5
Lessley 100 B8
Lexington▲ 2,227 D4
Liberty▲ 624 C8
Long 15,804 C4
Long Beach 7,967 F10
Longtown 150 D1
Longview 800 G4
Looxahoma 200 E1
Lorena 90 F6
Lorman 350 B7
Louin 289 F6
Louise 343 C5
Louisville▲ 7,169 G4
Lucedale▲ 2,592 G9
Ludlow 350 E5
Lula 224 C2
Lumberton 2,121 E8
Lyman 1,117 F10
Lyon 446 D2
Maben 752 F3
Macon▲ 2,256 G4
Madden 450 F5
Madison 7,471 D6
Magee 3,607 E7
Magnolia▲ 2,245 D8
Malvina 100 C3
Mantachie 651 H2
Mantee 134 F3
Marietta 287 H2
Marion 1,359 G6
Marks▲ 1,758 D2
Marydell 99 F5
Mashulaville 227 G4
Matherville 150 G7
Mathiston 818 F3
Mattson 200 C2
Maxie 233 F9
Mayersville▲ 329 B5
Mayhew 150 G4
McAdams 350 E4
McCall Creek 250 C7
McCarley 250 E3
McComb 11,591 D8
McCondy 150 G3
McCool 169 F4
McHenry 660 F9
McLain 536 G8
McLaurin 100 F8
McNeill 800 E9
Meadville▲ 453 C8
Meehan 100 G6
Mendenhall▲ 2,463 E7
Meridian▲ 41,036 G6
Merigold 572 C3
Merrill 100 G9
Metcalfe 1,092 B4
Michigan City 350 F1
Midnight 500 C4
Mineral Wells 250 E1
Minter City 150 D3
Mississippi State G4
Mize 312 E7
Money 350 D3
Monticello▲ 1,755 D7
Montpelier 175 G3
Montrose 106 F6
Mooreville 200 G2
Moorhead 2,417 C4
Morgan City 139 D4
Morgantown 32,880 B7
Morgantown 325 E8
Morton 3,212 E6
Moselle 525 F8
Moss 17,837 F7
Moss Point 18,998 G10
Mound Bayou 2,222 C3
Mount Olive 914 E7
Mount Pleasant 250 E1
Murphy 100 C4
Myrtle 358 F1
Natchez▲ 19,460 B7
Neely 270 G8
Nesbit 366 D1
Neshoba 250 F5
Nettleton 2,462 G2
New Albany▲ 6,775 G2
New Augusta▲ 668 F8
New Houlka (Houlka) 558 G2
New Site 100 H1
Newhebron 470 D7
Newton 3,701 F6
Nicholson 400 E10
Nitta Yuma 150 C4
Nola 120 D7
North Carrollton 578 E3
North Gulfport 4,966 F10
Noxapater 441 F5
Oak Ridge 350 C6
Oak Vale E8
Oakland 553 E2
Oakley 133 D6
Ocean Springs 14,658 G10
Ofahoma 350 E5
Okolona▲ 3,267 G2
Olive Branch 3,567 E1
Oloh 93 E8
Oma 200 D7
Ora 15,676 E7
Orange Grove H10
Osyka 483 D8
Ovett 600 F8
Oxford▲ 9,984 F2
Pace 354 C3
Pachuta 268 G6
Paden 123 H1
Palmers Crossing 2,765 F8
Panther Burn 300 C4
Parchman 200 D3
Paris 253 F2
Pascagoula▲ 25,899 G10
Pass Christian 5,557 F10
Pattison 540 C7
Paulding▲ 630 F6
Paulette 230 H4
Paynes 100 D3
Pearl 19,588 D6
Pearlington 1,603 E10
Pelahatchie 1,553 E6
Penton 175 D1
Peoria 100 C8
Perkinston 950 F9
Petal 7,883 F8
Pheba 280 G3
Philadelphia▲ 6,758 F5
Philipp 975 D3
Piave 150 G8
Picayune 10,633 E9
Pickens 1,285 E5
Pine Ridge 175 B7
Pineville 80 F6
Piney Woods 450 D6
Pinola E7
Pittsboro▲ 277 F3
Plantersville 1,046 G2
Pleasant Grove 100 D2
Pleasant Hill 400 E1
Polkville 129 E6

(continued on following page)

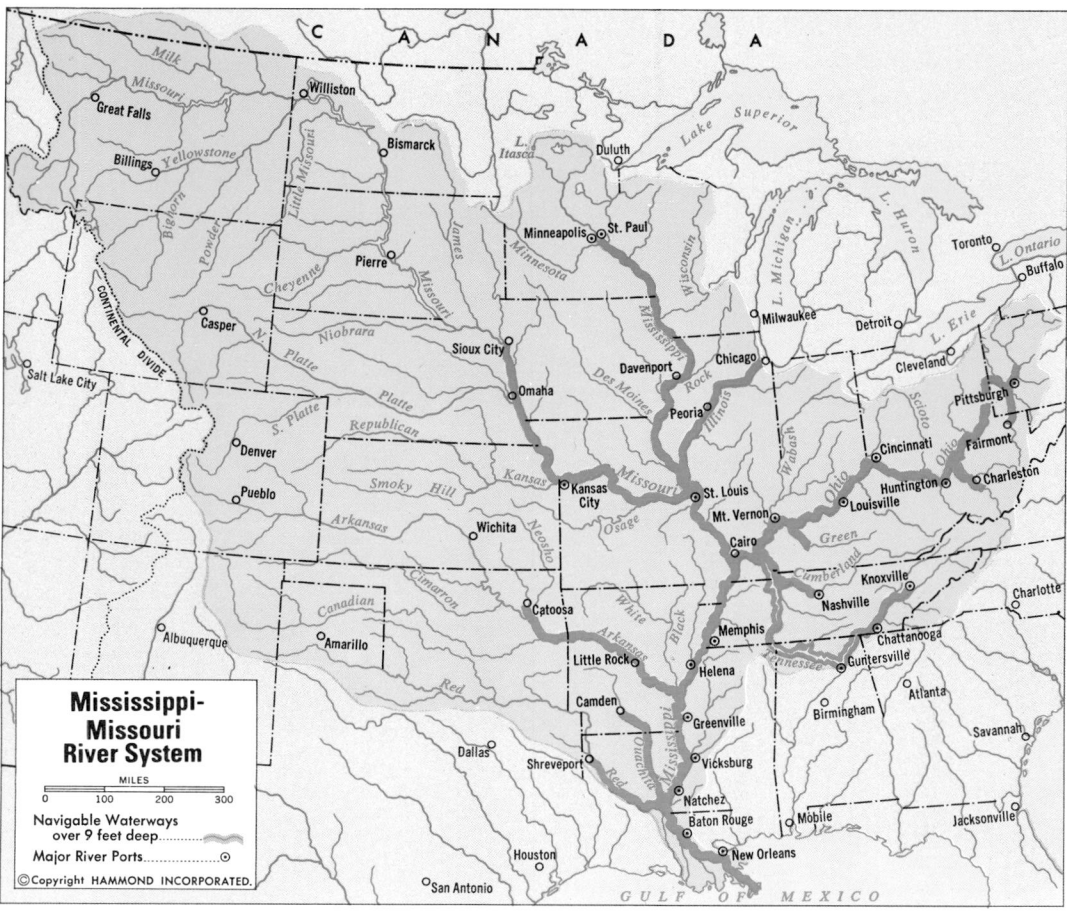

Mississippi-
Missouri
River System

MILES
0   100   200   300

Navigable Waterways
over 9 feet deep
Major River Ports.................⊙
©Copyright HAMMOND INCORPORATED.

Agriculture, Industry and Resources

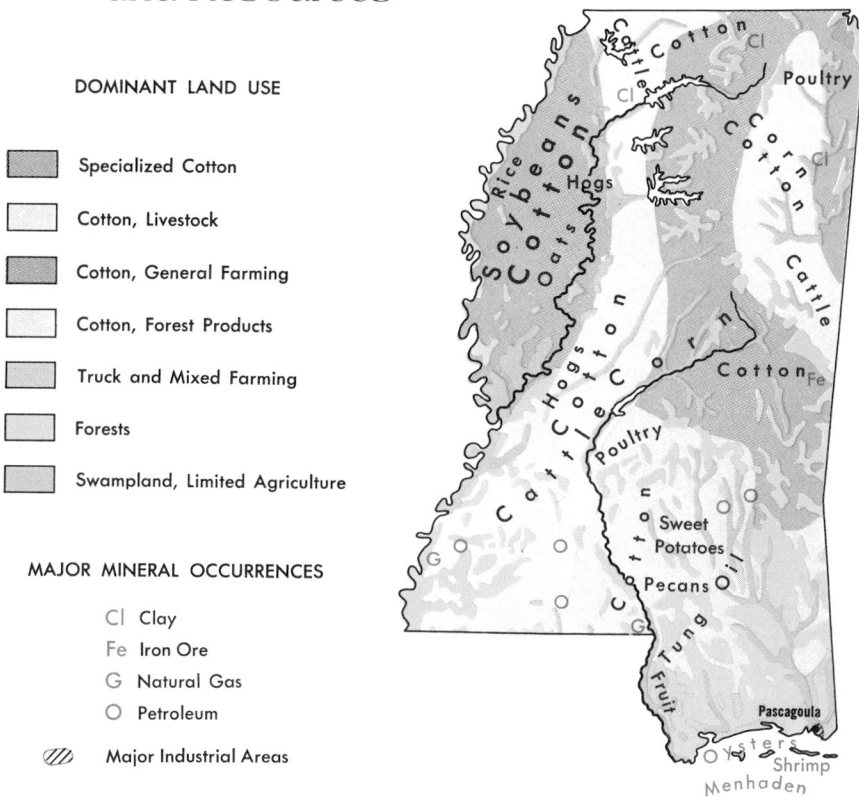

DOMINANT LAND USE

Specialized Cotton

Cotton, Livestock

Cotton, General Farming

Cotton, Forest Products

Truck and Mixed Farming

Forests

Swampland, Limited Agriculture

MAJOR MINERAL OCCURRENCES

Cl Clay

Fe Iron Ore

G Natural Gas

O Petroleum

//// Major Industrial Areas

Pontotoc▲ 4,570 ....G2
Pope 171 ....E2
Poplar Creek 100 ....E4
Poplarville▲ 2,561 ....E9
Port Gibson▲ 1,810 ....B7
Porterville 150 ....G5
Potts Camp 483 ....F1
Prairie G3
Prairie Point 150 ....H4
Prentiss▲ 1,487 ....E7
Preston 500 ....G5
Pricedale 400 ....D8
Puckett 294 ....E6
Pulaski 108 ....E6
Purvis▲ 2,140 ....F8
Pyland 120 ....F3
Quitman▲ 2,736 ....G6
Raleigh▲ 1,291 ....F6
Randolph F2
Raymond▲ 2,275 ....D6
Red Banks 350 ....F1
Red Lick 100 ....B7
Reform 100 ....F4
Rena Lara 350 ....C2
Renova 636 ....C3
Rich 4,014 ....D2
Richland 3,955 ....D6
Richton 1,034 ....G8
Ridgeland 11,714 ....D6
Rienzi 339 ....G1
Ripley▲ 5,371 ....G1
Robinsonville 285 ....D1
Rodney 100 ....B7
Rolling Fork▲ 2,444 ....C5
Rome C3
Rose Hill 500 ....F6
Rosedale▲ 2,595 ....B3
Rosetta 120 ....B8
Roundaway 175 ....C2
Roundlake 105 ....C2
Roxie 568 ....B8
Ruleville 3,245 ....C3
Runnelstown 200 ....F8
Russell 300 ....E6
Russum 200 ....B7
Ruth 400 ....D8
Sabougla 100 ....F3
Sallis 139 ....E4
Saltillo 1,782 ....G2
Sanatorium 400 ....E7
Sandersville 853 ....F7
Sandhill 100 ....E5
Sanford 150 ....F8
Sarah 150 ....D1
Sardis▲ 2,128 ....E2
Sarepta 120 ....F2
Saucier 100 ....F9
Savage 100 ....D1
Schlater 404 ....D3
Scobey 100 ....E3
Scooba 541 ....G5
Scott 400 ....B3
Sebastopol 281 ....F5
Seminary 231 ....E7
Senatobia▲ 4,772 ....E1
Sessums 150 ....G4
Sharon 200 ....E5
Shannon 1,419 ....G2
Shaw 2,349 ....C3
Shelby 2,806 ....C3
Sherard 150 ....C2
Sherman 528 ....G2
Shivers 100 ....E7
Shubuta 577 ....G7
Shuqualak 570 ....G5
Sibley 350 ....B8
Sidon 596 ....D4
Silver City 348 ....C4
Silver Creek 190 ....D7
Skene 250 ....C3
Slate Spring 118 ....F3
Slayden 310 ....F1
Sledge 577 ....D2
Smithdale 200 ....C8
Smithville 871 ....H2
Sontag 200 ....D7
Soso 366 ....F7
Southaven 17,949 ....E1
Springville 100 ....F2
Stallo 100 ....F5
Stanton 90 ....B7
Star 18,458 ....D6
Starkville▲ 15,169 ....G4
State Line 395 ....G8
Steens 125 ....H3
Stewart 350 ....F4
Stoneville 250 ....C4
Stonewall 1,148 ....G6
Strayhorn 275 ....D1
Stringer 350 ....F7
Stringtown 300 ....C3
Sturgis 198 ....G4
Summerland 150 ....F7
Summit 1,566 ....D8
Sumner▲ 368 ....D3
Sumrall 903 ....E8
Sunflower 729 ....C3
Swan Lake 325 ....D3
Swiftown 320 ....D4
Sylvarena 110 ....F6
Symonds 200 ....C3
Taylor 288 ....E2
Taylorsville 1,412 ....F7
Tchula 2,186 ....D4
Terry 613 ....D6
Thaxton 431 ....F2
Thomastown 400 ....E5
Thon 125 ....F3
Thornton 135 ....D4
Thrasher 100 ....G1
Thyatira 100 ....E1
Tie Plant 500 ....E3
Tilden 250 ....H2
Tillatoba 124 ....E3
Tiplersville 100 ....G1
Tippo 200 ....D3
Tishomingo 332 ....H1

Toccopola 154 ....F
Tomnolen 200 ....F
Toomsuba 500 ....G
Tougaloo 800 ....D
Tralake 200 ....D
Trebloc 100 ....H
Tremont 342 ....H
Tribbett 100 ....H
Troy 150 ....D
Tula 140 ....D
Tunica▲ 1,175 ....D
Tupelo▲ 30,685 ....D
Tutwiler 1,391 ....D
Tylertown▲ 1,938 ....D
Union 1,875 ....D
Utica 1,033 ....D
Vaiden▲ 789 ....D
Valley Park 400 ....D
Value 327 ....D
Van Vleet 400 ....G
Vance 200 ....D
Vancleave 3,214 ....G
Vardaman 920 ....F
Vaughan 210 ....D
Verona 2,893 ....G
Vicksburg▲ 20,908 C
Victoria 800 ....F
Vossburg 300 ....F
Wade 800 ....G
Wahalak 92 ....G
Waldrup 125 ....G
Walnut 523 ....G
Walnut Grove 389 ....F
Waltersville 150 C
Walthall▲ 167 ....F
Washington 250 ....B
Water Valley▲ 3,610 ....E
Waterford 400 ....F
Waveland 5,369 ....F1
Way 5,143 ....E
Waynesboro▲ 5,349 ....E
Wayside 500 C
Weathersby ....E
Webb 605 ....D
Weir 525 ....F
Wenasoga 175 ....G
Wesson 1,510 ....D
West 184 ....E
West Point▲ 8,489 ....H3
Wheeler 600 ....G
Whitfield 900 ....E
Wiggins▲ 3,185 ....F
Williamsville 250 ....E
Winona▲ 5,705 ....E
Winstonville 277 C
Winterville 200 C
Woodland 182 ....G
Woodville▲ 1,393 ....B
Wren 150 ....G
Yazoo City▲ 12,427 ....D5
Zama 100 ....E

OTHER FEATURES

Amite (riv.).....................C9
Arkabutla (lake)..............D1
Big Black (riv.)................C6
Black (creek)..................E8
Bogue Chitto (riv.)..........D8
Bogue Homo (lake).........E7
Bowie (creek)..................E7
Brices Cross Roads
   Nat'l Battlefield Site G2
Buttahatchee (riv.)..........H3
Cat (isl.)........................F10
Catalpa (creek)...............G4
Chickasaw Village,
   Natchez Trace Parkway.G2
Chickasawhay (riv.).........G7
Coldwater (riv.)...............D1
Columbus A.F.B. 2,890.....H3
Deer (creek)...................C4
Enid (lake).....................E2
Grenada (lake)................E3
Gulf Islands Nat'l Seashore..G10
Homochitto (riv.).............B8
Horn (isl.)......................G10
Keesler A.F.B. G10
Leaf (riv.).......................F8
Little Tallahatchie (riv.)....D2
Meridian Naval Air Sta.....G5
Mississippi (riv.)..............A8
Mississippi (sound)..........G11
Natchez Nat'l Hist. Park...A7
Noxubee (riv.).................G4
Okatibbee (lake).............G5
Pascagoula (riv.).............F8
Pearl (riv.)......................D8
Petit Bois (isl.)................H10
Pickwick (lake)................H1
Pierre (bayou).................C7
Ross Barnett (res.)..........D6
Round (isl.)....................G10
Saint Louis (bay).............F10
Sardis (lake)...................E2
Ship (isl.).......................G10
Skuna (riv.)....................E3
Strong (riv.)....................D7
Sunflower (riv.)................C5
Tallahaga (creek).............F4
Tallahala (creek)..............F7
Tallahatchie (riv.)............D3
Tchula (lake)...................D4
Tennessee-Tombigbee
   Waterway...................H2
Thompson (creek)............G8
Tombigbee (riv.)..............H4
Trim Cane (creek)............G4
Tupelo Nat'l Battlefield.....G2
Vicksburg Nat'l Mil. Park..C6
Wolf (riv.).......................E9
Woodall (mt.)..................H1
Yalobusha (riv.)...............E3
Yazoo (riv.).....................C5
Yockanookany (riv.).........E5

▲County seat

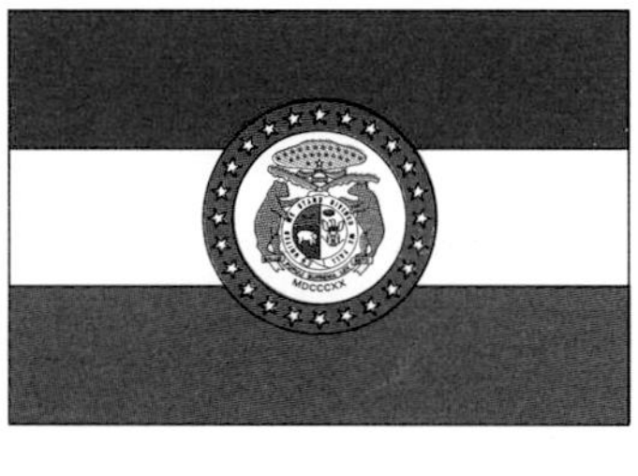

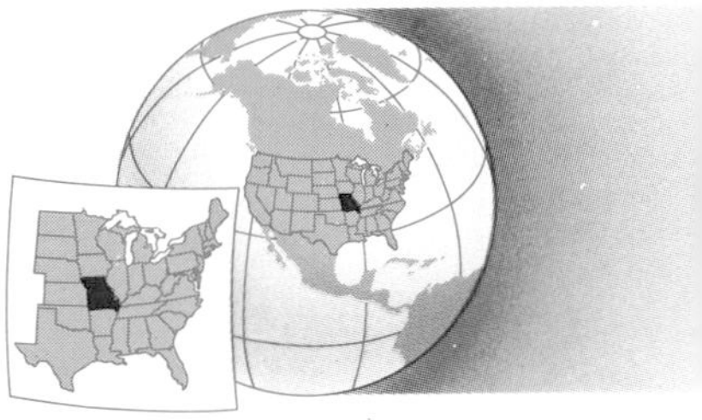

AREA 69,697 sq. mi. (180,515 sq. km.)
POPULATION 5,137,804
CAPITAL Jefferson City
LARGEST CITY St. Louis
HIGHEST POINT Taum Sauk Mtn. 1,772 ft. (540 m.)
SETTLED IN 1764
ADMITTED TO UNION August 10, 1821
POPULAR NAME Show Me State
STATE FLOWER Hawthorn
STATE BIRD Bluebird

COUNTIES

Adair 24,577 ... G2
Andrew 14,632 ... C3
Atchison 7,457 ... B2
Audrain 23,599 ... J4
Barry 27,547 ... E9
Barton 11,312 ... D7
Bates 15,025 ... D6
Benton 13,859 ... F6
Bollinger 10,619 ... M8
Boone 112,379 ... H4
Buchanan 83,083 ... C3
Butler 38,765 ... M9
Caldwell 8,380 ... E3
Callaway 32,809 ... J5
Camden 27,495 ... G6
Cape Girardeau 61,633 ... N8
Carroll 10,748 ... F4
Carter 5,515 ... L9
Cass 63,808 ... D5
Cedar 12,093 ... E7
Chariton 9,202 ... F3
Christian 32,644 ... F9
Clark 7,547 ... J2
Clay 153,411 ... D4
Clinton 16,595 ... D3
Cole 63,579 ... H6
Cooper 14,835 ... G5
Crawford 19,173 ... K7
Dade 7,449 ... E8
Dallas 12,646 ... F7
Daviess 7,865 ... E3
De Kalb 8,222 ... D3
Dent 13,702 ... J7
Douglas 11,876 ... G9
Dunklin 33,112 ... M1
Franklin 80,603 ... K6
Gasconade 14,006 ... J6
Gentry 6,843 ... D2
Greene 207,949 ... F8
Grundy 10,536 ... E2
Harrison 8,469 ... E2
Henry 20,044 ... E6
Hickory 7,335 ... F7
Holt 6,034 ... B2
Howard 9,631 ... G4
Howell 31,447 ... J9
Iron 10,726 ... L7
Jackson 633,232 ... R5
Jasper 90,465 ... D8
Jefferson 171,380 ... L6
Johnson 42,514 ... E5
Knox 4,482 ... H2
Laclede 27,158 ... G7
Lafayette 31,107 ... E4
Lawrence 30,236 ... E8
Lewis 10,233 ... J2
Lincoln 28,892 ... L4
Linn 13,885 ... F3
Livingston 14,592 ... E3
Macon 15,345 ... G3
Madison 11,127 ... M8
Maries 7,976 ... J6
Marion 27,682 ... J3
McDonald 16,938 ... D9
Mercer 3,723 ... E2
Miller 20,700 ... H6
Mississippi 14,442 ... O9
Moniteau 12,298 ... G5
Monroe 9,104 ... H3
Montgomery 11,355 ... K5
Morgan 15,574 ... G6
New Madrid 20,928 ... N9
Newton 44,445 ... D9
Nodaway 21,709 ... C2
Oregon 9,470 ... K9
Osage 12,018 ... J6
Ozark 8,598 ... H9
Pemiscot 21,921 ... N1
Perry 16,648 ... N7
Pettis 35,437 ... F5
Phelps 35,248 ... J7
Pike 15,969 ... K4
Platte 57,867 ... C4
Polk 21,826 ... F7
Pulaski 41,307 ... H7
Putnam 5,079 ... F2
Ralls 8,476 ... J3
Randolph 24,370 ... G3
Ray 21,971 ... E4
Reynolds 6,661 ... L8
Ripley 12,303 ... L9
Saint Charles 144,107 ... M2
Saint Clair 8,622 ... E6
Saint Francois 42,600 ... M7
Saint Louis 974,180 ... O3
Saint Louis (city county) 452,801 ... P3
Sainte Genevieve 15,180 ... M7
Saline 23,523 ... F4
Schuyler 4,236 ... G2
Scotland 4,822 ... H2
Scott 39,376 ... N8
Shannon 7,613 ... K8
Shelby 6,942 ... H3
Stoddard 28,895 ... N9
Stone 19,078 ... F9
Sullivan 6,326 ... F2
Taney 25,561 ... F9
Texas 21,476 ... J8
Vernon 19,041 ... D7
Warren 19,534 ... K5
Washington 20,380 ... L7
Wayne 11,543 ... L8
Webster 23,753 ... G8
Worth 2,440 ... D2
Wright 16,758 ... H8

CITIES and TOWNS

Adrian 1,582 ... D6
Advance 1,139 ... N8
Affton 21,106 ... P4
Agency 642 ... C3
Alba 465 ... D8
Albany▲ 1,958 ... D2
Alexandria 341 ... K2
Alma 446 ... E4
Altamont 188 ... D3
Altenburg 307 ... O7
Alton▲ 692 ... K9
Amazonia 257 ... C3
Amoret 212 ... C6
Amsterdam 237 ... D6
Anderson 1,432 ... D9
Annapolis 363 ... L8
Anniston 288 ... O9
Appleton City 1,280 ... D6
Arbyrd 597 ... M10
Arcadia 609 ... L7
Archie 799 ... D5
Argyle 178 ... J6
Armstrong 310 ... G4
Arnold 18,828 ... M6
Asbury 220 ... C8
Ash Grove 1,128 ... E8
Ashland 1,252 ... H5
Atlanta 411 ... H3
Augusta 263 ... L5
Aurora 6,459 ... E9
Auxvasse 821 ... J4
Ava▲ 2,938 ... G9
Avondale 550 ... P5
Bakersfield 292 ... H9
Ballwin 21,816 ... N3
Baring 182 ... H2
Barnard 234 ... C2
Barnett 215 ... G6
Bates City 197 ... E5
Battlefield 1,526 ... F8
Bel-Nor 2,935 ... P2
Bel-Ridge 3,199 ... P2
Bell City 469 ... N8
Bella Villa 708 ... R4
Belle 1,218 ... J6
Bellefontaine 10,922 ... N2
Bellefontaine Neighbors 12,082 ... R2
Bellflower 413 ... K4
Belton 18,150 ... C5
Benton City 139 ... J4
Benton▲ 575 ... O8
Berger 247 ... K5
Berkeley 12,450 ... P2
Bernie 1,847 ... M9
Bertrand 692 ... O9
Bethany▲ 3,005 ... E2
Beverly 660 ... O4
Bevier 643 ... G3
Billings 989 ... F8
Birch Tree 599 ... K9
Birmingham 222 ... R5
Bismarck 1,579 ... L7
Black 6,128 ... L7
Black Jack 5,293 ... R1
Blackburn 308 ... F4
Blackwater 221 ... G5
Blairstown 185 ... E5
Bland 651 ... J6
Blodgett 202 ... O8
Bloomfield▲ 1,800 ... M9
Bloomsdale 353 ... M6
Blue Springs 40,153 ... R6
Bogard 228 ... E4
Bolckow 253 ... C2
Bolivar▲ 6,845 ... F7
Bonne Terre 3,871 ... L7
Boonville▲ 7,095 ... G5
Bosworth 334 ... F4
Bourbon 1,188 ... K6
Bowling Green▲ 2,976 ... K4
Brandsville 167 ... J9
Branson 3,706 ... F9
Brashear 318 ... H2
Braymer 886 ... E3
Breckenridge 418 ... E3
Breckenridge Hills 5,40[illegible] ... O2
Brentwood 8,150 ... P3
Bridgeton 17,779 ... O2
Bridgeton Terrace 334 ... O2
Bronaugh 211 ... C7
Brookfield 4,888 ... F3
Browning 331 ... F2
Brunswick 1,074 ... F4
Bucklin 616 ... G3
Buckner 2,873 ... R5
Buffalo▲ 2,414 ... F7
Bunceton 341 ... G5
Bunker 390 ... K8
Burlington Junction 634 ... B2
Butler▲ 4,099 ... D6
Butterfield 248 ... E9
Cabool 2,006 ... H8
Cainsville 387 ... E2
Cairo 282 ... H4
Caledonia 142 ... L7
Calhoun 450 ... E6
California▲ 3,465 ... H5
Callao 332 ... G3
Calverton Park 1,404 ... P2
Camden 238 ... D4
Camden Point 373 ... C4
Camdenton▲ 2,561 ... G6
Cameron 4,831 ... D3
Campbell 2,165 ... M9
Canalou 319 ... N9
Canton 2,623 ... J2
Cape Girardeau 34,438 ... O8
Cardwell 792 ... M10
Carl Junction 4,123 ... C8
Carrollton▲ 4,406 ... E4
Carterville 2,013 ... D8
Carthage▲ 10,747 ... D8
Caruth 7,389 ... N10
Caruthersville▲ 7,958 ... N10
Carytown 149 ... D8
Cassville▲ 2,371 ... E9
Cedar City 427 ... H5
Cedar Hill Lakes 227 ... L6
Center 552 ... J3
Centertown 356 ... H5
Centerview 214 ... E5
Centerville▲ 89 ... L8
Centralia 3,414 ... H4
Chaffee 3,059 ... N8
Chamois 449 ... J5
Charlack 1,388 ... P2
Charleston▲ 5,085 ... O9
Chesterfield 37,991 ... N2
Chilhowee 335 ... E5
Chillicothe▲ 8,804 ... E3
Chula 183 ... F3
Circle City 154 ... N9
Clarence 1,026 ... H3
Clark 257 ... H4
Clarksburg 358 ... G5
Clarksdale 287 ... D3
Clarkson Valley 2,508 ... N3
Clarksville 480 ... K4
Clarkton 1,113 ... M10
Claycomo 1,668 ... P5
Clayton▲ 13,874 ... P3
Clearmont 175 ... C1
Cleveland 506 ... C5
Clever 580 ... F8
Clinton▲ 8,703 ... E6
Cobalt City 254 ... M7
Cole Camp 1,054 ... F6
Collins 144 ... E7
Columbia▲ 69,101 ... H5
Commerce 173 ... O8
Conception Junction 236 ... C2
Concord 19,859 ... P4
Concordia 2,160 ... E5
Conway 629 ... G7
Cool Valley 1,407 ... P2
Cooter 451 ... N10
Corder 485 ... E4
Cottleville 2,936 ... M2
Country Club Village 1,234 ... C3
Cowgill 257 ... E3
Craig 346 ... B2
Crane 1,218 ... E9
Creighton 289 ... D6
Crestwood 11,234 ... O3
Creve Coeur 12,304 ... O2
Crocker 1,077 ... H7
Cross Timbers 168 ... F6
Crystal City 4,088 ... M6
Crystal Lake Park 506 ... O3
Cuba 2,537 ... K6
Curryville 261 ... K4
Dadeville 220 ... E8
De Kalb 222 ... C3
De Soto 5,993 ... L6
Dearborn 480 ... C3
Deepwater 441 ... E6
Dellwood 5,245 ... R2
Delta 450 ... N8
Des Arc 173 ... L8
Des Peres 8,395 ... O3
Desloge 4,150 ... M7
Dexter 7,559 ... N9
Diamond 775 ... D9
Diehlstadt 145 ... N9
Diggins 258 ... G8
Dixon 1,585 ... H6
Doniphan▲ 1,713 ... L9
Doolittle 599 ... J7
Downing 359 ... H2
Drexel 936 ... C6
Dudley 271 ... M9
Duenweg 940 ... D8
Duquesne 1,229 ... D8
Eagleville 275 ... D2
East Lynne 289 ... D5
East Prairie 3,416 ... O9
Easton 232 ... C3
Edgar Springs 215 ... J7
Edgerton 565 ... C3
Edina▲ 1,283 ... H2
Edmundson 1,111 ... O2
El Dorado Springs 3,830 ... E7
Eldon 4,419 ... G6
Ellington 994 ... L8
Ellisville 7,545 ... M3
Ellsinore 405 ... L9
Elmo 179 ... B1
Elsberry 1,898 ... L4
Elvins 1,391 ... L7
Eminence▲ 582 ... K8
Emma 194 ... F5
Eolia 389 ... L4
Essex 531 ... N9
Esther 1,071 ... M7
Eugene 141 ... H6
Eureka 4,683 ... M4
Everton 325 ... E8
Ewing 463 ... J2
Excelsior Springs 10,354 ... R4
Exeter 597 ... D9
Fair Grove 919 ... F8
Fair Play 442 ... E7
Fairfax 699 ... B2
Fairview 298 ... D9
Farber 418 ... J4
Farley 217 ... O4
Farmington▲ 11,598 ... M7
Fayette▲ 2,888 ... G4
Fenton 3,346 ... O4
Ferguson 22,286 ... P2
Ferrelview 338 ... O4
Festus 8,105 ... M6
Fillmore 256 ... C2
Fisk 422 ... M9
Flat 4,823 ... J7
Flat River 4,443 ... M7
Fleming 130 ... D4
Flemington 141 ... F7
Flinthill 219 ... L5
Florissant 51,206 ... P1
Foley 209 ... L4
Fordland 523 ... G8
Forest City 380 ... B3
Foristell 144 ... L5
Forsyth▲ 1,175 ... F9
Foster 161 ... D6
Frankford 396 ... K4
Franklin 181 ... G4
Fredericktown▲ 3,950 ... M7
Freeburg 446 ... J6
Freeman 480 ... C5
Freistatt 166 ... E8
Fremont 201 ... K9
Frohna 162 ... N7
Frontenac 3,374 ... O3
Fulton▲ 10,033 ... J5
Gainesville▲ 659 ... G9
Galena▲ 401 ... F9
Gallatin▲ 1,864 ... E3
Galt 296 ... F2
Garden City 1,225 ... D5
Gasconade 253 ... J5
Gerald 888 ... K6
Gideon 1,104 ... N10
Gilliam 212 ... F4
Gilman City 393 ... D2
Gladstone 26,243 ... P5
Glasgow 1,295 ... G4
Glenaire 597 ... R5
Glendale 5,945 ... P3
Glenwood 195 ... G1
Golden 794 ... E9
Golden City 900 ... D8
Goodman 1,094 ... C9
Gordonville 345 ... N8
Gower 1,249 ... C3
Graham 204 ... C2
Grain Valley 1,898 ... S6
Granby 1,945 ... D9
Grandin 233 ... L9
Grandview 24,967 ... P6
Grant City▲ 998 ... D2
Grantwood 904 ... O4
Gray Summit 2,505 ... L6
Green Castle 285 ... G2
Green City 671 ... F2
Green Ridge 452 ... F5
Greenfield▲ 1,416 ... E8
Greentop 425 ... H2
Greenville▲ 437 ... M8
Greenwood 1,505 ... R6
Hale 480 ... F3
Half Way 157 ... F7
Hallsville 917 ... H4
Halltown 161 ... E8
Hamilton 1,737 ... E3
Hanley Hills 2,325 ... P2
Hannibal 18,004 ... K3
Hardin 598 ... E4
Harrisburg 169 ... H4
Harrisonville▲ 7,683 ... D5
Hartville▲ 495 ... G8
Hawk Point 472 ... K5
Hayti 3,280 ... N10
Hayti Heights 893 ... N10
Haywood City 263 ... N9
Hazelwood 15,324 ... P2
Henrietta 412 ... E4
Herculaneum 2,263 ... M6
Hermann▲ 2,754 ... K5
Hermitage▲ 512 ... F7
Higbee 639 ... H4
Higginsville 4,693 ... E4
High Hill 204 ... K5

(continued on following page)

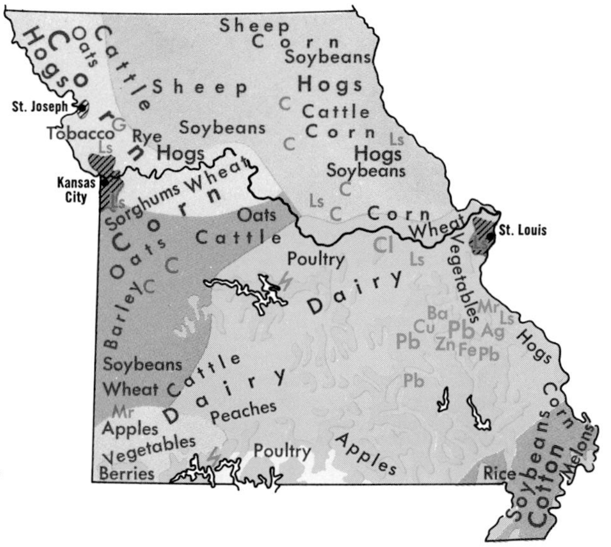

Agriculture, Industry and Resources

DOMINANT LAND USE

- Cattle Feed, Hogs
- Livestock, Cash Grain, Dairy
- Pasture Livestock
- Specialized Cotton
- General Farming, Dairy, Livestock, Poultry
- General Farming, Livestock, Truck Farming, Cotton
- Fruit and Mixed Farming
- Forests
- Urban Areas

MAJOR MINERAL OCCURRENCES

Ag	Silver	G	Natural Gas
Ba	Barite	Ls	Limestone
C	Coal	Mr	Marble
Cl	Clay	Pb	Lead
Cu	Copper	Zn	Zinc
Fe	Iron Ore		

Water Power — Major Industrial Areas

High Ridge 4,423	M6
Hillsboro▲ 1,625	L6
Hillsdale 1,948	R2
Holcomb 531	N10
Holden 2,389	E5
Holland 237	N10
Holliday 139	H3
Hollister 2,628	F9
Holt 311	D4
Holts Summit 2,292	H5
Homestown 230	N10
Hopkins 575	C1
Horine 1,043	M6
Hornersville 629	M10
Houston Lake 303	O5
Houston▲ 2,118	J8
Houstonia 283	F5
Howardville 440	N9
Hughesville 174	F5
Humansville 1,084	E7
Hume 287	C6
Hunnewell 219	J3
Huntleigh 392	R4
Huntsville▲ 1,567	H4
Hurdland 212	H2
Hurricane Deck 210	G6
Iberia 650	H6
Illmo 1,368	O8
Imperial 4,156	M6
Independence▲ 112,301	R5
Iron Gates 309	C8
Irondale 474	L7
Ironton▲ 1,539	L7
Jackson▲ 9,256	N8
Jameson 149	E2
Jamesport 570	E3
Jamestown 298	G5
Jasper 994	D8
Jefferson City (cap.)▲ 35,481	H5
Jennings 15,905	R2
Jerico Springs 247	E7
Jonesburg 630	K5
Joplin 40,961	C8
Junction City 326	M7
Kahoka▲ 2,195	J2
Kansas City 435,146	P5
Kearney 1,790	D4
Kelso 526	O8
Kennett▲ 10,941	M10
Keytesville▲ 564	G4
Kidder 241	D3
Kimberling City 1,590	F9
Kimmswick 135	M6
King City 986	D2
Kingston▲ 279	E3
Kingsville 279	D5
Kinloch 2,702	P2
Kirksville▲ 17,152	H2
Kirkwood 27,291	O3
Knob Noster 2,261	E5
Knox City 262	H2
Koshkonong 198	J9
La Belle 655	J2
La Grange 1,102	K2
La Monte 995	F5
La Plata 1,401	H2
Laclede 410	F3
Ladue 8,847	P3
Lake Lotawana 2,141	R6
Lake Ozark 681	G6
Lake Saint Louis 7,400	L5
Lake Tapawingo 761	R6
Lake Waukomis 1,027	P5
Lake Winnebago 748	R6
Lakeshire 1,467	P4
Lamar Heights 176	D8
Lamar▲ 4,168	D8
Lanagan 501	C9
Lancaster▲ 785	H1
Laredo 205	E2
Lathrop 1,794	D3
Laurie 507	G6
Lawson 1,876	D4
Leadington 201	M7
Leadwood 1,247	L7
Leasburg 289	K6
Lebanon▲ 9,983	G7
Lee's Summit 46,418	R6
Leeton 632	E5
Lemay 18,005	R4
Levasy 279	S5
Lewis 142	D9
Lewis and Clark Village 131	C3
Lewistown 453	J2
Lexington▲ 4,860	E4
Liberal 684	D7
Liberty▲ 20,459	R5
Licking 1,328	J8
Lilbourn 1,378	N9
Lincoln 874	F6
Linn Creek 232	G6
Linn▲ 1,148	J5
Linneus▲ 364	F3
Lockwood 1,041	E8
Lohman 154	H5
Lone Jack 392	S6
Louisiana 3,967	K3
Lowry City 723	E6
Ludlow 147	E3
Lutesville 865	M8
Mackenzie 148	P3
Macks Creek 272	G7
Macon▲ 5,571	H3
Madison 518	H4
Maitland 338	B2
Malden 5,123	N9
Malta Bend 289	F4
Manchester 6,542	O3
Mansfield 1,429	G8
Maplewood 9,962	P3
Marble Hill▲ 1,447	N8
Marceline 2,645	F3
Marionville 1,920	E8
Marlborough 1,949	P3
Marquand 278	L8
Marshall▲ 12,711	F4
Marshfield▲ 4,374	G8
Marston 691	N9
Marthasville 674	L5
Martinsburg 337	J4
Maryland Heights 25,407	O2
Maryville▲ 10,663	C2
Matthews 614	N9
Maysville▲ 1,176	D2
Mayview 279	E4
McFall 142	D2
Meadville 360	F3
Mehlville 27,557	P4
Memphis▲ 2,094	H2
Mendon 207	F3
Mercer 297	F2
Meta 249	H6
Mexico▲ 11,290	J4
Miami 142	F4
Middletown 217	J4
Milan▲ 1,767	F2
Mill Spring 252	L8
Miller 753	E8
Mindenmines 346	C8
Mine La Motte 125	M7
Miner 1,218	N9
Mineral Point 384	L7
Missouri City 348	R5
Moberly 12,839	G4
Mokane 186	J5
Moline Acres 2,710	R4
Monett 6,529	E9
Monroe City 2,701	J3
Montgomery City▲ 2,281	K5
Monticello▲ 106	J2
Montrose 440	E6
Morehouse 1,068	N9
Morley 683	N8
Morrison 160	J5
Morrisville 293	F8
Mosby 194	R4
Moscow Mills 924	K5
Mound City 1,273	B2
Mount Leonard 140	C7
Mount Vernon▲ 3,726	E8
Mountain Grove 4,182	H8
Mountain View 2,036	J8
Murphy 9,342	O4
Napoleon 233	E4
Naylor 642	L9
Neelyville 381	M9
Nelson 181	F4
Neosho▲ 9,254	D9
Nevada▲ 8,597	D7
New Bloomfield 480	J5
New Cambria 223	G3
New Florence 801	K5
New Franklin 1,107	G4
New Hampton 320	D2
New Haven 1,757	K5
New London▲ 988	K3
New Madrid▲ 3,350	O9
New Melle 486	L5
Newburg 589	J7
Newtonia 204	D8
Niangua 459	G8
Nixa 4,707	F8
Noel 1,169	D9
Norborne 856	E4
Normandy 4,480	R2
North Kansas City 4,130	P5
Northmoor 441	O5
Northwoods 5,106	R2
Norwood 449	H8
Novelty 143	H2
Novinger 542	G2
O'Fallon 18,698	L5
Oak Grove 4,067	S6
Oak Grove 402	K6
Oak Ridge 202	N7
Oakland 1,593	P3
Oaks 130	P5
Oakview 351	P5
Oakwood 212	P5
Oakwood Manor 137	P5
Oakwood Park 213	P5
Odessa 3,695	S6
Old Monroe 242	L5
Olivette 7,573	O2
Olympian Village 752	M6
Oran 1,164	N8
Oregon▲ 935	B2
Oronogo 595	D8
Orrick 935	E4
Osage Beach 2,599	G6
Osborn 400	D3
Osceola▲ 755	E6
Otterville 507	G5
Overland 17,987	O2
Owensville 2,325	K6
Ozark▲ 4,243	F8
Pacific 4,350	L5
Pagedale 3,771	P2
Palmyra▲ 3,371	J3
Paris▲ 1,486	J4
Parkdale 270	F6
Parkville 2,402	O5
Parkway 277	L6
Parma 995	N9
Parnell 157	C2
Patton 414	M8
Pattonsburg 502	D2
Peculiar 1,777	D5
Pevely 2,831	M6
Phillipsburg 170	G7
Pickering 171	C2
Piedmont 2,166	L8
Pierce City 1,382	E8
Pilot Grove 714	G5
Pilot Knob 783	L7
Pine 5,092	K9
Pine Lawn 6,600	R2
Pineville▲ 580	D9
Platte City▲ 2,947	C4
Platte Woods 427	O5
Plattsburg▲ 2,248	D3
Pleasant Hill 3,827	D5
Pleasant Hope 360	F8
Pleasant Valley 2,731	R5
Polo 539	D3
Poplar Bluff▲ 16,996	L9
Portage Des Sioux 503	M5
Portageville 3,401	N10
Potosi▲ 2,683	L7
Prairie Home 215	G5
Princeton▲ 1,021	E2
Purcell 359	D8
Purdin 217	F3
Purdy 977	E9
Puxico 819	M9
Queen City 704	H2
Qulin 384	M9
Ravenwood 409	C2
Raymondville 425	J8
Raymore 5,592	D5
Raytown 30,601	P6
Rayville 170	E4
Reeds Spring 411	F9
Renick 195	H4
Republic 6,292	E8
Rhineland 157	J5
Rich Hill 1,317	D6
Richland 2,029	H7
Richmond Heights 10,448	P3
Richmond▲ 5,738	D4
Ridgeway 379	D2
Risco 434	N9
Rivermines 459	L7
Riverside 3,010	O5
Riverview 3,242	R2
Rochepot 255	H5
Rock Hill 5,217	P3
Rock Port▲ 1,438	B2
Rockaway Beach 275	F9
Rockville 193	D6
Rogersville 995	G8
Rolla▲ 14,090	J7
Rosebud 380	K6
Rosendale 186	C2
Rushville 306	B3
Russellville 869	H6
Saginaw 384	D9
Saint Ann 14,489	O2
Saint Charles▲ 54,555	N1
Saint Clair 3,917	K6
Saint Elizabeth 257	H6
Saint George 1,270	P4
Saint James 3,256	J6
Saint John 7,466	R2
Saint Joseph▲ 71,852	C3
Saint Louis▲ 396,685	R3
Saint Martins 717	H5
Saint Mary's 461	M7
Saint Paul 1,192	L5
Saint Peters 45,779	M1
Saint Robert 1,730	H7
Saint Thomas 263	H6
Sainte Genevieve▲ 4,411	M6
Salem▲ 4,486	J7
Salisbury 1,881	G4
Sappington 10,917	O4
Sarcoxie 1,330	D8
Savannah▲ 4,352	C3
Schell City 292	D6
Scott City 4,292	O8
Sedalia▲ 19,800	F5
Sedgewickville 138	N7
Seligman 593	D9
Senath 1,622	M10
Seneca 1,885	D9
Seymour 1,636	G8
Shelbina 2,172	H3
Shelbyville▲ 582	H3
Sheldon 464	D7
Sheridan 174	C1
Shrewsbury 6,416	P3
Sibley 367	S5
Sikeston 17,641	N9
Silex 197	K4
Skidmore 404	B2
Slater 2,186	G4
Smithton 532	F5
Smithville 2,525	D4
South West City 600	D9
Spanish Lake 20,322	R1
Sparta 751	F9
Spickard 326	F2
Springfield▲ 140,494	F8
Stanberry 1,310	C2
Steele 2,395	N10
Steelville▲ 1,465	K7
Stewartsville 732	D3
Stockton▲ 1,579	E7
Stotts City 235	E8
Stoutland 207	H7
Stover 964	G6
Strafford 1,166	F8
Sturgeon 838	H4

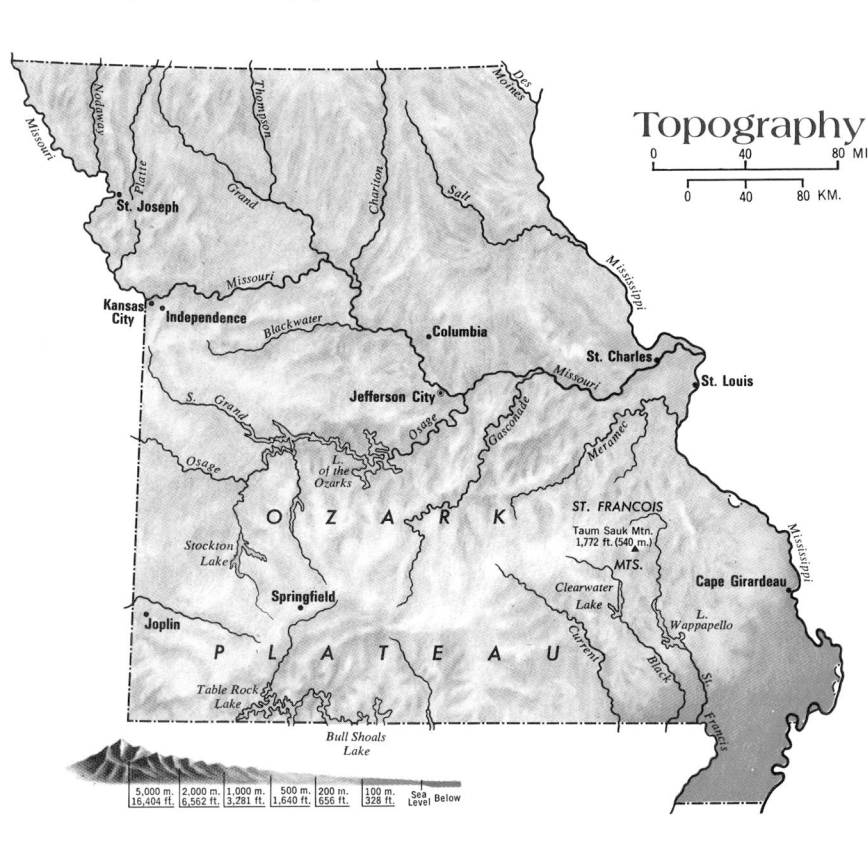

Topography

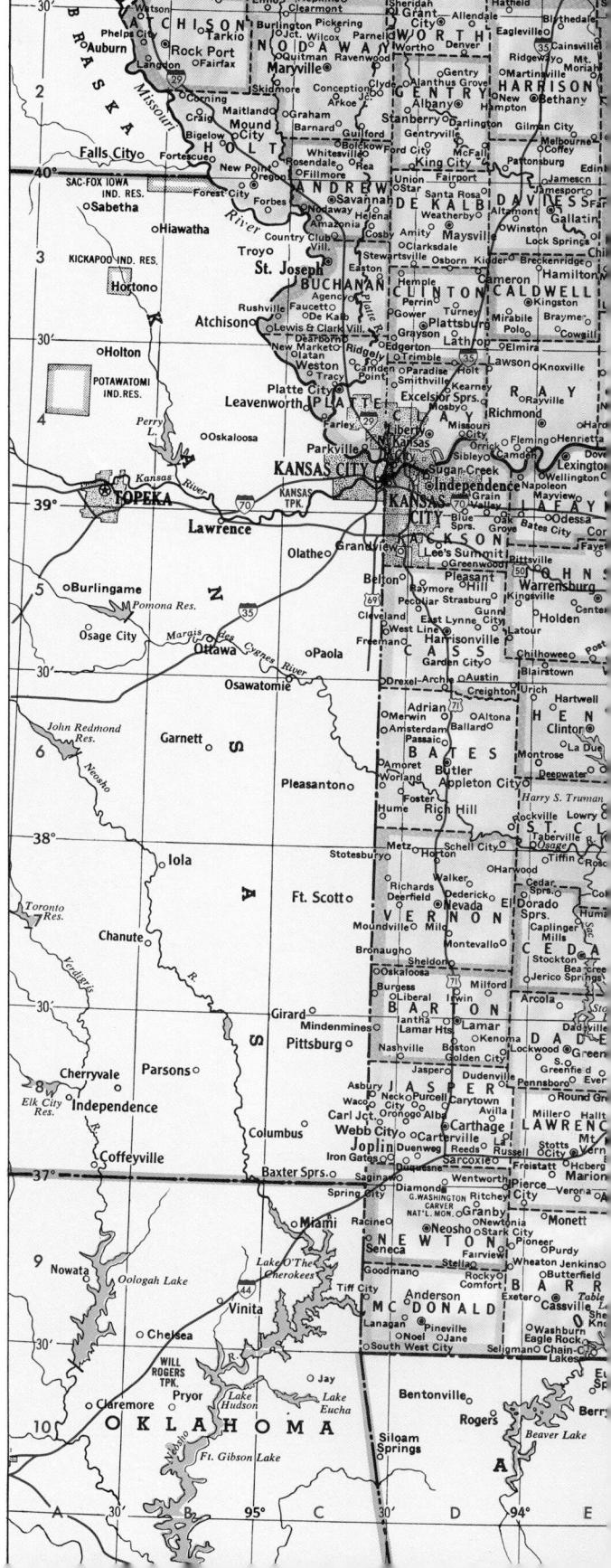

Sugar Creek 3,982 ....R5
Sullivan 5,661 ....K6
Summersville 571 ....J8
Sunrise Beach 181 ....G6
Sunset Hills 4,915 ....O4
Sweet Springs 1,595 ....H5
Sycamore 667 ....H9
Syracuse 185 ....G5
Tallapoosa 174 ....N9
Taneyville 279 ....F9
Taos 802 ....H5
Tarkio 2,243 ....B2
Tarsney Lakes 329 ....R6
Thayer 1,996 ....J9
Theodosia 235 ....G9
Tina 199 ....F3
Tipton 2,026 ....G5
Town and Country 9,519 ....O3
Tracy 287 ....C4
Trenton▲ 6,129 ....E2

Trimble 405 ....D4
Troy▲ 3,811 ....L5
Truesdale 285 ....K5
Tuscumbia▲ 148 ....H6
Twin Oaks 506 ....N3
Union Star 432 ....C2
Union▲ 5,909 ....L6
Unionville▲ 1,989 ....G2
Unity Village 138 ....R6
Urbana 350 ....F7
Urich 498 ....E6
Utica 299 ....E3
Valley Park 4,165 ....O3
Van Buren▲ 893 ....L5
Vandalia 2,683 ....J4
Vanduser 187 ....N10
Velda 1,597 ....P2
Verona 546 ....E9
Versailles▲ 2,365 ....G6

Viburnum 743 ....K7
Vienna▲ 611 ....H6
Vinita Park 2,001 ....P2
Walker 283 ....D7
Walnut Grove 549 ....F8
Wardell 325 ....N10
Wardsville 513 ....H6
Warren 15,244 ....J3
Warrensburg▲ 13,807 ....E5
Warrenton▲ 3,564 ....K5
Warsaw▲ 1,696 ....F6
Warson Woods 2,049 ....O3
Washburn 362 ....E9
Washington 10,704 ....K5
Waverly 837 ....E4
Wayland 391 ....J2
Waynesville▲ 3,207 ....H7
Weatherby Lake 1,613 ....O5
Weaubleau 436 ....F7
Webb City 7,449 ....C8

Webster Groves 22,987 ....P3
Wellington 779 ....E4
Wellston 3,612 ....R2
Wellsville 1,430 ....K4
Wentworth 138 ....D8
Wentzville 5,088 ....L5
West Plains▲ 8,913 ....J9
Westboro 182 ....B1
Weston 1,528 ....C4
Westphalia 287 ....J6
Westwood 309 ....O3
Wheatland 363 ....F7
Wheaton 637 ....D9
Wheeling 284 ....F3
Wilbur Park 522 ....P3
Willard 2,177 ....F8
Williamsville 391 ....L9
Willow Springs 2,038 ....H9
Wilson City 210 ....O9
Winchester 1,678 ....N3

Windsor 3,044 ....E5
Winfield 672 ....L5
Winona 1,081 ....K8
Winston 251 ....D3
Woods Heights 708 ....S4
Woodson Terrace 4,362 ....P2
Wright City 1,250 ....K5
Wyaconda 347 ....J2
Wyatt 376 ....O9

OTHER FEATURES

Bagnell (dam) G6
Big (riv.) L6
Black (riv.) L10
Bull Shoals (lake) G10
Chariton (riv.) G1
Clearwater (lake) L8
Cuivre (riv.) N2
Current (riv.) K8

Des Moines (riv.) J1
Fort Leonard Wood 15,863 ....H7
Gasconade (riv.) H7
George Washington Carver Nat'l Mon. D9
Grand (riv.) F3
Harry S Truman (res.) E6
Harry S Truman Nat'l Hist. Site R5
Jefferson Nat'l Expansion Mem. R3
Lake City Arsenal R5
Meramec (riv.) N3
Mississippi (riv.) L4
Missouri (riv.) H5
Norfork (lake) H10
Osage (riv.) E6
Ozark (plat.) F9
Ozark National Scenic Riverways K8

Ozarks, Lake of the (lake) F6
Platte (riv.) C3
Pomme de Terre (lake) E7
Richards Gebaur A.F.B. P6
Sac (riv.) E7
Saint Francis (riv.) M9
Saint Francis (mts.) L7
Salt (riv.) J3
Stockton (lake) E7
Table Rock Lake (res.) E9
Taneycomo (lake) F9
Taum Sauk (mt.) L7
Wappapello (lake) L8
White (riv.) G10
Whiteman A.F.B. 4,174 ....E5
Wilson's Creek Nat'l Battlefield F8

▲County seat

St. Louis and Vicinity

Kansas City and Vicinity

Missouri

SCALE
0 5 10   20   30   40   50 MI.
0 5 10   20   30   40   50 KM.

State Capitals ....⊛
County Seats ....◉
Major Limited Access Hwys. ——

1:2,250,000

© Copyright HAMMOND INCORPORATED, Maplewood, N.J.

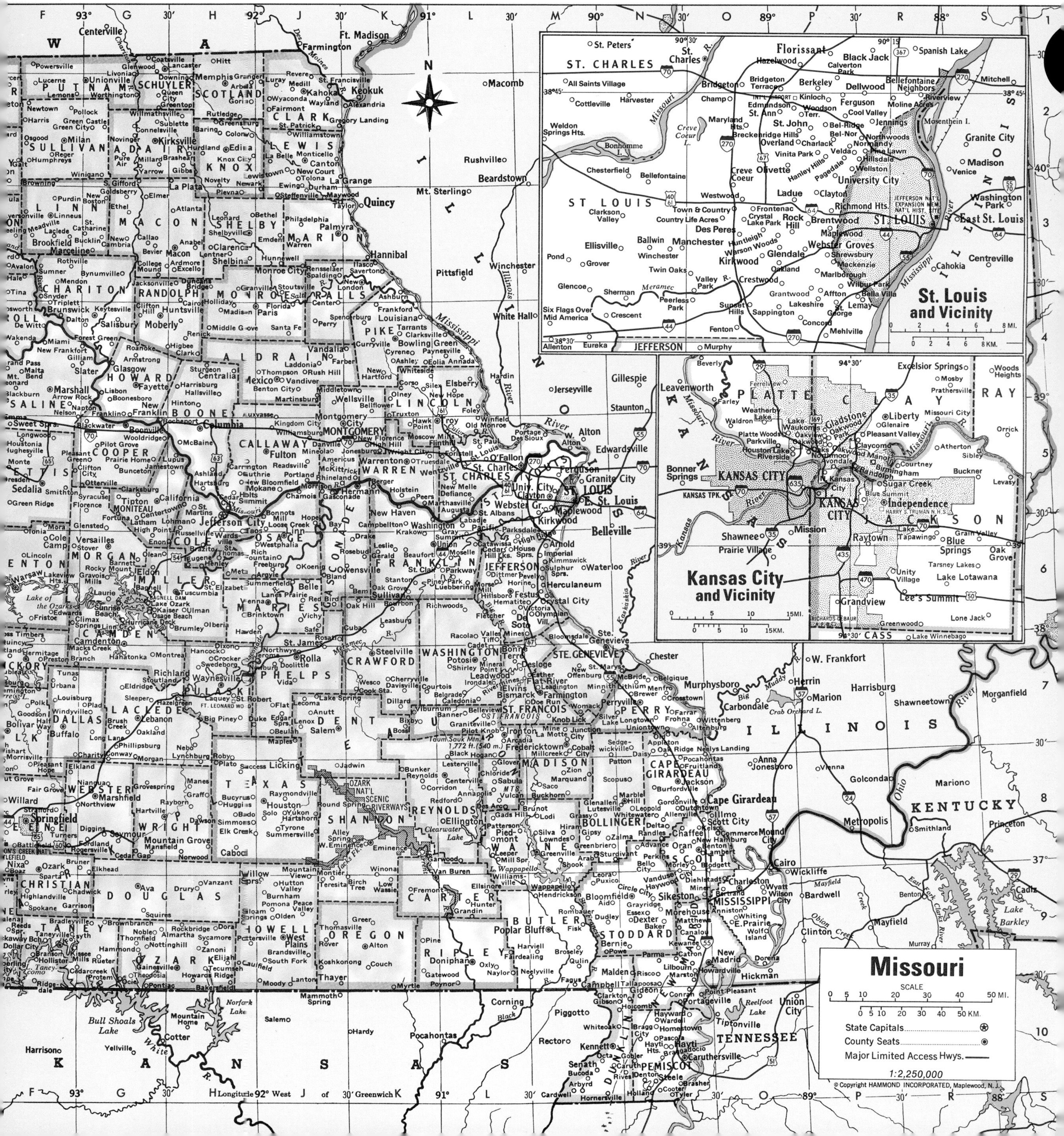

Agriculture, Industry and Resources

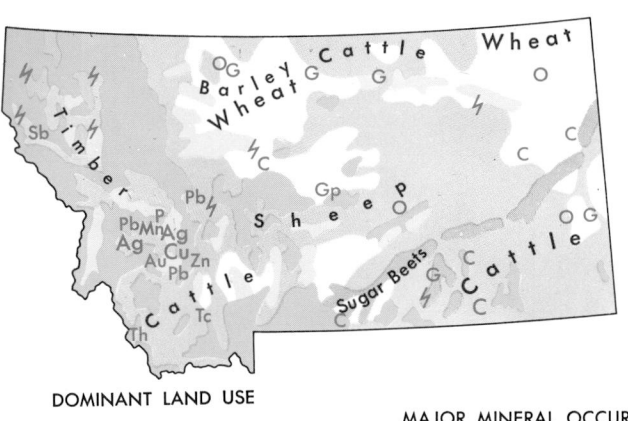

DOMINANT LAND USE

- Specialized Wheat
- Wheat, Range Livestock
- General Farming, Dairy, Range Livestock
- General Farming, Livestock, Special Crops
- Range Livestock
- Sugar Beets, Beans, Livestock, General Farming
- Forests

MAJOR MINERAL OCCURRENCES

Ag	Silver	O	Petroleum
Au	Gold	P	Phosphates
C	Coal	Pb	Lead
Cu	Copper	Sb	Antimony
G	Natural Gas	Tc	Talc
Gp	Gypsum	Th	Thorium
Mn	Manganese	Zn	Zinc

⚡ Water Power

COUNTIES

Beaverhead 8,424 ....C5
Big Horn 11,337 ....J5
Blaine 6,728 ....G2
Broadwater 3,318............E4
Carbon 8,080...................G5
Carter 1,503....................M5
Cascade 77,691 ....E3
Chouteau 5,452...............F3
Custer 11,697..................L4
Daniels 2,266 ....L2
Dawson 9,505..................M3
Deer Lodge 10,278 ....C5
Fallon 3,103.....................M4
Fergus 12,083 ....G3
Flathead 59,218...............B2
Gallatin 50,463................E5
Garfield 1,589..................J3
Glacier 12,121.................C2
Golden Valley 912............G4
Granite 2,548...................C4
Hill 17,654.......................F2
Jefferson 7,939................D4
Judith Basin 2,282...........F4
Lake 21,041.....................B3
Lewis and Clark 47,495.....D3
Liberty 2,295...................E2
Lincoln 17,481.................A2
Madison 5,989.................D5
McCone 2,276..................L3
Meagher 1,819................F4
Mineral 3,315..................B3
Missoula 78,687..............C3
Musselshell 4,106...........H4
Park 14,562.....................F5
Petroleum 519.................H3
Phillips 5,163...................J2
Pondera 6,433.................D2
Powder River 2,090..........L5
Powell 6,620....................D4
Prairie 1,383....................L4
Ravalli 25,010..................B4
Richland 10,716...............M3
Roosevelt 10,999.............L2
Rosebud 10,505..............K4
Sanders 8,669.................A3
Sheridan 4,732................M2
Silver Bow 33,941............D5
Stillwater 6,536...............G5

Sweet Grass 3,154 ....G5
Teton 6,271 ....D3
Toole 5,046.....................E2
Treasure 874...................J4
Valley 8,239.....................K2
Wheatland 2,246..............G4
Wibaux 1,191...................M4
Yellowstone 113,419........H4

CITIES and TOWNS

Absarokee 1,067..............G5
Acton 50 ....H5
Alberton 354...................B3
Alder 120.........................D5
Alzada 52.........................M5
Amsterdam 130...............E5
Anaconda-Deer Lodge
    County▲....................C4
Angela 50.........................K4
Antelope 83......................M2
Apgar 25..........................B2
Arlee 489.........................B3
Armington 75...................F3
Ashland 484.....................K5
Augusta 497.....................D3
Avon 125..........................D4
Babb 150..........................C2
Bainville 165....................M2
Baker▲ 1,818...................M4
Ballantine 380..................J5
Bannack 2........................C5
Basin 350.........................D4
Bearcreek 37...................G5
Becket 35.........................G4
Belfry 300.........................H5
Belgrade 3,411.................E5
Belt 571............................E3
Biddle 28..........................L5
Big Arm 250.....................B3
Big Sandy 740..................G2
Big Sky 50........................E5
Big Timber▲ 1,557...........G5
Bigfork 1,080....................C2
Billings▲ 81,151...............H5
Birney 100........................K5
Black Eagle 1,500............E3
Blackfoot 100...................D2
Bloomfield 28...................M3
Bonner-West Riverside 1,669.C4

Boulder▲ 1,316...............E4
Box Elder 300..................F2
Boyd 32............................H5
Bozeman▲ 22,660...........E5
Brady 450.........................E2
Bridger 692......................H5
Broadus▲ 572..................L5
Broadview 133..................H4
Brockton 365....................M2
Brockway 55.....................L3
Browning 1,170................C2
Busby 409.........................J5
Butte-Silver Bow
    County▲ 33,336...........D5
Bynum 49.........................D3
Camas Prairie 160............B2
Cameron 150....................E5
Canyon Creek 100............E4
Canyon Ferry 100.............E4
Cardwell 34......................D5
Carter 70..........................F3
Cartersville 115................K4
Cascade 729....................E3
Charlo 358........................B3
Chester▲ 942...................E2
Chinook▲ 1,512................G2
Choteau▲ 1,741...............D3
Christina 60......................G3
Circle▲ 805......................L3
Clancy 550.......................E4
Clinton 250.......................C4
Clyde Park 282.................F5
Coffee Creek 62...............F3
Colstrip 3,035...................K5
Columbia Falls 2,942........B2
Columbus▲ 1,573.............G5
Condon 300......................C3
Conner 420.......................B5
Conrad▲ 2,891.................D2
Coram 450........................C2
Corvallis 500....................B4
Craig 100..........................D4
Crane 163.........................M3
Creston 60........................C2
Crow Agency 1,446...........J5
Culbertson 796.................M2
Custer 300........................J4
Cut Bank▲ 3,329..............D2
Dagmar 35........................M2

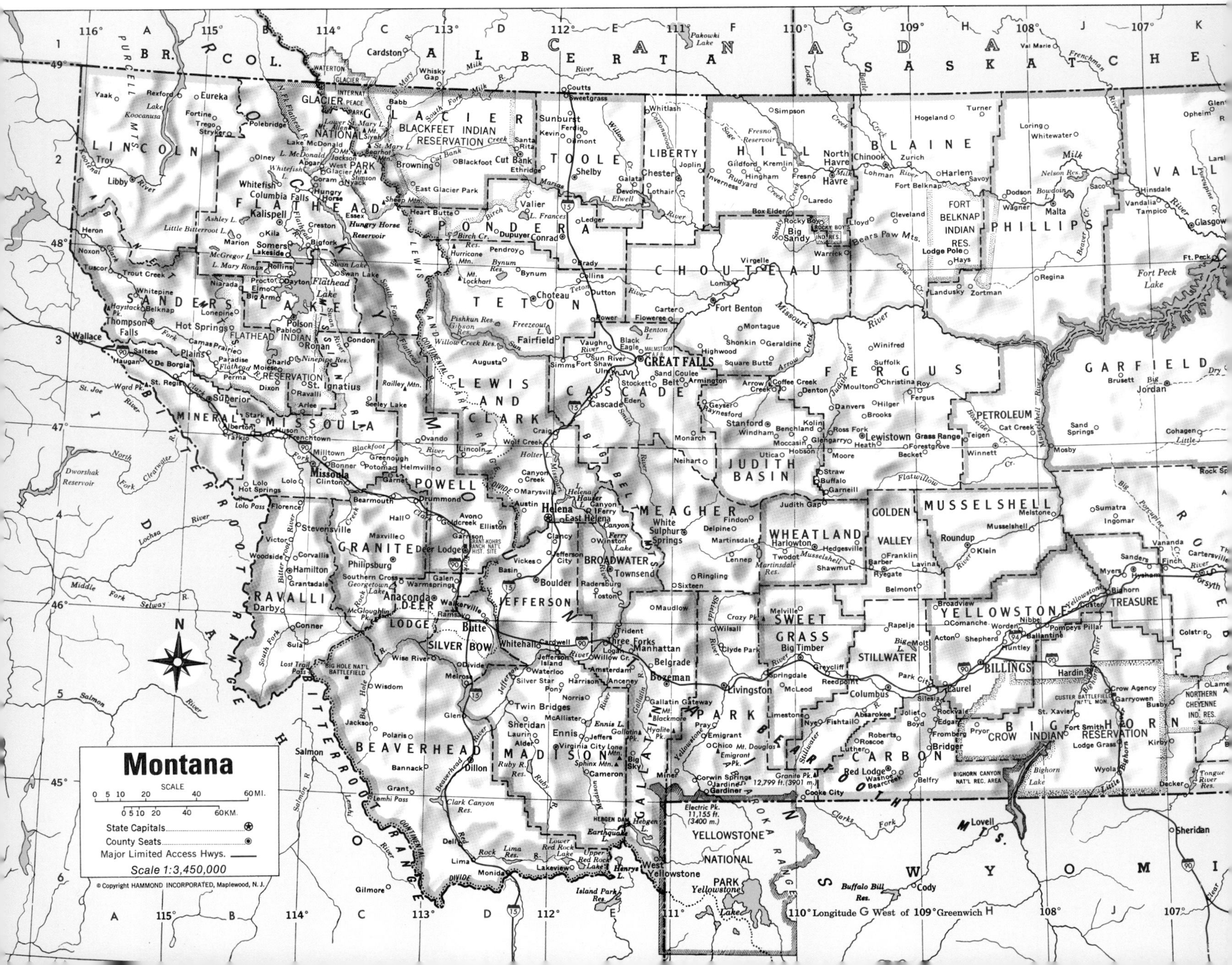

Topography

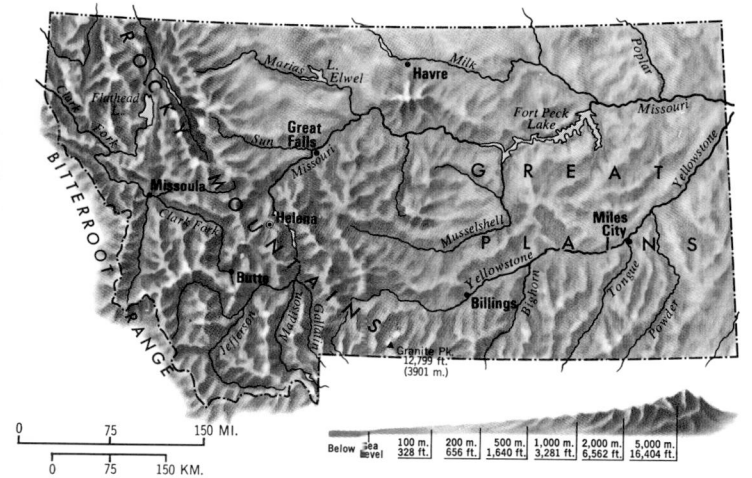

MONTANA

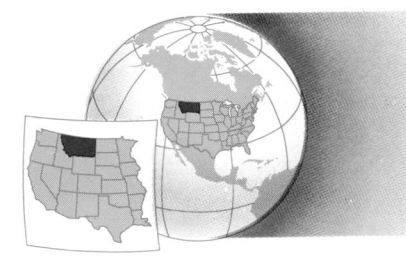

0   75   150 MI.
0   75   150 KM.

Below sea level | 100 m. 328 ft. | 200 m. 656 ft. | 500 m. 1,640 ft. | 1,000 m. 3,281 ft. | 2,000 m. 6,562 ft. | 5,000 m. 16,404 ft.

AREA 147,046 sq. mi. (380,849 sq. km.)
POPULATION 803,655
CAPITAL Helena
LARGEST CITY Billings
HIGHEST POINT Granite Pk. 12,799 ft.
(3901 m.)
SETTLED IN 1809
ADMITTED TO UNION November 8, 1889
POPULAR NAME Treasure State; Big Sky
Country
STATE FLOWER Bitterroot
STATE BIRD Western Meadowlark

Darby 625 ....B4
Dayton 140 ....B3
De Borgia 300 ....A3
Decker 150 ....K5
Deer Lodge▲ 3,378 ....D4
Dell 29 ....D6
Delpine 33 ....F4
Denton 350 ....G3
Dillon▲ 3,991 ....D5
Divide 275 ....D5
Dixon 550 ....B3

Dodson 137 ....H2
Drummond 264 ....D4
Dupuyer 105 ....D2
Dutton 392 ....E3
East Glacier Park 326 ....C2
East Helena 1,538 ....E4
Edgar 220 ....H5
Ekalaka▲ 439 ....M5
Elliston 250 ....D4
Elmo 250 ....B3
Emigrant 80 ....F5

Ennis 773 ....E5
Epsie 60 ....L5
Essex 48 ....C2
Eureka 1,043 ....B2
Fairfield 660 ....D3
Fairview 869 ....M3
Fallon 225 ....L4
Fishtail 46 ....G5
Flaxville 88 ....L2
Florence 700 ....B4
Floweree 48 ....E3
Forestgrove 100 ....H3
Forsyth▲ 2,178 ....K4
Fort Belknap 422 ....H2
Fort Benton▲ 1,660 ....F3
Fort Peck 325 ....K2
Fort Shaw 200 ....E3
Fort Smith 300 ....J5
Fortine 250 ....A2
Four Buttes 50 ....L2
Frazer 403 ....K2
Frenchtown 300 ....B3
Froid 195 ....M2
Fromberg 370 ....H5
Galata 100 ....E2
Galen 210 ....D4
Gallatin Gateway 600 ....E5
Gardiner 600 ....F5
Garneill 61 ....G4
Garrison 300 ....D4
Garryowen 200 ....J5
Geraldine 299 ....F3
Geyser 125 ....F3
Gildford 250 ....F2
Glasgow▲ 3,572 ....K2
Glen 4,802 ....D5
Glendive▲ 5,978 ....M3
Goldcreek 100 ....D4
Grant 25 ....C5
Grantsdale 500 ....B4
Grass Range 159 ....H3
Great Falls▲ 55,097 ....E3
Greenough 120 ....C4
Greycliff 37 ....G5
Hall 130 ....C4
Hamilton▲ 2,737 ....B4
Hardin▲ 2,940 ....J5
Harlem 882 ....H2
Harlowton▲ 1,049 ....F4
Harrison 94 ....E5
Hathaway 55 ....K4
Haugan 90 ....A3
Havre▲ 10,201 ....G2
Hays 333 ....H2
Heart Butte 499 ....C2
Helena (cap.)▲ 24,569 ....E4
Helmville 250 ....C4
Heron 79 ....A2
Highwood 150 ....F3
Hilger 38 ....G3
Hingham 181 ....F2
Hinsdale 260 ....K2
Hobson 226 ....G4
Hodges 50 ....M4
Hogeland 35 ....H2
Homestead 50 ....M2
Hot Springs 411 ....B3
Hungry Horse 700 ....C2
Huntley 250 ....H5
Huson 97 ....B3
Hysham▲ 361 ....J4
Ingomar 48 ....J4
Intake 60 ....M3
Inverness 150 ....F2
Jackson 210 ....C5
Jardine 30 ....F5
Jeffers 70 ....E5
Jefferson City 162 ....E4
Jefferson Island 25 ....E5
Joliet 522 ....G5
Joplin 300 ....F2
Jordan▲ 494 ....J3
Judith Gap 133 ....G4
Kalispell▲ 11,917 ....B2
Kevin 185 ....D2
Kila 250 ....B2
Kinsey 100 ....L4
Kirby 30 ....J5
Klein 250 ....H4

Kremlin 304 ....F2
Lakeside 663 ....B2
Lakeview 28 ....E6
Lambert 203 ....M3
Lame Deer 1,918 ....K5
Landusky 40 ....H3
Laurel 5,686 ....H5
Laurin 60 ....D5
Lavina 151 ....H4
Lewistown▲ 6,051 ....G3
Libby▲ 2,532 ....A2
Lima 265 ....D6
Lincoln 473 ....D4
Lindsay 50 ....L3
Livingston▲ 6,701 ....F5
Locate 55 ....L4
Lodge Grass 517 ....J5
Lodge Pole 292 ....H2
Logan 53 ....E5
Lohman 25 ....G2
Lolo 2,746 ....B4
Lolo Hot Springs 25 ....B4
Loma 200 ....F3
Lonepine 50 ....B3
Lothair 29 ....E2
Malta▲ 2,340 ....J2
Manhattan 1,034 ....E5
Marion 450 ....B2
Martinsdale 75 ....F4
Marysville 76 ....D4
Maxville 44 ....C4
McAllister 55 ....E5
McLeod 150 ....G5
Medicine Lake 357 ....M2
Melrose 350 ....D5
Melstone 166 ....H4
Melville 100 ....F4
Miles City▲ 8,461 ....L4
Mill Iron 96 ....M5
Milltown 300 ....C4
Missoula▲ 42,918 ....C4
Moccasin 57 ....F3
Molt 31 ....H5
Monarch 120 ....F3
Moore 211 ....G4
Musselshell 117 ....H4
Myers 120 ....J4
Nashua 375 ....K2
Neihart 53 ....F4
Nibbe 30 ....H4
Norris 55 ....E5
North Havre 1,230 ....G2
Noxon 800 ....A3
Nye 50 ....G5
Oilmont 50 ....E2
Olney 200 ....B2
Opheim 145 ....K2
Oswego 75 ....L2
Outlook 109 ....M2
Ovando 300 ....C3
Pablo 1,298 ....B3
Paradise 400 ....B3
Park City 800 ....H5
Peerless 110 ....L2
Pendroy 100 ....D2
Perma 50 ....B3
Philipsburg▲ 925 ....C4
Plains 992 ....B3
Plentywood▲ 2,136 ....M2
Plevna 140 ....M4
Polaris 53 ....C5
Polson▲ 3,283 ....B3
Pompeys Pillar 300 ....J5
Pony 130 ....E5
Poplar 881 ....L2
Potomac 80 ....C4
Power 159 ....E3
Pray 40 ....F5
Proctor 150 ....B3
Pryor 654 ....H5
Radersburg 104 ....E4
Ramsay 95 ....D4
Rapelje 50 ....G5
Ravalli 150 ....B3
Raymond 26 ....M2
Raynesford 35 ....F3
Red Lodge▲ 1,958 ....G5
Redstone 40 ....M2
Reedpoint 160 ....G5

Regina 83 ....J3
Reserve 80 ....M2
Rexford 132 ....A2
Richey 259 ....L3
Richland 48 ....K2
Ringling 102 ....F4
Roberts 312 ....G5
Rocky Boy 150 ....G2
Rollins 200 ....B3
Ronan 1,547 ....C3
Roscoe 40 ....G5
Rosebud 350 ....K4
Roundup▲ 1,808 ....H4
Roy 200 ....H3
Rudyard 450 ....F2
Ryegate▲ 260 ....G4
Saco 261 ....J2
Saint Ignatius 778 ....C3
Saint Regis 500 ....A3
Saint Xavier 200 ....J5
Saltese 90 ....A3
Sand Coulee 600 ....E3
Sanders 50 ....J4
Santa Rita 120 ....D2
Savage 300 ....M3
Scobey▲ 1,154 ....L2
Seeley Lake 900 ....C3
Shawmut 66 ....G4
Sheffield 49 ....K4
Shelby▲ 2,763 ....E2
Shepherd 200 ....H5
Sheridan 652 ....D5
Sidney▲ 5,217 ....M3
Silesia 90 ....H5
Silver Star 125 ....D5
Simms 200 ....E3
Simpson 70 ....F2
Somers 700 ....B2
Sonnette 42 ....L5
Springdale 45 ....F5
Square Butte 48 ....F3
Stanford▲ 529 ....F3
Stark 51 ....B3
Stevensville 1,221 ....C4
Stockett 500 ....E3
Stryker 96 ....B2
Suffolk 45 ....G3
Sula 200 ....B5
Sun River 300 ....E3
Sunburst 437 ....E2
Superior▲ 881 ....B3
Swan Lake 100 ....C3
Sweetgrass 250 ....E2
Terry▲ 659 ....L4
Thompson Falls▲ 1,319 ....A3
Three Forks 1,203 ....E5
Thurlow 84 ....K4
Toston 70 ....E4
Townsend▲ 1,635 ....E4
Trego 50 ....B2
Trident 50 ....E5
Trout Creek 300 ....A3
Troy 953 ....A2
Turner 150 ....H2
Twin Bridges 374 ....D5
Twodot 285 ....F4
Ulm 450 ....E3
Utica 30 ....F4
Valier 519 ....D2
Vananda 50 ....K4
Vandalia 35 ....J2
Vaughn 2,270 ....E3
Victor 700 ....B4
Vida 50 ....L3
Virgelle 28 ....F2
Virginia City▲ 142 ....E5
Volborg 125 ....L5
Wagner 32 ....H2
Walkerville 605 ....D4
Warmsprings 500 ....D4
Waterloo 50 ....D5
West Glacier 150 ....C2
West Yellowstone 913 ....E6
Westby 253 ....M2
White Sulphur Springs▲ 963 .E4
Whitefish 4,368 ....B2
Whitehall 1,067 ....D5
Whitetail 150 ....L2
Whitewater 100 ....J2

Whitlash 50 ....E2
Wibaux▲ 628 ....M3
Wickes 60 ....D4
Willow Creek 150 ....E5
Wilsall 250 ....F5
Windham 63 ....F3
Winifred 150 ....G3
Winnett▲ 188 ....H4
Winston 120 ....E4
Wisdom 140 ....C5
Wise River 150 ....C5
Wolf Creek 500 ....D3
Wolf Point▲ 2,880 ....L2
Woodside 75 ....B4
Worden 600 ....H5
Wyola 350 ....J5
Zurich 60 ....G2

OTHER FEATURES

Absaroka (range) F5
Allen (mt.) C2
Arrow (creek) F3
Ashley (lake) B2
Battle (creek) G1
Bearhat (mt.) C2
Bears Paw (mts.) H3
Beartooth (mts.) G5
Beaver (creek) J2
Beaverhead (riv.) D5
Benton (lake) E3
Big (lake) G5
Big Belt (mts.) E4
Big Dry (creek) K3
Big Hole (riv.) C5
Big Hole Nat'l Battlefield C5
Bighorn (lake) H5
Bighorn (riv.) J5
Bighorn Canyon Nat'l
Rec. Area H5
Big Muddy (riv.) M2
Big Porcupine (creek) J4
Birch (creek) D2
Birch Creek (res.) D2
Bitterroot (range) B4
Bitterroot (riv.) B4
Blackfeet Ind. Res. D2
Blackfoot (riv.) C4
Blackmore (mt.) F5
Bowdoin (lake) J2
Boxelder (creek) H3
Boxelder (creek) M5
Bynum (res.) D2
Cabinet (mts.) A2
Canyon Ferry (lake) E4
Clark Canyon (res.) D6
Clark Fork (riv.) A3
Clarks Fork, Yellowstone
(riv.) G6
Cottonwood (creek) E2
Cow (creek) G2
Crazy peak F4
Crow Ind. Res. H5
Cut Bank (creek) D2
Douglas (mt.) F5
Earthquake (lake) E6
Electric (peak) F6
Elwell (lake) E2
Emigrant (peak) F5
Ennis (lake) E5
Flathead (lake) C3
Flathead (riv.) B2
Flathead, North Fork (riv.) ...B2
Flathead, South Fork (riv.) ...C3
Flathead Ind. Res. B3
Flatwillow (creek) H4
Fort Belknap Ind. Res. H2
Fort Peck (lake) K3
Fort Union Trading Post
Nat'l Hist. Site N2
Frances (lake) D2
Freezeout (lake) D3
Frenchman (riv.) J1
Fresno (res.) F2
Gallatin (peak) E5
Gallatin (riv.) E5
Georgetown (lake) C4
Gibson (res.) D3
Glacier Nat'l Park C2

Granite (peak) F5
Grant-Kohrs Ranch
Nat'l Hist. Site D4
Hauser (lake) E4
Haystack (peak) A3
Hebgen (lake) E6
Helena (lake) E4
Holter (lake) D4
Hungry Horse (res.) C2
Hurricane (mt.) D2
Hyalite (peak) E5
Jackson (mt.) C2
Jefferson (riv.) D5
Judith (riv.) G3
Koocanusa (lake) A2
Kootenai (riv.) A2
Lemhi (pass) C6
Lewis and Clark (range) C3
Lima (res.) D6
Little Bighorn (riv.) J5
Little Bitterroot (lake) B2
Little Dry (creek) K3
Little Missouri (riv.) M5
Lockhart (mt.) D3
Lodge (creek) G1
Lolo (pass) B4
Lone (mt.) E5
Lost Trail (pass) B5
Lower Red Rock (lake) E6
Lower Saint Mary (lake) C2
Madison (riv.) E5
Malmstrom A.F.B. 5,938 ......E3
Marias (riv.) D2
Martinsdale (res.) F4
Mary Ronan (lake) B3
McDonald (lake) B2
McGloughlin (peak) C4
McGregor (lake) B3
Medicine (lake) M2
Milk (riv.) J2
Mission (range) C3
Missouri (riv.) L3
Musselshell (riv.) J3
Nelson (res.) J2
Ninepipe (res.) C3
Northern Cheyenne
Indian Reservation K5
O'Fallon (creek) L4
Pishkun (res.) D3
Poplar (riv.) L2
Porcupine (creek) K2
Powder (riv.) L4
Purcell (mts.) A2
Railley (mt.) C3
Red Rock (lakes) E6
Red Rock (riv.) D6
Redwater (riv.) L3
Rock (creek) C4
Rocky (mts.) D4
Rocky Boy's Ind. Res. G2
Rosebud (creek) K4
Ruby (riv.) D5
Ruby River (res.) D5
Sage (creek) F2
Saint Joseph (lake) C2
Saint Mary (lake) C1
Sandy (creek) F2
Sheep (mt.) C2
Shields (riv.) F4
Siyeh (mt.) C2
Smith (riv.) E3
Sphinx (mt.) E5
Stillwater (riv.) G5
Stimson (mt.) C2
Sun (riv.) D3
Swan (lake) C3
Teton (riv.) E3
Tongue (riv.) K5
Upper Red Rock (lake) E6
Ward (peak) A3
Waterton-Glacier Int'l
Peace Park C2
Whitefish (lake) B2
Willow (lake) E2
Willow Creek (res.) D3
Yellowstone (riv.) M3
Yellowstone National Park ...F6

▲County seat

COUNTIES

Adams 29,625 ....F4
Antelope 7,965 ....F2
Arthur 462 ....C3
Banner 852 ....A3
Blaine 675 ....E3
Boone 6,667 ....F3
Box Butte 13,130 ....A2
Boyd 2,835 ....F2
Brown 3,657 ....E2
Buffalo 37,447 ....E4
Burt 7,868 ....H3
Butler 8,601 ....G3
Cass 21,318 ....H4
Cedar 10,131 ....G2
Chase 4,381 ....C4
Cherry 6,307 ....C2
Cheyenne 9,494 ....A3
Clay 7,123 ....F4
Colfax 9,139 ....G3
Cuming 10,117 ....H3
Custer 12,270 ....E3
Dakota 16,742 ....H2
Dawes 9,021 ....A2
Dawson 19,940 ....E4
Deuel 2,237 ....B3
Dixon 6,143 ....H2
Dodge 34,500 ....H3
Douglas 416,444 ....H3
Dundy 2,582 ....C4
Fillmore 7,103 ....G4
Franklin 3,938 ....F4
Frontier 3,101 ....D4
Furnas 5,553 ....E4
Gage 22,794 ....H4
Garden 2,460 ....B3
Garfield 2,141 ....F3
Gosper 1,928 ....E4
Grant 769 ....C3
Greeley 3,006 ....F3
Hall 48,925 ....F4
Hamilton 8,862 ....F4
Harlan 3,810 ....E4
Hayes 1,222 ....C4
Hitchcock 3,750 ....C4
Holt 12,599 ....F2
Hooker 793 ....C3
Howard 6,055 ....F3
Jefferson 8,759 ....G4
Johnson 4,673 ....H4
Kearney 6,629 ....F4
Keith 8,584 ....C3
Keya Paha 1,029 ....E2
Kimball 4,108 ....A3
Knox 9,534 ....G2
Lancaster 213,641 ....H4
Lincoln 32,508 ....D4
Logan 878 ....D3
Loup 683 ....E3
Madison 32,655 ....G3
McPherson 546 ....C3
Merrick 8,042 ....F3
Morrill 5,423 ....A3
Nance 4,275 ....F3
Nemaha 7,980 ....J4
Nuckolls 5,786 ....F4
Otoe 14,252 ....H4
Pawnee 3,317 ....H4
Perkins 3,367 ....C4
Phelps 9,715 ....E4
Pierce 7,827 ....G2
Platte 29,820 ....G3
Polk 5,675 ....G3
Red Willow 11,705 ....D4
Richardson 9,937 ....J4
Rock 2,019 ....E2
Saline 12,715 ....G4
Sarpy 102,583 ....H3
Saunders 18,285 ....H3

Scotts Bluff 36,025 ......A3
Seward 15,450 ....G4
Sheridan 6,750 ....B2
Sherman 3,718 ....F3
Sioux 1,549 ....A2
Stanton 6,244 ....G3
Thayer 6,635 ....G4
Thomas 851 ....D3
Thurston 6,936 ....H2
Valley 5,169 ....E3
Washington 16,607 ......H3
Wayne 9,364 ....G2
Webster 4,279 ....F4
Wheeler 948 ....F3
York 14,428 ....G4

CITIES and TOWNS

Adams 472 ....H4
Ainsworth▲ 1,870 ....D2
Albion▲ 1,916 ....F3
Alda 540 ....F4
Alexandria 224 ....G4
Allen 331 ....H2
Alliance▲ 9,765 ....A2
Alma▲ 1,226 ....E4
Alvo 164 ....H4
Amherst 231 ....E4
Anselmo 189 ....E3
Ansley 555 ....E3
Arapahoe 1,001 ....E4
Arcadia 385 ....F3
Arlington 1,178 ....H3
Arnold 679 ....D3
Arthur▲ 128 ....C3
Ashland 2,136 ....H3
Ashton 251 ....F3
Atkinson 1,380 ....E2
Auburn▲ 3,443 ....J4
Aurora▲ 3,810 ....F4
Avoca 254 ....H4
Axtell 707 ....E4
Bancroft 494 ....H2
Bartlett▲ 131 ....F3
Bartley 339 ....D4
Bassett▲ 739 ....E2
Battle Creek 997 ....G3
Bayard 1,196 ....A3
Beatrice▲ 12,354 ....H4
Beaver City▲ 707 ....E4
Beaver Crossing 448 ....G4
Bee 209 ....H3
Beemer 672 ....H3
Belden 149 ....G2
Belgrade 157 ....G3
Bellevue 30,982 ....J3
Bellwood 395 ....G3
Benedict 230 ....G3
Benkelman▲ 1,193 ......C4
Bennet 544 ....H4
Bennington 866 ....H3
Bertrand 708 ....E4
Big Springs 495 ....B3
Bladen 280 ....F4
Blair▲ 6,860 ....H3
Bloomfield 1,181 ....G2
Blue Hill 810 ....F4
Blue Springs 431 ....H4
Boys Town 794 ....H3
Bradshaw 330 ....G4
Brady 331 ....D3
Brainard 326 ....G3
Brewster▲ 22 ....D3
Bridgeport▲ 1,581 ......A3
Broadwater 160 ....B3
Brock 143 ....H4
Broken Bow▲ 3,778 .....E3
Brownville 148 ....J4
Brule 411 ....C3
Bruning 332 ....G4

Bruno 141 ....G3
Brunswick 182 ....G2
Burwell▲ 1,278 ....E3
Butte▲ 452 ....F2
Cairo 733 ....F3
Callaway 539 ....D3
Cambridge 1,107 ....D4
Campbell 432 ....F4
Carleton 144 ....G4
Carroll 237 ....G2
Cedar Bluffs 591 ....H3
Cedar Creek 334 ....H3
Cedar Rapids 396 ....F3
Center▲ 112 ....G2
Central City▲ 2,868 .....F3
Ceresco 825 ....H3
Chadron▲ 5,588 ....B2
Chambers 341 ....F2
Chapman 292 ....F3
Chappell▲ 979 ....B3
Chester 351 ....G4
Clarks 379 ....G3
Clarkson 699 ....G3
Clatonia 296 ....H4
Clay Center▲ 825 ....F4
Clearwater 401 ....F2
Cody 177 ....C2
Coleridge 596 ....G2
Columbus▲ 19,480 ......G3
Concord 156 ....H2
Cook 333 ....H4
Cordova 147 ....G4
Cortland 393 ....H4
Cozad 3,823 ....E4
Craig 228 ....H3
Crawford 1,115 ....A2
Creighton 1,223 ....G2
Creston 220 ....G3
Crete 4,841 ....G4
Crofton 820 ....G2
Culbertson 795 ....C4
Curtis 791 ....D4
Dakota City▲ 1,470 .....H2
Dalton 282 ....B3
Dannebrog 324 ....F3
Davenport 383 ....G4
Davey 160 ....H4
David City▲ 2,522 ....G3
Dawson 157 ....J4
Daykin 188 ....G4
De Witt 598 ....G4
Decatur 641 ....H2
Denton 161 ....H4
Deshler 892 ....G4
Diller 298 ....H4
Dix 229 ....A3
Dodge 693 ....H3
Doniphan 736 ....F4
Dorchester 614 ....G4
Douglas 199 ....H4
Dunbar 171 ....J4
Duncan 387 ....G3
Dwight 397 ....G3
Eagle 1,047 ....H4
Edgar 600 ....F4
Edison 148 ....E4
Elba 196 ....F3
Elgin 731 ....F3
Elkhorn 1,398 ....H3
Elm Creek 852 ....E4
Elmwood 584 ....H4
Elsie 153 ....C4
Elwood▲ 679 ....E4
Emerson 791 ....H2
Endicott 163 ....G4
Eustis 452 ....D4
Ewing 449 ....F2
Exeter 661 ....G4
Fairbury▲ 4,335 ....G4
Fairfield 458 ....G4

Fairmont 708 ....G4
Falls City▲ 4,769 ....J4
Farnam 188 ....D4
Farwell 152 ....F3
Filley 157 ....H4
Firth 471 ....H4
Fordyce 190 ....G2
Fort Calhoun 648 ....J3
Franklin▲ 1,112 ....E4
Fremont▲ 23,680 ....H3
Friend 1,111 ....G4
Fullerton▲ 1,452 ....F3
Funk 198 ....E4
Garland 247 ....G4
Geneva▲ 2,310 ....G4
Genoa 1,082 ....G3
Gering▲ 7,946 ....A3
Gibbon 1,525 ....F4
Giltner 367 ....F4
Glenvil 304 ....F4
Goehner 192 ....G4
Gordon 1,803 ....B2
Gothenburg 3,232 ......D4
Grafton 167 ....G4
Grand Island 39,386 ...F4
Grant▲ 1,239 ....C4
Greeley▲ 562 ....F3
Greenwood 531 ....H3
Gresham 253 ....G3
Gretna 2,243 ....H3
Guide Rock 290 ....F4
Gurley 198 ....B3
Hadar 291 ....G2
Haigler 225 ....C4
Hallam 309 ....H4
Hampton 432 ....G4
Hardy 206 ....G4
Harrisburg▲ 75 ....A3
Harrison▲ 291 ....A2
Hartington▲ 1,583 ......G2
Harvard 976 ....F4
Hastings 22,837 ....F4
Hay Springs 693 ....B2
Hayes Center▲ 259 ....C4
Hebron▲ 1,765 ....G4
Hemingford 953 ....A2
Henderson 999 ....G4
Henry 145 ....A2
Herman 186 ....H3
Hershey 579 ....D3
Hickman 1,081 ....H4
Hildreth 364 ....E4
Holbrook 233 ....D4
Holdrege▲ 5,671 ....E4
Holstein 207 ....F4
Homer 553 ....H2
Hooper 830 ....H3
Hordville 164 ....G3
Hoskins 307 ....G2
Howells 615 ....H3
Hubbard 199 ....H2
Humboldt 1,003 ....J4
Humphrey 741 ....G3
Hyannis▲ 210 ....C3
Imperial▲ 2,007 ....C4
Indianola 672 ....D4
Inglewood 286 ....H3
Inman 159 ....F2
Jackson 230 ....H2
Johnson 323 ....J4
Juniata 811 ....F4
Kearney▲ 24,396 ....E4
Kenesaw 818 ....F4
Kennard 371 ....H3
Kimball▲ 2,574 ....A3
La Vista 9,840 ....J3
Laurel 981 ....G2
Lawrence 323 ....F4
Leigh 447 ....G3
Lewellen 307 ....B3

Lexington▲ 6,601 ....E4
Lincoln (cap.)▲ 191,972 ....H4
Lindsay 321 ....G3
Litchfield 314 ....E3
Lodgepole 368 ....B3
Long Pine 396 ....E2
Loomis 376 ....E4
Louisville 998 ....H3
Loup City▲ 1,104 ....E3
Lyman 452 ....A3
Lynch 296 ....F2
Lyons 1,144 ....H3
Macy 836 ....H2
Madison▲ 2,135 ....G3
Madrid 287 ....C4
Malcolm 181 ....H4
Manley 170 ....H4
Marquette 211 ....G4
Mason City 160 ....E3
Max 285 ....C4
Maxwell 410 ....D3
Maywood 313 ....D4
McCook▲ 8,112 ....D4
McCool Junction 372 ..G4
Mead 513 ....H3
Meadow Grove 332 ....G2
Merna 377 ....E3
Merriman 151 ....C2
Milford 1,886 ....H4
Milligan 328 ....G4
Minatare 807 ....A3
Minden▲ 2,749 ....F4
Mitchell 1,743 ....A3
Monroe 309 ....G3
Morrill 974 ....A3
Mullen▲ 554 ....C2
Murdock 267 ....H4
Murray 418 ....J4
Nebraska City▲ 6,547 ..J4
Nehawka 260 ....H4
Neligh▲ 1,742 ....G2
Nelson▲ 627 ....F4
Nemaha 188 ....J4
Newcastle 271 ....H2
Newman Grove 787 ....G3
Newport 136 ....E2
Nickerson 291 ....H3
Niobrara 376 ....G2
Norfolk 21,476 ....G2
North Bend 1,249 ....H3
North Loup 361 ....F3
North Platte▲ 22,605 ..D3

O'Neill▲ 4,049 ....F2
Oakdale 362 ....F2
Oakland 1,279 ....H3
Oconto 147 ....E3
Odell 291 ....H4
Ogallala▲ 5,095 ....C3
Ohiowa 146 ....G4
Omaha▲ 335,795 ....J3
Orchard 439 ....F2
Ord▲ 2,481 ....F3
Orleans 490 ....E4
Osceola▲ 879 ....G3
Oshkosh▲ 986 ....B3
Osmond 774 ....G2
Otoe 196 ....H4
Overton 547 ....E4
Oxford 949 ....E4
Page 191 ....F2
Palisade 381 ....C4
Palmer 753 ....F3
Palmyra 545 ....H4
Panama 207 ....H4
Papillion▲ 10,372 ....J3
Pawnee City▲ 1,008 ...H4
Paxton 536 ....C3
Pender▲ 1,208 ....H2
Peru 1,110 ....J4
Petersburg 388 ....G3
Phillips 316 ....F4
Pickrell 201 ....H4
Pierce▲ 1,615 ....G2
Pilger 361 ....G2
Plainview 1,333 ....G2
Platte Center 387 ....G3
Plattsmouth▲ 6,412 ...J3
Pleasant Dale 253 ......G4
Pleasanton 372 ....E4
Plymouth 455 ....G4
Polk 345 ....G3
Ponca▲ 877 ....H2
Potter 388 ....A3
Prague 282 ....H3
Ralston 6,236 ....J3
Randolph 983 ....G2
Ravenna 1,317 ....F3
Raymond 167 ....H4
Red Cloud▲ 1,204 ......F4
Republican City 199 ...E4
Rising City 341 ....G3
Riverdale 208 ....E4
Riverton 162 ....F4
Rosalie 178 ....H2

Rose 247 ....E2
Roseland 254 ....F4
Rulo 191 ....J4
Rushville▲ 1,127 ....B2
Ruskin 187 ....G4
Saint Edward 822 ....G3
Saint Paul▲ 2,009 ......F3
Salem 160 ....J4
Santee 365 ....G2
Sargent 710 ....E3
Schuyler▲ 4,052 ....G3
Scotia 318 ....F3
Scottsbluff 13,711 ......A3
Scribner 950 ....H3
Seward▲ 5,634 ....G4
Shelby 690 ....G3
Shelton 954 ....F4
Shickley 360 ....G4
Shubert 237 ....J4
Sidney▲ 5,959 ....A3
Silver Creek 625 ....G3
Snyder 280 ....H3
South Sioux City 9,677 ..H2
Spalding 592 ....F3
Spencer 536 ....F2
Sprague 157 ....H4
Springfield 1,426 ....H4
Springview▲ 304 ....E2
Stamford 188 ....E4
Stanton▲ 1,549 ....G3
Staplehurst 281 ....G4
Stapleton▲ 299 ....D3
Stella 248 ....J4
Sterling 451 ....H4
Stockville▲ 32 ....D4
Stratton 427 ....C4
Stromsburg 1,241 ......G3
Stuart 650 ....E2
Sumner 201 ....E4
Superior 2,397 ....F4
Sutherland 1,032 ....C3
Sutton 1,353 ....G4
Swanton 145 ....H4
Syracuse 1,646 ....H4
Table Rock 308 ....H4
Talmage 246 ....H4
Taylor▲ 186 ....E3
Tecumseh▲ 1,702 ......H4
Tekamah▲ 1,852 ....H3
Terrytown 656 ....A3
Thedford▲ 243 ....D3
Tilden 895 ....G2

Agriculture, Industry and Resources

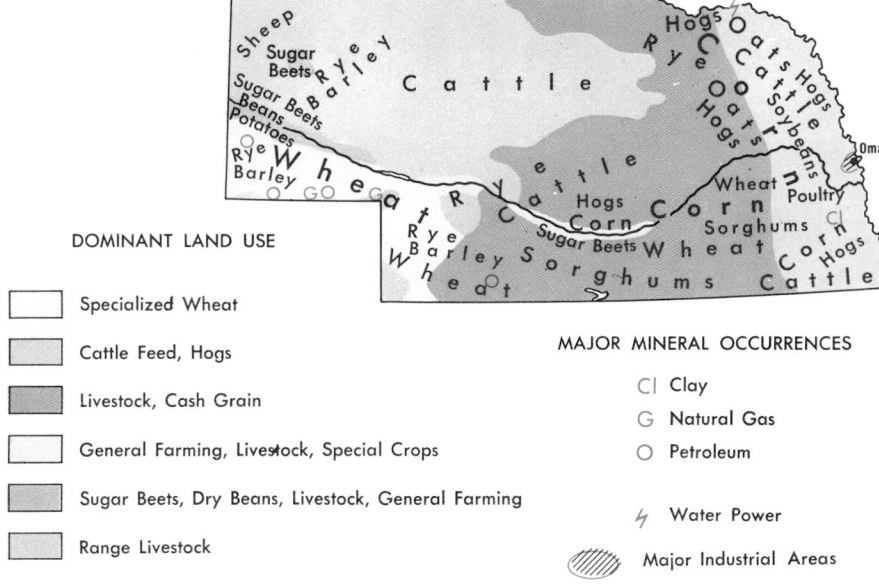

DOMINANT LAND USE

Specialized Wheat

Cattle Feed, Hogs

Livestock, Cash Grain

General Farming, Livestock, Special Crops

Sugar Beets, Dry Beans, Livestock, General Farming

Range Livestock

MAJOR MINERAL OCCURRENCES

Cl   Clay

G   Natural Gas

O   Petroleum

⚡   Water Power

Major Industrial Areas

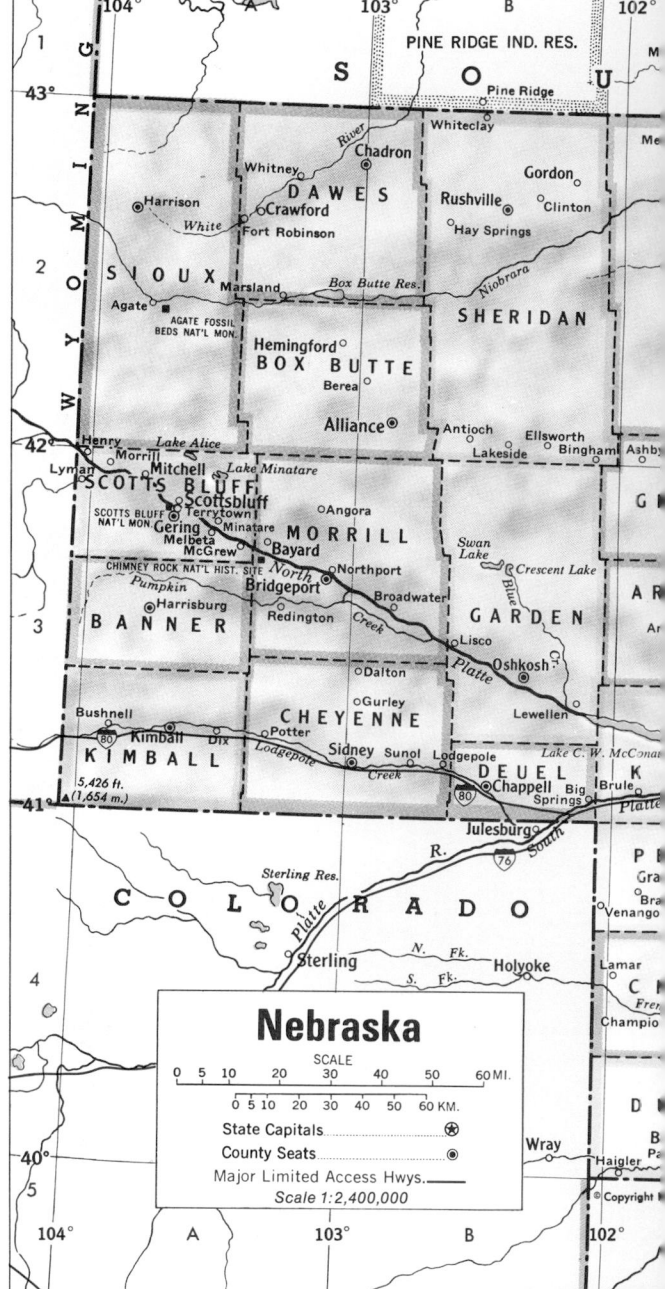

Nebraska

SCALE

0 5 10   20   30   40   50   60 MI.

0 5 10   20   30   40   60 KM.

State Capitals ....⊛

County Seats ....◉

Major Limited Access Hwys. _____

Scale 1:2,400,000

Trenton▲ 656	D4	Colamus (riv.)	E2
Trumbull 225	F4	Crescent (lake)	B3
Tryon▲ 139	C3	Dads (lake)	D2
Uehling 273	H3	Dismal (riv.)	C3
Ulysses 256	G3	Elkhorn (riv.)	G3
Unadilla 294	H4	Enders (res.)	C4
Union 299	J4	Frenchman (creek)	C4
Upland 169	F4	Gavins Point (dam)	G2
Utica 718	G4	Harlan County (lake)	E5
Valentine▲ 2,826	D2	Harry Strunk (lake)	D4
Valley 1,775	H3	Homestead Nat'l Mon.	H4
Valparaiso 431	H3	Hugh Butler (lake)	D4
Venango 192	C4	Jeffrey (res.)	D4
Verdigre 607	F2	Johnson (lake)	E4
Verdon 242	J4	Keya Paha (riv.)	D1
Waco 211	G4	Kingsley (dam)	C3
Wahoo▲ 3,681	H3	Lewis and Clark (lake)	G2
Wakefield 1,082	H2	Little Blue (riv.)	H5
Wallace 308	C4	Lodgepole (creek)	A3
Walthill 747	H2	Logan (creek)	H2
Waterloo 479	H3	Loup (riv.)	F3
Wauneta 675	C4	Maloney (res.)	D3
Wausa 598	G2	McConaughy, C. W. (lake)	C3
Waverly 1,869	H4	Medicine (creek)	D4
Wayne▲ 5,142	G2	Medicine Creek (dam)	D4
Weeping Water 1,008	J4	Merritt (res.)	D2
West Point▲ 3,250	H3	Middle Loup (riv.)	D3
Western 264	G4	Minatare (lake)	A3
Weston 299	H3	Missouri (riv.)	H3
Wilber▲ 1,527	G4	Moon (lake)	E2
Wilcox 349	E4	Niobrara (riv.)	E2
Wilsonville 136	D4	North Loup (riv.)	E3
Winnebago 705	H2	North Platte (riv.)	B3
Winside 434	G2	Offutt A.F.B.	J3
Wisner 1,253	H3	Omaha Ind. Res.	H2
Wolbach 280	F3	Pelican (lake)	D2
Wood River 1,156	F4	Platte (riv.)	E4
Wymore 1,611	H4	Pumpkin (creek)	A3
Wynot 213	G2	Republican (riv.)	G5
York▲ 7,884	G4	Santee Ind. Res.	G2
Yutan 626	H3	Scotts Bluff Nat'l Mon.	A3
		Sherman (res.)	E3
OTHER FEATURES		Snake (riv.)	C2
		South Loup (riv.)	E3
Agate Fossil Beds Nat'l Mon.	A2	South Platte (riv.)	C3
Alice (lake)	A2	Sutherland (res.)	C3
Beaver (creek)	D5	Swan (lake)	B3
Big Blue (riv.)	H4	Swanson (lake)	D4
Blue (creek)	B3	White (riv.)	A2
Box Butte (res.)	A2	Winnebago Ind. Res.	H2
Cedar (riv.)	F3		
Chimney Rock Nat'l Hist. Site	A3		

▲County seat

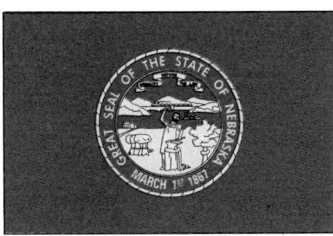

AREA 77,355 sq. mi. (200,349 sq. km.)
POPULATION 1,584,617
CAPITAL Lincoln
LARGEST CITY Omaha
HIGHEST POINT (Kimball Co.) 5,246 ft. (1654 m.)
SETTLED IN 1847
ADMITTED TO UNION March 1, 1867
POPULAR NAME Cornhusker State
STATE FLOWER Goldenrod
STATE BIRD Western Meadowlark

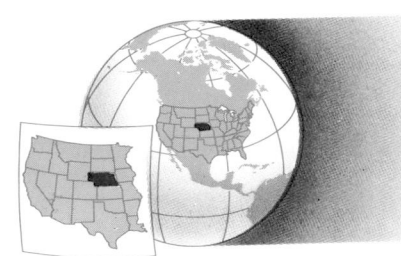

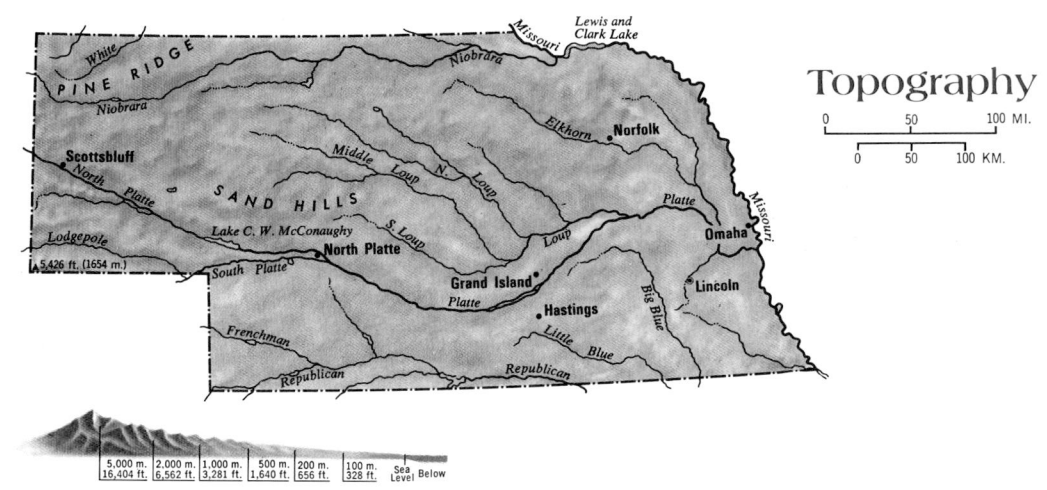

Topography

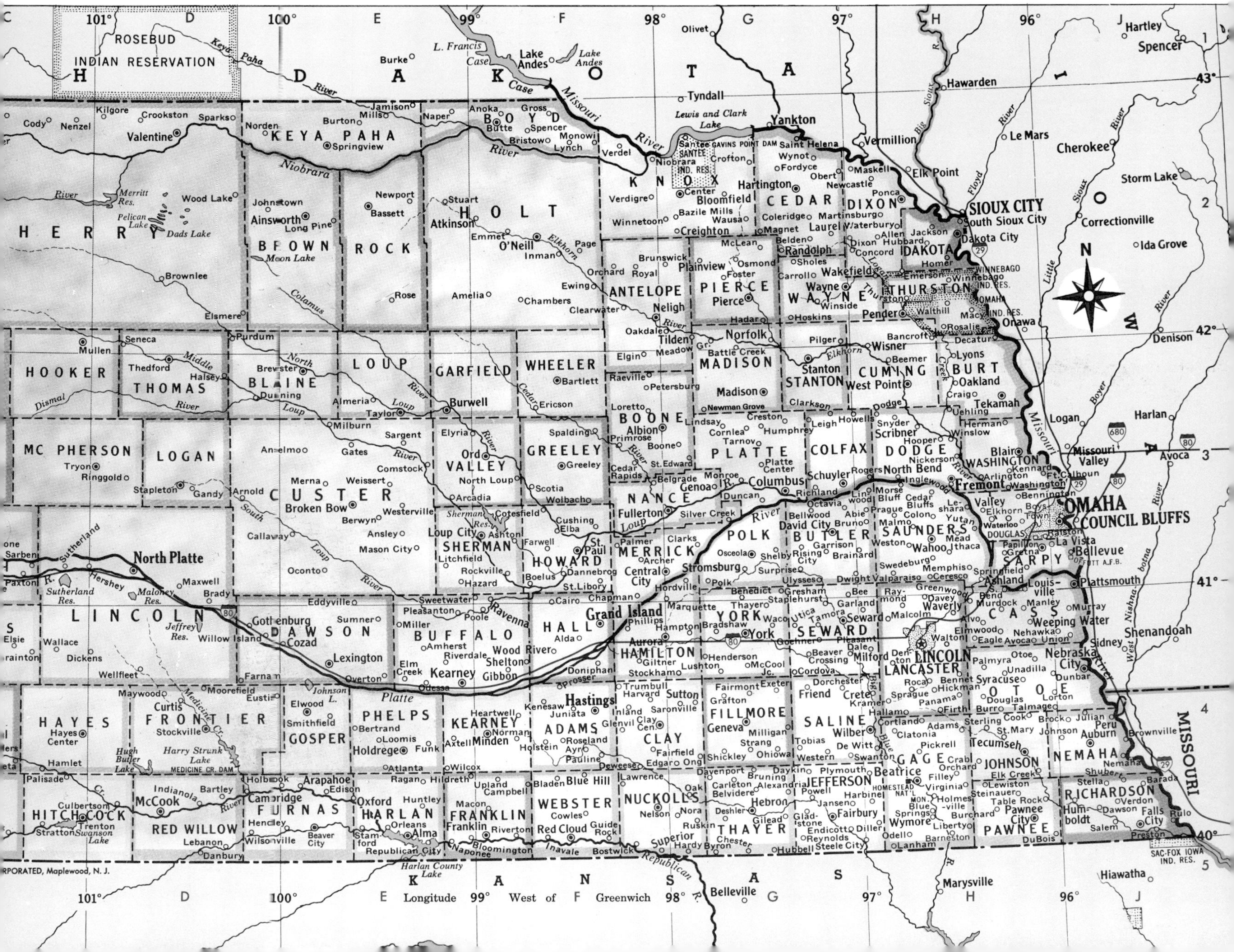

0	50	100 MI.

0	50	100 KM.

5,000 m.	2,000 m.	1,000 m.	500 m.	200 m.	100 m.	Sea	Below
16,404 ft.	6,562 ft.	3,281 ft.	1,640 ft.	656 ft.	328 ft.	Level	

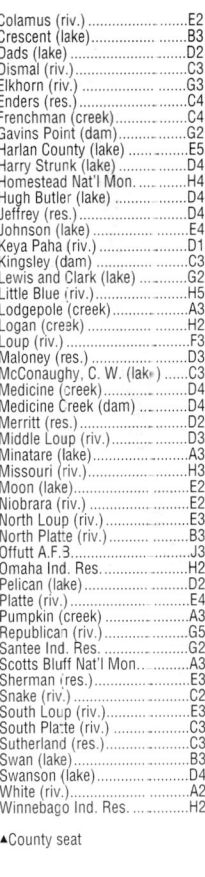

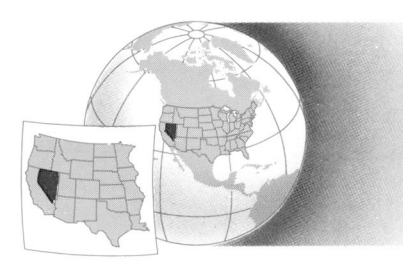

AREA 110,561 sq. mi. (286,353 sq. km.)
POPULATION 1,206,152
CAPITAL Carson City
LARGEST CITY Las Vegas
HIGHEST POINT Boundary Pk. 13,143 ft.
(4006 m.)
SETTLED IN 1850
ADMITTED TO UNION October 31, 1864
POPULAR NAME Silver State; Sagebrush
State
STATE FLOWER Sagebrush
STATE BIRD Mountain Bluebird

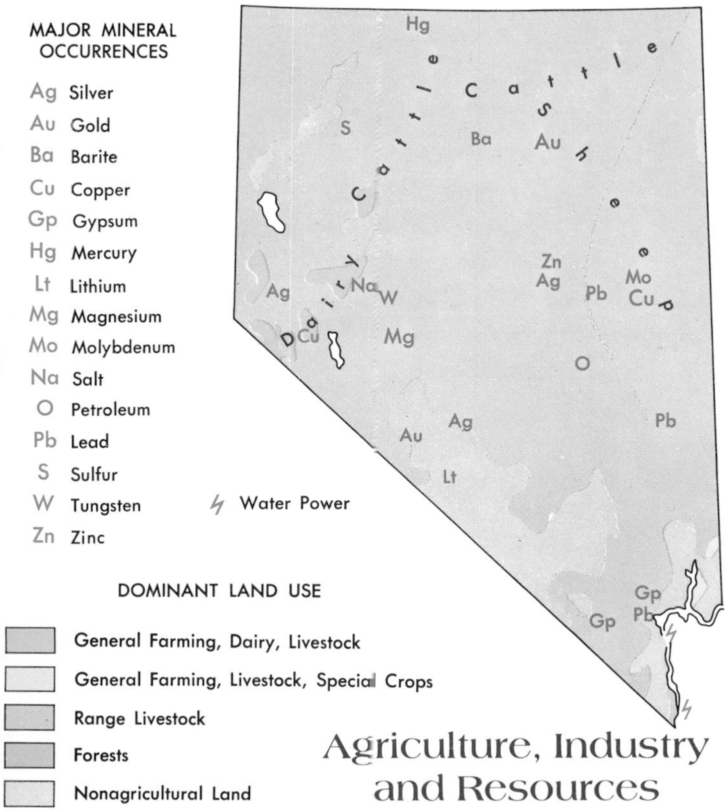

MAJOR MINERAL OCCURRENCES

Ag Silver
Au Gold
Ba Barite
Cu Copper
Gp Gypsum
Hg Mercury
Lt Lithium
Mg Magnesium
Mo Molybdenum
Na Salt
O   Petroleum
Pb Lead
S   Sulfur
W   Tungsten
Zn Zinc

⚡ Water Power

DOMINANT LAND USE

General Farming, Dairy, Livestock

General Farming, Livestock, Special Crops

Range Livestock

Forests

Nonagricultural Land

Agriculture, Industry and Resources

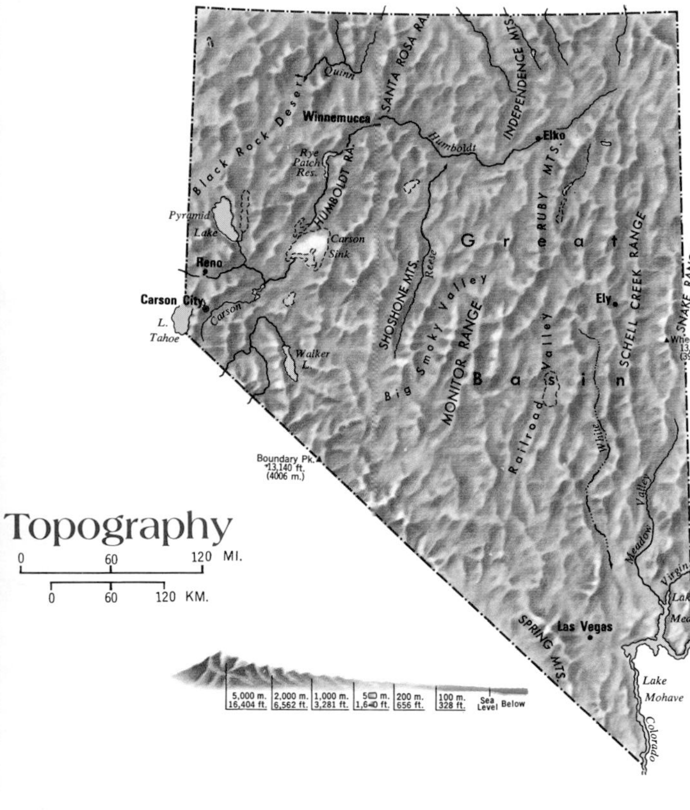

Topography

0   60   120 MI.

0   60   120 KM.

5,000 m. 2,000 m. 1,000 m. 5⃝ m. 200 m. 100 m. Sea
16,404 ft. 6,562 ft. 3,281 ft. 1,640 ft. 656 ft. 328 ft. Level
Below

COUNTIES

Carson City (city) 40,443	B3
Churchill 17,938	C3
Clark 741,459	F6
Douglas 27,637	B4
Elko 33,530	F1
Esmeralda 1,344	D5
Eureka 1,547	E3
Humboldt 12,844	C1
Lander 6,266	D3
Lincoln 3,775	F5
Lyon 20,001	B3
Mineral 6,475	C4
Nye 17,781	E4
Pershing 4,336	C2
Storey 2,526	B3
Washoe 254,667	B2
White Pine 9,264	F3

CITIES and TOWNS

Alamo 300	F5
Austin 300	E3
Babbitt	C4
Baker 140	G3
Battle Mountain▲ 3,542	D2
Beatty 1,623	E6
Beowawe 77	E2
Black Springs 180	B3
Boulder City 12,567	G7
Bunkerville 300	G6
Caliente 1,111	G5
Carlin 2,220	E2
Carp 30	G5
Carson City (cap.) 40,443	B3
Caselton	E5
Cherry Creek 80	G3
Coaldale 31	D4
Crystal Bay 6,225	A3
Currant 30	F4
Dayton 2,217	B3
Deeth 125	F1
Denio 35	C1
Duckwater 80	F4
Dunphy 25	E2
Dyer 56	C5
East Las Vegas 11,087	F6
Elko▲ 14,736	F2
Ely▲ 4,756	G3
Eureka▲ 300	E3
Fallon▲ 6,438	C3
Fernley 5,164	B3
Gabbs 667	D4
Gardnerville 2,177	B4
Genoa 254	B4
Gerlach 400	B2
Glenbrook 800	B3
Glendale 25	G6
Golconda 275	D2
Gold Hill 80	B3
Goldfield▲ 500	D5
Goodsprings 80	F7
Halleck 68	F2
Hawthorne▲ 4,162	C4
Hazen 76	C3
Henderson 64,942	G6
Hiko 210	F5
Imlay 250	C2
Indian Springs 1,164	F6
Jack Creek	E1
Jackpot 400	G1
Jean 125	F7
Lamoille 100	F2
Las Vegas▲ 258,295	F6
Lee 125	F2
Logandale 410	G6
Lovelock▲ 2,069	C2
Lund 380	F4
Luning 90	C4
Manhattan 93	E4
Mason 200	B4
McDermitt 373	D1
McGill 1,258	G3
Mercury 900	E6
Mesquite 1,871	G6
Mina 450	C4
Minden▲ 1,441	B4
Moapa 3,444	G6
Montello 100	G1
Mountain City 100	F1
Nelson 75	G7
Nixon 400	B3
North Las Vegas 47,707	F6
Oreana 45	C2
Orovada 200	D1
Overton 1,111	G6
Owyhee 908	F1
Pahrump 7,424	E6
Panaca 650	G5
Paradise Valley 115	D1
Paradise Valley 84,818	F6
Pioche▲ 850	G5
Preston 50	G4
Reno▲ 133,850	B3
Round Mountain 400	E4

Ruby Valley 150	F2
Ruth 455	F3
Schurz 617	C4
Searchlight 500	F7
Silver City 150	B3
Silverpeak 100	D5
Sloan 30	F7
Smith 1,033	B4
Sparks 53,367	B3
Stillwater 150	C3
Sulphur	D2
Sun Valley 11,391	B3
Sunrise Manor 95,362	F6
Thousand Springs	G1
Tonopah▲ 3,616	D4
Ursine 45	G5
Valmy 200	D2
Vegas Creek	G6
Verdi 100	B3
Virginia City▲ 750	B3
Wabuska 150	B3
Wadsworth 640	B3
Wellington 505	B4
Wells 1,256	G1
Winchester 23,365	F6
Winnemucca▲ 6,134	D2
Yerington▲ 2,367	B4
Zephyr Cove 1,434	A3

OTHER FEATURES

Alkali (lake)	B1
Antelope (range)	E3
Arc Dome (mt.)	D4
Arrow Canyon (range)	G6
Beaver Creek Fork, Humboldt (riv.)	F1
Belted (range)	E5
Berlin (mt.)	D4
Big (mt.)	B1
Big Smoky (valley)	D4
Bishop (creek)	F1
Black Rock (des.)	B2
Black Rock (range)	B1
Boundary (peak)	C5
Buffalo (creek)	B2
Butte (mts.)	F3
Cactus (range)	E5
Carson (lake)	C3
Carson (riv.)	B3
Carson (sink)	C3
Cedar (mt.)	D4
Charleston (peak)	F6
Clan Alpine (mts.)	D3
Columbus (salt marsh)	C4
Cortez (mts.)	E2
Crescent (valley)	E2
Davis (dam)	G7
Death Valley Nat'l Mon.	E6
Delamar (mts.)	G5
Desatoya (mts.)	D3
Desert (range)	F6
Desert (valley)	C1
Devil's Hole (Death Valley Nat'l Mon.)	E6
Division (peak)	B1
Duck (creek)	G3
Duck Valley Ind. Res.	E1
East (range)	D2
East Walker (riv.)	B4
Egan (range)	G4
Ely (range)	G4
Emigrant (peak)	C5
Excelsior (mts.)	C4
Fallon Ind. Res.	C3
Fallon Nav. Air Sta.	C3
Fish Creek (mts.)	D2
Fort McDermitt Ind. Res.	D1
Fort Mohave Ind. Res.	G7
Franklin (lake)	F2
Frenchman Flat (basin)	F6
Gillis (range)	C4
Golden Gate (range)	F5
Goshute (mts.)	G2
Goshute Ind. Res.	G3
Granite (peak)	B2
Granite (range)	B2
Grant (range)	F4
Great Basin Nat'l Park	G4
Great Salt Lake (des.)	H2
High Rock (creek)	B1
Highland (peak)	G5
Hoover (dam)	G7
Hot Creek (range)	E4
Hot Creek (valley)	E4
Humboldt (range)	C2
Humboldt (riv.)	E2
Humboldt (salt marsh)	C3
Humboldt (sink)	C2
Huntington (creek)	E6
Independence (mts.)	E1
Jackson (mts.)	C1
Job (peak)	C3
Kawich (range)	E5
Kelley (creek)	D1
Kings (riv.)	C1
Lahontan (res.)	B3

Lake Mead National Rec. Area	G6
Las Vegas (range)	F6
Little Humboldt (riv.)	D1
Little Smoky (valley)	E4
Lone (mt.)	D4
Long (valley)	B1
Marys (riv.)	F1
Mason (riv.)	F1
Massacre (lake)	B1
Mead (lake)	G6
Meadow Valley Wash (riv.)	G5
Moapa River Ind. Res.	G6
Mohave (lake)	G7
Monitor (range)	E4
Monte Cristo (range)	D4
Mormon (mts.)	G5
Muddy (mts.)	G6
Nellis A.F.B. 8,377	F6
Nellis Air Force Range and Nuclear Test Site	E5
Nelson (creek)	G2
New Pass (range)	D3
Nightingale (mts.)	B2
Owyhee (riv.)	E1
Pahranagat (range)	F5
Pahrock (range)	F5
Pah-rum (peak)	B2
Pahrump (valley)	E6
Pahute (mesa)	E5
Pancake (range)	F4
Pequop (mts.)	G2
Pilot (peak)	C4
Pine (creek)	E2
Pine Forest (range)	C1
Pintwater (range)	F6
Piper (peak)	D5
Potosi (mt.)	F7
Pyramid (lake)	B2
Pyramid Lake Ind. Res.	B2
Quinn (riv.)	D1
Quinn Canyon (range)	F4
Railroad (valley)	F4
Reese (riv.)	D3
Reveille (peak)	E5
Reveille (range)	E4
Ruby (lake)	F2
Ruby (mts.)	F2
Rye Patch (res.)	C2
Sand Springs (salt flat)	C3
Santa Rosa (range)	D1
Schell Creek (range)	G3
Sheep (range)	F6
Shoshone (mt.)	E6
Shoshone (mts.)	D3
Shoshone (range)	E2
Silver Peak (range)	D5
Simpson Park (mts.)	E3
Smith Creek (valley)	D3
Smoke Creek (des.)	B2
Snake (mts.)	F1
Snake (range)	G3
Snow Water (lake)	G2
Sonoma (range)	D2
Specter (range)	E6
Spotted (range)	F6
Spring (creek)	D2
Spring (mts.)	F6
Spring (valley)	G3
Stillwater (range)	C3
Sulphur Spring (range)	E3
Summit (lake)	C1
Summit Lake Ind. Res.	B1
Table (mt.)	C3
Tahoe (lake)	B3
Thousand Spring (creek)	G1
Timber (mt.)	E5
Timber (mt.)	F4
Timpahute (range)	F5
Toana (range)	G2
Toiyabe (range)	D4
Topaz (lake)	B4
Toquima (range)	E4
Trident (peak)	C1
Trinity (range)	C2
Truckee (riv.)	B3
Tule (des.)	G5
Tuscarora (mts.)	E1
Virgin (mts.)	G6
Virgin (peak)	G6
Virgin (riv.)	G6
Virginia (range)	B3
Walker (lake)	C4
Walker (riv.)	C3
Walker River Ind. Res.	C3
Washoe (lake)	B3
Wassuk (range)	C4
Wheeler (peak)	G4
White (riv.)	F4
White Pine (range)	F3
Wild Horse (res.)	E1
Winnemucca (lake)	B2
Winnemucca Ind. Res.	D2
Yerington Ind. Res.	B3
Yucca Flat (basin)	E6

▲County seat

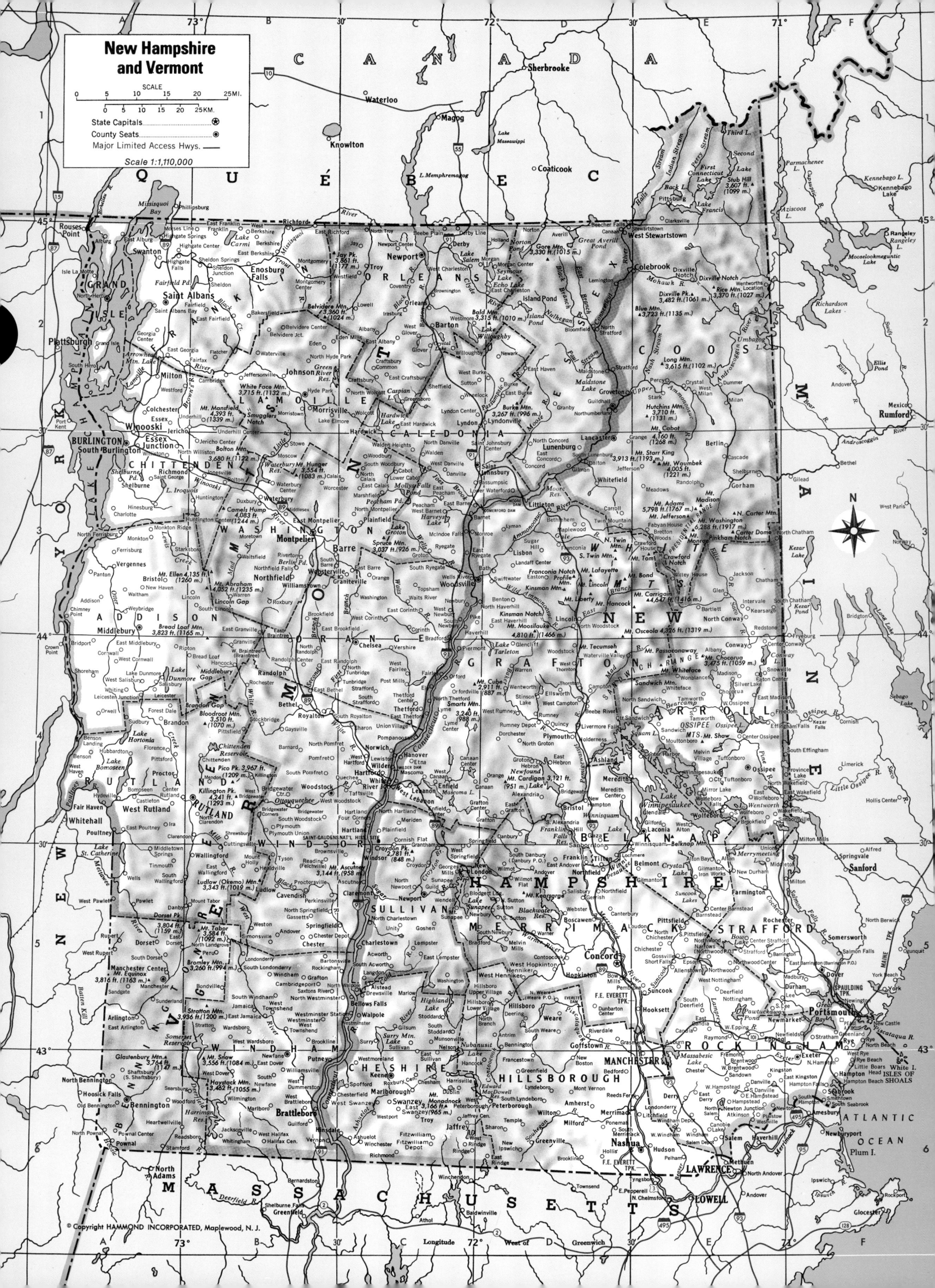

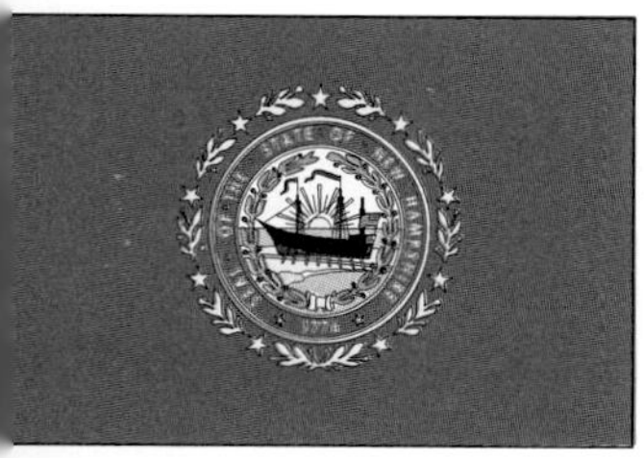

NEW HAMPSHIRE

AREA 9,279 sq. mi. (24,033 sq. km.)
POPULATION 1,113,915
CAPITAL Concord
LARGEST CITY Manchester
HIGHEST POINT Mt. Washington 6,288 ft. (1917 m.)
SETTLED IN 1623
ADMITTED TO UNION June 21, 1788
POPULAR NAME Granite State
STATE FLOWER Purple Lilac
STATE BIRD Purple Finch

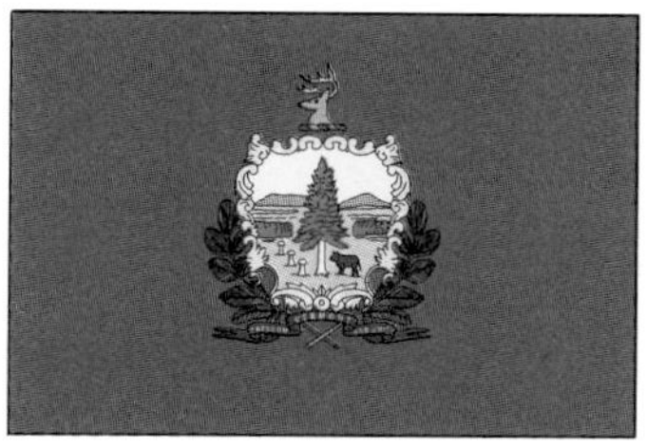

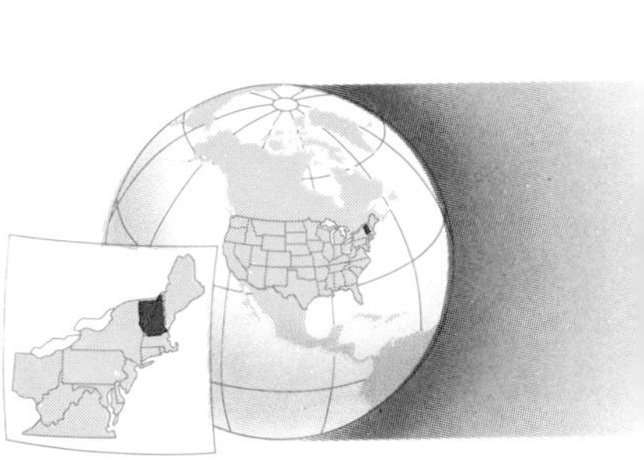

VERMONT

AREA 9,614 sq. mi. (24,900 sq. km.)
POPULATION 564,964
CAPITAL Montpelier
LARGEST CITY Burlington
HIGHEST POINT Mt. Mansfield 4,393 ft. (1339 m.)
SETTLED IN 1764
ADMITTED TO UNION March 4, 1791
POPULAR NAME Green Mountain State
STATE FLOWER Red Clover
STATE BIRD Hermit Thrush

Topography

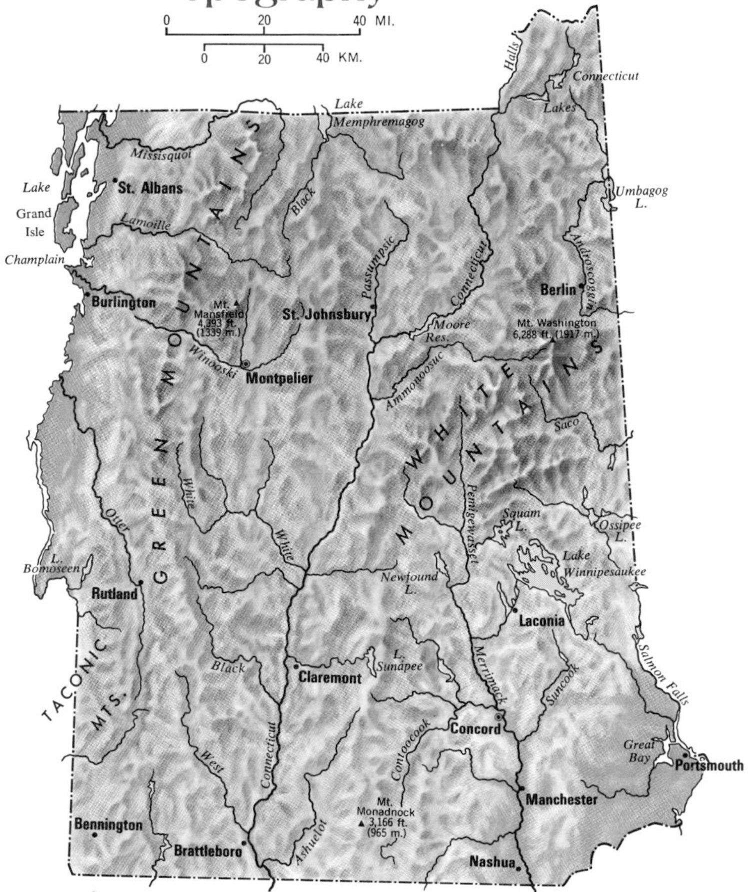
0 20 40 MI.
0 20 40 KM.
Lake Memphremagog
Missisquoi
Lake Champlain
Grand Isle
St. Albans
Lamoille
Burlington
Mt. Mansfield 4,393 ft. (1339 m.)
Winooski
Montpelier
Black
Passumpsic
St. Johnsbury
Connecticut Lakes
Halls
Umbagog L.
Androscoggin
Berlin
Moore Res.
Mt. Washington 6,288 ft. (1917 m.)
Ammonoosuc
Saco
WHITE MOUNTAINS
GREEN MOUNTAINS
White
Otter
L. Bomoseen
Rutland
Pemigewasset
Squam L.
Ossipee L.
Lake Winnipesaukee
Newfound L.
Laconia
TACONIC MTS.
Black
Claremont
L. Sunapee
Merrimack
Suncook
Salmon Falls
Concord
Contoocook
Great Bay
Portsmouth
West
Connecticut
Mt. Monadnock 3,166 ft. (965 m.)
Ashuelot
Manchester
Bennington
Brattleboro
Nashua

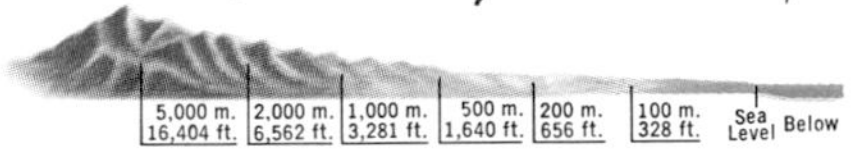
5,000 m. 16,404 ft.
2,000 m. 6,562 ft.
1,000 m. 3,281 ft.
500 m. 1,640 ft.
200 m. 656 ft.
100 m. 328 ft.
Sea Level
Below

NEW HAMPSHIRE

COUNTIES

Belknap 49,216.....D4
Carroll 35,410.....E4
Cheshire 70,121.....C6
Coos 34,828.....E2
Grafton 74,929.....D4
Hillsborough 336,073.....D6
Merrimack 120,005.....D5
Rockingham 245,845.....E5
Strafford 104,233.....E5
Sullivan 38,592.....C5

CITIES and TOWNS

Acworth• 776.....C5
Albany• 536.....E4
Alexandria• 1,190.....D4
Allenstown• 4,649.....E5
Alstead• 1,721.....C5
Alton Bay 500.....E5
Alton• 3,286.....E5
Amherst• 9,068.....D6
Andover• 1,883.....D5
Antrim 1,325.....D5
Antrim• 2,350.....D5
Ashland 1,915.....D4
Ashland• 1,807.....D4
Ashuelot 810.....C6
Atkinson• 5,188.....E6
Auburn• 4,085.....E5
Barnstead• 3,100.....E5
Barrington• 6,164.....F5
Bartlett• 2,290.....E3
Bath• 784.....D3
Bedford• 12,563.....D6
Beebe River 355.....D4
Belmont• 5,796.....E5
Bennington• 1,236.....D5
Benton• 330.....D3
Berlin 11,824.....E3
Bethlehem• 2,033.....D3
Boscawen• 3,586.....D5
Bow Mills 802.....D5
Bradford• 1,405.....D5
Brentwood• 2,590.....E6
Bretton Woods.....E3
Bridgewater• 796.....D4
Bristol 1,483.....D4
Bristol• 2,537.....D4
Brookfield• 518.....E4
Brookline• 2,410.....D6
Campton• 2,377.....D4
Canaan• 3,045.....C4
Candia• 3,557.....E5
Canobie Lake 500.....E6
Canterbury• 1,687.....D5
Carroll• 528.....D3
Cascade 350.....E3
Center Barnstead 400.....E5
Center Conway 558.....E4
Center Harbor• 996.....E4
Center Ossipee• 800.....E4
Center Tuftonboro 300.....E4
Charlestown 1,173.....C5
Charlestown• 4,630.....C5
Chatham• 268.....E3
Chester• 2,691.....E6
Chesterfield• 3,112.....C6
Chichester• 1,942.....E5
Chocorua 575.....E4
Claremont 13,902.....C5
Clarksville• 232.....E1
Colebrook 2,444.....E2
Colebrook• 2,459.....E2
Concord• (cap.) 36,006.....D5
Contoocook 1,334.....D5
Conway 1,604.....E4
Conway• 7,940.....E4
Cornish Flat 450.....C4
Croydon• 627.....C5
Dalton• 827.....D3
Danbury• 881.....D4
Danville• 2,534.....E6
Deerfield• 3,124.....E5
Deering• 1,707.....D5
Derry 20,446.....E6
Derry• 29,603.....E6
Dorchester• 392.....D4
Dover▲ 25,042.....F5
Dublin• 1,474.....C6
Dummer• 327.....E2
Durham 9,236.....F5
Durham• 11,818.....F5
East Andover 500.....D5
East Hampstead 900.....E6
East Kingston• 1,352.....F6
East Lempster 300.....C5
East Sullivan 300.....C6
East Swanzey 500.....C6
East Wolfeboro 400.....E4
Easton• 223.....D3
Eaton (Eaton Center) 362.....E4
Ellsworth• 74.....D4
Enfield 1,560.....C4
Enfield• 3,979.....C4
Epping 1,384.....E5
Epping• 5,162.....E5
Epsom• 3,591.....E5
Errol• 292.....E2
Etna 550.....C4
Exeter▲ 9,556.....F6
Exeter• 12,481.....F6
Farmington 3,567.....E5
Farmington• 5,739.....E5
Fitzwilliam• 2,011.....C6
Fitzwilliam Depot 350.....C6
Francestown• 1,217.....D6
Franconia• 811.....D3
Franklin 8,304.....D5
Freedom• 935.....E4
Fremont• 2,576.....E6
Georges Mills 375.....C5
Gerrish 500.....D5
Gilford• 5,867.....E4
Gilmanton• 2,609.....E5
Gilmanton Iron Works 300.....E5
Gilsum• 745.....C5
Glen 600.....E3
Goffstown• 14,621.....D5
Gorham 1,910.....E3
Gorham• 3,173.....E3
Goshen• 742.....C5
Grafton• 923.....D4
Grantham• 1,247.....C5
Grasmere 400.....D5
Greenfield• 1,519.....D6
Greenland• 2,768.....F5
Greenville 1,135.....D6
Greenville• 2,231.....D6
Groton• 318.....D4
Groveton 1,255.....D2
Guild 500.....C5
Hampstead• 6,732.....E6
Hampton 7,989.....F6
Hampton• 12,278.....F6
Hampton Beach 975.....F6
Hampton Falls• 1,503.....F6
Hancock• 1,604.....C6
Hanover 6,538.....C4
Hanover• 9,212.....C4
Harrisville• 981.....C6
Haverhill• 4,164.....C3
Hebron• 386.....D4
Henniker 1,693.....D5
Henniker• 4,151.....D5
Hill• 814.....D4
Hillsboro 1,826.....D5
Hillsboro• 4,498.....D5
Hinsdale 1,718.....C6
Hinsdale• 3,936.....C6
Holderness• 1,694.....D4
Hollis• 5,705.....D6
Hooksett 2,573.....E5
Hooksett• 8,767.....E5
Hopkinton• 4,806.....D5
Hudson 7,626.....E6
Hudson• 19,530.....E6
Intervale 725.....E3
Jackson• 678.....E3
Jaffrey 2,558.....C6
Jaffrey• 5,361.....C6
Jaffrey Center 340.....C6
Jefferson• 965.....D3
Kearsarge 350.....E3
Keene▲ 22,430.....C6
Kingston• 5,591.....E6
Laconia▲ 15,743.....E4
Lancaster▲ 1,859.....D3
Lancaster• 3,522.....D3
Landaff• 350.....D3
Langdon• 580.....C5
Lebanon 12,183.....C4
Lee• 3,729.....F5
Lempster• 947.....C5
Lincoln• 1,229.....D3
Lisbon 1,246.....D3
Lisbon• 1,664.....D3
Litchfield• 5,516.....D6
Littleton 4,633.....D3
Littleton• 5,827.....D3
Lochmere 300.....D5
Londonderry• 19,781.....E6
Loudon• 4,114.....E5
Lyman• 388.....D3
Lyme• 1,496.....C4
Lyndeborough• 1,294.....D6
Madbury• 1,404.....F5
Madison• 1,704.....E4
Manchester 99,567.....E6
Marlborough 1,211.....C6
Marlborough• 1,927.....C6
Marlow• 650.....C5
Melvin Village 450.....E4
Meredith 1,654.....D4
Meredith• 4,837.....D4
Meriden 800.....C4
Merrimack• 22,156.....D6
Middleton• 1,183.....E5
Milan• 1,295.....E2
Milford 8,015.....D6
Milford• 11,795.....D6
Milton• 3,691.....F5
Milton Mills 450.....F4
Mirror Lake 350.....E4
Monroe• 746.....C3
Mont Vernon• 1,812.....D6
Moultonboro• 2,956.....E4
Nashua▲ 79,662.....D6
Nelson• 535.....C5
New Boston• 3,214.....D6
New Castle• 840.....F5
New Durham• 1,974.....E5
New Hampton• 1,606.....D4
New Ipswich• 4,014.....D6
New London 3,180.....D5
New London• 2,935.....D5
Newbury• 1,347.....C5
Newfields• 888.....F5
Newington• 990.....F5
Newmarket 4,917.....F5
Newmarket• 7,157.....F5
Newport▲ 3,772.....C5
Newport• 6,110.....C5
Newton Junction 450.....E6
Newton• 3,473.....E6
North Chichester 450.....E5
North Conway 2,032.....E3
North Hampton• 3,637.....F6
North Haverhill 400.....D3
North Stratford 600.....D2
North Walpole 950.....C5
North Weare 400.....D5
North Woodstock 750.....D3
Northfield-Tilton.....D5
Northfield• 4,263.....D5
Northumberland• 2,492.....D2
Northwood• 3,124.....E5
Northwood Narrows 325.....E5
Nottingham• 2,939.....E5
Orange• 237.....D4
Orford• 1,008.....C4
Ossipee 3,309.....E4
Pelham• 9,408.....E6
Pembroke• 6,561.....E5
Peterborough 2,685.....D6
Peterborough• 5,239.....D6
Piermont• 624.....C4
Pike 433.....C3
Pittsburg• 901.....E1
Pittsfield 1,717.....E5
Pittsfield• 3,701.....E5
Plainfield• 2,056.....C4
Plaistow• 7,316.....E6
Plymouth 3,967.....D4
Plymouth• 5,811.....D4
Portsmouth 25,925.....F5
Randolph• 371.....E3
Raymond 2,516.....E5
Raymond• 8,713.....E5
Redstone 300.....E3
Richmond• 877.....C6
Rindge• 4,941.....C6
Rochester 26,630.....E5
Roxbury• 248.....C6
Rumney• 1,446.....D4
Rye• 4,612.....F5
Rye Beach 600.....F6
Rye North Beach 700.....F5
Salem• 25,746.....E6
Salem Depot 975.....E6
Salisbury• 1,061.....D5
Salmon Falls 950.....F5
Sanbornton• 2,136.....D5
Sanbornville 750.....F4
Sandown• 4,060.....E6
Sandwich• 1,066.....E4
Seabrook• 6,503.....F6
Sharon• 299.....D6
Shelburne 437.....E3
Shelburne• 318.....E3
Silver Lake 350.....E4
Somersworth 11,249.....F5
South Deerfield 500.....E5
South Hampton• 740.....F6
South Lyndeboro 300.....D6
South Merrimack 650.....D6
South Seabrook 500.....F6
South Weare 400.....D5
Spofford 750.....C6
Springfield• 788.....C4
Stark• 518.....E2
Stewartstown• 1,048.....E2
Stoddard• 622.....C5
Strafford• 2,965.....E5
Stratford• 927.....D2
Stratham• 4,955.....F5
Sugar Hill• 464.....D3
Sullivan• 706.....C5
Sunapee• 2,559.....C5
Suncook 5,214.....C5
Surry• 667.....C5
Sutton• 1,457.....D5
Swanzey• 6,236.....C6
Tamworth• 2,165.....E4
Temple• 1,194.....D6
Thornton• 1,505.....D4
Tilton-Northfield 3,081.....D5
Tilton• 3,240.....D5
Troy 2,097.....C6
Troy• 2,131.....C6
Tuftonboro• 1,842.....E4
Twin Mountain 500.....D3
Unity• 1,341.....C5
Wakefield• 3,057.....F4
Walpole• 3,210.....C5
Warner• 2,250.....D5
Warren• 820.....D4
Washington• 628.....C5
Waterville Valley• 151.....D4
Weare• 6,193.....D5
Webster• 1,405.....D5
Wentworth• 630.....D4
Wentworths Location 53.....E2
West Campton 400.....D4
West Epping 400.....E5
West Henniker 500.....D5
West Lebanon.....C4
West Milan 350.....E2
West Rye 350.....F6
West Stewartstown 700.....E2
West Swanzey 1,055.....C6
Westmoreland• 1,596.....C6
Westville 750.....E6
Whitefield 1,041.....D3
Whitefield• 1,909.....D3
Wilmot Flat 450.....D5
Wilmot• 935.....D5
Wilton 1,165.....D6
Wilton• 3,122.....D6
Winchester• 1,735.....C6
Windham• 9,000.....E6
Winnisquam 500.....E5
Wolfeboro 2,783.....E4
Wolfeboro• 4,807.....E4
Wolfeboro Falls 600.....E4
Woodstock• 1,167.....D4
Woodsville▲ 1,122.....C3

OTHER FEATURES

Adams (mt.).....E3
Ammonoosuc (riv.).....D3
Androscoggin (riv.).....E2
Ashuelot (riv.).....C6
Back (lake).....E1
Baker (riv.).....D4
Bearcamp (riv.).....E4
Beaver (brook).....E6
Belknap (mt.).....E5
Blackwater (res.).....D5
Blue (mt.).....E2
Bond (mt.).....E3
Bow (lake).....E5
Cabot (mt.).....E2
Cannon (mt.).....D3
Cardigan (mt.).....D4
Carrigain (mt.).....E3
Carter Dome (mt.).....E3
Chocorua (mt.).....E4
Cocheco (riv.).....E5
Cold (riv.).....C5
Comerford (dam).....D3
Connecticut (riv.).....B6
Contoocook (riv.).....D6
Conway (lake).....E4
Crawford Notch (pass).....E3
Croydon (peak).....C5
Croydon Branch, Sugar (riv.).....C5
Crystal (lake).....E5
Cube (mt.).....D4
Dixville (peak).....E2
Dixville Notch (pass).....E2
Edward MacDowell (res.).....D6
Ellis (riv.).....E3
Everett (dam).....D5
Exeter (riv.).....E6
First Connecticut (lake).....E1
Francis (lake).....E1
Franconia Notch (pass).....D3
Franklin Falls (res.).....D4
Gale (riv.).....D3
Great (bay).....F5
Halls (stream).....E1
Hancock (mt.).....D3
Highland (lake).....C5
Hutchins (mt.).....E2
Indian (stream).....E1
Jefferson (mt.).....E3
Kearsarge (mt.).....D5
Kinsman (mt.).....D3
Kinsman Notch (pass).....D3
Lafayette (mt.).....D3
Lamprey (riv.).....E5
Liberty (mt.).....D3
Lincoln (mt.).....D3
Long (mt.).....E2
Mad (riv.).....D4
Madison (mt.).....E3
Mascoma (lake).....C4
Massabesic (lake).....E6
Merrimack (riv.).....D5
Merrymeeting (lake).....E5
Mohawk (riv.).....E2
Monadnock (mt.).....C6
Monroe (mt.).....E3
Moore (dam).....D3
Moore (res.).....D3
Moosilauke (mt.).....D3
Nash (stream).....E2
Newfound (lake).....D4
North Carter (mt.).....E3
North Twin (mt.).....D3
Nubanusit (lake).....C5
Osceola (mt.).....E3
Ossipee (lake).....E4
Ossipee (mts.).....E4
Ossipee (riv.).....F4
Passaconaway (mt.).....E4
Pawtuckaway (pond).....E5
Pease A.F.B......F5
Pemigewasset (riv.).....D4
Perry (stream).....E1
Pine (riv.).....E4
Pinkham Notch (pass).....E3
Piscataqua (riv.).....F5
Piscataquog (riv.).....D5
Presidential (range).....E3
Rice (mt.).....E2
Saco (riv.).....E3

Agriculture, Industry and Resources

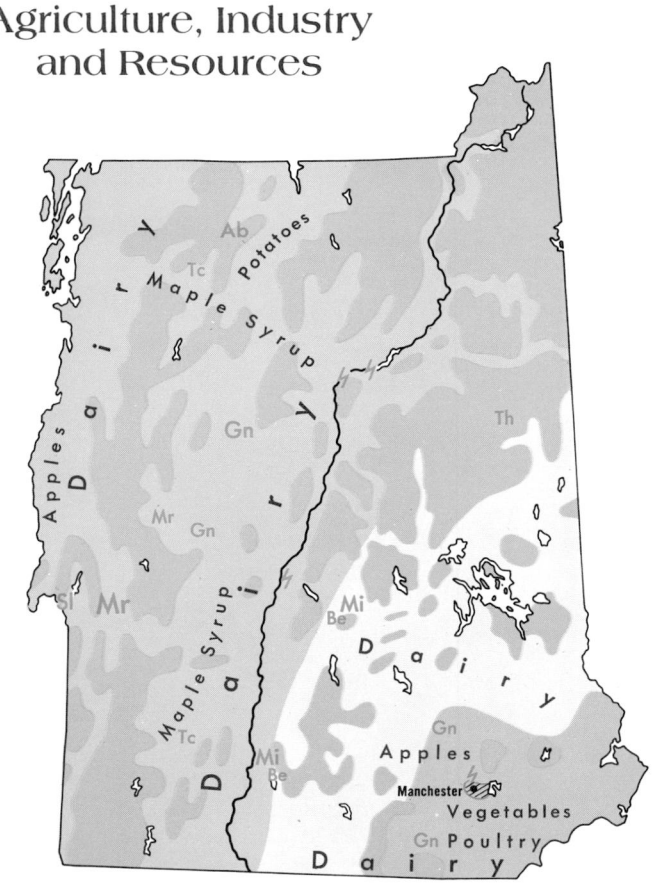

DOMINANT LAND USE

- Specialized Dairy
- Dairy, General Farming
- Dairy, Poultry, Mixed Farming
- Forests

⚡ Water Power
▨ Major Industrial Areas

MAJOR MINERAL OCCURRENCES

Ab	Asbestos	Mr	Marble
Be	Beryl	Sl	Slate
Gn	Granite	Tc	Talc
Mi	Mica	Th	Thorium

Saint-Gaudens Nat'l Hist. Site.B4
Salmon Falls (riv.) F5
Sandwich (mt.) E4
Sandwich (range)................E4
Second (lake) E1
Shaw (mt.) E4
Shoals (isls.) F6
Smarts (mt.) C4
Souhegan (riv.) D6
South Twin (mt.) D3
Squam (lake) E4
Starr King (mt.) E3
Stub Hill (mt.) E1
Sugar (riv.) C5
Sunapee (lake) C5
Suncook (lakes) E5
Suncook (riv.) E5
Surry Mountain (lake) C5
Tarleton (lake) D4
Tecumseh (mt.) D4
Third (lake) E1
Tom (mt.) E3
Umbagog (lake) E2
Upper Ammonoosuc (riv.) E2
Warner (riv.) D5
Washington (mt.) E3
Waumbek (mt.) E3
Wentworth (lake) E4
White (isl.) F6
White (mts.) E3
Whiteface (mt.) E4
Wild Ammonoosuc (riv.) D3
Wilder (dam) C4
Winnipesaukee (lake) E4
Winnipesaukee (riv.) D5
Winnisquam (lake) D4

VERMONT

COUNTIES

Addison 32,953 ....A3
Bennington 35,845 ....A6
Caledonia 27,846 ....C2
Chittenden 131,761 ....A3
Essex 6,405 ....D2
Franklin 39,980 ....B2
Grand Isle 5,318 ....A2
Lamoille 19,735 ....B2
Orange 26,149 ....C3
Orleans 24,053 ....C2
Rutland 62,142 ....A4
Washington 54,928 ....B3
Windham 41,588 ....B5
Windsor 54,055 ....B4

CITIES and TOWNS

Addison 1,023 ....A2
Albany 180 ....C2
Albany ● 782 ....C2
Alburg 436 ....A1
Alburg ● 1,362 ....A1
Andover ● 373 ....B5
Arlington 1,311 ....A5
Arlington ● 2,299 ....A5
Ascutney 274 ....C5
Averill ● 7 ....D2
Bakersfield ● 977 ....B1
Barnard ● 872 ....B4
Barnet ● 1,415 ....C2
Barre 9,482 ....C3
Barre ● 7,411 ....C3

Barton 908 ....C1
Barton ● 2,967 ....C1
Bartonsville 300 ....B5
Beebe Plain 500 ....C2
Beecher Falls 950 ....D1
Bellows Falls 3,313 ....C4
Belvidere ● 228 ....B2
Bennington▲ 9,532 ....A6
Bennington ● 16,451 ....A6
Benson ● 847 ....A4
Berkshire ● 1,190 ....B1
Bethel 1,866 ....B3
Bethel ● 1,715 ....B3
Bloomfield ● 253 ....D1
Bolton ● 971 ....B3
Bomoseen 700 ....A4
Bondville 500 ....B5
Bradford 672 ....C3
Bradford ● 2,522 ....C3
Braintree ● 1,174 ....B4
Brandon 1,902 ....A4
Brandon ● 4,223 ....A3
Brattleboro 8,612 ....B5
Brattleboro ● 12,241 ....B6
Bridgewater ● 895 ....B3
Bridport ● 1,137 ....A3
Bristol 1,801 ....A3
Bristol ● 3,762 ....A3
Brookfield ● 1,089 ....B3
Brookline ● 403 ....B5
Brownington ● 705 ....C2
Burke ● 1,406 ....D2
Burlington▲ 39,127 ....A3
Cabot 220 ....C2
Cabot ● 1,043 ....C3
Calais ● 1,521 ....B3

Cambridge 292 ....B2
Cambridge ● 2,667 ....B2
Canaan ● 1,121 ....D1
Castleton ● 4,278 ....A3
Cavendish ● 1,323 ....B5
Center Rutland 465 ....A4
Charlotte ● 3,148 ....A3
Chelsea ● 1,166 ....C3
Chester-Chester Depot 1,057..B4
Chester ● 2,832 ....B5
Chittenden ● 1,102 ....A4
Clarendon ● 2,835 ....A4
Colchester 14,731 ....A1
Concord ● 1,093 ....D2
Corinth ● 1,244 ....C3
Cornwall ● 1,101 ....A4
Coventry ● 806 ....C2
Craftsbury ● 994 ....C2
Cuttingsville 200 ....B4
Danby ● 1,193 ....A5
Danville ● 1,917 ....C2
Derby ● 4,479 ....C1
Derby (Derby Center) 684 ...C1
Derby Line 855 ....C1
Dorset ● 1,918 ....A5
Duxbury ● 976 ....B3
East Albany 250 ....C2
East Arlington 600 ....A5
East Barre-Graniteville C3
East Berkshire 200 ....B1
East Charleston 300 ....C2
East Dorset ● 550 ....A5
East Dover 275 ....B6
East Hardwick 200 ....C2
East Haven ● 269 ....D2
East Jamaica 200 ....B5

East Middlebury 550 ....A3
East Montpelier ● 2,239 ....B2
East Poultney 450 ....A4
East Ryegate 210 ....C3
East Wallingford 500 ....B5
Eden Mills 200 ....C2
Eden ● 840 ....B1
Enosburg Falls 1,350 ....B1
Essex Junction 8,396 ....A2
Essex ● 16,498 ....A1
Fair Haven 2,432 ....A3
Fair Haven ● 2,887 ....A4
Fairfax ● 2,486 ....B1
Fairfield ● 1,680 ....B2
Fairlee ● 883 ....C4
Ferrisburg ● 2,317 ....A3
Fletcher ● 941 ....B2
Florence 250 ....A4
Forest Dale 500 ....A3
Franklin ● 1,068 ....B2
Georgia ● 3,753 ....A2
Georgia Center 225 ....A2
Gilman 600 ....D2
Glover ● 820 ....C2
Grafton ● 602 ....B5
Granby ● 85 ....D2
Grand Isle ● 1,642 ....A1
Graniteville-East Barre 2,189 .B2
Granville ● 309 ....B3
Greensboro ● 717 ....C1
Groton ● 862 ....C2
Guildhall 270 ....D1
Guilford ● 1,941 ....B6
Halifax ● 588 ....B6
Hancock ● 340 ....B4
Hardwick 2,964 ....C2
Hardwick ● 2,613 ....C2
Hartford ● 9,404 ....C3
Hartland ● 2,988 ....C4
Hartland Four Corners 400 ...C4
Highgate ● 3,020 ....B2
Highgate Center 350 ....B2
Highgate Falls 400 ....A2
Hinesburg ● 3,780 ....A3
Holland ● 423 ....D2
Hubbardton ● 576 ....A4
Huntington ● 1,609 ....B3
Hyde Park 457 ....B2
Hyde Park ● 2,344 ....B2
Hydeville 500 ....A4
Ira ● 426 ....A4
Irasburg ● 907 ....C2
Island Pond 1,222 ....D2
Isle La Motte ● 408 ....A2
Jacksonville 244 ....B6
Jamaica ● 754 ....B5
Jay ● 381 ....C1
Jeffersonville 462 ....B2
Jericho ● 1,405 ....A2
Jericho ● 4,302 ....A2
Johnson 1,470 ....B2
Johnson ● 3,156 ....B2
Jonesville 300 ....B3
Killington 700 ....B4
Lake Elmore 250 ....B2
Leicester ● 871 ....A4
Lemington ● 102 ....D2
Lincoln ● 974 ....B3
Londonderry ● 1,506 ....B5
Lowell ● 594 ....C2
Ludlow ● 1,123 ....B5
Ludlow ● 2,302 ....B5
Lunenburg ● 1,176 ....D3
Lyndon ● 5,371 ....C2
Lyndon Center C2
Lyndonville ● 1,255 ....D2
Maidstone ● 131 ....D2
Manchester▲ 561 ....A5
Manchester ● 3,622 ....A5
Manchester Center 1,574 ...A5
Marlboro ● 924 ....B6
Marshfield 257 ....C2
Marshfield ● 1,331 ....C3
Mendon ● 1,049 ....B4
Middlebury▲ 6,007 ....A3
Middlebury ● 8,034 ....A3
Middlesex ● 1,514 ....B3
Middletown Springs ● 686 ...A4
Milton 1,578 ....A2
Milton ● 8,404 ....A2
Monkton ● 1,482 ....A3
Montgomery ● 823 ....B2
Montgomery Center 400 ...B2
Montpelier▲ (cap.) 8,247 ...B3
Moretown ● 1,415 ....B3
Morgan ● 497 ....D2
Morristown ● 4,733 ....B2
Morrisville 1,984 ....B2
Morses Line 200 ....B1
Moscow 250 ....B3
Mount Holly ● 1,093 ....B5
Mount Tabor ● 214 ....A5
New Haven ● 1,375 ....A3
Newark ● 354 ....D2
Newbury 412 ....C3
Newbury ● 1,985 ....C3
Newfane▲ 164 ....B6
Newfane ● 1,555 ....B6
Newport▲ 4,434 ....C2
Newport Center 250 ....B4
North Bennington 1,520 ...A6
North Clarendon 750 ....B4
North Concord 263 ....D2
North Hartland 500 ....C4
North Hero ● 502 ....A2
North Hyde Park 450 ....B2
North Pomfret 400 ....B4
North Pownal 700 ....A6
North Springfield 1,200 ...B5
North Thetford 350 ....C4
North Troy 723 ....C1
North Westminster 268 ...B5
North Williston 300 ....A3
Northfield 1,889 ....B3
Northfield ● 5,610 ....B3
Northfield Falls 600 ....B3
Norton ● 169 ....D2

Norwich ● 3,093 ....C4
Old Bennington 279 ....A6
Orange ● 915 ....C3
Orleans 806 ....C2
Orwell ● 1,114 ....A4
Panton ● 606 ....A3
Pawlet ● 1,314 ....A5
Peacham ● 627 ....C2
Perkinsville 148 ....B5
Peru ● 324 ....B5
Pittsfield ● 389 ....B4
Pittsford ● 2,919 ....A4
Plainfield ● 1,302 ....C3
Plainfield ● 1,249 ....C3
Plymouth ● 440 ....B4
Pomfret ● 874 ....B4
Post Mills 500 ....C3
Poultney 1,731 ....A4
Poultney ● 3,498 ....A4
Pownal ● 3,485 ....A6
Pownal Center 250 ....A6
Proctor ● 1,979 ....A4
Proctorsville 481 ....B5
Putney ● 2,352 ....B6
Quechee 900 ....C4
Randolph 4,764 ....B4
Randolph ● 4,689 ....B4
Reading ● 647 ....B4
Reading (Felchville) 614 ...B5
Readsboro ● 762 ....B6
Richford 1,425 ....B2
Richford ● 2,178 ....B2
Richmond ● 3,729 ....A3
Ripton ● 444 ....A4
Riverton 250 ....B3
Rochester ● 1,181 ....B4
Rockingham ● 5,484 ....B5
Roxbury ● 575 ....B3
Royalton ● 2,389 ....B4
Rupert ● 654 ....A5
Rutland▲ 18,230 ....B4
Rutland ● 3,781 ....B4
Ryegate ● 1,058 ....C3
Saint Albans▲ 7,339 ....A2
Saint Albans ● 4,606 ....A2
Saint Albans Bay 350 ....A2
Saint George ● 705 ....A2
Saint Johnsbury▲ 6,424 ....D3
Saint Johnsbury ● 7,608 ....D3
Saint Johnsbury Center 400 ..D3
Salisbury ● 1,024 ....A4
Sandgate ● 278 ....A5
Saxtons River 541 ....B5
Searsburg ● 85 ....A6
Shaftsbury ● 3,368 ....A5
Sharon ● 1,211 ....C4
Sheffield ● 541 ....C2
Shelburne ● 5,871 ....A3
Sheldon ● 1,748 ....B2
Sheldon Springs 300 ....A2
Shoreham ● 1,115 ....A4
Shrewsbury ● 1,107 ....B4
South Barre 1,314 ....B3
South Burlington 12,809 ...A3
South Hero ● 1,404 ....A2
South Londonderry 500 ...B5
South Pomfret 250 ....B4
South Royalton 700 ....C4
South Ryegate 400 ....C3
South Shaftsbury 650 ....A6
South Strafford 260 ....C4
South Woodstock 360 ....B4
Springfield 4,207 ....B5
Springfield ● 9,579 ....B5
Stamford ● 773 ....A6
Starksboro ● 1,511 ....A3
Stockbridge ● 618 ....B4
Stowe 450 ....B3
Stowe ● 3,433 ....B3
Strafford ● 902 ....C4
Stratton ● 121 ....B5
Sudbury ● 516 ....A4
Sunderland ● 872 ....A5
Sutton ● 854 ....C2
Swanton 2,360 ....A2
Swanton ● 5,636 ....A2
Taftsville 260 ....C4
Thetford ● 2,438 ....C4
Tinmouth ● 455 ....A5
Topsham ● 944 ....C3
Townshend ● 1,019 ....B5
Troy ● 1,609 ....C2
Tunbridge ● 1,154 ....C4
Underhill ● 2,799 ....B2
Underhill Center 575 ....B2
Vergennes 2,578 ....A3
Vernon ● 1,850 ....B6
Vershire ● 560 ....C4
Waitsfield ● 1,422 ....B3
Walden ● 703 ....C3
Wallingford 1,148 ....B5
Wallingford ● 2,184 ....B5
Waltham ● 454 ....A3
Wardsboro ● 654 ....B5
Warren ● 1,172 ....B3
Washington ● 937 ....C3
Waterbury 1,702 ....B3
Waterbury ● 4,589 ....B3
Waterbury Center 900 ....B3
Waterville ● 532 ....B2
Websterville 700 ....B3
Wells ● 902 ....A5
Wells River 424 ....C3
West Brattleboro 3,135 ...B6
West Burke 353 ....C2
West Cornwall 350 ....A4
West Danville 225 ....C3
West Dover 550 ....B6
West Fairlee ● 633 ....C4
West Glover 250 ....C2
West Hartford 300 ....C4
West Haven ● 273 ....A4
West Pawlet 300 ....A5
West Rupert 300 ....A5
West Rutland 2,246 ....A4
West Rutland ● 2,448 ....A4
West Townshend 500 ....B5

West Woodstock 250 ....B4
Westfield ● 422 ....C2
Westford ● 1,740 ....B2
Westminster 399 ....C5
Westminster ● 3,026 ....C5
Westminster West 400 ....B5
Westmore ● 305 ....C2
Weston ● 488 ....B5
Weybridge ● 749 ....A3
Wheelock ● 481 ....C2
White River Junction 2,521 .C4
Whiting ● 407 ....A4
Whitingham ● 1,177 ....B6
Wilder 1,576 ....C4
Williamstown ● 2,839 ....B3
Williston ● 4,887 ....A3
Wilmington ● 1,968 ....B6
Windham ● 251 ....B5
Windsor 3,714 ....C5
Windsor ● 4,084 ....C5
Winooski 6,649 ....A3
Wolcott ● 1,229 ....B2
Woodbury ● 766 ....B3
Woodford ● 331 ....A6
Woodstock▲ 1,037 ....B4
Woodstock ● 3,212 ....B4
Worcester ● 906 ....B3

OTHER FEATURES

Abraham (mt.) B3
Arrowhead Mountain (lake) ...A2
Ascutney (mt.) C5
Bald (mt.) D2
Barton (riv.) C2
Batten Kill (riv.) A5
Belvidere (mt.) B2
Black (riv.) B5
Black (riv.) C2
Bloodroot (mt.) B4
Bolton (mt.) B3
Bomoseen (lake) A4
Brandon Gap (pass) B4
Bread Loaf (mt.) B3
Bromley (mt.) A5
Brown's (riv.) A2
Burke (mt.) D2
Camels Hump (mt.) B3
Carmi (lake) B1
Caspian (lake) C2
Champlain (lake) A2
Chittenden (res.) B4
Clyde (riv.) C1
Comerford (dam) D3
Connecticut (riv.) C3
Crystal (lake) C2
Dorset (peak) A5
Dunmore (lake) A4
Echo (lake) C2
Ellen (mt.) B3
Equinox (mt.) A5
Fairfield (pond) B1
Glastenbury (mt.) A6
Gore (mt.) D2
Green (mts.) B4
Green River (res.) B6
Groton (lake) C3
Hardwick (lake) C2
Harriman (res.) B6
Harveys (lake) C3
Haystack (mt.) B6
Hoosic (riv.) A6
Hortonia (lake) A4
Hunger (mt.) B3
Iroquois (lake) A2
Island (pond) D2
Jay (peak) C1
Joes (brook) C2
Killington (peak) B4
Lamoille (riv.) A2
Lewis (creek) A3
Lincoln Gap (pass) B3
Little (riv.) B3
Mad (riv.) B3
Maidstone (lake) D2
Mansfield (mt.) B2
Memphremagog (lake) C1
Mettawee (riv.) A5
Middlebury Gap (pass) B4
Mill (riv.) B4
Missisquoi (riv.) B2
Mollys Falls (pond) C3
Moore (dam) D3
Moore (res.) D3
Moose (riv.) D2
Norton (pond) D2
Nulhegan (riv.) D2
Ottauquechee (riv.) C4
Otter (creek) A3
Passumpsic (riv.) C2
Pico (peak) B4
Poultney (riv.) A4
Saint Catherine (lake) A4
Salem (lake) D2
Seymour (lake) C2
Shelburne (pond) A3
Smugglers Notch (pass) B2
Snow (mt.) B6
Somerset (res.) B6
Spruce (mt.) C3
Stratton (mt.) B5
Tabor (mt.) A5
Trout (riv.) B2
Waits (riv.) C3
Waterbury (res.) B3
Wells (riv.) C3
West (riv.) B5
White (riv.) B4
White Face (mt.) B2
Wilder (dam) C4
Willoughby (lake) C2
Winooski (riv.) A3

▲County seat.
● Population of town or township.

AREA 7,787 sq. mi. (20,168 sq. km.)
POPULATION 7,748,634
CAPITAL Trenton
LARGEST CITY Newark
HIGHEST POINT High Point 1,803 ft. (550 m.)
SETTLED IN 1617
ADMITTED TO UNION December 18, 1787
POPULAR NAME Garden State
STATE FLOWER Purple Violet
STATE BIRD Eastern Goldfinch

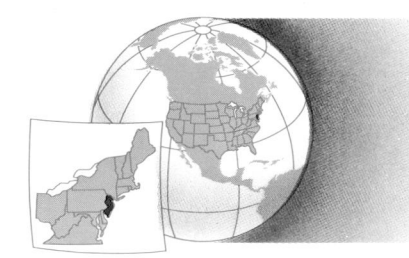

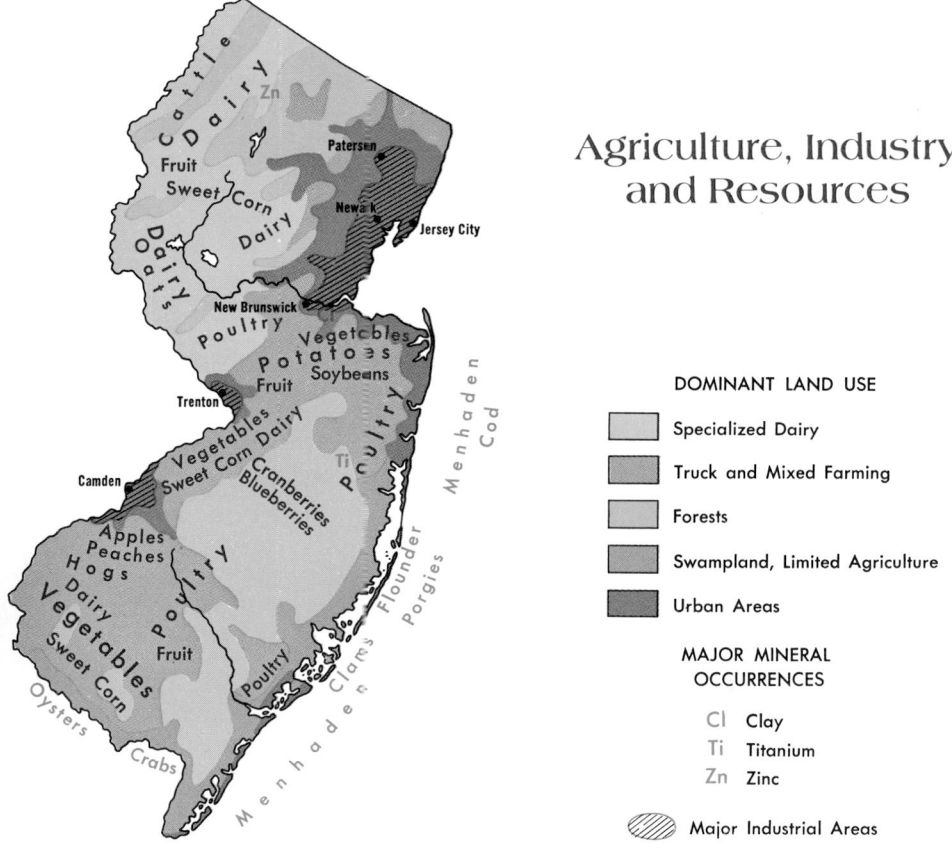

Agriculture, Industry and Resources

DOMINANT LAND USE

- Specialized Dairy
- Truck and Mixed Farming
- Forests
- Swampland, Limited Agriculture
- Urban Areas

MAJOR MINERAL OCCURRENCES

- Cl   Clay
- Ti   Titanium
- Zn   Zinc

▨ Major Industrial Areas

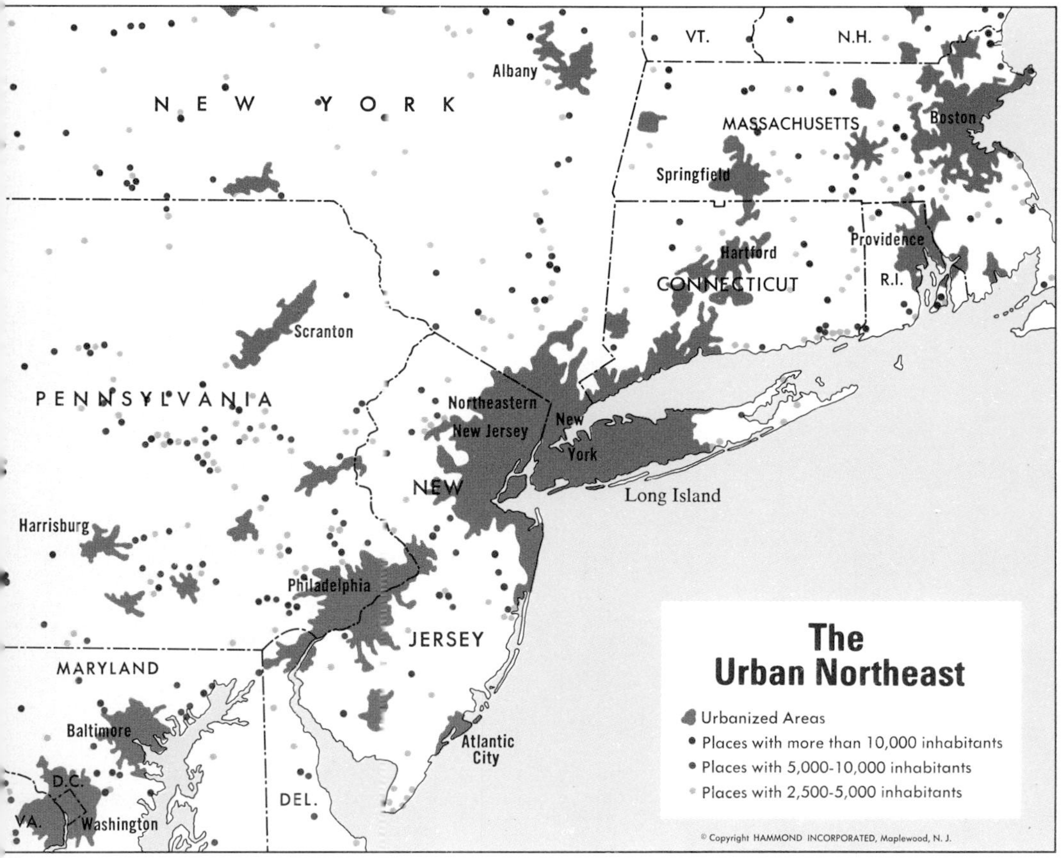

The Urban Northeast

- Urbanized Areas
- ● Places with more than 10,000 inhabitants
- ● Places with 5,000-10,000 inhabitants
- ● Places with 2,500-5,000 inhabitants

© Copyright HAMMOND INCORPORATED, Maplewood, N. J.

COUNTIES

Atlantic 224,327		D5
Bergen 825,380		E2
Burlington 395,066		D4
Camden 502,824		D4
Cape May 95,089		D5
Cumberland 138,053		C5
Essex 778,206		E2
Gloucester 230,082		C4
Hudson 553,099		E2
Hunterdon 107,776		D2
Mercer 325,824		D3
Middlesex 671,780		E3
Monmouth 553,124		E3
Morris 421,353		D2
Ocean 433,203		E4
Passaic 453,060		E1
Salem 65,294		C4
Somerset 240,279		D2
Sussex 130,943		D1
Union 493,819		E2
Warren 91,607		C2

CITIES and TOWNS

Aberdeen 17,235	E3
Absecon 7,298	D5
Allamuchy 600	D2
Allendale 5,900	B1
Allenhurst 759	F3
Allentown 1,828	D3
Allenwood 500	E3
Alloway 1,371	C4
Alpha 2,530	C2
Alpine 1,716	C1
Andover 700	D2
Annandale 1,074	D2
Asbury Park 16,799	F3
Ashland	B3
Atlantic City 37,986	E5
Atlantic Highlands 4,629	F3
Audubon 9,205	B3
Audubon Park 1,150	B3
Augusta 500	D1
Aura 500	C4
Avalon 1,809	D5
Avenel 15,504	E2
Avon By The Sea 2,165	E3
Barnegat 1,160	E4
Barnegat Light 675	E4
Barrington 6,774	B3
Basking Ridge	D2
Bay Head 1,226	E3
Bayonne 61,444	B2
Beach Haven 1,475	E4
Beach Haven Crest 500	E4
Beach Haven Terrace 500	E4
Beachwood 9,324	E4
Bedminster● 2,469	D2
Belford	E3
Belle Mead	D3
Belleplain 500	D5
Belleville 34,213	B2
Bellmawr 12,603	B3
Belmar 5,877	E3
Belvidere▲ 2,669	C2
Bergenfield 24,458	C1
Berkeley Heights ● 11,980	E2
Berlin 5,672	D4
Bernardsville 6,597	D2
Beverly 2,973	D3
Blackwood 5,120	C4
Blackwood Terrace	C4
Blairstown● 4,360	C2
Bloomfield 45,061	B2
Bloomingdale 7,530	E1
Bloomsbury 890	C2
Bogota 7,824	B2
Boonton 8,343	E2
Bordentown 4,341	D3
Bound Brook 9,487	D2
Bradley Beach 4,475	F3
Branchville 851	D1
Brant Beach 500	E4
Breton Woods	E3
Brick ● 66,473	E3
Bridgeport 750	C4
Bridgeton▲ 18,942	C5
Bridgewater ● 29,175	D2
Brielle 4,406	E3
Brigantine 11,354	E5
Brooklawn 1,805	B3
Brookside	D2
Browns Mills 11,429	D4
Budd Lake 7,272	D2
Buena 4,441	D4
Burlington 9,835	D3
Butler 7,392	E2
Caldwell 7,549	B2
Califon 1,073	D2
Camden▲ 87,492	B3
Candlewood 6,750	E3
Cape May 4,668	D6
Cape May Court House▲ 4,426	D5

Cape May Point 248	D6
Carlstadt 5,510	B2
Carneys Point 7,686	C4
Carteret 19,025	E2
Cedar Brook 600	C4
Cedar Grove● 12,053	B2
Cedar Knolls	E2
Cedarville 900	C5
Cedarwood Park	E3
Chatham 8,007	E2
Chatsworth 700	D4
Cheesequake	E3
Cherry Hill ● 69,319	B3
Chesilhurst 1,526	D4
Chester 1,214	D2
Chesterfield ● 3,867	D3
Cinnaminson ● 14,583	B3
Clark ● 14,629	A3
Clarksboro	C4
Clarksburg 800	E3
Clayton 6,155	C4
Clementon 5,601	D4
Cliffside Park 20,393	C2
Cliffwood	E3
Clifton 71,742	B2
Clinton 2,054	D2
Closter 8,094	C1
Cold Spring 500	D6
Collingswood 15,289	B3
Cologne 800	D4
Colonia 18,238	E2
Colts Neck 950	E3
Columbia 600	C2
Columbus 800	D3
Convent Station	E2
Corbin City 412	D5
Cranberry Lake 500	D2
Cranbury 1,255	E3
Cranford ● 22,624	E2
Cresskill 7,558	C1
Dayton 4,321	D3
Deal 1,179	F3
Deepwater 800	C4
Delanco ● 3,316	D3
Delran ● 14,811	B3
Demarest 4,800	C1
Dennisville 890	D5
Denville ● 14,380	E2
Deptford ● 23,473	B4
Dividing Creek 500	C5
Dorchester 500	D5
Dorothy 900	D5
Dover 15,115	D2
Dumont 17,187	C1
Dunellen 6,528	D2
East Brunswick ● 43,548	E3
East Hanover ● 9,926	E2
East Keansburg	E3
East Millstone 950	D3
East Newark 2,157	B2
East Orange 73,552	B2
East Rutherford 7,902	B2
Eatontown 13,800	E3
Edgewater 5,001	C2
Edgewater Park ● 8,388	D3
Edison ● 88,680	E2
Egg Harbor City 4,583	D4
Elberon	F3
Elizabeth▲ 110,002	B2
Elmer 1,571	C4
Elmwood Park 17,623	B2
Elwood 1,538	D4
Emerson 6,930	B1
Englewood 24,850	C2
Englewood Cliffs 5,634	C2
English Creek 500	D5
Englishtown 1,268	E3
Essex Fells 2,363	B2
Estell Manor 1,404	D5
Ewan 610	C4
Ewing 34,185	D3
Fair Haven 5,270	E3
Fair Lawn 30,548	B1
Fairfield ● 7,615	A2
Fairton 1,359	C5
Fairview 10,733	C2
Fanwood 7,115	E2
Far Hills 657	D2
Farmingdale 1,462	E3
Fieldsboro 579	D3
Flagtown 800	D2
Flanders	D2
Flemington▲ 4,047	D2
Florence-Roebling 8,564	D3
Florham Park 8,521	E2
Folsom 2,181	D4
Fords 14,392	E2
Forked River 4,243	E4
Fort Lee 31,997	C2
Franklin 4,977	D1
Franklin Lakes 9,873	B1
Franklin Park ● 31,358	D3
Franklinville	C4
Freehold ● 10,742	E3
Frenchtown 1,528	C2
Garfield 26,727	B2

(continued on following page)

Garwood 4,227 E2
Gibbsboro 2,383 B4
Gibbstown 3,902 C4
Gilford Park 8,668 E4
Gillette E2
Glassboro 15,614 C4
Glasser D2
Glen Gardner 1,665 D2
Glen Ridge 7,076 B2
Glen Rock 10,883 B1
Glendora 5,201 B4
Glenwood 500 D1
Gloucester City 12,649 B3
Green Brook D2
Green Creek 600 D5
Green Pond 800 E1
Green Village 800 D2
Greenwich• 973 C5
Grenloch 700 C4
Greystone Park D2
Groveville D3
Guttenberg 8,268 C2
Hackensack▲ 37,049 B2
Hackettstown 8,120 D2
Haddon Heights 7,860 B3
Haddonfield 11,628 B3
Hainesport• 3,236 D4
Haledon 6,951 B1
Hamburg 2,566 D1
Hamilton Square-Mercerville D3
Hammonton 12,208 D4
Hampton 1,515 D2
Harrington Park 4,623 C1
Harrison 13,425 B2
Hartford 650 D4
Harvey Cedars 362 E4
Hasbrouck Heights 11,488 B2
Haskell A1
Haworth 3,384 C1
Hawthorne 17,084 B2
Hazlet 23,013 E3
Helmetta 1,211 E3
Hewitt 950 E1
Hi-Nella 1,045 B4
High Bridge 3,886 D2
Highland Lakes 4,550 E1
Highland Park 13,279 D2
Highlands 4,849 F3
Hightstown 5,126 D3
Hillsdale 9,750 B1
Hillside• 21,044 B2
Ho Ho Kus 3,935 B1
Hoboken 33,397 C2
Holmdel• 8,447 E3
Hopatcong 15,586 D2
Hopewell 1,968 D3
Howell• 25,065 E3
Huntington C2
Interlaken 910 E3
Ironia D2
Irvington 59,774 B2
Iselin 16,141 E2
Island Heights 1,470 E4
Jackson• 25,644 E3
Jamesburg 5,294 E3
Jersey City▲ 228,537 B2
Johnsonburg 600 D2
Juliustown 500 D3
Keansburg 11,069 E3
Kearny 34,874 B2
Keasbey E2
Kendall Park 7,127 D3
Kenilworth 7,574 E2
Keyport 7,586 E3
Kingston 1,047 D3
Kinnelon 8,470 E2
Kirkwood 800 B4
Lafayette 900 D1
Lake Hiawatha E2
Lake Hopatcong D2
Lake Mohawk 8,930 D1
Lakehurst 3,078 E3
Lakewood 26,095 E3
Lambertville 3,927 D3
Landisville D4
Lanoka Harbor E4
Laurel Springs 2,341 B4
Laurence Harbor 6,361 E3
Lavallette 2,299 E4
Lawnside 2,841 B3
Lawrenceville 6,446 D3
Layton 700 D1
Lebanon 1,036 D2
Ledgewood D2
Leeds Point 500 E4
Leesburg 700 D5
Leonardo 3,788 E3
Leonia 8,365 C2
Liberty Corner D2
Lincoln Park 10,978 A1
Lincroft 6,193 E3
Linden 36,701 A3
Lindenwold 18,734 B4
Linwood 6,866 D5
Little Falls• 11,294 B2
Little Ferry 9,989 B2
Little Silver 5,721 F3
Livingston• 26,609 E2
Lodi 22,355 B2
Long Branch 28,658 F3
Long Valley 1,744 D2
Longport 1,224 D5
Lumberton 600 D4
Lyndhurst• 18,262 B2
Lyons D2
Madison 15,850 E2
Magnolia 4,861 B3
Mahwah• 12,127 E1
Malaga 950 C4
Manahawkin 1,594 E4
Manasquan 5,369 E3
Mantoloking 334 E3
Mantua• 9,193 C4
Manville 10,567 D2
Maple Shade• 19,211 B3
Maplewood• 21,756 E2
Marcella 540 E2
Margate City 8,431 E5
Marlboro• 17,560 E3
Marlton 10,228 D4
Marmora 650 D5
Martinsville D2
Matawan 9,270 E3
Mays Landing▲ 2,090 D5
Maywood 9,473 B2
McAfee 800 D1
McKee City 950 D5
Medford D4
Medford Lakes 4,462 D4
Mendham 4,890 D2
Menlo Park E2
Mercerville-Hamilton Square 26,873 D3
Merchantville 4,095 B3
Metuchen 12,804 E2
Mickleton 950 C4
Middlesex 13,055 E2
Middletown• 62,298 E3
Midland Park 7,047 B1
Milford 1,273 C2
Millburn• 18,630 E2
Millington 975 D2
Millstone 450 D2
Milltown 6,968 E3
Millville 25,992 C5
Milmay 798 D5
Milton D1
Mine Hill• 3,325 D2
Minotola D4
Mizpah 900 D5
Monmouth Beach 3,303 F3
Monmouth Junction 1,570 D3
Monroe• 15,858 D1
Montague 750 D1
Montclair 37,729 B2
Montvale 6,946 B1
Montville• 14,290 E2
Moonachie 2,817 B2
Moorestown 13,695 B3
Morganville E3
Morris Plains 5,219 D2
Morristown▲ 16,189 D2
Mount Arlington 3,630 D2
Mount Ephraim 4,517 B3
Mount Freedom D2
Mount Holly 10,639 D4
Mount Hope D2
Mount Laurel• 17,614 D4
Mount Olive• 18,748 D2
Mount Royal 900 C4
Mountain Lakes 3,847 E2
Mountain View B2
Mountainside 6,657 E2
Mullica Hill 1,117 C4
Mystic Islands 7,400 E4
National Park 3,413 B3
Navesink E3
Neptune City 4,997 E3
Neshanic Station D3
Netcong 3,311 D2
New Brunswick▲ 41,711 E3
New Egypt 2,327 E3
New Gretna 800 E4
New Milford 15,990 B1
New Providence 11,439 E2
New Vernon D2
Newark▲ 275,221 B2
Newfield 1,592 D4
Newfoundland 900 D1
Newport 700 C5
Newton▲ 7,521 D1
Newtonville 950 D4
Nixon E2
North Arlington 13,790 B2
North Bergen• 48,414 B2
North Branch 610 D2
North Brunswick• 31,287 D3
North Caldwell 6,706 B2
North Cape May 3,574 C6
North Haledon 7,987 B1
North Plainfield 18,820 E2
North Wildwood 5,017 D6
Northfield 7,305 D5
Northvale 4,563 F1
Norwood 4,858 C1
Nutley 27,099 B2
Oak Ridge 750 E1
Oakhurst 4,130 E3
Oakland 11,997 B1
Oaklyn 4,430 B3
Ocean City 15,512 D5
Ocean Gate 2,078 E4
Ocean Grove 4,818 F3
Ocean View 950 D5
Oceanport 6,146 F3
Oceanville 600 D5
Ogdensburg 2,722 D1
Old Bridge 22,151 E3
Old Tappan 4,254 C1
Oradell 8,024 B1
Orange 29,925 B2
Osbornsville E3
Oxford 1,767 C2
Packanack Lake B1
Palermo 600 D5
Palisades Park 14,536 C2
Palmyra 7,056 B3
Paramus 25,067 B1
Park Ridge 8,102 B1
Parsippany-Troy Hills• 48,478 E2
Passaic 58,041 B2
Paterson▲ 140,891 B2
Paulsboro 6,577 C4
Peapack-Gladstone 2,111 D2
Pedricktown C4
Pemberton 1,367 D4
Pennington 2,537 D3
Penns Grove 5,228 C4
Pennsauken• 34,733 B3
Pennsville 12,218 C4
Pequannock• 12,844 B1
Perth Amboy 41,967 E2
Petersburg 750 D5
Phillipsburg 15,757 C2
Pine Beach 1,954 E4
Pine Brook E2
Pine Hill 9,854 D4
Piscataway• 42,223 D2
Pitman 9,365 C4
Plainfield 46,567 E2
Plainsboro D3
Pleasantville 16,027 D5
Point Pleasant 18,177 E3
Point Pleasant Beach 5,112 E3
Pomona 2,624 D5
Pompton Lakes 10,539 A1
Pompton Plains B1
Port Monmouth 3,558 E3
Port Morris 616 D2
Port Norris 1,701 C5
Port Reading 3,977 E2
Port Republic 992 D4
Princeton 12,016 D3
Princeton Junction 2,362 D3
Prospect Park 5,053 B1
Quinton 750 C4
Rahway 25,325 E2
Ralston 650 D2
Ramblewood 6,181 D4
Ramsey 13,228 B1
Randolph• 17,828 D2
Raritan 5,798 D2
Red Bank 10,636 E3
Richland 950 D5
Ridgefield 9,996 B2
Ridgefield Park 12,454 B2
Ridgewood 24,152 B1
Ringoes 682 D3
Ringwood 12,623 E1
Rio Grande 2,505 D5
River Edge 10,603 B1
River Vale• 9,410 B1
Riverdale 2,370 A1
Riverside• 7,974 B3
Riverton 2,775 B3
Robbinsville 650 D3
Rochelle Park• 5,587 B2
Rockaway 6,243 D2
Rockleigh 270 C1
Rocky Hill 693 D3
Roebling-Florence D3
Roosevelt 884 E3
Roseland 4,847 A2
Roselle 20,314 B2
Roselle Park 12,805 A2
Rosenhayn 1,053 C5
Roxbury• 18,878 D2
Rumson 6,701 F3
Runnemede 9,042 B3
Rutherford 17,790 B2
Saddle Brook• 13,296 B1
Saddle River 2,950 B1
Salem▲ 6,883 C4
Sayreville 34,986 E3
Scotch Plains• 21,160 E2
Sea Bright 1,693 F3
Sea Girt 2,099 E3
Sea Isle City 2,692 D5
Seabrook 1,457 C5
Seaside Heights 2,366 E4
Seaside Park 1,871 E4
Secaucus 14,061 B2
Sewaren 2,569 E2
Sewell C4
Shiloh 408 C5
Ship Bottom 1,352 E4
Shore Acres E3
Short Hills E2
Shrewsbury 3,096 E3
Sicklerville D4
Singac B2
Skillman D3
Smithburg 750 E3
Somerdale 5,440 B4
Somers Point 11,216 D5
Somerville▲ 11,632 D2
South Amboy 7,863 E3
South Belmar 1,482 E3
South Bound Brook 4,185 E2
South Brunswick• 17,127 E3
South Orange• 16,390 A2
South Plainfield 20,489 E2
South River 13,692 E3
South Seaville 600 D5
South Toms River 3,869 E4
Sparta• 13,333 D1
Spotswood 7,983 E3
Spring Lake 3,499 F3
Spring Lake Heights 5,341 E3
Springfield• 13,420 E2
Stanhope 3,393 D2
Stanton 700 D2
Stewartsville 950 C2
Stirling E2
Stockholm D1
Stockton 629 D3
Stone Harbor 1,025 D5
Stratford 7,614 B4
Strathmore 7,060 E3
Succasunna 10,931 D2
Summit 19,757 E2
Surf City 1,375 E4
Sussex 2,201 D1
Swedesboro 2,024 C4
Teaneck• 37,825 B2
Tenafly 13,326 C1
Teterboro 22 B2
Thorofare B4
Three Bridges 750 D2
Tinton Falls 12,361 E3
Titusville 900 D3
Toms River▲ 7,524 E4
Totowa 10,177 B1
Towaco E2
Townsends Inlet D5
Trenton (cap.)▲ 88,675 D3
Tuckerton 3,048 E4
Turnersville 3,843 C4
Union Beach 6,156 E3

Topography

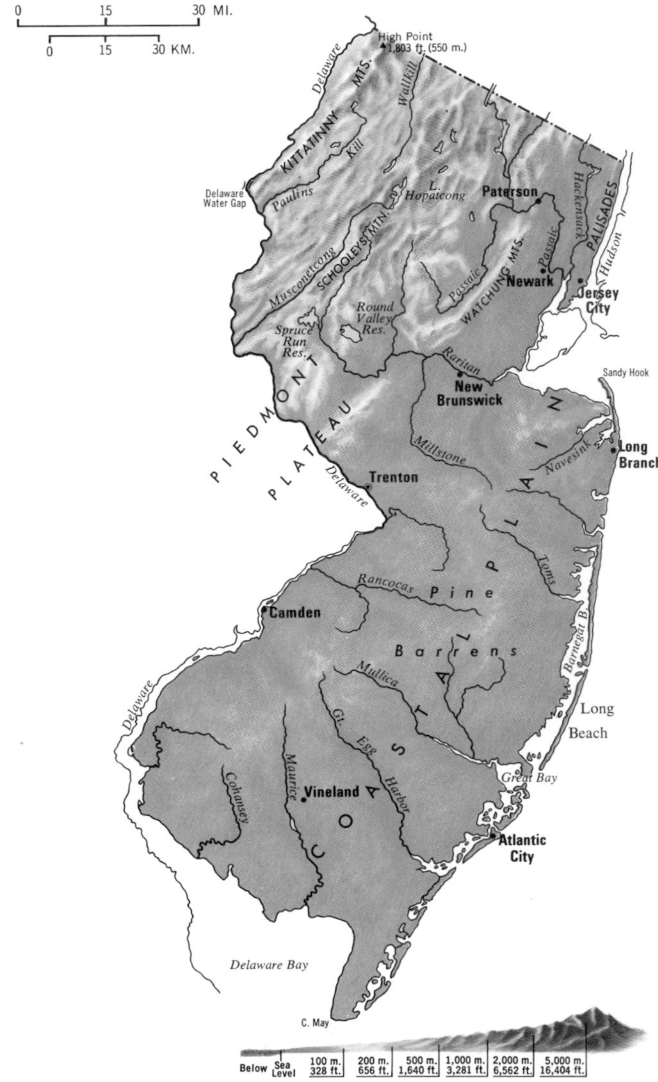

0 15 30 MI.
0 15 30 KM.
High Point 1,803 ft. (550 m.)
Delaware
KITTATINNY MTS.
Wallkill
Kill
Paulins
Delaware Water Gap
L. Hopatcong
SCHOOLEYS MTN.
Paterson
Hackensack
PALISADES
Hudson
Musconetcong
Passaic
WATCHUNG MTS.
Newark
Jersey City
Round Valley Res.
Spruce Run Res.
Raritan
Sandy Hook
New Brunswick
PIEDMONT PLATEAU
Millstone
Navesink
Long Branch
Trenton
Delaware
COASTAL PLAIN
Toms
Rancocas
Pine
Camden
Barrens
Barnegat B.
Mullica
Long Beach
Delaware
Gt. Egg Harbor
Great Bay
Cohansey
Maurice
Vineland
Atlantic City
Delaware Bay
C. May
Below Sea Level 100 m. 328 ft. 200 m. 656 ft. 500 m. 1,640 ft. 1,000 m. 3,281 ft. 2,000 m. 6,562 ft. 5,000 m. 16,404 ft.

Union City 58,012 C2
Union• 50,024 A2
Upper Greenwood Lake 2,734 E1
Upper Saddle River 7,198 B1
Vauxhall A2
Ventnor City 11,005 E5
Vernon 800 E1
Verona 13,597 B2
Villas 8,136 D5
Vincentown 900 D4
Vineland 54,780 C5
Voorhees• 12,919 B3
Waldwick 9,757 B1
Wall• 18,952 E3
Wallington 10,828 B2
Wanamassa 4,530 E3
Wanaque 9,711 B1
Waretown 1,283 E4
Warren• 9,805 D2
Washington 6,474 D2
Watchung 5,110 E2
Waterford Works 950 D4
Wayne• 47,025 A1
Weehawken• 12,385 C2
Wenonah 2,331 C4
West Berlin D4
West Caldwell 10,422 A2
West Cape May 1,026 D6
West Creek 827 E4
West Deptford• 18,002 B3
West Long Branch 7,690 F3
West Milford 25,430 E1
West New York 38,125 C2
West Orange 39,103 A2
West Paterson 10,982 B2
West Trenton D3
West Wildwood 453 D6
Westfield 28,870 E2
Westmont 15,875 B3
Westville 4,573 B3
Westwood 10,446 B1
Wharton 5,405 D2
Whippany E2
White House Station 1,287 D2
White Meadow Lake 8,002 D2
Whitehouse 852 D2
Whitesboro 1,583 D5
Whitesville 600 E3
Whiting 750 E4
Wickatunk 950 E3
Wildwood 4,484 D6
Wildwood Crest 3,631 D6
Williamstown 10,891 D4
Willingboro• 36,291 D3
Winfield• 1,785 B2
Winslow 950 D4
Wood-Lynne 2,578 B3
Wood-Ridge 7,506 B2
Woodbine 2,678 D5
Woodbridge• 90,074 E2
Woodbury Heights 3,392 B4
Woodbury▲ 10,904 B4
Woodcliff Lake 5,303 B1
Woodport D2
Woodstown 3,154 C4
Wrightstown 3,843 D3
Wyckoff• 15,372 B1
Yardville 9,414 D3

OTHER FEATURES

Absecon (inlet) E5
Alloways (creek) C4
Arthur Kill (str.) B3
Atlantic Highlands (ridge) E3
Barnegat (bay) E4
Batsto (riv.) D4
Bayonne Military Ocean Terminal B2
Beach Haven (inlet) E4
Beaver (brook) E2
Ben Davis (pt.) C5
Big Flat (brook) D1
Big Timber (creek) C4
Boonton (res.) E2
Brigantine (inlet) E5
Budd (lake) D2
Canistear (res.) E1
Cedar (creek) E4
Clinton (res.) E1
Cohansey (riv.) C5
Cooper (riv.) B3
Corson (inlet) D5
Crosswicks (creek) D3
Culvers (lake) D1
Delaware (bay) C5
Delaware (riv.) D3
Delaware Water Gap Nat'l Rec. Area C1
Earle Naval Weapons Sta. E3
Echo (lake) E1
Edison Nat'l Hist. Site A2
Egg Island (pt.) C5
Fort Dix 10,205 D3
Fort Hancock F3
Fort Monmouth E3
Gateway Nat'l Rec. Area E2
Great (bay) E4
Great Egg Harbor (inlet) E5
Greenwood (lake) E1
Hackensack (riv.) C1
Hereford (inlet) D5
High Point (mt.) D1
Hopatcong (lake) D2
Hudson (riv.) C1
Island (beach) E4
Kill Van Kull (str.) B2
Kittatinny (mts.) D1
Lakehurst Naval Air-Engineering Center E3
Lamington (riv.) D2
Landing (creek) D4
Little Egg (harb.) E4
Lockatong (creek) C3
Long (beach) E4
Long Beach (isl.) E4
Lower New York (bay) E2
Manasquan (riv.) E3
Manumuskin (riv.) D5
Maurice (riv.) C4
May (cape) C6
McGuire A.F.B. 7,580 D3
Metedeconk (riv.) E3
Mill (creek) E4
Millstone (riv.) D3
Mohawk (lake) D1
Morristown Nat'l Hist. Park D2
Mullica (riv.) D4
Musconetcong (riv.) C
Navesink (riv.) E
Newark (bay) B
Oak Ridge (res.) D
Oldmans (creek) C
Oradell (res.) B
Oswego (riv.) E
Owassa (lake) D
Palisades (cliffs) C
Passaic (riv.) E
Paulins Kill (riv.) D
Pennsauken (creek) B
Pequest (riv.) E
Picatinny Arsenal D
Pohatcong (creek) C
Pompton (lake) B
Raccoon (creek) C
Ramapo (riv.) E
Rancocas (creek) E
Raritan (bay) E
Raritan (riv.) D
Ridgeway Branch, Toms (riv.) E
Round Valley (res.) D
Saddle (riv.) B
Salem (riv.) C
Sandy Hook (split) F
Shoal Branch, Wading (riv.) D
Spruce Run (res.) D
Statue of Liberty Nat'l Mon. B
Stony (brook) D
Stow (creek) C
Swartswood (lake) D
Tappan (lake) C
The Narrows (str.) E
Toms (riv.) E
Townsend (inlet) D
Tuckahoe (riv.) D
Union (lake) C
Upper New York (bay) B
Wading (riv.) D
Wallkill (riv.) D
Wanaque (res.) E
Wawayanda (lake) E

▲County Seat
• Population of town or townshi

New Jersey

SCALE

0 ... 5 ... 10 ... 15 ... 20 MI.

0 ... 5 ... 10 ... 15 ... 20 KM.

State Capitals .... ⊛

County Seats .... ◉

Canals ....

Major Limited Access Hwys. ——

Scale 1:930,000

Copyright HAMMOND INCORPORATED, Maplewood, N.J.

Longitude 75° West of Greenwich

COUNTIES

Bernalillo 480,577 ....C4
Catron 2,563 ....A4
Chaves 57,849 ....E5
Cibola 23,794 ....A4
Colfax 12,925 ....E2
Curry 42,207 ....F4
De Baca 2,454 ....E4
Dona Ana 135,510 ....C6
Eddy 48,605 ....E6
Grant 27,676 ....A5
Guadalupe 4,156 ....E4
Harding 987 ....F3
Hidalgo 5,958 ....A7
Lea 55,765 ....F6

Lincoln 12,219 ....D5
Los Alamos 18,115 ....C3
Luna 18,110 ....B6
McKinley 60,686 ....A3
Mora 4,264 ....E3
Otero 51,928 ....D6
Quay 10,823 ....F3
Rio Arriba 34,365 ....B2
Roosevelt 16,702 ....F4
San Juan 91,605 ....A2
San Miguel 25,743 ....D3
Sandoval 34,799 ....C3
Santa Fe 98,928 ....C3
Sierra 9,912 ....B5
Socorro 14,764 ....C5
Taos 23,118 ....D2
Torrance 10,285 ....D4
Union 4,124 ....F2
Valencia 45,235 ....A4

CITIES and TOWNS

Abiquiu 500 ....C2
Acoma 150 ....B4
Acomita (Pueblo of Acoma) 975 ....B3
Alameda C3
Alamogordo▲ 27,596 ....C6
Albuquerque▲ 384,736 ....C3
Alcalde 308 ....C2
Algodones 195 ....C3
Allison A3
Alma 120 ....A5
Alto 285 ....D5
Amalia 200 ....D2
Animas 75 ....A7
Anthony 5,160 ....C6
Anton Chico 400 ....D3
Arrey 367 ....B6

Arroyo Hondo 400 ....D2
Arroyo Seco 500 ....D2
Artesia 10,610 ....E6
Aztec▲ 5,479 ....B2
Bayard 2,598 ....A6
Belen 6,547 ....C4
Bent 294 ....D5
Berino 600 ....C6
Bernalillo▲ 5,960 ....C3
Blanco 200 ....B2
Bloomfield 5,214 ....A2
Bluewater 300 ....A3
Bosque 3,791 ....C4
Bosque Farms C4
Buckhorn 85 ....A5
Buena Vista 178 ....D3
Caballo 225 ....B6
Canjilon 380 ....C2
Canones 300 ....C2

Capitan 842 ....D5
Capulin 100 ....F2
Carlsbad▲ 24,952 ....E6
Carrizozo▲ 1,075 ....D5
Casa Blanca 560 ....B4
Cebolla 100 ....C2
Cedar Crest 600 ....C3
Cedar Hill 145 ....B2
Central 1,835 ....A6
Cerrillos 500 ....D3
Cerro 400 ....D2
Chacon 310 ....D2
Chama 1,048 ....C2
Chamberino 700 ....C6
Chamisal 272 ....D2
Chilili 80 ....C4
Chimayo 2,789 ....D3
Cimarron 774 ....E2
Clayton▲ 2,484 ....F2

Cleveland 450 ....D2
Cliff 600 ....A6
Cloudcroft 636 ....D6
Clovis 30,954 ....F4
Cochiti 434 ....C3
Columbus 641 ....B7
Conchas Dam 240 ....E3
Cordova 750 ....D2
Corona 215 ....D4
Corrales 5,453 ....C3
Costilla 400 ....D2
Coyote 125 ....C2
Crownpoint 2,108 ....A3
Crystal 200 ....A2
Cuba 760 ....B2
Cubero 300 ....B3
Cuervo 80 ....E3
Cundiyo 200 ....D3
Datil 150 ....B4

Deming▲ 10,970 ....B6
Derry 175 ....B6
Des Moines 168 ....F2
Dexter 898 ....E5
Dilia 100 ....D3
Dixon 800 ....D2
Dona Ana 1,202 ....C6
Dora 167 ....F5
Dulce 2,438 ....B2
Duran 90 ....D4
Eagle Nest 189 ....D2
Edgewood 3,324 ....C3
El Porvenir 150 ....D3
El Prado 200 ....D2
El Rito 475 ....C2
Elephant Butte 500 ....B5
Elida 201 ....F5
Embudo 400 ....D2
Encino 131 ....D4

New Mexico

SCALE
0 5 10   20   30   40   50   60 MI.
0 5 10 20 30 40 50 60 KM.

State Capitals ....⊛
County Seats ....●
Major Limited Access Hwys. ——

Scale 1:2,910,000
© Copyright HAMMOND INCORPORATED, Maplewood, N.J.

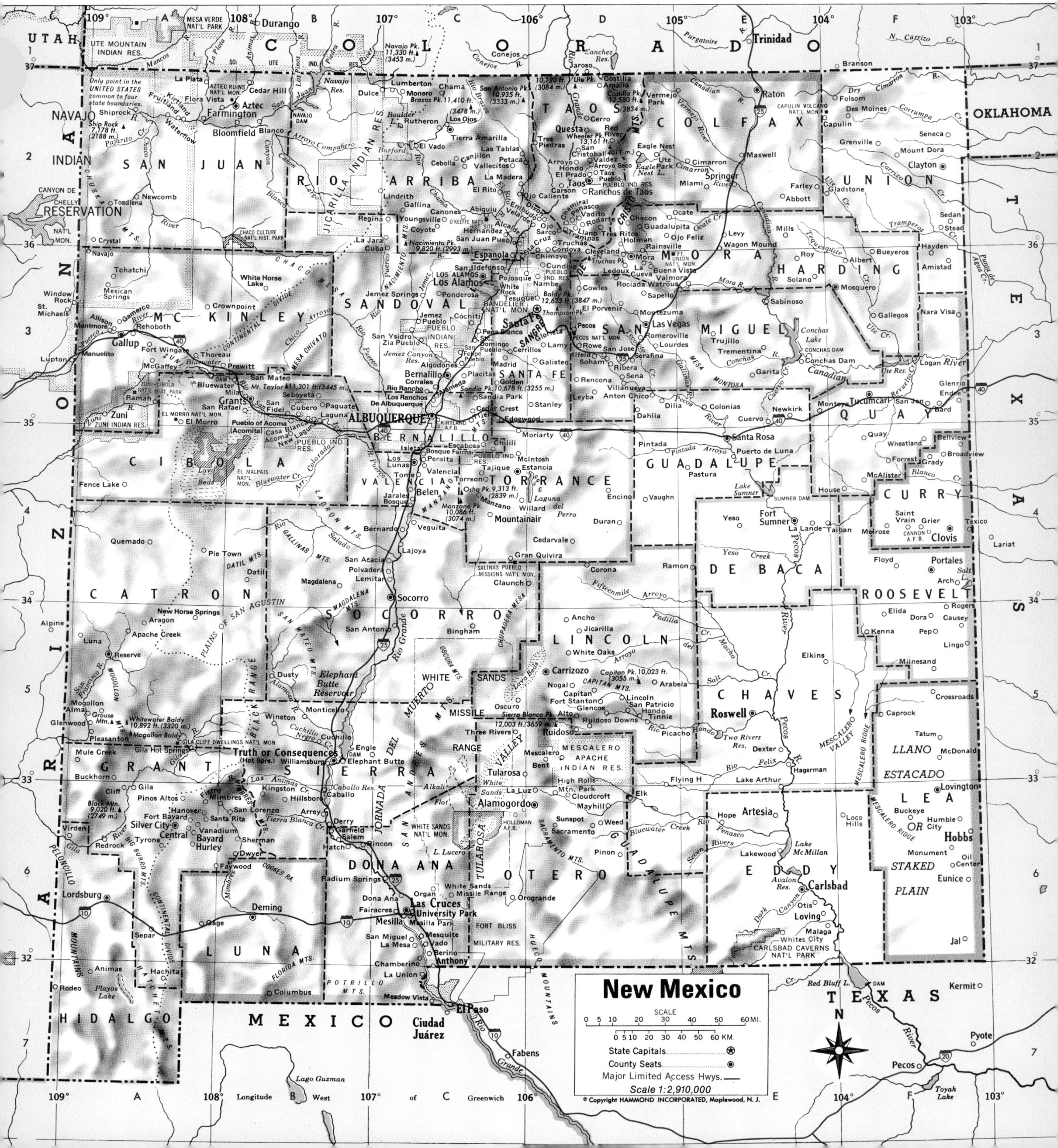

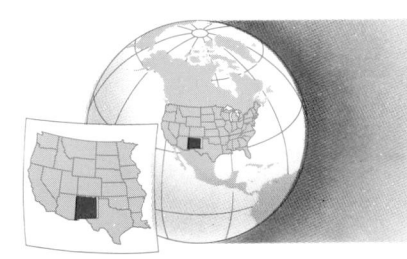

AREA 121,593 sq. mi. (314,926 sq. km.)
POPULATION 1,521,779
CAPITAL Santa Fe
LARGEST CITY Albuquerque
HIGHEST POINT Wheeler Pk. 13,161 ft. (4011 m.)
SETTLED IN 1605
ADMITTED TO UNION January 6, 1912
POPULAR NAME Land of Enchantment
STATE FLOWER Yucca
STATE BIRD Road Runner

Espanola 8,389 ...C3	Lordsburg▲ 2,951 ...A6	
Estancia▲ 792 ...D4	Los Alamos▲ 11,455 ...C3	
Eunice 2,676 ...F6	Los Lunas▲ 6,013 ...C4	
Fairacres 700 ...C6	Los Ojos ...C2	
Farmington 33,997 ...A2	Los Ranchos de Albuquerque	
Faywood 100 ...B6	3,955 ...C3	
Fence Lake 150 ...A4	Loving 1,243 ...E6	
Fierro 200 ...A6	Lovington▲ 9,322 ...F6	
Flora Vista 1,021 ...A2	Lumberton 175 ...C2	
Floyd 117 ...F4	Luna 200 ...A5	
Folsom 71 ...F2	Magdalena 861 ...B4	
Fort Bayard 400 ...A6	Malaga 300 ...E6	
Fort Stanton 50 ...D5	Manuelito 200 ...A3	
Fort Sumner▲ 1,269 ...E4	Manzano 65 ...C4	
Fort Wingate 800 ...A3	Maxwell 247 ...E2	
Fruitland 800 ...A2	Mayhill 300 ...D6	
Galisteo 125 ...D3	McAlister 320 ...F4	
Gallina 420 ...C2	McDonald 65 ...F5	
Gallup▲ 19,154 ...A3	McIntosh 325 ...D4	
Gamerco 800 ...A3	Meadow Vista 3,377 ...C7	

Red River 387 ...D2
Regina 80 ...B2
Rehoboth 200 ...A3
Reserve▲ 319 ...A5
Ribera 84 ...D3
Rincon 300 ...C6
Rio Rancho 32,505 ...C3
Rociada 140 ...D3
Rodarte 650 ...D2
Rodeo 200 ...A7
Roswell▲ 44,654 ...E5
Rowe 290 ...D3
Roy 362 ...E3
Ruidoso 4,600 ...D5
Ruidoso Downs 920 ...D5
Rutheron 95 ...C2
Salem 400 ...B6
San Acacia 286 ...B4
San Antonio 359 ...B5
San Cristobal 350 ...D2
San Felipe Pueblo 1,557 ...C3
San Fidel 150 ...B3
San Ildefonso 447 ...C3
San Jon 277 ...F3
San Jose 150 ...D3
San Juan Pueblo 4,107 ...C2
San Lorenzo 200 ...B6
San Mateo 200 ...B3
San Miguel 400 ...C6
San Patricio 300 ...D5
San Rafael 300 ...A3
San Ysidro 233 ...C3
Sandia Park 450 ...C3
Santa Cruz 2,504 ...D2
Santa Fe (cap.)▲ 55,859 ...C3
Santa Rita 600 ...B6
Santa Rosa▲ 2,263 ...E4
Santo Domingo Pueblo 2,866 ...C3
Sapello 600 ...D3
Seboyeta 125 ...B3
Sedan 60 ...F2
Sena 530 ...D3
Serafina 225 ...D3
Sherman 100 ...B6
Shiprock 7,687 ...A2
Silver City▲ 10,683 ...A6
Socorro▲ 8,159 ...C4
Soham 104 ...D3
Solano 114 ...E3
Springer 1,262 ...E2
Sunspot 78 ...D6
Taiban 120 ...F4
Tajique 145 ...C4
Taos Pueblo 1,187 ...D2
Taos▲ 4,065 ...D2

Tatum 768 ...F5
Tesuque 1,490 ...C3
Texico 966 ...F4
Thoreau 1,099 ...A3
Tierra Amarilla▲ 850 ...C2
Tijeras 340 ...C3
Tinnie 100 ...D5
Toadlena 200 ...A2
Tohatchi 661 ...A3
Tome 500 ...C4
Torreon 200 ...C4
Trampas 76 ...D2
Trementina 80 ...E3
Tres Piedras 200 ...D2
Truchas 275 ...D2
Truth or Consequences▲
  6,221 ...B5
Tucumcari▲ 6,831 ...F3
Tularosa 2,615 ...C5
Tyrone 100 ...A6
Ute Park 67 ...D2
Vadito 283 ...D2
Vado 325 ...C6
Valencia 150 ...C4
Vallecitos 450 ...C2
Vanadium 150 ...A6
Vaughn 633 ...D4
Velarde 950 ...C2
Vermejo Park 85 ...D2
Villanueva 500 ...D3
Virden 108 ...A6
Wagon Mound 319 ...E2
Waterflow 475 ...A2
Watrous 175 ...D3
White Horse Lake ...B3
White Rock 6,192 ...C3
White Sands Missile Range
  2,616 ...C6
Willard 183 ...D4
Williamsburg 456 ...B5
Yeso 200 ...E4
Youngsville 125 ...C2
Zia Pueblo 637 ...C3
Zuni 5,551 ...A3

OTHER FEATURES

Abiquiu (res.) ...C2
Alamosa (riv.) ...B5
Animas (riv.) ...B1
Avalon (res.) ...E6
Aztec Ruins Nat'l Mon. ...A2

Baldy (peak) ...D3
Bandelier Nat'l Mon. ...C3
Big Burro (mts.) ...A6
Black (mt.) ...A6
Black (range) ...B5
Blanco (creek) ...F4
Bluewater (creek) ...B4
Bluewater (creek) ...D6
Bluewater (lake) ...A3
Boulder (lake) ...C2
Brazos (peak) ...C2
Burford (lake) ...D2
Caballo (res.) ...B6
Canadian (riv.) ...F3
Cannon A.F.B. 3,312 ...F4
Canyon Blanco (creek) ...B2
Capitan (mts.) ...D5
Capitan (peak) ...D5
Capulin Volcano Nat'l Mon. ...E2
Carlsbad Caverns Nat'l Park ...F2
Carrizo (creek) ...F2
Chaco (creek) ...B3
Chaco (riv.) ...A2
Chaco Culture Nat'l Hist. Park ...B2
Chico Arroyo (creek) ...B3
Chivato (mesa) ...B3
Chupadera (mesa) ...C5
Chuska (mts.) ...A2
Cimarron (riv.) ...E2
Colorado, Arroyo (riv.) ...B4
Compañero, Arroyo (creek) ...B2
Conchas (lake) ...E3
Conchas (riv.) ...E3
Cookes (range) ...B6
Corrumpa (creek) ...F2
Costilla (peak) ...D2
Cuchillo Negro (creek) ...B5
Cuervo (creek) ...E3
Dark Canyon (creek) ...E6
Datil (mts.) ...B4
Dry Cimarron (riv.) ...F2
Eagle Nest (lake) ...D2
Elephant Butte (res.) ...B5
El Morro Nat'l Mon. ...A3
El Rito (creek) ...C2
Fifteenmile Arroyo (creek) ...D4
Florida (mts.) ...B7
Fort Bliss Mil. Res. ...C6
Fort Union Nat'l Mon. ...E3
Gallinas (mts.) ...B4
Gallinas (riv.) ...E3
Gila (riv.) ...A6
Gila Cliff Dwellings Nat'l Mon. ...A5
Grouse (riv.) ...A5
Guadalupe (mts.) ...D6

Hatchet (mts.) ...A7
Holloman A.F.B. 5,891 ...C6
Hueco (mts.) ...D6
Jemez (riv.) ...C3
Jemez Canyon (res.) ...C3
Jicarilla Ind. Res. ...B2
Jornada del Muerto (valley) ...C5
Kirtland A.F.B. ...C3
Ladron (mts.) ...B4
La Plata (riv.) ...A1
Lake Avalon (res.) ...E6
Largo, Cañon (creek) ...B2
Las Animas (creek) ...B5
Llano Estacado
  (Staked) (plain) ...F5
Lucero (lake) ...C6
Macho, Arroyo del (creek) ...D5
Magdalena (mts.) ...B4
Manzano (mts.) ...C4
Manzano (peak) ...C4
McMillan (lake) ...E6
Mescalero (ridge) ...F6
Mescalero (valley) ...F5
Mescalero Apache Ind. Res. ...C5
Mimbres (mts.) ...B6
Mimbres (riv.) ...B6
Mogollon (mts.) ...A5
Mogollon Baldy (peak) ...A5
Montosa (mesa) ...E3
Mora (riv.) ...E3
Nacimiento (mts.) ...C3
Nacimiento (peak) ...C2
Navajo (res.) ...B2
Navajo Ind. Res. ...A2
North Truchas (peak) ...D3
Ocate (creek) ...E2
O'Keeffe Nat'l Hist. Site ...C3
Oscura (mts.) ...C5
Osha (peak) ...C4
Padilla (creek) ...D5
Pajarito (creek) ...A2
Pecos (riv.) ...E5
Pecos Nat'l Mon. ...D3
Peloncillo (mts.) ...A6
Perro (lake) ...D4
Pinos, Rio de los (riv.) ...B2
Pintada Arroyo (creek) ...E4
Playas (lake) ...A7
Potrillo (mts.) ...B7
Pueblo Ind. Res. ...B4
Pueblo Ind. Res. ...C4
Pueblo Ind. Res. ...C3
Pueblo Ind. Res. ...D3
Puerco (riv.) ...A3
Red Bluff (lake) ...E7

Revuelto (creek) ...F3
Rio Brazos (riv.) ...C2
Rio Chama (riv.) ...C2
Rio Felix (riv.) ...E5
Rio Grande (riv.) ...C5
Rio Hondo (riv.) ...E5
Rio Penasco (riv.) ...E6
Rio Puerco (riv.) ...C4
Rio Salado (riv.) ...B4
Rocky (mts.) ...C1
Sacramento (mts.) ...D6
Salinas Pueblo Missions
  Nat'l Mon. ...C4
Salt (creek) ...E5
Salt (lake) ...F4
San Agustin (plains) ...B5
San Andres (mts.) ...C6
San Antonio (peak) ...C2
Sandia (peak) ...C3
San Francisco (riv.) ...A5
San Jose (riv.) ...B3
San Juan (riv.) ...B2
San Mateo (mts.) ...B5
Seven Rivers (creek) ...E6
Ship Rock (peak) ...A2
Sierra Blanca (peak) ...C5
Staked (Llano Estacado)
  (plain) ...F5
Sumner (lake) ...E4
Taylor (mt.) ...B3
Tecolote (creek) ...D3
Tequesquite (creek) ...E2
Thompson (peak) ...D3
Tierra Blanca (creek) ...B6
Tramperos (creek) ...F2
Tularosa (valley) ...C6
Ute (creek) ...F3
Ute (peak) ...D2
Ute (res.) ...F3
Ute Mountain Ind. Res. ...A1
Vermejo (riv.) ...E2
Wheeler (peak) ...D2
White Sands (des.) ...C5
White Sands Missile Range ...C5
White Sands Nat'l Mon. ...C6
Whitewater Baldy (mt.) ...A5
Wingate Army Depot ...A3
Yeso (creek) ...E4
Zuni (mts.) ...A3
Zuni (riv.) ...A3
Zuni-Cibola Nat'l Hist. Park ...A3
Zuni Ind. Res. ...A3

▲County seat

(Full index, columns 1–2:)

Espanola 8,389 ...C3
Estancia▲ 792 ...D4
Eunice 2,676 ...F6
Fairacres 700 ...C6
Farmington 33,997 ...A2
Faywood 100 ...B6
Fence Lake 150 ...A4
Fierro 200 ...A6
Flora Vista 1,021 ...A2
Floyd 117 ...F4
Folsom 71 ...F2
Fort Bayard 400 ...A6
Fort Stanton 50 ...D5
Fort Sumner▲ 1,269 ...E4
Fort Wingate 800 ...A3
Fruitland 800 ...A2
Galisteo 125 ...D3
Gallina 420 ...C2
Gallup▲ 19,154 ...A3
Gamerco 800 ...A3
Garfield 600 ...B6
Garita 66 ...E3
Gila 350 ...A6
Glencoe 125 ...D5
Glenwood 220 ...A5
Glorieta 300 ...D3
Golden 10C ...C3
Grady 110 ...F4
Grants▲ 8,626 ...B3
Guadalupita 300 ...D2
Hachita 75 ...A7
Hagerman 961 ...E5
Hanover 400 ...A6
Hatch 1,136 ...B6
Hernandez 500 ...C2
High Rolls-Mountain
  Park 555 ...D5
Hillsboro 175 ...B6
Hobbs 29,115 ...F6
Holman 400 ...D2
Hondo 425 ...D5
Hope 101 ...E6
Hot Springs▲ (Truth or
  Consequences) 6,221 ...B5
House 85 ...F4
Humble City 65 ...F6
Hurley 1,534 ...A6
Ilfeld 68 ...D3
Isleta 1,703 ...C4
Jal 2,156 ...F6
Jarales 700 ...C4
Jemez Pueblo 1,301 ...C3
Jemez Springs 413 ...C3
Kenna 100 ...F5
Kirtland 3,552 ...A2
La Cueva 200 ...D3
La Jara 210 ...B2
La Luz 1,625 ...C6
La Madera 200 ...C2
La Mesa 900 ...C6
La Plata 150 ...A2
La Union 200 ...C7
Laguna 434 ...B3
Lajoya 97 ...C4
Lake Arthur 336 ...E5
Lamy 66 ...D3
Las Cruces▲ 62,126 ...C6
Las Vegas▲ 14,753 ...D3
Ledoux 300 ...D3
Lemitar 800 ...B4
Lincoln 100 ...D5
Lindrith 349 ...C2
Llano 325 ...D2
Loco Hills 375 ...F6
Logan 870 ...F3

Loving 1,243 ...E6
Lovington▲ 9,322 ...F6
Lumberton 175 ...C2
Luna 200 ...A5
Magdalena 861 ...B4
Malaga 300 ...E6
Manuelito 200 ...A3
Manzano 65 ...C4
Maxwell 247 ...E2
Mayhill 300 ...D6
McAlister 320 ...F4
McDonald 65 ...F5
McIntosh 325 ...D4
Meadow Vista 3,377 ...C7
Melrose 662 ...F4
Mentmore 315 ...A3
Mescalero 1,159 ...D5
Mesilla 1,975 ...C6
Mesilla Park ...C6
Mesquite 500 ...C6
Mexican Springs 242 ...A3
Miami 112 ...E2
Milan 1,911 ...B3
Mimbres 300 ...B6
Montezuma 250 ...D3
Monticello 125 ...B5
Monument 300 ...F6
Mora▲ ...D3
Moriarty 1,399 ...D4
Mosquero▲ 164 ...F3
Mountainair 926 ...C4
Mule Creek 62 ...A5
Nambe 1,246 ...D3
Nara Visa 250 ...F3
Navajo 1,985 ...A3
New Laguna 250 ...B4
Newcomb 388 ...A2
Newkirk 54 ...E3
Nogal 150 ...D5
Ocate 75 ...E2
Oil Center 236 ...F6
Ojo Caliente 600 ...D2
Ojo Feliz 133 ...E2
Ojo Sarco 380 ...D2
Organ 300 ...C6
Orogrande 80 ...D6
Otis 200 ...E6
Paguate 492 ...B3
Pecos 1,012 ...D3
Pena Blanca 300 ...C3
Penasco 648 ...D2
Peralta 3,182 ...C4
Petaca 84 ...C2
Picacho 100 ...D5
Pie Town 90 ...A4
Pinos Altos 250 ...A6
Placitas 1,611 ...C3
Pleasanton 70 ...A5
Pojoaque 1,037 ...C3
Ponderosa 300 ...C3
Portales▲ 10,690 ...F4
Prewitt 300 ...B3
Puerto de Luna 175 ...E4
Questa 1,707 ...D2
Radium Springs 150 ...B6
Rainsville 350 ...D2
Ramah 574 ...A3
Ranchos de Taos 1,779 ...D2
Raton▲ 7,372 ...E2

Topography

0   50   100 MI.
0   50   100 KM.

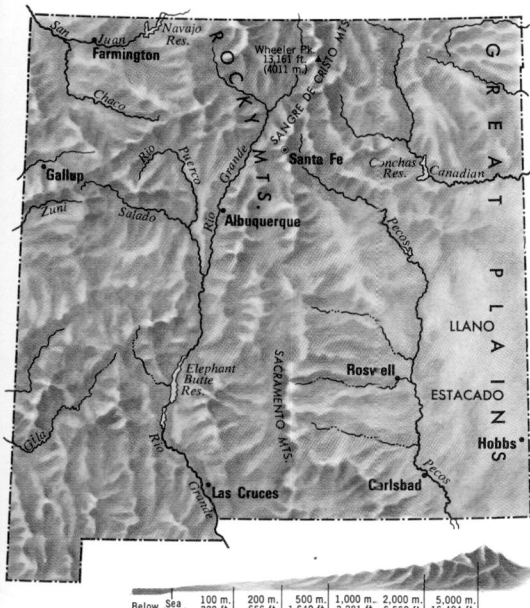

Below Sea Level | 100 m. 328 ft. | 200 m. 656 ft. | 500 m. 1,640 ft. | 1,000 m. 3,281 ft. | 2,000 m. 6,562 ft. | 5,000 m. 16,404 ft.

Agriculture, Industry and Resources

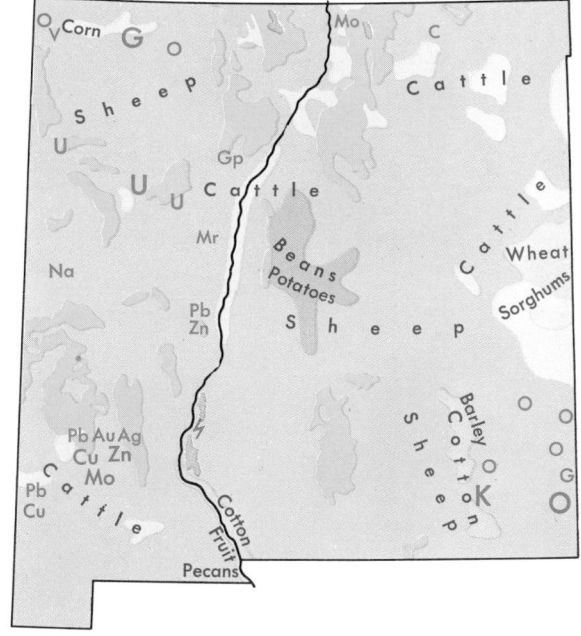

DOMINANT LAND USE

- Wheat, Grain Sorghums, Range Livestock
- General Farming, Livestock, Special Crops
- General Farming, Livestock, Cash Grain
- Dry Beans, General Farming
- Cotton, Forest Products
- Range Livestock
- Forests
- Nonagricultural Land

MAJOR MINERAL OCCURRENCES

Ag Silver	Gp Gypsum		
Au Gold	K Potash		
C Coal	Mo Molybdenum	U Uranium	
Cu Copper	Mr Marble	O Petroleum	V Vanadium	⚡ Water Power
G Natural Gas	Na Salt	Pb Lead	Zn Zinc

New York

SCALE

0 5 10   20   30   40 MI.

0 5 10   20   30   40 KM.

State Capitals................⊛
County Seats................⊙
Canals..........................
Major Limited Access Hwys. ——

Scale 1:1,920,000

COUNTIES

Albany 292,594	M5
Allegany 50,470	D6
Bronx 1,203,789	N9
Broome 212,160	J6
Cattaraugus 84,234	C6
Cayuga 82,313	G4
Chautauqua 141,895	B6
Chemung 95,195	G6
Chenango 51,768	J6
Clinton 85,969	N1
Columbia 62,982	N6
Cortland 48,963	H5
Delaware 47,225	K6
Dutchess 259,462	N7
Erie 968,532	C5
Essex 37,152	N2
Franklin 46,540	M1
Fulton 54,191	M4
Genesee 60,060	D4
Greene 44,739	M6
Hamilton 5,279	L3
Herkimer 65,797	L4
Jefferson 110,943	J2
Kings 2,300,664	N9
Lewis 26,796	K3
Livingston 62,372	E5
Madison 69,120	J5
Monroe 713,968	E4
Montgomery 51,981	M5
Nassau 1,287,348	N9
New York 1,487,536	M9
Niagara 220,756	C4
Oneida 250,836	J4
Onondaga 468,973	H5
Ontario 95,101	F5
Orange 307,647	M8

Orleans 41,846	D4
Oswego 121,771	H4
Otsego 60,517	K5
Putnam 83,941	N8
Queens 1,951,598	N9
Rensselaer 154,429	O5
Richmond 378,977	M9
Rockland 265,475	M8
Saint Lawrence 114,254	K2
Saratoga 181,276	N4
Schenectady 149,285	M5
Schoharie 31,859	M5
Schuyler 18,662	G6
Seneca 33,683	G5
Steuben 99,088	F6
Suffolk 1,321,864	P9
Sullivan 69,277	L7
Tioga 52,337	H6
Tompkins 94,097	H6
Ulster 165,304	M7
Warren 59,209	N3
Washington 59,330	O4
Wayne 89,123	G4
Westchester 874,866	N8
Wyoming 42,507	D5
Yates 22,810	F5

CITIES and TOWNS

Adams 1,753	J3
Adams Center 1,675	H3
Addison 1,842	F6
Afton 838	J6
Akron 2,906	C4
Albany (cap.)▲ 101,082	N5
Albion▲ 5,863	D4
Alden 2,457	C5
Alexandria Bay 1,194	J2

Alfred 4,559	E6
Allegany 1,980	C6
Altamont 1,519	M5
Altona 1,003	N1
Amagansett 2,188	R9
Amenia 1,058	N7
Amityville 9,286	O9
Amsterdam 20,714	M5
Andover 1,125	E6
Angelica 963	E6
Angola 2,231	C5
Angola on the Lake 1,719	C5
Antwerp 739	J2
Apalachin 1,208	H6
Arcade 2,081	D5
Ardsley 4,272	O6
Arkport 770	E6
Arlington 11,948	N7
Athens 1,708	N6
Atlantic Beach 1,933	P7
Attica 2,630	D5
Auburn▲ 31,258	G5
Aurora 687	G5
Averill Park 1,656	O5
Avoca 1,033	F6
Avon 2,995	E5
Babylon 12,249	O9
Bainbridge 1,550	J6
Baldwin 22,719	R7
Baldwinsville 6,591	H4
Ballston Spa▲ 4,937	N5
Balmville 2,963	M7
Bardonia 4,487	K8
Batavia▲ 16,310	D4
Bath▲ 5,801	F6
Bay Shore 21,279	O9
Bayport 7,702	O9
Bayville 7,193	R6

Beacon 13,243	N7
Belle Terre 839	O9
Bellerose 1,101	P7
Bellmore 16,438	R7
Bellport 2,572	P9
Belmont▲ 1,006	E6
Bergen 1,103	E4
Bethpage 15,761	R7
Big Flats 2,658	G6
Binghamton▲ 53,008	J6
Black River 1,349	J3
Blasdell 2,900	C5
Blauvelt 4,838	K8
Bloomingdale 608	M2
Bolivar 1,261	D6
Boonville 2,220	K4
Boysen Bay 1,160	J4
Brasher Falls-Winthrop 1,271	L1
Brentwood 45,218	O9
Brewerton 2,954	H4
Brewster 1,856	N8
Bridgehampton 1,997	R9
Bridgeport 2,107	J4
Brinckerhoff 2,756	N7
Broadalbin 1,397	M4
Brockport 8,749	D4
Brocton 1,387	B6
Bronx (borough)▲	N9
Bronxville 6,028	O7
Brooklyn (borough)▲	N9
Brookville 3,716	R6
Brownville 1,138	H3
Buchanan 1,970	N8
Buffalo▲ 328,123	B5
Cairo 1,273	M6
Caledonia 2,262	E5
Cambridge 1,906	O4

Camden 2,552	J4
Camillus 1,150	H4
Canajoharie 2,278	L5
Canandaigua▲ 10,725	F5
Canaseraga 700	E6
Canastota 4,673	J4
Candor 869	H6
Canisteo 2,421	E6
Canton▲ 6,379	K1
Cape Vincent 683	H2
Carmel▲ 27,948	N8
Carthage 4,344	J3
Cassadaga 768	B6
Castile 1,078	D5
Castleton-on-Hudson 1,491	N5
Catskill▲ 4,690	N6
Cattaraugus 1,100	C6
Cayuga Heights 3,457	H6
Cazenovia 3,007	J5
Cedarhurst 5,716	P7
Celoron 1,232	B6
Center Moriches 5,987	P9
Centereach 26,720	O9
Central Islip 26,028	O9
Central Square 1,671	H4
Central Valley 1,929	M8
Champlain 1,273	N1
Champlain Park 1,051	O1
Chateaugay 845	M1
Chatham 1,920	N6
Chautauqua 300	A6
Cheektowaga 84,387	C5
Chester 3,270	M8
Chittenango 4,734	J4
Churchville 1,731	E4
Clarence▲ 18,146	C5
Claverack 1,217	N6
Clayton 2,160	H2

Cleveland 784	J4
Clifton Park • 23,989	N5
Clifton Springs 2,175	F5
Clinton 2,238	K4
Clintondale 1,394	M7
Clyde 2,409	G4
Cobleskill 5,268	L5
Cohocton 859	F5
Cohoes 16,825	N5
Cold Spring 1,998	N8
Cold Spring Harbor 4,789	R6
Colonie 8,019	N5
Commack 36,124	O9
Constantia 1,140	J4
Cooperstown▲ 2,180	L5
Copenhagen 876	J3
Copiague 20,769	O9
Corfu 755	D5
Corinth 2,760	N4
Corning 11,938	F6
Cornwall On Hudson 3,093	M8
Cortland▲ 19,801	H5
Coxsackie 2,789	N6
Croghan 664	K3
Croton-on-Hudson 7,018	N8
Cuba 1,690	D6
Cutchogue-New Suffolk 2,788	P8
Dannemora 4,005	N1
Dansville 5,002	E5
DeWitt 8,244	H4
Deer Park 28,840	O9
Delavan 1,214	D6
Delhi▲ 3,064	L6
Delmar 8,360	N5
Depew 17,673	C5
Deposit 1,936	K6
Dexter 1,030	H2

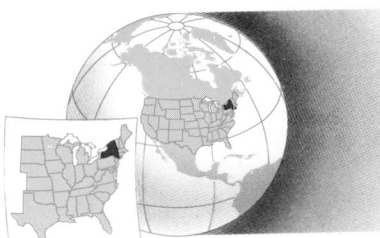

AREA   49,108 sq. mi. (127,190 sq. km.)
POPULATION   18,044,505
CAPITAL   Albany
LARGEST CITY   New York
HIGHEST POINT   Mt. Marcy 5,344 ft.
  (1629 m.)
SETTLED IN   1614
ADMITTED TO UNION   July 26, 1788
POPULAR NAME   Empire State
STATE FLOWER   Rose
STATE BIRD   Bluebird

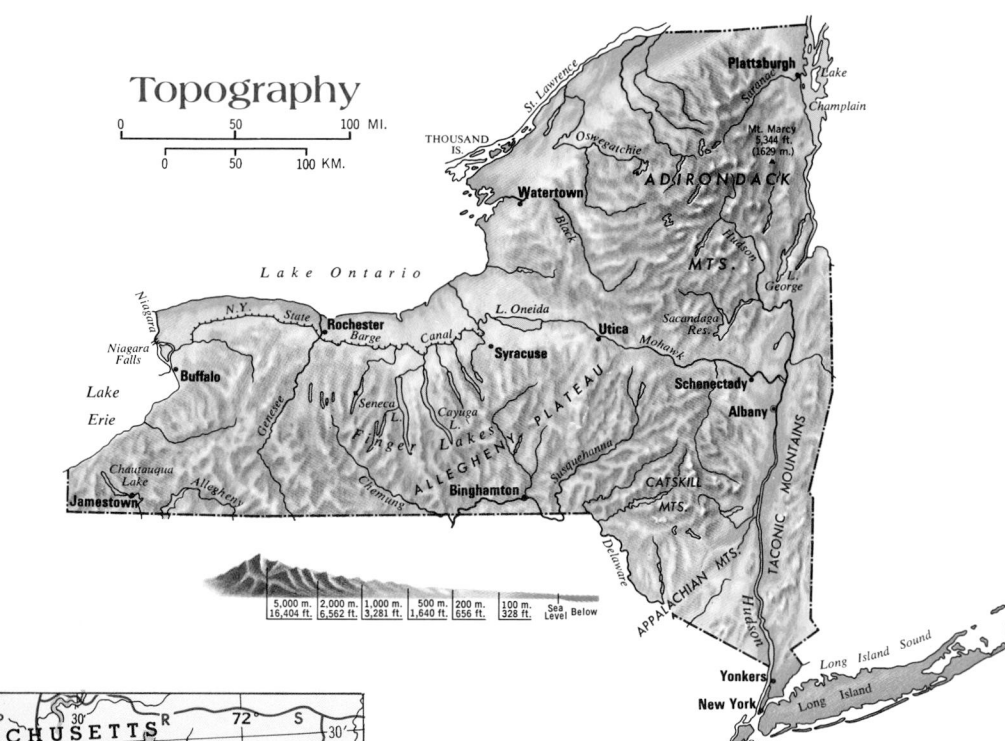

Topography

© Copyright HAMMOND INCORPORATED, Maplewood, N.J.

Dix Hills 25,849	O9	Gasport 1,336	C4
Dobbs Ferry 9,940	O6	Geneseo▲ 7,187	E5
Dolgeville 2,452	L4	Geneva 14,143	G5
Dover Plains 1,847	O7	Glasco 1,538	M6
Dryden 1,908	H6	Glen Cove 24,149	R6
Dundee 1,588	F5	Glens Falls 15,023	N4
Dunkirk 13,989	B5	Gloversville 16,656	M4
Earlville 883	J5	Golden's Bridge 1,589	N8
East Aurora 6,647	C5	Goshen▲ 5,255	M8
East Greenbush 3,784	N5	Gouverneur 4,604	K2
East Hampton 1,402	R9	Gowanda 2,901	B6
East Hills 6,746	R7	Granville 2,646	O4
East Meadow 36,909	R7	Great Neck 8,745	P6
East Moriches 4,021	O9	Greece 15,632	E4
East Northport 20,411	O9	Green Island 2,490	N5
East Rochester 6,932	F4	Greene 1,812	J6
East Rockaway 10,152	R7	Greenport 2,070	P8
East Syracuse 3,343	H4	Greenwich 1,961	O4
Eastchester 18,537	P6	Greenwood Lake 3,208	M8
Eden 3,088	C5	Groton 2,398	H5
Elba 703	D4	Hadley-Lake Luzerne 1,988	N4
Elbridge 1,099	G5	Hagaman 1,377	M5
Elizabethtown▲ 659	N2	Hamburg 10,442	C5
Ellenville 4,243	M7	Hamilton 3,790	J5
Elma 2,354	C5	Hammondsport 929	F6
Elmira Heights 4,359	G6	Hampton Bays 7,893	R9
Elmira▲ 33,724	G6	Hancock 1,330	K7
Elmont 28,612	P7	Hannibal 680	G4
Elmsford 3,938	O6	Harriman 2,288	M8
Elwood 10,916	O9	Harrison 23,308	P6
Endicott 13,531	H6	Harrisville 703	K2
Endwell 12,602	H6	Hartsdale 9,587	P6
Evans Mills 661	J2	Hastings On Hudson 8,000	O6
Fair Haven 895	G4	Hauppauge 19,750	O9
Fairport 5,943	F4	Haverstraw 9,438	M8
Fairview 4,811	N7	Hawthorne 4,764	O6
Falconer 2,653	B6	Hempstead 49,453	R7
Farmingdale 8,022	R7	Herkimer▲ 7,945	L4
Fayetteville 4,248	J4	Heuvelton 771	K1
Fernwood 3,640	N4	Hewlett 6,620	R7
Fishkill 1,957	N7	Hewlett Harbor 1,193	P7
Flanders-Riverside 5,400	P9	Hicksville 40,174	R7
Floral Park 15,947	P7	Highland 4,492	M7
Florida 2,497	M8	Highland Falls 3,937	M8
Fonda▲ 1,007	M5	Hillburn 892	M8
Forestville 738	B6	Hillcrest 6,447	K8
Fort Covington• 1,804	M1	Hilton 5,216	E4
Fort Edward 3,561	O4	Holcomb 790	F5
Fort Johnson 615	M5	Holland 1,288	C5
Fort Plain 2,416	L5	Holley 1,890	D4
Frankfort 2,693	K4	Homer 3,476	H5
Franklin Square 28,205	R7	Honeoye Falls 2,340	F5
Franklinville 1,739	D6	Hoosick Falls 3,490	O5
Fredonia 10,436	B6	Hopewell Junction 1,786	N7
Freeport 39,894	R7	Hornell 9,877	E6
Frewsburg 1,817	B6	Horseheads 6,802	G6
Friendship 1,423	D6	Houghton 1,740	D6
Fulton 12,929	H4	Hudson Falls▲ 7,651	O4
Fultonville 748	M5	Hudson▲ 8,034	N6
Garden City 21,686	R7	Huntington 18,243	R6

(continued on following page)

Huntington Station 28,247 .....R6
Hurley 4,644 .....M7
Hyde Park 2,550 .....N6
Ilion 8,888 .....K5
Interlaken 680 .....G5
Inwood 7,767 .....P7
Irondequoit 52,322 .....E4
Irvington 6,348 .....O6
Island Park 4,860 .....R7
Islip 18,924 .....O9
Ithaca▲ 29,541 .....G6
Jamestown 34,681 .....B6
Jericho 13,141 .....R6
Johnson City 16,890 .....J6
Johnstown▲ 9,058 .....M4
Jordan 1,325 .....H4
Keeseville 1,854 .....O2
Kenmore 17,180 .....B5
Kerhonkson 1,629 .....M7
Keuka Park 1,153 .....F5
Kinderhook 1,293 .....N6
Kings Park 17,773 .....O9
Kings Point 4,843 .....P6
Kingston▲ 23,095 .....M7
Lackawanna 20,585 .....B5
Lake Carmel 8,489 .....N8
Lake Erie Beach 4,509 .....B5
Lake George▲ 933 .....N4
Lake Katrine 1,998 .....M7
Lake Luzerne-Hadley 2,042 ...N4
Lake Placid 2,485 .....N2
Lake Pleasant▲ 700 .....M4
Lake Success 2,484 .....P7
Lakewood 3,564 .....B6
Lancaster 11,940 .....C5
Lansing 3,281 .....H5
Larchmont 6,181 .....P7
Latham 10,131 .....N5
Lattingtown 1,859 .....R6
Lawrence 6,513 .....P7
Le Roy 4,974 .....E5
Levittown 53,286 .....R7
Lewiston 3,048 .....B4
Liberty 4,128 .....L7
Lima 2,165 .....E5
Lindenhurst 26,879 .....O9
Little Falls 5,829 .....L4
Little Valley▲ 1,188 .....C6
Liverpool 2,624 .....H4
Livingston Manor 1,482 .....L7
Livonia 1,434 .....E5
Lloyd Harbor 3,343 .....R6
Lockport▲ 24,426 .....C4
Locust Grove 9,670 .....R6
Long Beach 33,510 .....R7
Lowville▲ 3,632 .....J3
Lynbrook 19,208 .....P7
Lyndonville 953 .....D4
Lyons Falls 698 .....K3
Lyons▲ 4,280 .....F4
Macedon 1,400 .....F4
Machias 1,191 .....D6
Mahopac 7,755 .....N8
Malone▲ 6,777 .....M1
Malverne 9,054 .....R7
Mamaroneck 17,325 .....P7
Manchester 1,598 .....F5
Manhasset 7,718 .....P7
Manhattan (borough) M9
Manlius 4,764 .....J5
Manorville 6,198 .....P9
Marathon 1,107 .....J6
Marcellus 1,840 .....H5
Margaretville 639 .....L6
Marion 1,080 .....F4
Marlboro 2,200 .....M7
Massapequa 22,018 .....R7
Massapequa Park 18,044 .....R7
Massena 11,719 .....L1
Mastic Beach 10,293 .....P9
Mattituck 3,902 .....P9
Maybrook 2,802 .....M8
Mayfield 817 .....M4
Mayville▲ 1,636 .....A6
McGraw 1,074 .....H5
Mechanicville 5,249 .....N5
Medina 6,686 .....D4
Melrose Park 2,091 .....G5
Melville 12,586 .....S7
Menands 4,333 .....N5
Merrick 23,042 .....R7
Mexico 1,555 .....H4
Middle Hope 3,229 .....M7
Middleburgh 1,436 .....M5
Middleport 1,876 .....C4
Middletown 24,160 .....L8
Middleville 624 .....K4
Mill Neck 977 .....R6
Millbrook 1,339 .....N7
Millerton 884 .....O7
Milton 1,140 .....N4
Milton 2,063 .....N4
Mineola▲ 18,994 .....R7
Minetto 1,252 .....H4
Mineville-Witherbee 1,740 ....O2
Minoa 3,745 .....H4
Mohawk 2,986 .....L4
Monroe 6,672 .....M8
Monsey 13,986 .....S8
Montauk 3,001 .....S9
Montgomery 2,696 .....M7
Monticello▲ 6,597 .....L7
Montour Falls 1,845 .....G6
Moravia 1,559 .....H5
Morris 642 .....K5
Morrisonville 1,742 .....N1
Morrisville 2,732 .....J5
Mount Kisco 9,108 .....N8
Mount Morris 3,102 .....E5
Mount Morris 3,102 .....E5
Mount Vernon 67,153 .....O7
Nanuet 14,065 .....K8
Napanoch 1,068 .....M7
Naples 1,237 .....F5
Nassau 1,254 .....N5
New Berlin 1,220 .....K5
New City▲ 33,673 .....K8

New Hartford 2,111 .....K4
New Hyde Park 9,728 .....M7
New Paltz 5,463 .....M7
New Rochelle 67,265 .....P7
New Square 2,605 .....K8
New Windsor 8,898 .....N8
New York Mills 3,534 .....K4
New York▲ 7,322,564 .....M9
Newark 9,849 .....G4
Newark Valley 1,082 .....H6
Newburgh 26,454 .....M7
Newfane 3,001 .....C4
Newport 676 .....K4
Niagara Falls 61,840 .....B4
Nichols 573 .....H6
Niskayuna 4,942 .....N5
Norfolk 1,412 .....K1
North Boston 2,581 .....C5
North Collins 1,335 .....C5
North Hornell 822 .....E6
North Syracuse 7,363 .....H4
North Tarrytown 8,152 .....O6
Northport 7,572 .....O9
Northville 1,180 .....M4
Norwich▲ 7,613 .....J5
Norwood 1,841 .....L1
Nunda 1,347 .....E5
Nyack 6,558 .....K8
Oakfield 1,818 .....D4
Oceanside 32,423 .....R7
Odessa 986 .....G6
Ogdensburg 13,521 .....K1
Olcott 1,432 .....C4
Old Forge 1,061 .....L3
Olean 16,946 .....D6
Oneida 10,850 .....J4
Oneonta 13,954 .....L6
Orangeburg 3,583 .....K8
Orchard Park 3,280 .....C5
Oriskany 1,450 .....K4
Oriskany Falls 795 .....J5
Ossining 22,582 .....N8
Oswego▲ 19,195 .....G4
Otego 1,068 .....K6
Otisville 1,078 .....L8
Ovid 660 .....G5
Owego▲ 4,442 .....H6
Oxford 1,738 .....J5
Oyster Bay 6,687 .....R6
Painted Post 1,950 .....F6
Palmyra 3,566 .....F4
Patchogue 11,060 .....P9
Pawling 1,974 .....N7
Pearl River 15,314 .....K8
Peconic 1,100 .....P8
Peekskill 19,536 .....N8
Pelham 6,413 .....O7
Pelham Manor 5,443 .....O7
Penn Yan▲ 5,248 .....F5
Perry 4,219 .....D5
Peru 1,565 .....N1
Phelps 1,978 .....F5
Philadelphia 1,478 .....J2
Philmont 1,623 .....N6
Phoenix 2,435 .....H4
Piermont 2,163 .....K8
Pine Bush 1,445 .....M7
Pine Plains 1,312 .....N7
Pine Valley 1,486 .....G6
Pittsford 1,488 .....E4
Plainview 26,207 .....R7
Plattsburgh▲ 21,255 .....O1
Pleasantville 6,592 .....N8
Port Byron 1,359 .....G4
Port Chester 24,728 .....P7
Port Dickinson 1,785 .....J6
Port Ewen 3,444 .....N7
Port Henry 1,263 .....O2
Port Jefferson 7,455 .....P9
Port Jervis 9,060 .....L8
Port Leyden 723 .....K3
Port Washington 15,387 .....R6
Portville 1,040 .....D6
Potsdam 10,251 .....K1
Poughkeepsie▲ 28,844 .....N7
Prattsburg • 1,657 .....F5
Pulaski 2,525 .....H3
Putnam Valley • 8,994 .....N8
Queens (borough) N9
Quogue 898 .....P9
Randolph 1,298 .....C6
Ransomville 1,542 .....C4
Ravena 3,547 .....N6
Red Hook 1,794 .....N7
Red Oaks Mill 4,906 .....N7
Rensselaer 8,255 .....N5
Rhinebeck 2,725 .....N7
Richfield Springs 1,565 .....K5
Richmond (borough) (Staten Island) M9
Richmondville 843 .....M5
Ripley 1,189 .....A6
Riverhead▲ 8,814 .....P9
Rochester▲ 231,636 .....E4
Rockville Centre 24,727 .....R7
Rome 44,350 .....J4
Ronkonkoma 20,391 .....O9
Roosevelt 15,030 .....R7
Rosendale 1,134 .....M7
Roslyn 1,965 .....R6
Rotterdam Junction 1,010 .....N5
Round Lake 765 .....N5
Rouses Point 2,377 .....O1
Rye 14,936 .....P6
Sackets Harbor 1,313 .....H3
Sag Harbor 2,134 .....R8
Saint James 12,703 .....O9
Saint Johnsville 1,825 .....L5
Salamanca 6,566 .....C6
Salem 958 .....O4
Sand Ridge 1,312 .....H4
Sands Point 2,477 .....P6
Sandy Creek 793 .....H3
Saranac Lake 5,377 .....M2
Saratoga Springs 25,001 .....N4
Saugerties 3,915 .....M6

Savannah • 1,905 .....G4
Savona 974 .....F6
Sayville 16,550 .....O9
Scarsdale 16,987 .....P6
Schaghticoke 794 .....N5
Schenectady▲ 65,566 .....M5
Schoharie▲ 1,045 .....M5
Schuylerville 1,364 .....N4
Scotia 7,359 .....M5
Scottsville 1,912 .....E4
Sea Cliff 5,054 .....R6
Seaford 15,597 .....R7
Seneca Falls 7,370 .....G5
Sherburne 1,531 .....K5
Sherman 694 .....A6
Sherrill 2,864 .....J4
Shortsville 1,485 .....F5
Sidney 4,720 .....K6
Silver Creek 2,927 .....B5
Silver Springs 852 .....E5
Sinclairville 708 .....B6
Skaneateles 2,724 .....H5
Sloan 3,830 .....C5
Sloatsburg 3,035 .....M8
Smithtown 25,638 .....O9
Sodus 1,904 .....G4
Sodus Point 1,190 .....G4
Solvay 6,717 .....H4
South Corning 1,025 .....F6
South Fallsburg 2,115 .....L7
South Glens Falls 3,506 .....N4
South Nyack 3,352 .....K8
Southampton 1,302 .....R9
Southold 5,192 .....P8
Southport 7,753 .....G6
Sparrow Bush 1,049 .....L8
Spencer 815 .....H6
Spencerport 3,606 .....E4
Spring Valley 21,802 .....K8
Springville 4,310 .....C5
Stamford 1,211 .....L6
Stannards 1,028 .....E6
Star Lake 1,092 .....K2
Staten Island (borough) M9
Stillwater 1,531 .....N5
Stony Brook 13,726 .....O9
Stony Point 10,587 .....N8
Stottville 1,369 .....N6
Suffern 11,055 .....J8
Sylvan Beach 1,119 .....J4
Syosset 18,967 .....R6
Syracuse▲ 163,860 .....H4
Tappan 6,867 .....K8
Tarrytown 10,739 .....O6
Theresa 889 .....J2
Thomaston 2,612 .....P7
Ticonderoga 2,770 .....N3
Tillson 1,688 .....M7
Tivoli 1,035 .....N6

Tonawanda 17,284 .....B4
Troy▲ 54,269 .....N5
Trumansburg 1,611 .....G5
Tuckahoe 6,302 .....O7
Tully 911 .....H5
Tupper Lake 4,087 .....M2
Tuxedo Park 706 .....M8
Unadilla 1,265 .....K6
Union Springs 1,142 .....G5
Uniondale 20,328 .....R7
Utica▲ 68,637 .....K4
Valatie 1,487 .....N6
Valley Cottage 9,007 .....K8
Valley Stream 33,946 .....P7
Vestal • 27,238 .....H6
Victor 2,308 .....F5
Victory Mills 571 .....N4
Viola 4,504 .....J8
Voorheesville 3,225 .....M5
Waddington 944 .....K1
Wading River 5,317 .....P9
Walden 5,836 .....M7
Wallkill 2,125 .....M7
Walton 3,326 .....K6
Wampsville▲ 501 .....J4
Wantagh 18,567 .....R7
Wappingers Falls 4,605 .....N7
Warrensburg 3,204 .....N3
Warsaw▲ 3,830 .....D5
Warwick 5,984 .....M8
Washingtonville 4,906 .....M8
Waterford 2,370 .....N5
Waterloo▲ 5,116 .....G5
Watertown▲ 29,429 .....J3
Waterville 1,664 .....K5
Watervliet 11,061 .....N5
Watkins Glen▲ 2,207 .....G6
Waverly 4,787 .....H6
Wayland 1,976 .....E5
Webster 5,464 .....F4
Weedsport 1,996 .....G4
Wellsburg 617 .....G6
Wellsville 5,241 .....E6
West Carthage 2,166 .....J3
West Elmira 5,218 .....G6
West Glens Falls 5,964 .....N4
West Hurley 2,252 .....M6
West Nyack 3,437 .....K8
West Point 8,024 .....M8
West Sayville 4,680 .....O9
West Seneca 47,866 .....C5
West Winfield 871 .....K5
Westbury 13,060 .....R7
Westhampton 2,129 .....P9
Westhampton Beach 1,571 ....P9
Westons Mills 1,837 .....D6
White Plains▲ 48,718 .....P6
Whitehall 3,071 .....O3
Whitesboro 4,195 .....K4

Whitney Point 1,054 .....J6
Willard 1,339 .....G5
Williamson 1,768 .....F4
Williamsville 5,583 .....C5
Williston Park 7,516 .....R7
Wilson 1,307 .....C4
Windsor 1,051 .....J6
Witherbee-Mineville 1,925 ....N2
Wolcott 1,544 .....G4
Woodmere 15,578 .....P7
Woodridge 783 .....L7
Woodstock 1,870 .....M6
Wurtsboro 1,048 .....L7
Wyandanch 8,950 .....N9
Yonkers 188,082 .....O6
Yorkshire 1,340 .....D5
Yorktown Heights 7,690 .....N8
Yorkville 2,972 .....K4
Youngstown 2,075 .....C4

OTHER FEATURES

Adirondack (mts.) M3
Algonquin (peak) M2
Allegany Ind. Res. C6
Allegheny (res.) C7
Allegheny (riv.) C6
Ashokan (res.) M7
Ausable (riv.) N2
Batten Kill (riv.) O4
Beaver (riv.) K3
Big Moose (lake) L3
Black (lake) J1
Black (riv.) J3
Block Island (sound) S8
Blue Mountain (lake) L3
Bonaparte (lake) K3
Brandreth (lake) L3
Brant (lake) N3
Brookhaven Nat'l Lab. P9
Butterfield (lakes) J2
Canandaigua (lake) F5
Canisteo (riv.) F6
Cannonsville (res.) K6
Catskill (lake) L6
Cattaraugus (creek) C6
Cattaraugus Ind. Res. C5
Cayuga (lake) G5
Champlain (lake) O1
Chateaugay, Upper (lake) ...M1
Chautauqua (lake) A6
Chazy (lake) N1
Chenango (riv.) J6
Cohocton (riv.) F6
Conesus (lake) E5
Conewango (creek) B6
Cranberry (lake) L2
Deer (riv.) J3
Deer (riv.) L1
Delaware (riv.) K7

East (riv.) N9
Erie (lake) A5
Fire Island Nat'l Seashore ...P9
Fishers (isl.) S8
Forked (lake) L3
Fort Drum 11,578 .....J2
Fort Niagara C4
Fort Stanwix Nat'l Mon. J4
Fulton Chain (lakes) K3
Galloo (isl.) H3
Gardiners (bay) R8
Gardiners (isl.) R8
Gateway Nat'l Rec. Area M9
Genesee (riv.) E4
George (lake) N4
Grand (isl.) B5
Great Sacandaga (lake) M4
Great South (bay) O9
Great South (beach) O9
Greenwood (lake) M8
Grenadier (isl.) H2
Griffiss A.F.B. K4
Haystack (mt.) M3
Hemlock (lake) E5
Hinckley (res.) K4
Honeoye (lake) E5
Honnedaga (lake) L3
Hudson (riv.) N7
Hunter (mt.) M6
Indian (lake) M3
Jones (beach) R7
Keuka (lake) F5
Lila (lake) L2
Little Tupper (lake) L2
Long (isl.) P9
Long (lake) M2
Long Island (sound) P9
Lower Saranac (lake) M2
Manhattan (isl.) P9
Marcy (mt.) N2
Martin Van Buren
   Nat'l Hist. Site N6
Meacham (lake) M1
Mohawk (riv.) L5
Montauk (pt.) S9
Moose (riv.) K3
Neversink (res.) L7
New York State Barge (canal) .C4
Niagara (riv.) B4
Oil Spring Ind. Res. D6
Oneida (lake) J4
Onondaga Ind. Res. H5
Ontario (lake) F3
Orient (pt.) R8
Oswegatchie (riv.) K2
Otisco (lake) H4
Otsego (lake) L5
Otselic (riv.) J5

Owasco (lake) .....G
Peconic (bay) .....R
Peninsula (pt.) L
Pepacton (res.) L
Piseco (lake) L
Placid (lake) .....N
Plattsburgh A.F.B. 5,483 ....O
Pleasant (lake) .....N
Plum (isl.) .....R
Poosepatuck Ind. Res. .....P
Raquette (lake) L
Rondout (pt.) .....R
Round (lake) .....N
Sacandaga (lake) .....M
Sagamore Hill Nat'l Hist. Site ..R
Saint Lawrence (lake) .....K
Saint Lawrence (riv.) .....J
Saint Regis (riv.) L
Saint Regis Ind. Res. L
Salmon (res.) .....H
Salmon (riv.) .....H
Salmon (riv.) .....N
Saranac (lakes) .....M
Saranac (riv.) .....N
Saratoga (lake) .....N
Saratoga Nat'l Hist. Park .....N
Schoharie (res.) L
Schroon (lake) .....N
Seneca (lake) .....G
Seneca (riv.) .....H
Shelter (isl.) .....R
Shinnecock Ind. Res. .....R
Silver (lake) .....N
Skaneateles (lake) .....H
Skylight (mt.) .....N
Slide (mt.) L
Staten (isl.) .....M
Statue of Liberty Nat'l Mon. ...M
Stony (isl.) .....H
Stony (pt.) .....R
Susquehanna (riv.) L
Thousand (isls.) .....J
Tioughnioga (riv.) .....M
Titus (lake) .....M
Tomhannock (res.) .....N
Tonawanda (creek) .....D
Toronto (res.) L
Tupper (lake) .....M
Tuscarora Ind. Res. L
Unadilla (riv.) .....K
Upper Chateaugay (lake) .....M
Valcour (isl.) .....N
Wallkill (riv.) L
Whiteface (mt.) .....N
Whitney Point (lake) L
Woodhull (lake) L

▲County seat
• Population of town or township

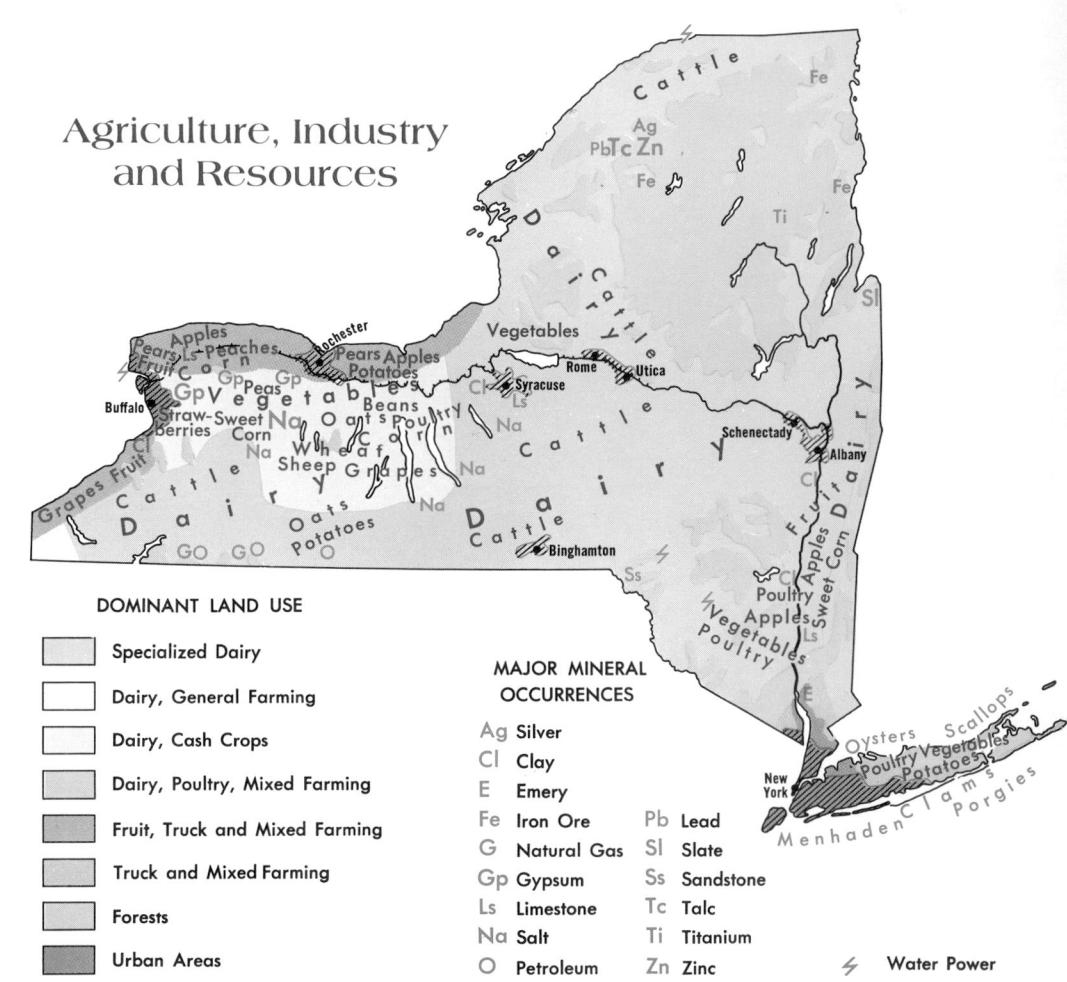

Agriculture, Industry and Resources

DOMINANT LAND USE

Specialized Dairy

Dairy, General Farming

Dairy, Cash Crops

Dairy, Poultry, Mixed Farming

Fruit, Truck and Mixed Farming

Truck and Mixed Farming

Forests

Urban Areas

MAJOR MINERAL OCCURRENCES

Ag   Silver
Cl   Clay
E   Emery
Fe   Iron Ore   Pb   Lead
G   Natural Gas   Sl   Slate
Gp   Gypsum   Ss   Sandstone
Ls   Limestone   Tc   Talc
Na   Salt   Ti   Titanium
O   Petroleum   Zn   Zinc

⚡   Water Power

▨   Major Industrial Areas

AREA 52,669 sq. mi. (136,413 sq. km.)
POPULATION 6,657,630
CAPITAL Raleigh
LARGEST CITY Charlotte
HIGHEST POINT Mt. Mitchell 6,684 ft. (2037 m.)
SETTLED IN 1650
ADMITTED TO UNION November 21, 1789
POPULAR NAME Tarheel State
STATE FLOWER Flowering Dogwood
STATE BIRD Cardinal

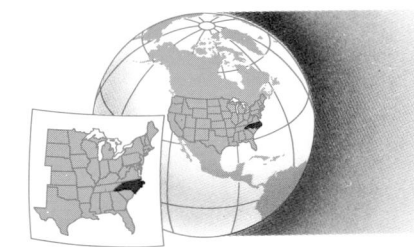

Great Smoky Mountains

MILES
0   5   10   15

COUNTIES

Alamance 108,213 ....L3
Alexander 27,544 ....G3
Alleghany 9,590 ....G1
Anson 23,474 ....J4
Ashe 22,209 ....F2
Avery 14,867 ....F2
Beaufort 42,283 ....R4
Bertie 20,388 ....P2
Bladen 28,663 ....M5
Brunswick 50,985 ....N6
Buncombe 174,821 ....D3
Burke 75,744 ....F3
Cabarrus 98,935 ....H4
Caldwell 70,709 ....F3
Camden 5,904 ....S2
Carteret 52,556 ....R5
Caswell 20,693 ....L2
Catawba 118,412 ....G3
Chatham 38,759 ....L3
Cherokee 20,170 ....A4
Chowan 13,506 ....R2
Clay 7,155 ....B4
Cleveland 84,714 ....F4
Columbus 49,587 ....M6
Craven 81,613 ....P4
Cumberland 274,566 ....L4
Currituck 13,736 ....S2
Dare 22,746 ....T3
Davidson 126,677 ....J3
Davie 27,859 ....H3
Duplin 39,995 ....O5
Durham 181,835 ....M3
Edgecombe 56,558 ....O3
Forsyth 265,878 ....J2
Franklin 36,414 ....N2
Gaston 175 093 ....G4
Gates 9,305 ....R2
Graham 7,196 ....B4
Granville 38,345 ....M2
Greene 15,384 ....O3
Guilford 347,420 ....K3
Halifax 55,516 ....O2
Harnett 67,822 ....M4
Haywood 46,942 ....C3
Henderson 69,285 ....D4
Hertford 22,523 ....P2
Hoke 22,856 ....L4
Hyde 5,411 ....S3
Iredell 92,931 ....H3
Jackson 26 846 ....C4
Johnston 81,306 ....N4
Jones 9,414 ....P4

Lee 41,374 ....L4
Lenoir 57,274 ....O4
Lincoln 50,319 ....G3
Macon 23,499 ....B4
Madison 16,953 ....D3
Martin 25,078 ....P3
McDowell 35,681 ....E3
Mecklenburg 511,433 ....H4
Mitchell 14,433 ....E2
Montgomery 23,346 ....K4
Moore 59,013 ....L4
Nash 76,677 ....O2
New Hanover 120,284 ......O6
Northampton 20,798 ....P2
Onslow 149,838 ....P5
Orange 93,851 ....L2
Pamlico 11,372 ....R4
Pasquotank 31,298 ....S2
Pender 28,855 ....O5
Perquimans 10,447 ....S2
Person 30,180 ....M2
Pitt 107,924 ....P3
Polk 14,416 ....E4
Randolph 106,546 ....K3
Richmond 44,518 ....K4
Robeson 105,179 ....L5
Rockingham 86,064 ....K2
Rowan 110,605 ....H3
Rutherford 56,918 ....E4
Sampson 47,297 ....N4
Scotland 33,754 ....L5
Stanly 51,765 ....J4
Stokes 37,223 ....J2
Surry 61,704 ....H2
Swain 11,268 ....C4
Transylvania 25,520 ....D4
Tyrrell 3,856 ....S3
Union 84,211 ....H4
Vance 38,892 ....N2
Wake 423,380 ....M3
Warren 17,265 ....N2
Washington 13,997 ....R3
Watauga 36,952 ....F2
Wayne 104,666 ....N4
Wilkes 59,393 ....G2
Wilson 66,061 ....N3
Yadkin 30,488 ....H2
Yancey 15,419 ....E2

CITIES and TOWNS

Abbottsburg 425 ....M5
Aberdeen 2,700 ....L4
Acme N6
Advance 4,391 ....J3
Ahoskie 4,391 ....P2
Alamance 258 ....K2
Alarka 900 ....C4
Albemarle▲ 14,939 ....J4
Alexander Mills 662 ....F4
Alliance 583 ....P4
Altamahaw 1,076 ....L2
Andrews 2,551 ....B4
Angier 2,235 ....M4
Ansonville 614 ....J4
Apex 4,968 ....M3
Arapahoe 430 ....R4
Archdale 6,913 ....K3
Arlington 795 ....H2
Ash 16,362 ....N6
Asheboro▲ 15,252 ....K3
Asheville▲ 61,607 ....D3
Askewville 201 ....R2
Atkinson 275 ....N5
Atlantic 1,938 ....S5
Atlantic Beach 941 ....R5

Aulander 1,209 ....P2
Aurora 654 ....R4
Autryville 166 ....M4
Avon 500 ....U4
Avondale F4
Ayden 4,740 ....N4
Badin 1,481 ....J4
Bahama 280 ....M2
Bailey 553 ....N3
Bakersville▲ 332 ....E2
Balfour 1,118 ....E3
Banner Elk 933 ....F2
Bannertown 1,028 ....H1
Barco 325 ....T2
Barker Heights 1,137 ....D4
Bat Cave 450 ....E4
Bath 154 ....P3
Battleboro 447 ....O2
Bayboro▲ 733 ....R4
Bear Creek 500 ....L3
Beargrass 77 ....P3
Beaufort▲ 3,808 ....R5

Belhaven 2,269 ....R3
Bellarthur 350 ....O3
Belmont 8,434 ....H4
Belvidere 275 ....S2
Belville 66 ....N6
Belwood 631 ....F4
Benham 400 ....G2
Bennett 254 ....K3
Benson 2,810 ....N4
Beta 500 ....C4
Bethel 1,842 ....P3
Beulaville 933 ....O5
Biltmore Forest 1,327 ....E3
Biscoe 1,484 ....K4
Black Creek 615 ....O3
Black Mountain 5,418 ......D3
Bladenboro 1,821 ....M5
Blowing Rock 1,257 ....F2
Boardman 250 ....M6
Boger City 1,373 ....G4
Boiling Spring Lakes 1,650 ...N7

Boiling Springs 2,445 ....F4
Bolivia▲ 228 ....N6
Bolton 531 ....N6
Bonlee 300 ....L3
Boomer 250 ....G2
Boone▲ 12,915 ....F2
Boonville 1,009 ....H2
Brevard▲ 5,388 ....D4
Bridgeton 453 ....R4
Broadway 973 ....L4
Brookford 451 ....G3
Browns Summit 500 ....K2
Brunswick 302 ....M6
Bryson City▲ 1,145 ....C4
Buies 2,805 ....M5
Buies Creek 1,939 ....M4
Bullock 525 ....M2
Bunn 364 ....N3
Bunnlevel M4
Burgaw▲ 1,807 ....O5
Burlington 39,498 ....K2
Burnsville▲ 1,482 ....E3
Butner 4,679 ....M2
Buxton 700 ....U4
Bynum 312 ....L3
Calabash 1,210 ....M7
Calypso 481 ....N4
Camden▲ 300 ....S2
Cameron 215 ....L4
Candler 950 ....D3
Candor 748 ....K4
Canton 3,790 ....D3
Cape Carteret 1,008 ....P5
Carolina Beach 3,630 ......O6
Carrboro 11,553 ....L3
Carthage▲ 976 ....K4
Cary 43,858 ....M3
Casar 328 ....F3
Cashiers 553 ....C4
Castalia 261 ....O2
Castle Hayne 1,182 ....O6
Caswell Beach 175 ....N7
Catawba 467 ....G3
Catharine Lake 500 ....O5
Cedar Falls 400 ....K3
Cedar Grove 250 ....L2
Cedar Island 310 ....S5
Cedar Mountain 250 ....D4
Centerville 115 ....N2
Cerro Gordo 227 ....M6
Chadbourn 2,005 ....M6
Chadwick Acres 15 ....P6
Chapel Hill 38,719 ....L3
Charlotte▲ 395,934 ....H4
Cherokee 975 ....C4
Cherry 4,756 ....R3
Cherryville 4,844 ....G4
China Grove 2,732 ....H3
Chinquapin 280 ....O5
Chocowinity 624 ....P4
Claremont 980 ....G3
Clarendon 300 ....M6
Clark 739 ....P4
Clarkton 664 ....M6
Clayton 4,756 ....N3
Clemmons 6,020 ....J2
Cleveland 696 ....H3
Cliffside 950 ....F4
Climax 475 ....K3
Clinton▲ 8,204 ....N5
Clyde 1,041 ....D3
Coats 1,493 ....M4
Cofield 407 ....R2
Coinjock 650 ....S2

Colerain 139 ....R2
Collettsville 275 ....F3
Columbia▲ 836 ....S3
Columbus▲ 812 ....E4
Comfort 325 ....O5
Como 71 ....P1
Concord▲ 27,347 ....H4
Conetoe 292 ....O3
Connellys Springs 500 .....F3
Conover 5,465 ....G3
Conway 759 ....P2
Cooleemee 971 ....H3
Cornelius 2,581 ....H4
Council M6
Cove City 497 ....P4
Cramerton 2,371 ....G4
Creedmoor 1,504 ....M2
Creswell 361 ....S3
Crisp 435 ....O3
Crossnore 271 ....F2
Cruso 800 ....D4
Culberson A4
Cullowhee 4,029 ....C4
Cumberland 400 ....M5
Currie 294 ....N6
Currituck▲ 700 ....T2
Dallas 3,012 ....G4
Dalton 400 ....J2
Danbury▲ 119 ....J2
Davidson 4,046 ....H4
Davis 612 ....R5
Delco 450 ....N6
Denton 1,292 ....J3
Dillsboro 95 ....C4
Dobson▲ 1,195 ....H2
Dortches 840 ....O2
Dover 451 ....P4
Drexel 1,746 ....F3
Dublin 246 ....M5
Dudley N4
Dulah 350 ....M6
Dundarrach L5
Dunn 8,336 ....M4
Durham▲ 136,611 ....M2
Dysartsville 950 ....F3
Eagle Springs 280 ....K4
Earl 230 ....F4
East Arcadia 468 ....N6
East Bend 619 ....H2
East Flat Rock 3,218 ....E4
East Laurinburg 302 ....L5
East Marion 1,851 ....F3
East Spencer 2,055 ....J3
Eden 15,238 ....K1
Edenton▲ 5,268 ....R2
Edward R4
Efland 600 ....L2
Elizabeth City▲ 14,292 ....S2
Elizabethtown▲ 3,704 ......M5
Elk Park 486 ....E2
Elkin 3,790 ....H2
Ellenboro 514 ....F4
Ellerbe 1,132 ....K4
Elm City 1,624 ....O3
Elon College 4,394 ....L2
Emerald Isle 2,434 ....P5
Enfield 3,082 ....O2
Engelhard 500 ....T3
Enka 5,567 ....D3
Ernul 350 ....P4
Erwin 4,061 ....M4
Ether 425 ....K4
Etowah 1,997 ....D4
Eure 282 ....R2

(continued on following page)

Agriculture, Industry and Resources

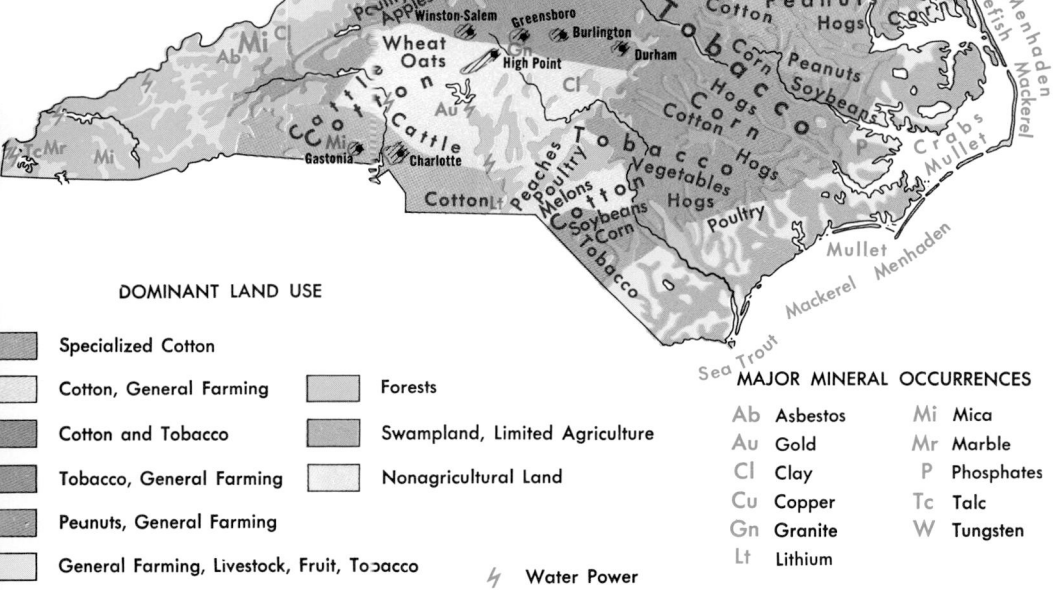

DOMINANT LAND USE

- Specialized Cotton
- Cotton, General Farming
- Cotton and Tobacco
- Tobacco, General Farming
- Peunuts, General Farming
- General Farming, Livestock, Fruit, Tobacco
- General Farming, Truck Farming, Tobacco, Livestock
- Forests
- Swampland, Limited Agriculture
- Nonagricultural Land

⚡ Water Power
▨ Major Industrial Areas

MAJOR MINERAL OCCURRENCES

Ab Asbestos
Au Gold
Cl Clay
Cu Copper
Gn Granite
Lt Lithium

Mi Mica
Mr Marble
P Phosphates
Tc Talc
W Tungsten

Eureka 303 ....O3
Everetts 143 ....P3
Evergreen 310 ....M6
Fair Bluff 1,068 ....M6
Fairfield 900 ....S3
Fairmont 2,489 ....L6
Fairview 1,830 ....D3
Faison 701 ....N4
Faith 553 ....J3
Falcon 216 ....M4
Falkland 108 ....O3
Fallston 498 ....G4
Farmington 300 ....H3
Farmville 4,392 ....O3
Fayetteville 75,695 ....M4
Flat Rock 1,812 ....E4
Fletcher 2,787 ....E4
Florence 500 ....R4
Forest City 7,475 ....E4
Fork 250 ....J3
Fountain 459 ....O3
Four Oaks 1,308 ....M4
Foxfire 334 ....K4
Francisco 350 ....J2
Franklin▲ 2,873 ....C4
Franklinton 1,615 ....N2
Franklinville 666 ....K3
Fremont 1,710 ....N3
Frisco 350 ....T4
Fuquay-Varina 4,562 ....M3
Garland 746 ....N5
Garner 14,967 ....M3
Garysburg 1,057 ....O2
Gaston 1,003 ....O1
Gastonia▲ 54,732 ....G4
Gates 308 ....R2
Gatesville▲ 363 ....R2
Gibson 532 ....K5
Gibsonville 3,441 ....K2
Glade Valley 650 ....G2
Glen Alpine 563 ....F3
Glen Raven 2,616 ....L2
Glendon 250 ....L4
Glenville 400 ....C4
Glenwood 400 ....F3
Gloucester 250 ....S5
Godwin 77 ....M4
Gold Hill 300 ....J3
Goldsboro▲ 40,709 ....O4
Goldston 299 ....L3
Graham▲ 10,426 ....L2
Grandy 425 ....T2
Granite Falls 3,253 ....G3
Granite Quarry 1,646 ....H3
Grantsboro 900 ....R4
Green Mountain 500 ....E3
Greenevers 512 ....O5
Greensboro▲ 183,521 ....K2
Greenville▲ 44,972 ....P3
Grifton 2,393 ....P4
Grimesland 469 ....P3
Grover 516 ....G4
Halifax▲ 327 ....O2
Hallsboro 600 ....M6
Hamilton 544 ....P3
Hamlet 6,196 ....K5
Hamptonville 250 ....H2
Harbinger 460 ....T2
Harkers Island 1,759 ....R5
Harmony 431 ....H3
Harrells 187 ....N5
Harrellsville 106 ....R2
Harrisburg 1,625 ....H4
Hassell 95 ....P3
Hatteras 800 ....T4
Havelock 20,268 ....P5
Hayesville▲ 279 ....B4
Hays 1,522 ....G2
Haywood 190 ....L3
Hazelwood 1,678 ....C4
Helton 250 ....G1
Henderson▲ 15,655 ....N2
Hendersonville▲ 7,284 ....E4
Henrietta 1,412 ....F4
Hertford▲ 2,105 ....S2
Hickory 28,301 ....G3
Hiddenite 800 ....G3
High Point 69,495 ....J3
High Shoals 605 ....G4
Highfalls 250 ....K4
Highlands 948 ....C4
Hildebran 790 ....F3
Hillsborough▲ 4,263 ....L2
Hobgood 435 ....P2
Hobucken 500 ....S4
Hoffman 348 ....K4
Holden Beach 625 ....N7
Hollister 750 ....O2
Holly Ridge 728 ....O6
Holly Springs 908 ....M3
Hookerton 422 ....O4
Hope Mills 8,184 ....M5
Hot Springs 478 ....D3
Hubert 980 ....P5
Hudson 2,819 ....G3
Huntersville 3,014 ....H4
Hurdle Mills 300 ....L2
Icard 2,553 ....G3
Indian Beach 153 ....R5
Indian Trail 1,942 ....H4
Iron Station 900 ....G4
Jackson Springs 300 ....K4
Jackson▲ 592 ....P2
Jacksonville▲ 30,013 ....O5
James City 4,279 ....P4
Jamestown 2,600 ....K3
Jamesville 612 ....P3
Jarvisburg 450 ....T2
Jason O4
Jefferson▲ 1,300 ....G2
Jonesville 1,549 ....H2
Julian 500 ....K3
Jupiter D3
Kannapolis 29,696 ....H3
Kelford 204 ....P2
Kenansville▲ 856 ....O5
Kenly 1,549 ....N3

Topography

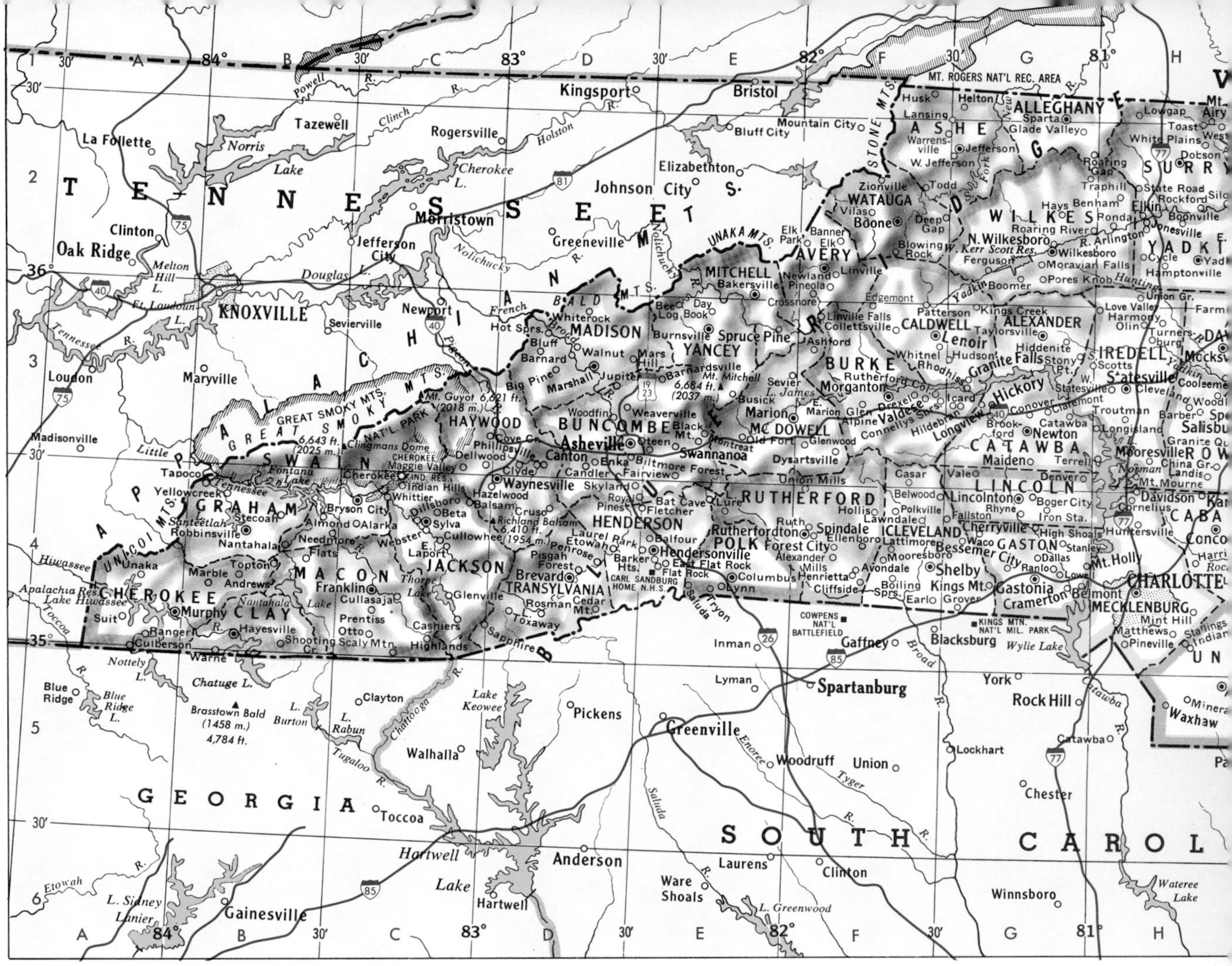

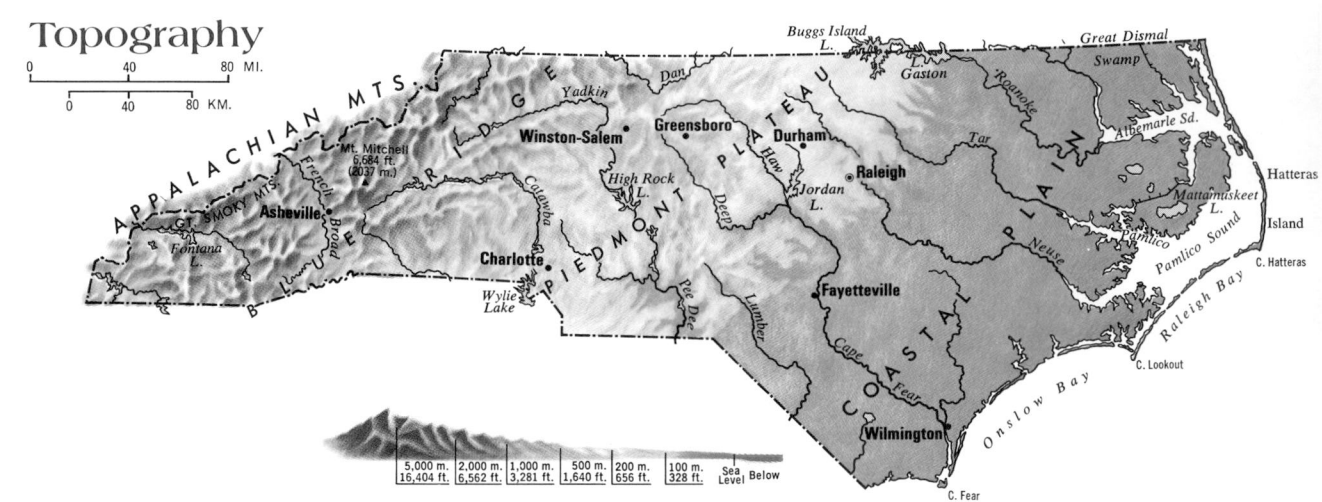

Kernersville 10,836 ....J2
Kill Devil Hills 4,238 ....T3
King 4,059 ....J2
Kings Mountain 8,763 ....G4
Kinston▲ 25,295 ....O4
Kittrell 228 ....M2
Kitty Hawk 1,937 ....T2
Knightdale 1,884 ....N3
Knotts Island 500 ....T2
Kure Beach 619 ....O7
La Grange 2,805 ....O4
Lake Lure 691 ....E4
Lake Toxaway 750 ....D4
Lake Waccamaw 954 ....M6
Lakeview 550 ....L4
Landis 2,333 ....H3
Lansing 171 ....F2
Lasker 139 ....P2
Lattimore 183 ....F4
Laurel Hill 2,314 ....K5
Laurel Park 1,322 ....D4
Laurinburg▲ 11,643 ....K5
Lawndale 573 ....F4
Leasburg 400 ....L2
Leggett 108 ....O3
Leland 1,801 ....N6
Lemon Springs 650 ....L4
Lenoir▲ 14,192 ....G3
Lewiston Woodville 1,000 ....P2
Lexington▲ 16,581 ....J3
Liberty 2,047 ....K3
Lilesville 468 ....K5

Lillington▲ 2,048 ....M4
Lincolnton▲ 6,847 ....G4
Linden 180 ....M4
Linville 244 ....F2
Linwood 300 ....J3
Littleton 691 ....O2
Locust 1,940 ....J4
Long Beach 3,816 ....N7
Longview 3,229 ....F3
Longwood 800 ....M7
Longwood Park K5
Louisburg▲ 3,037 ....N2
Love Valley 67 ....H3
Lowell 2,704 ....G4
Lowgap 660 ....H1
Lowland 600 ....S4
Lucama 931 ....N3
Lumber Bridge 109 ....L5
Lumberton▲ 18,601 ....L5
Lynn 650 ....E4
Macclesfield 493 ....O3
Mackeys 250 ....R3
Macon 154 ....O2
Madison 2,371 ....J2
Maggie Valley 185 ....C4
Magnolia 747 ....O5
Maiden 2,574 ....G3
Mamers 300 ....L4
Manly 500 ....L4
Manns Harbor 550 ....T3
Manteo▲ 991 ....T3
Marble 950 ....B4

Marietta 206 ....L6
Marion▲ 4,765 ....E3
Mars Hill 1,611 ....D3
Marshall▲ 809 ....D3
Marshallberg 400 ....S5
Marshville 2,020 ....J4
Matthews 13,651 ....H4
Maury O4
Maxton 2,373 ....L5
Mayodan 2,471 ....K2
Maysville 892 ....P5
McCain 700 ....L4
McDonald 88 ....L5
McFarlan 98 ....J5
Mebane 4,754 ....L2
Merrimon 500 ....R5
Mesic 310 ....R4
Micro 417 ....N3
Midland 950 ....J4
Midleburg 185 ....N2
Midway Park P5
Milton 185 ....L1
Milwaukee P2
Minnesott Beach 266 ....R4
Mint Hill 11,567 ....H4
Misenheimer 450 ....J4
Mocksville▲ 3,399 ....H3
Moncure 700 ....L3
Monroe▲ 16,127 ....J5
Montreat 693 ....E3
Mooresboro 294 ....F4

Mooresville 9,317 ....H3
Moravian Falls 1,736 ....G2
Morehead City 6,046 ....R5
Morganton▲ 15,085 ....F3
Morrisville 1,022 ....M3
Morven 590 ....J5
Mount Airy 7,156 ....H1
Mount Gilead 1,336 ....K4
Mount Holly 7,710 ....H4
Mount Mourne 950 ....H3
Mount Olive 4,567 ....O4
Mount Pleasant 1,027 ....J4
Moyock 500 ....S1
Murfreesboro 2,580 ....P2
Murphy▲ 1,575 ....B4
Nags Head 1,838 ....T3
Nashville▲ 3,617 ....N3
Navassa 445 ....N6
Neuse 1,110 ....M3
New Bern▲ 17,363 ....P4
New London 414 ....J4
New River 9,732 ....O6
Newland▲ 645 ....F2
Newport 2,516 ....R5
Newton▲ 9,304 ....G3
Newton Grove 511 ....N4
Norlina 996 ....N2
Norman 105 ....K4
North Cove 257 ....F3
North Harlowe 975 ....R5
North Roxboro L2
North Wilkesboro 3,384 ....G2

Northside 400 ....M2
Norwood 1,617 ....J4
Oak City 389 ....P3
Oak Ridge 675 ....K2
Oakboro 600 ....J4
Ocean Isle Beach 523 ....N7
Ocracoke 500 ....T4
Old Fort 720 ....E3
Old Trap 500 ....T2
Olivia 400 ....L4
Oriental 786 ....R4
Orrum 103 ....L5
Oteen E3
Otto 800 ....C4
Oxford▲ 7,913 ....M2
Pantego 171 ....R3
Parkton 367 ....M5
Parkwood 4,123 ....M3
Parmele 321 ....P3
Patterson 690 ....F3
Peachland 384 ....J5
Pelham 350 ....L1
Pembroke 2,241 ....L5
Penrose 500 ....D4
Phillipsville 1,642 ....C4
Pikeville 598 ....N4
Pilot Mountain 1,181 ....J2
Pine Hall 912 ....K2
Pine Knoll Shores 1,360 ....R5
Pine Level 1,217 ....N4
Pinebluff 876 ....K4
Pinehurst 5,103 ....K4

Pineola 500 ....F2
Pinetops 1,514 ....O3
Pinetown R3
Pineville 2,970 ....H4
Pink Hill 547 ....O4
Pinnacle 725 ....J2
Pisgah Forest 1,899 ....D4
Pittsboro▲ 1,436 ....L3
Pleasant Hill 1,114 ....O1
Plymouth▲ 4,328 ....R3
Point Harbor 250 ....T2
Polkton 662 ....J5
Polkville 1,514 ....F4
Pollocksville 299 ....P5
Poplar Branch 400 ....T2
Portsmouth S4
Powells Point 750 ....T2
Powellsville 103 ....R2
Princeton 1,181 ....N4
Princeville 1,652 ....P3
Proctorville 168 ....M6
Raeford▲ 3,469 ....L5
Raleigh (cap.)▲ 207,951 ....M3
Ramseur 1,181 ....K3
Randleman 2,612 ....K3
Ranger 500 ....B4
Ranlo 1,650 ....G4
Red Oak 280 ....N2
Red Springs 3,799 ....L5
Reidsville 12,183 ....K2
Rennert 217 ....L5

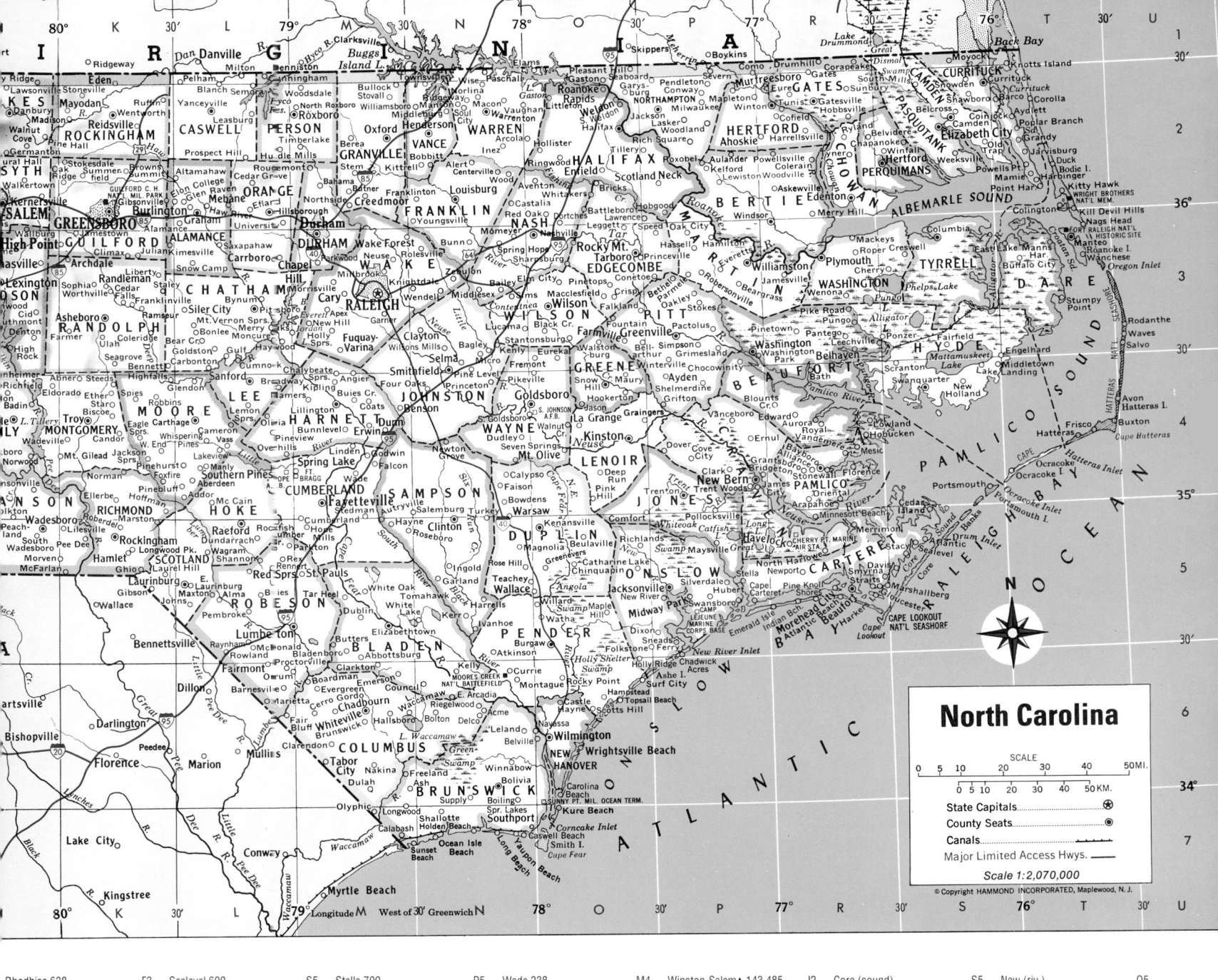

Rhodhiss 638 ...F3
Rich Square 1,058 ...P2
Richfield 535 ...J4
Richlands 996 ...O5
Ridgeway 500 ...N2
Riegelwood 459 ...N6
Roanoke Rapids 15,722 ...O2
Roaring Gap 450 ...H2
Roaring River 287 ...G2
Robbins 970 ...H4
Robbinsville▲ 709 ...B4
Robersonville 1,940 ...P3
Rockingham▲ 9,399 ...K5
Rockwell 1,598 ...J3
Rocky Mount 48,997 ...O3
Rocky Point 975 ...O6
Rolesville 572 ...N3
Ronda 367 ...H2
Roper 669 ...R3
Rose Hill 1,287 ...N5
Roseboro 1,441 ...M5
Rosman 385 ...D4
Rougemont 400 ...M2
Rowland 1,139 ...L5
Roxboro▲ 7,332 ...M2
Roxobel 244 ...P2
Royal 4,418 ...R4
Royal Pines ...D4
Ruffin 680 ...K2
Rural Hall 1,652 ...J2
Ruth 366 ...E4
Rutherford College 1,126 ...F3
Rutherfordton▲ 3,617 ...E4
Saint Pauls 1,992 ...M5
Salemburg 409 ...N4
Salisbury▲ 23,087 ...H3
Saluda 488 ...E4
Sandy Ridge 500 ...J1
Sanford▲ 14,475 ...L4
Sapphire 350 ...D4
Saxapahaw 1,178 ...J3
Scaly Mountain 250 ...C4
Scotland Neck 2,575 ...P2
Scotts 500 ...H3
Scranton 250 ...S4
Seaboard 791 ...O1
Seagrove 244 ...K3

Sealevel 600 ...S5
Selma 4,600 ...N3
Semora 500 ...L2
Seven Springs 163 ...O4
Severn 260 ...P2
Sevier 302 ...E3
Shallotte 965 ...N7
Sharpsburg 1,536 ...O3
Shawboro 300 ...S2
Shelby▲ 14,669 ...E4
Shoals 350 ...J2
Shooting Creek 250 ...B4
Siler City 4,808 ...L3
Silverdale 250 ...P5
Simpson 410 ...P3
Sims 124 ...N3
Skyland ...D4
Smithfield▲ 7,540 ...N3
Smyrna 291 ...R5
Sneads Ferry 2,031 ...P5
Snow Hill▲ 1,378 ...O4
Sophia 350 ...K3
South Goldsboro 2,53 ...O4
South Mills 950 ...S2
South Wadesboro ...
South Weldon 1,640 ...O2
Southern Pines 9,129 ...L4
Southmont 950 ...J3
Southport▲ 2,369 ...N7
Sparta▲ 1,957 ...G1
Speed 80 ...P3
Spencer 3,219 ...H3
Spindale 4,040 ...F4
Spring Hope 1,221 ...N3
Spring Lake 7,524 ...M4
Spruce Pine 2,010 ...E3
Stacy 410 ...S5
Staley 204 ...K3
Stallings 2,132 ...G4
Stanfield 517 ...J4
Stanley 2,823 ...G3
Stanleyville 4,779 ...J2
Stantonsburg 782 ...O3
Star 775 ...K4
Statesville▲ 17,567 ...H3
Stecoah 250 ...B4
Stedman 577 ...M4

Stella 700 ...P5
Stem 249 ...M2
Stokes 2,134 ...P3
Stokesdale 1,070 ...K2
Stoneville 1,109 ...K2
Stonewall 279 ...R4
Stony Point 1,286 ...G3
Stovall 409 ...M2
Stumpy Point 250 ...T3
Suit 350 ...A4
Summerfield 2,051 ...K2
Sunbury 400 ...R2
Sunset Beach 311 ...N7
Surf City 970 ...O6
Swannanoa 3,538 ...E3
Swanquarter▲ 550 ...S4
Swansboro 1,165 ...P5
Sylva▲ 1,809 ...C4
Tabor City 2,330 ...M6
Tar Heel 115 ...M5
Tarboro▲ 11,037 ...O3
Taylorsville▲ 1,566 ...G3
Teachey 244 ...N5
Terrell 319 ...G3
Thomasville 15,915 ...J3
Tillery 400 ...O2
Timberlake 500 ...M2
Todd ...F2
Topsail Beach 346 ...O6
Traphill 550 ...H2
Trenton▲ 248 ...P4
Troutman 1,493 ...H3
Troy▲ 3,404 ...J4
Tryon 1,680 ...E4
Turkey 234 ...N4
Tyner 264 ...R2
Ulah 350 ...K3
Union Grove 614 ...H3
Union Mills 500 ...F3
Valdese 3,914 ...F3
Vanceboro 946 ...P4
Vandemere 299 ...R4
Vass 670 ...L4
Waco 320 ...G4

Wade 238 ...M4
Wadesboro▲ 3,645 ...J5
Wagram 480 ...L5
Wake Forest 5,769 ...M3
Walkertown 1,200 ...J2
Wallace 2,939 ...N5
Wallburg 300 ...J3
Walnut 1,088 ...D3
Walnut Cove 1,147 ...J2
Walnut Creek 623 ...O4
Walstonburg 188 ...O3
Wanchese 1,380 ...T3
Warrensville ...F2
Warrenton▲ 949 ...N2
Warsaw 2,859 ...N4
Washington Park 403 ...R3
Washington 9,075 ...R3
Watha 99 ...O5
Waxhaw 1,294 ...H5
Waynesville▲ 6,758 ...D4
Weaverville 2,107 ...D3
Webster 410 ...C4
Weeksville 500 ...S2
Welcome 3,377 ...J3
Weldon 1,392 ...O2
Wendell 2,822 ...N3
Wentworth▲ 150 ...K2
West End 950 ...K4
West Jefferson 1,002 ...F2
West Statesville ...G3
Westfield 450 ...J2
Whispering Pines 1,243 ...L4
Whitakers 860 ...O2
White Lake 390 ...M5
White Plains 1,027 ...H2
Whiteville▲ 5,078 ...M6
Whitnel 975 ...F3
Wilkesboro▲ 2,573 ...G2
Willard 300 ...O5
Williamston▲ 5,503 ...P3
Wilmington▲ 55,530 ...N6
Wilson▲ 36,930 ...O3
Wilsons Mills ...M3
Windsor▲ 2,056 ...P2
Winfall 501 ...S2
Wingate 2,821 ...J5

Winston-Salem▲ 143,485 ...J2
Winterville 2,816 ...P3
Winton▲ 796 ...P2
Wise 500 ...N2
Wood 2,736 ...N2
Woodfin 3,260 ...D3
Woodland 760 ...P2
Woodleaf 350 ...H3
Worthville 350 ...K3
Wrightsville Beach 2,937 ...O6
Yadkinville▲ 2,525 ...H2
Yanceyville▲ 1,973 ...L2
Yaupon Beach 734 ...N7
Youngsville 424 ...N3
Zebulon 3,173 ...N3

OTHER FEATURES

Albemarle (sound) ...S2
Alligator (lake) ...S3
Alligator (riv.) ...S3
Angola (swamp) ...O5
Apalachia (res.) ...A4
Appalachian (mts.) ...D2
Ashe (isl.) ...P6
Bald (mts.) ...D3
Black (mts.) ...D3
Blue Ridge (mts.) ...E3
Bodie (isl.) ...T2
Broad (riv.) ...E4
Buggs Island (lake) ...M1
Camp Lejeune
  Marine Corps Base ...P5
Cape Fear (riv.) ...M5
Cape Hatteras Nat'l Seashore ...T4
Carl Sandburg Home
  Nat'l Hist. Site ...D4
Catawba (lake) ...G4
Catawba (riv.) ...H5
Catfish (lake) ...P5
Chatuge (lake) ...B5
Cherokee Ind. Res. ...C4
Cherry Point Marine Air Sta. ...R4
Chowan (riv.) ...R2
Clingmans Dome (mt.) ...C3
Contentnea (creek) ...N3
Core (banks) ...S5
Neuse (riv.) ...R5

Core (sound) ...S5
Corncake (inlet) ...O7
Croatan (sound) ...T3
Currituck (sound) ...T2
Dan (riv.) ...L1
Deep (riv.) ...K3
Drum (inlet) ...S5
Fear (cape) ...O7
Fishing (creek) ...O2
Fontana (lake) ...B4
Fort Bragg 34,744 ...M4
Fort Raleigh Nat'l Hist. Site ...T3
French Broad (riv.) ...D3
Gaston (res.) ...N2
Great (lake) ...P5
Great Dismal (swamp) ...S1
Great Smoky (mts.) ...B3
Great Smoky Mts. Nat'l Park ...B3
Green (swamp) ...N6
Guyot (mt.) ...D3
Hatteras (cape) ...U4
Hatteras (inlet) ...T4
Hatteras (isl.) ...U4
Haw (riv.) ...K2
High Rock (lake) ...J3
Hiwassee (lake) ...A4
Hiwassee (riv.) ...A4
Holly Shelter (swamp) ...O6
Hunting (riv.) ...O5
Hyco (riv.) ...L2
James (lake) ...E3
Jordan, B. Everett (lake) ...L3
Lanes (creek) ...J5
Little (creek) ...N3
Little (riv.) ...L4
Little Pee Dee (riv.) ...L5
Little Tennessee (riv.) ...B4
Long (lake) ...P5
Lookout (cape) ...S5
Lumber (riv.) ...L6
Mattamuskeet (lake) ...S3
Meherrin (riv.) ...P2
Mitchell (mt.) ...E3
Moores Creek
  Nat'l Battlefield ...N6
Nantahala (lake) ...B4

New (riv.) ...O5
New, South Fork (riv.) ...G2
New River (inlet) ...P6
Nolichucky (riv.) ...E2
Norman (lake) ...H3
North East Cape Fear (riv.) ...O4
Ocracoke (inlet) ...T5
Ocracoke (isl.) ...T4
Onslow (bay) ...P6
Oregon (inlet) ...U3
Pamlico (riv.) ...R4
Pamlico (sound) ...S4
Pee Dee (riv.) ...J4
Phelps (lake) ...S3
Pigeon (riv.) ...C3
Portsmouth (isl.) ...T5
Pungo (lake) ...S3
Pungo (riv.) ...R4
Raleigh (bay) ...S5
Richland Balsam (mt.) ...D4
Roanoke (isl.) ...T3
Roanoke (riv.) ...P2
Rocky (riv.) ...H4
Seanteetlah (lake) ...B4
Seymour Johnson A.F.B. ...O4
Six Run (creek) ...N4
Smith (isl.) ...O7
South Yadkin (riv.) ...H3
Stone (riv.) ...F2
Sunny Point
  Mil. Ocean Term. ...O6
Tar (riv.) ...O3
Thorpe (lake) ...C4
Tillery (lake) ...J4
Trent (riv.) ...P4
Unaka (mts.) ...E2
Unicoi (mts.) ...B4
Waccamaw (lake) ...N6
Waccamaw (riv.) ...M7
Whiteoak (swamp) ...P5
W. Scott Kerr (res.) ...G2
Wright Brothers Nat'l Mem. ...T2
Yadkin (riv.) ...J3
▲County seat.

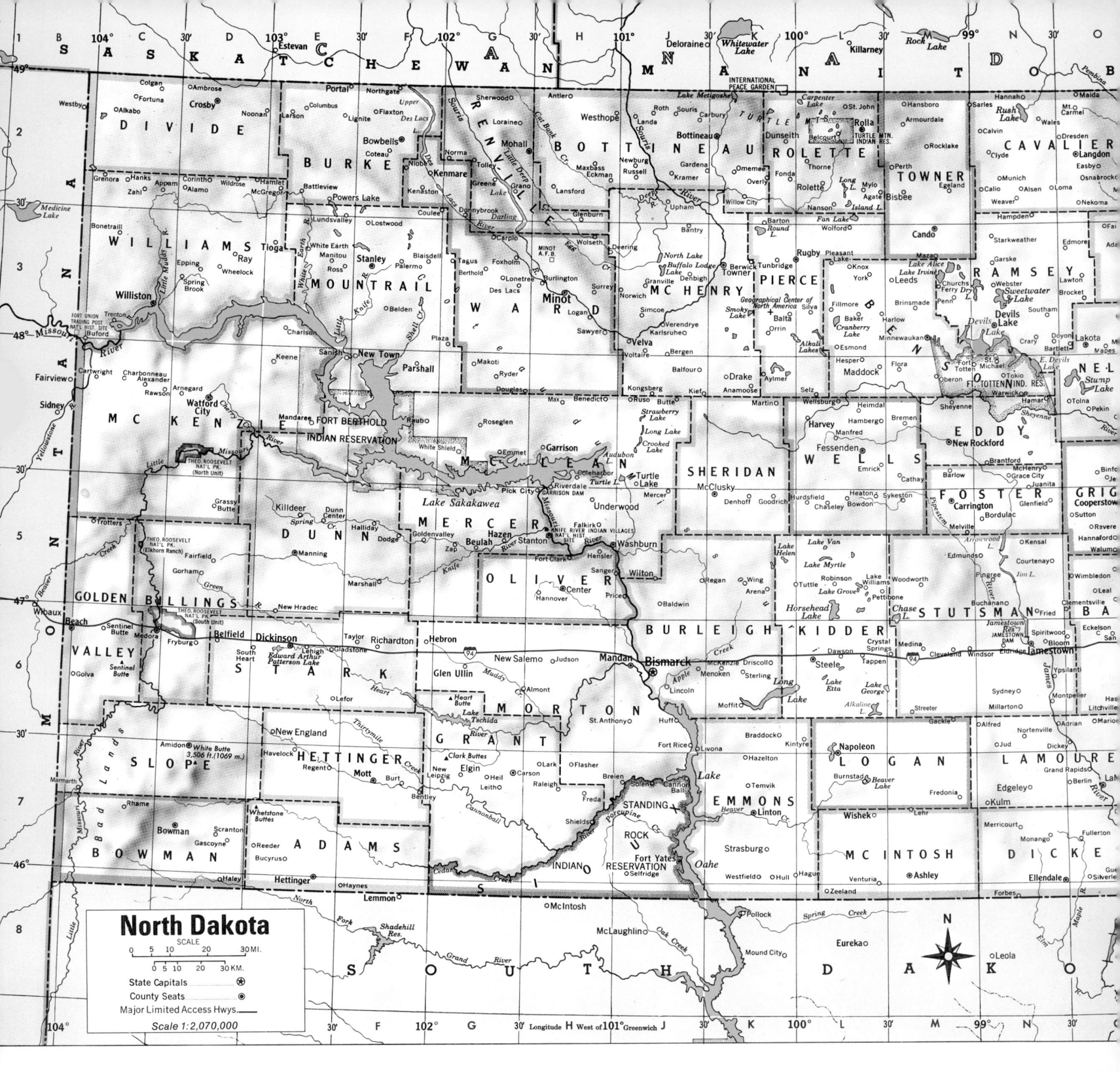

North Dakota

SCALE

0   5 10   20   30 MI.

0 5 10   20   30 KM.

State Capitals .... ⊛

County Seats .... ○

Major Limited Access Hwys. ____

Scale 1:2,070,000

COUNTIES

Adams 3,174 .... F7
Barnes 12,545 .... O5
Benson 7,198 .... M3
Billings 1,108 .... D5
Bottineau 8,011 .... J2
Bowman 3,596 .... C7
Burke 3,002 .... E2
Burleigh 60,131 .... J6
Cass 102,874 .... R5
Cavalier 6,064 .... N2
Dickey 6,107 .... N7
Divide 2,899 .... C2
Dunn 4,005 .... E5
Eddy 2,951 .... N4
Emmons 4,830 .... K7
Foster 3,983 .... N5
Golden Valley 2,108 .... B5
Grand Forks 70,633 .... P3
Grant 3,549 .... G6
Griggs 3,303 .... O5
Hettinger 3,445 .... E7
Kidder 3,332 .... L6
LaMoure 5,383 .... O7
Logan 2,847 .... L7
McHenry 6,528 .... J3
McIntosh 4,021 .... L7
McKenzie 6,383 .... D4
McLean 10,457 .... H4
Mercer 9,808 .... G5
Morton 23,700 .... H6

Mountrail 7,021 .... E3
Nelson 4,410 .... O4
Oliver 2,381 .... H5
Pembina 9,238 .... P2
Pierce 5,052 .... K3
Ramsey 12,681 .... N3
Ransom 5,921 .... P7
Renville 3,160 .... G2
Richland 18,148 .... R7
Rolette 12,772 .... L2
Sargent 4,549 .... P7
Sheridan 2,148 .... K4
Sioux 3,761 .... H7
Slope 907 .... C7
Stark 22,832 .... E6
Steele 2,420 .... P5
Stutsman 22,241 .... M5
Towner 3,627 .... M2
Traill 8,752 .... P4
Walsh 13,840 .... P3
Ward 57,921 .... G3
Wells 5,864 .... L4
Williams 21,129 .... C3

CITIES and TOWNS

Abercrombie 252 .... S7
Adams 248 .... O3
Alexander 216 .... C4
Almont 126 .... H6
Alsen 113 .... N2
Amidon 24 .... D7
Anamoose 277 .... K4
Aneta 314 .... P4

Argusville 161 .... R5
Arnegard 122 .... D4
Arthur 400 .... R5
Ashley▲ 1,052 .... M7
Beach▲ 1,205 .... C6
Belcourt 2,458 .... L2
Belfield 887 .... D6
Berthold 409 .... G3
Binford 233 .... P4
Bisbee 227 .... M2
Bottineau▲ 2,598 .... J2
Bowbells▲ 498 .... F2
Bowdon 196 .... K5
Bowman▲ 1,741 .... D7
Buffalo 204 .... R6
Burlington 995 .... H3
Butte 129 .... J4
Buxton 343 .... R4
Cando▲ 1,564 .... M3
Cannon Ball 702 .... J7
Carpio 178 .... G3
Carrington▲ 2,267 ...... L4
Carson▲ 383 .... H7
Casselton 1,601 .... R6
Cavalier▲ 1,508 .... P2
Center▲ 826 .... H6
Christine 140 .... S6
Church's Ferry 118 ..... N3
Cleveland 121 .... M6
Cogswell 184 .... P7
Colebarbor 88 .... H4

Columbus 223 .... E2
Cooperstown▲ 1,247 .. O5
Crary 145 .... N3
Crosby▲ 1,312 .... D2
Crystal 199 .... P2
Davenport 218 .... R6
Dazey 143 .... O5
Deering 99 .... J3
Des Lacs 216 .... G3
Devils Lake▲ 7,782 .... N3
Dickinson▲ 16,097 ..... E6
Dodge 135 .... G5
Donnybrook 106 .... G2
Drake 361 .... K4
Drayton 961 .... R2
Dunn Center 128 .... F5
Dunseith 723 .... K2
Edgeley 680 .... N7
Edinburg 284 .... P2
Edmore 196 .... N3
Egeland 103 .... M2
Elgin 765 .... G7
Ellendale▲ 1,798 ...... N7
Emerado 483 .... R4
Enderlin 997 .... P6
Esmond 196 .... L3
Fairmount 427 .... R7
Fargo 74,111 .... S6
Fessenden▲ 655 ...... L4
Fingal 138 .... P6
Finley▲ 543 .... P4
Flasher 317 .... H7
Flaxton 121 .... F2

Fordville 299 .... P3
Forest River 148 .... P3
Forman▲ 586 .... P7
Fort Ransom 111 ...... P6
Fort Totten 867 .... M4
Fort Yates▲ 183 .... J7
Frontier 218 .... H4
Fullerton 94 .... O7
Gackle 450 .... M6
Galesburg 161 .... P5
Garrison 1,530 .... H4
Gilby 262 .... R4
Gladstone 224 .... E6
Glen Ullin 927 .... G6
Glenburn 439 .... H2
Glenfield 118 .... N5
Goldenvalley 287 ...... G5
Golva 101 .... C6
Goodrich 192 .... K5
Grace City 108 .... N4
Grafton▲ 4,840 .... R3
Grand Forks▲ 49,425 . R4
Grandin 213 .... R5
Granville 236 .... J3
Great Bend 108 .... S7
Grenora 261 .... C2
Gwinner 585 .... P7
Hague 109 .... L7
Halliday 288 .... F5
Hankinson 1,038 ...... S7
Hannaford 204 .... O5
Harvey 2,263 .... L4
Harwood 590 .... S6

Hatton 800 .... R4
Havana 124 .... P8
Hazelton 240 .... K7
Hazen 2,818 .... G5
Hebron 888 .... G6
Hettinger▲ 1,574 ..... E8
Hillsboro▲ 1,488 ..... S5
Hoople 310 .... P3
Hope 281 .... P5
Horace 662 .... R5
Hunter 341 .... R5
Inkster 95 .... P3
Jamestown▲ 15,571 . N6
Karlsruhe 143 .... J3
Kenmare 1,214 .... G2
Kensal 194 .... M5
Killdeer 722 .... E5
Kindred 569 .... R6
Kulm 514 .... N7
LaMoure▲ 970 .... O7
Lakota▲ 898 .... O3
Langdon▲ 2,241 ..... O2
Lankin 152 .... P3
Lansford 249 .... H2
Larimore 1,464 ...... P4
Leeds 542 .... M3
Lehr 297 .... M7
Leonard 310 .... R6
Lidgerwood 799 ..... R7
Lignite 242 .... F2
Lincoln 1,132 .... J6
Linton▲ 1,410 .... K7
Lisbon▲ 2,177 .... P7

Litchville 205 .... O6
Maddock 559 .... L4
Makoti 145 .... G4
Mandan▲ 15,177 .... J6
Mandaree 367 .... E4
Manning 75 .... E5
Manvel 333 .... R3
Mapleton 682 .... R6
Marion 169 .... O6
Marmarth 144 .... B7
Martin 117 .... K4
Max 301 .... H4
Maxbass 123 .... H2
Mayville 2,092 ...... P5
McClusky▲ 492 ..... K4
McVille 559 .... O4
Medina 387 .... M6
Medora▲ 101 .... C6
Mercer 104 .... J5
Michigan 413 .... O3
Milnor 651 .... R7
Milton 133 .... O2
Minnewaukan▲ 401 . M3
Minot▲ 34,544 ..... H3
Minto 560 .... R3
Mohall▲ 931 .... G2
Mooreton 193 ..... S7
Mott▲ 1,019 .... F7
Mountain 134 ..... P2
Munich 310 .... N2
Napoleon▲ 930 ... L6
Neche 434 .... P2
New England 663 . E6

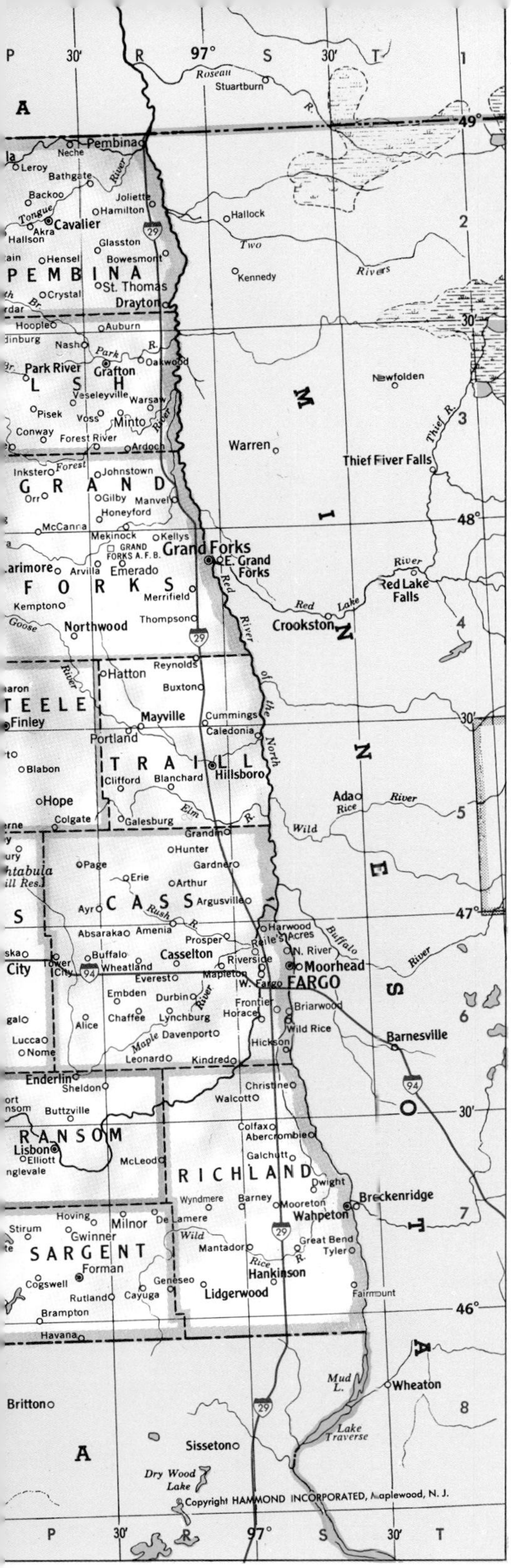

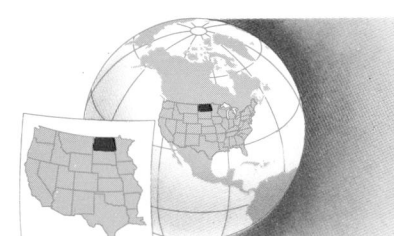

AREA 70,702 sq. mi. (183,118 sq. km.)
POPULATION 641,364
CAPITAL Bismarck
LARGEST CITY Fargo
HIGHEST POINT White Butte 3,506 ft.
　(1069 m.)
SETTLED IN 1780
ADMITTED TO UNION November 2, 1889
POPULAR NAME Flickertail State; Sioux
　State
STATE FLOWER Wild Prairie Rose
STATE BIRD Western Meadowlark

Topography

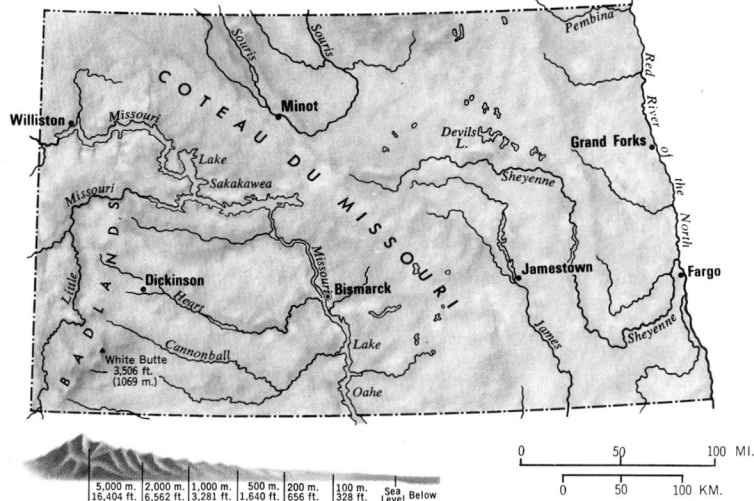

Towner▲ 669	K3
Turtle Lake 681	J4
Tuttle 160	L5
Underwood 976	H5
Upham 205	J2
Valley City▲ 7,163	P6
Velva 968	J3
Verona 103	O7
Wahpeton▲ 8,751	S7
Walcott 178	R6
Walhalla 1,131	P2
Washburn▲ 1,506	J5
Watford City▲ 1,784	D4
West Fargo 12,287	S6
Westhope 578	H2
White Shield 274	G4
Wildrose 193	D2
Williston▲ 13,131	C3
Willow City 281	K2
Wilton 728	J5
Wimbledon 275	O5
Wing 208	K5
Wishek 1,171	L7
Woodworth 102	M5
Wyndmere 501	R7
Zap 287	G5
Zeeland 197	L8

OTHER FEATURES

Alkali (lakes)	L3	Fan (lake)	L2	Little Missouri (riv.)	D4	Smoky (lake)	K3
Alkaline (lake)	L6	Forest (riv.)	P3	Little Muddy (riv.)	C3	Souris (riv.)	J2
Apple (creek)	J6	Fort Berthold Ind. Res.	E4	Long (lake)	J4	Spring (creek)	E5
Arrowwood (lake)	N5	Fort Totten Ind. Res.	N4	Long (lake)	K6	Standing Rock Ind. Res.	J7
Ashtabula (Baldhill Res.)		Fort Union Trading Post Nat'l		Long (lake)	L2	Strawberry (lake)	J4
(lake)	P5	Hist. Site	B3	Maple (lake)	O8	Stump (lake)	O4
Audubon (lake)	H4	Garrison (dam)	H5	Maple (riv.)	R6	Sweetwater (lake)	N3
Bad Lands (reg.)	C7	George (lake)	L6	Metigoshe (lake)	K2	Theodore Roosevelt
Baldhill (Ashtabula Lake)		Goose (riv.)	P4	Minot A.F.B. 9,095	H3	Nat'l Park	C5
(res.)	P5	Grand, North Fork (riv.)	E8	Missouri (riv.)	H5	Theodore Roosevelt
Bear (creek)	O7	Grand Forks A.F.B.9,343	R4	Muddy (creek)	G6	Nat'l Park	D4
Beaver (creek)	K7	Green (riv.)	D5	Myrtle (lake)	L5	Theodore Roosevelt
Beaver (creek)	B5	Grove (lake)	L5	North (lake)	J3	Nat'l Park	D6
Beaver (lake)	L7	Heart (butte)	G6	Oahe (lake)	J7	Thirty Mile (creek)	F6
Buffalo Lodge (lake)	J3	Heart (riv.)	F6	Oak (creek)	J8	Tongue (riv.)	P2
Cannonball (riv.)	G7	Helen (lake)	K5	Park (riv.)	R3	Tschida (lake)	G6
Carpenter (lake)	L2	Horsehead (lake)	L5	Patterson, Edward A. (lake)	E6	Turtle (lake)	H4
Cedar (creek)	G7	International Peace Garden	K1	Pembina (riv.)	O1	Turtle (mts.)	K2
Chase (lake)	M5	Irvine (lake)	L2	Pipestem (riv.)	M5	Turtle Mountain Ind. Res.	L2
Cherry (creek)	D4	Island (lake)	L2	Porcupine (creek)	J7	Upper Des Lacs (lake)	F2
Clark (buttes)	G7	James (riv.)	N6	Red River of the North (riv.)	S4	Van (lake)	L5
Coteau du Missouri (plain)	G3	Jamestown (res.)	M6	Round (lake)	K3	Whetstone (buttes)	E7
Cranberry (lake)	L3	Jim (lake)	N5	Rush (lake)	N2	White Butte (buttes)	D7
Crooked (lake)	J4	Knife (riv.)	G5	Rush (riv.)	R5	White Earth (riv.)	E3
Cut Bank (creek)	H2	Knife R. Indian Villages		Sakakawea (lake)	G5	Wild Rice (riv.)	R7
Darling (lake)	G2	Nat'l Hist. Site	H5	Sentinel (butte)	C6	Yellowstone (riv.)	B4
Deep (riv.)	J1	Little Deep (creek)	G2	Shell (creek)	F3
Des Lacs (riv.)	G3	Little Knife (riv.)	F3	Sheyenne (riv.)	O6
Devils (lake)	N3
Dry (lake)	M3
East Devils (lake)	N4
Egg (creek)	H3
Elm (riv.)	N8
Elm (riv.)	R5
Etta (lake)	L6

▲County seat

© Copyright HAMMOND INCORPORATED, Maplewood, N. J.

New Leipzig 326	G7	Rocklake 221	M2
New Rockford▲ 1,604	N4	Rolette 623	L2
New Salem 909	G6	Rolla 1,286	L2
New Town 1,388	F4	Rugby▲ 2,909	L3
Newburg 104	J2	Rutland 212	P7
Noonan 231	D2	Ryder 121	G4
Northwood 1,166	P4	Saint John 368	L2
Oakes 1,775	O7	Saint Thomas 444	R2
Oberon 103	M4	Sanborn 164	O6
Oriska 103	P6	Sanish	E4
Osnabrock 214	O2	Sawyer 319	H3
Page 266	P5	Scranton 294	D7
Palermo 95	F3	Selfridge 242	J7
Park River 1,725	P3	Sharon 119	P4
Parshall 943	F4	Sheldon 149	P6
Pekin 101	O4	Sherwood 286	G2
Pembina 642	R2	Sheyenne 272	M4
Petersburg 219	P3	Souris 97	J2
Pick City 203	G5	South Heart 322	D6
Pisek 130	P3	Stanley▲ 1,371	F3
Plaza 193	G3	Stanton▲ 517	H5
Portal 192	E2	Starkweather 197	N3
Portland 602	P5	Steele▲ 762	L6
Powers Lake 408	E2	Strasburg 553	K7
Ray 603	D3	Streeter 161	M6
Reeder 252	E7	Surrey 856	H3
Regent 268	E7	Sykeston 167	M5
Reile's Acres 210	S6	Tappen 239	L6
Reynolds 299	R4	Taylor 163	F6
Rhame 186	C7	Thompson 930	R4
Richardton 625	F6	Tioga 1,278	E3
Riverdale 283	H4	Tolna 230	O4
Riverside 465	S6	Tower City 233	P6

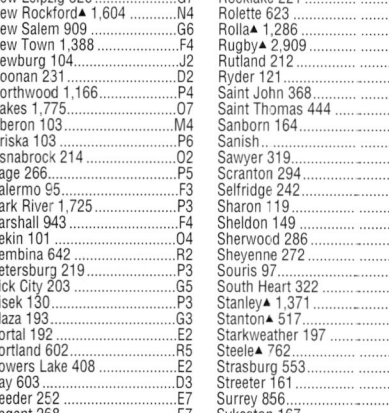

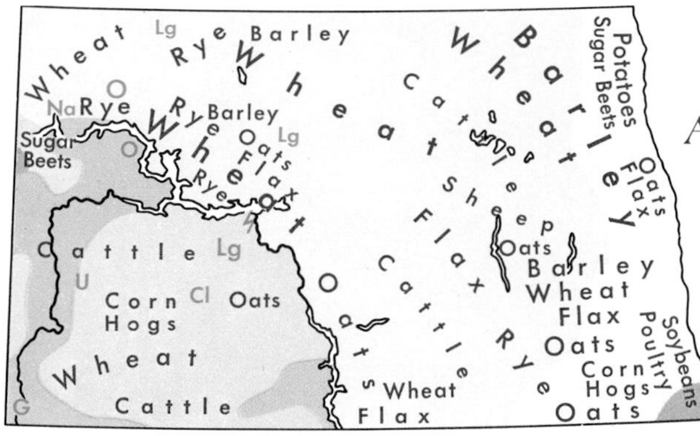

Agriculture, Industry and Resources

DOMINANT LAND USE

☐ Specialized Wheat

☐ Wheat, General Farming

☐ Wheat, Range Livestock

☐ Livestock, Cash Grain

☐ Sugar Beets, Dry Beans,
　Livestock, General Farming

☐ Range Livestock

⚡ Water Power

MAJOR MINERAL
OCCURRENCES

Cl Clay

G Natural Gas

Lg Lignite

Na Salt

O Petroleum

U Uranium

Ohio

SCALE

| 0 | 5 | 10 | 20 | 40 MI. |

| 0 | 5 | 10 | 20 | 40 KM. |

State Capitals............⊛
County Seats............◉
Major Limited Access Hwys. ▬▬▬

Scale 1:1,800,000

© Copyright HAMMOND INCORPORATED, Maplewood, N.J.

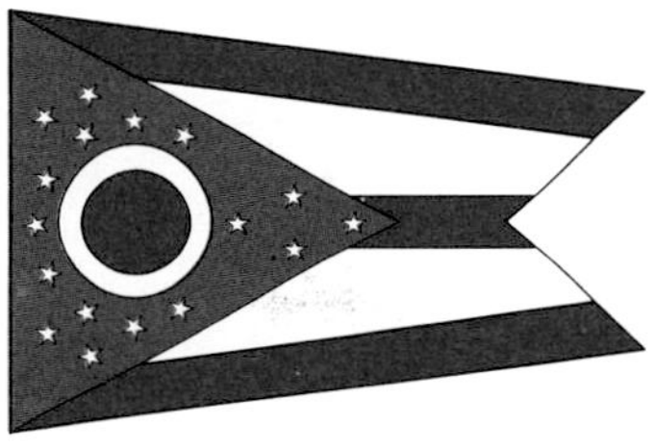

AREA 41,330 sq. mi. (107,045 sq. km.)
POPULATION 10,887,325
CAPITAL Columbus
LARGEST CITY Cleveland
HIGHEST POINT Campbell Hill 1,550 ft. (472 m.)
SETTLED IN 1788
ADMITTED TO UNION March 1, 1803
POPULAR NAME Buckeye State
STATE FLOWER Scarlet Carnation
STATE BIRD Cardinal

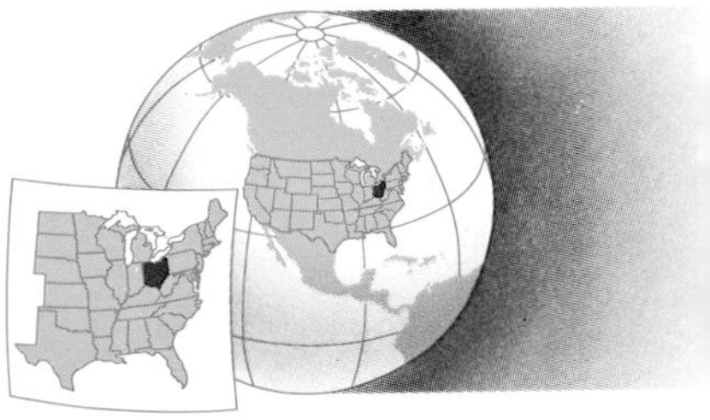

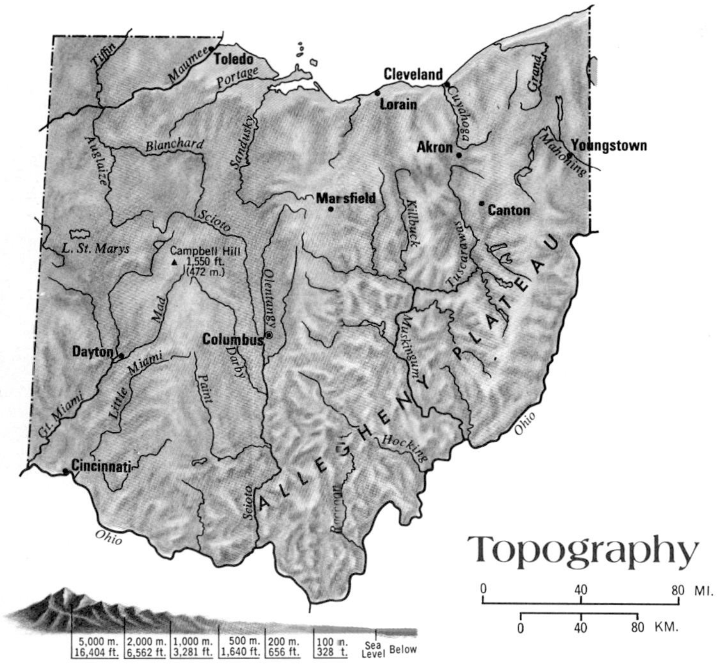
Toledo
Cleveland
Lorain
Akron
Youngstown
Mansfield
Canton
Columbus
Dayton
Cincinnati
Tiffin
Maumee
Portage
Blanchard
Sandusky
Auglaize
Cuyahoga
Grand
Mahoning
Scioto
L. St. Marys
Campbell Hill
▲ 1,550 ft.
(472 m.)
Killbuck
Tuscarawas
Olentangy
Mad
Muskingum
Darby
Little Miami
Gt. Miami
Paint
Hocking
Raccoon
Ohio
ALLEGHENY PLATEAU
0 40 80 MI.
0 40 80 KM.
5,000 m. 16,404 ft.
2,000 m. 6,562 ft.
1,000 m. 3,281 ft.
500 m. 1,640 ft.
200 m. 656 ft.
100 m. 328 ft.
Sea Level
Below

Topography

COUNTIES

dams 25,371 D8
llen 109,755 B4
shland 47,507 F4
shtabula 99,821 J2
thens 59,549 F7
uglaize 44,585 B4
elmont 71,074 J5
rown 34,966 C8
utler 291,479 A7
arroll 26,521 H4
hampaign 36,019 C5
lark 147,548 C6
lermont 150,187 B7
linton 35,415 C7
olumbiana 108,276 J4
oshocton 35,427 G5
rawford 47,870 E4
uyahoga 1,412,140 G3
arke 53,619 A5
efiance 39,350 A3
elaware 66,929 D5
rie 76,779 E3
airfield 103,461 E6
ayette 27,466 D6
ranklin 961,437 E5
ulton 38,498 B2
allia 30,954 F8
eauga 81,129 H3
reene 136,731 C6
uernsey 39,024 H5
amilton 866,228 A7
ancock 65,536 C3
ardin 31,111 C4
arrison 16,085 H5
enry 29,108 B3
ighland 35,728 C7
ocking 25,533 F6
olmes 32,849 G4
uron 56,240 E3
ackson 30,230 E7
efferson 80,298 J5
nox 47,473 F5
ake 215,499 H2
awrence 61,834 E8
cking 128,300 F5
ogan 42,310 C5
orain 271,126 F3
ucas 462,361 C2
adison 37,068 D6
ahoning 264,806 J4
arion 64,274 D4
edina 122,354 G3
eigs 22,987 F7
ercer 39,443 A4
iami 93,182 B5
onroe 15,497 H6
ontgomery 573,809 B6
organ 14,194 G6
orrow 27,749 E4
uskingum 82,068 G5
oble 11,336 G6
ttawa 40,029 D2
aulding 20,488 A3
erry 31,557 F6
Pickaway 48,255 D6
Pike 24,249 D7
Portage 142,585 H3
Preble 40,113 A6
Putnam 33,819 B3
Richland 126,137 E4
Ross 69,330 D7
Sandusky 61,963 D3
Scioto 80,327 D8
Seneca 59,733 D3
Shelby 44,915 B5
Stark 367,585 H4
Summit 514,990 G3
Trumbull 227,813 J3
Tuscarawas 84,090 H5
Union 31,969 D5
Van Wert 30,464 A4
Vinton 11,098 E7
Warren 113,909 B7
Washington 62,254 H7
Wayne 101,461 G4
Williams 36,956 A2
Wood 113,269 C3
Wyandot 22,254 D4

CITIES and TOWNS

Aberdeen 1,329 C8
Ada 5,413 C4
Adamsville 151 G5
Addyston 1,198 B9
Adelphi 398 E7
Adena 842 J5
Akron▲ 223,019 G3
Albany 795 F7
Alexandria 468 E5
Alger 864 C4
Alliance 23,376 H4
Alvordton 298 A2
Amanda 729 E6
Amberley 3,108 C9
Amelia 1,837 D10
Amesville 250 F7
Amherst 10,332 F3
Amsterdam 669 J5
Andover 1,216 J2
Anna 1,164 B5
Ansonia 1,279 A5
Antioch 68 H6
Antwerp 1,677 A3
Apple Creek 860 G4
Aquilla 360 H2
Arcadia 546 D3
Arcanum 1,953 A6
Archbold 3,440 B2
Arlington 1,267 C4
Arlington Heights 1,084 C9
Ashland▲ 20,079 F4
Ashley 1,059 E5
Ashtabula 21,633 J2
Ashville 2,254 E6
Athalia 346 F8
Athens▲ 21,265 F7
Attica 944 E3
Aurora 9,192 H3
Austintown 32,371 J3
Avon 7,337 F3
Avon Lake 15,066 F2
Bailey Lakes 367 F4
Bainbridge 968 D7
Bairdstown 130 C3
Ballville 3,083 D3
Baltic 659 G5
Baltimore 2,971 E6
Barberton 27,623 G4
Barnesville 4,326 H6
Barnhill 313 H5
Barton 1,039 J5
Batavia▲ 1,700 B7
Batesville 95 H6
Bay View 739 E3
Bay Village 17,000 G9
Beach City 1,051 G4
Beachwood 10,677 J9
Beallsville 464 J6
Beaver 336 E7
Beavercreek 33,626 C6
Beaverdam 467 C4
Bedford 14,822 H9
Bedford Heights 12,131 J9
Bellaire 6,028 J5
Bellbrook 6,511 C6
Belle Center 796 C4
Belle Valley 267 G6
Bellefontaine▲ 12,142 C5
Bellevue 8,146 E3
Bellville 1,568 E4
Belmont 471 J5
Belmore 161 B3
Beloit 1,037 J4
Belpre 6,796 G7
Bentleyville 674 J9
Benton 351 G4
Benton Ridge 343 C4
Berea 19,051 G10
Bergholz 713 J4
Berkey 264 C2
Berlin 691 G4
Berlin Heights 756 F3
Bethel 2,407 B8
Bethesda 1,161 H5
Bettsville 752 D3
Beverly 1,444 G6
Bexley 13,088 E6
Blakeslee 128 A2
Blanchester 4,206 B7
Bloomdale 632 D3
Bloomingburg 769 D6
Bloomingdale 227 J5
Bloomville 949 D3
Blue Ash 11,860 C9
Bluffton 3,367 C4
Boardman 38,596 J3
Bolivar 914 G4
Boston Heights 733 J10
Botkins 1,340 B5
Bowerston 343 H5
Bowersville 225 C6
Bowling Green▲ 28,176 C3
Bradford 2,005 B5
Bradner 1,093 C3
Brady Lake 490 H3
Brecksville 11,818 H10
Bremen 1,386 F6
Brewster 2,307 G4
Brice 109 E6
Bridgeport 2,318 J5
Bridgetown 11,748 B9
Brilliant 1,672 J5
Brimfield 3,223 H3
Broadview Heights 12,219 H10
Brook Park 22,865 G9
Brookfield 1,396 J3
Brooklyn 11,706 H9
Brooklyn Heights 1,450 H9
Brookside 703 J5
Brookville 4,621 B6
Broughton 151 B3
Brunswick 28,230 G3
Bryan▲ 8,348 A3
Buchtel 640 F7
Buckeye Lake 2,986 F6
Buckland 239 B4
Bucyrus▲ 13,496 E4
Burbank 289 F4
Burgoon 224 D3
Burkettsville 268 A5
Burlington 3,003 F9
Burton 1,349 H3
Butler 968 F4
Butlerville 188 B7
Byesville 2,435 G6
Cadiz▲ 3,439 J5
Cairo 473 B4
Calcutta 1,212 J4
Caldwell▲ 1,786 G6
Caledonia 644 D4
Cambridge▲ 11,748 G5
Camden 2,210 A6
Campbell 10,038 J3
Canal Fulton 4,157 H4
Canal Winchester 2,617 E6
Canfield 5,409 J3
Canton▲ 84,161 H4
Cardington 1,770 E5
Carey 3,684 D4
Carlisle 4,872 B6
Carroll 558 E6
Carrollton▲ 3,042 J4
Casstown 246 B5
Castalia 915 E3
Castine 163 A6
Catawba 268 C6
Cecil 249 A3
Cedarville 3,210 C6
Celina▲ 9,650 A4
Centerburg 1,323 E5
Centerville 128 B6
Chagrin Falls 4,146 J9
Chardon▲ 4,446 H2
Chatfield 206 E4
Chauncey 980 F7
Cherry Fork 178 C8
Cherry Grove 4,972 C10
Chesapeake 1,073 E9
Cheshire 250 F8
Chester 309 G7
Chesterhill 395 G6
Chesterland 2,078 H2
Chesterville 286 E5
Cheviot 9,616 B9
Chickasaw 378 A5
Chillicothe▲ 21,923 E7
Chilo 130 B8
Christiansburg 599 C5
Cincinnati▲ 364,040 B9
Circleville▲ 11,666 D6
Clarington 406 J6
Clark 523 G5
Clarksburg 483 D7
Clarksville 485 C7
Clay Center 289 D2
Clayton 713 B6
Cleveland Heights 54,052 H9
Cleveland▲ 505,616 H9
Cleves 2,208 B9
Clinton 1,175 G4
Cloverdale 270 B3
Clyde 5,776 E3
Coal Grove 2,251 E9
Coalton 553 E7
Coldwater 4,335 A5
College Corner 379 A6
Columbiana 4,961 J4
Columbus (cap.)▲ 632,910 E6
Columbus Grove 2,231 B4
Commercial Point 405 D6
Conesville 420 G5
Congress 162 F4
Conneaut 13,241 J2
Continental 1,214 B3
Convoy 1,200 A4
Coolville 663 G7
Corning 703 F6
Cortland 5,666 J3
Corwin 225 B6
Coshocton▲ 12,193 G5
Cove 6,669 E8
Covedale 5,830 B10
Covington 2,603 B5
Craig Beach 1,402 H3
Crestline 4,934 E4
Creston 1,848 G3
Cridersville 1,885 B4
Crooksville 2,601 F6
Crown City 445 F8
Cumberland 318 G6
Custar 209 C3
Cuyahoga Falls 48,950 G3
Cuyahoga Heights 682 H9
Cygnet 560 C3
Dalton 1,377 G4
Danville 1,001 F5
Darbydale 825 D6
Darbyville 272 D6
Dayton▲ 182,044 B6
Deer Park 6,181 C9
Deersville 186 H5
Defiance▲ 16,768 B3
Degraff 1,331 C5
Delaware▲ 20,030 E5
Dellroy 314 H4
Delphos 7,093 B4
Delta 2,849 B2
Dennison 3,282 H5
Dent 6,416 B9
Deshler 1,876 C3
Devola 2,736 H7
Dexter City 161 G6
Dillonvale 857 J5
Dover 11,329 G4
Doylestown 2,668 G4
Dresden 1,581 G5
Dublin 16,366 D5
Dunkirk 869 C4
Dupont 279 B3
East Canton 1,742 H4
East Cleveland 33,096 H9
East Liverpool 13,654 J4
East Palestine 5,168 J4
East Sparta 771 H4
Eastlake 21,161 J8
Eaton Estates 1,586 G3
Eaton▲ 7,396 A6
Edgerton 1,896 A3
Edgewood 5,189 J2
Edison 488 E4
Edon 880 A2
Eldorado 549 A6
Elgin 71 A4
Elida 1,486 B4
Elmore 1,334 D3
Elmwood Place 2,937 B9
Elyria▲ 56,746 F3
Empire 364 J5
Englewood 11,432 B6
Euclid 54,875 J9
Evendale 3,175 C9
Fairborn 31,300 B6
Fairfax 2,029 C9
Fairfield 39,729 A7
Fairlawn 5,779 G3
Fairport Harbor 2,978 H2
Fairview Park 18,028 G9
Farmer 932 A3
Farmersville 950 A6
Fayette 1,248 B2
Fayetteville 393 C7
Felicity 856 B8
Findlay▲ 35,703 C3
Fletcher 545 B5
Florida 304 B3
Flushing 1,042 J5
Forest 1,594 C4
Forest Park 18,609 B9
Forestville 9,185 C10
Fort Jennings 436 B4
Fort Loramie 1,042 B5
Fort McKinley 9,740 B6
Fort Recovery 1,313 A5
Fort Shawnee 4,128 B4
Fostoria 14,983 D3
Frankfort 1,065 D7
Franklin 11,026 B6
Franklin Furnace 1,212 E8
Frazeysburg 1,165 F5
Fredericksburg 502 G4
Fredericktown 2,443 F5
Freeport 475 H5
Fremont▲ 17,648 D3
Fulton 325 E5
Fultonham 178 F6
Gahanna 27,791 E5
Galena 361 E5
Galion 11,859 E4
Gallipolis▲ 4,831 F8
Gambier 2,073 F5
Garfield Heights 31,739 J9
Garrettsville 2,014 H3
Gates Mills 2,508 J9
Geneva 6,597 J2
Geneva-on-the-Lake 1,626 H2
Genoa 2,262 D2
Georgetown▲ 3,627 C8
Germantown 4,916 B6
Gettysburg 539 A5
Gibsonburg 2,579 D3
Gilboa 208 C3
Girard 11,304 J3
Glandorf 829 B3
Glendale 2,445 C9
Glenford 208 F6
Glenmont 233 F4
Glenwillow 455 J10
Glouster 2,001 F6
Gnadenhutten 1,226 G5
Golf Manor 4,154 C9
Gordon 206 B6
Grafton 3,344 F3
Grand Rapids 955 C3
Grand River H2
Grandview 1,301 H7
Grandview Heights 7,010 D6
Granville 4,353 E5
Gratiot 195 F6
Gratis 998 A6
Green Camp 393 D4
Green Springs 1,446 E3
Greenfield 5,172 D7
Greenhills 4,393 B9
Greensburg 3,306 G4
Greentown 1,856 H4
Greenville▲ 12,863 A5
Greenwich 1,442 E3
Groesbeck 6,684 B9
Grove City 19,661 D6
Groveport 2,948 E6
Grover Hill 518 B3
Hamden 877 F7
Hamersville 586 C8
Hamilton▲ 61,368 A7
Hamler 623 B3
Hanging Rock 306 E8
Hanover 803 F5
Hanoverton 434 J4
Harbor View 122 C2
Harpster 233 D4
Harrisburg 340 D6
Harrison 7,518 A9
Harrisville 308 J5
Harrod 537 C4
Hartford 418 J3
Hartford 444 E5
Hartville 2,031 H4
Harveysburg 437 C7
Haskins 549 C3
Haviland 210 A3
Hayesville 457 F4
Heath 7,231 F5
Hebron 2,076 E6
Helena 267 D3
Hemlock 203 F6
Hicksville 3,664 A3
Higginsport 298 C8
Highland 275 C7
Highland Heights 6,249 J9
Hilliard 11,796 D5
Hillsboro▲ 6,235 C7
Hiram 1,330 H3
Holgate 1,290 B3
Holland 1,210 C2
Hollansburg 300 A5
Holloway 354 H5
Holmesville 419 G4
Hopedale 685 J5
Hoytville 301 C3
Hubbard 8,248 J3
Huber Heights 38,696 B6
Hudson 5,159 H3
Hunting Valley 799 J9
Huntsville 343 C5
Huron 7,030 E3
Independence 6,500 H9
Indian Hill 5,383 C9
Irondale 382 J4
Ironton▲ 12,751 E8
Ithaca 119 A6
Jackson Center 1,398 B5
Jackson▲ 6,144 E7
Jacksonville 544 F7
Jamestown 1,794 C6
Jefferson (West Jefferson) 3,331 D6
Jefferson▲ 2,952 J2
Jeffersonville 1,281 C6
Jenera 285 C4
Jeromesville 582 F4
Jerry City 517 C3
Jerusalem 144 H6
Jewett 778 H5
Johnstown 3,237 E5
Junction City 770 F6
Kalida 947 B4
Kelleys Island 172 E2
Kent 28,835 H3
Kenton▲ 8,356 C4
Kettering 60,569 B6
Kettlersville 194 B5
Killbuck 809 G5
Kimbolton 134 G5
Kingston 1,153 E7
Kingsville 1,243 J2
Kipton 283 F3
Kirby 155 D4
Kirkersville 563 E6
Kirtland 5,881 H2
Kirtland Hills 628 H2
La Rue 802 D4
Lafayette 449 C4
Lagrange 1,199 F3
Lakeline 210 J8
Lakemore 2,684 H3
Lakeview 1,056 C4
Lakewood 59,718 G9
Lancaster▲ 34,507 E6
Latty 205 A3
Laura 483 B6
Laurelville 605 E7
Lawrenceville 304 C6
Lebanon▲ 10,453 B7
Leesburg 1,063 D7
Leesville 156 H5
Leetonia 2,070 J4
Leipsic 2,203 C3
Lewisburg 1,584 A6
Lewisville 261 H6
Lexington 4,124 E4
Liberty Center 1,084 B3
Lima▲ 45,549 B4
Limaville 152 H4
Lincoln Heights 4,805 C9
Lindsey 529 D3
Linndale 159 G9
Lisbon▲ 3,037 J4
Lithopolis 563 E6
Lockbourne 173 E6
Lockington 214 B5
Lockland 4,357 C9
Lodi 3,042 F3
Logan▲ 6,725 F6
London▲ 7,807 C6
Lorain 71,245 F3
Lordstown 3,404 J3
Lore City 384 H6
Loudonville 2,915 F4
Louisville 8,087 H4
Loveland 9,990 D9
Lowell 617 H6
Lowellville 1,349 J3
Lower Salem 103 H6
Lucas 730 F4
Lucasville 1,575 E8
Luckey 848 D3
Ludlow Falls 300 B6
Lynchburg 1,212 C7
Lyndhurst 15,982 J9
Lyons 579 B2
Macedonia 7,509 J10
Mack 2,816 B9
Macksburg 218 G6
Madeira 9,141 C9
Madison 2,477 H2
Magnetic Springs 373 D5
Magnolia 937 H4
Maineville 359 C9
Malinta 294 B3

(continued on following page)

Agriculture, Industry and Resources

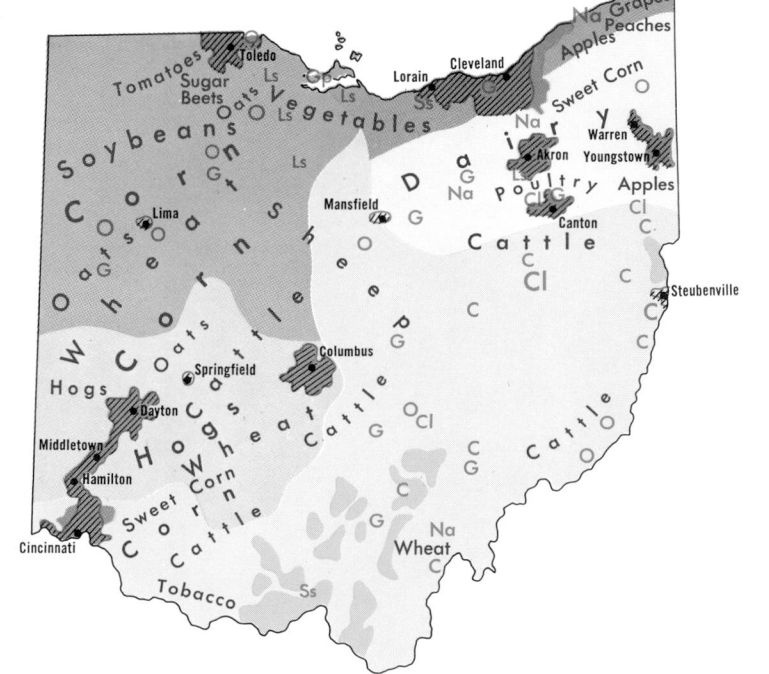

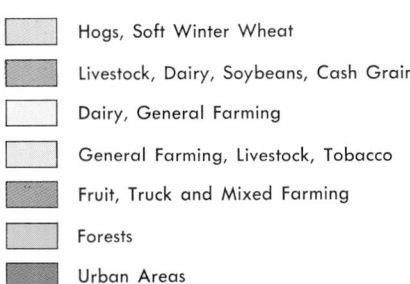

DOMINANT LAND USE

- Hogs, Soft Winter Wheat
- Livestock, Dairy, Soybeans, Cash Grain
- Dairy, General Farming
- General Farming, Livestock, Tobacco
- Fruit, Truck and Mixed Farming
- Forests
- Urban Areas

MAJOR MINERAL OCCURRENCES

C	Coal
Cl	Clay
G	Natural Gas
Gp	Gypsum
Ls	Limestone
Na	Salt
O	Petroleum
Ss	Sandstone

Major Industrial Area

Malta 802 ....G6
Malvern 1,112 ....H4
Manchester 2,223 ....C8
Mansfield▲ 50,627 ....F4
Mantua 1,178 ....H3
Maple Heights 27,089 ....H9
Marblehead 745 ....E2
Marengo 393 ....E5
Mariemont 3,118 ....C9
Marietta▲ 15,026 ....G7
Marion▲ 34,075 ....D4
Marseilles 130 ....D4
Marshall 758 ....C7
Marshallville 788 ....G4
Martin 7,990 ....D2
Martins Ferry 9,331 ....J5
Martinsburg 213 ....F5
Martinsville 476 ....C7
Marysville▲ 9,656 ....D5
Mason 11,452 ....B7
Massillon 31,007 ....H4
Masury 1,836 ....J3
Maumee 15,561 ....C2
Mayfield 3,462 ....J9
Mayfield Heights 19,847 ....J9
McArthur▲ 1,541 ....F7
McClure 781 ....C3
McComb 1,544 ....C3
McConnelsville▲ 1,804 ....G6
McDonald 3,526 ....J3
McGuffey 550 ....C4
Mechanicsburg 1,803 ....D5
Medina▲ 19,231 ....G3
Melrose 307 ....B3
Mendon 717 ....A4
Mentor 47,358 ....H2
Mentor-on-the-Lake 8,271 ....G2
Metamora 543 ....C2
Meyers Lake 493 ....H4
Miamisburg 17,834 ....B6
Middle Point 639 ....B4
Middleburg 14,702 ....C5
Middleburg Heights 16,218 ...G10
Middlefield 1,898 ....H3
Middleport 2,725 ....F7
Middletown 46,022 ....A6
Midland 319 ....C7
Midvale 575 ....H5
Mifflin 162 ....F4
Milan 1,464 ....E3
Milford 5,660 ....D9
Milford Center 651 ....D5
Millbury 1,081 ....D2
Milledgeville 120 ....C6
Miller 173 ....F8
Miller City 168 ....B3
Millersburg▲ 3,051 ....F4
Millersport 1,010 ....E6
Millville 755 ....A7
Milton Center 200 ....C3
Mineral 725 ....F7
Mineral City 884 ....H4
Minerva 4,318 ....H4
Minerva Park 1,463 ....E5
Mingo 4,297 ....C5
Mingo Junction 4,834 ....J5
Minster 2,650 ....B5
Mogadore 4,008 ....H3
Monroe 4,490 ....B7
Monroeville 1,381 ....E3
Montezuma 199 ....A4
Montgomery 9,753 ....C9
Montpelier 4,299 ....A2
Moraine 5,989 ....B6
Moreland Hills 3,354 ....J9
Morral 373 ....D4
Morristown 296 ....H5
Morrow 1,206 ....B7
Moscow 279 ....B8
Mount Blanchard 491 ....D4
Mount Carmel 4,462 ....C10
Mount Cory 245 ....C4
Mount Eaton 236 ....G4
Mount Gilead▲ 2,846 ....E4

Mount Healthy 7,580 ....B9
Mount Orab 1,929 ....C7
Mount Pleasant 498 ....J5
Mount Sterling 1,647 ....D6
Mount Vernon▲ 14,550 ....E5
Mount Victory 551 ....D4
Mowrystown 460 ....C7
Mulberry 2,856 ....B7
Munroe Falls 5,359 ....H3
Murray City 499 ....F6
Mutual 126 ....C5
Napoleon▲ 8,884 ....B3
Nashville 181 ....F4
Navarre 1,635 ....H4
Neffs 1,213 ....J5
Nellie 130 ....F5
Nelsonville 4,563 ....F7
Nevada 849 ....D4
Neville 226 ....B8
New Albany 1,621 ....E5
New Alexandria 257 ....J5
New Athens 370 ....H5
New Bloomington 282 ....D4
New Boston 2,717 ....E8
New Bremen 2,558 ....B5
New Carlisle 6,049 ....C6
New Concord 2,086 ....G6
New Holland 841 ....D6
New Knoxville 838 ....B4
New Lebanon 4,323 ....B6
New Lexington▲ 5,117 ....F6
New London 2,642 ....F3
New Madison 928 ....A6
New Miami 2,555 ....A7
New Middletown 1,912 ....J4
New Paris 1,801 ....A6
New Philadelphia▲ 15,698 ....G5
New Richmond 2,408 ....B8
New Riegel 298 ....D3
New Straitsville 865 ....F6
New Vienna 932 ....C7
New Washington 1,057 ....E4
New Waterford 1,278 ....J4
New Weston 148 ....A5
Newark▲ 44,389 ....F5
Newcomerstown 4,012 ....G5
Newton Falls 4,866 ....J3
Newtonsville 427 ....B7
Newtown 1,589 ....C10
Ney 331 ....B3
Niles 21,128 ....J3
North Baltimore 3,139 ....C3
North Bend 541 ....B9
North Canton 14,748 ....H4
North College Hill 11,002 ....B9
North Fairfield 504 ....E3
North Hampton 417 ....C5
North Kingsville 2,672 ....J2
North Lewisburg 1,160 ....C5
North Madison 8,699 ....H2
North Olmsted 34,204 ....G9
North Perry 824 ....H2
North Randall 977 ....H9
North Robinson 216 ....E4
North Royalton 23,197 ....H10
North Star 246 ....A5
North Zanesville 2,121 ....G6
Northfield 3,624 ....J10
Northridge 5,939 ....B6
Northwood 5,506 ....D2
Norton 11,477 ....G3
Norwalk▲ 14,731 ....E3
Norwich 133 ....G6
Norwood 23,674 ....C9
Oak Harbor 2,637 ....D2
Oak Hill 1,831 ....E8
Oakwood 709 ....H9
Oakwood 886 ....B6
Oakwood 9,372 ....B6
Oberlin 8,191 ....F3
Obetz 3,167 ....E6
Ohio City 899 ....A4

Olmsted Falls 6,741 ....G9
Ontario 4,026 ....E4
Orange 2,810 ....J5
Orangeville 253 ....J3
Oregon 18,334 ....D2
Orient 273 ....D6
Orrville 7,712 ....G4
Orwell 1,258 ....J2
Osgood 255 ....A5
Ostrander 431 ....D5
Ottawa Hills 4,543 ....C2
Ottawa▲ 3,999 ....B3
Ottoville 842 ....B4
Otway 105 ....D8
Owensville 1,019 ....B7
Oxford 18,937 ....A6
Painesville▲ 15,699 ....H2
Palestine 197 ....A5
Pandora 1,009 ....C4
Parma 87,876 ....H9
Parma Heights 21,448 ....G9
Parral 255 ....G4
Pataskala 3,046 ....E5
Patterson 145 ....C4
Paulding▲ 2,605 ....A3
Payne 1,244 ....A3
Peebles 1,782 ....C8
Pemberville 1,279 ....C3
Peninsula 562 ....G3
Pepper Pike 6,185 ....J9
Perry 1,012 ....H2
Perrysburg 12,551 ....C2
Perrysville 691 ....F4
Phillipsburg 644 ....B6
Philo 810 ....G6
Pickerington 5,668 ....E5
Piketon 1,717 ....E7
Pioneer 1,287 ....A2
Piqua 20,612 ....B5
Pitsburg 425 ....A6
Plain City 2,278 ....D5
Plainfield 178 ....G5
Pleasant City 419 ....G6
Pleasant Hill 1,066 ....B5
Pleasant Plain 138 ....B7
Pleasantville 926 ....F6
Plymouth 1,942 ....E4
Poland 2,992 ....J3
Polk 355 ....F4
Pomeroy▲ 2,259 ....G7
Port Clinton▲ 7,106 ....E2
Port Jefferson 381 ....C5
Port Washington 513 ....G5
Port Wiliam 242 ....C6
Portage 469 ....C3
Portsmouth▲ 22,676 ....D8
Potsdam 250 ....B6
Powell 2,154 ....D5
Powhatan Point 1,807 ....J6
Proctorville 765 ....F9
Prospect 1,148 ....D5
Put-in-Bay 141 ....E2
Quaker City 560 ....H6
Quincy 697 ....C5
Racine 729 ....G7
Rarden 184 ....D8
Ravenna▲ 12,069 ....H3
Rawson 482 ....C4
Ray 490 ....E7
Rayland 566 ....J5
Reading 12,038 ....C9
Reminderville 2,163 ....J10
Republic 611 ....D3
Reynoldsburg 25,748 ....E6
Richfield 3,117 ....G3
Richmond (Grand River) H2
Richmond 624 ....J5
Richmond Heights 9,611 ....H9
Richwood 2,186 ....D5
Ridgeway 378 ....D4
Rio Grande 995 ....F8
Ripley 1,816 ....C8
Risingsun 659 ....D3
Rittman 6,147 ....G4

Riverlea 503 ....D5
Rochester 206 ....F3
Rock Creek 553 ....J2
Rockford 1,119 ....A4
Rocky Ridge 425 ....D2
Rocky River 20,410 ....G9
Rogers 247 ....J4
Rome 99 ....J2
Rosemount 1,926 ....D8
Roseville 1,847 ....F6
Ross 2,124 ....B9
Rossburg 250 ....A5
Rossford 5,861 ....C2
Roswell 257 ....H5
Rushsylvania 573 ....C5
Rushville 229 ....F6
Russells Point 1,504 ....C5
Russellville 459 ....C8
Russia 442 ....B5
Rutland 469 ....F7
Sabina 2,662 ....C7
Saint Bernard 5,344 ....B9
Saint Clairsville▲ 5,162 ....J5
Saint Henry 1,907 ....A5
Saint Louisville 372 ....F5
Saint Martin 141 ....C7
Saint Marys 8,441 ....B4
Saint Paris 1,842 ....C5
Salem 12,233 ....J4
Salineville 1,474 ....J4
Sandusky▲ 29,764 ....E3
Sarahsville 162 ....H6
Sardinia 792 ....C7
Savannah 363 ....F4
Scio 856 ....H5
Sciotodale 1,128 ....E8
Scott 339 ....A4
Seaman 1,013 ....C8
Sebring 4,848 ....H4
Senecaville 434 ....H6
Seven Hills 12,339 ....H9
Seven Mile 804 ....A7
Seville 1,810 ....G3
Shadyside 3,934 ....J6
Shaker Heights 30,831 ....H9
Sharon 13,153 ....G6
Sharonville 10,108 ....C9
Shawnee 742 ....F6
Shawnee Hills 423 ....D5
Sheffield 1,943 ....F3
Sheffield Lake 9,825 ....F3
Shelby 9,564 ....E4
Sherrodsville 284 ....H4
Sherwood 828 ....A3
Shiloh 778 ....E4
Shreve 1,584 ....F4
Sidney▲ 18,710 ....B5
Silver Lake 3,052 ....H3
Silverton 5,859 ....C9
Sinking Spring 189 ....D7
Smithfield 722 ....J5
Smithville 1,354 ....G4
Solon 18,548 ....J9
Somerset 1,390 ....F6
Somerville 291 ....A6
South Amherst 1,765 ....F3
South Bloomfield 900 ....D6
South Charleston 1,626 ....C6
South Euclid 23,866 ....H9
South Lebanon 2,696 ....B7
South Point 3,823 ....E9
South Russell 3,402 ....H1
South Salem 227 ....D7
South Solon 379 ....C6
South Vienna 550 ....C6
South Webster 806 ....E8
South Zanesville 1,969 ....F6
Sparta 201 ....E5
Spencer 726 ....F3
Spencerville 2,288 ....B4
Spring Valley 567 ....C6
Springboro 6,590 ....B6
Springdale 10,621 ....B9
Springfield▲ 70,487 ....C6

Steubenville▲ 22,125 ....J5
Stockport 462 ....G6
Stone Creek 181 ....H5
Stout 518 ....D8
Stoutsville 537 ....E6
Stow 27,702 ....H3
Strasburg 1,995 ....G4
Stratton 278 ....J4
Streetsboro 9,932 ....H3
Strongsville 35,308 ....G10
Struthers 12,284 ....J3
Stryker 1,468 ....B3
Sugar Grove 465 ....E6
Sugarcreek 2,062 ....G5
Summerfield 295 ....H6
Summitville 125 ....J4
Sunbury 2,046 ....E5
Swanton 3,557 ....C2
Sycamore 919 ....D4
Sylvania 17,301 ....C2
Syracuse 827 ....G7
Tallmadge 14,870 ....H3
Tarlton 315 ....E6
Taylorsville (Philo) G6
Terrace Park 2,133 ....D9
The Plains 2,644 ....F7
Thornville 758 ....F6
Thurston 539 ....E6
Tiffin▲ 18,604 ....D3
Tiltonsville 1,517 ....J5
Timberlake 833 ....J8
Tipp City 6,027 ....B6
Tiro 246 ....E4
Toledo▲ 332,943 ....D2
Tontogany 364 ....C3
Toronto 6,127 ....J5
Tremont City 493 ....C5
Trenton 6,189 ....B7
Trimble 441 ....F7
Trotwood 8,816 ....B6
Troy▲ 19,478 ....B5
Tuscarawas 826 ....H5
Twinsburg 9,606 ....J10
Uhrichsville 5,604 ....H5
Union 5,501 ....B6
Union City 1,984 ....A5
Uniontown 3,074 ....H4
Unionville 238 ....J2
Unionville Center 272 ....D5
Uniopolis 261 ....B4
University Heights 14,790 ....H9
Upper Arlington 34,128 ....D6
Upper Sandusky▲ 5,906 ....D4
Urbana▲ 11,353 ....C5
Urbancrest 862 ....D6
Utica 1,997 ....F5
Valley Hi 217 ....C5
Valley View 2,137 ....H9
Valley View 730 ....H9
Van Buren 337 ....C3
Van Wert▲ 10,891 ....A4
Vandalia 13,882 ....B6
Vanlue 373 ....C4
Venedocia 158 ....B4
Vermilion 11,127 ....F3
Verona 472 ....A6
Versailles 2,351 ....A5
Vienna 1,067 ....J3
Vinton 293 ....F8
Wadsworth 15,718 ....G3
Waite Hill 454 ....H2
Wakeman 948 ....F3
Walbridge 2,736 ....C2
Waldo 340 ....D5
Walton Hills 2,371 ....J10
Wapakoneta▲ 9,214 ....B4
Warren▲ 50,793 ....J3
Warrensville Heights 15,745...H9
Warsaw 699 ....G5
Washington Court House▲
  12,682 ....D6
Washingtonville 894 ....J4
Waterville 4,517 ....C2
Wauseon▲ 6,322 ....B2

Waverly▲ 4,477 ....D7
Wayne 803 ....C3
Waynesburg 1,068 ....H4
Waynesfield 831 ....C4
Waynesville 1,949 ....B6
Wellington 4,140 ....F3
Wellston 6,049 ....F7
Wellsville 4,532 ....J4
West Alexandria 1,460 ....A6
West Carrollton 14,403 ....B6
West Elkton 208 ....A6
West Farmington 542 ....J3
West Jefferson 4,331 ....D6
West Leipsic 244 ....B3
West Liberty 1,613 ....C5
West Manchester 464 ....A6
West Mansfield 830 ....C5
West Millgrove 171 ....C3
West Milton 4,348 ....B6
West Portsmouth 3,551 ....D8
West Rushville 134 ....E6
West Salem 1,534 ....F4
West Union▲ 3,096 ....C8
West Unity 1,677 ....B2
Westerville 30,269 ....D5
Westfield Center 784 ....G3
Westlake 27,018 ....G9
Weston 1,716 ....C3
Wharton 378 ....D4
Wheelersburg 5,113 ....E8
Whitehall 20,572 ....E6
Whitehouse 2,528 ....C2
Wickliffe 14,558 ....J9
Wilberforce 2,639 ....C6
Wilkesville 151 ....F7
Willard 6,210 ....E3
Williamsburg 2,322 ....B7
Williamsport 851 ....D6
Willoughby 20,510 ....J8
Willoughby Hills 8,427 ....J9
Willowick 15,269 ....J8
Willshire 541 ....A4
Wilmington▲ 11,199 ....C7
Wilmot 261 ....G4
Wilson 136 ....H6
Winchester 978 ....C8
Windham 2,943 ....H3
Wintersville 4,102 ....J5
Withamsville 2,834 ....B7
Woodlawn 2,674 ....C9
Woodmere 834 ....J9
Woodsfield▲ 2,832 ....H6
Woodstock 296 ....C5
Woodville 1,953 ....D3
Wooster▲ 22,191 ....G4
Worthington 14,869 ....E5
Wren 190 ....A4
Wyoming 8,128 ....C9
Xenia▲ 24,664 ....C6
Yankee Lake 88 ....J3
Yellow Springs 3,973 ....C6
Yorkshire 126 ....B5
Yorkville 1,246 ....J5
Youngstown▲ 95,732 ....J3
Zaleski 294 ....F7
Zanesfield 183 ....C5
Zanesville▲ 26,778 ....G6
Zoar 177 ....H4

OTHER FEATURES

Atwood (lake) H4
Auglaize (riv.) B4
Berlin (lake) H4
Big Walnut (creek) E5
Black (riv.) F3
Black Fork, Mohican (riv.) F4
Blanchard (riv.) C4
Blennerhassett (isl.) G7
Buckeye (lake) F6
Campbell (hill) C5
Captina (creek) J6
Cedar (pt.) D2

Chagrin (riv.) J8
Clear Fork (res.) E4
Clear Fork, Mohican (riv.) E4
Clendening (lake) H5
Cuyahoga (riv.) H10
Cuyahoga Valley
  Nat'l Rec. Area H10
Darby (creek) D5
Deer (creek) D6
Deer Creek (lake) D6
Delaware (lake) E5
Dillon (lake) F5
Dover (lake) H6
Duck (creek) H6
Erie (lake) E2
Grand (riv.) J2
Great Miami (riv.) A6
Hocking (riv.) F7
Hoover (res.) E5
Huron (riv.) E3
Indian (lake) C5
James A. Garfield Nat'l
  Hist. Site G2
Kelleys (isl.) E2
Killbuck (creek) F4
Kokosing (riv.) E5
Leesville (lake) H5
Licking (riv.) F5
Little Beaver (creek) J4
Little Miami (riv.) B7
Little Miami, East Fork (riv.) C8
Little Muskingum (riv.) H6
Loramie (lake) B5
Mad (riv.) C5
Maumee (bay) D2
Maumee (riv.) B3
Middle Bass (isl.) E2
Mohican (riv.) F4
Mosquito Creek (lake) J3
Mound City Group Nat'l Mon. F7
Muskingum (riv.) G6
North Bass (isl.) E2
Ohio (riv.) G7
Ohio Brush (creek) C8
Olentangy (riv.) D5
Paint (creek) D7
Perry's Victory and
  Int'l Peace Mem. E2
Piedmont (lake) H5
Portage (riv.) D2
Pymatuning (res.) J3
Raccoon (creek) F8
Rattlesnake (creek) C6
Rickenbacker A.F.B. E6
Rocky (riv.) G9
Rocky Fork (lake) C7
Saint Joseph (riv.) A3
Saint Marys (lake) B4
Saint Marys (riv.) A4
Salt Fork (creek) H5
Sandusky (bay) E3
Sandusky (riv.) D3
Scioto (riv.) D7
Senecaville (lake) H6
Sevenmile (creek) A6
South Bass (isl.) E2
Stillwater (riv.) B5
Symmes (creek) F8
Tappan (lake) H5
Tiffin (riv.) B2
Tuscarawas (riv.) H4
Vermilion (riv.) F3
Wabash (riv.) A4
West Sister (isl.) D1
Whiteoak (creek) C8
William H. Taft
  Nat'l Hist. Site C10
Wills (creek) G5
Wills Creek (lake) G5
Wright-Patterson A.F.B.
  8,579 ....B6
Yellow (creek) J4

▲County seat

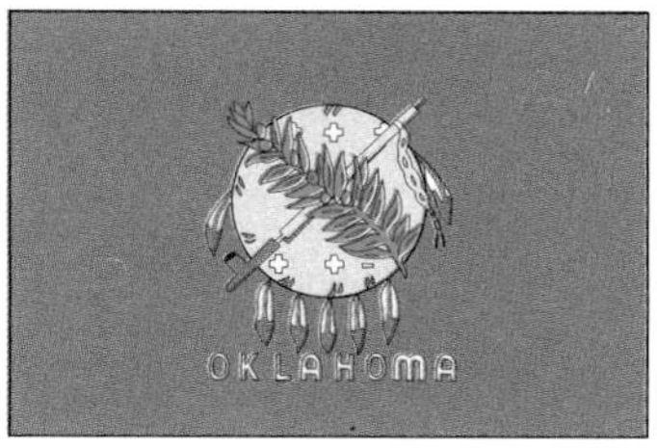

AREA 69,956 sq. mi. (181,186 sq. km.)
POPULATION 3,157,604
CAPITAL Oklahoma City
LARGEST CITY Oklahoma City
HIGHEST POINT Black Mesa 4,973 ft. (1516 m.)
SETTLED IN 1889
ADMITTED TO UNION November 16, 1907
POPULAR NAME Sooner State
STATE FLOWER Mistletoe
STATE BIRD Scissor-tailed Flycatcher

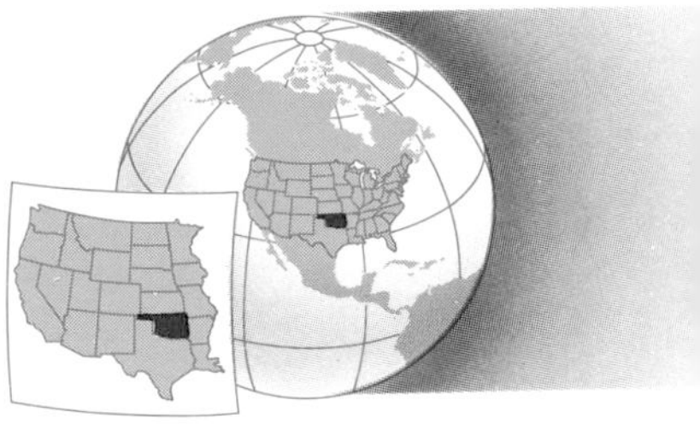

COUNTIES

Adair 18,421 ... S3
Alfalfa 6,416 ... K1
Atoka 12,778 ... O6
Beaver 6,023 ... E1
Beckham 18,812 ... G4
Blaine 11,470 ... K3
Bryan 32,089 ... O7
Caddo 29,550 ... K4
Canadian 74,409 ... K3
Carter 42,919 ... M6
Cherokee 34,049 ... R3
Choctaw 15,302 ... P6
Cimarron 3,301 ... A1
Cleveland 174,253 ... M4
Coal 5,780 ... O5
Comanche 111,486 ... K5
Cotton 6,651 ... K6
Craig 14,104 ... R1
Creek 60,915 ... O3
Custer 26,897 ... H3
Delaware 28,070 ... S2
Dewey 5,551 ... H2
Ellis 4,497 ... G2
Garfield 56,735 ... L2
Garvin 26,605 ... M5
Grady 41,747 ... L5
Grant 5,689 ... L1
Greer 6,559 ... G5
Harmon 3,793 ... G5
Harper 4,063 ... G1
Haskell 10,940 ... R4
Hughes 13,023 ... O4
Jackson 28,764 ... H5
Jefferson 7,010 ... L6
Johnston 10,032 ... N6
Kay 48,056 ... M1
Kingfisher 13,212 ... L3
Kiowa 11,347 ... J5
Latimer 10,333 ... R5
Le Flore 43,270 ... S5
Lincoln 29,216 ... N3
Logan 29,011 ... M3
Love 8,157 ... M7
Major 8,055 ... K2
Marshall 10,829 ... N6
Mayes 33,366 ... R2
McClain 22,795 ... L5
McCurtain 33,433 ... S6
McIntosh 16,779 ... P4
Murray 12,042 ... M6
Muskogee 68,078 ... R3
Noble 11,045 ... M2
Nowata 9,992 ... P1
Okfuskee 11,551 ... O3
Oklahoma 599,611 ... M3
Okmulgee 36,490 ... P3
Osage 41,645 ... O1
Ottawa 30,561 ... S1
Pawnee 15,575 ... N2
Payne 61,507 ... N2
Pittsburg 40,581 ... P5
Pontotoc 34,119 ... N5
Pottawatomie 58,760 ... N4
Pushmataha 10,997 ... R6
Roger Mills 4,147 ... G3
Rogers 55,170 ... P2
Seminole 25,412 ... N4
Sequoyah 33,828 ... S3
Stephens 42,299 ... L6
Texas 16,419 ... C1
Tillman 10,384 ... J6
Tulsa 503,341 ... P2
Wagoner 47,883 ... P3
Washington 48,066 ... P1
Washita 11,441 ... J4
Woods 9,103 ... J1
Woodward 18,976 ... H2

CITIES and TOWNS

Achille 491 ... O7
Ada▲ 15,820 ... N5
Adair 685 ... R2
Adams 150 ... D1
Adamson 150 ... P5
Addington 100 ... L6
Afton 915 ... S1
Agra 334 ... N3
Akins 250 ... S3
Albany 65 ... O7
Albert 100 ... K4
Albion 88 ... R5
Alderson 395 ... P5
Alex 639 ... L5
Alfalfa 70 ... J4
Aline 295 ... K1
Allen 972 ... O5
Altus▲ 21,910 ... H5
Alva▲ 5,495 ... J1
Amber 418 ... L4
Ames 268 ... K2
Amorita 56 ... K1
Anadarko▲ 6,586 ... K4
Antlers▲ 2,524 ... P6
Apache 1,591 ... K5
Apperson 30 ... N1
Aqua Park ... R3
Arapaho▲ 802 ... H3
Arcadia 320 ... M3
Ardmore▲ 23,079 ... M6
Arkoma 2,393 ... T4
Arnett▲ 547 ... G2
Asher 449 ... N5
Ashland 56 ... O5
Atoka▲ 3,298 ... O6
Atwood 225 ... O5
Avant 369 ... O2
Avard 37 ... J1
Avery 35 ... N3
Bache 100 ... P5
Bacone 786 ... R3
Baker 70 ... D1
Balko 100 ... E1
Barnsdall 1,316 ... O1
Baron 300 ... S3
Bartlesville▲ 34,256 ... O1
Battiest 250 ... S6
Bearden 142 ... O4
Beaver▲ 1,584 ... F1
Beggs 1,150 ... P3
Belzoni 50 ... R6
Bengal 300 ... R5
Bennington 251 ... P7
Bentley 75 ... O6
Berlin 50 ... G4
Bernice 330 ... S1
Bessie 248 ... H4
Bethany 20,075 ... L3
Bethel 2,505 ... S6
Bethel Acres 2,314 ... M4
Big Cabin 271 ... R1
Billings 555 ... M1
Binger 724 ... K4
Bison 103 ... L2
Bixby 9,502 ... P3
Blackburn 110 ... N2
Blackgum 150 ... S3
Blackwell 7,538 ... M1
Blair 922 ... H5
Blanchard 1,922 ... L4
Blanco 215 ... P5
Blocker 135 ... P4
Blue 175 ... O7
Bluejacket 247 ... R1
Boggy Depot 100 ... O6
Boise City▲ 1,509 ... B1
Bokchito 576 ... O6
Bokhoma 35 ... S7
Bokoshe 403 ... S4
Boley 908 ... O4
Boswell 643 ... P6
Bowlegs 398 ... N4
Bowring 115 ... O1
Boyd 10 ... E1
Boynton 391 ... P3
Braden 15 ... S4
Bradley 166 ... L5
Braggs 308 ... R3
Braman 251 ... M1
Bray 925 ... L5
Breckinridge 261 ... L2
Briartown 55 ... R4
Bridgeport 137 ... K3
Brinkman ... G4
Bristow 4,062 ... O3
Broken Arrow 58,043 ... P2
Broken Bow 3,961 ... S7
Bromide 162 ... N6
Brooksville 69 ... M4
Bryant 74 ... P4
Buffalo▲ 1,312 ... G1
Bunch 64 ... S3
Burbank 165 ... N1
Burlington 169 ... K1
Burneyville 150 ... M7
Burns Flat 1,027 ... H4
Butler 341 ... H3
Byars 263 ... N5
Byng 755 ... N5
Byron 57 ... K1
Cache 2,251 ... J5
Caddo 918 ... O6
Cairo 50 ... O5
Calera 1,536 ... O7
Calumet 560 ... K3
Calvin 251 ... O5
Camargo 185 ... H2
Cameron 327 ... T4
Canadian 261 ... P4
Canadian City ... L4
Caney 184 ... O6
Canton 632 ... J2
Canute 538 ... H4
Capron 38 ... J1
Cardin 165 ... S1
Carmen 459 ... J1
Carnegie 1,593 ... J4
Carney 558 ... N3
Carrier 171 ... K2
Carter 286 ... H4
Cartersville 79 ... S4
Cashion 430 ... L3
Castle 94 ... O4
Catoosa 2,954 ... P2
Cement 642 ... K5
Center 100 ... N5
Centrahoma 106 ... O5
Centralia ... R1
Chandler▲ 2,596 ... N3
Chattanooga 437 ... J6
Checotah 3,290 ... R4
Chelsea 1,620 ... P1
Cherokee▲ 1,787 ... K1
Chester 104 ... J2
Cheyenne▲ 948 ... G3
Chickasha▲ 14,988 ... L4
Chilocco 400 ... M1
Choctaw 8,545 ... M3
Chouteau 1,771 ... R2
Christie 375 ... S3
Cimarron 71 ... L3
Claremore▲ 13,280 ... R2
Clarita 72 ... O6
Clayton 636 ... R5
Clearview 47 ... O4
Clemscot 52 ... L6
Cleo Springs 359 ... K2
Cleora 45 ... S1
Cleveland 3,156 ... O2
Clinton 9,298 ... H3
Cloud Chief 12 ... J4
Cloudy 175 ... R6
Coalgate▲ 1,895 ... O5
Cogar 40 ... K4
Colbert 1,043 ... O7
Colcord 628 ... S2
Cold Springs 24 ... J5
Cole 355 ... L4
Coleman 200 ... O6
Collinsville 3,612 ... P2
Colony 163 ... J4
Comanche 1,695 ... L6
Commerce 2,426 ... R1
Concho 300 ... L3
Connerville 150 ... N6
Cooperton 15 ... J5
Copan 809 ... P1
Cordell▲ ... H4
Corinne 100 ... R6
Corn 548 ... J4
Cornish 164 ... L6
Council Hill 139 ... P3
Countyline 550 ... L6
Courtney 12 ... L7
Covington 590 ... L2
Coweta 6,159 ... P3
Cowlington 756 ... S4
Cox City 285 ... L5
Coyle 289 ... M3
Crawford 53 ... G3
Crescent 1,236 ... L3
Cromwell 268 ... N4
Crowder 339 ... P4
Cumberland 100 ... N6
Curtis 30 ... H2
Cushing 7,218 ... N3
Custer City 443 ... J3
Cyril 1,072 ... K5
Dacoma 182 ... J1
Daisy 250 ... P5
Dale 160 ... M4
Darwin 50 ... P6
Davenport 979 ... N3
Davidson 473 ... J6
Davis 2,543 ... M5
Deer Creek 124 ... L1
Del City 23,928 ... L4
Dela 434 ... P6
Delaware 544 ... P1
Delhi 41 ... G4
Depew 502 ... O3
Devol 165 ... J6
Dewar 921 ... P4
Dewey 3,326 ... P1
Dibble 181 ... L4
Dickson 942 ... M6
Dill City 622 ... H4
Disney 257 ... S2
Dougherty 138 ... M6
Douglas 55 ... L2
Douthat 30 ... S1
Dover 376 ... L3
Dow 300 ... P5
Driftwood ... K1
Drummond 408 ... L2
Drumright 2,799 ... N3
Duke (E. Duke) 360 ... G5
Duncan▲ 21,732 ... L5
Durant▲ 12,823 ... O6
Durham 30 ... G3
Dustin 429 ... O4
Eagle City 56 ... J3
Eagletown 650 ... S6
Eakly 277 ... K4
Earlsboro 535 ... N4
Edmond 52,315 ... M3
El Reno▲ 15,414 ... K3
Eldorado 573 ... G6
Elgin 975 ... K5
Elk City 10,428 ... G4
Elmer 132 ... H6
Elmore City 493 ... M5
Elmwood 300 ... F1
Empire City 219 ... L6
Enid▲ 45,309 ... L2
Enterprise 130 ... R4
Erick 1,083 ... G4
Eucha 210 ... S2
Eufaula▲ 2,652 ... P4
Fair Oaks 1,133 ... P2
Fairfax 1,749 ... N1
Fairland 916 ... S1
Fairmont 129 ... L2
Fairview▲ 2,936 ... J2
Fallis 49 ... M3
Fanshawe 331 ... S5
Fargo 299 ... G2
Farris 100 ... P6
Faxon 127 ... J6
Fay 140 ... J3
Featherston 75 ... P4
Felt 120 ... A1
Fillmore 60 ... N6
Finley 350 ... R6
Fittstown 500 ... N5
Fitzhugh 196 ... N5
Fleetwood 12 ... L7
Fletcher 1,002 ... K5
Foraker 25 ... O1
Forest Park 1,249 ... M3
Forgan 489 ... E1
Fort Cobb 663 ... K4
Fort Gibson 3,359 ... R3
Fort Supply 369 ... G1
Fort Towson 568 ... R7
Foss 148 ... H4
Foster 100 ... M5
Fox 400 ... M6
Foyil 86 ... R2
Francis 346 ... N5
Frederick▲ 5,221 ... H6
Freedom 264 ... H1
Gage 473 ... G2
Gans 218 ... S4
Garber 959 ... M2
Garvin 128 ... S7
Gate 159 ... F1
Geary 1,347 ... K3
Gene Autry 97 ... N6
Geronimo 990 ... K6
Gerty 95 ... O5
Glencoe 473 ... M2
Glenpool 6,688 ... P3
Glover 244 ... S6
Golden 300 ... S6
Goldsby 816 ... L4
Goltry 297 ... K1
Goodwater 240 ... S7
Goodwell 1,065 ... C1
Gore 690 ... R3
Gotebo 370 ... J4
Gould 237 ... G5
Gowen 75 ... R5
Gracemont 339 ... K4
Grady 85 ... L6
Graham 200 ... M6
Grainola 58 ... N1
Grand Lake Towne 58 ... S1
Grandfield 1,224 ... J6
Granite 1,844 ... H5
Grant ... R7
Gray Horse 60 ... N1
Grayson 66 ... P3
Greenfield 200 ... K3
Griggs 15 ... B1
Grove 4,020 ... S1
Guthrie▲ 10,518 ... M3
Guymon▲ 7,803 ... D1
Haileyville 918 ... P5
Hall Park 1,090 ... M4
Hallett 159 ... N2
Hammon 611 ... H3
Hanna 99 ... P4
Hanson 250 ... S4
Harden City 250 ... N5
Hardesty 228 ... D1
Hardy ... N1
Harjo 35 ... N4
Harmon 27 ... G2
Harrah 4,206 ... M4
Harris 192 ... S7
Hartshorne 2,120 ... R5
Haskell 2,143 ... P3
Hastings 164 ... K6
Haworth 293 ... S7
Haywood 175 ... P5
Headrick 183 ... H5
Healdton 2,872 ... M6
Heavener 2,601 ... S5
Helena 1,043 ... K1
Hendrix 108 ... O7
Hennepin 300 ... M5
Hennessey 1,902 ... L2
Henryetta 5,872 ... O4
Herd 18 ... O1
Hess 29 ... H6
Hester 25 ... H5
Hickory 77 ... N5
Hillsdale 96 ... K1
Hinton 1,233 ... K4
Hitchcock 139 ... K3
Hitchita 118 ... P3
Hobart▲ 4,305 ... J5
Hockerville 125 ... S1
Hodgen 150 ... S5
Hoffman 175 ... P4
Holdenville▲ 4,792 ... O4
Hollis▲ 2,584 ... G5
Hollister 59 ... J6
Homestead 35 ... K2
Hominy 2,342 ... O2
Honobia 80 ... R5
Hooker 1,551 ... D1
Hoot Owl 5 ... R2
Hopeton 42 ... J1
Howe 510 ... S5
Hoyt 160 ... R4
Hugo▲ 5,978 ... P7
Hulah 50 ... O1
Hulbert 499 ... R3
Humphreys 68 ... H5
Hunter 218 ... L1
Hydro 977 ... J3
Idabel▲ 6,957 ... S7
Indiahoma 337 ... J5

(continued on following page)

Agriculture, Industry and Resources

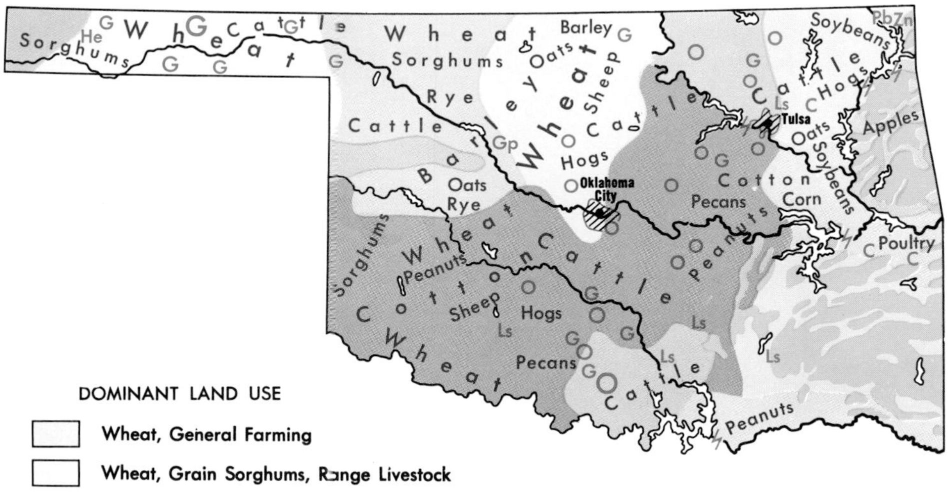

DOMINANT LAND USE

- Wheat, General Farming
- Wheat, Grain Sorghums, Range Livestock
- Wheat, Range Livestock
- General Farming, Livestock, Cash Grain
- General Farming, Livestock, Truck Farming, Cotton
- Cotton, General Farming
- Cotton, Wheat
- Fruit and Mixed Farming
- Range Livestock
- Forests

MAJOR MINERAL OCCURRENCES

C Coal
G Natural Gas
Gp Gypsum
He Helium
Ls Limestone
O Petroleum
Pb Lead
Zn Zinc

Water Power
Major Industrial Areas

Indianola 171 ....P4
Inola 1,444 ....P2
Isabella 113 ....K2
Jay▲ 2,220 ....S2
Jefferson 36 ....L1
Jenks 7,493 ....P2
Jennings 381 ....N2
Jet 272 ....K1
Jones 2,424 ....M3
Jumbo 40 ....P6
Kansas 556 ....S2
Kaw City 314 ....N1
Keefton 75 ....R3
Kellyville 984 ....O3
Kemp 138 ....O7
Kemp City (Hendrix) 106 ....O7
Kendrick 171 ....N3
Kenefic 147 ....O6
Kenton 21 ....A1
Kenwood 400 ....S2
Keota 625 ....S4
Ketchum 263 ....R1
Keyes 454 ....B1
Kiamichi 43 ....R5
Kiefer 962 ....O3
Kildare 94 ....M1
Kingfisher▲ 4,095 ....L3
Kingston 1,237 ....N7
Kinta 233 ....R4
Kiowa 718 ....P5
Knowles 18 ....F1
Konawa 1,508 ....N5
Kosoma 50 ....P6
Krebs 1,955 ....P5
Kremlin 243 ....L1
Lahoma 645 ....K2
Lamar 97 ....O4
Lambert 11 ....J1
Lamont 454 ....L1
Lane 218 ....O6
Langley 526 ....R2
Langston 1,471 ....M3
Laverne 1,269 ....G1
Lawton▲ 80,561 ....K5
Leach 350 ....S2
Lebanon 382 ....N7
Leedey 468 ....H3
Leflore 119 ....S5
Lehigh 303 ....O6
Lela 35 ....N2
Lenapah 253 ....P1
Leon 101 ....M7
Leonard 400 ....P3
Lequire 250 ....R4
Lexington 1,776 ....M4
Lima (New Lima) 133 ....O4
Lindsay 2,947 ....L5
Little Chief 35 ....N1
Loco 160 ....L6
Locust Grove 1,326 ....R2
Lone Grove 4,114 ....M6
Lone Wolf 576 ....H5
Longdale 281 ....K2
Lookeba 141 ....K4
Lotsee 7 ....O2
Loveland 13 ....J6
Lovell L2
Loyal 76 ....K3
Lucien 350 ....M2
Lula 100 ....O5
Luther 1,560 ....M3
Lutie 100 ....R5
Macomb 64 ....M4
Madill▲ 3,069 ....N6
Manchester 106 ....L1
Mangum▲ 3,344 ....G5
Manitou 244 ....J5
Mannford 1,826 ....O2
Mannsville 396 ....N6
Maramec 110 ....N2
Marble City 232 ....S3
Marietta▲ 2,306 ....M7
Marland 280 ....M1
Marlow 4,416 ....K5
Marshall 288 ....L2
Martha 217 ....H5
Mason 75 ....O3
Maud 1,204 ....N4
May 42 ....G1
Mayfield 17 ....G4
Maysville 1,203 ....M5
Mazie 118 ....R2

McAlester▲ 16,370 ....P5
McBride 80 ....N7
McCurtain 465 ....R4
McLoud 2,493 ....M4
McMillan 50 ....M6
Mead 109 ....O7
Medford▲ 1,172 ....L1
Medicine Park 285 ....J5
Meeker 1,003 ....N4
Mehan 60 ....M2
Meno 155 ....K2
Meridian 45 ....M3
Miami▲ 13,142 ....S1
Micawber 18 ....N3
Midwest City 52,267 ....M4
Milburn 264 ....O6
Milfay 200 ....N3
Mill Creek 336 ....N6
Millerton 234 ....S7
Milo 25 ....M6
Milton 55 ....S4
Minco 1,411 ....L4
Moffett 219 ....S4
Monroe 150 ....S4
Moodys 250 ....S2
Moon 50 ....S7
Moore 40,318 ....M4
Mooreland 1,157 ....H2
Morris 1,216 ....P3
Morrison 640 ....M2
Mounds 980 ....O3
Mountain Park 473 ....J5
Mountain View 1,086 ....J4
Moyers 312 ....P6

Muldrow 2,889 ....S4
Mulhall 199 ....M2
Muse 350 ....S5
Muskogee▲ 37,708 ....R3
Mustang 10,434 ....L4
Mutual 68 ....H2
Narcissa 100 ....S1
Nardin 75 ....M1
Nash 281 ....K1
Nashoba 50 ....R6
Nelagoney 62 ....O1
New Alluwe 83 ....R1
New Cordell▲ (Cordell) 2,903 ....H4
New Lima O4
New Prue (Prue) 554 ....O2
New Tulsa 272 ....P2
Newalla 350 ....M4
Newcastle 4,214 ....L4
Newkirk▲ 2,168 ....N1
Nichols Hills 4,020 ....L3
Nicoma Park 2,353 ....M4
Noble 4,710 ....M4
Norge 97 ....K4
Norman▲ 80,071 ....M4
North Enid 874 ....L2
North Miami 450 ....R1
Nowata▲ 3,896 ....P1
Oakhurst 3,030 ....P2
Oakland 602 ....N6
Oaks 431 ....S2
Oakwood 107 ....J3
Ochelata 441 ....P1
Octavia 30 ....S5
Oilton 1,060 ....N2

Okarche 1,160 ....L3
Okay 528 ....R3
Okeene 1,343 ....K2
Okemah▲ 3,085 ....O4
Okesa 165 ....O1
Oklahoma City (cap.)▲
      444,719 ....L4
Okmulgee▲ 13,441 ....O3
Oktaha 266 ....R3
Oleta 50 ....R6
Olive 100 ....O2
Olney 125 ....O6
Olustee 701 ....H5
Omega 50 ....K3
Oologah 828 ....P2
Optima 92 ....D1
Orienta 25 ....J2
Orlando 198 ....M2
Osage 163 ....O2
Oscar 60 ....L7
Overbrook 443 ....M6
Owasso 11,151 ....P2
Paden 400 ....N3
Page 20 ....S5
Panama 1,528 ....S4
Panola 75 ....R5
Paoli 574 ....M5
Paradise Hill 88 ....R3
Park Hill 100 ....R3
Parkland 60 ....N3
Pauls Valley▲ 6,150 ....M5
Pawhuska▲ 3,825 ....O1
Pawnee▲ 2,197 ....N2
Pearson 30 ....N4

Peckham 65 ....M1
Peggs R2
Pensacola 69 ....R2
Peoria 136 ....S1
Perkins 1,925 ....M3
Pernell 110 ....M5
Perry▲ 4,978 ....M2
Pershing 27 ....O1
Pharoah 100 ....O4
Phillips 161 ....O6
Picher 1,714 ....S1
Pickens 525 ....S6
Piedmont 2,522 ....L3
Pink 1,020 ....M4
Pittsburg 249 ....P5
Platter 275 ....O7
Plunkettville 125 ....S6
Pocasset 220 ....L4
Pocola 3,664 ....T4
Ponca City 26,359 ....M1
Pond Creek 982 ....L1
Pontotoc 150 ....N6
Pooleville 75 ....M6
Porter 588 ....R3
Porum 851 ....R4
Poteau▲ 7,210 ....S4
Prague 2,308 ....N4
Preston 350 ....P3
Proctor 175 ....S3
Prue 346 ....O2
Pryor▲ 8,327 ....R2
Purcell▲ 4,784 ....M4
Putnam 44 ....J3
Quapaw 928 ....S1

Quay 59 ....N2
Quinlan 23 ....J2
Quinton 1,133 ....R4
Ralston 405 ....N2
Ramona 508 ....P1
Ranchwood Manor 296 ....L4
Randlett 458 ....K6
Ratliff City 157 ....M6
Rattan 257 ....R6
Ravia 404 ....N6
Reagan 25 ....N6
Red Oak 602 ....R5
Red Rock 321 ....M2
Redbird 166 ....P3
Reed 48 ....G5
Remus N4
Renfrow 19 ....L1
Rentiesville 66 ....R4
Reydon 200 ....G3
Ringling 1,250 ....L6
Ringold 200 ....R6
Ringwood 394 ....K2
Ripley 376 ....N2
Rock Island 478 ....T4
Rocky 181 ....J4
Roff 717 ....N5
Roland 2,481 ....S4
Roosevelt 323 ....J5
Rose 48 ....R2
Rosedale 97 ....M5
Rosston 54 ....G1
Rubottom 35 ....M7
Rufe 150 ....R6
Rush Springs 1,229 ....L5

Ryan 945 ....L6
Saddle Mountain 16 ....J5
Saint Louis 181 ....N4
Salina 1,153 ....R2
Sallisaw▲ 7,122 ....S4
Sand Point 179 ....N7
Sand Springs 15,346 ....O2
Sapulpa▲ 18,074 ....O3
Sardis 58 ....R5
Sasakwa 169 ....N5
Savanna 869 ....P5
Sawyer 200 ....R6
Sayre▲ 2,881 ....G4
Schulter 600 ....P4
Scipio 100 ....P4
Scraper 80 ....S2
Scullin N5
Seiling 1,031 ....K3
Selman 25 ....G1
Seminole 7,071 ....N4
Sentinel 960 ....H4
Seward M3
Shady Point 597 ....S4
Shamrock 95 ....N3
Sharon 108 ....H2
Shattuck 1,454 ....G2
Shawnee▲ 26,017 ....N4
Sherwood 60 ....S6
Shidler 487 ....N1
Short 200 ....S4
Silo 249 ....N6
Skedee 96 ....N2
Skiatook 4,910 ....O2
Slaughterville 1,843 ....M4

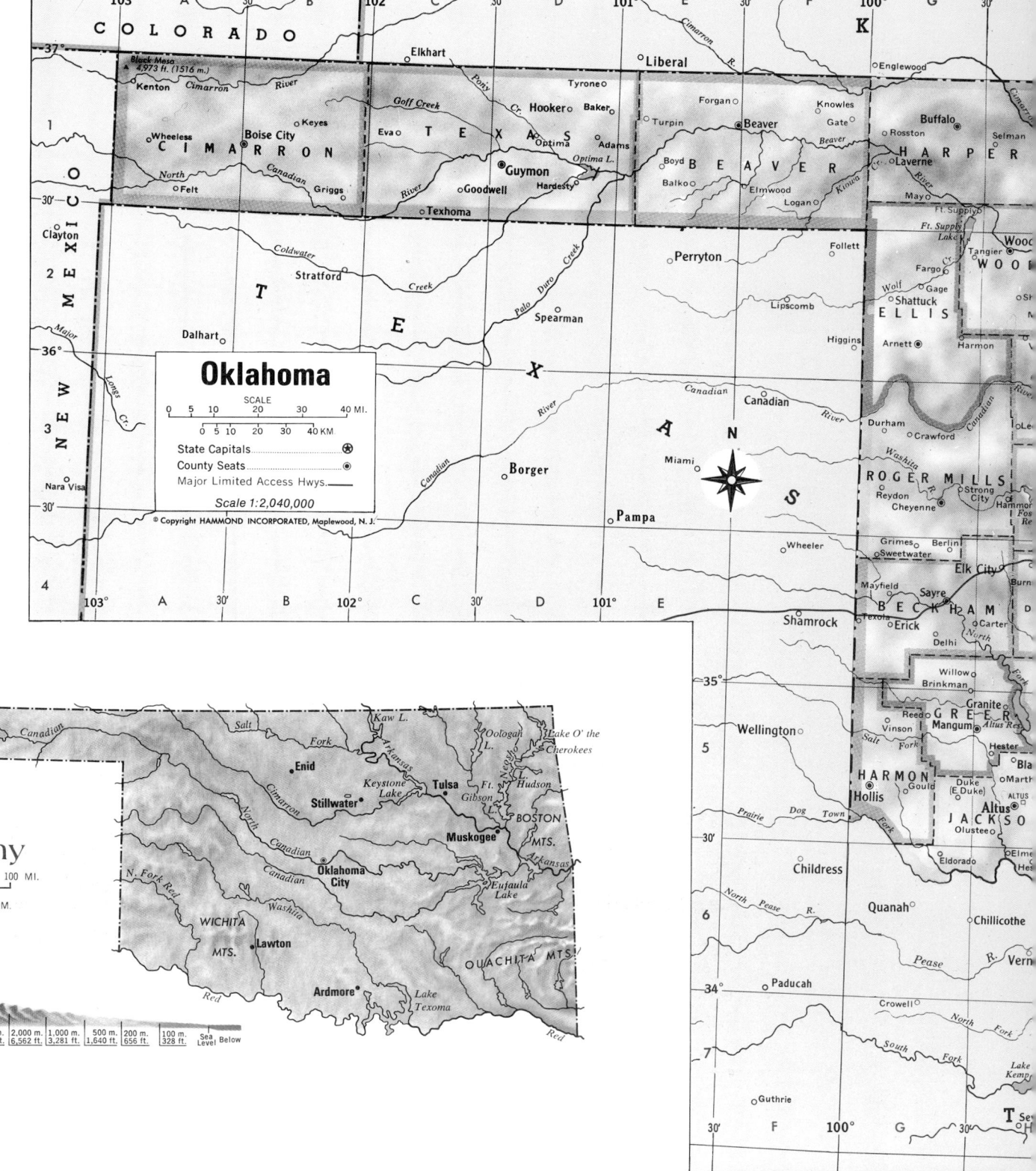

Slick 124	O3	Tabler 28	L4	Tuttle 2,807	L4	Waukomis 1,322	K2
Smithville 111	S6	Taft 400	R3	Tyrone 880	D1	Waurika▲ 2,088	L6
Snow 200	R6	Tahlequah▲ 10,398	R3	Union City 1,000	L4	Wayne 519	M5
Snyder 1,619	J5	Talala 206	P1	Utica 38	O7	Waynoka 947	J1
Soper 305	P6	Talihina 1,297	S5	Valley Brook 744	L4	Weatherford 10,124	J4
South Coffeyville 791	P1	Tallant 14	O1	Valliant 873	R6	Weathers 100	J4
Southard 130	K2	Taloga▲ 415	J2	Vanoss 130	N5	Webb City 99	N1
Sparks 202	N3	Tamaha 188	S4	Velma 661	L5	Webbers Falls 722	R3
Spavinaw 432	R2	Tatums 176	M6	Verden 546	K4	Welch 499	R1
Spencer 3,972	M3	Tecumseh 5,750	N4	Verdigris 150	P2	Weleetka 1,112	O4
Spencerville 275	R6	Temple 1,223	K6	Vernon 100	P2	Welling 115	S3
Sperry 937	P2	Terlton 121	O2	Vian 1,414	S4	Wellston 912	M3
Spiro 2,146	S4	Terral 469	L7	Vici 751	H3	Welty 80	O3
Springer 485	M6	Texhoma 746	C1	Vinson 42	G5	West Siloam Springs 539	S2
Stafford 18	H3	Texola 45	G4	Vinita▲ 5,804	R1	Westport 326	O2
Stanley 30	R5	The Village 10,353	L3	Wade 50	O7	Westville 1,374	S2
Sterling 684	K5	Thomas 1,246	J3	Wagoner▲ 6,894	R3	Wetumka 1,427	O4
Stidham 48	P4	Tiawah 125	P2	Wainwright 223	R3	Wewoka▲ 4,050	O4
Stigler▲ 2,574	R4	Tipton 1,043	H6	Wakita 453	L1	White Oak 200	R1
Stillwater▲ 36,676	N2	Tishomingo▲ 3,116	N6	Walters▲ 2,519	K6	Whitefield 253	R4
Stilwell▲ 2,663	S3	Tonkawa 3,127	M1	Wanette 346	M5	Whitesboro 450	S5
Stonebluff 50	P3	Tom 600	S7	Wann 126	P1	Wilburton▲ 3,092	R5
Stonewall 519	O5	Tonkawa 3,127	M1	Wapanucka 402	N6	Williams 110	T4
Strang 141	O2	Tribbey 288	M4	Wardville 52	P5	Willis 250	N7
Stratford 1,404	M5	Trousdale 38	N4	Warner 1,479	R4	Willow 142	H5
Stringtown 366	P6	Troy 92	N6	Warr Acres 9,288	L3	Wilson 1,639	M6
Strong City 49	G3	Trpin 450	E1	Warwick 160	M3	Wirt 350	L6
Stroud 2,666	N3	Tryon 514	N3	Washington 279	L4	Wister 956	S5
Stuart 228	O5	Tullahassee 92	P3	Washita 180	J4	Wolco 14	O1
Sugden 65	L6	Tulsa▲ 367,302	O2	Watonga▲ 3,408	K3	Wolf 200	N4
Sulphur▲ 4,824	N5	Tupelo 323	O5	Watova 35	P1	Woodford 30	M6
Summerfield 150	R4	Tushka 256	O6	Watson 48	S6	Woodville 31	N7
Sweetwater 85	G4	Tuskahoma 168	R5	Watson 48	S6	Woodward▲ 12,340	H2
Swink	R6	Tussy 150	L6	Watts 303	S2	Wright City 836	R6
						Wyandotte 366	S1
						Wynnewood 2,451	M5
						Wynona 531	O1
						Yale 1,392	N2
						Yanush 123	R5
						Yeager 40	O4
						Yuba 63	O7
						Yukon 20,935	L3

OTHER FEATURES

Altus (res.)	H5	Cimarron (riv.)	N2
Altus A.F.B.	H5	Clear Boggy (creek)	O6
Arbuckles, Lake of the (lake)	M6	Deep Fork, North	
Arbuckle Nat'l Rec. Area	N6	Canadian (riv.)	N3
Arkansas (riv.)	S4	Denison (dam)	H4
Atoka (res.)	P5	Elk (creek)	H4
Beaver (creek)	K6	Ellsworth (lake)	K1
Beaver (riv.)	F1	Ellsworth (lake)	K1
Bird (creek)	O1	Eucha (lake)	S2
Black Bear (creek)	M2	Eufaula (lake)	P4
Black Mesa (mt.)	A1	Fort Cobb (res.)	J4
Blue (riv.)	O6	Fort Gibson (lake)	R2
Bluestem (lake)	O1	Fort Sill 12,107	J5
Boston (mts.)	S3	Fort Supply (lake)	G1
Broken Bow (lake)	S6	Foss (res.)	H3
Cache (creek)	K6	Heyburn (res.)	O3
Canadian (riv.)	O4	Hudson (lake)	R2
Caney (riv.)	O1	Hugo (lake)	R6
Canton (lake)	J2	Hulah (lake)	O1
Carl Blackwell (lake)	M2	Illinois (riv.)	S3
Mountain Fork (riv.)	S6	Jackfork (mt.)	P5
Cherokees, Lake O'(lake)	S1	Kaw (lake)	N1
Chickasaw Nat'l Rec. Area	N6	Kerr, Robert S. (res.)	S4
Chickasha (lake)	K4	Keystone (lake)	O2
		Kiamichi (mt.)	S5
		Kiamichi (riv.)	R6
		Kiowa (creek)	F1
		Lawtonka (lake)	K5
		Little (riv.)	L4
		McAlester (lake)	P4
		Mountain Fork (riv.)	S6
		Mud (creek)	L6
		Muddy Boggy (creek)	O5
		Murray (lake)	M6

Neosho (riv.)	R1
North Canadian (riv.)	K3
North Carrizo (riv.)	A1
Oologah (lake)	P1
Optima (lake)	D1
Osage Ind. Res.	O1
Ouachita (mts.)	R5
Pine Creek (lake)	R6
Poteau (riv.)	S5
Prairie Dog Town Fork	
Red (riv.)	F5
Red (riv.)	R7
Red, North Fork (riv.)	H4
Salt Fork, Arkansas (riv.)	J1
Salt Fork, Red (riv.)	G5
Sans Bois (mts.)	R4
Scott (mt.)	K5
Spavinaw (lake)	S2
Tenkiller Ferry (lake)	S3
Texoma (lake)	N7
Thunderbird (lake)	M4
Tinker A.F.B.	M4
Tom Steed (res.)	J5
Vance A.F.B.	K2
Verdigris (riv.)	P2
Washita (riv.)	M5
Waurika (lake)	K6
Webbers Falls (res.)	R3
Wichita (riv.)	J5
Wildhorse (creek)	L5
Wister (lake)	S5
Wolf (creek)	G2

▲County seat.

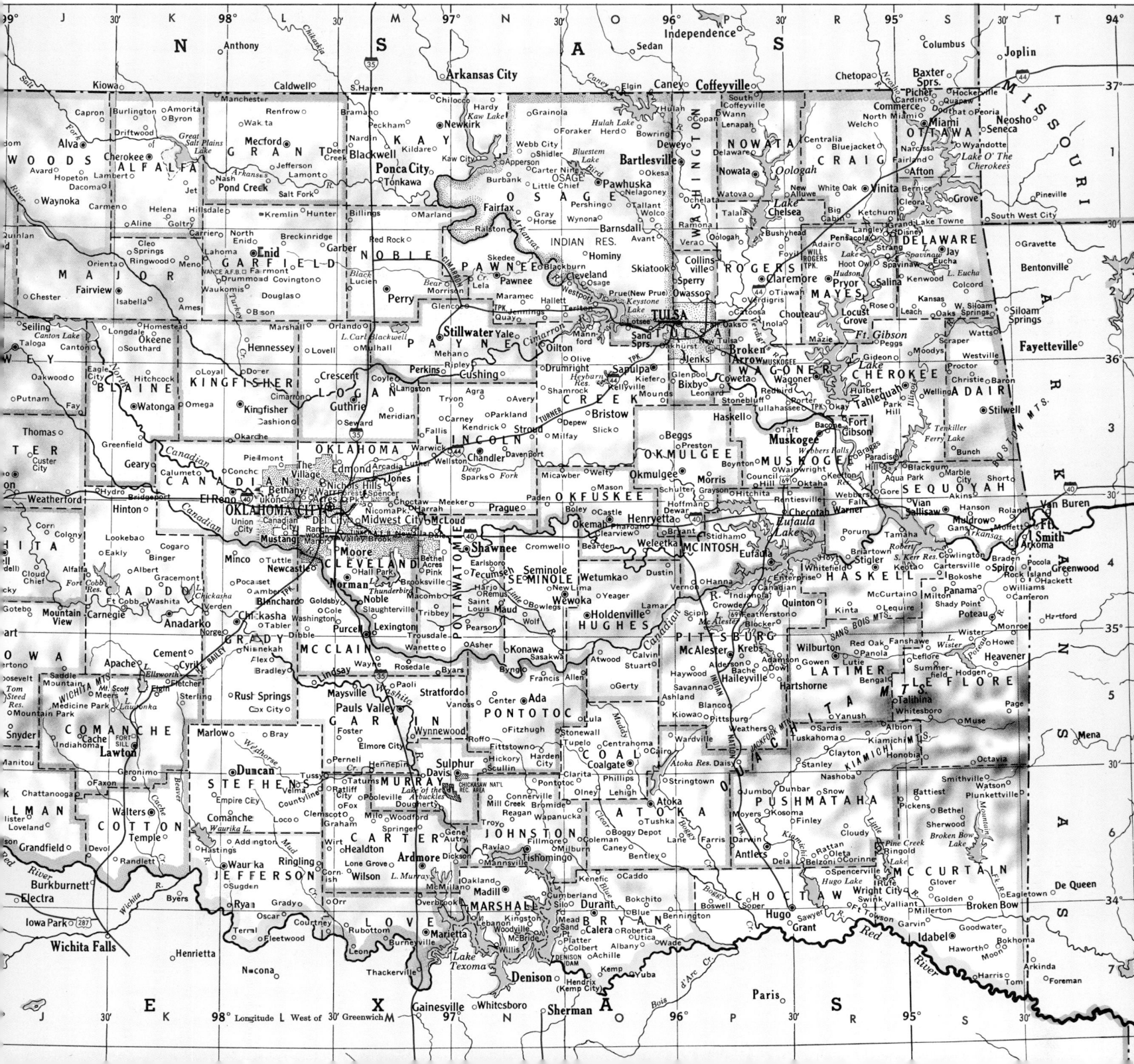

COUNTIES

Baker 15,317 ....K3
Benton 70,811 ....D3
Clackamas 278,850 ....E2
Clatsop 33,301 ....D1
Columbia 37,557 ....D2
Coos 60,273 ....C4
Crook 14,111 ....G3
Curry 19,327 ....C5
Deschutes 74,958 ....F4
Douglas 94,649 ....D4
Gilliam 1,717 ....G2
Grant 7,853 ....J3
Harney 7,060 ....H4
Hood River 16,903 ....F2
Jackson 146,389 ....E5
Jefferson 13,676 ....F3
Josephine 62,649 ....D5
Klamath 57,702 ....F5
Lake 7,186 ....G5
Lane 282,912 ....E4
Lincoln 38,889 ....D3
Linn 91,227 ....E3

Malheur 26,038 ....K4
Marion 228,483 ....E3
Morrow 7,625 ....H2
Multnomah 583,887 ....E2
Polk 49,541 ....D3
Sherman 1,918 ....G2
Tillamook 21,570 ....D2
Umatilla 59,249 ....J2
Union 23,598 ....J2
Wallowa 6,911 ....K2
Wasco 21,683 ....F2
Washington 311,554 ....D2
Wheeler 1,396 ....G3
Yamhill 65,551 ....D2

CITIES and TOWNS

Adair Village 554 ....D3
Adams 223 ....J2
Adel 24 ....H5
Adrian 131 ....K4
Agate Beach 975 ....C3
Agness 150 ....C5
Airlie 40 ....D3

Albany▲ 29,462 ....D3
Algoma 77 ....F5
Alicel 30 ....J2
Allegany 300 ....D4
Aloha 34,284 ....A2
Alpine 80 ....D3
Alsea 125 ....D3
Altamont 18,591 ....F5
Alvadore 800 ....D3
Amity 1,175 ....D2
Andrews 10 ....J5
Antelope 34 ....G3
Antone 40 ....H3
Applegate 150 ....D5
Arago 200 ....C4
Arch Cape 100 ....D2
Arlington 425 ....G2
Arock 40 ....K5
Ash 80 ....D4
Ashland 16,234 ....E5
Ashwood 98 ....G3
Astoria▲ 10,069 ....D1
Athena 997 ....J2
Aumsville 1,650 ....D3

Aurora 567 ....B2
Austin 19 ....J3
Azalea 900 ....D5
Baker▲ 9,140 ....K3
Ballston 120 ....D2
Bancroft 40 ....D5
Bandon 2,215 ....C4
Banks 563 ....A1
Bar View 170 ....C2
Barlow 118 ....B2
Barton 100 ....B2
Barview 1,402 ....C4
Bates 56 ....J3
Bay City 1,027 ....D2
Beatty 350 ....F5
Beaver 350 ....D2
Beavercreek 708 ....B2
Beaverton 53,310 ....A2
Bellfountain 50 ....D3
Bend▲ 20,469 ....F3
Beulah 4 ....J4
Biggs 50 ....G2
Birkenfeld 38 ....D1
Blachly 80 ....D3

Blaine 38 ....D2
Blodgett 250 ....D3
Blue River 318 ....E3
Bly 800 ....F5
Boardman 1,387 ....H2
Bonanza 323 ....F5
Bonneville 80 ....F2
Boring 150 ....E2
Boyd 20 ....F2
Breitenbush 50 ....F3
Bridal Veil 20 ....E2
Bridge 200 ....D4
Bridgeport 60 ....K3
Brighton 150 ....C2
Brightwood 200 ....E2
Broadacres 80 ....A3
Broadbent 400 ....C4
Brogan 130 ....K3
Brothers 11 ....G4
Brownlee 50 ....L3
Brownsboro 150 ....E5
Brownsville 1,281 ....E3

Buena Vista 130 ....D3
Bunker Hill 1,242 ....C4
Burns Junction 14 ....K5
Burns▲ 2,913 ....H4
Butte Falls 252 ....E5
Butteville 20 ....A2
Buxton 450 ....D2
Camas Valley 750 ....D4
Camp Sherman 350 ....F3
Canary 23 ....D4
Canby 8,983 ....B2
Cannon Beach 1,221 ....D2
Canyon City▲ 648 ....J3
Canyonville 1,219 ....D5
Carlton 1,289 ....D2
Carpenterville 30 ....C5
Cascade Locks 930 ....E2
Cascadia 250 ....E3
Cave Junction 1,126 ....D5
Cayuse 200 ....J2
Cecil 75 ....H2
Cedar Hills 9,294 ....A2
Cedar Mill 9,697 ....A2

Celilo 50 ....G2
Central Point 7,509 ....D5
Charleston 500 ....C4
Chemawa 400 ....A3
Chemult 800 ....F4
Chenoweth 3,246 ....F2
Cherry Grove 350 ....D2
Cherryville 75 ....E2
Cheshire 300 ....D3
Chiloquin 673 ....F5
Clackamas 2,578 ....B2
Clatskanie 1,629 ....D1
Cloverdale 260 ....D2
Coburg 763 ....D3
Colton 305 ....B2
Columbia City 1,003 ....D2
Condon▲ 635 ....G2
Coos Bay 15,076 ....C4
Coquille▲ 4,*21 ....C4
Cornelius 6,*48 ....A2
Corvallis▲ 44,757 ....D3
Cottage Grove 7,402 ....D4
Cove 507 ....K2
Cove Orchard 50 ....D2

Portland, Salem and Vicinity

Crabtree 200 .... E3
Crane 84 .... J4
Crater Lake 36 .... E5
Crawfordsville 350 .... E3
Crescent 750 .... F4
Crescent Lake 120 .... F4
Creswell 2,431 .... D4
Crow 200 .... D4
Culp Creek 600 .... E4
Culver 570 .... F3
Curtin 350 .... D4
Cushman 175 .... D4
Dairy 80 .... F5
Dale 85 .... J3
Dallas▲ 9,422 .... D3
Dalles, The▲ 11,060 .... F2
Danner 12 .... K5
Days Creek 550 .... D5
Dayton 1,526 .... A3
Dayville 144 .... H3
Deer Island 225 .... E2
Denmark 15 .... C5
Depoe Bay 870 .... C3
Detroit 331 .... E3

Dexter 500 .... E4
Diamond 6 .... J4
Diamond Lake 56 .... E4
Dillard 602 .... D4
Dilley 250 .... A2
Disston 123 .... E4
Donald 316 .... A3
Dora 100 .... D4
Dorena 200 .... E4
Drain 1,011 .... D4
Drew 60 .... E5
Drewsey J4
Dufur 527 .... F2
Dundee 1,663 .... A2
Dunes City (Westlake) C4
Durham 748 .... A2
Durkee 158 .... K3
Eagle Creek 250 .... E2
Eagle Point 3,008 .... E5
Echo 499 .... H2
Eddyville 564 .... D3
Elgin 1,586 .... K2
Elk City 30 .... D3
Elkton 172 .... D4

STATE OF OREGON
1859

AREA 97,073 sq. mi. (251,419 sq. km.)
POPULATION 2,853,733
CAPITAL Salem
LARGEST CITY Portland
HIGHEST POINT Mt. Hood 11,239 ft.
  (3426 m.)
SETTLED IN 1810
ADMITTED TO UNION February 14, 1859
POPULAR NAME Beaver State
STATE FLOWER Oregon Grape
STATE BIRD Western Meadowlark

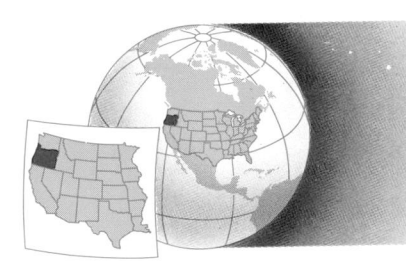

Topography

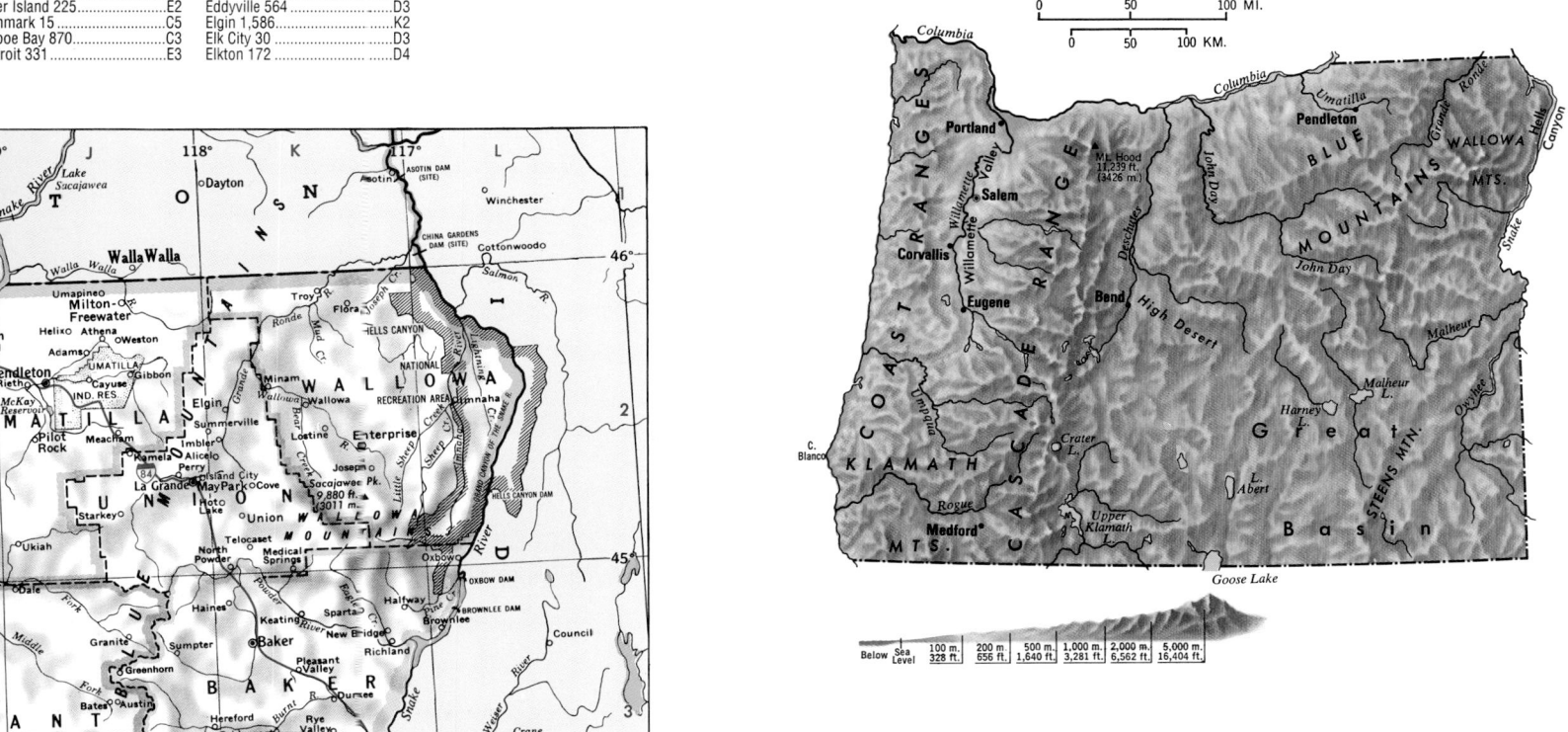

| | Below Sea Level | 100 m. 328 ft. | 200 m. 656 ft. | 500 m. 1,640 ft. | 1,000 m. 3,281 ft. | 2,000 m. 6,562 ft. | 5,000 m. 16,404 ft. |

Elmira 900 .... D3
Elsie 30 .... D2
Enterprise▲ 1,905 .... K2
Estacada 1,419 .... E2
Eugene▲ 112,669 .... D3
Fairview 2,391 .... B2
Falcon Heights F5
Fall Creek 58 .... E4
Falls City 818 .... D3
Farmington 100 .... A2
Fields 150 .... J5
Flora 45 .... K2
Florence 5,162 .... C4
Forest Grove 13,559 .... A2
Fort Klamath 200 .... E5
Fort Rock 150 .... G4
Fossil▲ 399 .... G2
Foster 850 .... E3
Four Corners 12,156 .... A3
Fox 30 .... H3
Frenchglen 45 .... H5
Fruitdale-Harbeck 4,733 ..... D5
Gales Creek 150 .... D2
Galice 30 .... D5
Garden Home-Whitford 6,652 . A2
Gardiner 750 .... C4
Garibaldi 877 .... D2
Gaston 563 .... D2
Gates 499 .... E3
Gateway 108 .... F3
Gaylord 80 .... C5
Gearhart 1,027 .... C1
Gervais 992 .... A3
Gibbon 100 .... J2
Gladstone 10,152 .... B2
Glenada 300 .... C4
Gleneden Beach 400 .... C3
Glenwood 225 .... D2
Glide 470 .... D4
Goble 108 .... E1
Gold Beach▲ 1,546 .... C5
Gold Hill 964 .... D5
Goshen 200 .... D4
Government Camp 230 .... F2
Grand Ronde 289 .... D2
Granite 8 .... J3
Grants Pass▲ 17,488 .... D5
Grass Valley 160 .... G2
Green 5,076 .... D4
Greenhorn 0 .... J3
Greenleaf 60 .... D3
Gresham 68,235 .... B2
Gunter 8 .... D4
Haines 405 .... J3
Halfway 311 .... K3
Halsey 667 .... D3
Hamilton 12 .... H3
Hammond 589 .... C1

Hampton 24 .... G4
Happy Valley 1,519 .... B2
Harbor 2,143 .... C5
Hardman H2
Harlan 200 .... D3
Harney 15 .... J4
Harper 400 .... K4
Harriman 250 .... E5
Harrisburg 1,939 .... D3
Hauser 400 .... C4
Hayesville 14,318 .... A3
Hebo 400 .... D2
Helix 150 .... J2
Heppner▲ 1,412 .... H2
Hereford 128 .... K3
Hermiston 10,040 .... H2
Hildebrand 50 .... F5
Hillsboro▲ 37,520 .... A2
Hines 1,452 .... H4
Holbrook 494 .... A1
Holley 75 .... E3
Hood River▲ 4,632 .... F2
Horton 175 .... D3
Hubbard 1,881 .... A3
Huntington 522 .... K3
Idanha 289 .... E3
Idleyld Park 300 .... D4
Illahe 30 .... C5
Imbler 299 .... J2
Imnaha 150 .... L2
Independence 4,425 .... D3
Ione 255 .... H2
Ironside 50 .... K3
Irrigon 737 .... H2
Island City 696 .... K2
Jacksonville 1,896 .... D5
Jamieson 120 .... K3
Jasper 231 .... E3
Jefferson 1,805 .... D3
Jennings Lodge 6,530 .... B2
Jewell 10 .... D2
John Day 2,012 .... H3
Johnson City 586 .... B2
Jordan Valley 364 .... K5
Joseph 1,073 .... K2
Junction City 3,670 .... D3
Juntura K4
Kah-Nee-Ta 100 .... F3
Kamela 11 .... J2
Keizer 21,884 .... A3
Keno 500 .... F5
Kent 200 .... G2
Kerby 650 .... D5
Kernville 450 .... C3
Kimberly 14 .... H3
King City 2,060 .... A2
Kings Valley 50 .... D3
Klamath Agency 10 .... F5
Klamath Falls▲ 17,737 ...... F5

Knappa 950 .... D1
La Grande▲ 11,766 .... J2
La Pine 850 .... F4
Lacomb 425 .... E3
Lafayette 1,292 .... A2
Lake Oswego 30,576 .... B2
Lakecreek 160 .... E5
Lakeside 1,437 .... C4
Lakeview▲ 2,526 .... G5
Langlois 150 .... C5
Latourell Falls 40 .... E2
Lawen 95 .... J4
Leaburg 150 .... E3
Lebanon 10,950 .... E3
Leland 70 .... D5
Lexington 286 .... H2
Liberal 300 .... B3
Lime 25 .... K3
Lincoln Beach 1,507 .... C3
Lincoln City 5,892 .... C3
Logan 450 .... B2
Logsden 55 .... D3
Lonerock 11 .... H2
Long Creek 249 .... H3
Lostine 231 .... K2
Lowell 785 .... E4
Lyons 938 .... E3
Madras▲ 3,443 .... F3
Malin 725 .... F5
Manzanita 513 .... C2
Mapleton 950 .... C3
Marcola 900 .... E3
Marion 200 .... D3
Marquam 40 .... B3
Marshland 30 .... D1
Maupin 456 .... F2
May Park J2
Mayger 35 .... D1
Mayville 150 .... G2
Maywood Park 781 .... B2
McCoy 40 .... D2
McKenzie Bridge 500 ...... E3
McMinnville▲ 17,894 .... D2
McNary 330 .... H2
McNulty 1,805 .... E2
Meacham 150 .... J2
Medford▲ 46,951 .... E5
Mehama 250 .... E3
Melrose 30 .... D4
Merlin 500 .... D5
Merrill 837 .... F5
Metolius 450 .... F3
Metzger 3,149 .... A2
Midland 520 .... F5
Mikkalo 40 .... G2
Mill City 1,555 .... E3
Millersburg 715 .... E3
Milo 600 .... E4
Milton-Freewater 5,533 .... J2

Milwaukie 18,692 .... B2
Mist 40 .... D1
Mitchell 163 .... G3
Modoc Point 65 .... F5
Mohawk 50 .... E3
Molalla 3,651 .... B3
Monitor 82 .... B3
Monmouth 6,288 .... D3
Monroe 448 .... D3
Monument 162 .... H3
Moro▲ 292 .... G2
Mosier 244 .... F2
Mount Angel 2,778 .... B3
Mount Hood 2,234 .... F2
Mount Vernon 538 .... H3
Mountaindale 25 .... A1
Mulino 720 .... B2
Murphy 500 .... D5
Myrtle Creek 3,063 .... D4
Myrtle Point 2,712 .... C4
Nashville 23 .... D3
Nehalem 232 .... D2
Neotsu 300 .... C2
Neskowin 250 .... D2
Netarts 975 .... C2
New Bridge 28 .... K3
New Era 27 .... B2
New Pine Creek 400 ...... G5
Newberg 13,086 .... A2
Newport▲ 8,437 .... C3
North Bend 9,614 .... C4
North Plains 972 .... A2
North Powder 448 .... K2
Norway 150 .... C4
Nyssa 2,629 .... K4
O'Brien 850 .... D5
Oak Grove 12,576 .... B2
Oakland 844 .... D3
Oakridge 3,063 .... E4
Oceanside 300 .... C2
Odell 450 .... F2
Olex 40 .... G2
Olney 75 .... D1
Ontario 9,392 .... K3
Ophir 275 .... C5
Oregon City▲ 14,698 ...... B2
Orenco 220 .... A2
Otis 200 .... D2
Otter Rock 450 .... C3
Oxbow 100 .... L2
Pacific City 500 .... C2
Paisley 350 .... G5
Park Place 500 .... B2
Parkdale 350 .... F2
Paulina 80 .... G3
Pecue 45 .... D3
Pendleton▲ 15,126 .... J2
Perry 50 .... J2
Perrydale 200 .... D2

(continued on following page)

Oregon

SCALE

0 5 10   20   30   40   50   60 MI.

0 5 10 20 30 40 50 60 KM.

State Capitals .... ⊛
County Seats .... ⊛
Major Limited Access Hwys. ....

Scale 1:2,750,000

© Copyright HAMMOND INCORPORATED, Maplewood, N.J.

Agriculture, Industry and Resources

DOMINANT LAND USE

Specialized Wheat

Wheat, Peas

Specialized Dairy

Dairy, Poultry, Mixed Farming

Fruit and Mixed Farming

Potatoes, General Farming

General Farming, Dairy, Hay, Sugar Beets

General Farming, Livestock, Special Crops

Range Livestock

Forests

Nonagricultural Land

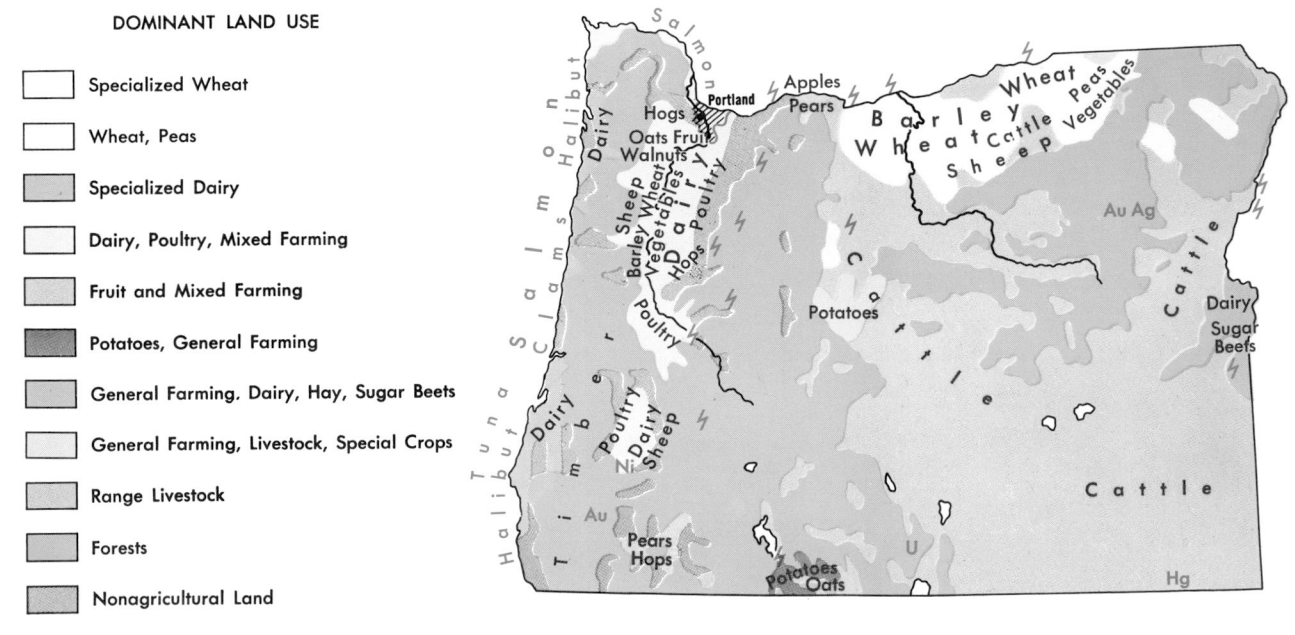

MAJOR MINERAL OCCURRENCES

Ag Silver   Hg Mercury   ⚡ Water Power

Au Gold   Ni Nickel   ▨ Major Industrial Areas

U Uranium

Philomath 2,983 ....D3
Phoenix 3,239 ....E5
Pilot Rock 1,478 ....J2
Pistol River 70 ....C5
Pleasant Valley 23 ....K3
Plush 150 ....H5
Port Orford 1,025 ....C5
Portland▲ 437,319 ....B2
Powell Butte 350 ....G3
Powers 682 ....D5
Prairie City 1,117 ....J3
Pratum 40 ....A3
Prescott 63 ....D1
Prineville▲ 5,355 ....G3
Progress 100 ....A2
Prospect 200 ....E5
Prosper 110 ....C4
Rainier 1,674 ....E1
Redland 700 ....B2
Redmond 7,163 ....F3
Reedsport 4,796 ....C4
Reedville 850 ....A2
Remote 84 ....D5
Rex 150 ....A2
Rhododendron F2
Richland 161 ....K3
Rickreall 700 ....D3
Riddle 1,143 ....D5
Rieth 300 ....J2
Riley 100 ....H4
Ritter 70 ....H3
River Grove 314 ....B2
Riverside 25 ....J4
Riverton 150 ....C4
Rockaway 906 ....C2
Rogue River 1,759 ....D5
Rome 8 ....K5
Rose Lodge 1,257 ....D3
Roseburg▲ 17,032 ....D4
Roy 200 ....A2
Ruch 25 ....E5
Rufus 295 ....G2
Rye Valley 15 ....K3
Saginaw 150 ....E4
Saint Benedict 70 ....B3
Saint Helens▲ 7,535 ....E2
Saint Louis 102 ....A3
Saint Paul 322 ....A3
Salem (cap.)▲ 107,786 .....A3
Sams Valley 100 ....E5
Sandy 4,152 ....E2
Scappoose 3,529 ....E2
Scholls 150 ....A2
Scio 623 ....E3
Scotts Mills 283 ....B3
Scottsburg 300 ....D4
Seal Rock 430 ....C3
Seaside 5,359 ....D2
Selma 150 ....D5
Seneca 191 ....J3

Service Creek 5 ....G3
Shady Cove 1,351 ....E5
Shaniko 26 ....G3
Shaw 800 ....A3
Sheaville 8 ....K4
Shedd 850 ....D3
Sheridan 3,979 ....D2
Sherwood 3,093 ....A2
Siletz 926 ....D3
Siltcoos 25 ....C4
Silver Lake 200 ....F4
Silverton 5,635 ....B3
Silvies 11 ....H3
Simnasho 25 ....F3
Sisters 679 ....F3
Sitkum 45 ....D4
Sixes 300 ....C5
Sodaville 192 ....E3
South Junction 20 ....F3
South Medford 2,898 ....E5
South Beach 300 ....C3
Sparta 30 ....K3
Sprague River 200 ....F5
Spray 149 ....H3
Springbrook 500 ....A2
Springfield 44,683 ....E3
Stanfield 1,568 ....H2
Starkey 60 ....J2
Stayton 5,011 ....E3
Sublimity 1,491 ....E3
Summer Lake 97 ....G5
Summerville 111 ....K2
Sumner 100 ....C4
Sumpter 119 ....J3
Sunny Valley 159 ....D5
Sutherlin 5,020 ....D4
Svensen 80 ....D1
Sweet Home 6,850 ....E3
Swisshome 350 ....D4
Sylvan B2
Talent 3,274 ....E5
Tangent 556 ....D3
Telocaset 50 ....K2
Tenmile 500 ....D4
Terrebonne 1,143 ....F3
The Dalles▲ 10,820 ....F2
Tidewater 100 ....C3
Tiernan 75 ....C3
Tigard 29,344 ....A2
Tillamook▲ 4,001 ....D2
Tiller 300 ....E4
Timber 175 ....D2
Toledo 3,174 ....D3
Tolovana Park 165 ....C2
Trail 350 ....E5
Trent 100 ....E4
Troutdale 7,852 ....E2
Troy 65 ....K2
Tualatin 15,013 ....A2
Tumalo 500 ....F3

Turner 1,281 ....E3
Twin Rocks 450 ....C2
Tygh Valley 663 ....F2
Ukiah 250 ....J2
Umapine 100 ....J2
Umatilla 3,046 ....H2
Umpqua 705 ....D4
Union 1,847 ....K2
Union Creek 35 ....E5
Unity 87 ....J3
Vale▲ 1,491 ....K4
Valley Falls 18 ....G5
Valsetz 320 ....D3
Veneta 2,519 ....D3
Verboort 280 ....A2
Vernonia 1,808 ....D2
Vida 300 ....E3
Wagontire 3 ....H4
Waldport 1,595 ....C3
Walker 50 ....D4
Wallowa 748 ....K2
Walterville 250 ....E3
Walton 300 ....D3
Wamic 255 ....F2
Wapinitia 10 ....F2
Warm Springs 2,287 ....F3
Warren 2,493 ....E2
Warrenton 2,681 ....C1
Wasco 374 ....G2
Waterloo 191 ....E3
Wauna 10 ....D1
Wedderburn 700 ....C5
Welches 100 ....E2
West Linn 16,367 ....B2
West Side 16 ....B2
West Woodburn 600 ....A3
Westfall 105 ....K3
Westfir 278 ....E4
Westlake 1,081 ....C4
Weston 606 ....J2
Westport 400 ....D1
Wheeler 335 ....D2
White City 5,891 ....E5
Whiteson 100 ....D2
Wilbur 476 ....D4
Wilderville 600 ....D5
Willamina 1,717 ....D2
Williams 750 ....D5
Willowcreek 20 ....K3
Willowdale 67 ....G3
Wilsonville 7,106 ....A2
Winchester 900 ....D4
Winchester Bay 535 ....C4
Winlock 25 ....H3
Winston 3,773 ....D4
Wolf Creek 500 ....D5
Wonder 200 ....D5
Wood Village 2,814 ....B2
Woodburn 13,404 ....A3
Worden 32 ....F5

Yachats 533 ....C3
Yamhill 867 ....D2
Yaquina 175 ....C3
Yoncalla 919 ....D4

OTHER FEATURES

Abert (lake) G5
Abiqua (creek) B3
Agency (lake) E5
Alsea (riv.) D3
Alvord (lake) J5
Arago (cape) C4
Aspen (lake) E5
Badger (creek) H3
Battle (creek) K5
Bear (creek) E5
Bear (creek) G4
Bear (creek) K2
Benjamin (lake) G4
Beulah (res.) J4
Big Antelope (creek) K5
Blacklock (pt.) C5
Blanco (cape) C5
Blue (mts.) J3
Bonneville (dam) E2
Brownlee (dam) L3
Buck Hollow (creek) G2
Bully (creek) K3
Burnt (riv.) K3
Butte (creek) B3
Butte (creek) E5
Butter (creek) H2
Calapooia (riv.) E3
Calapooya (mts.) E4
Camp (creek) J4
Campbells (lake) H5
Cascade (head) C2
Cascade (range) E4
Celilo (lake) G2
Chetco (riv.) C5
Clackamas (riv.) E2
Clover (creek) E5
Coal (pt.) C5
Coast (ranges) D5
Columbia (riv.) D1
Coos (riv.) D4
Coquille (riv.) C4
Cottage Grove (lake) E4
Cottonwood (creek) H5
Cougar (res.) E3
Cow (creek) K4
Crane (creek) J4
Crane Prairie (res.) F4
Crater (lake) E5
Crater Lake Nat'l Park E5
Crook (pt.) C5
Crooked (creek) K5
Crooked (riv.) G3
Cultus (lake) F4

Dalles, The (dam) F2
Davis (lake) F4
Deschutes (riv.) G2
Detroit (lake) E3
Diamond (lake) E4
Donner and Blitzen (riv.) ...J4
Dorena (lake) E4
Drews (res.) G5
Drift (creek) B3
Eagle (creek) K3
East (lake) F4
Elk (creek) E5
Ewauna (lake) F5
Falcon (cape) C2
Fern Ridge (lake) D3
Ferrelo (cape) C5
Fifteenmile (creek) F2
Fish (creek) E4
Fivemile (creek) F2
Fivemile (pt.) C4
Flagstaff (lake) C3
Fort Clatsop Nat'l Mem. C1
Foulweather (cape) C3
Fourmile (lake) E5
Gerber (res.) F5
Goose (lake) G5
Grand Canyon of the
  Snake River L2
Grande Ronde (riv.) K2
Green Peter (lake) E3
Guano (creek) H5
Guano (lake) H5
Harney (lake) H4
Hart (lake) H5
Hart (mt.) H5
Heads, The (prom.) C5
Heceta (head) C3
Hells Canyon (dam) L2
Hells Canyon Nat'l Rec. Area..K2
Hills Creek (lake) E4
Honey (creek) G5
Hood (mt.) F2
Hood (riv.) F2
Horse (creek) F3
Illinois (riv.) D5
Imnaha (riv.) L2
Indigo (creek) D5
Jackson (creek) E5
Jefferson (mt.) F3
Jenny (creek) E5
John Day (dam) G2
John Day (riv.) G2
John Day Fossil Beds
  Nat'l Mon. G3
Jordan (creek) K5
Joseph (creek) K2
Keeny (creek) K4
Kiger (creek) J5
Kincheloe (pt.) C2
Klamath (mts.) C5

Lake (creek) J3
Lava (lake) F4
Lightning (creek) L2
Little (riv.) E4
Little Butter (creek) H2
Little Sheep (creek) K2
Lookout (cape) C2
Lookout Point (lake) E4
Lost (riv.) F5
Malheur (lake) J4
Malheur (riv.) J4
McCoy (creek) J5
McKay (res.) J2
McKenzie, South Fork (riv.)....E3
McLoughlin (mt.) E5
McLoughlin House
  Nat'l Hist. Site B2
McNary (dam) H2
Meares (cape) C2
Metolius (riv.) F3
Miller (creek) F5
Molalla (riv.) B3
Mud (creek) K2
Murderers (creek) H3
Nehalem (riv.) D2
Nestucca (riv.) D2
North Santiam (riv.) E3
North Umpqua (riv.) E4
Oak Grove Fork,
  Clackamas (riv.) F2
Ochoco (creek) G3
Odell (lake) E4
Oregon Canyon (creek) K5
Oregon Caves Nat'l Mon. ..D5
Oregon Dunes
  Nat'l Rec. Area C4
Owyhee (dam) K4
Owyhee (lake) K4
Owyhee (mts.) K4
Owyhee (riv.) K5
Owyhee, North Fork (riv.) ..K4
Oxbow (dam) L3
Paulina (lake) F4
Perpetua (cape) C3
Pine (creek) J4
Pine (creek) L3
Portland Int'l Airport B2
Powder (riv.) K3
Prineville (res.) G3
Pudding (riv.) A3
Pueblo (mts.) J5
Rattlesnake (creek) K5
Rhea (creek) H2
Rock (creek) E4
Rock (creek) G2
Rock (creek) H3
Rogue (riv.) E4
Salt (creek) E4
Sebastian (cape) C5
Sheep (creek) L2

Shitike (creek) F3
Silver (creek) F4
Silver (creek) H4
Silver (lake) G4
Silver (lake) H4
Silvies (riv.) H4
Siskiyou (mts.) D6
Siuslaw (riv.) D4
Sixes (riv.) C5
Smith (riv.) D4
Snake (riv.) K3
South Santiam (riv.) E3
South Umpqua (riv.) E4
Sparks (lake) F3
Spencer (creek) E5
Sprague (riv.) F5
Squaw (creek) F3
Steens (mt.) J5
Succor (creek) K4
Summer (lake) G5
Summit (creek) J3
Sycan (riv.) F5
Tenmile (creek) J5
The Dalles (dam) F2
Thielsen (mt.) F4
Thirtymile (creek) G2
Thomas (creek) E3
Three Sisters (mt.) E4
Tillamook (head) C2
Trout (creek) F3
Trout (creek) J5
Tualatin (riv.) A2
Tumalo (creek) F3
Tumtum (lake) J5
Umatilla (lake) G2
Umatilla (riv.) H2
Umatilla Army Depot H2
Umatilla Ind. Res. H2
Umpqua (riv.) C4
Upper Klamath (lake) E5
Waldo (lake) E4
Walla Walla (riv.) H1
Wallowa (mts.) K2
Wallowa (riv.) K2
Wallula (lake) H1
Warm Springs (res.) F3
Warm Springs Ind. Res. F3
White (riv.) F2
Wickiup (res.) F4
Wiley (creek) E3
Willamette (riv.) B2
Willamette, Middle Fork
  (riv.) E4
Williamson (riv.) F5
Willow (creek) G2
Willow (creek) H3
Wilson (riv.) D2
Winchester (bay) C4

▲County seat

DOMINANT LAND USE

- Specialized Dairy
- Dairy, General Farming
- Fruit and Mixed Farming
- Fruit, Truck and Mixed Farming
- General Farming, Livestock, Tobacco
- General Farming, Livestock, Fruit, Tobacco
- Forests
- Urban Areas

AREA 45,308 sq. mi. (117,348 sq. km.)
POPULATION 11,924,710
CAPITAL Harrisburg
LARGEST CITY Philadelphia
HIGHEST POINT Mt. Davis 3,213 ft. (979 m.)
SETTLED IN 1682
ADMITTED TO UNION December 12, 1787
POPULAR NAME Keystone State
STATE FLOWER Mountain Laurel
STATE BIRD Ruffed Grouse

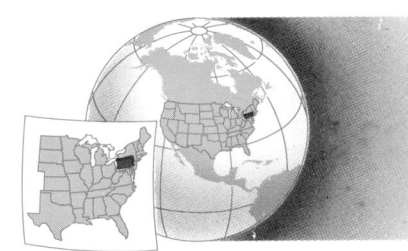

MAJOR MINERAL OCCURRENCES

C Coal	G Natural Gas	Sl Slate
Cl Clay	Ls Limestone	Ss Sandstone
Co Cobalt	O Petroleum	Zn Zinc
Fe Iron Ore		

⚡ Water Power

▨ Major Industrial Areas

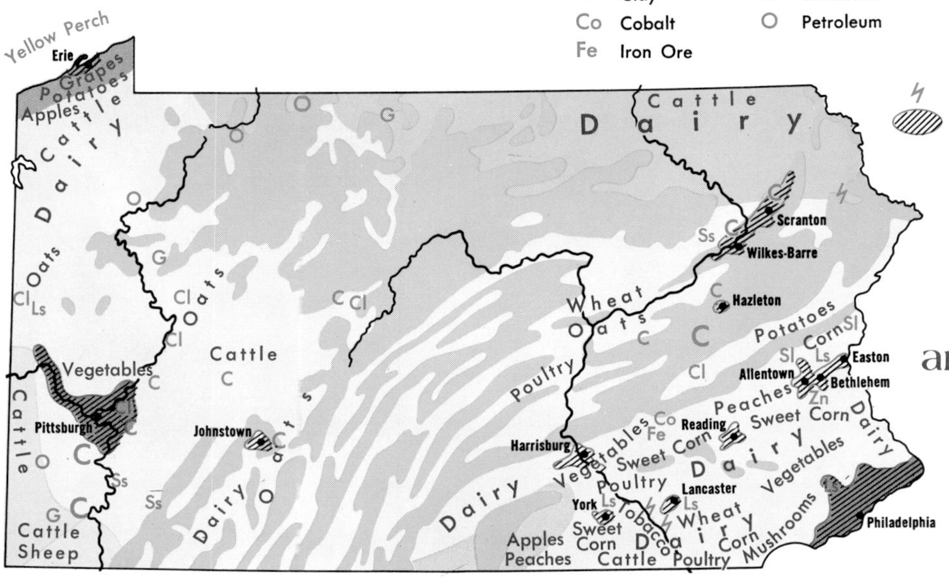

Agriculture, Industry and Resources

COUNTIES

Adams 78,274 ....H6
Allegheny 1,336,449 ......B5
Armstrong 73,478 ....D4
Beaver 186,093 ....B4
Bedford 47,919 ....E6
Berks 336,523 ....K5
Blair 130,542 ....F4
Bradford 60,967 ....J2
Bucks 541,174 ....M5
Butler 152,013 ....C4
Cambria 163,029 ....E4
Cameron 5,913 ....F3
Carbon 56,846 ....L4
Centre 123,786 ....G4
Chester 376,396 ....L6
Clarion 41,699 ....D3
Clearfield 78,097 ....F3
Clinton 37,182 ....G3
Columbia 63,202 ....K3
Crawford 86,169 ....B2
Cumberland 195,257 ....H5
Dauphin 237,813 ....J5
Delaware 547,651 ....M6
Elk 34,878 ....E3
Erie 275,572 ....C6
Fayette 145,351 ....C6
Forest 4,802 ....D2
Franklin 121,082 ....G6
Fulton 13,837 ....F6
Greene 39,550 ....B6
Huntingdon 44,164 ....F5
Indiana 89,994 ....D4
Jefferson 46,083 ....D3
Juniata 20,625 ....H4
Lackawanna 219,039 ....L3
Lancaster 422,822 ....K6
Lawrence 96,246 ....B4
Lebanon 113,744 ....K5
Lehigh 291,130 ....L4
Luzerne 323,149 ....L3
Lycoming 118,710 ....H3
McKean 50,635 ....E2
Mercer 121,003 ....B3
Mifflin 46,197 ....G4
Monroe 95,709 ....M3
Montgomery 678,111 ....M5
Montour 17,735 ....J4
Northampton 247,105 ......M4
Northumberland 96,771 ....J4
Perry 41,172 ....H5
Philadelphia (city county)
1,688,210 ....M6
Pike 27,966 ....M3
Potter 16,717 ....G2
Schuylkill 152,585 ....K4
Snyder 36,680 ....H4
Somerset 78,218 ....D6
Sullivan 6,104 ....J3
Susquehanna 40,380 ....L2
Tioga 41,126 ....H2
Union 36,176 ....H4
Venango 59,381 ....C3
Warren 45,050 ....D2
Washington 204,584 ....B5
Wayne 39,944 ....M2
Westmoreland 370,321 .....D5
Wyoming 28,076 ....K2
York 339,574 ....J6

CITIES and TOWNS

Abbottstown 539 ....J6
Abington • 58,836 ....M5
Adamstown 1,108 ....K5
Akron 3,869 ....K5
Albion 1,575 ....B2
Alburtis 1,415 ....L5
Aldan 4,549 ....M7
Alexandria 411 ....F4
Aliquippa 13,374 ....B4
Allentown▲ 105,090 ....L4
Allison Park 10,000 ......C6
Altoona 51,881 ....F4
Ambler 6,609 ....M5
Ambridge 8,133 ....B4
Annville 4,294 ....J5
Apollo 1,895 ....C4
Archbald 6,291 ....F6
Ardmore 12,646 ....M6
Arendtsville 693 ....H6
Arnold 6,113 ....C4
Ashland 3,859 ....K4
Ashley 3,291 ....E7
Aspinwall 2,880 ....C6
Atglen 825 ....K6
Athens 3,468 ....J2
Atlas 1,162 ....K4
Auburn 913 ....K4
Austin 591 ....F2
Avalon 5,784 ....B6
Avella 900 ....B5
Avis 1,506 ....H3
Avoca 2,897 ....F7
Avondale 954 ....L6
Avonmore 1,089 ....B5
Baden 5,074 ....B4
Bala-Cynwyd N6
Baldwin 21,923 ....B7
Bally 973 ....L5
Bangor 5,383 ....M4
Barnesboro 2,530 ....E4
Bath 2,358 ....M4
Beallsville 530 ....C5
Beaver Falls 10,687 .....B4
Beaver Meadows 985 ......L4
Beaver▲ 5,028 ....B4
Beaverdale 1,187 ....E5
Beavertown 853 ....H4
Bedford▲ 3,137 ....F5
Beech Creek 716 ....G3
Belle Vernon 1,213 ......C5
Bellefonte▲ 6,358 ....G4
Belleville 1,589 ....G4
Bellevue 9,126 ....B6
Bellwood 1,976 ....F4
Ben Avon 2,096 ....B6
Bendersville 560 ....H6
Bentleyville 2,673 ......B5
Benton 958 ....K3
Berlin 2,064 ....E6
Bernville 789 ....K5
Berrysburg 376 ....J4
Berwyn Devon 5,019 ......L5
Bessemer 1,196 ....B4
Bethel Park 33,823 ......B7
Bethlehem 71,428 ....M4
Big Run 699 ....E3
Biglerville 993 ....H6
Birdsboro 4,222 ....L5
Black Lick 1,100 ....D4
Blairsville 3,595 ....D4
Blakely 7,222 ....F6
Blawnox 1,626 ....C6
Bloomfield (New Bloomfield)▲
1,092 ....H5
Blooming Valley 391 .....B2
Bloomsburg▲ 12,439 ......J3
Blossburg 1,571 ....H2
Boalsburg 2,206 ....G4
Bobtown 1,008 ....B6
Boiling Springs 1,978 ...H5
Bolivar 544 ....D5
Boothwyn 5,069 ....L7
Boswell 1,485 ....E5
Bowmanstown 888 ....L4
Boyertown 3,759 ....L5
Brackenridge 3,784 ......C4
Braddock 4,682 ....C6
Bradford 9,625 ....E2
Brentwood 10,823 ....B7
Briar Creek 616 ....K3
Brickerville 1,265 ......K5
Bridgeport 4,292 ....M5
Bridgeville 5,445 ....B5
Bridgewater 751 ....B4
Brisbin 369 ....E4
Bristol 10,405 ....N5
Bristol • 587,330 ....N5
Broad Top 331 ....F5
Brockway 2,207 ....E2
Brodheadsville 1,389 ....M4
Brookhaven 8,567 ....M7
Brookville▲ 4,184 ....D3
Broomall 10,930 ....M6
Brownstown 937 ....K5
Brownsville 3,164 ....C5
Bruin 646 ....C3
Bryn Athyn 1,081 ....M5
Bryn Mawr 3,271 ....M5
Burgettstown 1,634 ......A5
Burlington 479 ....J2
Burnham 2,197 ....G4
Burnside 350 ....E4
Butler▲ 15,714 ....C4
Cadogan • 459 ....C4
Cairnbrook 1,081 ....E5
California 5,748 ....C5
Callery 420 ....C4
Cambridge Springs 1,837 .C2
Camp Hill 7,831 ....H5
Canonsburg 9,200 ....B5
Canton 1,966 ....H3
Carbondale 10,664 ....L2
Carlisle▲ 18,419 ....H5
Carmichaels 532 ....B6
Carnegie 9,278 ....B7
Carroll Valley 1,457 ...H6
Carrolltown 1,286 ......E4
Castle Shannon 9,135 ...B7
Catasauqua 6,662 ....M4
Catawissa 1,683 ....K4
Centerville 4,207 ......B6
Central City 1,246 .....E5
Centre Hall 1,203 ......G4
Chalfont 3,069 ....M5
Chambersburg▲ 16,647 ...G6
Charleroi 5,014 ....C5
Cherry Tree 431 ....E4
Chester 41,856 ....L7
Chester Heights 2,273 ..L7
Chester Hill 945 ....F4
Cheswick 1,971 ....C6
Chicora 1,058 ....C4
Christiana 1,045 ....K6
Churchill 3,883 ....C7
Clairton 9,656 ....C6
Clarendon 650 ....D2
Clarion▲ 6,457 ....D3
Clark (Clarksville) 610 .B3
Clarks Green 1,603 .....F6
Clarks Summit 5,433 ....F6
Claysburg 1,399 ....F5
Claysville 962 ....B5
Clearfield▲ 6,633 ......F3
Clifton Heights 7,111 ..M7
Clintonville 520 ....C3
Clymer 1,499 ....D4
Coalport 578 ....E4
Coatesville 11,038 .....L5
Cochranton 1,174 ....B2
Codorus (Jefferson) 685 .J6
Cokeburg 724 ....B5
Collegeville 4,227 .....M5
Collingdale 9,175 ......N7
Columbia 10,701 ....K5
Colver 1,024 ....E4
Colwyn 2,613 ....N7
Confluence 873 ....D6
Conneaut Lake 699 ......B2
Conneautville 822 ......A2
Connellsville 9,229 ....C5
Connoquenessing 507 ....B4
Conshohocken 8,064 .....M5
Conway 2,424 ....B4
Conyngham 2,060 ....K3
Coopersburg 2,599 ......M5
Cooperstown 506 ....C2
Coplay 3,267 ....L4
Coraopolis 6,747 ....B6
Cornwall 3,231 ....K5
Corry 7,216 ....C2
Coudersport▲ 2,854 .....G2
Crabtree 900 ....D5
Crafton 7,188 ....B7
Cranesville 598 ....B2
Cresson 1,784 ....E5
Cressona 1,694 ....K4
Cross Roads 322 ....J6
Curwensville 2,924 .....E4
Dale 1,642 ....E5
Dallas 2,567 ....E7
Dallastown 3,974 ....J6
Dalton 1,369 ....L2
Danville▲ 5,165 ....J4
Darby 10,955 ....M7
Dauphin 845 ....J5
Dayton 572 ....D4
Delaware Water Gap 733 .M4
Delmont 2,041 ....D5
Delta 761 ....K6
Denver 2,861 ....K5
Derry 2,950 ....D5
Dickson City 6,276 .....F7
Dillsburg 1,925 ....J5
Donora 5,928 ....C5
Dormont 9,772 ....B7
Dover 1,884 ....J6
Downingtown 7,749 ......L5
Doylestown▲ 8,575 ......M5
Dravosburg 2,377 ....C7
Drexel Hill 29,744 .....M6
Drifton 1,786 ....L3
Dublin 1,985 ....M5
DuBois 8,286 ....E3
Duboistown 1,201 ....H3
Dunbar 1,213 ....C5
Duncannon 1,450 ....H5
Duncansville 1,309 .....F5
Dunmore 15,403 ....F7
Dupont 2,984 ....F7
Duquesne 8,525 ....C7
Duryea 4,869 ....F7
Dushore 738 ....K2
East Bangor 1,006 ......M4
East Berlin 1,175 ......J6
East Berwick 2,128 .....K3
East Brady 1,047 ....C3
East Butler 725 ....C4
East Conemaugh 1,470 ...E5
East Faxon 3,951 ....J3
East Greenville 3,117 ..L5
East Lansdowne 2,691 ...M7
East Petersburg 4,197 ..K5
East Pittsburgh 2,160 ..C7
East Prospect 558 ......J6
East Stroudsburg 8,781 .M4
East Washington 2,126 ..B5
Easton▲ 26,276 ....M4
Eau Claire 391 ....C3
Ebensburg▲ 3,872 ....E5
Economy 9,519 ....B4
Eddystone 2,446 ....M7
Edgewood 2,719 ....B7
Edgeworth 1,670 ....B6
Edinboro 7,736 ....B2
Edwardsville 5,399 .....E7
Eldred 869 ....E2
Elizabeth 1,610 ....C5
Elizabethtown 9,952 ....J5
Elizabethville 1,467 ...J4
Elkland 1,849 ....H1
Ellsworth 1,048 ....B5
Ellwood City 8,894 .....B4
Elverson 470 ....L5
Elysburg 1,890 ....K4
Emigsville 2,580 ....J5
Emlenton 834 ....C3
Emmaus 11,157 ....M4
Emporium▲ 2,513 ....F2
Emsworth 2,892 ....B6
Enola 5,961 ....J5
Enon Valley 355 ....B4
Ephrata 12,133 ....K5
Erie▲ 108,718 ....B1
Ernest 492 ....D4
Espy 1,430 ....K4
Etna 4,200 ....B7
Etters (Goldsboro) 477 .J5
Evans City 2,054 ....B4
Everett 1,777 ....F5
Everson 939 ....C5
Exeter 5,691 ....F7
Export 981 ....C5
Factoryville 1,310 .....L2
Fairchance 1,918 ....C6
Fairfield 524 ....H6
Fairless Hills 9,026 ...N5
Falls Creek 1,087 ......E3
Farrell 6,841 ....A3
Fawn Grove 489 ....J6
Fayette City 713 ....C5
Fayetteville 3,033 .....G6
Felton 438 ....J6
Ferndale 2,020 ....E5
Finleyville 446 ....B5

Fleetwood 3,478 ....L5
Fleming (Unionville) 361 .G4
Flemington 1,321 ....G3
Folcroft 7,506 ....M7
Folsom 8,173 ....M7
Ford City 3,413 ....D4
Ford Cliff 450 ....D4
Forest City 1,846 ......L2
Forest Hills 7,335 .....C7
Forty Fort 5,049 ....F7
Fountain Hill 4,637 ....L4
Fox Chapel 5,319 ....C6
Frackville 4,700 ....K4
Franklin▲ 7,329 ....C3
Franklintown 373 ....H5
Fredericksburg 1,269 ...B2
Fredericktown 1,052 ....C6
Fredonia 683 ....B3
Freeburg 640 ....H4
Freedom 1,897 ....B4
Freeland 3,909 ....L3
Freemansburg 1,946 .....M4
Freeport 1,983 ....C4
Galeton 1,370 ....G2
Gallitzin 2,003 ....E4
Gap 1,226 ....L6
Garden View 2,687 ......H3
Garrett 520 ....D6
Geistown 2,749 ....E5
Gettysburg▲ 7,025 ......H6
Gilberton 953 ....K4
Girard 2,879 ....B2
Girardville 1,889 ......K4
Glassport 5,582 ....C7
Glen Lyon 2,082 ....E7
Glen Rock 1,688 ....J6
Glenolden 7,260 ....M7
Glenside 8,704 ....M5
Grampian 395 ....E4
Gratz 696 ....J4
Great Bend 704 ....L2
Greencastle 3,600 ......G6
Greensburg▲ 16,318 .....D5
Greentree 4,905 ....B7
Greenville 6,734 ....B3
Grove City 8,240 ....B3
Halifax 911 ....J5
Hallstead 1,274 ....L2
Hamburg 3,987 ....L4
Hanover 14,399 ....J6
Harmony 1,054 ....B4
Harrisburg (cap.)▲ 52,376 .H5
Harrisville 862 ....B3
Harveys Lake 2,746 .....E7
Hastings 1,431 ....E4
Hatboro 7,382 ....M5
Hatfield 2,650 ....M5
Haverford • 52,371 .....M6
Havertown M6
Hawley 1,244 ....M3
Hawthorn 528 ....D3
Hazleton 24,730 ....L4
Heidelberg 1,238 ....B7
Hellam (Hallam) 1,428 ..J6
Hellertown 5,662 ....M4
Herndon 422 ....J4
Hershey 11,860 ....J5
Highland Park 1,583 ....H4
Highspire 2,668 ....J5
Hollidaysburg▲ 5,624 ...F5
Homer City 1,809 ....D4
Homestead 4,179 ....B7
Honesdale▲ 4,972 ....M2
Honey Brook 1,184 ......L5
Hooversville 731 ....E5
Hop Bottom 345 ....L2
Hopwood 2,021 ....C6
Houston 1,445 ....B5
Houtzdale 1,204 ....F4
Howard 749 ....G3
Hughestown 1,734 ....F7
Hughesville 2,049 ......J3
Hummelstown 3,981 ......J5
Huntingdon▲ 6,843 ......G5
Hyde 1,643 ....F4
Hydetown 681 ....C2
Hyndman 1,019 ....E6
Imperial-Enlow 3,449 ...B5
Indian Lake 388 ....E6
Indiana▲ 15,174 ....D4
Industry 2,124 ....B7
Ingram 3,901 ....B7
Irvona 666 ....E4
Irwin 4,604 ....C5
Jacobus 1,370 ....J6
Jamestown 761 ....A3
Jeannette 11,221 ....C5
Jenkintown 4,574 ....M5
Jennerstown 635 ....D5
Jermyn 2,263 ....L2
Jerome 1,074 ....D5
Jersey Shore 4,353 .....H3
Jessup 4,605 ....F6
Jim Thorpe (Mauch Chunk)▲
5,048 ....L4

(continued on following page)

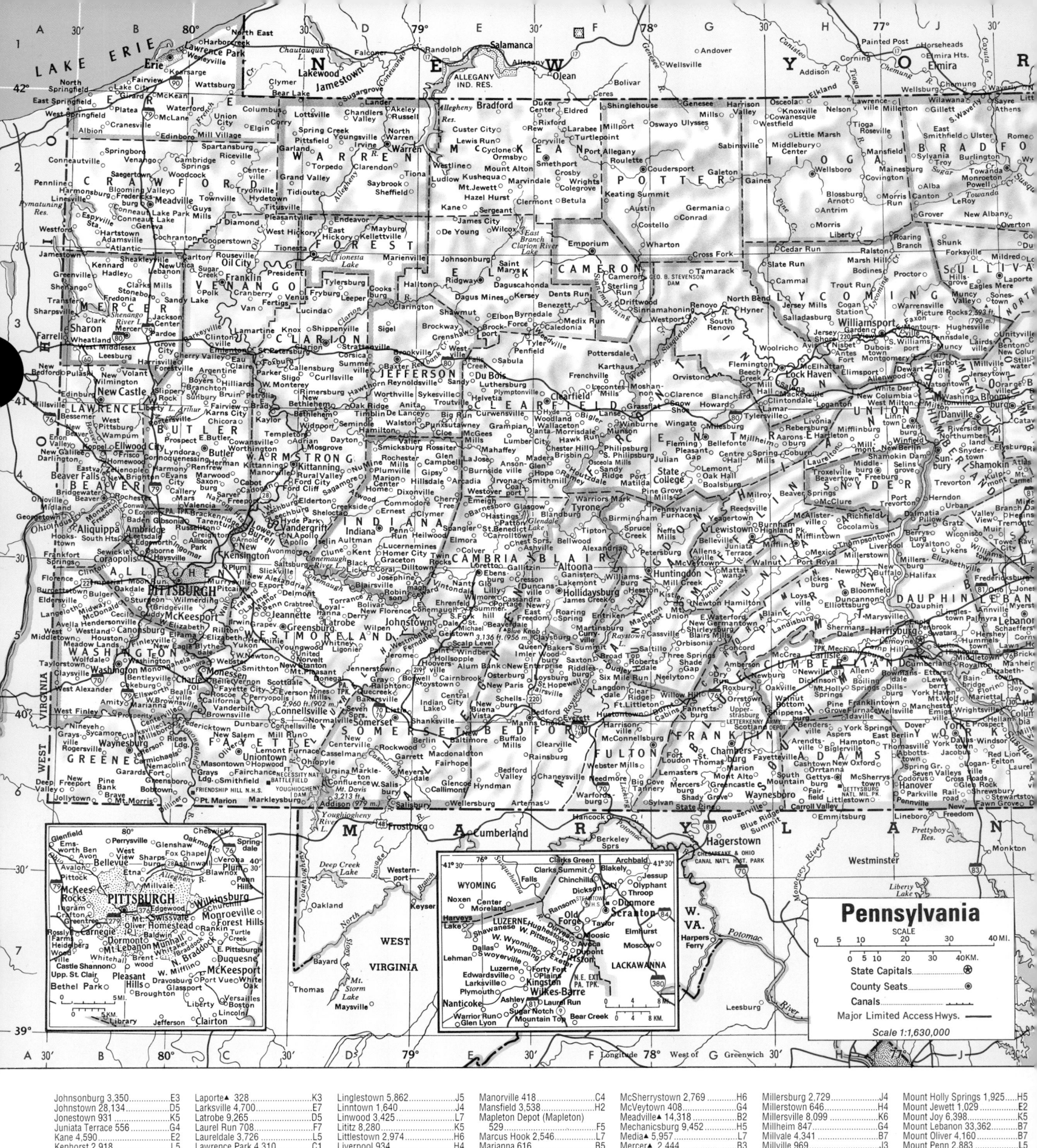

Pennsylvania

SCALE

0 5 10 20 30 40 MI.

0 5 10 20 30 40 KM.

State Capitals..............⊛

County Seats...............◉

Canals.........................

Major Limited Access Hwys. ——

Scale 1:1,630,000

Johnsonburg 3,350....E3	Laporte▲ 328....K3	Linglestown 5,862....J5	Manorville 418....C4	McSherrystown 2,769....H6	Millersburg 2,729....J4	Mount Holly Springs 1,925....H5
Johnstown 28,134....D5	Larksville 4,700....E7	Linntown 1,640....J4	Mansfield 3,538....H2	McVeytown 408....G4	Millerstown 646....H4	Mount Jewett 1,029....E2
Jonestown 931....K5	Latrobe 9,265....D5	Linwood 3,425....L7	Mapleton Depot (Mapleton)	Meadville▲ 14,318....B2	Millheim 847....G4	Mount Joy 6,398....K5
Juniata Terrace 556....G4	Laureldale 3,726....L5	Lititz 8,280....K5	529....F5	Mechanicsburg 9,452....H5	Millvale 4,341....B7	Mount Lebanon 33,362....B7
Kane 4,590....E2	Lawrence Park 4,310....C1	Littlestown 2,974....H6	Marcus Hook 2,546....L7	Media▲ 5,957....L7	Millville 969....J3	Mount Oliver 4,160....B7
Kenhorst 2,918....K5	Lawrenceville 481....H2	Liverpool 934....H4	Marianna 616....B5	Mercer▲ 2,444....B3	Milroy 1,456....G4	Mount Penn 2,883....L5
Kennett Square 5,218....L6	Leechburg 2,504....C4	Lock Haven▲ 9,230....H3	Marietta 2,778....J5	Mercersburg 1,640....G6	Milton 6,746....J3	Mount Pleasant 4,787....D5
Kingston 14,507....F7	Leetsdale 1,387....B4	Loganton 443....H3	Marion Center 476....D4	Merion Station....M6	Minersville 4,877....K4	Mount Pocono 1,795....M4
Kittanning▲ 5,120....D4	Lehighton 5,914....L4	Loganville 954....J6	Markleysburg 320....C6	Meshoppen 439....K2	Mohnton 2,484....L5	Mount Union 2,878....G5
Knox 1,182....C3	Lemont 2,613....G4	Loretto 1,072....E4	Mars 1,713....C4	Meyersdale 2,518....E6	Monaca 6,739....B4	Mount Wolf 1,365....J5
Knoxville 589....H2	Lemoyne 3,959....J5	Lower Burrell 12,251....C4	Martinsburg 2,119....F5	Middleburg▲ 1,422....H4	Monessen 9,901....C5	Mountainhome 1,042....M4
Koppel 1,024....B4	Levittown 55,362....N5	Loyalhanna 4,108....D5	Marysville 2,425....H5	Middletown 520....K4	Monongahela 4,928....B5	Mountainville 1,977....L4
Kulpmont 3,233....K4	Lewis Run 578....E2	Luzerne 3,206....E7	Masontown 3,759....C6	Middletown 9,254....J5	Monroeton (Monroe) 627....J2	Muncy 2,702....J3
Kulpsville 5,183....M5	Lewisburg▲ 5,785....J4	Lucernemines 1,074....D4	Matamoras 1,934....N3	Midland 3,321....A4	Monroeville 29,169....C7	Murrysville 17,240....C5
Kutztown 4,704....L4	Lewistown▲ 9,341....G4	Lykens 1,986....J4	Mauch Chunk (Jim Thorpe)▲	Midway 1,043....B5	Mont Alto 1,395....G6	Myerstown 3,236....K5
Laceyville 436....K2	Liberty 2,744....H2	Lyndora 8,333....B4	....L4	Mifflin 660....H4	Montgomery 1,631....H3	Nanticoke 12,267....E7
Lake City 2,519....B1	Ligonier 1,638....D5	Lyon Station (Lyons) 499....L5	Mayfield 1,890....L2	Mifflinburg 3,480....H4	Montoursville 4,983....J3	Nanty Glo 3,190....E5
Lancaster▲ 55,551....K5	Lilly 1,162....E5		McAdoo 2,459....L4	Mifflintown▲ 866....H4	Montrose▲ 1,982....K2	Narberth 4,278....M6
Lanesboro 659....L2	Lima 2,670....L7		McClure 1,070....H4	Milesburg 1,144....G4	Moosic 5,339....F7	Nazareth 5,713....M4
Langeloth 1,112....A5	Lincoln 1,187....C7		McConnellsburg▲ 1,106....F6	Milford▲ 1,064....N3	Morrisville 9,765....N5	Nemacolin 1,097....B6
Langhorne 1,361....N5	Linesville 1,166....A2		McDonald 2,252....B5	Mill Creek 392....G5	Morton 2,851....M7	Nescopeck 1,651....K3
Lansdale 16,362....M5			McKean (Middleboro) 418....B7	Mill Hall 1,702....G3	Moscow 1,527....F7	Nesquehoning 3,364....L4
Lansdowne 11,712....M7			McKees Rocks 7,691....B7	Mill Village 429....C2	Mount Carmel 7,196....K4	New Alexandria 571....C5
Lansford 4,583....L4			McKeesport 26,016....C7	Millbourne 831....M6		

Petersburg 469 ....G4
Philadelphia▲ 1,585,577 ....N6
Philipsburg 3,048 ....F4
Phoenixville 15,066 ....L5
Picture Rocks 660 ....J3
Pillow 341 ....J4
Pine Grove 2,118 ....K4
Pine Grove Mills 1,129 .....G4
Pitcairn 4,087 ....C5
Pittsburgh▲ 369,879 ....B7
Pittston 9,389 ....F7
Plains 4,694 ....F7
Platea 467 ....B2
Pleasant Gap 1,699 ....G4
Pleasant Hills 8,884 ......B7
Plum 25,609 ....C5
Plumville 390 ....D4
Plymouth 7,134 ....E7
Plymptonville 1,074 ....E3
Pocono Pines 824 ....M3
Point Marion 1,344 ....C6
Polk 1,267 ....C3
Port Allegany 2,391 ....F2
Port Carbon 2,134 ....K4
Port Matilda 669 ....F4
Port Royal 836 ....H4
Port Vue 4,641 ....C7
Portage 3,105 ....E5
Portland 516 ....M4
Pottstown 21,831 ....L5
Pottsville▲ 16,603 ....K4
Prospect 1,122 ....B4
Prospect Park 6,764 ....M7
Punxsutawney 6,782 ....E4
Quakertown 8,982 ....M5
Quarryville 1,642 ....K6
Ramey 536 ....F4
Rankin 2,503 ....C7
Reading▲ 78,380 ....L5
Reamstown 2,649 ....K5
Red Hill 1,794 ....L5
Red Lion 6,130 ....J6
Reedsville 1,023 ....G4
Renovo 1,526 ....G3
Reynoldsville 2,818 ....D3
Rices Landing 457 ....C6
Richland 1,457 ....K5
Richlandtown 1,195 ....M5
Ridgway▲ 4,793 ....E3
Ridley Park 7,592 ....M7
Riegelsville 912 ....M5
Rimersburg 1,053 ....D3
Ringtown 853 ....K4
Riverside 1,991 ....J4
Roaring Spring 2,615 ......F5
Robesonia 1,944 ....K5
Rochester 4,156 ....B4
Rockledge 2,679 ....M5
Rockwood 1,014 ....D6
Rome 475 ....K2
Roscoe 872 ....C5
Rose Valley 982 ....L7
Roseto 1,555 ....M4
Rosslyn Farms 483 ....B7
Rouseville 583 ....C3
Rouzerville 1,188 ....G6
Royalton 1,120 ....J5
Royersford 4,458 ....L5
Rural Valley 957 ....D4
Russellton 1,691 ....C4
Rutledge 843 ....M7
Saegertown 1,066 ....B2
Saint Clair 3,524 ....K4
Saint Marys 5,511 ....E3
Saint Michael-Sidman 1,189..E5
Saint Petersburg 349 ......C3
Salisbury 716 ....D6
Saltillo 347 ....G5
Saltsburg 990 ....C4
Sandy 1,795 ....E3
Sandy Lake 722 ....B3
Saxonburg 1,345 ....C4
Saxton 838 ....F5
Sayre 5,791 ....K2
Scalp Level 1,158 ....E5

Schnecksville 1,780 ....L4
Schuylkill Haven 5,610 ....K4
Schwenksville 1,326 ....L5
Scottdale 5,184 ....C5
Scranton▲ 81,805 ....F7
Selinsgrove 5,384 ....J4
Sellersville 4,479 ....M5
Seven Valleys 483 ....J6
Seward 522 ....E5
Sewickley 4,134 ....B4
Shamokin 9,184 ....J4
Shamokin Dam 1,690 ....J4
Sharon 17,493 ....B3
Sharon Hill 5,771 ....N7
Sharpsburg 3,781 ....B6
Sharpsville 4,729 ....A3
Sheffield 1,294 ....D2
Shenandoah 6,221 ....K4
Shickshinny 1,108 ....K3
Shillington 5,062 ....K5
Shinglehouse 1,243 ....F2
Shippensburg 5,331 ....H5
Shippenville 474 ....D3
Shoemakersville 1,443 .....K4
Shrewsbury 2,672 ....J6
Sinking Spring 2,467 ......K5
Skippack 2,042 ....M5
Slatington 4,678 ....L4
Slickville 1,178 ....C5
Sligo 706 ....D3
Slippery Rock 3,008 ....B3
Smethport▲ 1,734 ....F2
Smithfield 1,000 ....C6
Smithton 388 ....C5
Snow Shoe 800 ....G3
Snydertown 416 ....J4
Somerset▲ 6,454 ....D6
Souderton 5,957 ....M5
South Bethlehem 479 ....D4
South Connellsville 2,204..C6
South Fork 1,197 ....E5
South Heights 647 ....B4
South Philipsburg 438 .....F4
South Renovo 579 ....G3
South Waverly 1,049 ....J2
South Williamsport 6,496 ..J3
Spangler 2,068 ....E4
Spartansburg 403 ....C2
Spring City 3,433 ....L5
Spring Grove 1,863 ....J6
Springboro 557 ....B2
Springdale 3,992 ....C6
Springfield 24,160 ....M7
State College 38,923 ......G4
State Line 1,253 ....G6
Steelton 5,152 ....J5
Stewartstown 1,308 ....K6
Stockertown 641 ....M4
Stoneboro 1,091 ....B3
Stowe 3,598 ....L5
Stoystown 389 ....E5
Strasburg 2,568 ....K6
Strattanville 490 ....D3
Strausstown 353 ....K5
Stroudsburg▲ 5,312 ....M4
Sturgeon 1,312 ....B5
Sugar Creek 5,532 ....C3
Sugar Notch 1,044 ....E7
Sugargrove 630 ....D1
Summerhill 614 ....E5
Summerville 675 ....D3
Summit Hill 3,332 ....L4
Sunbury▲ 11,591 ....J4
Susquehanna 1,994 ....L2
Swatara • 18,796 ....J5
Swissvale 10,637 ....C7
Swoyerville 5,630 ....E7
Sykesville 1,387 ....E3
Tamaqua 7,943 ....L4
Tarentum 5,674 ....C4
Tatamy 873 ....M4
Taylor 6,941 ....F7
Telford 4,238 ....M5
Temple 1,491 ....L5

Terre Hill 1,282 ....L5
Thompsontown 582 ....H4
Three Springs 422 ....G5
Throop 4,070 ....F7
Tidioute 791 ....D2
Tioga 638 ....H2
Tionesta▲ 634 ....C2
Tipton 1,194 ....F4
Titusville 6,434 ....C2
Topton 1,987 ....L5
Toughkenamon 1,273 ....L6
Towanda▲ 3,242 ....J2
Tower City 1,518 ....J4
Townville 358 ....C2
Trafford 3,345 ....C5
Trainer 2,271 ....L7
Tremont 1,814 ....K4
Trescow 1,033 ....L4
Trevorton 2,058 ....J4
Troy 1,262 ....J2
Trumbauersville 894 ......M5
Tullytown 2,339 ....N5
Tunkhannock▲ 2,251 ....L3
Turbotville 675 ....J3
Turtle Creek 6,556 ....C7
Tyrone 5,743 ....F4
Ulysses (Lewisville) 653 ..G2
Union City 3,537 ....C2
Uniontown▲ 12,034 ....C6
Upland 3,334 ....L7
Upper Darby • 84,054 .....M6
Upper Saint Claire • 19,023..B7
Valencia 364 ....C4
Valley Forge 400 ....L5
Valley View 1,749 ....J4
Vanderbilt 545 ....C5
Vandergrift 5,904 ....D4
Vandling 660 ....M2
Verona 3,260 ....C6
Versailles 2,150 ....C7
Villanova M6
Vintondale 582 ....E5
Wall 853 ....C5
Walnutport 2,055 ....L4
Wampum 666 ....B4
Warren▲ 11,122 ....D2
Warrior Run 656 ....E7
Washington▲ 15,864 ....B5
Waterford 1,492 ....B2
Watsontown 2,310 ....J3
Wattsburg 486 ....C1
Waymart 1,337 ....M2
Wayne M6
Waynesboro 9,578 ....G6
Waynesburg▲ 4,270 ....B6
Weatherly 2,640 ....L4
Wellsboro▲ 3,430 ....H2
Wernersville 1,934 ....K5
Wesleyville 3,655 ....C1
West Brownsville 1,170 ....C5
West Chester▲ 18,041 .....L6
West Elizabeth 634 ....C5
West Grove 2,128 ....L6
West Hazleton 4,136 ......K4
West Kittanning 1,253 .....C4
West Lawn 1,606 ....K5
West Leechburg 1,359 .....C4
West Mifflin 23,644 ......C7
West Newton 3,152 ....C5
West Pittsburg 1,133 .....B4
West Pittston 5,590 ......F7
West View 7,734 ....B6
West Wyoming 3,117 ....E7
West York 4,283 ....J6
Westfield 1,119 ....H2
Westmont 5,789 ....D5
Westover 446 ....E4
Wheatland 760 ....B3
Whitaker 1,416 ....C7
White Haven 1,132 ....L3
White Oak 8,761 ....C7
Whitehall 14,451 ....B7
Wiconisco 1,321 ....J4
Wilkes-Barre▲ 47,523 .....F7

Wilkinsburg 21,080 ....C7
Williamsburg 1,456 ....F5
Williamsport▲ 31,933 .....H3
Williamstown 1,509 ....J4
Willow Grove 16,325 ......M5
Wilmerding 2,421 ....C5
Wilson 7,830 ....M4
Windber 4,756 ....E5
Windgap 2,651 ....M4
Windsor 1,355 ....J6
Wolfdale 2,906 ....B5
Womelsdorf 2,270 ....K5
Woodlyn 10,151 ....M7
Worthington 713 ....C4
Wrightsville 2,396 ....J5
Wyalusing 686 ....K2
Wyoming 3,255 ....E7
Wyomissing 7,332 ....K5
Yardley 2,288 ....N5
Yeadon 11,980 ....N7
Yeagertown 1,150 ....G4
York Haven 758 ....J5
York Springs 547 ....H6
York▲ 42,192 ....J6
Youngsville 1,775 ....D2
Youngwood 3,372 ....C5
Zelienople 4,158 ....B4

OTHER FEATURES

Allegheny (res.) E2
Allegheny (riv.) D2
Allegheny Front (mts.) E5
Appalachian (mts.) H4
Ararat (mt.) M2
Arthur (lake) A4
Beaver (riv.) B4
Blue (mt.) G5
Blue Knob (mt.) E5
Casselman (riv.) D6
Clarion (riv.) D3
Conemaugh (riv.) D5
Conemaugh River (lake) ...D4
Conewago (creek) D1
Davis (mt.) D6
Delaware (riv.) N3
Delaware Water Gap
  Nat'l Rec. N3
Erie (lake) B1
Fort Necessity Nat'l
  Battlefield C6
George B. Stevenson (dam)..G3
Gettysburg Nat'l Mil. Park.H6
Glendale (lake) F4
Juniata (riv.) G5
Laurel Hill (mt.) D5
Lehigh (riv.) L3
Letterkenny Army Depot ...G6
Licking (creek) F6
Little Tinicum (isl.) M7
Lycoming (creek) H3
Monongahela (riv.) C6
North (mt.) K3
Ohio (riv.) A4
Oil (creek) C2
Pine (creek) H2
Pine Grove (res.) K6
Pocono (mts.) M3
Pymatuning (res.) A2
Redbank (creek) E3
Schuylkill (riv.) M5
Shenango River (lake) B3
Sinnemahoning (creek) F3
South (mt.) H6
Steamtown Nat'l Hist. Site.K6
Susquehanna (riv.) K6
Tioga (riv.) H1
Tionesta Creek (lake) D3
Towanda (creek) J2
Tuscarora (mt.) G5
Wallenpaupack (lake) M3
Youghiogheny River (lake).D6

▲County seat
• Population of town or township

New Beaver 1,736 ....B4
New Berlin 892 ....J4
New Bethlehem 1,151 ....D3
New Bloomfield▲ H5
New Brighton 6,854 ....B4
New Britain 2,174 ....M5
New Castle▲ 28,334 ....B3
New Cumberland 7,665 ......J5
New Eagle 2,172 ....B5
New Florence 854 ....D5
New Freedom 2,920 ....J6
New Galilee 500 ....A4
New Holland 4,484 ....K5
New Hope 1,400 ....N5
New Kensington 15,894 .....C4
New Milford 953 ....L2
New Oxford 1,617 ....H6
New Philadelphia 1,283 ....K4
New Salem (Delmont) 669 ...D5
New Stanton 2,081 ....C5
New Wilmington 2,706 ......B3
Newport 1,568 ....H5
Newtown 2,565 ....N5
Newtown Square • 11,775 ...L6

Newville 1,349 ....H5
Nicholson 857 ....L2
Norristown▲ 30,749 ....M5
North Apollo 1,391 ....D4
North Braddock 7,036 .....C7
North Catasauqua 2,867 ....L4
North East 4,617 ....C1
North Wales 3,802 ....M5
North Warren 1,232 ....D2
Northampton 8,717 ....M4
Northumberland 3,860 .....J4
Norvelt 2,541 ....D5
Norwood 6,162 ....M7
Nuangola 701 ....L3
Oakdale 1,752 ....B5
Oakland 641 ....L2
Oakmont 6,961 ....C6
Ohioville 3,865 ....B4
Oil City 11,949 ....C3
Old Forge 8,834 ....F7
Oliver 3,271 ....C6
Olyphant 5,222 ....F7
Orangeville 504 ....K3
Orbisonia 447 ....G5

Orwigsburg 2,780 ....K4
Osborne 565 ....B4
Osceola Mills 1,310 ......F4
Oxford 3,769 ....K6
Paint 1,091 ....E5
Palmerton 5,394 ....L4
Palmyra 6,910 ....J5
Paoli 5,603 ....M5
Parker 853 ....C3
Parkesburg 2,981 ....L6
Parkside 2,369 ....M7
Parkville 6,014 ....J6
Patton 2,206 ....E4
Pen Argyl 3,492 ....M4
Penbrook 2,791 ....J5
Penn 511 ....C5
Penn Hills 51,430 ....C7
Penn Wynne 5,807 ....M6
Penndel 2,703 ....N5
Pennsburg 2,460 ....M5
Pennville 1,559 ....J6
Perkasie 7,878 ....M5
Perryopolis 1,833 ....C5

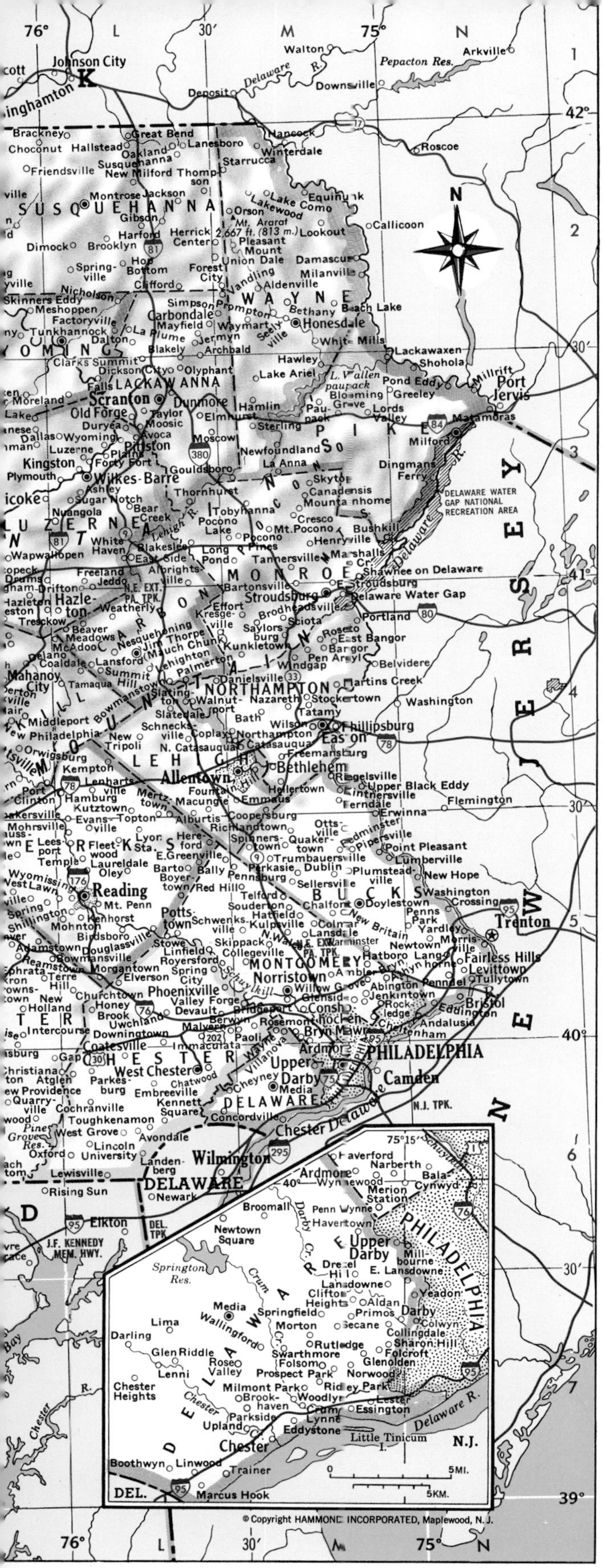

Topography

Erie — Allegheny Res. — Pymatuning Res. — ALLEGHENY PLATEAU — Williamsport — Scranton — L. Wallenpaupack — Wilkes-Barre — POCONO MTS. — Delaware Water Gap — Allentown — Reading — Philadelphia — Harrisburg — Altoona — Pittsburgh — York — Mt. Davis 3,213 ft. (979 m.) — LAUREL HILL — ALLEGHENY MOUNTAINS — APPALACHIAN MOUNTAINS — BLUE MOUNTAIN — SOUTH MTN. — PIEDMONT PLATEAU

0 30 60 MI.
0 30 60 KM.

| 5,000 m. 16,404 ft. | 2,000 m. 6,562 ft. | 1,000 m. 3,281 ft. | 500 m. 1,640 ft. | 200 m. 656 ft. | 100 m. 328 ft. | Sea Level Below |

© Copyright HAMMOND INCORPORATED, Maplewood, N.J.

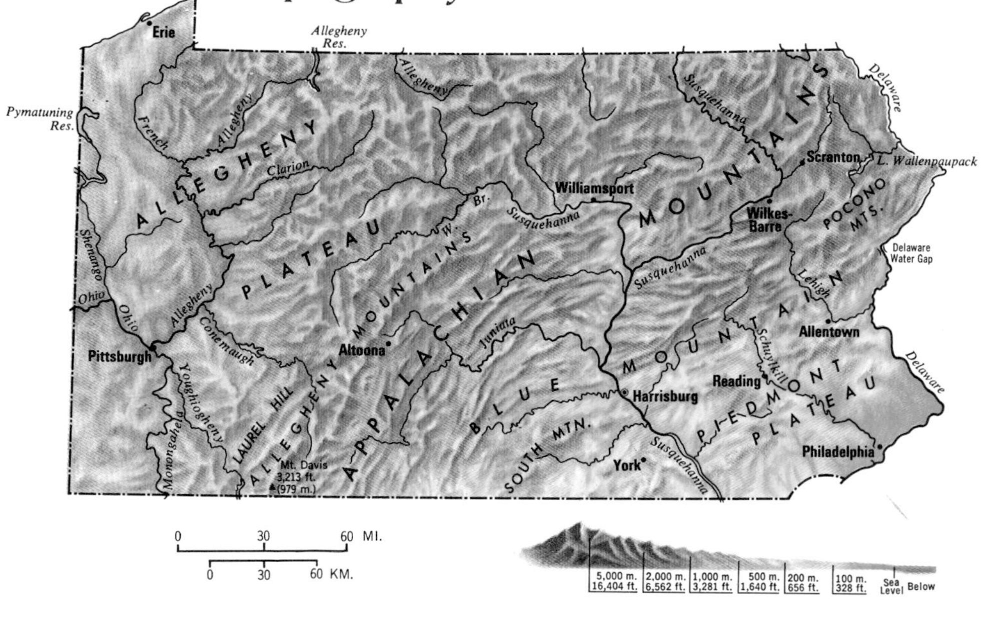

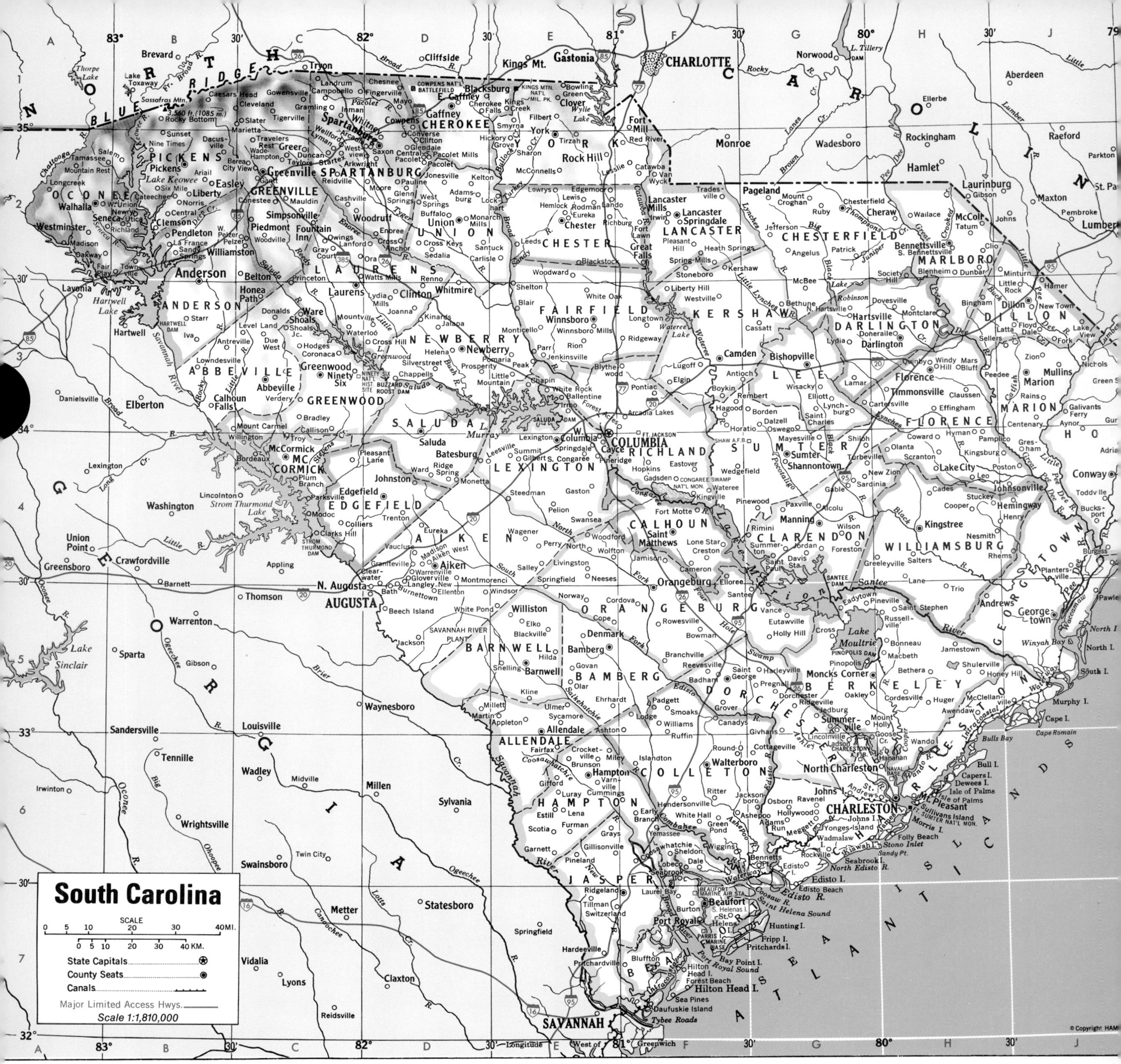

South Carolina

SCALE
0 5 10   20   30   40 MI.

0 5 10   20   30   40 KM.

State Capitals .... ⊗
County Seats .... ◉
Canals ....
Major Limited Access Hwys. ....
Scale 1:1,810,000

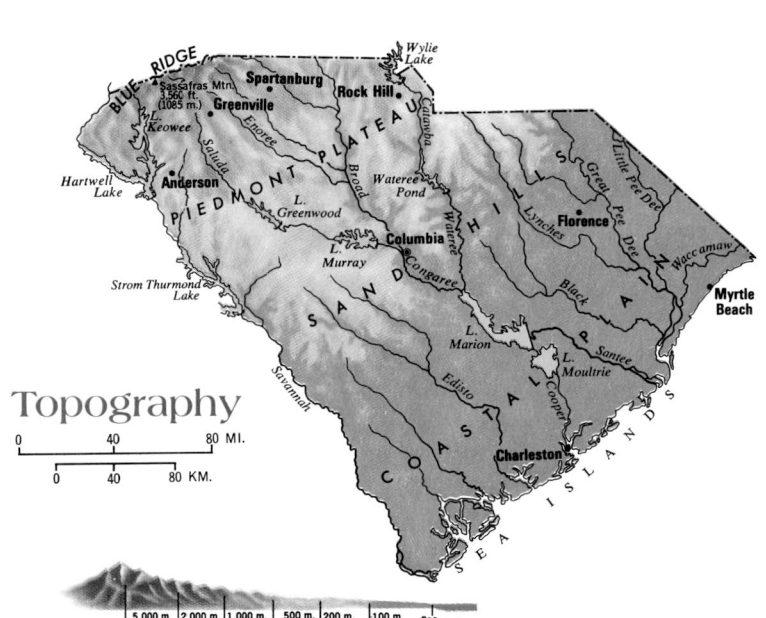

Topography

0   40   80 MI.

0   40   80 KM.

COUNTIES

Abbeville 23,862	B3
Aiken 120,940	D4
Allendale 11,722	E6
Anderson 145,196	B2
Bamberg 16,902	E5
Barnwell 20,293	E5
Beaufort 86,425	F7
Berkeley 128,776	G5
Calhoun 12,753	F4
Charleston 295,039	H6
Cherokee 44,506	D1
Chester 32,170	E2
Chesterfield 38,577	G2
Clarendon 28,450	G4
Colleton 34,377	F6
Darlington 61,851	H3
Dillon 29,114	J3
Dorchester 83,060	G5
Edgefield 18,375	D4
Fairfield 22,295	E3
Florence 114,344	H3
Georgetown 46,302	J5
Greenville 320,167	C2
Greenwood 59,567	C3
Hampton 18,191	E6
Horry 144,053	J4
Jasper 15,487	E6
Kershaw 43,599	F3
Lancaster 54,516	F2
Laurens 58,092	D2
Lee 18,437	G3

Lexington 167,611	E4
Marion 33,899	J3
Marlboro 29,361	H2
McCormick 8,868	C4
Newberry 33,172	D3
Oconee 57,494	A2
Orangeburg 84,803	F5
Pickens 93,894	B2
Richland 285,720	F4
Saluda 16,357	D3
Spartanburg 226,800	D2
Sumter 102,637	G4
Union 30,337	D2
Williamsburg 36,815	H4
York 131,497	E2

CITIES and TOWNS

Abbeville▲ 5,778	C3
Adams Run 500	G6
Adamsburg 300	D2
Aiken West 3,083	D4
Aiken▲ 19,872	D4
Alcolu 600	G4
Allendale▲ 4,410	E5
Allsbrook 100	K3
Anderson 26,184	B2
Andrews 3,050	H5
Antioch 500	F3
Antreville 500	B3
Appleton 200	E5
Arcadia 899	C2
Arcadia Lakes 611	F3

Ariail 2,419	B2
Arkwright 2,623	C2
Atlantic Beach 446	K4
Awendaw 200	H5
Aynor 470	J3
Ballentine 550	E3
Bamberg▲ 3,843	E5
Barnwell▲ 5,255	E5
Batesburg 4,082	D4
Bath 2,242	D5
Beaufort▲ 9,576	F7
Beech Island 400	D5
Belton 4,646	C2
Bennettsville▲ 9,345	H2
Berea 13,535	C2
Bethera 265	H5
Bethune 405	G3
Bingham 200	H3
Bishopville▲ 3,560	G3
Blacksburg 1,907	D1
Blackville 2,688	E5
Blenheim 191	H2
Bluffton 738	F7
Blythewood 164	E3
Bonneau 374	H5
Bowman 1,063	F5
Boykin 350	F3
Branchville 1,107	F5
Brunson 587	E6
Bucksport 1,022	J4
Buffalo 1,569	D2
Burgess 250	J4
Burnettown 493	D5

Burton 6,917	F7
Calhoun Falls 2,328	B3
Camden▲ 6,696	F3
Cameron 504	F4
Campobello 465	C1
Canadys 130	F5
Carlisle 470	D2
Cashville 200	C2
Catawba 607	F2
Cateechee 225	B2
Cayce 11,163	E4
Centenary 700	J3
Central 2,438	B2
Central Pacolet 257	D2
Chapin 282	D3
Chappells 45	D3
Charleston▲ 80,414	G6
Cheraw 5,505	H2
Cherokee Falls 250	D1
Chesnee 1,280	D1
Chester▼ 7,158	E2
Chesterfield▲ 1,373	G2
City View 1,490	C2
Clarks Hill 200	C4
Claussen 500	H3
Clearwater 4,731	D5
Clemson 11,096	B2
Cleveland 800	C1
Clifton 950	D2
Clinton 7,987	D2
Clio 882	H2
Clover 3,422	E2
Columbia (cap.)▲ 98,052	F4

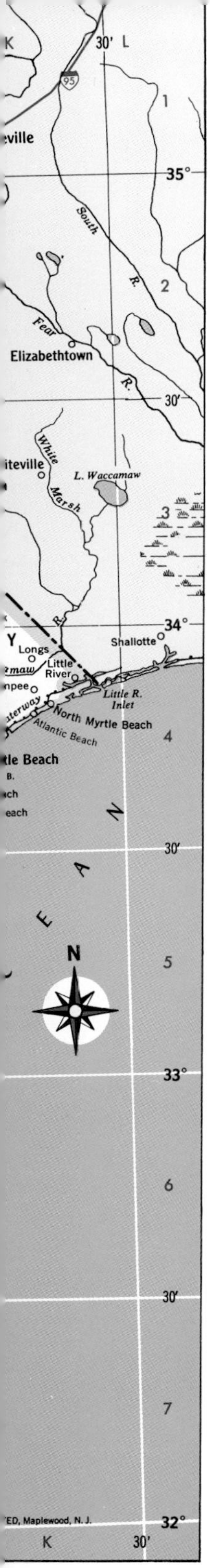

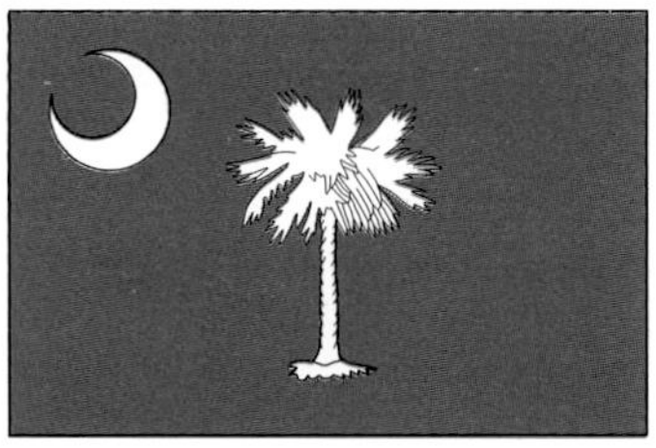

AREA 31,113 sq. mi. (80,583 sq. km.)
POPULATION 3,505,707
CAPITAL Columbia
LARGEST CITY Columbia
HIGHEST POINT Sassafras Mtn. 3,560 ft. (1085 m.)
SETTLED IN 1670
ADMITTED TO UNION May 23, 1788
POPULAR NAME Palmetto State
STATE FLOWER Carolina (Yellow) Jessamine
STATE BIRD Carolina Wren

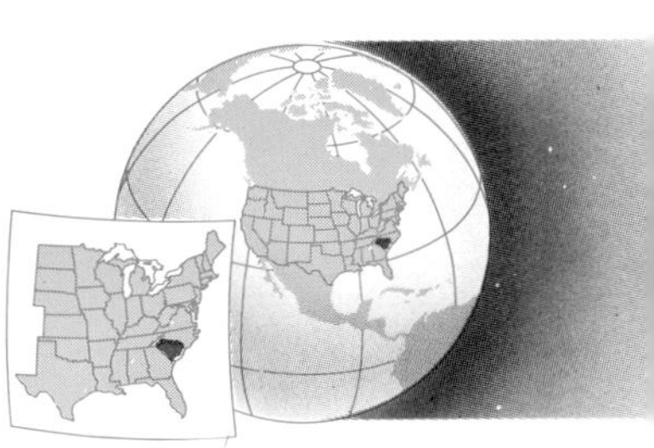

Conestee 500 C2
Converse 1,173 D2
Conway▲ 9,819 J4
Coosawhatchie 250 F6
Cope 124 E5
Cordesville 300 H5
Cordova 135 F5
Coronaca 200 C3
Cottageville 572 G6
Coward 532 H4
Cowpens 2,176 D1
Cross 469 G5
Cross Anchor 350 D2
Cross Hill 604 D3
Cross Keys 250 D2
Cummings 275 E6
Dacusville 350 B2
Dale 500 F6
Dalzell 625 G3
Darlington▲ 7,311 H3
Davis Station 300 G4
Denmark 3,762 E5
Dillon▲ 6,829 J3
Donalds 326 C3
Doneraile 1,276 H3
Dorchester 400 G5
Due West 1,220 C3
Duncan 2,152 C2
Easley 15,195 B2
East Gaffney 3,278 D1
Eastover 1,044 F4
Edgefield 2,563▲ C4
Edgemoor 500 E2
Edisto Beach 340 G7
Edisto Island 900 G6
Effingham 300 H3
Ehrhardt 442 E5
Elgin 622 F3
Elko 214 E5
Elliott 500 G3
Elloree 939 F4
Enoree 1,107 D2
Estill 2,387 E6
Eureka 1,738 E2
Eutawville 350 G5
Fair Play 500 A2
Fairfax 2,317 E6
Filbert 203 E1
Fingerville 320 D1
Florence▲ 29,813 H3
Floyd Dale 450 J3
Folly Beach 1,398 H6
Forest Acres 7,197 E3
Forest Beach 500 F7
Foreston 300 G4
Fort Lawn 718 F2
Fort Mill 4,930 F1
Fort Motte 700 F4
Fountain Inn 4,388 C2
Furman 260 E6
Gable 230 G4
Gadsden 500 F4
Gaffney▲ 13,145 D1
Gantt 13,891 C2
Garden City Beach 300 K4
Garnett 500 E6
Gaston 984 E4
Georgetown▲ 9,517 J5
Gifford 313 E6
Gilbert 324 E4
Gillisonville 350 E6
Givhans 400 G5
Glendale 1,049 D2
Glenn Springs 350 D2
Gloverville 2,753 D4
Goose Creek 24,692 H6
Govan 84 E5
Gowensville 200 C1
Gramling 400 C1
Graniteville 1,158 D4
Gray Court 914 C2
Great Falls 2,307 F2
Greeleyville 464 H4
Greenville▲ 58,282 C2
Greenwood▲ 20,807 C3
Greer 10,322 C2
Gresham 350 J4
Gurley 425 J3
Hamer 588 J3
Hampton 2,997▲ E6
Hanahan 13,176 H6
Hardeeville 1,583 E7
Harleyville 633 G5
Hartsville 8,372 G3
Heath Springs 907 F2
Helena 500 D3
Hemingway 829 J4
Hemlock (Eureka) E2
Hickory Grove 287 E2
Hilda 342 E5
Hilton Head Island 23,694 F7
Hodges 125 C3
Holly Hill 1,478 G5
Hollywood 2,094 G6
Honea Path 3,841 C3
Hopkins 300 F4
Horatio 500 F3
Huger 500 H5
Inman 1,742 C1
Irmo 11,280 D3
Irwin 1,296 E2
Isle of Palms 3,680 H6
Iva 1,174 B3
Jackson 1,681 D5
Jacksonboro 475 G6
Jamestown 84 H5
Jedburg 900 G5
Jefferson 745 G2
Joanna 1,735 D3
Johns Island 200 G6
Johnsonville 1,415 J4
Johnston 2,688 D4
Jonesville 1,205 D2
Kershaw 1,814 F3
Kinards 300 D3
Kingsburg 300 H4
Kingstree▲ 3,858 H4
Kingville 500 F4
Kline 285 E5
La France 875 B2
Ladson 13,540 G6
Lake City 7,153 H4
Lake View 872 J3
Lamar 1,125 G3
Lancaster Mills 2,096 F2
Lancaster▲ 8,914 F2
Lando 250 E2
Landrum 2,347 C1
Lane 523 H5
Langley 1,714 D4
Latta 1,565 J3
Laurel Bay 4,972 F7
Laurens▲ 9,694 C3
Leesville 2,025 E4
Lena 275 E6
Lesslie 1,102 E2
Level Land 100 C3
Lexington▲ 3,289 E4
Liberty 3,228 B2
Lincolnville 716 G6
Little Mountain 235 E3
Little River 3,470 K4
Little Rock 500 J3
Livingston 171 E4
Lobeco 345 F6
Lockhart 58 E2
Lodge 147 F5
Longcreek 200 A2
Longtown 400 F3
Loris 2,067 K3
Lowndesville 162 B3
Lowrys 200 E2
Lugoff 3,211 F3
Luray 102 E6
Lydia 500 G3
Lydia Mills 925 D3
Lyman 2,271 C2
Lynchburg 475 G3
Madison A2
Madison 1,150 D4
Manning▲ 4,428 G4
Marietta-Slater C1
Marion▲ 7,658 J3
Mars Bluff 500 H3
Mauldin 11,587 C2
Mayesville 694 G4
Mayo 1,569 D1
McBee 715 G3
McClellanville 333 H5
McColl 2,685 H2
McConnells 157 E2
McCormick▲ 1,659 C4
Meggett 787 G6
Modoc 300 C4
Monarch Mills 2,353 D2
Moncks Corner▲ 5,607 G5
Monetta 285 D4
Montmorenci 500 D4
Moore 500 D2
Mount Carmel 117 C3
Mount Croghan 131 G2
Mount Holly 200 H5
Mount Pleasant 30,108 H6
Mountain Rest 500 A2
Mullins 5,910 J3
Murrells Inlet 3,334 K4
Myrtle Beach 24,848 K4
Neeses 410 E4
Nesmith 350 H4
New Ellenton 2,515 D5
New Town 950 J3
New Zion 200 H4
Newberry▲ 10,542 D3
Newry 400 B2
Nichols 528 J3
Ninety Six 2,099 C3
Norris 884 B2
North 809 E4
North Augusta 15,351 C5
North Charleston 70,218 G6
North Hartsville 2,906 G3
North Myrtle Beach 8,636 K4
Norway 401 E5
Oakley 250 G5
Olanta 687 H4
Olar 391 E5
Ora 13,739 D2
Orangeburg▲ 14,933 F4
Oswego 500 G3
Pacolet 1,736 D2
Pacolet Mills 696 D2
Pageland 2,666 G2
Pamplico 1,314 H4
Parksville 193 C4
Parr 7,172 E3
Patrick 368 G2
Pauline 750 D2
Pawleys Island 176 J5
Paxville 218 G4
Peak 78 E3
Peedee 350 H3
Pelion 336 E4
Pelzer 81 B2
Pendleton 3,314 B2
Perry 241 E4
Pickens▲ 3,042 B2
Piedmont 4,143 C2
Pineland 800 E6
Pineridge 1,731 E4
Pineville 900 H5
Pinewood 600 G4
Pinopolis 788 G5
Plantersville 231 J4
Plum Branch 101 C4
Pomaria 267 E3
Port Royal 2,985 F7
Poston 250 J4
Princeton 300 C2
Prosperity 1,116 D3
Quinby 865 H3
Rains 450 J3
Ravenel 2,165 G6
Red River F2
Reevesville 244 F5
Reidville C2
Rembert 350 G3
Richburg 405 E2
Ridge Spring 861 D4
Ridgeland▲ 1,071 E7
Ridgeville 1,625 G5
Ridgeway 407 F3
Rimini 525 G4
Rion 300 E3
Ritter 300 F6
Rock Hill 41,643 E2
Rodman 500 E2
Rowesville 316 F5
Ruby 300 G2
Ruffin 400 F6
Saint Andrews 26,692 G6
Saint George▲ 2,077 F5
Saint Matthews▲ 2,345 F4
Saint Paul 725 G4
Saint Stephen 1,697 H5
Salem 192 A2
Salley 451 E4
Salters 300 H4
Saluda▲ 2,798 D4
Santee 638 F5
Sardinia 225 G4
Saxon 4,002 D2
Scotia 182 E6
Scranton 802 H4
Sea Pines 500 F7
Seabrook 948 F6
Sellers 358 H3
Seneca 7,726 A2
Shannontown G4
Sharon 270 E2
Sheldon 225 F6
Shulerville 375 H5
Silverstreet 156 D3
Simpsonville 11,708 C2
Six Mile 562 B2
Slater-Marietta 2,245 C1
Smoaks 142 F5
Smyrna 57 E1
Snelling 125 E5
Society Hill 686 H2
South Bennettsville 1,065 H2
South Congaree 2,406 E4
Spartanburg▲ 43,467 C1
Spring Mills 1,419 F2
Springdale 2,643 F2
Springdale 2,985 E4
Springfield 523 E4
Starr 164 B3
Startex 1,162 C2
Stuckey 311 H4
Sullivans Island 1,623 H6
Summerton 975 G4
Summerville 22,519 G5
Summit 242 E4
Sumter▲ 41,943 G4
Surfside Beach 3,845 K4
Swansea 527 E4
Sycamore 208 E5
Tamassee 320 A2
Tatum 49 H2
Taylors 19,619 C2
Tigerville 975 C1
Tillman 225 E7
Timmonsville 2,182 H3
Toddville 200 J4
Townville 300 B2
Tradesville 500 F2
Travelers Rest 3,069 C2
Trenton 303 D4
Trio 400 H5
Troy 140 C4
Turbeville 698 G4
Ulmer 90 E5
Union▲ 9,836 D2
Utica 1,478 B2
Van Wyck 500 F2
Vance 214 G5
Varnville 1,970 E6
Vaucluse 606 D4
Wade-Hampton 20,014 C2
Wagener 731 E4
Walhalla▲ 3,755 A2
Wallace 500 H2
Walterboro▲ 5,492 F6
Wampee 200 K4
Wando 500 H6
Ward 132 D4
Ware Shoals 2,497 C3
Warrenville 1,029 D4
Waterloo 122 C3
Watts Mill 1,535 D2
Wedgefield 550 F4
Wellford 2,511 C2
West Columbia 10,588 E4
West Pelzer 989 B2
West Springs 500 D2
West Union 260 B2
Westminster 3,120 A2
Westview 1,999 C2
Westville 440 F3
White Pond 200 D5
White Rock 600 E3
Whitmire 1,702 D3
Whitney 4,052 D1
Williams 188 F5
Williamston 3,876 B2
Williston 3,099 E5
Windsor 124 E5
Windy Hill 1,622 H3
Winnsboro Mills 2,275 E3
Winnsboro▲ 3,475 E3
Wisacky 250 G3
Woodford 200 E4
Woodruff 4,365 D2
Woodville C2
Yemassee 728 F6
Yonges Island 500 G6
York▲ 6,709 E1

OTHER FEATURES

Ashepoo (riv.) F6
Ashley (riv.) G6
Bay Point (isl.) F7
Beaufort Marine Air Sta. F7
Big Black (creek) G2
Black (riv.) H4
Blue Ridge (mts.) B1
Broad (riv.) E2
Broad (riv.) F7
Buck (creek) J3
Bull (isl.) H6
Bullock (creek) E2
Bulls (bay) H6
Bush (riv.) D3
Buzzard Roost (dam) D3
Cape (isl.) J5
Capers (isl.) H6
Catawba (riv.) F2
Catfish (creek) J3
Chattooga (riv.) A2
Combahee (riv.) F6
Congaree (riv.) F4
Congaree Nat'l Mon. F4
Cooper (riv.) H6
Coosaw (riv.) G7
Coosawhatchie (riv.) E6
Cowpens Nat'l Battlefield D1
Crooked (creek) H2
Deep (creek) B2
Dewees (isl.) H6
Donaldson A.F.B. C2
Edisto (isl.) G6
Edisto (riv.) G7
Enoree (riv.) C2
Fort Jackson F4
Fort Sumter Nat'l Mon. H6
Four Hole Swamp (creek) F5
Fripp (isl.) G7
Great Pee Dee (riv.) J4
Greenwood (lake) D3
Hartwell (dam) B3
Hartwell (lake) A3
Hilton Head (isl.) F7
Hunting (isl.) G7
Intracoastal Waterway H5
James (isl.) H6
Johns (isl.) G6
Juniper (creek) H2
Keowee (lake) B2
Keowee (riv.) B2
Kiawah (isl.) G6
Kings Mountain Nat'l Mil. Park E1
Little (riv.) C3
Little (riv.) D3
Little Lynches (riv.) G3
Little Pee Dee (riv.) J4
Little River (inlet) L4
Lumber (riv.) J3
Lynches (riv.) H3
Marion (lake) G5
Morris (isl.) H6
Moultrie (lake) G5
Murphy (isl.) J5
Murray (lake) D4
Myrtle Beach A.F.B. K4
Naval Base H6
New (riv.) E6
Ninety Six Nat'l Hist. Site C3
North (inlet) J5
North (isl.) J5
North Edisto (riv.) G6
Pacolet (riv.) D1
Palms, Isle of (isl.) H6
Parris Island Marine Base F7
Pee Dee (riv.) J4
Pocotaligo (riv.) G4
Port Royal (sound) F7
Pritchards (isl.) G7
Reedy (riv.) C2
Robinson (lake) G3
Romain (cape) J6
Saint Helena (isl.) F7
Saint Helena (sound) G7
Salkehatchie (riv.) E5
Saluda (riv.) D3
Sandy (pt.) H6
Sandy (riv.) E2
Santee (dam) G4
Santee (riv.) H5
Sassafras (mt.) B1
Savannah (riv.) E6
Savannah River Plant D5
Sea (isls.) G7
Seabrook (isl.) G6
Seneca (riv.) B2
Shaw A.F.B. F4
South (isl.) J5
Stevens (creek) C4
Stono (inlet) H6
Strom Thurmond (dam) C4
Strom Thurmond (lake) C4
Thompsons (creek) G2
Tugaloo (riv.) A2
Turkey (creek) E2
Tybee Roads (chan.) F7
Tyger (riv.) D2
Waccamaw (riv.) J5
Wadmalaw (isl.) G6
Wando (riv.) H6
Wateree (lake) F3
Winyah (bay) J5
Wylie (lake) E1

▲County seat

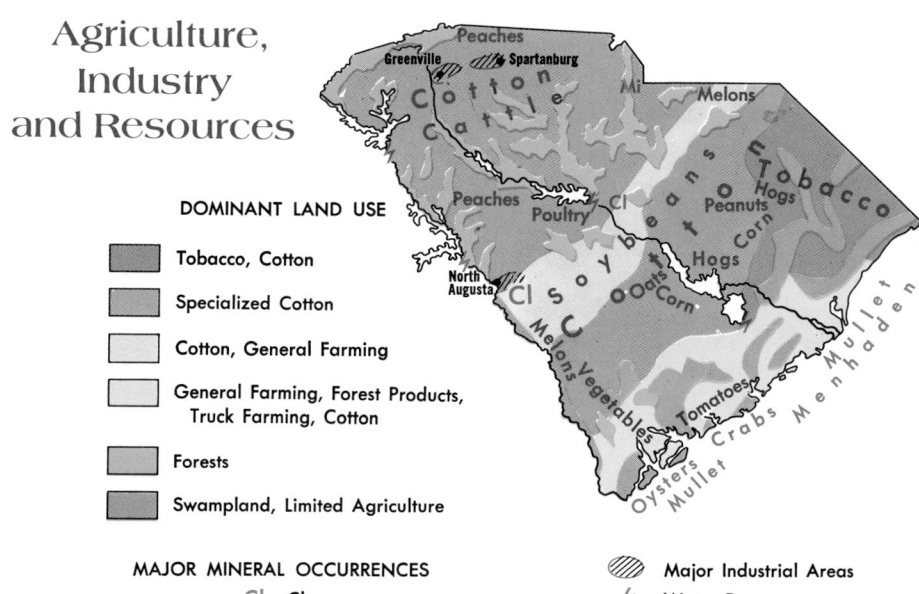

Agriculture, Industry and Resources

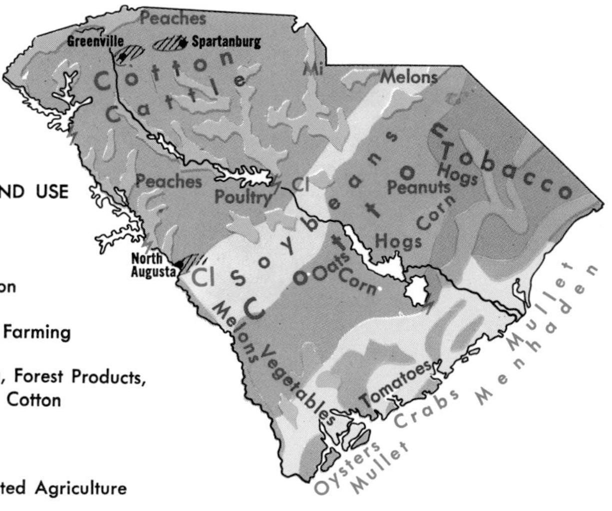

DOMINANT LAND USE

- Tobacco, Cotton
- Specialized Cotton
- Cotton, General Farming
- General Farming, Forest Products, Truck Farming, Cotton
- Forests
- Swampland, Limited Agriculture

MAJOR MINERAL OCCURRENCES

Cl Clay
Mi Mica

Major Industrial Areas
Water Power

COUNTIES

Aurora 3,135 ....M6
Beadle 18,253 ....N5
Bennett 3,206 ....F7
Bon Homme 7,089 ....O7
Brookings 25,207 ....R5
Brown 35,580 ....N2
Brule 5,485 ....L6
Buffalo 1,759 ....L5
Butte 7,914 ....B4
Campbell 1,965 ....J2
Charles Mix 9,131 ....M7
Clark 4,403 ....P4
Clay 13,186 ....P8
Codington 22,698 ....P4
Corson 4,195 ....G2
Custer 6,179 ....B6
Davison 17,503 ....N6
Day 6,978 ....O3
Deuel 4,522 ....R4
Dewey 5,523 ....G3

Douglas 3,746 ....N7
Edmunds 4,356 ....L3
Fall River 7,353 ....B7
Faulk 2,744 ....L3
Grant 8,372 ....R3
Gregory 5,359 ....L7
Haakon 2,624 ....F5
Hamlin 4,974 ....P4
Hand 4,272 ....L4
Hanson 2,994 ....O6
Harding 1,669 ....B2
Hughes 14,817 ....J5
Hutchinson 8,262 ....O7
Hyde 1,696 ....K4
Jackson 2,811 ....F6
Jerauld 2,425 ....M5
Jones 1,324 ....H6
Kingsbury 5,925 ....O5
Lake 10,550 ....P5
Lawrence 20,655 ....B5
Lincoln 15,427 ....R7
Lyman 3,638 ....J6

Marshall 4,844 ....O2
McCook 5,688 ....P6
McPherson 3,228 ....L2
Meade 21,878 ....D5
Mellette 2,137 ....H6
Miner 3,272 ....O5
Minnehaha 123,809 ....R6
Moody 6,507 ....R5
Pennington 81,343 ....C6
Perkins 3,932 ....D3
Potter 3,190 ....J3
Roberts 9,914 ....R3
Sanborn 2,833 ....N5
Shannon 9,902 ....D7
Spink 7,981 ....N4
Stanley 2,453 ....H5
Sully 1,589 ....J4
Todd 8,352 ....H7
Tripp 6,924 ....K7
Turner 8,576 ....P7
Union 10,189 ....R8
Walworth 6,087 ....J3

Yankton 19,252 ....P7
Ziebach 2,220 ....F4

CITIES and TOWNS

Aberdeen▲ 24,927 ....M3
Agar 82 ....J4
Akaska 52 ....J3
Alcester 843 ....R7
Alexandria▲ 518 ....O6
Allen 300 ....N5
Alpena 251 ....N5
Altamont 48 ....R4
Amherst 75 ....O2
Andover 106 ....O3
Ardmore 16 ....B7
Armour▲ 854 ....N7
Artas 28 ....K2
Artesian 217 ....N5
Ashton 148 ....N3

Astoria 155 ....S4
Aurora 619 ....R5
Avon 576 ....N8
Badger 114 ....P5
Baltic 666 ....R6
Bancroft 30 ....O4
Barnard 65 ....N2
Batesland 124 ....E7
Belle Fourche▲ 4,335 .....B4
Belvidere 63 ....F6
Beresford 1,849 ....R7
Big Stone City 669 ....S3
Bison▲ 451 ....E2
Black Hawk 1,995 ....C5
Blunt 342 ....J4
Bonesteel 297 ....M7
Bowdle 589 ....K3
Box Elder 2,680 ....D5
Bradley 117 ....O3
Brandon 3,543 ....R6
Brandt 123 ....R4

Brentford 69 ....N3
Bridgewater 533 ....P6
Bristol 419 ....O3
Britton▲ 1,394 ....O2
Broadland 40 ....N4
Brookings▲ 16,270 ....R5
Bruce 235 ....R5
Bryant 374 ....P4
Buffalo Gap 173 ....C6
Buffalo▲ 488 ....B2
Bullhead 178 ....G2
Burbank 90 ....R8
Burke▲ 756 ....L7
Butler 17 ....R5
Camp Crook 146 ....B2
Canistota 818 ....P6
Canning 40 ....L5
Canova 172 ....O6
Canton▲ 2,787 ....R7
Caputa 50 ....D5
Carter 7 ....J7

Carthage 221 ....O5
Castlewood 549 ....R4
Cavour 166 ....N5
Center 887 ....P6
Centerville 892 ....R7
Central City 185 ....B5
Chamberlain▲ 2,347 .....L6
Chancellor 276 ....R7
Chelsea 33 ....M3
Cherry Creek 500 ....F4
Chester 375 ....R6
Claire City 85 ....P2
Clark▲ 1,292 ....O4
Clear Lake▲ 1,247 ....R4
Colman 482 ....R6
Colome 309 ....K7
Colton 657 ....R6
Columbia 133 ....N2
Conde 203 ....N3
Corona 118 ....R3
Corsica 619 ....N7

South Dakota

SCALE

0 5 10   20   40   60 MI.

0 5 10   20   40   60 KM.

State Capitals ....⊛

County Seats ....⊙

Major Limited Access Hwys. ———

Scale 1:2,220,000

© Copyright HAMMOND INCORPORATED, Maplewood, N. J.

Corson 125	R6	
Cottonwood 12	F6	
Creighton 53	E5	
Cresbard 185	M3	
Crocker 70	O3	
Crooks 671	R6	
Custer▲ 1,741	B6	
Dallas 142	K7	
Dante 98	N7	
Davis 87	P7	
De Smet 1,172	O5	
Deadwood 1,830	B5	
Dell Rapids 2,484	R6	
Delmont 235	N7	
Dempster 62	R4	
Dimock 157	O7	
Dixon 125	L7	
Doland 306	N4	
Dolton 43	P7	
Draper 123	J6	
Dupree▲ 484	F3	
Eagle Butte 489	G4	
Eden 97	P2	
Edgemont 906	B7	
Egan 208	R6	
Elk Point▲ 1,423	R8	
Elkton 602	S5	
Emery 417	O6	
Epiphany 101	O6	
Erwin 42	P5	
Esmond	O5	
Estelline 658	R4	
Ethan 312	N6	
Eureka 1,197	K2	
Fairburn 62	C6	
Fairfax 144	M7	
Fairview 73	R7	
Faith 548	E4	
Farmer 23	O6	
Faulkton▲ 809	L3	
Fedora 80	O5	
Ferney 72	N3	
Flandreau 2,311	R5	
Florence 192	P3	

(continued on following page)

AREA 77,116 sq. mi. (199,730 sq. km.)
POPULATION 699,999
CAPITAL Pierre
LARGEST CITY Sioux Falls
HIGHEST POINT Harney Pk. 7,242 ft.
(2207 m.)
SETTLED IN 1856
ADMITTED TO UNION November 2, 1889
POPULAR NAME Coyote State; Sunshine
State
STATE FLOWER Pasqueflower
STATE BIRD Ring-necked Pheasant

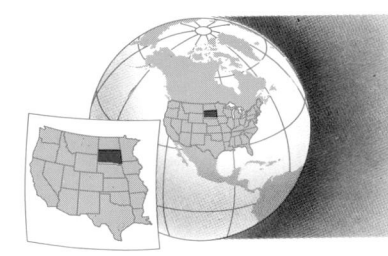

Topography

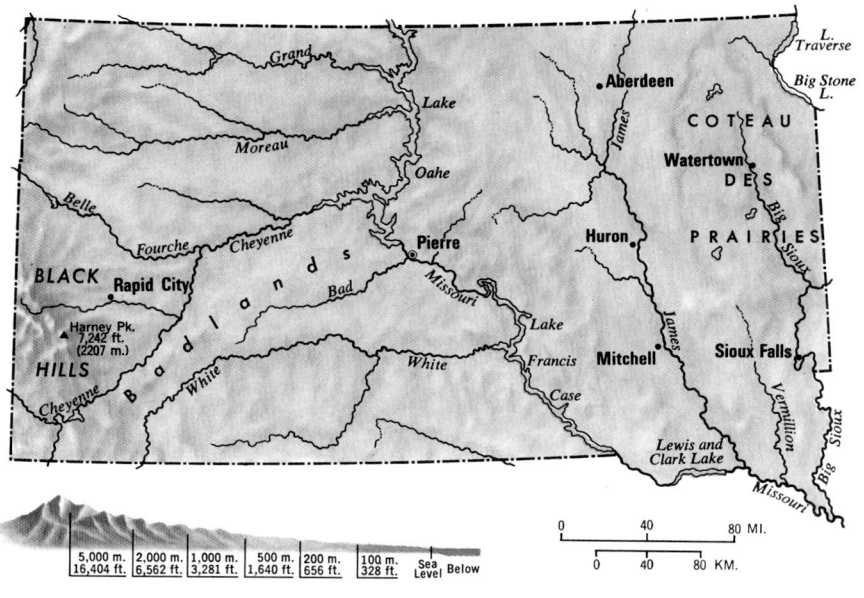

5,000 m. 16,404 ft.	2,000 m. 6,562 ft.	1,000 m. 3,281 ft.	500 m. 1,640 ft.	200 m. 656 ft.	100 m. 328 ft.	Sea Level	Below

0   40   80 MI.

0   40   80 KM.

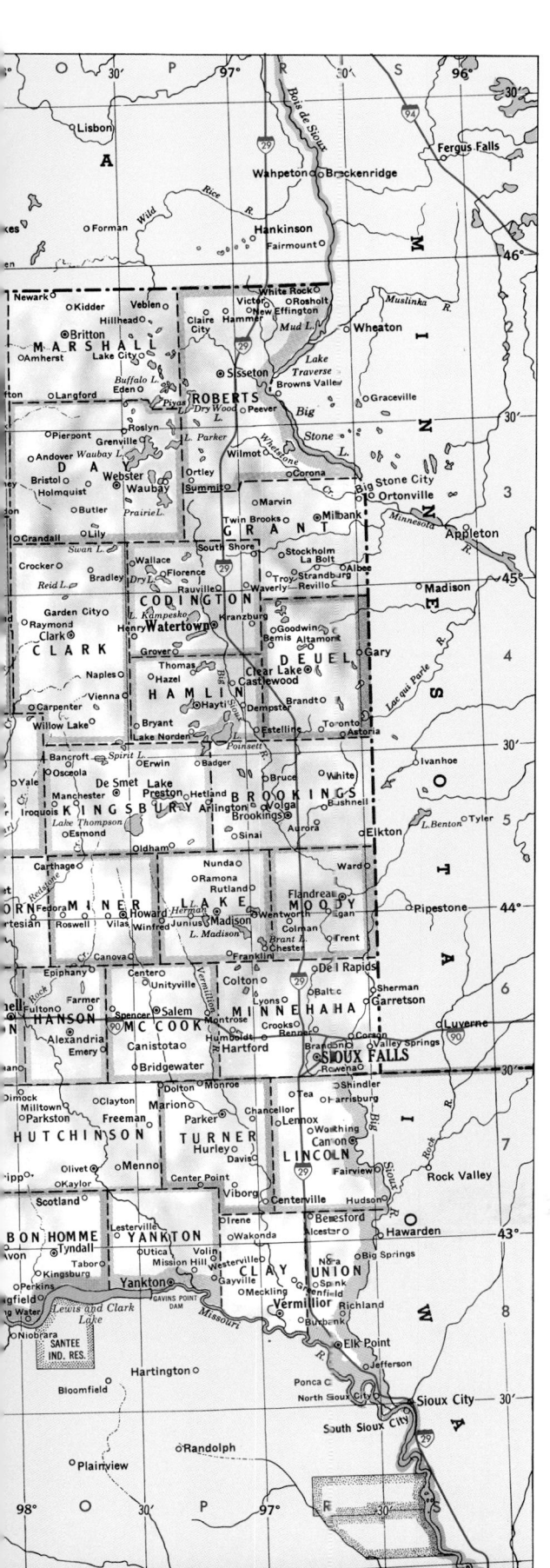

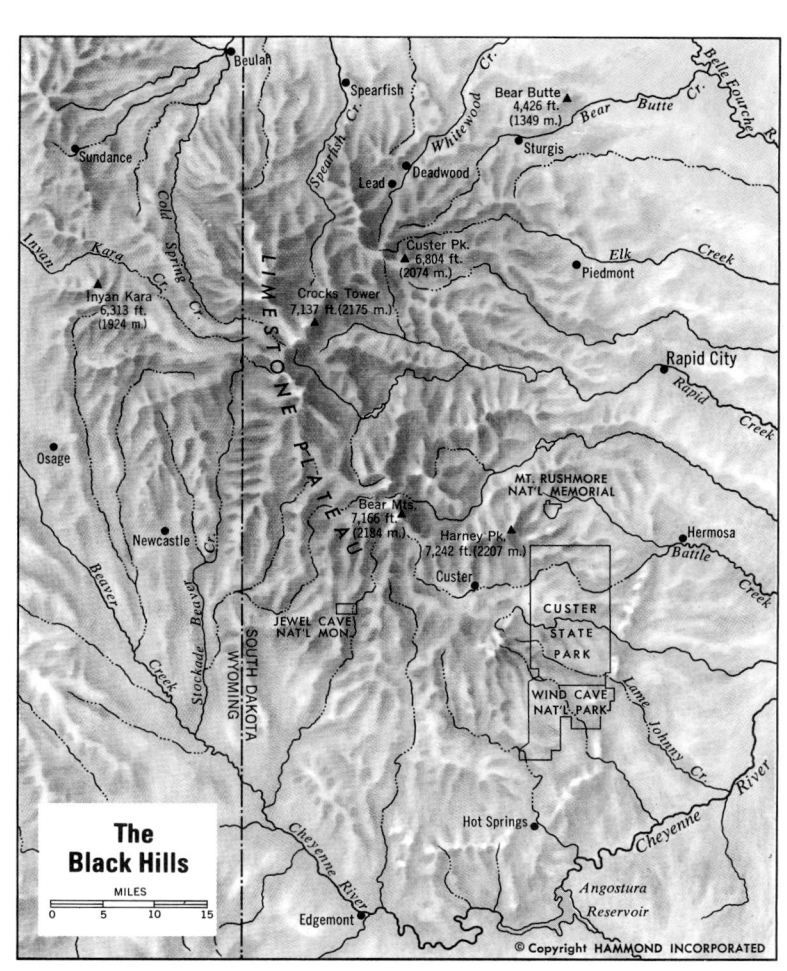

The Black Hills

MILES

0   5   10   15

© Copyright HAMMOND INCORPORATED

Agriculture, Industry and Resources

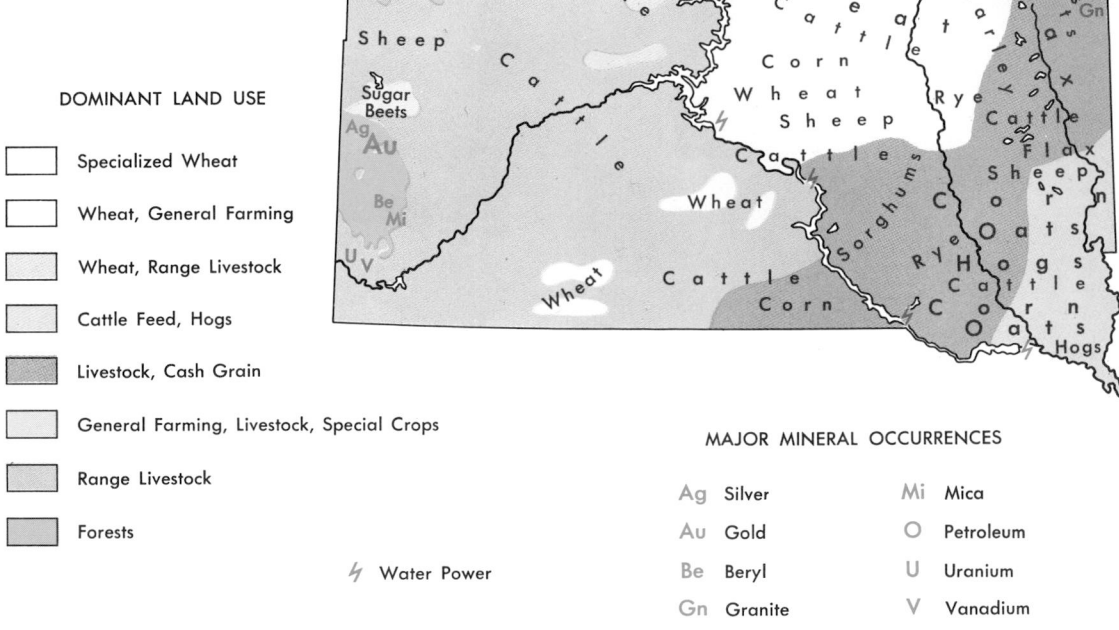

DOMINANT LAND USE

- Specialized Wheat
- Wheat, General Farming
- Wheat, Range Livestock
- Cattle Feed, Hogs
- Livestock, Cash Grain
- General Farming, Livestock, Special Crops
- Range Livestock
- Forests

⚡ Water Power

MAJOR MINERAL OCCURRENCES

Ag	Silver	Mi	Mica
Au	Gold	O	Petroleum
Be	Beryl	U	Uranium
Gn	Granite	V	Vanadium

Forestburg 100 ....N5
Fort Meade 900 ....C5
Fort Pierre▲ 1,854 ....H5
Fort Thompson 1,088 .....L5
Frankfort 192 ....N4
Frederick 241 ....N2
Freeman 1,293 ....O7
Fruitdale 43 ....B4
Fulton 70 ....O6
Gannvalley▲ 70 ....L5
Garden City 93 ....O4
Garretson 924 ....S6
Gary 274 ....S4
Gayville 401 ....P8
Geddes 280 ....M7
Gettysburg▲ 1,510 ....K3
Glad Valley 75 ....F3
Glencross 150 ....H3
Glenham 134 ....J2
Goodwin 126 ....R4
Greenway 57 ....K2
Greenwood 90 ....N8
Gregory 1,384 ....L7
Grenville 81 ....O3
Groton 1,196 ....N3
Harrington 54 ....G7
Harrisburg 727 ....R7
Harrison 89 ....M7
Harrold 167 ....K4
Hartford 1,262 ....P6
Hayti▲ 372 ....P4
Hazel 103 ....P4
Hecla 398 ....N2
Henry 215 ....P4
Hereford 50 ....D5
Hermosa 242 ....C6
Herreid 488 ....K2
Herrick 139 ....L7
Hetland 53 ....P5
Highmore▲ 835 ....L4
Hillsview 4 ....L2
Hitchcock 95 ....M4
Hosmer 310 ....L2
Hot Springs▲ 4,325 ....C7
Houghton 80 ....N2
Hoven 522 ....K3
Howard▲ 1,156 ....P5
Hudson 332 ....R7
Humboldt 468 ....P6
Hurley 372 ....P7
Huron▲ 12,448 ....N5
Ideal 250 ....K6
Interior 67 ....F6
Ipswich▲ 965 ....L3
Irene 464 ....P7
Iroquois 328 ....O5
Isabel 319 ....G3
Java 161 ....K3
Jefferson 527 ....S8
Junius 50 ....P6
Kadoka▲ 736 ....F6
Kaylor 120 ....O7
Kenel 245 ....H2
Kennebec▲ 284 ....K6
Keystone 232 ....C6
Kidder 75 ....O2
Kimball 743 ....M6
Kranzburg 132 ....R4
Kyle 914 ....E7
La Bolt 91 ....R3
La Plant 165 ....H3

Lake Andes▲ 846 ....M7
Lake City 43 ....O2
Lake Norden 427 ....P4
Lake Preston 663 ....P5
Lane 71 ....N5
Langford 298 ....O2
Lantry 200 ....G3
Lead 3,632 ....B5
Lebanon 115 ....K3
Lemmon 1,614 ....E2
Lennox 1,767 ....R7
Leola▲ 521 ....M2
Lesterville 168 ....O7
Letcher 164 ....N6
Lily 26 ....O3
Little Eagle 294 ....H2
Longlake 64 ....L2
Loomis 55 ....N6
Lower Brule 655 ....K5
Lowry 15 ....K3
Lyons 100 ....R6
Madison▲ 6,257 ....P6
Manderson 243 ....D7
Mansfield 120 ....N3
Marion 831 ....P7
Martin▲ 1,151 ....F7
Marty 436 ....N8
Marvin 38 ....R3
McIntosh▲ 302 ....G2
McLaughlin 780 ....H2
Meckling 108 ....R8
Mellette 184 ....N3
Menno 768 ....P7
Midland 233 ....G5
Milbank▲ 3,879 ....R3
Miller▲ 1,678 ....L4
Mission 730 ....H7
Mission Hill 180 ....P8
Mission Ridge 46 ....H4
Mitchell▲ 13,798 ....N6
Mobridge 3,768 ....J2
Monroe 151 ....P7
Montrose 420 ....P6
Morristown 64 ....F2
Mound City▲ 89 ....K2
Mount Vernon 368 ....N6
Murdo▲ 679 ....H6
Naples 35 ....O4
Nemo 42 ....B5
New Effington 219 ....R2
New Holland 125 ....M7
New Underwood 553 ......D5
New Witten 87 ....K7
Newell 675 ....C4
Nisland 174 ....C4
North Eagle Butte 1,423 .G3
North Sioux City 2,019 ..R8
Northville 105 ....M3
Nunda 45 ....P5
Oacoma 367 ....L6
Oelrichs 138 ....C7
Oglala 422 ....D7
Okreek 500 ....J7
Oldham 189 ....P5
Olivet▲ 74 ....O7
Onaka 52 ....L3
Onida▲ 761 ....K4
Oral 60 ....C7
Orient 59 ....L4
Ortley 63 ....P3
Parker▲ 984 ....P7

Parkston 1,572 ....O7
Parmelee 618 ....G7
Peever 195 ....R2
Philip▲ 1,077 ....F5
Pickstown 95 ....M7
Piedmont 500 ....C5
Pierpont 173 ....O3
Pierre (cap.)▲ 12,906 ....J5
Pine Ridge 2,596 ....E7
Plankinton▲ 604 ....N6
Platte 1,311 ....M7
Pollock 379 ....J2
Porcupine 783 ....E7
Potato Creek 40 ....F6
Prairie City 50 ....D2
Presho 654 ....J6
Pringle 96 ....B6
Provo 60 ....B7
Pukwana 263 ....L6
Quinn 72 ....E5
Ramona 194 ....P5
Ravinia 79 ....N7
Raymond 96 ....O4
Redfield▲ 2,770 ....N4
Redig 50 ....C3
Ree Heights 91 ....L4
Reliance 169 ....K6
Renner 320 ....R6
Revillo 152 ....R3
Richland 70 ....R8
Ridgeview 75 ....H3
Rockerville 28 ....C6
Rockham 48 ....M4
Roscoe 362 ....L3
Rosebud 1,538 ....H7
Rosholt 408 ....R2
Roslyn 251 ....P2
Roswell 19 ....O6
Rowena 100 ....R6
Saint Francis 815 ....H7
Saint Lawrence 223 ....M4
Saint Onge 250 ....B4
Salem▲ 1,289 ....P6
Sanator 150 ....B6
Scotland 968 ....O7
Selby▲ 707 ....J3
Seneca 81 ....L3
Shadehill 186 ....E2
Sherman 66 ....S6
Sinai 120 ....P5
Sioux Falls▲ 100,814 ....R6
Sisseton▲ 2,181 ....R2
Smithwick 50 ....C7
South Shore 260 ....P3
Spearfish 6,966 ....B5
Spencer 317 ....O6
Spink 75 ....R8
Springfield 834 ....N8
Stickney 323 ....M6
Stockholm 89 ....R3
Strandburg 74 ....R3
Stratford 85 ....N3
Sturgis▲ 5,330 ....B5
Summit 267 ....P3
Tabor 403 ....O8
Tea 786 ....R7
Tilford 75 ....C5
Timber Lake▲ 517 ....H3
Tolstoy 69 ....K3
Toronto 201 ....R4

Trail City 68 ....H3
Trent 211 ....R6
Tripp 664 ....N7
Trojan 40 ....B5
Tulare 194 ....N4
Turton 76 ....N3
Tuthill 75 ....G7
Twin Brooks 54 ....R3
Tyndall▲ 1,201 ....O8
Union Center 63 ....D4
Utica 115 ....P8
Vale 160 ....C4
Valley Springs 739 ....S6
Veblen 321 ....P2
Verdon 7 ....N3
Vermillion 10,034 ....R8
Viborg 763 ....P7
Vienna 93 ....O4
Vilas 28 ....O6
Villa Ranchaero 1,666 ....C5
Virgil 33 ....J6
Vivian 95 ....J6
Volga 1,263 ....R5
Volin 175 ....P8
Wagner 1,462 ....N7
Wakonda 329 ....P7
Wakpala 500 ....H2
Wall 834 ....E6
Wallace 83 ....P3
Wanblee 654 ....F6
Ward 35 ....R5
Warner 336 ....M3
Wasta 82 ....D5
Watauga 50 ....F2
Watertown▲ 17,592 ....P4
Waubay 647 ....P3
Webster▲ 2,017 ....P3
Wentworth 181 ....R6
Wessington 265 ....M5
Wessington Springs▲ 1,083 ..M5
Westport 112 ....M2
Wetonka 12 ....M2
White 536 ....R5
White Lake 419 ....M6
White River▲ 595 ....H6
White Rock 7 ....R2
Whitehorse 152 ....H3
Whitewood 891 ....B5
Willow Lake 317 ....O4
Wilmot 566 ....R3
Winfred 54 ....P6
Winner▲ 3,354 ....K7
Witten 134 ....J7
Wolsey 442 ....N5
Wood 73 ....J6
Woonsocket▲ 766 ....N5
Worthing 371 ....R7
Wounded Knee 18 ....D7
Yale 128 ....O5
Yankton▲ 12,703 ....P8

OTHER FEATURES

Aeber (creek) G4
Andes (lake) N7
Angostura (res.) B7
Antelope (creek) D3
Bad (riv.) G5
Badlands Nat'l Park E6
Battle (creek) C6
Bear in the Lodge (creek) ..F6

Beaver (creek) A6
Belle Fourche (res.) B4
Belle Fourche (riv.) C4
Big Bend (dam) K5
Big Sioux (riv.) S7
Big Stone (lake) R3
Black Hills (mts.) B5
Black Pine (creek) G6
Bois de Sioux (riv.) R1
Boxelder (creek) D5
Brant (lake) R6
Buffalo (creek) F6
Buffalo (lake) P2
Bull (creek) C2
Bull (creek) K6
Byron (lake) N4
Cain (creek) N5
Cherry (creek) F4
Cherry (creek) F5
Cheyenne (riv.) F4
Cheyenne River Ind. Res. ..F4
Choteau (creek) N7
Columbia Road (res.) N2
Cottonwood (creek) E5
Cottonwood (lake) M4
Crazy Horse Mon. B6
Crow (creek) A4
Crow Creek Ind. Res. L5
Dog Ear (creek) K6
Dry (creek) G4
Dry (lake) P3
Dry Wood (lake) P2
Elk (creek) C5
Ellsworth Air Force Base
  7,017 ....C5
Elm (creek) D4
Elm (riv.) M2
Firesteel (creek) N6
Flint Rock (creek) E3
Fort Randall (dam) N7
Foster (creek) N4
Francis Case (lake) L7
French (creek) C6
Gavins Point (dam) P8
Geographical Center of
  United States B4
Grand (riv.) F2
Harney (peak) B6
Hat (creek) B7
Hell Canyon (creek) B6
Herman (lake) P5
Horsehead (creek) C7
Indian (creek) B4
James (riv.) N5
Jewel Cave Nat'l Mon. B6
Kampeska (lake) P4
Keya Paha (riv.) K7
Lame Johnny (creek) C6
Lewis and Clark (lake) O8
Little Missouri (riv.) B1
Little Moreau (riv.) G3
Little White (riv.) H7
Long (lake) L2
Lower Brule Ind. Res. K5
Madison (lake) P6
Maple (riv.) M1
Medicine (lake) J6
Medicine Knoll (creek) J5
Minnechaduze (creek) H7
Minnesota (riv.) S3
Missouri (riv.) P8

Mitchell (creek) G5
Moreau (riv.) G3
Mount Rushmore Nat'l Mon. ..B6
Mud (creek) N3
Mud (lake) R2
Mud Lake (res.) N2
Nasty (creek) C2
Oahe (dam) J5
Oahe (lake) J1
Oak (creek) H2
Oak (creek) J6
Okobojo (creek) J4
Owl (creek) B4
Parker (lake) P3
Pearl (creek) N5
Pine Ridge Ind. Res. D7
Piyas (lake) P2
Platte (lake) M6
Pleasant Valley (creek) ...B6
Poinsett (lake) P4
Ponca (creek) L7
Prairie (lake) P3
Rabbit (creek) E3
Red (lake) L6
Red Owl (creek) E4
Red Scaffold (creek) F4
Redstone (creek) O5
Redwater (creek) A4
Reid (lake) O3
Rock (creek) O6
Rosebud Ind. Res. H7
Sand (creek) A4
Sand (creek) M5
Shadehill (res.) E3
Sharpe (lake) J5
Shue (creek) N5
Smith (creek) L6
Snake (creek) F4
Snake (creek) F5
Snake (creek) M3
Spirit (lake) O4
Spring (creek) C6
Spring (creek) J2
Squaw (creek) B3
Sulphur (creek) D4
Swan (creek) J3
Swan (lake) K3
Swan (lake) O3
Thompson (lake) O5
Thunder (creek) N4
Thunder Butte (creek) E3
Traverse (lake) R2
Turtle (creek) M4
Vermillion (riv.) P6
Virgin (creek) H3
Waubay (lake) P3
Whetstone (creek) R3
White (lake) M6
White (riv.) D7
Whitewood (creek) B4
Willow (creek) C4
Wind Cave Nat'l Park B6
Wolf (creek) L4
Wounded Knee (creek) E7

* ▲ County seat

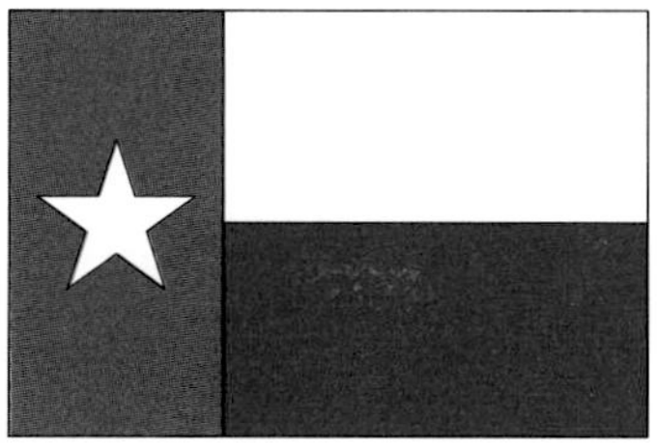

AREA 266,807 sq. mi. (691,030 sq. km.)
POPULATION 17,059,805
CAPITAL Austin
LARGEST CITY Houston
HIGHEST POINT Guadalupe Pk. 8,749 ft. (2667 m.)
SETTLED IN 1686
ADMITTED TO UNION December 29, 1845
POPULAR NAME Lone Star State
STATE FLOWER Bluebonnet
STATE BIRD Mockingbird

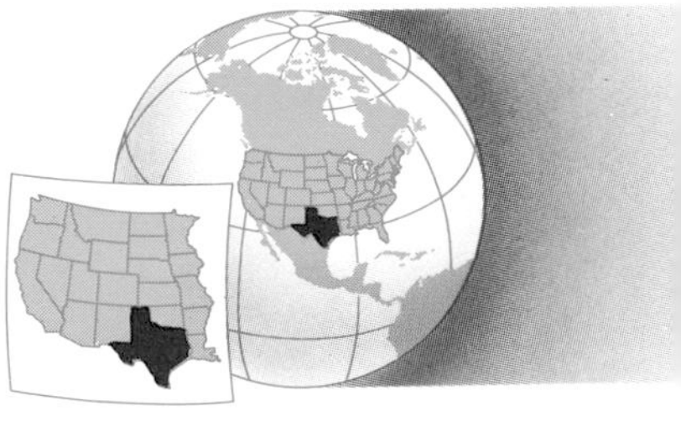

COUNTIES

Anderson 48,024 J6
Andrews 14,338 B5
Angelina 69,884 K6
Aransas 17,892 H10
Archer 7,973 F4
Armstrong 2,021 C3
Atascosa 30,533 F9
Austin 19,832 H8
Bailey 7,064 B3
Bandera 10,562 E8
Bastrop 38,263 G7
Baylor 4,385 E4
Bee 25,135 G9
Bell 191,088 G6
Bexar 1,185,394 F8
Blanco 5,972 F8
Borden 799 C5
Bosque 15,125 G6
Bowie 81,665 K4
Brazoria 191,707 J8
Brazos 121,862 H7
Brewster 8,681 A8
Briscoe 1,971 C3
Brooks 8,204 F11
Brown 34,371 F6
Burleson 13,625 H7
Burnet 22,677 F7
Caldwell 26,392 G8
Calhoun 19,053 H9
Callahan 11,859 E5
Cameron 260,120 G11
Camp 9,904 K5
Carson 6,576 C2
Cass 29,982 K4
Castro 9,070 B3
Chambers 20,088 K8
Cherokee 41,049 J6
Childress 5,953 D3
Clay 10,024 F4
Cochran 4,377 B4
Coke 3,424 D6
Coleman 9,710 E6
Collin 264,036 H4
Collingsworth 3,573 D3
Colorado 18,383 H8
Comal 51,832 F8
Comanche 13,381 F5
Concho 3,044 E6
Cooke 30,777 G4
Coryell 64,213 G6
Cottle 2,247 D3
Crane 4,652 B6
Crockett 4,078 C7
Crosby 7,304 C4
Culberson 3,407 C11
Dallam 5,461 B1
Dallas 1,852,810 H5
Dawson 14,349 C5
De Witt 18,903 G9
Deaf Smith 19,153 B3
Delta 4,857 J4
Denton 273,525 G4
Dickens 2,571 D4
Dimmit 10,433 E9
Donley 3,696 D2
Duval 12,918 F10
Eastland 18,488 F5
Ector 118,934 B6
Edwards 2,266 D7
El Paso 591,610 A10
Ellis 85,167 H5
Erath 27,991 F5
Falls 17,712 H6
Fannin 24,804 H4
Fayette 20,095 H8
Fisher 4,842 D5
Floyd 8,497 C3
Foard 1,794 E3
Fort Bend 225,421 J8
Franklin 7,802 J4
Freestone 15,818 H6
Frio 13,472 E9
Gaines 14,123 B5
Galveston 217,399 K8
Garza 5,143 C4
Gillespie 17,204 F7
Glasscock 1,447 C6
Goliad 5,980 G9
Gonzales 17,205 G8
Gray 23,967 D2
Grayson 95,021 H4
Gregg 104,948 K5
Grimes 18,828 J7
Guadalupe 64,873 G8
Hale 34,671 C3
Hall 3,905 D3
Hamilton 7,733 F6
Hansford 5,848 C1
Hardeman 5,283 E3
Hardin 41,320 K7
Harris 2,818,199 J8
Harrison 57,483 K5
Hartley 3,634 B2
Haskell 6,820 E4
Hays 65,614 F7
Hemphill 3,720 D2
Henderson 58,543 J5
Hidalgo 383,545 F11
Hill 27,146 G5
Hockley 24,199 B4
Hood 28,981 G5
Hopkins 28,833 J4
Houston 21,375 J6
Howard 32,343 C5
Hudspeth 2,915 B10
Hunt 64,343 H4
Hutchinson 25,689 C2
Irion 1,629 C6
Jack 6,981 F4
Jackson 13,039 H9
Jasper 31,102 K7
Jeff Davis 1,946 C11
Jefferson 239,397 K8
Jim Hogg 5,109 F11
Jim Wells 37,679 F10
Johnson 97,165 G5
Jones 16,490 E5
Karnes 12,455 G9
Kaufman 52,220 H5
Kendall 14,589 F8
Kenedy 460 G11
Kent 1,010 D4
Kerr 36,304 E7
Kimble 4,122 E7
King 354 D4
Kinney 3,119 D8
Kleberg 30,274 G10
Knox 4,837 E4
La Salle 5,254 E9
Lamar 43,949 J4
Lamb 15,072 B3
Lampasas 13,521 F6
Lavaca 18,690 H8
Lee 12,854 H7
Leon 12,665 J6
Liberty 52,726 K7
Limestone 20,946 H6
Lipscomb 3,143 D1
Live Oak 9,556 F9
Llano 11,631 F7
Loving 107 A6
Lubbock 222,636 C4
Lynn 6,758 C4
Madison 10,931 J6
Marion 9,984 K5
Martin 4,956 C5
Mason 3,423 E7
Matagorda 36,928 H9
Maverick 36,378 D9
McCulloch 8,778 E6
McLennan 189,123 G6
McMullen 817 F9
Medina 27,312 E8
Menard 2,252 E7
Midland 106,611 B6
Milam 22,946 H7
Mills 4,531 F6
Mitchell 8,016 D5
Montague 17,274 G4
Montgomery 182,201 J7
Moore 17,865 C2
Morris 13,200 K4
Motley 1,532 D3
Nacogdoches 54,753 K6
Navarro 39,926 H5
Newton 13,569 L7
Nolan 16,594 D5
Nueces 291,145 G10
Ochiltree 9,128 D1
Oldham 2,278 B2
Orange 80,509 L7
Palo Pinto 25,055 F5
Panola 22,035 K5
Parker 64,785 G5
Parmer 9,863 B3
Pecos 14,675 B7
Polk 30,687 K7
Potter 97,874 C2
Presidio 6,637 C12
Rains 6,715 J5
Randall 89,673 C2
Reagan 4,514 C6
Real 2,412 E8
Red River 14,317 J4
Reeves 15,852 D11
Refugio 7,976 G9
Roberts 1,025 D2
Robertson 15,511 H6
Rockwall 25,604 H5
Runnels 11,294 E6
Rusk 43,735 K5
Sabine 9,586 L6
San Augustine 7,999 K6
San Jacinto 16,372 J7
San Patricio 58,749 G10
San Saba 5,401 F6
Schleicher 2,990 D7
Scurry 18,634 D5
Shackleford 3,915 E5
Shelby 22,034 K6
Sherman 2,858 C1
Smith 151,309 J5
Somervell 5,360 G5
Starr 40,518 F11
Stephens 9,010 F5
Sterling 1,438 C6
Stonewall 2,013 D4
Sutton 4,135 D7
Swisher 8,133 C3
Tarrant 1,170,103 G5
Taylor 119,655 E5
Terrell 1,410 B7
Terry 13,218 B4
Throckmorton 1,880 E4
Titus 24,009 K4
Tom Green 98,458 D6
Travis 576,407 G7
Trinity 11,445 J6
Tyler 16,646 K7
Upshur 31,370 K5
Upton 4,447 B6
Uvalde 23,340 E8
Val Verde 38,721 C8
Van Zandt 37,944 J5
Victoria 74,361 H9
Walker 50,917 J7
Waller 23,390 J8
Ward 13,115 A6
Washington 26,154 H7
Webb 133,239 E10
Wharton 39,955 H8
Wheeler 5,879 D2
Wichita 122,378 F3
Wilbarger 15,121 E3
Willacy 17,705 G11
Williamson 139,551 G7
Wilson 22,650 F8
Winkler 8,626 A6
Wise 34,679 G4
Wood 29,380 J5
Yoakum 8,786 B4
Young 18,126 F4
Zapata 9,279 E11
Zavala 12,162 E9

CITIES and TOWNS

Abernathy 2,720 B4
Abilene▲ 106,654 E5
Addison 8,783 G2
Alamo 8,210 F11
Alamo Heights 6,502 K10
Albany▲ 1,962 E5
Alice▲ 19,788 F10
Allen 18,309 H1
Alpine▲ 5,637 D12
Alvarado 2,918 G5
Alvin 19,220 J3
Amarillo▲ 157,615 C2
Anahuac▲ 1,993 K8
Anderson▲ 500 J7
Andrews▲ 10,678 B5
Angleton▲ 17,140 J8
Anson▲ 2,644 E5
Anthony 3,328 A10
Aransas Pass 7,180 G10
Archer City▲ 1,748 F4
Arlington 261,721 F2
Aspermont▲ 1,214 D4
Athens▲ 10,967 J5
Atlanta 6,118 K4
Austin (cap.)▲ 465,622 G7
Azle 8,868 E2
Bacliff 5,549 K2
Baird▲ 1,658 E5
Balch Springs 17,406 H2
Balcones Heights 3,022 J10
Ballinger▲ 3,975 E6
Bandera▲ 877 F8
Barrett 3,052 K1
Bastrop▲ 4,044 G7
Bay City▲ 18,170 H9
Baytown 63,850 L2
Beaumont▲ 114,323 K7
Bedford 43,762 F2
Beeville▲ 13,547 G9
Bellaire 13,842 J2
Bellmead 8,336 H6
Bellville▲ 3,378 H8
Belton▲ 12,476 G7
Benavides 1,788 F10
Benbrook 19,564 E2
Benjamin▲ 225 E4
Big Lake▲ 3,672 C6
Big Spring▲ 23,093 C5
Bishop 3,337 G10
Bloomington 1,888 H9
Blue Mound 2,133 E2
Boerne▲ 4,274 J10
Bonham▲ 6,686 H4
Borger 15,675 C2
Boston▲ 400 K4
Bowie 4,990 G4
Brackettville▲ 1,740 D8
Brady▲ 5,946 E6
Brazoria 2,717 J9
Breckinridge▲ 5,665 F5
Brenham▲ 11,952 H7
Briar 3,899 E1
Bridge City 8,034 L7
Bridgeport 3,581 G4
Brookshire 2,922 J8
Brownfield▲ 9,560 B4
Brownsville▲ 98,962 G12
Brownwood▲ 18,387 F6
Bryan▲ 55,002 H7
Buda 1,795 G7
Buna 2,127 L7
Bunker Hill Village 3,391 J1
Burkburnett 10,145 F3
Burleson 16,113 F3
Burnet▲ 3,423 F7
Caldwell▲ 3,181 H7
Cameron▲ 5,580 H7
Canadian▲ 2,417 D2
Canton▲ 2,949 J5
Canutillo 4,442 A10
Canyon▲ 11,365 C3
Carrizo Springs▲ 5,745 E9
Carrollton 82,169 G2
Carthage▲ 6,496 K5
Castle Hills 4,198 J10
Castroville 2,159 J11
Cedar Hill 19,976 G3
Cedar Park 5,161 G7
Center▲ 4,950 K6
Centerville▲ 812 H6
Channelview 25,564 K1
Channing▲ 277 B2
Childress▲ 5,055 D3
Cisco 3,813 E5
Clarendon▲ 2,067 C3
Clarksville▲ 4,311 K4
Claude▲ 1,199 C2
Clear Lake Shores 1,096 K2
Cleburne▲ 22,205 G5
Cleveland 7,124 K7
Clifton 3,195 G6
Clute 8,910 J9
Clyde 3,002 E5
Cockrell Hill 3,746 G2
Coldspring▲ 538 J7
Coleman▲ 5,410 E6
College Station▲ 52,456 H7
Colleyville 12,724 F2
Colorado City▲ 4,749 C5
Columbus▲ 3,367 H8
Comanche▲ 4,087 F6
Commerce 6,825 J4
Conroe▲ 27,610 J7
Converse 8,887 K11
Cooper▲ 2,153 J4
Coppell 16,881 G2
Copperas Cove 24,079 G6
Corpus Christi▲ 257,453 G10
Corsicana▲ 22,911 H5
Cotulla▲ 3,694 E9
Crane▲ 3,533 B6
Crockett▲ 7,024 J6
Crosby 1,811 J8
Crosbyton▲ 2,026 C4
Crowell▲ 1,230 E4
Crowley 6,974 E3
Crystal City▲ 8,263 E9
Cuero▲ 6,700 G8
Daingerfield▲ 2,572 K4
Dalhart▲ 6,246 B1
Dallas▲ 1,006,877 G2
Dalworthington Gardens 1,758 F2
Dayton 5,151 J7
De Kalb 1,976 K4
De Leon 2,190 F5
De Soto 30,544 G3
Decatur▲ 4,252 G4
Deer Park 27,652 K2
Del Rio▲ 30,705 D8
Denison 21,505 H4
Denton▲ 66,270 G4
Denver City 5,145 B4
Devine 3,928 E8
Diboll 4,341 K6
Dickens▲ 322 D4
Dickinson 9,497 K3
Dilley 2,632 E9
Dimmitt▲ 4,408 B3
Donna 12,652 F11
Double Oak 1,664 F1

(continued on following page)

DOMINANT LAND USE

- Wheat, Grain Sorghums, Range Livestock
- Cotton, Wheat
- Specialized Cotton
- Cotton, General Farming
- Cotton, Forest Products
- Cotton, Range Livestock
- Rice, General Farming
- Peanuts, General Farming
- General Farming, Livestock, Cash Grain
- General Farming, Forest Products, Truck Farming, Cotton
- Fruit, Truck and Mixed Farming
- Range Livestock
- Forests
- Swampland, Limited Agriculture
- Nonagricultural Land
- Urban Areas

MAJOR MINERAL OCCURRENCES

At Asphalt
Cl Clay
Fe Iron Ore
G Natural Gas
Gn Granite
Gp Gypsum
Gr Graphite
He Helium
Ls Limestone
Na Salt
O Petroleum
S Sulfur
Tc Talc
U Uranium

Water Power
Major Industrial Areas

Agriculture, Industry and Resources

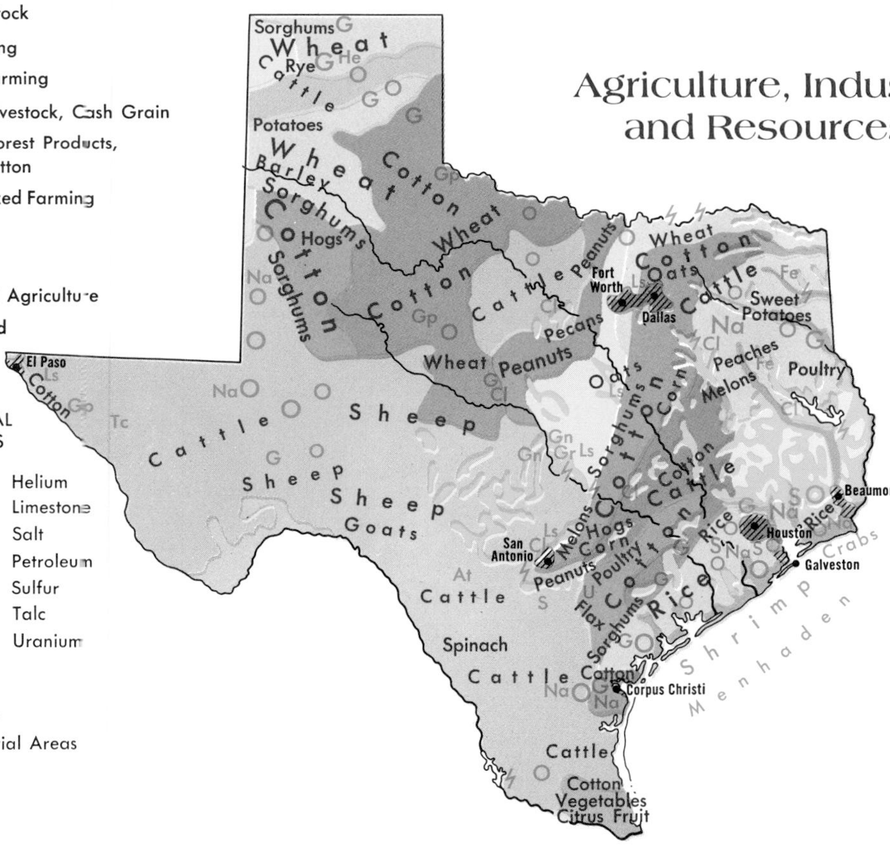

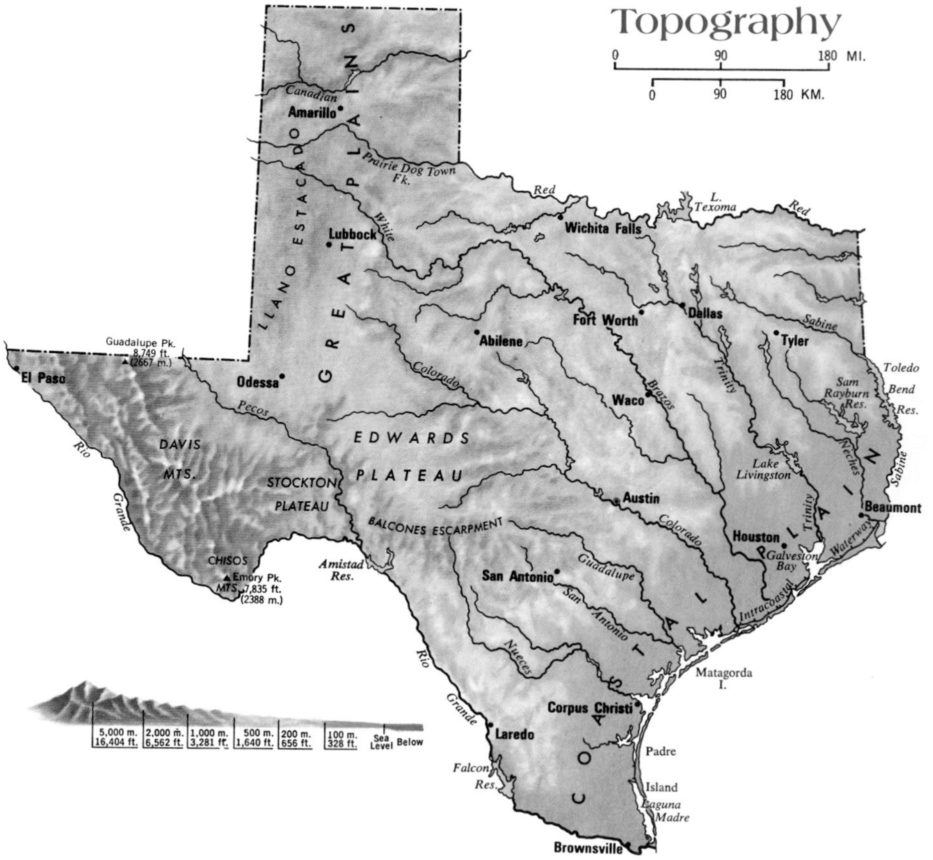
Topography
0 90 180 MI.
0 90 180 KM.
Amarillo
Canadian
Prairie Dog Town Fk.
LLANO ESTACADO
GREAT PLAINS
Red
L. Texoma
Red
Wichita Falls
Lubbock
White
Fort Worth
Dallas
Sabine
Tyler
Abilene
Guadalupe Pk. 8,749 ft. (2667 m.)
El Paso
Odessa
Colorado
Brazos
Trinity
Waco
Toledo Bend Res.
Sam Rayburn Res.
Pecos
EDWARDS PLATEAU
DAVIS MTS.
Rio Grande
STOCKTON PLATEAU
Neches
Lake Livingston
Sabine
Austin
Beaumont
BALCONES ESCARPMENT
Colorado
Houston
Trinity
Galveston Bay
Waterway
CHISOS MTS.
Emory Pk. 7,835 ft. (2388 m.)
Amistad Res.
San Antonio
Guadalupe
San Antonio
Intracoastal
COASTAL PLAIN
Nueces
Rio Grande
Matagorda I.
Corpus Christi
Laredo
5,000 m. 16,404 ft.
2,000 m. 6,562 ft.
1,000 m. 3,281 ft.
500 m. 1,640 ft.
200 m. 656 ft.
100 m. 328 ft.
Sea Level
Below
Padre Island
Falcon Res.
Laguna Madre
Brownsville

Dublin 3,190...F5
Dumas▲ 12,871...C2
Duncanville 35,748...G3
Eagle Lake 3,551...H8
Eagle Pass▲ 20,651...D9
Eastland▲ 3,690...F5
Edcouch 2,878...G11
Edgecliff 2,715...E2
Edinburg▲ 29,885...F11
Edna▲ 5,343...H9
El Campo 10,511...H8
El Lago 3,269...K2
El Paso▲ 515,342...A10
Eldorado▲ 2,019...D7
Electra 3,113...F4
Elgin 4,846...G7
Elsa 5,242...G11
Emory▲ 963...J5
Ennis 13,883...H5
Euless 38,149...F2
Everman 5,672...F3
Fabens 5,599...B10
Fairfield▲ 3,234...H6
Falfurrias▲ 5,788...F10
Farmers Branch 24,250...G2
Farmersville 2,640...H4
Farwell▲ 1,373...A3
Ferris 2,212...H3
Floresville▲ 5,247...K11
Flower Mound 15,527...F1
Floydada▲ 3,896...C3
Forest Hill 11,482...F2
Forney 4,070...H5
Fort Davis▲ 900...D11
Fort Stockton▲ 8,524...A7
Fort Worth▲ 447,619...F2
Franklin▲ 1,336...H7
Fredericksburg▲ 6,934...E7
Fredonia 50...E7
Freeport 11,389...J9
Freer 3,271...F10
Fresno 3,182...J2
Friendswood 22,814...J2
Friona 3,688...B3
Frisco 6,141...H4
Fritch 2,335...C2
Gail▲ 171...C5
Gainesville▲ 14,256...G4
Galena Park 10,033...J1
Galveston▲ 59,070...L3
Ganado 1,701...H8
Garden City▲ 350...C6
Garland 180,650...H2
Gatesville▲ 11,492...G6
George West▲ 2,586...F9
Georgetown▲ 14,842...G7
Giddings▲ 4,093...H7
Gilmer▲ 4,822...J5
Gladewater 6,027...K5
Glen Rose▲ 1,949...G5
Glenn Heights 4,564...G2
Goldthwaite▲ 1,658...F6
Goliad▲ 1,946...G9
Gonzales▲ 6,527...G8
Graham▲ 8,986...F4
Granbury▲ 4,045...G5
Grand Prairie 99,616...G2
Grand Saline 2,630...J5
Grapevine 29,202...F2
Greenville▲ 23,071...H4
Groesbeck▲ 3,185...H6
Groves 16,513...L8
Groveton▲ 1,071...J7
Guthrie▲ 170...D4
Hale Center 2,067...C3
Hallettsville▲ 2,718...G8
Hallsville 2,288...K5
Haltom City 32,856...F2
Hamilton▲ 2,937...G6
Hamlin 2,791...E5
Harlingen 48,735...G11
Haskell▲ 3,362...E4
Hearne 5,132...H7
Hebbronville▲ 4,465...F10
Hedwig Village 2,616...H1
Hemphill▲ 1,182...L6
Hempstead▲ 3,551...J7
Henderson▲ 11,139...K5
Henrietta▲ 2,896...F4
Hereford▲ 14,745...B3
Hickory Creek 1,893...F1
Hidalgo 3,292...F11
Highland Park 8,739...G2
Highland Village 7,027...F1
Highlands 6,632...K1
Hillsboro▲ 7,072...G5
Hitchcock 5,868...K3
Hollywood 3,231...K10
Hondo▲ 6,018...E8
Honey Grove 1,681...J4
Hooks 2,684...K4
Houston▲ 1,630,553...J2
Howe 2,173...H4
Hughes Springs 1,938...K5
Humble 12,060...J7
Hunters Creek Village 3,954...J1
Huntington 1,794...K6
Huntsville▲ 27,925...J7
Hurst 33,574...F2
Hutchins 2,719...G3
Idalou 2,074...C4
Iowa Park 6,072...F4
Irving 155,037...G2
Italy 1,699...H5
Jacinto City 9,343...J1
Jacksboro▲ 3,350...F4
Jacksonville 12,765...J5
Jasper▲ 6,959...L7
Jayton▲ 608...D4
Jefferson▲ 2,199...K5
Jersey Village 4,826...J1
Johnson City▲ 932...F7
Jones Creek 2,160...J9
Jourdanton▲ 3,220...F9
Junction▲ 2,654...E7
Karnes City▲ 2,916...G9
Katy 8,005...J8
Kaufman▲ 5,238...H5
Keene 3,944...G5
Keller 13,683...F2
Kenedy 3,763...G9
Kennedale 4,096...F3
Kerens 1,702...H5
Kermit▲ 6,875...B6
Kerrville▲ 17,384...E7
Kilgore 11,066...K5
Killeen 63,535...G6
Kingsland 2,725...F7
Kingsville▲ 25,276...G10
Kirby 8,326...K11
Kirbyville 1,871...K7
Kountze▲ 2,056...K7
Kyle 2,225...G8
La Feria 3,495...G11
La Grange▲ 3,951...G8
La Joya 2,604...F11
La Marque 14,120...K3
La Porte 27,910...K2
Lake Dallas 3,656...G1
Lake Jackson 22,776...J8
Lake Worth 4,591...E2
Lamesa▲ 10,809...C5
Lampasas▲ 6,382...F6
Lancaster 22,117...G3
Laredo▲ 122,899...E10
League City 30,159...K2
Leakey▲ 399...E8
Leon Valley 9,581...J10
Leonard 1,744...H4
Levelland▲ 13,986...B4
Lewisville 46,521...G1
Liberty▲ 7,733...K7
Lindale 2,428...J5
Linden▲ 2,375...K4
Lipscomb▲ 52...D1
Littlefield▲ 6,489...B4
Live Oak 10,023...K10
Livingston▲ 5,019...K7
Llano▲ 2,962...F7
Lockhart▲ 9,205...G8
Lockney 2,207...C3
Lomax 2,991...K2
Longview▲ 70,311...K5
Los Fresnos 2,473...G11
Lubbock▲ 186,206...C4
Lucas 2,205...H1
Lufkin▲ 30,206...K6
Luling 4,661...G8
Lumberton 6,640...K7
Lyford 1,674...G11
Lytle 2,255...J11
Mabank 1,739...H5
Madisonville▲ 3,569...J7
Malakoff 2,038...H5
Mansfield 15,607...F3
Manvel 3,733...J3
Marble Falls 4,007...F7
Marfa▲ 2,424...C12
Marlin▲ 6,386...H6
Marshall▲ 23,682...K5
Mart 2,004...H6
Mason▲ 2,041...E7
Matador▲ 790...D3
Mathis 5,423...G9
McAllen 84,021...F11
McCamey 2,493...B6
McGregor 4,683...G6
McKinney▲ 21,283...H4
Memphis▲ 2,465...D3
Menard▲ 1,606...E7
Mentone▲ 50...D10
Mercedes 12,694...F12
Meridian▲ 1,390...G6
Merkel 2,469...E5
Mertzon▲ 778...C6
Mesquite 101,484...H2
Mexia 6,933...H6
Miami▲ 675...D2
Midland▲ 89,443...C6
Midlothian 5,141...G5
Mineola 4,321...J5
Mineral Wells 14,870...F5
Mission 28,653...F11
Missouri City 36,176...J2
Monahans▲ 8,101...B6
Montague▲ 1,253...G4
Morton▲ 2,597...B4
Mount Pleasant▲ 12,291...K4
Mount Vernon▲ 2,219...J4
Muleshoe▲ 4,571...B3
Nacogdoches▲ 30,872...J6
Nash 2,162...K4
Nassau Bay 4,320...K2
Navasota 6,296...J7
Nederland 16,192...K8
Needville 2,199...J8
New Boston 5,057...J4
New Braunfels▲ 27,334...K10
Newton▲ 1,885...L7
Nixon 1,995...G8
Nocona 2,870...G4
North Richland Hills 45,895...F2
Odessa▲ 89,699...B6
Olmos Park 2,161...K11
Olney 3,519...F4
Olton 2,116...B3
Orange▲ 19,381...L7
Overton 2,105...K5
Ovilla 2,027...G3
Ozona▲ 3,181...C7
Paducah▲ 1,788...D4
Paint Rock▲ 227...E6
Palacios 4,418...H9
Palestine▲ 18,042...J6
Palo Pinto▲ 350...F5
Pampa▲ 19,959...D2
Panhandle▲ 2,353...C2
Pantego 2,371...F2
Paris▲ 24,699...J4
Pasadena 119,363...J2
Pearland 18,697...J2
Pearsall▲ 6,924...E9
Pecos▲ 12,069...D10
Perryton▲ 7,607...D1
Pflugerville 4,444...G7
Pharr 32,921...F11
Pickton 1,729...C2
Pilot Point 2,538...H4
Piney Point Village 3,197...J1
Pittsburg▲ 4,007...J4
Plains▲ 1,422...B4
Plainview▲ 21,700...C3
Plano 128,713...G1
Pleasanton 7,678...F9
Port Aransas 2,233...H10
Port Arthur 58,724...K8
Port Isabel 4,467...G11
Port Lavaca▲ 10,886...H9
Port Neches 12,974...K7
Portland 12,224...G10
Post▲ 3,768...C4
Poteet 3,206...F8
Prairie View 4,004...J7
Premont 2,914...F10
Presidio 3,072...C12
Quanah▲ 3,413...E3
Queen City 1,748...L4
Quitman▲ 1,684...J5
Ralls 2,172...C4
Ranger 2,803...F5
Rankin▲ 1,011...B6
Raymondville▲ 8,880...G11
Red Oak 3,124...H5
Refugio▲ 3,158...G9
Reno 1,784...E2
Richardson 74,840...G2
Richland Hills 7,978...F2
Richmond▲ 9,801...J8
Rio Grande City▲ 9,891...F11
Rio Hondo 1,793...G11
River Oaks 6,580...E2
Robert Lee▲ 1,276...D6
Robstown 12,849...G10
Roby▲ 616...D5
Rockdale 5,235...G7
Rockport▲ 4,753...H9
Rocksprings▲ 1,339...D8
Rockwall▲ 10,486...H5
Roma-Los Saenz 3,384...E11
Rosenberg 20,183...J8
Rotan 1,913...D5
Round Rock 30,923...G7
Rowlett 23,260...H2
Royse City 2,206...H4
Rusk▲ 4,366...J6
Sachse 5,346...H2
Saginaw 8,551...E2
San Angelo▲ 84,474...D6
San Antonio▲ 935,933...J11
San Augustine▲ 2,337...K6
San Benito 20,125...G12
San Diego▲ 4,983...F10
San Elizario 4,385...A10
San Juan 10,815...F11
San Leon 3,328...L2
San Marcos▲ 28,743...F8
San Saba▲ 2,626...E6
Sanderson▲ 1,128...B7
Sanger▲ 3,508...G4
Sansom Park Village 3,921...E2
Santa Fe 8,429...K3
Sarita▲ 200...G10
Schertz 10,555...K10
Schulenburg 2,455...H8
Seabrook 6,685...K2
Seagoville 8,969...H3
Seagraves 2,398...B5
Sealy 4,541...H8
Seguin▲ 18,853...G8
Seminole▲ 6,342...K10
Seymour▲ 3,185...E4
Shamrock 2,286...D2
Shepherd 1,812...K7
Sherman▲ 31,601...H4
Shiner 2,074...G8
Sierra Blanca▲ 800...B11
Silsbee 6,368...K7
Silverton▲ 779...C3
Sinton▲ 5,549...G9
Slaton 6,078...C4
Smithville 3,196...G7
Snyder▲ 12,195...D5
Sonora▲ 2,751...D7
South Houston 14,207...J2
South Padre Island 1,677...F11
Spearman▲ 3,197...C1
Spring 33,111...J7
Spring Valley 3,392...J1
Stafford 8,397...J2
Stamford 3,817...E5
Stanton▲ 2,576...C5
Stephenville▲ 13,502...F5
Sterling City▲ 1,096...D6
Stinnett▲ 2,166...C2
Stratford▲ 1,781...C1
Sugar Land 24,529...J8
Sulphur Springs▲ 14,062...J4
Sundown 1,759...B4
Sunnyvale 2,228...H2
Sweeny 3,297...J8
Sweetwater▲ 11,967...D5
Taft 3,222...G9
Tahoka▲ 2,868...C4
Taylor 11,472...G7
Taylor Lake Village 3,394...K2
Teague 3,268...H6
Temple 46,109...G6
Terlingua 100...D12
Terrell 12,490...H5
Terrell Hills 4,592...K11
Texarkana 31,656...L4
Texas City 40,822...K3
Texhoma 291...C1
The Colony 22,113...G1
Three Rivers 1,889...F9
Throckmorton▲ 1,036...F4
Tilden▲ 450...F9
Tomball 6,370...J7
Trinity 2,648...J7
Tulia▲ 4,699...C3
Tyler▲ 75,450...J5
Universal City 13,057...K10
University Park 22,259...F2
Uvalde▲ 14,729...E8
Van 1,854...J5
Van Alstyne 2,090...H4
Van Horn▲ 2,930...C11
Vega▲ 840...B2
Vernon▲ 12,001...E3
Victoria▲ 55,076...H9
Vidor 10,935...L7
Waco▲ 103,590...G6
Wake Village 4,757...K4
Waskom 1,812...L5
Watauga 20,009...E2
Waxahachie▲ 18,168...H5
Weatherford▲ 14,804...G5
Webster 4,678...K2
Weimar 2,052...H8
Wellington▲ 2,456...D3
Weslaco 21,877...F11
West 2,515...G6
West Columbia 4,372...J8
West Orange 4,187...L7
West University Place 12,920...J2
Westworth 2,350...E2
Wharton▲ 9,011...J8
Wheeler▲ 1,393...D2
White Oak 5,136...K5
White Settlement 15,472...E2
Whitesboro 3,209...H4
Whitewright 1,713...H4
Wichita Falls▲ 96,259...F4
Willis 2,764...J7
Wills Point 2,986...J5
Wilmer 2,479...H3
Windcrest 5,331...K11
Winnie 2,238...K8
Winnsboro 2,904...J5
Winters 2,905...E6
Wolfforth 1,941...C4
Woodsboro 1,731...G9
Woodville▲ 2,636...K7
Wylie 8,716...H1
Yoakum 5,611...G8
Yorktown 2,207...G9
Zapata▲ 7,119...E11

OTHER FEATURES

Alibates Flint Quarries Nat'l Mon....C2
Amistad (res.)...C8
Amistad Nat'l Rec. Area...D8
Angelina (riv.)...K6
Apache (mts.)...C11
Aransas (passage)...H10
Arlington (lake)...F2
Baffin (bay)...G10
Balcones Escarpment (plat.)...E8
Benbrook (lake)...E3
Bergstrom A.F.B....G7
Big Bend Nat'l Park...A8
Big Thicket Nat'l Preserve...K7
Bolivar (pen.)...K8
Brazos (riv.)...H7
Brooks A.F.B....K11
Brownwood (lake)...E6
Buchanan (lake)...F7
Caddo (lake)...L5
Calaveras (lake)...K11
Canadian (riv.)...D1
Carrizo (creek)...A1
Carswell A.F.B....E2
Cathedral (mt.)...D12
Cavallo (passage)...H9
Cedar (lake)...B5
Cerro Alto (mt.)...B10
Chamizal Nat'l Mon....A10
Chinati (mts.)...C12
Chinati (peak)...C12
Chisos (mts.)...A8
Cibolo (creek)...K11
Clear Fork, Brazos (riv.)...D5
Coldwater (creek)...B1
Colorado (riv.)...F6
Copano (bay)...G9
Corpus Christi (lake)...F9
Corpus Christi N.A.S....G10
Cottonwood Draw (dry riv.)...C10
Davis (mts.)...C11
Deep (creek)...C5
Delaware (creek)...C10
Delaware (mts.)...C10
Denison (dam)...H4
Devils (riv.)...D7
Double Mountain Fork, Brazos (riv.)...C4
Dyess A.F.B....D5
Eagle (peak)...C11
Eagle Mountain (lake)...E2
Edwards (plat.)...C7
Elephant (mt.)...D12
Elm Fork, Trinity (riv.)...G2
Emory (peak)...A8
Falcon (res.)...E11
Finlay (mts.)...B10
Fort Bliss 13,915...A10
Fort Davis Nat'l Hist. Site...D11
Fort Hood 35,580...G6
Fort Sam Houston...K11
Frio (riv.)...E8
Galveston (bay)...L2
Galveston (isl.)...K8
Glass (mts.)...A7
Goodfellow A.F.B....D6
Grapevine (lake)...F2
Guadalupe (mts.)...C10
Guadalupe (peak)...B10
Guadalupe (riv.)...G8
Guadalupe Mountains Nat'l Park...C10
Houston (lake)...J8
Houston Ship (chan.)...K2
Howard (creek)...C7
Hubbard Creek (lake)...F5
Hueco (mts.)...B10
Intracoastal Waterway...J9
Johnson Draw (dry riv.)...C7
Kelly A.F.B....J11
Kemp (lake)...E4
Kingsville N.A.S....G10
Kiowa (creek)...D1
Lackland A.F.B. 9,352...J11
Lake Meredith Nat'l Rec. Area...C2
Lampasas (riv.)...G6
Laughlin A.F.B. 2,556...D8
Lavon (lake)...H1
Leon (riv.)...F6
Livermore (mt.)...C11
Livingston (lake)...K7
Llano (riv.)...D7
Llano Estacado (plain)...B4
Locke (mt.)...D11
Los Olmos (creek)...F10
Los Olmos (creek)...F11
Lyndon B. Johnson Nat'l Hist. Site...F7
Lyndon B. Johnson Space Ctr...K2
Madre (lag.)...G11
Maravillas (creek)...A8
Matagorda (bay)...H9
Matagorda (isl.)...H9
Matagorda (pen.)...J9
Medina (lake)...E8
Medina (riv.)...J11
Mexico (gulf)...K9
Middle Concho (riv.)...C6
Mountain Creek (lake)...G2
Mustang (creek)...A1
Mustang (isl.)...G10
Mustang Draw (dry riv.)...B5
Navasota (riv.)...H7
Navidad (riv.)...H8
Neches (riv.)...K6
North Concho (riv.)...C6
North Pease (riv.)...D3
Nueces (riv.)...F9
Padre (isl.)...G10
Padre Island Nat'l Seashore...G11
Palo Duro (creek)...B2
Palo Duro (creek)...C1
Pease (riv.)...D3
Pecos (riv.)...C7
Pedernales (riv.)...F7
Possum Kingdom (lake)...F5
Prairie Dog Town Fork, Red (riv.)...C3
Quitman (mts.)...B11
Randolph A.F.B....K10
Ray Hubbard (lake)...H2
Red (riv.)...F3
Red Bluff (lake)...D10
Reese A.F.B....B4
Rio Grande (riv.)...D9
Rita Blanca (creek)...B2
Sabine (riv.)...L7
Salt Fork, Red (riv.)...D3
Sam Rayburn (res.)...K6
San Antonio (bay)...H9
San Antonio (mt.)...B10
San Antonio Missions Nat'l Hist. Park...J11
San Francisco (creek)...B8
San Luis (passage)...K8
San Martine Draw (dry riv.)...C11
San Saba (riv.)...D7
Santa Isabel (creek)...E10
Santiago (mts.)...A8
Santiago (peak)...D12
Sheppard A.F.B....F3
Sierra Diablo (mts.)...C10
Sierra Vieja (mts.)...C11
Staked (Llano Estacado) (plain)...B4
Stamford (lake)...E4
Stockton (plat.)...B7
Sulphur (riv.)...J4
Sulphur Draw (dry riv.)...B4
Sulphur Springs (creek)...B4
Tenmile (creek)...G3
Terlingua (creek)...D12
Texoma (lake)...H3
Thomas (lake)...C5
Tierra Blanca (creek)...B3
Toledo Bend (res.)...L6
Toyah (creek)...D11
Toyah (lake)...A6
Travis (lake)...G7
Trinity (bay)...L2
Trinity (riv.)...H5
Trinity, West Fork (riv.)...G2
Trujillo (creek)...A2
Washita (riv.)...D2
West (bay)...K3
White (riv.)...C3
White River (lake)...C4
White Rock (creek)...G2
Wichita (riv.)...F4
Wolf (creek)...D1
Worth (lake)...E2
Wright Patman (lake)...K4

▲County seat

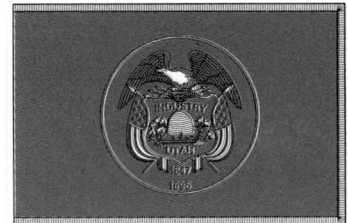

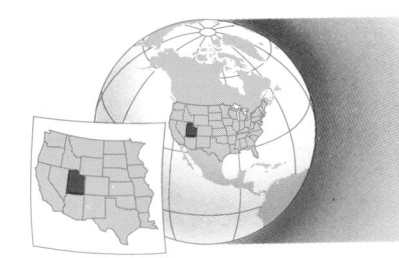

AREA 84,899 sq. mi. (219,888 sq. km.)
POPULATION 1,727,784
CAPITAL Salt Lake City
LARGEST CITY Salt Lake City
HIGHEST POINT Kings Pk. 13,528 ft. (4123 m.)
SETTLED IN 1847
ADMITTED TO UNION January 4, 1896
POPULAR NAME Beehive State
STATE FLOWER Sego Lily
STATE BIRD Sea Gull

COUNTIES

Beaver 4,765..............A5
Box Elder 36,485..........A2
Cache 70,183.............C2
Carbon 20,228............D4
Daggett 690..............D3
Davis 187,941............B3
Duchesne 12,645..........D3
Emery 10,332.............D4
Garfield 3,980...........C6
Grand 6,620.............E6
Iron 20,789.............A6
Juab 5,817.............A4
Kane 5,169.............B6
Millard 11,333..........A4
Morgan 5,528............C2
Piute 1,277............C5
Rich 1,725.............C2
Salt Lake 725,956.......B3
San Juan 12,621.........E6
Sanpete 16,259..........C4
Sevier 15,431...........C5
Summit 15,518...........C5
Tooele 26,601...........A3
Uintah 22,211...........E3
Utah 263,590............C3
Wasatch 10,089..........C3
Washington 48,560.......A6
Wayne 2,177............C5
Weber 158,330...........B2

CITIES and TOWNS

Alpine 3,492............C3
Alta 397...............C3
Amalga 366.............C2
American Fork 15,696....C3
Annabella 487...........B5
Aurora 911.............C5
Bear River City 700.....B2
Beaver▲ 1,998...........B5
Bicknell 327............C5
Big Water 326...........C6
Blanding 3,162..........E6
Bluffdale 2,152.........B3
Bountiful 36,659........C3
Brigham City▲ 15,644....C2
Brighton 150............C3
Castle Dale▲ 1,704......D4
Castle Rock............C2
Cedar City 13,443.......A6
Cedar Fort 284..........B3
Centerfield 766.........C4
Centerville 11,500......C3
Charleston 336..........C3
Circleville 417.........B5
Clarkston 645...........B2

Clearfield 21,435.......B2
Cleveland 522...........D4
Coalville▲ 1,065........C3
Corinne 639............B2
Delta 2,998............B4
Deweyville 318..........B2
Draper 7,257...........C3
Duchesne▲ 1,308.........D3
Dugway 1,761...........B3
East Carbon 1,270.......D4
East Millcreek 21,184...C3
Elmo 267...............D4
Elsinore 608...........B5
Elwood 575.............B2
Emery 300.............C5
Enoch 1,947............A6
Enterprise 936..........A6
Ephraim 3,363...........C4
Escalante 818...........C6
Eureka 562.............B4
Fairview 960............C4
Farmington▲ 9,028.......C4
Ferron 1,606............D4
Fielding 422............B2
Fillmore▲ 1,956.........B5
Fort Duchesne 655.......E3
Fountain Green 578......C4
Francis 381............C3
Fruit Heights 3,900.....C2
Garden City 193.........C2
Garland 1,637..........B2
Genola 803.............C4
Glendale 282...........B6
Glenwood 437...........C5
Goshen 578.............C4
Grantsville 4,500.......B3
Green River 866.........D4
Gunnison 1,298..........C4
Harrisville 3,004.......C2
Heber City▲ 4,782.......C3
Helper 2,148...........D4
Henefer 554............C2
Highland 5,002..........C3
Hildale 1,325...........A6
Hinckley 658...........B4
Holden 402.............B4
Holladay 22,189.........C3
Honeyville 1,112........B2
Hooper 3,468...........C2
Howell 237.............B2
Huntington 1,875........C4
Huntsville 561..........C2
Hurricane 3,915.........A6
Hyde Park 2,190.........C2
Hyrum 4,829............C2
Ivins 1,630............A6
Joseph 198.............B5
Junction▲ 132..........B5

Kamas 1,061............C3
Kanab▲ 3,289...........B6
Kanarraville 228........A6
Kanosh 386.............B5
Kaysville 13,961........C2
Kearns 28,374..........B3
Koosharem 266..........C5
La Verkin 1,771.........A6
Laketown 261...........C2
Layton 41,784..........C2
Leamington 253..........B4
Leeds 254.............C3
Lehi 8,475.............C3
Levan 416.............C4
Lewiston 1,532..........C2
Lindon 3,818...........C3
Loa▲ 444..............C5
Logan▲ 32,762..........C2
Lyman 198.............C5
Maeser 2,598...........E3
Magna 17,829...........B3
Manila▲ 207............E3
Manti▲ 2,268...........C4
Mantua 665.............C2
Mapleton 3,572.........C3
Marysvale 364..........B5
Mayfield 438...........C4
Meadow 250.............B5
Mendon 684............B2
Mexican Hat 259.........E6
Midvale 11,886.........B3
Midway 1,554...........C3
Milford 1,107..........A5
Millville 1,202........C2
Minersville 608........A5
Moab▲ 3,971............E5
Mona 584..............C4
Monroe 1,472...........B5
Montezuma Creek 345.....E6
Monticello▲ 1,806......E6
Morgan▲ 2,023..........C2
Moroni 1,115...........C4
Mount Pleasant 2,092....C4
Murray 31,282..........C3
Myton 468.............D3
Neola 511.............D3
Nephi▲ 3,515...........C4
Newton 659............C2
Nibley 1,167...........C2
North Ogden 11,668......C2
North Salt Lake 6,474...C3
Oak City 587...........B4
Oakley 522.............C3
Ogden▲ 63,909..........C2
Orangeville 1,459.......C4
Orderville 422..........B6
Orem 67,561............C3
Panguitch▲ 1,444.......B6

Paradise 561...........C2
Paragonah 307..........B6
Park City 4,468........C3
Parowan▲ 1,873.........B6
Payson 9,510...........C3
Perry 1,211............C2
Plain City 2,722........B2
Pleasant Grove 13,476...C3
Pleasant View 3,603.....B2
Plymouth 267...........B2
Price▲ 8,712...........D4
Providence 3,344........C2
Provo▲ 86,835..........C3
Randlett 283...........E3
Randolph▲ 488..........C2
Redmond 648............C4
Richfield▲ 5,593.......B5
Richmond 1,955.........C2
River Heights 1,274.....C2
Riverton 11,261........B3
Roosevelt 3,915........D3
Roy 24,603.............C2
Saint George▲ 28,502....A6
Salem 2,284............C3
Salina 1,943...........C5
Salt Lake City (cap.)▲
  159,936..............C3
Sandy 75,058...........C3
Santa Clara 2,322.......A6
Santaquin 2,386........C4
Scipio 291............B4
Sigurd 385............C5
Smithfield 5,566.......C2
South Jordan 12,220.....B3
South Ogden 12,105......C3
South Salt Lake 10,129..C3
Spanish Fork 11,272.....C3
Spring City 715........C4
Springdale 275.........B6
Springville 13,950......C3
Stockton 426...........B3
Sunnyside 339..........D4
Sunset 5,128...........B2
Syracuse 4,658.........B2
Taylorsville-Bennion 52,351..B3
Tooele▲ 13,887.........B3
Toquerville 488........A6
Tremonton 4,264........B2
Trenton 464............B2
Tropic 374.............B6
Uintah 760.............C2
Vernal▲ 6,644..........E3
Wallsburg 252..........C3
Washington 4,198.......A6
Washington Terrace 8,189...B2
Wellington 1,632.......D4
Wellsville 2,206.......C2
Wendover 1,127.........A3

West Bountiful 4,477....B3
West Jordan 42,892......B3
Whiterocks 312.........E3
Willard 1,298..........C2
Woods Cross 5,384......B3

OTHER FEATURES

Abajo (mts.)...........E6
Agassiz (mt.)..........D3
Antelope (isl.)........B3
Aquarius (plat.)........C5
Arches Nat'l Park.......E5
Assay (creek)..........D4
Bad Land (cliffs).......D4
Baldy (peak)...........B5
Bear (lake)............C2
Bear (riv.)............B2
Beaver (mts.)..........A5
Beaver (riv.)..........A5
Beaver Dam Wash (creek)..A6
Birch (creek)..........B5
Blue (creek)...........B2
Bonneville (salt flats)..A3
Book (cliffs)..........E4
Bryce Canyon Nat'l Park..B6
Canyonlands Nat'l Park..D5
Capitol Reef Nat'l Park..C5
Castle (valley)........D4
Cedar (mts.)...........B3
Cedar Breaks Nat'l Mon...B6
Chalk (creek)..........C3
Chinle (creek).........E6
Clear (lake)...........B4
Cliff (creek)..........E3
Coal (cliffs)..........C5
Colorado (riv.)........E5
Confusion (range)......A4
Cottonwood (creek)......C4
Cub (creek)............C1
Deep (creek)...........B1
Deep Creek (range).....A4
Delano (peak)..........B5
Desolation (canyon)....E4
Dinosaur Nat'l Mon......E3
Dirty Devil (riv.).....D5
Dolores (riv.).........E5
Dry Coal (creek).......A6
Duchesne (riv.)........D3
Dugway (range).........A3
Dugway Proving Grounds..B3
Dutton (mt.)...........B5
East Canyon (res.).....C3
Echo (res.)............C3
Elk (ridge)............E6
Ellen (mt.)............D5
Emmons (mt.)...........D3
Escalante (des.).......A6

Escalante (riv.)........C6
Fish (lake)............C5
Fish Springs (range)....A4
Flaming Gorge (res.)....E3
Flaming Gorge Nat'l
  Rec. Area.............E2
Fool Creek (res.).......B4
Fremont (isl.).........B2
Fremont (riv.).........C5
Glen Canyon Nat'l Rec. Area..D6
Golden Spike Nat'l Hist. Site...B2
Goshute Ind. Res........A4
Government (creek)......B3
Gray (canyon)..........D4
Great Salt (lake).......B2
Great Salt Lake (des.)..A3
Greeley (creek)........B3
Green (riv.)...........D4
Grouse (creek).........A2
Grouse Creek (mts.).....A2
Gunnison (res.)........C4
Henry (mts.)...........D6
Hilgard (mt.)..........C5
Hill (creek)...........E4
Hill A.F.B.............C2
Hill Creek Extension, Uintah
  and Ouray Ind. Res....E4
Hillers (mt.)..........D6
House (range)..........A4
Hovenweep Nat'l Mon.....E6
Hoyt (peak)............C3
Huntington (creek)......C4
Indian (creek).........B5
Jordan (riv.)..........C3
Kaiparowits (plat.).....C6
Kanab (creek)..........B7
Kanosh Ind. Res........B5
Kings (peak)...........D3
Koosharem Ind. Res......C5
Little Creek (peak).....B6
Little Salt (lake).....A6
Malad (riv.)...........B1
Marsh (peak)...........E3
Marvine (mt.)..........C5
Mineral (mts.).........B5
Mona (res.)............C4
Monroe (peak)..........B5
Montezuma (creek).......E6
Monument (valley)......D6
Muddy (creek)..........C4
Natural Bridges Nat'l Mon...E6
Navajo (mt.)...........D6
Navajo Ind. Res........D7
Nebo (mt.).............C4
Newfoundland (mts.).....A2
Nine Mile (creek)......D4
North (lake)...........B2
Orange (cliffs)........D5

Otter (creek)..........C5
Otter Creek (res.)......C5
Paria (riv.)...........B6
Paunsaugunt (plat.).....B6
Pahvant (range)........B5
Peale (mt.)............E5
Pennell (mt.)..........D6
Piute (res.)...........B5
Plumber (creek)........C2
Powell (lake)..........D6
Price (riv.)...........D4
Provo (peak)...........C3
Provo (riv.)...........C3
Raft River (mts.).......A2
Rainbow Bridge Nat'l Mon...C6
Roan (cliffs)..........E4
Rockport (lake)........C3
Salvation (creek)......C5
San Juan (riv.)........D6
San Pitch (riv.).......C4
San Rafael (riv.).......D4
San Rafael Swell (mts.)..D5
Santa Clara (riv.)......A6
Sevier (des.)..........B4
Sevier (lake)..........A5
Sevier (riv.)..........B4
Sevier (lake)..........B4
Sevier Bridge (res.)....C4
Shivwits Ind. Res.......A6
Silver Island (mts.)....A3
Skull Valley Ind. Res...B3
Spanish Fork (riv.).....C3
Strait (cliffs)........C6
Strawberry (res.)......C3
Strawberry (riv.)......D3
Swan (lake)............B4
Tavaputs (plat.).......D4
Thomas (range).........A4
Thousand Lake (mt.).....C5
Timpanogos Cave Nat'l Mon...C3
Tokewamna (peak).......D3
Tooele Army Depot.......B3
Two Water (creek)......E4
Uinta (mts.)...........D3
Uinta (riv.)...........D3
Uintah and Ouray Ind. Res...D3
Utah (lake)............C3
Virgin (riv.)..........A6
Waas (mt.).............E5
Wah Wah (mts.).........A5
Wasatch (range)........C3
Washakie Ind. Res.......B2
Waterpocket Fold (cliffs)..D6
Weber (riv.)...........C3
White (riv.)...........E3
Willow (creek).........E4
Zion Nat'l Park........A6

▲County seat

Agriculture, Industry and Resources

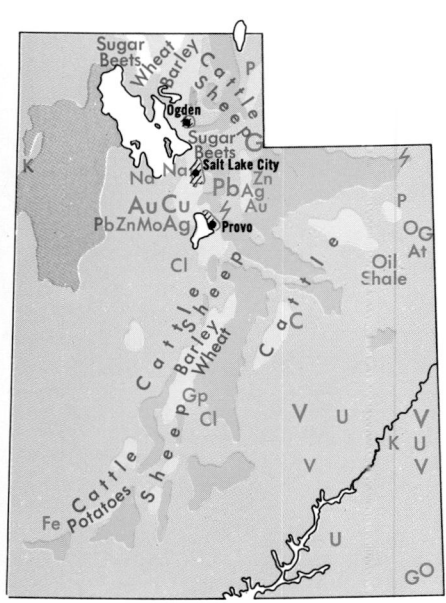

DOMINANT LAND USE

- Wheat, General Farming
- General Farming, Livestock, Special Crops
- Range Livestock
- Forests
- Nonagricultural Land

MAJOR MINERAL OCCURRENCES

Ag Silver
At Asphalt
Au Gold
C Coal
Cl Clay
Cu Copper

Fe Iron Ore
G Natural Gas
Gp Gypsum
K Potash
Mo Molybdenum
Na Salt

O Petroleum
P Phosphates
Pb Lead
U Uranium
V Vanadium
Zn Zinc

⚡ Water Power
▨ Major Industrial Areas

Topography

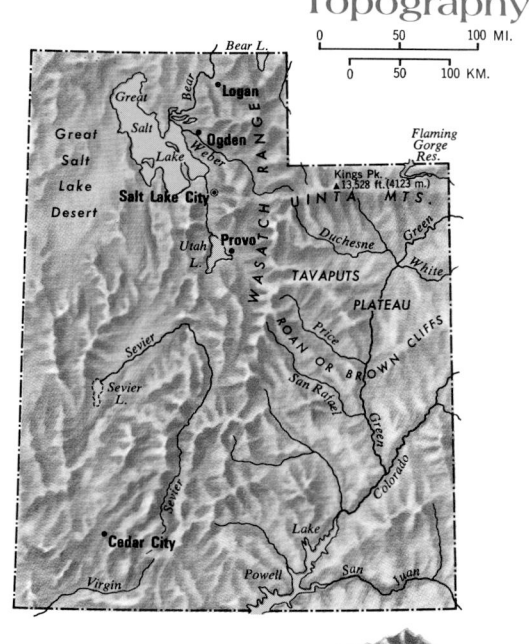

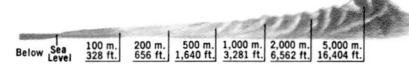

Topography

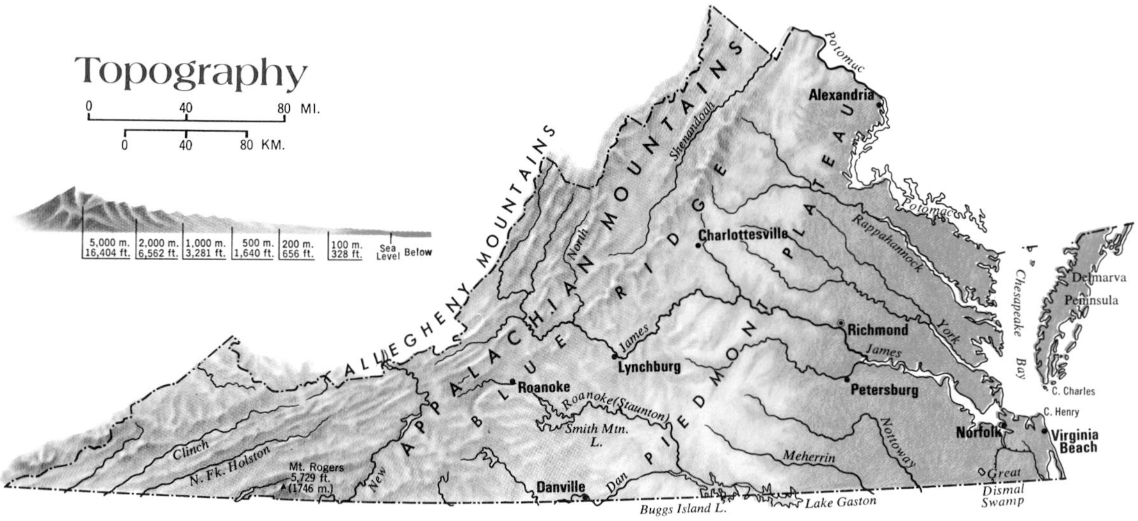

COUNTIES

Accomack 31,703 ..... S5
Albemarle 68,040 ..... L5
Alleghany 13,176 ..... H5
Amelia 8,787 ..... M6
Amherst 28,578 ..... K5
Appomattox 12,298 ..... L6
Arlington 170,936 ..... S2
Augusta 54,677 ..... K4
Bath 4,799 ..... J4
Bedford 45,656 ..... J6
Bland 6,514 ..... F6
Botetourt 24,992 ..... J5
Brunswick 15,987 ..... N7
Buchanan 31,333 ..... D6
Buckingham 12,873 ..... L5
Campbell 47,572 ..... K6
Caroline 19,217 ..... O4
Carroll 26,594 ..... G7
Charles City 6,282 ..... O6
Charlotte 11,688 ..... L6
Chesterfield 209,274 ..... N6
Clarke 12,101 ..... M2
Craig 4,372 ..... H6
Culpeper 27,791 ..... M3
Cumberland 7,825 ..... M6
Dickenson 17,620 ..... D6
Dinwiddie 20,960 ..... N6
Essex 8,689 ..... P5
Fairfax 818,584 ..... O3
Fauquier 35,889 ..... N3
Floyd 12,005 ..... H7
Fluvanna 12,429 ..... M5
Franklin 39,549 ..... J6
Frederick 45,723 ..... M2
Giles 16,366 ..... G6
Gloucester 30,131 ..... P6
Goochland 14,163 ..... N5
Grayson 16,278 ..... F7
Greene 10,297 ..... M4
Greensville 8,853 ..... N7
Halifax 29,033 ..... L7
Hanover 63,306 ..... N5
Henrico 217,881 ..... O6
Henry 56,942 ..... J7
Highland 2,635 ..... J4
Isle of Wight 25,053 ..... P7
James City 34,859 ..... P6
King George 13,527 ..... O4
King William 10,913 ..... O5
King and Queen 6,289 ..... P5
Lancaster 10,896 ..... R5
Lee 24,496 ..... B7
Loudoun 86,129 ..... N2
Louisa 20,325 ..... N5
Lunenburg 11,419 ..... M7
Madison 11,949 ..... M4
Mathews 8,348 ..... R6
Mecklenburg 29,241 ..... M7
Middlesex 8,653 ..... R5
Montgomery 73,913 ..... H6
Nelson 12,778 ..... L5
New Kent 10,445 ..... P5
Northampton 13,061 ..... S6
Northumberland 10,524 ..... R5
Nottoway 14,993 ..... M6
Orange 21,421 ..... M4
Page 21,690 ..... M3
Patrick 17,473 ..... H7
Pittsylvania 55,655 ..... K7
Powhatan 15,328 ..... N5
Prince Edward 17,320 ..... M6
Prince George 27,394 ..... O6
Prince William 215,686 ..... O3
Pulaski 34,496 ..... G6
Rappahannock 6,622 ..... M3
Richmond 7,273 ..... P5
Roanoke 79,332 ..... H6
Rockbridge 18,350 ..... K5
Rockingham 57,482 ..... L4
Russell 28,667 ..... D7
Scott 23,204 ..... C7
Shenandoah 31,636 ..... L3
Smyth 32,370 ..... E7
Southampton 17,550 ..... O7
Spotsylvania 57,403 ..... N4
Stafford 61,236 ..... O4
Surry 6,145 ..... P6
Sussex 10,248 ..... O7
Tazewell 45,960 ..... E6
Warren 26,142 ..... M3
Washington 45,887 ..... D7
Westmoreland 15,480 ..... P4
Wise 39,573 ..... C6
Wythe 25,466 ..... F7
York 42,422 ..... P6

CITIES and TOWNS

Abingdon▲ 7,003 ..... D7
Accomac▲ 466 ..... S5
Achilles 525 ..... R6
Afton 350 ..... L4
Alberene 200 ..... L5
Alberta 337 ..... N7
Alexandria (I.C.) 111,183 ..... S3
Allisonia 325 ..... G7
Altavista 3,686 ..... K6
Alton 500 ..... K7
Amelia Court House▲ 500 ..... N6
Amherst▲ 1,060 ..... K5
Ammissville 150 ..... M3
Amonate 350 ..... E6
Andover 180 ..... C7
Annandale 50,975 ..... S3
Appalachia 1,994 ..... C7
Appomattox▲ 1,707 ..... L6
Ararat 500 ..... G7
Arlington▲ 170,936 ..... T3
Arrington 500 ..... L5
Arvonia 500 ..... M5
Ashburn 3,393 ..... O2
Ashland 5,864 ..... N5
Atkins 1,130 ..... F7
Augusta Springs 600 ..... K4
Austinville 750 ..... F7
Axton 540 ..... J7
Bailey's Crossroads 19,507 ..... S3
Ballsville 150 ..... M6
Bandy 200 ..... E6
Banner 327 ..... D7
Barboursville 600 ..... M4
Barren Springs 125 ..... G7
Bassett 1,579 ..... J7
Bastian 600 ..... F6
Batesville 575 ..... L5
Bealeton 200 ..... N3
Beaverdam 500 ..... N5
Beaverlett 200 ..... R6
Bedford (I.C.)▲ 6,073 ..... J6
Belle Haven 526 ..... S5
Belle View T3
Ben Hur 400 ..... B7
Bent Mountain 140 ..... H6
Bentonville 500 ..... M3
Bergton 150 ..... L3
Berryville▲ 3,097 ..... M2
Big Island 500 ..... K5
Big Rock 900 ..... D6
Big Stone Gap 4,748 ..... C7
Birchleaf 650 ..... D6
Birdsnest 736 ..... S6
Bishop 600 ..... E6
Blacksburg 34,590 ..... H6
Blackstone 3,497 ..... N6
Blackwater 130 ..... B7
Blairs 500 ..... K7
Bland▲ 950 ..... F6
Bloxom 357 ..... S5
Blue Grass 200 ..... J3
Blue Ridge 2,840 ..... J6
Bluefield 5,363 ..... F6
Bluemont 200 ..... N2
Boissevain 975 ..... F6
Bolar 135 ..... J4
Bon Air 16,413 ..... N5
Boones Mill 239 ..... J6
Boston 400 ..... M3
Bowling Green▲ 727 ..... O4
Boyce 520 ..... M2
Boydton▲ 453 ..... M7
Boykins 658 ..... O7
Brandy Station 400 ..... N4
Breaks 550 ..... D6
Bremo Bluff 200 ..... M5
Bridgewater 3,918 ..... K4
Bristol (I.C.) 18,426 ..... D7
Broadford 500 ..... E7
Broadway 1,209 ..... L3
Brodnax 388 ..... N7
Brooke 245 ..... O4
Brookneal 1,344 ..... L6
Brownsburg 300 ..... K5
Browntown 300 ..... M3
Brucetown 250 ..... M2
Buchanan 1,222 ..... J5
Buckingham▲ 200 ..... L5
Buena Vista (I.C.) 6,406 ..... K5
Buffalo Junction 300 ..... L7
Burgess 200 ..... R5
Burke 57,734 ..... R3
Burkes Garden 2,687 ..... F6
Burkeville 535 ..... M6
Burnsville 140 ..... J4
Callao 500 ..... P5
Callaway 225 ..... H7
Calverton 500 ..... N3
Cana 168 ..... G7
Cape Charles 1,398 ..... R6
Capeville 325 ..... R6
Capron 144 ..... O7
Cardwell 200 ..... N5
Carrsville 300 ..... P7
Carson 500 ..... O6
Casanova 370 ..... N3
Cascade 835 ..... J7
Castlewood 2,110 ..... D7
Catawba 350 ..... H6
Catlett 500 ..... N3
Cedar Bluff 1,290 ..... E6
Cedar Springs 200 ..... F7
Cedarville 200 ..... M3
Center Cross 360 ..... P5
Ceres 200 ..... F6
Champlain 160 ..... O4
Chancellorsville 40 ..... N4
Chantilly 29,337 ..... O3
Charles City▲ 5 ..... O6
Charlotte Court House▲ 531 ..... L6
Charlottesville (I.C.)▲ 40,341 ..... M4
Chase City 2,442 ..... M7
Chatham▲ 1,354 ..... K7
Cheriton 515 ..... R6
Chesapeake 151,976 ..... R7
Chester 14,986 ..... O6
Chester Gap 400 ..... M3
Chesterfield▲ 950 ..... N6
Chilhowie 1,971 ..... E7
Chincoteague 3,572 ..... T5
Christiansburg▲ 15,004 ..... H6
Chula 150 ..... N6
Church View 200 ..... P5
Churchville 250 ..... K4
Claremont 380 ..... P6
Clarksville 1,243 ..... L7
Claudville 180 ..... H7
Clay Bank 200 ..... P6
Clayville 200 ..... N6
Clear Brook 300 ..... M2
Cleveland 214 ..... D7
Clifford 150 ..... K5
Clifton Forge (I.C.) 4,679 ..... J5
Clinchburg 250 ..... E7
Clinchco 900 ..... D6
Clintwood▲ 1,542 ..... D6
Clover 198 ..... L7
Cloverdale 1,689 ..... J6
Cluster Springs 350 ..... L7
Cobbs Creek 700 ..... R6
Coeburn 2,165 ..... D7
Coleman Falls 250 ..... K6
Collierstown 300 ..... J5
Collinsville 7,280 ..... J7
Colonial Beach 3,132 ..... P4
Colonial Heights (I.C.) 16,064 ..... O6
Concord 500 ..... K6
Copper Valley 425 ..... G7
Courtland▲ 819 ..... O7
Covesville 475 ..... L5
Covington (I.C.)▲ 6,991 ..... H5
Craigsville 812 ..... J4
Crandon 250 ..... G6
Crewe 2,276 ..... M6
Crimora 1,752 ..... L4
Cripple Creek 200 ..... F7
Critz 125 ..... H7
Crockett 200 ..... F7
Cross Junction 125 ..... M2
Crozet 2,256 ..... L4
Crozier 300 ..... N5
Crystal Hill 475 ..... L7
Cullen 725 ..... L6
Culpeper▲ 8,581 ..... M4
Cumberland▲ 300 ..... M6
Dahlgren 950 ..... O4
Dale City 47,170 ..... O3
Daleville 1,163 ..... J6
Damascus 918 ..... E7
Dante 1,083 ..... D7
Danville (I.C.) 53,056 ..... J7
Davenport 230 ..... D6

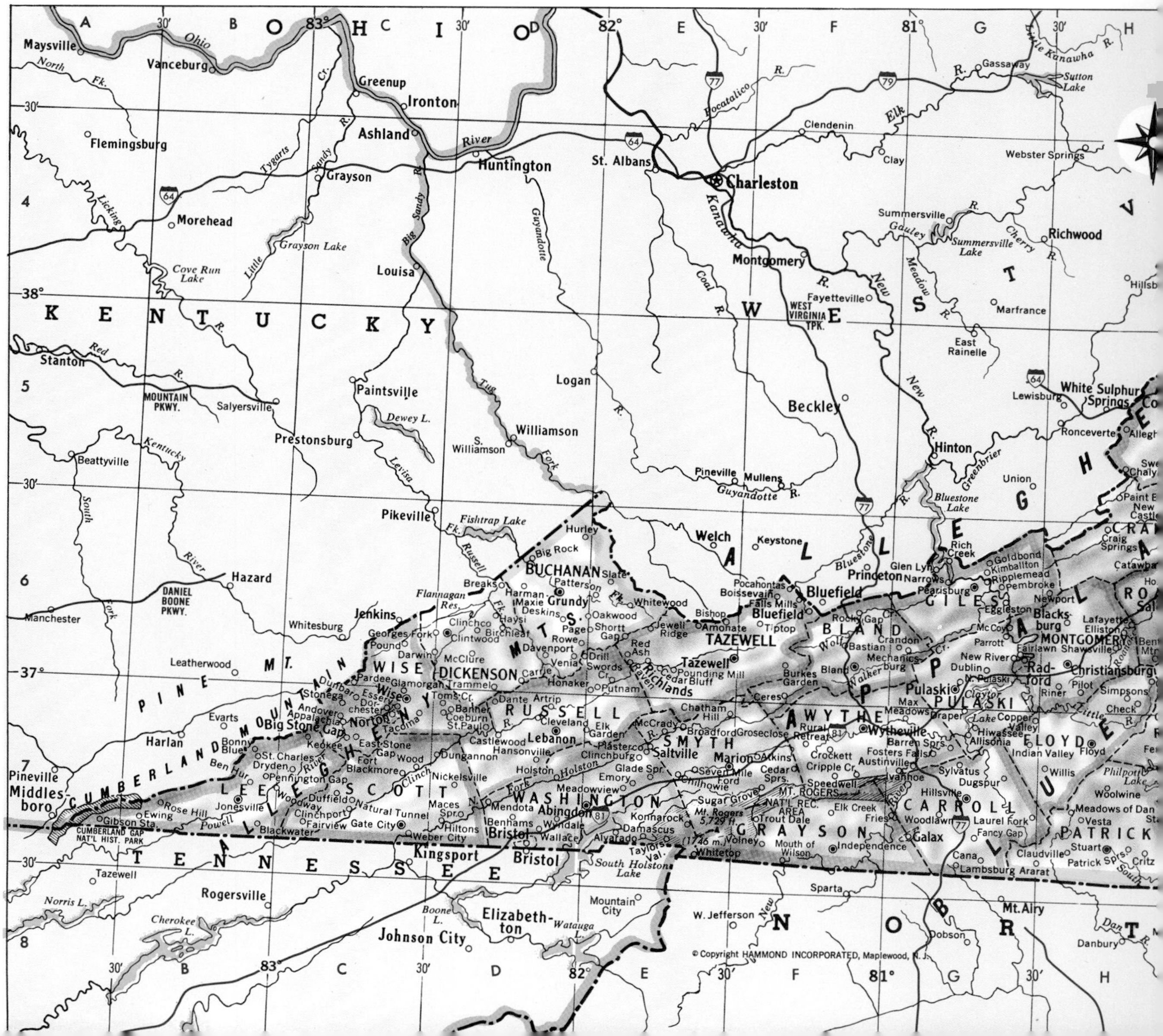

Dayton 921 ....L4	Emporia (I.C.)▲ 5,306.......N7						
Deerfield 500 ....K4	Esmont 950....................L5						
Deltaville 1,082 ....R5	Esserville 750.................C2						
Dendron 305 ....P6	Ettrick 5,290..................O6						
Denniston 200 ....L7	Evergreen 300.................L6						
Dewitt 140 ....N6	Evington 175..................K6						
Dillwyn 458 ....M5	Ewing 800.....................B7						
Dinwiddie▲ 500 ....N6	Exmore 1,115.................S5						
Disputanta 800 ....O6	Faber 125......................L5						
Drakes Branch 565 ....L7	Fairfax (I.C.)▲ 19,622.......R3						
Drewryville 200 ....O7	Fairfax Station................R3						
Drill 192 ....E6	Fairfield 465...................K5						
Dry Fork 200 ....K7	Fairlawn 2,399................G6						
Dryden 400 ....B7	Fairport 175...................R5						
Dublin 2,012 ....G6	Falls Church (I.C.) 9,573....S2						
Duffield 54 ....C7	Falls Mills 800................F6						
Dumfries 4 282 ....O3	Falmouth 3,541...............O4						
Dundas 200 ....M7	Fancy Gap 200................G7						
Dungannon 250 ....D7	Farmville▲ 6,046..............M6						
Dunn Loring 6,509 ....S2	Foxwells 400..........R5	Gasburg 150...........N7	Gloucester▲ 1,545.....P6	Greenbush 200..........S5	Hamilton 700..........N2
Dunnsville 800 ....P5	Franconia 19,882.....S3	Gate City▲ 2,214.....C7	Gloucester Point 8,509..R6	Greenville 400.........K5	Hampden-Sydney 1,240..L6
Eagle Rock 750 ....J5	Franklin (I.C.) 7,864..P7	Georges Fork 200....C6	Goldbond 250..........G6	Greenwood 800........L4	Hampton (I.C.) 133,793..R6
Earlysville 210 ....M4	Franktown 500........S6	Gibson Station 150...G6	Goldvein 500..........N4	Gretna 1,339..........K7	Hanover▲ 500..........O5
East Stone Gap 240 ....C7	Fredericksburg (I.C.) 19,027..N4	Glade Spring 1,435...E7	Goochland▲ 800........N5	Grottoes 1,455.........L4	Hansonville 150........D7
Eastville▲ 185 ....R6	Free Union 121........L4	Gladehill 150..........L6	Goode 200.............K6	Groveton 19,997.......T3	Harborton 200..........S5
Ebony 400 ....N7	Fries 690.............F7	Gladys 500............K6	Gordonsville 1,351....M4	Grundy▲ 1,305.........D6	Hardy 325.............J6
Edinburg 860 ....M3	Front Royal▲ 11,880..M3	Glasgow 1,140........K5	Gore 500..............M3	Gum Spring 125.......N5	Harman-Maxie 650.....D6
Eggleston 350 ....G6	Fork Union 350........M5	Glen Allen 9,010......N5	Goshen 366............K5	Gwynn 205............R5	Harrisonburg (I.C.)▲ 30,707..K4
Elkton 1,935 ....L4	Fulks Run 130.........L3	Glen Lyn 170..........G6	Grafton 500...........P6	Hague 425.............P4	Hartfield 700..........R5
Elliston-Lafayette 1,243 .....H6	Gainesville 600.......N3	Glen Wilton 190.......J5	Green Bay 500.........M6	Halifax▲ 772..........L7	Haymarket 483........N3
Emory-Meadowview 2,292...E7	Fort Mitchell 125......M7	Garrisonville 200.....N4	Glenwood 2,276.......K7	Greenbackville 300....T5	Hallwood 228..........S5	Haynesville 500........P5

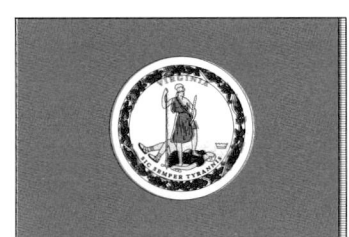

AREA 40,767 sq. mi. (105,587 sq. km.)
POPULATION 6,216,568
CAPITAL Richmond
LARGEST CITY Norfolk
HIGHEST POINT Mt. Rogers 5,729 ft. (1746 m.)
SETTLED IN 1607
ADMITTED TO UNION June 26, 1788
POPULAR NAME Old Dominion
STATE FLOWER Dogwood
STATE BIRD Cardinal

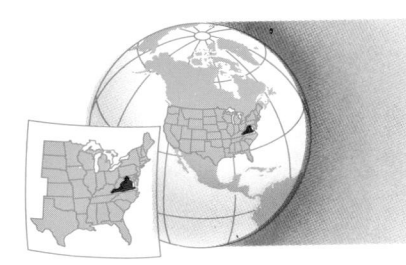

(continued on following page)

Agriculture, Industry and Resources

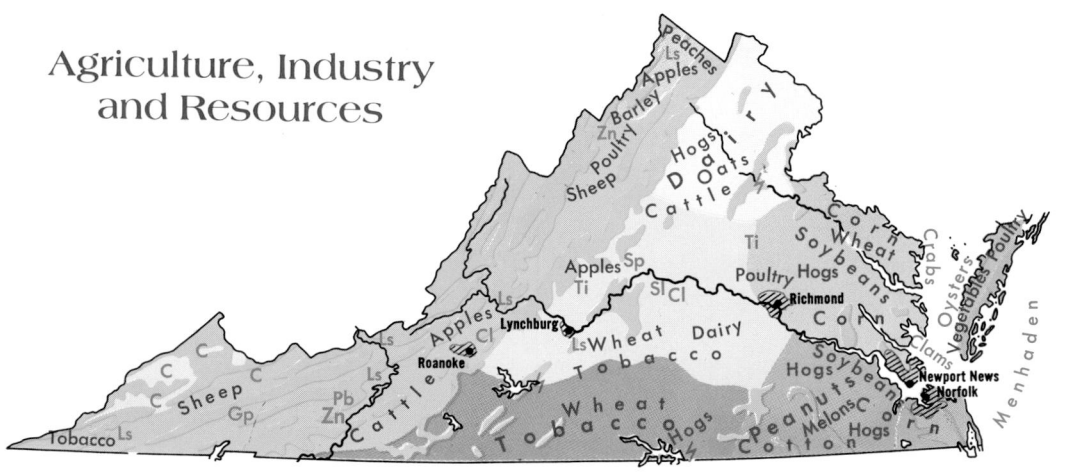

MAJOR MINERAL OCCURRENCES

C	Coal	Sl	Slate
Cl	Clay	Sp	Soapstone
Gp	Gypsum	Ti	Titanium
Ls	Limestone	Zn	Zinc
Pb	Lead		

↯ Water Power

▨ Major Industrial Areas

DOMINANT LAND USE

- Dairy, General Farming
- General Farming, Livestock, Dairy
- General Farming, Livestock, Tobacco
- General Farming, Livestock, Fruit, Tobacco
- General Farming, Truck Farming, Tobacco, Livestock
- Tobacco, General Farming
- Peanuts, General Farming
- Fruit and Mixed Farming
- Truck and Mixed Farming
- Forests
- Swampland, Limited Agriculture

Haysi 222 ....D6
Healing Springs 175 ....J5
Heathsville▲ 300 ....P5
Henry 300 ....J7
Herndon 16,139 ....O3
Highland Springs 13,823 .....H6
Hillsville▲ 2,008 ....G7
Hiltons 300 ....D7
Hiwassee 250 ....G7
Hoadly 400 ....O3
Hollins College 12,295 ......H6
Honaker 950 ....D6
Hopewell (I.C.) 23,101 ......T5
Horntown 400 ....T5
Hot Springs 300 ....J4
Huddleston 200 ....K6
Hume 350 ....N3
Huntington 7,489 ....S3
Hurley 850 ....D6
Hurt 1,294 ....K6
Independence▲ 988 ....F7
Indian Valley 300 ....G7
Iron Gate 417 ....J5
Irvington 496 ....R5
Isle of Wight▲ 185 ....P7
Ivanhoe 900 ....G7
Ivor 324 ....P7
Ivy 900 ....L4
Jamestown 12 ....P6
Jamesville 500 ....S5
Jarratt 556 ....O7
Jefferson 25,782 ....N5
Jefferson Manor S3
Jeffersonton 300 ....N3
Jewell Ridge 600 ....E6
Jonesville▲ 927 ....B7
Keeling 680 ....K7
Keezletown 975 ....L4
Keller 235 ....S5
Kenbridge 1,264 ....M7
Kents Store 130 ....M5
Keokee 300 ....C7
Keswick 300 ....M4
Keysville 606 ....M6
Kilmarnock 1,109 ....R5
King George▲ 575 ....O4
King William▲ 100 ....O5
King and Queen Court
  House▲ 500 ....P5
Kinsale 250 ....P4
La Crosse 549 ....M7

Lacey Spring 140 ....L3
Ladysmith 360 ....N4
Lafayette-Elliston H6
Lake Barcroft 8,686 ....S3
Lakeside 12,081 ....N5
Lambsburg 800 ....O5
Lancaster▲ 110 ....R5
Laurel Fork 300 ....G7
Lawrenceville▲ 1,486 ....N7
Lebanon Church 300 ....L2
Lebanon▲ 3,206 ....D7
Leesburg▲ 16,202 ....N2
Lewisetta 125 ....P4
Lexington (I.C.)▲ 6,959 .....J5
Lincolnia 13,041 ....S3
Linden 320 ....M3
Linville 500 ....L3
Little Plymouth 195 ....P5
Lively 400 ....P5
Loretto 150 ....O4
Lorton 15,385 ....O3
Louisa▲ 1,088 ....M5
Lovettsville 749 ....N2
Lovingston▲ 600 ....L4
Lowesville 500 ....K5
Lowmoor 700 ....J5
Lucketts 500 ....N2
Lunenburg▲ 13 ....M7
Luray▲ 4,587 ....M3
Lynch Station 500 ....K6
Lynchburg (I.C.) 66,049 .....K6
Machipongo 400 ....S6
Madison Heights 11,700 ......K6
Madison▲ 267 ....M4
Manakin-Sabot 200 ....N5
Manassas (I.C.)▲ 27,957 .....O3
Manassas Park (I.C.) 6,734 ..O3
Mannboro 175 ....N6
Manquin 576 ....O5
Mantua 6,804 ....S3
Mappsville 700 ....T5
Marion▲ 6,630 ....E7
Markham 300 ....N3
Marshall 800 ....N3
Martinsville (I.C.)▲ 16,162 .J7
Massies Mill 225 ....K5
Mathews▲ 500 ....R6
Matoaca 1,967 ....N6
Mattaponi 300 ....P5
Maurertown 158 ....L3
Max Meadows 782 ....G6

McClure 300 ....D6
McCoy 600 ....G6
McGaheysville 600 ....L4
McKenney 386 ....N7
McLean 38,168 ....S2
Meadows of Dan 150 ....H7
Meadowview-Emory 2,292 ......D7
Mechanicsburg 350 ....G6
Mechanicsville 22,027 ....O5
Meherrin 400 ....M6
Melfa 428 ....S5
Mendota 375 ....D7
Merrifield 8,399 ....S3
Middlebrook 125 ....K4
Middleburg 549 ....B3
Middletown 841 ....M2
Midland 600 ....N3
Mine Run 450 ....N4
Mineral 471 ....M5
Midlothian 950 ....N6
Milford 650 ....O4
Millboro 400 ....J5
Millboro Springs 200 ....J4
Millwood 400 ....M3
Mobjack 210 ....R6
Modest Town 225 ....S5
Mollusk 800 ....P5
Moneta 300 ....J6
Monroe 500 ....K6
Monterey▲ 222 ....J4
Montross▲ 359 ....P4
Montvale 900 ....J6
Morattico 225 ....P5
Moseley 210 ....N6
Mount Crawford 228 ....L4
Mount Holly 300 ....P4
Mount Jackson 1,583 ....L3
Mount Sidney 500 ....K4
Mount Solon 124 ....K4
Mount Vernon 27,485 ....O3
Mouth of Wilson 400 ....F7
Mustoe 150 ....K4
Narrows 2,082 ....G6
Naruna 175 ....L6
Nassawadox 564 ....S6
Nathalie 200 ....L7
Natural Bridge 200 ....J5
Natural Bridge Sta. 450 .....K5
Naxera 300 ....R6
Nellysford 290 ....L5
New Baltimore 125 ....N3

New Castle▲ 152 ....H5
New Church 427 ....S5
New Hope 200 ....L4
New Kent▲ 25 ....P5
New Market 1,435 ....L3
New River 500 ....G6
Newington 17,965 ....S3
Newport 600 ....H6
Newport News (I.C.) 170,045 .P6
Newsoms 337 ....O7
Nickelsville 411 ....D7
Nokesville 520 ....N3
Nora 550 ....D6
Norfolk (I.C.) 261,229 ......R7
Norge 750 ....P6
North Garden 300 ....L5
North Pulaski 1,405 ....G6
North Springfield 8,996 .....S3
Norton (I.C.) 4,247 ....C7
Nottoway▲ 170 ....M6
Oak Hall 221 ....S5
Oakpark 150 ....M4
Oakton 24,610 ....R3
Oakwood 715 ....E6
Occoquan 361 ....S3
Onancock 1,434 ....S5
Onley 532 ....S5
Orange▲ 2,582 ....M4
Owenton 400 ....O5
Oyster 200 ....S6
Paint Bank 235 ....H5
Painter 259 ....S5
Palmyra▲ 250 ....M5
Pamplin 273 ....L6
Pardee 190 ....C6
Parksley 779 ....S5
Parrott 750 ....G6
Patrick Springs 800 ....H7
Peaks 500 ....D6
Pearisburg▲ 2,064 ....G6
Pembroke 1,064 ....G6
Penhook 500 ....J7
Pennington Gap 1,922 ....C7
Petersburg (I.C.) 38,386 ....N6
Phenix 260 ....L6
Philomont 265 ....N2
Pilot 360 ....H6
Pimmit 6,658 ....S2
Piney River 778 ....L5
Pittsville 600 ....K7
Pleasant Valley 150 ....L4
Pocahontas 513 ....F6
Poquoson 11,005 ....R6
Port Royal 204 ....P4
Portsmouth (I.C.) 103,907 ..R7
Potomac Beach 200 ....P4
Pound 995 ....C6
Pounding Mill 399 ....F6
Powhatan▲ 600 ....N5
Prince George▲ 150 ....N6
Prospect 275 ....L6
Providence Forge 500 ....P6
Pulaski▲ 9,985 ....G6
Pungoteague 500 ....S5
Purcellville 1,744 ....N2
Purdy 350 ....N7
Quantico 670 ....N3
Quicksburg 160 ....L3
Quinby 350 ....S5
Radford (I.C.) 15,940 ......G6
Radiant 250 ....M4
Randolph 150 ....L7
Raphine 500 ....K5
Rapiden 176 ....M4

Raven 2,640 ....E6
Rawlings 200 ....N7
Rectortown 225 ....N3
Red Ash 500 ....E6
Red House 150 ....L6
Red Oak 250 ....L7
Reedville 400 ....R5
Reliance 150 ....M3
Remington 460 ....N3
Republican Grove 125 ....K7
Rice 194 ....M6
Rich Creek 746 ....G6
Richlands 4,456 ....E6
Richmond (cap.) (I.C.)▲
  203,056 ....O5
Ridgeway 752 ....J7
Riner 360 ....H6
Ringgold 150 ....K7
Ripplemead 600 ....G6
Riverton 500 ....M3
Rixeyville 350 ....M3
Roanoke (I.C.) 96,397 ......H6
Rockville 290 ....N5
Rocky Gap 200 ....F6
Rocky Mount▲ 4,098 ....J7
Rose Hill 12,675 ....B7
Rosedale 760 ....E7
Roseland 300 ....K5
Round Hill 514 ....N2
Rowe 150 ....F6
Ruby 188 ....N3
Rural Retreat 972 ....F7
Rushmere 1,064 ....P6
Rustburg▲ 650 ....K6
Ruther Glen 200 ....N4
Ruthville 300 ....P6
Saint Charles 206 ....C7
Saint Paul 1,007 ....D7
Saint Stephens Church 500 ..O5
Salem (I.C.)▲ 23,756 ....H6
Saltville 2,376 ....E7
Saluda▲ 150 ....P5
Sandy Hook 700 ....M5
Saxis 367 ....S5
Schuyler 250 ....L5
Scottsburg 152 ....L7
Scottsville 239 ....L5
Sealston 200 ....O4
Sebrell 160 ....O7
Sedley 523 ....P7
Selma 500 ....J5
Seven Corners 7,280 ....S3
Seven Mile Ford 425 ....E7
Shanghai 150 ....P5
Shawsville 1,260 ....H6
Shenandoah 2,213 ....L4
Shiloh 150 ....L5
Shipman 350 ....L5
Simpsons 150 ....K3
Singers Glen 155 ....K3
Skippers 150 ....O7
Skipwith 128 ....L7
Smithfield 4,686 ....P7
Snell 300 ....N4
Somerset 200 ....M4
South Boston (I.C.) 6,997 ..L7
South Hill 4,217 ....M7
Sparta 485 ....O4
Speedwell 650 ....F8
Spencer 500 ....H7
Sperryville 500 ....M3
Spotsylvania▲ 350 ....N4
Springfield 23,706 ....S3

Stafford▲ 750 ....O4
Stanardsville▲ 257 ....L4
Stanley 1,186 ....L3
Stanleytown 1,563 ....H7
Star Tannery 500 ....L2
Staunton (I.C.)▲ 24,461 ....K4
Steeles Tavern 200 ....K5
Stephens City 1,186 ....M2
Sterling 20,512 ....O2
Stevensburg 125 ....N4
Stonega 275 ....C7
Stony Creek 271 ....N7
Strasburg 3,762 ....M3
Stuart▲ 965 ....H7
Stuarts Draft 5,087 ....L4
Studley 500 ....O5
Suffolk (I.C.) 52,141 ......P7
Sugar Grove 1,027 ....E7
Surry▲ 192 ....P6
Susan 500 ....R6
Sussex▲ 75 ....O7
Sutherlin 180 ....K7
Sweet Briar 900 ....K5
Swords Creek 315 ....E6
Sylvatus 200 ....G7
Tacoma 150 ....C7
Tangier 659 ....R5
Tappahannock▲ 1,550 ....O5
Tazewell▲ 4,176 ....E6
Temperanceville 400 ....T5
Thaxton 450 ....J6
The Plains 219 ....N3
Thornburg 135 ....N4
Timberville 1,596 ....L3
Tiptop 175 ....F6
Toano 950 ....P6
Toms Brook 227 ....L3
Townsend 525 ....R6
Trammel 450 ....D6
Triangle 4,740 ....O3
Triplet 300 ....N7
Trout Dale 248 ....F7
Troutville 455 ....J6
Tyro 125 ....K5
Union Hall 125 ....J6
Unionville 500 ....N4
Upperville 250 ....N2
Urbanna 529 ....P5
Valentines 400 ....N7
Vansant 1,187 ....D6
Vera 150 ....L6
Vernon Hill 250 ....K7
Verona 3,479 ....K4
Vesta 350 ....H7
Vesuvius 500 ....K5
Victoria 1,830 ....M6
Vienna 14,852 ....R2
Vinton 7,665 ....H6
Virgilina 161 ....L7
Virginia Beach (I.C.) 393,069 ..S7
Wachapreague 291 ....S5
Wakefield 1,070 ....O7
Walkerton 985 ....O5
Warm Springs▲ 325 ....J4
Warrenton▲ 4,830 ....N3
Warsaw▲ 961 ....P5
Washington▲ 198 ....M3
Water View 265 ....P5
Waterford 350 ....N2
Waverly 2,223 ....O6
Waynesboro (I.C.) 18,549 ...K4
Weber City 1,377 ....C7
Weems 500 ....P5
Weirwood 300 ....S6
West Augusta 325 ....K4
West Point 2,938 ....P5
West Springfield 28,126 ....S3
Weyers Cave 300 ....K4
White Hall 250 ....L4
White Stone 372 ....P5
Whitetop 860 ....E7
Whitewood 350 ....E6
Wicomico Church 500 ....R5
Wilderness 200 ....N4
Williamsburg (I.C.)▲ 11,530 .P6
Williamsville 145 ....J4
Willis 170 ....H7
Willis Wharf 360 ....S5
Winchester (I.C.)▲ 21,947 ..M2
Windsor 1,025 ....P7
Wirtz 500 ....J6
Wise (I.C.)▲ 3,193 ....C7
Wolftown 350 ....M4
Woodberry Forest 450 ....M4
Woodbridge 26,401 ....O3
Woodlawn 1,689 ....G7
Woodstock▲ 3,182 ....L3
Woodville 500 ....C7
Woodway 400 ....C7
Woolwine 150 ....H7
Wylliesburg 213 ....L7
Wytheville▲ 8,038 ....F7
Zuni 300 ....P7

OTHER FEATURES

Aarons (creek) L7
Allegheny (mts.) H5
Anna (lake) N4
Appalachian (mts.) J5
Appomattox (riv.) M6
Appomattox Court House Nat'l
  Hist. Park M6
Arlington Nat'l Cemetery ...T3
Assateague Island
  Nat'l Seashore T4
Back (bay) S7
Back (creek) K3
Banister (riv.) K7
Big Otter (riv.) K6
Blackwater (riv.) J6
Blackwater (riv.) O7
Blue Ridge (mts.) J6
Bluestone (lake) G5
Booker T. Washington
  Nat'l Mon. J6
Buggs Island (lake) L8

Bull Run (creek) ....N
Cedar (isl.) ....
Central Intelligence Agency
  (C.I.A.) ....S
Charles (cape) ....
Chesapeake (bay) ....
Chesapeake and Ohio Canal
  Nat'l Hist. Park ....
Chincoteague (bay) ....
Chincoteague (inlet) ....
Claytor (lake) ....
Clinch (riv.) ....
Cobb (isl.) ....
Colonial Nat'l Hist. Park ..
Cowpasture (riv.) ....
Craig (creek) ....
Cub (creek) ....
Cumberland (mt.) ....
Cumberland Gap Nat'l
  Hist. Park ....
Dan (riv.) ....
Drummond (lake) ....
Fishermans (isl.) ....
Flannagan (res.) ....
Flat (creek) ....
Fort A.P. Hill ....
Fort Belvoir 8,590 ....
Fort Eustis ....
Fort Lee 6,595 ....
Fort Monroe ....
Fort Myer ....
Fort Pickett ....
Fort Story ....
Gaston (lake) ....
George Washington Birthplace
  Nat'l Mon. ....
Goose (creek) ....
Goose (creek) ....
Great Machipongo (inlet) ...S
Great North (mt.) ....
Henry (cape) ....
Hog (isl.) ....
Hog Island (bay) ....
Holston, North Fork (riv.) .
Hyco (riv.) ....K
Jackson (riv.) ....
James (riv.) ....
Jamestown Nat'l Hist. Site .F
John H. Kerr (dam) ....
Langley A.F.B. ....
Leesville (lake) ....
Levisa Fork (riv.) ....
Little (inlet) ....
Little (riv.) ....
Little (riv.) ....
Manassas Nat'l
  Battlefield Pk. ....
Massanutten (mt.) ....
Mattaponi (riv.) ....
Mattaponi Ind. Res. ....
Maury (riv.) ....
Meherrin (riv.) ....
Metompkin (inlet) ....
Metompkin (isl.) ....
Mobjack (bay) ....
Mount Rogers Nat'l Rec. Area.F
New (inlet) ....
New (riv.) ....
Ni (riv.) ....
North Anna (riv.) ....
Nottoway (riv.) ....
Oceana N.A.S. ....
Pamunkey (riv.) ....
Pamunkey Ind. Res. ....
Parramore (isl.) ....
Pentagon ....
Petersburg Nat'l Battlefield
Philpott (lake) ....
Piankatank (riv.) ....
Pigg (riv.) ....
Po (riv.) ....
Pocomoke (sound) ....
Potomac (riv.) ....
Powell (riv.) ....
Quantico Marine Corps
  Air Sta. ....
Quinby (inlet) ....
Rapidan (riv.) ....
Rappahannock (riv.) ....
Red Hill Patrick Henry
  Nat'l Mem. ....
Richmond Nat'l
  Battlefield Pk. ....
Rivanna (riv.) ....
Roanoke (riv.) ....
Rogers (mt.) ....
Russell Fork (riv.) ....
Sand Shoal (inlet) ....
Shenandoah (mt.) ....
Shenandoah (riv.) ....
Shenandoah Nat'l Park ......
Ship Shoal (isl.) ....
Slate (riv.) ....
Smith (isl.) ....
Smith Mountain (lake) ......
South Anna (riv.) ....
South Holston (lake) ....
South Mayo (riv.) ....
Stony (creek) ....
Swift (creek) ....
Tangier (isl.) ....
Tangier (sound) ....
Tug Fork (riv.) ....
U.S. Naval Base ....
Vint Hill Farms Mil. Res. ..
Wachapreague (inlet) ....
Walker (creek) ....
Wallops (isl.) ....
Willis (riv.) ....
Wolf (creek) ....
Wolf Trap Farm Park ....
York (riv.) ....

I.C. Independent City
▲ County seat

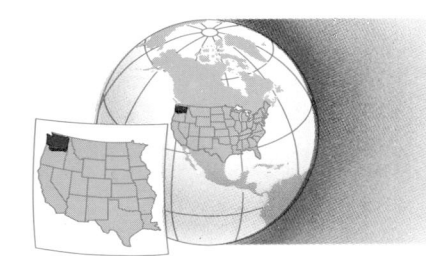

AREA 68,139 sq. mi. (176,480 sq. km.)
POPULATION 4,887,941
CAPITAL Olympia
LARGEST CITY Seattle
HIGHEST POINT Mt. Rainier 14,410 ft. (4392 m.)
SETTLED IN 1811
ADMITTED TO UNION November 11, 1889
POPULAR NAME Evergreen State
STATE FLOWER Western Rhododendron
STATE BIRD Willow Goldfinch

COUNTIES

dams 13,603	G3
sotin 17,605	H4
enton 112,560	F4
helan 52,250	E3
allam 56,464	B2
ark 238,053	C5
olumbia 4,024	H4
owlitz 82,119	C4
ouglas 26,205	F3
erry 6,295	G2
ranklin 37,473	G4
arfield 2,248	H4
rant 54,758	F3
rays Harbor 64,175	B3
sland 60,195	C2
efferson 20,146	B3
ing 1,507,319	D3
itsap 189,731	C3
ttitas 26,725	E3
lickitat 16,616	E5
ewis 59,358	C4
ncoln 8,864	G3
lason 38,341	B3
kanogan 33,350	F2
acific 18,882	B4
end Oreille 8,915	H2
erce 586,203	C3
an Juan 10,035	C2
kagit 79,555	D2
kamania 8,289	D5

CITIES and TOWNS

Aberdeen 16,565	B3
Acme 500	C2
Addy 180	H2
Airway Heights 1,971	H3
Albion 632	H4
Alder 300	C4
Algona 1,694	C3
Allyn 850	C3
Almira 310	G3
Aloha 140	A3
Amanda Park 495	A3
Amboy 480	C5
Anacortes 11,451	C2
Appleton 120	D5
Ardenvoir 150	E3
Ariel 386	C5
Arlington 4,037	C2
Ashford 300	C4
Asotin▲ 981	H4
Auburn 33,102	C3

Snohomish 465,642	D2
Spokane 361,364	H3
Stevens 30,948	H2
Thurston 161,238	C4
Wahkiakum 3,832	B4
Walla Walla 48,439	G4
Whatcom 127,780	D2
Whitman 38,775	H4
Yakima 188,823	E4

Azwell 152	F3
Bainbridge Island-Winslow (Winslow)	A2
Baring 200	D3
Battle Ground 3,758	C5
Bay Center 187	A4
Bay City 187	B4
Beaux Arts Village 303	B2
Beaver 450	A2
Belfair 500	C3
Bellevue 86,874	B2
Bellingham▲ 52,179	C2
Benton City 1,806	F4
Beverly 200	F4
Biglake 105	C2
Bingen 645	D5
Black Diamond 1,422	D3
Blaine 2,489	C2
Blanchard 125	C2
Bonney Lake 7,494	C3
Bothell 12,345	B1
Bow 200	C2
Boyds 125	G2
Bremerton 38,142	A2
Brewster 1,633	F2
Bridgeport 1,498	F3
Brier 5,633	C2
Brinnon 500	B3
Brownstown 200	E4
Brush Prairie 2,650	C5
Bryn Mawr-Skyway 12,514	B2
Buckley 3,516	C3

Bucoda 536	C4
Buena 590	E4
Burbank 1,745	G4
Burien 25,089	A2
Burley 300	C3
Burlington 4,349	C2
Burton 650	C3
Camas 6,442	C5
Carbonado 495	C3
Carlsborg 500	B2
Carlton 410	F2
Carnation 1,243	D3
Carson 500	D5
Cashmere 2,544	E3
Castle Rock 2,067	B4
Cathlamet▲ 508	B4
Cedar Falls 200	D3
Central Park 2,669	B3
Centralia 12,101	C4
Chattaroy 250	H3
Chehalis▲ 6,527	C4
Chelan 2,969	E3
Chelan Falls 250	E3
Cheney 7,723	H3
Chewelah 1,945	H2
Chimacum 275	C3
Chinook 928	A4
Cinebar 200	C4
Clallam Bay 600	A2
Clarkston 6,753	H4
Clayton 175	H3
Cle Elum 1,778	E3

Clearlake 750	C2
Clearwater 194	A3
Clinton 1,564	C3
Clyde	F4
Clyde Hill 2,972	B2
Coalfield 500	B2
Colbert 225	H3
Colby 150	A2
Colfax▲ 2,713	H4
College Place 6,308	G4
Colton 325	H4
Columbia Heights 2,515	C4
Colville▲ 4,360	H2
Conconully 153	F2
Concrete 735	D2
Connell 2,005	G4
Conway 150	C2
Copalis Beach 600	A3
Copalis Crossing 500	B3
Cosmopolis 1,372	B4
Coulee City 568	F3
Coulee Dam 1,087	G3
Coupeville▲ 1,377	C2
Cowiche 150	E4
Creston 230	G3
Cumberland 250	D3
Curlew 168	G2
Cusick 195	H2
Custer 300	C2
Dallesport 600	D5
Danville 215	G2
Darrington 1,042	D2

Davenport▲ 1,502	G3
Dayton▲ 2,468	H4
Deer Harbor 400	B2
Deer Park 2,278	H3
Deming 200	C2
Des Moines 17,283	B2
Dishman 9,671	H3
Dixie 210	G4
Doe Bay 150	C2
Doty 245	B4
Dryad 125	B4
Dryden 500	E3
Du Pont 592	C3
Dungeness 675	B2
Duvall 2,770	D3
East Olympia 300	B4
East Wenatchee 2,701	E3
Easton 250	D3
Eastsound 800	B2
Eatonville 1,374	C4
Edison 250	C2
Edmonds 30,744	C3
Edwall 150	H3
Electric City 910	F3
Ellensburg▲ 12,361	E3
Elma 3,011	B4
Elmer City 290	G2
Eltopia 200	G4
Endicott 320	H4
Enetai 2,638	A2
Entiat 449	E3
Enumclaw 7,227	D3
Ephrata▲ 5,349	F3
Erlands Point 1,254	A2
Ethel 180	C4
Everett▲ 69,961	C3
Everson 1,490	C2
Fairfield 446	H3
Fairview-Sumach 2,749	E4
Fall City 1,582	D3
Farmington 126	H3
Ferndale 5,398	C2
Fife 3,864	C3
Finley 4,897	F4
Fircrest 5,258	C3
Fords Prairie 2,480	B4
Forks 2,862	A3
Four Lakes 500	H3
Frances 144	B4
Freeland 1,278	C2
Freeman 150	H3
Friday Harbor▲ 1,492	B2
Fruitland 150	G2
Fruitvale 4,125	E4
Galvin 250	B4
Garfield 544	H3
Garrett 1,004	G4
Geiger Heights	H3
George 253	F3
Gig Harbor 3,236	C3
Glacier 150	D2
Glenoma 500	C4
Glenwood 626	D4
Gold Bar 1,078	D3
Goldendale▲ 3,319	E5
Gorst 750	C3
Grand Coulee 984	G3
Grand Mound 1,394	C4
Grandview 7,169	F4
Granger 2,053	E4
Granite Falls 1,060	D2
Grapeview 250	C3
Grayland 750	A4
Grays River 350	B4
Greenacres 4,626	J3
Greenbank 600	C2
Hadlock-Irondale 2,742	C2
Hamilton 228	D2
Hansville 250	C3
Harper 300	A2
Harrah 341	E4
Harrington 449	G3
Hartline 176	F3
Hatton 71	F4
Heisson 200	C5
Hobart 500	D3
Hoodsport 500	B3
Hoquiam 8,972	A3
Humptulips 275	A3
Hunters 200	G2
Hunts Point 513	B2
Husum 200	D5
Ilwaco 815	A4
Inchelium 393	G2
Index 139	D3
Indianola 1,729	A1
Ione 507	H2
Issaquah 7,786	C3
Joyce 375	B2
Juanita 17,232	B1
Kahlotus 167	B4
Kalama 1,210	C4
Kapowsin 500	C4
Keller 195	G2
Kelso▲ 11,820	C4

Kenmore 8,917	B1
Kennewick 42,155	F4
Kent 37,960	C3
Kettle Falls 1,272	H2
Keyport 900	A2
Kingston 1,270	C3
Kiona 230	F4
Kirkland 40,052	B2
Kittitas 843	E4
Klickitat 750	D5
Krupp (Marlin) 53	F3
La Center 451	C5
La Conner 656	C2
La Push 500	A3
Lacey 19,279	C3
Lacrosse 336	H4
Lake Forest Park 4,031	B1
Lake Stevens 3,380	D3
Lakewood 58,412	C3
Lamont 91	H3
Langley 845	C3
Latah 175	H3
Laurel 782	D5
Leavenworth 1,692	E3
Lebam 275	B4
Liberty Lake 2,015	J3
Lind 472	G4
Littlerock 850	B4
Long Beach 1,236	A4
Longbranch 640	C3
Longview 31,499	B4
Loomis 150	F2
Loon Lake 500	H2
Lummi Island 675	C2
Lyle 580	D5
Lyman 275	D2
Lynden 5,709	C2
Lynnwood 28,695	C3
Mabton 1,482	E4
Malaga 125	E3
Malden 189	H3
Malo 240	G2
Malone 175	B4
Malott 350	F2
Manchester 4,031	A2
Mansfield 311	F3
Manson 220	E3
Maple Falls 300	D2
Maple Valley 1,211	C3
Marblemount 300	D2
Marcus 135	H2
Marietta-Alderwood 2,766	C2
Markham 117	B4
Marlin	F3
Marysville 10,328	C2
Matlock 255	B3
Mattawa 941	F4
McCleary 1,235	B3
McKenna 300	C4
Mead	H3
Medical Lake 3,664	H3
Medina 2,981	B2
Menlo 237	B4
Mercer Island (city) 20,816	B2
Mesa 252	G4
Metaline 198	H2
Metaline Falls 210	H2
Mica 105	H3
Milan 150	H3
Millwood 1,559	H3
Milton 4,995	C3
Mineral 550	C4
Moclips 500	A3
Monitor 650	E3
Monroe 4,278	D3
Montesano▲ 3,064	B4
Moses Lake 11,235	F3
Mossyrock 452	C4
Mount Vernon▲ 17,647	C2
Mountlake Terrace 19,320	B1
Moxee City 814	E4
Mukilteo 7,007	C3
Naches 596	E4
Nahcotta 200	A4
Napavine 745	C4
Naselle 500	B4
Navy Yard City 2,905	A2
Neah Bay 916	A2
Neilton 250	B3
Nespelem 291	G2
Newhalem 350	D2
Newman Lake 102	J3
Newport▲ 1,691	H2
Nine Mile Falls 150	H3
Nisqually 558	C3
Nooksack 584	C2
Nordland 706	C2
Normandy Park 6,709	A2
North Bend 2,578	D3
North Bonneville 411	C5
Northport 308	H2
Oak Harbor 17,176	C2
Oakesdale 346	H3
Oakville 493	B4

Agriculture, Industry and Resources

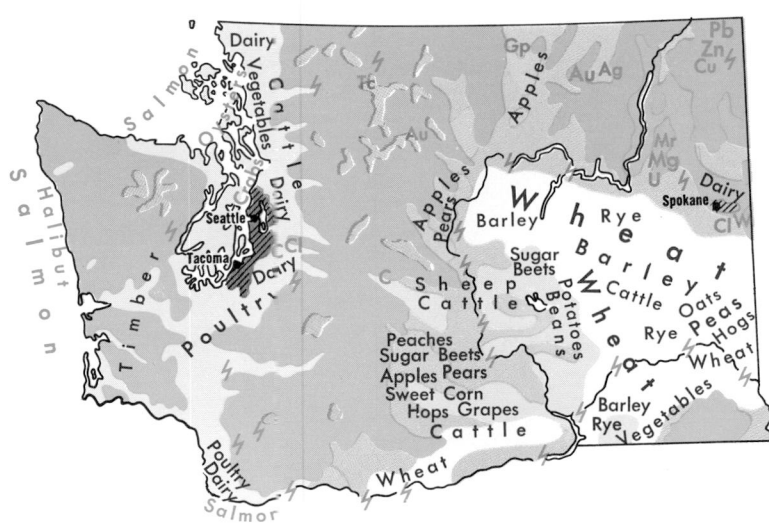

DOMINANT LAND USE

- Specialized Wheat
- Wheat, Peas
- Dairy, Poultry, Mixed Farming
- Fruit and Mixed Farming
- General Farming, Dairy, Range Livestock
- General Farming, Livestock, Special Crops
- Range Livestock
- Forests
- Urban Areas
- Nonagricultural Land

MAJOR MINERAL OCCURRENCES

Ag	Silver	Mr	Marble
Au	Gold	Pb	Lead
C	Coal	Tc	Talc
Cl	Clay	U	Uranium
Cu	Copper	W	Tungsten
Gp	Gypsum	Zn	Zinc
Mg	Magnesium		

⚡ Water Power

▨ Major Industrial Areas

(continued on following page)

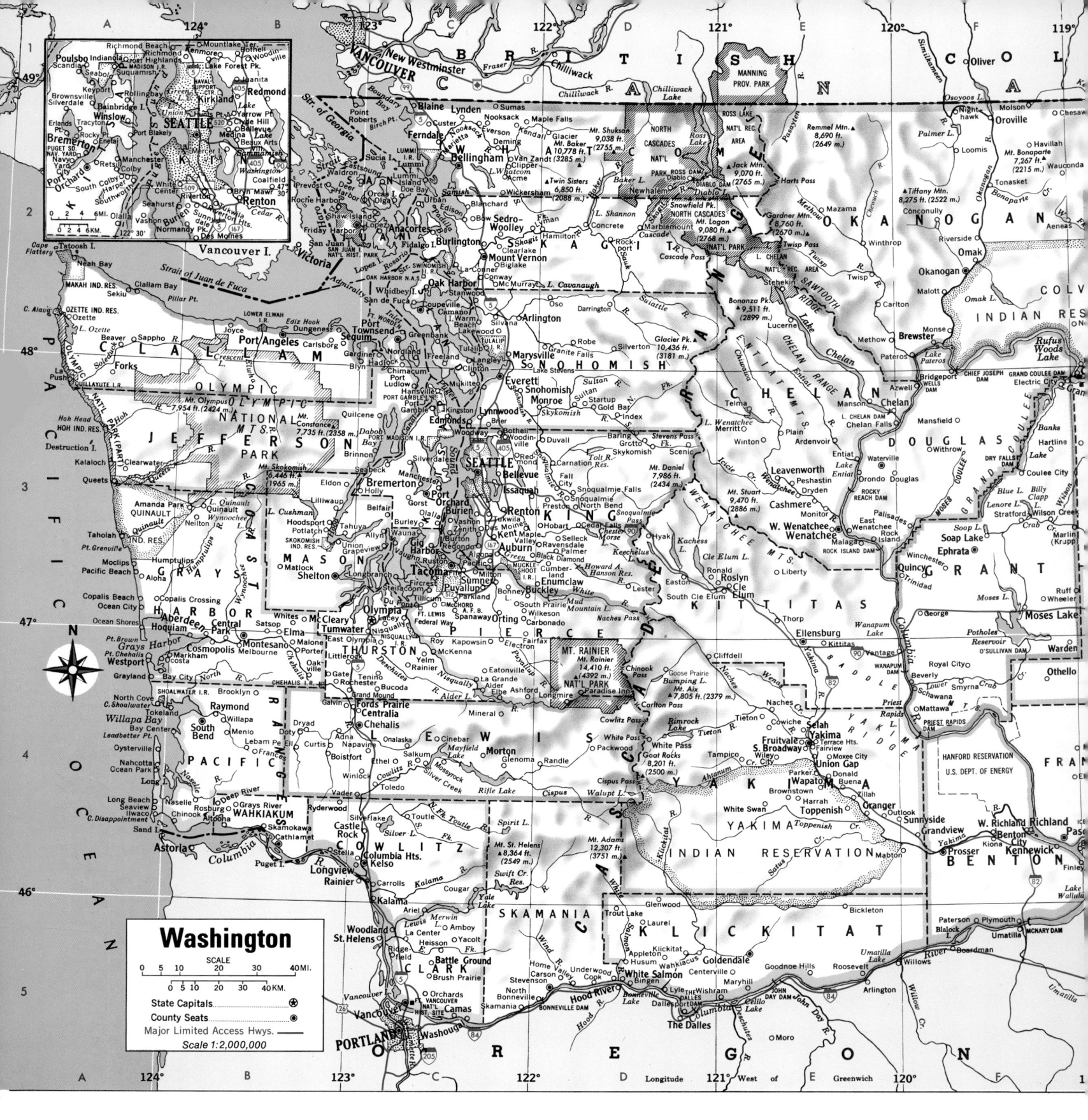

Washington

SCALE
0 5 10 20 30 40MI.
0 5 10 20 30 40KM.

State Capitals ⊛
County Seats ◉
Major Limited Access Hwys. ▬▬▬
Scale 1:2,000,000

Ocean City 350 ....A3
Ocean Park 1,409 ....A4
Ocean Shores 2,301 ....A3
Ocosta 369 ....B4
Odessa 935 ....G3
Okanogan▲ 2,370 ....F2
Olalla 500 ....A2
Olympia (cap.)▲ 33,840 ...C3
Omak 4,117 ....F2
Onalaska 600 ....C4
Opportunity 22,326 ....H3
Orchards 8,828 ....C5
Orondo 130 ....E3
Oroville 1,505 ....F2
Orting 2,106 ....C3
Oso 150 ....D2
Othello 4,638 ....F4
Otis Orchards-East
   Farms 5,811 ....H3
Outlook 300 ....E4
Oysterville 150 ....A4
Ozette 50 ....A2
Pacific 4,622 ....C3

Pacific Beach 900 ....A3
Packwood 800 ....D4
Palisades 150 ....E3
Palmer 200 ....D3
Palouse 915 ....H4
Parker 200 ....E4
Parkland 20,882 ....C3
Pasco▲ 20,337 ....F4
Pateros 570 ....E2
Paterson 250 ....F5
Pe Ell 547 ....B4
Peshastin 500 ....E3
Plymouth 220 ....F5
Point Roberts 500 ....B2
Pomeroy▲ 1,393 ....H4
Port Angeles▲ 17,710 ....B2
Port Blakely 600 ....A2
Port Gamble 122 ....C3
Port Ludlow 200 ....C3
Port Orchard▲ 4,984 ......C3
Port Townsend▲ 7,001 ....C2
Porter 200 ....B4
Poulsbo 4,848 ....A1

Prescott 267 ....G4
Preston 500 ....D3
Prosser▲ 4,476 ....F4
Pullman 23,478 ....H4
Puyallup 23,875 ....C3
Queets 450 ....A3
Quilcene 900 ....B3
Quinault 450 ....B3
Quincy 3,738 ....F3
Rainier 991 ....C4
Randle 500 ....D4
Ravensdale 400 ....D3
Raymond 2,901 ....B4
Reardan 482 ....H3
Redmond 35,800 ....B1
Redondo 950 ....C3
Renton 41,688 ....C3
Republic▲ 940 ....G2
Retsil 1,524 ....A2
Richland 32,315 ....F4
Richmond Beach-Innis
   Arden 7,242 ....A1
Richmond Highlands 26,037 ..A1

Ridgefield 1,297 ....C5
Riparia 210 ....G4
Ritzville▲ 1,725 ....G3
Riverside 223 ....F2
Riverton 14,182 ....B2
Riverton Heights B2
Roche Harbor 200 ....B2
Rochester 1,250 ....C4
Rock Island 524 ....E3
Rockford 481 ....H3
Rockport 200 ....D2
Rocky Point 1,495 ....A2
Rollingbay 950 ....A2
Ronald 200 ....E3
Rosalia 552 ....H3
Rosburg 419 ....B4
Roslyn 869 ....E3
Roy 258 ....C4
Royal City 1,104 ....F4
Ruston 693 ....A2
Ryderwood 367 ....B4
Saint John 499 ....H4
Salkum 390 ....C4

San de Fuca 150 ....C2
Satsop 300 ....B3
Schawana 150 ....F4
Seabeck 250 ....A1
Seabold 250 ....A1
Seahurst A2
Seattle▲ 516,259 ....A2
Seaview 500 ....A4
Sedro-Woolley 6,031 ....C2
Sekiu 328 ....A2
Selah 5,113 ....E4
Selleck 150 ....D3
Sequim 3,616 ....B2
Shaw Island 125 ....B2
Shelton▲ 7,241 ....B3
Silver Creek 175 ....C4
Silverdale 7,660 ....C3
Skamania 200 ....C5
Skamokawa 450 ....B4
Skykomish 273 ....D3
Snohomish 6,499 ....D3
Snoqualmie 1,546 ....D3
Snoqualmie Falls 250 ...D3

Soap Lake 1,149 ....F3
South Bend▲ 1,551 ......B4
South Broadway 2,735 ...E4
South Cle Elum 457 .....D3
South Colby 500 ....A2
South Prairie 180 ......D3
Southworth 175 ....A2
Spanaway 15,001 ....C3
Spangle 229 ....H3
Spokane▲ 177,196 ....H3
Sprague 410 ....G3
Springdale 260 ....H2
Stanwood 1,961 ....C2
Starbuck 170 ....G4
Startup 500 ....D3
Steilacoom 5,728 ....C3
Steptoe 215 ....H3
Stevenson▲ 1,147 ......C5
Sultan 2,236 ....D3
Sumas 744 ....C2
Sumner 6,281 ....C3
Sunnydale B2
Sunnyside 11,238 ....E4

Suquamish 3,105 ....A1
Tacoma▲ 176,664 ....C3
Taholah 788 ....A3
Tahuya 150 ....B3
Tekoa 750 ....H3
Tenino 1,292 ....C4
Terrace Heights 4,223 ..E4
Thorp 500 ....E3
Tieton 693 ....E4
Tillicum C3
Tokeland 500 ....A4
Toledo 586 ....C4
Tonasket 847 ....F2
Toppenish 7,419 ....E4
Touchet 450 ....G4
Town and Country 4,921 ..H3
Tracyton 2,621 ....A2
Trout Lake 900 ....D5
Tukwila 11,874 ....B2
Tulalip 250 ....C2
Tumtum 250 ....H3
Tumwater 9,976 ....B3

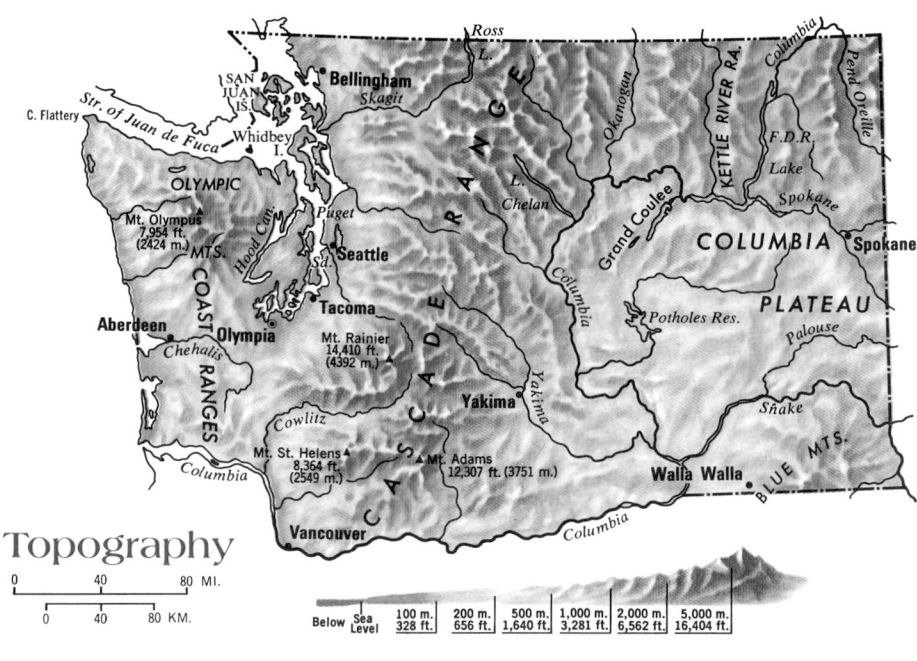

Topography

0   40   80 MI.
0   40   80 KM.

| Below Sea Level | 100 m. 328 ft. | 200 m. 656 ft. | 500 m. 1,640 ft. | 1,000 m. 3,281 ft. | 2,000 m. 6,562 ft. | 5,000 m. 16,404 ft. |

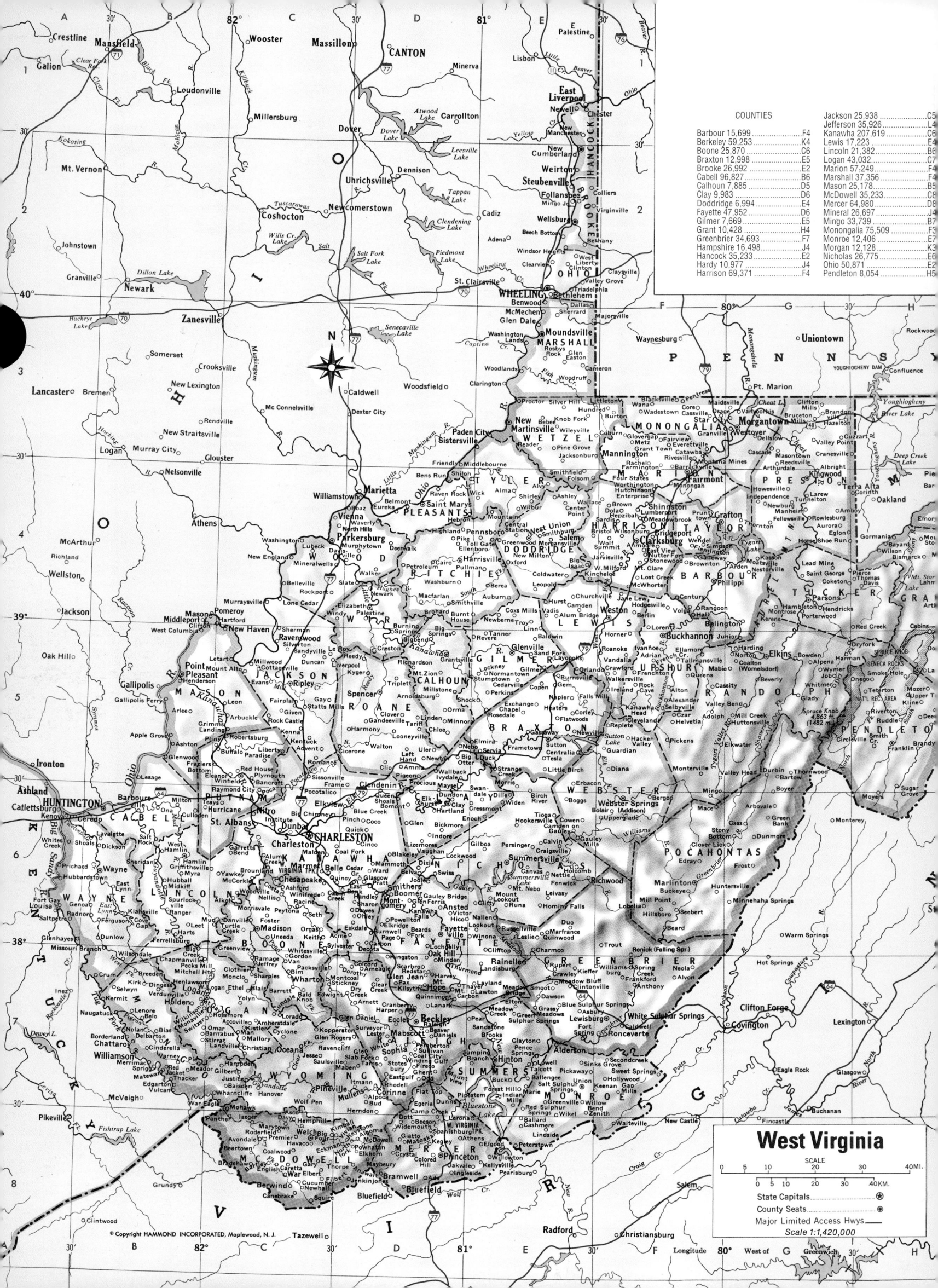

West Virginia

COUNTIES

Barbour 15,699 ....F4	Jackson 25,938 ....C5
Berkeley 59,253 ....K4	Jefferson 35,926 ....L4
Boone 25,870 ....C6	Kanawha 207,619 ....C6
Braxton 12,998 ....E5	Lewis 17,223 ....E4
Brooke 26,992 ....E2	Lincoln 21,382 ....B6
Cabell 96,827 ....B6	Logan 43,032 ....C7
Calhoun 7,885 ....D5	Marion 57,249 ....F4
Clay 9,983 ....D6	Marshall 37,356 ....F4
Doddridge 6,994 ....E4	Mason 25,178 ....B5
Fayette 47,952 ....D6	McDowell 35,233 ....C8
Gilmer 7,669 ....E5	Mercer 64,980 ....D8
Grant 10,428 ....H4	Mineral 26,697 ....J4
Greenbrier 34,693 ....F7	Mingo 33,739 ....B7
Hampshire 16,498 ....J4	Monongalia 75,509 ....F3
Hancock 35,233 ....E2	Monroe 12,406 ....E7
Hardy 10,977 ....J4	Morgan 12,128 ....K3
Harrison 69,371 ....F4	Nicholas 26,775 ....E6
	Ohio 50,871 ....E2
	Pendleton 8,054 ....H5

SCALE
0 5 10   20   30   40 MI.
0 5 10   20   30   40 KM.

State Capitals ....⊛

County Seats ....◉

Major Limited Access Hwys. _____

Scale 1:1,420,000

© Copyright HAMMOND INCORPORATED, Maplewood, N.J.

Longitude 80° West of Greenwich

Pleasants 7,546 ....D4
Pocahontas 9,008 ....F6
Preston 29,037 ....G4
Putnam 42,835 ....C6
Raleigh 76,819 ....D7
Randolph 27,803 ....G5
Ritchie 10,233 ....D4
Roane 15,120 ....D5
Summers 14,204 ....E7
Taylor 15,144 ....F4
Tucker 7,728 ....F4
Tyler 9,796 ....E4
Upshur 22,867 ....F5
Wayne 41,636 ....B6
Webster 10,729 ....F6
Wetzel 19,258 ....E3
Wirt 5,192 ....D4
Wood 86,915 ....D4
Wyoming 28,990 ....C7

AREA   24,231 sq. mi. (62,758 sq. km.)
POPULATION   1,801,625
CAPITAL   Charleston
LARGEST CITY   Charleston
HIGHEST POINT   Spruce Knob 4,863 ft.
   (1482 m.)
SETTLED IN   1774
ADMITTED TO UNION   June 20, 1863
POPULAR NAME   Mountain State
STATE FLOWER   Big Rhododendron
STATE BIRD   Cardinal

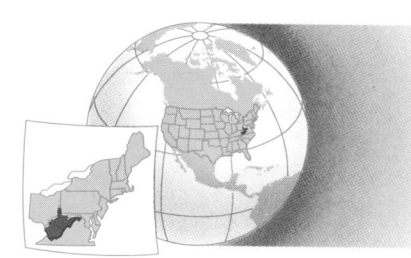

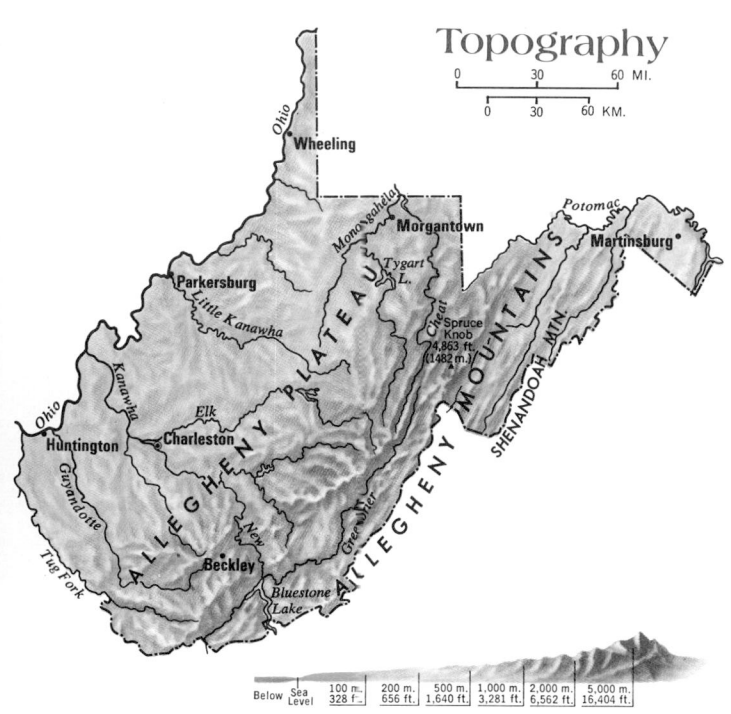

Topography

0   30   60 MI.

0   30   60 KM.

Below Sea Level | 100 m. 328 f. | 200 m. 656 ft. | 500 m. 1,640 ft. | 1,000 m. 3,281 ft. | 2,000 m. 6,562 ft. | 5,000 m. 16,404 ft.

CITIES and TOWNS

Accoville 975 ....C7
Acme 165 ....D6
Ada 250 ....D8
Addison▲ (Webster Springs)
   674 ....F6
Adrian 510 ....F5
Albright 195 ....G3
Algoma 200 ....D8
Alkol 500 ....C6
Alma 197 ....E4
Alpoca 200 ....D7
Alum Bridge 150 ....F5
Alum Creek 1,602 ....C6
Alvy 150 ....E4
Ameagle 230 ....D7
Amherstdale 1,057 ....C7
Amma 200 ....D5
Anawalt 329 ....D8
Anmoore 686 ....F4
Ansted 1,643 ....D6
Apple Grove 900 ....B5
Arbovale 610 ....G6
Arden 130 ....G4
Arnett 300 ....D7
Arnoldsburg 175 ....D5
Arthur 350 ....H4
Arthurdale 1,063 ....G3
Asbury 280 ....E7
Asco 175 ....C8
Ashford 400 ....C6
Ashton 259 ....B5
Athens 741 ....E8
Auburn 89 ....E4
Augusta 750 ....J4
Aurora 250 ....G4
Avondale 250 ....C8
Baisden 500 ....C7
Baker 200 ....J4
Bakerton 125 ....L4
Bald Knob 356 ....C7
Ballard 220 ....E8
Ballengee 170 ....E7
Bancroft 381 ....C5
Barboursville 2,774 ....B6
Barnabus 750 ....C7
Barrackville 1,443 ....F3
Barrett 950 ....C7
Bartley 900 ....C8
Bartow 500 ....G5
Bayard 414 ....H4
Beards Fork 400 ....D6
Beartown 500 ....C8
Beaver (Glen Hedrick) 1,244 ...D7
Bebee 125 ....E3
Beckley▲ 18,296 ....D7
Bedington 150 ....L3
Beech Bottom 415 ....E2
Beeson 300 ....D8
Belington 1,850 ....F4
Belle 1,421 ....C6
Belmont 912 ....D4
Belva 275 ....D6
Benwood 1,669 ....E2
Bergoo 220 ....F6
Berkeley 600 ....L4
Berkeley Springs▲ 789 ......K3
Berwind 615 ....C8
Bethany 1,139 ....E2
Bethlehem 2,694 ....E2
Beverly 696 ....G5
Bickmore 300 ....D6
Big Chimney 450 ....C6
Big Creek 500 ....B7
Big Four 150 ....C8
Big Otter 150 ....D5
Big Springs 485 ....D5
Bim 500 ....C7
Birch River 650 ....E6
Blacksville 168 ....F3
Blair 800 ....C7
Bloomery 200 ....K4
Blue Creek 650 ....D6
Bluefield 12,756 ....D8
Boaz 1,137 ....D4
Boggs 131 ....E6
Bolair 450 ....F6
Bolivar 1,013 ....L4
Bomont 300 ....D6
Boomer 1,051 ....D6
Borderland 250 ....B7
Bowden 135 ....G5
Bradshaw 394 ....C8
Bramwell 620 ....D8
Brandonville 73 ....G3
Brandywine 300 ....H5
Breeden 600 ....B7
Bridgeport 6,739 ....F4
Brooks 196 ....E7
Brounland 900 ....C6
Brownton 400 ....F4
Bruceton Mills 132 ....G3
Buck 150 ....E7
Buckhannon▲ 5,909 ....F5

Bud 400 ....D7
Buffalo 969 ....C5
Bunker Hill 600 ....K4
Burlington 300 ....J4
Burning Springs 137 ....D5
Burnsville 495 ....E5
Burnt House 175 ....D4
Burnwell 140 ....D6
Burton 200 ....F3
Cabin Creek 900 ....C6
Cairo 290 ....D4
Caldwell 795 ....F7
Calvin 400 ....E6
Camden on Gauley 171 .....E6
Cameron 1,177 ....E3
Camp Creek 200 ....D7
Canebrake 300 ....C8
Canvas 300 ....E6
Capon Bridge 192 ....K4
Capon Springs 580 ....K4
Carbon 300 ....D6
Caretta 650 ....C8
Cass 148 ....G6
Cassity 150 ....F5
Cassville 1,458 ....F3
Catawba 186 ....F3
Cedar Grove 1,213 ....D6
Center Point 250 ....E4
Central Station 200 ....E4
Ceredo 1,916 ....B6
Chapmanville 1,110 ....B7
Charles Town▲ 3,122 ....L4
Charleston (cap.)▲ 57,287 ...C6
Charmco 800 ....E6
Chattaroy 1,182 ....C7
Chesapeake 1,896 ....C6
Chester 2,905 ....E1
Christian 200 ....C7
Cinco 500 ....D6
Circleville 180 ....H5
Clarksburg▲ 18,059 ....F4
Clay▲ 592 ....D6
Clear Creek 300 ....D7
Clearview 622 ....E2
Clendenin 1,203 ....D5
Clifton 325 ....B5
Clifton Mills 136 ....G3
Clifty 250 ....E6
Clinton 350 ....E2
Clio 300 ....D5
Clothier 900 ....C7
Clover 350 ....D5
Clover Lick 250 ....F6
Coal City 1,876 ....D7
Coal Fork 2,100 ....D6
Coalton 277 ....G5
Coalwood 650 ....C8
Coburn 230 ....F3
Colcord 600 ....D7
Colliers 864 ....E2
Colored Hill 900 ....D8
Core 250 ....F3
Corinne 900 ....D7
Corinth 195 ....H4
Costa 250 ....D6
Cottageville 300 ....C5
Cove Gap 650 ....B6
Cowen 549 ....E6
Coxs Mills 275 ....E4
Craigsville 1,955 ....E6
Cranberry 315 ....D7
Crawley 395 ....E7
Crum 500 ....B7
Crystal 150 ....D8
Cucumber 274 ....C8
Culloden 2,907 ....C6
Cyclone 500 ....C7
Dallas 450 ....E2
Daniels 1,714 ....D7
Danville 595 ....C6
Darkesville 150 ....L4
Davis 799 ....H4
Davisville 200 ....C4
Davy 403 ....C8
Dawes 800 ....D6
Dawson 300 ....E7
Decota 800 ....D6
Deerwalk 150 ....D4
Delbarton 705 ....B7
Dellslow 300 ....F3
Diana 300 ....F5
Dickson 200 ....B6
Dille 300 ....E6
Dingess 600 ....B7
Dixie 985 ....D6
Dola 200 ....E4
Dorothy 400 ....D7
Dry Creek 441 ....D7
Dryfork 425 ....H4
Dunbar 8,697 ....C6
Dunlow 169 ....B6
Dunmore 280 ....G6
Durbin 278 ....G5
East Bank 892 ....D6

East Lynn 150 ....B6
East View 1,222 ....F4
Eastgulf 300 ....D7
Eccles 1,162 ....D7
Eckman 750 ....C8
Edgarton 415 ....B7
Edray 175 ....F6
Egeria 150 ....E7
Elbert 400 ....C8
Eleanor 1,256 ....C5
Elizabeth▲ 900 ....D4
Elk Garden 261 ....H4
Elkhorn 150 ....D8
Elkins▲ 7,420 ....G5
Elkridge 500 ....D6
Elkview 1,047 ....C6
Ellenboro 453 ....F5
Elton 200 ....E7
English 500 ....C8
Enterprise 1,058 ....F4
Erbacon 350 ....E6
Eskdale 400 ....D6
Ethel 450 ....C7
Evans 400 ....C5
Everettville 175 ....F3
Fairmont 20,210 ....F4
Fairplain 200 ....C5
Fairview 513 ....F3
Falling Spring (Renick) 191 ...F6
Falling Waters 130 ....L3
Farmington 414 ....F3
Fayetteville▲ 2,182 ....D6
Fenwick 500 ....E6
Ferguson 150 ....B6
Ferrellsburg 300 ....B6
Filbert 130 ....D8
Fireco 200 ....D7
Fisher 500 ....H4
Flat Top 550 ....D7
Flatwoods 324 ....E5
Flemington 352 ....F4
Follansbee 3,339 ....E2
Folsom 360 ....E4
Forest Hill 314 ....E7
Fort Ashby 1,288 ....J4
Fort Gay 852 ....A6
Fort Seybert 200 ....H5
Fort Spring 250 ....E7
Foster 500 ....C6
Four States 500 ....F4
Frametown 150 ....E5
Frankford 200 ....F6
Franklin▲ 914 ....H5
Fraziers Bottom 250 ....B5
French Creek 200 ....F5
Friendly 146 ....D3
Gallipolis Ferry 325 ....B5
Galloway 500 ....F4
Gandeeville 150 ....D5
Gap Mills 300 ....F7
Gary 1,355 ....C8
Gassaway 946 ....E5
Gauley Bridge 691 ....D6
Gauley Mills 165 ....E6
Gay 300 ....C5
Gerrardstown 240 ....K4
Ghent 500 ....D7
Giatto 400 ....D7
Gilbert 456 ....C7
Gilboa 500 ....E6
Glady 175 ....G5
Glasgow 906 ....D6
Glen 175 ....D6
Glen Dale 1,612 ....E3
Glen Daniel 300 ....D7
Glen Ferris 200 ....D6
Glen Hedrick (Beaver) D7
Glen Jean D7
Glen Rogers 500 ....D7
Glen White 300 ....D7
Glengary 250 ....K4
Glenhayes 175 ....A6
Glenville▲ 1,923 ....E5
Glenwood 400 ....B5
Gordon 300 ....C7
Grafton▲ 5,524 ....G4
Grant Town 694 ....F4
Grantsville▲ 671 ....D5
Granville 798 ....F3
Great Cacapon 750 ....K3
Green Bank 115 ....G6
Green Sulphur Springs 225 ...E7
Greenview 250 ....C6
Greenwood 750 ....E4
Griffithsville 300 ....B6
Grimms Landing 350 ....B5
Guardian 175 ....F5
Hacker Valley 440 ....F5
Halltown 375 ....L4
Hambleton 265 ....G4
Hamlin▲ 1,030 ....B6
Hampden 300 ....C7
Hancock 175 ....K3
Handley 334 ....D6
Hanover 300 ....C7
Harman 128 ....G5

(continued on following page)

DOMINANT LAND USE

- Dairy, General Farming
- General Farming, Livestock, Dairy
- General Farming, Livestock, Tobacco
- General Farming, Livestock, Fruit, Tobacco
- Fruit and Mixed Farming
- Forests

MAJOR MINERAL OCCURRENCES

- C   Coal
- Cl   Clay
- G   Natural Gas
- Ls   Limestone
- Na   Salt
- O   Petroleum
- ⚡   Water Power
- ▨   Major Industrial Areas

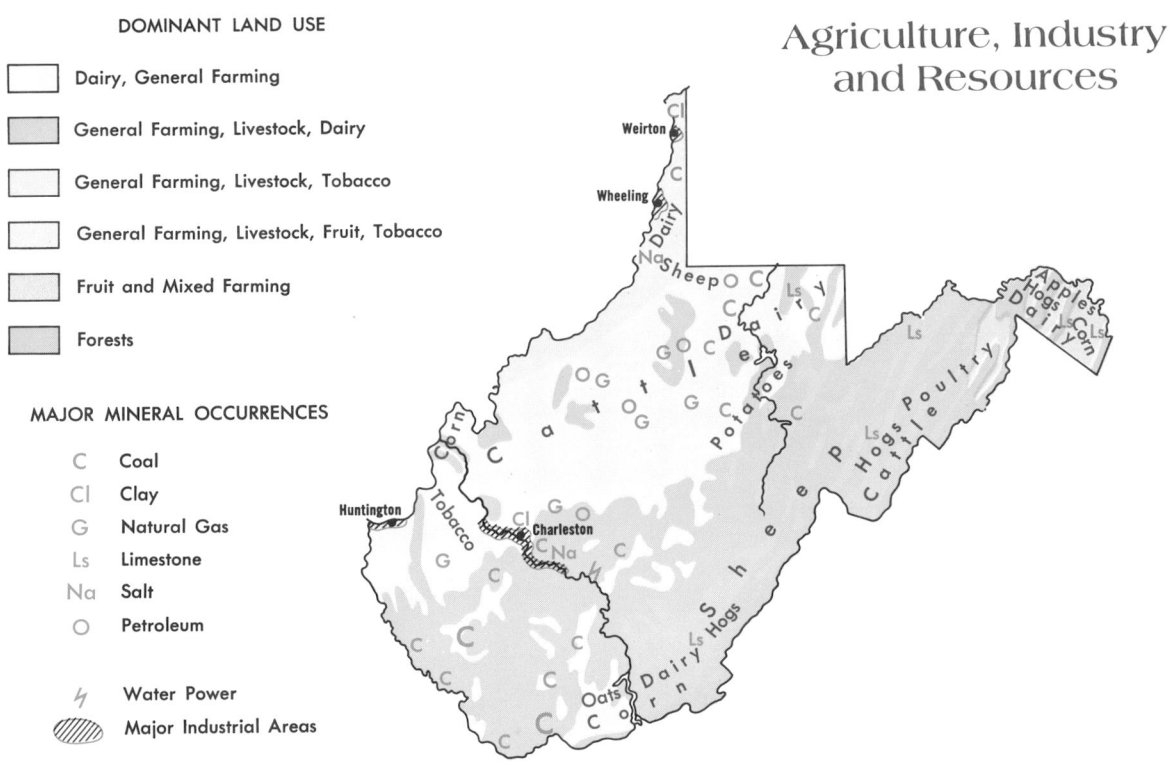

Agriculture, Industry and Resources

Harmony 600	D5	
Harper 400	D7	
Harpers Ferry 308	L4	
Harrisville▲ 1,839	E4	
Hartford 487	C4	
Harts 2,332	B6	
Harvey 300	D7	
Havaco 350	C8	
Heaters 440	E5	
Hedgesville 227	K3	
Helvetia 130	F5	
Hemphill 700	C8	
Henderson 549	B5	
Hendricks 303	G4	
Henlawson 900	B7	
Hepzibah 600	F4	
Herndon 500	D7	
Hico 750	D6	
Hillsboro 188	F6	
Hinton 3,433	E7	
Hodgesville 200	F4	
Holcomb 200	E6	
Holden 1,246	B7	
Hollywood 150	F7	
Hominy Falls 175	E6	
Hookersville 250	E6	
Horse Shoe Run 500	G4	
Howesville 600	G4	
Hubball 145	B6	
Hundred 386	E3	
Huntington▲ 54,844	A6	
Hurricane 4,461	C6	
Hutchinson 285	F4	
Huttonsville 211	G5	
Iaeger 551	C8	
Independence 200	G4	
Indian Mills 150	E7	
Indore 300	D6	
Inwood 1,360	K4	
Itmann 600	D7	
Ivanhoe 200	F5	
Ivydale 800	D5	
Jacksonburg 400	E3	
Jane Lew 439	F4	
Jarvisville 250	F4	
Jeffrey 900	C7	
Jenkinjones 750	D8	
Jesse 400	C7	
Jodie 440	D6	
Jumping Branch 700	E7	
Junior 542	G5	
Justice 600	C7	
Kearneysville 250	L4	
Kegley 900	D8	
Keith 175	C6	
Kellysville 165	E8	
Kenna 150	C5	
Kenova 3,748	A6	
Kentuck 200	C5	
Kermit 342	B7	
Keyser▲ 5,870	J4	
Keystone 627	D8	
Kieffer 135	E7	
Kilsyth 200	D7	
Kimball 550	C8	
Kingston 189	D7	
Kingwood▲ 3,243	G4	
Kirk 400	B7	
Kistler 200	C7	
Kopperston 700	C7	
Lahmansville 200	H4	
Lanark 559	D7	
Landisburg 250	E7	
Landville 400	C7	
Lavalette 600	B6	
Layland 500	E7	
Layopolis (Sand Fork)	E5	
Leet 175	B6	
Left Hand 700	D5	
Leivasy 200	E6	
Lenore 800	B7	
Leon 145	C5	
Lerona 550	D8	
Lesage 600	B5	
Leslie 350	E6	
Lester 420	D7	
Letart 350	C5	
Levels 180	J4	
Lewisburg▲ 3,598	E7	
Liberty 150	C5	
Lindside 225	E8	
Linn 165	E4	
Little Birch 400	E5	
Littleton 198	F3	
Lizemores 400	D6	
Lochgelly 250	D6	
Lockney 190	E5	
Lockwood 300	D6	
Logan▲ 2,206	B7	
Lookout 200	E6	
Lorado 400	C7	
Lorentz 200	F4	
Lost City 130	J5	
Lost Creek 413	F4	
Lost River 500	J5	
Lowell 140	E7	
Lubeck 1,579	C4	
Lumberport 1,014	F4	
Lundale 525	C7	
Maben 450	D7	
Mabie 550	F5	
Mabscott 1,543	D7	
Macfarlan 436	D4	
Madison▲ 3,051	C6	
Maidsville 500	F3	
Malden 900	C6	
Mallory 1,126	C7	
Mammoth 563	D6	
Man 914	C7	
Mannington 2,184	F3	
Marfrance 225	E6	
Marlinton▲ 1,148	F6	
Marmet 1,879	C6	
Martinsburg▲ 14,073	K4	
Mason 1,053	B4	
Masontown 737	G3	
Matewan 619	B7	
Matoaka 366	D8	
Maybeury 300	D8	
Maysel 350	D5	
Maysville 150	H4	
McCorkle 300	C6	
McDowell 500	D8	
McMechen 2,130	E3	
McWhorter 150	F4	
Meador 225	B7	
Meadow Bridge 325	E7	
Meadow Creek 300	E7	
Meadowbrook 500	F4	
Merrimac 140	B7	
Metz 150	F3	
Middlebourne▲ 922	E3	
Middleway 350	K4	
Midkiff 650	B6	
Mill Creek 685	G5	
Mill Point 148	F6	
Millstone 850	D5	
Millwood 800	C5	
Milton 2,242	B6	
Minden 800	D7	
Mineralwells 1,698	C4	
Mingo 350	F5	
Minnora 500	D5	
Missouri Branch 250	A7	
Mitchell Heights 265	B7	
Moatsville 150	G4	
Monaville 950	B7	
Monclo 242	C7	
Monomgah 1,132	F4	
Montana Mines 200	F3	
Montcoal 150	D7	
Monterville 250	F5	
Montgomery 2,449	D6	
Montrose 140	G4	
Moorefield▲ 2,148	J4	
Morgansville 164	E4	
Morgantown▲ 25,879	F3	
Morrisvale 450	C6	
Moundsville▲ 10,753	E3	
Mount Alto 200	C5	
Mount Carbon 450	D7	
Mount Clare 950	F4	
Mount Gay 4,366	C7	
Mount Hope 1,573	D7	
Mount Lookout 500	E6	
Mount Nebo 535	E6	
Mount Storm 500	H4	
Mount Zion 350	D5	
Mountain 200	E4	
Mud 143	C6	
Mullens 2,006	D7	
Murphytown 600	D4	
Nallen 250	E6	
Napier 158	E5	
Naugatuck 500	B7	
Nebo 200	D5	
Nellis 600	C6	
Neola 300	F7	
Nettie 500	E6	
New Cumberland▲ 1,363	E2	
New England 335	C4	
New Haven 1,632	C5	
New Manchester 800	E1	
New Martinsville▲ 6,705	E3	
Newburg 378	G4	
Newell 1,724	E1	
Newhall 400	C8	
Newton 390	D5	
Newville 160	E5	
Nitro 6,851	C6	
Nolan 250	B7	
North Hills 849	D4	
Northfork 656	D8	
Norton 400	G5	
Nutter Fort 1,819	F4	
Oak Hill 6,812	D6	
Oakvale 165	D8	
Oceana 1,791	C7	
Odd 500	D7	
Ohley 450	D6	
Omar 900	C7	
Ona 200	B6	
Onego 400	H5	
Orgas 500	C6	
Orlando 700	E5	
Orleans Cross Roads 150	K3	
Orma 183	D5	
Osage 183	F3	
Packsville 225	C7	
Paden City 2,862	D3	
Page 600	D6	
Panther 450	C8	
Parkersburg▲ 33,862	D4	
Parsons▲ 1,453	G4	
Patterson Creek 157	J3	
Paw Paw 538	K3	
Pax 167	D7	
Pecks Mill 350	B7	
Pemberton 300	D7	
Pence Springs 300	E7	
Pennsboro 1,282	E4	
Pentress 250	F3	
Petersburg▲ 2,360	H5	
Peterstown 550	E8	
Peytona 175	C6	
Philippi▲ 3,132	G4	
Pickaway 225	E7	
Pickens 240	F5	
Pie 250	B7	
Piedmont 1,094	H4	
Pinch 2,695	D6	
Pine Grove 701	E3	
Pineville▲ 865	C7	
Pliny 900	B5	
Poca 1,124	C6	
Pocatalico 2,420	C6	
Point Pleasant▲ 4,996	B5	
Points 250	J4	
Powellton 1,905	D6	
Powhatan 400	D8	
Pratt 640	D6	
Premier 400	C8	
Prichard 500	A6	
Princeton▲ 7,043	D8	
Procious 200	D5	
Proctor 350	E3	
Pruntytown 145	F4	
Pullman 109	D4	
Purgitsville 450	J4	
Quick 400	D6	
Quincy 150	C6	
Quinwood 559	E6	
Rachel 550	F3	
Racine 725	C6	
Radnor 300	A6	
Rainelle 1,681	E7	
Raleigh 900	D7	
Ramage 350	C7	
Ranger 300	B6	
Ranson 2,890	L4	
Ravencliff 350	D7	
Ravenswood 4,189	C5	
Raymond City 400	C6	
Reader 950	E3	
Red House 600	C5	
Red Jacket 760	B7	
Redstar 200	D7	
Reedsville 482	G3	
Reedy 271	D5	
Renick 200	F6	
Replete 200	F5	
Rhodell 221	D7	
Richwood 2,808	F6	
Ridgeley 779	J3	
Ridgeway 200	K4	
Rio 140	J4	
Ripley▲ 3,023	C5	
Rippon 500	L4	
Rivesville 1,064	F3	
Robertsburg 140	C5	
Rock Cave 400	F5	
Roderfield 900	C8	
Romney▲ 1,966	J4	
Ronceverte 1,754	F7	
Rosedale 400	E5	
Rossmore 200	C7	
Rowlesburg 648	G4	
Runa 150	E6	
Rupert 1,104	E7	
Russellville 280	E6	
Saint Albans 11,194	C6	
Saint George 150	F4	
Saint Marys▲ 2,148	D4	
Salem 2,063	E4	
Salt Rock 350	B6	
Sand Fork 196	E5	
Sandstone 300	E7	
Sandyville 500	C5	
Saulsville 250	C7	
Scarbo 800	D7	
Selwyn 500	B7	
Seth 950	C6	
Shanghai 200	K4	
Shanks 500	J4	
Sharon 450	D6	
Sharples 250	C7	
Shenandoah Junction 600	L4	
Shepherdstown 1,287	L4	
Sheridan 160	B6	
Sherrard 400	E3	
Shinnston 2,543	F4	
Shirley 275	E4	
Shoals 150	B6	
Shock 200	D5	
Silverton 250	C5	
Simpson 250	F4	
Sinks Grove 156	F7	
Sissonville 4,290	C5	
Sistersville 1,797	D3	
Slab Fork 210	D7	
Slaneville 250	K4	
Smithburg 130	E4	
Smithers 1,162	D6	
Smithfield 205	E4	
Smithville 200	D4	
Smoot 300	E7	
Sophia 1,182	D7	
South Charleston 13,645	C6	
Spanishburg 550	D8	
Spencer▲ 2,279	D5	
Sprigg 250	B7	
Springfield 250	J4	
Spurlockville 250	B6	
Squire 900	C8	
Star City 1,251	F3	
Statts Mills 400	C5	
Stickney 150	D7	
Stirrat 250	C7	
Stonewood 1,996	F4	
Stotesbury 199	D7	
Strange Creek 175	E5	
Sullivan 700	B7	
Summersville▲ 2,906	E6	
Summit Point 455	K4	
Surveyor 300	D7	
Sutton▲ 939	E5	
Swiss 500	E6	
Switzer 1,004	B7	
Sylvester 191	C6	
Talcott 800	E7	
Tallmansville 140	F5	
Tanner 375	E5	
Teays 200	B6	
Terra Alta 1,713	H4	
Tesla 300	E5	
Thacker 525	B7	
Thomas 573	H4	
Thornton 200	G4	
Thorpe 600	D8	
Three Churches 350	J4	
Thurmond 39	D7	
Tioga 825	E6	
Triadelphia 835	E2	
Troy 110	E4	
Tunnelton 331	G4	
Turtle Creek 566	C6	
Uneeda 700	C6	
Unger 300	K4	
Union▲ 566	E7	
Upper Tract 155	H5	
Upperglade 750	F6	
Vadis 130	E4	
Valley Bend 950	F5	
Valley Grove 569	E2	
Valley Head 900	G5	
Van 800	C7	
Varney 750	B7	
Vaughan 375	D6	
Verdunville 950	B7	
Victor 500	D6	
Vienna 10,862	D4	
Vivian 800	D8	
Vulcan 130	B7	
Wadestown 300	F3	
Waiteville 230	F8	
Walkersville 135	F5	
Wallace 325	E4	
Wallback 150	D5	
Walton 550	D5	
Wana 150	F3	
War 1,081	C8	
Ward 850	D6	
Wardensville 140	J4	
Washington 300	C4	
Washington Lands 400	E3	
Waverly 500	D4	
Wayne▲ 1,128	B6	
Webster Springs▲ 674	F6	
Weirton 22,124	E2	
Welch▲ 3,028	C8	
Wellsburg▲ 3,385	E2	
West Columbia 245	B5	
West Hamlin 423	B6	
West Liberty 1,434	E2	
West Logan 524	C7	
West Milford 519	F4	
West Union▲ 830	E4	
Weston▲ 4,994	F4	
Westover 4,201	F3	
Wharncliffe 900	C7	
Wharton 450	C7	
Wheeling▲ 34,882	E2	
White Sulphur Springs 2,779	F7	
Whites Creek 500	A6	
Whitesville 486	C6	
Whitmer 400	G5	
Widen 230	E6	
Wiley Ford 1,224	J3	
Wileyville 135	E3	
Wilkinson 975	B7	
Williamsburg 350	F7	
Williamson▲ 4,154	B7	
Williamstown 2,774		
Wilsonburg 350		
Wilsondale 250		
Windsor Heights 800		
Winfield▲ 1,164		
Winifrede 750		
Winona 250		
Wolf Pen 175		
Wolf Summit 750		
Womelsdorf (Coalton) 277		
Woodlands 200		
Woodville 300		
Worthington 233		
Yawkey 985		
Yellow Spring 280		
Yolyn 400		

OTHER FEATURES

Big Sandy (riv.)	H5
Bluestone (lake)	
Buckhannon (riv.)	
Cacapon (riv.)	
Cheat (riv.)	
Cherry (riv.)	
Chesapeake and Ohio Canal Nat'l Hist. Park	
Clear Fork, Guyandotte (riv.)	
Coal (riv.)	
Dry Fork (riv.)	
Dry Fork (riv.)	
East Lynn (lake)	
Elk (riv.)	
Fish (creek)	
Gauley (riv.)	
Greenbrier (riv.)	
Guyandotte (riv.)	
Harpers Ferry Nat'l Hist. Park	
Hughes (riv.)	
Kanawha (riv.)	
Little Kanawha (riv.)	
Meadow (riv.)	
Mill (creek)	
Monongahela (riv.)	
Mount Storm (lake)	
Mud (riv.)	
New (riv.)	
North (riv.)	
Ohio (riv.)	
Patterson (creek)	
Pigeon (creek)	
Pocatalico (riv.)	
Pond Fork (riv.)	
Potomac (riv.)	
Potts (creek)	
Reedy (creek)	
Shavers Fork (riv.)	
Shenandoah (riv.)	
Spruce Knob (mt.)	
Spruce Knob-Seneca Rocks Nat'l Rec. Area	
Stony (riv.)	
Summersville (lake)	
Sutton (lake)	
Tug Fork (riv.)	
Twelvepole (creek)	
Tygart (lake)	
Tygart Valley (riv.)	
West Fork (riv.)	
Williams (riv.)	

▲County seat

WISCONSIN
1848

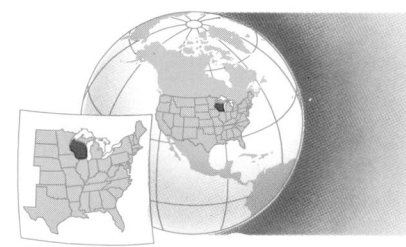

AREA   56.153 sq. mi. (145,436 sq. km.)
POPULATION   4,906,745
CAPITAL   Madison
LARGEST CITY   Milwaukee
HIGHEST POINT   Timms Hill 1,951 ft. (595 m.)
SETTLED IN   1670
ADMITTED TO UNION   May 29, 1848
POPULAR NAME   Badger State
STATE FLOWER   Wood Violet
STATE BIRD   Robin

COUNTIES

Adams 15,682 ....G7
Ashland 16,307 ....E3
Barron 40,750 ....C5
Bayfield 14,008 ....D3
Brown 194,594 ....L7
Buffalo 13,584 ....C6
Burnett 13,084 ....B4
Calumet 34,291 ....K7
Chippewa 52,360 ....D5
Clark 31,647 ....D6
Columbia 45,088 ....H9
Crawford 15,940 ....E9
Dane 367,085 ....H9
Dodge 76,559 ....J9
Door 25,690 ....M6
Douglas 41,758 ....C3
Dunn 35,909 ....C6
Eau Claire 85,183 ....D6
Florence 4,590 ....K4
Fond du Lac 90,083 ......K8
Forest 8,776 ....J4
Grant 49,264 ....E10
Green 30,339 ....G10
Green Lake 18,651 ....H8
Iowa 20,150 ....F9
Iron 6,153 ....F9
Jackson 16,588 ....F3
Jefferson 67,783 ....J9
Juneau 21,650 ....F8
Kenosha 128,181 ....K10
Kewaunee 18,878 ....L6
La Crosse 97,904 ....D8
Lafayette 16,076 ....F10
Langlade 19,505 ....H5
Lincoln 26,993 ....G5
Manitowoc 80,421 ....L7
Marathon 115,400 ....G6
Marinette 40,548 ....K5
Marquette 12,321 ....H8
Menominee 3,890 ....J5
Milwaukee 959,275 ......L9
Monroe 36,633 ....E8
Oconto 30,226 ....K6
Oneida 31,679 ....G4
Outagamie 140,510 ......K7
Ozaukee 72,831 ....L9
Pepin 7,107 ....C6
Pierce 32,765 ....B6
Polk 34,773 ....B5
Portage 61,405 ....G6
Price 15,600 ....F4
Racine 175,034 ....K10
Richland 17,521 ....F9
Rock 139,510 ....H10
Rusk 15,079 ....D5
Saint Croix 43,262 ....B5
Sauk 46,975 ....G8
Sawyer 14,181 ....D4
Shawano 37,157 ....J6
Sheboygan 103,877 ......L8
Taylor 18,901 ....E5
Trempealeau 25,263 .....D7
Vernon 25,617 ....E8
Vilas 17,707 ....G3
Walworth 75,000 ....J10
Washburn 13,772 ....C4
Washington 95,328 ......K9
Waukesha 304,715 ......K9
Waupaca 46,104 ....J6
Waushara 19,385 ....H7
Winnebago 140,320 ......J8
Wood 73,605 ....F7

CITIES and TOWNS

Abbotsford 1,916 ....F6
Abrams 300 ....L6
Adams 1,715 ....G8
Adell 510 ....L8
Afton 225 ....H10
Albany 1,140 ....G10
Albion 300 ....H10
Algoma 3,353 ....M6
Allenton 915 ....K9
Allouez 14,431 ....L7
Alma▲ 790 ....C7
Alma Center 416 ....E7
Almena 625 ....B5
Almond 455 ....G7
Alto 235 ....J8
Altoona 5,889 ....D6
Alvin 160 ....J4
Amberg 875 ....K5
Amery 2,657 ....B5
Amherst 792 ....H7
Amherst Junction 269 ....H7
Angelica 200 ....K6
Angelo 100 ....E3
Aniwa 249 ....H6
Antigo▲ 8,276 ....H5
Appleton▲ 65,695 ....J7
Arbor Vitae 900 ....G4
Arcadia 2,166 ....D7
Arena 525 ....G9

Argonne 600 ....G9
Argyle 798 ....G10
Arkansaw 400 ....B6
Arlington 440 ....H9
Armstrong Creek 615 ....K4
Arpin 312 ....G6
Ashippun 750 ....H1
Ashland▲ 8,695 ....E2
Ashwaubenon 16,376 ....K7
Athens 951 ....G5
Auburndale 665 ....F6
Augusta 1,510 ....D6
Auroraville 250 ....H7
Avoca 474 ....F9
Avon 120 ....H10
Babcock 250 ....F7
Bagley 306 ....D10
Baileys Harbor 250 ......M5
Baldwin 2,022 ....B6
Balsam Lake▲ 792 ....B5
Bancroft 355 ....G7
Bangor 1,076 ....E8
Baraboo▲ 9,203 ....G9
Barnes 225 ....D3
Barneveld 660 ....F10
Barron▲ 2,986 ....C5
Barronett 575 ....B4
Batavia 125 ....K8
Bay City 578 ....B6
Bayfield 686 ....E2
Bayside▲ M1
Bear Creek 418 ....J6
Beaver 100 ....K5
Beaver Dam 14,196 ......J9
Beetown 150 ....E10
Beldenville 175 ....A6
Belgium 928 ....L8
Bell Center 127 ....E9
Belleville 1,456 ....G10
Belmont 823 ....F10
Beloit 35,573 ....H10
Bennett 350 ....C3
Benton 898 ....F10
Berlin 5,371 ....H8
Bethel 210 ....F6
Bevent 200 ....H6
Big Bend 1,299 ....K2
Birchwood 443 ....C4
Birnamwood 693 ....H6
Biron 794 ....G7
Black Creek 1,152 ....K7
Black Earth 1,248 ....G9
Black River Falls▲ 3,490 .E7
Blackwell 550 ....K4
Blair 1,126 ....D7
Blanchardville 802 .....G10
Bloom City 167 ....E8
Bloomer 3,085 ....D5
Bloomington 776 ......E10
Blue Mounds 446 ....G9
Blue River 438 ....E9
Boardman 100 ....A5
Boaz 131 ....E9
Bohners Lake 1,553 ....K10
Bonduel 1,210 ....K6
Boscobel 2,706 ....E9
Boulder Junction 780 ...H3
Bowler 279 ....J6
Boyceville 913 ....C5
Boyd 683 ....E6
Brackett 150 ....D6
Bradley 100 ....G4
Branch 300 ....L7
Brandon 872 ....J8
Brantwood 500 ....F4
Bridgeport 250 ....D9
Briggsville 250 ....H8
Brighton 100 ....K3
Brill 200 ....C4
Brillion 2,840 ....L7
Brodhead 3,165 ....G10
Brokaw 224 ....G5
Brookfield 35,184 ....K1
Brooklyn 789 ....H10
Brooks 103 ....G8
Brothertown 100 ....K7
Brown Deer 12,236 ......L1
Brown's Lake 1,725 .....K3
Brownsville 415 ....J8
Browntown 256 ....G10
Bruce 844 ....D5
Brule 335 ....C2
Brussels 500 ....L6
Buffalo 915 ....C7
Burlington 8,855 ....K10
Burnett 260 ....J9
Butler 2,079 ....K1
Butte Des Morts J7
Butternut 416 ....E3

Cable 227 ....D3
Cadott 1,328 ....D6
Caldwell 101 ....J2
Caledonia 100 ....L2
Cambria 768 ....H8
Cambridge 963 ....H9
Cameron 1,273 ....C5

Camp Douglas 512 ......F8
Camp Lake 2,291 ....K10
Campbellsport 1,732 .....K8
Canton 100 ....C5
Caroline 450 ....J6
Carter 100 ....J5
Cascade 620 ....K8
Casco 544 ....L6
Cashton 780 ....E8
Cassville 1,144 ....E10
Cataract 200 ....E7
Catawba 178 ....F8
Cazenovia 288 ....F8
Cecil 373 ....K6
Cedar Grove 1,521 ......L8
Cedarburg 9,895 ....L9
Centuria 790 ....A5
Chaseburg 365 ....D8
Chelsea 120 ....E5
Chenequa 601 ....J1
Chetek 1,953 ....C5
Chili 185 ....F6
Chilton▲ 3,240 ....K7
Chippewa Falls▲ 12,727 .D6
City Point 110 ....F7
Clam Lake 140 ....E3
Clayton 450 ....B5
Clear Lake 932 ....B5
Clearwater Lake 200 ....H4
Cleveland 1,398 ....L8
Clinton 1,849 ....J10
Clintonville 4,351 ....J6
Clyman 370 ....J9
Cobb 440 ....F10
Cochrane 475 ....C7
Colby 1,532 ....F6
Coleman 839 ....L5
Colfax 1,110 ....C6
Coloma 383 ....H7
Columbus 4,093 ....H9
Combined Locks 2,190 ...K7
Commonwealth 240 .....K4
Como 1,353 ....K10
Comstock 160 ....C5
Concord 200 ....H1
Conover 480 ....H3
Conrath 92 ....E5
Coon Valley 817 ....E8
Cornell 1,541 ....D5
Cornucopia 250 ....D2
Couderay 92 ....D4
Crandon▲ 1,958 ....H4
Cream 120 ....C7
Crivitz 996 ....L5
Cross Plains 2,098 ......G9
Cuba City 2,024 ....F10
Cudahy 18,659 ....M2
Cumberland 2,163 ......C4
Curtiss 173 ....F6
Cushing 150 ....A4
Cylon 100 ....B5
Dale 410 ....J7
Dallas 452 ....C5
Dalton 300 ....H8
Danbury 350 ....B3
Dane 621 ....G9
Darien 1,158 ....J10
Darlington▲ 2,235 .....F10
De Forest 4,882 ....H9
De Pere 16,569 ....K7
De Soto 326 ....D9
Deer Park 237 ....B5
Deerfield 1,617 ....H9
Delafield 5,347 ....J1
Delavan 6,073 ....J10
Delavan Lake 2,177 ....J10
Dellwood 120 ....G7
Denmark 1,612 ....L7
Dexterville 100 ....F7
Diamond Bluff 100 .....A6
Dickeyville 862 ....E10
Dodge 185 ....D7
Dodgeville▲ 3,882 ....F10
Dorchester 697 ....F5
Dousman 1,277 ....J1
Downing 250 ....B5
Downsville 200 ....C6
Doylestown 316 ....H9
Draper 125 ....E4
Dresser 614 ....A5
Drummond 200 ....D3
Dunbar 106 ....K4
Durand▲ 2,003 ....C6
Dyckesville 300 ....L6
Eagle 1,182 ....H2
Eagle River▲ 1,374 .....H4
East Troy 2,664 ....J2
Eastman 369 ....D9
Easton 130 ....G8
Eau Claire▲ 56,856 .....D6
Eden 610 ....K8
Edgar 1,318 ....G6
Edgerton 4,254 ....H10
Egg Harbor 183 ....M5
Eland 247 ....H6
Elcho 500 ....H5

Elderon 175 ....H6
Eldorado 200 ....J8
Eleva 491 ....D6
Elk Mound 765 ....C6
Elkhart Lake 1,019 ......L8
Elkhorn▲ 5,337 ....J10
Ellison Bay 112 ....M5
Ellsworth▲ 2,706 ......A6
Elm Grove 6,261 ....K1
Elmwood 775 ....B6
Elmwood Park 534 ......M3
Elroy 1,533 ....F8
Elton 150 ....J5
Embarrass 461 ....J6
Emerald 128 ....B5
Endeavor 316 ....G8
Ephraim 261 ....M5
Ettrick 461 ....D7
Evansville 3,174 ....H10
Exeland 180 ....D4
Fair Water 310 ....J8
Fairchild 504 ....D6
Fall Creek 1,034 ....D6
Fall River 842 ....H9

Fence 200 ....K4
Fennimore 2,378 ....E9
Fenwood 214 ....F6
Ferryville 154 ....D9
Fifield 310 ....F4
Fish Creek 119 ....M5
Florence▲ 780 ....K4
Fond du Lac▲ 37,757 ....K8
Fontana 1,635 ....J10
Footville 764 ....H10
Forest Junction 140 ....K7
Forestville 470 ....L6
Fort Atkinson 10,227 ...J10
Fountain City 938 ......C7
Fox Lake 1,269 ....J8
Fox Point 7,238 ....M1
Foxboro 360 ....B2
Francis Creek 562 ......L7
Franklin 21,855 ....L2
Franksville 375 ....M3
Frederic 1,124 ....B4
Fredonia 1,558 ....L8
Fremont 632 ....J7
Friendship▲ 728 ....G8

Friesland 271 ....H8
Galesville 1,278 ....D7
Galloway 200 ....H6
Gays Mills 578 ....E9
Genesee 375 ....J2
Genesee Depot 350 ....J2
Genoa 266 ....D8
Genoa City 1,277 .....K11
Germantown 13,658 .....K1
Gibbsville 408 ....L8
Gillett 1,303 ....K6
Gilman 412 ....E5
Gilmanton 300 ....C7
Gleason 200 ....G5
Glen Flora 108 ....E4
Glen Haven 160 ....E10
Glenbeulah 386 ....L8
Glendale 14,088 ....M1
Glenwood City 1,026 ....B5
Glidden 940 ....E3
Goodman 875 ....K4
Gordon 600 ....C3
Gotham 250 ....F9
Grafton 9,340 ....L9

Grand Marsh 725 ....G8
Grand View 447 ....D3
Granton 379 ....E6
Grantsburg▲ 1,144 .....A4
Gratiot 207 ....F10
Green Bay▲ 96,466 .....K6
Green Lake▲ 1,064 .....H8
Green Valley 104 ....K6
Greendale 15,128 ......L2
Greenfield 33,403 ......L2
Greenleaf 300 ....L7
Greenville 900 ....J7
Greenwood 969 ....E6
Gresham 515 ....J6
Gurney 145 ....F3
Hager City 110 ....A6
Hales Corners 7,623 ....K2
Hallie D6
Hamburg 170 ....G5
Hammond 1,097 ....A6
Hancock 382 ....G7
Hartford 8,188 ....K9
Hartland 6,906 ....J1
Hatfield 500 ....E7

(continued on following page)

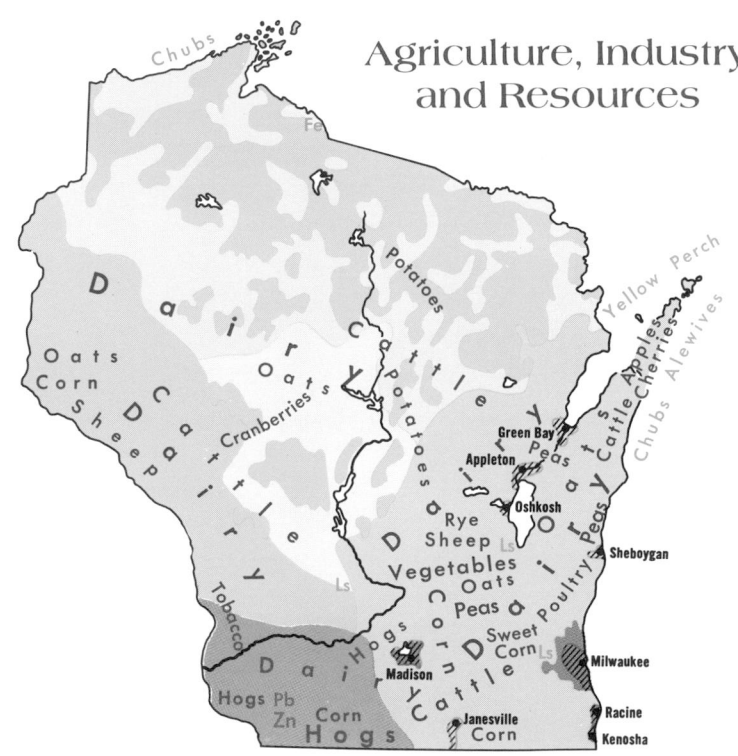

Agriculture, Industry and Resources

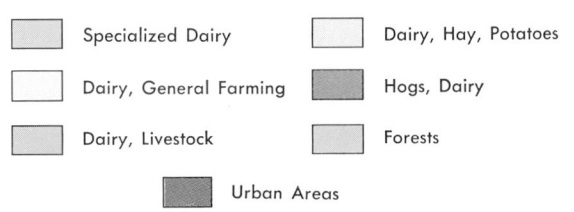

DOMINANT LAND USE

Specialized Dairy

Dairy, General Farming

Dairy, Livestock

Dairy, Hay, Potatoes

Hogs, Dairy

Forests

Urban Areas

MAJOR MINERAL OCCURRENCES

Fe Iron Ore   Pb Lead
Ls Limestone   Zn Zinc

 Major Industrial Areas

Hatley 295 ....H6
Haugen 305 ....C4
Hawkins 375 ....E4
Hawthorne 200 ....C3
Hayward▲ 1,897 ....D3
Hazel Green 1,171 ....F11
Hazelhurst 630 ....G4
Heafford Junction 110 ....G4
Hebron 450 ....J10
Helenville 300 ....J10
Hersey 125 ....B6
Hewitt 595 ....F6
High Bridge 525 ....E3
Highland 799 ....F9
Hilbert 1,211 ....K7
Hiles 350 ....J4
Hillsboro 1,288 ....F8
Hillsdale 160 ....C5
Hingham 250 ....K8
Hixton 345 ....E7
Holcombe 200 ....D5
Hollandale 256 ....G10
Holmen 3,220 ....D8
Holy Cross 150 ....L9
Honey Creek 300 ....J3
Horicon 3,873 ....J9
Hortonville 2,029 ....J7
Houlton 915 ....A5
Howard 9,874 ....K6
Howards Grove-Millersville 1,838 ....L8
Hubertus 600 ....K1
Hudson▲ 6,378 ....A6
Humbird 190 ....E6
Hurley▲ 1,782 ....F3
Hustisford 979 ....J9
Hustler 156 ....F8
Independence 1,041 ....D7
Ingram 91 ....E5
Iola 1,125 ....H6
Iron Belt 300 ....F3
Iron Ridge 887 ....K9
Iron River 878 ....D2
Ironton 200 ....F8
Ithaca 160 ....F9
Ixonia 525 ....H1
Jackson 2,486 ....K9
Jacksonport 150 ....M6
Janesville▲ 52,133 ....H10
Jefferson▲ 6,078 ....J10
Johnson Creek 1,259 ....J9
Juda 500 ....H10
Junction City 502 ....G6
Juneau▲ 2,157 ....J9
Kansasville 150 ....L3
Kaukauna 11,982 ....K7
Kekoskee 188 ....J8
Kellnersville 350 ....L7
Kempster 121 ....H5
Kendall 453 ....F8
Kennan 169 ....F5
Kenosha▲ 80,352 ....M3
Keshena 685 ....J6
Kewaskum 2,515 ....K8
Kewaunee▲ 2,750 ....M7
Kiel 2,910 ....L8
Kieler 800 ....E10
Kimberly 5,406 ....K7
King H7
Kingston 346 ....H8
Knapp 419 ....B6
Knowlton 127 ....G6
Kohler 1,817 ....L8
Krakow 345 ....K6
La Crosse▲ 51 003 ....D8
La Farge 766 ....E8
La Pointe 300 ....E2
La Valle 446 ....F8
Lac La Belle 258 ....H1
Lac du Flambeau 1,423 ....G4
Ladysmith▲ 3,938 ....D5
Lake Church 175 ....L9
Lake Delton 1,470 ....G8
Lake Geneva 5 979 ....K10
Lake Mills 4,143 ....H9
Lake Nebagamon 900 ....C3
Lake Tomahawk 600 ....H4
Lake Wazeecha 2,278 ....G7
Lake Wissota 2,175 ....D6
Lakewood 425 ....K5
Lamartine 190 ....J8
Lancaster▲ 4,192 ....E10
Land O'Lakes 786 ....H3
Lannon 950 ....K1
Lebanon 250 ....H1
Lena 590 ....K6
Leopolis 200 ....J6
Lewis 200 ....B4
Lily 125 ....J5
Lima Center 175 ....J10
Limeridge 152 ....F9
Linden 429 ....F10
Little Chute 9,207 ....K7
Little Suamico 190 ....L6
Livingston 576 ....E10
Lodi 2,093 ....G9
Loganville 228 ....F9
Lohrville 368 ....H7
Lomira 1,542 ....J8
London 317 ....H9
Lone Rock 641 ....F9
Long Lake 150 ....J4
Loretta 200 ....E4
Lowell 300 ....J9
Loyal 1,244 ....E6
Lublin 129 ....E5
Luck 1,022 ....B4
Luxemburg 1,151 ....L6
Lyndon Station 474 ....F8
Lynn 117 ....F6
Lynxville 153 ....D9
Lyons 550 ....K10
Madison (cap.)▲ 191,262 ....H9
Maiden Rock 146 ....B6
Manawa 1,169 ....J7
Manchester 160 ....J8
Manitowoc▲ 32,520 ....L7

Maple 596 ....C2
Maplewood 200 ....M6
Marathon 1,606 ....G6
Marengo 130 ....E3
Maribel 372 ....L7
Marinette▲ 11,843 ....L5
Marion 1,242 ....J6
Markesan 1,496 ....J8
Marquette 182 ....H8
Marshall 2,329 ....H9
Marshfield 19,291 ....F6
Martell 200 ....B6
Mason 102 ....D3
Mattoon 431 ....G5
Mauston▲ 3,439 ....F8
Mayville 4,374 ....K9
Mazomanie 1,377 ....G9
McFarland 5,232 ....H10
McNaughton 450 ....H4
Medford▲ 4,283 ....F5
Mellen 935 ....E3
Melrose 551 ....E7
Melvina 115 ....E8
Menasha 14,711 ....J7
Menomonee Falls 26,840 ....K1
Menomonie▲ 13,547 ....C6
Mequon 18,885 ....L1
Mercer V3
Merrill▲ 9,860 ....G5
Merrillan 553 ....E7
Merrimac 392 ....G9
Merton 1,199 ....K1
Middle Inlet 200 ....K5
Middleton 13,289 ....G9
Mikana 200 ....C4
Milan 153 ....F6
Milladore 314 ....G6
Millston 110 ....E7
Milltown 786 ....J10
Milton 4,434 ....J10
Milwaukee▲ 628,088 ....M1
Mindoro 200 ....D7
Mineral Point 2,428 ....F10
Minocqua 950 ....G4
Minong 521 ....C3
Mishicot 1,296 ....L7
Mondovi 2,491 ....C6
Monico 250 ....H4
Monona 8,637 ....G10
Monroe▲ 10,241 ....G10
Montello▲ 1,329 ....H8
Monterey 150 ....J1
Montfort 676 ....E10
Monticello 1,140 ....G10
Montreal 838 ....F3
Morrisonville 375 ....G9
Mosinee 3,820 ....G6
Mount Calvary 558 ....K8
Mount Hope 173 ....D10
Mount Horeb 4,182 ....G10
Mount Sterling 217 ....D9
Mount Vernon 138 ....G10
Mountain 250 ....K5
Mukwonago 4,457 ....J2
Muscoda 1,287 ....F9
Muskego 16,813 ....K2
Nashotah 567 ....J1
Navarino 140 ....J6
Necedah 743 ....F7
Neenah 23,219 ....J7
Neillsville▲ 2,680 ....E6
Nekoosa 2,557 ....G7
Nelson 388 ....C7
Nelsonville 171 ....H6
Neopit 615 ....J6
Neosho 658 ....J9
Neshkoro 384 ....H8
New Amsterdam 120 ....C8
New Auburn 485 ....D5
New Berlin 33,592 ....K2
New Franken 150 ....L6
New Glarus 1,899 ....G10
New Holstein 3,342 ....K8
New Lisbon 1,491 ....F8
New London 6,658 ....J7
New Richmond 5,106 ....A5
Newald 375 ....J4
Newburg 875 ....K9
Niagara 1,999 ....K4
Nichols 254 ....K6
North Bay 246 ....M3
North Bend 200 ....D7
North Fond du Lac 4,292 ....J8
North Freedom 591 ....G9
North Hudson 3,101 ....A5
North Lake 400 ....J1
North Prairie 1,322 ....J2
North Shore 14,272 ....M1
Norwalk 564 ....E8
Oak Creek 19,513 ....M2
Oakdale 162 ....F8
Oakfield 1,003 ....J8
Oconomowoc 10,993 ....H1
Oconomowoc Lake 493 ....H1
Oconto Falls 2,584 ....K6
Oconto▲ 4,474 ....L6
Odanah 190 ....E2
Ogdensburg 220 ....J7
Ogema 238 ....F5
Okauchee 3,958 ....J1
Okee 250 ....H9
Oliver 269 ....B2
Omro 2,836 ....J7
Onalaska 11,284 ....C8
Oneida 808 ....K7
Ontario 407 ....E8
Oostburg 1,931 ....L8
Oregon 4,519 ....H10
Orfordville 1,219 ....H10
Osceola 2,075 ....A5
Oshkosh▲ 55,006 ....J8
Osseo 1,551 ....D6
Owen 895 ....F6
Oxford 499 ....H8
Packwaukee 271 ....H8
Paddock Lake 2,662 ....K10
Palmyra 1,539 ....H2

Pardeeville 1,630 ....H8
Park Falls 3,104 ....F4
Park Ridge 546 ....H6
Patch Grove 202 ....D10
Pearson 102 ....H5
Peeksville 250 ....E3
Pell Lake 2,018 ....K10
Pembine 500 ....L4
Pence 234 ....F3
Pensaukee 225 ....L6
Pepin 873 ....B7
Perrygo Place J10
Peshtigo 3,154 ....L5
Pewaukee 4,941 ....K1
Phelps 950 ....H3
Phillips▲ 1,592 ....E4
Phlox 250 ....J5
Pickerel 107 ....J5
Pickett 120 ....J8
Pigeon Falls 289 ....D7
Pine River 110 ....H7
Pittsville 838 ....F7
Plain 691 ....F9
Plainfield 839 ....G7
Plat 120 ....K1
Platteville 9,708 ....F10
Pleasant Prairie 11,961 ....L10
Plover 8,176 ....G7
Plum City 534 ....B6
Plymouth 6,769 ....L8
Polonia 200 ....H6
Poplar 516 ....C2
Port Edwards 1,848 ....G7
Port Washington▲ 9,338 ....L9
Port Wing 290 ....C2
Portage▲ 8,640 ....G8
Potosi 654 ....E10
Potter 252 ....K7
Pound 434 ....L5
Poy Sippi 425 ....J7
Poynette 1,662 ....G9
Prairie Farm 494 ....C5
Prairie du Chien▲ 5,659 ....D9
Prairie du Sac 2,380 ....G9
Prentice 571 ....F4
Prescott 3,243 ....A6
Presque Isle 251 ....G3
Princeton 1,458 ....H8
Pulaski 2,200 ....K6
Racine▲ 84,298 ....M3
Radisson 237 ....D4
Randolph 1,729 ....H8
Random Lake 1,439 ....K8
Raymond 300 ....L2
Readfield 200 ....J7
Readstown 420 ....E9
Red Cliff 250 ....E2
Redgranite 1,009 ....H7
Reedsburg 5,834 ....G8
Reedsville 1,182 ....L7
Reeseville 673 ....J9
Reserve 371 ....D4
Rewey 210 ....F10
Rhinelander▲ 7,427 ....H4
Rib Falls 145 ....G6
Rice Lake 7,998 ....F5
Richfield 247 ....K1
Richland Center▲ 5,018 ....F9
Ridgeland 246 ....B5
Ridgeway 577 ....F10
Rio 768 ....H9
Rio Creek 200 ....L6
Ripon 7,241 ....J8
River Falls 10,610 ....A6
River Hills 1,612 ....M1
Roberts 1,043 ....A6
Rochester 978 ....K3
Rock Falls 200 ....C6
Rock Springs 432 ....G8
Rockdale 235 ....J10
Rockfield 200 ....L1
Rockland 509 ....D8
Rome 200 ....H1
Rosendale 777 ....J8
Rosholt 512 ....H6
Rothschild 3,310 ....G6
Roxbury 260 ....G9
Royalton 200 ....J7
Rozellville 150 ....G6
Rubicon 261 ....K9
Rudolph 451 ....G7
Saint Cloud 494 ....K8
Saint Croix Falls 1,640 ....A5
Saint Francis 9,245 ....M2
Saint Joseph Ridge 450 ....D8
Saint Nazianz 693 ....L7
Sand Creek 225 ....C5
Sauk City 3,019 ....G9
Saukville 3,695 ....L9
Saxon 375 ....F3
Sayner 300 ....H4
Scandinavia 298 ....H7
Schofield 2,415 ....G6
School Hill 228 ....L8
Seneca 235 ....E9
Sextonville 225 ....F9
Seymour 1,557 ....K6
Sharon 1,250 ....J11
Shawano▲ 7,598 ....J6
Sheboygan▲ 49,676 ....L8
Sheboygan Falls 5,823 ....L8
Sheldon 268 ....E5
Shell Lake▲ 1,161 ....C4
Sherry 115 ....G6
Sherwood 837 ....K7
Shiocton 805 ....K7
Shopiere 350 ....H10
Shorewood 14,116 ....M1
Shorewood Hills 1,680 ....G9
Shullsburg 1,236 ....F10
Silver Lake 1,801 ....K10
Siren 863 ....B4
Sister Bay 675 ....M5
Slinger 2,340 ....K9
Soldiers Grove 564 ....E9
Solon Springs 575 ....C3
Somers 400 ....M3

Somerset 1,065 ....A5
South Milwaukee 20,958 ....M2
South Range 149 ....B2
South Wayne 478 ....G10
Sparta▲ 7,788 ....E8
Spencer 1,757 ....F6
Spirit 400 ....F5
Spooner 2,464 ....B4
Spring Green 1,283 ....G9
Spring Valley 1,051 ....B6
Springbrook 150 ....C4
Stangelville 150 ....L7
Stanley 2,011 ....E6
Star Prairie 507 ....A5
Stetsonville 511 ....F5
Steuben 161 ....E9
Stevens Point▲ 23,006 ....G7
Stiles 300 ....L6
Stitzer 190 ....E10
Stockbridge 579 ....K7
Stoddard 775 ....D8
Stone Bank 390 ....J1
Stone Lake 210 ....C4
Stoughton 8,786 ....H10
Stratford 1,515 ....F6
Strum 949 ....D6
Sturgeon Bay▲ 9,176 ....M6
Sturtevant 3,803 ....M3
Suamico 900 ....K6
Sullivan 432 ....H1
Summit Lake 250 ....H5
Sun Prairie 15,333 ....H9
Superior▲ 27,134 ....C2
Superior Village 481 ....B2
Suring 626 ....K5
Sussex 5,039 ....K1
Symco 102 ....J6
Taycheedah 350 ....K8
Taylor 419 ....E7
Tennyson 378 ....E10
Theresa 771 ....K8
Thiensville 3,301 ....L1
Thorp 1,657 ....E6
Three Lakes 950 ....H4
Tichigan Lake 500 ....K2
Tigerton 815 ....H6
Tilleda 102 ....J6
Tisch Mills 315 ....L7
Tomah 7,570 ....F8
Tomahawk 3,328 ....G5
Tony 114 ....E5
Townsend 450 ....K5
Trego 280 ....C4
Trempealeau 1,039 ....C8
Troy Center 200 ....J2
Tunnel City 200 ....E7
Turtle Lake 817 ....B4
Tustin 101 ....J7
Twin Lakes 3,989 ....K11
Two Rivers 13,030 ....M7
Union Center 197 ....F8
Union Grove 4,322 ....L3
Unity 452 ....F6

Upson 115 ....F3
Valders 905 ....L7
Verona 5,374 ....G9
Vesper 598 ....F7
Viola 644 ....E8
Viroqua▲ 3,922 ....D8
Wabeno 800 ....J5
Waldo 442 ....L8
Wales 2,471 ....J1
Walworth 1,614 ....J10
Warrens 343 ....E7
Washburn▲ 2,285 ....D2
Washington Island 550 ....M5
Waterford 2,431 ....K3
Waterloo 2,712 ....J9
Watertown 19,142 ....J9
Waubeka 450 ....L9
Waukesha▲ 56,958 ....K1
Waumandee 115 ....C7
Waunakee 5,897 ....G9
Waupaca▲ 4,957 ....H7
Waupun 8,207 ....J8
Wausau▲ 37,060 ....G6
Wausaukee 656 ....K5
Wautoma▲ 1,784 ....H7
Wauwatosa 49,366 ....L1
Wauzeka 595 ....E9
Wayside 127 ....L7
Webster 623 ....B4
West Allis 63,221 ....L1
West Baraboo 1,021 ....G9
West Bend▲ 23,916 ....K9
West Milwaukee 3,973 ....L1
West Salem 3,611 ....D8
Westboro 750 ....F5
Westby 1,866 ....E8
Westfield 1,125 ....H8
Weston 8,775 ....G6
Weston 9,714 ....C6
Weyauwega 1,665 ....H7
Weyerhaeuser 283 ....D5
Wheeler 348 ....C5
White Lake 304 ....J5
Whitefish Bay 14,272 ....M1
Whitehall▲ 1,494 ....D7
Whitelaw 700 ....L7
Whitewater 12,636 ....J10
Whiting 1,835 ....H6
Wild Rose 676 ....H7
Williams Bay 2,108 ....J10
Wilson 163 ....B6
Wilton 478 ....E8
Winchester 300 ....G3
Windsor 2,182 ....H9
Wind Lake 3,748 ....K2
Wind Point 1,941 ....M2
Winneconne 2,059 ....J7
Winter 383 ....E4
Wiota 125 ....G10
Wisconsin Dells 2,393 ....G8
Wisconsin Rapids▲ 18,245 ....G7
Withee 503 ....E6

Wittenberg 1,145 ....H6
Wonewoc 793 ....F8
Woodford 107 ....G10
Woodman 120 ....E9
Woodruff 850 ....G4
Woodville 942 ....B6
Wrightstown 1,262 ....K7
Wyeville 154 ....F7
Wyocena 620 ....H9
Yuba 77 ....F8

OTHER FEATURES

Apostle (isls.) F2
Apostle Islands Nat'l Lakeshore E1
Apple (riv.) A5
Bad River Ind. Res. E2
Bardon (lake) B2
Bear (isl.) E1
Beaver Dam (lake) J9
Beulah (lake) J2
Big Eau Pleine (res.) G6
Big Muskego (lake) L2
Big Rib (riv.) G5
Black (riv.) E7
Butternut (lake) J4
Castle Rock (lake) G8
Cat (isl.) E1
Chambers (isl.) M5
Chequamegon (bay) E2
Chetac (lake) C4
Chippewa (lake) D4
Chippewa (riv.) B7
Clam (lake) B3
Clam (riv.) A4
Dells, The (valley) G8
Denoon (lake) K2
Door (pen.) M6
Du Bay (lake) G6
Eagle (lake) K3
Eagle (lake) K3
Eau Claire (riv.) D6
Flambeau (lake) G3
Flambeau Flowage (res.) F3
Fox (riv.) K2
Fox (riv.) K7
General Mitchell Field M2
Geneva (lake) K10
Golden (lake) J1
Green (bay) L6
Grindstone (lake) C4
Holcombe Flowage (res.) D5
Jump (riv.) E5
Kegonsa (lake) H10
Kickapoo (riv.) E9
Koshkonong (lake) H10
La Belle (lake) H1
Lac Court Oreilles Ind. Res. C4
Lac du Flambeau Ind. Res. G3
Long (lake) C4
Madeline (isl.) E2
Mendota (lake) H9

Menominee (riv.) L5
Menominee Ind. Res. J5
Metonga (lake) J4
Michigan (isl.) F2
Michigan (lake) M9
Mississippi (riv.) D10
Montreal (riv.) F2
Moose (lake) E3
Moose (lake) F3
Nagawicka (lake) J1
Namekagon (lake) D3
Namekagon (riv.) C3
North (lake) J1
Oak (isl.) E2
Oconomowoc (lake) H1
Oconto (riv.) K5
Okauchee (lake) J1
Outer (isl.) F1
Owen (lake) D3
Pecatonica (riv.) H11
Pelican (lake) H4
Pepin (lake) B7
Peshtigo (lake) K5
Petenwell (lake) G7
Pewaukee (lake) K1
Phantom (lake) J1
Pine (lake) J1
Poygan (lake) J7
Puckaway (lake) H8
Red Cedar (riv.) C5
Red Cliff Ind. Res. E2
Rock (riv.) J9
Round (lake) J4
Round (lake) C4
Saint Croix (lake) A6
Saint Croix (riv.) A4
Saint Croix Flowage (res.) C3
Saint Louis (riv.) A2
Sand (isl.) D2
Shawano (lake) K6
Shell (lake) C4
Spider (lake) C4
Stockbridge Ind. Res. K7
Stockton (isl.) E2
Sugar (riv.) H10
Sugarbush Hill (mt.) J4
Superior (lake) D2
Thunder (lake) H4
Tichigan (lake) K2
Timms Hill (mt.) F5
Trempealeau (riv.) C7
Trout (lake) G3
Washington (isl.) M5
Willow (res.) G4
Wind (lake) K2
Winnebago (lake) K7
Wisconsin (riv.) B4
Wolf (riv.) J5
Yellow (lake) B4
Yellow (riv.) B4

▲County-seat

Topography

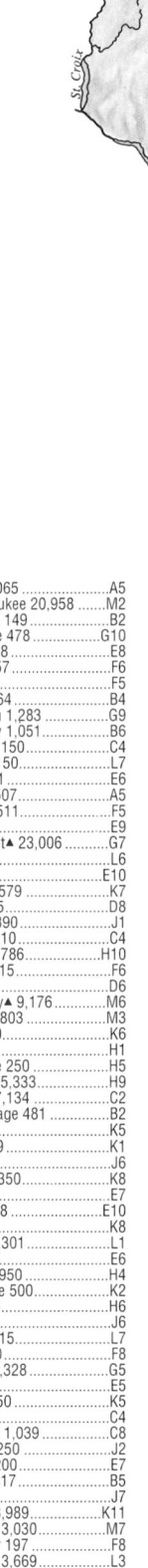

0   40   80 MI.

0   40   80 KM.

| Below Sea Level | Sea Level | 100 m. 328 ft. | 200 m. 656 ft. | 500 m. 1,640 ft. | 1,000 m. 3,281 ft. | 2,000 m. 6,562 ft. | 5,000 m. 16,404 ft. |

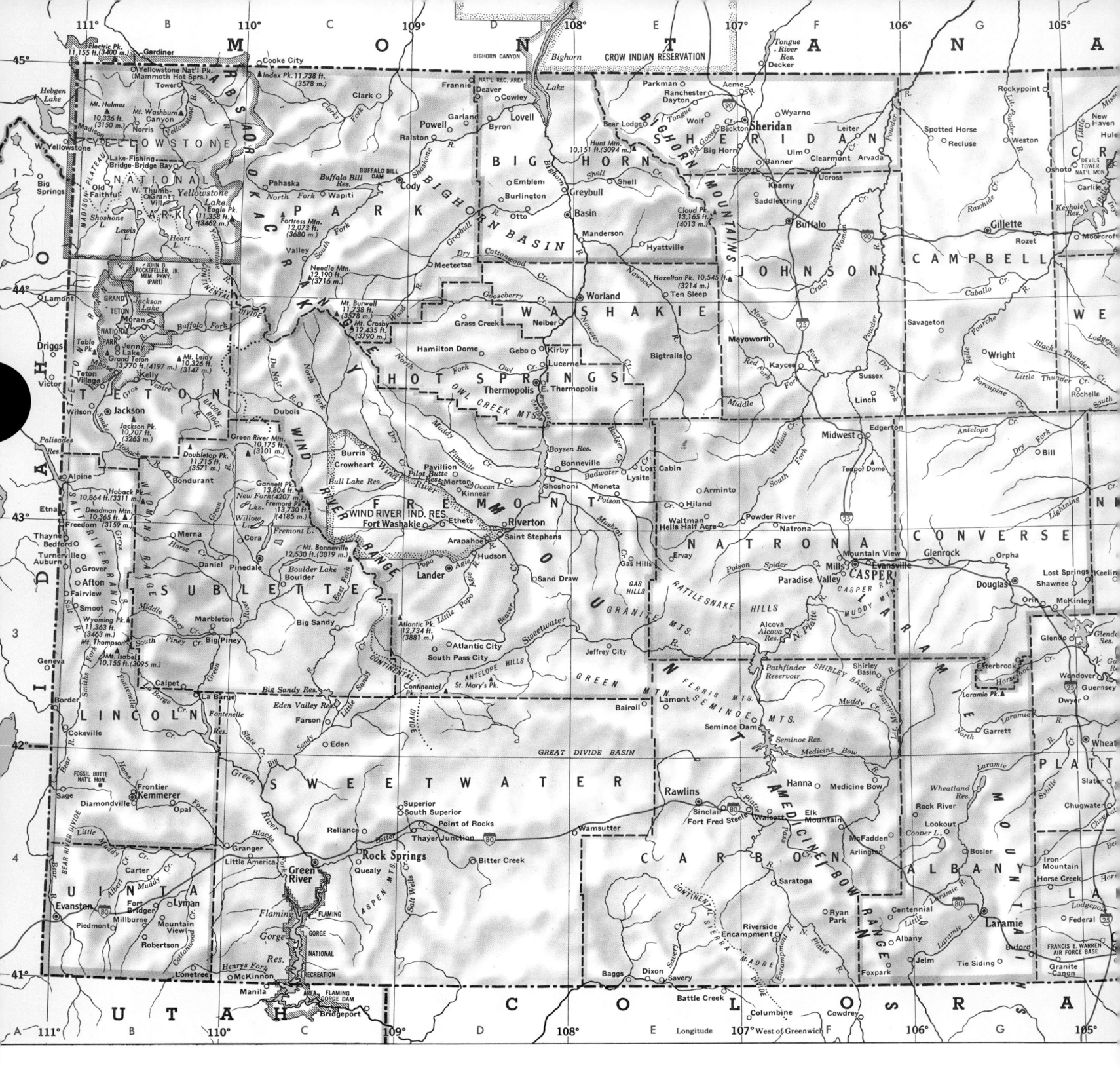

Agriculture, Industry and Resources

DOMINANT LAND USE

Specialized Wheat

Specialized Dairy

General Farming, Livestock, Special Crops

Sugar Beets, Dry Beans, Livestock, General Farming

Range Livestock

Forests

Nonagricultural Land

MAJOR MINERAL OCCURRENCES

C Coal	G Natural Gas	So Soda Ash
Cl Clay	O Petroleum	U Uranium
Fe Iron Ore	P Phosphates	V Vanadium
	⚡ Water Power	

COUNTIES

Albany 30,797 .... G4
Big Horn 10,525 .... E1
Campbell 29,370 .... G1
Carbon 16,659 .... F4
Converse 11,128 .... G3
Crook 5,294 .... H1
Fremont 33,662 .... D2
Goshen 12,373 .... H4
Hot Springs 4,809 .... D2
Johnson 6,145 .... F2
Laramie 73,142 .... H4
Lincoln 12,625 .... B3
Natrona 61,226 .... F3
Niobrara 2,499 .... H2
Park 23,178 .... C1
Platte 8,145 .... H3
Sheridan 23,562 .... F1
Sublette 4,843 .... C3
Sweetwater 38,823 .... D4
Teton 11,172 .... B2
Uinta 18,705 .... B4
Washakie 8,388 .... E2
Weston 6,518 .... H2

CITIES and TOWNS

Acme 98 .... E1
Afton 1,394 .... B3
Albany 25 .... G4
Albin 120 .... H4

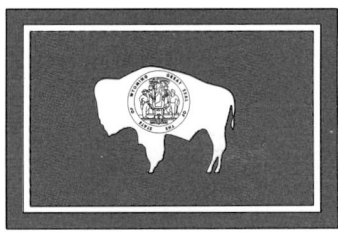

Wyoming

SCALE
0 5 10 20 30 40 MI.
0 5 10 20 30 40 KM.

State Capitals............⊛
County Seats.............◉
Major Limited Access Hwys._____

Scale 1:2,410,000

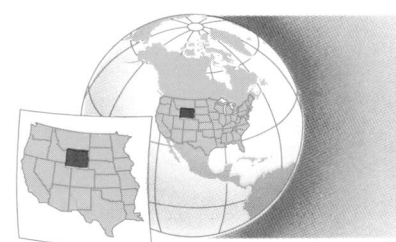

AREA 97,809 sq. mi. (253,325 sq. km.)
POPULATION 455,975
CAPITAL Cheyenne
LARGEST CITY Casper
HIGHEST POINT Gannett Pk. 13,804 ft. (4207 m.)
SETTLED IN 1834
ADMITTED TO UNION July 10, 1890
POPULAR NAME Equality State
STATE FLOWER Indian Paintbrush
STATE BIRD Meadowlark

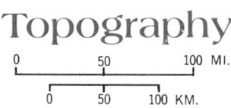

Topography

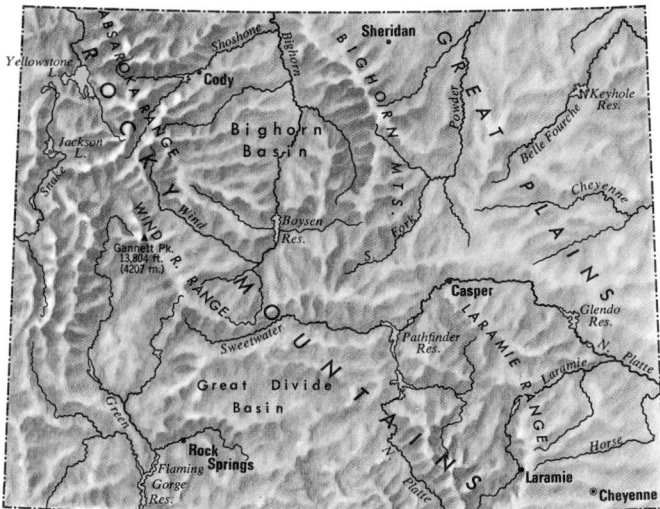

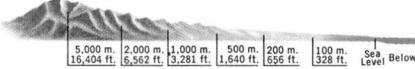

5,000 m. | 2,000 m. | 1,000 m. | 500 m. | 200 m. | 100 m. | Sea | Below
16,404 ft. | 6,562 ft. | 3,281 ft. | 1,640 ft. | 656 ft. | 328 ft. | Level |

© Copyright HAMMOND INCORPORATED, Maplewood, N.J.

Alcova 275.................F3
Alpine 200.................B2
Alva 50....................H1
Arapahoe 393.............D3
Arvada 30.................F1
Atlantic City 25...........D3
Auburn 360...............A3
Baggs 272.................E4
Bairoil 228................E3
Banner 40.................F1
Basin▲ 1,180.............E1
Beckton 110...............E1
Bedford 350...............A3
Beulah 184................H1
Big Horn 350..............E1
Big Piney 454.............B3
Bondurant 90.............B2
Border 25..................B3
Bosler 195.................G4
Boulder 50.................C3
Buffalo▲ 3,302...........F1
Buford 36..................G4
Burlington 184............D1
Burns 254.................H4
Burris 30...................C2
Byron 470..................D1
Carpenter 75..............H4
Carter 33...................B4
Casper▲ 46,742..........F3
Centennial 140............F4
Cheyenne (cap.)▲ 50,008..H4
Chugwater 192............H4

Clearmont 119............F1
Cody▲ 7,897..............D1
Cokeville 493..............B3
Colony 50..................H1
Cowley 477................D1
Crowheart 200............C2
Daniel 130..................B3
Dayton 565.................E1
Deaver 199.................D1
Devils Tower 28............H1
Diamondville 864..........B4
Dixon 70....................E4
Douglas▲ 5,076..........G3
Dubois 895..................C2
East Thermopolis 22.......D2
Eden 198....................C3
Edgerton 247...............F2
Egbert 75...................H4
Elk Mountain 174..........F4
Encampment 611..........F4
Ethete 1,059...............D2
Etna 200....................A2
Evanston▲ 10,903.......B4
Evansville 1,403...........F3
Fairview 150................B3
Farson 350..................C3
Fort Bridger 300...........B4
Fort Laramie 243..........H3
Fort Washakie 1,334......C2
Fox Farm 2,850...........H4
Foxpark 78.................F4
Frannie 148.................D1

Freedom 400...............B3
Frontier 150.................B4
Garland 57..................D1
Gas Hills 150...............E3
Gillette▲ 17,635..........G1
Glendo 195.................G3
Glenrock 2,153............G3
Granger 126................C4
Granite Canon 80..........G4
Grass Creek 152...........D2
Green River▲ 12,711....C4
Greybull 1,789.............E1
Grover 425..................B3
Guernsey 1,155...........H3
Hamilton Dome 80.........D2
Hanna 1,076...............F4
Hartville 78.................H3
Hawk Springs 84..........H4
Hillsdale 160...............H4
Horse Creek 225...........G4
Hudson 392.................D3
Hulett 429...................H1
Huntley 50..................H4
Hyattville 110...............E1
Iron Mountain 45..........G4
Jackson▲ 4,472...........B2
Jeffrey City 1,882..........E3
Jelm 29......................G4
Kaycee 256.................F2
Kearny 49....................F1

Kelly 100.....................B2
Kemmerer▲ 3,020.........B4
Kinnear 145.................D2
Kirby 59......................D2
La Barge 493...............B3
Lagrange 224...............H4
Lamont 30...................E3
Lance Creek 100...........H2
Lander▲ 7,023............D3
Laramie▲ 26,687.........G4
Leiter 46.....................F1
Linch 75......................F2
Lingle 473...................H3
Little America 175..........C4
Lost Cabin 25...............E2
Lovell 2,131.................D1
Lucerne 240.................D2
Lusk▲ 1,504...............H3
Lyman 1,896...............B4
Lysite 175...................E2
Mammoth Hot Springs
  (Yellowstone Nat'l Park)
  350.........................B1
Manderson 83..............E1
Manville 97..................H3
Marbleton 634..............B3
Mayoworth 72..............F2
McFadden 47...............F4
McKinnon 135..............C4
Medicine Bow 389.........F4
Meeteetse 368.............D1
Meriden 55..................H4

Midwest 495................F2
Millburne 54................B4
Mills 1,574..................F3
Moorcroft 768..............H1
Moose 150...................B2
Moran 200...................B2
Morrisey 28.................H2
Morton 35....................D2
Mountain View 1,345.....B4
Mountain View 76.........F3
Neiber.........................D2
New Haven 35..............H1
Newcastle▲ 3,003........H2
Old Faithful 75.............B1
Opal 95.......................B4
Orchard Valley 3,327.....H4
Osage 500...................H2
Otto 50.......................D1
Pahaska 75..................C1
Paradise Valley............F3
Parkman 30.................E1
Pavillion 126................D2
Piedmont 25................B4
Pine Bluffs 1,054..........H4
Pinedale▲ 1,181..........C3
Point of Rocks 425........D4
Powder River 70...........F2
Powell 5,292...............D1
Ralston 50...................D1
Ranchester 676............E1
Rawlins▲ 9,380..........E4
Recluse 225.................G1
Reliance 325................C4
Riverside 85.................F4
Riverton 9,202.............D2
Robertson 142..............B4
Rock River 190............G4
Rock Springs 19,050......C4
Rozet 30.....................G1
Saddlestring 100...........F1
Sage 45......................B4
Saint Stephens 80.........D3
Sand Draw 40..............D3
Saratoga 1,969............F4
Savageton 30...............G2
Savery 29....................E4
Shell 80.......................E1
Sheridan▲ 13,900.......F1
Shirley Basin 400..........F3
Shoshoni 497...............D2
Sinclair 500..................E4
Smoot 310...................B3
South Superior 586........D4
Story 637....................F1
Sundance▲ 1,139........H1
Sunrise 29...................H3
Superior 273................D4
Sussex 25....................F2
Ten Sleep 311..............E1
Teton Village................B2
Thayne 267.................A3
Thermopolis▲ 3,247....D2

Torrington▲ 5,651........H3
Turnerville 65...............A3
Ulm 25.......................F1
Upton 980...................H1
Veteran 60...................H4
Walcott 200.................F4
Wamsutter 240............E4
Wapiti 130...................C1
Wheatland▲ 3,271.......H3
Wilson 480...................B2
Worland▲ 5,742.........E1
Wright 1,236...............G2
Wyarno 101.................F1
Yellowstone National Park
  350.........................B1
Yoder 136...................H4

OTHER FEATURES

Absaroka (range)..........C1
Antelope (creek)...........G2
Antelope (hills).............D3
Atlantic (peak)..............D3
Bear (creek).................H4
Bear (riv.)....................B4
Bear Lodge (mts.).........H1
Bear River Divide (mts.)..B4
Beaver (creek)..............D3
Beaver (creek)..............H2
Belle Fourche (riv.)........H1
Big Goose (creek)..........E1
Bighorn (basin).............D1
Bighorn (lake)...............D1
Bighorn (mts.)..............E1
Bighorn (riv.)................D1
Bighorn Canyon Nat'l
  Rec. Area..................D1
Big Sandy (riv.).............C3
Bitter (creek)................C4
Blacks Fork, Green (riv.)..C4
Black Thunder (creek).....G2
Bonneville (mt.)............C3
Boysen (res.)...............D2
Buffalo Bill (dam)..........C1
Buffalo Bill (res.)...........C1
Buffalo Fork, Snake (riv.)..B2
Burwell (mt.)................C2
Caballo (creek).............G1
Casper (range).............F3
Cheyenne (riv.).............H2
Chugwater (creek).........H4
Clarks Fork (riv.)...........C1
Clear (creek)................F1
Cloud (peak)................E1
Cottonwood (creek).......B4
Crazy Woman (creek).....F1
Crosby (mt.)................C2
Crow (creek)................H4
Deadman (mt.)............B2
Devils Tower Nat'l Mon...H1
Doubletop (peak)..........B2

Dry (creek)...................C2
Dry Cottonwood (creek)..D1
Eagle (peak).................B1
Fivemile (creek).............D2
Flaming Gorge (res.)......C4
Flaming Gorge Nat'l
  Rec. Area..................C4
Fontenelle (creek)..........B3
Fontenelle (res.)............B3
Fort Laramie Nat'l Hist. Site..H3
Fortress (mt.)...............C1
Fossil Butte Nat'l Mon....B4
Francis E. Warren
  A.F.B. 3,832..............G4
Fremont (lake)..............C3
Fremont (peak).............C2
Gannett (peak).............C2
Gas (hills)....................E3
Glendo (res.)................H3
Gooseberry (creek)........D1
Grand Teton (mt.).........B2
Grand Teton Nat'l Park...B2
Granite (mts.)...............E3
Great Divide (basin).......E3
Green (mt.)..................E3
Green (riv.)...................C4
Green, East Fork (riv.).....C3
Green River (mt.)...........C2
Greybull (riv.)...............D1
Greys (riv.)...................B3
Gros Ventre (riv.)..........B2
Guernsey (res.).............H3
Hams Fork (riv.)............B4
Hazelton (peak).............E1
Henrys Fork, Green (riv.)..C4
Hoback (peak)..............B2
Hoback (riv.).................B2
Holmes (mt.)................B1
Horse (creek)...............H4
Horseshoe (creek).........G3
Hunt (mt.)...................E1
Index (peak).................C1
Inyan Kara (creek).........H1
Inyan Kara (mt.)...........H1
Isabel (mt.)..................B3
Jackson (lake)..............B2
Jackson (peak)..............B2
John D. Rockefeller, Jr.,
  Mem. Pkwy...............B1
Keyhole (res.)...............H1
Lamar (riv.)..................B1
Lance (creek)................H2
Laramie (mts.)..............G3
Laramie (peak)..............G3
Laramie (riv.)................G4
Leidy (mt.)...................B2
Lewis (lake).................B1
Lightning (creek)...........G2
Little Missouri (riv.).......H1
Little Muddy (creek).......B4
Little Powder (riv.).........G1
Little Sandy (creek)........C3

Little Thunder (creek).....G2
Lodgepole (creek)..........H2
Lodgepole (creek)..........H4
Madison (plat.)..............B1
Medicine Bow (range).....F4
Medicine Bow (riv.)........F3
Middle Piney (creek).......B3
Muddy (creek)..............D2
Muskrat (creek).............E2
Needle (mt.).................C1
Niobrara (riv.)...............J3
North Laramie (riv.).......G3
North Platte (riv.)..........H3
Nowater (creek)............E2
Nowood (riv.)................E1
Owl, North Fork (creek)...D2
Owl Creek (mts.)...........D2
Palisades (res.)..............A2
Pass (creek).................F4
Pathfinder (res.)............F3
Poison (creek)..............E2
Poison Spider (creek)......F3
Popo Agie (riv.)............D3
Powder (riv.)................F2
Rattlesnake (hills)..........E3
Rawhide (creek)............G1
Rocky (mts.).................C1
Salt (riv.).....................B3
Salt River (range)..........B3
Salt Wells (creek)..........D4
Seminoe (mts.).............E3
Seminoe (res.)..............F3
Shell (creek).................E1
Shirley (mts.)...............F3
Shoshone (lake)............B1
Shoshone (riv.).............D1
Sierra Madre (mts.).......E4
Slate (creek).................C3
Smiths Fork (riv.)..........B3
Snake (riv.)..................B2
South Cheyenne (riv.).....H2
South Piney (creek)........B3
Sweetwater (riv.)..........D3
Sybille (creek)..............G4
Teapot Dome (mt.)........F2
Teton (range)...............B2
Tongue (riv.).................E1
Washburn (mt.)............B1
Wheatland (res.)...........G4
Willow (creek)..............F2
Wind (riv.)...................C2
Wind River (canyon)......D2
Wind River (range).........C2
Wind River Ind. Res.......C2
Wood (riv.)...................C2
Wyoming (peak)...........B3
Wyoming (range)..........B2
Yellowstone (lake).........B1
Yellowstone (riv.)..........B1
Yellowstone Nat'l Park....B1

▲County seat

Acquisitions of Territory

WASHINGTON

OREGON COUNTRY

OREGON 1846
Treaty with Great Britain

IDAHO

MONTANA

NORTH DAKOTA

RED RIVER
Title Established 1818

L O U I S I A N A

MINNESOTA

WISCONSIN

MICHIGAN

MAINE

VT. N.H.

NEW YORK

MASS.
CONN.
R.I.

WYOMING

SOUTH DAKOTA

NEBRASKA

IOWA

PENNSYLVANIA

NEW JERSEY

CALIFORNIA

NEVADA

UTAH

MEXICAN CESSION 1848

COLORADO

KANSAS

Purchased from France 1803

MISSOURI

ILLINOIS

INDIANA

OHIO

WEST VIRGINIA

VIRGINIA

MD.

DEL.

UNITED STATES

KENTUCKY

1783

ARIZONA

NEW MEXICO

GADSDEN PURCHASE 1853

Annexed in 1845

OKLAHOMA

TEXAS

ARKANSAS

TENNESSEE

NORTH CAROLINA

SOUTH CAROLINA

MISSISSIPPI

ALABAMA

GEORGIA

LOUISIANA

F L O R I D A

1819
Treaty with Spain

ALASKA

1867
Purchased from Russia

The United States in 1783 comprised the thirteen original states and included lands acquired by conquest during the Revolution and by the Treaty of 1783.

H A W A I I

Annexed in 1898

Rank by Area

20 · 9

4

17

43 · 39
44
45
50
46 · 48
49
42

10

13

9

16

12

26

30

3

7

11

15

25

24

38

35

33

8

14

19

41

36

6

5

18

37

34

28

1

32

29

21

40

31

2

22

47

MAP COLORS INDICATE RANKINGS IN GROUPS OF TEN

Rank by Population
1990

18

29

44

47

20

16

48 · 38
41
13
43

42

50

45

2

39

35

36

30

8

14

7

5

9 · 27
46
19

26

32

15

6

23

34

12

10

24

37

28

33

17

3

21

22

11

25

49

40

YEAR OF ADMISSION TO THE UNION

DELAWARE ☆ — 1787
PENNSYLVANIA ☆
NEW JERSEY ☆
GEORGIA ☆ — 1788
CONNECTICUT ☆
MASSACHUSETTS ☆
MARYLAND ☆
SOUTH CAROLINA ☆
NEW HAMPSHIRE ☆
VIRGINIA ☆
NEW YORK ☆
NORTH CAROLINA ☆ — 1789
RHODE ISLAND ☆ — 1790
VERMONT ☆ — 1791
KENTUCKY ☆ — 1792

TENNESSEE ☆ — 1796

OHIO ☆ — 1803

LOUISIANA ☆ — 1812

INDIANA ☆ — 1816
MISSISSIPPI ☆ — 1817
ILLINOIS ☆ — 1818
ALABAMA ☆ — 1819
MAINE ☆ — 1820
MISSOURI ☆ — 1821

1959 ☆ HAWAII
     ☆ ALASKA

1912 ☆ ARIZONA
     ☆ NEW MEXICO

1907 ☆ OKLAHOMA

☆ NORTH DAKOTA
☆ SOUTH DAKOTA
☆ MONTANA

UTAH ☆ IDAHO ☆ ☆ WASHINGTON
☆ WYOMING

WEST VIRGINIA ☆
NEVADA ☆ KANSAS ☆

MINNESOTA ☆
OREGON ☆

CALIFORNIA ☆

WISCONSIN ☆
IOWA ☆

FLORIDA ☆
TEXAS ☆

ARKANSAS ☆
MICHIGAN ☆

COLORADO

NEBRASKA

1896   1889   1876   1867 1864 1861 1858   1848 1845   1836
     1890   1863   1859   1850   1846   1837

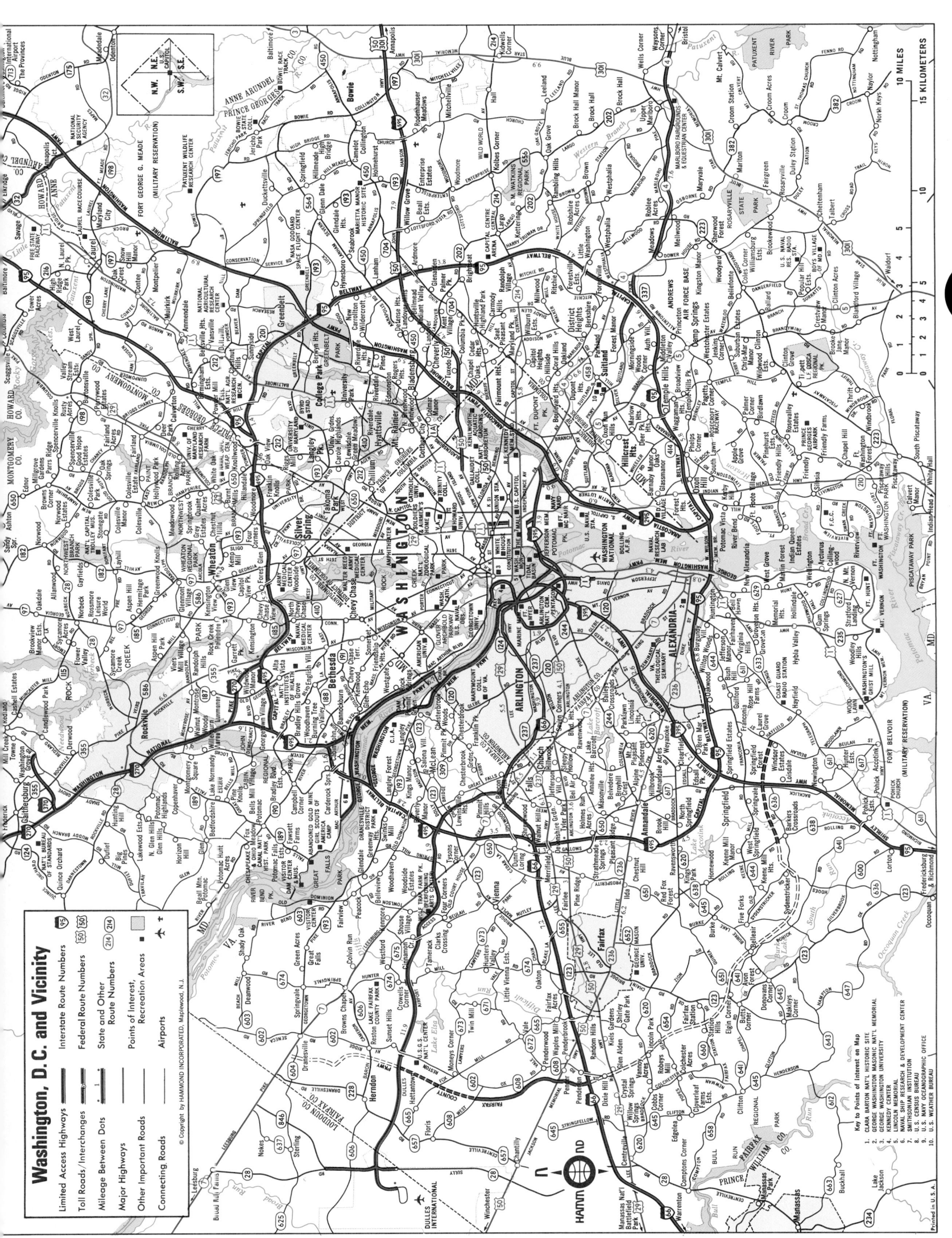

Washington, D.C. and Vicinity

Limited Access Highways
Toll Roads/Interchanges
Mileage Between Dots
Major Highways
Other Important Roads
Connecting Roads

Interstate Route Numbers
Federal Route Numbers
State and Other Route Numbers
Points of Interest, Recreation Areas
Airports

© Copyright by HAMMOND INCORPORATED, Maplewood, N.J.

Key to Points of Interest on Map
1. CLARA BARTON NAT'L HISTORIC SITE
2. GEORGE WASHINGTON MASONIC NAT'L MEMORIAL
3. GEORGE WASHINGTON UNIVERSITY
4. KENNEDY CENTER
5. LINCOLN MEMORIAL
6. NAVAL SHIP RESEARCH & DEVELOPMENT CENTER
7. SMITHSONIAN INSTITUTION
8. U.S. CENSUS BUREAU
9. U.S. NAVY OCEANOGRAPHIC OFFICE
10. U.S. WEATHER BUREAU

Printed in U.S.A.

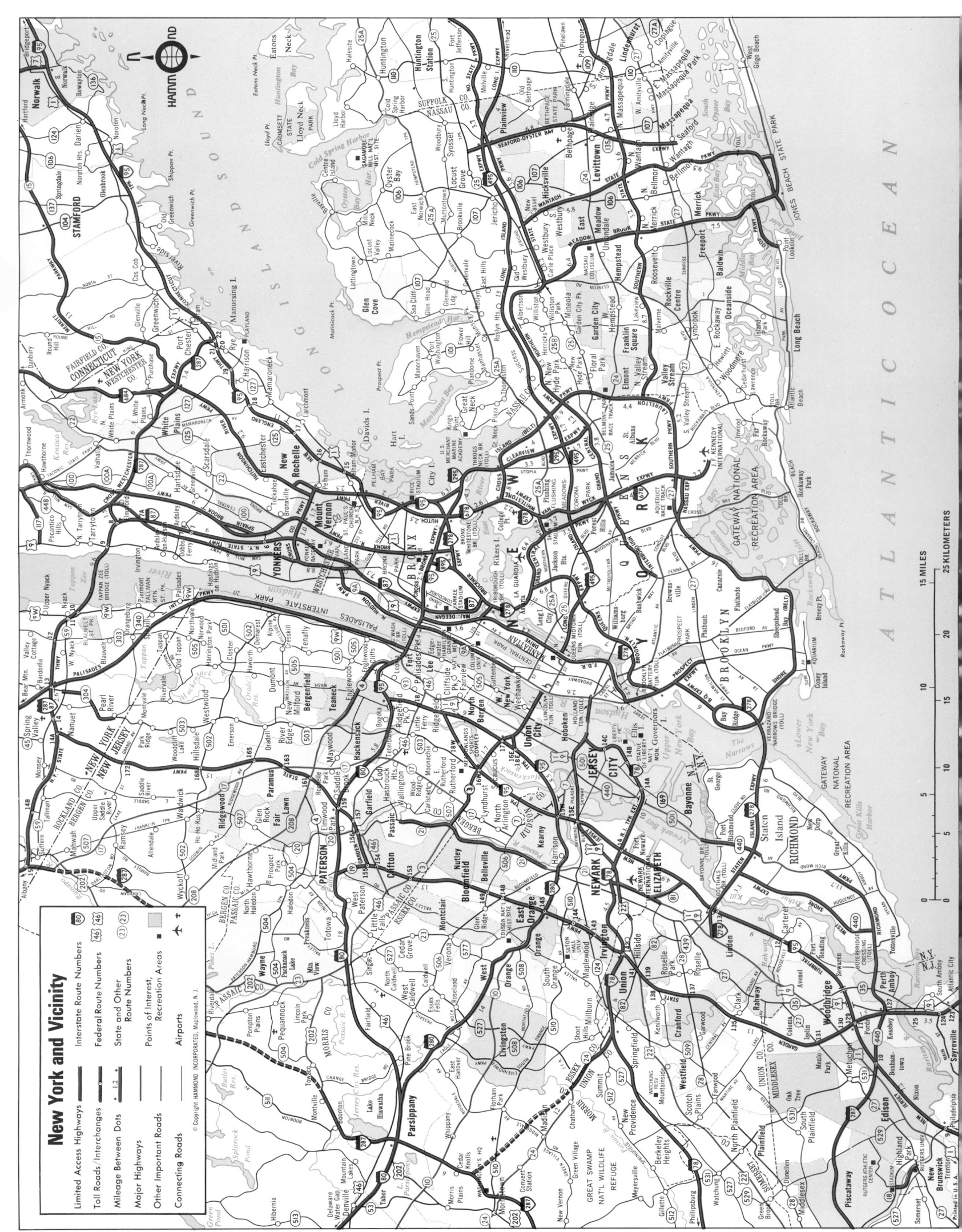

New York and Vicinity

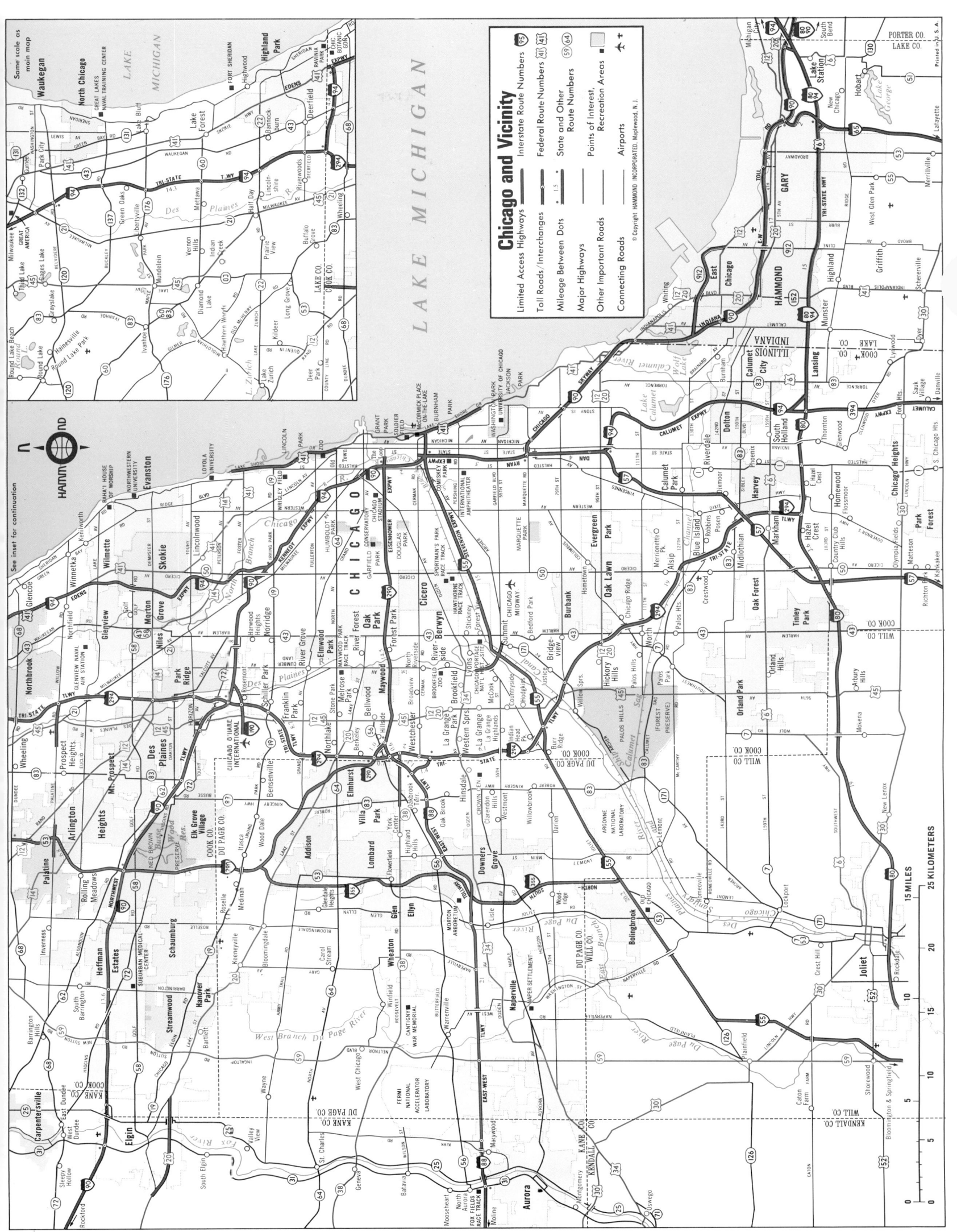

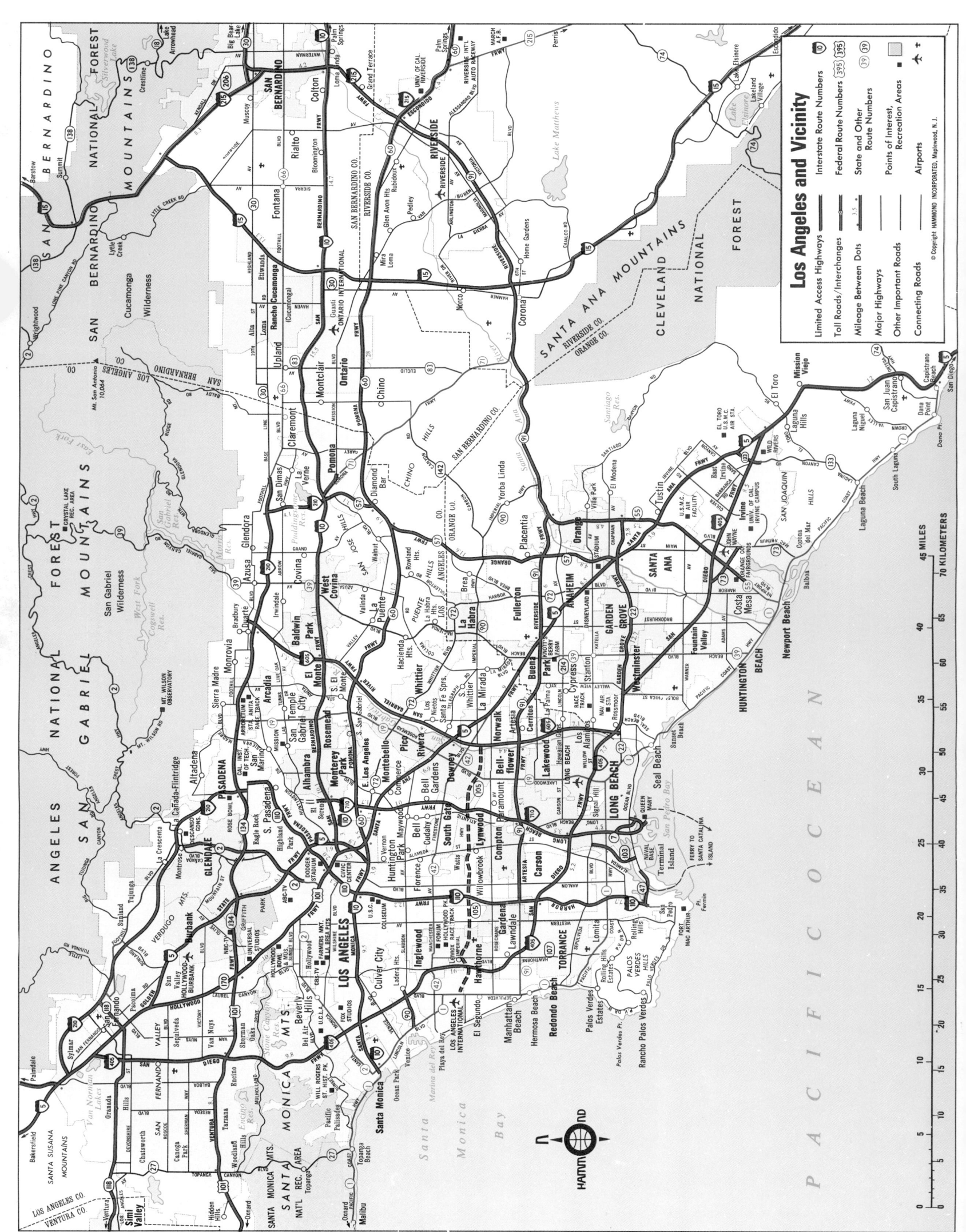

Los Angeles and Vicinity

Limited Access Highways	Interstate Route Numbers
Toll Roads/Interchanges	Federal Route Numbers
Mileage Between Dots	State and Other Route Numbers
Major Highways	Points of Interest, Recreation Areas
Other Important Roads	Airports
Connecting Roads	

© Copyright HAMMOND INCORPORATED, Maplewood, N.J.

INDEX OF THE WORLD

Introduction

This index contains a complete alphabetical listing of more than one hundred thousand names shown on all the maps included in this atlas. Names not found in the individual indexes accompanying the maps appear here. The user who is unfamiliar with the location of a country, town, or physical feature, or who is in doubt as to which country, state or province a place belongs will find the answers to his questions in this index. Entries are indexed to all maps or insets showing the place.

The name of the feature sought will be found in its proper alphabetical sequence, followed by the name of the political division in which it is located, the page number of the map on which it will be found, and the key reference necessary for finding its location on the map. After noting the key reference letter-number combination for the place name, turn to the page number indicated. The place name will be found within the square formed by the two lines of latitude and the two lines of longitude which enclose the coordinates—i.e., the marginal letters and numbers. A bullet (●) after the name signifies a township—better known as a town—in the northeastern U.S.

Because of limitations of space on the map, place names do not always appear in their complete form on the map. The complete forms are, however, given in the index. Variant spellings of names and alternate names are also given in this index. The alternate form or spelling of the name appears first, followed in parentheses by the name as it appears on the map. Physical features are usually listed under their proper names and not according to their generic terms; that is to say, Rio Negro will be found under Negro and not under Rio Negro. Exceptions are familiar names such as Rio Grande.

The abbreviations for the political division names and geographical features are explained on page VI of the atlas. In addition, reference can be made to the Gazetteer-Index appearing on pages I through V in which area, population, capital, map reference and type of government may be found for all major political and physical divisions of the world. Population figures for most entries are also included in the comprehensive individual indexes accompanying each map.

A

Aa (riv.), Switzerland 39/F3
Aachen, Germany 22/B3
Aadorf, Switzerland 39/G2
Aalen, Germany 22/D4
Aalsmeer, Netherlands 27/F4
Aalst, Belgium 27/D7
Aalten, Netherlands 27/K5
Aalter, Belgium 27/C6
Äänekoski, Finland 18/O5
Aarau, Switzerland 39/F2
Aarberg, Switzerland 39/D2
Aarburg, Switzerland 39/E2
Aardenburg, Netherlands 27/C6
Aare (riv.), Switzerland 39/E3
Aargau (canton), Switzerland 39/F2
Aarlen (Arlon), Belgium 27/H9
Aarons (creek), Va. 307/L7
Aaronsburg, Pa. 294/H4
Aarschot, Belgium 27/F7
Aat (Ath), Belgium 27/D7
Aba, China 77/F5
Aba, Hungary 41/E3
Aba, Nigeria 106/F7
Aba, Nigeria 102/C4
Aba, Zaire 115/F3
Aba as Sa'ud, Saudi Arabia 59/D6
Abacaxis (riv.), Brazil 132/B4
Abadan, Iran 54/F6
Abadan, Iran 66/F5
Abadan, Iran 59/E3
Abadeh, Iran 66/H5
Abadeh, Iran 59/F3
Abadla, Algeria 100/D2
Abádszalók, Hungary 41/F3
Abaeté, Brazil 132/E7
Abaetetuba, Brazil 132/D3
Abaetetuba, Brazil 120/E3
Abagnar (Silinhot), China 77/J3
Abai, Paraguay 144/E4
Abaiang (atoll), Kiribati 87/H5
'Abaila, Saudi Arabia 59/F5
Abajo (mts.), Utah 304/E6
Abakan, U.S.S.R. 54/L4
Abakan, U.S.S.R. 48/K4
Abala, Congo 115/C4
Abalos (pt.), Cuba 158/A2
Abana, Turkey 63/F2
Abancay, Peru 120/B4
Abancay, Peru 128/F9
Abapó, Bolivia 136/D6
Abaq, China 77/J3
Abarqu, Iran 59/F3
Abarqu, Iran 66/H5
'Abasan, Gaza Strip 65/A5
Abashiri, Japan 81/M1
Abashiri (riv.), Japan 81/M1
Abau, Papua N.G. 85/C7
Abaújszántó, Hungary 41/F2
Abay (riv.), Ethiopia 111/G5

Abay, U.S.S.R. 43/H5
Abaya (lake), Ethiopia 111/G6
Abaza, U.S.S.R. 48/J4
Abbaye (pt.), Mich. 250/B2
Abbe (lake), Djibouti 111/H5
Abbeville, Ala. 195/H7
Abbeville, France 28/D2
Abbeville, Georgia 217/F7
Abbeville, La. 238/F7
Abbeville, Miss. 256/F2
Abbeville (co.), S.C. 296/B3
Abbeville, S.C. 236/C3
Abbey (head), Scotland 15/E6
Abbeydorney, Ireland 17/B7
Abbeyfeale, Ireland 10/B4
Abbeyfeale, Ireland 17/C7
Abbeylara, Ireland 17/F4
Abbeyleix, Ireland 17/G6
Abbotsford, Br. Col. 184/L3
Abbotsford, Wis. 317/F6
Abbott, Ark. 202/B3
Abbott, N. Mex. 274/E2
Abbott, Texas 303/G6
Abbottabad, Pakistan 68/C2
Abbottabad, Pakistan 59/K3
Abbottsburg, N.C. 281/M5
Abbottsford, Georgia 217/B4
Abbottstown, Pa. 294/J6
Abbot Village ●, Maine 243/D5
Abbyville, Kansas 232/D4
'Abdul 'Aziz, Jebel (mts.), Syria 63/J4
Abdulino, U.S.S.R. 52/H4
Abéché, Chad 102/D3
Abéché, Chad 1 1/D5
Abee, Alberta 182/D2
Abell, Md. 245/M8
Abemama (atoll), Kiribati 87/H5
Abengourou, Ivory Coast 106/D7
Abengourou, Ivory Coast 102/B4
Åbenrå, Denmark 18/F9
Åbenrå, Denmark 21/C7
Abeokuta, Niger 106/E7
Abeokuta, Nigeria 102/C4
Aberaeron, Wales 13/C5
Aberaeron, Wales 10/D4
Abercarn, Wales 13/B6
Aberchirder, Scotland 15/F3
Abercorn, Québec 172/E4
Abercorn (Mbala), Zambia 115/F5
Abercrombie, N. Dak. 282/S7
Abercrombie, Nova Scotia 168/F3
Abercrombie (mt.), Wash. 310/H2
Aberdare, Wales 13/A6
Aberdare, Wales 10/E5
Aberdaron, Wales 13/C5
Aberdeen, Idaho 220/F7
Aberdeen, Ky. 237/H6
Aberdeen, Md. 245/O2
Aberdeen, Miss. 256/H3
Aberdeen (dam), Miss. 256/H3
Aberdeen ●, N.... 273/E3
Aberdeen, N.S. Wales 97/F3

Aberdeen, N.C. 281/L4
Aberdeen (lake), N.W. Terr. 187/J3
Aberdeen, Ohio 284/C8
Aberdeen, Sask. 181/E3
Aberdeen, Scotland 7/D3
Aberdeen, Scotland 15/F3
Aberdeen, Scotland 10/F2
Aberdeen (trad. co.), Scotland 15/B5
Aberdeen, S. Africa 118/C6
Aberdeen, S. Dak. 146/J5
Aberdeen, S. Dak. 188/G1
Aberdeen, S. Dak. 298/M3
Aberdeen, Wash. 188/B1
Aberdeen, Wash. 310/B3
Aberdeen Proving Ground, Md. 245/N3
Aberdour, Scotland 15/D1
Aberfeldy, Sask. 181/B2
Aberfeldy, Scotland 10/D2
Aberfeldy, Scotland 15/E4
Aberfoyle, Scotland 15/D4
Abergavenny, Wales 13/B6
Abergavenny, Wales 10/E5
Abergele, Wales 13/D4
Aberlady, Scotland 15/F4
Aberlour, Scotland 15/E3
Abernant, Ala. 195/D4
Abernathy, Texas 303/B4
Abernethy, Sask. 181/H5
Abernethy, Scotland 15/E4
Aberporth, Wales 13/C5
Abert (lake), Oreg. 188/C2
Abert (lake), Oreg. 291/B3
Abertillery, Wales 13/B6
Abertillery, Wales 10/E5
Aberystwyth, Wales 13/C5
Aberystwyth, Wales 10/D4
Abez', U.S.S.R. 52/K1
Abha, Saudi Arabia 59/D6
Abha, Saudi Arabia 54/F8
Abhar, Iran 66/F2
Abiad, Ras el (Blanc) (cape), Tunisia 106/G1
Abibe, Serranía de (mts.), Colombia 126/B3
'Abidiya, Sudan 59/B6
Abidjan, Ivory Coast 2/J5
Abidjan, Ivory Coast 102/B4
Abidjan, Ivory Coast 106/D7
Abie, Nebr. 264/H3
Abilene, Kansas 232/E3
Abilene, Texas 146/J6
Abilene, Texas 303/E5
Abilene, Texas 188/G4
Abingdon, England 10/F5
Abingdon, England 13/F6
Abingdon, Ill. 222/C3
Abingdon, Iowa 229/J6
Abingdon, Md. 245/N3
Abingdon, Va. 307/D7
Abingdon Downs, Queensland 95/B3
Abington, Conn. 210/G1
Abington, Ind. 227/H5
Abington ●, Mass. 249/L4

Abington, Pa. 294/M5
Abington, Scotland 15/E5
Abiqua (creek), Oreg. 291/B3
Abiquiu, N. Mex. 274/C2
Abiquiu (res.), N. Mex. 274/C2
Abita Springs, La. 238/L6
Abitibi (lake), Ont. 162/H6
Abitibi (lake), Ontario 175/E3
Abitibi (riv.), Ontario 162/H5
Abitibi (riv.), Ontario 175/D3
Abitibi (riv.), Ontario 175/D2
Abitibi (riv.), Ontario 177/J5
Abitibi (county), Québec 174/B2
Abitibi (terr.), Québec 174/B3
Abkhaz A.S.S.R., U.S.S.R. 48/E5
Abkhaz A.S.S.R., U.S.S.R. 52/F6
Abminga, S. Australia 94/D2
Abner, N.C. 281/K4
Abnûb, Egypt 111/J4
Åbo (Turku), Finland 18/N6
Aboisso, Ivory Coast 106/D7
Aboite, Ind. 227/G3
Abomey, Benin 106/E7
Abong-Mbang, Cameroon 115/B3
Abony, Hungary 41/E3
Abor (hills), India 68/G3
Aborlan, Philippines 82/B6
Abou Deïa, Chad 111/C5
Aboyne, Scotland 15/F3
Abqaiq, Saudi Arabia 59/E4
Abra (prov.), Philippines 82/C2
Abra (riv.), Philippines 82/C2
Abraham (lake), Alberta 182/B3
Abraham (mt.), Maine 243/C5
Abraham, Utah 304/B4
Abraham (mt.), Vt. 268/B3
Abraham Lincoln Birthplace Nat'l Hist. Site, Ky. 237/K5
Abrams, Wis. 317/L6
Abrantes, Portugal 33/B3
Abra Pampa, Argentina 143/C1
Abreus, Cuba 158/D2
'Abri, Sudan 111/F3
Abricots, Haiti 158/A6
Abruzzi (reg.), Italy 34/D3
Absaraka, N. Dak. 282/P6
Absaroka (range), Mont. 262/F5
Absaroka (range), Wyo. 319/C1
Absarokee, Mont. 262/G5
Absecon, N.J. 273/D5
Absecon (inlet), N.J. 273/E5
Abu, India 68/C4
Abu 'Arish, Saudi Arabia 59/D6
Abu Dara, Ras (cape), Sudan 59/C5
Abu Dara, Ras (cape), Sudan 111/G3
Abu Deleiq, Sudan 59/B6
Abu Dhabi (cap.), U.A.E. 54/G7
Abu Dhabi (cap.), U.A.E. 59/F5
Abu ed Duhur, Syria 63/G5
Abu Habl, Wadi (dry riv.), Sudan 111/F5
Abu Hadriya, Saudi Arabia 59/E4
Abu Hamed, Sudan 111/F4
Abu Hamed, Sudan 59/B6
Abuja, Nigeria 106/F7

Abuja, Nigeria 102/C4
Abu Cap. Terr., Nigeria 106/F7
Abu Kemal, Syria 59/D3
Abu Kemal, Syria 63/J5
Abukuma (riv.), Japan 81/K4
Abu-Mad, Ras (cape), Saudi Arabia 59/C5
Abu Matariq, Sudan 111/E5
Abumombazi, Zaire 115/D3
Abuná (riv.), Bolivia 136/B2
Abuná, Brazil 132/H10
Abuná (riv.), Brazil 132/G10
Abu Qir (bay), Egypt 111/J2
Abu Qurqās, Egypt 111/J4
Abu Road, India 68/C4
Abu Rujmein, Jebel (mts.), Syria 63/H5
Abu Shagara, Ras (cape), Sudan 111/G3
Abu Shagara, Ras (cape), Sudan 59/C5
Abut (head), N. Zealand 100/B5
Abu Tabari (well), Sudan 111/E4
Abuyog, Philippines 82/E5
Abu Zabad, Sudan 59/A7
Abu Zabad, Sudan 111/E5
Abwong, Sudan 111/F6
Aby (lag.), Ivory Coast 106/D8
Åbybro, Denmark 21/C3
Abydos (ruins), Egypt 111/F2
Abydos (ruins), Turkey 63/B6
Abyei, Sudan 111/E6
Acacías, Colombia 126/C3
Acaciaville, Nova Scotia 168/C4
Academy, S. Dak. 298/M7
Acadia (par.), La. 238/F6
Acadia Nat'l Park, Maine 243/G7
Acadia Siding, New Bruns. 170/E2
Acadieville, New Bruns. 170/E2
Acahay, Paraguay 144/B5
Acajutla, El Salvador 154/B4
Acala, Mexico 150/N8
Acala, Texas 303/B10
Acámbaro, Mexico 150/J7
Acampo, Calif. 204/C9
Acandí, Colombia 126/B3
Acaponeta, Mexico 150/G5
Acapulco de Juárez, Mexico 146/H8
Acapulco de Juárez, Mexico 150/K8
Acaraí, Serra do (range), Brazil 132/B2
Acarai (mts.), Guyana 131/B5
Acaraú, Brazil 132/F3
Acaray (riv.), Paraguay 144/E4
Acarí, Peru 128/E10
Acarí (riv.), Peru 128/E10
Acarigua, Venezuela 124/D3
Acatlán de Osorio, Mexico 150/K7
Acatzingo de Hidalgo, Mexico 150/N2
Acayucan, Mexico 150/M8
Acchilla, Bolivia 136/C7
Accident, Md. 245/A2
Accokeek, Md. 245/L6
Accomac, Va. 307/S5

Accomack (co.), Va. 307/S5
Accord, Mass. 249/E8
Accord, N.Y. 276/M7
Accoville, W. Va. 312/C7
Accra (cap.), Ghana 102/B4
Accra (cap.), Ghana 106/D7
Accra (cap.), Ghana 2/J5
Accrington, England 10/G1
Accrington, England 13/H1
Aceguá, Uruguay 145/E2
Acequia, Idaho 220/E7
Acevedo, Argentina 143/F6
Achacachi, Bolivia 136/A5
Achalpur, India 68/D4
Achao, Chile 138/D4
Achar, Uruguay 145/C3
Acharacle, Scotland 15/C4
Achégour (well), Niger 106/G5
Achenkirch, Austria 41/A3
Achill (head), Ireland 10/A4
Achill (head), Ireland 17/A4
Achill (isl.), Ireland 10/A4
Achill (isl.), Ireland 17/A4
Achille, Okla. 288/O7
Achilles, Va. 307/R6
Achill Sound, Ireland 17/A4
Achiltibuie, Scotland 15/C3
Achinsk, U.S.S.R. 48/K4
Achnasheen (butte), Scotland 10/D2
Achnasheen, Scotland 15/C3
Achourat (well), Mali 106/D4
A'Chralaig (mt.), Scotland 15/C3
Acı (lake), Turkey 63/C4
Acıgöl, Turkey 63/F3
Acıpayam, Turkey 63/C4
Acireale, Italy 34/E6
Ackerly, Texas 303/C5
Ackerman, Miss. 256/F4
Ackerville, Ala. 195/D6
Ackley, Iowa 229/G3
Acklins (isl.), Bahamas 146/L7
Acklins (isl.), Bahamas 156/C2
Ackworth, Iowa 229/G6
Aclare, Ireland 17/D3
Acle, England 13/J5
Acme, Alberta 182/D4
Acme, La. 238/G4
Acme, Mich. 250/D4
Acme, N.C. 281/N6
Acme, Texas 303/E3
Acme, Wash. 310/C2
Acme, W. Va. 312/D6
Acme, Wyo. 319/E1
Acoaxet, Mass. 249/K7
Acobamba, Peru 128/E9
Acolla, Peru 128/E8
Acoma, N. Mex. 274/B4
Acomayo, Cuzco, Peru 128/F9
Acomayo, Huánuco, Peru 128/E7
Acomita (Pueblo of Acoma), N. Mex. 274/B3
Acona, Miss. 256/D4

Aconcagua (mt.) 120/C6
Aconcagua, Cerro (mt.), Argentina 143/C3
Aconcagua, Chile 138/G4
Aconcagua (riv.), Chile 138/F2
Aconchi, Mexico 150/D2
Acopiara, Brazil 132/G4
Acora, Peru 128/H11
Acorizal, Brazil 132/C6
Acoyapa, Nicaragua 154/E5
Acqui Terme, Italy 34/B2
Acraman (lake), S. Australia 94/D5
Acre (state), Brazil 132/G10
Acre (riv.), Brazil 132/G10
Acre, Israel 65/C2
Acree, Georgia 217/D7
Acri, Italy 34/F5
Ács, Hungary 41/E3
Actinolite, Ontario 177/G3
Acton, Maine 243/B8
Acton•, Maine 243/B8
Acton•, Mass. 249/J3
Acton, Mont. 262/H5
Acton Vale, Québec 172/E4
Actopan, Hidalgo, Mexico 150/K6
Actopan, Veracruz, Mexico 150/Q1
Açu, Brazil 120/F3
Açu, Brazil 132/G4
Aculeo, Chile 138/G4
Aculeo (lag.), Chile 138/G4
Acuña, Argentina 143/G5
Acuracay, Peru 128/F5
Acushnet•, Mass. 249/L6
Acworth•, N.H. 268/C5
Acy, La. 238/L3
Ada, Ghana 106/E7
Ada (co.), Idaho 220/B6
Ada, Kansas 232/E2
Ada, Minn. 255/B3
Ada, Ohio 284/C4
Ada, Okla. 188/G4
Ada, Okla. 288/N5
Ada, W. Va. 312/D8
Adadle, Somalia 115/H2
Adafer (reg.), Mauritania 106/B5
Adair, Ill. 222/C3
Adair (co.), Iowa 229/E6
Adair, Iowa 229/E6
Adair (co.), Ky. 237/L6
Adair (co.), Mo. 261/G2
Adair (cape), N.W. Terr. 187/L2
Adair (co.), Okla. 288/S3
Adair, Okla. 288/R2
Adair, Tenn. 237/D9
Adairsville, Georgia 217/C2
Adair Village, Oreg. 291/D3
Adairville, Ky. 237/H7
Adaja (riv.), Spain 33/D3
Adak (isl.), Alaska 196/L4
Adak (str.), Alaska 196/K4
Adak Naval Air Station, Alaska 196/L4
Adalar (isl.), Turkey 63/D6
Adalia (Antalya), Turkey 63/D4
Adam, Oman 59/G5
Adamawa (reg.), Cameroon 115/B2
Adamawa (reg.), Nigeria 106/G7
Adaminaby, N.S. Wales 97/E5
Adams (lake), Br. Col. 184/H4
Adams (co.), Cclo. 208/L3
Adams (riv.), Br. Col. 184/H4
Adams (co.), Idaho 220/B5
Adams (co.), Ill. 222/B4
Adams (co.), Ind. 227/H3
Adams, Ind. 227/F6
Adams (co.), Iowa 229/D6
Adams, Kansas 232/E4
Adams, Ky. 237/R4
Adams, Mass. 249/B2
Adams•, Mass. 249/B2
Adams, Minn. 255/F7
Adams (co.), Miss. 256/B8
Adams (co.), Nebr. 264/F4
Adams, Nebr. 264/H4
Adams (mt.), N.H. 268/E3
Adams, N.Y. 276/J3
Adams (co.), N. Dak. 282/F7
Adams, N. Dak. 282/O3
Adams (co.), Ohio 284/D8
Adams, Okla. 288/D1
Adams, Oreg. 291/J2
Adams (co.), Pa. 294/H6
Adam's (peak), Sri Lanka 68/E7
Adams, Tenn. 237/G7
Adams (co.), Wash. 310/G3
Adams (mt.), Wash. 310/D4
Adams (co.), Wis. 317/G7
Adams, Wis. 317/G8
Adamsboro, Ind. 227/E3
Adam's Bridge (sound), India 68/D7
Adam's Bridge (shoals), Sri Lanka 68/D7
Adamsburg, S.C. 296/D2
Adams Center, N.Y. 276/H3
Adams Lake, Br. Col. 184/G5
Adams Mills, Ohio 284/G5
Adams Nat'l Hist. Site, Mass. 249/D7
Adamson, Okla. 288/P5
Adams Run, S.C. 296/G6
Adamstown, Md. 245/H3
Adamstown, Pa. 294/K5
Adamstown (cap.), Pitcairn Is. 87/N8
Adamsville, Ala. 195/D4
Adamsville, New Bruns. 170/E2
Adamsville, Ohio 284/G5
Adamsville, Pa. 294/B2
Adamsville, Québec 172/E4
Adamsville, R.I. 249/K6
Adamsville, Tenn. 237/E10
Adamsville, Texas 303/F6
Adamsville, Utah 304/B5
Adana (prov.), Turkey 63/F4
Adana, Turkey 59/C2
Adana, Turkey 63/F4
Adana, Turkey 54/E6
Adanac, Sask. 181/B3
Adapazarı, Turkey 63/D2

Adapazarı, Turkey 59/B1
Adarama, Sudan 111/G4
Adarama, Sudan 59/C6
Adare (cape), Ant. 2/T10
Adare (cape), Ant. 5/B9
Adare, Ireland 17/D6
Adar Qaga, Jebel (mt.), Sudan 59/C5
Adaut, Indonesia 85/J7
Adavale, Queensland 88/G5
Adavale, Queensland 95/C5
Adaza, Iowa 229/E4
Adda (riv.), Italy 34/B2
Adda (riv.), Sudan 111/D6
Addanki, India 68/D5
Addieville, Ill. 222/D5
Addington, Okla. 288/L6
Addis, La. 238/J2
Addis Ababa (cap.), Ethiopia 102/F4
Addis Ababa (cap.), Ethiopia 2/L5
Addis Ababa (cap.), Ethiopia 111/G6
Addis Alam, Ethiopia 111/G6
Addison, Ala. 195/D2
Addison, Conn. 210/E2
Addison, Ill. 222/B5
Addison, Maine 243/H6
Addison•, Maine 243/H6
Addison, Mich. 250/E7
Addison, N.Y. 276/F6
Addison, Ohio 284/D5
Addison, Pa. 294/D6
Addison, Texas 303/N9
Addison (co.), Vt. 268/A3
Addison, Vt. 268/A3
Addison (Webster Springs), W. Va. 312/F6
Addi Ugri, Ethiopia 59/C7
Ad Diwaniya, Iraq 66/D5
Addo Nat'l Park, S. Africa 118/D6
Addor, N.C. 281/L4
Addy, Wash. 310/H2
Addyston, Ohio 284/B9
Ade, Ind. 227/C3
Adel, Georgia 217/F8
Adel, Iowa 229/E5
Adel, Oreg. 291/H5
Adelaide (isl.), Ant. 5/C15
Adelaide, Australia 87/D9
Adelaide, Australia 2/S7
Adelaide (pen.), N.W. Terr. 187/J3
Adelaide, S. Africa 118/D6
Adelaide (cap.), S. Australia 88/D8
Adelaide Airport, Australia 88/D8
Adelaide River, North. Terr. 88/E2
Adelaide River, North. Terr. 93/B2
Adelanto, Calif. 204/H9
Adelboden, Switzerland 39/E3
Adele (isl.), W. Australia 88/C3
Adele (isl.), W. Australia 92/C1
Adélie Coast (reg.), Ant. 5/C7
Adeline, Ill. 222/D1
Adeline, La. 238/G7
Adell, Wis. 317/L8
Adelong, N.S. Wales 97/D4
Adelphi, Jamaica 158/H5
Adelphi, Ohio 284/E7
Adelphia, N.J. 273/E3
Aden (gulf) 54/F8
Aden (gulf) 2/M5
Aden (gulf) 102/G3
Aden, Alberta 182/E5
Aden (gulf), Djibouti 111/J5
Aden (gulf), Somalia 115/J1
Aden, Yemen 54/F8
Aden, Yemen 59/E7
Adena, Ohio 284/J5
Adenau, Germany 22/B3
Adger, Ala. 195/D4
Adhaim (riv.), Iraq 66/D3
Adi (isl.), Indonesia 85/J6
Adícora, Venezuela 124/D2
Adige (riv.), Italy 34/C2
Adigrat, Ethiopia 111/G5
Adilabad, India 68/D5
Adilcevaz, Turkey 63/K3
Adin, Calif. 204/E2
Adirondack, N.Y. 276/N3
Adirondack (mts.), N.Y. 276/M3
Adi Ugri, Ethiopia 111/G5
Adiyaman (prov.), Turkey 63/H4
Adıyaman, Turkey 63/H4
Adjuntas, P. Rico 161/B2
Adjuntas, P. Rico 156/F1
Adkins, Texas 303/K11
Adlatok (bay), Newf. 166/B2
Adlavik (isls.), Newf. 166/C2
Adliswil, Switzerland 39/F2
Admiral, Sask. 181/C6
Admiral's Beach, Newf. 166/D2
Admiral's Cove, Newf. 166/D2
Admiralty (inlet) 162/H1
Admiralty (isl.), Alaska 196/M1
Admiralty (isls.), N.S. Wales 97/J1
Admiralty (inlet), N.W. Terr. 187/K2
Admiralty, Papua N.G. 86/A1
Admiralty (inlet), Papua N.G. 87/E6
Admiralty (inlet), Wash. 310/B2
Admiralty (gulf), W. Australia 88/D2
Admiralty (gulf), W. Australia 92/D1
Admiralty Island Nat'l Mon., Alaska 196/M1
Admire, Kansas 232/F3
Admont, Austria 41/C3
Adna, Wash. 310/B4
Ado, Nigeria 106/E7
Adobe Creek (res.), Colo. 208/N6
Adok, Sudan 111/F6
Adolfo Alsina, Argentina 143/D4
Adolph, Minn. 255/F4
Adolph, W. Va. 312/F5
Adolphus, Ky. 237/J7
Adona, Ark. 202/E3
Adonara (isl.), Indonesia 85/G7
Adoni, India 68/D5
Adorf, Germany 22/E3
Adour (riv.), France 28/C4
Adra, Spain 33/F4
Adrano, Italy 34/E6
Adrar, Algeria 102/B2
Adrar, Algeria 106/D3

Adrar, Algeria 106/D3
Adrar, Mauritania 106/B4
Adrar des Iforas (plat.), Algeria 106/E5
Adrar des Iforas (plat.), Mali 106/E5
Adré, Chad 111/D5
Adria, Italy 34/D2
Adrian, Georgia 217/G5
Adrian, Ill. 222/B3
Adrian, Mich. 250/F7
Adrian, Minn. 255/C7
Adrian, Mo. 261/D6
Adrian, N. Dak. 282/O6
Adrian, Ohio 284/D3
Adrian, Oreg. 291/K4
Adrian, Pa. 294/D4
Adrian, S.C. 296/J4
Adrian, Texas 303/B2
Adrian, W. Va. 312/F5
Adriatic (sea) 7/F4
Adriatic (sea), Albania 45/B4
Adriatic (sea), Italy 34/E3
Adriatic (sea), Yugoslavia 45/B4
Aduwa, Ethiopia 59/C7
Advance, Ind. 227/D5
Advance, Mich. 250/D3
Advance, Mo. 261/N8
Advance, N.C. 281/J3
Advent, W. Va. 312/C5
Adventure (sound), 143/E7
Adventure (bay), Chile 138/D5
Adventure, Guyana 131/B2
Adventure Bay, Tasmania 99/D5
Advocate (bay), Nova Scotia 168/D3
Advocate Harbour, Nova Scotia 168/D3
Adwa, Ethiopia 111/G5
Adwick le Street, England 13/K2
Adygey Aut. Obl., U.S.S.R. 52/F6
Adygey Aut. Obl., U.S.S.R. 48/D5
Adzhar A.S.S.R., U.S.S.R. 52/F6
Adzhar A.S.S.R., U.S.S.R. 48/E5
Ae, Scotland 15/E5
Aeber (creek), S. Dak. 298/G4
Aegean (sea), Greece 7/G5
Aegean (sea), Greece 45/G6
Aegean (sea), Turkey 63/A3
Aegean Islands (reg.), Greece 45/G6
Aeneas, Wash. 310/F2
Aerial, Alberta 182/D4
AErø (isl.), Denmark 21/D8
AErøskøbing, Denmark 21/D8
Aeschi bei Spiez, Switzerland 39/E3
Aetna, Alberta 182/D5
Aetna, Tenn. 237/G9
Afaq, Iraq 66/D4
Afareaitu, Fr. Poly. 86/S13
Afayan (pt.), Guam 86/K7
Afdem, Ethiopia 111/H6
Affolé (reg.), Mauritania 106/B5
Affoltern am Albis, Switzerland 39/F2
Affoltern im Emmental, Switzerland 39/E2
Affric, Loch (lake), Scotland 15/D3
Affton, Mo. 261/N4
Afghanistan 2/N4
Afghanistan 54/H6
AFGHANISTAN 68/A2
Afgoi, Somalia 102/G4
Afgoi, Somalia 115/J3
Afif, Saudi Arabia 59/D5
Afikpo, Nigeria 106/F7
Afiqim, Israel 65/D2
Afjord, Norway 18/G5
Aflex, Ky. 237/S5
Afmadu, Somalia 115/H3
Afognak (isl.), Alaska 196/H3
Africa 2/K4
AFRICA 102
Afşin, Turkey 63/G3
Afton, Iowa 229/E6
Afton, La. 238/H2
Afton, Mich. 250/E3
Afton, Minn. 255/F6
Afton, N.Y. 276/J6
Afton, Okla. 288/S1
Afton, Tenn. 237/R8
Afton, Texas 303/D4
Afton, Va. 307/L4
Afton, Wis. 317/H10
Afton, Wyo. 319/B3
Afuá, Brazil 132/D3
'Afula, Israel 65/C2
Afyonkarahisar (prov.), Turkey 63/D3
Afyonkarahisar, Turkey 63/D3
Afyonkarahisar, Turkey 59/A2
Agadem (well), Niger 106/F5
Agadès, Niger 106/F5
Agadès, Niger 102/C3
Agadir, Morocco 106/C2
Agadir, Morocco 102/B2
Agaña (cap.), Guam 87/E4
Agaña (cap.), Guam 86/K7
Agano (riv.), Japan 81/J4
Agar, S. Dak. 298/J4
Agartala, India 68/G4
Agassiz (peak), Ariz. 198/D3
Agassiz (mt.), Utah 304/D3
Agat, Guam 86
Agat (bay), Guam 86/K7
Agata, U.S.S.R. 48/K3
Agate, Colo. 208/M4
Agate, Nebr. 264/A2
Agate, N. Dak. 282/L2
Agate Beach, Oreg. 291/C3
Agate Fossil Beds Nat'l Mon., Nebr. 264/A2
Agats, Indonesia 85/K7
Agatti (isl.), India 68/C6
Agattu (isl.), Alaska 196/J3
Agattu (str.), Alaska 196/J3
Agawa Bay, Ontario 177/J5
Agawa Bay, Ontario 175/D3
Agawam•, Mass. 249/D4
Agawam (riv.), Mass. 249/M5
Agawam (pt.), Mass. 249/M5
Agboville, Ivory Coast 102/B4
Agboville, Ivory Coast 106/D7
Agdam, U.S.S.R. 52/G6
Agde, France 28/E6

Agen, France 28/D5
Agency, Iowa 229/J7
Agency (lake), Oreg. 291/E5
Agency (lake), Oreg. 291/E5
Agenda, Kansas 232/E2
Ageo, Japan 81/O2
Agerbaek, Denmark 21/B6
Agerisee (lake), Switzerland 39/G2
Ages, Ky. 237/P7
Aghada-Farsid-Rostellan, Ireland 17/E8
Aghadoe, Ireland 17/B7
Aghagower, Ireland 17/C4
Agha Jari, Iran 66/F5
Aginsk Buryat Aut. Okr., U.S.S.R. 48/M4
Aginskoye, U.S.S.R. 48/M4
Agiobampo (bay), Mexico 150/E3
Agira, Italy 34/E6
Ağlasun, Turkey 63/D4
Ağlı, Turkey 63/E2
Agno, Philippines 82/B2
Agnone, Italy 34/E4
Agnos, Ark. 202/G1
Agoo, Philippines 82/C2
Agordat, Ethiopia 111/G4
Agordat, Ethiopia 59/C6
Agra, India 54/J7
Agra, India 68/D3
Agra, Kansas 232/C2
Agra, Okla. 288/N3
Agraciada, Uruguay 145/A4
Agrado, Colombia 126/C6
Agramonte, Cuba 158/D1
Agreda, Spain 33/E2
Ağrı (prov.), Turkey 63/K3
Ağrı, Büyük (Ararat) (mt.), Turkey 63/L3
Ağrı (Karaköse), Turkey 63/K3
Agricola, Kansas 232/G3
Agricola, Miss. 256/G9
Agrigento (prov.), Italy 34/D6
Agrigento, Italy 34/D6
Agrihan (isl.), No. Marianas 87/E4
Agrínion, Greece 45/E6
Agropoli, Italy 34/E4
Agryz, U.S.S.R. 52/H3
Agua Caliente, Ariz. 198/B4
Agua Caliente Ind. Res., Calif. 204/J10
Aguachica, Colombia 126/D3
Aguada, P. Rico 161/A1
Aguada de Pasajeros, Cuba 158/D2
Aguada Grande, Venezuela 124/D2
Aguadas, Colombia 126/C5
Agua de Dios, Colombia 126/C5
Aguadilla (dist.), P. Rico 161/A1
Aguadilla, P. Rico 156/F1
Aguadilla, P. Rico 161/A1
Aguadilla (bay), P. Rico 161/A1
Agua Dulce, Mexico 150/M7
Aguadulce, Panama 154/G6
Agua Dulce, Texas 303/F10
Agua Fria (riv.), Ariz. 198/C5
Agua Fría, Venezuela 124/D2
Agualeguas, Mexico 150/J3
Agua Linda, Venezuela 124/E5
Aguán (riv.), Honduras 154/E3
Aguanaval (riv.), Mexico 150/H4
Aguanish, Québec 174/B2
Aguanus (riv.), Newf. 166/B3
Aguanus (riv.), Québec 174/E2
Agua Prieta, Mexico 150/E1
Aguaray, Argentina 143/D1
Aguarico (riv.), Colombia 126/B7
Aguarico (riv.), Ecuador 128/D3
Aguasay, Venezuela 124/G3
Aguas Blancas, Chile 138/B4
Aguas Buenas, P. Rico 161/E2
Aguas Calientes, Cerro (mt.), Chile 138/C4
Aguascalientes (state), Mexico 150/H6
Aguascalientes, Mexico 150/H6
Aguascalientes, Mexico 146/H7
Aguas Corrientes, Uruguay 145/A6
Agua Vermelha (res.), Brazil 135/B3
Aguaytía (riv.), Peru 128/E7
Agudos, Brazil 135/B3
Águeda, Portugal 33/B2
Agueda (riv.), Spain 33/C2
Aguedaueda (riv.), Portugal 33/C2
Agueraktem (well), Mali 106/C4
Agueraktem (well), Mauritania 106/C4
Aguila, Ariz. 198/B5
Aguilar, Colo. 208/K8
Aguilar, Spain 33/F4
Aguilares, Argentina 143/C2
Aguilas, Spain 33/F4
Aguililla, Mexico 150/H7
Aguja, La (cape), Colombia 126/C2
Aguja (pt.), Peru 120/A2
Aguja (pt.), Peru 128/A5
Aguja (pt.), Peru 120/A3
Agulhas (cape), S. Africa 102/D8
Agulhas (cape), S. Africa 118/B6
Agusan (riv.), Philippines 82/E6
Agusan, Philippines 82/E6
Agusan del Norte (prov.), Philippines 82/E6
Agusan del Sur (prov.), Philippines 82/E6
Agustín Codazzi, Colombia 126/D3
Agutaya, Philippines 82/C5
Agutaya (isl.), Philippines 82/C5
Ahaggar (range), Algeria 102/C2
Ahaggar (range), Algeria 106/F4
Ahangaran, Afghanistan 111/J3
Ahar, Iran 66/E1
Ahascragh, Ireland 17/E5
Ahau, Fiji 87/H7
Ahaura, N. Zealand 100/C5
Ahaus, Germany 22/B2
Aherlow (riv.), Ireland 17/E7
Ah-Gwah-Ching, Minn. 255/D3
Ahipara, N. Zealand 100/D1
Ahlat, Turkey 63/K3
Ahlbeck, Germany 22/F2
Ahlen, Germany 22/B3
Ahmadabad, India 2/N4

Ahmadabad, India 68/C4
Ahmadabad, India 54/J7
Ahmadnagar, India 68/C5
Ahmadpur East, Pakistan 68/C3
Ahmeek, Mich. 250/A1
Ahmic (lake), Ontario 177/E2
Ahoghill, N. Ireland 17/J2
Ahome, Mexico 150/E4
Ahoskie, N.C. 281/P2
Ahousat, Br. Col. 184/D5
Ahrensburg, Germany 22/D2
Ahsahka, Idaho 220/B3
Ähtäri, Finland 18/N5
Ahtanum (creek), Wash. 310/D4
Ähtäri, Finland 18/N5
Ahuacatitlán, Mexico 150/L1
Ahuacatlán, Mexico 150/G6
Ahuachapán, El Salvador 154/B4
Ahuás, Honduras 154/E3
Ahumada, Mexico 150/F1
Ahurei, Fr. Poly. 87/M8
Åhus, Sweden 18/J9
Ahuzzam, Israel 65/B4
Ahvaz, Iran 54/F3
Ahvaz, Iran 59/E3
Ahvaz (Ahwaz), Iran 66/F5
Ahvenanmaa (prov.), Finland 18/L6
Ahwahnee, Calif. 204/F6
Ahwar, Yemen 59/E7
Ai-Ais, Namibia 118/B5
Aialik (bay), Alaska 196/C1
Aiama (lake), Brazil 132/H9
Aibonito, P. Rico 161/E2
Aichi (pref.), Japan 81/H6
Aid, Ohio 284/F8
Aid, Mo. 261/M9
Aiea, Hawaii 218/B3
Aigen im Mühlkreis, Austria 41/B2
Aigle (riv.), Québec 172/A3
Aigle, Switzerland 39/C4
Aiguá, Uruguay 145/E5
Aiguá (riv.), Uruguay 145/E4
Aigues-Mortes, France 28/F6
Aiguille d'Argentière (mt.), Switzerland 39/C5
Aihui (Aigun) (Heihe), China 77/L1
Aija, Peru 128/D7
Aikawa, Japan 81/H4
Aiken (co.), S.C. 296/D4
Aiken, S.C. 296/D4
Aikens (lake), Manitoba 179/G3
Aiken West, S.C. 296/D4
Aikin, Md. 245/O2
Aileron, North. Terrs. 93/C7
Ailey, Georgia 217/G6
Ailingalapalap (atoll), Marshall Is. 87/G5
Aillon (lake), Québec 172/C2
Ailsa Craig, Ontario 177/C4
Ailsa Craig (isl.), Scotland 15/C5
Ailuk (atoll), Marshall Is. 87/H4
Aimogasta, Argentina 143/C2
Aimwell, La. 238/G3
Ain (dept.), France 28/F4
Ain (riv.), France 28/F4
Ainabo, Somalia 115/J2
Aina Haina, Hawaii 218/F2
'Ain al Mubarrak, Saudi Arabia 59/C5
Ainaži, U.S.S.R. 53/C2
Aïn Beïda, Algeria 106/F1
Aïn ben Tili (well), Mauritania 106/C3
'Ain el 'Arab, Syria 63/H4
Ain-Galakka, Chad 111/F6
Aïn Sefra, Algeria 106/D2
Ainslie (lake), Nova Scotia 168/G3
Ainsworth, Br. Col. 184/J5
Ainsworth, Iowa 229/K6
Ainsworth, Nebr. 264/D2
Aïn Temouchent, Algeria 106/D1
Aïn Zueira (well), Libya 111/D3
Aïoun el Atrous, Mauritania 106/C5
Aïoun el Atrous, Mauritania 102/B3
Aipe, Colombia 126/C6
Aiquile, Bolivia 136/C6
Aiquina, Chile 138/C4
Air (mts.), Niger 106/F5
Airdrie, Alberta 182/C4
Airdrie, Scotland 10/B1
Airdrie, Scotland 15/C2
Aire (riv.), England 10/F4
Aire (riv.), England 13/G2
Aire-sur-l'Adour, France 28/C6
Airey, Md. 245/O6
Air Force (isl.), N.W. Terr. 187/L3
Air Force Academy, Colo. 208/K5
Airlie, Oreg. 291/D3
Airolo, Switzerland 39/G3
Air Ronge, Sask. 181/M3
Airville, Pa. 294/K6
Airway Heights, Wash. 310/H3
Aisén del General Carlos Ibáñez del Campo (terr.), Chile 138/E6
Aišiškes, U.S.S.R. 53/C3
Aisne (dept.), France 28/E3
Aisne (riv.), France 28/E3
Aitape, Papua N.G. 85/B6
Aith, Scotland 15/G2
Aitkin (co.), Minn. 255/E4
Aitkin, Minn. 255/E4
Aitutaki (atoll), Cook Is. 87/K7
Aiud, Romania 45/G3
Aix, France 7/E4
Aix (mt.), Wash. 310/D4
Aix-en-Provence, France 28/F6
Aix-les-Bains, France 28/F4
Aíyina, Greece 45/F7
Aíyion, Greece 45/F6
Aizpute, U.S.S.R. 53/A2
Aizuwakamatsu, Japan 81/J5
Ajaccio, France 7/E4
Ajaccio, France 28/B7
Ajaccio (gulf), France 28/B7
Ajalpan, Mexico 150/N2
Ajana, W. Australia 92/A5
Ajanta, India 68/D4
Ajax, La. 238/F5
Ajax, Ontario 177/E4
Ajdabia, Libya 111/D1
Aji Chai (riv.), Iran 66/E1

Ajigasawa, Japan 81/J3
'Ajja, West Bank 65/C3
Ajka, Hungary 41/D3
'Ajlun, Jordan 65/D3
'Ajlun (range), Jordan 65/D3
'Ajman, U.A.E. 59/G4
Ajmer, India 68/C3
Ajmer, India 54/J7
Ajo, Ariz. 198/C6
Ajoewa, Suriname 131/C4
Ajoupa-Bouillon, Martinique 161/C3
Akan National Park, Japan 81/M2
Akaroa, N. Zealand 100/D5
Akasha, Sudan 111/F3
Akashi, Japan 81/H8
Akaska, S. Dak. 298/J3
Akbaba Tepesi (mt.), Turkey 63/H3
Akçaabat, Turkey 63/H2
Akçadağ, Turkey 63/G3
Akçakale, Turkey 63/H4
Akçakoca, Turkey 63/D2
Akçay, Turkey 63/B4
Akçay (riv.), Turkey 63/C4
Akdağ (mt.), Turkey 59/A2
Akdağ (mt.), Turkey 63/E4
Akdağ (mt.), Turkey 63/D4
Akdağ (mt.), Turkey 63/C4
Akdağmadeni, Turkey 63/F3
Akeley, Minn. 255/D3
Akeley, Pa. 294/D2
Aken, Germany 22/D3
Akers, La. 238/L3
Akershus (co.), Norway 18/H6
Aketi, Zaire 102/E4
Aketi, Zaire 115/D3
Akhaltsikhe, U.S.S.R. 52/F6
Akhdar, Jebel (mts.), Libya 111/D1
Akhdar, Jebel (range), Oman 59/G5
Akhdar, Saudi Arabia 59/C4
Akhisar, Turkey 63/B3
Akhmim, Egypt 111/F2
Akhmim, Egypt 59/B4
Akhtopol, Bulgaria 45/H4
Akhtubinsk, U.S.S.R. 52/G5
Akhty, U.S.S.R. 52/G6
Akhtyrka, U.S.S.R. 52/E4
Aki, Japan 81/F7
Akiachak, Alaska 196/F2
Akimiski (isl.), N.W.T. 162/H5
Akins, Okla. 288/S3
Akirkeby, Denmark 21/F9
Akita (pref.), Japan 81/J3
Akita, Japan 81/J3
Akita, Japan 54/P6
Akitio, N. Zealand 100/F4
Akjoujt, Mauritania 106/B5
Akkerman (Belgorod-Dnestrovskiy), U.S.S.R. 52/E5
Akkeshi, Japan 81/M2
Akko (Acre), Israel 65/C2
Akkrum, Netherlands 27/H2
Aklan (prov.), Philippines 82/D5
Aklavik, Canada 4/C16
Aklavik, N.W.T. 162/C2
Aklavik, N.W. Terr. 187/E3
Akmolinsk (Tselinograd), U.S.S.R. 48/H4
Akobo (riv.), Ethiopia 111/F6
Akobo, Sudan 111/F6
Akobo (riv.), Sudan 111/F6
Akola, India 68/D4
Akolmiut (Kasigluk), Alaska 196/F2
Akpatok (isl.), N.W.T. 162/K3
Akpatok (isl.), N.W. Terr. 187/M3
Akpazar, Turkey 63/H3
Akpınar, Turkey 63/D5
Akqi, China 77/A3
Akra, N. Dak. 282/P2
Akranes, Iceland 21/B1
Akreïjit, Mauritania 106/C5
Akrítas (cape), Greece 45/E7
Akron, Ala. 195/C5
Akron, Colo. 208/N2
Akron, Ind. 227/E2
Akron, Iowa 229/A3
Akron, Mich. 250/F5
Akron, N.Y. 276/C4
Akron, Ohio 188/K2
Akron, Ohio 284/G5
Akron, Ohio 146/K5
Akron, Pa. 294/K5
Aksai Chin (reg.), Pakistan 68/D2
Aksaray, Turkey 63/F3
Aksay, U.S.S.R. 48/F4
Aksay, China 77/D4
Akşehir, Turkey 63/D3
Akşehir, Turkey 59/B2
Akşehir (lake), Turkey 63/D3
Akseki, Turkey 63/D4
Aksu, China 54/K5
Aksu (riv.), Turkey 63/D4
Aksum, Ethiopia 102/F3
Aksum, Ethiopia 111/G5
Aksum, Ethiopia 59/C7
Aktas, U.S.S.R. 48/J5
Aktash, U.S.S.R. 48/J4
Aktí (pen.), Greece 45/G5
Aktyubinsk, U.S.S.R. 54/G4
Aktyubinsk, U.S.S.R. 48/F4
Aku, Nigeria 106/F7
Akun (isl.), Alaska 196/E4
Akune, Japan 81/E7
Akure, Ghana 106/E7
Akureyri, Iceland 21/C1
Akureyri, Iceland 7/C2
Akuse, Ghana 106/E7
Akutan (isl.), Alaska 196/E4
Akutan, Alaska 196/E4
Akutan (passage), Alaska 196/E4
Akviran, Turkey 63/D4
Akyab (Sittwe), Burma 72/B2
Akyazı, Turkey 63/D2
Ål, Norway 18/F6
Alabam, Ark. 202/C1

Alley 327

abama 188/J4
_ABAMA 195
abama (riv.), Ala. 188/J4
abama (riv.), Ala. 195/C8
abama (state), U.S. 146/K6
abaster, Ala. 195/E4
abaster, Mich. 250/F4
abat, Philippines 82/D3
abat (isl.), Philippines 82/D3
aca, Turkey 63/F2
acahan, Turkey 63/G3
açam, Turkey 63/F2
achua (co.), Fla. 212/D2
achua, Fla. 212/D2
acrán (reef), Mexico 150/P5
acranes, Cuba 158/D1
adağ (mt.), Turkey 63/F4
adagh, Kuh-e (mts.), Iran 66/K2
adagh, Kuh-i- (mt.), Iran 59/G2
addin, Wyo. 319/H1
aejos, Spain 33/D2
agir, U.S.S.R. 52/F6
agoa Grande, Brazil 132/H4
agoas (state), Brazil 132/G5
agoinhas, Brazil 120/F4
agoinhas, Brazil 132/G6
agón, Spain 33/F2
agón (riv.), Spain 33/C2
ah (riv.), Philippines 82/E7
Ahqaf (Bahr es Safi) (des.), Saudi Arabia 59/E6
'Ain, Saudi Arabia 59/C4
ajuela, C. Rica 154/E6
akanuk, Alaska 196/E2
akol' (lake), U.S.S.R. 48/J5
'Ala, Saudi Arabia 59/C4
alakeiki (chan.), Hawaii 218/J3
alapadu, Suriname 131/C4
amagan (isl.), No. Marianas 87/E4
amance (co.), N.C. 281/L3
amance, N.C. 281/K2
ameda (co.), Calif. 204/D6
ameda, Calif. 204/J2
ameda (creek), Calif. 204/K3
ameda, N. Mex. 274/C3
ameda, Sask. 181/J6
amikamba, Nicaragua 154/E4
'amo (lake), Ariz. 198/B4
amo (riv.), Calif. 204/K10
amo, Georgia 217/G6
amo, Ind. 227/C5
amo, Mexico 150/L6
amo, Nev. 266/F5
amo, N. Dak. 282/D2
amo, Tenn. 237/C9
amo, Texas 303/F11
la Moana, Hawaii 218/C4
amo-Danville, Calif. 204/K2
amogordo, N. Mex. 188/E4
amogordo, N. Mex. 274/C6
amo Heights, Texas 303/K10
amos, Mexico 150/E3
amosa (co.), Colo. 208/H7
amosa, Colo. 208/H8
'amosa (creek), Colo. 208/G8
amosa (riv.), N. Mex. 274/B5
amota, Kansas 232/B3
and (Ahvenanmaa) (prov.), Finland 18/L6
and (isls.), Finland 7/F2
and (isls.), Finland 18/L6
anje, Panama 154/F6
anreed, Texas 303/D2
anson, Mich. 250/E3
anthus Grove, Mo. 261/D2
anya, Turkey 59/B2
anya, Turkey 63/D4
laotra (lake), Madagascar 118/H3
lapaha (riv.), Fla. 212/C1
lapaha, Georgia 217/F8
lapaha (riv.), Georgia 217/F7
laqua (creek), Fla. 212/C6
larcón (res.), Spain 33/E3
larka, N.C. 281/C4
las (str.), Indonesia 85/F7
aşehir, Turkey 63/C3
lashtar, Iran 66/E4
laska (reg.) 4/C17
aska 188/C5
LASKA 196
aska (gulf), Alaska 146/D4
aska (gulf), Alaska 188/D6
aska (gulf), Alaska 196/K3
aska (pen.), Alaska 188/C6
laska (pen.), Alaska 146/C4
laska (pen.), Alaska 196/G3
laska (range), Alaska 188/C6
laska (range), Alaska 146/C3
laska (range), Alaska 196/H2
laska, Mich. 250/D6
laska (state), U.S. 2/B2
laska (state), U.S. 146/C3
laska (gulf), U.S. 4/D17
laska (pen.), U.S. 4/D18
laska (range), U.S. 4/C17
laska Highway, Yukon 187/E3
lassio, Italy 34/A2
atna, Alaska 196/H1
atna (riv.), Alaska 196/H1
atri, Italy 34/D4
atyr', U.S.S.R. 52/G4
l 'Áuda, Saudi Arabia 59/E4
lausí, Ecuador 128/C4
lava (prov.), Spain 33/E1
lava (cape), Wash. 188/A1
lava (cape), Wash. 310/A2
laverdi, U.S.S.R. 52/F6
lavus, Finland 18/N5
layor, Spain 33/J3
l 'Azair, Iraq 66/E5
lazeya (riv.), U.S.S.R. 48/Q3
l 'Aziziya, Iraq 59/E3
l 'Aziziya, Iraq 66/D4
lba, Italy 34/B2
lba, Mich. 250/E4
lba, Mo. 261/D8
lba, Pa. 294/J2
lba, Texas 303/J5
Albacete (prov.), Spain 33/E3
Albacete, Spain 7/D5
Albacete, Spain 33/F3
Alba de Tormes, Spain 33/D2
Albaida, Spain 33/F3
Alba Iulia, Romania 45/F2
Albalate del Arzobispo, Spain 33/F2
Alban, Ontario 177/E1
Albanel, Québec 172/E1
Albanel (lake), Québec 174/C2
Albania 2/K3
Albania 7/G4
ALBANIA 45/E5
Albano (lake), Italy 34/F7
Albano Laziale, Italy 34/F7
Albany, Australia 87/B9
Albany, Calif. 204/J2
Albany, Ga. 146/K6
Albany, Georgia 217/D7
Albany, Ill. 222/C2
Albany, Ind. 227/G4
Albany, Jamaica 158/J6
Albany, Ky. 237/L7
Albany, La. 238/M1
Albany, Minn. 255/D5
Albany, Mo. 261/D2
Albany•, N.H. 268/E4
Albany (cap.), N.Y. 188/M2
Albany (cap.), N.Y. 146/L5
Albany (co.), N.Y. 276/M5
Albany (cap.), N.Y. 276/N5
Albany, N. Zealand 100/B1
Albany, Nova Scotia 168/C4
Albany, Ohio 284/F7
Albany, Okla. 288/O7
Albany (riv.), Ont. 146/K4
Albany (riv.), Ont. 162/H5
Albany (riv.), Ontario 175/C2
Albany, Oreg. 188/B2
Albany, Oreg. 291/D3
Albany, Pr. Edward I. 168/E2
Albany, Texas 303/E5
Albany, Vt. 268/C2
Albany•, Vt. 268/C2
Albany, W. Australia 88/B6
Albany, W. Australia 92/B6
Albany, Wis. 317/G10
Albany (co.), Wyo. 319/G4
Albany, Wyo. 319/F4
Albany Creek, Queensland 88/J2
Albardón, Argentina 143/C3
Albarracín, Spain 33/F2
Albatross (pt.), N. Zealand 100/E3
Albatross (bay), Queensland 88/G2
Albatross (bay), Queensland 95/B2
Albay (prov.), Philippines 82/D4
Albay (gulf), Philippines 82/D4
Albee, S. Dak. 298/R3
Albemarle (pt.), Ecuador 128/B9
Albemarle (sound), N.C. 188/L3
Albemarle, N.C. 281/J4
Albemarle (sound), N.C. 281/S2
Albemarle (co.), Va. 307/L5
Albenga, Italy 34/B3
Albeni Falls (dam), Idaho 220/B1
Alberdi, Paraguay 144/D5
Alberene, Va. 307/L5
Alberga, S. Australia 94/D2
Alberga, The (riv.), S. Australia 94/D2
Alberga, The (riv.), S. Australia 88/E5
Alberhill, Calif. 204/E11
Alberni (inlet), Br. Col. 184/H3
Albers, Ill. 222/D5
Albert (canal), Belgium 27/F6
Albert, France 28/E2
Albert, Kansas 232/C3
Albert (co.), New Bruns. 170/F3
Albert, N. Mex. 274/F3
Albert, N.S. Wales 97/D3
Albert, Okla. 288/K4
Albert (lake), Québec 172/C3
Albert (Mobuto Sese Seko) (lake), Uganda 115/F3
Albert (creek), Wyo. 319/B4
Albert (Mobuto Sese Seko) (lake), Zaire 115/F3
ALBERTA 182
Alberta (prov.) 162/E5
Alberta, Ala. 195/C5
Alberta (mt.), Alberta 182/B3
Alberta (mt.), Alta. 162/E5
Alberta (prov.), Canada 146/G4
Alberta, La. 238/D2
Alberta, Minn. 255/B5
Alberta, Va. 307/N7
Alberta Beach, Alberta 182/C3
Albert City, Iowa 229/C3
Albert Edward (bay), N.W. Terr. 187/H3
Albert Head, Br. Col. 184/J4
Alberti, Argentina 143/G7
Albertirsa, Hungary 41/E3
Albert Lea, Minn. 255/E7
Albert Mines, New Bruns. 170/F3
Alberton, Mont. 262/B3
Alberton, Pr. Edward I. 168/E2
Alberton, S. Africa 118/H6
Albert Town, Jamaica 158/H6
Albertville, Ala. 195/F2
Albertville, France 28/G5
Albertville, Minn. 255/E5
Albertville, Sask. 181/F2
Albeuve, Switzerland 39/D3
Albi, France 28/E6
Albia, Iowa 229/H6
Albin, Wyo. 319/H4
Albina, Suriname 131/D3
Albino, Italy 34/B2
Albion, Calif. 204/B4
Albion, Idaho 220/E7
Albion (mts.), Idaho 220/E7
Albion, Ill. 222/E5
Albion, Ind. 227/G2
Albion, Iowa 229/H4
Albion•, Maine 243/E6
Albion, Mich. 250/E6
Albion, Nebr. 264/F3
Albion, N.Y. 276/D4
Albion, Okla. 288/R5
Albion, Pa. 294/B2
Albion, R.I. 249/H5
Albion, Wash. 310/H4
Albion, Wis. 317/H10
Al Birk, Saudi Arabia 59/D6
Albocácer, Spain 33/F2
Alborán (isl.), Spain 7/D5
Alborán (isl.), Spain 33/E5
Ålborg, Denmark 7/F3
Ålborg, Denmark 18/G8
Ålborg,Ålborg (bay), Denmark 21/D4
Alborn, Minn. 255/F4
Albox, Spain 33/E4
Albreda, Br. Col. 184/H4
Albright, W. Va. 312/G3
Albrightsville, Pa. 294/L3
Albristhorn (mt.), Switzerland 39/D4
Albstadt, Germany 22/C4
Albufeira, Portugal 33/B4
Albuñol, Spain 33/E4
Albuquerque (cays), Colombia 126/A10
Albuquerque, N. Mex. 146/H6
Albuquerque, N. Mex. 188/E3
Albuquerque, N. Mex. 274/C3
Alburg, Vt. 268/A2
Alburg•, Vt. 268/A2
Alburnett, Iowa 229/K4
Alburquerque, Spain 33/C3
Alburtis, Pa. 294/L5
Albury, Australia 87/E9
Albury, N. S. Wales 88/H7
Albury, N.S. Wales 97/D5
Albury, N. Zealand 100/C6
Alca, Peru 128/F10
Alcácer do Sal, Portugal 33/B3
Alcalá, Bolivia 136/C6
Alcalá de Chivert, Spain 33/G2
Alcalá de Guadaira, Spain 33/D4
Alcalá de Henares, Spain 33/G4
Alcalá de los Gazules, Spain 33/D4
Alcalá la Real, Spain 33/E4
Alcalde, N. Mex. 274/C2
Alcamo, Italy 34/D6
Alcanar, Spain 33/G2
Alcañices, Spain 33/C2
Alcañiz, Spain 33/F2
Alcàntara, Portugal 33/A1
Alcántara, Spain 33/C3
Alcántara (res.), Spain 33/C3
Alcántaratara (res.), Portugal 33/C3
Alcantarilla, Spain 33/F4
Alcaraz, Argentina 143/G5
Alcaraz, Spain 33/E3
Alcaraz, Sierra de (range), Spain 33/E3
Alcatraz (isl.), Calif. 204/J2
Alcaudete, Spain 33/E4
Alcázar de San Juan, Spain 33/E3
Alcester, S. Dak. 298/R7
Alcida, New Bruns. 170/E1
Alcira, Spain 33/F3
Alco, Ark. 202/F2
Alco, La. 238/D4
Alcoa, Tenn. 237/N9
Alcobaça, Brazil 132/G7
Alcobaça, Portugal 33/B3
Alcolu, S.C. 296/G4
Alcomdale, Alberta 182/C3
Alcona (co.), Mich. 250/F4
Alcona Beach, Ontario 177/E3
Alcones, Chile 138/F5
Alcony, Ohio 284/B5
Alcora, Spain 33/F2
Alcorisa, Spain 33/F2
Alcorn, Ky. 237/O5
Alcorn (co.), Miss. 256/G1
Alcorn State University, Miss. 256/B7
Alcorta, Argentina 143/F6
Alcoutim, Portugal 33/C4
Alcova, Wyo. 319/F3
Alcova (res.), Wyo. 319/F3
Alcoy, Spain 33/F3
Alcudia (bay), Spain 33/H3
Alda, Nebr. 264/F4
Aldabra (isls.), Seychelles 102/G5
Aldabra (isls.), Seychelles 118/H1
Aldama, Chihuahua, Mexico 150/G2
Aldama, Tamaulipas, Mexico 150/L5
Aldan, Pa. 294/M7
Aldan, U.S.S.R. 54/O4
Aldan (riv.), U.S.S.R. 54/P3
Aldan, U.S.S.R. 48/N4
Aldan (plat.), U.S.S.R. 48/N4
Aldan (riv.), U.S.S.R. 48/O3
Aldeburgh, England 13/J5
Aldeburgh, England 10/G4
Aldeia Carajá, Brazil 132/D6
Aldeia Nova de São Bento, Portugal 33/C4
Alden, Ill. 222/E1
Alden, Iowa 229/G4
Alden, Kansas 232/D3
Alden, Mich. 250/D4
Alden, Minn. 255/E7
Alden, N.Y. 276/C5
Alden Bridge, La. 238/C1
Aldenville, Pa. 294/M2
Alder, Mont. 262/D5
Alder, Wash. 310/C4
Alder (lake), Wash. 310/C4
Alder Creek, N.Y. 276/K4
Alder Flats, Alberta 182/C3
Alderley, Wis. 317/J1
Alderney (isl.), Chan. Is. 10/E6
Alderney (isl.), Chan. Is. 13/E8
Alderpoint, Calif. 204/B3
Alder Point, Nova Scotia 168/H2
Aldershot, England 10/F5
Aldershot, England 13/G8
Aldershot, Nova Scotia 168/D3
Alderson, Okla. 288/P5
Alderson, W. Va. 312/E7
Aldersyde, Alberta 182/C4
Aldine, Ind. 227/D2
Aldora, Georgia 217/D4
Aldouane, New Bruns. 170/E2
Aldrich, Ala. 195/E4
Aldrich, Minn. 255/C4
Aldrich, Mo. 261/F7
Aldridge Brownhills, England 10/G3
Aldridge Brownhills, England 13/E5
Aledo, Ill. 222/C2
Aledo, Texas 303/E2
Aleg, Mauritania 106/B5
Alegre, Brazil 135/F2
Alegre, Brazil 132/F8
Alegrete, Brazil 132/B10
Alegrete, Brazil 120/D5
'Aleih, Lebanon 63/F6
Alejandra, Argentina 143/F5
Alejandría, Bolivia 136/C3
Alejandro Selkirk (isl.), Chile 120/A6
Aleknagik, Alaska 196/G3
Aleksandriya, U.S.S.R. 52/D5
Aleksandrov Gay, U.S.S.R. 52/G4
Aleksandrovsk, U.S.S.R. 52/J3
Aleksandrovsk-Sakhalinsky, U.S.S.R. 54/R4
Aleksandrovsk-Sakhalinskiy, U.S.S.R. 48/P5
Aleksandrów Kujawski, Poland 47/D2
Aleksandrów Łodzki, Poland 47/D3
Alekseyevka, U.S.S.R. 48/H4
Alekseyevka, U.S.S.R. 52/E4
Aleksin, U.S.S.R. 52/E4
Aleksinac, Yugoslavia 45/E4
Além Paraíba, Brazil 135/E2
Alençon, France 28/D3
Alenquer, Brazil 132/C3
Alenquer, Brazil 120/D3
Alenuihaha (chan.), Hawaii 218/E7
Aleppo (prov.), Syria 63/G4
Aleppo, Syria 54/E6
Aleppo, Syria 59/C2
Aleppo, Syria 63/G4
Aléria, France 28/B6
Alert, Canada 4/A12
Alert, Ind. 227/F6
Alert, N.C. 281/N2
Alert, N.W.T. 162/N3
Alert, N.W. Terr. 187/M1
Alert (pt.), N.W. Terr. 187/K1
Alert Bay, Br. Col. 184/D5
Alès, France 28/E5
Alessandria (prov.), Italy 34/B2
Alessandria, Italy 34/B2
Ålestrup, Denmark 21/C4
Ålesund, Norway 7/E2
Ålesund, Norway 18/D5
Aletschhorn (mt.), Switzerland 39/F4
Aleutian (isls.), Alaska 188/D6
Aleutian (isls.), Alaska 196/J4
Aleutian (range), Alaska 196/G3
Aleutian (isls.), U.S. 4/D18
Aleutian (isls.), U.S. 2/A3
Alex, Okla. 288/L5
Alexander (arch.), Alaska 146/E4
Alexander (arch.), Alaska 196/L1
Alexander (isl.), Ant. 5/B15
Alexander, Ark. 202/F4
Alexander (lake), Conn. 210/H1
Alexander, Georgia 217/J4
Alexander (co.), Ill. 222/D6
Alexander, Ill. 222/D4
Alexander, Iowa 229/G3
Alexander, Kansas 232/C3
Alexander•, Maine 243/H5
Alexander, Manitoba 179/B5
Alexander, N.Y. 276/D5
Alexander (co.), N.C. 281/G3
Alexander, N. Dak. 282/C4
Alexander (cape), Solomon Is. 86/D2
Alexander (arch.), U.S. 4/D16
Alexander, W. Va. 312/F5
Alexander Bay, S. Africa 102/D7
Alexander Bay, S. Africa 118/B5
Alexander City, Ala. 195/G5
Alexander Mills, N.C. 281/F4
Alexandra, N. Zealand 100/B6
Alexandra, S. Africa 118/H6
Alexandra, Victoria 97/C5
Alexandra Land (isl.), U.S.S.R. 4/A8
Alexandra Land (isl.), U.S.S.R. 48/E1
Alexandretta (Iskenderun), Turkey 63/G4
Alexandretta (gulf), Turkey 63/F4
Alexandria, Ala. 195/G3
Alexandria, Br. Col. 184/F4
Alexandria, Egypt 2/L4
Alexandria, Egypt 102/E1
Alexandria, Egypt 59/A3
Alexandria, Egypt 111/J2
Alexandria, Ind. 227/F4
Alexandria, Jamaica 158/J6
Alexandria, Ky. 237/N3
Alexandria, La. 146/J6
Alexandria, La. 188/H4
Alexandria, La. 238/E4
Alexandria, Minn. 255/C5
Alexandria, Mo. 261/K2
Alexandria, Nebr. 264/G4
Alexandria•, N.H. 268/D4
Alexandria, North. Terr. 93/E5
Alexandria, Ohio 284/E5
Alexandria, Ontario 177/K2
Alexandria, Pa. 294/F4
Alexandria, Romania 45/G3
Alexandria, Scotland 15/A1
Alexandria, Scotland 10/A1
Alexandria, S. Dak. 298/O6
Alexandria, Tenn. 237/J8
Alexandria, Va. 188/L3
Alexandria (I.C.), Va. 307/S3
Alexandria Bay, N.Y. 276/J2
Alexandrina (lake), S. Australia 94/F6
Alexandroúpolis, Greece 45/H5
Alexis, Ill. 222/C2
Alexis (riv.), Newf. 166/C3
Alexis Creek, Br. Col. 184/F4
Aleysk, U.S.S.R. 48/J4
Aleza Lake, Br. Col. 184/G3
Alfalfa (co.), Okla. 288/K1
Alfalfa, Okla. 288/J4
Al Falluja, Iraq 59/D3
Al Falluja, Iraq 66/C4
Alfaro, Spain 33/F1
Alfatar, Bulgaria 45/H4
Al Fatha, Iraq 59/D2
Al Fatha, Iraq 66/C3
Alfeld, Germany 22/C2
Alfenas, Brazil 135/D2
Alférez (riv.), Uruguay 145/E5
Alford, England 13/H4
Alford, Fla. 212/D6
Alford•, Mass. 249/A4
Alford, Scotland 15/F3
Alford, Scotland 10/E2
Alfordsville, Ind. 227/C7
Alfred, Maine 243/B9
Alfred•, Maine 243/B9
Alfred, N.Y. 276/E6
Alfred, N. Dak. 282/N6
Alfred, Ontario 177/K2
Alfredton, N. Zealand 100/F4
Alfreton, England 13/F4
Alga, U.S.S.R. 48/F5
Ålgård, Norway 18/D7
Algarrobo, Chile 138/F3
Algarrobo (pt.), P. Rico 161/A2
Algarrobo del Águila, Argentina 143/C4
Algeciras, Colombia 126/C6
Algeciras, Spain 33/D4
Algemesí, Spain 33/F3
Alger (co.), Mich. 250/C2
Alger, Mich. 250/E4
Alger, Ohio 284/C4
Algeria 2/J4
Algeria 102/C2
ALGERIA 106/D3
Algés, Portugal 33/A1
Algete, Spain 33/G4
Alghero, Italy 34/B4
Algiers (cap.), Algeria 102/C1
Algiers (cap.), Algeria 106/E1
Algiers (cap.), Algeria 2/K4
Algiers, Ind. 227/C7
Algoa, Ark. 202/H3
Algoa (bay), S. Africa 118/D6
Algoa, Texas 303/K3
Algodones, N. Mex. 274/C3
Algoma, Miss. 256/G2
Algoma (terr. dist.), Ontario 177/J5
Algoma (terr. dist.), Ontario 175/D3
Algoma, Oreg. 291/F5
Algoma, W. Va. 312/D8
Algoma, Wis. 317/M6
Algoma Mills, Ontario 177/B1
Algona, Iowa 229/E2
Algona, Wash. 310/C3
Algonac, Mich. 250/G6
Algonquin, Ill. 222/E1
Algonquin (peak), N.Y. 276/M2
Algonquin Park, Ontario 177/F2
Algonquin Prov. Park, Ontario 177/F2
Algonquin Prov. Park, Ontario 175/E3
Algood, Tenn. 237/K8
Algorta, Uruguay 145/B3
Algrove, Sask. 181/H3
Alhama de Granada, Spain 33/E4
Alhama de Murcia, Spain 33/F4
Alhambra, Alberta 182/C3
Alhambra, Calif. 204/C10
Alhambra, Ill. 222/D5
Al Hawtiah, Yemen 59/E6
Al Hilla, Saudi Arabia 59/E5
Al Hoceima, Morocco 106/D1
Alhos Vedros, Portugal 33/B3
Alhué, Estero de (riv.), Chile 138/F4
Alia, Spain 33/D3
'Aliabad, Kuh-e (mt.), Iran 59/F3
'Aliabad, Kuh-e (mt.), Iran 66/G3
Aliağa, Turkey 63/B3
Alibag, India 68/C5
Alibates Flint Quarries Nat'l Mon., Texas 303/C2
Ali-Bayramly, U.S.S.R. 52/G7
Alibeyköyü, Turkey 63/D6
Alicante (prov.), Spain 33/F3
Alicante, Spain 33/F3
Alicante, Spain 7/D5
Alice (lake), Nebr. 264/A2
Alice, N. Dak. 282/P6
Alice (lake), N. Dak. 282/M3
Alice, Ontario 177/G2
Alice (chan.), Philippines 82/B8
Alice (riv.), Queensland 95/C4
Alice, Texas 303/F10
Alice Arm, Br. Col. 184/C2
Alicel, Oreg. 291/J2
Alice Springs, Australia 87/D8
Alice Springs, North. Terr. 88/E4
Alice Springs, North. Terr. 93/D7
Aliceville, Ala. 195/B4
Aliceville (dam), Ala. 195/B4
Aliceville, Kansas 232/G3
Alicia, Ark. 202/H2
Alicia (bank), Colombia 126/B8
Alicudi (isl.), Italy 34/E5
Alida, Minn. 255/C3
Alida, Sask. 181/K6
Aligarh, India 68/D3
'Ali Gharbi, Iraq 66/E4
Alijó, Portugal 33/C2
Alima (riv.), Congo 115/B4
Alimodian, Philippines 82/D5
Alindao, Cent. Afr. Rep. 115/D2
Aline, Georgia 217/H6
Aline, Okla. 288/K1
Alingly, Sask. 181/E2
Alingsås, Sweden 18/H7
Alipore, India 68/F2
Aliquippa, Pa. 294/B4
Ali Sabieh, Djibouti 111/H5
'Ali Sharqi, Iraq 66/E4
Aliskerovo, U.S.S.R. 48/R3
Alivérion, Greece 45/G6
Aliwal North, S. Africa 118/D6
Alix, Alberta 182/D3
Alix, Ark. 202/C3
Aljezur, Portugal 33/B4
Aljojuca, Mexico 150/O1
Aljustrel, Portugal 33/B4
Alkabo, N. Dak. 282/C2
Alkali (lakes), Calif. 204/E2
Alkali (lake), Nev. 266/B1
Alkali (lakes), N. Dak. 282/L3
Alkali Lake, Br. Col. 184/F4
Alkaline (lake), N. Dak. 282/L6
Alken, Belgium 27/G7
Alkmaar, Netherlands 27/F3
Alkmaardermeer (lake), Netherlands 27/F3
Alkol, W. Va. 312/C6
Al Kufa, Iraq 66/D4
Al Kumait, Iraq 66/E4
Al Kuwait (cap.), Kuwait 59/E4
Al Kuwait (cap.), Kuwait 54/F7
Allagash•, Maine 243/F1
Allagash (lake), Maine 243/D3
Allagash (riv.), Maine 243/E2
Allahabad, India 68/E3
Allahabad, India 54/K7
Allaine (riv.), Switzerland 39/D2
Allaire, N.J. 273/E3
Allakaket, Alaska 196/H1
Allakh-Yun', U.S.S.R. 48/O3
Allamakee (co.), Iowa 229/L2
Allaman, Switzerland 39/B4
All American (canal), Calif. 204/K11
Allamoore, Texas 303/C11
Allamuchy, N.J. 273/D2
Allan (mt.), Idaho 220/D4
Allan, Sask. 181/E4
Allan (hills), Sask. 181/E4
Allanmyo, Burma 72/B3
Allanwater, Ontario 175/C2
Allanwater, Ontario 177/G4
'Allaqi, Wadi (dry riv.), Egypt 111/F3
Allard (lake), Québec 174/E2
Allardt, Tenn. 237/M8
Allardville, New Bruns. 170/E1
Allariz, Spain 33/C1
Allatoona (lake), Georgia 217/C2
Alle, Switzerland 39/D2
Alleene, Ark. 202/B6
Allegan (co.), Mich. 250/D6
Allegan, Mich. 250/D6
Allegany (co.), Md. 245/C2
Allegany (co.), N.Y. 276/D6
Allegany, N.Y. 276/C6
Allegany, Oreg. 291/D4
Allegany Ind. Res., N.Y. 276/C6
Alleghany, Calif. 204/E4
Alleghany (co.), N.C. 281/G1
Alleghany (co.), Va. 307/H5
Alleghany, Va. 307/H5
Allegheny (res.), N.Y. 276/C7
Allegheny (riv.), N.Y. 276/C6
Allegheny (co.), Pa. 294/B5
Allegheny (res.), Pa. 294/E2
Allegheny (riv.), Pa. 294/D2
Allegheny (mts.), Va. 307/H5
Allegheny Front (mts.), Md. 245/C2
Allegheny Front (mts.), Pa. 294/E5
Allègre (pt.), Guadeloupe 161/A6
Allegre, Ky. 237/G7
Alleman, Iowa 229/F5
Allemands (lake), La. 238/M4
Allen, Ala. 195/C7
Allen, Argentina 143/C4
Allen (co.), Ind. 227/G2
Allen, Lough (lake), Ireland 10/C3
Allen (lake), Ireland 17/E3
Allen, Bog of (marsh), Ireland 17/H5
Allen (co.), Kansas 232/G4
Allen, Kansas 232/F3
Allen (co.), Ky. 237/J7
Allen, Ky. 237/R5
Allen (par.), La. 238/E5
Allen, La. 238/D3
Allen, Md. 245/R7
Allen, Mich. 250/E7
Allen, Miss. 256/C7
Allen (mt.), Mont. 262/C2
Allen, Nebr. 264/H2
Allen (co.), Ohio 284/B4
Allen, Okla. 288/O5
Allen, Pa. 294/H5
Allen, S. Dak. 298/F7
Allen, Texas 303/H1
Allendale, England 13/E3
Allendale, Ill. 222/F5
Allendale, Mo. 261/D2
Allendale, N.J. 273/B1
Allendale (co.), S.C. 296/E6
Allendale, S.C. 296/E5
Allende, Coahuila, Mexico 150/J2
Allende, Nuevo León, Mexico 150/J4
Allendorf, Iowa 229/B2
Allenford, Ontario 177/C3
Allenhurst, Georgia 217/J7
Allenhurst, N.J. 273/F3
Allen Park, Mich. 250/B7
Allens Mills, Maine 243/C6
Allenspark, Colo. 208/J2
Allen Springs, Ky. 237/J7
Allenstein (Olsztyn), Poland 47/E2
Allenstown•, N.H. 268/E5
Allensville, Ky. 237/G7
Allensville, Ohio 284/E7
Allensville, Pa. 294/G4
Allenton, Mo. 261/M4
Allenton, R.I. 249/H6
Allenton, Wis. 317/K9
Allentown, Georgia 217/F5
Allentown, N.J. 273/D3
Allentown, N.Y. 276/E6
Allentown, Ohio 284/B4
Allentown, Pa. 188/L2
Allentown, Pa. 294/L4
Allentsteig, Austria 41/C2
Allenville, Ill. 222/E4
Allenville, Mo. 261/N8
Allenwood, N.J. 273/E3
Allenwood, Pa. 294/H3
Alleppey-Cochin, India 68/D7
Aller (riv.), Germany 22/C2
Allerton, Ill. 222/F4
Allerton, Iowa 229/G7
Allerton, Mass. 249/E7
Allerton (pt.), Mass. 249/E7
Alley, Jamaica 158/J7

Alley Spring, Mo. 261/J8
Allgäu (reg.), Germany 22/D5
Allgäu Alps (mts.), Austria 41/A3
Allgood, Ala. 195/F3
Alliance, Alberta 182/E3
Alliance, Nebr. 264/A2
Alliance, N.C. 281/R4
Alliance, Ohio 284/H4
Al Lidam, Saudi Arabia 59/D5
Allier (dept.), France 28/E4
Allier (riv.), France 28/E5
Alligator (lake), Fla. 212/E3
Alligator (pt.), Fla. 212/E3
Alligator (lake), La. 238/L6
Alligator (lake), N.C. 281/S3
Alligator (riv.), N.C. 281/S3
Alligator Pond, Jamaica 158/H6
Allingåbro, Denmark 21/D5
Allinge-Sandvig, Denmark 18/J9
Allinge-Sandvig, Denmark 21/F8
Allingham, Alberta 182/E3
Allingtown, Conn. 210/D3
Allison, Iowa 229/H3
Allison, N. Mex. 274/A3
Allison, Texas 303/D2
Allisona, Tenn. 237/H9
Allisonia, Va. 307/G7
Alison Park, Pa. 294/C4
Alliston, Ontario 177/E3
Al Lith, Saudi Arabia 59/C5
Alloa, Scotland 10/B1
Alloa, Scotland 15/C1
Alloa, W. Va. 312/G6
Allock, Ky. 237/P6
Allons, Tenn. 237/L8
Allouez, Mich. 250/A1
Allouez, Wis. 317/L7
Allow (riv.), Ireland 17/C
Alloway, N.J. 273/C4
Alloways (creek), N.J. 273/C4
Allport, Ark. 202/G4
Allred, Tenn. 237/L8
All Saints, Ant. & Bar. 161/E11
All Saints Village, Mo. 261/M2
Allsboro, Ala. 195/B1
Allsbrook, S.C. 296/K3
Allschwil, Switzerland 39/D1
Allyn, Wash. 310/C3
Alma, Ala. 195/C8
Alma, Ark. 202/B3
Alma, Colo. 208/G4
Alma, Georgia 217/G7
Alma, Ill. 222/E6
Alma, Kansas 232/F2
Alma, Mich. 250/E6
Alma, Mo. 261/E4
Alma, Nebr. 264/E4
Alma, New Bruns. 170/F3
Alma, N. Mex. 274/A5
Alma, N.C. 281/L5
Alma, Ontario 177/D4
Alma, Québec 174/C3
Alma, Québec 172/F1
Alma, W. Va. 312/E4
Alma, Wis. 317/C7
Alma-Ata, U.S.S.R. 2/N3
Alma-Ata, U.S.S.R. 54/J5
Alma-Ata, U.S.S.R. 48/H5
Alma Center, Wis. 317/E7
Alma City, Minn. 255/E6
Almada, Portugal 33/A1
Almadén, Spain 33/D3
Almagro, Spain 33/E3
Almaguer, Colombia 126/B7
Almanor (lake), Calif. 204/D3
Almansa, Spain 33/F3
Almanza, Spain 33/D1
Almanzor (mt.), Spain 33/D2
Almanzora (riv.), Spain 33/F4
Almartha, Mo. 261/H4
Almazán, Spain 33/E2
Almaznyy, U.S.S.R. 48/M3
Almeida, Sierra (mts.), Chile 138/C4
Almeida, Portugal 33/C2
Almeirim, Portugal 33/B3
Almelo, Netherlands 27/K4
Almelund, Minn. 255/F5
Almena, Kansas 232/C2
Almena, Wis. 317/B5
Almenara, Brazil 120/E4
Almendra (res.), Spain 33/C2
Almendralejo, Spain 33/C3
Almere, Netherlands 27/G4
Almería, Nebr. 264/E4
Almería (prov.), Spain 33/E4
Almería, Spain 7/D5
Almeriá, Spain 33/E4
Almería (gulf), Spain 33/E4
Al'met'yevsk, U.S.S.R. 52/H3
Älmhult, Sweden 18/H8
Almira, Wash. 310/G3
Almirantazgo (bay), Chile 138/F11
Almirante, Panama 154/F6
Almirante Montt (gulf), Chile 138/D9
Almirós, Greece 45/F6
Almo, Idaho 220/E7
Almo, Ky. 237/E7
Almodôvar, Portugal 33/B4
Almodóvar del Campo, Spain 33/D3
Almoharin, Spain 33/D3
Almoloya del Rió, Mexico 150/K1
Almon, Georgia 217/E3
Almond, N.Y. 276/G4
Almond, N.C. 281/B4
Almond (riv.), Scotland 15/E4
Almond, Wis. 317/G7
Almont, Colo. 208/G4
Almont, Mich. 250/F6
Almont, N. Dak. 282/H6
Almonte, Ontario 177/H2
Almonte, Spain 33/C4
Almora, India 68/D3
Almora, Minn. 255/C4
Almorox, Spain 33/D2
Almota, Wash. 310/H4
Al Muadhdham, Saudi Arabia 59/C4
Almudévar, Spain 33/F1
Almuñécar, Spain 33/E4

Almus, Turkey 63/G2
Al Musaiyib, Iraq 59/D3
Al Musaiyib, Iraq 66/D4
Almyra, Ark. 202/H5
Alna•, Maine 243/D7
Alness, Scotland 15/D3
Alness (riv.), Scotland 15/D3
Alnwick, England 10/F3
Alnwick, England 13/F2
Alofi (cap.), Niue 87/K7
Aloha, Oreg. 291/A2
Aloha, Wash. 310/A3
Alon, Burma 72/B2
Along, India 68/G3
Alonsa, Manitoba 179/C4
Alonso Rojas, Cuba 158/B2
Alor (isl.), Indonesia 85/G7
Alora, Spain 33/D4
Alor Gajah, Malaysia 72/D7
Alor Setar, Malaysia 72/D6
Alorton, Ill. 222/B2
Alost (Aalst), Belgium 27/D7
Alotau, Papua N.G. 87/E7
Aloysius (mt.), W. Australia 92/E4
Alpachiri, Argentina 143/D4
Alpaugh, Calif. 204/F8
Alpena, Ark. 202/D1
Alpena (co.), Mich. 250/F4
Alpena, Mich. 250/F3
Alpena, S. Dak. 298/N5
Alpena, W. Va. 312/G5
Alpen Siding, Alberta 182/D2
Alpera, Spain 33/F3
Alpes-de-Haute-Provence (dept.), France 28/G5
Alpes-Maritimes (dept.), France 28/G6
Alpha, Ill. 222/C2
Alpha, Georgia 217/E2
Alpha, Ky. 237/L7
Alpha, Mich. 250/A2
Alpha, Minn. 255/D7
Alpha, N.J. 273/C2
Alpha, Queensland 88/H4
Alpharetta, Georgia 217/D2
Alphen aan de Rijn, Netherlands 27/F4
Alpiarça, Portugal 33/B3
Alpine, Ala. 195/F4
Alpine, Ariz. 198/F5
Alpine (co.), Calif. 204/F5
Alpine, Calif. 204/J11
Alpine, Ind. 227/G5
Alpine, Ky. 237/M7
Alpine, N.J. 273/C1
Alpine, N.Y. 276/G6
Alpine, Oreg. 291/D3
Alpine, Tenn. 237/L8
Alpine, Texas 303/D12
Alpine, Utah 304/C3
Alpine, Wyo. 319/B2
Alpirsbach, Germany 22/C4
Alpnach, Switzerland 39/F3
Alpoca, W. Va. 312/D7
Alportel, Portugal 33/C4
Alps (mts.) 7/E4
Alpu, Turkey 63/D3
Al Q'aim, Iraq 66/B3
Al Qaiyara, Iraq 66/C3
Al Qosh, Iraq 66/C2
Alquina, Ind. 227/G5
Alquízar, Cuba 158/C1
Al Qurna, Iraq 66/E5
Al Qurna, Iraq 59/E3
Alroy Downs, North. Terr. 93/E5
Als (isl.), Denmark 21/C8
Alsace (trad. prov.), France, 29
Alsager, England 13/E4
Alsager, England 10/G2
Alsask, Sask. 181/B4
Alsatia, La. 238/H1
Alsdorf, Germany 22/B3
Alsea, Oreg. 291/D3
Alsea (riv.), Oreg. 291/D3
Alsek (riv.), Alaska 196/L3
Alsek (riv.), Br. Col. 184/H1
Alsek (riv.), Yukon 187/E3
Alsen, N. Dak. 282/N4
Alsey, Ill. 222/C4
Alsfeld, Germany 22/C3
Alsip, Ill. 222/B6
Alsózsolca, Hungary 41/F2
Alstead•, N.H. 268/C5
Alsten (isl.), Norway 18/H4
Alstfjorden (fjord), Norway 18/H3
Alston, England 13/E3
Alston, Georgia 217/H6
Alston, Mich. 250/G1
Alstonville, N.S. Wales 97/G1
Alta, Iowa 229/C3
Alta, Norway 18/P2
Alta, Utah 304/C3
Altadena, Calif. 204/C10
Altaelv (riv.), Norway 18/N2
Alta Gracia, Argentina 143/D3
Altagracia, Cuba 158/G3
Altagracia, Venezuela 124/C2
Altagracia de Orituco, Venezuela 124/E3
Altai (mts.) 54/K5
Altai (mts.), Mongolia 77/C2
Alta Loma, Calif. 204/E10
Alta Loma, Texas 303/K3
Altamachi (riv.), Bolivia 136/B5
Altamaha (riv.), Ga. 188/K3
Altamaha (riv.), Georgia 217/H7
Altamaha (sound), Georgia 217/K8
Altamahaw, N.C. 281/L2
Altamira, Brazil 132/C3
Altamira, Chile 138/B5
Altamira, Dom. Rep. 158/D5
Altamira, Mexico 150/L5
Altamont, Ill. 222/E4
Altamont, Kansas 232/G4
Altamont, Manitoba 179/D5
Altamont, Mo. 261/D3
Altamont, N.Y. 276/M5
Altamont, Oreg. 291/F7
Altamont, S. Dak. 298/R4

Altamont (canton), Tenn. 237/K10
Altamont, Utah 304/D3
Altamonte Springs, Fla. 212/E3
Altamura, Italy 34/F4
Altar, Mexico 150/D1
Altario, Alberta 182/E4
Altata, Mexico 150/E4
Alt Aussee, Austria 41/B3
Alta Vista, Iowa 229/J2
Alta Vista, Kansas 232/F3
Altavista, Va. 307/K6
Altay, China 77/C2
Altay, Mongolia 77/E2
Altay (mts.), U.S.S.R. 48/J5
Altdorf, Switzerland 39/G3
Altea, Spain 33/G3
Altena, Germany 22/B3
Altenburg, Germany 22/E3
Altenburg, Mo. 261/O7
Altepexi, Mexico 150/L7
Alter do Chão, Portugal 33/C3
Altevatn (lake), Norway 18/L2
Altha, Fla. 212/A1
Altheim, Austria 41/B2
Altheimer, Ark. 202/G5
Althofen, Austria 41/C3
Alticane, Sask. 181/D3
Altinağ, Turkey 63/E2
Altinova, Turkey 63/B3
Altinözü, Turkey 63/G4
Altıntaş, Turkey 63/D3
Altiplano (plat.) 120/C4
Altkirch, France 28/G4
Altmar, N.Y. 276/J3
Altmark (reg.), Germany 22/D2
Altmühl (riv.), Germany 22/D4
Altnaharra, Scotland 15/D2
Alto, Georgia 217/E2
Alto, La. 238/G2
Alto, Mich. 250/D6
Alto, N. Mex. 274/D5
Alto, Tenn. 237/K10
Alto, Texas 303/J6
Alto, Wis. 317/J8
Alto Araguaia, Brazil 132/C7
Alto Chicapa, Angola 115/C6
Alto Cuale, Angola 115/C5
Alto Cuale, Angola 115/C5
Alto de Cantillana (mt.), Chile 138/G4
Alto Lucero, Mexico 150/P1
Alto Molócuè, Mozambique 118/F3
Alton, Ala. 195/E3
Alton, Calif. 204/A3
Alton, England 13/G6
Alton, England 10/F5
Alton, Ill. 188/J3
Alton, Ill. 222/A2
Alton, Ind. 227/E8
Alton, Iowa 229/A3
Alton, Kansas 232/D2
Alton, Ky. 237/M4
Alton, La. 238/L6
Alton•, Maine 243/F5
Alton, Mo. 261/K9
Alton•, N.H. 268/E5
Alton, N.Y. 276/H4
Alton, Nova Scotia 168/E3
Alton, R.I. 249/G7
Alton, Utah 304/B6
Alton, Va. 307/K7
Alton, W. Va. 312/F5
Altona, Ill. 222/C2
Altona, Ind. 227/G2
Altona, Manitoba 179/E5
Altona, Mich. 250/D5
Altona, Mo. 261/D6
Altona, N.Y. 276/N1
Altona, Victoria 97/H5
Altona, Victoria 88/K7
Altona (bay), Victoria 97/H5
Altona (bay), Victoria 88/K7
Altona (lag.), Virgin Is. (U.S.) 161/F4
Altona, Germany 22/C2
Altonah, Utah 304/D3
Alton Bay, N.H. 268/E5
Alton Downs, S. Australia 94/F2
Alto Nevado, Cerro (mt.), Chile 138/E5
Altoona, Ala. 195/F2
Altoona, Fla. 212/E3
Altoona, Iowa 229/G5
Altoona, Kansas 232/G4
Altoona, Pa. 188/L2
Altoona, Pa. 294/F4
Altoona, Wash. 310/B4
Altoona, Wis. 317/C6
Alto Paraguay, Paraguay 144/C2
Alto Paraná, Paraguay 144/E4
Alto Paraná (riv.), Paraguay 144/D5
Alto Park, Georgia 217/B2
Alto Parnaíba, Brazil 132/E5
Alto Pass, Ill. 222/D6
Alto Ritacuva (mt.), Colombia 120/D4
Alto Ritacuva (mt.), Colombia 126/D4
Altos, Brazil 132/F4
Altos, Paraguay 144/B4
Alto Seco, Bolivia 136/D6
Alto Songo, Cuba 158/J4
Altotonga, Mexico 150/P1
Altötting, Germany 22/E4
Alto Velo (chan.), Dom. Rep. 158/C7
Alto Velo (isl.), Dom. Rep. 158/D7
Altrincham, England 13/H2
Altrincham, England 10/G2
Altro, Ky. 237/P6
Altstätten, Switzerland 39/J2
Altun Ha, Belize 154/C2
Altun Shan (range), China 54/K6
Altun Shan (range), China 77/C4
Altura, Minn. 255/G6
Alturas, Calif. 204/E2
Alturas, Fla. 212/E4
Altus, Ark. 202/C2
Altus, Okla. 288/H5
Altus (res.), Okla. 288/H5
Altus A.F.B., Okla. 288/H5
Alubijid, Philippines 82/E6
Alucra, Turkey 63/H2
Alūksne, U.S.S.R. 53/D2

Alula, Somalia 115/K1
Alula, Somalia 102/H3
Alum Bank, Pa. 294/E5
Alum Bridge, W. Va. 312/E4
Alum Creek, W. Va. 312/C6
Alum Rock, Calif. 204/L3
Alus, Iraq 66/C3
Alushta, U.S.S.R. 52/D6
Alva, Fla. 212/E5
Alva, Ky. 237/P7
Alva (lake), New Bruns. 170/D3
Alva, Okla. 288/J1
Alva, Scotland 10/B1
Alva, Scotland 15/C1
Alva, Wyo. 319/H1
Alva B. Adams (tunnel), Colo. 208/H2
Alvada, Ohio 284/D3
Alvadore, Oreg. 291/D3
Alvalade, Portugal 33/B4
Alvaneu, Switzerland 39/J3
Alvarado, Mexico 150/M7
Alvarado, Minn. 255/B2
Alvarado, Texas 303/G5
Álvaro S. Lima (res.), Brazil 135/B3
Alvaton, Georgia 217/C4
Alvaton, Ky. 237/J7
Ålvdal, Norway 18/G5
Älvdalen, Sweden 18/J6
Alvear, Argentina 143/E2
Alvena, Sask. 181/E3
Alvesta, Sweden 18/J8
Alvin, Colo. 184/L2
Alvin, Ill. 222/F3
Alvin, Texas 303/J3
Alvin, Wis. 317/J4
Alvinston, Ontario 177/B5
Alvito, Portugal 33/B3
Alvo, Nebr. 264/H4
Alvord, Iowa 229/A2
Alvord, Texas 303/G4
Alvordton, Ohio 284/A2
Álvsborg (co.), Sweden 18/H7
Älvsbyn, Sweden 18/M4
Alvwood, Minn. 255/D3
Alvy, W. Va. 312/E4
Alwar, India 68/D3
Alxa Shamo (des.), China 77/F4
Alxa Youqi, China 77/F4
Alxa Zuoqi, China 77/F4
Aly, Ark. 202/D4
Alyangula, North. Terr. 88/F2
Alyangula, North. Terr. 93/E2
Alyth, Scotland 10/E2
Alyth, Scotland 15/E4
Alytus, U.S.S.R. 53/C3
Alz (riv.), Germany 22/E4
Alzada, Mont. 262/M5
Alzette (riv.), Luxembourg 27/J9
Alzey, Germany 22/C4
Amacuro (riv.), Venezuela 124/H4
Amadeus (lake), Australia 87/D8
Amadeus (lake), North. Terr. 88/E4
Amadeus (lake), North. Terr. 93/B8
Amadi, Sudan 111/F6
'Amadiya, Iraq 59/D2
'Amadiya, Iraq 66/C2
Amadjuak, N.W.T. 162/J3
Amadjuak (lake), N.W.T. 162/K3
Amadjuak, N.W. Terr. 187/L3
Amadjuak, N.W. Terr. 187/L3
Amado, Ariz. 198/D7
Amador (co.), Calif. 204/E5
Amadora, Portugal 33/A1
Amador City, Calif. 204/C9
Amagansett, N.Y. 276/R9
Amagasaki, Japan 81/H8
Amager (isl.), Denmark 21/F6
Amagi, Japan 81/E7
Amagon, Ark. 202/H2
Amahai, Indonesia 85/H6
Amak (isl.), Alaska 196/F5
Amakura (riv.), Guyana 131/A2
Amakusa (isls.), Japan 81/D7
Åmål, Sweden 18/H7
Amalfi, Colombia 126/C4
Amalfi, Italy 34/E4
Amalga, Utah 304/C2
Amalia, N. Mex. 274/D2
Amaliás, Greece 45/E7
Amalner, India 68/C4
Amambaí, Brazil 132/C8
Amambaí, Serra de (range), Brazil 132/C7
Amambay, Paraguay 144/C2
Amambay, Cordillera de (mts.), Paraguay 144/D-E3
Amami (isls.), Japan 54/P7
Amami (isls.), Japan 81/N5
Amami-O-Shima (isl.), Japan 81/N5
Amana, Iowa 229/K5
Amananvé, Colombia 126/G6
Amanda, Ohio 284/E6
Amanda Park, Wash. 310/A3
Amanos (mts.), Turkey 63/G4
Amantea, Italy 34/F5
Amanu (atoll), Fr. Poly. 87/N7
Amapá (terr.), Brazil 132/D2
Amapá, Brazil 120/D2
Amapá, Brazil 132/D2
Amapala, Honduras 154/D4
Amapari (riv.), Brazil 132/C2
'Amara, Iraq 66/E5
'Amara, Iraq 59/E3
Amarante, Brazil 132/F4
Amarante, Portugal 33/B2
Amaranth, Manitoba 179/D4
Amarapura, Burma 72/B2
Amarete, Bolivia 136/A4
Amargosa, Brazil 132/F6
Amargosa (range), Calif. 204/J7
Amargosa (riv.), Calif. 204/J7
Amarillas, Cuba 158/D2
Amarillo, Texas 188/F3

Amarillo, Texas 146/H6
Amarillo, Texas 303/C2
Amasa, Mich. 250/G2
Amasra, Turkey 63/E2
Amasya (prov.), Turkey 63/F2
Amasya, Turkey 59/C1
Amasya, Turkey 63/F2
Amatignak (isl.), Alaska 196/K4
Amatitlán, Guatemala 154/B3
Amatlán de los Reyes, Mexico 150/P2
Amay, Belgium 27/G7
Amazon (riv.) 2/G6
Amazon (riv.), Brazil 120/D3
Amazon (riv.), Brazil 132/C3
Amazon (riv.), Colombia 126/E9
Amazon (riv.), Peru 128/F3
Amazon, Sask. 181/F4
Amazonas (state), Brazil 132/G9
Amazonas (comm.), Colombia 126/D8
Amazonas, Cuba 158/F2
Amazonas (dept.), Peru 128/C5
Amazonas (terr.), Venezuela 124/E5
Amazonia, Mo. 261/C3
Ambala, India 68/D2
Ambalavao, Madagascar 118/H4
Ambam, Cameroon 115/B3
Ambanja, Madagascar 118/H2
Ambarchik, U.S.S.R. 4/B1
Ambarchik, U.S.S.R. 48/R3
Ambato, Ecuador 120/B4
Ambato, Ecuador 128/C3
Ambato Boeny, Madagascar 118/H3
Ambatofinandrahana, Madagascar 118/H4
Ambatolampy, Madagascar 102/G6
Ambatolampy, Madagascar 118/H3
Ambatomainty, Madagascar 118/H3
Ambatondrazaka, Madagascar 118/H3
Ambatondrazaka, Madagascar 102/G6
Ambelau (isl.), Indonesia 85/H6
Amber, Iowa 229/K4
Amber (Bobaomby) (cape), Madagascar 118/H2
Amber, Okla. 288/L4
Amber, Wash. 310/H3
Amberg, Germany 22/D4
Amberg, Wis. 317/K5
Ambergris (cay), Belize 154/D1
Ambergris (cay), Turks & Caicos 156/D2
Ambérieu-en-Bugey, France 28/F5
Amberley, N. Zealand 100/D3
Amberley, Ohio 284/C9
Amberson, Pa. 294/G5
Ambert, France 28/E5
Ambia, Ind. 227/C4
Ambikapur, India 68/E4
Ambil (isl.), Philippines 82/C4
Ambilobe, Madagascar 118/H2
Amble, England 13/F2
Amble, Mich. 250/D5
Ambler, Alaska 196/G1
Ambler, Pa. 294/M5
Ambo, Peru 128/D8
Amboasary, Madagascar 118/H4
Ambodifototra, Madagascar 118/J3
Ambohimahasoa, Madagascar 118/H4
Amboise, France 28/D4
Ambon (Amboina), Indonesia 85/H6
Ambon, Indonesia 54/O10
Ambositra, Madagascar 102/G7
Ambositra, Madagascar 118/H4
Ambovombe, Madagascar 118/H5
Amboy, Calif. 204/K9
Amboy, Georgia 217/E7
Amboy, Ill. 222/D2
Amboy, Ind. 227/F3
Amboy, Minn. 255/D7
Amboy, Wash. 310/C5
Amboy, W. Va. 312/D5
Amboyna (cay), Philippines 85/E4
Ambridge, Pa. 294/B4
Ambriz, Angola 115/B5
Ambrose, Georgia 217/G2
Ambrose, N. Dak. 282/D2
Ambrym (isl.), Vanuatu 87/G7
Ambunti, Papua N.G. 85/B6
Amburgey, Ky. 237/R6
Amchitka (isl.), Alaska 188/D6
Amchitka (isl.), Alaska 196/K4
Amchitka (passage), Alaska 196/K4
Am-Dam, Chad 111/J5
Amderma, U.S.S.R. 52/K1
Amderma, U.S.S.R. 48/F3
Amdo, China 77/D5
Ameagle, W. Va. 312/D7
Amealco, Mexico 150/K6
Ameca, Mexico 150/H6
Amecameca de Juárez, Mexico 150/L1
Ameghino, Argentina 143/D3
Amel, Belgium 27/J8
Ameland (isl.), Netherlands 27/H2
Amelia (isl.), Fla. 212/E1
Amelia, Italy 34/D3
Amelia, La. 238/H7
Amelia, Nebr. 264/F2
Amelia, Ohio 284/D10
Amelia (co.), Va. 307/M6
Amelia City, Fla. 212/E1
Amelia Court House, Va. 307/N6
Amenia, N.Y. 276/N7
Amenia, N. Dak. 282/R6
America, Ill. 222/D6
American (highlands), Ant. 2/N10
American (riv.), Calif. 204/C8
American Falls, Idaho 220/E7
American Falls (res.), Idaho 188/D2
American Falls (res.), Idaho 220/E7
American Fork, Utah 304/C3
American Highland, Ant. 5/B2
American Samoa 2/A6
AMERICAN SAMOA 86/N9
American Samoa 87/J7
Americus, Georgia 217/D6
Americus, Ind. 227/D3
Americus, Kansas 232/F3

Americus, Mo. 261/J5
Amersfoort, Netherlands 27/G4
Amersham, England 13/G7
Amery, Man. 162/G4
Amery, Manitoba 179/J2
Amery, Wis. 317/B5
Amery Ice Shelf, Ant. 2/N9
Amery Ice Shelf, Ant. 5/C4
Ames, Iowa 229/F4
Ames, Kansas 232/E2
Ames, N.Y. 276/L5
Ames, Okla. 288/K2
Ames, Texas 303/K7
Amesbury, England 13/F6
Amesbury, Mass. 249/L1
Amesbury•, Mass. 249/L1
Amesville, Conn. 210/B1
Amesville, Ohio 284/F7
Amet (sound), Nova Scotia 168/E3
Amfilokhiá, Greece 45/E6
Amfissa, Greece 45/F6
Amga (riv.), U.S.S.R. 48/O3
Amgun' (riv.), U.S.S.R. 48/O4
Amherst, Burma 72/C3
Amherst, Colo. 208/P1
Amherst•, Maine 243/G6
Amherst, Mass. 249/E3
Amherst•, Mass. 249/E3
Amherst, Nebr. 264/E4
Amherst•, N.H. 268/D6
Amherst, N.Y. 276/C4
Amherst, N.S. 162/K6
Amherst, Nova Scotia 168/D3
Amherst, Ohio 284/F3
Amherst (isl.), Ontario 177/H3
Amherst, S. Dak. 298/O2
Amherst, Texas 303/B3
Amherst (co.), Va. 307/K5
Amherst, Va. 307/K5
Amherst (mt.), W. Australia 92/D2
Amherst, Wis. 317/H7
Amherstdale, W. Va. 312/C7
Amherstburg, Ontario 177/A5
Amherst Junction, Wis. 317/H7
Amherst View, Ontario 177/H3
Amidon, N. Dak. 282/D7
Amiens, France 7/E4
Amiens, France 28/D3
Amindini (isl.), India 68/C6
Amindivi (isls.), India 68/C6
Aminga, Argentina 143/C2
Amini (Amindiri) (isl.), India 68/C6
'Amir, Ras (cape), Libya 111/D1
Amiret, Minn. 255/C6
Amisk, Alberta 182/E3
Amisk (lake), Sask. 181/M4
Amissville, Va. 307/N3
Amistad (res.), Mexico 150/J2
Amistad, N. Mex. 274/F3
Amistad (dam), Texas 303/C8
Amistad (res.), Texas 303/C8
Amistad Nat'l Rec. Area, Texas 303/D8
Amite, La. 238/K5
Amite (riv.), La. 238/L2
Amite (co.), Miss. 256/C8
Amite (riv.), Miss. 256/C9
Amity, Ark. 202/D5
Amity, Georgia 217/G3
Amity, Ind. 227/E6
Amity, Mo. 261/D3
Amity, Oreg. 291/D2
Amity, Pa. 294/E5
Amityville, N.Y. 276/O9
Åmli, Norway 18/F7
Amlia (isl.), Alaska 196/L4
Amlia (passage), Alaska 196/L4
Amlwch, Wales 10/D4
Amlwch, Wales 13/C2
Amma, W. Va. 312/D5
Amman (distr.), Jordan 65/D4
Amman (cap.), Jordan 54/C2
Amman (cap.), Jordan 65/D4
Amman (cap.), Jordan 59/C3
Ammanford, Wales 13/C6
Ammassalik, Greenl. 4/C11
Ammassalik, Greenland 146/Q3
Ammersee (lake), Germany 22/D4
Ammie, Ky. 237/O6
Ammon, Idaho 220/G6
Ammon, Va. 307/N6
Ammonoosuc (riv.), N.H. 268/D3
Amnat, Thailand 72/E4
Amo, Ind. 227/D5
Amol, Iran 59/F2
Amol, Iran 66/H2
Amonate, Va. 307/E6
Amor, Minn. 255/C4
Amora, Portugal 33/A1
Amorbach, Germany 22/C4
Amoret, Mo. 261/C6
Amorgós (isl.), Greece 45/G7
Amorita, Okla. 288/K1
Amory, Miss. 256/H3
Amos, Que. 162/G4
Amos, Québec 174/B3
Åmotfors, Sweden 18/H7
Amoy (Xiamen), China 77/J7
Amozoc de Mota, Mexico 150/N2
Ampana, Indonesia 85/G6
Ampanihy, Madagascar 118/G4
Amparo, Brazil 135/C3
Amper (riv.), Germany 22/D4
Amphitrite (isls.), China 85/E2
Amposta, Spain 33/G2
Ampthill, England 13/G5
Amqui, Québec 172/G2
'Amran, Yemen 59/D6
Amravati, India 68/D4
Amreli, India 68/C4
Amriswil, Switzerland 39/H1
Amritsar, India 54/J6
Amritsar, India 68/C2
Amrum (isl.), Germany 22/C1
Amsden, Ohio 284/D3
Amstelveen, Netherlands 27/B5

Anvik 329

msterdam (isl.) 2/N7
msterdam, Georgia 217/D9
msterdam, Mo. 261/D6
msterdam, Mont. 262/E5
msterdam (cap.), Netherlands 27/B4
msterdam (cap.), Netherlands 7/E3
msterdam, N.Y. 276/M5
msterdam, Ohio 284/J5
msterdam, Sask. 181/J4
mstetten, Austria 41/C2
mston, Conn. 210/F2
m-Timan, Chad 111/D5
muay, Venezuela 124/C2
mudar'ya (riv.) 2/N3
mudar'ya (riv.), U.S.S.R. 54/H5
mudar'ya (riv.), U.S.S.R. 48/G5
mukta (isl.), Alaska 196/D4
mukta (passage), Alaska 196/D4
muku (mts.), Guyana 131/B4
mulet, Sask. 181/G6
mund Ringnes (isl.), N.W.T. 162/M3
mund Ringnes (isl.), N.W. Terr. 187/J2
mundsen (sea) 2/D10
mundsen (bay), Ant. 5/C3
mundsen (sea), Ant. 5/B13
mundsen (gulf), Canada 4/B16
mundsen (gulf), N.W.T. 162/D1
mundsen (gulf), N.W.T. 146/F2
mundsen (gulf), N.W. Terr. 187/F2
mundsen-Scott Station, Ant. 5/A14
muntai, Indonesia 85/F6
mur (riv.) 2/R3
mur (riv.) 54/P5
mur (Heilong Jiang) (riv.), China 77/L2
mur, Wadi (dry riv.), Sudan 111/G4
mur (riv.), U.S.S.R. 48/O4
murang, Indonesia 85/G5
mursk, U.S.S.R. 48/O4
my, Kansas 232/B3
nya (pass), Burma 72/C4
nya (pass), Thailand 72/C4
nyun, Lebanon 63/F5
n, Burma 72/B3
na, Iraq 66/B3
na, Iraq 59/D3
naa (atoll), Fr. Poly. 87/M7
nabar (riv.), U.S.S.R. 48/M2
nabel, Mo. 261/H3
na Branch, Darling (riv.), N.S. Wales 97/A3
nabta, West Bank 65/C3
nacapa (isl.), Calif. 204/F10
naco, Venezuela 124/F3
nacoco, La. 238/D4
nacoco (lake), La. 238/D4
naconda, Mont. 188/D1
naconda-Deer Lodge County, Mont. 262/C4
nacortes, Wash. 310/C2
nacostia, D.C. 245/F5
nacostia (riv.), D.C. 245/F5
nadarko, Okla. 288/K4
nanea, Peru 128/H10
nadia, Portugal 33/B2
nadolufeneri, Turkey 63/D5
nadoluhisarı, Turkey 63/D6
nadyr', U.S.S.R 2/T2
nadyr', U.S.S.R. 4/C1
nadyr', U.S.S.R. 48/S3
nadyr', U.S.S.R. 54/U3
nadyr' (gulf), U.S.S.R. 4/C18
nadyr' (gulf), U.S.S.R. 54/V3
nadyr' (gulf), U.S.S.R. 48/T3
nadyr' (range), U.S.S.R. 48/S3
nadyr' (riv.), U.S.S.R. 4/C1
nadyr' (riv.), U.S.S.R. 48/S3
nadyr' (riv.), U.S.S.R. 54/U3
náfi (isl.), Greece 45/G7
nagance, New Bruns. 170/E3
naheim, Calif. 188/C4
naheim, Calif. 204/D11
nahim Lake, Br. Col. 184/E4
nahola, Hawaii 218/C1
náhuac, Chihuahua, Mexico 150/F2
náhuac, Nuevo León, Mexico 150/J3
nahuac, Texas 303/K8
naï (well), Algeria 106/G4
nai Mudi (mt.), India 68/D6
naiza, Saudi Arabia 59/D4
naiza, Saudi Arabia 54/F7
nak, N. Korea 81/B4
nakapalle, India 68/E5
naktalik Brook (riv.), Newf. 166/B2
naktuvuk Pass, Alaska 196/H1
nalalava, Madagascar 118/H2
na María (gulf), Cuba 158/F3
nambas (isls.), Indonesia 85/D5
nambra (state), Nigeria 106/F7
namoose, N. Dak. 282/K4
namosa, Iowa 229/L4
namur, Turkey 63/E4
namur (cape), Turkey 59/B2
namur (cape), Turkey 63/E5
nan, Japan 81/G7
nandale, La. 238/F4
nanea, Bolivia 136/A4
nanea, Peru 128/H10
nantapur, India 68/D6
nantnag, India 68/D2
napa, U.S.S.R. 52/E6
nápolis, Brazil 132/D7
nápolis, Brazil 120/E4
nar, Iran 66/J5
nar, Iran 59/G3
narak, Iran 66/H4
narak, Iran 59/F3
nar Darreh, Afghanistan 59/H3
nar Darreh, Afghanistan 68/A2
ñasco, P. Rico 161/A1
ñasco, P. Rico 156/F1
ñasco (bay), P. Rico 161/A1
nastasia (isl.), Fla. 212/E2
natahan (isl.), No. Marianas 87/E4
natolia (reg.), Turkey 63/D3
natone, Wash. 310/H4
ñatuya, Argentina 143/D2
nauá (riv.), Brazil 132/B2
Anawalt, W. Va. 312/D8
Anaye (well), Niger 106/G5
Anbar (gov.), Iraq 66/B4
Ancash (dept.), Peru 128/D7
Ancaster, Ontario 177/D4
Anceney, Mont. 262/E5
Ancenis, France 28/C4
Anchieta, Brazil 132/F8
Ancho, N. Mex. 274/D5
Anchor, Ill. 222/E3
Anchorage, Alaska 188/D6
Anchorage, Alaska 146/D3
Anchorage, Alaska 196/B1
Anchorage, Ky. 237/L2
Anchorage, U.S. 2/B2
Anchorage, U.S. 4/D17
Anchorena, Argentina 143/C4
Anchor Point, Alaska 196/B2
Anchor Point, Newf. 166/C3
Anchorville, Mich. 250/G6
Anchovy, Jamaica 158/H5
Ancienne-Lorette, Québec 172/H3
Anclitas (cay), Cuba 158/F3
Anclote (keys), Fla. 212/D3
Anco, Ky. 237/P6
Ancohuma (mt.), Bolivia 120/C4
Ancohuma, Nevada (mt.), Bolivia 136/A4
Ancón, Peru 128/D8
Ancona, Ill. 222/E2
Ancona (prov.), Italy 34/D3
Ancona, Italy 34/D3
Ancona, Italy 7/F4
Ancón de Sardinas (bay), Colombia 126/A7
Ancón de Sardinas (bay), Ecuador 128/C2
Ancoraimes, Bolivia 136/A4
Ancram, N.Y. 276/N6
Ancroft, England 13/F2
Ancrum, Scotland 15/F5
Ancud, Chile 120/B7
Ancud, Chile 138/D4
Ancud (gulf), Chile 138/D4
Anda (Anta), China 77/L2
Andacollo, Argentina 143/B4
Andacollo, Chile 138/A8
Andado, North. Terr. 93/D8
Andahuaylas, Peru 128/F9
Andale, Kansas 232/E4
Andalgalá, Argentina 143/C2
Åndalsnes, Norway 18/F5
Andalusia, Ala. 195/E8
Andalusia, Ill. 222/C2
Andalusia, Pa. 294/N5
Andalusia (reg.), Spain 33/C4
Andaman (sea) 54/L8
Andaman (sea), Burma 72/B4
Andaman (isls.), India 2/P5
Andaman (isls.), India 54/L8
Andaman (isls.), India 68/G6
Andaman (sea), India 68/G6
Andaman and Nicobar Isls. (terr.), India 68/G6
Andamarca, Bolivia 136/B6
Andamarca, Peru 128/E8
Andamooka, S. Australia 94/E4
Andapa, Madagascar 118/H2
Andaraí, Brazil 132/F5
Andau, Austria 41/D3
Andeer, Switzerland 39/H3
Andelfingen, Switzerland 39/G1
Andenne, Belgium 27/G8
Anderlecht, Belgium 27/B9
Anderlues, Belgium 27/E8
Andermatt, Switzerland 39/G3
Andernach, Germany 22/B3
Anderson, Ala. 195/E1
Anderson, Alaska 196/H2
Anderson, Argentina 143/F7
Anderson, Calif. 204/C3
Anderson, Ind. 188/J2
Anderson, Ind. 227/F4
Anderson (riv.), Ind. 227/D8
Anderson, Iowa 229/B7
Anderson (co.), Kansas 232/G3
Anderson (co.), Ky. 237/M5
Anderson (lake), Manitoba 179/D2
Anderson (pt.), Manitoba 179/F3
Anderson, Mo. 261/D9
Anderson (riv.), N.W.T. 162/D2
Anderson (riv.), N.W. Terr. 187/F3
Anderson, S.C. 188/E4
Anderson (co.), S.C. 296/B2
Anderson, S.C. 296/B2
Anderson (bay), Tasmania 99/D2
Anderson (co.), Tenn. 237/N8
Anderson, Tenn. 237/K10
Anderson (co.), Texas 303/J6
Anderson, Texas 303/J7
Anderson Ranch (res.), Idaho 220/C6
Andersonville, Georgia 217/D6
Andersonville, Ind. 227/G5
Andersonville, Tenn. 237/O8
Andersonville, Va. 307/L6
Andersonville Nat'l Hist. Site, Georgia 217/D6
Andes (range) 120/B-26
Andes, Cordillera de los (mts.), Argentina 143/C2
Andes, Cordillera de los (mts.), Chile 138/C5,E
Andes, Colombia 126/C5
Andes, Mont. 262/M5
Andes, N.Y. 276/L6
Andes, Cordillera de los (mts.), Peru 128/F10
Andes (lake), S. Dak. 298/N7
Andheri, India 68/B7
Andhra Pradesh (state), India 68/D5
Andijk, Netherlands 27/G3
Andikíthira (isl.), Greece 45/F8
Andilamena, Madagascar 118/H3
Andimeshk, Iran 66/F4
Anding, Miss. 256/D5
Andirın, Turkey 63/G4
Ándissa, Greece 45/H6
Andizhan, U.S.S.R. 54/J5
Andizhan, U.S.S.R. 48/H5
Andkhvoy, Afghanistan 68/A1
Andkhvoy, Afghanistan 59/H2
Andoas Nuevo, Ecuador 128/D4
Andoma, Zaire 115/E3
Andong, S. Korea 81/D5
Andorra 7/E4
ANDORRA 33/G1
Andorra, Spain 33/F2
Andorra la Vella (cap.), Andorra 33/G1
Andover•, Conn. 210/F2
Andover, England 10/F5
Andover, England 13/F6
Andover, Ill. 222/C2
Andover, Iowa 229/N5
Andover, Kansas 232/E4
Andover, Maine 243/B6
Andover•, Maine 243/B6
Andover, Mass. 249/K2
Andover•, Mass. 249/K2
Andover, Minn. 255/E5
Andover•, N.H. 268/D5
Andover, N.J. 273/D2
Andover, N.Y. 276/E6
Andover, Ohio 284/J2
Andover, S. Dak. 298/O3
Andover•, Vt. 268/B5
Andover, Va. 307/C7
Andøya (isl.), Norway 18/J2
Andradas, Brazil 135/C3
Andradina, Brazil 132/D8
Andraitx, Spain 33/H3
Andravídha, Greece 45/E6
Andre (lake), Newf. 166/A3
Andreafski (Saint Marys), Alaska 196/F2
Andreanof (isls.), Alaska 196/L4
Andreas (cape), Cyprus 63/F5
Andrelândia, Brazil 135/D2
Andrés, Nicaragua 154/F3
Andrespol, Poland 47/D3
Andrew, Alberta 182/D3
Andrew, Iowa 229/M4
Andrew, La. 238/F6
Andrew (co.), Mo. 261/C3
Andrew (isl.), Nova Scotia 168/H3
Andrew Johnson Nat'l Hist. Site, Tenn. 237/R8
Andrews, 245/O7
Andrews, Ind. 227/F3
Andrews, N.C. 281/B4
Andrews, Oreg. 291/J5
Andrews, S.C. 296/H5
Andrews (co.), Texas 303/B5
Andrews, Texas 303/B5
Andrews A.F.B., Md. 245/G5
Andreyevka, U.S.S.R. 52/H4
Andria, Italy 34/F4
Androka, Madagascar 118/G5
Andros (isl.), Bahamas 146/L7
Andros (isl.), Bahamas 156/B1
Ándros, Greece 45/G7
Ándros (isl.), Greece 45/G7
Androscoggin (co.), Maine 243/C7
Androscoggin (riv.), Maine 243/C7
Androscoggin (riv.), N.H. 268/E2
Androth (isl.), India 68/C6
Andrychów, Poland 47/D4
Andsfjorden (fjord), Norway 18/K2
Andújar, Spain 33/D3
Andul, India 68/F2
Andulo, Angola 102/D6
Andulo, Angola 115/C6
Anéfis, Mali 106/E5
Anegada (isl.), Virgin Is. (U.K.) 156/H1
Anegada (passage), Virgin Is. (U.K.) 156/F3
Aného (Anecho), Togo 106/E7
Aneityum (Anatom) (isl.), Vanuatu 87/H8
Aneiza, Jebel (mt.), Iraq 66/A4
'Aneiza, Jebel (mt.), Iraq 59/C3
'Aneiza, Jebel (mt.), Jordan 59/C3
'Aneiza, Jebel (mt.), Saudi Arabia 59/C3
Añelo, Argentina 143/C4
Anerley, Sask. 181/D4
Aneroid, Sask. 181/D6
Aneta, N. Dak. 282/P4
Aneth, Utah 304/E6
Aneto (peak), Spain 33/G1
Angaki (Quirino), Philippines 82/C2
Angamos (isl.), Chile 138/D8
Angamos (pt.), Chile 138/A4
Angara (riv.), U.S.S.R. 54/L4
Angara (riv.), U.S.S.R. 48/K4
Angarsk, U.S.S.R. 54/M4
Angarsk, U.S.S.R. 48/L4
Angas Downs, North. Terr. 93/C8
Angaston, S. Australia 94/F6
Angaur (isl.), Belau 87/D5
Ånge, Sweden 18/J5
Ange-Gardien, Québec 172/E4
Angel (isl.), Calif. 204/J2
Angel (falls), Venezuela 120/C2
Angel (fall), Venezuela 124/G5
Angela, Mont. 262/K4
Ángel de la Guarda (isl.), Mexico 150/C2
Angeles, Philippines 82/C3
Ángeles, P. Rico 161/B2
Ängelholm, Sweden 18/H8
Angélica, Argentina 143/E5
Angelica, N.Y. 276/E6
Angelica, Wis. 317/K6
Angelina (co.), Texas 303/K6
Angelina (riv.), Texas 303/K6
Angelo, Wis. 317/E8
Angels Camp, Calif. 204/E5
Angelus, S.C. 296/G2
Angerman (riv.), Sweden 7/F2
Ångermanälven (riv.), Sweden 18/K5
Angermünde, Germany 22/E2
Angers, France 7/D4
Angers, France 28/C4
Angers, Québec 172/B4
Angicos, Brazil 132/G4
Angie, La. 238/L5
Angier, N.C. 281/M4
Angijak (isl.), N.W. Terr. 187/M3
Angikuni (lake), N.W. Terr. 187/J3
Angkor Wat (ruins), Cambodia 72/E4
Angle, Utah 304/C5
Angle Inlet, Minn. 255/C1
Anglem (mt.), N. Zealand 100/A7
Anglesey (isl.), Wales 13/C4
Anglesey (isl.), Wales 10/D4
Angleton, Texas 303/J8
Anglia, Sask. 181/C4
Angliers, Québec 174/B3
Ango, Zaire 115/E3
Angoche, Mozambique 118/G3
Angoche, Mozambique 102/G6
Angoche (isl.), Mozambique 118/G3
Angol, Chile 138/D1
Angola 2/K6
Angola 102/D6
ANGOLA 115/C6
Angola, Del. 245/T6
Angola, Ind. 227/G1
Angola, Kansas 232/G4
Angola, La. 238/G5
Angola, N.Y. 276/C5
Angola (swamp), N.C. 281/O5
Angola on the Lake, N.Y. 276/B5
Angoon, Alaska 196/M1
Angora, Minn. 255/F3
Angora, Nebr. 264/A3
Angoram, Papua N.G. 85/B6
Angostura (falls), Colombia 120/B2
Angostura (falls), Colombia 126/E6
Angostura, Mexico 150/E4
Angostura (res.), S. Dak. 298/B7
Angoulême, France 28/D5
Angoulnois (trad. prov.), France, 29
Angra do Heroísmo (dist.), Portugal 33/C1
Angra do Heroísmo, Portugal 33/C1
Angra dos Reis, Brazil 135/D3
Angren, U.S.S.R. 48/H5
Ang Thong, Thailand 72/C4
Anguil, Argentina 143/D4
Anguilla (isl.) 146/M8
ANGUILLA 156
Anguilla, Anguilla 156/F3
Anguilla, Miss. 256/C5
Anguillara Sabazia, Italy 34/F6
Anguille (cape), Newf. 166/C4
Angurugu, North. Terr. 93/E3
Angus, Iowa 229/E5
Angus, Minn. 255/B2
Angus, Ontario 177/E3
Angus (trad. prov.), Scotland, 15/B5
Angusville, Manitoba 179/A4
Angwin, Calif. 204/C5
Anheé, Belgium 27/F8
Anholt, Denmark 21/E4
Anholt (isl.), Denmark 21/E4
Anholt (isl.), Denmark 18/G8
Anhua, China 77/H6
Anhui (Anhwei), China 77/J5
Aniak, Alaska 196/G2
Aniakchak (vol.), Alaska 196/G3
Aniakchak Nat'l Mon., Alaska 196/G3
Aniakchak Nat'l Preserve, Alaska 196/G3
Anicuns, Brazil 132/D7
Aniene (riv.), Italy 34/F6
Animas (riv.), Colo. 208/D8
Animas, N. Mex. 274/A7
Animas (riv.), N. Mex. 274/B1
Añimbo, Bolivia 136/C7
Anin, Burma 72/C4
Anin, West Bank 65/C2
Anina, Romania 45/E3
Anita, Iowa 229/D6
Anita, Pa. 294/D3
Aniva (cape), U.S.S.R. 48/P5
Aniwa, Wis. 317/H6
Anjalankoski, Finland 18/P6
'Anjara, Jordan 65/D3
Anjidiv (Angediva) (isl.), India 68/C6
Anjou (trad. prov.), France, 29
Anjou, Québec 172/H4
Anju, N. Korea 81/B4
Anjum, Netherlands 27/J2
Ankang, China 77/G5
Ankara (prov.), Turkey 63/E3
Ankara (cap.), Turkey 63/E3
Ankara (cap.), Turkey 2/L4
Ankara (cap.), Turkey 54/E5
Ankara (cap.), Turkey 59/B2
Ankara (riv.), Turkey 63/D3
Ankazoabo, Madagascar 118/G4
Ankeny, Iowa 229/F5
Anker (riv.), England 10/G3
Ankerton, Alberta 182/D3
Ankhor, Somalia 115/J1
Anking (Anqing), China 77/J5
Anklam, Germany 22/E2
Ankober, Ethiopia 111/H6
Ankona, Fla. 212/F4
Ankoro, Zaire 115/E5
An Loc (Binh Long), Vietnam 72/E5
Anlu, China 77/H5
Anmoore, W. Va. 312/F4
Ann (cape), Mass. 249/M2
Anna, Ill. 222/D6
Anna, Ky. 237/J6
Anna, Ohio 284/B5
Anna, Texas 303/H4
Anna (lake), Va. 307/N4
Annaba, Algeria 102/C1
Annaba, Algeria 106/F1
Annabella, Utah 304/B5
Annaberg-Buchholz, Germany 22/E3
Anna Creek, S. Australia 94/D3
Annada, Mo. 261/L4
Annadel, Tenn. 237/M8
Annagry, Ireland 17/E1
Annaheim, Sask. 181/G3
Annai, Guyana 131/B4
An Najaf (gov.), Iraq 66/C5
An Najaf, Iraq 59/D3
An Najaf, Iraq 66/D5
An Najaf, Iraq 54/F6
Annalee (riv.), Ireland 17/G3
Annalong, N. Ireland 17/K3
Annaly (bay), Virgin Is. (U.S.) 161/E3
Anna Maria, Fla. 212/D4
Annan, Scotland 15/E6
Annan, Scotland 10/E3
Annan (riv.), Scotland 15/E5
Annandale, Minn. 255/D5
Annandale, N.J. 273/D2
Annandale, Va. 307/S3
Annandale-on-Hudson, N.Y. 276/N6
Anna Plains, W. Australia 92/C2
Annapolis, Calif. 204/B5
Annapolis, Ill. 222/F4
Annapolis (cap.), Md. 245/M5
Annapolis (cap.), Md. 188/L3
Annapolis, Mo. 261/L8
Annapolis (co.), Nova Scotia 168/C4
Annapolis (basin), Nova Scotia 168/C4
Annapolis (riv.), Nova Scotia 168/C4
Annapolis Junction, Md. 245/M4
Annapolis Royal, Nova Scotia 168/C4
Annapurna (mt.), Nepal 68/E3
Ann Arbor, Mich. 188/K2
Ann Arbor, Mich. 250/F6
Anna Regina, Guyana 131/B2
Annascaul, Ireland 17/B7
An Nasiriya, Iraq 59/E3
An Nasiriya, Iraq 66/D5
Annat, Scotland 15/C3
Annaville, Québec 172/E3
Annawan, Ill. 222/C2
Annbank Station, Scotland 15/D5
Anne (mt.), Tasmania 99/C4
Anne Arundel (co.), Md. 245/M4
Annecy, France 28/G5
Annemanie, Ala. 195/D6
Anner (riv.), Ireland 17/F7
Anneta, Ky. 237/J6
Annette, Alaska 196/N2
An Nhon, Vietnam 72/F4
Annieopscotch (mts.), Newf. 166/C4
Anniston, Ala. 188/J4
Anniston, Ala. 195/G3
Anniston, Mo. 261/O9
Anniston Army Depot, Ala. 195/F3
Annobon (isl.), Equat. Guinea 102/C5
Annona, Texas 303/K4
Annonay, France 28/F5
Annotto Bay, Jamaica 156/C3
Annotto Bay, Jamaica 158/K6
Annville, Ky. 237/O6
Annville, Pa. 294/J5
Annweiler am Trifels, Germany 22/B4
Anoka (co.), Minn. 255/E5
Anoka, Minn. 255/E5
Anoka, Nebr. 264/F2
Anola, Manitoba 179/F5
Año Nuevo (pt.), Calif. 204/J4
Áno Viánnos, Greece 45/G8
Anóyia, Greece 45/G8
Anqing (Anking), China 77/J5
Ans, Belgium 27/H7
Ansager, Denmark 21/B6
Ansai, China 77/G4
Ansbach, Germany 22/D4
Anse à Galets, Haiti 158/B6
Anse-à-Pitre, Haiti 158/C6
Anse-au-Griffon, Québec 172/D1
Anse-aux-Gascons, Québec 172/D2
Anse-à-Veau, Haiti 158/B6
Anse-Bertrand, Guadeloupe 161/A5
Anse-Bleue, New Bruns. 170/E1
Anse Boileau, Seychelles 118/H5
Anse-d'Hainault, Haiti 158/A6
Anse la Raye, St. Lucia 161/F6
Anselmo, Nebr. 264/E3
Anser Group (isls.), Tasmania 99/C1
Anserma, Colombia 126/B5
Anse Rouge, Haiti 158/B5
Anse Royale, Seychelles 118/H5
Anshan, China 77/K3
Anshan, China 54/O5
Anshun, China 77/G6
Ansley, Ala. 195/F7
Ansley, La. 238/E2
Ansley, Nebr. 264/E3
Anson, Kansas 232/E4
Anson, Maine 243/D6
Anson•, Maine 243/D6
Anson (pt.), Norfolk I. 88/K5
Anson (bay), Norfolk I. 88/K5
Anson (bay), North. Terr. 88/D2
Anson (co.), N.C. 281/J4
Anson, Texas 303/E5
Ansŏng, S. Korea 81/C5
Ansongo, Mali 106/E5
Ansonia, Conn. 210/C3
Ansonia, Ohio 284/A5
Ansonville, N.C. 281/J4
Ansonville, Pa. 294/E4
Ansted, W. Va. 312/D6
Anta, Peru 128/F9
Antabamba, Peru 128/F10
Antakya, Turkey 59/C2
Antakya, Turkey 63/G4
Antalaha, Madagascar 118/J2
Antalaha, Madagascar 102/H6
Antalya (prov.), Turkey 63/D4
Antalya, Turkey 54/D6
Antalya, Turkey 63/D4
Antalya, Turkey 59/B2
Antalya (gulf), Turkey 63/D4
Antalya (gulf), Turkey 59/B2
Antananarivo (prov.), Madagascar 118/H3
Antananarivo (cap.), Madagascar 2/M6
Antananarivo (cap.), Madagascar 102/G6
Antananarivo (cap.), Madagascar 118/H3
Antarctic (pen.), Ant. 2/G9
Antarctic (pen.), Ant. 5/C15
Antarctica 2/E11
ANTARCTICA 5
Antarctic Circle 2/A9
An Teallach (mt.), Scotland 15/C3
Antelope (creek), Idaho 220/E6
Antelope, Kansas 232/F3
Antelope, Mont. 262/M2
Antelope (co.), Nebr. 264/F2
Antelope (range), Nev. 266/E3
Antelope, Oreg. 291/G3
Antelope (creek), Oreg. 291/K5
Antelope (res.), Oreg. 291/K5
Antelope, Sask. 181/C5
Antelope (lake), Sask. 181/C5
Antelope, Texas 303/F4
Antelope (isl.), Utah 304/B3
Antelope (creek), Wyo. 319/G2
Antelope (hills), Wyo. 319/D3
Antequera, Paraguay 144/D4
Antequera, Spain 33/D4
Antero (mt.), Colo. 208/G5
Antero (res.), Colo. 208/H5
Antes Fort, Pa. 294/H3
Anthon, Iowa 229/B4
Anthony, Fla. 212/D2
Anthony, Ind. 227/G4
Anthony, Kansas 232/D4
Anthony, N. Mex. 274/C6
Anthony, R.I. 249/H6
Anthony, Texas 303/A10
Anthony, W. Va. 312/F7
Anthony Lagoon, North. Terr. 88/E3
Anthony Lagoon, North. Terr. 93/D4
Anthracite, Alberta 182/C4
Anti-Atlas (ranges), Morocco 106/C3
Antibes, France 28/G6
Anticosti (isl.), Que. 146/M5
Anticosti (isl.), Que. 162/K6
Anticosti (isl.), Québec 174/E3
Antietam, Md. 245/H3
Antietam (creek), Md. 245/H2
Antietam Nat'l Battlefield, Md. 245/H3
Antigo, Wis. 317/H5
Antigonish (co.), Nova Scotia 168/F3
Antigonish, Nova Scotia 168/F3
Antigonish (harb.), Nova Scotia 168/G3
Antigua (isl.) 146/M8
ANTIGUA & BARBUDA 156
ANTIGUA & BARBUDA 161
Antigua (isl.), Ant. & Bar. 161/E11
Antigua (isl.), Ant. & Bar. 156/G3
Antigua, Guatemala 154/B3
Antigua (riv.), Mexico 150/Q1
Antigua, Spain 33/B4
Antigues (pt.), Guadeloupe 161/A5
Antiguo Morelos, Mexico 150/K5
Antilla, Cuba 156/C2
Antilla, Cuba 158/J3
Antilles, Greater (isls.), W. Indies 156/B2
Antilles, Lesser (isls.), W. Indies 156/E4
Antimony, Utah 304/C5
Antioch, Calif. 204/L1
Antioch, Georgia 217/B4
Antioch, Ill. 222/E1
Antioch, Nebr. 264/B2
Antioch, Ohio 284/H6
Antioch, S.C. 296/F3
Antioch (Antakya), Turkey 63/G4
Antioch, W. Va. 312/H4
Antioquia (dept.), Colombia 126/B4
Antioquia, Colombia 126/B4
Antique (prov.), Philippines 82/D5
Antiquity, Ohio 284/G8
Antisana (mt.), Ecuador 128/D3
Anti-Taurus (mts.), Turkey 63/G3
Antler, N. Dak. 282/H2
Antler, Sask. 181/K6
Antler (riv.), Sask. 181/K6
Antler Lake, Alberta 182/D3
Antlers, Okla. 288/P6
Antofagasta (reg.), Chile 138/B4
Antofagasta, Chile 120/B5
Antofagasta, Chile 2/F7
Antofagasta, Chile 138/A4
Antofagasta de la Sierra, Argentina 143/C2
Antoine, Ark. 202/D5
Antoing, Belgium 27/C7
Anton, Colo. 208/N3
Antón, Panama 154/G6
Anton, Texas 303/B4
Anton Chico, N. Mex. 274/D3
Antone, Oreg. 291/H3
Antongil (bay), Madagascar 118/J3
Antonina, Brazil 135/B4
Antonino, Kansas 232/C3
Antonito, Colo. 208/H8
Antony, France 28/B2
Antora (peak), Colo. 208/G6
Antreville, S.C. 296/B3
Antrim (co.), Mich. 250/D3
Antrim, Mich. 250/D4
Antrim, N.H. 268/D5
Antrim•, N.H. 268/D5
Antrim (dist.), N. Ireland 17/J2
Antrim, N. Ireland 10/C3
Antrim, N. Ireland 17/J2
Antrim, Ohio 284/H5
Antrim, Pa. 294/H2
Antsalova, Madagascar 118/G3
Antsirabe, Madagascar 102/G7
Antsirabe, Madagascar 118/H3
Antsiranana (prov.), Madagascar 118/H2
Antsiranana, Madagascar 118/H2
Antsiranana, Madagascar 102/G6
Antsla, U.S.S.R. 53/D2
Antsohihy, Madagascar 118/H2
Antu, China 77/L3
An Tuc (An Khe), Vietnam 72/F4
Antwerp (prov.), Belgium 27/F6
Antwerp, Belgium 7/E3
Antwerp, Belgium 27/E6
Antwerp, N.Y. 276/J2
Antwerp, Ohio 284/A3
Antwerpen (Antwerp), Belgium 27/E6
An Uaimh, Ireland 10/C4
An Uaimh, Ireland 17/H4
Anuenue (Sand) (isl.), Hawaii 218/C4
Anuradhapura, Sri Lanka 68/E7
Anutt, Mo. 261/J7
Anvik, Alaska 196/F2

Anvil (peak), Alaska 196/K4
Anxi, China 77/E3
Anxious (bay), S. Australia 94/D5
Anyang, China 77/H4
A'nyêmaqên Shan (mts.), China 77/E5
Anykščiai, U.S.S.R. 53/C3
Anzá, Colombia 126/C4
'Anza, West Bank 65/C3
Anzaldo, Bolivia 136/C5
Anzhero-Sudzhensk, U.S.S.R. 54/K4
Anzhero-Sudzhensk, U.S.S.R. 48/J4
Anzio, Italy 34/D4
Anzóategui (state), Venezuela 124/F3
Aoiz, Spain 33/F1
Aoji-ri, N. Korea 81/E2
Aomori (pref.), Japan 81/K3
Aomori, Japan 54/R5
Aomori, Japan 81/K3
Ao Paray (riv.), Paraguay 144/A5
Aosta (prov.), Italy 34/A2
Aosta (reg.), Italy 34/A2
Aosta, Italy 34/A2
Aouara, Fr. Guiana 131/E3
Aoulef, Algeria 106/C3
Aoulef, Algeria 106/E3
Aozou, Chad 111/C3
Apa (riv.), Paraguay 144/D3
Apache (co.), Ariz. 198/F3
Apache (lake), Ariz. 198/D5
Apache, Okla. 288/K5
Apache (mts.), Texas 303/C11
Apache Creek, N. Mex. 274/A5
Apache Junction, Ariz. 198/D5
Apalachee (bay), Fla. 188/K5
Apalachee (bay), Fla. 212/B2
Apalachee, Georgia 217/E3
Apalachia (res.), N.C. 281/A4
Apalachicola, Fla. 212/A2
Apalachicola (bay), Fla. 212/B2
Apalachicola (riv.), Fla. 212/A1
Apalachin, N.Y. 276/H6
Apalona, Ind. 227/D8
Apan, Mexico 150/M1
Apaporis (riv.), Colombia 126/F8
Aparri, Philippines 82/C1
Aparri, Philippines 85/G2
Aparureñ, Venezuela 124/G5
Apataki (atoll), Fr. Poly. 87/M7
Apatin, Yugoslavia 45/D3
Apatity, U.S.S.R. 52/D1
Apatzingán de la Constitución, Mexico 150/H7
Ape, U.S.S.R. 53/D2
Apeldoorn, Netherlands 27/H4
Apennines (mts.), Italy 7/F4
Apennines, Central (range), Italy 34/D3
Apennines, Northern (range), Italy 34/B2
Apennines, Southern (range), Italy 34/E4
Apere (riv.), Bolivia 136/C4
Apex, N.C. 281/M3
Apgar, Mont. 262/B2
Apia (cap.), W. Samoa 2/A6
Apia (cap.), W. Samoa 87/J7
Apia (cap.), W. Samoa 86/M8
Apiaí, Brazil 135/B4
Apishapa (riv.), Colo. 208/L8
Apison, Tenn. 237/L10
Ap Iwan, Cerro (mt.), Chile 138/E6
Apizaco, Mexico 150/N1
Aplao, Peru 128/F11
Aplin, Ark. 202/E4
Aplington, Iowa 229/H3
Ap Long Ha, Vietnam 72/F5
Apo (vol.), Philippines 82/E7
Apohaqui, New Bruns. 170/E3
Apolda, Germany 22/D3
Apolima (str.), W. Samoa 86/L8
Apollo, Georgia 217/F4
Apollo, Pa. 294/C4
Apollo Bay, Victoria 97/B6
Apollo Beach, Fla. 212/C3
Apoo, Bolivia 136/A4
Aponguao (riv.), Venezuela 124/H5
Apopka, Fla. 212/E3
Apopka (lake), Fla. 212/E3
Aporé (riv.), Brazil 132/D7
Apostle (isls.), Wis. 317/F2
Apostle Islands Nat'l Lakeshore, Wis. 317/E1
Apóstoles, Argentina 143/E2
Apoteri, Guyana 131/B3
Appalachia, W. Va. 307/C7
Appalachian (mts.) 188/K3
Appalachian (mts.), N.C. 281/D2
Appalachian (mts.), Pa. 294/H4
Appalachian (mts.), Tenn. 237/M10
Appalachian (mts.), U.S. 146/K6
Appalachian (mts.), Va. 307/J5
Appam, N. Dak. 282/C2
Appanoose (co.), Iowa 229/H7
Appelscha, Netherlands 27/J3
Appenzell, Ausser Rhoden (canton), Switzerland 39/H2
Appenzell, Inner Rhoden (canton), Switzerland 39/H2
Appenzell, Switzerland 39/H2
Apperson, Okla. 288/N1
Appin, Ontario 177/C5
Appin (dist.), Scotland 15/C4
Appingedam, Netherlands 27/K2
Apple (creek), Ill. 222/C4
Apple (riv.), Ill. 222/C1
Apple (creek), N. Dak. 282/J6
Apple (riv.), Wis. 317/A5
Appleby, England 13/E3
Appleby, England 10/E3
Appleby, Texas 303/K6
Apple Creek, Ohio 284/G4
Applecross, Scotland 15/C3
Appledale, Br. Col. 184/J5
Applegate, Calif. 204/E5
Applegate, Mich. 250/G4
Applegate, Oreg. 291/D5

Apple Grove, W. Va. 312/B5
Apple Hill, Ontario 177/K2
Apple River, Ill. 222/C1
Apple River, Nova Scotia 168/D3
Apples, Switzerland 39/B3
Appleton, Ark. 202/E3
Appleton, Maine 243/E7
Appleton•, Maine 243/E7
Appleton, Minn. 255/D5
Appleton (Old Appleton), Mo. 261/N7
Appleton, N.Y. 276/C4
Appleton, Ontario 177/H2
Appleton, S.C. 296/F5
Appleton, Wash. 310/D5
Appleton, Wis. 188/G2
Appleton, Wis. 317/J7
Appleton City, Mo. 261/D6
Appling (co.), Georgia 217/H7
Appling, Georgia 217/H3
Appomattox (co.), Va. 307/L6
Appomattox, Va. 307/L6
Appomattox (riv.), Va. 307/M6
Appomattox Court House Nat'l Hist. Park, Va. 307/K6
Apponaug, R.I. 249/J6
Approuague (riv.), Fr. Guiana 131/E4
Apra (harb.), Guam 86/K7
Aprilia, Italy 34/D4
Apsheron (pen.), U.S.S.R. 52/H6
Apsheronsk, U.S.S.R. 52/F6
Apsley, Ontario 177/F3
Apsley, Victoria 97/A5
Apt, France 28/F6
Aptos, Calif. 204/K4
Apua (pt.), Hawaii 218/J6
Apulia (Puglia) (reg.), Italy 34/F4
Apulia Station, N.Y. 276/H5
Apure (state), Venezuela 124/D4
Apure (riv.), Venezuela 124/F3
Apurímac (dept.), Peru 128/F10
Apurímac (riv.), Peru 120/B4
Apurímac (riv.), Peru 128/F9
Apurito, Venezuela 124/D3
Ap Vinh Hao, Vietnam 72/F5
Aqaba (gulf) 54/E7
Aqaba (gulf), Egypt 111/G2
Aqaba (gulf), Egypt 59/C4
Aqaba (gulf), Israel 65/D6
'Aqaba, Jordan 65/D6
'Aqaba, Jordan 59/C4
Aqaba (gulf), Jordan 65/D6
Aqaba (gulf), Okla. 288/H3
Aqaba (gulf), Saudi Arabia 59/C4
Aqchen, Afghanistan 68/B1
Aqchen, Afghanistan 59/J2
Aq Darband, Iran 66/M2
'Aqiq, Sudan 111/G4
'Aqqaba, West Bank 65/C3
Aqqikkol Hu (lake), China 77/C4
'Aqra, Iraq 66/D2
'Aqraba, West Bank 65/C3
Aquades Beach, Sask. 181/C2
Aquaforte, Newf. 166/D2
Aqua Park, Okla. 288/R3
Aquarius (range), Ariz. 198/B4
Aquarius (plat.), Utah 304/C5
Aquasco, Md. 245/L6
Aquia, Peru 128/D8
Aquidabán (riv.), Paraguay 144/D3
Aquidauana, Brazil 120/D5
Aquidauana, Brazil 132/C8
Aquila, Mexico 150/H7
Aquila, Switzerland 39/G3
Aquiles Serdán, Mexico 150/G2
Aquilla, Ohio 284/H2
Aquin, Haiti 158/B6
Ara (riv.), Japan 81/O2
Arab, Ala. 195/B7
'Arab, Shatt-al- (riv.), Iran 59/E4
'Arab, Shatt-al- (riv.), Iran 66/F5
'Arab, Shatt-al- (riv.), Iran 59/E4
'Arab, Shatt-al- (riv.), Iraq 66/F5
Arab, Mo. 261/M8
'Araba, Wadi (valley), Israel 65/D5
'Araba, Wadi (valley), Jordan 65/D5
Arabela, N. Mex. 274/D4
Arabella, Sask. 181/K3
Arabi, Georgia 217/E7
'Arabi (isl.), Iran 66/G7
Arabi, La. 238/P4
Arabia, Ky. 237/M6
Arabia, Ohio 284/F8
Arabian (sea) 54/H8
Arabian (sea) 2/N5
Arabian (des.), Egypt 111/F2
Arabian (des.), Egypt 59/B4
Arabian (sea), India 68/B5
Arabian (sea), Pakistan 68/B5
Arabian (sea), Yemen 59/H5
Arabopó, Venezuela 124/H5
Araç, Turkey 63/E2
Araca, Bolivia 136/B5
Aracaju, Brazil 120/F4
Aracaju, Brazil 132/G5
Aracataca, Colombia 126/D2
Aracati, Brazil 132/G4
Araçatuba, Brazil 132/D8
Araçatuba, Brazil 135/A2
Araceli, Philippines 82/C5
Aracena, Spain 33/C4
Araçuaí, Brazil 132/F7
Arad, Israel 65/C5
Arad, Romania 7/G4
Arad, Romania 45/E2
Arada, Chad 111/D4
'Aradah, U.A.E. 59/F5
Aradan, Iran 66/H3
Arafat, Jebel (mt.), Saudi Arabia 59/D5
Arafura (sea) 87/D6
Arafura (sea) 2/R6
Arafura (sea) 88/E2
Arafura (sea), Indonesia 85/J8
Arafura (sea), North. Terr. 93/D1
Arago, Minn. 255/E4
Arago, Oreg. 291/C4
Arago (cape), Oreg. 291/C4

Aragon, Georgia 217/B2
Aragon, N. Mex. 274/A5
Aragón (reg.), Spain 33/F2
Aragón (riv.), Spain 33/F1
Aragona, Italy 34/D6
Aragua (state), Venezuela 124/E3
Araguacema, Brazil 132/D5
Aragua de Barcelona, Venezuela 124/F3
Aragua de Maturiñ, Venezuela 124/G3
Araguaia (riv.), Brazil 120/E3
Araguaia (riv.), Brazil 132/D4
Araguaiana, Brazil 132/C6
Araguaína, Brazil 120/E3
Araguari, Brazil 120/E4
Araguari, Brazil 132/D7
Araguari (riv.), Brazil 132/D2
Araioses, Brazil 132/F3
Arak, Algeria 106/E3
Arak, Iran 54/G6
Arak, Iran 59/E3
Arak, Iran 66/F3
Arakan Yoma (mts.), Burma 72/B3
Araks (riv.) 54/F6
Araks (riv.), Iran 59/E2
Araks (Aras) (riv.), Iran 66/E1
Araks (riv.), Turkey 63/K2
Araks (riv.), U.S.S.R. 7/J5
Araks (riv.), U.S.S.R. 52/G7
Araks (riv.), U.S.S.R. 48/F5
Aralık, Turkey 63/L3
Aral (sea), U.S.S.R. 54/G5
Aral (sea), U.S.S.R. 48/F5
Aral Sea (lake), U.S.S.R. 2/M3
Aral'sk, U.S.S.R. 54/H5
Aral'sk, U.S.S.R. 48/G5
Aramac, Queensland 95/C4
Aramberri, Mexico 150/J5
Arampampa, Bolivia 136/B5
Aran (isl.), Ireland 10/B3
Aran (isl.), Ireland 17/D2
Aran (isls.), Ireland 17/B5
Aran (isls.), Ireland 10/B3
Aranda de Duero, Spain 33/E2
Arandas, Mexico 150/H6
Aran Fawddwy (mt.), Wales 13/C5
Arani, Bolivia 136/C5
Aranjuez, Spain 33/E2
Aransas (co.), Texas 303/H10
Aransas (passage), Texas 303/H10
Aransas Pass, Texas 303/G10
Araoua (mts.), Fr. Guiana 131/E4
Araouane, Mali 106/D5
Araouane, Mali 102/B3
Arapaho, Okla. 288/H3
Arapahoe (co.), Colo. 208/L3
Arapahoe, Colo. 208/P5
Arapahoe (peak), Colo. 208/H2
Arapahoe, Nebr. 264/F4
Arapahoe, N.C. 281/R4
Arapahoe, Wyo. 319/D3
Arapaho Nat'l Rec. Area, Colo. 208/G2
Arapey, Uruguay 145/B1
Arapey Chico (riv.), Uruguay 145/B1
Arapey Grande (riv.), Uruguay 145/B2
Arapicos, Ecuador 128/D3
Arapiraca, Brazil 120/F3
Arapkir, Turkey 63/H3
Arapkir, Turkey 59/C2
'Ar'ar, Wadi (dry riv.), Iraq 66/B5
'Ar'ar, Wadi (dry riv.), Iraq 59/D3
'Ar'ar, Wadi (dry riv.), Saudi Arabia 59/D3
Araracuara, Colombia 126/E8
Araracuara, Cerros de (mts.), Colombia 126/E7
Araranguá, Brazil 132/D10
Araraquara, Brazil 132/E8
Araraquara, Brazil 135/B2
Araras, Brazil 135/C3
Ararat, Brazil 132/F4
Ararat, N.C. 281/H2
Ararat (mt.), Pa. 294/M2
Ararat (mt.), Turkey 54/F6
Ararat (mt.), Turkey 63/L3
Ararat (mt.), Turkey 59/D2
Ararat, Victoria 88/G7
Ararat, Victoria 97/B5
Ararat, Va. 307/G7
Arari, Brazil 132/E3
Araruama (lake), Brazil 135/E3
Aras (Araks) (riv.), Iran 66/E1
Aras (Araks) (riv.), Iran 59/E2
Aratürük (Yiwu), China 77/D3
Arauca (riv.) 120/C2
Arauca (inten.), Colombia 126/E4
Arauca, Colombia 120/B2
Arauca, Colombia 126/E4
Arauca (riv.), Colombia 126/E4
Arauca (riv.), Venezuela 124/E4
Arauco, Chile 138/D1
Arauco (gulf), Chile 138/D1
Arauquita, Colombia 126/E4
Araure, Venezuela 124/D3
Aravaca, Spain 33/F4
Aravaipa (creek), Ariz. 198/E6
Arawa, Papua N.G. 86/C2
Arawe, Papua N.G. 86/C2
Arax (Araks) (riv), Asia 59/E2
Araxá, Brazil 132/E7
Araya, Venezuela 124/F2
Arba, Ind. 227/H4
Arba Mench, Ethiopia 111/G6
Arba Mench, Ethiopia 102/F4
Arbeca, Spain 33/G2
Arbedo-Castione, Switzerland 39/G4
Arbela (Erbil), Iraq 59/D2
Arbela (Erbil), Iraq 66/D2
Arbela, Mo. 261/M1
Arboga, Sweden 18/J7
Arbois, France 28/F4
Arbon, Idaho 220/F7
Arbon, Switzerland 39/H1
Arborea, Italy 34/B5
Arborfield, Sask. 181/H2
Arborg, Manitoba 179/H4
Arbor Vitae, Wis. 317/G4
Arbovale, W. Va. 312/G5
Arbrá, Sweden 18/K6
Arbroath, Scotland 15/F4
Arden, Ark. 202/B6

Arbroath, Scotland 10/E2
Arbroth, La. 238/H5
Arbucias, Spain 33/H2
Arbuckle, Calif. 204/C4
Arbuckle, W. Va. 312/G2
Arbuckle (lake), Fla. 212/E4
Arbuckles, Lake of the (lake), Okla. 288/M6
Arbuthnot, Sask. 181/E6
Arbutus, Md. 245/M4
Arbyrd, Mo. 261/M10
Arcachon, France 28/C5
Arcachon (bay), France 28/C5
Arcade, Georgia 217/E2
Arcade, N.Y. 276/D5
Arcadia, Calif. 204/C10
Arcadia, Fla. 212/E4
Arcadia, Ind. 227/E4
Arcadia, Iowa 229/C4
Arcadia, La. 238/E1
Arcadia, Mich. 250/C4
Arcadia, Mo. 261/L7
Arcadia, Nebr. 264/F3
Arcadia, Nova Scotia 168/B5
Arcadia, Ohio 284/D3
Arcadia, Okla. 288/M3
Arcadia, Pa. 294/F4
Arcadia, R.I. 249/H6
Arcadia, S.C. 296/B2
Arcadia, Texas 303/K3
Arcadia, Utah 304/D3
Arcadia, Wis. 317/D7
Arcadia Lakes, S.C. 296/F3
Aramac, Queensland 95/C4
Aramco, Haiti 158/C6
Arcanum, Ohio 284/A6
Arcas (cay), Mexico 150/N6
Arcata, Calif. 204/A3
Arc Dome (mt.), Nev. 266/D4
Arcelia, Mexico 150/J7
Arch, N. Mex. 274/F4
Archambault (lake), Québec 172/C3
Archangel, U.S.S.R. 4/C7
Archangel, U.S.S.R. 7/J2
Archangel (Arkhangel'sk), U.S.S.R. 48/E3
Archangel (Arkhangel'sk), U.S.S.R. 52/F2
Archbald, Pa. 294/F6
Archbold, Ohio 284/B2
Arch Cape, Oreg. 291/D2
Archdale, N.C. 281/K3
Archena, Spain 33/F3
Archer, Fla. 212/D2
Archer, Iowa 229/B2
Archer, Nebr. 264/F3
Archer (fiord), N.W. Terr. 187/M1
Archer (riv.), Queensland 95/B2
Archer (co.), Texas 303/F4
Archer City, Texas 303/F4
Archerfield, Queensland 88/K3
Archerfield, Queensland 95/D3
Archerwill, Sask. 181/H3
Arches Nat'l Park, Utah 304/E5
Archidona, Ecuador 128/D3
Archidona, Spain 33/D4
Archie, La. 238/F2
Archie, Mo. 261/D5
Archiestown, Scotland 15/E3
Archuleta (co.), Colo. 208/E8
Archydal, Sask. 181/F5
Arcis-sur-Aube, France 28/F3
Arckaringa (creek), S. Australia 94/D2
Arco, Georgia 217/J8
Arco, Idaho 220/E6
Arco, Idaho 188/D2
Arco, Minn. 255/B6
Arcola, Ill. 222/E4
Arcola, Ind. 227/G2
Arcola, La. 238/K5
Arcola, Miss. 256/C4
Arcola, Mo. 261/E7
Arcola, N.C. 281/N2
Arcola, Sask. 181/J6
Arcopongo, Bolivia 136/B5
Arcos de la Frontera, Spain 33/D4
Arcos de Jalón, Spain 33/E2
Arcos de Valdevez, Portugal 33/B2
Arcot, India 68/D6
Arcoverde, Brazil 132/G5
Arctic (ocean) 54/C1
Arctic (ocean) 146/B2
Arctic (plain), Alaska 196/G1
Arctic, R.I. 249/A6
Arctic Bay, Canada 4/B14
Arctic Bay, N.W.T. 162/H1
Arctic Bay, N.W. Terr. 187/K2
Arctic Circle 2/J2
Arctic Ocean 2/B2
Arctic Ocean 4/A15
Arctic Ocean, U.S.S.R. 48/K1
Arctic Red (riv.), N.W. Terr. 187/E3
Arctic Red River, N.W.T. 162/C2
Arctic Red River, N.W. Terr. 187/E3
Arctic Village, Alaska 196/K1
Arda (riv.), Greece 45/G5
Ardabil, Iran 54/F6
Ardabil, Iran 59/E2
Ardabil, Iran 66/F2
Ardagh, Limerick, Ireland 17/C7
Ardagh, Longford, Ireland 17/F4
Ardahan, Turkey 59/D1
Ardahan, Turkey 63/K2
Årdal, Iran 66/G4
Årdal, Norway 18/E7
Ardalstangen, Norway 18/F6
Ardanuç, Turkey 63/K2
Ardara, Ireland 17/E2
Ardath, Sask. 181/D4
Ardavasar, Scotland 15/B3
Ardbeg, Ontario 177/D2
Ardèche (dept.), France 28/F5
Ardee, Ireland 17/H4
Ardee, Ireland 10/D4
Arden, Ark. 202/B6

Arden, Del. 245/R1
Arden, Denmark 21/C4
Arden, Manitoba 179/C4
Arden, Ontario 177/G3
Arden, Wash. 310/H2
Arden, W. Va. 312/G4
Arden-Arcade, Calif. 204/B8
Ardencroft, Del. 245/R1
Ardennes (for.), Belgium 27/F9
Ardennes (dept.), France 28/F3
Ardennes (dept.), France 28/F3
Ardenode, Alberta 182/D4
Ardentown, Del. 245/S1
Ardenvoir, Wash. 310/H3
Ardersier, Scotland 15/E3
Ardeşen, Turkey 63/J2
Ardestan, Iran 59/F3
Ardestan, Iran 66/H4
Ardez, Switzerland 39/K3
Ardfert, Ireland 17/B7
Ardgay, Scotland 15/D3
Ardglass, N. Ireland 17/K3
Ardgour (dist.), Scotland 15/C4
Ardheá, Greece 45/F5
Ardila (riv.), Spain 33/C3
Ardill, Sask. 181/F6
Ardino, Bulgaria 45/G5
Ardivachar (pt.), Scotland 15/A3
Ardle (riv.), Scotland 15/E4
Ardlethan, N.S. Wales 97/D4
Ardmore, Ala. 195/E1
Ardmore, Alberta 182/E2
Ardmore, Ind. 227/E1
Ardmore, Ireland 17/F8
Ardmore, Md. 245/G4
Ardmore, Mo. 261/H3
Ardmore, Okla. 188/G4
Ardmore, Okla. 288/M6
Ardmore, Pa. 294/N5
Ardmore, S. Dak. 298/B7
Ardmore, Tenn. 237/H10
Ardnamurchan (pen.), Scotland 15/B4
Ardnamurchan (pt.), Scotland 15/B4
Ardoch, N. Dak. 282/R3
Ardooie, Belgium 27/C7
Ardrahan, Ireland 17/D5
Ardrishaig, Scotland 15/C4
Ardrossan, Alberta 182/D3
Ardrossan, Scotland 10/D3
Ardrossan, Scotland 15/D5
Ards (dist.), N. Ireland 17/K2
Ardsley, N.Y. 276/O6
Åre, Sweden 18/H5
Arecibo (riv.), P. Rico 161/C1
Arecibo, P. Rico 156/G1
Arecibo, P. Rico 161/B1
Aredale, Iowa 229/H3
Areguá, Paraguay 144/B4
Areia Branca, Brazil 132/G4
Arelee, Sask. 181/D3
Arena (pt.), Calif. 188/B3
Arena (pt.), Calif. 204/B5
Arena (pt.), Mexico 150/E5
Arena, N. Dak. 282/K5
Arena (isl.), Philippines 82/C6
Arena, Wis. 317/G9
Arenac (co.), Mich. 250/F4
Arenas (pt.), Argentina 143/C7
Arenas (cay), Mexico 150/O5
Arenas (pt.), P. Rico 156/F2
Arenas de San Pedro, Spain 33/D2
Arendal, Norway 18/F7
Arendelovac, Yugoslavia 45/E3
Arendonk, Belgium 27/G6
Arendtsville, Pa. 294/H6
Arenillas, Ecuador 128/B4
Arenys de Mar, Spain 33/H2
Arenzville, Ill. 222/C4
Areópolis, Greece 45/F7
Arequipa (dept.), Peru 128/F10
Arequipa, Peru 120/B4
Arequipa, Peru 2/F6
Arequipa, Peru 128/G11
Arequipa, Peru 128/72
Aresji, Neth. Ant. 161/D9
Arese (riv.), Switzerland 39/C3
Arévalo, Spain 33/D2
Areyonga, North. Terr. 88/E4
Areyonga, North. Terr. 93/C8
Arezzo (prov.), Italy 34/C3
Arezzo, Italy 34/C3
Arfa Deh, Iran 66/H3
Arga (riv.), Spain 33/F1
Argadargada, North. Terr. 93/E6
Argalant, Mongolia 77/G3
Argalastí, Greece 45/F6
Argamasilla de Alba, Spain 33/E3
Arganda, Spain 33/G4
Argao, Philippines 82/D6
Argao, Philippines 82/D6
Argenta, Br. Col. 184/J5
Argenta, Ill. 222/E4
Argenta, Italy 34/C2
Argentan, France 28/D3
Argentat, France 28/D5
Argenteuil, France 28/A1
Argenteuil (co.), Québec 172/C4
Argentia, Newf. 166/D2
Argentina 120/C6
ARGENTINA 143
Argentina, Pa. 294/C3
Argentino (lake), Argentina 143/B7
Argenton-sur-Creusot, France 28/D4
Argeş (riv.), Romania 45/G3
Argo, Ala. 195/C5
Argo, Sudan 111/F4
Argo Fay, Ill. 222/C2
Argoliś (gulf), Greece 45/F7
Argonia, Kansas 232/E4
Argonne, Ill. 222/B6
Argonne Nat'l Laboratory, Ill. 222/B6
Argos, Greece 45/F7
Argos, Ind. 227/E2
Argos (cape), Nova Scotia 168/G3
Argostólion, Greece 45/E6

Arguello (pt.), Calif. 204/E9
Arguin (bay), Mauritania 106/A4
Argun (riv.) 54/N4
Argun (Ergun He) (riv.), China 77/K1
Argun (riv.), U.S.S.R. 48/M4
Argungu, Nigeria 106/E6
Argus (range), Calif. 204/H7
Argusville, N. Dak. 282/R5
Arguvan, Turkey 63/H3
Argyle, Fla. 212/C6
Argyle, Georgia 217/G8
Argyle, Iowa 229/K7
Argyle, Maine 243/F5
Argyle, Manitoba 179/E4
Argyle, Mich. 250/G5
Argyle, Minn. 255/B2
Argyle, Mo. 261/J6
Argyle, New Bruns. 170/C2
Argyle, N.Y. 276/O4
Argyle, Texas 303/F1
Argyle (lake), W. Australia 88/D3
Argyle (lake), W. Australia 92/E2
Argyle, Wis. 317/G10
Argyle Downs, W. Australia 92/E2
Argyll (dist.), Scotland 15/C4
Argyll (trad. co.), Scotland 15/B5
Arhangay, Mongolia 77/F2
Arhavi, Turkey 63/J2
Arhli (Arlit), Niger 106/F4
Ar Horqin, China 77/K3
Århus (co.), Denmark 21/D5
Århus, Denmark 7/E3
Århus, Denmark 21/D5
Århus, Denmark 18/F8
Aria, N. Zealand 100/E3
Ariah Park, N.S. Wales 97/D4
Ariaïl, S.C. 296/B2
Ariamsvlei, Namibia 118/B5
Ariano Irpino, Italy 34/E4
Ariari (riv.), Colombia 126/D6
Aribinda, Burkina Faso 106/D6
Arica, Chile 120/B4
Arica, Chile 138/A1
Arica, Colombia 126/E9
Aricagua, Venezuela 124/C3
Ariccia, Italy 34/F7
Arichat, Nova Scotia 168/H3
Arichuna, Venezuela 124/D4
Arichuna (riv.), Venezuela 124/D4
Arid (cape), W. Australia 88/C6
Arid (cape), W. Australia 92/C6
Ariège (dept.), France 28/D6
Ariguaní (riv.), Colombia 126/D3
Ariha (Jericho), West Bank 65/C4
Arikaree (riv.), Colo. 208/O3
Arima, Trin. & Tob. 156/G5
Arima, Trin. & Tob. 161/B10
Arimo, Idaho 220/F7
Arinagour, Scotland 15/B4
Arinos (riv.), Brazil 132/B5
Ario de Rosales, Mexico 150/J7
Arinos (riv.), Brazil 120/D3
Aripuaná (riv.), Brazil 132/A4
Arisaig, Scotland 15/C4
Arisaig (sound), Scotland 15/C4
Arismendi, Venezuela 124/D3
Arispe, Iowa 229/E7
Aristazabal (isl.), Br. Col. 184/C4
Ariton, Ala. 195/G7
Arivonimamo, Madagascar 118/H3
Arixang (Wenquan), China 77/B3
Ariza, Spain 33/E2
Arizaro, Salar de (salt dep.), Argentina 143/C2
Arizona 188/D4
ARIZONA 198
Arizona (state), U.S. 146/G6
Arizona City, Ariz. 198/D6
Arizona Sunsites, Ariz. 198/F7
Arjäng, Sweden 18/H7
Arjay, Ky. 237/O7
Arjeplog, Sweden 18/L3
Arjona, Colombia 126/C2
Arkabutla, Miss. 256/D1
Arkabutla (dam), Miss. 256/D1
Arkabutla (lake), Miss. 256/D1
Arkadelphia, Ala. 195/E3
Arkadelphia, Ark. 202/D5
Arkaig, Loch (lake), Scotland 15/C4
Arkaig, Loch (lake), Scotland 10/D2
Arkalyk, U.S.S.R. 48/G4
Arkansas 188/H3
ARKANSAS 202
Arkansas (riv.) 188/H3
Arkansas (co.), Ark. 202/H5
Arkansas (riv.), Ark. 202/G5
Arkansas (riv.), Colo. 208/Pf
Arkansas (riv.), Kansas 232/D4
Arkansas (riv.), Okla. 288/S4
Arkansas (state), U.S. 146/J6
Arkansas (riv.), U.S. 146/J6
Arkansas (riv.), U.S. 2/E4
Arkansas City, Ark. 202/H6
Arkansas City, Kans. 188/G3
Arkansas City, Kansas 232/E4
Arkansas City, Kansas 232/F2
Arkansas Divide (mts.), Colo. 208/L4
Arkansas Post Nat'l Mem., Ark. 202/H5
Arkansaw, Wis. 317/B7
Arkdale, Wis. 317/G7
Arkhángelos, Greece 45/J7
Arkhipo-Osipovka, U.S.S.R. 52/E6
Arkinda, Ark. 202/B6
Arklow, Ireland 10/C4
Arklow, Ireland 17/J6

Athelstan 331

Arklow (bank), Ireland 17/K6
Arkoe, Mo. 261/C2
Arkoma, Okla. 288/T4
Arkona (cape), Germany 22/E1
Arkona, Ontario 177/C4
Arkport, N.Y. 276/E6
Arkticheskiy Institut (isls.), U.S.S.R. 48/H2
Arkville, N.Y. 276/L6
Arkwright, S.C. 296/C2
Arlee, Mont. 262/B3
Arlee, W. Va. 312/B5
Arles, France 28/F6
Arley, Ala. 195/D2
Arlington, Ala. 195/C6
Arlington, Ariz. 198/C5
Arlington, Colo. 208/N6
Arlington, Georgia 217/C8
Arlington, Ill. 222/D2
Arlington, Ind. 227/F5
Arlington, Iowa 229/K3
Arlington, Kansas 232/D4
Arlington, Ky. 237/D7
Arlington•, Mass. 249/C6
Arlington, Minn. 255/D6
Arlington, Nebr. 264/H3
Arlington, N.Y. 276/N7
Arlington, N.C. 281/H2
Arlington, Ohio 284/C4
Arlington, Oreg. 291/G2
Arlington, S. Dak. 298/P5
Arlington, Tenn. 237/B10
Arlington, Tex. 188/G4
Arlington, Texas 303/F2
Arlington (lake), Texas 303/F2
Arlington, Vt. 268/A5
Arlington•, Vt. 268/A5
Arlington (co.), Va. 307/S2
Arlington, Va. 307/T3
Arlington, Wash. 310/C2
Arlington, Wis. 317/H9
Arlington, Wyo. 319/F4
Arlington Beach, Sask. 181/F4
Arlington Heights, Ill. 222/B5
Arlington Heights, Ohio 284/C9
Arlington Nat'l Cemetery, Va. 307/T3
Arlit (Arhli), Niger 106/F4
Arló, Hungary 41/F2
Arlon, Belgium 27/H9
Arltunga, North. Terr. 93/D7
Arm (riv.), Sask. 181/F5
Arma, Kansas 232/H4
Arma (plat.), Saudi Arabia 59/E4
Armada, Alberta 182/D4
Armada, Mich. 250/G6
Armadale, Scotland 15/C2
Armadale, Scotland 10/B1
Armagh (dist.), N. Ireland 17/H3
Armagh, N. Ireland 10/C3
Armagh, N. Ireland 17/H3
Armagh, Pa. 294/E5
Armagh, Québec 172/G3
Armathwaite, Tenn. 237/M8
Armavir, U.S.S.R. 7/J4
Armavir, U.S.S.R. 48/E5
Armavir, U.S.S.R. 52/F5
Armena, Alberta 182/D3
Armenia, Colombia 120/B2
Armenia, Colombia 126/B5
Armenian S.S.R., U.S.S.R. 7/J4
Armenian S.S.R., U.S.S.R. 52/F6
Armenian S.S.R., U.S.S.R. 48/E6
Armentières, France 28/E2
Armeriá, Mexico 150/G7
Armero, Colombia 126/C5
Armidale, Australia 87/F9
Armidale, N.S. Wales 88/J6
Armidale, N.S. Wales 97/F2
Armington, Ill. 222/D3
Armington, Mont. 262/F3
Arminto, Wyo. 319/E2
Armistead, La. 238/D3
Armit (lake), Manitoba 179/A2
Armley, Sask. 181/G2
Armona, Calif. 204/F7
Armorel, Ark. 202/L2
Armour, S. Dak. 298/N7
Armourdale, N. Dak. 282/M2
Armoy, N. Ireland 17/J1
Armstrong, Br. Col. 184/H5
Armstrong, Ill. 222/F3
Armstrong, Ind. 227/B8
Armstrong, Iowa 229/D2
Armstrong, Mo. 261/G4
Armstrong, Ont. 162/H5
Armstrong, Ontario 175/C2
Armstrong, Ontario 177/H4
Armstrong (co.), Pa. 294/D4
Armstrong (co.), Texas 303/C3
Armstrong, Texas 303/G11
Armstrong Brook, New Bruns. 170/E1
Armstrong Creek, Wis. 317/K4
Armstrongs Mills, Ohio 284/J6
Armuchee, Georgia 217/B2
Army Chemical Center, Md. 245/O3
Army Med. Ctr. Annex (Walter Reed), Md. 245/E4
Arnaiá, Greece 45/F5
Arnaud, Manitoba 179/E5
Arnaud (riv.), Québec 174/F1
Arnaudville, La. 238/G6
Arnauti (cape), Cyprus 59/B2
Arnauti (cape), Cyprus 63/E5
Arnavutköy, Turkey 63/D6
Arnedo, Spain 33/E1
Arnegard, N. Dak. 282/D4
Årnes, Norway 18/G6
Arnett, Okla. 288/G2
Arnett, W. Va. 312/D7
Arney (riv.), N. Ireland 17/F3
Arnheim, Mich. 250/G1
Arnhem (cape), Australia 87/D7
Arnhem, Netherlands 27/H4
Arnhem (cape), North. Terr. 88/F2
Arnhem (cape), North. Terr. 93/E2
Arnhem Land (reg.), Australia 87/D7
Arnhem Land (reg.), North. Terr. 88/E2
Arnhem Land (reg.), North. Terr. 93/D2
Arnhem Land Aboriginal Res., North. Terr. 88/E2
Arnhem Land Aboriginal Res., North. Terr. 93/C2
Arno (riv.), Italy 34/C3
Arno (atoll), Marshall Is. 87/H5
Arnold, Calif. 204/E5
Arnold, England 13/F4
Arnold, Kansas 232/B3
Arnold, Mich. 250/B2
Arnold, Minn. 255/F4
Arnold, Mo. 261/M6
Arnold, Nebr. 264/D3
Arnold (riv.), North. Terr. 93/D3
Arnold, Pa. 294/C4
Arnold Mills, R.I. 249/J5
Arnoldsburg, W. Va. 312/D5
Arnold's Cove, Newf. 166/C2
Arnolds Park, Iowa 229/C2
Arnoldstein, Austria 41/B3
Arnoldsville, Georgia 217/F3
Arnot, Pa. 294/H2
Arnøya (isl.), Norway 18/M1
Arnprior, Ontario 177/H2
Arnsberg, Germany 22/C3
Arnstadt, Germany 22/D3
Ærø (isl.), Denmark 21/C7
Aro (riv.), Venezuela 124/F4
Aroa, Venezuela 124/D2
Aroab, Namibia 118/B5
Aroche, Spain 33/C4
Arock, Oreg. 291/K5
Aroland, Ontario 177/H4
Aroland, Ontario 175/C2
Arolla, Switzerland 39/E4
Arolsen, Germany 22/C3
Aroma, Bolivia 136/B6
Aroma, Sudan 111/G4
Aroma Park, Ill. 222/F2
Aromas, Calif. 204/D7
Aroostook (co.), Maine 243/F2
Aroostook (riv.), Maine 243/G2
Aroostook, New Bruns. 170/C2
Arorae (atoll), Kiribati 87/H6
Aroroy, Philippines 82/D4
Arosa, Ria de (est.), Spain 33/B1
Arosa, Switzerland 39/J3
Aroser Rothorn (mt.), Switzerland 39/J3
Årøsund, Denmark 21/C7
Arouca, Trin. & Tob. 161/B10
Arp, Georgia 217/F7
Arp, Texas 303/J5
Arpa (riv.), Turkey 63/K2
Arpaçay, Turkey 63/K2
Arpin, Wis. 317/G6
Arque, Bolivia 136/B5
'Arraba, West Bank 65/C3
'Arrabe, Israel 65/C2
Arrah, India 68/E3
Ar Rahhaliya, Iraq 66/C4
Ar Rahhaliya, Iraq 59/D3
Arraias, Brazil 132/E6
Arran, Fla. 212/E1
Arran, Sask. 181/K4
Arran (isl.), Scotland 15/C5
Arran (isl.), Scotland 10/D3
Arras, Br. Col. 184/G2
Arras, France 28/E2
Arrecifal, Colombia 126/F6
Arrecife, Spain 106/B3
Arrecife, Spain 33/C4
Arrecife de la Media Luna (reefs), Honduras 154/F3
Arrecifes, Argentina 143/F7
Arrecifes (riv.), Argentina 143/G6
Arrey, N. Mex. 274/B6
Arriaga, Mexico 150/N8
Arriba, Colo. 208/N4
Arribeños, Argentina 143/F7
Arrington, Kansas 232/G2
Arrington, Tenn. 237/H9
Arrington, Va. 307/L5
Arriola, Colo. 208/B8
Arrochar, Scotland 15/D4
Arronches, Portugal 33/C3
Arrow (lake), Ireland 17/E3
Arrow (creek), Mont. 262/F3
Arrow Canyon (range), Nev. 266/G6
Arrow Creek, Mont. 262/F3
Arrowhead Mountain (lake), Vt. 268/A2
Arrow River, Manitoba 179/B4
Arrowrock (res.), Idaho 220/C6
Arrow Rock, Mo. 261/F4
Arrowsmith, Ill. 222/E3
Arrowtown, N. Zealand 100/B6
Arrowwood, Alberta 182/D4
Arrowwood (lake), N. Dak. 282/N5
Arroyas, Los (lake), Bolivia 136/C3
Arroyo, P. Rico 161/E3
Arroyo, P. Rico 156/G1
Arroyo Blanco, Cuba 158/F2
Arroyo de la Luz, Spain 33/C3
Arroyo del Valle (dry riv.), Calif. 204/L3
Arroyo Grande, Bolivia 136/A2
Arroyo Grande, Calif. 204/E8
Arroyo Hondo (dry riv.), Calif. 204/L3
Arroyo Hondo, N. Mex. 274/D2
Arroyo Mocho (dry riv.), Calif. 204/L2
Arroyo Seco, Argentina 143/F6
Arroyo Seco (dry riv.), Calif. 204/K10
Arroyo Seco, N. Mex. 274/D2
Arroyos y Esteros, Paraguay 144/B4
Ar Rumaila, Iraq 66/E5
Års, Denmark 21/C4
Ars-en-Ré, France 28/C4
Arsen'yev, U.S.S.R. 48/O5
Arsin, Turkey 63/H2
Arslanköy, Turkey 63/F4
Árta, Greece 45/E6
Artá, Spain 33/H3
Artas, S. Dak. 298/K2
Artawiya, Saudi Arabia 59/E4
Arteaga, Mexico 150/H7
Artem, U.S.S.R. 48/O5
Artemas, Pa. 294/E6
Artemisa, Cuba 158/B1
Artemisa, Cuba 156/A2
Artemovskiy, U.S.S.R. 48/M4
Artemus, Ky. 237/O7
Artena, Italy 34/F7
Artesia, Calif. 204/C11
Artesia, Miss. 256/G4
Artesia, N. Mex. 188/F4
Artesia, N. Mex. 274/E6
Artesian, S. Dak. 298/O6
Artesia Wells, Texas 303/E9
Arth, Switzerland 39/F2
Arthabaska (co.), Québec 172/E4
Arthabaska, Québec 172/F3
Arthur, Ill. 222/E4
Arthur, Ind. 227/C8
Arthur, Iowa 229/C4
Arthur (co.), Nebr. 264/C3
Arthur, Nebr. 264/C3
Arthur (range), N. Zealand 100/D4
Arthur, N. Dak. 282/R5
Arthur, Ontario 177/D4
Arthur (lake), Pa. 294/C4
Arthur (lake), Tasmania 99/D4
Arthur (range), Tasmania 99/C5
Arthur (riv.), Tasmania 99/B3
Arthur, Tenn. 237/O7
Arthur (riv.), W. Australia 92/B2
Arthur, W. Va. 312/H4
Arthurdale, W. Va. 312/G3
Arthuret, England 13/E2
Arthurette, New Bruns. 170/C2
Arthur Kill (str.), N.J. 273/B3
Arthur's (pass), N. Zealand 100/C5
Arthurstown, Ireland 17/H7
Artibonite (dept.), Haiti 158/C5
Artibonite (riv.), Haiti 158/C5
Artigas (dept.), Uruguay 145/B1
Artigas, Uruguay 145/C1
Artillery (lake), N.W. Terr. 187/H3
Artland, Sask. 181/B3
Artois, Calif. 204/C4
Artois (trad. prov.), France 29
Artova, Turkey 63/G2
Artux (Atushi), China 77/A4
Artvin (prov.), Turkey 63/J2
Artvin, Turkey 59/D1
Artvin, Turkey 63/J2
Aru (isls.), Indonesia 85/K7
Aru, Zaire 115/F3
Arua, Uganda 115/F3
Aruba (isl.), Netherlands 161/E9
Aruba (isl.), Netherlands 156/E4
Arucas, Spain 33/B5
Arunachal Pradesh (terr.), India 68/G3
Arundel, England 13/G7
Arundel, England 10/F5
Arundel, Québec 172/C4
Årup, Denmark 21/D7
Aruppukkottai, India 68/D7
'Arura, West Bank 65/C3
Arus, P. Rico 161/C3
Arusha (reg.), Tanzania 115/G4
Arusha, Tanzania 102/F5
Arusha, Tanzania 115/G4
Arusi (prov.), Ethiopia 111/G6
Aruwimi (riv.), Zaire 115/E3
Arva, Ireland 17/F4
Arva, Ontario 177/C4
Arvada, Colo. 208/J3
Arvada, Wyo. 319/F1
Arvayheer, Mongolia 77/F2
Arvel, Ky. 237/O5
Arvi, India 68/D4
Arvida, Québec 172/F1
Arvidsjaur, Sweden 18/L4
Arvika, Sweden 18/H7
Arvilla, N. Dak. 282/P4
Arvin, Calif. 204/G8
Arvonia, Va. 307/M5
Arwad (Ruad) (isl.), Syria 63/F5
Arxan, China 77/K2
Arys', U.S.S.R. 48/G5
Arzamas, U.S.S.R. 48/E4
Arzamas, U.S.S.R. 52/F3
Arzuá, Spain 33/B1
As, Belgium 27/H6
Aš, Czech. 41/B1
Aså, Denmark 21/D3
Asaba, Nigeria 106/F7
Asadabad, Iran 66/F3
Asahan (riv.), Indonesia 85/B5
Asahi, Japan 81/K6
Asahi (mt.), Japan 81/J4
Asahikawa, Japan 81/L2
Asahikawa, Japan 54/P5
Asama (mt.), Japan 81/J5
Asansol, India 68/F4
Åsarna, Sweden 18/J5
Asau, W. Samoa 86/L8
Asbest, U.S.S.R. 48/G4
Asbestos, Québec 172/F4
Asbury, Iowa 229/M4
Asbury, Mo. 261/C8
Asbury, N.J. 273/C2
Asbury, W. Va. 312/E7
Asbury Park, N.J. 273/F3
As Busaiya, Iraq 66/E5
Ascención (Áñez), Bolivia 136/D4
Ascensión, Argentina 143/F7
Ascension (par.), La. 238/J6
Ascensión, Mexico 150/E1
Ascension, Neth. Ant. 161/F8
Ascension (isl.), St. Helena 102/A5
Ascension (isl.), St. Helena 2/J6
Aschaffenburg, Germany 22/C4
Aschendorf, Germany 22/B2
Aschersleben, Germany 22/D3
Asco, W. Va. 312/C8
Ascog, Scotland 15/A2
Ascoli Piceno (prov.), Italy 34/D3
Ascoli Piceno, Italy 34/D3
Ascona, Switzerland 39/G4
Ascope, Peru 128/C6
Ascot, Queensland 88/K2
Ascot, Queensland 95/E2
Ascotán, Chile 138/B3
Ascotán, Salar de (salt dep.), Chile 138/B3
Ascot Corner, Québec 172/F4
Ascrib (isls.), Scotland 15/B3
Ascutney, Vt. 268/C5
Ascutney (mt.), Vt. 268/C5
Åseda, Sweden 18/J8
Åsele, Sweden 18/K4
Asenovgrad, Bulgaria 45/G5
Asèr, Ras (cape), Somalia 2/M5
Asèr, Ras (cape), Somalia 115/K1
Ash (riv.), Minn. 255/F2
Ash, N.C. 281/N6
Ash, Oreg. 291/D4
Ash (creek), Utah 304/A6
'Ashaira, Saudi Arabia 59/D5
Ashanti (reg.), Ghana 102/B4
Ashanti (reg.), Ghana 106/D7
Ashaway, R.I. 249/G7
Ashboro, Ind. 227/C6
Ashburn, Georgia 217/E7
Ashburn, Mo. 261/K3
Ashburn, Va. 307/O2
Ashburnham, Mass. 249/G2
Ashburnham•, Mass. 249/G2
Ashburton (riv.), Australia 87/B8
Ashburton, England 13/D7
Ashburton, N. Zealand 100/C5
Ashburton (riv.), W. Australia 88/B4
Ashburton (riv.), W. Australia 92/A3
Ashburton Downs, W. Australia 88/B4
Ashby, Ala. 195/E4
Ashby•, Mass. 249/G2
Ashby, Minn. 255/C4
Ashby, Nebr. 264/C2
Ashbyburg, Ky. 237/G5
Ash Creek, Minn. 255/B7
Ashcroft, Br. Col. 184/G5
Ashdale, Maine 243/D8
Ashdod, Israel 65/B4
Ashdot Ya'aqov, Israel 65/D2
Ashdown, Ark. 202/B6
Ashe (co.), N.C. 281/F2
Ashe (isl.), N.C. 281/P6
Asheboro, N.C. 281/K3
Ashepoo, S.C. 296/G6
Ashepoo (riv.), S.C. 296/F6
Asher, Okla. 288/N5
Ashern, Manitoba 179/D3
Asherton, Texas 303/E9
Asherville, Ind. 227/C6
Asherville, Kansas 232/D2
Asheville, N.C. 188/K3
Asheville, N.C. 281/D3
Asheweig (riv.), Ontario 175/C2
Ashfield•, Mass. 249/C2
Ashfield, N. S. Wales 88/K4
Ashfield, N.S. Wales 97/J3
Ash Flat, Ark. 202/G1
Ashford, Ala. 195/H8
Ashford•, Conn. 210/G1
Ashford, England 10/G5
Ashford, England 13/H6
Ashford, Ireland 17/J5
Ashford, N.S. Wales 97/F1
Ashford, N.C. 281/F3
Ashford, Wash. 310/C4
Ashford, W. Va. 312/C6
Ashford P.O. (Warrenville), Conn. 210/G1
Ash Fork, Ariz. 198/C3
Ash Grove, Kansas 232/D2
Ash Grove, Mo. 261/E8
Ashgrove, Queensland 88/K2
Ashhurst, N. Zealand 100/E4
Ashibetsu, Japan 81/L2
Ashikaga, Japan 81/J5
Ashington, England 13/F2
Ashington, England 10/F3
Ashippun, Wis. 317/H1
Ashiya, Japan 81/H8
Ashizuri (cape), Japan 81/F7
Ashkhabad, U.S.S.R. 54/G6
Ashkhabad, U.S.S.R. 48/F6
Ashkum, Ill. 222/E3
Ash Lake, Minn. 255/F2
Ashland, Ala. 195/G4
Ashland, Calif. 204/K2
Ashland, Georgia 217/F2
Ashland, Ill. 222/C4
Ashland, Kansas 232/C4
Ashland, Ky. 237/R4
Ashland, Ky. 188/K3
Ashland, La. 238/D2
Ashland, Maine 243/G2
Ashland•, Maine 243/G2
Ashland•, Mass. 249/J3
Ashland, Miss. 256/F1
Ashland, Mo. 261/H5
Ashland, Mont. 262/K5
Ashland, Nebr. 264/H3
Ashland, N.H. 268/D4
Ashland•, N.H. 268/D4
Ashland, N.J. 273/B3
Ashland, N.Y. 276/M6
Ashland (co.), Ohio 284/F4
Ashland, Ohio 284/F4
Ashland, Okla. 288/O5
Ashland, Oreg. 291/E5
Ashland, Pa. 294/K4
Ashland, Va. 307/N5
Ashland (co.), Wis. 317/E3
Ashland, Wis. 317/E2
Ashland City, Tenn. 237/G8
Ashley (co.), Ark. 202/G7
Ashley, Ill. 222/D5
Ashley, Ind. 227/G1
Ashley, Mich. 250/E5
Ashley, Mo. 261/K4
Ashley (lake), Mont. 262/B2
Ashley, N.S. Wales 97/E1
Ashley, N. Dak. 282/M7
Ashley, Ohio 284/E5
Ashley, Pa. 294/E7
Ashley (riv.), S.C. 296/G6
Ashley, W. Va. 312/E4
Ashley Falls, Mass. 249/A4
Ashmere (lake), Mass. 249/B3
Ashmont, Alberta 182/E2
Ashmore, Ill. 222/F4
Ashmore, Nova Scotia 168/C4
Ashmore (isls.), Terr. of Ashmore and Cartier Is. 88/C2
Ashmore and Cartier Is., Terr. of, 88/C2
Ashokan, N.Y. 276/M7
Ashokan (res.), N.Y. 276/M7
Ashport, Tenn. 237/B9
Ashqelon, Israel 65/A4
Ash Shabicha, Iraq 66/C5
Ashtabula (lake), N. Dak. 282/P5
Ashtabula (co.), Ohio 284/J2
Ashtabula, Ohio 284/J2
Ashton, Idaho 220/G5
Ashton, Ill. 222/D2
Ashton, Iowa 229/B2
Ashton, Kansas 232/E4
Ashton, Mich. 250/D5
Ashton, Nebr. 264/F3
Ashton, R.I. 249/J5
Ashton, S.C. 296/E5
Ashton, S. Dak. 298/N3
Ashton, W. Va. 312/B5
Ashton Creek, Br. Col. 184/H5
Ashton-under-Lyne, England 13/H2
Ashton-under-Lyne, England 10/G2
Ashuanipi (lake), Newf. 166/A3
Ashuanipi (riv.), Newf. 166/A3
Ashuanpi, Newf. 166/A3
Ashuelot, N.H. 268/C6
Ashuelot (riv.), N.H. 268/C6
Ash Valley, Kansas 232/C3
Ashville, Ala. 195/F3
Ashville, Maine 243/G7
Ashville, Manitoba 179/B3
Ashville, Ohio 284/E6
Ashville, Pa. 294/F4
Ashwaubenon, Wis. 317/K7
Ashwood, Oreg. 291/G3
'Asi (Orontes) (riv.), Syria 63/G5
Asia 2/P3
Asia (isls.), Indonesia 85/J5
Asid (gulf), Philippines 82/D4
Asidonhoppo, Suriname 131/D4
Asilah, Morocco 106/C1
Asinara (gulf), Italy 34/B4
Asinara (isl.), Italy 34/B4
Asino, U.S.S.R. 48/J4
'Asir (reg.), Saudi Arabia 59/D6
Aşkale, Turkey 63/J3
Askeaton, Ireland 17/D6
Askew, Miss. 256/D1
Askewville, N.C. 281/R2
Askim, Norway 18/E4
Askim, Sweden 18/G8
Aski Mosul, Iraq 66/C2
Askival (mt.), Scotland 15/B4
Askov, Denmark 21/C7
Askov, Minn. 255/F4
Askvoll, Norway 18/D6
Asmara, Ethiopia 111/G4
Asmara, Ethiopia 59/C6
Asmara, Ethiopia 102/F3
Åsnaes, Denmark 21/E6
Åsnen (lake), Sweden 18/J8
Asnières-sur-Seine, France 28/A1
Aso (mt.), Japan 81/E7
Aso National Park, Japan 81/E7
Asosa, Ethiopia 111/F5
Asoteriba, Jebel (mt.), Sudan 111/G3
Asotin (co.), Wash. 310/H4
Asotin, Wash. 310/H4
Asotin (creek), Wash. 310/H4
Asotin (dam), Wash. 310/J4
Aspang Markt, Austria 41/D3
Aspatria, England 13/D3
Aspe, Spain 33/F3
Aspelund, Minn. 255/F6
Aspen, Colo. 208/F4
Aspen, Nova Scotia 168/F3
Aspen (lake), Oreg. 291/E5
Aspen (mts.), Wyo. 319/C4
Aspen Grove, Br. Col. 184/G5
Aspen Hill, Md. 245/K4
Aspermont, Texas 303/D4
Aspers, Pa. 294/H6
Aspetuck, Conn. 210/B4
Aspetuck (res.), Conn. 210/B4
Aspetuck (riv.), Conn. 210/B3
Aspinwall, Iowa 229/C5
Aspinwall, Pa. 294/C6
Aspiring (mt.), N. Zealand 100/B6
Aspley, Queensland 88/K2
Aspy (bay), Nova Scotia 168/H2
Asquith, Sask. 181/D3
Assab, Ethiopia 59/D7
Assab, Ethiopia 111/H5
Assaba (reg.), Mauritania 106/B5
Assabet (riv.), Mass. 249/H3
Assad, Bahrat (lake), Syria 63/H4
Assakarai (dry riv.), Niger 106/F5
Assal (lake), Djibouti 110/H5
Assal (lake), Djibouti 114/H5
Assale (lake), Ethiopia 111/H5
As Salman, Iraq 59/E3
As Salman, Iraq 66/D5
Assam (state), India 68/G3
Assapan (riv.), Manitoba 179/G2
Assaria, Kansas 232/E3
Assateague Island Nat'l Seashore, Va. 307/T4
Assawompset (pond), Mass. 249/L5
Assay (creek), Utah 304/B6
Asse, Belgium 27/E7
Asselar (well), Mali 106/D5
Asselle, Ethiopia 102/F4
Asselle, Ethiopia 111/G6
Assen, Netherlands 27/K3
Assenede, Belgium 27/D6
Assens, Århus, Denmark 21/D4
Assens, Fyn, Denmark 21/D7
Assesse, Belgium 27/G8
Assigny (lake), Newf. 166/A3
Assiniboia, Sask. 181/E6
Assiniboine (mt.), Alberta 182/C4
Assiniboine (mt.), Br. Col. 184/K5
Assiniboine (riv.), Manitoba 179/C5
Assiniboine (riv.), Sask. 181/J3
Assinica (lake), Québec 174/C3
Assinika (lake), Manitoba 179/G2
Assinika (riv.), Manitoba 179/G2
Assinippi, Mass. 249/E8
Assis, Brazil 132/D8
Assis, Brazil 135/A3
Assisi, Italy 34/D3
Assonet, Mass. 249/K5
Assumption, Ill. 222/E4
Assumption (par.), La. 238/H7
Assumption, Ohio 284/B2
Assumption (isl.), Seychelles 118/H1
Assynt (dist.), Scotland 15/C2
Assynt, Loch (lake), Scotland 15/D2
Assyria, Mich. 250/D6
Astara, U.S.S.R. 52/G7
Astatula, Fla. 212/E3
Asten, Netherlands 27/H6
Asterabad (Gorgan), Iran 59/F2
Asterabad (Gorgan), Iran 66/J2
Asti, Calif. 204/C5
Asti (prov.), Italy 34/B2
Asti, Italy 34/B2
Astillero, Peru 128/H9
Astipálaia, Greece 45/H7
Astipálaia (isl.), Greece 45/H7
Astle, New Bruns. 170/D2
Aston (bay), N.W. Terr. 187/J2
Aston-Jonction, Québec 172/E3
Astor, Fla. 212/E2
Astorga, Spain 33/C1
Astoria, Ill. 222/C3
Astoria, Oreg. 188/B1
Astoria, Oreg. 291/D1
Astoria, S. Dak. 298/S4
Astorville, Ontario 177/E1
Astove (isl.), Seychelles 102/G6
Astove (isl.), Seychelles 118/H2
Astra, Argentina 143/C6
Astrakhan', U.S.S.R. 7/J4
Astrakhan', U.S.S.R. 52/G5
Astrakhan', U.S.S.R. 48/E5
Astray (lake), Newf. 166/A3
Astudillo, Spain 33/D1
Asturias (reg.), Spain 33/C1
Asunción, Bolivia 136/B2
Asuncion (isl.), No. Marianas 87/E4
Asunción, Paraguay 144/A4
Asunción (cap.), Paraguay 2/F7
Asunción (cap.), Paraguay 144/A4
Asunción (cap.), Paraguay 120/D5
Asuncion (passage), Philippines 82/D5
Asunción Mita, Guatemala 154/C3
Asunción Nochixtlán, Mexico 150/L8
Asunta, Bolivia 136/B5
Aswad, Ras al (cape), Saudi Arabia 59/C5
Aswân, Egypt 111/F3
Aswân, Egypt 59/B5
Aswân, Egypt 102/F2
Aswân (dam), Egypt 59/B5
Aswân (dam), Egypt 111/F3
Aswân High (dam), Egypt 102/F2
Aswân High (dam), Egypt 111/F3
Asyût, Egypt 111/J4
Asyût, Egypt 102/F2
Asyût, Egypt 59/B4
Aszód, Hungary 41/E3
Atabapo (riv.), Colombia 126/G6
Atabapo (riv.), Venezuela 124/E6
Atacama, Puna de (reg.), Argentina 143/C2
Atacama (reg.), Chile 138/B6
Atacama (des.), Chile 120/C5
Atacama (des.), Chile 138/B4
Atacama, Salar de (salt dep.), Chile 138/C4
Atafu (atoll), Tokelau Is. 87/J6
Atahona, Uruguay 145/B4
Atakora (mts.), Benin 106/E6
Atakpamé, Togo 106/E7
Atalándi, Greece 45/F6
Atalaya, Peru 128/E8
Atalissa, Iowa 229/L5
Atambua, Indonesia 85/G7
Atami, Japan 81/J6
Atapirire, Venezuela 124/F3
Atar, Mauritania 106/B4
Atar, Mauritania 102/A2
Ataran (riv.), Burma 72/C4
Atascadero, Calif. 204/E8
Atascosa (co.), Texas 303/F9
Atascosa, Texas 303/J11
Atbara (riv.), Ethiopia 111/G4
Atbara, Sudan 111/F4
Atbara, Sudan 59/B6
Atbara, Sudan 102/F3
Atbara (riv.), Sudan 59/C6
Atbara (riv.), Sudan 111/G4
Atbasar, U.S.S.R. 48/G4
Atchafalaya (bay), La. 238/H8
Atchafalaya (riv.), La. 238/G6
Atchison, Kans. 188/G3
Atchison (co.), Kansas 232/G2
Atchison, Kansas 232/G2
Atchison (co.), Mo. 261/B2
Atco, N.J. 273/D4
Ateca, Spain 33/F2
Atén, Bolivia 136/A4
Atenas, C. Rica 154/E6
Atessa, Italy 34/E3
Atglen, Pa. 294/K6
Ath, Belgium 27/D7
Athabasca (lake) 162/F4
Athabasca, Alberta 162/E5
Athabasca, Alberta 182/D2
Athabasca (lake), Alberta 182/C5
Athabasca (riv.), Alberta 182/D1
Athabasca (riv.), Alberta 162/E4
Athabasca (riv.), Alberta 146/G4
Athabasca (lake), Canada 146/H4
Athabasca (lake), Sask. 181/L2
Athalia, Ohio 284/F8
Athalmer, Br. Col. 184/K5
Athboy, Ireland 17/H4
Athea, Ireland 17/C4
Athelstan, Iowa 229/D7

Athelstan, Québec 172/C4
Athelstane, Wis. 317/K5
Athena, Oreg. 291/J2
Athenry, Ireland 17/D5
Athens, Ala. 195/E1
Athens, Ark. 202/C5
Athens, Ga. 188/K4
Athens, Georgia 217/F3
Athers (cap.), Greece 7/G5
Athers (cap.), Greece 2/K4
Athers (cap.), Greece 45/F7
Athers, Greater, Greece 45/F7
Athens, Ill. 222/D4
Athens, Ind. 227/E2
Athens, La. 238/E1
Athens, Maine 243/D6
Athens•, Maine 243/D6
Athens, Mich. 250/D6
Athens, N.Y. 276/N6
Athens (co.), Ohio 284/F7
Athens, Ohio 284/F7
Athens, Ontario 177/J3
Athens, Pa. 294/K2
Athens, Tenn. 237/M10
Athens, Texas 303/J5
Athens, W. Va. 312/E8
Athens, Wis. 317/G5
Athensville, Ill. 222/C4
Atherley, Ontario 177/E3
Atherton, Calif. 204/K3
Atherton, Mo. 261/H6
Atherton, Queensland 95/C3
Atherton, Queensland 88/G3
Athertonville, Ky. 237/K5
Athleague, Ireland 17/E4
Athlone, Ireland 10/C4
Athlone, Ireland 17/F5
Athok, Burma 72/B3
Athol, Idaho 220/B2
Athol, Kansas 232/D2
Athol, Mass. 249/F2
Athol•, Mass. 249/F2
Athol, N.Y. 276/N4
Athol, N. Zealand 100/B6
Athol, Nova Scotia 168/D3
Athol (dist.), Scotland 15/D4
Athol, S. Dak. 298/H4
Atholville, New Bruns. 170/D1
Áthos (mt.), Greece 45/G5
Athy, Ireland 17/H6
Athy, Ireland 10/C4
Ati, Chad 111/C5
Ati, Chad 102/D3
Atibaia, Brazil 135/C3
Atico, Peru 128/F11
Atienza, Spain 33/E2
Atikameg, Alberta 182/C2
Atikokan, Ont. 162/G6
Atikokan, Ontario 177/G5
Atikokan, Ontario 175/B3
Atikonak (lake), Newf. 166/B3
Atim (lake), Manitoba 179/C2
Atiquizaya, El Salvador 154/E3
Atitlán (lake), Guatemala 154/B3
Atitlán (vol.), Guatemala 154/B3
Atiu (isl.), Cook Is. 87/L8
Atka, Alaska 196/D4
Atka, Alaska 188/D6
Atka (isl.), Alaska 196/L4
Atka, U.S.S.R. 48/Q3
Atkarsk, U.S.S.R. 52/G4
Atkins, Ark. 202/E3
Atkins, Iowa 204/E6
Atkins, Va. 307/F7
Atkinson (co.), Georgia 217/G8
Atkinson, Georgia 217/J8
Atkinson, Ill. 222/C2
Atkinson•, Maine 243/E5
Atkinson, Minn. 255/F4
Atkinson, Nebr. 264/E2
Atkinson•, N.H. 268/E6
Atkinson, N.C. 281/N5
Atkinson (pt.), N.W. Terr. 187/E2
Atlanta, Ark. 202/D7
Atlanta, C. Rica 154/F6
Atlanta (cap.), Ga. 188/K4
Atlanta (cap.), Ga. 146/K6
Atlanta (cap.), Georgia 217/K1
Atlanta, Idaho 220/C6
Atlanta, Ill. 222/D3
Atlanta, Ind. 227/E4
Atlanta, Kansas 232/F4
Atlanta, La. 238/E3
Atlanta, Mich. 250/E3
Atlanta, Mo. 261/H3
Atlanta, Nebr. 264/E4
Atlanta, N.Y. 276/F5
Atlanta, Ohio 284/D6
Atlanta, Texas 303/K4
Atlanta, U.S. 2/E4
Atlanta Nav. Air Sta., Georgia 217/J1
Atlantic (ocean) 102/B5
Atlantic (ocean) 146/M6
Atlantic, Iowa 229/D6
Atlantic, Maine 243/G7
Atlantic (co.), N.J. 273/D5
Atlantic, N.C. 281/S5
Atlantic, Pa. 294/B3
Atlantic (peak), Wyo. 319/D3
Atlantic Beach, Fla. 212/E4
Atlantic Beach, N.Y. 276/P7
Atlantic Beach, N.C. 281/R5
Atlantic Beach, S.C. 296/K4
Atlantic City, N.J. 188/M3
Atlantic City, N.J. 273/E5
Atlantic City, Wyo. 319/D3
Atlantic Highlands, N.J. 273/E3
Atlantic Highlands (ridge), N.J. 273/E3
Atlantic Mine, Mich. 250/G1
Atlántico (dept.), Colombia 126/C2
Atlantic Ocean 4/D11
Atlantic Ocean 7/C4
Atlantic Ocean 13/A7
Atlantic Ocean 15/B2
Atlantic Ocean 33/A3
Atlántida, Uruguay 145/B6
Atlas (mts.) 102/B1
Atlas (mts.), Algeria 106/E2

Atlas (mts.), Morocco 106/C2
Atlas, Pa. 294/K4
Atlas, Wis. 317/A4
Atlin, Br. Col. 184/J1
Atlin (lake), Br. Col. 184/J1
Atlit, Israel 65/B2
Atlixco, Mexico 150/M2
Atmore, Ala. 195/C8
Atmore, Alberta 182/D2
Atnarko, Br. Col. 184/E4
Atocha, Bolivia 136/B7
Atoka (co.), Okla. 288/O6
Atoka, Okla. 288/O6
Atoka (res.), Okla. 288/P5
Atoka, Tenn. 237/B10
Atomic City, Idaho 220/F6
Atotonilco el Alto, Mexico 150/H6
Atoui, Wadi (dry riv.), Mauritania 106/B4
Atoui, Wadi (dry riv.), Western Sahara 106/B4
Atoyac (riv.), Mexico 150/N2
Atoyac (riv.), Mexico 150/O2
Atoyac de Álvarez, Mexico 150/J8
Atrato (riv.), Colombia 126/B4
Atrak (Atrek) (riv.), Iran 66/J2
Atrek (riv.), Iran 59/G2
Atrek (Atrak) (riv.), Iran 66/J2
Atrek (riv.), U.S.S.R. 48/F6
Atri, Italy 34/D3
Atsugi, Japan 81/O2
Atsumi (bay), Japan 81/H6
Attachie, Br. Col. 184/G2
Attala (co.), Miss. 256/E4
Attalens, Switzerland 39/C3
Attalla, Ala. 195/F2
Attapu, Laos 72/E4
Attapulgus, Georgia 217/D9
Attawapiskat (riv.), Ont. 146/K4
Attawapiskat (riv.), Ont. 162/H5
Attawapiskat, Ontario 175/D2
Attawapiskat (lake), Ontario 175/C2
Attawapiskat (riv.), Ontario 175/C2
Attawaugan, Conn. 210/H1
Atteam (pond), Maine 243/C4
Attebubu, Ghana 106/D7
Atterberry, Ill. 222/D3
Atter See (lake), Austria 41/B3
Attert, Belgium 27/H9
Attica, Ind. 227/C4
Attica, Iowa 229/G6
Attica, Kansas 232/D4
Attica, Mich. 250/F5
Attica, N.Y. 276/D5
Attica, Ohio 284/E3
Attikamagen (lake), Newf. 166/A3
Attil, West Bank 65/C3
Attleboro, Mass. 249/J5
Attleboro Falls, Mass. 249/J5
Attleborough, England 13/H5
Attnang-Puchheim, Austria 41/B2
Attock, Pakistan 68/C2
Attu (isl.), Alaska 188/D6
Attu (isl.), Alaska 196/J3
Attu (isl.), U.S. 4/D1
Attunga, N.S. Wales 97/F2
Atuel (riv.), Argentina 143/C4
Atuntaqui, Ecuador 128/C2
Atuona, Fr. Poly. 87/M7
Atura, Uganda 115/F3
Atushi (bay), China 77/A4
Åtvidaberg, Sweden 18/K7
Atwater, Calif. 204/F6
Atwater, Minn. 255/D5
Atwater, Ohio 284/H3
Atwater, Sask. 181/J5
Atwood (Samana) (cay), Bahamas 156/D2
Atwood, Colo. 208/N1
Atwood, Ill. 222/E4
Atwood, Ind. 227/F2
Atwood, Kansas 232/B2
Atwood, Mich. 250/D3
Atwood (lake), Ohio 284/H4
Atwood, Okla. 288/O5
Atwood, Ontario 177/D4
Atwood, Pa. 294/D4
Atwood, Tenn. 237/D9
Atwoodville, Conn. 210/G1
Atyrá, Paraguay 144/B4
Au, Switzerland 39/J2
Auasbila, Honduras 154/E3
Auau (chan.), Hawaii 218/H2
Aubá, Indonesia 85/H7
Aubagne, France 28/F6
Aubange, Belgium 27/H9
Aube (dept.), France 28/F3
Aube (riv.), France 28/F3
Aubenas, France 28/F5
Auberry, Calif. 204/F6
Aubervilliers, France 28/B1
Aubigny, Manitoba 179/E5
Aubonne, Switzerland 39/B4
Aubrey (cliffs), Ariz. 198/B3
Aubrey, Ark. 202/J4
Auburn, Ala. 195/H5
Auburn, Georgia 217/E2
Auburn, Ill. 222/D4
Auburn, Ind. 227/G2
Auburn (mt.), Ind. 227/G5
Auburn, Iowa 229/D4
Auburn, Kansas 232/G3
Auburn, Ky. 237/H7
Auburn, Maine 243/C7
Auburn, Maine 188/M2
Auburn•, Mass. 249/G4
Auburn, Mich. 250/F5
Auburn, Miss. 256/D3
Auburn, Nebr. 264/J4
Auburn•, N.H. 268/E5
Auburn, N.S. Wales 88/K4
Auburn, N.S. Wales 97/J3
Auburn, N.Y. 188/L2
Auburn, N.Y. 276/G5
Auburn, N. Dak. 282/R2
Auburn, Nova Scotia 168/D3
Auburn, Ontario 177/C4

Auburn, Pa. 294/K4
Auburn, Wash. 310/C3
Auburn, W. Va. 312/E4
Auburn, Wyo. 319/A3
Auburndale, Fla. 212/E3
Auburndale, Mass. 249/B7
Auburndale, Wis. 317/F6
Auburn Heights, Mich. 250/F6
Auburntown, Tenn. 237/J9
Aubusson, France 28/E4
Aucanquilcha, Cerro (mt.), Chile 138/B3
Auce, U.S.S.R. 53/B2
Auch, France 28/D6
Auchenblae, Scotland 15/F4
Auchencairn, Scotland 15/E6
Auchinleck, Scotland 15/D5
Auchterarder, Scotland 10/D2
Auchterarder, Scotland 15/E4
Auchtermuchty, Scotland 15/E4
Aucilla, Fla. 212/C1
Aucilla (riv.), Fla. 212/C1
Auckland, N. Zealand 2/S8
Auckland, N. Zealand 2/T7
Auckland, N. Zealand 100/B1
Auckland, N. Zealand 87/B1
Auclair, Québec 172/J2
Aude (dept.), France 28/E6
Audegle, Somalia 115/J3
Auden, Ontario 177/H4
Auden, Ontario 175/C2
Audenarde (Oudenaarde), Belgium 27/D7
Auderghem, Belgium 27/C9
Audet, Québec 172/G4
Audincourt, France 28/G4
Audrain (co.), Mo. 261/J4
Audubon (co.), Iowa 229/D5
Audubon, Iowa 229/D5
Audubon, Minn. 255/C4
Audubon, N.J. 273/B3
Audubon (lake), N. Dak. 282/H4
Audubon Park, Ky. 237/J2
Audubon Park, N.J. 273/B3
Aue, Germany 22/E3
Auerbach, Germany 22/E3
Augathella, Queensland 95/C5
Augathella, Queensland 88/H5
Auger (falls), Idaho 220/D7
Augher, N. Ireland 17/G3
Aughnacloy, N. Ireland 17/H3
Aughrabies (falls), S. Africa 118/B5
Aughrim, Ireland 17/J6
Auglaize (co.), Ohio 284/B4
Auglaize (riv.), Ohio 284/B4
Au Gres, Mich. 250/F4
Augsburg, Germany 7/E4
Augsburg, Germany 22/D4
Augusta, Ark. 202/H3
Augusta (cape), Colombia 126/C2
Augusta, Ga. 188/K4
Augusta, Ga. 146/K6
Augusta, Georgia 217/J4
Augusta, Ill. 222/C3
Augusta, Ind. 227/C8
Augusta, Iowa 229/L7
Augusta, Italy 34/E6
Augusta, Kansas 232/F4
Augusta, Ky. 237/N3
Augusta (cap.), Maine 146/M5
Augusta (cap.), Maine 243/D7
Augusta (cap.), Maine 188/N2
Augusta, Mich. 250/E6
Augusta, Mo. 261/L5
Augusta, Mont. 262/D3
Augusta, N.J. 273/D1
Augusta, Ohio 284/J4
Augusta (co.), Va. 307/K4
Augusta, W. Australia 92/A6
Augusta, W. Va. 312/J4
Augusta, Wis. 317/D6
Augusta Springs, Va. 307/K4
Au Train, Mich. 250/C2
Au Train (bay), Mich. 250/C2
Augustenborg, Denmark 21/D8
Augustine (isl.), Alaska 196/H3
Augustów, Poland 47/F2
Augustus (isl.), W. Australia 92/D1
Augustus (mt.), W. Australia 92/B4
Aujila, Libya 102/E2
Aujila, Libya 111/D2
Auki, Solomon Is. 86/E3
Auki, Solomon Is. 87/G6
Aulac, New Bruns. 170/F3
Aulander, N.C. 281/P2
Auld (lake), W. Australia 88/C4
Auldearn, Scotland 15/E3
Aulencia (riv.), Spain 33/F4
Aullville, Mo. 261/H4
Aulnay-sous-Bois, France 28/B1
Ault, Colo. 208/K1
Ault (peak), Switzerland 39/H3
Aultbea, Scotland 15/C3
Aultman, Pa. 294/D4
Aumsville, Oreg. 291/B2
Auning, Denmark 21/D5
Aunis (trad. prov.), France 29
Aur, Pulau (isl.), Malaysia 72/E7
Aura, Mich. 250/A2
Aura, N.J. 273/C4
Aurangabad, Bihar, India 68/E4
Aurangabad, Maharashtra, India 68/D5
Auraria, Georgia 217/E1
Auray, France 28/B4
Aurelia, Iowa 229/C3
Aurès (lag.), Algeria 106/F1
Aurich, Germany 22/B2
Aurignac, France 28/D6
Aurillac, France 28/E5
Aurland, Norway 18/E6
Aurora, Ark. 202/C2
Aurora, Brazil 132/G4
Aurora, Colo. 188/F3
Aurora, Colo. 208/K3
Aurora, Guyana 131/B2
Aurora, Ill. 222/E2
Aurora, Ind. 227/H6
Aurora, Iowa 229/K3
Aurora, Kansas 232/E2
Aurora•, Maine 243/G6
Aurora, Minn. 255/F3

Aurora, Mo. 261/E9
Auburn, Nebr. 264/F4
Aurora, N.Y. 276/G5
Aurora, N.C. 281/R4
Aurora, Ohio 284/H3
Aurora, Ontario 177/J3
Aurora, Philippines 82/D4
Aurora, Philippines 82/C3
Aurora (co.), S. Dak. 298/M6
Aurora, S. Dak. 298/R5
Aurora, Texas 303/E1
Aurora, Utah 304/D5
Aurora, W. Va. 312/G4
Aurora Lodge, Alaska 196/J2
Auroraville, Wis. 317/H7
Aus, Namibia 118/B5
Au Sable, Mich. 250/F4
Au Sable (pt.), Mich. 250/F4
Au Sable (pt.), Mich. 250/C2
Au Sable (riv.), Mich. 250/E4
Ausable (riv.), N.Y. 276/N2
Au Sable Forks, N.Y. 276/N2
Auschwitz (Oświęcim), Poland 47/D3
Ausert (well), Western Sahara 106/B4
Auskerry (isl.), Scotland 15/F1
Austell, Georgia 217/J1
Austerlitz (Slavkov), Czech. 41/D2
Austin, Ark. 202/G4
Austin, Colo. 208/D5
Austin, Ky. 237/K7
Austin, Manitoba 179/D5
Austin, Minn. 188/H2
Austin, Minn. 255/E7
Austin, Mo. 261/D5
Austin, Nev. 188/C3
Austin, Nev. 266/E3
Austin, Oreg. 291/J3
Austin, Pa. 294/F2
Austin (co.), Texas 303/H8
Austin (cap.), Texas 146/G7
Austin (cap.), Texas 303/G7
Austin (cap.), Texas 188/G4
Austin (lake), W. Australia 88/B5
Austin (lake), W. Australia 92/B4
Austinburg, Ohio 284/J2
Austintown, Ohio 284/J3
Austinville, Iowa 229/H3
Austinville, Va. 307/F7
Austonio, Texas 303/J6
Austral (isls.), Fr. Polynesia 2/B7
Austral (isls.), Fr. Poly. 87/L8
Australia 2/R7
Australia 87/E8
AUSTRALIA 88
Australia Aboriginal Reserve, W. Australia 88/B5
Australia Aboriginal Res., W. Australia 92/E4
Australian, Br. Col. 184/F4
Australian Alps (mts.), N.S. Wales 97/D5
Australian Alps (mts.), Victoria 97/D5
Australian Alps (mts.), Victoria 88/H7
Australian Capital Territory 88/H7
AUSTRALIAN CAPITAL TERRITORY 97/E4
Australian Capital Terr., Australia 87/F9
Australind, W. Australia 92/A2
Austria 2/K3
Austria 7/F4
AUSTRIA 41
Austwell, Texas 303/H9
Autauga (co.), Ala. 195/E5
Autaugaville, Ala. 195/E6
Autlán de Navarro, Mexico 150/G7
Au Train, Mich. 250/C2
Au Train (bay), Mich. 250/C2
Autreyville, Georgia 217/E8
Autryville, N.C. 281/M4
Autun, France 28/F4
Auvelais, Belgium 27/F8
Auvergne, Ark. 202/H2
Auvergne (mts.), France 28/E5
Auvergne (trad. prov.), France 29
Auvergne, North. Terr. 93/B3
Auvergne, Québec 172/F3
Auxerre, France 28/E4
Auxier, Ky. 237/R5
Auxonne, France 28/F4
Auxvasse, Mo. 261/J4
Auyantepui (mt.), Venezuela 124/G5
Auyuittug Nat'l Park, N.W. Terr. 187/M3
Auyuittuq Nat'l Park, Que. 162/K2
Ava, Ill. 222/D6
Ava, Mo. 261/G9
Ava, N.Y. 276/K4
Ava, Ohio 284/G6
Avallon, France 28/E4
Avalon, Calif. 204/G10
Avalon, Georgia 217/F1
Avalon, Miss. 256/D3
Avalon, Mo. 261/F3
Avalon (pen.), Newf. 166/D2
Avalon, N.J. 273/D5
Avalon (res.), N. Mex. 274/E6
Avalon, Pa. 294/B6
Avanos, Turkey 63/F3
Avans, Georgia 217/A1
Avant, Okla. 288/O2
Avard, Okla. 288/J1
Avaré, Brazil 132/D8
Avaré, Brazil 135/B3
Avarua (cap.), Cook Is. 87/L8
Avayalik (isls.), Newf. 166/B1
Avaz, Iran 66/M4
Aveiro (dist.), Portugal 33/B2
Aveiro, Portugal 33/B2
Avej, Iran 66/F3
Avella, Pa. 294/B5
Avellaneda, Argentina 143/G7
Avellino (prov.), Italy 34/E4
Avellino, Italy 34/E4

Avenches, Switzerland 39/D3
Avenel, N.J. 273/E2
Aventon, N.C. 281/O2
Avera, Georgia 217/G4
Avera, Miss. 256/G8
Averiás, Uruguay 145/E4
Averill, Mich. 250/E5
Averill, Minn. 255/B4
Averill•, Vt. 268/D2
Averill Park, N.Y. 276/O5
Aversa, Italy 34/E4
Avery, Idaho 220/C2
Avery, Iowa 229/H6
Avery (co.), N.C. 281/F2
Avery, Ohio 284/E3
Avery, Okla. 288/N3
Avery, Texas 303/K4
Avery Island, La. 238/G7
Aves (Bird) (isl.), Venezuela 156/F4
Avesnes-sur-Helpe, France 28/E2
Avesta, Sweden 18/J6
Aveyron (riv.), France 28/E5
Avezzano, Italy 34/D3
Aviemore, Scotland 15/E3
Avigliano, Italy 34/E4
Avignon, France 28/F6
Avignon, France 7/E4
Avihayil, Israel 65/B2
Avila (prov.), Spain 33/D2
Ávila, Spain 33/D2
Avila de los Caballeros, Spain 33/D2
Avilés, Spain 33/C1
Avilla, Ind. 227/G2
Avilla, Mo. 261/D8
Avinger, Texas 303/K5
Avion, France 28/E2
Avis, Pa. 294/H3
Avis, Portugal 33/C3
Aviston, Ill. 222/D5
Avize, France 28/F3
Avlum, Denmark 21/B5
Avoca, Ark. 202/B1
Avoca, Ind. 227/D7
Avoca, Iowa 229/C6
Avoca, Mich. 250/G5
Avoca, Minn. 255/C7
Avoca, Nebr. 264/H4
Avoca, N.Y. 276/F6
Avoca, Pa. 294/F7
Avoca (dam), Tasmania 99/D3
Avoca, Texas 303/E5
Avoca, Victoria 97/B5
Avoca (riv.), Victoria 97/B5
Avoch, Scotland 15/D3
Avola, Br. Col. 184/H4
Avola, Italy 34/E6
Avon, Colo. 208/F3
Avon, Colo. 210/D1
Avon•, Conn. 210/D1
Avon (co.), England 13/E6
Avon (riv.), England 13/F7
Avon (riv.), England 13/F5
Avon (riv.), England 10/F4
Avon, Idaho 220/B3
Avon, Ill. 222/C3
Avon•, Mass. 249/K4
Avon, Minn. 255/D5
Avon, Miss. 256/B4
Avon, Mont. 262/D4
Avon, N.Y. 276/E5
Avon, N.C. 281/U4
Avon (riv.), Nova Scotia 168/D4
Avon, Ohio 284/F3
Avon (riv.), Scotland 15/C1
Avon (riv.), Scotland 15/E3
Avon (riv.), W. Australia 88/B3
Avon (riv.), W. Australia 92/A1
Avon, S. Dak. 298/N8
Avon, Wis. 317/H10
Avon By The Sea, N.J. 273/E3
Avondale, Ariz. 198/C5
Avondale, Colo. 208/L6
Avondale, Mich. 250/D4
Avondale, Mo. 261/P5
Avondale, Newf. 166/D2
Avondale, N.S. Wales 97/F3
Avondale, N.C. 281/F4
Avondale, Pa. 294/L6
Avondale, W. Va. 312/C8
Avondale Estates, Georgia 217/L1
Avon Downs, North. Terr. 88/F4
Avon Downs, North. Terr. 93/E5
Avonhurst, Sask. 181/H5
Avon Lake, Ohio 284/F2
Avonlea, Sask. 181/G5
Avonmore, Pa. 294/C4
Avon Park, Fla. 212/E4
Avon Water (riv.), Scotland 15/D5
Avoyelles (par.), La. 238/G4
Avranches, France 28/C3
Awa (isl.), Japan 81/J4
Awaji, Japan 81/H8
Awaji (isl.), Japan 81/H8
Awanui, N. Zealand 100/D1
Awareh, Ethiopia 111/H6
Awarua (bay), N. Zealand 100/A6
Awasa, Ethiopia 114/G6
Awasa, Ethiopia 102/F4
Awash, Ethiopia 115/H5
Awash (riv.), Ethiopia 111/H5
Awaso, Ghana 106/D7
Awat, China 77/A3
Awatere (riv.), N. Zealand 100/D5
Awbeg (riv.), Ireland 17/D7
Awe, Loch (lake), Scotland 10/D2
Awe, Loch (lake), Scotland 15/C4
Aweil, Sudan 111/E6
Awendaw, S.C. 296/H5
Awosting, N.J. 273/E1
Axe Edge (mt.), England 13/F3
Axel, Netherlands 27/D6
Axel Heiberg (isl.), Canada 4/A14
Axel Heiberg (isl.), N.W.T. 146/J1
Axel Heiberg (isl.), N.W. Terr. 187/J2

Axel Heiberg (isl.), N.W.T. 162/N3
Axim, Ghana 106/D8
Axis, Ala. 195/B9
Ax-les-Thermes, France 28/D6
Axminster, England 13/D7
Axminster, England 10/E5
Axochiapan, Mexico 150/M2
Axson, Georgia 217/G8
Axtell, Kansas 232/F2
Axtell, Nebr. 264/E4
Axtell, Utah 304/C4
Axton, Va. 307/J7
Axum (Aksum), Ethiopia 111/G5
Ayabaca, Peru 128/C5
Ayabe, Japan 81/G6
Ayacucho, Argentina 143/E4
Ayacucho, Bolivia 136/B7
Ayacucho (dept.), Peru 128/C4
Ayacucho, Peru 128/F9
Ayacucho, Peru 128/B4
Ayaguz, U.S.S.R. 54/P4
Ayaguz, U.S.S.R. 48/J5
Ayakkum Hu (lake), China 77/C4
Ayamonte, Spain 33/C4
Ayan, U.S.S.R. 54/P4
Ayan, U.S.S.R. 48/O4
Ayancik, Turkey 63/F1
Ayapel, Colombia 126/C3
Ayapel, Serranía de (mts.), Colombia 126/C4
Ayaş, Turkey 63/E2
Ayata, Bolivia 136/A4
Ayaviri, Peru 128/G10
Aybak, Afghanistan 68/B1
Aybak, Afghanistan 59/J2
Aybastı, Turkey 63/G2
Aycliffe, England 13/F3
Ayden, N.C. 281/P4
Aydın (prov.), Turkey 63/B4
Aydin, Turkey 59/A2
Aydın, Turkey 63/B4
Aydıncık, Turkey 63/E4
Aydlett, N.C. 281/T2
Aydyrlinskiy, U.S.S.R. 52/K4
Ayer, Mass. 249/H2
Ayer•, Mass. 249/H2
Ayer, Switzerland 39/E4
Ayer, Wash. 310/G4
Ayers, Maine 243/J6
Ayer's Cliff, Québec 172/E4
Ayers Rock (Uluru) (mt.), North. Terr. 88/F5
Ayersville, Ohio 284/B3
Ayiá, Greece 45/F6
Áyion Óros (aut. dist.), Greece 45/G5
Áyios Evstrátios (isl.), Greece 45/G6
Áyios Kírikos, Greece 45/H7
Áyios Matthaíos, Greece 45/D6
Áyios Nikólaos, Greece 45/G8
Áyios Yeóryios (cape), Greece 45/G5
Aykhal, U.S.S.R. 48/M3
Aylen (lake), Ontario 177/G2
Aylesbury, England 13/G7
Aylesbury, England 10/F5
Aylesbury, Sask. 181/F5
Aylesford, England 13/J3
Aylesford, Nova Scotia 168/D3
Aylett, Va. 307/L5
Ayllón, Spain 33/E2
Aylmer, N. Dak. 282/K4
Aylmer (lake), N.W. Terr. 187/H3
Aylmer, Ontario 177/C5
Aylmer, Québec 172/B4
Aylmer (lake), Québec 172/F4
Aylsham, England 13/J5
Aylsham, Sask. 181/H2
Aynor, S.C. 296/J3
Ayod, Sudan 111/F6
Ayolas, Paraguay 144/D5
Ayon (isl.), U.S.S.R. 48/R2
Ayora, Spain 33/F3
Ayr, Nebr. 264/F4
Ayr, N. Dak. 282/P5
Ayr, Ontario 177/D4
Ayr, Queensland 95/C3
Ayr, Queensland 88/H3
Ayr, Scotland 15/D5
Ayr, Scotland 10/D3
Ayr, Heads of (cape), Scotland 15/D5
Ayr (trad. prov.) Scotland 15/A5
Ayr (riv.), Scotland 15/D5
Ayrancı, Turkey 63/E4
Ayre (pt.), I. of Man 13/A3
Ayre (pt.), I. of Man 10/D3
Ayrshire, Iowa 229/D2
Ayshire, Iowa 229/D2
Ayton, Ontario 177/D3
Ayton, Scotland 15/F5
Aytos, Bulgaria 45/H4
Ayu (isls.), Indonesia 85/J5
Ayun, Saudi Arabia 59/D4
Ayutla de los Libres, Mexico 150/K8
Ayutthaya (Phra Nakhon Si Ayutthaya), Thailand 72/D4
Ayvacık, Turkey 63/B3
Ayvalık, Turkey 59/A2
Ayvalık, Turkey 63/B3
Aywaille, Belgium 27/H8
Azalea, Oreg. 291/D5
Azalea Park, Fla. 212/E3
Azalia, Ind. 227/F6
Azalia, Mich. 250/F6
Azamgarh, India 68/E3
Azángaro, Peru 128/H10
Azángaro (riv.), Peru 128/G10
Azaoua (reg.), Niger 106/E5
Azaouad (reg.), Mali 106/D5
Azaouak (riv.), Mali 106/E5
Azapa, Chile 138/A1
Azaran, Iran 66/E2
Azapa, Quebrada (riv.), Chile 138/B1
Azare, Nigeria 106/G6
Azaz, Syria 63/G4
Azbine (Air) (mts.), Niger 106/F5
Azcapotzalco, Mexico 150/L1
Azdavay, Turkey 63/E2
Azemmour, Morocco 106/C2
Azerbaidzhan S.S.R., U.S.S.R. 7/J4
Azerbaidzhan S.S.R., U.S.S.R. 48/E5

Azerbaidzhan S.S.R., U.S.S.R. 52/G6
Azerbaijan, East (prov.), Iran 66/E1
Azerbaijan, West (prov.), Iran 66/D1
Azerbaijan (reg.), Iran 66/D1
Aziscoos (lake), Maine 243/A5
Azle, Texas 303/E2
Azogues, Ecuador 128/C4
AZORES 33
Azores (isls.), Portugal 2/H4
Azores (isls.), Portugal 33/A2
Azoum, Bahr, Chad 111/D5
Azov (sea), U.S.S.R. 7/H4
Azov, U.S.S.R. 52/E5
Azov (sea), U.S.S.R. 52/E5
Azov (sea), U.S.S.R. 48/D5
Azoyú, Mexico 150/K8
Azpeitia, Spain 33/E1
Azrou, Morocco 106/C2
Aztec, Ariz. 198/B6
Aztec, N. Mex. 274/B2
Aztec Ruins Nat'l Mon., N. Mex. 274/A2
Azua (prov.), Dom. Rep. 158/D6
Azua, Dom. Rep. 156/D3
Azua, Dom. Rep. 158/D6
Azuaga, Spain 33/D3
Azuara, Spain 33/F2
Azuay (prov.), Ecuador 128/C4
Azuero (pen.), Panama 154/G7
Azul, Argentina 143/E4
Azul, Argentina 120/D6
Azul (riv.), Guatemala 154/C2
Azul, Cordillera (mts.), Peru 128/E7
Azurduy, Bolivia 136/C6
Azure (lake), Br. Col. 184/G4
Azusa, Calif. 204/D10
Azwell, Wash. 310/F3
Azzel Mati, Sebkha (lake), Algeria 106/E3
Az Zubair, Iraq 66/E5

B

Ba, Fiji 86/P10
Baa, Indonesia 85/G8
Baaba (isl.), New Caled. 86/G4
Ba'albek, Lebanon 63/G5
Baan Baa, N.S. Wales 97/E2
Baar, Switzerland 39/F2
Baarle-Nassau, Netherlands 27/F6
Baarn, Netherlands 27/G4
Baatsagaan, Mongolia 77/E2
Baba, Ecuador 128/C3
Baba (cape), Turkey 63/D2
Baba (cape), Turkey 63/A3
Babadag, Romania 45/J3
Babadağ, Turkey 63/C4
Babaeski, Turkey 63/B2
Babahoyo, Ecuador 128/C3
Babanusa, Sudan 111/E5
Babaomby (cape), Madagascar 102/C6
Babaomby (cape), Madagascar 118/H2
Babar (isl.), Indonesia 85/H7
Babar (isls.), Indonesia 85/H7
Babati, Tanzania 115/G4
Babayevo, U.S.S.R. 52/E3
Babb, Mont. 262/C2
Babbie, Ala. 195/F8
Babbitt, Minn. 255/G3
Babbitt, Nev. 266/C4
Babcock, Wis. 317/F7
Babel (isls.), Tasmania 99/E1
Bab el Mandeb (str.) 102/G3
Bab el Mandeb (str.), Djibouti 111/H5
Babelthuap (isl.), Belau 87/D5
Babia (riv.), Mexico 150/J2
Babil (heads), Iraq 66/D4
Babine (lake), Br. Col. 162/D5
Babine, Br. Col. 184/D2
Babine (lake), Br. Col. 184/E3
Babine (riv.), Br. Col. 184/D2
Babo, Indonesia 85/K7
Babol, Iran 54/G6
Babol, Iran 59/F2
Babol, Iran 66/H2
Babol Sar, Iran 66/H2
Baboquivari (mts.), Ariz. 198/D7
Baboua, Cent. Afr. Rep. 115/C2
Babson Park, Fla. 212/E4
Babuyan (isls.), Philippines 54/O8
Babuyan (chan.), Philippines 82/A3
Babuyan (isl.), Philippines 82/B2
Babuyan (isls.), Philippines 85/G2
Babuyan (isls.), Philippines 82/A2
Babylon (ruins), Iraq 66/D4
Babylon, N.Y. 276/O9
Baca (co.), Colo. 208/O8
Bacabal, Brazil 120/E3
Bacabal, Maranhão, Brazil 132/E4
Bacabal, Pará, Brazil 132/B4
Bacadéhuachi, Mexico 150/E2
Bacalar, Mexico 150/P7
Bacalar (lake), Mexico 150/P7
Bacan (isls.), Indonesia 85/H6
Bacanora, Mexico 150/E2
Bacarra, Philippines 82/C1
Bacău, Romania 7/G4
Bacău, Romania 45/H2
Baccalieu (isl.), Newf. 166/D2
Bac Can, Vietnam 72/E2
Baccaro (pt.), Nova Scotia 168/C5
Bacchus Marsh, Victoria 97/C5
Bacerac, Mexico 150/E1
Bac Giang, Vietnam 72/E2
Bach, Mich. 250/F5
Bachaquero, Venezuela 124/C3
Bache (pen.), N.W. Terr. 187/L2
Bache, Okla. 288/P5
Bachíniva, Mexico 150/F2
Bach Long Vi, Dao (isl.), Vietnam 72/F2
Bachu (Maralwexi), China 77/A4
Back (bay), India 68/B7
Back (riv.), Md. 245/N4
Back (lake), N.H. 268/E1
Back (riv.), N.W.T. 146/H3
Back (riv.), N.W.T. 162/G2
Back (riv.), N.W. Terr. 187/J3
Back (bay), Va. 307/S7
Back (creek), Va. 307/J4
Bačka Topola, Yugoslavia 45/D3
Back Bay, New Bruns. 170/D3
Backbone (mt.), Md. 245/A3
Backnang, Germany 22/C4
Backoo, N. Dak. 282/P2
Backus, Minn. 255/D4
Backway, The (inlet), Newf. 166/C3
Bac Lieu, Vietnam 72/E5
Bacliff, Texas 303/K2
Bac Ninh, Vietnam 72/E2
Baco (mt.), Philippines 82/C4
Bacolod, Philippines 85/G3
Bacolod, Philippines 54/O8
Bacolod, Philippines 82/D5
Bacon (co.), Georgia 217/G7
Bacone, Okla. 288/R3
Bacon Ridge (mts.), Wyo. 319/B2
Bacons, Del. 245/R6
Baconton, Georgia 217/D8
Bácsalmás, Hungary 41/E3
Bács-Kiskun (co.), Hungary 41/E3
Bácum, Mexico 150/D3
Bacuna, Neth. Ant. 161/E8
Bacup, England 13/H1
Bacup, England 10/G1
Bad (riv.), Mich. 250/E5
Bad (hills), Sask. 181/C4
Bad (lake), Sask. 181/C4
Bad (riv.), S. Dak. 298/G5
Badacsonytomaj, Hungary 41/D3
Badagara, India 68/D6
Bad Aibling, Germany 22/D5
Badajoz (prov.), Spain 33/C3
Badajoz, Spain 33/C3
Badalona, Spain 33/H2
Bad Aussee, Austria 41/B3
Bad Axe, Mich. 250/G5
Bad Berleburg, Germany 22/C3
Bad Berneck, Germany 22/D3
Bad Bramstedt, Germany 22/C2
Bad Brückenau, Germany 22/C3
Baddeck, Nova Scotia 168/H2
Baddeck (riv.), Nova Scotia 168/H2
Bad Doberan, Germany 22/D1
Bad Driburg, Germany 22/C3
Bad Dürkheim, Germany 22/C4
Bad Dürrenberg, Germany 22/D3
Bad Ems, Germany 22/B3
Baden, Austria 41/D2
Baden, Manitoba 179/A2
Baden, Md. 245/M6
Baden, Ontario 177/D4
Baden, Pa. 294/B4
Baden, Switzerland 39/F2
Ba Den, Nui (mt.), Vietnam 72/E5
Baden-Baden, Germany 22/C4
Badenoch (dist.), Scotland 15/D4
Badenweiler, Germany 22/B5
Baden-Württemberg (state), Germany 22/C4
Bad Freienwalde, Germany 22/F2
Bad Gandersheim, Germany 22/D3
Badgastein, Austria 41/B3
Badger (peak), Idaho 220/E7
Badger, Iowa 229/E3
Badger, Minn. 255/B2
Badger, Newf. 166/C4
Badger (creek), Oreg. 291/H3
Badger, S. Dak. 298/P5
Badger (creek), Wyo. 319/E2
Badger's Quay, Newf. 166/D4
Bad Goisern, Austria 41/B3
Badham, S.C. 296/F5
Bad Harzburg, Germany 22/D3
Bad Hersfeld, Germany 22/C3
Badhoevedorp, Netherlands 27/B5
Bad Hofgastein, Austria 41/B3
Bad Homburg vor der Höhe, Germany 22/C3
Bad Honnef, Germany 22/B3
Badian, Philippines 82/D6
Badin, N.C. 281/J4
Badin, Pakistan 68/B4
Badiraguato, Mexico 150/F4
Bad Ischl, Austria 41/B3
Bad Kissingen, Germany 22/D3
Bad Kreuznach, Germany 22/B4
Bad Land (cliffs), Utah 304/D4
Bad Lands (reg.), N. Dak. 282/C7
Badlands Nat'l Park, S. Dak. 298/E6
Bad Langensalza, Germany 22/D3
Bad Lauterberg im Harz, Germany 22/D3
Bad Leonfelden, Austria 41/C2
Bad Liebenwerda, Germany 22/E3
Bad Lippspringe, Germany 22/C3
Bad Mergentheim, Germany 22/C4
Bad Münster-Ebernburg, Germany 22/B4
Bad Münstereifel, Germany 22/B3
Bad Muskau, Germany 22/F3
Bad Nauheim, Germany 22/C3
Bad Neuenahr-Ahrweiler, Germany 22/B3
Bad Neustadt an der Saale, Germany 22/D3
Bado, Mo. 261/H8
Bad Oldesloe, Germany 22/D2
Ba Don, Vietnam 72/E3
Bad Orb, Germany 22/C3
Bad Pyrmont, Germany 22/C3
Badr, Saudi Arabia 59/C5
Badra, Iraq 66/D4
Bad Ragaz, Switzerland 39/H2
Bad Reichenhall, Germany 22/E5
Bad River Ind. Res., Wis. 317/E2
Bad Sachsa, Germany 22/D3
Bad Salzschlirf, Germany 22/C3
Bad Salzuflen, Germany 22/C2
Bad Salzungen, Germany 22/C3
Bad Sankt-Leonhard im Lavanttal, Austria 41/C3
Bad Schwartau, Germany 22/D2
Bad Segeberg, Germany 22/D2
Bad Tölz, Germany 22/D5
Baduen, Somalia 115/J2
Badulla, Sri Lanka 68/E7
Bad Vilbel, Germany 22/C3
Bad Waldsee, Germany 22/C5
Badwater (creek), Wyo. 319/E2
Bad Wildungen, Germany 22/C3
Bad Wimpfen, Germany 22/C4
Baelum, Denmark 21/D4
Baena, Spain 33/D4
Baerle-Hertog, Belgium 27/F6
Báez, Cuba 158/E2
Baeza, Ecuador 128/D3
Baeza, Spain 33/E4
Bafa (lake), Turkey 63/B4
Baffin (bay) 4/B13
Baffin (bay) 146/M2
Baffin (bay), Canada 2/F2
Baffin (isl.), Canada 2/F2
Baffin (isl.), Canada 4/C13
Baffin (bay), N.W.T. 162/J1
Baffin (bay), N.W.T. 187/M2
Baffin (isl.), N.W.T. 146/L2
Baffin (isl.), N.W.T. 162/J1
Baffin (isl.), N.W.T. 187/L2
Baffin (reg.), N.W.T. 186/J2
Baffin (bay), Texas 303/G10
Bafia, Cameroon 115/B3
Bafing (riv.), Guinea 106/B6
Bafing (riv.), Mali 106/B6
Bafoulabé, Mali 106/B6
Bafoussam, Cameroon 115/B2
Bafq, Iran 59/G3
Bafq, Iran 66/J5
Bafra, Turkey 59/C1
Bafra, Turkey 63/F2
Bafra (cape), Turkey 59/C1
Bafra (cape), Turkey 63/G2
Baft, Iran 66/K6
Baft, Iran 59/G4
Baga, Nigeria 106/G6
Bagabag, Philippines 82/C2
Bagac, Philippines 82/C3
Bagaces, C. Rica 154/E5
Bagadó, Colombia 126/B5
Bagalkot, India 68/D5
Bagam (well), Niger 106/F5
Bagamoyo, Tanzania 115/G5
Baganga, Philippines 82/F7
Baganian (pen.), Philippines 82/D7
Bagansiapiapi, Indonesia 85/C5
Bagata, Zaire 115/C4
Bagdad, Ariz. 198/B4
Bagdad, Fla. 212/B6
Bagdad, Ky. 237/L4
Bagdad, Tasmania 99/D4
Bagdarin, U.S.S.R. 48/M4
Bagé, Brazil 120/D6
Bagé, Brazil 132/C10
Bagenalstown, Ireland 10/C4
Bagenalstown (Muinebeag), Ireland 17/H6
Bagenkop, Denmark 21/D8
Baggs, Wyo. 319/E4
Baghbaghu, Iran 66/M3
Baghdad (heads), Iraq 66/D4
Baghdad (cap.), Iraq 59/E3
Baghdad (cap.), Iraq 54/F6
Baghdad (cap.), Iraq 2/M4
Baghdad (cap.), Iraq 66/D4
Bagheria, Italy 34/D5
Baghlan, Afghanistan 54/H6
Baghlan, Afghanistan 59/J2
Baghlan, Afghanistan 68/B1
Baghu, Iran 66/K7
Bağırpaşa Dağı (mt.), Turkey 59/D2
Bağırpaşa Dağı (mt.), Turkey 63/J3
Bagley, Iowa 229/E5
Bagley, Minn. 255/C3
Bagley, N.C. 281/N3
Bagley, Wis. 317/D10
Bagnell, Mo. 261/G6
Bagnell (dam), Mo. 261/G6
Bagnères-de-Bigorre, France 28/D6
Bagnères-de-Luchon, France 28/D6
Bagnolet, France 28/B2
Bagnols-sur-Cèze, France 28/F5
Bågø (isl.), Denmark 21/C7
Bago, Philippines 82/D5
Bagoé (riv.), Ivory Coast 106/C6
Bagoé (riv.), Mali 106/C6
Bagot, Manitoba 179/D5
Bagot (co.), Québec 172/E4
Bagrax (Bosten Hu) (lake), China 77/C3
Bagua, Peru 128/C5
Báguanos, Cuba 158/J3
Baguio, Philippines 54/N8
Baguio, Philippines 85/G2
Baguio, Philippines 82/C2
Baguirmi (reg.), Chad 111/C5
Bagwell, Texas 303/J4
Bahama, N.C. 281/M2
Bahamas 2/F4
Bahamas 146/L7
BAHAMAS 156/C1
Bahariya (oasis), Egypt 111/E2
Bahariya (oasis), Egypt 59/A4
Bahawalnagar, Pakistan 68/C2
Bahawalpur, Pakistan 54/J7
Bahawalpur, Pakistan 68/C3
Bahawalpur, Pakistan 59/K4
Bahçe, Turkey 63/G4
Bahçesaray, Turkey 63/K3
Bahia (state), Brazil 132/F6
Bahia (Salvador), Brazil 132/G6
Bahía (isls.), Honduras 154/D2
Bahía Blanca, Argentina 2/F7
Bahía Blanca, Argentina 143/D4
Bahía Blanca, Argentina 120/C6
Bahía Bustamante, Argentina 143/C6
Bahía de Caráquez, Ecuador 128/B3
Bahía Honda, Cuba 158/B1
Bahía Kino, Mexico 150/C2
Bahía San Blas, Argentina 143/D5
Bahía Thetis, Argentina 143/C7
Bahía Tortugas, Mexico 150/B3
Bahir Dar, Ethiopia 111/G5
Bahomamey, P. Rico 161/A1
Bahoruco (prov.), Dom. Rep. 158/D6
Bahoruco, Sierra de (mts.), Dom. Rep. 158/D6
Bahraich, India 68/E3
Bahrain 54/G7
BAHRAIN 59/F4
Bahramabad (Rafsanjan), Iran 66/K5
Bahr Azoum (riv.), Sudan 111/D5
Bahr el 'Arab (riv.), Sudan 111/E6
Bahr el Ghazal (dry riv.), Chad 111/C5
Bahr El Ghazal (prov.), Sudan 111/E6
Bahr es Safi (des.), Saudi Arabia 59/E6
Bahr ez Zeraf (riv.), Sudan 111/F6
Bahr Yusef (stream), Egypt 111/J4
Baia de Aramă, Romania 45/F3
Baía dos Tigres, Angola 115/B7
Baia Farta, Angola 115/B6
Baia Mare, Romania 45/F2
Baião, Brazil 132/D3
Baibiene, Argentina 143/G4
Baibokoum, Chad 111/C6
Bai Bung, Mui (Ca Mau) (pt.), Vietnam 72/E5
Baicheng (Bay), Xinjiang Uygur, China 7/B3
Baicheng, Jilin, China 77/K2
Baida, Libya 102/E1
Baida, Libya 111/D1
Baidyabati, India 68/F1
Baie-Comeau, Québec 172/A1
Baie-Comeau, Québec 174/D3
Baie de Henne, Haiti 158/B5
Baie-des-Bacons, Québec 172/H1
Baie-des-Moutons, Québec 174/F2
Baie-des-Rochers, Québec 172/H2
Baie-des-Sables, Québec 172/A1
Baie-du-Poste, Québec 174/C2
Baie-d'Urfé, Québec 172/G4
Baie-du-Vieux-Fort, Québec 174/F2
Baie-Johan-Beetz, Québec 174/E2
Baie-Mahault, Guadeloupe 161/A6
Baiersbronn, Germany 22/C4
Baie-Sainte-Anne, New Bruns. 170/F1
Baie-Sainte-Catherine, Québec 172/H1
Baie-Saint-Paul, Que. 162/J6
Baie-Saint-Paul, Québec 174/C3
Baie-Saint-Paul, Québec 172/G2
Baie-Trinité, Québec 172/B1
Baie-Verte, New Bruns. 170/F2
Baie Verte, Newf. 166/C4
Baieville, Québec 172/E3
Baigorrita, Argentina 143/F7
Baiji, Iraq 66/C3
Baildon, Sask. 181/F5
Baile Átha Cliath (Dublin) (cap.), Ireland 17/K5
Baile Átha Cliath (Dublin) (cap.), Ireland 10/C4
Băile Herculane, Romania 45/F3
Bailén, Spain 33/E3
Băileşti, Romania 45/F3
Bailey, Colo. 208/H4
Bailey, Iowa 229/H2
Bailey, Mich. 250/D5
Bailey, Miss. 256/G6
Bailey, N.C. 281/N3
Bailey (co.), Texas 303/B3
Baileyboro, Texas 303/B3
Bailey Island, Maine 243/D8
Bailey Lakes, Ohio 284/F4
Bailey's Crossroads, Va. 307/S3
Baileys Harbor, Wis. 317/M5
Baileyton, Ala. 195/E2
Baileyton, Tenn. 237/R8
Baileyville, Conn. 210/E2
Baileyville, Ill. 222/D1
Baileyville, Kansas 232/F2
Bailieborough, Ireland 17/G4
Bailique (isl.), Brazil 132/D2
Bailivanish, Scotland 15/A3
Baillie (isls.), N.W. Terr. 187/F2
Baillieston, Scotland 15/B2
Baillif, Guadeloupe 161/A7
Bailundo, Angola 115/C6
Baima, China 77/E5
Bainbridge (isl.), Alaska 196/C1
Bainbridge, Georgia 217/C9
Bainbridge, Ind. 227/D5
Bainbridge, N.Y. 276/J6
Bainbridge (dist.), N. Ireland 17/J3
Bainbridge, Ohio 284/D7
Bainbridge, Pa. 294/J5
Bainbridge (isl.), Wash. 310/A2
Bainbridge Island-Winslow (Winslow), Wash. 310/A2
Bainbridge N.T.C., Md. 245/O2
Bainet, Haiti 158/B6
Baingoin, China 77/D5
Bains, La. 238/H5
Bainville, Mont. 262/M2
Baird (inlet), Alaska 196/F2
Baird (mts.), Alaska 196/F1
Baird, Miss. 256/C4
Baird (pen.), N.W. Terr. 187/L3
Baird, Texas 303/E5
Bairdstown, Ohio 284/C3
Bairdsville, New Bruns. 170/C2
Baire, Cuba 158/H4
Bairiki (cap.), Kiribati 87/H5
Bairin Zuoqi, China 77/J3
Bairnsdale, Victoria 88/H7
Bairnsdale, Victoria 97/D5
Bairoil, Wyo. 319/E3
Bais, Philippines 82/D6
Baisden, W. Va. 312/C7
Baïse (riv.), France 28/D6
Baisha, China 77/G8
Baitadi, Nepal 68/E3
Bait al Faqih, Yemen 59/D7
Bai Thuong, Vietnam 72/E3
Baixa da Banheira, Portugal 33/B3
Baixoaixo (isl.), Portugal 33/B2
Baixo Guandu, Brazil 132/F7
Baja, Hungary 41/E3
Baja California (state), Mexico 150/B1
Baja California Sur (state), Mexico 150/C3
Bajadero, P. Rico 161/C1
Bajgiran, Iran 66/L2
Bajo Boquete, Panama 154/F6
Bajo Nuevo (shoal), Colombia 126/C8
Bajos de Haina, Dom. Rep. 158/E6
Bajram Curri, Albania 45/D4
Bakala, Cent. Afr. Rep. 115/D2
Bakar, Yugoslavia 45/B3
Bakel, Senegal 106/B6
Baker (isl.), Alaska 196/M2
Baker, Calif. 204/J8
Baker (riv.), Chile 138/D7
Baker (mt.), Colo. 208/H2
Baker (co.), Fla. 212/D1
Baker, Fla. 212/C5
Baker (co.), Georgia 217/D8
Baker, Idaho 220/E4
Baker, La. 238/K1
Baker (lake), Maine 243/D3
Baker, Minn. 255/B4
Baker, Mo. 261/N9
Baker, Mont. 262/M4
Baker, Nev. 266/G3
Baker (riv.), N.H. 268/D4
Baker, N. Dak. 282/L3
Baker (lake), N.W. Terr. 187/J3
Baker, Okla. 288/D1
Baker, Oreg. 188/C2
Baker (co.), Oreg. 291/K3
Baker, Oreg. 291/K3
Baker (isl.), Pacific 87/J5
Baker (creek), Utah 304/A4
Baker (lake), Wash. 310/D2
Baker (mt.), Wash. 310/D2
Baker (riv.), Wash. 310/D2
Baker, W. Va. 312/J4
Baker Brook, New Bruns. 170/B1
Baker Butte (mt.), Ariz. 198/D4
Baker Hill, Ala. 195/H7
Baker Lake, N.W.T. 162/G3
Baker Lake, N.W. Terr. 187/J3
Bakers (isl.), Mass. 249/F5
Bakersfield, Calif. 146/G6
Bakersfield, Calif. 188/C3
Bakersfield, Calif. 204/G8
Bakersfield, Mo. 261/H9
Bakersfield, Texas 303/B7
Bakersfield•, Vt. 268/B2
Bakers Summit, Pa. 294/F5
Bakersville, Conn. 210/C1
Bakersville, N.C. 281/E2
Bakersville, Ohio 284/G5
Bakersville, Pa. 294/D5
Bakerton, Ky. 237/L7
Bakerton, W. Va. 312/L4
Bakerville, Tenn. 237/F9
Bakewell, England 10/G2
Bakewell, England 13/J2
Bakewell, Tenn. 237/L10
Bakharz, Kuhha-ye (mt.), Iran 66/M3
Bakhchisaray, U.S.S.R. 52/D6
Bakhmach, U.S.S.R. 52/D4
Bakhtaran (prov.), Iran 54/F6
Bakhtaran (prov.), Iran 58/E3
Bakhtaran (prov.), Iran 66/E3
Bakhtaran, Iran 54/F6
Bakhtaran, Iran 58/E3
Bakhtaran, Iran 66/E3
Bakhtegan (lake), Iran 66/J6
Bakhtiari (gov.), Iran 66/F4
Bakhun, Kuh-e (mt.), Iran 66/K6
Bakhuys (mts.), Suriname 131/C3
Bakia, Cent. Afr. Rep. 115/E2
Bakırköy, Turkey 63/D6
Baklan, Turkey 63/C4
Bako, Ethiopia 111/G6
Bakony (mts.), Hungary 41/D3
Bakool (prov.), Somalia 115/H3
Bakouma, Cent. Afr. Rep. 115/D2
Bakoy (riv.), Guinea 106/B6
Bakoy (riv.), Mali 106/B6
Bakraband, Kuh-e (mts.), Iran 66/M7
Baktalórántháza, Hungary 41/G2
Baktu (Paektu) (mt.), N. Korea 81/C3
Baku, U.S.S.R. 2/M3
Baku, U.S.S.R. 7/J4
Baku, U.S.S.R. 48/F5
Baku, U.S.S.R. 52/H6
Bala, Kansas 232/F2
Bala, Ontario 177/E2
Balâ, Turkey 63/E3
Bala, Wales 13/D5
Bala, Wales 10/E4
Balabac, Philippines 82/A7
Balabac (isl.), Philippines 85/F4
Balabac (isl.), Philippines 82/A7
Balabac (str.), Philippines 85/F4
Balabac (str.), Philippines 82/A7
Balabalagan (isls.), Indonesia 85/F6
Balabio (isl.), New Caled. 86/G4
Balaclava, Jamaica 158/H6
Bala-Cynwyd, Pa. 294/N6
Balad, Somalia 115/J3
Balaghat, India 68/E4
Balaguer, Spain 33/G2
Balaïtous (mt.), Spain 33/F1
Balakai (mesa), Ariz. 198/F3
Balakhna, U.S.S.R. 52/F3
Balaklava, S. Australia 94/F6
Balaklava, U.S.S.R. 52/D6
Balakovo, U.S.S.R. 7/J3
Balakovo, U.S.S.R. 48/E4
Balakovo, U.S.S.R. 52/G4
Balallan, Scotland 15/B2
Bal'ama, Jordan 65/E3
Balambangan (isl.), Malaysia 85/F4
Balancán de Domínguez, Mexico 150/O8
Balandra (pt.), Dom. Rep. 158/F5
Balanga, Philippines 82/C3
Balangala, Zaire 115/D3
Ba Lang An, Mui (cape), Vietnam 72/F4
Balangiga, Philippines 82/E5
Balao, Ecuador 128/C4
Balashi, Neth. Ant. 161/E10
Balashov, U.S.S.R. 7/J3
Balashov, U.S.S.R. 52/F4
Balashov, U.S.S.R. 48/E4
Balasore, India 68/F4
Balassagyarmat, Hungary 41/E2
Balaton (lake), Hungary 7/F4
Balaton (lake), Hungary 41/D3
Balaton, Minn. 255/C6
Balatonfüred, Hungary 41/D3
Balatonszentgyörgy, Hungary 41/D3
Balayan (bay), Philippines 82/C4
Balbi (mt.), Papua N.G. 86/C2
Balboa, Panama 154/H6
Balbriggan, Ireland 17/J4
Balbriggan, Ireland 10/C4
Balcarce, Argentina 143/E4
Balcarres, Sask. 181/H5
Balchik, Bulgaria 45/H4
Balch Springs, Texas 303/H2
Balclutha, N. Zealand 100/B7
Balcones Escarpment (plat.), Texas 303/E8
Balcones Heights, Texas 303/J10
Bald (mt.), Colo. 208/H4
Bald (hill), Conn. 210/G1
Bald (mt.), Idaho 220/D5
Bald (mt.), New Bruns. 170/C1
Bald (mts.), N.C. 281/D3
Bald (mts.), Tenn. 237/R9
Bald (mt.), Utah 304/C3
Bald (mt.), Vt. 268/D2
Bald (head), W. Australia 88/B7
Bald (head), W. Australia 92/B6
Bald Eagle (lake), Minn. 255/G3
Baldeggersee (lake), Switzerland 39/F2
Baldhill (Ashtabula) (res.), N. Dak. 282/P5
Bald Hill Branch (riv.), Md. 245/G4
Bald Hills, Queensland 88/K2
Bald Knob, Ark. 202/G3
Bald Knob, W. Va. 312/C7
Baldonnel, Br. Col. 184/G2
Baldur, Manitoba 179/C5
Baldwin (co.), Ala. 195/C9
Baldwin, Fla. 212/E1
Baldwin (co.), Georgia 217/F4
Baldwin, Georgia 217/E2
Baldwin, Ill. 222/D5
Baldwin, Iowa 229/M4
Baldwin, La. 238/H7
Baldwin, Mich. 250/D5
Baldwin, N.Y. 276/R7
Baldwin, N. Dak. 282/J5
Baldwin, Pa. 294/B7
Baldwin, W. Va. 312/E5
Baldwin, Wis. 317/B6
Baldwin City, Kansas 232/G3
Baldwin Park, Calif. 204/D10
Baldwinsville, N.Y. 276/H4
Baldwinton, Sask. 181/B3
Baldwinville, Mass. 249/F2
Baldwyn, Miss. 256/G2
Baldy (peak), Ariz. 198/F5
Baldy (mt.), Manitoba 179/B3
Baldy (peak), N. Mex. 274/D3
Baldy (peak), Utah 304/B5
Bale (prov.), Ethiopia 111/H6
Bale (mt.), Ethiopia 111/G6
Baleares (prov.), Spain 33/H3
Balearic (isls.), Spain 7/E5
Balearic (Baleares) (isls.), Spain 33/H3
Baleine (riv.), Québec 174/D1
Baleine, Grande R. de la (riv.), Que. 162/J4
Baleine, Grand Rivière de la (riv.), Québec 174/B1
Baleine, Petite Rivière de la (riv.), Québec 174/B1
Baleine, R. à la (riv.), Que. 162/K4
Balen, Belgium 27/G6
Baler, Philippines 82/C3
Baler (bay), Philippines 82/C3
Balerna, Switzerland 39/G5
Balerno, Scotland 15/D2
Baleshare (isl.), Scotland 15/A3
Balestrand, Norway 18/E6
Baley, U.S.S.R. 48/M4
Balfate, Honduras 154/D3
Balfour, Br. Col. 184/J5
Balfour, N.C. 281/E4
Balfour, N. Dak. 282/J4
Balfron, Scotland 15/B1
Balgonie, Sask. 181/G5
Balhaf, Yemen 59/E7
Bal Harbour, Fla. 212/C4
Bali, Cameroon 115/A2
Bali (isl.), Indonesia 54/N10
Bali (isl.), Indonesia 85/F7
Bali (sea), Indonesia 85/F7
Bali (str.), Indonesia 85/E7
Baliangao, Philippines 82/D6
Balicuatro (isls.), Philippines 82/E4
Balige, Indonesia 85/B5
Balıkesir (prov.), Turkey 63/B3
Balıkesir, Turkey 63/B3
Balıkesir, Turkey 59/A2
Balikpapan, Indonesia 54/N10
Balikpapan, Indonesia 85/F6
Balık-Uzun (lake), Turkey 63/G2
Balimbing (Bato-Bato), Philippines 82/C8
Baling, Malaysia 72/D6
Balingasag, Philippines 82/E6
Balingen, Germany 22/C4
Balintang (chan.), Philippines 82/A2
Balintang (isls.), Philippines 82/A2
Baljennie, Sask. 181/C3
Balk, Netherlands 27/H3
Balkan (mts.) 7/G4
Balkan (mts.), Bulgaria 45/G4
Balkan, Ky. 237/O7
Balkány, Hungary 41/G3
Balkbrug, Netherlands 27/J3
Balkh, Afghanistan 68/B1
Balkh, Afghanistan 59/J2
Balkhash, U.S.S.R. 48/H5
Balkhash, U.S.S.R. 54/J5
Balkhash (lake), U.S.S.R. 2/N3
Balkhash (lake), U.S.S.R. 48/H5
Balkhash (lake), U.S.S.R. 54/J5
Balko, Okla. 288/E1
Ball (mt.), Conn. 210/C1
Ball (pond), Conn. 210/A3

334 Ball

Ball, La. 238/F4
Ball (bay), Norfolk I. 88/L6
Balla, Ireland 17/C4
Balladonia, W. Australia 92/D6
Ballaghaderreen, Ireland 17/E4
Ballaigues, Switzerland 39/B3
Ballantine, Mont. 262/J5
Ballantrae, Scotland 15/C5
Ballantyne (str.), N.W. Terr. 187/G2
Ballarat, Australia 87/E9
Ballarat, Victoria 88/G7
Ballarat, Victoria 97/C5
Ballard (co.), Ky. 237/C6
Ballard, Mo. 261/D6
Ballard (cape), Newf. 166/D2
Ballard (lake), W. Australia 88/B5
Ballard, W. Va. 312/E8
Ballardsville, Miss. 256/H2
Ballardvale, Mass. 249/K2
Ballater, Scotland 10/E2
Ballater, Scotland 15/F3
Ball Club, Minn. 255/E3
Ballenas (bay), Mexico 150/C3
Ballenero (chan.), Chile 138/E11
Ballengee, W. Va. 312/E7
Ballens, Switzerland 39/B3
Ballenstedt, Germany 22/D3
Ballentine, S.C. 296/E3
Balleny (isls.), Ant. 2/S9
Balleny (isls.), Ant. 5/C9
Ballerup, Denmark 21/F6
Ballesteros, Philippines 82/C1
Balleza, Mexico 150/F3
Ball Ground, Georgia 217/D2
Ballground, Miss. 256/C5
Ballia, India 68/E3
Ballidu, W. Australia 92/B5
Ballina, Mayo, Ireland 17/C3
Ballina, Tipperary, Ireland 17/E6
Ballina, Ireland 10/B3
Ballina, N.S. Wales 97/G1
Ballinagh, Ireland 17/G4
Ballinakill, Ireland 17/G6
Ballinamore, Ireland 17/F3
Ballinasloe, Ireland 10/B4
Ballinasloe, Ireland 17/E5
Ballincollig-Carrigrohane, Ireland 17/D8
Ballindine, Ireland 17/C4
Ballineen, Ireland 17/D8
Ballingarry, Limerick, Ireland 17/D7
Ballingarry, Tipperary, Ireland 17/F6
Ballinger, Texas 303/E6
Ballingry, Scotland 15/D1
Ballinlough, Ireland 17/D4
Ballinluig, Scotland 15/E4
Ballinrobe, Ireland 10/B4
Ballinrobe, Ireland 17/C4
Ballinskelligs (bay), Ireland 17/A8
Ballintober, Ireland 17/E4
Ballintra, Ireland 17/E2
Ballisodare, Ireland 17/E3
Ballivor, Ireland 17/H4
Balloch, Highland, Scotland 15/D3
Balloch, Strathclyde, Scotland 15/B1
Ballouville, Conn. 210/H1
Ballston, Oreg. 291/D2
Ballston Spa, N.Y. 276/N5
Ballsville, Va. 307/M6
Balltown, Iowa 229/M3
Ballville, Ohio 284/D3
Ballwin, Mo. 261/N3
Bally, India 68/F1
Bally, Pa. 294/L5
Ballybay, Ireland 17/G3
Ballybofey-Stranorlar, Ireland 17/F2
Ballybunion, Ireland 10/B4
Ballybunion, Ireland 17/B7
Ballycanew, Ireland 17/J6
Ballycarney, Ireland 17/J6
Ballycarry, N. Ireland 17/K2
Ballycastle, Ireland 17/C3
Ballycastle, N. Ireland 10/C3
Ballycastle, N. Ireland 17/J1
Ballyclare, N. Ireland 17/J2
Ballyconnell, Ireland 17/F3
Ballycotton, Ireland 17/F8
Ballycotton (bay), Ireland 17/F8
Ballydehob, Ireland 17/C8
Ballyduff, Ireland 17/B7
Ballygally, N. Ireland 17/K2
Ballygar, Ireland 17/E4
Ballygawley, N. Ireland 17/G3
Ballygeary, Ireland 17/J7
Ballygrant, Scotland 15/B5
Ballyhaise, Ireland 17/G3
Ballyhaunis, Ireland 17/D4
Ballyheige (bay), Ireland 17/B7
Ballyheigue, Ireland 17/B7
Ballyhoura (hills), Ireland 17/E7
Ballyjamesduff, Ireland 17/G4
Ballykelly, N. Ireland 17/G1
Ballylanders, Ireland 17/E7
Ballylongford, Ireland 17/B6
Ballymahon, Ireland 17/F4
Ballymakeery, Ireland 17/C8
Ballymena (dist.), N. Ireland 17/J2
Ballymena, N. Ireland 17/J2
Ballymena, N. Ireland 10/C3
Ballymoney (dist.), N. Ireland 17/J1
Ballymoney, N. Ireland 10/C3
Ballymoney, N. Ireland 17/J1
Ballymore, Ireland 17/F5
Ballymore Eustace, Ireland 17/J5
Ballymote, Ireland 17/D3
Ballymote, Ireland 10/B3
Ballynahinch, N. Ireland 17/J3
Ballynakill (harb.), Ireland 17/A4
Ballyporeen, Ireland 17/E7
Ballyragget, Ireland 17/G6
Ballyroan, Ireland 17/G6
Ballysadare (bay), Ireland 17/D3
Ballyshannon, Ireland 10/B3
Ballyshannon, Ireland 17/E3
Ballyteige (bay), Ireland 17/H7
Ballytore, Ireland 17/H5
Ballywalter, N. Ireland 17/K2
Balmaceda, Chile 138/E6
Balmat, N.Y. 276/K2
Balmazújváros, Hungary 41/F3
Balmertown, Ontario 175/B2
Balmhorn (mt.), Switzerland 39/E4
Balmoral, Manitoba 179/E4
Balmoral, New Bruns. 170/D1
Balmoral, Queensland 88/K2
Balmoral, Queensland 95/E2
Balmoral, Victoria 97/A5
Balmoral Castle, Scotland 10/E2
Balmoral Castle, Scotland 15/E3
Balmorhea, Texas 303/D11
Balmville, N.Y. 276/M7
Balnearia, Argentina 143/D3
Balneario El Tesoro, Uruguay 145/E5
Balneario La Barra, Uruguay 145/E5
Balneario Solís, Uruguay 145/D5
Balombo, Angola 115/B6
Balonne (riv.), Queensland 88/H5
Balonne (riv.), Queensland 95/D6
Balotra, India 68/C3
Baloy (mt.), Philippines 82/D5
Balpunga, N.S. Wales 97/A3
Balrampur, India 68/E3
Balranald, N. S. Wales 88/G6
Balranald, N.S. Wales 97/B4
Balş, Romania 45/G3
Balsam, N.C. 281/C4
Balsam (lake), Ontario 177/F3
Balsam Creek, Ontario 177/E1
Balsam Lake, Wis. 317/B5
Balsapuerto, Peru 128/D5
Balsas, Brazil 120/E3
Balsas, Brazil 132/E4
Balsas (riv.), Brazil 132/E5
Balsas (riv.), Mexico 146/H8
Balsas (riv.), Mexico 150/J7
Bålsta, Sweden 18/G1
Balsthal, Switzerland 39/E2
Balta, N. Dak. 282/K3
Baltanás, Spain 33/D2
Baltasar Brum, Uruguay 145/B1
Baltasound, Scotland 15/G2
Baltic (sea) 2/K3
Baltic (sea) 7/F3
Baltic, Conn. 210/G2
Baltic (sea), Denmark 21/E9
Baltic (sea), Finland 18/K9
Baltic (sea), Germany 22/E1
Baltic, Mich. 250/G1
Baltic, Ohio 284/G5
Baltic (sea), Poland 47/B1
Baltic, S. Dak. 298/R6
Baltic (sea), Sweden 18/K9
Baltic (sea), U.S.S.R. 52/B3
Baltic (sea), U.S.S.R. 48/B4
Baltimore, Ireland 10/B5
Baltimore, Ireland 17/C9
Baltimore (city county), Md. 245/M3
Baltimore (co.), Md. 245/M3
Baltimore, Md. 245/M3
Baltimore, Md. 188/L3
Baltimore, Md. 146/L6
Baltimore, Ohio 284/E6
Baltimore, Ontario 177/F3
Baltinglass, Ireland 17/H6
Baltistan (reg.), Pakistan 68/D1
Baltit, Pakistan 68/C1
Baltiysk, U.S.S.R. 52/A4
Baltra (isl.), Ecuador 128/B9
Baltray, Ireland 17/J4
Baltrum (isl.), Germany 22/B2
Balty, Va. 307/O5
Baluchistan (reg.), Iran 66/M7
Baluchistan (prov.), Pakistan 68/B3
Baluchistan (reg.), Pakistan 59/J4
Balurghat, India 68/F3
Balvi, U.S.S.R. 53/D2
Balwina Aboriginal Res., W. Australia 88/D4
Balwina Aboriginal Res., W. Australia 92/E3
Balya, Turkey 63/B3
Balykshi, U.S.S.R. 48/F5
Balzac, Alberta 182/C4
Balzar, Ecuador 128/C3
Bam, Iran 54/G7
Bam, Iran 66/L6
Bam, Iran 59/G4
Bam, U.S.S.R. 48/N4
Bama, Nigeria 106/G6
Bamako (cap.), Mali 2/J5
Bamako (cap.), Mali 106/C6
Bamako (cap.), Mali 102/B3
Bamba, Mali 106/D5
Bambamarca, Peru 128/C6
Bamban, Philippines 82/C3
Bambari, Cent. Afr. Rep. 102/E4
Bambari, Cent. Afr. Rep. 115/D2
Bamberg (co.), S.C. 296/E5
Bamberg, S.C. 296/E5
Bamberg, Germany 22/D4
Bambesa, Zaire 115/E3
Bambili, Zaire 115/E3
Bambio, Cent. Afr. Rep. 115/C3
Bamble, Norway 18/F7
Bamboo, Jamaica 158/J6
Bamboo Creek, W. Australia 92/C3
Bambuí, Brazil 132/E8
Bambuí, Brazil 135/C2
Bamenda, Cameroon 115/B2
Bamfield, Br. Col. 184/E6
Bamian, Afghanistan 59/J3
Bamian, Afghanistan 68/B2
Bamingui, Cent. Afr. Rep. 115/D2
Bamingui (riv.), Cent. Afr. Rep. 115/C2
Bamoa, Mexico 150/E4
Bampur, Iran 59/H4
Bampur, Iran 66/M7
Bampur (riv.), Iran 66/M7
Bamyili-Beswick, North. Terr. 93/C3
Banaba (isl.), Kiribati 87/G6
Bañado de Medina, Uruguay 145/E3
Bañado de Rocha, Uruguay 145/C2
Banagher, Ireland 17/F5
Banagüises, Cuba 158/D1
Banahao (mt.), Philippines 82/C3
Banalia, Zaire 115/E3
Banam, Cambodia 72/E5
Banamba, Mali 106/C6
Banamba, Mali 102/B3
Banamichi, Mexico 150/D2
Banana (riv.), Fla. 212/F3
Banana, Zaire 115/B5
Bananal (isl.), Brazil 120/D4
Bananal (isl.), Brazil 132/D5
Bananier, Guadeloupe 161/A7
Banao, Cuba 158/F2
Ban Aranyaprathet, Thailand 72/D4
Bânâs, Ras (cape), Egypt 111/G3
Bânâs, Ras (cape), Egypt 59/C5
Banas (riv.), India 68/D3
Banaz, Turkey 63/C3
Banaz (riv.), Turkey 63/C3
Banbar, China 77/E5
Ban Boun Tai, Laos 72/D2
Banbridge, N. Ireland 17/J3
Banbury, England 10/F4
Banbury, England 13/F5
Bancalan (isl.), Philippines 82/A6
Bancannia (lake), N.S. Wales 97/A2
Banchory, Scotland 10/E2
Banchory, Scotland 15/F3
Bancoran (isl.), Philippines 82/B7
Bancroft, Idaho 220/G7
Bancroft, Iowa 229/E2
Bancroft, Kansas 232/G2
Bancroft, Ky. 237/K1
Bancroft, La. 238/C5
Bancroft, Maine 243/H4
Bancroft•, Maine 243/H4
Bancroft, Mich. 250/E6
Bancroft, Nebr. 264/H2
Bancroft, Ontario 177/G2
Bancroft, Oreg. 291/D5
Bancroft, S. Dak. 298/O4
Bancroft, W. Va. 312/C5
Bancroft, Wis. 317/G7
Bancroft (Chililabombwe), Zambia 115/E6
Banda, Gabon 115/B4
Banda, India 68/D3
Banda (isls.), Indonesia 85/H6
Banda (sea), Indonesia 54/O10
Banda (sea), Indonesia 85/H7
Banda Aceh, Indonesia 85/A4
Banda Aceh, Indonesia 54/L9
Bandai (mt.), Japan 81/K5
Bandai-Asahi National Park, Japan 81/J4
Bandama (riv.), Ivory Coast 106/C7
Bandana, Ky. 237/D6
Bandanaira, Indonesia 85/H6
Bandar (Machilipatnam), India 68/E5
Bandar 'Abbas, Iran 66/J7
Bandar 'Abbas, Iran 54/G7
Bandar 'Abbas, Iran 59/G4
Bandar Behesti (Bahar), Iran 66/M8
Bandar-e Anzali (Enzeli), Iran 66/E2
Bandar-e Bushehr (Bushire), Iran 66/G6
Bandar-e Deylam, Iran 66/G5
Bandar-e Khomeyni, Iran 58/E3
Bandar-e Khomeyni, Iran 66/E3
Bandar-e Lengeh, Iran 66/J7
Bandar-e Lengeh, Iran 59/F4
Bandar-e Ma'shur, Iran 66/F5
Bandar-e Pahlavi (Enzeli), Iran 59/E2
Bandar-e Pahlavi (Enzeli), Iran 66/F2
Bandar-e Rig, Iran 59/F4
Bandar-e Rig, Iran 66/G6
Bandar-e Torkeman, Iran 66/H2
Bandar-e Torkeman, Iran 59/F2
Bandar Khomeini, Iran 66/F5
Bandar Khomeini, Iran 59/E3
Bandar Maharani (Muar), Malaysia 72/D7
Bandar Penggaram (Batu Pahat), Malaysia 72/D7
Bandar Seri Begawan (cap.), Brunei 85/E4
Bandar Seri Begawan (cap.), Brunei 54/N9
Bandar Shahpur, Iran 66/F5
Bandawe, Malawi 115/F6
Bande, Spain 33/B1
Bandeira (mt.), Brazil 120/E5
Bandeira, Pico da (mt.), Brazil 132/F8
Bandeira (mt.), Brazil 135/E2
Bandelier Nat'l Mon., N. Mex. 274/C3
Bandera, Argentina 143/D2
Bandera (co.), Texas 303/E8
Bandera, Texas 303/F8
Banderas (bay), Mexico 150/G6
Banderilla, Mexico 150/P1
Bandholm, Denmark 21/E8
Bandiagara, Mali 106/D6
Bandırma, Turkey 59/A1
Bandırma, Turkey 63/B2
Bandon, Ireland 10/B5
Bandon, Ireland 17/D8
Bandon (riv.), Ireland 17/D8
Bandon, Oreg. 291/C4
Bandra, India 68/B7
Bandundu (prov.), Zaire 115/C4
Bandundu, Zaire 102/D5
Bandundu, Zaire 115/C4
Bandung, Indonesia 54/M10
Bandung, Indonesia 85/H2
Bandy, Va. 307/E6
Bandya, W. Australia 92/C4
Banes, Cuba 156/C2
Banes, Cuba 158/J3
Banff, Alberta 182/C4
Banff, Alta. 162/E5
Banff, Scotland 15/F3
Banff, Scotland 10/E2
Banff (trad. co.), Scotland 15/A5
Banff Nat'l Park, Alberta 182/B4
Banff Nat'l Park, Alta. 162/E5
Banfora, Burkina Faso 106/D6
Bangalore, India 2/N5
Bangalore, India 54/J8
Bangalore, India 68/D6
Bangalow, N.S. Wales 97/G1
Bangar, Philippines 82/C2
Bangassou, Centr. Afr. Rep. 102/E4
Bangassou, Cent. Afr. Rep. 115/D3
Banggai, Indonesia 85/G6
Banggai (arch.), Indonesia 85/G6
Banggi (isl.), Malaysia 85/F4
Bangil, Indonesia 85/K2
Bangka (isl.), Indonesia 54/M10
Bangka (isl.), Indonesia 85/D6
Bangka (str.), Indonesia 85/C6
Bangkalan, Indonesia 85/K2
Bangkok (cap.), Thailand 2/P5
Bangkok (cap.), Thailand 72/D4
Bangkok (cap.), Thailand 54/M8
Bangladesh 2/P4
Bangladesh 54/L7
BANGLADESH 68/G4
Bang Lamung, Thailand 72/D4
Bangong Co (lake), China 77/A5
Bangor, Calif. 204/D4
Bangor, Maine 146/M5
Bangor, Maine 243/F6
Bangor, Maine 188/N2
Bangor, Mich. 250/C6
Bangor, N.Y. 276/M1
Bangor, N. Ireland 17/K2
Bangor, Pa. 294/M4
Bangor, Sask. 181/J5
Bangor, Wales 13/C4
Bangor, Wales 10/D4
Bangor, Wis. 317/E8
Bangs, Texas 303/E6
Bang Saphan, Thailand 72/C5
Bangued, Philippines 85/G2
Bangued, Philippines 82/C2
Banguezane (mt.), Niger 106/F5
Bangui (cap.), Cent. Afr. Rep. 102/D4
Bangui (cap.), Centr. Afr. Rep. 2/K5
Bangui (cap.), Cent. Afr. Rep. 115/C3
Bangui, Philippines 85/G2
Bangui, Philippines 82/C1
Bangui (bay), Philippines 82/C1
Bangweulu (lake), Zambia 115/F6
Ban Houayxay, Laos 72/D2
Baní, Dom. Rep. 158/E6
Baní, Dom. Rep. 156/D3
Bani (riv.), Mali 106/C6
Bani, Jebel (mts.), Morocco 106/C3
Bani, Philippines 82/B2
Bania, Cent. Afr. Rep. 115/C3
Baniara, Papua N.G. 85/C7
Bánica, Dom. Rep. 156/D3
Bánica, Dom. Rep. 158/D5
Banida, Idaho 220/G7
Banister (riv.), Va. 307/K7
Bani Suheila, Gaza Strip 65/A5
Baniyas, Syria 63/F5
Banja Luka, Yugoslavia 7/F4
Banja Luka, Yugoslavia 45/C3
Banjarmasin, Indonesia 54/N10
Banjarmasin, Indonesia 85/E6
Banjul (cap.), Gambia 102/A3
Banjul (cap.), Gambia 106/A6
Banka Banka, North. Terr. 93/C5
Ban Kantang, Thailand 72/C6
Ban Kapong, Thailand 72/C5
Bankass, Mali 106/D6
Bankend, Sask. 181/H4
Ban Kèngkok, Laos 72/E3
Bankfoot, Scotland 15/E4
Bankhead (lake), Ala. 195/D4
Bankhead, Scotland 15/F3
Ban Khlong Yai, Thailand 72/D5
Ban Khon, Laos 72/E4
Banks, Ala. 195/G7
Banks (pt.), Alaska 196/H3
Banks, Ark. 202/F6
Banks (isl.), Br. Col. 184/B3
Banks (isl.), Canada 2/C2
Banks (isl)., Canada 4/B16
Banks (bay), Ecuador 128/B9
Banks (co.), Georgia 217/E2
Banks (lake), Georgia 217/F9
Banks, Idaho 220/B5
Banks, Miss. 256/D1
Banks (cape), N. S. Wales 88/L4
Banks (cape), N.S. Wales 97/K4
Banks (pen.), N. Zealand 100/D5
Banks (isl.), N.W.T. 146/F2
Banks (isl.), N.W.T. 162/D1
Banks (isl.), N.W. Terr. 187/F2
Banks, Oreg. 291/A1
Banks (isl.), Queensland 88/G2
Banks (isl.), Queensland 95/B1
Banks (str.), Tasmania 88/H8
Banks (str.), Tasmania 99/D2
Banks (isls.), Vanuatu 87/G7
Banks (lake), Wash. 310/F3
Bankston, Ala. 195/C3
Bankston, Iowa 229/L3
Bankstown, N.S. Wales 88/K4
Bankstown, N.S. Wales 97/J3
Ban Kui Nua, Thailand 72/D4
Bankura, India 68/F4
Ban Lahanam, Laos 72/E3
Ban Me Thuot, Vietnam 72/F4
Bann (riv.), Ireland 17/J6
Bann (riv.), N. Ireland 17/H2
Bannack, Mont. 262/C5
Banner, Ill. 222/D3
Banner, Ky. 237/R5
Banner, Miss. 256/F2
Banner, Mo. 261/L7
Banner (co.), Nebr. 264/A3
Banner, Va. 307/D7
Banner, Wyo. 319/F1
Banner Elk, N.C. 281/F2
Banner Hill, Tenn. 237/R8
Banner Springs, Tenn. 237/M8
Bannertown, N.C. 281/H1
Ban Ngon, Thailand 72/D3
Banning, Calif. 204/J10
Banning, Georgia 217/C3
Bannister, Mich. 250/E5
Bannock (co.), Idaho 220/F7
Bannock (creek), Idaho 220/F7
Bannock (peak), Idaho 220/F7
Bannock (range), Idaho 220/F7
Bannockburn, Ill. 222/B5
Bannockburn, Ontario 177/G3
Bannockburn, Scotland 15/C1
Bannockburn, Scotland 10/B1
Bannow, Ireland 17/H7
Bannu, Pakistan 59/K3
Bannu, Pakistan 68/C2
Bañolas, Spain 33/H1
Bánovce nad Bebravou, Czech. 41/E2
Ban Pak Phanang, Thailand 72/D5
Banphot Phisai, Thailand 72/C3
Ban Pua, Thailand 72/D3
Banquo, Ind. 227/F3
Ban Sattahip, Thailand 72/D4
Bansberia, India 68/F1
Bansha, Ireland 17/E7
Banská Bystrica, Czech. 41/E2
Banská Štiavnica, Czech. 41/E2
Bansko, Bulgaria 45/F5
Banstead, England 13/H8
Banstead, England 10/B6
Bansud, Philippines 82/C4
Banswara, India 68/C4
Bantam, Conn. 210/B2
Bantam (lake), Conn. 210/C2
Bantam (riv.), Conn. 210/B2
Bantayan, Philippines 82/D5
Bantayan (isl.), Philippines 82/D5
Ban Tha Uthen, Thailand 72/D3
Banton, Philippines 82/D4
Banton (isl.), Philippines 82/D4
Bantry, Ireland 10/B5
Bantry, Ireland 17/C8
Bantry (bay), Ireland 10/A5
Bantry (bay), Ireland 17/B8
Bantry, N. Dak. 282/J3
Bantul, Indonesia 85/J2
Bañuelo (mt.), Spain 33/D3
Banyak (isls.), Indonesia 85/B5
Banyo, Cameroon 115/B2
Banyo, Queensland 88/K2
Banyumas, Indonesia 85/J2
Banyuwangi, Indonesia 85/L2
Banzare Coast (reg.), Ant. 5/C7
Baode, China 77/H4
Baoding (Paoting), China 77/J4
Bao Ha, Vietnam 72/D2
Baoji, China 54/M6
Baoji (Paoki), China 77/G5
Bao Lac, Vietnam 72/E2
Baoshan, China 77/E7
Baoting, China 77/G8
Baotou (Paotow), China 77/G3
Baotou, China 54/M5
Baoulé (riv.), Ivory Coast 106/C6
Baoulé (dry riv.), Mali 106/C6
Baoulé (riv.), Mali 106/C6
Bapaume, Sask. 181/D2
Bapchule, Ariz. 198/D5
Bapsfontein, S. Africa 118/J6
Baptist, La. 238/M1
Baptiste (lake), Ontario 177/G2
Baptistown, N.J. 273/D2
Baqên, China 77/D5
Ba'quba, Iraq 59/D3
Ba'quba, Iraq 66/D4
Baquedano, Chile 138/A4
Baquerizo Moreno, Ecuador 128/C9
Baqura, Jordan 65/D2
Bar, Yugoslavia 45/D4
Bara, Sudan 111/F5
Bara, Sudan 59/B7
Barabai, Indonesia 85/F6
Barabinsk, U.S.S.R. 48/H4
Baraboo, Wis. 317/G9
Baracaldo, Spain 33/E1
Barachois, New Bruns. 170/F2
Barachois (pt.), Nova Scotia 168/G4
Barachois, Québec 172/D1
Barachois Pond Prov. Park, Newf. 166/C4
Baracoa, Cuba 158/K4
Baracoa, Cuba 156/C2
Barada, Nebr. 264/J4
Baradères, Haiti 158/B6
Baradères (bay), Haiti 158/B6
Baradero, Argentina 143/G6
Baradine, N.S. Wales 97/E2
Baradine (creek), N.S. Wales 97/E2
Baraga (co.), Mich. 250/A2
Baraga, Mich. 250/G1
Baragoi, Kenya 115/G3
Baraguá, Cuba 158/F2
Baragua, Venezuela 124/D2
Barahona (prov.), Dom. Rep. 158/D6
Barahona, Dom. Rep. 158/D6
Barahona, Dom. Rep. 156/D3
Barajas, Spain 33/F4
Barak, Turkey 63/G4
Baraka (riv.), Ethiopia 111/G4
Baraka (riv.), Sudan 111/G4
Baraka (riv.), Sudan 59/C6
Baraka, Zaire 115/E4
Baraki Barak, Afghanistan 59/J3
Baraki Barak, Afghanistan 68/B2
Baralzon (lake), Manitoba 179/J1
Barama (riv.), Guyana 131/A2
Baramanni, Guyana 131/B2
Baramati, India 68/C5
Baramita, Guyana 131/A2
Baramula, India 68/C2
Baranagar, India 68/F1
Barankwa, Sudan 59/B7
Baranoa, Colombia 126/C2
Baranof (isl.), Alaska 196/M1
Baranovichi, U.S.S.R. 7/G3
Baranovichi, U.S.S.R. 48/C4
Baranovichi, U.S.S.R. 52/C4
Baranya (co.), Hungary 41/E4
Barão de Cocais, Brazil 135/E1
Baras, Philippines 82/E4
Barasat, India 68/F1
Baratang (isl.), India 68/G6
Barataria, La. 238/L7
Barataria (bay), La. 238/L8
Barataria (passage), La. 238/L8
Barawa (Brava), Somalia 115/H3
Baraya, Colombia 126/C6
Barbacena, Brazil 120/E5
Barbacena, Brazil 135/E2
Barbacena, Brazil 132/F8
Barbacoas, Colombia 126/A7
Barbacoas, Venezuela 124/E3
Barbados 2/G5
Barbados 146/N8
BARBADOS 156/G4
BARBADOS 161/B8
Barbar (isls.), Indonesia 85/J7
Barbas (cape), Western Sahara 106/A4
Barbastro, Spain 33/F1
Barbate (riv.), Spain 33/D4
Barbeau, Mich. 250/E2
Barbeau (peak), N.W. Terr. 187/L1
Barber, Ark. 202/B3
Barber (co.), Kansas 232/D4
Barber, Mont. 262/G4
Barber, N.C. 281/H3
Barbers (pt.), Hawaii 218/E2
Barbers Point, Hawaii 218/E2
Barbers Point Nav. Air Sta., Hawaii 218/E2
Barberton, Ohio 284/G4
Barberton, S. Africa 118/E5
Barberville, Fla. 212/E2
Barbezieux-St-Hilaire, France 28/C5
Barbil, India 68/F4
Barbizon, France 28/E3
Barbosa, Colombia 126/D5
Barbour (co.), Ala. 195/H7
Barbour (co.), W. Va. 312/F4
Barbourmeade, Ky. 237/K1
Barboursville, Va. 307/M4
Barboursville, W. Va. 312/B6
Barbourville, Ky. 237/O7
Barbuda (isl.) 146/M8
Barbuda (isl.), Ant. & Bar. 156/G3
Barcaldine, Queensland 88/G4
Barcaldine, Queensland 95/C4
Barcaldine, Scotland 15/C4
Barcarrota, Spain 33/C3
Barce (El Marj), Libya 111/D1
Barcellona Pozzo di Gotto, Italy 34/E5
Barcelona (prov.), Spain 33/G2
Barcelona, Spain 7/E4
Barcelona, Spain 33/H2
Barcelona, Venezuela 124/F2
Barcelona, Venezuela 120/C2
Barceloneta, P. Rico 161/C1
Barcelonnette, France 28/G5
Barcelos, Brazil 120/C3
Barcelos, Brazil 132/H9
Barcelos, Portugal 33/B2
Barclay, Md. 245/P4
Barco, N.C. 281/T2
Barcoo (creek), Queensland 88/G4
Barcoo (creek), Queensland 95/B5
Barcoo (creek), S. Australia 88/F5
Barcoo (creek), S. Australia 94/F3
Barcos (pt.), Cuba 158/B2
Barcs, Hungary 41/D4
Barczewo, Poland 47/E2
Bard, Calif. 204/L11
Bard, N. Mex. 274/F3
Bardai, Chad 111/C3
Bardai, Chad 102/D2
Bardejov, Czech. 41/F2
Bardera, Somalia 115/H3
Bardera, Somalia 102/G4
Bardney, England 13/G4
Bardolph, Ill. 222/C3
Bardon (lake), Wis. 317/C3
Bardonia, N.Y. 276/K8
Bardsey (isl.), Wales 13/C5
Bardstown, Ky. 237/L5
Barduelv (riv.), Norway 18/L2
Bardwell, Ky. 237/D7
Bardwell, Texas 303/H5
Bareilly, India 54/K7
Bareilly, India 68/D3
Barellan, N.S. Wales 97/D4
Bärenhorn (mt.), Switzerland 39/H3
Barents (sea) 2/L2
Barents (sea) 7/J1
Barents (sea) 4/B8
Barents (sea), U.S.S.R. 48/D2
Barents (sea), U.S.S.R. 52/E1
Barentsburg, Norway 18/C2
Barentsøya (isl.), Norway 18/D2
Bäretswil, Switzerland 39/G2
Barfield, Ark. 202/L2
Barfleur, France 28/C3
Barfleur (pt.), France 28/C3
Barga, China 77/B5
Bargal, Somalia 115/K1
Bargamin (creek), Idaho 220/C4
Bargersville, Ind. 227/E5
Bargo, N.S. Wales 97/F4
Bargrax (Bohu), China 77/C3
Barham, N.S. Wales 97/C4
Bar Harbor, Maine 243/G7
Bar Harbor•, Maine 243/G7
Bari (prov.), Italy 34/F4
Bari, Italy 34/F4
Bari, Italy 7/F4
Bari (prov.), Somalia 115/J1
Baria (riv.), Venezuela 124/E7
Barich, Alberta 182/D2
Barichara, Colombia 126/D4
Barida, Ras (cape), Saudi Arabia 59/C5
Barima (riv.), Guyana 131/B2
Barinas (state), Venezuela 124/D3
Barinas, Venezuela 124/C3
Barinas, Venzuela 120/C2
Baring, Maine 243/J5
Baring•, Maine 243/J5
Baring, Mo. 261/H2
Baring (head), N. Zealand 100/B3
Baring (cape), N.W. Terr. 187/G3
Baring, Sask. 181/J5
Baring, Wash. 310/D3
Barinitas, Venezuela 124/C3
Baripada, India 68/F4
Bariri, Brazil 135/B3
Bariri (res.), Brazil 135/B3
Bâris, Egypt 111/F3
Barisal, Bangladesh 68/G4
Barisan (mts.), Indonesia 85/C6
Baritbog (riv.), New Bruns. 170/E1

Bayburt 335

Barito (riv.), Indonesia 85/E6
Bark (lake), Ontario 177/G2
Barkam, China 77/F5
Barker, N.Y. 276/C4
Barker Heights, N.C. 281/D4
Barkeyville, Pa. 294/C3
Barkhamsted•, Conn. 210/D1
Barkhamsted (res.), Conn. 210/D1
Barkhan, Pakistan 68/B3
Barkhan, Pakistan 59/J4
Barking, England 10/C5
Barking, England 13/H8
Barkley (sound), Br. Col. 184/E6
Barkley (dam), Ky. 237/E6
Barkley (lake), Ky. 237/F7
Barkley (lake), Tenn. 237/F7
Barkly Downs, Queensland 95/A4
Barkly East, S. Africa 118/D6
Barkly Tableland (plat.), Australia 87/D7
Barkly Tableland, North. Terr. 88/F3
Barkly Tableland, North. Terr. 93/D4
Barkly Tableland, Queensland 95/A4
Barkmere, Québec 172/C3
Barkol, China 77/D3
Bark River, Mich. 250/B3
Barksdale, Texas 303/D8
Barksdale A.F.B., La. 238/C2
Barlby, England 13/G4
Bar-le-Duc, France 28/F3
Barlee (lake), Australia 87/B8
Barlee (lake), W. Australia 88/B5
Barlee (lake), W. Australia 92/B5
Barletta, Italy 34/F4
Barlinek, Poland 47/B2
Barling, Ark. 202/B3
Barlow, Br. Col. 184/F3
Barlow, Ky. 237/D6
Barlow, Miss. 256/C7
Barlow, N. Dak. 282/M4
Barlow, Ohio 284/G7
Barlow, Oreg. 291/B2
Barlow Bend, Ala. 195/C8
Barmedman, N.S. Wales 97/D4
Barmer, India 68/C3
Barmera, S. Australia 94/G6
Bar Mills, Maine 243/C8
Barmouth, Wales 10/D4
Barmouth, Wales 13/C5
Barna, Ireland 17/C5
Barnabus, W. Va. 312/C7
Barnaby (riv.), New Bruns. 170/E2
Barnaby River, New Bruns. 170/E2
Barnard, Kansas 232/D2
Barnard, Mo. 261/C2
Barnard, N.C. 281/D3
Barnard, S. Dak. 298/N2
Barnard•, Vt. 268/B4
Barnard Castle, England 13/E3
Barnardsville, N.C. 281/E3
Barnaul, U.S.S.R. 54/K4
Barnaul, U.S.S.R. 48/J4
Barn Bluff (mt.), Tasmania 99/B3
Barnegat, Alberta 182/E2
Barnegat, N.J. 273/E4
Barnegat (bay), N.J. 273/E4
Barnegat (inlet), N.J. 273/E4
Barnegat Light, N.J. 273/E4
Barnes (sound), Fla. 212/F6
Barnes, Kansas 232/F2
Barnes (co.), N. Dak. 282/O5
Barnes, Wis. 317/D3
Barnesboro, Pa. 294/E4
Barnes City, Iowa 229/H6
Barnes Corners, N.Y. 276/J3
Barneston, Nebr. 264/H4
Barnesville, Colo. 208/L2
Barnesville, Georgia 217/D
Barnesville, Md. 245/J4
Barnesville, Minn. 255/B4
Barnesville, N.C. 281/L6
Barnesville, Ohio 284/H6
Barnet, England 13/H7
Barnet, England 10/B5
Barnet•, Vt. 268/C3
Barnett, Georgia 217/G3
Barnett, Miss. 256/G7
Barnett, Mo. 261/G6
Barnettville, New Bruns. 170/E2
Barneveld, Netherlands 27/H4
Barneveld, N.Y. 276/K4
Barneveld, Wis. 317/F10
Barneville-Carteret, France 28/C3
Barney, Georgia 217/E8
Barney, N. Dak. 282/S7
Barnhart, Texas 303/C6
Barnhill, Ohio 284/H5
Barnoldswick, England 13/H1
Barnrock, Ky. 237/R5
Barnsdall, Okla. 288/O1
Barnsley, England 13/J2
Barnsley, England 10/F4
Barnstable (co.), Mass. 249/N6
Barnstable, Mass. 249/N6
Barnstable•, Mass. 249/N6
Barnstaple, England 10/E5
Barnstaple, England 13/D6
Barnstaple (bay), England 10/D5
Barnstaple (bay), England 13/C6
Barnstead•, N.H. 268/E5
Barnum, Iowa 229/E3
Barnum, Minn. 255/F4
Barnum, W. Va. 312/H4
Barnum, Wis. 317/E9
Barnwell, Ala. 195/C10
Barnwell, Alberta 182/D5
Barnwell (co.), S.C. 296/E5
Barnwell, S.C. 296/E5
Baro (riv.), Ethiopia 111/G6
Baro, Nigeria 106/F7
Baroda (Vadodara), India 68/C4
Baroda, India 54/J7
Baroda, Mich. 250/C7
Baroghil (pass), Afghanistan 68/C1
Baroghil (pass), Pakistan 68/C1
Baron, Okla. 288/S3
Baron Bluff (prom.), Virgin Is. (U.S.) 161/E3
Barons, Alberta 182/D4
Barooga, N.S. Wales 97/C4
Barossa (res.), S. Australia 94/C6
Barotseland (reg.), Zambia 115/D7
Barpeta, India 68/G3
Barqa (Cyrenaica) (reg.), Libya 111/
Barques (pt.), Mich. 250/C3
Barquisimeto, Venezuela 124/D2
Barquisimeto, Venezuela 120/C2
Barr, Scotland 15/D5
Barr, Tenn. 237/B9
Barra, Brazil 132/F5
Barra (head), Scotland 10/C2
Barra (head), Scotland 15/A4
Barra (isl.), Scotland 15/A4
Barra (isl.), Scotland 10/C2
Barra (isls.), Scotland 10/C2
Barra (sound), Scotland 15/A3
Barraba, N.S. Wales 97/F2
Barra Bonita (res.), Brazil 135/B3
Barrackpore, India 68/F1
Barrackville, W. Va. 312/F3
Barra de Río Grande, Nicaragua 154/F4
Barra do Bugres, Brazil 132/B6
Barra do Corda, Brazil 132/E4
Barra do Piraí, Brazil 132/E8
Barra do Piraí, Brazil 135/E3
Barra Isles (isls.), Scotland 15/A4
Barra Mansa, Brazil 135/D3
Barranca, Lima, Peru 128/C8
Barranca, Loreto, Peru 128/D5
Barrancabermeja, Colombia 126/C4
Barranca de Upía, Colombia 126/D5
Barrancas, Argentina 143/F6
Barrancas (riv.), Argentina 143/G5
Barrancas, Chile 138/G3
Barrancas, Colombia 126/D2
Barrancas, Barinas, Venezuela 124/C3
Barrancas, Monagas, Venezuela 124/G3
Barranco de Loba, Colombia 126/C3
Barrancos, Cerro (mt.), Chile 138/D7
Barrancos, Portugal 33/C3
Barranqueras, Argentina 143/E2
Barranquilla, Colombia 120/B1
Barranquilla, Colombia 126/C2
Barranquitas, P. Rico 161/D2
Barras (riv.), Bolivia 136/B6
Barras, Brazil 132/F4
Barras, Colombia 126/D8
Barraute, Québec 174/B3
Barre, Mass. 249/F3
Barre•, Mass. 249/F3
Barre, Québec 172/G3
Barre, Vt. 268/C3
Barre•, Vt. 268/C3
Barreal, Argentina 143/C3
Barreau (pt.), New Bruns. 170/F1
Barre Center, N.Y. 276/D4
Barreiras, Brazil 120/E4
Barreiras, Brazil 132/E6
Barreirinha, Brazil 132/B3
Barreirinhas, Brazil 132/F3
Barreiro, Portugal 33/B1
Barreiros, Brazil 132/H5
Barren (isls.), Alaska 196/B2
Barren (isl.), India 68/G6
Barren (co.), Ky. 237/K7
Barren (riv.), Ky. 237/H6
Barren (isls.), Madagascar 118/G3
Barren (isl.), Nova Scotia 168/G4
Barren (cape), Tasmania 99/E2
Barren Plains, Tenn. 237/H7
Barren River (lake), Ky. 237/J7
Barren Springs, Va. 307/G7
Barre Plains, Mass. 249/F3
Barrera, Bolivia 136/B3
Barretos, Brazil 132/D8
Barretos, Brazil 135/B2
Barrett, Minn. 255/B5
Barrett, Texas 303/K1
Barrett, W. Va. 312/C7
Barretts, Georgia 217/F8
Barrhead, Alberta 182/C2
Barrhead, Scotland 10/A1
Barrhead, Scotland 15/B2
Barrhill, Scotland 15/D5
Barrie, Ontario 177/E3
Barrie (isl.), Ontario 177/B1
Barrière, Br. Col. 184/H4
Barrineau Park, Fla. 212/B6
Barrington, Ill. 222/A5
Barrington•, N.H. 268/F5
Barrington, N.J. 273/B3
Barrington, Nova Scotia 168/C5
Barrington (bay), Nova Scotia 168/C5
Barrington•, R.I. 249/J6
Barrington, Tasmania 99/C3
Barrington Hills, Ill. 222/A5
Barrington P.O. (East Barrington), N.H. 268/F5
Barrington Passage, Nova Scotia 168/C5
Barrington Tops (mt.), N.S. Wales 97/F2
Barringun, N.S. Wales 97/C1
Barron (co.), Wis. 317/C5
Barron, Wis. 317/C5
Barronett, Wis. 317/B4
Barrouallie, St. Vin. & Grens. 161/A9
Barroui, Dominica 161/E6
Barrow, Alaska 196/G1
Barrow, Alaska 188/C5
Barrow, Alaska 146/C2
Barrow (pt.), Alaska 146/C2
Barrow (pt.), Alaska 196/G1
Barrow (isl.), Australia 87/B8
Barrow (co.), Georgia 217/E2
Barrow (riv.), Ireland 17/H7
Barrow (riv.), Ireland 10/C4
Barrow (str.), N.W.T. 162/G1
Barrow (str.), N.W. Terr. 187/J2
Barrow (bay), Ontario 177/C2
Barrow, U.S. 4/B17
Barrow (pt.), U.S. 2/B2
Barrow (pt.), U.S. 4/B18
Barrow (isl.), W. Australia 88/A4
Barrow (isl.), W. Australia 92/A3
Barrow Creek, North. Terr. 93/D6
Barrow-in-Furness, England 10/E3
Barrow-in-Furness, England 13/D3
Barrows, Manitoba 179/A2
Barrowsville, Mass. 249/K5
Barr Smith (mt.), Ant. 5/C5
Barruelo de Santullán, Spain 33/D1
Barry, Ill. 222/B4
Barry (co.), Mich. 250/D6
Barry, Minn. 255/B5
Barry (co.), Mo. 261/E9
Barry (mts.), Victoria 97/D5
Barry, Wales 13/B7
Barry, Wales 10/E5
Barry's Bay, Ontario 177/G2
Barryton, Mich. 250/D5
Barryville, N.Y. 276/L8
Barsi, India 68/D5
Barsinghausen, Germany 22/C2
Barss Corners, Nova Scotia 168/D4
Barstow, Calif. 204/H9
Barstow, Md. 245/M6
Barstow, Texas 303/A6
Bar-sur-Aube, France 28/F3
Bar-sur-Seine, France 28/F3
Bartelso, Ill. 222/D5
Barterville, Ky. 237/N4
Barth, Germany 22/E1
Barth, Fla. 212/B6
Barthel, Sask. 181/B2
Bartholomew (bayou), Ark. 202/G6
Bartholomew (co.), Ind. 227/F6
Bartibog Bridge, New Bruns. 170/E1
Bartica, Guyana 120/D2
Bartica, Guyana 131/B2
Bartın, Turkey 63/E2
Bartle, Cuba 158/H3
Bartle Frere (mt.), Queensland 88/H3
Bartle Frere (mt.), Queensland 95/C3
Bartlesville, Okla. 288/O1
Bartlett (dam), Ariz. 198/D5
Bartlett (res.), Ariz. 198/D5
Bartlett, Ill. 222/A5
Bartlett, Iowa 229/B7
Bartlett, Kansas 232/G4
Bartlett, Nebr. 264/F3
Bartlett•, N.H. 268/E3
Bartlett, N. Dak. 282/N3
Bartlett, Ohio 284/G7
Bartlett, Tenn. 237/B10
Bartlett, Texas 303/G7
Bartlett Deep, Cayman Is. 156/B3
Bartletts Ferry (dam), Ala. 195/H5
Bartletts Ferry (dam), Georgia 217/B5
Bartley, Nebr. 264/D4
Bartley, W. Va. 312/C8
Barto, Pa. 294/L5
Bartolomeu Dias, Mozambique 118/F4
Barton, Ala. 195/C1
Barton, Ark. 202/J4
Barton (co.), Kansas 232/D3
Barton, Md. 245/B2
Barton (co.), Mo. 261/D7
Barton, N. Dak. 282/K2
Barton, Ohio 284/J5
Barton, Oreg. 291/B2
Barton, Vt. 268/C2
Barton•, Vt. 268/C2
Barton (riv.), Vt. 268/C2
Barton City, Mich. 250/F4
Barton Hills, Mich. 250/F6
Bartonsville, Pa. 294/M4
Bartonsville, Vt. 268/B5
Barton-upon-Humber, England 13/G4
Barton-upon-Humber, England 10/F4
Bartonville, Ill. 222/D3
Bartonville, Texas 303/F1
Bartoszyce, Poland 47/E1
Bartow, Fla. 212/E4
Bartow (co.), Georgia 217/C2
Bartow, Georgia 217/G5
Bartow, W. Va. 312/G5
Bartra Antiguo, Peru 128/E4
Bartra Nuevo, Peru 128/E4
Barú (isl.), Colombia 126/C2
Barú (vol.), Panama 154/F6
Baruipur, India 68/F2
Barus, Indonesia 85/B5
Barut, Tanjong (cape), Malaysia 85/E5
Baruun-Urt, Mongolia 77/H2
Barvas, Scotland 10/C1
Barvas, Scotland 15/B2
Barview, Oreg. 291/C4
Bar View, Oreg. 291/C2
Barville, Québec 174/B3
Barwani, India 68/D4
Barwick, Georgia 217/E9
Barwick, Ontario 175/B3
Barwick, Ontario 177/F5
Barwon (riv.) 88/H5
Barwon (riv.), N.S. Wales 97/D2
Barysh, U.S.S.R. 52/G4
Baryulgil, N.S. Wales 97/G1
Basalt, Colo. 208/E4
Basalt, Idaho 220/F6
Basankusu, Zaire 115/C3
Basavilbaso, Argentina 143/G6
Bas-Caraquet, New Bruns. 170/F1
Bascharage, Luxembourg 27/H9
Basco, Ill. 222/B3
Basco, Philippines 82/A2
Bascom, Fla. 212/A1
Bascom, Ohio 284/D3
Bascuñán (cape), Chile 138/A7
Basehor, Kansas 232/G2
Basel, Switzerland 39/E1
Basel, Switzerland 7/E4
Baselland (canton), Switzerland 39/E2
Baselstadt (canton), Switzerland 39/E1
Basey, Philippines 82/E5
Bashan, Conn. 210/F2
Bashan (lake), Conn. 210/F3
Bashaw, Alberta 182/D3
Bashi, Ala. 195/C7
Bashi (chan.), China 77/K7
Bashi (chan.), Philippines 82/A1
Bashkir A.S.S.R., U.S.S.R. 48/F4
Bashkir A.S.S.R., U.S.S.R. 52/J4
Basht, Iran 66/G5
Basic, Miss. 256/G6
Basilan (prov.), Philippines 82/D7
Basilan (isl.), Philippines 85/G4
Basilan (isl.), Philippines 82/D7
Basilan (str.), Philippines 82/C7
Basildon, England 13/J8
Basildon, England 10/G5
Basile, La. 238/E5
Basilicata (reg.), Italy 34/F4
Basim, India 68/D4
Basin, Mont. 262/D4
Basin (lake), Sask. 181/F3
Basin, Wyo. 319/E1
Basinger, Fla. 212/F4
Basingstoke, England 10/F5
Basingstoke, England 13/F6
Basirhat, India 68/F4
Basit (cape), Syria 63/F5
Baskahegan (lake), Maine 243/H5
Başkale, Turkey 63/K3
Baskatong (res.), Que. 162/J6
Baskatong (res.), Québec 172/B3
Baskerville, Va. 307/M7
Basket (lake), Manitoba 179/C3
Baskett, Ky. 237/F5
Baskil, Turkey 63/H3
Baskin, La. 238/G2
Basking Ridge, N.J. 273/D2
Başmakçı, Turkey 63/C4
Basodino (peak), Switzerland 39/G4
Basoko, Zaire 115/D3
Basom, N.Y. 276/D4
Basongo, Zaire 115/D4
Basora (pt.), Neth. Ant. 161/E10
Basra (gov.), Iraq 66/E5
Basra, Iraq 2/M4
Basra, Iraq 66/E5
Basra, Iraq 59/E3
Basra, Iraq 54/F6
Bas-Rhin (dept.), France 28/G3
Bass (str.) 88/H7
Bass (str.), Australia 87/E9
Bass (isls.), Fr. Poly. 87/M8
Bass (lake), Ind. 227/D2
Bass (str.), Tasmania 99/C1
Bassano, Alberta 182/D4
Bassano del Grappa, Italy 34/C2
Bassas da India (isl.), Réunion 102/F7
Bassas da India (isl.), Réunion 118/F4
Bassecourt, Switzerland 39/D2
Bassein, Burma 54/L8
Bassein, Burma 72/B3
Bassein, India 68/C5
Basse-Pointe, Martinique 161/C5
Basse-Sambre, Belgium 27/F8
Basse Santa Su, Gambia 106/B6
Basse-Terre (cap.), Guadeloupe 161/A7
Basse-Terre (cap.), Guadeloupe 156/F4
Basse-Terre (isl.), Guadeloupe 161/A6
Basseterre (cap.), St. Kitts & Nevis 161/C10
Basseterre (cap.), St. Kitts & Nevis 156/F3
Basse Terre, Trin. & Tob. 161/B11
Bassett, Ark. 202/K2
Bassett, Iowa 229/J2
Bassett, Kansas 232/G4
Bassett, Nebr. 264/E2
Bassett, Va. 307/J7
Bassfield, Miss. 256/E8
Bass Harbor, Maine 243/G7
Bassikounou, Mauritania 106/C5
Bassin Bleu, Haiti 158/B5
Bass River, New Bruns. 170/E2
Bass River, Nova Scotia 168/E3
Bassum, Germany 22/C2
Basswood, Manitoba 179/B4
Basswood (lake), Minn. 255/G2
Basswood (lake), Ontario 175/B3
Båstad, Sweden 18/H8
Bastak, Iran 66/J7
Bastam, Iran 66/J2
Bastar, India 68/E5
Bastelica, France 28/B6
Bastenaken (Bastogne), Belgium 27/H9
Bastia, France 7/E4
Bastia, France 28/B6
Bastian, Va. 307/F6
Bastimentos (isl.), Panama 154/G6
Bastogne, Belgium 27/H9
Bastrop, La. 238/G1
Bastrop (co.), Texas 303/G7
Bastrop, Texas 303/G7
Bastuträsk, Sweden 18/L4
Basye, Va. 307/L3
Bas-Zaïre (prov.), Zaire 115/B4
Bata, Equat. Guinea 102/C4
Bata, Equat. Guinea 115/B3
Bataan (prov.), Philippines 82/C3
Batabanó (gulf), Cuba 158/C2
Batabanó (gulf), Cuba 156/A2
Batag (isl.), Philippines 82/E4
Batagay, U.S.S.R. 48/O3
Batala, India 68/D2
Batalha, Brazil 132/F3
Batalha, Portugal 33/B3
Batan (isls.), Philippines 54/O7
Batan, Albay (isl.), Philippines 82/E4
Batan, Batanes (isl.), Philippines 82/B2
Batan (isls.), Philippines 85/G1
Batan (isls.), Philippines 82/A2
Batanes (prov.), Philippines 82/A2
Batang, China 77/E5
Batang, China 54/L6
Batang, Indonesia 85/J2
Batangafo, Cent. Afr. Rep. 115/C2
Batangas (prov.), Philippines 82/C4
Batangas, Philippines 82/C4
Batangas, Philippines 85/G3
Batas (isl.), Philippines 82/B5
Bátaszék, Hungary 41/E3
Batatais, Brazil 135/C2
Batavia, Ill. 222/E2
Batavia (Jakarta) (cap.), Indonesia 85/H1
Batavia, Iowa 229/J7
Batavia, Mich. 250/D7
Batavia, N.Y. 276/D5
Batavia, Ohio 284/B7
Batavia, Wis. 317/K8
Batawa, Ontario 177/G3
Bataysk, U.S.S.R. 52/E5
Bat Cave, N.C. 281/E4
Batchelor, La. 238/G5
Batchelor (brook), Mass. 248/D3
Batchelor, North. Terr. 93/B2
Batchtown, Ill. 222/C4
Batchwana Bay, Ontario 177/J5
Batdambang, Cambodia 54/M8
Batdambang (Battambang), Cambodia 72/D4
Bateman, Sask. 181/E5
Batemans Bay, N.S. Wales 97/F4
Bates, Ark. 202/B4
Bates, Mich. 250/D4
Bates (co.), Mo. 261/D6
Bates (mt.), Norfolk I. 88/L5
Bates, Oreg. 291/J3
Batesburg, S.C. 296/D4
Bates City, Mo. 261/E5
Batesland, S. Dak. 298/E7
Batesville, Ala. 195/H6
Batesville, Ark. 202/G2
Batesville, Ind. 227/G6
Batesville, Miss. 256/E2
Batesville, Ohio 284/H6
Batesville, Texas 303/E9
Batesville, Va. 307/L5
Bath, England 13/E6
Bath, England 10/E5
Bath, Ill. 222/C3
Bath, Ind. 227/H5
Bath, Jamaica 158/K6
Bath (co.), Ky. 237/O4
Bath, Maine 243/D8
Bath, Mich. 250/E6
Bath, Netherlands 27/E6
Bath, New Bruns. 170/C2
Bath•, N.H. 268/D3
Bath, N.Y. 276/F6
Bath, N.C. 281/R4
Bath, Ontario 177/H3
Bath, Pa. 294/M4
Bath, S.C. 296/D5
Bath, S. Dak. 298/N3
Bath (co.), Va. 307/J4
Batha (riv.), Chad 111/C5
Bathgate, N. Dak. 282/P2
Bathgate, Scotland 15/C2
Bathgate, Scotland 10/C1
Bathsheba, Barbados 161/B8
Bath Springs, Tenn. 237/E10
Bathurst (isl.), Australia 87/C7
Bathurst (isl.), Canada 4/B14
Bathurst (Banjul) (cap.), Gambia 106/A6
Bathurst, N. Br. 162/K6
Bathurst, New Bruns. 170/E1
Bathurst, N.S. Wales 88/H6
Bathurst, N.S. Wales 97/E3
Bathurst (isl.), North. Terr. 88/D2
Bathurst (isl.), North. Terr. 93/A1
Bathurst (cape), N.W.T. 162/D1
Bathurst (cape), N.W.T. 187/F2
Bathurst (inlet), N.W.T. 187/H3
Bathurst (isl.), N.W.T. 162/F1
Bathurst (isl.), N.W.T. 146/H2
Bathurst (isl.), N.W.T. 187/H2
Bathurst (harb.), Tasmania 99/C5
Bathurst Inlet, N.W. Terr. 187/H3
Bathurst Island, North. Terr. 93/B1
Bathurst Island Mission, North. Terr. 88/E2
Bathurst Mines, New Bruns. 170/E1
Batié, Burkina Faso 106/D7
Batı Fırat (riv.), Turkey 63/H3
Batin, Wadi al (dry riv.), Iraq 59/E4
Batin, Wadi al (dry riv.), Iraq 66/E6
Batin, Wadi al (dry riv.), Saudi Arabia 59/E4
Batina (reg.), Oman 59/G5
Batini (mt.), Fiji 86/Q10
Batiscan, Québec 172/E3
Batiscan (lake), Québec 172/E2
Batiscan (riv.), Québec 172/E2
Batley, England 13/J1
Batlow, N.S. Wales 97/E4
Batman, Turkey 63/J4
Batna, Algeria 102/C1
Batna, Algeria 106/F1
Bato, Catanduanes, Philippines 82/E4
Bato, Leyte, Philippines 82/E5
Bato-Bato, Philippines 82/C8
Batobato, Philippines 82/E7
Batoche, Sask. 181/E3
Batoche Nat'l Hist. Site, Sask. 181/E3
Baton Rouge (cap.), La. 146/J6
Baton Rouge (cap.), La. 188/H4
Baton Rouge (cap.), La. 238/K2
Bátonyterenye, Hungary 40/E3
Batopilas, Mexico 150/F3
Batouri, Cameroon 115/B3
Batovi, Uruguay 145/D2
Batrun, Lebanon 63/F5
Bat Shelomo, Israel 65/B2
Batson, Texas 303/K7
Batsto, N.J. 273/D4
Batsto (riv.), N.J. 273/D4
Batten Kill (riv.), N.Y. 276/O4
Batten Kill (riv.), Vt. 268/A5
Batterbee (cape), Ant. 2/N9
Batterbee (cape), Ant. 5/C3
Bätterkinden, Switzerland 39/E2
Battersea, Ontario 177/H3
Batticaloa, Sri Lanka 68/E7
Battiest, Okla. 288/S6
Batti Malv (isl.), India 68/G7
Battle (riv.) 162/E5
Battle (riv.), Alberta 182/D3
Battle, England 13/H7
Battle, England 10/G5
Battle (creek), Idaho 220/B7
Battle (riv.), Minn. 255/D3
Battle (creek), Mont. 262/G1
Battle (creek), Oreg. 291/K5
Battle (creek), Sask. 181/B6
Battle (riv.), Sask. 181/B3
Battle (creek), S. Dak. 298/C6
Battleboro, N.C. 281/O2
Battle Creek, Iowa 229/B4
Battle Creek, Mich. 188/J2
Battle Creek, Mich. 250/D6
Battle Creek, Nebr. 264/G3
Battlefield, Mo. 261/F8
Battleford, Sask. 162/E5
Battleford, Sask. 181/C3
Battle Ground, Ind. 227/D3
Battle Ground, Wash. 310/C5
Battle Harbour, Newf. 166/C3
Battle Harbour, Newf. 162/L5
Battle Lake, Alberta 182/C3
Battle Lake, Minn. 255/C4
Battle Mountain, Nev. 266/E2
Battles Wharf, Ala. 195/C10
Battletown, Ky. 237/J4
Battleview, N. Dak. 282/E2
Battock (mt.), Scotland 15/F4
Battonya, Hungary 41/F3
Battrum, Sask. 181/C5
Batu (isls.), Indonesia 85/B6
Batuco, Chile 138/G3
Batu Gajah, Malaysia 72/D6
Batulaki, Philippines 82/E8
Batumi, U.S.S.R. 48/E5
Batumi, U.S.S.R. 52/F6
Batu Pahat, Malaysia 72/D7
Baturaja, Indonesia 85/C6
Baturité, Brazil 132/G4
Batusangkar, Indonesia 85/C6
Bat Yam, Israel 65/B3
Bauang, Philippines 82/C2
Baubau, Indonesia 85/G7
Bauchi (state), Nigeria 106/F6
Bauchi, Nigeria 106/F6
Baudette, Minn. 255/D2
Baudette (riv.), Minn. 255/D2
Baudh, India 68/E4
Baudó, Serranía de (mts.), Colombia 126/B5
Baudó (riv.), Colombia 126/B5
Baugé, France 28/D4
Baukau, Indonesia 85/H7
Bauld (cape), Newf. 166/C3
Bauld (cape), Newf. 162/L5
Bauline, Newf. 166/D2
Baulkham Hills, N.S. Wales 88/K4
Baulkham Hills, N.S. Wales 97/H3
Baulmes, Switzerland 39/C3
Bauma, Switzerland 39/G2
Baumann (fjord), N.W. Terr. 187/K2
Baume-les-Dames, France 28/G4
Baures, Bolivia 136/D3
Baures (riv.), Bolivia 136/D3
Bauria, India 68/E2
Baurtregaum (mt.), Ireland 17/A7
Bauru, Brazil 120/E5
Bauru, Brazil 135/B3
Bauru, Brazil 132/D8
Bauska, U.S.S.R. 53/B2
Bauta, Cuba 158/C1
Bauta (riv.), P. Rico 161/C2
Bautzen, Germany 22/F3
Bauxite, Ark. 202/F4
Bavaria, Kansas 232/E3
Bavaria (state), Germany 22/D4
Bavarian (for.), Germany 22/E4
Bavarian Alps (mts.), Austria 41/A3
Bavarian Alps (range), Germany 22/D5
Baviácora, Mexico 150/E2
Bavispe, Mexico 150/E1
Bavispe, Río de (riv.), Mexico 150/E1
Bawean (isl.), Indonesia 85/K1
Bawku, Ghana 106/D6
Bawlf, Alberta 182/D3
Ba Xian, China 77/J4
Baxley, Georgia 217/H7
Baxoi, China 77/E5
Baxter (co.), Ark. 202/F1
Baxter, Iowa 229/G5
Baxter, Minn. 255/D4
Baxter, Miss. 256/F6
Baxter, Pa. 294/D3
Baxter, Tenn. 237/K8
Baxter Springs, Kansas 232/H4
Baxterville, Miss. 256/E8
Bay, Ark. 202/J2
Bay (Baicheng), China 77/B3
Bay (co.), Fla. 212/C6
Bay (co.), Mich. 250/E5
Bay, Mo. 261/J5
Bay, Laguna de (lake), Philippines 82/C3
Bay (prov.), Somalia 115/H3
Bayag (Calanasan), Philippines 82/C1
Bayaguana, Dom. Rep. 158/E6
Bayamhongor, Mongolia 77/E2
Bayamo, Cuba 156/C2
Bayamo, Cuba 158/H4
Bayamón (dist.), P. Rico 161/D1
Bayamón, P. Rico 161/D1
Bayamón, P. Rico 156/G1
Bayamón (riv.), P. Rico 161/D1
Bayanbaraat, Mongolia 77/G2
Bayandalay, Mongolia 77/F3
Bayan Dobo Suma, Mongolia 77/G3
Bayang, Philippines 82/E7
Bayangovĭ, Mongolia 77/F3
Bayan Har Shan (range), China 77/E5
Bayanhongor, Mongolia 77/E2
Bayan Mod, China 77/F3
Bayan Obo, China 77/G3
Bayan-Ölgiy, Mongolia 77/C2
Bayan-Öndör, Mongolia 77/E3
Bayan-Uul, Mongolia 77/E2
Bayard, Del. 245/T6
Bayard, Iowa 229/D5
Bayard, Nebr. 264/A3
Bayard, N. Mex. 274/A6
Bayard, Sask. 181/F5
Bayard, W. Va. 312/H4
Bayat, Turkey 63/F2
Baybay, Philippines 82/E5
Baybay, Philippines 85/H3
Bayble, Scotland 15/B2
Bayboro, N.C. 281/R4
Bay Bulls, Newf. 166/D2
Bayburt, Turkey 59/D1

336 Bayburt

Bayburt, Turkey 63/J2
Bay Center, Wash. 310/A4
Bay City, Mich. 188/K2
Bay City, Mich. 250/F5
Bay City, Oreg. 291/D2
Bay City, Texas 303/H9
Bay City, Wash. 310/B4
Bay City, Wis. 317/B6
Baydarata (bay), U.S.S.R. 52/L1
Bay de Verde, Newf. 166/D2
Baydhabo, Somalia 115/H3
Baydhabo, Somalia 102/G4
Baydrag, Mongolia 77/E2
Bay du Vin (riv.), New Bruns. 170/E2
Bayerischer Wald Nat'l Park, Germany 22/E4
Bayeux, France 28/C3
Bayfield, Colo. 208/D8
Bayfield, New Bruns. 170/G2
Bayfield, Ontario 177/C4
Bayfield (sound), Ontario 177/B2
Bayfield (co.), Wis. 317/D3
Bayfield, Wis. 317/E2
Bayham, Ontario 177/D5
Bay Harbor Islands, Fla. 212/B4
Bay Head, N.J. 273/E3
Bayhead, Nova Scotia 168/E3
Bayındır, Turkey 63/B3
Bayırköy, Turkey 63/B6
Baykal (lake), U.S.S.R. 54/N4
Baykal (lake), U.S.S.R. 2/Q3
Baykal (lake), U.S.S.R. 48/L4
Baykal (mts.), U.S.S.R. 48/L4
Baykan, Turkey 63/J3
Baykit, U.S.S.R. 48/K3
Baykonyr, U.S.S.R. 48/G5
Bay Lake, Fla. 212/E3
Bay Lake, Minn. 255/E4
Bay L'Argent, Newf. 166/D4
Baylis, Ill. 222/C4
Baylor (co.), Texas 303/E4
Bay Minette, Ala. 195/C9
Bay Mission, W. Australia 88/C3
Baynes Lake, Br. Col. 184/K5
Bayombong, Philippines 82/C2
Bayombong, Philippines 85/G2
Bayonne, France 28/C6
Bayonne, N.J. 273/B2
Bayonne Military Ocean Terminal, N.J. 273/B2
Bayou, Ky. 237/E6
Bayou Barbary, La. 238/M2
Bayou Bodcau (res.), Ark. 202/C7
Bayou Cane, La. 238/J7
Bayou Chicot, La. 238/F5
Bayou Current, La. 238/G5
Bayou D'Arbonne (lake), La. 238/F1
Bayou Des Arc (riv.), Ark. 202/G3
Bayou Goula, La. 238/J3
Bayou La Batre, Ala. 195/B10
Bayou Meto, Ark. 202/H5
Bayou Vista, La. 238/H7
Bayóvar, Peru 128/B5
Bay Pines, Fla. 212/B3
Bay Point, Maine 243/D8
Bay Point (isl.), S.C. 296/F7
Bayport, Fla. 212/D3
Bay Port, Mich. 250/F5
Bayport, Minn. 255/F5
Bayport, N.Y. 276/O9
Bayram-Ali, U.S.S.R. 48/G6
Bayramiç, Turkey 63/B3
Bayreuth, Germany 22/D4
Bayrischzell, Germany 22/E5
Bay Roberts, Newf. 166/D2
Bays, Ky. 237/P5
Bays (lake), Ontario 177/F2
Bay Saint Lawrence, Nova Scotia 168/H1
Bay Saint Louis, Miss. 256/F10
Bayshore, Fla. 212/E5
Bayshore, Mich. 250/D3
Bay Shore, N.Y. 276/O9
Bayshore Gardens, Fla. 212/D4
Bayside, Calif. 204/B3
Bayside, Maine 243/F7
Bayside, New Bruns. 170/C3
Bayside, Ontario 177/G3
Bayside, Texas 303/G9
Bayside, Wis. 317/M1
Bay Springs, Fla. 212/B6
Bay Springs, Miss. 256/F7
Bay Springs (dam), Miss. 256/H1
Bay Springs (lake), Miss. 256/H1
Bayston Hill, England 13/E5
Baysville, Ontario 177/E2
Baytown, Texas 303/L2
Bay Tree, Alberta 182/A2
Bayuca, Spain 33/B1
Bayview, Calif. 204/A3
Bayview, Idaho 220/B2
Bayview, Md. 245/P2
Bay View, Mich. 250/E3
Bay View, N. Zealand 100/F3
Bay View, Ohio 284/E3
Bay Village, Ohio 284/G9
Bayville, N.J. 273/E4
Bayville, N.Y. 276/R6
Baywood, La. 238/K1
Baywood Park-Los Osos, Calif. 204/E8
Baza, Spain 33/E4
Bazaar, Kansas 232/F3
Bazaruto, Ilha do (isl.), Mozambique 118/F4
Bazas, France 28/C5
Bazhong, China 77/G5
Bazile Mills, Nebr. 264/G2
Bazine, Kansas 232/C3
Bazman, Iran 66/M7
Bazman, Kuh-e (mt.), Iran 66/H4
Bazman, Kuh-e (mt.), Iran 59/H4
Beach (pond), Conn. 210/H2
Beach, Georgia 217/G8
Beach, N. Dak. 282/C6
Beachburg, Ontario 177/H2
Beach City, Ohio 284/G4
Beach City, Texas 303/L2
Beach Haven, N.J. 273/E4
Beach Haven (inlet), N.J. 273/E4
Beach Haven Crest, N.J. 273/E4
Beach Haven Terrace, N.J. 273/E4
Beach Lake, Pa. 294/M2
Beach Meadows, Nova Scotia 168/D4
Beachport, S. Australia 94/F7
Beachton, Georgia 217/D9
Beachville, Ontario 177/D4
Beachwood, N.J. 273/E4
Beachwood, Ohio 284/J9
Beachy (head), England 10/G5
Beachy (head), England 13/H7
Beacon, Iowa 229/H6
Beacon, N.Y. 276/N7
Beacon, Tenn. 237/E9
Beacon Falls•, Conn. 210/C3
Beaconia, Manitoba 179/F4
Beaconsfield, England 13/G8
Beaconsfield, Iowa 229/E7
Beaconsfield, Québec 172/H4
Beaconsfield, Tasmania 99/C3
Beadle, Sask. 181/B4
Beadle (co.), S. Dak. 298/N5
Beagle (chan.), Chile 138/E11
Beagle, Kansas 232/G3
Beagle (gulf), North. Terr. 93/A2
Beagle, W. Australia 88/C3
Beaglebay Aboriginal Res., W. Australia 92/C2
Beagle Bay Mission, W. Australia 92/C2
Beal (range), Queensland 95/B5
Bealanana, Madagascar 118/H2
Beal City, Mich. 250/D5
Beale (cape), Br. Col. 184/E6
Beale A.F.B., Calif. 204/D4
Bealeton, Va. 307/N3
Beallsville, Ohio 284/J6
Beallsville, Pa. 294/C5
Beals, Ky. 237/G5
Beals•, Maine 243/H7
Beals (creek), Texas 303/C5
Beaman, Iowa 229/H4
Beaminster, England 13/E7
Beanblossom, Ind. 227/E6
Beanblossom (creek), Ind. 227/D6
Bean City, Fla. 212/F5
Bean Station, Tenn. 237/P8
Bear (mt.), Alaska 196/K2
Bear (lake), Alberta 182/A2
Bear (lake), Br. Col. 184/D2
Bear (creek), Colo. 208/P8
Bear (hill), Conn. 210/B2
Bear (mt.), Conn. 210/B1
Bear, Del. 245/R2
Bear, Idaho 220/B4
Bear (lake), Idaho 220/G7
Bear (riv.), Idaho 220/G7
Bear (isl.), Ireland 17/B8
Bear (riv.), Maine 243/B6
Bear (riv.), Minn. 255/E3
Bear (creek), N. Dak. 282/O7
Bear (isl.), Norway 4/B9
Bear (creek), Oreg. 291/K2
Bear (creek), Oreg. 291/E5
Bear (creek), Oreg. 291/G4
Bear (hills), Sask. 181/C4
Bear (isls.), U.S.S.R. 4/B1
Bear (lake), Utah 304/C2
Bear (riv.), Utah 304/B2
Bear (isl.), Wis. 317/E1
Bear (creek), Wyo. 319/H4
Bear (riv.), Wyo. 319/B4
Bear Branch, Ind. 227/G7
Bearcamp (riv.), N.H. 268/E4
Bear Canyon, Alberta 182/A1
Bear Creek, Ala. 195/C2
Bearcreek, Mo. 261/E7
Bearcreek, Mont. 262/G5
Bear Creek, N.C. 281/L3
Bear Creek, Pa. 294/F7
Bear Creek, Sask. 181/K5
Bear Creek, Wis. 317/J6
Beard, Ind. 227/E4
Beard, W. Va. 312/F6
Bearden, Ark. 202/E6
Bearden, Okla. 288/O4
Beardmore (glac.), Ant. 5/A8
Beardmore, Ontario 177/H5
Beardmore, Ontario 175/C3
Beards Fork, W. Va. 312/D6
Beardsley, Kansas 232/A2
Beardsley, Minn. 255/B5
Beardstown, Ill. 222/C3
Beardstown, Ind. 227/D2
Beardstown, Tenn. 237/F9
Beargrass, N.C. 281/P3
Bearhat (mt.), Mont. 262/C2
Bear in the Lodge (creek), S. Dak. 298/F6
Bear Island, Ontario 177/K5
Bear Lake, Br. Col. 184/F3
Bear Lake (co.), Idaho 220/G7
Bear Lake, Mich. 250/C4
Bear Lake, Pa. 294/C1
Bear Lodge, Wyo. 319/E1
Bear Lodge (mts.), Wyo. 319/H1
Bearmouth, Mont. 262/C4
Béarn (trad. prov.), France 29
Bear River (range), Idaho 220/G7
Bear River, Minn. 255/E3
Bear River, Nova Scotia 168/C4
Bear River, Pr. Edward I. 168/F2
Bear River (range), Utah 304/C1
Bear River City, Utah 304/B2
Bear River Divide (mts.), Wyo. 319/B4
Bearsden, Scotland 15/B2
Bearskin Lake, Ontario 175/B2
Bears Paw (mts.), Mont. 262/G2
Bear Spring, Tenn. 237/F8
Beartooth (mts.), Mont. 262/G5
Beartown, W. Va. 312/C8
Beas de Segura, Spain 33/E3
Beason, Ill. 222/D3
Beata (cape), Dom. Rep. 158/D7
Beata (cape), Dom. Rep. 156/D3
Beata (chan.), Dom. Rep. 158/C7
Beata (isl.), Dom. Rep. 158/C7
Beata (isl.), Dom. Rep. 156/D3
Beatenberg, Switzerland 39/E3
Beaton, Br. Col. 184/J5
Beatrice, Ala. 195/D7
Beatrice, Nebr. 188/G2
Beatrice, Nebr. 264/H4
Beatrice (cape), North. Terr. 88/F2
Beatrice (cape), North. Terr. 93/E3
Beattie, Kansas 232/F2
Beattock, Scotland 15/E5
Beatton (riv.), Br. Col. 184/G1
Beatton River, Br. Col. 184/G1
Beatty, Nev. 266/E6
Beatty, Oreg. 291/F5
Beatty, Sask. 181/G3
Beattyville, Ky. 237/O5
Beau (lake), Québec 172/H2
Beaubier, Sask. 181/G6
Beaubois, New Bruns. 170/E1
Beaucaire, France 28/F6
Beauce (co.), Québec 172/G3
Beauceville, Québec 172/G3
Beaucoup, Ill. 222/D5
Beaudesert, Queensland 95/E6
Beauford, Minn. 255/D7
Beaufort (sea) 4/B16
Beaufort (sea) 146/D2
Beaufort (sea), Alaska 196/K1
Beaufort, Malaysia 85/F4
Beaufort, Mo. 261/K6
Beaufort (co.), N.C. 281/R4
Beaufort, N.C. 281/R5
Beaufort (sea), N.W.T. 162/C1
Beaufort (sea), N.W. Terr. 187/D2
Beaufort (co.), S.C. 296/F7
Beaufort, S.C. 296/F7
Beaufort, Victoria 97/B5
Beaufort (sea), Yukon 187/E2
Beaufort Marine Air Sta., S.C. 296/F7
Beaufort West, S. Africa 118/C6
Beauharnois (co.), Québec 172/C4
Beauharnois, Québec 172/D4
Beaulac, Québec 172/F4
Beaulieu, Minn. 255/C3
Beauly, Scotland 10/D2
Beauly, Scotland 15/D3
Beauly (riv.), Scotland 15/D3
Beaumaris (bay), Victoria 97/J6
Beaumaris (bay), Victoria 88/L8
Beaumaris, Wales 13/C4
Beaumaris, Wales 10/D4
Beaumont, Alberta 182/D3
Beaumont, Belgium 27/E8
Beaumont, Calif. 204/J10
Beaumont, Kansas 232/F4
Beaumont, Miss. 256/G8
Beaumont, N. Zealand 100/B6
Beaumont, Québec 172/F3
Beaumont (pt.), St. Lucia 161/F6
Beaumont, Texas 146/J6
Beaumont, Texas 188/H4
Beaumont, Texas 303/K7
Beaune, France 28/F4
Beauport, Québec 172/J3
Beaupré, Québec 172/G2
Beauraing, Belgium 27/F8
Beauregard (par.), La. 238/D5
Beauregard, Miss. 256/D7
Beauséjour, Manitoba 179/F4
Beauty, Ky. 237/S5
Beauty Point, Tasmania 99/C3
Beauvais, France 28/E3
Beauval, Sask. 181/L3
Beauvallon, Alberta 182/E3
Beaux Arts Village, Wash. 310/B2
Beaver (riv.) 162/F5
Beaver, Alaska 196/J1
Beaver (creek), Alaska 196/J1
Beaver (riv.), Alberta 182/E2
Beaver, Ark. 202/C1
Beaver (lake), Ark. 202/C1
Beaver (creek), Colo. 208/M3
Beaver (creek), Idaho 220/F5
Beaver, Iowa 229/E4
Beaver, Kansas 232/D3
Beaver (creek), Kansas 232/A2
Beaver, La. 238/E5
Beaver (isl.), Mich. 250/D3
Beaver (lake), Mich. 250/F4
Beaver (creek), Mont. 262/J2
Beaver (creek), Nebr. 264/D5
Beaver (riv.), Newf. 166/B3
Beaver (brook), N.H. 268/E6
Beaver (brook), N.J. 273/C2
Beaver (riv.), N.Y. 276/K3
Beaver (creek), N. Dak. 282/K7
Beaver (creek), N. Dak. 282/B5
Beaver (lake), N. Dak. 282/L7
Beaver, Ohio 284/E7
Beaver (co.), Okla. 288/E1
Beaver, Okla. 288/F1
Beaver (creek), Okla. 288/K6
Beaver (riv.), Okla. 288/F1
Beaver, Oreg. 291/D2
Beaver (co.), Pa. 294/B4
Beaver, Pa. 294/B4
Beaver (riv.), Pa. 294/B4
Beaver (hills), Sask. 181/H4
Beaver (riv.), Sask. 181/L4
Beaver (creek), S. Dak. 298/A6
Beaver (co.), Utah 304/A5
Beaver, Utah 304/B5
Beaver (mts.), Utah 304/A5
Beaver (riv.), Utah 304/A5
Beaver, Wash. 310/A2
Beaver (Glen Hedrick), W. Va. 312/D7
Beaver, Wis. 317/K5
Beaver (creek), Wyo. 319/H2
Beaver (creek), Wyo. 319/D3
Beaverbank, Nova Scotia 168/E4
Beaver Bay, Minn. 255/G3
Beaver Brook Station, New Bruns. 170/E1
Beaver City, Nebr. 264/E4
Beaver Cove, Br. Col. 184/D5
Beaver Creek, Md. 245/H2
Beaver Creek, Minn. 255/B7
Beavercreek, Ohio 284/C6
Beavercreek, Oreg. 291/B2
Beaver Creek, Yukon 187/D3
Beaver Creek Fork, Humboldt (riv.), Nev. 266/F1
Beaver Crossing, Nebr. 264/G4
Beaverdale, Pa. 294/E5
Beaverdam, Alberta 182/E2
Beaver Dam, Ky. 237/H6
Beaverdam, Ohio 284/C4
Beaverdam, Va. 307/N5
Beaver Dam, Wis. 317/J9
Beaver Dam (lake), Wis. 317/J9
Beaver Dams, N.Y. 276/F6
Beaver Dam Wash (creek), Utah 304/A6
Beaverdell, Br. Col. 184/H5
Beaver Falls, N.Y. 276/K3
Beaver Falls, Pa. 294/B4
Beaver Harbour, New Bruns. 170/D3
Beaverhead (mts.), Idaho 220/E4
Beaverhead (co.), Mont. 262/C5
Beaverhead (riv.), Mont. 262/D5
Beaverhill (lake), Alberta 182/D3
Beaverhill (lake), Manitoba 179/J3
Beaver Lake, Alberta 182/E2
Beaver Lake, N.J. 273/D1
Beaverlett, Va. 307/R6
Beaverlodge, Alberta 182/A2
Beaverlodge (lake), Sask. 181/L2
Beaver Meadows, Pa. 294/L4
Beaver Mines, Alberta 182/C5
Beaver Park, Sask. 181/J6
Beaver River, N.Y. 276/L3
Beaver River Flow (lake), N.Y. 276/K3
Beaver Springs, Pa. 294/H4
Beaverton, Ala. 195/B3
Beaverton, Mich. 250/E5
Beaverton, Ontario 177/E3
Beaverton, Oreg. 291/A2
Beavertown, Pa. 294/H4
Beaverville, Ill. 222/F3
Beawar, India 68/C3
Beazer, Alberta 182/D5
Beazley, Argentina 143/C3
Bebedouro, Brazil 132/D8
Bebedouro, Brazil 135/B2
Bebee, W. Va. 312/E3
Bebington, England 10/F2
Bebington, England 13/G2
Bebra, Germany 22/C3
Bécancour, Québec 172/E3
Bécancour (riv.), Québec 172/F3
Beccles, England 13/J5
Beccles, England 10/G4
Bečej, Yugoslavia 45/E3
Becerréa, Spain 33/C1
Béchar, Algeria 102/B1
Béchar, Algeria 106/D2
Bechar (pt.), W. Australia 88/A3
Bechard, Sask. 181/G5
Becharof (lake), Alaska 196/G3
Bechyn, Minn. 255/C6
Bechyně, Czech. 41/C2
Becida, Minn. 255/C3
Beckemeyer, Ill. 222/D5
Becker (co.), Minn. 255/C4
Becker, Minn. 255/E5
Becker, Miss. 256/G3
Becket•, Mass. 249/B3
Becket, Mont. 262/G4
Beckham (co.), Okla. 288/G4
Beckley, W. Va. 312/D7
Beckton, Wyo. 319/E1
Beckville, Texas 303/K5
Beckwourth, Calif. 204/E4
Bečva (riv.), Czech. 41/E2
Bedale, England 13/F3
Bédarieux, France 28/E6
Beddington•, Maine 243/H6
Beddouza, Ras (cape), Morocco 106/C2
Bedele, Ethiopia 111/G6
Bedeque (bay), Pr. Edward I. 168/E2
Bedessa, Ethiopia 111/H6
Bedford, England 10/F4
Bedford, England 13/G5
Bedford (pt.), Grenada 161/D8
Bedford, Ind. 227/E7
Bedford, Iowa 229/D7
Bedford, Ky. 237/L3
Bedford•, Mass. 249/B6
Bedford, Mich. 250/D6
Bedford, Mo. 261/F3
Bedford•, N.H. 268/D6
Bedford (basin), Nova Scotia 168/E4
Bedford, Ohio 284/H9
Bedford (co.), Pa. 294/E6
Bedford, Pa. 294/F5
Bedford, Québec 172/E4
Bedford (co.), Tenn. 237/J9
Bedford, Texas 303/F2
Bedford (co.), Va. 307/J6
Bedford (I.C.), Va. 307/J6
Bedford, Wyo. 319/A3
Bedford Heights, Ohio 284/J9
Bedford Hills, N.Y. 276/N8
Bedford Park, Ill. 222/B6
Bedfordshire (co.), England 13/G5
Bedford Valley, Pa. 294/E6
Bedias, Texas 303/J7
Bedington, W. Va. 312/L3
Bedlington, England 13/F2
Bedlington, England 10/E3
Bedminster•, N.J. 273/D2
Bedminster, Pa. 294/M5
Bedouaram (well), Niger 106/G5
Bedourie, Queensland 95/A5
Bedourie, Queensland 88/F4
Bedretto, Switzerland 39/G4
Bedrock, Colo. 208/B6
Bedsted, Denmark 21/B4
Bedwas and Machen, Wales 13/B6
Bedwellty, Wales 13/B6
Bedworth, England 13/F5
Bedworth, England 10/F4
Będzin, Poland 47/B3
Bee, Nebr. 264/H3
Bee (co.), Texas 303/G9
Beebe, Ark. 202/G3
Beebe Plain, Québec 172/E4
Beebe Plain, Vt. 268/C2
Beebe River, N.H. 268/D4
Bee Branch, Ark. 202/F3
Beech Bluff, Tenn. 237/D9
Beech Bottom, W. Va. 312/E2
Beech Creek, Ky. 237/G6
Beech Creek, Pa. 294/G3
Beecher, Ill. 222/F2
Beecher City, Ill. 222/E4
Beecher Falls, Vt. 268/D2
Beecher Island, Colo. 208/P3
Beech Fork (riv.), Ky. 237/L5
Beech Grove, Ind. 227/E5
Beech Grove, Ky. 237/G5
Beechgrove, Tenn. 237/J9
Beech Island, S.C. 296/D5
Beechwood, Mass. 249/F8
Beechwood, Mich. 250/C6
Beechwood, New Bruns. 170/C2
Beechwood, N.S. Wales 97/G2
Beechwood Village, Ky. 237/K2
Beechworth, Victoria 97/D5
Beechy, Sask. 181/D5
Beechy Point, Alaska 196/H1
Beedeville, Ark. 202/H3
Beekman, La. 238/G1
Beeler, Kansas 232/B3
Bee Log, N.C. 281/E3
Beemer, Nebr. 264/H3
Beenleigh, Queensland 88/J5
Beer Ef'e (well), Israel 65/C5
Be'eri, Israel 65/A5
Bee Ridge, Fla. 212/D4
Be'er Menuha, Israel 65/D5
Beernem, Belgium 27/C6
Be'er Ora, Israel 65/D5
Beersheba (Be'er Sheva'), Israel 65/B5
Beersheba Springs, Tenn. 237/K10
Beer Sheva' (dry riv.), Israel 65/B5
Beersville, New Bruns. 170/E2
Be'er Tuveya, Israel 65/B4
Beeskow, Germany 22/F2
Beesleys Point, N.J. 273/D5
Beeson, W. Va. 312/D8
Bee Spring, Ky. 237/J6
Beeston and Stapleford, England 13/F5
Beeton, Ontario 177/E3
Beetown, Wis. 317/E10
Beeville, Texas 303/G9
Befale, Zaire 115/D3
Befandriana, Madagascar 118/H3
Beg (lake), N. Ireland 17/J2
Bega, N. S. Wales 88/J7
Bega, N.S. Wales 97/E5
Begemdir (prov.), Ethiopia 111/G5
Beger, Mongolia 77/E2
Beggs, Okla. 288/P3
Begnins, Switzerland 39/B4
Béhague (pt.), Fr. Guiana 131/F3
Behan (lake), Alberta 182/E2
Behbehan, Iran 66/G5
Behistun (ruins), Iran 66/E3
Behm Canal (inlet), Alaska 196/N2
Behshahr, Iran 66/H2
Bei'an (Pehan), China 77/L2
Beica, Ethiopia 111/F6
Beihai (Pakhoi), China 77/G7
Beijing (Peking) (cap.), Peoples Rep. of China 54/N5
Beijing (Peking) (cap.), Peoples Rep. of China 77/J3
Beilen, Netherlands 27/K3
Beinn a Ghlo (mt.), Scotland 15/E4
Beinn Bhan (mt.), Scotland 15/C3
Beinn Bheigeir (mt.), Scotland 15/B5
Beinn Dearg (mt.), Scotland 15/D3
Beinn Dearg (mt.), Scotland 15/E4
Beinn Dhorain (mt.), Scotland 15/E2
Beinn Dorain (mt.), Scotland 15/D4
Beinn Eighe (mt.), Scotland 15/C3
Beinwil am See, Switzerland 39/F2
Beira, Mozambique 118/F3
Beira, Mozambique 102/F7
Beira, Somalia 115/J2
Beirne, Ark. 202/D6
Beirut (cap.), Lebanon 54/E6
Beirut (cap.), Lebanon 59/C3
Beirut (cap.), Lebanon 63/F6
Beiseker, Alberta 182/D4
Beishan, China 77/E3
Beitbridge, Zimbabwe 118/E4
Beit Fajjar, West Bank 65/C4
Beit Guvrin, Israel 65/B4
Beith, Scotland 10/A1
Beith, Scotland 15/D5
Beit Hanina, West Bank 65/C4
Beit Hanun, Gaza Strip 65/A4
Beit Jala, West Bank 65/C4
Beit Lahm (Bethlehem), West Bank 65/C4
Beit Sahur, West Bank 65/C4
Beiuş, Romania 45/F2
Beja (dist.), Portugal 33/C3
Beja, Portugal 33/C3
Béja, Tunisia 106/F1
Bejaïa, Algeria 106/F1
Bejaïa, Algeria 102/C1
Béjar, Spain 33/D2
Bejestan, Iran 59/G3
Bejestan, Iran 66/K3
Bejhi (riv.), Pakistan 68/B3
Bejou, Minn. 255/B3
Bejucal, Cuba 158/C1
Bejucal, Cuba 156/A2
Bekasi, Indonesia 85/H2
Békés (co.), Hungary 41/F3
Békés, Hungary 41/F3
Békéscsaba, Hungary 41/F3
Bekily, Madagascar 118/G4
Bekwai, Ghana 106/D7
Bel, La. 238/D6
Bela, Pakistan 68/B3
Bela, Pakistan 59/J4
Bélabo, Cameroon 115/B3
Bela Crkva, Yugoslavia 45/E3
Bélair, Manitoba 179/F4
Bel Air, Md. 245/N2
Bélair, Québec 172/H3
Bel Alton, Md. 245/L7
Belas, Portugal 33/A1
Bela Vista, Brazil 120/D5
Bela Vista, Mato Grosso, Brazil 132/C8
Bela Vista, Rondônia, Brazil 132/H10
Bela Vista, Mozambique 118/E5
Bela Vista de Goiás, Brazil 132/D7
Belawan, Indonesia 85/B5
Belaya (riv.), U.S.S.R. 7/K3
Belaya (riv.), U.S.S.R. 52/H3
Belaya Tserkov', U.S.S.R. 52/C5
Belbeck, Sask. 181/F5
Belbutte, Sask. 181/D2
Belchatów, Poland 47/D3
Belcher, Ky. 237/S6
Belcher, La. 238/C1
Belcher (isls.), N.W.T. 146/K4
Belcher (isl.), N.W.T. 162/H4
Belcher (chan.), N.W. Terr. 187/J2
Belcheragh, Afghanistan 68/B1
Belcheragh, Afghanistan 59/J2
Belchertown, Mass. 249/E3
Belchertown•, Mass. 249/E3
Belchite, Spain 33/F2
Belcourt, N. Dak. 282/L2
Belcross, N.C. 281/S2
Belden, Calif. 204/D3
Belden, Miss. 256/G2
Belden, Nebr. 264/G2
Belden, N. Dak. 282/F3
Beldenville, Wis. 317/A6
Belding, Mich. 250/D5
Belebey, U.S.S.R. 52/H4
Belém, Brazil 2/G6
Belém, Brazil 120/E3
Belém, Brazil 132/E3
Belém, Portugal 33/A1
Belén, Argentina 143/C2
Belén, Chile 138/B1
Belén, Honduras 154/C3
Belen, Miss. 256/D2
Belen, N. Mex. 274/C4
Belén, Panama 154/G6
Belén, Paraguay 144/D3
Belén, Uruguay 145/B1
Belén (range), Uruguay 145/C1
Belén de los Andaquíes, Colombia 126/C7
Belep (isls.), New Caled. 87/G7
Belet Weyne, Somalia 115/J3
Belet Weyne, Somalia 102/G4
Belev, U.S.S.R. 52/E4
Belfair, Wash. 310/C3
Belfast, Maine 243/F7
Belfast, N.Y. 276/D6
Belfast (dist.), N. Ireland 17/J2
Belfast (cap.), N. Ireland 7/D3
Belfast (cap.), N. Ireland 10/D3
Belfast (cap.), N. Ireland 17/J2
Belfast (inlet), N. Ireland 17/K2
Belfast, Tenn. 237/H10
Belfast Lough (inlet), N. Ireland 10/D3
Belfaux, Switzerland 39/D3
Belfield, N. Dak. 282/D6
Belford, England 13/F2
Belford, N.J. 273/E3
Belfort (terr.), France 28/G4
Belfort, France 28/G4
Belfry, Ky. 237/S5
Belfry, Mont. 262/H5
Belgaum, India 68/C5
Belgique, Mo. 261/N7
Belgium 2/J3
Belgium 7/E3
BELGIUM 27
Belgium, Ill. 222/F3
Belgium, Wis. 317/L8
Belgorod, U.S.S.R. 7/H3
Belgorod, U.S.S.R. 52/E4
Belgorod, U.S.S.R. 48/D4
Belgorod-Dnestrovskiy, U.S.S.R. 52/D5
Belgrade, Maine 243/D7
Belgrade•, Maine 243/D7
Belgrade, Minn. 255/C5
Belgrade, Mo. 261/L7
Belgrade, Mont. 262/E5
Belgrade, Nebr. 264/G3
Belgrade (cap.), Yugoslavia 7/G4
Belgrade (cap.), Yugoslavia 2/K3
Belgrade (cap.), Yugoslavia 45/E3
Belgrade Lakes, Maine 243/D6
Belgrave, Ontario 177/C4
Belgrave Heights, Victoria 97/J5
Belgrave South, Victoria 97/K5
Belgreen, Ala. 195/C2
Belhaven, N.C. 281/R3
Belic, Cuba 158/G4
Belice (riv.), Italy 34/D6
Beli Manastir, Yugoslavia 45/D3
Belington, W. Va. 312/F4
Belitung (Billiton) (isl.), Indonesia 85/D6
Belize 2/E5
Belize 146/K8
BELIZE 154/C2
Belize (riv.), Belize 154/C2
Belize City, Belize 154/C2
Bélizon, Fr. Guiana 131/E3
Belk, Ala. 195/C3
Belknap, Ill. 222/E6
Belknap, Iowa 229/J7
Belknap, Mont. 262/A3
Belknap (co.), N.H. 268/D4
Belknap (mt.), N.H. 268/E5
Belknap (peak), Utah 304/B5
Belkofski, Alaska 196/F3
Bell, Calif. 204/C11
Bell, Fla. 212/D2
Bell (co.), Ky. 237/O7
Bell (isl.), Newf. 166/D2
Bell (isl.), Newf. 166/C3
Bell (isl.), Newf. 162/L5
Bell (pen.), N.W. Terr. 187/K3
Bell (riv.), Que. 162/J6
Bell (riv.), Québec 174/B3
Bell (co.), Texas 303/G6
Bella Bella, Br. Col. 184/D4
Bellac, France 28/D4

Berlin 337

Bellaco, Uruguay 145/B3
Bella Coola, Br. Col. 184/D4
Bella Coola (riv.), Br. Col. 184/D4
Belladère, Haiti 158/C6
Bella Flor, Bolivia 136/A2
Bellaghy, N. Ireland 17/H2
Bellagio, Italy 34/B2
Bellaire, Kansas 232/D2
Bellaire, Mich. 250/D4
Bellaire, Ohio 284/J5
Bellaire, Texas 303/J2
Bellamy, Ala. 195/B6
Bellarmin, Québec 172/G4
Bellarthur, N.C. 281/O3
Bellary, India 68/D5
Bellata, N.S. Wales 97/E1
Bella Unión, Uruguay 145/B1
Bella Villa, Mo. 261/R4
Bella Vista, Corrientes, Argentina 143/E2
Bella Vista, Tucumán, Argentina 143/D2
Bella Vista, Ark. 202/B1
Bella Vista, Bolivia 136/E3
Bella Vista, Salar de (salt dep.), Chile 138/B3
Bella Vista, Paraguay 144/D3
Bella Vista, Paraguay 144/E5
Bellavista, Peru 128/C5
Bell Bay, Tasmania 99/C3
Bellbird-Cessnock, N.S. Wales 97/F3
Bellbrook, Ohio 284/C6
Bell Buckle, Tenn. 237/J9
Bellburns, Newf. 166/C3
Bell Center, Wis. 317/E9
Bell City, La. 238/D6
Bell City, Mo. 261/N8
Belle (riv.), Mich. 250/G6
Belle, Mo. 261/J6
Belle, W. Va. 312/C6
Belleair, Fla. 212/B2
Belleair Beach, Fla. 212/B2
Belleair Bluffs, Fla. 212/B3
Belleair Shore, Fla. 212/B3
Belle-Anse, Haiti 158/C6
Belle Center, Ohio 284/C4
Belle Chasse, La. 238/O4
Bellechasse (co.), Québec 172/G3
Bellechester, Minn. 255/F6
Belle Côte, Nova Scotia 168/G2
Belle D'Eau, La. 238/F4
Belledune, New Bruns. 170/E1
Belleek, N. Ireland 17/E3
Bellefleur, New Bruns. 170/C1
Bellefond, New Bruns. 170/E1
Bellefont, Kansas 232/C4
Bellefontaine, Martinique 161/C6
Bellefontaine, Miss. 256/F3
Bellefontaine, Mo. 261/N2
Bellefontaine, Ohio 284/C5
Bellefontaine Neighbors, Mo. 261/R2
Bellefonte, Ark. 202/D1
Bellefonte, Del. 245/S1
Bellefonte, Pa. 294/G4
Belle Fourche (riv.) 188/F2
Belle Fourche, S. Dak. 298/B4
Belle Fourche (res.), S. Dak. 298/B4
Belle Fourche (riv.), S. Dak. 298/C4
Belle Fourche (riv.), Wyo. 319/H1
Bellegarde, Sask. 181/K6
Belle Glade, Fla. 212/F5
Belle Glade Camp, Fla. 212/F5
Belle Haven, Va. 307/S5
Belle-Île (isl.), France 28/B4
Belle Isle (str.), Canada 146/N5
Belle Isle (str.), Canada 2/G3
Belle Isle, Fla. 212/E3
Belleisle (bay), New Bruns. 170/E3
Belle Isle (isl.), Newf. 166/C3
Belle Isle (str.), Newf. 166/C3
Belle Isle (str.), Newf. 162/L5
Belleisle Creek, New Bruns. 170/E3
Belle-Marche, Nova Scotia 168/H2
Belle Mead, N.J. 273/D3
Bellemeade, Ky. 237/K2
Belle Meade, Tenn. 237/H8
Belle Mina, Ala. 195/E1
Bellemont, Ariz. 198/D3
Belleoram, Newf. 166/C4
Belleplain, N.J. 273/D5
Belleplaine, Barbados 161/B8
Belle Plaine, Iowa 229/J5
Belle Plaine, Kansas 232/E4
Belle Plaine, Minn. 255/E6
Belle Plaine, Sask. 181/F5
Belle Prairie City, Ill. 222/E5
Belle Rive, Ill. 222/E5
Belle River, Minn. 255/C5
Belle River, Ontario 177/B5
Belle Rose, La. 238/K3
Bellerose, N.Y. 276/P7
Belle Terre, N.Y. 276/O9
Belleterre, Québec 174/B3
Belle Union, Ind. 227/D5
Belle Valley, Ohio 284/G6
Belle Vernon, Pa. 294/C5
Belleview, Fla. 212/D2
Belleview, Manitoba 179/B5
Belleview, Mo. 261/L7
Belle View, Va. 307/T3
Belleville, Ark. 202/D3
Belleville, Fla. 212/C1
Belleville, France 28/F4
Belleville, Ill. 188/J3
Belleville, Ill. 222/B3
Belleville, Kansas 232/E2
Belleville, Mich. 250/F6
Belleville, N.J. 273/B2
Belleville, N.Y. 276/H3
Belleville, Ontario 177/G3
Belleville, Pa. 294/G4
Belleville, W. Va. 312/C4
Belleville, Wis. 317/G10
Bellevue, Alberta 182/C5
Bellevue, Idaho 220/D6
Bellevue, Iowa 229/M4
Bellevue, Ky. 237/S1
Bellevue, Md. 245/O6
Bellevue, Mich. 250/E6
Bellevue, Nebr. 264/J3
Bellevue, Newf. 166/D2
Bellevue, Ohio 284/E3
Bellevue, Pa. 294/B6
Bellevue, Sask. 181/F3
Bellevue, Texas 303/F4
Bellevue, Wash. 310/B2
Belley, France 28/F5
Bell Farm, Ky. 237/M7
Bellflower, Calif. 204/C11
Bellflower, Ill. 222/E3
Bellflower, Mo. 261/K4
Bellfountain, Oreg. 291/D3
Bell Gardens, Calif. 204/C11
Bellingen, N.S. Wales 97/G2
Bellingham, England 13/E2
Bellingham, Mass. 249/J4
Bellingham•, Mass. 249/J4
Bellingham, Minn. 255/B5
Bellingham, Wash 188/B1
Bellingham, Wash 310/C2
Bellingham, Wash 310/80
Bellingshausen (sea), Ant. 2/E9
Bellingshausen (sea), Ant. 5/C14
Bellinzona, Switzerland 39/H4
Bell-Irving (riv.), Br. Col. 184/C2
Bellis, Alberta 182/D2
Belliveau Cove, Nova Scotia 168/B4
Bellmawr, N.J. 273/B3
Bellmead, Texas 303/H6
Bellmont, Ill. 222/F5
Bellmore, Ind. 227/C5
Bellmore, N.Y. 276/R7
Bello, Colombia 126/C4
Bello, Colombia 120/B2
Bellona (reefs), New Caled. 87/G8
Bellona (isl.), Solomon Is. 86/D3
Bellot (str.), N.W.T. 162/G1
Bellot (str.), N.W. Terr. 187/J2
Bellows Falls, Vt. 268/C5
Belloy, Alberta 182/A2
Bellport, N.Y. 276/P9
Bell Rock, N.W. Terr. 187/G3
Bell Rock (isl.), Scotland 15/F4
Bells, Tenn. 237/C9
Bells, Texas 303/H4
Bellsbank, Scotland 15/D5
Bellshill, Scotland 15/C2
Bellsite, Manitoba 179/B2
Bellsund, Norway 18/C2
Belluno (prov.), Italy 34/D1
Belluno, Italy 34/D1
Bellview, Ala. 195/D7
Bellview, N. Mex. 274/F4
Bell Villé, Argentina 143/D3
Bell Ville, Argentina 120/C6
Bellville, Georgia 217/H6
Bellville, Ohio 284/E4
Bellville, S. Africa 118/F6
Bellville, Texas 303/H8
Bellvue, Colo. 208/J1
Bellwald, Switzerland 39/F4
Bellwood, Ala. 195/G8
Bellwood, Ill. 222/B5
Bellwood, La. 238/D3
Bellwood, Nebr. 264/G3
Bellwood, Pa. 294/F4
Belly (riv.), Alberta 182/D5
Belmar, N.J. 273/E3
Bélmez, Spain 33/D3
Belmond, Iowa 229/F3
Belmont, Ala. 195/C5
Belmont, Calif. 204/J3
Belmont, Georgia 217/E2
Belmont, Kansas 232/D4
Belmont, Ky. 237/K5
Belmont, La. 238/C3
Belmont•, Maine 243/E7
Belmont, Manitoba 179/C5
Belmont•, Mass. 249/C6
Belmont, Miss. 256/H1
Belmont, Mont. 262/G4
Belmont•, N.H. 268/E5
Belmont, N.Y. 276/E6
Belmont, N. Zealand 100/B2
Belmont, N.C. 281/H4
Belmont, Nova Scotia 168/E3
Belmont (co.), Ohio 284/J5
Belmont, Ohio 284/J5
Belmont, Ontario 177/C5
Belmont, Wash. 310/H3
Belmont, W. Va. 312/D4
Belmont, Wis. 317/F10
Belmonte, Brazil 132/G6
Belmonte, Portugal 33/C2
Belmonte, Spain 33/E3
Belmopan (cap.), Belize 146/K8
Belmopan (cap.), Belize 154/C2
Belmore, N.S. Wales 97/J3
Belmore, Ohio 284/B3
Belmullet, Ireland 17/B3
Bel-Nor, Mo. 261/P2
Belo, W. Va. 312/B7
Beloeil, Belgium 27/D7
Beloeil, Québec 172/D4
Belogorsk, U.S.S.R. 54/O4
Belogorsk, U.S.S.R. 48/N4
Belogradchik, Bulgaria 45/F4
Belo Horizonte, Brazil 2/G6
Belo Horizonte, Brazil 120/E4
Belo Horizonte, Brazil 132/F7
Belo Horizonte, Brazil 135/D1
Beloit, Ala. 195/C6
Beloit, Kansas 232/D2
Beloit, Ohio 284/J4
Beloit, Wis. 188/J2
Beloit, Wis. 317/H10
Belomorsk, U.S.S.R. 48/D3
Belomorsk, U.S.S.R. 52/D2
Belorado, Spain 33/E1
Belorechensk, U.S.S.R. 52/E6
Beloretsk, U.S.S.R. 52/J4
Beloretsk, U.S.S.R. 48/F4
Belorussian S.S.R., U.S.S.R. 7/G3
Belorussian S.S.R., U.S.S.R. 48/C4
Belorussian S.S.R., U.S.S.R. 52/C4
Belo-Tsiribihina, Madagascar 118/G3
Belovo, U.S.S.R. 48/J4
Beloye (lake), U.S.S.R. 48/D3
Beloye (lake), U.S.S.R. 52/E2
Belozersk, U.S.S.R. 52/E3
Belp, Switzerland 39/D3
Belpre, Kansas 232/C4
Belpre, Ohio 284/G7
Bel-Ridge, Mo. 261/P2
Belshaw, Ind. 227/C2
Belt, Mont. 262/E3
Belted (range), Nev. 266/E5
Belterra, Brazil 132/C3
Belton, Ky. 237/H6
Belton, Mo. 261/C5
Belton, S.C. 296/C2
Belton, Texas 303/G7
Beltra (lake), Ireland 17/C4
Beltrami (co.), Minn. 255/C2
Beltrami, Minn. 255/B3
Beltsville, Md. 245/G3
Bel'tsy, U.S.S.R. 7/G4
Bel'tsy, U.S.S.R. 52/C5
Belturbet, Ireland 17/G3
Beluga (lake), Alaska 196/B1
Belumut, Gunong (mt.), Malaysia 72/D7
Belush'ya Guba, U.S.S.R. 4/B7
Belush'ya Guba, U.S.S.R. 52/H1
Belva, W. Va. 312/D6
Belvedere, Calif. 204/H2
Belvedere, Georgia 217/L1
Belvidere, Ill. 222/E1
Belvidere, Kansas 232/C4
Belvidere, Nebr. 264/G4
Belvidere, N.J. 273/C2
Belvidere, N.C. 281/S2
Belvidere, S. Dak. 298/G6
Belvidere, Tenn. 237/J10
Belvidere•, Vt. 268/B2
Belvidere (mt.), Vt. 268/B2
Belvidere Center, Vt. 268/B2
Belvidere Junction, Vt. 268/B2
Belview, Minn. 255/C6
Belville, N.C. 281/N6
Belvue, Kansas 232/F2
Belwood, N.C. 281/F4
Belwood, Ontario 177/D4
Belyando (riv.), Queensland 88/H4
Belyando (riv.), Queensland 95/C4
Belyy (isl.), U.S.S.R. 4/B6
Belyy (isl.), U.S.S.R. 48/G2
Belzoni, Miss. 256/C4
Belzoni, Okla. 288/R6
Bełżyce, Poland 47/F3
Bem, Mo. 261/K6
Bembe, Angola 115/B5
Bemboka, N.S. Wales 97/E5
Bement, Ill. 222/E4
Bemersyde, Sask. 181/J5
Bemidji, Minn. 255/D3
Bemidji (lake), Minn. 255/D3
Bemis, S. Dak. 298/R4
Bemiss, Georgia 217/F9
Bemmel, Netherlands 27/H5
Bemus Point, N.Y. 276/B6
Bena, Minn. 255/D3
Benabarre, Spain 33/G1
Bena-Dibele, Zaire 115/D4
Ben Alder (mt.), Scotland 15/D4
Benalla, Victoria 97/D5
Benalto, Alberta 182/C3
Benanee, N.S. Wales 97/B4
Benares (Varanasi), India 68/E3
Benavente, Spain 33/D1
Benavides, Texas 303/F10
Ben Avon, Pa. 294/B6
Ben Avon (mt.), Scotland 15/E3
Ben Barvas (mt.), Scotland 15/B2
Benbecula (isl.), Scotland 15/A3
Benbecula (isl.), Scotland 10/C2
Benbrook, Texas 303/E2
Benbrook (lake), Texas 303/E3
Benchland, Mont. 262/F3
Ben Cruachan (mt.), Scotland 15/C4
Bencubbin, W. Australia 92/B5
Bend, Oreg. 188/B2
Bend, Oreg. 291/F3
Bend, Texas 303/F7
Ben Dash (hill), Ireland 17/C6
Ben Davis (pt.), N.J. 273/C5
Bendel (state), Nigeria 106/F7
Bendemeer, N.S. Wales 97/F2
Bendena, Kansas 232/G2
Bender Beila, Somalia 115/K2
Bender Beila, Somalia 102/G4
Bender Cassim (Bosaso), Somalia 115/J1
Bendersville, Pa. 294/H6
Bendery, U.S.S.R. 52/C5
Bendigo, Australia 87/E9
Bendigo, Victoria 88/G7
Bendigo, Victoria 97/C5
Bendoc, Victoria 97/E5
Bendon, Mich. 250/D4
Bendorf, Germany 22/B3
Bene Beraq, Israel 65/B3
Benedict (pond), Conn. 210/C1
Benedict, Kansas 232/G4
Benedict, Md. 245/M6
Benedict, Minn. 255/D3
Benedict, Nebr. 264/G3
Benedict (mt.), Newf. 166/C3
Benedict, N. Dak. 282/H4
Benedicta•, Maine 243/G4
Beneditinos, Brazil 132/F4
Benenitra, Madagascar 118/H4
Benešov, Czech. 41/C2
Beneveian, Loch (lake), Scotland 15/D3
Benevento (prov.), Italy 34/E4
Benevento, Italy 34/E4
Benevolence, Georgia 217/C7
Benewah (co.), Idaho 220/B2
Benezett, Pa. 294/F3
Benfica, Portugal 33/A1
Benfleet, England 13/J8
Benga, Mozambique 118/E3
Bengal (bay) 54/K8
Bengal, Bay of (sea) 2/P5
Bengal, Bay of (sea), Bangladesh 68/F5
Bengal, Bay of (sea), Burma 72/B3
Bengal, Bay of (sea), India 68/F5
Bengal, Ind. 227/F6
Bengal, Okla. 288/R5
Ben Gardane, Tunisia 106/G2
Bengbis, Cameroon 115/B3
Bengbu (Pengpu), China 77/J5
Benge, Wash. 310/G4
Benggala (str.), Indonesia 85/A4
Benghazi, Libya 2/L4
Benghazi, Libya 102/D1
Benghazi, Libya 111/C1
Ben Ghnema, Jebel (mts.), Libya 111/C2
Bengkalis, Indonesia 85/C5
Bengkayang, Indonesia 85/E5
Bengkulu, Indonesia 85/C6
Bengo (prov.), Angola 115/B5
Bengough, Sask. 181/F6
Ben Griam More (mt.), Scotland 15/D2
Bengtsfors, Sweden 18/H7
Benguela (prov.), Angola 115/B6
Benguela, Angola 115/B6
Benguela, Angola 102/D6
Ben Guerdane (well), Mauritania 106/B3
Benguet (prov.), Philippines 82/C2
Benha, Egypt 111/J3
Benham, Ky. 237/R7
Benham, N.C. 281/G2
Benhams, Va. 307/D7
Ben Hee (mt.), Scotland 15/D2
Ben Hill (co.), Georgia 217/F7
Ben Hope (mt.), Scotland 15/D2
Ben Horn (mt.), Scotland 15/D2
Ben Hur, Va. 307/B7
Beni, El (dept.), Bolivia 136/C3
Beni (riv.), Bolivia 120/C4
Beni (riv.), Bolivia 136/B2
Beni, Zaire 115/E3
Beni Abbès, Algeria 106/D2
Benicarló, Spain 33/G2
Benicia, Calif. 204/K1
Benicito (riv.), Bolivia 136/C3
Beni Mazar, Egypt 111/J4
Beni Mellal, Morocco 106/C2
Beni Mellal, Morocco 102/B1
Benin 2/K5
Benin 102/C4
BENIN 106/E7
Benin (bight), Benin 106/E8
Benin (bight), Ghana 106/E8
Benin (bight), Nigeria 106/E8
Benin (bight), Togo 106/E8
Benin City, Nigeria 106/F7
Benin City, Nigeria 102/C4
Beni Ounif, Algeria 106/D2
Beni Saf, Algeria 106/D1
Beni Suef, Egypt 111/J3
Beni Suef, Egypt 102/E2
Beni Suef, Egypt 59/B4
Benito, Manitoba 179/A3
Beni Ulid, Libya 111/B1
Benjamín (isl.), Chile 138/D5
Benjamin, New Bruns. 170/D1
Benjamin (lake), Oreg. 291/G4
Benjamin, Texas 303/E4
Benjamin, Utah 304/C3
Benjamín Aceval, Paraguay 144/C4
Benjamin Constant, Brazil 132/G9
Benjamin Constant, Brazil 120/B3
Benjamín Hill, Mexico 150/D1
Benkelman, Nebr. 264/C4
Ben Kilbreck (mt.), Scotland 15/D2
Ben Lawers (mt.), Scotland 15/D4
Benld, Ill. 222/D4
Ben Lomond, Ark. 202/B6
Ben Lomond, Calif. 204/K4
Ben Lomond, New Bruns. 170/E3
Ben Lomond (mt.), Scotland 15/D4
Ben Loyal (mt.), Scotland 15/D2
Ben Lui (mt.), Scotland 15/D4
Ben Macdhui (mt.), Scotland 15/E3
Ben Mhor (mt.), Scotland 15/A3
Ben More (mt.), Scotland 15/D4
Ben More (mt.), Scotland 15/B4
Ben More Assynt (mt.), Scotland 15/D2
Bennan (head), Scotland 15/C5
Bennane (head), Scotland 15/C5
Benndale, Miss. 256/G9
Bennet, Nebr. 264/H4
Bennett, Br. Col. 184/J1
Bennett, W.A.C. (dam), Br. Col. 184/F2
Bennett, Colo. 208/L3
Bennett (peak), Colo. 208/G7
Bennett (creek), Idaho 220/C6
Bennett, Iowa 229/L5
Bennett, N.C. 281/K3
Bennett (lake), North. Terr. 93/B7
Bennett (co.), S. Dak. 298/F7
Bennett, Wis. 317/C3
Bennettsbridge, Ireland 17/G6
Bennetts Point, S.C. 296/G6
Bennetts Switch, Ind. 227/E3
Bennettsville, S.C. 296/H2
Bennettville, Minn. 255/E4
Ben Nevis (mt.), Scotland 7/D3
Ben Nevis (mt.), Scotland 15/D4
Ben Nevis (mt.), Scotland 10/D2
Benning, D.C. 245/F5
Bennington, Idaho 220/G7
Bennington, Ind. 227/G7
Bennington, Kansas 232/E2
Bennington, Nebr. 264/H3
Bennington•, N.H. 268/D5
Bennington, Okla. 288/P7
Bennington (co.), Vt. 268/A6
Bennington, Vt. 268/A6
Bennington•, Vt. 268/A6
Benns Church, Va. 307/P7
Benoit, Miss. 256/C3
Benoit, Wis. 317/D3
Benom, Gunong (mt.), Malaysia 72/D7
Benoni, S. Africa 118/J6
Bensenville, Ill. 222/B5
Bensheim, Germany 22/C4
Benson, Ariz. 198/E7
Benson, Ill. 222/D3
Benson, La. 238/C3
Benson, Minn. 255/C5
Benson, N.C. 281/N4
Benson (co.), N. Dak. 282/M3
Benson (Hollsopple), Pa. 294/E5
Benson, Sask. 181/J6
Benson•, Vt. 268/A4
Benson Landing, Vt. 268/A4
Bens Run, W. Va. 312/D4
Bent (co.), Colo. 208/N7
Bent, N. Mex. 274/D5
Bent Creek, Va. 307/L5
Benteng, Indonesia 85/F7
Bentham, England 13/E3
Bentheim, Germany 22/B2
Bentiaba, Angola 114/B6
Bentinck (isl.), Burma 72/C5
Bentinck (isl.), Queensland 88/F3
Bentinck (isl.), Queensland 95/A3
Bentiu, Sudan 111/E6
Bentley, Alberta 182/C3
Bentley, Ill. 222/B3
Bentley, Iowa 229/B6
Bentley, Kansas 232/E4
Bentley, La. 238/E3
Bentley, Mich. 250/E5
Bentley, N. Dak. 282/F7
Bentley, Okla. 288/O6
Bentley Springs, Md. 245/M2
Bentleyville, Ohio 284/J9
Bentleyville, Pa. 294/B5
Bentley with Arksey, England 13/F4
Bent Mountain, Va. 307/H6
Bento Gonçalves, Brazil 132/C10
Benton, Ala. 195/E6
Benton, Alberta 182/E4
Benton (co.), Ark. 202/B1
Benton, Ark. 202/E4
Benton, Calif. 204/G6
Benton, Ill. 222/E6
Benton (co.), Ind. 227/C3
Benton, Ind. 227/F2
Benton (co.), Iowa 229/J4
Benton, Iowa 229/E7
Benton, Kansas 232/E4
Benton, Ky. 237/E7
Benton, La. 238/C1
Benton•, Maine 243/D6
Benton (co.), Minn. 255/D5
Benton, Minn. 255/F6
Benton (lake), Minn. 255/B6
Benton (co.), Miss. 256/F1
Benton, Miss. 256/D5
Benton (co.), Mo. 261/F6
Benton, Mo. 261/O8
Benton (lake), Mont. 262/E3
Benton, New Bruns. 170/C3
Benton•, N.H. 268/D3
Benton, Ohio 284/G4
Benton (co.), Oreg. 291/D3
Benton, Pa. 294/K3
Benton (co.), Tenn. 237/E8
Benton, Tenn. 237/M10
Benton (co.), Wash. 310/F4
Benton, Wis. 317/F10
Benton City, Mo. 261/J4
Benton City, Wash. 310/F4
Bentong, Malaysia 72/D7
Benton Harbor, Mich. 250/C6
Benton Heights, Mich. 250/C6
Bentonia, Miss. 256/D5
Benton Ridge, Ohio 284/C4
Bentonsport, Iowa 229/K7
Bentonville, Ark. 202/B1
Bentonville, Ind. 227/G5
Bentonville, Ohio 284/C8
Bentonville, Va. 307/M3
Bent's Old Fort Nat'l Hist. Site, Colo. 208/M6
Benué (riv.), Cameroon 115/A2
Benue (state), Nigeria 106/F7
Benue (riv.), Nigeria 102/C4
Benue (riv.), Nigeria 106/F7
Ben Vorlich (mt.), Scotland 15/D4
Ben Vrackie (mt.), Scotland 15/E4
Benwee (head), Ireland 17/B3
Benwood, W. Va. 312/E2
Ben Wyvis (mt.), Scotland 15/D3
Benxi (Penki), China 77/K3
Benxi, China 54/O5
Benzie (co.), Mich. 250/C4
Benzonia, Mich. 250/D4
Beo, Indonesia 85/H5
Beograd (Belgrade) (cap.), Yugoslavia 45/E3
Beowawe, Nev. 266/E2
Beppu, Japan 81/E7
Bequia (isl.), St. Vin. & Grens. 156/G4
Beragh, N. Ireland 17/G2
Berar (reg.), India 68/D4
Berat, Albania 45/D5
Berau (bay), Indonesia 85/J6
Berber, Sudan 111/F4
Berber, Sudan 59/B6
Berber, Sudan 102/F3
Berbera, Somalia 115/J1
Berbera, Somalia 102/G3
Berberati, Cent. Afr. Rep. 102/D4
Berberati, Cent. Afr. Rep. 115/C3
Berbice (riv.), Guyana 131/B3
Berchem, Belgium 27/F6
Berchem-Sainte-Agathe, Belgium 27/B9
Bercher, Switzerland 39/C3
Berchtesgaden, Germany 22/E5
Berck, France 28/D2
Berclair, Texas 303/G9
Berdichev, U.S.S.R. 48/C5
Berdichev, U.S.S.R. 52/C5
Berdsk, U.S.S.R. 48/J4
Berdyansk, U.S.S.R. 7/H4
Berdyansk, U.S.S.R. 52/E5
Berea, Ky. 237/N5
Berea, Nebr. 264/A2
Berea, N.C. 281/M2
Berea, Ohio 284/G10
Berea, S.C. 296/C2
Berea, Spain 33/C1
Berea, W. Va. 312/E4
Bereda, Somalia 115/K1
Bereda, Somalia 102/H3
Beregovo, U.S.S.R. 52/B5
Berekum, Ghana 106/D7
Berenguela, Bolivia 136/A5
Berenice (ruins), Egypt 111/F3
Berens (riv.), Man. 162/G5
Berens (isl.), Manitoba 179/E2
Berens (riv.), Manitoba 179/F2
Berens (riv.), Ontario 175/A2
Berens River, Man. 162/G5
Berens River, Manitoba 179/F2
Beresford (lake), Fla. 212/E3
Beresford, New Bruns. 170/E1
Beresford, S. Dak. 298/R7
Beresford Lake, Manitoba 179/G4
Bereşti Tîrg, Romania 45/H2
Berettyó (riv.), Hungary 41/F3
Berettyóújfalu, Hungary 41/F3
Berezina (riv.), U.S.S.R. 52/C4
Bereznik, U.S.S.R. 52/F2
Berezniki, U.S.S.R. 7/K3
Berezniki, U.S.S.R. 48/F4
Berezniki, U.S.S.R. 52/J3
Berezovo, U.S.S.R. 48/G3
Berg, Norway 18/K2
Berg, Switzerland 39/H1
Berga, Algeria 106/E3
Berga, Spain 33/G1
Bergama, Turkey 63/B3
Bergama, Turkey 59/A2
Bergamo (prov.), Italy 34/B2
Bergamo, Italy 34/B2
Bergeijk, Netherlands 27/G6
Bergen (Mons), Belgium 27/E8
Bergen, Germany 22/E1
Bergen, Minn. 255/D7
Bergen, Netherlands 27/F3
Bergen (co.), N.J. 273/E2
Bergen, N.Y. 276/E4
Bergen, N. Dak. 282/J3
Bergen, Norway 18/D6
Bergen, Norway 7/E2
Berg en Dal, Suriname 131/D3
Bergenfield, N.J. 273/C1
Bergen op Zoom, Netherlands 27/E5
Berger, Mo. 261/K5
Bergerac, France 28/D5
Bergholz, Ohio 284/J4
Bergisch Gladbach, Germany 22/B3
Bergland, Mich. 250/F1
Bergman, Ark. 202/E1
Bergoo, W. Va. 312/F6
Bergos (riv.), Turkey 63/C6
Bergshamra, Sweden 18/L7
Bergsjö, Sweden 18/K5
Bergstrom A.F.B., Texas 303/G7
Bergton, Va. 307/L3
Berguent, Morocco 106/D2
Bergum, Netherlands 27/H2
Bergumermeer (lake), Netherlands 27/J2
Bergün-Bravuogn, Switzerland 39/J3
Berhala (str.), Indonesia 85/C6
Berhampore, India 68/F4
Berhampur, India 68/F5
Berhida, Hungary 41/E3
Bering (sea) 2/A3
Bering (sea) 54/V4
Bering (sea) 146/A3
Bering (str.) 4/C18
Bering (str.) 54/W3
Bering (str.) 146/B3
Bering (glac.), Alaska 196/K2
Bering (sea), Alaska 188/C6
Bering (sea), Alaska 196/D2
Bering (str.), Alaska 188/C5
Bering (str.), Alaska 196/E1
Bering (isl.), U.S.S.R. 48/R4
Bering (sea), U.S.S.R. 48/S4
Bering (str.), U.S.S.R. 48/U3
Beringen, Belgium 27/G6
Bering Land Bridge Nat'l Pres., Alaska 196/F1
Beringovskiy, U.S.S.R. 48/T3
Berino, N. Mex. 274/C6
Berja, Spain 33/E4
Berkåk, Norway 18/G5
Berkel, Netherlands 27/F5
Berkeley, Calif. 188/B3
Berkeley, Calif. 204/J2
Berkeley, Ill. 222/B5
Berkeley, Mo. 261/P2
Berkeley (co.), S.C. 296/G5
Berkeley (co.), W. Va. 312/K4
Berkeley, W. Va. 312/L4
Berkeley Heights•, N.J. 273/E2
Berkeley Lake, Georgia 217/D3
Berkeley Springs, W. Va. 312/K3
Berken, Libya 111/B2
Berkey, Ohio 284/C2
Berkhamsted, England 13/G7
Berkhout, Netherlands 27/F3
Berkley, Iowa 229/E5
Berkley•, Mass. 249/K5
Berkley, Mich. 250/B6
Berkner (isl.), Ant. 2/G10
Berkner (isl.), Ant. 5/B16
Berkovitsa, Bulgaria 45/F4
Berks (co.), Pa. 294/K5
Berkshire, Conn. 210/B3
Berkshire (co.), England 13/F6
Berkshire (co.), Mass. 249/B3
Berkshire (hills), Mass. 249/B4
Berkshire, N.Y. 276/H6
Berkshire•, Vt. 268/B2
Berland (riv.), Alberta 182/A3
Berlanga de Duero, Spain 33/E2
Berleburg (Bad Berleburg), Germany 22/C3
Berlevåg, Norway 18/Q1
Berlin•, Conn. 210/E2
Berlin, Georgia 217/E8
Berlin (cap.), Germany 7/F3
Berlin (cap.), Germany 2/K3
Berlin (cap.), Germany 22/F4
Berlin (state), Germany 22/F4
Berlin, Ill. 222/D4

338 Berlin

Berlin, Md. 245/T7
Berlin•, Mass. 249/H3
Berlin (mt.), Nev. 266/D4
Berlin, N.H. 188/M2
Berlin, N.H. 268/E3
Berlin, N.J. 273/D4
Berlin, N.Y. 276/O5
Berlin, N. Dak. 282/O7
Berlin, Ohio 284/G4
Berlin (lake), Ohio 284/H4
Berlin, Okla. 288/G4
Berlin, Pa. 294/E6
Berlin (pond), Vt. 268/B3
Berlin, W. Va. 312/F4
Berlin, Wis. 317/H8
Berlin Center, Ohio 284/J3
Berlin Heights, Ohio 284/F3
Bermagui, N.S. Wales 97/F5
Bermeja (pt.), Argentina 143/D5
Bermejo (riv.), Argentina 120/C5
Bermejo (riv.), Argentina 143/E2
Bermejo (riv.), Bolivia 136/C8
Bermen (lake), Québec 174/D2
Bermeo, Spain 33/E1
Bermillo de Sayago, Spain 33/D2
Bermuda (isl.) (U.K.) 2/F4
Bermuda (isls.) 146/M6
BERMUDA 156/G3
Bermuda, Ala. 195/D8
Bermuda (isl.), Bermuda 156/H3
Bermuda, La. 238/D3
Bern, Idaho 220/G7
Bern, Kansas 232/F2
Bern (canton), Switzerland 39/D2
Bern (cap.), Switzerland 7/E4
Bern (cap.), Switzerland 39/D3
Bernabé Rivera, Uruguay 145/B1
Bernadotte, Minn. 255/D6
Bernalillo (co.), N. Mex. 274/C4
Bernalillo, N. Mex. 274/C3
Bernard, Iowa 229/M4
Bernardino de Sahagún, Mexico 150/M1
Bernardo, N. Mex. 274/C4
Bernardo de Irigoyen, Argentina 143/F2
Bernardston•, Mass. 249/D2
Bernardsville, N.J. 273/D2
Bernasconi, Argentina 143/D4
Bernau bei Berlin, Germany 22/E2
Bernay, France 28/D3
Bernburg, Germany 22/D3
Berndorf, Austria 41/C3
Berne, Ind. 227/H3
Berne, N.Y. 276/M5
Bernera (isl.), Scotland 15/B2
Berneray (isl.), Scotland 15/A4
Berneray (isl.), Scotland 15/A3
Bernese Oberland (reg.), Switzerland 39/E3
Bernhards Bay, N.Y. 276/J4
Bernic (lake), Manitoba 179/G4
Bernice, La. 238/E1
Bernice, Okla. 288/S1
Bernic Lake, Manitoba 179/G4
Bernie, Mo. 261/M9
Bernier (bay), N.W. Terr. 187/K2
Bernier (isl.), W. Australia 88/A4
Bernier (isl.), W. Australia 92/A4
Bernierville, Québec 172/F3
Bernina (pass), Italy 34/C1
Bernina, Piz (peak), Italy 34/B1
Bernina (mts.), Switzerland 39/J4
Bernina (pass), Switzerland 39/K4
Bernina (peak), Switzerland 39/J4
Bernina (riv.), Switzerland 39/J4
Bernkastel-Kues, Germany 22/B4
Bernstadt, Ky. 237/N6
Bernville, Pa. 294/K5
Bero (riv.), Angola 115/B7
Beromünster, Switzerland 39/F2
Beroroha, Madagascar 118/G4
Beroun, Czech. 41/B2
Beroun, Minn. 255/F5
Berounka (riv.), Czech. 41/C2
Berovo, Yugoslavia 45/F5
Berre (lag.), France 28/F6
Berri, S. Australia 88/G6
Berri, S. Australia 94/G6
Berridale, N.S. Wales 97/E5
Berriedale, Scotland 15/E2
Berrien (co.), Georgia 217/F8
Berrien (co.), Mich. 250/C7
Berrien Springs, Mich. 250/C7
Berrigan, N.S. Wales 97/C4
Berrondo, Uruguay 145/C5
Berry, Ala. 195/C3
Berry (creek), Alberta 182/E4
Berry (isls.), Bahamas 156/B1
Berry (head), England 13/D7
Berry (trad. prov.) France 29
Berry, Ky. 237/N3
Berry, N.S. Wales 97/F4
Berry (head), Nova Scotia 168/G3
Berryessa (lake), Calif. 204/D5
Berry Hill, Tenn. 237/H8
Berry Mills, New Bruns. 170/E2
Berrymoor, Alberta 182/C3
Berrysburg, Pa. 294/J4
Berry's Chapel, Tenn. 237/H9
Berrys Lick, Ky. 237/H6
Berryton, Georgia 217/B2
Berryton, Kansas 232/G3
Berryville, Ark. 202/C1
Berryville, Va. 307/M2
Berseba, Namibia 118/B5
Bertha, Minn. 255/C4
Berthier (co.), Québec 172/C3
Berthier (county), Québec 174/B3
Berthier-en-Bas, Québec 172/G3
Berthierville, Québec 172/D3
Berthold, N. Dak. 282/G3
Berthoud, Colo. 208/J2
Berthoud Pass, Colo. 208/H3
Bertie (co.), N.C. 281/P2
Bertogne, Belgium 27/H8
Bertolinia, Brazil 132/F4
Bertoua, Cameroon 115/B3
Bertraghboy (bay), Ireland 17/A5
Bertram, Iowa 229/K5
Bertram, Texas 303/F7
Bertrand, Cerro (mt.), Chile 138/D8
Bertrand, Mo. 261/O9
Bertrand, Nebr. 264/E4
Bertrand, New Bruns. 170/E1
Bertrandville, La. 238/L7
Bertrix, Belgium 27/G9
Bertwell, Sask. 181/J3
Beru (atoll), Kiribati 87/H6
Beruni, U.S.S.R. 48/G5
Bervie, Ontario 177/C3
Berwick, Ill. 222/C3
Berwick, Iowa 229/G5
Berwick, Kansas 232/G2
Berwick, La. 238/H7
Berwick, Maine 243/B9
Berwick•, Maine 243/B9
Berwick, New Bruns. 170/E3
Berwick, N. Dak. 282/K3
Berwick, Nova Scotia 168/D4
Berwick, Pa. 294/K3
Berwick (trad. co.), Scotland 15/B5
Berwick, Victoria 97/K6
Berwick-upon-Tweed, England 13/F2
Berwick-upon-Tweed, England 10/F3
Berwind, W. Va. 312/C8
Berwyn, Alberta 182/B1
Berwyn, Ill. 222/B6
Berwyn, Nebr. 264/E3
Berwyn, Pa. 294/L5
Berwyn (mts.), Wales 13/D5
Berwyn Heights, Md. 245/G4
Beryl, Utah 304/A6
Beryl, W. Va. 312/H4
Berzence, Hungary 41/D3
Besalampy, Madagascar 118/G3
Besançon, France 28/G4
Besançon, France 7/E4
Beşiktaş, Turkey 63/D6
Beşiri, Turkey 63/J4
Beskids, West (mts.), Czech. 41/E2
Beskids, East (mts.), Czech. 41/F1
Beskids (range), Poland 47/D4
Beslan, U.S.S.R. 52/F6
Besni, Turkey 63/G4
Besor (riv.), Israel 65/B5
Bessbrook, N. Ireland 17/J3
Bessèges, France 28/F5
Bessemer, Ala. 188/J4
Bessemer, Ala. 195/D4
Bessemer, Mich. 250/F2
Bessemer, Pa. 294/B4
Bessemer City, N.C. 281/G4
Bessie, Okla. 288/H4
Best, Texas 303/C6
Beswick, North. Terr. 88/E2
Beswick Aboriginal Res., North. Terr. 88/E2
Beswick Aboriginal Res., North. Terr. 93/C3
Beta, N.C. 281/C4
Betanzos, Bolivia 136/C6
Betanzos, Spain 33/B1
Bétaré-Oya, Cameroon 115/B2
Bete Grise (bay), Mich. 250/B1
Bethalto, Ill. 222/B2
Bethanie, Namibia 118/B5
Bethany (res.), Calif. 204/L2
Bethany•, Conn. 210/C3
Bethany, Ill. 222/E4
Bethany, Ind. 227/E5
Bethany, La. 238/B2
Bethany, Manitoba 179/C4
Bethany, Minn. 255/F6
Bethany, Mo. 261/E2
Bethany, Ohio 284/B7
Bethany, Okla. 288/L3
Bethany, Ontario 177/F3
Bethany, Pa. 294/M2
Bethany, Sask. 181/F3
Bethany, W. Va. 312/E2
Bethany Beach, Del. 245/T6
Bethel, Alaska 188/C6
Bethel, Alaska 196/F2
Bethel, Conn. 210/B3
Bethel•, Conn. 210/B3
Bethel, Del. 245/R6
Bethel, Ky. 237/O4
Bethel, Maine 243/B7
Bethel•, Maine 243/B7
Bethel, Minn. 255/E5
Bethel, Mo. 261/J3
Bethel, N.Y. 276/L7
Bethel, N.C. 281/P3
Bethel, Ohio 284/B8
Bethel, Okla. 288/S6
Bethel, Pa. 294/K5
Bethel, Vt. 268/B4
Bethel•, Vt. 268/B4
Bethel, Wis. 317/F6
Bethel Acres, Okla. 288/M4
Bethel Heights, Ark. 202/B1
Bethel Island, Calif. 204/L1
Bethel Park, Pa. 294/B7
Bethelridge, Ky. 237/M6
Bethel Springs, Tenn. 237/D10
Bethel Town, Jamaica 158/G6
Bethera, S.C. 296/H5
Bethesda, Ark. 202/G2
Bethesda, Md. 245/E4
Bethesda, Ohio 284/H5
Bethesda, Wales 13/D4
Bethlehem, Conn. 210/C2
Bethlehem•, Conn. 210/C2
Bethlehem, Georgia 217/E3
Bethlehem, Ind. 227/G7
Bethlehem, Iowa 229/G7
Bethlehem, Ky. 237/L4
Bethlehem, Md. 245/P6
Bethlehem, Miss. 256/F1
Bethlehem•, N.H. 268/D3
Bethlehem, Pa. 294/M4
Bethlehem, S. Africa 102/E7
Bethlehem, S. Africa 118/D5
Bethlehem, Virgin Is. (U.S.) 161/E4
Bethlehem, West Bank 65/C4
Bethlehem, W. Va. 312/E2
Bethpage, N.Y. 276/R7
Bethpage, Tenn. 237/J7
Bethulie, S. Africa 118/D6
Bethune, Colo. 208/P4
Béthune, France 28/E2
Bethune, Sask. 181/F5
Bethune, S.C. 296/G3
Betijoque, Venezuela 124/C3
Betim, Brazil 135/D2
Betioky, Madagascar 118/G4
Betoota, Queensland 95/B5
Bet-Pak-Dala (des.), U.S.S.R. 48/H5
Bet Qama, Israel 65/B5
Betroka, Madagascar 118/H4
Bet She'an, Israel 65/D3
Bet Shemesh, Israel 65/B4
Betsiamites (riv.), Que. 162/J5
Betsiamites, Québec 174/D3
Betsiamites (riv.), Québec 174/C2
Betsiboka (riv.), Madagascar 118/H3
Betsy Layne, Ky. 237/R5
Bette (peak), Libya 102/D2
Bette (peak), Libya 111/C3
Bettendorf, Iowa 229/N5
Betteravia, Calif. 204/E9
Betterton, Md. 245/O3
Bettiah, India 68/E3
Bettlach, Switzerland 39/D2
Bettles, Alaska 196/H1
Bettles Field, Alaska 196/H1
Bettsville, Ohio 284/D3
Bettyhill, Scotland 15/D2
Betul, India 68/D4
Betula, Pa. 294/F2
Betwa (riv.), India 68/D4
Between, Georgia 217/E3
Betws-y-Coed, Wales 13/D4
Betzdorf, Germany 22/B3
Beulah, Ala. 195/H5
Beulah, Colo. 208/K6
Beulah, Manitoba 179/A4
Beulah, Mich. 250/C4
Beulah, Miss. 256/B3
Beulah, Mo. 261/J7
Beulah, N. Dak. 282/G5
Beulah, Oreg. 291/J4
Beulah (res.), Oreg. 291/J4
Beulah, Victoria 97/B4
Beulah (lake), Wis. 317/J2
Beulah, Wyo. 319/H1
Beulaker Wijde (lake), Netherlands 27/H3
Beulaville, N.C. 281/O5
Beuthen (Bytom), Poland 47/A3
Bevans, N.J. 273/D1
Bevent, Wis. 317/H6
Beveren, Belgium 27/E6
Beverin (peak), Switzerland 39/H3
Beverley, England 10/F4
Beverley, England 13/G4
Beverley, Sask. 181/C5
Beverley, W. Australia 92/B1
Beverly, C. Rica 154/F6
Beverly, Kansas 232/E2
Beverly, Ky. 237/P7
Beverly, Mass. 249/E5
Beverly, Mo. 261/O4
Beverly, N.J. 273/D3
Beverly (lake), N.W. Terr. 187/H3
Beverly, Ohio 284/G6
Beverly, Wash. 310/F4
Beverly, W. Va. 312/G5
Beverly Beach, Fla. 212/E2
Beverly Hills, Calif. 204/B10
Beverly Hills, Mich. 250/B6
Beverly Shores, Ind. 227/C1
Beverwijk, Netherlands 27/F4
Bevier, Mo. 261/G3
Bevington, Iowa 229/F6
Bewdley, England 13/E5
Bewdley, England 10/F3
Bewdley, Ontario 177/F3
Bex, Switzerland 39/D4
Bexar, Ala. 195/B2
Bexar (co.), Texas 303/F8
Bexhill, England 13/H7
Bexhill, England 10/G5
Bexley, England 13/H8
Bexley, England 10/C5
Bexley, Miss. 256/G9
Bexley, Ohio 284/E6
Bey (mts.), Turkey 63/D4
Bey el Kebir, Wadi (dry riv.), Libya 111/B1
Beykoz, Turkey 63/D5
Beyla, Guinea 106/C7
Beylerbeyi, Turkey 63/D6
Beynon, Alberta 182/D4
Beyoğlu, Turkey 63/D6
Beypazarı, Turkey 59/B1
Beypazarı, Turkey 63/D2
Beyşehir, Turkey 59/B2
Beyşehir, Turkey 63/D4
Beyşehir (lake), Turkey 63/D4
Beytüşşebap, Turkey 63/K4
Bezanson, Alberta 182/A2
Bezhetsk, U.S.S.R. 52/E3
Béziers, France 7/E4
Béziers, France 28/E6
Bhadrak, India 68/F4
Bhadravati, India 68/D6
Bhadreswar, India 68/F1
Bhag, Pakistan 68/B3
Bhag, Pakistan 59/J4
Bhagalpur, India 68/F4
Bhaktapur, Nepal 68/F3
Bhaktapur, Nepal 68/F3
Bhamo, Burma 72/C1
Bhandara, India 68/E4
Bhandup, India 68/B7
Bhanjanagar, India 68/E4
Bharatpur, India 68/D3
Bharuch, India 68/C4
Bhatapara, India 68/E4
Bhatinda, India 68/C2
Bhatkal, India 68/C6
Bhatpara, India 68/F1
Bhavnagar, India 68/C4
Bhavnagar, India 54/J7
Bhawanipatna, India 68/E5
Bhera, Pakistan 68/C2
Bheri (riv.), Nepal 68/E3
Bhilai, India 68/E4
Bhilwara, India 68/C3
Bhima (riv.), India 68/D5
Bhimavaram, India 68/E5
Bhimunipatnam, India 68/E5
Bhind, India 68/D3
Bhinmal, India 68/C3
Bhir (Bir), India 68/D5
Bhiwandi, India 68/C5
Bhiwani, India 68/D3
Bhojpur, Nepal 68/F3
Bhopal, India 54/J7
Bhopal, India 68/D4
Bhor, India 68/C5
Bhubaneswar, India 68/F4
Bhuj, India 68/B4
Bhusawal, India 68/D4
Bhutan 2/P4
Bhutan 54/L7
BHUTAN 68/G3
Biafra (bight), Cameroon 115/A3
Biafra (bight), Equat. Guinea 115/A3
Biafra (bight), Nigeria 106/F8
Biak, Indonesia 85/K6
Biak (isl.), Indonesia 85/K6
Biała Podlaska (prov.), Poland 47/F3
Biała Podlaska, Poland 47/F3
Białogard, Poland 47/C1
Białystok (prov.), Poland 47/F2
Białystok, Poland 47/F2
Białystok, Poland 7/G3
Biancavilla, Italy 34/E6
Biarritz, France 28/C6
Bias, W. Va. 312/B7
Biasca, Switzerland 39/H4
Biba, Egypt 111/J4
Bibai, Japan 81/L2
Bibala, Angola 115/B6
Bibb (co.), Ala. 195/D5
Bibb (co.), Georgia 217/E5
Bibb City, Georgia 217/B5
Bibbenluke, N.S. Wales 97/E5
Biberach an der Riss, Germany 22/C4
Biberist, Switzerland 39/D2
Bible Grove, Ill. 222/E5
Bible Hill, Nova Scotia 168/E3
Bic, Québec 172/J1
Bic (isl.), Québec 172/J1
Bicas, Brazil 135/E2
Bicaz, Romania 45/G2
Bicester, England 13/F6
Biche (lake), Alberta 182/E2
Biche, Trin. & Tob. 161/B10
Bicheno, Tasmania 99/E3
Bickerdike, Alberta 182/B3
Bickerton (isl.), North. Terr. 93/E2
Bickerton West, Nova Scotia 168/G3
Bickleigh, Sask. 181/C4
Bickleton, Wash. 310/E5
Bickmore, W. Va. 312/D6
Bicknell, Ind. 227/C7
Bicknell, Utah 304/C5
Bicske, Hungary 41/E3
Bida, Nigeria 106/F7
Bidar, India 68/D5
Biddeford, Maine 243/B9
Biddeford, Maine 188/N2
Biddeford Pool, Maine 243/C9
Biddinghuizen, Netherlands 27/H4
Biddle, Mont. 262/L5
Biddu, West Bank 65/C4
Biddulph, England 13/H2
Bidean nam Bian (mt.), Scotland 15/D4
Bide Arm, Newf. 166/C3
Bideford, England 13/C6
Bideford, England 10/D5
Bidokht, Iran 66/L3
Bidon 5 (Poste Maurice Cordier), Algeria 106/E4
Bidwell, Ohio 284/F8
Bidyadhari (riv.), India 68/F2
Bié (prov.), Angola 115/C6
Bieber, Calif. 204/D2
Biebrza (riv.), Poland 47/F2
Biel, Switzerland 39/D2
Bielawa, Poland 47/C3
Bield, Manitoba 179/A3
Bieldside, Scotland 15/F3
Bielefeld, Germany 22/C2
Bieler (lake), N.W. Terr. 187/L2
Bielersee (lake), Switzerland 39/D2
Biella, Italy 34/B2
Bielsko (prov.), Poland 47/D4
Bielsko-Biała, Poland 47/D4
Bielsk Podlaski, Poland 47/F2
Biencourt, Québec 172/J2
Bienfait, Sask. 181/J6
Bien Hoa, Vietnam 72/E5
Bienvenue, Fr. Guiana 131/E4
Bienville, Lac (lake), Que. 162/J4
Bienville (par.), La. 238/D2
Bienville, La. 238/D2
Bienville (lake), Québec 174/C2
Bière, Switzerland 39/B3
Bietigheim-Bissingen, Germany 22/C4
Bietschhorn (mt.), Switzerland 39/E4
Bièvre, Belgium 27/F9
Bièvres, France 28/A2
Big (isl.), Alberta 182/B5
Big (creek), Ontario 220/C4
Big (creek), Ind. 227/B8
Big (brook), Maine 243/E2
Big (lake), Maine 243/H5
Big (pond), Mass. 249/B4
Big (riv.), Mo. 261/L6
Big (lake), Mont. 262/G5
Big (mt.), Nev. 266/B1
Big (bay), Newf. 166/B2
Big (isl.), Newf. 166/B2
Big (riv.), Newf. 166/C3
Big (isl.), N.W. Terr. 187/L3
Biga, Turkey 63/B2
Bigadiç, Turkey 63/C3
Bigalı, Turkey 63/B6
Big Annemessex (riv.), Md. 245/P8
Big Antelope (creek), Oreg. 290/K5
Big Arm, Mont. 262/B3
Big Bald (mt.), New Bruns. 170/D1
Big Bar, Calif. 204/B3
Big Bar Creek, Br. Col. 184/F4
Big Basin, Calif. 204/J4
Big Bay, Mich. 250/B2
Big Bay (pt.), Mich. 250/B2
Big Bay de Noc (bay), Mich. 250/C3
Big Bear City, Calif. 204/J9
Big Bear Lake, Calif. 204/J9
Big Beaver, Sask. 181/F6
Bigbee, Ala. 195/B7
Bigbee Valley, Miss. 256/H4
Big Bell, W. Australia 92/B4
Big Belt (mts.), Mont. 262/E4
Big Bend (dam), S. Dak. 298/K5
Bigbend, W. Va. 312/D5
Big Bend, Wis. 317/K2
Big Bend City, Minn. 255/C5
Big Bend National Park, Texas 303/A8
Big Bend Nat'l Park, Texas 303/A8
Big Black (riv.), Maine 243/D2
Big Black (riv.), Miss. 256/C6
Big Black (creek), S.C. 296/G2
Big Black River, Manitoba 179/E1
Big Blue (riv.), Ind. 227/F5
Big Blue (riv.), Kansas 232/F1
Big Blue (riv.), Nebr. 264/H4
Big Boulder (creek), Idaho 220/B7
Big Bow, Kansas 232/A4
Big Bras d'Or, Nova Scotia 168/H2
Big Bureau (riv.), Ill. 222/D2
Big Burro (mts.), N. Mex. 274/A6
Bigbury (bay), England 13/C7
Big Cabin, Okla. 288/R1
Big Canoe (creek), Ala. 195/F3
Big Chimney, W. Va. 312/C6
Big Chino Wash (dry riv.), Ariz. 198/C3
Big Clifty, Ky. 237/J5
Big Coulee, Alberta 182/D2
Big Cove Tannery, Pa. 294/F6
Big Creek (lake), Ala. 195/B9
Big Creek, Calif. 204/F6
Big Creek, Idaho 220/C4
Big Creek, Ky. 237/O6
Big Creek, Miss. 256/F3
Big Creek, W. Va. 312/B7
Big Cypress (swamp), Fla. 212/E5
Big Cypress Nat'l Pres., Fla. 212/E5
Big Dry (creek), Mont. 262/K3
Big Eau Pleine (res.), Wis. 317/G6
Big Eddy, Br. Col. 184/H4
Big Elk (peak), Idaho 220/G6
Bigelow, Ark. 202/E3
Bigelow (brook), Conn. 210/G1
Bigelow (bight), Maine 243/C9
Bigelow (mt.), Maine 243/C5
Bigelow (bight), Mass. 249/M1
Bigelow, Minn. 255/C7
Bigelow, Mo. 261/B2
Big Falls, Minn. 255/E2
Big Falls, Wis. 317/H6
Big Flat, Ark. 202/F1
Big Flat (brook), N.J. 273/D1
Big Flats, N.Y. 276/G6
Bigfoot, Texas 303/F9
Big Fork, Ark. 202/B5
Bigfork, Minn. 255/E3
Big Fork (riv.), Minn. 255/E2
Bigfork, Mont. 262/C2
Big Four, W. Va. 312/C8
Bigga, N.S. Wales 97/E4
Biggar, Sask. 162/F5
Biggar, Sask. 181/C3
Biggar, Scotland 10/E3
Biggar, Scotland 15/E5
Bigge (range), Queensland 95/D5
Bigge (isl.), W. Australia 92/D1
Biggers, Ark. 202/J1
Biggleswade, England 10/F4
Biggleswade, England 13/G5
Big Goose (creek), Wyo. 319/E1
Big Grizzly (creek), Colo. 208/G1
Biggs, Calif. 204/D4
Biggs, Oreg. 291/G2
Biggs Field, Texas 303/A10
Biggsville, Ill. 222/C3
Big Hole (mts.), Idaho 220/G6
Big Hole (riv.), Mont. 262/C5
Big Hole Nat'l Battlefield, Mont. 262/C5
Bighorn (riv.) 188/E2
Big Horn (dam), Alberta 182/B3
Bighorn (range), Alberta 182/B3
Big Horn (mts.), Ariz. 198/B5
Big Horn (co.), Mont. 262/J5
Bighorn, Mont. 262/J4
Bighorn (lake), Mont. 262/H5
Bighorn (riv.), Mont. 262/J5
Big Horn (co.), Wyo. 319/E1
Big Horn, Wyo. 319/E1
Bighorn (basin), Wyo. 319/D1
Bighorn (lake), Wyo. 319/D1
Bighorn (mts.), Wyo. 319/E1
Bighorn (riv.), Wyo. 319/D1
Bighorn Canyon Nat'l Rec. Area, Mont. 262/H5
Bighorn Canyon Nat'l Rec. Area, Wyo. 319/D1
Big Indian, N.Y. 276/M6
Big Iron (riv.), Mich. 250/F1
Big Isaac, W. Va. 312/E4
Big Island, Ontario 177/G3
Big Island, Va. 307/K5
Big Lake, Alaska 196/B1
Big Lake, Alaska 196/J1
Big Lake, Minn. 255/E5
Big Lake, Texas 303/C6
Biglake, Wash. 310/C2
Big Lake Ranch, Br. Col. 184/G4
Bigler, Pa. 294/F4
Biglerville, Pa. 294/H6
Big Lick, Tenn. 237/L9
Big Lost (riv.), Idaho 220/E6
Big Moose, N.Y. 276/L3
Big Moose (lake), N.Y. 276/L3
Big Muddy (riv.), Ill. 222/D6
Big Muddy (riv.), Mont. 262/M2
Big Muddy (lake), Sask. 181/G6
Big Muskego (lake), Wis. 317/L2
Bignona, Senegal 106/A6
Big Oak Flat, Calif. 204/E6
Big Otter (riv.), Va. 307/K6
Big Otter, W. Va. 312/D5
Big Pine, Calif. 204/G6
Big Pine (key), Fla. 212/E7
Big Pine (creek), Ind. 227/C3
Big Pine, N.C. 281/D3
Big Piney, Mo. 261/H7
Big Piney, Wyo. 319/B3
Big Pipe (creek), Md. 245/K2
Big Plain, Ohio 284/D6
Bigpoint, Miss. 256/H9
Big Pond, Newf. 166/D2
Big Pond, Nova Scotia 168/H3
Big Pool, Md. 245/F2
Big Porcupine (creek), Mont. 262/J4
Big Prairie, Ohio 284/F4
Big Raccoon (creek), Ind. 227/C5
Big Rapids, Mich. 250/D5
Big Rib (riv.), Wis. 317/G5
Big Rideau (lake), Ontario 177/H3
Big River, Sask. 162/F5
Big River, Sask. 181/D2
Big Rock, Ill. 222/E2
Big Rock, Iowa 229/M5
Big Rock, Tenn. 237/F7
Big Rock, Va. 307/D6
Big Run, Pa. 294/E4
Big Sable (pt.), Mich. 250/C4
Big Sable (riv.), Mich. 250/C4
Big Sage (res.), Calif. 204/E2
Big Salmon (riv.), New Bruns. 170/E3
Big Sand (lake), Manitoba 179/H2
Big Sandy (riv.), Ariz. 198/B4
Big Sandy (creek), Colo. 208/N4
Big Sandy (riv.), Ky. 237/R4
Big Sandy (lake), Minn. 255/E4
Big Sandy, Mont. 262/G2
Big Sandy, Tenn. 237/E8
Big Sandy (riv.), Tenn. 237/E9
Big Sandy, Texas 303/J5
Big Sandy (riv.), W. Va. 312/A6
Big Sandy, Wyo. 319/C3
Big Sandy (res.), Wyo. 319/C3
Big Sandy (riv.), Wyo. 319/C3
Big Sioux (riv.), Iowa 229/A3
Big Sioux (riv.), S. Dak. 188/G2
Big Sioux (riv.), S. Dak. 298/S7
Big Sky, Mont. 262/E5
Big Smoky (valley), Nev. 266/D4
Big Southern (butte), Idaho 220/E6
Big Spencer (mt.), Maine 243/E4
Big Spring, Georgia 217/C5
Big Spring, Ky. 237/J5
Big Spring, Md. 245/G2
Big Spring, Tenn. 237/M10
Big Spring, Texas 188/F4
Big Spring, Texas 303/C5
Big Springs, Nebr. 264/B3
Big Springs, S. Dak. 298/S8
Big Springs, W. Va. 312/D5
Big Star (lake), Mich. 250/C5
Bigstick (lake), Sask. 181/B5
Big Stone, Alberta 182/E4
Bigstone (lake), Manitoba 179/J3
Bigstone (pt.), Manitoba 179/E2
Bigstone (riv.), Manitoba 179/J3
Big Stone (co.), Minn. 255/B5
Big Stone (lake), Minn. 255/B5
Big Stone (lake), S. Dak. 298/R3
Big Stone City, S. Dak. 298/S3
Big Stone Gap, Va. 307/C7
Big Sur, Calif. 204/D7
Big Thicket Nat'l Preserve, Texas 303/K7
Big Thompson (riv.), Colo. 208/H2
Big Timber, Mont. 262/G5
Big Timber (creek), N.J. 273/C4
Big Tracadie (riv.), New Bruns. 170/E1
Bigtrails, Wyo. 319/E2
Big Trout (lake), Ontario 177/F2
Big Trout (lake), Ontario 175/B2
Big Trout Lake, Ontario 175/C2
Big Valley, Alberta 182/D3
Big Walnut (creek), Ind. 227/D5
Big Walnut (creek), Ohio 284/E5
Big Water, Utah 304/C6
Big Wells, Texas 303/E9
Big Whiteshell Lake, Manitoba 179/G4
Big Wood (riv.), Idaho 220/D6
Bihać, Yugoslavia 45/B3
Bihar (state), India 68/F4
Bihar, India 68/F3
Biharamulo, Tanzania 115/F4
Biharkeresztes, Hungary 41/F3
Biharnagybajom, Hungary 41/F3
Bijagós (isls.), Guinea-Biss. 106/A6
Bijagós (isls.), Guinea-Biss. 102/A3
Bijapur, Karnataka, India 68/D5
Bijapur, Madhya Pradesh, India 68/E5
Bijar, Iran 66/E3
Bijeljina, Yugoslavia 45/D3
Bijelo Polje, Yugoslavia 45/D4
Bijiang, China 77/E6
Bijie, China 77/G6
Bijnor, India 68/D3
Bijou (creek), Colo. 208/L3
Bijou Hills, S. Dak. 298/L6
Bikaner, India 54/J7
Bikaner, India 68/C3
Bikar (atoll), Marshall Is. 87/H4
Bikin, U.S.S.R. 48/O5
Bikini (atoll), Marshall Is. 87/G4
Bikoro, Zaire 115/C4
Bikoro, Zaire 102/D5
Bilaspur, India 68/E4
Bilauktaung (range), Burma 72/C4
Bilauktaung (range), Thailand 72/C4
Bilbao, Spain 33/E1
Bilbao, Spain 7/D4
Bilecá, Yugoslavia 45/D4
Bilecik (prov.), Turkey 63/D2
Bilecik, Turkey 59/A1
Bilecik, Turkey 63/D2

Block Island 339

Biłgoraj, Poland 47/F3
Bilibino, U.S.S.R. 4/C1
Bilibino, U.S.S.R. 48/R3
Bilin, Burma 72/C3
Bílina, Czech. 41/B1
Biliran (isl.), Philippines 82/E5
Bill, Wyo. 319/G2
Billate (riv.), Ethiopia 111/G6
Billerica•, Mass. 249/J2
Billings (lake), Conn. 210/H2
Billings, Mo. 261/F8
Billings, Mont. 146/H5
Billings, Mont. 188/E1
Billings, Mont. 262/H5
Billings (co.), N. Dak. 282/D5
Billings, Okla. 288/M1
Billingsgate (isl.), Mass. 249/O5
Billingshurst, England 13/G6
Billingsley, Ala. 195/E5
Billiton (isl.), Indonesia 54/M10
Billiton (isl.), Indonesia 85/D6
Bill Williams (riv.), Ariz. 198/B4
Billy Clapp (lake), Wash. 310/F3
Bilma, Niger 102/D3
Bilma, Niger 106/G5
Biloela, Queensland 88/J4
Biloela, Queensland 95/D5
Biloku, Guyana 131/B5
Biloxi, Miss. 146/K6
Biloxi, Miss. 188/J4
Biloxi, Miss. 256/G10
Biltine, Chad 111/D5
Biltine, Chad 102/D3
Biltmore Forest, N.C. 281/E3
Bilwaskarma, Nicaragua 154/F3
Bilzen, Belgium 27/G7
Bim, W. Va. 312/C7
Biminis, The (isls.), Bahamas 156/B1
Bina-Itawa, India 68/D4
Binalbagan, Philippines 82/D5
Binalong, N.S. Wales 97/E4
Binboğa (mts.), Turkey 63/G3
Binbrook, Ontario 177/E4
Binche, Belgium 27/E8
Binda, N.S. Wales 97/E4
Bindloss, Alberta 182/E4
Bindoon, W. Australia 92/B1
Bindura, Zimbabwe 118/E3
Binéfar, Spain 33/G2
Binevenagh (mt.), N. Ireland 17/H1
Binford, N. Dak. 282/O4
Binga (mt.), Mozambique 118/E3
Bingara, N.S. Wales 97/F1
Bingen, Wash. 310/D5
Bingen, Germany 22/B4
Binger, Okla. 288/K4
Bingerville, Ivory Coast 106/D7
Bingham (co.), Idaho 220/F6
Bingham, Ill. 222/D4
Bingham, Maine 243/D5
Bingham•, Maine 243/D5
Bingham, Nebr. 264/B2
Bingham, N. Mex. 274/C5
Bingham, S.C. 296/H3
Bingham (canyon), Utah 304/B3
Bingham Lake, Minn. 255/C7
Binghamton, N.Y. 188/L2
Binghamton, N.Y. 276/J6
Bingöl (prov.), Turkey 63/J3
Bingöl (Çapakçur), Turkey 63/J3
Bingöl Dağları (mts.), Turkey 63/J3
Binhai, China 77/K5
Binh Long (An Loc), Vietnam 72/E5
Binh Son, Vietnam 72/F4
Binjai, Indonesia 85/B5
Binn, Switzerland 39/F4
Binnaway, N.S. Wales 97/E2
Binningen, Switzerland 39/D1
Binongko (isl.), Indonesia 85/G7
Binscarth, Manitoba 179/A4
Bintan (isl.), Indonesia 85/C5
Bintuhan, Indonesia 85/C6
Bintulu, Malaysia 85/E5
Binyamina, Israel 65/B2
Binyang, China 77/G7
Biobío (reg.), Chile 138/E1
Bío-Bío (riv.), Chile 138/E2
Biograd, Yugoslavia 45/B4
Bioko (isl.), Equat. Guinea 102/C4
Bioko (isl.), Equat. Guinea 115/A3
Bioko (terr.), Equat. Guinea 115/A3
Biola, Calif. 204/E7
Bippus, Ind. 227/F3
Bir, India 68/D5
Bira, U.S.S.R. 48/O5
Birag, Kuh-e (mts.), Iran 66/M7
Bir 'Ali, Yemen 59/E7
Birama (pt.), Cuba 158/G4
Birao, Cent. Afr. Rep. 115/D1
Biratnagar, Nepal 68/F3
Biratori, Japan 81/L2
Bir Bala, Iran 66/L8
Bir Bala, Iran 59/G4
Bircao, Somalia 115/H4
Birch (creek), Alaska 196/J1
Birch (hills), Alberta 182/A2
Birch (lake), Alberta 182/E3
Birch (mts.), Alberta 182/B5
Birch (riv.), Alberta 182/B5
Birch (creek), Idaho 220/F5
Birch (isl.), Manitoba 179/C2
Birch (lake), Minn. 255/G3
Birch (creek), Mont. 262/D2
Birch (lake), Sask. 181/C2
Birch (creek), Utah 304/B5
Birch (pt.), Wash. 310/C2
Birch Creek, Alaska 196/J1
Birch Creek (valley), Idaho 220/E5
Birch Creek (res.), Mont. 262/D2
Birchdale, Minn. 255/D2
Birch Harbor, Maine 243/H7
Birch Hills, Sask. 181/F3
Birchip, Victoria 97/B4
Birch Island, Br. Col. 184/H4
Birchleaf, Va. 307/D6
Birch River, Manitoba 179/A2
Birch River, W. Va. 312/E6
Birch Run, Mich. 250/F5
Birchtown, Nova Scotia 168/C5
Birch Tree, Mo. 261/K9
Birchwood, Tenn. 237/M10
Birchwood, Wis. 317/C4
Birchy Bay, Newf. 166/D4
Bird (isl.), La. 238/M8
Bird (creek), Okla. 288/O1
Bird City, Kansas 232/A2
Bird Cove, Newf. 166/C3
Bird Island, Minn. 255/D6
Birds, Ill. 222/F5
Birdsboro, Pa. 294/L5
Birdseye, Ind. 227/D8
Birds Hill, Manitoba 179/F4
Birdsnest, Va. 307/S6
Birdsong, Ark. 202/K3
Birdsville, Ky. 237/D6
Birdsville, Queensland 88/F5
Birdsville, Queensland 95/A5
Birdtail, Manitoba 179/B4
Birdum, North. Terr. 93/C3
Birdwood, S. Australia 94/C7
Birecik, Turkey 63/H4
Bir el Khzaim (well), Mauritania 106/C4
Bireuen, Indonesia 85/B4
Bir Ganduz (well), Western Sahara 106/A4
Birganj, Nepal 68/F3
Bir Hakeim (ruins), Libya 111/D1
Birigui, Brazil 135/A2
Birjand, Iran 66/L4
Birjand, Iran 59/G3
Birjand, Iran 54/G6
Birken, Br. Col. 184/F5
Birkenfeld, Oreg. 291/D1
Birkenfeld, Germany 22/B4
Birkenhead, England 13/G2
Birkenhead, England 10/F2
Birkenhead, N. Zealand 100/B1
Birkenhead Lake Prov. Park, Br. Col. 184/F5
Birkerød, Denmark 21/F6
Birket Qârûn (lake), Egypt 111/J3
Bir Ksaib Ounane (well), Mali 106/C4
Birksgate (range), S. Australia 94/A2
Bîrlad, Romania 45/H2
Bîrlad (riv.), Romania 45/H2
Birmingham, Ala. 146/K6
Birmingham, Ala. 188/J4
Birmingham, Ala. 195/D3
Birmingham, England 7/D3
Birmingham, England 10/G3
Birmingham, England 13/F5
Birmingham, Iowa 229/K7
Birmingham, Mich. 250/B6
Birmingham, Mo. 261/R5
Birmingham, N.J. 273/D4
Birmingham, Ohio 284/F3
Birmingham, Pa. 294/F4
Birmingham, Sask. 181/H5
Birmitrapur, India 68/E4
Bir Mogreïn, Mauritania 106/B3
Birnam, Scotland 15/E4
Birnamwood, Wis. 317/H6
Birney, Mont. 262/K5
Birnie, Manitoba 179/C4
Birnin Kebbi, Nigeria 106/E6
Birni-N'Konni, Niger 106/E6
Birni-N'Konni, Niger 102/C3
Bir Nzaran (well), Western Sahara 106/B4
Birobidzhan, U.S.S.R. 54/O5
Birobidzhan, U.S.S.R. 48/O5
Biron, Wis. 317/G7
Bir Ounane (well), Mali 106/D4
Birqin, West Bank 65/C3
Birr, Ireland 17/F5
Birr, Ireland 10/E4
Birregurra, Victoria 97/B6
Birrie (riv.), N.S. Wales 88/H5
Birrie (riv.), N.S. Wales 97/D1
Birrimbah, North. Terr. 93/C3
Birrindudu, North. Terr. 93/A5
Birriwa, N.S. Wales 97/E3
Birs (riv.), Switzerland 39/D2
Birsay, Sask. 181/D4
Birsk, U.S.S.R. 52/J3
Birta, Ark. 202/D3
Bir Taba, Egypt 59/B4
Bir Taba (well), Egypt 111/F2
Birtle, Manitoba 179/B4
Biru, China 77/D5
Biruaca, Venezuela 124/E4
Biržai, U.S.S.R. 53/C2
Bir Zeit, West Bank 65/C4
Bisbee, Ariz. 188/E4
Bisbee, Ariz. 198/F7
Bisbee, N. Dak. 282/M2
Biscarrosse (lake), France 28/C5
Biscay (bay) 2/J3
Biscay (bay) 7/D4
Biscay (bay), France 28/B5
Biscay, Minn. 255/D6
Biscay (bay), Spain 33/E1
Biscay Bay (riv.), Newf. 166/D2
Biscayne (bay), Fla. 212/F6
Biscayne (key), Fla. 212/B5
Biscayne Nat'l Park, Fla. 212/F6
Biscayne Park, Fla. 212/B4
Bisceglie, Italy 34/F4
Bischofshofen, Austria 41/B3
Bischofswerda, Germany 22/F3
Bischofszell, Switzerland 39/H1
Biscoe (isls.), Ant. 5/C15
Biscoe, Ark. 202/H4
Biscoe, N.C. 281/K4
Biscotasing, Ontario 177/J5
Biscotasing, Ontario 175/D3
Biscucuy, Venezuela 124/D3
Bisha, Saudi Arabia 59/D5
Bisha, Wadi (dry riv.), Saudi Arabia 59/D5
Bishiara (well), Libya 111/D3
Bisho, South Africa 118/D6
Bisho (cap.), Ciskei, S. Africa 102/E8
Bishop, Calif. 204/G6
Bishop, Georgia 217/F3
Bishop, Md. 245/S7
Bishop (creek), Nev. 266/F1
Bishop, Texas 303/G10
Bishop (creek), Utah 304/E3
Bishop, Va. 307/E6
Bishop Auckland, England 10/E3
Bishop Auckland, England 13/E3
Bishopbriggs, Scotland 15/B2
Bishop Hill, Ill. 222/C2
Bishopric, Sask. 181/F5
Bishop's Falls, Newf. 166/C4
Bishops Head, Md. 245/O7
Bishops Mitre (mt.), Newf. 166/B2
Bishop's Stortford, England 10/G5
Bishop's Stortford, England 13/H6
Bishopton, Québec 172/F4
Bishopton, Scotland 15/B2
Bishopville, Md. 245/T7
Bishopville, S.C. 296/G3
Bishri, Jebel el (mts.), Syria 63/H5
Biskra, Algeria 106/F2
Biskra, Algeria 102/C1
Biskupiec, Poland 47/E2
Bislig, Philippines 85/H4
Bislig, Philippines 82/F6
Bismarck, Ark. 202/D5
Bismarck, Ill. 222/F3
Bismarck, Mo. 261/L7
Bismarck (cap.), N. Dak. 146/H5
Bismarck (cap.), N. Dak. 188/G1
Bismarck (cap.), N. Dak. 282/J6
Bismarck (arch.), Papua N.G. 2/S6
Bismarck (arch.), Papua N.G. 87/E6
Bismarck (arch.), Papua N.G. 86/B1
Bismarck (sea), Papua N.G. 86/B1
Bismarck, W. Va. 312/H4
Bismil, Turkey 63/J4
Bison (lake), Alberta 182/B1
Bison, Kansas 232/C3
Bison, Okla. 288/L2
Bison, S. Dak. 298/E2
Bispgården, Sweden 18/K5
Bissau (cap.), Guinea-Biss. 106/A6
Bissau (cap.), Guinea-Biss. 102/A3
Bissett, Manitoba 179/G4
Bistineau (lake), La. 238/D2
Bistrița, Romania 45/G2
Bita (riv.), Colombia 126/F5
Bitagron, Suriname 131/C3
Bitam, Gabon 115/B3
Bitburg, Germany 22/B4
Bitely, Mich. 250/D5
Bithlo, Fla. 212/E3
Bitkine, Chad 111/C5
Bitlis (prov.), Turkey 63/J3
Bitlis, Turkey 63/J3
Bitlis, Turkey 59/D2
Bitola, Yugoslavia 45/E5
Bitola, Yugoslavia 7/G4
Bitonto, Italy 34/F4
Bitter (lakes), Egypt 111/K3
Bitter (lake), Sask. 181/B5
Bitter (creek), Wyo. 319/C4
Bitter Creek, Wyo. 319/D4
Bitterfeld, Germany 22/E3
Bitterfontein, S. Africa 118/B6
Bittern (lake), Alberta 182/D3
Bittern Lake, Alberta 182/D3
Bitterroot (range) 188/D1
Bitterroot (range), Idaho 220/D3
Bitterroot (range), Mont. 262/B4
Bitterroot (riv.), Mont. 262/B4
Bitterroot (range), U.S. 146/G5
Bitti, Italy 34/B4
Bitumount, Alberta 182/E1
Bitung, Indonesia 85/H5
Biu, Nigeria 106/G6
Biu (plat.), Nigeria 106/G6
Bivalve, Md. 245/P7
Bivalve, N.J. 273/C5
Bivolari, Romania 45/H2
Biwa (lake), Japan 81/H6
Biwabik, Minn. 255/F3
Bixby, Minn. 255/E7
Bixby, Mo. 261/K7
Bixby, Okla. 288/P3
Biyang, China 77/H5
Biysk, U.S.S.R. 54/K4
Biysk, U.S.S.R. 48/J4
Bizcocho, Uruguay 145/B4
Bizerte, Tunisia 106/F1
Bizerte, Tunisia 102/C1
Bjargtangar (pt.), Iceland 21/A1
Bjelovar, Yugoslavia 45/C3
Bjerringbro, Denmark 21/C5
Bjorkdale, Sask. 181/H3
Bjørnafjorden (fjord), Norway 18/D6
Bjorne (pen.), N.W. Terr. 187/K2
Bjørnøya (isl.), Norway 18/D3
Blabon, N. Dak. 282/P5
Blachly, Oreg. 291/D3
Black (sea) 2/L3
Black (sea) 54/E5
Black (sea) 7/H4
Black, Ala. 195/G8
Black (riv.), Alaska 196/K1
Black (mesa), Ariz. 198/E2
Black (mts.), Ariz. 198/A3
Black (riv.), Ariz. 198/E5
Black (riv.), Ark. 202/H2
Black (sea), Bulgaria 45/J4
Black (pt.), Conn. 210/G3
Black (pond), Conn. 210/G1
Black (mts.), England 13/D6
Black (creek), Fla. 212/E1
Black (for.), Germany 22/C4
Black (head), Ireland 17/C5
Black (riv.), Jamaica 158/H6
Black (mt.), Ky. 237/R7
Black (lake), La. 238/D3
Black (pond), Maine 243/D3
Black (isl.), Manitoba 179/F3
Black (riv.), Manitoba 179/F4
Black (lake), Mich. 250/E3
Black (riv.), Mich. 250/E3
Black (riv.), Mich. 250/G5
Black (riv.), Minn. 255/D2
Black (creek), Miss. 256/F8
Black, Mo. 261/L7
Black (riv.), Mo. 261/L10
Black (mt.), N. Mex. 274/A6
Black (range), N. Mex. 274/B5
Black (lake), N.Y. 276/J1
Black (riv.), N.Y. 276/K3
Black (riv.), N.C. 281/N5
Black (riv.), Ohio 284/F3
Black (riv.), Ontario 177/E3
Black (sea), Romania 45/J4
Black (lake), Sask. 181/M2
Black (riv.), S.C. 296/H4
Black (sea), Turkey 63/E1
Black (sea), U.S.S.R. 48/D5
Black (sea), U.S.S.R. 52/D6
Black (creek), Vt. 268/B2
Black (riv.), Vt. 268/C2
Black (riv.), Vt. 268/B5
Black (riv.), Vietnam 72/D2
Black (mts.), Wales 13/D6
Black (riv.), Wis. 317/E7
Black (riv.), Yukon 187/D3
Blackall, Australia 87/E8
Blackall, Queensland 88/H4
Blackall, Queensland 95/C5
Black Bear (creek), Okla. 288/M2
Blackberry (riv.), Conn. 210/B1
Blackbird, Del. 245/R3
Blackbourne (pt.), Norfolk I. 88/L6
Black Branch, Nulhegan (riv.), Vt. 268/D2
Blackburn (mt.), Alaska 196/K2
Blackburn, England 13/H1
Blackburn, England 10/G1
Blackburn, La. 238/D1
Blackburn, Mo. 261/F4
Blackburn, Okla. 288/N2
Blackburn, Ontario 177/J2
Blackburn, Scotland 15/C2
Black Butte (lake), Calif. 204/C4
Black Canyon City, Ariz. 198/C4
Black Canyon of the Gunnison Nat'l Mon., Colo. 208/D5
Black Creek, Br. Col. 184/E5
Black Creek, N.C. 281/O3
Black Creek, Wis. 317/K7
Black Diamond, Alberta 182/C4
Black Diamond, Wash. 310/D3
Blackduck, Minn. 255/D3
Black Duck (riv.), Ontario 175/C1
Black Eagle, Mont. 262/E3
Black Earth, Wis. 317/G9
Black Elster (riv.), Germany 22/E3
Blackey, Ky. 237/R6
Blackfalds, Alberta 182/D3
Blackfeet Ind. Res., Mont. 262/D2
Blackfoot, Alberta 182/E3
Blackfoot, Idaho 220/F6
Blackfoot (res.), Idaho 220/G7
Blackfoot (riv.), Idaho 220/G6
Blackfoot, Mont. 262/D2
Blackfoot (riv.), Mont. 262/C4
Blackford (co.), Ind. 227/G4
Blackford, Ky. 237/F6
Blackford, Scotland 15/E4
Black Forest, Colo. 208/K4
Blackfork, Ohio 284/E8
Black Fork, Mohican (riv.), Ohio 284/F4
Blackgum, Okla. 288/S3
Black Hall, Conn. 210/F3
Black Hawk, Colo. 208/J3
Blackhawk, Ind. 227/C6
Black Hawk (co.), Iowa 229/J4
Black Hawk, Miss. 256/E4
Black Hawk, S. Dak. 298/C5
Blackhead (bay), Newf. 166/D2
Blackhead Road, Newf. 166/D2
Black Hills (mts.) 188/F2
Black Hills (mts.), S. Dak. 298/B5
Blackie, Alberta 182/D4
Black Isle (pen.), Scotland 15/D3
Black Jack, Mo. 261/R1
Black Lake (bayou), La. 238/D1
Black Lake, Québec 172/F3
Black Lake, Sask. 181/M2
Blackledge (riv.), Conn. 210/F2
Black Lick, Pa. 294/D4
Blacklock (pt.), Oreg. 291/C5
Black Mesa (mt.), Okla. 288/A1
Blackmore (mt.), Mont. 262/F5
Black Mountain, N.C. 281/E3
Black Oak, Ark. 202/K2
Black Oak, Ind. 227/C1
Black Pine (mts.), Idaho 220/E7
Black Pine (peak), Idaho 220/E7
Black Pine (creek), S. Dak. 298/G6
Black Point, Calif. 204/J1
Black Point, Conn. 210/G3
Black Point, New Bruns. 170/D1
Blackpool, England 13/G1
Blackpool, England 10/F1
Blackridge, Va. 307/M7
Black River, Jamaica 158/H6
Black River, Jamaica 156/B3
Black River (bay), Jamaica 158/G6
Black River, Mich. 250/F4
Black River, New Bruns. 170/E3
Black River (pond), Newf. 166/C2
Black River, N.Y. 276/J3
Black River Bridge, New Bruns. 170/E2
Black River Falls, Wis. 317/E7
Black Rock, Ark. 202/H1
Black Rock (des.), Nev. 266/B2
Black Rock (range), Nev. 266/B1
Black Rock (pt.), R.I. 249/H8
Black Rock, Utah 304/B5
Blacksburg, S.C. 296/D1
Blacksburg, Va. 307/H6
Blacks Fork, Green (riv.), Wyo. 319/C4
Blacks Harbour, New Bruns. 170/D3
Blackshear, Georgia 217/H8
Blackshear (lake), Georgia 217/E7
Blacksher, Ala. 195/C8
Blacksod (bay), Ireland 17/A3
Black Springs, Ark. 202/C5
Black Springs, Nev. 266/B3
Black Squirrel (creek), Colo. 208/L5
Blackstairs (mt.), Ireland 17/H6
Blackstock, Ontario 177/F3
Blackstock, S.C. 296/E2
Blackstone•, Mass. 249/H4
Blackstone (riv.), Mass. 249/G3
Blackstone, Va. 307/N6
Blacksville, W. Va. 312/F3
Black Thunder (creek), Wyo. 319/G2
Black Tickle, Newf. 166/C3
Blackton, Ark. 202/H4
Blacktown, N.S. Wales 88/K4
Blacktown, N.S. Wales 97/H3
Blackville, New Bruns. 170/E2
Blackville, S.C. 296/E5
Black Volta (riv.) 102/B3
Black Volta (Mouhoun) (riv.), Burkina Faso 106/D6
Black Volta (riv.), Ghana 106/D6
Black Volta (riv.), Ivory Coast 106/D6
Black Warrior (riv.), Ala. 195/C5
Blackwater (riv.), England 13/H6
Blackwater (riv.), Fla. 212/B6
Blackwater, Ireland 17/J7
Blackwater (riv.), Ireland 10/B4
Blackwater (riv.), Ireland 17/D7
Blackwater (riv.), Ireland 17/H4
Blackwater, Mo. 261/G5
Blackwater (res.), N.H. 268/D5
Blackwater (riv.), N. Ireland 17/H3
Blackwater, Queensland 95/D4
Blackwater, Queensland 88/H4
Blackwater (res.), Scotland 15/D4
Blackwater, Va. 307/B7
Blackwater (riv.), Va. 307/J6
Blackwater (riv.), Va. 307/O6
Blackwell, Ark. 202/E3
Blackwell (brook), Conn. 210/H1
Blackwell, Okla. 288/M1
Blackwell, Texas 303/D5
Blackwell, Wis. 317/J4
Blackwood (Ngundju) (cape), Indonesia 85/F8
Blackwood, N.J. 273/C4
Blackwood Terrace, N.J. 273/C4
Bladen, Nebr. 264/F4
Bladen (co.), N.C. 281/M5
Bladenboro, N.C. 281/M5
Bladensburg, Md. 245/G4
Bladensburg, Ohio 284/F5
Blades, Del. 245/R6
Bladon Springs, Ala. 195/B7
Bladworth, Sask. 181/E4
Blaeberry, Br. Col. 184/J4
Blaenavon, Wales 13/B6
Blagodarnoye, U.S.S.R. 52/F5
Blagoevgrad, Bulgaria 45/F5
Blagoveshchensk, U.S.S.R. 54/O4
Blagoveshchensk, U.S.S.R. 48/N4
Blagoveshchensk, U.S.S.R. 52/J4
Blain, France 28/C4
Blain, Pa. 294/H5
Blaine, Georgia 217/C1
Blaine (co.), Idaho 220/D6
Blaine, Kansas 232/F2
Blaine, Ky. 237/R4
Blaine•, Maine 243/H2
Blaine, Mich. 250/G5
Blaine, Minn. 255/G5
Blaine, Miss. 256/C3
Blaine (co.), Mont. 262/G2
Blaine (co.), Nebr. 264/E3
Blaine, Ohio 284/J5
Blaine (co.), Okla. 288/K3
Blaine, Oreg. 291/D2
Blaine, Tenn. 237/O8
Blaine, Wash. 310/C2
Blaine Lake, Sask. 181/D3
Blaine-Mars Hill, Maine 243/H2
Blainville, Québec 172/H4
Blair, Kansas 232/H2
Blair, Nebr. 264/H3
Blair, Okla. 288/H5
Blair (co.), Pa. 294/F4
Blair, S.C. 296/E3
Blair, W. Va. 312/C7
Blair, Wis. 317/D7
Blair Athol, Queensland 95/C4
Blair Atholl, Scotland 10/E2
Blair Atholl, Scotland 15/E4
Blairgowrie and Rattray, Scotland 15/E4
Blairgowrie and Rattray, Scotland 10/E2
Blairmore, Alberta 182/C5
Blairs, Va. 307/K7
Blairsburg, Iowa 229/F4
Blairsden, Calif. 204/E4
Blairs Mills, Ky. 237/P4
Blairs Mills, Pa. 294/G5
Blairstown, Iowa 229/J5
Blairstown, Mo. 261/E5
Blairstown•, N.J. 273/C2
Blairsville, Georgia 217/E1
Blairsville, Pa. 294/D5
Blaisdell, N. Dak. 282/F3
Blaj, Romania 45/F2
Blake (pt.), Mich. 250/E1
Blakeley, Minn. 255/E6
Blakeley, W. Va. 312/D6
Blakely, Georgia 217/C8
Blakely, Pa. 294/F6
Blakesburg, Iowa 229/H7
Blakeslee, Ohio 284/A2
Blakeslee, Pa. 294/L3
Blaketown, Newf. 166/D2
Blalock, Ala. 195/D6
Blalock, Georgia 217/E1
Blalock (isl.), Wash. 310/F5
Blanc (cape) 2/J4
Blanc (mt.), France 7/E4
Blanc (mt.), France 28/G5
Blanc (mt.), Italy 34/A2
Blanc (cape), Mauritania 102/A2
Blanc (cape), Mauritania 106/A4
Blanc (cape), Tunisia 106/G1
Blanc (cape), Western Sahara 106/A4
Blanca (bay), Argentina 120/C6
Blanca (bay), Argentina 143/D4
Blanca (lag.), Chile 138/E10
Blanca (peak), Colo. 188/F3
Blanca, Colo. 208/H8
Blanca (peak), Colo. 208/H7
Blanca (pt.), C. Rica 154/F5
Blanca, Cordillera (mts.), Peru 128/D7
Blanch, N.C. 281/L2
Blanchard, Idaho 220/A1
Blanchard, Iowa 229/C7
Blanchard, La. 238/C1
Blanchard•, Maine 243/D5
Blanchard, Mich. 250/D5
Blanchard, N. Dak. 282/R5
Blanchard (riv.), Ohio 284/C4
Blanchard, Okla. 288/L4
Blanchard, Pa. 294/G3
Blanchard, Wash. 310/C2
Blanchardstown, Ireland 17/H5
Blanchardville, Wis. 317/G10
Blanche, Ky. 237/O7
Blanche (riv.), Québec 172/E2
Blanche (lake), S. Australia 88/F5
Blanche (lake), S. Australia 94/F3
Blanche, Tenn. 237/H10
Blanche (lake), W. Australia 88/C4
Blanche Marie (fall), Suriname 131/C3
Blanchester, Ohio 284/B7
Blanchisseuse, Trin. & Tob. 161/B10
Blanco (riv.), Argentina 143/C2
Blanco (riv.), Bolivia 136/D4
Blanco (lake), Chile 138/F10
Blanco (cape), C. Rica 154/E6
Blanco (peak), C. Rica 154/F6
Blanco (riv.), Mexico 150/Q2
Blanco, N. Mex. 274/B2
Blanco (creek), N. Mex. 274/F4
Blanco, Okla. 288/P5
Blanco (cape), Oreg. 188/A2
Blanco (cape), Oreg. 291/C5
Blanco (cape), Peru 128/B5
Blanco (riv.), Peru 128/F6
Blanco (co.), Texas 303/F8
Blanco, Texas 303/F7
Blanc-Sablon, Québec 174/F2
Bland, Mo. 261/J6
Bland (co.), Va. 307/F6
Bland, Va. 307/F6
Blandburg, Pa. 294/F4
Blandford•, Mass. 249/C4
Blandford, Nova Scotia 168/D4
Blandford Forum, England 13/E7
Blandford Forum, England 10/E5
Blanding, Utah 304/E6
Blandinsville, Ill. 222/C3
Blandville, Ky. 237/D7
Blanefield, Scotland 15/B1
Blanes, Spain 33/H2
Blaney Park, Mich. 250/D2
Blanford, Ind. 227/B5
Blankenberge, Belgium 27/C6
Blankenburg am Harz, Germany 22/D3
Blanket, Texas 303/F6
Blanquillo, Uruguay 145/D3
Blansko, Czech. 41/D2
Blanton, Ala. 195/H5
Blanton, Fla. 212/D3
Blantyre, Malawi 115/F7
Blantyre, Malawi 102/F6
Blantyre, Scotland 15/B2
Blarney, Ireland 10/B5
Blarney, Ireland 17/D8
Blas (peak), Switzerland 39/G3
Blasdell, N.Y. 276/C5
Blasket (isls.), Ireland 10/A4
Blasket (isls.), Ireland 17/A7
Blatná, Czech. 41/B2
Blato, Yugoslavia 45/C4
Blatten, Switzerland 39/E4
Blaubeuren, Germany 22/C4
Blauvelt, N.Y. 276/K8
Blåvands Huk (pt.), Denmark 21/A6
Blawenburg, N.J. 273/D3
Blawnox, Pa. 294/C6
Blaydon, England 10/F3
Blaydon, England 13/H3
Blaye, France 28/C5
Blayney, N.S. Wales 97/E3
Blaze (pt.), North. Terr. 88/D2
Blaze (pt.), North. Terr. 93/A2
Bleckley (co.), Georgia 217/F6
Bled, Yugoslavia 45/A2
Bledsoe (co.), Tenn. 237/L9
Bledsoe, Texas 303/A4
Bleecker, Ala. 195/H5
Blekinge (co.), Sweden 18/J8
Blencoe, Iowa 229/A5
Blenheim, N. Zealand 100/D4
Blenheim, Ontario 177/C5
Blenheim, S.C. 296/H2
Blenker, Wis. 317/F6
Blennerhassett (isl.), Ohio 284/G7
Blerick, Netherlands 27/J6
Blesbok (riv.), S. Africa 118/J7
Blessing, Texas 303/H9
Blessington, Ireland 17/J5
Blevins, Ark. 202/C6
Blewett, Texas 303/D8
Blida, Algeria 106/E1
Blida, Algeria 102/C1
Bligh (sound), N. Zealand 100/A6
Bligh Water (bay), Fiji 86/P10
Blind Channel, Br. Col. 184/E5
Blind River, Ont. 162/H6
Blind River, Ontario 177/J5
Blind River, Ontario 175/D3
Blinman, S. Australia 88/F6
Blinman, S. Australia 94/F4
Blinnenhorn (mt.), Switzerland 39/F4
Bliss, Idaho 220/D7
Bliss, N.Y. 276/D5
Blissfield, Mich. 250/F7
Blissfield, New Bruns. 170/D2
Blissfield, Ohio 284/G5
Blitar, Indonesia 85/K2
Blitchton, Georgia 217/J6
Blocher, Ind. 227/F7
Block (isl.), R.I. 249/H8
Blocker, Okla. 288/P4
Block House, Nova Scotia 168/D4
Block Island (sound), N.Y. 276/S8
Block Island, R.I. 249/H8
Block Island (sound), R.I. 249/H8

Blockton, Iowa 229/D7
Blodgett, Mo. 261/O8
Blodgett, Oreg. 291/D3
Blodgett Landing, N.H. 268/D5
Bloemendaal, Netherlands 27/E4
Bloemfontein, S. Africa 102/E7
Bloemfontein, S. Africa 118/C5
Blois, France 28/D4
Blokzijl, Netherlands 27/H3
Bl'onie, Poland 47/E2
Bloodroot (mt.), Vt. 268/B4
Bloodsworth (isl.), Md. 245/O8
Bloodvein (riv.), Manitoba 179/F3
Bloodvein (riv.), Ontario 175/A2
Bloodvein River, Manitoba 179/F3
Bloody Foreland (prom.), Ireland 17/E1
Bloody Foreland (prom.), Ireland 10/B3
Bloom, Kansas 232/C4
Bloom, N. Dak. 282/N6
Bloomburg, Texas 303/L4
Bloom City, Wis. 317/E8
Bloomdale, Ohio 284/D3
Bloomer, Ark. 202/B3
Bloomer, Wis. 317/D5
Bloomery, W. Va. 312/K4
Bloomfield, Sierra (mts.), Bolivia 136/D4
Bloomfield•, Conn. 210/E1
Bloomfield, Ind. 227/D6
Bloomfield, Iowa 229/J7
Bloomfield, Ky. 237/L5
Bloomfield, Mo. 261/M9
Bloomfield, Mont. 262/M3
Bloomfield, Nebr. 264/G2
Bloomfield, Newf. 166/D2
Bloomfield, N.J. 273/B2
Bloomfield, N. Mex. 274/A2
Bloomfield, Ontario 177/G4
Bloomfield (New Bloomfield), Pa. 294/H5
Bloomfield•, Vt. 268/D2
Bloomfield Hills, Mich. 250/B6
Bloomfield Ridge, New Bruns. 170/D2
Bloomfield Station, New Bruns. 170/E3
Bloomingburg, N.Y. 276/L7
Bloomingburg, Ohio 284/D6
Bloomingdale, Georgia 217/K6
Bloomingdale, Ill. 222/A5
Bloomingdale, Ind. 227/C5
Bloomingdale, Mich. 250/C6
Bloomingdale, N.J. 273/E1
Bloomingdale, N.Y. 276/M2
Bloomingdale, Ohio 284/J5
Bloomingdale, Tenn. 237/R7
Bloomingdale, Wis. 317/E8
Blooming Grove, Pa. 227/G5
Blooming Grove, Pa. 294/M3
Blooming Grove, Texas 303/H5
Bloomingport, Ind. 227/G5
Blooming Prairie, Minn. 255/E7
Bloomington, Calif. 204/E10
Bloomington, Idaho 220/G7
Bloomington, Ill. 188/J2
Bloomington, Ill. 222/D3
Bloomington, Ind. 227/D6
Bloomington, Md. 245/B3
Bloomington, Minn. 255/G6
Bloomington, Nebr. 264/F4
Bloomington, Texas 303/H9
Bloomington, Wis. 317/E10
Bloomington Springs, Tenn. 237/K8
Blooming Valley, Pa. 294/B2
Bloomsburg, Pa. 294/J3
Bloomsbury, Alberta 182/C2
Bloomsbury, N.J. 273/C2
Bloomsdale, Mo. 261/M6
Bloomville, N.Y. 276/L6
Bloomville, Ohio 284/D3
Blora, Indonesia 85/K2
Blossburg, Pa. 294/H2
Blossom, Texas 303/J4
Bloubergstrand, S. Africa 118/E6
Blount (co.), Ala. 195/E2
Blount (co.), Tenn. 237/O9
Blounts Creek, N.C. 281/P4
Blount Springs, Ala. 195/E3
Blountstown, Fla. 212/A1
Blountsville, Ala. 195/E2
Blountsville, Ind. 227/G4
Blountville, Tenn. 237/S7
Blowering (res.), N.S. Wales 97/E4
Blowing Rock, N.C. 281/F2
Bloxom, Va. 307/S5
Bludenz, Austria 41/A3
Blue, Ariz. 198/F5
Blue (riv.), Ariz. 198/F5
Blue (mt.), Colo. 208/B2
Blue (riv.), Colo. 208/G3
Blue (riv.), Ind. 227/E8
Blue (riv.), Jamaica 158/J6
Blue (mt.), Maine 243/C6
Blue (hills), Mass. 249/C8
Blue (creek), Nebr. 264/B3
Blue (mt.), New Bruns. 170/D1
Blue (riv.), N.H. 268/C2
Blue (mts.), N.S. Wales 88/H6
Blue (mts.), N.S. Wales 97/F3
Blue, Okla. 288/O7
Blue (riv.), Okla. 288/O6
Blue (mts.), Oreg. 291/J3
Blue (mt.), Pa. 294/E5
Blue (creek), Utah 304/B2
Blue (lake), Utah 304/B4
Blue (lake), Wash. 310/F3
Blue (mts.), Wash. 310/H4
Blue Ash, Ohio 284/C9
Blue Ball, Ark. 202/C4
Blue Bell, S. Dak. 298/C6
Bluebell, Utah 304/D3
Blueberry Creek, Br. Col. 184/J5
Blueberry Mountain, Alberta 182/A2
Blue Creek, Ohio 284/D8
Blue Creek, Utah 304/B2
Bluecreek, Wash. 310/H2
Blue Creek, W. Va. 312/D6
Blue Cypress (lake), Fla. 212/F4
Blue Diamond, Ky. 237/P6

Blue Earth (co.), Minn. 255/D6
Blue Earth, Minn. 255/D7
Blue Earth (riv.), Minn. 255/D7
Blue Eye, Ark. 202/D1
Blue Eye, Mo. 261/F9
Bluefield, Va. 307/F6
Bluefield, W. Va. 188/K3
Bluefield, W. Va. 312/D8
Bluefields, Jamaica 158/G6
Bluefields, Nicaragua 154/F4
Bluegrass, Ind. 227/E3
Blue Grass, Iowa 229/M5
Blue Grass, Minn. 255/C4
Blue Grass, Va. 307/J3
Blue Heron, Sask. 181/E2
Blue Hill, Maine 243/F7
Blue Hill•, Maine 243/F7
Blue Hill (bay), Maine 243/G7
Blue Hill, Nebr. 264/F4
Blue Hill Falls, Maine 243/F7
Blue Hills, Conn. 210/E1
Blue Island, Ill. 222/B6
Bluejacket, Okla. 288/R1
Blue Jay, Calif. 204/H9
Blue Joint (lake), Oreg. 291/H5
Blue Knob (mt.), Pa. 294/E5
Blue Lake, Calif. 204/A3
Blue Mesa (res.), Colo. 208/E5
Bluemont, Va. 307/N2
Blue Mound, Ill. 222/D4
Blue Mound, Kansas 232/H3
Blue Mound, Texas 303/E2
Blue Mounds, Wis. 317/G9
Blue Mountain, Ala. 195/G3
Blue Mountain, Ark. 202/C3
Blue Mountain (lake), Ark. 202/C3
Blue Mountain (peak), Jamaica 158/K6
Blue Mountain (peak), Jamaica 156/C3
Blue Mountain, Miss. 256/G1
Blue Mountain (riv.), N.Y. 276/M3
Blue Mountain Lake, N.Y. 276/M3
Blue Mountains, Australia 87/E9
Blue Mountains, N.S. Wales 88/J6
Blue Mountains, N.S. Wales 97/F3
Blue Nile (riv.) 102/F3
Blue Nile (Abay) (riv.), Ethiopia 111/G5
Blue Nile (prov.), Sudan 111/F5
Blue Nile (riv.), Sudan 59/B4
Blue Nile (riv.), Sudan 111/F5
Blue Nose (mt.), Idaho 220/D4
Bluenose (lake), N.W. Terr. 187/G3
Blue Rapids, Kansas 232/F2
Blue Ridge, Alberta 182/C2
Blue Ridge, Georgia 217/D1
Blue Ridge (lake), Georgia 217/D1
Blue Ridge (mts.), Georgia 217/D1
Blue Ridge, Ind. 227/F5
Blue Ridge (mts.), Md. 245/H3
Blue Ridge (mts.), N.C. 281/E3
Blue Ridge (mts.), S.C. 296/B1
Blue Ridge, Va. 307/J6
Blue Ridge (mts.), Va. 307/J6
Blue Ridge Manor, Ky. 237/L2
Blue Ridge Summit, Pa. 294/G6
Blue River, Br. Col. 184/H4
Blue River, Colo. 208/G4
Blue River, Oreg. 291/E3
Blue River, Wis. 317/E9
Blue Rock, Nova Scotia 168/D4
Blue Rock (Gaysport), Ohio 284/G6
Blue Sea Lake, Québec 172/A3
Bluesky, Alberta 182/A1
Blue Spring (hills), Utah 304/B1
Blue Springs, Ala. 195/G7
Blue Springs, Miss. 256/G2
Blue Springs, Mo. 261/R6
Blue Springs, Nebr. 264/H4
Blue Stack (mts.), Ireland 17/E2
Bluestem (lake), Okla. 288/O1
Bluestone (lake), Va. 307/G5
Bluestone (lake), W. Va. 312/E7
Blue Sulphur Springs, W. Va. 312/E7
Blue Summit, Mo. 261/R5
Bluevale, Ontario 177/E3
Bluewater, N. Mex. 274/A3
Bluewater (creek), N. Mex. 274/B4
Bluewater (creek), N. Mex. 274/D6
Bluewater (lake), N. Mex. 274/A3
Bluff (cape), Newf. 166/B5
Bluff, N. Zealand 100/B7
Bluff, N.C. 281/J5
Bluff, Utah 304/E6
Bluff City, Ark. 202/D6
Bluff City, Ill. 222/E5
Bluff City, Kansas 232/E4
Bluff City, Tenn. 237/S8
Bluff Dale, Texas 303/F5
Bluffdale, Utah 304/B9
Bluff Knoll (mt.), W. Australia 92/B6
Bluff Park, Ala. 195/E4
Bluffs, Ill. 222/C4
Bluffsprings, Fla. 212/B5
Bluffton, Alberta 182/C3
Bluffton, Ark. 202/C4
Bluffton, Georgia 217/C7
Bluffton, Ind. 227/G3
Bluffton, Minn. 255/C4
Bluffton, Ohio 284/C4
Bluffton, S.C. 296/F7
Bluford, Ill. 222/E5
Blum, Texas 303/G5
Blumenau, Brazil 132/D9
Blumenau, Brazil 120/E5
Blumenfeld, Manitoba 179/D5
Blumenheim, Sask. 181/E3
Blumenhof, Sask. 181/D5
Blumenort, Manitoba 179/E5
Blumenort, Manitoba 179/F5
Blumenort, Sask. 181/D5
Blumenstein, Switzerland 39/E3
Blumenthal, Sask. 181/E3
Blümlisalp (mt.), Switzerland 39/E3
Blunt, S. Dak. 298/J4
Bly, Oreg. 291/F5
Blying (sound), Alaska 196/C1
Blyn, Wash. 310/B3
Blyth, England 13/F2
Blyth, England 10/D5
Blyth, England 10/F3

Blyth, Ontario 177/C4
Blyth Bridge, Scotland 15/E5
Blythe, Calif. 204/L10
Blythe, Georgia 217/H4
Blythedale, Md. 245/O2
Blythedale, Mo. 261/E2
Blythedale, Pa. 294/C5
Blytheswood, Ontario 177/B5
Blytheville, Ark. 188/H3
Blytheville, Ark. 202/L2
Blytheville A.F.B., Ark. 202/K2
Blythewood, S.C. 296/E3
Bo, S. Leone 102/A4
Bo, S. Leone 106/B7
Boac, Philippines 82/C4
Boaco, Nicaragua 154/E4
Boa Esperança, Brazil 135/D2
Boalsburg, Pa. 294/G4
Boano (isl.), Indonesia 85/H6
Boa Nova, Brazil 132/B5
Board Camp, Ark. 202/B4
Boardman (riv.), Mich. 250/D4
Boardman, N.C. 281/M6
Boardman, Ohio 284/J3
Boardman, Oreg. 291/H2
Boardman, Wis. 317/A5
Boardmans Bridge, Conn. 210/B2
Boas (riv.), N.W. Terr. 187/K3
Boat Basin, Br. Col. 184/D5
Boat Harbour, Tasmania 99/B2
Boat of Garten, Scotland 15/E3
Boa Vista, Brazil 120/C2
Boa Vista, Brazil 132/H8
Boa Vista (isl.), C. Verde 106/B8
Boayan (isl.), Philippines 82/B5
Boaz, Ala. 195/F2
Boaz, Ky. 237/D7
Boaz, Mo. 261/F8
Boaz, W. Va. 312/D4
Boaz, Wis. 317/E9
Bobadah, N.S. Wales 97/D3
Bobai, China 77/H7
Bobaomby (cape), Madagascar 102/G6
Bobaomby (Amber) (cape), Madagascar 118/H2
Bobare, Venezuela 124/D2
Böblingen, Germany 22/C4
Bobo, Miss. 256/C2
Bobo Dioulasso, Burkina Faso 106/D6
Bobo Dioulasso, Burkina Faso 102/B3
Bobon, Philippines 82/F7
Bobonaza (riv.), Ecuador 128/D3
Bobonong, Botswana 118/D4
Bobotov Kuk (mt.), Yugoslavia 45/D4
Bobr (riv.), Poland 47/B3
Bobrov, U.S.S.R. 52/F4
Bobruysk, U.S.S.R. 7/G3
Bobruysk, U.S.S.R. 52/C4
Bobruysk, U.S.S.R. 48/C3
Bobs (lake), Ontario 177/H3
Bobtown, Pa. 294/B6
Bobures, Venezuela 124/C3
Boby, Pic (mt.), Madagascar 118/H4
Bocabec, New Bruns. 170/C3
Boca Chica, Dom. Rep. 158/E6
Boca Chica (key), Fla. 212/E7
Boca Ciega (bay), Fla. 212/B3
Boca de Aroa, Venezuela 124/D2
Boca del Mangle, Venezuela 124/D2
Boca del Pao, Venezuela 124/F3
Boca del Pepé, Colombia 126/B5
Boca del Río, Mexico 150/Q2
Boca del Soco, Dom. Rep. 158/F6
Boca do Acre, Brazil 120/C2
Boca Grande, Fla. 212/D5
Boca Grande (key), Fla. 212/D7
Boca Grande (passage), Trin. & Tob. 161/A10
Boca Grande (gulf), Venezuela 124/H3
Bocaiúva, Brazil 132/E7
Bocaranga, Cent. Afr. Rep. 115/C2
Boca Raton, Fla. 212/F5
Bocas del Toro, Panama 154/F6
Bocay, Nicaragua 154/E3
Bochnia, Poland 47/E4
Bocholt, Belgium 27/H6
Bocholt, Germany 22/B3
Bochov, Czech. 41/B1
Bochum, Germany 22/B3
Bock, Minn. 255/E5
Boco, Chile 138/F2
Boconó, Venezuela 124/C3
Boda, Cent. Afr. Rep. 115/C3
Boddam, Scotland 15/G3
Boddington, W. Australia 92/B2
Bode, Iowa 229/E3
Bodega (bay), Calif. 204/B5
Bodega (head), Calif. 204/B5
Bodega Bay, Calif. 204/B5
Bodegraven, Netherlands 27/F4
Bodélé (depr.), Chad 102/D3
Bodélé (depr.), Chad 111/D3
Boden, Sweden 18/M4
Bodensee (Constance) (lake), Austria 41/A3
Bodensee (Constance) (lake), Switzerland 39/H1
Bodensee (Constance) (lake), Germany 22/C5
Boderg (lake), Ireland 17/E4
Bodfish, Calif. 204/G8
Bodhan, India 68/D5
Bodie (isl.), N.C. 281/T2
Bodinayakkanur, India 68/D6
Bodines, Pa. 294/H3
Bodio, Switzerland 39/G4
Bodkin (pt.), Md. 245/N4
Bodmin, England 13/C7
Bodmin, England 10/D5
Bodmin, Sask. 181/D2

Bodo, Alberta 182/E3
Bodø, Norway 18/J3
Bodø, Norway 7/F2
Bodrum, Turkey 63/B4
Bodrum, Turkey 59/A2
Bo Duc, Vietnam 72/E4
Bódvaszilas, Hungary 41/F2
Boelus, Nebr. 264/F3
Boende, Zaire 115/D4
Boerne, Texas 303/J10
Boeuf (lake), La. 238/J7
Boeuf (riv.), La. 238/G1
Boffa, Guinea 106/B6
Bog (lake), Maine 243/H6
Bogalusa, La. 188/H4
Bogalusa, La. 238/L5
Bogan (riv.), N.S. Wales 97/D2
Bogandé, Burkina Faso 106/E6
Bogan Gate, N.S. Wales 97/D3
Bogantungan, Queensland 95/C4
Bogard, Mo. 261/F4
Bogart, Georgia 217/E3
Bogata, Texas 303/J4
Bogatynia, Poland 47/B3
Boğazlıyan, Turkey 63/F3
Bogen, Germany 22/E4
Bogenfels, Namibia 118/B5
Boger City, N.C. 281/G4
Boggabilla, N.S. Wales 97/F1
Boggabri, N.S. Wales 97/F2
Boggeragh (mts.), Ireland 17/D7
Boggs, W. Va. 312/E6
Boggstown, Ind. 227/F5
Boggy (peak), Ant. & Bar. 161/D11
Boggy Creek, Manitoba 179/A3
Boggy Depot, Okla. 288/O6
Bogia, Papua N.G. 85/B6
Bogie (riv.), Scotland 15/F3
Bognor Regis, England 13/G7
Bognor Regis, England 10/F5
Bogny-sur-Meuse, France 28/F3
Bogo, Philippines 82/E5
Bogon (riv.), N.S. Wales 88/H6
Bogong (mt.), Victoria 97/J6
Bogor, Indonesia 54/M10
Bogor, Indonesia 85/H2
Bogoslof (isl.), Alaska 196/E4
Bogotá (cap.), Colombia 126/D5
Bogotá (cap.), Colombia 120/B2
Bogota, Ill. 222/E5
Bogota, N.J. 273/B2
Bogota, Tenn. 237/C8
Bogra, Bangladesh 68/F4
Boguchar, U.S.S.R. 52/F5
Bogue, Kansas 232/C2
Bogué, Mauritania 106/B5
Bogue Chitto, Miss. 256/D8
Bogue Chitto (riv.), Miss. 256/D8
Bogue Homo (lake), Miss. 256/F7
Boguszów-Gorce, Poland 47/B3
Bog Walk, Jamaica 158/J6
Bo Hai (gulf), China 77/J4
Boharm, Sask. 181/F5
Bohemian (for.), Czech. 41/B2
Bohemian (for.), Germany 22/E4
Bohemian-Moravian Heights (hills), Czech. 41/C2
Boherbue, Ireland 17/C7
Bohners Lake, Wis. 317/K10
Bohodleh, Somalia 115/J2
Bohol (prov.), Philippines 82/E6
Bohol (isl.), Philippines 85/G4
Bohol (isl.), Philippines 82/E6
Bohol (sea), Philippines 82/E6
Bohol (str.), Philippines 82/D6
Böhönye, Hungary 41/D3
Bohu (Bagrax), China 77/C3
Boicourt, Kansas 232/H3
Boiestown, New Bruns. 170/D2
Boiling Spring Lakes, N.C. 281/N7
Boiling Springs, N.C. 281/F4
Boiling Springs, Pa. 294/H5
Bois Blanc (isl.), Mich. 250/E4
Boischatel, Québec 172/J3
Bois-des-Filion, Québec 172/H4
Bois de Sioux (riv.), Minn. 255/B4
Bois de Sioux (riv.), S. Dak. 298/R1
Boise (co.), Idaho 220/D6
Boise (cap.), Idaho 146/G5
Boise (cap.), Idaho 220/B6
Boise (cap.), Idaho 188/C2
Boise (mts.), Idaho 220/B6
Boise (riv.), Idaho 220/B6
Boise City, Okla. 288/B1
Boissevain, Man. 162/G6
Boissevain, Manitoba 179/C5
Boissevain, Va. 307/F6
Boistfort, Wash. 310/B4
Boisvert (pt.), Québec 172/J1
Boizenburg an der Elbe, Germany 22/D2
Bojador (cape), W. Sahara 102/A2
Bojador (cape), Western Sahara 106/B3
Bojeador (cape), Philippines 82/C1
Bojnurd, Iran 66/K2
Bojnurd, Iran 59/G2
Bojonegoro, Indonesia 85/J2
Bokchito, Okla. 288/O6
Boké, Guinea 106/B6
Bokeelia, Fla. 212/D5
Bokel (cay), Belize 154/D2
Bokhara (riv.), N.S. Wales 97/D1
Bokhoma, Okla. 288/S7
Boknafjord (fjord), Norway 18/D7
Boko, Congo 115/B4
Bokoro, Chad 111/C3
Bokoshe, Okla. 288/S4
Bokote, Zaire 115/D4
Bokpyin, Burma 72/C5
Boksburg, S. Africa 118/J6
Bokungu, Zaire 115/D4
Bol, Chad 111/B5

Bol, Chad 102/D3
Bolair, W. Va. 312/F6
Bolama, Guinea-Biss. 106/A6
Bolan (pass), Pakistan 68/B3
Bolangir, India 68/E4
Bolar, Va. 307/J4
Bolatusha, Miss. 256/E5
Bolbec, France 28/D3
Bolckow, Mo. 261/C2
Bolderslev, Denmark 21/C8
Bolding, Ark. 202/F7
Boldman, Ky. 237/R5
Boldon, England 13/J3
Bolduc, Québec 172/G4
Bole, China 77/B3
Bole, Ghana 106/D7
Boles, Ark. 202/B4
Bolesławiec, Poland 47/B3
Boley, Okla. 288/O4
Bolgatanga, Ghana 106/D6
Boli, China 77/M2
Boligee, Ala. 195/C5
Bolinao, Philippines 82/B2
Bolinao (cape), Philippines 82/B2
Bolinas, Calif. 204/H1
Boling, Texas 303/H8
Bolingbroke, Georgia 217/E5
Bolingbrook, Ill. 222/A6
Bolinger, Ala. 195/B7
Bolinger, La. 238/C1
Bolívar, Argentina 143/D4
Bolívar, Bolivia 136/B5
Bolívar (dept.), Colombia 126/C3
Bolívar, Antioquia, Colombia 126/C5
Bolívar, Cauca, Colombia 126/B5
Bolívar (prov.), Ecuador 128/C3
Bolívar, Ecuador 128/C2
Bolivar (co.), Miss. 256/C3
Bolivar, Mo. 261/F7
Bolivar, N.Y. 276/D6
Bolivar, Ohio 284/G4
Bolivar, Pa. 294/D5
Bolivar, Peru 128/B6
Bolivar, Tenn. 237/C10
Bolivar (pen.), Texas 303/K8
Bolivar (state), Venezuela 124/F7
Bolívar, Cerro (mt.), Venezuela 124/G4
Bolívar, Pico (peak), Venezuela 124/C3
Bolivar, W. Va. 312/L4
Bolivia 2/F6
Bolivia 120/C4
BOLIVIA 136
Bolivia, N.C. 281/N6
Bolkar (mts.), Turkey 63/F4
Bolkhov, U.S.S.R. 52/E5
Bolligen, Switzerland 39/E3
Bolling, Ala. 195/E7
Bollinger (co.), Mo. 261/M8
Bollington, England 13/H2
Bollnäs, Sweden 18/K6
Bollon, Queensland 95/C6
Bollon, Queensland 88/H5
Bollstabruk, Sweden 18/L5
Bollnen (lake), Sweden 18/H8
Bolobo, Zaire 115/C4
Bologna (prov.), Italy 34/C2
Bologna, Italy 7/F4
Bologna, Italy 34/C2
Bolognesi, Peru 128/F8
Bolognesi, Peru 128/B6
Bologoye, U.S.S.R. 52/D3
Bolomba, Zaire 115/C3
Bolonchén de Rejón, Mexico 150/O7
Bolondrón, Cuba 156/B2
Bolondrón, Cuba 158/D1
Bolovens (plat.), Laos 72/E4
Bolpebra, Bolivia 136/A2
Bolsena, Italy 34/C3
Bol'shevik (isl.) U.S.S.R. 54/N2
Bol'shevik (isl.), U.S.S.R. 4/A4
Bol'shevik, U.S.S.R. 48/K2
Bol'shoy Lyakhov (isl.), U.S.S.R. 54/R2
Bol'shoy Lyakhovskiy (isl.), U.S.S.R. 48/P2
Bolsover, England 13/J2
Bolsters Mills, Maine 243/B7
Bolsward, Netherlands 27/H2
Boltaña, Spain 33/F1
Bolton•, Conn. 210/F1
Bolton, England 10/G2
Bolton, England 13/H2
Bolton•, Mass. 249/H3
Bolton, Miss. 256/D6
Bolton, N.C. 281/N6
Bolton•, Vt. 268/B3
Bolton (mt.), Vt. 268/B3
Bolton Landing, N.Y. 276/N3
Bolu (prov.), Turkey 63/D2
Bolu, Turkey 59/B1
Bolu, Turkey 63/D2
Bolus (head), Ireland 17/A8
Bolvadin, Turkey 63/D3
Bolvanskiy Nos (cape), U.S.S.R. 52/K1
Bolvanskiy Nos (cape), U.S.S.R. 48/G2
Bolzano (Bolzen), Italy 34/C1
Bolzano, Italy 7/F4
Bolzano-Bozen (prov.), Italy 34/C1
Bolzen (Bolzano), Italy 34/C1
Boma, Zaire 115/B5
Boma, Zaire 115/C5
Bomaderry-Nowra, N.S. Wales 97/F4
Bomarton, Texas 303/F4
Bomba (gulf), Libya 111/D1
Bombala, N.S. Wales 97/E5
Bombardopolis, Haiti 158/D3
Bombay, India 2/N5
Bombay, India 54/J8
Bombay, India 68/B7
Bombay (Greater), India 68/B7
Bombay (harb.), India 68/B7
Bombay, Minn. 255/F6
Bombay, N.Y. 276/M1
Bomboma, Zaire 115/C3
Bom Conselho, Brazil 132/G5

Bom Despacho, Brazil 135/D1
Bom Despacho, Brazil 132/E7
Bomdila, India 68/G3
Bom Futuro, Brazil 120/C4
Bom Futuro, Brazil 132/A5
Bomi, China 77/E6
Bom Jesus, Brazil 132/E5
Bom Jesus da Lapa, Brazil 120/E4
Bom Jesus da Lapa, Brazil 132/E5
Bom Jesus do Itabapoana, Brazil 135/F2
Bomongo, Zaire 115/C3
Bomont, W. Va. 312/D6
Bomoseen, Vt. 268/A4
Bomoseen (lake), Vt. 268/A4
Bom Retiro, Brazil 132/D10
Bom Sucesso, Brazil 135/D2
Bomu (riv.), Centr. Afr. Rep. 102/E4
Bomu (riv.), Cent. Afr. Rep. 115/D3
Bomu (riv.), Zaire 115/D3
Bon (cape), Tunisia 102/D1
Bon (cape), Tunisia 106/G1
Bona (mt.), Alaska 196/K2
Bonabéri, Cameroon 115/A3
Bonacca (Guanaja) (isl.), Honduras 154/E2
Bon Accord, Alberta 182/D3
Bonaduz, Switzerland 39/H3
Bon Air, Ala. 195/F4
Bonair, Iowa 229/J2
Bon Air, Tenn. 237/L9
Bon Air, Va. 307/N5
Bonaire (isl.), Neth. Ant. 156/E4
Bonaire (isl.), Neth. Ant. 161/E9
Bonalbo, N.S. Wales 97/G1
Bonanza, Alberta 182/A2
Bonanza, Ark. 202/B3
Bonanza, Colo. 208/G6
Bonanza, Nicaragua 154/E4
Bonanza, Oreg. 291/F5
Bonanza, Utah 304/E3
Bonanza (peak), Wash. 310/E2
Bonao, Dom. Rep. 158/E6
Bonaparte, Iowa 229/K7
Bonaparte (lake), N.Y. 276/K2
Bonaparte (creek), Wash. 310/F2
Bonaparte (riv.), Wash. 310/F2
Bonaparte (arch.), W. Australia 88/C2
Bonaparte (arch.), W. Australia 92/D1
Bon Aqua, Tenn. 237/G9
Bonar Bridge, Scotland 15/D3
Bonaventure (cape), Newf. 166/D2
Bonaventure (co.), Québec 172/C2
Bonaventure (county), Québec 174/D3
Bonaventure, Québec 172/C2
Bonaventure (isl.), Québec 172/C2
Bonaventure (riv.), Québec 172/C1
Bonavista, Newf. 162/L6
Bonavista, Newf. 166/D2
Bonavista (bay), Newf. 166/D1
Bonavista (bay), Newf. 166/D1
Boncarbo, Colo. 208/K8
Bonchester Bridge, Scotland 15/F5
Boncourt, Switzerland 39/C2
Bond, Colo. 208/F3
Bond (co.), Ill. 222/D5
Bond, Ky. 237/N6
Bond, Miss. 256/F9
Bond (mt.), N.H. 268/E3
Bondeno, Italy 34/C2
Bond Falls (res.), Mich. 250/G2
Bondi (beach), N.S. Wales 97/K3
Bondiss, Alberta 182/D2
Bondo, Zaire 115/D3
Bondoukou, Ivory Coast 106/D7
Bondowoso, Indonesia 85/L2
Bondsville, Mass. 249/E4
Bonduel, Wis. 317/K6
Bondurant, Iowa 229/G5
Bondurant, Wyo. 319/B2
Bondville, Ill. 222/E3
Bondville, Ky. 237/M5
Bondville, Vt. 268/B5
Bondy, France 28/B1
Bône (Annaba), Algeria 106/F1
Bone, Idaho 220/G6
Bone (gulf), Indonesia 54/O10
Bone (gulf), Indonesia 85/G7
Bone Cave, Tenn. 237/L9
Bone Gap, Ill. 222/F6
Bo'ness, Scotland 15/D1
Bo'ness, Scotland 15/C1
Bonesteel, S. Dak. 298/M7
Bonet (riv.), Ireland 17/E3
Boneta, Utah 304/D3
Bonete (dam), Uruguay 145/C3
Bonetraill, N. Dak. 282/C3
Boneville, Georgia 217/G4
Bonfield, Ill. 222/E2
Bonfield, Ontario 177/E1
Bonfol, Switzerland 39/D2
Bong (range), Liberia 106/B7
Bongabong, Philippines 82/C4
Bongandanga, Zaire 115/D3
Bonggaw, Philippines 82/B8
Bongo (isl.), Philippines 82/D7
Bongo (isl.), Philippines 82/D7
Bongor, Chad 111/C5
Bongor, Chad 102/D3
Bong Son (Hoai Nhon), Vietnam 72/F4
Bonham, Texas 303/H4
Bonhill, Scotland 15/B1
Bonhomme (co.), S. Dak. 298/O7
Bon Homme (co.), S. Dak. 298/O7
Bonifacio, France 28/B7
Bonifacio (str.), France 28/B7
Bonifacio (str.), Italy 34/B4
Bonifay, Fla. 212/C6
Bönigen, Switzerland 39/E3
Bonilla, S. Dak. 298/N4
Bonin (isls.), Japan 2/S4
Bonin (isls.), Japan 54/R7
Bonin (isls.), Japan 81/M3
Bonita, Ariz. 198/E6
Bonita (riv.), Calif. 204/H2
Bonita, La. 238/G1
Bonita, Miss. 256/G6
Bonita Springs, Fla. 212/E5

Brady 341

Bonlee, N.C. 281/L3
Bonn (cap.), Germany 7/E3
Bonn (cap.), Germany 22/B3
Bonne (bay), Newf. 166/C4
Bonneau, S.C. 296/H5
Bonner (co.), Idaho 220/B1
Bonners Ferry, Idaho 220/B1
Bonner Springs, Kansas 232/H2
Bonner-West Riverside, Mont. 262/C4
Bonnet (lake), Manitoba 179/G4
Bonnétable, France 28/D3
Bonnet Carré Spillway and Floodway, La. 238/N3
Bonne Terre, Mo. 261/L7
Bonnet Plume (riv.), Yukon 187/E3
Bonneville, France 28/G4
Bonneville (co.), Idaho 220/G6
Bonneville, Oreg. 291/F2
Bonneville (dam), Oreg. 291/E2
Bonneville (salt flats), Utah 304/A3
Bonneville (dam), Wash. 310/D5
Bonneville (lake), Wash. 310/D5
Bonneville (mt.), Wyo. 319/C3
Bonneville, Wyo. 319/E2
Bonney Lake, Wash. 310/C3
Bonnie, Ill. 222/E5
Bonnieville, Ky. 237/K6
Bonnots Mill, Mo. 261/J5
Bonny (res.), Colo. 208/P3
Bonny, Nigeria 106/F8
Bonny (bight), Nigeria 106/F8
Bonnybridge, Scotland 15/C1
Bonnyman, Ky. 237/P6
Bonnyrigg, N.S. Wales 88/K4
Bonnyrigg, N.S. Wales 97/H3
Bonnyrigg and Lasswade, Scotland 10/C1
Bonnyrigg and Lasswade, Scotland 15/D2
Bonny River, New Bruns. 170/D3
Bonnyville, Alberta 182/E2
Bono, Ark. 202/J2
Bono, Ohio 284/D2
Bonorva, Italy 34/B4
Bonpas (creek), Ill. 222/F5
Bonpland (mt.), N. Zealand 100/A6
Bon Secour, Ala. 195/C10
Bon Secour (bay), Ala. 195/C10
Bonsecours, Québec 172/E4
Bonshaw, Pr. Edward I. 168/E2
Bonthain, Indonesia 85/F7
Bonthe, S. Leone 106/B7
Bontoc, Philippines 85/G2
Bontoc, Philippines 82/C2
Bon Wier, Texas 303/L7
Bonyhád, Hungary 41/E3
Boody, Ill. 222/D4
Book (cliffs), Utah 304/E4
Booker, Texas 303/D1
Booker T. Washington Nat'l Mon., Va. 307/J6
Boolaloo, W. Australia 92/B3
Booligal, N.S. Wales 97/C3
Boom, Belgium 27/E6
Boom, Tenn. 237/L7
Boomer, N.C. 281/G2
Boomer, W. Va. 312/D6
Boomi, N.S. Wales 88/H5
Boomi, N.S. Wales 97/E1
Boon (pt.), Ant. & Bar. 161/E11
Boon, Mich. 250/D4
Boondall, Queensland 88/K2
Boone (co.), Ark. 202/D1
Boone, Colo. 208/L6
Boone (co.), Ill. 222/E1
Boone (co.), Ind. 227/E4
Boone (co.), Iowa 229/F5
Boone, Iowa 229/F4
Boone (co.), Ky. 237/M3
Boone, Ky. 237/N5
Boone (co.), Mo. 261/H4
Boone (co.), Nebr. 264/F3
Boone, Nebr. 264/F3
Boone, N.C. 281/F2
Boone (lake), Tenn. 237/S8
Boone (co.), W. Va. 312/C6
Boone Grove, Ind. 227/C2
Boonesboro, Mo. 261/G4
Boones Mill, Va. 307/J6
Boonesville, Va. 307/L4
Booneville, Ark. 202/C3
Booneville, Ky. 237/O6
Booneville, Miss. 256/G1
Boonsboro, Md. 245/H2
Boonton, N.J. 273/E2
Boonton (res.), N.J. 273/E2
Boonville, Calif. 204/B5
Boonville, Ind. 227/C8
Boonville, Mo. 261/G5
Boonville, N.Y. 276/K4
Boonville, N.C. 281/H2
Boopi (riv.), Bolivia 136/B4
Boorooban, N.S. Wales 97/C4
Boorowa, N.S. Wales 97/E4
Boort, Victoria 97/B5
Booth, Ala. 195/E6
Boothbay, Maine 243/D8
Boothbay•, Maine 243/D8
Boothbay Harbor, Maine 243/D8
Boothia (pen.), Canada 4/B14
Boothia (gulf), Canada 4/B14
Boothia (gulf), N.W.T. 146/J2
Boothia (gulf), N.W.T. 162/G1
Boothia (gulf), N.W.T. 187/K3
Boothia (isthmus), N.W.T. 162/G2
Boothia (pen.), N.W.T. 146/J2
Boothia (pen.), N.W.T. 162/G1
Boothia (pen.), N.W.T. 187/J2
Boothville, La. 238/M8
Boothwyn, Pa. 294/L7
Bootle, England 10/F2
Bootle, England 13/G2
Booué, Gabon 115/B3
Bophuthatswana (bantustan), S. Africa 102/E7
Bophuthatswana (rep.), S. Africa 118/D5
Boppard, Germany 22/B3
Boquerón, Cuba 158/K4
Boquerón, Cuba 156/C3
Boquerón, Paraguay 144/B3
Boquerón, El (pass), Peru 128/E7
Boquerón, P. Rico 156/F1
Boquerón, P. Rico 161/A3
Boquerón (bay), P. Rico 161/A3
Boquilla del Carmen, Mexico 150/H2
Bor, Czech. 41/B2
Bor, Sudan 111/F6
Bor, Turkey 63/F4
Bor, U.S.S.R. 52/F3
Bor, Yugoslavia 45/E3
Bora-Bora (isl.) Fr. Poly. 87/L7
Borah (peak), Idaho 188/D2
Borah (peak), Idaho 220/E5
Borama, Somalia 115/H1
Borås, Sweden 7/F3
Borås, Sweden 18/H8
Borazjan, Iran 66/G6
Borazjan, Iran 59/F4
Borba, Brazil 120/D3
Borba, Brazil 132/H9
Borba, Portugal 33/C3
Borbón, Venezuela 124/F4
Borçka, Turkey 63/J2
Borculo, Netherlands 27/J4
Bordeaux, France 28/C5
Bordeaux, France 7/D4
Bordeaux, S.C. 296/C4
Bordeaux (mt.) Virgin Is. (U.S.) 161/C4
Bordelonville, La. 238/G4
Borden (isl.), Canada 4/B15
Borden, Ind. 227/F8
Borden (isl.), N.W. Terr. 187/G2
Borden (pen.), N.W. Terr. 187/K2
Borden, Pr. Edward I. 168/E2
Borden, Sask. 181/D3
Borden, S.C. 296/G3
Borden (co.), Texas 303/C5
Borden, W. Australia 92/B6
Borden Shaft, Md. 245/B2
Borden Springs, Ala. 195/H3
Bordentown, N.J. 273/D3
Border, Minn. 255/D2
Border, Wyo. 319/B3
Borderland, W. Va. 312/B7
Borders (reg.), Scotland 15/E5
Bordertown, S. Australia 88/F7
Bordertown, S. Australia 94/G7
Bordighera, Italy 34/A3
Bordj Bou Arreridj, Algeria 106/E1
Bordj Fly Sainte Marie, Algeria 106/D3
Bordj Omar Driss, Algeria 106/F3
Bordj Omar Driss, Algeria 102/C2
Bordulac, N. Dak. 282/N5
Boreing, Ky. 237/N6
Boreray (isl.), Scotland 15/A2
Boreray (isl.), Scotland 15/A3
Borgå, Finland 18/O6
Borge, Norway 18/H2
Borger, Netherlands 27/K3
Borger, Texas 303/C2
Borger, Texas 188/F3
Borgerhout, Belgium 27/E6
Borgholm, Sweden 18/K8
Borghorst, Germany 22/B2
Borgloon, Belgium 27/G7
Borgne (lake), La. 238/L7
Borgne (riv.), Switzerland 39/D4
Borgo, Italy 34/C1
Borgomanero, Italy 34/B2
Borgo San Lorenzo, Italy 34/C2
Borgworm (Waremme), Belgium 27/G7
Borikan, Laos 72/D3
Boring, Md. 245/L2
Boring, Oreg. 291/E2
Borinquen (pt.), P. Rico 156/F1
Borinquen (pt.), P. Rico 161/A1
Borislav, U.S.S.R. 52/B5
Borisoglebsk, U.S.S.R. 48/E4
Borisoglebsk, U.S.S.R. 52/F4
Borisov, U.S.S.R. 52/C4
Borisovka, U.S.S.R. 52/E4
Bo River Post, Sudan 111/E6
Borja, Peru 128/D5
Borja, Spain 33/F2
Borjas Blancas, Spain 33/G2
Borken, Germany 22/B3
Børkop, Denmark 21/C6
Borku, Chad 111/C4
Borkum, Germany 22/B2
Borkum (isl.), Germany 22/B2
Borlänge, Sweden 18/J6
Borna, Germany 22/E3
Borndiep (chan.), Netherlands 27/H2
Borne, Netherlands 27/K4
Borneo (isl.) 2/Q6
Borneo (isl.) 54/N9
Borneo (isl.), Indonesia 85/E5
Borneo (isl.), Malaysia 85/E5
Bornheim, Germany 22/B3
Bornholm (co.), Denmark 21/F9
Bornholm (isl.), Denmark 7/F3
Bornholm (isl.), Denmark 18/J9
Bornholm (isl.), Denmark 21/F9
Borno (state), Nigeria 106/G6
Bornova, Turkey 63/B3
Borocay (isl.), Philippines 82/D5
Borojó, Venezuela 124/C2
Boron, Calif. 204/H8
Borongan, Philippines 82/E5
Borot Kidod (well), Israel 65/C5
Borovichi, U.S.S.R. 52/D3
Borradaile, Alberta 182/E3
Borre, Norway 18/D4
Borrego Springs, Calif. 204/J10
Borris, Ireland 17/H6
Borris-in-Ossory, Ireland 17/F6
Borrisokane, Ireland 17/E6
Borrisoleigh, Ireland 17/E6
Borroloola, North. Terr. 88/F3
Borroloola, North. Terr. 93/E4
Borşa, Romania 45/G2
Borsod-Abaúj-Zemplén (co.), Hungary 41/F2
Bortala (Bole) China 77/B3
Borth, Wales 13/C5
Bort-les-Orgues, France 28/E5
Boruca, C. Rica 154/F6
Borujerd, Iran 59/E3
Borujerd, Iran 66/F4
Borup, Denmark 21/E7
Borup, Minn. 255/B3
Börzsöny (mts.), Hungary 41/E3
Borzya, U.S.S.R. 48/M4
Bosa, Italy 34/B4
Bosanska Dubica, Yugoslavia 45/C3
Bosanska Gradiška, Yugoslavia 45/C3
Bosanska Kostajnica, Yugoslavia 45/B3
Bosanska Krupa, Yugoslavia 45/C3
Bosanski Brod, Yugoslavia 45/D3
Bosanski Novi, Yugoslavia 45/C3
Bosanski Petrovac, Yugoslavia 45/C3
Bosanski Šamac, Yugoslavia 45/D3
Bosaso, Somalia 115/J1
Bosaso, Somalia 102/G3
Boscawen•, N.H. 268/D5
Bosch, van den (cape), Indonesia 85/J6
Bosco, La. 238/F2
Boscobel, Wis. 317/E9
Bose, China 77/G7
Boshan, China 77/J4
Boskoop, Netherlands 27/F4
Boskovice, Czech. 41/D2
Bosler, Wyo. 319/G4
Bosna (riv.), Yugoslavia 45/D3
Bosnia and Hercegovina (rep.), Yugoslavia 45/C3
Boso (pen.), Japan 81/K6
Bosobolo, Zaire 115/D3
Bosporus (str.), Turkey 7/G4
Bosporus (str.), Turkey 59/A1
Bosporus (str.), Turkey 63/C2
Bosque, N. Mex. 274/C4
Bosque (co.), Texas 303/G6
Boss, Mo. 261/K7
Bossangoa, Centr. Afr. Rep. 102/D4
Bossangoa, Cent. Afr. Rep. 115/C2
Bossburg, Wash. 310/H2
Bossé, New Bruns. 170/B1
Bossembele, Cent. Afr. Rep. 115/C2
Bossier (par.), La. 238/C1
Bossier City, La. 238/C1
Bosso, Niger 106/G6
Bostan, Iran 66/F5
Bostan, Pakistan 68/B2
Bostanabad-e-Bala, Iran 66/E2
Bosten (Bagrax) Hu (lake), China 77/C3
Boston (mts.), Ark. 202/B2
Boston, England 13/G5
Boston, England 10/F4
Boston, Georgia 217/E9
Boston, Ind. 227/H5
Boston, Ky. 237/K5
Boston (cap.), Mass. 146/L5
Boston (cap.), Mass. 188/M2
Boston (cap.), Mass. 249/D7
Boston (bay), Mass. 249/E6
Boston (harb.), Mass. 249/D7
Boston, Mo. 261/D8
Boston, N.Y. 276/C5
Boston (mts.), Okla. 288/S3
Boston, Pa. 294/C7
Boston, Tenn. 237/G9
Boston, Texas 303/K4
Boston, U.S. 2/F3
Boston, Va. 307/M3
Boston Bar, Br. Col. 184/G5
Boston Heights, Ohio 284/J10
Bostonnais (isl.), Québec 172/E2
Bostonnais, Grand Lac (lake), Québec 172/E2
Bostonnais (riv.), Québec 172/E2
Boston Nat'l Hist. Park, Mass. 249/D6
Bostwick, Fla. 212/E2
Bostwick, Georgia 217/E3
Bostwick, Nebr. 264/F4
Boswell, Ark. 202/F1
Boswell, Br. Col. 184/J5
Boswell, Ind. 227/C3
Boswell, Okla. 288/P6
Boswell, Pa. 294/E5
Boswell Bay, Alaska 196/J2
Boswil, Switzerland 39/F2
Bosworth, Mo. 261/F4
Bot (riv.), S. Africa 118/G7
Botany, N.S. Wales 88/L4
Botany (bay), N.S. Wales 88/L4
Botany, N.S. Wales 97/J4
Botany (bay), N.S. Wales 97/J4
Botene, Laos 72/D3
Botetourt (co.), Va. 307/J5
Botevgrad, Bulgaria 45/F4
Botha, Alberta 182/D3
Botha (riv.), Alberta 182/B1
Bothell, Wash. 310/B1
Bothnia (gulf) 7/G2
Bothnia (gulf), Finland 18/M5
Bothnia (gulf), Sweden 18/N4
Bothwell, Ontario 177/C5
Bothwell, Tasmania 99/C4
Bothwell, Utah 304/B2
Botkins, Ohio 284/B5
Botna, Iowa 229/C5
Botoşani, Romania 45/H2
Botrange (mt.), Belgium 27/J8
Botrivier, S. Africa 118/F7
Botsford, Conn. 210/C3
Botswana 2/L7
Botswana 102/E7
BOTSWANA 118/C4
Bottesford, England 13/G4
Bottineau (co.), N. Dak. 282/J2
Bottineau, N. Dak. 282/J2
Bottrel, Alberta 182/C4
Bottrop, Germany 22/B3
Botucatu, Brazil 135/B3
Botucatu, Brazil 132/D8
Botwood, Newf. 166/C4
Bouaflé, Ivory Coast 106/C7
Bouaké, Ivory Coast 102/B4
Bouaké, Ivory Coast 106/D7
Bouali, Cent. Afr. Rep. 115/C3
Bouar, Cent. Afr. Rep. 102/D4
Bouar, Cent. Afr. Rep. 115/C2
Bou Arfa, Morocco 106/D2
Bouca, Cent. Afr. Rep. 115/C2
Boucaut (bay), North. Terr. 93/D1
Boucherville, Québec 172/J4
Boucherville (isl.), Québec 172/J4
Bouches-du-Rhône (dept.), France 28/F6
Bouchette, Québec 172/A3
Bouckville, N.Y. 276/J5
Bou Djebeha, Mali 106/D5
Boudreau (bay), La. 238/M7
Boudreaux, La. 238/J8
Boudreaux (lake), La. 238/J8
Boudry, Switzerland 39/C3
Boufarik, Algeria 106/E1
Bougainville (reef), Coral Sea Is. Terr. 95/C2
Bougainville (reef), Coral Sea Is. Terr. 88/H3
Bougainville (isl.), Papua N.G. 87/F6
Bougainville (isl.), Papua N.G. 86/C2
Bougainville (str.), Papua N.G. 86/D2
Bougainville (str.), Solomon Is. 86/D2
Bougainville (cape), W. Australia 88/D2
Bougainville (cape), W. Australia 92/D1
Bougaroun (cape), Algeria 106/F1
Boughton (isl.), Pr. Edward I. 168/F2
Bougie (Béjaïa), Algeria 106/F1
Bougouni, Mali 106/C6
Bouillante, Guadeloupe 161/A6
Bouillon, Belgium 27/G9
Bou Izakarn, Morocco 106/C3
Boujad, Morocco 106/C2
Boula, Cent. Afr. Rep. 115/C3
Boulanger, Québec 172/E1
Boularderie (isl.), Nova Scotia 168/H2
Boulder, Australia 87/C9
Boulder, Colo. 188/E2
Boulder, Colo. 146/H6
Boulder (co.), Colo. 208/J2
Boulder, Colo. 208/J2
Boulder (mts.), Idaho 220/D6
Boulder, Mont. 262/E4
Boulder (lake), N. Mex. 274/C2
Boulder, Utah 304/C6
Boulder (creek), Utah 304/C6
Boulder, W. Australia 88/C6
Boulder, Wyo. 319/C3
Boulder (lake), Wyo. 319/C3
Boulder City, Nev. 266/G7
Boulder Creek, Calif. 204/J4
Boulder Junction, Wis. 317/G3
Boulder-Kalgoorlie, W. Australia 92/C5
Boulevard, Calif. 204/J11
Boulevard Heights, Md. 245/F5
Boulia, Queensland 95/A4
Boulia, Queensland 88/F4
Boulogne, Fla. 212/E1
Boulogne-Billancourt, France 28/A2
Boulogne-sur-Mer, France 28/D2
Bouna, Ivory Coast 106/D7
Boundary, Alaska 196/K2
Boundary (co.), Idaho 220/B1
Boundary (peak), Nev. 266/C5
Boundary (plat.), Sask. 181/B6
Boundary (bay), Wash. 310/C1
Boundary (dam), Wash. 310/H2
Boundary (lake), Wash. 310/H2
Boundary Bend, Victoria 97/B4
Bound Brook, N.J. 273/D2
Boundiali, Ivory Coast 106/C7
Boundji, Congo 115/C4
Boun Nua, Laos 72/D2
Bountiful, Utah 304/C3
Bounty (isls.), N. Zealand 87/H10
Bounty, Sask. 181/D4
Bourail, New Caled. 87/G8
Bourail, New Caled. 86/G4
Bourbon, Ill. 222/E4
Bourbon, Ind. 227/E2
Bourbon (co.), Kansas 232/H4
Bourbon (co.), Ky. 237/N4
Bourbon, Miss. 256/C4
Bourbon, Mo. 261/K6
Bourbonnais (trad. prov.), France 29
Bourbonnais, Ill. 222/F2
Bourem, Mali 106/E5
Bourg, La. 238/J7
Bourganeuf, France 28/D5
Bourg-des-Saintes, Guadeloupe 161/A7
Bourg-en-Bresse, France 28/F4
Bourgeois, New Bruns. 170/F2
Bourges, France 28/E4
Bourget, Ontario 177/J2
Bourg-Léopold (Leopoldsburg), Belgium 27/G6
Bourgoin-Jallieu, France 28/F5
Bourg Saint-Pierre, Switzerland 39/D5
Bourke, N.S. Wales 88/H6
Bourke, N.S. Wales 97/D2
Bourne, England 13/G5
Bourne, Mass. 249/M6
Bourne•, Mass. 249/M6
Bournedale, Mass. 249/M5
Bournemouth, England 13/F7
Bournemouth, England 10/F5
Bourneville, Ohio 284/D7
Bou Saâda, Algeria 106/E1
Bouse, Ariz. 198/A5
Bouse Wash (dry riv.), Ariz. 198/A4
Boussac, France 28/D4
Bousso, Chad 111/C5
Boussu, Belgium 27/D8
Boutilimit, Mauritania 106/B5
Boutilimit, Mauritania 102/A3
Bouton, Iowa 229/E5
Boutte, La. 238/N4
Bouvard (cape), W. Australia 92/A2
Bouvet (isl.), Ant. 5/D1
Bouvetøya (Bouvet) (isl.), Ant. 5/D1
Boven Bolivia, Neth. Ant. 161/E8
Boves, Italy 34/A2
Bovey, Minn. 255/E3
Bovey Tracey, England 13/D7
Bovill, Idaho 220/B3
Bovina, Miss. 256/C6
Bovina, Texas 303/A3
Bovril, Argentina 143/G5
Bow (riv.), Alberta 182/D4
Bow (riv.), Alta. 162/E5
Bow (lake), N.H. 268/E5
Bow, Wash. 310/C2
Bowbells, N. Dak. 282/F2
Bow City, Alberta 182/D4
Bowden, Alberta 182/C4
Bowden, Jamaica 158/K6
Bowden, W. Va. 312/G5
Bowdens, N.C. 281/N4
Bowdle, S. Dak. 298/K3
Bowdoin (lake), Mont. 262/J2
Bowdoinham•, Maine 243/D7
Bowdon, Georgia 217/B3
Bowdon, N. Dak. 282/L5
Bowdon Junction, Georgia 217/B3
Bowell, Alberta 182/E4
Bowen, Australia 87/E7
Bowen, Ill. 222/B3
Bowen, Ky. 237/O5
Bowen, Queensland 95/D3
Bowen, Queensland 88/H3
Bowen Island, Br. Col. 184/K3
Bowens, Md. 245/M6
Bowerbank•, Maine 243/E5
Bowers, Ind. 227/D4
Bowers Beach, Del. 245/S4
Bowerston, Ohio 284/H5
Bowersville, Georgia 217/G2
Bowersville, Ohio 284/C6
Bowes, England 13/F3
Bowesmont, N. Dak. 282/R2
Bowie, Ariz. 198/F6
Bowie, Colo. 208/D5
Bowie, Md. 245/L4
Bowie (creek), Miss. 256/E7
Bowie (co.), Texas 303/K4
Bowie, Texas 303/G4
Bow Island, Alberta 182/E5
Bowkan, Iran 66/E2
Bowlegs, Okla. 288/N4
Bowler, Wis. 317/J6
Bowling Green, Fla. 212/E4
Bowling Green, Ind. 227/D6
Bowling Green, Ky. 237/H7
Bowling Green, Ky. 188/J3
Bowling Green, Mo. 261/K4
Bowling Green, Ohio 284/C3
Bowling Green (cape), Queensland 88/H3
Bowling Green (cape), Queensland 95/C3
Bowling Green, S.C. 296/E1
Bowling Green, Va. 307/O4
Bowlus, Minn. 255/D5
Bowman, Calif. 204/C8
Bowman, Georgia 217/G2
Bowman (co.), N. Dak. 282/C7
Bowman, N. Dak. 282/D7
Bowman (bay), N.W.T. 162/J2
Bowman (bay), N.W. Terr. 187/L3
Bowman (dam), Oreg. 291/G3
Bowman, S.C. 296/F5
Bowmansdale, Pa. 294/J5
Bowmanstown, Pa. 294/L4
Bowmansville, Pa. 294/L5
Bow Mills, N.H. 268/D5
Bowmont, Idaho 220/B6
Bowmore, Scotland 15/B5
Bowmore, Scotland 10/C3
Bowral, N.S. Wales 97/F4
Bowraville, N.S. Wales 97/G2
Bowring, Okla. 288/O1
Bowron Lake Prov. Park, Br. Col. 184/G3
Bowser, Br. Col. 184/H2
Bowser (lake), Br. Col. 184/C2
Bowsman, Manitoba 179/A2
Bowstring, Minn. 255/E3
Bowstring (lake), Minn. 255/E3
Boxborough•, Mass. 249/H3
Box Butte (co.), Nebr. 264/A2
Box Butte (res.), Nebr. 264/A2
Box Canyon (dam), Wash. 310/H2
Box Elder (creek), Colo. 208/K4
Box Elder, Mont. 262/F2
Boxelder (creek), Mont. 262/M5
Boxelder (creek), Mont. 262/H3
Box Elder, S. Dak. 298/D5
Boxelder (creek), S. Dak. 298/D5
Box Elder (co.), Utah 304/A2
Boxford, Mass. 249/L2
Boxford•, Mass. 249/L2
Box Hill, Victoria 97/J5
Box Hill, Victoria 88/L7
Boxholm, Iowa 229/E4
Bo Xian (Pohsien), China 77/J5
Boxley, Ark. 202/D2
Boxmeer, Netherlands 27/H5
Box Springs, Georgia 217/C5
Boxtel, Netherlands 27/G5
Boyabat, Turkey 63/F2
Boyacá (dept.), Colombia 126/D5
Boyama (Stanley) (falls), Zaire 102/E5
Boyama (Stanley) (falls), Zaire 115/D3
Boyanup, W. Australia 92/A2
Boyce, La. 238/E4
Boyce, Va. 307/M2
Boyceville, Wis. 317/C5
Boyd, Ala. 195/B5
Boyd, Fla. 212/C1
Boyd (co.), Ky. 237/R4
Boyd, Minn. 255/C6
Boyd, Mont. 262/G5
Boyd (co.), Nebr. 264/F2
Boyd, Okla. 288/E1
Boyd, Oreg. 291/F2
Boyd, Texas 303/E1
Boyd, Wis. 317/E6
Boydell, Ark. 202/H7
Boyden, Iowa 229/B2
Boyd Lake, Maine 243/F5
Boyds, Md. 245/J4
Boyds, Wash. 310/G2
Boydton, Va. 307/M7
Boyer (riv.), Alberta 182/A5
Boyer, Iowa 229/C4
Boyer (riv.), Iowa 229/B5
Boyer, W. Va. 312/G5
Boyero, Colo. 208/N5
Boyers, Pa. 294/C3
Boyertown, Pa. 294/L5
Boyes, Mont. 262/M5
Boykin, Georgia 217/C8
Boykin, S.C. 296/F3
Boykins, Va. 307/O7
Boyle, Alberta 182/D2
Boyle, Ireland 17/E4
Boyle, Ireland 10/B3
Boyle (co.), Ky. 237/M5
Boyle, Miss. 256/C3
Boyleston, Ind. 227/E4
Boylston•, Mass. 249/H3
Boylston, Nova Scotia 168/G3
Boyne (riv.), Ireland 17/J4
Boyne City, Mich. 250/E3
Boyne Falls, Mich. 250/E3
Boyne Lake, Alberta 182/E5
Boynton, Okla. 288/P3
Boynton Beach, Fla. 212/F5
Boy River, Minn. 255/D3
Boysen (res.), Wyo. 319/D2
Boysen Bay, N.Y. 276/H4
Boys Ranch, Texas 303/B2
Boys Town, Nebr. 264/H3
Boyuibe, Bolivia 136/D7
Bozcaada (isl.), Turkey 63/A3
Bozdoğan, Turkey 63/C4
Bozeman, Mont. 188/D1
Bozeman, Mont. 262/E5
Bozkır, Turkey 63/E4
Bozkurt, Turkey 63/F2
Bozman, Md. 245/N5
Bozoum, Cent. Afr. Rep. 115/C2
Bozova, Turkey 63/H4
Bozqush, Kuh-e (mts.), Iran 66/E2
Bozüyük, Turkey 59/B2
Bozüyük, Turkey 63/C3
Bra, Italy 34/A2
Brabant (prov.), Belgium 27/F7
Brabant Lake, Sask. 181/M3
Brač (isl.), Yugoslavia 45/C4
Bracadale, Loch (inlet), Scotland 15/B3
Bracciano, Italy 34/C3
Bracciano (lake), Italy 34/D3
Bracebridge, Ontario 177/E2
Braceville, Ill. 222/E2
Bracey, Va. 307/M7
Bräcke, Sweden 18/J5
Bracken (co.), Ky. 237/N3
Bracken, Sask. 181/C6
Brackendale, Br. Col. 184/F5
Brackenridge, Pa. 294/C4
Brackett, Wis. 317/D6
Brackettville, Texas 303/D8
Brackley, England 10/F4
Brackley, England 13/F5
Bracknell, England 13/G8
Bracknell, Tasmania 99/C3
Brackney, Pa. 294/K2
Braço Maior do Araguaia (riv.), Brazil 132/D5
Braço Menor do Araguaia (riv.), Brazil 132/D6
Brad, Romania 45/F2
Bradbury, Calif. 204/D10
Braddock, N. Dak. 282/K6
Braddock, Pa. 294/C7
Braddock, Sask. 181/D5
Braddyville, Iowa 229/D7
Braden, Okla. 288/S4
Braden, Tenn. 237/B10
Bradenton, Fla. 212/D4
Bradenton Beach, Fla. 212/D4
Bradford, Ark. 202/G3
Bradford, England 13/J1
Bradford, England 10/H1
Bradford (co.), Fla. 212/D2
Bradford, Ill. 222/D2
Bradford, Ind. 227/E8
Bradford, Iowa 229/G3
Bradford, Ky. 237/N3
Bradford, Maine 243/F5
Bradford•, Maine 243/F5
Bradford•, N.H. 268/D5
Bradford, Ohio 284/B5
Bradford, Ontario 177/E3
Bradford (co.), Pa. 294/J2
Bradford, Pa. 294/E2
Bradford, R.I. 249/H7
Bradford, Tenn. 237/D8
Bradford, Vt. 268/C3
Bradford•, Vt. 268/C3
Bradford Center, Maine 243/F5
Bradford-on-Avon, England 13/E6
Bradfordsville, Ky. 237/L6
Bradgate, Iowa 229/E3
Bradley (co.), Ark. 202/F7
Bradley, Ark. 202/C7
Bradley, Calif. 204/E8
Bradley, Fla. 212/D4
Bradley, Georgia 217/E4
Bradley, Ill. 222/F2
Bradley•, Maine 243/F6
Bradley, Miss. 256/G4
Bradley, Ohio 284/J5
Bradley, Okla. 288/L5
Bradley, S.C. 296/C3
Bradley, S. Dak. 298/O3
Bradley (co.), Tenn. 237/M10
Bradley, Wis. 317/G4
Bradley Beach, N.J. 273/F3
Bradleyton, Ala. 195/F7
Bradleyville, Mo. 261/F9
Bradner, Ohio 284/C3
Bradshaw, Nebr. 264/G4
Bradshaw, Texas 303/D5
Bradshaw, W. Va. 312/C8
Bradwardine, Manitoba 179/B5
Bradwell, Sask. 181/E4
Brady (glac.), Alaska 196/M1
Brady, Mont. 262/E2
Brady, Nebr. 264/D3
Brady (mt.), S. Australia 94/D3
Brady, Texas 303/E6

342 Brady Lake

Brady Lake, Ohio 284/H3
Bradyville, Tenn. 237/J9
Brae, Scotland 15/G2
Braedstrup, Denmark 21/C6
Braemar, Scotland 15/E3
Braemar, Scotland 10/E2
Braemar (dist.), Scotland 15/E3
Braemar, Tenn. 237/S8
Braeside, Ontario 177/H2
Braeside, W. Australia 92/C3
Braga (dist.), Portugal 33/B2
Braga, Portugal 7/D4
Braga, Portugal 33/B2
Bragado, Argentina 143/F7
Bragança, Brazil 120/E3
Bragança, Brazil 132/E3
Bragança (dist.), Portugal 33/C2
Bragança, Portugal 33/C2
Bragança Paulista, Brazil 135/C3
Bragança Paulista, Brazil 132/E8
Braggadocio, Mo. 261/N10
Bragg City, Mo. 261/N10
Bragg Creek, Alberta 182/C4
Braggs, Ala. 195/E6
Braggs, Okla. 288/R3
Bragman's Bluff (Puerto Cabezas), Nicaragua 154/F3
Braham, Minn. 255/E5
Brahmaputra (riv.) 54/L7
Brahmaputra (riv.), Bangladesh 68/G3
Brahmaputra (riv.), India 68/G3
Braich-y-Pwll (prom.), Wales 10/D4
Braich-y-Pwll (prom.), Wales 13/C5
Braidwood, Ill. 222/E2
Braidwood, N.S. Wales 97/E4
Brăila, Romania 7/G4
Brăila, Romania 45/H3
Brăila (marshes), Romania 45/H3
Brainard, Nebr. 264/G3
Brainards, N.J. 273/C2
Braine-l'Alleud, Belgium 27/E7
Braine-le-Comte, Belgium 27/D7
Brainerd, Minn. 188/H1
Brainerd, Minn. 255/D4
Braintree•, Mass. 249/D8
Braintree (West Braintree), Vt. 268/B4
Braintree•, Vt. 268/B4
Braintree and Bocking, England 13/H6
Braintree and Bocking, England 10/G5
Braithwaite, La. 238/P4
Brak, Libya 102/D2
Brak, Libya 111/B2
Brake, Germany 22/C2
Brakna (reg.), Mauritania 106/B5
Brakpan, S. Africa 118/J6
Bralorne, Br. Col. 184/F5
Braman, Okla. 288/M1
Bramber, Nova Scotia 168/D3
Bramberg am Wildkogel, Austria 41/B3
Bramble (bay), Queensland 95/E2
Bramming, Denmark 21/B7
Bramon, Venezuela 124/B4
Brampton, England 13/E3
Brampton, Mich. 250/B3
Brampton, N. Dak. 282/P7
Brampton, Ontario 177/J4
Bramsche, Germany 22/B2
Bramwell, W. Va. 312/D8
Bran (riv.), Scotland 15/D3
Brancepeth, Sask. 181/F2
Branch, Ark. 202/C3
Branch, La. 238/F6
Branch (co.), Mich. 250/D7
Branch, Mich. 250/D5
Branch, Minn. 255/F5
Branch, Mo. 261/G7
Branch, Newf. 166/D2
Branch (riv.), Newf. 166/C2
Branch, Wis. 317/L7
Branch Dale, Pa. 294/K4
Branchport, N.Y. 276/F5
Branchton, Pa. 294/C3
Branchville, Ala. 195/F3
Branchville, Conn. 210/B3
Branchville, Ind. 227/D8
Branchville, N.J. 273/D1
Branchville, S.C. 296/F5
Branchville, Va. 307/O7
Branco (riv.), Brazil 120/C2
Branco (riv.), Brazil 132/H8
Brandberg (mt.), Namibia 118/A4
Brande, Denmark 21/B6
Brandenburg, Germany 22/E2
Brandenburg (state), Germany 22/E2
Brandenburg, Ky. 237/J4
Brandon, Colo. 208/P6
Brandon, England 13/H5
Brandon, Fla. 212/D4
Brandon, Iowa 229/K4
Brandon (bay), Ireland 17/A7
Brandon (head), Ireland 17/A7
Brandon (mt.), Ireland 17/A7
Brandon, Man. 146/H4
Brandon, Man. 162/F6
Brandon, Manitoba 179/C5
Brandon, Minn. 255/C5
Brandon, Miss. 256/E6
Brandon, Nebr. 264/C4
Brandon, Ohio 284/F5
Brandon, S. Dak. 298/R6
Brandon, Vt. 268/A4
Brandon•, Vt. 268/A4
Brandon, Wis. 317/J8
Brandon Gap (pass), Vt. 268/B4
Brandonville, W. Va. 312/G3
Brandreth (lake), N.Y. 276/L3
Brandsville, Mo. 261/J9
Brandt, Ohio 284/B6
Brandt, S. Dak. 298/R4
Brandvlei, S. Africa 118/B6
Brandýs nad Labem-Stará Boleslavv, Czech. 41/C1
Brandy Station, Va. 307/N4
Brandywine, Md. 245/L6
Brandywine, W. Va. 312/H5
Branford, Conn. 210/D3
Branford•, Conn. 210/D3
Branford (harb.), Conn. 210/D4
Branford (riv.), Conn. 210/D3
Branford, Fla. 212/D2
Braniewo, Poland 47/D1
Brannock (isls.), Ireland 17/A5
Bransfield (str.), Ant. 5/C16
Branson, Colo. 208/M8
Branson, Mo. 261/F9
Brant, Alberta 182/D4
Brant, Mich. 250/E5
Brant, N.Y. 276/B5
Brant (lake), N.Y. 276/N3
Brant (county), Ontario 177/D4
Brant (lake), S. Dak. 298/R6
Brant Beach, N.J. 273/E4
Brantford, Kansas 232/E2
Brantford, N. Dak. 282/N4
Brantford, Ontario 177/D4
Brant Lake, N.Y. 276/N3
Brantley, Ala. 195/F7
Brantley (co.), Georgia 217/J8
Brant Rock-Ocean Bluff, Mass. 249/M4
Brantville, New Bruns. 170/E1
Brantwood, Wis. 317/F4
Branxholm, Tasmania 99/D3
Branxholme, Victoria 97/A5
Branxton-Greta, N.S. Wales 97/F3
Bras d'Or, Nova Scotia 168/H2
Bras d'Or (lake), Nova Scotia 168/H3
Braselton, Georgia 217/E2
Brasfield, Ark. 202/H4
Brashear, Mo. 261/H2
Brasher, Mo. 261/N10
Brasher Falls-Winthrop, N.Y. 276/L1
Brasiléia, Brazil 132/G10
Brasília (cap.), Brazil 2/G6
Brasília (cap.), Brazil 120/E4
Brasília (cap.), Brazil 132/E6
Brasília de Minas, Brazil 132/F7
Braşov, Romania 45/G3
Braşov, Romania 7/G4
Brass, Nigeria 106/F8
Brass (isls.), Virgin Is. (U.S.) 161/A4
Brassey (range), W. Australia 92/C4
Brasstown Bald (mt.), Georgia 217/E1
Brassua (lake), Maine 243/D4
Braswell, Georgia 217/C3
Brate, Norway 18/G7
Bratenahl, Ohio 284/H9
Bratislava, Czech. 7/F4
Bratislava (city), Czech. 41/D2
Bratislava, Czech. 41/D2
Bratsk, U.S.S.R. 54/M4
Bratsk, U.S.S.R. 48/L4
Bratsk (res.), U.S.S.R. 48/L4
Brattleboro, Vt. 268/B6
Brattleboro•, Vt. 268/B6
Bratton, Sask. 181/D4
Braunau am Inn, Austria 41/B2
Braunlage, Germany 22/D3
Braunschweig (Brunswick), Germany 22/D2
Braunton, England 13/C6
Brava (isl.), C. Verde 106/B8
Brava, Somalia 115/H3
Brava, Somalia 102/G4
Brava (pt.), Uruguay 145/B7
Brave, Pa. 294/B6
Bravo (riv.), Chile 138/D7
Bravo (Grande) (riv.), Mexico 150/G2
Brawley, Calif. 188/C4
Brawley, Calif. 204/K11
Braxton, Miss. 256/D6
Braxton (co.), W. Va. 312/E5
Bray, Ireland 17/K5
Bray, Ireland 10/C4
Bray (head), Ireland 17/A8
Bray (isl.), N.W. Terr. 187/L3
Bray, Okla. 288/L5
Braymer, Mo. 261/E3
Brayton, Iowa 229/D5
Brazeau (dam), Alberta 182/C3
Brazeau (mt.), Alberta 182/B3
Brazeau (riv.), Alberta 182/B3
Brazil 2/F6
Brazil 120/D4
BRAZIL 132, 135
Brazil, Ind. 227/C5
Brazil, Miss. 256/D2
Brazil, Tenn. 237/C9
Brazilian Highlands (plat.), Brazil 120/E4
Brazilton, Kansas 232/H4
Brazito, Mo. 261/H6
Brazoria (co.), Texas 303/J8
Brazoria, Texas 303/J9
Brazos (peak), N. Mex. 274/C2
Brazos (co.), Texas 303/H7
Brazos (riv.), Texas 188/G4
Brazos (riv.), Texas 146/J6
Brazos (riv.), Texas 303/H7
Brazo Sur, Pilcomayo (riv.), Argentina 143/E1
Brazzaville (cap.), Congo 115/C4
Brazzaville (cap.), Congo 2/K6
Brazzaville (cap.), Congo 102/D5
Brčko, Yugoslavia 45/D3
Brda (riv.), Poland 47/C2
Brea, Calif. 204/D11
Breadalbane (dist.), Scotland 15/D4
Bread Loaf, Vt. 268/B4
Bread Loaf (mt.), Vt. 268/A3
Breakabeen, N.Y. 276/M5
Breakeyville, Québec 172/J3
Breaks, Va. 307/D6
Breaksea (sound), N. Zealand 100/A6
Bream (bay), N. Zealand 100/E1
Brasclete, Scotland 15/B2
Breathitt (co.), Ky. 237/P5
Breau-Village, New Bruns. 170/F2
Breaux Bridge, La. 238/G6
Brebes, Indonesia 85/H2
Brébeuf, Québec 172/C3
Brébeuf (lake), Québec 172/G1
Brechin, Ontario 177/E3
Brechin, Scotland 10/E2
Brechin, Scotland 15/F4
Brecht, Belgium 27/F6
Breckenridge, Colo. 208/G4
Breckenridge, Mich. 250/E5
Breckenridge, Minn. 255/B4
Breckenridge, Mo. 261/E3
Breckenridge, Texas 303/F5
Breckenridge Hills, Mo. 261/O2
Breckinridge (co.), Ky. 237/H5
Breckinridge, Okla. 288/L2
Brecknock (Brecon), Wales 13/D6
Brecksville, Ohio 284/H10
Břeclav, Czech. 41/D2
Brecon, Wales 13/D6
Brecon, Wales 10/E5
Brecon Beacons (mt.), Wales 13/D6
Brecon Beacons National Park, Wales 13/D6
Breda, Iowa 229/C4
Breda, Netherlands 27/F5
Bredasdorp, S. Africa 118/B6
Bredasdorp Nat'l Park, S. Africa 118/C6
Bredbo, N.S. Wales 97/E4
Bredbyn, Sweden 18/L5
Bredebro, Denmark 21/B7
Bredenbury, Sask. 181/K5
Bredene, Belgium 27/B6
Bredstedt, Germany 22/C1
Bree, Belgium 27/H6
Breed, Wis. 317/K5
Breeden, W. Va. 312/B7
Breeding, Ky. 237/L7
Breedsville, Mich. 250/C6
Breese, Ill. 222/D5
Breesport, N.Y. 276/G6
Breezand, Netherlands 27/F3
Breezy Point, Minn. 255/D4
Bregenz, Austria 41/A3
Bregovo, Bulgaria 45/F3
Breidhafjördhur (fjord), Iceland 7/B2
Breidhafjördhur (fjord), Iceland 21/B1
Breien, N. Dak. 282/H7
Breil-Brigels, Switzerland 39/H3
Breil-sur-Roya, France 28/G6
Breisach am Rhein, Germany 22/B4
Breisgau (reg.), Germany 22/B5
Breitenbach, Switzerland 39/E2
Breitenbush, Oreg. 291/F3
Breithorn (mt.), Switzerland 39/E5
Breithorn (mt.), Switzerland 39/E4
Brejo, Brazil 132/F3
Bremanger (isl.), Norway 18/D6
Bremen, Ala. 195/E3
Bremen, Georgia 217/B3
Bremen, Ill. 222/D6
Bremen, Ind. 227/E2
Bremen, Kansas 232/F2
Bremen, Ky. 237/G6
Bremen, N. Dak. 282/M4
Bremen, Ohio 284/F6
Bremen, Sask. 181/F3
Bremen (state), Germany 22/C2
Bremen, Germany 7/E3
Bremen, Germany 22/C2
Bremer (co.), Iowa 229/J3
Bremer, Iowa 229/J3
Bremerhaven, Germany 22/C2
Bremerton, Wash. 188/B1
Bremerton, Wash. 310/A2
Bremervörde, Germany 22/C2
Bremgarten, Switzerland 39/F2
Bremo Bluff, Va. 307/M5
Bremond, Texas 303/H6
Brenham, Texas 303/H7
Brenner (pass), Austria 41/A3
Brenner (pass), Italy 34/C1
Brent, Ala. 195/D5
Brent, England 13/H8
Brent, England 10/B5
Brent, Ontario 177/F1
Brentford, S. Dak. 298/N3
Brenton (pt.), R.I. 249/J7
Brentwood, Ark. 202/B2
Brentwood, Calif. 204/L2
Brentwood, England 10/C5
Brentwood, England 13/J8
Brentwood, Md. 245/F4
Brentwood, Mo. 261/P3
Brentwood•, N.H. 268/E6
Brentwood, N.Y. 276/O9
Brentwood, Pa. 294/B7
Brentwood, Tenn. 237/H8
Brentwood Park, S. Africa 118/J6
Brereton Lake, Manitoba 179/G5
Bresaylor, Sask. 181/C3
Brescia (prov.), Italy 34/C2
Brescia, Italy 7/E4
Brescia, Italy 34/C2
Breskens, Netherlands 27/C6
Breslau (Wrocław), Poland 47/C3
Bressanone, Italy 34/C1
Bressay (isl.), Scotland 15/G2
Bressay (isl.), Scotland 10/G1
Bressuire, France 28/C4
Brest, France 7/D4
Brest, France 28/A3
Brest, Georgia 217/D8
Brest, New Bruns. 170/E2
Brest, U.S.S.R. 7/G3
Brest, U.S.S.R. 48/C4
Brest, U.S.S.R. 52/B4
Bretaña, Peru 128/E5
Brethren, Mich. 250/D4
Breton, Alberta 182/C3
Breton (isls.), La. 238/M8
Breton (sound), La. 238/M7
Breton (cape), Nova Scotia 168/J3
Breton Cove, Nova Scotia 168/H2
Breton Woods, N.J. 273/E3
Brett (cape), N. Zealand 100/E1
Bretten, Germany 22/C4
Bretton Woods, N.H. 268/E3
Brevard (co.), Fla. 212/F3
Brevard, N.C. 281/D4
Breves, Brazil 132/D3
Brevig Mission, Alaska 196/E1
Brevik, Minn. 255/D3
Brevoort (lake), Mich. 250/D3
Brevoort (isl.), N.W. Terr. 187/M3
Brevort, Mich. 250/E2
Brewarrina, N. S. Wales 88/H5
Brewarrina, N.S. Wales 97/D1
Brewer, Maine 243/F6
Brewer, Mo. 261/N7
Brewers, Ky. 237/E7
Brewers Mills, New Bruns. 170/C2
Brewersville, Ind. 227/F6
Brewerton, N.Y. 276/H4
Brewster (pond), Conn. 210/F2
Brewster, Kansas 232/A2
Brewster, Mass. 249/O5
Brewster•, Mass. 249/O5
Brewster (isls.), Mass. 249/E7
Brewster, Minn. 255/C7
Brewster, Nebr. 264/D3
Brewster (lake), N.S. Wales 97/D3
Brewster, N.Y. 276/N8
Brewster, Ohio 284/G4
Brewster, Cerro (mt.), Panama 154/H6
Brewster (co.), Texas 303/A8
Brewster, Wash. 310/F2
Brewton, Ala. 195/D8
Breynat, Alberta 182/D2
Brežice, Yugoslavia 45/B3
Brezina, Algeria 106/E2
Březnice, Czech. 41/B2
Breznik, Bulgaria 45/F4
Brezno, Czech. 41/E2
Bria, Cent. Afr. Rep. 102/E4
Bria, Cent. Afr. Rep. 115/D2
Briançon, France 28/G5
Brian Head, Utah 304/B6
Briar, Texas 303/E1
Briar Creek, Pa. 294/K3
Briare, France 28/E4
Briartown, Okla. 288/R4
Briarwood, 282/S6
Bribbaree, N.S. Wales 97/D3
Brice, Ohio 284/E6
Bricelyn, Minn. 255/E7
Brices Cross Roads Nat'l Battlefield Site, Miss. 256/G2
Briceville, Tenn. 237/N8
Brí Chualann (Bray), Ireland 17/K5
Brick•, N.J. 273/E3
Brickaville (Vohibinany), Madagascar 118/H3
Brickerville, Pa. 294/K5
Brickeys, Ark. 202/J4
Bricks, N.C. 281/O2
Brickton, Nova Scotia 168/C4
Bridal Veil, Oreg. 291/E2
Bride (riv.), Ireland 17/E7
Bridesville, Br. Col. 184/H6
Bridge, Idaho 220/E7
Bridge, Oreg. 291/D4
Bridgeboro, Georgia 217/E8
Bridge City, Texas 303/L7
Bridgedale, New Bruns. 170/F3
Bridgeford, Sask. 181/E5
Bridgehampton, N.Y. 276/R9
Bridge Lake, Br. Col. 184/G4
Bridgeland, Utah 304/D3
Bridgend, Wales 13/A7
Bridgenorth, Ontario 177/F3
Bridge of Allan, Scotland 10/B1
Bridge of Allan, Scotland 15/C1
Bridge of Don, Scotland 15/F3
Bridge of Weir, Scotland 15/A2
Bridgeport, Ala. 195/G1
Bridgeport, Calif. 204/F5
Bridgeport, Conn. 188/M2
Bridgeport, Conn. 210/C4
Bridgeport, Ill. 222/F5
Bridgeport, Kansas 232/E3
Bridgeport, Mich. 250/F5
Bridgeport, Nebr. 264/A3
Bridgeport, N.J. 273/C4
Bridgeport, N.Y. 276/J4
Bridgeport, Ohio 284/J5
Bridgeport, Okla. 288/K3
Bridgeport, Oreg. 291/K3
Bridgeport, Pa. 294/M5
Bridgeport, Texas 303/G4
Bridgeport, Wash. 310/F3
Bridgeport, W. Va. 312/F4
Bridgeport, Wis. 317/D9
Bridger, Mont. 262/H5
Bridgeton, Ind. 227/C5
Bridgeton, Mich. 250/D5
Bridgeton, Mo. 261/O2
Bridgeton, N.J. 273/C5
Bridgeton, N.C. 281/R4
Bridgeton Terrace, Mo. 261/O2
Bridgetown (cap.), Barbados 156/G4
Bridgetown (cap.), Barbados 161/B9
Bridgetown, Md. 245/P4
Bridgetown, Nova Scotia 168/C4
Bridgetown, Ohio 284/B9
Bridgetown, W. Australia 88/B6
Bridgetown, W. Australia 92/B6
Bridgeview, Ill. 222/B6
Bridgeville, Calif. 204/B3
Bridgeville, Del. 245/R6
Bridgeville, Nova Scotia 168/F3
Bridgeville, Pa. 294/B5
Bridgeville, Québec 172/D1
Bridgewater•, Conn. 210/B2
Bridgewater, Iowa 229/D6
Bridgewater•, Maine 243/H3
Bridgewater, Mass. 249/K5
Bridgewater•, Mass. 249/K5
Bridgewater•, N.H. 268/D4
Bridgewater•, N.J. 273/D2
Bridgewater, N.Y. 276/K5
Bridgewater, N.S. 162/K7
Bridgewater, Nova Scotia 168/D4
Bridgewater, Pa. 294/B4
Bridgewater, S. Dak. 298/P6
Bridgewater, Tasmania 99/D4
Bridgewater•, Vt. 268/B4
Bridgewater (cape), Victoria 97/A6
Bridgewater, Va. 307/K4
Bridgewater Center, Vt. 268/B4
Bridgewater Corners, Vt. 268/B4
Bridgman, Mich. 250/C7
Bridgnorth, England 13/E5
Bridgnorth, England 10/E4
Bridgton, Maine 243/B7
Bridgton•, Maine 243/B7
Bridgwater, England 10/E5
Bridgwater, England 13/E6
Bridlington, England 13/G3
Bridlington, England 10/F3
Bridlington (bay), England 13/G3
Bridport, England 13/E7
Bridport, England 10/E5
Bridport, Tasmania 99/D3
Bridport•, Vt. 268/A4
Brieg (Brzeg), Poland 47/C3
Brielle, Netherlands 27/E5
Brielle, N.J. 273/E3
Briensburg, Ky. 237/E7
Brienz, Switzerland 39/F3
Brienzer Rothorn (mt.), Switzerland 39/F3
Brienzersee (lake), Switzerland 39/F3
Brier (isl.), Nova Scotia 168/B4
Brier, Wash. 310/C3
Briercrest, Sask. 181/F5
Brierfield, Ala. 195/E4
Brier Hill, N.Y. 276/J1
Brig, Switzerland 39/F4
Brigantine, N.J. 273/E5
Brigantine (inlet), N.J. 273/E5
Brigden, Ontario 177/B5
Brigg, England 13/G4
Briggs, Texas 303/F7
Briggs Corner, New Bruns. 170/E2
Briggsdale, Colo. 208/L1
Briggsville, Ark. 202/C4
Briggsville, Wis. 317/H8
Brigham City, Utah 188/D2
Brigham City, Utah 304/C2
Brighowe, England 13/J1
Bright, Ind. 227/H6
Bright, Victoria 97/D5
Brightlingsea, England 13/J6
Brightlingsea, England 10/G5
Brighton, Ala. 195/D4
Brighton, Colo. 208/K3
Brighton, England 10/F5
Brighton, England 13/G7
Brighton, Fla. 212/E4
Brighton, Ill. 222/C4
Brighton, Ind. 227/G1
Brighton, Iowa 229/K6
Brighton•, Maine 243/D5
Brighton, Mich. 250/F6
Brighton, Mo. 261/F8
Brighton, Nova Scotia 168/C4
Brighton, Ohio 284/F3
Brighton, Ontario 177/G3
Brighton, Oreg. 291/C2
Brighton, S. Australia 88/D8
Brighton, S. Australia 94/A8
Brighton, Tasmania 99/D4
Brighton, Tenn. 237/B10
Brighton, Utah 304/C3
Brighton, Victoria 97/J5
Brighton, Victoria 88/L7
Brighton, Wis. 317/K3
Brightons, Scotland 15/C1
Brightsand (lake), Sask. 181/B2
Brights Grove, Ontario 177/B4
Brightshade, Ky. 237/O7
Brightstar, Ark. 202/C7
Brightwood, D.C. 245/F4
Brightwood, Oreg. 291/E2
Brightwood, Va. 307/M4
Brignoles, France 28/G6
Brigus, Newf. 166/D2
Brihuega, Spain 33/E2
Brikama, Gambia 106/A6
Brill, Wis. 317/C4
Brilliant, Ala. 195/C2
Brilliant, Ohio 284/J5
Brillion, Wis. 317/L7
Brilon, Germany 22/C3
Brimfield, Ill. 222/D3
Brimfield, Ind. 227/G2
Brimfield•, Mass. 249/F4
Brimfield, Ohio 284/H3
Brimley, Mich. 250/E2
Brimson, Minn. 255/F3
Brimson, Mo. 261/E2
Brimstone (hill), St. Kitts & Nevis 161/C10
Brinckerhoff, N.Y. 276/N7
Brindakit, U.S.S.R. 48/O4
Brindisi (prov.), Italy 34/G4
Brindisi, Italy 7/F4
Brindisi, Italy 34/G4
Binghurst, Ind. 227/E3
Brinkhaven, Ohio 284/F5
Brinkley, Ark. 202/H4
Brinkman, Okla. 288/G4
Brinktown, Mo. 261/J6
Brinnon, Wash. 310/B3
Brinsmade, N. Dak. 282/M3
Brinson, Georgia 217/C9
Briny Breezes, Fla. 212/G5
Brione, Switzerland 39/G4
Brioude, France 28/E5
Brisbane, Australia 2/S7
Brisbane, Calif. 204/J2
Brisbane (cap.), Queensland 95/D2
Brisbane (cap.), Queensland 88/K3
Brisbane (riv.), Queensland 88/J3
Brisbane (riv.), Queensland 95/D2
Brisbane Airport, Queensland 95/E2
Brisbane International Airport, Queensland 88/K2
Brisbane Water, N.S. Wales 88/J6
Brisbane Water, N.S. Wales 97/F3
Brisbin, Pa. 294/F4
Brisco, Br. Col. 184/J5
Briscoe (co.), Texas 303/C3
Briscoe, Texas 303/D2
Brisighella, Italy 34/C2
Brissago, Switzerland 39/G4
Bristol (bay), Alaska 188/C6
Bristol (bay), Alaska 146/D4
Bristol (bay), Alaska 196/F3
Bristol (lake), Calif. 204/K9
Bristol, Colo. 208/P6
Bristol, Conn. 210/D2
Bristol, England 13/E6
Bristol, England 7/D3
Bristol, England 10/E5
Bristol (chan.), England 13/C6
Bristol (chan.), England 10/E5
Bristol, Fla. 212/B1
Bristol, Georgia 217/H8
Bristol, Ind. 227/F1
Bristol, Maine 243/D8
Bristol•, Maine 243/D8
Bristol, Md. 245/M5
Bristol (co.), Mass. 249/K5
Bristol, Mich. 250/D4
Bristol, New Bruns. 170/C2
Bristol, N.H. 268/D4
Bristol•, N.H. 268/D4
Bristol, Pa. 294/N5
Bristol•, Pa. 294/N5
Bristol (co.), R.I. 249/J6
Bristol, R.I. 249/J6
Bristol, S. Dak. 298/O3
Bristol, Tenn. 188/K3
Bristol, Tenn. 237/S7
Bristol (bay), U.S. 4/D18
Bristol, Va. 188/K3
Bristol, Vt. 268/A3
Bristol•, Vt. 268/A3
Bristol (I.C.), Va. 307/D7
Bristol (chan.), Wales 13/C6
Bristol (chan.), Wales 10/E5
Bristol, W. Va. 312/F4
Bristolville, Ohio 284/J3
Bristow, Ind. 227/D8
Bristow, Iowa 229/H3
Bristow, Nebr. 264/F2
Bristow, Okla. 288/O3
Bristow, Va. 307/N3
Britannia Beach, Br. Col. 184/K2
British (mts.), Alaska 196/K1
British (mts.), Yukon 187/D3
British Columbia (prov.) 162/D4
BRITISH COLUMBIA 184
British Columbia (prov.), Canada 146/F4
British Empire (range), N.W.T. 186/L1
British Indian Ocean Territory 2/N6
British Indian Ocean Territory 54/J10
British Isles 7/D3
Brits, S. Africa 118/D5
Britstown, S. Africa 118/C6
Britt, Iowa 229/F2
Britt, Minn. 255/F3
Britt, Ontario 177/D2
Brittany (trad. prov.), France 29
Brittany, La. 238/L3
Brittnau, Switzerland 39/E2
Britton, Mich. 250/F6
Britton, S. Dak. 298/O2
Brive-la-Gaillarde, France 28/D5
Briviesca, Spain 33/E1
Brno, Czech. 7/F4
Brno, Czech. 41/D2
Broa (inlet), Cuba 158/C1
Broach (Bharuch), India 68/C4
Broad (brook), Conn. 210/H2
Broad (creek), Del. 245/R6
Broad (riv.), N.C. 281/E4
Broad (sound), Queensland 88/H4
Broad (sound), Queensland 95/D4
Broad (bay), Scotland 15/B2
Broad (riv.), S.C. 296/F7
Broad (riv.), S.C. 296/E2
Broadacres, Oreg. 291/A3
Broadacres, Sask. 181/B3
Broadalbin, N.Y. 276/M4
Broad Arrow, W. Australia 88/C6
Broad Arrow, W. Australia 92/C5
Broadback (riv.), Québec 174/B2
Broadbent, Oreg. 291/C4
Broad Brook, Conn. 210/E1
Broad Cove, Newf. 166/D2
Broad Cove, Nova Scotia 168/D4
Broaddus, Texas 303/K6
Broadfields, Ky. 237/K2
Broadford, Ireland 17/C7
Broadford, Scotland 15/B3
Broadford, Victoria 97/C5
Broadford, Va. 307/E7
Broad Haven (harb.), Ireland 17/B3
Broadhurst, Georgia 217/J8
Broadkill (riv.), Del. 245/S5
Broadland, S. Dak. 298/N4
Broadlands, Ill. 222/E4
Broad Law (mt.), Scotland 15/E5
Broadmeadows, Victoria 88/L6
Broadmeadows, Victoria 97/H4
Broadstairs and Saint Peter's, England 13/J6
Broad Top, Pa. 294/F5
Broadus, Mont. 262/L5
Broad Valley, Manitoba 179/E4
Broadview, Ill. 222/B6
Broadview, Mont. 262/H4
Broadview, N. Mex. 274/F4
Broadview, Sask. 181/J5
Broadview Heights, Ohio 284/H10
Broadview Park, Fla. 212/B4
Broadwater (co.), Mont. 262/E4
Broadwater, Nebr. 264/B3
Broadway, N.J. 273/C2
Broadway, N.C. 281/L4
Broadway, Ohio 284/C5
Broadway, Va. 307/L3
Broadwell, Ill. 222/D3
Broager, Denmark 21/C8
Broc, Switzerland 39/D3
Brochet, Man. 162/F4
Brochet, Manitoba 179/H2
Brock (isl.), N.W.T. 162/M3
Brock, Nebr. 264/H4
Brock (isl.), N.W. Terr. 187/G2
Brock, Sask. 181/C4
Brockdell, Tenn. 237/L10
Brocken (mt.), Germany 22/D3
Brocket, Alberta 182/D5
Brocket, N. Dak. 282/O3
Brockington, Sask. 181/G2
Brockport, N.Y. 276/D4

Buffalo Narrows 343

Brockport, Pa. 294/E3
Brockton, Mass. 249/K4
Brockton, Mont. 262/M2
Brockville, Ontario 177/J3
Brockway, Mont. 262/L3
Brockway, New Bruns. 170/C3
Brockway, Pa. 294/E3
Brocton, Ill. 222/F4
Brocton, N.Y. 276/B6
Broderick, Sask. 181/E4
Broderick-Bryte, Calif. 204/B8
Brodeur (pen.), Canada 4/B14
Brodeur (pen.), N.W.T. 146/K2
Brodeur (pen.), N.W.T. 162/H1
Brodeur (pen.), N.W. Terr. 187/K2
Brodhead, Ky. 237/N6
Brodhead, Wis. 317/G10
Brodheadsville, Pa. 294/M4
Brodick, Scotland 15/C5
Brodick, Scotland 10/D3
Brodnax, Va. 307/N7
Brodnica, Poland 47/D2
Broek in Waterland, Netherlands 27/C4
Brogan, Oreg. 291/K3
Brohard, W. Va. 312/D4
Brohman, Mich. 250/D5
Brokaw, Wis. 317/G5
Broken (bay), N.S. Wales 97/F3
Broken Arrow, Okla. 288/P2
Broken Bow, Nebr. 264/E3
Broken Bow, Okla. 288/S7
Broken Bow (lake), Okla. 288/S6
Broken Hill, Australia 87/E9
Broken Hill, N.S. Wales 88/G6
Broken Hill, N.S. Wales 97/A3
Broken Hill (Kabwe), Zambia 115/E6
Brokensword, Ohio 284/E4
Brokopondo (dist.), Suriname 131/D4
Brokopondo, Suriname 131/D3
Brome (co.), Québec 172/E4
Brome, Québec 172/E4
Brome (lake), Québec 172/E4
Bromer, Ind. 227/E7
Bromhead, Sask. 181/H6
Bromide, Okla. 288/N6
Bromley, England 13/H8
Bromley, England 10/C5
Bromley, Ky. 237/S2
Bromley (mt.), Vt. 268/B5
Bromont, Québec 172/E4
Brompton (lake), Québec 172/E4
Bromptonville, Québec 172/F4
Bromsgrove, England 13/E5
Bromyard, England 13/E5
Bronaugh, Mo. 261/D7
Bronco, Texas 303/B4
Brønderslev, Denmark 18/F8
Brønderslev, Denmark 21/C3
Brønnøysund, Norway 18/G4
Brøns, Denmark 21/B7
Bronson, Fla. 212/D2
Bronson, Iowa 229/A4
Bronson, Kansas 232/H4
Bronson, Mich. 250/D7
Bronson (lake), Sask. 181/B2
Bronson, Texas 303/L6
Bronston, Ky. 237/M7
Bronte, Italy 34/E6
Bronte, Texas 303/D6
Bronwood, Georgia 217/D7
Bronx (co.), N.Y. 276/N9
Bronx (borough), N.Y. 276/N9
Bronxville, N.Y. 276/O7
Brook, Ind. 227/C3
Brookdale, Calif. 204/J4
Brookdale, Manitoba 179/C4
Brookdale, Nova Scotia 168/D3
Brooke, Va. 307/O4
Brooke (co.), W. Va. 312/E2
Brookeborough, N. Ireland 17/G3
Brookeland, Texas 303/L6
Brooker, Fla. 212/D2
Brooke's Point, Philippines 82/A6
Brookeville, Md. 245/K4
Brookfield•, Conn. 210/B3
Brookfield, Georgia 217/F8
Brookfield, Ill. 222/B6
Brookfield, Mass. 249/F4
Brookfield•, Mass. 249/F4
Brookfield, Mo. 261/F3
Brookfield•, N.H. 268/E4
Brookfield, N.Y. 276/K5
Brookfield, Nova Scotia 168/E3
Brookfield, Ohio 284/J3
Brookfield•, Vt. 268/B3
Brookfield, Wis. 317/K1
Brookfield Center, Conn. 210/B3
Brookford, N.C. 281/G3
Brookhaven, Georgia 217/K1
Brookhaven, Miss. 256/C7
Brookhaven, Pa. 294/M7
Brookhaven Nat'l Lab., N.Y. 276/P9
Brookings, Oreg. 291/C5
Brookings (co.), S. Dak. 298/R5
Brookings, S. Dak. 298/R5
Brookland, Ark. 202/J2
Brookland, D.C. 245/F4
Brooklawn, N.J. 273/B3
Brooklet, Georgia 217/J6
Brooklin•, Maine 243/F7
Brookline•, Mass. 249/C7
Brookline•, N.H. 268/D6
Brookline•, Vt. 268/B5
Brookline Station (Brookline), Mo. 261/F8
Brooklyn, Ala. 195/E8
Brooklyn•, Conn. 210/H1
Brooklyn, Georgia 217/C6
Brooklyn (Lovejoy), Ill. 222/A2
Brooklyn, Ill. 222/C3
Brooklyn, Ind. 227/E5
Brooklyn, Iowa 229/J5
Brooklyn, Ky. 237/H6
Brooklyn, Mich. 250/E6
Brooklyn, Miss. 256/F8
Brooklyn, Newf. 166/D2
Brooklyn (borough), N.Y. 276/N9
Brooklyn, Nova Scotia 168/D4
Brooklyn, Ohio 234/H9
Brooklyn, Pa. 294/L2
Brooklyn, Wash. 310/B4
Brooklyn, Wis. 317/H10
Brooklyn Center, Minn. 255/G5
Brooklyn Heights, Ohio 284/H9
Brooklyn Park, Md. 245/M4
Brooklyn Park, Minn. 255/G5
Brookmere, Br. Col. 184/G5
Brookneal, Va. 307/L6
Brook Park, Minn. 255/F5
Brook Park, Ohio 284/G9
Brookport, Ill. 222/E6
Brooks (range), Alaska 146/C3
Brooks (range), Alaska 188/C5
Brooks (range), Alaska 196/G1
Brooks, Alberta 182/E4
Brooks (pen.), Br. Col. 184/D5
Brooks, Calif. 204/C5
Brooks (co.), Georgia 217/E9
Brooks, Georgia 217/D4
Brooks, Iowa 229/D7
Brooks, Ky. 237/K4
Brooks•, Maine 243/E6
Brooks, Minn. 255/B3
Brooks, Mont. 262/G3
Brooks, Oreg. 291/A3
Brooks (co.), Texas 303/F11
Brooks (range), U.S. 4/C17
Brooks, W. Va. 312/E7
Brooks, Wis. 317/G8
Brooks A.F.B., Texas 303/K11
Brooksburg, Ind. 227/G7
Brooksby, Sask. 181/G2
Brookshire, Texas 303/J8
Brookside, Ala. 195/E3
Brookside, Colo. 208/J6
Brookside, Del. 245/R2
Brookside, N.J. 273/D2
Brookside, Ohio 284/J5
Brookside Village, Texas 303/J2
Brookston, Ind. 227/D3
Brookston, Minn. 255/F4
Brooksville, Ala. 195/F2
Brooksville, Fla. 212/D3
Brooksville, Ky. 237/N3
Brooksville, Maine 243/F7
Brooksville•, Maine 243/F7
Brooksville, Miss. 256/G4
Brooksville, Okla. 288/M4
Brookton, Georgia 217/E2
Brookton, Maine 243/H4
Brookton, W. Australia 92/B2
Brooktondale, N.Y. 276/H6
Brookview, Md. 245/P6
Brook Village, Nova Scotia 168/G2
Brookville, Ind. 227/G6
Brookville (lake), Ind. 227/G6
Brookville, Kansas 232/E3
Brookville, Mass. 249/K4
Brookville, N.Y. 276/R6
Brookville, Ohio 284/B6
Brookville, Pa. 294/D3
Brookwood, Ala. 195/D4
Broom, Loch (inlet), Scotland 15/C3
Broomall, Pa. 294/M6
Broome, Australia 87/C7
Broome (co.), N.Y. 276/J6
Broome, W. Australia 88/C3
Broome, W. Australia 92/C2
Broomfield, Colo. 208/J3
Broomhill, Manitoba 179/B5
Brooten, Minn. 255/C5
Brora, Scotland 15/E2
Brora (riv.), Scotland 15/D2
Brørup, Denmark 21/C7
Broseley, Mo. 261/M9
Brosna, Ireland 17/C7
Brosna (riv.), Ireland 17/F5
Brossard, Québec 172/H4
Brosseau, Alberta 182/E3
Brothers, Oreg. 291/G4
Brotherton, Tenn. 237/L8
Brothertown, Wis. 317/K7
Brou, France 23/D3
Brough (head), Scotland 15/E1
Brough Ness (prom.), Scotland 15/F2
Broughshane, N. Ireland 17/J2
Broughton, Ill. 222/E6
Broughton, Ohio 284/B3
Broughton, Pa. 294/B7
Broughton, Scotland 15/E5
Broughton Island, N.W. Terr. 187/M3
Broumov, Czech. 41/D1
Brounland, W. Va. 312/C6
Brouse, Br. Col. 184/J5
Broussard, La. 238/F6
Brouwershaven, Netherlands 27/D5
Brovst, Denmark 21/C3
Broward (co.), Fla. 212/F5
Browardale, Fla. 212/B4
Browder, Ky. 237/H6
Browerville, Minn. 255/D4
Brown (co.), Ill. 222/C4
Brown (co.), Ind. 227/E6
Brown (co.), Kansas 232/G2
Brown (co.), Minn. 255/D6
Brown (co.), Nebr. 264/E2
Brown (lake), N.W. Terr. 187/J3
Brown (co.), Ohio 284/C8
Brown (reefs), Philippines 85/F3
Brown (co.), S. Dak. 298/N2
Brown (co.), Texas 303/F6
Brown (Roan) (cliffs), Utah 304/E4
Brown (pt.), Wash. 310/A4
Brown, W. Va. 312/F4
Brown (co.), Wis. 317/L7
Brownbranch, Mo. 261/G9
Brown City, Mich. 250/G5
Brown Deer, Wis. 317/L1
Browndell, Texas 303/L7
Browne (bay), N.W. Terr. 187/J2
Brownell, Kansas 232/C3
Browney (riv.), England 13/H3
Brownfield, Alberta 182/E3
Brownfield, Ill. 222/E6
Brownfield, Maine 243/B8
Brownfield•, Maine 243/B8
Brownfield, Miss. 256/G1
Brownfield, Texas 303/B4
Browning, Ill. 222/C3
Browning, Mo. 261/F2
Browning, Mont. 262/C2
Browning, N.S. Wales 97/E4
Browning, Sask. 181/J6
Browning Entrance (str.), Br. Col. 184/B3
Brownington, Mo. 261/E6
Brownington•, Vt. 268/C2
Brownlee (dam), Idaho 220/B5
Brownlee, Nebr. 264/D2
Brownlee, Oreg. 291/L3
Brownlee (dam), Oreg. 291/L3
Brownlee, Sask. 181/F5
Browns, Ala. 195/D6
Browns, Ill. 222/F5
Brown's (riv.), Vt. 268/A2
Brownsboro, Ala. 195/F1
Brownsboro, Oreg. 291/E5
Brownsboro, Texas 303/J5
Brownsboro Farm, Ky. 237/L1
Brownsburg, Ind. 227/E5
Brownsburg, Québec 172/C4
Brownsburg, Va. 307/K5
Brownsdale, Minn. 255/F7
Brownsdale, Newf. 166/D2
Browns Flat, New Bruns. 170/D3
Brown's Lake, Wis. 317/K3
Browns Mills, N.J. 273/D4
Browns Spring, Mo. 261/F9
Browns Summit, N.C. 281/K2
Brownstown, Ill. 222/E5
Brownstown, Ind. 227/F7
Browns Town, Jamaica 158/J6
Brownstown, Pa. 294/K5
Brownstown, Wash. 310/E4
Browns Valley, Ind. 227/C5
Browns Valley, Minn. 255/B5
Browns Village, Fla. 212/B4
Brownsville, Ind. 227/H5
Brownsville, Ky. 237/J6
Brownsville, Md. 245/H3
Brownsville, Minn. 255/G7
Brownsville, Miss. 256/D6
Brownsville, Oreg. 291/E3
Brownsville, Pa. 294/C5
Brownsville, Tenn. 237/C9
Brownsville, Texas 303/G12
Brownsville, Texas 188/G5
Brownsville, Texas 146/J7
Brownsville, Vt. 268/B5
Brownsville, Wash. 310/A2
Brownsville, Wis. 317/J8
Brownton, Minn. 255/D6
Brownton, W. Va. 312/F4
Browntown, Va. 307/M3
Browntown, Wis. 317/G10
Brownvale, Alberta 182/B1
Brownville, Ala. 195/C4
Brownville, Fla. 212/E4
Brownville, Maine 243/E5
Brownville•, Maine 243/E5
Brownville, Nebr. 264/J4
Brownville, N.Y. 276/H3
Brownville Junction, Maine 243/E5
Brown Willy (mt.), England 13/C7
Brownwood, Texas 303/F6
Brownwood (lake), Texas 303/E6
Browse (isl.), W. Australia 88/C2
Browse (isl.), W. Australia 92/C1
Broxburn, Scotland 15/D1
Broxton, Georgia 217/G7
Broye (riv.), Switzerland 39/C3
Broyle (cape), Newf. 166/D2
Brozas, Spain 33/C3
Brozville, Miss. 256/D4
Brtnice, Czech. 41/C2
Bruay-en-Artois, France 28/E2
Bruce, Alberta 182/E3
Bruce (mt.), Australia 87/C8
Bruce, Fla. 212/C6
Bruce, Miss. 256/F3
Bruce (mts.), N.W. Terr. 187/L2
Bruce (county), Ontario 177/C3
Bruce (pen.), Ontario 177/C2
Bruce, S. Dak. 298/R5
Bruce (mt.), W. Australia 88/B4
Bruce (mt.), W. Australia 92/B3
Bruce, Wis. 317/D5
Bruce Crossing, Mich. 250/G2
Brucefield, Ontario 177/C4
Bruce Lake, Ontario 175/B2
Bruce Mines, Ontario 177/J5
Bruce Mines, Ontario 175/D3
Bruce Rock, W. Australia 88/B6
Bruce Rock, W. Australia 92/B5
Bruceton, Tenn. 237/E8
Bruceton Mills, W. Va. 312/G3
Brucetown, Va. 307/M2
Bruceville, Ind. 227/C7
Bruchsal, Germany 22/C4
Bruck an der Leitha, Austria 41/D2
Bruck an der Mur, Austria 41/C3
Bruderheim, Alberta 182/D3
Bruff, Ireland 17/D7
Bruges, Belgium 27/C6
Brugg, Switzerland 39/F2
Brugge (Bruges), Belgium 27/C6
Brühl, Germany 22/B3
Bruin, Ky. 237/P4
Bruin (cape), New Bruns. 170/G2
Bruin, Pa. 294/C3
Bruins, Ark. 202/K4
Brûlé, Alberta 182/B3
Brule (riv.), Mich. 250/A3
Brule, Nebr. 264/C3
Brule, Nova Scotia 168/E3
Brûlé (lake), Québec 172/C3
Brûlé (lake), Québec 172/B2
Brule (co.), S. Dak. 298/L6
Brule (mt.), Switzerland 39/D4
Brule, Wis. 317/C2
Brumado, Brazil 120/E4
Brumado, Brazil 132/F6
Brumley, Mo. 261/H6
Brummen, Netherlands 27/J4
Brundidge, Ala. 195/G7
Bruneau, Idaho 220/C7
Bruneau (riv.), Idaho 220/C7
Brunei 2/Q5
Brunei 54/N9
BRUNEI 85/E4
Bruner, Mo. 261/F8
Brunete, Spain 33/F4
Brunette (isl.), Newf. 166/C4
Brunflo, Sweden 18/J5
Bruni, Texas 303/F10
Brunico, Italy 34/D1
Bruning, Nebr. 264/G4
Brunkild, Manitoba 179/E5
Brunner, N. Zealand 100/C5
Brunner (lake), N. Zealand 100/C5
Bruno, Ark. 202/E1
Bruno, Minn. 255/F4
Bruno, Nebr. 264/G3
Bruno, Sask. 181/F3
Brunot, Mo. 261/M8
Brunsbüttel, Germany 22/C2
Brunson, S.C. 296/E6
Brunssum, Netherlands 27/J7
Brunsville, Iowa 229/A3
Brunswick (pen.), Chile 138/E10
Brunswick, Ga. 188/K4
Brunswick, Georgia 217/K8
Brunswick, Germany 7/E3
Brunswick, Germany 22/D2
Brunswick, Maine 243/C8
Brunswick•, Maine 243/C8
Brunswick, Md. 245/H3
Brunswick, Minn. 255/E5
Brunswick, Miss. 256/C5
Brunswick, Mo. 261/F4
Brunswick, Nebr. 264/G2
Brunswick (co.), N.C. 281/N6
Brunswick, N.C. 281/M6
Brunswick, Ohio 284/G3
Brunswick, Tenn. 237/B10
Brunswick, Victoria 88/K7
Brunswick, Victoria 97/H5
Brunswick (co.), Va. 307/N7
Brunswick (bay), W. Australia 88/C3
Brunswick (bay), W. Australia 92/D1
Brunswick Heads, N.S. Wales 97/G1
Brunswick Junction, W. Australia 92/A2
Bruntál, Czech. 41/D2
Bruree, Ireland 17/D7
Brus (lag.), Honduras 154/E2
Brusett, Mont. 262/J3
Brush, Colo. 208/M2
Brush Creek, Minn. 255/E7
Brush Creek, Mo. 261/G7
Brush Creek, Tenn. 237/J8
Brush Prairie, Wash. 310/C5
Brushton, N.Y. 276/L1
Brushy Prairie, Ind. 227/G1
Brusio, Switzerland 39/K4
Brus Laguna, Honduras 154/E3
Brusly, La. 238/J2
Brusque, Brazil 132/D9
Brussels (cap.), Belgium 7/E3
Brussels, Ill. 222/C5
Brussels, Ontario 177/C4
Brussels, Wis. 317/L6
Bruthen, Victoria 97/D5
Brutus, Mich. 250/E3
Bruxelles, Manitoba 179/C5
Bruzual, Venezuela 124/D3
Bryan (co.), Georgia 217/K6
Bryan, Ohio 284/A3
Bryan (co.), Okla. 288/O7
Bryan, Texas 188/G4
Bryan, Texas 303/H7
Bryan (lake), Wash. 310/H4
Bryansk, U.S.S.R. 7/H3
Bryansk, U.S.S.R. 52/D4
Bryansk, U.S.S.R. 48/D4
Bryanston, Ontario 177/C4
Bryant, Ala. 195/G1
Bryant, Ark. 202/F4
Bryant, Fla. 212/F5
Bryant (lake), Fla. 212/E2
Bryant, Ill. 222/C3
Bryant, Ind. 227/G3
Bryant, Iowa 229/N5
Bryant, Okla. 288/P4
Bryant, S. Dak. 298/P4
Bryant, Wis. 317/J5
Bryant Pond, Maine 243/B7
Bryantsburg, Ind. 227/G7
Bryantsville, Ky. 237/M5
Bryantville, Mass. 249/L4
Bryce (mt.), Br. Col. 184/J4
Bryce, Utah 304/B6
Bryce Canyon, Utah 304/B6
Bryce Canyon Nat'l Park, Utah 304/B6
Bryceland, La. 238/E2
Bryceville, Fla. 212/D1
Bryn Athyn, Pa. 294/M5
Brynica (riv.), Poland 47/B4
Bryn Mawr, Pa. 294/M5
Brynmawr, Wales 10/E5
Brynmawr, Wales 13/B6
Bryn Mawr-Skyway, Wash. 310/B2
Bryrup, Denmark 21/C5
Bryson, Texas 303/F4
Bryson City, N.C. 281/C4
Bryte-Broderick, Calif. 204/B8
Brzeg, Poland 47/C3
Brzeg Dolny, Poland 47/C3
Brzesko, Poland 47/E3
Brzozów, Poland 47/F4
B-Say-Tah, Sask. 181/G5
Bua Chum, Thailand 72/D4
Buad (isl.), Philippines 82/E5
Buba, Guinea-Biss. 106/B6
Bubali, Neth. Ant. 161/D10
Bubaque, Guinea-Biss. 106/A6
Bubendorf, Switzerland 39/E2
Bubikon, Switzerland 39/G2
Bubiyan (isl.), Kuwait 59/E4
Bucak, Turkey 63/D4
Bucaramanga, Colombia 120/B2
Bucaramanga, Colombia 126/D4
Bucareli (bay), Alaska 196/M2
Bucas Grande (isl.), Philippines 82/F6
Bucasia, Queensland 95/D4
Buccaneer (arch.), W. Australia 88/C3
Buccaneer (arch.), W. Australia 92/C2
Buchan (gulf), N.W. Terr. 187/L2
Buchan (dist.), Scotland 15/F3
Buchanan, Georgia 217/B3
Buchanan (co.), Iowa 229/K4
Buchanan, Iowa 229/L5
Buchanan, Ky. 237/R4
Buchanan, Liberia 106/B7
Buchanan, Liberia 102/A4
Buchanan, Mich. 250/C7
Buchanan (co.), Mo. 261/C3
Buchanan, N.Y. 276/N8
Buchanan, N. Dak. 282/N5
Buchanan, Sask. 181/J4
Buchanan, Tenn. 237/E8
Buchanan (lake), Texas 303/F7
Buchanan (co.), Va. 307/D6
Buchanan, Va. 307/J5
Buchan Ness (prom.), Scotland 15/G3
Buchans, Newf. 166/C4
Bucharest (cap.), Romania 7/G4
Bucharest (cap.), Romania 2/L3
Bucharest (București) (cap.), Romania 45/G3
Buchegg (mts.), Switzerland 39/D2
Buchholz in der Nordheide, Germany 22/C2
Buchlyvie, Scotland 15/B1
Buchon (pt.), Calif. 204/D8
Buchs, Switzerland 39/H2
Buchtel, Ohio 284/F7
Buck (creek), Ind. 227/E8
Buck (creek), S.C. 296/J3
Buck (creek), Texas 303/D3
Buck (isl.), Virgin Is. (U.S.) 161/G3
Buck, W. Va. 312/E7
Buckatunna, Miss. 256/G7
Buck Creek, Alberta 182/C3
Buck Creek, Ind. 227/D4
Bückeburg, Germany 22/C2
Buckeye, Ariz. 198/C5
Buckeye, Iowa 229/G4
Buckeye, La. 238/F4
Buckeye, N. Mex. 274/F6
Buckeye (lake), Ohio 284/F6
Buckeye, W. Va. 312/F6
Buckeye Lake, Ohio 284/F6
Buckeystown, Md. 245/J3
Buckfastleigh, England 13/C7
Buckfield•, Maine 243/C7
Buck Grove, Iowa 229/C5
Buckhannon, W. Va. 312/F5
Buckhannon (riv.), W. Va. 312/F5
Buckhaven and Methil, Scotland 15/F4
Buckhaven and Methil, Scotland 10/E2
Buckhead, Georgia 217/F3
Buck Hollow (creek), Oreg. 291/G2
Buckholts, Texas 303/H7
Buckhorn (lake), Ky. 237/O6
Buckhorn, Mo. 261/M8
Buckhorn, N. Mex. 274/A5
Buckhorn, Ontario 177/F3
Buckhorn (lake), Ontario 177/F3
Buckie, Scotland 15/E3
Buckie, Scotland 10/E2
Buckingham, Colo. 208/L1
Buckingham, Conn. 210/E2
Buckingham, England 13/G6
Buckingham, England 10/F5
Buckingham, Ill. 222/E2
Buckingham, Iowa 229/J4
Buckingham, Québec 172/B4
Buckingham, Texas 303/H2
Buckingham (co.), Va. 307/L5
Buckingham, Va. 307/L5
Buckinghamshire (co.), England 13/G6
Buck Island (chan.), Virgin Is. (U.S.) 161/F3
Buck Island Reef Nat'l Mon., Virgin Is. (U.S.) 161/G3
Buck Lake, Alberta 182/C3
Buckland, Alaska 196/F1
Buckland, Conn. 210/E1
Buckland•, Mass. 249/C2
Buckland, Ohio 284/B4
Buckland, Québec 172/G3
Buckley, Ill. 222/F3
Buckley, Mich. 250/D4
Buckley, Wales 13/G2
Buckley, Wash. 310/C3
Bucklin, Kansas 232/C4
Bucklin, Mo. 261/G3
Buckman, Minn. 255/D5
Buckner, Ark. 202/D7
Buckner, Ill. 222/E6
Buckner, Ky. 237/L4
Buckner, Mo. 261/R2
Bucks, Ala. 195/B8
Bucks (co.), Pa. 294/M5
Bucksburn, Scotland 15/F3
Bucks Harbor, Maine 243/J6
Buckskin (mts.), Ariz. 198/B4
Buckskin, Ind. 227/C8
Bucksport, Maine 243/F6
Bucksport•, Maine 243/F6
Bucksport, S.C. 296/J4
Buckville, Ark. 202/D4
Bucoda, Mo. 261/M10
Bucoda, Wash. 310/C4
Buco-Zau, Angola 115/B4
Buctouche, New Bruns. 170/F2
Buctouche (harb.), New Bruns. 170/F2
Buctouche (riv.), New Bruns. 170/F2
București (Bucharest) (cap.), Romania 45/G3
Bucyrus, Kansas 232/H3
Bucyrus, Mo. 261/H8
Bucyrus, N. Dak. 282/E7
Bucyrus, Ohio 284/E4
Bud, Ind. 227/E6
Bud, W. Va. 312/D7
Buda, Ill. 222/D2
Buda, Texas 303/G7
Budafok, Hungary 41/E3
Budakeszi, Hungary 41/E3
Budaörs, Hungary 41/E3
Budapest (co.), Hungary 41/E3
Budapest (cap.), Hungary 41/E3
Budapest (cap.), Hungary 7/F4
Budaun, India 68/D3
Budd (lake), N.J. 273/D2
Budd Coast (reg.), Ant. 5/C6
Budd Lake, N.J. 273/D2
Buddon Ness (prom.), Scotland 15/F4
Bude (bay), England 13/C7
Bude, Miss. 256/C8
Bude-Stratton, England 13/C7
Budge-Budge, India 68/F2
Budgewoi Lake, N.S. Wales 97/F3
Budia, Spain 33/E2
Büdingen, Germany 22/C3
Budišov, Czech. 41/D2
Budjala, Zaire 115/C3
Budleigh Salterton, England 13/D7
Budrio, Italy 34/C2
Budva, Yugoslavia 45/D4
Buea, Cameroon 115/A3
Buechel, Ky. 237/K2
Buel (lake), Mass. 249/A4
Buellton, Calif. 204/E9
Buena, N.J. 273/D4
Buena, Wash. 310/E4
Buena Esperanza, Argentina 143/C3
Buena Park, Calif. 204/D11
Buenaventura, Colombia 126/B6
Buenaventura, Colombia 120/B2
Buenaventura (bay), Colombia 126/B6
Buenaventura, Cuba 158/H3
Buenaventura, Mexico 150/F2
Buena Vista, Ala. 195/D7
Buena Vista, Ark. 202/D7
Buena Vista, Bolivia 136/D5
Buena Vista (lake), Calif. 204/F8
Buena Vista, Colo. 208/G5
Buenavista, Cuba 158/F2
Buenavista (bay), Cuba 158/F2
Buena Vista, Georgia 217/C6
Buena Vista (co.), Iowa 229/C3
Buena Vista, Miss. 256/G3
Buena Vista, N. Mex. 274/D3
Buena Vista, Ohio 284/D8
Buena Vista, Oreg. 291/D3
Buena Vista, Paraguay 144/D5
Buenavista, Philippines 82/E6
Buena Vista, Sask. 181/F5
Buena Vista, Tenn. 237/E9
Buena Vista, Uruguay 145/E3
Buena Vista, Anzoátegui, Venezuela 124/F3
Buena Vista, Apure, Venezuela 124/D4
Buena Vista, Falcón, Venezuela 124/D2
Buena Vista (I.C.), Va. 307/K5
Buendía (res.), Spain 33/E2
Bueno (riv.), Chile 138/D3
Buenos Aires (lake) 120/B7
Buenos Aires (prov.), Argentina 143/D4
Buenos Aires (cap.), Argentina 120/C6
Buenos Aires (cap.), Argentina 143/H7
Buenos Aires (cap.), Argentina 2/F7
Buenos Aires (lake), Argentina 143/B6
Buenos Aires (lake), Chile 138/E6
Buenos Aires, Amazonas, Colombia 126/F9
Buenos Aires, Caquetá, Colombia 126/D7
Buenos Aires, C. Rica 154/F6
Buesaco, Colombia 126/B7
Buey Arriba, Cuba 158/H4
Bueyeros, N. Mex. 274/F3
Buffalo, Ala. 195/H5
Buffalo, Alberta 182/E4
Buffalo (lake), Alberta 182/D3
Buffalo (riv.), Ark. 202/E2
Buffalo, Ill. 222/D4
Buffalo, Ind. 227/D3
Buffalo, Iowa 229/M6
Buffalo, Kansas 232/G4
Buffalo, Ky. 237/K6
Buffalo (bay), Manitoba 179/G5
Buffalo, Minn. 255/E5
Buffalo (riv.), Minn. 255/B4
Buffalo, Mo. 261/F7
Buffalo, Mont. 262/G4
Buffalo (co.), Nebr. 264/E4
Buffalo (creek), Nev. 266/B2
Buffalo, N.Y. 146/L5
Buffalo, N.Y. 188/L2
Buffalo, N.Y. 276/B5
Buffalo, N. Dak. 282/R6
Buffalo, Ohio 284/G6
Buffalo, Okla. 288/G1
Buffalo, S.C. 296/D2
Buffalo (co.), S. Dak. 298/L5
Buffalo, S. Dak. 298/B2
Buffalo (creek), S. Dak. 298/F6
Buffalo (lake), S. Dak. 298/P2
Buffalo (riv.), Tenn. 237/F9
Buffalo, Texas 303/J6
Buffalo, W. Va. 312/C5
Buffalo (co.), Wis. 317/C7
Buffalo, Wis. 317/C7
Buffalo, Wyo. 319/F1
Buffalo Bill (dam), Wyo. 319/C1
Buffalo Bill (res.), Wyo. 319/C1
Buffalo Center, Iowa 229/F2
Buffalo City, Ark. 202/E1
Buffalo City, N.C. 281/T3
Buffalo Creek, Br. Col. 184/G4
Buffalo Creek, Colo. 208/J4
Buffalo Fork, Snake (riv.), Wyo. 319/B2
Buffalo Gap, Sask. 181/F6
Buffalo Gap, S. Dak. 298/C6
Buffalo Gap, Texas 303/E5
Buffalo Grove, Ill. 222/B5
Buffalo Head (hills), Alberta 182/B5
Buffalo Junction, Va. 307/L7
Buffalo Lake, Minn. 255/D6
Buffalo Lodge (lake), N. Dak. 282/J3
Buffalo Mills, Pa. 294/E6
Buffalo Narrows, Sask. 181/L3

Buffalo Nat'l River, Ark. 202/E1
Buffalo Pound Prov. Park, Sask. 181/F5
Buffalo River Junction, N.W. Terr. 187/G3
Buffalo Valley, Tenn. 237/K8
Buffaloville, Ind. 227/D8
Buff Bay, Jamaica 158/K6
Buford, Alberta 182/D3
Buford, Georgia 217/D2
Buford, N. Dak. 282/C3
Buford, Ohio 284/C7
Buford, Wyo. 319/G4
Bug (riv.) 7/G3
Bug (riv.), Poland 47/F2
Bug (riv.), U.S.S.R. 7/G4
Bug (riv.), U.S.S.R. 52/B4
Bug (riv.), U.S.S.R. 52/D5
Buga, Colombia 126/B6
Bugaboo Glacier Prov. Park, Br. Col. 184/J5
Bugak, Hungary 41/E3
Bugaldie, N.S. Wales 97/E2
Bugasong, Philippines 82/C5
Buggs Island (lake), N.C. 281/M1
Buggs Island (lake), Va. 307/L8
Bugiougio (isl.), Portugal 33/B2
Bugojno, Yugoslavia 45/C3
Bugrino, U.S.S.R. 52/G1
Bugsuk (isl.), Philippines 85/F4
Bugsuk (isl.), Philippines 82/A6
Bugt, China 77/K2
Bugui (pt.), Philippines 82/D4
Bugul'ma, U.S.S.R. 7/K3
Bugul'ma, U.S.S.R. 52/H4
Bugul'ma, U.S.S.R. 48/F4
Buguruslan, U.S.S.R. 52/H4
Buhl, Ala. 195/C4
Bühl, Germany 22/C4
Buhl, Idaho 220/D7
Buhl, Minn. 255/F4
Buhler, Kansas 232/E3
Buhuşi, Romania 45/H2
Buie, Loch (inlet), Scotland 15/C4
Buies, N.C. 281/L5
Buies Creek, N.C. 281/M4
Buiksloot, Netherlands 27/C4
Builth Wells, Wales 13/D5
Builth Wells, Wales 10/E4
Buin, Chile 138/G4
Buin, Papua N.G. 86/C2
Buin (peak), Switzerland 39/K3
Buinsk, U.S.S.R. 52/G4
Bujalance, Spain 33/D4
Bujumbura (cap.), Burundi 102/F5
Bujumbura (cap.), Burundi 115/E4
Buka, Papua N.G. 87/F6
Buka (isl.), Papua N.G. 86/C2
Buka (passage), Papua N.G. 86/C2
Bukachacha, U.S.S.R. 48/M4
Bukama, Zaire 115/E5
Buka Passage, Papua N.G. 86/C2
Bukavu, Zaire 102/E5
Bukavu, Zaire 115/E4
Bukene, Tanzania 115/F4
Bukhara, U.S.S.R. 54/H5
Bukhara, U.S.S.R. 48/G5
Bukidnon (prov.), Philippines 82/E6
Bukittinggi, Indonesia 85/B6
Bükk (mts.), Hungary 41/F2
Bukoba, Tanzania 115/F4
Bukowno, Poland 47/C4
Bul, Kuh-e (mt.), Iran 66/H5
Bula, Indonesia 85/H4
Bula, Texas 303/B4
Bulacan (prov.), Philippines 82/C3
Bülach, Switzerland 39/G1
Bulahdelah, N.S. Wales 97/G3
Bulak (Bole), China 77/B3
Bulalakao, Philippines 82/C4
Bulan, Ky. 237/P6
Bulan, Philippines 82/D4
Bulancak, Turkey 63/H2
Buldan, Turkey 59/A4
Buldan, Turkey 63/C3
Buldibuyo, Peru 128/D7
Buldir (isl.), Alaska 196/J3
Bulgan, Mongolia 77/F2
Bulgan, Bulgan, Mongolia 77/F2
Bulgan, Hovd, Mongolia 77/D2
Bulgan, Ömnögovĭ, Mongolia 77/F3
Bulgaria 2/L3
Bulgaria 7/G4
BULGARIA 45/G4
Bulger, Pa. 294/B5
Bulgroo, Queensland 95/B5
Bulgroo, Queensland 88/G5
Bulhar, Somalia 115/H1
Buli, Indonesia 85/H5
Buliluyan (cape), Philippines 85/F4
Buliluyan (cape), Philippines 82/A6
Bulimba (creek), Queensland 95/E3
Bulkley (riv.), Br. Col. 184/D2
Bull, The (isl.), Ireland 17/A8
Bull (isl.), Newf. 166/D2
Bull (isl.), S.C. 296/H6
Bull (creek), S. Dak. 298/K6
Bull (creek), S. Dak. 298/C3
Bullard, Georgia 217/D5
Bullard, Texas 303/J5
Bull Arm (inlet), Newf. 166/D2
Bullas, Spain 33/F4
Bulldog (isl.), Newf. 166/C3
Bulle, Switzerland 39/D3
Bullen (bay), Neth. Ant. 161/F8
Buller (riv.), N. Zealand 100/D4
Buller (mt.), Victoria 97/C5
Bullfinch, W. Australia 92/B5
Bull Harbour, Br. Col. 184/C5
Bullhead, S. Dak. 298/G2
Bullhead City-Riviera, Ariz. 198/A3
Bullitt (co.), Ky. 237/K5
Bull Lake (res.), Wyo. 319/C2

Bulloch (co.), Georgia 217/J6
Bullock (co.), Ala. 195/G6
Bullock, N.C. 281/M2
Bullock (creek), S.C. 296/E2
Bulloo (lake), Queensland 95/B6
Bulloo (riv.), Queensland 88/G5
Bulloo (riv.), Queensland 95/B6
Bulloo Downs, Queensland 88/G5
Bull Run (creek), Va. 307/N3
Bulls, N. Zealand 100/E4
Bulls (bay), S.C. 296/H6
Bull Savanna-Junction, Jamaica 158/H6
Bulls Bridge, Conn. 210/B2
Bulls Gap, Tenn. 237/P8
Bull Shoals, Ark. 202/E1
Bull Shoals (lake), Ark. 202/E1
Bull Shoals (lake), Mo. 261/G10
Bully (creek), Oreg. 291/K3
Bulnes, Chile 138/E1
Bulo Burti, Somalia 115/J3
Bulolo, Papua N.G. 85/B7
Bulpitt, Ill. 222/D4
Buluan (lake), Philippines 82/E7
Bulukumba, Indonesia 85/G7
Bulun, U.S.S.R. 4/B3
Bulun, U.S.S.R. 48/N2
Bulungu, Zaire 115/C4
Bulusan, Philippines 82/E4
Bulusan (vol.), Philippines 82/D4
Bulyea, Sask. 181/G5
Bumba, Zaire 115/D3
Bumble Bee, Ariz. 198/C4
Bumiayu, Indonesia 85/H2
Bumpass, Va. 307/N5
Bumping (lake), Wash. 310/D2
Bumpus Mills, Tenn. 237/F7
Bumthang, Bhutan 68/G3
Buna, Kenya 115/G3
Buna, Papua N.G. 85/C7
Buna, Texas 303/L7
Bunavista, Texas 303/C2
Bunawan, Philippines 82/E6
Bunbeg-Derrybeg, Ireland 17/E1
Bunbury, Australia 87/B9
Bunbury, W. Australia 88/B6
Bunbury, W. Australia 92/A2
Bunbury, Pr. Edward I. 168/F2
Bunbury, Ky. 237/M5
Bunceton, Mo. 261/G5
Bunch, Iowa 229/H4
Bunch, Okla. 288/S3
Bunche Park, Fla. 212/B4
Bunclody-Carrickduff, Ireland 17/H6
Buncombe, Ill. 222/E6
Buncombe (co.), N.C. 281/D3
Buncrana, Ireland 17/G1
Buncrana, Ireland 10/C3
Bundaberg, Australia 87/E8
Bundaberg, Queensland 88/J4
Bundaberg, Queensland 95/D5
Bundanoon, N.S. Wales 97/E4
Bundarra, N.S. Wales 97/F2
Bünde, Germany 22/C2
Bundi, India 68/D3
Bundick (lake), La. 238/D5
Bundooma, North. Terr. 93/D8
Bundoora, Victoria 97/J4
Bundoran, Ireland 17/E3
Bunessan, Scotland 15/B4
Bunga (pt.), Philippines 82/E4
Bungalaut (chan.), Indonesia 85/B6
Bungay, England 10/G4
Bungay, England 13/J5
Bungee (brook), Conn. 210/G1
Bu Ngem, Libya 111/C1
Bungendore, N.S. Wales 97/E4
Bungo (str.), Japan 81/F7
Bunguran (Great Natuna) (isl.), Indonesia 85/D5
Bunguran (Natuna) (isls.), Indonesia 85/D5
Bunia, Zaire 115/E3
Bunia, Zaire 102/E4
Bunji, Pakistan 68/C1
Bunker, Mo. 261/K8
Bunker Group (isls.), Queensland 95/E4
Bunker Hill, Ill. 222/D4
Bunker Hill, Ind. 227/E3
Bunker Hill, Kansas 232/D3
Bunker Hill, Oreg. 291/C4
Bunker Hill, W. Va. 312/K4
Bunker Hill Village, Texas 303/J1
Bunkerville, Nev. 266/E6
Bunkeya, Zaire 115/E6
Bunkie, La. 238/F5
Bunn, N.C. 281/N3
Bunnell, Fla. 212/F4
Bunnlevel, N.C. 281/M4
Buntok, Indonesia 85/F6
Bunyala, Kenya 115/F3
Bünyan, Turkey 63/G3
Bunyan's Cove, Newf. 166/C2
Bunyu (isl.), Indonesia 85/F5
Buochs, Switzerland 39/F3
Buol, Indonesia 85/G5
Buq, Iran 66/M6
Bura, Kenya 115/H4
Bur Acaba, Somalia 115/H3
Bur Acaba, Somalia 102/G4
Buraida, Saudi Arabia 59/D4
Buraimi, Oman 59/G5
Buraimi, U.A.E. 59/G5
Buram, Sudan 111/E5
Burang, China 77/B5
Burao, Somalia 102/G4
Burao, Somalia 115/J2
Buras-Triumph, La. 238/L8
Burauen, Philippines 82/E5
Burbank, Calif. 204/C10
Burbank, Ill. 222/B6
Burbank, Ohio 284/H4
Burbank, Okla. 288/N1
Burbank, S. Dak. 298/R8
Burbank, Wash. 310/G4
Burchard, Minn. 255/C6
Burchard, Nebr. 264/H4
Burcher, N.S. Wales 97/D3
Burchinal, Iowa 229/G2

Burdekin (riv.), Queensland 88/H3
Burdekin (riv.), Queensland 95/C3
Burden, Kansas 232/F4
Burdett, Alberta 182/E5
Burdett, Kansas 232/C3
Burdett, N.Y. 276/G6
Burdette, Ark. 202/L2
Burdette, S. Dak. 298/M4
Burdick, Kansas 232/F3
Burdur (prov.), Turkey 63/D4
Burdur, Turkey 59/A2
Burdur, Turkey 63/D4
Burdur (lake), Turkey 63/D4
Burdwan, India 68/F4
Bureå, Sweden 18/M4
Bureau (co.), Ill. 222/D2
Bureau, Ill. 222/D2
Büren, Germany 22/C3
Büren an der Aare, Switzerland 39/D2
Bürentsogt, Mongolia 77/H2
Burford (lake), N. Mex. 274/C2
Burford, Ontario 177/D4
Burfordville, Mo. 261/N8
Burgas, Bulgaria 45/H4
Burgas, Bulgaria 7/G4
Burgaw, N.C. 281/N5
Burgaz, Turkey 63/B5
Burgaz (isl.), Turkey 63/D6
Burg bei Magdeburg, Germany 22/D2
Burgdorf, Switzerland 39/E2
Burgenland (prov.), Austria 41/D3
Burgeo, Newf. 166/C4
Burgersdorp, S. Africa 118/D6
Burgess, Mo. 261/C7
Burgess, S.C. 296/J4
Burgess, Va. 307/R5
Burgess (mt.), Yukon 187/D3
Burgess Hill, England 13/G7
Burgessville, Ontario 177/D4
Burgettstown, Pa. 294/A5
Burghausen, Germany 22/E4
Burghead, Scotland 10/E2
Burghead, Scotland 15/E3
Burghill, Ohio 284/J3
Burgin, Ky. 237/M5
Burgis, Sask. 181/J4
Bürglen, Thurgau, Switzerland 39/H1
Bürglen, Uri, Switzerland 39/G3
Burglengenfeld, Germany 22/D4
Burgoon, Ohio 284/D3
Burgos, Mexico 150/K4
Burgos (prov.), Spain 33/E1
Burgos, Spain 7/D4
Burgos, Spain 33/E1
Burg Stargard, Germany 22/E2
Burgsteinfurt, Germany 22/B2
Burgsvik, Sweden 18/K8
Burgundy (trad. prov.), France 29
Burhaniye, Turkey 63/B3
Burhanpur, India 68/D4
Buri, Brazil 135/B3
Buri (pen.), Ethiopia 111/H4
Burias (isl.), Philippines 82/D4
Burias (passage), Philippines 82/D4
Buribay, U.S.S.R. 52/J4
Burica (pt.), C. Rica 154/F6
Burica, Punta (cape), Panama 154/F6
Burien, Wash. 310/A2
Burin, Newf. 166/C4
Burin (pen.), Newf. 166/C4
Buriram, Thailand 72/D4
Buriti, Brazil 132/E4
Buriti Alegre, Brazil 132/D7
Buriti dos Lopes, Brazil 132/F3
Burj al Hattaba, Tunisia 106/F2
Burjassot, Spain 33/F3
Burke (chan.), Br. Col. 184/D4
Burke (co.), Georgia 217/J4
Burke, Idaho 220/D2
Burke, N.Y. 276/M1
Burke (co.), N.C. 281/F3
Burke (co.), N. Dak. 282/E2
Burke, S. Dak. 298/L7
Burke, Texas 303/K6
Burke •, Vt. 268/D2
Burke (mt.), Vt. 268/D2
Burke, Va. 307/R3
Bürkelkopf (mt.), Switzerland 39/K3
Burkes Garden, Va. 307/F6
Burkesville, Ky. 237/L7
Burket, Ind. 227/F2
Burketown, Queensland 95/A3
Burketown, Queensland 88/F3
Burkett, Texas 303/E5
Burkettsville, Ohio 284/A5
Burkettville, Maine 243/E7
Burkeville, Texas 303/L7
Burkeville, Va. 307/M6
Burkina Faso 102/B3
BURKINA FASO 106/D6
Burkittsville, Md. 245/H3
Burkley, Ky. 237/C7
Burk's Falls, Ontario 177/E2
Burkville, Ala. 195/E6
Burleigh (co.), N. Dak. 282/J6
Burleson (co.), Texas 303/H7
Burleson, Texas 303/F3
Burley, Idaho 220/E7
Burley, Wash. 310/C3
Burlingame, Calif. 204/J2
Burlingame, Kansas 232/G3
Burlington, Colo. 208/P4
Burlington •, Conn. 210/D1
Burlington, Ill. 222/E1
Burlington, Ind. 227/E4
Burlington, Iowa 229/L7
Burlington, Kansas 232/G3
Burlington, Ky. 237/R2
Burlington •, Maine 243/G5
Burlington •, Mass. 249/C5
Burlington (co.), N.J. 273/D3
Burlington, N.J. 273/D3
Burlington, N.C. 281/K3
Burlington, N. Dak. 282/H3
Burlington, Ohio 284/F9

Burlington, Okla. 288/K1
Burlington, Ontario 177/E4
Burlington, Pa. 294/J2
Burlington, Vt. 268/A3
Burlington, Vt. 146/L5
Burlington, Wash. 310/C2
Burlington, W. Va. 312/J4
Burlington, Wis. 317/K10
Burlington, Wyo. 319/D1
Burlington Flats, N.Y. 276/K5
Burlington Junction, Mo. 261/B2
Burlison, Tenn. 237/B9
Burma 2/P4
Burma (Myanmar) 72/B2
Burmis, Alberta 182/C5
Burna, Ky. 237/C8
Burnaby, Br. Col. 184/K3
Burnaby (isl.), Br. Col. 184/B4
Burnet (co.), Texas 303/F7
Burnet, Texas 303/F7
Burnett, Minn. 255/F4
Burnett (co.), Wis. 317/B4
Burnett, Wis. 317/J9
Burnettown, S.C. 296/D5
Burnettsville, Ind. 227/D3
Burney, Calif. 204/D3
Burney (mt.), Chile 138/D9
Burney, Ind. 227/F6
Burneyville, Okla. 288/M7
Burnham, Ill. 222/C6
Burnham •, Maine 243/E6
Burnham, Mo. 261/J9
Burnham, Pa. 294/H4
Burnham-on-Crouch, England 13/H6
Burnham-on-Sea, England 13/D6
Burnie, Tasmania 99/B3
Burnie-Somerset, Tasmania 88/H8
Burning Springs, Ky. 237/N6
Burning Springs, W. Va. 312/D5
Burnips, Mich. 250/D6
Burnley, England 10/G1
Burnley, England 13/H1
Burnmouth, Scotland 15/F5
Burns, Colo. 208/F3
Burns, Kansas 232/F3
Burns, Miss. 256/E6
Burns, N.S. Wales 97/A3
Burns, Oreg. 291/H4
Burns, Tenn. 237/G8
Burns, Wyo. 319/H4
Burns City, Ind. 227/D7
Burns Flat, Okla. 288/H4
Burns Harbor, Ind. 227/C1
Burnside, Conn. 210/E1
Burnside, Ill. 222/B3
Burnside, Iowa 229/E4
Burnside, Ky. 237/M6
Burnside, La. 238/L3
Burnside, Miss. 256/F5
Burnside (riv.), N.W. Terr. 187/G3
Burnside, Pa. 294/E4
Burnside, S. Australia 88/E8
Burnside, S. Australia 94/B8
Burnside, Suriname 131/C2
Burns Junction, Oreg. 291/K5
Burns Lake, Br. Col. 162/D5
Burns Lake, Br. Col. 184/D3
Burnstad, N. Dak. 282/L7
Burnsville, Ala. 195/E6
Burnsville, Ind. 227/F6
Burnsville, Minn. 255/E6
Burnsville, Miss. 256/H1
Burnsville, New Bruns. 170/E1
Burnsville, N.C. 281/E3
Burnsville, W. Va. 307/J4
Burnsville, W. Va. 312/E5
Burnt (lkes), Alberta 182/C1
Burnt (lake), Newf. 166/B3
Burnt (riv.), Ontario 177/F3
Burnt (riv.), Oreg. 291/K3
Burnt (lake), Québec 174/E2
Burnt Cabins, Pa. 294/G5
Burnt Corn, Ala. 195/D7
Burnt House, W. Va. 312/D4
Burnt Island (lake), Ontario 177/F2
Burntisland, Scotland 15/D1
Burntisland, Scotland 10/C1
Burnt Islands, Newf. 166/C4
Burnt Point, Newf. 166/D2
Burnt Prairie, Ill. 222/E5
Burnt River, Ontario 177/F3
Burntroot (lake), Ontario 177/F2
Burntside (lake), Minn. 255/F3
Burntwood, England 13/F5
Burntwood, England 10/G2
Burntwood (riv.), Manitoba 179/J2
Burnwell, W. Va. 312/D6
Burqa, West Bank 65/C3
Burqin, China 77/C2
Burr (pond), Conn. 210/C1
Burr, Minn. 255/A5
Burr, Nebr. 264/H4
Burr, Sask. 181/F3
Burra, S. Australia 94/F5
Burraboi, N.S. Wales 97/B3
Burramurra, North. Terr. 93/E6
Burray (isl.), Scotland 15/F2
Burrel, Albania 45/D5
Burren Junction, N.S. Wales 97/E2
Burriana, Spain 33/G3
Burringbar, N.S. Wales 97/G1
Burrinjuck (res.), N.S. Wales 97/E4
Burris, Wyo. 319/C2
Burro (creek), Ariz. 198/B4
Burro (mts.), Mexico 150/J2
Burr Oak, Ind. 227/E2
Burr Oak, Iowa 229/K2
Burr Oak, Kansas 232/D2
Burr Oak, Mich. 250/D7
Burro-Burro (riv.), Guyana 131/B3
Burrow (head), Scotland 15/D6
Burrows, Ind. 227/E3
Burrows, Wash. 310/C1
Burr Ridge, Ill. 222/B6
Burrsville, Md. 245/P5

Burrton, Kansas 232/E3
Burrville, Conn. 210/C1
Burrville, Tenn. 237/M8
Burrville, Utah 304/C5
Burrwood, La. 238/M8
Burry Port, Wales 13/C6
Bursa (prov.), Turkey 63/C2
Bursa, Turkey 63/C2
Bursa, Turkey 59/A1
Bursa, Turkey 54/D5
Bur Sa'id (Port Said), Egypt 111/K2
Bur Said (Port Said), Egypt 59/B3
Burstall, Sask. 181/B5
Burt, Iowa 229/E2
Burt, Mich. 250/F5
Burt (lake), Mich. 250/E3
Burt (co.), Nebr. 264/H3
Burt, N.Y. 276/C4
Burt, N. Dak. 282/J6
Burta, N.S. Wales 97/A3
Burt Lake, Mich. 250/E3
Burton, Br. Col. 184/H5
Burton (lake), Georgia 217/E1
Burton, Mich. 250/F6
Burton, Nebr. 264/E2
Burton, New Bruns. 170/D3
Burton, Ohio 284/H3
Burton, S.C. 296/F7
Burton, Texas 303/H7
Burton, Wash. 310/C3
Burton, W. Va. 312/F3
Burtonport, Ireland 17/E2
Burtonport, Ireland 10/B3
Burtonville, Ky. 237/P4
Burträsk, Sweden 18/M4
Burtrum, Minn. 255/D5
Burtts Corner, New Bruns. 170/D3
Buru (isl.), Indonesia 54/O10
Buru (isl.), Indonesia 85/H6
Buru (sea), Indonesia 85/H6
Burultokay (Fuhai), China 77/C2
Burundi 2/L6
BURUNDI 115/E4
Bururi, Burundi 115/F4
Burutu, Nigeria 106/F7
Burwash Landing, Yukon 187/D3
Burwell, Nebr. 264/E3
Burwood, N.S. Wales 88/K4
Burwood, N.S. Wales 97/J3
Bury, England 13/H2
Bury, England 10/G2
Bury, Québec 172/F4
Buryat A.S.S.R., U.S.S.R. 48/M4
Burye, Ethiopia 102/F3
Burye, Ethiopia 111/G5
Bury Saint Edmunds, England 13/H5
Bury Saint Edmunds, England 10/G4
Busby, Alberta 182/C3
Busby, Mont. 262/J5
Buseno, Switzerland 39/H4
Bush, Ill. 222/D6
Bush, Ky. 237/O6
Bush, La. 238/L5
Bush (creek), Md. 245/J3
Bush (riv.), N. Ireland 17/H1
Bush (riv.), S.C. 296/D3
Bush City, Kansas 232/G3
Bushehr (prov.), Iran 66/G6
Bushehr, Iran 59/F4
Bushell, Sask. 181/L2
Bushey, England 10/B5
Bushey, England 13/H7
Bushire, Iran 54/G5
Bushiribana, Neth. Ant. 161/E10
Bush Island, Nova Scotia 168/D4
Bushkill, Pa. 294/M3
Bushland, Texas 303/B2
Bushmills, N. Ireland 17/J1
Bushnell, Fla. 212/D3
Bushnell, Ill. 222/C3
Bushnell, Nebr. 264/A3
Bushnell, S. Dak. 298/R5
Bushong, Kansas 232/F3
Bushton, Ill. 222/D6
Bushton, Kansas 232/D3
Bushwood, Md. 245/L7
Bushyhead, Okla. 288/P2
Bushy Park, Tasmania 99/G3
Busick, N.C. 281/E3
Businga, Zaire 115/D3
Buskerud (co.), Norway 18/F4
Buskirk, Ky. 237/P5
Busko Zdrój, Poland 47/E3
Busra, Syria 63/G6
Busselton, W. Australia 88/A6
Busselton, W. Australia 92/A6
Busseron (creek), Ind. 227/C7
Busse Woods (res.), Ill. 222/B5
Bussey, Iowa 229/H6
Bussigny-près-Lausanne, Switzerland 39/B3
Bussum, Netherlands 27/G4
Bustard (isls.), Ontario 177/C2
Busti, N.Y. 276/B6
Bustinza, Argentina 143/F6
Busto Arsizio, Italy 34/B2
Busuanga (isl.), Philippines 82/B4
Busuanga (isl.), Philippines 85/F3
Busu-Djanoa, Zaire 115/D3
Büsum, Germany 22/C1
Buta, Zaire 102/E4
Buta, Zaire 115/D3
Buta-Ranquil, Argentina 143/C4
Butare, Rwanda 115/E4
Butaritari (atoll), Kiribati 87/H5
Butcher (co.), India 68/B7
Bute (inlet), Br. Col. 184/E5
Bute (isl.), Scotland 15/C5
Bute (sound), Scotland 15/C5
Bute (trad. co.), Scotland 15/A5
Butedale, Br. Col. 184/C3
Butembo, Zaire 115/E3
Butembo, Zaire 102/E5
Butha, China 77/K2

Butiaba, Uganda 115/F3
Butler (co.), Ala. 195/E7
Butler, Ala. 195/B6
Butler, Georgia 217/D5
Butler, Ill. 222/D4
Butler, Ind. 227/H2
Butler (co.), Iowa 229/H3
Butler (co.), Kansas 232/E4
Butler (co.), Ky. 237/H6
Butler, Ky. 237/N3
Butler, Md. 245/M2
Butler, Minn. 255/C4
Butler (co.), Mo. 261/M9
Butler, Mo. 261/D6
Butler (co.), Nebr. 264/G3
Butler, N.J. 273/E2
Butler (co.), Ohio 284/A7
Butler, Ohio 284/F4
Butler, Okla. 288/H3
Butler (co.), Pa. 294/C4
Butler, Pa. 294/C4
Butler, S. Dak. 298/Q3
Butler, Tenn. 237/T7
Butler (bay), Virgin Is. (U.S.) 161/E4
Butler, Wis. 317/K1
Butler Springs, Ala. 195/E7
Butlerville, Ark. 202/G4
Butlerville, Ind. 227/F6
Butlerville, Ohio 284/B7
Butner, N.C. 281/M2
Bütschelegg (mt.), Switzerland 39/D3
Bütschwil, Switzerland 39/H2
Buttahatchee (riv.), Ala. 195/A3
Buttahatchee (riv.), Miss. 256/H3
Butte (co.), Calif. 204/D4
Butte (co.), Idaho 220/E6
Butte, Mont. 146/G5
Butte, Mont. 188/D1
Butte, Nebr. 264/F2
Butte (mts.), Nev. 266/F3
Butte, N. Dak. 298/G4
Butte, Oreg. 291/G2
Butte (creek), Oreg. 291/B3
Butte (co.), S. Dak. 298/B4
Butte City, Calif. 204/C4
Butte City, Idaho 220/E6
Butte Des Morts, Wis. 317/J7
Butte Falls, Oreg. 291/E5
Butter (creek), Oreg. 291/H2
Butterfield, Minn. 255/D7
Butterfield, Mo. 261/E9
Butterfield (lake), N.Y. 276/J2
Butternut, Mich. 250/E5
Butternut, Wis. 317/E3
Butternut (lake), Wis. 317/J4
Butter Pot Prov. Park, Newf. 166/D2
Butters, N.C. 281/M5
Butterworth, Malaysia 72/D6
Butterworth (Gcuwa), S. Africa 118/D6
Buttes, Switzerland 39/C3
Butte-Silver Bow County, Mont. 262/F4
Buttevant, Ireland 17/D7
Buttlar, Germany 29/A2
Butt of Lewis (prom.), Scotland 15/B2
Button (isls.), N.W. Terr. 187/M3
Buttonwillow, Calif. 204/F8
Butts (co.), Georgia 217/E4
Buttzville, N.J. 273/D2
Buttzville, N. Dak. 282/P6
Butuan, Philippines 82/E6
Butuan, Philippines 85/H4
Butuan, Philippines 54/O9
Butuan (bay), Philippines 82/E6
Butumi, U.S.S.R. 7/J4
Butung (isl.), Indonesia 54/O10
Butung (isl.), Indonesia 85/G6
Buturlinovka, U.S.S.R. 52/F4
Butzbach, Germany 22/C3
Bützow, Germany 22/E2
Buxtehude, Germany 22/C2
Buxton, England 10/G2
Buxton, England 13/J2
Buxton •, Maine 243/A8
Buxton, N.C. 281/U4
Buxton, N. Dak. 282/R4
Buxton, Oreg. 291/D2
Buxton Center, Maine 243/B8
Buy, U.S.S.R. 52/F3
Buyck, Minn. 255/F2
Buynaksk, U.S.S.R. 52/G6
Büyükada, Turkey 63/D6
Büyük Ağrı (Ararat) (mt.), Turkey 63/L3
Büyük Ağrı (Ararat) (mt.), Turkey 59/D2
Büyükanafarta, Turkey 63/B6
Büyükdere, Turkey 63/D5
Büyük Hasan Dağı, Turkey 63/E3
Büyük Menderes (riv.), Turkey 59/A2
Buzău, Romania 45/H3
Buzău (riv.), Romania 45/H3
Buzeima (well), Libya 111/D3
Buzias, Romania 45/E3
Buzios (cape), Brazil 135/F3
Buzuluk, U.S.S.R. 52/H4
Buzuluk, U.S.S.R. 48/F4
Buzzard Roost (dam), S.C. 296/C5
Buzzards Bay, Mass. 249/L7
Buzzards Bay, Mass. 249/M5
Byala, Bulgaria 45/G4
Byala Slatina, Bulgaria 45/F4
Byam Martin (chan.), N.W. Terr. 187/H2
Byam Martin (isl.), N.W. Terr. 187/H2
Byars, Okla. 288/N5
Byars, Tenn. 237/P8
Bybee, Tenn. 237/P8
Bydgoszcz (prov.), Poland 47/C2
Bydgoszcz, Poland 47/C2
Bydgoszcz, Poland 7/F3
Byemoor, Alberta 182/D4
Byers, Colo. 208/L3
Byers, Kansas 232/D4
Byers, Texas 303/F3
Byesville, Ohio 284/G6
Byfield, Mass. 249/L1
Byford, W. Australia 88/B2
Bygland, Minn. 255/B3
Bygland, Norway 18/F7
Byhalia, Miss. 256/E1

Cambridge 345

Byknov, U.S.S.R. 52/C4
Bylas, Ariz. 198/E5
Bylot (isl.), N.W.T. 146/L2
Bylot (isl.), N.W.T. 162/J1
Bylot (isl.), N.W. Terr. 187/L2
Byng, Okla. 288/N5
Byng Inlet, Ontario 177/D2
Byng Inlet, Ontario 175/D3
Bynum, Mont. 262/D3
Bynum (res.), Mont. 262/D2
Bynum, N.C. 281/L3
Bynumville, Mo. 261/G3
Byram, Conn. 210/A4
Byram (pt.), Conn. 210/A4
Byram (riv.), Conn. 210/A4
Byram, Miss. 256/D6
Byrd Station, Ant. 5/A12
Byrdstown, Tenn. 237/L7
Byrnedale, Pa. 294/E3
Byrock, N.S. Wales 97/D2
Byromville, Georgia 217/E6
Byron, Calif. 204/L2
Byron (isl.), Chile 138/D7
Byron, Georgia 217/E5
Byron, Ill. 222/D1
Byron, Ind. 227/C5
Byron, Maine 243/B6
Byron•, Maine 243/B6
Byron, Mich. 250/E6
Byron, Minn. 255/F6
Byron, Nebr. 264/G4
Byron (bay), Newf. 166/C3
Byron (cape), N. S. Wales 88/J5
Byron (cape), N.S. Wales 97/G1
Byron, N.Y. 276/D4
Byron, Okla. 288/K1
Byron (lake), S. Dak. 298/N4
Byron, Wis. 317/K8
Byron, Wyo. 319/D1
Byron Bay, N.S. Wales 97/G1
Byron Center, Mich. 250/D6
Byrum, Denmark 21/E3
Byskeälv (riv.), Sweden 18/L4
Bystřice nad Pernštejnem, Czech. 41/D2
Bystřice pod Hostýnem, Czech. 41/D2
Bystrzyca Kłodzka, Poland 47/C3
Bytča, Czech. 41/E2
Bytom, Poland 47/A3
Bytów, Poland 47/C1

C

Caacupé, Paraguay 144/B5
Caaguazú, Paraguay 144/D-E4
Caaguazú, Paraguay 144/D4
Caála, Angola 115/C6
Caamaño (sound), Br. Col. 184/C4
Caapucú, Paraguay 144/D5
Caatingas (for.), Brazil 120/E3
Caazapá, Paraguay 144/D-E5
Caazapá, Paraguay 144/D5
Caba, Philippines 82/C2
Cabadbaran, Philippines 82/E6
Cabaiguán, Cuba 158/E2
Cabalasan (mt.), Philippines 82/E5
Caballero, Paraguay 144/B5
Caballo, N. Mex. 274/B6
Caballo (res.), N. Mex. 274/B6
Caballo (creek), Wyo. 319/G1
Caballococha, Peru 128/G4
Caballones (chan.), Cuba 158/F3
Cabana, Peru 128/C7
Cabañaquinta, Spain 33/D1
Cabañas, Cuba 158/B1
Cabanatuan, Philippines 54/O8
Cabanatuan, Philippines 82/C3
Cabanatuan, Philippines 85/G2
Cabanes, Spain 33/F2
Cabano, Québec 172/J2
Cabarroguis, Philippines 82/C2
Cabarrus (co.), N.C. 281/H4
Cabazon, Calif. 204/J10
Cabbage Tree (creek), Queensland 95/D2
Cabedelo, Brazil 132/H4
Cabell (co.), W. Va. 312/B6
Cabery, Ill. 222/E3
Cabet, Pitons du (mt.), Martinique 161/C6
Cabeza del Buey, Spain 33/D3
Cabezas, Bolivia 136/D6
Cabezas, Cuba 158/D1
Cabildo, Chile 138/A9
Cabimas, Venezuela 120/B1
Cabimas, Venezuela 124/C2
Cabin Creek, W. Va. 312/C6
Cabinda (prov.), Angola 115/B5
Cabinda, Angola 115/B5
Cabinda, Angola 102/D5
Cabinet (mts.), Mont. 262/A2
Cabin John (creek), Md. 245/E4
Cabin John-Brookmont, Md. 245/E4
Cabins, W. Va. 312/H4
Cable, Minn. 255/D5
Cable, Ohio 284/C5
Cable, Wis. 317/D3
Cabo Blanco, Peru 128/B5
Cabo Delgado (prov.), Mozambique 118/F2
Cabo Frio, Brazil 132/F8
Cabo Frio, Brazil 135/F3
Cabo Gracias a Dios, Nicaragua 154/F3
Cabonga (res.), Québec 174/B3
Cabool, Mo. 261/H8
Cabora Bassa (dam), Mozambique 118/E3
Caborn, Ind. 227/B9
Cabo Rojo, P. Rico 161/A2
Cabo San Lucas, Mexico 150/E5
Cabot (str.) 162/K6
Cabot, Ark. 202/F4
Cabot (str.), Canada 146/N5
Cabot (lake), Newf. 166/B2
Cabot (str.), Newf. 166/B4
Cabot (mt.), N.H. 268/E2
Cabot (head), Ontario 177/C2
Cabot, Pa. 294/C4
Cabot, Vt. 268/C3
Cabot•, Vt. 268/C3
Cabo Vírgenes, Argentina 143/C7
Cabra, Spain 33/D4
Cabra de Santo Cristo, Spain 33/E4
Cabral, Dom. Rep. 158/D6
Cabral (lag.), Paraguay 144/A5
Cabrera, Dom. Rep. 158/E5
Cabrera (isl.), Spain 33/H3
Cabri, Sask. 181/C5
Cabri (lake), Sask. 181/B4
Cabrillo Nat'l Mon., Calif. 204/H11
Cabrits (isl.), Martinique 161/D7
Cabrón (cape), Dom. Rep. 158/F5
Cabruta, Venezuela 124/E4
Cabudare, Venezuela 124/D3
Cabugao, Philippines 82/C2
Cabulauan (isls., Philippines 82/C5
Cabullones (pt.) P. Rico 161/C3
Caburai (mt.), Guyana 131/A3
Cabure, Venezuela 124/D2
Caçador, Brazil 132/D9
Cacahoatán, Mexico 150/N9
Čačak, Yugoslavia 45/E4
Caçapava, Brazil 135/D3
Caçapava do Sul, Brazil 132/C10
Cacapon (riv.), W. Va. 312/J4
Cáceres (lag.), Bolivia 136/G6
Cáceres, Brazil 132/B7
Cáceres, Brazil 120/D4
Cáceres, Colombia 126/C4
Cáceres (prov.) Spain 33/C3
Cáceres, Spain 33/C3
Cáceres, Spain 7/D5
Cachapoal (riv.), Chile 138/G5
Cache (riv.), Ark. 202/H3
Cache (riv.), Ill. 222/D6
Cache, Okla. 288/J5
Cache (creek), Okla. 288/K6
Cache (co.), Utah 304/C2
Cache Bay, Ontario 177/D1
Cache Creek, Br. Col. 184/G5
Cache Junction, Utah 304/C2
Cache la Poudre (riv.), Colo. 208/H1
Cacheu, Guinea-Biss. 106/A6
Cachi, Argentina 143/C2
Cachina, Quebrada (riv.), Chile 138/A5
Cachipo, Venezuela 124/G3
Cachoeira, Brazil 132/G6
Cachoeira de Itapemirim, Brazil 120/E5
Cachoeira do Arari, Brazil 132/D3
Cachoeira do Sul, Brazil 132/C10
Cachoeira do Sul, Brazil 120/D6
Cachoeiro de Itapemirim, Brazil 132/G8
Cachorras, Colombia 126/D8
Cachos (pt.), Chile 138/A6
Cachuela Esperanza, Bolivia 136/C2
Cachuma (lake , Calif. 204/F9
Cacocum, Cuba 158/H3
Cacocum, Cuba 156/C2
Cacolo, Angola 115/C6
Caconda, Angola 115/B6
Cacouna, Québec 172/H2
Cactus (range) Nev. 266/E5
Cactus (hills), Sask. 181/F5
Cactus, Texas 303/B1
Cactus Lake, Sask. 181/B3
Cacuri, Venezuela 124/F5
Cacuso, Angola 115/C5
Čadca, Czech. 41/E2
Caddo (riv.), Ark. 202/D5
Caddo (par.), La. 238/C1
Caddo (lake), La. 238/B1
Caddo (co.), Okla. 288/K4
Caddo, Okla. 288/O6
Caddo, Texas 303/F5
Caddo (lake), Texas 303/L5
Caddo Gap, Ark. 202/C5
Caddo Valley, Ark. 202/D5
Caddy Lake, Manitoba 179/G5
Cade, La. 238/G6
Cadereyta Jiménez, Mexico 150/K4
Cades, S.C. 296/H4
Cades, Tenn. 237/D9
Cades Cove, Tenn. 237/O9
Cadet, Mo. 261/L6
Cadibarrawirracanna (lake), S. Australia 94/D3
Cadillac, Mich. 250/D4
Cadillac, Québec 174/B3
Cadillac, Sask. 181/D6
Cadiz, Calif. 204/K9
Cadiz (lake), Calif. 204/K9
Cadiz, Ind. 227/G5
Cadiz, Ky. 237/F7
Cadiz, Ohio 284/J5
Cadiz, Philippines 82/D5
Cádiz (gulf), Portugal 33/C4
Cádiz (prov.), Spain 33/D4
Cádiz, Spain 33/C4
Cádiz, Spain 7/D5
Cádiz (gulf), Spain 33/C4
Cadogan, Alberta 182/E3
Cadogan•, Pa. 294/C4
Cadomin, Alberta 182/B3
Cadott, Wis. 317/D6
Cadotte (lake), Alberta 182/B1
Cadotte (riv.), Alberta 182/B1
Cadotte Lake, Alberta 182/B1
Cadron (creek), Ark. 202/F3
Caduruan (pt.), Philippines 82/D5
Cadwell, Georgia 217/G6
Cadyville, N.Y. 276/N1
Caen, France 28/C3
Caen, France 7/D4
Caerleon, Wales 13/B6
Caernarfon, Wales 13/C4
Caernarfon, Wales 10/D4
Caernarfon (bay), Wales 13/C4
Caernarfon (bay), Wales 10/D4
Caerphilly, Wales 13/B6
Caerphilly, Wales 10/E5
Caesar, Miss. 256/E9
Caesarea, Ontario 177/F3
Caesars Head, S.C. 296/B1
Caeté, Brazil 135/E1
Caetité, Brazil 132/F6
Cafayate, Argentina 143/C2
Cafelândia, Brazil 135/B2
Cagayan (prov.), Philippines 82/C1
Cagayan (isls.), Philippines 82/C6
Cagayan (isls.), Philippines 85/F4
Cagayan (riv.), Philippines 82/C2
Cagayancillo, Philippines 82/C6
Cagayan de Oro, Philippines 82/E6
Cagayan de Oro, Philippines 85/G4
Cagayan Sulu (isl.), Philippines 85/F4
Cagayan Sulu (isl.), Philippines 82/B7
Cagle, Tenn. 237/L10
Cagles Mill (lake), Ind. 227/D6
Cagli, Italy 34/D3
Cagliari (prov.), Italy 34/B5
Cagliari, Italy 7/E5
Cagliari, Italy 34/B5
Cagliari (gulf), Italy 34/B5
Cagua (vol.), Philippines 82/D1
Cagua, Venezuela 124/E2
Caguán (riv.), Colombia 126/C7
Caguas, P. Rico 161/E2
Caguas, P. Rico 156/G1
Caha (mts.), Ireland 17/B8
Cahaba, Ala. 195/D6
Cahaba (riv.), Ala. 195/D5
Cahabón, Guatemala 154/C3
Cahir, Ireland 10/B4
Cahir, Ireland 17/F7
Cahirciveen, Ireland 17/A8
Cahirciveen, Ireland 10/A5
Cahokia, Ill. 222/A3
Cahone, Colo. 208/B7
Cahore (pt.), Ireland 17/J6
Cahors, France 28/D5
Cahuapanas, Peru 128/D5
Cahuilla Ind. Res., Calif. 204/J10
Cahuinari (riv.), Colombia 126/E8
Cahuita (pt.), C. Rica 154/F6
Caia, Mozambique 114/G7
Caia, Mozambique 118/E3
Caiapônia, Brazil 132/C7
Caibarién, Cuba 158/F2
Caibarién, Cuba 156/B2
Caibiran, Philippines 82/E5
Caicara, Venezuela 124/G3
Caicara de Orinoco, Venezuela 124/E4
Caicedonia, Colombia 126/C5
Caicó, Brazil 120/F3
Caicó, Brazil 132/G4
Caicos (passage), Bahamas 156/D2
Caicos (bank), Turks & Caicos 156/D2
Caicos (isls.), Turks & Caicos 156/D2
Caicos (passage), Turks & Caicos 156/D2
Caile, Miss. 256/C4
Cailloma, Peru 128/G10
Caillou (bay), La. 238/J8
Caimanera, Cuba 158/J4
Caimanera, Cuba 156/C3
Cain (creek), S. Dak. 298/N5
Cainde, Angola 115/B7
Cains (riv.), New Bruns. 170/D2
Cains Store, Ky. 237/M6
Cainsville, Mo. 261/E2
Cainsville, Tenn. 237/J9
Caird Coast (reg.), Ant. 5/B17
Cairnbaan, Scotland 15/C4
Cairnbrook, Pa. 294/E5
Cairndow, Scotland 15/D4
Cairn Gorm (mt.), Scotland 15/E3
Cairngorm (mts.), Scotland 15/E3
Cairnryan, Scotland 15/D6
Cairns, Australia 87/E7
Cairns, Queensland 95/C3
Cairns, Queensland 88/H3
Cairnsmore (mt.), Scotland 15/D5
Cairn Toul (mt.), Scotland 15/E3
Cairo, Egypt 59/B4
Cairo (cap.), Egypt 102/F2
Cairo (cap.), Egypt 111/J3
Cairo (cap.), Egypt 2/L4
Cairo, Georgia 217/D9
Cairo, Ill. 188/J3
Cairo, Ill. 222/D6
Cairo, Kansas 232/D4
Cairo, Mo. 261/H4
Cairo, Nebr. 264/F3
Cairo, N.Y. 276/M6
Cairo, Ohio 284/B4
Cairo, Okla. 288/O5
Cairo, W. Va. 312/D4
Caissie (pt.), New Bruns. 170/F2
Caister-on-Sea, England 13/J5
Caistor, England 13/G4
Caithness (trad. co.), Scotland 15/B4
Caiundo, Angola 102/D6
Caiundo, Angola 115/C7
Caiza, Bolivia 136/C7
Cajabamba, Ecuador 128/C3
Cajabamba, Peru 128/C6
Cajacay, Peru 128/D8
Caja de Muertos (isl.), P. Rico 161/C3
Cajamarca (dept.), Peru 128/C6
Cajamarca, Peru 128/C6
Cajamarca, Peru 120/B3
Cajatambo, Peru 128/D8
Cajazeiras, Brazil 132/G4
Cajidiocan, Philippines 82/D4
Cajuata, Bolivia 136/B5
Cajuru, Brazil 135/C2
Čakovec, Yugoslavia 45/C2
Çal, Turkey 63/C3
Çala, Turkey 63/K2
Calabar, Nigeria 102/D4
Calabar, Nigeria 106/F7
Calabash, N.C. 281/M7
Calabazar de Sagua, Cuba 158/E1
Calabogie, Ontario 177/H2
Calabozo, Venezuela 124/E3
Calabria (reg.), Italy 34/F5
Cala Burras (pt.), Spain 33/D4
Calaceite, Spain 33/G2
Calacoto, Bolivia 136/A5
Caladesi (isl.), Fla. 212/B2
Calafat, Romania 45/F3
Calafate, Argentina 143/B7
Calafquén (lake), Chile 138/E3
Calagnaan (isl.), Philippines 82/D5
Calagua (isls.), Philippines 82/D3
Calahoo, Alberta 182/D3
Calahorra, Spain 33/E1
Calais, Alberta 182/B2
Calais, France 28/D2
Calais, France 7/E3
Calais (Dover) (str.), France 28/D2
Calais, Maine 188/N1
Calais, Maine 243/J5
Calais•, Vt. 268/B3
Calama, Brazil 132/H10
Calama, Chile 120/C5
Calama, Chile 138/B3
Calamar, Bolívar, Colombia 126/C2
Calamar, Vaupés, Colombia 126/D7
Calamarca, Bolivia 136/A5
Calamba, Laguna, Philippines 82/C3
Calamba, Misamis Occ., Philippines 82/D6
Calamian Group (isls.), Philippines 85/F3
Calamian Group (isls.), Philippines 82/B4
Calamine, Ark. 202/H1
Calamocha, Spain 33/F2
Calamus, Iowa 229/M5
Calanasan, Philippines 82/C1
Calancasca (riv.), Switzerland 39/H4
Calanda, Spain 33/F2
Calandula, Angola 114/C5
Calang, Indonesia 85/B5
Calansho, Serir (des.), Libya 111/D2
Calansho Sand Sea (des.), Libya 111/D2
Calapan, Philippines 82/C4
Calapan, Philippines 85/G3
Calapooia (riv.), Oreg. 291/E3
Calapooya (mts.), Oreg. 291/E4
Călăraşi, Romania 45/H3
Calarcá, Colombia 126/C5
Calasparra, Spain 33/F3
Calatayud, Spain 33/F2
Calatorao, Spain 33/F2
Calauag, Philippines 82/D4
Calaveras (co.), Calif. 204/E5
Calaveras (res.), Calif. 204/L3
Calaveras (riv.), Texas 303/K11
Calavite (cape), Philippines 82/C4
Calayan, Philippines 82/A2
Calayan (isl.), Philippines 82/A2
Calbayog, Philippines 82/E4
Calbe, Germany 22/D3
Calbuco, Chile 138/D4
Calca, Peru 128/G9
Calcasieu (par.), La. 238/D6
Calcasieu, La. 238/E4
Calcasieu (lake), La. 238/D7
Calcasieu (passage), La. 238/D7
Calcasieu (riv.), La. 238/E5
Calceta, Ecuador 128/C3
Calchaquí, Argentina 143/F5
Calcis, Ala. 195/F4
Calcutta, India 68/F2
Calcutta, India 54/K7
Calcutta, India 2/P4
Calcutta, Ohio 284/J4
Calcutta, Suriname 131/C3
Caldas (dept.), Colombia 126/C5
Caldas da Rainha, Portugal 33/B3
Caldas Novas, Brazil 132/D7
Calder, Idaho 220/B2
Calder, Sask. 181/K4
Calder, Loch (lake), Scotland 15/E2
Caldera, Chile 120/B5
Caldera, Chile 138/A6
Calderas (bay), Dom. Rep. 158/D6
Calderas, Venezuela 124/C3
Calderwood, Tenn. 237/N9
Caldicot, Wales 13/E6
Çaldıran, Turkey 63/K3
Caldwell, Ark. 202/J3
Caldwell, Idaho 220/B6
Caldwell, Idaho 188/C2
Caldwell, Kansas 232/E4
Caldwell (co.), Ky. 237/F6
Caldwell (par.), La. 238/F2
Caldwell (co.), Mo. 261/E3
Caldwell, N.J. 273/B2
Caldwell (co.), N.C. 281/F3
Caldwell, Ohio 284/G6
Caldwell (co.), Texas 303/G8
Caldwell, Texas 303/H7
Caldwell, W. Va. 312/F7
Caldwell, Wis. 317/J2
Caldy (isl.), Wales 13/C6
Cale, Ark. 202/D6
Cale, Ind. 227/D7
Caledon, N. Ireland 17/H3
Caledon, Ontario 177/E4
Caledon, S. Africa 118/G7
Caledonia, Ill. 222/E1
Caledonia, Mich. 250/D6
Caledonia, Minn. 255/G7
Caledonia, Miss. 256/H3
Caledonia, Mo. 261/L7
Caledonia, N.Y. 276/E5
Caledonia, N. Dak. 282/S5
Caledonia, Guysborough, Nova Scotia 168/F3
Caledonia, Queens, Nova Scotia 168/C4
Caledonia, Ohio 284/D4
Caledonia, Pa. 294/F3
Caledonia (co.), Vt. 268/C2
Caledonia, Wis. 317/L2
Caledonian (canal), Scotland 15/D3
Calella, Spain 33/H2
Calenzana, France 28/B6
Calera, Ala. 195/E4
Calera, Okla. 288/O7
Calera de Tango, Chile 138/G4
Caleta Barquito, Chile 138/A6
Caleta Clarencia, Chile 138/E10
Caleta Olivia, Argentina 143/C6
Caleta Olivia, Argentina 120/C7
Caleta Pan de Azúcar, Chile 138/A5
Caleu, Chile 138/G2
Caleufú, Argentina 143/C4
Calexico, Calif. 204/K11
Calf of Man (isl.), I. of Man 13/C3
Calfsound, Scotland 15/F1
Calgary (cap.), Alberta 182/C4
Calgary (cap.), Alta.. 146/G4
Calgary, Alta. 162/E5
Calgary, Canada 2/D3
Calhan, Colo. 208/L4
Calheta, Portugal 33/A2
Calhoun (co.), Ala. 195/G3
Calhoun, Ala. 195/F6
Calhoun (co.), Ark. 202/E6
Calhoun (co.), Fla. 212/D6
Calhoun (co.), Georgia 217/C7
Calhoun, Georgia 217/C1
Calhoun (co.), Ill. 222/C4
Calhoun, Ill. 222/E5
Calhoun (co.), Iowa 229/D4
Calhoun, Ky. 237/G5
Calhoun, La. 238/F2
Calhoun (co.), Mich. 250/D6
Calhoun (co.), Miss. 256/F3
Calhoun, Mo. 261/E6
Calhoun (co.), S.C. 296/F4
Calhoun, Tenn. 237/M10
Calhoun (co.), Texas 303/H9
Calhoun (co.), W. Va. 312/D5
Calhoun City, Miss. 256/F3
Calhoun Falls, S.C. 296/B3
Cali, Colombia 126/B6
Cali, Colombia 120/B2
Calicito, Cuba 158/H4
Calicoan (isl.), Philippines 82/E5
Calico Rock, Ark. 202/F1
Calicut (Kozhikode), India 68/D6
Caliente, Nev. 266/G5
Califon, N.J. 273/D2
California 188/B3
CALIFORNIA 204
California, Ky. 237/N3
California, Md. 245/M7
California (gulf), Mexico 146/G7
California (gulf), Mexico 150/D3
California, Mo. 261/H5
California, Pa. 294/C5
California, Trin. & Tob. 161/A11
California (state), U.S. 146/G6
California Aqueduct, Calif. 204/E7
California City, Calif. 204/H8
California Hot Springs, Calif. 204/G8
California Junction, Iowa 229/B5
Calimete, Cuba 158/D1
Calio, N. Dak. 282/N2
Calion, Ark. 202/E7
Calipatria, Calif. 204/K10
Calistoga, Calif. 204/C5
Calixa-Lavallée, Québec 172/J4
Calkiní, Mexico 150/O6
Çalköy, Turkey 63/C3
Call, Texas 303/L7
Callabonna (lake), S. Australia 88/G5
Callabonna (lake), S. Australia 94/F3
Callafo, Ethiopia 111/H6
Callahan, Calif. 204/C2
Callahan, Fla. 212/E1
Callahan (co.), Texas 303/E5
Callalli, Peru 128/G10
Callan, Ireland 17/G7
Callan, Ireland 10/C4
Callander, Ont. 162/H6
Callander, Ontario 177/E1
Callander, Scotland 10/D2
Callander, Scotland 15/D4
Callands, Va. 307/J7
Callantsoog, Netherlands 27/F3
Callao, Mo. 261/G3
Callao (prov.), Peru 128/D9
Callao, Peru 128/D9
Callao, Peru 2/F6
Callao, Peru 120/B4
Callao, Utah 304/A4
Callao, Va. 307/P5
Callapa, Bolivia 136/A5
Callaway, Fla. 212/D6
Callaway, Minn. 255/C3
Callaway (co.), Mo. 261/J5
Callaway, Nebr. 264/D3
Callaway, Va. 307/H7
Calle Larga, Chile 138/G2
Callender, Iowa 229/E4
Callensburg, Pa. 294/D3
Callery, Pa. 294/C4
Calleuque, Chile 138/F5
Calliaqua, St. Vin. & Grens. 161/A9
Callicoon, N.Y. 276/K7
Callicoon Center, N.Y. 276/L7
Calliham, Texas 303/F9
Callimont, Pa. 294/E6
Calling (lake), Alberta 182/D2
Callis, Somalia 115/J2
Callison, S.C. 296/C3
Callosa de Ensarriá, Spain 33/G3
Calloway (co.), Ky. 237/E7
Calmar, Alberta 182/D3
Calmar, Iowa 229/K2
Calmer, Ark. 202/F6
Calnali, Mexico 150/K6
Calne, England 13/F6
Calobre, Panama 154/G6
Caloosahatchee (riv.), Fla. 212/E5
Caloundra, Queensland 88/J5
Caloundra, Queensland 95/E5
Čalovo, Czech. 41/D3
Calpella, Calif. 204/B4
Calpet, Wyo. 319/B3
Calpulálpan, Mexico 150/M1
Calstock, England 13/C7
Caltagirone, Italy 34/E6
Caltanissetta (prov.), Italy 34/D6
Caltanissetta, Italy 34/D6
Caluire-et-Cuire, France 28/F5
Calulo, Angola 115/C6
Calumet (lake), Ill. 222/C6
Calumet, Iowa 229/B3
Calumet, La. 238/H7
Calumet, Mich. 188/J1
Calumet, Mich. 250/A1
Calumet, Minn. 255/E3
Calumet, Okla. 288/K3
Calumet, Québec 172/C4
Calumet (co.), Wis. 317/K7
Calumet City, Ill. 222/C6
Calumet Park, Ill. 222/C6
Calumetville, Wis. 317/K8
Caluquembe, Angola 102/D6
Caluquembe, Angola 115/B6
Calva, Ariz. 198/E5
Calvados (dept.), France 28/C3
Calvary, Georgia 217/D9
Calvary, Ky. 237/L6
Calvert, Ala. 195/B8
Calvert (isl.), Br. Col. 184/C4
Calvert, Kansas 232/C2
Calvert (co.), Md. 245/M6
Calvert, Md. 245/O2
Calvert, Newf. 166/D2
Calvert, Texas 303/H7
Calvert City, Ky. 237/E6
Calvert Hills, North. Terr. 93/E4
Calverton, Md. 245/L4
Calverton, Va. 307/N3
Calverton Park, Mo. 261/P2
Calvertville, Ind. 227/D6
Calvi, France 28/B6
Calvillo, Mexico 150/H6
Calvin, Ky. 237/O7
Calvin, La. 238/E3
Calvin, N. Dak. 282/N2
Calvin, Okla. 288/O5
Calvin, W. Va. 312/E6
Calvinia, S. Africa 102/E8
Calvinia, S. Africa 118/B6
Calwa, Calif. 204/F7
Calypso, N.C. 281/N4
Calzada de Calatrava, Spain 33/E3
Camabatela, Angola 115/C5
Camacho, Bolivia 136/C7
Camacupa, Angola 115/C6
Camaguán, Venezuela 124/E3
Camagüey (prov.), Cuba 158/G2
Camagüey, Cuba 158/G3
Camagüey, Cuba 146/L7
Camagüey, Cuba 156/B2
Camagüey (arch.), Cuba 158/G2
Camaiore, Italy 34/C3
Camajuaní, Cuba 158/E2
Camak, Georgia 217/G4
Camaná, Peru 128/F11
Camanche (res.), Calif. 204/C9
Camanche, Iowa 229/N5
Camano (isl.), Wash. 310/C2
Camanongue, Angola 115/D6
Camanongue, Angola 102/E6
Camaquã, Brazil 132/C10
Câmara de Lobos, Portugal 33/A2
Çamardı, Turkey 63/F4
Camargo, Bolivia 136/C7
Camargo, Ill. 222/E4
Camargo, Ky. 237/K4
Camargo, Okla. 288/H2
Camarillo, Calif. 204/F9
Camarines Norte (prov.), Philippines 82/D3
Camarines Sur (prov.), Philippines 82/D4
Camarón (cape), Honduras 154/E2
Camarones, Argentina 143/C5
Camarones, Chile 138/B2
Camarones (riv.), Chile 138/A2
Camas (co.), Idaho 220/D6
Camas (creek), Idaho 220/D6
Camas (creek), Idaho 220/F5
Camas (creek), Idaho 220/D5
Camas, Wash. 310/C5
Camas Prairie, Mont. 262/B3
Camas Valley, Oreg. 291/D4
Camatagua, Venezuela 124/E3
Camatindi, Bolivia 136/D7
Ca Mau (Mui Bai Bung) (pt.), Vietnam 72/E5
Cambará, Brazil 135/A3
Cambará, Brazil 132/D8
Cambay, India 68/C4
Cambay (gulf), India 54/J7
Cambay (gulf), India 68/C4
Camberwell, Victoria 88/L7
Camberwell, Victoria 97/J5
Cambodia 2/Q5
Cambodia 54/M8
CAMBODIA (KAMPUCHEA) 72
Camborne-Redruth, England 10/D5
Camborne-Redruth, England 13/B7
Cambra, Pa. 294/K3
Cambrai, France 28/E2
Cambria, Alberta 182/D4
Cambria, Calif. 204/D8
Cambria, Ill. 222/D6
Cambria, Ind. 227/D4
Cambria, Iowa 229/G7
Cambria, Mich. 250/E7
Cambria, Minn. 255/D6
Cambria (co.), Pa. 294/E4
Cambria, Wis. 317/H8
Cambrian (mts.), Wales 13/D5
Cambridge, England 13/G5
Cambridge, England 10/G4
Cambridge, Idaho 220/B5
Cambridge, Ill. 222/C2
Cambridge, Iowa 229/G5
Cambridge, Jamaica 158/H6
Cambridge, Kansas 232/F4
Cambridge•, Maine 243/E5
Cambridge, Md. 245/O6
Cambridge, Mass. 249/C7
Cambridge (res.), Mass. 249/B6
Cambridge, Minn. 255/E5
Cambridge, Nebr. 264/D4
Cambridge, N.Y. 276/O4
Cambridge, N. Zealand 100/E2
Cambridge, Ohio 284/G5
Cambridge, Ontario 177/D4
Cambridge, Tasmania 99/D4
Cambridge, Vt. 268/B2
Cambridge•, Vt. 268/B2
Cambridge, Wis. 317/H9

Cambridge Bay, Canada 4/B15
Cambridge Bay, N.W.T. 162/F2
Cambridge Bay, N.W. Terr. 187/H3
Cambridge City, Ind. 227/G5
Cambridge-Narrows, New Bruns. 170/E3
Cambridgeport, Vt. 268/B5
Cambridgeshire (co.), England 13/G5
Cambridge Springs, Pa. 294/C2
Cambridge Station, Nova Scotia 168/D3
Cambuí, Brazil 135/C3
Cambulo, Angola 115/D5
Cambulo, Angola 102/E5
Cambundi-Catembo, Angola 114/C5
Cambuslang, Scotland 15/B2
Camden, Ala. 195/D7
Camden (bay), Alaska 196/K1
Camden, Ark. 202/E6
Camden, Del. 245/R4
Camden, England 13/H8
Camden, England 10/B5
Camden (co.), Georgia 217/J9
Camden, Ill. 222/C4
Camden, Ind. 227/D3
Camden, Maine 243/F7
Camden•, Maine 243/F7
Camden, Mich. 250/E7
Camden, Miss. 256/E5
Camden (co.), Mo. 261/G6
Camden, Mo. 261/J4
Camden, N.J. 188/M3
Camden, N.J. 273/D4
Camden, N.J. 273/B3
Camden, N.S. Wales 97/F4
Camden, N.Y. 276/J4
Camden (co.), N.C. 281/S2
Camden, N.C. 281/S2
Camden, Ohio 284/A6
Camden, S.C. 296/F3
Camden, Tenn. 237/E8
Camden, Texas 303/K7
Camden, W. Va. 312/F4
Camden Haven, N.S. Wales 97/G2
Camden on Gauley, W. Va. 312/E6
Camden Park, St. Vin. & Grens. 161/A9
Camden Point, Mo. 261/C4
Camdenton, Mo. 261/G6
Cameia, Angola 115/D6
Camelford, England 13/C7
Çameli, Turkey 63/C4
Camels Hump (mt.), Vt. 268/B3
Camerino, Italy 34/E4
Cameron, Ariz. 198/D5
Cameron (peak), Colo. 208/H1
Cameron, Ill. 222/C3
Cameron (par.), La. 238/D7
Cameron, La. 238/D7
Cameron, Mo. 261/D3
Cameron, Mont. 262/E5
Cameron, N.Y. 276/F6
Cameron (mts.), N. Zealand 100/A7
Cameron, N.C. 281/L4
Cameron (isl.), N.W. Terr. 187/H2
Cameron, Ohio 284/J6
Cameron, Okla. 288/T4
Cameron (co.), Pa. 294/F3
Cameron, Pa. 294/F3
Cameron, S.C. 296/F4
Cameron (co.), Texas 303/G11
Cameron, Texas 303/H7
Cameron, W. Va. 312/F3
Cameron, Wis. 317/C5
Cameron Falls, Ontario 177/H5
Cameron Highlands, Malaysia 72/D6
Cameroon 2/K5
Cameroon 102/D4
CAMEROON 115/B2
Cameroon (mt.), Cameroon 102/C4
Cameroon (mt.), Cameroon 115/A3
Camerota, Italy 34/E4
Cametá, Brazil 132/D3
Camiguin (prov.), Philippines 82/E6
Camiguin, Cagayan (isl.), Philippines 82/B3
Camiguin, Camiguin (isl.), Philippines 82/E6
Camiling, Philippines 82/C3
Camilla, Georgia 217/D8
Camillus, N.Y. 276/H4
Camiña, Chile 138/B2
Camiña, Quebrada (riv.), Chile 138/B2
Caminha, Portugal 33/B2
Camino, Calif. 204/F5
Camiri, Bolivia 120/C5
Camirí, Bolivia 136/D7
Camlachie, Ontario 177/B4
Çamlıdere, Turkey 63/E2
Cammack, Ind. 227/G4
Cammack Village, Ark. 202/E4
Cammal, Pa. 294/H3
Camoapa, Nicaragua 154/E4
Camocim, Brazil 132/F3
Camolin, Ireland 17/J6
Camooweal, Queensland 88/F3
Camooweal, Queensland 95/A3
Camopi, Fr. Guiana 131/E4
Camopi (riv.), Fr. Guiana 131/E4
Camorta (isl.), India 68/G7
Camoruco, Colombia 126/E4
Camotes (isls.), Philippines 82/E5
Camotes (sea), Philippines 82/E5
Camp (creek), Georgia 217/J2
Camp (creek), Ind. 227/E6
Camp (creek), Oreg. 291/J4
Camp (co.), Texas 303/K5
Campaign, Tenn. 237/K9
Campamento, Uruguay 145/C1
Campana, Argentina 143/G6
Campana (isl.), Chile 120/B7
Campana (isl.), Chile 138/D7
Campanario, Cerro (mt.), Argentina 143/C4
Campanario, Cerro (mt.), Chile 138/A10
Campanario, Spain 33/D3
Campanha, Brazil 135/D2
Campania, Georgia 217/H4
Campania (reg.), Italy 34/E4
Campaspe (riv.), Victoria 97/C5

Campbell, Ala. 195/C7
Campbell, Alaska 196/M2
Campbell, Calif. 204/K3
Campbell (co.), Ky. 237/N3
Campbell, Minn. 255/B4
Campbell, Mo. 261/M9
Campbell, Nebr. 264/F4
Campbell, N.Y. 276/F6
Campbell (cape), N. Zealand 100/E4
Campbell (hill), Ohio 284/C5
Campbell (co.), S. Dak. 298/J2
Campbell (co.), Tenn. 237/N8
Campbell (co.), Va. 307/K6
Campbell (co.), Wyo. 319/G1
Campbell (mt.), Yukon 187/E3
Campbellford, Ontario 177/G3
Campbell Hall, N.Y. 276/K8
Campbell Hill, Ill. 222/D6
Campbell Island, Br. Col. 184/C4
Campbellpore, Pakistan 68/C2
Campbell River, Br. Col. 184/E5
Campbells (lake), Oreg. 291/H5
Campbellsburg, Ind. 227/E7
Campbellsburg, Ky. 237/L3
Campbellsport, Wis. 317/K8
Campbell Station, Ark. 202/H2
Campbellsville, Ky. 237/L6
Campbellton, Fla. 212/D5
Campbellton, Mo. 261/K5
Campbellton, N. Br. 162/K6
Campbellton, N. Br. 146/M5
Campbellton, New Bruns. 170/D1
Campbellton, Newfl. 166/C3
Campbellton, Pr. Edward I. 168/D2
Campbellton, Texas 303/F9
Campbelltown, N.S. Wales 97/F4
Campbelltown, S. Australia 88/E8
Campbelltown, S. Australia 94/E7
Campbell Town, Tasmania 99/D3
Campbeltown, Scotland 15/C5
Campbeltown, Scotland 10/C3
Camp Creek, Alberta 182/C2
Camp Creek, W. Va. 312/D7
Camp Crook, S. Dak. 298/B2
Camp David, Md. 245/J2
Camp Denton, Ohio 284/D9
Camp Dix, Ky. 237/P3
Camp Douglas, Wis. 317/F8
Campeche (state), Mexico 150/O7
Campeche, Mexico 146/J8
Campeche, Mexico 150/O7
Campeche (bank), Mexico 150/O6
Campeche (bay), Mexico 146/J7
Campeche (bay), Mexico 150/N7
Campechuela, Cuba 158/G4
Camper, Manitoba 179/D3
Camperdown, Victoria 97/C6
Camperville, Manitoba 179/B2
Camp Grove, Ill. 222/D2
Camp Hale, Colo. 208/G4
Camp Hill, Ala. 195/G5
Camp Hill, Pa. 294/H5
Camp Hill, Queensland 88/K3
Camp Hill, Queensland 95/E3
Campiglia Marittima, Italy 34/C3
Campile, Ireland 17/H7
Campillo de Altobuey, Spain 33/F3
Campillos, Spain 33/D4
Campina Grande, Brazil 120/F3
Campina Grande, Brazil 132/G4
Campinas, Brazil 120/E5
Campinas, Brazil 135/C3
Campinas, Brazil 132/E8
Campina Verde, Brazil 135/B1
Campina Verde, Brazil 132/D7
Camp Lake, Wis. 317/K10
Camp Lejeune Marine Corps Base, N.C. 281/P5
Campli, Italy 34/E4
Camp Morton, Manitoba 179/E4
Camp Nelson, Calif. 204/G7
Campo, Calif. 204/J11
Campo, Cameroon 115/B3
Campo, Colo. 208/O8
Campoalegre, Colombia 126/C6
Campobasso (prov.), Italy 34/E4
Campobasso, Italy 34/E4
Campobello (isl.), New Bruns. 170/D4
Campobello, S.C. 296/C1
Campo Belo, Brazil 132/E8
Campo Belo, Brazil 135/D2
Campo Claro, Venezuela 124/G2
Campo de Criptana, Spain 33/E3
Campo de la Cruz, Colombia 126/C2
Campo Florido, Brazil 135/B1
Campo Formoso, Brazil 132/F5
Campo Grande, Brazil 120/D5
Campo Grande, Brazil 132/C8
Campo Ind. Res., Calif. 204/J11
Campo Largo, Brazil 135/B4
Campo Maior, Brazil 132/F3
Campo Maior, Portugal 33/C3
Campos, Brazil 132/F8
Campos, Brazil 135/F2
Campos, Brazil 120/E5
Campos (reg.), Brazil 120/E4
Campos Altos, Brazil 135/C1
Campo Seco, Calif. 204/F5
Campo Tencia (peak), Switzerland 39/G4
Campo Tures, Italy 34/C1
Camp Pendleton, Calif. 204/H10
Camp Perrin, Haiti 158/A6
Camp Point, Ill. 222/B6
Camp Robinson, Ontario 177/G4
Camp Robinson, Ontario 175/B2
Camp Sherman, Oreg. 291/F4
Camp Springs, Md. 245/G6
Campti, La. 238/D3
Campton, Georgia 217/E3
Campton, Ky. 237/O5
Campton•, N.H. 268/D4
Camptown, Pa. 294/K2
Campus, Ill. 222/E2
Camp Verde, Ariz. 198/D4
Campville, Fla. 212/D2
Camp Wood, Texas 303/D8

Cam Ranh, Vietnam 72/F5
Cam Ranh, Vinh (bay), Vietnam 72/F5
Camrose, Alberta 182/D3
Camrose, Alta. 162/F5
Camsell (riv.), N.W. Terr. 187/G3
Camsell Portage, Sask. 181/L2
Camuy, P. Rico 161/B1
Camuy, P. Rico 156/F1
Camuy (riv.), P. Rico 161/B1
Çan, Turkey 63/B2
Caña, Czech. 41/F2
Cana (pt.), Dom. Rep. 158/F6
Cana, Sask. 181/J5
Cana, Va. 307/G7
Canaan, Conn. 210/B1
Canaan•, Conn. 210/B1
Canaan (mt.), Conn. 210/B1
Canaan, Ind. 227/G7
Canaan•, Maine 243/D6
Canaan, Miss. 256/E5
Canaan, New Bruns. 170/E2
Canaan (riv.), New Bruns. 170/E2
Canaan•, N.H. 268/C4
Canaan, N.Y. 276/O6
Canaan•, Vt. 268/D2
Canaan Center, N.H. 268/C4
Canaan Forks, N.B. 170/E2
Canaan Road, New Bruns. 170/E2
Canada 2/D3
Canada 4/C13
Canada 146/G4
CANADA 163
Cañada, La (mt.), Cuba 158/B2
Canada, Ky. 237/S5
Canada (bay), Newfl. 166/C3
Cañada de Gómez, Argentina 143/F6
Cañada Nieto, Uruguay 145/B4
Canadensis, Pa. 294/M3
Canadian (riv.) 188/F3
Canadian (riv.), N. Mex. 274/F3
Canadian (co.), Okla. 288/K3
Canadian, Okla. 288/P4
Canadian (riv.), Okla. 288/O4
Canadian, Texas 303/D2
Canadian (riv.), Texas 303/D1
Canadian (riv.), U.S. 146/H6
Canadian City, Okla. 288/L4
Canadice (lake), N.Y. 276/F5
Canadys, S.C. 296/F5
Canagua (riv.), Venezuela 124/C3
Canajoharie, N.Y. 276/L5
Canakkale (prov.), Turkey 63/B2
Çanakkale, Turkey 63/B6
Çanakkale, Turkey 59/A2
Çanakkale (bay), Turkey 59/A2
Çanakkale Boğazı (Dardanelles) (str.), Turkey 63/B6
Çanakkale Boğazı (str.), Turkey 59/A2
Canal (creek), N.J. 273/E1
Canala, New Caled. 86/G4
Canala (bay), New Caled. 86/H4
Canal Flats, Br. Col. 184/K5
Canal Fulton, Ohio 284/H4
Canalou, Mo. 261/N9
Canal Point, Fla. 212/F5
Canals, Argentina 143/F5
Canal Winchester, Ohio 284/E6
Canandaigua, N.Y. 276/F5
Canandaigua (lake), N.Y. 276/F5
Cananea, Mexico 150/D1
Cananéia, Brazil 132/E9
Cananéia, Brazil 135/C4
Cananova, Cuba 158/K3
Cañar (prov.), Ecuador 128/C4
Cañar, Ecuador 128/C4
Canaries, St. Lucia 161/G6
Canaries, Piton (mt.), St. Lucia 161/G6
Canarreos, Los (arch.), Cuba 158/C2
Canary, Oreg. 291/D4
Canary (isls.), Spain 102/A2
Canary (isls.), Spain 2/H4
Canary (isls.), Spain 33/B4
Canary (isls.), Spain 106/A3
Cañas, C. Rica 154/E5
Cañas, Cuba 158/B1
Cañas (range), Uruguay 145/C2
Canaseraga, N.Y. 276/E6
Cañasgordas, Colombia 126/B4
Canasí, Cuba 158/C1
Canastota, N.Y. 276/J4
Canatlán, Mexico 150/G4
Canaveral (cape), Fla. 146/L7
Canaveral (Kennedy) (cape), Fla. 188/L5
Canaveral (cape), U.S. 2/F4
Canavieiras, Brazil 132/G6
Cañazas, Panama 154/G6
Canbelego, N.S. Wales 97/F3
Canberra (cap.), Australia 87/F9
Canberra (cap.), Australia 2/S7
Canberra (cap.), Aust. Cap. Terr. Australia 97/E4
Canby, Calif. 204/E2
Canby, Minn. 255/B6
Canby, Oreg. 291/B2
Cancún, Mexico 150/Q6
Candala, Somalia 115/J1
Candarave, Peru 128/G11
Çandarlı (gulf), Turkey 63/B3
Candás, Spain 33/D1
Candéias, Brazil 120/F4
Candela, Mexico 150/J3
Candelaria, Bolivia 136/F5
Candelaria (riv.), Bolivia 136/F5
Candelaria, Cuba 158/B1
Candelaria, Mexico 150/O7
Candelaria (riv.), Mexico 150/O8
Candelaria, Philippines 82/B3
Candelaria, Texas 303/C12
Candelaria, Venezuela 124/F4
Candeleda, Spain 33/D2
Candelero (pt.), P. Rico 161/F2
Candelo, N.S. Wales 97/E5
Candia (Iráklion), Greece 45/G8
Candia•, N.H. 268/E5
Candiac, Québec 172/J4
Candiac, Sask. 181/H5
Cândido Mendes, Brazil 132/E3
Çandır, Turkey 63/F3

Candle (lake), Sask. 181/F2
Candle Lake, Sask. 181/F2
Candler, Fla. 212/E2
Candler (co.), Georgia 217/H6
Candler, N.C. 281/D3
Candlewood (lake), Conn. 210/A2
Candlewood, N.J. 273/E3
Cando, N. Dak. 282/M3
Cando, Sask. 181/C3
Candon, Philippines 82/C2
Candor, N.Y. 276/H6
Candor, N.C. 281/K4
Cane (creek), Utah 304/E5
Caneadea, N.Y. 276/D6
Canea (Khaniá), Greece 45/G8
Canebay, Virgin Is. (U.S.) 161/E3
Cane Beds, Ariz. 198/B2
Canebrake, W. Va. 312/C8
Caneel (bay), Virgin Is. (U.S.) 161/B4
Canehill, Ark. 202/B2
Canelones (dept.), Uruguay 145/D5
Canelones, Uruguay 120/E6
Canelones, Uruguay 145/B6
Canelos, Ecuador 128/D3
Canendiyu, Paraguay 144/E4
Cañete (riv.), Peru 128/D9
Cañete, Chile 138/D2
Cañete, Spain 33/F2
Cane Valley, Ky. 237/L6
Caney, Kansas 232/G4
Caney, Ky. 237/P6
Caney (riv.), Okla. 288/O1
Caney Fork (riv.), Tenn. 237/L9
Caneyville, Ky. 237/J6
Canfield, Ark. 202/C7
Canfield, Ohio 284/J3
Canford, Br. Col. 184/G5
Cangallo, Peru 128/E9
Cangamba, Angola 115/C6
Cangas, Spain 33/B1
Cangas de Narcea, Spain 33/C1
Cangas de Onís, Spain 33/D1
Canguaretama, Brazil 132/H4
Cangyuan, China 77/E7
Cangzhou (Tsangchow), China 77/J4
Caniapiscau (riv.), Que. 162/K4
Canto do Buriti, Brazil 132/F5
Caniapiscau, Québec 174/D1
Caniapiscau (res.), Québec 162/J3
Caniapiscau (riv.), Québec 174/D1
Canicatti, Italy 34/E6
Canigao (chan.), Philippines 82/E5
Canik (mts.), Turkey 63/G2
Caniles, Spain 33/E4
Canindé, Brazil 132/G4
Canistear (res.), N.J. 273/E1
Canisteo, N.Y. 276/E6
Canisteo (riv.), N.Y. 276/F6
Canistota, S. Dak. 298/P6
Cañitas de Felipe Pescador, Mexico 150/H5
Canjáyar, Spain 33/E4
Canje (riv.), Guyana 131/C2
Canjilon, N. Mex. 274/C2
Çankaya, Turkey 63/E3
Çankırı (prov.), Turkey 63/E2
Çankırı, Turkey 63/E2
Çankırı, Turkey 59/B1
Cankton, La. 238/F6
Canlaon, Philippines 82/D5
Canlaon (peak), Philippines 82/D5
Canmer, Ky. 237/K6
Canmore, Alberta 182/C4
Canna (isl.), Scotland 10/C2
Canna (isl.), Scotland 15/B3
Canna (sound), Scotland 15/B3
Cannalville, Ohio 284/F6
Cannanore, India 68/C6
Cannanore (Laccadive) (isls.), India 54/H8
Cannanore (Laccadive) (isls.), India 68/C6
Cannelburg, Ind. 227/C7
Cannel City, Ky. 237/P5
Cannelles (riv.), St. Lucia 161/G7
Cannelles (riv.), St. Lucia 161/G6
Cannelton, Ind. 227/D9
Cannes, France 28/G6
Cannich, Scotland 15/D3
Canning (riv.), Alaska 196/J1
Canning, Nova Scotia 168/D3
Canning, S. Dak. 298/K5
Canning (riv.), W. Australia 88/B3
Canning (res.), W. Australia 88/B2
Canning, W. Australia 92/A1
Cannington, Ontario 177/E3
Cannington Manon Hist. Park, Sask. 181/J6
Cannock, England 10/G2
Cannock, England 13/E5
Cannon, Del. 245/R5
Cannon (mt.), N.H. 268/D3
Cannon (co.), Tenn. 237/J9
Cannon A.F.B., N. Mex. 274/F4
Cannon Ball, N. Dak. 282/G7
Cannon Beach, Oreg. 291/D2
Cannondale, Conn. 210/A3
Cannon Falls, Minn. 255/F6
Cannonsburg, Miss. 256/B7
Cannonsville (res.), N.Y. 276/K6
Cannonville, Utah 304/B6
Cann River, Victoria 97/E5
Caño, C. Rica 154/F4
Canoas, Brazil 132/D10
Canobie Lake, N.H. 268/E6
Caño Colorado (riv.), Venezuela 124/H3
Canoe, Ala. 195/D8
Canoe (lake), Sask. 181/L3
Canoe Lake, Sask. 181/L3
Canoe Reach (riv.), Br. Col. 184/H4
Canoe River, Br. Col. 184/H4
Canoga Park, Calif. 204/B10
Canoinhas, Brazil 132/D9
Caño Macareo (riv.), Venezuela 124/H3

Caño Mánamo (riv.), Venezuela 124/G3
Canon, Georgia 217/F2
Canonbie, Scotland 15/F5
Canonchet, R.I. 249/H7
Canon City, Colo. 208/J6
Canones, N. Mex. 274/C2
Canonsburg, Pa. 294/B5
Canoochee, Georgia 217/H5
Canoose Flowage (lake), New Bruns. 170/C3
Canora, Sask. 181/J4
Canosa di Puglia, Italy 34/E4
Canouan (isl.), St. Vin. & Grens. 156/G4
Canova, S. Dak. 298/O6
Canovanas (riv.), P. Rico 161/E1
Canowindra, N.S. Wales 97/E3
Canquela, Bolivia 136/A7
Canso, Nova Scotia 168/H3
Canso (cape), Nova Scotia 168/H3
Canso (str.), Nova Scotia 168/G3
Canta, Peru 128/D8
Cantabrian (range), Spain 33/C1
Cantagalo, Brazil 135/E3
Cantal (dept.), France 28/E5
Cantal, Sask. 181/K6
Cantalejo, Spain 33/D2
Cantanhede, Portugal 33/B2
Cantaura, Venezuela 124/F3
Canterbury•, Conn. 210/H2
Canterbury, Del. 245/R4
Canterbury, England 10/G5
Canterbury, England 13/H6
Canterbury, New Bruns. 170/C3
Canterbury•, N.H. 268/D5
Canterbury, N.S. Wales 88/K4
Canterbury, N.S. Wales 97/F4
Canterbury (bight), N. Zealand 100/D6
Can Tho, Vietnam 72/D5
Can Tho, Vietnam 54/M9
Cantil, Calif. 204/H8
Cantiles (cay), Cuba 158/C3
Cantillana, Alto de (mt.), Chile 138/G4
Cantley, Québec 172/B3
Canto del Agua, Chile 138/A7
Canto do Buriti, Brazil 132/F5
Canton (Guangzhou), China 77/H7
Canton (Guangzhou), China 54/N7
Canton, China 2/Q4
Canton, Conn. 210/D1
Canton•, Conn. 210/D1
Canton, Georgia 217/C2
Canton, Ill. 222/C3
Canton, Kansas 232/E3
Canton•, Maine 243/C7
Canton•, Mass. 249/C8
Canton, Minn. 255/F7
Canton, Miss. 256/D5
Canton, Mo. 261/J2
Canton, N.J. 273/C5
Canton, N.Y. 276/K1
Canton, N.C. 281/D3
Canton (Hensel), N. Dak. 282/M3
Canton, Ohio 188/K2
Canton, Ohio 284/H4
Canton, Okla. 288/J2
Canton (lake), Okla. 288/J2
Canton, Pa. 294/J2
Canton, S. Dak. 298/R7
Canton, Texas 303/J5
Canton, Wis. 317/C5
Canton-Bégin, Québec 172/F1
Canton Bend, Ala. 195/D6
Canton Center, Conn. 210/D1
Cantonment, Fla. 212/B6
Canton-Patapédia, Québec 172/B2
Cantoria, Spain 33/E4
Cantrall, Ill. 222/D4
Cantril, Iowa 229/J7
Cantù, Italy 34/B2
Cantuar, Sask. 181/C5
Cantwell, Alaska 196/J2
Canuck, Sask. 181/C6
Cañuelas, Argentina 143/G7
Canumã (riv.), Brazil 132/B4
Canutama, Brazil 132/G9
Canute, Okla. 288/H3
Canutillo, Texas 303/A10
Canvas, W. Va. 312/E6
Canvey Island, England 13/J8
Canwood, Sask. 181/E2
Canyon (lake), Ariz. 198/D5
Canyon, Br. Col. 184/J5
Canyon, Calif. 204/K2
Canyon (co.), Idaho 220/B6
Canyon (creek), Idaho 220/C6
Canyon, Minn. 255/F3
Canyon, Texas 303/C3
Canyon, Wyo. 319/B1
Canyon Blanco (creek), N. Mex. 274/B2
Canyon City, Oreg. 291/J3
Canyon Creek, Alberta 182/C2
Canyon Creek, Mont. 262/D4
Canyon de Chelly Nat'l Mon., Ariz. 198/F2
Canyon Ferry, Mont. 262/E4
Canyon Ferry (lake), Mont. 262/E4
Canyonlands Nat'l Park, Utah 304/D5
Canyonville, Oreg. 291/D5
Cao Bang, Vietnam 72/E2
Caol, Scotland 15/C4
Cao Lanh, Vietnam 72/E5
Caonao, Cuba 158/F2
Caonillas (lake), P. Rico 161/C2
Cap (isl.), Philippines 82/C8
Cap (pt.), St. Lucia 161/G5
Capa, S. Dak. 298/H5
Capac, Mich. 250/G5
Capachica, Peru 128/H10
Çapakçur, Turkey 59/H3
Çapakçur, Turkey 63/J3
Capa-à-l'Aigle, Québec 172/G2
Capalonga, Philippines 82/D3

Canaparo (riv.), Venezuela 124/E4
Capanema, Brazil 132/E3
Capannori, Italy 34/C3
Capão Bonito, Brazil 132/D9
Capão Bonito, Brazil 135/B4
Caparica, Portugal 33/A1
Caparo (riv.), Venezuela 124/C4
Capasin, Sask. 181/D2
Capatárida, Venezuela 124/C2
Capay, Calif. 204/C5
Cap-Bateau, New Bruns. 170/F1
Cap-Chat, Que. 162/K6
Cap-Chat, Québec 172/B1
Cap-Chat, Québec 174/D3
Cap-de-la-Madeleine, Québec 172/E3
Cap-des-Rosiers, Québec 172/D1
Cap d'Or (cape), Nova Scotia 168/D3
Cape (pt.), S. Africa 118/F7
Cape (prov.), S. Africa 102/B4
Cape (prov.), S. Africa 118/C6
Cape (isl.), S.C. 296/J5
Cape Barren (isl.), Tasmania 88/H8
Cape Barren (isl.), Tasmania 99/E2
Cape Breton (co.), Nova Scotia 168/H3
Cape Breton (isl.), N.S. 146/N5
Cape Breton (isl.), N.S. 162/M8
Cape Breton (isl.), Nova Scotia 168/J2
Cape Breton Highlands Nat'l Park, Nova Scotia 168/H2
Cape Broyle, Newf. 166/D2
Cape Canaveral, Fla. 212/F3
Cape Carteret, N.C. 281/P5
Cape Charles, Newf. 166/D2
Cape Charles, Va. 307/R6
Cape Coast, Ghana 106/D7
Cape Coast, Ghana 102/B4
Cape Cod (bay), Mass. 249/N5
Cape Cod (canal), Mass. 249/N5
Cape Cod Nat'l Seashore, Mass. 249/P5
Cape Coral, Fla. 212/E5
Cape Dorset, N.W.T. 162/J3
Cape Dorset, N.W. Terr. 187/L3
Cape Dyer, N.W. Terr. 187/M3
Cape Fanshaw, Alaska 196/N1
Cape Fear (riv.), N.C. 188/L4
Cape Fear (riv.), N.C. 281/M5
Cape George, Nova Scotia 168/F3
Cape Girardeau (co.), Mo. 261/N8
Cape Girardeau, Mo. 261/O8
Cape Girardeau, Mo. 188/H3
Cape Hatteras Nat'l Seashore, N.C. 281/T4
Cape Horn (mt.), Idaho 220/C5
Cape Krusenstern Nat'l Mon., Alaska 196/F1
Capel, W. Australia 92/A2
Capela, Brazil 132/G5
Cape Lisburne, Alaska 196/E1
Capella, Queensland 95/D4
Capella (isls.), Virgin Is. (U.S.) 161/B5
Capelle, Netherlands 27/F5
Capelongo, Angola 115/C7
Cape Lookout Nat'l Seashore, N.C. 281/S5
Cape May (co.), N.J. 273/D5
Cape May, N.J. 273/D6
Cape May (inlet), N.J. 273/D6
Cape May Coastguard Ctr., N.J. 273/D5
Cape May Court House, N.J. 273/D5
Cape May Point, N.J. 273/D6
Capenda-Camulemba, Angola 115/C5
Capenda-Camulemba, Angola 102/D5
Cape Neddick, Maine 243/B9
Cape Negro (riv.), Nova Scotia 168/C5
Cape North, Nova Scotia 168/H2
Cape Pole, Alaska 196/M2
Cape Porpoise, Maine 243/C9
Cape Ray, Newf. 166/C4
Capers (isl.), S.C. 296/H6
Cape Sable (isl.), Nova Scotia 168/C5
Cape Saint Claire, Md. 245/N4
Cape Smith, N.W. Terr. 187/L3
Capesterre, Basse-Terre, Guadeloupe 161/A7
Capesterre, Marie-Galante, Guadeloupe 161/B7
Cape Tormentine, New Bruns. 170/G2
Cape Town (cap.), S. Africa 2/L7
Cape Town (cap.), S. Africa 102/B8
Cape Town (cap.), S. Africa 118/C6
Cape Verde 2/H5
CAPE VERDE 106/A8
Capeville, Va. 307/R6
Cape Vincent, N.Y. 276/H2
Cape York (pen.), Australia 87/E7
Cape York, Queensland 95/B1
Cape York (pen.), Queensland 88/G2
Cape York (pen.), Queensland 95/B2
Cap-Haïtien, Haiti 158/D3
Cap-Haïtien, Haiti 156/D3
Capiatá, Paraguay 144/B4
Capibara, Venezuela 124/E6
Capilla de Farruco, Uruguay 145/D3
Capim (riv.), Brazil 132/D3
Capinota, Bolivia 136/D7
Capira, Panama 154/G6
Capirenda, Bolivia 136/D7
Capistrano Beach, Calif. 204/H10
Capitan, Mts.), N. Mex. 274/D5
Capitan (peak), N. Mex. 274/D5
Capitán Aracena (isl.), Chile 138/E10
Capitán Bado, Paraguay 144/E3
Capitan Grande Ind. Res., Calif. 204/J11
Capitán Meza, Paraguay 144/E5
Capitán Ustarés, Cerro (mt.), Bolivia 136/E6
Capitol, Mont. 262/M5
Capitola, Calif. 204/K3
Capitola, Fla. 212/B1
Capitol Heights, Md. 245/G5
Capitol Hill (cap.), No. Marianas 87/E4
Capitol Reef Nat'l Park, Utah 304/C5

Capiz (prov.), Philippines 82/D5
Caplan, Québec 172/G2
Capleville, Tenn. 237/B10
Caplin Cove, Newf. 166/D2
Caplinger Mills, Mo. 261/E7
Cap Lumière, New Bruns. 170/F2
Capon Bridge, W. Va. 312/K4
Capon Springs, W. Va. 312/K4
Capotoan (mt.), Philippines 82/E4
Cappahayden, Newf. 166/D2
Cappamore, Ireland 17/E6
Cappawhite, Ireland 17/E6
Cap-Pelé, New Bruns. 170/F2
Cappoquin, Ireland 17/F7
Capps, Ala. 195/H8
Capraia (isl.), Italy 34/B3
Capreol, Ontario 175/D3
Capreol, Ontario 177/K5
Capri, Italy 34/E4
Capricorn (chan.), Queensland 95/D4
Capricorn Group (isls.), Queensland 88/J4
Capricorn Group (isls.), Queensland 95/E4
Caprivi Strip (reg.), Namibia 102/E6
Caprivi Strip (reg.), Namibia 118/C3
Caprock, N. Mex. 274/F5
Capron, Ill. 222/E1
Capron, Okla. 288/J1
Capron, Va. 307/O7
Cap-Rouge, Québec 172/H3
Cap-Saint-Ignace, Québec 172/G2
Cap-Santé, Québec 172/F3
Cap-Seize, Québec 172/C1
Capshaw, Ala. 195/E1
Capstan (cape), Nova Scotia 168/D3
Capstick, Nova Scotia 168/H1
Captain Bermúdez, Argentina 143/F6
Captain Cook, Hawaii 218/G5
Captains Flat, N.S. Wales 97/E4
Captieux, France 28/C5
Captina (creek), Ohio 284/J6
Captiva, Fla. 212/D5
Captiva (isl.), Fla. 212/D5
Capua, Italy 34/E4
Capuchin (cape), Dominica 161/E5
Capulhuac de Mirafuentes, Mexico 150/K1
Capulin, Colo. 208/G8
Capulin, N. Mex. 274/F2
Capulin Volcano Nat'l Mon., N. Mex. 274/E2
Caputa, S. Dak. 298/D5
Caquetá (dept.), Colombia 126/C7
Caquetá (riv.), Colombia 120/B2
Caquetá (riv.), Colombia 126/E8
Caquiaviri, Bolivia 136/A5
Carabao (isl.), Philippines 82/D4
Carabelas, Argentina 143/F6
Carabobo (state), Venezuela 124/D2
Carabobo, Bolívar, Venezuela 124/H4
Carabobo, Carabobo, Venezuela 124/D3
Carabuco, Bolivia 136/A4
Caracal, Romania 45/G3
Caracaraí, Brazil 120/C2
Caracas (bay), Neth. Ant. 161/G9
Caracas (cap.), Venezuela 120/C2
Caracas (cap.), Venezuela 124/D2
Caracas (cap.), Venuzuela 2/F5
Carache, Venezuela 124/C3
Caracollo, Bolivia 136/B5
Caraga, Philippines 82/F7
Caragabal, N.S. Wales 97/D3
Caraguatá, Uruguay 145/D3
Caraguatá (riv.), Uruguay 145/D3
Caraguatatuba, Brazil 135/D3
Caraguatay, Paraguay 144/B4
Carahue, Chile 138/D2
Carajás, Serra dos (range), Brazil 132/D4
Caramat, Ontario 177/H5
Caramat, Ontario 175/C3
Caramoan, Philippines 82/D4
Caranavi, Bolivia 136/B4
Carandaí, Brazil 135/E2
Carandaiti, Bolivia 136/D7
Carandotta, Queensland 95/A4
Carangola, Brazil 135/E2
Caransebeş, Romania 45/F3
Carapa (riv.), Paraguay 144/E4
Carapa, Venezuela 124/G3
Caraparaná (riv.), Colombia 126/D8
Caraparí, Bolivia 136/D7
Carapeguá, Paraguay 144/B5
Carapichaima, Trin. & Tob. 161/B10
Caraquet, New Bruns. 170/F1
Caraquet (isl.), New Bruns. 170/F1
Carás, Peru 128/D7
Caratasca, Honduras 154/F3
Caratasca (cays), Honduras 154/F2
Caratasca (lag.), Honduras 154/F2
Caratinga, Brazil 132/F7
Caratinga, Brazil 135/E1
Caratunk, Maine 243/C5
Caratunk •, Maine 243/C5
Carauari, Brazil 120/C3
Carauari, Brazil 132/G9
Caraúbas, Brazil 132/G4
Caravaca de la Cruz, Spain 33/E3
Caravaggio, Italy 34/B2
Caravelas, Brazil 132/G7
Caravelí, Peru 128/F10
Caravelle (pen.), Martinique 161/D6
Caraway, Ark. 202/K2
Carayaó, Paraguay 144/C4
Carazinho, Brazil 132/C10
Carballino, Spain 33/B1
Carballo, Spain 33/B1
Carberry, Manitoba 179/C5
Carbo, Mexico 150/C2
Carbon, Alberta 182/D4
Carbon (peak), Colo. 208/E5
Carbon, Ind. 227/C5
Carbon (co.), Mont. 262/G5
Carbon (co.), Pa. 294/L4

Carbon, Texas 303/F5
Carbon (co.), Utah 304/D4
Carbon, W. Va. 312/D6
Carbon (co.), Wyo. 319/F4
Carbonado, Wash. 310/D3
Carbonara (cape), Italy 34/B5
Carbon Cliff, Ill. 222/C2
Carbondale, Alberta 182/B1
Carbondale, Colo. 208/E4
Carbondale, Ill. 222/D6
Carbondale, Kansas 232/G3
Carbondale, Ohio 284/F7
Carbondale, Pa. 294/L2
Carbonear, Newf. 166/D2
Carbon Hill, Ala. 195/D3
Carbon Hill, Ill. 222/E2
Carbon Hill, Ohio 284/F7
Carbonia, Italy 34/B5
Carbonton, N.C. 281/L3
Carbost, Scotland 15/B3
Carbury, Ireland 17/H5
Carbury, N. Dak. 282/J2
Carcagente, Spain 33/F3
Carcans (lake), France 28/C5
Carcaraña, Argentina 143/F6
Carcaraña (riv.), Argentina 143/F6
Carcassonne, France 28/D6
Carchi (prov.), Ecuador 128/C2
Carcoar, N.S. Wales 97/E3
Carcross, Yukon 187/B3
Çardak, Turkey 63/C6
Cardal, Uruguay 145/C5
Cardale, Manitoba 179/B4
Cárdenas, Cuba 158/D1
Cárdenas, Cuba 156/B2
Cárdenas (bay), Cuba 158/D1
Cárdenas, San Luis Potosí, Mexico 150/K6
Cárdenas, Tabasco, Mexico 150/N8
Cardenden, Scotland 15/D1
Cardiel (lake), Argentina 143/B6
Cardiff, Ala. 195/E3
Cardiff, Md. 245/N2
Cardiff, Wales 7/D3
Cardiff, Wales 13/B7
Cardiff, Wales 10/C6
Cardiff-by-the-Sea, Calif. 204/H10
Cardigan (mt.), N.H. 268/D4
Cardigan, Pr. Edward I. 168/F2
Cardigan (bay), Pr. Edward I. 168/F2
Cardigan, Wales 13/C5
Cardigan, Wales 10/D4
Cardigan (bay), Wales 10/D4
Cardigan (bay), Wales 13/C5
Cardin, Okla. 288/S1
Cardinal (lake), Alberta 182/B1
Cardinal, Manitoba 179/D5
Cardinal, Ontario 177/J3
Cardington, Ohio 284/E5
Cardona, Uruguay 145/B4
Cardoso (isl.), Brazil 135/C4
Cardozo, Uruguay 145/C3
Cardross, Sask. 181/F6
Cardston, Alberta 182/D5
Cardston, Alta. 262/E6
Cardville, Maine 243/F5
Cardwell, Mo. 261/M10
Cardwell, Mont. 262/E5
Cardwell, Queensland 95/C3
Cardwell, Va. 307/N5
Carefree, Ariz. 198/D5
Carefree, Ind. 227/E8
Carei, Romania 45/F2
Carén, Chile 138/A8
Carencro, La. 238/G6
Carentan, France 28/C3
Caretta, W. Va. 312/C8
Carey, Idaho 220/E6
Carey, Ohio 284/D4
Carey (lake), W. Australia 88/C5
Carey (lake), W. Australia 92/C5
Careywood, Idaho 220/B1
Cargill, Ontario 177/J3
Carhués, Peru 128/D7
Cariaco, Venezuela 124/G2
Cariamanga, Ecuador 128/C5
Caribbean (sea) 2/F5
Caribbean (sea) 146/K8
Caribbean (sea) 156/B4
Caribbean (sea, Ant. & Bar. 156/B4
Caribbean (sea, Cayman Is. 156/B4
Caribbean (sea, Cuba 156/B4
Caribbean (sea, Dominica 156/B4
Caribbean (sea, Dom. Rep. 156/B4
Caribbean (sea, Grenada 156/B4
Caribbean (sea, Guadeloupe 156/B4
Caribbean (sea, Haiti 156/B4
Caribbean (sea, Jamaica 156/B4
Caribbean (sea, Martinique 156/B4
Caribbean (sea, Neth. Ant. 156/B4
Caribbean (sea, P. Rico 156/B4
Caribbean (sea, St. Kitts & Nevis 156/B4
Caribbean (sea, St. Lucia 156/B4
Caribbean (sea, St. Vin. & Grens. 156/B4
Caribbean (sea, Virgin Is. (U.S.) 156/B4
Caribbean (sea, Virgin Is. (U.K.) 156/B4
Caribén, Venezuela 124/E4
Cariboo (mts.) Br. Col. 184/G3
Caribou (mts.) Alberta 182/B5
Caribou (co.), Idaho 220/G7
Caribou (mt.), Idaho 220/G6
Caribou (range), Idaho 220/G6
Caribou, Maine 188/N1
Caribou, Maine 243/G2
Caribou (riv.), Manitoba 179/J1
Caribou, Nova Scotia 168/F3
Caribou (isl.), Nova Scotia 168/F3
Caribou (isl.), Ontario 177/H4
Caribou (lake), Ontario 177/H4
Caribou (lake), Québec 172/D3
Caribou River, Nova Scotia 168/F3
Carib Reserve, Dominica 161/F6
Caribrod (Dimitrovgrad), Yugoslavia 45/F4
Carichic, Mexico 150/F2
Carievale, Sask. 181/K6

Carigara, Philippines 82/E5
Carignan, France 28/F3
Carignan (lake), Québec 172/E2
Carillon, Québec 172/C4
Carina, Queensland 88/K3
Carinda, N.S. Wales 97/D2
Cariñena, Spain 33/F2
Carinhanha, Brazil 132/E6
Carini, Italy 34/D5
Carinthia (prov.), Austria 41/B3
Caripe, Venezuela 124/G2
Caripito, Venezuela 124/G2
Cariquima, Chile 138/B2
Carirubana, Venezuela 124/C2
Carite (lake), P. Rico 161/E2
Cark (mt.), Ireland 17/F2
Carl, Georgia 217/E3
Carl Blackwell (lake), Okla. 288/M2
Carlea, Sask. 181/H2
Carleton, Mich. 250/F6
Carleton, Nebr. 264/G4
Carleton (co.), New Bruns. 170/C2
Carleton (mt.), New Bruns. 170/D1
Carleton, Nova Scotia 168/C4
Carleton (riv.), Nova Scotia 168/C4
Carleton, Québec 172/C2
Carleton Place, Ontario 177/H2
Carlile, Wyo. 319/H1
Carlin, Nev. 266/E2
Carlingford, Ireland 17/J3
Carlingford (inlet), Ireland 17/J3
Carlingford (mt.), Ireland 17/J3
Carlingford, New Bruns. 170/C2
Carlinville, Ill. 222/D4
Carlisle, Ark. 202/G4
Carlisle (bay), Barbados 161/B9
Carlisle (bay), Barbados 161/B9
Carlisle, England 13/D3
Carlisle, England 10/E3
Carlisle, Ind. 227/C5
Carlisle, Iowa 229/H4
Carlisle (co.), Ky. 237/C7
Carlisle, Ky. 237/N4
Carlisle, La. 238/L7
Carlisle •, Mass. 249/J2
Carlisle, Minn. 255/B7
Carlisle, Miss. 256/C7
Carlisle, New Bruns. 170/C2
Carlisle, N.Y. 276/L5
Carlisle, Ohio 284/B6
Carlisle, Ontario 177/J3
Carlisle, Pa. 294/H5
Carlisle, S.C. 296/D2
Carl Junction, Mo. 261/C8
Carlock, Ill. 222/D3
Carlock, S. Dak. 298/L7
Carloforte, Italy 34/B5
Carlos, Ind. 227/E4
Carlos, Minn. 255/C5
Carlos Casares, Argentina 143/F7
Carlos Reyles, Uruguay 145/C4
Carlos Tejedor, Argentina 143/D4
Carlow (co.), Ireland 17/H6
Carlow, Ireland 17/H6
Carlow, Ireland 10/C4
Carloway, Scotland 15/B2
Carlowrie, Manitoba 179/E5
Carlowville, Ala. 195/D5
Carl Sandburg Home Nat'l Hist. Site, N.C. 281/D4
Carlsbad, Ca. 204/H10
Carlsbad, N. Mex. 188/F4
Carlsbad, N. Mexico 146/H6
Carlsbad, N. Mex. 274/E6
Carlsbad, Texas 303/D6
Carlsbad Caverns Nat'l Park, N. Mex. 274/E6
Carlsbad Springs, Ontario 177/J2
Carlsborg, Wash. 310/B2
Carlshend, Mich. 250/D2
Carlstadt, N.J. 273/B2
Carlton, Ala. 195/C6
Carlton, Barbados 161/B8
Carlton, England 13/F5
Carlton, Georgia 217/F2
Carlton, Kansas 232/E3
Carlton (co.), Minn. 255/F4
Carlton, Minn. 255/F4
Carlton, N.Y. 276/D4
Carlton, Oreg. 291/D2
Carlton, Pa. 294/C3
Carlton, Sask. 181/E3
Carlton, Texas 303/F6
Carlton, Wash. 310/F2
Carlton (pass), Wash. 310/D4
Carltonville, S. Africa 118/G7
Carluke, Scotland 15/D2
Carluke, Scotland 10/B1
Carlyle, Ill. 222/D5
Carlyle (lake), Ill. 222/D5
Carlyle, Kansas 232/G4
Carlyle, Mont. 262/M4
Carlyle, Sask. 181/J6
Carlyle Lake Resort, Sask. 181/J6
Carmacks, Yukon 187/E3
Carmagnola, Italy 34/A2
Carman, Ill. 222/B3
Carman, Man. 162/G6
Carman, Manitoba 179/D5
Carmangay, Alberta 182/D4
Carmanville, Newf. 166/D4
Carmarthen, Wales 13/C6
Carmarthen, Wales 10/D5
Carmarthen (bay), Wales 10/D5
Carmarthen (bay), Wales 13/C6
Carmaux, France 28/E5
Carmel, Calif. 204/D7
Carmel (cape), Israel 65/B2
Carmel (mt.), Israel 65/C2
Carmel •, Maine 243/F6
Carmel •, N.Y. 276/N8
Carmel, Sask. 181/F3
Carpio, N. Dak. 282/G3
Carmelo, Uruguay 145/A4
Carmelo, Venezuela 124/C2
Carmel Valley, Calif. 204/D7
Carmen, Ariz. 198/D7
Carmen, Bolivia 136/B2

Carmen (riv.), Chile 138/B7
Carmen, C. Rica 154/F5
Carmen, Idaho 220/E4
Carmen (isl.), Mexico 150/D3
Carmen, Okla. 288/J1
Carmen, Bohol, Philippines 82/E6
Carmen, North Cotabato, Philippines 82/E7
Carmen, Uruguay 145/A2
Carmen de Areco, Argentina 143/F7
Carmen del Paraná, Paraguay 144/D5
Carmen de Patagones, Argentina 143/D5
Carmensa, Argentina 143/C4
Carmi, Br. Col. 184/H5
Carmí, Ill. 222/E5
Carmi (lake), Vt. 268/B2
Carmichael, Calif. 204/C8
Carmichael, Miss. 256/G7
Carmichael, Sask. 181/C5
Carmichaels, Pa. 294/B6
Carmine, Texas 303/H4
Carmody Hills-Pepper Mill Village, Md. 245/G5
Carmona, Spain 33/D4
Carnac, France 28/B4
Carnadero (creek), Calif. 204/L4
Carnamah, W. Australia 87/B8
Carnamah, W. Australia 92/A5
Carnarvon, Iowa 229/C4
Carnarvon, W. Australia 88/A4
Carnarvon, W. Australia 92/A4
Carnarvon (range), Queensland 95/D5
Carnarvon, S. Africa 118/C6
Carnaxide, Portugal 33/A1
Carn Ban (mt.), Scotland 15/D3
Carndonagh, Ireland 17/G1
Carnduff, Sask. 181/K6
Carnegie, Georgia 217/C7
Carnegie, Okla. 288/J4
Carnegie, Pa. 294/B7
Carnegie (lake), W. Australia 88/C5
Carnegie (lake), W. Australia 92/C4
Carn Eige (mt.), Scotland 15/C3
Carneiro, Kansas 232/E3
Carnes, Miss. 256/F7
Carnesville, Georgia 217/F2
Carnew, Ireland 17/H6
Carney, Mich. 250/B3
Carney, Okla. 288/N3
Carneys Point, N.J. 273/C4
Carnic Alps (mts.), Austria 41/B3
Carnic Alps (range), Italy 34/D1
Car Nicobar (isl.), India 68/G2
Carnlough, N. Ireland 17/K2
Carn More (mt.), Scotland 15/E3
Carnot, Cent. Afr. Rep. 115/C3
Carnoustie, Scotland 15/F4
Carnoustie, Scotland 10/E2
Carnsore (pt.), Ireland 10/C4
Carnsore (pt.), Ireland 17/J7
Carnwath, Scotland 15/D2
Carnwood, Alberta 182/C3
Caro, Mich. 250/F5
Caroga Lake, N.Y. 276/L4
Carol City, Fla. 212/B4
Carolina, Ala. 195/D6
Carolina, Brazil 132/E4
Carolina, P. Rico 161/E1
Carolina, R.I. 249/H7
Carolina Beach, N.C. 281/O6
Caroline, Alberta 182/C3
Caroline (isl.), Kiribati 87/M7
Caroline (co.), Md. 245/P5
Caroline, N.Y. 276/H6
Caroline (isls.), Fed. States of Micronesia 87/E5
Caroline (isls.), Fed. States of Micronesia 2/S5
Caroline (co.), Va. 307/O4
Caroline, Wis. 317/J6
Carol Stream, Ill. 222/A5
Caron, Sask. 181/F5
Caron Brook, New Bruns. 170/B1
Carondelet, Ecuador 128/C2
Caroni (riv.), Venezuela 120/C2
Caroní (riv.), Venezuela 124/G4
Caroni, Trin. & Tob. 161/B10
Carora, Venezuela 124/C2
Carouge, Switzerland 39/A2
Carp, Ind. 227/D6
Carp, Minn. 255/D2
Carp, Nev. 266/G5
Carp, Ontario 177/H2
Carpathian (mts.) 7/G4
Carpathian (mts.), Romania 45/G2
Carpentaria (gulf) 88/D7
Carpentaria (gulf), Australia 87/D7
Carpentaria (gulf), North. Terr. 93/E3
Carpentaria (gulf), Queensland 95/A2
Carpenter (lake), Br. Col. 184/F3
Carpenter, Iowa 229/H2
Carpenter, Ky. 237/O7
Carpenter, Miss. 256/C6
Carpenter (lake), N. Dak. 282/L2
Carpenter, Ohio 284/F7
Carpenter, S. Dak. 298/O4
Carpenter, Wyo. 319/H4
Carpentersville, Ill. 222/E1
Carpentersville, N.J. 273/C2
Carpenterville, Oreg. 291/C5
Carpentras, France 28/F5
Carpertee (riv.), N.S. Wales 97/F3
Carpi, Italy 34/C2
Carpinteria, Calif. 204/F9
Carp Lake, Mich. 250/E3
Carp Lake Prov. Park, Br. Col. 184/F3
Carr, Colo. 208/K1
Carra (lake), Ireland 17/C4
Carrabassett Valley •, Maine 243/C5
Carrabelle, Fla. 212/B2

Carradale, Scotland 15/C5
Carraguana, Sask. 181/J3
Carraguao (pt.), Cuba 158/B2
Carraipía, Colombia 126/D1
Carraízo (lake), P. Rico 161/E1
Carranglan, Philippines 82/C3
Carrantuohill (mt.), Ireland 10/B5
Carrantuohill (mt.), Ireland 17/B7
Carranza, Venustiano (res.), Mexico 150/J3
Carrao (riv.), Venezuela 124/G5
Carrasco, Uruguay 145/B7
Carrasquero, Venezuela 124/B2
Carrathool, N. S. Wales 88/G6
Carrathool, N.S. Wales 97/C4
Carrbridge, Scotland 15/E3
Carrera de Yeguas, Dom. Rep. 158/D3
Carrera Pinto, Chile 138/B6
Carreta (pt.), C. Rica 154/F6
Carreto, Panama 154/J6
Carriacou (isl.), Grenada 156/G4
Carrick, Manitoba 179/F5
Carrick (dist.), Scotland 15/D5
Carrickfergus (dist.), N. Ireland 17/K2
Carrickfergus, N. Ireland 10/D3
Carrickfergus, N. Ireland 17/K2
Carrickmacross, Ireland 10/C3
Carrickmacross, Ireland 17/H4
Carrick-on-Shannon, Ireland 17/F4
Carrick-on-Shannon, Ireland 10/C3
Carrick-on-Suir, Ireland 17/F7
Carrick-on-Suir, Ireland 10/C3
Carrier, Okla. 288/K2
Carriere, Miss. 256/E9
Carrier Mills, Ill. 222/E6
Carrigaholt, Ireland 17/B6
Carrigaline (mt.), N.H. 268/E3
Carrigaline, Ireland 17/E8
Carrigallen, Ireland 17/F4
Carrigan (head), Ireland 17/D2
Carrigart, Ireland 17/F1
Carrigtwohill, Ireland 17/E8
Carrington, Mo. 261/H5
Carrington, N. Dak. 282/M5
Carrión de los Condes, Spain 33/D1
Carrizal, Colombia 126/D1
Carrizal Bajo, Chile 138/A7
Carrizo (creek), Ariz. 198/E4
Carrizo (mts.), Ariz. 198/G2
Carrizo (creek), N. Mex. 274/F2
Carrizo (creek), Texas 303/A1
Carrizo Springs, Texas 303/E9
Carrizozo, N. Mex. 274/D5
Carroll (co.), Ark. 202/C1
Carroll (co.), Georgia 217/B3
Carroll (co.), Ill. 222/D1
Carroll (co.), Ind. 227/D3
Carroll (co.), Iowa 229/D4
Carroll, Iowa 229/D4
Carroll (co.), Ky. 237/L3
Carroll •, Maine 243/G5
Carroll, Manitoba 179/B5
Carroll (lake), Manitoba 179/G3
Carroll (co.), Md. 245/K2
Carroll (co.), Miss. 256/E4
Carroll (co.), Mo. 261/F4
Carroll, Nebr. 264/G2
Carroll (co.), N.H. 268/E4
Carroll •, N.H. 268/D3
Carroll (co.), Ohio 284/H4
Carroll, Ohio 284/F5
Carroll (co.), Tenn. 237/E9
Carroll (co.), Va. 307/G7
Carrolls, Wash. 310/C4
Carrolls Crossing, New Bruns. 170/D2
Carrollton, Ala. 195/B4
Carrollton, Georgia 217/C3
Carrollton, Ill. 222/C4
Carrollton, Iowa 229/D5
Carrollton, Ky. 237/L3
Carrollton, Mich. 250/E5
Carrollton, Miss. 256/E4
Carrollton, Mo. 261/E4
Carrollton, Ohio 284/J4
Carrollton, Texas 303/G2
Carrolltown, Pa. 294/E4
Carroll Valley, Pa. 294/H6
Carron (riv.), Scotland 15/C3
Carron, Scotland 15/C1
Carron (riv.), Scotland 15/C3
Carron (riv.), Scotland 15/C3
Carron Valley (res.), Scotland 15/B1
Carrot (riv.), Sask. 181/J2
Carrot Creek, Alberta 182/B3
Carrot River, Sask. 181/J3
Carrowdore, N. Ireland 17/K2
Carrowkeel, Ireland 17/G1
Carrowmore (lake), Ireland 17/B3
Carrsville, Ky. 237/E6
Carrsville, Va. 307/P7
Carruthers, Sask. 181/B3
Carryduff, N. Ireland 17/K2
Carryville, Ark. 202/K1
Çarşamba, Turkey 63/G2
Carseland, Alberta 182/D4
Carson, Ala. 195/C8
Carson, Iowa 229/C5
Carson, Miss. 256/E7
Carson (lake), Nev. 266/C3
Carson (riv.), Nev. 266/B3
Carson (sink), Nev. 266/C3
Carson, N. Mex. 274/D2
Carson, N. Dak. 282/H7
Carson (co.), Texas 303/C3
Carson, Va. 307/O6
Carson, Wash. 310/D5
Carson City, Mich. 250/E5
Carson City (co.), Nev. 266/B3
Carson City (cap.), Nev. 266/B3
Carson City (cap.), Nev. 146/G6
Carson City (cap.), Nev. 188/C3
Carson City (cap.), Nev. 266/B3
Carson Lake, Ark. 202/K2

Carson Sink (depr.), Nev. 188/C3
Carsonville, Georgia 217/D5
Carsonville, Mich. 250/F5
Carsphairn, Scotland 15/D5
Carstairs, Alberta 182/D3
Carswell A.F.B., Texas 303/E2
Cartagena, Chile 138/A7
Cartagena, Colombia 120/B1
Cartagena, Colombia 126/C2
Cartagena, Cuba 158/C3
Cartagena, Spain 7/D5
Cartagena, Spain 33/F4
Cartago, Colombia 126/B5
Cartago, C. Rica 154/F6
Carta Valley, Texas 303/D8
Cartaxo, Portugal 33/B3
Cartecay, Georgia 217/D1
Carter (co.), Ky. 237/P4
Carter, Ky. 237/P4
Carter (co.), Mo. 261/L9
Carter (co.), Mont. 262/M5
Carter, Mont. 262/E3
Carter (co.), Okla. 288/M6
Carter, Okla. 288/H4
Carter, S. Dak. 298/J7
Carter (co.), Tenn. 237/S8
Carter, Tenn. 237/S8
Carter, Wis. 317/J5
Carter, Wyo. 319/B4
Carter Dome (mt.), N.H. 268/E3
Carteret, N.J. 273/E2
Carteret (co.), N.C. 281/R5
Carter Lake, Iowa 229/B6
Carter Nine, Okla. 288/N1
Carters, Georgia 217/C1
Carters (lake), Georgia 217/C1
Cartersburg, Ind. 227/E5
Cartersville, Georgia 217/C2
Cartersville, Iowa 229/G2
Cartersville, Mont. 262/K4
Cartersville, Okla. 288/S4
Cartersville, S.C. 296/H3
Cartersville, Va. 307/M5
Carterton, N. Zealand 100/E4
Carterton and Black Bourton, England 13/F6
Carterville, Ill. 222/D6
Carterville, Mo. 261/D8
Carthage, Ark. 202/E4
Carthage, Ill. 222/B3
Carthage, Ind. 227/F5
Carthage, Maine 243/C6
Carthage •, Maine 243/C6
Carthage, Miss. 256/E5
Carthage, Mo. 261/D8
Carthage, N.Y. 276/J3
Carthage, N.C. 281/L3
Carthage, S. Dak. 298/O5
Carthage, Tenn. 237/K8
Carthage, Texas 303/K5
Cartier, Ontario 177/J5
Cartier (isl.), Terr. Ashmore and Cartier Is. 88/C2
Cartwright, Manitoba 179/C5
Cartwright, Newf. 146/N4
Cartwright, Newf. 166/C3
Cartwright, Newf. 162/L5
Cartwright, N. Dak. 282/C4
Caruai (riv.), Venezuela 124/H5
Caruaru, Brazil 132/G5
Carumás, Peru 128/G11
Carúpano, Venezuela 120/C1
Carúpano, Venezuela 124/G2
Carurú, Colombia 126/E7
Carutapera, Brazil 132/E3
Caruth, Mo. 261/N10
Caruthers, Calif. 204/E7
Caruthersville, Mo. 261/N10
Carver •, Mass. 249/M5
Carver (co.), Minn. 255/E6
Carver, Minn. 255/E6
Carville, La. 238/K3
Carvoeiro (cape), Portugal 33/B3
Cary, Ill. 222/H4
Cary •, Maine 243/H4
Cary, Miss. 256/C5
Cary, N.C. 281/M3
Caryapundy (swamp), N.S. Wales 97/B1
Caryapundy (swamp), Queensland 95/D6
Carysbrook, Va. 307/M5
Carytown, Mo. 261/D8
Caryville, Fla. 212/C6
Caryville, Mass. 249/J4
Caryville, Tenn. 237/N8
Casa, Ark. 202/D3
Casa Agapito, Colombia 126/D6
Casablanca, Chile 138/F3
Casablanca, Estero de (riv.), Chile 138/F3
Casablanca, Morocco 102/B1
Casablanca, Morocco 106/C2
Casablanca, Morocco 2/J4
Casa Blanca, N. Mex. 274/B4
Casale Monferrato, Italy 34/B2
Casalmaggiore, Italy 34/C2
Casa Branca, Brazil 135/C2
Casa Cruz (cape), Trin. & Tob. 161/B11
Casa Grande, Ariz. 188/D4
Casa Grande, Ariz. 198/D6
Casa Grande Nat'l Mon., Ariz. 198/D6
Casamance (riv.), Senegal 106/A6
Casanare (inten.), Colombia 126/B3
Casanare (riv.), Colombia 126/E4
Casanay, Venezuela 124/G2
Casa Nova, Brazil 132/F5
Casanova, Va. 307/N3
Casa Piedra, Texas 303/C12
Casar, N.C. 281/F3
Casar de Cáceres, Spain 33/C3
Casas Grandes (riv.), Mexico 150/F1
Casas-Ibáñez, Spain 33/F3
Cascade (range) 188/B1
Cascade (range), Calif. 204/D1
Cascade, Colo. 208/K5

Cascade, Idaho 220/C5
Cascade (res.), Idaho 220/C5
Cascade, Iowa 229/L4
Cascade, Jamaica 158/G6
Cascade, N.S. Wales 97/E3
Cascade (co.), Mont. 262/E3
Cascade, Mont. 262/E3
Cascade, N.H. 268/E3
Cascade (pt.), N. Zealand 100/B6
Cascade, Norfolk I. 88/L5
Cascade (bay), Norfolk I. 88/L5
Cascade (head), Oreg. 291/E2
Cascade (range), Oreg. 291/E4
Cascade, Seychelles 118/H5
Cascade (range), U.S. 146/F5
Cascade, Va. 307/J7
Cascade (pass), Wash. 310/D2
Cascade (range), Wash. 310/D4
Cascade (riv.), Wash. 310/D2
Cascade, W. Va. 312/G3
Cascade, Wis. 317/K8
Cascade Locks, Oreg. 291/E2
Cascade Summit, Oreg. 291/F4
Cascadia, Oreg. 291/E3
Cascais, Portugal 33/B3
Cascajal, Cuba 158/E1
Cascapédia (riv.), Québec 172/C1
Cascas, Peru 128/C6
Cascavel, Brazil 120/G4
Cascilla, Miss. 256/D3
Cascina-Navacchio, Italy 34/C3
Casco, Maine 243/B7
Casco •, Maine 243/B7
Casco (bay), Maine 243/C8
Casco, Wis. 317/L6
Cascorro, Cuba 158/H3
Cascumpeque (bay), Pr. Edward I. 168/F2
Caselton, Nev. 266/G5
Case-Pilote, Martinique 161/C6
Caserta (prov.), Italy 34/E4
Caserta, Italy 34/E4
Caseville, Mich. 250/F5
Casey (key), Fla. 212/D4
Casey, Ill. 222/F4
Casey, Iowa 229/D5
Casey (co.), Ky. 237/M6
Casey, Québec 174/C3
Casey Creek, Ky. 237/L6
Caseyville, Ill. 222/B2
Caseyville, Ky. 237/E5
Cash, Ark. 202/J2
Cashel, Ireland 17/F7
Cashel, Ireland 10/C4
Cashiers, N.C. 281/C4
Cashion, Ariz. 198/C5
Cashion, Okla. 288/L3
Cashmere, Wash. 310/D3
Cashmere, W. Va. 312/E8
Cashton, Wis. 317/E8
Cashtown, Pa. 294/H6
Cashville, S.C. 296/C2
Casigua, Falcón, Venezuela 124/C2
Casigua, Zulia, Venezuela 124/B3
Casiguran, Philippines 82/C2
Casiguran (sound), Philippines 82/C2
Casilda, Argentina 143/F6
Casilda, Cuba 158/E2
Casilda (pt.), Cuba 158/E2
Casino, N.S. Wales 88/J5
Casino, N.S. Wales 97/G1
Casiquiare, Brazo (riv.), Venezuela 124/E6
Casitas Springs, Calif. 204/F9
Caslan, Alberta 182/D2
Cáslav, Czech. 41/C2
Casma, Peru 128/C7
Casma (riv.), Peru 128/C7
Casmalia, Calif. 204/E9
Casnovia, Mich. 250/D5
Caspar, Calif. 204/B4
Caspe, Spain 33/G2
Casper, Wyo. 188/E2
Casper, Wyo. 146/H5
Casper, Wyo. 319/F3
Casper (range), Wyo. 319/F3
Caspian (sea) 54/G5
Caspian (sea), Iran 66/G1
Caspian (sea), Mich. 250/B2
Caspian (sea), U.S.S.R. 7/J4
Caspian (sea), U.S.S.R. 52/G5
Caspian (sea), U.S.S.R. 48/F6
Caspian (lake), Vt. 268/C2
Caspiana, La. 238/C2
Cass, Ark. 202/C2
Cass (co.), Ill. 222/C4
Cass (co.), Ind. 227/E3
Cass, Ind. 227/C6
Cass (co.), Iowa 229/D6
Cass (co.), Mich. 250/C7
Cass (riv.), Mich. 250/F5
Cass (co.), Minn. 255/D4
Cass (lake), Minn. 255/D3
Cass (co.), Mo. 261/D5
Cass (co.), Nebr. 264/H4
Cass (co.), N. Dak. 282/R5
Cass (co.), Texas 303/K4
Cass, W. Va. 312/G6
Cassadaga, Fla. 212/E3
Cassadaga, N.Y. 276/B6
Cassá de la Selva, Spain 33/H2
Cassai, Angola 115/D6
Cassamba, Angola 115/D6
Cassandra, Georgia 217/B1
Cassandra, Pa. 294/E5
Cassano allo Ionio, Italy 34/F5
Cassatt, S.C. 296/E3
Cass City, Mich. 250/F5
Casscoe, Ark. 202/H4
Casselberry, Fla. 212/E3
Casselman (riv.), Md. 245/B2
Casselman, Ontario 177/J2
Casselman, Pa. 294/D6
Casselman (riv.), Pa. 294/D6
Casselton, N. Dak. 282/R6
Cássia, Brazil 135/C2
Cassia (co.), Idaho 220/E7
Cassiar, Br. Col. 184/K2

Cassiar (mts.), Br. Col. 184/K2
Cassiar (mts.), Yukon 187/E3
Cassidy, Br. Col. 184/J3
Cassilis, N.S. Wales 97/E3
Cassils, Alberta 182/D4
Cassinga, Angola 114/C7
Cassino, Italy 34/D4
Cassiporé (cape), Brazil 132/D2
Cassity, W. Va. 312/F5
Cass Lake, Minn. 255/D3
Cassoday, Kansas 232/F3
Cassopolis, Mich. 250/C7
Casstown, Ohio 284/B5
Cassville, Georgia 217/C2
Cassville, Ind. 227/E3
Cassville, Mo. 261/E9
Cassville, Pa. 294/G5
Cassville, W. Va. 312/F3
Cassville, Wis. 317/E10
Castagnola, Switzerland 39/G4
Castaic, Calif. 204/G9
Castalia, Iowa 229/K2
Castalia, New Bruns. 170/D4
Castalia, N.C. 281/O2
Castalia, Ohio 284/D3
Castalian Springs, Tenn. 237/J8
Castana, Iowa 229/B4
Castanhal, Brazil 120/E3
Castanhal, Brazil 132/E3
Castaños, Mexico 150/J3
Castelfranco Veneto, Italy 34/D2
Castel Gandolfo, Italy 34/F7
Casteljaloux, France 28/D5
Castella, Calif. 204/C2
Castellammare (gulf), Italy 34/D5
Castellammare del Golfo, Italy 34/D5
Castellammare di Stabia, Italy 34/E4
Castellane, France 28/G6
Castellanos, Uruguay 145/B6
Castelli, Buenos Aires, Argentina 143/H7
Castelli, Chaco, Argentina 143/D2
Castellón (prov.), Spain 33/G2
Castellón de la Plana, Spain 33/G2
Castellote, Spain 33/F2
Castelnaudary, France 28/E6
Castelo, Brazil 132/F8
Castelo Branco (dist.), Portugal 33/C3
Castelo Branco, Portugal 33/C3
Castelo de Vide, Portugal 33/C3
Castelo do Piauí, Brazil 132/F4
Castel San Pietro Terme, Italy 34/C2
Castelsarrasin, France 28/D6
Castelvetrano, Italy 34/D6
Casterton, Victoria 97/A5
Castiglione del Lago, Italy 34/C3
Castiglion Fiorentino, Italy 34/C3
Castile, N.Y. 276/D5
Castilla, Cerro (mt.), Chile 138/E6
Castillo, Dom. Rep. 158/E5
Castillo de San Marcos Nat'l Mon., Fla. 212/E2
Castillos, Uruguay 145/F5
Castillos (lag.), Uruguay 145/F5
Castine •, Maine 243/F7
Castine, Ohio 284/A6
Castle (harb.), Bermuda 156/H2
Castle (mt.), Br. Col. 184/A2
Castle (peak), Colo. 208/F5
Castle (creek), Idaho 220/B7
Castle (peak), Idaho 220/D5
Castle (pt.), N. Zealand 100/F4
Castle, Okla. 288/K4
Castle (valley), Utah 304/D4
Castle A.F.B., Calif. 204/E6
Castlebar, Ireland 17/C4
Castlebar, Ireland 10/B4
Castlebay, Scotland 15/A4
Castlebellingham, Ireland 17/J4
Castleberry, Ala. 195/D8
Castleblayney, Ireland 10/C3
Castleblayney, Ireland 17/H3
Castlebridge, Ireland 17/J7
Castle Bruce, Dominica 161/F6
Castlecomer-Donaguile, Ireland 17/G6
Castlecomer-Donaguile, Ireland 10/C4
Castle Dale, Utah 304/D4
Castle Danger, Minn. 255/N3
Castledawson, N. Ireland 17/H2
Castlederg, N. Ireland 17/F2
Castledermot, Ireland 17/H6
Castle Dome (mts.), Ariz. 198/A5
Castle Douglas, Scotland 15/E6
Castle Douglas, Scotland 10/D3
Castlefin, Ireland 17/F2
Castleford, Idaho 220/C7
Castlegar, Br. Col. 184/J3
Castlegregory, Ireland 17/B6
Castlegregory, Ireland 17/A7
Castle Hayne, N.C. 281/O6
Castle Hills, Texas 303/J10
Castle Hot Springs, Ariz. 198/C5
Castleisland, Ireland 17/B7
Castle Kennedy, Scotland 15/D6
Castlemaine, Victoria 97/C5
Castlemartyr, Ireland 17/E8
Castle Park, Mich. 250/C6
Castlepollard, Ireland 17/G4
Castlerea, Ireland 17/D4
Castlerea, Ireland 10/B4
Castlereagh (riv.), N.S. Wales 97/E2
Castlereagh (dist.), N. Ireland 17/K2
Castle Rock, Colo. 208/K4
Castle Rock, Minn. 255/E6
Castle Rock, S. Dak. 298/C4
Castle Rock, Utah 304/C2
Castle Rock, Wash. 310/B4
Castle Rock (lake), Wis. 317/G8
Castle Shannon, Pa. 294/B7
Castleton, Ill. 222/D2
Castleton, Jamaica 158/J6
Castleton, Md. 245/N2
Castleton, Ontario 177/F3
Castleton •, Vt. 268/A4
Castleton-on-Hudson, N.Y. 276/N5
Castletown, Ireland 17/H5
Castletown, I. of Man 13/C3
Castletown, Scotland 15/E2

Castletownbere, Ireland 17/B8
Castletownroche, Ireland 17/D7
Castletownshend, Ireland 17/C9
Castlewellan, N. Ireland 17/K3
Castlewood, S. Dak. 298/R4
Castlewood, Va. 307/D7
Castolon, Texas 303/D12
Castor, Alberta 182/D3
Castor, La. 238/D2
Castorland, N.Y. 276/J3
Castres, France 28/E6
Castries (cap.), St. Lucia 156/G4
Castries (cap.), St. Lucia 161/G6
Castro, Brazil 135/B4
Castro, Brazil 132/D9
Castro, Chile 138/D4
Castro (co.), Texas 303/B3
Castro Alves, Brazil 132/G6
Castro Daire, Portugal 33/C2
Castro del Río, Spain 33/D4
Castrojeriz, Spain 33/E1
Castro Marim, Portugal 33/C4
Castropol, Spain 33/C1
Castrop-Rauxel, Germany 22/B3
Castroreale, Italy 34/E5
Castro-Urdiales, Spain 33/E1
Castro Valley, Calif. 204/K2
Castro Verde, Portugal 33/B4
Castrovillari, Italy 34/F5
Castroville, Calif. 204/D7
Castroville, Texas 303/J11
Castrovirreyna, Peru 128/E9
Castuera, Spain 33/D3
Casualito, Colombia 126/G5
Casupá, Uruguay 145/D5
Caswell, Alaska 196/J1
Caswell (co.), N.C. 281/L2
Caswell Beach, N.C. 281/N7
Cat (isl.), Bahamas 146/L7
Cat (isl.), Bahamas 156/C1
Cat (isl.), Miss. 256/F10
Çat, Turkey 63/J3
Cat (isl.), Wis. 317/E1
Catacamas, Honduras 154/E3
Catacaos, Peru 128/B5
Catacocha, Ecuador 128/C5
Catadupa, Jamaica 158/H6
Cataguases, Brazil 135/E2
Catahoula (par.), La. 238/G3
Catahoula (lake), La. 238/F4
Cataingan, Philippines 82/E5
Çatak, Turkey 63/K4
Çatalão, Brazil 132/D7
Çatalca, Turkey 63/C2
Cataldo, Idaho 220/B2
Catalina, Chile 138/B5
Catalina (pt.), Chile 138/F10
Catalina (isl.), Dom. Rep. 158/F6
Catalina, Newf. 166/L3
Catalone, Nova Scotia 168/H3
Catalonia (reg.), Spain 33/G2
Catalpa (creek), Miss. 256/G4
Catalzeytin, Turkey 63/F1
Catamarca (prov.), Argentina 143/C2
Catamarca, Argentina 143/C2
Catamarca, Argentina 120/C5
Catamayo, Ecuador 128/C4
Catanauan, Philippines 82/D5
Catandica, Mozambique 118/E3
Catanduanes (prov.), Philippines 82/E4
Catanduanes (isl.), Philippines 82/E4
Catanduanes (isl.), Philippines 85/H3
Catanduva, Brazil 135/B2
Catanduva, Brazil 132/D8
Catania (prov.), Italy 34/E6
Catania, Italy 34/E6
Catania, Italy 7/F5
Cataño, P. Rico 156/G1
Cataño, P. Rico 161/D1
Catanzaro (prov.), Italy 34/F5
Catanzaro, Italy 34/F5
Cataouatche (lake), La. 238/N4
Cataract (creek), Ariz. 198/C3
Cataract, Ind. 227/D6
Cataract (canyon), Utah 304/D5
Cataract, Wis. 317/E7
Catarama, Ecuador 128/C3
Cataricahua, Bolivia 136/B6
Catarina, Texas 303/G6
Catarman, Philippines 82/E7
Catarman (pt.), Philippines 82/F7
Catasauqua, Pa. 294/M4
Catastrophe (cape), S. Australia 88/F7
Catastrophe (cape), S. Australia 94/D6
Catatumbo (riv.), Colombia 126/D3
Catatumbo (riv.), Venezuela 124/B3
Cataula, Georgia 217/C5
Cataumet, Mass. 249/M6
Catawba (co.), N.C. 281/G3
Catawba, N.C. 281/G3
Catawba (lake), N.C. 281/G4
Catawba (riv.), N.C. 281/H5
Catawba, Ohio 284/C6
Catawba, S.C. 296/F2
Catawba (riv.), S.C. 296/F2
Catawba, Va. 307/H6
Catawba, W. Va. 312/F3
Catawba, Wis. 317/F4
Catawba Island, Ohio 284/E2
Catawissa, Mo. 261/L6
Catawissa, Pa. 294/K4
Cat Ba, Dao (isl.), Vietnam 72/E2
Catbalogan, Philippines 85/H3
Catbalogan, Philippines 82/E5
Cat Creek, Mont. 262/H3
Cateechee, S.C. 296/B2
Cateel, Philippines 85/H4
Cateel, Philippines 82/F7
Catemaco, Mexico 150/M7
Catemu, Chile 138/G2
Cater, Sask. 181/C2
Caterham and Warlingham, England 13/H8
Caterham and Warlingham, England 10/B6
Cates, Ind. 227/C4
Catete, Angola 115/B5
Catfish (lake), N.C. 281/P5

Catfish (lake), Ontario 177/F2
Catfish (creek), S.C. 296/E4
Cathance (riv.), Maine 243/J6
Catharine, Kansas 232/C3
Catharine Lake, N.C. 281/O5
Cathay, N. Dak. 282/M4
Cathedral (mt.), Texas 303/D12
Cathedral City, Calif. 204/J10
Cathedral Prov. Park, Br. Col. 184/H5
Catherine, Ala. 195/D6
Catherine (lake), Ark. 202/E5
Catherine (mt.), Ecuador 128/D2
Cathlamet, Wash. 310/B4
Catlettsburg, Ky. 237/R4
Catlin, Ill. 222/F3
Catlin, Ind. 227/C5
Catmon, Philippines 82/E5
Cato, Ark. 202/F4
Cato (isl.), Australia 87/F8
Cato, Ind. 227/C8
Cato, N.Y. 276/G4
Cato, Wis. 317/L7
Catoche (cape), Mexico 150/Q6
Catoctin (creek), Md. 245/H3
Catoctin Furnace, Md. 245/J2
Catoctin Mt. Park, Md. 245/J2
Catolé do Rocha, Brazil 132/G4
Catonsville, Md. 245/M3
Catoosa (co.), Georgia 217/B1
Catoosa, Okla. 288/P2
Catriló, Argentina 143/D4
Catrimani, Brazil 132/H9
Catrine, Scotland 15/D5
Catron, Mo. 261/N9
Catron (co.), N. Mex. 274/A4
Catskill, N.Y. 276/N6
Catskill (mts.), N.Y. 276/L6
Cattaraugus (co.), N.Y. 276/C6
Cattaraugus, N.Y. 276/C6
Cattaraugus (creek), N.Y. 276/C6
Cattaraugus Ind. Res., N.Y. 276/C5
Catumbela, Angola 115/B6
Cauayan, Isabela, Philippines 82/C2
Cauayan, Negros Occ., Philippines 82/D6
Cauca (dept.), Colombia 126/B6
Cauca (riv.), Colombia 120/B2
Cauca (riv.), Colombia 126/C4
Caucagua, Venezuela 124/E2
Caucasia, Colombia 126/C4
Caucasus (mts.), U.S.S.R. 7/J4
Caucasus (mts.), U.S.S.R. 52/F6
Caucasus (mts.), U.S.S.R. 48/E5
Caucedo (pass), Dom. Rep. 158/E6
Caucete, Argentina 143/C3
Caucomgomoc (lake), Maine 243/D3
Caudete, Spain 33/F3
Caughnawaga, Québec 172/H4
Cauit (pt.), Philippines 82/F6
Cauldcleuch Head (mt.), Scotland 15/F5
Caulfield, Mo. 261/H9
Caulfield, Victoria 88/L7
Caulfield, Victoria 97/J5
Caulksville, Ark. 202/C3
Caulonia, Italy 34/F5
Caúngula, Angola 115/C5
Cauquenes, Chile 138/A11
Caura (riv.), Venezuela 120/D2
Caura (riv.), Venezuela 124/F5
Causapscal, Québec 172/B2
Causeway, Ireland 17/B7
Causey, N. Mex. 274/F5
Causses (mts.), France 28/D5
Cauterets, France 28/C6
Cauthron, Ark. 202/B4
Cauto (riv.), Cuba 158/H3
Cauto del Embarcadero, Cuba 158/H4
Cauto el Cristo, Cuba 158/J3
Cava de'Tirreni, Italy 34/E4
Cavaillon, France 28/F6
Cavaillon, Haiti 158/A6
Cavalier (co.), N. Dak. 282/N2
Cavalier, N. Dak. 282/P2
Cavalla (riv.), Liberia 106/C7
Cavalli (isls.), N. Zealand 100/E1
Cavallo (passage), Texas 303/H9
Cavally (riv.), Ivory Coast 106/C7
Cavan (co.), Ireland 17/G4
Cavan, Ireland 10/C4
Cavan, Ireland 17/G3
Cavan, Ontario 177/F3
Cavanaugh (lake), Wash. 310/D2
Cavari, Bolivia 136/B5
Cavarzere, Italy 34/D2
Cave City, Ark. 202/G2
Cave City, Ky. 237/K6
Cave Creek, Ariz. 198/D5
Cave Hill, Barbados 161/B9
Cave in Rock, Ill. 222/E6
Cave Junction, Oreg. 291/D5
Cave Spring, Georgia 217/B2
Cave Springs, Ark. 202/B1
Cavetown, Md. 245/H2
Caviana (i.), Brazil 120/E2
Caviana (isl.), Brazil 132/D2
Cavili (isl.), Philippines 82/C6
Cavinas, Bolivia 136/B3
Cavite (prov.), Philippines 82/C3
Cavite, Philippines 82/C3
Cavite, Philippines 85/G3
Cavour, S. Dak. 298/N5
Cavour, Wis. 317/J4
Cawdor, Scotland 15/E3
Cawker City, Kansas 232/D2
Cawndilla (lake), N.S. Wales 97/A3
Cawnpore (Kanpur), India 68/E3
Cawood, Ky. 237/P7
Cawston, Br. Col. 184/H5

Cawston, England 13/J5
Caxambu, Brazil 135/D2
Caxias, Brazil 120/L5
Caxias, Brazil 132/F4
Caxias do Sul, Brazil 120/D5
Caxias do Sul, Brazil 132/D10
Caxito, Angola 115/B5
Çay, Turkey 63/D3
Cayacoa, Dom. Rep. 158/E6
Cayamas (cays), Cuba 158/C2
Cayambe, Ecuador 128/D2
Cayambe (mt.), Ecuador 128/D2
Cayasta, Argentina 143/F5
Cayastacito, Argentina 143/F5
Cayce, Ky. 237/C7
Cayce, S.C. 296/E4
Çaycuma, Turkey 63/E2
Caycuse, Br. Col. 184/J3
Çayeli, Turkey 63/J2
Cayenne (dist.), Fr. Guiana 131/E3
Cayenne (cap.), Fr. Guiana 2/G5
Cayenne (cap.), Fr. Guiana 120/D2
Cayenne (cap.), Fr. Guiana 131/E3
Cayer, Manitoba 179/D3
Cayes Jacmel, Haiti 158/C6
Cayeux-sur-Mer, France 28/D2
Cayey, P. Rico 156/G1
Cayey, P. Rico 161/D2
Cayey, Sierra de (mts.), P. Rico 161/D2
Çayıralan, Turkey 63/F3
Çayırlı, Turkey 63/J3
Cayley, Alberta 182/D4
Cayman Brac (isl.), Cayman Is. 156/B3
Cayman (isl.), Cayman 146/K8
CAYMAN ISLANDS 156/B3
Cayo Costa (isl.), Fla. 212/D5
Cayon, St. Kitts & Nevis 161/C10
Cay Sal (bank), Bahamas 156/B2
Cayucos, Calif. 204/E8
Cayuga (co.), N.Y. 276/G4
Cayuga (co.), N.Y. 276/G4
Cayuga, N.Y. 276/G5
Cayuga (lake), N.Y. 276/G5
Cayuga, N. Dak. 282/R7
Cayuga, Texas 303/J6
Cayuga Heights, N.Y. 276/H6
Cayuga, Ind. 227/C5
Cayuse, Oreg. 291/J2
Cayuta (creek), N.Y. 276/G6
Cazadero, Calif. 204/B5
Cazalla de la Sierra, Spain 33/D4
Cazaux (lake), France 28/C5
Cazenovia, N.Y. 276/J5
Cazenovia, Wis. 317/F8
Cazin, Yugoslavia 45/B3
Cazis, Switzerland 39/H3
Cazma, Yugoslavia 45/C3
Cazombo, Angola 115/D6
Cazones (gulf), Cuba 158/C2
Cazorla, Spain 33/E4
Cazorla, Venezuela 124/E3
Cazot, Uruguay 145/B6
Cazuela (creek), Miss. 256/G4
Cazuleja, Cerro (mt.), Colombia 126/C6
Ceanannus Mór, Ireland 17/G4
Ceanannus Mór, Ireland 10/C4
Ceará (state), Brazil 132/G4
Ceará (Fortaleza), Brazil 132/G3
Ceará-Mirim, Brazil 132/H4
Ceará-Mirim, Brazil 120/F3
Cébaco (isl.), Panama 154/G7
Ceballos, Mexico 150/H3
Cebeci, Turkey 63/B1
Cebolla (creek), Colo. 208/E6
Cebolla, N. Mex. 274/C2
Cebollatí, Uruguay 145/F4
Cebollatí (riv.), Uruguay 145/F4
Cebreros, Spain 33/D2
Cebu (prov.), Philippines 82/D5
Cebu, Philippines 82/D5
Cebu, Philippines 85/G3
Cebu, Philippines 54/O8
Cebu, Philippines 2/P5
Cebu (isl.), Philippines 85/G3
Cebu (isl.), Philippines 82/D5
Cecelia, La. 238/G6
Cecil (co.), N. Dak. 282/N2
Cecil, Ala. 195/F6
Cecil, Ark. 202/C3
Cecil, Georgia 217/F8
Cecil (co.), Md. 245/P2
Cecil, Ohio 284/A3
Cecil, Oreg. 291/H2
Cecil, Pa. 294/B5
Cecil, Wis. 317/K6
Cecil Field Naval Air Sta., Fla. 212/E1
Cecil Lake, Br. Col. 184/G2
Cecil M. Harden (lake), Ind. 227/C5
Cecilton, Md. 245/P3
Cecilville, Calif. 204/B2
Cecina, Italy 34/C3
Ceclavín, Spain 33/C3
Cedar (creek), Colo. 208/M1
Cedar (creek), Ind. 227/F1
Cedar (co.), Iowa 229/L5
Cedar, Iowa 229/H6
Cedar (riv.), Iowa 188/H2
Cedar (riv.), Iowa 229/K4
Cedar, Kansas 232/D2
Cedar (riv.), Manitoba 179/B1
Cedar (pt.), Md. 245/N7
Cedar, Mich. 250/D4
Cedar (lake), Mich. 255/F7
Cedar (co.), Minn. 255/F7
Cedar (co.), Mo. 261/E7
Cedar (co.), Nebr. 264/G2
Cedar (riv.), Nebr. 264/F3
Cedar (mt.), Nev. 266/F3
Cedar (creek), N.J. 273/E4
Cedar (creek), N. Dak. 282/G7
Cedar (pt.), Ohio 284/D2
Cedar (lake), Ontario 177/F1
Cedar (isl.), Texas 303/B5
Cedar (mts.), Utah 304/B3
Cedar (isl.), Va. 307/S5
Cedar (lake), Va. 307/F1
Cedar (riv.), Wash. 310/B2

Cedar Bluff, Ala. 195/G2
Cedar Bluff, Iowa 229/L5
Cedar Bluff (res.), Kansas 232/C3
Cedarbluff, Miss. 256/G3
Cedar Bluff, Va. 307/E6
Cedar Bluffs, Kansas 232/B2
Cedar Bluffs, Nebr. 264/H3
Cedar Breaks Nat'l Mon., Utah 304/B6
Cedar Brook, N.J. 273/D4
Cedarburg, Wis. 317/L9
Cedarbutte, S. Dak. 298/H6
Cedar City, Mo. 261/H5
Cedar City, Utah 188/D3
Cedar City, Utah 304/A6
Cedar Cove, Ala. 195/D4
Cedar Creek, Ark. 202/C4
Cedar Creek (peak), Idaho 220/E7
Cedar Creek (res.), Idaho 220/D7
Cedarcreek, Mo. 261/G9
Cedar Creek, Nebr. 264/H3
Cedar Crest, N. Mex. 274/C3
Cedaredge, Colo. 208/D5
Cedar Falls, Iowa 229/H3
Cedar Falls, N.C. 281/K3
Cedar Falls, Wash. 310/D4
Cedar Falls, Wis. 317/C6
Cedar Fort, Utah 304/B3
Cedar Gap, Mo. 261/G8
Cedar Grove, Ant. & Bar. 161/E11
Cedar Grove, Fla. 212/D6
Cedar Grove, Georgia 217/L2
Cedar Grove, Ind. 227/H6
Cedar Grove, Md. 245/K4
Cedar Grove •, N.J. 273/E2
Cedar Grove, N.C. 281/L2
Cedar Grove, Tenn. 237/D9
Cedar Grove, W. Va. 312/D6
Cedar Grove, Wis. 317/L8
Cedar Heights, Md. 245/C2
Cedar Hill, N. Mex. 274/B2
Cedar Hill, Tenn. 237/H7
Cedar Hill, Texas 303/H6
Cedar Hill Lakes, Mo. 261/L6
Cedar Hills, Oreg. 291/A2
Cedarhurst, N.Y. 276/P7
Cedar Island, N.C. 281/S5
Cedar Key, Fla. 212/C2
Cedar Knolls, N.J. 273/E2
Cedar Lake, Ind. 227/C2
Cedar Lake, Minn. 255/E4
Cedar Mill, Oreg. 291/A2
Cedar Mills, Minn. 255/D6
Cedar Mountain, N.C. 281/D4
Cedar Park, Texas 303/G4
Cedar Point, Ill. 222/D2
Cedar Point, Kansas 232/F4
Cedar Rapids, Iowa 188/H2
Cedar Rapids, Iowa 229/K5
Cedar Rapids, Iowa 146/J5
Cedar Rapids, Nebr. 264/F3
Cedar River, Mich. 250/B3
Cedar Run, N.J. 273/E4
Cedar Run, Pa. 294/H4
Cedar Springs, Georgia 217/C8
Cedar Springs, Mich. 250/D5
Cedar Springs, Mo. 261/E7
Cedar Springs, Ontario 177/B5
Cedar Springs, Va. 307/F7
Cedar Swamp (pond), Conn. 210/G2
Cedartown, Georgia 217/B2
Cedarvale, Br. Col. 184/C2
Cedar Vale, Kansas 232/F4
Cedarvale, N. Mex. 274/C4
Cedar Valley, Utah 304/B3
Cedarville, Ark. 202/B2
Cedarville, Calif. 204/E2
Cedarville, Ill. 222/D1
Cedarville, Ind. 227/G2
Cedarville, Ky. 237/S6
Cedarville, Md. 245/L6
Cedarville, Mich. 250/E2
Cedarville, N.J. 273/C5
Cedarville, N.Y. 276/K5
Cedarville, Ohio 284/C6
Cedarville, Va. 307/M3
Cedarville, W. Va. 312/E5
Cedarwood Park, N.J. 273/E3
Cedonia, Wash. 310/G2
Cedoux, Sask. 181/H6
Cedral, Mexico 150/J5
Cedros, Honduras 154/D3
Cedros (isl.), Mexico 146/G7
Cedros (isl.), Mexico 150/B2
Cedros, Trin. & Tob. 161/A11
Ceduna, S. Australia 88/E6
Ceduna, S. Australia 94/D5
Cee Vee, Texas 303/D3
Cefalù, Italy 34/E5
Cegléd, Hungary 41/E3
Ceglie Messapico, Italy 34/F4
Cehegín, Spain 33/F3
Ceiba, P. Rico 161/F2
Çekerek, Turkey 63/F2
Çekerek (riv.), Turkey 63/F3
Celada Cué, Paraguay 144/D3
Celano, Italy 34/D3
Celanova, Spain 33/B1
Celaya, Mexico 150/J6
Celbridge, Ireland 17/H5
Celebes (sea) 54/O9
Celebes (isl.), Indonesia 54/N10
Celebes (isl.), Indonesia 2/R6
Celebes (Sulawesi) (isl.), Indonesia 85/G5
Celebes (sea), Indonesia 85/F5
Celebes (sea), Philippines 82/D8
Celendín, Peru 128/D6
Celerigna-Schlarigna, Switzerland 39/J3
Celeste, Texas 303/H4
Celestine, Ind. 227/D8
Celestún, Mexico 150/O6
Celica, Ecuador 128/B4
Céligny, Switzerland 39/B4
Çelikhan, Turkey 63/H3
Celilo, Oreg. 291/G2
Celilo (lake), Oreg. 291/G2
Celilo (lake), Wash. 310/E5

Charleville 349

Celina, Minn. 255/E3
Celina, Ohio 284/A4
Celina, Tenn. 237/K7
Celina, Texas 303/H4
Celista, Br. Col. 184/H5
Celje, Yugoslavia 45/B2
Cella, Spain 33/F2
Cellar (head), Scotland 15/B2
Celldömölk, Hungary 41/D3
Celle, Germany 22/D2
Celorico da Beira, Portugal 33/C2
Celoron, N.Y. 276/B6
Cement, Okla. 288/K5
Cement City, Mich. 250/E6
Çemişkezek, Turkey 63/H3
Cemmaes (head), Wales 13/C5
Cenderawasih (bay), Indonesia 85/K6
Ceneri (mt.), Switzerland 39/G4
Cenia, Spain 33/G2
Census Bureau, Md. 245/F5
Centenary, Ind. 227/B5
Centenary, S.C. 296/J3
Centennial (mts.), Idaho 220/F5
Centennial, Wyo. 319/F4
Centennial Wash (dry riv.), Ariz. 198/B5
Center, Colo. 208/G7
Center, Georgia 217/F2
Center, Ind. 227/E4
Center, Ky. 237/K6
Center (pond), Maine 243/E5
Center, Mo. 261/J3
Center, Nebr. 264/G2
Center, N. Dak. 282/H5
Center, Okla. 288/N5
Center, S. Dak. 298/P6
Center, Texas 303/K6
Center Barnstead, N.H. 268/E5
Center Belpre, Ohio 284/G7
Centerbrook, Conn. 210/F3
Centerburg, Ohio 284/E5
Center City, Minn. 255/F5
Center Conway, N.H. 268/E4
Center Cross, Va. 307/P5
Centerdale, R.I. 249/H5
Centereach, N.Y. 276/O9
Centerfield, Utah 304/C4
Center Groton, Conn. 210/G3
Center Harbor•, N.H. 268/E4
Center Hill, Ark. 202/G3
Center Hill, Fla. 212/D3
Center Hill (lake), Tenn. 237/K9
Center Junction, Iowa 229/L4
Center Line, Mich. 250/B6
Center Lovell, Maine 243/B7
Center Montville, Maine 243/E7
Center Moreland, Pa. 294/E7
Center Moriches, N.Y. 276/P9
Center Ossipee, N.H. 268/E4
Center Point, Ark. 202/C5
Centerpoint, Ind. 227/C6
Center Point, Iowa 229/K4
Center Point, La. 238/F4
Center Point, S. Dak. 298/P7
Center Point, Texas 303/E8
Center Point, W. Va. 312/E4
Center Ridge, Ark. 202/E3
Center Rutland, Vt. 268/A4
Center Sandwich, N.H. 268/D4
Center Square, Ind. 227/H7
Center Strafford, N.H. 268/E5
Centerton, Ark. 202/B1
Centerton, Ind. 227/E5
Centerton, N.J. 273/C4
Centertown, Ky. 237/G6
Centertown, Mo. 261/H5
Centertown, Tenn. 237/K9
Center Tuftonboro, N.H. 268/E4
Centerview, Mo. 261/E5
Center Village, Ohio 284/E5
Centerville, Ark. 202/D3
Centerville, Del. 245/R1
Centerville, Georgia 217/E5
Centerville, Ind. 227/H5
Centerville, Iowa 229/H7
Centerville, Kansas 232/H3
Centerville, Ky. 237/S6
Centerville, La. 238/H7
Centerville•, Maine 243/H6
Centerville, Mass. 249/N6
Centerville, Minn. 255/E5
Centerville, Mo. 261/L8
Centerville, N.C. 281/N2
Centerville, Ohio 284/B6
Centerville, Pa. 294/B6
Centerville, Pa. 294/C2
Centerville, S. Dak. 298/R7
Centerville, Tenn. 237/G9
Centerville, Texas 303/H6
Centerville, Utah 304/C3
Centerville, Wash. 310/D5
Centrahoma, Okla. 288/O5
Central, Ala. 195/F5
Central, Alaska 196/H2
Central, Alaska 196/J1
Central, Ariz. 198/F6
Central, Cordillera (range), Bolivia 136/C6
Central, Cordillera (range), Colombia 126/C5
Central, Cordillera (range), Dom. Rep. 158/D5
Central, Idaho 220/G7
Central, Ind. 227/E8
Central (Markazi) (prov.), Iran 66/G3
Central (dist.), Israel 65/B3
Central (prov.), Kenya 115/G4
Central, La. 238/L3
Central, N. Mex. 274/A6
Central, Paraguay 144/D4
Central (Baganga), Philippines 82/F7
Central, Cordillera (range), P. Rico 161/C2
Central (reg.), Scotland 15/D4
Central, S.C. 296/B2
Central, Utah 304/A6
Central, Utah 304/B5
Central Aboriginal Res., W. Australia 88/D4
Central Aboriginal Res., W. Australia 92/E3
Central African Republic 2/K5
Central African Republic 102/D4
CENTRAL AFRICAN REPUBLIC 115/C2
Central Aguirre, P. Rico 161/D3
Central Amancio Rodríguez, Cuba 158/G3
Central America 2/E5
Central América, Cuba 158/J4
Central Bedeque, Pr. Edward I. 168/E2
Central Blissville, New Bruns. 170/D3
Central Bolivia, Cuba 158/G2
Central Brasil, Cuba 158/G2
Central Bridge, N.Y. 276/M5
Central Butte, Sask. 181/E5
Central Cándido González, Cuba 158/G3
Central City, Ark. 202/B3
Central City, Colo. 208/J3
Central City, Ill. 222/D5
Central City, Iowa 229/K4
Central City, Ky. 237/G6
Central City, Nebr. 264/F3
Central City, Pa. 294/E5
Central City, S. Dak. 298/B5
Central Colombia, Cuba 158/G3
Central Falls, R.I. 249/J5
Central Frank País, Cuba 158/K3
Central Greece and Euboea (reg.), Greece 45/F6
Central Guatemala, Cuba 158/J3
Central Haití, Cuba 158/G3
Centralhatchee, Georgia 217/B4
Central Heights-Midland City, Ariz. 198/E5
Centralia, Ill. 222/D5
Centralia, Iowa 229/M4
Centralia, Kansas 232/F2
Centralia, Mo. 261/H4
Centralia, Okla. 288/R1
Centralia, Pa. 294/K4
Centralia, Texas 303/K6
Centralia, Wash. 288/B1
Centralia, Wash. 310/C4
Centralia, W. Va. 312/E5
Central Intelligence Agency (C.I.A.), Va. 307/S2
Central Islip, N.Y. 276/O9
Central Lake, Mich. 250/D3
Central Los Reynaldos, Cuba 158/J4
Central Loynaz Echevarría, Cuba 158/J3
Central Manuel Tames, Cuba 158/K4
Central Niágara, Cuba 158/B1
Central Pacolet, S.C. 296/D2
Central Park, Wash. 310/B3
Central Patricia, Ontario 175/B2
Central Point, Oreg. 291/D5
Central Point, Va. 307/O4
Central Saanich, Br. Col. 184/K3
Central Square, N.Y. 276/H4
Central Station, W. Va. 312/E4
Central Ural (mts.), U.S.S.R. 52/J2
Central Valley, Calif. 204/C3
Central Valley, N.Y. 276/M8
Central Village, Conn. 210/H2
Central Village, Mass. 249/K6
Central Wedge (mt.), North. Terr. 93/C7
Centre, Ala. 195/G2
Centre (co.), Pa. 294/G4
Centre Hall, Pa. 294/G4
Centre Island, N.Y. 276/R6
Centre-Saint-Simon, New Bruns. 170/E1
Centreville, Ala. 195/D5
Centreville, Ill. 222/B3
Centreville, Md. 245/O4
Centreville, Mich. 250/D7
Centreville, Miss. 256/B8
Centreville, New Bruns. 170/C2
Centreville, Digby, Nova Scotia 168/B4
Centreville, Kings, Nova Scotia 168/D3
Centreville (Thurman), Ohio 284/F8
Centuria, Wis. 317/A5
Centurión, Uruguay 145/F3
Century, Fla. 212/B5
Century, W. Va. 312/F4
Cephalonia (Kefallinía) (isl.), Greece 45/E6
Ceram (isl.), Indonesia 54/P10
Ceram (isl.), Indonesia 85/H6
Cerbat (mts.), Ariz. 198/A3
Cercal, Portugal 33/B4
Cerca la Source, Haiti 158/C5
Cereal, Alberta 182/E4
Ceredo, W. Va. 312/B6
Ceres, Argentina 143/D2
Ceres, Brazil 132/D6
Ceres, Brazil 120/E4
Ceres, Calif. 204/D6
Ceres, N.Y. 276/E6
Ceres, S. Africa 118/B6
Ceres, Va. 307/F6
Ceresco, Nebr. 264/H3
Céret, France 28/E6
Cereté, Colombia 126/C3
Cerf (lake), Québec 172/B3
Cerf (isl.), Seychelles 118/H5
Cerfontaine, Belgium 27/E8
Cerignola, Italy 34/E4
Çerkeş, Turkey 63/E2
Çerkezköy, Turkey 63/C2
Çermik, Turkey 63/H3
Cernavodă, Romania 45/J3
Cernier, Switzerland 39/C2
Cernobbio, Italy 34/B2
Cerralvo (isl.), Mexico 150/E4
Cerrillos, N. Mex. 274/D3
Cerrillos, Uruguay 145/A6
Cerrito, Paraguay 144/D5
Cerritos, Calif. 204/C11
Cerritos, Mexico 150/J5
Cerro, N. Mex. 274/D2
Cerro Aconcagua (mt.) 120/C6
Cerro Alto (mt.), Texas 303/B10
Cêrro Azul, Brazil 135/B4
Cerro Azul, Mexico 150/L6
Cerro Azul, Peru 128/D9
Cerro Castillo, Chile 138/E9
Cerro Chato, Cerro Largo, Uruguay 145/F3
Cerro Chato, Rivera, Uruguay 145/D2
Cerro Chato, Treinta y Tres, Uruguay 145/D2
Cerro Colorado, Uruguay 145/D4
Cerro Corá, Paraguay 144/E3
Cerro de las Armas, Uruguay 145/B5
Cerro de las Cuentas, Uruguay 145/E3
Cerro de Pasco, Peru 120/B4
Cerro de Pasco, Peru 128/D8
Cerro de San Antonio, Colombia 126/C2
Cerro Gordo, Ill. 222/E4
Cerro Gordo (co.), Iowa 229/G2
Cerro Gordo, N.C. 281/M6
Cerro Gordo (pt.), P. Rico 161/D1
Cerro Gordo, Tenn. 237/E10
Cerro Largo (dept.), Uruguay 145/E3
Cerro Manantiales, Chile 138/F10
Cerulean, Ky. 237/F7
Cervera, Spain 33/G2
Cervera del Río Alhama, Spain 33/E1
Cervera de Pisuerga, Spain 33/D1
Cerveteri, Italy 34/E6
Cervione, France 28/B6
Cesano, Italy 34/F6
Cesar (dept.), Colombia 126/D3
César (riv.), Colombia 126/D2
Cesena, Italy 34/D2
Cesenatico, Italy 34/D2
Cēsis, U.S.S.R. 53/C2
Cēsis, U.S.S.R. 52/C3
Česká Kamenice, Czech. 41/C1
Česká Lípa, Czech. 41/C1
Česká Třebová, Czech. 41/D2
České Budějovice, Czech. 41/C2
Český Brod, Czech. 41/C1
Český Krumlov, Czech. 41/C2
Český Těšín, Czech. 41/E2
Çeşme, Turkey 63/B3
Céspedes, Cuba 158/G2
Cessford, Alberta 182/E4
Cessnock-Bellbird, N.S. Wales 88/J6
Cessnock-Bellbird, N.S. Wales 97/F3
Cestos (riv.), Liberia 106/C7
Cetinje, Yugoslavia 45/D4
Çetinkaya, Turkey 63/G3
Ceuta, Spain 106/C1
Ceuta, Spain 7/D5
Ceuta, Spain 102/B1
Ceuta, Spain 33/D5
Cévennes (mts.), France 28/E5
Cevio, Switzerland 39/G4
Cevizli, Turkey 63/D4
Ceyhan, Turkey 63/F4
Ceyhan (riv.), Turkey 63/F4
Ceyhan (riv.), Turkey 59/C2
Ceylânpınar, Turkey 63/H4
Ceylon (Sri Lanka) 54/K9
Ceylon, Minn. 255/D7
Ceylon, Sask. 181/G6
Chabás, Argentina 143/F6
Chaca, Chile 138/B1
Chacabuco, Argentina 143/F7
Chacabuco, Chile 138/G2
Chacachacare (isl.), Trin. & Tob. 161/A10
Chacahoula, La. 238/J7
Chacalluta, Chile 138/A1
Chachacomani, Bolivia 136/A6
Chachapoyas, Peru 128/D6
Chachapoyas, Peru 120/B3
Chachoengsao, Thailand 72/D4
Chachro, Pakistan 68/C3
Chaco (prov.), Argentina 143/D2
Chaco (mesa), N. Mex. 274/B3
Chaco (riv.), N. Mex. 274/A2
Chaco, Paraguay 144/B-C2
Chaco Austral (reg.), Argentina 143/D2
Chaco Boreal (reg.), Paraguay 144/B2-3
Chaco Central (reg.), Argentina 143/D1
Chaco Culture Nat'l Hist. Park, N. Mex. 274/B2
Chacoma, Bolivia 136/A6
Chacon (cape), Alaska 196/N2
Chacon, N. Mex. 274/D2
Chacuaco (creek), Colo. 208/M8
Chad 2/K5
Chad 102/D3
CHAD 111/C4
Chad (lake) 102/D3
Chad (lake), Chad 111/C5
Chad (lake), Niger 106/G6
Chad (lake), Nigeria 106/G6
Chadan, U.S.S.R. 48/K4
Chadbourn, N.C. 281/M6
Chadron, Nebr. 264/B2
Chadwick, Ill. 222/D1
Chadwick, Mo. 261/G9
Chadwick Acres, N.C. 281/P6
Chadwicks, N.Y. 276/K4
Chadyr-Lunga, U.S.S.R. 52/C5
Chaffee (co.), Colo. 208/G5
Chaffee, Mo. 261/N8
Chaffee, N.Y. 276/C5
Chaffee, N. Dak. 282/R6
Chaffers (isl.), Chile 138/D5
Chafurray, Colombia 126/D6
Chagai (hills), Afghanistan 68/A3
Chagai, Pakistan 59/H4
Chagai, Pakistan 68/A3
Chagai (hills), Pakistan 68/A3
Chagai (hills), Pakistan 59/H4
Chagda, U.S.S.R. 48/O4
Chaghcharan, Afghanistan 68/B2
Chagoda, U.S.S.R. 52/E3
Chagoness, Sask. 181/G3
Chagos (arch.), Br. Ind. Ocean Terr. 2/N6
Chagos (arch.), Br. Ind. Ocean Terr. 54/J10
Chagrin (riv.), Ohio 284/J8
Chagrin Falls, Ohio 284/J9
Chaguanas, Trin. & Tob. 161/B10
Chaguaramas, Trin. & Tob. 161/A10
Chaguaramas, Venezuela 124/E3
Chaguaya, Bolivia 136/C7
Chagulak (isl.), Alaska 196/D4
Chahal, Guatemala 154/C3
Chahar Borjak, Afghanistan 59/H3
Chahar Borjak, Afghanistan 68/A2
Chah Bahar, Afghanistan 59/H4
Chahuites, Mexico 150/M8
Chai Badan, Thailand 72/D4
Chaibasa, India 68/F4
Chai Buri, Thailand 72/D3
Chainat, Thailand 72/D4
Chain-O-Lakes, Mo. 261/E9
Chaira, Laguna (lake), Colombia 126/C7
Chaires, Fla. 212/B1
Chaitén, Chile 138/E4
Chaiya, Thailand 72/C5
Chaiyaphum, Thailand 72/D4
Chajarí, Argentina 143/G5
Chajul, Guatemala 154/B3
Chake Chake, Tanzania 115/H5
Chala, Peru 128/E10
Chalais, Switzerland 39/E4
Chalatenango, El Salvador 154/C3
Chalchihuites, Mexico 150/G5
Chalco de Díaz Covarrubias, Mexico 150/M1
Chaleur (bay), New Bruns. 170/E1
Chaleur (bay), Québec 172/C2
Chaleur (bay), Québec 174/D3
Chalfont, Pa. 294/M5
Chalhuanca, Peru 128/F10
Chaling, China 77/H6
Chalk (creek), Utah 304/C3
Chalk River, Ontario 175/E3
Chalk River, Ontario 177/G1
Chalkyitsik, Alaska 196/K1
Challacollo, Bolivia 136/B6
Challana, Bolivia 136/A4
Challapata, Bolivia 136/B6
Challis, Idaho 220/D5
Challviri (salt dep.), Bolivia 136/B8
Chalmers, Ind. 227/D3
Chalmette, La. 238/P4
Chalna Port, Bangladesh 68/F4
Chalonnes-sur-Loire, France 28/C4
Châlons-sur-Marne, France 28/F3
Chalon-sur-Saône, France 28/F4
Chaltel, Cerro (mt.), Chile 138/E8
Chalus, Iran 59/F2
Chalus, Iran 66/G2
Chalybeate, Miss. 256/G1
Chalybeate Springs, Georgia 217/C5
Chalybeate Springs, N.C. 281/M3
Cham, Germany 22/E4
Cham, Switzerland 39/F2
Chama, Colo. 208/J8
Chama, N. Mex. 274/C2
Chaman, Pakistan 68/B2
Chaman, Pakistan 59/J3
Chamba, India 68/D2
Chambal (riv.), India 68/D3
Chambas, Cuba 158/F2
Chamberino, N. Mex. 274/C6
Chamberlain (creek), Idaho 220/C4
Chamberlain (lake), Maine 243/E3
Chamberlain, Sask. 181/F5
Chamberlain, S. Dak. 298/L6
Chamberlain, Uruguay 145/C3
Chamberlin, La. 238/J1
Chambers (co.), Ala. 195/H5
Chambers, Ariz. 198/F3
Chambers, Nebr. 264/F2
Chambers (co.), Texas 303/K8
Chambers (isl.), Wis. 317/M5
Chambersburg, Ill. 222/C4
Chambersburg, Ind. 227/E7
Chambersburg, Pa. 294/G6
Chambéry, France 28/F5
Chambeshi (riv.), Zambia 115/F6
Chambeyron (mt.), France 28/G5
Chambeyron (mt.), Italy 34/A2
Chambi, Jebel (mt.), Tunisia 106/F2
Chamblee, Georgia 217/K1
Chambly (co.), Québec 172/J4
Chambly, Québec 172/J4
Chambord, France 28/D4
Chambord, Québec 172/E1
Chamdo (Qamdo), China 77/E5
Chame (pt.), Panama 154/H6
Chamela (bay), Mexico 150/G7
Chamical, Argentina 143/C3
Chamisal, N. Mex. 274/D2
Chamizal Nat'l Mem., Texas 303/A10
Chamizo, Uruguay 145/D5
Chamo (lake), Ethiopia 111/G6
Chamois, Mo. 261/J5
Chamonix-Mont-Blanc, France 28/G5
Chamoson, Switzerland 39/D4
Champ, Mo. 261/O2
Champagne (trad. prov.), France 29
Champagne, Yukon 187/E3
Champaign (co.), Ill. 222/E3
Champaign, Ill. 188/J2
Champaign, Ill. 222/E3
Champaign (co.), Ohio 284/C5
Champasak, Laos 72/E4
Champdani, India 68/F1
Champerico, Guatemala 154/A3
Champéry, Switzerland 39/C4
Champex, Switzerland 39/D4
Champigny-sur-Marne, France 28/C2
Champion, Alberta 182/D4
Champion, Mich. 250/B2
Champion, Nebr. 264/C4
Champlain (lake) 188/M2
Champlain, N.Y. 276/N1
Champlain (lake), N.Y. 276/O1
Champlain (county), Québec 174/C3
Champlain (co.), Québec 172/E2
Champlain, Québec 172/E3
Champlain (lake), Québec 172/D4
Champlain (lake), Vt. 268/A2
Champlain, Va. 307/O4
Champlain Park, N.Y. 276/O1
Champlin, Minn. 255/G5
Champney's West, Newf. 166/D2
Champotón, Mexico 150/O7
Chamusa, Sierra (mts.), Colombia 126/C6
Chamusca, Portugal 33/B3
Chan, Ko (isl.), Thailand 72/C5
Chana, Ill. 222/D2
Chañaral, Chile 120/B5
Chañaral, Chile 138/A6
Chañaral (isl.), Chile 138/A7
Chancay, Peru 128/D8
Chance, Ala. 195/C7
Chance, Ky. 237/L7
Chance, Md. 245/P8
Chance Cove, Newf. 166/D2
Chance Cove (cape), Newf. 166/D2
Chance Harbour, New Bruns. 170/D3
Chancellor, Ala. 195/G8
Chancellor, Alberta 182/D4
Chancellor, S. Dak. 298/R7
Chancellorsville, Va. 307/N4
Chanco, Chile 138/A11
Chancy, Switzerland 39/A4
Chandalar, Alaska 196/J1
Chandalar (riv.), Alaska 196/J1
Chandalar, East Fork (riv.), Alaska 196/J1
Chandeleur (isls.), La. 238/N7
Chandeleur (sound), La. 238/M7
Chanderi, India 68/D4
Chandernagore, India 68/F1
Chandigarh (terr.), India 68/D2
Chandigarh, India 68/D2
Chandler, Ariz. 198/D5
Chandler, Ind. 227/C8
Chandler, Minn. 255/C7
Chandler, Okla. 288/N3
Chandler, Que. 162/K6
Chandler, Québec 174/E3
Chandler, Québec 172/D2
Chandler, Texas 303/J5
Chandler Springs, Ala. 195/F4
Chandlers Valley, Pa. 294/D2
Chandlersville, Ohio 284/G6
Chandlerville, Ill. 222/C3
Chandmanī, Mongolia 77/E2
Chandolin, Switzerland 39/E4
Chandos (lake), Ontario 177/G3
Chandrapur, India 68/D5
Chaneysville, Pa. 294/F6
Chang, Ko (isl.), Thailand 72/D4
Changane (riv.), Mozambique 118/E4
Changbaek-sanmaek (mts.), N. Korea 81/D2
Changchih (Changzhi), China 77/H4
Changchow (Changzhou), China 77/J5
Changchow (Zhangzhou), China 77/J7
Changchun, China 77/K3
Changchun, China 54/O5
Changchun, China 2/R3
Changde (Changteh), China 77/H6
Changde, China 54/N7
Change Islands, Newf. 166/D4
Changewater, N.J. 273/D2
Changhua, China 77/K7
Changhŭng, S. Korea 81/C6
Changji, China 77/C3
Changjiang, China 77/G8
Chang Jiang (Yangtze) (riv.), China 2/Q4
Chang Jiang (Yangtze) (riv.), China 54/N6
Chang Jiang (Yangtze) (riv.), China 77/K5
Changjin (res.), N. Korea 81/C3
Chang Khoeng, Thailand 72/C3
Changling, China 77/K3
Changsha, China 77/H6
Changsha, China 2/Q4
Changsha, China 54/N7
Changshun, China 77/G6
Changsŏng, S. Korea 81/C6
Changteh (Changde), China 77/H6
Changuinola, Panama 154/F6
Changwu, China 77/G4
Changyang, China 77/H5
Changyeh (Zhangye), China 77/F4
Changyŏn, N. Korea 81/B4
Changzhi (Changchih), China 77/H4
Changzhi, China 54/N6
Changzhou (Changchow), China 77/K5
Chanhassen, Minn. 255/F6
Chankiang (Zhanjiang), China 77/H7
Channahon, Ill. 222/E2
Channel (isls.) 7/D4
Channel (isl.), Manitoba 179/B2
CHANNEL ISLANDS 10/E6
CHANNEL ISLANDS 13/E8
Channel Islands Nat'l Park, Calif. 204/E11
Channel-Port aux Basques, Newf. 166/C4
Channel-Port aux Basques, Newf. 162/L6
Channelview, Texas 303/K1
Channing, Mich. 250/B2
Channing, Texas 303/B2
Chantada, Spain 33/C1
Chanthaburi, Thailand 72/D4
Chantilly, France 28/E3
Chantilly, Va. 307/O3
Chantonnay, France 28/C4
Chantrey (inlet), N.W. Terr. 187/J3
Chanute, Kansas 232/G4
Chanute A.F.B., Ill. 222/E3
Chao, Peru 128/C7
Chao'an (Chaochow), China 77/J7
Chao (isl.), Portugal 33/B2
Chao Phraya, Mae Nam (riv.), Thailand 72/D4
Chaotung (Zhaotung), China 77/F6
Chaoyang, Guangdong, China 77/J7
Chaoyang, Liaoning, China 77/J3
Chapa, Vietnam 72/E2
Chapacura, Bolivia 136/A2
Chapais, Québec 174/B3
Chapala (lake), Mexico 150/H6
Chapanoke, N.C. 281/S2
Chaparé (riv.), Bolivia 136/C5
Chaparra, Cuba 158/H3
Chaparral, Colombia 126/C6
Chapayevsk, U.S.S.R. 48/F4
Chapayevsk, U.S.S.R. 52/G4
Chapecó, Brazil 132/C9
Chapel, W. Va. 312/E5
Chapel Arm, Newf. 166/D2
Chapel en le Frith, England 13/J2
Chapel Hill, Ark. 202/B5
Chapel Hill, Ind. 227/E6
Chapel Hill, N.C. 281/L3
Chapel Hill, Tenn. 237/H9
Chapelton, Jamaica 158/J6
Chapicuy, Uruguay 145/B2
Chapin, Ill. 222/C4
Chapin, Iowa 229/G3
Chapin, S.C. 296/E3
Chapleau, Ont. 162/H6
Chapleau, Ontario 175/D3
Chapleau, Ontario 177/J5
Chaplin•, Conn. 210/G1
Chaplin, Ky. 237/L5
Chaplin (riv.), Ky. 237/L5
Chaplin, Sask. 181/E5
Chaplin (lake), Sask. 181/E5
Chapman, Ala. 195/E7
Chapman (pt.), Conn. 210/F3
Chapman, Kansas 232/E3
Chapman•, Maine 243/G2
Chapman, Nebr. 264/F3
Chapmansboro, Tenn. 237/G8
Chapmanville, W. Va. 312/B7
Chappaquiddick (isl.), Mass. 249/N7
Chappell, Ky. 237/P7
Chappell, Nebr. 264/B3
Chappell (isls.), Tasmania 99/D2
Chappell Hill, Texas 303/H7
Chappells, S.C. 296/D3
Chapra, India 68/F3
Chaptico, Md. 245/M7
Chapultepec, Mexico 150/A1
Chaquí, Bolivia 136/C6
Chara, U.S.S.R. 48/M4
Charadai, Argentina 143/D2
Charagua, Bolivia 136/D6
Charagua, Sierra de (mts.), Bolivia 136/D6
Charagua, Paraguay 144/D3
Charak, Iran 66/J7
Charambirá (pt.), Colombia 126/B5
Charaña, Bolivia 136/A5
Charata, Argentina 143/D2
Charbon, N.S. Wales 97/F3
Charbonneau, N. Dak. 282/C4
Charcas, Mexico 150/J5
Charcot (isl.), Ant. 5/C15
Chard, Alberta 182/E2
Chard, England 13/E7
Chard, England 10/E5
Chardon, Ohio 284/H2
Chardonnière, Haiti 158/A6
Chardzhou, U.S.S.R. 54/H6
Chardzhou, U.S.S.R. 48/G6
Charente (dept.), France 28/D5
Charente (riv.), France 28/C5
Charente-Maritime (dept.), France 28/C5
Charenton, La. 238/H7
Charenton-le-Pont, France 28/B2
Charette, Québec 172/D3
Charikar, Afghanistan 68/B1
Charikar, Afghanistan 59/J2
Charing, Georgia 217/D6
Charing Cross, Ontario 177/B5
Chariton, Iowa 229/G6
Chariton (riv.), Iowa 229/G7
Chariton (co.), Mo. 261/F3
Chariton (riv.), Mo. 261/G1
Charity, Guyana 131/B2
Charity, Mo. 261/G7
Charkhlia (Ruoqiang), China 77/C4
Charlack, Mo. 261/P2
Charlemagne, Québec 172/H4
Charlemont•, Mass. 249/C2
Charleroi, Belgium 27/E8
Charleroi, Pa. 294/C5
Charles, Georgia 217/H6
Charles (co.), Md. 245/K6
Charles (riv.), Mass. 249/C7
Charles (isl.), N.W. Terr. 187/L3
Charles (cape), Va. 188/L3
Charles (cape), Va. 307/R6
Charlesbourg, Québec 172/J3
Charles City, Iowa 229/H2
Charles City (co.), Va. 307/O6
Charles City, Va. 307/O6
Charles Mix (co.), S. Dak. 298/M7
Charles Mound (hill), Ill. 222/C1
Charleston, Ark. 202/B3
Charleston, Ill. 222/E4
Charleston, Kansas 232/B4
Charleston•, Maine 243/F5
Charleston, Miss. 256/D2
Charleston, Mo. 261/O9
Charleston, Nev. 266/F1
Charleston (peak), Nev. 266/F6
Charleston (lake), Ontario 177/J3
Charleston, Oreg. 291/C4
Charleston, S.C. 146/L6
Charleston, S.C. 188/L4
Charleston (co.), S.C. 296/H6
Charleston, S.C. 296/G6
Charleston, Tenn. 237/M10
Charleston, Utah 304/C3
Charleston (cap.), W. Va. 188/K3
Charleston (cap.), W. Va. 146/K6
Charleston (cap.), W. Va. 312/C6
Charleston A.F.B., S.C. 296/G6
Charlestown, Ind. 227/F8
Charlestown, Md. 245/P2
Charlestown, N.H. 268/C5
Charlestown•, N.H. 268/C5
Charlestown, R.I. 249/H7
Charlestown, St. Kitts & Nevis 161/C11
Charlestown (cap.), Nevis, St. Kitts & Nevis 156/F3
Charles Town, W. Va. 312/L4
Charlestown-Bellahy, Ireland 17/D4
Charleville, Australia 87/E8
Charleville (Rathluirc), Ireland 17/D7

350 Charleville

Charleville, Queensland 95/C5
Charleville, Queensland 88/H5
Charleville-Mézières, France 28/F3
Charlevoix (co.), Mich. 250/D3
Charlevoix, Mich. 250/D3
Charlevoix (lake), Mich. 250/D3
Charlevoix-Est (co.), Québec 172/G2
Charlevoix-Est (county), Québec 174/C3
Charlevoix-Ouest (co.), Québec 172/G2
Charlevoix-Ouest (county), Québec 174/C3
Charley, Ky. 237/R5
Charlie Lake, Br. Col. 184/G2
Charlo, Mont. 262/B3
Charlo, New Bruns. 170/D1
Charlo (riv.), New Bruns. 170/D1
Charlotte, Ark. 202/H2
Charlotte (lake), Br. Col. 184/E4
Charlotte (harb.), Fla. 188/K5
Charlotte (co.), Fla. 212/E5
Charlotte (harb.), Fla. 212/D5
Charlotte, Iowa 229/M5
Charlotte•, Maine 243/J5
Charlotte, Mich. 250/E6
Charlotte (co.), New Bruns. 170/C3
Charlotte, N.C. 281/H4
Charlotte, N.C. 188/L3
Charlotte, N.C. 146/K6
Charlotte (lake), Nova Scotia 168/F4
Charlotte, Tenn. 237/G8
Charlotte, Texas 303/F9
Charlotte•, Vt. 268/A3
Charlotte (co.), Va. 307/L6
Charlotte Amalie (cap.), Virgin Is. (U.S.) 156/H1
Charlotte Amalie (cap.), Virgin Is. (U.S.) 161/B4
Charlotte Court House, Va. 307/L6
Charlotte Hall, Md. 245/M7
Charlotte Harbor, Fla. 212/E5
Charlottenberg, Sweden 18/H6
Charlottenburg, Germany 22/E4
Charlottesville, Ind. 227/F5
Charlottesville, Va. 188/L3
Charlottesville (I.C.), Va. 307/M4
Charlottetown, Newf. 166/D2
Charlottetown, Newf. 166/C3
Charlottetown (cap.), P.E.I. 146/M5
Charlottetown (cap.), P.E.I. 162/K6
Charlottetown (cap.), Pr. Edward I. 168/E2
Charlotteville, N.Y. 276/L5
Charlotte Waters, North. Terr. 93/D8
Charlson, N. Dak. 282/E3
Charlton (co.), Georgia 217/H9
Charlton•, Mass. 249/F4
Charlton (isl.), N.W.T. 162/H5
Charlton, Ontario 177/K5
Charlton, Ontario 175/D3
Charlton, Victoria 97/B5
Charlton City, Mass. 249/F4
Charlton Depot, Mass. 249/F4
Charlton Kings, England 13/F6
Charmco, W. Va. 312/E6
Charmey, Switzerland 39/D3
Charny, Québec 172/J3
Charolles, France 28/F4
Charouine, Algeria 106/D3
Charqueada Aguas de São Pedro, Brazil 135/B3
Charron (lake), Manitoba 179/G2
Charsk, U.S.S.R. 48/J5
Charter Oak, Iowa 229/C4
Charters, Ky. 237/P3
Charters Towers, Australia 87/E7
Charters Towers, Queensland 95/C4
Charters Towers, Queensland 88/H4
Chartierville, Québec 172/F4
Chartley, Mass. 249/K5
Chartres, France 28/D3
Chascomús, Argentina 143/H7
Chase, Ala. 195/E1
Chase, Br. Col. 184/H5
Chase (co.), Kansas 232/F3
Chase, Kansas 232/D3
Chase, La. 238/G2
Chase, Md. 245/N3
Chase, Mich. 250/D5
Chase (co.), Nebr. 264/C4
Chase (lake), N. Dak. 282/M5
Chaseburg, Wis. 317/D8
Chase City, Va. 307/M7
Chaseley, N. Dak. 282/L5
Chase Mills, N.Y. 276/K1
Chase N.A.S., Texas 303/G9
Chaska, Minn. 255/F6
Chaska, Tenn. 237/N7
Chasm, Br. Col. 184/G4
Chasŏng, N. Korea 81/C3
Chasseron (mt.), Switzerland 39/C3
Chastang, Ala. 195/B8
Chastre, Belgium 27/F7
Chaswood, Nova Scotia 168/E3
Chataignier, La. 238/F5
Chatanika, Alaska 196/J1
Chatawa, Miss. 256/D8
Chatcolet, Idaho 220/B2
Chateaubelair, St. Vin. & Grens. 161/A8
Châteaubriant, France 28/C4
Château-Chinon, France 28/E4
Château-d'Oex, Switzerland 39/D4
Château-du-Loir, France 28/D4
Châteaudun, France 28/D3
Chateaugay, N.Y. 276/N1
Chateaugay, Upper (lake), N.Y. 276/M1
Château-Gontier, France 28/C4
Châteauguay (co.), Québec 172/D4
Châteauguay, Québec 172/H4
Châteauguay-Centre, Québec 172/H4
Châteauneuf-sur-Loire, France 28/E4
Château-Renault, France 28/D4
Château-Richer, Québec 172/F3
Châteauroux, France 28/D4
Château-Salins, France 28/G3
Château-Thierry, France 28/E3
Châteaux (pt.), Guadeloupe 161/B6
Chateh, Alberta 182/A5
Châtelet, Belgium 27/F8
Châtellerault, France 28/D4
Châtel-Saint-Denis, Switzerland 39/C3
Chater, Manitoba 179/C5
Chatfield, Ark. 202/K3
Chatfield, Manitoba 179/E4
Chatfield, Minn. 255/F7
Chatfield, Ohio 284/E4
Chatham (str.), Alaska 196/M1
Chatham (sound), Br. Col. 184/B3
Chatham (isl.), Chile 138/D9
Chatham, England 13/J8
Chatham, England 10/G5
Chatham (co.), Georgia 217/K6
Chatham, Ill. 222/D4
Chatham, La. 238/F2
Chatham, Mass. 249/P6
Chatham•, Mass. 249/P6
Chatham, Mich. 250/B2
Chatham, Miss. 256/B4
Chatham, N. Br. 162/K6
Chatham, New Bruns. 170/E1
Chatham•, N.H. 268/E3
Chatham, N.J. 273/E2
Chatham, N.Y. 276/N6
Chatham (isl.), N. Zealand 100/D7
Chatham (isls.), N. Zealand 87/J10
Chatham (isls.), N. Zealand 100/D7
Chatham (co.), N.C. 281/L3
Chatham, Ontario 177/B5
Chatham, Va. 307/K7
Chatham Center, N.Y. 276/N6
Chatham Head, New Bruns. 170/E2
Chatham Port, Mass. 249/P6
Châtillon, France 28/B2
Châtillon-sur-Indre, France 28/D4
Châtillon-sur-Seine, France 28/F4
Chato, Cerro (mt.), Argentina 143/B5
Chato, Cerro (mt.), Chile 138/E4
Chatom, Ala. 195/B8
Chatou, France 28/A1
Chatrapur, India 68/F5
Chatsworth, Calif. 204/B10
Chatsworth, Georgia 217/C1
Chatsworth, Ill. 222/E3
Chatsworth, Iowa 229/A3
Chatsworth, N.J. 273/D4
Chatsworth, Ontario 177/D3
Chattahoochee (riv.) 188/K4
Chattahoochee (riv.), Ala. 195/H8
Chattahoochee, Fla. 212/B1
Chattahoochee (riv.), Fla. 212/B1
Chattahoochee (co.), Georgia 217/C6
Chattahoochee (riv.), Georgia 217/B8
Chattahoochee River Nat'l Rec. Area, Georgia 217/K1
Chattanooga, Ohio 284/A4
Chattanooga, Okla. 288/J6
Chattanooga, Tenn. 188/J3
Chattanooga, Tenn. 146/K6
Chattanooga, Tenn. 237/K10
Chattaroy, Wash. 310/H3
Chattaroy, W. Va. 312/B7
Chatteris, England 13/H5
Chattooga (riv.), Ala. 195/H2
Chattooga (co.), Georgia 217/B1
Chattooga (riv.), Georgia 217/A2
Chattooga (riv.), Georgia 217/F1
Chattooga (riv.), S.C. 296/A2
Chatuge (lake), Georgia 217/E1
Chatuge (lake), N.C. 281/B5
Chatwood, Pa. 294/L6
Chaud (lake), Québec 172/C3
Chaudière (riv.), Québec 172/G4
Chauk, Burma 72/B2
Chauk, Burma 54/L7
Chaukan (pass), Burma 72/C1
Chaumont, France 28/F3
Chaumont, N.Y. 276/H2
Chauncey, Georgia 217/F6
Chauncey, Ohio 284/F7
Chauny, France 28/E3
Chau Phu, Vietnam 72/E5
Chauques (isls.), Chile 138/D4
Chautauqua, Ill. 222/C5
Chautauqua (co.), Kansas 232/F4
Chautauqua, Kansas 232/F4
Chautauqua (co.), N.Y. 276/B6
Chautauqua, N.Y. 276/A6
Chautauqua (lake), N.Y. 276/A6
Chauvin, Alberta 182/E3
Chauvin, La. 238/J8
Chavantes, Serra dos (range), Brazil 132/D5
Chaves, Brazil 132/D3
Chaves (Santa Cruz) (isl.), Ecuador 128/C9
Chaves (co.), N. Mex. 274/E5
Chaves, Portugal 33/C2
Chavies, Ky. 237/P6
Chavornay, Switzerland 39/C3
Chayanta, Bolivia 136/B6
Chaykovskiy, U.S.S.R. 52/H3
Chazelles-sur-Lyon, France 28/F5
Chazy, N.Y. 276/N1
Chazy (lake), N.Y. 276/N1
Cheadle, Alberta 182/D4
Cheadle, England 13/E5
Cheadle and Gatley, England 13/H2
Cheadle and Gatley, England 10/G2
Cheaha (mt.), Ala. 195/G4
Cheam View, Br. Col. 184/M3
Cheap (chan.), Chile 138/D7
Cheat (lake), W. Va. 312/G3
Cheat (riv.), W. Va. 312/G3
Cheatham (co.), Tenn. 237/G8
Cheatham (dam), Tenn. 237/G8
Cheatham (lake), Tenn. 237/H8
Cheb, Czech. 41/B1
Chebanse, Ill. 222/F3
Chebeague Island, Maine 243/C8
Chebogue (harb.), Nova Scotia 168/B5
Cheboksary, U.S.S.R. 7/J3
Cheboksary, U.S.S.R. 52/G3
Cheboksary, U.S.S.R. 48/E4
Cheboygan, Mich. 188/K1
Cheboygan (co.), Mich. 250/E3
Cheboygan, Mich. 250/E3
Chech, Erg (des.), Algeria 106/D3
Chech, Erg (des.) 102/B2
Chech, Erg (des.), Mali 106/D4
Chechaouene, Morocco 106/D1
Chechen-Ingush A.S.S.R., U.S.S.R. 48/E5
Chechen-Ingush A.S.S.R., U.S.S.R. 52/G6
Chech'ŏn, S. Korea 81/D5
Check, Va. 307/H6
Checker Hall, Barbados 161/B8
Checotah, Okla. 288/R4
Chedabucto (bay), Nova Scotia 168/G3
Cheduba (isl.), Burma 72/B3
Cheektowaga, N.Y. 276/C5
Cheekye, Br. Col. 184/F5
Cheesequake, N.J. 273/E3
Cheesman (lake), Colo. 208/J4
Chefoo (Yantai), China 77/K4
Chefornak, Alaska 196/F2
Chegdomyn, U.S.S.R. 48/O4
Chegga (well), Mauritania 106/C3
Chegutu, Zimbabwe 115/F7
Chegutu, Zimbabwe 118/E3
Chehalis (lake), Br. Col. 184/L3
Chehalis, Wash. 310/C4
Chehalis (pt.), Wash. 310/A4
Chehalis (riv.), Wash. 310/B4
Chehalis Ind. Res., Wash. 310/B4
Chehar Deh, Iran 66/K4
Cheju (isl.), S. Korea 54/O6
Cheju, S. Korea 81/C7
Cheju (isl.), S. Korea 81/C7
Cheju (str.), S. Korea 81/C7
Chekiang (Zhejiang), China 77/K6
Chelan, Sask. 181/H3
Chelan (lake), Wash. 188/B1
Chelan (co.), Wash. 310/E3
Chelan, Wash. 310/E3
Chelan (dam), Wash. 310/E3
Chelan (lake), Wash. 310/E2
Chelan (range), Wash. 310/E2
Chelan Falls, Wash. 310/E3
Cheleken, U.S.S.R. 48/F6
Chelia (mt.), Algeria 106/F1
Chelif (riv.), Algeria 106/E1
Chelkar, U.S.S.R. 48/F5
Chelles, France 28/C1
Chełm (prov.), Poland 47/F3
Chełm, Poland 47/F3
Chełmno, Poland 47/D2
Chelmsford, England 13/J7
Chelmsford, England 10/G5
Chelmsford•, Mass. 249/J2
Chełmza, Poland 47/D2
Chelsea, Ala. 195/E4
Chelsea, Ind. 227/F7
Chelsea, Iowa 229/J5
Chelsea•, Maine 243/D7
Chelsea, Mass. 249/D6
Chelsea, Mich. 250/E6
Chelsea, Okla. 288/P1
Chelsea, S. Dak. 298/M3
Chelsea, Vt. 268/C4
Chelsea, Victoria 88/L8
Chelsea, Victoria 97/J6
Chelsea, Wis. 317/F5
Cheltenham, England 13/E6
Cheltenham, England 10/F5
Cheltenham, Md. 245/L6
Cheltenham•, Pa. 294/M5
Chelva, Spain 33/F3
Chelyabinsk, U.S.S.R. 2/N3
Chelyabinsk, U.S.S.R. 54/H4
Chelyabinsk, U.S.S.R. 48/G4
Chelyuskin (cape), U.S.S.R. 54/N2
Chelyuskin (cape), U.S.S.R. 4/B4
Chelyuskin (cape), U.S.S.R. 48/M2
Chemainus, Br. Col. 184/J3
Chemawa, Oreg. 291/A3
Chemba, Mozambique 118/E3
Chembur, India 68/B7
Chemehuevi Valley Ind. Res., Calif. 204/L9
Chemeketa Park-Redwood Estates, Calif. 204/K4
Chemnitz, Germany 22/E3
Chemnitz, Germany 7/E3
Chemquasabamticook (lake), Maine 243/D3
Chemult, Oreg. 291/F4
Chemung, Ill. 222/E1
Chemung (co.), N.Y. 276/G6
Chemung, N.Y. 276/G6
Chenab (riv.), India 68/C2
Chenab (riv.), Pakistan 68/C2
Chenab (riv.), Pakistan 59/K4
Chenachane, Algeria 106/D3
Chena Hot Springs, Alaska 196/J1
Chenango (co.), N.Y. 276/J6
Chenango (riv.), N.Y. 276/J6
Chenango Bridge, N.Y. 276/J6
Chenango Forks, N.Y. 276/J6
Chen Barag, China 77/J2
Chêne-Bougeries, Switzerland 39/B4
Chenequa, Wis. 317/J1
Chénéville, Québec 172/B4
Cheney, Kansas 232/E4
Cheney (res.), Kansas 232/E4
Cheney, Wash. 310/H3
Cheneyville, Ill. 222/F3
Cheneyville, La. 238/F4
Chengchow (Zhengzhou), China 77/H5
Chengde (Chengteh), China 77/J3
Chengdu (Chengtu), China 77/F5
Chengdu, China 54/M6
Chengdu, China 2/P4
Chengkou, China 77/G5
Chengteh (Chengde), China 77/J3
Chengtu (Chengdu), China 77/F5
Chenier (lake), La. 238/F2
Chenoa, Ill. 222/E3
Chenoa, Ky. 237/O7
Chenoweth, Oreg. 291/F2
Chen Xian, China 77/H6
Chepachet, R.I. 249/H5
Chepén, Peru 128/C6
Chépénéhé, New Caled. 86/H4
Chepes, Argentina 143/C3
Chépica, Chile 138/A10
Chepo, Panama 154/H6
Chepo (riv.), Panama 154/H6
Chepstow, Ontario 177/C3
Chepstow, Wales 10/E5
Chepstow, Wales 13/E6
Chequamegon (bay), Wis. 317/E2
Cher (dept.), France 28/E4
Cher (riv.), France 28/D4
Cheraw, Colo. 208/N6
Cheraw, Miss. 256/E8
Cheraw, S.C. 296/H2
Cherbourg, France 28/C3
Cherbourg, France 7/D4
Cherbourg, Queensland 95/D5
Cherchell, Algeria 106/E1
Cherchen (Qiemo), China 77/C4
Cherdyn', U.S.S.R. 52/J2
Cheremkhovo, U.S.S.R. 54/L4
Cheremkhovo, U.S.S.R. 48/L4
Cherepovets, U.S.S.R. 7/H3
Cherepovets, U.S.S.R. 52/E3
Cherepovets, U.S.S.R. 48/D4
Chergui, Chott Ech (salt lake), Algeria 106/E2
Cherhill, Alberta 182/C3
Cherial (riv.), India 68/F2
Cheriton, Va. 307/R6
Cherkassy, U.S.S.R. 7/H4
Cherkassy, U.S.S.R. 52/D5
Cherkessk, U.S.S.R. 48/E5
Cherkessk, U.S.S.R. 52/F6
Chermside, Queensland 88/K2
Chermside, Queensland 95/D2
Chernigov, U.S.S.R. 7/H3
Chernigov, U.S.S.R. 48/D4
Chernigov, U.S.S.R. 52/D4
Chernobyl', U.S.S.R. 52/D4
Chernogorsk, U.S.S.R. 48/K4
Chernorechenskiy, U.S.S.R. 52/H2
Chernovtsy, U.S.S.R. 7/G4
Chernovtsy, U.S.S.R. 52/C5
Chernovtsy, U.S.S.R. 48/C5
Chernushka, U.S.S.R. 52/J3
Chernyshevsk, U.S.S.R. 48/M4
Chernyshevskiy, U.S.S.R. 48/M3
Cherokee (co.), Ala. 195/G2
Cherokee, Ala. 195/C1
Cherokee (co.), Georgia 217/D2
Cherokee (co.), Iowa 229/B3
Cherokee, Iowa 229/B3
Cherokee (co.), Kansas 232/H4
Cherokee, Kansas 232/H4
Cherokee, Ky. 237/R4
Cherokee (co.), N.C. 281/A4
Cherokee, N.C. 281/C4
Cherokee (co.), Okla. 288/R3
Cherokee, Okla. 288/K1
Cherokee (co.), S.C. 296/D1
Cherokee (dam), Tenn. 237/P8
Cherokee (lake), Tenn. 237/P8
Cherokee (co.), Texas 303/J6
Cherokee, Texas 303/F7
Cherokee City, Ark. 202/A1
Cherokee Falls, S.C. 296/D1
Cherokee Ind. Res., N.C. 281/C3
Cherokees, Lake O' The (lake), Okla. 288/S1
Cherokee Village, Ark. 202/G1
Cherrapunji, India 68/G3
Cherry, Ariz. 198/C4
Cherry (creek), Ariz. 198/E4
Cherry (brook), Conn. 210/D1
Cherry, Ill. 222/D2
Cherry (co.), Nebr. 264/C2
Cherry, N.C. 281/R3
Cherry (creek), N. Dak. 282/D4
Cherry (creek), S. Dak. 298/F5
Cherry (creek), S. Dak. 298/F4
Cherry, Tenn. 237/B9
Cherry (creek), Utah 304/B4
Cherry (riv.), W. Va. 312/E6
Cherry Creek, Br. Col. 184/G5
Cherry Creek, Nev. 266/G3
Cherry Creek, N.Y. 276/B6
Cherry Creek, S. Dak. 298/F4
Cherryfield•, Maine 243/H6
Cherry Fork, Ohio 284/C8
Cherry Grove, Alberta 182/E2
Cherry Grove, Minn. 255/F7
Cherry Grove, Ohio 284/C10
Cherry Grove, Oreg. 291/D2
Cherry Hill, Ark. 202/B4
Cherry Hill, Md. 245/P2
Cherry Hill•, N.J. 273/B3
Cherry Lake Farms, Fla. 212/C1
Cherryland, Calif. 204/K2
Cherrylog, Georgia 217/D1
Cherry Point, Alberta 182/A1
Cherry Point Marine Air Sta., N.C. 281/R5
Cherry Run, W. Va. 312/L3
Cherry Tree, Pa. 294/E4
Cherryvale, Kansas 232/G4
Cherry Valley, Ark. 202/J3
Cherry Valley, Ill. 222/D1
Cherry Valley, Mass. 249/G3
Cherry Valley, N.Y. 276/L5
Cherry Valley, Ontario 177/G4
Cherry Valley, Pa. 294/C3
Cherryville, Br. Col. 184/H5
Cherryville, Mo. 261/K7
Cherryville, N.C. 281/G4
Cherryville, Oreg. 291/E2
Cherskiy, U.S.S.R. 54/T3
Cherskiy, U.S.S.R. 4/C1
Cherskiy (range), U.S.S.R. 54/R3
Cherskiy, U.S.S.R. 48/Q3
Cherskiy (range), U.S.S.R. 48/P3
Cherta, Spain 33/G2
Chertsey, England 13/G8
Chertsey, England 10/B6
Chervonograd, U.S.S.R. 52/B4
Chesaning, Mich. 250/E5
Chesapeake (bay) 188/L3
Chesapeake (bay), Md. 245/N7
Chesapeake, Ohio 284/E9
Chesapeake (bay), U.S. 146/L6
Chesapeake (I.C.), Va. 307/R7
Chesapeake (bay), Va. 307/R5
Chesapeake, W. Va. 312/C6
Chesapeake and Delaware (canal), Del. 245/R2
Chesapeake and Delaware (canal), Md. 245/R2
Chesapeake and Ohio Canal Nat'l Hist. Park, Md. 245/J4
Chesapeake and Ohio Canal Nat'l Mon., Va. 307/O2
Chesapeake and Ohio Canal Nat'l Hist. Park, W. Va. 312/J3
Chesapeake Beach, Md. 245/N6
Chesapeake City, Md. 245/P2
Chesaw, Wash. 310/G2
Chésery, Pointe de (mt.), Switzerland 39/C4
Chesham, England 10/F5
Chesham, England 13/G7
Chesham, N.H. 268/C6
Cheshire, Conn. 210/D2
Cheshire•, Conn. 210/D2
Cheshire (co.), England 13/E4
Cheshire•, Mass. 249/B2
Cheshire (res.), Mass. 249/A2
Cheshire (co.), N.H. 268/C6
Cheshire, Ohio 284/F8
Cheshire, Oreg. 291/D3
Cheshskaya (bay), U.S.S.R. 7/J2
Cheshskaya (bay), U.S.S.R. 52/G1
Cheshunt, England 13/H7
Cheshunt, England 10/B5
Chesilhurst, N.J. 273/D4
Cheslatta, Br. Col. 184/E3
Chesley, Ontario 177/C3
Chesnaye, Manitoba 179/K2
Chesnee, S.C. 296/D1
Chester, Ark. 202/B2
Chester, Calif. 204/D3
Chester, Conn. 210/F3
Chester•, Conn. 210/F3
Chester, England 10/F2
Chester, England 13/G2
Chester, Georgia 217/F6
Chester, Idaho 220/G5
Chester, Ill. 222/D6
Chester, Ind. 227/H5
Chester, Iowa 229/J2
Chester•, Maine 243/F5
Chester, Md. 245/N5
Chester (riv.), Md. 245/O4
Chester•, Mass. 249/C3
Chester, Minn. 255/F6
Chester, Miss. 256/F4
Chester, Mont. 262/E2
Chester, Nebr. 264/G4
Chester•, N.H. 268/E6
Chester, N.J. 273/D2
Chester, N.Y. 276/M8
Chester, Nova Scotia 168/D4
Chester, Ohio 284/G7
Chester, Okla. 288/J2
Chester (co.), Pa. 294/L6
Chester, Pa. 294/L7
Chester (creek), Pa. 294/L7
Chester (co.), S.C. 296/E2
Chester, S.C. 296/E2
Chester, S. Dak. 298/R6
Chester (co.), Tenn. 237/D10
Chester, Texas 303/K7
Chester, Utah 304/C4
Chester•, Vt. 268/B5
Chester, Va. 307/O6
Chester, W. Va. 312/E1
Chester Basin, Nova Scotia 168/D4
Chester-Chester Depot, Vt. 268/B5
Chesterfield, Conn. 210/G3
Chesterfield, England 13/J2
Chesterfield, England 10/F4
Chesterfield, Idaho 220/G7
Chesterfield (res.), Idaho 220/F7
Chesterfield, Ill. 222/D4
Chesterfield, Ind. 227/F4
Chesterfield (isl.), Madagascar 118/G3
Chesterfield•, Mass. 249/C3
Chesterfield, Mo. 261/N2
Chesterfield (isls.), New Caled. 87/F7
Chesterfield•, N.H. 268/C6
Chesterfield•, N.J. 273/D3
Chesterfield (inlet), N.W.T. 146/J3
Chesterfield (inlet), N.W.T. 162/G2
Chesterfield (inlet), N.W. Terr. 187/J3
Chesterfield (co.), S.C. 296/G2
Chesterfield, S.C. 296/G2
Chesterfield, Tenn. 237/E9
Chesterfield (co.), Va. 307/N6
Chesterfield, Va. 307/N6
Chesterfield Inlet, N.W.T. 162/G3
Chesterfield Inlet, N.W. Terr. 187/K3
Chester Gap, Va. 307/M3
Chester Heights, Pa. 294/L7
Chesterhill, Ohio 284/G6
Chester Hill, Pa. 294/F4
Chesterland, Ohio 284/H2
Chester-le-Street, England 10/E3
Chester-le-Street, England 13/J3
Chester Morse (lake), Wash. 310/D3
Chesterton, Ind. 227/D1
Chestertown, Md. 245/O4
Chestertown, N.Y. 276/N3
Chesterville, Ill. 222/E4
Chesterville, Maine 243/C6
Chesterville•, Maine 243/C6
Chesterville, Md. 245/P3
Chesterville, Ohio 284/E5
Chesterville, Ontario 177/J2
Chesterville, Québec 172/F4
Chestnut, Ala. 195/D7
Chestnut, Ill. 222/D3
Chestnut, La. 238/D2
Chestnut Hill, Conn. 210/G2
Chestnut Mound, Tenn. 237/K8
Chest Springs, Pa. 294/E4
Chesuncook, Maine 243/D3
Chesuncook (lake), Maine 243/E3
Cheswick, Pa. 294/C4
Cheswold, Del. 245/R4
Chetac (lake), Wis. 317/D4
Chetco (riv.), Oreg. 291/C5
Chetek, Wis. 317/C5
Chéticamp, Nova Scotia 168/G2
Chéticamp (isl.), Nova Scotia 168/G2
Chetlat (isl.), India 68/C6
Chetopa, Kansas 232/G4
Chetumal, Mexico 150/Q7
Chetumal (bay), Mexico 150/P8
Chetwynd, Br. Col. 184/G2
Chevak, Alaska 196/E2
Cheval Blanc (pt.), Haiti 158/B5
Chevelon (creek), Ariz. 198/E4
Cheverly, Md. 245/G4
Cheville (pass), Switzerland 39/D4
Cheviot (hills), England 13/E2
Cheviot, The (mt.), England 13/E2
Cheviot, N. Zealand 100/D5
Cheviot, Ohio 284/B9
Cheviot (hills), Scotland 15/F5
Cheviot, The (mt.), Scotland 15/F5
Chevrolet, Ky. 237/P7
Chevy Chase, Md. 245/E4
Chevy Chase Section Four, Md. 245/E4
Chewuch (riv.), Wash. 310/E2
Chewalla, Tenn. 237/D10
Chewelah, Wash. 310/H2
Chewsville, Md. 245/H2
Chexbres, Switzerland 39/C3
Cheyenne (riv.) 188/F2
Cheyenne (co.), Colo. 208/O5
Cheyenne (co.), Kansas 232/A2
Cheyenne (co.), Nebr. 264/A3
Cheyenne, Okla. 288/G3
Cheyenne (riv.), S. Dak. 298/F4
Cheyenne (riv.), U.S. 146/H5
Cheyenne (cap.), Wyo. 146/H5
Cheyenne (cap.), Wyo. 188/E2
Cheyenne (cap.), Wyo. 319/H4
Cheyenne (riv.), Wyo. 319/H2
Cheyenne Bottoms (lake), Kansas 232/D3
Cheyenne River Ind. Res., S. Dak. 298/F4
Cheyenne Wells, Colo. 208/P5
Cheyne (bay), W. Australia 92/B6
Cheyney, Pa. 294/M6
Cheyres, Switzerland 39/C3
Chezacut, Br. Col. 184/F4
Chhatarpur, India 68/D4
Chhindwara, India 68/D4
Chi, Mae Nam (riv.), Thailand 72/D3
Chiai, China 77/K7
Chiambone, Somalia 115/H4
Chiang Dao, Thailand 72/C3
Chiange, Angola 115/B7
Chiang Khan, Thailand 72/D3
Chiang Mai, Thailand 72/C3
Chiang Mai, Thailand 54/L8
Chiang Rai, Thailand 72/C3
Chiang Saen, Thailand 72/C2
Chiapa de Corzo, Mexico 150/N8
Chiapas (state), Mexico 150/N8
Chiari, Italy 34/C2
Chiasso, Switzerland 39/G5
Chiatura, U.S.S.R. 52/F6
Chiautempan, Mexico 150/N1
Chiavari, Italy 34/B2
Chiba (pref.), Japan 81/P2
Chiba, Japan 81/P2
Chibabava, Mozambique 118/E4
Chibia, Angola 115/B7
Chiblow (lake), Ontario 177/A1
Chibougamau, Québec 174/C3
Chibougamau, Que. 162/J6
Chibukak (cape), Alaska 196/D2
Chibuto, Mozambique 118/E4
Chibwe, Zambia 115/E6
Chicago, Ill. 146/K5
Chicago, Ill. 188/J2
Chicago, Ill. 222/C5
Chicago, North Branch (riv.), Ill. 222/B5
Chicago, U.S. 2/E3
Chicago Heights, Ill. 222/C6
Chicago Portage Nat'l Hist. Site, Ill. 222/B6
Chicago Ridge, Ill. 222/B6
Chicama, Peru 128/C6
Chicamacomico (riv.), Md. 245/P7
Chicamocha (riv.), Colombia 126/D4
Chicanán (riv.), Venezuela 124/H4
Chicapa (riv.), Angola 115/D5
Chicapa (riv.), Zaire 115/D5
Chic-Chocs (mts.), Québec 172/C1
Chichagof (isl.) Alaska 188/D6
Chichagof (isl.), Alaska 196/M1
Chichén-Itzá (ruin), Mexico 150/P6
Chichester, England 13/G7
Chichester, England 10/F5
Chichester•, N.H. 268/E5
Chichester, N.Y. 276/M6
Chichi (isl.), Japan 87/E3
Chichi (isl.), Japan 81/M3
Chichibu, Japan 81/J5
Chichibu-Tama National Park, Japan 81/J6
Chichicaste, Honduras 154/E3
Chichicastenango, Guatemala 154/B3
Chichigalpa, Nicaragua 154/D4
Chichiriviche, Venezuela 124/D2
Chickalah, Ark. 202/D3
Chickaloon, Alaska 196/C1
Chickamauga, Georgia 217/B1
Chickamauga (dam), Tenn. 237/L10
Chickamauga (lake), Tenn. 188/J3
Chickamauga (lake), Tenn. 237/L10
Chickamauga and Chattanooga Nat'l Mil. Park, Georgia 217/B1
Chickamaw Beach, Minn. 255/D4
Chickasaw, Ala. 195/B9
Chickasaw (co.), Iowa 229/J2
Chickasaw (co.), Miss. 256/G3
Chickasaw, Ohio 284/A5
Chickasawhay (riv.), Miss. 256/G7
Chickasaw Village, Natchez Trace Pkwy., Miss. 256/G2
Chickasha, Okla. 188/G4

Chickasha, Okla. 288/L4
Chickasha (lake), Okla. 288/K4
Chicken, Alaska 196/K2
Chiclana de la Frontera, Spain 33/C4
Chiclayo, Peru 128/C6
Chiclayo, Peru 120/B3
Chico (riv.), Argentina 120/C7
Chico (riv.), Argentina 143/C6
Chico (riv.), Argentina 143/C5
Chico, Calif. 204/D4
Chico, Mont. 262/F5
Chico (riv.), Philippines 82/C2
Chico, Texas 303/G4
Chicoana, Argentina 143/C2
Chico Arroyo (creek), N. Mex. 274/B3
Chicopee, Kansas 232/H4
Chicopee, Mass. 249/D4
Chicopee (riv.), Mass. 249/D4
Chicora, Miss. 256/G7
Chicora, Pa. 294/C4
Chicot (co.), Ark. 202/H7
Chicot, Ark. 202/H7
Chicot (pt.), La. 238/M7
Chicoutimi, Que. 162/J6
Chicoutimi, Que. 146/L5
Chicoutimi (county), Québec 174/C2
Chicoutimi (co.), Québec 172/G1
Chicoutimi, Québec 172/G1
Chicoutimi, Québec 174/C3
Chicoutimi (riv.), Québec 172/F2
Chicoutimi-Nord, Québec 172/F1
Chicualacuala, Mozambique 118/E4
Chidambaram, India 68/E6
Chidley (cape), Canada 146/M3
Chidley (cape), Newf. 166/B1
Chidley (cape), Newf. 162/K3
Chidley (cape), N.W. Terr. 187/M3
Chidlow, W. Australia 88/B2
Chief Joseph (dam), Wash. 310/F3
Chiefland, Fla. 212/D2
Chiefs (riv.), Ontario 177/C3
Chiemsee (lake), Germany 22/E5
Chienti (riv.), Italy 34/D3
Chieri, Italy 34/A2
Chieti, Italy 34/E3
Chieti, Italy 34/E3
Chietla, Mexico 150/M2
Chièvres, Belgium 27/D7
Chifeng, China 77/J3
Chigasaki, Japan 81/O3
Chiginagak (mt.), Alaska 196/G3
Chignahuapan, Mexico 150/N1
Chignecto (bay), New Bruns. 170/F3
Chignecto (bay), Nova Scotia 168/D3
Chignecto (cape), Nova Scotia 168/D3
Chignecto (isth.), Nova Scotia 168/D3
Chignik, Alaska 196/G3
Chignik (bay), Alaska 196/G3
Chignik Lagoon, Alaska 196/G3
Chignik Lake, Alaska 196/G3
Chiguana, Bolivia 136/A7
Chigubo, Mozambique 118/E4
Chigwell, England 13/H8
Chigwell, England 10/C5
Chihuahua (state), Mexico 150/F2
Chihuahua, Mexico 150/F2
Chihuahua, Mexico 146/H7
Chikaskia (riv.), Kansas 232/E4
Chik Ballapur, India 68/D6
Chikmagalur, India 68/E6
Chilanga, Zambia 115/E7
Chilanko Forks, Br. Col. 184/E4
Chilapa de Alvarez, Mexico 150/K8
Chilas, Pakistan 68/C1
Chilas, Pakistan 59/K2
Chilca (Pucusana), Peru 128/D9
Chilcoot, Calif. 204/E4
Chilcotin (riv.), Br. Col. 184/E4
Childers, Queensland 88/J5
Childersburg, Ala. 195/F4
Childress (co.), Texas 303/D3
Childress, Texas 303/D3
Childs (lake), Manitoba 179/J4
Childs, Md. 245/P2
Childwold, N.Y. 276/L2
Chile 2/F7
Chile 120/B5
CHILE 138
Chile Chico, Chile 138/E6
Chilecito, Argentina 143/C2
Chiles, Colombia 126/A7
Chilete, Peru 128/C6
Chilga, Ethiopia 111/G5
Chilhowee, Mo. 261/E3
Chilhowee (mt.), Tenn. 237/O9
Chilhowie, Va. 307/E7
Chili, Ind. 227/E4
Chili, Wis. 317/F6
Chililabombwe, Zambia 115/E6
Chililabombwe, Zambia 102/E6
Chilili, N. Mex. 274/C4
Chilka (lake), India 68/F5
Chilko (lake), Br. Col. 184/F4
Chilko (riv.), Br. Col. 184/E4
Chilkoot (pass), Alaska 196/M1
Chilkoot (pass), Br. Col. 184/J1
Chillán, Chile 120/B6
Chillán, Chile 138/A11
Chillicothe, Ill. 222/D3
Chillicothe, Iowa 229/J6
Chillicothe, Mo. 261/E3
Chillicothe, Ohio 284/E7
Chillicothe, Texas 303/E3
Chilliwack, Br. Col. 162/D6
Chilliwack, Br. Col. 184/M3
Chillum, Md. 245/F4
Chilmark, Mass. 249/M7
Chilo, Ohio 284/B8
Chilocco, Okla. 288/M1
Chiloé (isl.), Chile 120/B7
Chiloé (isl.), Chile 138/D4
Chiloquin, Oreg. 291/F5
Chilpancingo de los Bravos, Mexico 150/K8
Chiltern (hills), England 13/G6
Chilton (co.), Ala. 195/E5
Chilton, Texas 303/G6
Chilton, Wis. 317/K7

Chiltonville, Mass. 249/M5
Chilumba, Malawi 115/F6
Chilwa (lake), Malawi 115/G7
Chilwa (lake), Mozambique 118/F3
Chimacum, Wash. 310/C3
Chimaltenango, Guatemala 154/B3
Chimán, Panama 154/H6
Chimanimani, Zimbabwe 118/E3
Chimantá-tepuí (mt.), Venezuela 124/G5
Chimay, Belgium 27/E8
Chimayo, N. Mex. 274/D3
Chimbarongo, Chile 138/A10
Chimbay, U.S.S.R. 48/F5
Chimborazo (prov.), Ecuador 128/C3
Chimborazo (mt.), Ecuador 120/B3
Chimborazo (mt.), Ecuador 128/C3
Chimbote, Peru 120/B3
Chimbote, Peru 128/C7
Chimbote (bay), Peru 128/C7
Chimichagua, Colombia 126/D3
Chimkent, U.S.S.R. 54/H5
Chimkent, U.S.S.R. 48/H5
Chimney Point, Vt. 268/A3
Chimney Rock, Colo. 208/E8
Chimney Rock Nat'l Hist. Site, Nebr. 264/A3
Chimoio, Mozambique 118/E3
Chimoio, Mozambique 102/F6
Chin, Alberta 182/D5
Chin (state), Burma 72/B2
Chin (hills), Burma 72/B2
Chin (cape), Ontario 177/C2
China 2/P4
China 54/L6
CHINA 77
CHINA 85
China, Maine 243/E7
China•, Maine 243/E7
Chiná, Campeche, Mexico 150/O7
Chiná, Nuevo León, Mexico 150/K4
Chinácota, Colombia 126/D4
China Gardens (dam), Wash. 310/J4
China Grove, Ala. 195/G7
China Grove, N.C. 281/H3
China Grove, Texas 303/K11
China Lake, Calif. 204/H8
China Lake Naval Weapons Center, Calif. 204/H8
Chinameca, El Salvador 154/C4
Chinandega, Nicaragua 154/D4
Chinati (mts.), Texas 303/C12
Chinati (peak), Texas 303/C12
Chincha (isls.), Peru 128/D9
Chincha Alta, Peru 128/D9
Chincha Alta, Peru 120/B4
Chinchaga (riv.), Alberta 182/A5
Chinchilla, Pa. 294/F6
Chinchilla, Queensland 88/J5
Chinchilla de Monte-Aragón, Spain 33/F3
Chinchiná, Colombia 126/C5
Chinchón, Spain 33/G5
Chinchoua, Gabon 115/A4
Chinchow (Jinzhou), China 77/K3
Chincoteague (bay), Md. 245/S8
Chincoteague, Va. 307/T4
Chincoteague (bay), Va. 307/T4
Chincoteague (inlet), Va. 307/T5
Chinde, Mozambique 118/F3
Chinde, Mozambique 102/F6
Chindu, China 77/E5
Chindwin (riv.) Burma 72/B2
Chinese Camp, Calif. 204/E6
Chingleput, India 68/E6
Chingola, Zambia 115/E6
Chingola, Zambia 102/E6
Chinguar, Angola 115/C6
Chinguetti, Mauritania 106/B4
Chinhae, S. Korea 81/D6
Chiniak (cape) Alaska 196/H3
Chinhoyi, Zimbabwe 115/F7
Chinhoyi, Zimbabwe 118/D3
Chiñijo, Bolivia 136/A4
Chiniot, Pakistan 68/C2
Chínipas, Mexico 150/E3
Chinju, S. Korea 81/D6
Chinkapin Knob (mt.), Ark. 202/C4
Chinkiang (Zhenjiang), China 77/J5
Chinle, Ariz. 198/F2
Chinle (creek), Ariz. 198/F2
Chinle (valley), Ariz. 198/F2
Chinle (creek), Utah 304/E6
Chinle Wash (dry riv.), Ariz. 198/F2
Chino (valley), Ariz. 198/C3
Chino, Calif. 204/D10
Chinon, France 28/C4
Chinook, Alberta 182/E4
Chinook, Mont. 262/G2
Chinook (lake) Oreg. 291/F3
Chinook, Wash. 310/B4
Chinook (pass), Wash. 310/D4
Chinook Valley, Alberta 182/B1
Chino Valley, Ariz. 198/C4
Chinquapin, N.C. 281/O5
Chinsali, Zambia 115/F6
Chinsi (Jinxi), China 77/K3
Chintheche, Malawi 115/F6
Chinú, Colombia 126/C3
Chinwangtao (Qinhuangdao), China 77/K4
Chiny, Belgium 27/G9
Chioggia, Italy 34/D2
Chip (lake), Alberta 182/C3
Chipamanu (riv.), Bolivia 136/A2
Chipata, Zambia 115/F6
Chipata, Zambia 102/F6
Chipewyan (lake), Alberta 182/D1
Chipewyan (riv.), Alberta 182/D1
Chipewyan Lake, Alberta 182/D1
Chipindo, Angola 102/D6
Chipinge, Zimbabwe 118/E4
Chipley, Fla. 212/D6
Chiplun, India 68/C5
Chipman, Alberta 182/D3
Chipman, New Bruns. 170/E2
Chipman (riv.), Sask. 181/M2

Chipoka, Malawi 115/F6
Chipola (riv.), Fla. 212/D6
Chipola, La. 238/J5
Chippenham, England 13/E6
Chippenham, England 10/F5
Chippewa (co.), Mich. 250/E2
Chippewa (riv.), Mich. 250/E2
Chippewa (co.), Minn. 255/C5
Chippewa (riv.), Minn. 255/C5
Chippewa (riv.), Wis. 188/H1
Chippewa (riv.), Wis. 317/D5
Chippewa (lake), Mich. 250/D5
Chippewa (lake), Wis. 317/D4
Chippewa Falls, Wis. 317/D6
Chipping Norton, England 13/F6
Chippis, Switzerland 39/E4
Chiputneticook (lakes), Maine 243/H4
Chiputneticook (lakes), New Bruns. 170/C3
Chiquián, Peru 128/D8
Chiquimula, Guatemala 154/C3
Chiquinquirá, Colombia 126/C5
Chiquita (lake), Argentina 120/C6
Chira (riv.), Ecuador 128/B5
Chira (riv.) 120/A3
Chirala, India 68/E5
Chirchik, U.S.S.R. 48/H5
Chireno, Texas 303/K6
Chirfa, Niger 106/G4
Chiri (mt.), S. Korea 81/C6
Chiribiquete, Sierra de (mts.), Colombia 126/D7
Chiricahua (mts.), Ariz. 198/F6
Chiricahua Nat'l Mon., Ariz. 198/F6
Chiriguaná, Colombia 126/D3
Chirikof (isl.), Alaska 196/G3
Chirinos, Peru 128/C5
Chiriquí (gulf), Panama 154/F7
Chiriquí (lag.), Panama 154/G6
Chiriquí Grande, Panama 154/F6
Chirk, Wales 13/D5
Chirnside, Scotland 15/F5
Chiromo, Malawi 115/F7
Chironico, Switzerland 39/G4
Chirpan, Bulgaria 45/G4
Chirripó Grande (mt.), C. Rica 154/F6
Chirundu, Zimbabwe 118/D3
Chisago (co.), Minn. 255/F5
Chisago City, Minn. 255/E6
Chisamba, Zambia 115/E6
Chisana, Alaska 196/K2
Chisasibi, Québec 162/J5
Chisasibi, Québec 174/B2
Chisec, Guatemala 154/B3
Chisholm, Maine 243/C7
Chisholm, Minn. 255/E3
Chisholm Mills, Alberta 182/C2
Chishui, China 77/G6
Chisimayu, Somalia 115/H4
Chisimayu, Somalia 102/G5
Chişineu Criş, Romania 45/E2
Chisismville, Ark. 202/C3
Chisos (mts.), Texas 303/A8
Chistochina, Alaska 196/K2
Chistopol', U.S.S.R. 52/H3
Chiswick, Ontario 177/E1
Chita, U.S.S.R. 54/N4
Chita, U.S.S.R. 48/N4
Chitado, Angola 115/B7
Chitado, Namibia 118/A3
Chitato, Angola 114/D3
Chitek (lake), Manitoba 179/G2
Chitek (lake), Sask. 181/D2
Chitek Lake, Sask. 181/D2
Chitembo, Angola 115/C6
Chitina, Alaska 196/K2
Chitina (riv.), Alaska 196/K2
Chitipa, Malawi 115/F5
Chitorgarh, India 68/C4
Chitose, Japan 81/K2
Chitradurga, India 68/D6
Chitral, Pakistan 59/K2
Chitral, Pakistan 68/C1
Chitré, Panama 154/G7
Chittagong, Bangladesh 54/L7
Chittagong, Bangladesh 68/G4
Chittenango, N.Y. 276/J4
Chittenden (co.), Vt. 268/A3
Chittenden•, Vt. 268/B4
Chittenden (res.), Vt. 268/B4
Chittering, W. Australia 88/B6
Chittoor, India 68/D6
Chiume (riv.), Angola 115/D6
Chiva, Spain 33/F3
Chivacoa, Venezuela 124/D2
Chivapure (riv.), Venezuela 124/E4
Chivasso, Italy 34/A2
Chivato (mesa), N. Mex. 274/B3
Chivay, Peru 128/G10
Chive, Bolivia 136/A3
Chivho, Zimbabwe 118/E3
Chivilcoy, Argentina 143/F7
Chivilcoy, Argentina 120/C6
Chivington, Colo. 208/O6
Chiwawa (riv.), Wash. 310/E2
Chixoy (riv.), Guatemala 154/B2
Chizha, U.S.S.R. 52/F1
Chloe, W. Va. 312/D5
Chloride, Ariz. 198/A3
Chloride, Mo. 261/L8
Chlumec, Czech. 41/C1
Choam Khsant, Cambodia 72/E4
Choapa, Chile 138/A9
Choapa (riv.), Chile 138/A9
Choate, Br. Col. 184/M3
Chobe (riv.), Botswana 118/C3
Chobe (riv.), Namibia 118/C3
Chobe Nat'l Park, Botswana 118/D3
Choc, St. Lucia 161/G5
Choc (bay), St. Lucia 161/G5
Chocalán, Chile 138/A10
Chocaya, Bolivia 136/B7
Choccolocco, Ala. 195/G3
Chocen, Czech. 41/D1
Choch'iwŏn, S. Korea 81/C5
Chocó (dept.), Colombia 126/B4

Chocó (bay), Colombia 126/B6
Chocolate (mts.), Ariz. 198/A5
Chocolate (mts.), Calif. 204/K10
Chocomán, Mexico 150/P2
Choconut, Pa. 294/K2
Chocorua, N.H. 268/E4
Chocorua (riv.), N.H. 268/E4
Chocowinity, N.C. 281/P4
Choctaw (co.), Ala. 195/B6
Choctaw, Ala. 195/B6
Choctaw, Ark. 202/F2
Choctaw (co.), Miss. 256/F4
Choctaw (co.), Okla. 288/P6
Choctaw, Okla. 288/M3
Choctaw Bluff, Ala. 195/C8
Choctawhatchee (riv.), Ala. 195/H8
Choctawhatchee (bay), Fla. 212/C6
Choctawhatchee (riv.), Fla. 212/C6
Choctaw Ind. Res., Miss. 256/F6
Chodov, Czech. 41/B1
Chodzież, Poland 47/C2
Choele-Choel, Argentina 143/C4
Choele-Choel, Argentina 120/C6
Choestoe, Georgia 217/E1
Chofu, Japan 81/O2
Choiceland, Sask. 181/G2
Choiseul (sound), Falkland Is. 143/E7
Choiseul, St. Lucia 161/F2
Choiseul (isl.), Solomon Is. 87/F6
Choiseul (isl.), Solomon Is. 86/D2
Choisy-le-Roi, France 28/B2
Choix, Mexico 150/E3
Chojna, Poland 47/B2
Chojnice, Poland 47/C2
Chojnów, Poland 47/B3
Chokai (mt.), Japan 81/J4
Chokio, Minn. 255/B5
Chokoloskee, Fla. 212/E6
Chokurdakh, U.S.S.R. 4/B2
Chokurdakh, U.S.S.R. 54/R2
Chokurdakh, U.S.S.R. 48/P2
Cholame, Calif. 204/E8
Cholet, France 28/C4
Choloma, Honduras 154/C3
Cholula de Rivadavia, Mexico 150/M1
Choluteca, Honduras 154/D4
Choluteca (riv.), Honduras 154/D4
Choma, Zambia 115/E7
Choma, Zambia 102/E6
Chomes, C. Rica 154/E5
Chomo Lhari (mt.), Bhutan 68/F3
Chomutov, Czech. 41/B1
Ch'ŏnan, S. Korea 81/C5
Chon Buri, Thailand 72/D4
Chonchi, Chile 138/D4
Chone, Ecuador 128/B3
Ch'ŏnch'ŏn, N. Korea 81/C3
Ch'ŏngjin, N. Korea 54/P5
Ch'ŏngjin, N. Korea 81/E2
Chŏngju, N. Korea 81/B4
Ch'ŏngju, S. Korea 81/C5
Chongqing (Chungking), China 77/G6
Chongqing, China 2/P4
Chongqing, China 54/M7
Ch'ŏngŭp, S. Korea 81/C6
Chongyang, China 77/H6
Chongzuo, China 77/G7
Chŏnju, S. Korea 81/C6
Chon May, Vung (bay), Vietnam 72/F3
Chonos (arch.), Chile 120/B7
Chonos (arch.), Chile 138/D6
Chopin, La. 238/E4
Chopin (lake), Québec 172/B2
Choptank (riv.), Del. 245/P5
Choptank, Md. 245/P6
Choptank (riv.), Md. 245/O6
Choquecota, Bolivia 136/A6
Chorley, England 10/G2
Chorley, England 13/G2
Chorleywood, England 13/G7
Chorleywood, England 10/A5
Choroní, Venezuela 124/E2
Choros (cape), Chile 138/A7
Choros, Los (riv.), Chile 138/A7
Chortitz, Sask. 181/D5
Chortkov, U.S.S.R. 52/B5
Ch'ŏrwŏn, S. Korea 81/C4
Chorzele, Poland 47/E2
Chorzów, Poland 47/B4
Ch'osan, N. Korea 81/C3
Choshi, Japan 81/K6
Chosica, Peru 128/D8
Chos-Malal, Argentina 143/C4
Choszczno, Poland 47/B2
Chota, Peru 128/C6
Choteau (creek), S. Dak. 298/N7
Choteau, Mont. 262/D3
Chotĕboř, Czech. 41/C2
Choudrant, La. 238/F1
Chouteau (co.), Mont. 262/F3
Chouteau, Okla. 288/N2
Chovoreca, Cerro (mt.), Bolivia 136/F6
Chovoreca (mt.), Paraguay 144/C1
Chowan (co.), N.C. 281/R2
Chowan (riv.), N.C. 281/R2
Chowchilla, Calif. 204/E6
Chowchilla (riv.), Wash. 310/E2
Choybalsan, Mongolia 54/N5
Choybalsan, Mongolia 77/J2
Chrastava, Czech. 41/C1
Chriesman, Texas 303/H7
Chrisman, Ill. 222/F4
Chrisney, Ind. 227/C8
Christchurch, England 10/F5
Christchurch, England 13/F7
Christchurch, N. Zealand 2/T8
Christchurch, N. Zealand 100/D5
Christian (sound), Alaska 196/M2
Christian (co.), Ill. 222/D4
Christian (co.), Ky. 237/B7
Christian (co.), Mo. 261/F9
Christian (cape), N.W. Terr. 187/M2
Christian (isl.), Ontario 177/D3
Christian, W. Va. 312/C7
Christiana, Jamaica 158/H6
Christiana, Pa. 294/K6
Christiana, S. Africa 118/D5
Christiana, Tenn. 237/J9

Church Point, La. 238/F6
Church Point, Nova Scotia 168/B4
Church's Ferry, N. Dak. 282/M3
Church Stretton, England 13/E5
Churchton, Md. 245/N5
Churchtown, Pa. 294/L5
Churchville, Md. 245/N2
Churchville, N.Y. 276/E4
Churchville, Va. 307/K4
Churchville, W. Va. 312/E4
Churdan, Iowa 229/D4
Churfirsten (mts.), Switzerland 39/H2
Churín, Peru 128/D8
Churu, India 68/D3
Churubusco, Ind. 227/G2
Churubusco, N.Y. 276/N1
Churuguara, Venezuela 124/D2
Churwalden, Switzerland 39/J3
Chushul, India 68/D2
Chuska (mts.), N. Mex. 274/A2
Chusovoy, U.S.S.R. 52/J3
Chute-à-Blondeau, Ontario 177/K2
Chute-aux-Outardes, Québec 172/A1
Chute-des-Passes, Québec 174/B3
Chute-Saint-Philippe, Québec 172/B3
Chuvash A.S.S.R., U.S.S.R. 48/E4
Chuvash A.S.S.R., U.S.S.R. 52/G3
Chu Xian, China 77/J5
Chuxiong, China 77/F7
Chuy, Uruguay 145/F4
Chvalšiny, Czech. 41/C2
Chwang, China 77/J7
Chyston, Scotland 15/C2
Ciales, P. Rico 161/C1
Ciamis, Indonesia 85/H2
Ciampino, Italy 34/F7
Cianjur, Indonesia 85/H2
Cianorte, Brazil 143/A5
Cibola (co.), N. Mex. 274/B3
Cibola, Texas 303/K10
Cibolo (creek), Texas 303/K11
Çiçekdağı, Turkey 63/F3
Cícero, Ill. 222/B5
Cicero, Ill. 222/B5
Cicero, Ind. 227/E4
Cícero Dantas, Brazil 132/G5
Cicerone, W. Va. 312/D5
Ciconsine (lake), Québec 172/D2
Cid, N.C. 281/J3
Cide, Turkey 63/E2
Cidlina (riv.), Czech. 41/C1
Cidra, Cuba 158/D1
Cidra, P. Rico 161/D2
Ciechanów (prov.), Poland 47/E2
Ciechanów, Poland 47/E2
Ciechocinek, Poland 47/D2
Ciego de Ávila (prov.), Cuba 158/F2
Ciego deÁvila, Cuba 156/F2
Ciego de Ávila, Cuba 158/F2
Ciempozuelos, Spain 33/F5
Ciénaga, Colombia 120/B1
Ciénaga, Colombia 126/C2
Ciénaga de Oro, Colombia 126/C3
Cienfuegos (prov.), Cuba 158/C2
Cienfuegos, Cuba 156/D2
Cienfuegos, Cuba 156/K7
Cienfuegos, Cuba 158/D2
Cienfuegos (bay), Cuba 158/D2
Cieplice Śląskie-Zdrój, Poland 47/B3
Cierny Balog, Czech. 41/E2
Cieszyn, Poland 47/D4
Cieza, Spain 33/F3
Çifteler, Turkey 63/D3
Cifuentes, Spain 33/E2
Cigánd, Hungary 41/F2
Cihanbeyli, Turkey 63/E3
Cihuatlán, Mexico 150/G7
Cijara (res.), Spain 33/D3
Cijulang, Indonesia 85/H2
Cilacap, Indonesia 85/H2
Çıldır, Turkey 63/K2
Çıldır (lake), Turkey 63/K2
Cilleros, Spain 33/C2
Cilo Daği (mt.), Turkey 63/K4
Cima, Calif. 204/K8
Cimahi, Indonesia 85/H2
Cimarron (riv.), N. Mex. 274/D2
Cimarron, Colo. 208/D6
Cimarron, Kansas 232/B4
Cimarron (riv.), Kansas 232/B4
Cimarron, N. Mex. 274/E2
Cimarron (riv.), N. Mex. 274/E2
Cimarron (co.), Okla. 288/A1
Cimarron, Okla. 288/L3
Cimarron (riv.), Okla. 288/N2
Cimin, Turkey 63/H3
Cimone (mt.), Italy 34/C2
Cîmpeni, Romania 45/F2
Cîmpia Turzii, Romania 45/F2
Cîmpina, Romania 45/H3
Cîmpulung, Romania 45/G3
Cîmpulung Moldovenesc, Romania 45/G2
Cinaruco (riv.), Colombia 126/F4
Cinaruco (riv.), Venezuela 124/D4
Cinca (riv.), Spain 33/G2
Cincinnati, Ark. 202/B1
Cincinnati, Iowa 229/G7
Cincinnati, Ohio 146/K6
Cincinnati, Ohio 284/B9
Cincinnati, Ohio 188/K3
Cincinnatus, N.Y. 276/H5
Cinclare, La. 238/J2
Cinco, W. Va. 312/D6
Cinco Balas (cays), Cuba 158/E3
Cinco Bayou, Fla. 212/B6
Cinco Saltos, Argentina 143/C4
Cinderella, W. Va. 312/B7
Cinderford, England 13/E6
Cine, Turkey 63/B4
Cinebar, Wash. 310/C4
Cinnaminson•, N.J. 273/B3
Cintalapa de Figueroa, Mexico 150/N8
Cinto (mt.), France 28/B6
Cipolletti, Argentina 143/C4
Circeo (cape), Italy 34/G4
Circle, Alaska 196/K1
Circle, Mont. 262/L3
Circle (cliffs), Utah 304/C6

Circle Back, Texas 303/B3
Circle City, Mo. 261/N9
Circle Pines, Minn. 255/G5
Circle Springs, Alaska 196/K1
Circleville, Kansas 232/G2
Circleville, Ohio 284/D6
Circleville, Utah 304/B5
Circleville, W. Va. 312/H5
Circular (head), Tasmania 99/B2
Cirebon, Indonesia 85/H2
Cirebon, Indonesia 54/M10
Ciremay (mt.), Indonesia 85/H2
Cirencester, England 10/F5
Cirencester, England 13/E6
Cirque (mt.), Newf. 166/B2
Cisco, Georgia 217/C1
Cisco, Ill. 222/E3
Cisco, Texas 303/E5
Cisco, Utah 304/E5
Cisco Springs Wash (creek), Utah 304/E4
Ciskei (bantustan), S. Africa 102/E8
Ciskei (prov.), South Africa 118/D6
Cismont, Va. 307/M4
Cisnădie, Romania 45/G3
Cisne, Ill. 222/E5
Cisneros, Colombia 126/C4
Cisnes (riv.), Chile 138/E5
Cispus (pass), Wash. 310/D4
Cispus (riv.), Wash. 310/D4
Cissna Park, Ill. 222/F3
Citlaltépeti (mt.), Mexico 150/O2
Citra, Fla. 212/D2
Citronelle, Ala. 195/B8
Citrus (co.), Fla. 212/D3
Citrus Center, Fla. 212/E5
Citrus Heights, Calif. 204/C8
Cittadella, Italy 34/C2
Città di Castello, Italy 34/C3
Cittanova, Italy 34/F5
City of Rocks Nat'l Reserve, Idaho 220/E7
City Mills, Mass. 249/J4
City Point, Wis. 317/F7
City View, Ontario 177/J2
City View, S.C. 296/C2
Ciudad Acuña (Villa Acuña), Mexico 150/J2
Ciudad Altamirano, Mexico 150/J7
Ciudad Bolívar, Venezuela 120/C2
Ciudad Bolívar, Venezuela 124/G3
Ciudad Bolivia, Venezuela 124/C3
Ciudad Camargo, Chihuahua, Mexico 150/G3
Ciudad Camargo, Tamaulipas, Mexico 150/K3
Ciudad Darío, Nicaragua 154/D4
Ciudad del Carmen, Mexico 150/N7
Ciudad Delicias, Mexico 150/G2
Ciudad del Maíz, Mexico 150/K5
Ciudad de Nutrias, Venezuela 124/D3
Ciudad de Río Grande, Mexico 150/H5
Ciudadela, Spain 33/H2
Ciudad Guayana, Venezuela 120/C2
Ciudad Guayana, Venezuela 124/G3
Ciudad Guerrero, Mexico 150/F2
Ciudad Guzmán, Mexico 150/H7
Ciudad Hidalgo, Chiapas, Mexico 150/N9
Ciudad Hidalgo, Michoacán, Mexico 150/J7
Ciudad Juárez, Mexico 146/H6
Ciudad Juárez, Mexico 150/F1
Ciudad Lerdo, Mexico 150/H4
Ciudad Madero, Mexico 150/L5
Ciudad Mante, Mexico 150/K5
Ciudad Mendoza, Mexico 150/O2
Ciudad Miguel Alemán, Mexico 150/K3
Ciudad Obregón, Mexico 146/H7
Ciudad Obregón, Mexico 150/E3
Ciudad Ojeda, Venezuela 120/B2
Ciudad Ojeda, Venezuela 124/C2
Ciudad Piar, Venezuela 124/G4
Ciudad Presidente Stroessner, Paraguay 144/E4
Ciudad Quesada, C. Rica 154/E5
Ciudad Real (prov.), Spain 33/D3
Ciudad Real, Spain 33/D3
Ciudad Río Bravo, Mexico 150/K4
Ciudad-Rodrigo, Spain 33/C2
Ciudad Satélite, Mexico 150/L1
Ciudad Serdán, Mexico 150/O2
Ciudad Valles, Mexico 150/K5
Ciudad Victoria, Mexico 150/K5
Civa (cape), Turkey 63/G2
Cividale del Friuli, Italy 34/D1
Civitavecchia, Italy 34/C3
Civitella del Tronto, Italy 34/D3
Civray, France 28/D4
Çivril, Turkey 63/C3
Cizre, Turkey 63/K4
Clachan, Scotland 15/C5
Clackamas (co.), Oreg. 291/E2
Clackamas, Oreg. 291/B2
Clackamas (riv.), Oreg. 291/E2
Clackmannan, Scotland 10/B1
Clackmannan, Scotland 15/C1
Clackmannan (trad. co.), Scotland 15/E5
Clacton, England 13/J6
Clacton, England 10/G5
Claflin, Kansas 232/D3
Claiborne, Ala. 195/D7
Claiborne (par.), La. 238/D1
Claiborne (lake), La. 238/E1
Claiborne, Md. 245/N5
Claiborne (co.), Miss. 256/C7
Claiborne (co.), Tenn. 237/O8
Clair, New Bruns. 170/B1
Clair, Sask. 181/G3
Claire (lake), Alberta 182/B5
Claire (lake), Alta. 162/E4
Claire City, S. Dak. 298/F2
Clairemont, Texas 303/D4
Clair Engle (lake), Calif. 204/C3
Clairette, Texas 303/F5
Clairfield, Tenn. 237/O7
Clairmont, Alberta 182/A2

Clairmont Springs, Ala. 195/G4
Clairton, Pa. 294/C7
Clallam (co.), Wash. 310/B2
Clallam Bay, Wash. 310/A2
Clam (bay), Nova Scotia 168/F4
Clam (lake), Wis. 317/B4
Clam (riv.), Wis. 317/A4
Clamart, France 28/A2
Clamecy, France 28/E4
Clam Falls, Wis. 317/B4
Clam Gulch, Alaska 196/B1
Clam Lake, Wis. 317/E3
Clan Alpine (mts.), Nev. 266/D3
Clancy, Mont. 262/E4
Clandeboye, Manitoba 179/E4
Clandeboye, Ontario 177/C4
Clandonald, Alberta 182/E3
Clanton, Ala. 195/E5
Clanwilliam, Manitoba 179/C4
Clanwilliam, S. Africa 118/B6
Clapperton (isl.), Ontario 177/B1
Clara, Ireland 10/C4
Clara, Ireland 17/F5
Clara, Miss. 256/G7
Clara, Uruguay 145/D3
Clara Barton Nat'l Hist. Site, Md. 245/E4
Clara City, Minn. 255/C6
Claravale, North. Terr. 93/B3
Clare, Ill. 222/E1
Clare, Ind. 227/F4
Clare, Iowa 229/E3
Clare (co.), Ireland 17/D6
Clare, Ireland 17/F5
Clarè (isl.), Ireland 10/A4
Clare (isls.), Ireland 17/A4
Clare (riv.), Ireland 17/D5
Clare (co.), Mich. 250/E5
Clare, Mich. 250/E5
Clare, N.S. Wales 97/B3
Clare, S. Australia 94/F5
Claregalway, Ireland 17/D5
Claremont, Calif. 204/D10
Claremont, Ill. 222/F5
Claremont; Jamaica 158/J6
Claremont, Minn. 255/E6
Claremont, N.H. 268/C5
Claremont, N.C. 281/G3
Claremont, S. Dak. 298/N2
Claremont, Va. 307/P6
Claremore, Okla. 288/R2
Claremorris, Ireland 17/C4
Claremorris, Ireland 10/B4
Clarence (str.), Alaska 196/N2
Clarence (isl.), Chile 120/B8
Clarence (isl.), Chile 138/E10
Clarence, Iowa 229/M5
Clarence, La. 238/E3
Clarence, Mo. 261/H3
Clarence (riv.), N.S. Wales 88/J5
Clarence (riv.), N.S. Wales 97/G1
Clarence•, N.Y. 276/C5
Clarence (riv.), N. Zealand 100/E5
Clarence (str.), North. Terr. 88/C3
Clarence (str.), North. Terr. 93/B2
Clarence (cape), N.W. Terr. 187/K2
Clarence (head), N.W. Terr. 187/L2
Clarence, Pa. 294/G3
Clarence Bridge, N. Zealand 100/E5
Clarence Creek, Ontario 177/J2
Clarenceville, Québec 172/D4
Clarendon, Ark. 202/H4
Clarendon, New Bruns. 170/D3
Clarendon, N.C. 281/M6
Clarendon (lake), Ontario 177/G3
Clarendon, Pa. 294/D2
Clarendon (co.), S.C. 296/G4
Clarendon, Texas 303/C3
Clarendon•, Vt. 268/A4
Clarendon Hills, Ill. 222/B6
Clarens, Switzerland 39/C4
Clarenville, Newf. 166/C2
Claresholm, Alberta 182/D4
Clariden (mt.), Switzerland 39/G3
Clarie Coast (reg.), Ant. 5/C7
Clarinda, Iowa 229/C7
Clarines, Venezuela 124/F3
Clarington, Ohio 284/J6
Clarington, Pa. 294/D2
Clarion, Iowa 229/F3
Clarión (isl.), Mexico 150/B7
Clarion, Mich. 250/E3
Clarion (co.), Pa. 294/D3
Clarion, Pa. 294/D3
Clarion (riv.), Pa. 294/D3
Clarion River, East Branch (lake), Pa. 294/E2
Clarissa, Minn. 255/C4
Clarita, Okla. 288/O6
Clark (lake), Alaska 196/H2
Clark (co.), Ark. 202/D5
Clark, Colo. 208/F1
Clark (co.), Idaho 220/F5
Clark (co.), Ill. 222/F4
Clark (co.), Ind. 227/F8
Clark (co.), Ky. 237/N4
Clark (co.), Mo. 261/J2
Clark, Mo. 261/H4
Clark•, N.J. 273/A4
Clark, N.C. 281/P4
Clark (buttes), N. Dak. 282/G7
Clark (co.), Ohio 284/B6
Clark, Ohio 284/G5
Clark (pt.), Ontario 177/C3
Clark, Pa. 294/B3
Clark (co.), S. Dak. 298/O4
Clark, S. Dak. 298/O4
Clark (co.), Wash. 310/C5
Clark (co.), Wis. 317/E6
Clark, Wyo. 319/C1
Clark Canyon (res.), Mont. 262/D6
Clark Center, Ill. 222/F4
Clarkdale, Ariz. 198/C4
Clarke (co.), Ala. 195/C7
Clarke (co.), Georgia 217/F3
Clarke (co.), Iowa 229/F6
Clarke (co.), Miss. 256/G6

Clarke (range), Queensland 95/C4
Clarke (isl.), Tasmania 99/E2
Clarke (co.), Va. 307/M2
Clarke City, Québec 174/D2
Clarkedale, Ark. 202/K3
Clarke's Beach, Newf. 166/D2
Clarkesville, Georgia 217/F1
Clarkfield, Minn. 255/C6
Clark Fork, Idaho 220/B1
Clark Fork (riv.), Mont. 188/D1
Clark Fork (riv.), Mont. 262/A3
Clarkia, Idaho 220/B2
Clark Island, Maine 243/E8
Clarklake, Mich. 250/E6
Clarkrange, Tenn. 237/L8
Clarks, East Fork (riv.), Ky. 237/E7
Clarks, La. 238/F2
Clarks, Nebr. 264/G3
Clarksboro, N.J. 273/C4
Clarksburg, Calif. 204/B9
Clarksburg, Ind. 227/G6
Clarksburg, Md. 245/J4
Clarksburg, Mo. 261/G5
Clarksburg, N.J. 273/E3
Clarksburg, Ohio 284/D7
Clarksburg, Ontario 177/D3
Clarksburg, Tenn. 237/E9
Clarksburg, W. Va. 188/K3
Clarksburg, W. Va. 312/F4
Clarks Corner, Conn. 210/G1
Clarksdale, Miss. 188/J4
Clarksdale, Miss. 256/D2
Clarksdale, Mo. 261/D3
Clarks Falls, Conn. 210/H3
Clarks Fork, Yellowstone (riv.), Mont. 262/G6
Clarks Fork (riv.), Wyo. 319/C1
Clarks Green, Pa. 294/F6
Clarks Grove, Minn. 255/E7
Clark's Harbour, Nova Scotia 168/C5
Clarks Hill, Ind. 227/D4
Clarks Hill, S.C. 296/C4
Clarks Mill, Maine 243/B8
Clarks Mills, Pa. 294/B3
Clarkson, Ky. 237/J6
Clarkson, Miss. 256/F3
Clarkson, Nebr. 264/G3
Clarkson, N.Y. 276/E4
Clarkson Valley, Mo. 261/N3
Clarks Point, Alaska 196/G3
Clarks Summit, Pa. 294/F6
Clarkston, Georgia 217/L1
Clarkston, Mich. 250/F6
Clarkston, Scotland 15/B2
Clarkston, Utah 304/B2
Clarkston, Wash. 310/H4
Clark's Town, Jamaica 158/H6
Clarksville, Ark. 202/D3
Clarksville, Del. 245/T6
Clarksville, Fla. 212/D6
Clarksville, Ind. 227/F8
Clarksville, Iowa 229/H3
Clarksville, Md. 245/L4
Clarksville, Mich. 250/D6
Clarksville, Mo. 261/K4
Clarksville•, N.H. 268/E1
Clarksville, N.Y. 276/M5
Clarksville, Ohio 284/B6
Clarksville (Clark), Pa. 294/B3
Clarksville, Pa. 294/B6
Clarksville, Tenn. 188/J3
Clarksville, Tenn. 237/G7
Clarksville, Texas 303/K4
Clarksville, Va. 307/L7
Clarkton, Mo. 261/M10
Clarkton, N.C. 281/M6
Clarno, Wis. 317/G10
Claro (riv.), Bolivia 136/A3
Claro (riv.), Brazil 132/B7
Claro (riv.), Chile 138/G5
Claro, Switzerland 39/G4
Clashmoor, Sask. 181/H3
Clashmore, Ireland 17/F8
Clatonia, Nebr. 264/H4
Clatskanie, Oreg. 291/D1
Clatsop (co.), Oreg. 291/D1
Claud, Ala. 195/F5
Claude, Texas 303/C2
Claudell, Kansas 232/C2
Claudville, Va. 307/H7
Claudy, N. Ireland 17/G2
Claussen, S.C. 296/H3
Clausthal-Zellerfeld, Germany 22/D3
Claverack-Red Mills, N.Y. 276/N6
Claveria, Philippines 82/C1
Clavet, Sask. 181/E4
Clawson, Mich. 250/B6
Clawson, Utah 304/C4
Claxton, Georgia 217/J6
Clay (co.), Ala. 195/G4
Clay (co.), Ark. 202/K1
Clay, Calif. 204/C9
Clay (creek), Colo. 208/O7
Clay (co.), Fla. 212/E2
Clay (co.), Georgia 217/B7
Clay (co.), Ill. 222/E5
Clay (co.), Ind. 227/C6
Clay (co.), Iowa 229/C2
Clay (co.), Kansas 232/E2
Clay (co.), Ky. 237/O6
Clay, Ky. 237/F6
Clay, La. 238/E2
Clay (co.), Minn. 255/B4
Clay (co.), Miss. 256/G3
Clay (co.), Mo. 261/D4
Clay (co.), Nebr. 264/F4
Clay (co.), N.C. 281/B4
Clay (co.), S. Dak. 298/P8
Clay (co.), Tenn. 237/K7
Clay (co.), Texas 303/H4
Clay (hills), Utah 304/D6
Clay (co.), W. Va. 312/D6
Clay, W. Va. 312/D6
Claybank, Sask. 181/F5
Clay Bank, Va. 307/O6
Clay Center, Kansas 232/E2
Clay Center, Nebr. 264/F4

Clay Center, Ohio 284/D2
Clay City, Ill. 222/E5
Clay City, Ind. 227/C6
Clay City, Ky. 237/O5
Claycomo, Mo. 261/P5
Clay Cross, England 13/J2
Claydon, Sask. 181/B6
Clayhatchee, Ala. 195/G8
Claymont, Del. 245/S1
Claymour, Ky. 237/G7
Clayoquot (sound), Br. Col. 184/D5
Claypool, Ariz. 198/E5
Claypool, Ind. 227/F2
Claypool, Ky. 237/J7
Clay Springs, Ariz. 198/E4
Claysville, Ohio 284/G6
Claysville, Pa. 294/B5
Claysburg, Pa. 294/F5
Clayton, Ala. 195/G7
Clayton, Calif. 204/K2
Clayton, Del. 245/R3
Clayton (co.), Georgia 217/D3
Clayton, Georgia 217/F1
Clayton, Idaho 220/D5
Clayton, Ill. 222/B3
Clayton, Ind. 227/D5
Clayton (co.), Iowa 229/L3
Clayton, Iowa 229/L3
Clayton, Kansas 232/C2
Clayton, La. 238/H3
Clayton (lake), Maine 243/D2
Clayton, Mich. 250/E7
Clayton, Miss. 256/D1
Clayton, Mo. 261/P3
Clayton, N.J. 273/C4
Clayton, N. Mex. 274/F2
Clayton, N.Y. 276/H2
Clayton, N.C. 281/N3
Clayton, Ohio 284/B6
Clayton, Okla. 288/R5
Clayton, S. Dak. 298/O7
Clayton, Victoria 97/L5
Clayton, Wash. 310/H3
Clayton, W. Va. 312/E7
Clayton, Wis. 317/B5
Clayton Lake, Maine 243/E2
Claytonville, Ill. 222/F3
Claytor (lake), Va. 307/G6
Clayville, R.I. 249/H5
Clayville, S. Africa 118/H6
Clayville, Va. 307/N6
Clear (cape), Alaska 196/D1
Clear (hills), Alberta 182/A1
Clear (creek), Ariz. 198/D4
Clear (lake), Calif. 188/B3
Clear (lake), Calif. 204/C4
Clear (lake), Iowa 229/G2
Clear (cape), Ireland 7/C3
Clear (cape), Ireland 17/B9
Clear (cape), Ireland 10/B5
Clear (isl.), Ireland 17/C9
Clear (lake), La. 238/D3
Clear (lake), Manitoba 179/C4
Clear (lake), Ontario 177/F3
Clear (lake), Ontario 177/G2
Clear (creek), Utah 304/B5
Clear (lake), Utah 304/B4
Clear (creek), Wyo. 319/F1
Clear Boggy (creek), Okla. 288/O6
Clearbrook, Br. Col. 184/L3
Clearbrook, Minn. 255/C3
Clear Brook, Va. 307/M2
Clear Creek, Calif. 204/B2
Clear Creek (co.), Colo. 208/H3
Clear Creek, Ind. 227/E6
Clearcreek, Utah 304/C4
Clear Creek, W. Va. 312/D7
Clearfield, Iowa 229/D7
Clearfield, Ky. 237/P4
Clearfield (co.), Pa. 294/F3
Clearfield, Pa. 294/F3
Clearfield, S. Dak. 298/K7
Clearfield, Utah 304/B2
Clear Fork (res.), Ohio 284/E4
Clear Fork, Mohican (riv.), Ohio 284/F4
Clear Fork, Brazos (riv.), Texas 303/D5
Clear Fork, Guyandotte (riv.), W. Va. 312/C7
Clear Hills, Alberta 182/B1
Clearlake, Calif. 204/C5
Clear Lake (res.), Calif. 204/D2
Clear Lake, Ind. 227/H1
Clear Lake, Iowa 229/G2
Clear Lake, La. 238/E3
Clear Lake, Minn. 255/E5
Clear Lake, S. Dak. 298/R4
Clearlake, Wash. 310/D2
Clearlake Oaks, Calif. 204/C5
Clear Lake Shores, Texas 303/K2
Clearmont, Mo. 261/C1
Clearmont, Wyo. 319/F1
Clear Ridge, Pa. 294/F5
Clear Spring, Ind. 227/F7
Clear Spring, Md. 245/G2
Clearview, Okla. 288/O4
Clearview, W. Va. 312/E7
Clearview City, Kansas 232/G3
Clearville, Pa. 294/F6
Clearwater (riv.), Alberta 182/C4
Clearwater (riv.), Alberta 182/E1
Clearwater, Br. Col. 184/G4
Clearwater (lake), Br. Col. 184/G4
Clearwater (riv.), Br. Col. 184/G3
Clearwater, Fla. 212/B2
Clearwater (co.), Idaho 220/C3
Clearwater, Idaho 220/C3
Clearwater (mts.), Idaho 220/D3
Clearwater (riv.), Idaho 220/B3
Clearwater, Kansas 232/E4
Clearwater, Manitoba 179/D5
Clearwater (co.), Minn. 255/C3
Clearwater, Minn. 255/D5
Clearwater (riv.), Minn. 255/C3
Clearwater (lake), Mo. 261/L8

Clearwater, Nebr. 264/F2
Clearwater (brook), New Bruns. 170/D2
Clearwater (riv.), Sask. 181/L3
Clearwater, S.C. 296/D4
Clearwater, Wash. 310/A3
Clearwater Beach (isl.), Fla. 212/B2
Clearwater Lake, Manitoba 179/H3
Clearwater Lake, Wis. 317/H4
Clearwater Lake Beach, Sask. 181/D5
Clearwater Lake Prov. Park, Manitoba 179/H3
Cleator Moor, England 13/D3
Cleburne (co.), Ala. 195/G3
Cleburne (co.), Ark. 202/F2
Cleburne, Texas 188/G4
Cleburne, Texas 303/G5
Cle Elum, Wash. 310/E3
Cle Elum (lake), Wash. 310/E3
Cleethorpes, England 13/H4
Cleethorpes, England 10/F4
Cleeves, Sask. 181/C2
Cleghorn, Iowa 229/B3
Cleghorn, Wis. 317/C6
Clem, Georgia 217/B3
Clemenceau, Ariz. 198/C4
Clemenceau, Sask. 181/J3
Clément, Fr. Guiana 131/E4
Clemente (isl.), Chile 138/D6
Clementon, N.J. 273/D4
Clements, Calif. 204/C9
Clements, Kansas 232/F3
Clements, Md. 245/L7
Clements, Minn. 255/D6
Clementson, Minn. 255/D2
Clementsport, Nova Scotia 168/C4
Clementsvale, Nova Scotia 168/C4
Clementsville, N. Dak. 282/O5
Clemmons, N.C. 281/J2
Clemons, Iowa 229/G4
Clemscot, Okla. 288/L6
Clemson, S.C. 296/B2
Clendenin, W. Va. 312/D5
Clendening (lake), Ohio 284/H5
Cleopatra Needle (mt.), Philippines 82/B1
Cleora, Okla. 288/S1
Cleo Springs, Okla. 288/K2
Clerf (riv.), Luxembourg 27/J8
Clermont, Fla. 212/E3
Clermont, Georgia 217/E2
Clermont, Iowa 229/K3
Clermont, Ky. 237/K5
Clermont, N.Y. 276/N6
Clermont (co.), Ohio 284/B7
Clermont, Pa. 294/E2
Clermont, Québec 172/G2
Clermont, Queensland 88/H4
Clermont, Queensland 95/C4
Clermont-Ferrand, France 7/E4
Clermont-Ferrand, France 28/E5
Clermont Harbor, Miss. 256/F10
Clervaux, Luxembourg 27/J8
Cleve, S. Australia 88/F6
Cleve, S. Australia 94/E5
Clevedon, England 13/D6
Cleveland, Ala. 195/E3
Cleveland (co.), Ark. 202/F6
Cleveland, Ark. 202/E3
Cleveland (co.), England 13/F3
Cleveland (hills), England 13/F3
Cleveland, Fla. 212/E6
Cleveland, Georgia 217/E1
Cleveland, Minn. 255/E6
Cleveland, Miss. 256/C3
Cleveland, Mo. 261/C5
Cleveland, Mont. 262/G2
Cleveland, N. Mex. 274/J4
Cleveland (co.), N.C. 281/F4
Cleveland, N.C. 281/H3
Cleveland, N. Dak. 282/M6
Cleveland, Ohio 188/K2
Cleveland, Ohio 284/H9
Cleveland, Ohio 146/K5
Cleveland (co.), Okla. 288/M4
Cleveland, Okla. 288/O2
Cleveland, S.C. 296/C1
Cleveland, Tenn. 237/M10
Cleveland, Texas 303/J6
Cleveland, Utah 304/C4
Cleveland, Va. 307/D7
Cleveland, W. Va. 312/F5
Cleveland Heights, Ohio 284/H9
Cleveland-Hopkins Mun. Airport, Ohio 284/G9
Clevelândia do Norte, Brazil 132/D2
Cleveland Park, D.C. 245/B4
Clever, Mo. 261/F8
Cleves, Iowa 229/G4
Cleves, Ohio 284/B9
Clew (bay), Ireland 17/B4
Clew (bay), Ireland 10/B4
Clewiston, Fla. 212/E5
Clichy, France 28/B1
Clifden, Ireland 10/B4
Clifden, Ireland 17/B3
Cliff, N. Mex. 274/A6
Cliff (cape), Nova Scotia 168/E3
Cliff (creek), Utah 304/E3
Cliffdell, Wash. 310/E4
Clifford, Ind. 227/F6
Clifford, Ky. 237/S4
Clifford (lake), Maine 243/H5
Clifford, Mich. 250/F5
Clifford, Ont. 177/D4
Clifford, Pa. 294/F6
Clifford, Va. 307/K5
Clifford, Wis. 317/F5
Cliffordvale, New Bruns. 170/C2
Cliffside, N.C. 281/F4
Cliffside Park, N.J. 273/C2
Clifftop, W. Va. 312/E6
Cliffwood, N.J. 273/E3

Clifton, Ariz. 198/F5
Clifton, Colo. 208/B3
Clifton, Idaho 220/F7
Clifton, Ill. 222/F3
Clifton, Kansas 232/E2
Clifton, La. 238/K5
Clifton•, Maine 243/G6
Clifton, New Bruns. 170/E1
Clifton, N.J. 273/B2
Clifton, S.C. 296/D2
Clifton, Tenn. 237/F10
Clifton, Texas 303/G6
Clifton, W. Va. 312/B5
Clifton, Wis. 317/F8
Clifton City, Mo. 261/G5
Clifton Dartmouth Hardness, England 10/E5
Clifton Dartmouth Hardness, England 13/D7
Clifton Forge (I.C.), Va. 307/J5
Clifton Heights, Pa. 294/M7
Clifton Hill, Mo. 261/G4
Clifton Hills, S. Australia 94/F2
Clifton Mills, W. Va. 312/G3
Clifton Park•, N.Y. 276/N5
Clifton Springs, N.Y. 276/F4
Cliftonville, Miss. 256/H4
Clifty, Ark. 202/C1
Clifty (creek), Ind. 227/F6
Clifty, Ky. 237/G7
Clifty, Tenn. 237/L9
Clifty, W. Va. 312/E6
Climax, Colo. 208/G3
Climax, Georgia 217/D9
Climax, Kansas 232/F4
Climax, Ky. 237/N6
Climax, Mich. 250/D6
Climax, Minn. 255/B3
Climax, N.C. 281/K3
Climax, Sask. 181/C6
Climax Springs, Mo. 261/G6
Climbing Hill, Iowa 229/B4
Clinch (co.), Georgia 217/G9
Clinch (riv.), Tenn. 237/N9
Clinch (riv.), Va. 307/C7
Clinchburg, Va. 307/E7
Clinchco, Va. 307/D6
Clinchfield, Georgia 217/E5
Clinchmore, Tenn. 237/N8
Clinchport, Va. 307/C7
Cline Settlement, Alberta 182/B3
Clingmans Dome (mt.), N.C. 281/C3
Clingmans Dome (mt.), Tenn. 237/P10
Clint, Texas 303/B10
Clinton, Ala. 195/C5
Clinton, Ark. 202/F2
Clinton, Br. Col. 184/G4
Clinton, Conn. 210/E3
Clinton•, Conn. 210/E3
Clinton (co.), Ill. 222/D5
Clinton, Ill. 222/E3
Clinton (co.), Ind. 227/E4
Clinton, Ind. 227/C5
Clinton (co.), Iowa 229/M5
Clinton, Iowa 229/N5
Clinton (co.), Ky. 237/L7
Clinton, Ky. 237/D7
Clinton, La. 238/J5
Clinton, Maine 243/D6
Clinton•, Maine 243/D6
Clinton, Md. 245/G6
Clinton•, Mass. 249/H3
Clinton (co.), Mich. 250/E6
Clinton, Mich. 250/F6
Clinton (co.), Minn. 255/B5
Clinton (co.), Miss. 256/D6
Clinton (co.), Mo. 261/D3
Clinton, Mo. 261/E6
Clinton (co.), Mo. 261/D3
Clinton, Mont. 262/C4
Clinton, Nebr. 264/B2
Clinton, N.J. 273/D2
Clinton (res.), N.J. 273/E1
Clinton (co.), N.Y. 276/N1
Clinton, N.Y. 276/K4
Clinton, N. Zealand 100/B7
Clinton (co.), N.C. 281/N5
Clinton, N.C. 281/M5
Clinton, Ohio 284/G4
Clinton (co.), Ohio 284/C7
Clinton, Okla. 288/H3
Clinton, Ontario 177/C4
Clinton (co.), Pa. 294/F3
Clinton, Pa. 294/B5
Clinton, S.C. 296/D3
Clinton, Tenn. 237/N8
Clinton, Wash. 310/C3
Clinton, W. Va. 312/D3
Clinton, Wis. 317/J10
Clinton-Colden (lake), N.W. Terr. 187/J1
Clinton Corners, N.Y. 276/N7
Clinton Creek, Yukon 187/D3
Clintondale, N.Y. 276/M7
Clintondale, Pa. 294/H3
Clinton Falls, Minn. 255/E6
Clintonville, Conn. 210/D3
Clintonville, Ky. 237/N4
Clintonville, Pa. 294/C3
Clintonville, W. Va. 312/E7
Clintonville, Wis. 317/J6
Clintwood, Va. 307/D6
Clio, Ala. 195/G7
Clio, Iowa 229/G6
Clio, La. 238/M2
Clio, Mich. 250/F5
Clio, S.C. 296/H2
Clio, W. Va. 312/D5
Clipper, Wash. 310/C2
Clipperton (isl.) 146/H8
Clipperton (isl.) 2/D5
Clisham (mt.), Scotland 15/B3
Clitheroe, Ireland 13/H1
Clitheroe, England 10/G1
Clive, Alberta 182/D3
Clive, Iowa 229/P5
Clive, N. Zealand 100/F3
Cliza, Bolivia 136/C5

Colombia 353

Cloan, Sask. 181/C3
Cloates (pt.), W. Australia 92/A3
Clode (sound), Newf. 166/D2
Cloe, Pa. 294/E4
Cloghan, Ireland 17/F5
Clogh-Chatsworth, Ireland 17/G6
Clogheen, Ireland 17/F7
Clogher, N. Ireland 17/G3
Clogherhead, Ireland 17/J4
Cloghy, N. Ireland 17/K3
Clonakilty, Ireland 10/B5
Clonakilty, Ireland 17/D8
Clonakilty (bay), Ireland 17/D8
Clonaslee, Ireland 17/F5
Cloncurry, Australia 87/E8
Cloncurry, Queensland 95/B4
Cloncurry, Queensland 88/G4
Cloncurry (riv.), Queensland 95/B4
Clondalkin, Ireland 17/J5
Clonegal, Ireland 17/H6
Clones, Ireland 10/C3
Clones, Ireland 17/G3
Clonfert, Ireland 17/E5
Clonmany, Ireland 17/G1
Clonmel, Ireland 17/F7
Clonmel, Ireland 10/C4
Clonmellon, Ireland 17/H4
Clonroche, Ireland 17/H7
Clontarf, Minn. 255/C5
Clontuskert, Ireland 17/E4
Cloone, Ireland 17/F4
Cloppenburg, Germany 22/B2
Clopton, Ala. 195/G7
Cloquet, Minn. 255/F4
Cloquet (riv.), Minn. 255/F4
Cloridorme, Québec 172/D1
Clorinda, Argentina 143/E2
Closeburn, Scotland 15/E5
Closplint, Ky. 237/P7
Closter, N.J. 273/C1
Clothier, W. Va. 312/C7
Clotho, Minn. 255/C4
Cloud (co.), Kansas 232/E2
Cloud (peak), Wyo. 319/E1
Cloud Chief, Okla. 288/J4
Cloudcroft, N. Mex. 274/D6
Cloudland, Georgia 217/A1
Cloudy (bay), N. Zealand 100/E4
Cloudy, Okla. 288/R6
Cloughjordan, Ireland 17/E6
Cloughmills, N. Ireland 17/J2
Cloutierville, La. 238/E3
Clova, Québec 174/B3
Clover (creek), Oreg. 291/K3
Clover, S.C. 296/E1
Clover, Va. 307/L7
Clover, W. Va. 312/D5
Clover Bar, Alberta 182/D3
Clover Bend, Ark. 202/H2
Clover Bottom, Ky. 237/N5
Cloverdale, Ala. 195/C1
Cloverdale, Calif. 204/B5
Cloverdale, Ind. 227/D5
Cloverdale, Minn. 255/F4
Cloverdale, Ohio 284/B3
Cloverdale, Oreg. 291/D2
Cloverdale, Va. 307/J6
Cloverland, Ind. 227/C6
Cloverland, Wash. 310/H4
Cloverleaf, Manitoba 179/F5
Clover Lick, W. Va. 312/F6
Clover Pass, Alaska 196/N2
Cloverport, Ky. 237/H5
Cloverton, Minn. 255/F4
Clovis, Calif. 204/F7
Clovis, N.Mex. 188/F4
Clovis, N. Mex. 274/F4
Clovulin, Scotland 15/C4
Cloyne, Ireland 17/E8
Cloyne, Ontario 177/G3
Cluanie, Loch (lake), Scotland 15/C3
Club (isl.), Ontario 177/C2
Cluff Lake, Sask. 181/L2
Cluj-Napoca, Romania 45/F2
Cluj-Napoca, Romania 7/G4
Clun, England 10/E4
Clun, England 13/D6
Clune, Pa. 294/D4
Clunes, Victoria 97/B5
Cluny, Alberta 182/D4
Cluny, France 28/F4
Cluses, France 28/G4
Clusone-Fiorine, Italy 34/C2
Cluster Springs, Va. 307/L7
Clute, Texas 303/J9
Clutha (riv.), N. Zealand 100/B6
Clutier, Iowa 229/J4
Clwyd (co.), Wales 13/D4
Clyattville, Georgia 217/F9
Clyde, Alberta 182/D2
Clyde (lake), Alberta 182/E2
Clyde, Canada 4/B13
Clyde (riv.), Dominica 161/F6
Clyde, Kansas 232/E2
Clyde, Mo. 261/C2
Clyde, N.Y. 276/G4
Clyde, N.C. 281/D3
Clyde, N. Dak. 282/N2
Clyde, N.W.T. 162/J1
Clyde (inlet), N.W.T. 162/K1
Clyde (inlet), N.W. Terr. 187/M2
Clyde (riv.), Nova Scotia 168/C5
Clyde, Ohio 284/E3
Clyde (firth), Scotland 15/D5
Clyde (firth), Scotland 10/D3
Clyde (riv.), Scotland 10/E3
Clyde (riv.), Scotland 15/D5
Clyde (riv.), Tasmania 99/D4
Clyde, Texas 303/E5
Clyde (riv.), Vt. 268/C2
Clyde, Wash. 310/G4
Clydebank, Scotland 15/B2
Clydebank, Scotland 10/A1
Clyde Hill, Wash. 310/B2
Clyde Park, Mont. 262/F5
Clyde River, N.W.T. 187/J7
Clyde River, N.W.T. 186/M2
Clyde River, Nova Scotia 168/C5
Clyman, Wis. 317/J9
Clymer, N.Y. 276/A6
Clymer, Pa. 294/E4
Clymers, Ind. 227/E3
Clyo, Georgia 217/K6
Cnoc May (mt.), Scotland 15/C5
Coachella, Calif. 204/J10
Coachella (canal), Calif. 204/K10
Coachford, Ireland 17/D8
Coahoma (co.), Miss. 256/C2
Coahoma, Miss. 256/C2
Coahoma, Texas 303/C5
Coahuila (state), Mexico 150/H3
Coakley, Ky. 237/K6
Coal (creek), Ind. 227/C4
Coal, Mo. 261/E6
Coal (co.), Okla. 288/O5
Coal (pt.), Oreg. 291/C5
Coal (cliffs), Utah 304/C5
Coal (creek), Wash. 310/G3
Coal (riv.), W. Va. 312/C6
Coal Bluff, Ind. 227/C5
Coal Branch, New Bruns. 170/E2
Coalburn, Scotland 15/E5
Coal City, Ill. 222/E2
Coal City, Ind. 227/D6
Coal City, W. Va. 312/D7
Coalcomán de Matamoros, Mexico 150/H7
Coal Creek, Alaska 196/K1
Coal Creek, Colo. 208/J6
Coal Creek, Ind. 227/C4
Coal Creek, New Bruns. 170/E2
Coaldale, Alberta 182/D5
Coaldale, Colo. 208/H6
Coaldale, Nev. 266/D4
Coaldale, Pa. 294/L4
Coaldale (Six Mile Run), Pa. 294/F5
Coalfield, Tenn. 237/N8
Coalfield, Wash. 310/B2
Coal Fork, W. Va. 312/D6
Coalgate, Okla. 288/O5
Coal Grove, Ohio 284/E9
Coal Harbour, Br. Col. 184/D5
Coal Hill, Ark. 202/C3
Coalhurst, Alberta 182/D5
Coaling, Ala. 195/D4
Coalinga, Calif. 204/E7
Coalisland, N. Ireland 17/H2
Coalmont, Br. Col. 184/G5
Coalmont, Colo. 208/F1
Coalmont, Ind. 227/C6
Coalmont, Tenn. 237/K10
Coalport, Pa. 294/E4
Coalridge, Mont. 262/M2
Coal Run, Ky. 237/R5
Coalspur, Alberta 182/B3
Coalton, Ill. 222/D4
Coalton, Ohio 284/E7
Coalton, W. Va. 312/G5
Coal Valley, Alberta 182/B3
Coal Valley, Ill. 222/C2
Coalville, England 13/F5
Coalville, Iowa 229/E4
Coalville, Utah 304/C3
Coalwood, Mont. 262/L5
Coalwood, W. Va. 312/C8
Coambo, Angola 115/C5
Coambo, Angola 102/D5
Coamo, P. Rico 161/D2
Coamo, P. Rico 156/G1
Coamo (res.), P. Rico 161/D3
Coamo (riv.), P. Rico 161/D3
Coari, Brazil 120/C3
Coari, Brazil 132/H9
Coarsegold, Calif. 204/F6
Coast (mts.) 162/C4
Coast (ranges) 188/B2
Coast (mts.), Alaska 196/N1
Coast (mts.), Br. Col. 146/E4
Coast (mts.), Br. Col. 184/D3
Coast (ranges), Calif. 204/D7
Coast (prov.), Kenya 115/G4
Coast (ranges), Oreg. 291/D5
Coast (ranges), U.S. 146/F5
Coast (ranges), Wash. 310/B3
Coast Guard Academy, Conn. 210/G3
Coatbridge, Scotland 10/B1
Coatbridge, Scotland 15/C2
Coatepec, Mexico 150/P1
Coatepeque, Guatemala 154/A3
Coates, Minn. 255/E6
Coatesville, Ind. 227/D5
Coatesville, Pa. 294/L5
Coatetelco, Mexico 150/L2
Coaticook, Québec 172/F4
Coatopa, Ala. 195/B6
Coats, Kansas 232/D4
Coats, N.C. 281/M4
Coats (isl.), N.W.T. 162/H3
Coats (isl.), N.W.T. 146/K3
Coats (isl.), N.W. Terr. 187/K3
Coatsburg, Ill. 222/B3
Coats Land (reg.), Ant. 2/H10
Coats Land (reg.), Ant. 5/B17
Coatsville, Mo. 261/G1
Coatzacoalcos, Mexico 146/J8
Coatzacoalcos, Mexico 150/M7
Coatzingo, Mexico 150/N2
Cobalt, Conn. 210/E2
Cobalt, Idaho 220/D4
Cobalt, Ont. 162/H6
Cobalt, Ontario 177/K5
Cobalt, Ontario 175/D3
Cobalt City, Mo. 261/M7
Cobán, Guatemala 154/B3
Cobar, N. S. Wales 88/H6
Cobar, N.S. Wales 97/C2
Cobargo, N.S. Wales 97/E5
Cobb (co.), Georgia 217/C3
Cobb, Georgia 217/E7
Cobb, Ky. 237/F6
Cobb (riv.), Minn. 255/E7
Cobb (isl.), Va. 307/S6
Cobb, Wis. 317/F10
Cobbadah, N.S. Wales 97/F2
Cobble Hill, Br. Col. 184/K3
Cobble Mountain (res.), Mass. 249/C4
Cobbs Creek, Va. 307/R6
Cobbtown, Georgia 217/H6
Cobden, Ill. 222/D6
Cobden, Minn. 255/D6
Cobden, Ontario 177/H2
Cobden, Victoria 97/B6
Cobequid (bay), Nova Scotia 168/E3
Cóbh, Ireland 10/B5
Cóbh, Ireland 17/E8
Cobham (riv.), Manitoba 179/G1
Cobham (riv.), Ontario 175/A2
Cobija, Bolivia 136/A2
Cobija, Brazil 120/C4
Coble, Tenn. 237/F9
Cobleskill, N.Y. 276/L5
Coboconk, Ontario 177/F3
Cobourg (pen.), North. Terr. 88/E2
Cobourg (pen.), North. Terr. 93/C1
Cobourg, Ontario 177/F4
Cobquecura, Chile 138/D1
Cobram, Victoria 97/C4
Cobre, Nev. 266/G1
Cóbuè, Mozambique 118/F2
Coburg, Germany 22/D3
Coburg, Iowa 229/C7
Coburg (isl.), N.W. Terr. 187/L2
Coburg, Oreg. 291/E3
Coburg, Victoria 88/K7
Coburg, Victoria 97/H5
Coburn, Pa. 294/H4
Coburn, W. Va. 312/F3
Coca, Ecuador 128/D3
Cocachacra, Peru 128/G11
Cocagne, New Bruns. 170/F2
Cocagne (isl.), New Bruns. 170/F2
Cocagne (riv.), New Bruns. 170/F2
Cocagne Cape, New Bruns. 170/F2
Cocama, Peru 128/G8
Cocanada (Kakinada), India 68/E5
Cocani, Bolivia 136/B7
Cocapata, Bolivia 136/B5
Cocentaina, Spain 33/F3
Cochabamba (dept.), Bolivia 136/C5
Cochabamba, Bolivia 120/C4
Cochabamba, Bolivia 136/C5
Cochamó, Chile 138/E3
Coche (isl.), Venezuela 124/F2
Cocheco (riv.), N.H. 268/E5
Cochecton, N.Y. 276/K7
Cochem, Germany 22/B3
Cochenour, Ontario 175/B2
Cochetopa (creek), Colo. 208/F6
Cochimbo, Serra do (mts.), Brazil 132/C5
Cochin, Sask. 181/C2
Cochin-Alleppey, India 68/D6
Cochinos (bay), Cuba 158/D2
Cochise (co.), Ariz. 198/F7
Cochise, Ariz. 198/F6
Cochiti, N. Mex. 274/C3
Cochituate, Mass. 249/A7
Cochituate (lake), Mass. 249/A7
Cochran, Georgia 217/F6
Cochran (co.), Texas 303/B4
Cochrane, Ala. 195/B4
Cochrane, Alberta 182/C4
Cochrane (lake), Chile 138/E7
Cochrane, Cerro (mt.), Chile 138/E7
Cochrane (riv.), Manitoba 179/H2
Cochrane, Ont. 146/K5
Cochrane, Ont. 162/H6
Cochrane (terr. dist.), Ontario 177/J4
Cochrane (terr. dist.), Ontario 175/D2
Cochrane, Ontario 177/K5
Cochrane, Ontario 175/D3
Cochrane (riv.), Sask. 181/N2
Cochrane, Wis. 317/C7
Cochranton, Pa. 294/B2
Cochranville, Pa. 294/L6
Cockburn (chan.), Chile 138/E11
Cockburn (isl.), Ontario 177/A2
Cockburn, S. Australia 94/G5
Cockburn (sound), W. Australia 88/B2
Cockburn Harbour, Turks & Caicos 156/D2
Cockburnspath, Scotland 15/F5
Cocke (co.), Tenn. 237/P9
Cockenoe (isl.), Conn. 210/B4
Cockenzie and Port Seton, Scotland 15/D1
Cockermouth, England 13/D3
Cockermouth, England 10/E3
Cockeysville, Md. 245/M3
Cockrell Hill, Texas 303/G2
Cockrum, Miss. 256/E1
Coclé del Norte, Panama 154/G6
Coco (chan.), Burma 72/B4
Coco (cay), Cuba 158/G1
Coco (riv.), Honduras 154/E3
Coco (chan.), India 68/G6
Coco (riv.), Nicaragua 154/E3
Coco, W. Va. 312/D6
Cocoa, Fla. 212/F3
Cocoa Beach, Fla. 212/F3
Cocobeach, Gabon 115/B3
Cocodrie (lake), La. 238/E5
Cocolamus, Pa. 294/H4
Coconino (co.), Ariz. 198/C3
Coconino (plat.), Ariz. 198/C3
Coconut Creek, Fla. 212/F5
Cocopah Ind. Res., Ariz. 198/A6
Cocorit, Mexico 150/E3
Cocos (isls.), Australia 2/P6
Cocos (isls.), Australia 54/L11
Cocos (isl.), C. Rica 146/K9
Cocos (isl.), Guam 86/K7
Cocos (bay), Trin. & Tob. 161/B10
Cocuy, Sierra Nevada del (mts.), Colombia 126/D4
Cod (cape), Mass. 146/M5
Cod (cape), Mass. 188/N2
Cod (cape), Mass. 249/O4
Cod (isl.), Newf. 166/B2
Codajás, Brazil 120/C3
Codajás, Brazil 132/H9
Coddle (harb.), Nova Scotia 168/G3
Codegua, Chile 138/G4
Codell, Kansas 232/C2
Coden, Ala. 195/B10
Codera (cape), Venezuela 124/F2
Coderre, Sask. 181/E5
Codesa, Alberta 182/B2
Codes Corner, Ontario 177/H3
Codette, Sask. 181/H2
Codfish (isl.), N. Zealand 100/A7
Codigua, Chile 138/F4
Codington (co.), S. Dak. 298/P4
Codó, Brazil 120/E3
Codó, Brazil 132/E4
Codorus, Pa. 294/J6
Codpa, Chile 138/B1
Codrington, Ant. & Bar. 156/G3
Codrington, Barbados 161/B8
Codroipo, Italy 34/D2
Codroy, Newf. 166/C4
Cody, Nebr. 264/C2
Cody, Wyo. 319/D1
Codys, New Bruns. 170/E3
Coe, Ind. 227/C8
Coeburn, Va. 307/D7
Coe Hill, Ontario 177/G3
Coelemu, Chile 138/D1
Coello, Ill. 222/D6
Coen, Queensland 88/G2
Coen, Queensland 95/B2
Coeroeni (riv.), Suriname 131/C4
Coesfeld, Germany 22/B3
Coesse, Ind. 227/G2
Coeur d'Alene, Idaho 220/B2
Coeur d'Alene, Idaho 188/C1
Coeur d'Alene (lake), Idaho 220/B2
Coeur d'Alene (mts.), Idaho 220/C2
Coeur d'Alene (riv.), Idaho 220/B2
Coevorden, Netherlands 27/K3
Coeymans, N.Y. 276/N6
Coffee (co.), Ala. 195/G8
Coffee (co.), Georgia 217/G8
Coffee (co.), Tenn. 237/J9
Coffee Creek, Mont. 262/F3
Coffeen, Ill. 222/D4
Coffee Springs, Ala. 195/G8
Coffeeville, Ala. 195/B7
Coffeeville (dam), Ala. 195/B7
Coffeeville, Miss. 256/E3
Coffey (co.), Kansas 232/G3
Coffey, Mo. 261/E2
Coffeyville, Kans. 188/G3
Coffeyville, Kansas 232/G4
Coffin (bay), S. Australia 94/D6
Coffin Bay (pen.), S. Australia 94/D6
Coffs Harbour, N. S. Wales 88/J6
Coffs Harbour, N.S. Wales 97/G2
Cofield, N.C. 281/R2
Cogan Station, Pa. 294/H3
Cogar, Okla. 288/K4
Cogdell, Georgia 217/G8
Cogealac, Romania 45/J3
Coggon, Iowa 229/L4
Coghinas (riv.), Italy 34/B4
Coglians (Hohe Warte) (mt.), Austria 41/B3
Cognac, France 28/C5
Cogolludo, Spain 33/E2
Cogotí, Chile 138/A8
Cogswell, N. Dak. 282/P7
Cogtong, Philippines 82/E6
Cohagen, Mont. 262/K3
Cohansey (riv.), N.J. 273/C5
Cohasset, Ala. 195/E8
Cohasset•, Mass. 249/F7
Cohasset, Minn. 255/E3
Cohoctah, Mich. 250/F6
Cohocton, N.Y. 276/F5
Cohocton (riv.), N.Y. 276/F6
Cohoe, Alaska 196/B1
Cohoes, N.Y. 276/N5
Cohoni, Bolivia 136/B5
Cohuna, Victoria 97/C4
Cohutta, Georgia 217/C1
Coiba, Isla de (isl.), Panama 154/F7
Coihaique, Chile 138/E6
Coihaique Alto, Chile 138/E6
Coihueco, Chile 138/A11
Coila, Miss. 256/E4
Coill Dubh, Ireland 17/H5
Coimbatore, India 54/J8
Coimbatore, India 68/D6
Coimbra (dist.), Portugal 33/B2
Coimbra, Portugal 7/D4
Coimbra, Portugal 33/B2
Coin, Iowa 229/C7
Coín, Spain 33/D4
Coinco, Chile 138/G5
Coinjock, N.C. 281/S2
Coipasa, Bolivia 136/A6
Coipasa (lake), Bolivia 136/B6
Coipasa (salt dep.), Bolivia 136/A6
Coire, Loch (lake), Scotland 15/D2
Cojata, Peru 128/H10
Cojedes (state), Venezuela 124/D3
Cojedes (riv.), Venezuela 124/D3
Cojimíes, Ecuador 128/B2
Cojoro, Venezuela 124/C2
Cojutepeque, El Salvador 154/C4
Cokato, Minn. 255/D5
Coke (co.), Texas 303/D6
Cokeburg, Pa. 294/B5
Cokedale, Colo. 208/K8
Coker, Ala. 195/C4
Cokercreek, Tenn. 237/N10
Coketon, W. Va. 312/G4
Cokeville, Wyo. 319/B3
Colaba (pt.), India 68/B7
Colac, Victoria 88/G7
Colac, Victoria 97/B6
Colachel, India 68/D7
Colair (lake), India 68/E5
Colamus (riv.), Nebr. 264/E2
Colasay, Peru 128/C5
Colatina, Brazil 120/E4
Colatina, Brazil 132/F7
Colbeck (cape), Ant. 5/B10
Colbert (co.), Ala. 195/C1
Colbert, Georgia 217/F2
Colbert, Okla. 288/O7
Colbert, Wash. 310/H3
Colborne, Ontario 177/G4
Colbún, Chile 138/A11
Colburn, Idaho 220/B1
Colburn, Ind. 227/D3
Colby, Kansas 232/A2
Colby, Wash. 310/A2
Colby, Wis. 317/F6
Colcamar, Peru 128/D6
Colchester, Conn. 210/F2
Colchester•, Conn. 210/F2
Colchester, England 13/H6
Colchester, England 10/G5
Colchester, Ill. 222/C3
Colchester (co.), Nova Scotia 168/E3
Colchester, Ontario 177/B6
Colchester•, Vt. 268/A2
Colcord, Okla. 288/S2
Colcord, W. Va. 312/D7
Cold (bay), Alaska 196/F4
Cold (lake), Alberta 182/E2
Cold (riv.), N.H. 268/C5
Cold Bay, Alaska 196/F4
Cold Brook, N.Y. 276/L4
Coldbrook Station, Nova Scotia 168/D3
Colden, N.Y. 276/C5
Coldingham, Scotland 15/F5
Cold Lake, Alberta 182/E2
Cold Spring, Ky. 237/T2
Cold Spring, Minn. 255/D5
Cold Spring, N.J. 273/D6
Cold Spring, N.Y. 276/N8
Coldspring (head), Nova Scotia 168/E3
Coldspring, Texas 303/J7
Cold Spring Harbor, N.Y. 276/R6
Cold Springs, Okla. 288/J5
Coldstream, Br. Col. 184/H5
Cold Stream (pond), Maine 243/G5
Coldstream, New Bruns. 170/C2
Coldstream, Scotland 10/E3
Coldstream, Scotland 15/F5
Coldstream, Victoria 97/K4
Coldwater, Kansas 232/C4
Coldwater, Mich. 250/D7
Coldwater, Miss. 256/E1
Coldwater (riv.), Miss. 256/D1
Coldwater, Ohio 284/A5
Coldwater, Ontario 177/E3
Coldwater, Tenn. 237/H10
Coldwater (creek), Texas 303/B1
Coldwater, W. Va. 312/E4
Cole (co.), Mo. 261/H6
Cole (harb.), Nova Scotia 168/E4
Cole, Okla. 288/L5
Colebrook•, Conn. 210/C1
Colebrook, N.H. 268/E2
Colebrook•, N.H. 268/E2
Colebrook, Ohio 284/J2
Colebrook, Tasmania 99/D4
Colebrook River (lake), Conn. 210/C1
Cole Camp, Mo. 261/F6
Coleen (riv.), Alaska 196/K1
Colegrove, Pa. 294/F2
Coleharbor, N. Dak. 282/H4
Coleman, Alberta 182/C5
Coleman, Alta. 162/E6
Coleman, Fla. 212/D3
Coleman, Georgia 217/C7
Coleman, Mich. 250/E5
Coleman, Okla. 288/O6
Coleman (riv.), Queensland 95/B2
Coleman (co.), Texas 303/E6
Coleman, Texas 303/E6
Coleman, Wis. 317/L5
Coleman Falls, Va. 307/K6
Colemans Lake, Georgia 217/H5
Çölemerik, Turkey 63/K4
Colerain, N.C. 281/R2
Coleraine, Minn. 255/E3
Coleraine (dist.), N. Ireland 17/H1
Coleraine, N. Ireland 17/H1
Coleraine, N. Ireland 10/C3
Coleraine, Québec 172/F4
Coleraine, Victoria 97/A5
Coleridge, Nebr. 264/G2
Coleridge (lake), N. Zealand 100/C5
Coleridge, N.C. 281/K3
Coles (co.), Ill. 222/E4
Coles, Miss. 256/C8
Coles (pt.), Peru 128/G11
Colesberg, S. Africa 118/D6
Colesburg, Georgia 217/J9
Colesburg, Iowa 229/L3
Colesburg, Ky. 237/K5
Coles Island, New Bruns. 170/E3
Coles Point, Va. 307/P4
Colesville, Md. 245/K4
Colesville, N.J. 273/D1
Coleta, Ill. 222/D2
Coleville, Calif. 204/F5
Coleville, Sask. 181/B4
Colfax, Calif. 204/E4
Colfax, Ill. 222/E3
Colfax, Ind. 227/D4
Colfax, Iowa 229/G5
Colfax, La. 238/E3
Colfax (co.), Nebr. 264/G3
Colfax (co.), N. Mex. 274/E2
Colfax, N. Dak. 282/S7
Colfax, Sask. 181/H6
Colfax, Wash. 310/H4
Colfax, Wis. 317/C6
Colgan, N. Dak. 282/C2
Colgate, N. Dak. 282/P5
Colgate (cape), N.W. Terr. 187/J1
Colgate, Sask. 181/H6
Colgate, Wis. 317/K1
Colhué Huapi (lake), Argentina 143/C6
Co Lieu, Vietnam 72/E3
Colignan, Victoria 97/B4
Colijnsplaat, Netherlands 27/D5
Colima (state), Mexico 150/G7
Colima, Mexico 150/H7
Colina, Chile 138/G3
Colina (riv.), Chile 138/G3
Colinas, Brazil 132/F4
Colinet, Newf. 166/D2
Colington, N.C. 281/T3
Colinton, Alberta 182/D2
Coll, Scotland 15/B2
Coll (isl.), Scotland 15/B4
Coll (isl.), Scotland 10/C2
Collaguasi, Chile 138/B3
Collamer, Ind. 227/F2
Collarenebri, N.S. Wales 97/E1
Collbran, Colo. 208/C4
Colle di Val d'Elsa, Italy 34/C3
College, Alaska 196/J1
College Bridge, New Bruns. 170/F3
College City, Ark. 202/J1
College Corner, Ohio 284/A6
Collegedale, Tenn. 237/M10
College Grove, Tenn. 237/H9
College Heights, Alberta 182/D3
College Hill, Ky. 237/N5
College Hill, Miss. 256/E2
College Mound, Mo. 261/G3
College Park, Georgia 217/K2
College Park, Md. 245/G4
College Place, Wash. 310/G4
College Springs, Iowa 229/C7
College Station, Texas 303/H7
Collegeville, Ind. 227/C3
Collegeville, Minn. 255/D5
Collegeville, Pa. 294/M5
Colle Sestriere, Italy 34/A2
Colleton (co.), S.C. 296/F6
Collett, Ind. 227/H4
Collette, New Bruns. 170/E2
Collettsville, N.C. 281/F3
Colley, Pa. 294/K2
Colleyville, Texas 303/F2
Collie, Australia 87/B9
Collie, N.S. Wales 97/E2
Collie, W. Australia 88/B6
Collie, W. Australia 92/B2
Collier (co.), Fla. 212/E5
Collier (bay), W. Australia 88/C3
Collier (bay), W. Australia 92/C1
Colliers, Newf. 166/D2
Colliers, S.C. 296/C4
Colliers, W. Va. 312/E2
Collierstown, Va. 307/J5
Collierville, Tenn. 237/B10
Colliguay, Chile 138/F3
Collin (co.), Texas 303/H4
Collingdale, Pa. 294/N7
Collingswood, N.J. 273/B3
Collingsworth (co.), Texas 303/D3
Collingwood, N. Zealand 100/D4
Collingwood, Ontario 177/D3
Collingwood, Victoria 97/J5
Collingwood, Victoria 88/L7
Collingwood Corner, Nova Scotia 168/E3
Collins, Ark. 202/G6
Collins, Georgia 217/H6
Collins, Iowa 229/G5
Collins, Miss. 256/E7
Collins, Mo. 261/E7
Collins, Mont. 262/E3
Collins, N.Y. 276/C6
Collins (head), Norfolk I. 88/L6
Collins, Ohio 284/E3
Collins, Ontario 177/G4
Collins (riv.), Tenn. 237/K9
Collins Bay, Ontario 177/H3
Collins Bay, Sask. 181/M2
Collins Center, N.Y. 276/C6
Collinston, La. 238/G1
Collinston, Utah 304/B2
Collinsville, Ala. 195/G2
Collinsville, Calif. 204/L1
Collinsville, Conn. 210/D1
Collinsville, Ill. 222/B2
Collinsville, Mass. 249/J2
Collinsville, Miss. 256/G6
Collinsville, Ohio 284/A6
Collinsville, Okla. 288/P2
Collinsville, Queensland 88/H4
Collinsville, Queensland 95/C4
Collinsville, Va. 307/J7
Collinwood, Tenn. 237/F10
Collipulli, Chile 138/E2
Collirene, Ala. 195/E6
Collis, Minn. 255/B5
Collison, Ill. 222/F3
Collista, Ky. 237/R5
Collombey-Muraz, Switzerland 39/C4
Collon, Ireland 17/J4
Collon (mt.), Switzerland 39/D5
Collonge-Bellerive, Switzerland 39/B4
Collooney, Ireland 17/E3
Collpa, Bolivia 136/C6
Collyer, Kansas 232/B2
Colma, Calif. 204/J2
Colman, S. Dak. 298/R6
Colmar, France 28/G3
Colmar, Pa. 294/M5
Colmar Manor, Md. 245/F4
Colmenar, Spain 33/D4
Colmenar de Oreja, Spain 33/G5
Colmenar Viejo, Spain 33/F4
Colmesneil, Texas 303/K7
Colmonell, Scotland 15/D5
Colne, England 10/G1
Colne, England 13/H1
Colne (riv.), England 10/B5
Colne (riv.), England 13/G8
Colne Valley, England 10/G2
Colne Valley, England 13/J2
Colo, Iowa 229/G4
Colo (riv.), N.S. Wales 97/F3
Cologne, Germany 7/E3
Cologne, Germany 22/B3
Cologne, Minn. 255/E6
Cologne, N.J. 273/D4
Coloma, Calif. 204/C5
Coloma, Mich. 250/C6
Coloma, Wis. 317/H7
Colombes, France 28/A1
Colombia 2/F5
Colombia 120/B2

COLOMBIA 126
Colombia, Colombia 126/C6
Colombo (cap.), Sri Lanka 54/J9
Colombo (cap.), Sri Lanka 2/N5
Colombo (cap.), Sri Lanka 68/D7
Colome, S. Dak. 298/K7
Colón, Buenos Aires, Argentina 143/F6
Colón, Entre Ríos, Argentina 143/G6
Colón, Colombia 126/B1
Colón, Colombia 126/B7
Colón, Cuba 158/D1
Colón, Cuba 156/B2
Colón, Archipiélago de (terr.), Ecuador 128/C8
Colón (mts.), Honduras 154/E3
Colón, Mexico 150/K6
Colon, Mich. 250/D7
Colon, Nebr. 264/H3
Colón, Pan. 146/K9
Colón, Panama 154/H6
Colón, Isla de (isl.), Panama 154/G6
Colón, Lavalleja, Uruguay 145/B7
Colón, Montevideo, Uruguay 145/B7
Colón, Venezuela 124/E6
Colona, Colo. 208/D6
Colona, Ill. 222/C2
Colonarie, St. Vin. & Grens. 161/A9
Colonarie (pt.), St. Vin. & Grens. 161/A9
Colonel Light Gardens, S. Australia 88/D8
Colonel Light Gardens, S. Australia 94/A8
Colonia, N.J. 273/E2
Colonia (dept.), Uruguay 145/B5
Colonia, Uruguay 145/B5
Colonia Agraciada, Uruguay 145/A4
Colonia Arrué, Uruguay 145/B5
Colonia Artigas, Uruguay 145/B1
Colonia Concordia, Uruguay 145/A4
Colonia Elisa, Argentina 143/E2
Colonia Itacumbú, Uruguay 145/B1
Colonia Josefa, Argentina 143/D4
Colonia Las Heras, Argentina 143/C6
Colonia Lavalleja, Uruguay 145/C2
Colonial Beach, Va. 307/M5
Colonial Heights, Tenn. 237/R8
Colonial Heights (I.C.), Va. 307/O6
Colonial Nat'l Hist. Park, Va. 307/P6
Colonia Neuland, Paraguay 144/B3
Colonia Palma, Paraguay 145/B1
Colonia Pte. Stroessner, Paraguay 144/D3
Colonia Rossel y Rius, Uruguay 145/D4
Colonias, N. Mex. 274/E3
Colonia San Alfredo, Paraguay 144/D3
Colonia Sgto. José E. López, Paraguay 144/D3
Colonia Valdense, Uruguay 145/B5
Colonia Yby Yu, Paraguay 144/E3
Colonie, N.Y. 276/N5
Colonne (cape), Italy 34/F5
Colonsay, Sask. 181/F4
Colonsay (isl.), Scotland 10/C2
Colonsay (isl.), Scotland 15/B4
Colony, Kansas 232/G3
Colony, Mo. 261/H2
Colony, Okla. 288/J4
Colony, Wyo. 319/H1
Colora, Md. 245/O2
Colorada (lag.), Bolivia 136/A8
Colorado 188/E3
COLORADO 208
Colorado (riv.) 188/D4
Colorado (riv.), Argentina 2/F5
Colorado (riv.), Argentina 120/C6
Colorado (riv.), Argentina 143/D4
Colorado (riv.), Ariz. 198/A5
Colorado (riv.), Calif. 204/L8
Colorado (riv.), Colo. 208/C2
Colorado (riv.), Mexico 150/D1
Colorado, Arroyo (riv.), N. Mex. 274/B4
Colorado (riv.), Texas 303/H8
Colorado (riv.), Texas 188/G4
Colorado (riv.), Texas 146/H6
Colorado (riv.), Texas 303/F7
Colorado (state), U.S. 146/H6
Colorado (riv.), U.S. 146/G6
Colorado (riv.), U.S. 2/D7
Colorado (riv.), Utah 304/E5
Colorado City, Ariz. 198/B2
Colorado City, Colo. 208/K6
Colorado City, Texas 303/F7
Colorado Nat'l Mon., Colo. 208/B4
Colorado River Aqueduct, Calif. 204/K10
Colorado River Ind. Res., Ariz. 198/A5
Colorado River Ind. Res., Calif. 204/L10
Colorados, Los (arch.), Cuba 158/A1
Colorado Springs, Colo. 146/H6
Colorado Springs, Colo. 188/F3
Colorado Springs, Colo. 208/K5
Colored Hill, W. Va. 312/H6
Colotlán, Mexico 150/H5
Colp, Ill. 222/D6
Colpoy (bay), Ontario 177/C3
Colpoys Bay, Ontario 177/C3
Colquechaca, Bolivia 136/B6
Colquiri, Bolivia 136/B5
Colquitt (co.), Georgia 217/E8
Colquitt, Georgia 217/C8
Colrain •, Mass. 249/D2
Colson, Ky. 237/R6
Colstrip, Mont. 262/K5
Colt, Ark. 202/J3
Coltauco, Chile 138/F5
Colton, Calif. 204/E10
Colton, N.Y. 276/L1
Colton, Ohio 284/C3
Colton, Oreg. 291/B3
Colton, S. Dak. 298/P6
Colton, Utah 304/C4
Colton, Wash. 310/H4
Coltons Point, Md. 245/M8
Colts Neck, N.J. 273/E3
Coluene (riv.), Brazil 120/D4
Columbia (riv.) 188/B1
Columbia, Ala. 195/H8

Columbia (glac.), Alaska 196/C1
Columbia (mt.), Alberta 182/B3
Columbia (co.), Ark. 202/D7
Columbia (lake), Br. Col. 184/K5
Columbia (mt.), Br. Col. 184/J4
Columbia (riv.), Br. Col. 184/H4
Columbia, Calif. 204/E5
Columbia (cape), Canada 4/A13
Columbia •, Conn. 210/F2
Columbia (co.), Fla. 212/D1
Columbia, Fla. 212/D1
Columbia (co.), Georgia 217/H3
Columbia, Ill. 222/C5
Columbia, Iowa 229/G6
Columbia, Ky. 237/L6
Columbia, La. 238/F2
Columbia •, Maine 243/H6
Columbia, Md. 245/L4
Columbia, Miss. 256/E8
Columbia, Mo. 261/H5
Columbia, Mo. 188/H3
Columbia, N.J. 273/C2
Columbia (co.), N.Y. 276/N6
Columbia, N.C. 281/S3
Columbia (cape), N.W.T. 162/N3
Columbia (cape), N.W. Terr. 187/M1
Columbia (co.), Oreg. 291/D2
Columbia City, Oreg. 291/D2
Columbia (riv.), Oreg. 291/D2
Columbia (co.), Pa. 294/K3
Columbia, Pa. 294/K5
Columbia (cap.), S.C. 146/M6
Columbia (cap.), S.C. 281/K4
Columbia (cap.), S.C. 188/K6
Columbia (cap.), S.C. 296/F4
Columbia, S. Dak. 298/N2
Columbia, Tenn. 188/J3
Columbia, Tenn. 237/G9
Columbia (riv.), U.S. 146/F5
Columbia, Utah 304/D4
Columbia, Va. 307/M5
Columbia (co.), Wash. 310/H4
Columbia (riv.), Wash. 310/B4
Columbia (riv.), Wis. 317/H9
Columbia City, Ind. 227/G2
Columbia City, Oreg. 291/C2
Columbia Falls •, Maine 243/H6
Columbia Falls, Mont. 262/B2
Columbia Furnace, Va. 307/L3
Columbia Heights, Minn. 255/G5
Columbia Heights, Wash. 310/C4
Columbiana, Ala. 195/E4
Columbiana (co.), Ohio 284/J4
Columbiana, Ohio 284/J4
Columbia Reach (riv.), Br. Col. 184/J4
Columbia Road (res.), S. Dak. 298/N2
Columbia Station, Ohio 284/G10
Columbiaville, Mich. 250/F5
Columbine, Colo. 208/E1
Columbretes (isl.), Spain 33/G3
Columbus (dam), 256/H3
Columbus, Ark. 202/C6
Columbus, Ga. 188/K4
Columbus, Ga. 146/K6
Columbus, Georgia 217/C6
Columbus, Ill. 222/B4
Columbus, Ind. 227/E6
Columbus, Ky. 237/C7
Columbus, Kansas 232/H4
Columbus, Miss. 188/J4
Columbus, Miss. 256/H3
Columbus, Mont. 262/G5
Columbus, Nebr. 264/G3
Columbus, N.J. 273/D3
Columbus, N. Mex. 274/D7
Columbus (co.), N.C. 281/M6
Columbus, N.C. 281/E4
Columbus, N. Dak. 282/E2
Columbus (cap.), Ohio 188/K3
Columbus (cap.), Ohio 146/K6
Columbus (cap.), Ohio 284/E6
Columbus, Pa. 294/C2
Columbus, Texas 303/H8
Columbus, Wis. 317/H9
Columbus A.F.B., Miss. 256/H3
Columbus City, Iowa 229/L6
Columbus Grove, Ohio 284/B4
Columbus Junction, Iowa 229/L6
Columbus Salt (marsh), Nev. 266/C4
Colusa (co.), Calif. 204/C4
Colusa, Calif. 204/C11
Colusa, Ill. 222/B3
Colver, Pa. 294/F4
Colville (riv.), Alaska 188/C5
Colville (riv.), Alaska 196/G1
Colville (cape), N. Zealand 100/E2
Colville (bay), N.W. Terr. 187/K3
Colville (lake), N.W. Terr. 187/F3
Colville, Wash. 310/H2
Colville (riv.), Wash. 310/H2
Colville Ind. Res., Wash. 310/G2
Colville Lake, N.W. Terr. 187/F3
Colwell, Iowa 229/H2
Colwich, Kansas 232/E4
Colwyn, Pa. 294/N7
Colwyn Bay, Wales 10/E4
Colwyn Bay, Wales 13/D4
Comacchio, Italy 34/D2
Comai, China 77/D6
Comal (co.), Texas 303/F8
Comala, Mexico 150/G7
Comalapa, Guatemala 154/B3
Comalapa, Nicaragua 154/E4
Comalcalco, Mexico 150/N7
Comanche (co.), Kansas 232/C4
Comanche, Mont. 262/H4
Comanche (co.), Okla. 288/K5
Comanche, Okla. 288/L6
Comanche (co.), Texas 303/F5
Comanche, Texas 303/F5
Comandante Fontana, Argentina 143/D2
Comandante Luis Piedrabuena, Argentina 143/C6
Comanești, Romania 45/H2
Comarapa, Bolivia 136/C5
Comayagua, Honduras 154/D3
Combahee (riv.), S.C. 296/F6
Comber, N. Ireland 17/K2

Comber, Ontario 177/B5
Combermere (bay), Burma 72/B3
Combermere, Ontario 177/G2
Combine, Texas 303/H9
Combined Locks, Wis. 317/K7
Comblain-au-Pont, Belgium 27/G8
Combourg, France 28/C3
Comboyne, N.S. Wales 97/G2
Combs, Ark. 202/C2
Comb Wash (creek), Utah 304/E6
Comeauville, Nova Scotia 168/B4
Come By Chance, Newf. 166/D2
Come-by-Chance, N.S. Wales 97/E2
Comendador, Dom. Rep. 158/C6
Comer, Ala. 195/H6
Comer, Georgia 217/F2
Comeragh (mts.), Ireland 17/F7
Comerford (dam), N.H. 268/D3
Comerford (dam), Vt. 268/D3
Comerío, P. Rico 161/G2
Comet (riv.), Queensland 88/H4
Comet (riv.), Queensland 95/B5
Comfort, N.C. 281/O5
Comfort (cape), N.W. Terr. 187/K3
Comfort, Texas 303/F7
Comfrey, Minn. 255/D6
Comilla, Bangladesh 68/G4
Comines, Belgium 27/B7
Comino (isl.), Malta 34/E7
Comins, Mich. 250/E4
Comiso, Italy 34/E6
Comitán de Domínguez, Mexico 150/O8
Comite, La. 238/K1
Commack, N.Y. 276/O9
Commentry, France 28/E4
Commerce, Calif. 204/C10
Commerce, Georgia 217/E2
Commerce, Mo. 261/O8
Commerce, Okla. 288/R1
Commerce, Texas 303/J4
Commerce City, Colo. 208/K3
Commercial Point, Ohio 284/E6
Commercy, France 28/F3
Commewijne (dist.), Suriname 131/D3
Commewijne (riv.), Suriname 131/D3
Commiskey, Ind. 227/F7
Commissaires (lake), Québec 172/E1
Commissioner (isl.), Manitoba 179/E2
Committee (bay), N.W.T. 162/H2
Committee (bay), N.W. Terr. 187/K3
Commodore, Pa. 294/D4
Commodore (reef), Philippines 85/F4
Commonwealth, Wis. 317/K4
Communism (mt.), U.S.S.R. 54/J6
Communism (peak), U.S.S.R. 48/H6
Como, Colo. 208/H4
Como (prov.), Italy 34/B2
Como, Italy 7/E4
Como, Italy 34/B2
Como (lake), Italy 34/B1
Como, La. 238/G2
Como, Miss. 256/E1
Como, N.C. 281/P1
Como, Tenn. 237/E8
Como, Texas 303/J4
Como, Wis. 317/K10
Comodoro Rivadavia, Argentina 143/C6
Comodoro Rivadavia, Argentina 2/G7
Comoé (riv.), Ivory Coast 106/D7
Comoé (riv.), Burkina Faso 106/D7
Comorin (cape), India 54/J9
Comorin (cape), India 2/N5
Comorin (cape), India 68/D7
Comoros 2/M6
Comoros 102/G2
COMOROS 118/G2
Comox, Br. Col. 184/H2
Compañero, Arroyo (creek), N. Mex. 274/B2
Compass Lake, Fla. 212/D6
Compeer, Alberta 182/E4
Compiègne, France 28/E3
Compostela, Mexico 150/G6
Comprida (isl.), Brazil 135/C4
Comptche, Calif. 204/B4
Compton, Calif. 204/C11
Compton, Ill. 222/D2
Compton, Md. 245/M7
Compton (co.), Québec 172/F4
Compton, Québec 172/F4
Comrie, Scotland 15/E4
Comstock (dam), Conn. 210/F2
Comstock, Minn. 255/B6
Comstock, Nebr. 264/E3
Comstock, N.Y. 276/O4
Comstock, Texas 303/C8
Comstock, Wis. 317/C5
Comstocks Bridge, Conn. 210/F2
Comté (riv.), Fr. Guiana 131/E3
Comunidad, Venezuela 124/E6
Cona, China 77/D6
Conaica, Peru 128/E9
Conakry (cap.), Guinea 102/A4
Conanicut (isl.), R.I. 249/J6
Conara Junction, Tasmania 99/D3
Conargo, N.S. Wales 97/C6
Conasauga, Tenn. 237/M10
Conasauga (riv.), Tenn. 237/M11
Concarneau, France 28/A4
Conceição da Barra, Brazil 132/G7
Conceição do Araguaia, Brazil 132/D5
Conceição do Araguaia, Brazil 120/D3
Concepción, Corrientes, Argentina 143/E2
Concepción, Tucumán, Argentina 143/C2
Concepción, El Beni, Bolivia 136/B2
Concepción, Santa Cruz, Bolivia 136/D5
Concepción (lag.), Bolivia 136/E5
Concepción, Chile 138/D1
Concepción, Chile 120/B6
Concepción (chan.), Chile 138/D9
Concepción (bay), Mexico 150/D3
Concepción, Paraguay 144/D3
Concepción, Paraguay 144/D3

Concepción, Paraguay 120/D5
Concepción, Peru 128/E8
Concepcion, Texas 303/F10
Concepción de la Sierra, Argentina 143/E2
Concepción del Oro, Mexico 150/J4
Concepción del Uruguay, Argentina 143/G6
Concepción de María, Honduras 154/D4
Conception (pt.), Calif. 188/B4
Conception (pt.), Calif. 204/E9
Conception (bay), Newf. 166/D2
Conception Harbour, Newf. 166/D2
Conception Junction, Mo. 261/C2
Conchas (res.), N. Mex. 188/F3
Conchas (dam), N. Mex. 274/E3
Conchas (lake), N. Mex. 274/E3
Conchas Dam, N. Mex. 274/E3
Conche, Newf. 166/C3
Conchi, Chile 138/B2
Conchillas, Uruguay 145/B5
Conchi Viejo, Chile 138/B3
Concho, Ariz. 198/F4
Concho, Okla. 288/L3
Concho (co.), Texas 303/E6
Conchos (riv.), Mexico 146/H7
Conchos (riv.), Mexico 150/G2
Concise, Switzerland 39/B2
Concón, Chile 138/F2
Conconully, Wash. 310/F2
Concord, Calif. 204/K1
Concord, Del. 245/R6
Concord, Fla. 212/B1
Concord, Georgia 217/D4
Concord, Ill. 222/C4
Concord, Ky. 237/P3
Concord •, Mass. 249/B6
Concord (riv.), Mass. 249/J2
Concord, Mich. 250/E6
Concord, Mo. 261/P4
Concord, Nebr. 264/H2
Concord (cap.), N.H. 146/L5
Concord (cap.), N.H. 188/M2
Concord (cap.), N.H. 268/D5
Concord, N.S. Wales 88/K4
Concord, N.S. Wales 97/J3
Concord, N.C. 281/H4
Concord, Pa. 294/G5
Concord, Tenn. 237/N9
Concord •, Vt. 268/D3
Concord, Va. 307/K6
Concord, Wis. 317/H1
Concordia, Argentina 143/G5
Concordia, Argentina 120/D6
Concórdia, Brazil 132/D9
Concordia, Honduras 154/D3
Concordia, Kansas 232/E2
Concordia, Ky. 237/J4
Concordia (par.), La. 238/G4
Concordia, Mexico 150/G5
Concordia, Mo. 261/E5
Concordia, Peru 128/E5
Concordville, Pa. 294/M6
Concrete, N. Dak. 282/P2
Concrete, Wash. 310/D2
Con Cuong, Vietnam 72/E3
Conda, Idaho 220/G7
Condado, Cuba 158/E2
Condamine (riv.), Queensland 88/H5
Condamine (riv.), Queensland 95/D5
Condar, Colombia 126/D8
Conde, Brazil 132/G5
Conde, S. Dak. 298/N3
Condega, Nicaragua 154/D4
Condit, Ohio 284/E5
Condo, Bolivia 136/B6
Condobolin, N.S. Wales 97/D3
Condobolin, N. S. Wales 88/H6
Condom, France 28/D6
Condon, Mont. 262/C3
Condon, Oreg. 291/G2
Condor, Alberta 182/C3
Cóndor, Cordillera del (range), Ecuador 128/C5
Cóndor, Cordillera del (range), Peru 128/C5
Condoto, Colombia 126/B5
Cone, Texas 303/C4
Conecuh (co.), Ala. 195/E8
Conecuh (riv.), Ala. 195/D8
Conegliano, Italy 34/D2
Conehatta, Miss. 256/F6
Conejos (co.), Colo. 208/G8
Conejos, Colo. 208/G8
Conejos (peak), Colo. 208/G8
Conejos (riv.), Colo. 208/G8
Conemaugh (riv.), Pa. 294/D5
Conemaugh River (lake), Pa. 294/D4
Conestee, S.C. 296/C2
Conestoga, Pa. 294/K6
Conesus, N.Y. 276/E5
Conesus (lake), N.Y. 276/E5
Conesville, Iowa 229/L6
Conesville, Ohio 284/G5
Conetoe, N.C. 281/O3
Conewango, N.Y. 276/C6
Conewango (creek), N.Y. 276/B6
Conewango (creek), Pa. 294/D1
Confidence, Iowa 229/G7
Confidence (riv.), Pa. 237/P6
Confluence, Pa. 294/D6
Confolens, France 28/D4
Confusion (range), Utah 304/A4
Confuso (riv.), Paraguay 144/C4
Cong, Ireland 17/C4
Congamond (lakes), Conn. 210/E1
Congamond (lakes), Mass. 249/D4
Congaree (riv.), S.C. 296/E4
Congaree Nat'l Mon., S.C. 296/F4
Contla, Mexico 150/M1
Contoocook, N.H. 268/D5
Contoocook (riv.), N.H. 268/D6
Contra Costa (co.), Calif. 204/D6
Contramaestre, Cuba 158/G3
Contratación, Colombia 126/D4
Contrecoeur, Québec 172/D4

Congo 102/D5
CONGO 115/C3
Congo (riv.) 102/D5
Congo (riv.) 2/L5
Congo (riv.), Angola 115/C4
Congo (riv.), Congo 115/C4
Congo, Ohio 284/F6
Congo (riv.), Zaire 115/C4
Congonhas, Brazil 135/E2
Congress, Ariz. 198/C4
Congress, Ohio 284/F4
Congress, Sask. 181/E6
Congress Heights, D.C. 245/F5
Cónico, Cerro (mt.), Argentina 143/B5
Cónico, Cerro (mt.), Chile 138/E4
Conimicut, R.I. 249/J6
Coningsby, England 13/G4
Coniston, North. Terr. 93/C7
Conjuror (bay), N.W. Terr. 187/G3
Conklin, Alberta 182/E2
Conklin, Mich. 250/D5
Conley, Georgia 217/K2
Conn, Lough (lake), Ireland 10/B3
Conn (lake), Ireland 17/C3
Conn (lake), N.W. Terr. 187/L2
Connacht (prov.), Ireland 17/C4
Connacht (trad. prov.), Ireland 17
Connah's Quay, Wales 13/G2
Connaught Heights, Sask. 181/G3
Conneaut, Ohio 284/J2
Conneaut Lake, Pa. 294/B2
Conneaut Lake Park, Pa. 294/B2
Conneautville, Pa. 294/A2
Connecticut 188/M2
CONNECTICUT 210
Connecticut (riv.) 188/M2
Connecticut (riv.), Conn. 210/E2
Connecticut (riv.), Mass. 249/D2
Connecticut (riv.), N.H. 268/B6
Connecticut (state), U.S. 146/L5
Connecticut (riv.), Vt. 268/C4
Connell, Scotland 15/D4
Connell, New Bruns. 170/C2
Connell, Wash. 310/G4
Connell Creek, Sask. 181/H3
Connellsville, Pa. 294/C5
Connellys Springs, N.C. 281/F3
Connelsville, Pa. 261/G2
Connemara (dist.), Ireland 17/B5
Conner, Mont. 262/B5
Conner (mt.), North. Terr. 93/B8
Connersville, Ind. 227/G5
Connerville, Okla. 288/N6
Connétable (isls.), Fr. Guiana 131/F3
Connoquenessing, Pa. 294/B4
Connors, New Bruns. 170/B1
Conoble, N.S. Wales 97/C3
Conococheague (creek), Md. 245/G1
Cononbridge, Scotland 15/E3
Conover, N.C. 281/G3
Conover, Ohio 284/B5
Conover, Wis. 317/H3
Conowingo, Md. 245/O2
Conowingo (dam), Md. 245/O2
Conquerall Bank, Nova Scotia 168/D4
Conquest, Sask. 181/D4
Conquista, Bolivia 136/B2
Conrad, Alberta 182/D5
Conrad, Iowa 229/H4
Conrad, Mont. 262/D2
Conran, Mo. 261/N10
Conrath, Wis. 317/E5
Conroe, Texas 303/J7
Conroy, Iowa 229/J5
Consecon, Ontario 177/G3
Conselheiro Lafaiete, Brazil 135/E2
Conselheiro Lafaiete, Brazil 132/E8
Consett, England 13/H3
Conshohocken, Pa. 294/M5
Consolación del Norte, Cuba 158/B1
Consolación del Sur, Cuba 158/B2
Consolación del Sur, Cuba 156/A2
Consort, Alberta 182/E3
Constable, N.Y. 276/M1
Constableville, N.Y. 276/J3
Constance (lake), Austria 41/A3
Constance (lake), Germany 22/C5
Constance, Ky. 237/R2
Constance, Sask. 181/F6
Constance (lake), Switzerland 39/H1
Constance (mt.), Wash. 310/B3
Constancia, Uruguay 145/B3
Constant, Morne (hill), Guadeloupe 161/B7
Constanța, Romania 7/G4
Constanța, Romania 45/J3
Constantia, N.Y. 276/H4
Constantia, S. Africa 118/E6
Constantine, Spain 33/D4
Constantine (bay), Alaska 196/G3
Constantine, Algeria 102/G1
Constantine, Algeria 106/F1
Constantine, Mich. 250/D7
Constanza, Argentina 143/G6
Constanza, Dom. Rep. 158/D6
Constitución, Chile 138/A11
Constitución, Uruguay 145/A2
Constitution, Georgia 217/K2
Constitution, Ohio 284/G7
Consuegra, Spain 33/E3
Consul, Ala. 195/C6
Consul, Sask. 181/B6
Contact, Nev. 266/G1
Contamana, Peru 128/E6
Contas (riv.), Brazil 132/F6
Contentnea (creek), N.C. 281/N3
Conthey, Switzerland 39/D4
Continental, Ariz. 198/D7
Continental, Ohio 284/B3
Continental (peak), Wyo. 319/G3

Contreras (isl.), Chile 138/D9
Contreras (isls.), Panama 154/F7
Controller (bay), Alaska 196/J3
Contulmo, Chile 138/D7
Contumazá, Peru 128/C6
Contwoyto (lake), N.W.T. 162/G2
Contwoyto (lake), N.W. Terr. 187/H3
Convención, Colombia 126/D3
Convent, La. 238/L3
Convent Station, N.J. 273/E2
Conversano, Italy 34/F4
Converse (hill), Conn. 210/F1
Converse, Ind. 227/F3
Converse, La. 238/C3
Converse, S.C. 296/D2
Converse, Texas 303/K11
Converse (co.), Wyo. 319/G3
Convoy, Ireland 17/F2
Convoy, Ohio 284/A4
Conway (co.), Ark. 202/E3
Conway, Ark. 202/F3
Conway (lake), Ark. 202/F3
Conway, Iowa 229/D7
Conway, Kansas 232/E3
Conway, Ky. 237/N6
Conway •, Mass. 249/D2
Conway, Mich. 250/E3
Conway, Miss. 256/E5
Conway, Mo. 261/G7
Conway, N.H. 268/E4
Conway •, N.H. 268/E4
Conway, N.C. 281/P2
Conway, N. Dak. 282/P3
Conway, Nova Scotia 168/C4
Conway, Pa. 294/B4
Conway, S.C. 296/J4
Conway, Texas 303/C2
Conway, Wash. 310/C2
Conway Springs, Kansas 232/E4
Conwy, Wales 10/E4
Conwy, Wales 13/D4
Conwy (bay), Wales 13/C4
Conyers, Georgia 217/D3
Conyngham, Pa. 294/K3
Coober Pedy, S. Australia 88/E5
Coober Pedy, S. Australia 94/D3
Cooch Behar, India 68/F3
Coogee, N.S. Wales 97/K3
Cook (isls.) 87/K7
Cook (inlet), Alaska 196/B1
Cook (mt.), Alaska 196/K2
Cook (cape), Br. Col. 184/C5
Cook (bay), Chile 138/E11
Cook (co.), Georgia 217/F8
Cook (co.), Ill. 222/F4
Cook (co.), Minn. 255/H3
Cook, Minn. 255/F3
Cook, Nebr. 264/H4
Cook (isls.), N. Zealand 2/B6
Cook (inlet), Alaska 196/B1
Cook (mt.), N. Zealand 87/G10
Cook (mt.), N. Zealand 100/C5
Cook (str.), N. Zealand 87/H10
Cook (str.), N. Zealand 100/D5
Cook, S. Australia 88/E6
Cook, S. Australia 94/B4
Cook (inlet), U.S. 4/D17
Cook (pt.), Victoria 97/H5
Cook (pt.), Victoria 88/K7
Cook, Wash. 310/D5
Cooke (co.), Texas 303/G4
Cooke City, Mont. 262/G6
Cookes (range), N. Mex. 274/B6
Cookeville, Tenn. 237/L8
Cooking Lake, Alberta 182/D3
Cook's (Paopao) (bay), Fr. Poly. 86/S12
Cooks, Mich. 250/C3
Cooksburg, Pa. 294/D3
Cooks Falls, N.Y. 276/K7
Cook's Harbour, Newf. 166/C3
Cookshire, Québec 172/F4
Cooks Mills, Ill. 222/E4
Cook Station, Mo. 261/K7
Cookstown, N.J. 273/D3
Cookstown (dist.), N. Ireland 17/H2
Cookstown, N. Ireland 10/H3
Cookstown, N. Ireland 17/H2
Cookstown, Ontario 177/E3
Cooksville, Ill. 222/E3
Cooksville, Md. 245/K3
Cooksville, Miss. 256/H5
Cooktown, Australia 87/E7
Cooktown, Queensland 95/C2
Cooktown, Queensland 88/H3
Cool, Texas 303/G5
Coolabah, N.S. Wales 97/D2
Cooladdi, Queensland 95/C5
Cooladdi, Queensland 88/H5
Coolah, N.S. Wales 97/E3
Coolamon, N.S. Wales 97/D4
Coolaney, Ireland 17/D3
Coolatai, N.S. Wales 97/F1
Cooleemee, N.C. 281/H3
Coolgardie, W. Australia 88/C6
Coolgardie, W. Australia 92/C5
Coolgreany, Ireland 17/J6
Coolibah, North. Terr. 93/B3
Coolidge, Ariz. 198/D6
Coolidge (dam), Ariz. 198/E5
Coolidge, Georgia 217/D8
Coolidge, Kansas 232/A3
Coolidge, Texas 303/H6
Coolidge Dam, Ariz. 198/E5
Coolin, Idaho 220/B1
Cool Spring, Del. 245/T6
Cool Valley, Mo. 261/P2
Coolville, Ohio 284/G7
Cooma, N.S. Wales 88/H7
Cooma, N.S. Wales 97/E5
Coombs, Br. Col. 184/H4
Coonabarabran, N.S. Wales 97/E2
Coonamble, N.S. Wales 88/H6
Coonamble, N.S. Wales 97/E2
Coondapoor, India 68/C6
Coon Rapids, Iowa 229/D5
Coon Rapids, Minn. 255/G5
Coon Valley, Wis. 317/E8

Coventry 355

Cooper, Ala. 195/E5
Cooper (pt.), Calif. 204/D7
Cooper, Iowa 229/E5
Cooper, Ky. 237/M7
Cooper, Maine 243/H6
Cooper•, Maine 243/H6
Cooper (co.), Mo. 261/G5
Cooper (riv.), N.J. 273/B3
Cooper, S.C. 296/H4
Cooper (riv.), S.C. 296/H6
Cooper, Texas 303/J4
Cooper (lake), Wyo. 319/G4
Co-Operative, Ky. 237/M7
Cooper City, Fla. 212/B4
Cooperdale, Ohio 284/F5
Cooper Landing, Alaska 196/C1
Coopers (Barcoo) (creek), Queensland 95/B5
Coopers (Barcoo) (creek), S. Australia 88/G5
Coopers (Barcoo) (creek), S. Australia 94/F3
Coopersburg, Pa. 294/M5
Coopers Mills, Maine 243/E7
Coopers Plains, N.Y. 276/F6
Coopers Plains, Queensland 95/D3
Coopers Plains, Queensland 88/K3
Cooperstown, N.Y. 276/L5
Cooperstown, N. Dak. 282/O5
Cooperstown, Pa. 294/C2
Coopersville, Ky. 237/M7
Coopersville, Mich. 250/C5
Cooperton, Okla. 288/J5
Coorabie, S. Australia 88/E6
Coorabie, S. Australia 94/B4
Coorong, The (lag.), S. Australia 94/F6
Coorow, W. Australia 92/B5
Coos (co.), N.H. 268/E2
Coos (co.), Oreg. 291/C4
Coos (riv.), Oreg. 291/D4
Coosa (co.), Ala. 195/F5
Coosa (riv.), Ala. 195/F4
Coosa, Georgia 217/B2
Coosa (riv.), Georgia 217/A2
Coosada, Ala. 195/F5
Coosaw (riv.), S.C. 296/G7
Coosawattee (riv.), Georgia 217/C1
Coosawhatchie, S.C. 296/F6
Coosawhatchie (riv.), S.C. 296/E6
Coos Bay, Oreg. 188/A2
Coos Bay, Oreg. 291/C4
Cootamundra, N.S. Wales 88/H6
Cootamundra, N.S. Wales 97/D4
Cootehill, Ireland 17/G3
Cootehill, Ireland 10/C3
Cooter, Mo. 261/N10
Copacabana, Argentina 143/C2
Copacabana, Bolivia 136/A5
Copake, N.Y. 276/N6
Copake Falls, N.Y. 276/N6
Copala, Mexico 150/K8
Copalis Beach, Wash. 310/A3
Copalis Crossing, Wash. 310/B3
Copan, Okla. 288/P1
Copano (bay), Texas 303/G9
Copco (lake), Calif. 204/C2
Cope, Colo. 208/O3
Cope, Ind. 227/E6
Cope, S.C. 296/E5
Cope (cape), Spain 33/F4
Copeland, Ala. 195/B7
Copeland, Fla. 212/E6
Copeland, Idaho 220/B1
Copeland, Kansas 232/B4
Copeland (isl.), N. Ireland 17/K2
Copemish, Mich. 250/D4
Copen, W. Va. 312/E5
Copenhagen (commune), Denmark 21/F6
Copenhagen (cap.), Denmark 7/F3
Copenhagen (cap.), Denmark 21/F6
Copenhagen (cap.), Denmark 18/G9
Copenhagen, N.Y. 276/J3
Copere, Bolivia 136/D6
Copiague, N.Y. 276/O9
Copiah (co.), Miss. 256/D7
Copiapó, Chile 120/B5
Copiapó, Chile 138/B6
Copiapó (bay), Chile 138/A6
Copiapó (riv.), Chile 138/A6
Copinsay (isl.), Scotland 15/F2
Coplay, Pa. 294/L4
Copley, S. Australia 94/F4
Copmanhurst, N.S. Wales 97/G1
Coporito, Venezuela 124/H3
Coporolo (riv.), Angola 115/B6
Coppell, Texas 303/G2
Coppename (riv.), Suriname 131/C3
Copper (riv.), Alaska 196/J2
Copper (mts.), Ariz. 198/B6
Copperas Cove, Texas 303/G6
Copper Canyon, Texas 303/F1
Copper Center, Alaska 196/J2
Copper City, Mich. 250/A1
Copperfield, W. Australia 88/C5
Copperfield, W. Australia 92/B5
Copper Harbor, Mich. 250/B1
Copperhill, Tenn. 237/N10
Copper Hill, Va. 307/H6
Coppermine, Canada 4/C15
Coppermine, N.W.T. 162/E2
Coppermine (riv.), N.W.T. 162/E2
Coppermine (riv.), N.W.T. 187/G3
Coppermine, N.W. Terr. 187/G3
Copper Mountain, Br. Col. 184/G5
Copperton, Utah 304/B3
Copper Valley, Va. 307/G7
Coppet, Switzerland 39/B4
Coppock, Iowa 229/K6
Coqên, China 77/C5
Coquet (riv.), England 13/F2
Coquí, P. Rico 161/D3
Coquille, Oreg. 291/C4
Coquille (pt.), Oreg. 291/C4
Coquimatlán, Mexico 150/G7
Coquimbo (reg.), Chile 138/A8
Coquimbo, Chile 120/B6
Coquimbo, Chile 138/A8
Coquitlam, Br. Col. 184/K3
Cora, Ill. 222/D6
Cora, Wyo. 319/C3
Corabia, Romania 45/G4
Coracora, Peru 128/F10
Corail, Haiti 158/A6
Coraki, N.S. Wales 97/G1
Coral (sea) 87/F7
Coral (sea) 88/H2
Coral (sea) 2/S6
Coral, Mich. 250/D5
Coral (sea), New Caled. 86/G4
Coral (sea), Papua N.G. 85/B7
Coral, Pa. 294/D5
Coral (bay), Philippines 82/A6
Coral (sea), Queensland 95/C1
Coral (bay), Virgin Is. (U.S.) 161/C4
Coral Cove, Fla. 212/D4
Coral Gables, Fla. 212/B5
Coral Harbour, N.W.T. 162/H2
Coral Harbour, N.W. Terr. 187/K3
Coral Hills, Md. 245/G5
Coral Sea Islands (terr.), Australia 87/E7
CORAL SEA ISLANDS TERR. 95/C2
Coral Sea Islands Territory, Australia 88/J3
Coral Springs, Fla. 212/F5
Coralville, Iowa 229/K5
Coralville (lake), Iowa 229/K5
Coram, Mont. 262/C2
Coramba, N.S. Wales 97/G2
Corangamite (lake), Victoria 97/B6
Corantijn (riv.), Suriname 131/C3
Coraopolis, Pa. 294/B4
Corapeake, N.C. 281/R1
Corato, Italy 34/F4
Corbeil, Ontario 177/E1
Corberrie, Nova Scotia 168/C4
Corbigny, France 28/E4
Corbin, Kansas 232/E4
Corbin, Ky. 237/N7
Corbin City, N.J. 273/D5
Corbridge, England 13/E3
Corby, England 13/G5
Corcelles-près-Payerne, Switzerland 39/C3
Corcoran, Calif. 204/F7
Corcoran, Minn. 255/F5
Corcovado (gulf), Chile 120/B7
Corcovado (gulf), Chile 138/D4
Corcovado (vol.), Chile 138/D5
Corcubión, Spain 33/B1
Cord, Ark. 202/H2
Cordaville, Mass. 249/H3
Cordele, Georgia 217/E7
Cordelia, Calif. 204/K1
Cordell, Okla. 288/H4
Cordell Hull (res.), Tenn. 237/K8
Corder, Mo. 261/E4
Cordesville, S.C. 296/H5
Cordillera, Paraguay 144/D4
Cordillo Grounds, S. Australia 94/G2
Córdoba (prov.), Argentina 143/D3
Córdoba, Argentina 2/F7
Córdoba, Argentina 143/D3
Córdoba, Argentina 120/C6
Córdoba (dept.), Colombia 126/C3
Córdoba, Mexico 150/P2
Córdoba (prov.), Spain 33/D3
Córdoba, Spain 33/D4
Córdoba, Spain 7/D5
Cordobés (riv.), Uruguay 145/D3
Cordova, Ala. 195/D3
Cordova, Alaska 196/D1
Cordova, Alaska 188/D6
Cordova, Alaska 146/D3
Cordova (bay), Alaska 196/M2
Cordova, Ill. 222/C2
Cordova, Manitoba 179/C4
Cordova, Md. 245/O5
Cordova, Nebr. 264/G4
Cordova, N. Mex. 274/D2
Córdova, Peru 128/E10
Cordova, S.C. 296/F5
Cordova, Tenn. 237/B10
Cordova, U.S. 4/C17
Cordova Mines, Ontario 177/G3
Core (banks), N.C. 281/S5
Core (sound), N.C. 281/S5
Core, W. Va. 312/F3
Corea, Maine 243/H7
Coredó (Humboldt) (bay), Colombia 126/B4
Coree South, N.S. Wales 97/C4
Corella, Spain 33/F1
Corey, La. 238/F2
Corfield, Queensland 88/G4
Corfield, Queensland 95/B4
Corfu (Kérkira) (isl.), Greece 45/D6
Corfu, N.Y. 276/D5
Corgémont, Switzerland 39/D2
Cori, Italy 34/F7
Coria, Spain 33/C3
Coria del Río, Spain 33/C4
Corigliano Calabro, Italy 34/F5
Corinda, Queensland 88/K3
Corinda, Queensland 95/A3
Corinda, Queensland 95/D3
Coringa (islets), Australia 87/F7
Coringa (isls.), Coral Sea Is. Terr. 88/H3
Corinna•, Maine 243/E6
Corinne, Okla. 288/R6
Corinne, Sask. 181/G5
Corinne, Utah 304/B2
Corinne, W. Va. 312/D7
Corinth, Ark. 202/C3
Corinth, Georgia 217/B4
Corinth, Greece 45/F7
Corinth (gulf), Greece 45/F6
Corinth, Ky. 237/M3
Corinth, Miss. 256/G1
Corinth, N.Y. 276/N4
Corinth, N. Dak. 282/D2
Corinth•, Vt. 268/C3
Corinth, W. Va. 312/H4
Corinto, Brazil 132/E7
Corinto, Colombia 126/B6
Corinto, Nicaragua 154/D4
Coriole, Somalia 115/H3
Coripata, Bolivia 136/B5
Corisco (isl.), Equat. Guinea 115/A3
Cork (co.), Ireland 17/D7
Cork, Ireland 7/D3
Cork, Ireland 10/B5
Cork, Ireland 17/E8
Cork (harb.), Ireland 17/E8
Cork (harb.), Ireland 10/B5
Cork, New Bruns. 170/D3
Corker (cay), Belize 154/D2
Corleone, Italy 34/D6
Corley, W. Va. 312/E5
Çorlu, Turkey 63/B2
Cormorant, Manitoba 179/H3
Cormorant (lake), Manitoba 179/H3
Cormorant, Minn. 255/B4
Corn (creek), Ariz. 198/E3
Corn, Okla. 288/J4
Cornaca, Bolivia 136/C7
Corncake (inlet), N.C. 281/O7
Cornelia, Georgia 217/E1
Cornélio Procópio, Brazil 132/D8
Cornelius, N.C. 281/H4
Cornelius, Oreg. 291/A2
Cornell, Ill. 222/E3
Cornell, Mich. 250/B3
Cornell, Wis. 317/D5
Corner (inlet), Victoria 97/D6
Corner Brook, Newf. 166/C4
Corner Brook, Newf. 162/K6
Cornerstone, Ark. 202/G5
Cornersville, Md. 245/O6
Cornersville, Miss. 256/F1
Cornersville, Tenn. 237/H10
Cornerville, Ark. 202/G6
Cornettes de Bise (mts.), Switzerland 39/C4
Cornfield (pt.), Conn. 210/F3
Cornfields, Ariz. 198/F3
Cornhill, New Bruns. 170/E3
Cornhill, Scotland 15/F3
Corning, Ark. 202/J1
Corning, Calif. 204/C4
Corning, Iowa 229/D7
Corning, Kansas 232/F2
Corning, Mo. 261/B2
Corning, N.Y. 276/F6
Corning, Ohio 284/F6
Corning, Sask. 181/J6
Cornish, Colo. 208/L2
Cornish•, Maine 243/B8
Cornish, Okla. 288/L6
Cornish, Utah 304/B2
Cornish Flat, N.H. 268/C4
Cornishville, Ky. 237/M5
Cornland, Ill. 222/D4
Cornlea, Nebr. 264/G3
Corno (mt.), Italy 34/D3
Cornucopia, Wis. 317/D2
Cornville, Ariz. 198/D4
Cornville•, Maine 243/D6
Cornwall•, Conn. 210/B1
Cornwall (co.), England 13/C7
Cornwall (cape), England 13/B7
Cornwall (isl.), N.W.T. 162/M3
Cornwall (isl.), N.W. Terr. 187/J2
Cornwall, Ont. 162/J7
Cornwall, Ontario 177/K2
Cornwall, Pa. 294/K5
Cornwall, Pr. Edward I. 168/E2
Cornwall, Tasmania 99/E3
Cornwall•, Vt. 268/A4
Cornwall Bridge, Conn. 210/B1
Cornwall Center, Conn. 210/B1
Cornwall Hollow, Conn. 210/B1
Cornwallis (isl.), N.W.T. 162/F1
Cornwallis (isl.), N.W. Terr. 187/J2
Cornwall On Hudson, N.Y. 276/M8
Cornwell, Fla. 212/E4
Coro, Venezuela 124/D2
Coro, Venezuela 120/C1
Coroatá, Brazil 132/F3
Corocoro, Bolivia 120/C4
Corocoro, Bolivia 136/A5
Corofin, Ireland 17/C6
Coroico, Bolivia 136/B5
Corolla, N.C. 281/T2
Coromandel, Brazil 132/E7
Coromandel, N. Zealand 100/E2
Coromandel (pen.), N. Zealand 100/F2
Coromandel (range), N. Zealand 100/E2
Coromandel Coast (reg.), India 68/E6
Coron, Philippines 82/C4
Coron (isl.), Philippines 82/C5
Corona, Ala. 195/C3
Corona, Calif. 204/E11
Corona, N. Mex. 274/D4
Corona, S. Dak. 298/R3
Coronaca, S.C. 296/C3
Coronach, Sask. 181/F6
Coronada (bay), C. Rica 154/F6
Coronado, Calif. 204/H11
Coronado (pt.), Philippines 82/C7
Coronado Nat'l Memorial, Ariz. 198/E7
Coronados (gulf), Chile 138/D4
Coronation (isl.), Alaska 196/M2
Coronation, Alberta 182/E3
Coronation (isl.), Ant. 5/C16
Coronation (gulf), N.W.T. 162/E2
Coronation (gulf), N.W. Terr. 187/G3
Coronda, Argentina 143/F6
Coronel, Chile 138/D1
Coronel, Chile 120/B6
Coronel Bogado, Argentina 143/F6
Coronel Bogado, Paraguay 144/D5
Coronel Brandsen, Argentina 143/H7
Coronel Dorrego, Argentina 143/D4
Coronel F. Cabrera, Bolivia 136/E6
Coronel F. Cabrera (mt.), Paraguay 144/B1
Coronel Martínez, Paraguay 144/B5
Coronel Moldes, Argentina 143/C2
Coronel Oviedo, Paraguay 144/C5
Coronel Pringles, Argentina 143/D4
Coronel Suárez, Argentina 143/D4
Coronel Vidal, Argentina 143/E4
Corongo, Peru 128/D7
Coronie (dist.), Suriname 131/C3
Coropuna, Nudo (mt.), Peru 128/F10
Cororooke, Victoria 97/B6
Çorovodë, Albania 45/E5
Corowa, N.S. Wales 97/D4
Corozal, Colombia 126/C3
Corozal, P. Rico 161/D1
Corozal Town, Belize 154/C1
Corozo Pando, Venezuela 124/E3
Corpach, Scotland 15/C4
Corpus Christi, Texas 188/G5
Corpus Christi, Texas 146/J7
Corpus Christi, Texas 303/G10
Corpus Christi (bay), Texas 188/G5
Corpus Christi (lake), Texas 303/F9
Corpus Christi N.A.S., Texas 303/G10
Corque, Bolivia 136/B6
Corquín, Honduras 154/C3
Corral, Chile 138/D3
Corral, Idaho 220/D6
Corral City, Texas 303/F1
Corral de Almaguer, Spain 33/E3
Corral de Bustos, Argentina 143/D3
Corrales, N. Mex. 274/C3
Corralillo, Cuba 158/D1
Corralitos, Calif. 204/L4
Corral Viejo, P. Rico 161/C2
Correct, Ind. 227/G7
Correctionville, Iowa 229/B4
Correggio, Italy 34/C2
Corregidor (isl.), Philippines 82/C3
Correll, Minn. 255/B5
Corrente, Brazil 132/E5
Corrente (riv.), Brazil 132/E6
Correntina, Brazil 132/E6
Corrèze (dept.), France 28/D5
Corrib (lake), Ireland 17/C5
Corrib, Lough (lake), Ireland 10/B4
Corridon, Mo. 261/L8
Corrie, Scotland 15/C5
Corrientes (prov.), Argentina 143/E2
Corrientes, Argentina 143/E2
Corrientes, Argentina 120/D5
Corrientes (riv.), Argentina 143/E2
Corrientes (cape), Colombia 120/B2
Corrientes (cape), Colombia 126/B5
Corrientes (cape), Cuba 158/A2
Corrientes (inlet), Cuba 158/A2
Corrientes (cape), Mexico 146/H7
Corrientes (cape), Mexico 150/F6
Corrientes (riv.), Peru 128/E4
Corrigan, Texas 303/K7
Corriganville, Md. 245/C2
Corrigin, W. Australia 92/B6
Corriverton, Guyana 131/C3
Corrumpa (creek), N. Mex. 274/F2
Corry, Pa. 294/C2
Corryong, Victoria 97/D5
Corryton, Tenn. 237/O8
Corse (cape), France 28/B6
Corse du Sud (dept.), France 28/B6
Corserine (mt.), Scotland 15/D5
Corsewall (pt.), Scotland 15/C5
Corsham, England 13/E6
Corsica (isl.), France 7/E4
Corsica (isl.), France 28/B6
Corsica, Pa. 294/D3
Corsica, S. Dak. 298/N7
Corsicana, Texas 188/G4
Corsicana, Texas 303/H5
Corso, Mo. 261/K4
Corson (inlet), N.J. 273/D5
Corson (co.), S. Dak. 298/G2
Corson, S. Dak. 298/R6
Cortaro, Ariz. 198/D6
Corte, France 28/B6
Corte Madera, Calif. 204/J2
Cortés, Cuba 158/A2
Cortés (inlet), Cuba 158/B2
Cortez, Colo. 208/B8
Cortez, Fla. 212/D4
Cortez (mts.), Nev. 266/E2
Cortina d'Ampezzo, Italy 34/D1
Cortland, Ill. 222/E2
Cortland, Ind. 227/F7
Cortland, Nebr. 264/H4
Cortland (co.), N.Y. 276/H5
Cortland, N.Y. 276/H5
Cortland, Ohio 284/J3
Cortona, Italy 34/C3
Coruche, Portugal 33/B3
Çoruh (riv.), Turkey 59/D1
Çoruh (riv.), Turkey 63/J2
Çorum (prov.), Turkey 63/F2
Çorum, Turkey 59/B1
Çorum, Turkey 63/F2
Çorum (riv.), Turkey 63/F2
Corumbá, Brazil 120/D4
Corumbá, Brazil 132/B7
Corunna, Ind. 227/G2
Corunna, Mich. 250/E6
Corunna, Ontario 177/B5
Corvallis, Mont. 262/C4
Corvallis, Oreg. 188/B2
Corvallis, Oreg. 291/D3
Corvo (isl.), Portugal 33/A1
Corvuso, Minn. 255/D6
Corwen (delta), Wales 10/E4
Corwen, Wales 13/D5
Corwin, Kansas 232/D4
Corwin, Ohio 284/B6
Corwin Springs, Mont. 262/F5
Corwith, Iowa 229/F3
Cory, Ind. 227/C6
Corydon, Ind. 227/E8
Corydon, Iowa 229/G7
Corydon, Ky. 237/F5
Coryell (co.), Texas 303/G6
Coryville, Pa. 294/F2
Corzoneso, Switzerland 39/G4
Cosalá, Mexico 150/F4
Cosamaloapan de Carpio, Mexico 150/M7
Cosapa, Bolivia 136/A6
Cosautlán de Carvajal, Mexico 150/P1
Cosby, Mo. 261/C3
Cosby, Tenn. 237/P9
Cos Cob, Conn. 210/A4
Coscomatepec de Bravo, Mexico 150/P2
Cosegüina (pt.), Nicaragua 154/D4
Cosenza (prov.), Italy 34/F5
Cosenza, Italy 34/F5
Cosenza, Italy 7/F5
Coshocton (co.), Ohio 284/G5
Coshocton, Ohio 284/G5
Cosine, Sask. 181/A3
Cosío, Mexico 150/H5
Cosmoledo (isls.), Seychelles 102/G5
Cosmoledo (isls.), Seychelles 118/H1
Cosmo Newbery Aboriginal Res., W. Australia 88/C5
Cosmo Newbery Aboriginal Res., W. Australia 92/C5
Cosmopolis, Wash. 310/B4
Cosmos, Minn. 255/D6
Cosne-Cours-sur-Loire, France 28/E4
Cosperville, Ind. 227/F1
Cosquín, Argentina 143/D3
Cossonay, Switzerland 39/B3
Costa, W. Va. 312/C6
Costa Azul, Uruguay 145/E5
Costa Brava (reg.), Spain 33/H2
Costa da Caparica, Portugal 33/A1
Costa de Sola (Costa del Sol) (reg.), Spain 33/D4
Costa Mesa, Calif. 204/D11
Costa Rica 2/E5
Costa Rica 146/K8
COSTA RICA 154/E5
Costa Rica, Bolivia 136/A2
Costa Rica, Mexico 150/F4
Costa Smeralda (reg.), Italy 34/B4
Costa Verde (reg.), Italy 34/B5
Costello, Pa. 294/G2
Costessey, England 13/J5
Costeşti, Romania 45/G3
Costigan, Maine 243/F5
Costilla (co.), Colo. 208/J8
Costilla, N. Mex. 274/D2
Costilla (peak), N. Mex. 274/D2
Cosumnes (riv.), Calif. 204/C9
Coswig, Dresden, Germany 22/E3
Coswig, Halle, Germany 22/E3
Cotabato, Philippines 85/G4
Cotabato, Philippines 82/D7
Cotacajes (riv.), Bolivia 136/B5
Cotagaita, Bolivia 136/C7
Cotahuasi, Peru 128/F10
Cotati, Calif. 204/C5
Coteau, N. Dak. 282/F2
Coteau (hills), Sask. 181/D4
Coteau-du-Lac, Québec 172/C4
Coteau du Missouri (plain), N. Dak. 282/G3
Coteau-Landing, Québec 172/C4
Coteaux, Haiti 158/A6
Côte-d'Or (dept.), France 28/F4
Côte-d'Or (mts.), France 28/F4
Cotentin (pen.), France 28/C3
Côte-Saint-Luc, Québec 172/H4
Côtes de Fer, Haiti 158/B6
Côtes-du-Nord (dept.), France 28/B3
Cotesfield, Nebr. 264/F3
Cotija de la Paz, Mexico 150/H7
Cotile (lake), La. 238/E4
Coto, Argentina 143/D2
Cotoca, Bolivia 136/D5
Coto Laurel, P. Rico 161/C2
Cotonou, Benin 102/C4
Cotonou, Benin 106/E7
Cotopaxi, Colo. 208/H6
Cotopaxi (prov.), Ecuador 128/C3
Cotopaxi (mt.), Ecuador 128/C3
Cotswold (hills), England 13/E6
Cottage City, Md. 245/F4
Cottage Grove, Ala. 195/F5
Cottage Grove, Ind. 227/H5
Cottage Grove, Minn. 255/F6
Cottage Grove, Oreg. 291/D4
Cottage Grove (lake), Oreg. 291/E4
Cottage Grove, Tenn. 237/E8
Cottagehill, Fla. 212/B6
Cottage Hills, Ill. 222/B2
Cottageville, S.C. 296/G6
Cottageville, W. Va. 312/C5
Cottam, Ontario 177/B5
Cottbus, Germany 22/F3
Cotter, Ark. 202/E1
Cotter, Iowa 229/L6
Cottesloe, W. Australia 88/B2
Cottian Alps (range), France 28/G5
Cottian Alps (range), Italy 34/A2
Cottica, Suriname 131/D4
Cottica (riv.), Suriname 131/D3
Cottle, Ky. 237/P5
Cottle (co.), Texas 303/D3
Cottleville, Mo. 261/M2
Cotton, Georgia 217/D8
Cotton, Minn. 255/F3
Cotton (co.), Okla. 288/K6
Cottonburg, Ky. 237/N5
Cotton Center, Texas 303/C4
Cottondale, Ala. 195/D4
Cottondale, Fla. 212/D6
Cotton Ground, St. Kitts & Nevis 161/C11
Cotton Plant, Ark. 202/H3
Cottonport, La. 238/F5
Cottonton, Ala. 195/H6
Cottontown, Tenn. 237/H8
Cotton Valley, La. 238/D1
Cottonwood, Ala. 195/H8
Cottonwood, Ariz. 198/D4
Cottonwood (cliffs), Ariz. 198/B3
Cottonwood, Br. Col. 184/G3
Cottonwood, Calif. 204/C3
Cottonwood (creek), Calif. 204/C3
Cottonwood, Idaho 220/B3
Cottonwood (butte), Idaho 220/C4
Cottonwood (riv.), Kansas 232/F3
Cottonwood (co.), Minn. 255/C6
Cottonwood, Minn. 255/C6
Cottonwood (riv.), Minn. 255/C6
Cottonwood (creek), Mont. 262/E2
Cottonwood (creek), Oreg. 291/K4
Cottonwood, S. Dak. 298/F6
Cottonwood (creek), S. Dak. 298/E5
Cottonwood (lake), S. Dak. 298/M4
Cottonwood, Texas 303/D5
Cottonwood (creek), Utah 304/C4
Cottonwood (creek), Utah 304/E4
Cottonwood (creek), Wyo. 319/B4
Cottonwood Draw (dry riv.), Texas 303/C10
Cottonwood Falls, Kansas 232/F3
Cottonwood Wash (dry riv.), Ariz. 198/E4
Cottonwood Wash (creek), Utah 304/E6
Cotuí, Dom. Rep. 158/E5
Cotuit, Mass. 249/N6
Cotulla, Texas 303/E9
Couch, Mo. 261/K9
Couchiching (lake), Ontario 177/E3
Couchwood, La. 238/D1
Coudekerque-Branche, France 28/E2
Couderay, Wis. 317/D4
Coudersport, Pa. 294/G2
Coudres (isl.), Québec 172/G2
Cougar (res.), Oreg. 291/E3
Cougar, Wash. 310/C4
Coughlan, New Bruns. 170/E2
Coulee, N. Dak. 282/F2
Coulee City, Wash. 310/F3
Coulee Dam, Wash. 310/G3
Coulee Dam Nat'l Rec. Area, Wash. 310/G2
Coulihaut, Dominica 161/E6
Coulommiers, France 28/E3
Coulter, Iowa 229/G3
Coulter, Manitoba 179/B5
Coulterville, Calif. 204/E6
Coulterville, Ill. 222/D5
Counamama, Fr. Guiana 131/E3
Counce, Tenn. 237/E10
Council, Alaska 196/F2
Council, Georgia 217/G9
Council, Idaho 220/B5
Council, N.C. 281/M6
Council Bluffs, Iowa 229/B6
Council Bluffs, Iowa 188/G2
Council Grove, Kansas 232/F3
Council Grove (lake), Kansas 232/F3
Council Hill, Okla. 288/P3
Countess, Alberta 182/D4
Country (harb.), Nova Scotia 168/G3
Country Club Hills, Ill. 222/B6
Country Club Village, Mo. 261/C3
Country Harbour Mines, Nova Scotia 168/G3
Country Life Acres, Mo. 261/N3
Countryside, Ill. 222/B6
County Line, Ala. 195/E3
Countyline, Okla. 288/L6
Coupar Angus, Scotland 10/E2
Coupar Angus, Scotland 15/E4
Coupeville, Wash. 310/C2
Courantyne (riv.) 120/D2
Courantyne (riv.), Guyana 131/C3
Courbevoie, France 28/A1
Courcelles, Belgium 27/E8
Courcelles, Québec 172/G4
Courgenay, Switzerland 39/D2
Courmayeur, Italy 34/A2
Courrendlin, Switzerland 39/D2
Courroux, Switzerland 39/D2
Courtelary, Switzerland 39/C2
Courtenay, Br. Col. 162/D6
Courtenay, Br. Col. 184/E5
Courtenay, N. Dak. 282/N5
Courtételle, Switzerland 39/D2
Courtland, Ala. 195/D1
Courtland, Calif. 204/B9
Courtland, Kansas 232/E2
Courtland, Minn. 255/D6
Courtland, Miss. 256/E2
Courtland, Ontario 177/D5
Courtland, Va. 307/O7
Courtmacsherry, Ireland 17/D8
Courtmacsherry (bay), Ireland 17/D8
Courtney, Mo. 261/R5
Courtney, Okla. 288/L7
Courtois, Mo. 261/K7
Courtown (Este Sudeste) (cays), Colombia 126/A10
Courtown Harbour, Ireland 17/J6
Courtrai (Kortrijk), Belgium 27/C7
Courtright, Ontario 177/B5
Courval, Sask. 181/E5
Courville, Québec 172/J3
Coushatta, La. 238/D2
Coutances, France 28/C3
Coutras, France 28/C5
Coutts, Alberta 182/D5
Coutts (inlet), N.W. Terr. 187/L2
Couva, Trin. & Tob. 161/B10
Couvet, Switzerland 39/C3
Couvin, Belgium 27/F8
Cova da Piedade, Portugal 33/A1
Cove, Ark. 202/B5
Cove (pt.), Md. 245/N7
Cove, Minn. 255/E4
Cove, Ohio 284/E8
Cove (isl.), Ontario 177/C2
Cove, Oreg. 291/K2
Cove, Texas 303/L1
Cove (creek), Utah 304/B5
Cove and Kilcreggan, Scotland 15/A1
Cove Bay, Scotland 15/F3
Cove City, N.C. 281/P4
Cove Creek, N.C. 281/D3
Covedale, Ohio 284/B10
Cove Fort, Utah 304/B5
Cove Gap, W. Va. 312/B6
Covelo, Calif. 204/B4
Covena, Georgia 217/H6
Covendo, Bolivia 136/B4
Cove Neck, N.Y. 276/R6
Coventry•, Conn. 210/F1
Coventry, England 13/F5

356 Coventry

Coventry, England 10/F4
Coventry•, R.I. 249/H6
Coventry•, Vt. 268/C2
Coventry Center, R.I. 249/H6
Cove Orchard, Oreg. 291/D2
Coverdale, Georgia 217/E7
Coverdale, Ontario 177/F4
Covert, Mich. 250/C6
Cove Run (lake), Ky. 237/O4
Covesville, Va. 307/L5
Covilhã, Portugal 33/C2
Covin, Ala. 195/C3
Covina, Calif. 204/D10
Covington (co.), Ala. 195/F8
Covington, Georgia 217/E3
Covington, Ind. 227/C4
Covington, Iowa 229/K5
Covington, Ky. 237/S2
Covington, Ky. 188/J3
Covington, La. 238/K5
Covington, Mich. 250/G2
Covington (co.), Miss. 256/E7
Covington, Ohio 284/B5
Covington, Okla. 288/L2
Covington, Pa. 294/J2
Covington, Tenn. 237/B9
Covington (I.C.), Va. 307/H5
Cow (creek), Mont. 262/G2
Cow (creek), Oreg. 291/K4
Cow (lake), Oreg. 291/K4
Cow (creek), Wash. 310/G3
Cowal (lake), N.S. Wales 97/D3
Cowal (dist.), Scotland 15/C4
Cowan, Ind. 227/G4
Cowan, Ky. 237/O4
Cowan, Manitoba 179/B2
Cowan (lake), Sask. 181/D2
Cowan, Tenn. 237/K10
Cowan (lake), W. Australia 88/C6
Cowan (lake), W. Australia 92/C5
Cowanesque, Pa. 294/H2
Cowangie, Victoria 97/A4
Cowansville, Pa. 294/C4
Cowansville, Québec 172/E4
Cowaramup, W. Australia 92/A6
Coward, S.C. 296/H4
Coward Springs, S. Australia 94/E3
Cowarie, S. Australia 94/F2
Cowarts, Ala. 195/H8
Cow Bay, Nova Scotia 168/E4
Cowbridge, Wales 13/A7
Cowcreek, Ky. 237/O6
Cowden, Ill. 222/E4
Cowdenbeath, Scotland 10/C1
Cowdenbeath, Scotland 15/D1
Cowdrey, Colo. 208/G1
Cowell, S. Australia 88/F6
Cowell, S. Australia 94/E5
Cowen, W. Va. 312/E6
Cowes, England 10/F5
Cowes, England 13/F7
Coweta (co.), Georgia 217/C4
Coweta, Okla. 288/P3
Cowgill, Mo. 261/E3
Cow Head, Newf. 166/C4
Cowichan (lake), Br. Col. 184/J3
Cowiche, Wash. 310/E4
Cowie, Scotland 15/C1
Cowikee, North Fork (creek), Ala. 195/H6
Cow Island, La. 238/F7
Cowles, Nebr. 264/F4
Cowles, N. Mex. 274/D3
Cowlesville, N.Y. 276/D5
Cowley, Alberta 182/D5
Cowley (co.), Kansas 232/F4
Cowley, Wyo. 319/D1
Cowley, Yukon 187/E3
Cowlington, Okla. 288/S4
Cowlitz (co.), Wash. 310/C4
Cowlitz (pass), Wash. 310/D4
Cowlitz (riv.), Wash. 310/C4
Cowpasture (riv.), Va. 307/J4
Cowpens, S.C. 296/D1
Cowpens Nat'l Battlefield, S.C. 296/D1
Cowra, N.S. Wales 88/H6
Cowra, N.S. Wales 97/E3
Cox (bight), Tasmania 99/C5
Coxburg, Miss. 256/D5
Cox City, Okla. 288/L5
Coxim, Brazil 132/C7
Coxsackie, N.Y. 276/N6
Cox's Bazar, Bangladesh 68/G4
Cox's Cove, Newf. 166/C4
Coxs Mills, W. Va. 312/E4
Cox Station (Bel Alton), Md. 245/L7
Coxton, Ky. 237/P7
Coy, Ala. 195/D7
Coy, Ark. 202/G4
Coyame, Mexico 150/G2
Coyle (riv.), Argentina 143/B7
Coyle, Okla. 288/M3
Coyoacán, Mexico 150/L1
Coyote (creek), Calif. 204/L3
Coyote (res.), Calif. 204/L4
Coyote, N. Mex. 274/C2
Coyotepec, Mexico 150/L1
Coyuca (riv.), Mexico 150/O1
Coyuca de Benítez, Mexico 150/J8
Coyuca de Catalán, Mexico 150/J7
Coyutla, Mexico 150/L6
Coyville, Kansas 232/G4
Cozad, Nebr. 264/E4
Cozumel, Mexico 150/Q6
Cozumel (isl.), Mexico 150/Q6
Crab (creek), Wash. 310/F3
Crab Hill, Barbados 161/B8
Crab Orchard (lake), Ill. 222/E6
Crab Orchard, Ky. 237/M6
Crab Orchard, Nebr. 264/H4
Crab Orchard, Tenn. 237/M9
Crabtree, Oreg. 291/E3
Crabtree, Pa. 294/D5
Crabtree, Québec 172/D4
Cracow (city prov.), Poland 47/E4
Cracow (Kraków) (prov.), Poland 47/E4
Cracow, Poland 47/E4
Cracow, Poland 7/F3
Cradle (mt.), Tasmania 99/B3
Cradle Mt. Lake St. Clair Nat'l Park, Tasmania 99/B3
Cradock, S. Africa 102/E8
Cradock, S. Africa 118/D6
Crafters-Bridgewater, S. Australia 88/E8
Crafters-Bridgewater, S. Australia 94/B8
Crafton, Pa. 294/B7
Craftsbury•, Vt. 268/C2
Craftsbury Common, Vt. 268/C2
Cragford, Ala. 195/G4
Craig, Alaska 196/M2
Craig, Colo. 208/D2
Craig (mts.), Idaho 220/B4
Craig, Iowa 229/A3
Craig, Mo. 261/B2
Craig, Mont. 262/D3
Craig, Nebr. 264/H3
Craig (co.), Okla. 288/R1
Craig (co.), Va. 307/H6
Craig (creek), Va. 307/H5
Craigavon (dist.), N. Ireland 17/J3
Craigavon, N. Ireland 10/C3
Craigavon, N. Ireland 17/J3
Craig Beach, Ohio 284/H3
Craigellachie, Scotland 15/E3
Craighead (co.), Ark. 202/J2
Craighouse, Scotland 15/C5
Craigieburn, Victoria 97/C5
Craigleath, Ontario 177/D3
Craigmont, Idaho 220/B3
Craigmyle, Alberta 182/D4
Craignish (hills), Nova Scotia 168/G3
Craignure, Scotland 15/C4
Craigs (Sainte Rita), Manitoba 179/F5
Craig Springs, Va. 307/H6
Craigsville, Va. 307/J4
Craigsville, W. Va. 312/E6
Craigville, Ind. 227/G3
Craigville, Minn. 255/E3
Craik, Sask. 181/F4
Crail, Scotland 15/F4
Crail, Scotland 10/E2
Crailsheim, Germany 22/D4
Craiova, Romania 45/F3
Craiova, Romania 7/G4
Cramerton, N.C. 281/G4
Cramond (isl.), Scotland 15/D1
Cranberry (lake), N.Y. 276/L2
Cranberry (lake), N. Dak. 282/L3
Cranberry, Pa. 294/C3
Cranberry, W. Va. 312/D7
Cranberry Isles, Maine 243/G7
Cranberry Isles•, Maine 243/G7
Cranberry Lake, N.J. 273/D2
Cranberry Lake, N.Y. 276/L2
Cranberry Portage, Manitoba 179/H3
Cranbourne, Victoria 97/C6
Cranbourne, Victoria 88/M8
Cranbrook, Br. Col. 162/E6
Cranbrook, Br. Col. 184/K5
Cranbrook, Tasmania 99/D4
Cranbrook, W. Australia 92/B6
Cranbury, Conn. 210/B4
Cranbury, N.J. 273/E3
Crandall, Georgia 217/C1
Crandall, Ind. 227/E8
Crandall, Manitoba 179/B4
Crandall, S. Dak. 298/O3
Crandall, Texas 303/H5
Crandon, Va. 307/G6
Crandon, Wis. 317/H4
Crane, Barbados 161/C9
Crane, Ind. 227/D7
Crane, Mo. 261/E9
Crane, Mont. 262/M3
Crane, Oreg. 291/J4
Crane (creek), Oreg. 291/J4
Crane (lake), Sask. 181/B5
Crane (co.), Texas 303/B6
Crane, Texas 303/B6
Crane Creek (res.), Idaho 220/B5
Crane Hill, Ala. 195/D2
Crane Lake, Minn. 255/F2
Crane Nest, Ky. 237/O7
Crane Prairie (res.), Oreg. 291/F4
Crane River, Manitoba 179/C3
Cranesville, Pa. 294/B2
Cranesville, W. Va. 312/G3
Crane Valley, Sask. 181/F6
Cranfills Gap, Texas 303/G6
Cranford•, N.J. 273/E2
Cranleigh, England 13/G6
Cransac, France 28/E5
Cranston, Iowa 229/L6
Cranston, R.I. 249/J5
Crapaud, Pr. Edward I. 168/E2
Crapo, Md. 245/O7
Crary, N. Dak. 282/N3
Craster, England 13/F2
Crater (lake), Oreg. 291/E5
Crater Lake, Oreg. 291/E5
Crater Lake Nat'l Park, Oreg. 291/E5
Craters of the Moon Nat'l Mon., Idaho 220/E6
Crateús, Brazil 132/F4
Crateús, Brazil 120/E3
Crati (riv.), Italy 34/F5
Crato, Brazil 132/G4
Crato, Brazil 120/E3
Crato e Mártires, Portugal 33/C3
Crauford (cape), N.W. Terr. 187/K2
Craven (co.), N.C. 281/P4
Craven, Sask. 181/G5
Cravens, La. 238/E5
Cravo Norte, Colombia 126/F4
Cravo Norte (riv.), Colombia 126/E4
Cravo Sur (riv.), Colombia 126/E5
Crawford (co.), Ark. 202/B2
Crawford, Colo. 208/D5
Crawford (co.), Georgia 217/E5
Crawford, Georgia 217/F3
Crawford (co.), Ill. 222/F4
Crawford (co.), Ind. 227/E8
Crawford (co.), Iowa 229/C4
Crawford (co.), Kansas 232/H4
Crawford, Kansas 232/E3
Crawford•, Maine 243/H5
Crawford (lake), Maine 243/H5
Crawford (co.), Mich. 250/E4
Crawford, Miss. 256/G4
Crawford (co.), Mo. 261/K7
Crawford, Nebr. 264/A2
Crawford (co.), Ohio 284/E4
Crawford, Okla. 288/G3
Crawford (co.), Pa. 294/B2
Crawford, Scotland 15/E5
Crawford, Tenn. 237/L8
Crawford, Texas 303/G6
Crawford, W. Va. 312/F5
Crawford (co.), Wis. 317/E9
Crawford Bay, Br. Col. 184/J5
Crawford House, N.H. 268/E3
Crawford Notch (pass), N.H. 268/E3
Crawfordsville, Ark. 202/K3
Crawfordsville, Ind. 227/D4
Crawfordsville, Iowa 229/K6
Crawfordsville, Oreg. 291/E3
Crawfordville, Fla. 212/B1
Crawfordville, Georgia 217/G3
Crawley, England 13/G6
Crawley, W. Va. 312/E7
Crayne, Ky. 237/E6
Crazy (peak), Mont. 262/F4
Crazy Horse Mon., S. Dak. 298/B6
Crazy Woman (creek), Wyo. 319/F1
Creach Bheinn (mt.), Scotland 15/C4
Creagerstown, Md. 245/J2
Creag Meagaidh (mt.), Scotland 15/D4
Creal Springs, Ill. 222/E6
Cream (hill), Conn. 210/B1
Cream, Wis. 317/C7
Creamridge, N.J. 273/E3
Crean (lake), Sask. 181/E1
Creciente (isl.), Mexico 150/D5
Credenhill, England 13/E5
Crediton, England 13/D7
Crediton, England 10/E5
Crediton, Ontario 177/C4
Cree (lake), Sask. 162/F4
Cree (lake), Sask. 181/L3
Cree (riv.), Sask. 181/M2
Cree (riv.), Scotland 15/D5
Creede, Colo. 208/E7
Creedmoor, N.C. 281/M2
Creek (co.), Okla. 288/O3
Creekside, Pa. 294/D4
Creek Stand, Ala. 195/G6
Creekville, Ky. 237/P6
Creel, Mexico 150/E3
Cree Lake, Sask. 181/L3
Creelman, Sask. 181/H6
Creelsboro, Ky. 237/L7
Creemore, Ontario 177/D3
Creeslough, Ireland 17/F1
Creetown, Scotland 15/D6
Creighton, Mo. 261/D6
Creighton, Nebr. 264/G2
Creighton, Pa. 294/C4
Creighton, Sask. 181/N4
Creighton, S. Dak. 298/E5
Creignish, Nova Scotia 168/G3
Creil, France 28/E3
Crellin, Md. 245/A3
Crema, Italy 34/B2
Cremona, Alberta 182/C4
Cremona (prov.), Italy 34/B2
Cremona, Italy 34/B2
Crenshaw (co.), Ala. 195/F7
Crenshaw, Miss. 256/D2
Crenshaw, Pa. 294/E3
Creola, Ala. 195/B9
Creola, Ohio 284/E7
Creole, La. 238/D7
Crépy-en-Valois, France 28/E3
Creran, Loch (inlet), Scotland 15/C4
Cres (isl.), Yugoslavia 45/B3
Cresaptown, Md. 245/C2
Cresbard, S. Dak. 298/M3
Crescent (isls.), China 85/E2
Crescent (lake), Fla. 212/E2
Crescent, Iowa 229/B6
Crescent, La. 238/J2
Crescent, Mo. 261/N4
Crescent (lake), Nebr. 264/B3
Crescent (valley), Nev. 266/E2
Crescent, Okla. 288/L3
Crescent, Oreg. 291/F4
Crescent (lake), Tasmania 99/D4
Crescent (lake), Wash. 310/B2
Crescent Beach, Conn. 210/G3
Crescent City, Calif. 204/A2
Crescent City, Fla. 212/E2
Crescent City, Ill. 222/F3
Crescent Head, N.S. Wales 97/G2
Crescent Lake, Maine 243/C7
Crescent Lake, Oreg. 291/F4
Crescent Lake, Sask. 181/J4
Crescent Mills, Calif. 204/E3
Crescent Springs, Ky. 237/R2
Cresco, Iowa 229/J2
Cresco, Pa. 294/M3
Crespo, Argentina 143/F6
Cresskill, N.J. 273/C1
Cressmont, W. Va. 312/E6
Cresson, Pa. 294/E5
Cresson, Texas 303/G5
Cressona, Pa. 294/K4
Cressy, Tasmania 99/C3
Crest, France 28/F5
Crest, Georgia 217/D5
Crested Butte, Colo. 208/E5
Crest Hill, Ill. 222/E2
Crestline, Calif. 204/H9
Crestline, Kansas 232/H4
Crestline, Ohio 284/E4
Creston, Br. Col. 184/J5
Creston, Calif. 204/E8
Creston, Ill. 222/D2
Creston, Ind. 227/C2
Creston, Iowa 229/E6
Creston, Ky. 237/L6
Creston, La. 238/E3
Creston, Mont. 262/C2
Creston, Nebr. 264/G3
Creston, Newf. 166/C4
Creston, Ohio 284/G3
Creston, S.C. 296/F4
Creston, Wash. 310/G3
Creston, W. Va. 312/D5
Crestone, Colo. 208/H7
Crestone (peak), Colo. 208/H7
Crestview, Fla. 212/C6
Crestview, Ky. 237/S2
Crestview Hills, Ky. 237/R2
Crestwood, Ill. 222/B6
Crestwood, Ky. 237/L4
Crestwood, Mo. 261/O3
Crestwynd, Sask. 181/F5
Creswell, N.C. 281/S3
Creswell (bay), N.W. Terr. 187/J2
Creswell, Oreg. 291/D4
Creswell Downs, North. Terr. 93/E4
Creswick, Victoria 97/B5
Crete (reg.), Greece 45/G8
Crete (isl.), Greece 7/G5
Crete (isl.), Greece 45/G8
Crete (sea), Greece 45/G7
Crete, Ill. 222/F2
Crete, Nebr. 264/G4
Crete, N. Dak. 282/P7
Créteil, France 28/B2
Cretin (cape), Papua N.G. 86/B2
Creus (cape), Spain 33/H1
Creuse (dept.), France 28/D4
Creuse (riv.), France 28/D4
Creve Coeur, Ill. 222/D3
Creve Coeur, Mo. 261/O2
Crevillente, Spain 33/F3
Crewe, Va. 307/M6
Crewe and Nantwich, England 13/E4
Crewe and Nantwich, England 10/F2
Crewkerne, England 13/E7
Crewkerne, England 10/E5
Crews, Ala. 195/B3
Crianlarich, Scotland 15/D4
Criccieth, Wales 13/C5
Criccieth, Wales 10/D4
Crichton, Sask. 181/D6
Criciúma, Brazil 132/D10
Crider, Ky. 237/F6
Cridersville, Ohio 284/B4
Crieff, Scotland 15/E4
Crieff, Scotland 10/E2
Criehaven, Maine 243/F8
Crillon (mt.), Alaska 196/L1
Crimea (pen.), U.S.S.R. 7/H4
Crimea (pen.), U.S.S.R. 48/D5
Crimea (pen.), U.S.S.R. 52/D5
Crimean Oblast, U.S.S.R. 52/D6
Crimmitschau, Germany 22/E3
Crimond, Scotland 15/G3
Crimora, Va. 307/L4
Crinan, Scotland 15/C4
Cripple Creek, Colo. 188/F3
Cripple Creek, Colo. 208/J5
Cripple Creek, Va. 307/F7
Crisfield, Md. 245/P9
Crisp (co.), Georgia 217/E7
Crisp (pt.), Mich. 250/D2
Crisp, N.C. 281/O3
Crissolo, Italy 34/A2
Cristal, Sierra del (mts.), Cuba 158/J3
Cristalina, Brazil 132/E7
Cristóbal (mt.), Colombia 120/B1
Cristóbal (pt.), Ecuador 128/B9
Cristóbal, Panama 154/G6
Cristóbal Colón, Pico (peak), Colombia 126/D2
Crişul Alb (riv.), Romania 45/F2
Crişul Repede (riv.), Romania 45/F2
Crittenden (co.), Ark. 202/K3
Crittenden (co.), Ky. 237/E6
Crittenden, Ky. 237/M3
Critz, Va. 307/H7
Crivitz, Wis. 317/L5
Croagh Patrick (mt.), Ireland 17/C4
Croatan (sound), N.C. 281/T3
Croatia (rep.), Yugoslavia 45/C3
Croche (riv.), Québec 172/E2
Crocheron, Md. 245/O8
Crochu, Grenada 161/D8
Crocker, Mo. 261/H7
Crocker, S. Dak. 298/O3
Crocketford, Scotland 15/E5
Crockett, Calif. 204/J1
Crockett (co.), Tenn. 237/C9
Crockett (co.), Texas 303/C7
Crockett, Texas 303/J6
Crockett, Va. 307/F7
Crockett Mills, Tenn. 237/C9
Crocketts Bluff, Ark. 202/H5
Crocketville, S.C. 296/E6
Crocodile (riv.), S. Africa 118/H6
Croft, Kansas 232/D4
Crofton, Br. Col. 184/J3
Crofton, Ky. 237/G6
Crofton, Md. 245/M4
Crofton, Nebr. 264/G2
Croghan, N.Y. 276/K3
Croix des Bouquets, Haiti 158/C6
Croker (cape), North. Terr. 88/E2
Croker (cape), North. Terr. 93/C1
Croker (bay), N.W. Terr. 187/K2
Croker (cape), Ontario 177/D3
Croker Island Mission, North. Terr. 88/E2
Croker Island Mission, North. Terr. 93/C1
Cromarty, Scotland 15/E3
Cromarty, Scotland 10/D2
Cromarty (firth), Scotland 15/D3
Cromdale, Scotland 15/E3
Cromer, England 13/J5
Cromer, England 10/G4
Cromer, Manitoba 179/A5
Cromwell, Ala. 195/B6
Cromwell•, Conn. 210/E2
Cromwell, Ind. 227/F2
Cromwell, Iowa 229/E6
Cromwell, Ky. 237/H6
Cromwell, Minn. 255/F4
Cromwell, N. Zealand 100/B6
Cromwell, Okla. 288/N4
Cronulla, N.S. Wales 88/L5
Cronulla, N.S. Wales 97/J4
Crook, Colo. 208/O1
Crook (co.), Oreg. 291/G3
Crook (pt.), Oreg. 291/C5
Crook (co.), Wyo. 319/H1
Crook and Willington, England 13/E3
Crooked (isl.), Bahamas 156/D2
Crooked (creek), Ind. 227/D2
Crooked (creek), Kansas 232/B4
Crooked (creek), Minn. 255/F4
Crooked (lake), Minn. 255/G2
Crooked (lake), N. Dak. 282/J4
Crooked (creek), Oreg. 291/K5
Crooked (riv.), Oreg. 291/G3
Crooked (creek), S.C. 296/H2
Crooked Creek, Alaska 196/G2
Crooked Creek, Alberta 182/B2
Crooked Island (passage), Bahamas 156/C2
Crooked River, Sask. 181/H3
Crookhaven, Ireland 17/B9
Crooks, S. Dak. 298/R6
Crookston, Minn. 188/G1
Crookston, Minn. 255/B3
Crookston, Nebr. 264/D2
Crooksville, Ohio 284/F6
Crookwell, N.S. Wales 97/E4
Croom, Ireland 17/D6
Cropper, Ky. 237/L4
Cropsey, Ill. 222/E3
Crosby, Ala. 195/H8
Crosby, England 13/G2
Crosby, England 10/F2
Crosby, Minn. 255/D4
Crosby, Miss. 256/B8
Crosby, N. Dak. 282/D2
Crosby, Pa. 294/F2
Crosby (co.), Texas 303/C4
Crosby, Texas 303/J8
Crosby (mt.), Wyo. 319/C2
Crosbyton, Texas 303/C4
Crosland, Georgia 217/E8
Cross (sound), Alaska 196/L1
Cross (co.), Ark. 202/J3
Cross (riv.), Cameroon 115/A2
Cross (lake), La. 238/C2
Cross (isl.), Maine 243/J6
Cross (lake), Maine 243/G1
Cross (bay), Manitoba 179/C1
Cross (lake), Manitoba 179/J3
Cross (cape), Namibia 118/A4
Cross (riv.), Nigeria 106/F7
Cross (isl.), Nova Scotia 168/D4
Cross, S.C. 296/G5
Cross Anchor, S.C. 296/D2
Crossapoll, Scotland 15/B4
Cross City, Fla. 212/C2
Cross Creek, New Bruns. 170/D2
Crossett, Ark. 202/G7
Crossfarnoge (pt.), Ireland 17/J7
Cross Fell (mt.), England 13/E3
Crossfield, Alberta 182/C4
Cross Fork, Pa. 294/G3
Crossgar, N. Ireland 17/K3
Crosshaven, Ireland 17/E8
Crosshill, Scotland 15/D5
Cross Hill, S.C. 296/D3
Cross Junction, Va. 307/M2
Cross Keys, S.C. 296/D2
Cross Lake, Manitoba 179/J3
Crosslake, Minn. 255/E4
Crossley (mt.), N. Zealand 100/D5
Crossmaglen, N. Ireland 17/H3
Crossmichael, Scotland 15/D6
Crossmolina, Ireland 17/C3
Crossnore, N.C. 281/F2
Cross Plains, Ind. 227/G7
Cross Plains, Tenn. 237/H7
Cross Plains, Texas 303/E5
Cross Plains, Wis. 317/G9
Cross River (state), Nigeria 106/F7
Cross Roads, Calif. 204/L9
Crossroads, N. Mex. 274/F5
Cross Roads, Pa. 294/J6
Cross Timbers, Mo. 261/F6
Crosstown, Mo. 261/N7
Cross Village, Mich. 250/D3
Crossville, Ala. 195/G2
Crossville, Ill. 222/F5
Crossville, Tenn. 237/L9
Crosswicks, N.J. 273/D3
Crosswicks (creek), N.J. 273/D3
Croswell, Mich. 250/G5
Crotch (lake), Ontario 177/H3
Crothersville, Ind. 227/F7
Croton (Hartford), Ohio 284/E5
Crotone, Italy 34/F5
Croton Falls, N.Y. 276/N8
Croton-on-Hudson, N.Y. 276/N8
Crouch, Idaho 220/B5
Crouseville, Maine 243/G2
Crow (creek), Colo. 208/L1
Crow (riv.), Minn. 255/F5
Crow, Oreg. 291/D4
Crow (creek), S. Dak. 298/A4
Crow (creek), Wyo. 319/H4
Crow Agency, Mont. 262/J5
Crowborough, England 13/H6
Crow Creek Ind. Res., S. Dak. 298/L5
Crowder, Miss. 256/D2
Crowder, Okla. 288/P4
Crowduck (lake), Manitoba 179/G4
Crowdy (head), N.S. Wales 97/G2
Crowell, Texas 303/E4
Crowfoot, Alberta 182/D4
Crowheart, Wyo. 319/C2
Crow Ind. Res., Mont. 262/H5
Crowl (creek), N.S. Wales 97/C2
Crow Lake, S. Dak. 298/M6
Crowle, England 13/G4
Crowley (lake), Calif. 204/G6
Crowley (co.), Colo. 208/M6
Crowley, Colo. 208/M6
Crowley, La. 238/F6
Crowley, Texas 303/E3
Crowley Lake, Calif. 204/G6
Crowley's Ridge (mt.), Ark. 202/J2
Crown, Minn. 255/E5
Crown (mt.), Virgin Is. (U.S.) 161/A4
Crown City, Ohio 284/F8
Crown King, Ariz. 198/C4
Crown Point, Ind. 227/C2
Crownpoint, N. Mex. 274/A3
Crown Point, N.Y. 276/N3
Crown Prince Frederik (isl.), N.W. Terr. 187/K3
Crownsville, Md. 245/M4
Crows Landing, Calif. 204/D6
Crowsnest (pass), Alberta 182/C5
Crowsnest, Br. Col. 184/K5
Crowsnest (pass), Br. Col. 184/K5
Crowville, La. 238/G2
Crow Wing (co.), Minn. 255/D4
Crow Wing (riv.), Minn. 255/D4
Croydon, England 13/H8
Croydon, England 10/B6
Croydon•, N.H. 268/C5
Croydon (peak), N.H. 268/C5
Croydon, Queensland 88/G3
Croydon, Queensland 95/B3
Croydon, Utah 304/C2
Croydon, Victoria 88/M7
Croydon, Victoria 97/K5
Croydon Branch, Sugar (riv.), N.H. 268/C5
Crozet (isls.) 2/M8
Crozet, Va. 307/L4
Crozier (chan.), N.W. Terr. 187/G2
Crozier, Va. 307/N5
Cruces, Cuba 158/E2
Cruces, Cuba 156/B2
Cruden Bay, Scotland 15/G3
Cruger, Miss. 256/D4
Cruillas, Mexico 150/K4
Crum (creek), Pa. 294/M7
Crum, W. Va. 312/B7
Crumlin, N. Ireland 17/J2
Crum Lynne, Pa. 294/M7
Crummies, Ky. 237/P7
Crump, Mich. 250/E5
Crump (lake), Oreg. 291/H5
Crump, Tenn. 237/E10
Crumpton (pt.), Dominica 161/F5
Crumpton, Md. 245/P4
Crumrod, Ark. 202/H5
Crumstown, Ind. 227/E1
Crusheen, Ireland 17/D6
Cruso, N.C. 281/D4
Cruta, Honduras 154/F3
Crutchfield, Ky. 237/D7
Crutwell, Sask. 181/E2
Cruz (cape), Cuba 156/C3
Cruz (cape), Cuba 158/G4
Cruz Alta, Brazil 120/D5
Cruz Alta, Brazil 132/C10
Cruz Bay, Virgin Is. (U.S.) 161/C4
Cruz del Eje, Argentina 143/C3
Cruz del Eje, Argentina 120/C6
Cruz de Piedra, Uruguay 145/E3
Cruz de San Pedro, Uruguay 145/E2
Cruzeiro, Brazil 135/D3
Cruzeiro do Sol, Brazil 120/B3
Cruzeiro do Sul, Brazil 132/G10
Cruz Grande, Chile 138/A7
Crysler, Ontario 177/J2
Crystal (mts.), Congo 115/B4
Crystal (lake), Conn. 210/F1
Crystal (pond), Conn. 210/G1
Crystal (bay), Fla. 212/D3
Crystal (mts.), Gabon 115/B4
Crystal, Ind. 227/D8
Crystal•, Maine 243/G4
Crystal, Mich. 250/E5
Crystal (lake), Mich. 250/C4
Crystal, Minn. 255/G5
Crystal, N.H. 268/E2
Crystal (lake), N.H. 268/E5
Crystal, N. Mex. 274/A2
Crystal, N. Dak. 282/P2
Crystal (lake), Vt. 268/C2
Crystal, W. Va. 312/D8
Crystal Bay (Orono), Minn. 255/F5
Crystal Bay, Nev. 266/A3
Crystal Beach, Texas 303/K8
Crystal Brook, S. Australia 94/E5
Crystal City, Manitoba 179/C5
Crystal City, Mo. 261/M6
Crystal City, Texas 303/E9
Crystal Falls, Mich. 250/A2
Crystal Falls, Ontario 177/E1
Crystal Hill, Va. 307/L7
Crystal Lake, Conn. 210/F1
Crystal Lake, Fla. 212/D6
Crystal Lake, Ill. 222/E1
Crystal Lake, Iowa 229/F2
Crystal Lake Park, Mo. 261/O3
Crystal River, Fla. 212/D3
Crystal Springs, Ark. 202/D5
Crystal Springs (res.), Calif. 204/J3
Crystal Springs, Fla. 212/D3
Crystal Springs, Georgia 217/B2
Crystal Springs, Kansas 232/D4
Crystal Springs, Miss. 256/D7
Crystal Springs, N. Dak. 282/L6
Crystal Springs, Sask. 181/F3
Crystal Valley, Mich. 250/C5
Csabrendek, Hungary 41/D3
Csákvár, Hungary 41/E3
Csanádpalota, Hungary 41/F3
Csenger, Hungary 41/G3
Csepel, Hungary 41/E3
Csepelsziget (isl.), Hungary 41/E3
Csepreg, Hungary 41/D3
Csongrád (co.), Hungary 41/F3
Csongrád, Hungary 41/E3
Csorna, Hungary 41/D3
Csorvás, Hungary 41/F3
Csurgó, Hungary 41/D3
Ctesiphon (ruins), Iraq 66/D4
Cúa, Venezuela 124/E2
Cuadro Nacional, Argentina 143/C3
Cuamba, Mozambique 118/F2
Cuando (riv.), Angola 115/C7
Cuando (riv.), Zambia 115/D7

Dalhousie East 357

Cuando Cubango (prov.), Angola 115/C7
Cuangar, Angola 115/C7
Cuango (riv.) 102/D5
Cuango, Angola 115/C5
Cuango (riv.), Angola 115/C5
Cuanza (riv.), Angola 102/D6
Cuanza (riv.), Angola 115/C5
Cuanza-Norte (prov.), Angola 115/B5
Cuanza-Sul (prov.), Angola 115/C6
Cuao (riv.), Venezuela 124/E5
Cua Rao, Vietnam 72/E3
Cuareim (riv.), Uruguay 145/B1
Cuaró, Uruguay 145/D2
Cuatrociénagas de Carranza, Mexico 150/H3
Cuatro Compañeros, Cuba 158/G3
Cuatro Ojos, Bolivia 136/D5
Cuauhtémoc, Mexico 150/F2
Cuautepec de Hinojosa, Mexico 150/K6
Cuautitlán de Romero Rubio, Mexico 150/L1
Cuautla Morelos, Mexico 150/L2
Cub (creek), Utah 304/C1
Cub (creek), Va. 307/L6
Cuba 2/E4
Cuba 146/L7
CUBA 156/B2
CUBA 158
Cuba, Ala. 195/B6
Cuba, Ill. 222/C3
Cuba, Ind. 227/D6
Cuba, Kansas 232/E2
Cuba, Mo. 261/K6
Cuba, N. Mex. 274/B2
Cuba, N.Y. 276/D6
Cuba (chan.), N. Zealand 100/D7
Cuba, Ohio 284/C7
Cuba, Portugal 33/C3
Cuba City, Wis. 317/F10
Cubage, Ky. 237/O7
Cubagua (isl.), Venezuela 124/F2
Cuballing, W. Australia 92/B2
Cubango (riv.), Angola 102/D6
Cubango (riv.), Angola 115/C7
Cubango (riv.), Namibia 118/B3
Cubatão, Brazil 135/C3
Cube (mt.), N.H. 268/D4
Cubero, N. Mex. 274/B3
Cubiro, Venezuela 124/D3
Cub Run, Ky. 237/J6
Çubuk, Turkey 63/E2
Cubulco, Guatemala 154/B3
Cuchara, Colo. 208/J8
Cuchi, Angola 115/C6
Cuchi, Angola 102/D6
Cuchillo, N. Mex. 274/B5
Cuchillo-Có, Argentina 143/D4
Cuchillo Negro (creek), N. Mex. 274/B5
Cuchivero, Venezuela 124/F4
Cuchivero (riv.), Venezuela 124/F4
Cuckfield, England 13/G6
Cuckfield, England 10/F5
Cucumber, W. Va. 312/C8
Cúcuta, Colombia 126/D4
Cúcuta, Colombia 120/B2
Cudahy, Calif. 204/C5
Cudahy, Wis. 317/M2
Cudal, N.S. Wales 97/E3
Cuddalore, India 68/E6
Cuddapah, India 68/D6
Cuddeback (lake), Calif. 204/H8
Cuddy, Pa. 294/B5
Cudgewa, Victoria 97/D5
Cudillero, Spain 33/C1
Cudjoe (key), Fla. 212/E7
Cudrefin, Switzerland 39/D3
Cudworth, Sask. 181/F3
Cue, W. Australia 88/B5
Cue, W. Australia 92/B4
Cuéllar, Spain 33/D2
Cuéllar-Baza, Spain 33/E4
Cuemaní (riv.), Colombia 126/D7
Cuenca, Ecuador 120/B3
Cuenca, Ecuador 128/C4
Cuenca (prov.), Spain 33/E2
Cuenca, Spain 33/E2
Cuenca, Sierra de (range), Spain 33/F3
Cuencamé de Ceniceros, Mexico 150/H4
Cuernavaca, Mexico 150/L2
Cuero, Texas 303/G8
Cuervo, N. Mex. 274/E3
Cuervo (creek), N. Mex. 274/E3
Cueto, Cuba 158/J3
Cuevas, Miss. 256/F10
Cuevas del Almanzora, Spain 33/F4
Cuevas de Vinromá, Spain 33/F2
Cuevo, Bolivia 136/D7
Cufré, Uruguay 145/B5
Cuiabá, Brazil 120/D4
Cuiabá, Brazil 132/C6
Cuiabá (riv.), Brazil 132/B7
Cuicatlán, Mexico 150/L8
Cuicuina, Nicaragua 154/E4
Cuilapa, Guatemala 154/B3
Cuilapa Miravalles (vol.), C. Rica 154/E5
Cuilcagh (mt.), Ireland 17/F3
Cuilco, Guatemala 154/B3
Cuillin (hills), Scotland 15/B3
Cuillin (sound), Scotland 10/C2
Cuillin (sound), Scotland 15/B3
Cuilo, Angola 115/C5
Cuitlahuac, Mexico 150/P2
Cuito (riv.), Angola 115/C7
Cuito-Cuanavale, Angola 115/C7
Cuitzeo (lake), Mexico 150/J7
Cuivre (riv.), Mo. 261/N2
Cujmir, Romania 45/F3
Cukmantl, Czech. 41/D1
Çukur, Turkey 63/F3
Çukurca, Turkey 63/K4
Culaba, Philippines 82/E5
Cu Lao, Hon (isls.), Vietnam 72/F5
Culberson, N.C. 281/A4
Culberson (co.), Texas 303/C11
Culbertson, Mont. 262/M2
Culbertson, Nebr. 264/C4
Culcairn, N.S. Wales 97/D4
Culdaff, Ireland 17/G1
Culdaff (bay), Ireland 17/G1
Culdesac, Idaho 220/B3
Cul-de-Sac du Marin (bay), Martinique 161/D7
Culebra (creek), Colo. 208/H8
Culebra (peak), Colo. 208/J8
Culebra, P. Rico 161/G1
Culebra (isl.), P. Rico 161/G1
Culebra (isl.), P. Rico 156/G1
Culebras, Peru 128/C7
Culebrinas (riv.), P. Rico 161/A1
Culebrita (isl.), P. Rico 161/G2
Culemborg, Netherlands 27/G5
Culgoa (riv.), N.S. Wales 97/D1
Culgoa (riv.), Queensland 95/C6
Culiacán, Mexico 150/F4
Culiacán, Mexico 146/H7
Culion, Philippines 82/C5
Culion (isl.), Philippines 82/B5
Cullasaja, N.C. 281/C4
Cullburra-Orient Point, N.S. Wales 97/F4
Cullen, La. 238/D1
Cullen, Sask. 181/J6
Cullen, Scotland 15/F3
Cullen, Va. 307/L6
Cullen Bullen, N.S. Wales 97/F3
Culleoka, Tenn. 237/G10
Cullera, Spain 33/F3
Cullin (lake), Ireland 17/C4
Cullison, Kansas 232/D4
Cullman (co.), Ala. 195/E2
Cullman, Ala. 195/E2
Culloden, Georgia 217/D5
Culloden, W. Va. 312/B6
Cullom, Ill. 222/E3
Cullomburg, Ala. 195/B7
Cullompton, England 13/D7
Cullowhee, N.C. 281/C4
Cully, Switzerland 39/C4
Cullybackey, N. Ireland 17/J2
Culotte (lake), Québec 172/C2
Culp, Alberta 182/B2
Culp Creek, Oreg. 291/E4
Culpeper (co.), Va. 307/M3
Culpeper, Va. 307/M4
Culpepper (isl.), Ecuador 128/B8
Culpina, Bolivia 136/C7
Culross, Manitoba 179/E5
Culross, Scotland 10/B1
Culross, Scotland 15/C1
Culta, Bolivia 136/B6
Cults, Scotland 15/F3
Cultus (lake), Oreg. 291/F4
Cultus Lake, Br. Col. 184/M3
Culuene (riv.), Brazil 132/C6
Culver, Ind. 227/E2
Culver, Kansas 232/E3
Culver, Minn. 255/F4
Culver, Oreg. 291/F3
Culver (pt.), W. Australia 88/D6
Culver (pt.), W. Australia 92/D6
Culver City, Calif. 204/B10
Culverden, N. Zealand 100/D5
Culvers (lake), N.J. 273/D1
Culverton, Georgia 217/G4
Cuma, Angola 115/B6
Cumaná, Venezuela 120/C2
Cumaná, Venezuela 124/F2
Cumanacoa, Venezuela 124/F2
Cumanayagua, Cuba 158/E2
Cumaria, Peru 128/F7
Cumback, Ind. 227/C7
Cumbal, Colombia 126/B7
Cumberland (riv.) 188/J3
Cumberland (plat.), Ala. 195/F1
Cumberland, Br. Col. 184/E5
Cumberland (sound), Canada 4/C13
Cumberland (isl.), Georgia 217/K9
Cumberland (co.), Ill. 222/E4
Cumberland, Ind. 227/E5
Cumberland, Iowa 229/D6
Cumberland (co.), Ky. 237/L7
Cumberland, Ky. 237/R6
Cumberland (lake), Ky. 237/M7
Cumberland (mt.), Ky. 237/P7
Cumberland (riv.), Ky. 237/K8
Cumberland (co.), Maine 243/C8
Cumberland, Md. 188/L3
Cumberland, Md. 245/D2
Cumberland (basin), New Bruns. 170/F3
Cumberland (co.), N.J. 273/C5
Cumberland (co.), N.C. 281/M4
Cumberland, N.C. 281/M5
Cumberland (pen.), N.W.T. 162/K2
Cumberland (pen.), N.W. Terr. 187/M3
Cumberland (sound), N.W.T. 146/N3
Cumberland (sound), N.W.T. 162/K2
Cumberland (sound), N.W. Terr. 187/M3
Cumberland (co.), Nova Scotia 168/D3
Cumberland (basin), Nova Scotia 168/D3
Cumberland, Ohio 284/G6
Cumberland, Okla. 288/N6
Cumberland, Ontario 177/J2
Cumberland (co.), Pa. 294/H5
Cumberland (isls.), Queensland 88/H4
Cumberland (isls.), Queensland 95/D4
Cumberland (bay), St. Vin. & Grens. 161/A8
Cumberland (lake), Sask. 181/J1
Cumberland (co.), Tenn. 237/L9
Cumberland (plat.), Tenn. 237/L9
Cumberland (riv.), Tenn. 237/K8
Cumberland (co.), Va. 307/M6
Cumberland, Va. 307/M6
Cumberland (mt.), Va. 307/B7
Cumberland, Wash. 310/D3
Cumberland, Wis. 317/C4
Cumberland Bay, New Bruns. 170/E2
Cumberland Beach, Ontario 177/E3
Cumberland Center, Maine 243/C8
Cumberland Center •, Maine 243/C8
Cumberland City, Tenn. 237/F8
Cumberland Furnace, Tenn. 237/G8
Cumberland Gap, Tenn. 237/O8
Cumberland Gap Nat'l Hist. Park, Ky. 237/P7
Cumberland Gap Nat'l Hist. Park, Tenn. 237/O7
Cumberland Gap Nat'l Hist. Park, Va. 307/A7
Cumberland House, Sask. 181/J2
Cumberland Island Nat'l Seashore, Georgia 217/K9
Cumbernauld, Scotland 15/C1
Cumbre del Laudo (mt.), Argentina 143/C2
Cumbre Negra, Cerro (mt.), Argentina 143/C5
Cumbre Negra, Cerro (mt.), Chile 138/E5
Cumbria (co.), England 13/D3
Cumbrian (mts.), England 13/D3
Cumbum, India 68/D5
Cumby, Texas 303/J4
Cuming (co.), Nebr. 264/H3
Cummaquid, Mass. 249/N6
Cumming, Georgia 217/D2
Cumming, Iowa 229/F6
Cummings, Kansas 232/G2
Cummings, N. Dak. 282/S4
Cummings, S.C. 296/E6
Cummingsville, Tenn. 237/L9
Cummington •, Mass. 249/C3
Cummins, S. Australia 94/D6
Cumnock, N.S. Wales 97/E3
Cumnock, N.C. 281/L3
Cumnock and Holmhead, Scotland 10/D3
Cumnock and Holmhead, Scotland 15/D5
Cumpas, Mexico 150/E1
Çumra, Turkey 63/E4
Cuñapirú, Uruguay 145/D2
Cuñapirú, Arroyo (riv.), Uruguay 145/D2
Cunapo, Trin. & Tob. 161/B10
Cuñare, Colombia 126/D7
Cunaviche, Venezuela 124/E4
Cunco, Chile 138/E2
Cuncumén, Coquimbo, Chile 138/A9
Cuncumén, Santiago, Chile 138/F4
Cundeelee Aboriginal Res., W. Australia 88/C6
Cundeelee Aboriginal Res., W. Australia 92/C5
Cunderdin, W. Australia 92/B5
Cundiff, Ky. 237/L7
Cundinamarca (dept.), Colombia 126/C5
Cundiyo, N. Mex. 274/D3
Cunduacán, Mexico 150/N7
Cundys Harbor, Maine 243/D8
Cunene (riv.) 102/D6
Cunene (prov.), Angola 115/C7
Cunene (dam), Angola 115/B7
Cunene (riv.), Angola 115/B7
Cuneo (prov.), Italy 34/A2
Cuneo, Italy 34/A2
Çüngüş, Turkey 63/H3
Cunnamulla, Australia 87/E8
Cunnamulla, Queensland 95/C5
Cunnamulla, Queensland 88/H5
Cunningham, Kansas 232/D4
Cunningham, Ky. 237/D7
Cunningham, N.C. 281/L1
Cunningham, Tenn. 237/G8
Cunningham, Wash. 310/G4
Cuorgnè, Italy 34/A2
Cupar, Sask. 181/G5
Cupar, Scotland 15/E4
Cupar, Scotland 10/E2
Cupertino, Calif. 204/K3
Cupica (gulf), Colombia 126/B4
Cupids, Newf. 166/D2
Ćuprija, Yugoslavia 45/E4
Cuprum, Idaho 220/B4
Cupsuptic (riv.), Maine 243/B5
Cuquenán (riv.), Venezuela 124/H5
Cuquiari (riv.), Colombia 126/E7
Curaçá, Brazil 132/G5
Curaçao (isl.), Neth. Ant. 161/G7
Curaçao (isl.), Neth. Ant. 156/E4
Curacautín, Chile 138/E2
Curacaví, Chile 138/G3
Curahuara de Carangas, Bolivia 136/A5
Curahuara de Pacajes, Bolivia 136/A5
Curanilahue, Chile 138/D1
Curaray (riv.), Ecuador 128/D3
Curaumilla (pt.), Chile 138/E2
Curdsville, Ky. 237/G5
Curecanti Nat'l Rec. Area, Colo. 208/F6
Curepipe, Mauritius 118/G5
Curepto, Chile 138/A10
Curiapo, Venezuela 124/H3
Curiche, Bolivia 136/D6
Curicó, Chile 120/B6
Curicó, Chile 138/A10
Curieuse (isl.), Seychelles 118/H5
Curitiba, Brazil 132/D9
Curitiba, Brazil 120/F5
Curitiba, Brazil 135/B4
Curlew, Iowa 229/D3
Curlew (isls.), La. 238/M7
Curlew, Wash. 310/G2
Curlew (lake), Wash. 310/G2
Curlewis, N.S. Wales 97/F2
Curllsville, Pa. 294/D3
Curnamona, S. Australia 94/F4
Curragh, The, Ireland 17/H5
Curragh, The (racecourse), Ireland 10/C4
Currais Novos, Brazil 132/G4
Curran, Ill. 222/D4
Curran, Mich. 250/F4
Currant, Nev. 266/F4
Currawilla, Queensland 95/B5
Current (riv.), Ark. 202/J1
Current (riv.), Mo. 261/K8
Currie, Minn. 255/C6
Currie, Nev. 266/G2
Currie, N.C. 281/N6
Currie, Scotland 15/D2
Currie, Tasmania 99/A1
Currituck (co.), N.C. 281/S2
Currituck, N.C. 281/T2
Currituck (sound), N.C. 281/T2
Curry, Alaska 196/J2
Curry (co.), N. Mex. 274/F4
Curry (co.), Oreg. 291/C5
Curryville, Mo. 261/K4
Curryville, Pa. 294/F5
Curtea de Argeș, Romania 45/G3
Curtice, Ohio 284/D2
Curtin, Oreg. 291/D4
Curtina, Uruguay 145/C3
Curtis, Ark. 202/D6
Curtis, La. 238/C2
Curtis, Mich. 250/D2
Curtis, Nebr. 264/D4
Curtis, Okla. 288/H2
Curtis (isl.), Queensland 88/J4
Curtis (isl.), Queensland 95/D4
Curtis, Wash. 310/B4
Curtis Group (isls.), Tasmania 99/C1
Curtiss, Wis. 317/F6
Curtis Station, Miss. 256/D2
Curtisville, Ind. 227/F4
Curuá (riv.), Brazil 132/C4
Curuçá, Brazil 132/E3
Curuguaty, Paraguay 144/E4
Curup, Indonesia 85/C6
Cururú, Bolivia 136/D4
Cururupu, Brazil 132/E3
Curutú (riv.), Venezuela 124/G5
Curuzú Cuatiá, Argentina 143/G5
Curuzú Cuatiá, Argentina 120/D5
Curve, Tenn. 237/B9
Curvelo, Brazil 132/E7
Curwensville, Pa. 294/E4
Curwood (mt.), Mich. 250/A2
Cusachón (isl.), Colombia 126/D1
Cusco, Peru 120/B4
Cusco (dept.), Peru 128/F9
Cusco (Cuzco), Peru 128/F9
Cushendall, N. Ireland 17/J1
Cushing, Iowa 229/B4
Cushing •, Maine 243/E7
Cushing, Minn. 255/D4
Cushing, Nebr. 264/F3
Cushing, Okla. 288/N3
Cushing, Texas 303/J6
Cushing, Wis. 317/A4
Cushman, Ark. 202/G2
Cushman, Mass. 249/D3
Cushman, Oreg. 291/D4
Cushman (lake), Wash. 310/B3
Cusiana (riv.), Colombia 126/D5
Cusick, Wash. 310/H2
Cuslett, Newf. 166/C2
Cusset, France 28/E4
Cusseta, Ala. 195/H5
Cusseta, Georgia 217/C6
Cusson, Minn. 255/F2
Custar, Ohio 284/C3
Custer (co.), Colo. 208/J6
Custer (co.), Idaho 220/D5
Custer, Ky. 237/J5
Custer, Mich. 250/C5
Custer (co.), Mont. 262/L4
Custer, Mont. 262/J4
Custer (co.), Nebr. 264/E3
Custer (co.), Okla. 288/H3
Custer (co.), S. Dak. 298/B6
Custer, S. Dak. 298/B6
Custer, Wash. 310/C2
Custer City, Okla. 288/J3
Custer City, Pa. 294/E2
Custer Park, Ill. 222/E2
Cut Bank, Mont. 262/D2
Cut Bank (creek), Mont. 262/D2
Cut Bank (creek), N. Dak. 282/H2
Cutbank, Sask. 181/E4
Cutchogue-New Suffolk, N.Y. 276/P8
Cutervo, Peru 128/C6
Cuthbert, Georgia 217/C7
Cut Knife, Sask. 181/B3
Cutler, Calif. 204/F7
Cutler, Ill. 222/D5
Cutler, Ind. 227/D4
Cutler, Maine 243/J6
Cutler •, Maine 243/J6
Cutler, Ohio 284/G7
Cutler Ridge, Fla. 212/F6
Cutlerville, Mich. 250/D6
Cut Off, La. 238/K7
Cutra (lake), Ireland 17/D5
Cutral-Có, Argentina 143/C4
Cutshin, Ky. 237/P6
Cuttaburra (creek), N.S. Wales 97/C1
Cuttack, India 54/K7
Cuttack, India 68/F4
Cutten, Calif. 204/A3
Cuttingsville, Vt. 268/B4
Cuttyhunk, Mass. 249/L7
Cuttyhunk (isl.), Mass. 249/L7
Cuvier (isl.), N. Zealand 100/E2
Cuvier (cape), W. Australia 88/A4
Cuvier (cape), W. Australia 92/A4
Cuvo (riv.), Angola 115/B6
Cuxhaven, Germany 22/C2
Cuya, Chile 138/B2
Cuyabeno, Ecuador 128/E3
Cuyahoga (co.), Ohio 284/G3
Cuyahoga (riv.), Ohio 284/H10
Cuyahoga Falls, Ohio 284/G3
Cuyahoga Heights, Ohio 284/H9
Cuyama, Calif. 204/F9
Cuyama (riv.), Calif. 204/E8
Cuyapaipe Ind. Res., Calif. 204/J11
Cuyk, Netherlands 27/H5
Cuylerville, N.Y. 276/E5
Cuyo, Philippines 82/C5
Cuyo (isl.), Philippines 82/C5
Cuyo (isls.), Philippines 82/C5
Cuyo (isls.), Philippines 85/G3
Cuyocuyo, Peru 128/H10
Cuyo East (passage), Philippines 82/C5
Cuyo West (passage), Philippines 82/C5
Cuyuna, Minn. 255/E4
Cuyuna (range), Minn. 255/D4
Cuyuni (riv.) 120/C2
Cuyuni (riv.), Guyana 131/B2
Cuyuni (riv.), Venezuela 124/H4
Cuyu Tigni, Nicaragua 154/F3
Cuzco, Ind. 227/D8
Cuzzart, W. Va. 312/H3
Čvrsnica (mt.), Yugoslavia 45/C4
Cwmamman, Wales 13/D6
Cwmbran, Wales 13/B6
Cyangugu, Rwanda 115/E4
Cyclades (isls.), Greece 45/G7
Cycle, N.C. 281/H2
Cyclone, Ind. 227/E4
Cyclone, Pa. 294/E2
Cyclone, W. Va. 312/C7
Cygnet, Ohio 284/C3
Cygnet, Tasmania 99/C5
Cylinder, Iowa 229/D2
Cylon, Wis. 317/B5
Cymric, Sask. 181/G4
Cynthia, Alberta 182/C3
Cynthiana, Ind. 227/B8
Cynthiana, Ky. 237/N4
Cynthiana, Ohio 284/D7
Cypert, Ark. 202/J5
Cypress, Ala. 195/C5
Cypress (hills), Alberta 182/E5
Cypress (bayou), Ark. 202/F3
Cypress, Calif. 204/D11
Cypress, Fla. 212/A1
Cypress (lake), Fla. 212/E3
Cypress, Ill. 222/D6
Cypress, Ind. 227/B9
Cypress (pond), Ind. 227/B8
Cypress, La. 238/D3
Cypress (hills), Sask. 181/B6
Cypress (lake), Sask. 181/B6
Cypress Gardens, Fla. 212/E3
Cypress Hills Prov. Park, Alberta 182/E5
Cypress Hills Prov. Park, Sask. 181/B6
Cypress Inn, Tenn. 237/F10
Cypress Prov. Park, Br. Col. 184/K3
Cypress Quarters, Fla. 212/F4
Cypress River, Manitoba 179/D5
Cyprus 2/L4
Cyprus 54/E6
CYPRUS 59/B2
CYPRUS 63/E5
Cyrenaica (reg.), Libya 102/E1
Cyrenaica (reg.), Libya 111/D1
Cyrene (Shahat), Libya 111/D1
Cyrene, Mo. 261/K4
Cyril, Okla. 288/K5
Cyrus, Minn. 255/C5
Czar, Alberta 182/E3
Czar, W. Va. 312/F5
Czarna Białostocka, Poland 47/F2
Czarnków, Poland 47/C2
Czechoslovakia 2/K3
Czechoslovakia 7/F4
CZECHOSLOVAKIA 41
Czechowice-Dziedzice, Poland 47/D4
Czech Republic, Czech. 41/B1
Czeladź, Poland 47/B4
Czersk, Poland 47/D2
Częstochowa (prov.), Poland 47/D3
Częstochowa, Poland 47/D3
Częstochowa, Poland 7/F3
Człuchów, Poland 47/C2

D

Da'an (Talai), China 77/K2
Daaquam, Québec 172/H3
Dabajuro, Venezuela 124/C2
Dabakala, Ivory Coast 106/D7
Dabas, Hungary 41/E3
Daba Shan (range), China 77/G5
Dabeiba, Colombia 126/B4
Dabhoi, India 68/C4
Dabney, Ind. 227/G6
Dabob (bay), Wash. 310/C3
Dabola, Guinea 106/B6
Dabou, Ivory Coast 106/D7
Daboya, Ghana 106/D7
Dąbrowa Górnicza, Poland 47/B3
Dąbrowa Tarnowska, Poland 47/E3
Dăbuleni, Romania 45/F4
Dachau, Germany 22/D4
Dačice, Czech. 41/C2
Dac Lac, Cao Nguyen (plat.), Vietnam 72/F4
Dacoma, Okla. 288/J1
Dacono, Colo. 208/K2
Dacre, Ontario 177/G2
Dacula, Georgia 217/E3
Dacusville, S.C. 296/B2
Dadanawa, Guyana 131/B4
Daday, Turkey 63/E2
Dade (co.), Fla. 212/F6
Dade (co.), Georgia 217/A1
Dade (co.), Mo. 261/E8
Dade City, Fla. 212/D3
Dadeville, Ala. 195/G5
Dadeville, Mo. 261/E8
Dadra and Nagar Haveli (terr.), India 68/C4
Dads (lake), Nebr. 264/D2
Dadu, Pakistan 68/B3
Dadu, Pakistan 59/J4
Dăeni, Romania 45/J3
Daer (res.), Scotland 15/E5
Daet, Philippines 85/G3
Daet, Philippines 82/D3
Dafang, China 77/G6
Dafna, Israel 65/D1
Dafoe, Sask. 181/G4
Dafter, Mich. 250/E2
Dagabur, Ethiopia 111/H6
Dagana, Senegal 106/A5
Dagda, U.S.S.R. 53/D2
Dagelet (Ullŭng) (isl.), S. Korea 81/E5
Dagestan A.S.S.R., U.S.S.R. 48/E5
Dagestan A.S.S.R., U.S.S.R. 52/G6
Dagestanskiye Ogni, U.S.S.R. 52/G6
Daggett, Calif. 204/H9
Daggett, Mich. 250/B3
Daggett (co.), Utah 304/E3
Dagmar, Mont. 262/M2
Dagö (Hiiumaa) (isl.), U.S.S.R. 52/B3
Dagsboro, Del. 245/S6
Dagua, Colombia 126/B6
Daguan, China 77/F6
D'Aguilar (range), Tasmania 99/B4
Dagupan, Philippines 82/C2
Daguscahonda, Pa. 294/E3
Dagus Mines, Pa. 294/E3
Dahab, Egypt 111/F2
Dahana (des.), Saudi Arabia 54/F7
Dahana (des.), Saudi Arabia 59/E4
Dahinda, Ill. 222/C3
Dahinda, Sask. 181/G6
Da Hingan Ling (Great Khingan) (range), China 54/O5
Da Hingan Ling (range), China 77/J3
Dahlak (arch.), Ethiopia 111/H4
Dahlak (arch.), Ethiopia 59/D6
Dahlak (isl.), Ethiopia 59/D6
Dahlak (isl.), Ethiopia 111/H4
Dahlem, Germany 22/E4
Dahlen, N. Dak. 282/P3
Dahlgren, Ill. 222/E5
Dahlgren, Va. 307/O4
Dahlia, N. Mex. 274/D3
Dahlonega, Georgia 217/D1
Dahme, Germany 22/E3
Dai (mt.), Japan 81/F6
Dailekh, Nepal 68/E3
Dailey, Colo. 208/O1
Dailly, Scotland 15/D5
Daimanji (mt.), Japan 81/F5
Daimiel, Spain 33/E3
Daingean, Ireland 17/G5
Daingerfield, Texas 303/K4
Daio (cape), Japan 81/H6
Daiquirí, Cuba 158/J4
Daireaux, Argentina 143/D4
Dairût, Egypt 111/J4
Dairy, Oreg. 291/F5
Dairy Flat-Redvale, N. Zealand 100/B1
Dairyland, Wis. 317/B3
Daisen-Oki Nat'l Park, Japan 81/F6
Daisetsu (mt.), Japan 81/L2
Daisetsu-Zan Nat'l Park, Japan 81/L2
Daisetta, Texas 303/K7
Daisy, Ark. 202/C5
Daisy, Georgia 217/J6
Daisy, Ky. 237/P6
Daisy, Mo. 261/N7
Daisy, Okla. 288/P5
Daisy, Wash. 310/G2
Daito, Japan 81/J8
Daito (isls.), Japan 54/P7
Dajabón (prov.), Dom. Rep. 158/D5
Dajabón, Dom. Rep. 158/D5
Dajarra, Queensland 88/F4
Dajarra, Queensland 95/A4
Dakar (cap.), Senegal 2/J5
Dakar (cap.), Senegal 102/A3
Dakar (cap.), Senegal 106/A6
Dakhla (oasis), Egypt 111/E2
Dakhla (oasis), Egypt 59/A4
Dakhla, W. Sahara 102/A2
Dakhla, Western Sahara 106/A4
Dakoro, Niger 106/F6
Dakota, Georgia 217/E7
Dakota, Ill. 222/D1
Dakota (co.), Minn. 255/E6
Dakota, Minn. 255/G7
Dakota (co.), Nebr. 264/H2
Dakota City, Iowa 229/E3
Dakota City, Nebr. 264/H2
Dal (riv.), Sweden 7/F2
Dala, Angola 115/D6
Dalaba, Guinea 106/B6
Dalälven (riv.), Sweden 18/K6
Dalaman (riv.), Turkey 63/C4
Dalandzadgad, Mongolia 77/G3
Dalanganem (isls.), Philippines 82/C5
Dalark, Ark. 202/E5
Da Lat, Vietnam 72/F5
Dalavich, Scotland 15/C4
Dalbandin, Pakistan 68/A3
Dalbandin, Pakistan 59/H4
Dalbeattie, Scotland 10/E3
Dalbeattie, Scotland 15/E6
Dalbo, Minn. 255/E5
Dalby, Queensland 95/D5
Dalby, Queensland 88/J5
Dalby, Sweden 18/H6
Dalcahue, Chile 138/D4
Dalcour, La. 238/P4
Dale (co.), Ala. 195/G8
Dale, Ill. 222/E6
Dale, Ind. 227/D8
Dale, Minn. 255/B4
Dale, Norway 18/E6
Dale, Okla. 288/M4
Dale, Oreg. 291/J3
Dale, Pa. 294/E5
Dale, S.C. 296/F6
Dale (mt.), W. Australia 88/B2
Dale (mt.), W. Australia 92/B1
Dale, Wis. 317/J7
Dale City, Va. 307/O3
Dale Hollow (lake), Ky. 237/L7
Dale Hollow (lake), Tenn. 237/L7
Dalemead, Alberta 182/D4
Dalen, Netherlands 27/K3
Daleside, S. Africa 118/H7
Daleville, Ala. 195/G8
Daleville, Ind. 227/F4
Daleville, Miss. 256/G5
Daleville, Va. 307/J6
Dale West, W. Australia 92/B2
Dalhart, Texas 303/B1
Dalhousie, New Bruns. 170/D1
Dalhousie (cape), N.W. Terr. 187/E2
Dalhousie (mt.), Nova Scotia 168/E3
Dalhousie East, Nova Scotia 168/D4

358 Dalhousie Junction

Dalhousie Junction, New Bruns. 170/D1
Dalhousie West, Nova Scotia 168/C4
Dali, China 77/E6
Dalian (Lüda), China 77/K4
Dalías, Spain 33/E4
Daliburgh, Scotland 15/A3
Dalizi, China 77/L3
Dalkeith, Ontario 177/K2
Dalkeith, Scotland 10/C1
Dalkeith, Scotland 15/D2
Dalkena, Wash. 310/H2
Dall (isl.), Alaska 196/M2
Dall (mt.), Alaska 196/H2
Dallam (co.), Texas 303/B1
Dallas (co.), Ala. 195/D6
Dallas (co.), Ark. 202/E6
Dallas, Georgia 217/C3
Dallas (co.), Iowa 229/E5
Dallas, Iowa 229/G6
Dallas, Manitoba 179/E3
Dallas (co.), Mo. 261/F7
Dallas, N.C. 281/G4
Dallas, Oreg. 291/D3
Dallas, Pa. 294/E7
Dallas, Scotland 15/E3
Dallas, S. Dak. 298/K7
Dallas (co.), Texas 303/H5
Dallas, Texas 303/G2
Dallas, Texas 188/G4
Dallas, Texas 146/J6
Dallas, U.S. 2/E4
Dallas, W. Va. 312/E2
Dallas, Wis. 317/C5
Dallas Center, Iowa 229/E5
Dallas City, Ill. 222/B3
Dallas Naval Air Sta., Texas 303/G2
Dallastown, Pa. 294/J6
Dalles, The, Oreg. 291/F2
Dalles, The (dam), Oreg. 291/F2
Dalles, The (dam), Wash. 310/D5
Dallesport, Wash. 310/D5
Dallol, Ethiopia 111/G5
Dallol Bosso (dry riv.), Niger 106/E6
Dalmaj, Hor (lake), Iraq 66/D4
Dalmally, Scotland 10/D2
Dalmally, Scotland 15/D4
Dalmatia, Pa. 294/J4
Dalmatia (reg.), Yugoslavia 45/C4
Dalmellington, Scotland 15/D5
Dalmellington, Scotland 10/D3
Dalmeny, Sask. 181/E3
Dal'negorsk, U.S.S.R. 48/O5
Dal'nerechensk, U.S.S.R. 48/O5
Daloa, Ivory Coast 106/C7
Daloa, Ivory Coast 102/B4
Dalroy, Alberta 182/D4
Dalry, Scotland 10/A1
Dalry, Scotland 15/D5
Dalrymple, Scotland 15/D5
Dalton, Ark. 202/H1
Dalton, Georgia 217/C1
Dalton, Ky. 237/F6
Dalton•, Mass. 249/B3
Dalton, Mich. 250/C5
Dalton, Minn. 255/C4
Dalton, Mo. 261/F4
Dalton, Nebr. 264/B3
Dalton•, N.H. 268/D3
Dalton, N.Y. 276/E5
Dalton, N.C. 281/J2
Dalton, Ohio 284/G4
Dalton, Pa. 294/L2
Dalton, Wis. 317/H8
Dalton City, Ill. 222/E4
Daltonganj, India 68/E4
Dalton Gardens, Idaho 220/B2
Dalton-in-Furness, England 13/D3
Dalupiri (isl.), Philippines 82/A3
Dalwallinu, W. Australia 88/B6
Dalwallinu, W. Australia 92/B5
Dalwhinnie, Scotland 15/D4
Dalworthington Gardens, Texas 303/F2
Daly (cape), Ant. 5/C4
Daly (riv.), North. Terr. 88/E2
Daly (riv.), North. Terr. 93/B2
Daly (bay), N.W. Terr. 187/K3
Dalyat al-Karmel, Israel 65/B2
Daly City, Calif. 204/H2
Daly River, North. Terr. 88/E2
Daly River, North. Terr. 93/B2
Daly River Aboriginal Res., North. Terr. 88/D2
Daly River Aboriginal Res., North. Terr. 93/A2
Dalyup, W. Australia 92/C6
Daly Waters, Australia 87/D7
Daly Waters, North. Terr. 88/E3
Daly Waters, North. Terr. 93/C4
Dalzell, Ill. 222/D2
Dalzell, S.C. 296/G3
Dam, Saudi Arabia 59/D5
Daman (dist.), India 68/C4
Daman & Diu (terr.), India 68/C4
Damanhur, Egypt 111/J3
Damanhur, Egypt 59/A3
Damar (isl.), Indonesia 85/H7
Damar (isls.), Indonesia 85/H7
Damar, Kansas 232/C2
Damara, Cent. Afr. Rep. 115/C2
Damaraland (reg.), Namibia 118/B4
Damariscotta•, Maine 243/E7
Damariscotta-Newcastle, Maine 243/E7
Damascus, Ark. 202/F3
Damascus, Georgia 217/C8
Damascus, Md. 245/K3
Damascus, Ohio 284/J4
Damascus, Pa. 294/M2
Damascus (prov.), Syria 63/G6
Damascus (cap.), Syria 59/C3
Damascus (cap.), Syria 54/E6
Damascus (cap.), Syria 63/G6
Damascus, Va. 307/E7
Damavand, Iran 66/H3
Damavand (mt.), Iran 54/G6
Damavand (mt.), Iran 59/F2
Damavend (Demavend) (mt.), Iran 66/G3
Damazin (Ed Damazin), Sudan 111/F5
Damba, Angola 115/B5
Dam Doi, Vietnam 72/E5
Dame Marie, Haiti 158/A6
Dame Marie (cape), Haiti 158/A6
Dame Marie (cape), Haiti 156/C3
Dameron, Md. 245/N8
Dames Ferry, Georgia 217/E4
Dames Quarter, Md. 245/P8
Damghan, Iran 59/F2
Damghan, Iran 66/J2
Damh, Loch (lake), Scotland 15/C3
Damietta, Egypt 102/F1
Damietta, Egypt 111/J3
Damietta, Egypt 59/B3
Damiya, Jordan 65/D3
Dammam, Saudi Arabia 59/F4
Dammastock (mt.), Switzerland 39/F3
Damme, Belgium 27/C6
Damodar (riv.), India 68/F4
Damoh, India 68/D4
Damongo, Ghana 106/D7
Dampier (str.), Indonesia 85/J6
Dampier (str.), Papua N.G. 86/B2
Dampier (str.), Papua N.G. 85/C7
Dampier, W. Australia 88/B4
Dampier, W. Australia 92/B3
Dampier (arch.), W. Australia 88/B4
Dampier (arch.), W. Australia 92/B3
Dampier Downs, W. Australia 92/C2
Dampier Land (reg.), W. Australia 88/C3
Dampier Land (reg.), W. Australia 92/C2
Damqut, Yemen 59/F6
Damvant, Switzerland 39/C2
Dan, Israel 65/D1
Dan (riv.), N.C. 281/L1
Dan (riv.), Va. 307/K7
Dana, Ill. 222/E3
Dana, Ind. 227/C5
Dana, Iowa 229/E4
Dana, Jordan 65/E5
Dana, Sask. 181/F3
Danakil (reg.), Ethiopia 111/H5
Danané, Ivory Coast 106/C7
Da Nang, Vietnam 72/E3
Da Nang, Vietnam 54/M8
Da Nang, Mui (cape), Vietnam 72/F3
Danao, Philippines 82/D5
Dana Point, Calif. 204/H10
Danba, China 77/F5
Danburg, Georgia 217/G3
Danbury, Conn. 210/B3
Danbury, Iowa 229/B4
Danbury, Nebr. 264/D4
Danbury•, N.H. 268/D4
Danbury, N.C. 281/J2
Danbury, Sask. 181/J4
Danbury, Texas 303/J8
Danbury, Wis. 317/B3
Danbury P.O. (South Danbury), N.H. 268/D5
Danby (lake), Calif. 204/K9
Danby•, Vt. 268/A5
Dancing (pt.), Manitoba 179/D2
Dancy, Ala. 195/B4
Dancy, Miss. 256/F3
Dancy, Wis. 317/G6
Dancyville, Tenn. 237/C10
Dand, Manitoba 179/B5
Dandaragan, W. Australia 88/B6
Dandaragan, W. Australia 92/A5
Dandenong, Victoria 97/K5
Dandenong, Victoria 88/M7
Dandenong (creek), Victoria 88/M7
Dandenong (creek), Victoria 97/K5
Dandenong (mt.), Victoria 97/K5
Danderyd, Sweden 18/H1
Dandong (Tantung), China 77/K3
Dandong, China 54/O5
Dandridge, Tenn. 237/O8
Dane (riv.), England 13/H2
Dane (co.), Wis. 317/H9
Dane, Wis. 317/G9
Daneborg, Greenl. 4/B10
Danford Lake, Québec 172/A4
Danforth, Ill. 222/E3
Danforth, Maine 243/H4
Danforth•, Maine 243/H4
Danger (Pukapuka) (atoll), Cook Is. 87/K7
Dangila, Ethiopia 111/G5
Dangrek (mts.), Cambodia 72/D4
Dangrek (Dong Rak) (mts.), Thailand 72/D4
Dangriga (Stann Creek), Belize 154/C2
Dania, Fla. 212/B4
Daniel (mt.), Wash. 310/D3
Daniel, Wyo. 319/B3
Daniel-Johnson (dam), Québec 174/D2
Daniels, Md. 245/L3
Daniels (co.), Mont. 262/L2
Daniels, W. Va. 312/D7
Daniel's Harbour, Newf. 166/C3
Danielson, Conn. 210/H1
Danielson Prov. Park, Sask. 181/E4
Danielstown, Guyana 131/B2
Danielsville, Georgia 217/F2
Danielsville, Pa. 294/M4
Danilov, U.S.S.R. 52/E3
Dankov, U.S.S.R. 52/E4
Danlí, Honduras 154/D3
Danmarks Havn, Greenl. 4/B10
Dannebrog, Nebr. 264/F3
Dannelly (res.), Ala. 195/D6
Dannemora, N.Y. 276/N1
Dannemora, Sweden 18/K6
Dannenberg, Germany 22/D2
Danner, Oreg. 291/K5
Dannevirke, N. Zealand 100/F4
Dan Sai, Thailand 72/D3
Dansville, Mich. 250/E6
Dansville, N.Y. 276/E5
Dante (Hafun), Somalia 115/K1
Dante, S. Dak. 298/N7
Dante, Va. 307/D7
Danube (riv.) 7/G4
Danube (riv.), Austria 41/C2
Danube (riv.), Bulgaria 45/H4
Danube (riv.), Czech. 41/C2
Danube (riv.), Hungary 41/E3
Danube, Minn. 255/C6
Danube (delta), Romania 45/J3
Danube (riv.), Romania 45/H4
Danube (riv.), Germany 22/C4
Danube (riv.), Yugoslavia 45/E3
Danubyu, Burma 72/B3
Danvers, Ill. 222/D3
Danvers•, Mass. 249/D5
Danvers, Minn. 255/C5
Danvers, Mont. 262/G3
Danversport, Mass. 249/E5
Danville, Ala. 195/D2
Danville, Ark. 202/D3
Danville, Calif. 204/K2
Danville, Georgia 217/F5
Danville, Ill. 188/J3
Danville, Ill. 222/F3
Danville, Ind. 227/D5
Danville, Iowa 229/L7
Danville, Kansas 232/E4
Danville, Ky. 237/M5
Danville, La. 238/E2
Danville, Mo. 261/J5
Danville•, N.H. 268/E6
Danville, Ohio 284/F5
Danville, Pa. 294/J4
Danville, Québec 172/E4
Danville•, Vt. 268/C3
Danville, Va. 188/L3
Danville, Va. 146/L6
Danville (I.C.), Va. 307/J7
Danville, Wash. 310/G2
Danville, W. Va. 312/C6
Danville, Wis. 317/J9
Dan Xian, China 77/G8
Danzig (Gdańsk), Poland 47/D1
Danzig (Gdańsk) (gulf), Poland 47/D1
Daocheng, China 77/F6
Dao Xian, China 77/H6
Dapa, Philippines 82/E6
Dapaong, Togo 106/E6
Daphne, Ala. 195/C9
Daphne, Sask. 181/G3
Dapitan, Philippines 82/D6
Dapoli, India 68/C5
Dapp, Alberta 182/C2
Da Qaidam, China 77/E4
Darab, Iran 59/G4
Darab, Iran 66/J6
Darabani, Romania 45/H1
Dar al Hamra, Saudi Arabia 59/C4
Daram (isl.), Philippines 82/E5
Daran, Iran 66/G4
Darbandikhan (dam), Iraq 66/D3
Darbhanga, India 68/F3
Darbun, Miss. 256/D8
Darby (cape), Alaska 196/F2
Darby, Mont. 262/B4
Darby (creek), Ohio 284/D5
Darby, Pa. 294/M7
Darby (creek), Pa. 294/M6
Darby, Victoria 97/D6
Darbydale, Ohio 284/D6
Darbyville, Ohio 284/D6
D'Arcy, Br. Col. 184/F5
D'Arcy, Sask. 181/C4
Dardanelle, Ark. 202/D3
Dardanelle (lake), Ark. 202/D3
Dardanelles (str.), Turkey 7/G5
Dardanelles (str.), Turkey 59/A2
Dardanelles (str.), Turkey 63/B6
Darden, Tenn. 237/E9
Dare (co.), N.C. 281/T3
Dar-el-Beida (Casablanca), Morocco 106/C2
Darende, Turkey 63/G3
Dar es Salaam (cap.), Tanzania 102/F5
Dar es Salaam (cap.), Tanzania 2/M6
Dar es Salaam (cap.), Tanzania 115/G5
Dareton, N.S. Wales 97/B4
Daretown, N.J. 273/C4
Darfur, Minn. 255/D6
Darfur, Northern (prov.), Sudan 111/D5
Darfur, Southern (prov.), Sudan 111/E5
Dargan, Md. 245/H3
Dargaville, N. Zealand 100/D1
Dar Hamid (reg.), Sudan 111/F5
Darham Muminggan Lianheqi, China 77/H3
Darhan (Darkhan), Mongolia 77/G2
Darien•, Conn. 210/B4
Darien, Georgia 217/K8
Darien, Ill. 222/B6
Darien, N.Y. 276/D5
Darién (mts.), Panama 154/J6
Darien, Wis. 317/J10
Darien Center, N.Y. 276/D5
Dariense, Cordillera (range), Nicaragua 154/E4
Darjeeling, India 68/F3
Dark (head), St. Vin. & Grens. 161/A8
Darkan, W. Australia 92/B2
Dark Canyon (creek), N. Mex. 274/E6
Dark Cove, Newf. 166/D4
Darke (co.), Ohio 284/A5
Darkesville, W. Va. 312/L4
Darkin (riv.), W. Australia 88/B2
Darlag, China 77/E5
Darling (river), Australia 87/E9
Darling, Miss. 256/D2
Darling (riv.), N.S. Wales 88/G6
Darling (riv.), N.S. Wales 97/B3
Darling (lake), N. Dak. 282/G2
Darling, Pa. 294/L7
Darling (range), W. Australia 88/B6
Darling (range), W. Australia 92/A1
Darling Downs, Queensland 95/D5
Darlingford, Manitoba 179/D5
Darlington, Ala. 195/D7
Darlington, England 10/F3
Darlington, England 13/F3
Darlington, Fla. 212/C5
Darlington, Idaho 220/E6
Darlington, Ind. 227/D4
Darlington, La. 238/J5
Darlington, Md. 245/N2
Darlington, Mo. 261/D2
Darlington, New Bruns. 170/D1
Darlington, Pa. 294/A4
Darlington (co.), S.C. 296/H3
Darlington, S.C. 296/H3
Darlington, Wis. 317/F10
Darlington Heights, Va. 307/L6
Darlington Point, N.S. Wales 97/C4
Darliston, Jamaica 158/H6
Darłowo, Poland 47/C1
Dar Masalit (reg.), Sudan 111/D5
Darmody, Sask. 181/E5
Darmstadt, Germany 22/C4
Darmstadt, Ill. 222/D5
Darmstadt, Ind. 227/B8
Darnell, La. 238/G1
Darnestown, Md. 245/J4
Darnick, N.S. Wales 97/B3
Darnley (cape), Ant. 5/C4
Darnley (bay), N.W. Terr. 187/F3
Daroca, Spain 33/F2
Darra, Queensland 88/K3
Darreh Gaz, Iran 66/L2
Darrington, Wash. 310/D2
Dar Rounga (reg.), Cent. Afr. Rep. 115/D2
Darrouzett, Texas 303/D1
Darrow, La. 238/K3
Darrtown, Ohio 284/A7
Darsser Ort (pt.), Germany 22/E1
Dart (cape), Ant. 5/B12
Dart (riv.), England 13/D7
D'Artagnan, Québec 172/J3
Dartford, England 13/J8
Dartford, England 10/C5
Dartmoor, Victoria 97/A5
Dartmoor Nat'l Park, England 13/C7
Dartmouth (Clifton Dartmouth Hardness), England 10/E5
Dartmouth (Clifton Dartmouth Hardness), England 13/D7
Dartmouth•, Mass. 249/K6
Dartmouth, Nova Scotia 162/K7
Dartmouth, Nova Scotia 168/E4
Dartmouth (riv.), Québec 172/D1
Darton, England 13/J2
Dartuch (cape), Spain 33/H3
Daru, Papua N.G. 87/E6
Daru, Papua N.G. 85/B7
Daruvar, Yugoslavia 45/C3
Darvel, Scotland 15/D5
Darwell, Alberta 182/C3
Darwen, England 10/G1
Darwen, England 13/H1
Darwin, Australia 2/R6
Darwin, Australia 87/D7
Darwin, Calif. 204/H7
Darwin (bay), Chile 138/D6
Darwin, Cordillera (mts.), Chile 138/D8
Darwin, Cordillera (mts.), Chile 138/E11
Darwin (Culpepper) (isl.), Ecuador 128/B8
Darwin, Ill. 222/F4
Darwin, Minn. 255/D5
Darwin (cap.), North. Terr. 88/E2
Darwin (cap.), North. Terr. 93/B2
Darwin, Okla. 288/P6
Das (isl.), U.A.E. 59/F4
Dash, Ben (hill), Ireland 17/C6
Dashan, Ras (mt.), Ethiopia 59/C7
Dashbalbar, Mongolia 77/H2
Dasher, Georgia 217/F9
Dashinchilen, Mongolia 77/F2
Dasht (riv.), Pakistan 68/A3
Dasht (riv.), Pakistan 59/H4
Dashtiari, Iran 66/M8
Dashtiari, Iran 59/H4
Dashwood, Br. Col. 184/H3
Dashwood, Ontario 177/C4
Dasol (bay), Philippines 82/B3
Dassel, Minn. 255/D5
Datça, Turkey 63/B4
Dateland, Ariz. 198/B6
Datia, India 68/D3
Datil, N. Mex. 274/B4
Datil (mts.), N. Mex. 274/B4
Datong, Qinghai, China 77/F4
Datong (Tatung), Shanxi, China 77/H3
Datto, Ark. 202/J1
Datu Piang, Philippines 82/E7
Daua (riv.), Kenya 115/H3
Daufuskie Island, S.C. 296/F7
Daugava (Western Dvina) (riv.), U.S.S.R. 53/D2
Daugavpils, U.S.S.R. 7/G3
Daugavpils, U.S.S.R. 53/D3
Daugavpils, U.S.S.R. 48/C4
Daugavpils, U.S.S.R. 52/C3
Daule, Ecuador 128/B3
Daulnay, New Bruns. 170/E1
Daun, Germany 22/B3
Daung Kyun (isl.), Burma 72/C4
Dauphin, Man. 162/F5
Dauphin, Manitoba 179/B3
Dauphin (lake), Manitoba 179/C3
Dauphin (riv.), Manitoba 179/D3
Dauphin (cape), Nova Scotia 168/H2
Dauphin (co.), Pa. 294/J5
Dauphin, Pa. 294/J5
Dauphin, St. Lucia 161/G5
Dauphiné (trad. prov.), France 29
Dauphin Island, Ala. 195/B10
Daus, Tenn. 237/L10
Davangere, India 68/D6
Davant, La. 238/L7
Davao, Philippines 85/H4
Davao, Philippines 54/O9
Davao, Philippines 2/R5
Davao, Philippines 82/E7
Davao (gulf), Philippines 82/E7
Davao (gulf), Philippines 85/H4
Davao del Norte (prov.), Philippines 82/E7
Davao del Sur (prov.), Philippines 82/E7
Davao Oriental (prov.), Philippines 82/F7
Daveluyville, Québec 172/E3
Davenport, Calif. 204/K4
Davenport, Fla. 212/E3
Davenport, Iowa 229/M5
Davenport, Iowa 188/H2
Davenport, Nebr. 264/G4
Davenport, N.Y. 276/L6
Davenport, N. Dak. 282/R6
Davenport (mt.), North. Terr. 93/B7
Davenport, Okla. 288/N3
Davenport, Va. 307/D6
Davenport, Wash. 310/G3
Daventry, England 13/F5
Davey, Nebr. 264/H4
Davey (riv.), Tasmania 99/B4
David (pt.), Grenada 161/D8
David, Ky. 237/R5
David, Panama 154/F6
David City, Nebr. 264/G3
Davidson (mts.), Alaska 196/K1
Davidson, Maine 243/F4
Davidson (co.), N.C. 281/J3
Davidson, N.C. 281/H4
Davidson, Okla. 288/J6
Davidson, Sask. 181/E4
Davidson (co.), Tenn. 237/H8
Davidson (mts.), Yukon 187/D3
Davidsonville, Md. 245/M5
Davie, Fla. 212/B4
Davie (co.), N.C. 281/H3
Daviess (co.), Ind. 227/C7
Daviess (co.), Ky. 237/G5
Daviess (co.), Mo. 261/E3
Davik, Norway 18/D6
Davilla, Texas 303/G7
Davin, Sask. 181/H5
Daviot, Scotland 15/D3
Davis (str.) 2/G2
Davis (str.) 146/N3
Davis (str.) 4/C12
Davis (sea), Ant. 5/C5
Davis (dam), Ariz. 198/A3
Davis, Calif. 204/B8
Davis (isl.), Fla. 212/C3
Davis, Ill. 222/D1
Davis (co.), Iowa 229/J7
Davis (dam), Nev. 266/G7
Davis, N.C. 281/R5
Davis (str.), N.W.T. 162/K1
Davis (str.), N.W. Terr. 187/M3
Davis, Okla. 288/M5
Davis (lake), Oreg. 291/F4
Davis (mt.), Pa. 294/D6
Davis, Sask. 181/F2
Davis, S. Dak. 298/P7
Davis (mts.), Texas 303/C11
Davis (co.), Utah 304/B3
Davis, W. Va. 312/H4
Davisboro, Georgia 217/G5
Davis City, Iowa 229/F7
Davis Cove, Newf. 166/D4
Davis Creek, Calif. 204/E2
Davis Dam, Ariz. 198/A3
Davis Inlet, Newf. 166/B2
Davis Junction, Ill. 222/D1
Davis-Monthan A.F.B., Ariz. 198/E6
Davison, Mich. 250/F5
Davison (co.), S. Dak. 298/N6
Davis Station, Ant. 5/C4
Davis Station, S.C. 296/G4
Daviston, Ala. 195/G4
Davisville, Mo. 261/K7
Davisville, R.I. 249/H6
Davisville, W. Va. 312/C4
Davlekanovo, U.S.S.R. 52/H4
Davos, Switzerland 39/J3
Davos (valley), Switzerland 39/J3
Davy, W. Va. 312/C8
Dawa (riv.), Ethiopia 111/G7
Dawasir, Hadhb (range), Saudi Arabia 59/D5
Dawasir, Wadi (dry riv.), Saudi Arabia 59/E5
Dawes (co.), Nebr. 264/A2
Dawes, W. Va. 312/D6
Dawlish, England 13/D7
Dawn, Mo. 261/E3
Dawn, Texas 303/B3
Dawna (range), Burma 72/C3
Dawson, Ala. 195/G2
Dawson, Canada 4/C16
Dawson (isl.), Chile 138/E10
Dawson (co.), Georgia 217/D2
Dawson, Georgia 217/D7
Dawson, Ill. 222/D4
Dawson, Iowa 229/E5
Dawson (bay), Manitoba 179/B2
Dawson, Minn. 255/B6
Dawson, Mo. 261/H8
Dawson (co.), Mont. 262/M3
Dawson (co.), Nebr. 264/E4
Dawson, Nebr. 264/J4
Dawson, N. Dak. 282/L6
Dawson (inlet), N.W. Terr. 187/J3
Dawson (riv.), Queensland 88/H4
Dawson (riv.), Queensland 95/D5
Dawson (co.), Texas 303/C5
Dawson, Texas 303/H6
Dawson, W. Va. 312/E7
Dawson, Yukon 146/E3
Dawson, Yukon 162/C3
Dawson, Yukon 187/E3
Dawson Bay, Manitoba 179/B2
Dawson Creek, Br. Col. 146/F4
Dawson Creek, Br. Col. 162/D4
Dawson Creek, Br. Col. 184/G2
Dawson Springs, Ky. 237/F6
Dawsonville, Georgia 217/D2
Dawsonville, New Bruns. 170/C1
Dawu, China 77/H5
Dawu, China 77/F5
Dax, France 28/C6
Da Xian, China 77/G5
Day, Fla. 212/C1
Day, Minn. 255/E5
Day (co.), S. Dak. 298/O3
Day Book, N.C. 281/E3
Daykin, Nebr. 264/G4
Daylesford, Victoria 97/C5
Daylight, Tenn. 237/K9
Daymán, Uruguay 145/B2
Daymán (range), Uruguay 145/B2
Daymán (riv.), Uruguay 145/B2
Dayong, China 77/H6
Days Creek, Oreg. 291/D5
Daysland, Alberta 182/D3
Daysville, Ky. 237/G7
Dayton, Ala. 195/C6
Dayton, Idaho 220/F7
Dayton, Ill. 222/E2
Dayton, Ind. 227/D4
Dayton, Iowa 229/E4
Dayton, Ky. 237/T1
Dayton, Mich. 250/C7
Dayton, Minn. 255/E5
Dayton, Mont. 262/B3
Dayton, Nev. 266/B3
Dayton, N.J. 273/D3
Dayton, N.Y. 276/C6
Dayton, Ohio 284/B6
Dayton, Ohio 146/K6
Dayton, Ohio 188/K3
Dayton, Oreg. 291/A3
Dayton, Pa. 294/D4
Dayton, Tenn. 237/L9
Dayton, Texas 303/J7
Dayton, Va. 307/L4
Dayton, Wash. 310/H4
Dayton, Wis. 317/H10
Dayton, Wyo. 319/E1
Daytona Beach, Fla. 188/K5
Daytona Beach, Fla. 146/K7
Daytona Beach, Fla. 212/F2
Daytona Beach Shores, Fla. 212/F2
Dayu, China 77/H6
Dayville, Conn. 210/H1
Dayville, Oreg. 291/H3
Dazey, N. Dak. 282/O5
Dazhai, China 77/H4
Dazkırı, Turkey 63/D4
De Aar, S. Africa 118/C6
Dead (lake), Fla. 212/D6
Dead (sea), Israel 65/C4
Dead (sea), Israel 59/C3
Dead (sea), Jordan 59/C3
Dead (sea), Jordan 65/C4
Dead (riv.), Maine 243/C5
Dead (riv.), Mich. 250/B2
Dead (lake), Minn. 255/C4
Dead (sea), West Bank 59/C3
Deadhorse, Alaska 196/J1
Deadman (creek), Wash. 310/H4
Deadman (mt.), Wyo. 319/B2
Deadwood, Alberta 182/B1
Deadwood (res.), Idaho 220/C5
Deadwood (riv.), Idaho 220/C5
Deadwood, S. Dak. 298/B5
Deaf Smith (co.), Texas 303/B3
Deal, England 13/J6
Deal, England 10/G5
Deal, N.J. 273/F3
Deal (isl.), Tasmania 99/D1
Deale, Md. 245/M5
Deal Island, Md. 245/P8
Dean (chan.), Br. Col. 184/D4
Dean (riv.), Br. Col. 184/D4
Dean, Nova Scotia 168/F3
Deán Funes, Argentina 143/D3
Deanville, Texas 303/H7
Dearborn (co.), Ind. 227/H6
Dearborn, Mich. 250/B7
Dearborn, Mo. 261/C3
Dearborn Heights, Mich. 250/B7
Dearing, Georgia 217/H4
Dearing, Kansas 232/G4
De Armanville, Ala. 195/G3
Dearne, England 13/K2
Deary, Idaho 220/B3
Dease (inlet), Alaska 196/H1
Dease (lake), Br. Col. 184/K2
Dease (riv.), Br. Col. 184/K2
Dease (str.), N.W.T. 146/G3
Dease (str.), N.W.T. 162/F2
Dease (str.), N.W. Terr. 187/H3
Dease Arm (inlet), N.W. Terr. 187/F3
Death (valley), Calif. 204/H7
Death Valley, Calif. 204/J7
Death Valley (depr.), Calif. 188/C3
Death Valley Junction, Calif. 204/J7
Death Valley Nat'l Mon., Calif. 204/H7
Death Valley Nat'l Mon., Nev. 266/E6
Deatsville, Ala. 195/F5
Deauville, France 28/C3
Deauville, Québec 172/E4
Deaver, Wyo. 319/D1
Deavertown, Ohio 284/G6
De Baca (co.), N. Mex. 274/E4
Deba Habe, Nigeria 106/G6
Debar, Yugoslavia 45/E5
De Bary, Fla. 212/E3
Debden, Sask. 181/E2
Débé, Trin. & Tob. 161/B11
Debec, New Bruns. 170/C2
De Beque, Colo. 208/C4
De Berry, Texas 303/L5
Debert, Nova Scotia 168/E3
Dębica, Poland 47/E3
De Bilt, Netherlands 27/G4
Dęblin, Poland 47/E3
Deblois•, Maine 243/H6
Dębno, Poland 47/B2
Débo (lake), Mali 106/D5
Debolt, Alberta 182/B2
De Borgia, Mont. 262/A3
Debra Birhan, Ethiopia 111/G6
Debra Markos, Ethiopia 111/G5
Debra Markos, Ethiopia 102/F3
Debra Tabor, Ethiopia 111/G5
Debrecen, Hungary 41/F3
Debrecen, Hungary 7/G4
Decatur, Ala. 195/D1
Decatur, Ark. 202/A1
Decatur (co.), Georgia 217/C9
Decatur, Georgia 217/K1
Decatur, Ill. 188/J3
Decatur, Ill. 146/K6
Decatur, Ill. 222/E4
Decatur (lake), Ill. 222/E4

De Soto 359

)ecatur (co.), Ind. 227/G6
)ecatur, Ind. 227/H3
)ecatur (co.), Iowa 229/F7
)ecatur, Iowa 229/F7
)ecatur (co.), Kansas 232/B2
)ecatur, Mich. 250/C6
)ecatur, Miss. 256/F6
)ecatur, Nebr. 264/H2
)ecatur, Ohio 284/C8
)ecatur (co.), Tenn. 237/E9
)ecatur, Tenn. 237/M9
)ecatur, Texas 303/G4
)ecaturville, Tenn. 237/E9
)ecazeville, France 28/E5
)eccan (plat.), India 68/D6
)echerd, Tenn. 237/J10
)ěčín, Czech. 41/C1
)ecision (cape), Alaska 196/M2
)ecize, France 28/E4
)ecker, Ind. 227/B7
)ecker, Manitoba 179/B4
)ecker, Mich. 250/F5
)ecker, Mont. 262/K5
)ecker Lake, Br. Col. 184/E3
)eckers, Colo. 208/J4
)eckerville, Ark. 202/K3
)eckerville, Mich. 250/G5
)eclo, Idaho 220/E7
)ecorah, Iowa 229/K2
)ecota, W. Va. 312/D6
)ecoy, Ky. 237/P5
)ededo, Guam 86/K6
)edegül Dağı (mt.), Turkey 63/D4
)edemsvaart, Netherlands 27/J3
)ederick, Mo. 261/D7
)edham, Iowa 229/D5
)edham, Maine 243/F6
)edham•, Maine 243/F6
)edham, Mass. 249/C7
)édougou, Burkina Faso 106/D6
)edza, Malawi 115/F6
)ee (riv.), England 13/D4
)ee (riv.), England 10/E4
)ee (riv.), Ireland 17/H4
)ee (riv.), Scotland 15/D5
)ee (riv.), Scotland 15/F3
)ee (riv.), Scotland 10/E2
)ee (riv.), Tasmania 99/C4
)ee (riv.), Wales 10/E4
)ee (riv.), Wales 13/D4
)eedsville, Ind. 227/E3
)eel (riv.), Ireland 17/C3
)eel (riv.), Ireland 17/G4
)eel (riv.), Ireland 17/D7
)eele (riv.), Ireland 17/F2
)eenwood, Georgia 217/H8
)eep (creek), Idaho 220/F7
)eep (creek), Idaho 220/B7
)eep (inlet), Newf. 166/B2
)eep (riv.), N.C. 281/K3
)eep (riv.), N. Dak. 282/J1
)eep (creek), S.C. 296/B2
)eep (creek), Texas 303/C5
)eep (creek), Utah 304/B1
)eep (creek), Utah 304/A3
)eep Bight, Newf. 166/C2
)eep Brook, Nova Scotia 168/C4
)eep Creek (mts.), Idaho 220/F7
)eep Creek (lake), Md. 245/A3
)eep Creek (range), Utah 304/A4
)eepcreek, Wash. 310/H3
)eepdale, Manitoba 179/A3
)eep Fork, North Canadian (riv.), Okla. 288/N3
)eep Gap, N.C. 281/F2
)eephaven, Minn. 255/G5
)eeping Saint James, England 13/G5
)eep River, Conn. 210/F3
)eep River•, Conn. 210/F3
)eep River (res.), Conn. 210/F2
)eep River, Iowa 229/J5
)eep River, Ontario 177/G1
)eep River, Ontario 175/E3
)eep River, Wash. 310/B4
)eep Run, N.C. 281/O4
)eep Springs, Calif. 204/H6
)eepstep, Georgia 217/G4
)eep Valley, Pa. 294/A6
)eep Water (pt.), Del. 245/S4
)eepwater, Mo. 261/E6
)eepwater, N.J. 273/C4
)eepwater, N.S. Wales 97/F1
)eer (isl.), Alaska 196/F4
)eer, Ariz. 202/D2
)eer (creek), Ind. 227/D5
)eer (creek), Ind. 227/E3
)eer (isl.), Maine 243/F7
)eer (creek), Md. 245/N2
)eer (isl.), Mass. 249/E7
)eer (riv.), Mich. 250/A2
)eer (lake), Minn. 255/E3
)eer (creek), Miss. 256/C4
)eer (isl.), New Bruns. 170/D4
)eer (harb.), Newf. 166/D2
)eer (riv.), N.Y. 276/L1
)eer (riv.), N.Y. 276/J3
)eer (creek), Ohio 284/D6
)eer (lake), Wash. 310/H2
)eerbrook, Miss. 256/G4
)eerbrook, Wis. 317/H5
)eer Creek, Ill. 222/D3
)eer Creek, Ind. 227/E3
)eer Creek, Minn. 255/C4
)eer Creek (lake), Ohio 284/D6
)eer Creek, Okla. 288/L1
)eerfield, Ill. 222/B5
)eerfield, Ind. 227/H4
)eerfield, Kansas 232/A4
)eerfield•, Mass. 249/D2
)eerfield (riv.), Mass. 249/C2
)eerfield, Mich. 250/F7
)eerfield, Mo. 261/D7
)eerfield•, N.H. 268/E5
)eerfield, Ohio 284/H3
)eerfield (riv.), Vt. 268/B6
)eerfield, Va. 307/K4
)eerfield, Wis. 317/H9
)eerfield Beach, Fla. 212/F5
Deerfield Street, N.J. 273/C4
Deerford, La. 238/K1
Deer Grove, Ill. 222/D2
Deer Harbor, Wash. 310/B2
Deerhorn, Manitoba 179/E4
Deering, Alaska 196/F1
Deering•, N.H. 268/D5
Deering, N. Dak. 282/J3
Deer Island, Oreg. 291/E2
Deer Isle, Maine 243/F7
Deer Isle•, Maine 243/F7
Deer Lake, Newf. 166/C4
Deer Lake, Ontario 175/B2
Deer Lodge (co.), Mont. 262/C5
Deer Lodge, Mont. 262/D4
Deer Lodge, Tenn. 237/M8
Deer Park, Ala. 195/B8
Deer Park, Calif. 204/C5
Deer Park, Fla. 212/F3
Deer Park, Ill. 222/A5
Deer Park, Md. 245/A3
Deer Park, N.Y. 276/O9
Deer Park, Ohio 284/C9
Deer Park, Texas 303/K2
Deer Park, Wash. 310/H3
Deer Park, Wis. 317/B5
Deer River, Minn. 255/E3
Deer River, N.Y. 276/J3
Deer Run, W. Va. 312/H5
Deersville, Ohio 284/H5
Deerton, Mich. 250/B2
Deer Trail, Colo. 208/M3
Deerwalk, W. Va. 312/D4
Deerwood, Minn. 255/E4
Deesa, India 68/C4
Deeson, Miss. 256/C2
Deeth, Nev. 266/F
Dee Why, N.S. Wales 88/L4
Dee Why, N.S. Wales 97/K3
Defense Heights, Md. 245/G4
Deferiet, N.Y. 276/J2
Defiance (plat.), Ariz. 198/F3
Defiance, Iowa 229/C5
Defiance, Mo. 261/L5
Defiance (co.), Ohio 284/A3
Defiance, Ohio 284/B3
De Fluessen (lake), Netherlands 27/G3
Defoe, Ky. 237/L4
Deford, Mich. 250/F5
De Forest, Wis. 317/H9
Defoy, Québec 172/E3
De Funiak Springs, Fla. 212/C6
Dégelis, Québec 172/J2
Degema, Nigeria 106/F8
Degersheim, Switzerland 39/H2
Deggendorf, Germany 22/E4
De Graff, Kansas 232/F4
De Graff, Minn. 255/C5
Degraff, Ohio 284/C5
Degrasse, N.Y. 276/L2
De Gray (lake), Ark. 202/D5
De Grey, W. Australia 88/B4
De Grey, W. Australia 92/B3
De Grey (riv.), W. Australia 88/C4
De Grey (riv.), W. Australia 92/B3
De Haan, Belgium 27/C6
Deh Bid, Iran 66/H5
Dehdez, Iran 66/G5
Deheq, Iran 66/G4
Dehiwala-Mt. Lavinia, Sri Lanka 68/D7
Dehkhvareqan, Iran 66/D2
Dehlco, La. 238/G2
De Honte (bay), Netherlands 27/D6
Dehra Dun, India 68/D2
Dehua, China 77/J6
Deim Zubeir, Sudan 111/E6
Deinze, Belgium 27/C7
Deir Abu Sa'id, Jordan 65/D3
Deir Ballut, West Bank 65/C3
Deir el Balah, Gaza Strip 65/A5
Deir ez Zor (prov.), Syria 63/H5
Deir ez Zor, Syria 63/H5
Deir ez Zor, Syria 59/C2
Deir Sharaf, West Bank 65/C3
Dej, Romania 45/F2
De Kalb (co.), Ala. 195/G2
De Kalb (co.), Georgia 217/D3
De Kalb (co.), Ill. 222/E2
De Kalb, Ill. 222/E2
De Kalb (co.), Ind. 227/H2
De Kalb, Miss. 256/G5
De Kalb (co.), Mo. 261/D3
De Kalb, Mo. 261/C3
De Kalb (co.), Tenn. 237/K9
De Kalb, Texas 303/K4
De Kalb Junction, N.Y. 276/K2
Dekese, Zaire 115/D4
Dekoa, Cent. Afr. Rep. 115/C2
De Koog, Netherlands 27/F2
De Koven, Ky. 237/E5
Dela, Okla. 288/P6
Delacour, Alberta 182/D4
Delacroix, La. 238/L7
Delafield, Ill. 222/E5
Delafield, Wis. 317/J1
Delagoa (bay), Mozambique 118/E5
Delair, N.J. 273/B3
Delamar (mts.), Nev. 266/G5
De Lamere, N. Dak. 282/R7
DeLancey, Pa. 294/D4
Delanco•, N.J. 273/D3
De Land, Fla. 212/E2
De Land, Ill. 222/E3
Delaney, Ark. 202/C2
Delano, Calif. 204/F8
Delano, Minn. 255/E5
Delano, Pa. 294/K4
Delano, Tenn. 237/M10
Delano (peak), Utah 304/B5
Delanson, N.Y. 276/M5
Delaplaine, Ark. 202/J1
Delaplane, Va. 307/N3
Delaram, Afghanistan 59/H3
Delaram, Afghanistan 68/A2
Delaronde (lake), Sask. 181/E1
Delavan, Ill. 222/D3
Delavan, Kansas 232/F3
Delavan, Minn. 255/D7
Delavan, Wis. 317/J10
Delavan Lake, Wis. 317/J10
Delaware 188/L3
DELAWARE 245
Delaware (bay) 188/M3
Delaware, Ark. 202/D3
Delaware (bay), Del. 245/T5
Delaware (riv.), Del. 245/R3
Delaware (co.), Ind. 227/G4
Delaware, Ind. 227/G6
Delaware (co.), Iowa 229/L4
Delaware, Iowa 229/L4
Delaware, N.J. 273/C2
Delaware (bay), N.J. 273/C5
Delaware (riv.), N.J. 273/D3
Delaware (co.), N.Y. 276/K6
Delaware (riv.), N.Y. 276/K7
Delaware (co.), Ohio 284/D5
Delaware, Ohio 284/E5
Delaware (lake), Ohio 284/E5
Delaware (co.), Okla. 288/S2
Delaware, Okla. 288/P1
Delaware, Ontario 177/C5
Delaware (co.), Pa. 294/M6
Delaware (riv.), Pa. 294/N3
Delaware (creek), Texas 303/C10
Delaware (mts.), Texas 303/C10
Delaware (state), U.S. 146/L6
Delaware City, Del. 245/R2
Delaware Water Gap, Pa. 294/M4
Delaware Water Gap Nat'l Rec. Area, N.J. 273/C1
Delaware Water Gap Nat'l Rec. Area, Pa. 294/N3
Delbarton, W. Va. 312/B7
Del Bonita, Alberta 182/D5
Delburne, Alberta 182/D3
Delcambre, La. 238/G7
Del City, Okla. 288/L4
Delco, N.C. 281/N6
Deldoul, Algeria 106/E3
Deleau, Manitoba 179/B5
Delegate, N.S. Wales 97/E5
Delémont, Switzerland 39/D2
De Leon, Texas 303/F5
De Leon Springs, Fla. 212/E2
Delevan, N.Y. 276/D6
Delfi, Greece 45/F6
Delft, Minn. 255/C7
Delft, Netherlands 27/E4
Delfzijl, Netherlands 27/K2
Delgada (pt.), Argentina 143/D5
Delgada (pt.), Calif. 204/A3
Delgada (pt.), Mexico 150/L7
Delgado (cape), Mozambique 102/G6
Delgado (cape), Mozambique 118/G2
Delgado Chalbaud, Cerro (mt.), Venezuela 124/G6
Delgertsogt, Mongolia 77/G2
Delgo, Sudan 111/F3
Delhi, Calif. 204/E6
Delhi, Colo. 208/M7
Delhi, Ill. 222/C4
Delhi (terr.), India 68/D3
Delhi, India 68/D3
Delhi, India 54/J7
Delhi, India 2/N4
Delhi, Iowa 229/L4
Delhi, La. 238/H2
Delhi, Minn. 255/C6
Delhi, N.Y. 276/L6
Delhi, Okla. 288/G4
Delhi, Ontario 177/D5
Delia, Alberta 182/D4
Delia, Kansas 232/G2
Delice, Dominica 161/F7
Delice, Turkey 63/E3
Delice (riv.), Turkey 63/F3
Délices, Fr. Guiana 131/E3
Delicias, Cuba 158/H3
Delicias, Venezuela 124/B4
Delight, Ark. 202/C5
Delijan, Iran 66/G4
Delingha, China 77/E4
De Lisle, Miss. 256/F10
Delisle, Québec 172/F1
Delisle, Sask. 181/D4
Delitzsch, Germany 22/E3
Dell, Ark. 202/K2
Dell, Mont. 262/D6
Dell City, Texas 303/C10
Dell Rapids, S. Dak. 298/R6
Dellrose, Tenn. 237/H10
Dellroy, Ohio 284/H4
Dells, The (valley), Wis. 317/G8
Dellslow, W. Va. 312/G3
Dellwood, Minn. 255/F5
Dellwood, Mo. 261/R2
Dellwood, N.C. 281/C3
Dellwood, Wis. 317/G7
Dellys, Algeria 106/E1
Delmar, Ala. 195/C2
Del Mar, Calif. 204/H11
Delmar, Del. 245/R7
Delmar, Iowa 229/M4
Delmar, Md. 245/R7
Delmar, N.Y. 276/N5
Delmas, Sask. 181/C3
Delmas, S. Africa 118/J6
Delmenhorst, Germany 22/C2
Delmont, N.J. 273/C5
Delmont, Pa. 294/D5
Delmont, S. Dak. 298/N7
Del Norte (co.), Calif. 204/B2
Del Norte, Colo. 208/G7
Del Norte (peak), Colo. 208/F7
Deloit, Iowa 229/C4
DeLong (mts.), Alaska 196/F1
De Long, Ill. 222/C3
Delong, Ind. 227/E2
Deloraine, Man. 162/G6
Deloraine, Manitoba 179/B5
Deloraine, Tasmania 99/C3
Delorme (lake), Québec 174/C2
Deloro, Ontario 177/G3
Delphi, Ind. 227/D3
Delphia, Ky. 237/P6
Delphos, Iowa 229/E7
Delphos, Kansas 232/E2
Delphos, Ohio 284/B4
Delpine, Mont. 262/F4
Delran•, N.J. 273/B3
Delray Beach, Fla. 212/F5
Del Rey Oaks, Calif. 204/D7
Del Rio, Tenn. 237/P9
Del Rio, Texas 188/F5
Del Rio, Texas 146/H7
Del Rio, Texas 303/D8
Del Rosa, Calif. 204/E10
Delson, Québec 172/H4
Delta, Ala. 195/G4
Delta, Br. Col. 184/K3
Delta (co.), Colo. 208/D5
Delta, Colo. 208/D5
Delta, Iowa 229/J6
Delta, La. 238/J2
Delta, Manitoba 179/D4
Delta (co.), Mich. 250/C2
Delta, Mo. 261/N8
Delta, Ohio 284/B2
Delta, Ontario 177/H3
Delta, Pa. 294/K6
Delta (co.), Texas 303/J4
Delta, Utah 304/B4
Delta, Wis. 317/D3
Delta Amacuro (terr.), Venezuela 124/H3
Delta City, Miss. 256/C4
Delta Junction, Alaska 196/J2
Deltaville, Va. 307/R5
Delton, Mich. 250/D6
Deltona, Fla. 212/E3
Delungra, N.S. Wales 97/F1
Del Valle, Argentina 143/F7
Del Valle (lake), Calif. 204/L3
Delvin, Ireland 17/G4
Delvinákion, Greece 45/E6
Delvinë, Albania 45/D6
Delwin, Mich. 250/E5
Demaine, Sask. 181/D5
Demak, Indonesia 85/J2
Demanda, Sierra de la (range), Spain 33/E1
Demarcation (pt.), Alaska 196/K1
Demarest, N.J. 273/C1
Demavend (Damavend) (mt.), Iran 66/G3
Demba, Zaire 115/D5
Dembidollo, Ethiopia 111/F6
Demchok, India 68/D2
Demerara (riv.), Guyana 131/B3
Demidov, U.S.S.R. 52/D3
Deming, N. Mex. 274/B6
Deming, Wash. 310/C2
Demini (riv.), Brazil 132/H8
Demirci, Turkey 63/C3
Demirkent, Turkey 63/E4
Demirköy, Turkey 63/B2
Demir Qapu, Syria 63/J4
Demmin, Germany 22/E2
Democracia, Venezuela 124/E6
Demopolis, Ala. 195/C6
Demopolis (dam), Ala. 195/C5
Demopolis (lake), Ala. 195/C5
Demorest, Georgia 217/F1
De Mossville, Ky. 237/N3
Demotte, Ind. 227/C2
Dempo (mt.), Indonesia 85/C6
Dempster, S. Dak. 298/R4
Demster, N.Y. 276/H3
Demta, Indonesia 85/L6
Denain, France 28/E2
Denali, Alaska 196/J2
Denali Nat'l Park, Alaska 196/H2
Denali Nat'l Preserve, Alaska 196/H2
Denare Beach, Sask. 181/M4
Denau, U.S.S.R. 48/G6
Denbigh (cape), Alaska 196/F2
Denbigh, N. Dak. 282/J3
Denbigh, Ontario 177/G2
Denbigh, Wales 13/D4
Denbigh, Wales 10/E4
Den Burg, Netherlands 27/F2
Denby, S. Dak. 298/E7
Denby Dale, England 13/J2
Den Chai, Thailand 72/C3
Dender (riv.), Belgium 27/D7
Denderleeuw, Belgium 27/E7
Dendermonde, Belgium 27/E6
Dendron, Va. 307/P6
Denekamp, Netherlands 27/L4
Denezhkin Kamen' (mt.), U.S.S.R. 52/J2
Dengkou, China 77/G3
Dêngqên, China 77/E5
Denham, Ind. 227/D2
Denham, Minn. 255/F4
Denham, W. Australia 92/A4
Denham Springs, La. 238/L2
Den Helder, Netherlands 27/F3
Denhoff, N. Dak. 282/K5
Denholm, Sask. 181/C3
Denholm, Scotland 15/F5
Denia, Spain 33/G3
Deniliquin, N.S. Wales 88/G7
Deniliquin, N.S. Wales 97/C4
Denio, Nev. 266/C1
Denison, Iowa 229/C4
Denison, Kansas 232/G2
Denison (dam), Okla. 288/O7
Denison (range), Tasmania 99/C4
Denison, Texas 188/G4
Denison, Texas 303/H4
Denison (dam), Texas 303/H4
Denison, Wash. 310/H3
Denizli (prov.), Turkey 63/C4
Denizli, Turkey 63/C4
Denizli, Turkey 59/A2
Denman, N.S. Wales 97/F3
Denman Island, Br. Col. 184/H2
Denmark 2/K3
Denmark 7/E3
DENMARK 18/D9
DENMARK 21/E6
Denmark (str.) 4/C11
Denmark (str.) 146/S3
Denmark (str.) 7/B2
Denmark, Iowa 229/L7
Denmark, Kansas 232/D2
Denmark•, Maine 243/B8
Denmark, Miss. 256/F2
Denmark (bay), N.W. Terr. 187/H2
Denmark, Oreg. 291/C5
Denmark, S.C. 296/E5
Denmark, Tenn. 237/D9
Denmark, W. Australia 88/B7
Denmark, W. Australia 92/B6
Denmark, Wis. 317/L7
Dennard, Ark. 202/E2
Dennehotso, Ariz. 198/F2
Dennery, St. Lucia 161/G6
Denning, Ark. 202/C3
Dennis (hill), Conn. 210/C1
Dennis, Kansas 232/G4
Dennis•, Mass. 249/O5
Dennis, Miss. 256/H1
Dennis (head), Scotland 15/F1
Dennison, Minn. 255/E6
Dennison, Ohio 284/H5
Dennis Port, Mass. 249/O6
Denniston, Va. 307/L7
Dennisville, N.J. 273/D5
Dennisville, Sask. 181/K6
Denny and Dunipace, Scotland 10/B1
Denny and Dunipace, Scotland 15/C1
Dennysville•, Maine 243/J6
Den Oever, Netherlands 27/G3
Denoon (lake), Wis. 317/K2
Denpasar, Indonesia 85/E7
Densmore, Kansas 232/C2
Dent, Minn. 255/C4
Dent (co.), Mo. 261/J7
Dent, Ohio 284/B9
Dent Blanche (mt.), Switzerland 39/E4
Dent de Lys (mt.), Switzerland 39/D4
Dent de Ruth (mt.), Switzerland 39/D3
Dent d'Hérens (mt.), Switzerland 39/E5
Denton, England 13/H2
Denton, Georgia 217/G7
Denton, Kansas 232/G2
Denton, Ky. 237/R4
Denton, Md. 245/P5
Denton, Mo. 261/N10
Denton, Mont. 262/G3
Denton, Nebr. 264/H4
Denton, N.C. 281/J3
Denton (co.), Texas 303/G4
Denton, Texas 188/G4
Denton, Texas 303/G4
D'Entrecasteaux (isls.), Papua N.G. 87/F6
D'Entrecasteaux (isls.), Papua N.G. 85/C7
D'Entrecasteaux (chan.), Tasmania 99/D5
D'Entrecasteaux (pt.), W. Australia 88/B7
D'Entrecasteaux (pt.), W. Australia 92/A6
Dents du Midi (mt.), Switzerland 39/C4
Dents Run, Pa. 294/F3
Dentville, Miss. 256/C7
Denver, Ark. 202/D1
Denver (co.), Colo. 208/K3
Denver (cap.), Colo. 208/K3
Denver (cap.), Colo. 188/F3
Denver (cap.), Colo. 146/H6
Denver, Ill. 222/B3
Denver, Ind. 227/E3
Denver, Iowa 229/J3
Denver, Mo. 261/D2
Denver, N.C. 281/G3
Denver, Pa. 294/K5
Denver, Tenn. 237/F8
Denver, U.S. 2/D3
Denver City, Texas 303/B4
Denville•, N.J. 273/E2
Denzil, Sask. 181/B3
Deogarh, India 68/E4
Deoghar, India 68/F4
Deolali, India 68/C5
Deora, Colo. 208/O7
Deoria, India 68/E3
De Panne, Belgium 27/B6
Depauville, N.Y. 276/H2
Depauw, Ind. 227/E8
De Peel (reg.), Netherlands 27/H6
Dependencias Federales (terr.), Venezuela 124/E2
De Pere, Wis. 317/K7
Depew, N.Y. 276/C5
Depew, Okla. 288/O3
De Peyster, N.Y. 276/K1
Depoe Bay, Oreg. 291/C3
Deport, Texas 303/J4
Deposit, N.Y. 276/K6
Dépôt Lézard, Fr. Guiana 131/E3
Depoy, Ky. 237/G6
Deptford•, N.J. 273/B4
Depue, Ill. 222/D2
Deputy, Ind. 227/F7
Dêqên, China 77/E6
De Queen, Ark. 202/B5
De Quincy, La. 238/D6
Der'a (prov.), Syria 63/G6
Der'a, Syria 63/G6
Dera Bugti, Pakistan 68/B3
Dera Bugti, Pakistan 59/J4
Dérac, Haiti 158/C5
Dera Ghazi Khan, Pakistan 68/C3
Dera Ghazi Khan, Pakistan 59/J3
Dera Ismail Khan, Pakistan 59/K3
Dera Ismail Khan, Pakistan 68/C2
Derbent, U.S.S.R. 7/J4
Derbent, U.S.S.R. 52/G6
Derby, Australia 87/C7
Derby, Conn. 210/C3
Derby, England 13/F5
Derby, England 10/F4
Derby, Ind. 227/D8
Derby, Iowa 229/G7
Derby, Kansas 232/E4
Derby, Maine 243/E5
Derby, Miss. 256/E9
Derby, N.Y. 276/B5
Derby, Ohio 284/D6
Derby, Tasmania 99/D3
Derby, Texas 303/E9
Derby (Derby Center), Vt. 268/C2
Derby•, Vt. 268/C2
Derby, W. Australia 88/C3
Derby, W. Australia 92/C2
Derby Line, Vt. 268/C2
Derbyshire (co.), England 13/F5
Derecske, Hungary 41/F3
Dereli, Turkey 63/H2
Derendingen, Switzerland 39/E2
Derg (lake), Ireland 17/E6
Derg (lake), Ireland 17/F2
Derg, Lough (lake), Ireland 10/B4
Derg (riv.), N. Ireland 17/F2
De Ridder, La. 238/D5
Derik, Turkey 63/J4
Dering Harbor, N.Y. 276/R8
Derinkuyu, Turkey 63/F3
Derj, Libya 111/B1
Derma, Miss. 256/F3
Dermott, Ark. 202/H7
Derna, Libya 102/E1
Derna, Libya 111/D1
Dernic, Sask. 181/J4
Dernieres (isls.), La. 238/J8
Deroche, Br. Col. 184/L3
Deronda, Wis. 317/B5
De Rossett, Tenn. 237/L9
Déroute (passage), Chan. Is. 13/F8
Derravaragh (lake), Ireland 17/G4
Derrinallum, Victoria 97/B5
Derry, La. 238/E3
Derry, N.H. 268/E6
Derry•, N.H. 268/E6
Derry, N. Mex. 274/B6
Derry, Pa. 294/D5
Derrygonnelly, N. Ireland 17/F3
Derryveagh (mts.), Ireland 17/E2
Derudeb, Sudan 111/G4
De Ruyter, N.Y. 276/J5
Dervaig, Scotland 15/B4
Derventa, Yugoslavia 45/C3
Dervock, N. Ireland 17/J1
Derwent, Alberta 182/E3
Derwent (riv.), England 13/H3
Derwent (riv.), England 13/G3
Derwent (riv.), England 10/F3
Derwent (riv.), Tasmania 99/C4
Derwent Bridge, Tasmania 99/C4
Derwood, Md. 245/K4
Desaguadero (riv.), Argentina 143/C3
Desaguadero, Bolivia 136/A5
Desaguadero (riv.), Bolivia 136/B5
Desaguadero, Peru 128/H11
De Salis (bay), N.W. Terr. 187/F2
Des Allemands, La. 238/N4
Des Arc, Ark. 202/G4
Des Arc (bayou), Ark. 202/G3
Des Arc, Mo. 261/L8
Desatoya (mts.), Nev. 266/D3
Desbiens, Québec 172/E1
Des Bois (lake), N.W. Terr. 187/F3
Desboro, Ontario 177/C3
Desborough, England 13/G5
Descanso, Calif. 204/J11
Deschaillons-sur-Saint-Laurent, Québec 172/E3
Deschambault, Québec 172/E3
Deschambault Lake, Sask. 181/M3
Descharme Lake, Sask. 181/L3
Deschênes, Québec 172/B4
Deschênes (lake), Québec 172/A4
Deschutes (co.), Oreg. 291/F4
Deschutes (riv.), Oreg. 291/G2
Deschutes (riv.), Wash. 310/C4
Deseado (riv.), Argentina 120/C7
Deseado (riv.), Argentina 143/C6
Deseado (cape), Chile 138/D10
Desemboque Seris, Mexico 150/C2
Desengaño (pt.), Argentina 143/C6
Desenzano del Garda, Italy 34/C2
Deseret, Utah 304/B4
Deseronto, Ontario 177/G3
Desert (range), Nev. 266/F6
Desert (valley), Nev. 266/C1
Deserta Grande (isl.), Portugal 33/B2
Desertas (isl.), Portugal 102/A1
Desertas (isls.), Portugal 106/A2
Desertas (isls.), Portugal 33/A2
Desert Center, Calif. 204/K10
Desert Hot Springs, Calif. 204/J9
Desert View Highlands, Calif. 204/G9
Desha (co.), Ark. 202/H6
Deshaies, Guadeloupe 161/A6
Deshler, Nebr. 264/G4
Deshler, Ohio 284/C3
Désirade, La (isl.), Guadeloupe 161/B6
Des Lacs, N. Dak. 282/G3
Des Lacs (riv.), N. Dak. 282/G3
Desloge, Mo. 261/M7
Desmarais, Alberta 182/D2
Desmaraisville, Québec 174/B3
Desmet, Idaho 220/B2
De Smet, S. Dak. 298/O5
Desmochados, Paraguay 144/C5
Des Moines (riv.) 188/H2
Des Moines (co.), Iowa 229/L7
Des Moines (cap.), Iowa 146/J5
Des Moines (cap.), Iowa 188/H2
Des Moines (cap.), Iowa 229/G5
Des Moines (riv.), Iowa 229/J7
Des Moines (riv.), Minn. 255/C7
Des Moines (riv.), Mo. 261/J1
Des Moines, N. Mex. 274/F2
Des Moines, Wash. 310/B2
Desna (riv.), U.S.S.R. 52/D4
Desolación (isl.), Chile 120/B8
Desolación (isl.), Chile 138/D10
Desolation (canyon), Utah 304/E4
De Soto (co.), Fla. 212/E4
De Soto, Georgia 217/D7
De Soto, Ill. 222/D6
Desoto, Ind. 227/G4
De Soto, Iowa 229/E5
De Soto, Kansas 232/H3
De Soto (par.), La. 238/C2
De Soto (co.), Miss. 256/E1

De Soto, Miss. 256/G7
De Soto, Mo. 261/L6
De Soto, Texas 303/G3
De Soto, Wis. 317/D9
De Soto Nat'l Mem., Fla. 212/D4
Des Peres, Mo. 261/O3
Des Plaines, Ill. 222/B5
Des Plaines (riv.), Ill. 222/A6
Dessa, Niger 106/E6
Dessalines, Haiti 158/C5
Dessau, Germany 22/E3
Dessel, Belgium 27/G6
Dessye, Ethiopia 102/G3
Dessye, Ethiopia 111/G5
Destelbergen, Belgium 27/D6
Destin, Fla. 212/C6
Destrehan, La. 238/C4
Destruction (isl.), Wash. 310/A3
Destruction Bay, Yukon 187/E3
Deta, Romania 45/E3
Detah, N.W. Terr. 187/G3
Dete, Zimbabwe 118/D3
Detlor, Ontario 177/G2
Detmold, Germany 22/C3
De Tour (passage), Mich. 250/E3
Detour (pt.), Mich. 250/C3
De Tour Village, Mich. 250/E3
Detrital Wash (dry riv.), Ariz. 198/A3
Detroit, Ala. 195/B2
Detroit, Ill. 222/C4
Detroit, Kansas 232/E3
Detroit•, Maine 243/E6
Detroit, Mich. 146/K5
Detroit, Mich. 188/K2
Detroit, Mich. 250/B7
Detroit (riv.), Mich. 250/B7
Detroit, Oreg. 291/E3
Detroit (lake), Oreg. 291/E3
Detroit, Texas 303/J4
Detroit, U.S. 2/E3
Detroit Beach, Mich. 250/F7
Detroit Lakes, Minn. 255/C4
Detva, Czech. 41/E2
De Twente (reg.), Netherlands 27/K4
Deuel (co.), Nebr. 264/B3
Deuel (co.), S. Dak. 298/F4
Deûle (riv.), Belgium 27/B7
Deurne, Belgium 27/F6
Deurne, Netherlands 27/H6
Deustua, Peru 128/G10
Deutsch Feistritz, Austria 41/C3
Deutschkreutz, Austria 41/D3
Deutsch Landsberg, Austria 41/C4
Deutsch Wagram, Austria 41/D2
Deux Frères, Les (isls.), Vietnam 72/E5
Deux-Montagnes (co.), Québec 172/C4
Deux-Montagnes, Québec 172/H4
Deux Montagnes (lake), Québec 172/C4
Deux Rivières, Ontario 177/F1
Deux-Sèvres (dept.), France 28/C4
Deva, Romania 45/F3
De Valls Bluff, Ark. 202/H4
Devault, Pa. 294/L5
Dévaványa, Hungary 41/F3
Devecser, Hungary 41/D3
Develi, Turkey 59/C2
Develi, Turkey 63/F3
Deventer, Netherlands 27/J4
Devenyns (lake), Québec 172/D2
Devereux, Georgia 217/F4
Deveron (riv.), Scotland 15/F3
De View (bayou), Ark. 202/J3
Deville, La. 238/F4
Devil River (peak), N. Zealand 100/D4
Devils (isl.), Fr. Guiana 120/D2
Devil's (isl.), Fr. Guiana 131/E3
Devils (lake), N. Dak. 282/N3
Devils (riv.), Texas 303/D7
Devilsbit (mt.), Ireland 17/F6
Devil's Hole (Death Valley Nat'l Mon.), Nev. 266/E6
Devils Lake, N. Dak. 188/G1
Devils Lake, N. Dak. 282/N3
Devils Paw (mt.), Alaska 196/N1
Devils Postpile Nat'l Mon., Calif. 204/F6
Devils Slide, Utah 304/C2
Devils Thumb (mt.), Br. Col. 184/A1
Devils Tower, Wyo. 319/H1
Devils Tower Nat'l Mon., Wyo. 319/H1
Devin, Bulgaria 45/G5
Devine, Texas 303/E8
Devizes, England 13/F6
Devizes, England 10/F5
Devol, Okla. 288/J6
Devola, Ohio 284/H7
De Volet (pt.), St. Vin. & Grens. 161/A8
Devon, Alberta 182/D3
Devon (isl.), Canada 4/B14
Devon, Conn. 210/C4
Devon (co.), England 13/D7
Devon, Jamaica 158/H6
Devon, Kansas 232/H4
Devon, Mont. 262/E2
Devon (isl.), N.W.T. 162/M3
Devon (isl.), N.W.T. 146/K2
Devon (isl.), N.W. Terr. 187/K2
Devondale, Ky. 237/T2
Devonia, Tenn. 237/N8
Devonport, Australia 87/E10
Devonport, N. Zealand 100/C1
Devonport, Tasmania 88/H8
Devonport, Tasmania 99/B8
Devrek, Turkey 63/D2
Devrekâni, Turkey 63/E2
Devrez (riv.), Turkey 63/E2
Dewar, Iowa 229/J3
Dewar, Okla. 288/P4
Dewart, Pa. 294/J3
Dewas, India 68/D4
Dewberry, Alberta 182/E3
Dewees (isl.), S.C. 296/H6
De Weese (plat.), Colo. 208/J6
Dewey, Ariz. 198/C4
Dewey, Ill. 222/E3
Dewey (lake), Ky. 237/R5

Dewey (co.), Okla. 288/H2
Dewey, Okla. 288/P1
Dewey (Culebra), P. Rico 161/G1
Dewey (co.), S. Dak. 298/G3
Dewey Park, Ill. 222/B7
Deweyville, Texas 303/L7
Deweyville, Utah 304/B2
De Wijk, Netherlands 27/J3
De Winton, Alberta 182/C4
De Witt, Ark. 202/H5
De Witt (co.), Ill. 222/E3
Dewitt, Ill. 222/E3
De Witt, Iowa 229/N5
De Witt, Ky. 237/O7
De Witt, Mich. 250/E6
De Witt, Mo. 261/F4
De Witt, Nebr. 264/G4
DeWitt, N.Y. 276/H4
De Witt (co.), Texas 303/G9
Dewitt, Va. 307/N6
Dewittville, Québec 172/C4
Dewsbury, England 10/H2
Dewsbury, England 13/J1
Dewy Rose, Georgia 217/G2
Dexter (lake), Fla. 212/E2
Dexter, Georgia 217/G6
Dexter, Iowa 229/E5
Dexter, Kansas 232/F4
Dexter, Ky. 237/E7
Dexter, Maine 243/E5
Dexter•, Maine 243/E5
Dexter, Mich. 250/F6
Dexter, Minn. 255/F7
Dexter, Mo. 261/N9
Dexter, N. Mex. 274/E5
Dexter, N.Y. 276/H2
Dexter, Oreg. 291/E4
Dexter City, Ohio 284/G6
Dexterville, Wis. 317/E10
Deyang, China 77/F5
Dey Dey (lake), S. Australia 88/E5
Dey Dey (lake), S. Australia 94/B3
DeYoung, Pa. 294/E2
Dez (riv.), Iran 59/E3
Dez (riv.), Iran 66/F4
De Zaan (riv.), Netherlands 27/B4
Dezful, Iran 59/E3
Dezful, Iran 54/F6
Dezful, Iran 66/F4
Dezhnev (cape), U.S.S.R. 4/C18
Dezhnev (cape), U.S.S.R. 48/T3
Dezhou (Tehchow), China 77/J4
Dezh Shahpur, Iran 66/E3
Dezh Shahpur, Iran 59/E2
Dhaba, Saudi Arabia 59/D5
Dhahiriya, West Bank 65/B5
Dhahran, Saudi Arabia 54/F7
Dhahran, Saudi Arabia 59/E4
Dhaka (Dacca) (cap.), Bengladesh 68/G4
Dhaka (Dacca) (cap.), Bengladesh 54/L7
Dhali, Cyprus 63/E5
Dhamar, Yemen 59/D7
Dhamtari, India 68/E4
Dhanbad, India 68/F4
Dhangarhi, Nepal 68/E3
D'Hanis, Texas 303/E8
Dhank, Oman 59/G5
Dhankuta, Nepal 68/F3
Dhar, India 68/D4
Dharma, Saudi Arabia 59/E5
Dharmsala, India 68/D2
Dharwar-Hubli, India 68/C5
Dhaulagiri (mt.), Nepal 68/E3
Dhenkanal, India 68/E4
Dhidhimótikhon, Greece 45/H5
Dhíkaia, Greece 45/H5
Dhimitsána, Greece 45/F7
Dhi Qar (heads), Iraq 66/E5
Dhira', Jordan 65/D5
Dhofar (reg.), Oman 59/F6
Dholpur, India 68/D3
Dhomokós, Greece 45/F6
Dhond, India 68/C5
Dhoraji, India 68/C4
Dhubri, India 68/G3
Dhulia, India 68/C4
Día (isl.), Greece 45/G8
Diable (pt.), Martinique 161/D5
Diablerets (mt.), Switzerland 39/D4
Diablo (canyon), Ariz. 198/D4
Diablo, Calif. 204/K2
Diablo, Sierra (mts.), Texas 303/C10
Diablo, Wash. 310/D2
Diablo (dam), Wash. 310/D2
Diablo (lake), Wash. 310/D2
Diablotin, Morne (mt.), Dominica 161/E6
Diadema, Brazil 135/C3
Diagonal, Iowa 229/E7
Dial, Georgia 217/D1
Diamant, Rocher du (isl.), Martinique 161/C7
Diamante, Argentina 143/F6
Diamante (riv.), Argentina 143/C3
Diamantina, Brazil 132/F7
Diamantina (riv.), Queensland 88/G4
Diamantina (riv.), Queensland 95/B4
Diamantina Lakes, Queensland 95/B4
Diamantino, Brazil 132/B6
Diamond (lake), Conn. 210/F2
Diamond (head), Hawaii 218/C5
Diamond (peak), Idaho 220/E5
Diamond, Ind. 227/C5
Diamond, La. 238/L7
Diamond, Mo. 261/D9
Diamond, Ohio 284/H3
Diamond, Oreg. 291/J4
Diamond (lake), Oreg. 291/E4
Diamond (peak), Oreg. 291/E4
Diamond, Pa. 294/C2
Diamond, Virgin Is. (U.S.) 161/F4
Diamond, Wash. 310/H2
Diamond (lake), Wash. 310/H2
Diamond Bluff, Wis. 317/A6
Diamond City, Alberta 182/D5

Diamond City, Ark. 202/E1
Diamond Coast (reg.), Namibia 118/A5
Diamond Lake, Oreg. 291/E4
Diamond Point, N.Y. 276/N4
Diamond Springs, Calif. 204/D8
Diamondville, Wyo. 319/B4
Diana, W. Va. 312/F5
Dian Chi (lake), China 77/F7
Dianjiang, China 77/G5
Diano Marina, Italy 34/B3
Dianópolis, Brazil 132/E5
Diapaga, Burkina Faso 106/E6
Dias Creek, N.J. 273/D5
Díaz, Argentina 143/F6
Diaz, Ark. 202/H2
Dibaya, Zaire 115/D5
Dibaya-Lubue, Zaire 115/C4
Dibeng, S. Africa 118/C5
D'Iberville, Miss. 256/G10
Dibete, Botswana 118/D4
Diboll, Texas 303/K6
Dibrugarh, India 68/G3
Dibulla, Colombia 126/D2
Dickens, Iowa 229/C2
Dickens, Nebr. 264/C4
Dickens (pt.), R.I. 249/H8
Dickens (co.), Texas 303/D4
Dickens, Texas 303/D4
Dickenson (co.), Va. 307/D6
Dickerson, Md. 227/G4
Dickey, Georgia 217/C7
Dickey (co.), N. Dak. 282/N7
Dickey, N. Dak. 282/N6
Dickeyville, Wis. 317/E10
Dickinson, Ala. 195/C7
Dickinson (co.), Iowa 229/C2
Dickinson (co.), Kansas 232/E3
Dickinson (co.), Mich. 250/B2
Dickinson, N. Dak. 188/F1
Dickinson, N. Dak. 282/E6
Dickinson, Pa. 294/H5
Dickinson, Texas 303/K3
Dickinson Center, N.Y. 276/M1
Dickson, Alberta 182/C3
Dickson, Okla. 288/M6
Dickson (lake), Ontario 177/F2
Dickson (co.), Tenn. 237/G8
Dickson, Tenn. 237/G8
Dickson, W. Va. 312/B6
Dickson City, Pa. 294/F7
Dicle, Turkey 63/J3
Dicle (riv.), Turkey 63/J4
Didam, Netherlands 27/J5
Didcot, England 13/F6
Dido, La. 238/C5
Didsbury, Alberta 182/C4
Didsbury, Alta. 162/C4
Didyme, Québec 172/E1
Die, France 28/F5
Diébougou, Burkina Faso 106/D6
Diefenbaker (lake), Sask. 181/H4
Diego de Almagro (isl.), Chile 138/D9
Diego Garcia (isl.), Br. Ind. Ocean Terr. 54/J10
Diego Lamas, Uruguay 145/C1
Diego Pérez (cay), Cuba 158/C2
Diégo-Suarez (Antsiranana), Madagascar 118/H2
Diehlstadt, Mo. 261/N9
Diekirch, Luxembourg 27/J9
Dielsdorf, Switzerland 39/F1
Diemen, Netherlands 27/C5
Diemtigen, Switzerland 39/D3
Dien Bien Phu, Vietnam 72/D2
Diep (riv.), S. Africa 118/F6
Diepholz, Germany 22/C2
Diepoldsau, Switzerland 39/J2
Dieppe, France 28/D3
Dieppe, New Bruns. 170/F2
Dieppe Bay, St. Kitts & Nevis 161/C10
Dieren, Netherlands 27/J4
Dierks, Ark. 202/B5
Diessenhofen, Switzerland 39/G1
Diest, Belgium 27/F7
Dieterich, Ill. 222/E4
Dietikon, Switzerland 39/F2
Dietrich, Idaho 220/D7
Diever, Netherlands 27/J3
Diez y Nueve de Abril, Uruguay 145/E5
Diez y Ocho de Julio, Uruguay 145/F4
Dif, Somalia 115/H3
Diffa, Niger 106/G6
Differdange, Luxembourg 27/H9
Difficult, Tenn. 237/K8
Difficult (mt.), Victoria 97/B5
Digboi, India 68/H3
Digby (co.), Nova Scotia 168/C4
Digby, Nova Scotia 168/C4
Digby Gut (chan.), Nova Scotia 168/C4
Digby Neck (pen.), Nova Scotia 168/B4
Digdeguash (riv.), New Bruns. 170/C3
Digges (isls.), N.W. Terr. 187/L3
Diggins, Mo. 261/G8
Dighton, Kansas 232/B3
Dighton•, Mass. 249/K5
Dighton, Mich. 250/D4
Digne, France 28/G5
Digoin, France 28/F4
Digor, Turkey 63/K2
Digos, Philippines 82/E7
Digul (riv.), Indonesia 85/K7
Dijon, France 28/F4
Dijon, France 7/F4
Dike, Iowa 229/H4
Dikhil, Djibouti 111/H5
Dikili, Turkey 63/B3
Diksmuide, Belgium 27/B6
Dikson, U.S.S.R. 4/B5
Dikson, U.S.S.R. 48/J2
Dikwa, Nigeria 106/G6
Dikwa, Nigeria 102/D3
Dilam, Saudi Arabia 59/E5
Dilbeek, Belgium 27/B9
Dildo, Newf. 166/D2
Dili, Indonesia 54/O10
Dili, Indonesia 85/H7
Dilia, N. Mex. 274/D3

Diligent River, Nova Scotia 168/D3
Di Linh, Vietnam 72/F5
Dilke, Sask. 181/J5
Dilkon, Ariz. 198/E3
Dilla, Ethiopia 111/G6
Dillabough, Sask. 181/J3
Dillard, Georgia 217/F1
Dillard, Mo. 261/K7
Dillard, Oreg. 291/D4
Dille, W. Va. 312/E6
Dillenburg, Germany 22/C3
Diller, Nebr. 264/H4
Dilley, Oreg. 291/A2
Dilley, Texas 303/E9
Dillia (dry riv.), Niger 106/G5
Dilling, Sudan 111/E5
Dillingen, Germany 22/B4
Dillingen an der Donau, Germany 22/D4
Dillingham, Alaska 188/C6
Dillingham, Alaska 196/G4
Dillion (riv.), Alberta 182/E2
Dillon, Colo. 208/H3
Dillon, Kansas 232/E3
Dillon, Mont. 262/D5
Dillon (lake), Ohio 284/F5
Dillon, S.C. 296/J3
Dillon (co.), S.C. 296/J3
Dillon, S.C. 296/J3
Dillonvale, Ohio 284/J5
Dillsboro, Ind. 227/G6
Dillsboro, N.C. 281/C4
Dillsburg, Pa. 294/H5
Dilltown, Pa. 294/E5
Dillwyn, Va. 307/M5
Dilolo, Zaire 115/D6
Dilsen, Belgium 27/H6
Dilworth, Minn. 255/B4
Dimas, Cuba 158/A2
Dimas, Mexico 150/F5
Dimbelenge, Zaire 115/D5
Dimbokro, Ivory Coast 106/D7
Dimboola, Victoria 97/B5
Dime Box, Texas 303/H7
Dimitrovgrad, Bulgaria 45/G4
Dimitrovgrad, U.S.S.R. 52/G4
Dimitrovgrad, Yugoslavia 45/F4
Dimlang (mt.), Nigeria 106/F7
Dimmit (co.), Texas 303/E9
Dimmitt, Texas 303/B3
Dimock, Pa. 294/L2
Dimock, S. Dak. 298/O7
Dimona, Israel 65/C5
Dimona (mt.), Israel 65/C5
Dimondale, Mich. 250/E6
Dimsdale, Alberta 182/A2
Dinagat (isls.), Philippines 82/E5
Dinagat (isls.), Philippines 85/H3
Dinagat (sound), Philippines 82/E5
Dinajpur, Bangladesh 68/F3
Dinan, France 28/B3
Dinant, Belgium 27/G8
Dinar, Kuh-e (mts.), Iran 66/G5
Dinar, Turkey 63/D3
Dinard, France 28/B3
Dinaric Alps (mts.), Yugoslavia 45/B3
Dinas Powis, Wales 13/B7
Dinder (riv.), Ethiopia 111/F5
Dinder (riv.), Sudan 59/B7
Dinder (riv.), Sudan 111/F5
Dindigul, India 68/D6
Dingalan (bay), Philippines 82/C3
Dingbian, China 77/G4
Dingess, W. Va. 312/B7
Dinggye, China 77/C6
Dinghai, China 77/K5
Dingle, Idaho 220/G7
Dingle, Ireland 10/A4
Dingle, Ireland 17/A7
Dingle (bay), Ireland 10/A4
Dingle (bay), Ireland 17/A7
Dingmans Ferry, Pa. 294/N2
Dingolfing, Germany 22/E4
Dinguiraye, Guinea 106/B6
Dingwall, Nova Scotia 168/H2
Dingwall, Scotland 15/D3
Dingwall, Scotland 10/D2
Dingxi, China 77/F4
Dingxing, China 77/H4
Dinh, Mui (cape), Vietnam 72/F5
Dinkelsbühl, Germany 22/D4
Dinnebito Wash (dry riv.), Ariz. 198/E3
Dinokwe, Botswana 118/D4
Dinorwic, Ontario 177/G5
Dinorwic, Ontario 175/B3
Dinosaur, Colo. 208/B2
Dinosaur Nat'l Mon., Colo. 208/B2
Dinosaur Nat'l Mon., Utah 304/E3
Dinsdale, Iowa 229/H4
Dinsmore, Sask. 181/H4
Dinsor, Somalia 115/H3
Dinuba, Calif. 204/F7
Dinwiddie (co.), Va. 307/N6
Dinwiddie, Va. 307/N6
Dinxperlo, Netherlands 27/K5
Diogo (isl.), Philippines 82/B2
Dioila, Mali 106/C6
Diomede, Alaska 196/E1
Diourbel, Senegal 106/A6
Diphu, India 68/G3
Dipilto, Cordillera (range), Nicaragua 154/D4
Diplo, Pakistan 68/B4
Dipolog, Philippines 82/D6
Dipper Harbour, New Bruns. 170/D3
Dir, Pakistan 68/C1
Dir, Pakistan 59/K2
Dire, Mali 106/D5
Direction (cape), Queensland 88/G2
Direction (cape), Queensland 95/B2
Dire Dawa, Ethiopia 102/G4
Dire Dawa, Ethiopia 111/H6

Diriamba, Nicaragua 154/D5
Dirico, Angola 115/D7
Dirico, Namibia 118/D3
Dirk Hartogs (isl.), Australia 87/B3
Dirk Hartogs (isl.), W. Australia 88/A5
Dirk Hartogs (isl.), W. Australia 92/A4
Dirksland, Netherlands 27/E5
Dirmil, Turkey 63/C4
Dirranbandi, Queensland 88/H5
Dirranbandi, Queensland 95/D6
Dirty Devil (riv.), Utah 304/D5
Disappointment (lake), Australia 87/C8
Disappointment (creek), Colo. 208/B7
Disappointment (isls.), Fr. Poly. 87/N7
Disappointment (cape), Newf. 166/B3
Disappointment (cape), Wash. 188/A1
Disappointment (cape), Wash. 310/A4
Disappointment (cape), W. Australia 88/C4
Disappointment (lake), W. Australia 92/C3
Discovery (bay), Victoria 88/E7
Discovery (bay), Victoria 97/A6
Discovery Bay, Jamaica 158/H5
Disentis-Mustér, Switzerland 39/G3
Dishman, Wash. 310/H3
Disko (isl.), Greenl. 4/C12
Disko (isl.), Greenland 146/N3
Disko, Ind. 227/E2
Disley, Sask. 181/J5
Dismal (riv.), Nebr. 264/C3
Dismal (Great) (swamp), N.C. 281/S1
Disney, China 288/S2
Dison, Belgium 27/H7
Dispur, India 68/G3
Disputanta, Va. 307/O6
Disraeli (fiord), N.W. Terr. 187/L1
Disraëli, Québec 172/F4
Diss, England 13/J5
Diss, England 10/G4
Disston (lake), Fla. 212/E2
Disston, Oreg. 291/E4
District Heights, Md. 245/G5
District of Columbia 146/L6
District of Columbia 188/L3
DISTRICT OF COLUMBIA 245
Distrito Especial, Colombia 126/C5
Distrito Federal, Argentina 143/H7
Distrito Federal, Mexico 150/L1
Distrito Federal, Venezuela 124/E2
Distrito Nacional, Dom. Rep. 158/E6
Disûq, Egypt 111/J3
Dittmer, Mo. 261/L6
Ditton (riv.), Québec 172/F4
Diu (dist.), India 68/C4
Diu, India 68/C4
Diuata (mts.), Philippines 82/E6
Divernon, Ill. 222/D4
Divide, Colo. 208/J5
Divide, Mont. 262/D5
Divide (co.), N. Dak. 282/C2
Dividing (creek), Md. 245/R8
Dividing Creek, N.J. 273/C5
Divino, Brazil 135/E2
Divinópolis, Brazil 132/E8
Divinópolis, Brazil 120/E5
Divinópolis, Brazil 135/D2
Divis (mt.), N. Ireland 17/J2
Divisa Nova, Brazil 135/C2
Division (peak), Nev. 266/B1
Divo, Ivory Coast 106/C7
Divriği, Turkey 63/H3
Divriği, Turkey 59/C2
Dix, Ill. 222/E5
Dix (riv.), Ky. 237/M5
Dix, Nebr. 264/A3
Dixfield, Maine 243/C6
Dixfield•, Maine 243/C6
Dix Hills, N.Y. 276/O9
Dixie, Ala. 195/E8
Dixie (co.), Fla. 212/C2
Dixie, Georgia 217/E9
Dixie, Idaho 220/C4
Dixie, La. 238/C1
Dixie, Wash. 310/G4
Dixie, W. Va. 312/D6
Dixie Inn, La. 238/D1
Dixmont, Maine 243/E5
Dixmont•, Maine 243/E6
Dixmoor, Ill. 222/C6
Dixmude (Diksmuide), Belgium 27/B6
Dixon, Calif. 204/B9
Dixon, Ill. 222/D2
Dixon, Iowa 229/M5
Dixon, Ky. 237/F5
Dixon, Miss. 256/F5
Dixon, Mo. 261/H6
Dixon, Mont. 262/D3
Dixon (co.), Nebr. 264/H2
Dixon, Nebr. 264/H3
Dixon, N.C. 281/O5
Dixon, Ohio 284/A4
Dixon, S. Dak. 298/L7
Dixon, Wyo. 319/E4
Dixon Entrance (chan.) 146/E4
Dixon Entrance (chan.), Alaska 196/M2
Dixon Entrance (chan.), Br. Col. 184/A3
Dixons Mills, Ala. 195/C6
Dixon Springs, Ill. 222/E6
Dixon Springs, Tenn. 237/J8
Dixonville, Ala. 195/E8
Dixonville, Alberta 182/B1
Dixonville, Pa. 294/D4
Dixville (peak), N.H. 268/E2
Dixville, Québec 172/F4
Dixville Notch (pass), N.H. 268/E2
Diyadin, Turkey 63/K3
Diyala (heads), Iraq 66/D4
Diyala (riv.), Iraq 66/D4
Diyarbakir (prov.), Turkey 63/H4
Diyarbakir, Turkey 54/F6
Diyarbakir, Turkey 63/H4
Diyarbakir, Turkey 59/C2
Dizful (Dezful), Iran 66/F4
Dja (riv.), Cameroon 115/B3
Dja (riv.), Congo 115/B3

Djado (plat.) 102/D2
Djado, Niger 102/D2
Djado, Niger 106/G4
Djado (plat.), Niger 106/G4
Djakarta (Jakarta) (cap.), Indonesia 85/H1
Djakovica, Yugoslavia 45/E4
Djakovo, Yugoslavia 45/D3
Djambala, Congo 115/B4
Djambi (Jambi), Indonesia 85/C6
Djanet, Algeria 106/F4
Djanet, Algeria 102/D2
Djelfa, Algeria 106/E2
Djema, Cent. Afr. Rep. 115/E2
Djemaa, Algeria 106/F2
Djenné, Mali 102/B3
Djenné, Mali 106/D6
Djerba (isl.), Tunisia 106/G2
Djerid, Shott el (salt lake), Tunisia 106/F2
Djibo, Burkina Faso 106/D6
Djibouti 2/L5
Djibouti 102/G3
DJIBOUTI 111/H5
Djibouti (cap.), Djibouti 111/H5
Djibouti (cap.), Djibouti 102/G3
Djokjakarta (Yogyakarta), Indonesia 85/J2
Djolu, Zaire 115/D3
Djouf, El (des.), Mauritania 106/C4
Djougou, Benin 106/E7
Djoum, Cameroon 115/B3
Djugu, Zaire 115/F3
D'Lo, Miss. 256/E7
Dmitriya Lapteva (str.), U.S.S.R. 4/B2
Dmitriya Lapteva (str.), U.S.S.R. 48/O2
Dneprodzerzhinsk, U.S.S.R. 7/H4
Dneprodzerzhinsk, U.S.S.R. 52/D5
Dnepropetrovsk, U.S.S.R. 7/H4
Dnepropetrovsk, U.S.S.R. 48/D5
Dnepropetrovsk, U.S.S.R. 52/D5
Dnieper (riv.), U.S.S.R. 7/H3
Dnieper (riv.), U.S.S.R. 48/D5
Dnieper (riv.), U.S.S.R. 52/D5
Dniester (riv.), U.S.S.R. 7/G4
Dniester (riv.), U.S.S.R. 52/B5
Dniester (riv.), U.S.S.R. 48/C5
Dno, U.S.S.R. 52/C3
Doaghbeg, Ireland 17/F1
Doaktown, New Bruns. 170/D2
Doans, Ind. 227/D7
Doba, Chad 111/C6
Doba, Chad 102/D4
Dobbie (mt.), North. Terr. 93/E7
Dobbin (bay), N.W. Terr. 187/L2
Dobbins A.F.B., Georgia 217/J1
Dobbs Ferry, N.Y. 276/O6
Dobbyn, Queensland 95/A3
Dobele, U.S.S.R. 53/B2
Döbeln, Germany 22/E3
Doberai (pen.), Indonesia 85/J6
Dobiegniew, Poland 47/B2
Doblas, Argentina 143/D4
Dobo, Indonesia 85/J7
Doboj, Yugoslavia 45/C3
Doboy (sound), Georgia 217/K8
Dobra, Czech. 41/B2
Dobre Miasto, Poland 47/E2
Dobrich (Tolbukhin), Bulgaria 45/H4
Dobrush, U.S.S.R. 52/D4
Dobruška, Czech. 41/D1
Dobryanka, U.S.S.R. 52/J3
Dobšiná, Czech. 41/F2
Dobson, N.C. 281/H2
Doce (riv.), Brazil 135/E2
Doce (riv.), Brazil 132/F7
Doce Leguas (cays), Cuba 158/D3
Docker River, North. Terr. 93/A8
Docking, England 13/J5
Dock Junction (Arco), Georgia 217/J8
Doctor Arroyo, Mexico 150/K5
Doctor Cecilio Báez, Paraguay 144/D4
Doctor Juan L. Mallorquín, Paraguay 144/F4
Doctor Juan Manuel Frutos, Paraguay 144/F4
Doctor M. Irala, Paraguay 144/F4
Doctor Pedro P. Peña, Paraguay 144/A3
Doctors Inlet, Fla. 212/E1
Doctortown, Georgia 217/J7
Doddridge, Ark. 202/C7
Doddridge (co.), W. Va. 312/E4
Dodds, Alberta 182/D3
Doddsville, Miss. 256/C3
Dodecanese (isls.), Greece 45/H4
Dodge (co.), Georgia 217/F6
Dodge, Mass. 249/K4
Dodge (co.), Minn. 255/F7
Dodge (co.), Nebr. 264/H3
Dodge, Nebr. 264/H3
Dodge, N. Dak. 282/F5
Dodge, Texas 303/J7
Dodge (co.), Wis. 317/J9
Dodge, Wis. 317/D7
Dodge Center, Minn. 255/F6
Dodge City, Kans. 188/F3
Dodge City, Kansas 232/B4
Dodgeville, Wis. 317/F10
Dodgingtown, Conn. 210/B3
Dodman (pt.), England 13/C7
Dodoma, Tanzania 102/F5
Dodoma, Tanzania 115/G5
Dodsland, Sask. 181/C4
Dodson, La. 238/E2
Dodson, Mont. 262/H2
Dodson, Texas 303/D3
Doe (lake), Ontario 177/E2
Doe (bay), Wash. 310/C2
Doe Bay, Wash. 310/C2
Doe Hill, Va. 307/K4
Doering, Wis. 317/G5
Doerun, Georgia 217/E8
Doe Run, Mo. 261/M7
Doesburg, Netherlands 27/J4
Doetinchem, Netherlands 27/J5

Druzhina 361

Dog (pond), Conn. 210/C1
Dog (isl.), Fla. 212/B2
Dog (lake), Manitoba 179/D3
Dog (isl.), Newf. 166/B2
Dog (lake), Ontario 177/G5
Dogai Coring (lake), China 77/C5
Doğanbey, Turkey 63/D4
Doğanhisar, Turkey 63/D3
Doğanşehir, Turkey 63/G3
Dog Creek, Br. Col. 184/G4
Dog Ear (creek), S. Dak. 298/K6
Döger, Turkey 63/D3
Dogo (isl.), Japan 81/F5
Dogondoutchi, Niger 106/E6
Dogondoutchi, Niger 102/C3
Dogpatch, Ark. 202/D1
Dog Pound, Alberta 182/C4
Dogskin (lake), Manitoba 179/G3
Doğubeyazıt, Turkey 63/K3
Dogwood (pt.), St. Kitts & Nevis 161/D11
Doha (cap.), Qatar 54/G7
Doha (cap.), Qatar 59/F4
Dohad, India 68/C4
Doheny, Québec 172/E2
Dohuk (gov.), Iraq 66/C2
Dohuk, Iraq 66/C2
Doi Inthanon (mt.), Thailand 72/C3
Doilungdêqên, China 77/C6
Doi Pha Hom Pok (mt.), Thailand 72/C2
Doi Pia Fai (mt.), Thailand 72/D4
Doische, Belgium 27/F8
Dois Córregos, Brazil 135/B3
Dois Irmãos, Serra (range), Brazil 132/F5
Dokkum, Netherlands 27/H2
Doksy, Czech. 41/C1
Dokterstuin, Neth. Ant. 161/F8
Dola, Ohio 284/C4
Dola, W. Va. 312/F4
Dolan, Ind. 227/E6
Doland, S. Dak. 298/N4
Dolan Springs, Ariz. 198/A3
Dolavon, Argentina 143/C5
Dolbeau, Québec 174/C3
Dolbeau, Québec 172/E1
Doldenhorn (mt.), Switzerland 39/E4
Dôle, France 28/F4
Dolega, Panama 154/F6
Dolent (mt.), Switzerland 39/C5
Doles, Georgia 217/E7
Dolgellau, Wales 13/D5
Dolgellau, Wales 10/E4
Dolgeville, N.Y. 276/L4
Dolgiy (isl.), U.S.S.R. 52/J1
Dolinsk, U.S.S.R. 48/P5
Dollar, Scotland 10/B1
Dollar, Scotland 15/E4
Dollar Bay, Mich. 250/G1
Dollard (bay), Netherlands 27/L2
Dollard, Sask. 181/C6
Dollard-des-Ormeaux, Québec 172/H4
Dollart (est.), Germany 22/B2
Dollarville, Mich. 250/D2
Dolliver, Iowa 229/D2
Dolný Kubín, Czech. 41/E2
Dolo, Ethiopia 111/H7
Dolomite, Ala. 195/D4
Dolomite Alps (range), Italy 34/C1
Dolores, Argentina 143/E4
Dolores, Argentina 120/D6
Dolores (co.), Colo. 208/C7
Dolores, Colo. 208/C8
Dolores (riv.), Colo. 208/B5
Dolores, Guatemala 154/C2
Dolores, Philippines 82/E4
Dolores, Spain 33/F3
Dolores, Uruguay 145/A4
Dolores (riv.), Utah 304/E5
Dolores, Venezuela 124/D3
Dolores Hidalgo de la Independencia Nacional, Mexico 150/J6
Dolphin and Union (str.), N.W. Terr. 187/G3
Dölsach, Austria 41/B3
Dolton, Ill. 222/C6
Dolton, S. Dak. 298/P7
Dom (mt.), Switzerland 39/E4
Domain, Manitoba 179/E5
Domaniç, Turkey 63/C3
Domar (dry riv.), Chad 111/C4
Domat-Ems, Switzerland 39/H3
Domažlice, Czech. 41/B2
Dombås, Norway 18/F5
Dombe Grande, Angola 115/B6
Dombóvár, Hungary 41/E3
Dombrád, Hungary 41/F2
Dombresson, Switzerland 39/C2
Domburg, Netherlands 27/C5
Domburg, Suriname 131/D3
Dome, Ariz. 198/A6
Dome Creek, Br. Col. 184/G3
Domeiko, Chile 138/A7
Domeyko, Cordillera (mts.), Chile 138/B4
Domínguez, Argentina 143/G6
Dominica 2/F5
Dominica 146/M8
DOMINICA 156/G4
DOMINICA 161/E7
Dominica (passage), Dominica 161/E5
Dominican Republic 2/F4
Dominican Republic 146/L8
DOMINICAN REPUBLIC 156/D3
DOMINICAN REPUBLIC 158
Dominion (lake), Newf. 166/B3
Dominion (cape), N.W. Terr. 187/L3
Dominion, Nova Scotia 168/J2
Dominion City, Manitoba 179/E5
Domino, Newf. 166/C3
Dömitz, Germany 22/D2
Domjor, India 68/F1
Domleschg (valley), Switzerland 39/E2
Dommel (riv.), Netherlands 27/H6
Domo, Ethiopia 111/J6
Domodossola, Italy 34/A1
Dom Pedrito, Brazil 132/C10
Dompu, Indonesia 85/F7
Domremy, Sask. 181/F3
Domrémy-la-Pucelle, France 28/F3
Dom Silvério, Brazil 135/E2
Dömsöd, Hungary 41/E3
Domuyo (vol.), Argentina 143/B4
Don (riv.), England 10/F4
Don (riv.), England 13/F4
Don (riv.), Ontario 177/J4
Don (riv.), Scotland 15/F3
Don (riv.), Scotland 10/E2
Don (riv.), U.S.S.R. 7/J4
Don (riv.), U.S.S.R. 48/E5
Don (riv.), U.S.S.R. 52/F5
Dona Ana (Mutarara), Mozambique 118/F3
Dona Ana (co.), N. Mex. 274/C6
Dona Ana, N. Mex. 274/C6
Donabate, Ireland 17/J5
Donaghadee, N. Ireland 17/K2
Donahue, Iowa 229/M5
Donald, Br. Col. 184/J4
Donald, Oreg. 291/A3
Donald, Victoria 97/B5
Donald, Wash. 310/E4
Donald, Wis. 317/E5
Donalda, Alberta 182/D3
Donalds, S.C. 296/C3
Donaldson, Ark. 202/E5
Donaldson, Ind. 227/E2
Donaldson, Minn. 255/B2
Donaldson A.F.B., S.C. 296/C2
Donaldsonville, La. 238/K3
Donalsonville, Georgia 217/C8
Donansburg, Ky. 237/K6
Donath, Switzerland 39/H3
Donatville, Alberta 182/D2
Donau (Danube) (riv.), Austria 41/D2
Donau (Danube) (riv.), Germany 22/C4
Donaueschingen, Germany 22/C5
Donauwörth, Germany 22/D4
Donavon, Sask. 181/D4
Donbar, Queensland 95/B3
Don Benito, Spain 33/C3
Doncaster, England 13/F4
Doncaster, England 10/F4
Doncaster, Md. 245/K7
Doncaster and Templestowe, Victoria 88/L7
Doncaster and Templestowe, Victoria 97/J5
Dondo, Angola 115/B5
Dondo, Mozambique 118/F3
Dondra (head), Sri Lanka 68/E7
Dondra Head (cape), Sri Lanka 54/K9
Donegal (co.), Ireland 17/K2
Donegal, Ireland 10/B3
Donegal, Ireland 17/F2
Donegal (bay), Ireland 17/D3
Donegal (bay), Ireland 10/B3
Donegal (harb.), Ireland 17/E2
Donegal (pt.), Ireland 17/B6
Donegal, Pa. 294/D5
Donel, Honduras 154/E3
Doneraile, Ireland 17/D7
Doneraile, S.C. 296/H3
Donets (riv.), U.S.S.R. 7/H4
Donets (riv.), U.S.S.R. 48/D5
Donets (riv.), U.S.S.R. 52/E5
Donetsk, U.S.S.R. 7/H4
Donetsk, U.S.S.R. 48/D5
Donetsk, U.S.S.R. 52/E5
Donga (riv.), Cameroon 115/B2
Donga, Nigeria 106/G7
Donga (riv.), Nigeria 106/G7
Dongara, W. Australia 92/A5
Dongchuan, China 77/F6
Dongen, Netherlands 27/F5
Dongfang, China 77/G8
Dongfanghong, China 77/M2
Donggala, Indonesia 85/F6
Dônghén, Laos 72/E3
Dong Hoi, Vietnam 72/E3
Dongio, Switzerland 39/H4
Dongning, China 77/M3
Dongo, Zaire 115/C3
Dongola, Ill. 222/D6
Dongola, Sudan 102/E3
Dongola, Sudan 59/B6
Dongola, Sudan 111/F4
Dongou, Congo 115/C3
Dong Rak (mts.), Thailand 72/D4
Dongsha (isl.), China 77/J7
Dongsheng, China 77/H4
Dongtai, China 77/K5
Dongting (lake), China 54/N7
Dongting Hu (riv.), China 77/H6
Dong Ujimqin, China 77/J2
Dongwe (riv.), Zambia 115/D6
Donie, Texas 303/H5
Doñihue, Chile 138/G5
Doniphan (co.), Kansas 232/G2
Doniphan, Mo. 261/L9
Doniphan, Nebr. 264/F4
Donji Vakuf, Yugoslavia 45/C3
Donkin, Nova Scotia 168/J2
Donley (co.), Texas 303/D2
Dønna (isl.), Norway 18/H3
Donna, Texas 303/F11
Donnacona, Québec 172/F3
Donnellson, Ill. 222/D4
Donnellson, Iowa 229/K7
Donnelly, Alberta 182/B2
Donnelly, Idaho 220/B5
Donnelly, Minn. 255/B5
Donner (pass), Calif. 204/E4
Donner, La. 238/J7
Donner and Blitzen (riv.), Oreg. 291/J4
Donnybrook, N. Dak. 282/G2
Donnybrook, Queensland 95/D5
Donnybrook, W. Australia 92/A2
Donora, Pa. 294/C5
Donovan, Georgia 217/G5
Donovan, Ill. 222/F3
Donsol, Philippines 82/D4
Donwell, Sask. 181/J4
Donzère, France 28/F5
Dooagh-Keel, Ireland 17/A4
Doole, Texas 303/E6
Dooling, Georgia 217/E6
Doolittle (pond), Conn. 210/C1
Doolittle, Mo. 261/J7
Doolittle Mills, Ind. 227/D8
Dooly (co.), Georgia 217/E6
Doon, Iowa 229/A2
Doon, Ireland 17/E6
Doon, Loch (lake), Scotland 15/D5
Doon (riv.), Scotland 15/D5
Doonerak (mt.), Alaska 196/H1
Doonside, Sask. 181/K6
Door (pt.), La. 238/M6
Door (co.), Wis. 317/M6
Door (pen.), Wis. 317/M6
Doorn, Netherlands 27/G4
Doornik (Tournai), Belgium 27/C7
Doqa, Saudi Arabia 59/D6
Dor, Israel 65/B2
Dora, Ala. 195/D3
Dora, Mo. 261/H9
Dora, N. Mex. 274/F5
Dora, Oreg. 291/D4
Dora (lake), W. Australia 88/C4
Dora (lake), W. Australia 92/C3
Dora Baltea (riv.), Italy 34/A2
Dorado, P. Rico 161/D1
Dora Lake, Minn. 255/D3
Doran, Minn. 255/B4
Dora Riparia (riv.), Italy 34/A2
Doraville, Georgia 217/K1
D'Orbigny, Bolivia 136/D7
Dorbiljin (Emin), China 77/B2
Dorbod, China 77/K2
Dorcas, W. Va. 312/H5
Dorchester, England 10/E5
Dorchester, England 13/E7
Dorchester, Georgia 217/K7
Dorchester, Ill. 222/D4
Dorchester, Iowa 229/L2
Dorchester (co.), Md. 245/O7
Dorchester, Mass. 249/D7
Dorchester, Nebr. 264/G4
Dorchester, New Bruns. 170/F3
Dorchester•, N.H. 268/D4
Dorchester, N.J. 273/D5
Dorchester (cape), N.W. Terr. 187/L3
Dorchester, Ontario 177/C5
Dorchester (co.), Québec 172/C3
Dorchester (co.), S.C. 296/G5
Dorchester, S.C. 296/G5
Dorchester, Wis. 317/F5
Dorchester Crossing, New Bruns. 170/F2
Dordogne (dept.), France 28/D5
Dordogne (riv.), France 7/E4
Dordogne (riv.), France 28/D5
Dordrecht, Netherlands 27/F5
Doré (lake), Ontario 177/G2
Doré (lake), Sask. 181/L3
Dore Alps (mts.), France 28/E5
Doré Lake, Sask. 181/L4
Dorena, Mo. 261/O9
Dorena, Oreg. 291/E4
Dorena (lake), Oreg. 291/E4
Dorenlee, Alberta 182/D3
Dores, Scotland 15/D3
Dores do Indaiá, Brazil 132/E7
Dorgali, Italy 34/B4
Dörgön Nuur (lake), Mongolia 77/D2
Dori, Mali 102/B3
Dori, Burkina Faso 106/D6
Doring (riv.), S. Africa 118/B6
Dorintosh, Sask. 181/L4
Dorion, Ontario 177/H5
Dorion, Québec 172/C4
Dorking, England 13/G8
Dorking, England 10/F5
Dormont, Pa. 294/B7
Dornach, Switzerland 39/E2
Dornbirn, Austria 41/A3
Dornie, Scotland 15/C3
Dornoch, Scotland 10/D2
Dornoch, Scotland 15/D3
Dornoch (firth), Scotland 15/E3
Dornoch (firth), Scotland 10/E2
Dornod, Mongolia 77/H2
Dornogovĭ, Mongolia 77/G3
Dorog, Hungary 41/E3
Dorohoi, Romania 45/H2
Dorotea, Sweden 18/K4
Dorothy, Alberta 182/D4
Dorothy, Minn. 255/B3
Dorothy, N.J. 273/D5
Dorothy, W. Va. 312/D7
Dorr (lake), Fla. 212/E2
Dorr, Mich. 250/D6
Dorrance, Kansas 232/D3
Dorre (isl.), W. Australia 88/A5
Dorre (isl.), W. Australia 92/A4
Dorreen, Br. Col. 184/C3
Dorrigo, N.S. Wales 97/G2
Dorris, Calif. 204/D2
Dorset (co.), England 13/E7
Dorset, Minn. 255/D4
Dorset, Ohio 284/J2
Dorset•, Vt. 268/A5
Dorset (peak), Vt. 268/A5
Dorset Heights (hills), England 13/E7
Dorsey, Miss. 256/H2
Dorsten, Germany 22/B3
Dortches, N.C. 281/O2
Dortmund, Germany 7/E3
Dortmund, Germany 22/B3
Dorton, Ky. 237/R6
Dörtyol, Turkey 63/F4
Doruma, Zaire 115/E3
Dorval, Québec 172/H4
Dory Point, N.W. Terr. 187/G3
Dos Bahías (cape), Argentina 143/D5
Dos Cabezas, Ariz. 198/F6
Dos Caminos, Cuba 158/J4
Dos de Mayo, Peru 128/E6
Dos Hermanas, Spain 33/D4
Dos Palos, Calif. 204/E6
Dosquet, Québec 172/F3
Dos Reyes (pt.), Chile 138/A5
Dos Ríos, Cuba 158/J4
Dosso, Niger 106/E6
Dossor, U.S.S.R. 48/F5
Dossville, Miss. 256/F5
Doswell, Va. 307/N5
Dothan, Ala. 188/J4
Dothan, Ala. 195/H8
Doti, Nepal 68/E3
Dot Klish (canyon), Ariz. 198/E2
Dot Lake, Alaska 196/K2
Dott, W. Va. 312/D8
Döttingen, Switzerland 39/F1
Doty, Wash. 310/B4
Douai, France 28/E2
Douala, Cameroon 115/B3
Douala, Cameroon 102/D4
Douarnenez, France 28/A3
Double Branches, Georgia 217/H3
Double Mer (lake), Newf. 166/C3
Double Mountain Fork, Brazos (riv.), Texas 303/C4
Double Oak, Texas 303/F1
Double Springs, Ala. 195/D2
Doubletop (peak), Wyo. 319/B2
Doubs (dept.), France 28/G4
Doubs (riv.), France 28/G4
Doubs, Md. 245/J3
Doubs (riv.), Switzerland 39/C2
Doubtful (sound), N. Zealand 100/A6
Doubtless (bay), N. Zealand 100/D1
Doucette, Texas 303/K7
Douds, Iowa 229/J7
Doué-la-Fontaine, France 28/C4
Douentza, Mali 106/D6
Douentza, Mali 102/B3
Dougherty (co.), Georgia 217/D7
Dougherty, Iowa 229/G3
Dougherty, Okla. 288/M6
Dougherty, Texas 303/C4
Douglas, Ala. 195/F2
Douglas (mt.), Alaska 196/H3
Douglas, Ariz. 146/G6
Douglas, Ariz. 188/E4
Douglas, Ariz. 198/F7
Douglas (chan.), Br. Col. 184/C3
Douglas (co.), Colo. 208/K4
Douglas (creek), Colo. 208/B3
Douglas (bay), Dominica 161/E5
Douglas (co.), Georgia 217/C3
Douglas, Georgia 217/G7
Douglas (co.), Ill. 222/E4
Douglas, Ireland 17/D8
Douglas (cap.), I. of Man 13/C3
Douglas (cap.), I. of Man 10/D3
Douglas (co.), Kansas 232/G3
Douglas, Manitoba 179/C5
Douglas•, Mass. 249/H4
Douglas, Mich. 250/C6
Douglas (co.), Minn. 255/C5
Douglas, Minn. 255/F6
Douglas (co.), Mo. 261/G9
Douglas (mt.), Mont. 262/F5
Douglas (co.), Nebr. 264/H3
Douglas, Nebr. 264/H4
Douglas (co.), Nev. 266/B4
Douglas, N. Dak. 282/G4
Douglas, North. Terr. 93/B2
Douglas, Okla. 288/L2
Douglas, Ontario 177/H2
Douglas (pt.), Ontario 177/C3
Douglas (co.), Oreg. 291/D4
Douglas, Scotland 15/E5
Douglas, S. Africa 118/C5
Douglas (co.), S. Dak. 298/N7
Douglas (lake), Tenn. 237/P9
Douglas (co.), Wash. 310/F3
Douglas, Wash. 310/F3
Douglas (co.), Wis. 317/C3
Douglas, Wyo. 319/G3
Douglas Harbour, New Bruns. 170/D3
Douglas Lake, Br. Col. 184/H5
Douglas Prov. Park, Sask. 181/E4
Douglass, Kansas 232/F4
Douglass, Texas 303/K6
Douglass Hills, Ky. 237/L2
Douglassville, Pa. 294/L5
Douglastown, New Bruns. 170/E1
Douglastown, Québec 172/D1
Douglasville, Georgia 217/C3
Doullens, France 28/E2
Doulus (head), Ireland 17/A8
Doumé, Cameroon 115/B3
Dounby, Scotland 15/E1
Doune, Scotland 15/D4
Dour, Belgium 27/D8
Dourados, Brazil 120/D5
Dourados, Brazil 132/C8
Douro (riv.), Portugal 7/D4
Douro (riv.), Portugal 33/B2
Douro (riv.), Spain 33/C2
Dousman, Wis. 317/J1
Douthat, Okla. 288/S1
Douville, Québec 172/D4
Dove (riv.), England 13/J2
Dove (creek), Utah 304/A2
Dove Creek, Colo. 208/A7
Dover, Ark. 202/D3
Dover (cap.), Del. 146/L6
Dover (cap.), Del. 188/L3
Dover (cap.), Del. 245/R4
Dover, England 7/E3
Dover, England 10/G5
Dover, England 13/J6
Dover (str.), England 13/J7
Dover (str.), England 10/G5
Dover, Fla. 212/D4
Dover, Georgia 217/J5
Dover, Idaho 220/B1
Dover, Ill. 222/D2
Dover, Ind. 227/H6
Dover, Kansas 232/G3
Dover, Ky. 237/O3
Dover, Mass. 249/B7
Dover•, Mass. 249/B7
Dover, Minn. 255/F7
Dover, Mo. 261/E4
Dover, N.H. 268/F5
Dover, N.J. 273/D2
Dover, N.C. 281/P4
Dover, Ohio 284/G4
Dover (lake), Ohio 284/H4
Dover, Okla. 288/L3
Dover, Pa. 294/J6
Dover, Tasmania 99/C5
Dover, Tenn. 237/F8
Dover (pt.), W. Australia 88/D6
Dover (pt.), W. Australia 92/D6
Dover A.F.B., Del. 245/S4
Doverel, Georgia 217/D7
Dover-Foxcroft, Maine 243/E5
Dover-Foxcroft•, Maine 243/E5
Dover Hill, Ind. 227/D7
Dover Plains, N.Y. 276/O7
Dover South Mills, Maine 243/E5
Dovesville, S.C. 296/H3
Dovey (riv.), Wales 10/D4
Dovey (riv.), Wales 13/D5
Dovns Klint (cliff), Denmark 21/D8
Dovray, Minn. 255/C6
Dovre, Norway 18/F6
Dovrefjell (hills), Norway 18/F5
Dow (Xau) (lake), Botswana 118/C4
Dow, Ill. 222/C4
Dow, Okla. 288/P5
Dowa, Malawi 115/F6
Dowagiac, Mich. 250/D6
Dow City, Iowa 229/B5
Dowell, Ill. 222/D6
Dowelltown, Tenn. 237/K8
Dowlatabad, Afghanistan 59/H3
Dowlatabad, Afghanistan 68/A2
Dowlatabad, Kerman, Iran 66/K6
Dowlatabad, Khorasan, Iran 66/M2
Dowlat Yar, Afghanistan 59/J3
Dowlat Yar, Afghanistan 68/B2
Dowling, Alberta 182/E4
Dowling (lake), Alberta 182/D4
Dowling, Mich. 250/D6
Dowling Park, Fla. 212/C1
Down (dist.), N. Ireland 17/K3
Downe, Sask. 181/C4
Downer, Minn. 255/B4
Downers Grove, Ill. 222/A6
Downey, Calif. 204/C11
Downey, Idaho 220/F7
Downey, Iowa 229/L5
Downfall (creek), Queensland 95/D2
Downham Market, England 13/H5
Downham Market, England 10/G4
Downieville, Calif. 204/E4
Downing, Mo. 261/H2
Downing, Wis. 317/B5
Downings, Va. 307/P5
Downingtown, Pa. 294/L5
Downpatrick (head), Ireland 17/C3
Downpatrick, N. Ireland 10/C3
Downpatrick, N. Ireland 17/K3
Downs, Ill. 222/E3
Downs, Kansas 232/D2
Downsville, La. 238/F1
Downsville, Md. 245/G2
Downsville, N.Y. 276/L6
Downsville, Wis. 317/C6
Downton, England 13/F6
Dows, Iowa 229/F3
Dowshi, Afghanistan 59/J2
Dowshi, Afghanistan 68/B1
Doyle, Calif. 204/E3
Doyle, Georgia 217/D6
Doyle, Tenn. 237/K9
Doylestown, Ohio 284/G4
Doylestown, Pa. 294/M5
Doylestown, Wis. 317/H9
Doyleville, Colo. 208/F6
Doyline, La. 238/D1
Doyon, N. Dak. 282/O3
Dozen (isls.), Japan 81/F5
Dozier, Ala. 195/F7
Dozier, Texas 303/D2
Dozois (res.), Québec 174/B3
Dra, Wadi (dry riv.), Morocco 106/C3
Drachten, Netherlands 27/J2
Dracut•, Mass. 249/J2
Drăgănești Olt, Romania 45/G3
Drăgășani, Romania 45/F3
Dragonera (isl.), Spain 33/H3
Dragons Mouth (str.), Trin. & Tob. 156/F5
Dragons Mouth (str.), Trin. & Tob. 161/A10
Dragons Mouth (str.), Venezuela 124/H2
Dragoon, Ariz. 198/F6
Dragoon (mts.), Ariz. 198/F7
Draguignan, France 28/G6
Drain, Oreg. 291/D4
Drake (passage) 2/F8
Drake (passage), Ant. 5/C15
Drake (passage), Chile 138/E11
Drake, Colo. 208/J2
Drake, Mo. 261/K6
Drake, N. Dak. 282/K4
Drake, Sask. 181/G4
Drakensberg (range), Lesotho 118/D6
Drakensberg (range), S. Africa 118/D6
Drakensberg (range), Swaziland 118/D6
Drakes (creek), Ky. 237/J7
Drakesboro, Ky. 237/H6
Drakes Branch, Va. 307/L7
Drakesville, Iowa 229/J7
Draketown, Georgia 217/B3
Dráma, Greece 45/F5
Drammen, Norway 7/E3
Drammen, Norway 18/C4
Drance (riv.), Switzerland 39/D4
Drancy, France 28/B1
Drang, Ia (riv.), Cambodia 72/E4
Draper, S. Dak. 298/J6
Draper, Utah 304/C3
Draper, Va. 307/G7
Draper, Wis. 317/E4
Draperstown, N. Ireland 17/H2
Draperstown, N. Ireland 10/C3
Drasco, Ark. 202/G2
Drau (riv.), Austria 41/C3
Drava (riv.) 7/F4
Dráva (riv.), Hungary 41/D3
Drava (riv.), Yugoslavia 45/C3
Dravosburg, Pa. 294/C7
Drawsko Pomorskie, Poland 47/B2
Drax Hall, Barbados 161/B8
Drayden, Md. 245/N8
Drayton, N. Dak. 282/R2
Drayton, Ontario 177/D4
Drayton Plains, Mich. 250/F6
Drayton Valley, Alberta 182/C3
Drenthe (prov.), Netherlands 27/K3
Dresbach, Minn. 255/G7
Dresden, Germany 7/F3
Dresden, Germany 22/E3
Dresden, Kansas 232/B2
Dresden•, Maine 243/D7
Dresden, Mo. 261/F5
Dresden, N.Y. 276/F5
Dresden, N. Dak. 282/O2
Dresden, Ohio 284/G5
Dresden, Ontario 177/B5
Dresden, Tenn. 237/D8
Dresden Station, N.Y. 276/O3
Dresser, Wis. 317/A5
Dreux, France 28/D3
Drew (co.), Ark. 202/G6
Drew, Miss. 256/C3
Drew, Oreg. 291/E5
Drewry, Ala. 195/D8
Drewryville, Va. 307/O7
Drews (res.), Oreg. 291/G5
Drewsey, Oreg. 291/J4
Drewsville, N.H. 268/C5
Drexel, Mo. 261/C6
Drexel, N.C. 281/F3
Drexel Hill, Pa. 294/M6
Dreyfus, Ky. 237/N5
Drezdenko, Poland 47/B2
Driebergen, Netherlands 27/G4
Driffield, England 13/G3
Driffield, England 10/F4
Drift (creek), Oreg. 291/B3
Drifton, Pa. 294/L3
Driftwood, Okla. 288/K1
Driftwood, Pa. 294/F3
Driggs, Ark. 202/C3
Driggs, Idaho 220/G6
Drill, Va. 307/E6
Drimoleague, Ireland 17/C8
Drin (riv.), Albania 45/E4
Drina (riv.), Yugoslavia 45/D3
Drinkwater, Sask. 181/F5
Dripping Springs, Texas 303/F7
Driscoll, N. Dak. 282/K6
Driscoll, Texas 303/G10
Drishane, Ireland 17/C7
Driskill (mt.), La. 238/E2
Drøbak, Norway 18/D4
Drobeta-Turnu Severin, Romania 45/F3
Drogenbos, Belgium 27/B10
Drogheda, Ireland 17/J4
Drogheda, Ireland 10/C4
Drogobych, U.S.S.R. 52/B5
Drogobych, U.S.S.R. 48/C5
Droichead Nua, Ireland 10/C4
Droichead Nua, Ireland 17/H5
Droitwich, England 13/E5
Dromahair, Ireland 17/E3
Drôme (dept.), France 28/F5
Drôme (riv.), France 28/F5
Dromore, Bainbridge, N. Ireland 17/J3
Dromore, Omagh, N. Ireland 17/G3
Dromore West, Ireland 17/D3
Dronfield, England 13/J2
Drongan, Scotland 15/D5
Dronne (riv.), France 28/D5
Dronninglund, Denmark 21/D3
Dronten, Netherlands 27/H3
Dropmore, Manitoba 179/A3
Drouin, Victoria 97/C6
Druid, Sask. 181/C4
Druif, Neth. Ant. 161/D10
Drum (hills), Ireland 17/F7
Drum (bay), La. 238/M7
Drum (inlet), N.C. 281/S5
Drumaness, N. Ireland 17/K3
Drumbeg, Scotland 15/C2
Drumbo, Ontario 177/D4
Drumcar, Ireland 17/J4
Drumconrath, Ireland 17/H4
Drumheller, Alberta 182/D4
Drumheller, Alta. 162/E5
Drumhill, N.C. 281/R1
Drumkeerin, Ireland 17/E3
Drumlish, Ireland 17/F4
Drummond, Idaho 220/G5
Drummond (isl.), Mich. 250/F2
Drummond, Mont. 262/D4
Drummond, New Bruns. 170/C1
Drummond (mt.), North. Terr. 93/E5
Drummond, Okla. 288/L2
Drummond (co.), Québec 172/E4
Drummond (range), Queensland 88/H4
Drummond (range), Queensland 95/C5
Drummond (lake), Va. 307/P7
Drummond, Wis. 317/D3
Drummond Island, Mich. 250/F3
Drummonds, Tenn. 237/A10
Drummondville, Québec 172/E4
Drummondville-Nord, Québec 172/E4
Drummondville-Sud, Québec 172/E4
Drummore, Scotland 15/D6
Drummoyne, N.S. Wales 88/K4
Drummoyne, N.S. Wales 97/J3
Drumnadrochit, Scotland 15/D3
Drumquin, N. Ireland 17/F2
Drumright, Okla. 288/N3
Drums, Pa. 294/K3
Drumshanbo, Ireland 17/E3
Drury, Mo. 261/H9
Druskininkai, U.S.S.R. 53/C3
Druten, Netherlands 27/H5
Druz, Jebel ed (mts.), Syria 63/G6
Druzhba, U.S.S.R. 48/J5
Druzhina, U.S.S.R. 48/P3

362 Drvar

Drvar, Yugoslavia 45/C3
Dry (bay), Alaska 196/L3
Dry (creek), Ky. 237/R3
Dry (lake), N. Dak. 282/M3
Dry (riv.), North. Terr. 88/E3
Dry (riv.), North. Terr. 93/C3
Dry (creek), S. Dak. 298/G4
Dry (lake), S. Dak. 298/P3
Dry (creek), Wyo. 319/C2
Dryad, Wash. 310/B4
Dryanovo, Bulgaria 45/G4
Dry Branch, Georgia 217/F5
Dry Cimarron (riv.), N. Mex. 274/F2
Dry Coal (creek), Utah 304/A6
Dry Cottonwood (creek), Wyo. 319/D1
Dry Creek, La. 238/D5
Dry Creek, W. Va. 312/D7
Dryden, Ark. 202/J2
Dryden, Maine 243/C6
Dryden, Mich. 250/F6
Dryden, N.Y. 276/H6
Dryden, Ontario 177/G4
Dryden, Ontario 175/B3
Dryden, Texas 303/C7
Dryden, Va. 307/B7
Dryden, Wash. 310/E3
Dry Falls (dam), Wash. 310/F3
Dry Fork, Va. 307/K7
Dryfork, W. Va. 312/H5
Dry Fork (riv.), W. Va. 312/G5
Dry Fork (riv.), W. Va. 312/C8
Dry Fork, Cheyenne (riv.), Wyo. 319/G2
Dry Fork, Powder (riv.), Wyo. 319/F2
Dry Lake, Nev. 266/G6
Drymen, Scotland 15/B1
Dry Mills, Maine 243/C8
Dry Prong, La. 238/E3
Dry Ridge, Ky. 237/M3
Dry Run, Pa. 294/G5
Drysdale (riv.), W. Australia 88/D3
Drysdale (riv.), W. Australia 92/D1
Dry Tortugas (keys), Fla. 212/D7
Drytown, Calif. 204/C8
Dry Wood (lake), S. Dak. 298/P2
Dschang, Cameroon 115/A2
Duaca, Venezuela 124/D2
Duaringa, Queensland 95/D4
Duart, Ontario 177/C5
Duarte, Calif. 204/D10
Duarte (prov.), Dom. Rep. 158/E5
Duarte (peak), Dom. Rep. 158/D5
Dubach, La. 238/E1
Dubai, U.A.E. 59/F4
Dubawnt (lake), N.W.T. 162/F3
Dubawnt (lake), N.W.T. 146/H3
Dubawnt (lake), N.W. Terr. 187/H3
Dubawnt (riv.), N.W.T. 162/F3
Dubawnt (riv.), N.W. Terr. 187/H3
Du Bay (lake), Wis. 317/G6
Dubberly, La. 238/D1
Dubbo, N. S. Wales 88/H6
Dubbo, N.S. Wales 97/E3
Dubbs, Miss. 256/D1
Dübendorf, Switzerland 39/G2
Dublin, Calif. 204/K2
Dublin, Georgia 217/G5
Dublin, Ind. 227/G5
Dublin (co.), Ireland 17/J5
Dublin (cap.), Ireland 7/D3
Dublin (cap.), Ireland 17/K5
Dublin (cap.), Ireland 10/C4
Dublin (bay), Ireland 10/C4
Dublin (bay), Ireland 17/J5
Dublin, Ky. 237/D7
Dublin, Md. 245/N2
Dublin, Mich. 250/D4
Dublin, Miss. 256/C2
Dublin•, N.H. 268/C6
Dublin, N.C. 281/M5
Dublin, Ohio 284/D5
Dublin, Ontario 177/C4
Dublin, Pa. 294/M5
Dublin, Texas 303/F5
Dublin, Va. 307/G6
Dubna, U.S.S.R. 52/E4
Dubna, U.S.S.R. 52/E3
Dubnica nad Váhom, Czech. 41/E2
Dubno, U.S.S.R. 52/C4
Dubois, Idaho 220/F5
Dubois, Ill. 222/D5
Dubois (co.), Ind. 227/D8
Dubois, Ind. 227/D8
Du Bois, Nebr. 264/H4
DuBois, Pa. 294/E3
Dubois, Wyo. 319/C2
Duboistown, Pa. 294/H3
Dubréka, Guinea 106/B7
Dubreuilville, Ontario 177/J5
Dubrovnik, Yugoslavia 45/C4
Dubrueilville, Ontario 175/D3
Dubuc, Sask. 181/J5
Dubuque (co.), Iowa 229/M4
Dubuque, Iowa 188/H2
Dubuque, Iowa 229/M3
Duchcov, Czech. 41/B1
Duchesne (co.), Utah 304/D3
Duchesne, Utah 304/D3
Duchesne (riv.), Utah 304/D3
Duchess, Alberta 182/E4
Duchess, Queensland 88/F4
Duchess, Queensland 95/A4
Ducie (isl.), Pitcairn Is. 87/O8
Duck (isls.), Maine 243/G7
Duck (lake), Mich. 250/F4
Duck (creek), Nev. 266/G3
Duck, N.C. 281/T2
Duck (creek), Ohio 284/H6
Duck (isl.), Ontario 177/H4
Duck (isls.), Ontario 177/A2
Duck (riv.), Tenn. 237/F9
Duck, W. Va. 312/E5
Duck Bay, Manitoba 179/B2
Duck Hill, Miss. 256/E3
Duck Lake, Sask. 181/E3
Duck Lake Hist. Park, Sask. 181/E3
Duck Lake Post, Manitoba 179/J2
Duck Mountain Prov. Park, Manitoba 179/B3
Duck Mountain Prov. Park, Sask. 181/K4
Duck River, Tenn. 237/G9
Ducktown, Georgia 217/D2
Ducktown, Tenn. 237/N10
Duck Valley Indian Res., Idaho 220/B7
Duck Valley Indian Res., Nev. 266/E1
Duckwater, Nev. 266/F4
Duclos, Québec 172/A4
Ducor, Calif. 204/G8
Ducos, Martinique 161/D6
Dudelange, Luxembourg 27/J10
Dudenville, Mo. 261/D8
Duderstadt, Germany 22/D3
Dudhi, India 68/E4
Dudignac, Argentina 143/F7
Düdingen, Switzerland 39/D3
Dudinka, U.S.S.R. 54/K3
Dudinka, U.S.S.R. 4/B5
Dudinka, U.S.S.R. 48/J3
Dudley, England 13/E5
Dudley, England 10/G3
Dudley, Georgia 217/F5
Dudley•, Mass. 249/G4
Dudley, Mo. 261/M9
Dudley, N.C. 281/N4
Dudley, Pa. 294/F5
Dudley (lake), Québec 172/B3
Dudleytown, Ind. 227/F7
Dudváh (riv.), Czech. 41/D2
Dueñas, Spain 33/D2
Duenweg, Mo. 261/D8
Duero (Douro) (riv.), Spain 33/C2
Due West, S.C. 296/C3
Duff, Sask. 181/H5
Duff, Tenn. 237/N8
Duffee, Miss. 256/G6
Duffel, Belgium 27/F6
Dufferin (county), Ontario 177/D3
Duffield, Alberta 182/C3
Duffield, Va. 307/C7
Dufftown, Scotland 10/E2
Dufftown, Scotland 15/E3
Dufourspitze (mt.), Switzerland 39/E5
Dufresne, Manitoba 179/F5
Dufrost, Manitoba 179/E5
Dufur, Oreg. 291/F2
Dugald, Manitoba 179/F5
Dugger, Ind. 227/C6
Dugi Otok (isl.), Yugoslavia 45/B3
Dugspur, Va. 307/G7
Duguayville, New Bruns. 170/E1
Du Gué (riv.), Québec 174/C1
Dugway, Utah 304/B3
Dugway (range), Utah 304/A3
Dugway Proving Grounds, Utah 304/B3
Duhamel, Alberta 182/D3
Duhamel, Québec 172/B3
Duich, Loch (inlet), Scotland 15/C3
Duida, Cerro (mt.), Venezuela 124/F6
Duifken (pt.), Queensland 88/G2
Duifken (pt.), Queensland 95/B2
Duiker (pt.), S. Africa 118/E6
Duinain (riv.), Scotland 15/D3
Duirinish (dist.), Scotland 15/B3
Duisburg, Germany 22/B3
Duitama, Colombia 126/D5
Duiveland (isl.), Netherlands 27/D5
Duivendrecht, Netherlands 27/C5
Duke, Ala. 195/G3
Duke (isl.), Alaska 196/N2
Duke, Mo. 261/H7
Duke (East Duke), Okla. 288/G5
Duke Center, Pa. 294/F2
Dukedom, Tenn. 237/D8
Duke of Gloucester (isls.), Fr. Poly. 87/M8
Dukes (co.), Mass. 249/M7
Dukes, Mich. 250/B2
Dukhan, Qatar 59/F4
Duki, Pakistan 68/B2
Dukla (pass), Czech. 41/F2
Dukla (pass), Poland 47/E4
Dukou, China 77/F6
Dulac, La. 238/J8
Dulah, N.C. 281/M6
Dulan, China 77/E4
Dulce (riv.), Argentina 143/D2
Dulce (gulf), C. Rica 154/F6
Dulce, N. Mex. 274/B2
Duleek, Ireland 17/J4
Dulgalakh (riv.), U.S.S.R. 48/O3
Dülmen, Germany 22/B3
Dulunguin (pt.), Philippines 82/C7
Duluth, Georgia 217/D2
Duluth, Kansas 232/F2
Duluth, Minn. 146/J5
Duluth, Minn. 188/H1
Duluth, Minn. 255/F4
Dulverton, England 13/D6
Duma, Syria 63/G6
Duma, West Bank 65/C3
Dumagasa (pt.), Philippines 82/C7
Dumaguete, Philippines 82/D6
Dumaguete, Philippines 85/G4
Dumanquilas (bay), Philippines 82/D7
Dumaran (isl.), Philippines 85/G3
Dumaran (isl.), Philippines 82/C5
Dumaresq (riv.), N.S. Wales 97/F1
Dumas, Ark. 202/H6
Dumas, Miss. 256/G1
Dumas, Sask. 181/J6
Dumas, Texas 303/C2
Dumbarton, New Bruns. 170/C3
Dumbarton, Scotland 10/A1
Dumbarton, Scotland 15/B1
Dum Dum, India 68/F1
Dume (pt.), Calif. 204/G10
Dumeir, Syria 63/G6
Dumfounding (bay), Fla. 212/C4
Dumfries, New Bruns. 170/C3
Dumfries, Scotland 15/E5
Dumfries, Scotland 10/E3
Dumfries (trad. co.), Scotland, 15/B5
Dumfries, Va. 307/O3
Dumfries and Galloway (reg.), Scotland 15/E5
Dumlu, Turkey 63/J2
Dummer•, N.H. 268/E2
Dummer, Sask. 181/G6
Dümmersee (lake), Germany 22/C2
Dumont, Iowa 229/H3
Dumont, Minn. 255/B5
Dumont, N.J. 273/C1
Dumont, Texas 303/D4
Dumont d'Urville Station, Ant. 5/C7
Dumyât (Damietta), Egypt 111/J3
Dumyat (Damietta), Egypt 59/B3
Dun (isl.), Scotland 15/A2
Duna (Danube) (riv.), Hungary 41/E3
Dunaff (head), Ireland 17/F1
Dunaföldvár, Hungary 41/E3
Dunaharaszti, Hungary 41/E3
Dunajec (riv.), Czech. 41/F2
Dunajec (riv.), Poland 47/E4
Dunajská Streda, Czech. 41/D3
Dunakeszi, Hungary 41/E3
Dunalley, Tasmania 99/D4
Dunany (pt.), Ireland 17/J4
Dunaszekcső, Hungary 41/E3
Dunaújváros, Hungary 41/E3
Dunav (Danube) (riv.), Bulgaria 45/H4
Dunavecse, Hungary 41/E3
Dunbar, Iowa 229/H5
Dunbar, Nebr. 264/J4
Dunbar, Okla. 288/P6
Dunbar, Pa. 294/C6
Dunbar, Scotland 10/E2
Dunbar, Scotland 15/F4
Dunbar, S.C. 296/H2
Dunbar, W. Va. 312/C6
Dunbar, Wis. 317/K4
Dunbarton•, N.H. 268/D5
Dunbarton (trad. co.), Scotland 15/A5
Dunbarton Center, N.H. 268/D5
Dunbeath, Scotland 15/E2
Dunbeg, Scotland 15/C4
Dunblane, Sask. 181/D4
Dunblane, Scotland 15/E4
Dunblane, Scotland 10/D2
Dunbridge, Ohio 284/C3
Duncan, Ariz. 198/F6
Duncan, Br. Col. 184/J3
Duncan (riv.), Br. Col. 184/J5
Duncan (isls.), China 85/E2
Duncan, Ill. 222/D3
Duncan (passage), India 68/G6
Duncan, Miss. 256/C2
Duncan, Nebr. 264/G3
Duncan, Okla. 288/L5
Duncan (lake), Québec 174/B2
Duncan, S.C. 296/C2
Duncan, W. Va. 312/C5
Duncan Falls, Ohio 284/G6
Duncannon, Ireland 17/H7
Duncannon, Pa. 294/H5
Duncans, Jamaica 158/H5
Duncans Bridge, Mo. 261/H3
Duncansby (head), Scotland 15/F2
Duncansby (head), Scotland 10/E1
Duncansville, Pa. 294/F5
Duncanville, Ala. 195/D4
Duncanville, Texas 303/G3
Dunchurch, Ontario 177/E2
Duncombe, Iowa 229/E4
Duncombe (bay), Norfolk I. 88/L5
Dundaga, U.S.S.R. 53/B2
Dundalk, Ireland 17/H3
Dundalk, Ireland 10/C4
Dundalk (bay), Ireland 10/C4
Dundalk (bay), Ireland 17/J4
Dundalk, Md. 245/N3
Dundalk, Ontario 177/D3
Dundarrach, N.C. 281/L5
Dundas (isl.), Br. Col. 184/B3
Dundas, Ill. 222/E5
Dundas, Minn. 255/E6
Dundas (str.), North. Terr. 88/E2
Dundas (str.), North. Terr. 93/B1
Dundas (pen.), N.W. Terr. 187/G2
Dundas, Ohio 284/E7
Dundas (county), Ontario 177/J2
Dundas, Ontario 177/D4
Dundas, Va. 307/M7
Dundas (lake), W. Australia 88/C6
Dundas (lake), W. Australia 92/C6
Dundee, Fla. 212/E3
Dundee (East and West Dundee), Ill. 222/E1
Dundee, Ind. 227/F4
Dundee, Iowa 229/L3
Dundee, Ky. 237/H5
Dundee, Mich. 250/F7
Dundee, Minn. 255/C7
Dundee, Miss. 256/D1
Dundee, N.Y. 276/F5
Dundee, Oreg. 291/A2
Dundee, Scotland 7/D3
Dundee, Scotland 15/F4
Dundee, Scotland 10/E2
Dundee, S. Africa 118/E5
Dundee, Texas 303/F4
Dundgovĭ, Mongolia 77/G2
Dundon, W. Va. 312/D6
Dundonald, Scotland 15/D5
Dundrum, N. Ireland 17/K3
Dundrum (bay), N. Ireland 17/K3
Dundurn, Sask. 181/E4
Dundy (co.), Nebr. 264/C4
Dune Acres, Ind. 227/C1
Dunedin, Fla. 212/B2
Dunedin, N. Zealand 2/T8
Dunedin, N. Zealand 100/C6
Dunedoo, N.S. Wales 97/E3
Dunellen, N.J. 273/D2
Dunes (Westlake), Oreg. 291/C4
Dunfanaghy, Ireland 17/F1
Dunfee, Ind. 227/G2
Dunfermline, Ill. 222/D3
Dunfermline, Sask. 181/D3
Dunfermline, Scotland 15/D1
Dunfermline, Scotland 10/C1
Dungalear Station, N.S. Wales 97/D1
Dungannon (dist.), N. Ireland 17/H3
Dungannon, N. Ireland 17/H3
Dungannon, Ontario 177/C4
Dungannon, Va. 307/D7
Dungarpur, India 68/C4
Dungarvan, Ireland 10/C4
Dungarvan, Ireland 17/F7
Dungarvan (harb.), Ireland 10/C4
Dungarvan (harb.), Ireland 17/G7
Dungarvon (riv.), New Bruns. 170/D2
Dungeness (pt.), Argentina 143/C7
Dungeness (pt.), Chile 138/F10
Dungeness (prom.), England 13/J7
Dungeness (prom.), England 10/G5
Dungeness, Wash. 310/B2
Dungiven, N. Ireland 17/H2
Dungloe, Ireland 17/E2
Dungog, N.S. Wales 97/F3
Dungu, Zaire 115/E3
Dungunab, Sudan 59/C5
Dungunab, Sudan 111/G3
Dunham, Québec 172/E4
Dunhua (Tunhwa), China 77/L3
Dunhuang, China 77/E3
Dunkeld, Queensland 95/D5
Dunkeld, Scotland 15/E4
Dunkeld, Victoria 97/B5
Dunkellin (riv.), Ireland 17/D5
Dunkerton, Iowa 229/J3
Dunkery (hill), England 13/D6
Dunkineely, Ireland 17/E2
Dunkirk (riv.), Alberta 182/D1
Dunkirk (Dunkerque), France 28/E2
Dunkirk, France 28/E2
Dunkirk, Ind. 227/G4
Dunkirk, N.Y. 276/B5
Dunkirk, Ohio 284/C4
Dunkley, Br. Col. 184/F3
Dunklin (co.), Mo. 261/M10
Dunkwa, Ghana 106/D7
Dún Laoghaire, Ireland 10/D4
Dún Laoghaire, Ireland 17/K5
Dunlap, Ill. 222/D3
Dunlap, Ind. 227/F1
Dunlap, Iowa 229/B5
Dunlap, Kansas 232/F3
Dunlap, Tenn. 237/L10
Dunlavin, Ireland 17/H5
Dunleath, Sask. 181/K4
Dunleer, Ireland 17/J4
Dunleith, Miss. 256/C4
Dunlow, W. Va. 312/B6
Dunloy, N. Ireland 17/J1
Dunmanus (bay), Ireland 17/B8
Dunmanway, Ireland 17/C8
Dunmanway, Ireland 10/B5
Dunmor, Ky. 237/G6
Dunmore, Alberta 182/E5
Dunmore, Ireland 17/D4
Dunmore, Pa. 294/F7
Dunmore (lake), Vt. 268/A4
Dunmore, W. Va. 312/G6
Dunmore East, Ireland 17/G7
Dunn, La. 238/G2
Dunn, N.C. 281/M4
Dunn (co.), N. Dak. 282/E5
Dunn, Texas 303/D5
Dunn (co.), Wis. 317/C6
Dunnamanagh, N. Ireland 17/G2
Dunn Center, N. Dak. 282/E5
Dunnegan, Mo. 261/E7
Dunnell, Minn. 255/D7
Dunnellon, Fla. 212/D2
Dunnet, Scotland 15/E2
Dunnet (bay), Scotland 15/E2
Dunnet (head), Scotland 10/E1
Dunnet (head), Scotland 15/E2
Dunnigan, Calif. 204/C5
Dunning, Nebr. 264/D3
Dunning, Scotland 15/E4
Dunn Loring, Va. 307/S2
Dunnottar, Manitoba 179/E4
Dunnottar, S. Africa 118/J6
Dunns, W. Va. 312/D7
Dunnsville, Va. 307/P5
Dunnville, Ky. 237/M6
Dunnville, Ontario 177/E5
Du Noir (riv.), Wyo. 319/C2
Dunolly, Victoria 97/B5
Dunoon, Scotland 15/A2
Dunoon, Scotland 10/A1
Dunphy, Nev. 266/E2
Dunragit, Scotland 15/D6
Dunrea, Manitoba 179/C5
Dunreith, Ind. 227/F5
Duns, Scotland 10/E3
Duns, Scotland 15/F5
Dunscore, Scotland 15/E5
Dunseith, N. Dak. 282/K2
Dunshaughlin, Ireland 17/H5
Dunsmuir, Calif. 204/C2
Dunstable, England 10/F5
Dunstable, England 13/G6
Dunstable•, Mass. 249/J2
Dunster, Br. Col. 184/G3
Duntochter, Scotland 15/B2
Dunure, Scotland 15/D5
Dunvegan, Nova Scotia 168/F4
Dunvegan, Scotland 15/B3
Dunvegan, Loch (inlet), Scotland 15/B3
Dunville, Newf. 166/D2
Dunwoody, Georgia 217/K1
Duo, W. Va. 312/E6
Duolun, China 77/J3
Duong Dong, Vietnam 72/D5
Du Page (co.), Ill. 222/E2
Du Page (riv.), Ill. 222/E2
Du Page, East Branch (riv.), Ill. 222/A6
Du Page, West Branch (riv.), Ill. 222/A6
Duparquet, Québec 174/B3
Duperow, Sask. 181/C4
Duplessis, La. 238/K2
Duplin (co.), N.C. 281/O5
Dupo, Ill. 222/A3
Du Pont, Georgia 217/G9
Dupont, Ind. 227/G7
Dupont, Ohio 284/B3
Dupont, Pa. 294/F7
Du Pont, Wash. 310/C3
Dupont Manor, Del. 245/R4
Dupree, S. Dak. 298/F3
Dupuis Corner, New Bruns. 170/F2
Dupuy, Québec 174/B3
Dupuyer, Mont. 262/D2
Duque de Caxias, Brazil 135/E3
Duque de York (isl.), Chile 138/C9
Duquesne, Mo. 261/D8
Duquesne, Pa. 294/C7
Duquette, Minn. 255/F4
Du Quoin, Ill. 222/D5
Duquoin, Kansas 232/D4
Dura, West Bank 65/C4
Durack (range), W. Australia 88/D3
Durağan, Turkey 63/F2
Duran, N. Mex. 274/D4
Durance (riv.), France 28/F6
Durand, Georgia 217/C5
Durand, Ill. 222/D1
Durand, Mich. 250/E6
Durand, Wis. 317/C6
Durango, Colo. 188/E3
Durango, Colo. 208/D8
Durango, Iowa 229/M3
Durango (state), Mexico 150/G4
Durango, Mexico 146/H7
Durango, Mexico 150/G4
Durango, Spain 33/E1
Duranillin, W. Australia 92/B2
Durant, Iowa 229/M5
Durant, Miss. 256/E4
Durant, Okla. 188/G4
Durant, Okla. 288/O6
Duratón (riv.), Spain 33/E2
Durazno (dept.), Uruguay 145/C3
Durazno, Uruguay 145/C4
Durazno, Grande del (range), Uruguay 145/D4
Durban, Manitoba 179/A3
Durban, S. Africa 2/L7
Durban, S. Africa 102/F7
Durban, S. Africa 118/E5
Durbanville, S. Africa 118/F6
Durbe, U.S.S.R. 53/A2
Durbin, Ind. 227/F4
Durbin, N. Dak. 282/R6
Durbin, W. Va. 312/G5
Durbuy, Belgium 27/H8
Düren, Germany 22/B3
Durfee (hill), R.I. 249/G5
Durg, India 68/E4
Durgapur, India 68/F4
Durgerdam, Netherlands 27/C4
Durham, Ark. 202/C2
Durham, Calif. 204/D4
Durham, Conn. 210/E3
Durham•, Conn. 210/E3
Durham (co.), England 13/F3
Durham, England 13/J3
Durham, England 10/F3
Durham, Kansas 232/E3
Durham, Mo. 261/J3
Durham, N.H. 268/F5
Durham•, N.H. 268/F5
Durham (pt.), N. Zealand 100/D7
Durham (co.), N.C. 281/M3
Durham, N.C. 188/L3
Durham, N.C. 281/M2
Durham, Okla. 288/G3
Durham (reg. munic.), Ontario 177/F3
Durham, Ontario 177/D3
Durham, Oreg. 291/A2
Durham Bridge, New Bruns. 170/D2
Durham Center, Conn. 210/E3
Durham Downs, Queensland 95/B5
Durham-Sud, Québec 172/E4
Durhamville, N.Y. 276/J4
Duri, N.S. Wales 97/F2
Durkee, Oreg. 291/K3
Durness, Scotland 15/D2
Durnford (pt.), Western Sahara 106/A4
Dürnten, Switzerland 39/G2
Duror, Scotland 15/C4
Durrell, Newf. 166/D4
Dürrenroth, Switzerland 39/E2
Durrës (Durazzo), Albania 45/D5
Durrës, Albania 7/F4
Durrington, England 13/F6
Durrow, Laois, Ireland 17/G6
Durrow, Offaly, Ireland 17/F5
Dursey (isl.), Ireland 17/A8
Dursunbey, Turkey 63/C3
Duruh, Iran 59/H3
Duruh, Iran 66/M4
D'Urville (isl.), N. Zealand 100/D4
Duryea, Pa. 294/F7
Dusa Marreb, Somalia 115/J2
Dûsh, Egypt 59/B5
Dûsh, Egypt 111/F3
Dushan, China 77/G6
Dushanbe, U.S.S.R. 54/H6
Dushanbe, U.S.S.R. 2/N4
Dushanbe, U.S.S.R. 48/G6
Dushore, Pa. 294/K2
Dusky (sound), N. Zealand 100/A6
Duson, La. 238/F6
Düsseldorf, Germany 7/E3
Düsseldorf, Germany 22/B3
Dustin, Okla. 288/O4
Dusty, N. Mex. 274/B5
Dusty, Wash. 310/H4
Dutch (creek), Ark. 202/C4
Dutch Cap (cay), Virgin Is. (U.S.) 161/A4
Dutchess (co.), N.Y. 276/N7
Dutch Flat, Calif. 204/E4
Dutch Harbor, Alaska 196/E4
Dutch John, Utah 304/E3
Dutch Mills, Ark. 202/B2
Dutch Neck, N.J. 273/D3
Dutchtown, Mo. 261/N8
Dutton, Ala. 195/G1
Dutton, Ark. 202/C2
Dutton (mt.), Conn. 210/C1
Dutton, Mont. 262/E3
Dutton, Ontario 177/C5
Dutton (mt.), Utah 304/B5
Duval (co.), Fla. 212/E1
Duval, Sask. 181/G4
Duval (co.), Texas 303/F10
Duvalierville, Haiti 158/C6
Duvall, Wash. 310/D3
Duvergé, Dom. Rep. 158/D6
Duvernay, Alberta 182/E3
Duwadami, Saudi Arabia 59/D5
Duxbury (pt.), Calif. 204/H2
Duxbury, Mass. 249/M4
Duxbury•, Mass. 249/M4
Duxbury•, Vt. 268/B3
Duyun (Tuyün), China 77/G6
Düzce, Turkey 63/D2
Duzdab (Zahedan), Iran 66/M6
Dvina (bay), U.S.S.R. 52/E2
Dvina, Northern (riv.), U.S.S.R. 4/C7
Dvina, Northern (riv.), U.S.S.R. 7/J2
Dvina, Northern (riv.), U.S.S.R. 48/E3
Dvina, Northern (riv.), U.S.S.R. 52/F2
Dvina, Western (riv.), U.S.S.R. 48/C4
Dvina, Western (riv.), U.S.S.R. 52/C3
Dvina, Western (riv.), U.S.S.R. 53/C2
Dvina, Western (riv.), U.S.S.R. 7/G3
Dvinsk (Daugavpils), U.S.S.R. 52/C3
Dvory nad Žitavou, Czech. 41/E3
Dvůr Králové nad Labem, Czech. 41/C1
Dwale, Ky. 237/R5
Dwarka, India 68/B4
Dwellingup, W. Australia 92/B2
Dwight, Ill. 222/E2
Dwight, Kansas 232/F3
Dwight, Nebr. 264/G3
Dwight, N. Dak. 282/S7
Dwight, Ontario 177/F2
Dworshak (res.), Idaho 220/C3
Dwyer, N. Mex. 274/B6
Dwyer, Wyo. 319/G3
Dyas, Ala. 195/C9
Dyat'kovo, U.S.S.R. 52/D4
Dybvad, Denmark 21/D3
Dyce, Scotland 15/F3
Dyckesville, Wis. 317/L6
Dycusburg, Ky. 237/E6
Dyer, Ark. 202/B3
Dyer, Ind. 227/C1
Dyer, Ky. 237/J5
Dyer, Nev. 266/C5
Dyer (cape), N.W.T. 162/K2
Dyer (cape), N.W. Terr. 187/M3
Dyer (co.), Tenn. 237/C8
Dyer, Tenn. 237/D8
Dyer Brook•, Maine 243/G3
Dyersburg, Tenn. 237/C8
Dyersville, Iowa 229/L3
Dyess, Ark. 202/K2
Dyess A.F.B., Texas 303/D5
Dyfed, Wales 13/C6
Dyje (riv.), Czech. 41/D2
Dyke (lake), Newf. 166/A3
Dykh-Tau (mt.), U.S.S.R. 52/F6
Dyle (riv.), Belgium 27/F7
Dysart, Iowa 229/J4
Dysart, Sask. 181/H5
Dysartsville, N.C. 281/F3
Dzamïn üüd, Mongolia 77/H3
Dzaoudzi (cap.), France 118/H2
Dzavhan, Mongolia 77/E2
Dzavhan Gol (riv.), Mongolia 77/D2
Dzerzhinsk, U.S.S.R. 7/J3
Dzerzhinsk, U.S.S.R. 48/E4
Dzerzhinsk, U.S.S.R. 52/F3
Dzhalal-Abad, U.S.S.R. 48/H5
Dzhalilabad, U.S.S.R. 52/G7
Dzhalinda, U.S.S.R. 48/N4
Dzhambul, U.S.S.R. 54/J5
Dzhambul, U.S.S.R. 48/H5
Dzhankoy, U.S.S.R. 52/D5
Dzhelinda, U.S.S.R. 48/M2
Dzhetygara, U.S.S.R. 48/G4
Dzhezkazgan, U.S.S.R. 54/H5
Dzhezkazgan, U.S.S.R. 48/G5
Dzhugdzhur (range), U.S.S.R. 54/P4
Dzhugdzhur (range), U.S.S.R. 48/O4
Dzhul'fa, U.S.S.R. 52/G7
Dzhusaly, U.S.S.R. 48/G5
Działdowo, Poland 47/E2
Dzibalchén, Mexico 150/P7
Dzibichaltún (ruin), Mexico 150/P6
Dzidzantún, Mexico 150/P6
Dzierżoniów, Poland 47/C3
Dzilam de Bravo, Mexico 150/P6
Dzitbalché, Mexico 150/P6
Dzurh, Mongolia 77/E2
Dzüünharaa, Mongolia 77/G2
Dzuunmod, Mongolia 77/G2

E

Eabamet (lake), Ontario 175/C2
Eads, Colo. 208/O6
Eads, Tenn. 237/B10
Eadytown, S.C. 296/G5
Eagan, Minn. 255/G6
Eagan, Tenn. 237/O7
Eagar, Ariz. 198/F4
Eagarville, Ill. 222/D4
Eagle, Alaska 188/D5
Eagle, Alaska 196/K2
Eagle (creek), Ariz. 198/F5
Eagle (lake), Calif. 204/E3
Eagle (peak), Calif. 204/E2
Eagle (co.), Colo. 208/F3
Eagle, Colo. 208/F3
Eagle (riv.), Colo. 208/E3
Eagle, Idaho 220/B6
Eagle (creek), Ind. 227/E4
Eagle (lake), Iowa 229/F2
Eagle (creek), Ky. 237/M3
Eagle (lake), Maine 243/F1
Eagle (lake), Maine 243/E3
Eagle, Mich. 250/E6
Eagle (mt.), Minn. 255/G2
Eagle, Nebr. 264/H4

Edenvale 363

Eagle (riv.), Newf. 166/C3
Eagle, Ontario 177/C5
Eagle (lake), Ontario 177/F5
Eagle (lake), Ontario 177/E2
Eagle (creek), Oreg. 291/K3
Eagle (hills), Sask. 181/C3
Eagle (peak), Texas 303/C11
Eagle (mt.), Virgin Is. (U.S.) 161/E4
Eagle, Wis. 317/H2
Eagle (lake), Wis. 317/H2
Eagle (lake), Wis. 317/K3
Eagle (peak), Wyo. 319/B1
Eagle Bay, N.Y. 276/L3
Eagle Bend, Minn. 255/D4
Eagle Bridge, N.Y. 276/O5
Eagle Butte, S. Dak. 298/G4
Eagle City, Okla. 288/J3
Eagle Crags (mt.), Calif. 204/J8
Eagle Creek, Oreg. 291/E2
Eagle Grove, Iowa 229/F3
Eagle Harbor, Md. 245/M6
Eagle Harbor, Mich. 250/A1
Eaglehawk, Victoria 97/C5
Eaglehill (creek), Sask. 181/D4
Eagle Lake, Fla. 212/E4
Eagle Lake, Maine 243/F1
Eagle Lake•, Maine 243/F1
Eagle Lake, Minn. 255/E6
Eagle Lake, Ontario 177/F2
Eagle Lake, Texas 303/H8
Eagle Mills, Ark. 202/E6
Eagle Mountain (lake), Texas 303/E2
Eagle Nest, N. Mex. 274/D2
Eagle Nest (lake), N. Mex. 274/D2
Eagle Pass, Texas 303/D9
Eagle Point, Oreg. 291/E5
Eagle River, Alaska 196/C1
Eagle River, Mich. 250/A1
Eagle River, Wis. 317/H4
Eagle Rock, Mo. 261/E9
Eagle Rock, Va. 307/J5
Eaglesfield, Scotland 15/E5
Eaglesham, Alberta 182/B2
Eaglesham, Scotland 15/D5
Eagles Mere, Pa. 294/J3
Eagle Springs, N.C. 281/K4
Eagleton Village, Tenn. 237/O9
Eagletown, Ind. 227/E4
Eagletown, Okla. 288/S6
Eagleville, Calif. 204/E2
Eagleville, Conn. 210/F1
Eagleville, Mo. 261/D2
Eagleville, Tenn. 237/H9
Eakly, Okla. 288/K4
Ealing, England 13/H8
Ealing, England 10/B5
Ear (lake), Sask. 181/B3
Earby, England 13/H1
Eardley (lake), Manitoba 179/F2
Ear Falls, Ontario 175/B2
Earl (lake), Calif. 204/A2
Earl, N.C. 281/F4
Earl, Wis. 317/C4
Earle, Ark. 202/K3
Earle Naval Weapons Sta., N.J. 273/E3
Earleton, Fla. 212/D2
Earleville, Md. 245/P3
Earl Grey, Sask. 181/G5
Earlham, Iowa 229/E6
Earlimart, Calif. 204/F8
Earling, Iowa 229/C5
Earlington, Ky. 237/F6
Earl Park, Ind. 227/C3
Earlsboro, Okla. 288/N4
Earlston, Scotland 15/F5
Earlton, Kansas 232/G4
Earlton, Ontario 177/K5
Earltown, Nova Scotia 168/E3
Earlville, Ill. 222/E2
Earlville, Iowa 229/L4
Earlville, N.Y. 276/J5
Early (co.), Georgia 217/C8
Early, Iowa 229/C4
Early Branch, S.C. 296/F6
Earlysville, Va. 307/M4
Earn, Loch (lake), Scotland 15/D4
Earn (riv.), Scotland 15/E4
Earnslaw (mt.), N. Zealand 100/B6
Earp, Calif. 204/L9
Earth, Texas 303/B3
Earthquake (lake), Mont. 262/E6
Easby, N. Dak. 282/O2
Easington, England 13/J3
Easingwold, England 13/F3
Eask (lake), Ireland 17/E2
Easky, Ireland 17/D3
Easley, S.C. 296/B2
East (cape), Alaska 196/K4
East (riv.), Conn. 210/E3
East (pt.), Fla. 212/E6
East (bay), La. 238/M8
East (pt.), Mass. 249/E6
East (range), Nev. 266/D2
East (pt.), N.S. Wales 97/J2
East (riv.), N.Y. 276/N9
East (cape), N. Zealand 87/H9
East (cape), N. Zealand 100/G2
East (bay), Nova Scotia 168/H3
East (riv.), Nova Scotia 168/F3
East (lake), Oreg. 291/F4
East (pt.), Pr. Edward I. 168/G2
East (Dezhnev) (cape), U.S.S.R. 4/C18
East (pt.), Virgin Is. (U.S.) 161/G4
Eastaboga, Ala. 195/F3
Eastabuchie, Miss. 256/F8
East Albany, Vt. 268/C2
East Alburg, Vt. 268/A2
East Aldfield, Québec 172/A4
East Alligator (riv.), North. Terr. 93/C2
East Alton, Ill. 222/A2
East Andover, Maine 243/B6
East Andover, N.H. 268/D5
East Angus, Québec 172/F4
Eastanollee, Georgia 217/F1
East Arcadia, N.C. 281/N6
East Arlington, Vt. 268/A5
East Arrow Park, Br. Col. 184/J5
East Aspetuck (riv.), Conn. 210/B2
East Aurora, N.Y. 276/C5
East Baldwin, Maine 243/B8
East Bangor, Pa. 294/M4
East Bank, W. Va. 312/D6
East Barnet, Vt. 268/C3
East Barre-Graniteville, Vt. 268/C3
East Barrington, N.H. 268/F5
East Baton Rouge (par.), La. 238/K1
East Bay, Nova Scotia 168/H2
East Bay (hills), Nova Scotia 168/H3
East Bend, N.C. 281/H2
East Berbice-Corantyne (dist.), Guyana 131/C3
East Berkshire, Vt. 268/B2
East Berlin, Conn. 210/E2
East Berlin, Pa. 294/J6
East Bernard, Texas 303/H8
East Bernstadt, Ky. 237/N6
East Berwick, Pa. 294/K3
East Bethany, N.Y. 276/D5
East Bethel, Minn. 255/E5
East Bethel, Vt. 268/B4
East Bloomfield, N.Y. 276/E5
East Blue Hill, Maine 243/G7
East Blythe, Calif. 204/L10
East Boothbay, Maine 243/D8
Eastborough, Kansas 232/E4
Eastbourne, England 13/H7
Eastbourne, England 10/G5
Eastbourne, N. Zealand 100/B3
East Brady, Pa. 294/C4
East Braintree, Manitoba 179/G5
East Braintree, Mass. 249/D8
East Braintree, Vt. 268/B3
East Branch, N.Y. 276/K7
East Branch, Rocky (riv.), Ohio 284/G10
East Brewster, Mass. 249/O5
East Brewton, Ala. 195/E8
East Bridgewater•, Mass. 249/L4
East Brisbane, Queensland 88/K3
East Brisbane, Queensland 95/E3
East Brookfield, Mass. 249/G4
East Brookfield•, Mass. 249/G4
East Brookfield, Vt. 268/C3
East Brooklyn, Conn. 210/H1
East Broughton, Québec 172/F3
East Broughton Station, Québec 172/F3
East Brownfield, Maine 243/B8
East Brunswick•, N.J. 273/E3
East Burke, Vt. 268/D2
East Butler, Pa. 294/C4
East Calais, Vt. 268/C3
East Calder, Scotland 15/D2
East Camden, Ark. 202/E6
East Canaan, Conn. 210/B1
East Candia, N.H. 268/E5
East Canton, Ohio 284/H4
East Canyon (res.), Utah 304/C3
East Cape Girardeau, Ill. 222/D6
East Carbon, Utah 304/D4
East Carondelet, Ill. 222/A3
East Carroll (par.), La. 238/H1
East Chain, Minn. 255/D7
East Charleston, Vt. 268/D2
Eastchester, N.Y. 276/P6
East Chester, Nova Scotia 168/D4
East Chevington, England 13/F2
East Chezzetcook, Nova Scotia 168/E4
East Chicago, Ind. 227/C1
East China (sea) 54/O7
East China (sea), China 77/L6
East China (sea), Japan 81/C8
East China (sea), S. Korea 81/C8
East Chop (pt.), Mass. 249/M7
East Claridon, Ohio 284/H2
East Cleveland, Ohio 284/H9
East Coast Bays, N. Zealand 100/B1
East Concord, Vt. 268/D3
East Conemaugh, Pa. 294/E5
East Corinth, Maine 243/F5
East Corinth, Vt. 268/C3
East Cote Blanche (bay), La. 238/G7
East Coulée, Alberta 182/D4
East Craftsbury, Vt. 268/C2
East Dedham, Mass. 249/C8
East Demerara-West Coast Berbice (dist.), Guyana 131/C2
East Dennis, Mass. 249/O5
East Dereham, England 13/H5
East Dereham, England 10/G4
East Derry, N.H. 268/E6
East Detroit, Mich. 250/B6
East Devils (lake), N. Dak. 282/N4
East Dixfield, Maine 243/C6
East Dixmont, Maine 243/E6
East Dorset, Vt. 268/A5
East Douglas, Mass. 249/G4
East Dover, Vt. 268/B6
East Dublin, Georgia 217/G5
East Dubuque, Ill. 222/C1
East Dundee (Dundee), Ill. 222/E1
East Durham, N.Y. 276/M6
East Eddington, Maine 243/F6
East Ellijay, Georgia 217/C1
Eastend, Sask. 181/C6
Eastend, Virgin Is. (U.S.) 161/D4
East Enterprise, Ind. 227/H7
Easter (isl.), Chile 87/Q8
Easter (isl.), Chile 2/D7
Eastern (pt.), Conn. 210/G3
Eastern (Arabian) (des.), Egypt 111/F2
Eastern (prov.), Kenya 115/G4
Eastern (bay), Md. 245/N5
Eastern (pt.), Mass. 249/M2
Eastern (creek), N.S. Wales 97/H3
Eastern Channel (str.), Japan 81/D7
Eastern Ghats (mts.), India 68/D6
Eastern Samar (prov.), Philippines 82/E5
Eastern Scheldt (est.), Netherlands 27/D5
Eastern Taurus (mts.), Turkey 63/J3
Eastern Wolf (isl.), New Bruns. 170/D4
Easterville, Manitoba 179/C1
East Fairfield, Vt. 268/B2
East Falkland (isl.), Falk. Is. 143/E7
East Falkland (isl.), Falk. Is. 120/D8
East Falmouth (Teaticket), Mass. 249/M6
East Farnham, Québec 172/E4
East Faxon, Pa. 294/J3
East Feliciana (par.), La. 238/H5
East Ferry, Nova Scotia 168/B4
East Flanders (prov.), Belgium 27/D7
East Flat Rock, N.C. 281/E4
Eastford•, Conn. 210/G1
East Fork, Little Miami (riv.), Ohio 284/C7
East Fork, Green (riv.), Wyo. 319/C3
East Foxboro, Mass. 249/K4
East Franklin, Maine 243/G6
East Franklin, Vt. 268/B2
East Freedom, Pa. 294/E5
East Freetown, Mass. 249/L5
East Friesland (reg.), Germany 22/B2
East Frisian (isls.), Germany 22/B2
East Gaffney, S.C. 296/D1
East Galesburg, Ill. 222/C3
Eastgate, Nev. 266/D3
East Georgia, Vt. 268/A2
East Germantown (Pershing), Ind. 227/G5
East Gillespie, Ill. 222/D4
East Glacier Park, Mont. 262/C2
East Glastonbury, Conn. 210/E2
East Grafton, N.H. 268/D4
East Granby•, Conn. 210/E1
East Grand Forks, Minn. 255/B3
East Grand Rapids, Mich. 250/D6
East Granville, Vt. 268/B3
East Greenbush, N.Y. 276/N5
East Green Harbour, Nova Scotia 168/C5
East Greenville, Ohio 284/G4
East Greenville, Pa. 294/L5
East Greenwich, R.I. 249/H6
East Grinstead, England 10/G5
East Grinstead, England 13/G6
Eastgulf, W. Va. 312/D7
East Gull Lake, Minn. 255/D4
East Haddam•, Conn. 210/F3
Eastham•, Mass. 249/O5
East Hampstead, N.H. 268/E6
East Hampton, Conn. 210/E2
East Hampton•, Conn. 210/E2
Easthampton•, Mass. 249/D3
East Hampton, N.Y. 276/R9
East Hanover•, N.J. 273/E2
East Hardin, Ill. 222/C4
East Hardwick, Vt. 268/C2
East Hartford•, Conn. 210/E1
East Hartland, Conn. 210/D1
East Harwich, Mass. 249/O6
East Haven•, Conn. 210/D3
East Haven•, Vt. 268/D2
East Haverhill, N.H. 268/D3
East Hazelcrest, Ill. 222/C6
East Hebron, N.H. 268/D4
East Helena, Mont. 262/E4
East Hereford, Québec 172/F4
East Hickory, Pa. 294/D2
East Hills, N.Y. 276/R7
East Hiram, Maine 243/B8
East Hodge, La. 238/E2
East Holden, Maine 243/F6
East Hope, Idaho 220/B1
East Jackson, Maine 243/E6
East Jamaica, Vt. 268/B5
East Jordan, Mich. 250/D3
East Juliette, Georgia 217/E4
East Keansburg, N.J. 273/E3
East Kelowna, Br. Col. 184/H5
East Kent, Conn. 210/B2
East Kilbride, Scotland 15/B2
East Killingly, Conn. 210/H1
East Kingsford, Mich. 250/A3
East Kingston•, N.H. 268/F6
East Knox, Maine 243/E7
East Korea (bay), N. Korea 81/D4
East Lake, Mich. 250/C4
East Lake, Minn. 255/E4
East Lake, N.C. 281/S3
Eastlake, Ohio 284/J8
East Lake-Orient Park, Fla. 212/C2
Eastland, Tenn. 237/L9
Eastland (co.), Texas 303/F5
Eastland, Texas 303/F5
East Lansdowne, Pa. 294/M7
East Lansing, Mich. 250/E6
East Laport, N.C. 281/C4
East Las Vegas, Nev. 266/F6
East Laurinburg, N.C. 281/L5
East Lebanon, Maine 243/B9
East Lee, Mass. 249/B3
Eastleigh, England 13/F7
Eastleigh, England 10/F5
East Lempster, N.H. 268/C5
East Limington, Maine 243/B8
East Linton, Scotland 15/F5
East Litchfield, Conn. 210/C1
East Livermore, Maine 243/C7
East Liverpool, Ohio 284/J4
East Loch (inlet), Hawaii 218/B3
East Loch Tarbert (inlet), Scotland 15/B3
East London, S. Africa 102/E8
East London, S. Africa 118/D6
East Longmeadow•, Mass. 249/E4
East Los Angeles, Calif. 204/C10
East Lowell, Maine 243/G5
East Lyme•, Conn. 210/G3
East Lynn, Ill. 222/F3
East Lynn, W. Va. 312/B6
East Lynn (lake), W. Va. 312/B6
East Lynne, Mo. 261/D5
East Machias, Maine 243/J6
East Machias•, Maine 243/J6
East Machias (riv.), Maine 243/H6
East Madison, Maine 243/D6
East Madison, N.H. 268/E4
Eastmain, Que. 162/J5
Eastmain, Québec 174/B2
Eastmain (riv.), Que. 146/L4
Eastmain (riv.), Que. 162/J5
Eastmain (riv.), Que. 174/B2
Eastman, Georgia 217/F6
Eastman, Québec 172/E4
Eastman, Wis. 317/D9
East Marion, N.C. 281/F3
East Meadow, N.Y. 276/R7
East Meredith, N.Y. 276/L6
East Middlebury, Vt. 268/A4
East Millcreek, Utah 304/C3
East Millinocket, Maine 243/F4
East Millinocket•, Maine 243/F4
East Millstone, N.J. 273/D3
East Milton, Mass. 249/D7
East Mines, Nova Scotia 168/E3
East Moline, Ill. 222/C2
East Montpelier•, Vt. 268/B3
East Moriches, N.Y. 276/P9
East Morris, Conn. 210/C2
East Murton, England 13/J3
East Musquash (lake), Maine 243/H5
East Naples, Fla. 212/E5
East Newark, N.J. 273/B2
East New Market, Md. 245/P6
East Newnan, Georgia 217/C4
East New Portland, Maine 243/D6
East Nishnabotna (riv.), Iowa 229/C6
East Northfield, Mass. 249/E2
East Northport, N.Y. 276/O9
East Norton, Mass. 249/K5
East Norwalk, Conn. 210/B4
East Olympia, Wash. 310/B4
Easton, Calif. 204/F7
Easton•, Conn. 210/B4
Easton (res.), Conn. 210/B3
Easton, Ill. 222/D3
Easton, Kansas 232/G2
Easton, La. 238/F5
Easton•, Maine 243/H2
Easton, Md. 245/O5
Easton•, Mass. 249/K4
Easton, Minn. 255/E7
Easton, Mo. 261/C3
Easton•, N.H. 268/D3
Easton, Pa. 294/M4
Easton, Wash. 310/D3
Easton, Wis. 317/G8
Eastondale, Mass. 249/K4
East Orange, N.J. 273/B2
East Orland, Maine 243/F6
East Orleans, Mass. 249/P5
East Otis, Mass. 249/B4
East Otisfield, Maine 243/B7
East Otto, N.Y. 276/C6
Eastover, S.C. 296/F4
East Palatka, Fla. 212/E2
East Palestine, Ohio 284/J4
East Park (res.), Calif. 204/C4
East Parsonfield, Maine 243/B8
East Peacham, Vt. 268/C3
East Pembroke, Mass. 249/M4
East Pembroke, N.Y. 276/D5
East Peoria, Ill. 222/D3
East Pepperell, Mass. 249/H2
East Peru (Peru), Iowa 229/F6
East Peru, Maine 243/C7
East Petersburg, Pa. 294/K5
East Pleasant Plain, Iowa 229/K6
Eastpoint, Fla. 212/B2
East Point, Georgia 217/K2
East Point, Ky. 237/R5
East Point, La. 238/D2
East Poland, Maine 243/C7
East Poplar, Sask. 181/F6
Eastport, Idaho 220/B1
Eastport, Maine 188/N2
Eastport, Maine 243/K6
Eastport, Mich. 250/D3
Eastport, Newf. 166/D1
Eastport, N.Y. 276/P9
East Poultney, Vt. 268/A4
East Prairie, Mo. 261/O9
East Preston, England 13/G7
East Prospect, Pa. 294/J6
East Providence, R.I. 249/J5
East Putnam, Conn. 210/H1
East Randolph, N.Y. 276/C6
East Randolph, Vt. 268/B4
East Retford, England 13/G4
East Retford, England 10/F4
East Richford, Vt. 268/B2
East Ridge, Tenn. 237/L11
Eastriggs, Scotland 15/E5
East Rindge, N.H. 268/D6
East River, Conn. 210/E3
East River Saint Marys, Nova Scotia 168/F3
East Riverside-Kingshurst, New Bruns. 170/E3
East Rochester, N.Y. 276/F4
East Rochester, Ohio 284/H4
East Rockaway, N.Y. 276/R7
East Rutherford, N.J. 273/B2
Eastry, England 13/J6
East Ryegate, Vt. 268/C3
East Saint Louis, Ill. 188/J3
East Saint Louis, Ill. 222/A2
East Sandwich, Mass. 249/N6
East Saugus, Mass. 249/D6
East Sebago, Maine 243/B8
East Selkirk, Manitoba 179/F4
East Shoal (lake), Manitoba 179/E4
East Siberian (sea), U.S.S.R. 4/B1
East Siberian (sea), U.S.S.R. 54/T2
East Siberian (sea), U.S.S.R. 48/S2
East Side, Pa. 294/L3
East Sister (peak), Idaho 220/C2
East Sister (isl.), Tasmania 99/E1
East Smithfield, Pa. 294/J2
Eastsound, Wash. 310/B2
East Sparta, Ohio 284/H4
East Spencer, N.C. 281/J3
East Springfield, N.Y. 276/L5
East Springfield, Pa. 294/A2
East Stone Gap, Va. 307/C7
East Stoneham, Maine 243/B7
East Stroudsburg, Pa. 294/M4
East Sullivan, Maine 243/G6
East Sullivan, N.H. 268/C6
East Sumner, Maine 243/C7
East Sussex (co.), England 13/H7
East Swan (riv.), Minn. 255/F3
East Swanzey, N.H. 268/C6
East Syracuse, N.Y. 276/H4
East Tawas, Mich. 250/F4
East Templeton, Mass. 249/G2
East Thermopolis, Wyo. 319/D2
East Thetford, Vt. 268/C4
East Thompson, Conn. 210/H1
East Tintic (creek), Utah 304/B4
East Tohopekaliga (lake), Fla. 212/E3
East Troy, Wis. 317/J2
East Union, Maine 243/E7
Eastvale, Pa. 294/B4
Eastvale, Texas 303/G1
East Vassalboro, Maine 243/D7
East Verde (riv.), Ariz. 198/D4
Eastview, Tenn. 237/D10
East View, W. Va. 312/F4
East Village, Conn. 210/C3
Eastville, Georgia 217/E3
Eastville, Va. 307/R6
East Wakefield, N.H. 268/E4
East Walker (riv.), Nev. 266/B4
East Wallingford, Vt. 268/B5
East Walpole, Mass. 249/C8
East Wareham, Mass. 249/M5
East Washington, Pa. 294/B5
East Waterboro, Maine 243/B8
East Waterford, Pa. 294/G5
East Wenatchee, Wash. 310/E3
East Weymouth, Mass. 249/E8
East Whately, Mass. 249/D3
East Williamson, N.Y. 276/F4
East Willington, Conn. 210/G1
East Wilton, Maine 243/C6
East Windsor•, Conn. 210/E1
East Windsor Hill, Conn. 210/E1
East Winn, Maine 243/G5
East Wolfeboro, N.H. 268/E4
Eastwood, Mich. 250/D6
Eastwood, N.S. Wales 88/K4
Eastwood, N.S. Wales 97/J3
Eastwood, Ontario 177/D4
East Woodstock, Conn. 210/H1
East Worcester, N.Y. 276/L5
East York, Ontario 177/J4
Eaton, Colo. 208/K1
Eaton, Ill. 222/F4
Eaton, Ind. 227/G4
Eaton, Maine 243/H4
Eaton (co.), Mich. 250/E6
Eaton (Eaton Center)•, N.H. 268/E4
Eaton, N.Y. 276/J5
Eaton, Ohio 284/A6
Eaton, Tenn. 237/C9
Eaton Center, N.H. 268/E4
Eaton Estates, Ohio 284/G3
Eatonia, Sask. 181/B4
Eaton Rapids, Mich. 250/E6
Eatonton, Georgia 217/F4
Eatontown, N.J. 273/E3
Eatonville, Fla. 212/E3
Eatonville, Wash. 310/C4
Eau Claire, Mich. 250/C6
Eau Claire, Pa. 294/C3
Eau Claire (lake), Québec 174/C1
Eau Claire, Lac à l' (lake), Que. 162/J4
Eau Claire (co.), Wis. 317/D6
Eau Claire, Wis. 188/H2
Eau Claire, Wis. 317/D6
Eau Claire (riv.), Wis. 317/D6
Eau Galle, Wis. 317/B6
Eauripik (atoll), Micronesia 87/E5
Ebal (mt.), Jordan 65/C3
Ebano, Mexico 150/K5
Ebb, Fla. 212/C1
Ebb and Flow (lake), Manitoba 179/C3
Ebbw Vale, Wales 13/B6
Ebbw Vale, Wales 10/E5
Ebeltoft, Denmark 21/D5
Ebeltoft, Denmark 18/G8
Ebenezer, Miss. 256/D5
Ebenezer, Sask. 181/J4
Ebenfurth, Austria 41/D3
Eben Junction, Mich. 250/B2
Ebensburg, Pa. 294/E5
Ebensee, Austria 41/B3
Eberbach, Germany 22/C4
Ebersbach, Germany 22/F3
Eberswalde-Finow, Germany 22/E2
Ebetsu, Japan 81/K2
Ebinur Hu (lake), China 77/B2
Ebnat-Kappel, Switzerland 39/H2
Eboli, Italy 34/E4
Ebolowa, Cameroon 102/D4
Ebolowa, Cameroon 115/B3
Ebon (atoll), Marshall Is. 87/G5
Ebony, Va. 307/N7
Ebor, Manitoba 179/A5
Ebrach, Germany 22/D4
Ebrié (lag.), Ivory Coast 106/D8
Ebro, Fla. 212/C6
Ebro, Minn. 255/C3
Ebro (riv.), Spain 7/D4
Ebro (riv.), Spain 33/G2
Ecatepec de Morelos, Mexico 150/L1
Ecaussinnes, Belgium 27/E7
Ecclefechan, Scotland 15/E5
Eccles, W. Va. 312/D7
Ecclesville, Trin. & Tob. 161/B11
Eceabat, Turkey 63/B6
Echallens, Switzerland 39/C3
Echarate, Peru 128/F9
Ech Cheliff (El Asnam), Algeria 106/E1
Echeconnee, Georgia 217/E5
Echmiadzin, U.S.S.R. 52/F6
Echo, Ala. 195/G8
Echo (cliffs), Ariz. 198/D2
Echo, La. 238/F4
Echo, Minn. 255/C6
Echo (lake), N.J. 273/E1
Echo, Oreg. 291/H2
Echo (lake), Tasmania 99/C4
Echo, Utah 304/C3
Echo (res.), Utah 304/C3
Echo (lake), Vt. 268/D2
Echo Bay (Port Radium), Canada 4/C15
Echo Bay (Port Radium), N.W.T. 146/G3
Echo Bay (Port Radium), N.W.T. 162/E3
Echo Bay (Port Radium), N.W.T. 187/G3
Echo Bay, Ontario 177/J5
Echo Bay, Ontario 175/D3
Echola, Ala. 195/C4
Echo Lake, N.J. 273/E1
Echo Lake, Nova Scotia 168/E4
Echols (co.), Georgia 217/G9
Echols, Ky. 237/H6
Echo Valley Prov. Park, Sask. 181/G5
Echt, Netherlands 27/H6
Echternach, Luxembourg 27/J9
Echuca, Victoria 97/C5
Echuca, Victoria 88/G7
Ecija, Spain 33/D4
Eck, Loch (lake), Scotland 15/A1
Eckelson, N. Dak. 282/O6
Eckerman, Mich. 250/E2
Eckernförde, Germany 22/D1
Eckerty, Ind. 227/D8
Eckhart Mines, Md. 245/C2
Eckley, Colo. 208/P2
Eckman, N. Dak. 282/H2
Eckman, W. Va. 312/C8
Eckville, Alberta 182/C3
Eclectic, Ala. 195/F5
Eclipse (harb.), Newf. 166/B2
Eclipse (sound), N.W. Terr. 187/L2
Economy, Ind. 227/G5
Economy, Nova Scotia 168/D3
Economy, Pa. 294/B4
Ecorce (lake), Québec 172/A2
Ecorces (riv.), Québec 172/F1
Ecorse, Mich. 250/B7
Ecrins, Les (mt.), France 28/G5
Ecru, Miss. 256/F2
Ector (co.), Texas 303/B6
Ecuador 2/D6
Ecuador 120/B3
ECUADOR 128
Ecublens, Switzerland 39/B3
Ecum Secum, Nova Scotia 168/F3
Ecum Secum Bridge, Nova Scotia 168/F4
Edam, Sask. 181/C2
Edam-Volendam, Netherlands 27/G4
Eday (isl.), Scotland 10/E1
Eday (isl.), Scotland 15/F1
Edberg, Alberta 182/D3
Edcouch, Texas 303/G11
Edd, Ethiopia 111/H5
Edd, Ethiopia 59/D7
Ed Da'ein, Sudan 111/E5
Ed Damazin, Sudan 111/F5
Ed Damer, Sudan 111/F4
Ed Damer, Sudan 59/B6
Ed Damer, Sudan 102/F3
Ed Debba, Sudan 111/F4
Ed Debba, Sudan 59/B6
Edderton, Scotland 15/D3
Eddiceton, Miss. 256/C8
Eddington, Maine 243/F6
Eddington•, Maine 243/F6
Eddington, Pa. 294/N5
Eddleston, Scotland 15/E5
Eddontenajon, Br. Col. 184/K2
Eddrachillis (bay), Scotland 15/C2
Ed Dueim, Sudan 59/B7
Ed Dueim, Sudan 111/F5
Ed Dueim, Sudan 102/F3
Eddy (co.), N. Mex. 274/E6
Eddy (co.), N. Dak. 282/N4
Eddy, Texas 303/G6
Eddystone (rocks), England 13/C7
Eddystone (rocks), England 10/D5
Eddystone, Manitoba 179/C3
Eddystone, Pa. 294/M7
Eddystone (pt.), Tasmania 88/H8
Eddystone (pt.), Tasmania 99/E2
Eddyville, Ill. 222/E6
Eddyville, Iowa 229/H6
Eddyville, Ky. 237/E6
Eddyville, Nebr. 264/E3
Eddyville, Oreg. 291/D3
Ede, Netherlands 27/H4
Ede, Nigeria 106/E7
Edéa, Cameroon 115/B3
Edelény, Hungary 41/F2
Edelstein, Ill. 222/D3
Eden, Ariz. 198/F6
Edén, Ecuador 128/E3
Eden (riv.), England 13/E3
Eden (riv.), England 10/E3
Eden, Georgia 217/K6
Eden, Idaho 220/D7
Eden, Ind. 227/F5
Eden, Manitoba 179/C4
Eden, Md. 245/R7
Eden, Miss. 256/D5
Eden, Mont. 262/E3
Eden, N.S. Wales 97/E5
Eden, N.Y. 276/C5
Eden, N.C. 281/K1
Eden (riv.), Scotland 15/F4
Eden, S. Dak. 298/P2
Eden, Texas 303/E6
Eden, Utah 304/C2
Eden•, Vt. 268/B2
Eden, Wis. 317/K8
Eden, Wyo. 319/C3
Edenburg, Sask. 181/E3
Edenburg, S. Africa 118/D5
Edendale, S. Africa 118/D5
Edenderry, Ireland 10/C4
Edenderry, Ireland 17/G5
Edenhope, Victoria 97/A5
Eden Mills, Ontario 177/D4
Eden Mills, Vt. 268/C2
Eden Prairie, Minn. 255/G6
Edenton, N.C. 281/R2
Edenton, Ohio 284/C7
Edenvale, S. Africa 118/H6

Eden Valley, Minn. 255/D5
Eden Valley (res.), Wyo. 319/C3
Edenville, Mich. 250/E5
Edenwold, Sask. 181/G5
Eder (res.), Germany 22/C3
Eder (riv.), Germany 22/C3
Ederney and Kesh, N. Ireland 17/F2
Edgar (co.), Ill. 222/F4
Edgar, Mont. 262/H5
Edgar, Nebr. 264/F4
Edgar, Wis. 317/G6
Edgard, La. 238/M3
Edgar Springs, Mo. 261/J7
Edgarton, W. Va. 312/B7
Edgartown, Mass. 249/M7
Edgartown•, Mass. 249/M7
Edge (isl.), Norway 4/B8
Edgecliff, Texas 303/E2
Edgecomb•, Maine 243/D8
Edgecombe (co.), N.C. 281/O3
Edgecumbe (cape), Alaska 196/L1
Edgecumbe, N. Zealand 100/F2
Edgefield, La. 238/D2
Edgefield (co.), S.C. 296/D4
Edgefield, S.C. 296/C4
Edge Hill, Georgia 217/G4
Edgehill, Va. 307/O4
Edgeley, N. Dak. 282/N7
Edgeley, Sask. 181/H5
Edgell (isl.), N.W. Terr. 187/M3
Edgemere, Idaho 220/C1
Edgemere, Md. 245/N4
Edgemont, Ark. 202/F2
Edgemont, N.C. 281/F2
Edgemont, S. Dak. 298/B7
Edgemoor, Del. 245/S1
Edgemoor, S.C. 296/E2
Edgeøya (isl.), Norway 18/E2
Edgerly, La. 238/C6
Edgerton, Alberta 182/E3
Edgerton, Ind. 227/H2
Edgerton, Kansas 232/H3
Edgerton, Minn. 255/B7
Edgerton, Mo. 261/C3
Edgerton, Ohio 284/A3
Edgerton, Va. 307/N7
Edgerton, Wis. 317/H10
Edgerton, Wyo. 319/F2
Edgewater, Br. Col. 184/J5
Edgewater, Colo. 208/J3
Edgewater, Fla. 212/F3
Edgewater, N.J. 273/C2
Edgewater, Wis. 317/D4
Edgewater Park•, N.J. 273/D3
Edgewood, Br. Col. 184/H5
Edgewood, Calif. 204/C2
Edgewood, Fla. 212/E3
Edgewood, Ill. 222/E5
Edgewood, Ind. 227/F4
Edgewood, Iowa 229/N4
Edgewood, Ky. 237/S2
Edgewood, Md. 245/N3
Edgewood, N. Mex. 274/C3
Edgewood, Ohio 284/J2
Edgewood, Pa. 294/B7
Edgeworth, Pa. 294/B4
Edgington, Ill. 222/C2
Edhessa, Greece 45/F5
Edievale, N. Zealand 100/B6
Edina, Minn. 255/G5
Edina, Mo. 261/H2
Edinboro, Pa. 294/B2
Edinburg, Miss. 256/F5
Edinburg, Mo. 261/E2
Edinburg, N. Dak. 282/P3
Edinburg, Pa. 294/B3
Edinburg, Texas 303/F11
Edinburg, Va. 307/M3
Edinburgh, Ind. 227/E6
Edinburgh (cap.), Scotland 7/D3
Edinburgh (cap.), Scotland 15/D1
Edinburgh (cap.), Scotland 10/C1
Edingen (Enghien), Belgium 27/D7
Edirne (prov.), Turkey 63/B2
Edirne, Turkey 7/G4
Edirne, Turkey 63/B2
Edirne, Turkey 59/A1
Edison, Calif. 204/G8
Edison (lake), Calif. 204/F6
Edison, Georgia 217/C7
Edison, Nebr. 264/E4
Edison•, N.J. 273/E2
Edison, Ohio 284/E4
Edison, Wash. 310/C2
Edison Nat'l Hist. Site, N.J. 273/A2
Edisto (isl.), S.C. 296/G6
Edisto (riv.), S.C. 296/G7
Edisto Beach, S.C. 296/G7
Edisto Island, S.C. 296/G6
Edith, Georgia 217/G9
Edithburgh, S. Australia 94/E6
Ediz Hook (pen.), Wash. 310/B2
Edjeleh, Algeria 106/F3
Edmeston, N.Y. 276/K5
Edmond, Kansas 232/C2
Edmond, Okla. 288/M3
Edmonds, Wash. 310/C3
Edmondson, Ark. 202/K3
Edmondt, Fr. Guiana 131/E3
Edmonson (co.), Ky. 237/J6
Edmonson, Texas 303/D3
Edmonston, Md. 245/F4
Edmonton (cap.), Alberta 182/D3
Edmonton (cap.), Alta. 146/G4
Edmonton (cap.), Alta. 162/E5
Edmonton, Canada 2/D3
Edmonton, Ky. 237/K7
Edmonton Beach, Alberta 182/C3
Edmore, Mich. 250/E6
Edmore, N. Dak. 282/O3
Edmore, Sask. 181/H4
Edmund, Wis. 317/F9
Edmunds, Maine 243/J6
Edmunds, N. Dak. 282/M5
Edmunds (co.), S. Dak. 298/L3
Edmundson, Mo. 261/O2
Edmundston, N. Br. 162/K6

Edmundston, New Bruns. 170/B1
Edna, Ala. 195/B6
Edna, Iowa 229/A2
Edna, Kansas 232/G4
Edna, Texas 303/H9
Edna Bay, Alaska 196/M2
Edo (riv.), Japan 81/P2
Edolo, Italy 34/C1
Edom, Texas 303/J5
Edon, Ohio 284/A2
Edouard (lake), Québec 172/E2
Edrans, Manitoba 179/C4
Edray, W. Va. 312/F6
Edremit, Turkey 63/B3
Edremit, Turkey 59/A2
Edremit (gulf), Turkey 63/B3
Edri, Libya 111/B2
Edsbyn, Sweden 18/J6
Edson, Alberta 182/B3
Edson, Alta. 162/E5
Edson, Kansas 232/A2
Eduardo Castex, Argentina 143/D4
Edwall, Wash. 310/H3
Edwand, Alberta 182/D2
Edward (lake) 102/E5
Edward, N.C. 281/R4
Edward (lake), Uganda 115/E4
Edward (lake), Zaire 115/E4
Edward MacDowell (res.), N.H. 268/D6
Edwards, Colo. 208/F3
Edwards (co.), Ill. 222/E5
Edwards, Ill. 222/D3
Edwards (riv.), Ill. 222/C2
Edwards (co.), Kansas 232/C4
Edwards (lake), La. 238/C2
Edwards, Miss. 256/C6
Edwards, Mo. 261/F6
Edwards, N.Y. 276/K2
Edwards (co.), Texas 303/D7
Edwards (plat.), Texas 303/C7
Edwards A.F.B., Calif. 204/H9
Edwardsburg, Mich. 250/E7
Edwardsport, Ind. 227/C7
Edwardsville, Ala. 195/H3
Edwardsville, Ill. 222/B3
Edwardsville, Ill. 227/F8
Edwardsville, Kansas 232/H2
Edwardsville, Pa. 294/E7
Edward VII (pen.), Ant. 5/B11
Edward VIII (bay), Ant. 5/C4
Edwight, W. Va. 312/C7
Edwin, Ala. 195/H7
Edwin, Manitoba 179/D5
Edzell, Scotland 15/F4
Eefde, Netherlands 27/J4
Eek, Alaska 196/F2
Eeklo, Belgium 27/D6
Eel (riv.), Calif. 204/B4
Eel (riv.), Ind. 227/C6
Eel (riv.), Ind. 227/F3
Eel River Bridge, New Bruns. 170/F1
Eel River Crossing, New Bruns. 170/D1
Eems (riv.), Netherlands 27/K2
Eersterivier, S. Africa 118/F6
Efate (isl.), Vanuatu 87/G7
Eferding, Austria 41/B2
Effie, La. 238/F4
Effie, Minn. 255/E3
Effigy Mounds Nat'l Mon., Iowa 229/L2
Effingham (co.), Georgia 217/K6
Effingham (co.), Ill. 222/E4
Effingham, Ill. 222/E4
Effingham, Kansas 232/G2
Effingham, S.C. 296/F5
Effingham Falls, N.H. 268/E4
Effort, Pa. 294/M4
Efland, N.C. 281/L2
Eflâni, Turkey 63/E2
Egadi (isls.), Italy 34/C6
Egan, Ill. 222/D1
Egan (range), Nev. 266/G4
Egan, S. Dak. 298/R6
Egaña, Uruguay 145/B4
Eganville, Ontario 177/G2
Egbert, Wyo. 319/H4
Ege, Ind. 227/G2
Egegik, Alaska 196/G3
Egeland, N. Dak. 282/M2
Eger, Hungary 41/F3
Egeria, W. Va. 312/D7
Egernsund, Denmark 21/C8
Egerton (mt.), W. Australia 92/B4
Egg (isl.), Manitoba 179/E3
Egg (creek), N. Dak. 282/H3
Egg, Switzerland 39/G2
Eggenburg, Austria 41/C2
Eggertsville, N.Y. 276/C5
Egg Harbor, Wis. 317/M6
Egg Harbor City, N.J. 273/D4
Egg Island (pt.), N.J. 273/C5
Eggiwil, Switzerland 39/E3
Egg Lagoon, Tasmania 99/A1
Eggleston, Va. 307/G6
Egham, England 13/G8
Egham, England 10/B5
Eghezée, Belgium 27/F7
Egilsay (isl.), Scotland 15/F1
Eglin A.F.B., Fla. 212/C4
Eglington (isl.), N.W.T. 162/G1
Eglinton (cape), N.W. Terr. 187/M2
Eglinton (isl.), N.W. Terr. 187/F2
Eglisau, Switzerland 39/G1
Eglon, W. Va. 312/G4
Egmond aan Zee, Netherlands 27/E3
Egmondville, Ontario 177/C4
Egmont (key), Fla. 212/D4
Egmont (cape), N. Zealand 100/D3
Egmont (mt.), N. Zealand 100/D3
Egmont (cape), Nova Scotia 168/H2
Egmont (bay), Pr. Edward I. 168/D2
Egmont (cape), Pr. Edward I. 168/D2
Egnach, Switzerland 39/H1
Egnar, Colo. 208/B7
Egremont, Alberta 182/D2
Egremont, England 13/D3
Eğridir, Turkey 63/D4
Eğridir (lake), Turkey 59/B2

Eğridir (lake), Turkey 63/D4
Egtved, Denmark 21/C6
Egvekinot, U.S.S.R. 48/S3
Egyek, Hungary 41/F3
Egypt 2/L4
Egypt 102/E2
EGYPT 111/E2
EGYPT 59/A4
Egypt, Georgia 217/K6
Egypt, Miss. 256/G3
Egypt Lake, Fla. 212/C2
Eha Amufu, Nigeria 106/F7
Ehime (pref.), Japan 81/F7
Ehingen, Germany 22/C4
Ehrenberg (range), North. Terr. 93/B7
Ehrenburg, Ariz. 198/A5
Ehrenfeld, Pa. 294/E5
Ehrhardt, S.C. 296/E5
Ehrwald, Austria 41/A3
Eiao (isl.), Fr. Poly. 87/M6
Eibar, Spain 33/E1
Eichstätt, Germany 22/D4
Eider (riv.), Germany 22/C1
Eidfjord, Norway 18/E6
Eidsfoss, Norway 18/C4
Eidson, Tenn. 237/P7
Eidsvold, Queensland 95/D5
Eidsvoll, Norway 18/G6
Eielson A.F.B., Alaska 196/J2
Eigenbrakel (Braine-l'Alleud), Belgium 27/E7
Eigersund, Norway 18/D7
Eigg (mt.), Nova Scotia 168/F3
Eigg (isl.), Scotland 15/B4
Eigg (isl.), Scotland 10/C2
Eigg (sound), Scotland 15/B4
Eight Degree (chan.), India 68/C7
Eighteen Mile (peak), Idaho 220/E5
Eight Mile (brook), Conn. 210/C3
Eight Mile (riv.), Conn. 210/F3
Eights Coast (reg.), Ant. 5/B14
Eighty Eight, Ky. 237/K7
Eighty Mile (beach), W. Australia 88/C3
Eighty Mile (beach), W. Australia 92/C2
Eijerlandsche Gat (str.), Netherlands 27/F2
Eil, Loch (lake), Scotland 15/C4
Eil, Somalia 115/J2
Eildon, Victoria 97/C5
Eildon (lake), Victoria 97/C5
Eileen (lake), N.W.T. 162/F3
Eilenburg, Germany 22/E3
Eilerts de Haan (mts.), Suriname 131/C4
Eina, Norway 18/G6
Einbeck, Germany 22/C3
Eindhoven, Netherlands 27/G6
'Ein Gedi, Israel 65/C5
'Ein Harod, Israel 65/C2
'Ein Netafim (well), Israel 65/D5
Einsiedeln, Switzerland 39/G2
Eirunepé, Brazil 132/G10
Eirunepé, Brazil 120/B3
Eisenach, Germany 22/D3
Eisenberg, Germany 22/D3
Eisenerz, Austria 41/C3
Eisenhower (mt.), Alberta 182/C4
Eisenhüttenstadt, Germany 22/F2
Eisenkappel-Vellach, Austria 41/C3
Eisenstadt, Austria 41/D3
Eishort (inlet), Scotland 15/B3
Eisleben, Germany 22/D3
Eisling (mts.), Luxembourg 27/H9
Eitzen, Minn. 255/G7
Ejby, Denmark 21/C7
Ejea de los Caballeros, Spain 33/F1
Ejido, Venezuela 124/C3
Ejin, China 77/F3
Ejin Horo, China 77/H4
Ejutla de Crespo, Mexico 150/L8
Ekalaka, Mont. 262/M5
Ekenäs, Finland 18/N6
Ekeren, Belgium 27/E6
Eketahuna, N. Zealand 100/E4
Ekibastuz, U.S.S.R. 48/H4
Ekibin, Queensland 88/K3
Ekimchan, U.S.S.R. 48/O4
Ekin, Ind. 227/E4
Ekonk, Conn. 210/H2
Ekron, Ky. 237/J5
Eksjö, Sweden 18/J8
Ekuk, Alaska 196/G3
Ekwan (riv.), Ont. 162/H5
Ekwan (riv.), Ontario 175/C2
Ekwok, Alaska 196/G3
El Aaiún (Laayoune), Western Sahara 102/A2
El Aaiún (Laayoune), Western Sahara 106/B3
El Abiar, Libya 111/D1
El Abbasiya, Sudan 111/F5
El Abiod Sidi Cheikh, Algeria 106/E2
El Agheila, Libya 111/C1
Elaine, Ark. 202/J5
El 'Al, Jordan 65/D4
El 'Alamein, Egypt 111/E1
El 'Alamein, Egypt 59/A3
El Almacén, Venezuela 124/G4
El Amparo de Apure, Venezuela 124/C4
Elams, N.C. 281/O1
Elamton, Ky. 237/P5
Elamville, Ala. 195/G7
Eland, Wis. 317/H6
El Angel, Ecuador 128/C2
El Arahal, Spain 33/D4
El 'Arish, Egypt 59/B3
El 'Arish, Egypt 111/F1
El Asiento, Bolivia 136/B6
Elassón, Greece 45/F6
Elat, Israel 65/D6
Elath (Elat), Israel 65/D6
Elath, Israel 59/B4
El Athale (Itala), Somalia 115/J3
Elato (atoll), Micronesia 87/E5
El 'Atrun (oasis), Sudan 111/E4
El 'Auja, Egypt 59/B3
Elâzığ (prov.), Turkey 63/H3
Elâzığ, Turkey 59/C2

Elâzığ, Turkey 63/H3
El Azizia, Libya 111/B1
El Azúcar (res.), Mexico 150/K3
Elba, Ala. 195/F8
Elba, Idaho 220/E7
Elba (isl.), Italy 7/E4
Elba (isl.), Italy 34/C3
Elba, Minn. 255/F6
Elba, Nebr. 264/F3
Elba, N.Y. 276/D4
Elba, Ohio 284/H6
El Bab, Syria 63/G4
El Balga (dist.), Jordan 65/D4
El Banco, Colombia 126/D3
El Barco, Spain 33/C1
El Barco de Ávila, Spain 33/D2
El Bardi, Libya 111/B3
El Barkat, Libya 111/B3
El Baúl, Venezuela 124/D3
El Bawiti, Egypt 111/E2
El Bawiti, Egypt 102/E2
El Bawiti, Egypt 59/A4
El Bayadh, Algeria 106/E2
El Bayadh, Algeria 102/C1
El Beida, Yemen 59/E7
El Beni (dept.), Bolivia 136/C3
Elberfeld, Ind. 227/C8
Elberon, Iowa 229/J4
Elberon, N.J. 273/F3
Elberon, Va. 307/P6
Elbert (mt.), Colo. 188/E3
Elbert (co.), Colo. 208/G4
Elbert, Colo. 208/L4
Elbert, Colo. 208/G4
Elbert (co.), Georgia 217/G2
Elbert, Texas 303/F5
Elbert, W. Va. 312/C8
Elberta, Georgia 217/E5
Elberta, Mich. 250/C4
Elberta, Utah 304/D4
Elberton, Georgia 217/G2
Elberton, Wash. 310/H4
Elbeuf, France 28/D3
Elbing, Kansas 232/E3
Elbing (Elbląg), Poland 47/D1
El Bira, West Bank 65/C4
Elbistan, Turkey 63/G3
Elbląg (prov.), Poland 47/D1
Elbląg, Poland 47/D1
Elbląg, Poland 7/F3
El Bolsón, Argentina 143/B5
El Bonillo, Spain 33/E3
El Boquerón (pass), Peru 128/E7
El Borma, Tunisia 106/F2
Elbow (riv.), Alberta 182/C4
Elbow (lake), Manitoba 179/G4
Elbow (lake), Minn. 255/C3
Elbow, Sask. 181/E4
Elbow Lake, Minn. 255/B5
Elbridge, N.Y. 276/G5
Elbridge, Tenn. 237/C8
El'brus (mt.), U.S.S.R. 7/J4
El'brus (mt.), U.S.S.R. 52/F6
Elburz (mts.), Iran 59/F2
Elburz (mts.), Iran 66/G2
El Burgo de Osma, Spain 33/E2
Elburn, Ill. 222/E2
Elburz (mts.), Iran 59/F2
El Cajon, Calif. 204/J11
El Callao, Venezuela 124/G4
El Calvario, Venezuela 124/E3
El Campo, Texas 303/H8
El Caney, Cuba 158/J4
El Carmen, El Beni, Bolivia 136/D3
El Carmen, Santa Cruz, Bolivia 136/F6
El Carmen, Bíobío, Chile 138/A11
El Carmen, O'Higgins, Chile 138/F5
El Carmen, Chocó, Colombia 126/B5
El Carmen, Nariño, Colombia 126/A6
El Carmen, Norte de Santander, Colombia 126/D3
El Carmen de Bolívar, Colombia 126/C3
El Carre, Ethiopia 111/H6
El Centro, Calif. 188/C4
El Centro, Calif. 204/K11
El Centro, Colombia 126/D4
El Cercado, Dom. Rep. 158/D6
El Cerrito, Calif. 204/J2
El Cerrito, Colombia 126/B6
El Cerro, Bolivia 136/E5
El Chaparro, Venezuela 124/F3
Elche, Spain 33/F3
Elche de la Sierra, Spain 33/E3
El Chichón (vol.), Mexico 150/O8
El Chocó (isl.), North. Terr. 93/D1
Elcho, Wis. 317/H5
El Chocón (res.), Argentina 143/C4
Elcho Island Mission, North. Terr. 93/D1
El Choro, Bolivia 136/B6
El Chorro, Argentina 143/D1
Elco, Ill. 222/D6
El Cobre, Chile 138/A4
El Cobre, Cuba 158/J4
El Cocuy, Colombia 126/D4
El Convento, Chile 138/F4
El Corazón, Ecuador 128/C3
El Cristo, Venezuela 124/G4
El Cuey, Dom. Rep. 158/F6
El Cuy, Argentina 143/C4
Elda, Spain 33/F3
El Dara, Ill. 222/C4
Elde (riv.), Germany 22/D2
Eldén (mt.), Ariz. 198/D3
El Der, Ethiopia 111/H6
Elderbank, Nova Scotia 168/G4
El Dere, Somalia 115/J3
El Dere, Somalia 102/G4
Elderon, Wis. 317/H6
Eldersburg, Md. 245/L3

Eldersley, Sask. 181/H3
Elderslie, Scotland 15/B2
Eldersville, Pa. 294/A5
Elderton, Pa. 294/C4
El Diente (peak), Colo. 208/C7
El'dikan, U.S.S.R. 48/O3
Eldivan, Turkey 63/E2
El Diviso, Colombia 126/A7
El Djem, Tunisia 106/G1
El Djezair (Algiers) (cap.), Algeria 106/E1
El Djouf (des.) 102/B2
Eldon, Iowa 229/A7
Eldon, Mo. 261/G6
Eldon, Wash. 310/B3
Eldora, Colo. 208/H3
Eldora, Iowa 229/G4
Eldora, N.J. 273/D5
El Dorado, Ark. 188/H4
El Dorado, Ark. 202/E7
Eldorado, Brazil 135/B4
El Dorado (co.), Calif. 204/E5
El Dorado, Calif. 204/C8
Eldorado (Fender), Georgia 217/E8
Eldorado, Ill. 222/E6
Eldorado, Iowa 229/K2
El Dorado, Kansas 232/F4
Eldorado, Md. 245/P6
Eldorado, Mexico 150/E4
Eldorado, Miss. 256/C5
El Dorado, N.C. 281/K4
Eldorado, Ohio 284/A6
Eldorado, Okla. 288/G6
Eldorado, Sask. 181/L2
Eldorado, Texas 303/D7
El Dorado, Venezuela 124/H4
Eldorado, Wis. 317/J8
El Dorado Hills, Calif. 204/C8
El Dorado Springs, Mo. 261/E7
Eldorendo, Georgia 217/C8
Eldoret, Kenya 102/F4
Eldoret, Kenya 115/G3
Eldred, Ill. 222/C4
Eldred, Minn. 255/B3
Eldred, Pa. 294/F2
El Dulce Nombre, Honduras 154/D1
Eleanor, W. Va. 312/C5
Electra, Texas 303/F5
Electric (peak), Mont. 262/F6
Electric City, Wash. 310/F3
Electric Mills, Miss. 256/G5
Electron, Wash. 310/C4
Elefantes (gulf), Chile 138/D6
Elek, Hungary 41/F3
Elektrostal', U.S.S.R. 7/H3
Elektrostal', U.S.S.R. 52/E3
El Empedrado, Venezuela 124/C3
Elena, Bulgaria 45/G4
Elephant (isl.), Ant. 5/D16
Elephant (riv.), Namibia 118/B5
Elephant (mt.), Texas 303/D12
Elephanta (isl.), India 68/B7
Elephant Butte, N. Mex. 274/C4
Elephant Butte (res.), N. Mex. 188/E4
Elephant Butte (res.), N. Mex. 274/B5
Eleroy, Ill. 222/D1
Eleskirt, Turkey 63/K3
El Espinar, Spain 33/D2
El Estor, Guatemala 154/C3
Eleuthera (isl.), Bahamas 146/L7
Eleuthera (isl.), Bahamas 156/C1
Eleva, Wis. 317/D6
Eleven Mile Canyon (res.), Colo. 208/H5
Elevtheroúpolis, Greece 45/G5
El Faiyûm, Egypt 111/J3
El Faiyûm, Egypt 59/B4
El Faiyûm, Egypt 102/E2
El Fasher, Sudan 111/E5
El Fasher, Sudan 102/E3
El Fashn, Egypt 111/J4
El Ferrol, Spain 7/D4
El Ferrol, Spain 32/B1
El Fifi, Sudan 111/D5
El Fogaha, Libya 111/C2
Elfrida, Ariz. 198/F7
Elfros, Sask. 181/H4
El Fuerte, Mexico 150/D4
El Furat (riv.), Syria 63/H4
El Gallo, Nicaragua 154/E4
El Gatrun, Libya 111/B3
El Gatrun, Libya 102/D2
El Geneina, Sudan 111/D5
El Geneina, Sudan 102/E3
El Geteina, Sudan 111/F5
El Geteina, Sudan 59/B7
El Gezira (prov.), Sudan 111/F5
El Gezira, Libya 111/D2
Elgg, Switzerland 39/G2
El Gheria esh Shergia, Libya 111/B1
El Ghor (reg.), Jordan 65/C6
Elgin, Ariz. 198/E7
El Cobre, Chile 138/A4
Elgin, Ill. 146/J2
Elgin, Ill. 222/E1
Elgin, Iowa 229/K3
Elgin, Kansas 232/F5
Elgin, Manitoba 179/B5
Elgin, Minn. 255/F6
Elgin, Nev. 266/G5
Elgin, New Bruns. 170/E3
Elgin, N. Dak. 282/G7
Elgin, Ohio 284/A4
Elgin, Okla. 288/K5
Elgin, Oreg. 291/K2
Elgin, Pa. 294/C2
Elgin, Scotland 10/E2
Elgin, Scotland 15/E3

Elgin, S.C. 296/F3
Elgin, Tenn. 237/M8
Elgin, Texas 303/G7
El Golea, Algeria 102/C1
El Goléa, Algeria 106/E2
Elgon (mt.) 102/F4
Elgon (mt.), Kenya 115/F3
Elgon (mt.), Uganda 115/F3
Elgood, W. Va. 312/E8
El Granada, Calif. 204/H3
El Guapo, Venezuela 124/F2
El Guayabo, Dom. Rep. 158/E5
El Hamad (des.), Iraq 59/D3
El Hammam, Egypt 111/E1
El Hammam, Egypt 59/A3
El Hamurre, Somalia 115/J2
El Haseke, Syria 59/D2
El Haseke, Syria 63/J4
El Hilla, Sudan 111/E5
El Huecu, Argentina 143/B4
El Husn, Jordan 65/D3
Eli, Nebr. 264/C2
Elias, Ky. 237/O6
Elida, N. Mex. 274/F5
Elida, Ohio 284/B4
Elie, Manitoba 179/E5
Elie and Earlsferry, Scotland 15/F4
Elihu, Ky. 237/M6
Elijah, Mo. 261/H9
Elila (riv.), Zaire 115/E4
Elim, Alaska 196/F2
Elimsport, Pa. 294/H3
El Indio, Texas 303/D9
Eling, England 13/F7
Elin Pelin, Bulgaria 45/F4
Eliot•, Maine 243/B9
Eliot (mt.), Newf. 166/B2
Elisa, Argentina 143/F5
Eliska, Ala. 195/C8
El Iskandariya (Alexandria), Egypt 59/A3
El Iskandariya (Alexandria), Egypt 111/J2
Elista, U.S.S.R. 7/J4
Elista, U.S.S.R. 48/E5
Elista, U.S.S.R. 52/F5
Elizabeth, Ark. 202/F5
Elizabeth, Colo. 208/K4
Elizabeth, Georgia 217/J1
Elizabeth, Ill. 222/C1
Elizabeth, Ind. 227/F8
Elizabeth, La. 238/D4
Elizabeth (cape), Maine 243/C9
Elizabeth (isls.), Mass. 249/L7
Elizabeth, Minn. 255/B4
Elizabeth, Miss. 256/C4
Elizabeth (mt.), New Bruns. 170/D1
Elizabeth, N.J. 273/E2
Elizabeth, Pa. 294/C5
Elizabeth, S. Australia 88/E7
Elizabeth, W. Australia 94/B7
Elizabeth City, N.C. 281/S2
Elizabethton, Tenn. 237/S8
Elizabethton, Ill. 222/E6
Elizabethtown, Ind. 227/F6
Elizabethtown, Ky. 237/K5
Elizabethtown, N.Y. 276/N2
Elizabethtown, Ohio 284/A9
Elizabethtown, N.C. 281/M5
Elizabethville, Pa. 294/J4
Elizaville, Ind. 227/E4
Elizaville, Ky. 237/O4
Elizondo, Spain 33/F1
El Jadida, Morocco 102/B1
El Jadida, Morocco 106/C2
El Jauf, Libya 102/B1
El Jauf, Libya 111/D3
El Jicaral, Nicaragua 154/D4
El Jícaro, Nicaragua 154/E4
Elk (riv.), Ala. 195/D1
Elk (riv.), Br. Col. 184/K5
Elk, Calif. 204/B4
Elk (riv.), Colo. 208/F1
Elk (co.), Kansas 232/F4
Elk (riv.), Kansas 232/F4
Elk (isl.), Manitoba 179/F4
Elk, Md. 245/P3
Elk (lake), Mich. 250/D4
Elk, N. Mex. 274/D6
Elk (creek), Okla. 288/H4
Elk (creek), Oreg. 291/H5
Elk (co.), Pa. 294/E3
Elk, Poland 47/F2
Elk (creek), S. Dak. 298/C5
Elk (riv.), Tenn. 237/H10
Elk (ridge), Utah 304/E6
Elk, Wash. 310/H2
Elk (riv.), W. Va. 312/D6
Elkader, Iowa 229/L3
Elk Bath, Sudan 59/B7
El Karak (dist.), Jordan 65/E5
El Karak, Jordan 59/C3
El Karak, Jordan 65/E4
El Karnak, Egypt 111/F2
El Karnak, Egypt 59/B4
Elkatawa, Ky. 237/P5
Elk City, Idaho 220/C4
Elk City, Kansas 232/G4
Elk City (lake), Kansas 232/F4
Elk City, Okla. 288/G4
Elk City, Oreg. 291/D3
Elk Creek, Calif. 204/C4
Elk Creek, Mo. 261/H8
Elk Creek, Nebr. 264/H4
Elk Creek, W. Va. 307/F9
Elk Creek, Wis. 317/C7
El Kef, Tunisia 106/F1
El Kelaa des Srarhna, Morocco 106/C2
Elk Falls, Kansas 232/F4
Elkford, Br. Col. 184/K5
Elk Garden, Va. 307/F2
Elk Garden, W. Va. 312/H4
Elk Grove, Calif. 204/B9
Elk Grove Village, Ill. 222/B5

Engelhard 365

El Khalil (Hebron), West Bank 65/C4
El Khandaq, Sudan 59/B6
El Khandaq, Sudan 111/E4
El Khârga, Egypt 111/F2
El Khârga, Egypt 102/E2
El Khârga, Egypt 59/B4
Elkhart, Ill. 222/D3
Elkhart (co.), Ind. 227/F1
Elkhart, Ind. 188/J2
Elkhart, Ind. 227/F1
Elkhart (riv.), Ind. 227/F1
Elkhart, Iowa 229/F5
Elkhart, Kansas 232/A4
Elkhart, Texas 303/J6
Elkhart Lake, Wis. 317/L8
Elkhead, Mo. 261/G8
Elk Horn, Iowa 229/C5
Elkhorn, Manitoba 179/A5
Elkhorn, Nebr. 264/H3
Elkhorn (riv.), Nebr. 264/G3
Elkhorn, W. Va. 312/D8
Elkhorn, Wis. 317/J10
Elkhorn City, Ky. 237/S6
Elkhovo, Bulgaria 45/H4
Elkhurst, W. Va. 312/D6
Elkin, N.C. 281/H2
Elkins, Ark. 202/C1
Elkins, N. Mex. 274/E5
Elkins, W. Va. 312/G5
Elkinsville, Ind. 227/E6
Elk Island Nat'l Park, Alberta 182/D3
Elk Island Nat'l Pk., Alta 162/E5
El Kitta, Jordan 65/D3
Elk Lake, Ontario 177/K5
Elk Lake, Ontario 175/D3
Elk Lakes Prov. Park, Br. Col. 184/K5
Elkland, Mo. 261/F8
Elkland, Pa. 294/H1
Elk Mills, Md. 245/P2
Elkmont, Ala. 195/E1
Elkmont, Tenn. 237/O9
Elk Mound, Wis. 317/C6
Elk Mountain, Wyo. 319/F4
Elk Neck, Md. 245/P2
Elko, Br. Col. 184/K5
Elko, Georgia 217/E6
Elko, Minn. 255/E6
Elko (co.), Nev. 266/F1
Elko, Nev. 188/C2
Elko, Nev. 146/G6
Elko, Nev. 266/F2
Elko, S.C. 296/E5
Elk Park, N.C. 281/E2
Elk Point, Alberta 182/E3
Elk Point, S. Dak. 298/R8
Elkport, Iowa 229/L3
Elk Rapids, Mich. 250/D4
Elkridge, Md. 245/M4
Elkridge, W. Va. 312/D6
Elk River, Idaho 220/B3
Elk River, Minn. 255/E5
Elk Run Heights, Iowa 229/J4
Elk Springs, Colo. 208/C2
Elkton, Alberta 182/C4
Elkton, Fla. 212/E2
Elkton, Ky. 237/G7
Elkton, Md. 245/P2
Elkton, Mich. 250/F5
Elkton, Minn. 255/F7
Elkton, Mo. 261/F7
Elkton, Oreg. 291/D4
Elkton, S. Dak. 298/S5
Elkton, Tenn. 237/H10
Elkton, Va. 307/L4
Elk Valley, Tenn. 237/N7
Elkview, W. Va. 312/C6
Elkville, Ill. 222/D6
Elkwater, Alberta 182/E5
Elkwater, W. Va. 312/G5
Ellabell, Georgia 217/K6
El Ladhiqiya (Latakia), Syria 59/C2
El Ladhiqiya (Latakia), Syria 63/F5
El Lago, Texas 303/K2
Ellamar, Alaska 196/D1
Ellamore, W. Va. 312/F5
Ellaville, Fla. 212/C1
Ellaville, Georgia 217/D6
Ellef Ringnes (isl.), Canada 4/B15
Ellef Ringnes (isl.), N.W.T. 146/H2
Ellef Ringnes (isl.), N.W.T. 162/M3
Ellef Ringnes (isl.), N.W.T. 187/H2
Ellen (mt.), Utah 304/D5
Ellen (mt.), Vt. 268/B3
Ellenboro, N.C. 281/F4
Ellenboro, W. Va. 312/D4
Ellenboro, Wis. 317/E10
Ellenburg Center, N.Y. 276/N1
Ellenburg Depot, N.Y. 276/N1
Ellendale, Del. 245/S5
Ellendale, Minn. 255/E7
Ellendale, N. Dak. 282/N7
Ellendale, Tasmania 99/C4
Ellendale, Tenn. 237/B10
Ellendale, W. Australia 92/D2
Ellensburg, Wash. 310/E3
Ellenton, Georgia 217/E8
Ellenville, N.Y. 276/M7
Ellenwood, Georgia 217/L2
Ellerbe, N.C. 281/K4
Ellershouse, Nova Scotia 168/D4
Ellerslie, Georgia 217/C5
Ellerslie, Md. 245/C2
Ellerslie, N. Zealand 100/C1
Ellerslie, Pr. Edward I. 168/D2
Ellerton, Barbados 161/B9
Ellerton, Md. 245/H2
Ellery, Ill. 222/E5
Ellesmere (isl.), Canada 4/B14
Ellesmere (isl.), Canada 2/F1
Ellesmere, England 13/E5
Ellesmere (lake), N. Zealand 100/D5
Ellesmere (isl.), N.W.T. 146/K1
Ellesmere (isl.), N.W.T. 162/N3
Ellesmere (isl.), N.W. Terr. 187/K2
Ellesmere Island Nat'l Pk. Res., N.W.T. 162/N3
Ellesmere Island Nat'l Pk. Res., N.W.T. 187/L1
Ellesmere Port, England 13/G2
Ellesmere Port, England 10/F2
Ellettsville, Ind. 227/D6
Ellezelles, Belgium 27/D7
El Libertador General Bernardo O'Higgins (reg.), Chile 138/A10
Ellice (riv.), N.W. Terr. 187/H3
Ellicott City, Md. 245/L3
Ellicottville, N.Y. 276/C6
Ellijay, Georgia 217/C1
El Limón, Nicaragua 154/E4
Ellington•, Conn. 210/F1
Ellington, Mo. 261/L8
Ellington, N.Y. 276/B6
Ellington A.F.B., Texas 303/K2
Ellinwood, Kansas 232/D3
Elliot (lake), Manitoba 179/G2
Elliot, S. Africa 118/D6
Elliot Lake, Ontario 177/B1
Elliot Lake, Ontario 175/D3
Elliott, Ark. 202/E7
Elliott (key), Fla. 212/F6
Elliott, Ill. 222/E3
Elliott, Iowa 229/C6
Elliott (co.), Ky. 237/P4
Elliott, Md. 245/P7
Elliott, Miss. 256/E3
Elliott, N. Dak. 282/P7
Elliott, North. Terr. 88/E3
Elliott, North. Terr. 93/C4
Elliott, S.C. 296/G3
Elliott, Tasmania 99/B3
Elliott (bay), Tasmania 99/B5
Elliottsburg, Pa. 294/H5
Elliottville, Ky. 237/P4
Ellis, Idaho 220/D5
Ellis (co.), Kansas 232/C3
Ellis, Kansas 232/C3
Ellis (pond), Maine 243/B6
Ellis (riv.), Maine 243/B6
Ellis (riv.), N.H. 268/E3
Ellis (co.), Okla. 288/G2
Ellis (co.), Texas 303/H5
El Lisan (pen.), Jordan 65/C5
Ellisburg, N.Y. 276/H3
Ellis Grove, Ill. 222/D5
Ellison Bay, Wis. 317/M5
Elliston, Mont. 262/D4
Elliston, Newf. 166/D2
Elliston, Ohio 284/D2
Elliston, S. Australia 88/E6
Elliston, S. Australia 94/D5
Elliston-Lafayette, Va. 307/H6
Ellisville, Ill. 222/C3
Ellisville, Miss. 256/F7
Ellisville, Mo. 261/M3
Ellisville, Wis. 317/L7
Ellon, Scotland 10/E2
Ellon, Scotland 15/F3
Elloree, S.C. 296/F4
Elloughton, England 13/G4
Ells (riv.), Alberta 182/D1
Ellscott, Alberta 182/D2
Ellsinore, Mo. 261/L9
Ellston, Iowa 229/E7
Ellsworth (hill), Conn. 210/B1
Ellsworth, Ill. 222/E3
Ellsworth, Iowa 229/F4
Ellsworth (co.), Kansas 232/D3
Ellsworth, Kansas 232/D3
Ellsworth, Maine 243/F6
Ellsworth, Mich. 250/D3
Ellsworth, Minn. 255/C7
Ellsworth, Nebr. 264/B2
Ellsworth•, N.H. 268/D4
Ellsworth (lake), Okla. 288/K5
Ellsworth, Pa. 294/B5
Ellsworth, Wis. 317/A6
Ellsworth A.F.B., S. Dak. 298/C5
Ellsworth Land (reg.), Ant. 5/B14
Ellwangen, Germany 22/D4
Ellwood City, Pa. 294/B4
Elm (riv.), N. Dak. 282/R5
Elm (riv.), N. Dak. 282/N8
Elm (creek), S. Dak. 298/D4
Elm (riv.), S. Dak. 298/M2
Elm, Switzerland 39/H3
Elma, Iowa 229/J2
Elma, Manitoba 179/G5
Elma, N.Y. 276/C5
Elma, Wash. 310/B4
El Macao, Dom. Rep. 158/F6
El Madwar, Jordan 65/E3
El Mafraq, Jordan 65/E3
El Mahalla el Kubra, Egypt 111/J3
El Maitén, Argentina 143/B5
El Majdal, Jordan 65/D3
Elmalı, Turkey 63/C4
El Manaqil, Sudan 111/F5
El Mansûra, Egypt 111/K3
El Mansûra, Egypt 59/B3
El Manteco, Venezuela 124/G4
El Manzano, Chile 138/F5
El Ma'qil, Iraq 66/E5
El Marj, Libya 102/E1
El Marj, Libya 111/D1
El Marmol, Mexico 150/B2
Elm City, N.C. 281/O3
Elm Creek, Manitoba 179/E5
Elm Creek, Nebr. 264/E4
Elmdale, Kansas 232/F3
Elmdale, Minn. 255/D5
Elmendorf, Texas 303/K11
Elmendorf A.F.B., Alaska 196/B1
Elmer, La. 238/E4
Elmer, Minn. 255/F3
Elmer, Mo. 261/G3
Elmer, N.J. 273/C4
Elmer, Okla. 288/H6
Elmer City, Wash. 310/G2
Elm Fork, Trinity (riv.), Texas 303/G2
Elm Grove, La. 238/C2
Elm Grove, Wis. 317/K1
Elmhurst, Ill. 222/B5
Elmhurst, Pa. 294/F7
El Miamo, Venezuela 124/H4
El Milagro, Argentina 143/C3
Elmina, Ghana 106/D8
El Minya, Egypt 102/F2
El Minya, Egypt 59/B4
El Minya, Egypt 111/J4
Elmira, Ill. 222/D2
Elmira, Mich. 250/E3
Elmira, Mo. 261/D3
Elmira, N.Y. 188/L2
Elmira, N.Y. 276/G6
Elmira, Ontario 177/D4
Elmira, Oreg. 291/D3
Elmira, Pr. Edward I. 168/F2
Elmira, W. Va. 312/E5
El Mirage, Ariz. 198/C5
Elmira Heights, N.Y. 276/G6
El Misti (mt.), Peru 128/G11
Elmo, Kansas 232/E3
Elmo, Mo. 261/B1
Elmo, Mont. 262/B3
Elmo, Texas 303/H5
Elmo, Utah 304/D4
Elmodel, Georgia 217/D8
Elmont, Kansas 232/G2
Elmont, N.Y. 276/P7
El Monte, Calif. 204/D10
El Monte, Chile 138/G4
Elmora, Pa. 294/E4
Elmore (co.), Ala. 195/F5
Elmore, Ala. 195/F5
Elmore (co.), Idaho 220/C6
Elmore, Minn. 255/D7
Elmore, Ohio 284/D3
Elmore City, Okla. 288/M5
El Morro, N. Mex. 274/A3
El Morro Nat'l Mon., N. Mex. 274/A3
Elm Park, La. 238/H5
El Mraiti (well), Mali 106/D5
El Mrayer (well), Mauritania 106/C4
El Mreïti (well), Mauritania 106/C4
Elmrock, Ky. 237/P6
Elmsdale, Nova Scotia 168/E4
Elmsdale, Pr. Edward I. 168/D2
Elmsford, N.Y. 276/O6
Elmshorn, Germany 22/C2
Elm Springs, Ark. 202/B1
Elm Springs, S. Dak. 298/D5
Elmsvale, Nova Scotia 168/E3
Elmvale, Ontario 177/E3
Elmville, Conn. 210/H1
Elmwood, Conn. 210/D2
Elmwood, Ill. 222/D3
Elmwood, Mass. 249/L4
Elmwood, Nebr. 264/H4
Elmwood, Okla. 288/F1
Elmwood, Ontario 177/C3
Elmwood, Wis. 317/B6
Elmwood Park, Ill. 222/B5
Elmwood Park, N.J. 273/B2
Elmwood Park, Wis. 317/M3
Elmwood Place, Ohio 284/B9
Elmworth, Alberta 182/A2
Elne, France 28/E6
El Nido, Calif. 204/E6
El Nido, Philippines 82/B5
El Ñilhue, Chile 138/G2
Elnora, Alberta 182/D3
Elnora, Ind. 227/C7
El Obeid, Sudan 102/E3
El Obeid, Sudan 59/B7
El Obeid, Sudan 111/E5
Elobey (isls.), Equat. Guinea 115/A3
El Odaiya, Sudan 111/E5
Eloff, S. Africa 118/J6
Eloi (bay), La. 238/M7
Elon, Ala. 195/F1
Elon College, N.C. 281/L2
Elora, Ontario 177/D4
Elora, Tenn. 237/J10
El Oro (prov.), Ecuador 128/C4
Elortondo, Argentina 143/F6
Elorza, Venezuela 124/D4
El Oso, Venezuela 124/H5
El Oued, Algeria 106/F2
Eloy, Ariz. 198/D6
El Pájaro, Colombia 126/D2
El Palmar, Chuquisaca, Bolivia 136/D7
El Palmar, Santa Cruz, Bolivia 136/D5
El Palmar, Tarija, Bolivia 136/D7
El Palmar, Venezuela 124/G4
El Pao, Anzoátegui, Venezuela 124/F3
El Pao, Bolívar, Venezuela 124/G3
El Pao, Cojedes, Venezuela 124/D3
El Paraíso, Colombia 126/C7
El Paraíso, Copán, Honduras 154/C3
El Paraíso, El Paraíso, Honduras 154/D3
El Pardo, Spain 33/F4
El Paso, Ark. 202/F3
El Paso (co.), Colo. 208/K5
El Paso, Ill. 222/D3
El Paso (co.), Texas 303/A10
El Paso, Texas 146/H6
El Paso, Texas 188/E4
El Paso, Texas 303/A10
El Paso, U.S. 2/D4
El Pato, Colombia 126/C6
El Perú, Bolivia 136/B3
El Perú, Venezuela 124/H4
Elphin, Ireland 17/E4
Elphinstone, Manitoba 179/B4
El Pico, Bolivia 136/C4
El Pilar, Cuba 158/G3
El Pilar, Venezuela 124/G2
El Pintado, Argentina 143/D1
El Piquete, Argentina 143/D1
El Portal, Calif. 204/F6
El Portal, Fla. 212/B4
El Portugués, Peru 128/C7
El Porvenir, Honduras 154/D3
El Porvenir, Mexico 150/G1
El Porvenir, N. Mex. 274/D3
El Porvenir, Panama 154/H6
El Potosí, Mexico 150/J4
El Pozo, Dom. Rep. 158/E5
El Prado, N. Mex. 274/D2
El Progreso, Ecuador 128/C9
El Progreso, Guatemala 154/B3
El Progreso, Honduras 154/D3
El Puente, Santa Cruz, Bolivia 136/D5
El Puente, Tarija, Bolivia 136/C7
El Puerto de Santa María, Spain 33/C4
El Pun, Ecuador 128/D2
El Qâhira (Cairo) (cap.), Egypt 59/B4
El Qâhira (Cairo) (cap.), Egypt 111/J3
El Qantara, Egypt 111/K3
El Qantara, Egypt 59/B3
El Qasr, Egypt 111/E2
El Qasr, Egypt 59/A4
El Quadmus, Syria 63/F5
El Quebrachal, Argentina 143/D2
Elqui (riv.), Chile 138/A8
El Quisco, Chile 138/E3
El Quneitra (prov.), Syria 63/F6
El Quneitra, Syria 63/F6
El Quryatein, Syria 63/G5
El Quseir, Egypt 102/F2
El Quseir, Egypt 59/B4
El Quseir, Egypt 111/F2
El Quseir, Syria 63/G5
El Quweira, Jordan 65/E5
Elrama, Pa. 294/C5
El Rashid, Syria 63/H5
El Rashid, Syria 59/C2
El Rastro, Venezuela 124/E3
El Real de Santa María, Panama 154/J6
El Realejo, Nicaragua 154/D4
El Reno, Okla. 288/K3
El Rio, Calif. 204/F9
El Rito, N. Mex. 274/C2
El Rito (riv.), N. Mex. 274/C2
Elrod, Ala. 195/C4
Elrod, Ind. 227/G6
El Roque, Venezuela 124/E2
Elrosa, Minn. 255/C5
El Rosario, Estero (riv.), Chile 138/F3
El Rosario, Mexico 150/B1
Elrose, Sask. 181/D4
Elroy, Wis. 317/F8
Elsa, Texas 303/G11
Elsa, Yukon 187/E3
Elsah, Ill. 222/C5
El Salado, Dom. Rep. 158/F6
El Salto, Mexico 150/G5
El Salvador 2/E5
El Salvador 146/J8
EL SALVADOR 154/C4
El Salvador, C. Rica 154/F5
El Samán de Apure, Venezuela 124/D4
El Santo, Cuba 158/E1
Elsas, Ontario 175/D3
El Sauce, Nicaragua 154/D4
Elsberry, Mo. 261/L4
Elsburg, S. Africa 118/H6
El Segundo, Calif. 204/B11
El Seibo (prov.), Dom. Rep. 158/F6
El Seibo, Dom. Rep. 158/F6
Elsey, Mo. 261/E9
Elsie, Mich. 250/E5
Elsie, Nebr. 264/C4
Elsie, Oreg. 291/D2
Elsiesrivier, S. Africa 118/F6
Elsinore (lake), Calif. 204/E11
Elsinore, Utah 304/B5
Elsmere, Del. 245/R2
Elsmere, Ky. 237/R2
Elsmere, Nebr. 264/D2
Elsmore, Kansas 232/G4
El Socorro, Venezuela 124/F3
El Sollum (gulf), Egypt 111/E1
El Sombrero, Venezuela 124/E3
Elst, Netherlands 27/H5
Elster, Black (riv.), Germany 22/E3
Elster, White (riv.), Germany 22/E3
Elston, Ind. 227/D4
Elstow, Sask. 181/E4
El Tabo, Chile 138/F3
El Tambo, Colombia 126/B6
El Teleno (mt.), Spain 33/C1
Eltham, N. Zealand 100/E3
Eltham, Victoria 97/J4
Eltham, Victoria 88/L6
El Tiemblo, Spain 33/D2
El Tigre, Venezuela 120/C2
El Tigre, Venezuela 124/F3
El Tocuyo, Venezuela 124/C3
El Tofo, Chile 138/A7
Elton, La. 238/E6
El'ton, U.S.S.R. 52/G5
Elton, W. Va. 312/E7
Elton, Wis. 317/J5
Eltopia, Wash. 310/G4
El Toro, Calif. 204/E11
El Toro (mt.), P. Rico 161/F2
El Toro, Venezuela 124/H3
El Toro Marine Air Sta., Calif. 204/D11
El Tránsito, Chile 138/B7
El Triunfo, Honduras 154/D4
El Tucuche (mt.), Trin. & Tob. 161/B10
El Tûr, Egypt 111/F2
El Tur, Egypt 59/B4
Eluru, India 68/E5
El' Uweinat, Libya 111/B2
Elva, Manitoba 179/A5
Elva, U.S.S.R. 53/D1
El Vado, N. Mex. 274/C2
Elvas, Portugal 33/C3
Elvaston, Ill. 222/B3
Elverson, Pa. 294/L5
Elverum, Norway 18/G6
El Viejo, Nicaragua 154/D4
El Vigía, Venezuela 124/C3
El Vinculo, Venezuela 124/D1
Elvins, Mo. 261/L7
Elvira, Iowa 229/N5
Elvira (isl.), N.W. Terr. 187/H2
El Volcán, Chile 138/B10
El Wak, Kenya 115/H3
El War (well), Niger 106/G4
El Wasta, Egypt 111/J3
Elwell, Mich. 250/E5
Elwell (lake), Mont. 262/E2
Elwha (riv.), Wash. 310/B3
Elwood, Ill. 222/E2
Elwood, Ind. 227/F4
Elwood, Iowa 229/M4
Elwood, Kansas 232/H2
Elwood, Nebr. 264/E4
Elwood, N.J. 273/D4
Elwood, N.Y. 276/O9
Elwood, Utah 304/B2
Ely, England 13/H5
Ely, England 10/G4
Ely, Iowa 229/K5
Ely, Minn. 255/G3
Ely, Nev. 188/D3
Ely, Nev. 266/G3
Ely (range), Nev. 266/G4
Ely, Vt. 268/C4
Ely (riv.), Wales 13/B7
El Yaduda, Jordan 65/D4
El Yagual, Venezuela 124/D4
Elyakim, Israel 65/C2
Elyashiv, Israel 65/B3
Elyria, Kansas 232/E3
Elyria, Nebr. 264/E3
Elyria, Ohio 284/F3
Elysburg, Pa. 294/K4
Elysian, Minn. 255/E6
Elysian Fields, Texas 303/L5
Elysian Grove, Tenn. 237/F8
El Yunque (mt.), P. Rico 161/F1
El Zacatón, Mexico 150/J5
Elze, Germany 22/C2
Emamshahr (Shahrud), Iran 66/G2
Emanguk (Emmonak), Alaska 196/E2
Emanuel (co.), Georgia 217/H5
Emba, U.S.S.R. 48/F5
Emba (riv.), U.S.S.R. 48/F5
Embar, Newf. 166/A3
Embarcación, Argentina 143/D1
Embarras (riv.), Ill. 222/E4
Embarras Airport, Alberta 182/C5
Embarrass, Minn. 255/F3
Embarrass, Wis. 317/J6
Embden (pond), Maine 243/D6
Embden, N. Dak. 282/R6
Emblem, Wyo. 319/D1
Embo, Scotland 15/E3
Emboscada, Paraguay 144/B4
Embree, Newf. 166/C4
Embreeville, Pa. 294/L6
Embreeville Junction, Tenn. 237/R8
Embro, Ontario 177/C4
Embrun, France 28/G5
Embrun, Ontario 177/J2
Embu, Kenya 115/G4
Embudo, N. Mex. 274/C2
Emden, Germany 22/B2
Emden, Ill. 222/D3
Emden, Mo. 261/J3
Emeigh, Pa. 294/E4
Emelle, Ala. 195/B5
Emerado, N. Dak. 282/R4
Emerald (isl.), N.W. Terr. 187/G2
Emerald, Queensland 88/H4
Emerald, Queensland 95/C4
Emerald, Wis. 317/B5
Emerald Isle, N.C. 281/P5
Emero (riv.), Bolivia 136/B3
Emerson, Ark. 202/D7
Emerson, Georgia 217/C2
Emerson, Iowa 229/C6
Emerson, Man. 162/G6
Emerson, Manitoba 179/E5
Emerson, Nebr. 264/H2
Emerson, N.J. 273/B1
Emerson, N.C. 281/M6
Emery, S. Dak. 298/O6
Emery (co.), Utah 304/D4
Emery, Utah 304/C5
Emery Mills, Maine 243/B8
Emeryville, Calif. 204/J2
Emeryville, Ontario 177/B5
Emet, Turkey 63/C3
Emida, Idaho 220/B2
Emigrant, Mont. 262/F5
Emigrant (peak), Mont. 262/F5
Emigrant (peak), Nev. 266/C5
Emigsville, Pa. 294/J5
Emi Koussi (mt.), Chad 102/D3
Emi Koussi (mt.), Chad 111/C4
Emilia-Romagna (reg.), Italy 34/C2
Emilio Ayarza, Argentina 143/F7
Emily, Minn. 255/E4
Emily (lake), Minn. 255/C5
Emin (Dorbiljin), China 77/B2
Emine (cape), Bulgaria 45/J4
Eminence, Ind. 227/D5
Eminence, Ky. 237/L4
Eminence, Mo. 261/K8
Emington, Ill. 222/E3
Emirau (isl.), Papua N.G. 86/B1
Emirdağ, Turkey 63/D3
Emir Daği (mt.), Turkey 63/D3
Emir Daği (mt.), Turkey 59/B2
Emirgazi, Turkey 63/E4
Emison, Ind. 227/C7
Emita, Tasmania 99/D2
Emlenton, Pa. 294/C3
Emlyn, Ky. 237/N7
Emma, Ill. 222/E6
Emma, Ind. 227/F1
Emma, Ky. 237/R5
Emma, Mo. 261/F5
Emma (range), Suriname 131/C4
Emmaboda, Sweden 18/J8
Emmalane, Georgia 217/H5
Emmastad, Neth. Ant. 161/F9
Emmaus, Pa. 294/M4
Emmaus, Virgin Is. (U.S.) 161/C4
Emmaville, N.S. Wales 97/F1
Emmeloord, Netherlands 27/H3
Emmen, Netherlands 27/K3
Emmen, Switzerland 39/F2
Emmendingen, Germany 22/B4
Emmental (riv.), Switzerland 39/E3
Emmerich, Germany 22/B3
Emmet, Ark. 202/D6
Emmet (co.), Iowa 229/D2
Emmet (co.), Mich. 250/E3
Emmet, Nebr. 264/F2
Emmet, N. Dak. 282/G4
Emmet, Queensland 88/G4
Emmet, Queensland 95/C5
Emmetsburg, Iowa 229/D2
Emmett, Idaho 220/B6
Emmett, Kansas 232/F2
Emmett, Mich. 250/G6
Emmitsburg, Md. 245/J2
Emmonak, Alaska 196/E2
Emmons, Minn. 255/E7
Emmons (co.), N. Dak. 282/K7
Emmons (mt.), Utah 304/D3
Emneth, England 13/H5
Emo, Ontario 175/B3
Emo, Ontario 177/F5
Emory (riv.), Tenn. 237/M8
Emory, Texas 303/J5
Emory (peak), Texas 303/A8
Emory Gap, Tenn. 237/M9
Emory-Meadowview, Va. 307/E7
Emoryville, W. Va. 312/H4
Empalme, Mexico 150/D2
Empalme Olmos, Uruguay 145/B6
Empangeni, S. Africa 118/E5
Empedrado, Argentina 143/E2
Empedrado, Chile 138/A11
Empexa (salt dep.), Bolivia 136/A7
Empire, Ala. 195/D3
Empire, Calif. 204/D6
Empire, Colo. 208/H3
Empire (res.), Colo. 208/L2
Empire, Georgia 217/F6
Empire, La. 238/L8
Empire, Mich. 250/C4
Empire, Ohio 284/J5
Empire City, Okla. 288/L6
Empire Landing, Ariz. 198/A4
Empoli, Italy 34/C3
Emporia, Fla. 212/E2
Emporia, Ind. 227/F5
Emporia, Kans. 188/G3
Emporia, Kansas 232/F3
Emporia (I.C.), Va. 307/N7
Emporium, Pa. 294/F2
Empress, Alberta 182/E4
Empress Augusta (bay), Papua N.G. 86/C2
'Emrani, Iran 66/L3
Emrick, N. Dak. 282/L4
Ems (riv.), Germany 22/B2
Emsdale, Ontario 177/E2
Emsdetten, Germany 22/B2
Emsworth, Pa. 294/B6
Emyvale, Ireland 17/G3
Enaratoli, Indonesia 85/K6
Enard (bay), Scotland 15/C2
Enaville, Idaho 220/B2
Encampment, Wyo. 319/F4
Encampment (riv.), Wyo. 319/F4
Encarnación, Paraguay 120/D5
Encarnación, Paraguay 144/E5
Encarnación de Díaz, Mexico 150/H6
Enchant, Alberta 182/D4
Enchi, Ghana 106/D7
Encinal, Texas 303/E9
Encinitas, Calif. 204/H10
Encino, Calif. 204/B10
Encino, N. Mex. 274/D4
Encino, Texas 303/F11
Enciso, Colombia 126/E7
Encontrados, Venezuela 124/B3
Encounter (bay), S. Australia 88/F7
Encounter (bay), S. Australia 94/F6
Encrucijada, Cuba 158/E1
Endako, Br. Col. 184/E3
Ende, Indonesia 85/G7
Endeavor, Pa. 294/D2
Endeavor (str.), Queensland 88/G2
Endeavor, Wis. 317/G8
Endeavour (str.), Queensland 95/B1
Endeavour, Sask. 181/J3
Endee, N. Mex. 274/F3
Endelave (isl.), Denmark 21/D6
Enderbury (isl.), Kiribati 87/J6
Enderby, Br. Col. 184/H5
Enderby Land (reg.), Ant. 2/M9
Enderby Land (reg.), Ant. 5/B3
Enderlin, N. Dak. 282/P6
Enders, Nebr. 264/C4
Enders (res.), Nebr. 264/C4
Endiang, Alberta 182/D4
Endicott (mts.), Alaska 196/H1
Endicott, Nebr. 264/G4
Endicott, N.Y. 276/H6
Endicott, S. Africa 118/J6
Endicott, Wash. 310/H4
Endless (lake), Maine 243/F5
Endrick Water (riv.), Scotland 15/B1
Endrőd, Hungary 41/F3
Endwell, N.Y. 276/H6
Ene (riv.), Peru 128/E8
Energy, Ill. 222/E6
Enes, Hungary 41/F2
Enetai, Wash. 310/A2
Enewetak (Eniwetok) (atoll), Marshall Is. 87/G4
Enez, Turkey 63/B2
Enfield, Conn. 210/E1
Enfield•, Conn. 210/E1
Enfield, England 13/H7
Enfield, England 10/B5
Enfield, Ill. 222/E5
Enfield, Maine 243/F5
Enfield•, Maine 243/F5
Enfield, Minn. 255/E5
Enfield, N.H. 268/C4
Enfield•, N.H. 268/C4
Enfield, N.C. 281/O2
Enfield, Nova Scotia 168/E4
Enfield, S. Australia 88/D7
Enfield, S. Australia 94/B7
Enfield Center, N.H. 268/C4
Enfield P.O. (Thompsonville), Conn. 210/E1
Engadine, Mich. 250/D2
Engadine (valley), Switzerland 39/K3
Engaño (cape), Dom. Rep. 158/F6
Engaño (cape), Philippines 82/D1
Engaño (cape), Philippines 54/O8
Engelberg, Switzerland 39/F3
Engelhard, N.C. 281/T3

Engelhartszell, Austria 41/B2
Engel's, U.S.S.R. 7/J3
Engel's, U.S.S.R. 52/G4
Engel's, U.S.S.R. 48/E4
Engen, Br. Col. 184/D4
Enggano (isl.), Indonesia 85/C7
Enghien, Belgium 27/D7
Engi, Switzerland 39/H3
ENGLAND 10/F5
ENGLAND 13
England, Ark. 202/G4
England, U.K. 7/D3
England A.F.B., La. 238/E4
Engle, N. Mex. 274/B5
Englee, Newf. 166/C4
Englefeld, Sask. 181/G3
Englehart, Ont. 162/H6
Englehart, Ontario 177/K5
Englehart, Ontario 175/E3
Englevale, Kansas 232/H4
Englevale, N. Dak. 282/P7
Englewood, Colo. 208/K3
Englewood, Fla. 212/D5
Englewood, Kansas 232/C4
Englewood, N.J. 273/C2
Englewood, Ohio 284/B6
Englewood, Tenn. 237/M10
Englewood Cliffs, N.J. 273/C2
English (chan.) 7/D4
English (chan.), Chan. Is. 13/D8
English (chan.), England 13/B8
English (chan.), England 10/E6
English (chan.), France 28/B3
English (chan.), Ind. 227/E8
English, Ky. 237/L3
English (riv.), Ontario 175/B2
English, W. Va. 312/C8
English Bay, Alaska 196/B2
English Bazar, India 68/E3
English Coast (reg.), Ant. 5/B15
English Creek, N.J. 273/D5
English Harbour, Newf. 166/D2
English Harbour West, Newf. 166/C4
English Lake, Ind. 227/D2
Englishman (bay), Maine 243/J6
English River, Ontario 177/G5
English River, Ontario 175/B3
Englishtown, N.J. 273/E3
Englishtown, Nova Scotia 168/H2
Enguera, Spain 33/F3
Enid, Miss. 256/E2
Enid (lake), Miss. 256/E2
Enid, Mont. 262/M3
Enid, Okla. 188/G3
Enid, Okla. 288/L2
Enid (mt.), W. Australia 92/B3
Enigma, Georgia 217/F8
Enilda, Alberta 182/E4
Eniwa, Japan 81/K2
Enka, N.C. 281/D3
Enkhuizen, Netherlands 27/G3
Enköping, Sweden 18/G1
Enmore, Guyana 131/C2
Enna (prov.), Italy 34/E6
Enna, Italy 34/E6
Ennadai (lake), N.W. Terr. 187/H3
En Nahud, Sudan 111/E5
En Nahud, Sudan 102/E3
En Naqura, Lebanon 63/F6
En Nebk, Syria 59/C3
En Nebk, Syria 63/G5
Ennedi (plat.), Chad 111/D4
Ennell (lake), Ireland 17/G5
Ennenda, Switzerland 39/H2
Ennery, Haiti 158/D5
Enngonia, N.S. Wales 97/C1
Enning, S. Dak. 298/E4
Ennis, Ireland 10/B4
Ennis, Ireland 17/D6
Ennis, Ky. 237/H6
Ennis, Mont. 262/E5
Ennis (lake), Mont. 262/E5
Ennis, Texas 303/H5
Enniscorthy, Ireland 17/J7
Enniscorthy, Ireland 10/C4
Enniskerry, Ireland 17/J5
Enniskillen, New Bruns. 170/D3
Enniskillen, N. Ireland 10/C3
Enniskillen, N. Ireland 17/F3
Ennistymon, Ireland 10/B4
Ennistymon, Ireland 17/C6
Enns, Austria 41/C2
Enns (riv.), Austria 41/C3
Enoch, Utah 304/A6
Enoch, W. Va. 312/C6
Enochs, Texas 303/B4
Enoggera, Queensland 88/K2
Enoggera (creek), Queensland 95/D2
Enola, Ark. 202/F3
Enola, Pa. 294/J5
Enon, Mo. 261/G6
Enon, Ohio 284/C6
Enontekiö, Finland 18/N2
Enon Valley, Pa. 294/B4
Enoree, S.C. 296/D2
Enoree (riv.), S.C. 296/C2
Enos, Ind. 227/D2
Enosburg Falls, Vt. 268/B2
Enrage (cape), New Bruns. 170/F3
Enrile, Philippines 82/C2
Enrique Carbó, Argentina 143/G6
Enriquillo, Dom. Rep. 158/D7
Enriquillo, Dom. Rep. 156/D3
Enriquillo (lake), Dom. Rep. 158/C6
Ens, Sask. 181/F3
Enschede, Netherlands 27/K4
Ensenada, Argentina 143/H7
Ensenada, Mexico 150/A1
Ensenada, P. Rico 161/B3
Enshi, China 77/G5
Ensign, Alberta 182/D4
Ensign, Kansas 232/B4
Ensign, Mich. 250/C3
Ensley, Fla. 212/B6
Ent A.F.B., Colo. 208/K5
Entebbe, Uganda 115/F4
Entebbe, Uganda 102/F5
Enterprise, Ala. 195/G8

Enterprise, Calif. 204/C3
Enterprise, Guyana 131/B2
Enterprise, Kansas 232/E3
Enterprise, La. 238/G3
Enterprise, Miss. 256/G6
Enterprise, N.W. Terr. 187/G3
Enterprise, Ohio 284/B4
Enterprise, Okla. 288/R4
Enterprise, Ontario 177/H3
Enterprise, Utah 304/A6
Enterprise, W. Va. 312/F4
Entiat, Wash. 310/E3
Entiat (lake), Wash. 310/E3
Entiat (mts.), Wash. 310/E2
Entiat (riv.), Wash. 310/E3
Entlebuch, Switzerland 39/F3
Entrance, Alberta 182/B3
Entrejo, Neth. Ant. 161/E8
Entrelacs, Québec 172/C3
Entrepñas (res.), Spain 33/E2
Entre Ríos (prov.), Argentina 143/E3
Entre Ríos, Bolivia 136/C7
Entre Ríos, Kansas 232/G4
Entre Rios de Minas, Brazil 135/D2
Entriken, Pa. 294/F5
Entwistle, Alberta 182/C3
Enugu, Nigeria 102/C4
Enugu, Nigeria 106/F7
Enumclaw, Wash. 310/D3
Envigado, Colombia 126/C4
Enville, Tenn. 237/E10
Enwarak (mt.), Guyana 131/B3
Enyellé, Congo 115/C3
Enying, Hungary 41/E3
Eola, La. 238/F5
Eola, Texas 303/E6
Eolia, Ky. 237/R6
Eolia, Mo. 261/L4
Eoline, Ala. 195/D4
Epe, Netherlands 27/H4
Epéna, Congo 115/C3
Epéna, Congo 102/D4
Epenarra, North. Terr. 93/D6
Epernay, France 28/E3
Epes, Ala. 195/B5
Ephesus, Georgia 217/B4
Ephesus (ruins), Turkey 63/B3
Ephraim, Utah 304/C4
Ephraim, Wis. 317/M5
Ephrata, Pa. 294/K5
Ephrata, Wash. 310/F3
Ephratah, N.Y. 276/L4
Epinal, France 28/G3
Epinay-sur-Seine, France 28/B1
Epiphany, S. Dak. 298/O6
Epira, Guyana 131/C3
Epirus (reg.), Greece 45/E6
Episkopi, Cyprus 63/E5
Eport, Loch (inlet), Scotland 15/A3
Epoufette, Mich. 250/D2
Epping, England 13/H7
Epping, England 10/C5
Epping, N.H. 268/E5
Epping•, N.H. 268/E5
Epping, N. Dak. 282/D3
Epps, La. 238/G1
Epsie, Mont. 262/L5
Epsom, Ind. 227/C7
Epsom•, N.H. 268/E5
Epsom and Ewell, England 13/G8
Epsom and Ewell, England 10/B6
Epukiro, Namibia 118/B4
Epworth, Georgia 217/D1
Epworth, Iowa 229/M4
Equality, Ala. 195/F5
Equality, Ill. 222/E6
Equateur (prov.), Zaire 115/D3
Equator 2/H5
Equatoria, Eastern (prov.), Sudan 111/F6
Equatoria, Western (prov.), Sudan 111/E6
Equatorial Guinea 2/K5
Equatorial Guinea 102/C4
EQUATORIAL GUINEA 115/A3
Equinox (mt.), Vt. 268/A5
Equinunk, Pa. 294/M2
Era, Ohio 284/D6
Era, Texas 303/G4
Era (peak), Switzerland 39/J3
Er Rachidia, Morocco 106/C2
Er Rafid, Jordan 65/D2
Erath, La. 238/F7
Erath (co.), Texas 303/F5
Erbaa, Turkey 63/G2
Erbach, Germany 22/C4
Erbacon, W. Va. 312/E5
Erbil (gov.), Iraq 66/C3
Erbil, Iraq 59/D2
Erbil, Iraq 54/F6
Erbil, Iraq 66/D2
Erçek (lake), Turkey 63/K3
Ercilla, Chile 143/D3
Erciş, Turkey 59/D2
Erciş, Turkey 63/K3
Erciyas Daği (mt.), Turkey 63/F3
Érd, Hungary 41/E3
Erdahl, Minn. 255/C5
Erdek, Turkey 63/B2
Erdemli, Turkey 63/F4
Erdentsagaan, Mongolia 77/J2
Erdőtelek, Hungary 41/F3
Erebato (riv.), Venezuela 124/F5
Ereen, Mongolia 77/H2
Ereğli, Turkey 63/D2
Ereğli, Turkey 59/B2
Ereğli, Turkey 63/F4
Ertai, China 77/C2
Ertil', U.S.S.R. 52/F4
Eruh, Turkey 63/K4
Erval, Brazil 132/C11
Ervay, Wyo. 319/E3
Erving•, Mass. 249/E2
Erwin, N.C. 281/M4
Erwin, S. Dak. 298/P5
Erwin, Tenn. 237/S8
Erwinna, Pa. 294/N5
Erwinville, La. 238/H5
Erwood, Sask. 181/J3
Eryuan, China 77/F6
Erzgebirge (mts.), Czech. 41/B†

Ergun He (Argun') (riv.), China 77/K1
Ergun Youqi, China 77/K1
Ergun Zuoqi, China 77/K1
Ergun Zuoqi, China 54/O4
Er Hai (lake), China 77/F6
Erhard, Minn. 255/B4
Eriboll, Loch (inlet), Scotland 15/D2
Erica, Netherlands 27/K3
Erica, Victoria 97/D5
Erice, Italy 34/D5
Ericeira, Portugal 33/B3
Erichsen (lake), N.W. Terr. 187/K2
Ericht, Loch (lake), Scotland 15/D4
Erick, Okla. 288/G4
Erickson, Br. Col. 184/J5
Erickson, Manitoba 179/C4
Ericsburg, Minn. 255/E2
Ericson, Nebr. 264/F3
Erie (lake) 146/K5
Erie (lake) 188/K2
Erie (lake) 162/H7
Erie, Colo. 208/K2
Erie, Ill. 222/C2
Erie, Kansas 232/G4
Erie, Mich. 250/F7
Erie (lake), Mich. 250/G7
Erie, N. Dak. 282/R5
Erie (co.), N.Y. 276/C5
Erie (lake), N.Y. 276/A5
Erie, Ohio 284/H1
Erie (lake), Ohio 284/E3
Erie (lake), Ontario 177/E5
Erie (co.), Pa. 294/B2
Erie, Pa. 188/K2
Erie, Pa. 146/L5
Erie (lake), Pa. 294/B1
Erie, Pa. 294/B1
Erie, Tenn. 237/M9
Erieau, Ontario 177/C5
Erie Beach, Ontario 177/B5
Erieville, N.Y. 276/J5
Erigabo, Somalia 115/J1
Eriksdale, Manitoba 179/D4
Erimo (cape), Japan 81/L3
Erin, Ontario 177/D4
Erin, Tenn. 237/E9
Erin (bay), Trin. & Tob. 161/A11
Erin (pt.), Trin. & Tob. 161/A11
Erinferry, Sask. 181/D2
Eriskay (isl.), Scotland 15/A3
Erisort, Loch (inlet), Scotland 15/B2
Erith, Alberta 182/B3
Eritrea (prov.), Ethiopia 111/G4
Eritrea (reg.), Ethiopia 102/F3
Eritrea (reg.), Ethiopia 59/C6
Erkilet, Turkey 63/F3
Erkina (riv.), Ireland 17/G6
Erkowit, Sudan 59/C6
Erlach, Switzerland 39/D2
Erlands Point, Wash. 310/A2
Erlangen, Germany 22/D4
Erlanger, Ky. 237/R2
Erldunda, North. Terr. 93/C8
Erlenbach im Simmental, Switzerland 39/E3
Erling (lake), Ark. 202/C7
Ermatingen, Switzerland 39/H1
Ermelo, Netherlands 27/H4
Ermelo, S. Africa 118/E5
Ermenak, Turkey 63/E4
Ermeran Station, N.S. Wales 97/C3
Ermoúpolis, Greece 45/G7
Ernabella, S. Australia 94/C2
Ernakulam, India 54/J8
Erne (riv.), Ireland 17/F3
Erne, Lough (lake), N. Ireland 10/C3
Ernée, France 28/C3
Ernen, Switzerland 39/F4
Ernest, Pa. 294/D4
Ernfold, Sask. 181/D5
Ernul, N.C. 281/N4
Erode, India 68/D6
Eromanga, Queensland 88/G5
Eromanga, Queensland 95/B5
Eros, La. 238/F2
Erquelinnes, Belgium 27/E8
Err (peak), Switzerland 39/J3
Er Rachidia, Morocco 106/C2
Er Rafid, Jordan 65/D2
Er Rahad, Sudan 111/F5
Er Rahad, Sudan 59/B7
Er Ramtha, Jordan 65/E2
Er Ras, Saudi Arabia 59/D4
Errata, Miss. 256/F7
Errego, Mozambique 118/F3
Er Rif (range), Morocco 106/D2
Errigal (mt.), Ireland 17/E1
Er Rihiya, West Bank 65/C5
Errington, Br. Col. 184/J3
Erris (head), Ireland 10/A3
Erris (head), Ireland 17/A3
Errol•, N.H. 268/E2
Errol, Scotland 15/E4
Erromanga (isl.), Vanuatu 87/H7
Er Roseires, Sudan 111/F5
Er Rumman, Jordan 65/D3
Er Ruseifa, Jordan 65/E3
Ersekë, Albania 45/E5
Erskine, Alberta 182/D3
Erskine, Minn. 255/B3
Erstein, France 28/G3
Erstfeld, Switzerland 39/G3

Erzgebirge (mts.), Germany 22/E3
Erzin, Turkey 63/G4
Erzincan (prov.), Turkey 63/H3
Erzincan, Turkey 59/C2
Erzurum (prov.), Turkey 63/J3
Erzurum, Turkey 59/D2
Erzurum, Turkey 54/E5
Erzurum, Turkey 63/J3
Esan (pt.), Japan 81/K3
Esashi, Iwate, Japan 81/K4
Esashi, Hokkaido, Japan 81/J3
Esashi, Hokkaido, Japan 81/L1
Esbjerg, Denmark 21/B7
Esbjerg, Denmark 7/B3
Esbjerg, Denmark 18/F9
Esbon, Kansas 232/D2
Escabosa, N. Mex. 274/C4
Escalante, Philippines 82/D5
Escalante, Utah 304/C6
Escalante (des.), Utah 304/A6
Escalante (riv.), Utah 304/C6
Escalon, Calif. 204/E6
Escalón, Mexico 150/G3
Escalona, Spain 33/D2
Escambia (co.), Ala. 195/D8
Escambia (creek), Ala. 195/D8
Escambia (riv.), Ala. 195/D8
Escambia (co.), Fla. 212/B6
Escambia (co.), Fla. 212/B6
Escanaba, Mich. 250/C3
Escanaba (riv.), Mich. 250/B2
Escarcega, Mexico 150/O7
Escatawpa (riv.), 256/H8
Escatawpa, Ala. 195/B8
Escatawpa (riv.), Ala. 195/B9
Escatawpa, Miss. 256/G10
Eschenbach, Switzerland 39/G2
Escholzmatt, Switzerland 39/E3
Esch-sur-Alzette, Luxembourg 27/J9
Esch-sur-Sûre, Luxembourg 27/H9
Eschwege, Germany 22/C3
Eschweiler, Germany 22/B3
Escobar, Argentina 143/G7
Escobar, Paraguay 144/B5
Escocesa (bay), Dom. Rep. 158/E5
Escoma, Bolivia 136/A4
Escondido, Calif. 204/J10
Escondido (riv.), Nicaragua 154/F4
Escoumins, Québec 172/H1
Escudo de Veraguas (isl.), Panama 154/G6
Escuinapa de Hidalgo, Mexico 150/G5
Escuintla, Guatemala 154/B3
Escuintla, Mexico 150/N9
Escuminac, New Bruns. 170/F1
Escuminac (bay), New Bruns. 170/D1
Escuminac (pt.), New Bruns. 170/F1
Esdaile, Wis. 317/A6
Eséka, Cameroon 115/B3
Eşen, Turkey 63/C4
Esfahan (Isfahan) (prov.), Iran 66/H4
Esfahan (Isfahan), Iran 66/G4
Esfandak, Iran 66/N7
Esh, England 13/H3
Esher, England 13/H8
Esher, England 10/B6
Eshowe, S. Africa 118/E5
Esh Shaubak (interm. str.), Jordan 65/D5
Esk (riv.), England 13/D2
Esk, Queensland 95/E5
Esk, Sask. 181/G4
Esk (riv.), Scotland 15/F5
Eska, Alaska 196/B1
Eskdale, W. Va. 312/D6
Esker, Newf. 166/A3
Eskilstuna, Sweden 18/K7
Eskimalatya, Turkey 63/H3
Eskimo (lakes), N.W. Terr. 187/E2
Eskimo Point, N.W.T. 162/G3
Eskimo Point, N.W. Terr. 187/J3
Eskipazar, Turkey 63/E2
Eskişehir (prov.), Turkey 63/D3
Eskişehir, Turkey 54/D6
Eskişehir, Turkey 59/B2
Eskişehir, Turkey 63/D3
Esko, Minn. 255/F4
Eskridge, Kansas 232/F3
Eskutassis (pond), Maine 243/G5
Esla (riv.), Spain 33/D2
Eslamabad, Iran 66/E3
Eslöv, Sweden 18/H9
Esme, Sask. 181/D6
Eşme, Turkey 63/C3
Esslingen am Neckar, Germany 22/C4
Essonne (dept.), France 28/E3
Es Sukhna, Jordan 65/E4
Es Sukhne, Syria 59/C3
Es Sukhne, Syria 63/H5
Es Suki, Sudan 59/B7
Es Suweida (prov.), Syria 63/G6
Es Suweida, Syria 59/C3
Es Suweide, Syria 63/H5
Es Suweide, Syria 63/G6
Est (pt.), Haiti 158/C4
Esmond, N. Dak. 282/L3
Esmond, Ill. 222/E1
Esmond, R.I. 249/H5
Esmond, S. Dak. 298/O5
Esmont, Va. 307/L5
Esmoraca, Bolivia 136/B7
Esneux, Belgium 27/H7
Esom Hill, Georgia 217/B3
Espada (pt.), Colombia 126/E1
Espada (pt.), Dom. Rep. 158/F6
Espagnol (pt.), St. Vin. & Grens. 161/A8
Espaillat (prov.), Dom. Rep. 158/D5
Espalion, France 28/E5
Española (isl.), Ecuador 128/C10
Española, Fla. 212/E2
Española, N. Mex. 274/C3
Espanola, Ontario 177/J5
Espanola, Ontario 175/D3
Espanola, Wash. 310/H3
Esparta, C. Rica 154/E5
Esparto, Calif. 204/C5
Espejo, Chile 138/G3
Espejo, Spain 33/D4
Espelkamp, Germany 22/C2
Espenberg (cape), Alaska 196/F1
Esperança, Brazil 132/G4

Esperance, Australia 87/C9
Esperance, N.Y. 276/M5
Esperance, W. Australia 88/C6
Esperance, W. Australia 92/C6
Esperance (bay), W. Australia 92/C6
Esperanza, Argentina 143/F5
Esperanza, Br. Col. 184/D5
Esperanza, Cuba 158/E2
Esperanza, Dom. Rep. 158/D5
Esperanza (mts.), Honduras 154/E3
Esperanza, Puebla, Mexico 150/O2
Esperanza, Sonora, Mexico 150/D4
Esperanza, Peru 128/G7
Esperanza, P. Rico 161/G2
Esperanza, Texas 303/B11
Esperanza, Venezuela 124/E6
Espichel (cape), Portugal 33/B3
Espigão Mestre (Geral de Goiás) (range), Brazil 132/E6
Espinal, Colombia 126/C3
Espinar, Peru 128/G10
Espino (pt.), Uruguay 145/A7
Espinhaço (mts.), Brazil 120/E4
Espinhaço, Serra do (range), Brazil 132/F7
Espinho, Portugal 33/B2
Espinillo, Argentina 143/E2
Espinillo (pt.), Uruguay 145/A7
Espino, Venezuela 124/F3
Espírito Santo (state), Brazil 132/F7
Espírito Santo (state), Brazil 135/F2
Espírito Santo (isl.), Mexico 150/D4
Espiritu Santo (cape), Philippines 85/H3
Espiritu Santo (cape), Philippines 82/E4
Espiritu Santo (isl.), Vanuatu 87/G7
Espita, Mexico 150/O6
Espiye, Turkey 63/H2
Esplanada, Brazil 132/G5
Espluga de Francolí, Spain 33/G2
Espoir (bay), Newf. 166/C4
Espoo, Finland 18/O6
Esposende, Portugal 33/B2
Esprit-Saint, Québec 172/J1
Espungabera, Mozambique 118/E4
Espy, Pa. 294/K4
Espyville Station, Pa. 294/B2
Esqueda, Mexico 150/E1
Esquel, Argentina 143/B5
Esquel, Argentina 120/B7
Esquimalt, Br. Col. 184/K4
Esquina, Argentina 143/G5
Esquipulas, Guatemala 154/C3
Esquipulas, Nicaragua 154/E4
Es Sahab, Jordan 65/E4
Es Salt, Jordan 65/D3
Es Salt, Jordan 59/C3
Essaouira, Morocco 106/B2
Essaouira, Morocco 102/A1
Essé, Cameroon 115/B3
Essen, Belgium 27/F6
Essen, Germany 27/E3
Essen, Germany 7/E3
Essen, Germany 22/B3
Essendon, Victoria 88/K7
Essendon, Victoria 97/H5
Essequibo (riv.), Guyana 120/D2
Essequibo (riv.), Guyana 131/B3
Esserville, Va. 307/G2
Essex, Calif. 204/K9
Essex, Conn. 210/F3
Essex•, Conn. 210/F3
Essex (co.), England 13/H6
Essex, Ill. 222/E2
Essex, Iowa 229/C7
Essex, Md. 245/N3
Essex (co.), Mass. 249/L2
Essex•, Mass. 249/L2
Essex, Mo. 261/N9
Essex, Mont. 262/C2
Essex (co.), N.J. 273/E2
Essex (co.), N.Y. 276/N2
Essex, N.Y. 276/O2
Essex (county), Ontario 177/B5
Essex, Ontario 177/B5
Essex (co.), Vt. 268/D2
Essex•, Vt. 268/A2
Essex (co.), Va. 307/P5
Essex Fells, N.J. 273/B2
Essex Junction, Vt. 268/A3
Essexville, Mich. 250/F5
Es Sidr, Libya 111/C1
Essie, Ky. 237/P6
Essig, Minn. 255/D6
Essington, Pa. 294/M7

Estampuis, Belgium 27/C7
Estância, Brazil 132/G5
Estância, Brazil 120/F4
Estancia, N. Mex. 274/C4
Estancia Caleta Josefina, Chile 138/F10
Estancia Laguna Blanca, Chile 138/E9
Estancia Morro Chico, Chile 138/E9
Estancia Punta Delgada, Chile 138/E9
Estancia San Gregorio, Chile 138/E9
Estancia Springhill (Cerro Manantiales), Chile 138/F10
Estanzuela, Uruguay 145/B5
Estanzuelas, El Salvador 154/C4
Estarca, Bolivia 136/C7
Estats (peak), Spain 33/G1
Estavayer-le-Lac, Switzerland 39/C3
Estcourt, S. Africa 118/D5
Este (pt.), Cuba 158/C3
Este, Italy 34/C2
Este (pt.), P. Rico 161/G2
Este (pt.), Uruguay 120/D6
Este (pt.), Uruguay 145/D6
Esteban Rams, Argentina 143/F5
Esteli, Nicaragua 154/D4
Estella, Spain 33/E1
Estelline, S. Dak. 298/R4
Estelline, Texas 303/D3
Estell Manor, N.J. 273/D5
Estepa, Spain 33/D4
Estepona, Spain 33/D4
Ester, Alaska 196/J2
Esterbrook, Wyo. 319/G3
Estérel, Québec 172/C3
Esterhazy, Sask. 181/K5
Estero (bay), Calif. 204/D8
Estero (pt.), Calif. 204/D8
Estero, Fla. 212/E5
Estero (isl.), Fla. 212/E5
Estes Park, Colo. 208/J2
Este Sudeste (cays), Colombia 126/A10
Estevan, Sak. 162/F6
Estevan, Sask. 181/K6
Estevan Point, Br. Col. 184/D5
Estey, Mich. 250/E5
Esther (isl.), Alaska 196/C1
Esther, Alberta 182/E4
Esther, La. 238/F7
Esther, Mo. 261/M7
Estherville, Iowa 229/D2
Estherwood, La. 238/F6
Estill (co.), Ky. 237/O5
Estill, Miss. 256/C4
Estill, S.C. 296/F6
Estillfork, Ala. 195/F1
Estill Springs, Tenn. 237/J10
Estlin, Sask. 181/G5
Esto, Fla. 212/C5
Eston, England 13/F3
Eston, Sask. 162/F5
Eston, Sask. 181/C4
ESTONIA 53
Estonian S.S.R., U.S.S.R. 7/G3
Estonian S.S.R., U.S.S.R. 48/C4
Estonian S.S.R., U.S.S.R. 52/G3
Estoril, Portugal 33/B3
Estral Beach, Mich. 250/F7
Estreito (res.), Brazil 135/C2
Estrela, Serra da (mts.), Portugal 33/C2
Estrella (riv.), Calif. 204/D8
Estremadura (reg.), Spain 33/C3
Estremoz, Portugal 33/C3
Estrondo, Serra do (range), Brazil 132/D4
Estuary, Sask. 181/B5
Esztergom, Hungary 41/E3
Etadunna, S. Australia 94/F3
Étalle, Belgium 27/H9
Étampes, France 28/E3
Étaples, France 28/D2
Etawah, India 68/D3
Etawney (lake), Manitoba 179/J2
Etchojoa, Mexico 150/E3
Ethan, S. Dak. 298/N6
Ethel, Ark. 202/H5
Ethel (mt.), Colo. 208/F1
Ethel, La. 238/H5
Ethel, Miss. 256/F4
Ethel, Mo. 261/G3
Ethel, Ontario 177/C4
Ethel, Wash. 310/C4
Ethel, W. Va. 312/C7
Ethelbert, Manitoba 179/B3
Ethel Creek, W. Australia 92/C3
Ethelsville, Ala. 195/B4
Ethelton, Sask. 181/G3
Ether, N.C. 281/K4
Ethete, Wyo. 319/D2
Ethiopia 2/L5
ETHIOPIA 59/C7
Ethiopia 102/F4
ETHIOPIA 111/G5
Ethridge, Mont. 262/D2
Ethridge, Tenn. 237/G10
Etive, Loch (inlet), Scotland 15/C4
Etiwanda, Calif. 204/E10
Etna, Calif. 204/C2
Etna, Calif. 204/C2
Etna (vol.), Italy 7/F5
Etna (vol.), Italy 34/E6
Etna•, Maine 243/E6
Etna, N.H. 268/C3
Etna, Ohio 284/E6
Etna, Pa. 294/B6
Etna, Utah 304/A2
Etna, Wyo. 319/A2
Etna Green, Ind. 227/E2
Etobicoke, Ontario 177/J4
Etoile, Ky. 237/L7
Etoile, Zaire 115/E6
Etolin (isl.), Alaska 196/N2
Etolin (str.), Alaska 196/E2
Etomami (riv.), Manitoba 179/F2
Etomami (riv.), Sask. 181/J3
Eton, England 10/F5
Eton, England 13/G8
Eton, Georgia 217/C1
Etorofu (Iturup) (isl.), Japan 81/N1
Etosha Pan (salt pan), Namibia 118/B3

Farallon 367

Etosha Salt Pan, Namibia 102/D6
Etoumbi, Congo 115/B3
Etowah (co.), Ala. 195/F2
Etowah, Ark. 202/K2
Etowah (riv.), Georgia 217/C2
Etowah, N.C. 281/D4
Etowah, Tenn. 237/M10
Étretat, France 28/D3
Etta, Miss. 256/F2
Etta (lake), N. Dak. 282/L6
Et Tafila, Jordan 65/E5
Et Taiyiba, Jordan 65/D2
Ettelbruck, Luxembourg 27/J9
Et Tell el Abyad, Syria 63/H4
Etten-Leur, Netherlands 27/F5
Etter, Minn. 255/F6
Etterbeek, Belgium 27/B9
Etters, Pa. 294/J5
Etters Beach, Sask. 181/F4
Ettington, Sask. 181/F6
Ettlingen, Germany 22/C4
Ettrick, Scotland 15/E5
Ettrick, Va. 307/O6
Ettrick, Wis. 317/D7
Ettrick Pen (mt.), Scotland 15/E5
Etty, Ky. 237/R6
Etzatlán, Mexico 150/G6
Etzikom, Alberta 182/E5
Etzikom Coulee (riv.), Alberta 182/E5
Eu, France 28/D3
Euabalong, N.S. Wales 97/D3
Eubank, Ky. 237/M6
Euboea (Évvoia) (isl.), Greece 45/G6
Eucha, Okla. 288/S2
Eucha (lake), Okla. 288/S2
Eucla, W. Australia 92/E5
Euclid, Minn. 255/B3
Euclid, Ohio 284/J9
Eucumbene (lake), N.S. Wales 97/E5
Eucutta, Miss. 256/G7
Eudora, Ark. 202/H7
Eudora, Kansas 232/G3
Eudora, Miss. 256/D1
Eudora, Mo. 261/E7
Eufaula, Ala. 195/H7
Eufaula (Walter F. George Res.) (lake), Ala. 195/H7
Eufaula (Walter F. George Res.) (lake), Georgia 217/B7
Eufaula (res.), Ohio 284/L4
Eufaula, Okla. 288/P4
Eufaula (lake), Okla. 288/P4
Eugene, Ind. 227/B5
Eugene, Mo. 261/H6
Eugene, Oreg. 188/B2
Eugene, Oreg. 146/F5
Eugene, Oreg. 291/D3
Eugene O'Neill Nat'l Hist. Site, Calif. 204/K2
Eugowra, N.S. Wales 97/E3
Euharlee, Georgia 217/C2
Euless, Texas 303/F2
Eulo, Queensland 95/C6
Eulonia, Georgia 217/K7
Eumungerie, N.S. Wales 97/E2
Eunice, La. 238/F6
Eunice, N. Mex. 274/F6
Eunola, Ala. 195/G8
Eupen, Belgium 27/J7
Euphrates (riv.) 54/F6
Euphrates (riv.), Iran 59/E3
Euphrates (riv.), Iraq 59/E3
Euphrates (riv.), Iraq 66/D4
Euphrates (riv.), Syria 59/E3
Euphrates (El Furat) (riv.), Syria 63/H4
Euphrates (Firat) (riv.), Turkey 63/G4
Eupora, Miss. 256/F3
Eure (dept.), France 28/D3
Eure (riv.), France 28/D3
Eure, N.C. 281/R2
Eure-et-Loir (dept.), France 28/D3
Eureka, Calif. 188/B2
Eureka, Calif. 146/F5
Eureka, Calif. 204/A3
Eureka, Canada 4/A14
Eureka, Colo. 208/D7
Eureka (res.), Fla. 212/E2
Eureka, Ill. 222/D3
Eureka, Ind. 227/C9
Eureka, Kansas 232/F4
Eureka, Mo. 261/M4
Eureka, Mont. 262/B2
Eureka (co.), Nev. 266/E3
Eureka, Nev. 266/E3
Eureka, N.C. 281/O3
Eureka, N.W.T. 146/K2
Eureka, N.W.T. 162/N3
Eureka, N.W. Terr. 187/K2
Eureka (sound), N.W. Terr. 187/K2
Eureka, Nova Scotia 168/F3
Eureka, S.C. 296/E2
Eureka, S.C. 296/D4
Eureka, S. Dak. 298/K2
Eureka, Utah 304/B4
Eureka, Wash. 310/G4
Eureka, W. Va. 312/D4
Eureka Lodge, Alaska 196/C1
Eureka Springs, Ark. 202/C1
Euroa, Victoria 97/C5
Europa (pt.), Gibraltar 33/D4
Europa (isl.), Réunion 102/G7
Europa (isl.), Réunion 118/G4
Europe 2/K3
Europoort, Netherlands 27/E5
Eusebio Ayala, Paraguay 144/B4
Euskirchen, Germany 22/B3
Eustace, Texas 303/H5
Eustis, Fla. 212/E3
Eustis, Maine 243/B5
Eustis•, Maine 243/B5
Eustis, Nebr. 264/D4
Euston, N.S. Wales 97/B4
Eutaw, Ala. 195/C5
Eutawville, S.C. 296/G5
Eutin, Germany 22/D1
Eutsuk (lake), Br. Col. 184/D3
Eva, Ala. 195/E2
Eva (lake), Alberta 182/B5
Eva, La. 238/G4
Eva, Okla. 288/C1
Eva, Tenn. 237/E8
Evadale, Texas 303/L7
Eva Downs, North. Terr. 93/D5
Évain, Québec 174/B3
Evan, Minn. 255/D6
Evan (lake), Québec 174/B2
Evandale, New Bruns. 170/D3
Evandale, Tasmania 99/D3
Evangeline (par.), La. 238/F5
Evangeline, La. 238/F6
Evangeline, New Bruns. 170/F1
Evans, Colo. 208/K2
Evans (mt.), Colo. 208/H3
Evans (co.), Georgia 217/J6
Evans, Georgia 217/H3
Evans, La. 238/D5
Evans (head), N.S. Wales 97/G1
Evans (str.), N.W.T. 162/H3
Evans (str.), N.W. Terr. 187/K3
Evans, Wash. 310/H2
Evans, W. Va. 312/C5
Evansburg, Alberta 182/C3
Evans Center, N.Y. 276/B5
Evans City, Pa. 294/B4
Evansdale, Iowa 229/J4
Evans Head, N.S. Wales 97/G1
Evans Mills, N.Y. 276/J2
Evansport, Ohio 284/B3
Evanston, Ill. 222/B5
Evanston, Ind. 227/D8
Evanston, Wyo. 188/D2
Evanston, Wyo. 319/B4
Evansville (Bettles Field), Alaska 196/H1
Evansville, Ark. 202/B2
Evansville, Ill. 222/D5
Evansville, Ind. 138/J3
Evansville, Ind. 146/K6
Evansville, Ind. 227/C9
Evansville, Minn. 255/C4
Evansville, Miss. 256/D1
Evansville, Pa. 294/L5
Evansville, Wis. 317/H10
Evansville, Wyo. 319/F3
Evant, Texas 303/G6
Evanton, Scotland 15/D3
Evart, Mich. 250/D5
Evarts, Ky. 237/P7
Evaton, S. Africa 118/H7
Evaz, Iran 66/J7
Eveleth, Minn. 255/F3
Evelyn, La. 238/D3
Evendale, Ohio 284/C9
Evening Shade, Ark. 202/G1
Evenki Aut. Okr., U.S.S.R. 48/K3
Evensk, U.S.S.R. 4/C1
Evensk, U.S.S.R. 48/Q3
Evensville, Tenn. 237/M9
Even Yehuda, Israel 65/B3
Everard (lake), S. Australia 88/E6
Everard (lake), S. Australia 94/D4
Everard (ranges), S. Australia 94/C2
Evere, Belgium 27/C9
Everest (mt.) 54/K7
Everest (mt.), China 77/C6
Everest, Kansas 232/G2
Everest (mt.), Nepal 68/F3
Everest, N. Dak. 282/R6
Everett, Georgia 217/J8
Everett, Mass. 249/D6
Everett (mt.), Mass. 249/A4
Everett, New Bruns. 170/C1
Everett (dam), N.H. 268/D5
Everett (mts.), N.W. Terr. 187/M3
Everett, Ontario 177/E3
Everett, Pa. 294/F5
Everett, Wash. 188/B1
Everett, Wash. 310/C3
Everetts, N.C. 281/P3
Everettville, W. Va. 312/F3
Evergem, Belgium 27/D6
Everglades, The (swamp), Fla. 212/F6
Everglades, The (swamp), Fla. 188/K5
Everglades City, Fla. 212/E6
Everglades Nat'l Park, Fla. 212/F6
Evergreen, Ala. 195/E8
Evergreen, Colo. 208/J3
Evergreen, La. 238/F5
Evergreen, N.C. 281/M6
Evergreen, Va. 307/L6
Evergreen Park, Ill. 222/B6
Everly, Iowa 229/C2
Everman, Texas 303/F3
Everson, Pa. 294/C5
Everson, Wash. 310/C2
Eversonville, Mo. 261/F3
Everton, Ark. 202/E1
Everton, Ind. 227/G5
Everton, Mo. 261/E8
Evesham, England 10/E4
Evesham, England 13/F5
Evesham, Sask. 181/B3
Evington, Va. 307/K6
Evolène, Switzerland 39/D4
Évora (dist.), Portugal 33/C3
Évora, Portugal 7/D5
Évora, Portugal 33/C3
Évreux, France 28/D3
Évros (riv.), Greece 45/H5
Évry, France 28/E3
Évvoia (isl.), Greece 7/G5
Évvoia (isl.), Greece 45/G6
Ewa, Hawaii 218/A4
Ewab (Kai) (isls.), Indonesia 85/J7
Ewa Beach, Hawaii 218/A4
Ewan, N.J. 273/C4
Ewan, Wash. 310/H3
Ewaninga, North. Terr. 93/D7
Ewart, Iowa 229/H5
Ewarton, Jamaica 156/C3
Ewarton, Jamaica 158/J6
Ewauna (lake), Oreg. 291/F5
Ewe, Loch (inlet), Scotland 15/C3
Ewell, Md. 245/O9
Ewen, Mich. 250/F2
Ewing, Ill. 222/E5
Ewing, Ky. 237/O4
Ewing, Mo. 261/J2
Ewing, Nebr. 264/F2
Ewing, N.J. 273/D3
Ewing (mt.), North. Terr. 93/E7
Ewing, Va. 307/B7
Ewington, Ohio 284/F8
Ewo, Congo 115/B4
Exaltación, Bolivia 136/C3
Excel, Ala. 195/D8
Excel, Alberta 182/E4
Excello, Mo. 261/H3
Excello, Ohio 284/B7
Excelsior, Minn. 255/E6
Excelsior (mts.), Nev. 266/C4
Excelsior, Wis. 317/E9
Excelsior Springs, Mo. 261/R4
Exchange, W. Va. 312/E5
Excursion Inlet, Alaska 196/M1
Exe (riv.), England 13/D7
Exe (riv.), England 10/E5
Executive Committee (range), Ant. 5/B12
Exeland, Wis. 317/D4
Exeter, Calif. 204/F7
Exeter, Conn. 210/F2
Exeter, England 13/D7
Exeter, England 10/E5
Exeter, Ill. 222/C4
Exeter, Maine 243/E6
Exeter•, Maine 243/E6
Exeter, Mo. 261/D9
Exeter, Nebr. 264/G4
Exeter, N.H. 268/F6
Exeter•, N.H. 268/F6
Exeter (riv.), N.H. 268/E6
Exeter (sound), N.W. Terr. 187/M3
Exeter, Ontario 177/C4
Exeter•, R.I. 249/H6
Exeter, Tasmania 99/C3
Exira, Iowa 229/D5
Exline, Iowa 229/H7
Exminster, England 13/D7
Exmoor National Park, England 13/D6
Exmore, Va. 307/S5
Exmouth, England 13/D7
Exmouth, England 10/E5
Exmouth, W. Australia 88/A4
Exmouth, W. Australia 92/A3
Exmouth (gulf), W. Australia 88/A4
Exmouth (gulf), W. Australia 92/A3
Expanse, Sask. 181/E6
Experiment, Georgia 217/D4
Exploits (riv.), Newf. 166/C4
Export, Pa. 294/C5
Exshaw, Alberta 182/C4
Extension, Br. Col. 184/J3
Extension, La. 238/G3
Exu, Brazil 132/G4
Exuma (cays), Bahamas 156/C1
Exuma (sound), Bahamas 156/C1
Eyasi (lake), Tanzania 115/F4
Eye, England 10/G4
Eye, England 13/J5
Eye (pen.), Scotland 15/B2
Eyebrow, Sask. 181/E5
Eyebrow (lake), Sask. 181/E5
Eyehill (creek), Sask. 181/B3
Eyemouth, Scotland 15/F5
Eyemouth, Scotland 10/F3
Eynesil, Turkey 63/H2
Eynhallow (sound), Scotland 15/E1
Eynort, Loch (inlet), Scotland 15/A3
Eyota, Minn. 255/F7
Eyre (lake), Australia 87/D8
Eyre (bay), Chile 138/D8
Eyre (mts.), N. Zealand 100/B6
Eyre (riv.), Queensland 88/F5
Eyre (lake), S. Australia 88/F5
Eyre (pen.), S. Australia 88/F6
Eyre (pen.), S. Australia 94/D5
Eyre, W. Australia 92/D6
Eyrecourt, Ireland 17/E5
Eyre North (lake), S. Australia 94/E3
Eyre South (lake), S. Australia 94/E3
Eysturoy (isl.), Denmark 21/B3
Eyüp, Turkey 63/D6
Ezel, Ky. 237/P5
Ezequiel Montes, Mexico 150/K6
Ezibider, Turkey 63/H2
Ezine, Turkey 63/B3
Ezna, Iran 66/F4
Ez Zababida, West Bank 65/C3
Ez Zarqa', Jordan 65/E3
Ez Zuetina, Libya 111/D1

F

Faaa, Fr. Poly. 86/S13
Fabens, Texas 303/B10
Faber (lake), N.W. Terr. 187/G3
Faber, Va. 307/L5
Fabius, Ala. 195/G1
Fabius, N.Y. 276/J5
Fåborg, Denmark 21/D7
Fåborg, Denmark 18/G9
Fabriano, Italy 34/D3
Fabyan, Alberta 182/E3
Fabyan, Conn. 210/H1
Fabyan House, N.H. 268/E3
Facatativá, Colombia 126/C5
Faceville, Georgia 217/C9
Fachi, Niger 106/G5
Fackler, Ala. 195/G1
Factoryville, Pa. 294/L2
Facundo, Argentina 143/C6
Fada, Chad 111/D4
Fada-N'Gourma, Burkina Faso 106/E6
Fadd, Hungary 41/E3
Faddeyevskiy (isl.), U.S.S.R. 4/B2
Faddeyevskiy (isl.), U.S.S.R. 48/P2
Faden, Newf. 166/A3
Faenza, Italy 34/D2
Fafan (riv.), Ethiopia 111/H6
Fafe, Portugal 33/B2
Fagan, Ky. 237/O5
Făgăraş, Romania 45/G3
Fagernes, Norway 18/F6
Fagersta, Sweden 18/J6
Fagnano (lake), Argentina 143/C7
Fagnano (lake), Chile 138/F11
Faguibine (lake), Mali 106/D5
Fagundes, Brazil 132/C4
Fagus, Mo. 261/M9
Fahan, Ireland 17/G1
Fahrej (Iranshahr), Iran 66/M7
Fahrej (Iranshahr), Iran 59/H4
Faial (isl.), Portugal 33/B1
Faid, Saudi Arabia 59/D4
Faido, Switzerland 39/G4
Fainaven (mt.), Scotland 15/D2
Fair (head), N. Ireland 17/J1
Fair (isl.), Scotland 10/F1
Fairacres, N. Mex. 274/C6
Fairbank, Ariz. 198/E7
Fairbank, Iowa 229/K3
Fairbank, Md. 245/N6
Fairbanks, Alaska 146/D3
Fairbanks, Alaska 196/J2
Fairbanks, Alaska 188/D5
Fairbanks, Fla. 212/D2
Fairbanks, Ind. 227/B6
Fairbanks, La. 238/F1
Fairbanks, Maine 243/C6
Fairbanks, Minn. 255/G3
Fairbanks, U.S. 4/C17
Fairbanks, U.S. 2/C2
Fair Bluff, N.C. 281/M6
Fairborn, Ohio 284/B6
Fairburn, Georgia 217/J2
Fairburn, S. Dak. 298/C6
Fairbury, Ill. 222/E3
Fairbury, Nebr. 264/G4
Fairchance, Pa. 294/C6
Fairchild, Wis. 317/D6
Fairchild A.F.B., Wash. 310/H3
Fairdale, Ill. 222/E1
Fairdale, Ky. 237/K4
Fairdale, N. Dak. 282/O3
Fairdealing, Mo. 261/L9
Fairfax, Calif. 204/H1
Fairfax, Iowa 229/K5
Fairfax, Manitoba 179/B5
Fairfax, Minn. 255/D6
Fairfax, Mo. 261/B2
Fairfax, Ohio 284/C9
Fairfax, Okla. 288/N1
Fairfax, S.C. 296/E6
Fairfax, S. Dak. 298/M7
Fairfax•, Vt. 268/B2
Fairfax (co.), Va. 307/O3
Fairfax (I.C.), Va. 307/R3
Fairfax, Wash. 310/C4
Fairfax Station, Va. 307/R3
Fairfield, Ala. 195/E4
Fairfield, Calif. 204/K1
Fairfield (co.), Conn. 210/B3
Fairfield•, Conn. 210/B4
Fairfield, Fla. 212/D2
Fairfield, Idaho 220/D6
Fairfield, Ill. 222/E5
Fairfield, Iowa 229/J6
Fairfield, Ky. 237/L5
Fairfield, Maine 243/D6
Fairfield•, Maine 243/D6
Fairfield, Mont. 262/D3
Fairfield, Nebr. 264/G4
Fairfield, New Bruns. 170/E3
Fairfield•, N.J. 273/A2
Fairfield, N.S. Wales 88/K4
Fairfield, N.S. Wales 97/H3
Fairfield, N. Zealand 100/C6
Fairfield, N.C. 281/S3
Fairfield, N. Dak. 282/D5
Fairfield (co.), Ohio 284/E6
Fairfield, Ohio 284/A7
Fairfield, Pa. 294/H6
Fairfield (co.), S.C. 296/E3
Fairfield, Tenn. 237/J9
Fairfield, Texas 303/H6
Fairfield, Utah 304/B3
Fairfield•, Vt. 268/B2
Fairfield (pond), Vt. 268/A2
Fairfield, Va. 307/K5
Fairfield, Wash. 310/H3
Fairfield Center, Maine 243/D6
Fairford, Ala. 195/B8
Fairford, Manitoba 179/D3
Fairgrange, Ill. 222/E4
Fairgrove, Mich. 250/F5
Fair Grove, Mo. 261/F8W
Fair Harbour, Br. Col. 184/D5
Fairhaven•, Mass. 249/L6
Fair Haven, Mich. 250/G6
Fairhaven, Minn. 255/D5
Fairhaven, New Bruns. 170/C4
Fair Haven, N.J. 273/E3
Fair Haven, N.Y. 276/G4
Fairhaven, Ohio 284/A6
Fair Haven, Vt. 268/A4
Fair Haven•, Vt. 268/A4
Fair Hill, Md. 245/P2
Fairholme, Sask. 181/C2
Fairhope, Ala. 195/C10
Fairhope, Pa. 294/E6
Fairisle, New Bruns. 170/E1
Fair Isle (isl.), Scotland 15/F3
Fairland, Ind. 227/F5
Fairland, Okla. 288/S1
Fair Lawn, N.J. 273/B1
Fairlawn, Ohio 284/G3
Fairlawn, Va. 307/G6
Fairlee, Md. 245/O4
Fairlee•, Vt. 268/C4
Fairless Hills, Pa. 294/N5
Fairlie, N. Zealand 100/C6
Fairlie, Scotland 15/D5
Fairlight, Sask. 181/K6
Fairmead, Calif. 204/E6
Fairmont, Ill. 222/A2
Fairmont, Minn. 255/D7
Fairmont, Mo. 261/J2
Fairmont, Nebr. 264/G4
Fairmont, N.C. 281/L6
Fairmont, Okla. 288/L2
Fairmont, W. Va. 188/K3
Fairmont, W. Va. 312/F4
Fairmont City, Ill. 222/B2
Fairmont Hot Springs, Br. Col. 184/J5
Fairmount, Georgia 217/C2
Fairmount, Ill. 222/F3
Fairmount, Ind. 227/F4
Fairmount, Md. 245/P8
Fairmount, N. Dak. 282/S7
Fairmount, Sask. 181/B4
Fairmount Heights, Md. 245/G5
Fair Oaks, Ark. 202/J3
Fair Oaks, Calif. 204/C8
Fair Oaks, Georgia 217/J1
Fair Oaks, Ind. 227/C2
Fair Oaks, Okla. 288/P2
Fair Plain, Mich. 250/C6
Fairplain, W. Va. 312/C5
Fairplay, Colo. 208/H4
Fairplay, Ky. 237/L7
Fair Play, Mo. 261/E7
Fair Play, S.C. 296/A2
Fairpoint, Ohio 284/J5
Fairpoint, S. Dak. 298/D4
Fairport, Iowa 229/M6
Fairport, Kansas 232/C2
Fairport, Mo. 261/D2
Fairport, N.Y. 276/F4
Fairport, Va. 307/R5
Fairport Harbor, Ohio 284/H2
Fairton, N.J. 273/C5
Fairvale, New Bruns. 170/E3
Fairview, Ala. 195/E2
Fairview, Alberta 182/A1
Fairview, Ill. 222/B3
Fairview, Ind. 227/G5
Fairview, Ind. 227/G7
Fairview, Kansas 232/G2
Fairview, Ky. 237/S2
Fairview, Ky. 237/G7
Fairview, Mich. 250/F4
Fairview, Mo. 261/D9
Fairview, Mont. 262/M3
Fairview, N.J. 273/C2
Fairview, N.Y. 276/N7
Fairview, N.C. 281/D3
Fairview, Ohio 284/H5
Fairview, Okla. 288/J2
Fairview, Oreg. 291/B2
Fairview, Pa. 294/B1
Fairview, Pa. 294/C3
Fairview, S. Dak. 298/R7
Fairview, Tenn. 237/G9
Fairview, Utah 304/C4
Fairview, W. Va. 312/F3
Fairview, Wyo. 319/B3
Fairview Heights, Ill. 222/B3
Fairview Park, Ind. 227/C5
Fairview Park, Ohio 284/G9
Fairview-Sumach, Wash. 310/E4
Fair Water, Wis. 317/J8
Fairway, Kansas 232/H2
Fairweather (cape), Alaska 196/L1
Fairweather (mt.), Alaska 196/L1
Fairweather (mt.), Br. Col. 184/H1
Fairy Glen, Sask. 181/G2
Fais (isl.), Micronesia 87/E5
Faisalabad, Pakistan 54/J6
Faisalabad, Pakistan 59/K3
Faisalabad, Pakistan 68/C2
Faison, N.C. 281/N4
Faith, Minn. 255/B3
Faith, N.C. 281/J3
Faith, S. Dak. 298/E4
Faithorn, Mich. 250/B3
Faizabad-cum-Ayodhya, India 68/E3
Fajami, Syria 63/J5
Fajardo, P. Rico 161/F1
Fajardo (riv.), P. Rico 161/F1
Fajou (isl.), Guadeloupe 161/A6
Fakaofo (atoll), Tokelau Is. 87/J6
Fakarava (atoll), Fr. Poly. 87/M7
Fakenham, England 13/H5
Fakfak, Indonesia 85/J6
Fakılı, Turkey 63/F3
Fakse, Denmark 21/F7
Fakse (bay), Denmark 21/F7
Fakse Ladeplads, Denmark 21/F7
Falaise, France 28/C3
Falam, Burma 72/B2
Falama, West Bank 65/C3
Falcarragh, Ireland 17/E1
Fălçiu, Romania 45/J2
Falcon, Ky. 237/P5
Falcon (lake), Manitoba 179/G5
Falcón (res.), Mexico 150/K3
Falcon, Miss. 256/D2
Falcon, N.C. 281/M4
Falcon (cape), Oreg. 291/C2
Falcon (dam), Texas 303/E11
Falcon (res.), Texas 188/G5
Falcon (res.), Texas 303/E11
Falcón (state), Venezuela 124/D2
Falcone (cape), Italy 34/B4
Falconer, N.Y. 276/B6
Falcon Heights, Minn. 255/G5
Falcon Heights, Oreg. 291/F5
Falcon Lake, Manitoba 179/G5
Falémé (riv.), Mali 106/B6
Falémé (riv.), Senegal 106/B6
Faleolo, W. Samoa 86/L8
Falfurrias, Texas 303/F10
Falher, Alberta 182/B2
Falkenberg, Sweden 18/H8
Falkensee, Germany 22/E3
Falkenstein, Germany 22/E3
Falkirk, N. Dak. 282/H5
Falkirk, Scotland 10/B1
Falkirk, Scotland 15/C1
Falkland (isls.) 2/G8
Falkland (isls.) 143/D7
Falkland (sound), Falk. Is. 143/D7
Falkland, Br. Col. 184/H5
Falkland, N.C. 281/O3
Falkland, Scotland 15/E4
Falkland Islands 120/D8
FALKLAND ISLANDS 143
Falkner, Miss. 256/G1
Falknov (Sokolov), Czech. 41/B1
Falköping, Sweden 18/H7
Falkville, Ala. 195/E2
Fall (riv.), Kansas 232/G4
Falla, Cuba 158/F2
Fall Branch, Tenn. 237/R8
Fallbrook, Calif. 204/H10
Fall City, Wash. 310/D3
Fall Creek, Oreg. 291/E4
Fall Creek, Wis. 317/D6
Fallin, Scotland 15/C1
Falling Spring (Renick), W. Va. 312/F6
Falling Waters, W. Va. 312/L3
Fallis, Okla. 288/M3
Fall Mills, Tenn. 237/J10
Fallon (co.), Mont. 262/M4
Fallon, Mont. 262/L4
Fallon, Nev. 266/C3
Fallon Ind. Res., Nev. 266/C3
Fallon Nav. Air Sta., Nev. 266/C3
Fall River, Kansas 232/G4
Fall River (lake), Kansas 232/F4
Fall River, Mass. 188/M2
Fall River, Mass. 249/K6
Fall River, Nova Scotia 168/E4
Fall River (co.), S. Dak. 298/B7
Fall River, Tenn. 237/G10
Fall River, Wis. 317/H9
Fall River Mills, Calif. 204/D3
Falls (riv.), Mass. 249/D2
Falls, Pa. 294/E6
Falls (co.), Texas 303/H6
Falls Church (I.C.), Va. 307/S2
Falls City, Nebr. 264/J4
Falls City, Oreg. 291/D3
Falls City, Texas 303/G9
Falls Creek, Pa. 294/E3
Falls Mill, W. Va. 312/E5
Falls Mills, Va. 307/F6
Falls of Rough, Ky. 237/J5
Fallston, Md. 245/N2
Fallston, N.C. 281/G4
Falls Village, Conn. 210/B1
Fallsville, Ark. 202/D2
Falmouth, Ant. & Bar. 161/E11
Falmouth, Ant. & Bar. 156/F3
Falmouth, England 10/D5
Falmouth, England 13/B7
Falmouth (bay), England 13/B7
Falmouth, Ind. 227/G5
Falmouth, Jamaica 158/H5
Falmouth, Jamaica 156/C3
Falmouth, Ky. 237/N3
Falmouth, Maine 243/C8
Falmouth•, Maine 243/C8
Falmouth, Mass. 249/M6
Falmouth•, Mass. 249/M6
Falmouth, Mich. 250/E4
Falmouth, Nova Scotia 168/D3
Falmouth, Va. 307/O4
False (bay), S. Africa 118/F7
False Detour (chan.), Mich. 250/F3
False Divi (pt.), India 68/E5
False Pass, Alaska 196/F4
Falso (cape), Dom. Rep. 158/C7
Falso (cape), Honduras 154/F3
Falso (cape), Mexico 150/D5
Falster (isl.), Denmark 21/F8
Fălticeni, Romania 45/H2
Falun, Kansas 232/E3
Falun, Sweden 18/J6
Falun, Sweden 7/F2
Falun, Wis. 317/A4
Famagusta, Cyprus 63/F5
Famagusta, Cyprus 59/B3
Famagusta (bay), Cyprus 63/F5
Famaka, Sudan 111/F5
Famatina, Argentina 143/C2
Famatina, Sierra de (mts.), Argentina 143/C2
Family (lake), Manitoba 179/G3
Famoso, Calif. 204/F8
Fan (lake), N. Dak. 282/L2
Fanad (head), Ireland 17/F1
Fancy Farm, Ky. 237/D7
Fancy Gap, Va. 307/G7
Fancy Prairie, Ill. 222/D4
Fandriana, Madagascar 118/H4
Fangak, Sudan 111/F6
Fang Xian, China 77/G5
Fangzheng, China 77/L2
Fannettsburg, Pa. 294/G5
Fannich, Loch (lake), Scotland 15/D3
Fannin (co.), Georgia 217/D1
Fannin, Miss. 256/E6
Fannin (co.), Texas 303/H4
Fannin, Texas 303/G9
Fanning (Tabuaeran) (isl.), Kiribati 87/L5
Fanning (Tabuaeran) (isl.), Kiribati 2/B5
Fanning Springs, Fla. 212/D2
Fanny Bay, Br. Col. 184/H2
Fannystelle, Manitoba 179/E5
Fanø (isl.), Denmark 21/B7
Fanø (isl.), Denmark 18/F9
Fano, Italy 34/D3
Fanshawe, Okla. 288/S5
Fan Si Pan (mt.), Vietnam 72/D2
Fantasque (pt.), Haiti 158/B6
Fanwood, N.J. 273/E2
Fao, Iraq 66/F6
Faradje, Zaire 115/E3
Faradofay, Madagascar 102/G7
Faradofay, Madagascar 118/H5
Farafangana, Madagascar 102/G7
Farafangana, Madagascar 118/H4
Farâfra (oasis), Egypt 111/E2
Farâfra (oasis), Egypt 59/A4
Farah, Afghanistan 68/A2
Farah, Afghanistan 54/H6
Farah, Afghanistan 59/H3
Farah Rud (riv.) 54/H6
Farah Rud (riv.), Afghanistan 59/H3
Farah Rud (riv.), Afghanistan 68/A2
Farallon (isls.), Calif. 204/B6

Farallon de Pajaros (isl.), No. Marianas 87/E3
Farallons, The (gulf), Calif. 204/H2
Faranah, Guinea 106/B6
Farasan (isls.), Saudi Arabia 59/D6
Faraulep (atoll), Micronesia 87/E5
Farber, Mo. 261/J4
Farciennes, Belgium 27/E8
Fareham, England 10/F5
Fareham, England 13/F7
Farewell, Alaska 196/H2
Farewell (cape), Greenl. 4/D12
Farewell (cape), Greenland 146/P4
Farewell (cape), Greenland 2/G3
Farewell (cape), N. Zealand 100/D4
Farfa, Italy 34/D3
Farfán, Ecuador 128/D2
Fargo, Ark. 202/H4
Fargo, Georgia 217/G9
Fargo, Mich. 250/G5
Fargo, N. Dak. 146/J5
Fargo, N. Dak. 188/G1
Fargo, N. Dak. 282/S6
Fargo, Okla. 288/G2
Fargo, Texas 303/E3
Far Hills, N.J. 273/D2
Faribault (co.), Minn. 255/D7
Faribault, Minn. 188/H2
Faribault, Minn. 255/E6
Faridpur, Bangladesh 68/F4
Fariman, Iran 66/L3
Farina, Ill. 222/E5
Farisita, Colo. 208/J7
Fariston, Ky. 237/N6
Färjestaden, Sweden 18/K8
Farler, Ky. 237/P6
Farley, Iowa 229/L4
Farley, Mo. 261/O4
Farley, N. Mex. 274/E2
Farlin, Iowa 229/K4
Farlington, Kansas 232/H4
Farm (riv.), Conn. 210/D3
Farmdale, Ohio 284/J3
Farmer, N.C. 281/K3
Farmer (isl.), N.W. Terr. 187/K4
Farmer, Ohio 284/A3
Farmer, S. Dak. 298/O6
Farmer City, Ill. 222/E3
Farmers, Ky. 237/P4
Farmers Branch, Texas 303/G2
Farmersburg, Ind. 227/C6
Farmersburg, Iowa 229/L3
Farmersville, Ala. 195/E6
Farmersville, Calif. 204/F7
Farmersville, Ill. 222/D4
Farmersville, Mo. 261/E3
Farmersville, Ohio 284/A6
Farmersville, Texas 303/H4
Farmerville, La. 238/F1
Farmhaven, Miss. 256/E5
Farmili (riv.), Conn. 210/C3
Farmingdale•, Maine 243/D7
Farmingdale•, Maine 243/D7
Farmingdale, N.J. 273/D3
Farmingdale, N.Y. 276/R7
Farmingdale, S. Dak. 298/D6
Farmington, Ark. 202/B1
Farmington, Br. Col. 184/G2
Farmington, Calif. 204/E6
Farmington•, Conn. 210/D2
Farmington (riv.), Conn. 210/D1
Farmington, Del. 245/R5
Farmington, Georgia 217/F3
Farmington, Ill. 222/C3
Farmington, Iowa 229/K7
Farmington, Ky. 237/D7
Farmington, Maine 243/C6
Farmington•, Maine 243/C6
Farmington, Md. 245/O2
Farmington, Mich. 250/F6
Farmington, Minn. 255/E6
Farmington, Mo. 261/M7
Farmington, N.H. 268/E5
Farmington•, N.H. 268/E5
Farmington, N. Mex. 188/E3
Farmington, N. Mex. 274/A2
Farmington, N.C. 281/H3
Farmington, Oreg. 291/A2
Farmington, Tenn. 237/H9
Farmington, Utah 304/C3
Farmington, Wash. 310/H3
Farmington, W. Va. 312/F3
Farmington, Wis. 317/F4
Farmington Falls, Maine 243/C6
Farmington Hills, Mich. 250/F6
Farmland, Ind. 227/G4
Farmville, N.C. 281/O3
Farmville, Va. 307/M6
Farnam, Nebr. 264/D4
Farnams, Mass. 249/B2
Farnborough, England 13/G8
Farner, Tenn. 237/N10
Farnham, England 13/G8
Farnham, England 10/F5
Farnham, N.Y. 276/B6
Farnham, Québec 172/E4
Farnham, Va. 307/P5
Farnhamville, Iowa 229/D4
Farnsworth, Texas 303/C1
Farnworth, England 13/H2
Faro, Brazil 132/B3
Faro (dist.), Portugal 33/B4
Faro, Portugal 7/D5
Faro, Portugal 33/B4
Fårö (isl.), Sweden 18/L8
Faro, Yukon 187/E3
Faro, Yukon 162/G4
Faroe (isls.), Den. 4/C10
Faroe (isls.), Denmark 7/D2
Faroe (isls.), Denmark 21/B2
FAROE ISLANDS, 21/B2
Faroe Islands, Denmark 21/B2
Fårösund, Sweden 18/L8
Farquhar (cape), W. Australia 88/A4
Farquhar (cape), W. Australia 92/A3
Farr (bay), Ant. 5/C5
Farragut, Iowa 229/C7

Farrar, Georgia 217/E4
Farrar, Iowa 229/G5
Farrar, Mo. 261/N7
Farrar (riv.), Scotland 15/D3
Farrashband, Iran 66/G6
Farrell (lake), Alberta 182/D4
Farrell, Miss. 256/C2
Farrell, Pa. 294/A3
Farrellton, Québec 172/A4
Farris, Okla. 288/P6
Farrow, Alberta 182/D4
Farrukhabad-cum-Fatehgarh, India 68/D3
Fars (prov.), Iran 66/H6
Fársala, Greece 45/F6
Farsi, Afghanistan 68/A2
Farsi, Afghanistan 59/H3
Farsi (isl.), Iran 66/G7
Farsø, Denmark 21/C4
Farson, Iowa 229/J6
Farson, Wyo. 319/C3
Farsund, Norway 18/E7
Fartak, Ras (cape), Yemen 59/F6
Farum, Denmark 21/F6
Farwell, Mich. 250/E5
Farwell, Minn. 255/C5
Farwell, Nebr. 264/F3
Farwell, Texas 303/A3
Fasa, Iran 66/H6
Fasa, Iran 59/F4
Fasano, Italy 34/F4
Fashoda (Kodok), Sudan 111/F6
Fassett, Québec 172/C4
Fastnet Rock (isl.), Ireland 17/B9
Fastov, U.S.S.R. 52/C4
Fatagar Tuting (cape), Indonesia 85/J6
Fatehpur, Rajasthan, India 68/C3
Fatehpur, Uttar Pradesh, India 68/E3
Fatih, Turkey 63/D6
Fátima, Portugal 33/B3
Fatsa, Turkey 63/G2
Fatshan (Foshan), China 77/H7
Fatuhiva (isl.), Fr. Poly. 87/N7
Faubush, Ky. 237/M6
Faucett, Mo. 261/C3
Faucilles (mts.), France 28/G3
Fauldhouse, Scotland 10/C1
Fauldhouse, Scotland 15/C2
Fauik (riv.), S. Dak. 298/L3
Faulkner, Iowa 229/G3
Faulkner (co.), Ark. 202/F8
Faulkton, S. Dak. 298/L3
Faunsdale, Ala. 195/C6
Fauquier, Ontario 177/J5
Fauquier, Ontario 177/J5
Fauquier (co.), Va. 307/N3
Făurei, Romania 45/H3
Faust, Alberta 182/C2
Favara, Italy 34/D6
Faversham, England 13/H6
Faversham, England 10/G5
Favignana (isl.), Italy 34/D6
Fawcett, Alberta 182/C2
Fawn (riv.), Ind. 227/G1
Fawn (riv.), Mich. 250/D7
Fawn (lake), Ont. 162/H5
Fawn (riv.), Ontario 175/C2
Fawn Grove, Pa. 294/J6
Fawnskin, Calif. 204/J9
Faxaflói (bay), Iceland 21/B1
Faxon, Okla. 288/J6
Fay, Okla. 288/J3
Faya-Largeau, Chad 102/D3
Faya-Largeau, Chad 111/C4
Fayette (co.), Ala. 195/C3
Fayette, Ala. 195/C3
Fayette (co.), Georgia 217/C4
Fayette (co.), Ill. 222/D4
Fayette (co.), Ind. 227/G5
Fayette, Ind. 227/E5
Fayette (co.), Iowa 229/K3
Fayette, Iowa 229/K3
Fayette (co.), Ky. 237/N4
Fayette•, Maine 243/C7
Fayette, Miss. 256/B7
Fayette, Mo. 261/G4
Fayette (co.), Ohio 284/D6
Fayette, Ohio 284/B2
Fayette (co.), Pa. 294/C6
Fayette (co.), Tenn. 237/C10
Fayette (co.), Texas 303/H8
Fayette, Utah 304/C4
Fayette (co.), W. Va. 312/D6
Fayette City, Pa. 294/C5
Fayetteville, Ala. 195/F4
Fayetteville, Ark. 188/H3
Fayetteville, Ark. 202/B1
Fayetteville, Georgia 217/C4
Fayetteville, Ill. 222/D5
Fayetteville, Ind. 227/D7
Fayetteville, Mo. 261/E5
Fayetteville, N.Y. 276/J4
Fayetteville, N.C. 281/L3
Fayetteville, N.C. 281/M4
Fayetteville, Ohio 284/C7
Fayetteville, Pa. 294/G6
Fayetteville, Tenn. 237/H10
Fayetteville, Texas 303/H8
Fayetteville, W. Va. 312/D6
Fayville, Mass. 249/H3
Faywood, N. Mex. 274/B6
Fderik (Fort-Gouraud), Mauritania 106/B4
Feakle, Ireland 17/C6
Feale (riv.), Ireland 17/C7
Fear (cape), N.C. 184/L7
Fear (cape), N.C. 281/O7
Fearer, Md. 245/J2
Fearns Springs, Miss. 256/G4
Feather (riv.), Calif. 204/D4
Feather Falls, Calif. 204/D4
Featherston, N. Zealand 100/E4
Featherston, Okla. 288/P4
Fécamp, France 28/D3
Fédala (Mohammedia), Morocco 106/C2
Federación, Argentina 143/G5

Federal, Alberta 182/E3
Federal, Wyo. 319/G4
Federal Dam, Minn. 255/D3
Federal District, Brazil 132/E6
Federal Heights, Colo. 208/J3
Federalsburg, Md. 245/P6
Federal Territory (state), Laos 72/D7
Federated States of Micronesia 86/D-G5
Fedora, S. Dak. 298/O5
Fedscreek, Ky. 237/S6
Feeagh (lake), Ireland 17/B4
Feeding Hills, Mass. 249/D4
Feeny, N. Ireland 17/H2
Feesburg, Ohio 284/B8
Fegyvernek, Hungary 41/F3
Fehérgyarmat, Hungary 41/G3
Fehmarn (str.), Germany 22/D1
Fehmarn (isl.), Germany 22/D1
Fehmarn (str.), Germany 22/D1
Feia (lake), Brazil 135/F3
Feijó, Brazil 132/G10
Feilding, N. Zealand 100/E4
Feio (riv.), Brazil 135/B2
Feira, Portugal 33/B2
Feira de Santana, Brazil 132/G5
Feira de Santana, Brazil 120/F4
Fejér (co.), Hungary 41/E3
Fejø (isl.), Denmark 21/E8
Feke, Turkey 63/G4
Felanitx, Spain 33/H3
Felch, Mich. 250/B3
Felchville (Reading), Vt. 268/B5
Felda, Fla. 212/E5
Feldbach, Austria 41/C3
Feldberg (mt.), Germany 22/C5
Feldkirch, Austria 41/A3
Feldkirchen in Kärnten, Austria 41/B3
Feliciano (riv.), Argentina 143/G5
Felicité (isl.), Seychelles 118/J5
Felicity, Ohio 284/B8
Felipe Carillo Puerto, Mexico 150/P7
Felipe Matiauda, Paraguay 144/D4
Felipe Yofré, Argentina 143/G4
Felix (cape), N.W. Terr. 187/K4
Felixstowe, England 10/G5
Felixstowe, England 13/J6
Fellbach, Germany 22/C4
Felletin, France 28/E5
Felling, England 13/J3
Fellows, Calif. 204/F8
Fellowsville, W. Va. 312/G4
Fellsburg, Kansas 232/C4
Fellsmere, Fla. 212/F4
Fels am Wagram, Austria 41/C2
Felsberg, Switzerland 39/H3
Felsenthal, Ark. 202/F7
Felt, Idaho 220/G6
Felt, Okla. 288/A1
Felton, Ark. 202/J4
Felton, Calif. 204/K4
Felton, Del. 245/R4
Felton, Georgia 217/B3
Felton, Minn. 255/B3
Felton, Pa. 294/J6
Feltre, Italy 34/C1
Felts Mills, N.Y. 276/J3
Feltwell, England 13/H5
Felty, Ky. 237/O6
Femø (isl.), Denmark 21/E8
Femundsjø (lake), Norway 18/G5
Fence (riv.), Mich. 250/A2
Fence, Wis. 317/F6
Fence Lake, N. Mex. 274/A4
Fender, Georgia 217/E8
Fenelon Falls, Ontario 177/F3
Fengcheng, China 77/K3
Fengjie, China 77/G5
Fengning, China 77/J3
Fengqing, China 77/E7
Fengtai, China 77/J5
Feng Xian, China 77/G5
Fengyang, China 77/J4
Fengxiang, China 77/G5
Fengzhen, China 77/H3
Fen He (riv.), China 77/H4
Fenholloway (riv.), Fla. 212/C1
Feni (isls.), Papua N.G. 86/C2
Fenimore (passage), Alaska 196/L4
Fenit, Ireland 17/B7
Fenn, Alberta 182/D3
Fenn, Idaho 220/B4
Fenner, Calif. 204/K9
Fennimore, Wis. 317/E9
Fennville, Mich. 250/C6
Fenoarivo, Fianarantsoa, Madagascar 118/H4
Fenoarivo, Toamasina, Madagascar 118/H3
Fens, The (reg.), England 13/G5
Fenton (riv.), Conn. 210/G1
Fenton, Ill. 222/C2
Fenton, Iowa 229/E2
Fenton, La. 238/E6
Fenton, Mich. 250/F6
Fenton, Mo. 261/O4
Fenton, Sask. 181/F2
Fentress (co.), Tenn. 237/M8
Fenwick, Conn. 210/F3
Fenwick, Mich. 250/D5
Fenwick, Nova Scotia 168/D3
Fenwick, W. Va. 312/E6
Fenwick Island, Del. 245/T7
Fenwood, Sask. 181/H4
Fenwood, Wis. 317/F6
Feodosiya, U.S.S.R. 52/D5
Ferbane, Ireland 17/F5
Ferdig, Mont. 262/F2
Feversham, Ontario 177/D3
Fevzipaşa, Turkey 63/G4
Ferdinand, Idaho 220/B3
Ferdinand, Ind. 227/D8
Ferdows, Iran 59/G3
Ferdows, Iran 66/K3
Ferfer, Somalia 115/J2
Fergana, U.S.S.R. 54/J6
Fergana, U.S.S.R. 48/H5
Fergus (riv.), Ireland 17/D6
Fergus (co.), Mont. 262/G3
Fergus, Mont. 262/H3

Fergus, Ontario 177/D4
Fergus Falls, Minn. 255/B4
Ferguson, Br. Col. 184/J5
Ferguson, Iowa 229/H5
Ferguson, Ky. 237/M6
Ferguson, Mo. 261/P2
Ferguson, N.C. 281/G2
Ferguson, W. Va. 312/B6
Ferintosh, Alberta 182/D3
Ferlach, Austria 41/C3
Ferland, Ontario 177/H4
Ferland, Ontario 175/C2
Ferland, Québec 172/G1
Ferland, Sask. 181/D6
Ferlo, Senegal 106/B6
Ferme-Neuve, Québec 172/B3
Fermeuse, Newf. 166/C3
Fermo, Italy 34/D3
Fermont, Québec 174/D2
Fermoselle, Spain 33/C2
Fermoy, Ireland 17/E7
Fermoy, Ireland 10/B4
Fernald, Iowa 229/H5
Fernández, Argentina 143/D2
Fernandina (isl.), Ecuador 128/B9
Fernandina Beach, Fla. 212/E1
Fernando de la Mora, Paraguay 144/B4
Fernando Po (Bioko) (isl.), Equat. Guinea 102/C4
Fernando Po (Bioko) (isl.), Equat. Guinea 115/A3
Fernandópolis, Brazil 135/A2
Fernan Lake, Idaho 220/B2
Fernbank, Ala. 195/B3
Fernberg, Queensland 88/K3
Ferndale, Calif. 204/A3
Ferndale, Md. 245/M4
Ferndale, Mich. 250/B6
Ferndale, Pa. 294/M4
Ferndale, Pa. 294/E5
Ferndale, Wash. 310/C2
Fernelmont, Belgium 27/F7
Ferness, Scotland 15/E3
Ferney, S. Dak. 298/N3
Fernie, Br. Col. 162/E6
Fernie, Br. Col. 184/K5
Fernley, Nev. 266/B3
Fern Ridge (lake), Oreg. 291/D3
Ferns, Ireland 17/J6
Fern Tree Gully, Victoria 97/K5
Fernwood, Idaho 220/B2
Fernwood, Miss. 256/D8
Fernwood, N.Y. 276/N4
Fernwood, N.Y. 276/H4
Ferolle (pt.), Newf. 166/C3
Ferrandina, Italy 34/F4
Ferrara (prov.), Italy 34/C2
Ferrara, Italy 34/C2
Ferré (cape), Martinique 161/E7
Ferreira do Alentejo, Portugal 33/B3
Ferreira Gomes, Brazil 132/D2
Ferrellsburg, W. Va. 312/B6
Ferrelo (cape), Oreg. 291/C5
Ferrelview, Mo. 261/O4
Ferreñafe, Peru 128/C6
Ferriday, La. 238/G3
Ferrier, Alberta 182/C3
Ferrières, Belgium 27/H8
Ferris, Ill. 222/B3
Ferris, Texas 303/H3
Ferris (mts.), Wyo. 319/E3
Ferrisburg•, Vt. 268/A3
Ferron, Utah 304/C4
Ferron (creek), Utah 304/C4
Ferros, Brazil 132/F7
Ferrum, Va. 307/H7
Ferry, Guadeloupe 161/A6
Ferry, Mich. 250/C5
Ferry (co.), Wash. 310/G2
Ferryden, Scotland 15/F4
Ferryland, Newf. 166/D2
Ferryland (cape), Newf. 166/D2
Ferry Road, New Bruns. 170/E1
Ferrysburg, Mich. 250/C5
Ferryville, Wis. 317/D9
Fertigs, Pa. 294/C3
Fertile, Iowa 229/G2
Fertile, Minn. 255/B3
Fertile, Sask. 181/K6
Fertilia, Italy 34/B4
Fertő tó (Neusiedler See) (lake), Austria 41/D3
Fertő tó (Neusiedler See) (lake), Hungary 41/D3
Fès, Morocco 102/B1
Fès (Fez), Morocco 106/D2
Feshi, Zaire 115/C5
Fessenden, N. Dak. 282/L4
Fesserton, Ontario 177/E3
Festina, Iowa 229/K2
Festus, Mo. 261/M6
Fetești, Romania 45/H3
Fethard, Tipperary, Ireland 17/F7
Fethard, Wexford, Ireland 17/H7
Fethiye, Turkey 63/C4
Fethiye, Turkey 59/A2
Fetlar (isl.), Scotland 15/G2
Fetlar (isl.), Scotland 10/H1
Feudal, Sask. 181/D4
Feuerkogel (mt.), Austria 41/B3
Feuerthalen, Switzerland 39/G1
Feuilles (riv.), Que. 162/J4
Feuilles (riv.), Que. 146/L4
Feuilles (riv.), Québec 174/C1
Feversham, Ontario 177/D3
Fevzipaşa, Turkey 63/G4

Fianarantsoa (prov.), Madagascar 118/H4
Fianarantsoa, Madagascar 102/G7
Fianarantsoa, Madagascar 118/H4
Fianga, Chad 111/C6
Fiat, Ind. 227/G3
Fiatt, Ill. 222/C3
Fichtelberg (mt.), Germany 22/E3
Fichtelgebirge (range), Germany 22/D3
Fickle, Ind. 227/G4
Ficklin, Georgia 217/G3
Ficksburg, S. Africa 118/D5
Fidalgo (isl.), Wash. 310/C2
Fidelity, Ill. 222/C4
Fidenza, Italy 34/B2
Field, Br. Col. 184/J4
Field, Ky. 237/O7
Field, Ontario 177/E1
Fieldale, Va. 307/H7
Field Creek, Texas 303/F7
Fielding, N.S. Wales 88/H7
Fielding, Sask. 181/D3
Fielding, Utah 304/B2
Fieldon, Ill. 222/C4
Fields, La. 238/C5
Fields (lake), La. 238/J7
Fields, Oreg. 291/J5
Fieldsboro, N.J. 273/D3
Fieldton, Texas 303/B3
Fier, Albania 45/D5
Fierro, N. Mex. 274/A6
Fiesch, Switzerland 39/F4
Fiesole, Italy 34/C3
Fife (co.), Sask. 181/K6
Fife (reg.), Scotland 15/E4
Fife (trad. co.), Scotland 15/B5
Fife, Wash. 310/C3
Fife Lake, Mich. 250/D4
Fife Lake, Sask. 181/F6
Fife Ness (prom.), Scotland 15/F4
Fifield, N.S. Wales 97/G3
Fifield, Wis. 317/F4
Fifteenmile (creek), Oreg. 291/F2
Fifteenmile Arroyo (creek), N. Mex. 274/D4
Fifth (lake), Maine 243/H1
Fifth Cataract, Sudan 111/F4
Fifth Cataract, Sudan 59/B6
Fifth Cataract (dam), Sudan 102/F3
Fifty Lakes, Minn. 255/D4
Fifty-Six, Ark. 202/F7
Fig (riv.), Newf. 166/B3
Figeac, France 28/D5
Figueira da Foz, Portugal 33/B2
Figueras, Spain 33/H1
Figuig, Morocco 102/B1
Figuig, Morocco 106/D2
Figuras (pt.), P. Rico 161/E3
Fiji 2/A6
Fiji 87/H8
FIJI (isls.) 86/P11
Fiji (bay), Tasmania 99/E3
Filadelfia, Bolivia 136/A2
Filadelfia, C. Rica 154/E5
Filadelfia, Paraguay 144/B3
Fil'akovo, Czech. 41/E2
Filbert, S.C. 296/E1
Filbert, W. Va. 312/D8
Filchner Ice Shelf, Ant. 2/H10
Filchner Ice Shelf, Ant. 5/B16
Fil di Remia (peak), Switzerland 39/H4
File (hills), Sask. 181/H5
Filer, Idaho 220/F6
Filer City, Mich. 250/C4
Filey, England 13/G3
Filey, England 10/F3
Filiátes, Greece 45/E6
Filiatrá, Greece 45/E7
Filicudi (isl.), Italy 34/E5
Filingué, Niger 106/E6
Filion, Mich. 250/G5
Filippiás, Greece 45/E6
Filipstad, Sweden 18/H7
Filisur, Switzerland 39/J3
Filley, Nebr. 264/H4
Fillmore, Calif. 204/G9
Fillmore, Ill. 222/D4
Fillmore, Ind. 227/D5
Fillmore (co.), Minn. 255/F7
Fillmore, Minn. 255/F7
Fillmore, Mo. 261/C2
Fillmore (co.), Nebr. 264/G4
Fillmore, N.Y. 276/D6
Fillmore, N. Dak. 282/L3
Fillmore, Okla. 288/N6
Fillmore, Sask. 181/H6
Fillmore, Utah 304/B5
Filtu, Ethiopia 111/H6
Filyos (riv.), Turkey 63/D2
Fimi (riv.), Zaire 115/C4
Finale Emilia, Italy 34/C2
Finale Ligure, Italy 34/B2
Fiñana, Spain 33/E4
Fincastle, Ind. 227/D5
Fincastle, Ky. 237/L1
Fincastle, Va. 307/J6
Finch, Mont. 262/K4
Finch, Ontario 177/J2
Finchburg, Ala. 195/D7
Finchville, Ky. 237/L4
Findhorn, Scotland 15/E3
Findhorn (riv.), Scotland 15/E3
Findıklı, Turkey 63/J2
Findlater, Sask. 181/F5
Findlay, Ill. 222/E4
Findlay, Ohio 284/C3
Findley Lake, N.Y. 276/A6
Findochty, Scotland 15/E3
Findon, Mont. 262/F4
Fine, N.Y. 276/K2
Finesville, N.J. 273/C2
Fingal, N. Dak. 282/N6
Fingal, Ontario 177/C5
Fingal, Tasmania 99/E3
Finger (lake), Ontario 175/B2
Finger, Tenn. 237/D10
Fingerville, S.C. 296/D1
Fingoè, Mozambique 118/E2

Finhaut, Switzerland 39/C4
Finike, Turkey 63/C4
Finistère (dept.), France 28/A3
Finisterre (cape), Spain 7/C4
Finisterre (cape), Spain 33/B1
Finke (riv.), North. Terr. 88/E5
Finke (riv.), North. Terr. 93/C8
Finke (riv.), S. Australia 94/C1
Finksburg, Md. 245/L3
Finland 2/L2
Finland 4/C8
Finland 7/G2
FINLAND 18
Finland (gulf), Finland 18/P7
Finland (gulf), Minn. 255/G3
Finland (gulf), U.S.S.R. 52/C3
Finland (gulf), U.S.S.R. 53/D1
Finlay (riv.), Br. Col. 162/D4
Finlay (riv.), Br. Col. 184/E1
Finlay (mts.), Texas 303/B10
Finlayson, Minn. 255/E4
Finley, Ky. 237/L6
Finley, N.S. Wales 88/H7
Finley, N.S. Wales 97/C4
Finley, N. Dak. 282/N4
Finley, Okla. 288/R6
Finley, Tenn. 237/B8
Finley, Wash. 310/F4
Finleyson, Georgia 217/F6
Finleyville, Pa. 294/B5
Finly, Ind. 227/F5
Finn (riv.), Ireland 17/F2
Finn (riv.), Ireland 17/G3
Finnegan, Alberta 182/E4
Finney (co.), Kansas 232/B3
Finnmark (co.), Norway 18/O2
Finnschhafen, Papua N.G. 86/B2
Finnschhafen, Papua N.G. 85/C7
Finspång, Sweden 18/J7
Finsteraarhorn (mt.), Switzerland 39/F3
Finstermünz (pass), Switzerland 39/K3
Finsterwalde, Germany 22/E3
Fintown, Scotland 15/E1
Fintona, N. Ireland 17/G3
Fintry, Scotland 15/B1
Fionn Loch (lake), Scotland 15/C3
Fir (riv.), Sask. 181/J2
Firat (riv.), Turkey 63/G4
Fircrest, Wash. 310/C3
Fire (isl.), Alaska 196/B1
Firebag (riv.), Alberta 182/E1
Firebaugh, Calif. 204/E7
Firebrick, Ky. 237/P3
Fire, Va. 312/D7
Fire Island Nat'l Seashore, N.Y. 276/P9
Firenze (Florence), Italy 34/C3
Fires (bay), Tasmania 99/E3
Firesteel (riv.), Mich. 250/G1
Firesteel, S. Dak. 298/G3
Firesteel (creek), S. Dak. 298/N6
Firestone, Colo. 208/K2
Firgrove, S. Africa 118/F6
Firmat, Argentina 143/F6
Firminy, France 28/F5
Fir Mountain, Sask. 181/E6
Firozabad, India 68/D3
Firozpur, India 68/C2
First (lake), New Bruns. 170/B1
First Cataract, Egypt 59/B5
First Connecticut (lake), N.H. 268/E1
First Eel (lake), New Bruns. 170/C3
Firstview, Colo. 208/O5
Firth (riv.), Alaska 196/K1
Firth, Idaho 220/F6
Firth, Nebr. 264/H4
Firth (riv.), Yukon 187/D3
Firuzabad, Iran 66/H6
Firuzkuh, Iran 66/H3
Firuzkuh, Iran 59/F3
Fischot Islands, Newf. 166/C3
Fish (creek), Ind. 227/H2
Fish (riv.), Maine 243/F1
Fish (riv.), Namibia 118/B5
Fish (creek), Oreg. 291/E4
Fish (lake), Utah 304/C5
Fish (creek), W. Va. 312/E3
Fish Camp, Calif. 204/F6
Fish Creek (res.), Idaho 220/E6
Fish Creek (mts.), Nev. 266/D2
Fish Creek, Wis. 317/M5
Fisher, Ark. 202/J2
Fisher (isl.), Fla. 212/B5
Fisher, Ill. 222/E3
Fisher, La. 238/D4
Fisher (bay), Manitoba 179/E3
Fisher (riv.), Manitoba 179/E3
Fisher, Minn. 255/B3
Fisher (str.), N.W.T. 162/H3
Fisher (str.), N.W. Terr. 187/K3
Fisher (lake), Nova Scotia 168/C4
Fisher, S. Australia 94/B4
Fisher (co.), Texas 303/D5
Fisher, W. Va. 312/H4
Fisher Bay, Manitoba 179/E3
Fisher Branch, Manitoba 179/E3
Fishermans (isl.), Va. 307/S6
Fishers, Ind. 227/E5
Fishers (isl.), N.Y. 276/S8
Fishers Island, N.Y. 276/R8
Fishersville, Va. 307/K4
Fisherville (South Grafton), Mass. 249/H4
Fishguard and Goodwick, Wales 13/B5
Fishguard and Goodwick, Wales 10/D4
Fish Haven, Idaho 220/G7
Fishing (bay), Md. 245/O7
Fishing (creek), N.C. 281/O2
Fishing Creek, Md. 245/N7
Fishing Lake, Alberta 182/E3
Fishing Ships Harbour, Newf. 166/C3
Fishkill, N.Y. 276/N7
Fish River (lake), Maine 243/F2
Fishs Eddy, N.Y. 276/K8

Fort Bridger 369

Fish Springs (range), Utah 304/A4
Fishtail, Mont. 262/G5
Fishtoft, England 13/H5
Fishtrap, Ky. 237/S6
Fishtrap (lake), Ky. 237/S6
Fisk, Mo. 261/M9
Fiskdale, Mass. 249/F4
Fiske, Sask. 181/C4
Fiskeville, R.I. 249/H6
Fitch Bay, Québec 172/E4
Fitchburg, Mass. 249/G2
Fitchville, Conn. 210/G2
Fitchville, Ohio 284/E3
Fithian, Ill. 222/F3
Fitler, Miss. 256/B5
Fittri (lake), Chad 111/C5
Fittstown, Okla. 288/N5
Fitzcarrald, Peru 128/G8
Fitzgerald, Alberta 182/C4
Fitzgerald, Georgia 217/F7
Fitzgerald, N.W.T. 162/E4
Fitzhugh (sound), Br. Col. 184/D4
Fitzhugh, Okla. 288/N5
Fitzmaurice (riv.), North. Terr. 93/B3
Fitzpatrick, Ala. 195/G6
Fitzpatrick, Georgia 217/F5
Fitzroy (riv.), Australia 87/C7
Fitz Roy (Chaltel) (mt.), Chile 138/E8
Fitzroy, North. Terr. 93/B4
Fitzroy (riv.), Queensland 88/J4
Fitzroy (riv.), Queensland 95/D4
Fitzroy, Victoria 97/H5
Fitzroy, Victoria 88/L7
Fitzroy (riv.), W. Australia 88/C3
Fitzroy (riv.), W. Australia 92/D2
Fitzroy Crossing, W. Australia 88/D3
Fitzroy Crossing, W. Australia 92/D2
Fitzroy Harbour, Ontario 177/H2
Fitzwilliam•, N.H. 268/C6
Fitzwilliam (isl.), Ontario 177/C2
Fitzwilliam Depot, N.H. 268/C6
Fiume (Rijeka), Yugoslavia 45/B3
Fiumicino, Italy 34/F7
Five (isls.), Nova Scotia 168/D3
Five Fingers, New Bruns. 170/C1
Five Island (lake), Iowa 229/D2
Five Islands, Maine 243/D8
Five Islands, Nova Scotia 168/D3
Five Mile (riv.), Conn. 210/H1
Fivemile (creek), Oreg. 291/F2
Fivemile (pt.), Oreg. 291/C4
Fivemile (creek), Wyo. 319/D2
Fivemiletown, N. Ireland 17/G3
Five Points, Ala. 195/H4
Five Points, Fla. 212/D1
Five Points, Tenn. 237/G10
Five Stars, Guyana 131/A2
Fivizzano, Italy 34/B2
Fizi, Zaire 115/E4
Fjerritslev, Denmark 21/C3
Flagler, Colo. 208/N4
Flagler (co.), Fla. 212/E2
Flagler Beach, Fla. 212/E2
Flag Pond, Tenn. 237/R8
Flagstaff, Ariz. 146/G6
Flagstaff, Ariz. 188/D3
Flagstaff, Ariz. 198/D3
Flagstaff (lake), Maine 243/C5
Flagstaff (lake), Oreg. 291/H5
Flagtown, N.J. 273/D2
Flambeau (riv.), Wis. 317/E4
Flambeau Flowage (res.), Wis. 317/F3
Flamborough (head), England 13/G3
Flamborough (head), England 10/G3
Flamenco de San Pedro, Cuba 158/F3
Flaming Gorge (dam), Utah 304/E3
Flaming Gorge (res.), Utah 304/E3
Flaming Gorge (res.), Wyo. 319/C4
Flaming Gorge Nat'l Rec. Area, Utah 304/E2
Flaming Gorge Nat'l Rec. Area, Wyo. 319/C4
Flamingo (cay), Bahamas 156/C2
Flanagan, Ill. 222/E3
Flanagan (passage), Virgin Is. (U.S.) 161/D4
Flanagan (passage), Virgin Is. (U.K.) 161/D4
Flanagin Town, Trin. & Tob. 161/B10
Flanders, Conn. 210/B1
Flanders (trad. prov.) France 29
Flanders, N.J. 273/D2
Flanders, Ontario 175/B3
Flanders-Riverside, N.Y. 276/P9
Flandreau, S. Dak. 298/R5
Flanigan, Nev. 266/B2
Flannagan (res.), Va. 307/C6
Flannan (isls.), Scotland 15/A2
Flannan (isls.), Scotland 10/C1
Flasher, N. Dak. 282/H7
Flat, Ky. 237/O5
Flat, Mo. 261/J7
Flat (isl.), Philippines 85/F3
Flat, Texas 303/G6
Flat (cays), Virgin Is. (U.S.) 161/A4
Flat (creek), Va. 307/M6
Flat Bay, Newf. 166/C4
Flatbrookville, N.J. 273/D1
Flatbush, Alberta 182/C2
Flat Creek, Tenn. 237/H10
Flat Creek-Wegra, Ala. 195/D3
Flat Fork, Ky. 237/P5
Flatgap, Ky. 237/R5
Flathead (riv.), Br. Col. 184/K6
Flathead (co.), Mont. 262/B2
Flathead (lake), Mont. 188/D1
Flathead (lake), Mont. 262/C3
Flathead (riv.), Mont. 262/B2
Flathead, North Fork (riv.), Mont. 262/B2
Flathead, South Fork (riv.), Mont. 262/C3
Flathead Ind. Res., Mont. 262/B3
Flatlands, New Bruns. 170/D1
Flat Lick, Ky. 237/O7
Flatonia, Texas 303/G8
Flat River, Mo. 261/M7
Flat Rock, Ala. 195/G1
Flat Rock, Ill. 222/F5
Flat Rock, Ind. 227/F6
Flatrock (creek), Ind. 227/F5
Flat Rock, Ky. 237/M7
Flat Rock, Mich. 250/F6
Flat Rock, Newf. 166/D2
Flat Rock, N.C. 281/E4
Flat Rock, Ohio 284/E3
Flats, N.C. 281/B4
Flattery (cape), Br. Col. 162/D6
Flattery (cape), Queensland 88/H2
Flattery (cape), Queensland 95/C2
Flattery (cape), Wash. 146/F5
Flattery (cape), Wash. 188/A1
Flattery (cape), Wash. 310/A2
Flat Top, W. Va. 312/D7
Flatwillow (creek), Mont. 262/H4
Flatwood, Ala. 195/C6
Flatwoods, Ky. 237/R4
Flatwoods, La. 238/E4
Flatwoods, Tenn. 237/F9
Flatwoods, W. Va. 312/E5
Flawil, Switzerland 39/H2
Flaxcombe, Sask. 181/B4
Flaxman (isl.), Alaska 196/J1
Flaxton, N. Dak. 282/F2
Flaxville, Mont. 262/L2
Fleet, Alberta 182/E3
Fleet, England 13/G8
Fleet, Loch (inlet), Scotland 15/D3
Fleetwood, England 10/E4
Fleetwood, England 13/D4
Fleetwood, Okla. 288/L7
Fleetwood, Pa. 294/L5
Fleischmanns, N.Y. 276/L6
Flekkefjord, Norway 18/E7
Flémalle, Belgium 27/G7
Fleming, Colo. 208/O1
Fleming, Georgia 217/K7
Fleming (co.), Ky. 237/O4
Fleming, Mo. 261/D4
Fleming, Pa. 294/G4
Fleming, Sask. 181/K5
Fleming-Neon, Ky. 237/R6
Flemingsburg, Ky. 237/O4
Flemington, Georgia 217/K7
Flemington, Mo. 261/F7
Flemington, N.J. 273/D2
Flemington, Pa. 294/G3
Flemington, W. Va. 312/F4
Flen, Sweden 18/K7
Flensburg, Minn. 255/D5
Flensburg, Germany 22/C1
Flers, France 28/C3
Flesherton, Ontario 177/D3
Flesk (riv.), Ireland 17/C7
Fleta, Ala. 195/F6
Fletcher (pond), Mich. 250/F4
Fletcher, Mo. 261/L6
Fletcher, N.C. 281/E4
Fletcher, Ohio 284/B5
Fletcher, Okla. 288/K5
Fletcher•, Vt. 268/B2
Fletschhorn (mt.), Switzerland 39/F4
Fleurance, France 28/D6
Fleur de Lys, Newf. 166/C3
Fleur-de-May (lake), Newf. 166/B3
Fleurier, Switzerland 39/C3
Fleurus, Belgium 27/E8
Flevoland Polders, Netherlands 27/G4
Flims, Switzerland 39/H3
Flinders (reef), Coral Sea Is. Terr. 88/H3
Flinders (reefs), Coral Sea Is. Terr. 95/D3
Flinders (riv.), Australia 87/E7
Flinders (riv.), Queensland 88/G3
Flinders (riv.), Queensland 95/B3
Flinders (range), S. Australia 88/F6
Flinders (range), S. Australia 94/F4
Flinders (isl.), Tasmania 88/H7
Flinders (isl.), Tasmania 99/D1
Flinders (bay), W. Australia 88/A6
Flinders (bay), W. Australia 92/A6
Flin Flon, Man. 146/H4
Flin Flon, Manitoba 179/H3
Flin Flon, Man.-Sask. 162/F4
Flin Flon, Sask. 181/N4
Flint (riv.), Ga. 188/K4
Flint (riv.), Georgia 217/D8
Flint, Georgia 217/D8
Flint, Ind. 227/G[illegible]
Flint (isl.), Kiribati 87/L7
Flint, Mich. 146/K5
Flint, Mich. 188/K2
Flint, Mich. 250/F5
Flint (riv.), Mich. 250/F5
Flint (lake), N.W. Terr. 187/L3
Flint, Wales 13/G2
Flint City, Ala. 195/D1
Flinthill, Mo. 261/L5
Flint Hill, Va. 307/M3
Flinton, Ontario 177/G3
Flint Rock (creek), S. Dak. 298/E3
Flintstone, Georgia 217/B1
Flintstone (lake), Manitoba 179/G4
Flintstone, Md. 245/D2
Flintville, Tenn. 237/H10
Flippen, Georgia 217/D3
Flippin, Ark. 202/E1
Flippin, Ky. 237/K7
Flix, Spain 33/G2
Flom, Minn. 255/B3
Flomaton, Ala. 195/D8
Flomot, Texas 303/D3
Flood, Br. Col. 184/M3
Floodwood, Minn. 255/E4
Flora, Ill. 222/E5
Flora, Ind. 227/E3
Flora, La. 238/D3
Flora, Miss. 256/D5
Flora, N. Dak. 282/M4
Flora (riv.), North. Terr. 93/B3
Flora, Norway 18/D6
Flora, Oreg. 291/K2
Florac, France 28/E5
Florahome, Fla. 212/E2
Floral, Ark. 202/G2
Florala, Ala. 195/F8
Floral City, Fla. 212/D3
Floral Park, N.Y. 276/P7
Floraville, Queensland 95/B3
Flora Vista, N. Mex. 274/A2
Floreana (Sta. Maria), Ecuador 128/B10
Floreana (Santa María) (isl.), Ecuador 128/B10
Florence, Ala. 188/J4
Florence, Ala. 195/C1
Florence, Ariz. 198/D5
Florence, Ark. 202/G6
Florence (lake), Calif. 204/G6
Florence, Colo. 208/J6
Florence, Ill. 222/C4
Florence, Ind. 227/H7
Florence (prov.), Italy 34/C3
Florence, Italy 7/F4
Florence, Italy 34/C3
Florence, Kansas 232/E3
Florence, Ky. 237/R2
Florence, Minn. 255/B6
Florence, Miss. 256/D6
Florence, Mo. 261/G5
Florence, Mont. 262/B4
Florence, N.Y. 276/J4
Florence, N.C. 281/R4
Florence, Nova Scotia 168/H2
Florence, Ontario 177/B5
Florence, Oreg. 291/C4
Florence, Pa. 294/A5
Florence (co.), S.C. 296/H3
Florence, S.C. 188/L4
Florence, S.C. 296/H3
Florence, S. Dak. 298/P3
Florence (riv.), Tasmania 99/C4
Florence, Tenn. 237/H9
Florence, Texas 303/G7
Florence, Vt. 268/A4
Florence (co.), Wis. 317/K4
Florence, Wis. 317/K4
Florence Junction, Ariz. 198/D5
Florence-Roebling, N.J. 273/D3
Florenceville, New Bruns. 170/C2
Florencia, Colombia 126/C7
Florencia, Colombia 120/B2
Florencia, Cuba 158/F2
Florennes, Belgium 27/F8
Florenton, Minn. 255/F3
Florenville, Belgium 27/G9
Flores, Las (riv.), Argentina 143/G7
Flores, Brazil 132/G4
Flores (isl.), Br. Col. 184/D5
Flores, Guatemala 154/C2
Flores (isl.), Indonesia 54/O10
Flores (isl.), Indonesia 85/G7
Flores (sea), Indonesia 2/Q6
Flores (sea), Indonesia 54/N10
Flores (sea), Indonesia 85/F7
Flores (isl.), Portugal 33/A1
Flores (dept.), Uruguay 145/C4
Flores (isl.), Uruguay 145/D5
Floresville, Texas 303/K11
Florey, Texas 303/B5
Florham Park, N.J. 273/E2
Floriano, Brazil 132/F4
Floriano, Brazil 120/E3
Florianópolis, Brazil 132/E9
Florianópolis, Brazil 120/E5
Florida 188/K5
FLORIDA 212
Florida (strs.) 146/K7
Florida, Bolivia 136/D6
Florida, Cuba 158/G3
Florida (str.), Cuba 156/B1
Florida (bay), Fla. 188/K6
Florida (bay), Fla. 212/F6
Florida (cape), Fla. 212/F6
Florida (keys), Fla. 188/K6
Florida (keys), Fla. 212/E7
Florida (strs.), Fla. 188/K6
Florida (strs.), Fla. 212/F7
Florida•, Mass. 249/B2
Florida, Mo. 261/J4
Florida (mts.), N. Mex. 274/B7
Florida, N.Y. 276/M8
Florida, Ohio 284/B3
Florida, P. Rico 161/C1
Florida (isls.), Solomon Is. 86/E3
Florida (state), U.S. 146/K7
Florida (dept.), Uruguay 145/D4
Florida, Uruguay 145/C5
Florida City, Fla. 212/F6
Florida Ridge, Fla. 212/F4
Floridia, Italy 34/E6
Florien, La. 238/D4
Florin, Calif. 204/B8
Florin, Pa. 294/J5
Flórina, Greece 45/E5
Floris, Iowa 229/J7
Florissant, Colo. 208/J5
Florissant, Mo. 261/P1
Florissant Fossil Beds Nat'l Mon., Colo. 208/J5
Flossmoor, Ill. 222/B6
Flovilla, Georgia 217/E4
Flowerdale, Tasmania 99/B2
Floweree, Mont. 262/E3
Flower Mound, Texas 303/F1
Flowerpot (isl.), Ontario 177/C2
Flowers (bay), Newf. 166/B2
Flowers Cove, Newf. 166/C3
Flowery Branch, Georgia 217/E2
Flowood, Miss. 256/D6
Floyd (co.), Georgia 217/B2
Floyd, Georgia 217/J1
Floyd (co.), Ind. 227/F8
Floyd (co.), Iowa 229/H2
Floyd, Iowa 229/H2
Floyd (riv.), Iowa 229/A3
Floyd (co.), Ky. 237/R5
Floyd, La. 238/H1
Floyd, N. Mex. 274/F4
Floyd (co.), Texas 303/C3
Floyd (co.), Va. 307/H7
Floyd, Va. 307/H7
Floydada, Texas 303/C3
Floyd Dale, S.C. 296/J3
Floyds Knobs, Ind. 227/F8
Fluchthorn (mt.), Switzerland 39/K3
Flüela (pass), Switzerland 39/J3
Flüelen, Switzerland 39/G3
Fluhberg (mt.), Switzerland 39/G2
Fluker, La. 238/K5
Flums, Switzerland 39/H2
Flushing, Mich. 250/F5
Flushing, Netherlands 27/C6
Flushing, Ohio 284/J5
Fluvanna, Texas 303/D5
Fluvanna (co.), Va. 307/M5
Fly, Ohio 284/H6
Fly (riv.), Papua N.G. 87/E6
Fly (riv.), Papua N.G. 85/A7
Fly Creek, N.Y. 276/K5
Flying H, N. Mex. 274/E5
Flying Shot, Alberta 182/A2
Flynns Lick, Tenn. 237/K8
Foam Lake, Sask. 181/H4
Foard (co.), Texas 303/E3
Foça, Turkey 63/B3
Foča, Yugoslavia 45/D4
Fochabers, Scotland 15/E3
Focşani, Romania 45/H3
Foge (isl.), Nigeria 106/E6
Foggia (prov.), Italy 34/E4
Foggia, Italy 7/F4
Foggia, Italy 34/E4
Fogo (isl.), C. Verde 106/B8
Fogo, Newf. 166/D4
Fogo (isl.), Newf. 166/D4
Fogo (isl.), Newf. 162/L6
Fohnsdorf, Austria 41/C3
Föhr (isl.), Germany 22/C1
Foisy, Alberta 182/E3
Foix, France 28/D6
Foix (trad. prov.) France 29
Folcroft, Pa. 294/M7
Folda (fjord), Norway 18/J3
Folda (fjord), Norway 18/G4
Földeák, Hungary 41/F3
Földes, Hungary 41/F2
Foley, Ala. 195/C10
Foley, Fla. 212/C1
Foley, Minn. 255/D5
Foley, Mo. 261/L4
Foley (isl.), N.W. Terr. 187/L3
Foleyet, Ontario 177/J5
Foleyet, Ontario 175/D3
Foligno, Italy 34/D3
Folkestone, England 13/J6
Folkestone, England 10/G5
Folkston, Georgia 217/H9
Folkstone, N.C. 281/O5
Follansbee, W. Va. 312/E2
Follett, Texas 303/D1
Föllinge, Sweden 18/J5
Folly Beach, S.C. 296/H6
Folsom, Calif. 204/C8
Folsom (lake), Calif. 204/C8
Folsom, La. 238/K5
Folsom, N.J. 273/D4
Folsom, N. Mex. 274/F2
Folsom, Pa. 294/M7
Folsom, W. Va. 312/E4
Folsomville, Ind. 227/C8
Folteşti, Romania 45/H3
Fomboni, Comoros 118/G2
Fomento, Cuba 158/E2
Fonda, Iowa 229/D3
Fonda, N.Y. 276/M5
Fonda, N. Dak. 282/K2
Fond d'Or (bay), St. Lucia 161/G6
Fond du Lac, Sask. 181/L2
Fond-du-Lac (riv.), Sask. 162/F4
Fond du Lac (riv.), Sask. 181/M2
Fond du Lac (co.), Wis. 317/K8
Fond du Lac, Wis. 188/J2
Fond du Lac, Wis. 317/K8
Fond du Lac Ind. Res., Minn. 255/F4
Fonde, Ky. 237/O7
Fondi, Italy 34/D4
Fond-Lahaye, Martinique 161/C6
Fond-Saint-Denis, Martinique 161/C6
Fond Verrettes, Haiti 158/C6
Fonehill, Sask. 181/J4
Fongafale (cap.), Tuvalu 87/H6
Fonsagrada, Spain 33/C1
Fonseca, Colombia 126/D2
Fonseca (gulf), El Salvador 154/D4
Fonseca (gulf), Honduras 154/D4
Fonseca (gulf), Nicaragua 154/D4
Fontaine, New Bruns. 170/F2
Fontainebleau, France 28/E3
Fontainebleau, Québec 172/F4
Fontana, Calif. 204/E10
Fontana, Kansas 232/H3
Fontana (lake), N.C. 281/B4
Fontana, Wis. 317/J10
Fontanelle, Iowa 229/E6
Fontanet, Ind. 227/C5
Fontas (riv.), Br. Col. 184/M2
Fonte Boa, Brazil 132/G9
Fontein, Neth. Ant. 161/E8
Fontenay-le-Comte, France 28/C4
Fontenay-sous-Bois, France 28/C2
Fonteneau (lake), Newf. 166/B3
Fontenelle, Québec 172/D1
Fontenelle (creek), Wyo. 319/B3
Fontenelle (res.), Wyo. 319/B3
Fontibón, Colombia 126/C5
Fontur (prom.), Iceland 7/C2
Fontur (pt.), Iceland 21/D1
Fonyód, Hungary 41/D3
Foochow (Fuzhou), China 77/J6
Fool Creek (res.), Utah 304/B4
Foosland, Ill. 222/E3
Foothills, Alberta 182/B3
Footscray, Victoria 97/H5
Footscray, Victoria 88/K7
Footville, Ohio 284/J2
Footville, Wis. 317/H10
Foping, China 77/G5
Forada, Minn. 255/C5
Foraker (mt.), Alaska 196/H2
Foraker, Ind. 227/F1
Foraker, Ohio 284/C4
Foraker, Okla. 288/O1
Forbach, France 28/G3
Forbes (mt.), Alberta 182/B4
Forbes (mt.), Br. Col. 184/J4
Forbes (isl.), Fla. 212/D6
Forbes, Minn. 255/F3
Forbes, Mo. 261/B3
Forbes, N.S. Wales 88/H6
Forbes, N.S. Wales 97/E3
Forbes, N. Dak. 282/N8
Forbes (lake), Québec 172/C3
Forbing, La. 238/C2
Forbus, Tenn. 237/M7
Forcados, Nigeria 106/E7
Forcalquier, France 28/F6
Force, Pa. 294/E3
Forchheim, Germany 22/D4
Forchu (bay), Nova Scotia 168/H3
Forchu (cape), Nova Scotia 168/B5
Ford, England 13/F2
Ford (isl.), Hawaii 218/B3
Ford (co.), Ill. 222/E3
Ford (co.), Kansas 232/C4
Ford, Kansas 232/C4
Ford, Ky. 237/N5
Ford (riv.), Mich. 250/B2
Ford (cape), North. Terr. 88/D2
Ford (cape), North. Terr. 93/A2
Ford, Va. 307/N6
Ford, Wash. 310/H3
Ford City, Calif. 204/F8
Ford City, Mo. 261/C2
Ford City, Pa. 294/D4
Ford Cliff, Pa. 294/D4
Ford Heights, Ill. 222/C6
Fordland, Mo. 261/G8
Fordoche, La. 238/G5
Ford Ranges (mts.), Ant. 5/B11
Fords, N.J. 273/E2
Ford's Bridge, N.S. Wales 97/C1
Fords Prairie, Wash. 310/B4
Fordsville, Ky. 237/H5
Fordville, N. Dak. 282/P3
Fordwich, Ontario 177/C4
Fordyce, Ark. 202/F6
Fordyce, Nebr. 264/G2
Forécariah, Guinea 106/B7
Foreman, Ark. 202/B6
Foremost, Alberta 182/E5
Foresman, Ind. 227/C3
Forest, Belgium 27/B9
Forest, Ind. 227/E4
Forest, La. 238/H1
Forest, Miss. 256/F6
Forest (riv.), N. Dak. 282/P3
Forest, Ohio 284/C4
Forest, Ontario 177/C4
Forest (co.), Pa. 294/D2
Forest, Va. 307/K6
Forest (co.), Wis. 317/J4
Forest Acres, S.C. 296/E3
Forest Beach, S.C. 296/F7
Forestburg, Alberta 182/E3
Forestburg, S. Dak. 298/N5
Forestburg, Texas 303/G4
Forest City, Ill. 222/D3
Forest City, Iowa 229/F2
Forest City, Maine 243/H4
Forest City, Mo. 261/B3
Forest City, New Bruns. 170/C3
Forest City, N.C. 281/E4
Forest City, Pa. 294/L2
Forestdale, Ala. 195/E3
Forestdale, R.I. 249/H5
Forest Dale, Vt. 268/A4
Forester, Mich. 250/G5
Foresters Falls, Ontario 177/H2
Forest Glen, Georgia 217/F7
Forest Green, Mo. 261/G4
Forest Grove, Br. Col. 184/G4
Forestgrove, Mont. 262/H3
Forest Grove, Oreg. 291/A2
Forest Heights, Md. 245/F5
Foresthill, Calif. 204/E4
Forest Hill, Ind. 227/F6
Forest Hill, La. 238/E4
Forest Hill, Md. 245/N2
Forest Hill, N.S. Wales 97/D4
Forest Hill, Texas 303/F2
Forest Hill, W. Va. 312/E7
Forest Hills, Ky. 237/L2
Forest Hills, Pa. 294/C7
Forest Hills, Tenn. 237/H8
Forest Home, Ala. 195/E7
Forest Homes, Ill. 222/B2
Forestier (cape), Tasmania 99/E4
Forestier (pen.), Tasmania 99/E4
Forest Junction, Wis. 317/K7
Forest Knolls-Lagunitas, Calif. 204/H1
Forest Lake, Mich. 250/C2
Forest Lake, Minn. 255/F5
Foreston, Minn. 255/E5
Foreston, S.C. 296/G4
Forest Park, Georgia 217/K2
Forest Park, Ill. 222/B5
Forest Park, Ohio 284/B9
Forest Park, Okla. 288/M3
Forestport, N.Y. 276/K4
Forest River, N. Dak. 282/P3
Forest Station, Maine 243/H4
Forest View, Ill. 222/B6
Forestville, Conn. 210/D2
Forestville, Md. 245/G5
Forestville, Mich. 250/G5
Forestville, N.Y. 276/B6
Forestville, Ohio 284/C10
Forestville, Pa. 294/B3
Forestville, Québec 172/H1
Forestville, Québec 174/D3
Forestville, Wis. 317/L6
Forez (mts.), France 28/E5
Forfar, Scotland 10/E2
Forfar, Scotland 15/F4
Forgan, Okla. 288/E1
Forgan, Sask. 181/D4
Forget, Sask. 181/J6
Forge Village, Mass. 249/H2
Forillon Nat'l Park, Que. 162/K6
Forillon Nat'l Park, Québec 172/D1
Foristell, Mo. 261/L5
Fork, N.C. 281/J3
Fork, S.C. 296/J3
Forked (lake), N.Y. 276/L3
Forked Deer (riv.), Tenn. 237/C9
Forked Deer, Middle Fork (riv.), Tenn. 237/C9
Forked Deer, North Fork (riv.), Tenn. 237/C8
Forked Deer, South Fork (riv.), Tenn. 237/C9
Forked River, N.J. 273/E4
Fork Lake, Alberta 182/E2
Forkland, Ala. 195/C5
Fork Mountain, Tenn. 237/N8
Fork River, Manitoba 179/B3
Forks, Wash. 310/A3
Forks of Buffalo, Va. 307/K5
Forks of Elkhorn, Ky. 237/M4
Forks of Salmon, Calif. 204/B2
Forksville, Pa. 294/J3
Fork Union, Va. 307/M5
Forkville, Miss. 256/E6
Forlì (prov.), Italy 34/D2
Forlì, Italy 34/D2
Forman, N. Dak. 282/P7
Formartine (dist.), Scotland 15/F3
Formby, England 13/G2
Formby, England 10/F2
Formby (head), England 13/G2
Formentera (isl.), Spain 33/G3
Formentor (cape), Spain 33/H2
Formia, Italy 34/D4
Formiga, Brazil 135/D2
Formiga, Brazil 132/E8
Formosa (prov.), Argentina 143/D1
Formosa, Argentina 143/E2
Formosa, Argentina 120/D5
Formosa, Ark. 202/E3
Formosa, Brazil 132/E6
Formosa, Serra (range), Brazil 132/C5
Formosa (Taiwan) (isl.), China 2/R4
Formosa (Taiwan) (isl.), China 77/K7
Formosa (Taiwan) (str.), China 77/J7
Formosa (bay), Kenya 115/H4
Formosa, Ontario 177/C3
Formosa, Paraguay 144/C5
Formoso, Kansas 232/D2
Forney, Ala. 195/H2
Forney, Texas 303/H5
Forres, Scotland 10/E2
Forres, Scotland 15/E3
Forrest, Ill. 222/E3
Forrest (co.), Miss. 256/F8
Forrest, N. Mex. 274/F4
Forrest (lake), Sask. 181/L3
Forrest, W. Australia 88/D6
Forrest (lakes), W. Australia 88/D5
Forrest, W. Australia 92/D5
Forrest City, Ark. 202/J3
Forreston, Ill. 222/D1
Forrest River Aborginal Res., W. Australia 92/D1
Forrest River Mission, W. Australia 92/D1
Forrest Station, Manitoba 179/C5
Forsan, Texas 303/C5
Forsayth, Queensland 95/B3
Forsayth, Queensland 88/G3
Forshaga, Sweden 18/H7
Forssa, Finland 18/N6
Forst, Germany 22/F3
Forster-Tuncurry, N.S. Wales 97/G3
Forsyth (co.), Georgia 217/D2
Forsyth, Georgia 217/E4
Forsyth, Ill. 222/D4
Forsyth, Mo. 261/F9
Forsyth, Mont. 262/K4
Forsyth (co.), N.C. 281/J2
Fort (pt.), St. Kitts and Nevis 161/C11
Fort (mt.), Switzerland 39/D4
Fort A.P. Hill, Va. 307/O4
Fort Adams, Miss. 256/B8
Fort à la Corne, Sask. 181/G2
Fort Albany, Ont. 146/K4
Fort Albany, Ont. 162/H5
Fort Albany, Ontario 175/D2
Fort Alexander, Manitoba 179/F4
Fortaleza, Bolivia 136/C1
Fortaleza, Bolivia 136/B3
Fortaleza, Brazil 132/G3
Fortaleza, Brazil 120/F3
Fortaleza, Brazil 2/H6
Fortaleza de Santa Teresa, Uruguay 145/F5
Fort Ann, N.Y. 276/N4
Fort Apache, Ariz. 198/F5
Fort Apache Ind. Res., Ariz. 198/E5
Fort Ashby, W. Va. 312/J4
Fort Assiniboine, Alberta 182/C2
Fort Atkinson, Iowa 229/J2
Fort Atkinson, Wis. 317/J10
Fort Augustus, Scotland 10/D2
Fort Augustus, Scotland 15/D3
Fort Battleford Nat'l Hist. Park, Sask. 181/C3
Fort Bayard, N. Mex. 274/A6
Fort Beaufort, S. Africa 118/D6
Fort Beauséjour Nat'l Hist. Park, New Bruns. 170/F3
Fort Belknap, Mont. 262/H2
Fort Belknap Ind. Res., Mont. 262/H2
Fort Belvoir, Va. 307/O3
Fort Bend (co.), Texas 303/J8
Fort Benjamin Harrison, Ind. 227/E5
Fort Benning, Georgia 217/B6
Fort Benton, Mont. 262/F3
Fort Berthold Ind. Res., N. Dak. 282/E4
Fort Bidwell, Calif. 204/E2
Fort Bidwell Ind. Res., Calif. 204/E2
Fort Blackmore, Va. 307/C7
Fort Bliss, Texas 303/A10
Fort Bliss Mil. Res., N. Mex. 274/C6
Fort Bowie Nat'l Hist. Site, Ariz. 198/F6
Fort Bragg, Calif. 204/B4
Fort Bragg, N.C. 281/M4
Fort Branch, Ind. 227/B8
Fort Bridger, Wyo. 319/B4

Fort Calhoun, Nebr. 264/J3
Fort Campbell, Ky. 237/G7
Fort Campbell, Tenn. 237/G7
Fort Carlton Hist. Park, Sask. 181/E3
Fort Caroline Nat'l Mem., Fla. 212/E1
Fort Carson, Colo. 208/K5
Fort Chaffee, Ark. 202/B3
Fort Chambly Nat'l Hist. Park, Québec 172/J4
Fort Chipewyan, Alberta 182/C5
Fort Chipewyan, Alta. 162/E4
Fort Chipewyan, Alta. 146/G4
Fort Churchill, Manitoba 179/K2
Fort Clark, N. Dak. 282/H5
Fort Clatsop Nat'l Mem., Oreg. 291/C1
Fort Cobb, Okla. 288/K4
Fort Cobb (res.), Okla. 288/J4
Fort Collins, Colo. 146/H6
Fort Collins, Colo. 188/E2
Fort Collins, Colo. 208/J1
Fort Covington•, N.Y. 276/M1
Fort-Dauphin (Faradofay), Madagascar 118/H5
Fort Davis, Ala. 195/G6
Fort Davis, Alaska 196/E2
Fort Davis, Texas 303/D11
Fort Davis Nat'l Hist. Site, Texas 303/D11
Fort Defiance, Ariz. 198/F3
Fort Defiance, Va. 307/L4
Fort-de-France (cap.), Martinique 161/C6
Fort-de-France (cap.), Martinique 156/G4
Fort-de-France (bay), Martinique 161/C6
Fort Denaud, Fla. 212/E5
Fort Deposit, Ala. 195/E7
Fort-Desaix, Martinique 161/D6
Fort Detrick, Md. 245/J3
Fort Devens, Mass. 249/H2
Fort Dick, Calif. 204/A2
Fort Dix, N.J. 273/D3
Fort Dodge, Iowa 229/E3
Fort Dodge, Iowa 188/H2
Fort Dodge, Kansas 232/C4
Fort Donelson Nat'l Mil. Park, Tenn. 237/F8
Fort Drum, Fla. 212/F4
Fort Drum, N.Y. 276/J2
Fort Duchesne, Utah 304/E4
Forteau, Newf. 166/C3
Fort Edward, N.Y. 276/O4
Forte República, Angola 115/C5
Forte Republica, Angola 102/D5
Fort Erie, Ontario 177/E5
Fortescue, Mo. 261/B2
Fortescue, N.J. 273/C5
Fortescue (riv.), W. Australia 88/B4
Fortescue (riv.), W. Australia 92/B3
Fort Eustis, Va. 307/P6
Fort Fairfield, Maine 243/H2
Fort Fairfield•, Maine 243/H2
Fort Foote, Md. 245/P6
Fort-Foureau (Kousseri), Cameroon 115/B1
Fort Frances, Ont. 162/G6
Fort Frances, Ontario 177/F5
Fort Frances, Ontario 175/B3
Fort Franklin, N.W.T. 162/D3
Fort Franklin, N.W. Terr. 187/F3
Fort Fraser, Br. Col. 184/E3
Fort Frederica Nat'l Mon., Georgia 217/K8
Fort Fred Steele, Wyo. 319/E4
Fort Gaines, Ala. 195/B10
Fort Gaines, Georgia 217/C7
Fort Garland, Colo. 208/J8
Fort Gay, W. Va. 312/A6
Fort George G. Meade, Md. 245/L4
Fort Gibson, Okla. 288/R3
Fort Gibson (lake), Okla. 288/R2
Fort Good Hope, N.W.T. 162/D2
Fort Good Hope, N.W. Terr. 187/F3
Fort Gordon, Georgia 217/H4
Fort-Gouraud (Fderik), Mauritania 106/B4
Fort Grant, Ariz. 198/E6
Fort Greely, Alaska 196/J2
Fort Green, Fla. 212/E4
Forth, Scotland 15/C2
Forth (firth), Scotland 10/E2
Forth (firth), Scotland 15/F4
Forth (riv.), Scotland 15/B1
Forth (riv.), Scotland 10/C1
Forth, Tasmania 99/C3
Forth (riv.), Tasmania 99/C3
Fort Hall, Idaho 220/F6
Fort Hall, Kenya 115/G4
Fort Hall Ind. Res., Idaho 220/F6
Fort Hancock, N.J. 273/F3
Fort Hancock, Texas 303/B11
Forth and Clyde (canal), Scotland 10/B1
Forth and Clyde (canal), Scotland 15/B2
Fort Hertz (Putao), Burma 72/C1
Fort Hood, Texas 303/G6
Fort Howard, Md. 245/N4
Fort Huachuca, Ariz. 198/E7
Fort Hunter Liggett, Calif. 204/D8
Fortierville, Québec 172/F3
Fortín 10 de Octubre, Paraguay 144/A2
Fortín Avalos Sánchez, Paraguay 144/C4
Fortín Boquerón, Paraguay 144/C3
Fortín Buenos Aires, Paraguay 144/B3
Fortín Campero, Bolivia 136/C8
Fortín Capitán Escobar, Paraguay 144/B3
Fortín Carlos Antonio López (Pitiantuta), Paraguay 144/C2
Fortín Casanillo, Paraguay 144/C3
Fortín Coronel Bogado, Paraguay 144/C2
Fortín Coronel Sánchez, Paraguay 144/C1
Fortín de las Flores, Mexico 150/P2
Fort Independence Ind. Res., Calif. 204/G7

Fortine, Mont. 262/A2
Fortín Falcon, Paraguay 144/C3
Fortín Florida, Paraguay 144/C2
Fortín Galpón, Paraguay 144/C1
Fortín General Bruguez, Paraguay 144/C4
Fortín General Caballero, Paraguay 144/C4
Fortín General Delgado, Paraguay 144/B4
Fortín General Díaz, Paraguay 144/B3
Fortín Guaraní, Paraguay 144/C3
Fortín Hernandarias, Paraguay 144/A2
Fortín Infante Rivarola, Paraguay 144/A2
Fortín Isla Poi, Paraguay 144/C3
Fortín Lagerenza i, Paraguay 144/B2
Fortín Madrejón, Paraguay 144/B2
Fortín Max Paredes, Bolivia 136/F6
Fortín Mayor Alberto Gardel, Paraguay 144/A4
Fortín Mayor Rodríguez, Paraguay 144/B3
Fortín Mutum, Bolivia 136/F6
Fortín Nueva Asunción (Picuiba), Paraguay 144/B2
Fortín Olmos, Argentina 143/F4
Fortín Palmar de las Islas, Paraguay 144/B1
Fortín Pilcomayo, Paraguay 144/B3
Fortín Presidente Ayala, Paraguay 144/C3
Fortín Presidente Cardozo, Paraguay 144/B5
Fortín Ravelo, Bolivia 136/E6
Fortín Santiago Rodríguez, Paraguay 144/A2
Fortín Suárez Arana, Bolivia 136/F6
Fortín Teniente Américo Picco, Paraguay 144/C1
Fortín Teniente E. Ochoa, Paraguay 144/B2
Fortín Teniente Esteban Martínez, Paraguay 144/C3
Fortín Teniente Gabino Mendoza, Paraguay 144/B2
Fortín Teniente Juan E. López, Paraguay 144/B2
Fortín Teniente Martínez, Paraguay 144/C2
Fortín Teniente Montenia, Paraguay 144/B3
Fortín Teniente Primero Anselmo Escobar, Paraguay 144/A3
Fortín Teniente Primero M. Cabello, Paraguay 144/B3
Fortín Teniente Primero Ramiro Espínola, Paraguay 144/B2
Fortín Toledo, Paraguay 144/B3
Fortín Torres, Paraguay 144/C2
Fortín Vanguardia, Bolivia 136/F6
Fortín Zalazar, Paraguay 144/C3
Fort Jackson, N.Y. 276/L1
Fort Jackson, S.C. 296/F4
Fort Jefferson Nat'l Mon., Fla. 212/C7
Fort Jennings, Ohio 284/B4
Fort Jesup, La. 238/C3
Fort Johnson, N.Y. 276/M5
Fort Jones, Calif. 204/C2
Fort Kent, Alberta 182/E2
Fort Kent, Maine 243/F1
Fort Kent•, Maine 243/F1
Fort Kent Mills, Maine 243/F1
Fort Klamath, Oreg. 291/E5
Fort Knox, Ky. 237/K5
Fort Lallemand, Algeria 106/F2
Fort Lamar, Georgia 217/F2
Fort Langley, Br. Col. 184/L3
Fort Laramie, Wyo. 319/H3
Fort Laramie Nat'l Hist. Site, Wyo. 319/H3
Fort Larned Nat'l Hist. Site, Kansas 232/C4
Fort Lauderdale, Fla. 188/K5
Fort Lauderdale, Fla. 212/C4
Fort Lawn, S.C. 296/F2
Fort Lawrence, Nova Scotia 168/D3
Fort Leavenworth, Kansas 232/H2
Fort Lee, N.J. 273/F2
Fort Lee, Va. 307/O6
Fort Leonard Wood, Mo. 261/H7
Fort Lesley J. McNair, D.C. 245/E5
Fort Lewis, Wash. 310/C3
Fort Liard, N.W.T. 146/F3
Fort Liard, N.W.T. 162/D3
Fort Liard, N.W.T. 187/F3
Fort Liberté, Haiti 156/D3
Fort Liberté, Haiti 158/C5
Fort Littleton, Pa. 294/F5
Fort Loramie, Ohio 284/B5
Fort Loudon, Pa. 294/G6
Fort Loudoun (lake), Tenn. 237/N9
Fort Lupton, Colo. 208/K2
Fort Lyon, Colo. 208/N5
Fort MacArthur, Calif. 204/C11
Fort Mackay, Alta. 162/E4
Fort Macleod, Alberta 182/D5
Fort Macleod, Alta. 162/E6
Fort MacMahon, Algeria 106/E3
Fort Madison, Iowa 188/H2
Fort Madison, Iowa 229/L7
Fort Matanzas Nat'l Mon., Fla. 212/E2
Fort McClellan Mil. Res., Ala. 195/G3
Fort McCoy, Fla. 212/E2
Fort McCoy, Wis. 317/J3
Fort McDermitt Ind. Res., Nev. 266/D1
Fort McDowell Ind. Res., Ariz. 198/D5
Fort McHenry Nat'l Mon., Md. 245/M3
Fort McKavett, Texas 303/E7
Fort McKay, Alberta 182/E1
Fort McKinley, Ohio 284/B6
Fortín McMurray, Alberta 182/E1
Fortín McMurray, Alta. 146/G4
Fortín McMurray, Alta. 162/E4
Fortín McPherson, Georgia 217/K1
Fort McPherson, N.W.T. 146/E3
Fort McPherson, N.W.T. 162/C2
Fort McPherson, N.W. Terr. 187/E3

Fort Meade, Fla. 212/E4
Fort Meade, Uruguay 298/C5
Fort Mill, S.C. 296/F1
Fort Miribel, Algeria 106/E3
Fort Mitchell, Ala. 195/H6
Fort Mitchell, Ky. 237/S2
Fort Mitchell, N. Dak. 307/M7
Fort Mohave Ind. Res., Ariz. 198/A4
Fort Mohave Ind. Res., Calif. 204/L9
Fort Mohave Ind. Res., Nev. 266/G7
Fort Monmouth, N.J. 273/E3
Fort Monroe, Va. 307/R6
Fort Morgan, Ala. 195/C10
Fort Morgan, Colo. 208/M2
Fort Motte, S.C. 296/F4
Fort Myer, Va. 307/T2
Fort Myers, Fla. 188/K5
Fort Myers, Fla. 212/E5
Fort Myers Beach, Fla. 212/E5
Fort Necessity, La. 238/G2
Fort Necessity Nat'l Battlefield, Pa. 294/C6
Fort Nelson, Br. Col. 146/F4
Fort Nelson, Br. Col. 162/D4
Fort Nelson, Br. Col. 184/M2
Fort Nelson (riv.), Br. Col. 184/M2
Fort Niagara, N.Y. 276/H3
Fort Norman, N.W.T. 162/D3
Fort Norman, N.W.T. 146/E3
Fort Norman, N.W. Terr. 187/F3
Fort Ogden, Fla. 212/E4
Fort Oglethorpe, Georgia 217/B1
Fort Ord, Calif. 204/D7
Fort Payne, Ala. 195/G2
Fort Pearce Wash (dry riv.), Ariz. 198/B2
Fort Pearce Wash (creek), Utah 304/A6
Fort Peck, Mont. 262/K2
Fort Peck (dam), Mont. 262/K3
Fort Peck (lake), Mont. 146/N5
Fort Peck (lake), Mont. 188/E1
Fort Peck (lake), Mont. 262/K3
Fort Pickett, Va. 307/N6
Fort Pierce, Fla. 188/K5
Fort Pierce, Fla. 212/F4
Fort Pierre, S. Dak. 298/H5
Fort Pillow, Tenn. 237/B9
Fort Pitt Hist. Park, Sask. 181/B2
Fort Plain, N.Y. 276/L5
Fort Point Nat'l Hist. Site, Calif. 204/J2
Fort Polk, La. 238/D4
Fort Portal, Uganda 115/F3
Fort Providence, N.W.T. 162/E3
Fort Providence, N.W. Terr. 187/G3
Fort Pulaski Nat'l Mon., Georgia 217/L6
Fort Qu'Appelle, Sask. 181/H5
Fort Raleigh Nat'l Hist. Site, N.C. 281/T3
Fort Randall (dam), S. Dak. 298/N7
Fort Ransom, N. Dak. 282/P6
Fort Recovery, Ohio 284/A5
Fort Resolution, N.W.T. 146/G3
Fort Resolution, N.W.T. 162/E3
Fort Resolution, N.W. Terr. 187/G3
Fortress (mt.), Wyo. 319/C1
Fort Rice, N. Dak. 282/J6
Fort Richardson, Alaska 196/C1
Fort Riley-Camp Whiteside, Kansas 232/F2
Fort Ripley, Minn. 255/D4
Fort Ritchie, Md. 245/H2
Fort Ritner, Ind. 227/E7
Fort Rock, Oreg. 291/G4
Fort Rodman, Mass. 249/L6
Fortrose, Scotland 10/D2
Fortrose, Scotland 15/D3
Fort Rosebery (Mansa), Zambia 115/E6
Fort Ross, Calif. 204/B5
Fort Rucker, Ala. 195/G8
Fort-Rupert, Que. 146/L4
Fort Rupert (Rupert House), Québec 174/B2
Fort Saint James, Br. Col. 162/D5
Fort Saint James, Br. Col. 184/E3
Fort Saint John, Br. Col. 162/D4
Fort Saint John, Br. Col. 184/G2
Fort Sam Houston, Texas 303/K11
Fort San, Sask. 181/H5
Fort Sandeman, Pakistan 68/B2
Fort Sandeman, Pakistan 59/J3
Fort Saskatchewan, Alberta 182/D3
Fort Saskatchewan, Alta. 162/E5
Fort Scott, Kans. 188/H3
Fort Scott, Kansas 232/H4
Fort Seneca, Ohio 284/D3
Fort Severn, Ontario 175/C1
Fort Seward, Calif. 204/B3
Fort Seybert, W. Va. 312/H5
Fort Shafter, Hawaii 218/C3
Fort Shaw, Mont. 262/E3
Fort Shawnee, Ohio 284/B4
Fort Sheridan, Ill. 222/B5
Fort-Shevchenko, U.S.S.R. 48/F5
Fort Sill, Okla. 288/K5
Fort Simpson, Canada 4/C15
Fort Simpson, N.W.T. 146/F3
Fort Simpson, N.W.T. 162/D3
Fort Simpson, N.W. Terr. 187/F3
Fort Smith, Ark. 188/H3
Fort Smith, Ark. 146/J6
Fort Smith, Ark. 202/B3
Fort Smith, Mont. 262/J5
Fort Smith (reg.), N.W.T. 187/G3
Fort Smith, N.W.T. 146/G3
Fort Smith, N.W.T. 162/E3
Fort Smith, N.W.T. 187/G4
Fort Smith Nat'l Hist. Site, Ark. 202/B3
Fort Spring, W. Va. 312/E7
Fort Stanton, N. Mex. 274/D5
Fort Stanwix Nat'l Mon., N.Y. 276/J4
Fort Steele, Br. Col. 184/K5
Fort Stewart, Georgia 217/J7
Fort Stewart, Ontario 177/G2
Fort Stockton, Texas 303/A7
Fort Story, Va. 307/S7
Fort Sumner, N. Mex. 274/E4
Fort Sumter Nat'l Mon., S.C. 296/H6

Fort Supply, Okla. 288/G1
Fort Supply (lake), Okla. 288/G1
Fort Tarat, Algeria 106/F3
Fort Thomas, Ariz. 198/E5
Fort Thomas, Ky. 237/S2
Fort Thompson, S. Dak. 298/L5
Fort Ticonderoga, N.Y. 276/O3
Fort Totten, N. Dak. 282/M4
Fort Totten Ind. Res., N. Dak. 282/N4
Fort Towson, Okla. 288/R7
Fortuna, Calif. 204/A3
Fortuna, Mo. 261/G5
Fortuna, N. Dak. 282/C2
Fortuna, Spain 33/F3
Fortuna Ledge, Alaska 196/F2
Fortune, Newf. 166/C4
Fortune (bay), Newf. 166/C4
Fort Union Nat'l Mon., N. Mex. 274/E3
Fort Union Trading Post Nat'l Hist. Site, Mont. 262/N2
Fort Union Trading Post Nat'l Hist. Site, N. Dak. 282/B3
Fort Valley, Georgia 217/E5
Fort Vancouver Nat'l Hist. Site, Wash. 310/C6
Fort Vermilion, Alberta 182/B5
Fort Vermilion, Alta. 162/E4
Fort Vermilion, Alta. 146/G4
Fortville, Ind. 227/F5
Fort Wainwright, Alaska 196/J1
Fort Walsh Nat'l Hist. Park, Sask. 181/A6
Fort Walton Beach, Fla. 212/C6
Fort Washakie, Wyo. 319/C2
Fort Washington, Md. 245/L6
Fort Washington Park, Md. 245/L6
Fort Wayne, Ind. 188/G3
Fort Wayne, Ind. 227/G2
Fort Wellington, Guyana 131/C2
Fort White, Fla. 212/D2
Fort William, Scotland 10/D2
Fort William, Scotland 15/C4
Fort Wingate, N. Mex. 274/C3
Fort Worden, Wash. 310/C2
Fort Worth, Texas 146/J6
Fort Worth, Texas 303/F2
Fort Worth, Texas 188/G4
Fort Wright, Ky. 237/S2
Fort Yates, N. Dak. 282/J7
Fort Yukon, Alaska 146/D3
Fort Yukon, Alaska 196/J1
Fort Yukon, Alaska 188/D5
Fort Yukon, U.S. 4/C17
Forum, Ark. 202/C1
Fosforescente (bay), P. Rico 161/A3
Foshan (Fatshan), China 77/H7
Fosheim (pen.), N.W.T. 187/K1
Foss, Okla. 288/H3
Foss (res.), Okla. 288/H3
Fossano, Italy 34/A2
Fosses-La-Ville, Belgium 27/F8
Fossil (creek), Ariz. 198/D4
Fossil, Oreg. 291/G2
Fossil Butte Nat'l Mon., Wyo. 319/B4
Fossombrone, Italy 34/D3
Fosston, Minn. 255/C3
Fosston, Sask. 181/H3
Foster, Ind. 227/C4
Foster, Ky. 237/N3
Foster, Mo. 261/D6
Foster, Nebr. 264/G2
Foster (co.), N. Dak. 282/N5
Foster, Okla. 288/M5
Foster, Oreg. 291/E3
Foster•, R.I. 249/H5
Foster (riv.), Sask. 181/M3
Foster (creek), S. Dak. 298/N4
Foster, W. Va. 312/C6
Foster, Wis. 317/D6
Foster Center (Foster P.O.), R.I. 249/H5
Foster City, Calif. 204/J2
Foster City, Mich. 250/B3
Fosters, Ala. 195/C4
Fosters, Mich. 250/F5
Fosters Falls, Va. 307/G7
Fosterton, Sask. 181/C5
Fosterville, New Bruns. 170/C3
Fosterville, Tenn. 237/J9
Fostoria, Ala. 195/E6
Fostoria, Iowa 229/G2
Fostoria, Kansas 232/F2
Fostoria, Mich. 250/F5
Fostoria, Ohio 284/D3
Fougamou, Gabon 115/A4
Fougères, France 28/C3
Fouke, Ark. 202/C7
Foul (bay), Egypt 111/G3
Foul (sound), Ireland 17/B5
Foula (isl.), Scotland 15/F2
Foula (isl.), Scotland 10/G1
Foules, La. 238/G3
Foulness Island (pen.), England 13/J6
Foulpointe, Madagascar 118/H3
Foulweather (cape), Oreg. 291/C4
Foulwind (cape), N. Zealand 100/C4
Foumban, Cameroon 115/B2
Foumban, Cameroon 102/D2
Fountain, Ala. 195/D7
Fountain, Colo. 208/K5
Fountain (creek), Colo. 208/K5
Fountain (co.), Ind. 227/C4
Fountain, Ind. 227/C4
Fountain, Minn. 255/F7
Fountain, N.C. 281/O3
Fountain City, Ind. 227/H5
Fountain City, Wis. 317/C7
Fountain Green, Ill. 222/C3
Fountain Green, Utah 304/C4
Fountain Head, Md. 245/G2
Fountain Head, Tenn. 237/J7
Fountain Hill, Ark. 202/E7
Fountain Hill, Pa. 294/L4
Fountain Hills, Ariz. 198/D5

Fountain Inn, S.C. 296/C2
Fountain Run, Ky. 237/K7
Fountaintown, Ind. 227/F5
Fountain Valley, Calif. 204/D11
Four (peaks), Newf. 166/B3
Four Buttes, Mont. 262/L2
Fourche, Ariz. 198/E5
Fourche LaFave (riv.), Ark. 202/D4
Four Corners, Oreg. 291/A3
Four Corners, Wyo. 319/H1
Four Falls, New Bruns. 170/C2
Four Lakes, Wash. 310/H9
Four Mile, Conn. 210/F3
Fourmile (lake), Oreg. 291/E5
Fourmies, France 28/F2
Four Mile, Conn. 210/F3
Four Mountains (isls.), Alaska 196/E4
Fournier (cape), N. Zealand 100/E7
Fournier, Ontario 177/K2
Four Oaks, N.C. 281/N4
Four Paths, Jamaica 158/J6
Four Peaks (mt.), Ariz. 198/D5
Four States, W. Va. 312/F4
Fourteen Mile (pt.), Mich. 250/F1
Fourth (lake), Maine 243/H5
Fourth Cataract, Sudan 107/E4
Fourth Cataract, Sudan 59/B6
Fourth Cataract (dam), Sudan 102/F3
Foveaux (str.), N. Zealand 87/G10
Foveaux (str.), N. Zealand 100/A7
Fowler, Calif. 204/F7
Fowler, Colo. 208/L6
Fowler, Ill. 222/B3
Fowler, Ind. 227/C3
Fowler, Ind. 227/C3
Fowler, Kansas 232/B4
Fowler, Mich. 250/E5
Fowlerton, Ind. 227/F4
Fowlerton, Texas 303/F9
Fowlerville, Mich. 250/F6
Fowlkes, Tenn. 237/C9
Fowlstown, Georgia 217/D9
Fowman, Iran 66/F2
Fowyang (Fuyang), China 77/J5
Fox (isls.), Alaska 196/E4
Fox, Ark. 202/F2
Fox (lake), Ill. 222/A4
Fox (riv.), Ill. 222/E5
Fox (riv.), Ill. 222/E2
Fox (riv.), Manitoba 179/K2
Fox, Mich. 250/B3
Fox, Okla. 288/M6
Fox, Oreg. 291/H3
Fox (riv.), Wis. 317/K7
Fox (riv.), Wis. 317/K2
Fox (isl.), S. Dak. 4/C17
Fox, Okla. 288/M6
Foxboro, Mass. 249/J4
Foxboro•, Mass. 249/J4
Foxboro, Ontario 177/G3
Foxboro, Wis. 317/B2
Foxburg, Pa. 294/C4
Fox Chapel, Pa. 294/C6
Fox Creek, Alberta 182/B2
Foxe (basin), Canada 4/C13
Foxe (basin), N.W.T. 146/L3
Foxe (basin), N.W.T. 162/J2
Foxe (basin), N.W.T. 187/L3
Foxe (chan.), N.W.T. 162/H2
Foxe (chan.), N.W.T. 146/K3
Foxe (chan.), N.W.T. 187/K3
Foxe (pen.), N.W.T. 146/L3
Foxe (pen.), N.W.T. 162/J3
Foxe (pen.), N.W.T. 187/L3
Fox Farm, Wyo. 319/H4
Foxfire, N.C. 281/K4
Foxford, Ireland 17/C4
Foxford, Sask. 181/F2
Fox Glacier, N. Zealand 100/B5
Fox Harbour, Newf. 166/D2
Fox Harbour, Newf. 166/C3
Foxholm, N. Dak. 282/G3
Foxhome, Minn. 255/B4
Fox Lake, Alberta 182/B5
Fox Lake, Ill. 222/A4
Fox Lake, Wis. 317/J8
Foxon, Conn. 210/D3
Foxpark, Wyo. 319/F4
Fox Point, Wis. 317/M1
Fox River, Nova Scotia 168/D3
Fox River Grove, Ill. 222/A5
Foxton, Colo. 208/J4
Foxton, N. Zealand 100/E4
Fox Valley, Sask. 181/B5
Foxville, Md. 245/H2
Foxwarren, Manitoba 179/A4
Foxwells, Va. 307/R5
Foxworth, Miss. 256/E8
Foyers, Scotland 15/D3
Foyil, Okla. 288/R2
Foyle (inlet), Ireland 17/G1
Foyle, Lough (inlet), Ireland 10/C3
Foyle, Lough (inlet), N. Ireland 10/C3
Foyle (inlet), N. Ireland 17/G1
Foyle (riv.), Ireland 17/G2
Foynes, Ireland 10/B4
Foynes, Ireland 17/C6
Foz do Breu, Brazil 132/F10
Foz do Cunene, Angola 115/B7
Foz do Iguaçu, Brazil 132/C9
Frackville, Pa. 294/K4
Fraga, Spain 33/G2
Fragoso (cay), Cuba 158/F1
Fraile Muerto, Uruguay 145/E5
Fraile, Paraguay 144/E5
Frailes, Los (isl.), Dom. Rep. 158/C7
Fram, Paraguay 144/E5
Framboise, Nova Scotia 168/H3
Framboise Cove (bay), Nova Scotia 168/H3
Frame, W. Va. 312/C5
Frameries, Belgium 27/D8
Frametown, W. Va. 312/E5
Framingham, Mass. 249/J3
Framingham•, Mass. 249/J4
Framingham Center, Mass. 249/J3
Framlingham, England 13/J5
Frampton, Québec 172/G3
Franca, Brazil 135/C2
Franca, Brazil 132/E8
Francavilla Fontana, Italy 34/F4

France 2/J3
France 7/E4
FRANCE 28
Francés (cape), Cuba 158/B2
Francés (cape), Cuba 158/A2
Frances (lake), Mont. 262/D2
Frances, Wash. 310/B4
Frances (lake), Yukon 187/E3
Francestown•, N.H. 268/D3
Francés Viejo (cape), Dom. Rep. 158/E5
Francesville, Ind. 227/D3
Franceville, Gabon 115/B4
Franche Comté (trad. prov.), France 29
Francia, Uruguay 145/C3
Francis (lake), N.H. 268/E1
Francis, Okla. 288/N5
Francis, Sask. 181/H5
Francis, Utah 304/E3
Francis Case (lake), S. Dak. 188/F2
Francis Case (lake), S. Dak. 146/J5
Francis Case (lake), S. Dak. 298/M5
Francisco, Ala. 195/F1
Francisco, Ind. 227/B8
Francisco, N.C. 281/J2
Francisco de Orellana, Peru 128/F4
Francis Creek, Wis. 317/L1
Francis E. Warren A.F.B., Wyo. 319/H4
Francistown, Botswana 118/D4
Francoeur, Québec 172/J4
Francois (lake), Br. Col. 162/D5
François (lake), Br. Col. 184/D3
François, Newf. 166/C4
François Lake, Br. Col. 184/D3
Franconia•, N.H. 268/D3
Franconia, Va. 307/S3
Franconian Jura (range), Germany 22/D4
Franconia Notch (pass), N.H. 268/D3
Franeker, Netherlands 27/H2
Frank, Alberta 182/C5
Frankel City, Texas 303/B5
Frankenberg-Eder, Germany 22/C3
Frankenmarkt, Austria 41/B3
Frankenmuth, Mich. 250/F5
Frankenthal, Germany 22/C4
Frankenwald (for.), Germany 22/D3
Frankewing, Tenn. 237/H10
Frankfield, Jamaica 158/H6
Frankford, Del. 245/S6
Frankford (Kilcormac), Ireland 17/F5
Frankford, Mo. 261/K4
Frankford, Ontario 177/G3
Frankford, W. Va. 312/F7
Frankfort, Ala. 195/C1
Frankfort, Ill. 222/B3
Frankfort, Ind. 227/E4
Frankfort, Kansas 232/F2
Frankfort (cap.), Ky. 237/M4
Frankfort (cap.), Ky. 188/K3
Frankfort (cap.), Ky. 146/M3
Frankfort•, Maine 243/H5
Frankfort, Mich. 250/C4
Frankfort, N.Y. 276/K4
Frankfort, Ohio 284/D7
Frankfort, S. Dak. 298/M4
Frankfort Springs, Pa. 294/A4
Frankfurt, Germany 7/E3
Frankfurt am Main, Germany 22/C3
Frankfurt an der Oder, Germany 22/F2
Frankland (cape), Tasmania 99/D1
Frankland (range), Tasmania 99/B3
Franklin (co.), Ala. 195/C2
Franklin, Ala. 195/G6
Franklin (pt.), Alaska 196/G1
Franklin, Ariz. 198/F6
Franklin (co.), Ark. 202/C2
Franklin, Ark. 202/G1
Franklin•, Conn. 210/G2
Franklin (co.), Fla. 212/B2
Franklin (co.), Georgia 217/F2
Franklin, Georgia 217/B4
Franklin (co.), Idaho 220/G7
Franklin, Idaho 220/G7
Franklin (co.), Ill. 222/E5
Franklin, Ill. 222/C4
Franklin (co.), Ind. 227/G6
Franklin, Ind. 227/E6
Franklin (co.), Iowa 229/G3
Franklin, Iowa 229/L7
Franklin (co.), Kansas 232/G3
Franklin, Kansas 232/H4
Franklin (co.), Ky. 237/M4
Franklin, Ky. 237/J7
Franklin (par.), La. 238/G2
Franklin, La. 238/F5
Franklin (co.), Maine 243/B5
Franklin, Maine 243/G6
Franklin•, Maine 243/G6
Franklin, Manitoba 179/C4
Franklin (co.), Mass. 249/D2
Franklin, Mass. 249/J4
Franklin•, Mass. 249/J4
Franklin, Mich. 250/B6
Franklin, Minn. 255/D6
Franklin, Minn. 255/D6
Franklin (co.), Miss. 256/C8
Franklin (co.), Mo. 261/K6
Franklin, Mo. 261/H5
Franklin, Mont. 262/G4
Franklin (co.), Nebr. 264/E4
Franklin, Nebr. 264/E4
Franklin (lake), Nev. 266/F2
Franklin, N.H. 268/D3
Franklin, N.J. 273/D1
Franklin (co.), N.Y. 276/M1
Franklin, N.Y. 276/K6
Franklin (co.), N.C. 281/N2
Franklin, N.C. 281/C4
Franklin (bay), N.W. Terr. 187/F2
Franklin (lake), N.W. Terr. 187/J3
Franklin (mts.), N.W. Terr. 187/F3
Franklin (str.), N.W.T. 162/G1
Franklin (str.), N.W. Terr. 187/J2
Franklin (co.), Ohio 284/E5
Franklin, Ohio 284/B6

Gagnon 371

Franklin (co.), Pa. 294/G6
Franklin, Pa. 294/C3
Franklin, S. Dak. 298/P6
Franklin, Tasmania 99/C5
Franklin (riv.), Tasmania 99/B4
Franklin (co.), Tenn. 237/J10
Franklin, Tenn. 237/H9
Franklin (co.), Texas 303/J4
Franklin, Texas 303/H7
Franklin (co.), Vt. 268/B2
Franklin•, Vt. 268/B2
Franklin (co.), Va. 307/J6
Franklin (I.C.), Va. 307/P7
Franklin (co.), Wash. 310/G4
Franklin, W. Va. 312/H5
Franklin, Wis. 317/L2
Franklin D. Roosevelt (lake), Wash. 310/G2
Franklin Falls (res.), N.H. 268/D4
Franklin Furnace, Ohio 284/E8
Franklin Grove, Ill. 222/D2
Franklin Lakes, N.J. 273/B1
Franklin Park, Ill. 222/B5
Franklin Park•, N.J. 273/D3
Franklin River, Br. Col. 184/H3
Franklin Springs, Georgia 217/F2
Franklin Square, N.Y. 276/R7
Franklinton, La. 238/K5
Franklinton, N.C. 281/N2
Franklintown, Pa. 294/H5
Franklinville, N.J. 273/C4
Franklinville, N.Y. 276/D6
Franklinville, N.C. 281/K3
Franks (pond), Newf. 166/D2
Frankslake, Sask. 181/G5
Frankston, Texas 303/J5
Franksville, Wis. 317/M3
Frankton, Ind. 227/F4
Franktown, Colo. 208/K4
Franktown, Ontario 177/H2
Franktown, Va. 307/S6
Frankville, Ala. 195/B7
Frankville, Iowa 229/K2
Frankville, Nova Scotia 168/G3
Frankville, Ontario 177/J2
Frannie, Wyo. 319/D1
Franquelin, Québec 172/B1
Franquia, Uruguay 145/B1
Franschhoek, S. Africa 118/F6
Fransfontein, Namibia 118/A4
Františkovy Lázně, Czech. 41/B1
Franz, Ontario 177/J5
Franz, Ontario 175/D3
Franz Josef Land (isls.), U.S.S.R. 2/L1
Franz Josef Land (isls.), U.S.S.R. 4/A7
Franz Josef Land (isls.), U.S.S.R. 48/F1
Frascati, Italy 34/F7
Fraser (isl.), Australia 87/F8
Fraser (lake), Br. Col. 184/E3
Fraser (riv.), Br. Col. 146/F4
Fraser (riv.), Br. Col. 162/D5
Fraser (riv.), Br. Col. 184/F4
Fraser, Colo. 208/H3
Fraser, Iowa 229/E4
Fraser, Mich. 250/B6
Fraser, Minn. 255/F3
Fraser (riv.), Newf. 166/B2
Fraser (isl.), Queensland 88/J4
Fraser (isl.), Queensland 95/E5
Fraserburgh, Scotland 15/G3
Fraserburgh, Scotland 10/E2
Fraserdale, Ontario 175/D3
Fraserdale, Ontario 177/J5
Fraser Lake, Br. Col. 184/E3
Fraser Mills, Br. Col. 184/K3
Fraser Reach (chan.), Br. Col. 184/C3
Frasertown, N. Zealand 100/F3
Fraserwood, Manitoba 179/E4
Frasnes-lez Anvaing, Belgium 27/D7
Frauenfeld, Switzerland 39/G1
Frauenkirchen, Austria 41/D3
Fray Benito, Cuba 158/J3
Fray Bentos, Uruguay 145/A4
Fray Marcos, Uruguay 145/D5
Frazee, Minn. 255/C4
Frazer, Mont. 262/K2
Frazeysburg, Ohio 284/F5
Frazier Park, Calif. 204/F9
Fraziers Bottom, W. Va. 312/B5
Frechen, Germany 22/B3
Fred, Texas 303/K7
Freda, N. Dak. 282/H7
Fredensborg, Denmark 21/F6
Fredensdal, Virgin Is. (U.S.) 161/F4
Frederic, Mich. 250/E4
Frederic, Wis. 317/B4
Frederica, Del. 245/S4
Fredericia, Denmark 21/C6
Fredericia, Denmark 18/F9
Frederick (sound), Alaska 196/N1
Frederick, Colo. 208/K2
Frederick, Ill. 222/C3
Frederick, Kansas 232/D3
Frederick (co.), Md. 245/J3
Frederick, Md. 245/J3
Frederick, Okla. 288/H6
Frederick, S. Dak. 298/N2
Frederick (co.), Va. 307/M2
Fredericksburg, Ind. 227/E8
Fredericksburg, Iowa 229/J3
Fredericksburg, Ohio 284/G4
Fredericksburg, Pa. 294/J5
Fredericksburg, Pa. 294/B2
Fredericksburg, Texas 303/E7
Fredericksburg (I.C.), Va. 307/N4
Fredericks Hall, Va. 307/N4
Frederickton, N.S. Wales 97/G2
Fredericktown, Mo. 261/M7
Fredericktown, Ohio 284/F5
Fredericktown, Pa. 294/C6
Fredericton (cap.), N. Br. 146/M5
Fredericton, N. Br. 162/K6
Fredericton (cap.), New Bruns. 170/D3
Fredericton Junction, New Bruns. 170/D3
Frederika, Iowa 229/J3
Frederik Hendrik (Kolepom) (isl.), Indonesia 85/K7
Frederiksberg (commune), Denmark 21/F6
Frederiksberg, Denmark 21/F6
Frederiksborg (co.), Denmark 21/E5
Frederikshåb (Paamiut), Greenl. 4/C12
Frederikshåb (Paamiut), Greenl. 146/N3
Frederikshavn, Denmark 18/G8
Frederikshavn, Denmark 21/D3
Frederikssund, Denmark 21/E6
Frederiksted, Virgin Is. (U.S.) 161/E4
Frederiksted, Virgin Is. (U.S.) 156/G2
Frederiksvaerk, Denmark 21/E6
Frederiksvaerk, Denmark 18/G8
Frederik Willem IV (falls), Suriname 131/C4
Fredonia, Ala. 195/H5
Fredonia, Ariz. 198/C2
Fredonia (Biscoe), Ark. 202/H4
Fredonia, Ind. 227/E8
Fredonia, Iowa 229/L6
Fredonia, Kansas 232/G4
Fredonia, Ky. 237/E6
Fredonia, N.Y. 276/B6
Fredonia, N. Dak. 282/M7
Fredonia, Pa. 294/B3
Fredonia, Texas 303/E7
Fredonia, Wis. 317/L8
Fredric, Iowa 229/H6
Fredrika, Sweden 18/L4
Fredrikstad, Norway 18/D4
Freeborn (co.), Minn. 255/E7
Freeborn, Minn. 255/E7
Freeburg, Ill. 222/D5
Freeburg, Minn. 255/G7
Freeburg, Mo. 261/J6
Freeburg, Pa. 294/H4
Freeburn, Ky. 237/S5
Freedhem, Minn. 255/D4
Freedom, Calif. 204/L4
Freedom, Ind. 227/D6
Freedom, Ky. 237/K7
Freedom•, Maine 243/E7
Freedom•, N.H. 268/E4
Freedom, Okla. 288/H1
Freedom, Pa. 294/B4
Freedom, Wyo. 319/B3
Freehold, N.J. 273/E3
Freehold, N.Y. 276/N6
Freel (peak), Calif. 204/F5
Freeland, Md. 245/M2
Freeland, Mich. 250/E5
Freeland, N.C. 281/N6
Freeland, Pa. 294/L3
Freeland, Wash. 310/C2
Freeland Park, Ind. 227/C3
Freelandville, Ind. 227/C7
Freels (cape), Newf. 166/D3
Freelton, Ontario 177/D4
Freeman (riv.), Alberta 182/C2
Freeman, Ind. 227/D6
Freeman (lake), Ind. 227/D3
Freeman, Mo. 261/C5
Freeman, S. Dak. 298/O7
Freeman, Wash. 310/H3
Freemansburg, Pa. 294/M4
Freemanville, Ala. 195/D8
Free Mason (isls.), La. 238/M7
Freemont, Calif. 188/B3
Freemont, Sask. 181/B3
Freeport, Bahamas 156/B1
Freeport, Fla. 212/C6
Freeport, Ill. 188/J2
Freeport, Ill. 222/D1
Freeport, Ind. 227/F5
Freeport, Kansas 232/E4
Freeport, Maine 243/C8
Freeport•, Maine 243/C8
Freeport, Mich. 250/D6
Freeport, Minn. 255/D5
Freeport, N.Y. 276/R7
Freeport, Nova Scotia 168/B4
Freeport, Ohio 284/H5
Freeport, Pa. 294/C4
Freeport, Texas 303/J9
Freer, Texas 303/F10
Free Soil, Mich. 250/C4
Freestone (co.), Texas 303/H6
Freetown, Ant. & Bar. 161/E11
Freetown, Ind. 227/E7
Freetown, N.Y. 276/R9
Freetown (cap.) S. Leone 102/A4
Freetown (cap.) S. Leone 106/B7
Free Union, Va. 307/L4
Freeville, N.Y. 276/H5
Freezeout (lake), Mont. 262/D3
Fregenal de la Sierra, Spain 33/C3
Fregene, Italy 34/F6
Freiberg, Germany 22/E3
Freiburg, Germany 7/E4
Freiburg im Breisgau, Germany 22/B5
Freidberg, Austria 41/D3
Freienbach, Switzerland 39/G2
Freire, Chile 138/E2
Freirina, Chile 138/A7
Freising, Germany 22/D4
Freistadt, Austria 41/C2
Freistatt, Mo. 261/E8
Freital, Germany 22/E3
Freixo de Espada à Cinta, Portugal 33/C2
Fréjus, France 28/G6
Fréjus (pass), France 28/G5
Fréjus (pass), Italy 34/A2
Frelighsburg, Québec 172/E4
Fremantle, Australia 2/Q7
Fremantle, Australia 87/B9
Fremantle, W. Australia 88/B6
Fremantle, W. Australia 92/A1
Fremington, England 13/C6
Fremont, Calif. 204/K3
Fremont (peak), Calif. 204/H8
Fremont (co.), Colo. 208/J5
Fremont (co.), Idaho 220/G5
Fremont, Ind. 227/H1
Fremont (co.), Iowa 229/B7
Fremont, Iowa 229/H6
Fremont, Mich. 250/D5
Fremont, Mo. 261/K9
Fremont, Nebr. 188/G2
Fremont, Nebr. 264/H3
Fremont•, N.H. 268/E6
Fremont, N.C. 281/N3
Fremont, Ohio 284/D3
Fremont, Utah 304/C5
Fremont (isl.), Utah 304/B2
Fremont (riv.), Utah 304/C5
Fremont, Wis. 317/J7
Fremont (co.), Wyo. 319/D2
Fremont (lake), Wyo. 319/C3
Fremont (peak), Wyo. 319/C2
French, Argentina 143/F7
French (riv.), Conn. 210/H1
French (riv.), Ontario 177/D1
French (creek), Pa. 294/C2
French (creek), S. Dak. 298/C6
French (isl.), Victoria 97/C6
Frenchboro•, Maine 243/G7
French Broad (riv.), N.C. 281/D3
French Broad (riv.), Tenn. 237/R9
Frenchburg, Ky. 237/O5
French Camp, Miss. 256/F4
French Creek, W. Va. 312/F5
French Frigate (shoal), Hawaii 188/F6
French Frigate (shoals), Hawaii 87/K3
French Frigate (shoals), Hawaii 218/C6
Frenchglen, Oreg. 291/H5
French Guiana 2/G5
French Guiana 120/D2
FRENCH GUIANA 131/E3
French Lick, Ind. 227/D7
Frenchman (creek), Colo. 208/P1
Frenchman (bay), Maine 243/G7
Frenchman (riv.), Mont. 188/E1
Frenchman (riv.), Mont. 262/J1
Frenchman (creek), Nebr. 264/C4
Frenchman (riv.), Sask. 181/C6
Frenchman (cay), Virgin Is. (U.K.) 161/C4
Frenchman Butte, Sask. 181/B2
Frenchman Flat (basin), Nev. 266/F6
Frenchmans Cap (mt.), Tasmania 99/B4
Frenchmans Island, Newf. 166/C3
Frenchpark, Ireland 17/E4
French Polynesia 87/L8
French River, Minn. 255/G4
French River, Ontario 177/D1
French Settlement, La. 238/L2
Frenchton, W. Va. 312/F5
Frenchtown, Mont. 262/B3
Frenchtown, N.J. 273/C2
Frenchville, Maine 243/G1
Frenchville•, Maine 243/G1
Frenchville, Pa. 294/F3
Frenštát pod Radhoštěm, Czech. 41/E2
Fresco, Ivory Coast 106/C7
Fresh (pond), Mass. 249/C6
Freshford, Ireland 17/G6
Freshwater, Calif. 204/B3
Freshwater (Guffey), Colo. 208/H5
Freshwater, England 13/F7
Freshwater, Newf. 166/D2
Fresia, Chile 138/D3
Fresillo, Mexico 146/H7
Fresnillo de González Echererría, Mexico 150/H5
Fresno (co.), Calif. 204/E7
Fresno, Calif. 146/G6
Fresno, Calif. 188/C3
Fresno, Calif. 204/F7
Fresno (riv.), Calif. 204/E7
Fresno, Colombia 126/C5
Fresno, Mont. 262/G2
Fresno (res.), Mont. 262/F2
Fresno, Texas 303/J2
Freudenstadt, Germany 22/C4
Frew, Ky. 237/P6
Frewena, North. Terr. 93/D5
Frewsburg, N.Y. 276/B6
Freycinet (pen.), Tasmania 99/E4
Fria, Guinea 106/B6
Fria (cape), Namibia 102/D6
Fria (cape), Namibia 118/A3
Friant, Calif. 204/F7
Friant-Kern (canal), Calif. 204/F8
Friars Point, Miss. 256/C2
Frias, Argentina 143/D2
Fribourg (canton), Switzerland 39/D3
Fribourg, Switzerland 39/D3
Frick, Switzerland 39/E1
Friday Harbor, Wash. 310/B2
Fridley, Minn. 255/G5
Fried, N. Dak. 282/N5
Friedberg, Germany 22/C3
Friedland, Germany 22/E2
Friedrichshafen, Germany 22/C5
Friedrichstadt, Germany 22/C1
Friend, Kansas 232/B3
Friend, Nebr. 264/G4
Friend, Oreg. 291/F2
Friendly, W. Va. 312/D3
Friendship, Ark. 202/E5
Friendship, Ind. 227/G7
Friendship, Maine 243/E7
Friendship•, Maine 243/E7
Friendship, Md. 245/M6
Friendship, N.Y. 276/D6
Friendship, Ohio 284/D8
Friendship, Tenn. 237/C9
Friendship, Wis. 317/G8
Friendship Hill Nat'l Hist. Site, Pa. 294/C6
Friendsville, Ill. 222/F5
Friendsville, Md. 245/A2
Friendsville, Pa. 294/L2
Friendsville, Tenn. 237/N9
Friendswood, Texas 303/J2
Frienisberg (mt.), Switzerland 39/D2
Frierson, La. 238/C2
Fries, Va. 307/F7
Friesach, Austria 41/C3
Friesche Gat (chan.), Netherlands 27/J2
Friesland, Minn. 255/E4
Friesland (prov.), Netherlands 27/H2
Friesland, Wis. 317/H8
Frigate (isl.), Seychelles 118/J5
Frigate Bay, St. Kitts & Nevis 161/C10
Frimley and Camberley, England 13/G8
Frink, Fla. 212/D6
Frinton and Walton, England 10/G5
Frinton and Walton, England 13/J6
Frio (cape), Brazil 120/E5
Frio (cape), Brazil 135/F3
Frio (co.), Texas 303/E9
Frio (riv.), Texas 303/E8
Friockheim, Scotland 15/F4
Friol, Spain 33/C1
Friona, Texas 303/B3
Fripp (isl.), S.C. 296/G7
Frisches Haff (lag.), Poland 47/D1
Frisco, Colo. 208/G3
Frisco, N.C. 281/T4
Frisco, Pa. 294/B4
Frisco, Texas 303/H4
Frisco City, Ala. 195/D8
Frisian (isls.) 7/E3
Frisian, North (isls.), Denmark 21/B7
Frisian, East (isls.), Germany 22/B2
Frisian, North (isls.), Germany 22/B1
Frisian, West (isls.), Netherlands 27/G2
Frissell (mt.), Conn. 210/B1
Fristoe, Mo. 261/F6
Fritch, Texas 303/C2
Fritchton, Ind. 227/C7
Fritz Creek, Alaska 196/B2
Fritzlar, Germany 22/C3
Friuli-Venezia Giulia (reg.), Italy 34/D1
Frizzellburg, Md. 245/K2
Frobisher (bay), N.W.T. 162/K3
Frobisher (bay), N.W. Terr. 187/M3
Frobisher, Sask. 181/J6
Frobisher (lake), Sask. 181/L3
Froelich, Iowa 229/L2
Frog (lake), Alberta 182/E3
Frog Lake, Alberta 182/E3
Frogue, Ky. 237/L7
Frohavet (bay), Norway 18/F5
Frohna, Mo. 261/N7
Frohnleiten, Austria 41/C3
Froid, Mont. 262/M2
Froidchapelle, Belgium 27/E8
Frolovo, U.S.S.R. 48/E5
Frolovo, U.S.S.R. 52/F5
Fromberg, Mont. 262/H5
Frome (lake), Australia 87/E9
Frome, England 10/E5
Frome, England 13/E6
Frome, Jamaica 158/G6
Frome (lake), S. Australia 88/G6
Frome (lake), S. Australia 94/G4
Front (range), Colo. 208/H1
Fronteira, Portugal 33/C3
Fronteiras, Brazil 132/F4
Frontenac, Kansas 232/H4
Frontenac, Minn. 255/F6
Frontenac, Mo. 261/O3
Frontenac (county), Ontario 177/H3
Frontenac (co.), Québec 172/G4
Frontera, Mexico 150/N7
Frontier, Mich. 250/E7
Frontier (co.), Nebr. 264/D4
Frontier, N. Dak. 282/S6
Frontier, Sask. 181/C6
Frontier, Wyo. 319/B4
Front Royal, Va. 307/M3
Frosinone (prov.), Italy 34/D4
Frosinone, Italy 34/D4
Frösö, Sweden 18/J5
Frost, La. 238/L2
Frost, Minn. 255/D7
Frost, Texas 303/H5
Frost, W. Va. 312/G6
Frostburg, Md. 245/C2
Frostproof, Fla. 212/E4
Froude, Sask. 181/H6
Frövi, Sweden 18/J7
Frøya (isl.), Norway 18/F5
Frozen (str.), N.W.T. 162/H2
Frozen (str.), N.W. Terr. 187/K3
Fruita, Colo. 208/B4
Fruita, Utah 304/C5
Fruitdale, Ala. 195/B8
Fruitdale, S. Dak. 298/B4
Fruitdale-Harbeck, Oreg. 291/D5
Fruitgrove, Queensland 88/K3
Fruit Heights, Utah 304/C2
Fruithurst, Ala. 195/G3
Fruitland, Idaho 220/B6
Fruitland, Iowa 229/L6
Fruitland, Md. 245/R7
Fruitland, Mo. 261/N8
Fruitland, N. Mex. 274/A2
Fruitland, Tenn. 237/D9
Fruitland, Utah 304/D3
Fruitland, Wash. 310/G2
Fruitland Park, Fla. 212/D3
Fruitland Park, Miss. 256/F9
Fruitport, Mich. 250/C5
Fruitvale, Br. Col. 184/J5
Fruitvale, Idaho 220/B5
Fruitvale, Tenn. 237/C9
Fruitvale, Wash. 310/E4
Fruitville, Fla. 212/D4
Frunze, U.S.S.R. 54/J5
Frunze, U.S.S.R. 48/H5
Frutal, Brazil 135/B2
Frutigen, Switzerland 39/E3
Frutillar, Chile 138/D3
Fry, Georgia 217/D1
Fryburg, N. Dak. 282/D6
Fryburg, Ohio 284/B4
Fryburg, Pa. 294/D3
Fry Canyon, Utah 304/D6
Frýdek-Místek, Czech. 41/E2
Frýdlant nad Ostravicí, Czech. 41/E2
Frýdlant v. Čechách, Czech. 41/C1
Frye, Maine 243/B6
Fryeburg, La. 238/D2
Fryeburg, Maine 243/A7
Fryeburg•, Maine 243/A7
Fu'an, China 77/K6
Fuchu, Hiroshima, Japan 81/F6
Fuchu, Tokyo, Japan 81/O2
Fuding, China 77/K6
Fuengirola, Spain 33/D4
Fuensalida, Spain 33/D2
Fuente-Álamo, Spain 33/F4
Fuente de Cantos, Spain 33/C3
Fuentelapeña, Spain 33/D2
Fuente Obejuna, Spain 33/D3
Fuenterrabía, Spain 33/E1
Fuentesaúco, Spain 33/D2
Fuentes de Andalucía, Spain 33/D4
Fuentes de Oñoro, Spain 33/C2
Fuerte (isl.), Colombia 126/B3
Fuerte (riv.), Mexico 150/E3
Fuerte Bulnes, Chile 138/E10
Fuerte Olimpo, Argentina 120/D5
Fuerte Olimpo, Paraguay 144/C2
Fuerteventura (isl.), Spain 102/A2
Fuerteventura (isl.), Spain 106/B3
Fuerteventura (isl.), Spain 33/C4
Fuga (isl.), Philippines 82/A3
Fuglebjerg, Denmark 21/E7
Fugu, China 77/H4
Fuhai (Burultokay), China 77/C2
Fuik, Neth. Ant. 161/G9
Fujairah, U.A.E. 59/G4
Fuji, Japan 81/J6
Fuji (mt.), Japan 81/J6
Fuji (riv.), Japan 81/J6
Fujian (Fukien), China 77/J6
Fujieda, Japan 81/J6
Fuji-Hakone-Izu Nat'l Park, Japan 81/H6
Fujin, China 77/M2
Fujisawa, Japan 81/O3
Fukagawa, Japan 81/L2
Fukang, China 77/C3
Fukuchiyama, Japan 81/G6
Fukue, Japan 81/D7
Fukui (pref.), Japan 81/G5
Fukui, Japan 81/G5
Fukuoka (pref.), Japan 81/D7
Fukuoka, Japan 54/O6
Fukuoka, Japan 81/D7
Fukushima (pref.), Japan 81/K5
Fukushima, Japan 81/K5
Fukuyama, Japan 81/F6
Fulbourn, England 13/H5
Fulbright, Texas 303/J4
Fulda, Germany 22/C3
Fulda, Ind. 227/D8
Fulda, Minn. 255/C7
Fulda, Sask. 181/F3
Fulda (riv.), Germany 22/C3
Fulford, England 13/F4
Fulford Harbour, Br. Col. 184/K3
Fuling, China 77/G6
Fulks Run, Va. 307/L3
Fullarton, Trin. & Tob. 161/A11
Fullerton, Calif. 204/D11
Fullerton, Ky. 237/P3
Fullerton, La. 238/D4
Fullerton, Nebr. 264/F3
Fullerton, N. Dak. 282/O7
Fully, Switzerland 39/D4
Fulnek, Czech. 41/D2
Fulpmes, Austria 41/A3
Fulton, Ala. 195/C7
Fulton (co.), Ark. 202/G1
Fulton, Ark. 202/C6
Fulton (co.), Georgia 217/D3
Fulton (co.), Ill. 222/C3
Fulton, Ill. 222/C2
Fulton (co.), Ind. 227/E2
Fulton, Ind. 227/E3
Fulton, Iowa 229/M4
Fulton, Kansas 232/H4
Fulton (co.), Ky. 237/C7
Fulton, Ky. 237/D7
Fulton, Mich. 250/D6
Fulton, Miss. 256/H2
Fulton, Mo. 261/J5
Fulton (co.), N.Y. 276/M4
Fulton, N.Y. 276/H4
Fulton (co.), Ohio 284/B2
Fulton, Ohio 284/E5
Fulton (co.), Pa. 294/F6
Fulton, S. Dak. 298/O6
Fulton, Tenn. 237/B9
Fulton, Texas 303/H9
Fulton Chain (lakes), N.Y. 276/K3
Fultondale, Ala. 195/E3
Fultonham, Ohio 284/F6
Fultonville, N.Y. 276/M5
Fults, Ill. 222/C5
Fulwood, England 10/G1
Fulwood, England 13/G1
Funabashi, Japan 81/P2
Funafuti (atoll), Tuvalu 87/H6
Funchal, Portugal 33/A2
Funchal (cap.), Madeira, Port. 102/A1
Funchal (cap.), Madeira, Portugal 106/A2
Fundación, Colombia 126/C2
Fundão, Portugal 33/C2
Fundy (bay) 162/K7
Fundy (bay), New Bruns. 170/E3
Fundy (bay), Nova Scotia 168/C3
Fundy Nat'l Park, New Bruns. 170/E3
Funhalouro, Mozambique 118/E4
Funing, China 77/K5
Funk, Nebr. 264/E4
Funk (isl.), Newf. 166/D4
Funkley, Minn. 255/D3
Funkstown, Md. 245/H2
Funston, Georgia 217/E8
Funter, Alaska 196/M1
Funtua, Nigeria 106/F6
Fuping, China 77/H4
Fuquay-Varina, N.C. 281/M3
Furancungo, Mozambique 118/E2
Furka (pass), Switzerland 39/F3
Furman, Ala. 195/E6
Furman, S.C. 296/E6
Furmanov, U.S.S.R. 52/F3
Furnace, Ky. 237/O5
Furnace, Mass. 249/F3
Furnace, Scotland 15/C4
Furnas (res.), Brazil 120/E5
Furnas (dam), Brazil 135/C2
Furnas (co.), Nebr. 264/E4
Furneaux Group (isls.), Australia 87/E9
Furneaux Group (isls.), Tasmania 88/H8
Furneaux Group (isls.), Tasmania 99/E1
Furnes (Veurne), Belgium 27/B6
Furness, Sask. 181/B2
Furry Creek, Br. Col. 184/K2
Fürstenberg, Germany 22/E2
Fürstenfeld, Austria 41/C3
Fürstenfeldbruck, Germany 22/D4
Fürstenwalde, Germany 22/F2
Fürth, Germany 22/D4
Furth im Wald, Germany 22/E4
Furukawa, Japan 81/K4
Fury and Hecla (str.), N.W.T. 162/H2
Fury and Hecla (str.), N.W. Terr. 187/K3
Fusagasugá, Colombia 126/C5
Fushun, China 77/K3
Fushun, China 54/O5
Fusilier, Sask. 181/B4
Fusin (Fuxin), China 77/K3
Fusingchen (Simao), China 77/F7
Fusio, Switzerland 39/G4
Fusong, China 77/L3
Füssen, Germany 22/D5
Futa Jallon (lag.), Guinea 106/B6
Futaleufú, Chile 138/E4
Futrono, Chile 138/E3
Futuna (Hoorn) (isls.), Wallis and Futuna 87/J7
Fu Xian, Liaoning, China 77/K4
Fu Xian, Shaanxi, China 77/G4
Fuxin (Fusin), China 77/K3
Fuxin, China 54/O5
Fuyang (Fowyang), China 77/J5
Fuyu, Heilongjiang, China 77/K2
Fuyu, Jilin, China 77/L2
Fuyuan, Heilongjiang, China 77/M2
Fuyuan, Yunnan, China 77/F6
Fuyun, China 77/C2
Füzesabony, Hungary 41/F3
Füzesgyarmat, Hungary 41/F3
Fuzhou, Jiangxi, China 77/J6
Fuzhou, China 2/R4
Fuzhou, China 54/N7
Fuzhou (Foochow), Fujian, China 77/J6
Fyffe, Ala. 195/G2
Fylingdales, England 13/G3
Fyn (co.), Denmark 21/D7
Fyn (isl.), Denmark 21/D7
Fyn (isl.), Denmark 18/G9
Fyne, Loch (inlet), Scotland 10/D2
Fyne, Loch (inlet), Scotland 15/C5
Fyns Hoved (pt.), Denmark 21/D6
Fyvie, Scotland 15/F3
Fyzabad, Trin. & Tob. 161/A11

G

Gaastra, Mich. 250/G2
Gabarus, Nova Scotia 168/H3
Gabarus (bay), Nova Scotia 168/H3
Gabarus (cape), Nova Scotia 168/J3
Gabbettville, Georgia 217/B5
Gabbs, Nev. 266/D4
Gabela, Angola 115/B6
Gabès, Tunisia 106/F2
Gabès, Tunisia 102/D1
Gabès (gulf), Tunisia 106/G2
Gabgaba, Wadi (dry riv.), Sudan 111/F3
Gable, S.C. 296/G4
Gabon 2/K6
Gabon 102/D4
GABON 115/B4
Gaborone (cap.), Botswana 2/L7
Gaborone (cap.), Botswana 118/D4
Gaborone (cap.), Botswana 102/E7
Gabras, Sudan 111/E5
Gabredarre, Ethiopia 111/H6
Gabriel (str.), N.W. Terr. 187/M3
Gabrik (riv.), Iran 66/L7
Gabriola, Br. Col. 184/J3
Gabrovo, Bulgaria 45/G4
Gachalá, Colombia 126/D5
Gach Saran, Iran 59/F3
Gach Saran, Iran 66/G5
Gackle, N. Dak. 282/M6
Gacko, Yugoslavia 45/D4
Gadag-Betgeri, India 68/D5
Gäddede, Sweden 18/J4
Gadê, China 77/E5
Gadebusch, Germany 22/D2
Gadmen, Switzerland 39/F3
Gadsby, Alberta 182/D3
Gadsden, Ala. 188/J4
Gadsden, Ala. 195/G2
Gadsden, Ariz. 198/A6
Gadsden (co.), Fla. 212/B1
Gadsden, S.C. 296/F4
Gadsden, Tenn. 237/D9
Gads Hill, Mo. 261/L8
Gadston (pt.), Fla. 212/C3
Gadwal, India 68/D5
Gadyach, U.S.S.R. 52/D4
Găeşti, Romania 45/G3
Gaeta, Italy 34/D4
Gaeta (gulf), Italy 34/D4
Gaferut (isl.), Micronesia 87/E5
Gaffney, S.C. 296/D1
Gafsa, Tunisia 106/F2
Gagarin, U.S.S.R. 52/D3
Gage, Alberta 182/A1
Gage (co.), Nebr. 264/H4
Gage, N. Mex. 274/A6
Gage, Okla. 288/G2
Gagetown, Mich. 250/F5
Gagetown, New Bruns. 170/D3
Gaggenau, Germany 22/C4
Gagnoa, Ivory Coast 102/B4
Gagnoa, Ivory Coast 106/C7
Gagnon, Que. 162/K5
Gagnon, Québec 174/D2

Gagnon (lake), Québec 172/B3
Gagny, France 28/C1
Gagra, U.S.S.R. 52/E6
Gahanna, Ohio 284/E5
Gaiba (lag.), Bolivia 136/F5
Gail, Saudi Arabia 59/E5
Gail, Texas 303/C5
Gaillac, France 28/D6
Gaillard (lake), Conn. 210/D3
Gaillard, Georgia 217/D5
Gaima, Papua N.G. 85/B7
Gaiman, Argentina 143/C5
Gaines, Mich. 250/F6
Gaines (co.), Texas 303/B5
Gainesboro, Tenn. 237/K8
Gainesboro, Va. 307/M2
Gainestown, Ala. 195/C8
Gainesville, Ala. 195/B5
Gainesville (dam), Ala. 195/B5
Gainesville, Fla. 188/K5
Gainesville, Fla. 212/D2
Gainesville, Georgia 217/E2
Gainesville, Mo. 261/G9
Gainesville, N.Y. 276/D5
Gainesville, Texas 303/G4
Gainesville, Va. 307/N3
Gainsborough, England 10/F4
Gainsborough, England 13/G4
Gainsborough, Sask. 181/K6
Gairdner (lake), Australia 87/D9
Gairdner (lake), S. Australia 88/F6
Gairdner (lake), S. Australia 94/D4
Gairloch, Scotland 15/C3
Gairloch, Loch (inlet), Scotland 15/C3
Gais, Switzerland 39/H2
Gaithersburg, Md. 245/K4
Gajdel, Czech. 41/E2
Gakona, Alaska 196/K2
Galadi, Ethiopia 111/J6
Galahad, Alberta 182/E3
Galana (riv.), Kenya 115/G4
Galand, Iran 66/J2
Galanta, Czech. 41/D2
Galápagos (isls.), Ecuador 2/E6
Galápagos (isls.), Ecuador 128/C8
Galashiels, Scotland 10/E3
Galashiels, Scotland 15/F5
Galata, Mont. 262/E2
Galata, Turkey 63/C6
Galați, Romania 7/G4
Galați, Romania 45/H3
Galatia, Ill. 222/E6
Galatia, Kansas 232/D3
Galatina, Italy 34/G4
Galatone, Italy 34/F4
Galax (I.C.), Va. 307/G7
Galbally, Ireland 17/E7
Galbraith, La. 238/E4
Galcaio, Somalia 102/G4
Galcaio, Somalia 115/J2
Galchutt, N. Dak. 282/S7
Gale, Ill. 222/D6
Gale (riv.), N.H. 268/D3
Galeana, Chihuahua, Mexico 150/F1
Galeana, Nuevo León, Mexico 150/J4
Galela, Indonesia 85/H5
Galen, Mont. 262/D4
Galena, Alaska 196/G2
Galena, Ill. 222/C1
Galena, Ind. 227/F8
Galena, Kansas 232/H4
Galena, Md. 245/P3
Galena, Mo. 261/F9
Galena, Ohio 284/E5
Galena Park, Texas 303/J1
Galeota (pt.), Trin. & Tob. 161/B11
Galera (pt.), Chile 138/C3
Galera (pt.), Ecuador 128/B2
Galera (pt.), Trin. & Tob. 161/C10
Galera (pt.), Trin. & Tob. 156/G5
Galesburg, Ill. 188/H2
Galesburg, Ill. 222/C3
Galesburg, Kansas 232/G4
Galesburg, Mich. 250/D6
Galesburg, N. Dak. 282/R5
Gales Creek, Oreg. 291/D2
Gales Ferry, Conn. 210/G3
Galestown, Md. 245/P6
Galesville, Md. 245/M5
Galesville, Wis. 317/D7
Galeton, Colo. 208/K1
Galeton, Pa. 294/G2
Galetta, Ontario 177/H2
Galgenberg (hill), Netherlands 27/H4
Galguduud (prov.), Somalia 115/J2
Galiano, Br. Col. 184/K3
Galiano (isl.), Br. Col. 184/K3
Galice, Oreg. 291/D5
Galich, U.S.S.R. 52/F3
Galicia (reg.), Spain 33/B1
Galien, Mich. 250/C7
Galilee (reg.), Israel 65/C2
Galilee, Sea of (lake), Israel 59/C3
Galilee, Sea of (Tiberias) (lake), Israel 65/D2
Galilee (lake), Queensland 95/C4
Galina (pt.), Jamaica 158/J6
Galion (bay), Martinique 161/D6
Galion, Ohio 284/E4
Galisteo, N. Mex. 274/D3
Galivants Ferry, S.C. 296/J3
Gallabat, Sudan 111/H5
Gallan (head), Scotland 15/A2
Gallant, Ala. 195/F2
Gallarate, Italy 34/B2
Gallatin (co.), Ill. 222/E6
Gallatin (co.), Ky. 237/M3
Gallatin, Mo. 261/E3
Gallatin (co.), Mont. 262/E5
Gallatin (peak), Mont. 262/E5
Gallatin (riv.), Mont. 262/E5
Gallatin, Tenn. 237/H8
Gallatin Gateway, Mont. 262/E5
Gallaway, Tenn. 237/B10
Galle, Sri Lanka 54/J9
Galle, Sri Lanka 68/D7

Gallegos (riv.), Argentina 143/B7
Gallegos, N. Mex. 274/F3
Galley (head), Ireland 17/D9
Gallia (co.), Ohio 284/F8
Galliano, La. 238/K8
Gallina, N. Mex. 274/C2
Gallinas (pt.), Colombia 120/B1
Gallinas (pt.), Colombia 126/E1
Gallinas (mts.), N. Mex. 274/B4
Gallinas (pt.), N. Mex. 274/E3
Gallion, Ala. 195/C6
Gallion, La. 238/G1
Gallipoli, Italy 34/F4
Gallipoli, Turkey 59/A1
Gallipoli, Turkey 63/C5
Gallipolis, Ohio 284/F8
Gallipolis Ferry, W. Va. 312/B5
Gallitzin, Pa. 294/F4
Gallo (pt.), Chile 138/E3
Gallo (int.), Dom. Rep. 158/D5
Gällö, Sweden 18/J5
Galloo (isl.), N.Y. 276/N1
Galloway, Ark. 202/F4
Galloway, Br. Col. 184/K5
Galloway (dist.), Scotland 15/D5
Galloway, Mull of (prom.), Scotland 15/D6
Galloway, Mull of (prom.), Scotland 10/D3
Galloway, W. Va. 312/F4
Galloway, Wis. 317/H6
Gallup, N. Mex. 188/E3
Gallup, N. Mex. 274/A3
Gallur, Spain 33/F2
Galole, Kenya 115/G4
Gal'on, Israel 65/B4
Galston, Scotland 10/D3
Galston, Scotland 15/D5
Galt, Calif. 204/C9
Galt, Iowa 229/F3
Galt, Mo. 261/F2
Galtee (mts.), Ireland 17/E7
Galtymore (mt.), Ireland 17/E7
Galva, Ill. 222/D2
Galva, Iowa 229/C3
Galva, Kansas 232/E3
Galván (mt.), Paraguay 144/C3
Galvarino, Chile 138/D2
Galveston, Ind. 227/E3
Galveston (co.), Texas 303/K8
Galveston, Texas 188/H5
Galveston, Texas 188/H5
Galveston, Texas 303/L3
Galveston (bay), Texas 188/H5
Galveston (bay), Texas 303/L2
Galveston (isl.), Texas 303/K8
Gálvez, Argentina 143/F6
Gálvez, La. 238/L2
Gálvez, Spain 33/D3
Galvin, Wash. 310/B4
Galway (co.), Ireland 17/D5
Galway, Ireland 17/C5
Galway, Ireland 7/D3
Galway, Ireland 10/B4
Galway (bay), Ireland 17/C5
Galway (bay), Ireland 10/B4
Galway, N.Y. 276/N4
Gamaliel, Ky. 237/K7
Gamarra, Colombia 126/D3
Gamas Ab (riv.), Iran 66/E3
Gamay, Philippines 82/E4
Gamay (bay), Philippines 82/E4
Gamba, China 77/C6
Gambaga, Ghana 106/D6
Gambela, Ethiopia 111/F6
Gambell, Alaska 196/D2
Gamber, Md. 245/L3
Gambia 2/J5
Gambia 102/A3
GAMBIA 106/A6
Gambia (riv.), Gambia 106/B6
Gambia (riv.), Senegal 106/B6
Gambier (isls.), Fr. Poly. 87/N8
Gambier, Ohio 284/F5
Gambo, Newf. 166/D4
Gamboma, Congo 115/C4
Gambos, Angola 115/B6
Gambrills, Md. 245/M4
Gamerco, N. Mex. 274/A3
Gaming, Austria 41/C3
Gamleby, Sweden 18/K8
Gammon (riv.), Manitoba 179/G3
Gammon (pt.), Mass. 249/N6
Gampel, Switzerland 39/E4
Gamu-Gofa (prov.), Ethiopia 111/G6
Gamvik, Norway 18/Q1
Ganado, Ariz. 198/F3
Ganado, Texas 303/H8
Ganale Dorya (riv.), Ethiopia 111/H6
Gananoque, Ontario 177/H3
Ganassi, Philippines 82/D7
Ganaveh, Iran 66/G6
Ganda, Angola 115/B6
Gandajika, Zaire 115/D5
Gandara, Philippines 82/E4
Gándara, Spain 33/C1
Gandava, Pakistan 68/B3
Gandava, Pakistan 59/J4
Gandeeville, W. Va. 312/D5
Gander, Newf. 162/L6
Gander, Newf. 166/D4
Gander (lake), Newf. 166/D4
Gander (riv.), Newf. 166/D4
Gandesa, Spain 33/G2
Gandi, Georgia 217/J7
Gandhinagar, India 68/C4
Gandía, Spain 33/F3
Gandy, Nebr. 264/D3
Gandy, Utah 304/A4
Ganga (Ganges) (riv.), India 68/F3
Gan Gan, Argentina 143/C5
Ganganagar, India 68/C3
Gangapur, India 68/D3
Gangara, Niger 106/F6
Gangaw, Burma 72/B2
Gangca, China 77/F4
Gangdisê Shan (range), China 77/B5

Ganges (riv.) 54/K7
Ganges (riv.) 2/P4
Ganges, Mouths of the (delta), Bangladesh 68/F3
Ganges (riv.), Bangladesh 68/F3
Ganges, Br. Col. 184/K3
Ganges, Mouths of the (delta), India 68/F4
Ganges (riv.), India 68/F3
Gangtok, India 68/F3
Gan He (riv.), China 77/K2
Gani, Indonesia 85/H6
Ganister, Pa. 294/F5
Ganmain, N.S. Wales 97/D4
Gann (Brinkhaven), Ohio 284/F5
Gannat, France 28/E4
Gannett, Idaho 220/D6
Gannett (peak), Wyo. 188/D2
Gannett (peak), Wyo. 319/C2
Gannvalley, S. Dak. 298/L5
Ganquan, China 77/H4
Gans, Okla. 288/S4
Gänserndorf, Austria 41/D2
Gansevoort, N.Y. 276/N4
Ganshoren, Belgium 27/B9
Gansu (Kansu), China 77/E3
Gansville, La. 238/E2
Gantt, Ala. 195/E8
Gantt, S.C. 296/C2
Ganzhou (Kanchow), China 77/H6
Gao (mt.), Cent. Afr. Rep. 115/C2
Gao, Mali 102/C3
Gao, Mali 106/E5
Gao'an, China 77/H6
Gaolan, China 77/F4
Gaotai, China 77/F4
Gaoua, Burkina Faso 106/D6
Gaoual, Guinea 106/B6
Gaoyou Hu (lake), China 77/J5
Gap, France 28/G5
Gap, Pa. 294/L6
Gap (creek), Sask. 181/B6
Gapan, Philippines 82/C3
Gapcreek, Ky. 237/M7
Gap Mills, W. Va. 312/F7
Gar, China 77/B5
Gara (lake), Ireland 17/D4
Gara, Lough (lake), Ireland 10/B4
Garadice (lake), Ireland 17/F3
Garah, N.S. Wales 97/E1
Garamba Nat'l Park, Zaire 115/E3
Garanhuns, Brazil 120/D3
Garanhuns, Brazil 132/G5
Garards Fort, Pa. 294/C7
Garbahaarrey, Somalia 115/H3
Garba Tula, Kenya 115/G3
Garber, Iowa 229/L3
Garber, Okla. 288/M2
Garberville, Calif. 204/B3
Garbosh, Kuh-e (mt.), Iran 66/G4
Garbsen, Germany 22/C2
Garça, Brazil 135/B3
Garcia, Colo. 208/J8
García de Sola (res.), Spain 33/D3
Garcitas, Venezuela 124/C3
Gard (dept.), France 28/F6
Gard (riv.), France 28/F5
Garda (lake), Italy 34/C2
Gardanne, France 28/F6
Gardar, N. Dak. 282/P2
Gardelegen, Germany 22/D2
Garden, Mich. 250/C3
Garden (isl.), Mich. 250/D3
Garden (pen.), Mich. 250/C3
Garden (co.), Nebr. 264/B3
Garden (isl.), W. Australia 88/A2
Garden (isl.), W. Australia 92/A1
Gardena, Calif. 204/C11
Gardena, Idaho 220/B5
Gardena, N. Dak. 282/J2
Garden City, Ala. 195/E2
Garden City, Georgia 217/K6
Garden City, Idaho 220/B6
Garden City, Iowa 229/G4
Garden City, Kans. 188/F3
Garden City, Kansas 232/B4
Garden City, La. 238/H7
Garden City, Mich. 250/F6
Garden City, Minn. 255/D6
Garden City, Mo. 261/D5
Garden City, N.Y. 276/R7
Garden City, S. Dak. 298/O4
Garden City, Texas 303/C6
Garden City, Utah 304/C2
Garden City Beach, S.C. 296/K4
Gardendale, Ala. 195/E3
Garden Grove, Calif. 204/D11
Garden Grove, Iowa 229/F7
Garden Home-Whitford, Oreg. 291/A2
Garden Island (bay), La. 238/M8
Garden Plain, Kansas 232/E4
Garden Prairie, Ill. 222/E1
Garden Reach, India 68/F2
Garden River, Alberta 182/B5
Gardenstown, Scotland 15/F3
Gardenton, Manitoba 179/F5
Garden Valley, Idaho 220/C5
Garden View, Pa. 294/H3
Garden Village, Ontario 177/E1
Gardez, Afghanistan 59/J3
Gardez, Afghanistan 68/B2
Gardi, Georgia 217/J7
Gardiner, Maine 243/D7
Gardiner, Mont. 262/F5
Gardiner, Oreg. 291/C4
Gardiner (dam), Sask. 181/D4
Gardiner, Wash. 310/B2
Gardiners (bay), N.Y. 276/R8
Gardiners (isl.), N.Y. 276/R8
Gardner (canal), Br. Col. 184/C3
Gardner, Colo. 208/J7
Gardner (lake), Conn. 210/G2
Gardner, Fla. 212/E4
Gardner, Ill. 222/E2
Gardner, Kansas 232/H3

Gardner (Nikumaroro) (isl.), Kiribati 87/J6
Gardner (lake), Maine 243/J6
Gardner, Mass. 249/G2
Gardner, N. Dak. 282/R5
Gardner, Tenn. 237/D8
Gardner (mt.), Wash. 310/E2
Gardner Creek, New Bruns. 170/E3
Gardner Pinnacles (isls.), Hawaii 87/K3
Gardner Pinnacles (isls.), Hawaii 188/F6
Gardner Pinnacles (isls.), Hawaii 218/C6
Gardnerville, Nev. 266/B4
Gardo, Somalia 115/J2
Gardula, Ethiopia 111/G6
Gare Loch (inlet), Scotland 15/A1
Garelochhead, Scotland 15/A1
Garelochhead, Scotland 10/A1
Gareloi (isl.), Alaska 196/K4
Garessio, Italy 34/A2
Garfield (co.), Colo. 208/C3
Garfield, Colo. 208/G5
Garfield, Georgia 217/H5
Garfield, Kansas 232/C3
Garfield, Ky. 237/J5
Garfield, Minn. 255/C5
Garfield (co.), Mont. 262/J3
Garfield (co.), Nebr. 264/F3
Garfield, N.J. 273/B2
Garfield, N. Mex. 274/B6
Garfield (co.), Okla. 288/L2
Garfield (co.), Utah 304/C6
Garfield (co.), Wash. 310/H4
Garfield (co.), Wash. 310/H4
Garfield Heights, Ohio 284/J9
Gargaliánoi, Greece 45/E7
Gargunnock, Scotland 15/B1
Garibaldi, Br. Col. 184/F5
Garibaldi, Oreg. 291/C2
Garibaldi Prov. Park, Br. Col. 184/F5
Garies, S. Africa 118/B6
Garioch (dist.), Scotland 15/F3
Garissa, Kenya 115/G4
Garita, N. Mex. 274/E3
Garland, Ala. 195/E7
Garland (co.), Ark. 202/D4
Garland, Kansas 232/H4
Garland, Maine 243/E5
Garland •, Maine 243/E5
Garland, Manitoba 179/G3
Garland, Nebr. 264/G4
Garland, N.C. 281/N5
Garland, Pa. 294/C2
Garland, Tenn. 237/B9
Garland, Tex. 188/G4
Garland, Texas 303/H2
Garland, Utah 304/B2
Garland, Wyo. 319/D1
Garland City, Ark. 202/C7
Garlandville, Miss. 256/F6
Garlieston, Scotland 15/D6
Garlin, Ky. 237/L6
Garmisch-Partenkirchen, Germany 22/D5
Garmouth, Scotland 15/E3
Garmsar, Iran 59/F2
Garmsar, Iran 66/H3
Garnavillo, Iowa 229/L3
Garneill, Mont. 262/G4
Garner, Ark. 202/G3
Garner, Iowa 229/F2
Garner (lake), Manitoba 179/G4
Garner, N.C. 281/M3
Garnet, Mich. 250/D2
Garnet, Mont. 262/C4
Garnet (bay), N.W. Terr. 187/L3
Garnett, Kansas 232/G3
Garnett, S.C. 296/E6
Garnish, Newf. 166/C4
Garoe, Somalia 115/J2
Garonne (riv.), France 7/D4
Garonne (riv.), France 28/C5
Garoua, Cameroon 102/D4
Garoua, Cameroon 115/B2
Garrabost, Scotland 15/B2
Garrard (co.), Ky. 237/M5
Garretson, S. Dak. 298/S6
Garrett, Ill. 222/E4
Garrett, Ind. 227/G2
Garrett, Ky. 237/R6
Garrett (co.), Md. 245/A2
Garrett, Pa. 294/D6
Garrett, Wash. 310/G4
Garrett, Wyo. 319/G5
Garrett Park, Md. 245/E3
Garretts Bend, W. Va. 312/C6
Garrettsville, Ohio 284/H3
Garrick, Sask. 181/G2
Garrison, Iowa 229/J4
Garrison, Ky. 237/P3
Garrison, Md. 245/L3
Garrison, Minn. 255/E4
Garrison, Mo. 261/F9
Garrison, Mont. 262/D4
Garrison, Nebr. 264/G3
Garrison, N.Y. 276/N8
Garrison, N. Dak. 282/H4
Garrison (dam), N. Dak. 282/H5
Garrison, Texas 303/K6
Garrison, Utah 304/A5
Garrisonville, Va. 307/N4
Garron (pt.), N. Ireland 17/K1
Garrovillas, Spain 33/C3
Garry (lake), Canada 4/C14
Garry (lake), N.W.T. 162/G2
Garry (lake), N.W. Terr. 187/H3
Garry, Loch (lake), Scotland 15/D3
Garry (riv.), Scotland 15/D4
Garryowen, Mont. 262/J5
Garsen, Kenya 115/G4
Garske, N. Dak. 282/N3
Garson (lake), Alberta 182/E1
Garson, Manitoba 179/F4
Garstang, England 13/G1
Gartan (lake), Ireland 17/F2
Gartmore, Scotland 15/B1

Garulia, India 68/F1
Garut, Indonesia 85/H2
Garvagh, N. Ireland 17/H2
Garvan (isls.), Ireland 17/G1
Garvin, Minn. 255/C6
Garvin (co.), Okla. 288/M5
Garvin, Iowa 229/H4
Garwolin, Poland 47/E3
Garwood, Mo. 261/L8
Garwood, N.J. 273/E2
Garwood, Texas 303/H8
Gary, Ind. 146/K5
Gary, Ind. 188/J2
Gary, Ind. 227/C1
Gary, Minn. 255/C6
Gary, S. Dak. 298/S4
Gary, W. Va. 312/C8
Gary, Texas 303/K5
Garyarsa (Gartok), China 77/B5
Garyarsa, China 54/K6
Garyville, La. 238/M3
Garza, Colombia 126/C6
Garza (co.), Texas 303/C4
Garzê, China 77/F5
Garzón, Colombia 126/C6
Garzón, Uruguay 145/E5
Garzón (lag.), Uruguay 145/E5
Gas, Kansas 232/G4
Gas (hills), Wyo. 319/E3
Gasan-Kuli, U.S.S.R. 48/F6
Gasburg, Va. 307/N7
Gas City, Ind. 227/F4
Gasconade (co.), Mo. 261/J6
Gasconade, Mo. 261/J5
Gasconade (riv.), Mo. 261/H7
Gascony (trad. prov.), France 29
Gascoyne (riv.), Australia 87/B8
Gascoyne, N. Dak. 282/D7
Gascoyne (riv.), W. Australia 88/A4
Gascoyne (riv.), W. Australia 92/B4
Gascoyne Junction, W. Australia 92/A4
Gash (Mareb) (riv.), Ethiopia 59/C4
Gash (riv.), Sudan 59/C6
Gashaka, Nigeria 106/G7
Gash Hills, Wyo. 319/E3
Gash Mareb (riv.), Ethiopia 111/G5
Gasht, Iran 66/M7
Gasker (isl.), Scotland 15/A3
Gaskiers, Newf. 166/D2
Gasmata, Papua N.G. 86/B2
Gaspar, Cuba 158/F2
Gaspar Hernández, Dom. Rep. 158/E5
Gasparilla (isl.), Fla. 212/D5
Gaspé, Que. 162/L6
Gaspé, Québec 172/D1
Gaspé, Québec 174/E3
Gaspé (bay), Québec 172/D1
Gaspé (cape), Québec 172/D1
Gaspé (cape), Québec 174/E3
Gaspé (pen.), Québec 172/D2
Gaspé-Est (county), Québec 174/E3
Gaspé-Est (co.), Québec 172/D1
Gaspé-Ouest (co.), Québec 172/C1
Gaspé-Ouest (county), Québec 174/D3
Gaspereau (riv.), New Bruns. 170/E3
Gaspereau (lake), Nova Scotia 168/D4
Gaspésie Prov. Park, Québec 174/D3
Gaspésie Prov. Park, Québec 172/C1
Gasport, N.Y. 276/C4
Gasque, Ala. 195/C10
Gassan (mt.), Japan 81/J4
Gassaway, Tenn. 237/K9
Gassaway, W. Va. 312/E5
Gassetts, Vt. 268/B5
Gassville, Ark. 202/F1
Gaston, Ind. 227/G4
Gaston (co.), N.C. 281/G4
Gaston, N.C. 281/O1
Gaston (res.), N.C. 281/O2
Gaston, Oreg. 291/D2
Gaston, S.C. 296/E4
Gastonburg, Ala. 195/C6
Gastonia, N.C. 188/K3
Gastonia, N.C. 281/G4
Gastonville, Pa. 294/B5
Gat, Israel 65/B4
Gata (cape), Cyprus 59/B3
Gata (cape), Cyprus 63/E5
Gata (cape), Spain 33/F4
Gata (mts.), Spain 33/C2
Gatchel, Ind. 227/D8
Gatchina, U.S.S.R. 52/C3
Gate, Okla. 288/F1
Gate City, Va. 307/C7
Gatehouse-of-Fleet, Scotland 10/E3
Gatehouse-of-Fleet, Scotland 15/D6
Gates, Nebr. 264/E3
Gates (co.), N.C. 281/R2
Gates, N.C. 281/R2
Gates, Oreg. 291/E3
Gates, Tenn. 237/C9
Gateshead, England 10/F3
Gateshead, England 13/H3
Gateshead (isl.), N.W. Terr. 187/J2
Gates Mills, Ohio 284/J9
Gates of the Arctic Nat'l Park, Alaska 196/H1
Gates of the Arctic Nat'l Pres., Alaska 196/H1
Gatesville, N.C. 281/R2
Gatesville, Texas 303/G6
Gateswood, Ala. 195/C9
Gateway, Ark. 202/B1
Gateway, Colo. 208/B5
Gateway, Oreg. 291/E3
Gateway Nat'l Rec. Area, N.J. 273/E2
Gateway Nat'l Rec. Area, N.Y. 276/M9
Gatewood, Mo. 261/K9
Gatico, Chile 138/A4
Gatineau (co.), Québec 172/B3
Gatineau (county), Québec 174/B3
Gatineau, Québec 172/B3
Gatineau (riv.), Québec 172/B3
Gatliff, Ky. 237/O7
Gatlinburg, Tenn. 237/O9
Gatooma (Kadoma), Zimbabwe·118/D3

Gatooma, Zimbabwe 102/E6
Gatow, Germany 22/E4
Gatteville-le-Phare, France 28/C3
Gattman, Miss. 256/H3
Gatton, Queensland 88/J5
Gatton, Queensland 95/C5
Gatun (lake), Panama 154/G6
Gatzke, Minn. 255/C2
Gaucín, Spain 33/D4
Gauhati, India 68/G3
Gauhati, India 54/L7
Gauja (riv.), U.S.S.R. 53/C2
Gauley (riv.), W. Va. 312/D6
Gauley Bridge, W. Va. 312/D6
Gauley Mills, W. Va. 312/E6
Gaultois, Newf. 166/C4
Gausdale, Ky. 237/N7
Gause, Texas 303/H7
Gaussberg (mt.), Ant. 5/C5
Gautier, Miss. 256/G10
Gautier, Iran 66/M8
Gávdhos (isl.), Greece 45/F8
Gave de Pau (riv.), France 28/C6
Gavião, Portugal 33/C3
Gavins Point (dam), Nebr. 264/G2
Gavins Point (dam), S. Dak. 298/P8
Gaviota (lag.), Calif. 204/E9
Gavkhuni (lake), Iran 59/F3
Gavkhuni (marsh), Iran 66/H4
Gävle, Sweden 7/F2
Gävle, Sweden 18/K6
Gävleborg (co.), Sweden 18/K6
Gawai, Burma 72/C1
Gawler, S. Australia 88/F6
Gawler (ranges), S. Australia 88/F6
Gawler, S. Australia 94/B6
Gawler (riv.), S. Australia 94/B6
Gawler (ranges), S. Australia 94/E5
Gay, Georgia 217/C4
Gay, Mich. 250/A1
Gay, U.S.S.R. 52/J4
Gay, W. Va. 312/C5
Gaya, India 68/F4
Gaya, Niger 106/E6
Gay Head •, Mass. 249/L7
Gay Head (prom.), Mass. 249/L7
Gay Hill, Texas 303/H7
Gayle, Jamaica 158/J6
Gaylesville, Ala. 195/G2
Gaylord, Kansas 232/D2
Gaylord, Mich. 250/E4
Gaylord, Minn. 255/D6
Gaylord, Oreg. 291/C5
Gaylord, Va. 307/M2
Gaylordsville, Conn. 210/A2
Gayndah, Queensland 95/D5
Gayndah, Queensland 88/J5
Gayny, U.S.S.R. 52/H2
Gays, Ill. 222/E4
Gaysin, U.S.S.R. 52/C5
Gays Mills, Wis. 317/E9
Gaysport, Ohio 284/G6
Gaysville, Vt. 268/B4
Gayville, S. Dak. 298/P8
Gaza, Cent. Afr. Rep. 115/C3
Gaza, Egypt 59/B3
Gaza, Gaza Strip 65/A5
Gaza, Iowa 229/B2
Gaza (prov.), Mozambique 118/E4
Gaza, N.H. 268/D4
Gaza Strip 65/A5
GAZA STRIP 59/B3
Gazelle, Calif. 204/C2
Gazelle (pen.), Papua N.G. 86/B2
Gaziantep (prov.), Turkey 63/G4
Gaziantep, Turkey 54/E6
Gaziantep, Turkey 63/G4
Gaziantep, Turkey 59/C2
Gazik, Iran 66/L4
Gazipaşa, Turkey 63/E4
Gbarnga, Liberia 106/C7
Gbarnga, Liberia 102/B4
Gbogo, Nigeria 106/F7
Gcuwa, S. Africa 118/D6
Gdańsk, Poland 47/D1
Gdańsk, Poland 7/F3
Gdańsk, Poland 7/F3
Gdańsk (gulf), Poland 47/D1
Gdov, U.S.S.R. 52/C3
Gdynia, Poland 7/F3
Gdynia, Poland 47/D1
Gearhart, Oreg. 291/C1
Geary (co.), Kansas 232/F3
Geary, New Bruns. 170/D3
Geary, Okla. 288/K3
Geashill, Ireland 17/G5
Geauga (co.), Ohio 284/H3
Gebe (isl.), Indonesia 85/H6
Gebeit Mine, Sudan 111/H3
Gebo, Wyo. 319/D2
Gebze, Turkey 63/C2
Gedaref, Sudan 111/G5
Gedaref, Sudan 59/C7
Gedaref, Sudan 102/F3
Geddes, S. Dak. 298/M7
Gede (mt.), Indonesia 85/H2
Gedera, Israel 65/B4
Gedi (ruins), Kenya 115/G4
Gedinne, Belgium 27/F9
Gediz, Turkey 63/C3
Gediz (riv.), Turkey 63/C3
Gedo, Ethiopia 111/G6
Gedo (prov.), Somalia 115/H3
Gedser, Denmark 21/F8
Gedser Odde (pt.), Denmark 21/E8
Gedsted, Denmark 21/C4
Geebung, Queensland 88/K2
Geebung, Queensland 95/E2
Geel, Belgium 27/F6
Geelong, Victoria 88/L7
Geelong, Victoria 97/C6
Geelong West, Victoria 88/G7
Geelong West, Victoria 97/C6
Geelvink (Cenderawasih) (bay), Indonesia 85/K6
Geelvink (chan.), W. Australia 88/A5
Geelvink (chan.), W. Australia 92/A5

Glacier 373

Geertruidenberg, Netherlands 27/F5
Geesthacht, Germany 22/D2
Geetingsville, Ind. 227/D4
Geeveston, Tasmania 99/C5
Geff, Ill. 222/E5
Ge'gyai, China 77/B5
Geh, Iran 59/H4
Geh, Iran 66/L7
Gehua, Papua N.G. 85/C8
Geidam, Nigeria 106/G6
Geiger, Ala. 195/B5
Geiger Heights, Wash. 310/H3
Geikie (riv.), Sask. 181/M3
Geilo, Norway 18/F6
Geiranger, Norway 18/E5
Geislingen an der Steige, Germany 22/C4
Geismar, La. 238/K3
Geist (res.), Ind. 227/F5
Geistown, Pa. 294/E5
Geita, Tanzania 115/F4
Gejiu (Kokiu), China 77/F7
Gejiu, China 54/M7
Gela, Italy 34/E6
Gelang, Tanjong (pt.), Malaysia 72/D6
Geldenaken (Jodoigne), Belgium 27/F7
Gelderland (prov.), Netherlands 27/H4
Geldermalsen, Netherlands 27/G5
Geldern, Germany 22/B3
Geldrop, Netherlands 27/H6
Geleen, Netherlands 27/H7
Gelendzhik, U.S.S.R. 52/E6
Gelgia (riv.), Switzerland 39/J3
Gelibolu (Gallipoli), Turkey 63/C5
Gelidonya (cape), Turkey 59/B2
Gelidonya (cape), Turkey 63/D4
Gelligaer, Wales 13/A6
Gelnhausen, Germany 22/C3
Gelnica, Czech. 41/F2
Gelså (riv.), Denmark 21/C7
Gelsenkirchen, Germany 22/B3
Gelsted, Denmark 21/C7
Gelterkinden, Switzerland 39/E2
Gem, Alberta 182/D4
Gem (co.), Idaho 220/B6
Gem, Idaho 220/C2
Gem, Ind. 227/F5
Gem, Kansas 232/B2
Gem (lake), Manitoba 179/G4
Gem, W. Va. 312/E5
Gemas, Malaysia 72/D7
Gembloux-sur-Orneau, Belgium 27/F7
Gemena, Zaire 115/D3
Gemena, Zaire 102/E4
Gemerek, Turkey 63/G3
Gemert, Netherlands 27/H5
Gemlik, Turkey 63/C2
Gemmell, Minn. 255/D3
Gemona, Italy 34/D1
Gemsa, Egypt 111/F2
Genç, Turkey 63/J3
Gendringen, Netherlands 27/J5
Gene Autry, Okla. 288/N6
Genemuiden, Netherlands 27/H3
General Acha, Argentina 143/C4
General Alvear, Buenos Aires, Argentina 143/F7
General Alvear, Mendoza, Argentina 143/C3
General Arenales, Argentina 143/F7
General Artigas, Paraguay 144/D5
General Belgrano, Argentina 143/G7
General Bravo, Mexico 150/K4
General Campos, Argentina 143/G5
General Cepeda, Mexico 150/J4
General Conesa, Argentina 143/C5
General Elizardo Aquino, Paraguay 144/D4
General Enrique Martínez, Uruguay 145/F4
General Eugenio A. Garay, Paraguay 144/A2
General Galarza, Argentina 143/C6
General Grant Grove Section (King's Canyon), Calif. 204/G7
General Güemes, Argentina 143/D1
General Guido, Argentina 143/E4
General José de San Martín, Argentina 143/E2
General Juan Madariaga, Argentina 143/E4
General Lagos, Chile 138/B1
General La Madrid, Argentina 143/D4
General Las Heras, Argentina 143/G7
General Lavalle, Argentina 143/E4
General Manuel Belgrano, Cerro (mt.), Argentina 143/C2
General Mitchell Field, Wis. 317/M2
General O'Brien, Argentina 143/F7
General Paz, Argentina 143/E2
General Paz, Argentina 143/H7
General Paz (lake), Chile 138/E5
General Pico, Argentina 143/D4
General Ramírez, Argentina 143/F6
General Roca, Argentina 143/C4
General Saavedra, Bolivia 136/D5
General San Martín, Buenos Aires, Argentina 143/G4
General San Martín, La Pampa, Argentina 143/D4
General Santos, Philippines 82/E7
General Terán, Mexico 150/K4
General Tinio, Philippines 82/C3
General-Toshevo, Bulgaria 45/H4
General Viamonte, Argentina 143/F7
General Villegas, Argentina 143/D4
Generoso (mt.), Switzerland 39/H5
Genesee, Idaho 220/B3
Genesee (co.), Mich. 250/F5
Genesee (co.), N.Y. 276/D4
Genesee (riv.), N.Y. 276/E5
Genesee, Pa. 294/G2
Genesee, Wis. 317/J2
Genesee Depot, Wis. 317/J2
Geneseo, Ill. 222/C2
Geneseo, Kansas 232/D3
Geneseo, N.Y. 276/E5
Geneseo, N. Dak. 282/R7
Geneva (lake) 7/E4
Geneva (co.), Ala. 195/G8
Geneva, Ala. 195/G8
Geneva, Fla. 212/E3
Geneva (lake), France 28/G4
Geneva, Georgia 217/C5
Geneva, Idaho 220/G7
Geneva, Ill. 222/E2
Geneva, Ind. 227/H3
Geneva, Iowa 229/G3
Geneva, Ky. 237/F5
Geneva, Minn. 255/E7
Geneva, Nebr. 264/G4
Geneva, N.Y. 276/G5
Geneva, Ohio 284/J2
Geneva, Pa. 294/B2
Geneva (Genève) (canton), Switzerland 39/B4
Geneva (Genève), Switzerland 39/B4
Geneva, Switzerland 7/E4
Geneva (lake), Switzerland 39/C4
Geneva, Texas 303/L6
Geneva (lake), Wis. 317/K10
Geneva-on-the-Lake, Ohio 284/H2
Genezin, Turkey 63/F3
Genichesk, U.S.S.R. 52/E5
Genil (riv.), Spain 33/D4
Genk, Belgium 27/H7
Gennargentu, Monti del (mt.), Italy 34/B5
Gennep, Netherlands 27/H5
Gennevilliers, France 28/B1
Genoa, Ark. 202/C7
Genoa, Colo. 208/N4
Genoa, Ill. 222/E1
Genoa (prov.), Italy 34/B2
Genoa, Italy 7/E4
Genoa, Italy 34/B2
Genoa (gulf), Italy 34/B2
Genoa, Nebr. 264/G3
Genoa, Nev. 266/B4
Genoa, N.Y. 276/G5
Genoa, Ohio 284/D2
Genoa, W. Va. 312/A6
Genoa, Wis. 317/D8
Genoa City, Wis. 317/K11
Genola, Minn. 255/D5
Genola, Utah 304/C4
Genova (Genoa), Italy 34/B2
Genovesa (isl.), Ecuador 128/C9
Gent (Ghent), Belgium 27/D6
Genthin, Germany 22/E2
Gentilly, France 28/B2
Gentilly, Minn. 255/B3
Genting, Indonesia 85/D5
Gentofte, Denmark 21/F6
Gentry, Ark. 202/A1
Gentry (co.), Mo. 261/D2
Gentry, Mo. 261/D2
Gentryville, Ind. 227/C8
Gentryville, Mo. 261/D2
Genzano di Roma, Italy 34/F7
Geographe (bay), W. Australia 92/A6
Geographe (chan.), W. Australia 88/A4
Geographe (chan.), W. Australia 92/A4
Geographical Center of North America, N. Dak. 282/K3
Geographical Center of U.S., S. Dak. 298/B4
George (isl.), Falk. Is. 143/E7
George (lake), Fla. 212/E2
George, Iowa 229/B2
George (isl.), Manitoba 179/E2
George (lake), Manitoba 179/G4
George (co.), Miss. 256/G9
George (isl.), Newf. 166/C3
George (lake), N.S. Wales 97/E4
George (lake), N.Y. 276/N4
George (sound), N. Zealand 100/A6
George (lake), N. Dak. 282/L6
George (cape), Nova Scotia 168/G3
George (lake), Nova Scotia 168/B5
George (riv.), Que. 162/K4
George (riv.), Que. 146/M4
George (riv.), Québec 174/F2
George, S. Africa 118/C6
George (lake), Uganda 115/F4
George, Wash. 310/F3
George A.F.B., Calif. 204/H9
George B. Stevenson (dam), Pa. 294/G3
George Land (isl.), U.S.S.R. 4/B7
George Land (isl.), U.S.S.R. 48/E1
George Rogers Clark Nat'l Hist. Park, Ind. 227/B7
Georges (isls.), Maine 243/E8
Georges (riv.), N.S. Wales 88/K4
Georges (riv.), N.S. Wales 97/H4
Georges Brook, Newf. 166/D2
George's Cove, Newf. 166/C3
Georges Fork, Va. 307/C6
Georges Mills, N.H. 268/C5
Georgetown, Ark. 202/G3
Georgetown, Calif. 204/E5
George Town (cap.), Cayman Is. 156/B3
Georgetown, Colo. 208/H3
Georgetown, Conn. 210/B4
Georgetown, Del. 245/S6
Georgetown, D.C. 245/E5
Georgetown, Fla. 212/E2
Georgetown, Gambia 106/A6
Georgetown, Georgia 217/B7
Georgetown (cap.), Guyana 2/G5
Georgetown (cap.), Guyana 131/C2
Georgetown (cap.), Guyana 120/D2
Georgetown, Idaho 220/G7
Georgetown, Ill. 222/F4
Georgetown, Ind. 227/F8
Georgetown, Ky. 237/M4
Georgetown, La. 238/F3
Georgetown, Maine 243/D8
Georgetown•, Maine 243/D8
George Town (Pinang), Malaysia 72/C6
George Town, Malaysia 54/M9
Georgetown, Mass. 249/L2
Georgetown•, Mass. 249/L2
Georgetown, Minn. 255/B3
Georgetown, Miss. 256/D7
Georgetown (lake), Mont. 262/C4
Georgetown, Ohio 284/C8
Georgetown, Pa. 294/A4
Georgetown, Pr. Edward I. 168/F2
Georgetown, Queensland 88/G3
Georgetown, Queensland 95/B3
Georgetown, St. Vin. & Grens. 161/A8
Georgetown, St. Vin. & Grens. 156/G4
Georgetown, S.C. 188/L4
Georgetown (co.), S.C. 296/J5
Georgetown, S.C. 296/J5
George Town, Tasmania 99/C3
George Town, Tasmania 88/H8
Georgetown, Tenn. 237/L10
Georgetown, Texas 303/G7
George V Coast (reg.), Ant. 5/C8
Georgeville, Minn. 255/C5
Georgeville, Nova Scotia 168/F3
George Washington Carver Nat'l Mon., Mo. 261/D9
George Washington Birthplace Nat'l Mon., Va. 307/P4
George West, Texas 303/F9
Georgia 188/K4
GEORGIA 217
Georgia (str.), Br. Col. 184/J3
Georgia (state), U.S. 146/K6
Georgia•, Vt. 268/A2
Georgia (str.), Wash. 310/B2
Georgia Center, Vt. 268/A2
Georgian (bay), Ont. 162/H6
Georgian (bay), Ontario 177/D2
Georgian (bay), Ontario 175/D3
Georgiana, Ala. 195/E7
Georgian Bay Is. Nat'l Park, Ontario 177/C2,D3
Georgian S.S.R., U.S.S.R. 7/J4
Georgian S.S.R., U.S.S.R. 52/F6
Georgian S.S.R., U.S.S.R. 48/D5
Georgiaville, R.I. 249/H5
Georgina (riv.), North. Terr. 93/E6
Georgina (isl.), Ontario 177/E3
Georgina (riv.), Queensland 88/F4
Georgina (riv.), Queensland 95/A4
Georgiu-Dezh, U.S.S.R. 52/E4
Georgsmarienhütte, Germany 22/B2
Gera, Germany 22/E3
Geraardsbergen, Belgium 27/D7
Gerald, Mo. 261/K6
Gerald, Sask. 181/K5
Geral de Goiás, Serra (range), Brazil 132/E6
Geraldine, Ala. 195/G2
Geraldine, Mont. 262/F3
Geraldine, N. Zealand 100/C6
Geraldton, Australia 87/B8
Geraldton, Ont. 162/H6
Geraldton, Ontario 177/H5
Geraldton, Ontario 175/C3
Geraldton, W. Australia 88/A5
Geraldton, W. Australia 92/A5
Gerar (dry riv.), Israel 65/B5
Gerber, Calif. 204/C3
Gerber (res.), Oreg. 291/F5
Gercüş, Turkey 63/J4
Gerdine (mt.), Alaska 196/A1
Gerede, Turkey 63/E2
Gereshk, Afghanistan 59/H3
Gereshk, Afghanistan 68/A2
Geretsried, Germany 22/D5
Gérgal, Spain 33/E4
Gerger, Turkey 63/H3
Gerik, Malaysia 72/D6
Gering, Nebr. 264/A3
Gerlach, Nev. 266/B2
Gerlachovka (mt.), Czech. 41/E2
Gerlogubi, Ethiopia 111/H6
Germania, Miss. 256/C5
Germania, Pa. 294/G2
Germania, Wis. 317/H8
Germano, Ohio 284/J5
Germansen (lake), Br. Col. 184/E2
Germansen Landing, Br. Col. 184/E2
Germanton, N.C. 281/J2
Germantown, Ill. 222/D5
Germantown, Ky. 237/O3
Germantown, Md. 245/J4
Germantown, New Bruns. 170/F3
Germantown, N.Y. 276/N6
Germantown, Ohio 284/B6
Germantown, Tenn. 237/B10
Germantown, Wis. 317/K1
German Valley, Ill. 222/D1
Germany 2/K3
Germany 7/F3
GERMANY 22
Germencik, Turkey 63/B4
Germersheim, Germany 22/C4
Germfask, Mich. 250/C2
Germiston, S. Africa 102/E7
Germiston, S. Africa 118/H6
Gerofit, Israel 65/D5
Gerolstein, Germany 22/B3
Gerona (Girona) (prov.), Spain 33/H1
Gerona (Girona), Spain 33/H2
Geronimo, Ariz. 198/F5
Geronimo, Okla. 288/K6
Gerpinnes, Belgium 27/F8
Gerpir (cape), Iceland 21/D1
Gerra, Switzerland 39/G4
Gerrardstown, W. Va. 312/K4
Gerringong, N.S. Wales 97/F4
Gerrish, N.H. 268/D5
Gerry, N.Y. 276/B6
Gers (dept.), France 28/D6
Gers (riv.), France 28/D6
Gersau, Switzerland 39/G2
Gersfeld, Germany 22/C3
Gerster, Mo. 261/E7
Gerty, Okla. 288/O5
Gervais, Oreg. 291/A3
Gervasio, Uruguay 145/F4
Gërzë, China 77/B5
Gerze, Turkey 63/F2
Geser, Indonesia 85/J6
Gesher, Israel 65/C2
Gesher Haziv, Israel 65/C1
Gessie, Ind. 227/C4
Getafe, Spain 33/F4
Getaway, Ohio 284/F9
Gettysburg, Ohio 284/A5
Gettysburg, Pa. 294/H6
Gettysburg, S. Dak. 298/K3
Gettysburg Nat'l Mil. Park, Pa. 294/H6
Getulio Vargas, Uruguay 145/F3
Getz Ice Shelf, Ant. 5/B12
Geuda Springs, Kansas 232/E4
Geurie, N.S. Wales 97/E3
Gevar'am, Israel 65/B4
Gevaş, Turkey 63/K3
Gevgelija, Yugoslavia 45/F5
Gex, France 28/G4
Geyser, Mont. 262/F3
Geyserville, Calif. 204/B5
Geyve, Turkey 63/D2
Gezira, El (reg.), Sudan 111/F5
Ghabaghib, Syria 63/H5
Ghadames, Libya 102/D2
Ghadames, Libya 111/A2
Ghaemshar, Iran 66/H2
Ghaghra (riv.), India 68/E3
Ghaida, Yemen 59/F6
Ghalla, Wadi el (dry riv.), Sudan 111/E5
Ghana 2/J5
Ghana 102/B4
GHANA 106/D7
Ghanzi, Botswana 118/C4
Ghard Abu Muharik (des.), Egypt 111/J4
Ghardaïa, Algeria 106/E2
Ghardaïa, Algeria 102/C1
Gharīan, Libya 102/D1
Gharīan, Libya 111/B1
Gharib, Jebel (mt.), Egypt 59/B4
Ghat, Libya 102/D2
Ghat, Libya 111/B3
Ghat Kopar, India 68/B7
Ghazaouet, Algeria 106/D2
Ghaziabad, India 68/D3
Ghazipur, India 68/E3
Ghazni, Afghanistan 68/B2
Ghazni, Afghanistan 59/J3
Ghea (riv.), India 68/F1
Gheen, Minn. 255/F3
Gheens, La. 238/K7
Ghemines, Libya 111/C1
Ghenghis Khan Wall (ruin), China 77/H2
Ghenghis Khan Wall (ruins), Mongolia 77/H2
Ghent, Belgium 27/D6
Ghent, Ky. 237/L3
Ghent, Minn. 255/C6
Ghent, N.Y. 276/N6
Ghent, W. Va. 312/D7
Gheorghe Gheorghiu-Dej, Romania 45/H2
Gheorghieni, Romania 45/G2
Gherla, Romania 45/G2
Ghimbi, Ethiopia 111/G6
Ghio, N.C. 281/K5
Ghisonaccia, France 28/B7
Ghizar, Pakistan 68/C1
Gholson, Miss. 256/G5
Ghost Dam, Alberta 182/C4
Ghost Lake, Alberta 182/C4
Ghurian, Afghanistan 68/A2
Ghurian, Afghanistan 59/H3
Giacomo (pass), Switzerland 39/G4
Gia Dinh, Vietnam 72/E5
Giannutri (isl.), Italy 34/C3
Giant's Causeway, N. Ireland 17/H1
Giarre, Italy 34/E6
Giatto, W. Va. 312/D8
Gibara, Cuba 156/C2
Gibara, Cuba 158/J3
Gibbon, Minn. 255/D6
Gibbon, Nebr. 264/F4
Gibbon, Oreg. 291/J2
Gibbons, Alberta 182/D3
Gibbonsville, Idaho 220/E4
Gibb River, W. Australia 92/D2
Gibbs, Mo. 261/H2
Gibbs, Sask. 181/G5
Gibbsboro, N.J. 273/B4
Gibbs City, Mich. 250/G2
Gibbstown, N.J. 273/C4
Gibbsville, Wis. 317/L8
Gibeon, Namibia 118/B5
Gibloux (mt.), Switzerland 39/D3
Gibraltar 7/D5
Gibraltar (str.) 2/J4
Gibraltar (str.) 102/B1
Gibraltar (str.) 7/D5
Gibraltar 2/J4
GIBRALTAR 33
Gibraltar, Gibraltar 33/D4
Gibraltar (pt.), England 13/H4
Gibraltar, Mich. 250/F6
Gibraltar (str.), Morocco 106/C1
Gibraltar (str.), Spain 33/D5
Gibsland, La. 238/E1
Gibson (desert), Australia 87/C8
Gibson, Georgia 217/G4
Gibson (co.), Ind. 227/B8
Gibson, Iowa 229/J6
Gibson, La. 238/J7
Gibson, Miss. 256/G3
Gibson, Mo. 261/M10
Gibson (res.), Mont. 262/D3
Gibson, N.C. 281/K5
Gibson, Pa. 294/L2
Gibson (co.), Tenn. 237/D9
Gibson, Tenn. 237/D9
Gibson, W. Australia 88/C6
Gibson, W. Australia 92/C6
Gibson (des.), W. Australia 88/C4
Gibson (des.), W. Australia 92/D3
Gibsonburg, Ohio 284/D3
Gibson City, Ill. 222/E3
Gibsonia, Pa. 294/B4
Gibsons, Br. Col. 184/K3
Gibson Station, Va. 307/A7
Gibsonton, Fla. 212/C3
Gibsonville, N.C. 281/K2
Giddings, Texas 303/H7
Gideälv (riv.), Sweden 18/L5
Gideon, Mo. 261/N10
Gideon, Okla. 288/R2
Gien, France 28/E4
Giese, Minn. 255/E4
Giessendam-Hardinxveld, Netherlands 27/F5
Giethoorn, Netherlands 27/J3
Gif, France 28/E3
Gifan, Iran 66/K2
Giffard, Québec 172/J3
Giffnock, Scotland 15/B2
Gifford, Fla. 212/F4
Gifford, Ill. 222/E3
Gifford, Iowa 229/G4
Gifford (riv.), N.W. Terr. 187/K2
Gifford, Scotland 15/F5
Gifford, S.C. 296/E6
Gifford, Wash. 310/G2
Gifhorn, Germany 22/D2
Gift Lake, Alberta 182/C2
Gifu (pref.), Japan 81/H6
Gifu, Japan 81/H6
Giganta, Sierra de la (mts.), Mexico 150/D4
Gigante, Colombia 126/C6
Gigha (isl.), Scotland 15/C5
Gigha (sound), Scotland 15/C5
Gig Harbor, Wash. 310/C3
Giglio (isl.), Italy 34/C3
Gijón, Spain 7/D4
Gijón, Spain 33/D1
Gil (isl.), Br. Col. 184/C3
Gila (riv.) 188/D4
Gila (co.), Ariz. 198/E5
Gila (mts.), Ariz. 198/A6
Gila (mts.), Ariz. 198/F5
Gila (riv.), Ariz. 198/B6
Gila, N. Mex. 274/A6
Gila (riv.), N. Mex. 274/A6
Gila (riv.), U.S. 146/G6
Gila Bend, Ariz. 198/C6
Gila Bend (mts.), Ariz. 198/B5
Gila Bend Ind. Res., Ariz. 198/C6
Gila Cliff Dwellings Nat'l Mon., N. Mex. 274/A5
Gila Hot Springs, N. Mex. 274/A5
Gilan (prov.), Iran 66/F2
Gilan (reg.), Iran 66/F2
Gila River Ind. Res., Ariz. 198/C5
Gilat, Israel 65/B5
Gilbert, Ariz. 198/D5
Gilbert, Ark. 202/E2
Gilbert, Iowa 229/F4
Gilbert (isls.), Kiribati 2/T5
Gilbert (isls.), Kiribati 87/H6
Gilbert, La. 238/G2
Gilbert, Minn. 255/F3
Gilbert (riv.), Newf. 166/C3
Gilbert (riv.), Queensland 88/G3
Gilbert (riv.), Queensland 95/B3
Gilbert, S.C. 296/E4
Gilbert (peak), Utah 304/D3
Gilbert, W. Va. 312/C7
Gilberton, Pa. 294/K4
Gilbertown, Ala. 195/B7
Gilbert Plains, Manitoba 179/B3
Gilberts, Ill. 222/E1
Gilbertsville, Ky. 237/E7
Gilbertsville, N.Y. 276/K6
Gilbertville, Iowa 229/J4
Gilbertville, Mass. 249/F3
Gilbjerg Hoved (pt.), Denmark 21/F5
Gilboa, N.Y. 276/M6
Gilboa, Ohio 284/C3
Gilboa, W. Va. 312/E6
Gilbués, Brazil 132/E5
Gilby, N. Dak. 282/R3
Gilchrist (co.), Fla. 212/D2
Gilchrist (creek), Manitoba 179/F2
Gilchrist (lake), Manitoba 179/G2
Gilcrest, Colo. 208/K2
Gildford, Mont. 262/F2
Gilé, Mozambique 118/F3
Gilead, Conn. 210/F2
Gilead, Ind. 227/E3
Gilead•, Maine 243/B7
Gilead, Nebr. 264/G4
Giles (co.), Tenn. 237/G10
Giles (co.), Va. 307/G6
Gilf Kebir (plat.), Egypt 111/E3
Gilford, Mich. 250/F5
Gilford•, N.H. 268/E4
Gilford, N. Ireland 17/J3
Gilford Park, N.J. 273/E4
Gilgai, N.S. Wales 97/F1
Gilgandra, N. S. Wales 88/H6
Gilgandra, N.S. Wales 97/E2
Gilgil, Kenya 115/G4
Gilgit, Pakistan 68/C1
Gilgit, Pakistan 59/K2
Gilgunnia, N.S. Wales 97/C3
Gill, Colo. 208/L2
Gill (lake), Ireland 17/E3
Gill•, Mass. 249/D2
Gillam, Manitoba 179/K2
Gilleleje, Denmark 21/F5
Gilles (lake), S. Australia 94/E5
Gillespie, Ill. 222/D4
Gillespie, New Bruns. 170/C2
Gillespie (co.), Texas 303/F7
Gillett, Ark. 202/H5
Gillett, Pa. 294/J2
Gillett, Texas 303/G8
Gillett, Wis. 317/K6
Gillette, N.J. 273/E2
Gillette, Wyo. 319/G1
Gillette Grove, Iowa 229/C2
Gilleyville, La. 238/G2
Gillham, Ark. 202/B5
Gilliam, La. 238/C1
Gilliam, Mo. 261/F4
Gilliam (co.), Oreg. 291/G2
Gillies Bay, Br. Col. 184/H2
Gillingham, Dorset, England 13/E6
Gillingham, Kent, England 13/J8
Gillis (range), Nev. 266/C4
Gillisonville, S.C. 296/E6
Gillsburg, Miss. 256/C8
Gillsville, Georgia 217/E2
Gilly, Switzerland 39/B4
Gilman, Colo. 208/G3
Gilman, Conn. 210/G2
Gilman, Ill. 222/E3
Gilman, Ind. 227/F4
Gilman, Iowa 229/H5
Gilman, Minn. 255/E5
Gilman, Vt. 268/D3
Gilman, Wis. 317/E5
Gilman City, Mo. 261/D2
Gilmanton•, N.H. 268/E5
Gilmanton, Wis. 317/C7
Gilmanton Iron Works, N.H. 268/E5
Gilmer (co.), Georgia 217/D1
Gilmer, Texas 303/J5
Gilmer (co.), W. Va. 312/E5
Gilmer, W. Va. 312/E5
Gilmore, Ark. 202/K3
Gilmore, Georgia 217/J1
Gilmore City, Iowa 229/D3
Gilpin (co.), Colo. 208/H3
Gilroy, Calif. 204/D6
Gilson, Ill. 222/C3
Gilsum•, N.H. 268/C5
Gilt Edge, Tenn. 237/B9
Giltner, Nebr. 264/F4
Gilze, Netherlands 27/F5
Gimel, Switzerland 39/B3
Gimie (mt.), St. Lucia 161/G6
Gimlet, Ky. 237/P4
Gimli, Manitoba 179/F4
Gimo, Sweden 18/K6
Gingerland, St. Kitts and Nevis 161/D11
Gingin, W. Australia 92/A1
Gingoog, Philippines 82/E6
Gingoog (bay), Philippines 82/E6
Gings, Ind. 227/G5
Ginir, Ethiopia 111/H6
Ginnosar, Israel 65/D2
Ginzo de Limia, Spain 33/C1
Gio, Hon (isl.), Vietnam 72/E3
Giohar, Somalia 102/G4
Giohar, Somalia 115/J3
Gioia del Colle, Italy 34/F4
Gioiosa Ionica, Italy 34/F5
Giornico, Switzerland 39/G4
Giovinazzo, Italy 34/F4
Gi-Paraná (riv.), Brazil 132/H10
Gippsland (reg.), Victoria 97/D6
Gipsy (lake), Alberta 182/E1
Gipsy, Mo. 261/M8
Gipsy, Pa. 294/E4
Giraltovce, Czech. 41/F2
Girard, Ill. 222/D4
Girard, Georgia 217/J4
Girard, Kansas 232/H4
Girard, La. 238/G2
Girard, Mich. 250/E6
Girard, Ohio 284/J3
Girard, Pa. 294/B2
Girard, Texas 303/D4
Girardot, Colombia 126/C5
Girardville, Pa. 294/K4
Girardville, Québec 172/E1
Girdle Ness (prom.), Scotland 15/G3
Girdler, Ky. 237/O7
Girdletree, Md. 245/S8
Giresun (prov.), Turkey 63/H2
Giresun, Turkey 59/C1
Giresun, Turkey 63/H2
Girga, Egypt 59/B4
Girga, Egypt 111/F2
Girga, Egypt 102/F2
Giri (riv.), Zaire 115/C3
Girilambone, N.S. Wales 97/D2
Girón, Ecuador 128/C4
Girona (prov.), Spain 33/H1
Girona, Spain 33/H2
Gironde (dept.), France 28/C5
Gironde (riv.), France 28/C5
Giroux, Manitoba 179/F5
Girouxville, Alberta 182/B2
Girvan, Scotland 15/D5
Girvan, Scotland 10/D3
Girvin, Sask. 181/F4
Girvin, Texas 303/B6
Gisborne, N. Zealand 100/G3
Giscome, Br. Col. 184/F3
Gisenyi, Rwanda 115/E4
Gislaved, Sweden 18/H8
Gisors, France 28/D3
Gistel, Belgium 27/B6
Giswil, Switzerland 39/F3
Gitega, Burundi 115/F4
Giuba (riv.), Somalia 115/H3
Giubiasco, Switzerland 39/H4
Giulianova, Italy 34/E3
Giurgiu, Romania 45/G3
Giv'atayim, Israel 65/B3
Giv'at Brenner, Israel 65/B4
Giv'at Hayyim, Israel 65/B3
Give, Denmark 21/C6
Given, W. Va. 312/C5
Givet, France 28/F2
Givhans, S.C. 296/G5
Givors, France 28/F5
Giza, Egypt 111/J3
Giza, Egypt 59/B4
Gizab, Afghanistan 59/J3
Gizab, Afghanistan 68/B2
Gizhiga (bay), U.S.S.R. 48/Q3
Gizo, Solomon Is. 86/D3
Giżycko, Poland 47/E1
Gjerlev, Denmark 21/D4
Gjerrild Klint (cliff), Denmark 21/D5
Gjirokastër, Albania 45/D5
Gjoa Haven, N.W.T. 162/G2
Gjoa Haven, N.W. Terr. 187/J3
Gjøvik, Norway 18/G6
Gjøvik, Norway 7/E2
Glace Bay, Nova Scotia 162/L6
Glace Bay, Nova Scotia 168/J2
Glacier (bay), Alaska 196/M1
Glacier, Br. Col. 184/J4
Glacier (co.), Mont. 262/C2

Glacier, Wash. 310/D2
Glacier (peak), Wash. 310/D2
Glacier Bay Nat'l Park, Alaska 196/M1
Glacier Bay Nat'l Pres., Alaska 196/L1
Glacier Nat'l Pk., Br. Col. 162/D5
Glacier Nat'l Park, Br. Col. 184/J4
Glacier Nat'l Park, Mont. 188/D1
Glacier Nat'l Park, Mont. 262/C2
Gladbrook, Iowa 229/H4
Glade, Kansas 232/C2
Glade, La. 238/G4
Gladehill, Va. 307/J7
Glade Park, Colo. 208/B5
Glades (co.), Fla. 212/E5
Glade Spring, Va. 307/E7
Glade Valley, N.C. 281/G2
Gladeville, Tenn. 237/J8
Gladewater, Texas 303/K5
Gladmar, Sask. 181/G6
Gladstone, Ill. 222/B3
Gladstone, Manitoba 179/D4
Gladstone, Mich. 250/C3
Gladstone, Mo. 261/P5
Gladstone, Nebr. 264/G4
Gladstone, N. Mex. 274/F2
Gladstone, N. Dak. 282/F6
Gladstone, Oreg. 291/D5
Gladstone, Queensland 88/J4
Gladstone, Queensland 95/D4
Gladstone, S. Australia 94/F5
Gladstone, Tasmania 99/D2
Gladstone, Va. 307/L5
Glad Valley, S. Dak. 298/F3
Gladwin (co.), Mich. 250/E4
Gladwin, Mich. 250/E5
Glady, W. Va. 312/G5
Gladys, Va. 307/K6
Glåma (riv.), Norway 7/F2
Glåma (riv.), Norway 18/G6
Glamis, Calif. 204/K11
Glamis, Sask. 181/D4
Glamoč, Yugoslavia 45/C3
Glamsbjerg, Denmark 21/D7
Glan, Philippines 85/G4
Glan, Philippines 82/E8
Glancy, Miss. 256/C4
Gland, Switzerland 39/B4
Glandore, Ireland 17/C8
Glandore (harb.), Ireland 17/C9
Glandorf, Ohio 284/B3
Glåne (riv.), Switzerland 39/C3
Glanmire-Riverstown, Ireland 17/E8
Glanworth, Ireland 17/E7
Glärnisch (mt.), Switzerland 39/H2
Glarus (canton), Switzerland 39/H3
Glarus, Switzerland 39/H2
Glarus Alps (mts.), Switzerland 39/H3
Glasco, Kansas 232/E2
Glasco, N.Y. 276/M6
Glascock (co.), Georgia 217/G4
Glasford, Ill. 222/B3
Glasgo, Conn. 210/H2
Glasgow, Del. 245/N4
Glasgow, Ill. 222/C4
Glasgow, Ky. 237/J7
Glasgow, Mo. 261/G4
Glasgow, Mont. 262/K2
Glasgow, Pa. 294/E4
Glasgow, Scotland 7/D3
Glasgow, Scotland 10/B1
Glasgow, Scotland 15/B2
Glasgow, Va. 307/K5
Glasgow, W. Va. 312/D6
Glasier (lake), New Bruns. 170/A1
Glaslyn, Sask. 181/C2
Glas Maol (mt.), Scotland 15/E4
Glasnevin, Sask. 181/F6
Glass, Manitoba 179/F5
Glass (riv.), Scotland 15/D3
Glass (mts.), Texas 303/A7
Glassboro, N.J. 273/C4
Glasscock (co.), Texas 303/C6
Glasser, N.J. 273/D2
Glassport, Pa. 294/C7
Glasston, N. Dak. 282/R2
Glassville, New Bruns. 170/C2
Glastenbury (mt.), Vt. 268/A6
Glastonbury, Conn. 210/E2
Glastonbury •, Conn. 210/E2
Glastonbury, England 13/E6
Glastonbury, England 10/E5
Glatt (riv.), Switzerland 39/G2
Glattfelden, Switzerland 39/F1
Glauchau, Germany 22/E3
Glazier, Texas 303/D2
Glazov, U.S.S.R. 7/K3
Glazov, U.S.S.R. 52/H3
Gleason, Tenn. 237/D8
Gleason, Wis. 317/G5
Gleasondale, Mass. 249/J3
Gleeson, Ariz. 198/F7
Gleichen, Alberta 182/D4
Gleisdorf, Austria 41/C3
Gleiwitz (Gliwice), Poland 47/A4
Glen (lake), Ireland 17/F1
Glen (lake), Mich. 250/C4
Glen, Minn. 255/E4
Glen, Miss. 256/H1
Glen, Mont. 262/D5
Glen, N.H. 268/E3
Glen (canyon), Utah 304/D6
Glen, W. Va. 312/D6
Glenada, Oreg. 291/C4
Glenaire, Mo. 261/R5
Glen Alice, Tenn. 237/M9
Glen Allan, Miss. 256/B4
Glen Allen, Ala. 195/C3
Glenallen, Mo. 261/M8
Glen Allen, Va. 307/N5
Glen Almond, Québec 172/B4
Glen Alpine, N.C. 281/F3
Glen Arbor, Mich. 250/C4
Glenarden, Md. 245/G4
Glen Arm, Md. 245/N3
Glenarm, N. Ireland 17/J2
Glenavon, Sask. 181/J5

Glen Avon Heights, Calif. 204/E10
Glenavy, N. Zealand 100/C6
Glenavy, N. Ireland 17/J2
Glen Bain, Sask. 181/E6
Glenbarr, Scotland 15/C5
Glenbeigh, Ireland 17/B7
Glenbeulah, Wis. 317/L8
Glenboro, Manitoba 179/C5
Glenbrook, Nev. 266/B3
Glenburn •, Maine 243/F6
Glenburn, N. Dak. 282/H2
Glen Burnie, Md. 245/M4
Glenbush, Sask. 181/D2
Glen Campbell, Pa. 294/E4
Glen Canyon (dam), Ariz. 198/D2
Glen Canyon Nat'l Rec. Area, Ariz. 198/D1
Glen Canyon Nat'l Rec. Area, Utah 304/D6
Glencaple, Scotland 15/E5
Glen Carbon, Ill. 222/B2
Glencliff, N.H. 268/D4
Glencoe, Ala. 195/G3
Glencoe, Ill. 222/B5
Glencoe, Ky. 237/M3
Glencoe, La. 238/G7
Glencoe, Minn. 255/D6
Glencoe, Mo. 261/M3
Glencoe, New Bruns. 170/D1
Glencoe, N. Mex. 274/D5
Glencoe, Ohio 284/J6
Glencoe, Okla. 288/M2
Glencoe, Ontario 177/C5
Glencoe, Pa. 294/E6
Glencoe, Scotland 15/C4
Glencoe, S. Africa 118/E5
Glencolumbkille, Ireland 17/D2
Glen Cove, Maine 243/E7
Glen Cove, N.Y. 276/B9
Glencross, S. Dak. 298/H3
Glendale, Ariz. 198/C5
Glendale, Calif. 188/C4
Glendale, Calif. 204/C10
Glendale, Fla. 212/C5
Glendale, Ind. 227/C7
Glendale, Kansas 232/K4
Glendale, Ky. 237/K5
Glendale, Mass. 249/A3
Glendale, Mo. 261/P3
Glendale, Nev. 266/G6
Glendale, N.H. 268/E4
Glendale, Nova Scotia 168/G3
Glendale, Ohio 284/C9
Glendale, Oreg. 291/D5
Glendale (lake), Pa. 294/F4
Glendale, R.I. 249/H5
Glendale, S.C. 296/D2
Glendale, Utah 304/B6
Glen Dale, W. Va. 312/E2
Glendale, Wis. 317/M1
Glendale Heights, Ill. 222/A5
Glen Daniel, W. Va. 312/D7
Glen Dean, Ky. 237/J5
Glendevey, Colo. 208/H1
Glendive, Mont. 262/M3
Glendo, Wyo. 319/G3
Glendo (res.), Wyo. 319/H3
Glendon, Alberta 182/F2
Glendon, N.C. 281/L4
Glendora, Calif. 204/D10
Glendora, Miss. 256/D3
Glendora, N.J. 273/B4
Glen Easton, W. Va. 312/E3
Glen Echo, Md. 245/F4
Glen Eden, N. Zealand 100/B1
Gleneden Beach, Oreg. 291/C3
Glen Elder, Kansas 232/D2
Glenelg, Md. 245/L3
Glenelg (cay), Scotland 10/D2
Glenelg, Scotland 15/C3
Glenelg, S. Australia 88/D8
Glenelg, S. Australia 94/A8
Glenelg (riv.), Victoria 97/A5
Glenella, Manitoba 179/C4
Glen Ellyn, Ill. 222/A5
Glenevis, Alberta 182/C3
Glen Ewen, Sask. 181/K6
Glen Ferris, W. Va. 312/D6
Glenfield, N.Y. 276/K3
Glenfield, N. Zealand 100/B1
Glenfield, N. Dak. 282/N5
Glenfield, Pa. 294/B6
Glen Flora, Texas 303/H8
Glen Flora, Wis. 317/E4
Glenford, Ohio 284/F6
Glen Gardner, N.J. 273/D2
Glengarriff, Ireland 17/C8
Glengarry, Mont. 262/B3
Glengarry (county), Ontario 177/K2
Glengary, W. Va. 312/K4
Glenham, S. Dak. 298/J2
Glen Harbour, Sask. 181/G5
Glen Haven, Colo. 208/H2
Glen Haven, Mich. 250/C4
Glen Haven, Wis. 317/E10
Glenhayes, W. Va. 312/C7
Glen Hedrick (Beaver), W. Va. 312/D7
Glen Hope, Pa. 294/F4
Glen Innes, N. S. Wales 88/J5
Glen Innes, N. S. Wales 97/F1
Glen Jean, W. Va. 312/D7
Glen Kerr, Sask. 181/D5
Glenlea, Manitoba 179/E5
Glenlivet, New Bruns. 170/D1
Glenluce, Scotland 15/D6
Glen Lyn, Va. 307/G6
Glen Lyon, Pa. 294/K4
Glenmary, Tenn. 237/M8
Glenmere, Sask. 181/J5
Glen Miller, Ontario 177/G3
Glenmont, Ohio 284/F4
Glenmora, La. 238/E5
Glen More (dist.), Scotland 15/D3
Glenmörgan, Queensland 95/D5
Glenn (co.), Calif. 204/C4
Glenn, Georgia 217/B4
Glenn, Mich. 250/C6
Glennallen, Alaska 196/D1

Glenn Heights, Texas 303/G3
Glennie, Mich. 250/F4
Glenns Ferry, Idaho 220/C7
Glenn Springs, S.C. 296/D2
Glennville, Calif. 204/G8
Glennville, Georgia 217/J7
Glenolden, Pa. 294/M7
Glenoma, Wash. 310/C4
Glenora, Br. Col. 184/K2
Glenorchy, Tasmania 88/H8
Glenorchy, Tasmania 99/D4
Glenormiston, Queensland 95/A4
Glen Park, N.Y. 276/J3
Glenpool, Okla. 288/P3
Glen Raven, N.C. 281/L2
Glenreagh, N.S. Wales 97/G2
Glen Riddle, Pa. 294/L7
Glen Ridge, N.J. 273/B2
Glenrio, N. Mex. 274/F3
Glen Robertson, Ontario 177/K2
Glen Rock, N.J. 273/B1
Glen Rock, Pa. 294/J6
Glenrock, Wyo. 319/G3
Glen Rogers, W. Va. 312/D7
Glen Rose, Texas 303/G5
Glenrothes, Scotland 15/E4
Glen Roy, Ohio 284/E7
Glen Saint Mary, Fla. 212/D1
Glens Falls, N.Y. 276/N4
Glens Fork, Ky. 237/L6
Glenshaw, Pa. 294/C6
Glenside, Pa. 294/M5
Glenside, Sask. 181/E4
Glenside-Churton Park, N. Zealand 100/B2
Glensted, Mo. 261/G5
Glentana, Mont. 262/K2
Glenties, Ireland 10/B3
Glenties, Ireland 17/E2
Glentrool, Scotland 15/D5
Glentworth, Sask. 181/E6
Glen Ullin, N. Dak. 282/G6
Glenview, Ill. 222/B5
Glenview, Ky. 237/K1
Glenview Nav. Air. Sta., Ill. 222/B5
Glenvil, Nebr. 264/F4
Glenville, Conn. 210/A4
Glenville, Ireland 17/D7
Glenville, Minn. 255/F7
Glenville, N.C. 281/C4
Glenville, W. Va. 312/E5
Glen Walter, Ontario 177/K2
Glen White, W. Va. 312/D7
Glenwillow, Ohio 284/J10
Glen Wilton, Va. 307/J5
Glenwood, Ala. 195/F7
Glenwood, Alberta 182/D5
Glenwood, Ark. 202/C5
Glenwood, Fla. 212/E4
Glenwood, Georgia 217/L1
Glenwood, Ill. 222/C6
Glenwood, Ind. 227/G5
Glenwood, Iowa 229/B6
Glenwood, Mich. 250/C6
Glenwood, Minn. 255/C5
Glenwood, Mo. 261/G1
Glenwood, Newf. 166/D4
Glenwood, N.J. 273/D1
Glenwood, N. Mex. 274/A5
Glenwood, N.C. 281/F3
Glenwood, Oreg. 291/D2
Glenwood, Utah 304/C5
Glenwood, Va. 307/K7
Glenwood, W. Va. 312/B5
Glenwood City, Wis. 317/B5
Glenwood Springs, Colo. 208/E4
Glezen, Ind. 227/C8
Glidden, Iowa 229/D4
Glidden, Sask. 181/B4
Glidden, Wis. 317/E3
Glide, Oreg. 291/D4
Glin, Ireland 17/C6
Glinde, Ind. 227/C8
Glis, Switzerland 39/E4
Glittertinden (mt.), Norway 7/E2
Glittertinden (mt.), Norway 18/F6
Gliwice, Poland 47/A4
Globe, Ariz. 188/D4
Globe, Ariz. 198/E5
Gloggnitz, Austria 41/D3
Głogów (Glogau), Poland 47/C3
Glomawr, Ky. 237/P6
Glomfjord, Norway 18/J3
Gloria (bay), Cuba 158/G2
Glorieta, N. Mex. 274/D3
Glorioso (isls.), Réunion 118/H2
Glory, Minn. 255/E4
Glory of Russia (cape), Alaska 196/D2
Glossop, England 13/J2
Glossop, England 10/G2
Gloster, La. 238/C2
Gloster, Miss. 256/B8
Glostrup, Denmark 21/F6
Gloucester, England 13/E6
Gloucester, England 10/E5
Gloucester, Mass. 249/M2
Gloucester (co.), New Bruns. 170/E1
Gloucester (co.), N.J. 273/C4
Gloucester, N.S. Australia 97/F2
Gloucester, N.C. 281/S5
Gloucester (cape), Papua N.G. 86/B2
Gloucester (co.), Va. 307/P6
Gloucester, Va. 307/P6
Gloucester City, N.J. 273/B3
Gloucester Junction, New Bruns. 170/E1
Gloucester Point, Va. 307/P6
Gloucestershire (co.), England 13/E6
Glouster, Ohio 284/F6
Glover (reef), Belize 154/D2
Glóis, Portugal 33/B2
Glover, Mo. 261/L8
Glover (isl.), Newf. 166/C4
Glover, N. Dak. 282/O7
Glover, Okla. 288/S6
Glover •, Vt. 268/C2
Glovergap, W. Va. 312/F3
Gloversville, N.Y. 276/M4
Glovertown, Newf. 166/C1

Gloverville, S.C. 296/D4
Głowno, Poland 47/D2
Głubczyce, Poland 47/C3
Glubokoye, U.S.S.R. 52/C3
Głuchołazy, Poland 47/C3
Glücksburg, Germany 22/C1
Gluckstadt, Miss. 256/D5
Glückstadt, Germany 22/C2
Glukhov, U.S.S.R. 52/D4
Glumsø, Denmark 21/E7
Glyde (riv.), Ireland 17/H4
Glynco, Georgia 217/J8
Glyncorrwg, Wales 13/D6
Glyndon, Md. 245/L3
Glyndon, Minn. 255/B4
Glynn (co.), Georgia 217/J8
Glynn, La. 238/H5
Glynn, N. Ireland 17/K2
Gmünd, Carinthia, Austria 41/B3
Gmünd, Lower Austria, Austria 41/C2
Gmunden, Austria 41/B3
Gnadenhutten, Ohio 284/G5
Gnaw Bone, Ind. 227/E6
Gnesta, Sweden 18/G2
Gniew, Poland 47/F7
Gniewkowo, Poland 47/D2
Gniezno, Poland 47/C2
Gnjilane, Yugoslavia 45/E4
Gnowangerup, W. Australia 88/B6
Gnowangerup, W. Australia 92/B6
Goa (state), India 68/C5
Goalpara, India 68/G3
Goascorán, Honduras 154/D4
Goat Fell (mt.), Scotland 15/C5
Goat Rock (dam), Ala. 195/H5
Goat Rock (lake), Ala. 195/H5
Goat Rock (dam), Georgia 217/B5
Goat Rock (lake), Georgia 217/B5
Goat Rocks (mt.), Wash. 310/D4
Goba, Ethiopia 111/H6
Goba, Ethiopia 102/G4
Goba, Mozambique 118/E5
Gobabis, Namibia 118/B4
Gobabis, Namibia 102/D7
Gobernador Crespo, Argentina 143/F5
Gobernador Gregores, Argentina 143/C6
Gobernador Mansilla, Argentina 143/G6
Gobi (des.) 54/M5
Gobi (des.), China 77/G3
Gobi (des.), Mongolia 77/G3
Goble, Oreg. 291/E1
Gobler, Mo. 261/N10
Gobles, Mich. 250/D6
Gobo, Japan 81/G7
Gobwen, Somalia 115/H4
Goch, Germany 22/B3
Go Cong, Vietnam 72/E5
Godahl, Minn. 255/D6
Godalming, England 13/G8
Godalming, England 10/F5
Godavari (riv.), India 54/J8
Godavari (riv.), India 68/D5
Godbout, Québec 174/D3
Godbout (riv.), Québec 174/D1
Goddard, Kansas 232/E4
Godech, Bulgaria 45/F4
Goderich, Ontario 177/C4
Godfrey, Georgia 217/F4
Godfrey, Ill. 222/A2
Godhavn (Qeqertarsuaq), Greenland 4/C12
Godhavn (Qeqertarsuaq), Greenland 146/N3
Godhra, India 68/C4
Gödöllő, Hungary 41/E3
Godoy Cruz, Argentina 143/C3
Gods (lake), Man. 162/G5
Gods (lake), Manitoba 179/K3
Gods (riv.), Man. 162/G4
Gods (riv.), Manitoba 179/K3
Gods Mercy (bay), N.W. Terr. 187/K3
Gods River, Manitoba 179/K3
Godthåb (Nuuk) (cap.), Greenl. 4/C12
Godthåb (Nuuk) (cap.), Greenland 2/G2
Godthåb (Nuuk) (cap.), Greenland 146/N3
Godwin, N.C. 281/M4
Godwin Austen (mt.), Pakistan 68/D1
Godwinsville, Georgia 217/F6
Goehner, Nebr. 264/K4
Goéland (lake), Québec 174/B3
Goélands (lake), Québec 174/E1
Goeree (isl.), Netherlands 27/D5
Goes, Netherlands 27/D5
Goessel, Kansas 232/E3
Goetzville, Mich. 250/E2
Goff, Kansas 232/G2
Goff (creek), Okla. 288/C1
Goffstown •, N.H. 268/D5
Gogama, Ontario 175/D3
Gogama, Ontario 177/C2
Gogebic (co.), Mich. 250/F2
Gogebic (lake), Mich. 250/F2
Gogrial, Sudan 111/K6
Goi, Ben (bay), Vietnam 72/F4
Goiana, Brazil 132/M4
Goiandira, Brazil 132/D7
Goiânia, Brazil 132/D7
Goiânia, Brazil 120/D4
Goiás (state), Brazil 132/D6
Goiás, Brazil 132/D6
Goiás, Brazil 120/D7
Goil, Loch (lake), Scotland 15/A1
Goin, Tenn. 237/O8
Goirle, Netherlands 27/G5
Góis, Portugal 33/B2
Gojjam (prov.), Ethiopia 111/G5
Gökçe, Turkey 63/B2
Gökçeada (isl.), Turkey 59/A1
Gökçeada (isl.), Turkey 63/A2
Gökirmak (riv.), Turkey 63/F2
Göksu (riv.), Turkey 63/E4
Göksun, Turkey 63/G3
Gokteik, Burma 72/C2
Gol, Norway 18/F6

Gola (isl.), Ireland 17/E1
Golan Heights, West Bank 65/D1
Gölbaşı, Turkey 63/G4
Golborne, England 13/B4
Gol'chikha, U.S.S.R. 48/J2
Golconda, Ill. 222/E6
Golconda, Nev. 266/D2
Golconda (ruins), India 68/D5
Golconda, Nev. 266/D2
Gölcük, Turkey 63/C2
Golčuv Jeníkov, Czech. 41/C2
Gold (riv.), Nova Scotia 168/G3
Gold Bar, Wash. 310/D3
Goldboro, Nova Scotia 168/G3
Gold Bridge, Br. Col. 184/F5
Gold Coast (reg.), Ghana 106/D8
Gold Coast, Queensland 95/D5
Gold Coast, Queensland 88/J5
Goldcreek, Mont. 262/D4
Golden, Br. Col. 184/J4
Golden, Colo. 208/J3
Golden, Idaho 220/C4
Golden, Ill. 222/B3
Golden, Ireland 17/F7
Golden, Miss. 256/H2
Golden, Mo. 261/E9
Golden, N. Mex. 274/C3
Golden (bay), N. Zealand 100/D4
Golden, Okla. 288/S6
Golden (lake), Ontario 177/G2
Golden (lake), Wash. 317/H1
Golden Beach, Fla. 212/C4
Golden City, Mo. 261/D8
Golden Ears Prov. Park, Br. Col. 184/L2
Golden Gate (chan.), Calif. 188/B3
Golden Gate (chan.), Calif. 204/H2
Golden Gate, Fla. 212/E5
Golden Gate, Ill. 222/E5
Golden Gate (range), Nev. 266/F5
Golden Gate Nat'l Rec. Area, Calif. 204/H2
Golden Grove, Jamaica 158/K6
Golden Hill, Md. 245/O7
Golden Lake, Ontario 177/G2
Golden Meadow, La. 238/K8
Golden Prairie, Sask. 181/B5
Golden Rock, St. Kitts & Nevis 161/C10
Golden's Bridge, N.Y. 276/N8
Golden Shores, Ariz. 198/A4
Golden Spike Nat'l Hist. Site, Utah 304/B2
Golden Vale (plain), Ireland 17/E7
Golden Valley, Minn. 255/G5
Golden Valley (co.), Mont. 262/G4
Golden Valley (co.), N. Dak. 282/C5
Golden Valley, Ontario 177/E2
Goldenville, N. Dak. 282/F5
Goldfield, Iowa 229/F3
Goldfield, Nev. 188/C3
Goldfield, Nev. 266/D5
Gold Hill, Nev. 266/B3
Gold Hill, N.C. 281/J3
Gold Hill, Oreg. 291/D5
Goldonna, La. 238/D2
Gold Point, Nev. 266/D5
Gold River, Br. Col. 184/D5
Goldsberry, Mo. 261/G3
Goldsboro, Md. 245/P4
Goldsboro, N.C. 188/L3
Goldsboro, N.C. 281/O4
Goldsboro (Etters), Pa. 294/J5
Goldsby, Okla. 288/L4
Goldsmith, Ind. 227/E4
Goldsmith, Texas 303/B5
Goldston, N.C. 281/L3
Goldstone (mt.), Idaho 220/E4
Goldsworthy, W. Australia 88/C4
Goldsworthy, W. Australia 92/C4
Goldthwaite, Texas 303/F6
Goldvein, Va. 307/N4
Goldville, Ala. 195/G4
Göle, Turkey 63/K2
Goleniów, Poland 47/B2
Goleta, Calif. 204/F9
Golf, Fla. 212/F5
Golf, Ill. 222/B5
Golfito, C. Rica 154/F6
Golf Manor, Ohio 284/C9
Golfo Santa Clara, Mexico 150/B1
Goliad (co.), Texas 303/G9
Goliad, Texas 303/G9
Golingen in der Salzach, Austria 41/B3
Gölmarmara, Turkey 63/C3
Golmud (Golmo), China 77/D4
Golmud, China 54/L6
Golo (riv.), France 28/B6
Golo (isl.), Philippines 82/C4
Golovin, Alaska 196/D2
Gölpazarı, Turkey 63/D2
Golpayegan, Iran 59/F3
Golpayegan, Iran 66/G4
Gölpazarı, Turkey 63/D2
Golshan (Tabas), Iran 66/K4
Golspie, Scotland 15/E3
Golts, Md. 245/P3
Golub-Dobrzyn, Poland 47/D2
Golungo Alto, Angola 115/B5
Golva, N. Dak. 282/C6
Goma, Zaire 115/E4
Goma, Zaire 102/E5
Gombari, Zaire 115/E3
Gombe, Nigeria 106/G6
Gomel', U.S.S.R. 7/H3
Gomel', U.S.S.R. 48/D1
Gomer, Ohio 284/B4
Gomera (isl.), Spain 106/A3
Gomera (isl.), Spain 33/B5
Gomez, Fla. 212/F4
Gómez Farías, Mexico 150/F2
Gómez Palacio, Mexico 150/G4

Gomishan, Iran 66/J2
Goms (valley), Switzerland 39/F4
Gona, Papua N.G. 85/C7
Gonabad, Iran 59/G3
Gonabad, Iran 66/L3
Gonaïves, Haiti 158/B5
Gonaïves, Haiti 156/D3
Gonâve (gulf), Haiti 158/B5
Gonâve (isl.), Haiti 158/B6
Gonâve (isl.), Haiti 156/D3
Gonbad-e Kavus, Iran 66/J2
Gonbadli, Iran 66/M2
Gönc, Hungary 41/F2
Gonda, India 68/E3
Gondal, India 68/C4
Gondar, Ethiopia 102/F3
Gondar, Ethiopia 59/C7
Gondar, Ethiopia 111/G5
Gondia, India 68/E4
Gondola Point, New Bruns. 170/D3
Gondomar, Portugal 33/B2
Gönen, Turkey 63/B2
Gonggar, China 77/D6
Gongga Shan (mt.), China 77/F6
Gonghe, China 77/F4
Gongliu, China 77/B3
Gongola (state), Nigeria 106/G7
Gongola (riv.), Nigeria 106/G6
Gongolgan, N.S. Wales 97/D2
Góngora, C. Rica 154/E5
Goñi, Uruguay 145/C4
Gonjo, China 77/E5
Gonvick, Minn. 255/C3
Gonzaga, Philippines 82/D1
Gonzales, Calif. 204/D7
Gonzales, La. 238/L2
Gonzales (co.), Texas 303/G8
Gonzales, Texas 303/G8
Gonzalez, Fla. 212/B6
González, Mexico 150/K5
González, Riacho (riv.), Paraguay 144/C3
Goobies, Newf. 166/D2
Goochland (co.), Va. 307/N5
Goochland, Va. 307/N5
Goodbee, La. 238/K6
Goode (mt.), Alaska 196/C1
Goode, Va. 307/K6
Goodell, Iowa 229/F3
Goodenough (cape), Ant. 5/C7
Gooderham, Ontario 177/F3
Gooderham, Ontario 177/F3
Gooderham, Ontario 177/F3
Gooderham, Ontario 177/F3
Gooderham, Ontario 177/F3
Goodeve, Sask. 181/H4
Goodfare, Alberta 182/A2
Goodfellow A.F.B., Texas 303/D6
Goodfield, Ill. 222/D3
Good Harbor (bay), Mich. 250/D3
Good Hart, Mich. 250/D3
Good Hope, Ala. 195/E2
Goodhope (bay), Alaska 196/F1
Good Hope, Georgia 217/E3
Good Hope, Ill. 222/C3
Good Hope, La. 238/K3
Good Hope, Miss. 256/E5
Good Hope, Ohio 284/E7
Good Hope (cape), S. Africa 102/D8
Good Hope (cape), S. Africa 2/K7
Good Hope (cape), S. Africa 118/K7
Goodhue (co.), Minn. 255/F6
Goodhue, Minn. 255/F6
Gooding (co.), Idaho 220/D6
Gooding, Idaho 220/D7
Goodland, Fla. 212/E6
Goodland, Ind. 227/C3
Goodland, Kansas 232/A2
Goodland, Minn. 255/F3
Goodlands, Manitoba 179/B5
Goodlettsville, Tenn. 237/H8
Goodlow, Br. Col. 184/G2
Good Luck, Md. 245/G4
Goodman, Miss. 256/E5
Goodman, Mo. 261/C9
Goodman, Wis. 317/K4
Goodnews Bay, Alaska 196/F3
Goodnight, Texas 303/C3
Goodnoe Hills, Wash. 310/E5
Goodooga, N.S. Wales 97/D1
Good Pine, La. 238/F3
Goodrich, Colo. 208/M2
Goodrich, Mich. 250/F6
Goodrich, N. Dak. 282/K5
Goodrich, Texas 303/K7
Goodrich, Wis. 317/G5
Goodridge, Alberta 182/E2
Goodridge, Minn. 255/C2
Goodsoil, Sask. 181/L4
Goodson, Mo. 261/F7
Good Spirit (lake), Sask. 181/J4
Goodspirit Lake Prov. Park, Sask. 181/J4
Goodspring, Tenn. 237/G10
Goodsprings, Ala. 195/D3
Goodsprings, Nev. 266/F7
Good Thunder, Minn. 255/D6
Goodview, Minn. 255/G6
Goodwater, Ala. 195/F4
Goodwater, Okla. 288/S7
Goodwater, Sask. 181/H6
Goodway, Ala. 195/D8
Goodwell, Okla. 288/C1
Goodwin, Ark. 202/J4
Goodwin, S. Dak. 298/R4
Goodwins Mills, Maine 243/B8
Goodwood, Ontario 177/E3
Goodwood, S. Africa 118/F6
Goodyear, Ariz. 198/C5
Gooik, Belgium 27/E7
Goole, England 10/H4
Goole, England 13/G4
Googowi, N.S. Wales 97/C3
Goolgowi, N.S. Australia 97/E3
Goomalling, W. Australia 88/B6
Goomalling, W. Australia 92/B6
Goombalie, N.S. Wales 97/C1
Goondiwindi, Queensland 88/H5
Goondiwindi, Queensland 95/D6
Goor, Netherlands 27/K4
Goose (lake) 188/B3
Goose (lake) 188/B3
Goose (lake), Calif. 204/E1

Granite 375

Goose (creek), Idaho 220/E7
Goose (riv.), Newf. 166/B3
Goose (riv.), N. Dak. 282/P4
Goose (isl.), Nova Scotia 168/F4
Goose (isl.), Nova Scotia 168/G3
Goose (lake), Oreg. 291/G5
Goose (creek), Va. 307/J6
Goose (creek), Va. 307/N3
Goose Airport P.O. (Goose Bay), Newf. 162/K5
Goose Bay, Newf. 162/K5
Goose Bay, Newf. 146/M4
Goose Bay-Happy Valley, Newf. 166/B3
Gooseberry (creek), Wyo. 319/D1
Gooseberry Cove, Newf. 166/C2
Goose Cove, Newf. 166/C2
Goose Cove, Newf. 166/C3
Goose Cove, Nova Scotia 168/H2
Goose Creek (mts.), Idaho 220/E7
Goose Creek, Ky. 237/L1
Goose Creek, S.C. 296/H6
Goose Lake, Iowa 229/N5
Goose Prairie, Wash. 310/D4
Goose Rock, Ky. 237/O6
Goose Rocks Beach, Maine 243/C9
Göppingen, Germany 22/C4
Góra, Poland 47/C3
Gorakhpur, India 68/E3
Gorchs, Argentina 143/G7
Gorda (pt.), Cuba 158/C2
Gorda (bank), Honduras 154/F3
Gorda (cay), Honduras 154/F3
Gorda (pt.), Nicaragua 154/F5
Gorda (pt.), Panama 154/H6
Gördes, Turkey 63/C3
Gordevio, Switzerland 39/G4
Gørding, Denmark 21/B7
Gordo, Ala. 195/C4
Gordola, Switzerland 39/G4
Gordon, Ala. 195/H8
Gordon (lake), Alberta 182/E1
Gordon (riv.), Br. Col. 184/H3
Gordon (isl.), Chile 138/E11
Gordon (co.), Georgia 217/C2
Gordon, Georgia 217/F5
Gordon, Kansas 232/F4
Gordon, Nebr. 264/B2
Gordon, Ohio 284/B6
Gordon, Scotland 15/F5
Gordon, Tasmania 99/G5
Gordon (lake), Tasmania 99/C4
Gordon (riv.), Tasmania 99/B4
Gordon, Texas 303/F5
Gordon, W. Va. 312/C7
Gordon, Wis. 317/C3
Gordondale, Alberta 182/A2
Gordon Downs, W. Australia 92/E2
Gordon's Bay, S. Africa 118/F7
Gordonsburg, Tenn. 237/F9
Gordonsville, Ala. 195/E6
Gordonsville, Minn. 255/E7
Gordonsville, Tenn. 237/K8
Gordonsville, Va. 307/M4
Gordonvale, Queensland 88/H3
Gordonvale, Queensland 95/C3
Gordonville, Mo. 261/N8
Gore (pt.), Alaska 196/C2
Goré, Chad 111/C6
Gore (range), Colo. 208/G3
Gore, Ethiopia 111/G6
Gore, Ethiopia 102/F4
Gore, N. Zealand 100/B7
Gore, Ohio 284/F6
Gore, Okla. 288/R3
Gore (mt.), Vt. 268/D2
Gore, Va. 307/M2
Gore Bay, Ontario 177/B2
Gorebridge, Scotland 10/C1
Gorebridge, Scotland 15/D2
Goree, Texas 303/E4
Goregaon, India 68/B7
Görele, Turkey 63/H2
Gore Springs, Miss. 256/E3
Goreville, Ill. 222/E6
Gorey, Chan. Is. 13/F8
Gorey, Ireland 17/J6
Gorey, Ireland 10/C4
Gorgan, Iran 54/G6
Gorgan, Iran 59/F2
Gorgan (Gurgan), Iran 66/J2
Gorgan (riv.), Iran 66/J2
Gorgan (riv.), Iran 59/F2
Gorgas, Ala. 195/D3
Gorgol (reg.), Mauritania 106/B5
Gorgona (isl.), Colombia 126/A6
Gorgona (isl.), Italy 34/B3
Gorham, Ill. 222/D6
Gorham, Kansas 232/D3
Gorham, Maine 243/C8
Gorham •, Maine 243/C8
Gorham, N.H. 268/E3
Gorham •, N.H. 268/E3
Gorham, N.Y. 276/F5
Gorham, N. Dak. 282/D5
Gori, U.S.S.R. 52/F6
Gorin, Mo. 261/H2
Gorinchem, Netherlands 27/G5
Gorizia (prov.), Italy 34/D2
Gorizia, Italy 34/D2
Gorki, U.S.S.R. 52/D4
Gørlev, Denmark 21/E7
Gorlice, Poland 47/E4
Görlitz, Germany 22/F3
Görlitz, Germany 7/F3
Gorlitz, Sask. 181/J4
Gorlovka, U.S.S.R. 7/H4
Gorlovka, U.S.S.R. 52/E5
Gorman, Calif. 204/G9
Gorman, Tenn. 237/F8
Gorman, Texas 303/F5
Gormania, W. Va. 312/H4
Gormanston, Ireland 17/J4
Gormanston, Tasmania 99/B4
Gorna Oryakhovitsa, Bulgaria 45/G4
Gornji Milanovac, Yugoslavia 45/D3
Gornji Vakuf, Yugoslavia 45/C4
Gorno-Altay Aut. Obl., U.S.S.R. 48/J4
Gorno-Altaysk, U.S.S.R. 48/J4
Gorno-Badakhshan Aut. Obl., U.S.S.R. 48/H6
Gornyak, U.S.S.R. 48/J4
Gorodets, U.S.S.R. 52/F3
Gorodok, U.S.S.R. 52/D3
Goroka, Papua N.G. 85/B7
Goroke, Victoria 97/A5
Gorong (isl.), Indonesia 85/J6
Gorong (isls.), Indonesia 85/J6
Gorongosa Nat'l Park, Mozambique 118/E3
Gorongoza, Mozambique 118/E3
Gorontalo, Indonesia 85/G5
Gorrahei, Ethiopia 111/H6
Gorredijk, Netherlands 27/J2
Gorrie, Ontario 177/C4
Gorst, Wash. 310/C3
Gort, Ireland 10/B4
Gort, Ireland 17/D5
Gortin, N. Ireland 17/G2
Gorum, La. 238/E4
Gorumna (isl.), Ireland 17/B5
Goryn' (riv.), U.S.S.R. 52/C4
Gorzów (prov.), Poland 47/B2
Gorzów Wielkopolski, Poland 47/B2
Gorzów Wielkopolski, Poland 7/F3
Göschenen, Switzerland 39/G3
Gose, Japan 81/J8
Gosen, Japan 81/J5
Goshen, Ala. 195/F7
Goshen, Ark. 202/C1
Goshen, Calif. 204/F7
Goshen •, Conn. 210/C1
Goshen (pt.), Conn. 210/G3
Goshen, Ind. 227/F1
Goshen, Ky. 237/K4
Goshen •, Mass. 249/C3
Goshen •, N.H. 268/C5
Goshen, N.J. 273/D5
Goshen, N.Y. 276/M8
Goshen, Nova Scotia 168/G3
Goshen, Ohio 284/B7
Goshen, Oreg. 291/D4
Goshen, Utah 304/C4
Goshen, Va. 307/K5
Goshen (co.), Wyo. 319/H4
Goshen Springs, Miss. 256/E6
Goshogawara, Japan 81/K3
Goshute (mts.), Nev. 266/G2
Goshute Ind. Res., Nev. 266/G3
Goshute Ind. Res., Utah 304/A4
Gosier, Guadeloupe 161/B6
Goslar, Germany 22/D3
Gosnell, Ark. 202/K2
Gosper (co.), Nebr. 264/E4
Gospić, Yugoslavia 45/B3
Gosport, Ala. 195/C7
Gosport, England 13/F7
Gosport, England 10/F5
Gosport, Ind. 227/D6
Goss, Miss. 256/E8
Gossau, Switzerland 39/H2
Gossville, N.H. 268/E5
Gostivar, Yugoslavia 45/E5
Gostyń, Poland 47/C3
Gostynin, Poland 47/D2
Göta (canal), Sweden 18/J7
Göta (riv.), Sweden 18/H7
Gotebo, Okla. 288/J4
Göteborg, Sweden 7/F3
Göteborg, Sweden 18/G8
Göteborg och Bohus (co.), Sweden 18/G7
Gotha, Germany 22/D3
Gotham, Wis. 317/F9
Gothenburg, Nebr. 264/D4
Gothic (mesa), Ariz. 198/F2
Gotland (co.), Sweden 18/L8
Gotland (isl.), Sweden 7/F3
Gotland (isl.), Sweden 18/L8
Goto (isls.), Japan 81/D7
Goto (lake), Neth. Ant. 161/D8
Gotse Delchev, Bulgaria 45/F5
Gotska Sandön (isl.), Sweden 18/L7
Gotsu, Japan 81/F6
Göttingen, Germany 22/D3
Gottwaldov, Czech. 41/D2
Götzis, Austria 41/A3
Goubere, Cent. Afr. Rep. 115/E2
Gouda, Netherlands 27/F4
Goudeau, La. 238/G5
Gough (lake), Alberta 182/D3
Gough, Georgia 217/H4
Gough (isl.), St. Helena 2/J8
Gouin (res.), Que. 162/J6
Gouin (res.), Québec 174/C3
Goulburn, N.S. Wales 88/J6
Goulburn, N.S. Wales 97/E4
Goulburn (isls.), North. Terr. 88/E2
Goulburn (isls.), North. Terr. 93/C1
Goulburn (riv.), Victoria 97/C5
Goulburn Island, North. Terr. 93/C1
Gould, Ark. 202/G6
Gould, Colo. 208/G2
Gould, Okla. 288/G5
Gould, Québec 172/F4
Gould City, Mich. 250/D2
Goulding, Fla. 212/B6
Goulds, Fla. 212/F6
Goulds, Newf. 166/D2
Gouldsboro, Maine 243/H7
Gouldsboro •, Maine 243/H7
Gouldsboro, Pa. 294/L3
Gouldtown, Sask. 181/D5
Goulmima, Morocco 106/C2
Goumbou, Mali 106/C6
Gounamitz (riv.), New Bruns. 170/C1
Goundam, Mali 106/D5
Goundam, Mali 102/B3
Gourara (oasis), Algeria 106/E3
Gourbeyre, Guadeloupe 161/A7
Gourdon, France 28/D5
Gouré, Niger 106/G6
Gourma-Rharous, Mali 106/D5
Gournay-en-Bray, France 28/D3
Gouro, Chad 111/C4
Gourock, Scotland 10/A1
Gourock, Scotland 15/A1
Gouveia, Portugal 33/C2
Gouverneur, N.Y. 276/K2
Gouvy, Belgium 27/H8
Gouyave, Grenada 161/C8
Gouyave, Grenada 156/F4
Govan, Sask. 181/G4
Govan, S.C. 296/E5
Gove (co.), Kansas 232/B3
Gove, Kansas 232/B3
Gove (Nhulunbuy), North. Terr. 93/E2
Govena (cape), U.S.S.R. 48/R4
Govenlock, Sask. 181/B6
Governador Valadares, Brazil 132/F7
Governador Valadares, Brazil 120/E4
Government (mt.), Ariz. 198/C3
Government (peak), Mich. 250/F1
Government (creek), Utah 304/B3
Government Camp, Oreg. 291/F2
Governor (lake), Nova Scotia 168/F3
Govĭ-Altay, Mongolia 77/E3
Gowan, Minn. 255/F4
Gowanda, N.Y. 276/B6
Gowd-e Zerreh (depr.), Afghanistan 59/H4
Gowen, Mich. 250/D5
Gowen, Okla. 288/R5
Gowensville, S.C. 296/C1
Gower, Mo. 261/C3
Gower (isl.), N.S. Wales 97/J2
Gower (mt.), N.S. Wales 97/J2
Gower (pen.), Wales 13/C6
Gowna (lake), Ireland 17/G4
Gowran, Ireland 17/G6
Gowrie, Iowa 229/E4
Gowrie Park, Tasmania 99/C3
Goya, Argentina 120/D5
Goya, Argentina 143/G4
Goyave, Guadeloupe 161/A6
Goyder (riv.), North. Terr. 93/D2
Goyders (lag.), S. Australia 94/F2
Göynücek, Turkey 63/F2
Göynük, Turkey 63/D2
Goz Beïda, Chad 111/D5
Gozo (isl.), Malta 34/E6
Goz Regeb, Sudan 111/G4
Graaff-Reinet, S. Africa 118/C6
Graal-Müritz, Germany 22/E1
Graauw, Netherlands 27/E6
Grabill, Ind. 227/H2
Grabouw, S. Africa 118/F7
Grabs, Switzerland 39/H2
Gračac, Yugoslavia 45/B3
Gračanica, Yugoslavia 45/D3
Grace, Idaho 220/G7
Grace (mt.), Mass. 249/E2
Grace, Miss. 256/C5
Grace (pt.), R.I. 249/H8
Grace City, N. Dak. 282/N4
Gracefield, Québec 172/A3
Graceham, Md. 245/J2
Gracemont, Okla. 288/K4
Graceton, Minn. 255/D2
Graceton, Pa. 294/D4
Graceville, Fla. 212/D5
Graceville, Minn. 255/B5
Graceville, Queensland 88/K3
Gracewood, Georgia 217/H4
Gracey, Ky. 237/F7
Grächen, Switzerland 39/E4
Gracias, Honduras 154/C3
Gracias a Dios (cape), Nic. 146/K8
Gracias a Dios (cape), Nicaragua 154/F3
Graciosa (isl.), Portugal 33/C1
Gradačac, Yugoslavia 45/D3
Gradaús, Brazil 120/D3
Gradaús, Brazil 132/D4
Gradaús, Serra dos (range), Brazil 132/D4
Grado, Spain 33/D1
Grady, Ala. 195/F7
Grady, Ark. 202/G5
Grady (co.), Georgia 217/D9
Grady (isl.), Newf. 166/C3
Grady, N. Mex. 274/F4
Grady (co.), Okla. 288/L5
Grady, Okla. 288/L6
Gradyville, Ky. 237/L6
Graeagle, Calif. 204/E4
Graested, Denmark 21/F5
Graettinger, Iowa 229/D2
Graf, Iowa 229/M3
Grafenau, Germany 22/E4
Grafenwöhr, Germany 22/D4
Graff, Mo. 261/H8
Graff-Reinet, S. Africa 102/E8
Graford, Texas 303/F5
Grafton, Australia 87/F8
Grafton (isls.), Chile 138/D10
Grafton, Ill. 222/C5
Grafton, Ind. 227/B9
Grafton, Iowa 229/G2
Grafton •, Mass. 249/H4
Grafton, Nebr. 264/G4
Grafton, New Bruns. 170/C2
Grafton (co.), N.H. 268/D4
Grafton •, N.H. 268/D4
Grafton, N.S. Wales 88/J5
Grafton, N.S. Wales 97/G1
Grafton, N.Y. 276/N5
Grafton, N. Dak. 282/R3
Grafton, Ohio 284/F3
Grafton, Ontario 177/G4
Grafton •, Vt. 268/B5
Grafton, Va. 307/P6
Grafton, W. Va. 312/G4
Grafton, Wis. 317/L9
Grafton Center, N.H. 268/D4
Graham, Ala. 195/H4
Graham (lake), Alberta 182/C1
Graham (co.), Ariz. 198/E6
Graham (mt.), Ariz. 198/F6
Graham (isl.), Br. Col. 184/A3
Graham (peak), Colo. 208/E8
Graham, Fla. 212/D2
Graham, Georgia 217/H7
Graham (creek), Ind. 227/F7
Graham (co.), Kansas 232/C2
Graham, Ky. 237/G6
Graham (lake), Maine 243/G6
Graham, Mo. 261/C2
Graham (co.), N.C. 281/B4
Graham, N.C. 281/L2
Graham (isl.), N.W.T. 162/M3
Graham (isl.), N.W. Terr. 187/J2
Graham, Okla. 288/M6
Graham, Ontario 175/B3
Graham, Ontario 177/G5
Graham, Texas 303/F4
Graham Bell (isl.), U.S.S.R. 4/A6
Graham Bell (isl.), U.S.S.R. 48/G1
Grahamdale, Manitoba 179/D3
Graham Land (reg.), Ant. 2/G9
Graham Land (reg.), Ant. 5/C15
Graham Reach (chan.), Br. Col. 184/C3
Grahamstown, S. Africa 102/E8
Grahamstown, S. Africa 118/D6
Grahamsville, N.Y. 276/L7
Grahn, Ky. 237/P4
Graian Alps (range), France 28/G5
Graian Alps (range), Italy 34/A2
Graiguenamanagh-Tinnahinch, Ireland 17/H6
Grain Coast (reg.), Liberia 106/B8
Grainfield, Kansas 232/B2
Grainger (co.), Tenn. 237/O8
Graingers, N.C. 281/O4
Grainola, Okla. 288/N1
Grainton, Nebr. 264/C4
Grain Valley, Mo. 261/S6
Grajaú, Brazil 132/E4
Grajaú (riv.), Brazil 132/E4
Grajewo, Poland 47/F2
Gram, Denmark 21/C7
Gramalote, Colombia 126/D4
Gramat, France 28/D5
Grambling, La. 238/E1
Gramercy, La. 238/M3
Gramling, S.C. 296/C1
Grammer, Ind. 227/F6
Grammont (Geraardsbergen), Belgium 27/D7
Grampian, Pa. 294/E4
Grampian (reg.), Scotland 15/F3
Grampian (mts.), Scotland 15/D4
Gramsbergen, Netherlands 27/K3
Gran, Norway 18/G6
Granada, Colo. 208/P6
Granada, Minn. 255/D7
Granada, Nicaragua 154/E5
Granada (prov.), Spain 33/E4
Granada, Spain 33/E4
Granada, Spain 7/D5
Granada Hills, Calif. 204/B10
Granados, Mexico 150/E2
Granard, Ireland 17/F4
Granbury, Texas 303/G5
Granby, Colo. 208/H2
Granby (lake), Colo. 208/G2
Granby, Conn. 210/D1
Granby •, Conn. 210/D1
Granby, Mass. 249/E3
Granby •, Mass. 249/E3
Granby, Mo. 261/D9
Granby, Québec 172/E4
Granby •, Vt. 268/D2
Gran Canaria (isl.), Spain 33/B5
Gran Chaco (reg.) 120/C5
Gran Chaco (reg.), Argentina 143/D1
Gran Chaco (reg.), Paraguay 144/B2-3
Gran Couva, Trin. & Tob. 161/B11
Grand (canal), China 54/N6
Grand (canal), China 77/J4
Grand (co.), Colo. 208/G2
Grand (bay), Dominica 161/F7
Grand (canal), Ireland 17/G5
Grand (lake), La. 188/H4
Grand (lake), La. 238/H8
Grand (lake), La. 238/E7
Grand (lake), Maine 243/H4
Grand (isl.), Mich. 250/C2
Grand (lake), Mich. 250/F3
Grand (riv.), Mich. 250/D6
Grand (riv.), Mo. 261/F3
Grand (bay), New Bruns. 170/D3
Grand (lake), New Bruns. 170/D3
Grand (lake), New Bruns. 170/C3
Grand (lake), Newf. 166/B3
Grand (lake), Newf. 166/C4
Grand (isl.), N.Y. 276/B5
Grand (riv.), Ohio 284/H2
Grand (riv.), Ontario 177/D4
Grand (riv.), S. Dak. 298/F2
Grand (co.), Utah 304/E5
Grand Anse, Grenada 161/C9
Grand Bahama (isl.), Bahamas 146/L7
Grand Bahama (isl.), Bahamas 156/B1
Grand Bank, Newf. 166/C4
Grand-Bassam, Ivory Coast 106/D7
Grand Bay, Ala. 195/B10
Grand Bay, Dominica 161/F7
Grand Bay, New Bruns. 170/D3
Grand Bayou, La. 238/C2
Grand Beach, Manitoba 179/F4
Grand Beach, Mich. 250/C7
Grand Bend, Ontario 177/C4
Grand Blanc, Mich. 250/F6
Grand-Bourg, Guadeloupe 161/B7
Grand Bruit, Newf. 166/C4
Grand Caicos (isl.), Turks & Caicos 156/D2
Grand Caille (pt.), St. Lucia 161/F6
Grand Canary (isl.), Spain 102/A2
Grand Canary (isl.), Spain 106/A3
Grand Cane, La. 238/C2
Grand Canyon, Ariz. 198/D2
Grand Canyon, Ariz. 198/C2
Grand Canyon, Snake R. (canyon), Oreg. 291/L2
Grand Canyon Nat'l Mon., Ariz. 198/C2
Grand Canyon Nat'l Park, Ariz. 188/D3
Grand Canyon Nat'l Park, Ariz. 198/C2
Grand Canyon of the Snake River (canyon), Idaho 220/B4
Grand Cayman (isl.), Cayman Is. 156/B3
Grand Centre, Alberta 182/E2
Grand Cess, Liberia 106/C8
Grand Chain, Ill. 222/E6
Grand Chenier, La. 238/E7
Grand Combin (mt.), Switzerland 39/D5
Grand Comoro (Njazidja) (isl.), Comoros 102/G6
Grand Comoro (Njazidja) (isl.), Comoros 118/G2
Grand Coteau, La. 238/G6
Grand Coulee, Sask. 181/G5
Grand Coulee, Wash. 310/G3
Grand Coulee (canyon), Wash. 310/F3
Grand Coulee (dam), Wash. 310/F3
Grandcour, Switzerland 39/C3
Grand Cul de Sac (riv.), St. Lucia 161/G6
Grand Cul-de-Sac Marin (bay), Guadeloupe 161/A6
Grand Desert, Nova Scotia 168/E4
Grand Detour, Ill. 222/D2
Grande (bay), Argentina 120/C8
Grande (bay), Argentina 143/C7
Grande (falls), Argentina 143/E3
Grande (riv.), Argentina 143/C4
Grande (marsh), Bolivia 136/F5
Grande (riv.), Bolivia 136/C6
Grande (riv.), Bolivia 136/C4
Grande (isl.), Brazil 132/C8
Grande (isl.), Brazil 135/D3
Grande (riv.), Brazil 120/E5
Grande (riv.), Brazil 132/D8
Grande (riv.), Brazil 132/E5
Grande (riv.), Brazil 135/B2
Grande (isl.), Chile 138/A6
Grande (riv.), Chile 138/F10
Grande, Salar (salt dep.), Chile 138/B3
Grande, Salto (falls), Colombia 126/D8
Grande (isl.), Colombia 126/B4
Grande (riv.), Guatemala 154/A3
Grande (riv.), Jamaica 158/K6
Grande (riv.), Mexico 150/J7
Grande (riv.), Mexico 150/N8
Grande (riv.), New Bruns. 170/C1
Grande (riv.), Nicaragua 154/E4
Grande (riv.), Peru 128/E10
Grande (range), Uruguay 145/D4
Grande, Arroyo (riv.), Uruguay 145/B4
Grande-Anse, New Bruns. 170/E1
Grande-Anse, Québec 172/E2
Grande Cache, Alberta 182/A3
Grande-Cascapédia, Québec 172/C2
Grande Cayemite (isl.), Haiti 158/B6
Grande-Clairière, Manitoba 179/B5
Grande de Añasco (riv.), P. Rico 161/B2
Grande de Arecibo (riv.), P. Rico 161/C1
Grande de Lípez (riv.), Bolivia 136/B7
Grande de Loíza (riv.), P. Rico 161/E1
Grande de Manatí (riv.), P. Rico 161/C1
Grande de Santiago (riv.), Mexico 150/G6
Grande de Tierra del Fuego (isl.), Argentina 143/C7
Grande de Tierra del Fuego (isl.), Chile 138/E11
Grande Dixence (dam), Switzerland 39/D4
Grande-Grève, Québec 172/D1
Grande Inferior (range), Uruguay 145/C4
Grande Pointe, Manitoba 179/F5
Grande Prairie, Alberta 182/A2
Grande Prairie, Alta. 162/E4
Grande-Prairie, Alta. 146/G4
Grande Prairie, Texas 303/G2
Grand Erg Occidental (des.), Algeria 102/C1
Grand Erg Occidental (des.), Algeria 106/E2
Grand Erg Oriental (des.), Algeria 102/C1
Grand Erg Oriental (des.), Algeria 106/F2
Grand Erg Oriental (des.), Tunisia 106/F2
Grande' Rivière, Martinique 161/C5
Grande-Rivière, Québec 172/D2
Grande-Rivière, La (riv.), Que. 146/L4
Grande Rivière, La (riv.), Québec 174/B2
Grande Rivière, Trin. & Tob. 161/B10
Grande Rivière du Nord, Haiti 158/C5
Grande Ronde (riv.), Oreg. 291/K2
Grande Ronde (riv.), Wash. 310/H5
Grande Saline, Haiti 158/B5
Grandes-Bergeronnes, Québec 172/H1
Grandes-Piles, Québec 172/E3
Grand-Étang, Nova Scotia 168/G2
Grande-Terre, Guadeloupe 161/B6
Grande-Vallée, Québec 172/D1
Grande Vigie, Guadeloupe 161/B5
Grand Falls (lake), Maine 243/H5
Grand Falls, New Bruns. 170/C1
Grand Falls, Newf. 166/C4
Grand Falls, Newf. 146/N5
Grand Falls, Newf. 162/L6
Grandfalls, Texas 303/B6
Grand Falls Hill, New Bruns. 170/C1
Grandfield, Okla. 288/J6
Grand Forks, Br. Col. 184/H6
Grand Forks, N. Dak. 146/J5
Grand Forks, N. Dak. 188/G1
Grand Forks (co.), N. Dak. 282/P3
Grand Forks, N. Dak. 282/R4
Grand Forks A.F.B., N. Dak. 282/R4
Grand Glaise, Ark. 202/G3
Grand Goâve, Haiti 158/B6
Grand Gorge, N.Y. 276/L6
Grand Gosier, Haiti 158/C6
Grand Gulf, Miss. 256/B6
Grand Harbour, New Bruns. 170/D4
Grand Haven, Mich. 250/C5
Grand-Îlet (isl.), Guadeloupe 161/A7
Grandin, Fla. 212/E2
Grandin, Mo. 261/L9
Grandin, N. Dak. 282/R5
Grand Island, Nebr. 146/J5
Grand Island, Nebr. 188/G2
Grand Island, Nebr. 264/F4
Grand Island, N.Y. 276/B5
Grand Isle, La. 238/L8
Grand Isle, Maine 243/G1
Grand Isle (co.), Vt. 268/A2
Grand Isle •, Vt. 268/A2
Grand Junction, Colo. 146/H6
Grand Junction, Colo. 188/E3
Grand Junction, Colo. 208/B4
Grand Junction, Iowa 229/E4
Grand Junction, Mich. 250/C6
Grand Junction, Tenn. 237/C10
Grand-Lahou, Ivory Coast 106/C8
Grand Lake, Ark. 202/H7
Grand Lake, Colo. 208/H2
Grand Lake, La. 238/D6
Grand Lake, Nova Scotia 168/E4
Grand Lake Seboeis (lake), Maine 243/F3
Grand Lake Stream •, Maine 243/H5
Grand Lake Towne, Okla. 288/S1
Grand Ledge, Mich. 250/E6
Grand-Lieu (lake), France 28/C4
Grand Manan (chan.), Maine 243/K6
Grand Manan (chan.), New Bruns. 170/C4
Grand Manan (isl.), New Bruns. 170/D4
Grand Marais, Manitoba 179/F4
Grand Marais, Mich. 250/D2
Grand Marais, Minn. 255/G2
Grand Marsh, Wis. 317/G8
Grand Meadow, Minn. 255/F7
Grand'Mère, Québec 172/E3
Grand Mound, Iowa 229/M5
Grand Mound, Wash. 310/C4
Grand Muveran (mt.), Switzerland 39/D4
Grand Narrows, Nova Scotia 168/H3
Grândola, Portugal 33/B3
Grandora, Sask. 181/E3
Grand Pass, Mo. 261/E4
Grand-Popo, Benin 106/E7
Grand Portage, Minn. 255/G2
Grand Portage Ind. Res., Minn. 255/G2
Grand Portage Nat'l Mon., Minn. 255/G2
Grand Pré, Nova Scotia 168/D3
Grand Rapids, Manitoba 179/C1
Grand Rapids, Mich. 146/K5
Grand Rapids, Mich. 188/K2
Grand Rapids, Mich. 250/D5
Grand Rapids, Minn. 255/E3
Grand Rapids, N. Dak. 282/N7
Grand Rapids, Ohio 284/C3
Grand-Remous, Québec 172/B3
Grand Ridge, Fla. 212/A1
Grand Ridge, Ill. 222/E2
Grand River, Iowa 229/F7
Grand River, Nova Scotia 168/H3
Grand River, Ohio 284/H2
Grand River (valley), Utah 304/E4
Grand Rivers, Ky. 237/E7
Grand Ronde, Oreg. 291/D2
Grand Roy, Grenada 161/C8
Grand Saline, Texas 303/J5
Grand Santi, Fr. Guiana 131/D3
Grandson, Switzerland 39/C3
Grand Terrace, Calif. 204/E10
Grand Terre (isls.), La. 238/L8
Grand Teton (mt.), Wyo. 319/B2
Grand Teton Nat'l Park, Wyo. 319/B2
Grand Tower, Ill. 222/D6
Grand Traverse (co.), Mich. 250/D4
Grand Traverse (bay), Mich. 250/D3
Grand Turk (isl.), Turks & Caicos 156/D2
Grand Valley, Ontario 177/D4
Grand Valley, Pa. 294/C2
Grandview, Ark. 202/C1
Grand View, Idaho 220/B7
Grandview, Ill. 222/D4
Grand View, Ill. 222/F4
Grandview, Ind. 227/C9
Grandview, Iowa 229/L6
Grandview, Manitoba 179/B3
Grandview, Mo. 261/P6
Grandview, Ohio 284/H7
Grandview, Tenn. 237/M9
Grandview, Texas 303/G5
Grandview, Wash. 310/F4
Grand View, Wis. 317/D3
Grandview Heights, Ohio 284/D6
Grand View-on-Hudson, N.Y. 276/K8
Grandview Plaza, Kansas 232/F2
Grandville, Mich. 250/D6
Grand Wash (butte), Ariz. 198/B2
Grand Wash (riv.), Ariz. 198/B2
Grandy, Minn. 255/E5
Grandy, N.C. 281/T2
Graneros, Chile 138/G5
Grange, England 13/E3
Grange, N.H. 268/E3
Grangeburg, Ala. 195/H8
Grange City, Ky. 237/O4
Grangemouth, Scotland 10/B1
Grangemouth, Scotland 15/C1
Granger, Ind. 227/E1
Granger, Iowa 229/F5
Granger, Minn. 255/F7
Granger, Mo. 261/H2
Granger, Texas 303/G7
Granger, Wash. 310/E4
Granger, Wyo. 188/D2
Granger, Wyo. 319/C4
Grangeville, Idaho 220/B4
Grangeville, La. 238/J5
Granisle, Br. Col. 184/D3
Granite, Colo. 208/G4
Granite, Md. 245/L3
Granite (pt.), Mich. 250/B2
Granite (co.), Mont. 262/C4
Granite (peak), Mont. 262/F5
Granite (peak), Nev. 266/B2
Granite (range), Nev. 266/B2
Granite, Okla. 288/H5

Granite, Oreg. 291/J3
Granite (mts.), Wyo. 319/E3
Granite Bay, Br. Col. 184/E5
Granite Canon, Wyo. 319/G4
Granite, Ill. 222/A2
Granite City Army Depot, Ill. 222/A2
Granite Falls, Minn. 255/C6
Granite Falls, N.C. 281/G5
Granite Falls, Wash. 310/D2
Granite Quarry, N.C. 281/H5
Graniteville, Mass. 249/J2
Graniteville, Mo. 261/L7
Graniteville, S.C. 296/C4
Graniteville-East Barre, Vt. 268/C3
Granitique, Chaîne (range), Fr. Guiana 131/E4
Granity, N. Zealand 100/C4
Granja, Brazil 132/F3
Granma (prov.), Cuba 158/H4
Gränna, Sweden 18/J8
Grannis, Ark. 202/B5
Grano, N. Dak. 282/G2
Granollers, Spain 33/H2
Gran Paradiso (mt.), Italy 34/A2
Gran Piedra (mt.), Cuba 158/J4
Gran Quivira, N. Mex. 274/D4
Gran Sabana, La (plain), Venezuela 124/G5
Grant, Ala. 195/F1
Grant (co.), Ark. 202/F5
Grant, Colo. 208/H4
Grant, Fla. 212/F4
Grant (co.), Ind. 227/F3
Grant, Iowa 229/C6
Grant (co.), Kansas 232/A4
Grant (co.), Ky. 237/M3
Grant, Ky. 237/M3
Grant (par.), La. 238/E3
Grant, La. 238/E5
Grant, Mich. 250/D5
Grant (co.), Minn. 255/B5
Grant, Mont. 262/C5
Grant (co.), Nebr. 264/C3
Grant, Nebr. 264/C4
Grant (range), Nev. 266/F4
Grant (co.), N. Mex. 274/A5
Grant (co.), N. Dak. 282/G6
Grant (co.), Okla. 288/L1
Grant, Okla. 288/R7
Grant (co.), Oreg. 291/J3
Grant, Oreg. 291/J3
Grant (co.), S. Dak. 298/R3
Grant (co.), Wash. 310/F3
Grant (co.), W. Va. 312/H4
Grant (co.), Wis. 317/E10
Grant Center, Iowa 229/A4
Grant City, Mo. 261/D2
Grantfork, Ill. 222/D5
Grantham, Alberta 182/E4
Grantham, England 13/G5
Grantham, England 10/F4
Grantham•, N.H. 268/C5
Granthams Landing, Br. Col. 184/J3
Grant-Kohrs Ranch Nat'l Hist. Site, Mont. 262/D4
Granton, Ontario 177/C4
Granton, Wis. 317/E6
Grantown-on-Spey, Scotland 10/E2
Grantown-on-Spey, Scotland 15/E3
Grant Park, Ill. 222/F2
Grants, N. Mex. 274/B3
Grantsboro, N.C. 281/R4
Grantsburg, Ill. 222/E6
Grantsburg, Ind. 227/E8
Grantsburg, Wis. 317/A4
Grantsdale, Mont. 262/B4
Grants Pass (chan.), Ala. 195/B10
Grants Pass, Oreg. 188/B2
Grants Pass, Oreg. 291/D5
Grantsville, Md. 245/B2
Grantsville, Utah 304/B3
Grantsville, W. Va. 312/D5
Grant Town, W. Va. 312/F3
Grantville, Alberta 182/D4
Grantville, Georgia 217/C4
Grantville, Kansas 232/C4
Grantwood, Mo. 261/O4
Granum, Alberta 182/D5
Granville, France 28/C3
Granville, Ill. 222/D2
Granville, Iowa 229/B3
Granville (lake), Man. 162/G4
Granville (lake), Manitoba 179/H2
Granville•, Mass. 249/C4
Granville, Mo. 261/M3
Granville, N.Y. 276/O4
Granville (co.), N.C. 281/M2
Granville, N. Dak. 282/J3
Granville, Ohio 284/E5
Granville, Tenn. 237/K8
Granville•, Vt. 268/B4
Granville, W. Va. 312/F3
Granville Centre, Nova Scotia 168/C4
Granville Ferry, Nova Scotia 168/C4
Granville Lake, Manitoba 179/H2
Grapeland, Miss. 256/B3
Grapeland, Texas 303/J6
Grapeview, Wash. 310/C3
Grapeville, Pa. 294/C6
Grapevine, Ark. 202/F5
Grapevine (mts.), Calif. 204/H7
Grapevine, Texas 303/F2
Grapevine (lake), Texas 303/F2
Grasmere, Br. Col. 184/K5
Grasmere, N.H. 268/D5
Grasmere, S. Africa 118/H7
Gråsö (isl.), Sweden 18/L6
Grasonville, Md. 245/O5
Grass (riv.), Manitoba 179/J3
Grass (riv.), N.Y. 276/K1
Grass (pt.), Virgin Is. (U.S.) 161/G4
Grass Creek, Ind. 227/E3
Grass Creek, Wyo. 319/D2
Grasse, France 28/G6
Grassflat, Pa. 294/F3
Grassington, England 13/F3
Grass Lake, Mich. 250/E6
Grassland, Alberta 182/D2

Grasslands Nat'l Park, Sask. 185/D6
Grass Patch, W. Australia 92/C6
Grass Range, Mont. 262/H3
Grass River Prov. Park, Manitoba 179/H3
Grasston, Minn. 255/E5
Grass Valley, Calif. 188/B3
Grass Valley, Calif. 204/D4
Grass Valley, Oreg. 291/G2
Grassy (key), Fla. 212/F7
Grassy, Mo. 261/M8
Grassy Butte, N. Dak. 282/D5
Grassy Lake, Alberta 182/E5
Grassy Meadows, W. Va. 312/E7
Grassy Park, S. Africa 118/E6
Grassy Plains, Br. Col. 184/E3
Gråsten, Denmark 21/C8
Grates (pt.), Newf. 166/D2
Grates Cove, Newf. 166/D2
Gratiot (co.), Mich. 250/E5
Gratiot, Ohio 284/F6
Gratiot, Wis. 317/F10
Gratis, Ohio 284/A6
Graton, Calif. 204/C5
Gratwein, Austria 41/C3
Gratz, Ky. 237/M4
Gratz, Pa. 294/J4
Graubünden (Grisons) (canton), Switzerland 39/H3
Grauehörner (mts.), Switzerland 39/H3
Graulhet, France 28/E6
Graus, Spain 33/G1
Grauspitz (mt.), Liecht. 39/J2
Grave (pt.), France 28/D5
Grave, Netherlands 27/H5
Gravelbourg, Sask. 181/E6
Gravelly, Ark. 202/C4
Gravelly Beach, Tasmania 99/C3
Gravelly Branch, Nanticoke (riv.), Del. 245/R6
Gravel Switch, Ky. 237/L5
Gravelton, Ind. 227/F2
Gravenhurst, Ontario 177/E3
Graves, Georgia 217/C7
Graves (co.), Ky. 237/D7
Gravesend, England 13/J8
Gravesend, England 10/C5
Gravette, Ark. 202/B1
Gravina (isl.), Alaska 196/N4
Gravina in Puglia, Italy 34/F4
Gravity, Iowa 229/D7
Gravois (pt.), Haiti 158/A7
Gravois Mills, Mo. 261/G6
Grawn, Mich. 250/D4
Gray, France 28/F4
Gray, Georgia 217/F4
Gray, Iowa 229/D5
Gray (co.), Kansas 232/B4
Gray, Ky. 237/O7
Gray, La. 238/J7
Gray, Maine 243/C8
Gray•, Maine 243/C8
Gray, Pa. 294/D5
Gray, Sask. 181/G5
Gray (co.), Texas 303/D2
Gray, W. 307/O7
Grayback (mt.), Oreg. 291/D5
Gray Court, S.C. 296/C2
Gray Hawk, Ky. 237/N6
Gray Horse, Okla. 288/N1
Grayland, Wash. 310/A4
Grayling, Alaska 196/G2
Grayling, Mich. 250/E4
Graymont, Ill. 222/E3
Graymoor, Ky. 237/K1
Gray Rapids, New Bruns. 170/E2
Grayridge, Mo. 261/N9
Grays, Ark. 202/H3
Grays (lake), Idaho 220/G6
Grays, S.C. 296/E6
Grays (harb.), Wash. 310/A4
Graysbranch, Ky. 237/R3
Grays Harbor (co.), Wash. 310/B3
Grayslake, Ill. 222/B4
Grays Lake Outlet (creek), Idaho 220/G6
Grays Landing, Pa. 294/C6
Grayson, Georgia 217/E3
Grayson (co.), Ky. 237/J5
Grayson, Ky. 237/R4
Grayson (lake), Ky. 237/P4
Grayson, La. 238/F2
Grayson, Mo. 261/G3
Grayson, Okla. 288/P3
Grayson, Sask. 181/J5
Grayson (co.), Texas 303/H4
Grayson (co.), Va. 307/F7
Grays River, Wash. 310/B4
Gray Summit, Mo. 261/L6
Graysville, Ala. 195/D3
Graysville, Georgia 217/B1
Graysville, Ind. 227/B6
Graysville, Manitoba 179/D5
Graysville, Ohio 284/H6
Graysville, Pa. 294/B6
Graysville, Tenn. 237/L10
Graytown, Ohio 284/D2
Grayville, Ill. 222/B4
Graz, Austria 7/F4
Graz, Austria 41/C3
Grazalema, Spain 33/D4
Greaney, Minn. 255/F3
Great (lakes) 2/E3
Great (sound), Bermuda 156/G3
Great (fall), Guyana 131/E3
Great (chan.), India 68/G7
Great (riv.), Jamaica 158/G6
Great (pond), Mass. 249/D8
Great (pt.), Mass. 249/O7
Great (bay), N.H. 268/F5
Great (bay), N.J. 273/E4
Great (isl.), N. Zealand 100/D1
Great (lake), N.C. 281/R3
Great (lake), Tasmania 99/C3
Great (pond), Virgin Is. (U.S.) 161/F4
Great Abaco (isl.), Bahamas 146/L7

Great Abaco (isl.), Bahamas 156/C1
Great Alföld (plain), Hungary 41/F3
Great Australian (bight) 88/D6
Great Australian (bight), Australia 87/C9
Great Australian (bight), S. Australia 94/A5
Great Australian (bight), W. Australia 92/E6
Great Averill (pond), Vt. 268/D2
Great Bacolet (pt.), Grenada 161/D8
Great Baddow (creek), England 13/J7
Great Bahama (bank), Bahamas 156/B1
Great Barrier (reef) 88/H2
Great Barrier (reef), Australia 95/C2
Great Barrier (reef), Australia 87/E7
Great Barrier (isl.), N. Zealand 100/E2
Great Barrington, Mass. 249/A4
Great Barrington•, Mass. 249/A4
Great Barton (cay), England 13/H5
Great Basin Nat'l Park, Nev. 266/F4
Great Bear (lake), Canada 4/C16
Great Bear (lake), N.W.T. 162/D2
Great Bear (lake), N.W.T. 146/H3
Great Bear (lake), N.W.T. 187/F3
Great Bear (riv.), N.W.T. 187/F3
Great Bend, Kansas 232/D3
Great Bend, N.Y. 276/J2
Great Bend, N. Dak. 282/S7
Great Bend, Pa. 294/L2
Great Blasket (isl.), Ireland 17/A7
Great Bras d'Or (chan.), Nova Scotia 168/H2
Great Burnt (lake), Newf. 166/C4
Great Cacapon, W. Va. 312/K3
Great Coco (isl.), Burma 72/B4
Great Colinet (isl.), Newf. 166/D2
Great Corn (isl.), Nicaragua 154/F2
Great Cornard, England 13/H5
Great Cumbrae (isl.), Scotland 15/A2
Great Dismal (swamp), N.C. 281/S1
Great Dismal (swamp), Va. 307/R8
Great Divide (basin), Wyo. 319/E3
Great Dividing (range), N. S. Wales 88/J3
Great Dividing (range), N.S. Wales 97/E3
Great Dividing (range), Queensland 88/H4
Great Dividing (range), Queensland 95/C4
Great Egg Harbor (inlet), N.J. 273/E5
Great Egg Harbor (riv.), N.J. 273/D4
Greater Antilles (isls.) 146/K7
Greater London, England 13/H8
Greater Manchester (co.), England 13/H2
Greaterville, Ariz. 198/E7
Great Exhibition (bay), N. Zealand 100/D1
Great Exuma (isl.), Bahamas 146/L7
Great Exuma (isl.), Bahamas 156/C2
Great Falls, Manitoba 179/F4
Great Falls, Mont. 188/D1
Great Falls, Mont. 146/G5
Great Falls, Mont. 262/E3
Great Falls, S.C. 296/F2
Great Falls (dam), Tenn. 237/K9
Great Fish (riv.), S. Africa 118/D6
Great Grimsby, England 10/F4
Great Grimsby, England 13/G4
Great Harwood, England 13/H1
Greathead (bay), St. Vin. & Grens. 161/A9
Great Inagua (isl.), Bahamas 146/L7
Great Inagua (isl.), Bahamas 156/D2
Great Indian (des.), India 68/C3
Great Isaac (isl.), Bahamas 156/B1
Great Kai (isl.), Indonesia 85/J7
Great Karoo (reg.), S. Africa 118/C6
Great Kei (riv.), S. Africa 118/D6
Great Khingan (range), China 54/O5
Great Lakes Nav. Trng. Ctr., Ill. 222/B4
Great Machipongo (inlet), Va. 307/S6
Great Meadows, N.J. 273/D2
Great Mercury (isl.), N. Zealand 100/F2
Great Miami (riv.), Ohio 284/A7
Great Misery (isl.), Mass. 249/F5
Great Moose (lake), Maine 243/D6
Great Namaland (reg.), Namibia 118/B4
Great Natuna (isl.), Indonesia 85/D5
Great Neck, N.Y. 276/P6
Great Nicobar (isl.), India 68/G7
Great North (mt.), Va. 307/L2
Great Ormes (head), Wales 13/C4
Great Ouse (riv.), England 13/H5
Great Ouse (riv.), England 10/G4
Great Pedro Bluff (prom.), Jamaica 158/H6
Great Pee Dee (riv.), S.C. 296/J4
Great Pond•, Maine 243/G6
Great Pond (bay), Virgin Is. (U.S.) 161/F4
Great Pubnico (lake), Nova Scotia 168/C5
Great Ruaha (riv.), Tanzania 115/G5
Great Sacandaga (lake), N.Y. 276/M4
Great Saint Bernard (pass), Italy 34/A2
Great Saint Bernard (mt.), Switzerland 39/D5
Great Saint Bernard (pass), Switzerland 39/D5
Great Saint Bernard (tunnel), Switzerland 39/D5
Great Salt (pond), St. Kitts and Nevis 161/D10
Great Salt (lake), Utah 188/D2
Great Salt (lake), Utah 146/G6
Great Salt (lake), Utah 304/B2
Great Salt Lake (des.), Nev. 266/H2
Great Salt Lake (des.), Utah 304/A3
Great Salt Plains (lake), Okla. 288/K1
Great Sand (hills), Sask. 181/B5
Great Sand Dunes Nat'l Mon., Colo. 208/H7
Great Sand Sea (des.), Egypt 111/D2
Great Sand Sea (des.), Libya 111/D2
Great Sandy (desert), Australia 87/C8

Great Sandy (Fraser) (isl.), Queensland 88/J5
Great Sandy (Fraser) (isl.), Queensland 95/K5
Great Sandy (des.), W. Australia 88/C4
Great Sandy (des.), Australia 92/C3
Great Seneca (creek), Md. 245/J4
Great Sitkin (isl.), Alaska 196/L4
Great Slave (lake), Canada 4/C15
Great Slave (lake), N.W.T. 162/D1
Great Slave (lake), N.W.T. 146/H3
Great Slave (lake), N.W. Terr. 187/G3
Great Slave Lake Highway, N.W. Terr. 187/G3
Great Smoky (mts.), N.C. 281/B3
Great Smoky (mts.), Tenn. 237/P9
Great Smoky Mountains Nat'l Park, Tenn. 237/P9
Great Smoky Mts. Nat'l Park, N.C. 281/B3
Great South (bay), N.Y. 276/O9
Great South (beach), N.Y. 276/O9
Great Tenasserim (riv.), Burma 72/C4
Great Thatch (isl.), Virgin Is. (U.K.) 161/C4
Great Tobago (isl.), Virgin Is. (U.K.) 161/B3
Great Torrington, England 10/D5
Great Torrington, England 13/C7
Great Valley, N.Y. 276/C6
Great Victoria (desert), Australia 87/C8
Great Victoria (des.), S. Australia 94/B3
Great Victoria (des.), W. Australia 92/D5
Great Village, Nova Scotia 168/E3
Great Wall (ruins), China 54/N5
Great Wall (ruins), China 77/G4,J3
Great Wass (isl.), Maine 243/J7
Great Western Tiers (mts.), Tasmania 99/C3
Great Yarmouth, England 13/J5
Great Yarmouth, England 10/G4
Great Zab (riv.), Iraq 66/C2
Grecco, Uruguay 145/B3
Grecia, C. Rica 154/E5
Greco (cape), Cyprus 63/F5
Gredos, Sierra de (range), Spain 33/D2
Greece 2/L4
Greece 7/G5
GREECE 45/F6
Greece, N.Y. 276/E4
Greeley, Colo. 188/F2
Greeley, Colo. 208/K2
Greeley, Iowa 229/L3
Greeley (co.), Kansas 232/A3
Greeley, Kansas 232/G3
Greeley (co.), Nebr. 264/F3
Greeley, Nebr. 264/F3
Greeley, Pa. 294/N3
Greeley (creek), Utah 304/B3
Greeleyville, S.C. 296/H4
Greely (fjord), N.W. Terr. 187/K1
Greely, Ontario 177/J2
Green (bay) 188/J1
Green (riv.) 188/D3
Green (isl.), Ant. & Bar. 161/E11
Green (riv.), Colo. 208/A2
Green (isl.), Grenada 161/D8
Green (riv.), Ill. 222/D2
Green (isl.), Maine 243/F8
Green (riv.), Mass. 249/B2
Green, Mich. 250/B4
Green (bay), Mich. 250/B4
Green (lake), Minn. 255/D5
Green (riv.), New Bruns. 170/B1
Green (cape), N.S. Wales 97/F5
Green (swamp), N.C. 281/N6
Green (riv.), N. Dak. 282/D5
Green (pt.), Nova Scotia 168/C5
Green (isl.), Ontario 177/A2
Green, Oreg. 291/D4
Green (isls.), Papua N.G. 86/C2
Green (lake), Sask. 181/D1
Green (riv.), Tenn. 237/F10
Green (riv.), U.S. 146/H6
Green (riv.), Utah 304/D4
Green (mts.), Vt. 268/B4
Green (cay), Virgin Is. (U.S.) 161/F4
Green (lake), Wash. 310/A2
Green (riv.), Wash. 310/D3
Green (co.), Wis. 317/G10
Green (bay), Wis. 317/L6
Green (riv.), Wyo. 319/E3
Green (riv.), Wyo. 319/C4
Greenacres, Calif. 204/F8
Green Acres, Ark. 181/F2
Greenacres, Wash. 310/J3
Greenacres City, Fla. 212/F5
Greenan, Sask. 181/F3
Greenback, Tenn. 237/N9
Greenbackville, W. Va. 307/T5
Green Bank, N.J. 273/D4
Greenbank, Wash. 310/C2
Green Bank, W. Va. 312/G6
Green Bay, N. Zealand 100/B1
Green Bay, Va. 307/M6
Green Bay, Wis. 188/J2
Green Bay, Wis. 146/J5
Green Bay, Wis. 317/K6
Greenbelt, Md. 245/G4
Greenbelt Park, Md. 245/G4
Green Boulder•, St. Kitts and Nevis 161/D10
Greenbrier, Ala. 195/E1
Greenbrier, Ark. 202/F3
Greenbrier, Mo. 261/M8
Greenbrier, Tenn. 237/H8
Greenbrier (co.), W. Va. 312/F7
Greenbrier, W. Va. 312/F6
Green Brook, N.J. 273/D2
Greenbush, Mass. 249/F8
Greenbush, Mich. 250/F4
Greenbush, Minn. 255/B2
Greenbush, Va. 307/S5
Green Camp, Ohio 284/D4
Greencastle, Ind. 227/D5
Greencastle, Ireland 17/H1

Green Castle, Mo. 261/G2
Greencastle, Pa. 294/G6
Green Center, Ind. 227/G2
Green City, Mo. 261/H2
Green Court, Alberta 182/C2
Green Cove Springs, Fla. 212/E2
Greencreek, Idaho 220/B3
Green Creek, N.J. 273/D5
Greendale, Ind. 227/H6
Greendale, Wis. 317/L2
Greendell, N.J. 273/D2
Greene (co.), Ala. 195/C5
Greene (co.), Ark. 202/J1
Greene (co.), Georgia 217/F3
Greene (co.), Ill. 222/C4
Greene (co.), Ind. 227/D6
Greene (co.), Iowa 229/E5
Greene, Iowa 229/H3
Greene•, Maine 243/C7
Greene (co.), Miss. 256/G7
Greene (co.), Mo. 261/F8
Greene (co.), N.Y. 276/M6
Greene, N.Y. 276/J6
Greene (co.), N.C. 281/O3
Greene, N. Dak. 282/G2
Greene (co.), Ohio 284/C6
Greene (co.), Pa. 294/B6
Greene, R.I. 249/G6
Greene (co.), Tenn. 237/R8
Greene (co.), Va. 307/M4
Greenevers, N.C. 281/O5
Greeneville, Tenn. 237/R8
Greenfield (calif. 204/D7
Greenfield, Ill. 222/C4
Greenfield, Ind. 227/F5
Greenfield, Iowa 229/D6
Greenfield, Mass. 249/C2
Greenfield•, Mass. 249/D2
Greenfield•, N.H. 268/D6
Greenfield, Nova Scotia 168/D4
Greenfield, Ohio 284/D7
Greenfield, Okla. 288/K3
Greenfield, S. Dak. 298/F4
Greenfield, Tenn. 237/F8
Greenfield, Wis. 317/L2
Greenfield Hill, Conn. 210/B4
Greenfield Park, Québec 172/J4
Greenford, Ohio 284/J4
Green Forest, Ark. 202/D1
Green Hall, Ky. 237/O6
Green Harbor, Mass. 249/M4
Green Haven, Md. 245/M4
Greenhills, Ohio 284/B9
Greenhorn, Oreg. 291/J3
Green Island, Iowa 229/N4
Green Island, Jamaica 158/G6
Green Island, N.Y. 276/N6
Green Island, N. Zealand 100/C7
Greenisland, N. Ireland 17/K2
Green Island (bay), Philippines 82/B5
Green Island Cove, Newf. 166/C3
Green Isle, Minn. 255/E6
Green Lake, Maine 243/F6
Green Lake, Sask. 181/L4
Green Lake, Wis. 317/H8
Green Lake, Wis. 317/J7
Greenland 2/G2
Greenland 4/B12
Greenland 146/P2
Greenland (sea) 146/T2
Greenland (sea) 4/B10
Greenland, Ark. 202/B1
Greenland, Barbados 161/B8
Greenland, Colo. 208/K4
Greenland, Mich. 250/G1
Greenland•, N.H. 268/F5
Greenlaw, Scotland 15/F5
Greenleaf, Idaho 220/B6
Greenleaf, Kansas 232/E2
Greenleaf, Minn. 255/D6
Greenleaf, Oreg. 291/D3
Greenleaf, Wis. 317/K1
Greenleafton, Minn. 255/F7
Greenlee (co.), Ariz. 198/F5
Green Lowther (mt.), Scotland 15/E5
Greenmanville, Conn. 210/D4
Greenmount, Ky. 237/N6
Greenmount, Md. 245/L2
Green Mountain (res.), Colo. 208/G3
Green Mountain, Iowa 229/H4
Green Mountain, N.C. 281/E3
Green Mountain Falls, Colo. 208/K5
Green Oaks, Ill. 222/B4
Greenock, Scotland 10/A1
Greenock, Scotland 15/A2
Greenore, Ireland 17/J4
Greenore (pt.), Ireland 17/J7
Green Peter (lake), Oreg. 291/E3
Green Pond, Ala. 195/D4
Green Pond, N.J. 273/E1
Green Pond, S.C. 296/F6
Greenport, N.Y. 276/P8
Green Ridge (mts.), Md. 245/E2
Green Ridge, Mo. 261/F5
Green River (lake), Ky. 237/L6
Green River, Utah 304/D4
Green River (res.), Vt. 268/B2
Green River, Wyo. 188/E2
Green River, Wyo. 319/D3
Green River (mt.), Wyo. 319/C2
Green Rock, Ill. 222/C2
Greens (peak), Ariz. 198/F4
Greensboro, Ala. 195/C5
Greensboro, Fla. 212/B1
Greensboro, Georgia 217/F3
Greensboro, Ind. 227/G5
Greensboro, Md. 245/P5
Greensboro, N.C. 146/K3
Greensboro, N.C. 188/K3
Greensboro, N.C. 281/K2
Greensboro, Pa. 294/B6
Greensboro•, Vt. 268/C2
Greensburg, Ind. 227/G6
Greensburg, Kansas 232/C4

Greensburg, Ky. 237/K6
Greensburg, La. 238/J5
Greensburg, Mo. 261/H2
Greensburg, Ohio 284/G4
Greensburg, Pa. 294/D5
Green Sea, La. 212/J2
Green Sea, S.C. 296/J3
Greens Farms, Conn. 210/B4
Greens Fork, Ind. 227/H5
Green's Harbour, Newf. 166/D2
Greenshields, Alberta 182/E3
Greenslopes, Queensland 88/K3
Greenslopes, Queensland 95/E3
Greenspond, Newf. 166/D4
Green Springs, Ohio 284/E3
Greenstone (pt.), Scotland 15/C3
Greenstreet, Sask. 181/A2
Green Sulphur Springs, W. Va. 312/E7
Greensville (co.), Va. 307/N7
Greentop, Mo. 261/H2
Greentown•, Ind. 227/E4
Greentown, Ohio 284/H4
Greentree, Pa. 294/B7
Greenup, Ill. 222/E4
Greenup (co.), Ky. 237/R3
Greenup, Ky. 237/R3
Greenvale, Queensland 95/C3
Green Valley, Ariz. 198/D7
Green Valley, Ill. 222/D3
Green Valley, Minn. 255/C6
Green Valley, Ontario 177/K2
Green Valley, Wis. 317/K6
Greenview, Calif. 204/B2
Greenview, Ill. 222/D3
Greenview, W. Va. 312/C6
Green Village, N.J. 273/D2
Greenville, Ala. 195/E7
Greenville, Calif. 204/E3
Greenville, Del. 245/R1
Greenville, Fla. 212/C1
Greenville, Georgia 217/C4
Greenville, Ill. 222/D5
Greenville, Ind. 227/F8
Greenville, Iowa 229/C3
Greenville, Ky. 237/G6
Greenville, Liberia 106/C8
Greenville, Maine 243/D5
Greenville•, Maine 243/D5
Greenville, Mich. 250/D5
Greenville, Miss. 188/H4
Greenville, Miss. 256/B4
Greenville, Mo. 261/M8
Greenville, N.H. 268/D6
Greenville•, N.H. 268/D6
Greenville, N.C. 281/P3
Greenville, Ohio 284/A5
Greenville, Pa. 294/B3
Greenville, R.I. 249/H5
Greenville, S.C. 146/K6
Greenville, S.C. 188/K4
Greenville (co.), S.C. 296/C2
Greenville, S.C. 296/C2
Greenville, Texas 188/G4
Greenville, Texas 303/H4
Greenville, Utah 304/B5
Greenville, Va. 307/K5
Greenville, W. Va. 312/E7
Greenville, Wis. 317/J7
Greenville Junction, Maine 243/D5
Greenwald, Minn. 255/D5
Greenwater Lake, Sask. 181/H3
Greenwater Lake Prov. Park, Sask. 181/H3
Greenway, Ark. 202/K1
Greenway, Manitoba 179/C5
Greenway, S. Dak. 298/K2
Greenwell Springs, La. 238/K1
Greenwich•, Conn. 210/A4
Greenwich (pt.), Conn. 210/A4
Greenwich, England 13/H8
Greenwich, England 10/B5
Greenwich (Kapingamarangi) (atoll), Micronesia 87/F5
Greenwich•, N.J. 273/C5
Greenwich, N.Y. 276/O4
Greenwich, Ohio 284/E3
Greenwich, Utah 304/B5
Greenwood, Br. Col. 184/H5
Greenwood, Calif. 204/K5
Greenwood, Del. 245/R5
Greenwood, Fla. 212/A1
Greenwood, Ind. 227/E5
Greenwood (co.), Kansas 232/F4
Greenwood, Ky. 237/N7
Greenwood, La. 238/B2
Greenwood, Mass. 249/D6
Greenwood (lake), Minn. 255/G3
Greenwood, Miss. 256/D4
Greenwood, Mo. 261/R6
Greenwood, Nebr. 264/H3
Greenwood, N.J. 273/E1
Greenwood, N.Y. 276/E6
Greenwood (lake), N.Y. 276/M8
Greenwood, S.C. 188/K4
Greenwood (co.), S.C. 296/C3
Greenwood, S.C. 296/C3
Greenwood (lake), S.C. 296/D3
Greenwood, S. Dak. 298/N8
Greenwood, Va. 307/L4
Greenwood, W. Va. 312/E4
Greenwood, Wis. 317/E6
Greenwood, Wis. 276/M8
Greenwood Springs, Miss. 256/H3
Greer, Ariz. 198/F4
Greer, Idaho 220/B3
Greer, Mo. 261/K9
Greer, Ohio 284/E3
Greer (co.), Okla. 288/G5
Greer, S.C. 296/C2
Greers Ferry, Ark. 202/F2
Greers Ferry (lake), Ark. 202/G2
Greeson (lake), Ark. 202/C5
Gregg (co.), Texas 303/K5
Gregory, Ark. 202/H3
Gregory, Mich. 250/E6
Greggs, Georgia 217/F8
Gregory (range), Queensland 95/B3

egory (riv.), Queensland 88/F3
egory (riv.), Queensland 95/A3
egory (lake), S. Australia 88/F5
egory (lake), S. Australia 94/F3
egory (co.), S. Dak. 298/L7
egory, S. Dak. 298/L7
egory (lake), W. Australia 92/C4
egory Landing, Mo. 261/K2
egory's (sound), Ireland 17/B5
eian (head), Scotland 15/A3
eifensee (lake), Switzerland 39/G2
eifswald, Germany 22/E1
ein, Austria 41/C2
eina (pass), Switzerland 39/G3
eiz, Germany 22/E3
elton, Ohio 284/C3
emikha, U.S.S.R. 52/E1
emyachinsk, U.S.S.R. 52/J3
enå, Denmark 21/D5
enå, Denmark 18/G8
enada 2/F5
enada 146/M8
RENADA 161/D9
RENADA 156/G4
enada, Calif. 204/C2
enada (isl.), Grenada 156/G4
enada (co.), Miss. 256/E3
enada, Miss. 256/E3
enada (lake), Miss. 256/E3
enada-Tobago (passage), Grenada 156/G5
enadier (isl.), N.Y. 276/H2
enadines (isls.), Grenada 156/G4
enadines (isls.), St. Vin. & Grens. 156/G4
enchen, Switzerland 39/D2
enfell, N.S. Wales 97/F3
enfell, Sask. 181/J5
enloch, N.J. 273/C4
enoble, France 7/E4
enoble, France 28/F5
enola, Kansas 232/F4
enora, N. Dak. 282/F5
enville (chan.), Br. Col. 184/C3
enville, Grenada 161/D8
enville, N. Mex. 274/F2
enville (county), Ontario 177/J3
enville, Québec 172/C4
enville (cape), Queensland 88/G2
enville (cape), Queensland 95/B1
enville, S. Dak. 298/D3
enville (pt.), Wash. 310/A3
esham, Nebr. 264/G3
esham, Oreg. 291/B2
esham, S.C. 296/J4
esham, Wis. 317/J6
eeshamville, Georgia 217/F3
esik, Indonesia 85/K2
esston, Georgia 217/F6
eta-Branxton, N.S. Wales 97/F3
eta East, N.S. Wales 97/F3
etna, Fla. 212/B1
etna, La. 238/C4
etna, Manitoba 179/E5
etna, Nebr. 264/H3
etna, Scotland 10/E3
etna, Scotland 15/E5
etna, Tasmania 99/D4
etna, Va. 307/K7
revelingen (str.), Netherlands 27/E5
even, Germany 22/B2
evená, Greece 45/E5
evenbroich, Germany 22/B3
evenmacher, Luxembourg 27/J9
evesmühlen, Germany 22/D2
eville (bay), Nova Scotia 168/D3
ey (isls.), Newf. 166/C3
ey (riv.), N. Zealand 100/C5
ey (cape), North. Terr. 88/F2
ey (cape), North. Terr. 93/F2
ey (county), Ontario 177/D3
ey (range), Queensland 88/G5
ey (range), Queensland 95/B5
rey Abbey, N. Ireland 17/K2
reybull, Wyo. 319/E1
reybull (riv.), Wyo. 319/D1
reycliff, Mont. 262/G5
rey Eagle, Minn. 255/D5
rey Forest, Texas 303/J10
rey Islands, Newf. 166/C3
reylock (mt.), Idaho 220/C6
reylock (mt.), Mass. 249/B2
reymouth, N. Zealand 100/C4
reymouth, N. Zealand 87/G10
rey River, Newf. 166/C4
reys (riv.), Wyo. 319/B3
reystone, Colo. 208/B7
reystone, Conn. 210/C2
reystone Park, N.J. 273/D2
reystones-Delgany, Ireland 10/D4
reystones-Delgany, Ireland 17/K5
reytown, N. Zealand 100/E4
reytown (San Juan del Norte), Nicaragua 154/F5
reytown, S. Africa 118/E5
rez-Doiceau, Belgium 27/F7
ribbles Settlement, North. Terr. 93/B1
ridley, Calif. 204/D4
ridley (mt.), Conn. 210/B1
ridley, Ill. 222/E3
ridley, Kansas 232/G3
ridone (mt.), Switzerland 39/G4
riend (isl.), Netherlands 27/G2
rier, N. Mex. 274/F7
ries am Brenner, Austria 41/A3
riesham, Germany 22/C4
riesheim, Germany 22/C3
rieskirchen, Austria 41/B2
riffin, Georgia 217/D4
riffin, Ind. 227/B8
riffin, Sask. 181/H6
riffith A.F.B., N.Y. 276/K4
riffith, Ind. 227/C1
riffith, N.S. Wales 88/H6
riffith, N.S. Wales 97/C4
riffith (isl.), Ontario 177/D3
riffithsville, W. Va. 312/B6

Griffithville, Ark. 202/G3
Grifton, N.C. 281/P4
Griggs (lake), N. Dak. 282/O5
Griggs, Okla. 288/B1
Griggsville, Ill. 222/C4
Grigston, Kansas 232/B3
Grijalva (riv.), Mexico 150/N7
Grim (cape), Tasmania 99/A2
Grimari, Cent. Afr. Rep. 115/C2
Grimbergen, Belgium 27/E7
Grimes, Ala. 195/H8
Grimes, Calif. 204/C
Grimes, Iowa 229/FE
Grimes, Okla. 288/G
Grimes (co.), Texas 303/J7
Grimesland, N.C. 28 /P3
Griminish, Scotland 15/A3
Grimma, Germany 22/E3
Grimmen, Germany 22/E1
Grimms Landing, W. Va. 312/B5
Grimsby, Ontario 177/F4
Grimsel (pass), Switzerland 39/F3
Grímsey (isl.), Iceland 21/C1
Grimstad, Norway 1 /F7
Grindelwald, Switzerland 39/E3
Grindrod, Br. Col. 184/H5
Grindsted, Denmark 21/B6
Grindstone, Maine 243/F4
Grindstone (isl.), New Bruns. 170/F3
Grindstone (lake), Wis. 317/C4
Grind Stone City, Mich. 250/G4
Grindstone Prov. Rec. Park, Manitoba 179/F3
Grinnell, Iowa 229/H 5
Grinnell, Kansas 232/B2
Grinnell (pen.), N.W. Terr. 187/J2
Grippon, Guadeloupe 161/B6
Griqualand West (reg.), S. Africa 118/C5
Griquatown, S. Africa 118/C5
Grise Fiord, Canada 4/B13
Grise Fiord, N.W.T. 162/H1
Grise Fiord, N.W. Terr. 187/K2
Gris-Nez (cape), France 28/D2
Grisons (Graubünden) (elec. div.), Switzerland 39/H3
Grissom A.F.B., Ind. 227/E3
Griswold, Iowa 229/C6
Griswold, Manitoba 179/B5
Griswoldville, Mass. 249/C2
Grïva, U.S.S.R. 53/D3
Grizzly (bay), Calif. 204/K1
Grizzly Flats, Calif. 204/E5
Groais (isl.), Newf. 166/C3
Grobiņa, U.S.S.R. 53/A2
Grodno, U.S.S.R. 7/G3
Grodno, U.S.S.R. 43/C4
Grodno, U.S.S.R. 52/B4
Grodzisk Mazowiecki, Poland 47/E2
Grodzisk Wielkopolski, Poland 47/C2
Groenlo, Netherlands 27/K4
Groesbeck, Ohio 284/B9
Groesbeck, Texas 303/H6
Groesbeek, Netherlands 27/H5
Groix (isl.), France 28/B4
Grójec, Poland 47/E3
Grömitz, Germany 22/D1
Gronau, Germany 22/B2
Grondines, Québec 172/E3
Grong, Norway 18/H4
Grong Grong, N.S. Wales 97/D4
Groningen, Minn. 255/E4
Groningen (prov.), Netherlands 27/K2
Groningen, Netherlands 27/K4
Groningen, Netherlands 27/K2
Groningen, Suriname 131/D2
Groninger Wad (sound), Netherlands 27/J2
Gronlid, Sask. 181/G2
Grono, Switzerland 39/H4
Groom, Texas 303/C2
Groomsport, N. Ireland 17/K2
Groot-Drakenstein, S. Africa 118/F6
Groote (isl.), North. Terr. 88/F2
Groote (riv.), S. Africa 118/C6
Groote Eylandt (isl.), Australia 87/D7
Groote Eylandt (isl.), North. Terr. 93/E3
Groote IJ Polder, Netherlands 27/B4
Grootfontein, Namibia 118/B3
Groot Sint Joris, Neth. Ant. 161/G9
Gros (pt.), Grenada 161/C8
Gros Islet, St. Lucia 161/G5
Gros Islet (bay), St. Lucia 161/G5
Grosmont (Island Lake), Alberta 182/D2
Gros Morne, Haiti 158/B5
Gros-Morne, Martinique 161/D6
Gros Morne (mt.), Newf. 166/C4
Gros-Morne, Québec 172/C1
Gros Morne Nat'l Park, Newf. 166/C4
Gros Piton (mt.), St. Lucia 161/G6
Gross, Nebr. 264/E2
Grosse Ile, Mich. 250/B7
Grosse Isle, Manitoba 179/E4
Gross Emme (riv.), Switzerland 39/E3
Grossenbrode, Germany 22/D1
Grossenhain, Germany 22/E3
Grosse Pointe, Mich. 250/B7
Grosse Pointe Farms, Mich. 250/B6
Grosse Pointe Park, Mich. 250/B6
Grosse Pointe Shores, Mich. 250/B6
Grosse Pointe Woods, Mich. 250/B6
Grosser Arber (mt.), Germany 22/E4
Grosser Peilstein (mt.), Austria 41/C2
Grosses Coques, Nova Scotia 168/B4
Grosses-Roches, Québec 172/B1
Grosse Tete, La. 238/G6
Grosseto (prov.), Italy 34/C3
Grosseto, Italy 34/C3
Grossglockner (mt.), Austria 41/B3
Gross Litzner (mt.), Switzerland 39/K3
Grossräschen, Germany 22/E3
Grosssieghart s, Austria 41/C2
Grosswangen, Switzerland 39/F2
Grosvenor Dale, Conn. 210/H1
Gros Ventre (riv.), Wyo. 319/B2
Groswater (bay), Newf. 166/C3
Groton, Conn. 210/G3
Groton •, Conn. 210/G3
Groton, Mass. 249/H2

Groton •, Mass. 249/H2
Groton •, N.H. 268/D4
Groton, N.Y. 276/H5
Groton, S. Dak. 298/N3
Groton •, Vt. 268/C3
Groton (lake), Vt. 268/C3
Groton Long (pt.), Conn. 210/H3
Groton Long Point, Conn. 210/H3
Grottaferrata, Italy 34/F7
Grottaglie, Italy 34/F4
Grotto, Wash. 310/D3
Grottoes, Va. 307/L4
Grouard, Alberta 182/B2
Grouard Mission, Alberta 182/C2
Grouard Mission, Alta. 162/E4
Groundhog (riv.), Ontario 175/D3
Grouse (Lost River), Idaho 220/E6
Grouse (mt.), N. Mex. 274/A5
Grouse (creek), Utah 304/A2
Grouse Creek, Utah 304/A2
Grouse Creek (mts.), Utah 304/A2
Grouw, Netherlands 27/H2
Grovania, Georgia 217/E6
Grove, Maine 243/J5
Grove (lake), N. Dak. 282/L5
Grove, Okla. 288/S1
Grove Beach, Conn. 210/E3
Grove Center, Ky. 237/F5
Grove City, Fla. 212/D5
Grove City, Minn. 255/D5
Grove City, Ohio 284/D6
Grove City, Pa. 294/B3
Grovedale, Alberta 182/A2
Grove Hill, Ala. 195/C7
Groveland, Calif. 204/E6
Groveland, Fla. 212/E3
Groveland, Georgia 217/J6
Groveland, Ind. 227/D2
Groveland •, Mass. 249/L1
Groveland, N.Y. 276/E5
Groveoak, Ala. 195/F2
Grove Place, Virgin Is. (U.S.) 161/E4
Groveport, Ohio 284/E6
Grover, Colo. 208/H1
Grover, Mo. 261/M3
Grover, N.C. 281/E4
Grover, Pa. 294/J2
Grover, S.C. 296/F5
Grover, S. Dak. 298/P4
Grover, Utah 304/C5
Grover, Wyo. 319/B3
Grover City, Calif. 204/E8
Grover Hill, Ohio 284/B3
Grovertown, Ind. 227/D2
Groves, Texas 303/L8
Grovespring, Mo. 261/G8
Groveton, N.H. 268/D2
Groveton, Texas 303/J7
Groveton, Va. 307/T3
Grovetown, Georgia 217/H4
Groveville, N.J. 273/C3
Growler (mts.), Ariz. 198/B6
Groznyy, U.S.S.R. 7/J4
Groznyy, U.S.S.R. 48/E5
Groznyy, U.S.S.R. 52/G6
Grubbs, Ark. 202/H2
Grubišno Polje, Yugoslavia 45/C3
Grudovo, Bulgaria 45/H4
Grudziądz, Poland 47/D2
Gruenthal, Sask. 181/E3
Gruetli, Tenn. 237/K10
Gruinard (bay), Scotland 15/C3
Grulla, Texas 303/F11
Grünberg (Zielona Góra), Poland 47/B3
Grünburg, Austria 41/C3
Grundy (co.), Ill. 222/E2
Grundy (co.), Iowa 229/H4
Grundy (co.), Mo. 261/E2
Grundy (co.), Tenn. 237/K10
Grundy, Va. 307/O6
Grundy Center, Iowa 229/H4
Grunthal, Manitoba 179/F5
Gruver, Iowa 229/D2
Gruver, Texas 303/C1
Gruyères, Switzerland 39/D4
Gryazi, U.S.S.R. 52/F4
Gryazovets, U.S.S.R. 52/F3
Gryfice, Poland 47/B2
Gryfino, Poland 47/B2
Gryla, Minn. 255/C2
Gryon, Switzerland 39/D4
Grytviken, South Georgia I. 5/D17
Gstaad, Switzerland 39/D4
Gsteig, Switzerland 39/D4
Guacamaya, Colombia 126/C6
Guacamayo, Colombia 126/F6
Guacanayabo (gulf), Cuba 156/C2
Guacanayabo (gulf), Cuba 158/G4
Guacara, Venezuela 124/D2
Guachara, Venezuela 124/D4
Gu Achi, Ariz. 198/C6
Guácimo, C. Rica 154/F5
Guacuí, Brazil 135/F2
Guadalajara, Mexico 2/D5
Guadalajara, Mexico 150/H6
Guadalajara, Mexico 146/H7
Guadalajara (prov.), Spain 33/E2
Guadalajara, Spain 33/E2
Guadalcanal (isl.), Solomon Is. 87/F7
Guadalcanal (isl.), Solomon Is. 86/D3
Guadalcanal, Spain 33/D3
Guadalimar (riv.), Spain 33/E3
Guadaloupe (isl.), Mexico 146/G7
Guadalquivir (riv.), Spain 7/D5
Guadalquivir (riv.), Spain 33/C4
Guadalupe, Potosí, Bolivia 136/B7
Guadalupe, Santa Cruz, Bolivia 136/C6
Guadalupe, Calif. 204/E9
Guadalupe, Calif. 204/C8
Guadalupe, Nuevo León, Mexico 150/K4
Guadalupe, Zacatecas, Mexico 150/H5
Guadalupe (co.), N. Mex. 274/E4
Guadalupe (mts.), N. Mex. 274/D6
Guadalupe, Peru 128/E9
Guadalupe, Spain 33/D3

Guadalupe, Sierra de (range), Spain 33/D3
Guadalupe (co.), Texas 303/G8
Guadalupe (mts.), Texas 303/C10
Guadalupe (peak), Texas 303/B10
Guadalupe (riv.), Texas 303/G8
Guadalupe Bravo, Mexico 150/F1
Guadalupe Mts. Nat'l Park, Texas 303/C10
Guadalupe Victoria, Durango, Mexico 150/H4
Guadalupe Victoria, Puebla, Mexico 150/O1
Guadalupe y Calvo, Mexico 150/F3
Guadalupita, N. Mex. 274/D2
Guadarrama, Sierra de (range), Spain 33/E2
Guadarrama (riv.), Spain 33/F4
Guadarrama, Venezuela 124/D3
Guadeloupe (isl.) 146/M8
GUADELOUPE 161/A5
GUADELOUPE 156/F3
Guadeloupe (isl.), Guadeloupe 161/B6
Guadeloupe (isl.), Guadeloupe 156/F3
Guadeloupe (passage), Guadeloupe 161/A5
Guadeloupe Natural Park, Guadeloupe 161/A6
Guadiana (riv.) 7/D5
Guadiana (riv.), Portugal 33/C4
Guadiana (riv.), Spain 33/D3
Guadix, Spain 33/E4
Guafo (gulf), Chile 138/D5
Guafo (isl.), Chile 138/D5
Guage, Ky. 237/P5
Guaicanamar, Cuba 158/E2
Guaico, Trin. & Tob. 161/B10
Guaimaca, Honduras 154/D3
Guáimaro, Cuba 158/G3
Guaina, Venezuela 124/G5
Guainía (riv.) 120/C2
Guainía (comm.), Colombia 126/F6
Guainía (riv.), Colombia 126/F6
Guainía (riv.), Venezuela 124/E6
Guaira, Paraguay 144/D4
Guairá (falls), Paraguay 144/E4
Guaitecas (isls.), Chile 138/D5
Guajaba (cay), Cuba 158/G3
Guajará-Mirim, Brazil 132/H10
Guajará-Mirim, Brazil 120/C4
Guajataca (lake), P. Rico 161/B1
Guajira (pen.) 120/C2
Guajira, La (dept.), Colombia 126/D2
Guajira (pen.), Colombia 126/E1
Gualaca, Panama 154/F6
Gualaceo, Ecuador 128/C4
Gualala, Calif. 204/B5
Gualán, Guatemala 154/C3
Gualaquiza, Ecuador 128/C4
Guale, Ecuador 128/B3
Gualeguay, Argentina 143/G6
Gualeguay (riv.), Argentina 143/G5
Gualeguaychú, Argentina 143/G6
Gualpatanta, Honduras 154/E3
Guam (isl.) 87/E4
GUAM 86/K7
Guam (isl.), U.S. 2/S5
Guamal, Magdalena, Colombia 126/C3
Guamal, Meta, Colombia 126/D5
Guamblin (isl.), Chile 138/D5
Guamo, Cuba 158/H3
Guamote, Ecuador 128/C4
Guampí, Sierra de (mts.), Venezuela 124/F4
Guamúchil, Mexico 150/E4
Guana, Venezuela 124/D3
Guanabacoa, Cuba 158/C1
Guanabacoa, Cuba 158/D1
Guanabara (bay), Brazil 135/E3
Guanacevi, Mexico 150/G4
Guanahacabibes (gulf), Cuba 158/A2
Guanahacabibes (pen.), Cuba 158/A2
Guanaja, Honduras 154/E2
Guanaja (isl.), Honduras 154/E2
Guanajay, Cuba 158/B1
Guanajay, Cuba 156/G2
Guanajibo (pt.), P. Rico 161/A2
Guanajibo (riv.), P. Rico 161/A2
Guanajuato (state), Mexico 150/H6
Guanajuato, Mexico 150/J6
Guanambi, Brazil 135/F4
Guañape (isls.), Peru 128/C7
Guanare, Venezuela 124/D3
Guanare (riv.), Venezuela 124/D3
Guanare Viejo (riv.), Venezuela 124/D3
Guanarito, Venezuela 124/D3
Guandacol, Argentina 143/C2
Guane, Cuba 158/A2
Guane, Cuba 156/A2
Guangdong (Kwangtung), China 77/H7
Guangnam, China 77/G7
Guangshan, China 77/H6
Guangxi Zhuangzu (Kwangsi Chuang Aut. Reg.), China 77/G7
Guangyuan, China 77/G5
Guangze, China 77/J6
Guangzhou, China 77/H7
Guangzhou, China 54/N7
Guánica, P. Rico 161/B3
Guánica, P. Rico 156/F1
Guánica (lake), P. Rico 161/B3
Guanipa (riv.), Venezuela 124/G3
Guaniquilla (pt.), P. Rico 161/A2
Guano, Ecuador 128/C3
Guano (creek), Oreg. 291/H5
Guano (lake), Oreg. 291/H5
Guanoco, Venezuela 124/G2
Guanta, Venezuela 124/F2
Guantánamo (prov.), Cuba 158/K4
Guantánamo, Cuba 156/L7
Guantánamo, Cuba 158/K4
Guantánamo (bay), Cuba 158/J4
Guantánamo (bay), Cuba 156/C3
Guantánamo Bay U.S. Nav. Reserve, Cuba 158/K4
Guan Xian, China 77/F5
Guape, Colombia 126/D6

Guapí, Colombia 126/B6
Guapi (bay), Colombia 126/A6
Guápiles, C. Rica 154/F5
Guapo (bay), Trin. & Tob. 161/A11
Guaporé (riv.) 120/C4
Guaporé (riv.), Bolivia 136/C3
Guaporé, Brazil 132/H10
Guaqui, Bolivia 136/A5
Guaramabaré, Paraguay 144/B5
Guaranda, Ecuador 128/C3
Guarapuava, Brazil 132/C9
Guaratinguetá, Brazil 135/D3
Guaratinguetá, Brazil 132/E8
Guarda (dist.), Portugal 33/C2
Guarda, Portugal 33/C2
Guardamar, Sierra de (range), Spain 33/E2
Guardatinajas, Venezuela 124/E3
Guardiagrele, Italy 34/E3
Guardia Mitre, Argentina 143/D5
Guardian (bank), C. Rica 154/D6
Guardian, W. Va. 312/B5
Guareña, Spain 33/C3
Guarenésia, Brazil 135/C2
Guarero, Venezuela 124/B2
Guárico (pt.), Cuba 158/K3
Guárico (state), Venezuela 124/E3
Guarico, Venezuela 124/D3
Guárico (res.), Venezuela 124/E3
Guárico (riv.), Venezuela 124/E3
Guariquén, Venezuela 124/G2
Guarita, Honduras 154/C3
Guaro, Cuba 158/J3
Guarujá, Brazil 135/C4
Guarulhos, Brazil 135/C3
Guasave, Mexico 150/E4
Guasdualito, Venezuela 124/C4
Guasimal, Cuba 158/E2
Guasimal, Venezuela 124/D4
Guasipati, Venezuela 124/H4
Guastalla, Italy 34/C2
Guatemala 2/D5
Guatemala 146/J8
Guatemala (cap.), Guat. 146/J8
GUATEMALA 154/B3
Guatemala (cap.), Guatemala 154/B3
Guateque, Colombia 126/D5
Guatuaro (pt.), Trin. & Tob. 161/B11
Guaviare (comm.), Colombia 126/D6
Guaviare (riv.), Colombia 120/C2
Guaviare (riv.), Colombia 126/F6
Guaxupé, Brazil 135/C2
Guayabal, Cuba 158/G3
Guayabal (lake), P. Rico 161/C2
Guayabal, Amazonas, Venezuela 124/E6
Guayabal, Guárico, Venezuela 124/E3
Guayabero (riv.), Colombia 126/D6
Guayacán, Chile 138/A8
Guayaguayare, Trin. & Tob. 161/B11
Guayama, P. Rico 161/E3
Guayama, P. Rico 156/G1
Guayaneco (arch.), Chile 138/D7
Guayanés (pt.), P. Rico 161/E3
Guayanés (riv.), P. Rico 161/E2
Guayanilla, P. Rico 161/B3
Guayanilla, P. Rico 156/F1
Guayanilla (bay), P. Rico 161/B3
Guayape, Honduras 154/D3
Guayapo, Serranía (mts.), Venezuela 124/E5
Guayaquil, Ecuador 2/E6
Guayaquil, Ecuador 128/B4
Guayaquil, Ecuador 120/A3
Guayaquil (gulf), Ecuador 120/A3
Guayaquil (gulf), Ecuador 128/B4
Guayaquilaró (riv.), Argentina 143/G4
Guayaramerín, Bolivia 136/C2
Guayas (prov.), Ecuador 128/B4
Guayas (riv.), Ecuador 128/C4
Guaymas, Mexico 146/G7
Guaymas, Mexico 150/D3
Guaynabo, P. Rico 161/D1
Guayo (lake), P. Rico 161/B2
Guayos, Cuba 158/F2
Guayubín, Dom. Rep. 158/D5
Guazú-cuá, Paraguay 144/D5
Gubakha, U.S.S.R. 48/F4
Gubakha, U.S.S.R. 52/J3
Guban (reg.), Somalia 115/H1
Gubat, Philippines 82/E4
Gubbio, Italy 34/E4
Guben, Germany 22/F3
Guben (Gubin), Poland 47/B3
Gubin, Poland 47/B3
Gubkin, U.S.S.R. 52/E4
Guckeen, Minn. 255/D7
Gúdar, Sierra de (range), Spain 33/F2
Gudauta, U.S.S.R. 52/F6
Gudenå (riv.), Denmark 21/C5
Gudermes, U.S.S.R. 52/G6
Güdül, Turkey 63/D2
Gudur, India 68/D6
Guebwiller, France 28/G4
Guéckédou, Guinea 106/B7
Guelma, Algeria 106/F1
Guelph, N. Dak. 282/O7
Guelph, Ont. 162/H7
Guelph, Ontario 177/D4
Guelta de Zemmur (well), Western Sahara 106/B3
Guemar, Algeria 102/C1
Guemar, Algeria 106/F2
Güémez, Mexico 150/K5
Güeppi, Peru 128/E5
Guerara, Algeria 106/E2
Güere (riv.), Venezuela 124/F3
Guéret, France 28/D4
Guernesville, Calif. 204/C6
Guernica y Luno, Spain 33/E1
Guernsey (isl.), Chan. Is. 13/E8
Guernsey (isl.), Chan. Is. 10/E6
Guernsey, Iowa 229/J5
Guernsey (co.), Ohio 284/H5
Guernsey, Sask. 181/F4
Guernsey, Wyo. 319/H3
Guernsey (res.), Wyo. 319/H3
Guerra, Texas 303/F11
Guerrero (state), Mexico 150/J8

Guerzim, Algeria 106/D3
Gueydan, La. 238/E6
Guffey, Colo. 208/H5
Gugerd, Kuh-e (mts.), Iran 66/H3
Guggisberg, Switzerland 39/D3
Gughe (mt.), Ethiopia 111/G6
Guiana, Cent। & Bar. 161/E11
Guiana Highlands (plat.) 120/C2
Guichi, China 77/J5
Guichón, Uruguay 145/B3
Guidder, Cameroon 115/B2
Guide, China 77/F4
Guide Rock, Nebr. 264/F4
Guidonia, Italy 34/F6
Guiglo, Ivory Coast 106/C7
Guihulngan, Philippines 82/D5
Güija (lake), El Salvador 154/C3
Güija (lake), Guatemala 154/C3
Guija, Mozambique 118/E4
Guijuelo, Spain 33/D2
Guilarte (mt.), P. Rico 161/B2
Guild, N.H. 268/C5
Guildford, England 13/G8
Guildford, England 10/F5
Guildford Junction, Tasmania 99/B3
Guildhall, Vt. 268/D2
Guilford, Conn. 210/E3
Guilford •, Conn. 210/E3
Guilford, Ind. 227/H6
Guilford, Maine 243/F4
Guilford •, Maine 243/F5
Guilford, Mo. 261/C2
Guilford, N.Y. 276/J6
Guilford (co.), N.C. 281/K3
Guilford •, Vt. 268/B6
Guilin, China 77/G6
Guilin, China 54/N7
Guillaume-Delisle (lake), Québec 174/B1
Guimarães, Brazil 132/E3
Guimarães, Portugal 33/B2
Guimaras (isl.), Philippines 82/D5
Guimaras (str.), Philippines 82/D5
Guimba, Philippines 82/C3
Guin, Ala. 195/C3
Guinan, China 77/F4
Guinea 2/J5
Guinea 102/A3
GUINEA 106/B6
Guinea (gulf) 2/K5
Guinea (gulf) 102/C4
Guinea (gulf), Benin 106/E8
Guinea (gulf), Ghana 106/E8
Guinea (gulf), Guinea-Biss. 106/E8
Guinea (gulf), Ivory Coast 106/E8
Guinea (gulf), Nigeria 106/E8
Guinea (gulf), Togo 106/E8
Guinea, Va. 307/N5
Guinea-Bissau 2/H5
Guinea-Bissau 102/A3
GUINEA-BISSAU 106/A6
Guinea-Bissau 102/A3
GUINEA-BISSAU 106/A6
Güines, Cuba 158/C1
Güines, Cuba 156/B2
Guingamp, France 28/B3
Guion, Ark. 202/G2
Guionos (pt.), C. Rica 154/E6
Guiping, China 77/G7
Guipúzcoa (prov.), Spain 33/E1
Güira de Melena, Cuba 158/C1
Güiratinga, Brazil 132/C7
Güiria, Venezuela 124/G2
Guisa, Cuba 158/H4
Guisanbourg, Fr. Guiana 131/F3
Guisborough, England 13/F4
Guise, France 28/E3
Guitiriz, Spain 33/C1
Guiuan, Philippines 82/E5
Guixi, China 77/J6
Gui Xian, China 77/G7
Guiyang (Kweiyang), Guizhou, China 77/G6
Guiyang, Hunan, China 77/H7
Guiyang, China 54/M7
Guizhou (Kweichow), China 77/G6
Gujarat (state), India 68/C4
Gujranwala, Pakistan 59/K3
Gujranwala, Pakistan 68/C2
Gujrat, Pakistan 59/K3
Gujrat, Pakistan 68/C2
Gukovo, U.S.S.R. 52/F5
Gulang, China 77/F4
Gulargambone, N.S. Wales 97/E2
Gulbarga, India 68/D5
Gulbene, U.S.S.R. 53/D2
Gulch (cape), Newf. 166/B2
Gulen, Norway 18/D6
Gulf (co.), Fla. 212/D7
Gulf, N.C. 281/L3
Gulf Breeze, Fla. 212/B6
Gulf Crest, Ala. 195/B8
Gulf Hammock, Fla. 212/D2
Gulf Harbors, Fla. 212/D3
Gulf Island Nat'l Seashore, Fla. 212/B6
Gulf Islands Nat'l Seashore, Miss. 256/G10
Gulfport, Fla. 212/B3
Gulf Port, Ill. 222/B3
Gulfport, Miss. 188/J4
Gulfport, Miss. 256/F10
Gulf Shores, Ala. 195/C10
Gulf Stream, Fla. 212/B3
Gulgong, N.S. Wales 97/E3
Gulian, China 77/K1
Gulin, China 77/G6
Gulistan, U.S.S.R. 48/G5
Gulja (Yining), China 77/B3
Gulkana, Alaska 196/J2
Gull (lake), Alberta 182/C3
Gull (isl.), Newf. 166/D2
Gull Bay, Ontario 177/H5
Gull Bay, Ontario 175/H3
Gullfoot (lake), Ontario 177/F3
Gull Island, Newf. 166/D2
Gull Island (pt.), Newf. 166/D2

378 Gulliver

Gulliver, Mich. 250/D2
Gull Lake, Alberta 182/D3
Gull Lake, Sask. 181/C5
Gully, Minn. 255/C3
Gülnar, Turkey 63/E4
Gulnare, Colo. 208/K8
Gulnare, Ky. 237/S5
Gulquac (lake), New Bruns. 170/D2
Gulquac (riv.), New Bruns. 170/C2
Gülşehir, Turkey 63/F3
Gulu, Uganda 115/F3
Gulvain (mt.), Scotland 15/C4
Guma (Pishan), China 77/A4
Gumaca, Philippines 82/D4
Gumare, Botswana 118/C3
Gumbranch, Georgia 217/J7
Gumel, Nigeria 106/F6
Gumeracha, S. Australia 94/C7
Gumma (pref.), Japan 81/J5
Gummersbach, Germany 22/B3
Gummi, Nigeria 106/F6
Gum Spring, Va. 307/N5
Gum Springs, Ark. 202/D5
Gümüş, Turkey 63/F2
Gümüşhacıköy, Turkey 63/F2
Gümüşhane (prov.), Turkey 63/H2
Gümüşhane, Turkey 59/C1
Gümüşhane, Turkey 63/H2
Gun (cay), Bahamas 156/B1
Gun (lake), Mich. 250/D6
Guna, India 68/D4
Gunbower, Victoria 97/C4
Gundagai, N.S. Wales 97/D4
Gunderbooka (ranges), N.S. Wales 97/C2
Gündoğmuş, Turkey 63/D4
Güney, Turkey 63/C3
Gunflint Trail, Minn. 255/F1
Gungu, Zaire 115/C5
Gunisao (lake), Manitoba 179/J3
Gunlock, Utah 304/A6
Gunn, Alberta 182/C3
Gunna (isl.), Scotland 15/B4
Gunnbjørn (mt.), Greenl. 4/C11
Gunn City, Mo. 261/D5
Gunnedah, N. S. Wales 88/H6
Gunnedah, N.S. Wales 97/F2
Gunning, N.S. Wales 97/E4
Gunnison (co.), Colo. 208/E5
Gunnison, Colo. 208/E5
Gunnison (riv.), Colo. 208/C5
Gunnison (tunnel), Colo. 208/D6
Gunnison, Miss. 256/C3
Gunnison, Utah 304/C4
Gunnison (res.), Utah 304/C4
Gunnworth, Sask. 181/C4
Gunpowder (riv.), Md. 245/N3
Gunpowder, Queensland 95/A3
Gunpowder, Queensland 88/F3
Gunpowder Falls (creek), Md. 245/M2
Guntakal, India 68/D5
Gunter, Ontario 177/G3
Gunter, Oreg. 291/D4
Gunter Air Force Base, Ala. 195/F6
Guntersville, Ala. 195/F2
Guntersville (dam), Ala. 195/F2
Guntersville (lake), Ala. 195/F2
Gunton, Manitoba 179/E4
Guntown, Miss. 256/G2
Guntur, India 54/K8
Guntur, India 68/D5
Gunungapi (isl.), Indonesia 85/H7
Günzburg, Germany 22/D4
Gunzenhausen, Germany 22/D4
Gurabo, P. Rico 161/E2
Gurais, India 68/D2
Gurdon, Ark. 202/D6
Gurgan (Gorgan), Iran 66/J2
Gurguéia (riv.), Brazil 132/E5
Guri, Venezuela 124/G4
Guri (dam), Venezuela 120/C2
Guri (res.), Venezuela 120/C2
Guri (res.), Venezuela 124/G4
Gurk, Austria 41/C3
Gurla Mandhada (mt.), China 77/B5
Gurley, Ala. 195/F1
Gurley, La. 238/H5
Gurley, Nebr. 264/B3
Gurley, N.S. Wales 97/E1
Gurley, S.C. 296/J3
Gurleyville, Conn. 210/G1
Gurnee, Ill. 222/B4
Gurnet (pt.), Mass. 249/M4
Gurney, Wis. 317/F3
Gurneyville, Alberta 182/E2
Guro, Mozambique 118/E3
Gürpınar, Turkey 63/K3
Gurteen, Ireland 17/D3
Gurtnellen, Switzerland 39/G3
Gürün, Turkey 63/G3
Gurupá, Brazil 132/D3
Gurupi, Brazil 132/D5
Gurupi, Brazil 120/E4
Gurupi, Serra do (range), Brazil 132/E4
Gurupi (riv.), Brazil 132/E3
Gur'yev, U.S.S.R. 54/G5
Gur'yev, U.S.S.R. 48/F5
Gusau, Nigeria 106/F6
Gusau, Nigeria 102/C3
Gusher, Utah 304/E3
Gusinje, Yugoslavia 45/D4
Gusinoozersk, U.S.S.R. 48/L4
Gus'-Khrustal'nyy, U.S.S.R. 52/F3
Güssing, Austria 41/D3
Gustavo Díaz Ordaz, Mexico 150/K3
Gustavus, Alaska 196/M1
Gustavus, Ohio 284/J3
Gustine, Calif. 204/D6
Gustine, Texas 303/F6
Guston, Ky. 237/J5
Güstrow, Germany 22/E2
Gütersloh, Germany 22/C3
Guthrie, Ind. 227/D7
Guthrie (co.), Iowa 229/D5
Guthrie, Ky. 237/G7
Guthrie, Minn. 255/D3
Guthrie, Mo. 261/H5
Guthrie, Okla. 188/G3
Guthrie, Okla. 288/M3
Guthrie, Texas 303/D4
Guthrie Center, Iowa 229/D5
Gutiérrez Zamora, Mexico 150/L6
Guttannen, Switzerland 39/F3
Guttenberg, Iowa 229/L3
Guttenberg, N.J. 273/C2
Guttingen, Switzerland 39/H1
Gu-Win, Ala. 195/C3
Guy, Alberta 182/B2
Guy, Ark. 202/F3
Guyana 2/G5
Guyana 120/D2
GUYANA 131/B3
Guyandotte (riv.), W. Va. 312/B6
Guyang, China 77/G3
Guymon, Okla. 288/D1
Guyot (glac.), Alaska 196/K2
Guyot (mt.), N.C. 281/C3
Guyot (mt.), Tenn. 237/P9
Guyra, N.S. Wales 97/F2
Guys, Tenn. 237/D10
Guysborough (co.), Nova Scotia 168/F3
Guysborough, Nova Scotia 168/G3
Guysborough (riv.), Nova Scotia 168/G3
Guys Mills, Pa. 294/C2
Guysville, Ohio 284/G7
Guyton, Georgia 217/K6
Guyuan, China 77/G4
Guzmán (lake), Mexico 150/F1
Guzmán Blanco, Venezuela 124/E6
Guzmanes (cays), Cuba 158/B2
Gwa, Burma 72/B3
Gwaai, Zimbabwe 118/D3
Gwabegar, N.S. Wales 97/E2
Gwadabawa, Nigeria 106/F6
Gwadar, Pakistan 59/H5
Gwadar, Pakistan 68/A4
Gwalior, India 54/J7
Gwalior, India 68/D3
Gwanda, Zimbabwe 118/D4
Gwda (riv.), Poland 47/C2
Gweebarra (bay), Ireland 17/D2
Gweebarra (riv.), Ireland 17/E2
Gwelo, (Gweru) Zimbabwe 118/D3
Gwent, Wales 13/D6
Gwersyllt, Wales 13/E4
Gweru, Zimbabwe 118/D3
Gweru, Zimbabwe 102/F6
Gwinn, Mich. 250/B2
Gwinner, N. Dak. 282/P7
Gwinnett (co.), Georgia 217/D2
Gwydir (riv.), N.S. Wales 97/E1
Gwynedd, Wales 13/C4
Gwynn, Va. 307/R5
Gwynne, Alberta 182/D3
Gwynneville, Ind. 227/F5
Gyaca, China 77/D6
Gyandzhe, U.S.S.R. 7/J4
Gyandzhe, U.S.S.R. 48/E5
Gyandzhe, U.S.S.R. 52/G6
Gyangzê, China 77/C6
Gyaring Co (lake), China 77/C5
Gyaring Hu (lake), China 77/E5
Gyasikan, Ghana 106/D7
Gyda (pen.), U.S.S.R. 54/J2
Gyda (pen.), U.S.S.R. 4/C6
Gyda, U.S.S.R. 48/H2
Gyda (pen.), U.S.S.R. 48/H2
Gydan (Kolyma) (range), U.S.S.R. 48/Q3
Gyirong, China 77/B6
Gylling, Denmark 21/D6
Gympie, Australia 87/F8
Gympie, Queensland 88/J5
Gympie, Queensland 95/E5
Gyobingauk, Burma 72/C3
Gyoma, Hungary 41/F3
Gyöngyös, Hungary 41/E3
Gyönk, Hungary 41/E3
Győr, Hungary 7/F4
Győr, Hungary 41/D3
Győr-Sopron (co.), Hungary 41/D3
Gypsum, Colo. 208/F3
Gypsum, Kansas 232/E3
Gypsum (lake), Manitoba 179/D3
Gypsum, Ohio 284/E2
Gypsumville, Manitoba 179/D3
Gyrfalcon (isls.), N.W. Terr. 187/M4
Gyula, Hungary 41/F3

H

Haacht, Belgium 27/F7
Haag, Austria 41/C2
Haakon (co.), S. Dak. 298/F5
Haamstede, Netherlands 27/D5
Ha'apai Group (isls.), Tonga 87/J8
Haapajärvi, Finland 18/O5
Haapamäki, Finland 18/O5
Haapsalu, U.S.S.R. 53/B1
Haar, Germany 22/D4
Haarlem, Netherlands 27/F4
Haarlemmermeer (Hoofddorp), Netherlands 27/F4
Haarlemmermeer Polder, Netherlands 27/B5
Haast, N. Zealand 100/B5
Haast (pass), N. Zealand 100/B6
Haast (riv.), N. Zealand 100/B5
Haasts Bluff, North. Terr. 88/E4
Haasts Bluff, North. Terr. 93/B7
Haasts Bluff Aboriginal Reserve, North. Terr. 88/E5
Haasts Bluff Aboriginal Res., North. Terr. 93/B7
Hab (riv.), Pakistan 68/B3
Hab (riv.), Pakistan 59/J4
Habahe, China 77/C2
Habana, Ciudad de La (prov.), Cuba 158/C1
Habana, La (Havana) (prov.), Cuba 158/C1
Habana (Havana) (cap.), Cuba 158/C1
Habay, Alberta 182/A5
Habay, Belgium 27/H9
Habban, Yemen 59/E7
Habbaniya, Iraq 59/D3
Habbaniya, Iraq 66/C4
Habbaniya, Hor al (lake), Iraq 66/C4
Habersham (co.), Georgia 217/E1
Habersham, Georgia 217/F1
Habersham, Tenn. 237/N8
Habiganj, Bangladesh 68/G4
Habikino, Japan 81/J8
Habomai (isls.), Japan 81/N2
Habonim, Israel 65/B2
Haboro, Japan 81/K1
Hachenburg, Germany 22/B3
Hachinohe, Japan 81/K3
Hachioji, Japan 81/O2
Hachiro (lag.), Japan 81/J3
Hachita, N. Mex. 274/A7
Hacıbektaş, Turkey 63/F3
Hacılar, Turkey 63/F3
Hack (mt.), S. Australia 94/F4
Hackberry, Ariz. 198/B3
Hackberry, La. 238/D7
Hackensack, Minn. 255/D4
Hackensack, N.J. 273/B2
Hackensack (riv.), N.J. 273/C1
Hacker Valley, W. Va. 312/F5
Hacketstown, Ireland 17/H6
Hackett, Ark. 202/B3
Hacketts Cove, Nova Scotia 168/E4
Hackettstown, N.J. 273/D2
Hackleburg, Ala. 195/C2
Hackleman, Ind. 227/F4
Hackney, England 13/H8
Hackney, England 10/B5
Hacksneck, Va. 307/S5
Hacoda, Ala. 195/F8
Hadano, Japan 81/O3
Hadar, Nebr. 264/G2
Hadarba, Ras (cape), Sudan 111/G3
Hadashville, Manitoba 179/G5
Hadd, Ras al (cape), Oman 59/G5
Hadd, Ras al (cape), Oman 54/H7
Haddam•, Conn. 210/E3
Haddam, Kansas 232/E2
Haddam Neck, Conn. 210/E2
Haddar, Saudi Arabia 59/E5
Haddington, Scotland 10/E3
Haddington, Scotland 15/F5
Haddix, Ky. 237/P6
Haddock, Georgia 217/F4
Haddonfield, N.J. 273/B3
Haddon Heights, N.J. 273/B3
Hadejia, Nigeria 106/G6
Hadejia (riv.), Nigeria 106/F6
Hadensville, Ky. 237/G7
Hadera, Israel 65/B3
Hadera (dry riv.), Israel 65/B3
Haderslev, Denmark 21/C7
Haderslev, Denmark 18/F9
Hadhar, Iraq 66/C3
Hadhramaut (reg.), Yemen 54/F8
Hadhramaut (dist.), Yemen 59/E7
Hadhramaut, Wadi (dry riv.), Yemen 59/F7
Hadibu, Yemen 54/G8
Hadibu, Yemen 59/F7
Hadım, Turkey 63/E4
Haditha, Iraq 66/C3
Haditha, Iraq 59/D3
Hadiya, Saudi Arabia 59/C4
Hadleigh, England 13/H5
Hadley, Ind. 227/D5
Hadley, Ky. 237/H6
Hadley•, Mass. 249/D3
Hadley, Minn. 255/C7
Hadley (bay), N.W. Terr. 187/H2
Hadley, Pa. 294/B3
Hadley-Lake Luzerne, N.Y. 276/N4
Hadlock-Irondale, Wash. 310/C2
Hadlyme, Conn. 210/F3
Hadselfjorden (fjord), Norway 18/J2
Hadspen, Tasmania 99/D3
Hadsten, Denmark 21/C5
Hadsund, Denmark 21/D4
Haedo (range), Uruguay 145/C2
Haeju, N. Korea 81/B4
Haena, Hawaii 218/C1
Haena (pt.), Hawaii 218/C1
Hafar al Batin, Saudi Arabia 59/E4
Haffe, Syria 63/G5
Hafford, Sask. 181/D3
Hafik, Turkey 63/G3
Haflong, India 68/G3
Hafnarfjördhur, Iceland 21/B2
Haft Gel, Iran 66/F5
Hafun, Somalia 115/K1
Hafun, Ras (cape), Somalia 115/K1
Hagaman, N.Y. 276/M5
Hagan, Georgia 217/J6
Hagar, Ontario 177/D1
Hagari (riv.), India 68/D6
Hagarstown, Ill. 222/D5
Hagarville, Ark. 202/D2
Hagemeister (isl.), Alaska 196/F3
Hagen, Germany 22/B3
Hagen, Sask. 181/F3
Hagenow, Germany 22/D2
Hagensborg, Br. Col. 184/D4
Hager City, Wis. 317/A6
Hagerman, Idaho 220/D7
Hagerman, N. Mex. 274/E5
Hagerman Fossil Beds Nat'l Monument, Idaho 220/D7
Hagerstown, Ind. 227/G5
Hagerstown, Md. 245/G2
Hagerstown, Md. 188/L3
Hagfors, Sweden 18/H6
Hagi, Japan 81/E6
Ha Giang, Vietnam 72/E2
Hagley, Tasmania 99/C3
Hagood, S.C. 296/F3
Hags (head), Ireland 17/B6
Hague, Fla. 212/D2
Hague (cape), France 28/C3
Hague, The (cap.), Netherlands 7/E3
Hague, The (cap.), Netherlands 27/E4
Hague, N.Y. 276/N3
Hague, N. Dak. 282/L7
Hague, Sask. 181/E3
Hague, Va. 307/P4
Haguenau, France 28/G3
Haha (isl.), Japan 87/E3
Haha (isl.), Japan 81/M3
Ha! Ha! (lake), Qué. 172/G1
Ha! Ha! (riv.) Qué. 172/G1
Hahatonka, Mo. 261/G7
Hahira, Georgia 217/F9
Hahndorf, S. Australia 94/C8
Hahnville, La. 238/N4
Hai, Iraq 59/E3
Hai, Iraq 66/E4
Haifa (dist.), Israel 65/C2
Haifa, Israel 65/B2
Haifa, Israel 59/B3
Haifa (bay), Israel 65/C2
Haifeng, China 77/J7
Haig (lake), Alberta 182/B1
Haight, Alberta 182/D3
Haigler, Nebr. 264/C4
Haikang, China 77/G7
Haikou (Hoihow), China 77/H7
Haikou, China 54/N8
Haiku, Hawaii 218/J2
Hail, Saudi Arabia 54/F7
Hail, Saudi Arabia 59/D4
Hailar, China 77/J2
Hailar He (riv.), China 77/K2
Haile, La. 238/F1
Hailesboro, N.Y. 276/K2
Hailey, Idaho 220/D6
Haileybury, Ontario 177/K5
Haileybury, Ontario 175/D3
Haileyville, Okla. 288/P5
Hailong, China 77/L3
Hailsham, England 13/H7
Hailun, China 77/L2
Hailuoto, Finland 18/O4
Hailuoto (isl.), Finland 18/O4
Haina, Hawaii 218/H3
Hainan (prov.), China 77/H8
Hainan (isl.), China 2/Q5
Hainan (isl.), China 54/N8
Hainan (isl.), China 77/H8
Hainaut (prov.), Belgium 27/D7
Hainburg an der Donau, Austria 41/D2
Haines, Alaska 196/M1
Haines, Oreg. 291/J3
Hainesburg, N.J. 273/C2
Haines City, Fla. 212/E3
Haines Junction, Yukon 187/E3
Haines Landing, Maine 243/B6
Hainesport•, N.J. 273/D4
Hainesville, Ill. 222/A4
Hainesville, N.J. 273/D1
Hainfeld, Austria 41/C2
Haiphong, Vietnam 54/M7
Hairy Hill, Alberta 182/D3
Haiti 2/F5
Haiti 146/L8
HAITI 158
HAITI 156/D3
Haiwee, Calif. 204/H7
Haiya Junction, Sudan 59/C6
Haiya Junction, Sudan 111/G4
Haiyan, China 77/F4
Haiyang, China 77/K4
Haiyuan, China 77/E4
Hajara, Al (plain), Iraq 66/D5
Hajarain, Yemen 59/E6
Hajdú-Bihar (co.), Hungary 41/F3
Hajdúböszörmény, Hungary 41/F3
Hajdúdorog, Hungary 41/F3
Hajdúhadház, Hungary 41/F3
Hajdúnánás, Hungary 41/F3
Hajdúsámson, Hungary 41/F3
Hajdúszoboszló, Hungary 41/F3
Haji Ibraham (mt.), Iraq 66/D2
Hajja, Yemen 59/D6
Hajnowka, Poland 47/F2
Hajós, Hungary 41/E3
Haka, Burma 72/B2
Hakalau, Hawaii 218/J4
Hakkâri (prov.), Turkey 63/K4
Hakkâri (Çölemerik), Turkey 63/K4
Hakkâri (mts.), Turkey 63/K4
Hakken (mt.), Japan 81/H6
Hakodate, Japan 81/K3
Hakodate, Japan 54/R5
Haku (mt.), Japan 81/H5
Hakui, Japan 81/H5
Hakusan National Park, Japan 81/H5
Hal (Halle), Belgium 27/E7
Halabja, Iraq 66/D3
Halachó, Mexico 150/O6
Halaib, Sudan 59/C5
Halaib, Sudan 111/G3
Halalii (lake), Hawaii 218/A2
Halaula, Hawaii 188/G5
Halawa, Hawaii, Hawaii 218/G3
Halawa, Molokai, Hawaii 218/H1
Halawa (bay), Hawaii 218/H1
Halawa (cape), Hawaii 218/H1
Halawa (stream), Hawaii 218/B3
Halawa Heights, Hawaii 218/B3
Halberstadt, Germany 22/D3
Halbrite, Sask. 181/H6
Halbur, Iowa 229/D4
Halcon (mt.), Philippines 82/C4
Halcyon Dale, Georgia 217/J5
Haldane, Ill. 222/D1
Haldeman, Ky. 237/P4
Halden, Norway 18/G7
Haldensleben, Germany 22/D2
Haldimand, Ontario 177/E5
Haldimand-Norfolk (reg. munic.), Ontario 177/E5
Hale (co.), Ala. 195/C5
Hale, Argentina 143/F7
Hale, Colo. 208/P3
Hale, Camp, Colo. 208/G4
Hale, England 13/H2
Hale, Iowa 229/L4
Hale, Mich. 250/F4
Hale, Mo. 261/F3
Hale (riv.), North. Terr. 93/D8
Hale (co.), Texas 303/C3
Hale (mt.), W. Australia 92/B4
Haleakala (crater), Hawaii 218/K2
Haleakala Nat'l Park, Hawaii 218/K2
Haleb (Aleppo), Syria 59/C2
Haleb (Aleppo), Syria 63/G4
Haleburg, Ala. 195/H8
Hale Center, Texas 303/C3
Haledon, N.J. 273/B1
Haleiwa, Hawaii 218/E1
Halen, Belgium 27/G7
Hales Corners, Wis. 317/K2
Halesowen, England 13/E5
Halesowen, England 10/G3
Hales Point, Tenn. 237/B9
Halesworth, England 13/J5
Haley, N. Dak. 282/D8
Haley Station, Ontario 177/H2
Haleyville, Ala. 195/C2
Haleyville, N.J. 273/C5
Half Assini, Ghana 106/D8
Halfeti, Turkey 63/H4
Half Island Cove, Nova Scotia 168/G3
Half Moon (cay), Belize 154/D2
Halfmoon Bay, Alberta 182/C3
Halfmoon Bay, Br. Col. 184/J2
Half Moon Bay, Calif. 204/H3
Half Moon Bay (Oban), N. Zealand 100/B7
Half Moon Lake, Alberta 182/D2
Halford, Kansas 232/B3
Halfway (riv.), Br. Col. 184/F2
Halfway, Ky. 237/J7
Halfway, Md. 245/G2
Half Way, Mo. 261/F7
Halfway, Oreg. 291/K3
Halfway House, Hawaii 218/H6
Halfway House, S. Africa 118/H6
Halfweg, Netherlands 27/B4
Halhul, West Bank 65/C4
Haliburton (county), Ontario 177/F2
Haliburton, Ontario 177/F2
Haliburton (lake), Ontario 177/F2
Halieli, Turkey 63/B6
Halifax, Canada 2/F3
Halifax, England 13/J1
Halifax, England 10/G1
Halifax (harb.), Grenada 161/C8
Halifax•, Mass. 249/L5
Halifax (co.), N.C. 281/O2
Halifax, N.C. 281/O2
Halifax (co.), Nova Scotia 168/E4
Halifax (cap.), Nova Scotia 162/K7
Halifax (cap.), Nova Scotia 146/M5
Halifax (cap.), Nova Scotia 168/E4
Halifax (harb.), Nova Scotia 168/E4
Halifax, Pa. 294/J5
Halifax (bay), Queensland 88/H3
Halifax (bay), Queensland 95/C3
Halifax•, Vt. 268/B6
Halifax (co.), Va. 307/L7
Halifax, Va. 307/L7
Halifax Center, Vt. 268/B6
Haliimaile, Hawaii 218/J2
Halil (riv.), Iran 59/G4
Halin, Somalia 115/J2
Halkett (cape), Alaska 196/H1
Halkirk, Alberta 182/D3
Halkirk, Scotland 10/E1
Halkirk, Scotland 15/E2
Hall (isl.), Alaska 196/D2
Hall (co.), Georgia 217/E2
Hall, Ind. 227/D5
Hall, Ky. 237/R6
Hall, Md. 245/L5
Hall (isls.), Micronesia 87/F5
Hall, Mont. 262/C4
Hall (co.), Nebr. 264/F4
Hall (basin), N.W.T. 187/M1
Hall (lake), N.W.T. 187/K3
Hall (pen.), N.W.T. 162/K3
Hall (pen.), N.W. Terr. 187/M3
Hall (riv.), Québec 172/C2
Hall (co.), Texas 303/D3
Hall, W. Va. 312/F4
Halla (mt.), S. Korea 81/C7
Hallam, Nebr. 264/H4
Hallam, Victoria 97/K5
Halland (co.), Sweden 18/H8
Hallandale, Fla. 212/B4
Hallandale (riv.), Scotland 15/E2
Hallaniya (isl.), Yemen 59/G6
Hallau, Switzerland 39/F1
Hall Beach, N.W. Terr. 187/K3
Hallboro, Manitoba 179/C4
Halle, Belgium 27/E7
Halle, Germany 7/F3
Halle, Germany 22/D3
Halleck, Nev. 266/F2
Hällefors, Sweden 18/J7
Hallein, Austria 41/B3
Halle-Neustadt, Germany 22/D3
Hallett, Okla. 288/N2
Hallettsville, Texas 303/G8
Halley, Ark. 202/H6
Halliday, N. Dak. 282/F5
Hallie, Wis. 317/D6
Halligen (isls.), Germany 22/C1
Hall Meadow (brook), Conn. 210/C1
Hallock, Minn. 255/A2
Hallonquist, Sask. 181/D5
Hallowell, Kansas 232/H4
Hallowell, Maine 243/D7
Hall Park, Okla. 288/M4
Halls (stream), N.H. 268/E1
Halls, Tenn. 237/C9
Halls (creek), Utah 304/D6
Hallsberg, Sweden 18/J7
Hallsboro, N.C. 281/M6
Halls Creek, Australia 87/C7
Halls Creek, W. Australia 88/D3
Halls Creek, W. Australia 92/D2
Halls Crossroads, Tenn. 237/O8
Hallson, N. Dak. 282/P2
Halls Summit, Kansas 232/G3
Hallstahammar, Sweden 18/K7
Hallstatt, Austria 41/B3
Hallstavik, Sweden 18/L6
Hallstead, Pa. 294/L2
Hall Summit, La. 238/D2
Hallsville, Ill. 222/D3
Hallsville, Mo. 261/H4
Hallsville, Ohio 284/E7
Hallsville, Texas 303/K5
Hallton, Pa. 294/E3
Halltown, Mo. 261/E8
Halltown, W. Va. 312/L4
Hallum, Netherlands 27/H2
Hallwilersee (lake), Switzerland 39/F2
Hallwood, Va. 307/S5
Halma, Minn. 255/B2
Halmahera (isl.), Indonesia 54/O9
Halmahera (isl.), Indonesia 85/H5
Halmahera (sea), Indonesia 85/H5
Halmstad, Sweden 18/H8
Halq el Oued, Tunisia 106/G1
Hals, Denmark 21/D3
Halsell, Ala. 195/B6
Halsey, Nebr. 264/D3
Halsey, Oreg. 291/D3
Halstad, Minn. 255/B3
Halstead, England 13/H6
Halstead, England 10/G5
Halstead, Kansas 232/E4
Haltdalen, Norway 18/G5
Haltemprice, England 13/G4
Haltemprice, England 10/F4
Haltern, Germany 22/B3
Haltiatunturi (mt.), Finland 18/M2
Haltom City, Texas 303/F2
Halton (reg. munic.), Ontario 177/E4
Halton Hills, Ontario 177/E4
Haltwhistle, England 13/E2
Halulu (lake), Hawaii 218/A2
Ham, Chad 111/C5
Ham, France 28/E3
Hama (prov.), Syria 63/G5
Hama, Syria 63/G5
Hama, Syria 59/C2
Hamada, Jebel (mt.), Egypt 59/B5
Hamada, Japan 81/E6
Hamadan (gov.), Iran 66/F3
Hamadan, Iran 66/J3
Hamadan, Iran 59/E3
Hamadan, Iran 54/F6
Hamamatsu, Japan 54/P6
Hamamatsu, Japan 81/H6
Hamar, N. Dak. 282/N4
Hamar, Norway 18/G6
Hamar, Saudi Arabia 59/E5
Hambantota, Sri Lanka 68/E7
Hamberg, N. Dak. 282/L4
Hamber Prov. Park, Br. Col. 184/H4
Hamblen (co.), Tenn. 237/P8
Hambleton, W. Va. 312/G4
Hamburg, Ark. 202/G7
Hamburg, Conn. 210/F3
Hamburg (state), Germany 22/D2
Hamburg, Germany 7/F3
Hamburg, Germany 22/D2
Hamburg, Ill. 222/C4
Hamburg, Iowa 229/B7
Hamburg, Mich. 250/F6
Hamburg, Minn. 255/D6
Hamburg, Miss. 256/B7
Hamburg, N.J. 273/D1
Hamburg, N.Y. 276/C5
Hamburg, Pa. 294/L4
Hamburg, Wis. 317/G5
Hamda, Saudi Arabia 59/D6
Hamden•, Conn. 210/D3
Hamden, N.Y. 276/K6
Hamden, Ohio 284/F7
Häme (prov.), Finland 18/O6
Hämeenlinna, Finland 18/O6
Hamel, Ill. 222/D2
Hamel, Minn. 255/F5
Hamel, Québec 172/G3
Hamelin Pool, W. Australia 88/A5
Hamelin Pool, W. Australia 92/A4
Hameln, Germany 22/C2
Hamer, Idaho 220/F6
Hamer, S.C. 296/J3
Hamersley (range), W. Australia 88/B4
Hamersley (range), W. Australia 92/B3
Hamersville, Ohio 284/C8
Hamhŭng, N. Korea 81/C4
Hami (Kumul), China 77/D3
Hami, China 54/L5
Hamill, S. Dak. 298/K6
Hamilton, Ala. 195/C2
Hamilton (lake), Ark. 202/D5
Hamilton (cap.), Bermuda 156/G3
Hamilton (mt.), Calif. 204/L3
Hamilton, Colo. 208/D2
Hamilton (co.), Fla. 212/D1
Hamilton, Georgia 217/C5
Hamilton (co.), Ill. 222/E5
Hamilton, Ill. 222/B3
Hamilton (co.), Ind. 227/E4
Hamilton, Ind. 227/H1
Hamilton (co.), Iowa 229/F4
Hamilton, Iowa 229/H6
Hamilton (co.), Kansas 232/A3
Hamilton, Kansas 232/F4
Hamilton•, Mass. 249/L2
Hamilton, Mich. 250/C6
Hamilton, Miss. 256/H3
Hamilton, Mo. 261/E3
Hamilton, Mont. 262/B4
Hamilton (co.), Nebr. 264/F4
Hamilton (inlet), Newf. 166/C3
Hamilton (inlet), Newf. 146/N4
Hamilton (inlet), Newf. 162/L5
Hamilton (sound), Newf. 166/D4
Hamilton (co.), N.Y. 276/L3
Hamilton, N.Y. 276/J5
Hamilton, N. Zealand 100/E2
Hamilton, N.C. 281/P3
Hamilton, N. Dak. 282/R2
Hamilton (co.), Ohio 284/A7
Hamilton, Ohio 188/K3
Hamilton, Ohio 284/A7
Hamilton, Ont. 146/K5
Hamilton, Ont. 162/H7

Hartsville 379

milton, Ontario 177/E4
milton, Oreg. 291/H3
milton, Pa. 294/D4
milton (riv.), Queensland 95/B4
milton, R.I. 249/J6
milton, Scotland 15/C2
milton, Scotland 10/B1
milton, The (riv.), S. Australia 94/D2
milton, The (riv.), S. Australia 88/E5
milton, Tasmania 99/C4
milton (co.), Tenn. 237/L10
milton (co.), Texas 303/F6
milton, Texas 303/G6
milton, Victoria 88/G7
milton, Victoria 97/B5
milton, Va. 307/N2
milton, Wash. 310/D2
milton City, Calif. 204/C4
milton Dome, Wyo. 319/D2
milton Square-Mercerville, N.J. 273/D3
milton-Wentworth (reg. munic.), Ontario 177/D4
mina, Finland 18/P6
miota, Manitoba 179/B4
m Lake, Minn. 255/E5
mler, Ohio 284/B3
mlet, Ind. 227/D2
mlet, Nebr. 264/C4
mlet, N.Y. 276/B6
mlet, N.C. 281/K5
mlet, N. Dak. 282/E2
mlet, Ohio 284/B8
mletsburg, Ill. 222/E6
mlin, Alberta 182/D2
mlin, Iowa 229/D5
mlin, Kansas 232/G2
mlin, Ky. 237/E7
mlin•, Maine 243/H1
mlin (lake), Mich. 250/C4
mlin, N.Y. 276/E4
mlin, Pa. 294/M3
mlin, Sask. 181/C3
mlin (co.), S. Dak. 298/P4
mlin, Texas 303/E5
mlin, W. Va. 312/B6
mm, Germany 22/B3
mmamet (gulf), Tunisia 106/G1
mmar, Hor al (lake), Iraq 66/E5
mmarstrand, Sweden 18/J5
mme, Belgium 27/E6
mmel, Denmark 21/C5
mmelburg, Germany 22/C3
mmer, S. Dak. 298/R2
mmerdal, Sweden 18/J5
mmerfest, Norway 4/B9
mmerfest, Norway 18/N1
mmerfest, Norway 7/G1
mmersmith, England 10/B5
mmersmith, England 13/H8
mmerum, Denmark 21/C5
mmett, Idaho 220/C7
mmon, Okla. 288/H3
mmonasset (pt.), Conn. 210/E3
mmonasset (res.), Conn. 210/E3
mmonasset (riv.), Conn. 210/E3
mmond, Ill. 222/E4
mmond, Ind. 227/B1
mmond, Ky. 237/O7
mmond, La. 238/N1
mmond, Minn. 255/F6
mmond, Mo. 261/G9
mmond, Mont. 262/M5
mmond (riv.), New Bruns. 170/E3
mmond, N.Y. 276/J2
mmond, Oreg. 291/C1
mmond, Wis. 317/A6
mmondsport, N.Y. 276/F6
mmondsville, Ohio 284/J4
mmondvale, New Bruns. 170/E3
mmondville, Ala. 195/G1
mmonton, N.J. 273/D4
mnavoe, Scotland 15/G2
m-Nord, Québec 172/F4
moa, Hawaii 218/K2
mois, Belgium 27/G8
mont-Achel, Belgium 27/H6
mpden, Maine 243/F6
mpden•, Maine 243/F6
mpden (co.), Mass. 249/D4
mpden•, Mass. 249/E4
mpden, Newf. 166/C4
mpden, N. Zealand 100/C6
mpden, N. Dak. 282/N2
mpden, W. Va. 312/C7
mpden Highlands, Maine 243/F6
mpden-Sydney, Va. 307/L6
mpshire (co.), England 13/F6
mpshire, Ill. 222/E1
mpshire (co.), Mass. 249/D3
mpshire, Tenn. 237/G9
mpshire (co.), W. Va. 312/J4
mpshire, Wyo. 319/H2
mpstead, Dominica 161/E5
mpstead, Md. 245/L2
mpstead, New Bruns. 170/D3
mpstead•, N.H. 268/E6
mpstead, N.C. 281/O6
mpstead, Québec 172/H4
mpton, Ark. 202/F6
mpton•, Conn. 210/G1
mpton, Fla. 212/D2
mpton, Georgia 217/D4
mpton, Ill. 222/C2
mpton, Iowa 229/G3
mpton, Ky. 237/E6
mpton, Minn. 255/E6
mpton, Miss. 256/B4
mpton, Nebr. 264/G4
mpton, New Bruns. 170/E3
mpton, N.H. 268/F6
mpton•, N.H. 268/F6
mpton, N.J. 273/D2
mpton, N.Y. 276/O3
mpton, Nova Scotia 168/C4
mpton, Oreg. 291/G4
mpton, Pa. 294/H6
mpton (co.), S.C. 296/E6
Hampton, S.C. 296/E6
Hampton, Tenn. 237/S8
Hampton (I.C.), Va. 307/R6
Hampton Bays, N.Y. 276/R9
Hampton Beach, N.H. 268/F6
Hampton Falls•, N.H. 268/F6
Hampton Nat'l Hist. Site, Md. 245/M3
Hampton Park, Victoria 97/K6
Hampton Park, Victoria 88/M8
Hampton Roads (est.), Va. 307/R7
Hampton Springs, Fla. 212/C1
Hamptonville, N.C. 281/H2
Hamrat esh Sheikh, Sudan 111/E5
Hamrin, Jabal (mts.) Iraq 66/D3
Hams Bluff (prom.), Virgin Is. (U.S.) 161/E3
Hams Fork (riv.), Wyo. 319/B4
Ham-Sud, Québec 172/F4
Hamton, Sask. 181/C4
Hamtramck, Mich. 250/B6
Hamur, Turkey 63/K3
Han (riv.), China 54/J6
Han (riv.), S. Korea 81/C5
Hana, Hawaii 188/F5
Hana, Hawaii 218/K2
Hanac, Turkey 63/K2
Hanaford (Logan), Ill. 222/E6
Hanagita (peak), Alaska 196/K2
Hanahan, S.C. 296/H6
Hanakiya, Saudi Arabia 59/D5
Hanalei, Hawaii 218/C1
Hanalei (bay), Hawaii 218/C1
Hanalei (riv.), Hawaii 218/C1
Hanamaki, Japan 81/K4
Hanamalo (pt.), Hawaii 218/F7
Hanamaulu, Hawaii 218/C1
Hanapepe, Hawaii 218/C2
Hanapepe (bay), Hawaii 218/C2
Hanau, Germany 22/C3
Hanbogd, Mongolia 77/G3
Hanceville, Ala. 195/E2
Hancheng, China 77/H4
Hanchung (Hanzhong), China 77/G5
Hancock, Conn. 210/C2
Hancock (co.), Georgia 217/G4
Hancock (co.), Ill. 222/B3
Hancock (co.), Ind. 227/F5
Hancock (co.), Iowa 229/F2
Hancock, Iowa 229/C6
Hancock (co.), Ky. 237/H5
Hancock (co.), Maine 243/G6
Hancock•, Maine 243/G6
Hancock, Md. 245/F2
Hancock•, Mass. 249/A2
Hancock, Mich. 250/G1
Hancock, Minn. 255/C5
Hancock (co.), Miss. 256/E10
Hancock, Mo. 261/K7
Hancock•, N.H. 268/C6
Hancock (mt.), N.H. 268/D3
Hancock, N.Y. 276/L7
Hancock (co.), Ohio 284/C3
Hancock (co.), Tenn. 237/P7
Hancock•, Vt. 268/B4
Hancock (co.), W. Va. 312/E2
Hancock, W. Va. 312/K3
Hancock, Wis. 317/G7
Hancocks Bridge, N.J. 273/C4
Hand (co.), S. Dak. 298/L4
Handa (isl.), Scotland 15/C2
Handan (Hantan), China 77/H4
Handan, China 54/N6
Handel, Sask. 181/C3
Handeni, Tanzania 115/G5
Handies (peak), Colo. 208/E7
Handley, W. Va. 312/D6
Handlová, Czech. 41/E2
Handsom, Va. 307/O7
Handsworth, Sask. 181/J6
Haney, Br. Col. 184/L3
Hanford, Calif. 204/F7
Hanford Reservation, Wash. 310/F4
Hangayn Nuruu (mts.), Mongolia 77/E2
Hangchow (Hangzhou), China 77/J5
Hanggin, China 77/G4
Hanging Rock, Ohio 284/E8
Hangklip (cape), S. Africa 118/F7
Hangman (creek), Wash. 310/H3
Hangö, Finland 18/N7
Hangöudd (prom.) Finland 18/N7
Hangzhou (Hangchow), China 77/J5
Hangzhou, China 54/N6
Hangzhou Wan (bay), China 77/K5
Hanh, Mongolia 77/F1
Hani, Turkey 63/J3
Haniqra, Rosh (cape), Israel 65/C1
Hanish (isls.), Yemen 59/D7
Hankinson, N. Dak. 282/S7
Hanko (Hangö), Finland 18/N7
Hanks, N. Dak. 282/C2
Hanksville, Utah 304/D5
Hanle, India 68/D2
Hanley, Sask. 181/E4
Hanley Falls, Minn. 255/C6
Hanley Hills, Mo. 261/P2
Hanlontown, Iowa 229/G2
Hanmer, N. Zealand 100/D5
Hann (mt.), W. Australia 92/D1
Hanna, Alberta 182/E4
Hanna, Alta. 162/E5
Hanna, Ind. 227/D2
Hanna, La. 238/D3
Hanna, Okla. 288/P4
Hanna, Utah 304/D3
Hanna, Wyo. 319/F4
Hanna City, Ill. 222/D3
Hannaford, N. Dak. 282/O5
Hannah, N. Dak. 282/N2
Hannah (bay), Ontario 175/D2
Hannawa Falls, N.Y. 276/L1
Hannibal, Mo. 261/K3
Hannibal, Mo. 188/H3
Hannibal, N.Y. 276/G4
Hannibal, Ohio 284/J6
Hannibal, Wis. 317/E5
Hanno, Japan 81/O2
Hannover, Germany 7/E3
Hannover, Germany 22/C2
Hannover, N. Dak. 282/H5
Hannuit (Hannut), Belgium 27/G7
Hannut, Belgium 27/G7
Hanöbukten (bay), Sweden 18/J9
Hanoi (cap.), Vietnam 2/Q4
Hanoi (cap.), Vietnam 54/M7
Hanoi (cap.), Vietnam 72/E2
Hanover (isl.), Chile 120/B8
Hanover (isl.), Chile 138/D9
Hanover, Conn. 210/G2
Hanover, Ill. 222/C1
Hanover, Ind. 227/F7
Hanover, Kansas 232/F2
Hanover•, Maine 243/B7
Hanover, Md. 245/M4
Hanover•, Mass. 249/L4
Hanover, Mich. 250/E6
Hanover, Minn. 255/E5
Hanover, N.H. 268/C4
Hanover•, N.H. 268/C4
Hanover, N. Mex. 274/A6
Hanover, Ohio 284/F5
Hanover, Ontario 177/C3
Hanover, Pa. 294/J6
Hanover (co.), Va. 307/N5
Hanover, Va. 307/O5
Hanover, W. Va. 312/C7
Hanover Park, Ill. 222/A5
Hanoverton, Ohio 284/J4
Hansboro, N. Dak. 282/M2
Hansell, Iowa 229/G3
Hansen, Idaho 220/D7
Hansford (co.), Texas 303/C1
Han Shui (riv.), China 77/H5
Hanska, Minn. 255/D6
Hans Lollik (isls.), Virgin Is. (U.S.) 161/B4
Hanson, Ky. 237/G6
Hanson, Mass. 249/L4
Hanson•, Mass. 249/L4
Hanson (bay), N. Zealand 100/E7
Hanson (riv.), North. Terr. 93/C6
Hanson, Okla. 288/S4
Hanson (co.), S. Dak. 298/O6
Hansonville, Va. 307/D7
Hanstholm, Denmark 21/B3
Hanston, Kansas 232/C3
Hansville, Wash. 310/C3
Hantan (Handan), China 77/H4
Hants (co.), Nova Scotia 168/D4
Hant's Harbour, Newf. 166/D2
Hantsport, Nova Scotia 168/D3
Hantzsch (riv.), N.W. Terr. 187/L3
Hanumangarh, India 68/C3
Hanwood, N.S. Wales 97/C4
Hanyuan, China 77/F6
Hanzhong (Hanchung), China 77/G5
Hao (atoll), Fr. Poly. 87/N7
Haouach, Wadi (dry riv.), Chad 111/C4
Haparanda, Sweden 18/N4
Hapeville, Georgia 217/K2
Happy, Ky. 237/P6
Happy, Texas 303/C3
Happy Adventure, Newf. 166/D2
Happy Camp, Calif. 204/B2
Happy Jack, Ariz. 198/D4
Happy Jack, La. 238/L7
Happy Valley, Oreg. 291/B2
Happy Valley-Goose Bay, Newf. 166/B3
Haql, Saudi Arabia 59/C4
Harad, Saudi Arabia 59/E5
Harads, Sweden 18/M3
Harahan, La. 238/O4
Haraja, Saudi Arabia 59/D6
Haralson (co.), Georgia 217/B3
Haralson, Georgia 217/C4
Haramachi, Japan 81/K5
Harar (prov.), Ethiopia 111/H6
Harar, Ethiopia 111/H6
Harar, Ethiopia 102/G4
Harardera, Somalia 115/J3
Harare (Salisbury) (cap.), Zimbabwe 102/E6
Harare (cap.), Zimbabwe 118/E3
Haraz, Chad 111/C5
Harbel, Liberia 106/B7
Harbeson, Del. 245/S6
Harbin, China 77/L2
Harbin, China 2/R3
Harbin, China 54/O5
Harbine, Nebr. 264/G4
Harbinger, N.C. 281/T2
Harbøør, Denmark 21/B4
Harbor, Oreg. 291/C5
Harbor Beach, Mich. 250/G5
Harbor City, Calif. 204/C11
Harborcreek, Pa. 294/C1
Harbor Springs, Mich. 250/D3
Harborton, Va. 307/S5
Harbor View, Ohio 284/C2
Harbour (isl.), Bahamas 156/C1
Harbour Breton, Newf. 166/C4
Harbour Deep, Newf. 166/C3
Harbour Grace, Newf. 166/D2
Harbour Grace, Newf. 162/L6
Harbour Main, Newf. 166/D2
Harbourton, N.J. 273/D3
Harbourville, Nova Scotia 168/D3
Harburg-Wilhelmsburg, Germany 22/C2
Hårby, Denmark 21/D7
Harco, Ill. 222/E6
Harcourt, Iowa 229/E4
Harcourt, New Bruns. 170/E2
Harcourt, Ontario 177/F2
Harcuvar (mts.), Ariz. 198/B5
Harda, India 68/D4
Hardangerfjord (fjord), Norway 18/D7
Hardangerfjorden (fjord), Norway 7/E3
Hardangervidda (plat.), Norway 18/E6
Hardaway, Ala. 195/G6
Hardburly, Ky. 237/P6
Hardee (co.), Fla. 212/E4
Hardee, Miss. 256/C5
Hardeeville, S.C. 296/E7
Hardeman (co.), Tenn. 237/C10
Hardeman (co.), Texas 303/E3
Hardenberg, Netherlands 27/J3
Harden City, Okla. 288/N5
Harderwijk, Netherlands 27/H4
Hardesty, Okla. 288/D1
Hardieville, Alberta 182/D5
Hardin (co.), Ill. 222/E6
Hardin, Ill. 222/C4
Hardin (co.), Iowa 229/G4
Hardin (co.), Ky. 237/K5
Hardin, Ky. 237/E7
Hardin, Mo. 261/E4
Hardin, Mont. 262/J5
Hardin (co.), Ohio 284/C4
Hardin (co.), Tenn. 237/E10
Hardin (co.), Texas 303/K7
Harding (lake), Ala. 195/H5
Harding (lake), Georgia 217/B5
Harding, Manitoba 179/B5
Harding, Minn. 255/E4
Harding (co.), N. Mex. 274/F3
Harding (pt.), Nova Scotia 168/D5
Harding (co.), S. Dak. 298/B2
Harding, W. Va. 312/G5
Harding Icefield, Alaska 196/C2
Hardingville, N.J. 273/C4
Hardinsburg, Ind. 227/E8
Hardinsburg, Ky. 237/H5
Hardin Springs, Ky. 237/J5
Hardinville, Ill. 222/F5
Hardinxveld-Giessendam, Netherlands 27/G5
Hardisty, Alberta 182/E3
Hardisty (lake), N.W. Terr. 187/G3
Hardman, Oreg. 291/H2
Hardoi, India 68/E3
Hardshell, Ky. 237/P6
Hardt (mts.), Germany 22/C4
Hardtner, Kansas 232/D4
Hardwar, India 68/D2
Hardwick (Midway-Hardwick), Georgia 217/F4
Hardwick•, Mass. 249/F3
Hardwick, Minn. 255/B7
Hardwick, Vt. 268/C2
Hardwick•, Vt. 268/C2
Hardwick (lake), Vt. 268/C2
Hardwicke, New Bruns. 170/E1
Hardwicke Island, Br. Col. 184/E5
Hardwood Ridge, New Bruns. 170/D2
Hardy, Ark. 202/H1
Hardy (pen.), Chile 138/F11
Hardy, Iowa 229/E3
Hardy, Ky. 237/S5
Hardy, Miss. 256/E3
Hardy, Nebr. 264/G4
Hardy, Okla. 288/N1
Hardy, Sask. 181/G6
Hardy, Va. 307/J6
Hardy (co.), W. Va. 312/J4
Hardyville, Ky. 237/K6
Hare (bay), Newf. 166/C3
Hare (fjord), N.W. Terr. 187/K1
Hare Bay, Newf. 166/D4
Harelbeke, Belgium 27/C7
Harfleur, France 28/D3
Harford (co.), Md. 245/N2
Harford, N.Y. 276/H6
Harford, Pa. 294/L2
Hargeysa, Somalia 115/H2
Hargeysa, Somalia 102/G4
Hargill, Texas 303/F11
Hargrave, Manitoba 179/A5
Hargwen, Alberta 182/B3
Har Hu (lake), China 77/E4
Hari (riv.), Indonesia 85/C6
Harib, Yemen 59/E7
Haricha Hamada (des.), Mali 106/D4
Harim, Syria 63/G4
Harima (sea), Japan 81/G6
Harima, Jordan 65/D2
Haringey, England 10/B5
Haringey, England 13/H8
Haringvliet (str.), Netherlands 27/E5
Hariq, Saudi Arabia 59/E5
Harirud (riv.), Afghanistan 68/A1
Harirud (riv.), Afghanistan 59/H3
Hari Rud (riv.), Iran 66/M3
Haris, West Bank 65/C3
Harjavalta, Finland 18/M6
Harjo, Okla. 288/N4
Harkaway, Victoria 97/K5
Harkers Island, N.C. 281/R5
Harkiko, Ethiopia 111/G4
Harlan, Ind. 227/H2
Harlan, Iowa 229/C5
Harlan, Kansas 232/D2
Harlan (co.), Ky. 237/P7
Harlan, Ky. 237/P7
Harlan (co.), Nebr. 264/E4
Harlan, Oreg. 291/D3
Harlan County (lake), Nebr. 264/E5
Harlech (comm.), Wales 10/E4
Harlech, Wales 13/C5
Harlem, Fla. 212/F5
Harlem, Georgia 217/H4
Harlem, Mont. 262/H2
Harlem Springs, Ohio 284/J4
Harleston, England 13/J5
Harleton, Texas 303/K5
Hårlev, Denmark 21/F7
Harleyville, S.C. 296/G5
Harlingen, Netherlands 27/G2
Harlingen, N.J. 273/D3
Harlingen, Texas 303/G11
Harlingen, Texas 188/G5
Harlow, England 13/H7
Harlow, N. Dak. 282/M3
Harlowton, Mont. 262/F4
Harman, W. Va. 312/G5
Harman-Maxie, Va. 307/D6
Harmans, Md. 245/M4
Harmattan, Alberta 182/C4
Harmon, Ill. 222/D2
Harmon (co.), Okla. 288/G5
Harmon, Okla. 288/G2
Harmonsburg, Pa. 294/B2
Harmony, Ark. 202/D2
Harmony, Ind. 227/C5
Harmony, Maine 243/D6
Harmony•, Maine 243/D6
Harmony, Minn. 255/F7
Harmony, N.C. 281/H3
Harmony, Pa. 294/B4
Harmony, R.I. 249/H5
Harmony, W. Va. 312/D5
Harms, Tenn. 237/H10
Harned, Ky. 237/J5
Harnett (co.), N.C. 281/M4
Harney (lake), Fla. 212/F3
Harney, Md. 245/K2
Harney (co.), Oreg. 291/H4
Harney, Oreg. 291/J4
Harney (lake), Oreg. 291/H4
Harney (peak), S. Dak. 298/B6
Härnösand, Sweden 18/L5
Haro, Spain 33/E1
Haro (str.), Wash. 310/B2
Harold, Fla. 212/B6
Harold, Ky. 237/R5
Harp (lake), Newf. 166/B2
Harper, Ill. 222/D1
Harper, Iowa 229/J6
Harper (co.), Kansas 232/D4
Harper, Kansas 232/D4
Harper, Liberia 106/C8
Harper, Liberia 102/B4
Harper (co.), Okla. 288/G1
Harper, Oreg. 291/K4
Harper, Texas 303/E7
Harper, Wash. 310/A2
Harper, W. Va. 312/D7
Harpers Ferry, Iowa 229/L2
Harpers Ferry, W. Va. 312/L4
Harpers Ferry Nat'l Hist. Park, Md. 245/G3
Harpers Ferry Nat'l Hist. Park, W. Va. 312/L4
Harpersville, Ala. 195/F4
Harperville, Miss. 256/E6
Harper Woods, Mich. 250/B6
Harpeth (riv.), Tenn. 237/G8
Harpster, Idaho 220/C4
Harpster, Ohio 284/D4
Harpswell•, Maine 243/D8
Harpswell Center, Maine 243/D8
Harpursville, N.Y. 276/J6
Harput, Turkey 63/H3
Harquahala (mts.), Ariz. 198/B5
Harrah, Okla. 288/M4
Harrah, Wash. 310/E4
Harran, Turkey 63/H4
Harrell, Ark. 202/F7
Harrells, N.C. 281/N5
Harrellsville, N.C. 281/R2
Harricana (riv.), Québec 174/B3
Harriet, Ark. 202/E2
Harrietsfield, Nova Scotia 168/E4
Harrietta, Mich. 250/D4
Harriettsville, Ohio 284/H6
Harrigan Cove, Nova Scotia 168/F4
Harriman, N.Y. 276/M8
Harriman, Oreg. 291/E5
Harriman, Tenn. 237/M9
Harriman (res.), Vt. 268/B6
Harrington (sound), Bermuda 156/G3
Harrington, Del. 245/R5
Harrington•, Maine 243/H6
Harrington (lake), Maine 243/E4
Harrington, N.S. Wales 97/G2
Harrington, S. Dak. 298/G7
Harrington, Wash. 310/G3
Harrington Harbour, Québec 174/F2
Harrington Park, N.J. 273/C1
Harris, Calif. 204/B3
Harris (co.), Georgia 217/C5
Harris, Iowa 229/C2
Harris, Kansas 232/G3
Harris, Mich. 250/B3
Harris, Minn. 255/F5
Harris, Mo. 261/F2
Harris, Okla. 288/S7
Harris, Sask. 181/D4
Harris (dist.), Scotland 15/B3
Harris (dist.), Scotland 10/C2
Harris (sound), Scotland 15/A3
Harris (sound), Scotland 10/C2
Harris (lake), S. Australia 94/D4
Harris, Tenn. 237/C8
Harris (co.), Texas 303/J8
Harrisburg, Ark. 202/J2
Harrisburg, Ill. 222/E6
Harrisburg, Ind. 227/G5
Harrisburg, Mo. 261/H4
Harrisburg, Nebr. 264/A3
Harrisburg, N.C. 281/H4
Harrisburg, Ohio 284/D6
Harrisburg, Oreg. 291/D3
Harrisburg (cap.), Pa. 188/L2
Harrisburg (cap.), Pa. 146/L5
Harrisburg (cap.), Pa. 294/H5
Harrisburg, S. Dak. 298/R7
Harrismith, S. Africa 118/D5
Harrison (bay), Alaska 196/H1
Harrison, Ark. 202/D1
Harrison (lake), Br. Col. 184/M2
Harrison, Georgia 217/G5
Harrison, Idaho 220/B2
Harrison, Ill. 222/D1
Harrison (co.), Ind. 227/E8
Harrison (co.), Iowa 229/B5
Harrison (co.), Ky. 237/N4
Harrison•, Maine 243/B7
Harrison, Mich. 250/E4
Harrison (co.), Miss. 256/F10
Harrison (co.), Mo. 261/E2
Harrison, Mont. 262/E5
Harrison, Nebr. 264/A2
Harrison (cape), Newf. 166/C3
Harrison, N.J. 273/B2
Harrison, N.Y. 276/P6
Harrison (co.), Ohio 284/H5
Harrison, Ohio 284/A9
Harrison, S. Dak. 298/M7
Harrison, Tenn. 237/L10
Harrison (co.), Texas 303/K5
Harrison (co.), W. Va. 312/F4
Harrison, Wis. 317/G5
Harrisonburg, La. 238/G3
Harrisonburg (I.C.), Va. 307/K4
Harrison Hot Springs, Br. Col. 184/M3
Harrison Valley, Pa. 294/G2
Harrisonville, Ill. 222/C5
Harrisonville, Mo. 261/D5
Harrisonville, N.J. 273/C4
Harrisonville, Ohio 284/F7
Harrisonville, Pa. 294/F6
Harriston, Miss. 256/C7
Harriston, Ontario 177/D4
Harristown, Ill. 222/D4
Harrisville, Ind. 227/H4
Harrisville, Mich. 250/F4
Harrisville, Miss. 256/D7
Harrisville•, N.H. 268/C6
Harrisville, N.Y. 276/K2
Harrisville, Ohio 284/J5
Harrisville, Pa. 294/B3
Harrisville, R.I. 249/H5
Harrisville, Utah 304/C2
Harrisville, W. Va. 312/E4
Harris Wash (creek), Utah 304/C6
Harrod, Ohio 284/C4
Harrodsburg, Ind. 227/D6
Harrodsburg, Ky. 237/M5
Harrods Creek, Ky. 237/K4
Harrogate, Br. Col. 184/J5
Harrogate, England 13/J1
Harrogate, England 10/F4
Harrogate-Shawanee, Tenn. 237/O8
Harrold, S. Dak. 298/K4
Harrold, Texas 303/F3
Harrop (lake), Manitoba 179/G2
Harrow, England 13/G8
Harrow, England 10/B5
Harrow, Ontario 177/B5
Harrow, Victoria 97/A5
Harrowby, Manitoba 179/A4
Harrowsmith, Ontario 177/H3
Harry S. Truman Nat'l Hist. Site, Mo. 261/R5
Harry Strunk (lake), Nebr. 264/D4
Harsens Island, Mich. 250/G6
Harshaw, Wis. 317/G4
Harstad, Norway 18/K2
Hart (lake), Fla. 212/E3
Hart (co.), Georgia 217/G2
Hart (co.), Ky. 237/K6
Hart, Mich. 250/C5
Hart (lake), Oreg. 291/H5
Hart (mt.), Oreg. 291/H5
Hart, Texas 303/B3
Hart (riv.), Yukon 187/E3
Hartbees (riv.), S. Africa 118/C5
Hartberg, Austria 41/C3
Harte, Manitoba 179/C4
Harte (mt.), Manitoba 179/A2
Hartell, Alberta 182/C4
Hartfield, Va. 307/R5
Hartford, Ala. 195/G8
Hartford (cape), Newf. 162/L5
Hartford, Ark. 202/B3
Hartford (co.), Conn. 210/D1
Hartford (cap.), Conn. 146/L5
Hartford (cap.), Conn. 188/M2
Hartford (cap.), Conn. 210/E1
Hartford, Ill. 222/A2
Hartford, Iowa 229/G6
Hartford, Kansas 232/F3
Hartford, Ky. 237/H6
Hartford•, Maine 243/C7
Hartford, Mich. 250/C6
Hartford, N.J. 273/D4
Hartford, N.Y. 276/O4
Hartford, Ohio 284/E5
Hartford, Ohio 284/J3
Hartford, S. Dak. 298/P6
Hartford, Tenn. 237/P9
Hartford•, Vt. 268/C4
Hartford, W. Va. 312/C4
Hartford, Wis. 317/K9
Hartford City, Ind. 227/G4
Harthill, Scotland 15/C2
Hartington, Nebr. 264/G2
Hartington, Ontario 177/H3
Hartland•, Conn. 210/D1
Hartland, England 13/C7
Hartland (pt.), England 13/C6
Hartland (pt.), England 10/D5
Hartland, Maine 243/D6
Hartland•, Maine 243/D6
Hartland, Mich. 250/F6
Hartland, Minn. 255/E7
Hartland, New Bruns. 170/C2
Hartland•, Vt. 269/C4
Hartland, W. Va. 312/D6
Hartland, Wis. 317/J1
Hartland Four Corners, Vt. 268/C4
Hartlepool, England 10/F3
Hartlepool, England 13/F3
Hartleton, Pa. 294/H4
Hartley, Iowa 229/C2
Hartley (co.), Texas 303/B2
Hartley, Texas 303/B2
Hartleyville, Alberta 182/D5
Hartline, Wash. 310/F3
Hartly, Del. 245/R4
Hartman, Ark. 202/C3
Hartman, Colo. 208/P6
Hartney, Manitoba 179/B5
Harts (pass), Wash. 310/E2
Harts, W. Va. 312/B6
Hartsburg, Ill. 222/D3
Hartsburg, Mo. 261/H5
Hartsdale, N.Y. 276/P6
Hartsel, Colo. 208/H4
Hartselle, Ala. 195/E2
Hartsfield, Georgia 217/E8
Hartsgrove, Ohio 284/J2
Hartshorn, Mo. 261/J8
Hartshorne, Okla. 288/R5
Harts Range, North. Terr. 88/F4
Harts Range, North. Terr. 93/D7
Hartstown, Pa. 294/B2
Hartsville, Ind. 227/F6
Hartsville, Mass. 249/B4
Hartsville, S.C. 296/G3
Hartsville, Tenn. 237/J8

Hartville, Mo. 261/G8
Hartville, Ohio 284/H4
Hartville, Wyo. 319/H3
Hartwell, Georgia 217/G2
Hartwell (dam), Georgia 217/G2
Hartwell (lake), Georgia 217/G2
Hartwell, Mo. 261/E6
Hartwell (dam), S.C. 296/B3
Hartwell (lake), S.C. 296/A3
Hartwick, Iowa 229/J5
Hartwick, N.Y. 276/K5
Hartz (mt.), Tasmania 99/C5
Harug el Asued, El (mts.), Libya 111/C2
Haruniye, Turkey 63/G4
Har Us Nuur (lake), Mongolia 77/D2
Harvard (mt.), Colo. 208/G5
Harvard, Idaho 220/B5
Harvard, Ill. 222/E1
Harvard, Iowa 229/G7
Harvard•, Mass. 249/H2
Harvard, Nebr. 264/F4
Harvel, Ill. 222/D4
Harvester, Mo. 261/N2
Harvey, Ill. 222/B6
Harvey, Iowa 229/H6
Harvey (co.), Kansas 232/E3
Harvey, La. 238/O4
Harvey, Albert, New Bruns. 170/F3
Harvey (lake), New Bruns. 170/C3
Harvey (mt.), New Bruns. 170/D3
Harvey, N. Dak. 282/L4
Harvey, W. Australia 88/B6
Harvey, W. Australia 92/A2
Harvey, W. Va. 312/D7
Harvey Cedars, N.J. 273/E4
Harveys (lake), Vt. 268/C3
Harveysburg, Ohio 284/C7
Harveys Lake, Pa. 294/E7
Harveyton, Ky. 237/P6
Harveyville, Kansas 232/F3
Harviell, Mo. 261/M9
Harwich, England 13/J6
Harwich, England 10/G5
Harwich, Mass. 249/O6
Harwich•, Mass. 249/O6
Harwich Port, Mass. 249/O6
Harwinton, Conn. 210/C1
Harwinton•, Conn. 210/C1
Harwood, Mo. 261/D7
Harwood, N. Dak. 282/S6
Harwood, Ontario 177/F3
Harwood, Texas 303/G8
Harwood Heights, Ill. 222/B5
Harwood Island, N.S. Wales 97/G1
Harworth, England 13/F4
Haryana (state), India 68/D3
Harz (mts.), Germany 22/D3
Harzgerode, Germany 22/D3
Hasa, Wadi el (dry riv.), Jordan 65/E5
Hasan Daği, Büyük (mt.), Turkey 63/E3
Hasbrouck Heights, N.J. 273/B2
Hase (riv.), Germany 22/B2
Haseke (prov.), Syria 63/J4
Haselünne, Germany 22/B2
Hasenkamp, Argentina 143/F5
Hashtpar, Iran 66/F2
Haskeir (isl.), Scotland 15/A3
Haskell, Ark. 202/E4
Haskell, N.J. 273/A1
Haskell (co.), Kansas 232/B4
Haskell, Okla. 288/P3
Haskell (co.), Okla. 288/R4
Haskell, Texas 303/E4
Haskett, Manitoba 179/D5
Haskins, Iowa 229/K6
Haskins, Ohio 284/C3
Haslach an der Mühl, Austria 41/C2
Hasle, Denmark 21/F8
Haslemere, England 13/G6
Haslemere, England 10/F5
Haslet, Texas 303/E2
Haslett, Mich. 250/E6
Haslev, Denmark 21/E7
Haslingden, England 13/H1
Hassa, Turkey 63/G4
Hassan, India 68/D6
Hassayampa (riv.), Ariz. 198/C5
Hasse, Texas 303/F6
Hassel (sound), N.W. Terr. 187/J2
Hassel (isl.), Virgin Is. (U.S.) 161/B4
Hassell, N.C. 281/P3
Hasselt, Belgium 27/G7
Hasselt, Netherlands 27/J3
Hassfurt, Germany 22/D3
Hassi Messaoud, Algeria 106/F2
Hassi R'Mel, Algeria 106/E2
Hässleholm, Sweden 18/H8
Hassloch, Germany 22/C4
Haster, Scotland 15/E2
Hastière, Belgium 27/F8
Hastings, England 10/G5
Hastings, England 13/H7
Hastings, Fla. 212/E2
Hastings, Ill. 222/B6
Hastings, Iowa 229/C6
Hastings, Mich. 250/D6
Hastings, Minn. 255/F6
Hastings, Nebr. 188/G2
Hastings, Nebr. 264/F4
Hastings, N. Zealand 100/F3
Hastings, N. Dak. 282/O6
Hastings, Okla. 288/K6
Hastings (county), Ontario 177/G3
Hastings, Ontario 177/G3
Hastings, Pa. 294/E4
Hastings On Hudson, N.Y. 276/O6
Hasty, Ark. 202/D1
Hasty, Colo. 208/O6
Hasvik, Norway 18/M1
Haswell, Colo. 208/N6
Hat (peak), Calif. 204/E2
Hat (creek), S. Dak. 298/B7
Hatay (prov.), Turkey 63/G4
Hatay (Antakya), Turkey 63/G4

Hatboro, Pa. 294/M5
Hatch, N. Mex. 274/B6
Hatch, Utah 304/B6
Hatchechubbee, Ala. 195/H6
Hatcher, Georgia 217/B7
Hatches Creek, North. Terr. 88/F4
Hatches Creek, North. Terr. 93/D6
Hatchet (mt.), N. Mex. 274/A7
Hatchie (riv.), Tenn. 237/B9
Hatchineha (lake), Fla. 212/E3
Hateg, Romania 45/F3
Hatfield, Ark. 202/B5
Hatfield, England 13/H7
Hatfield, England 13/H7
Hatfield, Ind. 227/C9
Hatfield, Mass. 249/D3
Hatfield•, Mass. 249/D3
Hatfield, Minn. 255/B7
Hatfield, Mo. 261/D1
Hatfield, N.S. Wales 97/B3
Hatfield, Pa. 294/M5
Hatfield, Sask. 181/F4
Hatfield, Wis. 317/E7
Hatfield Point, New Bruns. 170/E3
Hatgal, Mongolia 77/E1
Hathaway, Mont. 262/K4
Hatherleigh, Sask. 181/C2
Hathras, India 68/D3
Hatiba, Ras (cape), Saudi Arabia 59/C5
Ha Tien, Vietnam 72/E5
Hatillo, P. Rico 161/B1
Ha Tinh, Vietnam 72/E3
Hatira (mt.), Israel 65/B6
Hatley, Miss. 256/E3
Hatley, Québec 172/F4
Hatley, Wis. 317/H6
Hato, Neth. Ant. 161/G8
Hato del Volcán, Panama 154/F6
Hato Mayor, Dom. Rep. 158/F6
Hato Rey, P. Rico 161/E1
Hatseva, Israel 65/D5
Hattem, Netherlands 27/H4
Hatteras (cape), N.C. 146/L6
Hatteras (cape), N.C. 188/M3
Hatteras, N.C. 281/T4
Hatteras (cape), N.C. 281/U4
Hatteras (inlet), N.C. 281/T4
Hatteras (isl.), N.C. 281/U4
Hatteras (cape), U.S. 2/F4
Hattiesburg, Miss. 188/H4
Hattiesburg, Miss. 256/F8
Hattieville, Ark. 202/E3
Hattieville, Belize 154/C2
Hatton, Ala. 195/D1
Hatton, N. Dak. 282/R4
Hatton, Sask. 181/B4
Hatton, Scotland 15/G3
Hatton, Sask. 181/E4
Hatton, Wash. 310/G4
Hatuey, Cuba 158/G3
Hatvan, Hungary 41/E3
Hat Yai, Thailand 72/C6
Hatzic, Br. Col. 184/L3
Hau Bon, Vietnam 72/E4
Haubstadt, Ind. 227/B8
Haud (reg.), Ethiopia 111/J6
Haud (plat.), Somalia 115/J2
Haugan, Mont. 262/A3
Hauge, Norway 18/D7
Haugen, Wis. 317/C4
Haugesund, Norway 7/E3
Haugesund, Norway 18/D7
Haughton, La. 238/C1
Hauhungaroa (range), N. Zealand 100/E3
Haukivesi (lake), Finland 18/Q5
Haultain (riv.), Sask. 181/L3
Hauppauge, N.Y. 276/O9
Haura, Yemen 59/E7
Hauraki (gulf), N. Zealand 100/C1
Hauran, Wadi (dry riv.), Iraq 59/D3
Hauran, Wadi (dry riv.), Iraq 66/B4
Hauroko (lake), N. Zealand 100/A6
Haruru (pt.), Fr. Poly. 86/S12
Hauser, Idaho 220/A2
Hauser (lake), Mont. 262/E4
Hauser, Oreg. 291/C4
Hausstock (mt.), Switzerland 39/H3
Haut (isl.), Maine 243/G7
Haute, Nova Scotia 168/C3
Haute-Corse (dept.), France 28/B6
Haute-Garonne (dept.), France 28/D5
Haute-Loire (dept.), France 28/E5
Haute-Marne (dept.), France 28/F3
Hauterive, Québec 172/A1
Hauterive, Québec 174/A2
Hautes-Alpes (dept.), France 28/G5
Haute-Saône (dept.), France 28/G4
Haute-Savoie (dept.), France 28/G5
Hautes-Pyrénées (dept.), France 28/D6
Haute-Vienne (dept.), France 28/D5
Hautmont, France 28/F2
Haut-Rhin (dept.), France 28/G4
Hauts-de-Seine (dept.), France 28/A2
Hauts-Zaïre (prov.), Zaire 115/E3
Hauula, Hawaii 218/E1
Havaco, W. Va. 312/C8
Havana, Ala. 195/C5
Havana, Ark. 202/D3
Havana (prov.), Cuba 158/C1
Havana (cap.), Cuba 2/E4
Havana (cap.), Cuba 158/C1
Havana (cap.), Cuba 156/A2
Havana (cap.), Cuba 158/C1
Havana, Fla. 212/B1
Havana, Ill. 222/D3
Havana, Kansas 232/G4
Havana, Minn. 255/E6
Havana, N. Dak. 282/P8
Havana, Ohio 284/E3
Havannah (chan.), New Caled. 86/H5
Havant and Waterloo, England 13/G7
Havasu (lake) 188/D4
Havasu (lake), Ariz. 198/A4
Havasu (lake), Calif. 204/L9
Havasu (lake), U.S. 146/G6

Havasupai Ind. Res., Ariz. 198/C2
Havdrup, Denmark 21/F6
Havel (riv.), Germany 22/E2
Havelange, Belgium 27/G8
Havelberg, Germany 22/D2
Havelock, Iowa 229/D3
Havelock, New Bruns. 170/E3
Havelock, N. Zealand 100/D4
Havelock, N.C. 281/P5
Havelock, N. Dak. 282/E7
Havelock, Ontario 177/G3
Havelock North, N. Zealand 100/F3
Havelock West, Md. 245/O2
Haven, Kansas 232/E4
Havensville, Kansas 232/F2
Haverford•, Pa. 294/M6
Haverfordwest, Wales 10/D5
Haverfordwest, Wales 13/B6
Haverhill, England 13/H5
Haverhill, Iowa 229/H5
Haverhill, Mass. 249/K1
Haverhill•, N.H. 268/C3
Haverhill, Ohio 284/E8
Havering, England 10/C5
Havering, England 13/J8
Haverstraw, N.Y. 276/M8
Havertown, Pa. 294/M6
Haviland, Kansas 232/C4
Haviland, Ohio 284/A3
Havillah, Wash. 310/F2
Havířov, Czech. 41/E2
Havran, Turkey 63/B3
Havre, Mont. 146/G5
Havre, Mont. 188/E1
Havre, Mont. 262/G2
Havre Boucher, Nova Scotia 168/G3
Havre de Grace, Md. 245/O2
Havre-Saint-Pierre, Québec 174/E2
Havre-St-Pierre, Que. 162/K5
Havsa, Turkey 63/B2
Havza, Turkey 63/F2
Haw (riv.), N.C. 281/K2
HAWAII 218
Hawaii 188/F5
Hawaii (co.), Hawaii 218/K7
Hawaii (isl.), Hawaii 87/L4
Hawaii (isl.), Hawaii 188/F6
Hawaii (isl.), Hawaii 218/H5
Hawaii (state), U.S. 188/F5
Hawaii (state), U.S. 87/K4
Hawaiian (isls.) 87/J3
Hawaii Kai, Hawaii 218/F2
Hawaii Nat'l Park, Hawaii 218/J6
Hawaii Volcanoes Nat'l Park, Hawaii 218/H6
Hawara, Jordan 65/D2
Hawarden, Iowa 229/A2
Hawarden, N. Zealand 100/D5
Hawarden, Sask. 181/E4
Hawarden, Wales 13/G2
Hawea (lake), N. Zealand 100/B6
Hawera, N. Zealand 100/E4
Hawes, England 13/E3
Hawesville, Ky. 237/H5
Hawi, Hawaii 218/G3
Hawick, Minn. 255/D5
Hawick, Scotland 10/E3
Hawick, Scotland 15/E5
Hawk (hills), Alberta 182/B1
Hawke (hills), Newf. 166/D2
Hawke (isl.), Newf. 166/C3
Hawke (riv.), Newf. 166/C3
Hawke (bay), N. Zealand 100/F3
Hawker, S. Australia 88/F6
Hawker, S. Australia 94/F4
Hawke's Bay, Newf. 166/C3
Hawke's Bay (isl.), Br. Col. 184/C3
Hawkesbury, Ontario 177/K2
Hawkestone, Ontario 177/E3
Hawkeye, Iowa 229/J3
Hawkins, Mich. 250/D5
Hawkins (co.), Tenn. 237/P8
Hawkins, Texas 303/J5
Hawkins, Wis. 317/E4
Hawkinsville, Georgia 217/E6
Hawk Junction, Ontario 175/D3
Hawk Junction, Ontario 177/J5
Hawk Point, Mo. 261/K5
Hawk Run, Pa. 294/F4
Hawks, Mich. 250/F3
Hawk Springs, Wyo. 319/H4
Hawley, Minn. 255/B4
Hawley, Pa. 294/M3
Hawley, Texas 303/E5
Hawleyville, Conn. 210/B3
Haworth, N.J. 273/C1
Haworth, Okla. 288/S7
Hawston, S. Africa 118/G7
Hawthorn, La. 238/D4
Hawthorn, Pa. 294/D3
Hawthorn, Victoria 97/J5
Hawthorne, Calif. 204/C11
Hawthorne, Fla. 212/D2
Hawthorne, N.J. 273/B2
Hawthorne, N.Y. 276/O6
Hawthorne, Victoria 88/L7
Hawthorne, Wis. 317/C3
Hawthorn Woods, Ill. 222/B5
Haxby, England 13/F3
Haxtun, Colo. 208/O1
Hay (riv.) 162/E4
Hay (lake), Alberta 182/A5
Hay (riv.), Alberta 182/A5
Hay (riv.), Canada 146/G4
Hay, N.S. Wales 88/H6
Hay, N.S. Wales 97/C4
Hay (dry riv.), North. Terr. 88/F4
Hay (dry riv.), North. Terr. 93/E7
Hay (isl.), Ontario 177/F2
Hay, Wales 10/E4
Hay, Wales 13/D5
Hay, Wash. 310/H4
Hayama, Japan 81/O3
Hayange, France 28/F3
Haycock, Alaska 196/F1
Hayden, Ala. 195/E3

Hayden, Ariz. 198/E5
Hayden, Colo. 208/E2
Hayden, Idaho 220/B2
Hayden (lake), Idaho 220/B2
Hayden, Ind. 227/F7
Hayden, Mo. 261/H6
Hayden, N. Mex. 274/F3
Hayden (peak), Utah 304/C3
Hayden Lake, Idaho 220/B2
Haydenburg, Tenn. 237/K8
Haydenville, Mass. 249/C3
Haydenville, Ohio 284/F7
Hayes (mt.), Alaska 196/J2
Hayes (pen.), Greenl. 4/B13
Hayes, La. 238/E6
Hayes (riv.), Man. 162/G4
Hayes (co.), Nebr. 264/C4
Hayes (riv.), Manitoba 179/K3
Hayes (co.), N.W. Terr. 187/J3
Hayes, S. Dak. 298/H5
Hayes, Wis. 317/J5
Hayes Center, Nebr. 264/C4
Hayesville, Iowa 229/J6
Hayesville, New Bruns. 170/D2
Hayesville, N.C. 281/B4
Hayesville, Ohio 284/F4
Hayesville, Oreg. 291/A3
Hayfield, Iowa 229/F2
Hayfield, Minn. 255/F7
Hayfork, Calif. 204/B3
Hay Fork, Trinity (riv.), Calif. 204/B3
Hay Lakes, Alberta 182/D3
Hayle, England 13/B7
Haylow, Georgia 217/G9
Haymana, Turkey 63/E3
Haymarket, Va. 307/N3
Hayne, N.C. 281/M5
Haynes, Alberta 182/D3
Haynes, Ark. 202/J4
Haynes, N. Dak. 282/F8
Haynesville, La. 238/D1
Haynesville•, Maine 243/G4
Haynesville, Va. 307/P5
Hayneville, Ala. 195/E6
Hayrabolu, Turkey 63/B2
Hay River, N.W.T. 162/E3
Hay River, N.W. Terr. 146/G3
Hay River, N.W. Terr. 187/G3
Hays, Alberta 182/E3
Hays, Kansas 232/D4
Hays, Mont. 262/H2
Hays, N.C. 281/G2
Hays (co.), Texas 303/F7
Haysi, Va. 307/D6
Hay Springs, Nebr. 264/B2
Haystack (mt.), Conn. 210/C1
Haystack (peak), Mont. 262/A3
Haystack (mt.), N.Y. 276/N2
Haystack (mt.), Vt. 268/C3
Haysville, Ind. 227/B8
Haysville, Kansas 232/E4
Haysville, Pa. 294/P4
Hayter, Alberta 182/E3
Hayti, Mo. 261/N10
Hayti, S. Dak. 298/P5
Hayti Heights, Mo. 261/N10
Hayton, Wis. 317/K2
Hayward, Calif. 204/K2
Hayward (lake), Conn. 210/F2
Hayward, Minn. 255/F7
Hayward, Mo. 261/N10
Hayward, Wis. 317/D3
Haywards-Manor Park, N. Zealand 100/B2
Haywood, Manitoba 179/D5
Haywood (co.), N.C. 281/C3
Haywood, N.C. 281/L3
Haywood, Okla. 288/P5
Haywood (co.), Tenn. 237/C9
Haywood City, Mo. 261/N9
Hazar (lake), Turkey 63/H3
Hazaran, Kuh-e (mt.), Iran 66/K6
Hazard, Ky. 237/P6
Hazard, Nebr. 264/F3
Hazardville, Conn. 210/E1
Hazaribagh, India 68/F4
Hazar Qadam, Afghanistan 59/J3
Hazar Qadam, Afghanistan 68/B2
Hazebrouck, France 28/E2
Hazel, Ky. 237/E7
Hazel, S. Dak. 298/P4
Hazel Cliffe, Sask. 181/J5
Hazel Crest, Ill. 222/B6
Hazeldean, New Bruns. 170/C2
Hazel Dell, Ill. 222/F4
Hazel Dell, Sask. 181/H4
Hazeldine, Alberta 182/E3
Hazel Green, Ala. 195/E1
Hazel Green, Ky. 237/O5
Hazelgreen, Mo. 261/H7
Hazel Green, Wis. 317/F11
Hazel Grove and Bramhall, England 13/H2
Hazel Hill, Nova Scotia 168/G3
Hazelhurst, Ill. 222/F8
Hazel Hurst, Pa. 294/E2
Hazelhurst, Wis. 317/G4
Hazelridge, Manitoba 179/F5
Hazelrigg, Ind. 227/D4
Hazel Run, Minn. 255/C6
Hazelton, Br. Col. 162/D5
Hazelton, Br. Col. 184/D2
Hazelton (mts.), Br. Col. 184/C2
Hazelton, Idaho 220/E7
Hazelton, Kansas 232/D4
Hazelton, N. Dak. 282/K7
Hazelton, W. Va. 312/G3
Hazelton (peak), Wyo. 319/E1
Hazelwood, Ind. 227/D5
Hazelwood, Mo. 261/P2
Hazelwood, N.C. 281/C4
Hazen (bay), Alaska 196/E2
Hazen, Ark. 202/G4
Hazen, Nev. 266/C3
Hazen, N. Dak. 282/G5

Hazen (lake), N.W. Terr. 187/L1
Hazen (str.), N.W. Terr. 187/G2
Hazenmore, Sask. 181/D6
Hazerim, Israel 65/B5
Hazlehurst, Georgia 217/G7
Hazlehurst, Miss. 256/D7
Hazlet, N.J. 273/E3
Hazlet, Sask. 181/C5
Hazleton, Ind. 227/B8
Hazleton, Iowa 229/K3
Hazleton, Pa. 294/L4
Hazlett (lake), W. Australia 88/D4
Hazlettville, Del. 245/R4
Heacham, England 13/H5
Headford, Ireland 17/C5
Headland, Ala. 195/H8
Headlee, Ind. 227/F7
Head of Amherst, Nova Scotia 168/E3
Head of Bay d'Espoir, Newf. 166/C4
Head of Bight (bay), S. Australia 94/B4
Head of Grassy, Ky. 237/P4
Head of Island, La. 238/L2
Head of Jeddore, Nova Scotia 168/E4
Head of Millstream, New Bruns. 170/E3
Head of Saint Margarets Bay, Nova Scotia 168/E4
Headquarters, Idaho 220/C3
Headrick, Okla. 288/H5
Heads, The (prom.), Oreg. 291/C5
Head Waters, Va. 307/K4
Heafford Junction, Wis. 317/G4
Healdsburg, Calif. 204/B5
Healdton, Okla. 288/M6
Healdville, Vt. 268/B5
Healesville, Victoria 97/C5
Healing Springs, Ala. 195/D5
Healing Springs, Va. 307/J5
Healy, Alaska 196/H2
Healy, Kansas 232/B3
Healys, Va. 307/R5
Heanor, England 13/F4
Heard (isl.), Australia 2/N8
Heard (co.), Georgia 217/B4
Hearne, Sask. 181/F5
Hearne, Texas 303/H7
Hearst (isl.), Ant. 5/B16
Hearst, Ont. 162/H6
Hearst, Ontario 177/J5
Hearst, Ontario 175/D3
Heart (lake), Alberta 182/E2
Heart (butte), N. Dak. 282/G6
Heart (riv.), N. Dak. 282/F6
Heart (lake), Wyo. 319/B1
Heart Butte, Mont. 262/D2
Heart River Settlement, Alberta 182/B2
Heart's Content, Newf. 166/D2
Heart's Delight, Newf. 166/D2
Heart's Desire, Newf. 166/D2
Hearts Hill, Sask. 181/B4
Heartwell, Nebr. 264/F4
Heartwellville, Vt. 268/A6
Heaters, W. Va. 312/E5
Heath, Ala. 195/F8
Heath, Alberta 182/E3
Heath (riv.), Bolivia 136/A3
Heath•, Mass. 249/C2
Heath, Mont. 262/G3
Heath, Ohio 284/F5
Heath (riv.), Peru 128/H9
Heath (pt.), Québec 174/F3
Heathcote, Victoria 97/C5
Heatherton, Newf. 166/C4
Heatherton, Nova Scotia 168/G3
Heathhall, Scotland 15/E5
Heath Springs, S.C. 296/F2
Heath Steele, New Bruns. 170/D1
Heathsville, Va. 307/P5
Heaton, N. Dak. 282/L5
Heavener, Okla. 288/S5
Hebbardsville, Ky. 237/G5
Hebbronville, Texas 303/F10
Hebbs Cross, Nova Scotia 168/D4
Hebei (Hopei), China 77/J4
Hebel, Queensland 95/C6
Heber, Ariz. 198/E4
Heber, Calif. 204/K7
Heber City, Utah 304/C3
Heber Springs, Ark. 202/G2
Hébert, La. 238/G2
Hébert (riv.), Nova Scotia 168/D3
Hébertville, Québec 172/F1
Hébertville-Station, Québec 172/F1
Hebgen (dam), Mont. 262/E6
Hebgen (lake), Mont. 262/E6
Hebi, China 77/H4
Hebo, Oreg. 291/C3
Hebrides, Inner (isls.), Scotland 10/C1
Hebrides, Inner (isls.), Scotland 15/B4
Hebrides, Outer (isls.), Scotland 10/C2
Hebrides, Outer (isls.), Scotland 15/A3
Hebrides (sea), Scotland 15/B3
Hebrides (sea), Scotland 10/C2
Hebron•, Conn. 210/F2
Hebron, Ill. 222/E1
Hebron, Ind. 227/C2
Hebron, Ky. 237/R2
Hebron, Md. 245/R7
Hebron•, Maine 243/C7
Hebron, Nebr. 264/G4
Hebron (fjord), Newf. 166/B2
Hebron•, N.H. 268/C3
Hebron, N. Dak. 282/G6
Hebron, Nova Scotia 168/B5
Hebron, Ohio 284/E6
Hebron, Texas 303/D5
Hebron, West Bank 65/C4
Hebron, West Bank 59/C3
Hebron, W. Va. 312/D4
Hebron, Wis. 317/J10
Hecate (str.), Br. Col. 162/C5
Hecate (str.), Br. Col. 184/B3
Hecate (str.), Br. Col. 184/B3
Hecelchakán, Mexico 150/O6
Heceta (isl.), Alaska 196/M2

Heceta (head), Oreg. 291/C3
Hechi, China 77/G7
Hechingen, Germany 22/C4
Hechuan (Hochwan), China 77/G5
Hecker, Ill. 222/D5
Hecla, Manitoba 179/F3
Hecla, Miss. 256/D7
Hecla (isl.), Manitoba 179/F3
Hecla, S. Dak. 298/N2
Hecla Prov. Park, Manitoba 179/F3
Hector, Ark. 202/E3
Hector, Minn. 255/D6
Hector, N.Y. 276/G5
Hede, Sweden 18/H5
Hedemora, Sweden 18/K6
Hedenäset, Sweden 18/N3
Hedensted, Denmark 21/C6
Hedgesville, Mont. 262/E4
Hedgesville, W. Va. 312/K3
Hedley, Br. Col. 184/G5
Hedley, Texas 303/D3
Hedmark (co.), Norway 18/G6
Hedon, England 13/G4
Hedrick, Iowa 229/J6
Hedville, Kansas 232/E3
Hedwig Village, Texas 303/H1
Heemskert, Netherlands 27/F4
Heemstede, Netherlands 27/F4
Heer, Netherlands 27/H7
Heerde, Netherlands 27/H4
Heerenveen, Netherlands 27/H3
Heerhugowaard, Netherlands 27/F4
Heerlen, Netherlands 27/J7
Heesch, Netherlands 27/G5
Hefei (Hofei), China 77/J5
Hefei, China 54/N6
Heffley Creek, Br. Col. 184/G5
Heflin, Ala. 195/G3
Heflin, La. 238/D2
Hegang (Hokang), China 77/L2
Hegang, China 54/O5
Hegau (reg.), Germany 22/C5
Hegeler, Ill. 222/F3
Hegins, Pa. 294/K4
Heiban, Sudan 111/F5
Heiberger, Ala. 195/D5
Heide, Germany 22/C1
Heidelberg, Germany 22/C4
Heidelberg, Ky. 237/O5
Heidelberg, Minn. 255/E6
Heidelberg, Miss. 256/F7
Heidelberg, Pa. 294/B7
Heidelberg, S. Africa 118/J2
Heidelberg, Victoria 97/J5
Heidelberg, Victoria 88/L7
Heiden, Switzerland 39/H2
Heidenau, Germany 22/E3
Heidenheim an der Brenz, Germany 22/D4
Heidenreichstein, Austria 41/C2
Heidrick, Ky. 237/O7
Heihe (Aihui) (Aigun), China 77/L1
Heijo (P'yŏngyang) (cap.), N. Korea 81/C4
Heil, N. Dak. 282/G7
Heilbron, S. Africa 118/D5
Heilbronn, Germany 22/C4
Heiligenblut, Austria 41/B3
Heiligenhafen, Germany 22/D1
Heiligenstadt, Germany 22/D3
Heilman, Ind. 227/C8
Heilongjiang (Heilungkiang), China 77/K2
Heilong Jiang (Amur) (riv.), China 77/L2
Heiloo, Netherlands 27/F3
Heilwood, Pa. 294/E4
Heimberg, Switzerland 39/E4
Heimdal, N. Dak. 282/L4
Heinola, Finland 18/P6
Heinola, Minn. 255/C4
Heinsburg, Alberta 182/E3
Heinze Chaung (bay), Burma 72/C4
Heise, Idaho 220/H2
Heiskell, Tenn. 237/O8
Heisler, Alberta 182/D3
Heislerville, N.J. 273/D5
Heisson, Wash. 310/C5
Heist-Knokke, Belgium 27/C6
Heist-op-den-Berg, Belgium 27/F6
Heizer, Kansas 232/D3
Hejaz (reg.), Saudi Arabia 59/C4
Hejian, China 77/J4
Hejing, China 77/C3
Hekimhan, Turkey 63/G3
Hekla (mt.), Iceland 4/C11
Hekla (mt.), Iceland 7/C2
Hekla (vol.), Iceland 21/B1
Hekou, China 77/F7
Hel, Poland 47/D1
Hel (pen.), Poland 47/D1
Helan, China 77/G4
Heldens (pt.), St. Kitts & Nevis 161/C10
Helechawa, Ky. 237/P5
Helen, Georgia 217/E1
Helen, Md. 245/M7
Helen (lake), N. Dak. 282/K5
Helena, Ala. 195/E4
Helena, Ark. 202/J4
Helena, Calif. 204/B3
Helena, Georgia 217/G6
Helena, Mo. 261/C3
Helena (cap.), Mont. 146/G5
Helena (cap.), Mont. 188/D1
Helena (cap.), Mont. 262/E4
Helena (lake), Mont. 262/E4
Helena, N.Y. 276/L1
Helena, Ohio 284/D3
Helena, Okla. 288/K1
Helena, S.C. 296/D3
Helensburgh, N.S. Wales 97/F1A
Helensburgh, Scotland 10/A1
Helensburgh, Scotland 15/D4
Helen Springs, North. Terr. 93/C5
Helensville, N. Zealand 100/B1
Helenville, Wis. 317/J10
Helenwood, Tenn. 237/M8
Helez, Israel 65/B4

Hillsborough 381

Helgoland (bay), Germany 22/C1
Helgoland (isl.), Germany 22/B1
Heliopolis, Egypt 111/J3
Helix, Oreg. 291/J2
Hellam, Pa. 294/J6
Hell Canyon (creek), S. Dak. 298/B6
Hellebaek, Denmark 21/F5
Hellendoorn, Netherlands 27/J4
Hellertown, Pa. 294/M4
Helles (cape), Turkey 63/B6
Hellevoetsluis, Netherlands 27/E5
Hellier, Ky. 237/S6
Hellín, Spain 33/F3
Hells (canyon), Idaho 220/B4
Hells Canyon (dam), Idaho 220/B4
Hells Canyon (dam), Oreg. 291/L2
Hells Canyon Nat'l Rec. Area, Idaho 220/B4
Hells Canyon Nat'l Rec. Area, Oreg. 291/K2
Hells Canyon Nat'l Rec. Area, Wash. 310/H5
Hells Half Acre, Wyo. 319/E2
Hell-Ville, Madagascar 102/G6
Hell-Ville, Madagascar 118/H2
Helm, Miss. 256/C4
Helmand (riv.), Afghanistan 54/H6
Helmand (riv.), Afghanistan 59/J3
Helmand (riv.), Afghanistan 68/B2
Helmand (Sistan, Daryacheh-ye) (lake), Iran 66/M5
Helmer, Ind. 227/G1
Helmetta, N.J. 273/E3
Helmond, Netherlands 27/H6
Helmsburg, Ind. 227/E6
Helmsdale, Scotland 10/E1
Helmsdale, Scotland 15/E2
Helmsdale (riv.), Scotland 15/E2
Helmsley, England 13/G3
Helmstedt, Germany 22/D2
Helmville, Mont. 262/C4
Helotes, Texas 303/J10
Helper, Utah 304/D4
Helsenhorn (mt.), Switzerland 39/F4
Helsingborg, Sweden 18/H8
Helsingborg, Sweden 7/F3
Helsinge, Denmark 21/F6
Helsingør, Denmark 21/F6
Helsingør, Denmark 18/H8
Helsinki (cap.), Finland 18/O6
Helsinki (cap.), Finland 7/G2
Helsinki (cap.), Finland 2/L2
Helston, England 13/B7
Helston, England 10/D5
Helston, Manitoba 179/C4
Helton, Ky. 237/P7
Helton, N.C. 281/G1
Heltonville, Ind. 227/E7
Helvecia, Argentina 143/F5
Helvetia, Pa. 294/E3
Helvetia, W. Va. 312/F5
Helvick (head), Ireland 17/G7
Helwân, Egypt 59/B4
Helwân, Egypt 111/J3
Hemar (dry riv.), Israel 65/C5
Hemaruka, Alberta 182/E4
Hematite, Mo. 261/L6
Hemel Hempstead, England 10/F5
Hemel Hempstead, England 13/G7
Hemet, Calif. 204/H10
Hemford, Nova Scotia 168/D4
Hemingford, Nebr. 264/A2
Hemingway, S.C. 296/J4
Hemlock, Ind. 227/F4
Hemlock, Mich. 250/E5
Hemlock, N.Y. 276/E5
Hemlock (lake), N.Y. 276/E5
Hemlock, Ohio 284/F6
Hemlock (Eureka), S.C. 296/E2
Hemlock Grove, Ohio 284/F7
Hemmingford, Québec 172/D4
Hemnes, Norway 18/J3
Hemphill (co.), Texas 303/D2
Hemphill, Texas 303/L6
Hemphill, W. Va. 312/C8
Hemple, Mo. 261/D3
Hempstead (co.), Ark. 202/C6
Hempstead, N.Y. 276/R7
Hempstead, Texas 303/J7
Hemse, Sweden 18/L8
Henagar, Ala. 195/G1
Henan (Honan), China 77/H5
Henan, China 77/F5
Hen and Chickens (isls.), N. Zealand 100/E1
Henares (riv.), Spain 33/G4
Henbury, North. Terr. 93/C8
Hendaye, France 28/C6
Hendek, Turkey 63/D2
Henderson, Ala. 195/F7
Henderson (co.), Ill. 222/C3
Henderson, Ill. 222/C2
Henderson (riv.), Ill. 222/C2
Henderson, Ind. 227/F5
Henderson, Iowa 229/B6
Henderson (co.), Ky. 237/F5
Henderson, Ky. 237/F5
Henderson, La. 238/G6
Henderson, Md. 245/P4
Henderson, Minn. 255/E6
Henderson, Nebr. 264/G4
Henderson, Nev. 266/G6
Henderson, N.Y. 276/H3
Henderson, N. Zealand 100/B1
Henderson (co.), N.C. 281/D4
Henderson, N.C. 281/N2
Henderson (isl.), Pitcairn Is. 87/O8
Henderson (co.), Tenn. 237/E9
Henderson, Tenn. 237/D10
Henderson (co.), Texas 303/J5
Henderson, Texas 303/K5
Henderson, W. Va. 312/B5
Hendersonville, N.C. 281/E4
Hendersonville, Pa. 294/B5
Hendersonville, S.C. 296/F6
Hendersonville, Tenn. 237/H8
Hendley, Nebr. 264/D4
Hendon, Sask. 181/H3
Hendorabi (isl.), Iran 66/H7
Hendra, Queensland 88/K2
Hendricks (co.), Ind. 227/D5
Hendricks, Ky. 237/P5
Hendricks, Minn. 255/B6
Hendricks, W. Va. 312/G4
Hendrickson, Mo. 261/M9
Hendrix, Okla. 288/O7
Hendrix Lake, Br. Col. 184/G4
Hendrum, Minn. 255/B3
Hendry (co.), Fla. 212/E5
Hendrysburg, Ohio 284/H5
Henefer, Utah 304/C2
Hengchun, China 77/K7
Hengduan Shan (mts.), China 77/E6
Hengelo, Gelderland, Netherlands 27/J4
Hengelo, Overijssel, Netherlands 27/K4
Hengshan, China 77/G4
Hengshui, China 77/J4
Heng Xian, China 77/G7
Hengyang, China 77/H6
Hengyang, China 54/N7
Henik (lakes), N.W. Terr. 187/J3
Hénin-Beaumont, France 28/E2
Henjam (isl.), Iran 66/J7
Henlawson, W. Va. 312/B7
Henley, Mo. 261/H5
Henley and Grange, S. Australia 88/D8
Henley Harbour, Newf. 166/C3
Henley on Klip, S. Africa 118/H7
Henley-on-Thames, England 13/G8
Henlopen (cape), Del. 245/T5
Henlopen Acres, Del. 245/T6
Henne, Denmark 21/B6
Hennebont, France 28/B4
Hennef, Germany 22/B3
Hennepin, Ill. 222/D2
Hennepin (co.), Minn. 255/E5
Hennepin, Okla. 288/M5
Hennessey, Okla. 288/L2
Hennigsdorf bei Berlin, Germany 22/E3
Henniker, N.H. 268/D5
Henniker•, N.H. 268/D5
Henning, Ill. 222/F3
Henning, Minn. 255/C4
Henning, Tenn. 237/B9
Henribourg, Sask. 181/F2
Henrico (co.), Va. 307/O6
Henrietta, Mo. 261/E4
Henrietta, N.Y. 276/E4
Henrietta, N.C. 281/F4
Henrietta, Texas 303/F4
Henrietta Maria (cape), Ont. 162/H4
Henrietta Maria (cape), Ontario 175/D1
Henriette, Minn. 255/E5
Henrieville, Utah 304/C6
Henry (co.), Ala. 195/H7
Henry (co.), Georgia 217/D4
Henry, Idaho 220/G7
Henry (co.), Ill. 222/C2
Henry, Ill. 222/D2
Henry (co.), Ind. 227/G5
Henry (co.), Iowa 229/K6
Henry (co.), Ky. 237/L4
Henry (co.), Mo. 261/E6
Henry, Nebr. 264/A2
Henry (isl.), Nova Scotia 168/G3
Henry (co.), Ohio 284/B3
Henry, S.C. 296/J4
Henry, S. Dak. 298/P4
Henry (co.), Tenn. 237/E8
Henry, Tenn. 237/E8
Henry (mts.), Utah 304/D6
Henry (co.), Va. 307/J7
Henry, Va. 307/J7
Henry (cape), Va. 307/R7
Henryetta, Okla. 288/O4
Henry House, Alberta 182/B3
Henry Kater (cape), N.W. Terr. 187/M3
Henrys (lake), Idaho 220/G5
Henrys Fork, Snake (riv.), Idaho 220/G5
Henrys Fork, Green (riv.), Wyo. 319/C4
Henryton, Md. 245/L3
Henryville, Ind. 227/F7
Henryville, Pa. 294/M3
Henryville, Québec 172/D4
Henryville, Tenn. 237/G10
Hensall, Ontario 177/C4
Hensel, N. Dak. 282/P2
Henshaw, Ky. 237/F5
Hensies, Belgium 27/D8
Hensler, N. Dak. 282/H5
Hensley, Ark. 202/F4
Henson (creek), Md. 245/F6
Hentiy, Mongolia 77/H2
Henty, N.S. Wales 97/D4
Henzada, Burma 72/B3
Henzada, Burma 54/L8
Hepburn, Iowa 229/C7
Hepburn, Ohio 284/D4
Hepburn, Sask. 181/E3
Hephzibah, Georgia 217/H4
Hepler, Kansas 232/H4
Heppner, Oreg. 291/H2
Hepu (Hoppo), China 77/G7
Hepworth, Ontario 177/C3
Hepzibah, W. Va. 312/F4
Hequ, China 77/H4
Herald, Calif. 204/C9
Heralds (cays), Australia 95/D3
Herat, Afghanistan 54/H6
Herat, Afghanistan 59/H3
Herat, Afghanistan 68/A2
Hérault (dept.), France 28/E6
Hérault (riv.), France 28/E6
Herbert, Ala. 195/E8
Herbert (riv.), Queensland 88/H3
Herbert, Sask. 181/D5
Herbert Hoover Nat'l Hist. Site, Iowa 229/L5
Herbes (isl.), Ala. 195/B10
Herbeumont, Belgium 27/G9
Herb Lake, Manitoba 179/H3
Herborn, Germany 22/C3
Herbst, Ind. 227/F3
Herbster, Wis. 317/D2
Herceg Novi, Yugoslavia 45/D4
Herchmer, Man. 162/G4
Herchmer, Manitoba 179/K2
Herculaneum, Mo. 261/M6
Hercules, Calif. 204/J1
Herd, Okla. 288/O1
Heredia, C. Rica 154/E5
Hereford, Ariz. 198/E7
Hereford, Colo. 208/L1
Hereford, England 13/E5
Hereford, England 10/E4
Hereford, Md. 245/M2
Hereford (inlet), N.J. 273/D5
Hereford, Oreg. 291/K3
Hereford, Pa. 294/L5
Hereford, S. Dak. 298/D5
Hereford, Texas 303/B3
Hereford and Worcester (co.), England 13/E5
Hérémence, Switzerland 39/D4
Herencia, Spain 33/E3
Herentals, Belgium 27/F6
Heretaunga-Pinehaven, N. Zealand 100/C2
Herford, Germany 22/C2
Hergiswil, Switzerland 39/F3
Héricourt, France 28/G4
Heringsdorf, Germany 22/F1
Herington, Kansas 232/E3
Heriot Bay, Br. Col. 184/E5
Herisau, Switzerland 39/H2
Herkimer, Kansas 232/F2
Herkimer (co.), N.Y. 276/L4
Herkimer, N.Y. 276/L4
Herlen Gol (Kerulen) (riv.), Mongolia 77/H2
Herlong, Calif. 204/E3
Herm (isl.), Chan. Is. 13/E8
Hermagor-Presеggersee, Austria 41/B3
Herman, Mich. 250/A2
Herman, Minn. 255/B5
Herman, Nebr. 264/H3
Herman, Pa. 294/C4
Herman (lake), S. Dak. 298/P5
Herma Ness (prom.), Scotland 15/G2
Hermann, Mo. 261/K5
Hermannsburg, North. Terr. 88/E4
Hermannsburg, North. Terr. 93/C7
Hermansverk, Norway 18/E6
Hermansville, Mich. 250/B3
Hermantown, Minn. 255/F4
Hermanus, S. Africa 118/G7
Hermanville, Miss. 256/C7
Hermidale, N.S. Wales 97/D2
Hermil, Lebanon 63/G5
Herminie, Pa. 294/C5
Hermiston, Oreg. 291/H2
Hermitage, Ark. 202/F7
Hermitage, Grenada 161/D8
Hermitage, Mo. 261/F7
Hermitage, Newf. 166/C4
Hermitage (bay), Newf. 166/C4
Hermitage Springs, Tenn. 237/K7
Hermite (isls.), Chile 138/F11
Hermleigh, Texas 303/D5
Hermon, Ill. 222/C3
Hermon•, Maine 243/F6
Hermon, N.Y. 276/K2
Hermon (mt.), Syria 63/F6
Hermosa (peak), Colo. 208/D7
Hermosa, S. Dak. 298/C6
Hermosa Beach, Calif. 204/B11
Hermosillo, Mexico 146/G7
Hermosillo, Mexico 150/D2
Hermsdorf, Germany 22/E3
Hernád (riv.), Hungary 41/F2
Hernandarias, Argentina 143/F5
Hernandarias, Paraguay 144/E4
Hernández, Argentina 143/F6
Hernandez, N. Mex. 274/C2
Hernando, Argentina 143/D3
Hernando (co.), Fla. 212/D3
Hernando, Fla. 212/D3
Hernando, Miss. 256/E1
Herndon, Georgia 217/H5
Herndon, Iowa 229/E5
Herndon, Kansas 232/B2
Herndon, Ky. 237/G7
Herndon, Pa. 294/J4
Herndon, Va. 307/O3
Herndon, W. Va. 312/D7
Herne, Belgium 27/E7
Herne, Germany 22/B3
Herning, Denmark 18/F8
Herning, Denmark 21/B5
Herod, Georgia 217/D7
Herod, Ill. 222/E6
Heroica Caborca, Mexico 150/C1
Heroica Nogales, Mexico 150/D1
Heron (lake), Minn. 255/C7
Heron, Mont. 262/A2
Heron (isl.), New Bruns. 170/D1
Heron Bay, Ontario 177/H5
Heron Bay, Ontario 175/C3
Heron Lake, Minn. 255/C7
Hérouxville, Québec 172/E3
Herradura, Argentina 143/E2
Herradura, Cuba 158/B1
Herreid, S. Dak. 298/K2
Herrera, Argentina 143/D2
Herrera del Duque, Spain 33/D3
Herrera de Pisuerga, Spain 33/D1
Herrero (pt.), Mexico 150/Q7
Herrick, Ill. 222/D4
Herrick, S. Dak. 298/L7
Herrick, Tasmania 99/D3
Herrick Center, Pa. 294/L2
Herrin, Ill. 222/E6
Herring Cove, Nova Scotia 168/E4
Herrings, N.Y. 276/J2
Herrington (lake), Ky. 237/M5
Herron, Mich. 250/F3
Herronton, Alberta 182/D4
Hersbruck, Germany 22/D4
Herschel, Sask. 181/C4
Herschel (isl.), Yukon 187/E3
Herscher, Ill. 222/E2
Herselt, Belgium 27/F6
Hersey, Mich. 250/D5
Hersey, Wis. 317/B6
Hershey, Nebr. 264/D3
Hershey, Pa. 294/J5
Hersman, Ill. 222/C4
Herstal, Belgium 27/H7
Hertel, Wis. 317/B4
Hertford, England 13/H7
Hertford, England 10/G5
Hertford (co.), N.C. 281/P2
Hertford, N.C. 281/S2
Hertfordshire (co.), England 13/G6
Hervás, Spain 33/D2
Herve, Belgium 27/H7
Hervey, Queensland 88/J4
Hervey (bay), Queensland 95/E5
Hervey Bay, Queensland 88/J5
Hervey Bay, Queensland 95/E5
Herzberg, Germany 22/E3
Herzeliyya, Israel 65/B3
Herzogenbuchsee, Switzerland 39/E2
Herzogenburg, Austria 41/C2
Heshui, China 77/G4
Hesketh, Alberta 182/D4
Hesper, Iowa 229/K2
Hesper, N. Dak. 282/L4
Hesperange, Luxembourg 27/J9
Hesperia, Calif. 204/H9
Hesperia, Mich. 250/D5
Hespero, Alberta 182/C3
Hesperus, Colo. 208/C8
Hesperus (mt.), Colo. 208/C8
Hess, Okla. 288/H6
Hess (riv.), Yukon 187/E3
Hesse (state), Germany 22/C3
Hessel, Mich. 250/E2
Hessmer, La. 238/F4
Hesston, Kansas 232/E3
Hesston, Pa. 294/F5
Hester, La. 238/L3
Hester, Okla. 288/H5
Hesterville, Miss. 256/E4
Hetch Hetchy (res.), Calif. 204/F6
Heth, Ark. 202/K3
Het IJ (est.), Netherlands 27/C4
Hetland, S. Dak. 298/P5
Hettick, Ill. 222/C4
Hettinger (co.), N. Dak. 282/E7
Hettinger, N. Dak. 282/E8
Hetton, England 13/J3
Hettstedt, Germany 22/D3
Heusden, Netherlands 27/G5
Heuvelland, Belgium 27/B7
Heuvelton, N.Y. 276/K1
Heves (co.), Hungary 41/F3
Heves, Hungary 41/F3
Heward, Sask. 181/H6
Hewins, Kansas 232/F4
Hewitt, Minn. 255/C4
Hewitt, N.J. 273/E1
Hewitt, Wis. 317/F6
Hewlett, N.Y. 276/P7
Hewlett Harbor, N.Y. 276/P7
Hexham, England 13/E3
Hexham, England 10/E3
He Xian, China 77/H7
Hexigten, China 77/J3
Hext, Texas 303/E7
Heybeli (isl.), Turkey 63/D6
Heybridge, Tasmania 99/C3
Heyburn, Idaho 220/E7
Heyburn (res.), Okla. 288/O3
Heyden, Ontario 177/J5
Heyfield, Victoria 97/D6
Heyuan, China 77/H7
Heywood (chan.), Burma 72/B3
Heywood, England 13/H2
Heywood, Victoria 97/A6
Heyworth, Ill. 222/E3
Heze, China 77/J4
Hezuo, China 77/F5
Hialeah, Fla. 188/K5
Hialeah, Fla. 212/B4
Hialeah Gardens, Fla. 212/B4
Hiattville, Kansas 232/H4
Hiawassee, Georgia 217/E1
Hiawatha, Iowa 229/K4
Hiawatha, Kansas 232/G2
Hiawatha, Mich. 250/C2
Hiawatha, Utah 304/D4
Hibbard, Ind. 227/E2
Hibbing, Minn. 188/H1
Hibbing, Minn. 255/F3
Hibbs (pt.), Tasmania 99/B4
Hibernia, N.J. 273/E2
Hibuson (isl.), Philippines 82/E5
Hicacos (pen.), Cuba 158/D1
Hicacos (pt.), Cuba 158/D1
Hickam A.F.B., Hawaii 218/B4
Hickam Housing, Hawaii 218/B4
Hickman, Ark. 202/L2
Hickman, Del. 245/R5
Hickman (co.), Ky. 237/C7
Hickman, Ky. 237/C7
Hickman, Nebr. 264/H4
Hickman (co.), Tenn. 237/G9
Hickman, Tenn. 237/K8
Hickman's Harbour, Newf. 166/D2
Hickok, Kansas 232/A4
Hickory, Ky. 237/D7
Hickory, Miss. 256/F6
Hickory (co.), Mo. 261/F7
Hickory, N.C. 281/G3
Hickory, Okla. 288/N5
Hickory Corners, Mich. 250/D6
Hickory Creek, Texas 303/F1
Hickory Flat, Ala. 195/H4
Hickory Flat, Miss. 256/F1
Hickory Grove, S.C. 296/E2
Hickory Hills, Ill. 222/B6
Hickory Plains, Ark. 202/G3
Hickory Ridge, Ark. 202/J3
Hickory Valley, Tenn. 237/C10
Hickory Withe, Tenn. 237/B10
Hickox, Georgia 217/H8
Hicks, La. 238/E4
Hickson, N. Dak. 282/S6
Hickson, Ontario 177/D4
Hicksville, N.Y. 276/R7
Hicksville, Ohio 284/A3
Hico, La. 238/E1
Hico, Texas 303/F6
Hico, W. Va. 312/D6
Hida (riv.), Japan 81/H6
Hidalgo, Ill. 222/E4
Hidalgo, Ky. 237/M7
Hidalgo (state), Mexico 150/K6
Hidalgo, Coahuila, Mexico 150/K3
Hidalgo, Tamaulipas, Mexico 150/K4
Hidalgo (co.), N. Mex. 274/A7
Hidalgo (co.), Texas 303/F11
Hidalgo, Texas 303/F11
Hidalgo del Parral (Parral), Mexico 150/G3
Hidden Hills, Calif. 204/B10
Hiddenite, N.C. 281/G3
Hiddensee (isl.), Germany 22/E1
Hieflau, Austria 41/C3
Hienghene, New Caled. 86/G4
Hierro (isl.), Spain 106/A3
Hierro (isl.), Spain 33/A5
Higashiosaka, Japan 81/J8
Higbee, Mo. 261/H4
Higden, Ark. 202/F2
Higdon, Ala. 195/G1
Higganum, Conn. 210/E2
Higgins (lake), Mich. 250/E4
Higgins, Texas 303/D1
Higgins Lake, Mich. 250/E4
Higginson, Ark. 202/G3
Higginsport, Ohio 284/C8
Higginsville, Mo. 261/E4
Higgston, Georgia 217/G6
High, Iowa 229/K5
High (isl.), Ireland 17/A4
High (isl.), Mich. 250/D3
High Atlas (ranges), Morocco 106/C2
High Bluff, Manitoba 179/D4
High Bridge, Ky. 237/M5
High Bridge, N.J. 273/D2
High Bridge, Wis. 317/E3
Highbury, W. Australia 92/B2
High Falls, N.Y. 276/M7
Highfalls, N.C. 281/K4
Highfield-Cascade, Md. 245/J2
Highfill, Ark. 202/B1
Highgate, Jamaica 158/J6
Highgate, Ontario 177/C5
Highgate•, Vt. 268/B2
Highgate Center, Vt. 268/B2
Highgate Falls, Vt. 268/A2
Highgate Springs, Vt. 268/A2
Highgrove, Calif. 204/E10
High Hill, Mo. 261/K5
High Island, Texas 303/K8
Highland, Calif. 204/H9
Highland (lake), Conn. 210/C1
Highland (pt.), Fla. 212/E6
Highland, Ill. 222/D5
Highland, Ind. 227/B1
Highland, Kansas 232/G2
Highland (peak), Nev. 266/G5
Highland (lake), N.H. 268/C5
Highland, N.Y. 276/M7
Highland (co.), Ohio 284/C7
Highland, Ohio 284/C7
Highland (reg.), Scotland 15/D3
Highland, Utah 304/C3
Highland (co.), Va. 307/J4
Highland, W. Va. 312/D4
Highland, Wis. 317/F9
Highland Beach, Fla. 212/F5
Highland Beach, Md. 245/M5
Highland Center, Iowa 229/J6
Highland City, Fla. 212/E4
Highland Falls, N.Y. 276/M8
Highland Heights, Ky. 237/T2
Highland Heights, Ohio 284/J9
Highland Home, Ala. 195/F7
Highland Lake, Ala. 195/F3
Highland Lake, Maine 243/C8
Highland Lakes, N.J. 273/E1
Highland Park, Conn. 210/F1
Highland Park, Fla. 212/E4
Highland Park, Ill. 222/B5
Highland Park, Mich. 250/B6
Highland Park, N.J. 273/D2
Highland Park, Pa. 294/H4
Highland Park, Texas 303/G2
Highlands (co.), Fla. 212/E4
Highlands, N.J. 273/F3
Highlands, N.C. 281/C4
Highlands, Texas 303/K1
Highland Springs, Va. 307/O5
Highland Village, Texas 303/F1
Highlandville, Iowa 229/K2
Highlandville, Mo. 261/F9
High Level, Alberta 182/A5
Highmore, S. Dak. 298/L4
Highpine, Maine 243/B9
High Plateaus (ranges), Algeria 106/D2
High Point, Fla. 212/B3
Highpoint, Miss. 256/F4
High Point, Mo. 261/G5
High Point (mt.), N.J. 273/D1
High Point, N.C. 188/K3
High Point, N.C. 281/J3
High Prairie, Alberta 182/B2
Highridge, Alberta 182/D2
High Ridge, Mo. 261/M6
High River, Alberta 182/D4
High River, Alta. 162/E5
High Rock (creek), Nev. 266/B1
High Rock, N.C. 281/J3
High Rock (lake), N.C. 281/J3
High Rocky (pt.), Tasmania 99/B4
High Rolls-Mountain Park, N. Mex. 274/D5
High Shoals, N.C. 281/G4
Highspire, Pa. 294/J5
Highsplint, Ky. 237/P7
High Springs, Fla. 212/D2
High Tatra (range), Poland 47/D4
Hightower, Ala. 195/H3
Hightown, Va. 307/J4
Hightstown, N.J. 273/D3
Highway, Ky. 237/L7
High Willhays (mt.), England 13/C7
Highwood (riv.), Alberta 182/C4
Highwood, Ill. 222/B5
Highwood, Mont. 262/F3
Highworth, England 13/F6
High Wycombe, England 13/G8
High Wycombe, England 10/F5
Higley, Ariz. 198/D5
Higuerote, Venezuela 124/F2
Higüey, Dom. Rep. 158/F6
Hiiraan (prov.), Somalia 115/J3
Hiiumaa (isl.), U.S.S.R. 7/G3
Hiiumaa (isl.), U.S.S.R. 52/B3
Hiiumaa (isl.), U.S.S.R. 53/B1
Hiiumaa (isl.), U.S.S.R. 48/C4
Híjar, Spain 33/F2
Hijuelas, Chile 138/F2
Hiko, Nev. 266/F5
Hikone, Japan 81/H6
Hikueru (atoll), Fr. Poly. 87/M7
Hikurangi, N. Zealand 100/E1
Hikurangi (mt.), N. Zealand 100/G2
Hiland, Wyo. 319/E2
Hiland Park, Fla. 212/C6
Hilbert, Wis. 317/K7
Hilbre, Manitoba 179/D3
Hilda, Alberta 182/E4
Hilda, S.C. 296/E5
Hildale, Utah 304/A6
Hildburghausen, Germany 22/D3
Hildebran, N.C. 281/F3
Hildebrand, Oreg. 291/F5
Hilden, Nova Scotia 168/E3
Hildesheim, Germany 22/D2
Hildreth, Nebr. 264/E4
Hiles, Wis. 317/J4
Hilgard (mt.), Utah 304/C5
Hilger, Mont. 262/G3
Hilham, Tenn. 237/L8
Hill (riv.), Minn. 255/C3
Hill (co.), Mont. 262/F2
Hill•, N.H. 268/D4
Hill (co.), Texas 303/G5
Hill (creek), Utah 304/E4
Hilla, Iraq 66/D4
Hilla, Iraq 59/D3
Hill A.F.B., Utah 304/C2
Hillaby (mt.), Barbados 161/B8
Hillandale, Md. 245/F4
Hill Bank, Belize 154/C2
Hillburn, N.Y. 276/M8
Hill City, Idaho 220/D6
Hill City, Kansas 232/C2
Hill City, Minn. 255/E4
Hill City, S. Dak. 298/B6
Hill Country Village, Texas 303/K10
Hill Creek Ext., Uintah and Ouray Ind. Res., Utah 304/E4
Hillcrest, Alberta 182/C5
Hillcrest, Ill. 222/D2
Hillcrest, N.Y. 276/K8
Hillcrest, Texas 303/J3
Hillcrest Heights, Fla. 212/E4
Hillcrest Heights, Md. 245/F5
Hillegom, Netherlands 27/E4
Hillemann, Ark. 202/H3
Hill End, N.S. Wales 97/E3
Hillerød, Denmark 18/H9
Hillerød, Denmark 21/F6
Hillers (mt.), Utah 304/D6
Hillham, Ind. 227/D7
Hillhead, S. Dak. 298/O2
Hillhouse, Miss. 256/C2
Hilliard, Alberta 182/D3
Hilliard, Fla. 212/E1
Hilliard, Ohio 284/D5
Hilliards, Pa. 294/C3
Hilliardville, Fla. 212/B1
Hillingdon, England 10/B5
Hillingdon, England 13/G8
Hillisburg, Ind. 227/E4
Hill Island (lake), N.W. Terr. 187/H3
Hillman, Mich. 250/F3
Hillman, Minn. 255/E4
Hillman, New Bruns. 170/C2
Hillmond, Sask. 181/B2
Hill of Fearn, Scotland 15/D3
Hillridge, Manitoba 179/C3
Hillrose, Colo. 208/N2
Hills, Iowa 229/K5
Hills, Minn. 255/B7
Hillsboro, Ala. 195/D1
Hillsboro, Georgia 217/E4
Hillsboro, Ill. 222/D4
Hillsboro, Ind. 227/C4
Hillsboro, Iowa 229/K7
Hillsboro, Kansas 232/E3
Hillsboro, Ky. 237/O4
Hillsboro, Md. 245/P5
Hillsboro, Miss. 256/E6
Hillsboro, Mo. 261/L6
Hillsboro, N.H. 268/D5
Hillsboro•, N.H. 268/D5
Hillsboro, N. Mex. 274/B6
Hillsboro, N. Dak. 282/S5
Hillsboro, Ohio 284/C7
Hillsboro, Oreg. 291/A2
Hillsboro, Tenn. 237/K10
Hillsboro, Texas 303/G5
Hillsboro, Va. 307/N2
Hillsboro, W. Va. 312/F6
Hillsboro, Wis. 317/F8
Hillsboro Beach, Fla. 212/F5
Hillsboro Lower Village, N.H. 268/D5
Hillsborough, Calif. 204/J2
Hillsborough (co.), Fla. 212/D4
Hillsborough (bay), Fla. 212/C3
Hillsborough (canal), Fla. 212/F5
Hillsborough (riv.), Fla. 212/C2
Hillsborough, New Bruns. 170/F3
Hillsborough (co.), N.H. 268/D6
Hillsborough, N.C. 281/L2
Hillsborough, N. Ireland 17/J3

382 Hillsborough

Hillsborough (bay), Pr. Edward I. 168/E2
Hillsboro Upper Village, N.H. 268/D5
Hillsburgh, Ontario 177/D4
Hillsburn, Nova Scotia 168/C4
Hills Creek (lake), Oreg. 291/E4
Hillsdale, Ill. 222/C2
Hillsdale, Ind. 227/C5
Hillsdale, Kansas 232/H3
Hillsdale (co.), Mich. 250/E7
Hillsdale, Mich. 250/E7
Hillsdale, Mo. 261/R2
Hillsdale, N.J. 273/B1
Hillsdale, N.Y. 276/O6
Hillsdale, Okla. 288/K1
Hillsdale, Ontario 177/E3
Hillsdale, Pa. 294/E4
Hillsdale, Wis. 317/C5
Hillsdale, Wyo. 319/H4
Hillsgrove, Pa. 294/J3
Hillsgrove, R.I. 249/J6
Hillside, Ariz. 198/B4
Hillside, Colo. 208/H6
Hillside, Ill. 222/B5
Hillside•, N.J. 273/B2
Hillside, Scotland 15/F4
Hillside, S. Dak. 298/N7
Hillside Beach, Manitoba 179/F4
Hillsport, Ontario 175/C3
Hillsport, Ontario 177/H5
Hill Spring, Alberta 182/D5
Hillston, N.S. Wales 88/G6
Hillston, N.S. Wales 97/C3
Hillsview, S. Dak. 298/L2
Hillsville, Pa. 294/A4
Hillsville, Va. 307/G7
Hillswick, Scotland 15/G2
Hilltonia, Georgia 217/J5
Hilltop, Ariz. 198/F6
Hilltown, N. Ireland 17/J3
Hillview, Ill. 222/C4
Hillview, Minn. 255/C4
Hillview, Newf. 166/D2
Hilmar-Irwin, Calif. 204/E6
Hilo, Hawaii 87/L4
Hilo, Hawaii 218/J5
Hilo, Hawaii 188/G6
Hilo (bay), Hawaii 218/J5
Hilongos, Philippines 82/E5
Hilshire Village, Texas 303/J1
Hilt, Calif. 204/C2
Hilterfingen, Switzerland 39/E3
Hilton (inlet), Ant. 5/B16
Hilton, Georgia 217/C8
Hilton, Manitoba 179/C5
Hilton, N.Y. 276/E4
Hilton Beach, Ontario 177/J5
Hilton Head (isl.), S.C. 296/F7
Hilton Head Island, S.C. 296/F7
Hiltons, Va. 307/D7
Hilvan, Turkey 63/H4
Hilvarenbeek, Netherlands 27/G6
Hilversum, Netherlands 27/G4
Hima, Ky. 237/O6
Himachal Pradesh (state), India 68/D2
Himalaya (mts.) 54/L7
Himalaya (mts.), Bhutan 68/E2
Himalaya (mts.), China 77/C6
Himalaya (mts.), India 68/D2
Himalaya (mts.), Nepal 68/D2
Himanka, Finland 18/N5
Himeji, Japan 81/G6
Himi, Japan 81/H5
Himlerville (Beauty), Ky. 237/S5
Himrod, N.Y. 276/F5
Himyar, Ky. 237/O7
Hinatuan, Philippines 82/F6
Hinchcliff, Miss. 256/D2
Hinche, Haiti 158/C5
Hinche, Haiti 156/D3
Hinchinbrook (isl.), Alaska 196/D1
Hinchinbrook (isl.), Queensland 88/H3
Hinchinbrook (isl.), Queensland 95/C3
Hinchinbrook Entrance (chan.), Alaska 196/J3
Hinchliffe, Sask. 181/J3
Hinckley, England 10/F4
Hinckley, England 13/F5
Hinckley, Ill. 222/E2
Hinckley, Maine 243/D6
Hinckley, Minn. 255/E4
Hinckley, N.Y. 276/K4
Hinckley (res.), N.Y. 276/K4
Hinckley, Ohio 284/G3
Hinckley, Utah 304/B4
Hindeloopen, Netherlands 27/G3
Hindenburg (Zabrze), Poland 47/A4
Hinderwell, England 13/G3
Hindiya, Iraq 66/C4
Hindman, Ky. 237/R6
Hindmarsh, S. Australia 88/D8
Hindmarsh, S. Australia 94/A7
Hindmarsh (lake), Victoria 97/A5
Hinds (co.), Miss. 256/D6
Hinds, N. Zealand 100/C6
Hindsboro, Ill. 222/E4
Hindsville, Ark. 202/C1
Hindubagh, Pakistan 68/B2
Hindu Kush (mts.) 54/J6
Hindu Kush (mts.), Afghanistan 68/B1
Hindu Kush (mts.), Afghanistan 59/J2
Hindu Kush (mts.), India 68/C1
Hindu Kush (mts.), Pakistan 68/B1
Hindupur, India 68/D6
Hi-Nella, N.J. 273/B4
Hines, Minn. 255/D3
Hines, Oreg. 291/H4
Hinesburg•, Vt. 268/A3
Hines Creek, Alberta 182/A1
Hines Creek, Alta. 162/E4
Hineston, La. 238/E4
Hinesville, Georgia 217/J7
Hinganghat, India 68/D4
Hingham, Mass. 249/E8
Hingham•, Mass. 249/E8
Hingham (bay), Mass. 249/E7
Hingham, Mont. 262/F2
Hingham, Wis. 317/K8
Hingoli, India 68/D5
Hinigaran, Philippines 82/D5
Hinis, Turkey 63/J3
Hinkley, Calif. 204/H9
Hinkston (creek), Ky. 237/N4
Hinlopenstreten (str.), Norway 18/C1
Hinnerup, Denmark 21/D5
Hinnøya (isl.), Norway 18/K2
Hino, Japan 81/O2
Hinojosa del Duque, Spain 33/D3
Hinsdale (co.), Colo. 208/E7
Hinsdale, Ill. 222/B6
Hinsdale•, Mass. 249/B3
Hinsdale, Mont. 262/K2
Hinsdale, N.H. 268/C6
Hinsdale•, N.H. 268/C6
Hinsdale, N.Y. 276/D6
Hinson, Fla. 212/B1
Hinsonton, Georgia 217/D8
Hinterrhein (riv.), Switzerland 39/H3
Hinton, Alberta 182/B3
Hinton, Iowa 229/A3
Hinton, Mo. 261/H4
Hinton, Okla. 288/K4
Hinton, W. Va. 312/E7
Hintonville, Miss. 256/F8
Hinwil, Switzerland 39/G2
Hinze, Miss. 256/F4
Hippolytushoef, Netherlands 27/G3
Hipswell, England 13/F3
Hirakata, Japan 81/J7
Hiram, Georgia 217/C3
Hiram, Ky. 237/P7
Hiram, Maine 243/B8
Hiram•, Maine 243/B8
Hiram, Mo. 261/M8
Hiram, Ohio 284/H3
Hirara, Japan 81/L7
Hirata, Japan 81/F6
Hiratsuka, Japan 81/O3
Hîrlău, Romania 45/H2
Hiroo, Japan 81/L2
Hirosaki, Japan 81/K3
Hiroshima (pref.), Japan 81/E6
Hiroshima, Japan 54/P6
Hiroshima, Japan 81/E6
Hirsch, Sask. 181/J6
Hirschberg (Jelenia Góra), Poland 47/B3
Hirson, France 28/F3
Hîrşova, Romania 45/J3
Hirtshals, Denmark 21/C2
Hisarönü, Turkey 63/E2
Hisban, Jordan 65/D4
Hisega, S. Dak. 298/C5
Hiseville, Ky. 237/K6
Hisle, S. Dak. 298/F7
Hispaniola (isl.) 146/L7
Hispaniola (isl.), Dom. Rep. 156/D2
Hispaniola (isl.), Haiti 156/D2
Hispaniola (isl.), W. Indies 156/D2
Hissar, India 68/D3
Hissop, Ala. 195/F5
Hit, Iraq 59/D3
Hit, Iraq 66/C4
Hitachi, Japan 81/K5
Hitachiota, Japan 81/K5
Hitchcock (lakes), Conn. 210/D2
Hitchcock (co.), Nebr. 264/C4
Hitchcock, Okla. 288/K3
Hitchcock, Sask. 181/J6
Hitchcock, S. Dak. 298/M4
Hitchcock, Texas 303/K3
Hitchin, England 13/G6
Hitchin, England 10/F5
Hitchins, Ky. 237/R4
Hitchita, Okla. 288/P3
Hiteman, Iowa 229/H6
Hitoyoshi, Japan 81/E7
Hitra (isl.), Norway 18/F5
Hitt, Mo. 261/H1
Hitterdal, Minn. 255/B4
Hitzacker, Germany 22/D2
Hitzkirch, Switzerland 39/F2
Hivaoa (isl.), Fr. Poly. 87/N6
Hiwannee, Miss. 256/G7
Hiwasse, Ark. 202/B1
Hiwassee (lake), N.C. 281/A4
Hiwassee (riv.), N.C. 281/A4
Hiwassee (riv.), Tenn. 237/O10
Hiwassee, Va. 307/G7
Hixon, Br. Col. 184/F3
Hixson, Tenn. 237/L10
Hixton, Wis. 317/E7
Hizan, Turkey 63/K3
Hjallerup, Denmark 21/C3
Hjälmaren (lake), Sweden 18/J7
Hjerm, Denmark 21/B5
Hjerting, Denmark 21/B6
Hjo, Sweden 18/J7
Hjørring, Denmark 18/F8
Hjørring, Denmark 21/C3
Hka, Nam (riv.), Burma 72/C2
Hkakabo Razi (mt.), Burma 72/C1
Hlinsko, Czech. 41/D2
Hlohovec, Czech. 41/D2
Hlučín, Czech. 41/E2
Hmawbi, Burma 72/C3
Hnúšť'a-Likier, Czech. 41/E2
Ho, Ghana 106/E7
Hoa Binh, Vietnam 72/E2
Hoa Da, Vietnam 72/F5
Hoadley, Alberta 182/C3
Hoadly, Va. 307/O3
Hoagland, Ind. 227/H3
Hoai Nhon, Vietnam 72/F4
Hoaksbergen, Netherlands 27/K4
Hoare (bay), N.W. Terr. 187/M3
Hoback (peak), Wyo. 319/B2
Hoback (riv.), Wyo. 319/B2
Hobart, Australia 2/S8
Hobart, Ind. 227/C1
Hobart, N.Y. 276/L6
Hobart, Okla. 288/J5
Hobart (cap.), Tasmania 88/H8
Hobart (cap.), Tasmania 99/D4
Hobart, Wash. 310/D3
Hobbema, Alberta 182/D3
Hobbs, Ind. 227/F4
Hobbs (lake), Manitoba 179/G3
Hobbs, Md. 245/P5
Hobbs, N. Mex. 188/F4
Hobbs, N. Mex. 274/F6
Hobbs Coast (reg.), Ant. 5/B12
Hobbs Island, Ala. 195/F1
Hobbsville, N.C. 281/R2
Hoberg, Mo. 261/E8
Hobe Sound, Fla. 212/F4
Hobgood, N.C. 281/P2
Hoboken, Belgium 27/E6
Hoboken, Georgia 217/H8
Hoboken, N.J. 273/C2
Hoboksar, China 77/C2
Hobro, Denmark 21/C4
Hobro, Denmark 18/F8
Hobson (lake), Br. Col. 184/H4
Hobson, Mont. 262/G4
Hobson City, Ala. 195/G3
Hobsons (bay), Victoria 97/H5
Hobsons (bay), Victoria 88/L7
Hobucken, N.C. 281/S4
Hoburgen (cliff), Sweden 18/L8
Hochdorf, Switzerland 39/F2
Hochfeld, Manitoba 179/E5
Hochgolling (mt.), Austria 41/B3
Ho Chi Minh City, Vietnam 2/Q5
Ho Chi Minh City, Vietnam 54/M8
Ho Chi Minh City, Vietnam 72/E5
Hochwan (Hechuan), China 77/G5
Hochwang (mt.), Switzerland 39/J3
Hockaday, Mich. 250/E4
Hockanum, Conn. 210/E2
Hockanum (riv.), Conn. 210/E1
Hockenheim, Germany 22/C4
Hockerville, Okla. 288/S1
Hockessin, Del. 245/R1
Hocking (co.), Ohio 284/F6
Hocking (riv.), Ohio 284/F7
Hockingport, Ohio 284/G7
Hockley (co.), Texas 303/B4
Hodaka (mt.), Japan 81/H5
Hodder (riv.), England 13/H1
Hoddesdon, England 13/H7
Hodeida, Yemen 54/F8
Hodeida, Yemen 59/D7
Hodgdon•, Maine 243/H3
Hodge, La. 238/E2
Hodge, Mo. 261/E4
Hodgeman (co.), Kansas 232/C3
Hodgen, Okla. 288/S5
Hodgenville, Ky. 237/K5
Hodges, Ala. 195/C2
Hodges, Mont. 262/M4
Hodges, S.C. 296/C3
Hodge's Cove, Newf. 166/D2
Hodgesville, W. Va. 312/F4
Hodgeville, Sask. 181/E5
Hodgkins, Ill. 222/B6
Hodgson, Manitoba 179/E3
Hodh (reg.), Mauritania 106/C5
Hod Hasharon, Israel 65/B3
Hodiyya, Israel 65/B4
Hódmezővásárhely, Hungary 41/F3
Hodonín, Czech. 41/D2
Hoehne, Colo. 208/L8
Hoei (Huy), Belgium 27/G8
Hoek, Netherlands 27/D6
Hoek van Holland (Hook of Holland), Netherlands 27/D4
Hoek van Holland (cape), Netherlands 27/D5
Hoensbroek, Netherlands 27/H7
Hoeryŏng, N. Korea 81/D2
Hoeselt, Belgium 27/G7
Hoey, Sask. 181/F3
Hof, Germany 22/D3
Hofei (Hefei), China 77/J5
Hoffman (mt.), Calif. 204/D2
Hoffman, Ill. 222/D5
Hoffman, Minn. 255/C5
Hoffman, N.C. 281/K4
Hoffman, Okla. 288/P4
Hoffman Estates, Ill. 222/A5
Hofgeismar, Germany 22/C3
Hofors, Sweden 18/K6
Hofs (glac.), Iceland 21/C1
Hofu, Japan 81/E6
Hofuf, Saudi Arabia 59/E4
Hofuf, Saudi Arabia 54/F7
Hog (isl.), Mich. 250/D3
Hog (isl.), Pr. Edward I. 168/E2
Hog (isl.), Va. 307/S6
Hogan, Mo. 261/L7
Hogan (lake), Ontario 177/F2
Höganäs, Sweden 18/H8
Hogan Group (isls.), Tasmania 99/D1
Hogansburg, N.Y. 276/L1
Hogansville, Georgia 217/C4
Hogarth (mt.), North. Terr. 93/E6
Hogatza, Alaska 196/G1
Hogeland, Mont. 262/H2
Hog Island (bay), Va. 307/S6
Hog River (Hogatza), Alaska 196/G1
Hogshead (pt.), Conn. 210/E3
Hőgyész, Hungary 41/E3
Hoh (head), Wash. 310/A3
Hoh (riv.), Wash. 310/A3
Hohenau, Paraguay 144/E5
Hohenau an der March, Austria 41/D2
Hohenberg, Austria 41/C3
Hohenems, Austria 41/A3
Hohenlinden, Miss. 256/F3
Hohen Neuendorf, Germany 22/E2
Hohen Solms, La. 238/K3
Hohenstollen (mt.), Switzerland 39/F3
Hohenwald, Tenn. 237/F9
Hohe Tauern (range), Austria 41/B3
Hohe Venn (plat.), Belgium 27/H8
Hohe Warte (mt.), Austria 41/B3
Hohhot (Huhehot), China 77/H3
Hohhot, China 54/N5
Hoh Ind. Res., Wash. 310/A3
Hohokam Pima Nat'l Mon., Ariz. 198/D5
Ho Ho Kus, N.J. 273/B1
Hoholitna (riv.), Alaska 196/G2
Hoh Xil Shan (mts.), China 77/C4
Hoi An, Vietnam 72/F4
Hoihow (Haikou), China 77/H7
Hoima, Uganda 115/F3
Hoisington, Kansas 232/D3
Hoi Xuan, Vietnam 72/E2
Højer, Denmark 21/B8
Højslev, Denmark 21/C4
Hokah, Minn. 255/G7
Hokang (Hegang), China 77/L2
Hoke (co.), N.C. 281/L4
Hokes Bluff, Ala. 195/G3
Hokianga (harb.), N. Zealand 100/D1
Hokitika, N. Zealand 100/C5
Hokkaido (pref.), Japan 81/K2
Hokkaido (isl.), Japan 2/S3
Hokkaido (isl.), Japan 54/R5
Hokkaido (isl.), Japan 81/L2
Holabird, S. Dak. 298/K4
Holbaek, Denmark 21/E6
Holbaek, Denmark 18/G9
Holbeach, England 10/F4
Holbeach, England 13/H5
Holbein, Sask. 181/E2
Holberg, Br. Col. 184/C5
Holbrook, Ariz. 198/E4
Holbrook, Idaho 220/F7
Holbrook, Iowa 229/K5
Holbrook•, Mass. 249/D8
Holbrook, Nebr. 264/D4
Holbrook, N.S. Wales 97/D4
Holbrook, Oreg. 291/A1
Holcomb, Ill. 222/D1
Holcomb, Kansas 232/B3
Holcomb, Miss. 256/D3
Holcomb, Mo. 261/N10
Holcomb, N.Y. 276/F5
Holcomb, W. Va. 312/E6
Holcombe, Wis. 317/D5
Holcombe Flowage (res.), Wis. 317/D5
Holden, Alberta 182/D3
Holden, La. 238/M1
Holden•, Mass. 249/G3
Holden, Mo. 261/E5
Holden, Utah 304/B4
Holden, W. Va. 312/B7
Holden Beach, N.C. 281/N7
Holdenville, Okla. 288/O4
Holder, Fla. 212/D3
Holderness (dist.), England 13/G4
Holderness•, N.H. 268/D4
Holdfast, Sask. 181/F5
Holdingford, Minn. 255/D5
Holdrege, Nebr. 264/E4
Holeby, Denmark 21/E8
Hølen, Norway 18/D4
Holešov, Czech. 41/D2
Holetown, Barbados 161/B8
Holgate, Ohio 284/B3
Holguín (prov.), Cuba 158/J3
Holguín, Cuba 146/L7
Holguín, Cuba 158/J3
Holguín, Cuba 156/C2
Holíč, Czech. 41/D2
Holice, Czech. 41/C1
Holiday Hills, Ill. 222/A4
Holijsloot, Netherlands 27/C4
Holitna (riv.), Alaska 196/G2
Hollabrunn, Austria 41/D2
Holladay, Tenn. 237/E9
Holladay, Utah 304/C3
Hollam's Bird (isl.), Namibia 118/A4
Holland, Georgia 217/B2
Holland, Ind. 227/C8
Holland, Iowa 229/H4
Holland, Ky. 237/J7
Holland, Manitoba 179/D5
Holland•, Mass. 249/F4
Holland, Mich. 250/C6
Holland, Minn. 255/B6
Holland, Mo. 261/N10
Holland, N.Y. 276/C5
Holland, Ohio 284/C2
Holland, Texas 303/G7
Holland•, Vt. 268/D2
Hollandale, Minn. 255/E7
Hollandale, Miss. 256/C4
Hollandale, Wis. 317/G10
Holland Centre, Ontario 177/D3
Hollandia (Jayapura), Indonesia 85/K6
Holland Landing, Ontario 177/E3
Holland Park, Queensland 88/K3
Holland Park, Queensland 95/E3
Holland Patent, N.Y. 276/K4
Hollandsburg, Ind. 227/C5
Hollandstoun, Scotland 15/F1
Hollansburg, Ohio 284/A5
Hollenbeck (riv.), Conn. 210/B1
Hollenberg, Kansas 232/F2
Holley, N.Y. 276/D4
Holley, Oreg. 291/E3
Hollick-Kenyon (plat.), Ant. 5/B13
Holliday, Mo. 261/H3
Holliday, Texas 303/F4
Hollidaysburg, Pa. 294/F5
Hollins, Ala. 195/F4
Hollins College, Va. 307/H6
Hollis, Ark. 202/D4
Hollis, Kansas 232/E2
Hollis•, N.H. 268/D6
Hollis, N.C. 281/F4
Hollis, Okla. 288/G5
Hollis Center•, Maine 243/B8
Hollister, Calif. 204/D7
Hollister, Fla. 212/E2
Hollister, Idaho 220/D7
Hollister, Mo. 261/F9
Hollister, N.C. 281/O2
Hollister, Okla. 288/J6
Hollister, Wis. 317/J5
Holliston•, Mass. 249/A8
Holloman A.F.B., N. Mex. 274/C6
Holloway, Minn. 255/C5
Holloway, Ohio 284/H5
Hollowayville, Ill. 222/D2
Hollow Creek, Ky. 237/K4
Hollow Rock, Tenn. 237/E8
Hollsopple, Pa. 294/E5
Hollum, Netherlands 27/H2
Holly, Colo. 208/P6
Holly, Mich. 250/F6
Holly, Wash. 310/C3
Holly Bluff, Miss. 256/C5
Holly Grove, Ark. 202/H4
Holly Hill, Fla. 212/E2
Holly Hill, S.C. 296/G5
Holly Oak, Del. 245/S1
Holly Pond, Ala. 195/E2
Holly Ridge, La. 238/G2
Holly Ridge, Miss. 256/C4
Holly Ridge, N.C. 281/O6
Holly Shelter (swamp), N.C. 281/O6
Holly Springs, Ark. 202/E6
Holly Springs, Georgia 217/D2
Holly Springs, Miss. 256/E1
Holly Springs, N.C. 281/M3
Hollytree, Ala. 195/F1
Hollyville, Del. 245/T6
Hollywood, Ala. 195/G1
Hollywood, Ark. 202/D5
Hollywood, Calif. 204/C10
Hollywood, Fla. 188/K5
Hollywood, Fla. 212/B4
Hollywood, Georgia 217/E1
Hollywood, La. 238/D6
Hollywood, Md. 245/M7
Hollywood, Miss. 256/D1
Hollywood, S.C. 296/G6
Hollywood, W. Va. 312/F7
Hollywood Park, Texas 303/K10
Holman, N. Mex. 274/D2
Holman (isl.), N.W.T. 187/G2
Holman (isl.), N.W.T. 162/D1
Holman, Canada 4/B15
Holman, N.W. Terr. 187/G2
Holmdel•, N.J. 273/E3
Holmen, Wis. 317/D8
Holmes (reef), Australia 95/C3
Holmes (reef), Coral Sea Is. Terr. 88/H3
Holmes (co.), Fla. 212/C5
Holmes (creek), Fla. 212/D5
Holmes, Iowa 229/F3
Holmes (co.), Miss. 256/D4
Holmes (co.), Ohio 284/G4
Holmes (mt.), Wyo. 310/B1
Holmes Beach, Fla. 212/D4
Holmes City, Minn. 255/C5
Holmeson, N.J. 273/E3
Holmestrand, Norway 18/C4
Holmesville, Miss. 256/D8
Holmesville, Nebr. 264/H4
Holmesville, New Bruns. 170/C2
Holmesville, Ohio 284/G4
Holmesville, Ontario 177/C4
Holmfield, Manitoba 179/C5
Holmfirth, England 13/J2
Holmquist, S. Dak. 298/O3
Holmsbu, Norway 18/D4
Holmsund, Sweden 18/M5
Holmwood, La. 238/D6
Holon, Israel 65/B3
Holopaw, Fla. 212/E3
Holroyd, N.S. Wales 97/H3
Holroyd (riv.), Queensland 95/B2
Holstebro, Denmark 18/F8
Holstebro, Denmark 21/B5
Holsted, Denmark 21/B6
Holstein, Iowa 229/B4
Holstein, Mo. 261/K5
Holstein, Nebr. 264/F4
Holstein, Ontario 177/D3
Holsteinsborg (Sisimiut), Greenl. 4/C12
Holston (riv.), Tenn. 237/O8
Holston, Va. 307/D7
Holston, North Fork (riv.), Va. 307/D7
Holston Valley, Tenn. 237/S7
Holsworthy, England 10/D5
Holsworthy, England 13/C7
Holt, Ala. 195/D4
Holt (dam), Ala. 195/D4
Holt, Calif. 204/D6
Holt, England 13/J5
Holt, Fla. 212/C6
Holt, Mich. 250/E6
Holt, Minn. 255/B2
Holt (co.), Mo. 261/B2
Holt, Mo. 261/D4
Holt (co.), Nebr. 264/F2
Holte, Denmark 21/F6
Holter (lake), Mont. 262/D4
Holtland, Tenn. 237/H9
Holton, Ind. 227/G6
Holton, Kansas 232/G2
Holton, La. 238/K5
Holton, Mich. 250/C5
Holton, Newf. 166/C3
Holts Summit, Mo. 261/H5
Holtville, Ala. 195/F5
Holtville, Calif. 204/K11
Holtville, New Bruns. 170/D2
Holtwood, Pa. 294/K6
Holualoa, Hawaii 218/G5
Holualoa, Hawaii 188/F6
Holwerd, Netherlands 27/H2
Holy (isl.), England 13/F2
Holy (isl.), England 10/F3
Holy (isl.), Scotland 15/C5
Holy (isl.), Wales 10/D4
Holy (isl.), Wales 13/C4
Holy City, Calif. 204/K4
Holy Cross, Alaska 196/G2
Holy Cross (mt.), Colo. 208/F4
Holy Cross, Iowa 229/L3
Holycross, Ireland 17/F6
Holy Cross, Wis. 317/L9
Holyhead, Wales 10/D4
Holyhead, Wales 13/C4
Holy Loch (inlet), Scotland 15/A1
Holyoke, Colo. 208/P1
Holyoke, Mass. 249/D4
Holyoke (range), Mass. 249/D3
Holyoke, Minn. 255/F4
Holyrood, Kansas 232/D3
Holyrood, Newf. 166/D2
Holyrood (bay), Newf. 166/D2
Holyrood (pond), Newf. 166/D2
Holyroyd, N. S. Wales 88/K4
Holy Trinity, Ala. 195/H6
Holywell, Wales 13/G2
Holywood, N. Ireland 17/K2
Holzminden, Germany 22/C3
Homalin, Burma 72/B1
Homathko (riv.), Br. Col. 184/E4
Hombori, Mali 106/D5
Hombori (mts.), Mali 106/D5
Homburg, Germany 22/B4
Home (bay) 162/K2
Home, Kansas 232/F2
Home (isl.), Newf. 166/B1
Home (bay), N.W. Terr. 187/M3
Home, Pa. 294/D4
Homedale, Idaho 220/A6
Home Gardens, Calif. 204/E11
Home Hill, Queensland 88/H3
Home Hill, Queensland 95/C3
Homeland, Calif. 204/H10
Homeland, Georgia 217/H9
Home Place, La. 238/L8
Homer, Alaska 196/B2
Homer, Georgia 217/F2
Homer, Ill. 222/F3
Homer, Ind. 227/F5
Homer, Ky. 237/H7
Homer, La. 238/D1
Homer, Mich. 250/E6
Homer, Minn. 255/G6
Homer, Nebr. 264/H2
Homer, N.Y. 276/H5
Homer, Ohio 284/E5
Homer City, Pa. 294/D4
Homerville, Georgia 217/G8
Homerville, Ohio 284/F3
Homestead, Fla. 212/F6
Homestead, Iowa 229/K5
Homestead, Mont. 262/M2
Homestead, Okla. 288/K2
Homestead, Pa. 294/B7
Homestead, Queensland 95/C4
Homestead A.F.B., Fla. 212/F6
Homestead Nat'l Mon., Nebr. 264/H4
Homestown, Mo. 261/N10
Hometown, Ill. 222/B6
Home Valley, Wash. 310/D5
Homewood, Ala. 195/E4
Homewood, Calif. 204/E4
Homewood, Ill. 222/B6
Homewood, Kansas 232/G3
Homewood, Manitoba 179/E5
Homewood, Miss. 256/E6
Homewood, Pa. 294/B4
Homeworth, Ohio 284/J4
Hominy, Okla. 288/O2
Hominy Falls, W. Va. 312/E6
Homochitto (riv.), Miss. 256/B8
Homoíne, Mozambique 118/E4
Homonhon (isl.), Philippines 82/E5
Homosassa, Fla. 212/D3
Homosassa (isls.), Fla. 212/D3
Homosassa Springs, Fla. 212/D3
Homra, Hamada el (des.), Libya 111/B2
Homs, Libya 102/D1
Homs, Libya 111/B1
Homs (prov.), Syria 63/G5
Homs, Syria 59/C3
Homs, Syria 63/G5
Homs, Syria 54/E6
Hon, Ark. 202/B4
Hon, Libya 102/D2
Hon, Libya 111/C2
Honaker, Va. 307/D6
Honan (Henan), China 77/H5
Honaunau, Hawaii 218/G6
Honavar, India 68/C6
Honaz Dağı (mt.), Turkey 63/C4
Hon Chong, Vietnam 72/E5
Honda, Colombia 126/C5
Honda (bay), Cuba 158/B1
Honda (bay), Philippines 82/B6
Honda (bay), P. Rico 161/F2
Hondo (riv.), Belize 154/C1
Hondo, Japan 81/E7
Hondo (riv.), Mexico 150/P7
Hondo, N. Mex. 274/D5
Hondo, Texas 303/E8
Hondsrug (hills), Netherlands 27/K3
Honduras 2/E5
Honduras 146/K8
Honduras 154/D3
Honduras (gulf) 146/K8
Honduras (gulf), Belize 154/D2
Honduras (gulf), Guatemala 154/D2
Honduras (cape), Honduras 154/E2
Honduras (gulf), Honduras 154/D2
Honea Path, S.C. 296/C3
Honegg (mt.), Switzerland 39/E3
Honeoye, N.Y. 276/F5
Honeoye (lake), N.Y. 276/F5
Honeoye Falls, N.Y. 276/F5
Honesdale, Pa. 294/M2
Honey (lake), Calif. 204/E3
Honey (creek), Ind. 227/C6
Honey (creek), Oreg. 291/G5
Honey Brook, Pa. 294/L5
Honey Creek, Ind. 227/F4
Honey Creek, Iowa 229/B6
Honey Creek, Wis. 317/J3
Honeydale, New Bruns. 170/C3
Honeyford, N. Dak. 282/R3
Honey Grove, Texas 303/J4
Honey Harbour, Ontario 177/E3
Honey Hill, S.C. 296/H5
Honey Island, Texas 303/K7
Honeymoon Bay, Br. Col. 184/J3
Honeyville, Utah 304/B2
Honeywood, Ontario 177/D3
Honfleur, France 28/D3
Honfleur, Québec 172/G3
Høng, Denmark 21/E7
Honga (riv.), Md. 245/O7
Hon Gai, Vietnam 72/E2
Hongch'ŏn, S. Korea 81/D5
Hong Kong 54/N7
Hong Kong 2/Q4
HONG KONG 77

Hudson 383

Hongliuhe, China 77/E3
Hongor, Mongolia 77/H2
Hongshui He (riv.), China 77/G7
Hongsŏng, S. Korea 81/C5
Hongtong, China 77/H4
Honguedo (passage), Québec 174/E3
Hongwŏn, N. Korea 81/C3
Hongze Hu (lake), China 77/J5
Honiara (cap.), Solomon Is. 86/D3
Honiara (cap.), Solomon Is. 87/F6
Honiton, England 10/E5
Honiton, England 13/D7
Honjo, Japan 81/J4
Honnedaga (lake), N.Y. 276/L3
Honnelles, Belgium 27/D8
Honningsvag, Norway 18/O1
Honobia, Okla. 288/R5
Honohina, Hawaii 218/J4
Honokaa, Hawaii 188/G5
Honokaa, Hawaii 218/H4
Honokahua, Hawaii 218/H1
Honokohau, Hawaii, Hawaii 218/G5
Honokohau, Maui, Hawaii 218/J1
Honolulu (co.), Hawaii 218/D3
Honolulu (cap.), Hawaii 87/L3
Honolulu (cap.), Hawaii 188/F5
Honolulu (cap.), Hawaii 218/C4
Honolulu (harb.), Hawaii 218/C4
Honolulu, U.S. 2/B5
Honolulu Int'l Airport, Hawaii 218/B4
Honomu, Hawaii 218/J4
Honor, Mich. 250/D4
Honoraville, Ala. 195/F7
Honouliuli, Hawaii 218/A3
Honshu (isl.), Japan 2/S4
Honshu (isl.), Japan 54/P6
Honshu (isl.), Japan 81/J5
Honuapo, Hawaii 218/H7
Hood, Calif. 204/B9
Hood (riv.), N.W. Terr. 187/G3
Hood (mt.), Oreg. 291/F2
Hood (riv.), Oreg. 291/F2
Hood (co.), Texas 303/G5
Hood (canal), Wash. 310/B3
Hood River (co.), Oreg. 291/F2
Hood River, Oreg. 291/F2
Hoodsport, Wash. 310/B3
Hoofddorp (Haarlemmermeer), Netherlands 27/F4
Hoogeveen, Netherlands 27/J3
Hoogezand-Sappemeer, Netherlands 27/K2
Hooghly (riv.), India 68/F2
Hooghly-Chinsura, India 68/F1
Hoogkarspel, Netherlands 27/G3
Hoogstraten, Belgium 27/F6
Hook (head), Ireland 17/H7
Hook (isl.), Queensland 88/H4
Hook (isl.), Queensland 95/D4
Hookena, Hawaii 218/G6
Hooker (co.), Nebr. 264/C3
Hooker, Okla. 288/D1
Hooker Creek, North. Terr. 88/E3
Hooker Creek, North. Terr. 93/B5
Hooker Creek Aboriginal Reserve, North. Terr. 88/E3
Hookersville, W. Va. 312/E6
Hookerton, N.C. 281/O4
Hook of Holland, Netherlands 27/D4
Hooks, Texas 303/K4
Hooksett, N.H. 268/E5
Hooksett•, N.H. 268/E5
Hookstown, Pa. 294/B4
Hoolehua, Hawaii 188/F5
Hoolehua, Hawaii 218/G1
Hoonah, Alaska 196/M1
Hoonah (sound), Alaska 196/M1
Hoopa, Calif. 204/B2
Hoopa Valley Ind. Res., Calif. 204/A2
Hooper, Colo. 208/H7
Hooper (str.), Md. 245/O8
Hooper, Nebr. 264/H3
Hooper, Utah 304/B2
Hooper, Wash. 310/G4
Hooper Bay, Alaska 196/E2
Hooper Bay, Alaska 188/C5
Hoopersville, Md. 245/O7
Hoopeston, Ill. 222/F3
Hoople, N. Dak. 282/P2
Hooppole, Ill. 222/D2
Hoorn, Netherlands 27/G3
Hoorn (isls.), Wallis and Futuna 87/J7
Hoosac (mts.), Mass. 249/B2
Hoosac Tunnel, Mass. 249/C2
Hoosic (riv.), Mass. 249/A1
Hoosic (riv.), Vt. 268/A6
Hoosick Falls, N.Y. 276/O5
Hoosier, Sask. 181/B4
Hoot Owl, Okla. 288/R2
Hooven, Ohio 284/A9
Hoover, Ala. 195/E4
Hoover (dam), Ariz. 198/A2
Hoover (dam), Nev. 266/G7
Hoover (res.), Ohio 284/E5
Hoover, S. Dak. 298/C3
Hooversville, Pa. 294/E5
Hop (riv.), Conn. 210/F1
Hopa, Turkey 63/J2
Hopatcong, N.J. 273/D2
Hopatcong (lake), N.J. 273/D2
Hop Bottom, Pa. 294/L2
Hope, Alaska 196/C1
Hope (pt.), Alaska 196/E1
Hope (bay), Ant. 5/C16
Hope, Ark. 202/C6
Hope, Br. Col. 162/D6
Hope, Br. Col. 184/M3
Hope, Idaho 220/B1
Hope, Ind. 227/F6
Hope, Kansas 232/E3
Hope, Ky. 237/O4
Hope, Maine 243/E7
Hope•, Maine 243/E7
Hope, Mich. 250/E5
Hope, Minn. 255/E7
Hope, Mo. 261/J5
Hope (lake), Newf. 166/B3
Hope, N.J. 273/D2
Hope, N. Mex. 274/E6
Hope, N. Dak. 282/P5
Hope (isl.), Norway 4/B8
Hope, R.I. 249/H6
Hope, Loch (lake), Scotland 15/D2
Hope Bay, Jamaica 158/K6
Hopedale, Ill. 222/D3
Hopedale, Mass. 249/H4
Hopedale•, Mass. 249/H4
Hopedale, Newf. 166/B2
Hopedale, Newf. 162/L4
Hopedale, Newf. 166/N4
Hopedale, Ohio 284/J5
Hope Hull, Ala. 195/F6
Hopei (Hebei), China 77/J4
Hopeland, Pa. 294/K5
Hopelchén, Mexico 150/P7
Hopeman, Scotland 15/E3
Hope Mills, N.C. 281/M5
Hopen (isl.), Norway 18/E2
Hopes Advance (cape), Québec 174/F1
Hopeton, Okla. 288/J1
Hopeton, Va. 307/S5
Hopetoun, Victoria 97/B4
Hopetoun, W. Australia 92/C6
Hopetown, Québec 172/D2
Hopetown, S. Africa 118/C5
Hopetown, W. Australia 88/C6
Hope Valley, R.I. 249/H6
Hope Valley (res.), S. Australia 88/E7
Hopeville, Iowa 229/F7
Hopewell, Ala. 195/H3
Hopewell, Jamaica 158/G5
Hopewell, Kansas 232/D4
Hopewell, Md. 245/P8
Hopewell, Miss. 256/D7
Hopewell, N.J. 273/D3
Hopewell (isls.), N.W. Terr. 187/L4
Hopewell, Nova Scotia 168/F3
Hopewell, Ohio 284/F6
Hopewell, Pa. 294/F5
Hopewell (I.C.), Va. 307/O6
Hopewell Cape, New Bruns. 170/F3
Hopewell Hill, New Bruns. 170/F3
Hopewell Junction, N.Y. 276/N7
Hopfgarten in Nordtirol, Austria 41/B3
Hopi (buttes), Ariz. 198/E3
Hopi Ind. Res., Ariz. 198/E2
Hopkins (co.), Ky. 237/F6
Hopkins, Mich. 250/D6
Hopkins, Minn. 255/G5
Hopkins, Mo. 261/C1
Hopkins (lake), North. Terr. 93/A8
Hopkins, S.C. 296/F4
Hopkins (co.), Texas 303/J4
Hopkins (riv.), Victoria 97/B5
Hopkins, Va. 307/S5
Hopkins (lake), W. Australia 88/D4
Hopkins (lake), W. Australia 92/E4
Hopkins Park, Ill. 222/F2
Hopkinsville, Ky. 237/F7
Hopkinton, Iowa 229/L4
Hopkinton, Mass. 249/J4
Hopkinton•, Mass. 249/J4
Hopkinton•, N.H. 268/D5
Hopkinton, N.Y. 276/L1
Hopkinton•, R.I. 249/H7
Hopland, Calif. 204/B5
Hoppo (Hepu), China 77/G7
Hop River, Conn. 210/F2
Hopwood, Pa. 294/C6
Hoquiam, Wash. 188/B1
Hoquiam, Wash. 310/A3
Horace, Kansas 232/A3
Horace, N. Dak. 282/S6
Horasan, Turkey 63/K2
Horatio, Ark. 202/B3
Horatio, S.C. 296/F3
Horažd'ovice, Czech. 41/B2
Horche, Spain 33/E2
Horconcitos, Panama 154/F6
Hordaland (co.), Norway 18/E6
Horden, England 13/J4
Hordio, Somalia 115/K1
Hordville, Nebr. 264/G3
Horgen, Switzerland 39/G2
Hořice v Podkrkonoší, Czech. 41/C1
Horicon, Wis. 317/J9
Horine, Mo. 261/M6
Horizon, Sask. 181/F6
Horley, England 13/H8
Hormigüeros, P. Rico 161/A2
Hormoz, Iran 66/J7
Hormoz (isl.), Iran 66/K7
Hormozgan (prov.), Iran 66/J7
Hormuz (str.), Iran 59/G4
Hormuz (str.), Iran 66/K7
Hormuz (str.), Oman 59/G4
Horn (cape) 2/F8
Horn, Austria 41/C2
Horn (cape), Chile 120/C8
Horn (cape), Chile 138/F11
Horn (cape), Iceland 7/B2
Horn (cape), Iceland 21/B1
Horn (head), Ireland 17/E1
Horn (isl.), Miss. 256/G10
Horn (mts.), N.W. Terr. 187/G3
Horn (riv.), N.W. Terr. 187/G3
Hornád (riv.), Czech. 41/F2
Hornaday (riv.), N.W. Terr. 187/F3
Hornafjördhur (fjord), Iceland 21/D1
Horná Štubňa, Czech. 41/E2
Horn-Bad Meinberg, Germany 22/C3
Hornbeak, Tenn. 237/C8
Hornbeck, Alberta 182/B3
Hornbeck, La. 238/D4
Hornbrook, Calif. 204/C2
Hornby, N. Zealand 100/D5
Hornby (bay), N.W. Terr. 187/G3
Hornby Island, Br. Col. 184/H2
Horncastle, England 13/G4
Horncastle, England 10/F4
Horndean, Manitoba 179/E5
Hörnefors, Sweden 18/L5
Hornell, N.Y. 276/E6
Hornepayne, Ontario 175/C3
Hornepayne, Ontario 177/J5
Horner, W. Va. 312/F5
Hornerstown, N.J. 273/E3
Hornersville, Mo. 261/M10
Horní Benešov, Czech. 41/D2
Hornick, Iowa 229/A4
Horní Libina, Czech. 41/D2
Hornings Mills, Ontario 177/D3
Hornitos, Calif. 204/E6
Horn Lake, Miss. 256/D1
Hörnli (mt.), Switzerland 39/G2
Hornos, Falso (cape), Chile 138/F11
Hornsby, N.S. Wales 88/K3
Hornsby, N.S. Wales 97/J3
Hornsby, Tenn. 237/D10
Hornsea, England 13/G4
Hornsea, England 10/F4
Hornslandet (pen.), Sweden 18/K6
Hornslet, Denmark 21/D5
Horns Road, Nova Scotia 168/H2
Hornsund (bay), Norway 18/C2
Horntown, Va. 307/T5
Hořovice, Czech. 41/C2
Horqin Youyi Qianqi (Ulanhot), China 77/K2
Horqueta, Paraguay 144/D3
Horry (co.), S.C. 296/J4
Horse (lake), Calif. 204/E3
Horse (creek), Colo. 208/M5
Horse (creek), Fla. 212/E4
Horse (isls.), Newf. 166/C3
Horse (creek), Oreg. 291/F3
Horse (creek), Wyo. 319/H4
Horse (creek), Wyo. 319/B3
Horse Branch, Ky. 237/H6
Horse Cave, Ky. 237/K6
Horse Chops (head), Newf. 166/D2
Horse Creek, Calif. 204/C2
Horse Creek (res.), Colo. 208/N6
Horse Creek, Wyo. 319/G4
Horsefly, Br. Col. 184/G4
Horsefly (lake), Br. Col. 184/G4
Horsehead (lake), N. Dak. 282/L5
Horsehead (creek), S. Dak. 298/C7
Horseheads, N.Y. 276/G6
Horsens, Denmark 18/F9
Horsens, Denmark 21/C6
Horsens (fjord), Denmark 21/D6
Horseshoe (lake), Ariz. 198/D5
Horseshoe (pt.), Fla. 212/C2
Horseshoe (lake), Manitoba 179/G2
Horse Shoe (pt.), St. Kitts and Nevis 161/C11
Horseshoe (creek), Wyo. 319/G3
Horseshoe Beach, Fla. 212/C2
Horseshoe Bend, Ark. 202/G1
Horseshoe Bend, Idaho 220/B6
Horseshoe Bend Nat'l Mil. Park, Ala. 195/G5
Horseshoe Lake, Ontario 177/E2
Horse Shoe Run, W. Va. 312/G4
Horsetooth (res.), Colo. 208/J1
Horsham, England 10/F5
Horsham, England 13/G6
Horsham, Sask. 181/B5
Horsham, Victoria 97/B5
Horsham, Victoria 88/G7
Hørsholm, Denmark 21/F6
Horšovský Týn, Czech. 41/B2
Horst, Netherlands 27/H6
Horta (dist.), Portugal 33/A1
Horta, Portugal 33/B1
Hortaleza, Spain 33/G4
Horten, Norway 18/D4
Hortense, Georgia 217/J8
Hortensfjord (fjord), Norway 18/G4
Horton, Ala. 195/F2
Horton, Iowa 229/J3
Horton, Kansas 232/G2
Horton, Mich. 250/E6
Horton, Mo. 261/D7
Horton (riv.), N.S. Wales 97/F2
Horton (riv.), N.W. Terr. 187/F3
Horton, Oreg. 291/D3
Horton Bay, Mich. 250/D3
Hortonia (lake), Vt. 268/A4
Hortonville, Ind. 227/E4
Hortonville, Mass. 249/K5
Hortonville, Wis. 317/J7
Hørve, Denmark 21/E6
Horwich, England 10/G2
Horwich, England 13/G2
Hoschton, Georgia 217/E2
Hoselaw, Alberta 182/E2
Hosenofu (well), Libya 111/D3
Hosford, Fla. 212/B1
Hoshab, Pakistan 68/A3
Hoshab, Pakistan 59/H4
Hoshangabad, India 68/D4
Hoskins, Nebr. 264/G2
Hosmer, Br. Col. 184/K5
Hosmer, S. Dak. 298/L2
Hospental, Switzerland 39/F3
Hospers, Iowa 229/B2
Hospet, India 68/D5
Hospital, Chile 138/G4
Hospital, Ireland 17/E7
Hospitalet, Spain 33/H2
Hosseina, Ethiopia 111/G6
Hosston, La. 238/C1
Hoste (isl.), Chile 120/B8
Hoste (isl.), Chile 138/F11
Hostinné, Czech. 41/C1
Hoswick, Scotland 15/G2
Hot, Thailand 72/C3
Hotan, China 77/B4
Hotan, China 54/K6
Hotan He (riv.), China 77/B4
Hotchkiss, Alberta 182/B1
Hotchkiss, Colo. 208/D5
Hotchkissville, Conn. 210/C2
Hot Creek (range), Nev. 266/E4
Hot Creek (valley), Nev. 266/E4
Hotevilla, Ariz. 198/E3
Hotham (inlet), Alaska 196/F1
Hoting, Sweden 18/K4
Hot Lake, Oreg. 291/K2
Hot Spring (co.), Ark. 202/E5
Hot Springs, Mont. 262/B3
Hot Springs (Truth or Consequences), N. Mex. 274/B5
Hot Springs, N.C. 281/D3
Hot Springs, S. Dak. 188/F2
Hot Springs, S. Dak. 298/C7
Hot Springs, Va. 307/J4
Hot Springs (co.), Wyo. 319/D2
Hot Springs Cove, Br. Col. 184/D5
Hot Springs National Park, Ark. 188/H4
Hot Springs National Park, Ark. 202/D4
Hot Springs Nat'l Park, Ark. 202/D4
Hot Sulphur Springs, Colo. 208/H2
Hottah (lake), N.W.T. 162/E2
Hottah (lake), N.W. Terr. 187/G3
Hottentot (bay), Namibia 118/A5
Hotton, Belgium 27/G8
Hou, Nam (riv.), Laos 72/D2
Houck, Ariz. 198/F3
Houcktown, Ohio 284/C4
Houffalize, Belgium 27/H8
Houghton, Iowa 229/K7
Houghton, Maine 243/B6
Houghton, Mich. 188/J1
Houghton (co.), Mich. 250/G1
Houghton, Mich. 250/G1
Houghton (lake), Mich. 250/E4
Houghton, N.Y. 276/D6
Houghton, S. Dak. 298/N2
Houghton Lake, Mich. 250/E4
Houghton Lake Heights, Mich. 250/E4
Houghton-le-Spring, England 13/J3
Houhoek, S. Africa 118/F7
Houlka, Miss. 256/G2
Houlton, Maine 188/N1
Houlton, Maine 243/H3
Houlton•, Maine 243/H3
Houlton, Wis. 317/A5
Houma, China 77/H4
Houma, La. 238/J7
Houndé, Burkina Faso 106/D6
Hounslow, England 13/G8
Hounslow, England 10/B5
Hourn, Loch (inlet), Scotland 15/C3
Housatonic (riv.), Conn. 210/C3
Housatonic, Mass. 249/A3
Housatonic (riv.), Mass. 249/A4
House (mt.), Alberta 182/C2
House (riv.), Alberta 182/D2
House, N. Mex. 274/F4
House (range), Utah 304/A4
House Springs, Mo. 261/L6
Houston (co.), Ala. 195/H8
Houston, Ala. 195/D2
Houston, Alaska 196/B1
Houston, Ark. 202/E3
Houston, Br. Col. 184/D3
Houston, Del. 245/S5
Houston, Fla. 212/D1
Houston (co.), Georgia 217/E6
Houston, Ind. 227/E6
Houston (co.), Minn. 255/G7
Houston, Minn. 255/G7
Houston, Miss. 256/G3
Houston, Mo. 261/J8
Houston, Ohio 284/B5
Houston, Pa. 294/B5
Houston (co.), Tenn. 237/F8
Houston (co.), Texas 303/J6
Houston, Texas 303/J2
Houston, Texas 188/G5
Houston, Texas 146/J7
Houston (lake), Texas 303/J8
Houston, U.S. 2/E4
Houston Acres, Ky. 237/K2
Houstonia, Mo. 261/F5
Houston Lake, Mo. 261/O5
Houston Ship (chan.), Texas 303/K2
Hout (bay), S. Africa 118/E6
Houtbaai, S. Africa 118/E6
Houtman Abrolhos (isls.), W. Australia 88/A5
Houtman Abrolhos (isls.), W. Australia 92/A5
Houtrak Polder, Netherlands 27/A4
Houtzdale, Pa. 294/F4
Hov, Denmark 21/D6
Hovd, Mongolia 77/D2
Hovd (Kobdo, Jirgalanta), Mongolia 77/D2
Hovd, Mongolia 54/L5
Hovd Gol (riv.), Mongolia 77/D2
Hove, England 13/G7
Hove, England 10/F5
Hoven, S. Dak. 298/K3
Hovenweep Nat'l Mon., Colo. 208/A8
Hovenweep Nat'l Mon., Utah 304/E6
Hoving, N. Dak. 282/P7
Hovland, Minn. 255/G2
Hövsgöl, Mongolia 77/E1
Hövsgöl Nuur (lake), Mongolia 77/F1
Howar, Wadi (dry riv.), Sudan 111/E4
Howard (pass), Alaska 196/G1
Howard (co.), Ark. 202/C5
Howard, Colo. 208/H6
Howard, Georgia 217/D5
Howard (co.), Ind. 227/E4
Howard (co.), Iowa 229/J2
Howard, Kansas 232/F4
Howard (co.), Md. 245/L4
Howard (co.), Mo. 261/G4
Howard (co.), Nebr. 264/F3
Howard, New Bruns. 170/E2
Howard, Ohio 284/F5
Howard, Pa. 294/G3
Howard, S. Dak. 298/P5
Howard (co.), Texas 303/C5
Howard (creek), Texas 303/C7
Howard, Wis. 317/K6
Howard A. Hanson (res.), Wash. 310/D3
Howard City, Mich. 250/D5
Howard City (Boelus), Nebr. 264/F3
Howard Lake, Minn. 255/D5
Howards Grove-Millersville, Wis. 317/L8
Howards Ridge, Mo. 261/H9
Howardstown, Ky. 237/K5
Howardsville, Va. 307/L5
Howardville, Mo. 261/N9
Howden, England 13/G4
Howe (cape), Australia 87/F9
Howe (sound), Br. Col. 184/K2
Howe, Idaho 220/F6
Howe, Ind. 227/G1
Howe (cape), N.S. Wales 88/J7
Howe (cape), N.S. Wales 97/F5
Howe, Okla. 288/S5
Howe, Texas 303/H4
Howell, Ark. 202/H3
Howell, Georgia 217/F9
Howell, Mich. 250/E6
Howell (co.), Mo. 261/J9
Howell•, N.J. 273/E3
Howell, Tenn. 237/H10
Howell, Utah 304/B2
Howells, Nebr. 264/H3
Howes, S. Dak. 298/E4
Howesville, Ind. 227/C6
Howesville, W. Va. 312/G4
Howey In The Hills, Fla. 212/E3
Howick, N. Zealand 100/C1
Howick, Québec 172/D4
Howick, S. Africa 118/E5
Howison, Miss. 256/F9
Howland, Maine 243/F5
Howland•, Maine 243/F5
Howland (isl.), Pacific 87/J5
Howland Ridge, New Bruns. 170/C2
Howley, Newf. 166/C4
Howlong, N.S. Wales 97/D4
Howrah, India 68/F2
Howrah, India 54/K7
Howser, Br. Col. 184/J5
Hoxeyville, Mich. 250/D4
Hoxie, Ark. 202/H1
Hoxie, Kansas 232/B2
Höxter, Germany 22/C3
Hoxud, China 77/C3
Hoy (isl.), Scotland 15/E2
Hoy (isl.), Scotland 10/E1
Hoy (sound), Scotland 15/E2
Hoyerswerda, Germany 22/F3
Hoylake, England 13/G2
Hoylake, England 10/F2
Hoyland Nether, England 13/J2
Hoyleton, Ill. 222/D5
Hoyos, Spain 33/C2
Hoyran (lake), Turkey 63/D3
Hoyt, Colo. 208/L2
Hoyt, Kansas 232/G2
Hoyt, New Bruns. 170/D3
Hoyt, Okla. 288/R4
Hoyt (peak), Utah 304/C3
Hoyt Lakes, Minn. 255/F3
Hoytsville, Utah 304/C3
Hoytville, Ohio 284/C3
Hozat, Turkey 59/C2
Hozat, Turkey 63/H3
Hradec Králové, Czech. 41/C1
Hranice, Czech. 41/D2
Hrinova, Czech. 41/E2
Hron (riv.), Czech. 41/E2
Hronov, Czech. 41/D1
Hrubieszów, Poland 47/F3
Hrušovany, Czech. 41/D2
Hsenwi, Burma 72/C2
Hsipaw, Burma 72/C2
Hsüchang (Xuchang), China 77/H5
Htawgaw, Burma 72/C1
Huacaraje, Bolivia 136/D3
Huacareta, Bolivia 136/C7
Huacaya, Bolivia 136/D7
Huachacalla, Bolivia 136/A6
Huachi, Bolivia 136/D4
Huachi, China 77/G4
Huachinango, Mexico 150/K7
Huachipato, Chile 138/D1
Huacho, Peru 120/B4
Huacho, Peru 128/D8
Huachuca (peak), Ariz. 198/E7
Huachuca City, Ariz. 198/E7
Huacrachuco, Peru 128/D7
Huade, China 77/H3
Huadian, China 77/L3
Hua Hin, Thailand 72/D4
Huahine (isl.), Fr. Poly. 87/L7
Huaibei, China 77/J5
Huaibin, China 77/H5
Huaide (Hwaiteh), China 77/K3
Huaiji, China 77/H7
Huainan, China 77/J5
Huainan, China 54/N6
Huairen, China 77/H4
Huajuapan de León, Mexico 150/L8
Hualaihué, Chile 138/E4
Hualalai (mt.), Hawaii 218/G5
Hualañé, Chile 138/A10
Hualapai (mts.), Ariz. 198/B4
Hualapai (peak), Ariz. 198/B3
Hualapai Ind. Res., Ariz. 198/B3
Hualgayoc, Peru 128/C7
Hualien, China 77/K7
Hualla, Peru 128/F9
Huallaga (riv.), Peru 120/B3
Huallaga (riv.), Peru 128/D5
Huallanca, Ancash, Peru 128/D7
Huallanca, Huánuco, Peru 128/D7
Huallen, Alberta 182/A2
Huamachuco, Peru 128/D6
Huamantla, Mexico 150/N1
Huambo (prov.), Angola 115/C6
Huambo, Angola 102/D6
Huambo, Angola 115/C6
Huambo, Angola 2/K6
Huanaqui, Bolivia 136/A7
Huanay, Bolivia 136/B4
Huancabamba, Peru 128/C5
Huancané, Bolivia 136/B6
Huancané, Peru 128/H10
Huancapi, Peru 128/E9
Huancavelica (dept.), Peru 128/E9
Huancavelica, Peru 120/B4
Huancavelica, Peru 128/E9
Huancayo, Peru 128/E9
Huancayo, Peru 120/B4
Huanchaca, Bolivia 136/B7
Huanchaca, Cerro (mt.), Bolivia 136/B7
Huanchaca, Serranía de (mts.), Bolivia 136/E4
Huanchaco, Peru 128/C7
Huanggang, China 77/J5
Huang He (riv.), China 2/Q4
Huang He (Hwang Ho) (riv.), China 54/N6
Huang He (Ma Qu) (riv.), China 77/F5
Huang He (Yellow) (riv.), China 77/J4
Huangling, China 77/G4
Huangliu, China 77/G8
Huangshi, China 77/J5
Huangzhong, China 77/F4
Huanqueros, Argentina 143/F5
Huanta, Peru 128/E9
Huánuco (dept.), Peru 128/D7
Huánuco, Peru 128/E7
Huánuco, Peru 120/B3
Huanuni, Bolivia 136/B6
Huanuni, Bolivia 120/C4
Huan Xian, China 77/G4
Huapai, N. Zealand 100/B1
Huapí (mts.), Nicaragua 154/E4
Huaquechula, Mexico 150/M2
Huara, Chile 138/B2
Huaral, Peru 128/D8
Huaráz, Peru 128/D7
Huaráz, Peru 120/B3
Huari, Bolivia 136/B6
Huari, Peru 128/D7
Huariaca, Peru 128/E8
Huarina, Bolivia 136/A5
Huarmey, Peru 128/C8
Huarochirí, Peru 128/D9
Huarocondo, Peru 128/F9
Huásabas, Mexico 150/E2
Huasaga (riv.), Peru 128/D4
Huascarán (mt.), Peru 120/B3
Huascarán (mt.), Peru 128/D7
Huasco, Chile 138/A7
Huasco (riv.), Chile 138/A7
Huatabampo, Mexico 150/D3
Huatunas (lag.), Bolivia 136/B3
Huatusco de Chicuellar, Mexico 150/P2
Huauchinango, Mexico 150/L6
Huaura, Peru 128/D8
Huautla de Jiménez, Mexico 150/L7
Huayabamba (riv.), Peru 128/D6
Huaylas, Peru 128/C7
Huayllas, Bolivia 136/C6
Hub, Miss. 256/E8
Hubball, W. Va. 312/B6
Hubbard, Iowa 229/G4
Hubbard (lake), Mich. 250/F4
Hubbard (co.), Minn. 255/D3
Hubbard, Minn. 255/C4
Hubbard, Nebr. 264/H2
Hubbard, Ohio 284/J3
Hubbard, Oreg. 291/A3
Hubbard, Sask. 181/H4
Hubbard, Texas 303/H6
Hubbard Creek (lake), Texas 303/F5
Hubbard Lake, Mich. 250/F4
Hubbards, Nova Scotia 168/D4
Hubbardston•, Mass. 249/F3
Hubbardston, Mich. 250/E5
Hubbardstown, W. Va. 312/A6
Hubbardsville, N.Y. 276/J5
Hubbardton•, Vt. 268/A4
Hubbart (pt.), Manitoba 179/K2
Hubbell, Mich. 250/A1
Hubbell, Nebr. 264/G4
Hubbell Trading Post Nat'l Hist. Site, Ariz. 198/F3
Hub City, Wis. 317/F9
Hubei (Hupei), China 77/H5
Huberdeau, Québec 172/C4
Huber Heights, Ohio 284/B6
Hubert, N.C. 281/P5
Hubertus, Wis. 317/K1
Hubli-Dharwar, India 68/C5
Hubli-Dharwar, India 54/J8
Huch'ang, N. Korea 81/C3
Hückelhoven, Germany 22/B3
Hucknall, England 13/F4
Huddersfield, England 10/G2
Huddersfield, England 13/J2
Huddinge, Sweden 18/H1
Huddleston, Va. 307/K6
Huddy, Ky. 237/S5
Hudiksvall, Sweden 18/K6
Hudson (bay) 162/H3
Hudson (str.) 162/J3
Hudson (bay), Canada 2/E3
Hudson (str.), Canada 146/L3
Hudson (bay), Canada 146/K3
Hudson, Colo. 208/K2
Hudson, Fla. 212/D3
Hudson, Ill. 222/E3
Hudson, Ind. 227/G1
Hudson, Iowa 229/H4
Hudson, Kansas 232/D3
Hudson, Ky. 237/J5
Hudson•, Maine 243/F5
Hudson (bay), Manitoba 179/K2
Hudson, Md. 245/N6
Hudson, Mass. 249/H3
Hudson•, Mass. 249/H3
Hudson, Mich. 250/E7
Hudson, N.H. 268/E6
Hudson•, N.H. 268/E6
Hudson (co.), N.J. 273/E2
Hudson (riv.), N.J. 273/C1
Hudson, N.Y. 276/N6
Hudson (riv.), N.Y. 276/N7
Hudson, N.C. 281/G3
Hudson (bay), N.W. Terr. 187/K3
Hudson (str.), N.W. Terr. 187/L3
Hudson, Ohio 284/H3
Hudson (lake), Okla. 288/R2
Hudson, Ontario 175/B2
Hudson, Ontario 177/G4
Hudson (bay), Ontario 175/D1
Hudson, Québec 172/C4
Hudson (bay), Québec 174/A1

384 Hudson

Hudson (str.), Québec 174/F1
Hudson, S. Dak. 298/R7
Hudson, Wis. 317/A6
Hudson, Wyo. 319/D3
Hudson Bay, Sask. 181/J3
Hudson Falls, N.Y. 276/O4
Hudson Hope, Br. Col. 184/F2
Hudson Lake, Ind. 227/D1
Hudsons Bay, Alberta 182/E4
Hudsonville, Mich. 250/D6
Hudspeth (co.), Texas 303/B10
Hudwin (lake), Manitoba 179/G1
Hue, Vietnam 54/M8
Hue, Vietnam 72/E3
Hueco (mts.), N. Mex. 274/D6
Hueco (mts.), Texas 303/B10
Huedin, Romania 45/F2
Huehue, Hawaii 218/G5
Huehuetenango, Guatemala 154/B3
Huehuetlán el Chico, Mexico 150/M2
Huejotzingo, Mexico 150/M1
Huejutla, Mexico 150/K6
Huelma, Spain 33/E4
Huelva (prov.), Spain 33/C4
Huelva, Spain 33/C4
Huelva, Spain 7/D5
Huelva (riv.), Spain 33/C4
Huentelauquén, Chile 138/A8
Huercal-Overa, Spain 33/F4
Huerfano (co.), Colo. 208/K7
Huerfano (riv.), Colo. 208/L7
Huesca (prov.), Spain 33/F1
Huesca, Spain 33/F1
Huéscar, Spain 33/E4
Huetamo, Mexico 150/J7
Huete, Spain 33/E2
Huetter, Idaho 220/B2
Huey, Ill. 222/D5
Hueyotlipan de Hidalgo, Mexico 150/M1
Hueytown, Ala. 195/D4
Huff, N. Dak. 282/J6
Huffman, Ark. 202/L2
Huffton, S. Dak. 298/N2
Huger, S.C. 296/H5
Huggins, Mo. 261/H8
Hugh Butler (lake), Nebr. 264/D4
Hughenden, Alberta 182/E3
Hughenden, Australia 87/E8
Hughenden, Queensland 88/G4
Hughenden, Queensland 95/B4
Hughes, Alaska 196/H1
Hughes, Ark. 202/J4
Hughes (co.), Okla. 288/O4
Hughes, S. Australia 94/A4
Hughes (co.), S. Dak. 298/J5
Hughes (riv.), W. Va. 312/D4
Hughes Springs, Texas 303/K5
Hughestown, Pa. 294/F7
Hughesville, Md. 245/L6
Hughesville, Mo. 261/F5
Hughesville, Pa. 294/J3
Hughson, Calif. 204/E6
Hughton, Sask. 181/D4
Hugh Town, England 13/A8
Hugo, Colo. 208/N4
Hugo, Minn. 255/E5
Hugo, Okla. 288/P7
Hugo (lake), Okla. 288/R6
Hugo Stroessner, Paraguay 144/C4
Hugoton, Kansas 232/A4
Huhehot (Hohhot), China 77/H3
Huiarau (range), N. Zealand 100/F3
Hŭich'ŏn, N. Korea 81/C3
Huíla (prov.), Angola 115/B7
Huila (dept.), Colombia 126/C6
Huila (mt.), Colombia 120/B2
Huila, Nevado del (mt.), Colombia 126/C6
Huimanguillo, Mexico 150/N8
Huimin, China 77/J4
Huinca Renancó, Argentina 143/D3
Huining, China 77/G4
Huissen, Netherlands 27/H5
Huitzilán, Mexico 150/O1
Huitzuco de los Figueroa, Mexico 150/K7
Huixcolotla, Mexico 150/N2
Huixtepec, Mexico 150/L8
Huixtla, Mexico 150/N9
Huize, China 77/F6
Huizen, Netherlands 27/G4
Huizhou, China 77/H7
Hulaco, Ala. 195/E2
Hulah (lake), Kansas 232/F5
Hulah, Okla. 288/O1
Hulah (lake), Okla. 288/O1
Hulan, China 77/L2
Hulbert, Mich. 250/D2
Hulbert, Okla. 288/R3
Hulberton, N.Y. 276/D4
Hulett, Wyo. 319/H1
Hulin, China 77/M2
Hull, England 7/E3
Hull, England 10/F4
Hull, England 13/G4
Hull, Fla. 212/E4
Hull, Georgia 217/F2
Hull, Ill. 222/B4
Hull, Iowa 229/A2
Hull (Orono) (isl.), Kiribati 87/J6
Hull•, Mass. 249/E7
Hull, N. Dak. 282/K7
Hull, Que. 162/J6
Hull (co.), Québec 172/B4
Hull, Québec 172/B4
Hulls Cove, Maine 243/G7
Hulopoe (bay), Hawaii 218/G2
Hulopoe Bay, Hawaii 218/H2
Hulst, Netherlands 27/E6
Hultsfred, Sweden 18/K8
Hulun Nur (lake), China 77/J2
Huma, China 77/L1
Humacao (dist.), P. Rico 161/E2
Humacao, P. Rico 161/E2
Humacao, P. Rico 156/G1
Humacao (riv.), P. Rico 161/E2
Huma He (riv.), China 77/K1
Humahuaca, Argentina 143/C1
Humaitá, Bolivia 136/B2
Humaitá, Brazil 132/H10
Humaitá, Brazil 120/C3
Humaitá, Brazil 132/G10
Humaitá, Paraguay 144/C5
Humansdorp, S. Africa 118/C6
Humansville, Mo. 261/E7
Humarock, Mass. 249/M4
Humber (riv.), England 13/G4
Humber (riv.), England 10/G4
Humber (riv.), Newf. 166/C4
Humber (riv.), Ontario 177/J3
Humberside (co.), England 13/G4
Humberto, Argentina 143/F5
Humbird, Wis. 317/E6
Humble, Texas 303/J7
Humble City, N. Mex. 274/F6
Humboldt, Ariz. 198/C4
Humboldt (co.), Calif. 204/B3
Humboldt (bay), Calif. 204/A3
Humboldt (bay), Colombia 126/B4
Humboldt, Ill. 222/E4
Humboldt (co.), Iowa 229/E3
Humboldt, Iowa 229/E3
Humboldt, Kansas 232/G4
Humboldt, Minn. 255/A2
Humboldt, Nebr. 264/J4
Humboldt (co.), Nev. 266/C1
Humboldt, Nev. 266/C2
Humboldt (range), Nev. 266/C2
Humboldt (riv.), Nev. 188/C2
Humboldt (riv.), Nev. 266/E2
Humboldt (sink), Nev. 266/C2
Humboldt (mt.), New Caled. 86/H4
Humboldt, Sask. 162/F5
Humboldt, Sask. 181/F3
Humboldt, S. Dak. 298/P6
Humboldt, Tenn. 237/D9
Humboldt Salt (marsh), Nev. 266/D3
Humbug (mt.), Oreg. 291/C5
Hume, Ill. 222/F4
Hume, Mo. 261/C6
Hume (res.), N.S. Wales 97/D4
Hume, N.Y. 276/D5
Hume, Sask. 181/H6
Hume (lake), Victoria 97/D4
Hume, Va. 307/N3
Humenné, Czech. 41/G2
Humeston, Iowa 229/G7
Humlum, Denmark 21/B4
Hummelstown, Pa. 294/J5
Hummock (isl.), Tasmania 99/D2
Humnoke, Ark. 202/G4
Humphrey (pt.), Alaska 196/K1
Humphrey, Ark. 202/G5
Humphrey, Idaho 220/F5
Humphrey, Nebr. 264/G3
Humphreys (peak), Ariz. 198/D3
Humphreys, La. 238/J7
Humphreys (co.), Miss. 256/C4
Humphreys, Mo. 261/F2
Humphreys, Okla. 288/H5
Humphreys (co.), Tenn. 237/F8
Humpolec, Czech. 41/C2
Humptulips, Wash. 310/A3
Humptulips (riv.), Wash. 310/B3
Humpty Doo, North. Terr. 93/B2
Húnaflói (bay), Iceland 7/B2
Húnaflói (bay), Iceland 21/B1
Hunan, China 77/H6
Hunchun, China 77/M3
Hundested, Denmark 21/E6
Hundred, W. Va. 312/E3
Hunedoara, Romania 7/G4
Hunedoara, Romania 45/F3
Hünfeld, Germany 22/C3
Hungary 2/K3
Hungary 7/F4
HUNGARY 41
Hunger (mt.), Vt. 268/B3
Hungerford, Queensland 95/B6
Hŭngnam, N. Korea 54/O6
Hungry Horse, Mont. 262/C2
Hungry Horse (res.), Mont. 262/C2
Hungtow (isl.), China 77/K7
Hunjiang, China 77/L3
Hunmanby, England 13/G3
Hunnewell, Kansas 232/E4
Hunnewell, Mo. 261/J3
Hunse (riv.), Netherlands 27/K3
Hunsrück (mts.), Germany 22/B4
Hunstanton, England 13/H5
Hunstanton, England 10/G4
Hunt, Ill. 222/E4
Hunt (co.), Texas 303/H4
Hunt (mt.), Wyo. 319/E1
Hunte (riv.), Germany 22/C2
Hunter, Ark. 202/H3
Hunter (isl.), Br. Col. 184/C4
Hunter (peak), Idaho 220/D3
Hunter, Kansas 232/D2
Hunter, Mo. 261/L9
Hunter (riv.), N.S. Wales 97/F3
Hunter, N.Y. 276/M6
Hunter (mt.), N.Y. 276/M6
Hunter (mts.), N. Zealand 100/A6
Hunter, N. Dak. 282/R5
Hunter, Okla. 288/L1
Hunter (isls.), Tasmania 88/G8
Hunter (isl.), Tasmania 99/A2
Hunter (isls.), Tasmania 99/B2
Hunterdon (co.), N.J. 273/D2
Hunter River, Pr. Edward I. 168/E2
Hunters, Wash. 310/G2
Hunters Creek Village, Texas 303/J1
Hunters Hill, N.S. Wales 88/K4
Hunters Hill, N.S. Wales 97/J3
Huntersville, Ky. 237/L7
Huntersville, Minn. 255/D4
Huntersville, N.C. 281/H4
Huntersville, W. Va. 312/G6
Huntertown, Ind. 227/G2
Hunterville, N. Zealand 100/E3
Hunting (riv.), N.C. 281/H2
Hunting (isl.), S.C. 296/G7
Huntingburg, Ind. 227/D8
Huntingdon, Br. Col. 184/L3
Huntingdon (isl.), Newf. 166/C3
Huntingdon (co.), Pa. 294/F5
Huntingdon, Pa. 294/G5
Huntingdon (co.), Québec 172/C4
Huntingdon, Québec 172/C4
Huntingdon, Tenn. 237/E8
Huntingdon and Godmanchester, England 13/G5
Huntingdon and Godmanchester, England 10/F4
Huntington, Ark. 202/B3
Huntington, Conn. 210/C3
Huntington, England 13/G3
Huntington (co.), Ind. 227/G3
Huntington, Ind. 227/G3
Huntington (lake), Ind. 227/F3
Huntington, Iowa 229/D2
Huntington•, Mass. 249/C4
Huntington (creek), Nev. 266/F2
Huntington, N.J. 273/C2
Huntington, N.Y. 276/R6
Huntington, Oreg. 291/K3
Huntington, Texas 303/K6
Huntington, Utah 304/C4
Huntington (creek), Utah 304/C4
Huntington•, Vt. 268/B3
Huntington, Va. 307/S3
Huntington, W. Va. 188/K3
Huntington, W. Va. 312/A6
Huntington Beach, Calif. 204/C11
Huntington Center, Vt. 268/B3
Huntington Park, Calif. 204/C11
Huntington Station, N.Y. 276/R6
Huntingtown, Md. 245/M6
Hunting Valley, Ohio 284/J9
Huntland, Tenn. 237/J10
Huntleigh, Mo. 261/O3
Huntley, Ill. 222/E1
Huntley, Minn. 255/D7
Huntley, Mont. 262/H5
Huntley, Nebr. 264/E4
Huntley, Wyo. 319/H4
Huntly, N. Zealand 100/E2
Huntly, Scotland 10/E2
Huntly, Scotland 15/F3
Huntoon, Sask. 181/H6
Huntsburg, Ohio 284/H2
Hunts Inlet, Br. Col. 184/B3
Hunts Point, Nova Scotia 168/D5
Hunts Point, Wash. 310/B2
Huntsville, Ala. 188/J4
Huntsville, Ala. 195/E1
Huntsville, Ark. 202/C1
Huntsville, Conn. 210/B1
Huntsville, Ind. 227/F4
Huntsville, Ind. 227/G4
Huntsville, Ky. 237/H6
Huntsville, Mo. 261/H4
Huntsville, Ohio 284/C5
Huntsville, Ontario 177/E2
Huntsville, Ontario 175/E3
Huntsville, Tenn. 237/N8
Huntsville, Texas 303/J7
Huntsville, Utah 304/C2
Huntsville, Wash. 310/G4
Hunucmá, Mexico 150/O6
Hunza (Baltit), Pakistan 68/C1
Huocheng, China 77/B3
Huon (isls.), New Caled. 87/G7
Huon (gulf), Papua N.G. 87/E6
Huon (gulf), Papua N.G. 85/C7
Huon (pen.), Papua N.G. 86/A2
Huon (riv.), Tasmania 99/C5
Huong Khe, Vietnam 72/E3
Huonville-Ranelagh, Tasmania 99/C5
Huoshan, China 77/J5
Huot, Minn. 255/B3
Huo Xian, China 77/H4
Hupei (Hubei), China 77/H5
Hurbanovo, Czech. 41/E3
Hurd (cape), Ontario 177/C2
Hurdland, Mo. 261/H2
Hurdle Mills, N.C. 281/L2
Hurdsfield, N. Dak. 282/L5
Hure, China 77/K3
Hureidha, Yemen 59/E6
Hurghada, Egypt 111/F2
Hurghada, Egypt 59/B4
Hurlburt, Fla. 212/B6
Hurley, Miss. 256/H9
Hurley, Mo. 261/F9
Hurley, N. Mex. 274/A6
Hurley, N.Y. 276/M7
Hurley, S. Dak. 298/P7
Hurley, Va. 307/D6
Hurley, Wis. 317/F3
Hurleyville, N.Y. 276/L7
Hurlford, Scotland 15/D5
Hurlock, Md. 245/P6
Huron (lake) 146/K5
Huron (lake) 162/H7
Huron, Calif. 204/E7
Huron, Ind. 227/D7
Huron, Kansas 232/G2
Huron (lake), Mich. 188/K2
Huron (co.), Mich. 250/F5
Huron (bay), Mich. 250/A2
Huron (lake), Mich. 250/G4
Huron (riv.), Mich. 250/F6
Huron (co.), Ohio 284/E3
Huron, Ohio 284/E3
Huron (riv.), Ohio 284/E3
Huron (county), Ontario 177/C4
Huron (lake), Ontario 177/B3
Huron (lake), Ontario 175/D3
Huron, S. Dak. 188/G2
Huron, S. Dak. 298/N5
Huron, Tenn. 237/E9
Huron City, Mich. 250/G4
Huron Mountain, Mich. 250/B2
Huron Park, Ontario 177/C4
Huron River (pt.), Mich. 250/B2
Hurricane, Ala. 195/C9
Hurricane (cliffs), Ariz. 198/B2
Hurricane (mt.), Mont. 262/D2
Hurricane, Utah 304/A6
Hurricane, W. Va. 312/C6
Hurricane Deck, Mo. 261/G6
Hurricane Mills, Tenn. 237/F9
Hurst, Georgia 217/D1
Hurst, Ill. 222/D6
Hurst, Texas 303/F2
Hurst, W. Va. 312/E4
Hurstville, Iowa 229/M4
Hurstville, N.S. Wales 88/K4
Hurstville, N.S. Wales 97/J4
Hurt, Va. 307/K6
Hürth, Germany 22/B3
Hurtsboro, Ala. 195/H6
Hurunui (riv.), N. Zealand 100/D5
Hurup, Denmark 21/B4
Húsavík, Iceland 21/C1
Husher, Wis. 317/L2
Hushpuckena, Miss. 256/C2
Huşi, Romania 45/J2
Husk, N.C. 281/F1
Huskisson, N.S. Wales 97/F4
Huslia, Alaska 196/G1
Huson, Mont. 262/B3
Hussar, Alberta 182/D4
Hustisford, Wis. 317/J9
Hustler, Wis. 317/F8
Hustontown, Pa. 294/F5
Hustonville, Ky. 237/M6
Hustopeče, Czech. 41/D2
Husum, Sweden 18/L5
Husum, Wash. 310/D5
Husum, Germany 22/C1
Hutchins (mt.), N.H. 268/E2
Hutchins, Texas 303/G3
Hutchinson, Kansas 188/G3
Hutchinson, Kansas 232/D3
Hutchinson, Kansas 146/J6
Hutchinson, Minn. 255/D6
Hutchinson (co.), S. Dak. 298/O7
Hutchinson (co.), Texas 303/C2
Hutchinson, W. Va. 312/F4
Huth, Yemen 59/D6
Hutsonville, Ill. 222/F4
Hutt (riv.), N. Zealand 100/C2
Hüttenberg, Austria 41/C3
Hutte Sauvage (lake), Québec 174/E1
Huttig, Ark. 202/F7
Hutto, Texas 303/G7
Hutton, La. 238/D4
Hutton, Md. 245/A3
Huttonsville, W. Va. 312/G5
Hutton Valley, Mo. 261/J9
Huttwil, Switzerland 39/E2
Hutubi, China 77/C3
Huumula, Hawaii 218/H5
Huutokoski, Finland 18/P5
Huwelijkszorg, Suriname 131/C2
Huxford, Ala. 195/D8
Hu Xian, China 77/G5
Huxley, Alberta 182/D4
Huxley, Iowa 229/F5
Huxley, Texas 303/L6
Huy, Belgium 27/G8
Huyton-with-Roby, England 13/G2
Huzgan, Iran 66/F5
Huzhou, China 77/K5
Hvannadalshnúkur (mt.), Iceland 21/C1
Hvar (isl.), Yugoslavia 45/C4
Hvidbjerg, Denmark 21/B4
Hvide Sande, Denmark 21/A6
Hviding, Denmark 21/B7
Hvítá (riv.), Iceland 21/B1
Hwainan (Huainan), China 77/J5
Hwaiteh (Huaide), China 77/K3
Hwange (Wankie), Zimbabwe 118/D3
Hwange (Wankie), Zimbabwe 102/E6
Hwang Ho (riv.), China 54/N6
Hwangju, N. Korea 81/C4
Hwangshih (Huangshi), China 77/J5
Hyak, Wash. 310/D3
Hyalite (peak), Mont. 262/E5
Hyannis, Mass. 249/N6
Hyannis, Nebr. 264/C3
Hyannis Port, Mass. 249/N6
Hyargas, Mongolia 77/D2
Hyargas Nuur (lake), Mongolia 77/D2
Hyas, Sask. 181/J4
Hyattstown, Md. 245/J3
Hyattsville, Md. 245/F4
Hyattville, Wyo. 319/E1
Hybart, Ala. 195/D7
Hybord, Manitoba 179/C1
Hyco (riv.), N.C. 281/L2
Hyco (riv.), Va. 307/K8
Hydaburg, Alaska 196/M2
Hyde, England 13/H2
Hyde, England 10/G2
Hyde, N. Zealand 100/C6
Hyde (co.), N.C. 281/S3
Hyde, Pa. 294/F4
Hyde (co.), S. Dak. 298/K4
Hyden, Ky. 237/P6
Hyden, W. Australia 92/B6
Hyde Park, Mass. 249/C7
Hyde Park, N.Y. 276/N6
Hyde Park, Ontario 177/C4
Hyde Park, Pa. 294/D4
Hyde Park, Utah 304/C2
Hyde Park, Vt. 268/B2
Hyde Park•, Vt. 268/B2
Hyder, Alaska 196/P2
Hyderabad, India 2/N5
Hyderabad, India 68/D5
Hyderabad, India 54/J8
Hyderabad, Pakistan 68/B3
Hyderabad, Pakistan 59/J4
Hyderabad, Pakistan 54/H7
Hydesville, Calif. 204/B3
Hydetown, Pa. 294/C2
Hydeville, Vt. 268/A4
Hydraulic, Br. Col. 184/F4
Hydro, Okla. 288/J3
Hye, Texas 303/F7
Hyères, France 28/G6
Hyères (isls.), France 28/G6
Hyesan, N. Korea 81/D3
Hygiene, Colo. 208/J2
Hyland (riv.), Yukon 187/F3
Hylo, Alberta 182/D2
Hyltebruk, Sweden 18/H8
Hyman, S.C. 296/H4
Hymer, Kansas 232/F3
Hymera, Ind. 227/C6
Hyndman (peak), Idaho 220/D6
Hyndman, Pa. 294/E6
Hyner, Pa. 294/G3
Hynish (bay), Scotland 15/B4
Hyogo (pref.), Japan 81/H7
Hypoluxo, Fla. 212/F5
Hyrra Banda, Cent. Afr. Rep. 115/D2
Hyrum, Utah 304/C2
Hyrynsalmi, Finland 18/Q4
Hysham, Mont. 262/J4
Hythe, Alberta 182/A2
Hythe, Alta. 162/E4
Hythe, England 10/G5
Hythe, England 13/H6
Hythe, Tasmania 99/C5
Hytop, Ala. 195/F1
Hyuga, Japan 81/E7
Hyvinkää, Finland 18/O6

I

Ia Drang (riv.), Vietnam 72/E4
Iaeger, W. Va. 312/C8
Ialomiţa (marshes), Romania 45/J3
Ialomiţa (riv.), Romania 45/H3
Iamonia (lake), Fla. 212/B1
Iantha, Mo. 261/D8
Iar Connacht (dist.), Ireland 17/C5
Iaşi, Romania 7/G4
Iaşi, Romania 45/H2
Iatan, Mo. 261/C4
Iatt (lake), La. 238/E3
Iba, Philippines 85/F2
Iba, Philippines 82/B3
Ibadan, Nigeria 2/K5
Ibadan, Nigeria 102/C4
Ibadan, Nigeria 106/E7
Ibagué, Colombia 126/C5
Ibagué, Colombia 120/B2
Ibaiti, Brazil 135/A3
Ibapah, Utah 304/A3
Ibar (riv.), Yugoslavia 45/E4
Ibaraki (pref.), Japan 81/K5
Ibaraki, Japan 81/J7
Ibarra, Ecuador 128/D2
Ibarra, Ecuador 120/B2
Ibarreta, Argentina 143/D2
Ibb, Yemen 59/D7
Ibbenbüren, Germany 22/B2
'Ibbin, Jordan 65/D3
Iberia (par.), La. 238/G7
Iberia, Mo. 261/H6
Iberia, Ohio 284/E4
Iberia, Peru 128/F5
Iberville (par.), La. 238/H6
Iberville, La. 238/K2
Iberville (co.), Québec 172/D4
Iberville, Québec 172/D4
Iberville, D' (lake), Québec 174/C1
Ibi, Nigeria 106/F7
Ibiá, Brazil 132/E7
Ibibobo, Bolivia 136/D7
Ibicaraí, Brazil 132/G6
Ibicuí (riv.), Brazil 132/C10
Ibicuy, Argentina 143/G6
Ibipetuba, Brazil 132/F5
Ibitinga, Brazil 135/B2
Ibiza, Spain 33/G3
Ibiza (isl.), Spain 7/E5
Ibiza (isl.), Spain 33/G3
Ibo, Bolivia 136/D7
Ibo, Mozambique 118/G2
Ibounzi (mt.), Gabon 115/B4
Ibra, Oman 59/G5
Ibra, Wadi (dry riv.), Sudan 111/D5
Ibrány, Hungary 41/F2
'Ibri, Oman 59/G5
Ibusuki, Japan 81/E8
Içá (riv.), Brazil 120/C3
Içá (riv.), Brazil 132/G9
Ica (dept.), Peru 128/E10
Ica, Peru 128/E10
Ica, Peru 120/B4
Ica (riv.), Peru 128/E10
Icabarú, Venezuela 124/H5
Icabarú (riv.), Venezuela 124/G5
Icacos (pt.), Trin. & Tob. 161/A11
Icaña, Catamarca, Argentina 143/C2
Icaño, Santiago del Estero, Argentina 143/D2
Icard, N.C. 281/G3
Ice Harbor (dam), Wash. 310/G4
İçel (prov.), Turkey 63/F4
İçel (Mersin), Turkey 63/F4
Iceland 2/J2
Iceland 7/C2
Iceland 4/C10
ICELAND 21/B1
Ichang (Yichang), China 77/H5
Ichchapuram, India 68/F5
Ichhapur, India 68/F1
Ichihara, Japan 81/P3
Ichikawa, Japan 81/P2
Ichilo (riv.), Bolivia 136/C5
Ichinohe, Japan 81/K3
Ichinomiya, Japan 81/H6
Ichinoseki, Japan 81/K4
Ichnya, U.S.S.R. 52/D4
Ichoa (riv.), Bolivia 136/C4
Ichoca, Bolivia 136/B5
Ichtegem, Belgium 27/B6
Ichun (Yichun), China 77/L2
Ichuña, Peru 128/G11
Icicle (creek), Wash. 310/E3
Ickesburg, Pa. 294/H5
Icla, Bolivia 136/C6
Içme, Turkey 63/H3
Icó, Brazil 132/G4
Iconium, Mo. 261/E6
Icy (bay), Alaska 196/K3
Icy (cape), Alaska 196/F1
Icy (cape), Alaska 196/K3
Icy (pt.), Alaska 196/L1
Icy (str.), Alaska 196/M1
Ida (co.), Iowa 229/C4
Ida, La. 238/C1
Ida, Mich. 250/F7
Idabel, Okla. 288/S7
Ida Grove, Iowa 229/B4
Idaho 188/D2
IDAHO 220
Idaho (co.), Idaho 220/C4
Idaho, Ohio 284/D7
Idaho (state), U.S. 146/G5
Idaho City, Idaho 220/C6
Idaho Falls, Idaho 146/G5
Idaho Falls, Idaho 188/D2
Idaho Falls, Idaho 220/F6
Idaho Springs, Colo. 208/H3
Idahue, Chile 138/F5
Idalia, Colo. 208/P3
Idalou, Texas 303/C4
Idana, Kansas 232/E2
Idanha, Oreg. 291/E3
Idanha-a-Nova, Portugal 33/C3
Idar-Oberstein, Germany 22/B4
Idaville, Ind. 227/D3
Idaville, Pa. 294/H5
Iddan, Somalia 115/J2
Iddesleigh, Alberta 182/E4
Ide, Japan 81/J7
Ideal, Georgia 217/D6
Ideal, S. Dak. 298/K6
Idehan Murzuk (des.), Libya 111/B2
Idehan Ubari (des.), Libya 111/B2
Idelès, Algeria 106/F4
Ider, Ala. 195/G1
Ider Gol (riv.), Mongolia 77/E2
Idfu, Egypt 111/F3
Idfu, Egypt 59/B5
Ídhi (mt.), Greece 45/G8
Ídhra, Greece 45/F7
Idi, Indonesia 85/B4
İdil, Turkey 63/J4
Idiofa, Zaire 115/C4
Idlewild, Mich. 250/D5
Idlewild, Tenn. 237/D8
Idleyld Park, Oreg. 291/D4
Idlib (prov.), Syria 63/G5
Idlib, Syria 63/G5
Idna, West Bank 65/B4
Idrigill (pt.), Scotland 15/B3
Idyllwild, Calif. 204/J10
Ie (isl.), Japan 81/N6
Ieper, Belgium 27/B7
Ierápetra, Greece 45/G8
Iet, Somalia 115/H3
Ifakara, Tanzania 115/G5
Ifalik (atoll), Micronesia 87/E5
Ifanadiana, Madagascar 118/H4
Ife, Nigeria 106/E7
Iférouane, Niger 102/C3
Iférouane, Niger 106/F5
Iffley, Sask. 181/C3
Ifni (Sidi Ifni), Morocco 106/B3
Ifni (Sidi Ifni), Morocco 102/B2
Ifugao (prov.), Philippines 82/C2
Igal, Hungary 41/D3
Igara-Paraná (riv.), Colombia 126/D8
Igarapava, Brazil 135/C2
Igarapé-Miri, Brazil 132/D3
Igarka, U.S.S.R. 4/C5
Igarka, U.S.S.R. 54/K3
Igarka, U.S.S.R. 48/J3
Iğdir, Turkey 63/K3
Iggesund, Sweden 18/K6
Igis, Switzerland 39/J3
Igiugig, Alaska 196/G3
Iglesias, Italy 34/B5
Igli, Algeria 106/D2
Igloo, S. Dak. 298/B7
Igloolik, Canada 4/B14
Igloolik, N.W.T. 162/H2
Igloolik, N.W. Terr. 187/K3
Iglosiatik (isl.), Newf. 166/B2
Ignace, Ont. 162/G6
Ignace, Ontario 175/B3
Ignace, Ontario 177/G5
Ignacio, Calif. 204/H1
Ignacio, Colo. 208/D8
Ignacio Agramonte, Cuba 158/G3
Ignacio de la Llave, Mexico 150/Q2
İğneada (cape), Turkey 63/C2
Igoumenitsa, Greece 45/E6
Igra, U.S.S.R. 52/H3
Igrim, U.S.S.R. 48/G3
Iguaçu (riv.) 120/D5
Iguaçu (riv.), Brazil 132/C9
Igualada, Spain 33/G2
Iguala de la Independencia, Mexico 150/K7
Iguape, Brazil 135/C4
Iguassú (falls) 120/D5
Iguatu, Brazil 120/F3
Iguatu, Brazil 132/G4
Iguazú (falls), Argentina 143/F2
Iguazú (falls), Brazil 132/C9
Iguazú (falls), Paraguay 144/E4
Iguazú Nat'l Park, Argentina 143/E2
Iguéla, Gabon 115/A4
Iguidi, Erg (des.) 102/B2
Iguidi, Erg (des.), Algeria 106/C3
Iguidi, Erg (des.), Mauritania 106/C3
Iheya (isl.), Japan 81/N6
Ihlen, Minn. 255/B7
Ihosy, Madagascar 118/H4
Ihu, Papua N.G. 85/B7
Ii (riv.), Finland 7/G2
Iida, Japan 81/H6
Iijoki (riv.), Finland 18/O4
Iisalmi, Finland 18/P5
Iizuka, Japan 81/E7
Ijamsville, Md. 245/J3
Ijebu-Ode, Nigeria 106/E7
IJlst, Netherlands 27/H2
IJmeer (bay), Netherlands 27/C4
IJmuiden, Netherlands 27/E4
IJssel (riv.), Netherlands 27/J4
IJsselmeer (lake), Netherlands 27/G3

sselstein, Netherlands 27/F4
ul, Brazil 132/C10
zendijke, Netherlands 27/D6
aalinen, Finland 18/N6
aría (isl.), Greece 45/G7
ast, Denmark 21/C5
eda, Hokkaido, Japan 81/L2
eda, Osaka, Japan 81/H7
eja, Nigeria 106/F7
ela, Zaire 115/D4
elemba, Congo 115/C3
htiman, Bulgaria 45/F4
i (isl.), Japan 81/D7
om, Nigeria 106/F7
oma, Japan 81/J8
opa (riv.), Madagascar 118/H3
pikpuk (riv.), Alaska 196/H1
sal, Israel 65/C2
i, Georgia 217/F2
agan, Philippines 82/C2
m (gov.), Iran 66/E4
am, Iran 66/E4
am, Nepal 68/F3
an, China 77/K7
inskiy, U.S.S.R. 48/K4
anz, Switzerland 39/H3
aro, Nigeria 106/E7
asco, Mo. 261/K3
ava, Czech. 41/E2
ave, Peru 128/H11
awa, Poland 47/D2
Jerton, Ontario 177/C4
e-à-la-Crosse, Sask. 181/L3
e-à-la-Crosse (lake), Sask. 181/L3
e-Bizard, Québec 172/H4
ebo, Zaire 115/C4
e de France (trad. prov.), France, 29
e-de-Montréal (co.), Québec 172/H4
e des Chênes, Manitoba 179/F5
e-Jésus (co.), Québec 172/H4
ek (riv.), U.S.S.R. 52/J4
e-Perrot, Québec 172/G4
es (lake), Québec 172/B3
esha, Nigeria 106/F7
eld, N. Mex. 274/D3
is (riv.), Switzerland 39/E3
ord, Manitoba 179/J2
ord, N.S. Wales 97/D4
racombe, England 13/F5
racombe, England 13/C6
gaz, Turkey 63/E2
gaz (mts.), Turkey 63/E2
gin, Turkey 63/D3
ha Grande (bay), Brazil 135/D3
havo, Portugal 33/B2
héus, Brazil 120/F4
héus, Brazil 132/G6
(riv.), U.S.S.R. 54/J5
(riv.), U.S.S.R. 48/H5
amna, Alaska 196/H1
amna (lake), Alaska 188/C6
amna (lake), Alaska 196/G3
amna (vol.), Alaska 196/H2
ç, Turkey 63/H3
ca, Turkey 63/J3
ff, Colo. 208/N1
gan, Philippines 82/E6
gan (bay), Philippines 82/E6
n (isl.), Philippines 82/E6
o (pt.), Hawaii 218/G1
on, N.Y. 276/K5
um (ruins), Turkey 63/B6
keston, England 13/F5
keston, England 10/F4
abo, N.S. Wales 97/D4
ahe, Oreg. 291/C5
ampu, Nevada (mt.), Bolivia 136/A4
ana (bay), Philippines 82/D7
ana, Spain 33/E2
apel, Chile 138/A8
e-et-Vilaine (dept.), France 28/C3
éla, Niger 106/F6
er (riv.), Germany 22/D4
escas, Spain 33/D2
escas, Uruguay 145/D4
e-sur-Têt, France 28/E6
imani, Nevada (mt.), Bolivia 136/B5
inois 188/J3
LINOIS 222
inois (bayou), Ark. 202/D3
inois (riv.), Colo. 208/G1
inois (riv.), Ill. 188/H2
inois (riv.), Ill. 222/C4
inois (riv.), Okla. 288/S3
inois (riv.), Oreg. 291/D5
inois (state), U.S. 146/K6
inois-Mississippi (canal), Ill. 222/C2
iopolis, Ill. 222/D4
izi, Algeria 106/F3
izi, Algeria 102/C2
mo, Mo. 261/O8
nau-Effretikon, Switzerland 39/G2
ora, Spain 33/E4
uka, N.S. Wales 97/G1
'men (lake), U.S.S.R. 7/H3
'men' (lake), U.S.S.R. 52/D3
menau, Germany 22/D4
menau (riv.), Germany 22/D2
minster, England 13/D7
o, Peru 128/G11
obasco, El Salvador 154/C4
ocos Norte (prov.), Philippines 82/C1
ocos Sur (prov.), Philippines 82/C1
oilo (prov.), Philippines 82/D5
oilo, Philippines 85/G3
oilo, Philippines 82/D5
oilo, Philippines 54/O8
oilo (str.), Philippines 82/D5
omantsi, Finland 18/R5
orin, Nigeria 106/F7
orin, Nigeria 106/F7
pendam, Netherlands 27/C4
sley, Ky. 237/F6
ubabor (prov.), Ethiopia 111/F6
ūkste, U.S.S.R. 53/D3
waco, Wash. 310/A4
za, Poland 47/E3

Imabari, Japan 81/F3
Imandra (lake), U.S.S.R. 48/D3
Imandra (lake), U.S.S.R. 52/D1
Imari, Japan 81/D7
Imataca, Serranía (mts.), Venezuela 124/H4
Imatra, Finland 18/C6
Imazu, Japan 81/G6
Imbâba, Egypt 111/J3
Imbabura (prov.), Ecuador 128/C2
Imbaimadai, Guyana 131/A3
Imbert, Dom. Rep. 158/D5
Imbituba, Brazil 132/D10
Imbituva, Brazil 135/A4
Imbler, Oreg. 291/J2
Imbocen, Ark. 202/H1
Imeri, Sierra (mts.), Venezuela 124/F7
Imese, Zaire 115/C2
Imi, Ethiopia 111/H6
Imías, Cuba 158/K4
Imilac, Chile 138/B4
Imishli, U.S.S.R. 52/G7
Imlay, Nev. 266/C2
Imlay, S. Dak. 298/E6
Imlay City, Mich. 250/F5
Imlaystown, N.J. 273/D3
Imler, Pa. 294/E5
Immaculata, Pa. 294/L6
Immenstadt im Allgäu, Germany 22/C5
Immingham, England 13/G4
Immokalee, Fla. 212/E6
Imnaha, Oreg. 291/J2
Imnaha (riv.), Oreg. 291/L2
Imo (state), Nigeria 106/F7
Imogene, Iowa 229/C7
Imola, Italy 34/C2
Impach, Wash. 310/G2
Imperatriz, Brazil 120/E3
Imperatriz, Brazil 132/E4
Imperia (prov.), Italy 34/B3
Imperia, Italy 34/B3
Imperial (dam), Ariz. 198/A6
Imperial (res.), Ariz. 198/A6
Imperial (co.), Calif. 204/K10
Imperial, Calif. 204/K11
Imperial (dam), Calif. 204/L11
Imperial (res.), Calif. 204/L10
Imperial (valley), Calif. 204/K10
Imperial (riv.), Chile 138/D2
Imperial, Mo. 261/M6
Imperial, Nebr. 264/C4
Imperial, Peru 128/D7
Imperial, Sask. 181/F4
Imperial, Texas 303/B6
Imperial Beach, Calif. 204/H11
Imperial Head, Md. 245/K6
Imperial Head, Sask. 162/F5
Imperial Head, Sask. 181/H5
Imperial Hill, Ohio 284/C9
Imperial Mills, Alberta 182/E2
Impfondo, Congo 115/C3
Imphal, India 54/L7
Imphal, India 68/G4
Impora, Bolivia 136/C7
Imral (isl.), Turkey 63/C2
Imranlı, Turkey 63/H2
Imroz (Gökçeada) (isl.), Turkey 63/A2
Imst, Austria 41/A3
Imuris, Mexico 150/D1
Imuruan (bay), Philippines 82/B5
Imuruk (basin), Alaska 196/E1
Ina, Ill. 222/E5
Ina, Japan 81/H6
Ina (riv.), Japan 81/H7
Inaha, Georgia 217/E7
Inala, Queensland 88/K3
Inala, Queensland 95/D3
Inambari, Peru 128/H9
Inambari (riv.), Peru 128/H9
In Amenas, Algeria 106/F3
In Amguel, Algeria 106/E4
Inançahua Junction, N. Zealand 100/C4
Iñapari, Peru 128/F8
Inarajan, Guam 86/K7
Inari, Finland 18/P2
Inari (lake), Finland 7/G2
Inari (lake), Finland 18/P2
Inavale, Nebr. 264/F4
Inawashiro (lake), Japan 81/K5
Inca, Spain 33/H3
Incacamachi, Cerro (mt.), Bolivia 136/A6
Inca de Oro, Chile 138/B6
Incaguasi, Nevada (mt.), Chile 138/C6
Incahuasi, Cerro de (mt.), Argentina 143/C2
Ince (cape), Turkey 63/F1
Incekum (cape), Turkey 63/F4
Incesu, Turkey 63/F3
Inchard, Loch (inlet), Scotland 15/C2
Inchcape (Bell Rock) (isl.), Scotland 15/F4
Inchelium, Wash. 310/G2
Inchigeelagh, Ireland 17/C8
Inchiri (reg.), Mauritania 106/A5
Inchkeith, Sask. 181/J5
Inchkeith (isl.), Scotland 15/D1
Inchnadamph, Scotland 15/D2
Inch'ŏn, S. Korea 54/O6
Inch'ŏn, S. Korea 81/C5
Indaal, Loch (inlet), Scotland 15/B5
In Dagouber (well) Mali 106/D4
Indalsälven (riv.), Sweden 18/H5
Indé, Mexico 150/G4
Independence (co.), Ark. 202/G2
Independence, Belize 154/C2
Independence, Calif. 204/H7
Independence, Iowa 229/K4
Independence, Kansas 232/G4
Independence, Ky. 237/M3
Independence (lake), Mich. 250/B2
Independence, Minn. 255/F5
Independence (lake), Minn. 255/F5
Independence, Miss. 256/E1
Independence, Mo. 261/R5
Independence (mts.), Nev. 266/E1
Independence, Ohio 284/H9
Independence, Oreg. 291/D3

Independence, Va. 307/F7
Independence, W. Va. 312/G4
Independence, Wis. 317/D7
Independencia, Bolivia 136/B5
Independencia, Brazil 132/C6
Independencia (prov.), Dom. Rep. 158/D6
Independencia (bay), Peru 128/D10
Independencia (isl.), Peru 128/D10
Independencia, Venezuela 124/H4
Index, Wash. 310/D3
Index (peak), Wyo. 319/C1
India 2/N4
India 54/J7
INDIA 68/D4
Indiahoma, Okla. 288/J5
Indialantic, Fla. 212/F3
India Muerta (riv.), Uruguay 145/E4
Indian (ocean) 54/H10
Indian (ocean) 102/G7
Indian (mt.) Conn. 210/B1
Indian (pond), Conn. 210/A1
Indian (riv.), Del. 245/S6
Indian (riv.), Fla. 212/F3
Indian (creek), Idaho 220/C5
Indian (creek), Ind. 227/D6
Indian (creek), Ind. 227/E8
Indian (creek), Md. 245/G4
Indian (lake), Mich. 250/C2
Indian (stream), N.H. 268/E1
Indian (lake), N.Y. 276/M3
Indian (harb.), Nova Scotia 168/G3
Indian (lake), Ohio 284/C5
Indian (creek), S. Dak. 298/B4
Indian (creek), Utah 304/B5
Indian (creek), Utah 304/E5
Indiana 188/J3
INDIANA 227
Indiana (co.), Pa. 294/D4
Indiana, Pa. 294/E4
Indiana (prov.), Italy 34/B3
Indiana (state), U.S. 146/K6
Indiana Dunes Nat'l Lakeshore, Ind. 227/C1
Indianapolis (cap.), Ind. 146/K5
Indianapolis (cap.), Ind. 188/J3
Indianapolis (cap.), Ind. 227/E5
Indian Bay, Manitoba 179/G5
Indian Beach, N.C. 281/R5
Indian Brook, Nova Scotia 168/H2
Indian Cabins, Alberta 182/B4
Indian Creek, Fla. 212/B4
Indian Creek, Ill. 222/B4
Indian Harbour Beach, Fla. 212/F3
Indian Head, Md. 245/K6
Indian Head, Sask. 162/F5
Indian Head, Sask. 181/H5
Indian Hill, Ohio 284/C9
Indian Hills, Ky. 237/K1
Indian Hills, N.C. 281/C4
Indian Lake, N.Y. 276/M3
Indian Lake, Pa. 294/E5
Indian Mills, W. Va. 312/E7
Indian Mound, Tenn. 237/F7
Indian Neck, Conn. 210/D3
Indian Neck, Va. 307/O5
Indian Ocean 2/N6
Indian Ocean, Ant. 5/C3
Indian Ocean, Indonesia 85/E8
Indian Ocean, S. Australia 94/E7
Indian Ocean, Tasmania 99/A4
Indian Ocean, Victoria 97/B6
Indian Ocean, W. Australia 92/A5
Indianola, Ill. 222/F4
Indianola, Iowa 229/F6
Indianola, Miss. 256/C4
Indianola, Nebr. 264/D4
Indianola, Okla. 288/P4
Indianola, Utah 304/C4
Indianola, Wash. 310/A1
Indian Pond (lake), Maine 243/D4
Indian River (bay), Del. 245/T6
Indian River (inlet), Del. 245/T6
Indian River (co.), Fla. 212/F4
Indian River, Maine 243/H6
Indian River, Mich. 250/D2
Indian River, Ontario 177/F3
Indian River Shores, Fla. 212/F4
Indian Rocks Beach, Fla. 212/B3
Indian Shores, Fla. 212/B3
Indian Springs, Georgia 217/E4
Indian Springs, Ind. 227/D7
Indian Springs, Nev. 266/F6
Indiantown, Fla. 212/F4
Indian Trail, N.C. 281/H4
Indian Valley, Idaho 220/B5
Indian Valley, Va. 307/G7
Indian Village, Ind. 227/E1
Indian Village, La. 238/D4
Indian Wells, Ariz. 198/E3
Indian Wells, Calif. 204/J10
Indiga, U.S.S.R. 48/E3
Indiga, U.S.S.R. 52/G1
Indigirka, U.S.S.R. 54/R3
Indigirka (riv.), U.S.S.R. 4/C2
Indigirka (riv.), U.S.S.R. 48/P3
Indigo (creek), Oreg. 291/D5
Indios (chan.), Cuba 158/B2
Indira (pt.), India 68/G7
Indispensable (str.), Solomon Is. 86/G3
Indochina (reg.), Asia 72/C1
Indonesia 2/Q6
Indonesia 54/M10
INDONESIA 85
Indooroopilly, Queensland 95/D3
Indooroopilly, Queensland 88/K3
Indore, India 68/D4
Indore, India 54/J7
Indore, W. Va. 312/D6
Indramayu, Indonesia 85/H2
Indramayu (pt.), Indonesia 85/H1
Indravati (riv.), India 68/E5
Indre (dept.), France 28/D4
Indre (riv.), France 28/D4
Indre-et-Loire (dept.), France 28/D4
Indus (riv.), 2/N4
Indus (riv.), 54/H7

Indus, Alberta 182/D4
Indus (riv.), India 68/B3
Indus, Minn. 255/E2
Indus, Mouths of the (delta), Pakistan 68/B4
Indus (riv.), Pakistan 59/J4
Indus (riv.), Pakistan 68/B3
Industrial City, Georgia 217/C1
Industry, Ill. 222/C4
Industry, Kansas 232/E2
Industry, Pa. 294/A4
Industry, Texas 303/H7
Inebolu, Turkey 59/B1
Inebolu, Turkey 63/E2
Inegöl, Turkey 63/C2
In Eker, Algeria 106/F4
Ineu, Romania 45/E2
Inez, Ky. 237/S5
Inez, N.C. 281/N2
Inezgane, Morocco 106/C2
In Ezzane (well), Algeria 106/G4
Infanta, Philippines 82/C3
Infieles (pt.), Chile 138/A6
Infiesto, Spain 33/D1
In-Gall, Niger 106/F5
Ingalls, Ark. 202/F4
Ingalls (mt.), Calif. 204/E3
Ingalls, Ind. 227/F5
Ingalls, Kansas 232/B4
Ingalls, Mich. 250/B3
Ingavi, Bolivia 136/B2
Ingelmunster, Belgium 27/C7
Ingelow, Manitoba 179/B5
Ingenbohl, Switzerland 39/G2
Ingende, Zaire 115/C4
Ingende, Zaire 102/D5
Ingeniero Huergo, Argentina 143/C4
Ingeniero Jacobacci, Argentina 143/C5
Ingeniero Luiggi, Argentina 143/D4
Ingeniero Montero Hoyos (Tocomechi), Bolivia 136/D6
Ingersoll, Ontario 177/D4
Ingham (co.), Mich. 250/E6
Ingham, Queensland 88/H3
Ingham, Queensland 95/C3
Inglefield, Ind. 227/B8
Inglés (pt.), Cuba 158/G4
Inglesa (bay), Chile 138/A6
Ingleside, Md. 245/P4
Ingleside, W. Va. 312/E8
Inglewood, Calif. 204/B11
Inglewood, Nebr. 264/H4
Inglewood, N. Zealand 100/E3
Inglewood, Victoria 97/B5
Inglis, Fla. 212/D2
Inglis, Manitoba 179/A4
Ingold, N.C. 281/N5
Ingoldsby, Ontario 177/F3
Ingolstadt, Germany 22/D4
Ingomar, Miss. 256/F2
Ingomar, Mont. 262/J4
Ingomar, Nova Scotia 168/C5
Ingomar, Pa. 294/C4
Ingonish, Nova Scotia 168/H2
Ingonish Beach, Nova Scotia 168/H2
Ingonish North (bay), Nova Scotia 168/H2
Ingornachoix (bay), Newf. 166/C2
Ingraham (lake), Fla. 212/E6
Ingraham, Ill. 222/E5
Ingram, Pa. 294/B7
Ingram, Texas 303/E7
Ingram, Va. 307/K7
Ingram, Wis. 317/E5
Ingre, Bolivia 136/D7
In Guezzam, Algeria 106/F5
Ingwavuma, S. Africa 118/E5
Inhambane (prov.), Mozambique 118/E4
Inhambane, Mozambique 118/F4
Inhambane, Mozambique 102/F7
Inhaminga, Mozambique 118/F3
Inharrime, Mozambique 118/F4
Inharrime, Mozambique 102/F7
Inhumas, Brazil 132/D7
Iniesta, Spain 33/F3
Inini, Fr. Guiana 131/E4
Inini (riv.), Fr. Guiana 131/E4
Inírida (riv.), Colombia 126/F6
Inishannon, Ireland 17/D8
Inishbofin (isl.), Ireland 17/A4
Inishbofin (isl.), Ireland 17/A4
Inishbofin (isl.), Ireland 17/E1
Inisheer (isl.), Ireland 17/B5
Inishmaan (isl.), Ireland 17/C5
Inishmore (isl.), Ireland 17/B5
Inishmurray (isl.), Ireland 17/D3
Inishowen (head), Ireland 17/H1
Inishowen (pen.), Ireland 17/G1
Inishshark (isl.), Ireland 17/A4
Inishtrahull (isl.), Ireland 17/G1
Inishtrahull (sound), Ireland 17/G1
Inishturk (isl.), Ireland 10/A4
Inishturk (isls.), Ireland 17/A4
Inistioge, Ireland 17/G7
Injune, Queensland 95/D5
Injune, Queensland 88/H5
Inkerman, New Bruns. 170/F1
Inklin (riv.), Br. Col. 184/J2
Inkom, Idaho 220/F5
Inkster, N.D. 282/P3
Inkster, N. Dak. 282/P3
Inland (lake), Ala. 195/G3
Inland (lake), Alaska 196/G1
Inland, Nebr. 264/F4
Inle (lake), Burma 72/C2
Inlet, N.Y. 276/L3
Inman, Georgia 217/D4
Inman, Kansas 232/E3
Inman, Nebr. 264/F2
Inman, S.C. 296/C1
Inn (riv.), Austria 41/B2
Inn (riv.), Germany 22/E4
Inn (riv.), Switzerland 39/K3
Innaminka, S. Australia 94/G3
Innellan, Scotland 15/A2
Inner (sound), Scotland 10/D2

Inner (sound), Scotland 15/C3
Inner Hebrides (isls.), Scotland 15/B4
Innerkip, Ontario 177/D4
Innerleithen, Scotland 10/E3
Innerleithen, Scotland 15/E5
Inner Mongolia (reg.), China 54/N5
Inner Mongolia (reg.), China 77/H3
Inner Mongolian Aut. Reg. (Nei Monggol), China 77/H3
Innerkirchen, Switzerland 39/F3
Innes (lake), N.S. Wales 97/G2
Innisfail, Alberta 182/D3
Innisfail, Queensland 95/C3
Innisfail, Queensland 88/H3
Innisfree, Alberta 182/E3
Inniscrone, Ireland 17/C3
Innisville, Ontario 177/H2
Innoko (riv.), Alaska 196/G2
Innsbruck, Austria 7/F4
Innsbruck, Austria 41/A3
Inny (riv.), Ireland 17/F4
Inny (riv.), Ireland 17/A8
Inola, Okla. 288/P2
Inongo, Zaire 115/C4
inönü, Turkey 63/D3
Inowrocław, Poland 47/D2
Inquisivi, Bolivia 136/B5
In Rhar, Algeria 106/E3
Ins, Switzerland 39/D2
In Salah, Algeria 106/E3
In Salah, Algeria 102/C2
Insch, Scotland 15/F3
Insein, Burma 72/C3
Insinger, Sask. 181/H4
Inspiration, Ariz. 198/D5
Institute, W. Va. 312/C6
Instow, Sask. 181/C6
Inta, U.S.S.R. 7/K2
Inta, U.S.S.R. 52/K1
Inta, U.S.S.R. 48/G3
Intake, Mont. 262/M3
Intelewa, Suriname 131/D4
Intendente Alvear, Argentina 143/D4
intepe, Turkey 63/B6
Intercession City, Fla. 212/E3
Intercourse, Pa. 294/K5
Interior, S. Dak. 298/F6
Interlachen, Fla. 212/E3
Interlaken, Mass. 249/A3
Interlaken, N.J. 273/E3
Interlaken, N.Y. 276/G5
Interlaken, Switzerland 39/E3
Interlochen, Mich. 250/D4
International Airport, Georgia 217/K2
International Airport, Mo. 261/P2
International Airport (Dallas-Ft. Worth), Texas 303/F2
International Falls, Minn. 188/H1
International Falls, Minn. 255/N2
International Peace Garden, Manitoba 179/B5
International Peace Garden, N. Dak. 282/K1
Intervale, N.H. 268/E3
Interview (isl.), India 68/G6
Inthanon, Doi (mt.), Thailand 72/C3
Intipucá, El Salvador 154/D4
Intracoastal Waterway, S.C. 296/H5
Intracoastal Waterway, Texas 303/J9
Intragna, Switzerland 39/G4
Intutu, Peru 128/E4
Inubo (cape), Japan 81/K6
Inukjuak, Québec 162/H4
Inukjuak, Québec 174/E1
Inútil (bay), Chile 138/E10
Inuvik, Canada 4/C16
Inuvik, N.W.T. 146/E2
Inuvik, N.W.T. 162/C2
Inuvik (reg.), N.W. Terr. 187/F3
Inuvik, N.W. Terr. 187/E3
Inver (bay), Ireland 17/E2
Inveraray, Scotland 10/D2
Inveraray, Scotland 15/C4
Inverbervie, Scotland 10/E2
Inverbervie, Scotland 15/F4
Invercargill, N. Zealand 100/B7
Invercassley, Scotland 15/D3
Inverell, N.S. Wales 88/J5
Inverell, N.S. Wales 97/F1
Invergarry, Scotland 15/D3
Invergordon, Scotland 10/D3
Invergordon, Scotland 15/D3
Invergowrie, Scotland 15/E4
Inver Grove Heights, Minn. 255/E6
Inverhuron, Ontario 177/C3
Inverie, Scotland 15/C3
Inverkeilor, Scotland 15/F4
Inverkeithing, Scotland 15/D1
Inverkeithing, Scotland 10/C1
Inverloch, Victoria 97/C6
Invermay, Ontario 177/C3
Invermay, Sask. 181/J4
Invermere, Br. Col. 184/J5
Invermoriston, Scotland 15/D3
Inverness, Ala. 195/G6
Inverness, Calif. 204/B5
Inverness, Fla. 212/D3
Inverness, Ill. 222/A5
Inverness, Miss. 256/C4
Inverness, Mont. 262/F2
Inverness, Nova Scotia 162/K6
Inverness (co.), Nova Scotia 168/G2
Inverness, Nova Scotia 168/G2
Inverness, Québec 172/F4
Inverness, Scotland 15/D3
Inverness, Scotland 7/D3
Inverness, Scotland 10/D2
Inverness, (trad. co.), Scotland, 15/A5
Inverurie, Scotland 15/F3
Inverurie, Scotland 10/E2
Inverway, North. Terr. 93/A4
Investigator (shoal), Philippines 85/E4
Investigator (str.), S. Australia 88/F7
Investigator (str.), S. Australia 94/E6
Investigator Group (isls.), S. Australia 88/E6

Investigator Group (isls.), S. Australia 94/D5
Inwood, Ind. 227/E2
Inwood, Iowa 229/A2
Inwood, Manitoba 179/E4
Inwood, N.Y. 276/P7
Inwood, Ontario 177/C5
Inwood, W. Va. 312/K4
Inyanga, Zimbabwe 118/E3
Inyanga Nat'l Park, Zimbabwe 118/E3
Inyan Kara (creek), Wyo. 319/H1
Inyan Kara (mt.), Wyo. 319/H1
Inyo (co.), Calif. 204/H7
Inyo (mts.), Calif. 204/G6
Inyokern, Calif. 204/H8
Inza, U.S.S.R. 52/G4
Inzana (lake), Br. Col. 184/E3
Ioánnina, Greece 7/G4
Ioánnina, Greece 45/E6
Ioco, Br. Col. 184/K3
Ioka, Utah 304/D3
Iola, Ill. 222/E5
Iola, Kansas 232/G4
Iola, Texas 303/H7
Iola, Wis. 317/H6
Iolotan', U.S.S.R. 48/G6
Ioma, Papua N.G. 85/C7
Iona, Angola 115/B7
Iona, Idaho 220/G6
Iona, Minn. 255/C7
Iona (isls.), Newf. 166/C2
Iona, N.J. 273/C4
Iona, Nova Scotia 168/H3
Iona, Ontario 177/C5
Iona (isl.), Scotland 15/B4
Iona (isl.), Scotland 10/C4
Iona, S. Dak. 298/L6
Ione, Calif. 204/C9
Ione, Nev. 266/D4
Ione, Oreg. 291/H2
Ione, Wash. 310/H2
Ionia, Iowa 229/G2
Ionia, Kansas 232/D2
Ionia (co.), Mich. 250/D6
Ionia, Mich. 250/D6
Ionia, Mo. 261/F6
Ionian (sea) 7/F5
Ionian (sea), Greece 7/F5
Ionian (sea), Greece 45/D7
Ionian (sea), Italy 34/F4
Ionian Islands (reg.), Greece 45/D6
los, Greece 45/G7
los (isl.), Greece 45/G7
Iosco, U.S.S.R. 52/F5
Iosegun (lake), Alberta 182/B2
Iosegun (riv.), Alberta 182/B2
Iota, La. 238/E6
Iowa 188/J4
IOWA 229
Iowa (co.), Iowa 229/J5
Iowa (riv.), Iowa 188/H2
Iowa (riv.), Iowa 229/H4
Iowa, La. 238/D6
Iowa (state), U.S. 146/J5
Iowa (co.), Wis. 317/F9
Iowa City, Iowa 188/H2
Iowa City, Iowa 229/L5
Iowa Colony, Texas 303/J2
Iowa Falls, Iowa 229/G3
Iowa Park, Texas 303/F4
Iowa Point, Kansas 232/G2
Ipala, Guatemala 154/C3
Ipameri, Brazil 132/E7
Ipanema, Brazil 135/F1
Iparia, Peru 128/E7
Ipatovo, U.S.S.R. 52/F5
Ipava, Ill. 222/C4
Ipel' (riv.), Czech. 41/E2
Iphigenia (bay), Alaska 196/M2
Ipiales, Colombia 126/B7
Ipil, Philippines 82/D7
Ipin (Yibin), China 77/F6
Ipoh, Malaysia 54/M9
Ipoh, Malaysia 72/D6
Ipoly (riv.), Hungary 41/E2
Iporá, Brazil 120/D4
Ipperwash Prov. Park, Ontario 177/C4
Ippy, Cent. Afr. Rep. 115/D2
ipsala, Turkey 63/B2
ipsile, Turkey 63/G2
Ipswich, Australia 87/F8
Ipswich, England 13/J5
Ipswich, England 10/G4
Ipswich, Mass. 249/L2
Ipswich ▪, Mass. 249/L2
Ipswich (riv.), Mass. 249/L2
Ipswich, Queensland 88/J3
Ipswich, Queensland 95/E5
Ipswich, S. Dak. 298/L3
Ipu, Brazil 132/F4
Iqaluit, N.W.T. 187/M3
Iqaluit, N.W.T. 162/K3
Iquique, Chile 120/B5
Iquique, Chile 138/A2
Iquitos, Peru 120/B3
Iquitos, Peru 128/F4
Ira, Iowa 229/G4
Ira, N.Y. 276/G4
Ira, Texas 303/C5
Ira ▪, Vt. 268/A4
Iraan, Texas 303/D7
Iracoubo, Fr. Guiana 131/E3
Israël, U.S.S.R. 52/H2
Iráklion, Greece 45/G8
Iráklion, Greece 7/G5
Iran 2/M4
Iran 54/G7
IRAN 66
Iran 59/F3
Iran (mts.), Malaysia 85/E5
Iranshahr, Iran 66/M7
Iranshahr, Iran 59/H4
Irapa, Venezuela 124/G2
Irapuato, Mexico 150/J6
Iraq 2/M4
Iraq 54/F6

IRAQ 59/D3
IRAQ 66
Irasburg •, Vt. 268/C2
Irati, Brazil 132/D9
Irati, Brazil 135/A4
Irawan, Philippines 82/B6
Irazú (mt.), C. Rica 154/F6
Irbid, Jordan 65/D2
Irby, Wash. 310/G3
Irecê, Brazil 120/E4
Iredell (co.), N.C. 281/H3
Iredell, Texas 303/G6
Ireland 2/J3
Ireland 7/D3
IRELAND 17
IRELAND 10/B4
IRELAND, NORTHERN 10, 17
Ireland (isl.), Bermuda 156/G3
Ireland, Ind. 227/C8
Ireland, Texas 303/F6
Ireland, W. Va. 312/F5
Ireland's Eye (isl.), Ireland 17/K5
Ireland's Eye (isl.), Newf. 166/D2
Irene, S. Africa 118/H6
Irene, S. Dak. 298/P7
Ireng (riv.), Guyana 131/B3
Ireton, Iowa 229/A3
Irharhar, Wadi (dry riv.), Algeria 106/F3
Iri, S. Korea 81/C6
Irian Jaya (reg.), Indonesia 82/K7
Irian Jaya (reg.), Indonesia 85/J6
Iriba, Chad 111/D4
Iriga, Philippines 82/D4
Iringa (reg.), Tanzania 115/G5
Iringa, Tanzania 102/F5
Iringa, Tanzania 115/G5
Iriomote (isl.), Japan 81/K7
Irion (co.), Texas 303/C6
Iriona, Honduras 154/E2
Iriri (riv.), Brazil 132/C4
Irish (sea) 7/D3
Irish (sea), England 13/B4
Irish (sea), England 10/D4
Irish (sea), Ireland 10/D4
Irish (sea), Ireland 17/K4
Irish (sea), I. of Man 13/B4
Irish (sea), Wales 13/B4
Irish (sea), Wales 10/D4
Irishtown, New Bruns. 170/F2
Irishtown, Tasmania 99/B2
Irish Vale, Nova Scotia 168/H3
Irkutsk, U.S.S.R. 2/O3
Irkutsk, U.S.S.R. 54/M4
Irkutsk, U.S.S.R. 48/L4
Irma, Alberta 182/E3
Irma, Wis. 317/G5
Irmo, S.C. 296/E3
Iro (cape), Japan 81/J6
Irois (cape), Haiti 158/A6
Iron (mt.), Fla. 212/E4
Iron (co.), Mich. 250/G2
Iron, Minn. 255/F3
Iron (co.), Mo. 261/L7
Iron (co.), Utah 304/A6
Iron (co.), Wis. 317/F3
Iron Belt, Wis. 317/F3
Ironbound (isls.), Newf. 166/C2
Iron Bridge, Ontario 177/A1
Iron City, Georgia 217/F4
Iron City, Tenn. 237/F10
Irondale, Ala. 195/E3
Irondale, Mo. 261/L7
Irondale, Ohio 284/J4
Irondequoit, N.Y. 276/E4
Iron Gate (res.), Calif. 204/C2
Iron Gate, Va. 307/J3
Iron Gates, Mo. 261/C8
Ironia, N.J. 273/D2
Iron Knob, S. Australia 94/F6
Iron Knob, S. Australia 88/F6
Iron Mountain, Mich. 250/B3
Iron Mountain, Wyo. 319/G4
Iron Range, Queensland 95/B2
Iron Ridge, Wis. 317/K9
Iron River, Alberta 182/E2
Iron River, Mich. 250/G2
Iron River, Wis. 317/D2
Irons, Mich. 250/D4
Ironshire, Md. 245/T7
Ironside, Oreg. 291/K3
Ironspring (creek), Sask. 181/G3
Iron Springs, Alberta 182/D5
Iron Springs, Ariz. 198/C4
Iron Station, N.C. 281/G4
Ironton, Minn. 255/D4
Ironton, Mo. 261/L7
Ironton, Ohio 284/E8
Ironton, Wis. 317/F8
Ironwood, Mich. 250/F2
Iroquois (co.), Ill. 222/F3
Iroquois, Ill. 222/F3
Iroquois (riv.), Ill. 222/F3
Iroquois (riv.), Ind. 227/B3
Iroquois, Ontario 177/J3
Iroquois, S. Dak. 298/O5
Iroquois (lake), Vt. 268/A3
Iroquois Falls, Ont. 162/H6
Iroquois Falls, Ontario 175/D3
Iroquois Falls, Ontario 177/J5
Iroquois Point, Hawaii 218/A4
'Irqa, Yemen 59/E7
Irrara (creek), N.S. Wales 97/C1
Irrawaddy (div.), Burma 72/B3
Irrawaddy, Mouths of the (delta), Burma 72/B4
Irrawaddy (riv.), Burma 54/L7
Irrawaddy (riv.), Burma 72/B3
Irricana, Alberta 182/D4
Irrigon, Oreg. 291/H2
Irtysh (riv.), U.S.S.R. 54/J4
Irtysh (riv.), U.S.S.R. 48/H4
Irumu, Zaire 115/E3
Irún, Spain 33/F1
Irupana, Bolivia 136/B5
Iruya, Argentina 143/D1
Irvine, Alberta 182/E5
Irvine, Calif. 204/D11

Irvine, Ky. 237/O5
Irvine (lake), N. Dak. 282/M3
Irvine, Pa. 294/D2
Irvine, Scotland 15/D5
Irvine, Scotland 10/D3
Irvinestown, N. Ireland 17/F3
Irving, Ill. 222/D4
Irving, Iowa 229/J5
Irving, N.Y. 276/B5
Irving, Texas 303/G2
Irvington, Ala. 195/B9
Irvington, Ill. 222/D5
Irvington, Iowa 229/E3
Irvington, Ky. 237/J5
Irvington, N.J. 273/B2
Irvington, N.Y. 276/O6
Irvington, Va. 307/R5
Irvin's (bay), Grenada 161/D8
Irvona, Pa. 294/E4
Irwin (co.), Georgia 217/F7
Irwin, Idaho 220/G6
Irwin, Iowa 229/C5
Irwin, Mo. 261/D7
Irwin, Ohio 284/D5
Irwin, Pa. 294/C5
Irwin, S.C. 296/F2
Irwin, Va. 307/N5
Irwin, W. Australia 88/A5
Irwinton, Georgia 217/F5
Irwinville, Georgia 217/F7
Isa, Nigeria 106/F6
Isaac (lake), Br. Col. 184/F3
Isaacs (riv.), Queensland 88/H4
Isaacs (riv.), Queensland 95/D4
Isaac's Harbour North, Nova Scotia 168/G3
Isabel (bay), Ecuador 128/B9
Isabel, Kansas 232/D4
Isabel, La. 238/K5
Isabel, S. Dak. 298/G3
Isabel (mt.), Wyo. 319/B3
Isabela (bay), Dom. Rep. 158/D5
Isabela (cape), Dom. Rep. 158/D5
Isabela (isl.), Ecuador 128/B9
Isabela (prov.), Philippines 82/C2
Isabela, Philippines 82/C7
Isabela, P. Rico 156/F1
Isabela, P. Rico 161/A1
Isabela de Sagua, Cuba 158/E1
Isabela, Cordillera (range), Nicaragua 154/E4
Isabella (lake), Calif. 204/G8
Isabella, Manitoba 179/B4
Isabella (co.), Mich. 250/E5
Isabella, Mich. 250/C3
Isabella, Minn. 255/G3
Isabella (lake), Minn. 255/G3
Isabella (riv.), Minn. 255/G3
Isabella, N.W. Terr. 187/M3
Isabella, Okla. 288/E2
Isabella, Tenn. 237/N10
Isabel Segunda, P. Rico 161/G2
Isaccea, Romania 45/J3
Isachsen, Canada 4/B15
Isachsen, N.W. Terr. 187/H2
Isachsen (cape), N.W. Terr. 187/H2
Isachsens, N.W.T. 146/H2
Isafjördhardjúp (fjord), Iceland 21/A1
Isafjördhur, Iceland 7/B2
Isafjördhur, Iceland 21/B1
Isahaya, Japan 81/D7
Isana (riv.), Colombia 126/F7
Isangi, Zaire 115/D3
Isanti (co.), Minn. 255/E5
Isanti, Minn. 255/E5
Isar (riv.), Germany 22/E4
Isarog (mt.), Philippines 82/D4
Isbell, Ala. 195/C2
Iscar, Spain 33/D2
Ischia (isl.), Italy 34/D4
Ischua, N.Y. 276/D6
Iscuandé, Colombia 126/A6
Ise, Japan 81/H6
Ise (bay), Japan 81/H6
Isefjord (fjord), Denmark 21/E6
Iselin, N.J. 273/E2
Iselin, Pa. 294/E4
Isenthal, Switzerland 39/F3
Iseo (lake), Italy 34/C2
Isère (dept.), France 28/F5
Isère (riv.), France 28/F5
Iserlohn, Germany 22/B3
Isernia (prov.), Italy 34/E4
Isernia, Italy 34/E4
Ise-Shima Nat'l Park, Japan 81/H6
Iseyin, Nigeria 106/E7
Isfahan (prov.), Iran 66/H4
Isfahan, Iran 54/E4
Isfahan, Iran 66/G4
Isfahan, Iran 59/F3
Isfjorden (fjord), Norway 18/C2
Isham, Sask. 181/C4
Isherton, Guyana 131/B4
Ishigaki, Japan 81/L7
Ishigaki (isl.), Japan 81/L7
Ishige, Japan 81/P2
Ishikari (bay), Japan 81/K2
Ishikari (riv.), Japan 81/L2
Ishikawa (pref.), Japan 81/H5
Ishim (riv.), U.S.S.R. 54/H4
Ishim, U.S.S.R. 48/H4
Ishim (riv.), U.S.S.R. 48/G4
Ishimbay, U.S.S.R. 52/J4
Ishinomaki, Japan 81/K4
Ishioka, Japan 81/K5
Ishizuchi (mt.), Japan 81/F7
Ishpeming, Mich. 250/B2
Isiboro (riv.), Bolivia 136/C5
Isil'kul' (lake), U.S.S.R. 54/J5
Isimu, Indonesia 85/G5
Isiolo, Kenya 115/G3
Isiro, Zaire 102/E4
Isiro, Zaire 115/E3
Isisford, Queensland 88/G4
Isisford, Queensland 95/C5
Iskenderun, Turkey 59/C2

Iskenderun, Turkey 63/G4
Iskilip, Turkey 63/F2
Iskür (riv.), Bulgaria 45/G4
Iskut (riv.), Br. Col. 184/B2
Isla, Salar de la (salt dep.), Chile 138/B5
Isla, Veracruz, Mexico 150/M7
Isla (riv.), Scotland 15/E4
Isla Cristina, Spain 33/C4
Isla de Aguada, Mexico 150/O7
Isla de Maipo, Chile 138/C4
Islâhiye, Turkey 63/G4
Isla Holbox, Mexico 150/Q6
Islamabad (cap.), Pakistan 68/C2
Islamabad (cap.), Pakistan 2/N4
Islamabad (cap.), Pakistan 54/J6
Islamabad (cap.), Pakistan 59/K3
Islamabad District, Pakistan 68/C2
Islamorada, Fla. 212/F7
Isla Mujeres, Mexico 150/Q6
Island, Ky. 237/G6
Island (lake), Man. 162/G5
Island (lake), Manitoba 179/K3
Island (beach), N.J. 273/E4
Island (lake), N. Dak. 282/L2
Island (bay), Colombia 126/C4
Itaí, Brazil 135/B3
Itaipu (dam) 120/D5
Itaipu (res.) 120/D5
Itaipu (dam), Brazil 132/C9
Itaipu (dam), Brazil 132/C9
Itaipu (dam), Paraguay 144/E4
Itaipu (res.), Paraguay 144/E4
Itaituba, Brazil 132/C4
Itajaí, Brazil 120/E5
Itajaí, Brazil 132/D9
Itajubá, Brazil 135/D3
Itajubá, Brazil 132/E8
Itala, Somalia 115/J3
Italy 2/K3
Italy 7/F4
ITALY 34
Italy, Texas 303/H5
Itamarandiba, Brazil 132/F7
Itami, Japan 81/H7
Itanagar, India 68/G3
Itanhaém, Brazil 135/C4
Itapagipe, Brazil 135/B1
Itapé, Paraguay 144/C5
Itapeby, Uruguay 145/B2
Itapecerica, Brazil 135/D2
Itapecuru (riv.), Brazil 132/F3
Itapecuru-Mirim, Brazil 132/F3
Itapemirim, Brazil 132/F8
Itapetinga, Brazil 120/F4
Itapetinga, Brazil 132/G6
Itapetininga, Brazil 135/B3
Itapetininga, Brazil 132/D8
Itapeva, Brazil 132/D8
Itapeva, Brazil 135/B3
Itapi (riv.), Brazil 132/D8
Itapicuru, Brazil 132/G3
Itapicuru (riv.), Brazil 132/G5
Itapipoca, Brazil 132/G3
Itapira, Brazil 135/C3
Itapiranga, Brazil 132/B3
Itápolis, Brazil 132/D8
Itápolis, Brazil 135/B2
Itaporanga, Brazil 132/G4
Itapúa (prov.), Paraguay 144/E5
Itaquí, Brazil 132/B10
Itaquyry, Paraguay 144/E4
Itararé, Brazil 132/D9
Itararé, Brazil 135/B4
Itararé (riv.), Brazil 135/B3
Itariri, Brazil 135/C4
Itarsi, India 68/D4
Itasca (co.), Minn. 255/E3
Itasca (lake), Minn. 255/C3
Itasca, Texas 303/G5
Itata (riv.), Chile 138/A11
Itatí, Argentina 143/E2
Itatiba, Brazil 135/C3
Itaú, Bolivia 136/D7
Itauguá, Paraguay 144/B5
Itaúna, Brazil 135/D2
Itawamba (co.), Miss. 256/H2
Itbayat (isl.), Philippines 82/A2
Itchen (riv.), N.W. Terr. 187/J1
Iténez (Guaporé) (riv.), Bolivia 136/C3
Ithaca, Mich. 250/E5
Ithaca, Nebr. 264/H3
Ithaca, N.Y. 276/G6
Ithaca, Ohio 284/A6
Ithaca, Queensland 88/K2
Ithaca, Wis. 317/G9
Itháki, Greece 45/E6
Itháki (Ithaca) (isl.), Greece 45/E6
Itigi, Tanzania 115/F5
Itimbiri (riv.), Zaire 115/D3
Itkillik (riv.), Alaska 196/H1
Itmann, W. Va. 312/D7
Itnay (riv.), Fr. Guiana 120/D2
Ito, Japan 81/J6
Itoigawa, Japan 81/H5
Itoman, Japan 81/N6
Itonamas (riv.), Bolivia 136/C3
Itta Bena, Miss. 256/D4
Ittoqqortoormiit, Greenland 4/B11
Ittre, Belgium 27/E7
Itu, Brazil 135/C3
Ituaçu, Brazil 132/F6
Ituango, Colombia 126/C4
Ituberá, Brazil 132/G6
Ituiutaba, Brazil 132/D7
Itumbiara, Brazil 120/E4
Itumbiara, Brazil 132/D7
Ituna, Sask. 181/H4
Ituni, Guyana 131/B3
Itupiranga, Brazil 132/D4
Iturama, Brazil 135/A1
Iturbe, Paraguay 144/C5
Ituri (for.), Zaire 115/E3
Ituri (riv.), Zaire 115/E3
Ituverava, Brazil 135/C2
Ituzaingó, Argentina 143/E2
Ituzaingó, Uruguay 145/A6
Itzehoe, Germany 22/C2

Isthmus (bay), Ontario 177/C2
Istiaía, Greece 45/F6
Istmina, Colombia 126/B5
Istok, Philippines 82/E7
Istranca (mts.), Turkey 63/B2
Istres, France 28/F6
Istria (pen.), Yugoslavia 45/A3
Itá, Paraguay 144/B5
Itabaiana, Paraíba, Brazil 132/H4
Itabaiana, Sergipe, Brazil 132/G5
Itaberaba, Brazil 132/F6
Itabira, Brazil 120/E4
Itabira, Brazil 132/F7
Itabirito, Brazil 135/E2
Itabuna, Brazil 132/G6
Itabuna, Brazil 120/F4
Itacoatiara, Brazil 132/B3
Itacoatiara, Brazil 132/B3
Itacurubí, Paraguay 144/B5
Itacurubí del Rosario, Paraguay 144/D4
Itaguara, Brazil 135/D2
Itaguatins, Brazil 132/E5
Itaguí, Colombia 126/C4

Iuka, Ill. 222/E5
Iuka, Kansas 232/D4
Iuka, Ky. 237/E6
Iuka, Miss. 256/H1
Iul'tin, U.S.S.R. 48/T3
Iva, S.C. 296/B3
Ivaí (riv.), Brazil 132/C8
Ivalo, Finland 18/P2
Ivalojoki (riv.), Finland 18/P2
Ivan, Ark. 202/F6
Ivanava, Belarus 41/D2
Ivancice, Czech. 41/D2
Ivangrad, Yugoslavia 45/E4
Ivanhoe, Calif. 204/F7
Ivanhoe, Minn. 255/B6
Ivanhoe, N. S. Wales 88/G6
Ivanhoe, N.S. Wales 97/C3
Ivanhoe, N.C. 281/N5
Ivanhoe, Va. 307/G7
Ivanhoe, W. Australia 92/E1
Ivanhoe, W. Va. 312/F5
Ivanjica, Yugoslavia 45/E4
Ivanof, Alaska 196/G3
Ivano-Frankovsk, U.S.S.R. 7/G4
Ivano-Frankovsk, U.S.S.R. 48/C5
Ivano-Frankovsk, U.S.S.R. 52/B5
Ivanovo, U.S.S.R. 7/J3
Ivanovo, U.S.S.R. 48/E3
Ivanovo, U.S.S.R. 52/E3
Ivarib, Namibia 118/B4
Ivaylovgrad, Bulgaria 45/H5
Ivdel, U.S.S.R. 48/G3
Ivel (riv.), Cameroon 115/B3
Ivindo (riv.), Congo 115/B3
Ivindo (riv.), Gabon 115/B3
Ivins, Utah 304/A6
Ivittuut, Greenl. 4/D12
Ivohibe, Madagascar 118/H4
Ivón, Bolivia 136/C2
Ivory Coast (Côte d'Ivoire) 2/J5
Ivory Coast (Côte d'Ivoire) 102/B4
IVORY COAST (Côte d'Ivoire) 106/C7
Ivory Coast (reg.), Ivory Coast 106/C8
Ivoryton, Conn. 210/F3
Ivrea, Italy 34/B2
Ivry-sur-Seine, France 28/B2
Ivujivik, Que. 162/J3
Ivujivik, Québec 174/E1
Ivy, Va. 307/L4
Ivybridge, England 13/D7
Ivydale, W. Va. 312/D6
Ivy Mountain (brook), Conn. 210/C1
Ivyton, Ky. 237/P5
Ivyton, Tenn. 237/L8
Iwaizumi, Japan 81/K4
Iwaki, Japan 54/R6
Iwaki, Japan 81/K5
Iwaki (mt.), Japan 81/K3
Iwakuni, Japan 81/F6
Iwami, Japan 81/G6
Iwamizawa, Japan 81/L2
Iwanai, Japan 81/K2
Iwasaki, Japan 81/J3
Iwata, Japan 81/H6
Iwate (pref.), Japan 81/K4
Iwate, Japan 81/K4
Iwatsuki, Japan 81/O2
Iwilei, Hawaii 218/C4
Iwo (isl.), Japan 87/E3
Iwo (isl.), Japan 81/H8
Iwo, Nigeria 106/E7
Iwón, N. Korea 81/D3
Ixelles, Belgium 27/C9
Ixiamas, Bolivia 136/A3
Ixmiquilpan, Mexico 150/K6
Ixonia, Wis. 317/H1
Ixtapa, Mexico 150/J8
Ixtapalapa, Mexico 150/L1
Ixtenco, Mexico 150/N1
Ixtepec, Mexico 150/M8
Ixtlán del Río, Mexico 150/G6
Iyo, Japan 81/F7
Iyo (sea), Japan 81/E7
Izabal (lake), Guatemala 154/C3
Izamal, Mexico 150/P6
Izard (co.), Ark. 202/G1
Izberbash, U.S.S.R. 52/G4
Izegem, Belgium 27/C7
Izeh, Iran 66/F5
Izhevsk, U.S.S.R. 7/K3
Izhevsk, U.S.S.R. 48/F4
Izhevsk, U.S.S.R. 52/H3
Izhma (riv.), U.S.S.R. 52/H2
Izhma, U.S.S.R. 48/F3
Izigan (cape), Alaska 196/E4
Izmail, U.S.S.R. 48/C5
Izmail, U.S.S.R. 52/C5
Izmir, Turkey 54/D6
Izmir, Turkey 63/B3
Izmir, Turkey 59/A2
Izmir (gulf), Turkey 63/B3
Izmit, Turkey 59/A1
Izmit, Turkey 63/C2
Iznájar, Spain 33/D4
Iznalloz, Spain 33/E4
Iznik, Turkey 63/C2
Iznik (lake), Turkey 63/C2
Izozog, Bolivia 136/D6
Izozog (swamp), Bolivia 136/E6
Izra, Syria 63/D3
Izsák, Hungary 41/E3
Izsófalva, Hungary 41/F2
Iztapa, Guatemala 154/B4
Izu (isls.), Japan 81/J6
Izu (pen.), Japan 81/J6
Izúcar de Matamoros, Mexico 150/M2
Izuhara, Japan 81/D6
Izumi, Japan 81/J8

Izumiotsu, Japan 81/J8
Izumisano, Japan 81/G6
Izumo, Japan 81/F6
Izyum, U.S.S.R. 52/E5

J

Jaba, West Bank 65/C3
Jabaliya, Gaza Strip 65/A4
Jabalpur, India 54/K7
Jabalpur, India 68/D4
Jaba Rud (riv.), Iran 66/L2
Jabbeke, Belgium 27/C6
Jabir, Jordan 65/E2
Jablonec nad Nisou, Czech. 41/C1
Jablonica, Czech. 41/D2
Jablunka (pass), Czech. 41/E2
Jablunkov, Czech. 41/E2
Jaboatão, Brazil 120/F3
Jaboatão, Brazil 132/H5
Jaboticabal, Brazil 135/B2
Jaboticabal, Brazil 132/D8
Jabrin, Saudi Arabia 59/E5
Jaca, Spain 33/F1
Jacaguas (riv.), P. Rico 161/C2
Jacaleapa, Honduras 154/D3
Jacaltenango, Guatemala 154/B3
Jacaréacanga, Brazil 132/B4
Jacareí, Brazil 132/E8
Jacareí, Brazil 135/D3
Jacarezinho, Brazil 135/A3
Jacarezinho, Brazil 132/D8
Jáchal, Argentina 143/C3
Jachin, Ala. 195/B6
Jáchymov, Czech. 41/B1
Jacinto, Miss. 256/H1
Jacinto City, Texas 303/J1
Jack, Ala. 195/F7
Jack (creek), Minn. 255/C7
Jack (lake), Ontario 177/F3
Jack (co.), Texas 303/F4
Jack Creek, Nev. 266/E1
Jack (mt.), Wash. 310/E1
Jackfish (riv.), Alberta 182/B5
Jackfish (lake), Sask. 181/C2
Jackfish Lake, Sask. 181/C2
Jackfork (mt.), Okla. 288/P5
Jackman, Maine 243/C4
Jackman •, Maine 243/C4
Jackpot, Nev. 266/G1
Jacksboro, Tenn. 237/N8
Jacksboro, Texas 303/F4
Jacks Creek, Tenn. 237/D10
Jacks Fork (riv.), Mo. 261/J8
Jackson (co.), Ala. 195/F1
Jackson, Ala. 195/C8
Jackson (co.), Ark. 202/H2
Jackson, Calif. 204/C9
Jackson (co.), Colo. 208/G1
Jackson (co.), Fla. 212/D5
Jackson (lake), Fla. 212/B1
Jackson (lake), Fla. 212/E4
Jackson (co.), Georgia 217/E2
Jackson, Georgia 217/E4
Jackson (lake), Georgia 217/E4
Jackson (co.), Ill. 222/D6
Jackson (co.), Ind. 227/E7
Jackson (co.), Iowa 229/M4
Jackson (co.), Kansas 232/G2
Jackson (co.), Ky. 237/N6
Jackson, Ky. 237/P5
Jackson (par.), La. 238/G3
Jackson, La. 238/H5
Jackson (co.), Mich. 250/E6
Jackson, Mich. 250/E6
Jackson (co.), Minn. 255/C7
Jackson, Minn. 255/C7
Jackson (co.), Miss. 256/G9
Jackson (cap.), Miss. 146/K6
Jackson (cap.), Miss. 188/J4
Jackson (cap.), Miss. 256/D6
Jackson, Mo. 261/N8
Jackson, Mont. 262/C5
Jackson (mt.), Mont. 262/C2
Jackson, Nebr. 264/H2
Jackson (mts.), Nev. 266/C1
Jackson •, N.H. 268/E3
Jackson •, N.J. 273/E3
Jackson (bay), N. Zealand 100/A6
Jackson (co.), N.C. 281/C4
Jackson, N.C. 281/P2
Jackson (co.), Ohio 284/E7
Jackson (co.), Okla. 288/H5
Jackson (co.), Oreg. 291/E5
Jackson (creek), Oreg. 291/E5
Jackson, Pa. 294/L2
Jackson, S.C. 296/D5
Jackson (co.), S. Dak. 298/F6
Jackson (co.), Tenn. 237/K8
Jackson, Tenn. 188/J3
Jackson, Tenn. 237/D9
Jackson (riv.), Va. 307/J4
Jackson (co.), Va. 312/C5
Jackson (co.), Wis. 317/E7
Jackson, Wis. 317/K9
Jackson (lake), Wyo. 188/E2
Jackson, Wyo. 319/B2
Jackson (lake), Wyo. 319/B2
Jackson (peak), Wyo. 319/B2
Jacksonboro, S.C. 296/G6
Jacksonburg, Ind. 227/G5
Jacksonburg, Ohio 284/B6
Jacksonburg, W. Va. 312/F4
Jackson Center, Ohio 284/B5
Jackson Center, Pa. 294/B3
Jackson Junction, Iowa 229/K2
Jackson Lake (res.), Colo. 208/L2
Jacksonport, Ark. 202/H2
Jacksonport, Wis. 317/M6
Jackson's Arm, Newf. 166/C4
Jacksons Gap, Ala. 195/G5

Jiayuguan 387

kson Springs, N.C. 281/K4
ksontown, Ohio 284/F6
ksonville, Ala. 195/G3
ksonville, Ark. 202/F4
ksonville, Fla. 146/K6
ksonville, Fla. 188/K4
ksonville, Fla. 212/E1
ksonville, Georgia 217/G7
ksonville, Ill. 222/C4
ksonville, Maine 243/J6
ksonville, Md. 245/M2
ksonville, Mo. 261/G3
ksonville, New Bruns. 170/C2
ksonville, N.C. 281/O5
ksonville, Ohio 284/F7
ksonville, Oreg. 291/D5
ksonville (Kent), Pa. 294/D4
ksonville, Texas 303/J5
ksonville, Vt. 268/B6
ksonville Beach, Fla. 212/E1
ksonville Naval Air Sta., Fla. 212/E1
cmel, Haiti 158/C6
cmel, Haiti 156/D3
cobabad, Pakistan 59/J4
cobabad, Pakistan 68/B3
cobina, Brazil 120/E4
cobina, Brazil 132/F5
cob Lake, Ariz. 198/C2
cobson, Minn. 255/E4
cobstown, N.J. 273/D3
cobsville, Mich. 250/A1
cobus, Pa. 294/J6
cques-Cartier (lake), Québec 172/F2
cques-Cartier (mt.), Québec 172/C1
cques-Cartier (passage), Québec 174/E3
cques-Cartier (riv.), Québec 172/F2
cquet (riv.), New Bruns. 170/D1
cquet River, New Bruns. 170/E1
cquinot (bay), Papua N.G. 86/B2
cuípe (riv.), Brazil 132/F5
cumba, Calif. 204/J11
cupiranga, Brazil 135/B4
ddi, Ras (cape), Pakistan 59/H4
ddi, Ras (pt.), Pakistan 68/A4
de (bay), Germany 22/C2
dwin, Mo. 261/K8
én, Peru 128/C5
én (prov.), Spain 33/E4
én, Spain 7/D5
én, Spain 33/E4
ffa (cape), S. Australia 94/F7
ffna, Sri Lanka 68/E7
ffna, Sri Lanka 54/K9
ffray, Br. Col. 184/K5
ffrey, N.H. 268/C6
ffrey•, N.H. 268/C6
ffrey Center, N.H. 268/C6
fura (des.), Saudi Arabia 59/F5
gdalpur, India 68/E5
gdaqi, China 77/K1
gersfontein, S. Africa 118/D5
gfontein, S. Africa 118/G7
ghbub (Jarabub), Libya 111/D2
gin (riv.), Iran 66/L8
gna, Philippines 82/E6
gtial, India 68/D5
gua, Cuba 158/D2
guaquara, Brazil 132/F6
guara (res.), Brazil 135/C2
guarão, Brazil 132/C11
guariaíva, Brazil 132/D9
guariaíva, Brazil 135/B4
guaribe (riv.), Brazil 132/G4
güey Grande, Cuba 158/D2
güey Grande, Cuba 156/B2
hrom, Iran 59/F4
hrom, Iran 66/H6
icoa, Cordillera (mts.), P. Rico 161/B1
icós, Brazil 132/F4
ilolo, Indonesia 85/H5
inca, China 77/F4
ipur, India 54/J7
ipur, India 68/D3
isalmer, India 68/C3
jarm, Iran 66/K2
jce, Yugoslavia 45/C3
jpur, India 68/F4
karta (cap.), Indonesia 2/Q6
karta (cap.), Indonesia 54/M10
karta (cap.), Indonesia 85/H1
kin, Georgia 217/C8
kobstad, Finland 18/N5
kubany, Czech. 41/F2
l, N. Mex. 274/F6
la, Mexico 150/G6
lacingo, Mexico 150/P1
laid, China 77/K2
lalabad, Afghanistan 68/B2
lalabad, Afghanistan 59/K3
lama, West Bank 65/C3
lapa, Guatemala 154/B3
lapa, Ind. 227/F3
lapa, Nicaragua 154/E4
lapa, S.C. 296/D3
lapa Enríquez, Mexico 146/J8
lapa Enríquez, Mexico 150/P1
lbun, West Bank 65/C3
leswar, Nepal 68/F3
lgaon, India 68/D4
lingo, Nigeria 106/G7
lisco (state), Mexico 150/H6
lna, India 68/D4
lo, Libya 111/D2
lo (oasis), Libya 111/D2
lón (riv.), Spain 33/E2
lor, India 68/C3
lpa, Mexico 150/H6
lpa de Méndez, Mexico 150/N7
lpaiguri, India 68/F3
lpan, Mexico 150/K6
lq, Iran 66/N7
ltipan de Morelos, Mexico 150/M8
lud, West Bank 65/C3
luit (atoll), Marshall Is. 87/G5
Jam, Iran 66/H7
Jama, Ecuador 128/B3
Jamaica 2/F5
Jamaica 146/L8
JAMAICA 158
JAMAICA 156/C3
Jamaica, Cuba 158/K4
Jamaica (chan.), Haiti 156/C3
Jamaica, Iowa 229/E5
Jamaica (chan.), Jamaica 156/C3
Jamaica, N.Y. 276/N9
Jamaica•, Vt. 268/B5
Jamaica Plain, Mass. 249/C7
Jamaiké, Suriname 131/D4
Jamalpur, Bangladesh 68/F4
Jamalpur, India 68/F3
Jamama, Somalia 115/H3
Jamanota (mt.), Neth. Ant. 161/E10
Jamanxim (riv.), Brazil 132/C4
Jambi, Indonesia 85/C6
Jambi, Indonesia 54/M10
Jambuair (cape), Indonesia 85/B4
James (bay) 162/H5
James (riv.) 188/G2
James (bay), Canada 146/K4
James (isl.), Chile 138/D5
James (peak), Colo. 208/H3
James, Georgia 217/E5
James, Iowa 229/A3
James (pt.), Md. 245/N6
James, Miss. 256/B4
James (lake), N.C. 281/E3
James (riv.), N. Dak. 282/N6
James (bay), Ontario 175/D2
James (bay), Québec 174/A2
James (isl.), S.C. 296/H6
James (riv.), S. Dak. 298/N5
James (riv.), Va. 307/O6
James A. Garfield Nat'l Hist. Site, Ohio 284/G2
James Bay, Ontario 177/E2
Jamesburg, N.J. 273/E3
James City, N.C. 281/R4
James City, Pa. 294/E2
James City (co.), Va. 307/P6
James Creek, Pa. 294/F5
Jameson, Mo. 261/E2
Jameson Park, S. Africa 118/J7
Jamesport, Mo. 261/E3
James Ross (isl.), Ant. 5/C16
James Ross (str.), N.W.T. 162/G1
James Ross (str.), N.W. Terrs. 187/J3
Jamestown, Ala. 195/G2
Jamestown, Ark. 202/G2
Jamestown, Calif. 204/E6
Jamestown, Colo. 208/J2
Jamestown, Ill. 222/D5
Jamestown, Ind. 227/D5
Jamestown, Kansas 232/E2
Jamestown, Ky. 237/L7
Jamestown, La. 238/D2
Jamestown, Miss. 256/E8
Jamestown, Mo. 261/G5
Jamestown, N.Y. 188/L2
Jamestown, N.Y. 276/B6
Jamestown, N.C. 281/K3
Jamestown, N. Dak. 188/G1
Jamestown, N. Dak. 282/N6
Jamestown (dam), N. Dak. 282/N6
Jamestown (res.), N. Dak. 282/N6
Jamestown, Ohio 284/C6
Jamestown, Pa. 294/A3
Jamestown, R.I. 249/J6
Jamestown•, R.I. 249/J6
Jamestown, S. Australia 88/F6
Jamestown, S. Australia 94/F5
Jamestown, S.C. 296/H5
Jamestown, Tenn. 237/M8
Jamestown, Va. 307/P6
Jamestown Nat'l Hist. Site, Va. 307/P6
Jamesville, N.Y. 276/H5
Jamesville, N.C. 281/R3
Jamesville, Va. 307/S5
Jamieson, Fla. 212/B1
Jamieson, Oreg. 291/K3
Jamison, Nebr. 264/E2
Jamison, S.C. 296/F4
Jamma, Somalia 102/G4
Jammerbugt (bay), Denmark 21/C3
Jammu, India 54/J5
Jammu, India 68/C2
Jammu and Kashmir (state), India 68/D2
Jamnagar, India 68/B4
Jamnagar, India 54/H7
Jampur, Pakistan 59/K4
Jämsä, Finland 18/O6
Jamshedpur, India 54/K7
Jamshedpur, India 68/F4
Jämtland (co.), Sweden 18/J5
Jamursba (cape), Indonesia 85/J5
Janakpur, Nepal 68/F3
Jandaq, Iran 66/J3
Jandowae, Queensland 95/D5
Jane, Mo. 261/D9
Jane Lew, W. Va. 312/F4
Janesville, Calif. 204/E3
Janesville, Ill. 222/E4
Janesville, Iowa 229/J3
Janesville, Minn. 255/E6
Janesville (Smithmill), Pa. 294/F4
Janesville, Wis. 188/J2
Janesville, Wis. 317/H10
Janesville-Beloit, Wis. 317/H10
Janetstown, Scotland 15/E2
Janeville, New Bruns. 170/E1
Jánico, Dom. Rep. 158/D5
Janikowo, Poland 47/C2
Janiuay, Philippines 82/D5
Jan Mayen (isl.), Norway 4/B10
Jan Mayen (isl.), Norway 7/D1
Janos, Mexico 150/F1
Jánoshalma, Hungary 41/E3
Jánosháza, Hungary 41/D3
Janów Lubelski, Poland 47/F3
Jansen, Colo. 208/K8
Jansen, Nebr. 264/G4
Jansen, Sask. 181/G4
Jantetelco, Mexico 150/L2
Januária, Brazil 120/E4
Januária, Brazil 132/E6
Janvrin (isl.), Nova Scotia 168/G3
Jaora, India 68/D4
Japan 2/S4
Japan 54/R6
JAPAN 81
Japan (sea) 2/R4
Japan (sea) 54/P6
Japan (sea), Japan 81/G4
Japan (sea), N. Korea 81/G4
Japan (sea), S. Korea 81/G4
Japan (sea), U.S.S.R. 48/O6
Japurá, Brazil 132/G9
Japurá (riv.), Brazil 120/C3
Japurá (riv.), Brazil 132/G9
Jaquet (pt.), Dominica 161/E5
Jara, Cerrito (mt.), Bolivia 136/F6
Jara (hill), Paraguay 144/C1
Jarabacoa, Dom. Rep. 158/E5
Jarabub, Libya 102/E2
Jarabub, Libya 111/D2
Jaragua, Dom. Rep. 158/D6
Jaraíz de la Vera, Spain 33/D2
Jarales, N. Mex. 274/C4
Jarama (riv.), Spain 33/E2
Jaramillo, Argentina 143/C6
Jarandilla de la Vera, Spain 33/D2
Jarash, Jordan 65/D3
Jarbalo, Kansas 232/G2
Jarbidge (riv.), Idaho 220/C7
Jarbidge, Nev. 266/F1
Jardim, Brazil 132/G4
Jardine, Mont. 262/F5
Jardines de la Reina (arch.), Cuba 158/F3
Jardines de la Reina (arch.), Cuba 156/B2
Jargalant, Mongolia 77/J2
Jari (riv.), Brazil 120/D2
Jari (riv.), Brazil 132/C3
Järna, Sweden 18/G2
Jarnac, France 28/C5
Jaro, Philippines 82/E5
Jarocin, Poland 47/C3
Jaroměř, Czech. 41/C1
Jarosław, Poland 47/F4
Jaroso, Colo. 208/H8
Järpen, Sweden 18/H5
Jarrahdale, W. Australia 88/B3
Jarrahdale, W. Australia 92/B2
Jarratt, Va. 307/O7
Jarrettsville, Md. 245/M2
Jarrow, Alberta 182/E3
Jarrow, England 13/J3
Jarrow, England 10/F3
Jars (plain), Laos 72/D3
Jartai, China 77/G4
Jaruco, Cuba 158/C1
Jarud, China 77/K3
Järvenpää, Finland 18/O6
Jarvie, Alberta 182/D2
Jarvis (isl.), Pacific 87/K6
Jarvisburg, N.C. 281/T2
Jarvisville, W. Va. 312/F4
Järvsö, Sweden 18/K6
Jask, Iran 59/G4
Jask, Iran 54/G7
Jask, Iran 66/K8
Jasło, Poland 47/E4
Jasmin, Sask. 181/H4
Jasmine Estates, Fla. 212/D3
Jason (isls.), Falkland Is. 143/D7
Jason, Ky. 237/O6
Jason, N.C. 281/O4
Jasonville, Ind. 227/C6
Jasper, Ala. 195/D3
Jasper, Alberta 182/B3
Jasper, Alta. 162/E5
Jasper, Ark. 202/D1
Jasper, Fla. 212/D1
Jasper (co.), Georgia 217/E4
Jasper, Georgia 217/D2
Jasper (co.), Ill. 222/E4
Jasper (co.), Ind. 227/C2
Jasper, Ind. 227/D8
Jasper (co.), Iowa 229/G5
Jasper, Mich. 250/E7
Jasper, Minn. 255/B7
Jasper (co.), Miss. 256/F6
Jasper (co.), Mo. 261/D8
Jasper, Mo. 261/D8
Jasper, N.Y. 276/F6
Jasper, Ohio 284/D7
Jasper, Ontario 177/H3
Jasper, Oreg. 291/E3
Jasper (co.), S.C. 296/E6
Jasper, Tenn. 237/K10
Jasper (co.), Texas 303/K7
Jasper, Texas 303/L7
Jasper Nat'l Park, Alberta 182/A3
Jasper Nat'l Park, Alta. 162/E5
Jastrowie, Poland 47/C2
Jastrzębie Zdroj, Poland 47/D3
Jászapáti, Hungary 41/E3
Jászárokszállás, Hungary 41/E3
Jászberény, Hungary 41/E3
Jászfényszaru, Hungary 41/E3
Jászkarajenő, Hungary 41/E3
Jászkisér, Hungary 41/F3
Jászladány, Hungary 41/F3
Jataí, Brazil 120/D4
Jataí, Brazil 132/D7
Jatibonico, Cuba 158/F2
Jatibonico del Sur (riv.), Cuba 158/F3
Játiva, Spain 33/F3
Jaú, Brazil 132/D8
Jaú, Brazil 135/B3
Jauaperi (riv.), Brazil 132/A2
Jauari, Serra (mts.), Brazil 132/C3
Jauco, Cuba 158/K4
Jauf, Saudi Arabia 54/F7
Jauf, Saudi Arabia 59/C4
Jauja, Peru 128/E8
Jaumave, Mexico 150/K5
Jaun, Switzerland 39/D3
Jaunjelgava, U.S.S.R. 53/C2
Jaunpur, India 68/E3
Jauri, Iran 66/M6
Java (head), Indonesia 85/C7
Java (isl.), Indonesia 2/Q6
Java (isl.), Indonesia 54/M10
Java (isl.), Indonesia 85/J2
Java (sea), Indonesia 2/Q6
Java (sea), Indonesia 54/M10
Java (sea), Indonesia 85/D6
Java, S. Dak. 298/K3
Java, Va. 307/K7
Javari (riv.), Brazil 132/F9
Jávea, Spain 33/G3
Javier de Viana, Uruguay 145/C1
Jaworzno, Poland 47/B4
Jay, Fla. 212/B5
Jay (co.), Ind. 227/G4
Jay, Maine 243/C7
Jay•, Maine 243/C7
Jay, N.Y. 276/N2
Jay, Okla. 288/S2
Jay•, Vt. 268/C2
Jay (peak), Vt. 268/B2
Jaya, Puncak (mt.), Indonesia 85/K6
Jayanca, Peru 128/B6
Jayapura, Indonesia 85/L6
Jayawijaya (range), Indonesia 85/K6
Jay Creek, North. Terr. 88/E4
Jay Em, Wyo. 319/H3
Jayess, Miss. 256/D8
Jayton, Texas 303/D4
Jayuya, P. Rico 156/G1
Jayuya, P. Rico 161/C2
Jaz Murian, Hamun-e (marsh), Iran 66/L7
Jaz Murian, Hamun-e (marsh), Iran 59/G4
Jean, Nev. 266/F7
Jean, Texas 303/F4
Jean Côté, Alberta 182/B2
Jeanerette, La. 238/G7
Jeanette (bay), Newf. 166/C3
Jean Lafitte, La. 238/K7
Jean Lafitte Nat'l Hist. Park, La. 238/P4
Jean-Marie River, N.W. Terrs. 187/F3
Jeanne Mance, New Bruns. 170/E1
Jeannette, Pa. 294/C5
Jean-Rabel, Haiti 158/B5
Jean-Rabel (pt.), Haiti 158/B5
Jebba, Nigeria 106/E7
Jebel Abyad (plat.), Sudan 111/E4
Jebel Aulia (dam), Sudan 102/F3
Jebel Aulia (dam), Sudan 111/F4
Jebel Dhanna, U.A.E. 59/F5
Jeberos, Peru 128/D5
Jeble, Syria 63/F5
Jedburg, S.C. 296/G5
Jedburgh, Sask. 181/J4
Jedburgh, Scotland 10/E3
Jedburgh, Scotland 15/F5
Jeddah (Jidda), Saudi Arabia 59/C5
Jeddito, Ariz. 198/E3
Jeddo, Mich. 250/G5
Jeddo, Pa. 294/L3
Jeddore (cape), Nova Scotia 168/E4
Jeddore (harb.), Nova Scotia 168/F4
Jędrzejów, Poland 47/E3
Jefara (reg.), Libya 111/B1
Jefara (reg.), Tunisia 106/G2
Jeff, Ala. 195/E1
Jeff, Ky. 237/P6
Jeff Davis (co.), Georgia 217/G7
Jeff Davis (co.), Texas 303/C11
Jeffers, Minn. 255/C6
Jeffers, Mont. 262/E5
Jefferson (co.), Ala. 195/E3
Jefferson, Ala. 195/C6
Jefferson (co.), Ark. 202/G5
Jefferson, Ark. 202/F5
Jefferson (co.), Colo. 208/J3
Jefferson, Colo. 208/H4
Jefferson (co.), Fla. 212/C1
Jefferson (co.), Georgia 217/H4
Jefferson, Georgia 217/F2
Jefferson (co.), Idaho 220/F6
Jefferson (co.), Ill. 222/E5
Jefferson (co.), Ind. 227/G7
Jefferson, Ind. 227/D4
Jefferson (co.), Iowa 229/K6
Jefferson, Iowa 229/E4
Jefferson (co.), Kansas 232/G2
Jefferson (co.), Ky. 237/K4
Jefferson (par.), La. 238/K7
Jefferson•, Maine 243/D7
Jefferson, Md. 245/J3
Jefferson, Mass. 249/G3
Jefferson (co.), Miss. 256/B7
Jefferson (co.), Mo. 261/L6
Jefferson (co.), Mont. 262/D4
Jefferson (riv.), Mont. 262/D5
Jefferson (co.), Nebr. 264/G4
Jefferson•, N.H. 268/D3
Jefferson (mt.), N.H. 268/E3
Jefferson (co.), N.Y. 276/J2
Jefferson, N.Y. 276/L6
Jefferson, N.C. 281/G2
Jefferson (co.), Ohio 284/J5
Jefferson (West Jefferson), Ohio 284/D6
Jefferson, Ohio 284/J2
Jefferson (co.), Okla. 288/L6
Jefferson, Okla. 288/L1
Jefferson (co.), Oreg. 291/F3
Jefferson, Oreg. 291/D3
Jefferson (mt.), Oreg. 291/F3
Jefferson (co.), Pa. 294/D3
Jefferson, Pa. 294/B7
Jefferson, Pa. 294/B6
Jefferson (Codorus), Pa. 294/J6
Jefferson, S.C. 296/G2
Jefferson, S. Dak. 298/S8
Jefferson (co.), Tenn. 237/P8
Jefferson (co.), Texas 303/K8
Jefferson, Texas 303/K5
Jefferson, Va. 307/N5
Jefferson (co.), Wash. 310/B3
Jefferson (co.), W. Va. 312/L4
Jefferson (co.), Wis. 317/J9
Jefferson, Wis. 317/J10
Jefferson City (cap.), Mo. 261/H5
Jefferson City (cap.), Mo. 146/J6
Jefferson City (cap.), Mo. 188/H3
Jefferson City, Mont. 262/E4
Jefferson City, Tenn. 237/P8
Jefferson Davis (par.), La. 238/E6
Jefferson Davis (co.), Miss. 256/E7
Jefferson Heights, La. 238/O4
Jefferson Island, Mont. 262/E5
Jefferson Manor, Va. 307/S3
Jefferson Nat'l Expansion Mem. Nat'l Hist. Site, Mo. 261/R3
Jefferson Proving Ground, Ind. 227/G7
Jeffersonton, Va. 307/N3
Jeffersontown, Ky. 237/L2
Jeffersonville, Georgia 217/F5
Jeffersonville, Ind. 227/F8
Jeffersonville, Ky. 237/O5
Jeffersonville, N.Y. 276/L7
Jeffersonville, Ohio 284/C6
Jeffersonville, Vt. 268/B2
Jeffrey (res.), Nebr. 264/D4
Jeffrey, W. Va. 312/C7
Jeffrey City, Wyo. 319/E3
Jeffrey's, Newf. 166/C4
Jef Jef es Seghin (plat.), Chad 111/D3
Jef Jef es Seghin (plat.), Libya 111/D3
Jega, Nigeria 106/E6
Jegenstorf, Switzerland 39/D2
Jeinemeni, Cerro (mt.), Chile 138/E6
Jeiseyville, Ill. 222/D4
Jejuí-Guazú (riv.), Paraguay 144/D4
Jēkabpils, U.S.S.R. 53/C2
Jēkabpils, U.S.S.R. 52/C3
Jekyll (isl.), Georgia 217/K8
Jeleń, Poland 47/B4
Jelenia Góra (prov.), Poland 47/B3
Jelenia Góra, Poland 47/B3
Jelgava, U.S.S.R. 7/G3
Jelgava, U.S.S.R. 53/B2
Jelgava, U.S.S.R. 52/B3
Jellico, Tenn. 237/N7
Jellico Creek, Ky. 237/N7
Jellicoe, Ontario 177/H5
Jelling, Denmark 21/C6
Jelloway, Ohio 284/F4
Jelm, Wyo. 319/G4
Jelšava, Czech. 41/F2
Jemaja (isl.), Indonesia 85/D5
Jemappes, Belgium 27/D8
Jember, Indonesia 85/K2
Jemez (riv.), N. Mex. 274/C3
Jemez Canyon (res.), N. Mex. 274/C3
Jemez Pueblo, N. Mex. 274/C3
Jemez Springs, N. Mex. 274/C3
Jeminay, China 77/C2
Jemison, Ala. 195/E5
Jemnice, Czech. 41/C2
Jemseg, New Bruns. 170/D3
Jemtland, Maine 243/G1
Jena, Germany 22/D3
Jena, La. 238/F3
Jenaz, Switzerland 39/J3
Jenbach, Austria 41/A3
Jendouba, Tunisia 106/F1
Jeneponto, Indonesia 85/F7
Jenera, Ohio 284/C4
Jenifer, Ala. 195/G3
Jenin, West Bank 65/C3
Jenison, Mich. 250/D6
Jenkinjones, W. Va. 312/D8
Jenkins (co.), Georgia 217/J5
Jenkins, Ky. 237/R6
Jenkins, Minn. 255/D4
Jenkins, Mo. 261/E9
Jenkinsburg, Georgia 217/E4
Jenkinsville, S.C. 296/E3
Jenkintown, Pa. 294/M5
Jenks, Okla. 288/P2
Jenner, Alberta 182/E4
Jennersdorf, Austria 41/C3
Jennerstown, Pa. 294/D5
Jennie, Ark. 202/H7
Jennie, Suriname 131/C3
Jennings, Ant. & Bar. 161/D11
Jennings, Fla. 212/C1
Jennings (co.), Ind. 227/F7
Jennings, Kansas 232/B2
Jennings, La. 238/E6
Jennings, Md. 245/B2
Jennings, Mich. 250/D4
Jennings, Mo. 261/R2
Jennings, N.S. Wales 97/F1
Jennings, Okla. 288/N2
Jennings Lodge, Oreg. 291/B2
Jenny (creek), Oreg. 291/E5
Jenny Lake, Wyo. 319/B2
Jenny Lind, Calif. 204/C9
Jenny Lind (isl.), N.W. Terr. 187/H3
Jenolan Caves, N.S. Wales 97/E3
Jenpeg, Manitoba 179/J2
Jensen, Utah 304/E3
Jensen Beach, Fla. 212/F4
Jens Munk (isl.), N.W.T. 162/H2
Jens Munk (isl.), N.W. Terr. 187/K3
Jepara, Indonesia 85/J2
Jequié, Brazil 120/E4
Jequié, Brazil 132/F6
Jequitinhonha, Brazil 132/F7
Jequitinhonha (riv.), Brazil 120/E4
Jequitinhonha (riv.), Brazil 132/F7
Jerablus, Syria 63/G4
Jerada, Morocco 106/D2
Jerauld (co.), S. Dak. 298/M5
Jérémie, Haiti 156/C3
Jérémie, Haiti 158/A6
Jeremoabo, Brazil 132/G5
Jeremy (riv.), Conn. 210/F2
Jerez, Spain 7/D5
Jerez de García Salinas, Mexico 150/H5
Jerez de la Frontera, Spain 33/C4
Jerez de los Caballeros, Spain 33/C3
Jericho, Ark. 202/K3
Jericho, N.Y. 276/R6
Jericho, Queensland 95/C4
Jericho, Vt. 268/A2
Jericho•, Vt. 268/A2
Jericho, West Bank 65/C4
Jericho Center, Vt. 268/B3
Jerico Springs, Mo. 261/E7
Jeriel, Ky. 237/R4
Jerilderie, N.S. Wales 97/C4
Jerimoth (hill), R.I. 249/G5
Jermyn, Pa. 294/L2
Jermyn, Texas 303/F4
Jerome, Ariz. 198/C4
Jerome, Ark. 202/G7
Jerome (co.), Idaho 220/D7
Jerome, Idaho 220/D7
Jerome, Ill. 222/D4
Jerome, Mo. 261/J7
Jerome, Pa. 294/D5
Jeromesville, Ohio 284/F4
Jerry City, Ohio 284/C3
Jersey, Ark. 202/F7
Jersey (isl.), Chan. Is. 13/E8
Jersey (isl.), Chan. Is. 10/E6
Jersey, Georgia 217/E3
Jersey (co.), Ill. 222/C4
Jersey, Ohio 284/E5
Jersey (bay), Virgin Is. (U.S.) 161/B4
Jersey City, N.J. 188/M2
Jersey City, N.J. 273/B2
Jersey Mills, Pa. 294/H3
Jersey Shore, Pa. 294/H3
Jerseyside, Newf. 166/B3
Jerseytown, Pa. 294/J3
Jersey Village, Texas 303/J1
Jerseyville, Ill. 222/C4
Jerslev, Denmark 21/D3
Jerumenha, Brazil 132/F4
Jerusalem, Ark. 202/E3
Jerusalem (dist.), Israel 65/B4
Jerusalem (cap.), Israel 54/E6
Jerusalem (cap.), Israel 65/C4
Jerusalem (cap.), Israel 59/C3
Jerusalem, Ohio 284/H6
Jervis (inlet), Br. Col. 184/E5
Jervis (mt.), Chile 138/D8
Jervis Bay, Aust. Cap. Terr. 97/F4
Jervois Range, North. Terr. 88/F4
Jesenice, Yugoslavia 45/A2
Jeseník, Czech. 41/D1
Jeseníky (mts.), Czech. 41/D1
Jesenské, Czech. 41/F2
Jesi, Italy 34/D3
Jessamine (co.), Ky. 237/M5
Jesse, W. Va. 312/C7
Jessie, N. Dak. 282/O4
Jessieville, Ark. 202/D4
Jessnitz, Germany 22/E3
Jessore, Bangladesh 68/F4
Jessup, Pa. 294/F6
Jesterville, Md. 245/P7
Jesuit Bend, La. 238/K7
Jesup, Georgia 217/J7
Jesup, Iowa 229/J4
Jesús, Paraguay 144/E5
Jesús de Machaca, Bolivia 136/A5
Jesús de Otoro, Honduras 154/C3
Jesús María, Argentina 143/D3
Jesús María (reef), Mexico 150/L4
Jet, Okla. 288/K1
Jetersville, Va. 307/M6
Jetmore, Kansas 232/B3
Jett, Ky. 237/M4
Jette, Belgium 27/B9
Jetts Creek, Ky. 237/O6
Jever, Germany 22/B2
Jevíčko, Czech. 41/D2
Jewel Cave Nat'l Mon., S. Dak. 298/B6
Jewell, Georgia 217/G4
Jewell, Iowa 229/F4
Jewell (co.), Kansas 232/D2
Jewell, Kansas 232/D2
Jewell, Ohio 284/B3
Jewell, Oreg. 291/D2
Jewell Ridge, Va. 307/E6
Jewett, Ill. 222/E4
Jewett, Ohio 284/H5
Jewett, Texas 303/H6
Jewett City, Conn. 210/H2
Jewish Aut. Obl., U.S.S.R. 48/O5
Jeypore, India 68/E5
Jhalawar, India 68/D4
Jhal Jhao, Pakistan 59/H4
Jhal Jhao, Pakistan 68/B3
Jhang Sadar, Pakistan 59/K3
Jhang Sadar, Pakistan 68/C2
Jhansi, India 68/D3
Jharsuguda, India 68/E4
Jhelum (riv.), India 68/C2
Jhelum, Pakistan 68/C2
Jhelum, Pakistan 59/K3
Jhelum (riv.), Pakistan 68/C2
Jhudo, Pakistan 68/B3
Jhunjhunu, India 68/D3
Jialing (riv.), China 54/M6
Jiamusi (Kiamusze), China 77/M2
Ji'an (Kian), China 77/J6
Jiande, China 77/J6
Jiangcheng, China 77/F7
Jiangmen (Kongmoon), China 77/H7
Jiangsu (Kiangsu), China 77/K5
Jiangxi (Kiangsi), China 77/J6
Jiangyou, China 77/G5
Jian'ou, China 77/J6
Jianshi, China 77/H5
Jianshui, China 77/F7
Jianyang, China 77/J6
Jiaohe, China 77/L3
Jiao Xian, China 77/K4
Jiaozuo (Tsiaotso), China 77/H4
Jiashan, China 77/J5
Jia Xian, China 77/H4
Jiaxing (Kashing), China 77/K5
Jiayin, China 77/M2
Jiayu, China 77/H6
Jiayuguan, China 77/E4

Jíbaro, Cuba 158/F2
Jibhalanta (Uliastay), Mongolia 77/E2
Jibóia, Brazil 132/G8
Jibou, Romania 45/F2
Jibsh, Ras (cape), Oman 59/G5
Jicarilla, N. Mex. 274/D5
Jicarilla Ind. Res., N. Mex. 274/B2
Jicarón (isl.), Panama 154/F7
Jičín, Czech. 41/C1
Jico, Mexico 150/P1
Jidda, Saudi Arabia 54/E7
Jidda, Saudi Arabia 59/C5
Jiexiu, China 77/H4
Jifna, West Bank 65/C4
Jigalong Aboriginal Res., W. Australia 88/C4
Jigger, La. 238/G2
Jiggs, Nev. 266/F2
Jiguaní, Cuba 158/H4
Jiguero (pt.), P. Rico 156/F1
Jiguero (pt.), P. Rico 161/A1
Jigüey (bay), Cuba 158/G2
Jigzhi, China 77/F5
Jihlava, Czech. 41/C2
Jihlava (riv.), Czech. 41/D2
Jihočeský (reg.), Czech. 41/C2
Jihomoravský (reg.), Czech. 41/D2
Jijel, Algeria 106/F1
Jijia (riv.), Romania 45/H2
Jijiga, Ethiopia 111/H6
Jijona, Spain 33/F3
Jilemnice, Czech. 41/C1
Jilib, Somalia 115/H3
Jilin (Kirin), China 77/L3
Jilin, China 54/O5
Jilin, China 77/L3
Jilotepec de Abasolo, Mexico 150/K7
Jim (lake), N. Dak. 282/N5
Jimaní, Dom. Rep. 158/C6
Jimbolia, Romania 45/D3
Jimena de la Frontera, Spain 33/D4
Jiménez, Chihuahua, Mexico 150/G3
Jiménez, Coahuila, Mexico 150/J2
Jim Falls, Wis. 317/D5
Jim Hogg (co.), Texas 303/F11
Jimma, Ethiopia 111/G6
Jimma, Ethiopia 102/F4
Jimmy Carter Nat'l Hist. Site, Georgia 217/D6
Jimsar, China 77/C3
Jim Thorpe, Pa. 294/L4
Jim Wells (co.), Texas 303/F10
Jim Woodruff (dam), Georgia 217/C9
Jinan (Tsinan), China 77/J4
Jinan, China 54/N6
Jincheng, China 77/H4
Jinchuan, China 77/F5
Jind, India 68/D3
Jindabyne, N.S. Wales 97/E5
Jindabyne (lake), N.S. Wales 97/E5
Jindalee, N.S. Wales 97/E4
Jindřichův Hradec, Czech. 41/C2
Jingbian, China 77/G4
Jingdezhen (Kingtehchen), China 77/J6
Jingellic, N.S. Wales 97/C4
Jinggu, China 77/F7
Jinghe, China 77/B3
Jinghong, China 77/F7
Jingtai, China 77/F4
Jingxi, China 77/G7
Jing Xian, Anhui, China 77/J5
Jing Xian, Hunan, China 77/H6
Jingyuan, China 77/F4
Jinhua (Kinhwa), China 77/J6
Jining (Tsining), Nei Monggol, China 77/H3
Jining (Tsining), Shandong, China 77/J4
Jinja, Uganda 115/F3
Jinja, Uganda 102/F4
Jinmen (Quemoy) (isl.), China 77/J7
Jinotega, Nicaragua 154/E4
Jinotepe, Nicaragua 154/D5
Jinping, China 77/G6
Jinsha Jiang (Yangtze) (riv.), China 77/E5
Jinshi (Tsingshih), China 77/H6
Jintotolo (chan.), Philippines 82/D5
Jinxi (Chinsi), China 77/K3
Jin Xian, China 77/K4
Jinzhou (Chinchow), China 77/K3
Jinzhou, China 54/N5
Jipijapa, Ecuador 128/B3
Jiran, Ethiopia 111/H6
Jirgalanta (Hovd), Mongolia 77/D2
Jiřkov, Czech. 41/B1
Jish, Israel 65/C1
Jishou, China 77/H6
Jisr esh Shughur, Syria 63/G5
Jiu (riv.), Romania 45/F3
Jiujiang (Kiukiang), China 77/J6
Jiulong, China 77/F6
Jiuquan (Kiuchüan), China 77/E4
Jixi (Kisi), China 77/M2
Jixi, China 54/P5
Ji Xian, China 77/H4
Jizan (Qizan), Saudi Arabia 59/D6
Jizera (riv.), Czech. 41/C1
Joaçaba, Brazil 132/D9
Joachimsthal, Germany 22/E2
Joachin, Mexico 150/Q2
Joana Peres, Brazil 132/D3
Joanico, Uruguay 145/B6
Joanna, S.C. 296/D3
João Monlevade, Brazil 135/E1
João Pessoa, Brazil 120/F3
João Pessoa, Brazil 132/H4
João Pinheiro, Brazil 132/E7
Joaquim Távora, Brazil 135/B3
Joaquin, Texas 303/L5
Joaquín Suárez, Canelones, Uruguay 145/B6
Joaquín Suárez, Colonia, Uruguay 145/B5
Joaquín V. González, Argentina 143/D2
Job (peak), Nev. 266/C3
Job, W. Va. 312/G5
Jobabo, Cuba 158/H3

Jobos, P. Rico 161/D3
Jobos (bay), P. Rico 161/D3
Job's Cove, Newf. 166/D2
Jobstown, N.J. 273/D3
Joch (pass), Switzerland 39/F3
Jódar, Spain 33/E4
Jo Daviess (co.), Ill. 222/C1
Jodhpur, India 54/J7
Jodhpur, India 68/C3
Jodie, W. Va. 312/D6
Jodoigne, Belgium 27/F7
Joe Batt's Arm, Newf. 166/D4
Joensuu, Finland 7/H2
Joensuu, Finland 18/R5
Joes, Colo. 208/O3
Joes (brook), Vt. 268/C3
Joetsu, Japan 81/H5
Joffre, Alberta 182/D3
Jofra (oasis), Libya 111/C2
Jögeva, U.S.S.R. 53/D1
Joggins, Nova Scotia 168/D3
Joghatay, Kuh-e (mts.), Iran 66/K2
Jogjakarta (Yogyakarta), Indonesia 85/J2
Jogues, Ontario 175/D3
Johannesburg, Calif. 204/H8
Johannesburg, Mich. 250/E4
Johannesburg, S. Africa 102/E7
Johannesburg, S. Africa 2/L7
Johannesburg, S. Africa 118/H6
Johanngeorgenstadt, Germany 22/E3
John (riv.), Alaska 196/H1
John (cape), Nova Scotia 168/E3
John D. Rockefeller, Jr., Mem. Pkwy., Wyo. 319/B1
John Day, Oreg. 291/J3
John Day (dam), Oreg. 291/G2
John Day (dam), Oreg. 291/G2
John Day (dam), Wash. 310/E5
John Day Fossil Beds Nat'l Mon., Oreg. 291/G3
John d'Or Prairie, Alberta 182/B5
Johnetta, Ky. 237/N6
John F. Kennedy Space Center, Fla. 212/F3
John F. Kennedy Nat'l Hist. Site, Mass. 249/C7
John H. Kerr (dam), Va. 307/M7
John Jay (mt.), Br. Col. 184/B2
John Martin (res.), Colo. 208/N6
John Muir Nat'l Hist. Site, Calif. 204/K1
John O'Groats, Scotland 15/E2
John Redmond (res.), Kansas 232/G3
Johns, Miss. 256/E6
Johns, N.C. 281/K5
Johns (isl.), S.C. 296/G6
Johnsburg, Minn. 255/F7
Johnsburg, N.Y. 276/M3
Johnshaven, Scotland 15/F4
Johns Island, S.C. 296/G6
Johnson, Ark. 202/B1
Johnson (co.), Ark. 202/C2
Johnson (isl.), Chile 138/D5
Johnson (co.), Georgia 217/E5
Johnson (creek), Idaho 220/C5
Johnson (co.), Ill. 222/E6
Johnson (co.), Ind. 227/E6
Johnson, Ind. 227/B8
Johnson (co.), Iowa 229/K5
Johnson (co.), Kansas 232/H3
Johnson, Kansas 232/A4
Johnson (co.), Ky. 237/R5
Johnson, Minn. 255/B5
Johnson (co.), Mo. 261/E5
Johnson (co.), Nebr. 264/H4
Johnson, Nebr. 264/J4
Johnson (lake), Nebr. 264/E4
Johnson (co.), Tenn. 237/T7
Johnson (co.), Texas 303/G5
Johnson, Vt. 268/B2
Johnson•, Vt. 268/B2
Johnson (co.), Wyo. 319/F1
Johnsonburg, N.J. 273/D2
Johnsonburg, Pa. 294/E3
Johnson City, N.Y. 276/J6
Johnson City, Oreg. 291/B2
Johnson City, Tenn. 237/S8
Johnson City, Texas 303/F7
Johnson Creek, Wis. 317/J9
Johnsondale, Calif. 204/G8
Johnson Draw (dry riv.), Texas 303/C7
Johnsons (creek), Utah 304/B6
Johnsons Bayou, La. 238/C7
Johnson's Crossing, Yukon 187/E3
Johnsons Landing, Br. Col. 184/J5
Johnsons Point, Ant. & Bar. 161/D11
Johnsonville, Ill. 222/E5
Johnsonville, N.Y. 276/O5
Johnsonville, S.C. 296/J4
Johnston (key), Fla. 212/E7
Johnston, Iowa 229/F5
Johnston (co.), N.C. 281/N4
Johnston (co.), Okla. 288/N6
Johnston (atoll), Pacific 87/K4
Johnston, S.C. 296/D4
Johnston (lakes), W. Australia 88/C6
Johnston, The (lakes), W. Australia 92/C6
Johnston City, Ill. 222/E6
Johnstone (str.), Br. Col. 184/D5
Johnstone, Scotland 10/A1
Johnstone, Scotland 15/B2
Johnstons Station, Miss. 256/D8
Johnstown, Colo. 208/K2
Johnstown, Ireland 17/G6
Johnstown, Nebr. 264/F3
Johnstown, N.Y. 276/M4
Johnstown, N. Dak. 282/R3
Johnstown, Ohio 284/E5
Johnstown, Ontario 177/J3
Johnstown, Pa. 188/L2
Johnstown, Pa. 294/D5
Johnsville, Ark. 202/F7
Johnsville, Md. 245/N2
Johor (Johore) (state), Malaysia 72/D7
Johor, Sungai (riv.), Malaysia 72/F5
Johor Baharu (Johore Bharu), Malaysia 72/F5

Jobos, P. Rico 161/D3
Johore (str.), Malaysia 72/E6
Johore Baharu, Malaysia 54/M9
Joice, Iowa 229/G2
Joigny, France 28/E3
Joiner, Ark. 202/K3
Joinville, Brazil 120/E5
Joinville, Brazil 132/D9
Joinville (isl.), Ant. 5/C16
Joji, Philippines 82/E8
Jojutla de Juárez, Mexico 150/L2
Jokkmokk, Sweden 18/L3
Jökulsá (riv.), Iceland 21/C1
Joli (pt.), Nova Scotia 168/D5
Jolicure, New Bruns. 170/F3
Joliet, Ill. 188/J2
Joliet, Ill. 222/E2
Joliet, Mont. 262/G5
Joliette, N. Dak. 282/R2
Joliette (county), Québec 174/B3
Joliette (co.), Québec 172/C3
Joliette, Québec 172/D3
Jolietville, Ind. 227/E4
Jolley, Iowa 229/D4
Jollytown, Pa. 294/B6
Jolo, Philippines 82/C8
Jolo (isl.), Philippines 85/G4
Jolo (isl.), Philippines 82/C7
Jolon, Calif. 204/D7
Jomalig (isl.), Philippines 82/D3
Jo-Mary (lkes), Maine 243/E4
Jombang, Indonesia 85/K2
Jomda, China 77/E5
Jona, Switzerland 39/G2
Jonacatepec, Mexico 150/M2
Jonava, U.S.S.R. 53/C3
Joncs (plain), Cambodia 72/E5
Joncs (plain), Vietnam 72/E5
Jonesville, Sudan 111/F6
Jones, Ala. 195/E5
Jones (isls.), Alaska 196/J1
Jones (co.), Georgia 217/E5
Jones (co.), Iowa 229/L4
Jones, La. 238/G1
Jones, Mich. 250/C5
Jones (co.), Miss. 256/F7
Jones (beach), N.Y. 276/R7
Jones (co.), N.C. 281/P4
Jones, Okla. 288/M3
Jones (co.), S. Dak. 298/H6
Jones, Tenn. 237/C9
Jones (co.), Texas 303/E5
Jonesboro, Ark. 188/H3
Jonesboro, Ark. 202/J2
Jonesboro, Georgia 217/D4
Jonesboro, Ill. 222/D6
Jonesboro, Ind. 227/F4
Jonesboro, La. 238/E2
Jonesboro•, Maine 243/J6
Jonesborough, N. Ireland 17/J3
Jonesborough, Tenn. 237/R8
Jonesburg, Mo. 261/K5
Jones Creek, Texas 303/J9
Jonesdale, Wis. 317/F10
Jones Mills, Ark. 202/E5
Jones Mills, Pa. 294/D5
Jonesport, Maine 243/J6
Jonesport•, Maine 243/H6
Jones Springs, W. Va. 312/K4
Jonestown, Miss. 256/D2
Jonestown, Pa. 294/K5
Jonesville, Alaska 196/B1
Jonesville, Ind. 227/F6
Jonesville, Ky. 237/M3
Jonesville, La. 238/G3
Jonesville, Mich. 250/E6
Jonesville, N.C. 281/H2
Jonesville, S.C. 296/D2
Jonesville, Vt. 268/B3
Jonesville, Va. 307/B7
Jonglei, Sudan 111/F6
Jonglei (canal), Sudan 111/F6
Joniškis, U.S.S.R. 53/B2
Jönköping (co.), Sweden 18/H8
Jönköping, Sweden 18/H8
Jönköping, Sweden 7/F3
Jonquière, Québec 172/F1
Jonquière, Québec 174/C3
Jonuta, Mexico 150/N7
Jonzac, France 28/C5
Joplin, Mo. 261/C9
Joplin, Mo. 146/J6
Joplin, Mo. 188/H3
Joplin, Mont. 262/F2
Joppa, Ala. 195/E4
Joppa, Ill. 222/E6
Joppa, Tenn. 237/O8
Joppatowne, Md. 245/N3
Jora, Nigeria 106/F7
Jorat (mt.), Switzerland 39/C3
Jordan 2/L4
Jordan 54/E6
JORDAN 59/C3
Jordan (dam), Ala. 195/F5
Jordan (lake), Ala. 195/F5
Jordan (creek), Idaho 220/A7
Jordan, Iowa 229/F4
Jordan (riv.), Israel 65/D3
Jordan (co.), Jordan 65/D3
Jordan, Minn. 255/G6
Jordan, Mont. 262/J3
Jordan, N.Y. 276/H4
Jordan, B. Everett (lake), N.C. 281/M3
Jordan (bay), Nova Scotia 168/C5
Jordan (riv.), Nova Scotia 168/C4
Jordan (riv.), Nova Scotia 168/C5
Jordan (creek), Oreg. 291/K5
Jordan, S.C. 296/G4
Jordan (riv.), Utah 304/C3
Jordan Falls, Nova Scotia 168/C5
Jordan River, Sask. 181/H2
Jordan Valley, Oreg. 291/K5
Jorge Montt (isl.), Chile 138/D9
Jordt, India 68/G3
Jorm, Afghanistan 68/C1
Jorm, Afghanistan 59/K2
Jörn, Sweden 18/M4

Jornada del Muerto (valley), N. Mex. 274/C5
Jorquera (riv.), Chile 138/B6
Jörva-Jaani, U.S.S.R. 53/D1
Jos, Nigeria 106/F7
Jos, Nigeria 102/C4
Jos (plat.), Nigeria 106/F7
Jose Abad Santos, Philippines 82/E8
José Agustín Palacios, Bolivia 136/B3
José Batlle y Ordóñez, Uruguay 145/D4
José Cardel, Mexico 150/Q1
José de San Martín, Argentina 143/B5
José Enrique Rodó, Uruguay 145/B4
José Ignacio (lag.), Uruguay 145/E5
José M. Micheo, Argentina 143/G7
Jose Panganiban, Philippines 82/D3
José Pedro Varela, Uruguay 145/E4
Joseph (lake), Newf. 166/B3
Joseph (lake), Ontario 177/E2
Joseph, Oreg. 291/K2
Joseph (creek), Oreg. 291/K2
Joseph, Utah 304/B5
Joseph Bonaparte (gulf) 88/D2
Joseph Bonaparte (gulf), Australia 87/C7
Joseph Bonaparte (gulf), North. Terr. 93/A3
Joseph Bonaparte (gulf), W. Australia 92/E1
Joseph City, Ariz. 198/E4
Josephine, Ala. 195/C10
Josephine (co.), Oreg. 291/D5
Josephine, Pa. 294/D5
Joshinetsu-Kogen National Park, Japan 81/J5
Joshua (pt.), Conn. 210/E4
Joshua Tree, Calif. 204/J9
Joshua Tree Nat'l Mon., Calif. 204/J10
Jostedal, Norway 18/E6
Jostedalsbreen (glac.), Norway 18/E6
Jost Van Dyke (isl.), Virgin Is. (U.K.) 161/C3
Jost Van Dyke (isl.), Virgin Is. (U.K.) 156/G1
Joubert, S. Dak. 298/M7
Jourdanton, Texas 303/F9
Joure, Netherlands 27/H3
Joussard, Alberta 182/B2
Joux (lake), Switzerland 39/B3
Jovellanos, Cuba 156/B2
Jovellanos, Cuba 158/D1
Joveyn (riv.), Iran 66/K2
Joy, Ill. 222/C2
Joy, Ky. 237/E6
Joyce, La. 238/E3
Joyce, Wash. 310/B2
Joyce's Country (dist.), Ireland 17/B4
Joyo, Japan 81/J7
Juab (co.), Utah 304/A4
Juana Díaz, P. Rico 161/C3
Juan Aldama, Mexico 150/H4
Juan D. Jackson, Uruguay 145/C4
Juan de Fuca (str.), Br. Col. 162/D6
Juan de Fuca (str.), Br. Col. 184/J4
Juan de Fuca (str.), Wash. 188/A2
Juan de Fuca (str.), Wash. 310/A2
Juan de Mena, Paraguay 144/D4
Juan de Nova (isl.), Réunion 102/G6
Juan de Nova (isl.), Réunion 118/G3
Juan Fernández (isls.), Chile 2/E7
Juan Fernández (isls.), Chile 120/B6
Juangriego, Venezuela 124/G2
Juani (isl.), Tanzania 115/G5
Juanita, N. Dak. 282/N4
Juanita, Wash. 310/B1
Juanjuí, Peru 128/D6
Juan L. Lacaze, Uruguay 145/B5
Juan Stuven (isl.), Chile 138/D7
Juárez, Argentina 143/E7
Juárez, Mexico 150/J3
Juazeiro, Brazil 132/G5
Juàzeiro, Brazil 120/E3
Juazeiro do Norte, Brazil 132/F4
Juàzeiro do Norte, Brazil 120/F3
Juba, Sudan 111/F7
Juba, Sudan 111/F7
Jubail, Saudi Arabia 59/F4
Jubba, Saudi Arabia 59/D4
Jubbada Hoose (prov.), Somalia 115/H3
Jubbulpore (Jabalpur), India 68/D4
Jubilee (lake), W. Australia 88/D5
Juby (cape), Morocco 106/B3
Júcar (riv.), Spain 7/D5
Júcar (riv.), Spain 33/F3
Júcaro, Cuba 158/G2
Juchipila, Mexico 150/H6
Juchique de Ferrer, Mexico 150/Q1
Juchitán de Zaragoza, Mexico 150/M8
Jucuarán, El Salvador 154/C4
Jud, N. Dak. 282/N6
Juda, Wis. 317/H10
Judaea (reg.), Israel 65/B5
Judaea (reg.), Jordan 65/C4
Judas (pt.), C. Rica 154/E6
Judenburg, Austria 41/C3
Judibana, Venezuela 124/C2
Judique, Nova Scotia 168/G3
Judith (riv.), Mont. 262/G3
Judith (pt.), R.I. 249/J7
Judith Basin (co.), Mont. 262/F4
Judith Gap, Mont. 262/G4
Judson, Ind. 227/C4
Judson, Minn. 255/D6
Judson, N. Dak. 282/H6
Judyville, Ind. 227/C4
Juelsminde, Denmark 21/D6
Juhu, India 68/B7
Juichin (Ruijin), China 77/J6
Juigalpa, Nicaragua 154/E4
Juist (isl.), Germany 22/B2
Juruá, Brazil 120/C3
Juruá, Brazil 132/G10
Juruá (riv.), Brazil 120/D3
Juiz de Fora, Brazil 128/D7
Juiz de Fora, Brazil 135/E2
Juiz de Fora, Brazil 132/F8
Jujuy (prov.), Argentina 143/C1

Jujuy, Argentina 143/C1
Jujuy, Argentina 120/C5
Jukskei (riv.), S. Africa 118/H6
Julesburg, Colo. 208/P1
Juli, Peru 128/H11
Juliaca, Peru 120/B4
Juliaca, Peru 128/G10
Juliaetta, Idaho 220/B3
Julian, Calif. 204/J10
Julian, Nebr. 264/J4
Julian, N.C. 281/K3
Julian, Pa. 294/G4
Julian Alps (range), Italy 34/D1
Julianatop (mt.), Suriname 131/C4
Julianehåb (Qaqortoq), Greenl. 4/D12
Julianehåb (Qaqortoq), Greenland 2/G2
Julianehåb (Qaqortoq), Greenland 146/P3
Jülich, Germany 22/B3
Juliette, Georgia 217/E4
Juliff, Texas 303/J3
Julio María Sanz, Uruguay 145/E4
Juliustown, N.J. 273/D3
Jullundur, India 68/D2
Jumbilla, Peru 128/C5
Jumbo, Okla. 288/P6
Jumbo (isl.), China 77/J4
Jumilla, Spain 33/F3
Jumla, Nepal 68/E3
Jumna (riv.), India 68/E3
Jump (riv.), Wis. 317/E5
Jumpertown, Miss. 256/G1
Jumping Branch, W. Va. 312/F7
Jump River, Wis. 317/E5
Junagadh, India 68/B4
Junaina, Saudi Arabia 59/D5
Juncal, Argentina 143/F6
Juncos, P. Rico 161/E2
Juncos, P. Rico 156/G1
Junction, Ill. 222/E6
Junction, Texas 303/E7
Junction, Utah 304/B5
Junction, W. Va. 312/J4
Junction City, Ark. 202/E7
Junction City, Georgia 217/C5
Junction City, Ill. 222/D5
Junction City, Kansas 232/E2
Junction City, Ky. 237/M5
Junction City, La. 238/E1
Junction City, Mo. 261/M7
Junction City, Ohio 284/F6
Junction City, Oreg. 291/D3
Junction City, Wis. 317/G6
Jundah, Queensland 95/B5
Jundah, Queensland 88/G4
Jundiaí, Brazil 135/C3
Jundiaí, Brazil 132/E8
Juneau, Alaska 188/E4
Juneau (cap.), Alaska 188/E6
Juneau (cap.), Alaska 196/N1
Juneau, U.S. 4/D16
Juneau, U.S. 2/C3
Juneau (co.), Wis. 317/F8
Juneau, Wis. 317/J9
Juneda, Spain 33/G2
Junee, N.S. Wales 97/D4
June in Winter (lake), Fla. 212/F4
June Lake, Calif. 204/G6
June Park, Fla. 212/F3
Jungar, China 77/H4
Jungfrau (mt.), Switzerland 39/E3
Jungfraujoch, Switzerland 39/E3
Junggar Pendi (desert basin), China 77/C2
Jungli (prov.), Sudan 111/F6
Juniata (co.), Pa. 294/H4
Juniata, Nebr. 264/F4
Juniata (riv.), Pa. 294/G5
Juniata Terrace, Pa. 294/G4
Junín, Argentina 143/F7
Junín, Argentina 120/C6
Junín (dept.), Peru 128/E8
Junín, Peru 128/E8
Junín, Peru 128/E8
Junín de los Andes, Argentina 143/B4
Junior, W. Va. 312/G5
Juniper (mts.), Ariz. 198/C3
Juniper (mt.), Colo. 208/C1
Juniper, Georgia 217/C6
Juniper, New Bruns. 170/C2
Juniper (creek), S.C. 296/H2
Juniye, Lebanon 63/F5
Junlian, China 77/F6
Juno, Georgia 217/D2
Juno, North. Terr. 93/C5
Juno, Tenn. 237/E9
Juno, Texas 303/C7
Juno Beach, Fla. 212/F6
Junosuando, Sweden 18/N3
Juntura, Oreg. 291/K4
Juojärvi (lake), Finland 18/Q5
Jupiter, Fla. 212/F6
Jupiter, N.C. 281/D3
Jupiter Island, Fla. 212/F4
Juquiá, Brazil 135/C4
Jur (riv.), Sudan 111/E6
Jura (dept.), France 28/F4
Jura (isl.), Scotland 10/C3
Jura (isl.), Scotland 15/C5
Jura (sound), Scotland 15/C5
Jura (sound), Scotland 10/D3
Jura (canton), Switzerland 39/D2
Jura (mts.), Switzerland 39/D3
Jurado, Colombia 126/B4
Jurbarkas, U.S.S.R. 53/B3
Jurilovca, U.S.S.R. 53/B2
Jurmala, U.S.S.R. 52/B3
Jurong, Singapore 72/E6
Juruá, Brazil 120/D3
Juruá, Brazil 132/G10
Juruá (riv.), Brazil 120/D3
Juruena, Brazil 132/B6
Juruena (riv.), Brazil 120/D4
Juruena (riv.), Brazil 132/B5

Juruti, Brazil 132/B3
Jusepín, Venezuela 124/G3
Juskatla, Br. Col. 184/A3
Jussy, Switzerland 39/B4
Justice, Ill. 222/B6
Justice, Manitoba 179/C4
Justice, W. Va. 312/C7
Justiceburg, Texas 303/C5
Justin, Texas 303/F11
Justus, Ohio 284/G4
Jutaí (riv.), Brazil 132/G9
Jüterbog, Germany 22/E3
Jutiapa, Guatemala 154/D3
Jutiapa, Honduras 154/F3
Juticalpa, Honduras 154/E3
Jutland (pen.), Denmark 21/C5
Jutland (pen.), Denmark 18/F9
Jutland, N.J. 273/D2
Juuka, Finland 18/R5
Juventud (municipio especial), C 158/C2
Juventud (isl.), Cuba 146/K7
Juventud, Isla de la (Pines) (isl.), 158/B3
Juventud (Pines)' (isl.), Cuba 156 ..
Juwara, Oman 59/G6
Ju Xian, China 77/J4
Juye, China 77/J4
Jyderup, Denmark 21/E6
Jylland (Jutland) (pen.), Denmark 21/C5
Jyske Ås (hills), Denmark 21/D4
Jyväskylä, Finland 7/G2
Jyväskylä, Finland 18/O5

K

K2 (mt.) 54/J6
K2 (mt.), Pakistan 68/D1
Kaaawa, Hawaii 218/F1
Kaabong, Uganda 115/F3
Kaala (mt.), Hawaii 218/D1
Kaanapali, Hawaii 218/H2
Kaba (Habahe), China 77/C2
Kaba, Hungary 41/F2
Kabacan, Philippines 82/E7
Kabaena (isl.), Indonesia 85/G7
Kabala, S. Leone 106/B7
Kabale, Uganda 115/E4
Kabalega (falls), Uganda 115/F3
Kabalega Nat'l Park, Uganda 115/F
Kabalo, Zaire 115/E5
Kabambare, Zaire 115/E4
Kabardin-Balkar A.S.S.R., U.S.S.R. 48/E5
Kabardin-Balkar A.S.S.R., U.S.S.R. 52/F6
Kabare, Zaire 115/E4
Kabasalan, Philippines 82/D7
Kabba, Nigeria 106/F7
Kabetogama, Minn. 255/F2
Kabetogama (lake), Minn. 255/E2
Kabinakagami (riv.), Ontario 177/J5
Kabin Buri, Thailand 72/C4
Kabinda, Zaire 115/D5
Kabir Kuh (mts.), Iran 66/E4
Kabompo, Zambia 115/D6
Kabompo (riv.), Zambia 115/D6
Kabong, Malaysia 85/E5
Kabongo, Zaire 115/E5
Kabud Gonbad, Iran 66/L2
Kabul (cap.), Afghanistan 68/B2
Kabul (cap.), Afghanistan 59/J3
Kabul (cap.), Afghanistan 2/N4
Kabul (riv.), Afghanistan 68/C2
Kabul (riv.), Afghanistan 59/K3
Kabul (riv.), Pakistan 68/C2
Kabunda, Zaire 115/E6
Kabwe, Zambia 102/E6
Kabwe, Zambia 115/E6
Kabylia (reg.), Algeria 106/F1
Kachchh (gulf), India 68/B4
Kachchh (reg.), India 68/B4
Kachchh, Rann of (salt marsh), India 68/B4
Kachhch, Rann of (salt marsh), India 54/H7
Kachchh, Rann of (salt lake), Pakista 59/K5
Kachchh, Rann of (salt marsh), Pakistan 68/C4
Kachemak (bay), Alaska 196/B2
Kachemak City, Alaska 196/B2
Kachess (lake), Wash. 310/D3
Kachin (state), Burma 72/C1
Kachug, U.S.S.R. 48/L4
Kaçkar Dağı (mt.), Turkey 63/J2
Kackley, Kansas 232/E4
Kadan (Czech. 41/B1
Kadan Kyun (isl.), Burma 72/C4
Kadavu (Kandavu) (isl.), Fiji 87/H7
Kadayanallur, India 68/D7
Kadei (riv.), Cameroon 115/C3
Kadei (riv.), Cent. Afr. Rep. 115/C3
Kadei (riv.), Congo 115/C3
Kadina, S. Australia 88/F6
Kadina, S. Australia 94/F5
Kadınhanı, Turkey 63/D6
Kadıköy, Turkey 63/D6
Kadioli, Mali 106/C6
Kadiri, India 68/D5
Kadirli, Turkey 63/F4
Kadiyevka (Stakhanov), U.S.S.R. 52/F2
Kadmat (isl.), India 68/C6
Kadoka, S. Dak. 298/F6
Kadoma, Japan 81/J7
Kadoma, Zimbabwe 102/E6
Kadoma, Zimbabwe 113/D3
Kadugli, Sudan 111/E6
Kadugli, Sudan 102/E3
Kaduna (state), Nigeria 106/F6
Kaduna, Nigeria 102/C3
Kaduna, Nigeria 106/F6

Karlstad 389

Kaduna (riv.), Nigeria 106/F7
Kadzherom, U.S.S.R. 52/J2
Kaech'ŏn, N. Korea 81/B4
Kaédi, Mauritania 106/B5
Kaédi, Mauritania 102/A3
Kaélé, Cameroon 115/B1
Kaena (pt.), Hawaii 218/D1
Kaeo, N. Zealand 100/D1
Kaesŏng, N. Korea 81/C4
Kaf, Saudi Arabia 59/C3
Kafan, U.S.S.R. 52/G7
Kafar Kanna, Israel 65/C2
Kaffa (prov.), Ethiopia 111/G6
Kaffrine, Senegal 106/A6
Kafia Kingi, Sudan 111/D6
Kafirévs (cape), Greece 45/G6
Kafr Yasif, Israel 65/C2
Kafue, Zambia 115/E7
Kafue (riv.), Zambia 115/E7
Kafue Nat'l Park, Zambia 115/E6
Kaga, Japan 81/H5
Kaga Bandoro, Cent. Afr. Rep. 115/C2
Kagalaska (isl.), Alaska 196/L4
Kagan, U.S.S.R. 48/G6
Kagawa (pref.), Japan 81/G6
Kagawong, Ontario 177/B2
Kagawong (lake), Ontario 177/B2
Kagera (reg.), Tanzania 114/F4
Kagera Nat'l Park, Rwanda 115/F4
Kağithane, Turkey 63/D6
Kağizman, Turkey 63/K2
Kagoshima (pref.), Japan 81/E8
Kagoshima, Japan 81/E8
Kagoshima, Japan 54/O6
Kagoshima (bay), Japan 81/E8
Kagul, U.S.S.R. 52/C5
Kaguyak, Alaska 196/H3
Kahakuloa, Hawaii 218/J1
Kahala, Hawaii 218/D5
Kahala (pt.), Hawaii 218/D1
Kahaluu, Hawaii 218/E2
Kahama, Tanzania 115/F4
Kahana, Hawaii 218/F1
Kahana (bay), Hawaii 218/F1
Kahayan (riv.), Indonesia 85/E6
Kahemba, Zaire 115/C5
Kahiltna (riv.), Alaska 196/B1
Kahlotus, Wash. 310/G4
Kah-Nee-Ta, Oreg. 291/F3
Kahoka, Mo. 261/J2
Kahoolawe (isl.), Hawaii 188/F5
Kahoolawe (isl.), Hawaii 87/L4
Kahoolawe (isl.), Hawaii 218/H3
Kahouanne (isl.), Guadeloupe 161/A6
Kahramanmaraş (prov.), Turkey 63/G4
Kâhta, Turkey 63/H4
Kahuku, Hawaii 218/E1
Kahuku, Hawaii 188/F5
Kahuku (pt.), Hawaii 218/E1
Kahului, Hawaii 218/J2
Kahului, Hawaii 188/F5
Kahului (harb.), Hawaii 218/J1
Kai (isls.), Indonesia 85/J7
Kaiama, Nigeria 106/E7
Kaiapit, Papua N.G. 85/B7
Kaiapoi, N. Zealand 100/D5
Kaibab (plat.), Ariz. 198/C2
Kaibab Ind. Res., Ariz. 198/C2
Kaibito, Ariz. 198/D2
Kaibito (plat.), Ariz. 198/D2
Kaieteur (fall), Guyana 131/B3
Kaifeng, China 77/H5
Kaifeng, China 54/N6
Kaikohe, N. Zealand 100/D1
Kaikoura, N. Zealand 100/D5
Kaikoura (pen.), N. Zealand 100/E5
Kaikoura (range), N. Zealand 100/D5
Kaili, China 77/G6
Kailu, China 77/K3
Kailua (Kailua Kona), Hawaii, Hawaii 218/F5
Kailua, Oahu, Hawaii 218/F2
Kailua (bay), Hawaii 218/F2
Kailua (bay), Hawaii 218/F5
Kailua Kona, Hawaii 218/F5
Kaimana, Indonesia 85/J6
Kaimanawa (range), N. Zealand 100/E3
Kaimu, Hawaii 218/J6
Kaimuki, Hawaii 218/D4
Kainaliu, Hawaii 218/G5
Kainaliu, Hawaii 188/F6
Kainan (bay), Ant. 5/B10
Kaingaroa, N. Zealand 100/E7
Kainji (res.), Nigeria 106/E6
Kaipara (harb.), N. Zealand 100/D2
Kaipara (riv.), N. Zealand 100/A1
Kaiparowits (plat.), Utah 304/C6
Kaipokok (bay), Newf. 166/B2
Kaipokok (riv.), Newf. 166/B3
Kairouan, Tunisia 106/F1
Kairuku, Papua N.G. 85/B7
Kaiser, Mo. 261/G6
Kaiseregg (mt.), Switzerland 39/D3
Kaiserslautern, Germany 22/B4
Kaiserstuhl (mt.), Germany 22/B4
Kaitaia, N. Zealand 100/D1
Kaitangata, N. Zealand 100/C7
Kaitumälv (riv.), Sweden 18/M3
Kaiwi (chan.), Hawaii 218/E6
Kaiyuan, Liaoning, China 77/K3
Kaiyuan, Yunnan, China 77/F7
Kaiyuh (mts.), Alaska 196/G2
Kaizuka, Japan 81/H8
Kajaani, Finland 7/G2
Kajaani, Finland 18/P4
Kajabbi, Queensland 88/G3
Kajabbi, Queensland 95/A4
Kajiado, Kenya 115/G4
Kajok, Sudan 111/E6
Kaka, Cent. Afr. Rep. 115/E2
Kaka, Sudan 111/F5
Kakabeka Falls, Ontario 177/G5
Kakabeka Falls, Ontario 175/B3
Kakamega, Kenya 115/F3
Kake, Alaska 196/M1
Kakhk, Iran 66/L3
Kakhovka, U.S.S.R. 52/D5
Kakhovka (res.), U.S.S.R. 48/D5
Kakhovka (res.), U.S.S.R. 52/D5
Kakinada, India 54/K8
Kakinada, India 68/E5
Kakisa, N.W. Terr. 187/G3
Kakkiviak (cape), Newf. 166/B1
Kakogawa, Japan 81/G6
Kaktovik, Alaska 196/K1
Kakwa (riv.), Alberta 182/A2
Kalaa-Kebira, Tunisia 106/F1
Kalaallit-Nunaat (Greenland) 2/G2
Kalaallit-Nunaat (Greenland) 4/B12
Kalaallit-Nunaat (Greenland) 146/P2
Kalabahi, Indonesia 85/G7
Kalabo, Zambia 115/D6
Kalach, U.S.S.R. 52/F4
Kalachinsk, U.S.S.R. 48/H4
Kalach-na-Donu, U.S.S.R. 52/F5
Kaladan (riv.), Burma 72/B2
Kaladar, Ontario 177/H3
Kalae, Hawaii 218/G1
Ka Lae (cape), Hawaii 218/G7
Kalahari (des.) 102/E7
Kalahari (des.), Botswana 118/C4
Kalahari (des.), Namibia 118/C4
Kalahari Gemsbok Nat'l Park, S. Africa 118/C5
Kalaheo, Hawaii 218/C2
Kalajoki, Finland 18/N4
Kalajoki (riv.), Finland 18/O4
Kalakan, U.S.S.R. 48/M4
Kalaloch, Wash. 310/A3
Kalam, Pakistan 68/C1
Kalama, Wash. 310/C4
Kalama (riv.), Wash. 310/C4
Kalámai, Greece 7/G5
Kalámai, Greece 45/F7
Kalamazoo, Mich. 188/J2
Kalamazoo (co.), Mich. 250/D6
Kalamazoo, Mich. 250/D6
Kalamazoo (riv.), Mich. 250/C6
Kalambo (falls), Tanzania 115/F5
Kalambo (falls), Zambia 115/F5
Kalamo, Mich. 250/D6
Kalampáka, Greece 45/E6
Kalamunda, W. Australia 88/B2
Kalan, Turkey 63/H3
Kalao (isl.), Indonesia 85/G7
Kalaoa, Hawaii 218/G5
Kalaotoa (isl.), Indonesia 85/G5
Kalapana, Hawaii 218/J6
Kalasin, Thailand 72/D3
Kalat (Qalat), Afghanistan 68/B2
Kalat (Qalat), Afghanistan 59/J3
Kalat, Pakistan 54/H7
Kalat, Pakistan 59/J4
Kalat, Pakistan 68/B3
Kalaupapa, Hawaii 218/G1
Kalaupapa (pen.), Hawaii 218/H1
Kalaupapa Nat'l Hist. Park, Hawaii 218/H1
Kalávrita, Greece 45/F6
Kalawao (co.), Hawaii 218/G1
Kalbarri, W. Australia 92/A4
Kale, Turkey 63/C4
Kalecik, Turkey 63/E2
Kaleden, Br. Col. 184/H5
Kalegauk (isl.), Burma 72/C4
Kalehe, Zaire 115/E4
Kaleida, Manitoba 179/D5
Kalemie, Zaire 115/E5
Kalemie, Zaire 102/E5
Kalemyo, Burma 72/B2
Kaleva, Mich. 250/C4
Kalevala, U.S.S.R. 52/D1
Kalewa, Burma 72/B2
Kalgan (Zhangjiakou), China 77/J3
Kalgin (isl.), Alaska 196/B1
Kalgoorlie, Australia 2/R7
Kalgoorlie, W. Australia 88/C6
Kalgoorlie, W. Australia 92/C5
Kalgoorlie-Boulder, W. Australia 92/C5
Kaliakra (cape), Bulgaria 45/J4
Kalianda, Indonesia 85/D7
Kalibo, Philippines 82/D5
Kalida, Ohio 284/B4
Kalihi, Hawaii 218/C4
Kalihi (channel), Hawaii 218/B4
Kalihi (stream), Hawaii 218/C3
Kalihiwai, Hawaii 218/C1
Kalima, Zaire 115/E4
Kalimantan (reg.) Indonesia 85/E5
Kálimnos, Greece 45/H7
Kálimnos (isl.), Greece 45/H7
Kalinga, Queensland 88/K2
Kalinga-Apayao (prov.), Philippines 82/C1
Kalinin (Tver'), U.S.S.R. 7/H3
Kalinin (Tver'), U.S.S.R. 48/D4
Kalinin (Tver'), U.S.S.R. 52/E3
Kaliningrad, U.S.S.R. 7/G3
Kaliningrad, U.S.S.R. 48/B4
Kaliningrad, Kaliningrad, U.S.S.R. 52/B4
Kaliningrad, Moscow Oblast, U.S.S.R. 52/E3
Kalininsk, U.S.S.R. 52/F4
Kalinkovichi, U.S.S.R. 52/C4
Kalispel Ind. Res., Wash. 310/H2
Kalispell, Mont. 188/C1
Kalispell, Mont. 262/B2
Kalisz (prov.), Poland 47/D3
Kalisz, Poland 7/F3
Kalisz, Poland 47/D3
Kaliua, Tanzania 115/F5
Kalix, Sweden 18/N4
Kalixälv (riv.), Sweden 18/N3
Kalkaska (co.), Mich. 250/D4
Kalkaska, Mich. 250/D4
Kalkfeld, Namibia 118/B4
Kalkfontein, Botswana 118/C4
Kallaste, U.S.S.R. 53/D1
Kallavesi (lake), Finland 18/P5
Kallsjö (lake), Sweden 18/H5
Kalmalo, Nigeria 106/F6
Kalmar (co.), Sweden 18/K8
Kalmar, Sweden 7/F3
Kalmar, Sweden 18/K8
Kalmarsund (sound), Sweden 18/K8
Kalmthout, Belgium 27/F6
Kalmuck A.S.S.R., U.S.S.R. 52/F5
Kalmuck A.S.S.R., U.S.S.R. 48/E5
Kalmunai, Sri Lanka 68/E7
Kalmykovo, U.S.S.R. 48/F5
Kalo, Iowa 229/E4
Kalocsa, Hungary 41/E3
Kalohi (chan.), Hawaii 218/G1
Kaloko-Honokohau Nat'l Hist. Park, Hawaii 218/F6
Kaloli (pt.), Hawaii 218/K5
Kalomo, Zambia 115/E7
Kalona, Iowa 229/K6
Kalpeni (isl.), India 68/C7
Kalpin, China 77/A3
Kalskag, Alaska 196/F2
Kaltag, Alaska 196/G2
Kaltbrunn, Switzerland 39/H2
Kaluaaha, Hawaii 218/H1
Kaluga, U.S.S.R. 7/H3
Kaluga, U.S.S.R. 48/D4
Kaluga, U.S.S.R. 52/E4
Kalumburu Mission, W. Australia 88/D2
Kalumburu Mission, W. Australia 92/D1
Kalundborg, Denmark 21/D6
Kalundborg, Denmark 18/G9
Kalush, U.S.S.R. 52/B5
Kalutara, Sri Lanka 68/D7
Kalvarija, U.S.S.R. 53/B3
Kalvesta, Kansas 232/B3
Kalyan, India 68/C5
Kama, Burma 72/B3
Kama (res.), U.S.S.R. 52/J3
Kama (riv.), U.S.S.R. 7/K3
Kama (riv.), U.S.S.R. 52/H2
Kama, Zaire 115/E4
Kamaiki (pt.), Hawaii 218/H2
Kamaing, Burma 72/C1
Kamaishi, Japan 81/L4
Kamakou (peak), Hawaii 218/H1
Kamakura, Japan 81/O3
Kamakusa, Guyana 131/A3
Kamalino, Hawaii 218/A2
Kamalo, Hawaii 218/H1
Kaman, Turkey 63/E3
Kamaniskeg (lake), Ontario 177/G2
Kamanjab, Namibia 118/A3
Kamaran (isl.), Yemen 59/D6
Kamarang, Guyana 131/A3
Kamarhati, India 68/F1
Kamaria (falls), Guyana 131/B2
Kamas, Utah 304/C3
Kamay, Texas 303/F4
Kambalda, W. Australia 88/C6
Kambalda, W. Australia 92/C5
Kambia, S. Leone 106/B7
Kambove, Zaire 115/E6
Kambove, Zaire 102/E6
Kamchatka (pen.), U.S.S.R. 54/S4
Kamchatka (pen.), U.S.S.R. 2/T3
Kamchatka (pen.), U.S.S.R. 48/Q4
Kamela, Oreg. 291/J2
Kamenets-Podol'skiy, U.S.S.R. 52/C5
Kamenice, Czech. 41/C2
Kamenjak (cape), Yugoslavia 45/A3
Kamenka, Arkhangel, U.S.S.R. 52/F1
Kamenka, Penza, U.S.S.R. 52/F4
Kamen'-na-Obi, U.S.S.R. 48/H4
Kamenskoye, U.S.S.R. 48/R3
Kamensk-Shakhtinskiy, U.S.S.R. 52/F5
Kamensk-Ural'skiy, U.S.S.R. 48/G4
Kamenz, Germany 22/F3
Kameoka, Japan 81/J7
Kames, Scotland 15/C5
Kamet (mt.), India 68/D2
Kamiah, Idaho 220/B3
Kamienna Góra, Poland 47/B3
Kamień Pomorski, Poland 47/B2
Kamiisco, Japan 81/K3
Kamil, Oman 59/G5
Kamilo (pt.), Hawaii 218/H7
Kamilukuak (lake), N.W. Terr. 187/H3
Kamina, Zaire 102/E5
Kamina, Zaire 115/D5
Kaminak (lake), N.W. Terr. 187/J3
Kaminoyama, Japan 81/J4
Kaminuriak (lake), N.W. Terr. 187/J3
Kamishak (bay), Alaska 196/H3
Kamiyaku, Japan 81/E8
Kamloops, Br. Col. 162/D5
Kamloops, Br. Col. 146/G4
Kamloops, Br. Col. 184/G5
Kamo, Japan 81/J7
Kamoa (riv.), Guyana 131/B5
Kamouraska (co.), Québec 172/H2
Kamouraska, Québec 172/H2
Kamp (riv.), Austria 41/C2
Kampala (cap.), Uganda 2/L5
Kampala (cap.), Uganda 102/F4
Kampala (cap.), Uganda 115/F3
Kampar (riv.), Indonesia 85/C5
Kampar, Malaysia 72/D6
Kampen, Netherlands 27/H3
Kampen, Germany 22/C1
Kampene, Zaire 115/E4
Kampeska (lake), S. Dak. 298/P4
Kamphaeng Phet, Thailand 72/C3
Kampong Cham, Cambodia 54/M8
Kampong Cham, Cambodia 72/E4
Kampong Chhnang, Cambodia 72/D4
Kampong Khleang, Cambodia 72/E4
Kampong Kuala Besut, Malaysia 72/D6
Kampong Saom, Cambodia 72/D5
Kampong Sedenak, Malaysia 72/E5
Kampong Sibuti, Malaysia 85/E5
Kampong Spoe, Cambodia 72/E5
Kampong Thum, Cambodia 72/E4
Kampong Trabek, Cambodia 72/E5
Kampot, Cambodia 72/E5
Kampsville, Ill. 222/C4
Kamptee, India 68/D4
KAMPUCHEA (CAMBODIA) 72
Kampung Baru (Tolitoli), Indonesia 85/G5
Kamrar, Iowa 229/F4
Kamsack, Sask. 162/F5
Kamsack, Sask. 181/K4
Kamsack Beach, Sask. 181/K4
Kamsar, Guinea 106/B6
Kamuela, Hawaii 218/G3
Kamui (cape), Japan 81/K2
Kamyshin, U.S.S.R. 7/J3
Kamyshin, U.S.S.R. 52/F4
Kamyshin, U.S.S.R. 48/E4
Kanaaupscow (riv.), Québec 174/B2
Kanab (creek), Ariz. 198/C2
Kanab (plat.), Ariz. 198/C2
Kanab, Utah 304/B6
Kanab (creek), Utah 304/B7
Kanabec (co.), Minn. 255/E5
Kanaga (isl.), Alaska 196/L4
Kanagawa (pref.), Japan 81/O2
Kanaio, Hawaii 218/J3
Kanairiktok (riv.), Newf. 166/B3
Kanakanak, Alaska 196/G3
Kananaskis, Alberta 182/C4
Kananga, Zaire 115/D5
Kananga, Zaire 102/E5
Kanapou (bay), Hawaii 218/J3
Kanaranzi, Minn. 255/B7
Kanaranzi (creek), Minn. 255/C7
Kanarraville, Utah 304/A6
Kanash, U.S.S.R. 52/G3
Kanata, Ontario 177/J2
Kanauga, Ohio 284/F8
Kanawha, Iowa 229/F3
Kanawha (co.), W. Va. 312/C6
Kanawha (riv.), W. Va. 312/C5
Kanawha Falls, W. Va. 312/D6
Kanawha Head, W. Va. 312/F5
Kanazawa, Japan 81/H5
Kanazawa, Japan 54/P6
Kanbalu, Burma 72/B2
Kanchanaburi, Thailand 72/C4
Kanchenjunga (mt.), India 68/F3
Kanchenjunga (mt.), Nepal 68/F3
Kanchipuram, India 68/E6
Kanchow (Ganzhou), China 77/H6
Kanchrapara, India 68/F1
Kandahar (Qandahar), Afghanistan 59/J3
Kandahar (Qandahar), Afghanistan 68/B2
Kandahar, Sask. 181/G4
Kanda-Kanda, Zaire 115/D5
Kandalaksha, U.S.S.R. 7/H2
Kandalaksha, U.S.S.R. 52/D1
Kandalaksha, U.S.S.R. 48/C3
Kandalaksha (gulf), U.S.S.R. 52/D1
Kandangan, Indonesia 85/F6
Kándanos, Greece 45/F8
Kandava, U.S.S.R. 53/B2
Kandavu (Kadavu) (isl.), Fiji 87/H7
Kandavu (isl.), Fiji 86/Q11
Kandavu (passage), Fiji 86/Q11
Kander (riv.), Switzerland 39/C2
Kandersteg, Switzerland 39/E4
Kandi, Benin 106/E6
Kandıra, Turkey 63/D2
Kandiyohi (co.), Minn. 255/C5
Kandiyohi, Minn. 255/D5
Kandla, India 68/C4
Kandos, N.S. Wales 97/F3
Kandrach, Pakistan 68/A3
Kandrach, Pakistan 59/H4
Kandukur, India 68/E5
Kandy, Sri Lanka 54/K9
Kandy, Sri Lanka 68/E7
Kane (basin) 4/B13
Kane (co.), Ill. 222/E2
Kane, Ill. 222/C4
Kane, Manitoba 179/E5
Kane (basin), N.W.T. 162/N3
Kane (basin), N.W. Terr. 187/L2
Kane, Pa. 294/E2
Kane (co.), Utah 304/B6
Kanem (reg.), Chad 111/C5
Kaneohe, Hawaii 218/F2
Kaneohe (bay), Hawaii 218/F2
Kaneohe Bay U.S.M.C. Air Station, Hawaii 218/F2
Kaneville, Ill. 222/E2
Kang, Botswana 118/C4
Kanga, Tanzania 115/G5
Kangaba, Mali 106/C6
Kangal, Turkey 63/G3
Kangan, Iran 59/F4
Kangan, Iran 66/G7
Kangar, Malaysia 72/D6
Kangarilla, S. Australia 94/B8
Kangaroo (isl.), Australia 87/D9
Kangaroo (isl.), S. Australia 88/F7
Kangaroo (isl.), S. Australia 94/E7
Kangaroo Ground, Victoria 97/J4
Kangaruma, Guyana 131/B3
Kangavar, Iran 59/E3
Kangavar, Iran 66/F3
Kangding, China 77/F5
Kangean (isl.), Indonesia 85/F7
Kangean (isls.), Indonesia 85/F7
Kanggye, N. Korea 81/C3
Kanghwa (bay), N. Korea 81/B5
Kanghwa (bay), S. Korea 81/B5
Kangiqsualujjuaq, Québec 162/K4
Kangiqsualujjuaq, Québec 174/F2
Kangiqsujuaq, Québec 162/J3
Kangiqsujuaq, Québec 174/F1
Kangirsuk, Québec 162/J3
Kangsiruk, Québec 174/F1
Kangley, Ill. 222/E2
Kangnŭng, S. Korea 81/D5
Kango, Gabon 115/B3
Kangrinboqê Feng (mt.), China 77/B5
Kani, Burma 72/B2
Kaniama, Zaire 115/D5
Kanin (pen.), U.S.S.R. 7/J2
Kanin (pen.), U.S.S.R. 4/C7
Kanin (pen.), U.S.S.R. 48/E3
Kanin (pen.), U.S.S.R. 52/G1
Kaningo, Kenya 115/G4
Kanin Nos (cape), U.S.S.R. 48/E3
Kanin Nos (cape), U.S.S.R. 52/F1
Kaniva, Victoria 97/A5
Kanjiža, Yugoslavia 45/D2
Kankaanpää, Finland 18/M6
Kankakee, Ill. 188/J2
Kankakee (co.), Ill. 222/F2
Kankakee, Ill. 222/F2
Kankakee (riv.), Ill. 222/F2
Kankakee (riv.), Ind. 227/C2
Kankan, Guinea 106/C6
Kankan, Guinea 102/B3
Kanker, India 68/E4
Kankossa, Mauritania 102/A3
Kankossa, Mauritania 106/B5
Kannapolis, N.C. 281/H4
Kannata Valley, Sask. 181/G5
Kannauj, India 68/D3
Kano (state), Nigeria 106/F6
Kano, Nigeria 106/F6
Kano, Nigeria 102/C3
Kanon (pt.), Neth. Ant. 161/G9
Kanona, N.Y. 276/F6
Kanonji, Japan 81/F6
Kanopolis, Kansas 232/D3
Kanopolis (lake), Kansas 232/D3
Kanorado, Kansas 232/A2
Kanosh, Utah 304/B5
Kanosh Ind. Res., Utah 304/B5
Kanoya, Japan 81/E8
Kanpur, India 54/K7
Kanpur, India 68/E3
Kanrach, Pakistan 59/H4
Kansas 188/G3
KANSAS 232
Kansas, Ala. 195/C3
Kansas, Ill. 222/F4
Kansas (riv.), Kans. 188/G3
Kansas (riv.), Kansas 232/F2
Kansas, Ohio 284/D3
Kansas, Okla. 288/S2
Kansas (state), U.S. 146/J6
Kansas City, Kans. 188/G3
Kansas City, Kansas 232/H2
Kansas City, Mo. 261/P5
Kansas City, Mo. 188/H3
Kansas City, Mo. 146/J6
Kansasville, Wis. 317/L3
Kansk, U.S.S.R. 54/L4
Kansk, U.S.S.R. 48/K4
Kansu (Gansu), China 77/E3
Kantishna (riv.), Alaska 196/H2
Kanton (isl.), Kiribati 87/J6
Kantunilkin, Mexico 150/Q6
Kanturk, Ireland 10/B4
Kanturk, Ireland 17/D7
Kanuku (mts.), Guyana 131/B4
Kanuma, Japan 81/J5
Kanye, Botswana 102/E7
Kanye, Botswana 118/C5
Kanzi (cape), Tanzania 115/G5
Kaohsiung, China 77/J7
Kaohsiung, Taiwan 54/N7
Kaokoveld (reg.), Namibia 118/A3
Kaolack, Senegal 106/A6
Kaolack, Senegal 102/A3
Kaoma, Zambia 115/D6
Kao Prawa (mt.), Thailand 72/C3
Kapaa, Hawaii 218/D1
Kapaa, Hawaii 188/E5
Kapaahu, Hawaii 218/J6
Kapaau, Hawaii 218/G3
Kapalama, Hawaii 218/C4
Kapalong, Philippines 82/E7
Kapanga, Zaire 115/D5
Kapchagay, U.S.S.R. 48/H5
Kapellen, Belgium 27/E6
Kapenguria, Kenya 115/G3
Kapfenberg, Austria 41/C3
Kapingamarangi (atoll), Micronesia 87/F5
Kapiri Mposhi, Zambia 115/E6
Kapiskau (riv.), Ontario 175/D2
Kapit, Malaysia 85/E5
Kapiti (isl.), N. Zealand 100/E4
Kaplan, La. 238/F6
Kaplice, Czech. 41/C2
Kapoeta, Sudan 111/F7
Kapoho, Hawaii 218/K5
Kapos (riv.), Hungary 41/D3
Kaposvár, Hungary 41/D3
Kapowsin, Wash. 310/C4
Kappa, Ill. 222/D3
Kappl, Austria 41/A3
Kaprun, Austria 41/B3
Kapsan, N. Korea 81/C3
Kapsukas, U.S.S.R. 53/B3
Kapsukas, U.S.S.R. 52/B4
Kapuas (riv.), Indonesia 85/D6
Kapulena, Hawaii 218/H4
Kapunda, S. Australia 94/F6
Kapuskasing, Ont. 162/H6
Kapuskasing, Ontario 175/D3
Kapuskasing, Ontario 177/J5
Kapuskasing (riv.), Ontario 177/J5
Kapuskasing (riv.), Ontario 175/D3
Kapuvár, Hungary 41/D3
Kapydzhik (mt.), U.S.S.R. 52/G7
Kara, U.S.S.R. 48/G3
Kara, U.S.S.R. 52/L1
Kara (sea), U.S.S.R. 4/B6
Kara (sea), U.S.S.R. 54/H2
Kara (sea), U.S.S.R. 52/K1
Kara (sea), U.S.S.R. 48/G2
Kara-Bogaz-Gol (gulf), U.S.S.R. 48/F5
Karabük, Turkey 63/E2
Karaburun, Turkey 63/B3
Karacabey, Turkey 63/C2
Karaca Dağ (mt.), Turkey 63/H4
Karachay-Cherkess Aut. Obl., U.S.S.R. 48/E5
Karachay-Cherkess Aut. Obl., U.S.S.R. 52/F6
Karachayevsk, U.S.S.R. 52/F6
Karachev, U.S.S.R. 52/E4
Karachi, Pakistan 2/N4
Karachi, Pakistan 59/J5
Karachi, Pakistan 68/B4
Karachi, Pakistan 54/H7
Karád, Hungary 41/D3
Karad, India 68/C5
Karadağ (mt.), Turkey 59/B2
Karadağ (mt.), Turkey 63/E4
Karadeniz Boğazı (Bosporus) (str.), Turkey 63/C2
Karadeniz Boğazı (Bosporus) (str.), Turkey 59/A1
Karaganda, U.S.S.R. 2/N3
Karaganda, U.S.S.R. 54/J5
Karaganda, U.S.S.R. 48/H5
Karaginskiy (isl.), U.S.S.R. 54/T4
Karaginskiy (isl.), U.S.S.R. 48/R4
Karahallı, Turkey 63/C3
Karaikudi, India 68/D7
Karaisalı, Turkey 63/F4
Karaj, Iran 66/G3
Karakalpak A.S.S.R., U.S.S.R. 48/G5
Karakax (Kara Kash) (Moyu), China 77/A4
Karakax He (riv.), China 77/A4
Karakelong (isl.), Indonesia 85/H5
Karakhoto (ruins), China 77/F3
Karakoçan, Turkey 63/H3
Karakoram (mts.), India 68/D1
Karakoram (mts.), Pakistan 68/D1
Karakorum (ruins), Mongolia 54/M5
Karakorum (ruins), Mongolia 77/F2
Karaköse, Turkey 59/D2
Karaköse (Ağrı), Turkey 63/K3
Kara-Kum (canal), U.S.S.R. 48/F6
Kara-Kum (des.), U.S.S.R. 48/F5
Karakuwisa, Namibia 118/B3
Karaman, Turkey 59/B2
Karaman, Turkey 63/E4
Karamanlı, Turkey 63/C4
Karamay, China 77/B2
Karamay, China 54/K5
Karamea, N. Zealand 100/C4
Karamea (bight), N. Zealand 100/C4
Karamiran Shankou (pass), China 77/C4
Karan (state), Burma 72/C3
Karangasem, Indonesia 85/F7
Karanja, India 68/D4
Karapelit, Bulgaria 45/H4
Karapınar, Turkey 63/E4
Karas, Namibia 118/B5
Karasabai, Guyana 131/B4
Karasavey (cape), U.S.S.R. 4/B6
Karasburg, Namibia 118/B5
Karasjok, Norway 18/O2
Karasu, Turkey 63/D2
Karasu (riv.), Turkey 63/J3
Karasu-Aras (mts.), Turkey 63/J3
Karasuk, U.S.S.R. 48/H4
Karat, Iran 66/M3
Karataş, Turkey 63/F4
Karataş (cape), Turkey 63/F4
Karatau, U.S.S.R. 48/H5
Karathuri, Burma 72/C5
Karatsu, Japan 81/D7
Karawanken (range), Austria 41/C3
Karayaka, Turkey 63/G2
Karayazı, Turkey 63/J3
Karazhal, U.S.S.R. 48/H5
Karbala (gov.), Iraq 66/B4
Karbal'a, Iraq 59/D3
Karbala, Iraq 54/F6
Karbal'a, Iraq 66/C4
Karbers Ridge, Ill. 222/E6
Karby, Denmark 21/B4
Karcag, Hungary 41/F3
Kardhítsa, Greece 45/E6
Kärdla, U.S.S.R. 53/B1
Karelian A.S.S.R., U.S.S.R. 48/D3
Karelian A.S.S.R., U.S.S.R. 52/D2
Karema, Tanzania 115/F5
Karesuando, Sweden 18/M2
Kargasok, U.S.S.R. 48/J4
Kargı, Turkey 63/F2
Kargil, India 68/D2
Kargopol', U.S.S.R. 52/E2
Karhula, Finland 18/P6
Kariá, Greece 45/E6
Kariaí, Greece 45/G5
Kariba (lake) 102/E6
Kariba (mt.), Japan 81/K2
Kariba (dam), Zambia 115/E7
Kariba (lake), Zambia 115/E7
Kariba, Zimbabwe 118/D3
Kariba (dam), Zimbabwe 118/D3
Kariba (lake), Zimbabwe 118/D3
Karibib, Namibia 118/B4
Karikal, India 68/E6
Karikari (cape), N. Zealand 100/D1
Karima, Sudan 59/B6
Karima, Sudan 111/F4
Karimata (arch.), Indonesia 85/D6
Karimata (isl.), Indonesia 85/D6
Karimata (str.), Indonesia 85/D6
Karimunjawa (isls.), Indonesia 85/J1
Karin, Somalia 115/J1
Karis, Finland 18/N6
Karise, Denmark 21/F7
Karisimbi (mt.), Rwanda 115/E4
Karisimbi (mt.), Zaire 115/E4
Káristos, Greece 45/G6
Kariz, Iran 66/M3
Karjaa (Karis), Finland 18/N6
Karkabat, Ethiopia 111/G4
Karkal, India 68/C6
Karkar (isl.), Papua N.G. 85/B6
Karkas, Kuh-e (mt.), Iran 66/G4
Karkheh (riv.), Iran 66/E4
Karkkila, Finland 18/N6
Karkur-Pardes Hanna, Israel 65/C3
Karlıova, Turkey 63/J3
Karlö (Hailuoto) (isl.), Finland 18/O4
Karlovac, Yugoslavia 45/B3
Karlovo, Bulgaria 45/G4
Karlovy Vary, Czech. 41/B1
Karlshamn, Sweden 18/J8
Karlskoga, Sweden 18/J7
Karlskrona, Sweden 18/J8
Karlsruhe, N. Dak. 282/J3
Karlsruhe, Germany 7/E4
Karlsruhe, Germany 22/C4
Karlstad, Germany 22/C4
Karlstad, Minn. 255/B2
Karlstad, Sweden 7/F3
Karlstad, Sweden 18/H7

Karluk, Alaska 196/H3
Karnak (El Karnak), Egypt 111/F2
Karnak, Ill. 222/E6
Karnak, N. Dak. 282/O5
Karnal, India 68/D3
Karnataka (state), India 68/D6
Karnes (co.), Texas 303/G9
Karnes City, Texas 303/G9
Karnobat, Bulgaria 45/H4
Karns, Tenn. 237/N9
Karns City, Pa. 294/C4
Karonga, Malawi 115/F5
Karora, Sudan 111/G4
Karoro, N. Zealand 100/C5
Karosa, Indonesia 85/F6
Karpakora, N.S. Wales 97/B3
Kárpathos, Greece 45/H8
Kárpathos (isl.), Greece 45/H8
Karpenision, Greece 45/E6
Karpinsk, U.S.S.R. 48/F4
Karratha, W. Australia 88/B4
Karratha, W. Australia 92/B3
Kars, Ontario 177/J2
Kars (prov.), Turkey 63/K2
Kars, Turkey 59/D1
Kars, Turkey 63/K2
Kärsava, U.S.S.R. 53/D2
Karshi, U.S.S.R. 48/G6
Karşıyaka, Turkey 63/B3
Karskiye Vorota (str.), U.S.S.R. 4/B7
Karskiye Vorota (str.), U.S.S.R. 52/J1
Karskiye Vorota (str.), U.S.S.R. 48/F2
Kartal, Turkey 63/D6
Kartaly, U.S.S.R. 48/G4
Karthaus, Pa. 294/F3
Kartuzy, Poland 47/C1
Karumba, Queensland 88/G3
Karumba, Queensland 95/B3
Karun (riv.), Iran 59/G3
Karun (riv.), Iran 66/F5
Karunjie, W. Australia 92/D3
Karunki, Finland 18/O4
Karup, Denmark 21/C5
Karval, Colo. 208/N5
Karviná, Czech. 41/E2
Karwar, India 68/C6
Kaş, Turkey 63/C4
Kasaan, Alaska 196/N2
Kasabonika, Ontario 175/C2
Kasai (riv.) 102/E5
Kasai (riv.), Angola 115/D5
Kasai (riv.), Zaire 115/C4
Kasai-Occidental (prov.), Zaire 115/D4
Kasai-Oriental (prov.), Zaire 115/D5
Kasaji, Zaire 115/D6
Kasama, Zambia 102/F6
Kasama, Zambia 115/F6
Kasane, Botswana 118/D3
Kasanga, Tanzania 115/F5
Kasanga, Tanzania 102/F5
Kasangulu, Zaire 115/C4
Kasar, Ras (cape), Ethiopia 111/G4
Kasar, Ras (cape), Sudan 111/G4
Kasar, Ras (cape), Sudan 59/C6
Kasaragod, India 68/C6
Kasba (lake), N.W. Terr. 162/F3
Kasba (lake), N.W. Terr. 187/H3
Kasbeer, Ill. 222/D2
Kaseda, Japan 81/D8
Kasempa, Zambia 118/E6
Kasenga, Zaire 115/E6
Kasenyi, Zaire 115/E3
Kasese, Uganda 115/F3
Kasese, Zaire 115/E4
Kasganj, India 68/D3
Kashabowie, Ontario 177/G5
Kashaf Rud (riv.), Iran 66/M2
Kashan, Iran 59/F3
Kashan, Iran 66/G3
Kashechewan, Ontario 175/D2
Kashegelok, Alaska 196/G2
Kashi, China 77/A4
Kashi, China 54/A6
Kashihara, Japan 81/J8
Kashin, U.S.S.R. 52/E3
Kashing (Jiaxing), China 77/K5
Kashiwa, Japan 81/P2
Kashiwara, Japan 81/J8
Kashiwazaki, Japan 81/J5
Kashmar, Iran 66/L3
Kashmar, Iran 59/G2
Kashmor, Pakistan 68/C3
Kashunuk (riv.), Alaska 196/F2
Kasigluk, Alaska 196/F2
Kasilof, Alaska 196/B1
Kasimov, U.S.S.R. 52/F4
Kaskaskia, Ill. 222/C6
Kaskaskia (riv.), Ill. 222/E4
Kaskinen (Kaskö), Finland 18/M5
Kaskö, Finland 18/M5
Kaslo, Br. Col. 162/E6
Kaslo, Br. Col. 184/J5
Kasongo, Zaire 115/E4
Kasongo-Lunda, Zaire 115/C5
Kásos (isl.), Greece 45/H8
Kasota, Minn. 255/D6
Kasper Creek, Sask. 181/F6
Kaspiysk, U.S.S.R. 52/G6
Kaspiyskiy, U.S.S.R. 52/G5
Kassala (prov.), Sudan 111/F4
Kassala, Sudan 111/G4
Kassala, Sudan 59/C6
Kassala, Sudan 102/F3
Kassándra (pen.), Greece 45/F4
Kassel, Germany 7/E3
Kassel, Germany 22/C3
Kasserine, Tunisia 106/F1
Kasson, Minn. 255/F6
Kasson, W. Va. 312/F4
Kastamonu (prov.), Turkey 63/E2
Kastamonu, Turkey 59/B1
Kastamonu, Turkey 63/F2
Kastéllion, Greece 45/G3
Kastéllion (Kissamos), Greece 45/F8
Kasterlee, Belgium 27/F6
Kastoría, Greece 45/E5
Kastrup, Denmark 21/F6

Kastrup, Denmark 18/H9
Kasugai, Japan 81/H6
Kasukabe, Japan 81/O2
Kasulu, Tanzania 115/F4
Kasumiga (lag.), Japan 81/K5
Kasungu, Malawi 115/F6
Kasur, Pakistan 68/C2
Kasur, Pakistan 59/K3
Kataba, Zambia 115/D7
Katahdin (mt.), Maine 243/F4
Katako-Kombe, Zaire 115/D4
Katákolon, Greece 45/E7
Katanga (reg.), Zaire 102/E5
Katangi, U.S.S.R. 48/P4
Katanning, W. Australia 88/B6
Katanning, W. Australia 92/B6
Katarnian Ghat, India 68/E3
Kata Tjuta (Mt. Olga) (mt.), North. Terr. 93/B8
Katchall (isl.), India 68/G7
Katchiungo, Angola 115/D5
Katemcy, Texas 303/E7
Katenga, Zaire 115/E5
Katepwa Beach, Sask. 181/H5
Katepwa Prov. Park, Sask. 181/H5
Kateríni, Greece 45/F5
Kates Needle (mt.), Alaska 196/N1
Kates Needle (mt.), Br. Col. 184/A1
Katha, Burma 72/C1
Katherina, Jebel (mt.), Egypt 111/F2
Katherina, Jebel (mt.), Egypt 59/B4
Katherine, Ariz. 198/A3
Katherine, Australia 87/D7
Katherine, North. Terr. 88/E2
Katherine, North. Terr. 93/B3
Katherine (riv.), North. Terr. 93/C3
Kathiawar (pen.), India 68/B4
Kathleen, Alberta 182/B2
Kathleen, Fla. 212/D3
Kathleen, Georgia 217/E6
Kathmandu (cap.), Nepal 54/K7
Kathmandu (cap.), Nepal 68/E3
Kathryn, Alberta 182/D4
Kathryn, N. Dak. 282/P6
Kati, Mali 106/C6
Katihar, India 68/F3
Katima Mulilo, Namibia 118/C3
Katimik (lake), Manitoba 179/C2
Katiola, Ivory Coast 106/C7
Katipunan, Philippines 82/D6
Katmai (vol.), Alaska 196/H3
Katmai Nat'l Park, Alaska 196/H3
Katmai Nat'l Pres., Alaska 196/H3
Katni (Murwara), India 68/E4
Katonah, N.Y. 276/N8
Katoomba-Wentworth Falls, N.S. Wales 97/F3
Katowice (prov.), Poland 47/D3
Katowice, Poland 7/F3
Katowice, Poland 47/B4
Katrime, Manitoba 179/D4
Katrine, Ontario 177/E2
Katrine, Loch (lake), Scotland 15/D4
Katrineholm, Sweden 18/K7
Katsina, Nigeria 102/C3
Katsina, Nigeria 106/F6
Katsina Ala, Nigeria 106/F7
Katsuta, Japan 81/K5
Katsuura, Japan 81/K6
Kattakurgan, U.S.S.R. 48/G5
Kattegat (str.) 7/F3
Kattegat (str.), Denmark 21/E4
Kattegat (str.), Denmark 18/G8
Kattegat (str.), Sweden 18/G8
Katwe, Uganda 115/F4
Katwijk aan Zee, Netherlands 27/E4
Katy, Texas 303/J2
Kau (des.), Hawaii 218/J6
Kau, Indonesia 85/H5
Kauai (co.), Hawaii 218/A1
Kauai (isl.), Hawaii 87/L3
Kauai (isl.), Hawaii 188/E5
Kauai (chan.), Hawaii 218/B5
Kauai (isl.), Hawaii 218/C1
Kaufbeuren, Germany 22/D5
Kaufman (co.), Texas 303/H5
Kaufman, Texas 303/H5
Kauhola (pt.), Hawaii 218/G3
Kauiki (head), Hawaii 218/K2
Kaukauna, Wis. 317/K7
Kaukauveld (mts.), Botswana 118/C3
Kaukauveld (mts.), Namibia 118/C3
Kaukonahua (stream), Hawaii 218/E1
Kaula (isl.), Hawaii 188/M7
Kaula (isl.), Hawaii 218/D6
Kaulakahi (chan.), Hawaii 218/B2
Kauliranta, Finland 18/O3
Kaumajet (mts.), Newf. 166/B2
Kaumakani, Hawaii 218/C2
Kaumalapau (harb.), Hawaii 218/G2
Kaumalapau Harbor, Hawaii 218/G2
Kauna (pt.), Hawaii 218/J4
Kaunakakai, Hawaii 218/G1
Kaunakakai (harb.), Hawaii 218/G1
Kaunas, U.S.S.R. 7/G3
Kaunas, U.S.S.R. 53/C3
Kaunas, U.S.S.R. 48/C3
Kaunas, U.S.S.R. 52/B4
Kauniainen, Finland 18/O6
Kaunuopou (pt.), Hawaii 218/B2
Kaupakulua, Hawaii 218/K2
Kaupo, Hawaii 218/K2
Kaura Namoda, Nigeria 106/F6
Kauswagan, Philippines 82/E6
Kautokeino, Norway 18/N2
Kauttua, Finland 18/N6
Kavadarci, Yugoslavia 45/E5
Kavajë, Albania 45/D5
Kavak, Çanakkale, Turkey 63/C5
Kavak, Samsun, Turkey 63/F2
Kavalga (isl.), Alaska 196/K4
Kavali, India 68/D6
Kaválla, Greece 7/G4
Kaválla, Greece 45/G5
Kavanagh, Alberta 182/D3

Kavanayen, Venezuela 124/H5
Kavaratti, India 68/C6
Kavarna, Bulgaria 45/J4
Kaveri (riv.), India 68/D6
Kavieng, Papua N.G. 87/E6
Kavieng, Papua N.G. 86/B1
Kavir, Dasht-e (salt des.), Iran 59/G3
Kavir, Dasht-e (salt des.), Iran 66/J3
Kavir-e Namak (salt des.), Iran 59/G3
Kavirondo (gulf), Kenya 115/F4
Kavungo, Angola 114/D6
Kaw (lake), Okla. 288/N1
Kaw, Fr. Guiana 131/E3
Kawachinagano, Japan 81/J8
Kawagama (lake), Ontario 177/F2
Kawagoe, Japan 81/O2
Kawaguchi, Japan 81/J6
Kawaihae, Hawaii 218/G4
Kawaihae (bay), Hawaii 218/G4
Kawaihoa (cape), Hawaii 218/A2
Kawaikini (peak), Hawaii 218/C1
Kawailoa, Hawaii 218/E1
Kawakawa, N. Zealand 100/E1
Kawambwa, Zambia 115/E5
Kawanishi, Japan 81/H7
Kawardha, India 68/E4
Kawasaki, Japan 81/O3
Kawau (isl.), N. Zealand 100/E2
Kawerau, N. Zealand 100/F3
Kawhia, N. Zealand 100/E3
Kawhia (harb.), N. Zealand 100/E3
Kawi (mt.), Indonesia 85/K2
Kawich (peak), Nev. 266/E5
Kawich (range), Nev. 266/E5
Kawinaw (lake), Manitoba 179/C2
Kawio (isls.), Indonesia 85/H5
Kawkawlin, Mich. 250/F5
Kawlin, Burma 72/C2
Kawludo, Burma 72/C3
Kawthaung, Burma 72/C5
Kay (isl.), Alaska 196/K3
Kaw City, Okla. 288/M1
Kaya, Burkina Faso 106/D6
Kayah (state), Burma 72/C3
Kayak (isl.), Alaska 196/K3
Kayan (riv.), Indonesia 54/N9
Kayan (riv.), Indonesia 85/F5
Kaycee, Wyo. 319/F2
Kayenta, Ariz. 198/E2
Kayes, Mali 106/B6
Kayes, Mali 102/A3
Kayjay, Ky. 237/O7
Kaylor, Pa. 294/C4
Kaylor, S. Dak. 298/O7
Kayser (mts.), Suriname 131/C4
Kayseri (prov.), Turkey 63/F3
Kayseri, Turkey 59/C2
Kayseri, Turkey 63/F3
Kayseri, Turkey 54/E6
Kaysville, Utah 304/B2
Kayuagung, Indonesia 85/D6
Kayville, Sask. 181/F6
Kazabazua, Québec 172/A4
Kazakh, S.S.R., U.S.S.R. 54/H5
Kazakh, S.S.R., U.S.S.R. 48/G5
Kazan (riv.), N.W.T. 162/F3
Kazan (riv.), N.W. Terr. 187/H3
Kazan', U.S.S.R. 7/J3
Kazan', U.S.S.R. 48/F4
Kazan', U.S.S.R. 52/G3
Kazanli, Turkey 63/F4
Kazanlŭk, Bulgaria 45/G4
Kazan-retto (Volcano) (isls.), Japan 81/M4
Kazatin, U.S.S.R. 52/C5
Kazbek (mt.), U.S.S.R. 52/F6
Kazerun, Iran 66/G6
Kazerun, Iran 59/F4
Kazhim, U.S.S.R. 52/H2
Kazimierza Wielka, Poland 47/E3
Kazımkarabekir, Turkey 63/E4
Kazincbarcika, Hungary 41/F2
Kazlu-Rūda, U.S.S.R. 53/B3
Kazumba, Zaire 115/D5
Kazvin (Qazvin), Iran 66/F2
Kdyně, Czech. 41/B2
Kéa, Greece 45/G7
Kéa (isl.), Greece 45/G7
Keaau, Hawaii 188/G6
Keaau, Hawaii 218/J5
Keady, N. Ireland 17/H3
Keahi (pt.), Hawaii 218/F5
Keahole (pt.), Hawaii 218/F5
Kealaikahiki (chan.), Hawaii 218/H3
Kealakekua, Hawaii 218/G5
Kealakekua (bay), Hawaii 218/F6
Kealia, Hawaii, 218/G6
Kealia, Kauai, Hawaii 218/D1
Keams Canyon, Ariz. 198/E3
Keanae, Maui 218/K2
Keanapapa (pt.), Hawaii 218/G2
Keansburg, N.J. 273/E3
Kearney, Mo. 261/D4
Kearney, Nebr. 188/G2
Kearney, Nebr. 264/F4
Kearney (co.), Nebr. 264/F4
Kearney, Ontario 177/E2
Kearneysville, W. Va. 312/L4
Kearns, Utah 304/B3
Kearny (co.), Kansas 232/A3
Kearny, Ariz. 198/E5
Kearny, N.J. 273/B2
Kearny, Wyo. 319/F1
Kearsarge (mt.), N.H. 268/D5
Kearsarge, Mich. 250/B1
Kearsarge, Pa. 294/B1
Keasbey, N.J. 273/E2
Keatchie, La. 238/C2
Keating, Oreg. 291/K3
Keating Summit, Pa. 294/F2
Keatley, Sask. 181/D3
Keaton, Ky. 237/P5
Keats, Kansas 232/F2
Keats (isl.), W. Australia 92/A2
Keauhou, Hawaii 218/F5
Keaveny, Ky. 237/N6
Keawekaheka (pt.), Hawaii 218/F5
Keban, Turkey 63/H3

Kebang (mt.), S. Korea 81/D5
Ke Bao, Vietnam 72/E2
Kebbi (riv.), Nigeria 106/E6
Kebnekaise (mt.), Sweden 7/F2
Kebnekaise (mt.), Sweden 18/L3
Kebock (head), Scotland 15/B2
Kebumen, Indonesia 85/J2
Kechi, Kansas 232/E4
Kechika (riv.), Br. Col. 184/L2
Keçiborlu, Turkey 63/D4
Kecskemét, Hungary 7/F4
Kecskemét, Hungary 41/E3
Kedah (state), Malaysia 72/D6
Kedainiai, U.S.S.R. 53/C3
Keddie, Calif. 204/E3
Kedges (strs), Md. 245/O8
Kedgwick, New Bruns. 170/C1
Kedgwick Ouest, New Bruns. 170/C1
Kedgwick (riv.), New Bruns. 170/C1
Kedgwick River, New Bruns. 170/C1
Kediri, Indonesia 85/K2
Kédougou, Senegal 106/B6
Kedron (brook), Queensland 95/D2
Kedzierzyn-Koźle, Poland 47/C3
Keechelus (lake), Wash. 310/D3
Keedysville, Md. 245/H3
Keefers, Br. Col. 184/G5
Keefton, Okla. 288/N3
Keegan, Maine 243/G1
Keego Harbor, Mich. 250/F6
Keehi (lag.), Hawaii 218/B4
Keei, Hawaii 218/F6
Keel-Dooagh, Ireland 17/A4
Keele (peak), Yukon 187/E3
Keele (riv.), N.W. Terr. 187/F3
Keeler, Calif. 204/H7
Keeler, Sask. 181/F5
Keeline, Wyo. 319/H3
Keeling (Cocos) (isls.), Australia 2/P6
Keeling, Va. 307/K7
Keelung, China 77/K6
Keenan, W. Va. 312/F7
Keenan Siding, New Bruns. 170/E2
Keene, Calif. 204/G8
Keene, Ky. 237/M5
Keene, N.H. 268/C6
Keene, N.Y. 276/N2
Keene, N. Dak. 282/E4
Keene, Ohio 284/E5
Keene, Ontario 177/F3
Keene, Texas 303/G5
Keenes, Ill. 222/E5
Keener, Ala. 195/G2
Keenesburg, Colo. 208/L2
Keene Valley, N.Y. 276/N2
Keensburg, Ill. 222/F5
Keeny (hill), Ireland 17/E6
Keeper (hill), Ireland 17/E6
Keerweer (cape), Queensland 88/G2
Keerweer (cape), Queensland 95/B2
Keeseville, N.Y. 276/O2
Keesler A.F.B., Miss. 256/G10
Keetley, Utah 304/C3
Keetmanshoop, Namibia 118/B5
Keetmanshoop, Namibia 102/D7
Keewatin, Minn. 255/E3
Keewatin (reg.), N.W.T. 162/G3
Keewatin (reg.), N.W.T. 187/J3
Keewatin, Ontario 177/F5
Keewatin, Ontario 175/A3
Keewong, N.S. Wales 97/C3
Kefallinía (isl.), Greece 45/E6
Kefar Blum, Israel 65/D1
Kefar Gil'adi, Israel 65/C1
Kefar Ruppin, Israel 65/D3
Kefar Sava, Israel 65/B3
Kefar Vitkin, Israel 65/B3
Kefar Zekhariya, Israel 65/B4
Keffi, Nigeria 106/F7
Keflavík, Iceland 21/B1
Kégashka, Québec 174/E2
Kegley, W. Va. 312/D8
Kegonsa (lake), Wis. 317/H10
Keg River, Alberta 182/A5
Kehl, Germany 22/B4
Kehoe, Ky. 237/P4
Kehra, U.S.S.R. 53/C1
Keila, U.S.S.R. 53/C1
Keilor, Victoria 88/K7
Keilor, Victoria 97/H5
Keimoes, S. Africa 118/C5
Keirn, Miss. 256/D4
Keiser, Ark. 202/K2
Keiss, Scotland 15/E2
Keitele (lake), Finland 18/O5
Keith (co.), Nebr. 264/C3
Keith, Scotland 10/E2
Keith, Scotland 15/F2
Keith, S. Australia 94/G3
Keith, W. Va. 312/D8
Keith Arm (inlet), N.W. Terr. 187/F3
Keithley Creek, Br. Col. 184/G4
Keithsburg, Ill. 222/B2
Keith Sebelius (lake), Kansas 232/C2
Keithville, La. 238/C2
Keizer, Oreg. 291/A3
Kejimkujik (lake), Nova Scotia 168/C4
Kejimkujik Nat'l Park, Nova Scotia 168/C4
Kekaa (pt.), Hawaii 218/H2
Kekaha, Hawaii 188/D5
Kekaha, Hawaii 188/E5
Kekertaluk (isl.), N.W. Terr. 187/M3
Kékes (mt.), Hungary 41/E3
Kekoskee, Wis. 317/J8
Kelang, Malaysia 72/D7
Kelantan (state), Malaysia 72/D6
Kelantan, Sungai (riv.), Malaysia 72/D6
Kelasa (str.), Indonesia 85/D6
Keldron, S. Dak. 298/F2
Keldford, N.C. 281/P2
Kelheim, Germany 22/D4
Kelkit, Turkey 63/H2

Kelkit (riv.), Turkey 59/C1
Kelkit (riv.), Turkey 63/G2
Kell, Ill. 222/E5
Kellé, Congo 115/B4
Keller (lake), N.W. Terr. 187/F3
Keller, Texas 303/F2
Keller, Va. 307/S5
Keller, Wash. 310/G2
Kellerberrin, W. Australia 88/B6
Kellerberrin, W. Australia 92/B5
Kellerman, Ala. 195/D4
Kellerton, Iowa 229/E7
Kellettville, Iowa 229/E7
Kellett (cape), N.W.T. 162/D1
Kellett (cape), N.W. Terr. 187/F2
Kellett (str.), N.W. Terr. 187/G2
Kellettville, Pa. 294/D2
Kelley, Iowa 229/E5
Kelley (creek), Nev. 266/D1
Kelleys (isl.), Ohio 284/E2
Kelleys Island, Ohio 284/E2
Kelligrews, Newf. 166/D2
Kelliher, Minn. 255/D3
Kelliher, Sask. 181/H5
Kellnersville, Wis. 317/L7
Kellogg (mt.), Ariz. 198/E6
Kellogg, Idaho 220/B2
Kellogg, Iowa 229/H5
Kellogg, Minn. 255/G6
Kelloggsville, Ohio 284/J2
Kelloselkä, Finland 18/O3
Kells (Ceanannus Mór), Ireland 17/G4
Kells, Ireland 17/G6
Kells, N. Ireland 17/J2
Kelly, Georgia 217/E4
Kelly (creek), Idaho 220/C3
Kelly, Kansas 232/G2
Kelly, Ky. 237/D5
Kelly, La. 238/F3
Kelly, N.C. 281/N6
Kelly, Wyo. 319/B2
Kelly A.F.B., Texas 303/J11
Kelly Lake, Br. Col. 184/G4
Kelly Lake, Minn. 255/F3
Kellys, N. Dak. 282/K4
Kellyton, Ala. 195/F5
Kellyville, W. Va. 312/E8
Kelmė, U.S.S.R. 53/B3
Kélo, Chad 111/C6
Kélo, Chad 102/J4
Kelowna, Br. Col. 146/G4
Kelowna, Br. Col. 162/E6
Kelowna, Br. Col. 184/H5
Kelsey, Alberta 182/D3
Kelsey, Minn. 255/F3
Kelsey Bay, Br. Col. 184/D5
Kelseyville, Calif. 204/C5
Kelso, Ark. 202/H6
Kelso, Calif. 204/K8
Kelso, Mo. 261/O8
Kelso, Sask. 181/K6
Kelso, Scotland 10/F3
Kelso, Scotland 15/F5
Kelso, Tenn. 237/J10
Kelso, Wash. 310/D4
Kelstern, Sask. 181/E5
Kelston West, N. Zealand 100/B1
Keltie (cape), Ant. 5/C7
Kelty, Ky. 237/K6
Kelty, Scotland 10/C1
Kelty, Scotland 15/D1
Keluang, Malaysia 72/D7
Kelvington, Sask. 181/H3
Kelvin, Ariz. 198/E5
Kelwood, Manitoba 179/C4
Kem', U.S.S.R. 7/H2
Kem', U.S.S.R. 4/C8
Kem', U.S.S.R. 48/D3
Kem', U.S.S.R. 52/D2
Ké-Macina, Mali 106/C6
Kemah, Texas 303/K3
Kemah, Turkey 63/H3
Kemaliye, Turkey 63/H3
Kemalpaşa, Turkey 63/J2
Kemano, Br. Col. 184/D3
Kemasik, Malaysia 72/D6
Kembe, Cent. Afr. Rep. 115/D3
Kemble, Ontario 177/D3
Kemboma, Gabon 115/B3
Kemecse, Hungary 41/F2
Kemer, Turkey 63/D4
Kemerburgaz, Turkey 63/D5
Kemerovo, U.S.S.R. 54/K4
Kemerovo, U.S.S.R. 48/J4
Kemi, Finland 7/G2
Kemi, Finland 18/N4
Kemi (riv.), Finland 7/G2
Kemijärvi, Finland 18/P3
Kemijärvi (lake), Finland 18/O3
Kemijoki (riv.), Finland 18/P3
Kemikli, Büyük (cape), Turkey 63/B6
Kemirhisar, Turkey 63/F4
Kemmerer, Wyo. 319/B4
Kemnay, Manitoba 179/B5
Kemnay, Scotland 15/F3
Kemp, Ill. 222/E4
Kemp, Okla. 288/O7
Kemp, Texas 303/H5
Kemp (lake), Texas 303/E4
Kemp City (Hendrix), Okla. 288/O7
Kemp Coast (reg.), Ant. 5/C3
Kemper (co.), Miss. 256/G5
Kemp Mill, Md. 245/F3
Kempsey, N.S. Wales 88/J6
Kempsey, N.S. Wales 97/G2
Kempston, England 13/G5
Kempt, Nova Scotia 168/C4
Kempten, Germany 22/D5
Kempton, Ill. 222/E3
Kempton, Md. 245/A4
Kempton, N. Dak. 282/P4
Kempton, Pa. 294/L4
Kempton, Tasmania 99/D4

Kempton Park, S. Africa 118/J6
Kemptown, Md. 245/J3
Kemptown, Nova Scotia 168/E3
Kemptville, Nova Scotia 168/C4
Kemptville, Ontario 177/J2
Ken, Afghanistan 68/A2
Ken, Afghanistan 59/H3
Kenadsa, Algeria 106/D2
Kenai, Alaska 196/B1
Kenai (lake), Alaska 196/C1
Kenai (mt.), Alaska 195/C2
Kenai (pen.), Alaska 196/C2
Kenai Fjords Nat'l Park, Alaska 196/C2
Kenamu (riv.), Newf. 166/B3
Kenansville, Fla. 212/F4
Kenansville, N.C. 281/O5
Kenaston, N. Dak. 282/K3
Kenaston, Sask. 181/F4
Kenbridge, Va. 307/M7
Kendal, Barbados 161/B8
Kendal, England 13/E3
Kendal, England 10/E3
Kendal, Indonesia 85/J2
Kendal, Sask. 181/H5
Kendall, Fla. 212/B5
Kendall (co.), Ill. 222/E2
Kendall, Kansas 232/A4
Kendall, N.S. Wales 97/G2
Kendall, N.Y. 276/E4
Kendall (cape), N.W. Terr. 187/K3
Kendall (co.), Texas 3C3/F8
Kendall, Wash. 310/C2
Kendall, Wis. 317/F8
Kendall Park, N.J. 273/D3
Kendallville, Ind. 227/G2
Kendallville, Iowa 229/K2
Kendari, Indonesia 85/G6
Kendawangan, Indonesia 85/D6
Kendrapara, India 68/F4
Kendrick (peak), Ariz. 198/D3
Kendrick, Fla. 212/D2
Kendrick, Idaho 220/B3
Kendrick, Okla. 288/N3
Kenduskeag•, Maine 243/E6
Kenedy (co.), Texas 303/G11
Kenedy, Texas 303/G9
Kenefic, Okla. 288/O6
Kenel, S. Dak. 298/H2
Kenema, S. Leone 102/A4
Kenema, S. Leone 106/B7
Kenesaw, Nebr. 264/F4
Kengah (isls.), Indonesia 85/F7
Kenge, Zaire 115/C4
Keng Hkam, Burma 72/C2
Keng Tung, Burma 72/C2
Kenhardt, S. Africa 118/C5
Kenhorst, Pa. 294/L5
Kéniéba, Mali 106/B6
Kenilworth, England 13/F5
Kenilworth, Ill. 222/B5
Kenilworth, N.J. 273/E2
Kenilworth, Ontario 177/D4
Kenilworth, Utah 304/C4
Keningau, Malaysia 85/F4
Kenitra, Morocco 102/B1
Kenitra, Morocco 106/C2
Kenli, China 77/J4
Kenly, N.C. 281/N3
Kenmare, Ireland 10/B5
Kenmare, Ireland 17/B8
Kenmare (riv.), Ireland 17/A8
Kenmare, N. Dak. 282/G2
Kenmore, N.Y. 276/C5
Kenmore, Queensland 88/J3
Kenmore, Scotland 15/E4
Kenmore, Wash. 310/B1
Kenna, N. Mex. 274/F5
Kenna, W. Va. 312/C5
Kennan, Wis. 317/F5
Kennard, Ind. 227/G5
Kennard, Nebr. 264/H3
Kennard, Pa. 294/B3
Kennard, Texas 303/J6
Kennebago Lake, Maine 243/B5
Kennebec (co.), Maine 243/D7
Kennebec, Maine 243/D7
Kennebec, S. Dak. 298/K6
Kennebecasis (bay), New Bruns. 170/E2
Kennebecasis (riv.), New Bruns. 170/E2
Kennebunk, Maine 243/B9
Kennebunk•, Maine 243/B9
Kennebunk Beach, Maine 243/C9
Kennebunkport, Maine 243/C9
Kennebunkport•, Maine 243/C9
Kennedale, Texas 303/F2
Kennedy, Ala. 195/B3
Kennedy (Canaveral) (cape), Fla. 212/F3
Kennedy, Minn. 255/B2
Kennedy, N.Y. 276/B6
Kennedy (chan.), N.W.T. 162/N3
Kennedy (chan.), N.W. Terr. 187/M1
Kennedy, Sask. 181/J5
Kennedy Center, D.C. 245/A5
Kennedy Entrance (str.), Alaska 196/K3
Kennedyville, Md. 245/P3
Kenner, La. 238/N4
Kennesaw, Georgia 217/C2
Kennesaw Mtn. Nat'l Battlefield Park, Georgia 217/J1
Kennet (riv.), England 13/F6
Kennetcook, Nova Scotia 168/E3
Kennetcook (riv.), Nova Scotia 168/E3
Kenneth, Ind. 227/E3
Kenneth, Minn. 255/B7
Kennett, Mo. 261/M10
Kennett Square, Pa. 294/L6
Kennewick, Wash. 310/F4
Kenney (dam), Br. Col. 184/E3
Kenney (riv.), Ill. 222/D3
Kennisis (lake), Ontario 177/F2
Keno, Oreg. 291/F5
Kenogami (riv.), Ont. 162/H6
Kenogami (riv.), Ontario 177/H4
Kenogami (riv.), Ontario 175/C2
Kénogami (lake), Québec 172/F1

Keno Hill, Yukon 187/E3
Kenoma, Mo. 261/D8
Kenora, Ont. 146/J4
Kenora, Ont. 162/G5
Kenora (terr. dist.), Ontario 177/G5
Kenora (terr. dist.), Ontario 175/C2
Kenora, Ontario 175/B3
Kenora, Ontario 177/H4
Kenosee Park, Sask. 181/J6
Kenosha (co.), Wis. 317/K10
Kenosha, Wis. 317/M3
Kenova, W. Va. 312/A6
Kensal, N. Dak. 282/N5
Kenscoff, Haiti 158/C6
Kensett, Ark. 202/G3
Kensett, Iowa 229/G2
Kensington, Calif. 204/J2
Kensington, Conn. 210/D2
Kensington, Kansas 232/C2
Kensington, Md. 245/E4
Kensington, Minn. 255/C5
Kensington, N.S. Wales 97/J4
Kensington, Ohio 284/J4
Kensington, Pr. Edward I. 168/E2
Kensington and Chelsea, England 13/G8
Kensington and Chelsea, England 10/B5
Kensington and Norwood, S. Australia 88/E8
Kensington and Norwood, S. Australia 94/B8
Kent, Ala. 195/G5
Kent, Br. Col. 184/M3
Kent•, Conn. 210/B2
Kent (co.), Del. 245/R4
Kent (co.), England 13/H6
Kent, Ill. 222/D1
Kent, Ind. 227/F7
Kent, Iowa 229/E7
Kent (co.), Md. 245/O3
Kent (isl.), Md. 245/N5
Kent (pt.), Md. 245/N5
Kent (co.), Mich. 250/D5
Kent, Minn. 255/B4
Kent (co.), New Bruns. 170/E2
Kent (pen.), N.W. Terr. 187/H3
Kent, Ohio 284/H3
Kent (county), Ontario 177/B5
Kent, Oreg. 291/G2
Kent (co.), R.I. 249/H6
Kent (co.), Texas 303/D4
Kent, Texas 303/C11
Kent, Wash. 310/C3
Kentau, U.S.S.R. 48/G5
Kent Bridge, Ontario 177/B5
Kent City, Mich. 250/D5
Kent Furnace, Conn. 210/B2
Kent Group (isls.), Tasmania 99/D1
Kent Junction, New Bruns. 170/E2
Kent Lake, New Bruns. 170/E2
Kentland, Ind. 227/C3
Kenton, Del. 245/R4
Kenton (co.), Ky. 237/M3
Kenton, Ky. 237/N3
Kenton, Manitoba 179/B5
Kenton, Mich. 250/G2
Kenton, Ohio 284/C4
Kenton, Okla. 288/A1
Kenton, Tenn. 237/C8
Kenton Vale, Ky. 237/S2
Kents Hill, Maine 243/D7
Kents Store, Va. 307/M5
Kentuck, W. Va. 312/C5
Kentucky 188/J3
KENTUCKY 237
Kentucky (lake) 188/J3
Kentucky (dam), Ky. 237/E7
Kentucky (lake), Ky. 237/E8
Kentucky (riv.), Ky. 237/M3
Kentucky (lake), Tenn. 237/E8
Kentucky (state), U.S. 146/K6
Kentville, Nova Scotia 168/D3
Kentwood, La. 238/J5
Kentwood, Mich. 250/D6
Kenville, Manitoba 179/A3
Kenvir, Ky. 237/P7
Kenwood, Georgia 217/D3
Kenwood, Okla. 288/S2
Kenya 2/L5
Kenya 102/F4
KENYA 115/G3
Kenya (mt.), Kenya 102/F4
Kenya (mt.), Kenya 115/G4
Kenyon, Minn. 255/C6
Kenyon, R.I. 249/H7
Kenyonville, Conn. 210/G1
Keo, Ark. 202/G4
Keokea, Hawaii, Hawaii 218/G6
Keokea, Maui, Hawaii 218/J2
Keokee, Va. 307/C7
Keokuk (co.), Iowa 229/J6
Keokuk, Iowa 188/H2
Keokuk, Iowa 229/L8
Keoma, Alberta 182/D4
Keomah, Iowa 229/J6
Keomuku, Hawaii 218/H2
Keonjhar, India 68/F4
Keosauqua, Iowa 229/J7
Keota, Colo. 208/L1
Keota, Iowa 229/K6
Keota, Okla. 288/S4
Keowee (lake), S.C. 296/B2
Keowee (riv.), S.C. 296/B2
Kepez, Turkey 63/B6
Kepi, Indonesia 85/K7
Kępno, Poland 47/C3
Keppel (harb.), Singapore 72/F6
Kepsut, Turkey 63/C3
Kerala (state), India 68/D6
Kerama (isls.), Japan 81/M6
Kerang, Victoria 97/B4
Kerava, Finland 18/O6
Kerby, Oreg. 291/C6
Kerch', U.S.S.R. 7/H4
Kerch', U.S.S.R. 52/E5
Kerchoual, Mali 106/E5
Kerema, Papua N.G. 85/B7
Keremeos, Br. Col. 184/G5

Kerempe (cape), Turkey 63/E1
Keren, Ethiopia 59/C6
Keren, Ethiopia 111/G4
Kerens, Texas 303/H5
Kerens, W. Va. 312/G4
Keret', U.S.S.R. 52/D1
Kerguélen (isl.), Fr. 2/N8
Kerhonkson, N.Y. 276/M7
Kericho, Kenya 115/F4
Kerinci (mt.), Indonesia 85/C6
Keriya (Yutian), China 77/B4
Keriya He (riv.), China 77/B4
Keriya Shankou (pass), China 77/B4
Kerkdriel, Netherlands 27/G5
Kerkennah (isls.), Tunisia 106/G2
Kerkhoven, Minn. 255/C5
Kerki, U.S.S.R. 48/G6
Kérkira, Greece 45/D6
Kérkira (isl.), Greece 7/F5
Kérkira (isl.), Greece 45/D6
Kerkrade, Netherlands 27/J7
Kerlin, Ark. 202/D7
Kerma, Sudan 111/F4
Kerma, Sudan 59/B6
Kermadec (isls.), N. Zealand 2/T7
Kermadec (isls.), N. Zealand 87/J9
Kerman, Calif. 204/E7
Kerman (prov.), Iran 66/K6
Kerman, Iran 54/G6
Kerman, Iran 59/G3
Kerman, Iran 66/K5
Kerme (gulf), Turkey 63/B4
Kermit, Texas 303/B6
Kermit, W. Va. 312/B7
Kern (co.), Calif. 204/G8
Kern (riv.), Calif. 204/G8
Kernan, Ill. 222/E2
Kernersville, N.C. 281/J2
Kerns, Switzerland 39/F3
Kernville, Calif. 204/G8
Kernville, Oreg. 291/C3
Kérouané, Guinea 106/C7
Kerr (lake), Fla. 212/E2
Kerr, N.C. 281/N5
Kerr, W. Scott (res.), N.C. 281/G2
Kerr, Robert S. (res.), Okla. 288/S4
Kerr (co.), Texas 303/E7
Kerrera (isl.), Scotland 15/C4
Kerrick, Minn. 255/F4
Kerrick, Texas 303/B1
Kerrobert, Sask. 181/C4
Kerrville, Tenn. 237/B10
Kerrville, Texas 303/E7
Kerry (co.), Ireland 17/B7
Kerry (head), Ireland 17/A7
Kerry, Wales 13/D5
Kersey, Colo. 208/L2
Kersey, Ind. 227/C2
Kersey, Pa. 294/E3
Kershaw (co.), S.C. 296/F3
Kershaw, S.C. 296/G2
Kersley, Br. Col. 184/F4
Kerteminde, Denmark 21/D7
Kerulen (riv.), 54/N5
Kerulen (riv.), Mongolia 77/H2
Kerwood, Ontario 177/C5
Kerzaz, Algeria 106/D3
Kerzers, Switzerland 39/D3
Kesagami (lake), Ontario 175/E2
Keşan, Turkey 63/B2
Keşap, Turkey 63/H2
Kesch (peak), Switzerland 39/J3
Kesennuma, Japan 81/K4
Kesgrave, England 13/J5
Kesh, N. Ireland 17/F3
Keshena, Wis. 317/J6
Keşiş Tepesi (mt.), Turkey 63/H3
Keskin, Turkey 63/E3
Keski-Suomi (prov.), Finland 18/O5
Kesley, Iowa 229/H3
Kessel, W. Va. 312/H4
Kesten'ga, U.S.S.R. 52/D1
Kesteren, Netherlands 27/G5
Keswick, England 13/D3
Keswick, England 10/E3
Keswick, Iowa 229/J6
Keswick, New Bruns. 170/D3
Keswick (riv.), New Bruns. 170/C2
Keswick, Ontario 177/E3
Keswick, Va. 307/M4
Keswick Grove, N.J. 273/E4
Keszthely, Hungary 41/D3
Keta, Ghana 106/E7
Ketapang, Indonesia 85/E6
Ketchen, Sask. 181/J3
Ketch Harbour, Nova Scotia 168/E4
Ketchikan, Alaska 146/E4
Ketchikan, Alaska 188/E6
Ketchikan, Alaska 196/N2
Ketchum, Idaho 220/D6
Ketchum, Okla. 288/R1
Kétegyháza, Hungary 41/F3
Kete Krachi, Ghana 106/E7
Kętrzyn, Poland 47/E1
Kettering, England 13/G5
Kettering, England 10/F4
Kettering, Ohio 284/B6
Kettering, Tasmania 99/D5
Kettle (riv.), Br. Col. 184/H5
Kettle (riv.), Minn. 255/F4
Kettle (pt.), Ontario 177/B4
Kettle (riv.), Wash. 310/G2
Kettle Falls, Wash. 310/H2
Kettleman City, Calif. 204/E7
Kettle River, Minn. 255/F4
Kettle River (range), Wash. 310/G2
Kettlersville, Ohio 284/B5
Kettle Valley, Br. Col. 184/H5
Keuka, Lake, N.Y. 276/F5
Keuka Park, N.Y. 276/F5
Keuterville, Idaho 220/B3
Kevelaer, Germany 22/B3
Kevil, Ky. 237/D6
Kevin, Mont. 262/D2
Kevisville, Alberta 182/C4
Kew, Victoria 98/L7
Kew, Victoria 97/J5
Kewa, Wash. 310/G2

Kewanee, Ill. 222/C2
Kewanee, Miss. 256/H6
Kewanee, Mo. 261/N9
Kewanna, Ind. 227/E2
Kewaskum, Wis. 317/K8
Kewaunee (co.), Wis. 317/L6
Kewaunee, Wis. 317/M7
Keweenaw (co.), Mich. 250/A1
Keweenaw (bay), Mich. 250/A1
Keweenaw (pt.), Mich. 250/B1
Keweenaw Bay, Mich. 250/G1
Key, Ala. 195/G2
Key (lake), Ireland 17/E3
Keya Paha (co.), Nebr. 264/E2
Keya Paha (riv.), Nebr. 264/D1
Keyapaha, S. Dak. 298/J7
Keya Paha (riv.), S. Dak. 298/K7
Key Biscayne, Fla. 212/B5
Key Colony Beach, Fla. 212/F7
Keyes, Calif. 204/E6
Keyes, Manitoba 179/C4
Keyes, Okla. 288/B1
Keyesport, Ill. 222/D5
Keyhole (res.), Wyo. 319/H1
Key Largo, Fla. 212/F6
Key Largo (key), Fla. 212/F6
Keymar, Md. 245/K2
Keynsham, England 13/E6
Keyport, N.J. 273/E3
Keyport, Wash. 310/A2
Keysbrook, W. Australia 88/B3
Keyser, W. Va. 312/J4
Keyser, Iowa 229/J5
Keystone, Ind. 227/G3
Keystone, Iowa 229/J5
Keystone, Nebr. 264/C3
Keystone (res.), Ohio 284/K2
Keystone (lake), Okla. 288/O2
Keystone, S. Dak. 298/C6
Keystone, W. Va. 312/D8
Keystone Heights, Fla. 212/E2
Keystown, Sask. 181/F5
Keysville, Georgia 217/H4
Keysville, Va. 307/M6
Keytesville, Mo. 261/G4
Key Vaca (key), Fla. 212/E7
Key West, Fla. 146/K7
Key West, Fla. 188/K6
Key West, Fla. 212/E7
Key West Naval Air Sta., Fla. 212/E7
Kezar (lake), Maine 243/B7
Kezar (pond), Maine 243/B7
Kezar Falls, Maine 243/B8
Kežmarok, Czech. 41/F2
Khabake (Habahe), China 77/C2
Khabarovsk, U.S.S.R. 54/P5
Khabarovsk (co.), U.S.S.R. 2/R3
Khabarovsk, U.S.S.R. 48/O5
Khabur (riv.), Syria 63/J5
Khabur (riv.), Syria 59/D2
Khachmas, U.S.S.R. 52/G6
Khadyzhensk, U.S.S.R. 52/E6
Khaf, Iran 66/L3
Khaibar, 'Asir, Saudi Arabia 59/D6
Khaibar, Hejaz, Saudi Arabia 59/C4
Khairpur, Pakistan 68/B3
Khairpur, Pakistan 59/K4
Khakass Aut. Obl., U.S.S.R. 48/J4
Khalkhal, Iran 66/F2
Khálki (isl.), Greece 45/H7
Khalkis, Greece 45/F6
Khal'mer-Yu, U.S.S.R. 52/K1
Khaluf, Oman 59/G5
Khamgaon, India 68/D4
Khamis Mushait, Saudi Arabia 59/D6
Khamkeut, Laos 72/E3
Khamman, India 68/D5
Khanabad, Afghanistan 59/J2
Khanabad, Afghanistan 68/B1
Khanaqin, Iraq 59/D3
Khanaqin, Iraq 66/D3
Khancoban, N.S. Wales 97/E5
Khandwa, India 68/D4
Khandyga, U.S.S.R. 48/O3
Khan esh Shamat, Syria 63/G6
Khanewal, Pakistan 68/C2
Khanh Hoa, Vietnam 72/F4
Khanh Hung, Vietnam 72/E5
Khaniá, Greece 45/G8
Khaniá, Greece 7/G5
Khaniá (gulf), Greece 45/G8
Khanka (lake) 54/P5
Khanka (lake), China 77/M3
Khanka (lake), U.S.S.R. 48/O5
Khanpur, Pakistan 68/C3
Khanpur, Pakistan 59/K4
Khan Sheikhun, Syria 63/G5
Khanty-Mansi Aut. Okr., U.S.S.R. 48/H3
Khanty-Mansiysk, U.S.S.R. 54/J3
Khanty-Mansiysk, U.S.S.R. 48/H3
Khanu, Thailand 72/C3
Khan Yunis, Gaza Strip 65/A5
Khao Luang (mt.), Burma 72/C5
Khao Luang (mt.), Thailand 72/C5
Khapcheranga, U.S.S.R. 48/M5
Kharagpur, India 68/F4
Kharan, Pakistan 59/J4
Kharan Kalat, Pakistan 68/A3
Kharas, West Bank 65/C4
Kharasavey (cape), U.S.S.R. 48/G2
Khardah, India 68/F1
Khârga (oasis), Egypt 111/F2
Khârga (oasis), Egypt 59/B4
Khark (Kharg) (isl.), Iran 66/F5
Khark (Kharg) (isl.), Iran 66/G6
Khar'kov, U.S.S.R. 7/H4
Khar'kov, U.S.S.R. 2/L3
Khar'kov, U.S.S.R. 52/E5
Khar'kov, U.S.S.R. 48/D4
Kharmanli, Bulgaria 45/H5
Kharovsk, U.S.S.R. 48/D3
Kharovsk, U.S.S.R. 52/F3
Khartoum (prov.), Sudan 111/F4
Khartoum, Sudan 2/L5
Khartoum (cap.), Sudan 59/B6
Khartoum (cap.), Sudan 111/F4
Khartoum (cap.), Sudan 102/F3
Khartoum North, Sudan 102/F3

Khartoum North, Sudan 59/B6
Khartoum North, Sudan 111/F4
Khasab, Oman 59/G4
Khasavyurt, U.S.S.R. 52/G6
Khash, Afghanistan 68/A2
Khash, Afghanistan 59/H3
Khash, Iran 59/H4
Khash, Iran 66/M6
Khashm el Girba, Sudan 111/G5
Khashuri, U.S.S.R. 52/F6
Khasi (hills), India 68/G3
Khaskovo, Bulgaria 45/G5
Khatanga, U.S.S.R. 4/B4
Khatanga, U.S.S.R. 54/M2
Khatanga, U.S.S.R. 48/L2
Khatuniye, Syria 63/J4
Khay, Saudi Arabia 59/D6
Khedive, Sask. 181/G6
Khemis Miliana, Algeria 106/E1
Khemmarat, Thailand 72/E4
Khenifra, Morocco 106/C2
Kherson, U.S.S.R. 7/H4
Kherson, U.S.S.R. 48/D5
Kherson, U.S.S.R. 52/D5
Khe Sanh, Vietnam 72/E3
Kheta (riv.), U.S.S.R. 48/K2
Khilok, U.S.S.R. 48/M4
Khíos, Greece 45/G6
Khíos (isl.), Greece 45/G6
Khirbet Qumran (site), Jordan 65/D4
Khiva, U.S.S.R. 48/F5
Khiyav, Iran 66/E1
Khmel'nitskiy, U.S.S.R. 7/G4
Khmel'nitskiy, U.S.S.R. 52/C5
Khoai, Hon (isl.), Vietnam 72/E5
Khodzheyli, U.S.S.R. 48/F5
Kholm, Afghanistan 68/B1
Kholm, Afghanistan 59/J2
Kholm, U.S.S.R. 52/D3
Kholmsk, U.S.S.R. 48/P5
Khoman, Iran 66/F2
Khomeinshar, Iran 66/G4
Khon Kaen, Thailand 72/D3
Khoper (riv.), U.S.S.R. 52/F4
Khorasan (prov.), Iran 66/K3
Khoreyver, U.S.S.R. 52/J1
Khorixas, Namibia 118/A4
Khorog, U.S.S.R. 48/H6
Khorol, U.S.S.R. 52/D4
Khorramabad, Iran 59/E3
Khorramabad, Iran 66/F4
Khorramshahr, Iran 59/E3
Khorramshahr, Iran 66/F5
Khotan (Hotan), China 77/B4
Khotin, U.S.S.R. 52/C5
Khouribga, Morocco 106/C2
Khowst, Afghanistan 68/B2
Khromtau, U.S.S.R. 48/F4
Khuaf, Iran 66/L3
Khugiani, Afghanistan 68/B2
Khugiani, Afghanistan 59/J3
Khuis, Botswana 118/C5
Khu Khan, Thailand 72/E4
Khulna, Bangladesh 68/F4
Khurda, India 68/F4
Khurma, Saudi Arabia 59/D5
Khusf Rud (riv.), Iran 66/L4
Khushab, Pakistan 68/C2
Khust, U.S.S.R. 52/B5
Khuzdar, Pakistan 59/J4
Khuzestan (prov.), Iran 66/F5
Khvaf, Iran 66/L3
Khvalynsk, U.S.S.R. 52/G4
Khvojeh Lak, Kuh-e (mt.), Iran 66/E3
Khvonsar, Iran 66/F4
Khvor, Iran 66/H5
Khvor, Iran 66/J4
Khvoy, Iran 59/E2
Khvoy (Khoi), Iran 66/D1
Khwae Noi, Mae Nam (riv.), Thailand 72/C4
Khyber (pass) 54/J6
Khyber (pass), Pakistan 59/K3
Khyber (pass), Pakistan 68/C2
Kia, Solomon Is. 86/D2
Kiahsville, W. Va. 312/B6
Kiama, N.S. Wales 97/F4
Kiamba, Philippines 82/E8
Kiambi, Zaire 115/E5
Kiambu, Kenya 115/G4
Kiamichi (mts.), Okla. 288/R5
Kiamichi (riv.), Okla. 288/R5
Kiamika, Québec 172/B3
Kiamika (lake), Québec 172/B3
Kiamusze (Jiamusi), China 77/M2
Kian (Ji'an), China 77/J6
Kiana, Alaska 196/F1
Kiangsi (Jiangxi), China 77/K5
Kiangsu (Jiangsu), China 77/K5
Kiantajärvi (lake), Finland 18/Q4
Kiáton, Greece 45/F6
Kiawah (isl.), S.C. 296/G6
Kibaek, Denmark 21/B5
Kibangou, Congo 115/B4
Kibara, Tanzania 115/F4
Kibaya, Tanzania 115/G5
Kibbee, Georgia 217/H6
Kibler, Ark. 202/B3
Kibombo, Zaire 115/E4
Kibondo, Tanzania 115/F4
Kibre Mengist, Ethiopia 111/G6
Kibwezi, Kenya 115/G4
Kičevo, Yugoslavia 45/E5
Kickapoo (riv.), Wis. 317/E9
Kickapoo Ind. Res., Kansas 232/G2
Kickinghorse (pass), Alberta 182/B4
Kicking Horse (pass), Br. Col. 184/J4
Kidal, Mali 107/F4
Kidal, Mali 106/E5
Kidapawan, Philippines 82/E7
Kidder, Mo. 261/D3
Kidder (co.), N. Dak. 282/L6
Kidder, S. Dak. 298/O2
Killala, Ireland 17/C3

Kidderminster, England 10/G3
Kidderminster, England 13/E5
Kidepo Nat'l Park, Uganda 115/F3
Kidnappers (cape), N. Zealand 100/F3
Kidron, Ohio 284/G4
Kidsgrove, England 13/E4
Kidwelly, Wales 13/C6
Kidwelly, Wales 10/D5
Kief, N. Dak. 282/J4
Kiefer, Okla. 288/O3
Kieffer, W. Va. 312/E7
Kiel, Germany 7/E3
Kiel, Germany 22/D1
Kiel (bay), Germany 22/D1
Kiel (Nord-Ostsee) (canal), Germany 22/C1
Kiel, Wis. 317/L8
Kielce (prov.), Poland 47/E3
Kielce, Poland 47/E3
Kielce, Poland 7/G3
Kieler, Wis. 317/E10
Kien Hung, Vietnam 72/E5
Kienyang (Qianyang), China 77/H6
Kiester, Minn. 255/E7
Kieta, Papua N.G. 86/C2
Kieta, Papua N.G. 87/F6
Kiev, U.S.S.R. 2/L3
Kiev, U.S.S.R. 7/H3
Kiev, U.S.S.R. 48/D4
Kiev, U.S.S.R. 52/D4
Kiev (res.), U.S.S.R. 52/C4
Kiffa, Mauritania 106/B5
Kifri, Iraq 66/D3
Kigali (cap.), Rwanda 115/F4
Kigali (cap.), Rwanda 102/F5
Kiger (creek), Oreg. 291/J5
Kiği, Turkey 63/J3
Kiglapait (cape), Newf. 166/B2
Kiglapait (mts.), Newf. 166/B2
Kigoma (reg.), Tanzania 115/E5
Kigoma-Ujiji, Tanzania 115/E4
Kigoma-Ujiji, Tanzania 102/F5
Kihei, Hawaii 218/J2
Kihnu (isl.), U.S.S.R. 53/B1
Kiholo, Hawaii 218/G4
Kiholo (bay), Hawaii 218/F4
Kii (chan.), Japan 81/G7
Kiiminki, Finland 18/P4
Kikai (isl.), Japan 81/O5
Kikiktaksoak (isl.), Newf. 166/B2
Kikinda, Yugoslavia 45/E3
Kikino, Alberta 182/D2
Kikkertavak (isl.), Newf. 166/B2
Kikoira, N.S. Wales 97/D3
Kikonai, Japan 81/K3
Kikori, Papua N.G. 85/B7
Kikwit, Zaire 115/C5
Kikwit, Zaire 102/D5
Kila, Mont. 262/B2
Kilafors, Sweden 18/K6
Kilauea, Hawaii 218/B1
Kilauea, Hawaii 218/C1
Kilauea (crater), Hawaii 218/H6
Kilauea (pt.), Hawaii 218/C1
Kilbaha, Ireland 17/B6
Kilbarchan, Scotland 15/A2
Kilbeggan, Ireland 17/G5
Kilbirnie, Scotland 15/A2
Kilbourne, Ill. 222/D3
Kilbourne, La. 238/H1
Kilbrannan (sound), Scotland 15/C5
Kilbride, Newf. 166/D2
Kilbuck (mts.), Alaska 196/G2
Kilburn, New Bruns. 170/C2
Kilcar, Ireland 17/D2
Kilchoan, Scotland 15/B4
Kilchu, N. Korea 81/D3
Kilcock, Ireland 17/H5
Kilconnell, Ireland 17/E5
Kilcoole, Ireland 17/K5
Kilcormac, Ireland 17/G5
Kilcoy, Queensland 95/E5
Kilcullen, Ireland 17/H5
Kildare, Georgia 217/K5
Kildare (co.), Ireland 17/H5
Kildare, Ireland 10/C4
Kildare, Ireland 17/H5
Kildare, Okla. 288/M1
Kildare (cape), Pr. Edward I. 168/E2
Kildare, Texas 303/K5
Kildeer, Ill. 222/A5
Kildonan, Br. Col. 184/E5
Kildonan, Scotland 15/E2
Kildonan, Zimbabwe 118/E3
Kildurk, North. Terr. 93/A4
Kildysart, Ireland 17/C5
Kilembe, Uganda 115/F3
Kilembe, Zaire 115/C5
Kilfenora, Ireland 17/C5
Kilfinane, Ireland 17/D7
Kilgarvan, Ireland 17/B8
Kilgore, Idaho 220/F5
Kilgore, Nebr. 264/D1
Kilgore, Ohio 284/H5
Kilgore, Texas 303/K5
Kili (isl.), Marshall Is. 87/G5
Kilifi, Kenya 115/H4
Kilimanjaro (reg.), Tanzania 115/G4
Kilimanjaro (mt.), Tanzania 102/F5
Kilimanjaro (mt.), Tanzania 115/G4
Kilimli, Turkey 63/D2
Kilinailau (isls.), Papua N.G. 86/C2
Kilingi-Nõmme, U.S.S.R. 53/C1
Kilis, Turkey 63/G4
Kilitbahir, Turkey 63/B6
Kiliya, U.S.S.R. 52/C5
Kilkee, Ireland 10/B4
Kilkee, Ireland 17/B6
Kilkeel, N. Ireland 17/K3
Kilkelly, Ireland 17/D4
Kilkenny (co.), Ireland 17/G6
Kilkenny, Ireland 17/H6
Kilkenny, Ireland 17/G6
Kilkenny, Minn. 255/E6
Kilkieran (bay), Ireland 17/B5
Kilkis, Greece 45/F5
Killala, Ireland 17/C3

Killala (bay), Ireland 17/C3
Killaloe, Ireland 10/B4
Killaloe, Ireland 17/D6
Killaloe Station, Ontario 177/G2
Killaly, Sask. 181/J5
Killam, Alberta 182/E3
Killam, New Bruns. 170/E2
Killarney, Ireland 10/B4
Killarney, Ireland 17/C7
Killarney (lakes), Ireland 10/B4
Killarney, Man. 162/G6
Killarney, Manitoba 179/C5
Killarney, North. Terr. 93/B2
Killarney, Ontario 177/C2
Killarney Prov. Park, Ontario 177/C1
Killary (harb.), Ireland 17/A4
Killavullen, Ireland 17/D7
Killbear Point Prov. Park, Ontario 177/D2
Kill Buck, N.Y. 276/C6
Killbuck, Ohio 284/G5
Killbuck (creek), Ohio 284/G4
Killdeer, N. Dak. 282/E5
Killdeer, Sask. 181/E6
Kill Devil Hills, N.C. 281/T3
Killduff, Iowa 229/H5
Killearn, Scotland 15/B1
Killeen, Texas 303/G6
Killen, Ala. 195/D1
Killenaule, Ireland 17/F6
Killeshandra, Ireland 17/F3
Killian, La. 238/M2
Killimor, Ireland 17/E5
Killin, Scotland 15/B4
Killinaboy, Ireland 17/C6
Killingly•, Conn. 210/H1
Killington, Vt. 268/B4
Killington (peak), Vt. 268/B4
Killingworth•, Conn. 210/E3
Killona, Ireland 17/G5
Killorglin, Ireland 17/B7
Killough, N. Ireland 17/K3
Killucan-Rathwire, Ireland 17/G4
Kill Van Kull (str.), N.J. 273/B2
Killybegs, Ireland 17/E2
Killyclogher, N. Ireland 17/G2
Killyleagh, N. Ireland 17/K3
Kilmacolm, Scotland 15/A2
Kilmacrennan, Ireland 17/F1
Kilmacthomas, Ireland 17/G7
Kilmallock, Ireland 17/D7
Kilmarnock, Scotland 15/D5
Kilmarnock, Scotland 10/D5
Kilmarnock, Va. 307/R5
Kilmaurs, Scotland 15/D5
Kilmeadan, Ireland 17/G7
Kilmichael, Miss. 256/E4
Kilmihill, Ireland 17/C6
Kilmoganny, Ireland 17/G6
Kilmore, Victoria 97/C5
Kilmore Quay, Ireland 17/H7
Kilmurry, Ireland 17/C6
Kiln, Miss. 256/F10
Kilnaleck, Ireland 17/G4
Kilninver, Scotland 15/C4
Kilo, Zaire 115/E3
Kilombero (riv.), Tanzania 115/G5
Kilosa, Tanzania 115/G5
Kilpisjärvi (lake), Finland 18/M2
Kilpisjärvi (lake), Sweden 18/M2
Kilrea, N. Ireland 17/H3
Kilrenny and Anstruther, Scotland 15/F4
Kilrenny and Anstruther, Scotland 10/E2
Kilronan, Ireland 17/B5
Kilrush, Ireland 10/B4
Kilrush, Ireland 17/C6
Kilsheelan, Ireland 17/F7
Kilsyth, Scotland 15/B1
Kilsyth, Scotland 10/B1
Kilsyth, W. Va. 312/D7
Kiltan (isl.), India 68/C6
Kiltimagh, Ireland 17/C4
Kilwa, Zaire 115/E5
Kilwa Kivinje, Tanzania 115/G5
Kilwa Masoko, Tanzania 115/G5
Kilwinning, Sask. 181/E2
Kilwinning, Scotland 15/D5
Kilworth, Ireland 17/E7
Kilyos, Turkey 63/D5
Kim, Colo. 208/N8
Kimba, S. Australia 88/F6
Kimba, S. Australia 94/E5
Kimball (mt.), Alaska 196/K2
Kimball, Alberta 182/D5
Kimball, Kansas 232/G4
Kimball, Minn. 255/D5
Kimball (co.), Nebr. 264/A3
Kimball, Nebr. 264/A3
Kimball, S. Dak. 298/M6
Kimball, Tenn. 237/K10
Kimball, W. Va. 312/C8
Kimballton, Iowa 229/D5
Kimballton, Va. 307/G6
Kimbe, Papua N.G. 86/B2
Kimbe, Papua N.G. 87/F6
Kimberley, Br. Col. 184/K5
Kimberley, S. Africa 102/E7
Kimberley, S. Africa 118/D5
Kimberley (plat.), W. Australia 88/D3
Kimberley (plat.), W. Australia 92/D2
Kimberley Research Station, W. Australia 88/D3
Kimberling City, Mo. 261/F9
Kimberlin Heights, Tenn. 237/O9
Kimberly, Ala. 195/E3
Kimberly, Idaho 220/D7
Kimberly, Minn. 255/F5
Kimberly, Oreg. 291/H3
Kimberly, Wis. 317/K7
Kimble (co.), Texas 303/E7
Kimbolton, Ohio 284/G6
Kimbrough, Ala. 195/C6
Kimch'aek, N. Korea 81/D3
Kimch'ŏn, S. Korea 81/D5
Kimesville, N.C. 281/L3
Kimhae, Pakistan 81/D6

Kími, Greece 45/F6
Kimitsu, Japan 81/O3
Kimiwan (lake), Alberta 182/B2
Kimje, S. Korea 81/C6
Kimmell, Ind. 227/F2
Kimmins, Tenn. 237/F9
Kímolos (isl.), Greece 45/G7
Kimovsk, U.S.S.R. 52/E3
Kimry, U.S.S.R. 52/E3
Kimsquit, Br. Col. 184/D4
Kinabalu (mt.), Malaysia 85/F4
Kinalı (isl.), Turkey 63/D6
Kinalung, N.S. Wales 97/B3
Kinango, Kenya 115/G4
Kinard, Fla. 212/D6
Kinards, S.C. 296/D3
Kinbasket (lake), Br. Col. 184/H4
Kinbrace, Scotland 15/E2
Kinbrae, Minn. 255/C7
Kinburn, Ontario 177/H2
Kincaid, Ill. 222/D4
Kincaid, Kansas 232/G3
Kincaid, Sask. 181/D6
Kincardine, Ontario 177/C3
Kincardine, Scotland 10/B1
Kincardine, Scotland 15/C1
Kincheloe (pt.), Oreg. 291/C2
Kincheloe, W. Va. 312/E4
Kincolith, Br. Col. 184/B2
Kincraig, Scotland 15/E3
Kinda, Zaire 115/D5
Kindama, Congo 115/C4
Kindberg, Austria 41/C3
Kinde, Mich. 250/D4
Kinder, La. 238/E6
Kinderhook, Ill. 222/B4
Kinderhook, N.Y. 276/N6
Kindersley, Sask. 162/F5
Kindersley, Sask. 181/B4
Kindia, Guinea 106/B6
Kindia, Guinea 102/A3
Kindred, N. Dak. 282/R6
Kinel, U.S.S.R. 52/H4
Kinel' (riv.), U.S.S.R. 52/H4
Kineshma, U.S.S.R. 7/J3
Kineshma, U.S.S.R. 52/F3
King (isl.), Alaska 196/C4
King (isl.), Australia 87/E10
King (isl.), Br. Col. 184/D4
King, Ky. 237/O7
King (pt.), N.S. Wales 97/J2
King (cays), Nicaragua 154/F4
King, N.C. 281/J2
King (isl.), Tasmania 88/G7
King (isl.), Tasmania 99/A1
King (riv.), Tasmania 99/B4
King (co.), Texas 303/D4
King (co.), Wash. 310/D3
King (sound), W. Australia 88/C3
King (sound), W. Australia 92/C2
King, Wis. 317/H7
King and Queen (co.), Va. 307/P5
King and Queen Court House, Va.
  307/P5
Kingaroy, Queensland 95/D5
Kingaroy, Queensland 88/J5
King Christian (isl.), N.W. Terr.
  187/H2
King Christian IX Land (reg.), Greenl.
  4/C11
King Christian IX Land (reg.), Greenland
  146/Q3
King Christian X Land (reg.), Greenl.
  4/B11
King Christian X Land (reg.), Greenland
  146/R2
King City, Calif. 204/D7
King City, Mo. 261/D2
King City, Ontario 177/J3
King City, Oreg. 291/A2
Kingcome Inlet, Br. Col. 184/D4
King Cove, Alaska 196/F4
Kingdom City, Mo. 261/J5
King Ferry, N.Y. 276/G5
Kingfield•, Maine 243/C6
Kingfisher (co.), Okla. 288/L3
Kingfisher, Okla. 288/L3
King Frederik VI Coast (reg.), Greenland
  146/P3
King Frederik VIII Land (reg.), Greenl.
  4/B11
King Frederik VIII Land (reg.),
  Greenland 146/R2
King George (isl.), Ant. 5/C16
King George (isls.), N.W. Terr. 187/L4
King George (co.), Va. 307/O4
King George, Va. 307/O4
King Hill, Idaho 220/C6
Kinghorn, Scotland 15/D1
Kingisepp (Kuressaare), U.S.S.R. 53/B1
King Leopold (range), W. Australia
  88/D3
King Leopold (range), W. Australia
  92/D2
Kingman, Alberta 182/D3
Kingman, Ariz. 198/A3
Kingman, Ind. 227/C5
Kingman (co.), Kansas 232/D4
Kingman, Kansas 232/D4
Kingman, Maine 243/G4
Kingman (reef), Pacific 87/K5
Kingoonya, S. Australia 88/E6
Kingoonyah, S. Australia 94/C4
Kings (co.), Calif. 204/G4
Kings (riv.), Calif. 204/F7
Kings (riv.), Nev. 266/C1
King's (co.), New Bruns. 170/E3
Kings (co.), N.Y. 276/N9
Kings (co.), Nova Scotia 168/D4
Kings (co.), Pr. Edward I. 168/F2
Kings (peak), Utah 304/E3
King Salmon, Alaska 196/G3
Kings Beach, Calif. 204/F4
Kingsbridge, England 13/D7
Kingsburg, Calif. 204/F7
Kingsburg, S.C. 296/H4
Kingsburg, S. Dak. 298/O8

Kingsbury, Ind. 227/D1
Kingsbury•, Maine 243/D5
Kingsbury (pond), Maine 243/D5
Kingsbury, Québec 172/E4
Kingsbury (co.), S. Dak. 298/O5
Kingsbury, Texas 303/G8
Kingsclear, New Bruns. 170/D3
Kingscliff, N.S. Wales 97/J1
Kingscote, S. Australia 88/F7
Kingscote, S. Australia 94/E6
Kingscourt, Ireland 17/H4
Kingscourt, Ireland 10/C4
King's Cove, Newf. 166/D1
Kings Creek, N.C. 281/G3
Kings Creek, Ohio 284/C5
Kings Creek, S.C. 296/E1
Kingsdale, Minn. 255/F4
Kingsdown, Kansas 232/C4
Kingsey Falls, Québec 172/E4
Kingsford, Mich. 250/A3
Kingsford Heights, Ind. 227/D2
Kingsford Smith Airport, N.S. Wales
  88/L4
Kingsford Smith Airport, N.S. Wales
  97/J4
Kingsgate, Br. Col. 184/K5
Kingshill, Virgin Is. (U.S.) 161/F4
Kingsland, Ark. 202/F6
Kingsland, Georgia 217/J9
Kingsland, Texas 303/F7
Kings Landing, Ala. 195/D6
King's Landing, New Bruns. 170/C3
Kingsley (lake), Fla. 212/E2
Kingsley, Iowa 229/A3
Kingsley, Ky. 237/K2
Kingsley, Mich. 250/D4
Kingsley, New Bruns. 170/D2
King's Lynn, England 13/H5
King's Lynn, England 10/G4
Kingsmere (lake), Sask. 181/E1
Kingsmill, Texas 303/D2
Kings Mills, Ohio 284/B7
Kings Mountain, Ky. 237/M6
Kings Mountain, N.C. 281/G4
Kings Mountain Nat'l Mil. Park, S.C.
  296/E1
Kings Park, N.Y. 276/O9
King's Point, Newf. 166/C4
Kings Point, N.Y. 276/P6
Kingsport, Nova Scotia 168/D3
Kingsport, Tenn. 237/R7
Kingston, Ark. 202/C1
Kingston, Australia 87/G8
Kingston, Georgia 217/C2
Kingston, Ill. 222/E1
Kingston, Ind. 227/G6
Kingston, Iowa 229/L7
Kingston (cap.), Jamaica 146/L8
Kingston (cap.), Jamaica 158/K6
Kingston, La. 238/C2
Kingston, Md. 245/R8
Kingston, Mass. 249/M5
Kingston•, Mass. 249/M5
Kingston, Mich. 250/F5
Kingston, Minn. 255/D5
Kingston, Mo. 261/E3
Kingston•, N.H. 268/E6
Kingston, N.J. 273/D3
Kingston, N. Mex. 274/B6
Kingston, N. Zealand 100/B6
Kingston, Norfolk I. 88/L6
Kingston, Nova Scotia 168/D4
Kingston, Ohio 284/E7
Kingston, Okla. 288/N7
Kingston, Ont. 162/J7
Kingston, Ont. 146/L5
Kingston, Ontario 177/H3
Kingston, Pa. 294/F7
Kingston, R.I. 249/J7
Kingston, S. Australia 94/G7
Kingston, Tasmania 99/D4
Kingston, Tenn. 237/N9
Kingston, Utah 304/B5
Kingston, Wash. 310/C3
Kingston, W. Va. 312/D7
Kingston, Wis. 317/H6
Kingston Mines, Ill. 222/D4
Kingston Springs, Tenn. 237/G8
Kingston upon Thames, England 10/B6
Kingston upon Thames, England 13/H8
Kingstown (Dún Laoghaire), Ireland
  17/K5
Kingstown, N.S. Wales 97/F2
Kingstown, Ireland 17/K5
Kingstown (cap.), St. Vin. & Grens.
  161/A9
Kingstown (cap.), St. Vin. & Grens.
  156/G4
Kingstown (bay), St. Vin. & Grens.
  161/A9
Kingstree, S.C. 296/H4
Kings Valley, Oreg. 291/D3
Kingsville, Md. 245/N3
Kingsville, Mo. 261/E4
Kingsville, Ohio 284/J2
Kingsville, Ontario 177/B6
Kingsville, Texas 303/G10
Kingsville N.A.S., Texas 303/G10
Kingswood, England 13/E6
Kingswood, Ky. 237/J5
Kingtehchen (Jingdezhen), China 77/J6
Kington, England 13/E5
Kington, England 10/E4
Kingurutik (mesa), Newf. 166/B2
Kingussie, Scotland 15/D3
Kingussie, Scotland 10/D2
Kingville, S.C. 296/F4
King William (isl.), N.W.T. 162/G2
King William (isl.), N.W. Terr. 187/J3
King William (lake), Tasmania 99/C4
King William (co.), Va. 307/O5
King William, Va. 307/O5
King William's Town, S. Africa 102/E8
King William's Town, S. Africa 118/D6
Kingwood, W. Va. 312/G4

Kinhwa (Jinhua), China 77/J6
Kiniama, Zaire 115/E6
Kınık, Turkey 63/B3
Kinistino, Sask. 181/F3
Kinkala, Congo 115/B4
Kinkora, Pr. Edward I. 168/E2
Kinley, Sask. 181/D3
Kinloch, Mo. 261/P2
Kinlochbervie, Scotland 15/D2
Kinlochewe, Scotland 15/C3
Kinlochleven, Scotland 15/D4
Kinloch Rannoch, Scotland 15/D3
Kinloss, Scotland 15/E3
Kinlough, Ireland 17/E3
Kinmount, Minn. 255/F2
Kinmount, Ontario 177/F3
Kinmundy, Ill. 222/E5
Kinna, Sweden 18/H8
Kinnairds (head), Scotland 10/F2
Kinnairds (head), Scotland 15/G3
Kinnear, Wyo. 319/D2
Kinnegad, Ireland 17/G5
Kinnelon, N.J. 273/E2
Kinneret, Israel 65/D2
Kinney, Minn. 255/F3
Kinney (co.), Texas 303/D8
Kinnitty, Ireland 17/F5
Kino (riv.), Japan 81/G6
Kinoosao, Sask. 181/N3
Kinosota, Manitoba 179/D4
Kinrooi, Belgium 27/H6
Kinross, Iowa 229/K6
Kinross, Scotland 15/E4
Kinross, Scotland 10/E2
Kinross (trad. co.), Scotland 15/A5
Kinsale, Ireland 10/B5
Kinsale, Ireland 17/D8
Kinsale (harb.), Ireland 17/E8
Kinsale, Old Head of (head), Ireland
  17/E8
Kinsale, Va. 307/P4
Kinsella, Alberta 182/E3
Kinsey, Ala. 195/H8
Kinsey, Mont. 262/L4
Kinshasa (prov.), Zaire 115/C4
Kinshasa (cap.), Zaire 2/K6
Kinshasa (cap.), Zaire 115/C4
Kinshasa (cap.), Zaire 102/D5
Kinsley, Kansas 232/C4
Kinsman, Ill. 222/E2
Kinsman (mt.), N.H. 268/D3
Kinsman, Ohio 284/J3
Kinsman Notch (pass), N.H. 268/D3
Kinston, Ala. 195/F8
Kinston, N.C. 281/O4
Kinta, Okla. 288/R4
Kintampo, Ghana 106/D7
Kintnersville, Pa. 294/M4
Kintore, Scotland 15/F3
Kintyre, N. Dak. 282/L6
Kintyre (pen.), Scotland 15/C5
Kintyre, Mull of (prom.), Scotland 15/C5
Kinuso, Alberta 182/D2
Kinvara, Ireland 17/D5
Kinwow (bay), Manitoba 179/E2
Kinyangiri, Tanzania 115/G4
Kinyeti (mt.), Sudan 111/F7
Kinzel Springs, Tenn. 237/O9
Kinzua, Oreg. 291/H3
Kioa (isl.), Fiji 86/R10
Kioga (lake), Uganda 102/F4
Kioga (lake), Uganda 115/F3
Kiona, Wash. 310/F4
Kiosk, Ontario 177/F1
Kiowa (co.), Colo. 208/O6
Kiowa, Colo. 208/L4
Kiowa (creek), Colo. 208/L3
Kiowa (co.), Kansas 232/C4
Kiowa, Kansas 232/D4
Kiowa (co.), Okla. 288/J5
Kiowa, Okla. 288/P5
Kiowa (creek), Okla. 288/F1
Kiowa (co.), Texas 303/D1
Kipabiskau, Sask. 181/G3
Kipahulu, Hawaii 218/K2
Kiparissía, Greece 45/E7
Kiparissía (gulf), Greece 45/E7
Kipawa, Québec 174/B3
Kipili, Tanzania 115/F5
Kipini, Kenya 115/H4
Kipisa, N.W. Terr. 187/M3
Kipling, N.C. 281/M4
Kipling, Sask. 181/J5
Kipnuk, Alaska 196/F3
Kipp, Alberta 182/D5
Kipp, Kansas 232/E3
Kippel, Switzerland 39/E4
Kippen, Scotland 15/B1
Kippens, Newf. 166/B4
Kippure (mt.), Ireland 17/J5
Kipton, Ohio 284/D3
Kipushi, Zaire 115/E6
Kipushi, Zaire 102/E6
Kiput, Philippines 82/C8
Kira Kira, Solomon Is. 86/E3
Kiraz, Turkey 63/C3
Kirazlı, Turkey 63/C6
Kirby, Ark. 202/C5
Kirby, Mont. 262/J5
Kirby, Ohio 284/D4
Kirby, Texas 303/K11
Kirby, W. Va. 312/J4
Kirby, Wyo. 319/D2
Kirbyville, Texas 303/K7
Kirchberg, Bern, Switzerland 39/E2
Kirchberg, St. Gallen, Switzerland
  39/G2
Kirchdorf an der Krems, Austria 41/C3
Kirchheim unter Teck, Germany 22/C4
Kircubbin, N. Ireland 17/K3
Kirensk, U.S.S.R. 48/L4
Kirgiz S.S.R., U.S.S.R. 54/J5
Kirgiz S.S.R., U.S.S.R. 48/H5
Kiri, Zaire 115/C4
Kiribati 2/A6
Kiribati 87/J6
KIRIBATI 87/J6
Kiribati 2/T6
Kirigalpota (mt.), Sri Lanka 68/E7

Kırıkhan, Turkey 63/G4
Kırıkkale, Turkey 63/E3
Kirillov, U.S.S.R. 52/E2
Kirin (Jilin), (prov.) China 77/L3
Kirin (Jilin), China 77/L3
Kirishi, U.S.S.R. 52/D3
Kirishima-Yaku Nat'l Park, Japan
  81/F7
Kiritimati (isl.), Kiribati 87/L5
Kiriwina (isl.), Papua N.G. 85/C7
Kirk, Colo. 208/P3
Kirk, Ky. 237/H5
Kirk, W. Va. 312/B7
Kırkağaç, Turkey 63/B3
Kirkburton, England 13/J2
Kirkby, England 10/F2
Kirkby, England 13/G2
Kirkby Lonsdale, England 13/E3
Kirkbymoorside, England 13/F3
Kirkby Stephen, England 13/E3
Kirkcaldy, Alberta 182/D4
Kirkcaldy, Scotland 15/D1
Kirkcaldy, Scotland 10/C1
Kirkcolm, Scotland 15/C6
Kirkconnel, Scotland 15/E5
Kirkcowan, Scotland 15/D6
Kirkcudbright, Scotland 15/E6
Kirkcudbright, Scotland 10/D3
Kirkcudbright (trad. co.), Scotland
  15/A5
Kirkee, India 68/C5
Kirkella, Manitoba 179/A4
Kirkenes, Norway 18/Q2
Kirkersville, Ohio 284/E6
Kirkfield, Ontario 177/F3
Kirkham, England 13/G1
Kirkham, England 10/F1
Kirkhill, Scotland 15/D3
Kirkinner, Scotland 15/D6
Kirkintilloch, Scotland 10/B1
Kirkintilloch, Scotland 15/B2
Kirkland, Ariz. 198/C4
Kirkland, Georgia 217/G8
Kirkland, Ill. 222/E1
Kirkland, New Bruns. 170/C3
Kirkland, Québec 172/H4
Kirkland, Tenn. 237/H9
Kirkland, Texas 303/D3
Kirkland, Wash. 310/B2
Kirkland Lake, Ont. 162/H6
Kirkland Lake, Ont. 146/K5
Kirkland Lake, Ontario 177/K5
Kirkland Lake, Ontario 175/J3
Kırklareli (prov.), Turkey 63/B2
Kırklareli, Turkey 63/B2
Kirklin, Ind. 227/E4
Kirkman, Iowa 229/C5
Kirkmansville, Ky. 237/G6
Kirkmuirhill, Scotland 15/E5
Kirkpatrick (lake), Alberta 182/E4
Kirkpatrick (mt.), Ant. 5/A8
Kirkpatrick, Ind. 227/D4
Kirkpatrick, Ohio 284/D4
Kirksey, Ky. 237/E7
Kirksville, Ind. 227/D6
Kirksville, Ky. 237/N5
Kirksville, Mo. 261/H2
Kirkton of Glenisla, Scotland 15/E4
Kirkuk, Iraq 54/F6
Kirkuk, Iraq 59/D2
Kirkuk, Iraq 66/D3
Kirkville, Iowa 229/H6
Kirkville, Miss. 256/H2
Kirkwall, Scotland 10/E1
Kirkwall, Scotland 15/E2
Kirkwood, Del. 245/R2
Kirkwood, Ill. 222/C3
Kirkwood, Mo. 261/O3
Kirkwood, N.J. 273/B4
Kirkwood, N.Y. 276/J6
Kirkwood, Pa. 294/K6
Kirkwood, S. Africa 118/D6
Kırmastı (riv.), Turkey 63/C3
Kirn, Germany 22/B4
Kiron, Iowa 229/C4
Kirov, U.S.S.R. 7/J3
Kirov, U.S.S.R. 48/E4
Kirov, Kaluga, U.S.S.R. 52/D4
Kirov, Kirov, U.S.S.R. 52/G3
Kirovabad (Gyandzhe), U.S.S.R. 7/J4
Kirovabad (Gyandzhe), U.S.S.R. 52/G6
Kirovabad (Gyandzhe), U.S.S.R. 48/E5
Kirovakan, U.S.S.R. 52/G6
Kirovo-Chepetsk, U.S.S.R. 52/H3
Kirovograd, U.S.S.R. 7/H4
Kirovograd, U.S.S.R. 48/D5
Kirovograd, U.S.S.R. 52/D5
Kirovsk, U.S.S.R. 52/D1
Kirovskiy, U.S.S.R. 48/H5
Kirriemuir, Alberta 182/E4
Kirriemuir, Scotland 10/E2
Kirriemuir, Scotland 15/E4
Kirs, U.S.S.R. 52/H3
Kirsanov, U.S.S.R. 52/F4
Kırşehir (prov.), Turkey 63/F3
Kırşehir, Turkey 63/F3
Kırşehir, Turkey 59/B2
Kirte, Turkey 63/B6
Kirtland, N. Mex. 274/A2
Kirtland, Ohio 284/H2
Kirtland A.F.B., N. Mex. 274/C3
Kirtland Hills, Ohio 284/H2
Kirton, England 13/H5
Kiruna, Sweden 4/C8
Kiruna, Sweden 7/G2
Kiruna, Sweden 18/L3
Kirundu, Zaire 115/E4
Kirwin, Kansas 232/C2
Kirwin (res.), Kansas 232/C2
Kiryu, Japan 81/J5
Kisa, Sweden 18/J7
Kisangani, Zaire 115/E3
Kisangani, Zaire 102/E3
Kisar (isl.), Indonesia 85/H7
Kisarazu, Japan 81/P3
Kisatchie, La. 238/C4
Kisbér, Hungary 41/D3

Kisbey, Sask. 181/J6
Kishangarh, India 68/D3
Kishinev, U.S.S.R. 7/G4
Kishinev, U.S.S.R. 48/C5
Kishinev, U.S.S.R. 52/C5
Kishorganj, Bangladesh 68/G4
Kishtwar, India 68/D2
Kisi (Jixi), China 77/M2
Kisii, Kenya 115/F4
Kisiju, Tanzania 115/G5
Kiska (isl.), Alaska 188/D6
Kiska (isl.), Alaska 196/H4
Kiska (vol.), Alaska 196/J4
Kiskatinaw (riv.), Br. Col. 184/G2
Kiskissink, Québec 172/E2
Kiskissink (lake), Québec 172/E2
Kiskőrös, Hungary 41/E3
Kiskunfélegyháza, Hungary 41/E3
Kiskunhalas, Hungary 41/E3
Kiskunmajsa, Hungary 41/E3
Kislovodsk, U.S.S.R. 7/J4
Kislovodsk, U.S.S.R. 52/F6
Kismayu (Chisimayu), Somalia
  115/H4
Kismet, Kansas 232/B4
Kispest, Hungary 41/E3
Kissamos, Greece 45/G8
Kissee Mills, Mo. 261/G9
Kissidougou, Guinea 106/B7
Kissimmee, Fla. 212/E3
Kissimmee (lake), Fla. 212/E4
Kissimmee (riv.), Fla. 212/E4
Kissing (lake), Manitoba 179/H2
Kistelek, Hungary 41/E3
Kisten (pass), Switzerland 39/H3
Kisterenye, Hungary 41/E2
Kistler, Pa. 294/G5
Kistler, W. Va. 312/C7
Kistna (riv.), India 54/J8
Kistna (Krishna) (riv.), India 68/D5
Kistrand, Norway 18/O1
Kisújszállás, Hungary 41/F3
Kisumu, Kenya 115/F3
Kisumu, Kenya 102/F5
Kisvárda, Hungary 41/G2
Kita, Mali 102/B3
Kita, Mali 106/C6
Kitaibaraki, Japan 81/K5
Kita Iwo (isl.), Japan 87/D3
Kita Iwo (isl.), Japan 81/M4
Kitakami, Japan 81/K4
Kitakata, Japan 81/J5
Kitakyushu, Japan 81/E6
Kitakyushu, Japan 54/P6
Kitakyushu, Japan 2/R4
Kitale, Kenya 102/F4
Kitale, Kenya 115/G3
Kitami, Japan 81/L2
Kit Carson (co.), Colo. 208/O4
Kit Carson, Colo. 208/O5
Kit Carson (mt.), Colo. 208/H7
Kitchel, Ind. 227/B6
Kitchener (mt.), Alberta 182/B3
Kitchener, Ontario 177/D4
Kite, Georgia 217/F5
Kite, Ky. 237/R6
Kitgum, Uganda 115/F3
Kíthira, Greece 45/F7
Kíthira (isl.), Greece 45/F7
Kíthnos (isl.), Greece 45/G7
Kitikmeot (reg.), N.W.T. 187/G2
Kitim, Jordan 65/D3
Kitimat, Br. Col. 162/D5
Kitimat, Br. Col. 146/F4
Kitimat, Br. Col. 184/C3
Kitinen (riv.), Finland 18/P3
Kitsap (co.), Wash. 310/C3
Kitsault, Br. Col. 184/C2
Kitscoty, Alberta 182/E3
Kitt (peak), Ariz. 198/D7
Kittanning, Pa. 294/D4
Kittatinny (mts.), N.J. 273/D1
Kittery, Maine 243/B9
Kittery•, Maine 243/B9
Kittery Point, Maine 243/B9
Kittilä, Finland 18/O3
Kittitas (co.), Wash. 310/E3
Kittitas, Wash. 310/E4
Kittrell, N.C. 281/M2
Kitts, Ky. 237/P7
Kitts Hill, Ohio 284/E8
Kittson (co.), Minn. 255/B2
Kitty Hawk, N.C. 281/T2
Kitui, Kenya 115/G4
Kitunda, Tanzania 115/F5
Kitwanga, Br. Col. 184/C2
Kitwe, Zambia 115/E6
Kitwe, Zambia 102/E6
Kitzbühel, Austria 41/B3
Kitzingen, Germany 22/C4
Kitzmiller, Md. 245/D2
Kivijärvi (lake), Finland 18/O5
Kiviöli, U.S.S.R. 53/D1
Kivu (lake) 102/E3
Kivu (lake), Rwanda 115/E4
Kivu (prov.), Zaire 115/E4
Kivu (lake), Zaire 115/E4
Kiyiu (lake), Sask. 181/C4
Kizel, U.S.S.R. 48/F4
Kizel, U.S.S.R. 52/J3
Kızılcahamam, Turkey 63/E2
Kızılhisar, Turkey 63/C4
Kızılırmak (riv.), Turkey 63/F2
Kızılırmak (riv.), Turkey 59/B1
Kızıltepe, Turkey 63/H4
Kızıltoprak, Turkey 63/D3
Kızılviran, Turkey 63/E4
Kizimkazi, Tanzania 115/G5
Kizlyar, U.S.S.R. 52/G6
Kizu, Japan 81/J7

Kizyl-Arvat, U.S.S.R. 48/F6
Kjeller, Norway 18/E3
Kjellerup, Denmark 21/C5
Kjölen (mts.) 7/F2
Kjölen (mts.), Norway 18/K3
Kladanj, Yugoslavia 45/F3
Kladno, Czech. 41/B1
Kladovo, Yugoslavia 45/F3
Klagenfurt, Austria 41/C3
Klagetoh, Ariz. 198/F3
Klaipėda, U.S.S.R. 7/F3
Klaipėda, U.S.S.R. 53/A3
Klaipėda, U.S.S.R. 52/E3
Klaipėda, U.S.S.R. 48/E4
Klaksvík, Denmark 21/B2
Klamath (riv.), Calif. 188/B2
Klamath, Calif. 204/B2
Klamath (riv.), Calif. 204/B2
Klamath (co.), Oreg. 291/F5
Klamath (riv.), Oreg. 291/C5
Klamath (mts.), Oreg. 291/C5
Klamath (riv.), Oreg. 291/F5
Klamath Agency, Oreg. 291/F5
Klamath Falls, Oreg. 145/F5
Klamath Falls, Oreg. 183/B2
Klamath Falls, Oreg. 291/F5
Klapmuts, S. Africa 118/F6
Klar (riv.), Sweden 7/F2
Klarälv (riv.), Sweden 13/H6
Klaten, Indonesia 85/J2
Klatovy, Czech. 41/B2
Klausen (pass), Switzerland 39/G3
Klawock, Alaska 196/M2
Klazienaveen, Netherlands 27/L3
Kleberg (co.), Texas 303/G10
Kleefeld, Manitoba 179/F5
Kleena Kleene, Br. Col. 184/E4
Klein, Mont. 262/H4
Klein Bonaire (isl.), Neth. Ant. 161/E4
Kleine Emme (riv.), Switzerland 39/F3
Klein Karas, Namibia 118/B5
Kleinlützel, Switzerland 39/D2
Kleinmachnow, Germany 22/E4
Kleinmond, S. Africa 118/F7
Klemme, Iowa 229/F3
Klemtu, Br. Col. 184/C4
Klerksdorp, S. Africa 118/D5
Kleve, Germany 22/B3
Klickitat (riv.), Wash. 310/E5
Klickitat, Wash. 310/D5
Klickitat (riv.), Wash. 310/D4
Klides (isls.), Cyprus 63/F5
Klinaklini (riv.), Br. Col. 184/E4
Kline, S.C. 296/E5
Kline, W. Va. 312/H5
Kling, Philippines 82/E8
Klingenthal, Germany 22/E3
Klingnau, Switzerland 39/F1
Klintehamn, Sweden 18/K8
Klintsy, U.S.S.R. 52/D4
Klip (riv.), S. Africa 118/H6
Kliprivier, S. Africa 118/H7
Klitmøller, Denmark 21/B3
Ključ, Yugoslavia 45/C3
Kłobuck, Poland 47/D3
Kłoch (riv.), Br. Col. 184/E2
Kłodawa, Poland 47/D3
Kłodnica (riv.), Poland 47/A4
Kłodzko, Poland 47/C3
Klondike (riv.), Yukon 187/E3
Klondike Gold Rush Nat'l Hist. Park,
  Alaska 196/N1
Klondyke, Ariz. 198/E6
Klossner, Minn. 255/D6
Klosterneuburg, Austria 41/D2
Klosters-Serneus, Switzerland 39/J3
Kloten, N. Dak. 282/O4
Kloten, Switzerland 39/G2
Klotzville, La. 238/K3
Kluane (lake), Yukon 162/C3
Kluane (lake), Yukon 187/E3
Kluane Nat'l Park, Yukon 187/E3
Kluane Nat'l Park, Yukon 162/C3
Kluczbork, Poland 47/D3
Klukwan, Alaska 196/M1
Klutina (lake), Alaska 196/L2
Klyuchevskaya Sopka (vol.), U.S.S.R.
  48/U4
Knapdale (dist.), Scotland 15/C5
Knapp, Minn. 255/D5
Knapp, Wis. 317/B6
Knappa, Oreg. 291/D1
Knapp Creek, N.Y. 276/C6
Knaresborough, England 13/F4
Knaresborough, England 10/F3
Knee (lake), Manitoba 179/J3
Knierim, Iowa 229/D4
Knife (riv.), Minn. 255/G2
Knife (riv.), N. Dak. 282/G5
Knife R. Indian Villages Nat'l Hist. Site,
  N. Dak. 282/H5
Knife River, Minn. 255/G4
Knifley, Ky. 237/L6
Knight (isl.), Alaska 196/O1
Knight (inlet), Br. Col. 184/E5
Knightdale, N.C. 281/M3
Knight Inlet, Br. Col. 184/E5
Knighton, Wales 10/E4
Knighton, Wales 13/D5
Knightsen, Calif. 204/L1
Knights Landing, Calif. 204/B8
Knightstown, Ind. 227/T/A8
Knightstown, Ind. 227/C5
Knightsville (res.), Mass. 249/C3
Knik Arm (inlet), Alaska 196/B1
Kniman, Ind. 227/C2
Knin, Yugoslavia 45/C3
Knippa, Texas 303/E8
Knittelfeld, Austria 41/C3
Knjaževac, Yugoslavia 45/F4
Knobel, Ark. 202/J1
Knob Fork, W. Va. 312/E3
Knob Lick, Ky. 237/K6
Knob Lick, Mo. 261/M7
Knob Noster, Mo. 261/E5
Knock, Ireland 17/D4
Knockadoon (head), Ireland 17/F8
Knockanefune (mt.), Ireland 17/C7

Krotoszyn 393

ockboy (mt.), Ireland 17/B8
ocklayd (mt.), N. Ireland 17/J1
ocklong, Ireland 17/D7
ockmealdown (mts.), Ireland 17/F7
ocknagashel, Ireland 17/C7
oke, Iowa 229/D3
okke-Heist, Belgium 27/C6
osen (mt.), Denmark 21/D3
ott (co.), Ky. 237/R6
ott, Texas 303/C5
otts Island, N.C. 281/T2
ottsville, Ky. 237/H5
owles, Okla. 288/F1
owlesville, New Bruns. 170/C2
owlesville, N.Y. 276/D4
owlton, Mont. 262/L4
owlton, Québec 172/E4
owlton, Wis. 317/G6
ox (cape), Br. Col. 162/C5
ox (cape), Br. Col. 184/A3
ox (co.), Ill. 222/C3
ox (co.), Ind. 227/C7
ox, Ind. 227/D2
ox (co.), Ky. 237/O7
ox (co.), Maine 243/E7
ox•, Maine 243/E6
ox (co.), Mo. 261/H2
ox (co.), Nebr. 264/G2
ox (lake), Newf. 166/A3
ox, N. Dak. 282/L3
ox (co.), Ohio 284/F5
ox, Pa. 294/C3
ox (co.), Tenn. 237/O9
ox (co.), Texas 303/E4
ox, Victoria 97/K5
ox, Victoria 88/M7
oxboro, N.Y. 276/J5
ox Center, Maine 243/E6
ox City, Mo. 261/H2
ox City, Texas 303/E4
ox Coast (reg.), Ant. 5/C6
oxville, Ala. 195/C4
oxville, Ark. 202/D3
oxville, Georgia 217/E5
oxville, Ill. 222/C3
oxville, Iowa 229/G6
oxville, Md. 245/H3
oxville, Miss. 256/B8
oxville, Mo. 261/E4
oxville, Pa. 294/H2
oxville, Tenn. 146/K6
oxville, Tenn. 188/K3
oxville, Tenn. 237/O9
ud Rasmussen Land (reg.), Greenl. 4/B12
udshoved (pt.), Denmark 21/D7
urów, Poland 47/A4
utsford, Br. Col. 184/G5
utsford, England 13/H2
utsford, England 10/G2
utsford, Pr. Edward I. 168/D2
ysna, S. Africa 118/C6
ah Kong (isl.), Cambodia 72/D5
ah Nhek, Cambodia 72/E4
ah Rung (isl.), Cambodia 72/D5
ah Tang (isl.), Cambodia 72/D5
ali, Hawaii 218/K2
a Mill, Hawaii 218/G6
ani, Tanzania 115/G5
bayashi, Japan 81/E8
bbfjorden (fjord), Norway 18/O1
bdo (Hovd), Mongolia 77/D2
be, Japan 81/H7
be, Japan 54/P6
benhavn (Copenhagen) (cap.), Denmark 21/F6
benhavn (Copenhagen) (commune), Denmark 21/F6
benhavn (co.), Denmark 21/F6
blenz, Germany 22/B3
blenz, Switzerland 39/F1
brin, U.S.S.R. 52/B4
broor (isl.), Indonesia 85/K7
buk, Alaska 196/G1
buk (riv.), Alaska 188/C5
buk (riv.), Alaska 196/G1
buk Valley Nat'l Park, Alaska 196/F1
buleti, U.S.S.R. 52/F6
ca (riv.), Turkey 63/C3
ca (riv.), Turkey 63/C6
ca (riv.), Turkey 63/E2
caeli (prov.), Turkey 63/C2
caeli (Izmit), Turkey 63/D2
čani, Yugoslavia 45/F5
çarlı, Turkey 63/B4
čevje, Yugoslavia 45/B3
ch (isl.), N.W. Terr. 187/L3
ch'ang, S. Korea 81/C6
chevo, U.S.S.R. 52/J3
chi (pref.), Japan 81/F7
chi, Japan 81/F7
daira, Japan 81/O2
dak, Tenn. 237/O9
diak, Alaska 188/D6
diak, Alaska 196/H3
diak (isl.), Alaska 146/C4
diak (isl.), Alaska 196/H3
diak, U.S. 4/D17
diak (isl.), U.S. 4/D17
dok, Sudan 111/F6
dok, Sudan 102/F4
ekelare, Belgium 27/B6
ekelberg, Belgium 27/B9
enig, Mo. 261/J6
enton, Ala. 195/B7
es, Namibia 118/B5
fa (mts.), Ariz. 198/B5
fçaz, Turkey 63/B2
ffiefontein, S. Africa 118/D5
flach, Austria 41/C3
foridua, Ghana 106/D7
fu, Japan 81/J6
ga, Japan 81/J5
galuc (riv.), Québec 174/E1
galuk (riv.), Newf. 166/B2
ganei, Japan 81/O2
garah, N.S. Wales 88/K4
garah, N.S. Wales 97/J4
Køge, Denmark 21/F7
Køge (bay), Denmark 21/F7
Koggiung, Alaska 196/G3
Kogo, Equat. Guinea 106/F8
Kogo, Equat. Guinea 115/A3
Kohala (Kapaau), Hawaii 218/G3
Kohala (mts.), Hawaii 218/G4
Kohala (peak), Hawaii 218/G4
Kohat, Pakistan 59/K3
Kohat, Pakistan 68/C2
Kohila, U.S.S.R. 53/C1
Kohima, India 68/G3
Kohkiluyeh and Boyer Ahmediyeh (gov.), Iran 66/G5
Kohler, Wis. 317/L8
Kohls Ranch, Ariz. 198/D4
Kohtla-Järve, U.S.S.R. 52/C3
Kohtla-Järve, U.S.S.R. 53/D1
Kohŭng, S. Korea 81/C6
Koidern, Yukon 187/D3
Koitere (lake), Finland 18/R5
Kŏje (isl.), S. Korea 81/D6
Kojetín, Czech. 41/D2
Kojonup, W. Australia 88/B6
Kojonup, W. Australia 92/B6
Kokadjo, Maine 243/E4
Kokand, U.S.S.R. 48/H5
Kokanee Glacier Prov. Park, Br. Col. 184/J5
Kokava nad Rimavicou, Czech. 41/E2
Kokchetav, U.S.S.R. 54/J4
Kokchetav, U.S.S.R. 48/H4
Kokemäki, Finland 18/N6
Kokish, Br. Col. 184/D5
Kokiu (Gejiu), China 77/F7
Kokkola, Finland 18/N5
Koknanok, Alaska 196/H3
Koko (head), Hawaii 218/F2
Koko, Nigeria 106/F7
Kokoda, Papua N.G. 85/C7
Kokole (pt.), Hawaii 218/B2
Kokolik (riv.), Alaska 196/F1
Kokomo, Hawaii 218/K2
Kokomo, Ind. 188/J2
Kokomo, Ind. 227/E4
Kokomo, Miss. 256/E8
Kokonau, Indonesia 85/K6
Kokopo, Papua N.G. 86/B2
Kokosing (riv.), Ohio 284/E5
Kokrines, Alaska 196/G1
Kokrines (hills), Alaska 196/H1
Koksan, N. Korea 81/C4
Koksijde, Belgium 27/B6
Koksilah, Br. Col. 184/J3
Koksoak (riv.), Que. 162/K4
Koksoak (riv.), Québec 174/D1
Kokstad, S. Africa 118/D6
Kokubu, Japan 81/E8
Kola, Manitoba 179/A5
Kola (pen.), U.S.S.R. 7/H2
Kola (pen.), U.S.S.R. 4/C8
Kola (pen.), U.S.S.R. 52/E1
Kola (pen.), U.S.S.R. 48/D3
Kolahun, Liberia 106/C7
Kolaka, Indonesia 85/G6
Kolar, India 68/D6
Kolar Gold Fields, India 68/D6
Kolari, Finland 18/O3
Kolárovo, Czech. 41/D3
Kolašin, Yugoslavia 45/D4
Kolberg (Kołobrzeg), Poland 47/B1
Kolbio, Kenya 115/H4
Kolbuszowa, Poland 47/E3
Kolda, Senegal 106/B6
Kolding, Denmark 18/F9
Kolding, Denmark 21/C7
Kole, Haut-Zaïre, Zaire 115/E3
Kole, Kasai-Oriental, Zaire 115/D4
Koleen, Ind. 227/D7
Kolekole (stream), Hawaii 218/J4
Kölen (mts.), Sweden 18/K3
Kolepom (isl.), Indonesia 85/K7
Kolguyev (isl.), U.S.S.R. 7/J2
Kolguyev (isl.), U.S.S.R. 4/B7
Kolguyev (isl.), U.S.S.R. 52/G1
Kolguyev (isl.), U.S.S.R. 48/E3
Kolhapur, India 68/C5
Kolhapur, India 54/J8
Koliganek, Alaska 196/G3
Kolín, Czech. 41/C
Kolin, Mont. 262/G3
Kolind, Denmark 21/D5
Kölliken, Switzerland 39/F2
Kollum, Netherlands 27/J2
Kolmanskop, Namibia 118/B5
Köln (Cologne), Germany 22/B3
Kolno, Poland 47/E2
Koło, Poland 47/D2
Koloa, Hawaii 188/E5
Koloa, Hawaii 218/C2
Koloa Landing, Hawaii 218/C2
Kołobrzeg, Poland 47/B1
Kologriv, U.S.S.R. 52/F3
Kolokani, Mali 106/C6
Kolola Springs, Miss. 256/H3
Kolombangara (isl.), Solomon Is. 86/D2
Kolomiya, U.S.S.R. 52/B5
Kolomna, U.S.S.R. 7/H3
Kolomna, U.S.S.R. 48/D4
Kolomna, U.S.S.R. 52/E4
Kolondiéba, Mali 106/C6
Kolonia (cap.), Micronesia 87/F5
Kolonodale, Indonesia 85/G6
Kolovrat (mt.), Solomon Is. 86/E3
Kolpashevo, U.S.S.R. 54/K4
Kolpashevo, U.S.S.R. 48/J4
Kolpino, U.S.S.R. 52/D3
Kolva (riv.), U.S.S.R. 52/J1
Kolwezi, Zaire 102/E6
Kolwezi, Zaire 115/E6
Kolyma (range), U.S.S.R. 4/C1
Kolyma (riv.), U.S.S.R. 4/C2
Kolyma (range), U.S.S.R. 48/Q3
Kolyma (range), U.S.S.R. 54/S3
Kolyma (riv.), U.S.S.R. 54/S3
Kolyma (riv.), U.S.S.R. 48/Q3
Koma, Burma 72/C4
Komádi, Hungary 41/F3
Komadugu Yobe (riv.), Niger 106/G6
Komadugu Yobe (riv.), Nigeria 106/G6
Komaga (mt.), Japan 81/K2
Komagane, Japan 81/H6
Komandorskiye (isls.), U.S.S.R. 54/T4
Komandorskiye (isls.), U.S.S.R. 2/T3
Komandorskiye (isls.), U.S.S.R. 48/R4
Komárno, Czech. 41/D3
Komarno, Manitoba 179/E4
Komárom (co.), Hungary 41/E3
Komárom, Hungary 41/E3
Komatke, Ariz. 198/C5
Komatsu, Japan 81/H5
Komba, Zaire 115/D3
Kŏmdŏk (mt.), N. Korea 81/D3
Komi A.S.S.R., U.S.S.R. 48/F3
Komi A.S.S.R., U.S.S.R. 52/H2
Komi-Permyak Aut. Okr., U.S.S.R. 52/H3
Komi-Permyak Aut. Okr., U.S.S.R. 48/F4
Komló, Hungary 41/E3
Kommetjie, S. Africa 118/E7
Kommunarsk, U.S.S.R. 52/E5
Komodo (isl.), Indonesia 85/F7
Komoka, Ontario 177/C5
Kôm Ombo, Egypt 111/F3
Kôm Ombo, Egypt 59/B5
Komono, Congo 115/B4
Komoran (isl.), Indonesia 85/K7
Komotiní, Greece 45/G5
Komrat, U.S.S.R. 52/C5
Komsomolets (isl.), U.S.S.R. 4/A5
Komsomolets (isl.), U.S.S.R. 54/M1
Komsomolets (isl.), U.S.S.R. 48/L1
Komsomol'sk, U.S.S.R. 54/P4
Komsomol'sk, U.S.S.R. 48/G4
Komsomol'skiy, U.S.S.R. 52/K1
Komsomol'sk-na-Amure, U.S.S.R. 48/O4
Kona, Ky. 237/R6
Konahuanui (peaks), Hawaii 218/C3
Konar (riv.), Afghanistan 68/C1
Konar (riv.), Afghanistan 59/K2
Konar (riv.), Pakistan 68/C1
Konawa, Okla. 288/N5
Kondoa, Tanzania 115/G4
Kondopoga, U.S.S.R. 52/D2
Kondopoga, U.S.S.R. 48/D3
Kondoros, Hungary 41/F3
Konduz, Afghan. 58/J2
Konduz, Afghan. 68/B1
Konduz (riv.), Afghan. 58/J2
Konduz (riv.), Afghan. 68/B1
Koné, New Caled. 86/G4
Kong, Koh (isl.), Cambodia 72/D5
Kong, Ivory Coast 106/D7
Kongiganak, Alaska 196/F3
Kongju, S. Korea 81/C5
Kong Karls Land (isl.), Norway 18/E1
Kongmoon (Jiangmen), China 77/H7
Kongolo, Zaire 115/E5
Kongolo, Zaire 102/E5
Kongor, Sudan 111/F6
Kongsberg, N. Dak. 282/J4
Kongsberg, Norway 18/F7
Kongsfjorden (fjord), Norway 18/B2
Kongsvinger, Norway 18/H6
Kongur Shan (mt.), China 77/A4
Kongwa, Tanzania 115/G5
Koni (pen.), U.S.S.R. 48/Q4
Koniecpol, Poland 47/D3
Königsberg (Kaliningrad), U.S.S.R. 52/B4
Königssee (lake), Germany 22/E5
Königswiesen, Austria 41/C2
Königswinter, Germany 22/B3
Königs Wusterhausen, Germany 22/E2
Konin (prov.), Poland 47/D2
Konin, Poland 47/D2
Kónitsa, Greece 45/E5
Koniuji (isls.), Alaska 196/G3
Köniz, Switzerland 39/D3
Konjic, Yugoslavia 45/D4
Konkiep, Namibia 118/B5
Konnagar, India 68/F1
Konolfingen, Switzerland 39/E3
Konomoc (lake), Conn. 210/G3
Konosha, U.S.S.R. 52/F2
Konotop, U.S.S.R. 52/D4
Konqi He (riv.), China 77/C3
Końskie, Poland 47/E3
Konstantinovka, U.S.S.R. 52/E5
Konstantynów Łódzki, Poland 47/D3
Konstanz, Germany 22/C5
Kontagora, Nigeria 106/F6
Kontcha, Cameroon 115/B2
Kontich, Belgium 27/E6
Kontiomäki, Finland 18/Q4
Kon Tum, Vietnam 72/E4
Kon Tum (plat.), Vietnam 72/E4
Konya (prov.), Turkey 63/E4
Konya, Turkey 63/E4
Konya, Turkey 59/B2
Konya, Turkey 54/E6
Konza, Kenya 115/G4
Koocanusa (lake), Br. Col. 184/K6
Koocanusa (lake), Mont. 262/A2
Koochiching (co.), Minn. 255/E2
Koog aan de Zaan, Netherlands 27/A4
Koolan (isl.), W. Australia 88/C3
Koolan (isl.), W. Australia 92/C1
Koolau (range), Hawaii 218/E2
Kooline Station, W. Australia 92/B3
Koolpinyah, North. Terr. 93/B2
Koolyanobbing, W. Australia 88/B6
Koolyanobbing, W. Australia 92/B5
Koondrook, Victoria 97/B4
Koonibba, S. Australia 88/E6
Koonibba, S. Australia 94/C4
Koontz Lake, Ind. 227/D2
Koorawatha, N.S. Wales 97/E4
Koosharem, Utah 304/C5
Koosharem Ind. Res., Utah 304/C5
Kooskia, Idaho 220/C3
Koostatak, Manitoba 179/E3
Kootenai (co.), Idaho 220/B2
Kootenai, Idaho 220/B1
Kootenai (riv.), Idaho 220/C1
Kootenai (riv.), Mont. 262/A2
Kootenay (lake), Br. Col. 162/E5
Kootenay (lake), Br. Col. 184/J5
Kootenay (riv.), Br. Col. 184/K5
Kootenay Nat'l Park, Br. Col. 184/J4
Kootenay Nat'l Pk., Br. Col. 162/E5
Kootingal, N.S. Wales 97/F2
Kópavogur, Iceland 21/B1
Köpenick, Germany 22/F4
Koper, Yugoslavia 45/A3
Kopervik, Norway 18/D7
Kopeysk, U.S.S.R. 48/G4
Köping, Sweden 18/J7
Koppal, India 68/D5
Koppang, Norway 18/G6
Kopparberg (co.), Sweden 18/J6
Kopparberg, Sweden 18/J7
Koppel, Pa. 294/B4
Kopperston, W. Va. 312/C7
Koprivnica, Yugoslavia 45/C2
Köprü (riv.), Turkey 63/D4
Kor (riv.), Iran 66/H6
Korab (mt.), Albania 45/E5
Korab (mt.), Yugoslavia 45/E5
Koraka (cape), Turkey 63/B3
Koran, La. 238/D2
Koraput, India 68/E5
Korba, India 68/E4
Korbach, Germany 22/C3
Korbel, Calif. 204/B3
Korçë, Albania 45/E5
Korčula (isl.), Yugoslavia 45/C4
Kordestan (Kurdistan) (prov.), Iran 66/E3
Kord Kuy, Iran 66/J2
Kordofan, Southern (prov.), Sudan 111/E5
Kordofan, Northern (prov.), Sudan 111/E5
Korea (North) 2/R4
Korea (South) 2/R4
KOREA (NORTH) 81
KOREA (SOUTH) 81
Korea (bay), N. Korea 81/B4
Korea (str.), S. Korea 81/D6
Korenovsk, U.S.S.R. 52/E5
Korf, U.S.S.R. 54/T3
Korf, U.S.S.R. 4/C1
Korf, U.S.S.R. 48/R3
Korhogo, Ivory Coast 106/C7
Korhogo, Ivory Coast 102/B4
Kőrishegy (mt.), Hungary 41/D3
Koriyama, Japan 81/K5
Korkuteli, Turkey 63/D4
Korla, China 77/C3
Kormakiti (cape), Cyprus 59/B2
Kormakiti (cape), Cyprus 63/E5
Körmend, Hungary 41/D3
Kornat (isl.), Yugoslavia 45/B4
Korneuburg, Austria 41/D2
Kornsjø, Norway 18/G7
Kornwestheim, Germany 22/C4
Koro (isl.), Fiji 86/Q10
Koro (sea), Fiji 86/Q10
Köroğlu (mts.), Turkey 63/E2
Köroğlu Dağı (mt.), Turkey 63/E2
Korogwe, Tanzania 115/G5
Koroit, Victoria 97/B6
Korona, Fla. 212/E2
Koronadal, Philippines 82/E7
Koronowo, Poland 47/C2
Koropí, Greece 45/G7
Koror (cap.), Belau 87/D5
Kororoit (creek), Victoria 97/H5
Kororoit (creek), Victoria 88/K7
Körös (riv.), Hungary 41/F3
Körösladány, Hungary 41/F3
Korosten', U.S.S.R. 52/C4
Korostyshev, U.S.S.R. 52/C4
Koro Toro, Chad 111/C4
Korpilombolo, Sweden 18/N3
Korsakov, U.S.S.R. 48/P5
Korsnäs, Finland 18/M5
Korsør, Denmark 21/E7
Korsør, Denmark 18/G9
Kortemark, Belgium 27/C6
Korti, Sudan 111/F4
Korti, Sudan 59/B6
Kortrijk, Belgium 27/C7
Korumburra, Victoria 97/D6
Koryak (range), U.S.S.R. 54/U3
Koryak (range), U.S.S.R. 48/S3
Koryak Aut. Okr., U.S.S.R. 48/R3
Koryazhma, U.S.S.R. 52/G2
Kos, Greece 45/H7
Kos (isl.), Greece 45/H7
Kościan, Poland 47/C2
Kościerzyna, Poland 47/C1
Kosciusko (mt.), Australia 87/F9
Kosciusko (co.), Ind. 227/F2
Kosciusko, Miss. 256/E4
Kosciusko (mt.), N. S. Wales 88/H7
Kosciusko (mt.), N.S. Wales 97/E5
Koshigaya, Japan 81/P2
Koshiki (isls.), Japan 81/D8
Koshk-e Kohneh, Afghanistan 68/A2
Koshkonong, Mo. 261/J9
Koshkonong (lake), Wis. 317/H10
Košice, Czech. 7/G4
Košice, Czech. 41/F2
Koslan, U.S.S.R. 48/E3
Koslan, U.S.S.R. 52/G2
Köslin (Koszalin), Poland 47/C1
Kosoma, Okla. 288/P6
Kosŏng, N. Korea 81/D4
Kosovo (aut. reg.), Yugoslavia 45/E4
Kosovska Mitrovica, Yugoslavia 45/E4
Kosrae (isl.), Micronesia 87/G5
Kosse, Texas 303/H6
Kössen, Austria 41/B3
Kossou, Lac de (lake), Ivory Coast 106/C7
Kossuth, Ind. 227/E7
Kossuth (co.), Iowa 229/E2
Kossuth, Miss. 256/G1
Kostajnica, Yugoslavia 45/C3
Kostelec nad černými Lesy, Czech. 41/C2
Kostelec nad Orlicí, Czech. 41/D1
Kosti, Sudan 59/B7
Kosti, Sudan 111/F5
Kosti, Sudan 102/F3
Kostopol', U.S.S.R. 52/C4
Kostroma, U.S.S.R. 7/J3
Kostroma, U.S.S.R. 52/F3
Kostroma, U.S.S.R. 48/E4
Kostrzyń, Poland 47/B2
Koszalin (prov.), Poland 47/C1
Koszalin, Poland 7/F3
Koszalin, Poland 47/C1
Kőszeg, Hungary 41/D3
Koszta, Iowa 229/J5
Kota, India 68/D3
Kota, India 54/J7
Kotaagung, Indonesia 85/C7
Kotabaharu, Indonesia 85/E6
Kota Baharu, Malaysia 54/M9
Kota Baharu, Malaysia 72/D6
Kotabaru, Indonesia 85/F6
Kotabumi, Indonesia 85/C7
Kota Kinabalu, Malaysia 54/N9
Kota Kinabalu, Malaysia 85/F4
Kotamobagu, Indonesia 85/G5
Kota Tinggi, Malaysia 72/F5
Kotawaringin, Indonesia 85/E6
Kotcho (lake), Br. Col. 184/M2
Kotcho (riv.), Br. Col. 184/M2
Kotel, Bulgaria 45/H4
Kotel'nich, U.S.S.R. 52/G3
Kotel'nikovo, U.S.S.R. 52/F5
Kotel'nyy (isl.), U.S.S.R. 4/B2
Kotel'nyy (isl.), U.S.S.R. 48/O2
Köthen, Germany 22/E3
Kotido, Uganda 115/F3
Kotka, Finland 7/G2
Kotka, Finland 18/P6
Kotlas, U.S.S.R. 7/J2
Kotlas, U.S.S.R. 48/E3
Kotlas, U.S.S.R. 52/G2
Kotlik, Alaska 196/F2
Kotor, Yugoslavia 45/D4
Kotovo, U.S.S.R. 52/G4
Kotovsk, Odessa, U.S.S.R. 52/C5
Kotovsk, Tambov, U.S.S.R. 52/F4
Kotri, Pakistan 68/B3
Kötschach-Mauthen, Austria 41/B3
Kottaguden, India 68/E5
Kottayam, India 68/D7
Kotto (riv.), Cent. Afr. Rep. 115/D2
Kotturu, India 68/D6
Kotuy (riv.), U.S.S.R. 4/B4
Kotuy (riv.), U.S.S.R. 54/M2
Kotuy (riv.), U.S.S.R. 48/L3
Kotzebue, Alaska 196/F1
Kotzebue, Alaska 146/B3
Kotzebue, Alaska 188/C5
Kotzebue (sound), Alaska 196/F1
Kotzebue, U.S. 4/C18
Kouango, Cent. Afr. Rep. 115/D2
Kouchibouguac, New Bruns. 170/F2
Kouchibouguac (bay), New Bruns. 170/F2
Kouchibouguacis (riv.), New Bruns. 170/E2
Kouchobouguac Nat'l Park, New Bruns. 170/F2
Koudougou, Burkina Faso 106/D6
Kouilou (riv.), Congo 115/B4
Koukdjuak (riv.), N.W. Terr. 187/L3
Kouki, Cent. Afr. Rep. 115/C2
Koula-Moutou, Gabon 115/B4
Koula-Moutou, Gabon 102/D5
Koulikoro, Mali 106/C6
Koulikoro, Mali 102/B3
Koumala, Queensland 95/D4
Koumbi Saleh (ruins), Mauritania 106/C5
Koumra, Chad 102/D4
Koumra, Chad 111/C6
Koundara, Guinea 106/B6
Kounde, Cent. Afr. Rep. 115/B2
Kouno, Chad 111/C6
Kounradskiy, U.S.S.R. 48/H5
Kountze, Texas 303/K7
Koupela, Burkina Faso 106/D6
Kourou, Fr. Guiana 131/E3
Kourouba, Mali 106/B6
Kouroussa, Guinea 106/C6
Kousseri, Cameroon 115/B1
Koutiala, Mali 106/C6
Koutiala, Mali 102/B3
Kouts, Ind. 227/C2
Kouvola, Finland 18/P6
Kovdor, U.S.S.R. 52/D1
Kovel', U.S.S.R. 52/C4
Kovel', U.S.S.R. 48/C4
Kovrov, U.S.S.R. 52/F3
Kovrov, U.S.S.R. 48/E4
Kovur, India 68/E6
Kovylkino, U.S.S.R. 52/F4
Kowary, Poland 47/B3
Kowst, Afghanistan 59/J3
Kowt-e 'Ashrow, Afghanistan 68/B2
Koyama, Japan 81/E8
Köyceğiz, Turkey 63/C4
Köyceğiz (lake), Turkey 63/C4
Koyuk, Alaska 196/F1
Koyukuk, Alaska 196/G1
Koyukuk (riv.), Alaska 188/C5
Koyukuk (riv.), Alaska 196/G1
Koyulhisar, Turkey 63/G2
Kozaklı, Turkey 63/F3
Kozan, Turkey 63/F4
Kozáni, Greece 45/F5
Kozhevnikovo, U.S.S.R. 48/L2
Kozhikode, India 68/D6
Kozhikode, India 54/J8
Kozhva, U.S.S.R. 52/J1
Kozienice, Poland 47/E3
Kozlu, Turkey 63/D2
Kozluk, Turkey 63/J3
Kozmin, Poland 47/C3
Kożuchów, Poland 47/B3
Kpalimé, Togo 106/E7
Kpandu, Ghana 106/D7
Kpémé, Togo 106/E7
Kra (isth.), Thailand 72/C5
Kraaifontein, S. Africa 118/F6
Kraainem, Belgium 27/C9
Krabi, Thailand 72/C5
Kra Buri, Thailand 72/C5
Kracheh, Cambodia 72/E4
Kraemer, La. 238/M4
Kragan, Indonesia 85/K2
Kragerø, Norway 18/F7
Kragujevac, Yugoslavia 45/E3
Kragujevac, Yugoslavia 7/G4
Krakatau (Rakata) (isl.), Indonesia 85/C7
Krakow, Mo. 261/K6
Kraków (Cracow), Poland 47/E4
Krakow, Wis. 317/K6
Kralendijk (cap.), Bonaire, Neth. Ant. 161/E8
Kralendijk, Neth. Ant. 156/E4
Králíky, Czech. 41/D1
Kraljevo, Yugoslavia 45/E4
Kralovice, Czech. 41/B2
Kráľovský Chlmec, Czech. 41/G2
Kralupy nad Vltavou, Czech. 41/C1
Kramatorsk, U.S.S.R. 52/E5
Kramer, Ind. 227/C4
Kramer, Nebr. 264/H4
Kramer, N. Dak. 282/J2
Kramfors, Sweden 18/L5
Kranídhion, Greece 45/F7
Kranj, Yugoslavia 45/B2
Kranzburg, S. Dak. 298/R4
Krapkowice, Poland 47/D3
Krasino, U.S.S.R. 52/H1
Krasino, U.S.S.R. 48/F2
Krāslava, U.S.S.R. 53/D3
Kraslice, Czech. 41/B1
Krásná Lípa, Czech. 41/C1
Kraśnik Fabryczny, Poland 47/F3
Krasnoarmeysk, U.S.S.R. 52/G4
Krasnoborsk, U.S.S.R. 52/G2
Krasnodar, U.S.S.R. 7/H4
Krasnodar, U.S.S.R. 48/E5
Krasnodar, U.S.S.R. 52/E6
Krasnograd, U.S.S.R. 52/E5
Krasnokamensk, U.S.S.R. 48/M4
Krasnokamsk, U.S.S.R. 52/H3
Krasnokamsk, U.S.S.R. 48/F4
Krasnoperekopsk, U.S.S.R. 52/D5
Krasnoslobodsk, U.S.S.R. 52/G5
Krasnotur'insk, U.S.S.R. 48/G3
Krasnoural'sk, U.S.S.R. 48/G4
Krasnovishersk, U.S.S.R. 52/J2
Krasnovodsk, U.S.S.R. 54/G5
Krasnovodsk, U.S.S.R. 48/F5
Krasnoyarsk, U.S.S.R. 54/L4
Krasnoyarsk, U.S.S.R. 2/P3
Krasnoyarsk, U.S.S.R. 48/K4
Krasnystaw, Poland 47/F3
Krasnyy Kut, U.S.S.R. 52/G4
Krasnyy Luch, U.S.S.R. 52/E5
Krasnyy Sulin, U.S.S.R. 52/F5
Krasnyy Yar, U.S.S.R. 52/G5
Kraulshavn (Nussaq), Greenl. 4/B13
Krause Lagoon (chan.), Virgin Is. (U.S.) 161/F4
Krawang, Indonesia 85/H2
Krebs, Okla. 288/P5
Krefeld, Germany 22/B3
Kremenchug, U.S.S.R. 7/H4
Kremenchug, U.S.S.R. 48/D5
Kremenchug, U.S.S.R. 52/D5
Kremlin, Mont. 262/F2
Kremlin, Okla. 288/L1
Kremmling, Colo. 208/G2
Kremnica, Czech. 41/E2
Krems an der Donau, Austria 41/C2
Krenitzin (isls.), Alaska 196/E4
Kresgeville, Pa. 294/L4
Kress, Texas 303/C3
Kretinga, U.S.S.R. 53/A3
Kreutztal, Germany 22/C3
Kreuzlingen, Switzerland 39/H1
Kribi, Cameroon 115/B3
Krichev, U.S.S.R. 52/D4
Kriens, Switzerland 39/F2
Krimml, Austria 41/B3
Krimpen aan den IJssel, Netherlands 27/F5
Kriós (cape), Greece 45/F8
Krishna (Kistna) (riv.), India 68/D5
Krishnanagar, India 68/F4
Kristiansand, Norway 18/F8
Kristiansand, Norway 7/E3
Kristianstad (co.), Sweden 18/J8
Kristianstad, Sweden 18/J9
Kristiansund, Norway 7/E2
Kristiansund, Norway 18/E5
Kristiinankaupunki (Kristinestad), Finland 18/N5
Kristinehamn, Sweden 18/H7
Kristinestad, Finland 18/N5
Kriti (Crete) (isl.), Greece 45/G8
Krivoy Rog, U.S.S.R. 7/H4
Krivoy Rog, U.S.S.R. 48/D5
Krivoy Rog, U.S.S.R. 52/D5
Križevci, Yugoslavia 45/C2
Krk, Yugoslavia 45/B3
Krk (isl.), Yugoslavia 45/B3
Krnov, Czech. 41/D1
Krolevets, U.S.S.R. 52/D4
Kroměříž, Czech. 41/D2
Krompachy, Czech. 41/F2
Kronach, Germany 22/D3
Kronau, Sask. 181/G5
Krong Kaoh Kong, Cambodia 72/D4
Krong Keb, Cambodia 72/E5
Kronoberg (co.), Sweden 18/J8
Kronshtadt, U.S.S.R. 52/C3
Kroonstad, S. Africa 118/D5
Kropotkin, U.S.S.R. 52/F5
Kroschel, Minn. 255/E4
Krosno (prov.), Poland 47/E4
Krosno, Poland 47/E4
Krosno Odrzanskie, Poland 47/B2
Krotoszyn, Poland 47/C3

Krotz Springs, La. 238/G5
Krško, Yugoslavia 45/B3
Kru Coast (reg.), Liberia 106/C8
Kruger Nat'l Park, S. Africa 118/E4
Krugersdorp, S. Africa 118/H6
Krugloi (pt.), Alaska 196/J3
Kruis (riv.), S. Africa 118/F6
Krujë, Albania 45/D5
Krum, Texas 303/G4
Krumbach, Germany 22/D4
Krummenau, Switzerland 39/H2
Krumovgrad, Bulgaria 45/G5
Krung Thep (Bangkok) (cap.), Thailand 72/D4
Krupina, Czech. 41/E2
Krupka, Czech. 41/B1
Krupp (Marlin), Wash. 310/F3
Krusenstern (cape), Alaska 196/F1
Krusenstern (cape), N.W. Terr. 187/G3
Kruševac, Yugoslavia 45/E4
Krušné Hory (Erzgebirge) (mts.), Czech. 41/B1
Kruszwica, Poland 47/D2
Kruzof (isl.), Alaska 196/M1
Krydor, Sask. 181/D3
Krymsk, U.S.S.R. 52/E5
Krynica, Poland 47/E4
Krypton, Ky. 237/P6
Krzyż, Poland 47/C2
Ksar el Boukhari, Algeria 106/E1
Ksar el Kebir, Morocco 106/C2
Ktima, Cyprus 63/E5
Kuala Dungun, Malaysia 72/D6
Kualakapuas, Indonesia 85/E6
Kuala Kerai, Malaysia 72/D6
Kualakurun, Indonesia 85/E6
Kuala Lipis, Malaysia 72/D6
Kuala Lumpur (cap.), Malaysia 72/D7
Kuala Lumpur (cap.), Malaysia 54/M9
Kuala Lumpur (cap.), Malaysia 2/P5
Kuala Pilah, Malaysia 72/D7
Kualapuu, Hawaii 218/G1
Kuala Rompin, Malaysia 72/D7
Kuala Selangor, Malaysia 72/D7
Kuala Terengganu, Malaysia 72/D6
Kuancheng, China 77/J3
Kuantan, Malaysia 72/D7
Kuba, U.S.S.R. 52/G6
Kubachi, U.S.S.R. 52/G6
Kubaisa, Iraq 66/C4
Kuban (riv.), U.S.S.R. 7/J4
Kuban' (riv.), U.S.S.R. 52/E5
Kubbum, Sudan 111/D5
Kubeno (lake), U.S.S.R. 52/E3
Küblis, Switzerland 39/J3
Kubohama, Japan 81/F7
Kubrat, Bulgaria 45/H4
Kuching, Malaysia 54/N9
Kuching, Malaysia 85/E5
Kuchino (isl.), Japan 81/O4
Kuçovë (Stalin), Albania 45/D5
Küçükköy, Turkey 63/B3
Kudarebe (pt.), Neth. Ant. 161/D9
Kudat, Malaysia 85/F4
Kudowa Zdrój, Poland 47/B3
Kudus, Indonesia 85/J2
Kudymkar, U.S.S.R. 48/F4
Kudymkar, U.S.S.R. 52/H3
Kufra (oasis), Libya 102/E2
Kufra (oasis), Libya 111/D3
Kufrinja, Jordan 65/D3
Kufstein, Austria 41/A3
Kuh (cape), Iran 66/K8
Kuhak, Iran 66/N7
Kuhestan, Afghanistan 59/H3
Kuhestan, Afghanistan 68/A2
Kühlungsborn, Germany 22/D1
Kuhmo, Finland 18/Q4
Kuhpayeh, Iran 66/H4
Kuilsrivier, S. Africa 118/F6
Kuiseb (riv.), Namibia 118/B4
Kuito, Angola 115/C6
Kuiu (isl.), Alaska 196/M2
Kuivaniemi, Finland 18/O4
Kuji, Japan 81/K3
Kuju (mt.), Japan 81/E7
Kuk (riv.), Alaska 196/G1
Kukaiau, Hawaii 218/H4
Kukaklek (lake), Alaska 196/G3
Kukalar, Kuh-e (mt.), Iran 59/F3
Kukalar, Kuh-e (mt.), Iran 66/G5
Kukalaya (riv.), Nicaragua 154/E4
Kukawa, Nigeria 106/G6
Kukës, Albania 45/E4
Kuki, Japan 81/O2
Kukpowruk (riv.), Alaska 196/F1
Kukui (riv.), Guyana 131/A3
Kukuihaele, Hawaii 218/H3
Kula, Bulgaria 45/F4
Kula, Hawaii 218/J2
Kula, Turkey 63/C3
Kulai, Malaysia 72/F5
Kula Kangri (mt.), Bhutan 68/G3
Kuldīga, U.S.S.R. 53/A2
Kuldja (Yining), China 77/B3
Kulebaki, U.S.S.R. 52/F3
Kulen, Cambodia 72/E4
Kulen Vakuf, Yugoslavia 45/B3
Kulgera, North. Terr. 88/E5
Kulgera, North. Terr. 93/C8
Kulkyne (creek), N.S. Wales 97/C1
Kulm, N. Dak. 282/N7
Kulmbach, Germany 22/D3
Kuloy, U.S.S.R. 52/F2
Kulp, Turkey 63/J3
Kulpmont, Pa. 294/J4
Kulpsville, Pa. 294/M5
Kul'sary, U.S.S.R. 48/F5
Kulu, India 68/D2
Kulu, Turkey 63/D3
Kulunda, U.S.S.R. 48/H4
Kulyab, U.S.S.R. 48/H6
Küm (riv.), S. Korea 81/C5
Kuma (riv.), U.S.S.R. 7/H4
Kuma (riv.), U.S.S.R. 48/E5
Kuma (riv.), U.S.S.R. 52/G5
Kumagaya, Japan 81/J5
Kumai, Indonesia 85/E6

Kumai, Indonesia 85/E6
Kumaka, Guyana 131/B4
Kumamoto (pref.), Japan 81/E7
Kumamoto, Japan 54/P6
Kumamoto, Japan 81/E7
Kumano, Japan 81/G7
Kumanovo, Yugoslavia 45/E4
Kumara, N. Zealand 100/C5
Kumasi, Ghana 106/D7
Kumasi, Ghana 102/B4
Kumba, Cameroon 115/A3
Kumbakonam, India 68/D6
Kumbo, Cameroon 115/B2
Kum-Dag, U.S.S.R. 48/F6
Kume (isl.), Japan 81/M6
Kumertau, U.S.S.R. 52/J4
Kumeu, N. Zealand 100/B1
Kümgang (mt.), N. Korea 81/D4
Kumiyama, Japan 81/J7
Kumkale, Turkey 63/B6
Kumköy, Turkey 63/B6
Kumla, Sweden 18/J7
Kumluca, Turkey 63/D4
Kummerowersee (lake), Germany 22/E2
Kumo (riv.), Finland 7/G2
Kumo, Nigeria 106/G7
Kumphawapi, Thailand 72/D3
Kumta, India 68/C6
Kumukahi (cape), Hawaii 218/K5
Kumul (Hami), China 77/D3
Kuna, Idaho 220/B6
Kunágota, Hungary 41/F3
Kunashiri (isl.), Japan 81/N1
Kunda, U.S.S.R. 52/C3
Kunda, U.S.S.R. 53/D1
Kundiawa, Papua N.G. 85/B7
Kundl, Austria 41/A3
Künes (Xinyuan), China 77/B3
Künes He (riv.), China 77/B3
Kungälv, Sweden 18/G8
Kunghit (isl.), Br. Col. 184/B4
Kungsbacka, Sweden 18/G8
Kungu, Zaire 102/D4
Kungu, Zaire 115/C3
Kungur, U.S.S.R. 7/K3
Kungur, U.S.S.R. 48/F4
Kungur, U.S.S.R. 52/J3
Kunhegyes, Hungary 41/F3
Kunia, Hawaii 218/E2
Kuningan, Indonesia 85/H2
Kunkle, Ohio 284/A2
Kunkletown, Pa. 294/M4
Kunlong, Burma 72/C2
Kunlun (range), China 54/K6
Kunlun (range), India 68/D1
Kunlun Shan (range), China 77/B4
Kunmadaras, Hungary 41/F3
Kunming, China 77/F6
Kunming, China 2/Q4
Kunming, China 54/M7
Kunsan, S. Korea 81/C6
Kunszentmárton, Hungary 41/F3
Kunszentmiklós, Hungary 41/E3
Kununurra, W. Australia 88/D3
Kununurra, W. Australia 92/E2
Kuolayarvi, U.S.S.R. 18/S3
Kuopio (prov.), Finland 18/P5
Kuopio, Finland 7/G2
Kuopio, Finland 18/Q5
Kupa (riv.), Yugoslavia 45/B3
Kupang, Indonesia 54/O11
Kupang, Indonesia 85/G8
Kuparuk (riv.), Alaska 196/H1
Kupino, U.S.S.R. 48/H4
Kupiškis, U.S.S.R. 53/C3
Kupreanof (isl.), Alaska 196/N1
Kupreanov, Alaska 196/M2
Kupyansk, U.S.S.R. 52/E5
Kuqa, China 77/B3
Kur (isl.), Indonesia 85/J7
Kura (riv.), U.S.S.R. 48/E6
Kura (riv.), U.S.S.R. 52/G6
Kuraiyima, Jordan 65/D3
Kurang (riv.), Iran 66/G4
Kurashiki, Japan 81/F6
Kurayoshi, Japan 81/F6
Kurdistan (Kordestan) (prov.), Iran 66/E3
Kurdistan (reg.), Iran 59/D2
Kurdistan (reg.), Iran 66/D2
Kurdistan (reg.), Iraq 59/D2
Kurdistan (reg.), Iraq 66/C2
Kurdistan (reg.), Turkey 59/D2
Kürdzhali, Bulgaria 45/G5
Kure (atoll), Hawaii 187/J3
Kure (atoll), Hawaii 218/A5
Kure, Japan 81/F6
Küre, Turkey 63/E2
Küre (mts.), Turkey 63/E2
Kure Beach, N.C. 281/O7
Kuressaare, U.S.S.R. 53/B1
Kuressaare, U.S.S.R. 52/B3
Kurgan, U.S.S.R. 54/H4
Kurgan, U.S.S.R. 48/G4
Kurgan-Tyube, U.S.S.R. 48/G6
Kuria Muria (isls.), Oman 54/G8
Kuria Muria (isls.), Oman 59/G6
Kurikka, Finland 18/M5
Kuril (isls.), U.S.S.R. 2/S3
Kuril (isls.), U.S.S.R. 54/R5
Kuril (isls.), U.S.S.R. 48/P5
Kuril'sk, U.S.S.R. 48/P5
Ku-ring-gai, N. S. Wales 88/K4
Kurla, India 68/B7
Kurmuk, Sudan 111/F5
Kurnell (pen.), N.S. Wales 97/J4
Kurnool, India 54/J8
Kurnool, India 68/D5
Kuroiso, Japan 81/K5
Kuroki, Sask. 181/H4
Kurow, N. Zealand 100/C6
Kurri Kurri-Weston, N.S. Wales 97/F3
Kuršėnai, U.S.S.R. 53/B2
Kursk, U.S.S.R. 7/H3
Kursk, U.S.S.R. 48/D4
Kursk, U.S.S.R. 52/E4
Kurşunlu, Turkey 63/E2

Kurtalan, Turkey 63/J3
Kurthwood, La. 238/F4
Kurtistown, Hawaii 218/J5
Kurtz, Ind. 227/E7
Kurucaşile, Turkey 63/E2
Kuruçay (riv.), Turkey 63/K2
Kuruktag Shan (range), China 77/C3
Kuruman, S. Africa 118/C5
Kurume, Japan 81/E7
Kurundi, North. Terr. 93/D6
Kurunegala, Sri Lanka 68/E7
Kurungiku (mts.), Guyana 131/B3
Kurupukari, Guyana 131/B3
Kuş (lake), Turkey 63/B2
Kuşada (gulf), Turkey 63/B4
Kuşadası, Turkey 63/B4
Kushchevskaya, U.S.S.R. 52/E5
Kushequa, Pa. 294/F2
Kushikino, Japan 81/E8
Kushima, Japan 81/E8
Kushimoto, Japan 81/G7
Kushiro, Japan 54/R5
Kushiro, Japan 81/M2
Kushka, U.S.S.R. 48/G6
Kushog (lake), Ontario 177/F2
Kuskokwim (bay), Alaska 196/F3
Kuskokwim (mts.), Alaska 196/G2
Kuskokwim (riv.), Alaska 146/C3
Kuskokwim (riv.), Alaska 188/C6
Kuskokwim (riv.), Alaska 196/G2
Kuskokwim, North Fork (riv.), Alaska 196/H2
Kuskokwim, South Fork (riv.), Alaska 196/H2
Kuskokwim (riv.), U.S. 4/C17
Küsnacht, Switzerland 39/G2
Kusŏng, N. Korea 81/B4
Küssnacht am Rigi, Switzerland 39/F2
Kustanay, U.S.S.R. 54/H4
Kustanay, U.S.S.R. 48/G4
Kustatan, Alaska 196/B1
Küstrin, Poland 47/B2
Kut, Iraq 59/D3
Kut, Iraq 66/D4
Kut, Ko (isl.), Thailand 72/D5
Kuta, Nigeria 106/F7
Kütahya (prov.), Turkey 63/C3
Kütahya, Turkey 59/B2
Kütahya, Turkey 63/C3
Kutaisi, U.S.S.R. 7/J4
Kutaisi, U.S.S.R. 48/E5
Kutaisi, U.S.S.R. 52/F6
Kutaraja (Banda Aceh), Indonesia 85/A4
Kutari (riv.), Guyana 131/C4
Kutari (riv.), Suriname 131/C4
Kutch, Colo. 208/M5
Kutch (Kachchh), Rann of (salt marsh) 54/H7
Kutch (Kachchh) (gulf), India 68/B4
Kutch (Kachchh) (reg.), India 68/B4
Kutch (Kachchh), Rann of (salt marsh), India 68/B4
Kutch (Kachchh), Rann of (salt lake), Pakistan 59/K5
Kutch (Kachchh), Rann of (salt marsh), Pakistan 68/B4
Kutcharo (lake), Japan 81/M2
Kutina, Yugoslavia 45/C3
Kutná Hora, Czech. 41/C2
Kutno, Poland 47/D2
Kutoarjo, Indonesia 85/J2
Kuttawa, Ky. 237/E6
Kutu, Zaire 115/C4
Kutum, Sudan 111/D5
Kúty, Czech. 41/D2
Kutztown, Pa. 294/L4
Kuujjuac (Fort-Chimo), Québec 162/K4
Kuujjuac (Fort-Chimo), Québec 174/F2
Kuujjuarapik, Québec 162/J4
Kuujjuarapik, Québec 174/B1
Kuusamo, Finland 18/Q4
Kuusamojärvi (lake), Finland 18/Q4
Kuusankoski, Finland 18/P6
Kuvandyk, U.S.S.R. 52/J4
Kuwait 2/M4
Kuwait (cap.), Kuwait 59/E4
Kuwait 54/F7
KUWAIT 59/E4
Kuvango, Angola 115/C6
Kuybyshev (Samara), U.S.S.R. 2/M3
Kuybyshev (Samara), U.S.S.R. 7/K3
Kuybyshev (Samara), U.S.S.R. 48/F4
Kuybyshev (Samara), U.S.S.R. 52/H4
Kuybyshev (Samara), U.S.S.R. 48/H4
Kuybyshev (res.), U.S.S.R. 48/E4
Kuybyshev (res.), U.S.S.R. 52/G4
Kuybyshev (res.), U.S.S.R. 7/K3
Kuyto (lake), U.S.S.R. 52/D2
Kuytun, China 77/C3
Kuyucak, Turkey 63/C4
Kuyuwini (riv.), Guyana 131/B4
Kuznetsk, U.S.S.R. 52/G4
Kuzomen', U.S.S.R. 52/E1
Kvaenangen (fjord), Norway 18/N2
Kvaerndrup, Denmark 21/D7
Kvaløya (isl.), Norway 18/O1
Kvaløya (isl.), Norway 18/K2
Kvarner (gulf), Yugoslavia 45/B3
Kvichak, Alaska 196/G3
Kvichak (bay), Alaska 196/G3
Kvikkjokk, Sweden 18/K3
Kvinnherad, Norway 18/E7
Kvissleby, Sweden 18/K5
Kviteseid, Norway 18/F7
Kwa (riv.), Zaire 115/C4
Kwai (Mae Nam Khwae Noi) (riv.), Thailand 72/C4
Kwajalein (atoll), Marshall Is. 87/G5
Kwakoegron, Suriname 131/D3
Kwakwani, Guyana 131/C3
Kwale, Kenya 102/F5
Kwale, Kenya 115/G4
Kwamouth, Zaire 115/C4
Kwangchow (Canton), China 77/H7
Kwangju, S. Korea 54/O6
Kwangju, S. Korea 81/C6
Kwango (riv.), Zaire 115/C5

Kwangsi Chuang Aut. Reg. (Guangxi Zhuangzu), China 77/G7
Kwangtung (Guangdong), China 77/H7
Kwanmo (mt.), N. Korea 81/D3
Kwara (state), Nigeria 106/F7
Kwekwe, Zimbabwe 118/D3
Kwekwe, Zimbabwe 102/E6
Kweichow (Guizhou), China 77/G6
Kweilin (Guilin), China 77/H6
Kweisui (Hohhot), China 77/H3
Kweiyang (Guiyang), China 77/G6
Kwethluk, Alaska 196/F2
Kwidzin, Poland 47/D2
Kwigillingok, Alaska 196/F3
Kwilu (riv.), Angola 115/C5
Kwilu (riv.), Zaire 115/C4
Kwinana-Newtown, W. Australia 88/B2
Kwinana New Town, W. Australia 92/A1
Kwinitsa, Br. Col. 184/D3
Kwitaro (riv.), Guyana 131/B4
Kyabé, Chad 111/C6
Kyabram, Victoria 97/C5
Kyaikto, Burma 72/C3
Kyakhta, U.S.S.R. 54/M4
Kyakhta, U.S.S.R. 48/L4
Kyalite, N.S. Wales 97/B4
Kyana, Ind. 227/D8
Kyancutta, S. Australia 94/D5
Kyangin, Burma 72/B3
Kyaukme, Burma 72/C2
Kyaukpadaung, Burma 72/B2
Kyaukpyu, Burma 72/B3
Kyaukse, Burma 72/C2
Kybartai, U.S.S.R. 53/B3
Kyeburn, N. Zealand 100/C6
Kyger, Ohio 284/F8
Kyger, W. Va. 312/D5
Kyjov, Czech. 41/D2
Kykosmovi, Ariz. 198/E3
Kyle, Sask. 181/C5
Kyle, S. Dak. 298/E7
Kyle, Texas 303/E3
Kyleakin, Scotland 15/C3
Kylemore, Sask. 181/H4
Kyle of Lochalsh, Scotland 15/C3
Kyle of Tongue (inlet), Scotland 15/D2
Kyles Ford, Tenn. 237/R7
Kylestrome, Scotland 15/D2
Kymi (prov.), Finland 18/O6
Kyneton, Victoria 97/C5
Kynšperk, Czech. 41/B1
Kynuna, Queensland 95/B4
Kyogle, N.S. Wales 97/G1
Kyonan, Japan 81/O3
Kyŏnghŭng, N. Korea 81/E2
Kyŏngju, S. Korea 81/D6
Kyoto (pref.), Japan 81/J7
Kyoto, Japan 54/P6
Kyoto, Japan 81/J7
Kyrenia, Cyprus 63/E5
Kyritz, Germany 22/E2
Kysucké Nové Mesto, Czech. 41/E2
Kythrea, Cyprus 63/E5
Kyuquot, Br. Col. 184/D5
Kyuquot (sound), Br. Col. 184/D5
Kyushu (isl.), Japan 2/P4
Kyushu (isl.), Japan 54/P6
Kyushu (isl.), Japan 81/E7
Kyustendil, Bulgaria 45/F4
Kyusyur, U.S.S.R. 48/N2
Kywebwe, Burma 72/C3
Kyzyl (riv.), U.S.S.R. 54/L4
Kyzyl, U.S.S.R. 48/K4
Kyzyl-Kum (des.), U.S.S.R. 48/G5
Kzyl-Orda, U.S.S.R. 54/H5
Kzyl-Orda, U.S.S.R. 48/G5

L

Laa an der Thaya, Austria 41/D2
La Aduana, Venezuela 124/D3
Laager, Tenn. 237/K10
Laakirchen, Austria 41/B3
La Almunia de Doña Godina, Spain 33/F2
La Altagracia (prov.), Dom. Rep. 158/F6
La Anna, Pa. 294/M4
La Antigua Veracruz, Mexico 150/Q1
La Araucanía (reg.), Chile 138/E2
La Asunción, Venezuela 124/G2
Laau (pt.), Hawaii 218/G1
Lac-Frontière, Québec 172/H3
Lac Giao (Ban Me Thuot), Vietnam 72/E4
Laayoune, W. Sahara 102/A2
Laayoune, Western Sahara 106/B3
Labadie, Mo. 261/L5
Labadieville, La. 238/K4
La Baie, Québec 172/G1
La Baie-de-Shawinigan, Québec 172/E3
La Banda, Argentina 143/D2
La Bandera (pt.), P. Rico 161/F1
La Bañeza, Spain 33/C1
La Barca, Mexico 150/H6
La Barge, Wyo. 319/B3
La Barge (creek), Wyo. 319/B3
La Barra de Navidad, Mexico 150/G7
Labasheeda, Ireland 17/C6
La Baule-Escoublac, France 28/B4
L'Abbaye, Switzerland 39/B3
La Belle, Fla. 212/E5
La Bella (lake), Wis. 317/H1
Laberge (lake), Yukon 162/C3
Laberinto de las Doce Leguas (cays), Cuba 158/F3
La Berra (mt.), Switzerland 39/D3
Labette (co.), Kansas 232/G4
La Bella (lake), Wis. 317/H1
Laberge (lake), Yukon 162/C3

Labinsk, U.S.S.R. 52/F6
La Bisbal, Spain 33/H1
La Blanquilla (isl.), Venezuela 124/F2
La Bolsa, Uruguay 145/C1
La Bolt, S. Dak. 298/R3
La Bonita, Ecuador 128/D2
La Boquilla (res.), Mexico 150/G3
Laborec (riv.), Czech. 41/F2
Laborie, St. Lucia 161/G7
La Bostonnais, Québec 172/E2
Labougle, Argentina 143/G5
Laboulaye, Argentina 143/D3
Labrador (sea) 146/N4
Labrador (reg.), Canada 2/G3
Labrador (reg.), Newf. 166/B2
Labrador (sea), Newf. 166/C2
Labrador (reg.), Newf. 146/M4
Labrador (reg.), Newf. 162/K4
Labrador City, Newf. 166/A3
La Branche, Mich. 250/B3
Lábrea, Brazil 132/G10
La Brea, Trin. & Tob. 161/A11
Labrieville, Québec 174/C3
La Broquerie, Manitoba 179/F5
Labuan, Malaysia 85/E4
Labuan (isl.), Malaysia 85/E4
Labuan (state), Malaysia 85/F4
Labuha, Indonesia 85/H6
Labuhan, Indonesia 85/G2
Labuk (bay), Malaysia 85/F4
Labutta, Burma 72/B3
Labyrinth (canyon), Utah 304/D5
Labytnangi, U.S.S.R. 48/G3
Lac (bay), Neth. Ant. 161/D9
Lac-à-Beauce, Québec 172/E2
Lacadena, Sask. 181/C5
Lacadie, Québec 172/J4
La Cahouane, Haiti 158/H6
Lac-à-la-Croix, Québec 172/F1
Lac-Alouette, Québec 172/D4
Lacamp, La. 238/E4
La Canada Flintridge, Calif. 204/C10
Lacanau (lake), France 28/C5
La Canoa, Venezuela 124/G3
Lacantum (riv.), Mexico 150/O8
La Capilla, 136/C3
La Carlota, Argentina 143/D3
La Carlota, Philippines 82/D5
La Carlota, Spain 33/D4
La Carolina, Spain 33/E3
Lacassine, La. 238/E6
Lac-au-Saumon, Québec 172/B2
Lac-aux-Sables, Québec 172/E3
Lac Baker, New Bruns. 170/B1
Lac-Beauport, Québec 172/F3
Lac-Bouchette, Québec 172/E1
Lac-Carré, Québec 172/C3
Lac-Cayamant, Québec 172/A3
Lac-Chat, Québec 172/C2
Lac Court Oreilles Ind. Res., Wis. 317/D4
Lac de Gras (lake), N.W. Terr. 187/G3
Lac-Delage, Québec 172/F3
Lac-des-Aigles, Québec 172/J2
Lac des Arcs, Alberta 182/C4
Lac-des-Écorces, Québec 172/C3
Lac-des-Îles, Québec 172/B3
Lac-Drolet, Québec 172/G4
Lac du Bonnet, Manitoba 179/G4
Lac-du-Cerf, Québec 172/B3
Lac du Flambeau, Wis. 317/G4
Lac du Flambeau Ind. Res., Wis. 317/G3
Lac-Édouard, Québec 172/E2
La Ceiba, Hond. 146/K8
La Ceiba, Honduras 154/D3
La Ceiba, Apure, Venezuela 124/C4
La Ceiba, Trujillo, Venezuela 124/C4
La Center, Ky. 237/C6
La Center, Wash. 310/C5
Lacepede (bay), S. Australia 88/F7
Lacepede (bay), S. Australia 94/D7
Lacepede (range), W. Australia 88/D3
Lacepede (isls.), W. Australia 92/C2
Lac-Etchemin, Québec 172/G3
Lacey, Ark. 202/G7
Lacey, Wash. 310/C3
Lacey Spring, Va. 307/L3
Laceys Spring, Ala. 195/E1
Laceyville, Pa. 294/K2
Lacey, Ky. 237/R6
Lacha (lake), U.S.S.R. 52/E2
La Chapelle, Haiti 158/G5
La Charité-sur-Loire, France 28/E4
La Châtre, France 28/D4
La Chaux-de-Fonds, Switzerland 39/C2
Lachay (pt.), Peru 128/D8
Lachen, Switzerland 39/G2
Lachenaie, Québec 172/D4
Lachine, Mich. 250/F4
Lachine, Québec 172/J4
Lachlan (riv.), N.S. Wales 88/G6
Lachlan (range), N.S. Wales 97/C3
Lachlan (riv.), N.S. Wales 97/C3
La Chorrera, Colombia 126/C8
La Chorrera, Panama 154/H6
Lac-Humqui, Québec 172/B2
Lachute, Québec 172/C4
La Ciénaga, Dom. Rep. 158/D6
La Ciotat, France 28/F6
La Clarita, Argentina 143/G5

La Clarita, Argentina 143/G5
La Ronge Prov. Park, Sask. 181/M
Laclede, Idaho 220/B1
La Clede, Ill. 222/E5
Laclede (co.), Mo. 261/G7
Laclede, Mo. 261/F3
Lac-Mégantic, Québec 172/G4
Lacolle, Québec 172/D4
La Colmena, Paraguay 144/B5
La Coloma, Cuba 158/B2
La Colonia, Chile 138/D7
Lacomb, Oreg. 291/E3
Lacombe, Alberta 182/D3
Lacombe, Alta. 168/E5
Lacombe, La. 238/L6
Lacon, Ill. 222/D2
Lacona, Iowa 229/G6
Lacona, N.Y. 276/J3
La Concepción, Honduras 154/E3
La Concepción, Panama 154/F6
La Concepción, Venezuela 124/C2
La Concepción, Venezuela 124/B2
La Conception, Québec 172/C3
La Concordia, Mexico 150/N9
Laconia, Ind. 227/E8
Laconia, N.H. 268/E4
Laconia, Tenn. 237/C10
La Conner, Wash. 310/C2
La Conquista, Nicaragua 154/D5
Lacoochee, Fla. 212/D3
La Corey, Alberta 182/E2
La Coronilla, Uruguay 145/F4
La Coruña (prov.), Spain 33/B1
La Coruña, Spain 33/B1
La Coruña, Spain 7/D4
La Coste, Texas 303/J11
La Courneuve, France 28/B1
Lacovia, Jamaica 158/H6
Lac Pelletier, Sask. 181/C6
Lac-Poulin, Québec 172/G3
Lac qui Parle (co.), Minn. 255/B6
Lac qui Parle, Minn. 255/B5
Lac qui Parle (lake), Minn. 255/C5
Lac qui Parle (riv.), Minn. 255/B6
Lacre (pt.), Neth. Ant. 161/E9
La Crescent, Minn. 255/G7
La Crescenta-Montrose, Calif. 204/C10
La Crete, Alberta 182/35
La Croche, Québec 172/E2
La Croix (lake), Minn. 255/F2
La Crosse, Fla. 212/D2
La Crosse, Georgia 217/D6
La Crosse, Ind. 227/D2
La Crosse, Kansas 232/E3
La Crosse, Va. 307/M7
Lacrosse, Wash. 310/H4
La Crosse, Wis. 146/J5
La Crosse, Wis. 188/H2
La Crosse (co.), Wis. 317/D8
La Crosse, Wis. 317/D8
La Cruz, Argentina 143/E2
La Cruz, Chile 138/F2
La Cruz, Colombia 126/B7
La Cruz, Chihuahua, Mexico 150/G3
La Cruz, Sinaloa, Mexico 150/F5
La Cruz, Nicaragua 154/E4
La Cruz, Uruguay 145/E2
Lac-Saguay, Québec 172/B3
Lac-Saint-Charles, Québec 172/F3
Lac-Sainte-Marie, Québec 172/A4
Lac-Saint-Jean-Est (co.), Québec 172/E1
Lac-Saint-Jean-Est (county), Québec 174/C2
Lac-Saint-Jean-Ouest (co.), Québec 172/E1
Lac-Saint-Jean-Ouest (county), Québec 174/C2
Lac-Saint-Joseph, Québec 172/F3
Lac-Saint-Paul, Québec 172/B3
Lac-Sergent, Québec 172/F3
Lac Seul, Ontario 175/32
La Cuchilla, Uruguay 145/F3
La Cueva, N. Mex. 274/D3
La Cumbre, Argentina 143/C3
La Cure, Switzerland 39/B4
Lacuy (pen.), Chile 138/D4
Lac Vert, Sask. 181/G3
La Cygne, Kansas 232/H3
Ladakh (reg.), India 68/D2
Ladd, Ill. 222/D2
Ladder (creek), Kansas 232/A3
Ladder (hills), Scotland 15/E3
Laddonia, Mo. 261/J4
La Decharge, Québec 172/F1
Ladelle, Ark. 202/G7
Ladgasht (Qila Ladgasht), Pakistan 68/A3
Ladhar Bheinn (mt.), Scotland 15/C3
Ladiesburg, Md. 245/J2
La Digue (isl.), Seychelles 118/J5
Lâdik, Turkey 63/G2
Ladispoli, Italy 34/E6
Ladiz, Iran 66/M6
Ladner, S. Dak. 298/B2
Lado, Sudan 111/F6
Ladoga, Ind. 227/D5
Ladoga (lake), U.S.S.R. 7/H2
Ladoga (lake), U.S.S.R. 48/D3
Ladoga (lake), U.S.S.R. 52/D2
La Dôle (mt.), Switzerland 39/B4
Ladonia, Texas 303/J4
Ladora, Iowa 229/J5
La Dorada, Colombia 126/C3
Ladrillero (gulf), Chile 138/C8
Ladrillero (mt.), Chile 138/E10
Ladron (mts.), N. Mex. 274/D4
Ladrones (isls.), Panama 154/F7
Ladson, S.C. 296/G6
La Due, Mo. 261/F5
Ladue, Mo. 261/P3
La Durantaye, Québec 172/G3
Lady (pond), Newf. 166/D2
Lady Ann (str.), N.W. Terr. 187/K2
Ladybank, Scotland 15/E4
Lady Barrón, Tasmania 99/E2
Ladybrand, S. Africa 118/D5
Lady Franklin (bay), N.W. Terr. 187/M1

ady Franklin (isl.), N.W. Terr. 187/M3
ady Lake, Fla. 212/E3
ady Lake, Sask. 181/J3
ady's Island Lake (inlet), Ireland 17/J7
adysmith, Br. Col. 184/J3
adysmith, S. Africa 102/F7
adysmith, S. Africa 118/D5
adysmith, Va. 307/N4
adysmith, Wis. 317/D5
adywood, Manitoba 179/F4
ae, Papua N.G. 85/B7
ae, Papua N.G. 86/A2
ae, Papua N.G. 87/E6
ae, Thailand 72/D3
aem Chong Phra (cape), Thailand 72/C5
aem Pho (cape), Thailand 72/D6
aem Talumphuk (cape), Thailand 72/D5
ae o Kealaikahiki (pt.), Hawaii 218/H3
aerdal, Norway 18/E6
a Esmeralda, Argentina 143/G5
a Esmeralda, Bolivia 136/D8
a Esmeralda, Venezuela 124/F6
aesø (isl.), Denmark 18/G8
aesø (isl.), Denmark 21/D3
a Esperanza, Argentina 143/B7
a Esperanza, Bolivia 136/D4
a Esperanza, Honduras 154/C3
a Esperanza, Venezuela 124/H3
a Estrada, Spain 33/B1
a Estrella, Chile 138/F5
a Estrelleta (prov.), Dom. Rep. 158/C5
a Falda, Argentina 143/D3
a Farge, Wis. 317/E8
a Fargeville, N.Y. 276/M2
afayette, Ala. 195/H5
afayette (co.), Ark. 202/C7
afayette, Calif. 204/K2
afayette (co.), Fla. 212/C2
a Fayette, Georgia 217/B1
a Fayette, Ill. 222/C2
afayette, Ind. 188/J2
afayette, Ind. 227/D4
a Fayette, Ky. 237/F7
afayette (par.), La. 238/F6
afayette, La. 238/F6
afayette, Minn. 255/D6
afayette (co.), Miss. 256/E2
afayette (co.), Mo. 261/E4
afayette (mt.), N.H. 268/D4
afayette, N.J. 273/D1
a Fayette, N.Y. 276/H5
afayette, Ohio 284/C4
afayette, Oreg. 291/A2
a Fayette, R.I. 249/H6
afayette, Tenn. 237/J7
afayette (co.), Wis. 317/F10
afayette-Elliston, Va. 307/H6
afayette Springs, Miss. 256/F2
afe, Ark. 202/J1
a Fe, Cuba 158/A2
a Feria, Texas 303/G11
a Ferté-Macé, France 28/C3
afferty, Ohio 284/H5
afia, Nigeria 106/F7
afiagi, Nigeria 106/F7
afitte, La. 238/K7
a Flèche, France 28/C4
afleche, Sask. 181/E6
afnitz (riv.), Austria 41/D3
a Floresta, Uruguay 145/C7
a Follette, Tenn. 237/N8
a Fontaine, Ind. 227/F3
afontaine, Kansas 232/G4
afontaine, Québec 172/C4
afourche (par.), La. 238/K7
a Fourche, La. 238/J7
afourche (bayou), La. 238/K8
a France, S.C. 296/B2
a Fría, Venezuela 124/B3
aful, India 68/G7
agacéville, New Bruns. 170/E1
a Gallareta, Argentina 143/F5
agan (riv.), N. Ireland 17/K2
agarfljót (stream), Iceland 21/C1
a Garita, Colo. 208/G7
a Garita (mts.), Colo. 208/F7
agawe, Philippines 82/C2
agayan, Philippines 82/C2
age, Germany 22/C3
agen (riv.), Norway 18/G6
ages, Brazil 132/D9
ages, Brazil 120/D5
aggan, Scotland 15/D2
aggan, Scotland 10/D2
aggan (bay), Scotland 15/B5
aggan, Loch (lake), Scotland 15/D4
aghouat, Algeria 106/E2
aghouat, Algeria 102/C1
aghy, Ireland 17/E2
a Gineta, Spain 33/E3
agkadia, Greece 45/E7
a Glace, Alberta 182/A2
a Gloria, Colombia 126/D3
a Gloria, Cuba 158/G2
ago, Neth. Ant. 161/E10
agoa, Portugal 33/B4
agoa da Prata, Brazil 135/D2
agoa Dourada, Brazil 135/D2
ago Blanco, Argentina 143/B6
agoen, Neth. Ant. 161/F8
a Goleta, Colombia 126/B3
a Gomera, Guatemala 154/B3
agonegro, Italy 34/E4
agonoy (gulf), Philippines 82/E4
agoon (lake), S. Australia 88/F6
ago Ranco, Chile 138/G3
agos (state), Nigeria 106/E7
agos (cap.), Nigeria 2/K5
agos (cap.), Nigeria 102/C4
agos (cap.), Nigeria 106/E7
agos, Portugal 33/B4
ago Salto Grande (res.), Brazil 132/B10
agos de Moreno, Mexico 150/J6

Lagosta (Lastovo) (isl.), Yugoslavia 45/C4
La Goulette (Halq el Oued), Tunisia 106/G1
Lago Verde, Chile 138/E5
La Grand-Combe, France 28/E5
La Grande, Oreg. 188/C1
La Grande, Oreg. 291/J2
La Grande, Wash. 310/C4
La Grand Rivière (riv.), Que. 162/J5
La Grange, Ark. 202/J4
La Grange, Australia 87/C7
La Grange, Calif. 204/E6
La Grange, Ga. 188/K4
La Grange, Georgia 217/B4
La Grange (co.), Ind. 227/G1
Lagrange, Ind. 227/F1
La Grange, Ky. 237/L4
Lagrange, Maine 243/F5
Lagrange ●, Maine 243/F5
La Grange, Mo. 261/K2
La Grange, N.C. 281/O4
Lagrange, Ohio 284/F3
La Grange, Tenn. 237/C10
La Grange, Texas 303/G8
La Grange, W. Australia 92/C2
Lagrange, Wyo. 319/H4
La Grange Park, Ill. 222/B5
La Granja (San Ildefonso), Spain 33/E2
La Gran Sabana (plain), Venezuela 124/D3
La Grita, Venezuela 124/C3
Lagro, Ind. 227/F3
La Grue (bayou), Ark. 202/H5
La Guadeloupe, Québec 172/F4
La Guaira, Venezuela 124/E2
La Guaira, Venezuela 120/C1
La Guajira (dept.), Colombia 126/D2
La Guardia, Bolivia 136/D5
La Guardia, Spain 33/B2
Laguardia, Spain 33/E1
La Guata, Honduras 154/D3
Laguna (creek), Ariz. 198/E2
Laguna (dam), Ariz. 198/A6
Laguna (res.), Ariz. 198/A6
Laguna, Brazil 132/D10
Laguna (res.), Calif. 204/L11
Laguna, N. Mex. 274/B3
Laguna (prov.), Philippines 82/C3
Laguna Beach, Calif. 204/G10
Laguna de Perlas, Nicaragua 154/F4
Laguna Hills, Calif. 204/D11
Laguna Niguel, Calif. 204/H10
Laguna Paiva, Argentina 143/F5
Lagunas, Chile 138/B3
Lagunas, Peru 128/E5
Laguna Yema, Argentina 143/D1
Lagunetas, Venezuela 124/C3
Lagunillas, Bolivia 136/D6
Lagunillas, Chile 138/A7
Lagunillas, Venezuela 124/C2
Lagunitas, Calif. 204/H1
La Habana (Havana) (prov.), Cuba 158/C1
La Habana, Ciudad de (prov.), Cuba 158/C1
La Habra, Calif. 204/D11
Lahad Datu, Malaysia 85/F5
Lahaina, Hawaii 218/H2
Lahaina, Hawaii 188/F5
Laham, Indonesia 85/F5
Lahan, Nong (lake), Thailand 72/D3
La Harpe, Ill. 222/C3
La Harpe, Kansas 232/G4
Lahat, Indonesia 85/C6
La Have, Nova Scotia 168/D4
La Have (isl.), Nova Scotia 168/D4
La Have (riv.), Nova Scotia 168/D4
Lahej, Yemen 59/E7
La Higuera, Chile 138/A7
Lahijan, Iran 66/C2
Lahinch, Ireland 17/C6
Lahmansville, W. Va. 312/H4
Lahn, Germany 22/C3
Lahn (riv.), Germany 22/C3
Lahnstein, Germany 22/B3
Laholm, Sweden 18/H8
Lahoma, Okla. 288/K2
La Honda, Calif. 204/J3
Lahontan (res.), Nev. 266/B3
Lahore, Pakistan 59/K3
Lahore, Pakistan 68/C2
Lahore, Pakistan 54/J6
Lahore, Va. 307/M4
La Horqueta, Venezuela 124/G3
Lahr, Germany 22/B4
Lahri, Pakistan 63/B3
Lahti, Finland 7/C2
Lahti, Finland 18/O6
La Huaca, Peru 128/B5
La Huerta, Mexico 150/G7
Laï, Chad 111/C6
Laï, Chad 102/D4
Lai Chau, Vietnam 72/D2
Laidlaw, Br. Col. 184/M3
Laidon, Loch (lake), Scotland 15/D4
Laie, Hawaii 218/E1
Laie (pt.), Hawaii 218/E1
L'Aigle, France 23/D3
Lai-hka, Burma 72/C2
Laila, Saudi Arabia 59/E5
Lailan, Iraq 66/D3
La Inglesa, Venezuela 124/G3
Laings, Ohio 284/J6
Laingsburg, Mich. 250/E6
Lainioälv (riv.), Sweden 18/N3
Lair, Ky. 237/K4
Laird, Colo. 208/P2
Laird, Sask. 181/J3
Lairdsville, Pa. 294/J3
Lairg, Scotland 10/D1
Lairg, Scotland 15/D2
Lais, Philippines 82/E7
Laisamis, Kenya 115/G4
La Isla, Isla 3C3/A10
Laiwui, Indonesia 85/H6
Laiyang, China 77/K4

Laja (riv.), Chile 138/E1
La Jalca, Peru 128/D6
La Jara, Colo. 208/H8
La Jara, N. Mex. 274/B2
Lajas, P. Rico 161/A2
Lajes do Pico, Portugal 33/B1
Lajinha, Brazil 135/E2
La Jolla, Calif. 204/H11
La Jolla Ind. Res., Calif. 204/J10
Lajord, Sask. 181/G5
La Jose, Pa. 294/E4
Lajosmizse, Hungary 41/E3
La Joya, Bolivia 136/B5
La Joya, N. Mex. 274/C4
La Joya, Peru 128/G11
La Joya, Texas 303/F11
La Junta, Colo. 208/M7
La Junta, Colo. 208/M7
Lak Dera (dry riv.), Kenya 115/H3
Lak Dera (dry riv.), Somalia 115/H3
Lake (co.), Calif. 204/C4
Lake (co.), Colo. 208/G4
Lake (co.), Fla. 212/E3
Lake (co.), Ill. 222/E1
Lake (co.), Ind. 227/C2
Lake, Ky. 237/O6
Lake (co.), Mich. 250/D5
Lake, Mich. 250/E5
Lake (co.), Minn. 255/G3
Lake, Miss. 256/F6
Lake (co.), Mont. 262/B3
Lake (co.), Ohio 284/H2
Lake (co.), Oreg. 291/H5
Lake (creek), Oreg. 291/J3
Lake (co.), S. Dak. 298/P5
Lake (co.), Tenn. 237/B8
Lake (co.), Utah 304/A5
Lake (creek), Wash. 310/G3
Lake Alfred, Fla. 212/E3
Lake Alma, Sask. 181/G6
Lake Alpine, Calif. 204/F5
Lake Andes, S. Dak. 298/M7
Lake Ann, Mich. 250/B4
Lake Ariel, Pa. 294/M3
Lake Arrowhead, Calif. 204/H9
Lake Arthur, La. 238/E6
Lake Arthur, N. Mex. 274/E5
Lake Arthur, N.S. Wales 97/D3
Lake Barcroft, Va. 307/S3
Lake Barrington, Ill. 222/A5
Lake Benton, Minn. 255/B6
Lake Beulah, Wis. 317/J2
Lake Bluff, Ill. 222/B4
Lake Boga, Victoria 97/B4
Lake Bolac, Victoria 97/B5
Lake Bronson, Minn. 255/B2
Lake Bruce, Ind. 227/E2
Lake Buena Vista, Fla. 212/E3
Lake Butler, Fla. 212/D1
Lake Butte Des Morts (Butte Des Morts), Wis. 317/J7
Lake Cargelligo, N.S. Wales 97/D3
Lake Carmel, N.Y. 276/N8
Lake Carroll, Fla. 212/C2
Lake Catherine, Ill. 222/E1
Lake Charles, La. 188/H4
Lake Charles, La. 238/D6
Lake Chelan Nat'l Rec. Area, Wash. 310/E2
Lake Church, Wis. 317/L9
Lake Cicott, Ind. 227/D3
Lake City, Ark. 202/K2
Lake City, Calif. 204/E2
Lake City, Colo. 208/E6
Lake City, Fla. 212/D1
Lake City, Georgia 217/K2
Lake City, Ill. 222/E4
Lake City, Iowa 229/D4
Lake City, Kansas 232/D4
Lake City, Mich. 250/D4
Lake City, Minn. 255/F6
Lake City, Pa. 294/B1
Lake City, S.C. 296/J3
Lake City, Tenn. 237/N8
Lake Clark Nat'l Park, Alaska 196/H2
Lake Clark Nat'l Pres., Alaska 196/H2
Lake Clear, N.Y. 276/M2
Lake Como, Fla. 212/E2
Lake Como, Miss. 256/F6
Lake Como, Pa. 294/M2
Lake Cormorant, Miss. 256/D1
Lake Cowichan, Br. Col. 184/J3
Lakecreek, Oreg. 291/E5
Lake Crystal, Minn. 255/D6
Lake Dallas, Texas 303/G1
Lake Delton, Wis. 317/G8
Lake District Nat'l Park, England 13/D3
Lake Dunmore, Vt. 268/A4
Lake Elmo, Minn. 255/F6
Lake Elmore, Vt. 268/B2
Lake Elsinore, Calif. 204/F11
Lake End, La. 238/D3
Lake Erie Beach, N.Y. 276/B5
Lakefield, Minn. 255/C7
Lakefield, Ontario 177/F3
Lake-Fishing Bridge—Bridge Bay, Wyo. 319/B1
Lake Forest, Fla. 212/B4
Lake Forest, Ill. 222/B4
Lake Forest Park, Wash. 310/B1
Lake Fork, Gunnison (riv.), Colo. 208/E6
Lake Fork, Idaho 220/B5
Lake Fork, Ill. 222/D4
Lake Frances, Ark. 202/B1
Lake Francis, Manitoba 179/E4
Lake Fremont (Zimmerman), Minn. 255/E5
Lake Geneva, Wis. 317/K10
Lake George, Colo. 208/J5
Lake George, Mich. 250/D5
Lake George, Minn. 255/D3
Lake George, New Bruns. 170/C3
Lake George, N.Y. 276/N4

Lake Grace, W. Australia 88/B6
Lake Grace, W. Australia 92/B6
Lake Harbor, Fla. 212/F5
Lake Harbor, N.W.T. 162/J3
Lake Harbour, N.W. Terr. 187/L3
Lake Hart, Ind. 227/E5
Lake Havasu City, Ariz. 188/D4
Lake Havasu City, Ariz. 198/A4
Lakehead, Calif. 204/C3
Lake Helen, Fla. 212/E3
Lake Henry, Minn. 255/D5
Lake Hiawatha, N.J. 273/E2
Lake Hopatcong, N.J. 273/D2
Lake Hubert, Minn. 255/D4
Lake Hughes, Calif. 204/F8
Lake Huntington, N.Y. 276/L7
Lakehurst, N.J. 273/E3
Lakehurst Naval Air Engineering Center, N.J. 273/E3
Lake in the Hills, Ill. 222/E1
Lake Isabella, Calif. 204/G8
Lake Itasca, Minn. 255/C3
Lake Jackson, Texas 303/J8
Lake James, Ind. 227/H1
Lake Jem, Fla. 212/E3
Lake Katrine, N.Y. 276/M7
Lake King, W. Australia 88/C6
Lakeland, Fla. 188/K5
Lakeland, Fla. 212/D3
Lakeland, Georgia 217/F8
Lakeland, La. 238/H5
Lakeland, Manitoba 179/D4
Lakeland, Mich. 250/F6
Lakeland, Minn. 255/F6
Lakeland, Tenn. 237/B9
Lake Landing, N.C. 281/T4
Lakeland Village, Calif. 204/E11
Lake Leelanau, Mich. 250/C4
Lake Lillian, Minn. 255/C6
Lake Linden, Mich. 250/A1
Lakeline, Ohio 284/J8
Lake Lotawana, Mo. 261/R6
Lake Louise, Alberta 182/B4
Lake Louise, Alta. 162/E5
Lakelse Lake, Br. Col. 184/C3
Lake Lure, N.C. 281/E4
Lake Luzerne-Hadley, N.Y. 276/N4
Lake Mackay Aboriginal Reserve, North. Terr. 88/D4
Lake MacKay Aboriginal Res., North. Terr. 93/A6
Lake Macleod, W. Australia 92/A4
Lake Magdalene, Fla. 212/D3
Lake Mary, Fla. 212/E5
Lake McDonald, Mont. 262/B2
Lake Mead Nat'l Rec. Area, Ariz. 198/A2
Lake Mead Nat'l Rec. Area, Nev. 266/G6
Lake Meredith Nat'l Rec. Area, Texas 303/C2
Lake Michigan Beach, Mich. 250/C6
Lake Mills, Iowa 229/D2
Lake Mills, Wis. 317/H9
Lake Minchumina, Alaska 196/H2
Lake Minnewanka, Alberta 182/C4
Lake Mohawk, N.J. 273/D1
Lake Monroe, Fla. 212/E3
Lakemont, Georgia 217/F1
Lakemont, Pa. 294/F5
Lake Montezuma, Ariz. 198/D4
Lakemoor, Ill. 222/A4
Lakemore, Ohio 284/H3
Lake Moxie, Maine 243/D5
Lake Nash, North. Terr. 88/F4
Lake Nash, North. Terr. 93/E6
Lake Nebagamon, Wis. 317/C3
Lakenheath, Eng. 188/E6
Lakshadweep (terr.), India 68/C6
Lakshadweep (sea), India 68/C6
Lake Norden, S. Dak. 298/P4
Lake Odessa, Mich. 250/D6
Lake of the Woods (lake), Manitoba 179/H5
Lake of the Woods (co.), Minn. 255/D2
Lake of the Woods (lake), Minn. 255/D1
Lake of the Woods (lake), Ontario 177/F5
Lake of the Woods (lake), Ontario 175/B3
Lake Orion, Mich. 250/F6
Lake Oswego, Oreg. 291/B4
Lake Ozark, Mo. 261/G6
Lake Park, Fla. 212/F5
Lake Park, Georgia 217/F9
Lake Park, Iowa 229/C2
Lake Park, Minn. 255/B4
Lake Placid, Fla. 212/E4
Lake Placid, N.Y. 276/N2
Lake Pleasant, N.Y. 276/M4
Lake Pocotopaug, Conn. 210/F2
Lakeport, Calif. 204/C4
Lakeport, Fla. 212/E5
Lakeport, Ontario 177/G3
Lake Providence, La. 238/H1
Lakes, England 13/E3
Lakes, England 10/E3
Lake Saint Croix Beach, Minn. 255/F6
Lake Saint Louis, Mo. 261/N2
Lake Saint Peter, Ontario 177/F2
Lakes Entrance, Victoria 97/E5
Lakeshire, Mo. 261/N4
Lake Shore, Minn. 255/D4
Lakeshore, Miss. 256/F10
Lakeside, Ariz. 198/E4
Lake Side, Conn. 210/B2
Lakeside, Iowa 229/C3
Lakeside, Mont. 262/B2
Lakeside, Nebr. 264/B2
Lakeside, Ohio 284/E2
Lakeside, Oreg. 291/C4
Lakeside, Texas 303/E2
Lakeside, Va. 307/N5
Lakeside, Nova Scotia 168/E4
Lakeside Park, Ky. 237/R2
Lakesite, Tenn. 237/L10
Lake Spring, Mo. 261/J7
Lake Station, Ind. 227/C1
Lake Stevens, Wash. 310/D3

Lake Success, N.Y. 276/P7
Lake Superior Prov. Park, Ontario 175/D3
Lake Superior Prov. Park, Ontario 177/J5
Lakesville, Md. 245/O7
Lake Tapawingo, Mo. 261/R6
Lake Tomahawk, Wis. 317/H4
Laketon, Ind. 227/F3
Laketon, New Bruns. 170/E2
Laketown, Utah 304/C2
Lake Toxaway, N.C. 281/D4
Lakevale, Nova Scotia 168/G3
Lake Valley, Sask. 181/E5
Lakeview, Ala. 195/G2
Lakeview, Ark. 202/E1
Lakeview, Iowa 229/C4
Lake View ●, Mich. 250/D5
Lake View, Mich. 250/D5
Lake View, Miss. 256/D1
Lakeview, Mont. 262/E6
Lakeview, N.Y. 276/B5
Lakeview, N.C. 281/L4
Lakeview, Oreg. 291/G5
Lake View, S.C. 296/J3
Lakeview, Texas 303/D3
Lakeview Heights, Mo. 261/F6
Lake Villa, Ill. 222/A4
Lake Village, Ark. 202/H7
Lake Village, Ind. 227/C2
Lakeville, Conn. 210/B1
Lakeville, Ind. 227/E1
Lakeville, Mass. 249/L5
Lakeville ●, Mass. 249/L5
Lakeville, Minn. 255/E6
Lakeville, N.Y. 276/E5
Lakeville, Ohio 284/F4
Lake Waccamaw, N.C. 281/M6
Lake Wales, Fla. 212/E4
Lake Waukomis, Mo. 261/P5
Lake Way, W. Australia 88/C5
Lake Way, W. Australia 92/C4
Lake Wazeecha, Wis. 317/G7
Lake Williams, N. Dak. 282/L5
Lake Wilson, Minn. 255/B7
Lake Winnebago, Mo. 261/R6
Lake Wissota, Wis. 317/D6
Lakewood, Calif. 204/C11
Lakewood, Colo. 188/E4
Lakewood, Colo. 208/F7
Lakewood, Fla. 212/C5
Lakewood, Ill. 222/B4
Lakewood, N.J. 273/E3
Lakewood, N. Mex. 274/E6
Lakewood, N.Y. 276/B6
Lakewood, Ohio 284/G9
Lakewood, Pa. 294/M2
Lakewood, Tenn. 237/H8
Lakewood, Wash. 310/C2
Lakewood, Wis. 317/K5
Lakewood Club, Mich. 250/C5
Lake Worth, Fla. 212/G5
Lake Worth, Texas 303/E22
Lake Zurich, Ill. 222/A5
Lakhdenpokh'ya, U.S.S.R. 52/C2
Lakhish (dry riv.), Israel 65/B4
Lakin, Kansas 232/A4
Lakitusaki (riv.), Ontario 175/E2
Lakki, Greece 45/F6
Lakonía (gulf), Greece 45/F7
Lakor (isl.), Indonesia 85/H7
Lakota, Iowa 229/E2
Lakota, N. Dak. 282/O3
Laksefjorden (fjord), Norway 18/P1
Lakselv, Norway 18/O2
Lakshadweep (terr.), India 68/C6
Lakshadweep (sea), India 68/C6
La Laguna, Chile 138/F2
La Laguna, Spain 106/A3
La Laja (lag.), Chile 138/E1
La Lande, N. Mex. 274/E4
Lalapaşa, Turkey 63/D3
Lalara, Gabon 115/B3
La Lata, Uruguay 145/C3
Laleh Zar, Kuh-e (mt.), Iran 59/G4
Laleh Zar, Kuh-e (mt.), Iran 66/K6
La Leona, Venezuela 124/G3
Lalibela, Ethiopia 111/G5
La Libertad, Ecuador 128/B4
La Libertad, El Salvador 154/C4
La Libertad, Guatemala 154/B2
La Libertad, Nicaragua 154/E4
La Libertad (dept.), Peru 128/C6
La Ligua, Chile 138/A9
La Ligua (riv.), Chile 138/A9
Lalín, Spain 33/C1
La Línea de la Concepción, Spain 33/D4
Lalitpur, Nepal 68/E3
Lalitpur, Nepal 68/E3
La Loche, Sask. 181/L3
La Louvière, Belgium 27/E8
La Lune, Trin. & Tob. 161/B11
La Luz, N. Mex. 274/D5
La Luz, Venezuela 124/D3
La Macarena, Serranía de (mts.), Colombia 126/D6
La Macaza, Québec 172/C3
La Maddalena, Italy 34/B4
La Madera, N. Mex. 274/C2
Lamag, Malaysia 85/F4
Lama-Kara, Togo 106/E7
La Malbaie, Québec 172/G2
Lamaline, Newf. 166/C4
La Manche Valley Prov. Park, Newf. 166/D2
Lamar (co.), Ala. 195/B3
Lamar, Ark. 202/D3
Lamar, Colo. 208/O6
Lamar (co.), Georgia 217/D4
Lamar, Ind. 227/D8
Lamar, La. 238/G2
Lamar (co.), Miss. 256/E8
Lamar, Miss. 256/F1
Lamar, Mo. 261/D8
Lamar, Nebr. 264/C4
Lamar, Okla. 288/O4

Lamar, Pa. 294/H4
Lamar, S.C. 296/G3
Lamar (co.), Texas 303/J4
Lamar (riv.), Wyo. 319/B1
La Margarita, Venezuela 124/H3
Lamar Heights, Mo. 261/D8
La Marque, Texas 303/K3
Lamartine, Pa. 294/C3
Lamartine, Québec 172/G2
Lamartine, Wis. 317/J8
La Martre (lake), N.W. Terr. 187/G3
Lamas, Peru 128/D6
Lamasco, Ky. 237/F7
La Maurice Nat'l Park, Québec 172/D3
La Maya, Cuba 158/J4
La Mede, Mo. 261/F9
La Mede, Mo. 261/F9
Lambach, Austria 41/C2
Lambaréné, Gabon 115/B4
Lambaréné, Gabon 102/B5
Lambari, Brazil 135/D2
Lambasa, Fiji 86/Q10
Lambay (isl.), Ireland 17/K4
Lambayeque (dept.), Peru 128/B6
Lambayeque, Peru 128/B6
Lambeg, N. Ireland 17/J2
Lambert, Ark. 202/J5
Lambert, Miss. 256/D2
Lambert, Mo. 261/O8
Lambert, Mont. 262/M3
Lambert, Okla. 288/J1
Lambert Lake, Maine 243/H4
Lamberton, Minn. 255/C6
Lambert's Bay, S. Africa 118/B6
Lambertville, Mich. 250/F7
Lambertville, New Bruns. 170/C3
Lambertville, N.J. 273/D3
Lambeth, England 13/H8
Lambeth, England 10/B5
Lambeth, Ontario 177/D4
Lambric, Ky. 237/P5
Lamb's (head), Ireland 17/A8
Lambsburg, Va. 307/G7
Lambs Grove, Iowa 229/G5
Lambton (cape), N.W. Terr. 187/F2
Lambton (county), Ontario 177/B5
Lambton, Québec 172/F4
Lame Deer, Mont. 262/K5
Lamego, Portugal 33/C2
Lame Johnny (creek), S. Dak. 298/C6
Lamentin, Guadeloupe 161/F4
Lamèque, New Bruns. 170/F1
Lamèque (isl.), New Bruns. 170/F1
La Merced, Argentina 143/C2
La Merced, Bolivia 136/C8
Lameroo, S. Australia 94/G6
La Mesa, Calif. 204/H11
La Mesa, N. Mex. 274/C6
Lamesa, Texas 303/C5
Lamía, Greece 45/F6
La Minerve, Québec 172/C3
Lamington, N.J. 273/D2
Lamington (riv.), N.J. 273/D2
La Mirada, Calif. 204/D11
Lamison, Ala. 195/C6
Lamitan, Philippines 82/D7
Lamkin, Texas 303/F6
Lamlam (mt.), Guam 86/K7
Lamlash, Scotland 15/C5
Lammermuir (hills), Scotland 15/F5
Lamming Mills, Br. Col. 184/G3
La Moille, Ill. 222/D2
La Moille, Iowa 229/G4
La Moille, Minn. 255/G6
Lamoille, Nev. 266/F2
Lamoille (riv.), Vt. 268/B2
Lamoille (riv.), Vt. 268/A2
La Moine (riv.), Ill. 222/C3
Lamoine ●, Maine 243/G7
Lamon (bay), Philippines 82/C3
Lamona, Wash. 310/G3
Lamongan, Indonesia 85/K2
Lamoni, Iowa 229/E7
Lamont, Alberta 182/D3
Lamont, Calif. 204/G9
Lamont, Fla. 212/C1
Lamont, Idaho 220/H5
Lamont, Iowa 229/K3
Lamont, Kansas 232/F3
Lamont, Miss. 256/D9
Lamont, Okla. 288/L1
Lamont, Wash. 310/G10
Lamont, Wis. 317/G10
Lamont, Wyo. 319/E3
La Monte, Mo. 261/F5
Lamotrek (atoll), Micronesia 87/E5
La Motte, Iowa 229/M4
Lamotte (peak), Utah 304/D3
LaMoure (co.), N. Dak. 282/N7
LaMoure, N. Dak. 282/O7
Lampa, Chile 138/G3
Lampa, Peru 128/G8
Lampang, Thailand 72/C3
Lampard, Sask. 181/G4
Lampasas (co.), Texas 303/F6
Lampasas, Texas 303/F6
Lampasas (riv.), Texas 303/G6
Lampe, Mo. 261/F9
Lampedusa (isl.), Italy 34/D7
Lampertheim, Germany 22/C4
Lampeter, Pa. 294/K6
Lampeter, Wales 13/D5
Lampeter, Wales 10/C4
Lamphun, Thailand 72/C3
Lampman, Sask. 181/J6
Lamprey (riv.), N.H. 268/E5
Lampson, Wis. 317/C3
Lamu, Burma 72/B3
Lamu, Kenya 115/H4
Lamu, Kenya 102/G5
Lamud, Peru 128/C6
Lamy, N. Mex. 274/D3
Lamy, Québec 172/H2
Lanagan, Mo. 261/C9
Lanai (isl.), Hawaii 87/L3
Lanai (isl.), Hawaii 188/F5

Lanai (isl.), Hawaii 218/H2
Lanai City, Hawaii 188/F5
Lanai City, Hawaii 218/H2
Lanaihale (mt.), Hawaii 218/H2
Lanaken, Belgium 27/H7
Lanao (lake), Philippines 82/E7
Lanao del Norte (prov.), Philippines 82/E6
Lanao del Sur (prov.), Philippines 82/E7
Lanark, Ill. 222/D1
Lanark (county), Ontario 177/H3
Lanark, Ontario 177/H2
Lanark, Scotland 15/E5
Lanark, Scotland 10/E3
Lanark (trad. co.), Scotland 15/A5
Lanark, W. Va. 312/D7
Lanbi Kyun (isl.), Burma 72/C5
Lancang, China 77/E7
Lancang Jiang (riv.), China 77/F7
Lancashire (co.), England 13/E4
Lancaster, Calif. 204/G9
Lancaster, England 13/E3
Lancaster, England 10/E3
Lancaster, Ill. 222/F5
Lancaster, Ind. 227/F7
Lancaster, Kansas 232/G2
Lancaster, Ky. 237/M5
Lancaster •, Mass. 249/H3
Lancaster, Minn. 255/B2
Lancaster, Mo. 261/H1
Lancaster (co.), Nebr. 264/H4
Lancaster, N.H. 268/D3
Lancaster •, N.Y. 268/D3
Lancaster, N.Y. 276/C5
Lancaster (sound), N.W.T. 162/H1
Lancaster (sound), N.W.T. 146/K2
Lancaster (sound), N.W. Terr. 187/K2
Lancaster, Ohio 284/E6
Lancaster, Ontario 177/K2
Lancaster, Pa. 188/L2
Lancaster (co.), Pa. 294/K5
Lancaster, Pa. 294/K5
Lancaster (co.), S.C. 296/F2
Lancaster, S.C. 296/F2
Lancaster (co.), Va. 307/R5
Lancaster, Texas 303/G3
Lancaster, Va. 307/R5
Lancaster, Wis. 317/E10
Lancaster Mills, S.C. 296/F2
Lance (creek), Wyo. 319/H2
Lance Creek, Wyo. 319/H2
Lancer, Sask. 181/C5
Lanchester, England 13/H3
Lanciano, Italy 34/E3
Lancing, Tenn. 237/M8
Lanco, Chile 138/D2
Lancret, Cuba 158/D1
Lancut, Poland 47/F3
Lancy, Switzerland 39/B4
Land, Ala. 195/B6
Landa, N. Dak. 282/J2
Landaff •, N.H. 268/D3
Landaff Center, N.H. 268/D3
Landau an der Isar, Germany 22/E4
Landau in der Pfalz, Germany 22/C4
Landay, Afghanistan 68/A2
Landay, Afghanistan 59/H3
Land Between The Lakes Rec. Area, Ky. 237/E7
Land Between The Lakes Rec. Area, Tenn. 237/E7
Landeck, Austria 41/A3
Landeck, Ohio 284/B4
Landen, Belgium 27/G7
Landenberg, Pa. 294/L6
Lander (co.), Nev. 266/D3
Lander (dry riv.), North. Terr. 88/E4
Lander (riv.), North. Terr. 93/C6
Lander, Pa. 294/D2
Lander, Wyo. 188/E2
Lander, Wyo. 319/G2
Landerneau, France 28/B3
Landersville, Ala. 195/D2
Landes, W. Va. 312/H5
Landess, Ind. 227/F3
Landfall (isl.), India 68/G6
Landhi, Pakistan 59/J4
Landing, N.J. 273/D2
Landing (creek), N.J. 273/D4
Landis, N.C. 281/N4
Landis, Sask. 181/C3
Landisburg, Pa. 294/H5
Landisburg, W. Va. 312/E7
Landisville, N.J. 273/D4
Landisville, Pa. 294/K5
Landmark, Manitoba 179/F5
Lando, S.C. 296/E2
Land O'Lakes, Fla. 212/D3
Land O'Lakes, Wis. 317/H3
Landover, Md. 245/G4
Landover Hills, Md. 245/G4
Landquart (riv.), Switzerland 39/J3
Landrum, S.C. 296/C1
Landry, New Bruns. 170/E1
Landsberg (Gorzów Wielkopolski), Poland 47/B2
Landsberg am Lech, Germany 22/D4
Land's End (prom.), England 7/D3
Land's End (prom.), England 13/B7
Land's End (prom.), England 10/D5
Lands End (cape), N.W. Terr. 187/F2
Landshut, Germany 22/E4
Landskrona, Sweden 18/H9
Landsman (creek), Colo. 208/P4
Landsmeer, Netherlands 27/C4
Landstuhl, Germany 22/B4
Landusky, Mont. 262/H3
Landville, W. Va. 312/C7
Lane, Ill. 222/E3
Lane (co.), Kansas 232/B3
Lane, Kansas 232/G3
Lane, Okla. 288/O6
Lane (co.), Oreg. 291/E4
Lane, S.C. 296/H5

Lane, S. Dak. 298/N5
Lane, Tenn. 237/C8
Laneburg, Ark. 202/D6
Lane Cove, N.S. Wales 88/L4
Lane Cove (riv.), N.S. Wales 88/K4
Lane Cove, N.S. Wales 97/J3
Lane Cove (riv.), N.S. Wales 97/J3
Lanes (creek), N.C. 281/J5
Lanesboro, Iowa 229/D4
Lanesboro •, Mass. 249/A2
Lanesboro, Minn. 255/G7
Lanesboro, Pa. 294/L2
Lanesborough-Ballyleague, Ireland 17/E4
Lanes Prairie, Mo. 261/J6
Lanesville, Ind. 227/E8
Lanesville, Va. 307/P5
Lanett, Ala. 195/H5
La Neuveville, Switzerland 39/D2
Lanfine, Alberta 182/E4
Lanford, S.C. 296/C2
Lang, Ontario 177/F3
Lang, Sask. 181/G6
Langå, Denmark 21/C5
Langadhás, Greece 45/F5
Langádhia, Greece 45/F7
Langara (isl.), Br. Col. 184/A3
Langavat (lake), Scotland 15/B2
Langbank, Sask. 181/J5
Lang Bay, Br. Col. 184/E5
Lang Bian, Nui (mts.), Vietnam 72/E4
Langdon, Alberta 182/D4
Langdon, Iowa 229/C2
Langdon, Kansas 232/D4
Langdon, Mo. 261/A2
Langdon •, N.H. 268/C5
Langdon, N. Dak. 282/O2
Langdondale, Pa. 294/F5
Langeac, France 28/E5
L'Ange-Gardien, Québec 172/F3
Langeland (isl.), Denmark 21/D8
Langelands Baelt (chan.), Denmark 21/D8
Längelmävesi (lake), Finland 18/O6
Langeloth, Pa. 294/A5
Langemark-Poelkapelle, Belgium 27/B7
Langen, Germany 22/C4
Langenburg, Sask. 181/K5
Längenfeld, Austria 41/A3
Langenhagen, Germany 22/C2
Langenlois, Austria 41/C2
Langenthal, Switzerland 39/E2
Langenwang, Austria 41/C3
Langeoog (isl.), Germany 22/B2
Langford, Miss. 256/E6
Langford, S. Dak. 298/N2
Langham, Sask. 181/E3
Langholm, Scotland 15/E5
Langholm, Scotland 10/E3
Langhorne, Pa. 294/N5
Langjökull (glac.), Iceland 21/B1
Langkawi, Pulau (isl.), Malaysia 72/C6
Langlade (co.), Wis. 317/H5
Langlais, Québec 172/F1
Langley, Ark. 202/C5
Langley, Br. Col. 184/L3
Langley, Okla. 288/R2
Langley, S.C. 296/D4
Langley, Wash. 310/C2
Langley A.F.B., Va. 307/R6
Langley Park, Md. 245/F4
Langleyville, Ill. 222/D4
Langlois, Oreg. 291/C6
Langnau am Albis, Switzerland 39/G2
Langnau in Emmental, Switzerland 39/E3
Langness (prom.), I. of Man 13/C3
Langogne, France 28/E5
Langon, France 28/C5
Langøy (isl.), Norway 18/J2
Langres, France 28/F4
Langres (plat.), France 28/F4
Langruth, Manitoba 179/D4
Langsa, Indonesia 85/B5
Långsele, Sweden 18/K5
Långshyttan, Sweden 18/K6
Lang Son, Vietnam 72/E2
Lang Suan, Thailand 72/C5
Langston, Ala. 195/G1
Langston, Okla. 288/M3
Langsville, Ohio 284/E7
Langton, Ontario 177/D5
Langtry, Texas 303/C8
Languedoc (trad. prov.), France 29
L'Anguille (riv.), Ark. 202/J3
Langwies, Switzerland 39/J3
Langworthy, Iowa 229/L4
Lanham, Nebr. 264/H4
Lanham-Seabrook, Md. 245/G4
Lanier (co.), Georgia 217/F8
Lanigan, Sask. 181/F4
Lanigan (creek), Sask. 181/F4
Lanín (vol.), Argentina 143/B4
Lanín (vol.), Chile 138/E2
Lanín Nat'l Park, Argentina 143/B4
Lankin, N. Dak. 282/P3
Lanlacuni Bajo, Peru 128/G9
Lannion, France 28/B3
Lannon, Wis. 317/K1
L'Annonciation, Québec 172/C3
Lanoka Harbor, N.J. 273/E4
Lanoraie, Québec 172/D4
Lansdale, Pa. 294/M5
Lansdowne, India 68/D3
Lansdowne, Ontario 177/J3
Lansdowne, Pa. 294/M7
Lansdowne-Baltimore Highlands, Md. 245/M3
Lansdowne House, Ontario 175/C2
L'Anse, Mich. 250/G1
Lanse, Pa. 294/F4
L'Anse-Amour, Newf. 166/C3
L'Anse-au-Clair, Newf. 166/C3
L'Anse-au-Loup, Newf. 166/C3
L'Anse au Meadow, Newf. 166/C3
L'Anse Ind. Res., Mich. 250/A2
Lansford, N. Dak. 282/H2
Lansford, Pa. 294/L4

Lansing, Ill. 222/C6
Lansing, Iowa 229/L2
Lansing, Kansas 232/H2
Lansing (cap.), Mich. 146/K5
Lansing (cap.), Mich. 188/K2
Lansing (cap.), Mich. 250/E6
Lansing, Minn. 255/F3
Lansing, N.Y. 276/H5
Lansing, N.C. 281/F1
Lansing, Ohio 284/J5
Lańskroun, Czech. 41/D2
La Pointe, Wis. 317/E2
La Porte, Calif. 204/D4
Laporte, Colo. 208/J1
LaPorte (co.), Ind. 227/D1
LaPorte, Ind. 227/D1
Laporte, Mich. 250/B5
Laporte, Minn. 255/D3
Laporte, Pa. 294/J3
La Porte City, Iowa 229/J4
La Porte, Texas 303/K3
Lapaz, Ind. 227/E2
La Paz, Mexico 146/G2
La Paz, Baja California Sur, Mexico 150/D5
La Paz, San Luis Potosí, Mexico 150/J5
La Paz (bay), Mexico 150/D4
La Paz, Philippines 82/E6
La Paz (bay), Philippines 82/F6
La Paz, Canelones, Uruguay 145/B6
La Paz, Colonia, Uruguay 145/B5
La Paz Central, Nicaragua 154/E5
La Paz de Oriente, Nicaragua 154/E5
La Pêche, Québec 172/B4
La Pedrera, Colombia 126/F8
La Pedrera, Uruguay 145/F5
Lapeer (co.), Mich. 250/F5
Lapeer, Mich. 250/F5
Lapel, Ind. 227/F4
La Pelada, Argentina 143/F5
La Pérade, Québec 172/E3
La Pérouse (str.) 54/B5
La Perouse, N.S. Wales 88/L4
La Perouse, N.S. Wales 97/J4
La Pérouse (str.), U.S.S.R. 48/P5
La Pesca, Mexico 150/L4
Lapeyrère (lake), Québec 172/E2
La Piedad Cavadas, Mexico 150/H6
Lapine, Ala. 195/F7
La Pine, Oreg. 291/F4
Lapinin (isl.), Philippines 82/E5
La Pintada, Panama 154/G6
Lapithos, Cyprus 63/E5
La Place, Ill. 222/E4
La Place, La. 238/N3
La Plaine, Dominica 161/F6
Lapland 6 /
Lapland (reg.) 7/G2
Lapland (reg.), Finland 18/O2
Lapland (reg.), Norway 18/K2
Lapland (reg.), Sweden 18/M2
Lapland (reg.), U.S.S.R. 52/D1
La Plant, S. Dak. 298/H3
Laplante, New Bruns. 170/E1
La Plata (est.) 120/E6
La Plata, Argentina 143/H7
La Plata, Argentina 120/D6
La Plata, Río de (est.), Argentina 143/E4
La Plata, Colombia 126/C6
La Plata (co.), Colo. 208/D8
La Plata (peak), Colo. 208/C7
La Plata (riv.), Colo. 208/C8
La Plata, Md. 245/L6

La Plata, Mo. 261/H2
La Plata, N. Mex. 274/A2
La Plata (riv.), N. Mex. 274/A1
La Plume, Pa. 294/L2
La Pobla de Lillet, Spain 33/G1
La Pocatière, Québec 172/H2
La Poile, Newf. 166/C4
La Poile (bay), Newf. 166/C4
Lapoint, Utah 304/E3
La Pointe, Wis. 317/E2
La Porte, Calif. 204/D4
La Pobla de Montalbán, Spain 33/D3
La Prairie, Ill. 222/B3
La Prairie, Minn. 255/E3
Laprairie (co.), Québec 172/H4
La Prairie, Québec 172/J4
Laprida, Argentina 143/D4
La Protección, Honduras 154/D3
La Providence, Québec 172/E4
La Pryor, Texas 303/E9
Lâpseki, Turkey 63/C6
Laptev (sea), U.S.S.R. 4/B3
Laptev (sea), U.S.S.R. 54/O2
Laptev (sea), U.S.S.R. 48/N2
Lapua, Finland 18/N5
Lapuanjoki (riv.), Finland 18/N5
La Puebla, Spain 33/H3
La Puebla de Montalbán, Spain 33/D3
La Puente, Calif. 204/D10
La Puerto, Cuba 158/H3
La Puntilla (cape), Ecuador 128/B4
La Purísima, Mexico 150/D3
La Push, Wash. 310/A1
Lapwai, Idaho 220/B3
Lapy, Poland 47/F2
Laqiya 'Umran (well), Sudan 111/E3
Laquey, Mo. 261/H7
La Quiaca, Argentina 143/C1
L'Aquila (prov.), Italy 34/D3
L'Aquila, Italy 34/D3
La Pallice, France 28/C4
La Palma, Colombia 126/C5
La Palma, El Salvador 154/C3
La Palma, Panama 154/H6
La Palma (isl.), Spain 102/A2
La Palma (isl.), Spain 106/A3
La Palma (isl.), Spain 33/A4
La Palma del Condado, Spain 33/C4
La Paloma, Uruguay 145/F5
La Pampa (prov.), Argentina 143/C4
La Paragua, Venezuela 124/G4
Laparan (isl.), Philippines 82/B8
Laparan (isls.), Philippines 82/B8
La Passe, Ontario 177/H2
La Patrie, Québec 172/F4
La Paz, Entre Ríos, Argentina 143/G5
La Paz, Mendoza, Argentina 143/C3
La Paz (co.), Ariz. 198/A5
La Paz (dept.), Bolivia 136/A4
La Paz (cap.), Bolivia 136/B5
La Paz (cap.), Bolivia 2/F6
La Paz (cap.), Bolivia 120/C6
La Paz, Honduras 154/D3

Lark Harbour, Newf. 166/C4
Larkinburg, Kansas 232/G2
Larkinsville, Ala. 195/F1
Larkspur, Calif. 204/H1
Larkspur, Colo. 208/K4
Larksville, Pa. 294/F7
Larnaca, Cyprus 59/B3
Larnaca, Cyprus 63/B5
Larnaca (bay), Cyprus 63/E5
Larne (dist.), N. Ireland 17/K2
Larne, N. Ireland 17/K2
Larne, N. Ireland 10/D3
Larne (inlet), N. Ireland 17/K2
Larned, Kansas 232/C3
La Robla, Spain 33/D1
La Roche, Switzerland 39/D3
La Roche-en-Ardenne, Belgium 27/G8
La Rochelle, France 7/D4
La Rochelle, France 28/C4
La Rochelle, Manitoba 179/F5
La Roche-sur-Yon, France 28/C4
La Roda, Spain 33/E3
La Romana (prov.), Dom. Rep. 158/E3
La Romana, Dom. Rep. 158/F6
La Romana, Dom. Rep. 156/E3
La Ronge, Sask. 181/L3
La Rose, Ill. 222/D3
Larose, La. 238/K7
Larouche, Québec 172/F1
Larrabee, Iowa 229/B3
Larrimah, North. Terr. 88/E3
Larrimah, North. Terr. 93/C3
Larroque, Argentina 143/F5
Larry's River, Nova Scotia 168/G3
Larsen (sound), N.W. Terr. 187/J2
Larsen, Argentina 143/D2
Larsen Bay, Alaska 196/H3
Larsen Ice Shelf, Ant. 2/F9
Larsen Ice Shelf, Ant. 5/C16
Larslan, Mont. 262/K2
Larsmont, Minn. 255/G4
Larson, N. Dak. 282/E2
Larto, La. 238/G4
Larue (co.), Ky. 237/K5
La Rue, Ohio 284/D4
Laruns, France 28/C6
La Russell, Mo. 261/D8
Larvik, Norway 18/C4
Larwill, Ind. 227/F2
La Sal, Utah 304/E5
La Salle, Colo. 208/K2
La Salle (co.), Ill. 222/E2
La Salle, Ill. 222/E2
La Salle (par.), La. 238/F3
La Salle, Manitoba 179/E5
La Salle (riv.), Manitoba 179/E5
La Salle, Mich. 250/F7
La Salle, Minn. 255/D6
La Salle (riv.), Québec 172/H4
La Salle, Québec 172/H4
Lasalle (lake), Québec 172/E2
La Salle (co.), Texas 303/D9
Las Animas (co.), Colo. 208/L8
Las Animas, Colo. 208/N6
Las Animas (creek), N. Mex. 274/B5
Las And, Somalia 115/J2
La Sarraz, Switzerland 39/C3
La Sarre, Que. 162/J6
La Sarre, Québec 174/B3
Lasauces, Colo. 208/H8
Las Aves (isls.), Venezuela 124/E2
Las Bonitas, Venezuela 124/F4
Las Breas, Chile 138/B7
Lasca, Ala. 195/C6
Las Cabras, Chile 138/F5
Lascahobas, Haiti 156/D3
Lascahobas, Haiti 158/C6
Lascano, Uruguay 145/F5
Las Carreras, Bolivia 136/C7
Lascassas, Tenn. 237/J9
L'Ascension, Labelle, Québec 172/C3
L'Ascension, Lac-St-Jean-E., Québec 172/F1
L'Ascension-de-Patapédia, Québec 172/J2
Las Choapas, Mexico 150/M7
La Scie, Newf. 166/C4
Las Cruces, Chile 138/F3
Las Cruces, N. Mex. 146/H6
Las Cruces, N. Mex. 188/E4
Las Cruces, N. Mex. 274/C6
Las Dureh, Somalia 115/J1
La Selva Beach, Calif. 204/K4
La Serena, Chile 120/B5
La Serena, Chile 138/A8
La Seyne-sur-Mer, France 28/F6
Las Flores, Argentina 143/E4
Las Flores, Uruguay 145/D5
Las Hadas, Mexico 150/G7
Lashburn, Sask. 181/B3
Lash-e Joveyn, Afghanistan 68/A2
Lash-e Joveyn, Afghanistan 59/H3
Lashio, Burma 72/C2
Lashkar Gah, Afghanistan 68/A2
Lashkar Gah, Afghanistan 59/H3
La Sierra, Uruguay 145/D5
La Sierra (mt.), St. Lucia 161/G6
La Skhirra, Tunisia 106/G2
Las Khoreh, Somalia 115/J1
Las Lajas, Argentina 143/B4
Las Lajitas, Venezuela 124/F4
Las Lomitas, Argentina 143/D1
Las Marias, P. Rico 161/B2
Las Martinas, Cuba 158/A2
Las Matas de Farfán, Dom. Rep. 158/D6
Las Matas de Farfán, Dom. Rep. 156/D3
Las Mercedes, Venezuela 124/E3
Las Navas del Marqués, Spain 33/D2
Las Nieves, Mexico 150/G3
La Solana, Spain 33/E3
La Sorcière (mt.), St. Lucia 161/G6
La Souterraine, France 28/D4
Las Palmas (cap.), Canary Is., Spain 102/A2
Las Palmas, Argentina 143/E2
Las Palmas, Panama 154/G6
Las Palmas (prov.), Spain 33/C4

Las Palmas (cap.), Canary Is., Spain 102/A2
Las Palmas de Gran Canaria, Spain 33/B4
Las Palmas de Gran Canaria, Spain 106/B3
Las Pampitas, Bolivia 136/C3
Las Parejas, Argentina 143/F6
Las Pedroñeras, Spain 33/E3
Las Petas, Bolivia 136/F5
La Spezia (prov.), Italy 34/B2
La Spezia, Italy 34/B2
La Spezia, Italy 7/E4
Las Piedras, Peru 128/H9
Las Piedras, P. Rico 161/C2
Las Piedras, Uruguay 145/B6
Las Piedras, Falcón, Venezuela 124/C2
Las Piedras, Zulia, Venezuela 124/C2
Las Plumas, Argentina 143/C5
Lasqueti Island, Br. Col. 184/J2
Las Rosas, Argentina 143/F6
Las Rosas, Mexico 150/N8
Lassen (co.), Calif. 204/D3
Lassen (peak), Calif. 204/D3
Lassen Volcanic Nat'l Park, Calif. 204/D3
L'Assomption (co.), Québec 172/D4
L'Assomption, Québec 172/D4
L'Assomption (riv.), Québec 172/D3
Las Tablas, N. Mex. 274/C2
Las Tablas, Panama 154/G7
Lastarria (vol.), Chile 138/B5
La Station-du-Coteau, Québec 172/C4
Last Chance (creek), Utah 304/C6
Las Termas, Argentina 143/D2
Last Mountain (lake), Sask. 181/F4
La Toscas, Uruguay 145/E3
Lastoursville, Gabon 115/B4
Lastovo (Lagosta) (isl.), Yugoslavia 45/C4
Las Trincheras, Venezuela 124/F4
Las Truchas, Mexico 150/H7
Lastrup, Minn. 255/D4
Las Tunas (prov.), Cuba 158/H3
Las Varillas, Argentina 143/D3
Las Vegas, Nev. 146/B6
Las Vegas, Nev. 188/C3
Las Vegas, Nev. 266/F6
Las Vegas (range), Nev. 266/F6
Las Vegas, N. Mex. 183/C5
Las Vegas, N. Mex. 188/C3
Las Vegas, Venezuela 124/D3
Las Yaras, Peru 128/G11
Las Yungas (reg.), Bolivia 136/B5
La Tabatière, Québec 174/F2
Latacunga, Ecuador 128/C3
La Tagua, Colombia 126/C8
Latah (co.), Idaho 220/B3
Latah, Wash. 310/H3
Latakia (prov.), Syria 63/G5
Latakia, Syria 63/F5
Latakia, Syria 54/E6
Latakia, Syria 59/C2
La Taste, Grenada 161/D8
Latchford, Ontario 177/K5
Laterrière, Québec 172/F1
Latexo, Texas 303/J6
Latham, Ala. 195/C8
Latham, Ill. 222/D4
Latham, Kansas 232/F4
Latham, Mo. 261/G5
Latham, N.Y. 276/N5
Latham, Ohio 284/D7
Latham, Tenn. 237/D8
Lathrop, Calif. 204/D6
Lathrop, Mich. 250/B2
Lathrop, Mo. 261/D3
La Tigra, Venezuela 124/H4
Latimer, Iowa 229/G3
Latimer, Kansas 232/F3
Latimer (co.), Okla. 288/R5
Latimers (brook), Conn. 210/G3
Latina (prov.), Italy 34/D4
Latina, Italy 34/D4
La Tina, Peru 128/B5
Latium (Lazio) (reg.), Italy 34/D3
La Tola, Ecuador 128/C2
La Toma, Argentina 143/C3
Laton, Calif. 204/F7
Latorica (riv.), Czech. 41/F2
La Tortuga (isl.), Venezuela 124/F2
Latouche Treville (cape), W. Australia 88/C3
Latouche Treville (cape), W. Australia 92/C2
Latour, Mo. 261/D5
La Tour-de-Peilz, Switzerland 39/C4
La Tour-du-Pin, France 28/F5
Latourell Falls, Oreg. 291/E2
La Trinidad, Nicaragua 154/E4
La Trinidad, Philippines 82/C2
La Trinidad, Venezuela 124/F2
La Trinidad de Arauca, Venezuela 124/D4
La Trinidad de Orichuna, Venezuela 124/D4
La Trinité, Martinique 161/D6
La Trinité-des-Monts, Québec 172/J1
Latrobe, Pa. 294/D5
Latrobe, Tasmania 99/C3
Latta, S.C. 296/J3
Lattimore, N.C. 281/F4
Lattingtown, N.Y. 276/R6
Latty, Ohio 284/A3
La Tuque, Que. 162/J6
La Tuque, Québec 172/E2
La Tuque, Québec 174/C3
Latur, India 68/D5
LATVIA 53/B2
Latvian S.S.R., U.S.S.R. 7/G3
Latvian S.S.R., U.S.S.R. 52/B3
Latvian S.S.R., U.S.S.R. 48/C4
Lauca (riv.), Bolivia 136/A6
Lauca (riv.), Chile 138/B1
Lauchhammer, Germany 22/E3
Laud, Ind. 227/G2
Laudat, Dominica 161/E6
Lauder, Manitoba 179/E5

Lauder, Scotland 10/E3
Lauder, Scotland 15/F5
Lauderdale (co.), Ala. 195/C1
Lauderdale, Minn. 255/G5
Lauderdale (co.), Miss. 256/G6
Lauderdale, Miss. 256/F5
Lauderdale, Tasmania 99/D4
Lauderdale (co.), Tenn. 237/B9
Lauderdale-by-the-Sea, Fla. 212/C3
Lauderdale Lakes, Fla. 212/B3
Lauderhill, Fla. 212/B3
Lauenburg an der Elbe, Germany 22/D2
Lauenen, Switzerland 39/D4
Lauf an der Pegnitz, Germany 22/D4
Läufelfingen, Switzerland 39/E2
Laufen, Switzerland 39/D2
Laufen, Germany 22/E5
Laufenburg, Switzerland 39/F1
Laughery (creek), Ind. 227/G6
Laughing Fish (pt.), Mich. 250/B2
Laughlin A.F.B., Texas 303/D8
Lau Group (isls.), Fiji 87/J7
Lauingen, Germany 22/D4
Launceston, England 13/C7
Launceston, England 10/D5
Launceston, Tasmania 99/C3
Launceston, Tasmania 88/H8
Laune (riv.), Ireland 17/B7
Launglon Bok (isls.), Burma 72/C4
La Unión, Chile 138/D1
La Unión, Colombia 126/B7
La Unión, El Salvador 154/D4
La Union, Mexico 150/J8
La Union, N. Mex. 274/C7
La Unión, Peru 128/D7
La Unión (prov.), Philippines 82/C2
La Union, Spain 33/F4
La Unión, Venezuela 124/E3
Laupahoehoe, Hawaii 218/J4
Laupen, Switzerland 39/D3
Lauperswil, Switzerland 39/E3
Laura, Ill. 222/D3
Laura, Ohio 284/B6
Laura, Queensland 88/G3
Laura, Queensland 95/C2
Laura, Sask. 181/D4
Laura, S. Australia 94/F5
La Urbana, Venezuela 124/E4
Laurel, Del. 245/R6
Laurel, Fla. 212/D4
Laurel, Ind. 227/G6
Laurel, Iowa 229/H5
Laurel (co.), Ky. 237/N6
Laurel, Md. 245/L4
Laurel, Miss. 188/J4
Laurel, Miss. 256/F7
Laurel, Mont. 262/H5
Laurel, Nebr. 264/G2
Laurel, Oreg. 291/A2
Laurel, Pa. 294/K6
Laurel, Wash. 310/D5
Laurel (mt.), W. Va. 312/G4
Laurel Bay, S.C. 296/F7
Laurel Bloomery, Tenn. 237/T7
Laureldale, Pa. 294/L5
Laurel Dale, W. Va. 312/E5
Laureles, Paraguay 144/D5
Laurel Fork, Va. 307/G7
Laurel Hill, Fla. 212/C5
Laurel Hill, N.C. 281/K5
Laurel Hill (mt.), Pa. 294/D5
Laurel Park, N.C. 281/D4
Laurel River (lake), Ky. 237/N6
Laurel Run, Pa. 294/F7
Laurel Springs, N.J. 273/B4
Laurelton, Pa. 294/H4
Laurelville, Ohio 284/E7
Laurence G. Hanscom Field, Mass. 249/B6
Laurence Harbor, N.J. 273/E3
Laurencekirk, Scotland 10/E2
Laurencekirk, Scotland 15/F4
Laurens (co.), Georgia 217/G6
Laurens, Iowa 229/D3
Laurens, N.Y. 276/K5
Laurens (co.), S.C. 296/D2
Laurens, S.C. 296/C5
Laurentides, Québec 172/C4
Laurentides Prov. Park, Québec 174/C3
Laurentides Prov. Park, Québec 172/F2
Lauria, Italy 34/E4
Laurie (lake), Manitoba 179/A3
Laurie, Mo. 261/G6
Laurier, Manitoba 179/C4
Laurier, Wash. 310/G2
Laurier-Station, Québec 172/F3
Laurierville, Québec 172/F3
Laurieston, Scotland 15/D6
Laurin, Mont. 262/D5
Laurinburg, N.C. 281/K5
Lauritsala, Finland 18/Q6
Laurium, Mich. 250/A1
Laurot (Laut Kecil) (isls.), Indonesia 85/E7
Lausanne, Switzerland 39/C3
Lauscha, Germany 22/D3
Laut (isl.), Indonesia 85/F6
Laut (North Natuna) (isl.), Indonesia 85/D5
Lautaro, Chile 138/E2
Lauterbach, Germany 22/C3
Lauterbrunnen, Switzerland 39/E3
Lauterique, Honduras 154/D4
Laut Kecil (isls.), Indonesia 85/E7
Lautoka, Fiji 86/P10
Lauwers (chan.), Netherlands 27/J1
Lauwers Zee (bay), Netherlands 27/J2
Lauzon, Québec 172/J3
Lava (lake), Oreg. 291/F4
Lava Beds Nat'l Mon., Calif. 204/D2
Lavaca, Ala. 195/B6
Lavaca, Ark. 202/B3
Lavaca (co.), Texas 303/H8
Lavaca (riv.), Texas 303/H9
Lava Hot Springs, Idaho 220/F7
Laval, France 28/C3
Laval, Québec 172/H4

Laval (bay), Québec 172/J1
La Vale-Narrows Park, Md. 245/C2
Lavalette, W. Va. 312/B6
Lavalle, Argentina 143/G4
La Valle, Wis. 317/F8
Lavalleja (dept.) Uruguay 145/D5
Lavallette, N.J. 273/E4
Lavalley, Colo. 208/J8
Lavaltrie, Québec 172/D4
Lavamünd, Austria 41/C3
Lavapié (pt.), Chile 138/D1
Lavaur, France 28/D6
La Vecilla de Curueño, Spain 33/D1
Laveen, Ariz. 198/C5
La Vega (prov.), Dom. Rep. 158/D6
La Vega, Dom. Rep. 158/E5
La Vega, Dom. Rep. 156/D3
La Vega, Spain 33/C1
La Vela (cape), Colombia 126/D1
La Vela de Coro Venezuela 124/D2
Lavelanet, France 28/E6
Lavello, Italy 34/E4
Lavenham, Manitoba 179/D5
L'Avenir, Québec 172/E4
La Vergne, Tenn. 237/H9
La Verkin, Utah 304/A6
La Verne, Calif. 204/D10
Laverne, Okla. 288/G1
La Vernia, Texas 303/K11
Laverton, Australia 87/C8
Laverton, W. Australia 88/C5
Laverton, W. Australia 92/C5
La Veta, Colo. 208/J8
Lavey-Morcles, Switzerland 39/D4
Lavezares, Philippines 82/E4
La Victoria, Apure, Venezuela 124/D4
La Victoria, Aragua, Venezuela 124/E2
Lavieille (lake), Ontario 177/F2
La Vieja (pt.), Chile 138/A11
Lavik, Norway 18/D6
Lavillette, New Bruns. 170/E1
Lavina, Mont. 262/H4
Lavinia, Manitoba 179/B4
Lavinia, Tenn. 237/D9
La Vista, Nebr. 264/J3
Lavon (lake), Texas 303/H1
Lavongai (isl.), Papua N.G. 87/F6
Lavongai (isl.), Papua N.G. 86/B1
Lavonia, Georgia 217/F2
Lavos, Portugal 33/B2
Lavoy, Alberta 182/E3
Lavras, Brazil 132/E8
Lavras, Brazil 135/D2
Lávrion, Greece 45/G7
Lawa (riv.), Fr. Guiana 131/D4
Lawa (riv.), Suriname 131/D4
Lawai, Hawaii 218/C2
Lawang, Indonesia 85/K2
Lawen, Oreg. 291/J4
Lawler, Iowa 229/J2
Lawler, Minn. 255/E4
Lawlers, W. Australia 92/C5
Lawley, Ala. 195/E5
Lawn, Newf. 166/C4
Lawn, Pa. 294/J5
Lawn, Texas 303/E5
Lawndale, Calif. 204/B11
Lawndale, Ill. 222/D3
Lawndale, Minn. 255/B4
Lawndale, N.C. 281/C4
Lawnhill, Br. Col. 184/A3
Lawn Hill, Queensland 95/A3
Lawnside, N.J. 273/B3
Lawra, Ghana 106/D6
Lawrence (co.) Ala. 195/D1
Lawrence (co.) Ark. 202/H1
Lawrence (co.) Ill. 222/F5
Lawrence (co.) Ind. 227/E7
Lawrence, Ind. 227/E5
Lawrence, Kans. 188/G3
Lawrence, Kansas 232/G3
Lawrence (co.) Ky. 237/R4
Lawrence, Mass. 188/M2
Lawrence, Mass. 249/K2
Lawrence, Mich. 250/C6
Lawrence (co.) Miss. 256/D7
Lawrence (co.) Miss. 256/F6
Lawrence (co.) Mo. 261/E8
Lawrence, Nebr. 264/F4
Lawrence, N.Y. 276/N7
Lawrence, N. Zealand 100/B6
Lawrence, N.C. 281/O2
Lawrence (co.) Ohio 284/E8
Lawrence (co.) Pa. 294/B4
Lawrence (co.) S. Dak. 298/B5
Lawrence (co.) Tenn. 237/G10
Lawrenceburg Ind. 227/H6
Lawrenceburg Ky. 237/M4
Lawrenceburg Tenn. 237/G10
Lawrence Park, Pa. 294/C1
Lawrenceport, Ind. 227/D7
Lawrence Station, New Bruns. 170/C4
Lawrencetown Nova Scotia 168/C4
Lawrenceville, Georgia 217/D3
Lawrenceville, Ill. 222/F5
Lawrenceville, Ind. 227/H6
Lawrenceville, N.J. 273/D3
Lawrenceville, N.Y. 276/L1
Lawrenceville, Ohio 284/C6
Lawrenceville, Pa. 294/H2
Lawrenceville, Québec 172/E4
Lawrenceville, Va. 307/N7
Lawson, Ark. 202/F7
Lawson, Colo. 208/H3
Lawson, Mo. 261/D4
Lawson, Sask. 181/E5
Lawsonville, N.C. 281/J2
Lawtell, La. 238/F5
Lawtey, Fla. 212/D1
Lawton, Ind. 227/D2
Lawton, Iowa 229/A4
Lawton, Kansas 232/H4
Lawton, Ky. 237/P4
Lawton, Mich. 250/D6
Lawton, N. Dak. 282/O3
Lawton, Okla. 146/J6
Lawton, Okla. 188/G4

Lawton, Okla. 288/K5
Lawton, Pa. 294/K2
Lawton, W. Va. 312/E7
Lawtonka (lake), Okla. 288/K5
Lawu (mt.), Indonesia 85/J2
Lax, Georgia 217/F8
Lax, Switzerland 39/F4
Laxå, Sweden 18/J7
Laxey, I. of Man 13/C3
Laxford, Loch (inlet), Scotland 15/C2
Lay (dam), Ala. 195/E5
Lay (lake), Ala. 195/E5
Lay (pt.), Alaska 196/F1
Lay, Colo. 208/D2
Lay, Mui (cape), Vietnam 72/E3
Layang Layang, Malaysia 72/E5
Layland, W. Va. 312/E7
Layopolis (Sand Fork), W. Va. 312/E5
Layou (riv.), Dominica 161/E6
Layou, St. Vin. & Grens. 161/A9
Laysan (isl.), Hawaii 87/J3
Laysan (isl.), Hawaii 188/E6
Laysan (isl.), Hawaii 218/B5
Laysville, Conn. 210/F3
Layton, Fla. 212/F7
Layton, N.J. 273/C1
Layton, Utah 304/C2
Laytonsville, Md. 245/K4
Laytonville, Calif. 204/B4
Laytown-Bettystown-Mornington, Ireland 17/J4
Lazarev Station 5/C1
Lazdijai, U.S.S.R. 53/B3
Lazear, Colo. 208/D5
Lazi, Philippines 82/D6
Łaziska Górne, Poland 47/A4
Lazy Lake, Fla. 212/B3
Lea (riv.), England 13/G6
Lea (co.), N. Mex. 274/F6
Leaburg, Oreg. 291/D4
Leach, Okla. 288/S2
Leach, Tenn. 237/E9
Leachville, Ark. 202/K2
Leacross, Sask. 181/H2
Lead, S. Dak. 188/F2
Lead, S. Dak. 298/B5
Leadbetter (pt.), Wash. 310/A4
Leader, Minn. 255/D4
Leader, Sask. 181/B5
Lead Hill, Ark. 202/D1
Leadington, Mo. 261/M7
Leadmine (brook), Conn. 210/C1
Lead Mine, W. Va. 312/G4
Leadmine, Wis. 317/F10
Leadore, Idaho 220/E5
Leadpoint, Wash. 310/H1
Leadville, Colo. 188/E3
Leadville, Colo. 208/G4
Leadwood, Mo. 261/L7
Leaf, Georgia 217/E1
Leaf (riv.), Manitoba 179/F2
Leaf (riv.), Minn. 255/C4
Leaf, Miss. 256/G6
Leaf (riv.), Miss. 256/F8
Leaf (lake), Sask. 181/J2
Leaf River, Ill. 222/D1
Leaf Valley, Minn. 255/C4
League City, Texas 303/K2
Leah, Georgia 217/H3
Leake (co.), Miss. 256/E5
Leakesville, Miss. 256/G6
Leakey, Texas 303/E8
Leal, N. Dak. 282/N5
Lealui, Zambia 115/D6
Leamington, Ontario 177/B5
Leamington, Utah 304/B4
Leamington Spa, England 10/F4
Leander, La. 238/E4
Leane (lake), Ireland 17/G4
Leane (lake), Ireland 17/B7
Leapwood, Tenn. 237/E10
Learmonth, W. Australia 88/A4
Learmonth, W. Australia 92/A3
Learned, Miss. 256/C6
Leary, Georgia 217/C8
Leasburg, Mo. 261/K6
Leasburg, N.C. 281/L2
Leask, Sask. 181/E2
Leatherhead, England 13/G8
Leatherhead, England 10/B6
Leathersville, Georgia 217/G3
Leatherwood, Ky. 237/P6
Leavenworth, Ind. 227/E8
Leavenworth, Kans. 188/G3
Leavenworth (co.), Kansas 232/G2
Leavenworth, Kansas 232/H2
Leavenworth, Wash. 310/E3
Leavitt, Alberta 182/D5
Leavittsburg, Ohio 284/J3
Leawood, Kansas 232/H3
Łeba, Poland 47/C1
Lebam, Wash. 310/B4
Lebanon 2/L4
Lebanon 54/E6
LEBANON 59/C3
LEBANON 63/F6
Lebanon, Colo. 208/B8
Lebanon • , Conn. 210/G2
Lebanon, Georgia 217/D2
Lebanon, Ill. 222/D5
Lebanon, Ind. 227/D4
Lebanon, Kansas 232/D2
Lebanon, Ky. 237/L5
Lebanon, Mo. 261/G7
Lebanon, Nebr. 264/D2
Lebanon, N.H. 268/C4
Lebanon, Ohio 284/B7
Lebanon, Okla. 288/N7
Lebanon, Oreg. 291/E3
Lebanon, Pa. 294/K5
Lebanon, S. Dak. 298/K3
Lebanon, Tenn. 237/J8
Lebanon, Va. 307/D7

Lebanon, Wis. 317/H1
Lebanon Church, Va. 307/L2
Lebanon Junction, Ky. 237/K5
Lebanon Springs, N.Y. 276/O6
Lebeau, La. 238/F5
Lebec, Calif. 204/G9
Lebedin, U.S.S.R. 52/D4
Lebedinyy, U.S.S.R. 48/N4
Lebel-sur-Quévillon, Québec 174/B3
Lebesby, Norway 18/P1
Le Blanc, France 28/D4
Le Blanc, La. 238/E5
Le Blanc-Mesnil, France 28/B1
Lebo, Kansas 232/G3
Le Borgne, Haiti 158/C5
Le Bourget, France 28/B1
Le Brassus, Switzerland 39/B3
Lebret, Sask. 181/H5
Lebrija (riv.), Colombia 126/D4
Lebrija, Spain 33/C4
Lebu, Chile 138/D1
Lecanto, Fla. 212/D3
Le Carbet, Martinique 161/C6
Le Cateau, France 28/E2
Lecce (prov.), Italy 34/G4
Lecce, Italy 34/G4
Lecco, Italy 34/B2
Le Center, Minn. 255/E6
Le Châble, Switzerland 39/D4
Le Chasseral (mt.), Switzerland 39/D2
Leche (lag.), Cuba 158/F2
Le Chenit (Le Brassus), Switzerland 39/B3
Le Chesnay, France 28/A2
Lechiguanas (isls.), Argentina 143/G6
Lechuguilla (des.), Ariz. 198/A6
Le Claire, Iowa 229/N5
Leclercville, Québec 172/F3
Lecointre (lake), Québec 172/B2
Lecoma, Mo. 261/J7
Lecompte, La. 238/F4
Lecompton, Kansas 232/G2
Le Creusot, France 28/F4
Le Croisic, France 28/B4
Lecta, Ky. 237/K6
Łęczyca, Poland 47/D2
Ledang, Gunong (mt.), Malaysia 72/D7
Ledbury (cays), England 10/E5
Ledbury, England 13/E5
Lede, Belgium 27/D7
Ledeč, Czech. 41/C2
Ledesma, Spain 33/C2
Ledge, Bermuda 156/G2
Ledger, Mont. 262/E3
Ledgewood, N.J. 273/D2
Ledo, India 68/D2
Ledyard • , Conn. 210/G3
Ledyard, Iowa 229/E2
Lee (co.), Ala. 195/H5
Lee (co.), Georgia 217/D7
Lee (co.), Ill. 222/D2
Lee, Ill. 222/D2
Lee, Ind. 227/D3
Lee (co.), Iowa 229/L7
Lee (riv.), Ireland 17/D8
Lee (riv.), Ireland 10/B5
Lee (co.), Ky. 237/O5
Lee • , Maine 243/G5
Lee, Mass. 249/B3
Lee • , Mass. 249/B3
Lee (co.), Miss. 256/G2
Lee, Nev. 266/F2
Lee • , N.H. 268/F5
Lee (co.), N.C. 281/L4
Lee (co.), S.C. 296/G3
Lee (co.), Texas 303/H7
Lee (co.), Va. 307/B7
Lee Bayou, La. 238/D4
Lee Center, Ill. 222/D2
Lee Center, N.Y. 276/K4
Lee City, Ky. 237/P5
Leeco, Ky. 237/O5
Leecreek, Ark. 202/B2
Leedale, Alberta 182/C3
Leedey, Okla. 288/H3
Leeds, Ala. 195/E5
Leeds, England 13/J1
Leeds, England 10/F4
Leeds, England 10/F4
Leeds, Maine 243/C7
Leeds • , Maine 243/C7
Leeds, Md. 245/P2
Leeds, N.Y. 276/N6
Leeds, N. Dak. 282/M3
Leeds (county), Ontario 177/H3
Leeds, Québec 172/F3
Leeds, S.C. 296/E2
Leeds (mts.), Lebanon 63/F6
Leeds, Utah 304/A6
Leeds Junction, Maine 243/C7
Leeds Point, N.J. 273/E4
Leek, England 10/E4
Leek, England 13/F4
Leek, Netherlands 27/J2
Leelanau (co.), Mich. 250/D4
Leelanau (lake), Mich. 250/D4
Leenane, Ireland 17/B4
Leeper, Mo. 261/L8
Leeper, Pa. 294/D3
Leer, Germany 22/B2

Leerdam, Netherlands 27/F5
Leesburg, Ala. 195/G2
Leesburg, Fla. 212/E3
Leesburg, Georgia 217/D7
Leesburg, Ind. 227/F2
Leesburg, Miss. 256/E6
Leesburg, N.J. 273/D5
Leesburg, Ohio 284/D7
Leesburg, Pa. 294/B3
Leesburg, Va. 307/N2
Lees Creek, Ohio 284/C7
Lees Ferry, Ariz. 198/D2
Leesport, Pa. 294/K5
Lees Summit, Mo. 261/R6
Leeston, N. Zealand 100/D5
Leesville, Conn. 210/F2
Leesville, Ind. 227/E7
Leesville, La. 238/D4
Leesville, Ohio 284/H5
Leesville (lake), Ohio 284/H5
Leesville, S.C. 296/E4
Leesville, Va. 307/K6
Leesville (lake), Va. 307/K6
Leet, W. Va. 312/B6
Leetes Island, Conn. 210/E3
Leeton, Mo. 261/E5
Leeton, N. S. Wales 88/H6
Leeton, N.S. Wales 97/D4
Leeton, Utah 304/E3
Leetonia, Ohio 284/J4
Leetonia, Ohio 284/J4
Leetsdale, Pa. 294/B4
Leetsville, Mich. 250/D4
Leeuwarden, Netherlands 27/H2
Leeuwin (cape), Australia 87/B9
Leeuwin (cape), Australia 2/Q7
Leeuwin (cape), W. Australia 88/A6
Leeuwin (cape), W. Australia 92/A6
Lee Vining, Calif. 204/F6
Leeward (passage), Virgin Is. (U.S.) 161/B4
Leeward (isls.), W. Indies 156/F3
Lefaivre, Ontario 177/K2
Lefka, Cyprus 63/E5
Lefkara, Cyprus 63/E5
Leflore (co.), Miss. 256/D3
Le Flore, Miss. 256/D3
Leflore (co.), Okla. 288/S5
Leflore, Okla. 288/S5
Lefor, N. Dak. 282/F6
Lefors, Texas 303/D2
Le François, Martinique 161/D6
Lefroy, Ontario 177/E3
Lefroy (lake), W. Australia 88/C6
Lefroy (lake), W. Australia 92/C5
Left Hand, W. Va. 312/D5
Legal, Alberta 182/D3
Legana, Tasmania 99/C3
Leganés, Spain 33/F4
Legazpi, Philippines 82/D4
Legazpi, Philippines 85/G3
Legend, Alberta 182/E5
Legend (lake), Alberta 182/D1
Le Diamant, Martinique 161/D7
Léger Brook, New Bruns. 170/F2
Légerville, New Bruns. 170/F2
Legerwood, Tasmania 99/D3
Legges Tor (mt.), Tasmania 99/D3
Leggett, N.C. 281/O3
Leghorn (Livorno) (prov.), Italy 34/C3
Leghorn (Livorno), Italy 7/E4
Leghorn (Livorno), Italy 34/C3
Legionowo, Poland 47/E2
Léglise, Belgium 27/H9
Legnago, Italy 34/C2
Legnica (prov.), Poland 47/C4
Legnica, Poland 47/C3
Le Gore, Md. 245/J2
Le Goulet, New Bruns. 170/F1
Le Grand, Calif. 204/E6
Le Grand, Iowa 229/H5
Le Grand (cape), W. Australia 88/C6
Le Grand (cape), W. Australia 92/C6
Le Gros Crêt (mt.), Switzerland 39/B3
Leguan (isl.), Guyana 131/B2
Legune, North. Terr. 93/A3
Leh, India 68/D2
Le Havre, France 7/E4
Le Havre, France 28/C3
Lehew, W. Va. 312/K4
Lehi, Utah 304/C3
Lehigh, Alberta 182/D4
Lehigh, Iowa 229/E4
Lehigh, Kansas 232/E3
Lehigh, N. Dak. 282/E6
Lehigh, Okla. 288/O6
Lehigh (co.), Pa. 294/L4
Lehigh (riv.), Pa. 294/L4
Lehigh Acres, Fla. 212/E5
Lehighton, Pa. 294/L4
Lehman, Pa. 294/E7
Lehr, N. Dak. 282/M7
Lehrte, Germany 22/D2
Lehua (isl.), Hawaii 218/A2
Lehutu, Botswana 118/C4
Lehututu, Botswana 118/C4
Leiah, Pakistan 68/C2
Leibnitz, Austria 41/C3
Leicester, England 13/F5
Leicester, England 10/F4
Leicester • , Mass. 249/G4
Leicester, N.Y. 276/E5
Leicester • , Vt. 268/A4
Leicester Junction, Vt. 268/A4
Leicestershire (co.), England 13/F5
Leichhardt, N.S. Wales 97/J3
Leichhardt (range), Queensland 95/C4
Leichhardt (riv.), Queensland 88/F3
Leichhardt (riv.), Queensland 95/A3
Leiden, Netherlands 27/F4
Leidy (mt.), Wyo. 319/B2
Leigh, England 10/G2
Leigh, England 13/H2
Leigh, Nebr. 264/H3
Leigh Creek, S. Australia 88/F6
Leigh Creek, S. Australia 94/F4
Leighlinbridge, Ireland 17/H6
Leighton, Ala. 195/D1

Leighton, Iowa 229/H6
Leighton-Linslade, England 13/F7
Leijun, Yemen 59/G5
Leimebamba, Peru 128/D6
Leinan, Sask. 181/D5
Leine (riv.), Germany 22/C2
Leinster (prov.), Ireland 17/G5
Leinster (trad. co.), Ireland 17
Leinster (mt.), Ireland 17/H6
Leipers Fork, Tenn. 237/G9
Leipsic, Del. 245/S4
Leipsic (riv.), Del. 245/R4
Leipsic, Ind. 227/E7
Leipsic, Ohio 284/C3
Leipzig, Germany 7/F3
Leipzig, Germany 22/E3
Leipzig, Sask. 181/C3
Leiria (dist.), Portugal 33/B3
Leiria, Portugal 33/B3
Leisler (mt.), North. Terr. 93/A7
Leisure, Ind. 227/F4
Leisure City, Fla. 212/F6
Leitchfield, Ky. 237/J6
Leiter, Wyo. 319/F1
Leitersburg, Md. 245/H2
Leiters Ford, Ind. 227/E2
Leith, N. Dak. 282/G7
Leith, Ontario 177/D3
Leitrim (co.), Ireland 17/F4
Leitrim, Ireland 17/F3
Leivasy, W. Va. 312/E6
Leix (Laoighis) (co.), Ireland 17/G6
Leixlip, Ireland 17/J4
Leiyang, China 77/H6
Leizhou Bandao (pen.), China 77/G7
Lejunior, Ky. 237/P7
Lek (riv.), Netherlands 27/F5
Leka (isl.), Norway 18/G4
Le Kef (El Kef), Tunisia 106/F1
Lekitobi, Indonesia 85/G6
Lekoni, Gabon 102/D5
Lekoni, Gabon 115/B4
Leksand, Sweden 18/J6
Leksula, Indonesia 85/H6
Lela, Okla. 288/N2
Lela, Texas 303/D2
Le Lamentin, Martinique 161/D6
Leland, Georgia 217/J1
Leland, Ill. 222/E2
Leland, Iowa 229/F2
Leland, Mich. 250/D3
Leland, Miss. 256/C4
Leland, N.C. 281/N6
Leland, Oreg. 291/D5
Le Landeron, Switzerland 39/C2
Leleiwi (pt.), Hawaii 218/K5
Leleque, Argentina 143/B5
Lelia Lake, Texas 303/D3
Le Lieu, Switzerland 39/B3
Le Locle, Switzerland 39/C2
Le Lorrain, Martinique 161/D6
Le Loup, Kansas 232/G3
Lely (mts.), Suriname 131/D3
Lelydorp, Suriname 131/D3
Lelystad, Netherlands 27/H3
Lem, Denmark 21/B5
Léman (Geneva) (lake), Switzerland 39/C4
Le Mans, France 28/C3
Le Mans, France 7/E4
Le Marin, Martinique 161/D7
Le Mars, Iowa 229/A3
Lemasters, Pa. 294/G6
Lemay, Mo. 261/R4
Lemberg, Sask. 181/H5
Leme, Brazil 135/H5
Lemelerberg (hill), Netherlands 27/J4
Lemery, Philippines 82/C4
Lemesurier (isl.), Alaska 196/M1
Lemgo, Germany 22/C2
Lemhi (co.), Idaho 220/D4
Lemhi (pass), Idaho 220/E5
Lemhi, Idaho 220/E5
Lemhi (range), Idaho 220/E5
Lemhi (riv.), Idaho 220/E5
Lemhi (pass), Mont. 262/C6
Lemhi, India 68/D2
Lemieux (isls.), N.W. Terr. 187/M3
Lemington • , Vt. 268/D2
Lemitar, N. Mex. 274/B4
Lemmer, Netherlands 27/H3
Lemmon (mt.), Ariz. 198/E6
Lemmon, S. Dak. 298/E2
Lemon (lake), Ind. 227/E6
Lemon, Miss. 256/E6
Lemoncove, Calif. 204/G7
Lemon Grove, Calif. 204/J11
Lemons, Mo. 261/F2
Lemon Springs, N.C. 281/L4
Lemont, Ill. 222/B6
Lemont, Pa. 294/G4
Lemont Furnace, Pa. 294/C6
Le Mont-sur-Lausanne, Switzerland 39/C3
Lemoore, Calif. 204/F7
Lemoore N.A.S., Calif. 204/F7
Le Morne-Rouge, Martinique 161/C5
Le Morne-Vert, Martinique 161/C6
Lemoyne, Nebr. 264/C3
Lemoyne, Ohio 284/D3
Lemoyne, Pa. 294/J5
Le Moyne, Québec 172/J4
Le Moyne (lake), Québec 174/D1
Lempa (riv.), El Salvador 154/C4
Lempster • , N.H. 268/C5
Lemreway, Scotland 15/C2
Lemsford, Sask. 181/B5
Lemvig, Denmark 18/F8
Lemvig, Denmark 21/B4
Lena, Ill. 222/D1
Lena, La. 238/E4
Lena, Manitoba 179/C5
Lena, Miss. 256/E5
Lena, Ohio 284/B5
Lena, S.C. 296/E6
Lena (riv.), U.S.S.R. 4/C3
Lena (riv.), U.S.S.R. 9/R2
Lena (riv.), U.S.S.R. 54/O3

Lena (riv.), U.S.S.R. 48/N3
Lena, Wis. 317/K6
Lenapah, Okla. 288/P1
Lenawee (co.), Mich. 250/E7
Lençóis, Brazil 132/F6
Lendery, U.S.S.R. 52/D2
Lendinara, Italy 34/C2
Lenexa, Kansas 232/H2
Leney, Sask. 181/D3
Lengau, Switzerland 39/D2
Lengby, Minn. 255/C3
Lengerich, Germany 22/B2
Lenghu, China 77/D4
Lengshuijiang, China 77/H6
Lengua de Vaca (pt.), Chile 138/A8
Lengyeltóti, Hungary 41/D3
Lenhartsville, Pa. 294/L4
Leninabad, U.S.S.R. 48/G5
Leninakan, U.S.S.R. 7/J4
Leninakan, U.S.S.R. 48/E5
Leninakan, U.S.S.R. 52/F6
Leningrad, U.S.S.R. 2/L3
Leningrad, U.S.S.R. 48/D4
Leningrad, U.S.S.R. 52/C3
Leninogorsk, U.S.S.R. 48/J5
Leninogorsk, U.S.S.R. 52/H4
Leninsk, U.S.S.R. 54/H5
Leninsk, U.S.S.R. 48/G5
Leninsk-Kuznetskiy, U.S.S.R. 54/K4
Leninsk-Kuznetskiy, U.S.S.R. 48/J4
Leninskoye, U.S.S.R. 48/O5
Leninváros, Hungary 41/F3
Lenk, Switzerland 39/D4
Lenkoran', U.S.S.R. 48/E6
Lenkoran', U.S.S.R. 52/G7
Lennard, Manitoba 179/A4
Lennep, Mont. 262/F4
Lenni, Pa. 294/L7
Lennig, Va. 307/L7
Lennon, Mich. 250/E5
Lennox (isl.), Argentina 143/C8
Lennox (isl.), Chile 138/F11
Lennox (isl.), Pr. Edward I. 168/E2
Lennox (hills), Scotland 15/B1
Lennox, S. Dak. 298/R7
Lennox and Addington (county), Ontario 177/G3
Lennoxtown, Scotland 15/B1
Lennoxville, Québec 172/F4
Lenoir (co.), N.C. 281/O4
Lenoir, N.C. 281/G3
Lenoir City, Tenn. 237/N9
Le Noirmont, Switzerland 39/C2
Lenora, Kansas 232/C2
Lenora, Minn. 255/G7
Lenorah, Texas 303/B5
Lenore, Manitoba 179/B5
Lenore (lake), Sask. 181/G3
Lenore (lake), Wash. 310/F3
Lenore, W. Va. 312/B7
Lenox, Ala. 195/D8
Lenox, Georgia 217/F8
Lenox, Iowa 229/D7
Lenox, Mass. 249/A3
Lenox•, Mass. 249/A3
Lenox, Mo. 261/J7
Lenox, Tenn. 237/C5
Lenox Dale, Mass. 249/B3
Lens, Belgium 27/D7
Lens, France 28/E2
Lens, Switzerland 39/D4
Lensk, U.S.S.R. 54/N6
Lensk, U.S.S.R. 48/M3
Lenswood, Manitoba 179/B2
Lenswood, S. Australia 94/C8
Lent, Netherlands 27/H5
Lenti, Hungary 41/D3
Lentini, Italy 34/E6
Lentner, Mo. 261/H3
Lenvik, Norway 18/L2
Lenwood, Calif. 204/H9
Lenya, Burma 72/C5
Lenzburg, Ill. 222/D5
Lenzburg, Switzerland 39/F2
Lenzing, Austria 41/B3
Leo, Ind. 227/G2
Leo, S.C. 296/H4
Léo, Burkina Faso 106/D6
Leoben, Austria 41/C3
Léogâne, Haiti 156/D3
Léogâne, Haiti 158/C6
Leola, Ark. 202/E5
Leola, S. Dak. 298/M2
Leoma, Tenn. 237/G10
Leominster, England 13/E5
Leominster, England 10/E4
Leominster, Mass. 249/G2
Leon (co.), Fla. 212/B1
Leon, Iowa 229/F7
Leon, Kansas 232/F4
León, Mexico 146/H7
León, Mexico 150/J6
León, N.Y. 276/C6
León, Nic. 146/K8
León, Nicaragua 154/D4
Leon, Okla. 288/M7
León (mt.), Paraguay 144/B2
León (prov.), Spain 33/C1
León, Spain 7/D4
León, Spain 33/D1
León (reg.), Spain 33/C1
Leon (co.), Texas 303/J6
Leon (riv.), Texas 303/F6
Leon, W. Va. 312/C6
Leon, Wis. 317/E8
Leona, Kansas 232/G2
Leona, Texas 303/H6
Leonard, Mich. 250/F6
Leonard, Minn. 255/C3
Leonard, Mo. 261/H3
Leonard, N. Dak. 282/R6
Leonard, Okla. 288/P3
Leonard, Texas 303/H4
Leonardo, N.J. 273/E3
Leonardsburg, Ohio 284/D5
Leonardsville, N.Y. 276/K5
Leonardtown, Md. 245/M7

Leonardville, Kansas 232/F2
Leonardville, New Bruns. 170/C4
Leone (mt.), Switzerland 39/F4
Leonforte, Italy 34/E6
Leongatha, Victoria 97/C6
Leonia, Fla. 212/C5
Leonia, N.J. 273/C2
Leonidas, Mich. 250/D6
Leonidas, Minn. 255/F3
Leonídhion, Greece 45/F7
Leonora, W. Australia 88/C5
Leonora, W. Australia 92/C5
Leonore, Ill. 222/E2
Leon Springs, Texas 303/J10
Leonville, La. 238/G6
Leopold, Ind. 227/D8
Leopold, Mo. 261/N8
Leopold, W. Va. 312/E4
Leopoldina, Brazil 135/E2
Leopoldsburg, Belgium 27/G6
Leopolis, Wis. 317/G6
Leora, Mo. 261/M9
Leota, Minn. 255/C7
Leota, Utah 304/E3
Leoti, Kansas 232/A3
Leoville, Kansas 232/B2
Leoville, Sask. 181/D2
Lepanto, Ark. 202/K2
Lepel', U.S.S.R. 52/C4
Lephepe, Botswana 118/D4
Leping, China 77/J6
L'Épiphanie, Québec 172/D4
Lepontine Alps (range), Italy 34/B1
Lepontine Alps (range), Switzerland 39/G4
Le Port, Réunion 118/F5
Lepreau, New Bruns. 170/D3
Lepreau (pt.), New Bruns. 170/D3
Lepreau (riv.), New Bruns. 170/D3
Le Prêcheur, Martinique 161/C5
Leptis Magna (ruins), Libya 111/B3
Le Puy, France 28/F5
Lequille, Nova Scotia 168/C4
Lequire, Okla. 288/R4
Le Raimeux (mt.), Switzerland 39/D2
Le Raysville, Pa. 294/K2
Lerdal, Minn. 255/E7
Lerdo de Tejada, Mexico 150/M8
Léré, Chad 111/B6
Lere, Nigeria 106/F7
Leribe, Lesotho 118/D5
Lerici, Italy 34/B2
Lérida, Colombia 126/E7
Lérida (Lleida) (prov.), Spain 33/G2
Lérida (Lleida), Spain 7/D4
Lérida (Lleida), Spain 33/G2
Lérin, Spain 33/F1
Lerma, Mexico 150/O7
Lerma, Spain 33/E2
Lerna, Ill. 222/E4
Le Robert, Martinique 161/D6
Le Roeulx, Belgium 27/E8
Lerona, W. Va. 312/D8
Léros (isl.), Greece 45/H7
Leross, Sask. 181/H4
Leroy, Ala. 195/B8
Le Roy, Ill. 222/E3
Leroy, Ind. 227/C2
Le Roy, Iowa 229/F7
Le Roy, Kansas 232/G3
Leroy, La. 238/F6
Le Roy, Mich. 250/D4
Le Roy, Minn. 255/F7
Le Roy, N.Y. 276/E5
Le Roy, N. Dak. 282/P2
Le Roy, Pa. 294/J2
Leroy, Sask. 181/G4
Le Roy, Texas 303/G6
Le Roy, W. Va. 312/C6
Leroy Anderson (res.), Calif. 204/L4
Lerwick, Scotland 10/G1
Lerwick, Scotland 15/G2
Léry, Québec 172/J3
Les Abymes, Guadeloupe 161/B6
Lesage, W. Va. 312/B5
Le Saint-Esprit, Martinique 161/D6
Les Andelys, France 28/D3
Les Anglais, Haiti 158/A6
Les Anse-d'Arlets, Martinique 161/C7
Les Becquets, Québec 172/E3
Les Bois, Switzerland 39/C2
Les Cayes, Haiti 158/B6
Les Cayes, Haiti 156/C3
Les Éboulements, Québec 172/G2
Les Épey, Switzerland 39/E3
Les Étroits, Québec 172/J2
Leshan (Loshan), China 77/F6
Leshan, China 54/M6
Leshara, Nebr. 264/H3
Les Haudères, Switzerland 39/E4
Les Hauteurs-de-Rimouski, Québec 172/J1
Leshukonskoye, U.S.S.R. 52/G2
Lesina (lake), Italy 34/E3
Les Irois, Haiti 158/A6
Lesja, Norway 18/F5
Leskovac, Yugoslavia 45/E4
Leskovik, Albania 45/E5
Leslie, Ark. 202/F2
Leslie, Georgia 217/D7
Leslie, Idaho 220/F5
Leslie (co.), Ky. 237/P6
Leslie, Mich. 250/E6
Leslie, Mo. 261/K6
Leslie, Sask. 181/H4
Leslie, Scotland 15/E4
Leslie, W. Va. 312/E6
Leslieville, Alberta 182/C3
Lesmahagow, Scotland 15/E5

Les Méchins, Québec 172/B1
Lesnoy, U.S.S.R. 52/H3
Lesosibirsk, U.S.S.R. 48/K4
Lesotho 2/L7
Lesotho 102/E7
LESOTHO 118/D5
Le Vigan, France 28/E5
Lesozavodsk, U.S.S.R. 48/O5
Lesparre-Médoc, France 28/C5
Les Ponts-de-Martel, Switzerland 39/C2
Les Sables-d'Olonne, France 28/B4
Lesse (riv.), Belgium 27/F8
Lessebo, Sweden 18/J8
Lessen (Lessines), Belgium 27/D7
Lesser Antilles (isls.) 146/M8
Lesser Slave (lake), Alberta 182/C2
Lesser Slave (lake), Alta. 162/D2
Lessines, Belgium 27/D7
Lessley, Miss. 256/B8
Lesslie, S.C. 296/E2
Les Tantes (isls.), Grenada 161/D7
Lester, Ala. 195/D1
Lester, Iowa 229/A2
Lester, Pa. 294/M7
Lester, Wash. 310/D3
Lester, W. Va. 312/D7
Lester Prairie, Minn. 255/D6
Lesterville, Mo. 261/L8
Lesterville, S. Dak. 298/O7
Lestijärvi (lake), Finland 18/O5
Lestock, Sask. 181/H4
Les Trois-Îlets, Martinique 161/D6
Le Sueur (co.), Minn. 255/E6
Le Sueur, Minn. 255/E6
Les Verrières, Switzerland 39/B3
Lésvos (isl.), Greece 7/G5
Lésvos (isl.), Greece 45/G6
Leswalt, Scotland 15/C6
Leszcyny, Poland 47/A4
Leszno (prov.), Poland 47/C3
Leszno, Poland 47/C3
L'Étape, Québec 172/F2
Letart, W. Va. 312/C5
Letart Falls, Ohio 284/F8
Létavértes, Hungary 41/G3
Letcher (co.), Ky. 237/R6
Letcher, S. Dak. 298/N6
Letchworth, England 13/G6
Le Teil, France 28/F5
Letellier, Manitoba 179/E5
Letenye, Hungary 41/D3
Letha, Idaho 220/B6
Letham, Scotland 15/F4
Lethbridge, Alberta 182/D5
Lethbridge, Alta. 146/G4
Lethbridge, Alta. 162/E6
Lethbridge, Newf. 166/D2
Lethem, Guyana 120/D2
Lethem, Guyana 131/B4
Leti (isls.), Indonesia 85/H7
Leticia, Colombia 126/F10
Leticia, Colombia 120/B3
L'Etivaz, Switzerland 39/D4
Letka, U.S.S.R. 52/H3
Leto, Fla. 212/C2
Letohatchee, Ala. 195/E6
Leton, La. 238/D1
Letona, Ark. 202/G3
Letong, Indonesia 85/D5
Le Touquet-Paris-Plage, France 28/D2
Letpadan, Burma 72/C3
Le Tréport, France 28/D2
Letsôk-aw Kyun (isl.), Burma 72/C5
Lette, N.S. Wales 97/B4
Letterkenny, Ireland 10/B5
Letterkenny, Ireland 17/F2
Letterkenny Army Depot, Pa. 294/G6
Lettermullan (isl.), Ireland 17/B5
Letts, Ind. 227/F6
Letts, Iowa 229/L6
Lettsworth, La. 238/G5
Leucadia, Calif. 204/H10
Leucate (mts.), France 28/E6
Leuchars, Scotland 15/F4
Leuk, Switzerland 39/E4
Leukerbad, Switzerland 39/E4
Leupp, Ariz. 198/E3
Leurbost, Scotland 15/B2
Leuser (mt.), Indonesia 85/B5
Leuven, Belgium 27/F7
Leuze-en-Hainaut, Belgium 27/D7
Levádhia, Greece 45/F6
Levallois-Perret, France 28/A1
Levan, Utah 304/C4
Levanger, Norway 18/G5
Levant (co.), Kansas 232/A2
Levant•, Maine 243/F6
Levanzo (isl.), Italy 34/D5
Levasy, Mo. 261/S5
Le Vauclin, Martinique 161/D6
Levee, Ky. 237/O5
Level, Md. 245/O2
Level Green, Ky. 237/N6
Level Land, S.C. 296/C3
Levelland, Texas 303/B4
Levelock, Alaska 196/G3
Level Plains, Ala. 195/G8
Levels, W. Va. 312/H4
Leven, Scotland 10/E2
Leven, Scotland 15/F4
Leven, Loch (inlet), Scotland 15/D4
Leven (lake), Scotland 15/E4
Leven (riv.), Tasmania 99/B3
Leveque (cape), Australia 87/C7
L'Eveque (bay), N. Zealand 100/D7
Lévêque (cape), W. Australia 88/C3
Lévêque (cape), W. Australia 92/C2
Leverburgh, Scotland 15/B3
Le Verdon-sur-Mer, France 28/C5
Leverett•, Mass. 249/E3
Levering, Mich. 250/E3

Leverkusen, Germany 22/B3
Levesque, New Bruns. 170/C1
Levice, Czech. 41/E2
Levick (mt.) 5/B8
Levie, France 28/B7
Le Vigan, France 28/E5
Levin, N. Zealand 100/E4
Lévis (co.), Québec 172/J3
Lévis, Québec 172/J3
Lévis, Québec 174/C3
Levisa Fork (riv.), Va. 307/C5
Levítha (isl.), Greece 45/H7
Levittown, N.Y. 276/R7
Levittown, Pa. 294/N5
Levittown, P. Rico 161/D1
Levkás, Greece 45/E6
Levkás (isl.), Greece 45/E6
Levoča, Czech. 41/F2
Lévrier (bay), Mauritania 106/A3
Levuka, Fiji 87/H7
Levukaa, Fiji 86/Q10
Levy (co.), Fla. 212/D2
Levy (lake), Fla. 212/D2
Levy, N. Mex. 274/E2
Lewe, Burma 72/B3
Lewellen, Nebr. 264/B3
Lewes, Del. 245/T5
Lewes, England 13/H7
Lewes, England 10/G5
Lewis, Colo. 208/B8
Lewis (isl.), Fla. 212/B3
Lewis (co.), Idaho 220/B3
Lewis, Ind. 227/C6
Lewis, Iowa 229/C6
Lewis (co.), Ky. 237/P3
Lewis, Kansas 232/C4
Lewis (co.), Ky. 237/P3
Lewis, Manitoba 179/F5
Lewis (lake), Manitoba 179/G2
Lewis (co.), Mo. 261/J2
Lewis, Mo. 261/K6
Lewis (co.), N.Y. 276/K3
Lewis, N.Y. 276/N2
Lewis (dist.), Scotland 15/B2
Lewis (dist.), Scotland 10/C1
Lewis, Butt of (prom.), Scotland 15/B2
Lewis, Butt of (prom.), Scotland 10/C1
Lewis, S.C. 296/E2
Lewis (co.), Tenn. 237/F9
Lewis (creek), Vt. 268/A3
Lewis (co.), Wash. 310/C4
Lewis (riv.), Wash. 310/C5
Lewis, C. W. Va. 312/C4
Lewis, Wis. 317/B4
Lewis (lake), Wyo. 319/B1
Lewis and Clark (co.), Mont. 262/D3
Lewis and Clark (range), Mont. 262/C2
Lewis and Clark (lake), Nebr. 264/G2
Lewis and Clark (lake), S. Dak. 298/O8
Lewis and Clark Village, Mo. 261/O3
Lewisberry, Pa. 294/J5
Lewisburg, Ky. 237/G6
Lewisburg, La. 238/F6
Lewisburg, Ohio 284/A6
Lewisburg, Pa. 294/J4
Lewisburg, Tenn. 237/H10
Lewisburg, W. Va. 312/E7
Lewis Center, Ohio 284/D5
Lewis Creek, Ind. 227/F6
Lewisetta, Va. 307/R4
Lewisham, England 10/B5
Lewisham, England 13/H8
Lewis Hill (mt.), Newf. 166/C4
Lewisport, Ky. 237/H5
Lewisporte, Newf. 166/C4
Lewis Run, Pa. 294/E2
Lewis Smith (dam), Ala. 195/D3
Lewis Smith (lake), Ala. 195/D2
Lewiston, Calif. 204/C3
Lewiston, Idaho 188/C1
Lewiston, Idaho 220/A3
Lewiston, Maine 188/N2
Lewiston, Maine 243/C7
Lewiston, Mich. 250/E4
Lewiston, Minn. 255/G7
Lewiston, Nebr. 264/H4
Lewiston, N.Y. 276/B4
Lewiston, Utah 304/C2
Lewiston, Vt. 268/C4
Lewiston Woodville, N.C. 281/R7
Lewistown, Ill. 222/C3
Lewistown, Md. 245/J2
Lewistown, Mo. 261/J2
Lewistown, Mont. 262/G3
Lewistown, Ohio 284/C5
Lewistown, Pa. 294/G4
Lewisville, Ark. 202/C7
Lewisville, Idaho 220/F6
Lewisville, Ind. 227/G5
Lewisville, Minn. 255/D7
Lewisville, Ohio 284/H6
Lewisville (Ulysses), Pa. 294/G2
Lewisville, Pa. 294/L6
Lewisville (lake), Texas 303/G1
Lewisville (lake), Texas 303/G1
Lewvan, Sask. 181/H5
Lexa, Miss. 256/D8
Lexie, Miss. 256/D8
Lexington, Ala. 195/D1
Lexington, Ark. 202/F2
Lexington, Georgia 217/F3
Lexington, Ill. 222/E3
Lexington, Ind. 227/F7
Lexington, Ky. 237/N4
Lexington, Ky. 146/K6
Lexington, Ky. 188/K3
Lexington•, Mass. 249/B6
Lexington, Mich. 250/G5

Lexington, Minn. 255/G5
Lexington, Miss. 256/D4
Lexington, Mo. 261/E4
Lexington, Nebr. 264/E4
Lexington, N.Y. 276/M6
Lexington, N.C. 281/F3
Lexington, Ohio 284/E4
Lexington, Okla. 288/M4
Lexington, Oreg. 291/H2
Lexington (co.), S.C. 296/E4
Lexington, S.C. 296/E4
Lexington, Tenn. 237/E9
Lexington, Texas 303/G7
Lexington (I.C.), Va. 307/J5
Lexington Blue Grass Army Depot, Ky. 237/N5
Lexington Park, Md. 245/M7
Lexsy, Georgia 217/H6
Leyba, N. Mex. 274/D3
Leyburn, England 13/F3
Leyden•, Mass. 249/D2
Leyland, England 13/G1
Leyland, England 10/F1
Leyond (riv.), Manitoba 179/F3
Leysin, Switzerland 39/C4
Leyte (prov.), Philippines 82/E5
Leyte (isl.), Philippines 54/O8
Leyte (gulf), Philippines 82/E5
Leyte (isl.), Philippines 85/H3
Leyte (isl.), Philippines 82/E5
Lezajsk, Poland 47/F3
Lezama, Argentina 143/H7
Lézarde (riv.), Martinique 161/D6
Lezhë, Albania 45/D5
Lézignan-Corbières, France 28/E6
Lezuza, Spain 33/E3
L'gov, U.S.S.R. 52/E4
Lhanbryde, Scotland 15/E3
Lhari, China 77/D5
Lhasa, China 77/D6
Lhasa, China 2/P4
Lhasa, China 54/L7
Lhazê (Lhatse), China 77/C6
Lhazhong, China 77/C5
L'Hirondelle (Little Buffalo) (lake), Alta. 182/B1
Lhokseumawe, Indonesia 85/B4
Lhorong, China 77/E5
Lhozhag, China 77/D6
Lhünzê, China 77/D6
Lhünzhub, China 77/D5
Liancheng, China 77/J6
Lianga, Philippines 82/E6
Lianga (bay), Philippines 82/F6
Lianping, China 77/H7
Lian Xian, China 77/H7
Lianyungang (Lienyünkang), China 77/J5
Lianyunggang, China 54/N6
Liao (riv.), China 54/O5
Liaodong Bandao (pen.), China 77/K3
Liao He (riv.), China 77/K3
Liaoning (prov.), China 77/K3
Liaoyang, China 77/K3
Liaoyuan, China 77/K3
Liard (riv.) 162/D3
Liard (riv.), Br. Col. 184/L2
Liard (riv.), Canada 146/F3
Liard (riv.), N.W. Terr. 187/F4
Liard (riv.), Yukon 187/E3
Liard River, Br. Col. 184/L2
Libán, Czech. 41/C1
Líbano, Colombia 126/C5
Libau, Manitoba 179/F4
Libby, Minn. 255/F4
Libby, Mont. 262/A2
Libenge, Zaire 115/C3
Liberal, Kansas 232/B4
Liberal, Mo. 261/D7
Liberal, Oreg. 291/B3
Liberdade, Brazil 135/D3
Liberec (prov.), Czech. 41/C1
Liberia 2/J5
Liberia 106/C7
LIBERIA 106/C7
Liberia, C. Rica 154/E5
Liberta, Ant. & Bar. 161/E11
Libertad, Belize 154/C1
Libertad, Uruguay 145/C5
Libertad, Barinas, Venezuela 124/C3
Libertad, Cojedes, Venezuela 124/D3
Liberty, Ariz. 198/C5
Liberty (co.), Fla. 212/B1
Liberty (co.), Georgia 217/J7
Liberty, Ill. 222/B4
Liberty, Ind. 227/H5
Liberty, Kansas 232/G4
Liberty, Ky. 237/M6
Liberty, Maine 243/E7
Liberty•, Maine 243/E7
Liberty, Miss. 256/C8
Liberty, Mo. 261/R5
Liberty, Nebr. 264/H4
Liberty (mt.), N.H. 268/D3
Liberty, N.Y. 276/L7
Liberty, N.C. 281/K3
Liberty, Pa. 294/C7
Liberty, Pa. 294/C7
Liberty, S.C. 296/B3
Liberty, Tenn. 237/K8
Liberty (co.), Texas 303/K7
Liberty, Texas 303/K7
Liberty, Wash. 310/E3
Liberty, W. Va. 312/C5
Liberty Center, Ind. 227/G3
Liberty Center, Iowa 229/F6
Liberty Center, Ohio 284/B3
Liberty Corner, N.J. 273/D2
Liberty Grove, Md. 245/O2
Liberty Hill, Conn. 210/G2
Liberty Hill, La. 238/E2

Liberty Hill, S.C. 296/F3
Liberty Lake, Wash. 310/J3
Liberty Mills, Ind. 227/F2
Liberty Pole, Wis. 317/D3
Libertytown, Md. 245/J3
Libertyville, Ala. 195/F8
Libertyville, Iowa 229/K7
Libertyville, Ill. 222/B4
Libiaz, Poland 47/D3
Libin, Belgium 27/G9
Libiše, Louse. 238/F4
Libmanan, Philippines 82/D4
Libny, China 77/G7
Libon, Philippines 82/D4
Libong, Ko (isl.), Thailand 72/C6
Libourne, France 28/C5
Libramont-Chevigny, Belgium 27/G9
Library, Pa. 294/B7
Libres, Mexico 150/O1
Libreville (cap.), Gabon 2/K6
Libreville (cap.), Gabon 115/A3
Libreville (cap.), Gabon 102/C4
Libuse, La. 238/F4
Libya 2/K4
Libya 102/D2
LIBYA 111/B2
Libyan (des.) 102/E2
Libyan (des.), Egypt 111/E2
Libyan (plat.), Egypt 111/E1
Libyan (des.), Libya 111/B3
Libyan (plat.), Libya 111/D1
Libyan (des.), Sudan 111/E3
Licancábur, Cerro (mt.), Chile 138/B4
Licata, Italy 34/D6
Licantén, Chile 138/A10
Lice, Turkey 63/J3
Lichfield, England 13/F5
Lichfield, England 10/G2
Lichinga, Mozambique 102/F6
Lichinga, Mozambique 118/F2
Lichtenberg, Germany 22/F4
Lichtenfels, Germany 22/D3
Lichtenrade, Germany 22/F4
Lichterfelde, Germany 22/F4
Lichtervelde, Belgium 27/C6
Lick (creek), Tenn. 237/R8
Lick Creek, Ill. 222/E6
Licosa (cape), Italy 34/E4
Lida, Ky. 237/O6
Lida (lake), Minn. 255/C4
Lida, U.S.S.R. 52/C4
Lidcombe, N.S. Wales 97/J3
Liddel Water (riv.), Scotland 15/F5
Lidderdale, Iowa 229/D4
Liddes, Switzerland 39/D5
Liddon (gulf), N.W. Terr. 187/G4
Lidgerwood, N. Dak. 282/R7
Lidice, Czech. 41/C1
Lidingö, Sweden 18/H1
Lidköping, Sweden 18/H7
Lido di Ostia, Italy 34/F7
Lido di Venezia, Italy 34/C2
Lidzbark, Poland 47/D2
Lidzbark Warmiński, Poland 47/E1
Liebenthal, Kansas 232/C3
Liebenthal, Sask. 181/B5
Liechtensteig, Switzerland 39/H2
Liechtenstein 7/F4
LIECHTENSTEIN 39/J2
Liedekerke, Belgium 27/D7
Liège (riv.), Alberta 182/D1
Liège (prov.), Belgium 27/H7
Liège, Belgium 7/E3
Liège, Belgium 27/H7
Liegnitz (Legnica), Poland 47/C3
Lieksa, Finland 18/R5
Lienyünkang (Lianyungang), China 77/J5
Lienz, Austria 41/B3
Liepāja, U.S.S.R. 7/F3
Liepāja, U.S.S.R. 53/A2
Liepāja, U.S.S.R. 48/B3
Liepāja, U.S.S.R. 52/B3
Lier, Belgium 27/F6
Lierneux, Belgium 27/H8
Lierre (Lier), Belgium 27/F6
Liestal, Switzerland 39/E2
Liévin, France 28/E2
Lièvre (riv.), Québec 172/B4
Lièvres (isl.), Québec 172/H2
Liezen, Austria 41/C3
Liffey (riv.), Ireland 17/H5
Liffey (riv.), Ireland 10/C4
Lifford, Ireland 10/C3
Lifford, Ireland 17/F2
Lifu (isl.), New Caled. 87/G8
Lifu (isl.), New Caled. 86/H4
Ligao, Philippines 82/D4
Līgatne, U.S.S.R. 53/C2
Liggett, Ky. 237/P7
Lightfoot, Va. 307/P6
Lighthouse (pt.), Fla. 212/32
Light House (pt.), Mich. 250/D3
Lighthouse Point, Fla. 212/F5
Lightning (creek), Oreg. 291/J2
Lightning (creek), Wyo. 319/G2
Lightning Ridge, N.S. Wales 97/E1
Lightsville, Ohio 284/A5
Lignite, N. Dak. 282/F2
Ligon, Ky. 237/R6
Ligonha (riv.), Mozambique 118/F3
Ligonier, Ind. 227/G2
Ligonier, Pa. 294/D5
Liguria (reg.), Italy 34/B2

Ligurian (sea), Italy 34/B3
Lihir Group (isls.), Papua N.G. 86/C1
Lihou (cays), Coral Sea Is. Terr. 88/J3
Lihue, Hawaii 218/C2
Lihue, Hawaii 188/E5
Lihula, U.S.S.R. 53/C1
Lijiang, China 77/F6
Likasi, Panda-, Zaire 115/E6
Likati, Zaire 115/D3
Likely, Br. Col. 184/G4
Likely, Calif. 204/E2
Likhoslavl', U.S.S.R. 52/E3
Likouala (riv.), Congo 115/C3
Lila (lake), N.Y. 276/L2
Lilac, Sask. 181/D3
Lilbourn, Mo. 261/N9
Lilburn, Georgia 217/D3
Lileah, Tasmania 99/B2
L'Île-Rousse, France 28/B6
Liles (pt.), Chile 138/B3
Lilesville, N.C. 281/K5
Lilienfeld, Austria 41/C3
Lille, France 7/E3
Lille, France 28/E2
Lille, Maine 243/G1
Lilleå (riv.), Denmark 21/B5
Lille Baelt (chan.), Denmark 21/C7
Lillehammer, Norway 18/F6
Lillesand, Norway 18/F7
Lillestrøm, Norway 18/E3
Lillian, Ala. 195/D10
Lillie, La. 238/E1
Lilliesleaf, Scotland 15/F5
Lillington, N.C. 281/M4
Lillinonah (lake), Conn. 210/B3
Lilliwaup, Wash. 310/B3
Lillo, Spain 33/E3
Lillooet, Br. Col. 162/D5
Lillooet, Br. Col. 184/G5
Lillooet (riv.), Br. Col. 184/F5
Lilly, Georgia 217/E6
Lilly, Ill. 222/D3
Lilly, Pa. 294/E5
Lilly Chapel, Ohio 284/D6
Lillydale, Victoria 97/J4
Lilongwe (cap.), Malawi 2/L6
Lilongwe (cap.), Malawi 102/F6
Lilongwe (cap.), Malawi 115/E6
Liloy, Philippines 82/D6
Lily, Ky. 237/N6
Lily, S. Dak. 298/O3
Lily, Wis. 317/J5
Lily Dale, N.Y. 276/B6
Lilydale, Tasmania 99/D3
Lily Plain, Sask. 181/E2
Lim (fjord), Denmark 18/E8
Lim (riv.), Yugoslavia 45/D4
Lima, Ill. 222/B3
Lima (isls.), Indonesia 85/F7
Lima, Pulau (isl.), Malaysia 72/F4
Lima, Mont. 262/D6
Lima (res.), Mont. 262/D6
Lima, N.Y. 276/E5
Lima, Ohio 284/B4
Lima, Ohio 188/K2
Lima (New Lima), Okla. 288/D4
Lima, Paraguay 144/D3
Lima, Pa. 294/L7
Lima (dept.), Peru 128/D8
Lima (cap.), Peru 120/B4
Lima (cap.), Peru 128/D8
Lima (riv.), Portugal 33/B2
Lima (pt.), P. Rico 161/F2
Lima Center, Wis. 317/J10
Limache, Chile 138/F2
Lima Duarte, Brazil 135/E2
Limal, Bolivia 136/C4
Limanowa, Poland 47/E4
Limarí (riv.), Chile 138/A8
Limasawa (isl.), Philippines 82/E6
Limassol, Cyprus 59/B3
Limassol, Cyprus 63/E5
Limavady (dist.), N. Ireland 17/H1
Limavady, N. Ireland 10/C3
Limavady, N. Ireland 17/H1
Limaville, Ohio 284/H4
Limay (riv.), Argentina 120/C6
Limay (riv.), Argentina 143/C4
Limbach-Oberfrohna, Germany 22/E3
Limbani, Peru 128/H10
Limbaži, U.S.S.R. 53/C2
Limbe, Cameroon 106/F8
Limbe, Cameroon 115/A3
Limbé, Haiti 158/D2
Limbourg, Belgium 27/J7
Limbunya, North. Terr. 93/B4
Limburg (prov.), Belgium 27/G7
Limburg (Limbourg), Belgium 27/J7
Limburg (prov.), Netherlands 27/H6
Limburg an der Lahn, Germany 22/C3
Lime, Oreg. 291/K3
Limedsforsen, Sweden 18/H6
Limeira, Brazil 132/E8
Limeira, Brazil 135/E2
Lime Kiln, Md. 245/J3
Limekilns, Scotland 15/D1
Limenária, Greece 45/G5
Limerick (co.), Ireland 17/D7
Limerick, Ireland 17/D6
Limerick, Ireland 10/B4
Limerick, Ireland 7/D3
Limerick•, Maine 243/B8
Limerick, Sask. 181/E6
Limeridge, Wis. 317/F9
Lime Rock, Conn. 210/B1
Lime Springs, Iowa 229/J2
Limestone (co.), Ala. 195/E1
Limestone, Ark. 202/D2
Limestone, Fla. 212/E4

Limestone, Maine 243/H2
Limestone•, Maine 243/H2
Limestone, Mont. 262/F5
Limestone, N.Y. 276/C6
Limestone, Tenn. 237/R8
Limestone (co.), Texas 303/H6
Lime Village, Alaska 196/G2
Limfjorden (fjord), Denmark 21/D4
Limfjorden (fjord), Denmark 21/A4
Limington, Maine 243/B8
Limington•, Maine 243/B8
Limmat (riv.), Switzerland 39/F2
Limmen (bight) North. Terr. 88/F2
Limmen (bight) North. Terr. 93/D3
Limmen Bight (inv.), North. Terr. 88/F3
Limmen Bight (inv.), North. Terr. 93/D4
Límni, Greece 45/F6
Límnos (isl.), Greece 45/G6
Limoeiro, Brazil 132/H4
Limoeiro do Norte, Brazil 132/G4
Limoges, France 7/E4
Limoges, France 28/D5
Limoges, Ontario 177/J2
Limon, Colo. 208/M4
Limón, C. Rica 46/K8
Limón, C. Rica 54/F6
Limón, Honduras 154/E3
Limonade, Haiti 158/D2
Limonar, Cuba 58/D1
Limoquije, Bolivia 136/C4
Limousin (trad. prov.), France 29
Limousin (reg.) France 28/D5
Limoux, France 28/E6
Limpio, Paraguay 144/B4
Limpopo (riv.) 102/E7
Limpopo (riv.), Botswana 118/D4
Limpopo (riv.), Mozambique 118/E4
Limpopo (riv.), S. Africa 118/D4
Lim Rock, Ala. 195/F1
Linapacan (isl.), Philippines 82/B5
Linapacan (str.) Philippines 82/B5
Linard (peak), Switzerland 39/K3
Linares, Chile 138/A11
Linares, Chile 120/B6
Linares, Mexico 150/K4
Linares, Spain 33/E3
Linares, Spain 7/D5
Linaria, Alberta 82/C2
Lincang, China 77/F7
Linch, Wyo. 319/F2
Lincklaen, N.Y. 276/J5
Lincoln (sea) 14/M1
Lincoln (sea) 4/A12
Lincoln, Ala. 195/F3
Lincoln, Argentina 143/F7
Lincoln (co.), Ark. 202/G6
Lincoln, Ark. 202/B6
Lincoln, Calif. 204/B8
Lincoln (isl.), China 85/E2
Lincoln (co.), Colo. 208/M5
Lincoln (mt.), Colo. 208/G4
Lincoln, Del. 245/S5
Lincoln, England 13/G4
Lincoln, England 10/F4
Lincoln (co.), Georgia 217/H3
Lincoln (co.), Idaho 220/D6
Lincoln, Ill. 222/D3
Lincoln, Ind. 227/E3
Lincoln (co.), Kansas 232/D2
Lincoln, Kansas 232/D2
Lincoln (co.), Ky. 237/M6
Lincoln (par.), La. 238/E1
Lincoln (co.), Maine 243/D7
Lincoln, Maine 243/G5
Lincoln•, Maine 243/G5
Lincoln•, Mass. 249/B6
Lincoln, Mich. 250/F4
Lincoln (co.), Minn. 255/B6
Lincoln (co.), Miss. 256/D8
Lincoln (co.), Mo. 261/L4
Lincoln, Mo. 261/H7
Lincoln, Mont. 262/A2
Lincoln, Mont. 252/D4
Lincoln (co.), Nebr. 264/D4
Lincoln (cap.), Nebr. 146/J5
Lincoln (cap.), Nebr. 188/G2
Lincoln (cap.), Nebr. 264/H4
Lincoln (co.), Nev. 266/F5
Lincoln•, N.H. 268/D3
Lincoln (mt.), N.H. 268/D3
Lincoln (co.), N. Mex. 274/D5
Lincoln, N. Mex. 274/D5
Lincoln (co.), N.C. 281/G3
Lincoln, N. Dak. 282/D6
Lincoln (sea), N.W. Terr. 187/M1
Lincoln (co.), Okla. 288/N3
Lincoln, Ontario 177/E4
Lincoln (co.), Oreg. 291/C3
Lincoln, Pa. 294/C7
Lincoln (co.), S. Dak. 298/R7
Lincoln (co.), Tenn. 237/H10
Lincoln, Texas 303/H7
Lincoln (creek), Utah 304/C2
Lincoln•, Vt. 268/B3
Lincoln (co.), Wash. 310/G3
Lincoln, Wash. 310/G3
Lincoln (co.), W. Va. 312/B6
Lincoln (co.), Wis. 317/G5
Lincoln (co.), Wyo. 319/B3
Lincoln Beach, Oreg. 291/C3
Lincoln Boyhood Nat'l Mem., Ind. 227/C8
Lincoln Center, Maine 243/G5
Lincoln Center, Mass. 249/B6
Lincoln City, Ind. 227/C8
Lincoln City, Oreg. 291/C3
Lincoln Gap (pass), Vt. 268/B3
Lincoln Heights, Ohio 284/C9
Lincolnia, Va. 307/S3
Lincoln Park, Colo. 208/J6
Lincoln Park, Georgia 217/D5

Lincoln Park, Mich. 250/B7
Lincoln Park, N.J. 273/A1
Lincolnshire (co.), England 13/G4
Lincolnshire, Ill. 222/B5
Lincolnton, Georgia 217/G3
Lincolnton, N.C. 281/D4
Lincoln University, Pa. 294/L6
Lincolnville, Ind. 227/F3
Lincolnville, Kansas 232/F3
Lincolnville, Maine 243/E7
Lincolnville•, Maine 243/E7
Lincolnville, Nova Scotia 168/G3
Lincolnville, S.C. 296/G6
Lincolnville Center, Maine 243/E7
Lincoln Wolds (hills), England 13/G4
Lincolnwood, Ill. 222/B5
Lincroft, N.J. 273/E3
L'Incudine (mt.), France 28/B7
Lind, Wash. 310/G4
Linda, Calif. 204/D4
Lindale, Alberta 182/C3
Lindale, Georgia 217/B2
Lindale, Texas 303/J5
Lindau, Germany 22/C5
Lindberg, Alberta 182/E3
Linden, Ala. 195/C6
Linden, Alberta 182/D4
Linden, Ariz. 198/E4
Linden, Calif. 204/D5
Linden, Guyana 131/L2
Linden, Ind. 227/D4
Linden, Iowa 229/E5
Linden, Mich. 250/F6
Linden, N.J. 273/A3
Linden, N.C. 281/M4
Linden (mts.), Switzerland 39/F2
Linden, Tenn. 237/F9
Linden, Texas 303/K4
Linden, Va. 307/M3
Linden, W. Va. 312/D5
Linden, Wis. 317/F10
Linden Beach, Ontario 177/B6
Lindenhurst, Ill. 222/B4
Lindenhurst, N.Y. 276/O9
Lindenwold, N.J. 273/B4
Lindenwood, Ill. 222/D2
Lindesberg, Sweden 18/J7
Lindesnes (cape), Norway 7/E3
Lindesnes (cape), Norway 18/E8
Lindi (reg.), Tanzania 115/G5
Lindi, Tanzania 102/G7
Lindi, Tanzania 115/G6
Lindi (riv.), Zaire 115/E3
Lindisfarne (Holy) (dist.), England 13/F2
Lindisfarne (Holy) (isl.), England 10/F3
Lindley, N.Y. 276/F6
Lindon, Colo. 208/N3
Lindon, Utah 304/C3
Líndos, Greece 45/J7
Lindrith, N. Mex. 274/C2
Lindsay, Calif. 204/F7
Lindsay, La. 238/H5
Lindsay, Mont. 262/L3
Lindsay, Nebr. 264/G3
Lindsay, Okla. 288/L5
Lindsay, Ontario 177/F3
Lindsborg, Kansas 232/E3
Lindsey, Ohio 284/D3
Lindsey, Wis. 317/F6
Lindside, W. Va. 312/E8
Lindstrom, Minn. 255/F5
Line (isls.) 2/B6
Line (isls.), Pacific 87/K5
Lineboro, Md. 245/L2
Linesville, Pa. 294/A2
Lineville, Ala. 195/G4
Lineville, Iowa 229/G7
Linfen, China 77/H4
Linfield, Pa. 294/L5
Linganore (creek), Md. 245/J3
Lingao, China 77/G8
Lingayen, Philippines 85/F2
Lingayen, Philippines 82/C2
Lingayen (gulf), Philippines 82/C2
Lingen, Germany 22/B2
Lingga (arch.), Indonesia 85/D5
Lingga (isl.), Indonesia 85/D6
Lingle, Wyo. 319/J3
Linglestown, Pa. 294/J5
Lingling, China 77/H6
Lingo, N. Mex. 274/F5
Lingqiu, China 77/H4
Lingshan, China 77/G7
Lingshui, China 77/H8
Linguère, Senegal 106/B5
Lingwu, China 77/G4
Linhai, China 77/K6
Linhares, Brazil 132/F7
Linhe, China 77/G3
Linière, Québec 172/G3
Linkebeek, Belgium 27/C10
Linköping, Sweden 18/K7
Linköping, Sweden 7/C4
Linkou, China 77/M2
Linkwood, Md. 245/P6
Linlithgow, Scotland 10/B1
Linlithgow, Scotland 15/C1
Linn (co.), Iowa 229/K4
Linn (co.), Kansas 232/H3
Linn, Kansas 232/E2
Linn (co.), Mo. 261/F3
Linn, Mo. 261/J5
Linn (co.), Oreg. 291/E3
Linn, Texas 303/F11
Linn, W. Va. 312/E4
Linn Creek, Mo. 261/J5
Linndale, Ohio 284/G9
Linneus•, Maine 243/H3
Linneus, Mo. 261/F3
Linnhe, Loch (inlet), Scotland 10/D2

Linnhe, Loch (inlet), Scotland 15/C4
Linnsburg, Ind. 227/D5
Linntown, Pa. 294/J4
Lino Lakes, Minn. 255/G5
Linosa (isl.), Italy 34/D7
Linqing (Lintsing), China 77/J4
Lins, Brazil 132/D8
Lins, Brazil 135/B2
Linstead, Jamaica 158/A4
Linter, Belgium 27/G7
Linth (riv.), Switzerland 39/G3
Linthal, Switzerland 39/H3
Linthicum Heights, Md. 245/M4
Linton, Georgia 217/F4
Linton, Ind. 227/C6
Linton, Ky. 237/F7
Linton, N. Dak. 282/K7
Linville, La. 238/F1
Linville, N.C. 281/F3
Linville, Va. 307/L3
Linville Falls, N.C. 281/F3
Linwood, Georgia 217/B1
Linwood, Ind. 227/F4
Linwood, Kansas 232/G2
Linwood, Ky. 237/K6
Linwood, Md. 245/K2
Linwood, Mass. 249/H4
Linwood, Mich. 250/F5
Linwood, N.J. 273/D5
Linwood, N.C. 281/J3
Linwood, Ontario 177/D4
Linwood, Pa. 294/L7
Linwood, Scotland 15/B2
Linxi, China 77/J3
Linxia (Linsia), China 77/F4
Linyi, China 77/J4
Linz, Austria 7/F4
Linz, Austria 41/C2
Linze, China 77/F4
Linzee (cape), Nova Scotia 168/G2
Lionel, Scotland 15/B2
Lion Town, Jamaica 158/J7
Lions (gulf) 7/E4
Lions (gulf), France 28/F6
Lion's Bay, Br. Col. 184/K3
Lion's Head, Ontario 177/C2
Lipa, Philippines 82/C4
Lipan, Texas 303/F5
Lipari, Italy 34/E5
Lipari, Italy 34/E5
Lipari (isls.), Italy 34/E5
Lipetsk, U.S.S.R. 7/H3
Lipetsk, U.S.S.R. 48/E4
Lipetsk, U.S.S.R. 52/E4
Lipez, Cordillera de (range), Bolivia 136/B8
Liping, China 77/G6
Lipnik nad Bečvou, Czech. 41/D2
Lipno (res.), Czech. 41/C2
Lipno, Poland 47/D3
Lipoa (pt.), Hawaii 218/H1
Lipova, Romania 46/F2
Lippe (riv.), Germany 22/C3
Lippstadt, Germany 22/C3
Lipscomb, Ala. 195/E4
Lipscomb (co.), Texas 303/D1
Lipscomb, Texas 303/D1
Lipton, Sask. 181/H5
Liptovský Hrádok, Czech. 41/E2
Liptovský Mikuláš, Czech. 41/E2
Lipu, China 77/H7
Lira, Uganda 115/F3
Lircay, Peru 128/E9
Liri (riv.), Italy 34/D4
Liria, Spain 33/F3
Lisala, Zaire 115/D3
Lisbellaw, N. Ireland 17/K2
Lisbon•, Conn. 210/G2
Lisbon, Ill. 222/E2
Lisbon, Ind. 227/G2
Lisbon, Iowa 229/L5
Lisbon, La. 238/E1
Lisbon•, Maine 243/C7
Lisbon, Md. 245/K3
Lisbon, Mo. 261/G4
Lisbon, N.H. 268/D3
Lisbon•, N.H. 268/D3
Lisbon, N.Y. 276/K1
Lisbon, N. Dak. 282/P7
Lisbon, Ohio 284/J4
Lisbon (dist.), Portugal 33/A1
Lisbon (cap.), Portugal 2/J4
Lisbon (cap.), Portugal 7/D5
Lisbon (Lisboa) (cap.), Portugal 33/A1
Lisbon Falls, Maine 243/D7
Lisbon-Lisbon Center, Maine 243/C7
Lisburn, Alberta 182/C3
Lisburn (dist.), N. Ireland 17/J2
Lisburn, N. Ireland 17/J5
Lisburn, N. Ireland 17/J2
Lisburne (cape), Alaska 196/E1
Lisburne (pen.), Alaska 196/E1
Liscannor (bay), Ireland 17/B6
Liscarroll, Ireland 17/D7
Lisco, Nebr. 264/B3
Liscomb, Iowa 229/H4
Liscomb (isl.), Nova Scotia 168/G4
Lisdoonvarna, Ireland 17/C5
Lishi, China 77/H4
Lishui, China 77/K6
Lisianski (isl.), Hawaii 188/E6
Lisianski (isl.), Hawaii 87/J3
Lisianski (isl.), Hawaii 218/B5
Lisichansk, U.S.S.R. 52/E5
Lisieux, France 28/D3
Lisieux, Sask. 181/E6
Liskeard, England 13/C7
Liskeard, England 10/D5
Lisle, Ill. 222/A6
Lisle, N.Y. 276/H6
Lisle, Ontario 177/E3
L'Islet (co.), Québec 172/G2

L'Islet, Québec 172/G2
L'Islet-sur-Mer, Québec 172/G2
L'Isle-Verte, Québec 172/G1
Lisman, Ala. 195/B7
Lisman, Ky. 237/F6
Lismore, Australia 87/F8
Lismore, Ireland 10/B4
Lismore, Ireland 17/F7
Lismore, La. 238/G3
Lismore, Minn. 255/B7
Lismore, N. S. Wales 88/J5
Lismore, N.S. Wales 97/G1
Lismore (isl.), Scotland 15/C4
Lisnaskea, N. Ireland 17/G3
Lišov, Czech. 41/C2
Lispeszentadorján, Hungary 41/D3
Lisse, Netherlands 27/F4
Lista (pen.), Norway 18/E7
Lister (mt.) 5/B8
Listie, Pa. 294/D5
Listowel, Ireland 17/C7
Listowel, Ireland 10/B4
Listowel, Ontario 177/D4
Litang, China 77/F6
Litani (riv.), Fr. Guiana 131/D4
Litani (riv.), Lebanon 63/F6
Litani (riv.), Suriname 131/D4
Litchfield (co.), Conn. 210/B1
Litchfield•, Conn. 210/C2
Litchfield, Ill. 222/D4
Litchfield•, Maine 243/D7
Litchfield, Mich. 250/E6
Litchfield, Minn. 255/D5
Litchfield, Nebr. 264/E2
Litchfield•, N.H. 268/E6
Litchfield, North. Terr. 93/B2
Litchfield, Ohio 284/F3
Litchfield Park, Ariz. 198/C5
Litchville, N. Dak. 282/N5
Lith, Netherlands 27/G5
Litherland, England 13/G2
Litherland, England 10/F6
Lithgow, Australia 87/F9
Lithgow, N. S. Wales 88/J6
Lithgow, N.S. Wales 97/F3
Lithia, Va. 307/J6
Lithia Springs, Georgia 217/C3
Lithonia, Georgia 217/D3
Lithopolis, Ohio 284/E6
LITHUANIA 53/B3
Lithuanian S.S.R., U.S.S.R. 7/G3
Lithuanian S.S.R., U.S.S.R. 48/C4
Lithuanian S.S.R., U.S.S.R. 52/B3
Lititz, Pa. 294/K5
Litókhoron, Greece 45/F5
Litoměřice, Czech. 41/C1
Litomyšl, Czech. 41/D2
Litovel, Czech. 41/D2
Littau, Switzerland 39/F2
Littcarr, Ky. 237/R6
Little (riv.), Ala. 195/G2
Little (riv.), Ala. 195/C8
Little (riv.), Ark. 202/B6
Little (riv.), Conn. 210/G2
Little (riv.), Ind. 227/G3
Little (riv.), La. 238/F3
Little (riv.), Mass. 249/C4
Little (riv.), New Bruns. 170/D2
Little (riv.), N.C. 281/N3
Little (riv.), N.C. 281/L4
Little (riv.), Okla. 288/R6
Little (riv.), Oreg. 291/E4
Little (riv.), S.C. 296/D3
Little (riv.), S.C. 296/C3
Little (riv.), Vt. 268/B3
Little (inlet), Va. 307/S6
Little (riv.), Va. 307/N5
Little (riv.), Va. 307/H7
Little Alfold (plain), Hungary 41/D3
Little America, Ant. 2/B10
Little America 5/B10
Little America, Wyo. 319/C4
Little Andaman (isl.), India 68/G6
Little Arkansas (riv.), Kansas 232/E3
Little Barrier (isl.), N. Zealand 100/F5
Little Bay de Noc (bay), Mich. 250/B3
Little Bay Islands, Newf. 166/C4
Little Beaver (creek), Kansas 232/A2
Little Beaver (creek), Ohio 284/J4
Little Bighorn (riv.), Mont. 262/J5
Little Birch (lake), Manitoba 179/E3
Little Birch, W. Va. 312/E5
Little Bitterroot (lake), Mont. 262/B2
Little Black (riv.), Maine 243/E1
Little Black, Wis. 317/F5
Little Blue (riv.), Kansas 232/E1
Little Blue (riv.), Nebr. 264/H5
Little Boars Head, N.H. 268/F6
Little Bow (riv.), Alberta 182/D4
Little Britain, Ontario 177/F3
Little Brook, Nova Scotia 168/B4
Little Brosna (riv.), Ireland 17/E5
Little Buffalo Lake, Alberta 182/B1
Little Bullhead, Manitoba 179/F3
Little Butter (creek), Oreg. 291/H2
Little Cadotte (riv.), Alberta 182/B1
Little Cape, New Bruns. 170/D2
Little Catalina, Newf. 166/D2
Little Cayman (isl.), Cayman Is. 156/B3
Little Cedar, Iowa 229/H2
Little Chief, Okla. 288/N1
Little Choptank (riv.), Md. 245/N6
Little Chute, Wis. 317/K7
Little Coco (isl.), Burma 72/B4
Little Colorado (riv.), Ariz. 188/D3
Little Colorado (riv.), Ariz. 198/D3
Little Compton•, R.I. 249/K6
Little Corn (isl.), Nicaragua 154/F4
Little Creek, Del. 245/S4

Little Creek, La. 238/F3
Little Creek (peak), Utah 304/B6
Little Current, Ontario 177/B2
Little Current (riv.), Ontario 175/C2
Little Deep (creek), N. Dak. 282/G2
Little Deer Isle, Maine 243/F7
Little Diomede (isl.), Alaska 196/E1
Little Dover, Nova Scotia 168/G3
Little Dry (creek), Mont. 262/K3
Little Eagle, S. Dak. 298/H2
Little Egg (harb.), N.J. 273/E4
Little Egg (inlet), N.J. 273/E5
Little Elkhart (riv.), Ind. 227/F1
Little Falls, Minn. 255/D5
Little Falls, N.J. 273/B2
Little Falls•, N.J. 273/B2
Little Falls, N.Y. 276/L4
Little Falls-South Windham, Maine 243/C8
Little Farms, La. 238/N4
Little Ferry, N.J. 273/B2
Littlefield, Ariz. 198/B2
Littlefield, Texas 303/B4
Little Flock, Ark. 202/B1
Littlefork, Minn. 255/E2
Little Fork (riv.), Minn. 255/E2
Little Genesee, N.Y. 276/D6
Little Girl (pt.), Mich. 250/E1
Little Goose (dam), Wash. 310/G4
Little Grand Rapids, Manitoba 179/G2
Little Gunpowder Falls (creek), Md. 245/M2
Littlehampton, England 13/G7
Littlehampton, England 10/F5
Little Harbour, Nova Scotia 168/D5
Little Heart's Ease, Newf. 166/D2
Little Hocking, Ohio 284/G7
Little Humboldt (riv.), Nev. 266/D1
Little Inagua (isl.), Bahamas 156/D2
Little Kai (isl.), Indonesia 85/J7
Little Kanawha (riv.), W. Va. 312/D5
Little Knife (riv.), N. Dak. 282/C3
Little Lake, Calif. 204/H8
Little Lake, Mich. 250/B2
Little Laramie (riv.), Wyo. 319/G4
Little London, Jamaica 158/G4
Little Lorraine, Nova Scotia 168/J3
Little Lost (riv.), Idaho 220/E5
Littlelot, Tenn. 237/G9
Little Lynches (riv.), S.C. 296/G3
Little Madawaska (riv.), Maine 243/G2
Little Makin (atoll), Kiribati 87/H5
Little Manitou (lake), Sask. 181/F4
Little Marais, Minn. 255/G3
Little Marsh, Pa. 294/H2
Little Meadows, Pa. 294/K2
Little Mecatina (riv.), Newf. 166/B3
Little Medicine Bow (riv.), Wyo. 319/F3
Little Miami (riv.), Ohio 284/B6
Little Minch (sound), Scotland 10/C2
Little Minch (sound), Scotland 15/B3
Little Missouri (riv.) 188/F1
Little Missouri (riv.), Ark. 202/D6
Little Missouri (riv.), Mont. 262/M5
Little Missouri (riv.), N. Dak. 282/C3
Little Missouri (riv.), S. Dak. 298/B1
Little Missouri (riv.), Wyo. 319/H1
Littlemore, England 13/F6
Little Moreau (riv.), S. Dak. 298/G3
Little Mountain, S.C. 296/E3
Little Muddy (riv.), N. Dak. 282/C3
Little Muddy (creek), Wyo. 319/B4
Little Muskingum (riv.), Ohio 284/H6
Little Narrows, Nova Scotia 168/H3
Little Nicobar (isl.), India 68/G7
Little Orleans, Md. 245/E2
Little Owyhee (riv.), Idaho 220/B7
Little Paint Branch (riv.), Md. 245/H4
Little Para (riv.), S. Australia 88/D7
Little Para (riv.), S. Australia 94/B7
Little Patuxent (riv.), Md. 245/L4
Little Pee Dee (riv.), N.C. 281/L4
Little Pee Dee (riv.), S.C. 296/J4
Little Pigeon (creek), Ind. 227/C9
Little Plymouth, Va. 307/P5
Little Popo Agie (riv.), Wyo. 319/D4
Littleport, England 13/H5
Littleport, Iowa 229/L3
Little Powder (riv.), Wyo. 319/G1
Little Prairie, Wis. 317/H2
Little Red, Ark. 202/G3
Little River, Ala. 195/C8
Little River (co.), Ark. 202/B6
Littleriver, Calif. 204/B4
Little River, Kansas 232/E3
Little River, N. Zealand 100/D5
Little River, Nova Scotia 168/B4
Little River (harb.), Nova Scotia 168/B3
Little River, S.C. 296/K4
Little River (inlet), S.C. 296/L4
Little Rock, Ark. 188/H4
Little Rock (cap.), Ark. 146/J6
Little Rock (cap.), Ark. 202/F4
Little Rock, Iowa 229/B2
Little Rock, Minn. 255/D5
Little Rock, Miss. 256/F5
Little Rock, S.C. 296/J3
Littlerock, Wash. 310/B4
Little Rock A.F.B., Ark. 202/F4
Little Sable (pt.), Mich. 250/C5
Little Saint Bernard (pass), France 28/G5
Little Saint George (isl.), Fla. 212/B7
Little Salmon (riv.), Idaho 220/B4
Little Salt (lake), Utah 304/A6
Little Sandy (creek), Wyo. 319/C3
Little Sauk, Minn. 255/D5

Little Sevogle (riv.), New Bruns. 170/D1
Little Sheep (creek), Oreg. 291/K2
Little Shippegan, New Bruns. 170/F1
Little Silver, N.J. 273/F3
Little Sioux, Iowa 229/B5
Little Sioux (riv.), Iowa 229/B3
Little Sitkin (isl.), Alaska 196/K4
Little Smoky, Alberta 182/B2
Little Smoky (riv.), Alberta 182/B2
Little Smoky (valley), Nev. 266/E4
Little Southwest Miramichi (riv.), New Bruns. 170/D2
Little Spokane (riv.), Wash. 310/H3
Littlestown, Pa. 294/H6
Little Suamico, Wis. 317/L6
Little Summer (isl.), Mich. 250/C3
Little Tallahatchie (riv.), Miss. 256/D2
Little Tennessee (riv.), N.C. 281/B4
Little Tennessee (riv.), Tenn. 237/N10
Little Thunder (creek), Wyo. 319/G2
Little Tinicum (isl.), Pa. 294/M7
Little Tobago (isl.), Virgin Is. (U.K.) 161/B3
Little Tobique (riv.), New Bruns. 170/C1
Littleton, Colo. 208/K3
Littleton, Ill. 222/C3
Littleton, Iowa 229/K3
Littleton, Ireland 17/F6
Littleton•, Maine 243/H3
Littleton•, Mass. 249/H2
Littleton, N.H. 268/D3
Littleton•, N.H. 268/D3
Littleton, N.C. 281/O2
Littleton, W. Va. 307/O7
Littleton Common, Mass. 249/J2
Little Traverse (bay), Mich. 250/D3
Little Trout River (pond), Newf. 166/C4
Little Tupper (lake), N.Y. 276/L2
Little Valley, N.Y. 276/C6
Little Vermilion (riv.), Ind. 227/B5
Littleville, Ala. 195/C1
Little Wabash (riv.), Ill. 222/E5
Little Weiser (riv.), Idaho 220/B5
Little White (riv.), S. Dak. 298/H7
Little Wood (riv.), Idaho 220/D6
Little Yenisey (riv.), U.S.S.R. 48/K4
Little York, Ill. 222/C2
Little York, Ind. 227/F7
Little York, N.J. 273/C2
Little Zab (riv.), Iraq 66/C3
Lituya (bay), Alaska 196/L1
Litvínov, Czech. 41/B1
Liuba, China 77/G5
Liukang Tenggaja (isls.), Indonesia 85/F7
Liuli, Tanzania 115/F6
Liuzhou (Liuchow), China 77/G7
Liuzhou, China 54/M7
Līvāni, U.S.S.R. 53/D2
Livelong, Sask. 181/C2
Lively (isl.), Falkland Is. 143/E7
Lively, Va. 307/P5
Livengood, Alaska 196/J1
Live Oak, Calif. 204/K4
Live Oak, Calif. 204/D4
Live Oak, Fla. 212/D1
Live Oak (co.), Texas 303/F9
Live Oak, Texas 303/K10
Liveringa, W. Australia 88/C3
Liveringa, W. Australia 92/D2
Livermore, Calif. 204/L2
Livermore, Colo. 208/J1
Livermore, Iowa 229/E3
Livermore, Ky. 237/G5
Livermore, Maine 243/C7
Livermore•, Maine 243/C7
Livermore (mt.), Texas 303/C11
Livermore Falls, Maine 243/C7
Livermore Falls•, Maine 243/C7
Livermore Falls, N.H. 268/D4
Liverpool (swamp), Bolivia 136/D4
Liverpool, England 10/F2
Liverpool, England 13/G2
Liverpool, England 7/D3
Liverpool (bay), England 13/D4
Liverpool, Ill. 222/C3
Liverpool, N. S. Wales 88/K4
Liverpool, N.S. Wales 97/H4
Liverpool (range), N.S. Wales 97/F2
Liverpool, N.Y. 276/H4
Liverpool (bay), N.W. Terr. 187/E2
Liverpool (cape), N.W. Terr. 187/L2
Liverpool, Nova Scotia 168/D4
Liverpool (bay), Nova Scotia 168/D5
Liverpool, Pa. 294/H4
Liverpool, Texas 303/J3
Liverpool, W. Va. 312/C5
Livia, Ky. 237/G5
Livigno, Italy 34/C1
Livingston, Ala. 195/B5
Livingston, Calif. 204/E6
Livingston, Guatemala 154/C3
Livingston (co.), Ill. 222/E3
Livingston, Ill. 222/D5
Livingston (co.), Ky. 237/E6
Livingston, Ky. 237/N6
Livingston (par.), La. 238/L2
Livingston, La. 238/L1
Livingston (co.), Mich. 250/F6
Livingston (co.), Mo. 261/E3
Livingston, Mont. 188/D1
Livingston, Mont. 262/F5
Livingston•, N.J. 273/E2
Livingston (co.), N.Y. 276/E5
Livingston, Scotland 15/C2
Livingston, S.C. 296/E4
Livingston, Tenn. 237/L8

Livingston, Texas 303/K7
Livingston (lake), Texas 303/K7
Livingston, Wis. 317/E10
Livingstone (range), Alberta 182/C4
Livingstone (falls), Zaire 115/B5
Livingstone, Zambia 115/E7
Livingstone, Zambia 102/E6
Livingstonia, Malawi 115/F6
Livingston Manor, N.Y. 276/L7
Livingstonville, N.Y. 276/M6
Livno, Yugoslavia 45/C4
Livny, U.S.S.R. 52/E4
Livona, N. Dak. 282/K6
Livonia, Ind. 227/E7
Livonia, La. 238/G5
Livonia, Mich. 250/F6
Livonia, Mo. 261/G1
Livonia, N.Y. 276/E5
Livonia, Pa. 294/H4
Livorno, Italy 34/C3
Livorno, Italy 7/E4
Livorno, Italy 34/C3
Livry-Gargan, France 28/C1
Liwale, Tanzania 115/G5
Li Xian, China 77/H6
Lixoúrion, Greece 45/E4
Lizard, The (dist.), England 13/B8
Lizard (pt.), England 10/D6
Lizard (pt.), England 13/D8
Lizella, Georgia 217/E5
Lizemores, W. Va. 312/D6
Lizton, Ind. 227/D5
Ljubinje, Yugoslavia 45/D4
Ljubljana, Yugoslavia 45/B3
Ljubljana, Yugoslavia 7/F4
Ljubuški, Yugoslavia 45/C4
Ljugarn, Sweden 18/L8
Ljungan (riv.), Sweden 18/K5
Ljungby, Sweden 18/J8
Ljusdal, Sweden 18/J6
Ljusna (riv.), Sweden 7/F2
Ljusnan (riv.), Sweden 18/H5
Ljusne, Sweden 18/K6
Llagostera, Spain 33/H2
Llaima (vol.), Chile 138/E2
Llallagua, Bolivia 136/B6
Llallagua, Bolivia 120/C4
Llamara, Salar de (salt dep.), Chile 138/B3
Llanarth, Wales 13/C5
Llancanelo (lag.), Argentina 143/C3
Llancanelo, Salina y Laguna (salt dep.), Argentina 143/C4
Llandeilo, Wales 13/C6
Llandovery, Wales 13/D5
Llandovery, Wales 10/D5
Llandrindod Wells, Wales 10/E4
Llandrindod Wells, Wales 13/D5
Llandudno, Wales 13/D4
Llandudno, Wales 10/E4
Llandybie, Wales 13/C6
Llandyssul, Wales 13/C5
Llanelli, Wales 13/C6
Llanelli, Wales 10/D5
Llanes, Spain 33/D1
Llanfair Caereinion, Wales 13/D5
Llanfairfechan, Wales 13/D4
Llanfyllin, Wales 10/E4
Llanfyllin, Wales 13/D5
Llangefni, Wales 13/C4
Llangollen, Wales 13/D5
Llangollen, Wales 10/E4
Llanguicke, Wales 13/D6
Llanidloes, Wales 13/D5
Llanidloes, Wales 10/E4
Llanllyfni, Wales 13/C4
Llannon, Wales 13/C6
Llanos, Wales 13/C5
Llanrhaeadr, Wales 13/D5
Llanrhystyd, Wales 13/C5
Llanrian, Wales 13/B6
Llanrwst, Wales 13/D4
Llanrwst, Wales 10/E4
Llantrisant, Wales 13/A7
Llantwit Major, Wales 13/A7
Llanwnog, Wales 13/D5
Llanwrtyd Wells, Wales 13/D5
Llata, Peru 128/D7
Llay-Llay, Chile 138/G2
Llera de Canales, Mexico 150/K5
Llerena (pt.), C. Rica 154/F6
Llerena, Spain 33/C3
Lleyn (pen.), Wales 13/C5
Llica, Bolivia 136/A6
Llico, Chile 138/A10
Llivia, Spain 33/G1
Llobregat (riv.), Spain 33/H2
Llodio, Spain 33/E1
Llolleo, Chile 138/F4
Llorente, Philippines 82/E5
Loc Ninh, Vietnam 72/E5
Loco, Okla. 288/L6
Loco Hills, N. Mex. 274/F6
Locumba, Peru 128/G11
Locumba (riv.), Peru 128/G11
Locust, N.C. 281/J4
Locust Bayou, Ark. 202/E6
Locust Fork, Ala. 195/E3

Lloydminster, Sask. 181/A2
Lluchmayor, Spain 33/H3
Lluidas Vale, Jamaica 158/J6
Llullaillaco (mt.) 120/B3
Llullaillaco (vol.), Argentina 143/C1
Llullaillaco (vol.), Chile 138/B5
Lluta (riv.), Chile 138/B1
Llwchwr, Wales 13/D6
Loa (riv.), Chile 120/C5
Loa (riv.), Chile 138/B3
Loa, Utah 304/C5
Loachapoka, Ala. 195/G5
Loami, Ill. 222/D4
Loange (riv.), Angola 115/C5
Loange (riv.), Zaire 115/C5
Loanhead, Scotland 10/C1
Loanhead, Scotland 15/D2
Loatse, Botswana 118/D5
Lobatse, Botswana 118/D5
Löbau, Germany 22/F3
Lobaye (riv.), Cent. Afr. Rep. 115/C2
Lobdell, La. 238/J1
Lobeco, S.C. 296/F6
Lobelia, W. Va. 312/E7
Lobelville, Tenn. 237/F9
Lobenstein, Germany 22/D3
Lobería, Argentina 143/E4
Lobethal, S. Australia 94/C7
Łobez, Poland 47/B2
Lobito, Angola 115/B6
Lobito, Angola 102/D6
Lobitos, Peru 128/B5
Lobo, Philippines 82/C4
Lobo (cay), P. Rico 161/G1
Lobos, Argentina 143/G7
Lobos (pt.), Chile 138/A3
Lobos (cape), Mexico 150/C2
Lobos (pt.), Mexico 150/D3
Lobos (isl.), Uruguay 145/E6
Lobos de Afuera (isls.), Peru 128/B6
Lobos de Tierra (isl.), Peru 128/B6
Lobster (lake), Maine 243/E4
Locarno, Switzerland 39/G4
Locate, Mont. 262/L4
Lochaber, Nova Scotia 168/F3
Lochaber (dist.), Scotland 15/D4
Lochailort, Scotland 15/C4
Lochaline, Scotland 15/C4
Lochans, Scotland 15/D6
Locharbriggs, Scotland 15/E5
Lochawe, Scotland 15/C4
Lochboisdale, Scotland 15/A3
Lochbuie, Colo. 208/K2
Lochcarron, Scotland 10/D2
Lochcarron, Scotland 15/C3
Lochearnhead, Scotland 15/D4
Lochem, Netherlands 27/J4
Lochend, Scotland 15/C4
Loches, France 28/D4
Lochgelly, Scotland 10/C1
Lochgelly, Scotland 15/D1
Lochgelly, W. Va. 312/D6
Lochgilphead, Scotland 10/D2
Lochgilphead, Scotland 15/C4
Lochgoilhead, Scotland 15/D4
Lochindorb (lake), Scotland 15/E3
Lochinver, Scotland 10/D1
Lochinver, Scotland 15/C2
Lochloosa, Fla. 212/E2
Lochloosa (lake), Fla. 212/D2
Loch Lynn Heights, Md. 245/A3
Lochmaben, Scotland 10/E3
Lochmaben, Scotland 15/E5
Lochmaddy, Scotland 15/A3
Lochmere, N.H. 268/D5
Lochnagar (mt.), Scotland 15/E4
Lochore, Scotland 15/D1
Lochranza, Scotland 15/C5
Lochristi, Belgium 27/D3
Loch Raven (res.), Md. 245/M3
Lochwinnoch, Scotland 15/A2
Lochy, Loch (lake), Scotland 15/D3
Lochy, Loch (lake), Scotland 10/D2
Lock, S. Australia 94/D5
Lockatong (creek), N.J. 273/C3
Lockbourne, Ohio 284/E6
Locke, Calif. 204/B9
Locke, N.Y. 276/H5
Locke, Texas 303/D11
Lockeford, Calif. 204/C9
Locke Mills, Maine 243/B7
Lockeport, Nova Scotia 168/C5
Lockerbie, Scotland 10/E3
Lockerbie, Scotland 15/E5
Lockesburg, Ark. 202/B6
Lockhart, Ala. 195/F6
Lockhart, Minn. 255/B3
Lockhart (mt.), Mont. 262/D3
Lockhart, N.S. Wales 97/D4
Lockhart (riv.), N.W. Terr. 187/H3
Lockhart, S.C. 296/E2
Lockhart, Texas 303/G8
Lock Haven, Pa. 294/H3
Lockington, Ohio 284/B5
Lockland, Ohio 284/C9
Lockney, Texas 303/C3
Lockney, W. Va. 312/C6
Lockport, Ill. 222/B6
Lockport, Ky. 237/M4
Lockport, La. 238/K7
Lockport, Manitoba 179/F4
Lockport, N.Y. 276/C4
Lockridge, Iowa 229/K7
Lock Springs, Mo. 261/E3
Lockwood, Mo. 261/E8
Lockwood, Sask. 181/G4
Lockwood, W. Va. 312/D6
Locumba, Peru 128/G11
Locust, N.C. 281/J4
Locust Bayou, Ark. 202/E6
Locust Fork, Ala. 195/E3

Locust Fork (riv.), Ala. 195/E3
Locust Grove, Ark. 202/G2
Locust Grove, Georgia 217/D3
Locust Grove, N.Y. 276/R6
Locust Grove, Ohio 284/D8
Locust Grove, Okla. 288/R2
Locust Hill, Ky. 237/G5
Locustville, Va. 307/S5
Lod (Lydda), Israel 65/B4
Loda, Ill. 222/E3
Lodar, Yemen 59/E7
Loddon, England 13/J5
Loddon (riv.), Victoria 97/B5
Loddon (riv.), Victoria 88/G7
Lodève, France 28/E6
Lodeynoye Pole, U.S.S.R. 52/D2
Lodge (creek), Mont. 262/G1
Lodge (creek), Sask. 181/B6
Lodge, S.C. 296/F5
Lodge Bay, Newf. 166/C3
Lodge Grass, Mont. 262/J5
Lodge Hill, Barbados 161/B8
Lodgepole, Alberta 182/C3
Lodge Pole, Mont. 262/H2
Lodgepole, Nebr. 264/B3
Lodgepole (creek), Nebr. 264/A3
Lodgepole, S. Dak. 298/D2
Lodgepole (creek), Wyo. 319/H2
Lodgepole (creek), Wyo. 319/H4
Lodi, Calif. 188/B3
Lodi, Calif. 204/C9
Lodi, Italy 34/B2
Lodi, Italy 34/B2
Lodi, Miss. 256/E3
Lodi, Mo. 261/M8
Lodi, N.J. 273/B2
Lodi, N.Y. 276/G5
Lodi, Ohio 284/F3
Lodi (cape), Tasmania 99/E3
Lodi, Texas 303/K5
Lodi, Wis. 317/G9
Lødingen, Norway 18/J2
Lodja, Zaire 102/E5
Lodja, Zaire 115/D4
Lodosa, Spain 33/E1
Lodrino, Switzerland 39/G4
Lodwar, Kenya 115/G3
Łódź (prov.), Poland 47/D3
Łódź (city prov.), Poland 47/D3
Łódź, Poland 7/F3
Łódź, Poland 47/D3
Loei, Thailand 72/D3
Loen, Norway 18/E6
Lofer, Austria 41/B3
Lofoten (isls.), Norway 4/C9
Lofoten (isls.), Norway 7/F2
Lofoten (isls.), Norway 18/H2
Loftus, England 13/G3
Loftus, England 10/F3
Lofty (mt.), S. Australia 88/E8
Lofty (mt.), S. Australia 94/B8
Lofty (range), Tasmania 99/B3
Logan, Ala. 195/E2
Logan (lake), Alberta 182/E2
Logan (co.), Ark. 202/C3
Logan (mt.), Canada 4/C17
Logan (co.), Colo. 208/N1
Logan (co.), Ill. 222/D3
Logan, Ill. 222/E6
Logan, Ind. 227/H6
Logan, Iowa 229/B5
Logan (co.), Kansas 232/A3
Logan, Kansas 232/C2
Logan (co.), Ky. 237/H7
Logan, Mont. 262/E5
Logan (co.), Nebr. 264/D3
Logan (creek), Nebr. 264/H2
Logan, N. Mex. 274/F3
Logan (co.), N. Dak. 282/L7
Logan, N. Dak. 282/H3
Logan (co.), Ohio 284/C5
Logan, Ohio 284/F6
Logan (co.), Okla. 288/M3
Logan, Okla. 288/F1
Logan (co.), Oreg. 291/B2
Logan, Utah 304/D2
Logan, Utah 188/D2
Logan (mt.), Wash. 310/E2
Logan (co.), W. Va. 312/C7
Logan, W. Va. 312/B7
Logan (mt.), Yukon 162/B3
Logan (mt.), Yukon 187/D3
Logan (mts.), Yukon 187/F3
Logandale, Nev. 266/G6
Logan Internat'l Airport, Mass. 249/D7
Logan Lake, Br. Col. 184/G5
Logan Martin (lake), Ala. 195/F4
Logansport, Ind. 227/E3
Logansport, Ky. 237/H6
Logansport, La. 238/C3
Loganton, Pa. 294/H3
Loganville, Georgia 217/E3
Loganville, Pa. 294/J6
Loganville, Wis. 317/F9
Loge (riv.), Angola 115/B5
Loggieville, New Bruns. 170/E1
Log Lane Village, Colo. 208/M2
Logone (riv.) 102/D3
Logone (riv.), Cameroon 115/C2
Logone (riv.), Chad 111/J5
Logroño (prov.), Spain 33/E1
Logroño, Spain 7/D4
Logroño, Spain 33/E1
Logsden, Oreg. 291/D3
Løgstør, Denmark 21/C4
Løgstør, Denmark 18/F8
Løgstør Bredning (fjord), Denmark 21/C4
Løgumkloster, Denmark 21/B7
Lohals, Denmark 21/D7
Lohardaga, India 68/E4
Lohatlha, S. Africa 118/C5
Lohman, Mo. 261/H5
Lohman, Mont. 262/G2
Lohn, Texas 303/E6
Löhne, Germany 22/C2
Loho (Luohe), China 77/H5

Lohr am Main, Germany 22/C4
Lohrville, Iowa 229/D4
Lohrville, Wis. 317/H7
Loica, Chile 138/F4
Loi-kaw, Burma 72/C3
Loi Leng (mt.), Burma 72/C2
Loimaa, Finland 18/N6
Loir (riv.), France 28/D4
Loire (dept.), France 28/F5
Loire (riv.), France 7/E4
Loire (riv.), France 28/C4
Loire-Atlantique (dept.), France 28/C4
Loiret (dept.), France 28/E4
Loir-et-Cher (dept.), France 28/D4
Loíza, P. Rico 161/E1
Loíza Aldea, P. Rico 161/E1
Loja (prov.), Ecuador 128/C4
Loja, Ecuador 128/C4
Loja, Ecuador 120/B3
Loja, Spain 33/D4
Løjt Kirkeby, Denmark 21/C7
Loka, Sudan 111/F7
Lokeren, Belgium 27/D6
Lokitaung, Kenya 115/G3
Lokka (res.), Finland 18/Q3
Lokoja, Nigeria 106/F7
Lokolama, Zaire 115/D4
Lokoro (riv.), Zaire 115/C4
Lökösháza, Hungary 41/F3
Lokossa, Benin 106/E7
Loks Land (isl.), N.W.T. 187/M3
Lol (dry riv.), Sudan 111/E6
Lola, Ky. 237/E6
Loleta, Calif. 204/A3
Lolgorien, Kenya 115/G4
Lolita, Texas 303/H9
Lolland (isl.), Denmark 18/G9
Lolland (isl.), Denmark 21/E8
Lollie, Georgia 217/G6
Lolo (creek), Idaho 220/C3
Lolo (pass), Idaho 220/D3
Lolo, Mont. 262/B4
Lolo (pass), Mont. 262/B4
Lolo Hot Springs, Mont. 262/B4
Lom, Bulgaria 45/F4
Lom (riv.), Cameroon 115/B2
Lom, Norway 18/F6
Loma, Colo. 208/B4
Loma, Mont. 262/F3
Loma, N. Dak. 282/O2
Loma, Mansa (lag.), S. Leone 106/A7
Loma Alta, Bolivia 136/B2
Loma Bonita, Mexico 150/M7
Loma Linda, Calif. 204/F10
Loma Mar, Calif. 204/L3
Lomami (riv.), Zaire 115/D4
Loman, Minn. 255/F2
Loma Plata, Paraguay 144/C3
Lomas, Peru 128/E10
Lomas de Zamora, Argentina 143/G7
Lomax, Ala. 195/E5
Lomax, Ill. 222/B3
Lomax, S. Dak. 303/K2
Lombard, Ill. 222/B5
Lombardia, Serra (mts.), Brazil 132/D2
Lombardville, Ill. 222/D2
Lombardy (reg.), Italy 34/B2
Lombardy, S. Africa 118/H6
Lombez, France 28/D6
Lomblen (isl.), Indonesia 85/G7
Lombok (isl.), Indonesia 54/N10
Lombok (isl.), Indonesia 85/F7
Lombok (isl.), Indonesia 85/F7
Lomé (cap.), Togo 102/C4
Lomé (cap.), Togo 106/E7
Lomela, Zaire 115/D4
Lomela (riv.), Zaire 115/D4
Lometa, Texas 303/F6
Lomié, Cameroon 115/B3
Lomira, Wis. 317/J8
Lo Miranda, Chile 138/G5
Lomita, Calif. 204/C11
Lommel, Belgium 27/G6
Lomnice, Czech. 41/C2
Lomond, Alberta 182/D4
Lomond, Loch (lake), Nova Scotia 168/H3
Lomond, Loch (lake), Scotland 15/D4
Lomond, Loch (lake), Scotland 10/A1
Lompoc, Calif. 204/E9
Lom Sak, Thailand 72/D3
Łomża (prov.), Poland 47/F2
Łomża, Poland 47/F2
Lonaconing, Md. 245/C2
Loncoche, Chile 138/D2
Loncopué, Argentina 143/B4
London, Ark. 202/D3
London, Greater, England 13/H8
London (cap.), England 7/D3
London (cap.), England 10/B5
London (cap.), England 13/H8
London, Ind. 227/F5
London, Ky. 237/N6
London, Minn. 255/E7
London, Ohio 284/C6
London, Ont. 146/K5
London, Ont. 162/H7
London, Ont. 177/C5
London, Ontario 177/C5
London, Texas 303/E7
London (cap.), U.K. 2/J3
London, Wis. 317/H9
Londonderry (isl.), Chile 138/E11
Londonderry•, N.H. 268/E6
Londonderry, N. Ireland 7/D3
Londonderry (dist.), N. Ireland 17/G2
Londonderry (Derry), N. Ireland 10/C3

Londonderry (Derry), N. Ireland 17/G2
Londonderry, Nova Scotia 168/E3
Londonderry, Ohio 284/E7
Londonderry•, Vt. 268/B5
Londonderry (cape), W. Australia 88/D2
Londonderry (cape), W. Australia 92/D1
Londonderry Station, Nova Scotia 168/E3
London Mills, Ill. 222/C3
Londontowne, Md. 245/M4
Londrina, Brazil 132/D8
Londrina, Brazil 120/D5
Lone (mt.), Mont. 262/E5
Lone (mt.), Nev. 266/D4
Lone Butte, Br. Col. 184/G4
Lone Cedar, W. Va. 312/C4
Lone Cone (mt.), Colo. 208/C7
Lone Elm, Kansas 232/G3
Lone Grove, Okla. 288/M6
Lone Jack, Mo. 261/D5
Lone Oak, Ind. 227/D1
Lone Oak, Ky. 237/D6
Lone Oak, Texas 303/H5
Lone Pine, Alberta 182/C2
Lone Pine, Calif. 204/H7
Lone Pine (peak), Idaho 220/D5
Lonepine, La. 238/F5
Lonepine, Mont. 262/B3
Lone Prairie, Br. Col. 184/G2
Lone Rock, Iowa 229/E2
Lone Rock, Oreg. 291/H2
Lone Rock, Sask. 181/A2
Lone Rock, Wis. 317/F9
Lone Star, S.C. 296/F4
Lone Tree (creek), Colo. 208/K1
Lone Tree, Iowa 229/L6
Lonetree, N. Dak. 282/G3
Lonetree, Wyo. 319/B4
Lone Wolf, Okla. 288/H5
Long, Alaska 196/G2
Long (isl.), Maine 243/M2
Long (isl.), Ant. & Bar. 161/E11
Long (isl.), Bahamas 146/L7
Long (cay), Bahamas 156/C2
Long (isl.), Bahamas 156/C2
Long (bay), Barbados 161/B9
Long (mt.), Conn. 210/B2
Long (pond), Conn. 210/H3
Long (key), Fla. 212/F7
Long (key), Fla. 212/B3
Long (pond), Fla. 212/D2
Long (co.), Georgia 217/J7
Long (bay), Jamaica 158/H7
Long (lake), Maine 243/E6
Long (lake), Maine 243/G1
Long (lake), Maine 243/E7
Long (pond), Maine 243/E5
Long (pond), Maine 243/F6
Long (pond), Maine 243/D7
Long (lake), Manitoba 179/G4
Long (pt.), Manitoba 179/D1
Long (pt.), Manitoba 179/D4
Long (isl.), Martinique 161/D6
Long (isl.), Mass. 249/H7
Long (pond), Mass. 249/L5
Long (pt.), Mass. 249/O4
Long (lake), Mich. 250/D4
Long (lake), Minn. 255/C4
Long (lake), Minn. 255/C4
Long, Miss. 256/C4
Long (valley), Nev. 266/B1
Long (isl.), New Bruns. 170/D3
Long (isl.), Newf. 166/C2
Long (isl.), Newf. 166/D2
Long (isl.), Newf. 166/A3
Long (lake), Newf. 166/A3
Long (pt.), Newf. 166/C4
Long (mt.), N.H. 268/E2
Long (beach), N.J. 273/E4
Long (isl.), N.Y. 188/M2
Long (isl.), N.Y. 276/P9
Long (isl.), N.Y. 276/M2
Long (lake), N. Zealand 100/A7
Long (lake), N.C. 281/P5
Long (lake), N. Dak. 282/K6
Long (lake), N. Dak. 282/J4
Long (lake), N. Dak. 282/J3
Long (isl.), Nova Scotia 168/B4
Long (isl.), Ontario 177/H5
Long (isl.), Ontario 175/C3
Long (pt.), Ontario 177/D3
Long (isl.), Papua N.G. 85/B7
Long (isl.), Papua N.G. 86/A2
Long (creek), Sask. 181/H6
Long (str.), U.S.S.R. 48/S2
Long (pt.), Tasmania 99/E3
Long (pt.), Virgin Is. (U.S.) 161/E4
Long (pt.), Virgin Is. (U.S.) 161/K2
Long (isl.), Wash. 310/A4
Long (lake), Wash. 310/H3
Long (reef), W. Australia 92/D1
Long (lake), Wis. 317/C4
Longa, Angola 115/C6
Long (isl.), Scotland 15/C3
Longaví, Chile 138/A11
Long Bay, Jamaica 158/K6
Long Beach, Br. Col. 184/E5
Long Beach, Calif. 146/F5
Long Beach, Calif. 204/C11
Long Beach (pen.), Conn. 210/C4
Long Beach, Ind. 227/D1
Long Beach, Minn. 255/C5
Long Beach, Miss. 256/F10
Long Beach, N.J. 273/E4
Long Beach, N.Y. 276/R7
Long Beach, N.C. 281/N7

Long Beach, Ontario 177/E5
Long Beach, Wash. 310/A4
Longbenton, England 13/J3
Longboat (key), Fla. 212/D4
Longboat (key), Fla. 212/D4
Long Bottom, Ohio 284/G7
Long Branch, N.J. 273/F3
Longbranch, Wash. 310/C3
Longchuan, China 77/J7
Long Cove, Maine 243/E8
Long Creek, Oreg. 291/H3
Longdale, Okla. 288/K2
Longde, China 77/G4
Long Eaton, England 13/F5
Long Eddy, N.Y. 276/K7
Long Falls (dam), Maine 243/C5
Longfellow (mts.), Maine 243/B6
Longford (co.), Ireland 17/F4
Longford, Ireland 10/C4
Longford, Ireland 17/F4
Longford, Kansas 232/E2
Longford, Ontario 177/E3
Longford, Tasmania 99/C3
Longford, Virgin Is. (U.S.) 161/F4
Long Green, Md. 245/M3
Long Grove, Ill. 222/B5
Long Grove, Iowa 229/M5
Long Harbour, Newf. 166/D2
Long Hill, Conn. 210/C3
Longhua, China 77/J3
Longhui, China 77/H6
Longido, Tanzania 115/G4
Longiram, Indonesia 85/F5
Long Island (sound), Conn. 210/C4
Long Island (bay), Ireland 17/B9
Long Island, Kansas 232/C2
Long Island (sound), N.Y. 276/P9
Longisland, N.C. 281/H3
Long Island, Tenn. 237/S7
Longisland, Va. 307/K6
Longjiang, China 77/K2
Long Key, Fla. 212/F7
Longkou, China 77/J4
Longlac, Ontario 177/H5
Longlac, Ontario 175/F3
Long Lake, Mich. 250/F4
Long Lake, Minn. 255/F5
Long Lake, N.Y. 276/L3
Longlake, S. Dak. 298/L2
Long Lake, Wis. 317/J4
Long Lane, Mo. 261/G7
Longleaf, La. 238/E4
Long Meadow (pond), Conn. 210/C2
Longmeadow•, Mass. 249/D4
Longmire, Wash. 310/D4
Longmont, Colo. 188/E2
Longmont, Colo. 208/J2
Longnan, China 77/J7
Longnawan, Indonesia 85/F5
Long Neck (pt.), Conn. 210/B4
Long Pine, Nebr. 264/C2
Long Point, Ill. 222/E3
Long Point, Nova Scotia 168/G3
Long Point (bay), Ontario 177/D5
Long Point Beach, Ontario 177/D5
Long Pond, Maine 243/C4
Long Pond, Pa. 294/L3
Longport, N.J. 273/D5
Long Prairie, Minn. 255/D5
Long Prairie (riv.), Minn. 255/D4
Long Range (mts.), Newf. 166/C4
Long Rapids, Mich. 250/F3
Longreach, Australia 87/E8
Long Reach (inlet), New Bruns. 170/D3
Longreach, Queensland 88/G4
Longreach, Queensland 95/B4
Long Reef (pt.), N.S. Wales 97/K3
Longridge, England 13/H1
Longridge, England 10/G1
Longs (peak), Colo. 208/H2
Longs, S.C. 296/K4
Long Sault, Ontario 177/K2
Longshan, China 77/G6
Long Siding, Minn. 255/E5
Long Society, Conn. 210/G2
Long Spruce, Manitoba 179/K2
Longstreet, La. 238/B2
Longton, Kansas 232/F4
Longtown, Miss. 256/D1
Longtown, Mo. 261/N7
Longtown, S.C. 296/F4
Longueuil, Québec 172/J4
Long Valley, N.J. 273/D2
Longvalley, S. Dak. 298/F7
Longview, Ala. 195/F4
Longview, Alberta 182/C4
Longview, Colo. 208/J4
Longview, Ill. 222/F4
Longview, Miss. 256/G4
Longview, N.C. 281/F3
Longview, Texas 188/G4
Longview, Texas 303/K5
Longview, Wash. 188/B1
Longview, Wash. 310/B4
Longville, La. 238/D5
Longville, Minn. 255/D4
Longwood, Fla. 212/E3
Longwood, Mo. 261/F5
Longwood, N.C. 281/M7
Longwood Park, N.C. 281/K5
Longworth, Br. Col. 184/G3
Longworth, Texas 303/D5
Longwy, France 28/F3
Long Xian, China 77/G5
Long Xuyen, Vietnam 72/E5
Longyan, China 77/J6
Longyearbyen, Norway 18/D2
Longyearbyen, Norway 4/B8
Longzhen (Lungchen), China 77/L2
Loni Beach, Manitoba 179/F4
Lonigo, Italy 34/C2
Lonneker, Netherlands 27/K4

Lonoke (co.), Ark. 202/G4
Lonoke, Ark. 202/G4
Lonquimay, Chile 138/E2
Lonsdale, Ark. 202/F4
Lonsdale, Minn. 255/E6
Lonsdale, R.I. 249/J5
Lons-le-Saunier, France 28/F4
Lonton, Burma 72/B1
Lontzen, Belgium 27/H9
Looe, England 13/C7
Loogootee, Ind. 227/D7
Lookeba, Okla. 288/K4
Lookingglass (riv.), Mich. 250/E6
Lookout (mt.), Ala. 195/G2
Lookout (ridge), Alaska 196/G1
Lookout, Calif. 2C4/D2
Lookout (mt.), Idaho 220/F5
Lookout (mt.), Idaho 220/D5
Lookout, Ky. 237/S6
Lookout (pt.), Mc. 245/N8
Lookout (cape), N.C. 188/L4
Lookout (cape), N.C. 281/S5
Lookout, Okla. 288/H1
Lookout (cape), Oreg. 188/B1
Lookout (cape), Oreg. 291/C2
Lookout, Pa. 294/M2
Lookout, W. Va. 312/E6
Lookout, Wyo. 3·9/G4
Lookout Mountain, Georgia 217/B1
Lookout Mountain, Tenn. 237/L11
Lookout Point (cape), Oreg. 291/E4
Looma, Alberta 132/D3
Loomis, Calif. 204/C8
Loomis, Nebr. 264/E3
Loomis, Sask. 181/C6
Loomis, S. Dak. 298/N6
Loomis, Wash. 310/F2
Loomis, Wis. 317/K5
Loon (lake), Alberta 182/C1
Loon (riv.), Alberta 182/C1
Loon (lake), Maine 243/D3
Loon (lake), Ontario 177/F3
Loon (lake), Kansas 232/D3
Loon (creek), Sask. 181/G4
Loon (lake), Wash. 310/H2
Looneyville, W. Va. 312/D5
Loon Lake, Alberta 182/C1
Loon Lake, Maine 243/B5
Loon Lake, N.Y. 276/M1
Loon Lake, Sask. 181/B1
Loon Lake, Wash. 310/H2
Loon op Zand, Netherlands 27/G5
Loon Strait, Manitoba 179/F3
Loop (head), Ireland 17/A6
Loop (head), Ireland 10/A4
Loop, Texas 303/B5
Loos, Br. Col. 184/G3
Loosahatchie (riv.), Tenn. 237/B10
Loose Creek, Mo. 261/J5
Lo Ovalle, Chile 138/F3
Looxahoma, Miss. 256/E1
Looz (Borgloon), Belgium 27/G7
Lopatka (cape), U.S.S.R. 54/S4
Lopatka (cape), U.S.S.R. 48/Q4
Lop Buri, Thailand 72/D4
Lopeno, Texas 303/E11
Lopez (pt.), Calif. 204/D7
Lopez (cape), Gabon 102/C5
Lopez (cape), Gabon 115/A4
Lopez, Pa. 294/K3
Lopez, Wash. 310/C2
Lopez (isl.), Wash. 310/C2
Lopi, Congo 115/C3
Lop Nor (Lop Nur) (lake), China 77/D3
Lopnur (Yuli), China 77/C3
Lop Nur (lake), China 54/L5
Loophavet (bay) Norway 18/M1
Lora, Hamun-i- (swamp), Pakistan 58/B3
Lora, Hamun-i- (swamp), Pakistan 59/J4
Lora del Río, Spain 33/D4
Lorado, W. Va. 312/C7
Lorain (co.), Ohio 284/F3
Lorain, Ohio 284/F3
Loraine, Ill. 222/B3
Loraine, N. Dak. 282/G2
Loraine, Texas 303/D5
Loraine, Wis. 317/B4
Loralai, Pakistan 68/B2
Loralai, Pakistan 59/J3
Loramie (lake), Ohio 284/B5
Loranger, La. 238/N1
Lorca, Spain 33/F4
Lord Howe (isl.) Australia 87/G9
Lord Howe (isl.) Australia 2/T7
Lord Howe (isl.) N.S. Wales 97/J2
Lord Howe (Ontong Java) (isl.), Solomon Is. 87/G6
Lord Howe (ontong Java) (isls.), Solomon Is. 86/D2
Lord Mayor (bay), N.W. Terr. 187/J3
Lordsburg, N. Mex. 274/A6
Lords Point, Conn. 210/H3
Lordstown, Ohio 284/J3
Lords Valley, Pa. 294/M3
Loreauville, La. 238/G6
Loreburn, Sask. 181/F4
Lore City, Ohio 284/H6
Lorena, Brazil 135/D3
Lorena, Miss. 256/F6
Lorengau, Papua N.G. 86/A1
Lorengau, Papua N.G. 87/E6
Lo-Reninge, Belgium 27/B7
Lorentz, W. Va. 312/F4
Lorenzo, Idaho 220/G6
Lorenzo, Texas 303/C4
Lorenzo Geyres Uruguay 145/B3
Loreto, Bolivia 136/C4
Loreto, Colombia 126/E9
Loreto, Ecuador 128/D3
Loreto, Baja California, Mexico 150/D4

Loreto, Zacatecas, Mexico 150/J5
Loreto, Paraguay 144/D3
Loreto (dept.), Peru 128/E5
Loreto, Agusan del Sur, Philippines 82/E6
Loreto, Surigao del Norte, Philippines 82/E5
Loretta, Kansas 232/C3
Loretta, Wis. 317/E4
Lorette, Manitoba 179/F5
Loretteville, Québec 172/H3
Loretto, Ky. 237/L5
Loretto, Mich. 250/B3
Loretto, Minn. 255/F5
Loretto, Nebr. 264/F3
Loretto, Pa. 294/E4
Loretto, Tenn. 237/G10
Loretto, Va. 307/04
Lorian (swamp), Kenya 115/G3
Lorica, Colombia 126/C3
Lorida, Fla. 212/E4
Lorient, France 7/D4
Lorient, France 28/B4
L'Orignal, Ontario 177/K2
Lorimor, Iowa 229/E6
Lőrinci, Hungary 41/E3
Loring, Mont. 262/J2
Loring, Ontario 177/D2
Loring, Wash. 310/H2
Loring A.F.B., Maine 243/H2
Loris, S.C. 296/K3
Lorlie, Sask. 181/H5
Lorman, Miss. 256/B7
Lorne, New Bruns. 170/D1
Lorne, Nova Scotia 168/H3
Lorne (dist.), Scotland 15/C4
Lorne (firth), Scotland 10/D2
Lorne (firth), Scotland 15/C4
Loros (pt.), Chile 138/E3
Lörrach, Germany 22/B5
Lorrain (riv.), Martinique 161/D5
Lorraine, Kansas 232/D3
Lorraine, N.Y. 276/J3
Lorraine, Québec 172/H4
Lorrainville, Québec 174/B3
Lorrha, Ireland 17/E5
Lort (riv.), W. Australia 88/C6
Lorton, Nebr. 264/H4
Lorton, Va. 307/03
Lorze (riv.), Switzerland 39/F2
Los (isls.), Guinea 106/B7
Losada (riv.), Colombia 126/C6
Los Alamitos, Calif. 204/D11
Los Alamos, Calif. 204/B4
Los Alamos, N.Mex. 188/E3
Los Alamos (co.), N. Mex. 274/C3
Los Alamos, N. Mex. 274/C3
Los Alerces Nat'l Park, Argentina 143/C5
Los Algodones, Mexico 150/B1
Los Altos, Calif. 204/K3
Los Altos Hills, Calif. 204/J3
Los Amates, Guatemala 154/C3
Los Andes, Chile 138/B9
Los Andes, Colombia 126/B7
Los Angeles, Calif. 146/G6
Los Angeles, Calif. 188/C4
Los Angeles (co.), Calif. 204/G9
Los Angeles, Calif. 204/C10
Los Angeles, Chile 138/D1
Los Angeles, Chile 120/B6
Los Angeles, Texas 303/F9
Los Angeles, U.S. 2/D4
Los Angeles Aqueduct, Calif. 204/G8
Los Antiguos, Argentina 143/B6
Losantville, Ind. 227/G4
Los Arabos, Cuba 158/E1
Los Arroyos, Cuba 158/A2
Los Banos, Calif. 204/E6
Los Barcos (pt.), Cuba 158/B2
Los Canarreos (arch.), Cuba 158/C2
Los Castillos, Venezuela 124/G3
Los Choros (riv.), Chile 138/A7
Los Colorados (arch.), Cuba 158/A1
Los Conquistadores, Argentina 143/G5
Los Coyotes Ind. Res., Calif. 204/J10
Los Cusis, Bolivia 136/D4
Los Estados (isl.), Argentina 143/D7
Los Frailes (isl.), Dom. Rep. 158/C7
Los Fresnos, Texas 303/G11
Los Gatos, Calif. 204/K4
Los Glaciares Nat'l Park, Argentina 143/B6
Los Hermanos (isls.), Venezuela 124/F2
Losice, Poland 47/F2
Los Indios, Cuba 158/B2
Lošinj (isl.), Yugoslavia 45/B3
Los Lagos (reg.), Chile 138/D3
Los Lagos, Chile 138/D3
Los Llanos, Dom. Rep. 158/F6
Los Loros, Chile 138/B6
Los Lunas, N. Mex. 274/C4
Los Menucos, Argentina 143/C5
Los Mochis, Mexico 150/D4
Los Molinos, Calif. 204/C4
Los Monjes (isls.), Venezuela 124/C1
Los Muermos, Chile 138/D3
Los Navalmorales, Spain 33/D3
Los Navalucillos, Spain 33/D3
Los Negros, Cuba 158/F2
Los Novillos, Uruguay 145/D2
Los Ojos, N. Mex. 274/C2
Los Olivos, Calif. 204/E9
Los Olmos (creek), Texas 303/F10
Los Olmos (creek), Texas 303/F11
Los Osos-Baywood Park, Calif. 204/E8
Los Palacios, Cuba 158/B1
Los Palacios, Cuba 156/A2
Los Perales de Tapihue, Chile 138/F3

Los Pinos (riv.), Colo. 208/G8
Los Ranchos De Albuquerque, N. Mex. 274/C3
Los Reyes de Salgado, Mexico 150/H7
Los Ríos (prov.), Ecuador 128/C3
Los Roques (isls.), Venezuela 124/E2
Los Santos, Panama 154/G7
Los Santos de Maimona, Spain 33/C3
Los Sauces, Chile 138/D1
Losser, Netherlands 27/L4
Lossiemouth and Branderburgh, Scotland 15/E3
Lossiemouth and Branderburgh, Scotland 10/E2
Lost (riv.), Calif. 204/D1
Lost (riv.), Ind. 227/D7
Lost (riv.), Minn. 255/C3
Lost (riv.), Oreg. 291/F5
Lost (creek), Utah 304/C5
Lostant, Ill. 222/D2
Los Taques, Venezuela 124/C2
Lost Cabin, Wyo. 319/E2
Lost City, W. Va. 312/J5
Lost Creek, Ky. 237/P6
Lost Creek, Wash. 310/H2
Lost Creek, W. Va. 312/F4
Los Teques, Venezuela 120/C2
Los Teques, Venezuela 124/E2
Los Testigos (isls.), Venezuela 124/G2
Lost Hills, Calif. 204/F8
Lostine, Oreg. 291/K2
Lost Island (lake), Iowa 229/D2
Lost Nation, Iowa 229/M5
Lost River, Idaho 220/E5
Lost River (range), Idaho 220/E5
Lost River, W. Va. 312/J5
Lost Springs, Kansas 232/E3
Lost Springs, Wyo. 319/G3
Lost Trail (pass), Idaho 220/E4
Lost Trail (pass), Mont. 262/B5
Lostwood, N. Dak. 282/F3
Los Vilos, Chile 138/A9
Los Yébenes, Spain 33/E3
Lot (dept.), France 28/D5
Lot (riv.), France 28/D5
Lota, Chile 138/D1
Lotagipi Swamp (plain), Sudan 111/H6
Lotbinière (co.), Québec 172/F3
Lotbinière, Québec 172/F3
Lot-et-Garonne (dept.), France 28/D5
Lothair, Ky. 237/P6
Lothair, Mont. 262/E2
Lothian (co.), Scotland 15/E5
Lothian (reg.), Scotland 15/E5
Loto, Zaire 115/D4
Lötschberg (tunnel), Switzerland 39/E4
Lotsee, Okla. 288/O2
Lott, Texas 303/H6
Lottie, Ala. 195/C8
Lottie, La. 238/G5
Lottsville, Pa. 294/D2
Lotus, Calif. 204/C8
Lotzwil, Switzerland 39/E2
Louang Namtha, Laos 72/D2
Louangphrabang, Laos 72/D3
Louangprabang, Laos 54/M7
Louann, Ark. 202/E7
Loubomo, Congo 115/B4
Loubomo, Congo 102/D5
Loudéac, France 28/B3
Loudima, Congo 115/B4
Loudon•, N.H. 268/F5
Loudon (co.), Tenn. 237/N8
Loudon, Tenn. 237/N9
Loudonville, Ohio 284/F4
Loudoun (co.), Va. 307/N2
Louellen, Ky. 237/P7
Louga, Senegal 106/A5
Loughborough, England 13/F5
Loughborough, England 10/F4
Loughbrickland, N. Ireland 17/J3
Loughead, Alberta 182/E3
Lougheed (isl.), N.W. Terr. 187/H2
Loughman, Fla. 212/E3
Loughrea, Ireland 17/E5
Loughrea, Ireland 10/B4
Loughros More (bay), Ireland 17/D2
Louin, Miss. 256/F6
Louisa (co.), Iowa 229/L6
Louisa, Ky. 237/R4
Louisa, La. 238/G7
Louisa (lake), Ontario 177/E2
Louisa (co.), Va. 307/N5
Louisa, Va. 307/M4
Louisbourg, Nova Scotia 168/J3
Louisbourg Nat'l Hist. Park, Nova Scotia 168/J3
Louisburg, Kansas 232/H3
Louisburg, Minn. 255/B5
Louisburg, Mo. 261/F7
Louisburg, N.C. 281/N4
Louisburgh, Ireland 17/B4
Louis Creek, Br. Col. 184/H4
Louisdale, Nova Scotia 168/H3
Louise (lake), Alaska 196/C1
Louise (co.), Br. Col. 184/B4
Louise, Miss. 256/C5
Louise (lake), Québec 172/C4
Louise, Texas 303/H8
Louiseville, Québec 172/E3
Louisiade (arch.), Papua N.G. 87/F7
Louisiade (arch.), Papua N.G. 85/D8
Louisiana 188/H4
LOUISIANA 238
Louisiana (pt.), La. 238/C7
Louisiana, Mo. 261/K4

Louisiana (state), U.S. 146/J6
Louis Trichardt, S. Africa 118/E4
Louisville, Ala. 195/G7
Louisville, Colo. 208/J3
Louisville, Georgia 217/H4
Louisville, Ill. 222/E5
Louisville, Kansas 232/F2
Louisville, Ky. 237/J2
Louisville, Ky. 146/K6
Louisville, Miss. 256/G4
Louisville, Nebr. 264/H3
Louisville, Ohio 284/H4
Louisville, Tenn. 237/N9
Louisville, Ky. 188/J3
Loukhi, U.S.S.R. 52/D1
Loulé, Portugal 33/B4
Louny, Czech. 41/B1
Loup (co.), Nebr. 264/E3
Loup (riv.), Nebr. 264/E3
Loup (riv.), Québec 172/H2
Loup City, Nebr. 264/E3
Lourdes, France 28/C6
Lourdes, Newf. 166/C4
Lourdes, N. Mex. 274/D3
Lourdes, Québec 172/C4
Louriçal, Portugal 33/B3
Lourinhã, Portugal 33/B3
Lousã, Portugal 33/B2
Lousana, Alberta 182/D3
Louth, England 13/H4
Louth (co.), Ireland 17/J4
Louth, Ireland 17/J4
Louth, N.S. Wales 97/C2
Loutrá Aidhipsoú, Greece 45/F6
Louvain (Leuven), Belgium 27/F7
Louvale, Georgia 217/C6
Louviers, Colo. 208/K4
Louviers, France 28/D3
Lövånger, Sweden 18/M4
Lovango (cay), Virgin Is. (U.S.) 161/C4
Lovat' (riv.), U.S.S.R. 52/D3
Love, Miss. 256/D1
Love (co.), Okla. 288/M7
Love, Sask. 181/G2
Lovech, Bulgaria 45/G4
Lovejoy, Georgia 217/D4
Lovejoy, Ill. 222/A2
Lovelaceville, Ky. 237/D7
Lovelady, Texas 303/J6
Loveland, Colo. 188/E2
Loveland, Colo. 208/J2
Loveland, Iowa 229/B6
Loveland, Ohio 284/D9
Loveland, Okla. 288/J6
Lovell, Maine 243/B7
Lovell•, Mass. 249/B7
Lovell, Okla. 288/L2
Lovell, Wyo. 319/D1
Lovells, Mich. 250/E4
Lovelock, Nev. 266/C2
Lovely, Ky. 237/S5
Lovenia (mt.), Utah 304/D3
Love Point, Md. 245/N4
Loverna, Sask. 181/B4
Loves Park, Ill. 222/E1
Lovett, Georgia 217/G5
Lovett, Ind. 227/F7
Lovettsville, Va. 307/N2
Love Valley, N.C. 281/H3
Loveville, Md. 245/M7
Lovewell, Kansas 232/D2
Lovewell (res.), Kansas 232/D2
Lovilia, Iowa 229/H6
Loving, N. Mex. 274/E4
Loving (co.), Texas 303/A6
Lovingston, Va. 307/L5
Lovington, Ill. 222/E4
Lovington, N. Mex. 274/F6
Lovisa, Finland 18/P6
Lovisa (co.), Iowa 229/L6
Lővő, Hungary 41/D3
Lovosice, Czech. 41/C1
Lóvua, Angola 115/D5
Low (cape), N.W.T. 162/H3
Low (cape), N.W. Terr. 187/K3
Low, Québec 172/B4
Lowa (riv.), Zaire 115/E4
Low Bush River, Ontario 177/K5
Low Bush River, Ontario 175/C4
Lowden, Iowa 229/L5
Lowder, Ill. 222/D4
Lowe Farm, Manitoba 179/E5
Lowell, Ark. 202/B1
Lowell, Fla. 212/D2
Lowell, Idaho 220/C3
Lowell (lake), Idaho 220/B6
Lowell, Ind. 227/D2
Lowell, Iowa 229/L7
Lowell, Kansas 232/H4
Lowell, Maine 243/F5
Lowell•, Maine 243/F5
Lowell, Mass. 188/M2
Lowell, Mass. 249/J2
Lowell, Mich. 250/D6
Lowell, N.C. 281/G4
Lowell, Ohio 284/H6
Lowell, Oreg. 291/E4
Lowell•, Vt. 268/C2
Lowell, W. Va. 312/E7
Lowell, Wis. 317/J9
Lowell Nat'l Hist. Park, Mass. 249/J2
Lowellville, Ohio 284/J3
Lower Alkali (lake), Calif. 204/E2
Lower Argyle, Nova Scotia 168/C5
Lower Arrow (lake), Br. Col. 184/H5
Lower Austria (prov.), Austria 41/C2
Lower Bank, N.J. 273/E4
Lower Barneys River, Nova Scotia 168/H3
Lower Brule, S. Dak. 298/K5
Lower Brule Ind. Res., S. Dak. 298/K5
Lower Burrell, Pa. 294/C4
Lower Cabot, Vt. 268/C3
Lower California (pen.), Mexico 2/D4

Lower California (pen.), Mexico 146/G7
Lower California (pen.), Mexico 150/C3
Lower Cloverdale, New Bruns. 170/G2
Lower Crab (creek), Wash. 310/F4
Lower Derby, New Bruns. 170/E2
Lower Durham, New Bruns. 170/D2
Lower East Pubnico, Nova Scotia 168/C5
Lower Elwah Ind. Res., Wash. 310/B2
Lower Engadine (valley), Switzerland 39/K3
Lower Goose Creek (res.), Idaho 220/D7
Lower Granite (lake), Idaho 220/A3
Lower Granite (dam), Wash. 310/H4
Lower Granite (lake), Wash. 310/H4
Lower Hainesville, New Bruns. 170/C2
Lower Hutt, N. Zealand 100/B2
Lower Island Cove, Newf. 166/D2
Lower Kalskag, Alaska 196/F2
Lower Kars, New Bruns. 170/E3
Lower Klamath (lake), Calif. 204/D2
Lower Lake, Calif. 204/C5
Lower L'Ardoise, Nova Scotia 168/H3
Lower Marlboro, Md. 245/M6
Lower Matecumbe (key), Fla. 212/F7
Lower Millstream, New Bruns. 170/E3
Lower Montague, Pr. Edward I. 168/F2
Lower Monumental (dam), Wash. 310/G4
Lower Monumental (lake), Wash. 310/G4
Lower New York (bay), N.J. 273/E2
Lower Nicola, Br. Col. 184/G5
Lower Ohio, Nova Scotia 168/C5
Lower Paia, Hawaii 218/J1
Lower Peach Tree, Ala. 195/C7
Lower Post, Br. Col. 184/K1
Lower Red (lake), Minn. 255/C3
Lower Red Rock (lake), Mont. 262/E6
Lower Rhine (riv.), Netherlands 27/H5
Lower Roach (pond), Maine 243/E4
Lower Saint Mary (lake), Mont. 262/C2
Lower Salem, Ohio 284/H6
Lower Sapin, New Bruns. 170/F2
Lower Saranac (lake), N.Y. 276/M2
Lower Saxony (state), Germany 22/C2
Lower Southampton, New Bruns. 170/C2
Lower South River, Nova Scotia 168/H3
Lower Sysladobsis (lake), Maine 243/F5
Lower Tonsina, Alaska 196/D2
Lower Tunguska (riv.), U.S.S.R. 54/L3
Lower Tunguska (riv.), U.S.S.R. 48/K3
Lower Waterford, Vt. 268/D3
Lower Wedgeport, Nova Scotia 168/C5
Lower West Pubnico, Nova Scotia 168/C5
Lower Woods Harbour, Nova Scotia 168/C5
Lowery, Ala. 195/F8
Lowery (lake), Fla. 212/E3
Lowes, Ky. 237/D7
Lowestoft, England 13/J5
Lowestoft, England 10/J4
Lowesville, Va. 307/K5
Lowgap, N.C. 281/H1
Lowicz, Poland 47/D2
Lowland, N.C. 281/S4
Lowman, Idaho 220/C5
Lowmansville, Ky. 237/R5
Low Moor, Iowa 229/N5
Lowmoor, Va. 307/J5
Lowndes (co.), Ala. 195/E6
Lowndes (co.), Georgia 217/F9
Lowndes (co.), Miss. 256/H4
Lowndes, Mo. 261/M8
Lowndesboro, Ala. 195/E6
Lowndesville, S.C. 296/B3
Lowpoint, Ill. 222/D3
Low Rocky (pt.), Tasmania 99/B4
Lowry, Minn. 255/C5
Lowry, S. Dak. 298/K3
Lowry, Va. 307/K6
Lowry A.F.B., Colo. 208/K3
Lowry City, Mo. 261/E6
Lowrys, S.C. 296/E2
Lowther (isl.), N.W.T. 187/J2
Lowville, N.Y. 276/J3
Low Wassie, Mo. 261/K9
Loxahatchee, Fla. 212/F5
Loxley, Ala. 195/C9
Loxton, S. Australia 94/G6
Loxton North, S. Australia 94/G6
Loyal, Okla. 288/K3
Loyal, Loch (lake), Scotland 15/D2
Loyal, Wis. 317/E6
Loyalhanna, Pa. 294/D5
Loyalist, Alberta 182/E4
Loyall, Ky. 237/P7
Loyalton, Calif. 204/E4
Loyalton, Pa. 294/J4
Loyalty (isls.), New Caled. 87/G8
Loyalty (isls.), New Caled. 86/H4
Loyang (Luoyang), China 77/H5
Loyd, Wis. 317/F9
Loyne, Loch (lake), Scotland 15/C3
Loysburg, Pa. 294/F5
Loysville, Pa. 294/H5
Lozeau (lake), Newf. 166/B3
Lozère (dept.), France 28/E5
Loznica, Yugoslavia 45/D3

Lozovaya, U.S.S.R. 52/E5
Lua (riv.), Zaire 115/C3
Luacano, Angola 115/D6
Lualaba (riv.), Zaire 102/E5
Lualaba (riv.), Zaire 115/E4
Lu'an, China 77/J5
Luana, Iowa 229/K2
Luana (pt.), Jamaica 158/G6
Luanchuan, China 77/H5
Luanda (prov.), Angola 115/B5
Luanda (cap.), Angola 2/K6
Luanda (cap.), Angola 115/B5
Luanda (cap.), Angola 102/D5
Luang, Thale (lag.), Thailand 72/D6
Luang (mt.), Thailand 72/C5
Luang Prabang (Loungphrabang), Laos 72/D3
Luangwa, Zambia 115/E7
Luangwa, Zambia 118/D3
Luangwa (Feira), Zambia 115/E7
Luangwa (riv.), Zambia 115/F6
Luanshya, Zambia 115/E6
Luanshya, Zambia 102/E6
Luapula (riv.), Zaire 115/E6
Luapula (riv.), Zambia 115/E6
Luarca, Spain 33/C1
Luashi, Zaire 115/D6
Luau, Angola 115/D6
Luba, Equat. Guinea 115/A3
Lubaczów, Poland 47/F3
Lubań, Poland 47/B3
Lubāna (lake), U.S.S.R. 53/D2
Lubang, Philippines 82/C4
Lubang (isls.), Philippines 85/F3
Lubang (isls.), Philippines 82/B4
Lubango, Angola 115/B6
Lubango, Angola 102/D6
Lubartów, Poland 47/F3
Lubawa, Poland 47/D2
Lübben, Germany 22/E3
Lübbenau, Germany 22/F3
Lübbenau, Germany 22/F3
Lubbock (co.), Texas 303/C4
Lubbock, Texas 146/H6
Lubbock, Texas 303/C4
Lubbock, Texas 188/F4
Lubec, Maine 243/K6
Lubec •, Maine 243/K6
Lübeck, Germany 7/E3
Lübeck, Germany 22/D2
Lübeck, W. Va. 312/C4
Lubefu, Zaire 115/D4
Lubero, Zaire 115/E4
L'ubica, Czech. 41/F2
Lubicon (lake), Alberta 182/C1
Lubien Kujawski, Poland 47/D2
Lubilash (riv.), Zaire 115/D5
Lublin (prov.), Poland 47/F3
Lublin, Poland 47/F3
Lublin, Poland 7/G3
Lublin, Wis. 317/E5
Lubliniec, Poland 47/D3
Lubny, U.S.S.R. 52/D4
Luboń, Poland 47/C2
Lubrín, Spain 33/F4
Lubsko, Poland 47/B3
Lubuagan, Philippines 82/C2
Lubudi, Zaire 115/E5
Lubuklinggau, Indonesia 85/C6
Lubuksikaping, Indonesia 85/B5
Lubumbashi, Zaire 2/L6
Lubumbashi, Zaire 115/E6
Lubumbashi, Zaire 102/E6
Lubutu, Zaire 115/E4
Lübz, Germany 22/D2
Lucama, N.C. 281/N3
Lucan, Minn. 255/C6
Lucan, Ontario 177/C4
Luc An Chau, Vietnam 72/E2
Lucan-Doddsborough, Ireland 17/J5
Lucapa, Angola 114/D5
Lucas (co.), Iowa 229/G6
Lucas, Iowa 229/G6
Lucas, Kansas 232/D2
Lucas, Ky. 237/K7
Lucas, Mich. 250/D4
Lucas (co.), Ohio 284/C2
Lucas, Ohio 284/F4
Lucas, S. Dak. 298/C4
Lucas, Texas 303/H1
Lucas E. de Peña, Dom. Rep. 158/C4
Lucas González, Argentina 143/G6
Lucasville, Ohio 284/E8
Lucban, Philippines 82/C3
Lucca (prov.), Italy 34/C3
Lucca, Italy 34/C3
Lucca, N. Dak. 282/P6
Luce (co.), Mich. 250/D2
Luce, Minn. 255/C4
Luce (bay), Scotland 10/D3
Luce (bay), Scotland 15/D6
Lucea, Jamaica 158/G5
Lucedale, Miss. 256/G9
Lucena, Philippines 85/G3
Lucena, Philippines 82/C4
Lucena, Spain 33/D4
Lucena del Cid, Spain 33/F2
Lučenec, Czech. 41/E2
Lucens, Switzerland 39/C3
Lucera, Italy 34/E4
Lucerne, Peru 128/H9
Lucerne, Calif. 204/C4
Lucerne, Colo. 208/K2
Lucerne, Ind. 227/E3
Lucerne, Mo. 261/F2
Lucerne, Québec 172/B4
Lucerne (Luzern) (canton), Switzerland 39/F2
Lucerne (lake), Switzerland 39/F3
Lucerne, Wash. 310/C2
Lucerne, Wyo. 319/D2
Lucernemines, Pa. 294/D4
Lucerne Valley, Calif. 204/J9
Lucero (lake), N. Mex. 274/C6

Luceville, Québec 172/J1
Luchow (Luzhou), China 77/G6
Lüchow, Germany 22/D2
Lucia, Calif. 204/D7
Lucie (riv.), Suriname 131/C4
Lucien, Miss. 256/C7
Lucien, Okla. 288/M2
Lucile, Georgia 217/C8
Lucile, Idaho 220/B4
Lucile, Ky. 237/P4
Lucinda, Pa. 294/D3
Lucira, Angola 115/B6
Luck, Wis. 317/B4
Luckau, Germany 22/E3
Luckenwalde, Germany 22/E2
Lucketts, Va. 307/N2
Luckey, Ohio 284/D3
Lucknow, India 68/E3
Lucknow, India 54/K7
Lucknow, Ontario 177/C4
Lucky, La. 238/E2
Lucky Lake, Sask. 181/D5
Lucky Peak (lake), Idaho 220/B6
Luçon, France 28/C4
Lucrecia (cape), Cuba 158/J3
Lucy, La. 238/M3
Lucy, Tenn. 237/B10
Lucy Creek, North. Terr. 93/E7
Ludden, N. Dak. 282/O7
Ludell, Kansas 232/B2
Lüdenscheid, Germany 22/B3
Lüderitz, Namibia 118/A5
Lüderitz, Namibia 102/D7
Lüderitz (bay), Namibia 118/A5
Ludhiana, India 54/J6
Ludhiana, India 68/D2
Ludington, Mich. 250/C5
Ludlow, Calif. 204/J9
Ludlow (ridge), England 10/E4
Ludlow, England 13/E5
Ludlow, Ill. 222/E3
Ludlow, Ky. 237/S2
Ludlow •, Maine 243/G3
Ludlow •, Mass. 249/E4
Ludlow, Miss. 256/E5
Ludlow, Mo. 261/E3
Ludlow, New Bruns. 170/D2
Ludlow, Pa. 294/E2
Ludlow, S. Dak. 298/C2
Ludlow, Vt. 268/B5
Ludlow •, Vt. 268/B5
Ludlow (mt.), Vt. 268/B5
Ludlow Center, Mass. 249/E4
Ludlow Falls, Ohio 284/B6
Ludowici, Georgia 217/J7
Luduş, Romania 45/G2
Ludville, Georgia 217/C2
Ludwigsburg, Germany 22/C4
Ludwigshafen am Rhein, Germany 22/C4
Ludwigslust, Germany 22/D2
Ludza, U.S.S.R. 53/D2
Lue, N.S. Wales 97/E3
Luebbering, Mo. 261/L6
Luebo, Zaire 115/D5
Lueders, Texas 303/D5
Luella, Georgia 217/D4
Luena, Angola 102/D6
Luena, Angola 115/C6
Luepa, Venezuela 124/H5
Lüeyang, China 77/G5
Lufeng, China 77/J7
Lufira (riv.), Zaire 115/E5
Lufkin, Texas 303/K6
Luga, U.S.S.R. 52/C3
Luga, U.S.S.R. 48/D4
Lugano, Switzerland 39/G4
Lugano (lake), Switzerland 39/H5
Lugansk, U.S.S.R. 48/E5
Lugansk, U.S.S.R. 52/E5
Luganville, Vanuatu 87/G7
Lugareño, Cuba 158/G3
Lugenda (riv.), Mozambique 118/F2
Lugerville, Wis. 317/E4
Lugnaquillia (mt.), Ireland 17/J5
Lugo, Italy 34/D2
Lugo (prov.), Spain 33/C1
Lugo, Spain 33/C1
Lugoff, S.C. 296/F3
Lugoj, Romania 45/F3
Luhaiya, Yemen 59/D6
Luiana, Angola 119/D7
Luiana, Angola 102/E6
Luik (Liège), Belgium 27/H7
Luilaka (riv.), Zaire 115/C4
Luimneach (Limerick), Ireland 10/B4
Luimneach (Limerick), Ireland 17/D6
Luina, Tasmania 99/B3
Luing (isl.), Scotland 15/C4
Luís Correia, Brazil 132/F3
Luis de Saboya, Cerro (mt.), Chile 138/F11
Luishia, Zaire 115/E6
Luitpold Coast (reg.), 5/B17
Luiza, Zaire 115/D5
Luján, Argentina 143/G7
Lujiang, China 77/J5
Lukachukai, Ariz. 198/F1
Lukachukai (mts.), Ariz. 198/F2
Luke, Md. 245/B3
Luke A.F.B., Ariz. 198/C6
Lukenie (riv.), Zaire 115/D4
Lukeville, Ariz. 198/C7
Lukolela, Equateur, Zaire 115/C4
Lukolela, Kasai-Oriental, Zaire 115/D5
Lukovit, Bulgaria 45/G4
Łuków, Poland 47/F3
Lukuga (riv.), Zaire 115/E5
Lukula, Zaire 115/B5
Lukulu, Zambia 115/D6
Lula, Georgia 217/E2
Lula, Miss. 256/C2
Lula, Okla. 288/O5

Lule (riv.), Sweden 7/G2
Luleå, Sweden 7/G2
Luleå, Sweden 18/N4
Luleälv (riv.), Sweden 18/M4
Lüleburgaz, Turkey 63/B2
Lules, Argentina 143/C2
Luling, La. 238/N4
Luling, Texas 303/G8
Lulu, Fla. 212/D1
Lulua (riv.), Zaire 115/D5
Lum, Mich. 250/F5
Lumajang, Indonesia 85/K2
Lumajangdong Co (lake), China 77/B5
Lumbala N'guimbo, Angola 115/D6
Lumber (riv.), N.C. 281/L6
Lumber (riv.), S.C. 296/J3
Lumber Bridge, N.C. 281/L5
Lumber City, Georgia 217/G7
Lumber City, Pa. 294/E4
Lumberport, W. Va. 312/F4
Lumberton, Miss. 256/E8
Lumberton, N.J. 273/D4
Lumberton, N. Mex. 274/C2
Lumberton, N.C. 281/L5
Lumberton, Texas 303/K7
Lumberville, Pa. 294/N5
Lumbo, Mozambique 118/G3
Lumbrales, Spain 33/C2
Lumbrein, Switzerland 39/H3
Lumby, Br. Col. 184/H5
Lumding, India 68/G3
Lummen, Belgium 27/G7
Lummi (isl.), Wash. 310/C2
Lummi Ind. Res., Wash. 310/C2
Lummi Island, Wash. 310/C2
Lumphat, Cambodia 72/E4
Lumpkin (co.), Georgia 217/D1
Lumpkin, Georgia 217/C6
Lumsden, Newf. 166/D4
Lumsden, N. Zealand 100/B6
Lumsden, Sask. 181/F5
Lumsden, Scotland 15/F3
Lumsden Beach, Sask. 181/F5
Lumut, Malaysia 72/D6
Luna, Ark. 202/H7
Luna (co.), N. Mex. 274/B6
Luna, N. Mex. 274/A5
Luna Pier, Mich. 250/F7
Luncarty, Scotland 15/E4
Lund, Br. Col. 184/G5
Lund, Idaho 220/G7
Lund, Nev. 266/F4
Lund, Sweden 18/H9
Lund, Utah 304/A5
Lundale, W. Va. 312/C7
Lundar, Manitoba 179/D4
Lunda Sul (prov.), Angola 115/D5
Lundazi, Zambia 115/F6
Lundbreck, Alberta 182/C5
Lundby, Denmark 21/E7
Lundell, Ark. 202/H5
Lunderskov, Denmark 21/C7
Lundi (riv.), Zimbabwe 118/E5
Lunds Corner, Mass. 249/L6
Lundsvalley, N. Dak. 282/E3
Lundy, England 13/C6
Lundy (isl.), England 10/D5
Lune (riv.), England 13/E3
Lüneburg, Germany 22/D2
Lüneburger Heide (dist.), Germany 22/C2
Lunel, France 28/E6
Lünen, Germany 22/B3
Lunenburg, Mass. 249/H2
Lunenburg •, Mass. 249/H2
Lunenburg, N.S. 162/K7
Lunenburg (co.), Nova Scotia 168/D4
Lunenburg, Nova Scotia 168/D4
Lunenburg (bay), Nova Scotia 168/D4
Lunenburg •, Vt. 268/D3
Lunenburg (co.), Va. 307/M7
Lunenburg, Va. 307/M7
Lunéville, France 28/G3
Lung (riv.), Ireland 17/D4
Lungchen (Longzhen), China 77/L2
Lungdo, China 77/B5
Lungern, Switzerland 39/F3
Lungi, S. Leone 106/B7
Lungleh, India 68/G4
Lungwebungu (riv.), Angola 115/D6
Lungwebungu (riv.), Zambia 115/D6
Luni (riv.), India 68/C3
Luninets, U.S.S.R. 52/C4
Luning, Nev. 266/C4
Lunita, La. 238/C6
Lunsford, Ark. 202/K2
Luocheng, China 77/G7
Luodian, China 77/G6
Luoding, China 77/H7
Luohe, China 77/H5
Luoyang (Loyang), China 77/H5
Luoyang, China 54/N6
Luozi, Zaire 115/B5
Lupeni, Romania 45/F3
Luperón, Dom. Rep. 158/D5
Lupon, Philippines 82/E7
Lupton, Ariz. 198/F3
Lupton, Mich. 250/F4
Lupus, Mo. 261/H5
Luputa, Zaire 115/D5
Luqu, China 77/F5
Luquillo, P. Rico 161/F1
Luquillo, Sierra de (mts.), P. Rico 161/E2
Lurah (riv.), Afghanistan 68/B2
Lurah (riv.), Afghanistan 59/J3
Luray, Kansas 232/D2
Luray, Mo. 261/J2
Luray, S.C. 296/E6

Luray, Tenn. 237/D9
Luray, W. Va. 307/M3
Lure, France 28/G4
Lurgan, N. Ireland 17/J3
Luribay, Bolivia 136/B5
Lúrio, Mozambique 118/G2
Lúrio (riv.), Mozambique 118/F2
Luristan (Lorestan) (governorate), Iran 66/F4
Lurton, Ark. 202/D2
Lusaka (cap.), Zambia 115/E7
Lusaka (cap.), Zambia 102/E6
Lusaka (cap.), Zambia 2/L6
Lusambo, Zaire 102/E5
Lusambo, Zaire 115/D5
Lusatia (reg.), Germany 22/F3
Lusby, Md. 245/N7
Luseland, Sask. 181/B3
Lushi, China 77/H5
Lushnjë, Albania 45/D5
Lushoto, Tanzania 115/G4
Lushton, Nebr. 264/G4
Lushui, China 77/E6
Lüshun, China 77/K4
Lusk, Ireland 17/J4
Lusk, Wyo. 319/H3
Luss, Scotland 15/A1
Lustenau, Austria 41/A3
Lustre, Mont. 262/K2
Lut, Dasht-e (des.), Iran 59/G3
Lut, Dasht-e (des.), Iran 66/L5
Lüta (Lüda), China 77/K4
Lutcher, La. 238/L3
Lutesville, Mo. 261/M8
Luther, Iowa 229/F5
Luther, Mich. 250/D4
Luther, Mont. 262/G5
Luther, Okla. 288/M3
Luther, Tenn. 237/P8
Luthern, Switzerland 39/E2
Luthersburg, Pa. 294/E3
Luthersville, Georgia 217/C4
Lutherville-Timonium, Md. 245/M3
Lutie, Okla. 288/R5
Luton, England 13/G6
Luton, England 10/F5
Luton, Iowa 229/A4
Lutry, Switzerland 39/C3
Lutsen, Minn. 255/F2
Lutsk, U.S.S.R. 7/G3
Lutsk, U.S.S.R. 52/B4
Lutsk, U.S.S.R. 48/C4
Luttrell, Tenn. 237/O8
Lutts, Tenn. 237/F10
Lutz, Fla. 212/D3
Lützelflüh, Switzerland 39/E3
Lützow-Holm (bay) 5/C3
Luuq, Somalia 115/H3
Luverne, Ala. 195/F7
Lu Verne, Iowa 229/E3
Luverne, Minn. 255/B7
Luverne, N. Dak. 282/P7
Luvua (riv.), Zaire 115/E5
Luwingu, Zambia 115/E6
Luwuk, Indonesia 85/G6
Lux, Miss. 256/F8
Luxembourg 7/E4
Luxembourg (prov.), Belgium 27/G9
LUXEMBOURG 27/J9
Luxembourg (cap.), Luxembourg 27/J9
Luxemburg, Iowa 229/L3
Luxemburg, Minn. 255/D5
Luxemburg, Wis. 317/L6
Luxeuil-les-Bains, France 28/G4
Luxi, China 77/E7
Luxi, China 77/F7
Luxor, Egypt 102/F2
Luxor, Egypt 59/B4
Luxor, Egypt 111/F2
Luxora, Ark. 202/K2
Luz, Brazil 135/D1
Luz (isl.), Chile 138/D6
Luza, U.S.S.R. 52/G2
Luzein, Switzerland 39/J3
Luzenburg, Va. 307/M7
Luzern (canton), Switzerland 39/F2
Luzern (Lucerne), Switzerland 39/F2
Luzerne, Iowa 229/J5
Luzerne, Mich. 250/E4
Luzerne (co.), Pa. 294/L3
Luzerne, Pa. 294/E7
Luzhai, China 77/G7
Luzhi, China 77/G6
Luzhou (Luchow), China 77/G6
Luziânia, Brazil 132/E7
Luzilândia, Brazil 132/F3
Lužnice (riv.), Czech. 41/C2
Luzon (isl.), Philippines 2/R5
Luzon (isl.), Philippines 54/O8
Luzon (isl.), Philippines 82/C3
Luzon (isl.), Philippines 85/G2
Luzon (sea), Philippines 82/B4
Luzon (str.), Philippines 82/A2
Luz-Saint-Sauveur, France 28/C6
L'vov, U.S.S.R. 7/G4
L'vov, U.S.S.R. 48/C4
L'vov (Lwów), U.S.S.R. 52/B5
Lyakhov (isls.), U.S.S.R. 4/B3
Lyal (isl.), Ontario 177/C3
Lyallpur (Faisalabad), Pakistan 68/C2
Lyallpur (Faisalabad), Pakistan 59/K3
Lyalta, Alberta 182/D4
Lyatkhovskiye (isls.), U.S.S.R. 48/O2
Lybster, Scotland 10/E1
Lybster, Scotland 15/E2
Lycan, Colo. 208/P7
Lycksele, Sweden 18/L4
Lycoming, N.Y. 276/H3
Lycoming (co.), Pa. 294/H3
Lycoming (creek), Pa. 294/H3
Lydallville, Conn. 210/D1
Lydd, England 13/H7

Lydda, Israel 65/B4
Lydenburg, S. Africa 118/E4
Lydia, Minn. 255/E6
Lydia, S.C. 296/G3
Lydia Mills, S.C. 296/D3
Lydick, Ind. 227/E1
Lyell (mt.), Alberta 182/B4
Lyell (isl.), Br. Col. 184/B4
Lyell (mt.), Br. Col. 184/J4
Lyell (mt.), Tasmania 99/B4
Lyerly, Georgia 217/B2
Lyford, Ind. 227/C5
Lyford, Texas 303/G11
Lykens, Pa. 294/J4
Lyle, Minn. 255/F7
Lyle, Wash. 310/D5
Lyles, Tenn. 237/G9
Lyman, Miss. 256/F10
Lyman, Nebr. 264/A3
Lyman •, N.H. 268/D3
Lyman, S.C. 296/C2
Lyman (•), S. Dak. 298/J6
Lyman, Utah 304/C5
Lyman, Wash. 310/D2
Lyman, Wyo. 319/B4
Lyme (bay), England 13/D7
Lyme (bay), England 10/E5
Lyme •, N.H. 268/C4
Lyme Center, N.H. 268/C4
Lyme Regis, England 13/E7
Lyme Regis, England 10/E5
Lymington, England 10/F5
Lymington, England 13/F7
Lymm, England 13/H2
Lymm, England 10/G2
Lyn, Ontario 177/J3
Lyna (riv.), Poland 47/E1
Lynbrook, N.Y. 276/P7
Lynch, Ky. 237/R7
Lynch, Md. 245/O3
Lynch, Nebr. 264/F2
Lynchburg, Mo. 261/H7
Lynchburg, N. Dak. 282/R6
Lynchburg, Ohio 284/C7
Lynchburg, S.C. 296/G3
Lynchburg, Tenn. 237/J10
Lynchburg, Va. 188/L3
Lynchburg, Va. 146/K6
Lynchburg (I.C.), Va. 307/K6
Lynches (riv.), S.C. 296/H3
Lynch Station, Va. 307/K6
Lynd, Minn. 255/C6
Lynd, Queensland 95/C3
Lyndeborough •, N.H. 268/D6
Lynden, Ontario 177/D5
Lynden, Wash. 310/C2
Lyndhurst •, N.J. 273/B2
Lyndhurst, N.S. Wales 97/E3
Lyndhurst, Ontario 177/H3
Lyndhurst, S. Australia 88/F6
Lyndhurst, S. Australia 94/E4
Lyndoch, S. Australia 94/C6
Lyndon, Ill. 222/D2
Lyndon, Kansas 232/G3
Lyndon, Ohio 284/D7
Lyndon •, Vt. 268/C2
Lyndon, W. Australia 92/A3
Lyndon B. Johnson Nat'l Hist. Site, Texas 303/F7
Lyndon B. Johnson Space Ctr., Texas 303/K2
Lyndon Center, Vt. 268/C2
Lyndon Station, Wis. 317/F8
Lyndonville, N.Y. 276/D4
Lyndonville, Vt. 268/D2
Lyndora, Pa. 294/B4
Lyness, Scotland 15/E2
Lyngby, Denmark 21/F6
Lynhurst, Ontario 177/C5
Lynn, Ala. 195/C2
Lynn, Ark. 202/H2
Lynn, Ind. 227/H4
Lynn, Mass. 249/D6
Lynn, N.C. 281/C4
Lynn (co.), Texas 303/C4
Lynn, Wis. 317/F6
Lynn Canal (inlet), Alaska 196/M1
Lynn Center, Ill. 222/C2
Lynn Creek, Miss. 256/G4
Lynndyl, Utah 304/B4
Lynnfield •, Mass. 249/D5
Lynnfield Center (Lynnfield P.O.), Mass. 249/C5
Lynn Grove, Ky. 237/E7
Lynn Haven, Fla. 212/C6
Lynn Lake, Man. 162/G4
Lynn Lake, Man. 146/H4
Lynn Lake, Manitoba 179/H2
Lynnview, Ky. 237/K4
Lynnville, Ill. 222/C4
Lynnville, Ind. 227/C8
Lynnville, Iowa 229/H5
Lynnville, Ky. 237/D7
Lynnville, Tenn. 237/G10
Lynnwood, Wash. 310/C3
Lynton, England 13/D6
Lynton, England 10/D4
Lynwood, Calif. 204/C11
Lynwood, Ill. 222/C6
Lynx (lake), N.W. Terr. 187/H3
Lynxville, Wis. 317/D9
Lyon, France 7/E4
Lyon, France 28/F5
Lyon (co.), Iowa 229/A2
Lyon (co.), Kansas 232/F3
Lyon (co.), Ky. 237/E6
Lyon (co.), Minn. 255/C6
Lyon (co.), Nev. 266/B3
Lyon (inlet), N.W. Terr. 187/K3
Lyon, Loch (lake), Scotland 15/D4
Lyon Mountain, N.Y. 276/N1
Lyonnais (trad. prov.), France 29
Lyons, Colo. 208/J2

Lyons, Georgia 217/H6
Lyons, Ill. 222/B6
Lyons, Ind. 227/C7
Lyons, Kansas 232/D3
Lyons, Ky. 237/K5
Lyons, Mich. 250/E6
Lyons, Nebr. 264/H3
Lyons, N.J. 273/D2
Lyons, N.Y. 276/F4
Lyons, Ohio 284/B2
Lyons, Oreg. 291/E3
Lyons (Lyon Station), Pa. 294/L5
Lyons, S. Dak. 298/R6
Lyons (riv.), W. Australia 88/B4
Lyons (riv.), W. Australia 92/A4
Lyons, Wis. 317/K10
Lyons Brook, Nova Scotia 168/G3
Lyons Plain, Conn. 210/B4
Lyon Station, Pa. 294/L5
Lyra (reef), Papua N.G. 86/C1
Lys (riv.), Belgium 27/B7
Lys (riv.), France 28/E2
Lysaker, Norway 18/D3
Lysá nad Labem, Czech. 41/C1
Lysander, N.Y. 276/H4
Lysekil, Sweden 18/G7
Lysite, Wyo. 319/E2
Lyss, Switzerland 39/D2
Lyster, Québec 172/F3
Lys'va, U.S.S.R. 7/K3
Lys'va, U.S.S.R. 48/F4
Lys'va, U.S.S.R. 52/K3
Lytham Saint Anne's, England 13/G1
Lytham Saint Anne's, England 10/F1
Lytle, Texas 303/J11
Lyttelton, N. Zealand 100/D5
Lytton, Br. Col. 184/G5
Lytton, Iowa 229/D4
Lyubertsy, U.S.S.R. 52/E3
Lyubotin, U.S.S.R. 52/E4
Lyudinovo, U.S.S.R. 52/D4

M

Ma'ad, Jordan 65/D2
Maalaea, Hawaii 218/J2
Maalaea (bay), Hawaii 218/J2
Ma'alot-Tarshiha, Israel 65/C1
Ma'an (dist.), Jordan 65/D5
Ma'an, Jordan 65/E5
Ma'an, Jordan 59/C3
Ma'anshan, China 77/J5
Maarianhamina (Mariehamn), Finland 18/M7
Maarssen, Netherlands 27/F4
Maas (riv.), Netherlands 27/G5
Maasbree, Netherlands 27/H6
Maaseik, Belgium 27/H6
Maasin, Philippines 82/E5
Maasmechelen, Belgium 27/H7
Maassluis, Netherlands 27/E5
Maastricht, Netherlands 27/H7
Maatsuyker (isls.), Tasmania 99/C5
Mababe (depr.), Botswana 118/C3
Mabalane, Mozambique 118/E4
Mabank, Texas 303/H5
Mabaruma, Guyana 131/B1
Mabay, Cuba 158/H4
Mabel (lake), Br. Col. 184/H5
Mabel, Minn. 255/F7
Mabelvale, Ark. 202/F4
Maben, Miss. 256/F3
Maben, W. Va. 312/D7
Maberly, Ontario 177/H3
Mabie, W. Va. 312/F5
Mabille (lake), Newf. 166/B3
Mabini, Philippines 82/E6
Mablethorpe and Sutton, England 13/H4
Mablethorpe and Sutton, England 10/G4
Mableton, Georgia 217/J1
Mabote, Mozambique 118/E4
Mabou, Nova Scotia 163/G2
Mabou (harb.), Nova Scotia 168/G2
Mabou Highlands (hills), Nova Scotia 168/G2
Mabrouk, Mali 106/D5
Mabton, Wash. 310/E4
Macá (mt.), Chile 138/D5
Macachín, Argentina 143/D4
Macaé, Brazil 135/F3
Macaé, Brazil 132/F8
Macaíba, Brazil 132/H4
Macajalar (bay), Philippines 82/E6
Macalister, Br. Col. 184/F4
Macaloge, Mozambique 118/F2
MacAlpine (lake), N.W. Terr. 187/H3
Macamic, Québec 174/B3
Macan (isls.), Indonesia 85/F7
Macanao (pen.), Venezuela 124/F2
Mação, Portugal 33/B3
Macapá, Brazil 120/D2
Macapá, Brazil 132/D2
Macará, Ecuador 128/C5
Macaranaima, Colombia 126/E7
Macarena, Serranía de La (mts.), Colombia 126/D4
Macareo Santo Niño, Venezuela 124/H3
Macarthur, Victoria 97/A6
Macas, Ecuador 128/D4
Macassar, S. Africa 118/F6
Macau 54/N7
MACAU (MACAO) 77
Macau, Brazil 120/F3
Macau, Brazil 132/G4
Macau (Macao) (cap.), Macau 77/H7

Major 403

Macau, Portugal 2/Q4
Macaúbas, Brazil 132/F6
Macaya (mt.), Haiti 158/A6
Macbeth, S.C. 296/H5
Maccan, Nova Scotia 168/D3
Maccarese, Italy 34/F6
Macclenny, Fla. 212/D1
Maccles (lake), Newf. 166/C1
Macclesfield, England 10/G2
Macclesfield, England 13/H2
Macclesfield, N.C. 281/O3
Macdiarmid, Ontario 177/H5
MacDill A.F.B., Fla. 212/C3
Macdoel, Calif. 204/D2
Macdona, Texas 303/J11
Macdonald, Manitoba 179/D4
Macdonald (lake), North. Terr. 93/B7
Macdonald (lake), W. Australia 88/D4
Macdonald (lake), W. Australia 92/E3
Macdonaldton, Pa. 294/E6
Macdonnell (ranges), Australia 87/D8
Macdonnell (ranges), North. Terr. 88/E4
Macdonnell (ranges), North. Terr. 93/C7
Macdowall, Sask. 181/E2
Macduff, Scotland 10/E2
Macduff, Scotland 15/F3
Mace, Ind. 227/D4
Mace, W. Va. 312/F6
Macedon, N.Y. 276/F4
Macedonia, Ark. 202/D7
Macedonia, Conn. 210/A2
Macedonia (reg.), Greece 45/E5
Macedonia, Ill. 222/E5
Macedonia, Iowa 229/C6
Macedonia, Ohio 284/J10
Macedonia (rep.), Yugoslavia 45/E5
Maceió, Brazil 120/F3
Maceió, Brazil 132/H5
Macel, Miss. 256/D3
Macenta, Guinea 102/B4
Macenta, Guinea 106/C7
Maceo, Cuba 158/H3
Maceo, Ky. 237/H5
Macerata (prov.), Italy 34/D3
Macerata, Italy 34/D3
Maces (bay), New Bruns. 170/D3
Maces Bay, New Bruns. 170/D3
Macfarlan, W. Va. 312/D4
Macfarlane (lake), S. Australia 88/F6
Macfarlane (lake), S. Australia 94/E5
Macgillicuddy's Reeks (mts.), Ireland 17/B7
MacGregor, Manitoba 179/D5
MacGregor's Bay, Ontario 177/G2
Mach, Pakistan 59/J4
Mach, Pakistan 68/B3
Macha, Bolivia 136/B6
Machacamarca, Bolivia 136/B5
Machachi, Ecuador 128/C3
Machado, Brazil 135/C2
Machakos, Kenya 115/G4
Machala, Ecuador 120/B3
Machala, Ecuador 128/B4
Machalí, Chile 138/G5
Machalilla, Ecuador 128/B3
Machaneng, Botswana 118/D4
Machanga, Mozambique 118/F4
Machareti, Bolivia 136/D7
Machattie (lake), Queensland 88/G5
Machattie (lake), Queensland 95/B5
Machaze, Mozambique 118/E4
Machelen, Belgium 27/C9
Macheng, China 77/J5
Machers, The (pen.), Scotland 15/D6
Machesney Park, Ill. 222/D1
Machias, Maine 243/J6
Machias•, Maine 243/J6
Machias (bay), Maine 243/J6
Machias (riv.), Maine 243/H6
Machias (riv.), Maine 243/F2
Machias-Lime Lake, N.Y. 276/D6
Machiasport, Maine 243/H6
Machiasport•, Maine 243/H6
Machias Seal (isl.), Maine 243/J7
Machico, Portugal 33/A2
Machida, Japan 81/O2
Machilipatnam, India 68/E5
Machipongo, Va. 307/S6
Machiques, Venezuela 124/B3
Macho, Arroyo del (creek), N. Mex. 274/D5
Machrihanish, Scotland 15/C5
Machupicchu, Peru 128/F9
Machupo (riv.), Bolivia 136/C3
Machynlleth, Wales 13/D5
Machynlleth, Wales 10/D4
Macia, Mozambique 118/E4
Maciel, Argentina 143/F6
Maciel, Paraguay 144/D5
Maciel, Arroyo (riv.), Uruguay 145/C4
Macina (depr.), Mali 106/D6
Macintyre (riv.), N.S. Wales 88/J5
Macintyre (riv.), N.S. Wales 97/E1
Macintyre (riv.), Queensland 95/D6
Mack, Colo. 208/B4
Mack, Ohio 284/B9
MacKay, Alberta 182/C3
MacKay (riv.), Alberta 182/D1
Mackay, Australia 87/F8
Mackay (lake), Australia 87/D8
Mackay, Idaho 220/E6
Mackay (res.), Idaho 220/E6
Mackay (lake), North. Terr. 88/D4
MacKay (lake), North. Terr. 93/A7
MacKay (lake), N.W. Terr. 187/G3
Mackay, Queensland 88/H4
Mackay, Queensland 95/D4
Mackay (lake), W. Australia 92/E3
Mackenzie (bay), Ant. 5/C4
Mackenzie, Br. Col. 184/F2
Mackenzie, Br. Col. 184/F2
Mackenzie (bay), Canada 4/B16
Mackenzie (mts.), Canada 146/E3
Mackenzie (riv.), Canada 2/C2
Mackenzie (riv.), Canada 4/C16
Mackenzie (mts.), Canada 4/C16
Mackenzie, Mo. 261/P3
Mackenzie (bay), N.W.T. 187/E3
Mackenzie (mts.), N.W.T. 187/E3
Mackenzie (riv.), N.W.T. 162/C2
Mackenzie (riv.), N.W.T. 146/F3
Mackenzie (riv.), N.W.T. 187/F3
Mackenzie (bay), Yukon 162/C2
Mackenzie (bay), Yukon 187/E3
Mackenzie (mts.), Yukon 187/E3
Mackenzie King (isl.), Canada 4/B15
Mackenzie King (isl.), N.W.T. 162/M3
Mackenzie King (isl.), N.W. Terr. 187/G2
Mackey, Ind. 227/C8
Mackeys, N.C. 281/R3
Mackeyville, Pa. 294/H3
Mackinac (co.), Mich. 250/D2
Mackinac (isl.), Mich. 250/E3
Mackinac (str.), Mich. 250/E3
Mackinac Island, Mich. 250/E3
Mackinaw, Ill. 222/D3
Mackinaw (riv.), Ill. 222/E3
Mackinaw City, Mich. 250/E3
Macklin, Sask. 181/A3
Macks, Ark. 202/H2
Macksburg, Iowa 229/E6
Macksburg, Ohio 284/G6
Macks Creek, Mo. 261/G7
Macks Inn, Idaho 220/G5
Macksville, Kansas 232/D4
Macksville, N.S. Wales 97/G2
Mackville, Ky. 237/L5
Maclean, N.S. Wales 97/G1
Maclean (str.), N.W. Terr. 187/H2
Maclear, S. Africa 118/D6
Maclear (cape), S. Africa 118/F7
Macmillan (pass), N.W. Terr. 187/F3
Macmillan (pass), Yukon 187/F3
Macmillan (riv.), Yukon 187/E3
Macnean (lake), Ireland 17/F3
Macnean (lake), N. Ireland 17/F3
MacNutt, Sask. 181/K4
Macomb, Ill. 222/C3
Macomb (co.), Mich. 250/G6
Macomb, Okla. 288/M4
Macomer, Italy 34/B4
Macomia, Mozambique 118/F2
Macon (co.), Ala. 195/G6
Mâcon, France 28/F4
Macon (co.), Georgia 217/D6
Macon, Georgia 188/K4
Macon, Georgia 146/K6
Macon, Georgia 217/E5
Macon (co.), Ill. 222/E4
Macon, Ill. 222/E4
Macon (bayou), La. 238/H1
Macon, Miss. 256/G4
Macon (co.), Mo. 261/G3
Macon, Mo. 261/H3
Macon, Nebr. 264/E4
Macon (co.), N.C. 281/B4
Macon, N.C. 281/N2
Macon, Ohio 284/C8
Macon (co.), Tenn. 237/J7
Macon, Tenn. 237/B10
Macondo, Angola 115/D6
Macorís (cape), Dom. Rep. 158/E5
Macosquin, N. Ireland 17/H1
Macotera, Spain 33/D2
Macouba, Martinique 161/C5
Macoun, Sask. 181/H6
Macoupin (co.), Ill. 222/D4
Macoupin (riv.), Ill. 222/C4
Macouria, Fr. Guiana 131/E3
Macquarie (lake), N.S. Wales 97/F3
Macquarie (riv.), N.S. Wales 88/H6
Macquarie (riv.), N.S. Wales 97/D2
Macquarie (harb.), Tasmania 88/G8
Macquarie (harb.), Tasmania 99/B4
Macquarie (riv.), Tasmania 99/D3
Mac-Robertson Land (reg.) 5/B4
Macroom, Ireland 10/B5
Macroom, Ireland 17/C8
Macrorie, Sask. 181/E4
Mactan (isl.), Philippines 82/E5
Mactaquac (lake), New Bruns. 170/C3
MacTier, Ontario 177/E2
Macumba (riv.), S. Australia 88/F5
Macumba, The (riv.), S. Australia 94/E2
Macungie, Pa. 294/L4
Macurijes (pt.), Cuba 158/F3
Macuro, Venezuela 124/H2
Macusani, Peru 128/G10
Macuspana, Mexico 150/N8
Macuto, Venezuela 124/E2
Macwahoc•, Maine 243/G4
Macy, Ind. 227 E3
Macy, Nebr. 264/H2
Mad (riv.), Calif. 204/B3
Mad (riv.), Conn. 210/C2
Mad (riv.), Conn. 210/C1
Mad (riv.), N.H. 268/D4
Mad (riv.), Ohio 284/C6
Mad (riv.), Vt. 268/B3
Ma'daba, Jordan 65/D4
Madadi, Chad 111/D4
Madagascal (pond), Maine 243/G5
Madagascar 2/M6
Madagascar 102/G7
MADAGASCAR 118/H3
Madaket, Mass. 249/O7
Madama, Niger 106/G4
Madame (isl.), Nova Scotia 168/H3
Madang, Papua N.G. 85/B7
Madang, Papua N.G. 87/E6
Madaoua, Niger 106/F6
Madaras, Hungary 41/E3
Madaripur, Bangladesh 68/G4
Madauk, Burma 72/C3
Madawaska, Maine 243/G1
Madawaska•, Maine 243/G1
Madawaska (co.), New Bruns. 170/B1
Madawaska (riv.), New Bruns. 170/B1
Madawaska, Ontario 177/F2
Madawaska (riv.), Ontario 177/G2
Madawaska (riv.), Québec 172/J2
Madbury•, N.H. 268/F5
Maddela, Philippines 82/C2
Madden, Alberta 182/C4
Madden, Miss. 256/F5
Maddock, N. Dak. 282/L4
Maddy, Loch (inlet), Scotland 15/A3
Madeira (riv.), Brazil 2/F6
Madeira (riv.), Brazil 120/C3
Madeira (riv.), Brazil 132/A4
Madeira, Ohio 284/C9
Madeira (isl.), Portugal 33/A2
Madeira (isl.), Portugal 106/A2
Madeira (isls.), Portugal 2/H4
Madeira (isls.), Portugal 33/A2
Madeira (isls.), Portugal 102/A1
Madeira Beach, Fla. 212/B3
Madeira Park, Br. Col. 184/J2
Madeleine (cape), Québec 172/D1
Madelia, Minn. 255/D6
Madeline, Calif. 204/E2
Madeline (isl.), Wis. 317/E2
Maden, Turkey 63/H3
Madera (co.), Calif. 204/F6
Madera, Calif. 204/E7
Madera, Mexico 150/F2
Madera, Pa. 294/F4
Madera Canyon, Ariz. 198/E7
Madh, India 68/B7
Madhubani, India 68/F3
Madhya Pradesh (state), India 68/D4
Madidi (riv.), Bolivia 136/A3
Madill, Okla. 288/N6
Madinat ash Sha'b, Yemen 59/E7
Madinat el-Thawra, Syria 63/H5
Madingo-Kayes, Congo 115/B4
Madingou, Congo 115/B4
Madirovalo, Madagascar 118/H3
Madison (co.), Ala. 195/E1
Madison, Ala. 195/E1
Madison (co.), Ark. 202/C1
Madison, Ark. 202/J4
Madison, Calif. 204/D5
Madison, Conn. 210/E3
Madison•, Conn. 210/E3
Madison (co.), Fla. 212/C1
Madison, Fla. 212/C1
Madison (co.), Georgia 217/F2
Madison, Georgia 217/F3
Madison (co.), Idaho 220/G6
Madison (co.), Ill. 222/D5
Madison, Ill. 222/A2
Madison (co.), Ind. 227/F4
Madison, Ind. 227/G7
Madison (co.), Iowa 229/E6
Madison, Kansas 232/F3
Madison (co.), Ky. 237/N5
Madison (par.), La. 238/H2
Madison, Maine 243/D6
Madison•, Maine 243/D6
Madison, Md. 245/O6
Madison, Minn. 255/B5
Madison (co.), Miss. 256/D5
Madison, Miss. 256/D6
Madison (co.), Mo. 261/M8
Madison, Mo. 261/H4
Madison (co.), Mont. 262/D5
Madison (riv.), Mont. 262/E5
Madison (co.), Nebr. 264/G3
Madison, Nebr. 264/G3
Madison•, N.H. 268/E4
Madison (mt.), N.H. 268/E3
Madison, N.J. 273/E2
Madison (co.), N.Y. 276/J5
Madison, N.Y. 276/J5
Madison (co.), N.C. 281/D3
Madison, N.C. 281/J2
Madison (co.), Ohio 284/D6
Madison, Ohio 284/H2
Madison, Sask. 181/B4
Madison, S.C. 296/A2
Madison, S.C. 296/D4
Madison, S. Dak. 298/P6
Madison (lake), S. Dak. 298/P6
Madison (co.), Tenn. 237/D9
Madison (co.), Texas 303/J6
Madison (co.), Va. 307/M4
Madison, Va. 307/M4
Madison, W. Va. 312/C6
Madison (cap.), Wis. 146/K5
Madison (cap.), Wis. 188/H2
Madison (cap.), Wis. 317/H9
Madison, Wyo. 319/B1
Madison (plat.), Wyo. 319/B1
Madisonburg, Ohio 284/G4
Madison Heights, Mich. 250/B6
Madison Heights, Va. 307/K6
Madison Lake, Minn. 255/E6
Madisonville, Ky. 237/F6
Madisonville, La. 238/K6
Madisonville, Tenn. 237/N9
Madisonville, Texas 303/J7
Madiun, Indonesia 85/K2
Madley (mt.), W. Australia 92/D4
Madoc, Mont. 262/L2
Madoc, Ontario 177/G3
Mado Gashi, Kenya 115/G3
Madoi, China 77/E4
Madona, U.S.S.R. 53/C2
Madona, U.S.S.R. 52/C3
Madonna, Md. 245/M2
Madraka, Ras (cape), Oman 59/G6
Madran, New Bruns. 170/E1
Madras, India 68/E6
Madras, India 54/K8
Madras, India 2/P5
Madras, Oreg. 291/F3
Madre (lag.), Mexico 150/L4
Madre (lag.), Texas 188/G5
Madre (lag.), Texas 303/G11
Madre de Dios (riv.) 120/C4
Madre de Diós (riv.), Bolivia 136/A3
Madre de Dios (isl.), Chile 120/B8
Madre de Dios (isl.), Chile 138/D8
Madre de Dios (dept.), Peru 128/G8
Madre de Dios, Peru 128/G9
Madre de Dios (riv.), Peru 128/G9
Madre del Sur, Sierra (mts.), Mexico 150/K8
Madre Occidental, Sierra (mts.), Mexico 150/F3
Madre Oriental, Sierra (mts.), Mexico 150/J4
Madrid, Ala. 195/H8
Madrid, Iowa 229/F5
Madrid•, Maine 243/B6
Madrid, Nebr. 264/C4
Madrid, N. Mex. 274/C3
Madrid, N.Y. 276/K1
Madrid (prov.), Spain 33/E2
Madrid (cap.), Spain 7/D4
Madrid (cap.), Spain 33/F4
Madrid (cap.), Spain 2/J4
Madridejos, Spain 33/E3
Madrigal de las Altas Torres, Spain 33/D2
Madrigalejo, Spain 33/D3
Madrisahorn (mt.), Switzerland 39/J3
Madroñera, Spain 33/D3
Madsen, Ontario 175/B2
Madugula, India 68/E5
Madura (isl.), Indonesia 54/N10
Madura (isl.), Indonesia 85/K2
Madura (str.), Indonesia 85/K2
Madura, W. Australia 92/D5
Madurai, India 54/J9
Madurai, India 68/D7
Madvar, Kuh-e (mt.), Iran 59/F3
Madvar, Kuh-e (mt.), Iran 66/F3
Maebashi, Japan 81/J5
Mae Hong Son, Thailand 72/C3
Mae Klong, Mae Nam (riv.), Thailand 72/C4
Mael, Norway 18/F6
Maella, Spain 33/G2
Maeser, Utah 304/E3
Maesteg, Wales 13/D6
Maestra, Sierra (mts.), Cuba 158/H4
Maevatanana, Madagascar 118/H3
Maeystown, Ill. 222/C5
Mafeking, Manitoba 179/B2
Mafeking (Mafikeng), S. Africa 118/C5
Mafeteng, Lesotho 118/D5
Maffin (bay), Indonesia 85/K6
Maffra, Victoria 97/D5
Mafia (isl.), Tanzania 102/G5
Mafia (isl.), Tanzania 115/H5
Mafikeng, S. Africa 118/C5
Mafra, Brazil 132/D9
Mafra, Portugal 33/B3
Magadan, U.S.S.R. 2/S3
Magadan, U.S.S.R. 54/R4
Magadan, U.S.S.R. 48/P4
Magadi, Kenya 115/G4
Magadino, Switzerland 39/G4
Magaguadavic, New Bruns. 170/C3
Magaguadavic (lake), New Bruns. 170/C3
Magaguadavic (riv.), New Bruns. 170/C3
Magalia, Calif. 204/D4
Magaliesburg, S. Africa 118/G6
Magallanes (reg.), Chile 138/E10
Magallanes (Magellan) (str.), Chile 138/D10
Magallanes, Philippines 82/D4
Magallenes (Magellan) (str.), Argentina 143/C7
Magangué, Colombia 126/C3
Maganoy, Philippines 82/E7
Mağara, Turkey 63/G3
Magarabomba, Cuba 158/G2
Magaria, Niger 106/F6
Magazine, Ark. 202/C3
Magazine (mt.), Ark. 202/C3
Magdagachi, U.S.S.R. 48/N4
Magdala, Ethiopia 111/G5
Magdalen (isls.), Que. 162/K6
Magdalena, Argentina 143/H7
Magdalena, Bolivia 136/C3
Magdalena (isl.), Chile 138/D5
Magdalena (dept.), Colombia 126/C3
Magdalena (riv.), Colombia 120/B2
Magdalena (riv.), Colombia 126/C3
Magdalena (bay), Mexico 150/C4
Magdalena, N. Mex. 274/B4
Magdalena (mts.), N. Mex. 274/B4
Magdalena de Kino, Mexico 150/D1
Magdeburg, Germany 7/F3
Magdeburg, Germany 22/D2
Magdelaine (cays), Coral Sea Is. Terr. 88/H3
Magé, Brazil 135/E3
Magee, Miss. 256/E7
Magee, Island (pen.), N. Ireland 17/K2
Magelang, Indonesia 85/J2
Magellan (str.) 120/C8
Magellan (str.) 2/F8
Magellan (str.), Argentina 143/C7
Magellan (str.), Chile 138/D10
Magen, Israel 65/A5
Magens (bay), Virgin Is. (U.S.) 161/B4
Magerøya (isl.), Norway 18/P1
Magerrain (mt.), Switzerland 39/H2
Magetan, Indonesia 85/K2
Maggia, Switzerland 39/G4
Maggia (riv.), Switzerland 39/G4
Maggie Valley, N.C. 281/C3
Maggiore (lake), Fla. 212/B3
Maggiore (lake), Italy 34/B1
Maggiore (lake), Switzerland 39/G5
Maggotty, Jamaica 158/H6
Maghâgha, Egypt 59/B4
Maghâgha, Egypt 111/J4
Maghama, Mauritania 102/A3
Maghama, Mauritania 106/B5
Maghera, N. Ireland 17/H2
Magherafelt (dist.), N. Ireland 17/H2
Magherafelt, N. Ireland 10/C3
Magherafelt, N. Ireland 17/H2
Magic (res.), Idaho 220/D6
Magilligan (pt.), N. Ireland 17/H1
Maglaj, Yugoslavia 45/D3
Magley, Ind. 227/G3
Maglie, Italy 34/G4
Magna, Utah 304/B3
Magna Bay, Br. Col. 184/H4
Magness, Ark. 202/H2
Magnet, Ark. 202/E5
Magnet, Ind. 227/D8
Magnet, Manitoba 179/C3
Magnet, Nebr. 264/G2
Magnetawan, Ontario 177/E2
Magnetawan (riv.), Ontario 177/D2
Magnet Cove, Ark. 202/E5
Magnetic Springs, Ohio 284/D5
Magnitogorsk, U.S.S.R. 54/H4
Magnitogorsk, U.S.S.R. 48/G4
Magnolia, Ala. 195/C6
Magnolia, Ark. 202/D7
Magnolia, Del. 245/R4
Magnolia, Ill. 222/D2
Magnolia, Iowa 229/B5
Magnolia, Minn. 255/B7
Magnolia, Miss. 256/D8
Magnolia, N.J. 273/B3
Magnolia, N.C. 281/O5
Magnolia, Ohio 284/H4
Magnolia, Texas 303/J7
Magnolia, W. Va. 312/K3
Magnolia Springs, Ala. 195/C10
Màgoè, Mozambique 118/E3
Magoffin (co.), Ky. 237/P5
Magog, Québec 172/E4
Magpie, Québec 174/E2
Magpie (lake), Québec 174/E2
Magrath, Alberta 182/D5
Magude, Mozambique 118/E5
Maguindanao (prov.), Philippines 82/E7
Maguse (lake), N.W. Terr. 187/J3
Magwe (div.), Burma 72/B2
Magwe, Burma 72/B2
Mahabad, Iran 59/E2
Mahabad, Iran 66/D2
Mahabaleshwar, India 68/C5
Mahabo, Madagascar 118/G4
Mahaena, Fr. Poly. 86/T13
Mahaffey, Pa. 294/E4
Mahagi, Zaire 115/F3
Mahaica, Guyana 131/C2
Mahaicony Village, Guyana 131/C2
Mahajamba (bay), Madagascar 118/H2
Mahajanga (prov.), Madagascar 118/H3
Mahajanga, Madagascar 102/G6
Mahakam (riv.), Indonesia 85/F6
Mahalapye, Botswana 118/D4
Mahalapye, Botswana 102/E7
Mahalasville, Ind. 227/E6
Mahallat, Iran 66/G4
Mahan, Iran 66/K5
Mahanadi (riv.), India 68/E4
Mahanoro, Madagascar 118/H3
Mahanoy City, Pa. 294/K4
Maharashtra (state), India 68/C5
Maha Sarakham, Thailand 72/D3
Mahaska (co.), Iowa 229/H6
Mahaska, Kansas 232/E2
Mahaxai, Laos 72/E3
Mahbubnagar, India 68/D5
Mahdia, Guyana 131/B3
Mahdia, Tunisia 106/G1
Mahe, India 68/D6
Mahé (isl.), Seychelles 118/H5
Mahébourg, Mauritius 118/G5
Mahenge, Tanzania 115/G5
Maheno, N. Zealand 100/C6
Maher, Colo. 208/D5
Maheshkhali, Bangladesh 68/G4
Mahia (pen.), N. Zealand 100/G3
Mahim, India 68/C5
Mahim (bay), India 68/B7
Mahkonce, Minn. 255/C3
Mahlaing, Burma 72/B2
Mahmudiye, Turkey 63/D3
Mahnomen (co.), Minn. 255/C3
Mahnomen, Minn. 255/C3
Maho (bay), Virgin Is. (U.S.) 161/C4
Mahoba, India 68/D3
Mahomet, Ill. 222/E3
Mahón, Spain 33/J3
Mahone (bay), Nova Scotia 168/D4
Mahone Bay, Nova Scotia 168/D4
Mahoning (co.), Ohio 284/J4
Mahood (lake), Br. Col. 184/G4
Mahopac, N.Y. 276/N8
Mahout, Dominica 161/E6
Mahto, S. Dak. 298/H2
Mahtomedi, Minn. 255/F5
Mahtowa, Minn. 255/F4
Mahukona, Hawaii 218/G3
Mahuva, India 68/C4
Mahwah•, N.J. 273/E1
Maia, Portugal 33/B2
Maicao, Colombia 126/D2
Maicuru (riv.), Brazil 132/C2
Maida, N. Dak. 282/O2
Maida, Yemen 59/D6
Maidan, Iraq 66/D3
Maidan, Iraq 59/E3
Maidani, Ras (cape), Iran 59/G4
Maiden, N.C. 281/G3
Maidenhead, England 10/F5
Maidenhead, England 13/G8
Maiden Rock, Wis. 317/B6
Maidens, The (isls.), N. Ireland 17/K2
Maidens, Scotland 15/D5
Maidens, Va. 307/N5
Maidstone, England 13/J8
Maidstone, England 10/G5
Maidstone, Ontario 177/B5
Maidstone, Sask. 181/B2
Maidstone•, Vt. 268/D2
Maidstone (lake), Vt. 268/D2
Maidsville, W. Va. 312/F3
Maiduguri, Nigeria 106/G6
Maiduguri, Nigeria 102/D3
Maienfeld, Switzerland 39/J2
Maigatari, Nigeria 106/F6
Maigualida, Sierra (range), Venezuela 124/F4
Maigue (riv.), Ireland 17/D6
Maihara, Japan 81/G6
Maili, Hawaii 218/D2
Maillard, Québec 172/G2
Main (riv.), Germany 22/C4
Ma'in, Jordan 65/D4
Main (passage), La. 238/M8
Main (riv.), N. Ireland 17/J2
Main (chan.), Ontario 177/C2
Main (str.), Singapore 72/F6
Main-à-Dieu, Nova Scotia 168/J2
Main Barrier (range), N.S. Wales 88/G6
Main Barrier (range), N.S. Wales 97/A2
Main Brook, Newf. 166/C3
Main Centre, Sask. 181/D5
Mai-Ndombe (lake), Zaire 115/C4
Maine 188/N1
MAINE 241
Maine (gulf) 188/N2
Maine (gulf) 162/K7
Maine (trad. prov.), France 29
Maine (riv.), Ireland 17/C7
Maine (gulf), Mass. 249/M2
Maine, N.Y. 276/H6
Maine (state), U.S. 146/M5
Maine-et-Loire (dept.), France 28/C4
Mainesburg, Pa. 294/J2
Mainé-Soroa, Niger 106/G6
Maineville, Ohio 284/C9
Maingard (lake), Québec 172/G1
Maingkwan, Burma 72/C1
Mainit, Philippines 82/E6
Mainit (lake), Philippines 82/E6
Mainland, Orkney Is. (isl.), Scotland 10/E1
Mainland, Shetland Is. (isl.), Scotland 10/G1
Mainland (isl.), Scotland 15/G2
Mainland (isl.), Scotland 15/E1
Mainling, China 77/D6
Mainoru, North. Terr. 93/C3
Mainstream, Maine 243/D6
Maintirano, Madagascar 118/G3
Main Topsail (mt.), Newf. 166/C4
Mainz, Germany 22/C4
Maio (isl.), C. Verde 106/B8
Maipo (vol.), Argentina 143/C3
Maipo (riv.), Chile 138/F4
Maipú, Argentina 143/E4
Maipú, Chile 138/G3
Maipú (vol.), Chile 138/B10
Maipures, Colombia 126/F5
Maiquetía, Venezuela 120/C1
Maiquetía, Venezuela 124/E2
Mairana, Bolivia 136/D6
Maisí, Cuba 158/K4
Maisí (cape), Cuba 158/K4
Maisí (cape), Cuba 156/D2
Maison de Pierre (lake), Québec 172/C3
Maisonnette, New Bruns. 170/E1
Maisons-Alfort, France 28/B2
Maisons-Laffitte, France 28/A1
Maïssade, Haiti 158/C5
Maitencillo, Chile 138/A8
Maitland, Australia 87/F9
Maitland, Fla. 212/E3
Maitland, Mo. 261/B2
Maitland, N.S. Wales 88/J6
Maitland, N.S. Wales 97/F3
Maitland, Annapolis, Nova Scotia 168/C4
Maitland, Hants, Nova Scotia 168/E3
Maitland, Ontario 177/J3
Maitland, S. Australia 94/E6
Maitum, Philippines 82/E7
Maize, Kansas 232/E4
Maíz Grande (Great Corn) (isl.), Nicaragua 154/F4
Maizhokunggar, China 77/D6
Maíz Pequeña (Little Corn) (isl.), Nicaragua 154/F4
Maizuru, Japan 81/G6
Majagua, Cuba 158/F2
Majagual, Colombia 126/C3
Majalengka, Indonesia 85/H2
Majene, Indonesia 85/F6
Majenica, Ind. 227/F3
Majes (riv.), Peru 128/F11
Majestic, Ky. 237/S5
Maji, Ethiopia 111/G6
Majma'a, Saudi Arabia 59/D4
Majoli, Suriname 131/D4
Major (co.), Okla. 288/K2

Major, Sask. 181/B4
Majorca (isl.), Spain 7/E5
Majorca (isl.), Spain 33/H3
Majorsville, W. Va. 312/F3
Majunga, Madagascar 118/H3
Majuro (atoll) (cap.), Marshall Is. 87/H5
Makaha, Hawaii 218/D2
Makaha (pt.), Hawaii 218/B1
Makah Ind. Res., Wash. 310/A2
Makaiwa, Hawaii 218/H2
Makakilo, Hawaii 218/E2
Makale, Ethiopia 102/F3
Makale, Ethiopia 111/G5
Makallé, Argentina 143/E2
Makanda, Ill. 222/D6
Makanza, Zaire 115/C3
Makapala, Hawaii 218/G3
Makapuu (pt.), Hawaii 218/F2
Makara Beach, N. Zealand 100/A2
Makara-Ohariu, N. Zealand 100/A3
Makari, Cameroon 115/B1
Makaroff, Manitoba 179/A3
Makarov, U.S.S.R. 48/P5
Makarska, Yugoslavia 45/C4
Makar'yev, U.S.S.R. 52/F3
Makassar (Ujung Pandang), Indonesia 85/F7
Makassar (str.), Indonesia 54/N10
Makassar (str.), Indonesia 85/F6
Makatea (isl.), Fr. Poly. 87/L7
Makawao, Hawaii 218/K2
Makaweli, Hawaii 218/B2
Makena, Hawaii 218/J2
Makeni, S. Leone 102/A4
Makeni, S. Leone 106/B7
Makepeace, Alberta 182/D4
Makeyevka, U.S.S.R. 7/H4
Makeyevka, U.S.S.R. 52/E5
Makgadikgadi (salt pan), Botswana 102/E7
Makgadikgadi (salt pan), Botswana 118/D3
Makhachkala, U.S.S.R. 7/J4
Makhachkala, U.S.S.R. 48/E5
Makhachkala, U.S.S.R. 52/G6
Makharadze, U.S.S.R. 52/F6
Makhmur, Iraq 66/C3
Makiki, Hawaii 218/C4
Makin (Butaritari) (atoll), Kiribati 87/H5
Makinak, Manitoba 179/C4
Makinen, Minn. 255/F3
Makinsk, U.S.S.R. 48/H4
Makinson (inlet), N.W. Terr. 187/L2
Makkovik, Newf. 166/C2
Makkovik (cape), Newf. 166/C2
Makkum, Netherlands 27/G2
Makó, Hungary 41/F3
Makokou, Gabon 115/B3
Makoti, N. Dak. 282/G4
Makoua, Congo 115/C3
Maków Mazowiecki, Poland 47/E2
Makran (reg.), Iran 66/M8
Makteir (des.), Mauritania 106/B4
Maku, Iran 66/D1
Makubetsu, Japan 81/L2
Makumbako, Tanzania 115/G5
Makurazaki, Japan 81/O3
Makurdi, Nigeria 102/C4
Makurdi, Nigeria 106/F7
Makushin (vol.), Alaska 196/E4
Makwa, Sask. 181/C2
Makwa (lake), Sask. 181/B1
Makwa (riv.), Sask. 181/B1
Mal, Mauritania 106/B5
Mala, Punta (cape), Panama 154/H7
Malå, Sweden 18/L4
Malabang, Philippines 82/D7
Malabar, Fla. 212/F4
Malabar (hill), India 68/B7
Malabar (pt.), India 68/B7
Malabar Coast (reg.), India 68/C6
Malabo (cap.), Equat. Guinea 102/C4
Malabo (cap.), Equat. Guinea 115/A3
Malabrigo, Argentina 143/F4
Mal Abrigo, Uruguay 145/C5
Malabungan, Philippines 82/A6
Malacca (str.) 54/M9
Malacca (str.), Indonesia 85/C5
Malacca (Melaka), Malaysia 72/D7
Malacca (str.), Malaysia 72/D7
Malacky, Czech. 41/D2
Malad (riv.), Idaho 220/F7
Malad, India 68/B6
Malad (creek), India 68/B7
Malad (riv.), Utah 304/B1
Malad City, Idaho 220/F7
Maladers, Switzerland 39/J3
Málaga, Colombia 126/D4
Malaga, Ill. 273/C4
Malaga, N. Mex. 274/E6
Malaga, Ohio 284/H6
Málaga (prov.), Spain 33/D4
Málaga, Spain 7/D5
Málaga, Spain 33/D4
Malaga, Wash. 310/D5
Malagash, Nova Scotia 168/E3
Malagash (pt.), Nova Scotia 168/E3
Malagón, Spain 33/E3
Malagueta (bay), Cuba 158/H3
Malahide, Ireland 17/J5
Malaita (isl.), Solomon Is. 86/E3
Malaita (isl.), Solomon Is. 87/G3
Malakal, Sudan 111/F6
Malakal, Sudan 102/F4
Malakanagiri, India 68/E5
Malakand, Pakistan 68/C2
Malakand, Pakistan 59/K3
Malakoff, France 28/A2

Malakoff, Texas 303/H5
Malakwa, Br. Col. 184/H5
Malalag, Philippines 82/E7
Malamir (Izeh), Iran 66/F5
Malang, Indonesia 54/N10
Malang, Indonesia 85/K2
Malangka (cape), Indonesia 85/G5
Malanje (prov.), Angola 115/C6
Malanje, Angola 102/D3
Malanje, Angola 115/C5
Malans, Switzerland 39/J3
Malanville, Benin 106/E6
Mälaren (lake), Sweden 18/G1
Malargüe, Argentina 120/C6
Malargüe, Argentina 143/C4
Malartic, Québec 174/B3
Malaspina (glac.), Alaska 196/K3
Malaspina (str.), Br. Col. 184/J2
Malatya (prov.), Turkey 63/H3
Malatya, Turkey 59/C2
Malatya, Turkey 54/K6
Malatya, Turkey 63/H3
Malawi 2/L6
Malawi 102/F6
MALAWI 115/F6
Malawi (Nyasa) (lake), Malawi 115/F6
Malay (pen.), Malaysia 72/D6
Malay (pen.), Malaysia 85/B4
Malay (pen.), Thailand 72/D6
MALAYA, MALAYSIA 72
Malaya (reg.), Malaysia 54/M9
Malaya (West Malaysia) (reg.), Malaysia 72/E6
Malaya Vishera, U.S.S.R. 52/D3
Malaybalay, Philippines 82/E6
Malayer, Iran 66/F3
Malaysia 2/Q5
Malaysia 54/M9
MALAYSIA 85/D4
Malazgirt, Turkey 63/K3
Malbaie (riv.), Québec 172/G2
Malbon, Queensland 95/B4
Malbork (Marienburg), Poland 47/D1
Malchinersee (lake), Germany 22/E2
Malchow, Germany 22/E2
Malcolm, Ala. 195/B8
Malcolm, Nebr. 264/H4
Malcom, Iowa 229/H5
Maldegem, Belgium 27/C6
Malden, Ill. 222/D2
Malden, Ind. 227/C2
Malden (isl.), Kiribati 87/L6
Malden, Mass. 249/D6
Malden, Mo. 261/M9
Malden, New Bruns. 170/G2
Malden, Wash. 310/H3
Malden, W. Va. 312/C6
Maldives 2/N5
MALDIVES 68
Maldives 54/J9
Maldives (isls.) 68/C7
Maldon, England 10/G5
Maldon, England 13/G3
Maldon, Victoria 97/C5
Maldonado (pt.), Mexico 150/K8
Maldonado (dept.), Uruguay 145/E5
Maldonado, Uruguay 145/D6
Male (cap.), Maldives 54/J9
Male (cap.), Maldives 2/N5
Maléa (cape), Greece 45/F7
Malebo (Stanley Pool) (lake), Zaire 115/C4
Malegaon, India 54/J7
Malegaon, India 68/C4
Malekula (isl.), Vanuatu 87/G7
Malema, Mozambique 118/F2
Malemba-Nkulu, Zaire 115/E5
Malente, Germany 22/D1
Maler Kotla, India 68/D2
Malesus, Tenn. 237/D9
Malgobek, U.S.S.R. 52/F6
Malhão da Estrela (mt.), Portugal 33/C2
Malheur (co.), Oreg. 291/K4
Malheur (lake), Oreg. 188/C2
Malheur (lake), Oreg. 291/J4
Malheur (riv.), Oreg. 291/J4
Mali 2/J5
Mali 102/B2
MALI 106/D5
Mali (riv.), Burma 72/C1
Mali, Guinea 106/B6
Malibu, Calif. 204/B10
Malignant Cove, Nova Scotia 168/F3
Maligne (lake), Alberta 182/B3
Mali Kyun (isl.), Burma 72/C4
Malili, Indonesia 85/G6
Malin, Ireland 17/G1
Malin (head), Ireland 17/F1
Malin (head), Ireland 10/C3
Malin, Oreg. 291/F5
Malin, U.S.S.R. 52/C4
Malinau, Indonesia 85/F5
Malindang (mt.), Philippines 82/D6
Malindi, Kenya 102/B2
Malindi, Kenya 115/H4
Malines (Mechelen), Belgium 27/F6
Malinta, Ohio 284/B3
Malita, Philippines 82/E7
Maliwun, Burma 72/C5
Malkapur, India 68/D4
Malkara, Turkey 63/B2
Malkiya, Israel 65/D1
Malko Türnovo, Bulgaria 45/H4
Mallacoota, Victoria 97/E5
Mallaig, Alberta 182/K2
Mallaig, Scotland 10/D2
Mallaig, Scotland 15/C4
Mallanganee, N.S. Wales 97/G1
Mallard, Iowa 229/D3
Mallawi, Egypt 111/J4

Mallawi, Egypt 59/B4
Mallén, Spain 33/F2
Malleray, Switzerland 39/D2
Mallet Creek, Ohio 284/G3
Malling, Denmark 21/D5
Mallnitz, Austria 41/B3
Malloa, Chile 138/G5
Malloch (cape), N.W. Terr. 187/H2
Mallorca (Majorca) (isl.), Spain 33/H3
Mallory, N.Y. 276/H4
Mallory, W. Va. 312/C7
Mallorytown, Ontario 177/J3
Mallow, Ireland 17/D7
Mallow, Ireland 10/B4
Malmanoury, Fr. Guiana 131/E3
Malmberget, Sweden 18/M3
Malmédy, Belgium 27/J8
Malmesbury, England 13/E6
Malmesbury, S. Africa 118/B6
Malmköping, Sweden 18/F1
Malmo, Minn. 255/E4
Malmo, Nebr. 264/H3
Malmö, Sweden 18/H9
Malmöhus (co.), Sweden 18/H9
Malmok (mt.), Neth. Ant. 161/E8
Malmstrom A.F.B., Mont. 262/E3
Malo, Wash. 310/G2
Maloca, Brazil 132/C4
Maloca, Brazil 120/D3
Maloelap (atoll), Marshall Is. 87/H5
Malolos, Philippines 82/C3
Malone, Fla. 212/A1
Malone, Ky. 237/P5
Malone, N.Y. 276/M1
Malone, Texas 303/H5
Malone, Wash. 310/B4
Maloneton, Ky. 237/R3
Maloney (res.), Nebr. 264/D3
Malonton, Manitoba 179/E4
Malott, Wash. 310/F2
Maloy, Iowa 229/E7
Malpartida de Cáceres, Spain 33/C3
Malpartida de Plasencia, Spain 33/C2
Malpelo (isl.), Colombia 120/A2
Malpeque (bay), Pr. Edward I. 168/E2
Malta 2/K4
Malta 7/F5
MALTA 34
Malta, Colo. 208/G4
Malta, Idaho 220/E7
Malta, Ill. 222/E2
Malta (chan.), Italy 34/E6
Malta (isl.), Malta 34/E7
Malta, Mont. 262/J2
Malta, Ohio 284/G6
Malta Bend, Mo. 261/F4
Maltahöhe, Namibia 118/B4
Maltepe, Turkey 63/D6
Malters, Switzerland 39/F2
Malton, England 13/G3
Malton, England 10/F3
Maltrata, Mexico 150/O2
Malung, Sweden 18/H6
Malvaglia, Switzerland 39/H4
Malvan, India 68/C5
Malvern, Ala. 195/G8
Malvern, Ark. 202/E5
Malvern, England 13/E5
Malvern, England 10/E4
Malvern, Iowa 229/B7
Malvern, Jamaica 158/H6
Malvern, Ohio 284/H4
Malvern, Pa. 294/L5
Malvern, Victoria 88/L7
Malvern, Victoria 97/J5
Malverne, N.Y. 276/R7
Malvina, Miss. 256/C3
Malvinas (Falkland) (isls.), 143/D7
Malyye Karmakuly, U.S.S.R. 52/H1
Mama, U.S.S.R. 48/M4
Mamala (bay), Hawaii 218/B4
Mamalu (pt.), Hawaii 218/K3
Mamanguape, Brazil 132/H4
Mamaroneck, N.Y. 276/P7
Mambahenauhan (isl.), Philippines 82/B7
Mambajao, Philippines 82/E6
Mambasa, Zaire 115/E3
Mamberamo (riv.), Indonesia 85/K6
Mambrui, Kenya 115/H4
Mamburao, Philippines 82/C4
Ma-Me-O Beach, Alberta 182/D3
Mamer, Luxembourg 27/H9
Mamers, France 28/D3
Mamers, France 28/D3
Mamfé, Cameroon 115/A2
Mamie, N.C. 281/T2
Mamiña, Chile 138/B2
Mammoth, Ariz. 198/E6
Mammoth, Utah 304/B4
Mammoth (creek), Utah 304/B6
Mammoth, W. Va. 312/D6
Mammoth Cave Nat'l Park, Ky. 237/J6
Mammoth Hot Springs (Yellowstone Nat'l Park), Wyo. 319/B1
Mammoth Lakes, Calif. 204/G6
Mammoth Spring, Ark. 202/G1
Mamoré (riv.), Bolivia 120/C2
Mamoré (riv.), Bolivia 136/C2
Mamou, Guinea 106/B6
Mamou, La. 238/F5
Mampong, Ghana 106/D7
Mamry, Jezioro (lake), Poland 47/E1
Mamuju, Indonesia 85/F6
Man (isl.), I. of Man 13/C3
Man, Ivory Coast 106/C7
Man, Ivory Coast 102/B4

Man, W. Va. 312/C7
Mana, Fr. Guiana 131/E3
Mana (riv.), Fr. Guiana 131/E3
Mana (isl.), N. Zealand 100/B2
Manabí (prov.), Ecuador 128/B3
Manacacías (riv.), Colombia 126/D6
Manacapuru, Brazil 120/C3
Manacapuru, Brazil 132/H9
Manacas, Cuba 158/E1
Manacle (pt.), England 13/C7
Manacor, Spain 33/H3
Manado, Indonesia 54/O9
Manado, Indonesia 85/G5
Manage, Belgium 27/E7
Managua (cap.), Nic. 146/K8
Managua (cap.), Nicaragua 154/D4
Managua (lake), Nicaragua 154/D4
Manah, Oman 59/G5
Manahawkin, N.J. 273/E4
Manaia, N. Zealand 100/E3
Manakara, Madagascar 118/H4
Manakara, Madagascar 102/G7
Manakha, Yemen 59/D6
Manakin-Sabot, Va. 307/N5
Manalapan, N.J. 273/E3
Manama (cap.), Bahrain 59/F4
Manana (isl.), Hawaii 218/F2
Mananara, Madagascar 118/J3
Mananara (riv.), Madagascar 118/H4
Mananbao (riv.), Madagascar 118/G3
Mananjary, Madagascar 118/H4
Mananjary, Madagascar 102/G7
Manannah, Minn. 255/D5
Manapire (riv.), Venezuela 124/E3
Manapouri (lake), N. Zealand 100/A6
Manaqil, Sudan 59/B7
Manar, Jebel (mt.), Yemen 59/D7
Manare, Colombia 126/D4
Manas, China 77/C3
Manas Hu (lake), China 77/C3
Manas Hu (lake), China 77/C2
Manasquan, N.J. 273/E3
Manasquan (riv.), N.J. 273/E3
Manassa, Colo. 208/H8
Manassas, Georgia 217/H6
Manassas (I.C.), Va. 307/O3
Manassas Nat'l Battlefield Park, Va. 307/K3
Manassas Park (I.C.), Va. 307/O3
Manatee (co.), Fla. 212/D4
Manatee (riv.), Fla. 212/D4
Manatí, Cuba 158/H3
Manatí, P. Rico 156/G1
Manatí, P. Rico 161/C1
Manaus, Brazil 2/F6
Manaus, Brazil 120/D3
Manaus, Brazil 132/H9
Manavgat, Turkey 63/D4
Manawa, Wis. 317/J7
Manay, Philippines 82/F7
Mancelona, Mich. 250/E4
Mancha, La (reg.), Spain 33/E3
Manchac (passage), La. 238/N2
Manchaca, Texas 303/G7
Mancha Real, Spain 33/E4
Manchaug, Mass. 249/G4
Manche (dept.), France 28/C3
Manche, La (English) (chan.), France 28/B3
Manchester, Ala. 195/D3
Manchester, Calif. 204/B5
Manchester, Conn. 210/E1
Manchester •, Conn. 210/E1
Manchester, Greater (co.), England 13/H2
Manchester, England 7/D3
Manchester, England 10/G2
Manchester, England 13/H2
Manchester, Georgia 217/C5
Manchester, Ill. 222/C4
Manchester, Ind. 227/H6
Manchester, Iowa 229/L3
Manchester, Kansas 232/E2
Manchester, Ky. 237/O6
Manchester •, Maine 243/D7
Manchester, Md. 245/L2
Manchester, Mich. 250/E6
Manchester, Minn. 255/E7
Manchester, Mo. 261/O3
Manchester, N.H. 188/M2
Manchester, N.H. 268/E6
Manchester, N.Y. 276/F5
Manchester, Ohio 284/C8
Manchester, Okla. 288/L1
Manchester, Pa. 294/J5
Manchester, S. Dak. 298/O5
Manchester, Tenn. 237/J10
Manchester, Vt. 268/A5
Manchester, Wash. 310/A2
Manchester, Wis. 317/J8
Manchester-by-the-Sea •, Mass. 249/F5
Manchester Center, Vt. 268/A5
Manchioneal, Jamaica 158/K6
Manchouli (Manzhouli), China 77/J2
Máncora, Peru 128/B5
Mancos, Colo. 208/C8
Mancos (riv.), Colo. 208/B8
Mandabe, Madagascar 118/G4
Mandah, Mongolia 77/G3
Mandal, Norway 18/E7
Mandalay (div.), Burma 72/B2
Mandalay, Burma 54/L7
Mandalay, Burma 72/B2
Mandalgovi, Mongolia 77/G2
Mandali, Iraq 66/D3
Mandalya (gulf), Turkey 63/B4
Mandan, N. Dak. 188/F1
Mandan, N. Dak. 282/J6
Mandaon, Philippines 82/D4

Mandar (cape), Indonesia 85/F6
Mandaree, N. Dak. 282/E4
Mandaue, Philippines 82/E5
Mandeb, Bab el (str.), Saudi Arabia 59/D7
Mandeb, Bab el (str.), Yemen 59/D7
Mandera, Kenya 115/H3
Manderson, S. Dak. 298/D7
Manderson, Wyo. 319/E1
Mandeville, Ark. 202/C7
Mandeville, Jamaica 158/H6
Mandeville, La. 238/L6
Mandi, India 68/D2
Mandié, Mozambique 118/E3
Mandimba, Mozambique 118/F2
Mandinga, Panama 154/H6
Mandioré (lag.), Bolivia 136/F6
Mandla, India 68/E4
Mándok, Hungary 41/G2
Mandritsara, Madagascar 118/H3
Mand Rud (riv.), Iran 59/F4
Mand Rud (riv.), Iran 66/G6
Mandsaur, India 68/C4
Mandurah, W. Australia 88/B3
Mandurah, W. Australia 92/A2
Manduria, Italy 34/F4
Mandvi, India 68/B4
Manele (bay), Hawaii 218/H2
Manele Bay, Hawaii 218/H2
Manendragarh, India 68/E4
Manes, Mo. 261/H8
Manfalût, Egypt 111/J4
Manfalût, Egypt 59/B4
Manfred, N. Dak. 282/L4
Manfredonia, Italy 34/F4
Manfredonia (gulf), Italy 34/F4
Manga, Brazil 132/E6
Manga, Uruguay 145/B7
Mangai, Zaire 115/C4
Mangaia (isl.), Cook Is. 87/L8
Mangakino, N. Zealand 100/E3
Mangalia, Romania 45/J4
Mangalore, India 54/J9
Mangalore, India 68/C6
Mangareva (isl.), Fr. Poly. 87/N8
Mangaweka, N. Zealand 100/E3
Mangere (isl.), N. Zealand 100/F7
Mangham, La. 238/G2
Mangkalihat (cape), Indonesia 85/F5
Manglaralto, Ecuador 128/B3
Mangle (pt.), Cuba 158/J3
Manglillo (pt.), P. Rico 161/B3
Mangnai, China 77/D4
Mango, Fla. 212/D4
Mango, Togo 106/E6
Mangochi, Malawi 115/G6
Mangoky (riv.), Madagascar 102/G7
Mangoky (riv.), Madagascar 118/G4
Mangole (isl.), Indonesia 85/H6
Mangonui, N. Zealand 100/D1
Mangoro (riv.), Madagascar 118/H3
Mangotsfield, England 10/E5
Mangotsfield, England 13/E6
Mangrol, India 68/B4
Mangsee (isls.), Philippines 82/A7
Mangualde, Portugal 33/C2
Mangueigne, Chad 111/D5
Mangueira (lag.), Brazil 132/D11
Manguera Azul, Uruguay 145/D4
Mangui, China 77/K1
Manguito, Cuba 158/D1
Mangum, Okla. 288/G5
Mangyshlak (pen.), U.S.S.R. 48/F5
Manhan (riv.), Mass. 249/D4
Manhasset, N.Y. 276/P7
Manhattan, Ill. 222/F2
Manhattan, Ind. 227/D5
Manhattan, Kansas 232/E2
Manhattan, Mont. 262/E5
Manhattan, Nev. 265/E4
Manhattan (borough), N.Y. 276/M9
Manhattan (isl.), N.Y. 276/M9
Manhattan Beach, Calif. 204/B11
Manhattan Beach, Minn. 255/E4
Manhay, Belgium 27/H8
Manheim, Pa. 294/K5
Manheim, W. Va. 312/G4
Manhiça, Mozambique 118/E5
Man Hpang, Burma 72/C2
Manhuaçu, Brazil 132/F8
Manhuaçu, Brazil 135/E2
Manhumirim, Brazil 135/E2
Maní, Colombia 126/D4
Maniamba, Mozambique 118/F2
Maniamba, Mozambique 118/F2
Manibridge, Manitoba 179/J2
Manica (prov.), Mozambique 118/E3
Manica, Mozambique 118/E3
Manicani (isl.), Philippines 82/E5
Manicaragua, Cuba 158/E2
Manicoré, Brazil 120/C3
Manicoré, Brazil 132/H9
Manicouagan (riv.), Que. 162/K5
Manicouagan, Québec 174/D2
Manicouagan (res.), Québec 172/B1
Manicouagan (res.), Québec 174/D2
Manifest, La. 238/G3
Manifold (cape), Queensland 88/J4
Manifold (cape), Queensland 95/D4
Maniganggi, Indonesia 85/H6
Manigotagan, Manitoba 179/G4
Manigotagan (lake), Manitoba 179/G3
Manigotagan (riv.), Manitoba 179/G3
Manigouche, Québec 174/C3
Manihiki (atoll), Cook Is. 87/K7
Manitsoq, Greenland 4/C12
Manila, Ala. 195/C7
Manila, Ark. 202/K2

Manila (prov.), Philippines 82/C3
Manila (cap.), Philippines 2/R5
Manila (cap.), Philippines 85/G3
Manila (cap.), Philippines 82/C3
Manila (cap.), Philippines 54/N8
Manila (bay), Philippines 82/C3
Manila, Utah 304/E3
Manildra, N.S. Wales 97/E3
Manilla, Ind. 227/F5
Manilla, Iowa 229/C5
Manilla, N.S. Wales 97/F2
Maningrida, North. Terr. 93/C2
Manipa (str.), Indonesia 85/H6
Manipur (riv.), Burma 72/B2
Manipur (state), India 68/G4
Manisa (prov.), Turkey 63/B3
Manisa, Turkey 63/B3
Manisa, Turkey 59/A2
Manistee, Mich. 250/C4
Manistee, Mich. 250/C4
Manistee (riv.), Mich. 250/C4
Manistique, Mich. 250/C3
Manistique (lake), Mich. 250/D2
Manistique (riv.), Mich. 250/C2
Manito, Ill. 222/D3
Manito (lake), Sask. 181/B3
MANITOBA 179
Manitoba (prov.) 162/G5
Manitoba (lake), Canaca 146/J4
Manitoba (lake), Man. 146/H4
Manitoba (lake), Man. 152/G5
Manitoba (lake), Manitoba 179/D4
Manitou, Ky. 237/F6
Manitou, Manitoba 179/D5
Manitou (isl.), Mich. 250/B1
Manitou, N. Dak. 282/L2
Manitou, Okla. 288/J5
Manitou (lake), Ontario 177/C2
Manitou (lake), Québec 172/C3
Manitou Beach, Sask. 181/F4
Manitoulin (terr. dist.), Ontario 175/D3
Manitoulin (terr. dist.), Ontario 177/B2
Manitoulin (isl.), Ontario 162/H6
Manitoulin (isl.), Ontario 175/D3
Manitoulin (isl.), Ontario 177/B2
Manitou Springs, Colo. 208/J5
Manitouwadge, Ontario 177/H5
Manitouwadge, Ontario 175/D3
Manitowaning, Ontario 177/C2
Manitowish, Wis. 317/F3
Manitowish (co.), Wis. 317/L7
Manitowoc, Wis. 317/L7
Maniwaki, Québec 174/B3
Maniwaki, Québec 172/B3
Manizales, Colombia 126/C5
Manizales, Colombia 120/B2
Manja, Jordan 65/D4
Manja, Madagascar 118/G4
Manjacaze, Mozambique 118/E5
Manjimup, W. Australia 88/B6
Manjimup, W. Australia 92/B6
Mankato, Kansas 232/D1
Mankato, Minn. 188/H2
Mankato, Minn. 255/E6
Mankono, Ivory Coast 106/C7
Mankota, Sask. 181/D6
Manley, Nebr. 264/H4
Manley Hot Springs, Alaska 196/H2
Manlius, Ill. 222/D2
Manlius, N.Y. 276/J5
Manlleu, Spain 33/H1
Manly, Iowa 229/G2
Manly, N.S. Wales 88/L4
Manly, N.S. Wales 97/K3
Manly, N.C. 281/L4
Manly, Queensland 88/L2
Manmad, India 68/C4
Manmanoc (mt.), Philippines 82/C2
Mann (riv.), North. Terr. 93/D2
Manna, Indonesia 85/C6
Mannahill, S. Australia 94/F5
Mannar (gulf), India 68/D7
Mannar (gulf), Sri Lanka 68/D7
Mannar, Sri Lanka 68/D7
Mannargudi, India 68/E6
Mannboro, Va. 307/N6
Männedorf, Switzerland 39/G2
Mannersdorf am Leithagebirge, Austria 41/D3
Manners Sutton, New Bruns. 170/D3
Mannford, Okla. 288/O2
Mannheim, Germany 7/E4
Mannheim, Germany 22/C4
Manning, Alberta 182/B1
Manning, Ark. 202/C5
Manning, Iowa 229/C5
Manning, Kansas 232/B3
Manning (riv.), N.S. Wales 97/F2
Manning, N. Dak. 282/E5
Manning (cape), N.W. Terr. 187/F2
Manning (str.), Solomon Is. 86/D2
Manning, S.C. 296/G4
Manning Prov. Park, Br. Col. 184/G5
Mannington, Ky. 237/G6
Mannington, W. Va. 312/F3
Männlifluh (mt.), Switzerland 39/E3
Manns Choice, Pa. 294/E6
Manns Harbor, N.C. 281/T3
Mannsville, Ky. 237/L6
Mannsville, N.Y. 276/H3
Mannsville, Okla. 288/N6
Mannu (riv.), Italy 34/B5
Mannum, S. Australia 94/F6
Mannville, Alberta 182/K3
Mano (riv.), Liberia 106/B7
Mano (riv.), S. Leone 106/B7
Manoa, Bolivia 136/C1

Manokin, Md. 245/P8
Manokin (riv.), Md. 245/P8
Manokotak, Alaska 196/H5
Manokwari, Indonesia 85/J6
Manola, Alberta 182/C2
Manombo, Madagascar 118/G4
Manomet, Mass. 249/M5
Manomet (pt.), Mass. 249/N5
Manono, Zaire 115/E5
Manono, Zaire 102/E5
Manor, Georgia 217/G8
Manor, Pa. 294/C5
Manor, Sask. 181/K6
Manor, Texas 303/G7
Manorhamilton, Ireland 17/E3
Manori, India 68/B6
Manori (creek), India 68/B7
Manorville, N.Y. 276/P9
Manorville, Pa. 294/C4
Manosque, France 28/G6
Manotick, Ontario 177/J2
Manouane, Québec 172/C2
Manouane (lake), Québec 174/C2
Manp'o, N. Korea 81/B3
Manquin, Va. 307/O5
Manra (Sydney) (isl.), Kiribati 87/K6
Manresa, Spain 33/G2
Mansa, Zambia 115/E6
Mansa, Zambia 102/E6
Mansalay, Philippines 82/C4
Mansavillagra, Uruguay 145/D4
Manseau, Québec 172/E3
Mansel (isl.), N.W.T. 162/H3
Mansel (isl.), N.W.T. 146/K3
Mansel (isl.), N.W.T. 187/K3
Mansel'ka (mts.), U.S.S.R. 52/C1
Mansfield•, Conn. 210/F1
Mansfield, England 13/K2
Mansfield, England 10/F4
Mansfield, Georgia 217/E4
Mansfield, Ill. 222/E3
Mansfield, Ind. 227/C5
Mansfield, La. 238/C2
Mansfield, Mass. 249/J4
Mansfield•, Mass. 249/J4
Mansfield, Minn. 255/E7
Mansfield, Mo. 261/G8
Mansfield, Ohio 188/K2
Mansfield, Ohio 284/F4
Mansfield, Pa. 294/H2
Mansfield, S. Dak. 298/N3
Mansfield, Tenn. 237/E8
Mansfield, Texas 303/F3
Mansfield (mt.), Vt. 268/B2
Mansfield, Victoria 97/D5
Mansfield, Wash. 310/F3
Mansfield Center, Conn. 210/G1
Mansfield Depot, Conn. 210/F1
Mansfield Woodhouse, England 13/F4
Mansilla de las Mulas, Spain 33/D1
Manso (riv.), Brazil 132/C6
Manso (riv.), Chile 138/E4
Manson, Ind. 227/D4
Manson, Iowa 229/D3
Manson, Manitoba 179/A4
Manson, N.C. 281/N2
Manson, Wash. 310/E3
Manson Creek, Br. Col. 184/E2
Mansonville, Québec 172/E4
Mansura, La. 238/G4
Manta, Ecuador 128/B3
Manta, Ecuador 120/A3
Manta (bay), Ecuador 128/B3
Mantachie, Miss. 256/H2
Mantador, N. Dak. 282/R7
Mantagao (lake), Manitoba 179/E3
Mantagao (riv.), Manitoba 179/E3
Mantalingajan (mt.), Philippines 82/A6
Mantario, Sask. 181/B4
Mantaro (riv.), Peru 128/E8
Mantas (well), Niger 106/E5
Manteca, Calif. 204/D6
Mantecal, Apure, Venezuela 124/D4
Mantecal, Bolívar, Venezuela 124/F4
Mantee, Miss. 256/F3
Manteigas, Portugal 33/C2
Manteno, Ill. 222/F2
Manter, Kansas 232/A4
Mantes-la-Jolie, France 28/D3
Manti, Utah 304/C4
Mantiqueira (range), Brazil 135/D3
Manto, Honduras 154/D2
Mantoloking, N.J. 273/E3
Manton, Calif. 204/D3
Manton, Mich. 250/D4
Manton, R.I. 249/J5
Mantorville, Minn. 255/F6
Mänttä, Finland 18/O6
Mantua, Ala. 195/C4
Mantua, Cuba 158/A2
Mantua (prov.), Italy 34/C2
Mantua, Italy 34/C2
Mantua•, N.J. 273/C4
Mantua, Ohio 284/H3
Mantua, Utah 304/C2
Mantua•, Va. 307/S3
Manturovo, U.S.S.R. 52/F3
Manú, Peru 128/G9
Manú (riv.), Peru 128/G8
Manua (isls.), Amer. Samoa 87/K7
Manuae (atoll), Cook Is. 87/K7
Manuel Benavides, Mexico 150/H2
Manuelito, N. Mex. 274/A3
Manuel Rodríguez (isl.), Chile 138/D10
Manuels, New Bruns. 170/F1
Manuels, Newf. 166/D2
Manui (isl.), Indonesia 85/G6
Manukan, Philippines 82/D6
Manukau, N. Zealand 100/C1
Manukau (harb.), N. Zealand 100/B1
Manulla, Ireland 17/C4

Manumuskin (riv.), N.J. 273/D5
Manunui, N. Zealand 100/E3
Manuripi (riv.), Bolivia 136/B2
Manus (isl.), Papua N.G. 87/E6
Manus (isl.), Papua N.G. 86/A1
Manutuke, N. Zealand 100/F3
Manvel, N. Dak. 282/R3
Manvel, Texas 303/J3
Manville, N.J. 273/D2
Manville, R.I. 249/H5
Manville, Wyo. 319/H3
Many, La. 238/C2
Manyara (lake), Tanzania 115/G4
Manyas, Turkey 63/B3
Manyberries, Alberta 182/E5
Manych-Gudilo (lake), U.S.S.R. 52/F5
Many Farms, Ariz. 198/F2
Manyoni, Tanzania 115/G5
Manzai, Pakistan 59/K3
Manzanar, Chile 138/F2
Manzanares, Spain 33/E3
Manzanares (riv.), Spain 33/F4
Manzanillo, Cuba 158/H4
Manzanillo, Cuba 156/C2
Manzanillo (bay), Dom. Rep. 158/C5
Manzanillo (bay), Haiti 158/C5
Manzanillo (isl.), Brazil 132/D2
Manzanillo, Mexico 150/G7
Manzanillo, Mexico 146/H8
Manzanillo (pt.), Panama 154/H6
Manzanita, Oreg. 291/C2
Manzanita Ind. Res., Calif. 204/J11
Manzano, N. Mex. 274/C4
Manzano (mts.), N. Mex. 274/C4
Manzano (peak), N. Mex. 274/C4
Manzanola, Colo. 208/M6
Manzhouli (Manchouli), China 77/J2
Manzini, Swaziland 118/E5
Mao, Chad 111/C5
Mao, Dom. Rep. 158/D5
Maoke (mts.), Indonesia 85/K6
Maoming (Mowming), China 77/H7
Mapai, Mozambique 118/E4
Maparari, Venezuela 124/D2
Mapastepec, Mexico 150/N9
Mapes, N. Dak. 282/O3
Mapia (isls.), Indonesia 85/J5
Mapimí, Mexico 150/H4
Mapimí (depr.), Mexico 150/G3
Mapire, Venezuela 124/F4
Mapiri, Bolivia 136/B4
Mapiripán, Laguna (lake), Colombia 126/E6
Maple (peak), Ariz. 198/F5
Maple (riv.), Mich. 250/E5
Maple (lake), Minn. 255/B3
Maple (riv.), Minn. 255/F7
Maple (riv.), N. Dak. 282/O8
Maple (riv.), N. Dak. 282/R6
Maple (creek), Sask. 181/B5
Maple (riv.), S. Dak. 298/M1
Maple, Wis. 317/C2
Maple Bay, Br. Col. 184/K3
Maple Bay, Minn. 255/B3
Maple City, Kansas 232/F4
Maple City, Mich. 250/D4
Maple Creek, Sask. 162/F6
Maple Creek, Sask. 181/B6
Maple Falls, Wash. 310/D2
Maple Grove, Minn. 255/G5
Maple Grove, Ontario 177/F4
Maple Grove, Québec 172/H4
Maple Heights, Ohio 284/H9
Maple Hill, Iowa 229/D2
Maple Hill, Kansas 232/F2
Maple Hill, N.C. 281/O5
Maple Island, Minn. 255/E7
Maple Lake, Minn. 255/D5
Maple Park, Ill. 222/E2
Maple Plain, Minn. 255/F5
Maple Rapids, Mich. 250/E5
Maple Ridge, Br. Col. 184/L3
Maple River, Iowa 229/D4
Maples, Ind. 227/H2
Maples, Mo. 261/J7
Maple Shade•, N.J. 273/B3
Maplesville, Ala. 195/E5
Mapleton, Iowa 229/B4
Mapleton, Kansas 232/H3
Mapleton•, Maine 243/G2
Mapleton, Mich. 250/D4
Mapleton, Minn. 255/E7
Mapleton, N.C. 281/P2
Mapleton, N. Dak. 282/R6
Mapleton, Oreg. 291/C3
Mapleton (Mapleton Depot), Pa. 294/F5
Mapleton, Utah 304/C3
Mapleton, Wis. 317/J1
Mapleton Depot, Pa. 294/F5
Maple Valley, Wash. 310/C3
Mapleview, Minn. 255/E7
Mapleview, New Bruns. 170/C2
Mapleville, Md. 245/F2
Mapleville, R.I. 249/H5
Maplewood, La. 238/D4
Maplewood, Minn. 255/G5
Maplewood, Mo. 261/P3
Maplewood, N.J. 268/D3
Maplewood•, N.J. 273/E2
Maplewood, Ohio 284/B5
Maplewood, Wis. 317/M6
Mapocho (riv.), Chile 138/G3
Mapoon Mission Station, Queensland 88/G2
Mapoon Mission Station, Queensland 95/B1
Maporal, Venezuela 124/C4
Mapos (Amazonas), Cuba 158/F2
Mappsville, Va. 307/T5
Mapuera (riv.), Brazil 132/B3
Maputo (city) (prov.), Mozambique 118/E5
Maputo (prov.), Mozambique 118/E5
Maputo (cap.), Mozambique 2/L7

Maputo (cap.), Mozambique 118/E5
Maputo (cap.), Mozambique 102/F7
Maqatin (ruins), Yemen 59/E7
Maqên, China 77/F5
Magna, Saudi Arabia 59/C4
Ma Qu (Huang He) (riv.), China 77/F5
Maquapit (lake), New Bruns. 170/D3
Maqueda (chan.), Philippines 82/D3
Maquela do Zombo, Angola 102/D5
Maquela do Zombo, Angola 115/C5
Maquereau (pt.), Québec 172/D2
Maquinchao, Argentina 143/C5
Maquoketa, Iowa 229/M4
Maquon, Ill. 222/C3
Mar (mts.), Brazil 120/E5
Mar (range), Brazil 135/C4
Mar, Serra do (range), Brazil 132/G9
Mar (dist.), Scotland 15/F3
Mara, Guyana 131/F1
Mara (reg.), Tanzania 115/F4
Marabá, Brazil 132/D4
Marabá, Brazil 120/E2
Marabahan, Indonesia 85/E6
Marabella, Trin. & Tob. 161/All
Maracá (isl.), Brazil 120/E2
Maracá (isl.), Brazil 132/D2
Maracaibo, Venezuela 124/C1
Maracaibo, Venezuela 120/B1
Maracaibo (lake), Venezuela 120/B2
Maracaibo (lake), Venezuela 124/C3
Maracaju, Brazil 132/C8
Maracas (bay), Trin & Tob. 161/C10
Maracay, Venezuela 124/E2
Marada, Libya 111/C2
Maradi, Niger 106/F6
Maradi, Niger 102/G3
Maragheh, Iran 59/E2
Maragheh, Iran 66/E2
Maragogipe, Brazil 132/G6
Maraira (pt.), Philippines 82/C1
Marajó (bay), Brazil 132/E2
Marajó (est.), Brazil 120/E2
Marajó (isl.), Brazil 120/E3
Marajó (isl.), Brazil 132/D3
Maralal, Kenya 115/G3
Maralinga, S. Australia 88/E6
Maralwexi (Bachu), China 77/A4
Maramag, Philippines 82/E7
Maramec, Okla. 288/N2
Marampa, S. Leone 106/B7
Marana, Ariz. 198/D6
Marand, Iran 59/E2
Marand, Iran 66/D1
Marang, Malaysia 72/D6
Maranguape, Brazil 132/G3
Maranhão (state), Brazil 132/E4
Maranoa (riv.), Queensland 95/C4
Marañón (riv.), Peru 120/B3
Marañón (riv.), Peru 128/E5
Marapanim, Brazil 132/E2
Maras (mt.), Indonesia 85/D6
Maraş, Turkey 59/C2
Maraş (Kahramanmaraş), Turkey 63/G4
Marathon, Fla. 212/E7
Marathón, Greece 45/G6
Marathon, Iowa 229/C3
Marathon, N.Y. 276/J6
Marathon, Ohio 284/C7
Marathon, Ont. 162/H6
Marathon, Ontario 177/H5
Marathon, Ontario 175/C3
Marathon, Texas 303/A7
Marathon (co.), Wis. 317/G6
Marathon, Wis. 317/G6
Maratua (isl.), Indonesia 85/F5
Maravillas, Bolivia 136/B2
Maravillas (creek), Texas 303/A7
Marawi, Philippines 85/G4
Marawi, Philippines 82/E6
Marbach, Switzerland 39/E3
Marbach am Neckar, Germany 22/C4
Marbella, Spain 33/D4
Marble, Ark. 202/C1
Marble, Colo. 208/E4
Marble, Minn. 255/E3
Marble, N.C. 281/B4
Marble (isl.), N.W.T. 162/G3
Marble (isl.), N.W.T. 187/J3
Marble Bar, Australia 87/C8
Marble Bar, W. Australia 88/B4
Marble Bar, W. Australia 92/A6
Marble Canyon, Ariz. 198/D2
Marble Canyon Nat'l Mon., Ariz. 198/D2
Marble City, Okla. 288/S3
Marble Dale, Conn. 210/B2
Marble Falls, Texas 303/F7
Marblehead, Ill. 222/B4
Marblehead•, Mass. 249/F6
Marblehead (neck), Mass. 249/F6
Marblehead, Ohio 284/E2
Marble Hill, Georgia 217/D2
Marble Hill, Mo. 261/N8
Marblemount, Wash. 310/D2
Marble Rock, Iowa 229/H3
Marbleton, Québec 172/F4
Marbleton, Wyo. 319/B3
Marble Valley, Ala. 195/F4
Marburg an der Lahn, Germany 22/C3
Marbury, Ala. 195/E5
Marbury, Md. 245/K6
Marcala, Honduras 154/C3
Marcali, Hungary 41/D3
Marcapata, Peru 128/G9
Marcelin, Sask. 181/E3
Marceline, Mo. 261/F3
Marcell, Minn. 255/E3
Marcella, Ark. 202/G2
Marcella, N.J. 273/E2

Marcelline, Ill. 222/B3
Marcellus, Mich. 250/D6
Marcellus, N.Y. 276/H5
Marcelville, New Bruns. 170/E2
March (riv.), Austria 41/D2
March, England 13/H5
March, England 13/H5
March A.F.B., Calif. 204/E11
Marchand, Manitoba 179/F5
Marche, Ark. 202/F4
Marche (trad. prov.) France 29
Marche (reg.), Italy 34/D3
Marche-en-Famenne, Belgium 27/G8
Marchegg, Austria 41/D2
Marchena (isl.), Ecuador 128/B9
Marchena, Spain 33/D4
Marchfield, Barbados 161/B9
Marchigüe, Chile 138/F5
Marchin, Belgium 27/G8
Mar Chiquita (lake), Argentina 143/D3
Marchwell, Sask. 181/K5
Marco (Marco Island), Fla. 212/E6
Marco, Ind. 227/C7
Marco, La. 238/E3
Marcola, Oreg. 291/E3
Marcona, Peru 128/E10
Marcos Juárez, Argentina 143/D3
Marcus, Iowa 229/B3
Marcus (isl.), Japan 87/F3
Marcus, S. Dak. 298/E4
Marcus, Wash. 310/H2
Marcus Baker (mt.), Alaska 196/C1
Marcus Hook, Pa. 294/L7
Marcy, N.Y. 276/K4
Marcy (mt.), N.Y. 276/N2
Mardan, Pakistan 68/C2
Mardan, Pakistan 59/K3
Mardela Springs, Md. 245/P7
Mar del Plata, Argentina 143/E4
Mar del Plata, Argentina 120/D6
Mardin (prov.), Turkey 63/J4
Mardin, Turkey 59/D2
Maré (isl.), New Caled. 87/G8
Maré (isl.), New Caled. 86/J4
Mareb (riv.), Ethiopia 59/C5
Marechal Deodoro, Brazil 132/H5
Maree, Loch (lake), Scotland 10/D2
Mare, Loch (lake), Scotland 15/D3
Mareeba, Queensland 95/C3
Mareeba, Queensland 88/G3
Mare Island Navy Yard, Calif. 204/J1
Marengo (co.), Ala. 195/C6
Marengo, Ala. 195/C6
Marengo, Ill. 222/E1
Marengo, Ind. 227/E8
Marengo, Iowa 229/J5
Marengo, Ohio 284/D4
Marengo, Sask. 181/B4
Marengo, Wis. 317/E3
Marenisco, Mich. 250/F2
Marennes, France 28/C5
Mareth, Tunisia 106/F2
Marettimo (isl.), Italy 34/C6
Marfa, Texas 303/C12
Marfield, N.S. Wales 97/C3
Marfrance, W. Va. 312/E6
Margai Caka, China 77/C4
Marganets, U.S.S.R. 52/E5
Margao, India 68/C5
Margaree, Nova Scotia 168/G2
Margaree (isl.), Nova Scotia 168/F4
Margaree Centre, Nova Scotia 168/H2
Margaree Forks, Nova Scotia 168/H2
Margaree Harbour, Nova Scotia 168/H2
Margaree Valley, Nova Scotia 168/H2
Margaret, Ala. 195/F3
Margaret (lake), Alberta 182/B5
Margaret, Manitoba 179/C5
Margaret, Texas 303/E3
Margaret (riv.), W. Australia 88/D3
Margaret River, W. Australia 88/A6
Margaret River, W. Australia 92/A6
Margaret River Station, W. Australia 92/D2
Margaretsville, Nova Scotia 168/C3
Margaretville, N.Y. 276/L6
Margarita, Argentina 143/D3
Margarita (i.), Venezuela 120/C1
Margarita (isl.), Venezuela 124/F2
Margate, England 13/J6
Margate, England 10/G5
Margate, Fla. 212/B6
Margate, S. Africa 118/E6
Margate, Tasmania 99/D4
Margate City, N.J. 273/E5
Margento, Colombia 126/C4
Margerum, Ala. 195/B1
Margherita (Jamama), Somalia 115/H3
Margherita (mt.), Uganda 115/E3
Margherita (mt.), Zaire 102/E4
Margherita (mt.), Zaire 115/E3
Margherita, Minn. 255/E2
Margo, Sask. 181/H4
Margos, Peru 128/D8
Margosatubig, Philippines 82/D7
Margow, Dasht-e (des.), Afghanistan 59/H3
Margow, Dasht-e (des.), Afghanistan 68/A2
Margraten, Netherlands 27/H7
Margret, Georgia 217/D1
Margrethe (lake), Mich. 250/E4
Marguerite (bay) 5/C15
Mariá (isl.), Fr. Poly. 87/L8
Maria (creek), Ind. 227/C7

Maria, Québec 172/C2
Maria (isls.), St. Lucia 161/G7
Maria (isl.), Tasmania 99/E4
Mari A.S.S.R., U.S.S.R. 52/G3
Mari A.S.S.R., U.S.S.R. 48/E4
Maria Albina, Uruguay 145/E4
María Cleófas (isl.), Mexico 150/F6
María Elena, Chile 138/B3
Mariager, Denmark 21/D4
Mariager, Denmark 18/G8
Mariager (fjord), Denmark 21/D4
Mariah Hill, Ind. 227/D8
María Madre (isl.), Mexico 150/F6
María Magdalena (isl.), Mexico 150/F6
Marian (lake), Fla. 212/E4
Marian (lake), N.W. Terr. 187/G3
Marian, Queensland 88/H4
Marian, Queensland 95/D4
Mariana, Brazil 135/D2
Mariana Lake, Alberta 182/D2
Marianao, Cuba 158/C1
Marianao, Cuba 156/A2
Marianas, Northern 87/E4
Mariana Trench, Pacific 87/E4
Marianna, Ark. 202/J4
Marianna, Fla. 212/A1
Marianna, Pa. 294/B5
Mariano I. Loza, Argentina 143/G4
Mariano Roque Alonso, Paraguay 144/A4
Mariánské Lázně, Czech. 41/B2
María Pinto, Chile 138/G3
Mariapolis, Manitoba 179/C5
Marias, Islas (isls.), Mexico 150/F6
Marias (riv.), Mont. 188/D1
Marias (riv.), Mont. 262/D2
Maria Stein, Ohio 284/A5
Mariato, Punta (cape), Panama 154/G7
María Trinidad Sánchez (prov.), Dom. Republic 158/E5
Maria van Diemen (cape), N. Zealand 100/D1
Mariazell, Austria 41/C3
Marib, Saudi Arabia 59/E6
Marib, Yemen 59/E6
Mariba, Ky. 237/O5
Maribel, Wis. 317/L7
Maribo, Denmark 21/E8
Maribor, Yugoslavia 7/F4
Maribor, Yugoslavia 45/B2
Maribyrnong (riv.), Victoria 97/H5
Maribyrnong (riv.), Victoria 88/K7
Maricao, P. Rico 161/B2
Maricopa (co.), Ariz. 198/C5
Maricopa, Calif. 204/F8
Maricopa (mts.), Ariz. 198/C5
Maricopa Ind. Res., Ariz. 198/C6
Maricunga, Salar de (salt dep.), Chile 138/B6
Maridi, Sudan 111/E7
Marie (lake), Alberta 182/E2
Marie, Ark. 202/K2
Marie, W. Va. 312/E7
Marie Byrd Land (reg.), Ant. 2/D10
Marie Byrd Land (reg.) 5/B13
Mariefred, Sweden 18/F1
Marie-Galante (isl.), Guadeloupe 161/B7
Marie-Galante (isl.), Guadeloupe 156/G4
Mariehamn, Finland 18/M7
Mariel, Cuba 158/B1
Mariemont, Ohio 284/C9
Marienberg, Papua N.G. 85/B6
Marienburg (Malbork), Poland 47/D1
Mariënburg, Suriname 131/D2
Mariental, Namibia 118/B4
Mariental, Namibia 102/D7
Marienthal, Kansas 232/A3
Marienville, Pa. 294/D3
Marie-Reine, Alberta 182/B1
Maries (co.), Mo. 261/J6
Mariestad, Sweden 18/H7
Marietta, Georgia 217/J1
Marietta, Ill. 222/C3
Marietta, Ind. 227/F5
Marietta, Minn. 255/B5
Marietta, Miss. 256/H2
Marietta, N.C. 281/L6
Marietta, Ohio 284/G7
Marietta, Okla. 288/M7
Marietta, Pa. 294/J5
Marietta-Alderwood, Wash. 310/C2
Marietta-Slater, S.C. 296/C1
Marieval, Sask. 181/J5
Marieville, Québec 172/D4
Marigot, Dominica 161/F6
Marigot, Haiti 158/C6
Marigot, Martinique 161/D5
Marigot, St. Lucia 161/G6
Marigüitar, Venezuela 124/G2
Marihatag, Philippines 82/F6
Marília, Brazil 120/D5
Marília, Brazil 135/A3
Marilla, N.Y. 276/C5
Marín (co.), Calif. 204/C5
Marín, Spain 33/B1
Marina, Calif. 204/D7
Marinduque (prov.), Philippines 82/C4
Marinaduque (isl.), Philippines 82/C4
Marine, Ill. 222/D6
Marine City, Mich. 250/G6
Marineland, Fla. 212/F2
Marine on Saint Croix, Minn. 255/F5
Marinette (co.), Wis. 317/K5
Marinette, Wis. 317/L5
Maringá, Brazil 120/D5
Maringá, Brazil 132/D8
Maringouin, La. 238/G6

Marinha Grande, Portugal 33/B3
Marinhas, Portugal 33/B2
Marino, Italy 34/F7
Marion (reef) 95/E3
Marion (co.), Ala. 195/C2
Marion, Ala. 195/D5
Marion (lake), Alberta 182/D3
Marion (co.), Ark. 202/E1
Marion, Ark. 202/K3
Marion, Conn. 210/D2
Marion (co.), Fla. 212/D2
Marion (co.), Georgia 217/C6
Marion (co.), Ill. 222/E5
Marion, Ill. 222/E6
Marion (co.), Ind. 227/E5
Marion, Ind. 188/J2
Marion, Ind. 227/F3
Marion (co.), Iowa 229/G8
Marion, Iowa 229/K4
Marion (co.), Kansas 232/E3
Marion, Kansas 232/F3
Marion (lake), Kansas 232/E3
Marion (co.), Ky. 237/L5
Marion, Ky. 237/F6
Marion, La. 238/F1
Marion, Mass. 249/L6
Marion•, Mass. 249/L6
Marion, Mich. 250/D4
Marion (co.), Miss. 256/E6
Marion, Miss. 256/H3
Marion (co.), Mo. 261/J3
Marion, Mont. 262/B2
Marion (co.), Ohio 284/D4
Marion, Ohio 188/K2
Marion, Ohio 284/D4
Marion (co.), Oreg. 291/E3
Marion, Oreg. 291/D3
Marion, Pa. 294/G6
Marion (res.), Queensland 88/J3
Marion, S. Australia 88/D8
Marion, S. Australia 94/A8
Marion (lake), S.C. 188/K4
Marion (co.), S.C. 296/J3
Marion, S.C. 296/J3
Marion (lake), S.C. 296/G5
Marion, S. Dak. 298/P7
Marion (bay), Tasmania 99/E4
Marion (co.), Tenn. 237/K10
Marion (co.), Texas 303/K5
Marion, Va. 307/E7
Marion (co.), W. Va. 312/F4
Marion, Wis. 317/J6
Marion Bridge, Nova Scotia 168/H3
Marion Center, Pa. 294/D4
Marion Junction, Ala. 195/D6
Marion Station, Md. 245/R8
Marionville, Mo. 261/E8
Maripa, Fr. Guiana 131/E4
Maripa, Venezuela 124/F4
Maripasoula, Fr. Guiana 131/D4
Mariposa (co.), Calif. 204/E6
Mariposa, Calif. 204/E6
Mariscala, Uruguay 145/E5
Mariscal Estigarribia, Paraguay 120/C5
Mariscal Estigarribia, Paraguay 144/B3
Marismas, Las (marsh), Spain 33/C4
Marissa, Ill. 222/D5
Maritime Alps (range), France 28/G5
Maritime Alps (range), Italy 34/A2
Maritsa, Bulgaria 45/H4
Maritsa (riv.), Bulgaria 45/G4
Mariupol', U.S.S.R. 52/E5
Mariupol', U.S.S.R. 48/D5
Marivan (Dezh Shahpur), Iran 66/E3
Mariveles, Philippines 82/C3
Märjamaa, U.S.S.R. 53/C1
Mark (riv.), Belgium 27/F6
Mark, Ill. 222/D2
Mark (riv.), Netherlands 27/F6
Marka (Merka), Somalia 115/H3
Marka, Somalia 102/G4
Markam, China 77/E6
Markaryd, Sweden 18/H8
Mark Center, Ohio 284/A3
Markdale, Ontario 177/D3
Marked Tree, Ark. 202/K2
Marken (isl.), Netherlands 27/G4
Markerwaard Polder, Netherlands 27/G3
Markesan, Wis. 317/J8
Market Drayton, England 10/E4
Market Drayton, England 13/E5
Market Harborough, England 13/G5
Markethill, N. Ireland 17/H3
Market Rasen, England 13/G4
Market Weighton, England 13/G4
Markha (riv.), U.S.S.R. 48/M3
Markham (mt.) 5/A8
Markham, Ill. 222/B6
Markham (bay), N.W. Terr. 187/L3
Markham (inlet), N.W. Terr. 187/L1
Markham, Ontario 177/K4
Markham, Va. 307/N3
Markham, Wash. 310/B4
Markinch, Sask. 181/H5
Markinch, Scotland 15/F4
Markit, China 77/A4
Markkleeberg, Germany 22/E3
Markland, Ind. 227/G3
Markland, Newf. 166/D2
Markle, Ind. 227/G3
Markleeville, Calif. 204/F5
Marklesburg (James Creek), Pa. 294/F5
Markleton, Pa. 294/D6
Markleville, Ind. 227/F5

Markleysburg, Pa. 294/C6
Markounda, Cent. Afr. Rep. 115/C2
Markovo, U.S.S.R. 4/C1
Markovo, U.S.S.R. 48/S3
Marks, Miss. 256/G4
Marks, U.S.S.R. 52/G4
Markstay, Ontario 177/D1
Marksville, La. 238/C2
Marktredwitz, Germany 22/E4
Markville, Minn. 255/D6
Marl, Germany 22/B3
Marland, Okla. 288/M1
Marlbank, Ontario 177/G3
Marlboro, Alberta 182/B3
Marlboro •, N.J. 273/E3
Marlboro, N.Y. 276/M7
Marlboro (co.), S.C. 296/H2
Marlboro •, Vt. 268/B6
Marlborough, Conn. 210/F2
Marlborough •, Conn. 210/F2
Marlborough, England 13/F6
Marlborough, England 10/F5
Marlborough, Mass. 249/H3
Marlborough, Mo. 261/P3
Marlborough, N.H. 268/C6
Marlborough •, N.H. 268/C6
Marlborough, Queensland 95/D4
Marlette, Mich. 250/E3
Marlin, Texas 303/H6
Marlin, Wash. 310/F3
Marlinton, W. Va. 312/F6
Marlow, Ala. 195/C10
Marlow, England 13/G8
Marlow, Georgia 217/K6
Marlow •, N.H. 268/C5
Marlow, Okla. 288/K5
Marlton, N.J. 273/D4
Marmaduke, Ark. 202/K1
Marmagao, India 68/C5
Marmande, France 28/C4
Marmara (sea), Turkey 7/G4
Marmara (isl.), Turkey 63/B2
Marmara (sea), Turkey 63/C2
Marmara (sea), Turkey 59/A1
Marmaris, Turkey 63/C4
Marmarth, N. Dak. 282/B7
Mar Menor (lag.), Spain 33/F4
Marmet, W. Va. 312/C6
Marmolada (mt.), Italy 34/C1
Marmontana (mt.), Switzerland 39/H4
Marmora, N.J. 273/D5
Marmora, Ontario 177/G3
Marmot (bay), Alaska 196/H3
Marmot (isl.), Alaska 196/H3
Mar Muerto (lag.), Mexico 150/N9
Marne (dept.), France 28/F3
Marne (riv.), France 28/C2
Marne, Germany 22/C2
Marne, Iowa 229/C6
Marne, Mich. 250/D5
Maro (dry riv.), Chad 111/C4
Maro (reef), Hawaii 188/F6
Maro (reef), Hawaii 218/F6
Maroa, Ill. 222/E3
Maroa, Venezuela 124/E6
Maroantsetra, Madagascar 118/J3
Marolambo, Madagascar 118/H4
Maromokotro (mt.), Madagascar 102/G6
Maromokotro (mt.), Madagascar 118/H2
Marondera, Zimbabwe 118/E3
Maroni (riv.) 120/D2
Maroni (riv.), Fr. Guiana 131/D3
Maroochydore-Mooloolaba, Queensland 88/J5
Maroochydore-Mooloolaba, Queensland 95/E5
Maroon (peak), Colo. 208/F4
Maroon Town, Jamaica 158/H6
Maros (riv.), Hungary 41/F3
Maros, Indonesia 85/F6
Maroua, Cameroon 102/D3
Maroua, Cameroon 115/B1
Maroubra, N.S. Wales 97/K3
Marouini (riv.), Fr. Guiana 131/D4
Marovoay, Madagascar 102/G6
Marovoay, Madagascar 118/H3
Marowijne (dist.), Suriname 131/D4
Marowijne (riv.), Suriname 131/D3
Marquam, Oreg. 291/B3
Marquand, Mo. 261/M8
Marquesas (keys), Fla. 212/D7
Marquesas (isls.), Fr. Polynesia 2/B6
Marquesas (isls.), Fr. Poly. 87/N6
Marquette, Iowa 229/L2
Marquette, Kansas 232/E3
Marquette, Manitoba 179/E4
Marquette, Mich. 146/K5
Marquette, Mich. 188/J1
Marquette (co.), Mich. 250/B2
Marquette, Mich. 250/B2
Marquette (co.), Mich. 250/E3
Marquette, Nebr. 264/G4
Marquette (co.), Wis. 317/H8
Marquette, Wis. 317/H8
Marquette Heights, Ill. 222/D3
Marquez, Texas 303/H6
Marquis, Grenada 161/G8
Marquis, St. Lucia 161/G6
Marquis, Sask. 181/F5
Marra, Jebel (mt.), Sudan 102/E3
Marra (creek), N.S. Wales 97/D2
Marra, Jebel (mt.), Sudan 111/D3
Marracuene, Mozambique 118/E5
Marrakech, Morocco 102/B1
Marrakech, Morocco 106/C2
Marrawah, Tasmania 99/A2
Marree, S. Australia 88/F5
Marree, S. Australia 94/E3
Marrero, La. 238/O4
Marrickville, N.S. Wales 88/L4

Marrickville, N.S. Wales 97/J3
Marriott, Sask. 181/D4
Marromeu, Mozambique 118/F3
Marrowbone, Ky. 237/K7
Marrowie (creek), N.S. Wales 97/C3
Marrupa, Mozambique 118/F2
Mars, Pa. 294/C4
Mars (riv.), Québec 172/G1
Marsabit, Kenya 115/G3
Marsabit, Kenya 102/F4
Marsa el Brega, Libya 111/D1
Marsa el Hariga, Libya 111/D1
Marsala, Italy 34/D6
Marsa Oseif, Sudan 111/G3
Mars Bluff, S.C. 296/H3
Marsciano, Italy 34/D3
Marsden, N.S. Wales 97/D3
Marsden, Sask. 181/B3
Marsden Park, N.S. Wales 97/H3
Marsdiep (chan.), Netherlands 27/F3
Marseille, France 7/E4
Marseille, France 28/F6
Marseilles, Ill. 222/E2
Marseilles, Ohio 284/D4
Marsh (creek), Idaho 220/F7
Marsh (isl.), La. 238/G7
Marsh (lake), Minn. 255/B5
Marsh, Mont. 262/M4
Marsh (peak), Utah 304/E3
Marshall (co.), Ala. 195/F2
Marshall, Ark. 202/F2
Marshall (co.), Ill. 222/D2
Marshall, Ill. 222/F4
Marshall (co.), Ind. 227/E2
Marshall, Ind. 227/C5
Marshall (co.), Iowa 229/G4
Marshall (co.), Kansas 232/F2
Marshall (co.), Ky. 237/E7
Marshall, Liberia 106/B7
Marshall (isl.), Maine 243/G7
Marshall, Mich. 250/E6
Marshall (co.), Minn. 255/B2
Marshall, Minn. 255/C6
Marshall (co.), Miss. 256/E1
Marshall, Mo. 261/F4
Marshall, N.C. 281/D3
Marshall, N. Dak. 282/F5
Marshall (riv.), North. Terr. 88/F4
Marshall (riv.), North. Terr. 93/D7
Marshall, Ohio 284/C7
Marshall (co.), Okla. 288/N6
Marshall, Okla. 288/L2
Marshall (co.), S. Dak. 298/O2
Marshall (co.), Tenn. 237/H10
Marshall, Texas 188/G4
Marshall, Texas 303/K5
Marshall, Va. 307/N3
Marshall (isls.), U.S. 2/T5
Marshall (co.), W. Va. 312/E3
Marshall, Wis. 317/H9
Marshallberg, N.C. 281/S5
Marshall Hall, Md. 245/K6
Marshall Islands 87/G4
Marshalls Creeks, Pa. 294/M3
Marshallton, Del. 245/R2
Marshalltown, Iowa 229/G4
Marshalltown, Iowa 188/H2
Marshallville, Georgia 217/D6
Marshallville, Ohio 284/G4
Marshes Siding, Ky. 237/M7
Marshfield, Ind. 227/C4
Marshfield, Mass. 249/M4
Marshfield •, Mass. 249/M4
Marshfield, Mo. 261/G8
Marshfield, Vt. 268/C3
Marshfield •, Vt. 268/C3
Marshfield, Wis. 317/F6
Marshfield Hills, Mass. 249/M4
Marsh Hill, Pa. 294/J3
Mars Hill •, Maine 243/H2
Mars Hill, N.C. 281/D3
Mars Hill-Blaine, Maine 243/H2
Marshland, Oreg. 291/D1
Marshville, N.C. 281/J4
Marshy (lake), Manitoba 179/B5
Marshyhope (creek), Md. 245/P6
Marsing, Idaho 220/B6
Marsland, Nebr. 264/A2
Marsoui, Québec 172/C1
Märsta, Sweden 18/K7
Marstal, Denmark 21/D8
Marston, Mo. 261/N9
Marston, N.C. 281/K5
Marstons Mills, Mass. 249/N6
Marstrand, Sweden 18/G8
Mart, Texas 303/H6
Martaban, Burma 72/C3
Martaban (gulf), Burma 54/L8
Martaban (gulf), Burma 72/C4
Martapura, Indonesia 85/F6
Martel, Ohio 284/E4
Martel, Tenn. 237/N9
Martelange, Belgium 27/H9
Martell, Calif. 204/C9
Martell, Wis. 317/B6
Martelle, Iowa 229/L4
Marten (mt.), Alberta 182/C2
Martensdale, Iowa 229/F5
Martensville, Sask. 181/E3
Martha, Ky. 237/R4
Martha, Okla. 288/H5
Martha, Tenn. 237/J8
Marthaguy (creek), N.S. Wales 97/D2
Marthasville, Mo. 261/L5
Martha's Vineyard (isl.), Mass. 188/N2
Martha's Vineyard (isl.), Mass. 249/M7
Marthaville, La. 238/D3
Martí, Camagüey, Cuba 158/G3
Martí, Matanzas, Cuba 158/D1
Martí, Cuba 156/D2
Martigny, Switzerland 39/C4
Martigues, France 28/F6

Martin (dam), Ala. 195/G5
Martin (lake), Ala. 195/G5
Martin, Czech. 41/E2
Martin (co.), Fla. 212/F4
Martin •, Georgia 217/F2
Martin (co.), Ind. 227/D7
Martin (co.), Ky. 237/R5
Martin, Ky. 237/R5
Martin, La. 238/D2
Martin, Mich. 250/D6
Martin (co.), Minn. 255/D7
Martin, New Bruns. 170/E3
Martin (head), New Bruns. 170/E3
Martin (co.), N.C. 281/P3
Martin, N. Dak. 282/K4
Martin, Ohio 284/D2
Martin, S.C. 296/D5
Martin, S. Dak. 298/F7
Martin, Tenn. 237/D8
Martin (co.), Texas 303/C5
Martin, W. Va. 312/H4
Martina Franca, Italy 34/F4
Martinborough, N. Zealand 100/E4
Martín Chico, Uruguay 145/A5
Martinez, Calif. 204/K1
Martinez, Georgia 217/H3
Martínez de la Torre, Mexico 150/L6
Martín García (isl.), Argentina 143/H6
Martinique (isl.) 146/M8
MARTINIQUE 161/D5
MARTINIQUE 156/G4
Martinique (passage), Dominica 161/E7
Martinique (passage), Martinique 161/C5
Martin Luther King, Jr., Nat'l Hist. Site, Georgia 217/K1
Martinsburg, Ind. 227/E8
Martinsburg, Iowa 229/J6
Martinsburg, Mo. 261/J4
Martinsburg, Nebr. 264/H2
Martinsburg, N.Y. 276/J3
Martinsburg, Ohio 284/F5
Martinsburg, Pa. 294/F5
Martinsburg, W. Va. 312/K4
Martins Creek, Pa. 294/M4
Martinsdale, Mont. 262/F4
Martinsdale (res.), Mont. 262/F4
Martins Ferry, Ohio 284/J5
Martins Mills, Tenn. 237/F10
Martins River, Nova Scotia 168/D4
Martinsville, Ind. 222/F4
Martinsville, Ind. 227/D6
Martinsville, Miss. 256/D7
Martinsville, Mo. 261/D2
Martinsville, N.J. 273/D2
Martinsville, Ohio 284/C7
Martinsville (I.C.), Va. 307/J7
Martinton, Ill. 222/F3
Martintown, Ontario 177/K2
Martin Van Buren Nat'l Hist. Site, N.Y. 276/N6
Martinville, Ark. 202/F3
Martinville, Québec 172/F4
Martock, England 13/E7
Martofte, Denmark 21/D6
Marton, N. Zealand 100/E4
Martos, Spain 33/E4
Martre, Lac la (lake), N.W.T. 162/E3
Martwick, Ky. 237/H6
Marty, S. Dak. 298/N8
Marudi (mts.), Guyana 131/B5
Marudi, Malaysia 85/E5
Ma'ruf, Afghanistan 68/B2
Ma'ruf, Afghanistan 59/J3
Maruim, Brazil 132/G5
Marulan, N.S. Wales 97/E4
Marungu (mts.), Zaire 115/E5
Marutea (atoll), Fr. Poly. 87/N8
Marv Dasht, Iran 66/H6
Marvejols, France 28/E5
Marvel, Ala. 195/D4
Marvel, Colo. 208/C8
Marvell, Ark. 202/J4
Marvin, S. Dak. 298/R3
Marvindale, Pa. 294/E2
Marvine (mt.), Utah 304/C5
Marvyn, Ala. 195/H4
Marwayne, Alberta 182/E3
Marwood, Pa. 294/C4
Mary, Ky. 237/O5
Mary (lake), Minn. 255/C5
Mary (riv.), Queensland 95/E5
Mary, U.S.S.R. 54/H6
Mary (Merv), U.S.S.R. 48/G6
Maryborough, Australia 87/F8
Maryborough (Portlaoise), Ireland 17/G5
Maryborough (Portlaoise), Ireland 10/C4
Maryborough, Queensland 95/E5
Maryborough, Queensland 88/J5
Maryborough, Victoria 97/B5
Maryborough, Victoria 88/G7
Marydel, Md. 245/P4
Marydell, Miss. 256/E6
Mary Esther, Fla. 212/B6
Maryfield, Sask. 181/K6
Maryhill, Wash. 310/E5
Mary Kathleen, Queensland 88/G4
Mary Kathleen, Queensland 95/A4
Marykirk, Scotland 15/F4
Maryland 188/L3
MARYLAND 245
Maryland, N.Y. 276/L5
Maryland (state), U.S. 146/L6
Maryland City, Md. 245/L4
Maryland Heights, Mo. 261/O2
Maryland Line, Md. 245/M2
Maryneal, Texas 303/D5
Maryport, England 10/E3
Maryport, England 13/D3

Mary Ronan (lake), Mont. 262/B3
Marys (creek), Idaho 220/C7
Marys (riv.), Nev. 266/F1
Mary's Harbour, Newf. 166/C3
Marystown, Newf. 166/D4
Marysvale, Utah 304/B5
Marysvale (peak), Utah 304/B5
Marysville, Calif. 188/B3
Marysville, Calif. 204/D4
Marysville, Ind. 227/F7
Marysville, Iowa 229/H6
Marysville, Kansas 232/F2
Marysville, Mich. 250/G6
Marysville, Mont. 262/D4
Marysville, Ohio 284/D5
Marysville, Pa. 294/H5
Marysville, Wash. 310/C2
Marytown, W. Va. 312/C8
Maryvale, Queensland 95/D5
Maryvale, Queensland 88/H3
Maryville, Ill. 222/B2
Maryville, Mo. 261/C2
Maryville, Tenn. 237/O9
Marzo (pt.), Colombia 126/B4
Masagua, Guatemala 154/B3
Masahim, Kuh-e (mt.), Iran 66/J5
Masai (steppe), Tanzania 115/F4
Masaka, Uganda 115/F4
Masamba, Indonesia 85/G6
Masan, S. Korea 81/D6
Masardis •, Maine 243/G3
Masaryktown, Fla. 212/D3
Masasi, Tanzania 115/G6
Masatepe, Nicaragua 154/D5
Masaya, Nicaragua 154/D5
Masbate (prov.), Philippines 82/D4
Masbate, Philippines 82/D4
Masbate (isl.), Philippines 82/D4
Masbate (isl.), Philippines 85/G3
Mascara, Algeria 106/D1
Mascarene (isls.), Mauritius 118/F5
Mascarene (isls.), Réunion 118/F5
Mascoma, N.H. 268/C4
Mascoma (lake), N.H. 268/C4
Mascot, Tenn. 237/O8
Mascota, Mexico 150/G6
Mascotte, Fla. 212/E3
Mascouche, Québec 172/H4
Mascoutah, Ill. 222/D3
Masefield, Sask. 181/D6
Masela (isl.), Indonesia 85/H7
Maseru (cap.), Lesotho 102/E8
Maseru (cap.), Lesotho 118/D5
Mash'Abbe Sade, Israel 65/B6
Mashabi (isl.), Saudi Arabia 59/C4
Masham, England 13/F3
Mashapaug, Conn. 210/G1
Mashapaug (lake), Conn. 210/G1
Mashash, Wadi (dry riv.), Jordan 65/D4
Mashhad (Meshed), Iran 66/L2
Mashike, Japan 81/K2
Mashkel, Hamun-i- (swamp), Pakistan 68/A3
Mashkel, Hamun-i- (swamp), Pakistan 59/H4
Mashkid (riv.), Iran 66/N7
Mashkid (riv.), Iran 59/H4
Mashkid (riv.), Pakistan 59/H4
Mashkid (riv.), Pakistan 68/A3
Mashonaland (reg.), Zimbabwe 118/E3
Mashpee •, Mass. 249/M6
Mashulaville, Miss. 256/G4
Masi-Manimba, Zaire 115/C4
Masindi, Uganda 115/F3
Masinloc, Philippines 82/B3
Masío (cay), Cuba 158/C2
Masira (isl.), Oman 54/G7
Masira (gulf), Oman 54/G7
Masira (isl.), Oman 59/G5
Masisea, Peru 128/E7
Masisi, Zaire 115/E4
Masjed Soleyman, Iran 66/F5
Mask (lake), Ireland 17/C4
Mask, Lough (lake), Ireland 10/B4
Maskell, Nebr. 264/H2
Maskinongé (co.), Québec 172/D3
Maskinongé, Québec 172/B1
Maskinongé (county), Québec 174/C3
Maskinongé, Québec 172/E3
Maskinongé (riv.), Québec 172/D3
Masoala (pen.), Madagascar 118/J3
Masoller, Uruguay 145/C2
Mason (isl.), Conn. 210/H3
Mason (co.), Ill. 222/D3
Mason, Ill. 222/E5
Mason, Ky. 237/M3
Mason (co.), Mich. 250/C4
Mason, Mich. 250/E6
Mason, Nev. 266/B4
Mason (peak), Nev. 266/F1
Mason (bay), N. Zealand 100/A7
Mason, Ohio 284/B7
Mason, Okla. 288/O3
Mason, Tenn. 237/B10
Mason (co.), Texas 303/E7
Mason, Texas 303/E7
Mason (co.), Wash. 310/B3
Mason (co.), W. Va. 312/B5
Mason, W. Va. 312/B4
Mason, Wis. 317/D3
Mason City, Ill. 222/D3
Mason City, Iowa 229/G2
Mason City, Iowa 188/H2
Mason City, Nebr. 264/F3
Mason Hall, Tenn. 237/C8
Mason Springs, Md. 245/K6
Masontown, Pa. 294/C6
Masontown, W. Va. 312/G3
Masonville, Colo. 208/J2
Masonville, Iowa 229/K4
Masonville, N.Y. 276/M6
Masqat (Muscat) (cap.), Oman 59/G5
Massa, Italy 34/C2
Massabesic (lake), N.H. 268/E6

Massac (co.), Ill. 222/E6
Massa-Carrara (prov.), Italy 34/C2
Massachusetts 188/M2
MASSACHUSETTS 249
Massachusetts (bay), Mass. 249/M4
Massachusetts (state), U.S. 146/L5
Massacre (bay), Amer. Samoa 86/W4
Massacre (lake), Nev. 266/B1
Massafra, Italy 34/F4
Massakory, Chad 111/C5
Massa Marittima, Italy 34/C3
Massamgo (Forte República), Angola 115/C5
Massangena, Mozambique 118/E4
Massanutten (mt.), Va. 307/L3
Massapê, Brazil 132/G3
Massapeag, Conn. 210/G3
Massapequa, N.Y. 276/R7
Massapequa Park, N.Y. 276/R7
Massaponax, Va. 307/O4
Massawa, Ethiopia 59/C6
Massawa, Ethiopia 111/G4
Massawa, Ethiopia 102/F3
Massbach, Ill. 222/C1
Mass City, Mich. 250/G1
Massena, Iowa 229/D6
Massena, N.Y. 276/L1
Massénya, Chad 111/C5
Masset, Br. Col. 184/B3
Masset (inlet), Br. Col. 184/A3
Massey, Md. 245/P3
Massey, N. Zealand 100/B1
Massey, Ontario 177/C1
Massies Mill, Va. 307/K5
Massillon, Ala. 195/D6
Massillon, Iowa 229/L5
Massillon, Ohio 284/H4
Massina, Mozambique 118/F4
Massingir, Mozambique 118/E4
Massive (mt.), Colo. 208/F4
Masson, Québec 172/B4
Masson, Québec 172/E4
Massueville, Québec 172/D3
Mastaba, Saudi Arabia 59/C5
Mastens Corners, Del. 245/R5
Masterton, N. Zealand 100/E4
Masters, Colo. 208/L2
Mastic Beach, N.Y. 276/P9
Mastuj, Pakistan 59/K2
Mastung, Pakistan 59/J4
Mastung, Pakistan 68/B3
Mastura, Saudi Arabia 59/C5
Masuda, Japan 81/E6
Masurian (lakes), Poland 47/E2
Masury, Ohio 284/J3
Masvingo, Zimbabwe 118/E4
Masyaf, Syria 63/G5
Matabeleland (reg.), Zimbabwe 118/D3
Matachewan, Ontario 177/J5
Matachewan, Ontario 175/D3
Mata de São João, Brazil 132/G6
Matadi, Zaire 115/B5
Matadi, Zaire 102/D5
Matador, Sask. 181/D5
Matador, Texas 303/D3
Matagalpa, Nicaragua 154/E4
Matagami, Québec 174/B3
Matagami, Québec 174/B3
Matagorda (co.), Texas 303/H9
Matagorda, Texas 303/J9
Matagorda (bay), Texas 303/H9
Matagorda (isl.), Texas 303/H9
Matagorda (pen.), Texas 303/J9
Matagorda Isl. Bombing and Gunnery Range, Texas 303/H9
Matakana (isl.), N. Zealand 100/F2
Matala (dam), Angola 115/B6
Matam, Senegal 106/B5
Matamoros, Pa. 294/N3
Matamoros, Mexico 146/J7
Matamoros, Coahuila, Mexico 150/H4
Matamoros, Tamaulipas, Mexico 150/L4
Matane (co.), Québec 172/B1
Matane (county), Québec 174/D3
Matane, Québec 172/B1
Matane, Québec 174/D3
Matane (riv.), Québec 172/B1
Matane Prov. Park, Québec 172/B1
Matanuska (riv.), Alaska 196/C1
Matanza, Colombia 126/D4
Matanzas (prov.), Cuba 158/D1
Matanzas, Cuba 146/K7
Matanzas, Cuba 158/D1
Matanzas, Cuba 156/B2
Matanzas (bay), Cuba 158/C1
Matanzas (inlet), Fla. 212/E2
Matapalo (cape), C. Rica 154/F6
Matapan (Taínaron) (cape), Greece 45/F7
Matapédia (county), Québec 174/D3
Matapédia (co.), Québec 172/B2
Matapédia, Québec 172/B2
Matapédia (lake), Québec 172/B1
Matapédia (riv.), Québec 172/B2
Mataquito (riv.), Chile 138/A10
Matara, Sri Lanka 68/E7
Mataram, Indonesia 85/F7
Matarani, Peru 120/D4
Mataranka, North. Terr. 93/C3
Matarinao (bay), Philippines 82/E5
Mataró, Spain 33/H2
Matatiele, S. Africa 118/D6
Matatindoc (pt.), Philippines 82/D6
Mataura, N. Zealand 100/B7
Mataura (riv.), N. Zealand 100/B6
Mata Utu (cap.), Wallis and Futuna 87/J7
Matawai, N. Zealand 100/F3
Matawan, Minn. 255/E7
Matawan, N.J. 273/E3
Matawin (lake), Québec 172/C3
Matawin (riv.), Québec 172/C3
Mateare, Nicaragua 154/D4

Mateguá, Bolivia 136/D3
Matehuala, Mexico 150/J5
Matelot, Trin. & Tob. 161/B10
Matera (prov.), Italy 34/F4
Matera, Italy 34/F4
Maternillos (pt.), Cuba 158/H2
Matészalka, Hungary 41/G3
Matetsi, Zimbabwe 118/D3
Mateur, Tunisia 106/F1
Matewan, W. Va. 312/B7
Matfield Green, Kansas 232/F3
Mather, Manitoba 179/C5
Mather, Wis. 317/F7
Mather A.F.B., Calif. 204/C8
Matherville, Ill. 222/C2
Matherville, Miss. 256/G7
Matheson, Colo. 208/M4
Matheson, Ontario 177/K5
Matheson Island, Manitoba 179/E3
Mathews, Ala. 195/F6
Mathews (lake), Calif. 204/E11
Mathews, La. 238/J7
Mathews (co.), Va. 307/R6
Mathews, Va. 307/R6
Mathias, W. Va. 312/J5
Mathinna, Tasmania 99/E3
Mathis, Texas 303/G9
Mathis, Texas 303/G9
Mathiston, Miss. 256/F3
Mathoura, N.S. Wales 97/C4
Mathura, India 68/D3
Mati, Philippines 85/H4
Mati, Philippines 82/F7
Matías Romero, Mexico 150/M8
Matinenda (lake), Ontario 177/B1
Matinicus, Maine 243/F8
Matinicus Rock (isl.), Maine 243/F8
Matlock, England 10/F4
Matlock, England 13/J2
Matlock, Iowa 229/A2
Matlock, Wash. 310/B3
Matoaca, Va. 307/N6
Matoaka, W. Va. 312/D8
Matochkin Shar (str.), U.S.S.R. 48/F2
Mato Grosso (state), Brazil 132/B6
Mato Grosso, Brazil 120/D4
Mato Grosso, Brazil 132/B6
Mato Grosso (plat.), Brazil 120/D4
Mato Grosso, Planalto de (plat.), Brazil 132/B6
Mato Grosso del Sul (state), Brazil 132/C7
Matopos, Zimbabwe 118/D4
Matosinhos, Portugal 33/B2
Matoury, Fr. Guiana 131/E3
Mátra (mts.), Hungary 41/E3
Matrah, Oman 54/G7
Matrah, Oman 59/G5
Matrel in Osttirol, Austria 41/B3
Matruh, Egypt 59/A3
Matsqui, Br. Col. 184/L3
Matsu (Mazu) (isl.), China 77/K6
Matsubara, Japan 81/H8
Matsue, Japan 81/F6
Matsumae, Japan 81/J3
Matsumoto, Japan 81/H5
Matsusaka, Japan 81/H6
Matsuto, Japan 81/H5
Matsuyama, Japan 81/F7
Matsuyama, Japan 54/P6
Matt, Switzerland 39/H3
Mattabesset (riv.), Conn. 210/E2
Mattagami (riv.), Ontario 175/D3
Mattagami (riv.), Ontario 177/J5
Mattamiscontis (lake), Maine 243/F4
Mattamuskeet (lake), N.C. 281/S3
Mattapan, Mass. 249/C7
Mattapoisett, Mass. 249/L6
Mattapoisett •, Mass. 249/L6
Mattaponi, Va. 307/O5
Mattaponi (riv.), Va. 307/O5
Mattaponi Ind. Res., Va. 307/P5
Mattawa, Ont. 162/J6
Mattawa, Ontario 177/F1
Mattawa, Ontario 175/E3
Mattawa, Wash. 310/F4
Mattawamkeag •, Maine 243/G5
Mattawamkeag (lake), Maine 243/G4
Mattawamkeag (riv.), Maine 243/G4
Mattawan, Mich. 250/D6
Mattawana, Pa. 294/G5
Mattawoman (creek), Md. 245/K6
Matterhorn (mt.), Switzerland 39/E4
Mattersburg, Austria 41/D3
Matteson, Ill. 222/B6
Matthew, Ky. 237/P5
Matthews, Georgia 217/H4
Matthews, Ind. 227/F4
Matthews, Mo. 261/N9
Matthews, N.C. 281/H4
Matthews Ridge, Guyana 131/B2
Mattice, Ontario 175/D3
Mattice, Ontario 177/J5
Mattighofen, Austria 41/B2
Mattituck, N.Y. 276/P9
Mattoon, Ill. 222/E4
Mattoon, Wis. 317/G5
Mattson, Miss. 256/C2
Matu, Venezuela 124/F4
Matucana, Peru 128/D8
Matuku (isl.), Fiji 86/Q11
Matün, Cuba 158/D2
Matura, Trin. & Tob. 161/B10
Matura (bay), Trin. & Tob. 161/B10
Maturín, Venezuela 120/C2
Maturín, Venezuela 124/G3
Matutum (mt.), Philippines 82/E7
Matutum (mt.), Philippines 85/G4
Matveyev (isl.), U.S.S.R. 52/J1
Mau, India 68/E3
Maúa, Brazil 135/C3
Maúa, Mozambique 118/F2
Maubeuge, France 28/F2

Ma-ubin, Burma 72/B3
Mauch Chunk (Jim Thorpe), Pa. 294/L4
Mauchline, Scotland 15/D5
Mauckport, Ind. 227/E8
Maud, Ala. 195/B1
Maud, Ky. 237/L5
Maud, Miss. 256/D1
Maud, Ohio 284/B7
Maud, Okla. 288/N4
Maud, Scotland 15/F3
Maud, Texas 303/K4
Maude, N.S. Wales 97/C4
Maudlow, Mont. 262/E4
Mauerkirchen, Austria 41/B2
Maués, Brazil 132/B3
Maués, Brazil 120/D3
Maués-Açu (riv.), Brazil 132/B4
Maugansville, Md. 245/H2
Mauger (cay), Belize 154/D2
Maugerville, New Bruns. 170/D3
Maui (co.), Hawaii 218/J1
Maui (isl.), Hawaii 87/L3
Maui (isl.), Hawaii 188/F5
Maui (isl.), Hawaii 218/J2
Mauk, Georgia 217/D6
Mauke (isl.), Cook Is. 87/L8
Mauldin, S.C. 296/C2
Maule (reg.), Chile 138/A11
Maule (riv.), Chile 138/A11
Mauléon-Licharre, France 28/C6
Maullín, Chile 138/D4
Maullín (riv.), Chile 138/D5
Maumakeogh (mt.), Ireland 17/C3
Maumee (riv.), Ind. 227/H2
Maumee (bay), Mich. 250/F7
Maumee, Ohio 284/C2
Maumee (bay), Ohio 284/D2
Maumee (riv.), Ohio 284/A3
Maumelle (lake), Ark. 202/E4
Maumere, Indonesia 85/G7
Maumturk (mts.), Ireland 17/85
Maun, Botswana 118/C4
Maunabo, P. Rico 161/E3
Mauna Kea (mt.), Hawaii 87/L4
Mauna Kea (mt.), Hawaii 188/G6
Mauna Kea (mt.), Hawaii 218/H4
Maunaloa, Hawaii 218/G1
Mauna Loa (mt.), Hawaii 188/G6
Mauna Loa (mt.), Hawaii 188/G6
Mauna Loa (mt.), Hawaii 218/G6
Maunalua, Hawaii 218/F2
Maunawili, Hawaii 218/F2
Maungaturoto, N. Zealand 100/E1
Maungdaw, Burma 72/B2
Maunie, Ill. 222/E5
Maupin, Oreg. 291/F2
Maurepas, La. 238/M2
Maurepas (lake), La. 238/M2
Maurertown, Va. 307/J3
Mauriac, France 28/E5
Maurice (riv.), N.J. 273/C4
Maurice, La. 238/F6
Maurice (riv.), N.J. 273/C4
Maurice (lake), S. Australia 88/E5
Maurice (lake), S. Australia 94/B3
Mauricetown, N.J. 273/D5
Maurine, S. Dak. 298/E3
Mauritania 2/J4
Mauritania 102/A3
MAURITANIA 106/B5
Mauritius 2/M6
MAURITIUS 118/G5
Maury, N.C. 281/O4
Maury (co.), Tenn. 237/G9
Maury (riv.), Va. 307/K5
Maury City, Tenn. 237/C9
Mauston, Wis. 317/F8
Mautern in Steiermark, Austria 41/C3
Mauthausen, Austria 41/C2
Mauthen-Kötschach, Austria 41/B3
Mauvoisin (dam), Switzerland 39/D4
Mavaca (riv.), Venezuela 124/F6
Maverick, Ariz. 198/F5
Maverick (co.), Texas 303/D9
Mavila, Peru 128/H8
Mavillette, Nova Scotia 168/B4
Mavinga, Angola 115/D7
Mavora (mt.), N. Zealand 100/B6
Mavqi'im, Israel 65/B4
Mawai, Malaysia 72/F5
Mawbanna, Tasmania 99/B2
Mawer, Sask. 181/E5
Mawkmai, Burma 72/C2
Mawlaik, Burma 72/B2
Mawlu, Burma 72/C1
Mawson Station, Ant. 5/C4
Max, Minn. 255/G6
Max, Nebr. 264/C4
Max, N. Dak. 282/H4
Maxbass, N. Dak. 282/H2
Maxcanú, Mexico 150/O6
Maxeys, Georgia 217/F3
Maxie, La. 238/F6
Maxie, Miss. 256/F9
Máximo Gómez, Ciego de Ávila, Cuba 158/F2
Máximo Gómez, Matanzas, Cuba 158/D1
Máximo Paz, Argentina 143/F6
Maxinkuckee, Ind. 227/E2
Maxinkuckee (lake), Ind. 227/E2
Maxixe, Mozambique 118/F4
Max Meadows, Va. 307/G6
Maxstone, Sask. 181/F6
Maxton, N.C. 281/L5
Maxville, Mont. 262/C4
Maxville, Ontario 177/K2
Maxwell, Calif. 204/C4
Maxwell, Ind. 227/F5
Maxwell, Iowa 229/G5
Maxwell, Nebr. 264/D3
Maxwell, New Bruns. 170/C3
Maxwell, N. Mex. 274/E2
Maxwell (bay), N.W. Terr. 187/K2

Maxwell, Tenn. 237/J10
Maxwell Air Force Base, Ala. 195/F6
Maxwelton, Queensland 88/G4
May, Idaho 220/E5
May (cape), N.J. 188/M3
May (cape), N.J. 273/C6
May, Okla. 288/O7
May, Isle of (isl.) Scotland 15/F4
May, Texas 303/F5
Maya (mts.), Belize 154/C2
Maya (riv.), U.S.S.R. 54/P4
Maya (riv.), U.S.S.R. 48/O4
Maya Beach, Belize 154/C2
Mayaguana (isl.) Bahamas 146/L7
Mayaguana (isl.) Bahamas 156/D2
Mayaguana (passage), Bahamas 156/D2
Mayagüez (dist.) P. Rico 161/B2
Mayagüez, P. Rico 161/A2
Mayagüez, P. Rico 156/F1
Mayagüez (bay), P. Rico 161/A2
Mayajigua, Cuba 158/F2
Mayáis, Spain 35/G2
Mayarí, Cuba 158/J3
Mayari Arriba, Cuba 158/J4
Mayaro, Trin. & Tob. 161/B11
Mayaro (bay), Trin. & Tob. 161/B11
Maybee, Mich. 250/F6
Maybell, Colo. 208/B2
Mayberry, Sask. 181/K2
Maybeury, W. Va. 312/D8
Mayble, Scotland 10/D3
Maybole, Scotland 15/D5
Maybrook, N.Y. 276/M8
Mayburg, Pa. 294/D2
Maydena, Tasmania 99/C4
Mayen, Germany 22/B3
Mayenne (dept.) France 28/C3
Mayenne, France 28/C3
Mayenne (riv.), France 28/C4
Mayer, Ariz. 198/C4
Mayer, Chile 138/E7
Mayer, Minn. 255/E6
Mayersville, Miss. 256/B5
Mayerthorpe, Alberta 182/C3
Mayes (co.), Okla. 288/R2
Mayesville, S.C. 296/G4
Mayetta, Kansas 232/G2
Mayetta, N.J. 273/E4
Mayfair, Sask. 131/D2
Mayfield, Georgia 217/G4
Mayfield, Kansas 232/E4
Mayfield, Ky. 237/D7
Mayfield (creek) Ky. 237/C7
Mayfield, N.Y. 276/M4
Mayfield, Ohio 284/J9
Mayfield, Okla. 288/G4
Mayfield, Pa. 294/L2
Mayfield, Scotland 15/D2
Mayfield, Utah 304/C4
Mayfield (lake), Wash. 310/C4
Mayfield Heights, Ohio 284/J9
Mayflower, Ark. 202/F4
Mayger, Oreg. 291/D1
Mayhew, Miss. 256/G4
Mayhill, N. Mex. 274/D6
Maykop, U.S.S.R. 7/H4
Maykop, U.S.S.R. 48/O5
Maykop, U.S.S.R. 52/F6
Mayland, Tenn. 237/L8
Maylene, Ala. 195/E4
Maymont, Sask. 181/D3
Maymyo, Burma 72/C2
Mayna, La. 238/G4
Maynard, Ark. 202/J1
Maynard, Iowa 229/K3
Maynard •, Mass. 249/J3
Maynard, Minn. 255/C6
Maynardville, Tenn. 237/O8
Mayne, Br. Col. 184/K3
Maynooth, Ireland 17/H5
Maynooth, Ontario 177/H2
Mayo, Canada 4/C16
Mayo, Fla. 212/C1
Mayo (co.), Ireland 17/C4
Mayo, Md. 245/M5
Mayo (riv.), Peru 128/D6
Mayo (bay), Philippines 82/F7
Mayo, S.C. 296/D1
Mayo, Yukon 187/E3
Mayo, Yukon 162/C3
Mayo (lake), Yukon 187/E3
Mayodan, N.C. 281/K2
Mayon (vol.), Philippines 82/D4
Mayor (isl.), N. Zealand 100/F2
Mayor (cape), Spain 33/E1
Mayor Martínez Paraguay 144/C5
Mayor Pablo Lagerenza, Paraguay 144/B1
MAYOTTE 118/G2
Mayotte (isl.), France 102/G6
Mayoworth, Wyo. 319/F2
May Park, Oreg. 291/J2
May Pen, Jamaica 158/U6
Mayport Naval Air Sta., Fla. 212/E1
Mayrhofen, Austria 41/A3
Mays, Ind. 227/G5
Maysan (gov.), Iraq 66/E5
Maysel, W. Va. 312/D5
Mays Landing, N.J. 273/D5
Mays Lick, Ky. 237/O3
Maysville, Ark. 202/A1
Maysville, Calif. 204/D2
Maysville, Georgia 217/E2
Maysville, Iowa 229/M5
Maysville, Ky. 237/O3
Maysville, Mo. 261/D3
Maysville, N.C. 281/P5
Maysville, Okla. 288/M5
Maysville, W. Va. 312/H4
Maytiguid (isl.) Philippines 82/B5
Maytown, Ky. 237/O5
Mayumba, Gabon 115/A4
Mayuram, India 68/D6
Mayview, Mo. 261/E4
Mayville, Mich. 250/F5

Mayville, N.Y. 276/A6
Mayville, N. Dak. 282/R4
Mayville, Oreg. 291/G2
Mayville, Wis. 317/K9
Maywood, Calif. 204/C10
Maywood, Ill. 222/B5
Maywood, Mo. 261/J3
Maywood, Nebr. 264/D4
Maywood, N.J. 273/B2
Maywood Park, Oreg. 291/B2
Maza, N. Dak. 282/M3
Mazabuka, Zambia 115/E7
Mazabuka, Zambia 102/E6
Mazagan (El Jadida), Morocco 106/C2
Mazama, Wash. 310/E2
Mazamet, France 28/E6
Mazán, Peru 128/F4
Mazana (lake), Québec 172/C2
Mazana (riv.), Québec 172/C2
Mazandaran (prov.), Iran 66/H2
Mazangano, Uruguay 145/E3
Mazapil, Mexico 150/J4
Mazapil, Mexico 146/J5
Mazara del Vallo, Italy 34/D6
Mazar-e Sharif, Afghanistan 59/J2
Mazar-e Sharif, Afghanistan 68/B1
Mazarrón, Spain 33/F4
Mazaruni (riv.), Guyana 131/A2
Mazaruni-Potaro (dist.), Guyana 131/A2
Mazatán, Mexico 150/E2
Mazatenango, Guatemala 154/B3
Mazatlán, Mexico 146/H7
Mazatlán, Mexico 150/F5
Mazatzal (peak), Ariz. 198/D4
Mažeikiai, U.S.S.R. 53/A2
Mazenod, Sask. 181/E6
Mazeppa, Alberta 182/D5
Mazeppa, Minn. 255/F6
Mazgirt, Turkey 63/H3
Mazidağı, Turkey 63/J4
Mazie, Okla. 288/R2
Mazinaw (lake), Ontario 177/G3
Mazirbe, U.S.S.R. 53/B2
Mazocruz, Peru 128/H11
Mazomanie, Wis. 317/G9
Mazon, Ill. 222/E2
Mazowe (riv.), Mozambique 118/E3
Mazowe, Zimbabwe 118/E3
Mazowe (riv.), Zimbabwe 118/E3
Mazra'i, Israel 65/C3
Mazu (Matsu) (isl.), China 77/K6
Mazzarino, Italy 34/E6
Mbabane (cap.), Swaziland 118/E5
Mbabane (cap.), Swaziland 102/F7
Mbai'ki, Centr. Afr. Rep. 115/B3
Mbakou (res.), Cameroon 115/B2
Mbala, Zambia 102/F5
Mbala, Zambia 115/F5
Mbale, Uganda 115/F3
Mbale, Uganda 102/F4
Mbalmayo, Cameroon 115/B3
Mbamba Bay, Tanzania 115/G6
Mbandaka, Zaire 115/C3
Mbandaka, Zaire 115/C3
M'banza Congo, Angola 115/B5
Mbanza-Ngungu, Zaire 102/D5
Mbanza-Ngungu, Zaire 115/B5
Mbaracayú, Cordillera de (mts.), Paraguay 144/A3
Mbarangandu (riv.), Tanzania 115/G5
Mbarara, Uganda 115/F4
Mbemkuru (riv.), Tanzania 115/G5
Mbengga (isl.), Fiji 86/Q11
Mbéré (riv.), Cameroon 115/B2
Mbéré (riv.), Cent. Afr. Rep. 115/B2
Mbéré (riv.), Chad 111/C6
Mbeya (reg.), Tanzania 115/F5
Mbeya, Tanzania 102/F5
Mbeya, Tanzania 115/F5
M'Bigou, Gabon 115/B4
Mbinda, Equat. Guinea 115/A3
Mbini, Equat. Guinea 115/A3
Mbocayaty, Paraguay 144/C5
M'Bour, Senegal 106/A6
M'Bout, Mauritania 106/B5
Mbres, Cent. Afr. Rep. 115/D2
M'Bridge (riv.), Angola 115/B5
Mbuji-Mayi, Zaire 102/E5
Mbuji-Mayi, Zaire 115/D5
Mbulu, Tanzania 115/G4
Mburucuya, Argentina 143/E2
Mbuyapey, Paraguay 144/D5
McAdam, New Bruns. 170/C3
McAdams, Miss. 256/E4
McAdoo, Pa. 294/L4
McAdoo, Texas 303/D4
McAfee, N.J. 273/D1
McAlester, Okla. 188/G4
McAlester, Okla. 288/P5
McAlester (lake), Okla. 288/P4
McAlister, N. Mex. 274/F4
McAlisterville, Pa. 294/H4
McAllaster, Kansas 232/A3
McAllen, Texas 188/G5
McAllen, Texas 303/F11
McAllister, Mont. 262/E5
McAllister, Wis. 317/L5
McAlpin, Fla. 212/D1
McAndrews, Ky. 237/S5
McArthur, Calif. 204/D2
McArthur, Ohio 284/F7
McArthur River, North. Terr. 88/F3
McAuley, Manitoba 179/A4
McBain, Mich. 250/D4
McBaine, Mo. 261/H5
McBean, Georgia 217/H4
McBee, S.C. 296/G3
McBride, Br. Col. 184/G3
McBride, Miss. 256/C7
McBride, Mo. 261/N7
McBride, Okla. 288/N7
McBride Lake, Sask. 181/J3

McBrides, Mich 250/D5
McCabe, Mont. 262/M2
McCain, N.C. 281/L4
McCall, Idaho 220/C5
McCall, La. 238/K3
McCalla, Ala. 195/E4
McCall Creek, Miss. 256/C7
McCallsburg, Iowa 229/G4
McCallum, Newf. 166/C4
McCamey, Texas 303/B6
McCammon, Idaho 220/F7
McCanna, N. Dak. 282/P3
McCarley, Miss. 256/E3
McCarr, Ky. 237/S5
McCarthy, Alaska 196/K2
McCaskill, Ark. 202/C6
McCauley (isl.), Br. Col. 184/B3
McCaulley, Texas 303/E5
McCausland, Iowa 229/M5
McCaysville, Georgia 217/D1
McChord A.F.B., Wash. 310/C3
McClain (co.), Okla. 288/L5
McClave, Colo. 208/O6
McCleary, Wash. 310/B3
McClellan A.F.B., Calif. 204/B8
McClellan (lake), Alberta 182/E1
McClelland, Ark. 202/H3
McClelland, Iowa 229/B6
McClellandville, S.C. 296/H5
McCloud, Calif. 204/C2
McCloud, Tenn. 237/R8
McClure (lake), Calif. 204/E6
McClure, Ill. 222/D6
McClure, Ohio 284/C3
McClure, Pa. 294/H4
McClure, Va. 307/D6
McClusky, N. Dak. 282/K4
McColl, S.C. 296/H2
McComb, Miss. 256/D8
McComb, Ohio 284/C3
McConaughy, C.W. (lake), Nebr. 264/C3
McCondy, Miss. 256/G3
McCone (co.), Mont. 262/L3
McConnell, Ill. 222/D1
McConnell, Manitoba 179/B4
McConnell, Tenn. 237/D8
McConnell A.F.B., Kansas 232/E4
McConnells, S.C. 296/F6
McConnellsburg, Pa. 294/F6
McConnellsville, N.Y. 276/H4
McConnelsville, Ohio 284/G6
McCook, Nebr. 264/D4
McCook (co.), S. Dak. 298/P6
McCool, Miss. 256/F4
McCool Junction, Nebr. 264/G4
McCord, Sask. 181/E6
McCordsville, Ind. 227/F5
McCorkle, W. Va. 312/C6
McCormick (co.), S.C. 296/C4
McCormick, S.C. 296/C4
McCoy, Colo. 208/F3
McCoy, Oreg. 291/D2
McCoy (creek), Oreg. 291/J5
McCoy, Va. 307/G6
McCoy A.F.B., Fla. 212/E3
McCoysburg, Ind. 227/C3
McCracken, Kansas 232/C3
McCracken (co.), Ky. 237/B7
McCrea, Pa. 294/H5
McCreary (co.), Ky. 237/N7
McCreary, Manitoba 179/C4
McCrory, Ark. 202/H3
McCulloch (co.), Texas 303/E6
McCullom Lake, Ill. 222/E1
McCullough, Ala. 195/D8
McCune, Kansas 232/G4
McCurtain (co.), Okla. 288/S6
McCurtain, Okla. 288/R4
McCutchenville, Ohio 284/D4
McDade, Texas 303/G7
McDaniel, Md. 245/N5
McDaniels, Ky. 237/J5
McDavid, Fla. 212/B5
McDermitt, Nev. 266/D1
McDermott, Ohio 284/D8
McDonald, Kansas 232/A2
McDonald (co.), Mo. 261/D9
McDonald (lake), Mont. 262/B2
McDonald, N. Mex. 274/F5
McDonald, N.C. 281/L5
McDonald, Ohio 284/J3
McDonald, Pa. 294/B5
McDonald, Tenn. 237/M10
McDonalds Corners, Ontario 177/H3
McDonnell, Queensland 95/B1
McDonough (lake), Conn. 210/D1
McDonough, Del. 245/R3
McDonough, Georgia 217/D4
McDonough (co.), Ill. 222/C3
McDonough, N.Y. 276/J5
McDougal, Ark. 202/K1
McDougall (lake), New Bruns. 170/D3
McDowell, Ala. 195/C5
McDowell, Ky. 237/R6
McDowell (co.), N.C. 281/E3
McDowell, Va. 307/J4
McDowell (co.), W. Va. 312/C8
McDowell, W. Va. 312/D8
McDuffie (co.), Georgia 217/H4
McElhattan, Pa. 294/H3
McElmo (creek), Colo. 208/B8
McElmo (creek), Utah 304/E6
McEwen, Tenn. 237/F8
McFadden, Wyo. 319/H4
McFall, Mo. 261/D2
McFarland, Calif. 204/F7
McFarland, Kansas 232/F2
McFarland, Mich. 250/B2
McFarland, Wis. 317/H10
McFarlane (riv.), Sask. 181/L2
McGaffey, N. Mex. 274/A3

McGaheysville, Va. 307/L4
McGee, Sask. 181/C4
McGees Mills, Pa. 294/E4
McGehee, Ark. 202/H6
McGill, Nev. 266/G3
McGivney, New Bruns. 170/D2
McGloughlin (peak), Mont. 262/C4
McGrath, Alaska 188/C5
McGrath, Alaska 196/H2
McGrath, Minn. 255/F4
McGraw, N.Y. 276/H5
McGraw Brook, New Bruns. 170/D2
McGrawsville, Ind. 227/E3
McGregor (lake), Alberta 182/D4
McGregor, Br. Col. 184/F3
McGregor (riv.), Br. Col. 184/G3
McGregor, Iowa 229/L2
McGregor, Minn. 255/E4
McGregor (lake), Mont. 262/B3
McGregor, N. Dak. 282/D2
McGregor, Ontario 177/B5
McGregor, Texas 303/G6
McGrew, Nebr. 264/A3
McGuffey, Ohio 284/C4
McGuire (mt.), Idaho 220/D4
McGuire A.F.B., N.J. 273/D3
McHenry (co.), Ill. 222/E1
McHenry, Ill. 222/E1
McHenry, Ky. 237/H6
McHenry, Miss. 256/F9
McHenry (co.), N. Dak. 282/J3
McHenry, N. Dak. 282/N4
McHenry Shores, Ill. 222/E1
Mchinga, Tanzania 115/H5
Mchinji, Malawi 115/F6
McIlwraith (range), Queensland 95/B2
McIndoe Falls, Vt. 268/C3
McIntire, Iowa 229/H2
McIntosh, Ala. 195/B8
McIntosh, Fla. 212/D2
McIntosh (co.), Georgia 217/K7
McIntosh, Georgia 217/K7
McIntosh, Minn. 255/C3
McIntosh, N. Mex. 274/D4
McIntosh (co.), Okla. 288/P4
McIntosh, Ontario 177/A4
McIntosh, Ontario 175/B3
McIntosh, S. Dak. 298/G2
McIntyre, Georgia 217/F5
McIvor, Mich 250/F4
McKague, Sask. 181/G3
McKamie, Ark. 202/C7
McKay (lake), Manitoba 179/C2
McKay, Oreg. 291/J2
McKean (co.), Pa. 294/E2
McKean, Pa. 294/B2
McKeand (riv.), N.W. Terr. 187/M3
McKee (creek), Ill. 222/C4
McKee, Ky. 237/O6
McKee City, N.J. 273/D5
McKeesport, Pa. 188/L2
McKeesport, Pa. 294/C7
McKees Rocks, Pa. 294/B7
McKellar, Ontario 177/D2
McKendrick, New Bruns. 170/D1
McKenna, Wash. 310/C4
McKenney, Va. 307/N7
McKenzie (co.), N. Dak. 282/D4
McKenzie, N. Dak. 282/K6
McKenzie, South Fork (riv.), Oreg. 291/E3
McKenzie, Tenn. (38201 237/E8
McKenzie Bridge, Oreg. 291/F3
McKerrow, Ontario 177/C1
McKinlay, Queensland 95/B4
McKinlay, Queensland 88/G4
McKinley, Ala. 195/C6
McKinley (mt.), Alaska 146/C3
McKinley (mt.), Alaska 188/D5
McKinley (mt.), Alaska 196/H3
McKinley, Cuba 158/B2
McKinley, Minn. 255/F3
McKinley (co.), N. Mex. 274/A3
McKinley (mt.), U.S. 4/C17
McKinley Park, Alaska 196/J2
McKinleyville, Calif. 204/A3
McKinney (lake), Kansas 232/A3
McKinney, Ky. 237/M6
McKinney, Texas 303/H4
McKinnon, Georgia 217/J8
McKinnon, Tenn. 237/F8
McKinnon, Wyo. 319/C4
McKittrick, Calif. 204/F8
McKittrick, Mo. 261/J5
McLain, Miss. 256/G8
McLane, Pa. 294/B2
McLaughlin, Alberta 182/E3
McLaughlin, S. Dak. 298/H2
McLaurin, Miss. 256/F8
McLean (co.), Ill. 222/E3
McLean, Ill. 222/E3
McLean (co.), Ky. 237/G5
McLean, Nebr. 264/G2
McLean, N.Y. 276/H5
McLean (co.), N. Dak. 282/G4
McLean, Sask. 181/G5
McLean, Texas 303/D2
McLean, Va. 307/S2
McLeansboro, Ill. 222/E5
McLelan (str.), Newf. 166/B1
McLemoresville, Tenn. 237/D9
McLennan, Alberta 182/B2
McLennan (co.), Texas 303/G6
McLeod (co.), Minn. 255/D6
McLeod, Mont. 262/D5
McLeod, N. Dak. 282/R7
McLeod (bay), N.W. Terr. 187/L1
McLeod (lake), W. Australia 88/A4
McLeod (lake), W. Australia 92/A4

McLeod Lake, Br. Col. 184/F2
McLeod River, Alberta 182/B3
M'Clintock, Manitoba 179/K2
M'Clintock (chan.), N.W.T 146/H2
M'Clintock (chan.), N.W.T. 162/F1
M'Clintock (chan.), N.W. Terr. 187/H2
M'Clintock (inlet), N.W. Terr. 187/K1
McLoud, Okla. 288/M4
McLoughlin (mt.), Oreg. 291/E5
McLoughlin House Nat'l Hist. Site, Oreg. 291/B2
McLouth, Kansas 232/G2
McLure, Br. Col. 184/H4
M'Clure (str.), Canada 4/B15
M'Clure (str.), N.W.T. 162/D1
M'Clure (str.), N.W.T. 146/F1
M'Clure (cape), N.W.T. 187/F2
M'Clure (str.), N.W.T. 162/E1
M'Clure (str.), N.W.T. 187/G2
McMahon, Sask. 181/D5
McMechen, W. Va. 312/E3
McMillan, Mich. 250/D2
McMillan (lake), N. Mex. 274/E6
McMillan (lake), N. Mex. 188/F4
McMillan, Okla. 288/M6
McMinn (co.), Tenn. 237/M10
McMinnville, Oreg. 291/D2
McMinnville, Tenn. 237/K9
McMorran, Sask. 181/C4
McMullen (co.), Texas 303/F9
McMunn, Manitoba 179/G5
McMurdo (sound), Ant. 2/A10
McMurdo (sound) 5/B9
McMurdo, Br. Col. 184/J4
McMurray, Wash. 310/C2
McNab, Alberta 182/D5
McNab, Ark. 202/C6
McNabb, Ill. 222/D2
McNair, Texas 303/K1
McNairy (co.), Tenn. 237/D10
McNairy, Tenn. 237/D10
McNamee, New Bruns. 170/D2
McNary, Ariz. 198/F5
McNary, La. 238/E5
McNary, Oreg. 291/H2
McNary (dam), Oreg. 291/H2
McNary, Texas 303/B11
McNary (dam), Wash. 310/F5
McNaughton, Wis. 317/H4
McNeal, Ariz. 198/F7
McNeil, Ark. 202/D7
McNeill, Miss. 256/E9
McNulty, Oreg. 291/E2
McNutt (isl.), Nova Scotia 168/C5
McPhadyen (riv.), Newf. 166/A3
McPhall (riv.), Manitoba 179/F2
McPherson (co.), Kansas 232/E3
McPherson, Kansas 232/E3
McPherson (co.), Nebr. 264/C3
McPherson (range), N.S. Wales 97/G1
McPherson (co.), S. Dak. 298/L2
McQuady, Ky. 237/H5
McRae, Alberta 182/E2
McRae, Ark. 202/G3
McRae, Georgia 217/G6
McShan, Ala. 195/B8
McSherrystown, Pa. 294/H6
McTaggart, Sask. 181/H6
McTavish, Manitoba 179/E5
McTavish Arm (inlet), N.W. Terr. 187/F3
McVeigh, Ky. 237/S5
McVeytown, Pa. 294/G4
McVicar Arm (inlet), N.W. Terr. 187/F3
McVille, N. Dak 282/O4
McWhorter, W. Va. 312/F4
McWilliams, Ala. 195/D7
Meacham (lake), N.Y. 276/M1
Meacham, Oreg. 291/J2
Meacham, Sask. 181/F3
Mead (lake) 188/D3
Mead (lake), Ariz. 198/A2
Mead, Colo. 208/K2
Mead, Nebr. 264/H3
Mead (lake), Nev. 266/G6
Mead, Okla. 288/O7
Mead (lake), U.S. 146/G6
Mead, Wash. 310/H3
Meade (riv.), Alaska 196/G1
Meade (peak), Idaho 220/G7
Meade (co.), Kansas 232/B4
Meade, Kansas 232/B4
Meade (co.), Ky. 237/J5
Meade (co.), S. Dak. 298/D5
Meador, W. Va. 312/D8
Meadow (creek), Idaho 220/C4
Meadow (mt.), Md. 245/B2
Meadow (lake), Sask. 181/C1
Meadow, S. Dak. 298/E4
Meadow, Texas 303/B4
Meadow, Utah 304/B5
Meadow (riv.), W. Va. 312/E6
Meadow Bluff, W. Va. 312/E7
Meadow Bridge, W. Va. 312/E7
Meadowbrook, W. Va. 312/B2
Meadowbrook, W. Va. 312/F4
Meadow Creek, W. Va. 312/E7
Meadow Grove, Nebr. 264/G2
Meadow Lake, Sask. 181/C1
Meadow Lake Prov. Park, Sask. 181/K4
Meadowlands, Minn. 255/F3
Meadow Lands, Pa. 294/B5
Meadow Portage, Manitoba 179/C3
Meadows, Idaho 220/B5
Meadows, Ill. 222/E3
Meadows, Md. 245/G5
Meadows, N.H. 268/E3
Meadows, S. Australia 94/B8
Meadows of Dan, Va. 307/H7
Meadow Vale, Ky. 237/L1

Meadow Valley, Calif. 204/D4
Meadow Valley Wash (riv.), Nev. 266/G5
Meadowview-Emory, Va. 307/D7
Meadow Vista, N. Mex. 274/C7
Meadville, Miss. 256/C8
Meadville, Mo. 261/F3
Meadville, Pa. 188/L2
Meadville, Pa. 294/B2
Meaford, Ontario 177/D3
Meagher (co.), Mont. 262/F4
Meaghers Grant, Nova Scotia 168/E4
Meakan (mt.), Japan 81/L2
Mealhada, Portugal 33/B2
Mcally, Ky. 237/R5
Mealy (lake), Newf. 166/C3
Meander, Tasmania 99/C3
Meander River, Alberta 182/A5
Meanook, Alberta 182/D3
Means, Ky. 237/O5
Meansville, Georgia 217/D4
Meares (cape), Oreg. 291/C2
Mearim (riv.), Brazil 132/E4
Mearns, Alberta 182/D3
Mears, Mich. 250/C5
Meath (co.), Ireland 17/H4
Meathas Truim, Ireland 17/G4
Meath Park, Sask. 181/F2
Meaux, France 28/E3
Mebane, N.C. 281/L2
Mecca, Calif. 204/K10
Mecca, Ind. 227/C5
Mecca, Saudi Arabia 2/M4
Mecca, Saudi Arabia 59/C5
Mecca, Saudi Arabia 54/F7
Mechanic Falls, Maine 243/C7
Mechanic Falls•, Maine 243/C7
Mechanicsburg, Ill. 222/D4
Mechanicsburg, Ind. 227/G5
Mechanicsburg, Ohio 284/D5
Mechanicsburg, Pa. 294/H5
Mechanicsburg, Va. 307/G6
Mechanicstown, Ohio 284/H4
Mechanicsville, Conn. 210/H1
Mechanicsville, Georgia 217/L1
Mechanicsville, Iowa 229/L5
Mechanicsville, Md. 245/M7
Mechanicsville, Va. 307/O5
Mechanicville, N.Y. 276/N5
Mechelen, Belgium 27/F6
Mecheria, Algeria 106/D2
Mechernich, Germany 22/B3
Mecidiye, Turkey 63/B5
Mecitözü, Turkey 63/F2
Mecklenburg (bay), Germany 22/D1
Mecklenburg, N.Y. 276/G6
Mecklenburg (co.), N.C. 281/H4
Mecklenburg (co.), Va. 307/M7
Mecklenburg-West Pomerania (state), Germany 22/E2
Meckling, S. Dak. 298/R8
Meconta, Mozambique 118/F3
Mecosta (co.), Mich. 250/D5
Mecosta, Mich. 250/D5
Mecoya, Bolivia 136/C8
Mecsek (mts.), Hungary 41/D3
Mecúfi, Mozambique 118/G2
Mecula, Mozambique 118/G2
Medain Salih, Saudi Arabia 59/C4
Medan, Indonesia 54/L9
Medan, Indonesia 85/B5
Médanos, Buenos Aires, Argentina 143/D4
Médanos, Entre Ríos, Argentina 143/G6
Médanos (isth.), Venezuela 124/D2
Medanosa (pt.), Argentina 143/D6
Medaryville, Ind. 227/D2
Meddybemps•, Maine 243/J5
Meddybemps (lake), Maine 243/J5
Médéa, Algeria 106/E1
Medel (mt.), Switzerland 39/D2
Medellín, Colombia 120/B2
Medellín, Colombia 126/C4
Medellín de Bravo, Mexico 150/Q2
Medemblik, Netherlands 27/G3
Médenine, Tunisia 106/C2
Méderdra, Mauritania 106/A5
Mederville, Iowa 229/K3
Medetsiz Tepe (mt.), Turkey 63/F4
Medfield, Mass. 249/B8
Medfield•, Mass. 249/B8
Medford, Maine 243/F5
Medford•, Maine 243/F5
Medford, Mass. 249/C6
Medford, Minn. 255/E6
Medford, N.J. 273/D4
Medford, Okla. 288/L1
Medford, Oreg. 188/D2
Medford, Oreg. 146/D2
Medford, Oreg. 291/E5
Medford, Wis. 317/F5
Medford Center, Maine 243/F5
Medford Lakes, N.J. 273/D4
Medgidia, Romania 45/J3
Medgun (creek), N.S. Wales 97/E1
Medhishar, Iran 66/H3
Media, Ill. 222/C3
Media, Pa. 294/L7
Media Agua, Argentina 143/C3
Media Luna, Cuba 158/G4
Mediapolis, Iowa 229/L6
Medias, Romania 45/G2
Medical Lake, Wash. 310/H3
Medical Springs, Oreg. 291/K2
Medicine (lake), Mont. 262/M2
Medicine (creek), Nebr. 264/D4
Medicine (creek), S. Dak. 298/J6
Medicine Bow (range), Colo. 208/G1
Medicine Bow, Wyo. 319/F4
Medicine Bow (range), Wyo. 319/F4
Medicine Bow (riv.), Wyo. 319/F3

Medicine Creek (dam), Nebr. 264/D4
Medicine Hat, Alberta 182/E4
Medicine Hat, Alta. 146/H4
Medicine Hat, Alta. 162/E5
Medicine Knoll (creek), S. Dak. 298/J5
Medicine Lake, Minn. 255/F5
Medicine Lake, Mont. 262/M2
Medicine Lodge (creek), Idaho 220/F5
Medicine Lodge, Kansas 232/D4
Medicine Lodge (riv.), Kansas 232/D4
Medicine Mound, Texas 303/E3
Medicine Park, Okla. 288/J5
Medill, Mo. 261/J2
Medina, Colombia 126/D5
Medina (Hamel), Minn. 255/F5
Medina, N. Dak. 282/M6
Medina (co.), Ohio 284/G3
Medina, Ohio 284/G3
Medina, Saudi Arabia 54/F7
Medina, Saudi Arabia 59/D5
Medina, Tenn. 237/D9
Medina (co.), Texas 303/E8
Medina, Texas 303/E8
Medina (lake), Texas 303/E8
Medina (riv.), Texas 303/J11
Medina, Wash. 340/B2
Medinaceli, Spain 33/E2
Medina del Campo, Spain 33/D2
Medina de Rioseco, Spain 33/D2
Medina-Sidonia, Spain 33/D4
Mediodía, Colombia 126/D8
Mediterranean (sea) 2/K4
Mediterranean (sea) 7/E5
Mediterranean (sea), Algeria 106/E1
Mediterranean (sea), Egypt 111/E1
Mediterranean (sea), France 28/E7
Mediterranean (sea), Italy 34/B6
Mediterranean (sea), Libya 111/C1
Mediterranean (sea), Morocco 106/D1
Mediterranean (sea), Tunisia 106/F1
Medix Run, Pa. 294/F3
Medjerda (riv.), Algeria 106/F1
Medjerda (riv.), Tunisia 106/F1
Medley, Fla. 212/B4
Medley, W. Va. 312/H4
Mednogorsk, U.S.S.R. 52/J4
Mednogorsk, U.S.S.R. 48/F4
Médoc (reg.), France 28/C5
Mêdog, China 77/E6
Medon, Tenn. 237/D10
Medora, Ill. 222/C4
Medora, Ind. 227/E7
Medora, Kansas 232/E3
Medora, Manitoba 179/B5
Medora, N. Dak. 282/C6
Médouneu, Gabon 115/B3
Medstead, Sask. 181/C2
Meductic, New Bruns. 170/C3
Medveditsa (riv.), U.S.S.R. 52/J4
Medvezh'yegorsk, U.S.S.R. 48/F3
Medvezh'yegorsk, U.S.S.R. 52/D2
Medway•, Maine 243/G4
Medway•, Mass. 249/J4
Medway (harb.), Nova Scotia 168/D4
Medway (riv.), Nova Scotia 168/C4
Medzilaborce, Czech. 41/F2
Meeandah, Queensland 88/K2
Meehan, Miss. 256/G6
Meekatharra, Australia 87/B8
Meekatharra, W. Australia 88/B5
Meekatharra, W. Australia 92/B4
Meeker, Colo. 208/D2
Meeker, La. 238/F4
Meeker (co.), Minn. 255/D5
Meeker, Ohio 284/D4
Meeker, Okla. 288/N4
Meeks, Georgia 217/G5
Meeks Bay, Calif. 204/E5
Meelpaeg (lake), Newf. 166/C4
Meerane, Germany 22/E3
Meersburg, Germany 22/C5
Meerssen, Netherlands 27/H7
Meerut, India 54/J7
Meerut, India 68/D3
Meeteetse, Wyo. 319/D1
Meeting (lake), Sask. 181/D2
Meeting Creek, Alberta 182/D3
Mega, Ethiopia 111/G7
Mega (isl.), Indonesia 85/C6
Megalópolis, Greece 45/E7
Mégantic (co.), Québec 172/F3
Mégantic (lake), Québec 172/G4
Mégara, Greece 45/F6
Megargel, Ala. 195/D8
Megargel, Texas 303/E3
Meggett, S.C. 296/G6
Meghalaya (state), India 68/G3
Megiddo, Israel 65/C2
Mehama, Oreg. 291/E3
Mehan, Okla. 288/M2
Meherrin (riv.), N.C. 281/P1
Meherrin, Va. 307/M6
Meherrin (riv.), Va. 307/M7
Mehetia (isl.), Fr. Poly. 87/M7
Mehlville, Mo. 261/P4
Mehoopany, Pa. 294/K2
Mehran, Iran 66/E4
Mehran (riv.), Iran 59/F4
Mehran (riv.), Iran 66/J7
Mehsana, India 68/C4
Mehun-sur-Yèvre, France 28/E4
Meifa, Yemen 59/E7
Meiganga, Cameroon 115/B2
Meighen, U.S.S.R. 45/J3
Meighen (isl.), N.W.T. 162/M3
Meighen (isl.), N.W.T. 187/H1

Meigle, Scotland 15/E4
Meigs, Georgia 217/D8
Meigs (co.), Ohio 284/F7
Meigs (co.), Tenn. 237/M9
Meikle (riv.), Alberta 182/A1
Meiktila, Burma 72/B2
Meilen, Switzerland 39/G2
Meiners Oaks-Mira Monte, Calif. 204/F9
Meiningen, Germany 22/D3
Meire Grove, Minn. 255/C5
Meiringen, Switzerland 39/F3
Meiron (mt.), Israel 65/C1
Meise, Belgium 27/E7
Meissen, Germany 22/E3
Mei Xian, China 77/J7
Mejillones, Chile 120/B5
Mejillones, Chile 138/A4
Mejillones del Sur (bay), Chile 138/A4
Mekambo, Gabon 115/B3
Mekerrhane, Sebkha (salt lake), Algeria 106/E3
Mekili, Libya 111/D1
Mékinac (lake), Québec 172/E2
Mekinock, N. Dak. 282/R4
Meknès, Morocco 102/B1
Meknès, Morocco 106/C2
Mekong (riv.) 2/Q4
Mekong (riv.), Asia 54/M8
Mekong (riv.), Burma 72/D2
Mekong (riv.), Cambodia 72/E4
Mekong (Lancang Jiang) (riv.), China 77/F7
Mekong (riv.), Laos 72/D3
Mekong (riv.), Thailand 72/E3
Mekong, Mouths of the (delta), Vietnam 72/E5
Mekoryuk, Alaska 196/E2
Melaka (state), Malaysia 72/D7
Melaka, Malaysia 54/M9
Melaka, Malaysia 72/D7
Melanesia (reg.), Pacific 87/E5
Melaval, Sask. 181/E6
Melba, Idaho 220/B6
Melber, Ky. 237/N3
Melbern, Ohio 284/A3
Melbeta, Nebr. 264/A3
Melbourne, Ark. 202/G1
Melbourne, Australia 2/R7
Melbourne, Australia 87/E9
Melbourne, Fla. 188/F5
Melbourne, Fla. 212/F3
Melbourne, Iowa 229/G5
Melbourne, Ky. 237/T2
Melbourne, Mo. 261/E2
Melbourne (isl.), N.W. Terr. 187/H3
Melbourne, Ontario 177/C5
Melbourne, Québec 172/F3
Melbourne (cap.), Victoria 88/H7
Melbourne (cap.), Victoria 97/H5
Melbourne, Wash. 310/B4
Melbourne Airport, Victoria 88/K7
Melbourne Beach, Fla. 212/F3
Melby, Minn. 255/C4
Melcher, Honduras 154/D3
Melcher, Iowa 229/G6
Melchor (isl.), Chile 138/D6
Melchor Múzquiz, Mexico 150/H3
Melchor Ocampo, Mexico 150/H4
Melchor Ocampo del Balsas, Mexico 150/H8
Melder, La. 238/E4
Meldorf, Germany 22/C1
Meldrim, Georgia 217/K6
Meldrum Bay, Ontario 177/A2
Meldrum Creek, Br. Col. 184/F4
Meleb, Manitoba 179/E4
Melenki, U.S.S.R. 52/F3
Meleuz, U.S.S.R. 52/J4
Mélèzes (riv.), Québec 174/C1
Melfa, Va. 307/S5
Melfi, Chad 111/C5
Melfi, Italy 34/E4
Melfort, Sask. 162/F5
Melfort, Sask. 181/G3
Melfort, Loch (inlet), Scotland 15/C4
Melgaço, Portugal 33/B1
Melgar de Fernamental, Spain 33/D1
Melide, Switzerland 39/G5
Meligalá, Greece 45/F7
Melilla, Spain 106/D1
Melilla, Spain 106/B1
Melilla, Spain 7/D5
Melimoyu (mt.), Chile 138/D5
Melinca, Chile 138/D5
Melincué, Argentina 143/F6
Melipilla, Chile 138/F4
Melita, Manitoba 179/A5
Melitopol', U.S.S.R. 37/H4
Melitopol', U.S.S.R. 52/D5
Melitota, Md. 245/O4
Melk, Austria 41/C2
Melkbosstrand, S. Africa 118/B6
Melksham, England 13/E6
Melksham, England 10/E5
Mellansel, Sweden 18/L5
Melle, Germany 22/C2
Mellen, Wis. 317/E3
Mellerud, Sweden 18/H7
Mellette (co.), S. Dak. 298/H6
Mellette, S. Dak. 298/N3
Mellingen, Switzerland 39/F2
Mellott, Ind. 227/C4
Mellwood, Ark. 202/H5
Melmore, Ohio 284/D4
Melo, Uruguay 120/D6
Melo, Uruguay 145/G3
Melocheville, Québec 172/C4
Melozitna (riv.), Alaska 196/H1
Melrhir, Chott (salt lake), Algeria 106/F2

Melrose, Conn. 210/E1
Melrose, Fla. 212/D2
Melrose, Iowa 229/G7
Melrose, La. 238/E3
Melrose, Md. 245/L2
Melrose, Mass. 249/D6
Melrose, Minn. 255/D5
Melrose, Mont. 262/D5
Melrose, New Bruns. 170/F2
Melrose, Newf. 166/D2
Melrose, N. Mex. 274/F4
Melrose, Ohio 284/B3
Melrose, Oreg. 291/D4
Melrose, Scotland 15/F5
Melrose, Scotland 10/E3
Melrose, Wis. 317/E7
Melrose Park, Fla. 212/B4
Melrose Park, Ill. 222/B5
Melrose Park, N.Y. 276/G5
Melrude, Minn. 255/F3
Mels, Switzerland 39/H2
Melstone, Mont. 262/H4
Melsungen, Germany 22/C3
Melton, Victoria 97/C5
Melton Hill (lake), Tenn. 237/N9
Melton Mowbray, England 10/F4
Melton Mowbray, England 13/G5
Meltonville, Iowa 229/G2
Melun, France 28/E3
Melut, Sudan 111/F5
Melvaig, Scotland 15/C3
Melvern, Kansas 232/G3
Melvern (lake), Kansas 232/G3
Melvern Square, Nova Scotia 168/C3
Melvich, Scotland 15/E2
Melville (isl.), Australia 87/D7
Melville (isl.), Canada 4/B15
Melville (pen.), Canada 4/C14
Melville (bay), Greenl. 4/B13
Melville, La. 238/G5
Melville, Mont. 262/F4
Melville (lake), Newf. 166/C3
Melville, N.Y. 276/O9
Melville, N. Dak. 282/M5
Melville (bay), North. Terr. 88/F2
Melville (bay), North. Terr. 93/E2
Melville (isl.), North. Terr. 88/E2
Melville (isl.), North. Terr. 93/B1
Melville (isl.), N.W.T. 146/G2
Melville (isl.), N.W.T. 162/E1
Melville (isl.), N.W.T. 187/G2
Melville (lake), N.W.T. 162/L5
Melville (pen.), N.W.T. 146/K3
Melville (pen.), N.W.T. 162/H2
Melville (pen.), N.W.T. 187/K3
Melville (isl.), N.W. Terr. 187/H3
Melville (cape), Queensland 88/G2
Melville (cape), Queensland 95/C2
Melville, Sask. 162/F5
Melville, Sask. 181/J5
Melville, W. Australia 92/A1
Melvin, Ala. 195/B7
Melvin, Ill. 222/E3
Melvin, Iowa 229/B2
Melvin, Lough (lake), Ireland 10/B3
Melvin (lake), Ireland 17/E3
Melvin, Mich. 250/G5
Melvin, Minn. 255/B3
Melvin, Lough (lake), N. Ireland 10/B3
Melvin, Texas 303/E6
Melvina, Wis. 317/E6
Melvindale, Mich. 250/B7
Melvin Mills, N.H. 268/D5
Melvin Village, N.H. 268/E4
Mélykút, Hungary 41/E3
Memaliaj, Albania 45/D5
Memba, Mozambique 118/G2
Membij, Syria 63/G4
Memel (Klaipeda), U.S.S.R. 52/B3
Memel (Klaipeda), U.S.S.R. 53/A3
Memmingen, Germany 22/D5
Mempawah, Indonesia 85/D5
Memphis (ruins), Egypt 111/J3
Memphis, Fla. 212/D4
Memphis, Ind. 227/F8
Memphis, Mich. 250/G6
Memphis, Miss. 256/D1
Memphis, Mo. 261/H2
Memphis, Nebr. 264/H3
Memphis, Tenn. 146/K6
Memphis, Tenn. 188/D3
Memphis, Tenn. 237/B10
Memphis, Texas 303/D3
Memphis Naval Air Sta., Tenn. 237/B10
Memphrémagog (lake), Québec 172/F4
Memphremagog (lake), Vt. 268/C1
Memramcook, New Bruns. 170/F2
Mena, Ark. 202/B4
Menafra, Uruguay 145/B3
Menahga, Minn. 255/C3
Menai (str.), Wales 13/C4
Menaik, Alberta 182/D3
Menan, Idaho 220/F6
Menands, N.Y. 276/N5
Menaranda (riv.), Madagascar 118/H4
Menard (co.), Ill. 222/D3
Menard (co.), Texas 303/E7
Menard, Texas 303/E7
Menasalbas, Spain 33/D3
Menasha, Wis. 317/J7
Mencué, Argentina 143/C5
Mendak, Saudi Arabia 59/D5
Mende, France 28/E5
Mendenhall (cape), Alaska 196/E3

Mendenhall, Miss. 256/E7
Menderes, Büyük (riv.), Turkey 59/A2
Menderes, Büyük (riv.), Turkey 63/C4
Mendes, Georgia 217/H7
Méndez, Ecuador 128/C4
Mendham, N.J. 273/D2
Mendham, Sask. 181/B5
Mendi, Ethiopia 111/G6
Mendi, Papua N.G. 85/B7
Mendip (hills), England 13/E6
Mendocino (cape), Calif. 146/F5
Mendocino (cape), Calif. 188/A2
Mendocino (co.), Calif. 204/B4
Mendocino (co.), Calif. 204/A3
Mendocino, Calif. 204/B4
Mendon•, Mass. 249/H4
Mendon, Mich. 250/D7
Mendon, Mo. 261/F3
Mendon, N.Y. 276/E4
Mendon, Ohio 284/A4
Mendon, Utah 304/B2
Mendon•, Vt. 268/B4
Mendooran, N.S. Wales 97/E2
Mendota, Calif. 204/E7
Mendota, Ill. 222/D2
Mendota, Minn. 255/G5
Mendota, Va. 307/D7
Mendota (lake), Wis. 317/H9
Mendota Heights, Minn. 255/G6
Mendoza (prov.), Argentina 143/C4
Mendoza (riv.), Argentina 143/C3
Mendoza, Argentina 120/C6
Mendoza, Argentina 143/C3
Mendoza, Cuba 158/A2
Mendoza, Peru 128/D6
Mendoza, Uruguay 145/C5
Mene de Mauroa, Venezuela 124/C2
Mene Grande, Venezuela 124/C3
Menemen, Turkey 63/B5
Menemsha, Mass. 249/L7
Menen, Belgium 27/C7
Meneses, Cuba 158/F2
Menfi, Italy 34/D6
Menfro, Mo. 261/N7
Mengcheng, China 77/J5
Mengen, Turkey 63/D2
Menggala, Indonesia 85/D6
Menghai, China 77/F7
Mengla, China 77/F7
Mengshan, China 77/H7
Mengzi, China 77/F7
Menifee, Ark. 202/E3
Menifee (co.), Ky. 237/O5
Menihek, Newf. 166/A3
Menihek (lake), Newf. 166/A3
Menin (Menen), Belgium 27/C7
Menindee, N.S. Wales 97/B3
Menindee (lake), N.S. Wales 97/B3
Meningle, S. Australia 94/B5
Menisino, Manitoba 179/F5
Menistouc (lake), Newf. 166/A3
Menlo, Georgia 217/B2
Menlo, Iowa 229/E5
Menlo, Kansas 232/B2
Menlo, Wash. 310/B4
Menlo Park, Calif. 204/J3
Menlo Park, N.J. 273/E2
Menneval, New Bruns. 170/C1
Menno, S. Dak. 298/P7
Meno, Okla. 288/K2
Menoken, N. Dak. 282/J6
Menominee, Ill. 222/C1
Menominee (co.), Mich. 250/B3
Menominee, Mich. 250/B3
Menominee (riv.), Mich. 250/B3
Menominee (riv.), Wis. 317/J5
Menominee (riv.), Wis. 317/L5
Menominee Ind. Res., Wis. 317/J5
Menomonee Falls, Wis. 317/K1
Menomonie, Wis. 317/C6
Menongue, Angola 102/D6
Menongue, Angola 115/C6
Menorca (Minorca) (isl.), Spain 33/J2
Mentasta (pass), Alaska 196/K2
Mentasta Lake, Alaska 196/K2
Mentawai (isls.), Indonesia 54/L10
Mentawai (isls.), Indonesia 85/B6
Mentmore, N. Mex. 274/A3
Menton, France 28/G6
Mentone, Ala. 195/G1
Mentone, Calif. 204/H9
Mentone, Ind. 227/E2
Mentone, Texas 303/D10
Mentor, Kansas 232/E3
Mentor, Ky. 237/N3
Mentor, Minn. 255/B3
Mentor, Ohio 284/H2
Mentor-on-the-Lake, Ohio 284/G2
Menunketesuck (riv.), Conn. 210/E3
Menye, Turkey 63/C3
Menyuan, China 77/F4
Menzel Bourguiba, Tunisia 106/F1
Menzel Temime, Tunisia 106/G1
Menzie, Manitoba 179/B4
Menzies, W. Australia 88/C5
Menzies, W. Australia 92/C5
Menzingen, Switzerland 39/G2
Menznau, Switzerland 39/F2
Meoquí, Mexico 150/G2
Meota, Sask. 181/C2
Meppel, Netherlands 27/J3

Meppen, Germany 22/B2
Mequineza (res.), Spain 33/F2
Mequon, Wis. 317/L1
Mera, Ecuador 128/C3
Mera (riv.), Switzerland 39/E2
Merabéllou (gulf), Greece 45/H8
Meraia (reg.), Mauritania 106/C5
Meråker, Norway 18/G5
Meramangye (lake), S. Australia 94/C3
Meramec (riv.), Mo. 261/N3
Merano, Italy 34/C1
Merasheen (isl.), Newf. 166/C2
Merauke, Indonesia 85/K7
Merbein, Victoria 97/A4
Mercaderes, Colombia 126/B7
Mercara, India 68/D6
Merced (co.), Calif. 204/E6
Merced, Calif. 204/E6
Merced, Calif. 204/E6
Merced (riv.), Calif. 204/E6
Mercedario, Cerro (mt.), Argentina 143/B3
Mercedes, Buenos Aires, Argentina 143/G7
Mercedes, San Luis, Argentina 143/C3
Mercedes, Argentina 120/C6
Mercedes, Corrientes, Argentina 143/G4
Mercedes, Texas 303/F12
Mercedes, Uruguay 120/D6
Mercedes, Uruguay 145/B4
Merceditas, Chile 138/B7
Mercer (co.), Ill. 222/C2
Mercer (co.), Ky. 237/M5
Mercer•, Maine 243/D6
Mercer (co.), Mo. 261/E2
Mercer, Mo. 261/F2
Mercer (co.), N.J. 273/D3
Mercer, N. Zealand 100/E2
Mercer (co.), N. Dak. 282/G5
Mercer, N. Dak. 282/J5
Mercer (co.), Ohio 284/A4
Mercer, Ohio 284/A4
M... er (co.), Pa. 294/B3
Mercer, Pa. 294/B3
Mercer, Tenn. 237/D10
Mercer (co.), W. Va. 312/D6
Mercer, Wis. 317/F3
Mercer Island (city), Wash. 310/B2
Mercersburg, Pa. 294/G6
Mercerville-Hamilton Square, N.J. 273/D3
Merchantville, N.J. 273/E3
Merchtem, Belgium 27/E7
Mercier, Bolivia 136/B2
Mercier, Kansas 232/G2
Mercier, Québec 172/H4
Mercier (dam), Québec 172/A3
Mercoal, Alberta 182/B3
Mercury, Nev. 266/E6
Mercury (bay), N. Zealand 100/F2
Mercury (isls.), N. Zealand 100/F2
Mercury, Texas 303/E6
Mercy (bay), N.W. Terr. 187/G2
Mercy (cape), N.W. Terr. 187/M3
Mere, England 13/E6
Meredith, Colo. 208/F4
Meredith, N.H. 268/D4
Meredith• N.H. 268/D4
Meredith Center, N.H. 268/D4
Meredosia, Ill. 222/C4
Merefa, U.S.S.R. 52/E5
Meregh, Somalia 115/J3
Merelbeke, Belgium 27/D7
Merevari (riv.), Venezuela 124/F5
Mergui, Burma 54/L8
Mergui, Burma 72/C4
Mergui (arch.), Burma 72/C5
Meriç, Turkey 63/B2
Meriç, Turkey 63/B2
Merid, Sask. 181/B4
Mérida, Mexico 146/J7
Mérida, Mexico 150/P6
Mérida, Spain 7/D5
Mérida, Spain 33/C3
Mérida (state), Venezuela 124/C3
Mérida, Venezuela 120/B2
Mérida, Venezuela 124/C3
Mérida, Cordillera de (range), Venezuela 124/C3
Meriden, Conn. 210/D2
Meriden, Iowa 229/B3
Meriden, Kansas 232/G2
Meriden, Minn. 255/E6
Meriden, N.H. 268/C4
Meriden, Wyo. 319/H4
Meridian, Georgia 217/K8
Meridian, Idaho 220/B6
Meridian, Miss. 146/K6
Meridian, Miss. 188/J4
Meridian, Miss. 256/G6
Meridian, N.Y. 276/G4
Meridian, Okla. 288/M3
Meridian, Texas 303/G6
Meridian Naval Air Sta., Miss. 256/G5
Meridianville, Ala. 195/F1
Merigold, Miss. 256/C3
Merigomish, Nova Scotia 168/F3
Merigomish (harb.), Nova Scotia 168/F3
Merimbula, N.S. Wales 97/F5
Mérín (lag.), Uruguay 145/F4
Merino, Colo. 208/M2
Merino, Victoria 97/A5
Merino Jarpa (isl.), Chile 138/D7
Merinos, Uruguay 145/C3
Merino Village, Mass. 249/G4

Merion Station, Pa. 294/M6
Merir (isl.), Belau 87/D5
Meriwether (co.), Georgia 217/C4
Meriwether Lewis Park, Natchez
  Trace Pkwy., Tenn. 237/G10
Merj 'Uyun, Lebanon 63/F6
Merk, Hungary 41/G3
Merkel, Texas 303/E5
Merksem, Belgium 27/E6
Merksplas, Belgium 27/F6
Merlin, Ontario 177/B5
Merlin, Oreg. 291/D5
Merlo, Argentina 143/G7
Mermentau, La. 238/E6
Mermentau (riv.), La. 238/E7
Merna, Nebr. 264/E3
Merna, Wyo. 319/B3
Meroe (ruins), Sudan 111/F4
Merom, Ind. 227/B6
Merowe, Sudan 111/F4
Merowe, Sudan 59/B6
Merredin, W. Australia 88/B6
Merredin, W. Australia 92/B5
Merri (riv.), Victoria 88/L7
Merriam, Ind. 227/E2
Merriam, Kansas 232/H3
Merrick, N. Dak. 282/N7
Merrick (co.), Nebr. 264/F3
Merrick, N.Y. 276/R7
Merrick (mt.), Scotland 15/D5
Merrickville, Ontario 177/J3
Merricourt, N. Dak. 282/N7
Merrifield, Minn. 255/D4
Merrifield (bay), Newf. 166/B2
Merrifield, N. Dak. 282/N4
Merrifield, Va. 307/S3
Merrill (pass), Alaska 196/H2
Merrill, Iowa 229/A3
Merrill, Mich. 250/E5
Merrill, Miss. 256/G9
Merrill, N.Y. 276/N1
Merrill, Oreg. 291/F5
Merrill, Wis. 317/G5
Merrillan, Wis. 317/E7
Merrillville, Georgia 217/E9
Merrillville•, Ind. 227/C2
Merrimac, Ky. 237/K6
Merrimac•, Mass. 249/L1
Merrimac, W. Va. 312/B7
Merrimac, Wis. 317/G9
Merrimack (riv.), Mass. 249/K1
Merrimack (co.), N.H. 268/D5
Merrimack•, N.H. 268/D5
Merrimack (riv.), N.H. 268/D5
Merrimacport, Mass. 249/L1
Merriman, Nebr. 264/C2
Merrimon, N.C. 281/R5
Merrionette Park, Ill. 222/B6
Merritt, Br. Col. 162/D5
Merritt, Br. Col. 184/G5
Merritt (isl.), Fla. 212/F3
Merritt, Ill. 222/C4
Merritt, Mich. 250/D4
Merritt (res.), Nebr. 264/D2
Merritt, Wash. 310/E3
Merritt Island, Fla. 212/F3
Merriwa, N.S. Wales 97/F3
Merriwagga, N.S. Wales 97/C3
Merriweather, Mich. 250/F1
Mer Rouge, La. 238/G1
Merrow, Conn. 210/F1
Merry Hill, N.C. 281/R2
Merrymeeting (lake), N.H.
  268/E5
Merry Oaks, N.C. 281/L3
Merryville, La. 238/D5
Mersa Fatma, Ethiopia 111/H5
Mersá Matrûh, Egypt 111/E1
Mersá Matrûh, Egypt 102/E1
Mersch, Luxembourg 27/J9
Mersea (dist.), England 13/J6
Merseburg, Germany 22/D3
Mersey (riv.), England 10/F2
Mersey (riv.), England 13/G2
Mersey (riv.), Nova Scotia
  168/C4
Mersey (riv.), Tasmania 99/C3
Merseyside (co.), England 13/G2
Mershon, Georgia 217/H8
Mersin, Turkey 63/E4
Mersin, Turkey 59/D6
Mersin, Turkey 54/E6
Mersing, Malaysia 72/E7
Mersrags, U.S.S.R. 53/B2
Mertert, Luxembourg 27/J9
Merthyr Tydfil, Wales 13/A6
Merthyr Tydfil, Wales 10/E5
Mertola, Portugal 33/C4
Merton, England 10/B5
Merton, England 13/H8
Merton, Wis. 317/K1
Mertz Glacier Tongue, Ant.
  5/C8
Mertzon, Texas 303/C6
Mertztown, Pa. 294/L4
Meru, Kenya 115/G3
Meru (mt.), Tanzania 115/G4
Merv (Mary), U.S.S.R. 48/F8
Merville, Br. Col 184/E5
Mervin, Sask. 181/D3
Mervin, Mo. 261/C6
Merwin (lake), Wash. 310/C5
Merzifon, Turkey 63/F2
Merzig, Germany 22/B4
Mesa, Ariz. 146/G6
Mesa, Ariz. 198/D5
Mesa (co.), Colo. 208/B5
Mesa, Colo. 208/C4
Mesa, Idaho 220/B5
Mesa, Miss. 256/D8
Mesa, Wash. 310/E4
Mesabi (range), Minn. 255/E3
Mesachie Lake, Br. Col. 184/J3
Mesa del Seri, Mexico 150/D2
Mesagne, Italy 34/G4
Mesay (riv.), Colombia 126/D7
Mesará (gulf), Greece 45/G8

Mesa Verde National Park, Colo.
  208/C8
Mesa Verde Nat'l Park, Colo. 208/C8
Mescalero, N. Mex. 274/D5
Mescalero (ridge), N. Mex. 274/F6
Mescalero (valley), N. Mex. 274/F5
Mescalero Apache Ind. Res.,
  N. Mex. 274/D5
Meschede, Germany 22/C3
Mesena, Georgia 217/G4
Meservey, Iowa 229/G3
Meshed, Iran 54/G6
Meshed, Iran 66/L2
Meshed, Iran 59/H2
Meshed-i-Sar (Babol Sar), Iran
  66/H2
Meshik, Alaska 196/G3
Meshoppen, Pa. 294/L2
Meshra er Req, Sudan 111/E6
Mesic, N.C. 281/R4
Mesick, Mich. 250/D4
Mesilla, N. Mex. 274/C6
Mesilla Park, N. Mex. 274/C6
Mesita, Colo. 208/H8
Meskanaw, Sask. 181/F3
Meskene, Syria 59/C2
Meskene, Syria 63/H5
Mesocco, Switzerland 39/H4
Mesolóngion, Greece 45/E6
Mesopotamia (reg.), Iraq 66/B3
Mesopotamia (reg.), Iraq 59/D3
Mesopotamia, Ohio 284/J3
Mesquite (bay), Newf. 166/B2
Mesquite, Nev. 266/G6
Mesquite, N. Mex. 274/C6
Mesquite, Texas 303/H2
Messancy, Belgium 27/H9
Messina (prov.), Italy 34/E5
Messina, Italy 34/E5
Messina, Italy 7/F5
Messina (str.), Italy 34/E6
Messina, S. Africa 118/D4
Messines, Québec 172/B3
Messíni, Greece 45/E7
Messíni (gulf), Greece 45/E7
Mesta (riv.), Bulgaria 45/F5
Mestre, Italy 34/D2
Mesudiye, Turkey 63/F4
Meta (riv.) 120/B2
Meta (dept.), Colombia 126/D6
Meta (riv.), Colombia 126/D6
Meta, Ky. 237/S5
Meta, Mo. 261/H6
Meta (riv.), Venezuela 124/E4
Metabetchouan, Québec 172/F1
Métabetchouane (riv.), Québec
  172/F1
Metairie, La. 238/C4
Metaine, Wash. 310/H2
Metaline Falls, Wash. 310/H2
Metamma, Ethiopia 111/G5
Metamora, Ill. 222/D3
Metamora, Ind. 227/G6
Metamora, Mich. 250/F6
Metamora, Ohio 284/C2
Metán, Argentina 143/D2
Metangula, Mozambique
  118/F2
Metapán, El Salvador 154/C3
Métascouac (lake), Québec
  172/F2
Metasville, Georgia 217/G3
Metauro (riv.), Italy 34/D3
Metcalf, Georgia 217/E9
Metcalf, Ill. 222/F4
Metcalfe (co.), Ky. 237/K7
Metcalfe, Miss. 256/B4
Metcalfe, Ontario 177/J2
Metchin, Br. Col. 184/K4
Metchosin, Br. Col. 184/K4
Metea, Ind. 227/E3
Metedeconk (riv.), N.J. 273/E3
Meteghan, Nova Scotia 168/B4
Meteghan Centre, Nova Scotia
  168/B4
Meteghan River, Nova Scotia
  168/B4
Meteor (crater), Ariz. 198/E3
Metepec, Mexico 150/M2
Methlick, Scotland 15/F3
Methow, Wash. 310/E2
Methow (riv.), Wash. 310/E2
Methuen•, Mass. 249/K2
Methven, N. Zealand 100/C5
Methven, Scotland 15/E4
Metica (riv.), Colombia 126/D6
Metigoshe (lake), N. Dak.
  282/K2
Metinic (isl.), Maine 243/E8
Metinota, Sask. 181/C2
Metiskow, Alberta 182/E3
Métis-sur-Mer, Québec 172/A1
Metlakatla, Alaska 196/N2
Metlakatla, Br. Col. 184/B3
Metlatonoc, Mexico 150/K8
Metlili Chaamba, Algeria
  106/E2
Meto (bayou), Ark. 202/H5
Metolius, Oreg. 291/F3
Metolius (riv.), Oreg. 291/F3
Metompkin (inlet), Va. 307/T5
Metompkin (inlet), Va. 307/T5
Metonga (lake), Wis. 317/J4
Metropolis, Ill. 222/E6
Metropolitan, Mich. 250/A3
Métsovon, Greece 45/E6
Mettawa, Ill. 222/34
Mettawee (riv.), Vt. 268/A5
Metter, Georgia 217/H6
Mettet, Belgium 27/F8
Mettler, Calif. 204/G8
Metu, Ethiopia 111/G6
Metu, Ethiopia 115/G2
Metuchen, N.J. 273/E2
Metula, Israel 65/D1
Metz, France 7/E4
Metz, France 28/G3
Metz, Ind. 227/H1
Metz, Mo. 261/C6

Metz, W. Va. 312/F3
Metzger, Oreg. 291/A2
Metzingen, Germany 22/C4
Meudon, France 28/A2
Meulaboh, Indonesia 85/B5
Meulebeke, Belgium 27/C7
Meung-sur-Loire, France 28/D4
Meurthe-et-Moselle (dept.),
  France 28/G3
Meuse (riv.), Belgium 27/F8
Meuse (dept.), France 28/F3
Meuse (riv.), France 28/F3
Meuselwitz, Germany 22/E3
Mexia, Ala. 195/D8
Mexia, Texas 303/H6
Mexiana (isl.), Brazil 132/D2
Mexicali, Mexico 150/B1
Mexicali, Mexico 146/G6
Mexican Hat, Utah 304/E6
Mexican Springs, N. Mex.
  274/A3
Mexico 2/D4
Mexico 146/H7
MEXICO 150
Mexico (gulf) 188/J5
Mexico (gulf) 2/E4
Mexico (gulf) 146/K7
Mexico (gulf), Ala. 195/E10
Mexico (gulf), Cuba 158/A1
Mexico (gulf), Fla. 212/C4
Mexico, Ind. 227/E3
Mexico, Ky. 237/E6
Mexico (gulf), La. 238/F8
Mexico, Maine 243/B6
Mexico•, Maine 243/B6
México (state), Mexico 150/K7
Mexico (gulf), Mexico 150/N4
Mexico (gulf), N. Dak. 282/O3
Mexico, Mo. 261/J4
Mexico, N.Y. 276/H4
Mexico, Pa. 294/H4
Mexico (gulf), Texas 303/K9
Mexico Beach, Fla. 212/D6
Mexico City (cap.), Mexico 150/L1
Mexico City (cap.), Mexico 146/J7
Mexico City (cap.), Mexico 2/E5
Meyadin, Syria 59/C3
Meyadin, Syria 63/J5
Meybod, Iran 66/J4
Meydani, Ras-e (cape), Iran 59/G4
Meydani, Ras-e (cape), Iran 66/L8
Meyer, Iowa 229/H2
Meyers Chuck, Alaska 196/N2
Meyersdale, Pa. 294/E6
Meyers Lake, Ohio 284/H4
Meyerton, S. Africa 118/H7
Meymaneh, Afghanistan 68/A1
Meymaneh, Afghanistan 54/H6
Meymaneh, Afghanistan 59/H7
Meyrin, Switzerland 39/B4
Meyronne, Sask. 181/E6
Mezcala (riv.), Mexico 150/J8
Mezen', U.S.S.R. 4/C7
Mezen', U.S.S.R. 7/J2
Mezen', U.S.S.R. 48/E3
Mezen', U.S.S.R. 52/F1
Mezen' (bay), U.S.S.R. 52/F1
Mezen' (riv.), U.S.S.R. 48/E3
Mezen' (riv.), U.S.S.R. 52/G1
Mézenc (mt.), France 28/E5
Mezhdurechenskiy, U.S.S.R.
  48/G4
Mezhdusharskiy (isl.), U.S.S.R.
  52/G1
Meziadin (lake), Br. Col. 184/C2
Mézin, France 28/D5
Mezöberény, Hungary 41/F3
Mezöcsát, Hungary 41/F3
Mezöfalva, Hungary 41/E3
Mezöhegyes, Hungary 41/F3
Mezökovácsháza, Hungary 41/F3
Mezökövesd, Hungary 41/F3
Mezöszilas, Hungary 41/E3
Mezötúr, Hungary 41/F3
Mezquital, Mexico 150/G5
Mezquital (riv.), Mexico 150/G5
Mhor, Loch (lake), Scotland
  15/D3
Mhow, India 68/D4
Miacatlán, Mexico 150/K2
Miahuatlán de Porfirio Diaz, Mexico
  150/L8
Miajadas, Spain 33/D3
Miami, Ariz. 198/E5
Miami, Fla. 188/K5
Miami, Fla. 146/K7
Miami, Fla. 212/B5
Miami (canal), Fla. 212/F5
Miami (riv.), Fla. 212/B5
Miami (co.), Ind. 227/E3
Miami, Ind. 227/E3
Miami (co.), Kansas 232/H3
Miami, Manitoba 179/D5
Miami, Mo. 261/F4
Miami, N. Mex. 274/E2
Miami (co.), Ohio 284/B5
Miami, Okla. 288/S1
Miami, U.S. 2/F4
Miami Beach, Fla. 188/L5
Miami Beach, Fla. 212/C5
Miami Lakes, Fla. 212/B4
Miamisburg, Ohio 284/B6
Miami Shores, Fla. 212/B4
Miami Springs, Fla. 212/B5
Miamitown, Ohio 284/A9
Miamiville, Ohio 284/D9
Miandowab, Iran 66/E2
Miandrivazo, Madagascar
  118/G3
Mianeh, Iran 59/E2
Mianeh, Iran 66/F2
Mianus, Conn. 210/A4
Mianus (riv.), Conn. 210/A4
Mianwali, Pakistan 68/C2
Mianwali, Pakistan 59/K3
Mianyang, Hubei, China 77/H5
Mianyang, Sichuan, China
  77/G5

Mianzhu, China 77/F5
Miass, U.S.S.R. 48/G4
Miastko, Poland 47/C2
Miazal, Ecuador 128/D4
Mica (dam), Br. Col. 184/H4
Mica, Wash. 310/H3
Mica Creek, Br. Col. 184/H4
Micanopy, Fla. 212/D2
Micawber, Okla. 288/N3
Micay, Colombia 126/B6
Micco, Fla. 212/F4
Miccosukee, Fla. 212/B1
Miccosukee (lake), Fla. 212/B1
Michael, I. of Man 13/C3
Michael (lake), Newf. 166/C3
Michalovce, Czech. 41/G2
Michaud (pt.), Nova Scotia
  168/H3
Micheldean, N.S. Wales 97/E4
Michelson (mt.), Alaska 196/K1
Michelstadt, Germany 22/C4
Miches, Dom. Rep. 158/F6
Michiana, Mich. 250/C7
Michiana Shores, Ind. 227/D1
Michichi, Alberta 182/D4
Michie, Tenn. 237/E10
Michigamme, Mich. 250/B2
Michigamme (lake), Mich. 250/A2
Michigamme (res.), Mich. 250/B2
Michigamme (riv.), Mich. 250/A2
Michigan 188/J1
MICHIGAN 250/80
Michigan (lake) 188/J2
Michigan (lake), Ill. 222/F1
Michigan (lake), Ind. 227/C1
Michigan (lake), Mich. 250/B5
Michigan, N. Dak. 282/O3
Michigan (state), U.S. 146/K5
Michigan (state), U.S. 146/K5
Michigan (isl.), Wis. 317/F2
Michigan (lake), Wis. 317/M9
Michigan Bar, Calif. 204/C8
Michigan Center, Mich. 250/E6
Michigan City, Ind. 227/C1
Michigan City, Miss. 256/F1
Michigantown, Ind. 227/E4
Michigan Valley, Kansas
  232/G3
Michipicoten (isl.), Ontario 177/H5
Michipicoten (isl.), Ontario 175/C3
Michipicoten River, Ontario 177/H5
Michipicoten River, Ontario 177/C3
Michoacán (state), Mexico 150/H7
Michurin, Bulgaria 45/H4
Michurinsk, U.S.S.R. 52/F4
Michurinsk, U.S.S.R. 48/E4
Mickelton, N.J. 273/C4
Micotrin (mt.), Dominica 161/F6
Micoua, Québec 172/G1
Micoud, St. Lucia 161/G6
Micro, N.C. 281/N3
Micronesia, Federated States of
  2/S5
Micronesia, Federated States of
  87/F5
Micronesia (reg.), Pacific 87/E4
Midale, Sask. 181/H6
Midas, Nev. 266/E1
Middelburg, Netherlands 27/C6
Middelburg, Cape Prov.,
  S. Africa 118/C6
Middelburg, Transvaal,
  S. Africa 118/D5
Middelfart, Denmark 21/C7
Middelfart, Denmark 18/B9
Middelharnis, Netherlands 27/E5
Middelkerke, Belgium 27/B6
Middelvlei, S. Africa 118/G7
Middenmeer, Netherlands 27/F3
Middle (riv.), Conn. 210/F1
Middle (pt.), Fla. 212/E6
Middle, Iowa 229/K5
Middle (riv.), Minn. 255/B2
Middle Alkali (lake), Calif. 204/E2
Middle Andaman (isl.), India
  68/G4
Middle Arm, Newf. 166/C4
Middle Atlas (ranges), Morocco
  106/C2
Middle Bass, Ohio 284/E2
Middle Bass (isl.), Ohio 284/E2
Middle Beaver (creek), Colo. 208/P4
Middleboro, Mass. 249/L5
Middleboro•, Mass. 249/L5
Middleboro (McKean), Pa.
  294/B2
Middlebourne, W. Va. 312/F6
Middlebranch, Ohio 284/H4
Middlebro, Manitoba 179/G5
Middlebrook, Va. 307/K4
Middleburg, Fla. 212/E2
Middleburg, Ky. 237/M6
Middleburg, Md. 245/K2
Middleburg, N.C. 281/N2
Middleburg, Ohio 284/C5
Middleburg, Pa. 294/H4
Middleburg, Va. 307/N3
Middleburg, N.Y. 276/M5
Middleburg Heights, Ohio
  284/F10
Middlebury•, Conn. 210/C2
Middlebury, Ind. 227/F1
Middlebury•, Vt. 268/A3
Middlebury Center, Pa. 294/H2
Middlebury Gap (pass), Vt. 268/B4
Middlebush, N.J. 273/D3
Middlechurch, Manitoba 179/E4
Middle Concho (riv.), Texas 303/C6
Middledam, Maine 243/B6
Middle Falls, N.Y. 276/O4
Middlefield•, Conn. 210/E2
Middlefield•, Mass. 249/B3
Middlefield, Ohio 284/J3
Middle Fork (peak), Idaho 220/D5
Middlefork, Ind. 227/E4
Middle Fork, Powder (riv.), Wyo.
  319/F2

Middlegate, Norfolk Is. 88/L6
Middlegrove, Ill. 222/C3
Middle Grove, Mo. 261/H4
Middle Haddam, Conn. 210/E2
Middle Harbour (creek), N.S. Wales
  88/K3
Middle Harbour (creek), N.S. Wales
  97/J3
Middle Hope, N.Y. 276/M7
Middle Inlet, Wis. 317/K5
Middle Lake, Sask. 181/F3
Middle Loch (inlet), Hawaii
  218/A3
Middle Loup (riv.), Nebr. 264/D3
Middlemarch, N. Zealand 100/B6
Middle Musquodoboit, Nova Scotia
  168/E3
Middle Patuxent (riv.), Md.
  245/L3
Middle Piney (creek), Wyo.
  319/B3
Middle Point, Ohio 284/B4
Middleport, N.Y. 276/C4
Middleport, Ohio 284/F7
Middleport, Pa. 294/K4
Middle River, Md. 245/K2
Middle River, Minn. 255/B2
Middle River, Nova Scotia
  168/G2
Middle Saranac (lake), N.Y.
  276/M2
Middlesboro, Ky. 237/O7
Middlesboro, Ky. 188/K3
Middlesbrough, England 7/D3
Middlesbrough, England 13/F3
Middlesbrough, England 10/F3
Middlesex (co.), Conn. 210/E3
Middlesex (co.), Mass. 249/J3
Middlesex, N.J. 273/E2
Middlesex, N.Y. 276/F5
Middlesex, N.C. 281/N3
Middlesex (county), Ontario
  177/C4
Middlesex•, Vt. 268/B3
Middlesex•, Va. 307/R5
Middle Stewiacke, Nova Scotia
  168/E3
Middleton (isl.), Alaska 196/J3
Middleton, England 13/H2
Middleton, England 10/G2
Middleton, Georgia 217/G2
Middleton, Idaho 220/B6
Middleton•, Mass. 249/K2
Middleton, Mich. 250/E5
Middleton•, N.H. 268/E4
Middleton, Nova Scotia 168/C4
Middleton, Tenn. 237/D10
Middleton, Wis. 317/G9
Middletown, Calif. 204/C5
Middletown, Conn. 210/E2
Middletown, Del. 245/R3
Middletown, Ill. 222/D3
Middletown, Ind. 227/F4
Middletown, Iowa 229/L7
Middletown, Ky. 237/L2
Middletown, Md. 245/J3
Middletown, Mo. 261/J4
Middletown•, N.J. 273/E3
Middletown•, N.Y. 276/L8
Middletown, N.C. 281/T4
Middletown, N. Ireland 17/H3
Middletown, Ohio 284/A6
Middletown, Pa. 294/J5
Middletown•, R.I. 249/J6
Middletown, Va. 307/M2
Middletown Springs•, Vt.
  268/A5
Middle Valley, N.J. 273/D2
Middleville, Mich. 250/D6
Middleville, N.J. 273/D1
Middleville, N.Y. 276/K4
Middleville, Ontario 177/H2
Middle Water, Texas 303/B2
Middleway, W. Va. 312/K4
Middlewich, England 13/H2
Middlewich, England 10/G2
Middlewood, Nova Scotia
  168/D4
Midfield, Ala. 195/E4
Midgic Station, New Bruns.
  170/F3
Mid Glamorgan, Wales 13/D6
Midhurst, England 13/G6
Midian (dist.), Saudi Arabia 59/C4
Midkiff, W. Va. 312/B6
Midland, Ark. 202/B3
Midland, Ind. 227/C6
Midland, La. 238/E6
Midland, Md. 245/C2
Midland (co.), Mich. 250/E5
Midland, Mich. 250/E5
Midland, N.C. 281/J4
Midland, Ohio 284/C7
Midland, Ontario 177/D3
Midland, Oreg. 291/F5
Midland, Pa. 294/A4
Midland, S. Dak. 298/G5
Midland, Tex. 188/F4
Midland•, Texas 303/B6
Midland, Texas 303/C6
Midland City, Ala. 195/H8
Midland Park, N.J. 273/B1
Midlandvale, Alberta 182/D4
Midleton, Ireland 17/E8
Midleton, Ireland 10/B5
Midlothian, Ill. 222/B6
Midlothian (trad. co.), Scotland
  15/B5
Midlothian, Texas 303/G5
Midlothian, Va. 307/N6
Midnapore, India 68/F4
Midnight, Miss. 256/C4
Midnight (lake), Sask. 181/C2
Midongy Atsimo, Madagascar
  118/H4

Midvale, Idaho 220/B5
Midvale, Ohio 284/H5
Midvale, Utah 304/B3
Midville, Georgia 217/H5
Midway (isls.) 188/E6
Midway, Ala. 195/H6
Midway, Br. Col. 184/H6
Midway, Del. 245/T6
Midway, Fla. 212/B1
Midway, Georgia 217/K7
Midway, Ind. 227/C8
Midway, Ky. 237/M4
Midway (Sedalia), Ohio
  284/D6
Midway, Pa. 294/B5
Midway, Tenn. 237/P8
Midway (isls.), U.S. 87/J3
Midway, Utah 304/C3
Midway City, Calif. 204/D11
Midway Park, N.C. 281/O5
Midwest, Wyo. 319/F2
Midwest City, Okla. 288/M4
Midyat, Turkey 63/J4
Midye, Turkey 63/C2
Mid Yell, Scotland 15/G2
Midzhur (mt.), Bulgaria 45/F4
Midzhur (mt.), Yugoslavia
  45/F4
Mie (pref.), Japan 81/H6
Miechów, Poland 47/E3
Mięcychód, Poland 47/B2
Mięcyzlesie, Poland 47/C3
Mięcyzrec Podlaski, Poland
  47/F2
Mięcyzrzecz, Poland 47/B2
Mielec, Poland 47/E3
Mier, Ind. 227/F3
Mier, Mexico 150/K3
Miercurea Ciuc, Romania
  45/G2
Mieres, Spain 33/D1
Miesso, Ethiopia 111/H6
Miesso, Ethiopia 102/G4
Miesville, Minn. 255/F6
Miette, Alberta 182/B3
Mifflin, Ohio 284/F4
Mifflin (co.), Pa. 294/G4
Mifflin, Pa. 294/H4
Mifflin, Wis. 317/F10
Mifflinburg, Pa. 294/H4
Mifflintown, Pa. 294/H4
Miflin, Ala. 195/C10
Migdal, Israel 65/C2
Migdal Ha 'Emeq, Israel
  65/C2
Mignon, Ala. 195/F4
Migori, Kenya 115/F4
Miguel Alves, Brazil 132/F4
Miguel Auza, Mexico 150/H4
Miguel de la Borda, Panama
  154/G6
Miguelete, Uruguay 145/B5
Miguel Riglos, Argentina
  143/D4
Migues, Uruguay 145/C6
Mihajicçik, Turkey 63/D3
Mihara, Japan 81/F6
Mikado, Mich. 250/F4
Mikado, Sask. 181/J4
Mikana, Wis. 317/C4
Mikhaylovgrad, Bulgaria
  45/F4
Mikhaylovka, U.S.S.R. 52/F4
Mikhmoret, Israel 65/B3
Miki, Japan 81/H7
Mikinai, Greece 45/F7
Mikkalo, Oreg. 291/G2
Mikkeli (prov.), Finland 18/P6
Mikkeli, Finland 18/P6
Mikkwa (riv.), Alberta 182/B5
Miklów, Poland 47/B4
Mikonos (isl.), Greece 45/G7
Mikulov, Czech. 41/D2
Mikumi Nat'l Park, Tanzania
  115/G3
Mikun', U.S.S.R. 52/H2
Mikuni, Japan 81/G5
Milaca, Minn. 255/E5
Milagro, Ecuador 120/A3
Milagro, Ecuador 128/D4
Milagros, Philippines 82/D4
Milam (co.), Texas 303/H7
Milam, Texas 303/C4
Milam, W. Va. 312/H5
Milan, Georgia 217/G6
Milan (dist.), Saudi Arabia 59/C4
Milan, Ill. 222/C2
Milan, Ind. 227/G6
Milan (prov.), Italy 34/B2
Milan, Italy 2/K3
Milan, Italy 7/E4
Milan, Italy 34/B2
Milan, Kansas 232/E4
Milan, Mich. 250/F6
Milan, Minn. 255/C5
Milan, Mo. 261/F2
Milan•, N.H. 268/E2
Milan, N. Mex. 274/B3
Milan, Ohio 284/F3
Milan, Québec 172/F4
Milan, Tenn. 237/D9
Milan, Wash. 310/H3
Milan, Wis. 317/F6
Milanje, Mozambique
  118/F3
Milano, Texas 303/H7
Milanville, Pa. 294/M2
Milâs, Turkey 63/B4
Milazzo, Italy 34/E5
Milbank, S. Dak. 298/R3
Milbanke (sound), Br. Col.
  184/C4
Milberger, Kansas 232/D3
Milbridge•, Maine 243/H6
Milburn, Ky. 237/D7
Milburn, Nebr. 264/E3
Milburn, Okla. 288/O6
Milden, Sask. 181/D4
Mildenhall, England 13/H5

Mildmay, Ontario 177/C3
Mildred, Kansas 232/G3
Mildred, Mont. 262/M4
Mildred, Pa. 294/K3
Mildred Lake, Alberta
182/E1
Mildura, Victoria 88/G6
Mildura, Victoria 97/A4
Mile, China 77/F7
Miles, Iowa 229/N4
Miles, Queensland 88/H5
Miles, Texas 303/D6
Milesburg, Pa. 294/G4
Miles City, Mont. 188/E1
Milestone, Sask. 181/G5
Milesville, S. Dak. 298/F5
Milevsko, Czech. 41/C2
Miley, S.C. 296/E6
Milfay, Okla. 288/N3
Milford, Calif. 204/E3
Milford, Conn. 210/C4
Milford (pt.), Conn. 210/C4
Milford, Del. 245/S5
Milford, Georgia 217/C8
Milford, Ill. 222/F3
Milford, Ind. 227/F2
Milford, Ind. 227/F6
Milford, Iowa 229/C2
Milford, Ireland 17/F1
Milford, Kansas 232/F2
Milford (lake), Kansas
232/E2
Milford, Ky. 237/N3
Milford •, Maine 243/F6
Milford, Mass. 249/H4
Milford •, Mass. 249/H4
Milford, Mich. 250/F6
Milford, Mo. 261/D7
Milford, Nebr. 264/H4
Milford, N.H. 268/D6
Milford •, N.H. 268/D6
Milford, N.J. 273/C2
Milford (sound), N. Zealand
100/A6
Milford, Ohio 284/D9
Milford, Pa. 294/N3
Milford, Texas 303/D5
Milford, Utah 304/A5
Milford, Va. 307/O4
Milford, Wis. 317/J9
Milford Bay, Ontario 177/E2
Milford Center, Ohio 284/D5
Milford Haven, Wales 13/B6
Milford Haven, Wales 10/D5
Milford Haven (inlet), Wales 13/B6
Milford Haven (inlet), Wales 10/D5
Milford Station, Nova Scotia
168/E3
Milh, Bahr al (lake), Iraq 66/C4
Mili (atoll), Marshall Is. 87/H5
Miliana, Algeria 106/E1
Milicz, Poland 47/C3
Milieu (riv.), Québec 172/C3
Mililani Town, Hawaii 218/E2
Milingimbi, North. Terr. 93/D2
Milk (riv.) 146/H5
Milk (riv.), Alberta 182/D5
Milk (riv.), Mont. 188/D1
Milk (riv.), Mont. 262/J2
Milk, Wadi al (dry riv.), Sudan
59/A6
Milk, Wadi al (dry riv.), Sudan
111/E4
Milk River, Alberta 182/D5
Mill (creek), Calif. 204/D3
Mill (riv.), Conn. 210/C3
Mill (riv.), Conn. 210/B4
Mill (creek), Ind. 227/D5
Mill (riv.), Mass. 249/H3
Mill (riv.), Mass. 249/C3
Mill (creek), Mich. 250/G5
Mill (creek), N.J. 273/E4
Mill (isl.), N.W. Terr. 187/L3
Mill (riv.), Vt. 268/B4
Mill (creek), W. Va. 312/C5
Milladore, Wis. 317/G6
Millard, Ky. 237/S6
Millard, Mo. 261/G2
Millard (co.), Utah 304/A4
Millarton, N. Dak. 282/N6
Millarville, Alberta 182/C4
Millau, France 28/E5
Millbank, Ontario 177/D4
Mill Bay, Br. Col 184/K3
Millboro, S. Dak. 298/K7
Millboro, Va. 307/J5
Millboro Springs, Va. 307/J4
Millbourne, Pa. 294/M6
Millbrae, Calif. 204/J2
Millbridge, Ontario 177/G3
Millbrook, Ala. 195/F6
Millbrook, Ill. 222/E2
Millbrook, Mich. 250/D5
Millbrook, N.Y. 276/N7
Millbrook, N.C. 281/M3
Millbrook, Ontario 177/F3
Millburn •, N.J. 273/E2
Millburne, Wyo. 319/B4
Millbury •, Mass. 249/H4
Millbury, Ohio 284/D2
Mill City, Nev. 266/D2
Mill City, Oreg. 291/E3
Mill Cove, New Bruns. 170/D3
Mill Cove, Nova Scotia 168/D4
Millcreek, Ill. 222/D6
Mill Creek, Ind. 227/D1
Millcreek, Mo. 261/M7
Mill Creek, Okla. 288/N6
Mill Creek, Pa. 294/G5
Mill Creek, W. Va. 312/G5
Milldale, Conn. 210/D2
Millecoquins (lake), Mich.
250/D2
Milledgeville, Georgia 217/F4
Milledgeville, Ill. 222/D1

Milledgeville, Ohio 284/C6
Milledgeville, Tenn. 237/E10
Mille Iles (riv.), Québec 172/H4
Mille Lac Ind. Res., Minn. 255/E4
Mille Lacs (co.), Minn. 255/E5
Mille Lacs (lake), Minn. 188/H1
Mille Lacs (lake), Minn. 255/E4
Mille Lacs (lake), Ontario 177/G5
Mille Lacs (lake), Ontario 175/B3
Millen, Georgia 217/J5
Miller (peak), Ariz. 198/E7
Miller (co.), Ark. 202/C7
Miller (co.), Georgia 217/C8
Miller, Iowa 229/F2
Miller, Kansas 232/F3
Miller, Miss. 256/E1
Miller (co.), Mo. 261/H6
Miller, Mo. 261/E8
Miller, Nebr. 264/E4
Miller, Ohio 284/F8
Miller (creek), Oreg. 291/F5
Miller, S. Dak. 298/L4
Miller City, Ohio 284/B3
Miller Dam Flowage (res.), Wis.
317/E5
Miller House, Alaska 196/J1
Millerovo, U.S.S.R. 48/E5
Millerovo, U.S.S.R. 52/F5
Millers, Md. 245/L2
Millers (riv.), Mass. 249/E2
Millersburg, Ind. 227/F1
Millersburg, Iowa 229/J5
Millerburg, Ky. 237/N4
Millersburg, Mich. 250/F3
Millersburg, Ohio 284/F4
Millersburg, Oreg. 291/E3
Millersburg, Pa. 294/J4
Millers Falls, Mass. 249/E2
Millers Ferry, Ala. 195/D6
Millers Ferry, Fla. 212/C6
Millersport, Ohio 284/E6
Millerstown, Ky. 237/J6
Millerstown, Pa. 294/H4
Millersview, Texas 303/E6
Millersville, Md. 245/M4
Millersville, Ohio 284/D3
Millersville, Pa. 294/K6
Millerton (lake), Calif. 204/F6
Millerton, Iowa 229/G7
Millerton, New Bruns. 170/E2
Millerton, N.Y. 276/O7
Millerton, Okla. 288/S7
Millerton, Pa. 294/J2
Millertown, Newf. 166/C4
Millerville, Ala. 195/G4
Millerville, Minn. 255/C4
Millet, Alberta 182/D3
Millet, S.C. 296/D5
Millet, Texas 303/E9
Millgrove, Ind. 227/G4
Mill Grove, Mo. 261/E2
Mill Hall, Pa. 294/G3
Millhaven, Georgia 217/J5
Millhelm, Pa. 294/G4
Millhousen, Ind. 227/G6
Millican, Oreg. 291/F4
Millicent, Alberta 182/D3
Millicent, S. Australia 88/F7
Millicent, S. Australia 94/F7
Milligan, Fla. 212/C6
Milligan, Ind. 227/C5
Milligan, Nebr. 264/G4
Milligan College, Tenn.
237/S8
Milliken, Colo. 208/K2
Millikin, La. 238/H1
Millingen aan den Rijn,
Netherlands 27/J5
Millington, Conn. 210/F3
Millington, Ill. 222/E2
Millington, Md. 245/P3
Millington, Mich. 250/F5
Millington, N.J. 273/D2
Millington, Tenn. 237/B10
Millinocket •, Maine 243/F4
Millinocket (lake), Maine
243/F4
Millinocket (lake), Maine
243/F3
Mill Iron, Mont. 262/M5
Millis •, Mass. 249/A8
Millis-Clicquot, Mass. 249/A8
Millisle, N. Ireland 17/K2
Millmerran, Queensland 95/D5
Millmont, Pa. 294/H4
Millom, England 13/D3
Mill Plain, Conn. 210/A3
Mill Point, W. Va. 312/F6
Millport, Ala. 195/B3
Millport, N.Y. 276/M7
Millport, Pa. 294/F2
Millport, Scotland 15/A2
Millport, Scotland 10/A1
Millrift, Pa. 294/N3
Mill River, Mass. 249/A4
Mill Road, Nova Scotia
168/D4
Millrose, W. Australia 92/C4
Mill Run, Pa. 294/C6
Millry, Ala. 195/B7
Mills (co.), Iowa 229/B6
Mills, Ky. 237/O7
Mills, Nebr. 264/E2
Mills (lake), N.W. Terr.
187/G3
Mills, Pa. 294/G2
Mills (co.), Texas 303/F6
Mills, Utah 304/B4
Mills, Wyo. 319/F3
Millsap, Texas 303/G5
Millsboro, Del. 245/S6
Millsboro, Pa. 294/B6
Mill Shoals, Ill. 222/E5
Mill Spring, Mo. 261/M8
Mill Springs, Ky. 237/M7
Millstadt, Ill. 222/B3

Millston, Wis. 317/E7
Millstone, Ky. 237/R6
Millstone, N.J. 273/D2
Millstone (riv.), N.J. 273/D3
Millstone, W. Va. 312/D5
Millstream Station, W. Australia
92/B4
Millstreet, Ireland 17/D7
Millthorpe, N.S. Wales 97/E5
Milltown, Ala. 195/H4
Milltown, Ind. 227/E8
Milltown, Ireland 17/A7
Milltown, Ky. 237/L6
Milltown, Mont. 262/C4
Milltown, Newf. 166/C4
Milltown, N.J. 273/E3
Milltown, S. Dak 298/O7
Milltown, Wis. 317/B4
Millungera, Queensland
95/B3
Millvale, Pa. 294/B7
Mill Valley, Calif. 204/H2
Mill Village, Nova Scotia
168/D4
Mill Village, Pa. 294/C2
Millville, Del. 245/T6
Millville, Ind. 227/G5
Millville, Iowa 229/L3
Millville •, Mass. 249/H4
Millville, Minn. 255/F6
Millville, New Bruns. 170/C2
Millville, N.J. 273/C5
Millville, Ohio 284/A7
Millville, Pa. 294/J3
Millville, Utah 304/C2
Millwood (lake), Ark. 202/C6
Millwood, Georgia 217/G8
Millwood, Ky. 237/J6
Millwood, Manitoba 179/A4
Millwood, Ohio 284/E5
Millwood, Va. 307/N2
Millwood, Wash. 310/H3
Millwood, W. Va. 312/C5
Milly Milly, W. Australia 92/B4
Milmay, N.J. 273/D5
Milmine, Ill. 222/E4
Milmont Park, Pa. 294/M7
Milnathort, Scotland 15/E4
Milne (inlet), N.W. Terr. 187/K2
Milne (bay), Papua N.G. 85/C8
Milner, Colo. 208/F2
Milner, Georgia 217/D4
Milner Ridge, Manitoba 179/F4
Milnerton, S. Africa 118/F6
Milnesand, N. Mex. 274/F5
Milnes Landing, Br. Col.
184/J4
Milngavie, Scotland 10/B1
Milngavie, Scotland 15/B1
Milnor, N. Dak. 282/R7
Milo, Alberta 182/D3
Milo (riv.), Guinea 106/C7
Milo, Iowa 229/G6
Milo, Ky. 237/R5
Milo, Maine 243/F5
Milo •, Maine 243/F5
Milo, Mo. 261/D7
Milo, Okla. 288/M6
Milo, Oreg. 291/E5
Milo, Tenn. 237/L9
Milolii, Hawaii 218/G6
Milos, Greece 45/G7
Milos (isl.), Greece 45/G7
Milot, Québec 172/F1
Milpa, N.S. Wales 97/B2
Milparinka, N.S. Wales 97/A1
Milperra, N.S. Wales 97/H4
Milpitas, Calif. 204/L3
Milroy, Ind. 227/G6
Milroy, Minn. 255/C6
Milroy, Pa. 294/G4
Milstead, Ala. 195/G6
Milstead, Georgia 217/D3
Milton (res.), Colo. 208/K2
Milton, Conn. 210/C1
Milton, Del. 245/S5
Milton, Fla. 212/B6
Milton, Ill. 222/C4
Milton, Ind. 227/G5
Milton, Iowa 229/J7
Milton, Kansas 232/E4
Milton, Ky. 237/L3
Milton, La. 238/F6
Milton •, Mass. 249/D7
Milton, Newf. 166/C4
Milton •, N.H. 268/F5
Milton, N.J. 273/D1
Milton, N.S. Wales 97/F4
Milton, N.Y. 276/M7
Milton, N.Y. 276/N4
Milton, N. Zealand 100/B7
Milton, N.C. 281/L1
Milton, N. Dak. 282/O2
Milton, Nova Scotia 168/D4
Milton, Okla. 288/S4
Milton, Ontario 177/E4
Milton, Pa. 294/J3
Milton, Tenn. 237/J9
Milton, Vt. 268/A2
Milton •, Vt. 268/A2
Milton, Wash. 310/C3
Milton, W. Va. 312/B6
Milton, Wis. 317/J10
Miltona, Minn. 255/C4
Milton Center, Ohio 284/C3
Milton-Freewater, Oreg. 291/J2
Milton Keynes, England 13/F5
Milton Mills, N.H. 268/F4
Miltonsburg, Ohio 284/H6
Miltonvale, Kansas 232/E2
Miltownmalbay, Ireland 17/C6
Milverton, Ontario 177/D4
Milwaukee, N.C. 281/P2
Milwaukee, Wis. 146/K5
Milwaukee, Wis. 317/F10
Milwaukee (co.), Wis. 317/L9
Milwaukee, Wis. 317/M1

Milwaukie, Oreg. 291/B2
Mima, Ky. 237/P5
Mimbres, N. Mex. 274/B6
Mimbres (mts.), N. Mex.
274/B6
Mimbres (riv.), N. Mex.
274/B6
Mimasaka, Japan 81/E7
Mimigash, Pr. Edward I.
168/D2
Mimizan, France 28/C5
Mimongo, Gabon 115/B4
Mimosa Park, La. 238/N4
Mimoso do Sul, Brazil 135/F2
Mims, Fla. 212/F3
Mina, Nev. 266/C4
Mina, S. Dak. 298/M3
Mina al Ahmadi, Kuwait
59/E4
Mina al Fahal, Oman 59/G5
Minab, Iran 59/G2
Minab, Iran 66/K7
Minaki, Ontario 177/F4
Minaki, Ontario 175/A3
Minam, Oreg. 291/K2
Minamata, Japan 81/E7
Minami Iwo (isl.), Japan 87/D3
Minami Iwo (isl.), Japan 81/M5
Minapasuk, Philippines 82/D5
Minard, Ireland 17/A7
Minas, Cuba 158/G2
Minas (mts.), Guatemala 154/C3
Minas (basin), Nova Scotia 168/D3
Minas (chan.), Nova Scotia 168/D3
Minas, Uruguay 145/D5
Mina Saud, Kuwait 59/E4
Mina Sa'ud, Saudi Arabia 59/E4
Minas-Cué, Paraguay 144/C3
Minas de Corrales, Uruguay 145/D2
Minas de Matahambre, Cuba
158/A1
Minas de Ríotinto, Spain 33/C4
Minas Gerais (state), Brazil 135/D2
Minas Gerais (state), Brazil 132/E7
Minas Novas, Brazil 132/F7
Minatare, Nebr. 264/A3
Minatare (lake), Nebr. 264/A3
Minatitlán, Mexico 150/M8
Minbu, Burma 72/B2
Minburn, Alberta 182/E3
Minburn, Iowa 229/E5
Minbay, Burma 72/B2
Mincha, Chile 138/A8
Minchinmávida (vol.), Chile
138/C4
Mincio (riv.), Italy 34/C2
Minco, Okla. 288/L4
Mindanao (isl.), Philippines 54/O9
Mindanao (isl.), Philippines 2/R5
Mindanao (isl.), Philippines 85/H4
Mindanao (isl.), Philippines 82/D7
Mindanao (riv.), Philippines 85/H4
Mindanao (sea), Philippines 85/G4
Mindanao (sea), Philippines 82/D7
Mindelheim, Germany 22/D4
Mindelo, C. Verde 106/A7
Mindemoya, Ontario 177/B2
Mindemoya (lake), Ontario
177/B2
Minden, Germany 22/C2
Minden, Iowa 229/C6
Minden, La. 238/D1
Minden, Nebr. 264/F4
Minden, Nev. 266/B4
Minden, Ontario 177/F3
Minden, Texas 303/K5
Minden City, Mich. 250/G5
Mindenmines, Mo. 261/C8
Mindiptana, Indonesia 85/L7
Mindoro (isl.), Philippines
54/N8
Mindoro (isl.), Philippines
85/G3
Mindoro (isl.), Philippines 82/C4
Mindoro (isl.), Philippines 85/F3
Mindoro (str.), Philippines 82/C4
Mindoro, Wis. 317/D7
Mindouli, Congo 115/B4
Mindszent, Hungary 41/F3
Mine (head), Ireland 17/F8
Mine Centre, Ontario 177/F4
Mine Centre, Ontario 175/B3
Minehead, England 13/D6
Minehead, England 10/E5
Mine Hill •, N.J. 273/D2
Mineiros, Brazil 132/C7
Mineiros, Brazil 120/D4
Mine La Motte, Mo. 261/M7
Mineola, Iowa 229/B6
Mineola, Mo. 261/J5
Mineola, N.Y. 276/R7
Mineola, Texas 303/J5
Miner, Mo. 261/N9
Miner, Mont. 262/E5
Miner (co.), S. Dak. 298/O5
Mineral, Calif. 204/D3
Mineral (co.), Colo. 208/F7
Mineral, Ill. 222/D2
Mineral (co.), Mont. 262/B3
Mineral (co.), Nev. 266/C4
Mineral, Ohio 284/F7
Mineral, Texas 303/G9
Mineral (mts.), Utah 304/B5
Mineral, Va. 307/N4
Mineral, Wash. 310/C4
Mineral (co.), W. Va. 312/J4
Mineral Bluff, Georgia 217/D1
Mineral Center, Minn. 255/G2
Mineral del Monte, Mexico
150/K6
Mineral Hills, Mich. 250/G2
Mineral'nye Vody, U.S.S.R.
52/F6
Mineral Point, Mo. 261/L7
Mineral Point, Wis. 317/F10
Mineral Springs, Ark. 202/C5
Mineral Springs, N.C. 281/H5

Mineral Wells, Miss. 256/E1
Mineral Wells, Texas 303/F5
Mineralwells, W. Va. 312/C4
Minersville, Ohio 284/G7
Minersville, Pa. 294/K4
Minersville, Utah 304/A5
Mine Run, Va. 307/N4
Minerva, Ky. 237/O3
Minerva, N.Y. 276/N3
Minerva, Ohio 284/H4
Minerva Park, Ohio 284/E5
Minerva (reefs), Tonga 87/H8
Minetto, N.Y. 276/H4
Mineville-Witherbee, N.Y.
276/O2
Minfeng (Niya), China 77/B4
Minford, Ohio 284/E8
Mingan, Que. 162/K5
Mingan, Que. 162/K5
Mingechaur, U.S.S.R. 52/G6
Mingenew, W. Australia 88/B5
Mingenew, W. Australia 92/A5
Minginish (dist.), Scotland
15/B3
Minglanilla, Spain 33/F3
Mingo, Iowa 229/G5
Mingo, Kansas 232/B2
Mingo (lake), N.W. Terr.
187/L3
Mingo, Ohio 284/C5
Mingo (co.), W. Va. 312/B7
Mingo, W. Va. 312/F5
Mingo Junction, Ohio 284/J5
Mingshui, Gansu, China 77/E3
Mingshui, Heilongjiang, China
77/L2
Mingulay (isl.), Scotland 15/A4
Mingus, Texas 303/F5
Minhla, Burma 72/B3
Minho (riv.), Jamaica 158/J6
Minho (riv.), Portugal 33/B2
Minicoy (isl.), India 68/C7
Minidoka (co.), Idaho 220/E7
Minidoka, Idaho 220/E7
Minier, Ill. 222/D3
Minigwal (lake), W. Australia
88/C5
Minigwal (lake), W. Australia
92/C5
Minilya, W. Australia 92/A4
Miniota, Manitoba 179/B4
Minipi (lake), Newf. 166/B3
Minipi (riv.), Newf. 166/B3
Ministikwan (lake), Sask. 181/B1
Ministre (pt.), St. Lucia 161/G7
Minitonas, Manitoba 179/A4
Min Jiang (riv.), China 77/J6
Minlaton, S. Australia 94/E6
Minle, China 77/F4
Minna, Nigeria 106/F7
Minneapolis, Kansas 232/E2
Minneapolis, Minn. 146/J5
Minneapolis, Minn. 188/H1
Minneapolis, Minn. 255/G6
Minneapolis, U.S. 2/E3
Minneapolis-St. Paul Airport,
Minn. 255/G6
Minnechaduza (creek), S. Dak.
298/H7
Minnedosa, Manitoba 179/B4
Minnedosa (riv.), Manitoba
179/B4
Minnehaha (co.), S. Dak.
298/R6
Minnehaha Springs, W. Va.
312/G6
Minneiska, Minn. 255/G6
Minneola, Fla. 212/E3
Minneola, Kansas 232/C4
Minneota, Minn. 255/C6
Minnesota 188/H1
MINNESOTA 255
Minnesota (riv.), Minn. 188/G2
Minnesota (riv.), Minn. 255/E6
Minnesota (riv.), S. Dak. 298/S3
Minnesota (state), U.S. 146/J5
Minnesota City, Minn. 255/G6
Minnesota Lake, Minn. 255/E7
Minnesott Beach, N.C. 281/R5
Minnetonka, Minn. 255/G5
Minnetonka (lake), Minn. 255/F5
Minnetrista, Minn. 255/F5
Minnewaska (lake), Minn. 255/C5
Minnewaukan, N. Dak. 282/M3
Minnipa, S. Australia 88/F6
Minnipa, S. Australia 94/D5
Minnitaki (lake), Ontario 177/G4
Minnith, Mo. 261/M7
Minnora, W. Va. 312/D5
Miño, Spain 7/D4
Miño (riv.), Spain 33/B1
Minoa, N.Y. 276/H4
Minobu, Japan 81/J6
Minocqua, Wis. 317/G4
Minong, Wis. 317/C3
Minonk, Ill. 222/D3
Minoo, Japan 81/J7
Minooka, Ill. 222/E2
Minorca (isl.), Spain 7/H3
Minorca (isl.), Spain 33/J2
Minor Hill, Tenn. 237/G10
Minor Lane Heights, Ky.
237/K4
Minortown, Conn. 210/C2
Minot, Maine 243/C7
Minot •, Maine 243/C7
Minot, Mass. 249/F8
Minot, N. Dak. 188/F1
Minot, N. Dak. 146/H5
Minot, N. Dak. 282/H3
Minot A.F.B., N. Dak. 282/H3
Minotola, N.J. 273/D4
Minqin, China 77/F4

Miñsk Mazowiecki, Poland 47/E2
Minster, Ohio 284/B5
Minstrel Island, Br. Col. 184/D5
Minter, Ala. 195/D6
Minter City, Miss. 256/D3
Mint Hill, N.C. 281/H4
Mintlaw, Scotland 15/F3
Minto, Alaska 196/J2
Minto, Manitoba 179/B5
Minto, New Bruns. 170/D2
Minto, N. Dak. 282/R3
Minto (inlet), N.W. Terr. 187/G2
Minto (lake), Que. 162/J4
Minto (lake), Québec 174/E2
Minto, Yukon 187/E3
Minton, Sask. 181/G6
Minturn, Ark. 202/H2
Minturn, Colo. 208/G3
Minturn, Maine 243/G7
Minturn, S.C. 296/C2
Minturno, Italy 34/H4
Minûf, Egypt 111/J3
Minusinsk, U.S.S.R. 48/K4
Minusio, Switzerland 39/G4
Minute Man Nat'l Hist. Park,
Mass. 249/B6
Minvoul, Gabon 115/B3
Min Xian, China 77/F5
Minyip, Victoria 97/B5
Mio, Mich. 250/E4
Miocene, Br. Col. 184/G4
Miquan, China 77/C3
Miquelon (isl.), 166/C4
Miquihuana, Mexico 150/J5
Miquillo (pt.), P. Rico 161/H7
Mira (riv.), Colombia 126/A7
Mira (riv.), Ecuador 128/C2
Mira, La. 238/C1
Mira (bay), Nova Scotia 168/J2
Mira (riv.), Nova Scotia 168/H3
Mira, Portugal 33/B2
Mira (riv.), Portugal 33/B4
Mirabad, Afghanistan 68/A2
Mirabad, Afghanistan 59/H3
Mirabel, Québec 172/H4
Mirabile, Mo. 261/D3
Miracema, Brazil 135/E2
Miracema, Brazil 132/F8
Miraema do Norte, Brazil 132/D5
Mirador, Brazil 132/E4
Mirador Nacional (mt.), Uruguay
145/D5
Miraflores, Boyacá, Colombia
126/D5
Miraflores, Vaupés, Colombia
126/D7
Miragoâne, Haiti 158/B6
Miragoâne, Haiti 156/D3
Miraj, India 68/C5
Miraje, Salar del (salt dep.),
Chile 138/B5
Mira Loma, Calif. 204/E10
Miramar, Argentina 143/E4
Miramar, C. Rica 154/E5
Miramar, Fla. 212/B4
Miramar, Panama 154/H6
Miramichi (bay), New Bruns.
170/E1
Miram Shah, Pakistan 68/C2
Miranda, Brazil 132/B8
Miranda (riv.), Brazil 132/B8
Miranda, Colombia 126/B6
Miranda, S. Dak. 298/M4
Miranda (state), Venezuela
124/E2
Miranda de Ebro, Spain 33/E1
Miranda do Corvo, Portugal
33/B2
Miranda do Douro, Portugal
33/C2
Mirande, France 28/D6
Mirandela, Portugal 33/C2
Mirando City, Texas 303/E10
Mirandola, Italy 34/C2
Mira Por Vos (cays), Bahamas
156/C2
Mira Road, Nova Scotia 168/H2
Mirassol, Brazil 135/B2
Mira Taglio, Italy 34/D2
Mirebalais, Haiti 156/D3
Mirebalais, Haiti 158/C6
Mirecourt, France 28/G3
Mirgorod, U.S.S.R. 52/D5
Miri (hills), India 68/G3
Miri, Malaysia 85/E5
Mirik (Timiris) (cape), Mauritania
106/A5
Mirim (lake), Brazil 120/D6
Mirim (lag.), Brazil 132/C11
Mirirmire, Venezuela 124/D2
Mírina, Greece 45/G6
Miritiparaná (riv.), Colombia
126/E8
Mirjaveh, Iran 59/H4
Mirjaveh, Iran 66/M6
Mirjaveh, Pakistan 59/H4
Mirnyy Station, Ant. 5/C5
Mirnyy, U.S.S.R. 7/G3
Mirnyy, U.S.S.R. 32/L3
Mirnyy, U.S.S.R. 48/M3
Mirpur, Pakistan 68/C2
Mirpur Khas, Pakistan 68/B3
Mirror, Alberta 182/D3
Mirror Lake, N.H. 268/E4
Mirtóön (sea), Greece 45/F7
Miryang, S. Korea 81/D4
Mirzapur-cum-Vindhyachal,
India 68/E4
Misamis Occidental (prov.),
Philippines 82/D6
Misamis Oriental (prov.), Philippines
82/E4
Misantia, Mexico 150/P1
Misawa, Japan 81/K3
Miscou (isl.), New Bruns. 170/F1
Miscou (pt.), New Bruns. 170/F1
Miscou Centre, New Bruns.
170/F1
Miscouche, Pr. Edward I. 168/D2

Monkey 411

Miscou Harbour, New Bruns. 170/F1
Misenheimer, N.C. 281/J4
Misery (bay), Mich. 250/G1
Misery (riv.), Mich. 250/G1
Misery (mt.), St. Kitts & Nevis 161/C10
Misgar, Pakistan 68/C1
Misha'ab, Ras (cape), Saudi Arabia 59/E4
Mishagua, Peru 128/F8
Mishan, China 77/M2
Mishaum (pt.), Mass. 249/L6
Mishawaka, Ind. 227/E1
Misheguk (mt.), Alaska 196/F1
Mishicot, Wis. 317/L7
Mishmar Hanegev, Israel 65/B5
Mishmar Hayarden, Israel 65/D1
Mishmi (hills), India 68/H3
Misima (isl.), Papua N.G. 85/C8
Misiones (prov.), Argentina 143/F2
Misiones (dept.), Paraguay 144/D5
Miskitos (cays), Nicaragua 154/F3
Miskolc, Hungary 41/F2
Miskolc, Hungary 7/G4
Misool (isl.), Indonesia 85/J6
Mispec, New Bruns. 170/E3
Mispillion (riv.), Del. 245/S5
Misquah (hills), Minn. 255/F2
Missanable, Ontario 177/J5
Missanable, Ontario 175/D3
Missaukee (co.), Mich. 250/D4
Missi Falls, Manitoba 179/J2
Missinaibi (riv.), Ont. 162/H6
Missinaibi (lake), Ontario 175/D3
Missinaibi (riv.), Ontario 175/D2
Mission, Br. Col 184/L3
Mission, Kansas 232/H2
Mission (range), Mont. 262/C3
Mission, S. Dak. 298/H7
Mission, Texas 303/F11
Mission Beach, Alberta 182/C3
Mission City, Br. Col. 184/L3
Mission Hill, S. Dak. 298/P8
Mission Ridge, S. Dak. 298/H4
Mission Viejo, Calif. 204/D11
Missisa (lake), Ontario 175/D2
Missisquoi (co.), Québec 172/D4
Missisquoi (riv.), Vt. 268/B2
Mississagi (riv.), Ontario 177/A1
Mississagi (str.), Ontario 177/A2
Mississaugua, Ontario 177/J4
Mississinewa (lake), Ind. 227/F3
Mississinewa (riv.), Ind. 227/F3
Mississippi 188/J4
MISSISSIPPI 256
Mississippi (riv.) 188/H4
Mississippi (sound), Ala. 195/B10
Mississippi (co.), Ark. 202/K2
Mississippi (riv.), Ark. 202/H7
Mississippi (riv.), Ill. 222/C5
Mississippi (riv.), Iowa 229/L7
Mississippi (riv.), Ky. 237/A10
Mississippi (delta), La. 146/K7
Mississippi (delta), La. 188/J5
Mississippi (delta), La. 238/M8
Mississippi (riv.), La. 238/H3
Mississippi (sound), La. 238/M6
Mississippi (riv.), Minn. 255/D4
Mississippi (riv.), Miss. 256/A8
Mississippi (sound), Miss. 256/G10
Mississippi (co.), Mo. 261/O9
Mississippi (riv.), Mo. 261/L4
Mississippi (lake), Ontario 177/H2
Mississippi (riv.), Tenn. 237/A10
Mississippi (state), U.S. 146/K6
Mississippi (riv.), U.S. 2/E4
Mississippi (riv.), U.S. 146/J6
Mississippi (riv.), Wis. 317/D10
Mississippi River Gulf Outlet (canal), La. 238/L7
Mississippi State, Miss. 256/G4
Missoula, Mont. 146/G5
Missoula, Mont. 188/D1
Missoula (co.), Mont. 262/C3
Missoula, Mont. 262/C4
Missouri 188/H3
MISSOURI 261
Missouri (riv.) 188/H3
Missouri (riv.), Iowa 229/A4
Missouri (riv.), Kansas 232/G1
Missouri (riv.), Mo. 261/H5
Missouri (riv.), Mont. 262/L3
Missouri (riv.), Nebr. 264/H3
Missouri (riv.), N. Dak. 282/H5
Missouri (riv.), S. Dak. 298/P8
Missouri (state), U.S. 146/J6
Missouri (riv.), U.S. 2/D3
Missouri (riv.), U.S. 146/J5
Missouri Branch, W. Va. 312/A7
Missouri City, Mo. 261/R5
Missouri City, Texas 303/J2
Missouri Coteau (hills), Sask. 181/F5
Missouri Valley, Iowa 229/B5
Mist, Ark. 202/G7
Mist, Oreg. 291/D1
Mistake (bay), N.W. Terr. 187/J3
Mistake Creek, North. Terr. 93/A4
Mistaken (pt.), Newf. 166/D2
Mistassibi (riv.), Que. 162/J5
Mistassibi (riv.), Québec 174/C3
Mistassini (lake), Que. 162/J5
Mistassini (lake), Que. 146/L4
Mistassini (terr.), Québec 174/B2
Mistassini, Québec 172/E1
Mistassini, Québec 174/C3
Mistassini (Baie-du-Poste), Québec 174/C2
Mistassini (lake), Québec 174/C2
Mistastin (lake), Newf. 166/B2
Mistastin (riv.), Newf. 166/B2
Mistatim, Sask. 181/H3
Mistehae (lake), Alberta 182/C2
Mistelbach an der Zaya, Austria 41/D2
Misteriosa (bank), Cayman Is. 156/A3
Misti, El (mt.), Peru 120/B4
Misti, El (mt.), Peru 128/G11
Mistinippi (lake), Newf. 166/B3
Miston, Tenn. 237/B8
Mistretta, Italy 34/E6
Misty Fjords Nat'l Mon., Alaska 196/N2
Misurata, Libya 102/D1
Misurata, Libya 111/C1
Mita (pt.), Mexico 150/G6
Mitaka, Japan 81/O2
Mitcham, S. Australia 88/D8
Mitcham, S. Australia 94/B8
Mitchell (lake), Ala. 188/J4
Mitchell (dam), Ala. 195/E5
Mitchell (lake), Ala. 195/F5
Mitchell, Ark. 202/G1
Mitchell (co.), Georgia 217/D8
Mitchell, Georgia 217/G4
Mitchell, Ind. 227/E7
Mitchell (co.), Iowa 229/H2
Mitchell, Iowa 229/H2
Mitchell (co.), Kansas 232/D2
Mitchell, La. 238/C3
Mitchell, Nebr. 264/A3
Mitchell (co.), N.C. 281/E2
Mitchell (mt.), N.C. 188/K3
Mitchell (mt.), N.C. 281/E3
Mitchell, Ontario 177/C4
Mitchell, Oreg. 291/G3
Mitchell, Queensland 88/H5
Mitchell, Queensland 95/C5
Mitchell (riv.), Queensland 88/G3
Mitchell (riv.), Queensland 95/B2
Mitchell, S. Dak. 188/G2
Mitchell, S. Dak. 298/N6
Mitchell (creek), S. Dak. 298/G5
Mitchell (co.), Texas 303/D5
Mitchell (riv.), Victoria 97/D5
Mitchell Bay, Ontario 177/B5
Mitchell Heights, W. Va. 312/B7
Mitchells, Va. 307/N4
Mitchellsburg, Ky. 237/M5
Mitchellsville, Ill. 222/E6
Mitchellton, Sask. 181/F6
Mitchellville, Ark. 202/H6
Mitchellville, Iowa 229/G5
Mitchellville, Tenn. 237/J7
Mitchelstown, Ireland 10/B4
Mitchelstown, Ireland 17/E7
Mitchelton, Queensland 88/J2
Mitchelton, Queensland 95/D2
Mitchinamécus (res.), Québec 172/C2
Mithi, Pakistan 68/C4
Mithimna, Greece 45/G6
Mitiaro, Cook Is. 87/L7
Mitilini, Greece 45/H6
Mitkof (isl.), Alaska 196/N2
Mitla (ruin), Mexico 150/M8
Mito, Japan 81/K5
Mitrofania (isl.), Alaska 196/G3
Mitsamiouli, Comoros 118/G2
Mitsinjo, Madagascar 118/H3
Mitsue, Alberta 182/C2
Mitsukaido, Japan 81/P2
Mittagong, N.S. Wales 97/F4
Mitta Mitta (riv.), Victoria 97/D5
Mittenwald, Germany 22/D5
Mittersill, Austria 41/B3
Mittie, La. 238/E5
Mittweida, Germany 22/E3
Mitú, Colombia 126/E7
Mitú, Colombia 120/B2
Mituas, Colombia 126/F6
Mitwaba, Zaire 115/E5
Mitzic, Gabon 115/B3
Miura, Japan 81/C3
Miura (pen.), Japan 81/O3
Mivtahim, Israel 65/A5
Mix, La. 238/G5
Miyagi (pref.), Japan 81/K4
Miyako, Japan 81/L4
Miyako (isl.), Japan 81/L7
Miyako (isls.), Japan 81/L7
Miyakonojo, Japan 81/E8
Miyazaki (pref.), Japan 81/E8
Miyazaki, Japan 81/E8
Miyazu, Japan 81/G6
Miyoshi, Japan 81/F6
Mizan Teferi, Ethiopia 111/G6
Mizda, Libya 111/B1
Mize, Georgia 217/F2
Mize, Miss. 256/E7
Mizen (head), Ireland 10/A5
Mizen (head), Ireland 17/B9
Mizen (head), Ireland 17/K6
Mizhi, China 77/H4
Mizil, Romania 45/H3
Mizo (hill), India 68/G4
Mizoram (terr.), India 68/G4
Mizpah, Minn. 255/D3
Mizpah, N.J. 273/D5
Mizpe Ramon, Israel 65/D5
Mizque, Bolivia 136/C5
Mizque (riv.), Bolivia 136/C6
Mizusawa, Japan 81/K4
Mjölby, Sweden 18/J7
Mkokotoni, Tanzania 115/G5
Mkushi, Zambia 115/E6
Mladá Boleslav, Czech. 41/C1
Mladá Vožice, Czech. 41/C2
Mława, Poland 47/E2
Mljet (isl.), Yugoslavia 45/C4
Mmabatho (cap.), Bophuthatswana, S. Africa 102/E7
Mmabatho, S. Africa 118/D5
Mnichovo Hradiště, Czech. 41/C1
Mo, Norway 7/F2
Mo, Norway 18/J3
Moa, Cuba 158/K3
Moa (riv.), Guinea 106/B7
Moa (isl.), Indonesia 85/H7
Moa (riv.), S. Leone 106/B7
Moab, Utah 304/E5
Moak Lake, Manitoba 179/J2
Moala (isl.), Fiji 86/Q11
Moama, N.S. Wales 97/C5
Moamba, Mozambique 118/E5
Moanalua (stream), Hawaii 218/B3
Moanda, Gabon 115/B4
Moanda, Zaire 115/B5
Moapa, Nev. 266/G6
Moapa River Ind. Res., Nev. 266/G6
Moar (lake), Manitoba 179/G2
Moark, Ark. 202/J1
Moate, Ireland 17/F5
Moatsville, W. Va. 312/G4
Mobara, Japan 81/K6
Mobaye, Cent. Afr. Rep. 115/D3
Mobayi-Mbongo, Zaire 115/D3
Mobayi-Mbongo, Zaire 102/E4
Mobeetie, Texas 303/D2
Moberly, Br. Col. 184/J4
Moberly (lake), Br. Col. 184/F2
Moberly, Mo. 261/G4
Moberly, Mo. 188/H3
Moberly Lake, Br. Col. 184/G2
Mobile, Ala. 146/K6
Mobile, Ala. 188/J4
Mobile, Ala. 195/B9
Mobile (bay), Ala. 188/J5
Mobile (bay), Ala. 195/B10
Mobile (co.), Ala. 195/B9
Mobile (pt.), Ala. 195/B10
Mobile (riv.), Ala. 195/C9
Mobile, Ariz. 198/C5
Mobile, Newf. 166/D2
Mobile Big (pond), Newf. 166/D2
Mobjack, Va. 307/R6
Mobjack (bay), Va. 307/R6
Mobridge, S. Dak. 298/J2
Mobuto Sese Seko (lake), Africa 102/F4
Mobuto Sese Seko (lake), Uganda 115/F3
Mobuto Sese Seko (lake), Zaire 115/F3
Moca, Dom. Rep. 156/D3
Moca, Dom. Rep. 158/D5
Moca, P. Rico 161/A1
Mocajuba, Brazil 132/D3
Moçambique, Mozambique 118/G3
Moçambique, Mozambique 102/F6
Moçâmedes (Namibe), Angola 115/B7
Mocanaqua, Pa. 294/K3
Moccasin, Ariz. 198/C2
Moccasin, Mont. 262/F3
Mocha (isl.), Chile 138/B2
Mocha (isl.), Yemen 59/D7
Moc Hoa, Vietnam 72/E5
Mochudi, Botswana 118/D4
Mochudi, Botswana 102/E7
Mocímboa da Praia, Mozambique 118/G2
Mociu, Romania 45/G2
Mocksville, N.C. 281/H3
Moclips, Wash. 310/A3
Moco (mt.), Angola 115/C6
Mocoa, Colombia 126/B7
Mococa, Brazil 135/C2
Mocodome (cape), Nova Scotia 168/G3
Mocomoco, Bolivia 136/A4
Mocoretá, Argentina 143/G5
Mocorito, Mexico 150/F4
Moctezuma, San Luis Potosí, Mexico 150/J5
Moctezuma, Sonora, Mexico 150/E2
Moctezuma (riv.), Mexico 150/K6
Mocuba, Mozambique 118/F3
Modale, Iowa 229/B5
Modane, France 28/G5
Modasa, India 68/C4
Modderfontein, S. Africa 118/H6
Mode, Ill. 222/E4
Model, Colo. 208/L8
Modena (prov.), Italy 34/C2
Modena, Italy 7/F4
Modena, Italy 34/C2
Modena, Utah 304/A6
Modena, Wis. 317/C7
Modeste, La. 238/K3
Modesto, Calif. 188/B3
Modesto, Calif. 204/D6
Modesto, Ill. 222/D4
Modest Town, Va. 307/T5
Modica, Italy 34/E6
Mödling, Austria 41/D2
Modoc (co.), Calif. 204/E2
Modoc, Georgia 217/H5
Modoc, Ill. 222/C5
Modoc, Ind. 227/G4
Modoc, Kansas 232/A3
Modoc, S.C. 296/C4
Modoc Point, Oreg. 291/F5
Modra, Czech. 41/D2
Modriča, Yugoslavia 45/D3
Modrý Kameň, Czech. 41/E2
Mo Duc, Vietnam 72/F4
Moe, Victoria 88/H7
Moe, Victoria 97/D6
Moen (isl.), Micronesia 87/F5
Moencopi (plat.), Ariz. 198/D3
Moengo, Suriname 131/D3
Moenkopi, Ariz. 198/D2
Moenkopi Wash (dry riv.), Ariz. 198/D2
Moerai, Fr. Poly. 87/L8
Moerdijk, Netherlands 27/F5
Moerewa, N. Zealand 100/E1
Moësa (riv.), Switzerland 39/H4
Moeskroen (Mouscron), Belgium 27/C7
Moffat (co.), Colo. 208/C1
Moffat, Colo. 208/H6
Moffat, Scotland 15/E5
Moffat, Scotland 10/E3
Moffet (peak), N. Zealand 100/B6
Moffett, Okla. 288/S4
Moffett Nav. Air Sta., Calif. 204/K3
Moffit, N. Dak. 282/K6
Mogadiscio (prov.), Somalia 115/J3
Mogadishu (cap.), Somalia 2/M5
Mogadishu (cap.), Somalia 102/G4
Mogadishu (cap.), Somalia 115/J3
Mogador (Essaouira), Morocco 106/B2
Mogadore, Ohio 284/H3
Mogadouro, Portugal 33/C2
Mogami (riv.), Japan 81/K4
Mogaung, Burma 72/C1
Møgeltønder, Denmark 21/B8
Mogi das Cruzes, Brazil 132/E9
Mogi das Cruzes, Brazil 135/C3
Mogi Guaçu (riv.), Brazil 135/C2
Mogi-Guaçu, Brazil 135/C3
Mogilev, U.S.S.R. 7/G3
Mogilev, U.S.S.R. 52/C4
Mogilev, U.S.S.R. 48/D4
Mogilev-Podol'skiy, U.S.S.R. 52/C5
Mogil Mogil, N.S. Wales 97/E1
Mogilno, Poland 47/C2
Mogi-Mirim, Brazil 135/C3
Mogincual, Mozambique 118/G3
Mogocha, U.S.S.R. 48/N4
Mogok, Burma 72/C2
Mogollon (plat.), Ariz. 198/D4
Mogollon, N. Mex. 274/A5
Mogollon (mts.), N. Mex. 274/A5
Mogollon Baldy (peak), N. Mex. 274/A5
Mogollon Rim (cliffs), Ariz. 198/D4
Mogororo, Chad 111/D5
Mogotes (pt.), Argentina 143/E4
Moguer, Spain 33/C4
Mohács, Hungary 41/E4
Mohaka (riv.), N. Zealand 100/F3
Mohaleshoek, Lesotho 118/D6
Mohall, N. Dak. 282/G2
Mohammadia, Algeria 106/D1
Mohammedia, Morocco 106/C2
Mohave (co.), Ariz. 198/A3
Mohave (lake), Ariz. 198/A3
Mohave (mts.), Ariz. 198/A4
Mohave (lake), Nev. 266/G7
Mohawk (mts.), Ariz. 198/B6
Mohawk (mt.), Conn. 210/B1
Mohawk, Ind. 227/F5
Mohawk, Mich. 250/A1
Mohawk (riv.), N.H. 268/E2
Mohawk (lake), N.J. 273/D1
Mohawk, N.Y. 276/L4
Mohawk (riv.), N.Y. 276/L5
Mohawk, Oreg. 291/E3
Mohawk, Tenn. 237/P8
Mohawk, W. Va. 312/C7
Mohe, China 77/K1
Mohegan, Conn. 210/G3
Mohéli (Mwali) (isl.), Comoros 102/G6
Mohéli (Mwali) (isl.), Comoros 118/G2
Mohelnice, Czech. 41/D2
Mohenjo Daro (ruins), Pakistan 68/B3
Moher (cliffs), Ireland 17/B6
Mohican (cape), Alaska 196/E2
Mohican (riv.), Ohio 284/F4
Mohill, Ireland 17/F4
Mohler, Wash. 310/G3
Möhlin, Switzerland 39/E1
Mohnton, Pa. 294/L5
Mohnyin, Burma 72/C1
Moho, Peru 128/H10
Mohoro, Tanzania 115/G5
Mohrsville, Pa. 294/K5
Moi, Norway 18/E7
Moidart (dist.), Scotland 15/C4
Moiese, Mont. 262/B3
Moiliili, Hawaii 218/C4
Moineşti, Romania 45/H2
Moingona, Iowa 229/F4
Moira, N.Y. 276/M1
Moírai, Greece 45/G8
Moirones, Uruguay 145/E2
Mõisaküla, U.S.S.R. 53/C1
Moise (riv.), Que. 146/M4
Moisés Ville, Argentina 143/E5
Moisie (riv.), Que. 162/K5
Moisie, Québec 174/D2
Moisie (riv.), Québec 174/D2
Moissac, France 28/D5
Moïssala, Chad 111/C6
Moitaco, Venezuela 124/F4
Mojácar, Spain 33/F4
Mojave, Calif. 204/G8
Mojave (des.), Calif. 204/H9
Mojave (riv.), Calif. 204/J9
Mojo, Bolivia 136/C7
Mojocoya, Bolivia 136/C6
Mojokerto, Indonesia 85/K2
Mokane, Mo. 261/J5
Mokapu, Hawaii 218/F2
Mokapu (pen.), Hawaii 218/F2
Mokau (riv.), N. Zealand 100/E3
Mokelumne (riv.), Calif. 204/C9
Mokelumne Hill, Calif. 204/E5
Mokena, Ill. 222/B6
Mokil (atoll), Micronesia 87/G5
Moknine, Tunisia 106/G1
Mokohinau (isl.), N. Zealand 100/E1
Mokokchung, India 68/G3
Mokolo, Cameroon 115/B1
Mokp'o, S. Korea 81/C6
Moksha (riv.), U.S.S.R. 52/F4
Mokuaulua (isl.), Hawaii 218/E1
Mokuaweoweo (crater), Hawaii 218/H6
Mokuhoonki (isl.), Hawaii 218/J1
Mokuleia, Hawaii 218/D1
Mol, Belgium 27/G6
Mola di Bari, Italy 34/F4
Molalla, Oreg. 291/B3
Molalla (riv.), Oreg. 291/B3
Moland, Minn. 255/E6
Molanosa, Sask. 181/M4
Moláoi, Greece 45/F7
Molare (peak), Switzerland 39/G3
Mold, Wales 13/G2
Moldau (Vltava) (riv.), Czech. 41/C2
Moldava nad Bodvou, Czech. 41/F2
Moldavian S.S.R., U.S.S.R. 7/G4
Moldavian S.S.R., U.S.S.R. 52/C5
Moldavian S.S.R., U.S.S.R. 48/C5
Molde, Norway 18/E5
Moldova Nouă, Romania 45/E3
Modoveanul (mt.), Romania 45/G3
Mole (riv.), England 13/H8
Môle (cape), Haiti 158/B5
Mole Creek, Tasmania 99/C3
Molega (lake), Nova Scotia 168/D4
Molena, Georgia 217/D4
Molenbeek-Saint-Jean, Belgium 27/B9
Molepolole, Botswana 118/C4
Molepolole, Botswana 102/E7
Môle Saint Nicolas, Haiti 158/B5
Molfetta, Italy 34/F4
Molina, Chile 138/A10
Molina, Colo. 208/D4
Molina, Spain 33/F2
Molinas, Argentina 143/C2
Moline, Ill. 188/J2
Moline, Ill. 222/C2
Moline, Kansas 232/F4
Moline, Manitoba 179/B4
Moline, Mich. 250/D6
Moline Acres, Mo. 261/R2
Molinicos, Spain 33/F3
Molinière (pt.), Grenada 161/C8
Molino, Fla. 212/B6
Molinos (pt.), P. Rico 161/G1
Moliro, Zaire 115/E5
Molise (reg.), Italy 34/E4
Mollebjerg (mt.), Denmark 21/C6
Mollendo, Peru 120/B4
Mollendo, Peru 128/F11
Mollerusa, Spain 33/G2
Molles (pt.), Chile 138/A9
Mollis, Switzerland 39/H2
Mölln, Germany 22/D2
Mollusk, Va. 307/P5
Mollys Falls (pond), Vt. 268/C3
Mölndal, Sweden 18/H8
Moloaa, Hawaii 218/D1
Molodechno, U.S.S.R. 48/C4
Molodechno, U.S.S.R. 52/C4
Molokai (isl.), Hawaii 87/L3
Molokai (isl.), Hawaii 188/F5
Molokai (isl.), Hawaii 218/G1
Molokini (isl.), Hawaii 218/J2
Molong, N.S. Wales 97/E3
Molopo (riv.), Botswana 118/C5
Molopo (riv.), S. Africa 118/C5
Molotov (Perm'), U.S.S.R. 52/J3
Moloundou, Cameroon 115/C3
Molson (lake), Manitoba 179/J3
Molson, Wash. 310/F2
Molt, Mont. 262/H5
Molteno, S. Africa 118/D6
Molucca (isls.), Indonesia 54/O10
Molucca (sea), Indonesia 54/O10
Molucca (sea), Indonesia 85/H6
Moluccas (isls.), Indonesia 85/H6
Molunkus (lake), Maine 243/G4
Moma, Mozambique 118/F3
Mombasa, Kenya 115/G4
Mombasa, Kenya 102/G5
Mombetsu, Japan 81/L1
Mombo, Tanzania 115/G4
Momchilgrad, Bulgaria 45/G5
Momence, Ill. 222/F2
Momeyer, N.C. 281/N3
Momignies, Belgium 27/E8
Momostenango, Guatemala 154/B3
Mompog (passage), Philippines 82/D4
Mompós, Colombia 126/C3
Mon (state), Burma 72/C3
Mon (riv.), Burma 72/B2
Møn (isl.), Denmark 21/F8
Møn (isl.), Denmark 18/H9
Mona (passage) 146/M8
Mona, Cyprus 63/E5
Mona (passage), Dom. Rep. 156/E3
Mona (passage), Dom. Rep. 158/F6
Mona (isl.), P. Rico 156/E3
Mona (passage), P. Rico 156/E3
Mona (passage), P. Rico 161/A2
Mona, Utah 304/C4
Mona (res.), Utah 304/C4
Monaca, Pa. 294/B4
Monach (isls.), Scotland 15/A3
Monach (sound), Scotland 15/A3
Monaco 7/E4
MONACO 28/G6
Monadhliath (mts.), Scotland 15/D3
Monadnock (mt.), N.H. 268/C6
Monagas (state), Venezuela 124/G3
Monaghan (co.), Ireland 17/H3
Monaghan, Ireland 10/C3
Monaghan, Ireland 17/G3
Monahans, Texas 303/B6
Monango, N. Dak. 282/N7
Monapo, Mozambique 118/G2
Monar, Loch (lake), Scotland 15/C3
Monarch, Alberta 182/D5
Monarch, Mont. 262/F3
Monarch Mills, S.C. 296/D2
Monarda, Maine 243/G4
Monaro (range), N.S. Wales 97/E5
Monashee (mts.), Br. Col. 184/H4
Monasterevan, Ireland 17/H5
Monastery, Nova Scotia 168/G3
Monastir, Tunisia 106/G1
Monatélé, Cameroon 115/B3
Mona Vale, N.S. Wales 88/L3
Mona Vale, N.S. Wales 97/K2
Monaville, W. Va. 312/B7
Monavullagh (mts.), Ireland 17/F7
Monbetsu, Japan 81/L2
Moncalieri, Italy 34/A2
Monçao, Portugal 33/B1
Moncayo (mt.), Spain 33/F2
Moncayo, Sierra de (range), Spain 33/F2
Monchegorsk, U.S.S.R. 7/H2
Monchegorsk, U.S.S.R. 48/C3
Monchegorsk, U.S.S.R. 52/D1
Mönchengladbach, Germany 22/B3
Monches, Wis. 317/J1
Monchique, Portugal 33/B4
Monchique, Serra de (mts.), Portugal 33/B4
Monción, Dom. Rep. 158/D5
Moncks Corner, S.C. 296/G5
Monclo, W. Va. 312/C7
Monclova, Mexico 146/H7
Monclova, Mexico 150/J3
Monclova, Ohio 284/C2
Moncouche (lake), Québec 172/G1
Moncton, N. Br. 146/M5
Moncton, N. Br. 162/K6
Moncton, New Bruns. 170/F2
Moncure, N.C. 281/L3
Mondamin, Iowa 229/B5
Monday (riv.), Paraguay 144/E4
Mondego (cape), Portugal 33/B2
Mondego (riv.), Portugal 33/B2
Mondéjar, Spain 33/E2
Mondonac (lake), Québec 172/D2
Mondoñedo, Spain 33/C1
Mondovi, Wis. 317/C6
Mondovì Breo, Italy 34/A2
Mondragon, Philippines 85/H3
Mondragon, Philippines 82/E4
Mondsee, Austria 41/B3
Moneague, Jamaica 158/J6
Monee, Ill. 222/F2
Monero, N. Mex. 274/C2
Monessen, Pa. 294/C5
Monesterio, Spain 33/C3
Moneta, Iowa 229/C2
Moneta, Va. 307/J6
Moneta, Wyo. 319/E2
Monett, Mo. 261/E9
Monetta, S.C. 296/D4
Monette, Ark. 202/K2
Money (isl.), China 85/E2
Money, Miss. 256/D3
Moneygall, Ireland 17/F6
Moneymore, N. Ireland 17/H2
Monfalcone, Italy 34/D2
Monforte, Portugal 33/C3
Monforte, Spain 33/C1
Monga, Zaire 115/D3
Mongalla, Sudan 111/F6
Mong Cai, Vietnam 72/E2
Möng Hsat, Burma 72/C2
Monghyr, India 68/F3
Möng Maü, Burma 72/C3
Möng Mit, Burma 72/C2
Möng Tung, Burma 72/C2
Mongo, Chad 111/C5
Mongo, Chad 102/D3
Mongo, Ind. 227/G1
MONGOLIA 77
Mongolia 2/P3
Mongolia 54/M5
Mongoumba, Cent. Afr. Rep. 115/C3
Möng Pan, Burma 72/C2
Möng Si, Burma 72/C2
Möng Tön, Burma 72/C2
Möng Tung, Burma 72/C2
Mongu, Zambia 102/E6
Mongu, Zambia 115/D7
Monhegan •, Maine 243/E8
Monhegan (isl.), Maine 243/E8
Mönhhaan, Mongolia 77/H2
Moniac, Georgia 217/H9
Moniaive, Scotland 10/D3
Moniaive, Scotland 15/E5
Monica, Ill. 222/D3
Monico, Wis. 317/H4
Monida, Mont. 262/D6
Monie, Md. 245/P8
Monifieth, Scotland 15/F4
Moniquirá, Colombia 126/D5
Moniteau (co.), Mo. 261/G5
Monitor, Alberta 182/E4
Monitor, Ind. 227/D4
Monitor (range), Nev. 266/E4
Monitor, Oreg. 291/B3
Monitor, Wash. 310/E3
Monivea, Ireland 17/D5
Monkayo, Philippines 82/E7
Monkey (pt.), Nicaragua 154/F5

412 Monkey

Monkey (hill), St. Kitts & Nevis 161/C10
Monkey River Town, Belize 154/C2
Mońki, Poland 47/F2
Monkoto, Zaire 115/D4
Monkton, Md. 245/M2
Monkton, Ontario 177/C4
Monkton•, Vt. 268/A3
Monkton Ridge, Vt. 268/A3
Monmouth, Ill. 222/C3
Monmouth, Ind. 227/H3
Monmouth, Iowa 229/M4
Monmouth, Maine 243/D7
Monmouth•, Maine 243/D7
Monmouth (co.), N.J. 273/E3
Monmouth, Oreg. 291/D3
Monmouth, Wales 13/E6
Monmouth, Wales 10/E5
Monmouth Beach, N.J. 273/F3
Monmouth Junction, N.J. 273/D3
Monnickendam, Netherlands 27/C4
Mono (riv.), Benin 106/E7
Mono (co.), Calif. 204/F5
Mono (lake), Calif. 188/C3
Mono (lake), Calif. 204/G5
Mono (riv.), Togo 106/E7
Monocacy (riv.), Md. 245/J3
Monocacy Nat'l Battlefield, Md. 245/J3
Mono Lake, Calif. 204/F5
Monolith, Calif. 204/G8
Monólithos, Greece 45/H7
Monomonac (lake), Mass. 249/G2
Monomoy (isl.), Mass. 249/O6
Monomoy (pt.), Mass. 249/O6
Monon, Ind. 227/D3
Monona (co.), Iowa 229/B4
Monona, Iowa 229/L2
Monona, Wis. 317/H9
Monongah, W. Va. 312/F4
Monongahela, Pa. 294/B5
Monongahela (riv.), Pa. 294/C6
Monongahela (riv.), W. Va. 312/G3
Monongalia (co.), W. Va. 312/F3
Monopoli, Italy 34/F4
Monor, Hungary 41/E3
Monos (isl.), Trin. & Tob. 161/A10
Monóvar, Spain 33/F3
Monoville, Tenn. 237/K8
Monowi, Nebr. 264/F2
Monreal del Campo, Spain 33/F2
Monreale, Italy 34/D5
Monroe (co.), Ala. 195/D7
Monroe (co.), Ark. 202/H4
Monroe, Ark. 202/H4
Monroe•, Conn. 210/C3
Monroe (co.), Fla. 212/E7
Monroe (lake), Fla. 212/E3
Monroe (co.), Georgia 217/E4
Monroe, Georgia 217/E3
Monroe (co.), Ill. 222/C5
Monroe (co.), Ind. 227/D6
Monroe, Ind. 227/H3
Monroe (lake), Ind. 227/E6
Monroe (co.), Iowa 229/H7
Monroe, Iowa 229/G5
Monroe (co.), Ky. 237/K7
Monroe, La. 188/H4
Monroe, La. 146/J6
Monroe, La. 238/F1
Monroe•, Maine 243/E6
Monroe (co.), Mich. 250/F7
Monroe, Mich. 250/F7
Monroe (co.), Miss. 256/H3
Monroe (co.), Mo. 261/H3
Monroe, Nebr. 264/G3
Monroe•, N.H. 268/C3
Monroe (mt.), N.H. 268/E3
Monroe•, N.J. 273/E3
Monroe (co.), N.Y. 276/E4
Monroe, N.Y. 276/M8
Monroe, N.C. 281/J5
Monroe (co.), Ohio 284/H6
Monroe, Ohio 284/B7
Monroe, Okla. 288/S4
Monroe, Oreg. 291/D3
Monroe (co.), Pa. 294/M3
Monroe (Monroeton), Pa. 294/J2
Monroe, S. Dak. 298/P7
Monroe (co.), Tenn. 237/N10
Monroe, Tenn. 237/L8
Monroe, Utah 304/B5
Monroe (peak), Utah 304/B5
Monroe, Va. 307/K6
Monroe, Wash. 310/D3
Monroe (co.), W. Va. 312/E7
Monroe (co.), Wis. 317/E8
Monroe, Wis. 317/G10
Monroe Bridge, Mass. 249/C2
Monroe Center, Ill. 222/E1
Monroe City, Ind. 227/C7
Monroe City, Mo. 261/J3
Monroe P.O. (Stepney), Conn. 210/B3
Monroeton, Pa. 294/J2
Monroeville, Ala. 195/D7
Monroeville, Ind. 227/H3
Monroeville, N.J. 273/C4
Monroeville, Ohio 284/E3
Monroeville, Pa. 294/C7
Monrovia, Ala. 195/E1
Monrovia, Calif. 204/D10
Monrovia, Ind. 227/E5
Monrovia (cap.), Liberia 106/B7
Monrovia (cap.), Liberia 2/J5
Monrovia (cap.), Liberia 102/A4
Monrovia, Md. 245/J3
Mons, Belgium 27/E8
Monsanto, Portugal 33/C2
Monschau, Germany 22/B3
Monse, Wash. 310/F2
Monsefú, Peru 128/C6
Monselice, Italy 34/C2
Montserrate (isl.), Mexico 150/D4
Monsey, N.Y. 276/J8
Møns Klint (cliff), Denmark 21/F8
Monson•, Maine 243/E5
Monson, Mass. 249/E4
Monson•, Mass. 249/E4
Mönsterås, Sweden 18/K8
Montagu, S. Africa 118/C6
Montague (isl.), Alaska 196/D1
Montague (str.), Alaska 196/D1
Montague, Calif. 204/C2
Montague•, Mass. 249/E2
Montague (isl.), Mexico 150/B1
Montague, Mich. 250/C5
Montague, Mont. 262/F3
Montague, N.J. 273/D1
Montague, N.C. 281/N6
Montague, Pr. Edward I. 168/F2
Montague (co.), Texas 303/G4
Montague, Texas 303/G4
Montague (sound), W. Australia 88/C2
Montague (sound), W. Australia 92/D1
Montague City, Mass. 249/D2
Montalba, Texas 303/J6
Montalbán, Spain 33/F2
Montalcino, Italy 34/C3
Mont Alto, Pa. 294/G6
Montalto Uffugo, Italy 34/E5
Montalvão, Portugal 33/C3
Montalvo, Calif. 204/F9
Montana 188/E1
MONTANA 262
Montana, Alaska 196/B1
Montaña, La (reg.), Peru 128/F8
Montana, Switzerland 39/D4
Montana (state), U.S. 146/H5
Montana Mines, W. Va. 312/F3
Montánchez, Spain 33/D3
Montanja di Reij, Neth. Ant. 161/G9
Montara, Calif. 204/H3
Montargil, Portugal 33/B3
Montargis, France 28/E3
Montauban, France 28/D5
Montauban, Québec 172/E3
Montauk, N.Y. 276/S8
Montauk (pt.), N.Y. 276/S8
Montbard, France 28/F4
Montbéliard, France 28/G4
Mont Belvieu, Texas 303/L1
Montblanch, Spain 33/G2
Montbrison, France 28/E5
Montbrook, Fla. 212/D2
Montcalm (co.), Mich. 250/D5
Montcalm (co.), Québec 172/C3
Montcalm (co.), Québec 174/B3
Mont-Carmel, Québec 172/H2
Montceau-les-Mines, France 28/F4
Mont Cenis (tunnel), France 28/G5
Mont Cenis (tunnel), Italy 34/A2
Montcerf, Québec 172/A3
Montclair, Calif. 204/D10
Montclair, N.J. 273/B2
Montclare, S.C. 296/H3
Montcoal, W. Va. 312/D7
Mont-de-Marsan, France 28/C6
Montdidier, France 28/E3
Mont-Dore, France 28/E5
Monteagle, Tenn. 237/K10
Monteagudo, Bolivia 136/D6
Monte Alegre, Brazil 132/C3
Montealegre del Castillo, Spain 33/F3
Monte Alegre de Minas, Brazil 132/D7
Monte Aprazível, Brazil 135/A2
Monte Azul, Brazil 132/F6
Monte Bello (isls.), Australia 87/B8
Montebello, Calif. 204/C10
Montebello, Québec 172/B4
Monte Bello (isls.), W. Australia 88/A4
Monte Bello (isls.), W. Australia 92/A3
Montebelluna, Italy 34/D2
Monte Carlo, Monaco 28/G6
Monte Caseros, Argentina 143/G5
Montecito, Calif. 204/F9
Monte Comán, Argentina 143/C3
Monte Creek, Br. Col. 184/G5
Montecristi (prov.), Dom. Rep. 158/D5
Monte Cristi, Dom. Rep. 156/D2
Montecristi, Dom. Rep. 158/C5
Montecristi, Ecuador 128/B3
Monte Cristo, Bolivia 136/E4
Montecristo (isl.), Italy 34/C3
Monte Cristo (range), Nev. 266/D4
Monte Dourado, Brazil 132/C2
Montefiascone, Italy 34/D3
Montefrío, Spain 33/D4
Montego (bay), Jamaica 158/G5
Montego Bay, Jamaica 158/H5
Montego Bay, Jamaica 156/B3
Montego Bay (pt.), Jamaica 158/G5
Montegut, La. 238/J8
Montehermoso, Spain 33/C2
Monteiro, Brazil 132/G4
Monteith, Iowa 229/D5
Montejinnie, North. Terr. 93/C4
Monte Lake, Br. Col. 184/G5
Montélimar, France 28/F5
Montelindo (riv.), Paraguay 144/C3
Montellano, Spain 33/D4
Montello, Nev. 266/G1
Montello, Wis. 317/H8
Montemayor (plat.), Argentina 143/C5
Montemorelos, Mexico 150/K4
Montemoro-o-Novo, Portugal 33/B3
Montemoro-o-Velho, Portugal 33/B2
Monte Ne, Ark. 202/B1
Montenegro, Brazil 132/D10
Montenegro, Chile 138/G2
Montenegro (rep.), Yugoslavia 45/D4
Monte Patria, Chile 138/A8
Monte Plata, Dom. Rep. 158/E6
Montepuez, Mozambique 118/F2
Montepulciano, Italy 34/C3
Monte Quemado, Argentino 143/D2
Monte Real, Brazil 132/A5
Monterey, Ala. 195/E7
Monterey (co.), Calif. 204/D7
Monterey, Calif. 188/B3
Monterey, Calif. 204/D7
Monterey (bay), Calif. 188/B3
Monterey (bay), Calif. 204/K4
Monterey, Ind. 227/D2
Monterey, Ky. 237/M4
Monterey, La. 238/G4
Monterey•, Mass. 249/B4
Monterey, Tenn. 237/L8
Monterey, Va. 307/K4
Monterey, Wis. 317/J1
Monterey Park, Calif. 204/C10
Montería, Colombia 120/B2
Montería, Colombia 126/B3
Monte Rio, Calif. 204/B5
Montero, Bolivia 136/D5
Monteros, Argentina 143/C2
Monterotondo, Italy 34/f6
Monterrey, Mexico 2/D4
Monterrey, Mexico 146/J7
Monterrey, Mexico 150/J4
Monterville, W. Va. 312/F5
Montes, Uruguay 145/D5
Montesano, Wash. 310/B4
Monte Sant'Angelo, Italy 34/F4
Monte Santo, Brazil 132/G5
Montes Claros, Brazil 120/E4
Montes Claros, Brazil 132/E7
Monte Sereno, Calif. 204/K4
Montevallo, Ala. 195/E4
Montevallo, Mo. 261/D7
Montevarchi, Italy 34/C3
Montevideo, Minn. 255/C6
Montevideo (dept.), Uruguay 145/B7
Montevideo (cap.), Uruguay 145/B7
Montevideo (cap.), Uruguay 120/D6
Montevideo (cap.), Uruguay 2/G7
Montview, Idaho 220/F6
Monte Vista, Colo. 208/G7
Montezuma (co.), Colo. 208/B8
Montezuma, Colo. 208/H3
Montezuma (peak), Colo. 208/F8
Montezuma, Georgia 217/E6
Montezuma, Ind. 227/C5
Montezuma, Iowa 229/H5
Montezuma, Kansas 232/B4
Montezuma, N. Mex. 274/D3
Montezuma, Ohio 284/A4
Montezuma, Tenn. 237/D10
Montezuma (creek), Utah 304/E6
Montezuma Castle Nat'l Mon., Ariz. 198/D4
Montezuma Creek, Utah 304/E6
Montfoort, Netherlands 27/G4
Montfort, France 28/C3
Montfort, Wis. 317/E10
Montgomery (co.), Ala. 195/F6
Montgomery (cap.), Ala. 188/J4
Montgomery (cap.), Ala. 146/K6
Montgomery (cap.), Ala. 195/F6
Montgomery (co.), Ark. 202/C4
Montgomery (co.), Georgia 217/G6
Montgomery (co.), Ill. 222/D4
Montgomery, Ill. 222/E2
Montgomery (co.), Ind. 227/D4
Montgomery, Ind. 227/C7
Montgomery (co.), Iowa 229/C6
Montgomery, Iowa 229/C2
Montgomery (co.), Kansas 232/G4
Montgomery (co.), Ky. 237/O4
Montgomery, La. 238/E3
Montgomery (co.), Md. 245/J4
Montgomery, Mich. 250/E7
Montgomery, Minn. 255/E6
Montgomery (co.), Miss. 256/E4
Montgomery (co.), Mo. 261/K5
Montgomery (co.), N.Y. 276/M5
Montgomery, N.Y. 276/M7
Montgomery (co.), N.C. 281/K4
Montgomery (co.), Ohio 284/B6
Montgomery, Ohio 284/C9
Montgomery (co.), Pa. 294/M5
Montgomery, Pa. 294/H3
Montgomery (co.), Tenn. 237/G8
Montgomery (co.), Texas 303/J7
Montgomery, Texas 303/J7
Montgomery•, Vt. 268/B2
Montgomery (co.), Va. 307/H6
Montgomery, Wales 13/D5
Montgomery, Wales 10/E4
Montgomery, W. Va. 312/D6
Montgomery Center, Vt. 268/B2
Montgomery City, Mo. 261/K5
Monthey, Switzerland 39/C4
Monticello, Ark. 202/G6
Monticello, Fla. 212/C1
Monticello, Georgia 217/E4
Monticello, Ill. 222/E3
Monticello, Ind. 227/D3
Monticello, Iowa 229/L4
Monticello, Ky. 237/M7
Monticello•, Maine 243/H3
Monticello, Minn. 255/E5
Monticello, Miss. 256/D7
Monticello, Mo. 261/J2
Monticello, N. Mex. 274/B5
Monticello, N.Y. 276/L7
Monticello, Ohio 284/B4
Monticello, S.C. 296/E3
Monticello, Utah 304/E6
Monticello, Wis. 317/G10
Mont Ida, Kansas 232/G3
Montier, Mo. 261/J8
Montigny-les-Metz, France 28/G3
Montigny-le-Tilleul, Belgium 27/E8
Montijo, Panama 154/G6
Montijo (gulf), Panama 154/G7
Montijo, Portugal 33/B3
Montijo, Spain 33/C3
Montilla, Spain 33/D4
Montjoie (lake), Québec 172/B3
Mont-Joli, Québec 162/Kk6
Mont-Joli, Québec 174/D3
Mont-Joli, Québec 172/J1
Mont-Laurier, Québec 162/J6
Mont-Laurier, Québec 172/B3
Mont-Laurier, Québec 174/B3
Mont-Louis, Québec 172/C1
Montluçon, France 28/E4
Montmagny (co.), Québec 172/G3
Montmagny, Québec 174/C3
Montmagny, Québec 172/G3
Montmartre, Sask. 181/H5
Montmédy, France 28/F3
Montmorenci, Ind. 227/D4
Montmorenci, S.C. 296/D4
Montmorency (co.), Mich. 250/E3
Montmorency, Québec 172/J3
Montmorency (riv.), Québec 172/F2
Montmorency, Victoria 97/J4
Montmorency No. 1 (co.), Québec 172/F2
Montmorency No. 1 (co.), Québec 174/C3
Montmorency No. 2 (co.), Québec 172/G3
Montmorillon, France 28/D4
Mont Nebo, Sask. 181/E2
Montney, Br. Col. 184/G2
Monto, Queensland 95/D5
Monto, Queensland 88/J4
Montoire-sur-le-Loir, France 28/D4
Montor, Spain 33/D3
Montoso (mesa), N. Mex. 274/E3
Montour, Idaho 220/B6
Montour, Iowa 229/H5
Montour (co.), Pa. 294/J3
Montour Falls, N.Y. 276/G6
Montoursville, Pa. 294/J3
Montowese, Conn. 210/D3
Montoya, N. Mex. 274/F3
Montoz (mt.), Switzerland 39/D2
Montpelier, Idaho 188/D2
Montpelier, Idaho 220/G7
Montpelier, Ind. 227/G3
Montpelier, Iowa 229/M6
Montpelier, Jamaica 158/H6
Montpelier, La. 238/M1
Montpelier, Miss. 256/G3
Montpelier, N. Dak. 282/N6
Montpelier, Ohio 284/A2
Montpelier (cap.), Vt. 146/L5
Montpelier (cap.), Vt. 188/M2
Montpelier (cap.), Vt. 268/B3
Montpellier, France 7/E4
Montpellier, France 28/E6
Montpellier, Québec 172/B4
Montréal, Canada 2/F3
Montreal (riv.), Mich. 250/F1
Montreal, Mo. 261/G7
Montréal, Que. 146/L5
Montréal, Que. 162/J7
Montréal, Québec 172/H4
Montreal (lake), Sask. 181/F1
Montreal, Wis. 317/F3
Montreal (riv.), Wis. 317/F2
Montréal-Est, Québec 172/J4
Montreal Lake, Sask. 181/F1
Montréal-Nord, Québec 172/H4
Montreal River Harbor, Ontario 177/J5
Montreat, N.C. 281/E3
Montreuil, Pas-de-Calais, France 28/D2
Montreuil, Seine-Saint-Denis, France 28/B2
Montreux, Switzerland 39/C4
Montricher, Switzerland 39/B3
Mont-Rolland, Québec 172/C4
Montrose, Ala. 195/C9
Montrose, Ark. 202/H7
Montrose, Br. Col. 184/J5
Montrose (co.), Colo. 208/C6
Montrose, Colo. 208/D6
Montrose, Georgia 217/F5
Montrose, Ill. 222/E4
Montrose, Iowa 229/L7
Montrose, Kansas 232/D2
Montrose, La. 238/D3
Montrose, Md. 245/K4
Montrose, Mich. 250/F5
Montrose, Minn. 255/E5
Montrose, Miss. 256/F6
Montrose, Mo. 261/E6
Montrose, Pa. 294/L2
Montrose, Scotland 10/E2
Montrose, Scotland 15/F4
Montrose, S. Dak. 298/P6
Montrose, Victoria 97/K5
Montrose, W. Va. 312/G4
Montrose-La Crescenta, Calif. 204/C10
Montross, Va. 307/P4
Montrouge, France 28/B2
Mont-Royal, Québec 172/H4
Monts (pt.), Québec 172/B1
Mont-Saint-Hilaire, Québec 172/D4
Mont-Saint-Michel, France 28/C3
Mont-Saint-Michel, Québec 172/B3
Mont-Saint-Pierre, Québec 172/C1
MONTSERRAT 156/G3
Montserrat (mt.), Spain 33/G2
Montsinéry, Fr. Guiana 131/E3
Mont-Tremblant, Québec 172/C3
Mont-Tremblant Prov. Park, Québec 172/C3
Mont-Tremblant Prov. Park, Québec 174/C3
Montvale, N.J. 273/B1
Montvale, Va. 307/J6
Montverde, Fla. 212/E3
Mont Vernon•, N.H. 268/D6
Montville, Conn. 210/G3
Montville•, Conn. 210/G3
Montville, Maine 243/E7
Montville•, Maine 243/E7
Montville, Mass. 249/B4
Montville•, N.J. 273/E2
Montville, Ohio 284/H2
Montz, La. 238/M3
Monument, Colo. 208/K4
Monument (peak), Idaho 220/B4
Monument, Kansas 232/A2
Monument, N. Mex. 274/F6
Monument, Oreg. 291/H3
Monument (valley), Utah 304/D6
Monument Beach, Mass. 249/M6
Monument Valley, Utah 304/D6
Monywa, Burma 72/B2
Monza, Italy 34/B2
Monze, Zambia 115/E7
Monzón, Spain 33/G2
Mooar, Iowa 229/L8
Moodle (isl.), N.W. Terr. 187/M3
Moodus, Conn. 210/F2
Moodus (res.), Conn. 210/F2
Moody, Ala. 195/F3
Moody A.F.B., Georgia 217/F9
Moody, Maine 243/B9
Moody, Mo. 261/L9
Moody (co.), S. Dak. 298/R5
Moody, Texas 303/G6
Moodys, Okla. 288/S2
Moodyville, Tenn. 237/L7
Mooers, N.Y. 276/N1
Mooka, Japan 81/K5
Mooleyville, Ky. 237/H4
Mooloo Downs, W. Australia 92/B4
Moomin (creek), N.S. Wales 97/E1
Moon (lake), Calif. 204/E2
Moon (lake), Nebr. 264/E2
Moon, Okla. 288/S7
Moonachie, N.J. 273/B2
Moonah (creek), Queensland 95/A4
Moonbeam, Ontario 177/J5
Mooncoin, Ireland 17/G7
Moonie (riv.), N.S. Wales 97/E1
Moonie, Queensland 95/D5
Moon Run, Pa. 294/B5
Moonta, S. Australia 94/E5
Moora, W. Australia 88/B6
Moora, W. Australia 92/B5
Moorabbin, Victoria 88/L7
Moorabbin, Victoria 97/J5
Moorcroft, Wyo. 319/H1
Moore, Idaho 220/E6
Moore, Mont. 262/G4
Moore (dam), N.H. 268/D3
Moore (res.), N.H. 268/D3
Moore (co.), N.C. 281/L4
Moore, Okla. 288/M4
Moore, S.C. 296/D2
Moore (co.), Tenn. 237/J10
Moore (co.), Texas 303/C2
Moore, Texas 303/E9
Moore, Utah 304/C5
Moore (dam), Vt. 268/D3
Moore (res.), Vt. 268/D3
Moore (lake), W. Australia 88/B5
Moore (lake), W. Australia 92/B5
MOOREA, Fr. Poly. 86/S13
Moorea (isl.), Fr. Poly. 87/L7
Moorea (isl.), Fr. Poly. 86/S13
Moorefield, Ark. 202/G2
Moorefield, Ind. 227/G7
Moorefield, Ky. 237/O4
Moorefield, Nebr. 264/D4
Moorefield, Ontario 177/D4
Moorefield, W. Va. 312/J4
Moore Haven, Fla. 212/E5
Mooreland, Ind. 227/G5
Mooreland, Okla. 288/H2
Moore Park, Manitoba 179/C4
Mooresboro, N.C. 281/F4
Moores Bridge, Ala. 195/C4
Mooresburg, Tenn. 237/P8
Moores Creek, Ky. 237/O6
Moores Creek Nat'l Battlefield, N.C. 281/N6
Moores Hill, Ind. 227/G6
Moores Mills, New Bruns. 170/C3
Moorestown, Mich. 250/D4
Moorestown, N.J. 273/B3
Mooresville, Ala. 195/E1
Mooresville, Ind. 227/E5
Mooresville, Mo. 261/E3
Mooresville, N.C. 281/H3
Mooreton, N. Dak. 282/S7
Moore Town, Jamaica 158/K6
Mooretown, Ontario 177/B5
Mooreville, Miss. 256/G2
Moorfoot (hills), Scotland 15/E5
Moorhead, Iowa 229/B5
Moorhead, Minn. 188/G1
Moorhead, Minn. 255/B4
Moorhead, Miss. 256/C4
Mooringsport, La. 238/B1
Moorland, Iowa 229/E4
Moorland, Ky. 237/L2
Moorman, Ky. 237/G6
Moorooka, Queensland 88/K3
Moorooka, Queensland 95/D3
Mooroopna, Victoria 97/C5
Moorpark, Calif. 204/G9
Moorreesburg, S. Africa 118/B6
Moorslede, Belgium 27/B7
Moosburg an der Isar, Germany 22/D4
Moose (creek), Idaho 220/D3
Moose (pond), Maine 243/B7
Moose (riv.), Maine 243/D4
Moose (isl.), Manitoba 179/E3
Moose (riv.), Minn. 255/C2
Moose (riv.), N.Y. 276/K3
Moose (mt.), Sask. 181/J6
Moose (riv.), Vt. 268/D2
Moose (lake), Wis. 317/E3
Moose (lake), Wis. 317/F3
Moose, Wyo. 319/B2
Moose Creek, Ontario 177/K2
Moose Factory, Ontario 175/D2
Moosehead, Maine 243/D4
Moosehead (lake), Maine 243/D4
Mooseheart, Ill. 222/E2
Moose Heights, Br. Col. 184/F3
Moosehorn, Manitoba 179/D3
Moose Jaw, Sask. 146/H4
Moose Jaw, Sask. 162/F6
Moose Jaw, Sask. 181/F5
Moose Jaw (riv.), Sask. 181/G5
Moose Lake, Manitoba 179/H3
Moose Lake, Minn. 255/F4
Mooseland, Nova Scotia 168/F4
Mooseleuk (stream), Maine 243/F2
Mooselookmeguntic (lake), Maine 243/B6
Moose Mountain (creek), Sask. 181/J6
Moose Mountain Prov. Park, Sask. 181/J6
Moose Pass, Alaska 196/C1
Moose Range, Sask. 181/H2
Moose River•, Maine 243/C4
Moose River, Ontario 175/D2
Moosic, Pa. 294/F7
Moosilauke (mt.), N.H. 268/D3
Moosomin, Sask. 162/F5
Moosomin, Sask. 181/K5
Moosonee, Ont. 162/H5
Moosonee, Ont. 146/K4
Moosonee, Ontario 175/D2
Moosup, Conn. 210/H2
Moosup (riv.), Conn. 210/H2
Mopang (lake), Maine 243/H6
Mopeia, Mozambique 118/F3
Mopti, Mali 102/B3
Mopti, Mali 106/D6
Moqatta, Sudan 59/C7
Moqor, Afghanistan 68/B2
Moqor, Afghanistan 59/J3
Moquah, Wis. 317/D2
Moquegua (dept.), Peru 128/G11
Moquegua, Peru 120/B4
Moquegua, Peru 128/G11
Mór, Hungary 41/E3
Mora, Cameroon 115/B1
Mora, India 68/B7
Mora, La. 238/E4
Mora, Minn. 255/E5
Mora, Mo. 261/F5
Mora (co.), N. Mex. 274/E3
Mora, N. Mex. 274/D3
Mora (riv.), N. Mex. 274/E3
Mora, Portugal 33/B3
Mora, Spain 33/E3
Mora, Sweden 18/J6
Moradabad, India 54/J7
Moradabad, India 68/D3
Mora de Rubielos, Spain 33/F2
Morado, Quebrado (riv.), Chile 136/A6
Morafenobe, Madagascar 118/G3
Morąg, Poland 47/E2
Moraga, Calif. 204/K2
Moraine, Ohio 284/B6
Moraleda (chan.), Chile 138/D5
Morales, Guatemala 154/C3
Morales, Peru 128/D6
Moramanga, Madagascar 118/H3
Moramanga, Madagascar 102/G6
Moran, Ind. 227/D4
Moran, Kansas 232/G4
Moran, Mich. 250/E2
Moran, Texas 303/E5
Moran, Wyo. 319/B2
Moranbah, Queensland 95/C9
Morane (isl.), Fr. Poly. 87/N8
Morant (pt.), Jamaica 156/C3
Morant Bay, Jamaica 158/K7
Morar, Scotland 15/C4
Morar, Loch (lake), Scotland 15/C4
Morat (lake), Switzerland 39/D3
Morata de Tajuña, Spain 33/G4
Moratalla, Spain 33/F3
Morattico, Va. 307/P5
Moratuwa, Sri Lanka 68/D7
Morava (riv.), Czech. 41/D2
Morava (riv.), Yugoslavia 45/E3
Moravia, Iowa 229/H7
Moravia, N.Y. 276/H5
Moravian Falls, N.C. 281/G2
Moravská Třebová, Czech. 41/D2
Moravskaé Budějovice, Czech. 41/D2
Morawa, W. Australia 88/B5
Morawa, W. Australia 92/B5
Morawhanna, Guyana 120/D2
Morawhanna, Guyana 131/B1
Moray (firth), Scotland 7/D3
Moray (firth), Scotland 10/E2
Moray (firth), Scotland 15/E3
Moray (trad. co.), Scotland 15/A5
Morazán, Honduras 154/D3
Morbihan (dept.), France 28/B4
Mörbylånga, Sweden 18/K8
Morden, Man. 162/G6
Morden, Manitoba 179/D5
Mordialloc, Victoria 97/J6
Mordialloc, Victoria 88/L7
Mordvinian A.S.S.R., U.S.S.R. 52/G4
Mordvinian A.S.S.R., U.S.S.R. 48/E4
More, Loch (lake), Scotland 15/E2
More, Loch (lake), Scotland 15/D2

Mount Olive 413

Morea, Victoria 97/A5
Moreau (riv.), S. Dak. 298/G3
Moreauville, La. 238/G4
Morebattle, Scotland 15/F5
Morecambe, Alberta 182/E3
Morecambe (bay), England 10/E3
Morecambe (bay), England 13/D3
Moree, N.S. Wales 88/H5
Moree, N.S. Wales 97/E1
Morehead, Kansas 232/G4
Morehead, Ky. 237/P4
Morehead City, N.C. 281/R5
Morehouse (par.), La. 238/G1
Morehouse, Mo. 261/N9
Moreland, Ark. 202/E3
Moreland, Georgia 217/C4
Moreland, Idaho 220/F6
Moreland Hills, Ohio 284/J9
Morelia, Mexico 150/J7
Morelia, Mexico 146/H8
Morelia, Queensland 95/B4
Morell, Pr. Edward I. 168/F2
Morella, Queensland 88/G4
Morella, Spain 33/F2
Morelos (state), Mexico 150/K7
Morelos, Mexico 150/J2
Morelos Cañada, Mexico 150/O2
Morena, India 68/D3
Morena, Sierra (mts.), Spain 7/D5
Morena, Sierra (range), Spain 33/E3
Morenci, Ariz. 198/F5
Morenci, Mich. 250/E7
Moreni, Romania 45/G3
Moreno, Bolivia 136/B2
Moreno, Calif. 204/H10
Moreno (bay), Chile 138/A4
Møre og Romsdal (co.), Norway 18/E5
Mores (creek), Idaho 220/C6
Moresby, Br. Col. 184/B3
Moresby (isl.), Br. Col. 184/B4
Moreton (bay), Queensland 88/K2
Moreton (bay), Queensland 95/E5
Moreton (isl.), Queensland 88/J5
Moreton (isl.), Queensland 95/E5
Moretonhampstead, England 13/C7
Moreton-in-Marsh, England 13/F6
Moretown•, Vt. 268/B3
Morewood, Ontario 177/J2
Morgan (co.), Ala. 195/E2
Morgan (co.), Colo. 208/M2
Morgan (pt.), Conn. 210/D4
Morgan (co.), Georgia 217/F3
Morgan, Georgia 217/C7
Morgan (co.), Ill. 222/C4
Morgan (co.), Ind. 227/E6
Morgan (co.), Ky. 237/P5
Morgan, Ky. 237/N3
Morgan, Minn. 255/D6
Morgan (co.), Mo. 261/G6
Morgan, Mo. 261/G7
Morgan (co.), Ohio 284/G6
Morgan (co.), Tenn. 237/M8
Morgan, Texas 303/G5
Morgan (co.), Utah 304/C2
Morgan, Utah 304/C2
Morgan•, Vt. 268/D2
Morgan (co.), W. Va. 312/K3
Morgan Center, Vt. 268/D2
Morgan City, La. 238/H7
Morgan City, Miss. 256/D4
Morgan Falls (dam), Georgia 217/K1
Morganfield, Ky. 237/E5
Morgan Hill, Calif. 204/L4
Morganito, Venezuela 124/E5
Morgans Point, Texas 303/K2
Morgansville, W. Va. 312/E4
Morganton, Ark. 202/F3
Morganton, Georgia 217/D1
Morganton, N.C. 281/F3
Morgantown, Ind. 227/E6
Morgantown, Ky. 237/H6
Morgantown, Miss. 256/E8
Morgantown, Miss. 256/B7
Morgantown, Ohio 284/D7
Morgantown, Pa. 294/L5
Morgantown, W. Va. 312/G3
Morganville, Kansas 232/E2
Morganville, N.J. 273/E3
Morganza, La. 238/G5
Morges, Switzerland 39/B3
Morguilla (pt.), Chile 138/D1
Mori, China 77/D3
Mori, Japan 81/K2
Moriah, N.Y. 276/N2
Moriah Center, N.Y. 276/N2
Moriarty, N. Mex. 274/D4
Morice (lake), Br. Col. 184/D3
Morice (riv.), Br. Col. 184/D3
Morichal, Colombia 126/E6
Morichal Largo (riv.), Venezuela 124/G3
Morien (cape), Nova Scotia 168/J2
Moriguchi, Japan 81/J7
Morin Creek, Sask. 181/C1
Morin Dawa Daurzu, China 77/K2
Morin Heights, Québec 172/C4
Morinville, Alberta 182/D3
Morioka, Japan 81/K4
Morisset, N.S. Wales 97/F3
Morisset, Québec 172/G3
Moriston (riv.), Scotland 15/D3
Morjärv, Sweden 18/N3
Morlaix, France 28/B3
Morland, Kansas 232/B2
Morley, Alberta 182/C4
Morley, Iowa 229/L4
Morley, Mich. 250/D5
Morley, Mo. 261/N8
Morley, N.Y. 276/K1
Morley, Tenn. 237/O7
Mormon (lake), Ariz. 198/D4
Mormon (mt.), Idaho 220/D4
Mormon (mts.), Nev. 266/G5
Mormon Lake, Ariz. 198/D4
Morne-à-l'Eau, Guadeloupe 161/A6
Morne Seychellois (mt.), Seychelles 118/H5
Morningside, Alberta 182/D3
Morningside, Md. 245/G5
Morningside, Queensland 88/K2
Morningside Park, Conn. 210/G3
Morning Sun, Iowa 229/L6
Mornington (isl.) Chile 138/D8
Mornington (isl.) Queensland 88/F3
Mornington (isl.) Queensland 95/A3
Mornington, Victoria 97/C6
Mornington (pen.), Victoria 97/C6
Morning View, Ky. 237/N3
Moro, Ark. 202/H4
Moro (creek), Ark. 202/F7
Moro, Oreg. 291/G2
Moro (gulf), Philippines 82/D7
Moro (gulf), Philippines 85/G4
Moro (mt.), Switzerland 39/E5
Moro Bay, Ark. 202/F7
Morobe, Papua N.G. 85/C7
Morocco 2/J4
Morocco 102/B1
MOROCCO 106/C2
Morocco, Ind. 227/C3
Morocelí, Honduras 154/D3
Morochata, Bolivia 136/B5
Morococha, Peru 128/D8
Morogoro (reg.), Tanzania 115/G5
Morogoro, Tanzania 115/G5
Morogoro, Tanzania 102/F5
Moroleón, Mexico 150/J6
Morombe, Madagascar 118/G4
Moromoro, Bolivia 136/C6
Morón, Argentina 143/G7
Morón, Cuba 158/F2
Morón, Cuba 158/B2
Moron, Haiti 158/A6
Mörön (Muren), Mongolia 77/F2
Moron (mt.), Switzerland 39/D2
Morón, Venezuela 124/D2
Morona, Ecuador 128/D4
Morona (riv.), Peru 128/D5
Morona-Santiago (prov.), Ecuador 128/C4
Morondava, Madagascar 118/G3
Morondava, Madagascar 102/G7
Morón de la Frontera, Spain 33/D4
Morongo Ind. Res., Calif. 204/J10
Moroni (cap.), Comoros 118/G2
Moroni (cap.), Comoros 102/G6
Moroni, Utah 304/C4
Moron Us He (riv.), China 77/D5
Morotai (isl.), Indonesia 54/O9
Morotai (isl.), Indonesia 85/H5
Moroto, Uganda 115/F3
Morovis, P. Rico 161/D1
Morpeth, England 13/F2
Morpeth, England 10/F3
Morpeth, Ontario 177/C5
Morphou, Cyprus 63/E5
Morphou (bay), Cyprus 63/E5
Morral, Ohio 284/D4
Morrice, Mich. 250/E6
Morrill, Kansas 232/G2
Morrill•, Maine 243/E7
Morrill, Minn. 255/E5
Morrill (co.), Nebr. 264/A3
Morrill, Nebr. 264/A3
Morrillton, Ark. 202/E3
Morrin, Alberta 182/D4
Morrinhos, Brazil 132/D7
Morrinsville, N. Zealand 100/E2
Morris, Ala. 195/E3
Morris (res.), Calif. 204/D10
Morris•, Conn. 210/C2
Morris, Georgia 217/C7
Morris, Ill. 222/E2
Morris, Ind. 227/G6
Morris (co.), Kansas 232/F3
Morris, Manitoba 179/E5
Morris, Minn. 255/C5
Morris (co.), N.J. 273/D2
Morris, N.Y. 276/K5
Morris, Okla. 288/P3
Morris, Pa. 294/H2
Morris (mt.), S. Australia 94/B2
Morris (isl.), S.C. 296/H6
Morris (co.), Texas 303/K4
Morris, W. Va. 312/E5
Morrisburg, Ontario 177/J3
Morris Chapel, Tenn. 237/E10
Morrisdale, New Bruns. 170/D3
Morrisdale, Pa. 294/F4
Morrisey, Wyo. 319/H2
Morris Fork, Ky. 237/O6
Morris Jessup (cape), Greenl. 4/A11
Morrison, Colo. 208/J3
Morrison, Ill. 222/C2
Morrison, Iowa 229/H4
Morrison (lake), Manitoba 179/C1
Morrison (co.), Minn. 255/D4
Morrison, Mo. 261/J5
Morrison, Okla. 288/M2
Morrison, Tenn. 237/K9
Morrison Bluff, Ark. 202/D3
Morrison City, Tenn. 237/R7
Morrisonville, Ill. 222/D4
Morrisonville, N.Y. 276/N1
Morrisonville, Wis. 317/G9
Morris Plains, N.J. 273/D2
Morris Run, Pa. 294/J2
Morriston, Ark. 202/G1
Morriston, Fla. 212/D2
Morriston, Ontario 177/D4
Morristown, Ariz. 198/C5
Morristown, Ill. 222/D1
Morristown, Ind. 227/F5
Morristown, Minn. 255/E6
Morristown, N.J. 273/D2
Morristown, N.Y. 276/J1
Morristown, Ohio 284/H5
Morristown, S. Dak. 298/F2
Morristown, Tenn. 237/P8
Morristown•, Vt. 268/B2
Morristown Nat'l Hist. Park., N.J. 273/D2
Morrisvale, W. Va. 312/C6
Morrisville, Mo. 261/F8
Morrisville, N.Y. 276/J5
Morrisville, N.C. 281/M3
Morrisville, Pa. 294/N5
Morrisville, Vt. 268/B2
Morrito, Nicaragua 154/E5
Morro (pt.), Chile 138/A6
Morro Bay, Calif. 204/D8
Morro do Chapéu, Brazil 132/F5
Morropón, Peru 128/C5
Morros, Brazil 132/F3
Morrosquillo (gulf), Colombia 126/C3
Morrow, Ark. 202/B2
Morrow, Georgia 217/K2
Morrow, La. 238/F5
Morrow (co.), Ohio 284/E4
Morrow, Ohio 284/B7
Morrow (co.), Oreg. 291/H2
Morrow Point (res.), Colo. 208/E6
Morrowville, Kansas 232/E2
Morrumbala, Mozambique 118/F3
Morrumbene, Mozambique 118/F4
Mors (isl.), Denmark 21/B4
Morse (res.), Ind. 227/E4
Morse, La. 238/F6
Morse, Sask. 181/D5
Morse, Texas 303/C1
Morse, Wis. 317/E3
Morse Bluff, Nebr. 264/H3
Morse Mill, Mo. 261/L6
Morses Line, Vt. 268/A2
Morshank, U.S.S.R. 52/F4
Mortagne-au-Perche, France 28/D3
Mortara, Italy 34/B2
Morte (pt.), England 13/C6
Morteau, France 28/G4
Morteros, Argentina 143/D3
Mortes (Manso) (riv.), Brazil 132/D6
Mortlach, Sask. 181/E5
Mortlake, Victoria 97/B6
Morton, Ill. 222/D3
Morton (co.), Kansas 232/A4
Morton, Minn. 255/C6
Morton, Miss. 256/E6
Morton (co.), N. Dak. 282/H6
Morton, Ontario 177/H3
Morton, Pa. 294/M7
Morton, Texas 303/B4
Morton, Wash. 310/C4
Morton, Wyo. 319/D2
Morton Grove, Ill. 222/B5
Morton Mills, Iowa 229/C6
Mortons Gap, Ky. 237/F6
Mortsel, Belgium 27/E6
Moruga, Trin. & Tob. 161/B11
Moruka (riv.), Guyana 131/B2
Morundah, N.S. Wales 97/D4
Moruya, N.S. Wales 97/F4
Morvan (plat.), France 28/F4
Morven, Georgia 217/E9
Morven, N. Zealand 100/C6
Morven, N.C. 281/J5
Morven, Queensland 95/C5
Morven (dist.), Scotland 15/C4
Morven (mt.), Scotland 15/E2
Morvi, India 68/C4
Morvin, Ala. 195/C7
Morwell, Victoria 97/D5
Morwell, Victoria 88/H7
Mosbach, Germany 22/C4
Mosby, Mo. 261/R4
Mosby, Mont. 262/J4
Mosca, Colo. 208/H7
Moscavide, Portugal 33/A1
Moscow, Ark. 202/G5
Moscow, Idaho 220/B3
Moscow, Idaho 188/C1
Moscow, Ind. 227/F6
Moscow, Iowa 229/L5
Moscow, Kansas 232/A4
Moscow, Ky. 237/D7
Moscow, Miss. 256/G5
Moscow, Ohio 284/B8
Moscow, Pa. 294/F7
Moscow, Tenn. 237/C10
Moscow (cap.), U.S.S.R. 2/L3
Moscow (cap.), U.S.S.R. 7/H3
Moscow (cap.), U.S.S.R. 48/D4
Moscow (Moskva) (cap.), U.S.S.R. 52/E3
Moscow, Vt. 268/B3
Moscow Mills, Md. 245/B2
Moscow Mills, Mo. 261/K5
Mosel (riv.), Germany 22/B3
Mosel (riv.), Luxembourg 27/J9
Moseley, Sask. 181/G3
Moseley, Va. 307/N6
Moselle (dept.), France 28/G3
Moselle (riv.), France 28/G3
Moselle, Miss. 256/F8
Moselle, Mo. 261/L6
Moser River, Nova Scotia 168/F4
Moses (lake), Wash. 310/F3
Moses Coulee (canyon), Wash. 310/F3
Moses Lake, Wash. 310/F3
Moses Point, Alaska 196/F2
Mosetenes, Cordillera de (range), Bolivi 136/B5
Mosgiel, N. Zealand 100/C6
Mosgrove, Pa. 294/D4
Moshannon, Pa. 294/F3
Mosheim, Tenn. 237/R8
Mosher, S. Dak. 298/J7
Moshi, Tanzania 115/G4
Moshi, Tanzania 102/F5
Mosier, Oreg. 291/F2
Mosina, Poland 47/C2
Mosinee, Wis. 317/G6
Mosi-Oa-Tunya (falls), Africa 102/E6
Mosi-Oa-Tunya (Victoria) (falls), Zambia 115/E7
Mosi-Oa-Tunya (Victoria) (falls), Zimbabwe 118/C3
Mosjøen, Norway 18/H4
Moskenesøya (isl.), Norway 18/H3
Moskva (Moscow) (cap.), U.S.S.R 52/E3
Moskva (riv.), U.S.S.R. 52/E3
Mosler, Oreg. 291/C2
Mosman, N.S. Wales 88/L4
Mosman, N.S. Wales 97/J3
Mosonmagyaróvár, Hungary 41/D3
Mosquera, Colombia 126/A6
Mosquero, N. Mex. 274/F3
Mosquic (lake), Québec 172/C3
Mosquito (lag.), Fla. 212/F3
Mosquito, Riacho (riv.), Paraguay 144/C3
Mosquito Creek (lake), Ohio 284/J3
Mosquitos, Costa de (reg.), Nicaragua 154/E4
Mosquitos, Golfo de los (gulf), Panama 154/G6
Moss, Miss. 256/F7
Moss, Norway 18/D4
Moss, Tenn. 237/K7
Mossaka, Congo 115/C4
Mossbank, Sask. 181/E6
Moss Beach, Calif. 204/H3
Mossel Bay, S. Africa 102/E8
Mossel Bay, S. Africa 118/C6
Mossendjo, Congo 115/B4
Mossgiel, N.S. Wales 97/C4
Moss Landing, Calif. 204/C7
Mossleigh, Alberta 182/D4
Mossman, Queensland 88/G3
Mossman, Queensland 95/C3
Mossoró, Brazil 120/F3
Mossoró, Brazil 132/G4
Moss Point, Miss. 256/G10
Mossuril, Mozambique 118/G2
Moss Vale, N.S. Wales 97/F4
Mossville, Ill. 222/D3
Mossy (riv.), Manitoba 179/C3
Mossy (riv.), Sask. 181/H1
Mossy Head, Fla. 212/C6
Mossyrock, Wash. 310/C4
Most, Czech. 41/B1
Mostaganem, Algeria 102/C1
Mostaganem, Algeria 106/D1
Mostar, Yugoslavia 7/F4
Mostar, Yugoslavia 45/D4
Mosty, U.S.S.R. 52/B4
Mosul, Iraq 66/C2
Mosul, Iraq 59/D2
Mosul, Iraq 54/F6
Motacucito, Bolivia 136/E5
Mota del Cuervo, Spain 33/E3
Motagua (riv.), Guatemala 154/C3
Motala, Sweden 18/J7
Motherwell and Wishaw, Scotland 10/B1
Motherwell and Wishaw, Scotland 15/C2
Motilla del Palancar, Spain 33/E3
Motiti (isl.), N. Zealand 100/F2
Motley, Minn. 255/D4
Motley (co.), Texas 303/D3
Motobu, Japan 81/N6
Motozintla de Mendoza, Mexico 150/N9
Motril, Spain 33/E4
Motsuta (cape), Japan 81/J2
Mott, N. Dak. 282/F7
Motu (riv.), N. Zealand 100/F3
Motueka, N. Zealand 100/D4
Motuhora (isl.), N. Zealand 100/F2
Motuihe (isl.), N. Zealand 100/C1
Motul de Fielipe Carillo Puerto, Mexico 150/P6
Motupe, Peru 128/C6
Motutapu (isl.), N. Zealand 100/C1
Motygino, U.S.S.R. 48/K4
Mouchoir (passage), Turks & Caicos 156/D2
Moúdros, Greece 45/G6
Moudjéria, Mauritania 106/B5
Moudon, Switzerland 39/C3
Mouhoun (riv.), Burkina Faso 106/D6
Mouila, Gabon 115/B4
Mouka, Cent. Afr. Rep. 115/D2
Moulamein, N.S. Wales 97/C4
Moulamein (creek), N.S. Wales 97/C4
Mould Bay, Canada 4/B16
Mould Bay, N.W. Terr. 187/F2
Moule, Guadeloupe 161/B6
Moule à Chique (cape), St. Lucia 161/G7
Moulin-Morneault, New Bruns. 170/B1
Moulins, France 28/E4
Moulmein, Burma 72/C3
Moulmein, Burma 54/L8
Moulouya (riv.), Morocco 106/D2
Moulton, Ala. 195/D2
Moulton, Iowa 229/H7
Moulton, Mont. 262/G3
Moulton, Texas 303/H8
Moultonboro•, N.H. 268/E4
Moultrie, Fla. 212/E2
Moultrie, Georgia 217/E8
Moultrie (co.), Ill. 222/E4
Moultrie (lake), S.C. 188/K4
Moultrie (lake), S.C. 296/G5
Mounana, Gabon 115/B4
Mound, La. 238/H2
Mound, Minn. 255/E6
Mound Bayou, Miss. 256/C3
Mound City, Ill. 222/D6
Mound City, Kansas 232/H3
Mound City, Mo. 261/B2
Mound City, S. Dak. 298/K2
Mound City Group Nat'l Mon., Ohio 284/E7
Moundou, Chad 111/C6
Moundou, Chad 102/D4
Moundridge, Kansas 232/E3
Mounds, Ill. 222/D6
Mounds, Okla. 288/O3
Mound Station (Timewell), Ill. 222/C3
Mounds View, Minn. 255/G5
Moundsville, W. Va. 312/E3
Mound Valley, Kansas 232/G4
Moundville, Ala. 195/C5
Moundville, Mo. 261/C7
Moung Roussei, Cambodia 72/D4
Mouniapamôk, Laos 72/E4
Mount (cape), Liberia 106/B7
Mountain, N. Dak. 282/P2
Mountain (riv.), N.W. Terr. 187/F3
Mountain, Ontario 177/J2
Mountain (prov.), Philippines 82/C2
Mountain, W. Va. 312/E4
Mountain, Wis. 317/K5
Mountainair, N. Mex. 274/C4
Mountain Ash, Ky. 237/N7
Mountain Ash, Wales 13/A6
Mountain Ash, Wales 10/E5
Mountainboro, Ala. 195/F2
Mountain Brook, Ala. 195/E4
Mountainburg, Ark. 202/B2
Mountain City, Georgia 217/F1
Mountain City, Nev. 266/F1
Mountain City, Tenn. 237/T8
Mountain Creek, Ala. 195/E5
Mountain Creek (lake), Texas 303/G2
Mountaindale, Md. 245/J2
Mountain Dale, N.Y. 276/L7
Mountaindale, Oreg. 291/A1
Mountain Fork (riv.), Ark. 202/A5
Mountain Fork (riv.), Okla. 288/S6
Mountain Grove, Mo. 261/H8
Mountain Grove, Ontario 177/H3
Mountain Home, Ark. 202/F1
Mountain Home, Idaho 220/C6
Mountain Home (res.), Idaho 220/C6
Mountainhome, Pa. 294/M3
Mountain Home, Utah 304/D3
Mountain Home A.F.B., Idaho 220/C6
Mountain Iron, Minn. 255/F3
Mountain Lake, Minn. 255/D7
Mountain Lake Park, Md. 245/A3
Mountain Lakes, N.J. 273/E2
Mountain Meadows (res.), Calif. 204/E3
Mountain Park, Georgia 217/D2
Mountain Park, Okla. 288/J5
Mountain Pine, Ark. 202/D4
Mountain Point, Alaska 196/N2
Mountain Rest, S.C. 296/A2
Mountain Road, Manitoba 179/C4
Mountainside, N.J. 273/E2
Mountain Valley, Ark. 202/D4
Mountain View, Alberta 182/D5
Mountain View, Ark. 202/F2
Mountain View, Calif. 204/K3
Mountain View, Georgia 217/K2
Mountainview, Hawaii 218/J5
Mountain View, Mo. 261/J8
Mountain View, N.J. 273/B2
Mountain View, Okla. 288/J4
Mountain View, Wyo. 319/B4
Mountain View, Wyo. 319/F3
Mountain Village, Alaska 196/E2
Mountain Zebra Nat'l Park, S. Africa 118/C6
Mount Airy, Georgia 217/F1
Mount Airy, La. 238/M3
Mount Airy, Md. 245/K3
Mount Airy, N.C. 281/H1
Mount Airy, Tenn. 237/L10
Mount Albert, N. Zealand 100/B1
Mount Albert, Ontario 177/E3
Mount Alto, W. Va. 312/C5
Mount Alton, Pa. 294/E2
Mount Andrew, Ala. 195/H7
Mount Angel, Oreg. 291/B3
Mount Apo National Park, Philippine 82/E7
Mount Arlington, N.J. 273/D2
Mount Arrowsmith, N.S. Wales 97/A2
Mount Assiniboine Prov. Park, Br. Col. 184/K5
Mount Auburn, Ill. 222/D4
Mount Auburn, Ind. 227/G5
Mount Auburn, Iowa 229/J4
Mount Aukum, Calif. 204/E5
Mount Ayr, Ind. 227/C3
Mount Ayr, Iowa 229/E7
Mount Barker, S. Australia 94/C8
Mount Barker, W. Australia 88/B6
Mount Barker, W. Australia 92/B6
Mount Beauty, Victoria 97/D5
Mount Bellew, Ireland 17/D5
Mount Berry, Georgia 217/B2
Mount Bethel, Georgia 217/K1
Mount Blanchard, Ohio 284/D4
Mount Bold (res.), S. Australia 94/B8
Mount Brydges, Ontario 177/C5
Mount Calm, Texas 303/H6
Mount Calvary, Wis. 317/K8
Mount Carbon, W. Va. 312/D7
Mount Carleton Prov. Park, New Bruns. 170/D1
Mount Carmel, Ala. 195/F6
Mount Carmel, Ill. 222/F5
Mount Carmel, Ind. 227/H6
Mount Carmel, Miss. 256/E7
Mount Carmel, Newf. 166/D2
Mount Carmel, N. Dak. 282/O2
Mount Carmel, Ohio 284/C10
Mount Carmel, Pa. 294/K4
Mount Carmel, Pr. Edward I. 168/D2
Mount Carmel, S.C. 296/C3
Mount Carmel, Tenn. 237/R8
Mount Carmel, Utah 304/B6
Mount Carroll, Ill. 222/D1
Mount Cavenagh, North. Terr. 93/C8
Mountcharles, Ireland 17/E2
Mount Clare, W. Va. 312/F4
Mount Clemens, Mich. 250/G6
Mount Cory, Ohio 284/C4
Mount Crawford, Va. 307/L4
Mount Croghan, S.C. 296/G2
Mount Currie, Br. Col. 184/F5
Mount Darwin, Zimbabwe 118/E3
Mount Desert, Maine 243/G7
Mount Desert•, Maine 243/G7
Mount Desert (isl.), Maine 243/G7
Mount Desert Rock (isl.), Maine 243/G8
Mount Dora, Fla. 212/E3
Mount Dora, N. Mex. 274/F2
Mount Doreen, North. Terr. 93/B7
Mount Douglas, Queensland 95/C4
Mount Drysdale, N.S. Wales 97/C2
Mount Eaton, Ohio 284/G4
Mount Eba, S. Australia 94/D4
Mount Eden, Ky. 237/L4
Mount Eden, N. Zealand 100/B1
Mount Edziza Prov. Park and Rec. Area Br. Col. 184/B1
Mount Elgin, Ontario 177/D5
Mount Emu (creek), Victoria 97/B5
Mount Enterprise, Texas 303/K6
Mount Ephraim, N.J. 273/B3
Mount Erie, Ill. 222/E5
Mount Etna, Ind. 227/F3
Mount Etna, Iowa 229/D6
Mount Everard, Guyana 131/B2
Mount Forest, Mich. 250/F5
Mount Forest, Ontario 177/D4
Mount Freedom, N.J. 273/D2
Mount Gambier, Australia 87/D9
Mount Gambier, S. Australia 88/G7
Mount Gambier, S. Australia 94/G7
Mount Gay, W. Va. 312/C7
Mount Gilead, N.C. 281/K4
Mount Gilead, Ohio 284/E4
Mount Gravatt, Queensland 88/K3
Mount Hagen, Papua N.G. 85/B7
Mount Hamill, Iowa 229/K7
Mount Healthy, Ohio 284/B9
Mount Hermon, Calif. 204/K4
Mount Hermon, La. 238/K5
Mount Hermon, Mass. 249/D2
Mount Holly, Ark. 202/E7
Mount Holly•, N.J. 273/D4
Mount Holly, N.C. 281/H4
Mount Holly, S.C. 296/H5
Mount Holly•, Vt. 268/B5
Mount Holly, Va. 307/P4
Mount Holly Springs, Pa. 294/H5
Mount Hood, Oreg. 291/F2
Mount Hope, Ala. 195/D2
Mount Hope (riv.), Conn. 210/G1
Mount Hope, Kansas 232/E4
Mount Hope (bay), Mass. 249/K6
Mount Hope, N.J. 273/D2
Mount Hope, N.S. Wales 97/C3
Mount Hope, Ohio 284/G4
Mount Hope, Ontario 177/E4
Mount Hope (bay), R.I. 249/K6
Mount Hope, W. Va. 312/D7
Mount Hope, Wis. 317/D10
Mount Horeb, Wis. 317/G10
Mount Ida, Ark. 202/C4
Mount Ida, Wis. 317/E10
Mount Isa, Queensland 95/A4
Mount Isa, Queensland 88/F4
Mount Jackson, Va. 307/L3
Mount Jewett, Pa. 294/E2
Mount Joy, Pa. 294/K5
Mount Judea, Ark. 202/D2
Mount Juliet, Tenn. 237/H8
Mount Kisco, N.Y. 276/N8
Mount Kuring-gai, N.S. Wales 97/J3
Mountlake Terrace, Wash. 310/B1
Mount Laurel•, N.J. 273/D4
Mount Lebanon, La. 238/D2
Mount Lebanon•, Pa. 294/B7
Mount Lemmon, Ariz. 198/E6
Mount Leonard, Mo. 261/F4
Mount Liberty, Ohio 284/E5
Mount Lofty (range), S. Australia 88/F6
Mount Lookout, W. Va. 312/E6
Mount Magnet, W. Australia 88/B5
Mount Magnet, W. Australia 92/B5
Mount Margaret, Queensland 95/A3
Mount Margaret, W. Australia 88/C5
Mount Margaret, W. Australia 92/C5
Mount Maunganui, N. Zealand 100/E2
Mount Meigs, Ala. 195/F6
Mountmellick, Ireland 10/C4
Mountmellick, Ireland 17/G5
Mount Meridian, Ind. 227/D5
Mount Molloy, Queensland 95/C3
Mount Montgomery, Nev. 266/C5
Mount Morgan, Queensland 88/J4
Mount Morgan, Queensland 95/D4
Mount Moriah, Mo. 261/E2
Mount Morris, Ill. 222/D1
Mount Morris, Mich. 250/F5
Mount Morris, N.Y. 276/E5
Mount Morris, Pa. 294/B6
Mount Mourne, N.C. 281/H3
Mount Nebo, W. Va. 312/E6
Mount Olive, Ill. 222/D4

Mount Olive, Miss. 256/E7
Mount Olive •, N.J. 273/D2
Mount Olive, N.C. 281/O4
Mount Olive, Pa. 294/B7
Mount Olivet, Ky. 237/N3
Mount Orab, Ohio 284/C7
Mount Pearl, Newf. 166/D2
Mount Penn, Pa. 294/L5
Mount Pleasant, Ark. 202/G2
Mount Pleasant, Del. 245/R2
Mount Pleasant, Fla. 212/B1
Mount Pleasant, Ind. 227/D8
Mount Pleasant, Iowa 229/L7
Mount Pleasant, Md. 245/J3
Mount Pleasant, Mich. 250/E5
Mount Pleasant, Miss. 256/E1
Mount Pleasant, N.C. 281/J4
Mount Pleasant, Nova Scotia 168/C4
Mount Pleasant, Ohio 284/J5
Mount Pleasant, Ontario 177/D4
Mount Pleasant, Pa. 294/D5
Mount Pleasant, S.C. 296/H6
Mount Pleasant, Tenn. 237/G9
Mount Pleasant, Texas 303/K4
Mount Pleasant, Utah 304/C4
Mount Pocono, Pa. 294/M3
Mount Prospect, Ill. 222/B5
Mount Pulaski, Ill. 222/D3
Mountrail (co.), N. Dak. 282/E3
Mount Rainier, Md. 245/P4
Mount Rainier Nat'l Park, Wash. 310/D4
Mountrath, Ireland 17/F5
Mount Revelstoke Nat'l Park, Br. Col. 184/H4
Mount Robson, Br. Col. 184/H3
Mount Robson Prov. Park, Br. Col. 184/H3
Mount Rogers Nat'l Rec. Area, Va. 307/F7
Mount Roskill, N. Zealand 100/B1
Mount Royal, N.J. 273/C4
Mount Royal (range), N.S. Wales 97/F2
Mount Rushmore Nat'l Mem., S. Dak. 298/B6
Mounts (bay), England 10/D6
Mounts (bay), England 13/B7
Mount Saint Helens Nat'l Volcanic Mon., Wash. 310/C4
Mount Salem, Ky. 237/M6
Mount Savage, Md. 245/C2
Mount Shasta, Calif. 204/C5
Mount Sherman, Ala. 202/D1
Mount Sherman, Ky. 237/K6
Mount Sidney, Va. 307/K4
Mount Solon, Va. 307/K4
Mount Standfast, Barbados 161/B8
Mount Sterling, Ala. 195/B6
Mount Sterling, Ill. 222/C4
Mount Sterling, Ind. 227/G7
Mount Sterling, Iowa 229/J7
Mount Sterling, Ky. 237/N4
Mount Sterling, Ohio 284/D6
Mount Sterling, Wis. 317/D9
Mount Stewart, Pr. Edward I. 168/F2
Mount Storm, W. Va. 312/H4
Mount Storm (lake), W. Va. 312/H4
Mount Summit, Ind. 227/G4
Mount Sunapee, N.H. 268/C5
Mount Surprise, Queensland 95/C3
Mount Tabor, N.J. 273/E2
Mount Tabor •, Vt. 268/B5
Mount Tabor, Wis. 317/F8
Mount Tivoli, Grenada 161/D8
Mount Tom, Mass. 249/D3
Mount Trumbull, Ariz. 198/B2
Mount Uniacke, Nova Scotia 168/E4
Mount Union, Iowa 229/L6
Mount Union, Pa. 294/G5
Mount Upton, N.Y. 276/K6
Mount Vernon, Ala. 195/B8
Mount Vernon, Ark. 202/F3
Mount Vernon, Georgia 217/G6
Mount Vernon, Ill. 222/E5
Mount Vernon, Ind. 227/B9
Mount Vernon, Iowa 229/K5
Mount Vernon, Ky. 237/N6
Mount Vernon •, Maine 243/D7
Mount Vernon, Md. 245/P8
Mount Vernon, Mo. 261/E8
Mount Vernon, N.Y. 276/O7
Mount Vernon, Ohio 284/E5
Mount Vernon, Oreg. 291/H3
Mount Vernon, S. Dak. 298/N6
Mount Vernon, Tenn. 237/N10
Mount Vernon, Texas 303/J4
Mount Vernon, Va. 307/O7
Mount Vernon, Wash. 310/C2
Mount Vernon, W. Australia 92/B4
Mount Vernon, Wis. 317/G10
Mount Vernon Springs, N.C 281/L3
Mount Victory, Ohio 284/D4
Mountview, W. Va. 312/D7
Mountville, Georgia 217/C4
Mountville, Pa. 294/K5
Mountville, S.C. 296/C3
Mount Washington, Ky. 237/K4
Mount Washington •, Mass. 249/A4
Mount Wellington, N. Zealand 100/C1
Mount Willing, Ala. 195/E6
Mount Wolf, Pa. 294/J5
Mount Zion, Georgia 217/B3
Mount Zion, Ill. 222/E4
Mount Zion, Ind. 227/G3
Mount Zion, Iowa 229/K7
Mount Zion, W. Va. 312/D5
Moura, Portugal 33/C3
Moura, Queensland 88/J5
Moura, Queensland 88/D4
Mourão, Portugal 33/C3

Mourdi (depr.), Chad 111/D4
Mourne (Newry and Mourne) (dist.), N. Ireland 17/J3
Mourne (mts.), N. Ireland 17/J3
Mourne (riv.), N. Ireland 17/G2
Mouscron, Belgium 27/C7
Moussoro, Chad 111/C5
Mouthcard, Ky. 237/S6
Mouth of Wilson, Va. 307/F7
Moutier, Switzerland 39/D2
Moûtiers, France 28/G3
Mouton (isl.), Nova Scotia 168/D5
Mouydir (mts.), Algeria 106/E3
Moville, Iowa 229/A4
Moville, Ireland 17/G1
Mowbray, Manitoba 179/D5
Mowdok Mual (mt.), Bangladesh 68/G4
Moweaqua, Ill. 222/E4
Mower (co.), Minn. 255/F7
Mowming (Maoming), China 77/H7
Mowrystown, Ohio 284/C7
Moxahala, Ohio 284/F6
Moxee City, Wash. 310/E4
Moxico (prov.), Angola 115/D6
Moxie (lake), Maine 243/F5
Moxley, Georgia 217/H5
Moy (riv.), Ireland 17/C3
Moy, N. Ireland 17/H3
Moyale, Ethiopia 111/G7
Moyale, Kenya 115/G3
Moyamba, S. Leone 106/B7
Moycullen, Ireland 17/C5
Moyers, Okla. 288/P6
Moyers, W. Va. 312/H6
Moyeuvre-Grande, France 28/G3
Moygashel, N. Ireland 17/H3
Moyle, Br. Col. 184/K5
Moyle (riv.), Idaho 220/B1
Moyle (dist.), N. Ireland 17/J1
Moynalty, Ireland 17/H4
Moyo, Uganda 115/F3
Moyobamba, Peru 120/B3
Moyobamba, Peru 128/D6
Moyock, N.C. 281/S1
Moyogalpa, Nicaragua 154/E5
Moyu (Karakax), China 77/A4
Moza Illit, Israel 65/C4
Mozambique 2/L6
Mozambique 102/F6
MOZAMBIQUE 118/E4
Mozambique (chan.), Africa 2/L7
Mozambique (chan.), Africa 102/G6
Mozambique (pt.), La. 238/M7
Mozambique (chan.), Madagascar 118/G3
Mozambique (chan.), Mozambique 118/G3
Mozart, Sask. 181/G4
Mozer, W. Va. 312/H5
Mozhaysk, U.S.S.R. 52/E3
Mozhga, U.S.S.R. 52/H3
Mozier, Ill. 222/C4
Mozyr', U.S.S.R. 48/C4
Mozyr', U.S.S.R. 52/C4
Mpanda, Tanzania 115/F5
Mpika, Zambia 115/F6
Mporokoso, Zambia 115/F5
M'Pouya, Congo 115/C4
Mpraeso, Ghana 106/D7
Mpulungu, Zambia 115/F5
Mpwapwa, Tanzania 115/G5
Mrągowo, Poland 47/E2
Msaken, Tunisia 106/G1
M'Sila, Algeria 106/E1
Msta (riv.), U.S.S.R. 52/D3
Mtakuja, Tanzania 115/F5
Mtsensk, U.S.S.R. 52/E4
Mtwara (reg.), Tanzania 115/G5
Mtwara-Mikindani, Tanzania 102/G6
Mtwara-Mikindani, Tanzania 115/H6
Mu (riv.), Burma 72/B2
Mualama, Mozambique 118/F3
Muang Hinboun, Laos 72/E3
Muang Kènthao, Laos 72/E3
Muang Khammouan, Laos 72/E3
Muang Không, Laos 72/E4
Muang Khôngxédôn, Laos 72/E4
Muang Khoua, Laos 72/D2
Muang May, Laos 72/E4
Muang Ou Tai, Laos 72/D2
Muang Pak-Lay, Laos 72/D3
Muang Paktha, Laos 72/D2
Muang Pakxan, Laos 72/D2
Muang Phin, Laos 72/E3
Muang Sing, Laos 72/D2
Muang Tahoi, Laos 72/E3
Muang Vangviang, Laos 72/D3
Muang Vapi, Laos 72/D3
Muang Xaignabouri (Sayaboury), Laos 72/D3
Muang Xay, Laos 72/D3
Muang Xépôn, Laos 72/E3
Muang Xon, Laos 72/D2
Muar, Malaysia 72/D7
Muarabungo, Indonesia 85/C6
Muarasiberut, Indonesia 85/B6
Muaratewe, Indonesia 85/F6
Muarí, Ras (cape), Pakistan 68/B4
Muari, Ras (cape), Pakistan 59/J5
Mubarraz, Saudi Arabia 59/F4
Mubende, W. Australia 92/B5
Mubi, Nigeria 106/G6
Muchanes, Bolivia 136/B4
Müchein, Germany 22/D3
Muck (isl.), Scotland 10/C2
Muck (isl.), Scotland 15/B4
Muckamore, N. Ireland 17/J2
Muckle Flugga (isl.), Scotland 15/G2
Muckleshoot Ind. Res., Wash. 310/C3
Muckno (lake), Ireland 17/H3
Muco (riv.), Colombia 126/E5
Mucojo, Mozambique 118/G2
Mucondá, Angola 115/D6
Mucondá, Angola 118/C2

Mucope, Angola 115/B7
Mucuchachí, Venezuela 124/C3
Mucuchíes, Venezuela 124/C3
Mucugê, Brazil 132/F6
Mucur, Turkey 63/F3
Mucurapo, Trin. & Tob. 161/A10
Mucuri, Brazil 132/G7
Mucuripe (pt.), Brazil 132/G3
Mucusso, Angola 115/D7
Mud (lake), Idaho 220/F6
Mud (riv.), Ky. 237/H7
Mud (lake), La. 238/D7
Mud (lake), Minn. 255/C2
Mud (lake), Minn. 255/B5
Mud (riv.), Minn. 255/C2
Mud (isl.), Nova Scotia 168/B5
Mud (creek), Okla. 288/L6
Mud (creek), Oreg. 291/K2
Mud (creek), S. Dak. 298/N3
Mud (lake), S. Dak. 298/P2
Mud, W. Va. 312/C6
Mud (riv.), W. Va. 312/B6
Mud Bay, Br. Col. 184/H2
Mud Butte, S. Dak 298/D4
Muddy (creek), Colo. 208/E4
Muddy (brook), Conn. 210/H1
Muddy (pond), Conn. 210/G1
Muddy (riv.), Conn. 210/D3
Muddy, Ill. 222/E6
Muddy (creek), N. Dak. 282/G6
Muddy (creek), St. Kitts & Nevis 161/C10
Muddy (lake), Sask. 181/B3
Muddy (creek), Utah 304/A2
Muddy (creek), Utah 304/C4
Muddy (creek), Wyo. 319/F3
Muddy (creek), Wyo. 319/D2
Muddy (mt.), Wyo. 319/F3
Muddy Boggy (creek), Okla. 288/O7
Mudge (pond), Conn. 210/B1
Mudgee, N.S. Wales 88/J6
Mudgee, N.S. Wales 97/E3
Mudhnib, Saudi Arabia 59/D4
Mudjatik (riv.), Sask. 181/L3
Mud Lake, Idaho 220/F6
Mud Lake, Newf. 166/B3
Mud Lake (res.), S. Dak. 298/N2
Mud Mountain (lake), Wash. 310/D3
Mudon, Burma 72/C3
Mudug (prov.), Somalia 115/J2
Mudurnu, Turkey 63/D2
Muecate, Mozambique 118/F2
Mueda, Mozambique 118/F2
Muenster, Sask. 181/F3
Muenster, Texas 303/G4
Muerto, Mar (lag.), Mexico 150/N9
Muezerskiy, U.S.S.R. 52/D2
Muff, Ireland 17/G1
Mufulira, Zambia 102/E6
Mufulira, Zambia 115/E6
Muge, Portugal 33/B3
Mugford (cape), Newf. 166/B2
Mughar, Israel 65/C2
Mugla (prov.), Turkey 63/C4
Mugla, Turkey 59/A2
Mugla, Turkey 63/C4
Muglad, Sudan 111/E5
Muhammad Qol, Sudan 59/C5
Muhammad Qol, Sudan 111/G3
Muharraq, Bahrain 59/F4
Mühldorf am Inn, Germany 22/E4
Muhlenberg (co.), Ky. 237/G6
Mühlhausen, Germany 22/D3
Mühlviertel (reg.), Austria 41/C2
Muhu (isl.), U.S.S.R. 53/B1
Mui Bai Bung (pt.), Vietnam 54/M9
Muiden, Netherlands 27/G4
Muinebeag, Ireland 17/H6
Muir (glac.), Alaska 196/M1
Muir, Mich. 250/D5
Muir, Pa. 294/J4
Muirkirk, Md. 245/L4
Muirkirk, Scotland 15/E5
Muir of Ord, Scotland 15/D3
Muiron (isls.), W. Australia 88/A4
Muiron (isl.), W. Australia 92/A3
Muir Woods Nat'l Mon., Calif. 204/N2
Muizenberg, S. Africa 118/E7
Muju, S. Korea 81/C6
Mukachevo, U.S.S.R. 52/B5
Mukah, Malaysia 85/E5
Mukalla, Yemen 54/F8
Mukalla, Yemen 59/F7
Mukdahan, Thailand 72/E3
Mukden, Bolivia 136/A2
Mukden (Shenyang), China 77/K3
Mukilteo, Wash. 310/C3
Mukinbudin, W. Australia 92/B5
Muko, Japan 81/J7
Muko (isl.), Japan 81/M3
Muko (riv.), Japan 81/H7
Mukutawa (lake), Manitoba 179/G2
Mukutawa (riv.), Manitoba 179/E1
Mukwonago, Wis. 317/J2
Mula, Spain 33/F3
Mulaló, Ecuador 128/C3
Mulanje (mt.), Malawi 102/F6
Mulanje (mts.), Malawi 115/G7
Mulatos, Colombia 126/B3
Mulberry (creek), Ala. 195/E5
Mulberry, Ark. 202/B2
Mulberry (riv.), Ark. 202/C2
Mulberry, Calif. 204/D4

Mulberry, Fla. 212/E4
Mulberry, Ind. 227/D4
Mulberry, Kansas 232/H4
Mulberry, Ohio 284/B7
Mulberry, Tenn. 237/H10
Mulberry Fork (riv.), Ala. 195/E3
Mulberry Grove, Ill. 222/D5
Mulchatna (riv.), Alaska 196/G2
Mulchén, Chile 138/E1
Mulde (riv.), Germany 22/E3
Muldon, Miss. 256/G3
Muldoon, Texas 303/G8
Muldraugh, Ky. 237/J5
Muldrow, Okla. 288/S4
Mule (mts.), Ariz. 198/E7
Mule Creek, Kansas 232/C4
Mule Creek, N. Mex. 274/A5
Mule Creek, Wyo. 319/H2
Muleculus, Nicaragua 154/E4
Mulegé, Mexico 150/C3
Mulegns, Switzerland 39/J3
Muleshoe, Texas 303/B3
Mulgrave, Nova Scotia 168/G3
Mulgrave (lake), Nova Scotia 168/F3
Mulhacén (mt.), Spain 33/E4
Mulhall, Okla. 288/M2
Mülheim an der Ruhr, Germany 22/B3
Mulhouse, France 7/E4
Mulhouse, France 28/G4
Mulhurst, Alberta 182/D3
Muli, China 77/F6
Muli (str.), Indonesia 85/K7
Mulino, Oreg. 291/B2
Mulinu'u (cape), W. Samoa 86/L8
Mulkear (riv.), Ireland 17/E6
Mull (head), Scotland 15/F2
Mull (head), Scotland 15/F1
Mull (isl.), Scotland 10/D2
Mull (isl.), Scotland 15/C4
Mull (sound), Scotland 15/C4
Mullagh, Ireland 17/H4
Mullaghareirk (mts.), Ireland 17/C7
Mullaghearn (mt.), N. Ireland 17/G2
Mullaghmore, Ireland 17/D3
Mullaittivu, Sri Lanka 68/E7
Mullaley, N.S. Wales 97/E2
Mullan, Idaho 220/C2
Mullardoch, Loch (lake), Scotland 15/C3
Mullen, Nebr. 264/C2
Mullens, W. Va. 312/D7
Müller (mts.), Indonesia 85/E5
Mullet (key), Fla. 212/D4
Mullett (lake), Mich. 250/E3
Mullett Lake, Mich. 250/E3
Mullewa, W. Australia 88/B5
Mullewa, W. Australia 92/A5
Mullheim, Germany 22/B5
Müllheim, Switzerland 39/G1
Mullica (riv.), N.J. 273/D4
Mullica Hill, N.J. 273/C4
Mulliken, Mich. 250/E6
Mullin, Texas 303/F6
Mullinahone, Ireland 17/F7
Mullinavat, Ireland 17/G7
Mullingar, Ireland 10/C4
Mullingar, Ireland 17/G4
Mullingar, Sask. 181/D2
Mullins, S.C. 296/E3
Mullinville, Kansas 232/C4
Mullion, England 13/B7
Mull of Galloway (prom.), Scotland 15/D6
Mull of Kintyre (prom.), Scotland 15/C5
Mull of Oa (prom.), Scotland 15/B5
Mullumbimby, N.S. Wales 97/G1
Mulobezi, Zambia 115/E7
Mulongo, Zaire 115/E5
Mulroy (bay), Ireland 17/F1
Multan, Pakistan 54/J6
Multan, Pakistan 68/C2
Multan, Pakistan 59/K3
Multnomah (co.), Oreg. 291/F2
Mulund, India 68/B6
Mulungushi (dam), Zambia 115/E6
Mulvane, Kansas 232/E4
Mulvihill, Manitoba 179/D4
Mulwala, N.S. Wales 97/D4
Mumbwa, Zambia 115/E6
Mumford, N.Y. 276/E4
Mümliswil-Ramiswil, Switzerland 39/E2
Mumra, U.S.S.R. 52/G5
Mun, Mae Nam (riv.), Thailand 72/D4
Muna (isl.), Indonesia 85/G7
Muna, Mexico 150/P6
Munbura, Queensland 95/C2
Munbura, Queensland 95/D5
Müncheberg, Germany 22/F2
München (Munich), Germany 22/D4
Münchenbuchsee, Switzerland 39/E2
Muncho Lake, Br. Col. 184/L2
Muncho Lake Prov. Park, Br. Col. 184/L2
Muncie, Ill. 222/E2
Muncie, Ind. 188/J2
Muncie, Ind. 227/G4
Muncy, Pa. 294/J3
Muncy Valley, Pa. 294/J3
Munda, Solomon Is. 86/D3
Mundabullangana, W. Australia 92/B3
Mundare, Alberta 182/D3
Mundaring (res.), W. Australia 88/B2
Munday, Texas 303/E4
Mundelein, Ill. 222/A4
Mulberry, Kansas 232/E2
Münden, Germany 22/C3
Mundesley, England 13/J5

Mundijong, W. Australia 88/B3
Mundijong, W. Australia 92/A2
Mundo Novo, Brazil 132/F5
Mundrabilla, W. Australia 92/E5
Mundubbera, Queensland 88/J5
Munera, Spain 33/E3
Munford, Ala. 195/F3
Munford, Tenn. 237/B10
Munfordville, Ky. 237/J6
Mungbere, Zaire 115/F3
Munger, Mich. 250/F5
Mungindi, N.S. Wales 97/E1
Mungindi, Queensland 95/D6
Munguba, Brazil 132/C2
Munhall, Pa. 294/C7
Munhango, Angola 115/C6
Munich, Germany 7/F4
Munich, Germany 22/D4
Munich, N. Dak. 282/N2
Munith, Mich. 250/E6
Munjor, Kansas 232/C3
Munku-Sardyk (mt.), Mongolia 77/F1
Munnerlyn, Georgia 217/H5
Munning (pt.), N. Zealand 100/E7
Munnsville, N.Y. 276/J4
Muñoz Gamero (pen.), Chile 138/D10
Munro (mt.), Tasmania 99/E2
Munroe Falls, Ohio 284/H3
Münsingen, Switzerland 39/E3
Munson, Alberta 182/D4
Munson, Fla. 212/B5
Munson, Pa. 294/F4
Munsonville, N.H. 268/C5
Munster, Ind. 227/B1
Munster (prov.), Ireland 17/D7
Munster (trad. prov.), Ireland 17
Munster, Ontario 177/J2
Münster, Germany 22/B3
Münster, Switzerland 39/F4
Munsungan (lake), Maine 243/E3
Muntendam, Netherlands 27/K2
Muntok, Indonesia 85/D6
Munuscong (lake), Mich. 250/E2
Muojärvi (lake), Finland 18/R4
Muong Khoung, Vietnam 72/E2
Muonio (riv.) 7/G2
Muonio, Finland 18/O3
Muonio (riv.), Finland 18/M2
Muonioälven (riv.), Sweden 18/M2
Muota (riv.), Switzerland 39/G3
Muotathal, Switzerland 39/G3
Muqaddam, Wadi (dry riv.), Sudan 111/F4
Muqdadiyah, Iraq 66/D4
Muqdisho (Mogadishu) (cap.), Somalia 115/J3
Muqdisho (Mogadishu) (cap.), Somalia 102/G4
Muqeible, Israel 65/C2
Muqui, Brazil 132/F8
Mur (riv.), Austria 41/C3
Mur (riv.), Yugoslavia 45/B2
Mura (riv.), Hungary 41/D3
Muradiye, Turkey 63/K3
Murakami, Japan 81/J4
Murallón, Cerro (mt.), Argentina 143/B6
Murallón, Cerro (mt.), Chile 138/D8
Murarrie, Queensland 88/K2
Murashi, U.S.S.R. 52/G3
Murat, France 28/E5
Murat (riv.), Turkey 59/C2
Murat (riv.), Turkey 63/H3
Murat Daği (mt.), Turkey 63/C3
Murau, Austria 41/C3
Murbat, Oman 59/G6
Murchison, N. Zealand 100/D4
Murchison (range), North. Terr. 93/D6
Murchison (Kabalega) (falls), Uganda 115/F3
Murchison (mt.), W. Australia 92/B4
Murchison (mt.), W. Australia 88/B5
Murchison (riv.), W. Australia 92/B4
Murchison Downs, W. Australia 88/B5
Murcia (prov.), Spain 33/F4
Murcia, Spain 7/D5
Murcia, Spain 33/F4
Murcia (reg.), Spain 33/F3
Murderers (creek), Oreg. 291/H3
Murderkill (riv.), Del. 245/R5
Murdo, S. Dak. 298/H6
Murdochville, Québec 172/C1
Murdock, Fla. 212/D4
Murdock, Ill. 222/E4
Murdock, Kansas 232/E4
Murdock, Minn. 255/C5
Murdock, Nebr. 264/H4
Muren (Mörön), Mongolia 77/F2
Mureş (riv.), Romania 45/E2
Muret, France 28/D6
Muretto (pass), Switzerland 39/J4
Murfreesboro, Ark. 202/C5
Murfreesboro, N.C. 281/R2
Murfreesboro, Tenn. 237/J9
Murg (riv.), Switzerland 39/G1
Murgab, U.S.S.R. 48/H6
Murgab (riv.), U.S.S.R. 48/G6
Murghab (riv.), Afghanistan 59/H2
Murgon, Queensland 88/J5
Murgoo, W. Australia 92/B4
Muri, Switzerland 39/F2
Muriaé, Brazil 135/E2
Muriaé, Brazil 132/F8
Murias de Paredes, Spain 33/C1
Muri bei Bern, Switzerland 39/E3
Muriel (lake), Alberta 182/E2
Murindó, Colombia 126/B4
Müritzsee (lake), Germany 22/E2
Murjek, Sweden 18/M3

Murl, Ky. 237/M7
Murle, Ethiopia 111/G6
Murmansk, U.S.S.R. 2/L2
Murmansk, U.S.S.R. 4/C8
Murmansk, U.S.S.R. 7/H2
Murmansk, U.S.S.R. 48/D3
Murmansk, U.S.S.R. 52/D1
Murnau, Germany 22/D5
Murnpeowie, Australia 94/F3
Murom, U.S.S.R. 52/F3
Murongo, Tanzania 115/F4
Muroran, Japan 81/K2
Muros, Spain 33/B1
Muroto, Japan 81/G7
Muroto (pt.), Japan 81/G7
Murphy, Idaho 220/B6
Murphy, Miss. 256/C4
Murphy, Mo. 261/J7
Murphy, N.C. 281/B4
Murphy, Oreg. 291/D5
Murphy (isl.), S.C. 296/J5
Murphy, Texas 303/H1
Murphys, Calif. 204/E5
Murphysboro, Ill. 222/D6
Murphytown, W. Va. 312/D4
Murra Murra, Queensland 95/C6
Murray (riv.), Australia 88/G6
Murray (riv.), Australia 87/E9
Murray (riv.), Br. Col. 184/G3
Murray (co.), Georgia 217/C1
Murray, Idaho 220/C2
Murray, Ind. 227/G3
Murray, Iowa 229/F6
Murray, Ky. 237/E7
Murray (co.), Minn. 255/C6
Murray, Nebr. 264/J4
Murray (co.), Okla. 288/M6
Murray (lake), Okla. 288/M6
Murray (lake), Papua N.G. 85/B7
Murray (riv.), S. Australia 94/F6
Murray (lake), S.C. 188/K4
Murray (lake), S.C. 296/D4
Murray, Utah 304/C3
Murray (bay), Victoria 88/H7
Murray (riv.), Victoria 97/A4
Murray (riv.), W. Australia 92/A2
Murray Bridge, S. Australia 88/F7
Murray Bridge, S. Australia 94/F6
Murray City, Ohio 284/F6
Murray Corner, New Bruns. 170/G2
Murray Downs, North. Terr. 93/D6
Murray Harbour, Pr. Edward I. 168/F2
Murray Lake Hills, Tenn. 237/L10
Murray River, Pr. Edward I. 168/F2
Murraysville, W. Va. 312/C4
Murrayville, Georgia 217/E2
Murrayville, Ill. 222/C4
Murrayville, Victoria 97/A4
Murree, Pakistan 68/C2
Murrells Inlet, S.C. 296/K4
Mürren, Switzerland 39/F3
Murrieta, Calif. 204/H10
Murringo, N.S. Wales 97/E4
Murrumbidgee (riv.), N.S. Wales 88/H6
Murrumbidgee (riv.), N.S. Wales 97/C4
Murrumburrah, N.S. Wales 97/E4
Murrupula, Mozambique 118/F3
Murrurundi, N.S. Wales 97/F2
Murrysville, Pa. 294/C5
Murska Sobota, Yugoslavia 45/C2
Murtaröl (peak), Switzerland 39/K3
Murtaugh, Idaho 220/D7
Murten, Switzerland 39/D3
Murtle (lake), Br. Col. 184/H4
Murtoa, Victoria 97/B5
Murud, India 68/B4
Murupara, N. Zealand 100/F3
Mururoa (isl.), Fr. Poly. 87/M8
Murwara, India 68/E4
Murwillumbah, N.S. Wales 88/J5
Murwillumbah, N.S. Wales 97/G1
Muryo (mt.), Indonesia 85/J2
Mürz (riv.), Austria 41/C3
Murzuk, Libya 102/D2
Murzuk, Libya 111/B2
Mürzzuschlag, Austria 41/C3
Muş (prov.), Turkey 63/J3
Muş, Turkey 59/D2
Muş, Turkey 63/J3
Musa Khel Bazar, Pakistan 59/K3
Musa Khel Bazar, Pakistan 68/B2
Musala (mt.), Bulgaria 45/F4
Musan, N. Korea 81/D2
Musandam, Ras (cape), Oman 59/G4
Musashino, Japan 81/O2
Muscadine, Ala. 195/H3
Muscat (cap.), Oman 54/G7
Muscat (cap.), Oman 2/M4
Muscat (cap.), Oman 59/G5
Muscatatuck (riv.), Ind. 227/F7
Muscatine (co.), Iowa 229/L5
Muscatine, Iowa 188/H2
Muscatine, Iowa 229/L6
Muscle Shoals, Ala. 195/C1
Muscoda, Wis. 317/F9
Muscogee (co.), Georgia 217/C6
Musconetcong (riv.), N.J. 273/C2
Muscongus (bay), Maine 243/E6
Muscotah, Kansas 232/G2
Muscoy, Calif. 204/E10
Muse, Okla. 288/S5
Musella, Georgia 217/E5
Musgrave (ranges), Australia 87/D8
Musgrave, Queensland 95/B2
Musgrave (range), S. Australia 88/E5
Musgrave (ranges), S. Australia 94/B2
Musgrave Harbour, Newf. 166/D4
Musgravetown, Newf. 166/C2

Narrandera 415

Mushaboom, Nova Scotia 168/F4
Mushandike Nat'l Park, Zimbabwe 118/D4
Mushie, Zaire 102/D5
Mushie, Zaire 115/C4
Musi (riv.), Indonesia 85/C6
Musidora, Alberta 182/E3
Muskeg (bay), Manitoba 179/G6
Muskeg (bay), Minn. 255/C2
Muskeget (chan.), Mass. 249/N7
Muskeget (isl.), Mass. 249/N7
Muskego, Wis. 317/K2
Muskegon (co.), Mich. 250/C5
Muskegon, Mich. 188/J2
Muskegon, Mich. 250/C5
Muskegon (riv.), Mich. 250/C5
Muskegon Heights, Mich. 250/C5
Muskeg River, Alberta 182/A3
Muskingum (co.), Ohio 284/G5
Muskingum (riv.), Ohio 284/G6
Muskogee, Okla. 188/H3
Muskogee (co.), Okla. 288/R3
Muskogee, Okla. 288/R3
Muskoka (dist. munic.), Ontario 177/E3
Muskoka (lake), Ontario 177/E2
Muskrat (creek), Wyo. 319/E2
Muskwa (lake), Alberta 182/C1
Muskwa (riv.), Alberta 182/C1
Muskwa (riv.), Br. Col. 184/M2
Muslimiya, Syria 63/G4
Musmar, Sudan 111/G4
Musoma, Tanzania 115/F4
Musoma, Tanzania 102/F5
Musquacook (lakes), Maine 243/E2
Musquash (harb.), New Bruns. 170/D3
Musquodoboit (riv.), Nova Scotia 168/E4
Musquodoboit Harbour, Nova Scotia 168/E4
Mussau (isl.), Papua N.G. 86/B1
Musselburgh, Scotland 15/D2
Musselburgh, Scotland 10/C1
Musselshell (riv.) 188/E1
Musselshell (co.), Mont. 262/H4
Musselshell, Mont. 262/H4
Musselshell (riv.), Mont. 262/J3
Mustafakemalpaşa, Turkey 63/C3
Mustahil, Ethiopia 111/H6
Müstair, Switzerland 39/K3
Mustang, Nepal 68/E3
Mustang, Okla. 288/L4
Mustang (creek), Texas 303/A1
Mustang (isl.), Texas 303/G10
Mustang Draw (dry riv.), Texas 303/B5
Musters (lake), Argentina 143/C6
Mustinka (riv.), Minn. 255/B5
Mustoe, Va. 307/J4
Mustvee, U.S.S.R. 53/D1
Muswellbrook, N.S. Wales 88/J6
Muswellbrook, N.S. Wales 97/F3
Mût, Egypt 111/E2
Mût, Egypt 59/A4
Mût, Egypt 102/E2
Mut, Turkey 63/E4
Mutankiang (Mudanjiang), China 77/M3
Mutarara (Dona Ana), Mozambique 118/F3
Mutare (Umtali), Zimbabwe 118/E3
Muthanna (gov.), Iraq 66/D5
Muthill, Scotland 15/E4
Muting, Indonesia 85/K7
Mutki, Turkey 63/J3
Mutrie, Sask. 181/H5
Mutsamudu, Comoros 118/G2
Mutshatsha, Zaire 115/D6
Mutsu, Japan 81/K3
Mutsu (bay), Japan 81/K3
Muttaburra, Queensland 95/C4
Muttalip, Turkey 63/D3
Muttenz, Switzerland 39/E1
Muttler (mt.), Switzerland 39/K3
Mutton (isl.), Ireland 17/B6
Mutton Bird (isl.), N.S. Wales 97/J2
Muttonville, Mich. 250/G6
Mutual, Ohio 284/C5
Mutual, Okla. 288/H2
Mutum, Brazil 135/F1
Mu Us Shamo (des.), China 77/G4
Muwailih, Saudi Arabia 59/C4
Muwale, Tanzania 115/F5
Muxima, Angola 115/B5
Muy Muy, Nicaragua 154/E4
Muy Muy Viejo, Nicaragua 154/E4
Muynak, U.S.S.R. 48/F5
Muyumba, Zaire 115/E5
Muzaffarabad, Pakistan 68/C2
Muzaffarnagar, India 68/D3
Muzaffarpur, India 68/E3
Muzambinho, Brazil 135/C2
Muzo, Colombia 126/D5
Muzon (cape), Alaska 196/M2
Muztag (mt.), China 77/B4
Muztagata (mt.), China 77/A4
Mvadhi-Ousyé, Gabon 115/B3
M'Vouti, Congo 115/B4
Mvuma, Zimbabwe 118/D3
Mwadingusha, Zaire 115/E6
Mwadui, Tanzania 115/F4
Mwali (isl.), Comoros 118/G2
Mwali (isl.), Comoros 118/D3
Mwanza, Malawi 115/F7
Mwanza (reg.), Tanzania 115/F4
Mwanza, Tanzania 115/F4
Mwanza, Tanzania 102/F5
Mwanza, Zaire 115/E5
Mwaya, Tanzania 115/F5
Mweelrea (mt.), Ireland 17/B4
Mweenish (isl.), Ireland 17/B5
Mweka, Zaire 115/D4
Mwene-Ditu, Zaire 115/D5
Mwenezi, Zimbabwe 118/E4
Mwenga, Zaire 115/E4
Mweru (lake), 102/E5
Mweru (lake), Zaire 115/E5
Mweru (lake), Zambia 115/E5
Mwesi, Tanzania 115/F5
Mwinilunga, Zambia 115/D6
Mya, Wadi (dry riv.), Algeria 106/E2
Myakka (riv.), Fla. 212/D4
Myakka City, Fla 212/D4
Myall (lake), N.S. Wales 97/G3
Myanaung, Burma 72/B3
Myaungmya, Burma 72/B3
Myebon, Burma 72/B2
Myers, Ky. 237/O4
Myers, Mont. 262/J4
Myerstown, Pa. 294/K5
Myersville, Md. 245/H3
Myingyan, Burma 72/B2
Myitkyina, Burma 54/L7
Myitkyina, Burma 72/C1
Myitnge, Burma 72/C2
Myitnge (riv.), Burma 72/C2
Myjava, Czech. 41/D2
Mylo, N. Dak. 282/L2
Mymensingh (Nasirabad), Bangladesh 68/G4
Mynyddislwyn, Wales 13/B6
Myohaung, Burma 72/B2
Myohyang (mt.) N. Korea 81/C3
Myŏngch'ŏn, N. Korea 81/D3
Myra, Texas 303/G4
Myra, W. Va. 312/B6
Myricks, Mass. 249/K5
Myrnam, Alberta 182/E3
Myrtle, Idaho 220/B3
Myrtle, Manitoba 179/E5
Myrtle, Minn. 255/E7
Myrtle, Miss. 256/F1
Myrtle, Mo. 261/K9
Myrtle (lake), N. Dak. 282/L5
Myrtle Beach, S.C. 296/K4
Myrtle Beach A.F.B., S.C. 296/K4
Myrtle Creek, Oreg. 291/D4
Myrtleford, Victoria 97/D5
Myrtle Grove, Fla. 212/B6
Myrtle Grove, La. 238/K7
Myrtle Point, Oreg. 291/C4
Myrtlewood, Ala. 195/C6
Mysen, Norway 18/G7
Myślenice, Poland 47/E4
Myślibórz, Poland 47/B2
Mysłowice, Poland 47/C4
Mysore, India 68/D6
Mysore, India 54/J8
Mys Shmidta, U.S.S.R. 4/C1
Mys Shmidta, U.S.S.R. 48/T3
Mystery Lake, Manitoba 179/J2
Mystic, Conn. 210/H3
Mystic (riv.), Conn. 210/H3
Mystic, Georgia 217/F7
Mystic, Iowa 229/H7
Mystic (lake), Mass. 249/C6
Mystic (riv.), Mass. 249/C6
Mystic, S. Dak. 298/B5
Mystic Islands, N.J. 273/E4
Myszków, Poland 47/D3
My Tho, Vietnam 72/E5
Mytishchi, U.S.S.R. 52/E3
Myton, Utah 304/D3
M'zab (oasis), Algeria 106/E2
Mže (riv.), Czech. 41/B2
Mzimba, Malawi 115/F6
Mzimba, Malawi 102/F6

N

Naab (riv.), Germany 22/E4
Naafkopf (mt.), Switzerland 39/J2
Naaldwijk, Netherlands 27/E4
Naalehu, Hawaii 218/H7
Naalehu, Hawaii 188/G6
Naantali, Finland 18/M6
Naarden, Netherlands 27/G4
Naas, Ireland 10/C4
Naas, Ireland 17/H5
Naba, Burma 72/B1
Nababeep, S. Africa 118/B5
Nabari, Kiribati 87/J6
Nabb, Ind. 227/F7
Nabburg, Germany 22/E4
Naberezhnye Chelny, U.S.S.R. 52/H3
Nabesna, Alaska 196/K2
Nabeul, Tunisia 106/G1
Nabiac, N.S. Wales 97/G3
Nabire, Indonesia 85/K6
Nablus (Nabulus), West Bank 65/C3
Nabnasset, Mass. 249/J2
Nabua, Philippines 82/D4
Nacala, Mozambique 118/G2
Nacala, Mozambique 102/G6
Nacaome, Honduras 154/D4
Naches, Wash. 310/E4
Naches (pass), Wash. 310/D3
Naches (riv.), Wash. 310/E4
Nachikatsuura, Japan 81/H7
Nachingwea, Tanzania 115/G6
Náchod, Czech. 41/D1
Nachusa, Ill. 222/D2
Nachvak (fjord) Newf. 166/B2
Nacimiento (riv.), Calif. 204/D8
Nacimiento, Chile 138/D1
Nacimiento (mt.), N. Mex. 274/C3
Nacimiento (peak), N. Mex. 274/C2
Nacka, Sweden 18/H1
Nackawic, New Bruns. 170/C2
Nacmine, Alberta 182/D4
Naco, Ariz. 198/F7
Naco, Mexico 150/D1
Nacogdoches (co.), Texas 303/K6
Nacogdoches, Texas 303/J6
Nacozari, Mexico 150/E1
Nacunday, Paraguay 144/E5
Nadadores, Mexico 150/H3
Nadawah, Ala. 195/D7
Nadeau, Mich. 250/B3
Nadi, Fiji 86/P10
Nadi, Fiji 87/H7
Nadiad, India 68/C4
Nădlac, Romania 45/E2
Nador, Morocco 106/D1
Nádudvar, Hungary 41/F3
Nadvoitsy, U.S.S.R. 52/D2
Nadym, U.S.S.R. 48/H3
Nadym (riv.), U.S.S.R. 48/H3
Naestved, Denmark 21/E7
Naestved, Denmark 18/G9
Naf, Idaho 220/E7
Näfels, Switzerland 39/H2
Nafenen, Switzerland 39/H3
Naft-e Shah, Iran 66/D4
Naft Kaneh, Iraq 66/D3
Naga, Philippines 85/G3
Naga, Philippines 54/O8
Naga, Philippines 82/D4
Nagahama, Ehime, Japan 81/F7
Nagahama, Shiga, Japan 81/H6
Nagai (isl.), Alaska 196/F4
Nagaland (state), India 68/G3
Nagambie, Victoria 97/C5
Nagano (pref.), Japan 81/J5
Nagano, Japan 81/J5
Nagaoka, Kyoto, Japan 81/J7
Nagaoka, Niigata, Japan 81/J5
Nagaokakyo, Japan 81/J7
Nagapattinam, India 68/E6
Nagar, Pakistan 68/D1
Nagarote, Nicaragua 154/D4
Nagar Parkar, Pakistan 68/C4
Nagarzê, China 77/C6
Nagasaki (pref.), Japan 81/D7
Nagasaki, Japan 54/O6
Nagasaki, Japan 81/D7
Nagato, Japan 81/E6
Nagaur, India 68/C3
Nagawicka (lake), Wis. 317/J1
Nagele, Netherlands 27/H3
Nagercoil, India 68/D7
Nagina, India 68/D3
Nagishot, Sudan 111/F7
Nagles (mts.), Ireland 17/E7
Nago, Japan 81/N6
Nagold, Germany 22/C4
Nagorno-Karabakh Aut. Obl., U.S.S.R. 48/E5
Nagorno-Karabakh Aut. Obl., U.S.S.R. 52/G7
Nagornyy, U.S.S.R. 48/N4
Nagoya, Japan 81/H6
Nagoya, Japan 2/R4
Nagoya, Japan 54/P6
Nagpur, India 54/J7
Nagpur, India 68/D4
Nagqu, China 77/D5
Nags Head, N.C. 281/T3
Nagua, Dom. Rep. 158/E5
Naguabo, P. Rico 161/F2
Naguabo, P. Rico 156/G1
Nagyatád, Hungary 41/D3
Nagybajom, Hungary 41/D3
Nagyecsed, Hungary 41/G3
Nagyhalász, Hungary 41/F2
Nagykálló, Hungary 41/F3
Nagykanizsa, Hungary 41/D3
Nagykáta, Hungary 41/E3
Nagykőrös, Hungary 41/E3
Nagyszénás, Hungary 41/F3
Naha, Japan 54/O7
Naha, Japan 81/N6
Nahan, India 68/D2
Nahang (riv.), Iran 66/N7
Nahanni Butte, N.W.T. 187/F3
Nahanni Nat'l Park, N.W.T. 162/D3
Nahanni Nat'l Park, N.W.T. 187/F3
Nahant•, Mass. 249/E6
Nahant (bay), Mass. 249/E6
Nahariyya, Israel 65/C1
Nahavand, Iran 59/E3
Nahavand, Iran 66/F3
Nahcotta, Wash. 310/A4
Nahhalin, West Bank 65/C4
Nahiku, Hawaii 218/K2
Nahma, Mich. 250/C3
Nahmakanta (lake), Maine 243/E4
Nahuel Huapí (lake), Argentina 120/B7
Nahuel Huapí (lake), Argentina 143/B5
Nahuel Huapi Nat'l Park, Argentina 143/B5
Nahunta, Georgia 217/H8
Naica, Mexico 150/G2
Naicam, Sask. 181/G3
Naihati, India 68/F1
Nailsworth, England 13/E6
Naiman, China 77/K3
Na'in, Iran 66/H4
Na'in, Iran 59/F3
Nain, Jamaica 158/H6
Nain, Newf. 166/B2
Nain, Newf. 162/K4
Naini Tal, India 68/D3
Nainpur, India 68/E4
Naipo (isl.), Colombia 126/F6
Nairn, La. 238/L8
Nairn, Ontario 177/C1
Nairn, Scotland 15/E3
Nairn, Scotland 10/E2
Nairn (trad. co.), Scotland 15/B5
Nairn (riv.), Scotland 15/D3
Nairne, S. Australia 94/C8
Nairobi (cap.), Kenya 2/L6
Nairobi (cap.), Kenya 115/G4
Nairobi (cap.), Kenya 102/F5
Naivasha, Kenya 115/G4
Najafabad, Iran 59/F3
Najafabad, Iran 66/G4
Najayo Abajo, Dom. Rep. 158/E6
Najin, N. Korea 81/E2
Najran (Aba as Sa'ud), Saudi Arabia 59/D6
Naka (riv.), Japan 81/K5
Nakalele (pt.), Hawaii 218/J1
Nakaminato, Japan 81/K5
Nakamti, Ethiopia 102/F4
Nakamti, Ethiopia 111/G6
Nakamura, Japan 81/F7
Nakanbe (riv.), Burkina Faso 106/D6
Nakasato, Japan 81/K3
Nakatane (cape), Japan 81/E8
Nakatsu, Japan 81/E7
Na Keal, Loch (inlet), Scotland 15/B4
Naked (isl.), Alaska 196/D1
Nakfa, Ethiopia 111/G4
Nakhichevan', U.S.S.R. 7/J5
Nakhichevan', U.S.S.R. 48/E6
Nakhichevan', U.S.S.R. 52/F7
Nakhichevan' A.S.S.R., U.S.S.R. 52/F7
Nakhichevan' A.S.S.R., U.S.S.R. 48/E6
Nakhodka, U.S.S.R. 54/P5
Nakhodka, U.S.S.R. 48/O5
Nakhon Nayok, Thailand 72/D4
Nakhon Pathom, Thailand 72/C4
Nakhon Phanom, Thailand 72/D3
Nakhon Ratchasima, Thailand 72/D4
Nakhon Ratchasima, Thailand 54/M8
Nakhon Sawan, Thailand 72/D4
Nakhon Si Thammarat, Thailand 54/M9
Nakhon Si Thammarat, Thailand 72/D5
Nakina, N.C. 281/M6
Nakina, Ont. 162/H5
Nakina, Ontario 177/H4
Nakina, Ontario 175/C2
Nakło nad Notecia, Poland 47/C2
Naknek, Alaska 196/G3
Naknek (lake), Alaska 196/G3
Nakonde, Zambia 115/F5
Nakskov, Denmark 21/E8
Nakskov, Denmark 18/G9
Naktong (riv.), S. Korea 81/D6
Nakuru, Kenya 102/F5
Nakuru, Kenya 115/G4
Nakusp, Br. Col. 184/J5
Nal, Pakistan 59/J4
Nal, Pakistan 68/B3
Nal (riv.), Pakistan 59/J4
Nal (riv.), Pakistan 68/B3
Nalate, Turkey 63/G4
Nalayh (Nalaikha), Mongolia 77/G2
Nalcayec (isl.), Chile 138/D6
Nal'chik, U.S.S.R. 7/J4
Nal'chik, U.S.S.R. 48/E5
Nal'chik, U.S.S.R. 52/F6
Nalgonda, India 68/D5
Nallen, W. Va. 312/E6
Nallıhan, Turkey 63/D2
Nalut, Libya 111/B1
Namacurra, Mozambique 118/F3
Namak, Daryacheh-ye (salt lake), Iran 59/F3
Namak, Daryacheh-ye (salt lake), Iran 66/G3
Namaka, Alberta 182/D4
Namaksar (salt lake), Afghanistan 59/H3
Namaksar (salt lake), Afghanistan 68/A2
Namaksar (lake), Iran 66/M4
Namaksar (salt lake), Iran 59/H3
Namakzar-e Shahdad (salt lake), Iran 59/G3
Namakzar-e Shahdad (salt lake), Iran 66/L5
Namanga, Kenya 115/G4
Namangan, U.S.S.R. 48/H5
N'amaniya, Iraq 66/D4
Namapa, Mozambique 118/F2
Namaqualand (reg.), S. Africa 118/B5
Namarrói, Mozambique 118/F3
Namasagali, Uganda 115/F3
Namasigüe, Honduras 154/D4
Namatanai, Papua N.G. 87/F6
Namatanai, Papua N.G. 86/C1
Nambe, N. Mex. 274/D3
Nambour, Queensland 88/J5
Nambour, Queensland 95/E5
Nambucca Heads, N.S. Wales 97/G2
Nam Co (lake), China 77/D5
Nam Dinh (cliff), Vietnam 72/E2
Namekagon (lake), Wis. 317/D3
Namekagon (riv.), Wis. 317/C3
Namen (Namur), Belgium 27/F8
Námestovo, Czech. 41/E2
Nametil, Mozambique 118/F3
Namhkam, Burma 72/C2
Namib (des.), Namibia 118/A3
Namibe (prov.), Angola 115/B7
Namibe (Moçâmedes), Angola 115/B7
Namibe, Angola 102/D6
Namibia 2/K7
Namibia 102/D7
NAMIBIA 118/D3
Namibia (des.) 102/D6
Naminga, U.S.S.R. 48/M4
Namiquipa, Mexico 150/F2
Namlan, Burma 72/C2
Namlea, Indonesia 85/H6
Namoi (riv.), N.S. Wales 88/H6
Namoi (riv.), N.S. Wales 97/E2
Namonuito (atoll), Micronesia 87/E5
Namorik (atoll), Marshall Is. 87/G5
Nampa, Alberta 182/B1
Nampa, Idaho 146/G5
Nampa, Idaho 220/B6
Nampa, Idaho 188/C2
Nampala, Mali 106/C5
Namp'o, N. Korea 81/B4
Nampo-Shoto (isls.), Japan 81/M3
Nampula (prov.), Mozambique 118/F2
Nampula, Mozambique 118/F3
Nampula, Mozambique 102/F6
Namsen (riv.), Norway 18/H4
Namsos, Norway 7/F2
Namsos, Norway 18/G4
Nam Tram, Mui (cape), Vietnam 72/F4
Namtu, Burma 72/C2
Namu, Br. Col. 184/D4
Namuac, Philippines 82/C1
Namuli, Serra (mt.), Mozambique 118/F3
Namuno, Mozambique 118/F2
Namur (lake), Alberta 182/D1
Namur (prov.), Belgium 27/F8
Namur, Belgium 27/F8
Namur, Québec 172/C4
Namutoni, Namibia 118/B3
Namwala, Zambia 115/E7
Namwŏn, S. Korea 81/C6
Namysłów, Poland 47/C3
Namzha Parwa (mt.), China 77/E6
Nan, Thailand 72/D3
Nan, Mae Nam (riv.), Thailand 72/D3
Nanacamilpa, Mexico 150/M1
Nanafalia, Ala. 195/B6
Nanaimo, Br. Col. 146/F5
Nanaimo, Br. Col. 162/D6
Nanaimo, Br. Col. 184/J3
Nanakuli, Hawaii 218/D2
Nanao, Japan 81/H5
Nanay (riv.), Peru 128/E4
Nancagua, Chile 138/F6
Nance (co.), Nebr. 264/F3
Nanchang, China 77/J6
Nanchang, China 54/N7
Nancheng, China 77/J6
Nanchong (Nanchung), China 77/G5
Nanchong, China 54/M6
nan Clar, Loch (lake), Scotland 15/D2
Nancowry (isl.), India 68/G7
Nancy, France 28/G3
Nancy, France 7/E4
Nancy, Ky. 237/M6
Nanda Devi (mt.), India 68/D2
Nandaime, Nicaragua 154/E5
Nander, India 68/D5
Nandi (Nadi), Fiji 87/H7
Nando, Uruguay 145/F3
Nandurbar, India 68/C4
Nandyal, India 68/D5
Nanga-Eboko, Cameroon 115/B3
Nanga Parbat (mt.), Pakistan 68/D1
Nangapinoh, Indonesia 85/E6
Nangatayap, Indonesia 85/E6
Nangnim-sanmaek (range), N. Korea 81/C3
Nangong, China 77/H4
Nangqên, China 77/E5
Nang Rong, Thailand 72/D4
Nangwarry, S. Australia 94/G7
Nang Xian, China 77/D6
Nanika (dam), Br. Col. 184/D3
Nanika (lake), Br. Col. 184/D3
Nanisivik, N.W. Terr. 187/K2
Nanjemoy, Md. 245/K7
Nanjing (Nanking), China 77/J5
Nanjing, China 2/Q4
Nanjing, China 54/N6
Nanking (Nanjing), China 77/J5
Nankoku, Japan 81/F7
Nan Ling (mts.), China 77/H6
Nannine, W. Australia 92/B4
Nanning, China 77/G7
Nanning, China 54/M7
Nannup, W. Australia 92/B6
Nanoose Bay, Br. Col. 184/J3
Nanortalik, Greenl. 4/D12
Nanpan Jiang (riv.), China 77/F7
Nanping, China 77/J6
Nansei Shoto (Ryukyu) (isls.), Japan 81/M6
Nansen (sound), N.W. Terr. 187/J1
Nanson, N. Dak. 282/L2
Nantahala, N.C. 281/B4
Nantahala (lake), N.C. 281/B4
Nantai (mt.), Japan 81/J5
Nantasket Beach, Mass. 249/E7
Nanterre, France 28/A1
Nantes, France 28/C4
Nantes, France 7/D4
Nantes, Québec 172/F4
Nanticoke (riv.), Del. 245/R6
Nanticoke, Md. 245/P7
Nanticoke (riv.), Md. 245/P7
Nanticoke, Ontario 177/E5
Nanticoke, Pa. 294/E7
Nanton, Alberta 182/D4
Nantong, China 77/K5
Nantua, France 28/F4
Nantucket (co.), Mass. 249/O7
Nantucket, Mass. 249/O7
Nantucket•, Mass. 249/O7
Nantucket (isl.), Mass. 188/N2
Nantucket (isl.), Mass. 249/O8
Nantucket (sound), Mass. 249/N6
Nanty Glo, Pa. 294/E5
Nantyglo and Blaina, Wales 13/B6
Nanuet, N.Y. 276/K8
Nanuktok (isls.), Newf. 166/C2
Nanuku (passage), Fiji 86/R10
Nanumea (atoll), Tuvalu 87/H6
Nanuque, Brazil 132/F7
Nanuque, Brazil 120/E4
Nanxiong, China 77/H6
Nanyang, China 77/H5
Nanyuki, Kenya 115/G3
Nanzhang, China 77/H5
Nanzhao, China 77/H5
Nao (cape), Spain 33/G3
Naococane (lake), Québec 174/C2
Naolinco de Victoria, Mexico 150/P1
Naomi, Ky. 237/M6
Náousa, Greece 45/F5
Napa (co.), Calif. 204/C5
Napa, Calif. 188/B3
Napa, Calif. 204/C5
Napadogan, New Bruns. 170/D2
Napa Junction, Calif. 204/J1
Napakiak, Alaska 196/F2
Napaktok (bay), Newf. 166/B2
Napanee, Ontario 177/G3
Napanoch, N.Y. 276/M7
Napaskiak, Alaska 196/F2
Napata (ruins), Sudan 111/F4
Napavine, Wash. 310/C4
Napè, Laos 72/E3
Naper, Nebr. 264/E2
Naperville, Ill. 222/A6
Napf (mt.), Switzerland 39/E3
Napier, Ky. 237/P7
Napier, N. Zealand 100/F3
Napier, N. Zealand 87/H9
Napier (mt.), North. Terr. 93/A4
Napier, W. Va. 312/E5
Napier Field, Ala. 195/H8
Napierville (co.), Québec 172/D4
Napierville, Québec 172/D4
Napili-Honokowai, Hawaii 218/H1
Napinka, Manitoba 179/B5
Naplate, Ill. 222/E2
Naples, Fla. 212/E5
Naples, Idaho 220/B1
Naples, Ill. 222/C4
Naples (prov.), Italy 34/E4
Naples, Italy 7/F4
Naples, Italy 34/E4
Naples•, Maine 243/B8
Naples, N.Y. 276/F5
Naples, S. Dak. 298/O4
Naples, Texas 303/K4
Naples Park, Fla. 212/E5
Napo (riv.) 120/B3
Napo, China 77/G7
Napo (prov.), Ecuador 128/D3
Napo (riv.), Ecuador 128/D3
Napo (riv.), Peru 128/F4
Napoleon, Ind. 227/G6
Napoleon, Mich. 250/E6
Napoleon, Mo. 261/E4
Napoleon, N. Dak. 282/L6
Napoleon, Ohio 284/B3
Naponee, Nebr. 264/E4
Nappa Merri, Queensland 95/B5
Nappan, Nova Scotia 168/D3
Nappanee, Ind. 227/F2
Napperby, North. Terr. 93/C7
Napton, Mo. 261/F4
Naqa (ruins), Sudan 111/F4
Nara (pref.), Japan 81/J8
Nara, Japan 81/J8
Nara, Mali 106/C5
Naracoopa, Tasmania 99/B1
Naracoorte, S. Australia 88/F7
Naracoorte, S. Australia 94/G7
Naradhan, N.S. Wales 97/D3
Naramata, Br. Col. 184/H5
Naranja, Fla. 212/F6
Naranjal (riv.), Ecuador 128/C4
Naranjito, Honduras 154/C3
Naranjito, P. Rico 161/D1
Naranjos, Mexico 150/L6
Naraq, Iran 66/G3
Narashino, Japan 81/P2
Narathiwat, Thailand 72/D6
Nara Visa, N. Mex. 274/F3
Narayanganj, Bangladesh 68/G4
Narayanpet, India 68/D5
Narberth, Pa. 294/M6
Narberth, Wales 13/C6
Narbonne, France 28/E6
Narcissa, Okla. 288/S1
Narcisse, Manitoba 179/E4
Narcondam (isl.), India 68/G6
Narcoossee, Fla. 212/E3
Nardin, Okla. 288/M1
Nardò, Italy 34/F4
Naré, Argentina 143/F5
Nare, Colombia 126/C4
Narellan, N.S. Wales 97/F3
Nares (str.) 146/L2
Nares (str.), N.W.T. 162/N3
Nares (str.), N.W. Terr. 187/L2
Narew (riv.), Poland 47/E2
Naricual, Venezuela 124/F2
Narinda, Madagascar 118/H3
Nariño (dept.), Colombia 126/B7
Nariva (swamp), Trin. & Tob. 161/B10
Narka, Kansas 232/E2
Narmada (riv.), India 54/J7
Narmada (riv.), India 68/D4
Narman, Turkey 63/J2
Narnaul, India 68/D3
Narni, Italy 34/D3
Naro, Italy 34/D6
Narodnaya (mt.), U.S.S.R. 7/K2
Narodnaya (mt.), U.S.S.R. 48/G3
Narodnaya (mt.), U.S.S.R. 52/J1
Narok, Kenya 115/G4
Narooma, N.S. Wales 97/F5
Narrabeen, N.S. Wales 88/L3
Narrabeen, N.S. Wales 97/K3
Narrabri, N.S. Wales 88/J6
Narrabri, N.S. Wales 97/E2
Narragansett, R.I. 249/J7
Narragansett•, R.I. 249/J7
Narragansett (bay), R.I. 249/J6
Narran (lake), N.S. Wales 97/D1
Narran (riv.), N.S. Wales 97/D1
Narrandera, N.S. Wales 88/H6
Narrandera, N.S. Wales 97/D4

Narre Warren North, Victoria 97/K5
Narrogin, W. Australia 88/B6
Narrogin, W. Australia 92/B2
Narromine, N.S. Wales 88/H6
Narromine, N.S. Wales 97/E3
Narrows, Ky. 237/H5
Narrows, Oreg. 291/H4
Narrows, The (str.), St. Kitts & Nevis 161/D11
Narrows, The (str.), Virgin Is. (U.K.) 161/C4
Narrows, The (str.), Virgin Is. (U.S.) 161/C4
Narrows, Va. 307/G6
Narrowsburg, N.Y. 276/L7
Narrows Park-La Vale, Md. 245/C2
Narsaq, Greenl. 4/C12
Narsimhapur, India 68/D4
Narsinghgarh, India 68/D4
Naruna, Va. 307/L6
Narva, U.S.S.R. 52/C3
Narva, U.S.S.R. 53/E1
Narva (res.), U.S.S.R. 53/D1
Narvik, Norway 4/C9
Narvik, Norway 7/F2
Narvik, Norway 18/K3
Nary, Minn. 255/D3
Nar'yan-Mar, U.S.S.R. 4/C7
Nar'yan-Mar, U.S.S.R. 7/K2
Nar'yan-Mar, U.S.S.R. 48/F3
Nar'yan-Mar, U.S.S.R. 52/H1
Naryn, U.S.S.R. 48/H5
Nasarawa, Nigeria 106/F7
Năsăud, Romania 45/G2
Naseby, N. Zealand 100/C6
Naseby, Sask. 181/C3
Naselle, Wash. 310/B4
Naselle (riv.), Wash. 310/B4
Nash (stream), N.H. 268/E2
Nash (co.), N.C. 281/O2
Nash, N. Dak. 282/P3
Nash, Okla. 288/K1
Nash, Texas 303/K4
Nashawena (isl.), Mass. 249/L7
Nashoba, Okla. 288/M6
Nashoba, Wis. 317/J1
Nashport, Ohio 284/F5
Nashua, Iowa 229/J3
Nashua (riv.), Mass. 249/H3
Nashua, Minn. 255/B4
Nashua, Mont. 262/K2
Nashua, N.H. 188/M2
Nashua, N.H. 268/D6
Nashville, Ark. 202/C6
Nashville, Georgia 217/F8
Nashville, Ill. 222/D6
Nashville, Ind. 227/E6
Nashville, Kansas 232/D4
Nashville, Mich. 250/D6
Nashville, Mo. 261/D8
Nashville, N.C. 281/O3
Nashville, Ohio 284/F4
Nashville, Oreg. 291/D2
Nashville (cap.), Tenn. 146/K6
Nashville (cap.), Tenn. 188/J3
Nashville (cap.), Tenn. 237/H8
Nashwaak (riv.), New Bruns. 170/D2
Nashwaak Bridge, New Bruns. 170/D2
Nashwaak Village, New Bruns. 170/D2
Nashwauk, Minn. 255/E3
Našice, Yugoslavia 45/C3
Nasielsk, Poland 47/E2
Näsijärvi (lake), Finland 18/O6
Nasik, India 68/C5
Nasik, India 54/J8
Nasir, Sudan 111/F6
Nasirabad, Bangladesh 68/G4
Nasirabad, India 68/C3
Naskaupi (riv.), Newf. 166/B3
Naso (pt.), Philippines 82/C5
Nason, Ill. 222/D6
Nasonville, R.I. 249/H6
Nasratabad (Zabol), Iran 59/H3
Nasratabad (Zabol), Iran 66/M5
Nass (riv.), Br. Col. 184/C3
Nassau (cap.), Bahamas 146/L7
Nassau (cap.), Bahamas 156/C1
Nassau (bay), Chile 120/C8
Nassau (bay), Chile 138/F11
Nassau (isl.), Cook Is. 87/K7
Nassau, Del. 245/T6
Nassau (co.), Fla. 212/E1
Nassau (riv.), Fla. 212/E1
Nassau (isl.), Fla. 212/E1
Nassau (sound), Fla. 212/E1
Nassau, Minn. 255/B5
Nassau (co.), N.Y. 276/N9
Nassau, N.Y. 276/N5
Nassau Bay, Texas 303/K2
Nassawadox, Va. 307/S6
Nassawango (creek), Md. 245/S8
Nasser (lake), Egypt 102/F2
Nasser (lake), Egypt 111/F3
Nasser (lake), Egypt 59/F3
Nassereith, Austria 41/A3
Nässjö, Sweden 18/J8
Nassogne, Belgium 27/G8
Nasty (creek), Ariz. 198/F4
Nasu (mt.), Japan 81/J5
Nata, Botswana 118/D4
Natá, Panama 154/G6
Natagaima, Colombia 126/C6
Natal, Brazil 2/H6
Natal, Brazil 132/H4
Natal, Brazil 120/F3
Natal, Br. Col. 184/K5
Natal (prov.), S. Africa 102/F7
Natal (prov.), S. Africa 118/E5
Natalbany, La. 238/N1
Natalia, Texas 303/J11
Natalicio Talavera, Paraguay 144/D4
Natanz, Iran 59/F3

Natanz, Iran 66/H4
Natashquan (riv.) 162/K5
Natashquan (riv.), Newf. 166/B3
Natashquan, Québec 174/E3
Natashquan (riv.), Québec 174/E2
Natashquan-Est (riv.), Newf. 166/B3
Natchaug (riv.), Conn. 210/G1
Natchez, Ala. 195/E3
Natchez, La. 238/D3
Natchez, Miss. 188/H4
Natchez, Miss. 256/B7
Natchez Nat'l Historic Park, Miss. 256/B7
Natchitoches (par.), La. 238/D3
Natchitoches, La. 238/D3
Naters, Switzerland 39/E4
Natewa (bay), Fiji 86/Q10
Nathalia, Victoria 97/C5
Nathalie, Va. 307/L7
Nathan, Mich. 250/B3
Nathrop, Colo. 208/H5
Natick•, Mass. 249/A7
Natick, R.I. 249/H6
Natimuk, Victoria 97/A5
Nation (riv.), Br. Col. 184/F2
National Agricultural Research Center, Md. 245/G3
National Capital Region (Manila) (prov.), Philippines 82/C3
National City, Calif. 204/J11
National City, Mich. 250/F4
National Gardens, Fla. 212/E2
National Mills, Manitoba 179/A2
National Mine, Mich. 250/B2
National Park, N.J. 273/B3
National Park, Switzerland 39/K3
National Reactor Testing Sta. (U.S.A.E.C.), Idaho 220/F6
National Stock Yards, Ill. 222/A2
Natitingou, Benin 106/E6
Natividade, Brazil 132/E5
Natmauk, Burma 72/B2
Natoma, Kansas 232/D2
Natron (lake), Kenya 115/G4
Natron (lake), Tanzania 115/G4
Natrona (co.), Wyo. 319/F3
Natrona, Wyo. 319/F2
Natrona Heights, Pa. 294/C4
Nattavaara, Sweden 18/M3
Natuna (isls.), Indonesia 54/M9
Natuna (isls.), Indonesia 85/D5
Natural Bridge, Ala. 195/C2
Natural Bridge, N.Y. 276/K2
Natural Bridge, Va. 307/J3
Natural Bridges Nat'l Mon., Utah 304/E6
Natural Bridge Station, Va. 307/K5
Natural Dam, N.Y. 276/J2
Naturaliste (cape), Tasmania 99/E2
Naturaliste (cape), W. Australia 88/A6
Naturaliste (cape), W. Australia 92/A6
Naturaliste (chan.), W. Australia 88/A5
Naturaliste (chan.), W. Australia 92/A4
Natural Steps, Ark. 202/F4
Naturita, Colo. 208/B6
Naubinway, Mich. 250/D2
Naucalpan de Juárez, Mexico 150/L1
Nauders, Austria 41/A3
Nauen, Germany 22/E2
Naugatuck, Conn. 210/C3
Naugatuck (riv.), Conn. 210/C3
Naugatuck, W. Va. 312/B7
Nauhcampatépetl (mt.), Mexico 150/O1
Naujan (lake), Philippines 82/C4
Naujoji-Akmenė, U.S.S.R. 53/B2
Naumburg, Germany 22/D3
Na'ur, Jordan 65/D4
Nauru 2/T6
Nauru 87/G6
Naushon (isl.), Mass. 249/L7
Naustdal, Norway 18/E6
Nauta, Peru 128/F5
Nautla, Mexico 150/L6
Nauvoo, Ala. 195/D3
Nauvoo, Ill. 222/B3
Nauwigewauk, New Bruns. 170/E3
Nava, Mexico 150/J2
Nava del Rey, Spain 33/D2
Navajo, Ariz. 198/E3
Navajo (creek), Ariz. 198/E3
Navajo (peak), Colo. 208/F8
Navajo (res.), Colo. 208/E8
Navajo, Mont. 262/M2
Navajo, N. Mex. 274/A3
Navajo (dam), N. Mex. 274/B2
Navajo (res.), N. Mex. 274/B2
Navajo (mt.), Utah 304/D6
Navajo Ind. Res., Ariz. 198/D2
Navajo Ind. Res., N. Mex. 274/A2
Navajo Ind. Res., Utah 304/D7
Navajo Nat'l Mon., Ariz. 198/E2
Navajo Ord. Depot, Ariz. 198/D3
Naval Academy, U.S., Md. 245/N5
Naval Air Sta., La. 238/D4
Naval Air Station, Calif. 204/J2
Naval Air Station, Va. 307/R7
Naval Base, S.C. 296/H6
Navalcarnero, Spain 33/F4
Naval Medical Center, Md. 245/E4
Navalmoral de la Mata, Spain 33/D3
Naval Submarine Base, Conn. 210/G3
Naval Support Ctr., Wash. 310/B1
Naval Weapons Center, Md. 245/F3
Naval Yard, D.C. 245/F5
Navan (An Uaimh), Ireland 17/H4
Navan, Ontario 177/J2
Navarin (cape), U.S.S.R. 4/C18
Navarin (cape), U.S.S.R. 48/T3
Navarino (isl.), Chile 138/F11
Navarino, Wis. 317/J6

Navarre, Kansas 232/E3
Navarre, Ohio 284/H4
Navarro, Argentina 143/G7
Navarro, Calif. 204/B4
Navarro (riv.), Calif. 204/B4
Navarro (co.), Texas 303/H5
Navasota, Texas 303/J7
Navasota (riv.), Texas 303/H7
Navassa, N.C. 281/O6
Navassa (isl.), Virgin Is. (U.S.) 156/C3
Naver, Loch (lake), Scotland 15/D2
Naver (riv.), Scotland 15/D2
Navesink, N.J. 273/E3
Navesink (riv.), N.J. 273/E3
Navia (riv.), Spain 33/C1
Navidad, Chile 138/A10
Navidad (riv.), Texas 303/H8
Navin, Manitoba 179/F5
Navoi, U.S.S.R. 48/G6
Navojoa, Mexico 150/E3
Navolato, Mexico 150/E4
Návpaktos, Greece 45/F6
Návplion, Greece 45/F7
Navrongo, Ghana 106/D6
Navsari, India 68/C4
Navy Board (inlet), N.W. Terr. 187/K2
Navy Yard City, Wash. 310/A2
Nawabganj, Bangladesh 68/F4
Nawabshah, Pakistan 68/B3
Nawabshah, Pakistan 59/J4
Nawiliwili (bay), Hawaii 218/D2
Naxera, Va. 307/R6
Náxos, Greece 45/G7
Náxos (isl.), Greece 45/G7
Naya, Colombia 126/B6
Nayarit (state), Mexico 150/G6
Nayarit, Sierra (mts.), Mexico 150/G5
Nay Band, Iran 59/F4
Nay Band, Iran 59/G3
Nay Band, Bushehr, Iran 66/H7
Nay Band, Khorasan, Iran 66/K4
Naylor, Georgia 217/F9
Naylor, Mo. 261/L9
Nayoro, Japan 81/L1
Naythawaush, Minn. 255/C3
Nazaré, Brazil 132/G6
Nazaré, Portugal 33/B3
Nazareth, Belgium 27/D7
Nazareth, Israel 65/C2
Nazareth, Pa. 294/M4
Nazareth, Texas 303/B3
Nazarovo, U.S.S.R. 48/K4
Nazas, Mexico 150/G4
Nazas (riv.), Mexico 150/G4
Nazca, Peru 128/E10
Naze, (Phelps), England 13/J6
Naze, Japan 81/O5
Nazilli, Turkey 63/C4
Nazinon (riv.), Burkina Faso 106/D6
Nazko, Br. Col. 184/F3
Nazret, Ethiopia 111/G6
Nazret, Ethiopia 102/F4
Nazyvayevsk, U.S.S.R. 48/H4
Ncheu (Ntcheu), Malawi 115/F6
N'dalatando, Angola 115/B5
Ndele, Cent. Afr. Rep. 115/D2
N'Dendé, Gabon 115/B4
Ndeni (isl.), Solomon Is. 87/G7
N'Djamena (cap.), Chad 111/C5
N'Djamena (cap.), Chad 2/K5
N'Djamena (cap.), Chad 102/K3
N'Djolé, Gabon 115/B4
N'Dogo (lag.), Gabon 115/B4
Ndola, Zambia 115/E6
Ndola, Zambia 102/E6
Nead, Ind. 227/E3
Neagh (lake), N. Ireland 17/J2
Neagh, Lough (lake), N. Ireland 10/C3
Neah Bay, Wash. 310/A2
Neal, Kansas 232/F4
Neale (lake), North. Terr. 88/D4
Neale (lake), North. Terr. 93/A8
Neales, The (riv.), S. Australia 94/E3
Neales, The (riv.), S. Australia 88/F5
Neápolis, Greece 45/F7
Neapolis, Ohio 284/C3
Near (isls.), Alaska 196/H3
Neath, Wales 10/E5
Neath, Wales 13/D6
Neavitt, Md. 245/N6
Nebikon, Switzerland 39/F2
Nebish, Minn. 255/D3
Nebit-Dag, U.S.S.R. 48/F6
Neblina, Pico da (peak), Brazil 132/G8
Neblina (Phelps) (peak), Venezuela 124/E7
Nebo (mt.), Ark. 202/D3
Nebo, Ill. 222/C4
Nebo (mt.), Jordan 65/D4
Nebo, Ky. 237/D6
Nebo, La. 238/F3
Nebo, Mo. 261/H7
Nebo (mt.), Utah 304/C4
Nebo, W. Va. 312/D5
Nebraska 188/F2
NEBRASKA 264
Nebraska, Ind. 227/F6
Nebraska (state), U.S. 146/J5
Nebraska City, Nebr. 264/J4
Necedah, Wis. 317/F7
Nechako (riv.), Br. Col. 184/E3
Neche, N. Dak. 282/P2
Neches, Texas 303/J6
Neches (riv.), Texas 303/K6
Nechí (riv.), Colombia 126/C3
Neckar (riv.), Germany 22/C4
Neckarsulm, Germany 22/C4
Neck City, Mo. 261/C8
Necker (isl.), Hawaii 87/K3
Necker (isl.), Hawaii 188/F6
Necker (isl.), Hawaii 218/D6

Necochea, Argentina 143/E4
Necochea, Argentina 120/D6
Nectar, Ala. 195/E3
Necum Teuch (harb.), Nova Scotia 168/J4
Ned, Ky. 237/P6
Neded, Czech. 41/D2
Nederland, Colo. 208/H3
Nederland, Texas 303/K8
Nedgera (creek), N.S. Wales 97/E2
Nedlands, W. Australia 88/B2
Nedlands, W. Australia 92/A1
Neeb, Sask. 181/C1
Neebish (isl.), Mich. 250/E2
Neede, Netherlands 27/K4
Needham, Ala. 195/B7
Needham, Ind. 227/E5
Needham•, Mass. 249/B7
Needham Heights, Mass. 249/B7
Needle (mt.), Wyo. 319/C1
Needles, Calif. 188/C4
Needles, Calif. 204/L9
Needles (pt.), N. Zealand 100/E2
Needmore, Ind. 227/E7
Needmore, N.C. 281/B4
Needmore, Pa. 294/J6
Needmore, W. Va. 312/J4
Needville, Texas 303/J8
Neelin, Manitoba 179/C5
Neely, Miss. 256/G8
Neely Henry (lake), Ala. 195/F3
Neelys Landing, Mo. 261/O7
Neelyton, Pa. 294/G5
Neelyville, Mo. 261/M9
Neemuch, India 68/C4
Neembucú (dept.), Paraguay 144/C-D5
Neenah, Wis. 317/J7
Neepawa, Manitoba 179/C4
Neerlandia, Alberta 182/C2
Neerpelt, Belgium 27/G6
Neeses, S.C. 296/E4
Nee Soon, Singapore 72/F6
Neely (lake), Ala. 195/F3
Neffs, Ohio 284/J5
Neffs Mills, Pa. 294/G4
Nefta, Tunisia 106/F2
Neftekamsk, U.S.S.R. 52/J3
Nefteyugansk, U.S.S.R. 48/H3
Nefud (des.), Saudi Arabia 54/D4
Nefud (des.), Saudi Arabia 59/D4
Nefud Dahi (des.), Saudi Arabia 59/D5
Nefusa, Jebel (mts.), Libya 111/B1
Nefyn, Wales 13/C5
Negara, Indonesia 85/E7
Negaunee, Mich. 250/B2
Negba, Israel 65/B4
Negelli, Ethiopia 111/G6
Negeri Sembilan (state), Malaysia 72/D7
Negev (reg.), Israel 65/D5
Negley, Ohio 284/J4
Negomane, Mozambique 118/F2
Negombo, Sri Lanka 68/D7
Negotin, Yugoslavia 45/E3
Negra, Cordillera (mts.), Peru 128/D7
Negra (pt.), Peru 128/B6
Negra (pt.), P. Rico 161/G2
Negra (lag.), Uruguay 145/F5
Negra (range), Uruguay 145/F5
Negrais (cape), Burma 72/B3
Negreet, La. 238/D4
Negreiros, Chile 138/B2
Negreşti, Romania 45/H2
Negril, Jamaica 158/G6
Negrillos, Bolivia 136/A6
Negritos, Peru 128/B5
Negro (riv.) 2/F5
Negro (cape), Angola 115/B7
Negro (riv.), Argentina 120/C6
Negro (riv.), Argentina 143/D4
Negro (riv.), Bolivia 136/D4
Negro (riv.), Brazil 120/C3
Negro (riv.), Brazil 132/H9
Negro (riv.), Colombia 126/C3
Negro (riv.), Paraguay 144/C4
Negro (bay), Somalia 115/J2
Negro (riv.), Uruguay 120/D6
Negro, Arroyo (riv.), Uruguay 145/B3
Negro (riv.), Uruguay 145/B4
Negro (riv.), Venezuela 124/F7
Negro Bay, Virgin Is. (U.S.) 161/E4
Negros (isl.), Philippines 54/O9
Negros (isl.), Philippines 85/E6
Negros (isl.), Philippines 82/D6
Negros Occidental (prov.), Philippines 82/D6
Negros Oriental (prov.), Philippines 82/D6
Neguac, New Bruns. 170/E1
Nehalem, Oreg. 291/D2
Nehalem (riv.), Oreg. 291/D2
Nehawka, Nebr. 264/H4
Nehbandan, Iran 59/G4
Nehbandan, Iran 66/L5
Nehe, China 77/L2
Neiafu, Tonga 87/J7
Neiba, Dom. Rep. 158/D6
Neiba, Dom. Rep. 156/D3
Neiba (bay), Dom. Rep. 158/D6
Neiba, Sierra de (mts.), Dom. Rep. 158/D6
Neiber, Wyo. 319/D2
Neidpath, Sask. 181/D5
Neiges (lake), Québec 172/F2
Neigette, Québec 172/F1
Neihart, Mont. 262/F3
Neijiang (Neikiang), China 77/G6
Neilburg, Sask. 181/B3
Neillsville, Wis. 317/E6
Neil's Harbour, Nova Scotia 168/H2
Neilston, Scotland 15/B2
Neilton, Wash. 310/B3
Nei Monggol (Inner Mongolian Aut. Reg.), China 77/H3
Neis Beach, Sask. 181/E2

Neisse (riv.), Germany 22/F3
Neisse (Nysa), Poland 47/C3
Neisse (riv.), Poland 47/B3
Neiva, Colombia 120/B2
Neiva, Colombia 126/C6
Nejanilini (lake), Manitoba 179/J1
Nejd (reg.), Saudi Arabia 59/D4
Nejdek, Czech. 41/B1
Nejo, Ethiopia 111/G6
Nekoma, Kansas 232/C3
Nekoma, N. Dak. 282/O2
Nekoosa, Wis. 317/G7
Nekso, Denmark 18/J9
Nekso, Denmark 21/F9
Nelagoney, Okla. 288/O1
Nelchina, Alaska 196/C1
Nelidovo, U.S.S.R. 52/D3
Neligh, Nebr. 264/G2
Nel'kan, U.S.S.R. 48/O4
Nellie, Ohio 284/F5
Nellis, W. Va. 312/C6
Nellis A.F.B., Nev. 266/F6
Nellis Air Force Range and AEC Nuclear Testing Site, Nev. 266/E5
Nelliston, N.Y. 276/L5
Nellore, India 54/K8
Nellore, India 68/E6
Nellysford, Va. 307/L5
Nelma, Wis. 317/J3
Nelse, Ky. 237/R6
Nelson (isl.), Alaska 196/E2
Nelson, Argentina 143/F5
Nelson, Ariz. 198/B3
Nelson, Br. Col. 162/B3
Nelson, Br. Col. 184/J5
Nelson (str.), Chile 138/D9
Nelson, England 13/H1
Nelson, England 10/G1
Nelson, Georgia 217/D2
Nelson, Ill. 222/D2
Nelson (co.), Ky. 237/K5
Nelson, Ky. 237/G6
Nelson (riv.), Man. 146/J4
Nelson (riv.), Man. 162/G4
Nelson (riv.), Manitoba 179/J2
Nelson, Minn. 255/C5
Nelson, Mo. 261/F4
Nelson (res.), Mont. 262/J2
Nelson, Nebr. 264/F4
Nelson, Nev. 266/G7
Nelson (creek), Nev. 266/G2
Nelson•, N.H. 268/C5
Nelson, N. Zealand 87/H10
Nelson, N. Zealand 100/C4
Nelson (co.), N. Dak. 282/O4
Nelson, Pa. 294/H2
Nelson (cape), Victoria 97/A6
Nelson (co.), Va. 307/L5
Nelson, Wis. 317/C7
Nelson Forks, Br. Col. 184/M2
Nelson Head (prom.), N.W. Terr. 187/F2
Nelson House, Manitoba 179/J2
Nelson Lagoon, Alaska 196/G4
Nelson-Miramichi, New Bruns. 170/E2
Nelsonville, Ark. 202/H1
Nelsonville, Ky. 237/K5
Nelsonville, N.Y. 276/N8
Nelsonville, Ohio 284/E7
Nelsonville, Wis. 317/H7
Nelspruit, S. Africa 118/E5
Néma, Mauritania 106/C6
Néma, Mauritania 102/B3
Nemacolin, Pa. 294/B6
Nemadji (riv.), Minn. 255/F4
Nemaha, Iowa 229/C3
Nemaha (co.), Kansas 232/F2
Nemaha (co.), Kansas 232/G1
Nemaha (co.), Nebr. 264/J4
Nemaha, Nebr. 264/J4
Neméa, Greece 45/F7
Nemi, Italy 34/F7
Nemiskam, Alberta 182/E5
Nemo, S. Dak. 298/B5
Nemours, France 28/E3
Nemrut Daği (mt.), Turkey 63/J3
Nemunas (Niemen) (riv.), U.S.S.R. 53/A3
Nemuro, Japan 81/M2
Nemuro (str.), Japan 81/M1
Nen (riv.), China 54/O5
Nenagh, Ireland 10/B4
Nenagh, Ireland 17/E6
Nenagh (riv.), Ireland 17/E6
Nenana, Alaska 196/J2
Nendaz, Switzerland 39/D4
Nene (riv.), England 10/F4
Nene (riv.), England 13/H5
Nenets Aut. Okr., U.S.S.R. 48/F3
Nenets Aut. Okr., U.S.S.R. 52/H1
Nenjiang, China 77/L2
Nen Jiang (riv.), China 77/K2
Nenzel, Nebr. 264/C2
Neodesha, Kansas 232/G4
Neoga, Ill. 222/E4
Neola, Iowa 229/B6
Neola, Utah 304/D3
Neola, W. Va. 312/F7
Neon-Fleming, Ky. 237/R6
Neopit, Wis. 317/J6
Neópolis, Brazil 132/G5
Neosho, (riv.) 188/G2
Neosho (co.), Kansas 232/G4
Neosho (riv.), Kansas 232/G3
Neosho, Mo. 261/D9
Neosho, Wis. 317/J7
Neosho Falls, Kansas 232/G3
Neosho Rapids, Kansas 232/F3
Neotsu, Oreg. 291/C2
Nepa, U.S.S.R. 48/L4
Nepal 2/P4
Nepal 54/K7
NEPAL 68/E3
Nepalganj, Nepal 68/E3

Nepaug (res.), Conn. 210/D1
Nepaug (riv.), Conn. 210/C1
Nepean (isl.), Norfolk I. 88/L6
Nephi, Utah 304/C4
Nephin (mt.), Ireland 17/C3
Nephin Beg (mt.), Ireland 17/B3
Nephton, Ontario 177/J3
Nepisiguit (bay), New Bruns. 170/E1
Nepisiguit (lakes), New Bruns. 170/D1
Nepisiguit (riv.), New Bruns. 170/D1
Nepomuk, Czech. 41/B2
Neponset, Ill. 222/D2
Neponset, Mass. 249/D7
Neponset (riv.), Mass. 249/C8
Nepton, Ky. 237/O4
Neptune•, N.J. 273/E3
Neptune, Ohio 284/A4
Neptune (isls.), S. Australia 94/B6
Neptune Beach, Fla. 212/E1
Neptune City, N.J. 273/E3
Nera (riv.), Italy 34/D3
Nérac, France 28/D5
Nerekhta, U.S.S.R. 52/F3
Nerepis (riv.), New Bruns. 170/D3
Neresheim, Germany 22/D4
Nereta, U.S.S.R. 53/A3
Neretva (riv.), Yugoslavia 45/D4
Neriquinha, Angola 115/D7
Nerja, Spain 33/E4
Nerka (lake), Alaska 196/G3
Nermete (pt.), Peru 128/B5
Nerpio, Spain 33/E3
Nerstrand, Minn. 255/E6
Nerva, Spain 33/C4
Neryungri, U.S.S.R. 48/N4
Nes (Neskaupstadhur), Iceland 21/D1
Nes, Netherlands 27/H2
Nesbit, Miss. 256/D1
Nesbitt, Manitoba 179/C5
Nescopeck, Pa. 294/K3
Nesebŭr, Bulgaria 45/H4
Neshanic Station, N.J. 273/D3
Nesher, Israel 65/C2
Neshkoro, Wis. 317/H8
Neshoba (co.), Miss. 256/F5
Neshoba, Miss. 256/F5
Neskaupstadhur, Iceland 7/C2
Neskaupstadhur, Iceland 21/D1
Neskowin, Oreg. 291/C2
Nesmith, S.C. 296/H4
Nespelem, Wash. 310/G2
Nesquehoning, Pa. 294/L4
Ness (co.), Kansas 232/C3
Ness, Loch (lake), Scotland 15/D3
Ness, Loch (lake), Scotland 10/D2
Ness (riv.), Scotland 15/D3
Ness City, Kansas 232/C3
Nesselrode (mt.), Alaska 196/N1
Nesselwang, Germany 22/D5
Nesslau, Switzerland 39/H2
Neston, England 13/G2
Neston, England 10/E2
Nestor, Trin. & Tob. 161/B10
Nestor Falls, Ontario 177/F5
Nestor Falls, Ontario 175/B3
Nestoria, Mich. 250/A2
Nestórion, Greece 45/E5
Nestorville, W. Va. 312/G4
Néstos (riv.), Greece 45/G5
Nestow, Alberta 182/D2
Nesttun, Norway 18/D6
Nestucca (riv.), Oreg. 291/D2
Nesvady, Czech. 41/E3
Nes Ziyyona, Israel 65/B4
Net (riv.), Mich. 250/G2
Netanya, Israel 65/B3
Netarts, Oreg. 291/C2
Netawaka, Kansas 232/G2
Netcong, N.J. 273/D2
Nethe (riv.), Belgium 27/F6
Netherhill, Sask. 181/C4
Netherlands 2/K3
Netherlands 7/E3
NETHERLANDS 27/G4
Netherlands Antilles 120/C1
Netherlands Antilles 146/M8
NETHERLANDS ANTILLES 161
NETHERLANDS ANTILLES 156/E4
Nethy Bridge, Scotland 15/E3
Netivot, Israel 65/B5
Netolice, Czech. 41/C2
Netstal, Switzerland 39/H2
Nett (lake), Minn. 255/E2
Nettie, W. Va. 312/E6
Nettilling (lake), Canada 4/C13
Nettilling (fjord), N.W. Terr. 187/M3
Nettilling (lake), N.W. Terr. 187/L3
Nett Lake, Minn. 255/E2
Nett Lake Ind. Res., Minn. 255/E2
Nettleham, England 13/G4
Nettleton, Miss. 256/G2
Nettuno, Italy 34/F7
Netzahualcóyotl, Mexico 150/L1
Neuanlage, Sask. 181/E3
Neuberg an der Mürz, Austria 41/C3
Neubert, Tenn. 237/O9
Neubois, Québec 172/F3
Neubrandenburg, Germany 22/E2
Neuburg an der Donau, Germany 22/D4
Neuchâtel (canton), Switzerland 39/C3
Neuchâtel, Switzerland 39/C3
Neuchâtel (lake), Switzerland 39/C4
Neudorf, Sask. 181/J5
Neuenegg, Switzerland 39/D3
Neuenhagen bei Berlin, Germany 22/F4
Neufchâteau, Belgium 27/G9
Neufchâteau, France 28/F3
Neufchâtel-en-Bray, France 28/D3
Neugersdorf, Germany 22/F3
Neuhausen am Rheinfall, Switzerland 39/G1

euhorst, Sask. 181/E3
euilly-sur-Seine, France 28/A1
eu-Isenburg, Germany 22/C3
eumarkt am Wallersee, Austria 41/B3
eumarkt in der Oberpfalz, Germany 22/D4
eumarkt-Glewe, Germany 22/D2
eumarkt in Steiermark, Austria 41/C3
eumünster, Germany 22/C1
eunkirch, Switzerland 39/F1
eunkirchen, Austria 41/C3
eunkirchen, Germany 22/B4
euquén (prov.), Argentina 143/C4
euquén, Argentina 143/C4
euquén, Argentina 120/C6
euquén (riv.), Argentina 143/C4
euruppin, Germany 22/E2
euse, N.C. 281/M3
euse (riv.), N.C. 281/R5
eusiedl am See, Austria 41/D3
eusiedler See (lake), Austria 41/D3
eusiedler See (lake), Hungary 41/D3
euss, Germany 22/B3
eustadt, Ontario 177/D3
eustadt (Titisee-Neustadt), Germany 22/C5
eustadt an der Aisch, Germany 22/D4
eustadt an der Weinstrasse, Germany 22/B4
eustadt bei Coburg, Germany 22/D3
eustadt-Glewe, Germany 22/D2
eustadt in Holstein, Germany 22/D1
eustift im Stubaital, Austria 41/A3
eustrelitz, Germany 22/E2
EUTRAL ZONE 59/E4
eutral Zone 54/F7
eu-Ulm, Germany 22/D4
euville, Québec 172/F3
euwerk (isl.), Germany 22/C2
euwied, Germany 22/B3
eva, Tenn. 237/T8
evada 188/C3
EVADA 266
evada (co.), Ark. 202/D6
evada (co.), Calif. 204/E4
evada, Sierra (mts.), Calif. 204/E4
evada, Iowa 229/G5
evada, Mo. 261/D7
evada, Ohio 284/D4
evada, Sierra (mts.), Spain 33/E4
evada (state), U.S. 146/G6
evada City, Calif. 204/E4
evatim, Israel 65/B5
evel', U.S.S.R. 52/D3
evel'sk, U.S.S.R. 48/P5
evers, France 28/A2
eversink (res.), N.Y. 276/L7
evertire, N.S. Wales 97/D2
evesinje, Yugoslavia 45/D4
eville, Ohio 284/B8
eville, Sask. 181/D6
evils, Georgia 217/J6
evinnomyssk, U.S.S.R. 52/F6
evinville, Iowa 229/D6
evis, Alberta 182/D3
evis, Minn. 255/D4
evis (isl.), St. Kitts & Nevis 161/D11
evis (isl.), St. Kitts & Nevis 156/F3
evis (peak), St. Kitts & Nevis 161/D11
evis, Loch (inlet), Scotland 15/C3
evisdale, Ky. 237/N7
evşehir (prov.), Turkey 63/F3
evşehir, Turkey 59/B2
evşehir, Turkey 63/F3
ew (riv.), Belize 154/C2
ew (riv.), Calif. 204/K11
ew (for.), England 13/F6
ew (riv.), Fla. 212/D1
ew (riv.), Fla. 212/B1
ew (riv.), Guyana 131/C4
ew, South Fork (riv.), N.C. 281/G2
ew (riv.), N.C. 281/H5
ew (riv.), S.C. 296/E6
ew (inlet), Va. 307/S6
ew (riv.), Va. 307/F8
ew (riv.), W. Va. 312/E7
ew Abbey, Scotland 15/E6
ewagen, Maine 243/D8
ewala, Tanzania 115/G6
ew Albany, Ind. 188/J3
ew Albany, Ind. 227/F8
ew Albany, Kansas 232/G4
ew Albany, Miss. 256/G2
ew Albany, Ohio 284/E5
ew Albany, Pa. 294/J2
ew Albin, Iowa 229/L2
ewald, Wis. 317/J4
ew Alexandria, Ohio 284/J5
ew Alexandria, Pa. 294/C5
ewalla, Okla. 288/M4
ew Alluwe, Okla. 288/R1
ew Almaden, Calif. 204/L4
ew Almelo, Kansas 232/B2
ew Amsterdam, Guyana 120/D2
ew Amsterdam, Guyana 131/B2
ew Amsterdam, Ind. 227/E8
ew Amsterdam, Wis. 317/C8
ew Angledool, N.S. Wales 97/E1
ewark, Ark. 202/H2
ewark, Calif. 204/K3
ewark, Del. 245/P2
ewark, England 13/G4
ewark, England 10/F4
ewark, Ill. 222/D4
ewark, Md. 245/S7
ewark, Mo. 261/H2
ewark, N.J. 188/L2
ewark, N.J. 273/B2
ewark (bay), N.J. 273/B2
ewark, N.Y. 276/G4

Newark, Ohio 284/F5
Newark, S. Dak. 298/O2
Newark, Texas 303/E1
Newark•, Vt. 268/D2
Newark, W. Va. 312/D4
Newark Int'l Airport N.J. 273/B2
Newark Valley, N.Y. 276/H6
Newarthill, Scotland 15/C2
New Athens, Ill. 222/D5
New Athens, Ohio 284/H5
New Auburn, Minn. 255/D6
New Auburn, Wis. 317/D5
New Augusta, Miss. 256/F8
Newaygo (co.), Mich. 250/D5
Newaygo, Mich. 250/D5
New Baden, Ill. 222/D5
New Baltimore, Mich. 250/G6
New Baltimore, N.Y. 276/N6
New Baltimore, Pa. 294/E6
New Baltimore, Va. 307/N3
New Bavaria, Ohio 284/B3
New Beaver, Pa. 294/B4
New Bedford, Ill. 222/D2
New Bedford, Mass. 188/N2
New Bedford, Mass. 249/K6
New Bedford, Ohio 284/G5
New Bedford, Pa. 294/A3
New Bellsville, Ind. 227/E6
Newberg, Oreg. 291/A2
New Berlin, Ill. 222/D4
New Berlin, N.Y. 276/K5
New Berlin, Pa. 294/J4
New Berlin, Wis. 317/K2
Newbern, Ala. 195/C5
Newbern, Ind. 227/F6
New Bern, N.C. 188/L4
New Bern, N.C. 281/P4
Newbern, Tenn. 237/C8
Newberne, W. Va. 312/E4
Newberry, Fla. 212/D2
Newberry, Québec 172/F3
Newberry, Ind. 227/C7
Newberry, Mich. 250/D2
Newberry (co.), S.C. 296/D3
Newberry, S.C. 296/D3
Newberry Springs, Calif. 204/J9
New Bethlehem, Pa. 294/D3
Newbiggin-by-the-Sea, England 13/F2
New Blaine, Ark. 202/D3
Newbliss, Ireland 17/G3
New Bloomfield, Mo. 261/J5
New Bloomfield, Pa. 294/H5
New Bloomington, Ohio 284/D4
New Bonaventure, Newf. 166/D2
Newborn, Georgia 217/E3
Newboro, Ontario 177/H3
New Boston, Ill. 222/B2
New Boston, Mich. 250/F6
New Boston, Mo. 261/G3
New Boston•, N.H. 268/D6
New Boston, Ohio 284/E8
New Boston, Texas 303/K4
New Bothwell, Manitoba 179/F5
New Braintree•, Mass. 249/F3
New Braunfels, Texas 303/K10
New Bremen, N.Y. 276/K3
New Bremen, Ohio 284/B5
Newbridge (Droichead Nua), Ireland 17/H5
New Bridge, Oreg. 291/K3
New Brigden, Alberta 182/E4
New Brighton, Minn. 255/G5
New Brighton, Pa. 294/B4
New Britain, Conn. 210/E2
New Britain (isl.), Papua N.G. 87/F6
New Britain (isl.), Papua N.G. 85/C7
New Britain (isl.), Papua N.G. 86/B2
New Britain, Pa. 294/M5
New Brockton, Ala. 195/G8
Newbrook, Alberta 182/D2
NEW BRUNSWICK 170
New Brunswick (prov.) 162/K6
New Brunswick (prov.), Canada 146/M5
New Brunswick, N.J. 273/B3
New Buena Vista, Pa. 294/E5
New Buffalo, Mich. 250/C7
New Buffalo, Pa. 294/H5
Newburg, Ark. 202/G1
Newburg, Iowa 229/H5
Newburg, Md. 245/L7
Newburg, Mo. 261/J7
Newburg, N. Dak. 282/J2
Newburg, Pa. 294/G5
Newburg (La Jose), Pa. 294/E4
Newburg, W. Va. 312/G4
Newburg, Wis. 317/K9
Newburg, Ind. 227/C9
Newburgh•, Maine 243/F6
Newburgh, N.Y. 188/M2
Newburgh, N.Y. 276/M7
Newburgh, Ontario 177/H3
Newburgh, Scotland 10/E2
Newburgh, Grampian Scotland 15/G3
Newburgh, Fife, Scotland 15/E4
Newburgh Heights, Ohio 284/H9
New Burlington, Ind. 227/G4
New Burlington, Ohio 284/B9
New Burnside, Ill. 222/E6
Newbury, England 13/F6
Newbury, England 10/F6
Newbury•, Mass. 249/L1
Newbury•, N.H. 268/C5
Newbury, Ohio 284/H3
Newbury, Ontario 177/C5
Newbury, Vt. 268/C3
Newbury•, Vt. 268/D3
Newburyport, Mass. 249/L1
New Bussa, Nigeria 106/E6
NEW CALEDONIA 86/G4
New Caledonia 87/G8
New Caledonia (isl.), (Fr.) 2/T7
New Caledonia (isl.), New Caled. 87/G8
New Caledonia (isl.), New Caled. 86/G4
New Cambria, Kansas 232/E3

New Cambria, Mo. 261/G3
New Canaan•, Conn. 210/B4
New Canton, Ill. 222/B4
New Canton, Va. 307/M5
New Carlisle, Ind. 227/E1
New Carlisle, Ohio 284/C6
New Carlisle, Québec 172/D2
New Carlisle, Québec 174/E3
New Carrollton, Md. 245/G4
New Castile (reg.), Spain 33/E3
Newcastle, Australia 2/S7
Newcastle, Calif. 204/C8
New Castle, Colo. 208/E3
New Castle, Del. 245/R2
New Castle, Ind. 227/G5
Newcastle, Ireland 10/B4
Newcastle, Ireland 17/D7
New Castle, Ky. 237/L4
Newcastle•, Maine 243/D7
Newcastle, N. Br. 162/K6
Newcastle, N.S. Wales 88/J6
Newcastle, Nebr. 264/H2
Newcastle, New Bruns. 170/E2
New Castle•, N.H. 268/F5
Newcastle, N.S. Wales 97/F3
New Castle, Ohio 284/F5
Newcastle, Okla. 288/L4
New Castle, Ontario 177/F4
New Castle, Pa. 188/K2
New Castle, Pa. 294/B3
Newcastle, St. Kitts & Nevis 161/D11
Newcastle, S. Africa 118/E5
Newcastle, Texas 303/F4
Newcastle, Utah 304/A6
New Castle, Va. 307/H5
Newcastle, Wyo. 319/H2
Newcastle Creek, New Bruns. 170/D2
Newcastle-Damariscotta, Maine 243/E7
Newcastle Emlyn, Wales 13/C5
Newcastleton, Scotland 15/F5
Newcastle-under-Lyme, England 13/E4
Newcastle-under-Lyme, England 10/E4
Newcastle upon Tyne, England 7/D3
Newcastle upon Tyne, England 10/E3
Newcastle upon Tyne, England 13/H3
Newcastle Waters, North. Terr. 93/C4
New Centerville, Pa. 294/D6
New Chelsea, Newf. 166/D2
New Chicago, Ind. 227/C1
New Church, Va. 307/S5
New Cinema, Br. Col. 184/F3
New City, N.Y. 276/K8
New Columbia, Pa. 294/H3
New Columbus, Pa. 294/K3
Newcomb, N. Mex. 274/A2
Newcomb, N.Y. 276/M3
Newcomb, Tenn. 237/N7
Newcomerstown, Ohio 284/G5
New Concord, Ky. 237/E7
New Concord, Ohio 284/G6
New Cordell (Cordell), Okla. 288/H4
New Corydon, Ind. 227/H3
New Court, Mo. 261/J2
New Creek, W. Va. 312/J4
New Cumberland, Pa. 294/J5
New Cumberland, W. Va. 312/E2
New Cumnock, Scotland 15/D5
Newdale, Idaho 220/G6
Newdale, Manitoba 179/B4
New Dayton, Alberta 182/D5
New Deal, Texas 303/C4
New Deer, Scotland 15/H3
Newdegate, W. Australia 92/B6
New Delhi (cap.), India 2/N4
New Delhi, India 54/J7
New Delhi, India 68/D3
New Delhi (cap.), India 68/D3
New Denmark, New Bruns. 170/C1
New Denver, Br. Col. 184/J5
New Diggings, Wis. 317/F10
New Douglas, Ill. 222/D5
New Dover, Ohio 284/D5
New Durham•, N.H. 268/E5
New Eagle, Pa. 294/B5
New Edinburg, Ark. 202/F6
New Effington, S. Dak. 298/R2
New Egypt, N.J. 273/E3
Newell, Ala. 195/H4
Newell (lake), Alberta 182/E4
Newell, Iowa 229/D3
Newell, S. Dak. 298/C4
Newell, W. Va. 312/E1
New Ellenton, S.C. 296/D5
Newellton, La. 238/H2
Newellton, Nova Scotia 168/C5
New England (range), N.S. Wales 97/F3
New England, N. Dak. 282/E6
New England, W. Va. 312/C4
Newenham (cape), Alaska 196/H3
New Enterprise, Pa. 294/F5
New Era, La. 238/G4
New Era, Mich. 250/C5
New Era, Oreg. 291/B2
Newe Yam, Israel 65/B2
Newe Zohar, Israel 65/C5
New Fairfield•, Conn. 210/B3
Newfane, N.Y. 276/F4
Newfane, Vt. 268/B6
Newfane•, Vt. 268/B6
Newfield•, Maine 243/B8
Newfield•, Maine 243/B8
Newfield, N.J. 273/D4
Newfield, N.Y. 276/G6
Newfields•, N.H. 268/F5
New Fish Creek, Alberta 182/B2
New Florence, Mo. 261/K5
New Florence, Pa. 294/D5
Newfolden, Minn. 255/B2
New Fork (lakes), Wyo. 319/C2

Newfound (lake), N.H. 268/D4
NEWFOUNDLAND 166
Newfoundland (prov.) 162/L5
Newfoundland (isl.) 162/L6
Newfoundland (prov.), Canada 146/M4
Newfoundland (isl.), Canada 2/G3
Newfoundland, Ky. 237/P4
Newfoundland (isl.), Newf. 166/C4
Newfoundland (isl.), Newf. 146/N5
Newfoundland (isl.), Newf. 166/C4
Newfoundland, N.J. 273/D1
Newfoundland, Pa. 294/M3
Newfoundland (mts.), Utah 304/A2
New Franken, Wis. 317/L6
New Frankfort, Mo. 261/F4
New Franklin, Mo. 261/G4
New Freedom, Pa. 294/J6
New Freeport, Pa. 294/B6
New Galilee, Pa. 294/A4
New Galloway, Scotland 10/D3
New Galloway, Scotland 15/D5
Newgate, Br. Col. 184/K5
New Georgia (isl.), Solomon Is. 87/F6
New Georgia (isl.), Solomon Is. 86/D3
New Germantown, Pa. 294/G5
New Germany, Minn. 255/E6
New Germany, Nova Scotia 168/D4
New Glarus, Wis. 317/G10
New Glasgow, Nova Scotia 168/F3
New Glasgow, Québec 172/D4
New Gloucester, Maine 243/C8
New Gloucester•, Maine 243/C8
New Goshen, Ind. 227/B5
New Gretna, N.J. 273/E4
New Guinea (isl.) 2/S6
New Guinea (isl.) 54/P10
New Guinea (isl.) 87/E6
New Guinea (isl.), Papua N.G. 86/B2
Newgulf, Texas 303/J8
New Halem, Wash. 310/D2
Newhalen, Alaska 196/H3
Newhall, Calif. 204/G9
Newhall, Iowa 229/H5
Newhall, W. Va. 312/C8
New Hanover (co.), N.C. 281/O6
New Hanover (Lavongai) (isl.), Papua N.G. 87/F6
New Hanover (isl.), Papua N.G. 86/B1
New Harbor, Maine 243/E8
New Harbour, Newf. 166/C4
New Harbour, Newf. 166/D2
New Harbour, Nova Scotia 168/G3
New Harmony, Ind. 227/B8
New Harmony, Utah 304/A6
New Hartford, Conn. 210/C1
New Hartford•, Conn. 210/C1
New Hartford, Iowa 229/H3
New Hartford, N.Y. 276/K4
New Haven (co.), Conn. 210/D3
New Haven, Conn. 188/M2
New Haven, Conn. 210/D3
New Haven (harb.), Conn. 210/D3
New Haven, Ill. 222/E6
New Haven, Ind. 227/H2
New Haven, Ky. 237/K5
New Haven, Mich. 250/G6
New Haven, Mo. 261/K5
New Haven, N.Y. 276/H4
New Haven, Nova Scotia 168/H2
New Haven, Ohio 284/E3
New Haven•, Vt. 268/A3
New Haven, W. Va. 312/C8
New Haven, Wyo. 319/H1
New Hazelton, Br. Col. 184/D2
New Hebrides (Vanuatu) 87/G7
Newhebron, Miss. 256/D7
New Hill, N.C. 281/M3
New Holland, Georgia 217/E2
New Holland, Ill. 222/D3
New Holland, N.C. 281/S4
New Holland, Ohio 284/D6
New Holland, Pa. 294/K5
New Holland, S. Dak. 298/M7
New Holstein, Wis. 317/K8
New Home, Texas 303/C4
New Hope, Ala. 195/F1
New Hope, Ky. 237/K5
New Hope, Minn. 255/G5
New Hope, Ohio 284/A6
New Hope, Pa. 294/N5
New Hope, Tenn. 237/K11
New Hope, Va. 307/L4
New Horse Springs, N. Mex. 274/A5
New Houlka (Houlka), Miss. 256/G2
New Hradec, N. Dak. 282/E5
New Hyde Park, N.Y. 276/P7
New Iberia, La. 238/G6
Newington•, Conn. 210/E2
Newington, Georgia 217/J5
Newington•, N.H. 268/F5
Newington, Ontario 177/K2
Newington, Va. 307/S3
New Ipswich•, N.H. 268/D6
New Ireland (isl.), Papua N.G. 87/F6
New Ireland (isl.), Papua N.G. 86/B1
New Jenny Lind, Ark. 202/B3
New Jersey 188/M3
NEW JERSEY 273

New Jersey, New Bruns. 170/E1
New Jersey (state), U.S. 146/L5
New Johnsonville, Tenn. 237/E8
New Kensington, Pa. 294/C4
New Kent (co.), Va. 307/P5
New Kent, Va. 307/P5
Newkirk, N. Mex. 274/E3
Newkirk, Okla. 288/N1
New Knoxville, Ohio 284/B5
New Laguna, N. Mex. 274/B4
New Lancaster, Kansas 232/H3
Newland, N.C. 281/F2
New Lebanon, Ind. 227/C6
New Lebanon, N.Y. 276/O6
New Lebanon, Ohio 284/B6
New Lebanon, Pa. 294/B3
New Leipzig, N. Dak. 282/G7
New Lenox, Ill. 222/B6
New Lexington, Ohio 284/F6
New Liberty, Iowa 229/M5
New Liberty, Ky. 237/M3
New Lima, Okla. 288/O4
New Limerick•, Maine 243/G3
Newlin, Texas 303/D3
New Lisbon, Ind. 227/G5
New Lisbon, N.J. 273/D4
New Lisbon, Wis. 317/F8
New Liskeard, Ont. 162/H6
New Liskeard, Ontario 177/K5
New Liskeard, Ontario 175/E3
Newllano, La. 238/D4
New London, Ark. 202/F7
New London, Conn. 188/M2
New London, Conn. 210/G3
New London, Iowa 229/L7
New London, Minn. 255/C5
New London, Mo. 261/K3
New London, N.H. 268/D5
New London•, N.H. 268/D5
New London, N.C. 281/J4
New London, Ohio 284/D7
New London (bay), Pr. Edward I. 168/E2
New London, Texas 303/K5
New London, Wis. 317/J7
New Lothrop, Mich. 250/F5
New Lowell, Ontario 177/E3
New Lyme, Ohio 284/J2
New Lynn, N. Zealand 100/B1
New Madison, Ohio 284/A6
New Madrid (co.), Mo. 261/N9
New Madrid, Mo. 261/O9
Newmains, Scotland 15/C2
Newman, Calif. 204/D6
Newman, Ill. 222/B6
Newman, Ky. 237/G5
Newman (sound), Newf. 166/D2
Newman, W. Australia 88/C4
Newman (lake), Wash. 310/H3
Newman, W. Australia 92/B3
Newman Grove, Nebr. 264/G3
Newman Lake, Wash. 310/J3
Newmans Cove, Newf. 166/D2
New Marion, Ind. 227/G6
New Market, Ala. 195/F1
Newmarket, England 13/H4
Newmarket, England 10/G4
New Market, Ind. 227/D5
New Market, Iowa 229/D7
Newmarket, Ireland 10/B4
Newmarket, Ireland 17/C7
Newmarket, Jamaica 158/H6
New Market, Md. 245/J3
New Market, Minn. 255/E6
New Market, Mo. 261/C4
New Market, New Bruns. 170/D3
New Market•, N.H. 268/F5
New Market, Ohio 284/C7
Newmarket, Ontario 177/E3
Newmarket, Queensland 88/K2
Newmarket, Queensland 95/D2
Newmarket, Scotland 15/B2
Newmarket, Tenn. 237/O8
New Market, Va. 307/L3
Newmarket-on-Fergus, Ireland 17/D6
New Marlborough•, Mass. 249/B4
New Martinsburg, Ohio 284/D7
New Martinsville, W. Va. 312/E3
New Maryland, New Bruns. 170/D3
New Matamoras, Ohio 284/J6
New Meadows, Idaho 220/B4
New Melle, Mo. 261/L5
New Memphis, Ill. 222/D5
Newmerella, Victoria 97/E5
New Mexico 188/E4
NEW MEXICO 274
New Mexico (state), U.S. 146/H6
New Miami, Ohio 284/A7
New Middleton, Tenn. 237/J8
New Middletown, Ind. 227/E8
New Middletown, Ohio 284/J4
New Milford, Conn. 210/B2
New Milford•, Conn. 210/B2
New Milford, Ill. 222/D1
New Milford, N.J. 273/B1
New Milford, Ohio 284/H3
New Milford, Pa. 294/L2
Newmill, Scotland 15/E3
New Mills, England 13/J2
New Mills, England 10/G2
Newmilns and Greenholm, Scotland 15/D5
New Milton, W. Va. 312/E4
New Minas, Nova Scotia 168/D3
New Minden, Ill. 222/D5
Newington, Ontario 177/K2
New Mount Pleasant, Ind. 227/G4
New Munich, Minn. 255/D5
Newnan, Georgia 217/C4
Newnans (lake), Fla. 212/D2
New Norcia, W. Australia 92/A5
New Norfolk, Tasmania 88/H8
New Norfolk, Tasmania 99/C4
New Norway, Alberta 182/D3

New Offenburg, Mo. 261/M7
New Orleans, La. 188/H5
New Orleans, La. 146/K7
New Orleans, La. 238/O4
New Osgoode, Sask. 181/H3
New Oxford, Pa. 294/H6
New Palestine, Ind. 227/F5
New Pallas, Ireland 17/E6
New Paltz, N.Y. 276/M7
New Paris, Ind. 227/F2
New Paris, Ohio 284/A6
New Paris, Pa. 294/E5
New Pass (range), Nev. 266/D3
New Pekin, Ind. 227/F7
Perlican, Newf. 166/D2
New Petersburg, Ohio 284/D7
New Philadelphia, Ill. 222/C3
New Philadelphia, Ind. 227/F7
New Philadelphia, Ohio 284/G5
New Philadelphia, Pa. 294/K4
New Pine Creek, Oreg. 291/G5
New Pitsligo, Scotland 15/F3
New Pittsburg, Ohio 284/F4
New Plymouth, Idaho 220/B6
New Plymouth, N. Zealand 100/D3
New Plymouth, Ohio 284/F7
New Point, Ind. 227/G6
New Point, Mo. 261/B2
Newport, Ark. 202/H2
Newport, Del. 245/R2
Newport, England 13/F7
Newport, England 13/E5
Newport, England 10/F5
Newport, Ind. 227/C5
Newport, Mayo, Ireland 17/C4
Newport, Tipperary, Ireland 17/E6
Newport, Ky. 237/S2
Newport, Ky. 188/K3
Newport, Maine 243/E6
Newport•, Maine 243/E6
Newport, Md. 245/L7
Newport, Minn. 255/F6
Newport, Miss. 256/D1
Newport, Nebr. 264/E2
New Port, Neth. Ant. 161/G9
Newport, N.H. 268/C5
Newport•, N.H. 268/C5
Newport, N.J. 273/C5
Newport, N.Y. 276/K4
Newport, N.C. 281/R5
Newport, Nova Scotia 168/G3
Newport, Ohio 284/C6
Newport, Ohio 284/H7
Newport, Oreg. 291/C3
Newport, Pa. 294/H5
Newport, Québec 172/D2
Newport, R.I. 188/M2
Newport (co.), R.I. 249/K6
Newport, R.I. 249/J7
Newport, Tenn. 237/P9
Newport, Texas 303/F4
Newport, Vt. 268/C2
Newport•, Vt. 268/C2
Newport, Va. 307/H6
Newport, Wash. 310/H2
Newport, Dyfed, Wales 13/C5
Newport, Gwent, Wales 13/B6
Newport, Wales 10/E5
Newport, Wash. 310/H2
Newport Beach, Calif. 204/D11
Newport Center, Vt. 268/C2
New Portland, Maine 243/C6
New Portland•, Maine 243/C6
Newport News, Va. 188/L3
Newport News (I.C.), Va. 307/P6
Newport-on-Tay, Scotland 15/F4
Newport Pagnell, England 13/G5
New Port Richey, Fla. 212/D3
New Prague, Minn. 255/E6
New Preston, Conn. 210/B2
New Providence (isl.), Bahamas 156/C1
New Providence (Borden), Ind. 227/F8
New Providence, Iowa 229/G4
New Providence, N.J. 273/E2
New Providence, Pa. 294/K6
New Prue (Prue), Okla. 288/O2
Newquay, England 10/D5
Newquay, England 13/B7
New Quay, Wales 10/D4
New Quay, Wales 13/C5
New Raymer, Colo. 208/M1
New Richland, Minn. 255/E7
New Richmond, Ind. 227/D5
New Richmond, Ohio 284/B8
New Richmond, Québec 172/D2
New Richmond, Wis. 317/A5
New Riegel, Ohio 284/D3
New River, N.C. 281/O5
New River (inlet), N.C. 281/P6
New River, Tenn. 237/M8
New River, Va. 307/G6
New River Beach, New Bruns. 170/D3
New Road, Nova Scotia 168/E4
New Roads, La. 238/G5
New Rochelle, N.Y. 276/P7
New Rockford, N. Dak. 282/N4
New Romney, England 13/J7
New Ross, Ind. 227/D5
New Ross, Ireland 10/C4
New Ross, Ireland 17/H7
New Ross, Nova Scotia 168/D4
Newry, Maine 243/B6
Newry•, Maine 243/B6
Newry, N. Ireland 17/J3
Newry, N. Ireland 17/J3
Newry, North. Terr. 93/A3
Newry, Pa. 294/F5
Newry, S.C. 296/B2
New Salem, Ill. 222/C4
New Salem, Ind. 227/G5
New Salem, Kansas 232/G4
New Salem•, Mass. 249/E2
New Salem, N. Dak. 282/G6
New Salem, Nova Scotia 168/D3
New Salem, Ohio 284/E6

418 New Salem

New Salem, Pa. 294/C6
New Salem (Delmont), Pa. 294/D5
New Salisbury, Ind. 227/E8
New Sarepta, Alberta 182/D3
New Sarpy, La. 238/N4
New Schwabenland (reg.) 5/B1
New Scone, Scotland 15/E4
New Sharon, Iowa 229/H6
New Sharon•, Maine 243/C6
New Sharon, N.J. 273/D3
New Shoreham (Block Island)•, R.I. 249/H8
New Siberian (isls.), U.S.S.R. 54/R2
New Siberian (isls.), U.S.S.R. 4/B2
New Siberian (isls.), U.S.S.R. 2/S2
New Siberian (isls.), U.S.S.R. 48/P2
New Site, Ala. 195/G4
New Site, Miss. 256/H1
New Smyrna Beach, Fla. 212/F2
Newsoms, Va. 307/O7
New South Wales 88/H6
NEW SOUTH WALES 97
New South Wales (state), Australia 87/E9
New Spadra, Ark. 202/C3
New Square, N.Y. 276/K8
New Stanton, Pa. 294/C5
New Straitsville, Ohio 284/F6
New Strawn (Strawn), Kansas 232/G3
New Stuyahok, Alaska 196/G3
New Sweden, Maine 243/G2
New Sweden•, Maine 243/G2
New Tazewell, Tenn. 237/O8
Newtok, Alaska 196/F2
Newton, Ala. 195/G8
Newton (co.), Ark. 202/D2
Newton (co.), Georgia 217/E3
Newton, Georgia 217/D8
Newton, Ill. 222/E5
Newton (co.), Ind. 227/C3
Newton, Iowa 188/H2
Newton, Iowa 229/H5
Newton, Kansas 232/E3
Newton, Mass. 249/C7
Newton (co.), Miss. 256/F6
Newton, Miss. 256/F6
Newton (co.), Mo. 261/D9
Newton•, N.H. 268/E6
Newton, N.J. 273/D1
Newton, N.C. 281/G3
Newton, Québec 172/C4
Newton, Scotland 15/E5
Newton (co.), Texas 303/L7
Newton, Texas 303/L7
Newton, Utah 304/C2
Newton, W. Va. 312/D5
Newton Abbot, England 13/D7
Newton Abbot, England 10/E5
Newton Center, Mass. 249/C7
Newton Falls, N.Y. 276/K2
Newton Falls, Ohio 284/J3
Newtongrange, Scotland 15/D2
Newton Grove, N.C. 281/N4
Newton Hamilton, Pa. 294/G5
Newton Highlands, Mass. 249/C7
Newtonia, Mo. 261/D9
Newton Junction, N.H. 268/E6
Newton-le-Willows, England 13/H2
Newton Lower Falls, Mass. 249/B7
Newton Mearns, Scotland 15/B2
Newton Mills, Nova Scotia 168/F3
Newtonmore, Scotland 15/D3
Newton Siding, Manitoba 179/D5
Newton Stewart, Scotland 10/D3
Newton Stewart, Scotland 15/D6
Newtonsville, Ohio 284/B7
Newton Upper Falls, Mass. 249/C7
Newtonville, Ind. 227/D8
Newtonville, Mass. 249/C7
Newtonville, N.J. 273/D4
Newtown, Conn. 210/B3
Newtown•, Conn. 210/B3
Newtown, Ind. 227/C4
Newtown, Ky. 237/N4
Newtown, Mo. 261/F2
Newtown, New Bruns. 170/E3
Newtown, Newf. 166/D4
Newtown, N.S. Wales 97/C6
New Town, N. Dak. 282/F4
Newtown, Ohio 284/C10
Newtown, Pa. 294/N5
New Town, S.C. 296/J3
Newtown, Victoria 97/C6
Newtown, Wales 13/D5
Newtown, Wales 10/E4
Newtownabbey (dist.), N. Ireland 17/J2
Newtownabbey, N. Ireland 17/K2
Newtownards, N. Ireland 17/K2
Newtownbutler, N. Ireland 17/G3
Newtown Forbes, Ireland 17/F4
Newtownhamilton, N. Ireland 17/H3
Newtownmountkennedy, Ireland 17/J5
Newtown Saint Boswells, Scotland 15/F5
Newtownsandes, Ireland 17/C6
Newtown Square•, Pa. 294/L6
Newtownstewart, N. Ireland 17/G2
New Trenton, Ind. 227/H6
New Trier, Minn. 255/F6
New Tripoli, Pa. 294/L4
New Troy, Mich. 250/C7
New Tulsa, Okla. 288/P2
Newtyle, Scotland 15/E4
New Ulm, Minn. 255/D6
New Ulm, Texas 303/H8
New Underwood, S. Dak. 298/D5
New Vernon, N.J. 273/D2
New Victoria, Nova Scotia 168/H2
New Vienna, Iowa 229/L3
New Vienna, Ohio 284/C7
Newville, Ala. 195/H8
Newville, Ind. 227/H2
Newville, Pa. 294/H5
Newville, W. Va. 312/E5
New Vineyard•, Maine 243/C6
New Virginia, Iowa 229/F6
New Washington, Ind. 227/F7
New Washington, Ohio 284/E4
New Washington, Philippines 82/D5
New Waterford, Nova Scotia 168/J2
New Waterford, Ohio 284/J4
New Waverly, Ind. 227/E3
New Waverly, Texas 303/J7
New Westminster, Br. Col. 162/D6
New Westminster, Br. Col. 184/K3
New Weston, Ohio 284/A5
New Whiteland, Ind. 227/E5
New Wilmington, Pa. 294/B3
New Winchester, Ind. 227/D5
New Winchester, Ohio 284/D4
New Windsor, England 13/G8
New Windsor, England 10/F5
New Windsor, Ill. 222/C2
New Windsor, Md. 245/K2
New Windsor, N.Y. 276/N8
New Witten, S. Dak. 298/K7
New Woodstock, N.Y. 276/J5
New World (isl.), Newf. 166/C4
New York 188/L2
NEW YORK 276
New York (co.), N.Y. 276/M9
New York, N.Y. 146/L5
New York, N.Y. 188/M2
New York, N.Y. 276/M9
New York (state), U.S. 146/L5
New York, U.S. 2/F3
New York Mills, Minn. 255/C4
New York Mills, N.Y. 276/K4
New York State Barge (canal), N.Y. 276/C4
New Zealand 2/T8
New Zealand 87/G9
NEW ZEALAND 100
New Zion, New Bruns. 170/D2
New Zion, S.C. 296/H4
Ney, Ohio 284/B3
Neyagawa, Japan 81/J7
Neyland, Wales 13/B6
Neyriz, Iran 66/J6
Neyshabur, Iran 59/G2
Neyshabur, Iran 66/L2
Nezhin, U.S.S.R. 52/D4
Nez Perce (co.), Idaho 220/B3
Nezperce, Idaho 220/B3
Nez Perce Nat'l Hist. Park, Idaho 220/B-C3
Nezwar (mt.), Iran 66/H3
Ngabang, Indonesia 85/D5
N'gage, Angola 115/C5
N'gage, Angola 102/D5
Ngahere, N. Zealand 100/C5
Ngami (lake), Botswana 118/C4
Ngamiland (reg.), Botswana 118/C3
Ngamring, China 77/C6
Ngangla Ringco (lake), China 77/B5
Ngangzê Co (lake), China 77/C5
Ngao, Thailand 72/D3
Ngaoundéré, Cameroon 115/B2
Ngaoundéré, Cameroon 102/D4
Ngapara, N. Zealand 100/C6
Ngara, Tanzania 115/F4
Ngaruawahia, N. Zealand 100/E2
Ngatapa, N. Zealand 100/F3
Ngatik (atoll), Micronesia 87/F5
Ngau (isl.), Fiji 86/Q10
Ngauruhoe (mt.), N. Zealand 100/E3
Ngawi, Indonesia 85/K2
Nghia Lo, Vietnam 72/D2
Ngoc Linh (mt.), Vietnam 72/E4
Ngom Qu (riv.), China 77/E5
Ngong, Kenya 115/G4
Ngoring Hu (lake), China 77/E4
Ngorongoro (crater), Tanzania 115/F4
N'Gounié (riv.), Congo 115/B4
N'Gounié (riv.), Gabon 115/B4
Ngourou, Cent. Afr. Rep. 115/D2
N'Guigmi, Niger 106/G6
Ngulu (atoll), Micronesia 87/D5
Ngunju (cape), Indonesia 85/F8
Ngunza (Sumbe), Angola 102/D6
Ngunza (Sumbe), Angola 115/B6
Nguru, Nigeria 102/D3
Nguru, Nigeria 106/G6
Nhâmundá (riv.), Brazil 120/D3
Nhamundá (riv.), Brazil 132/B3
Nharêa, Angola 115/C6
Nharêa, Angola 102/D6
Nha Trang, Vietnam 72/F4
Nha Trang, Vietnam 54/M8
Nhava-Sheva, India 68/B7
Nhill, Victoria 88/G7
Nhill, Victoria 97/A5
Nhulunbuy, North. Terr. 88/F2
Nhulunbuy, North. Terr. 93/E2
Ni (riv.), Va. 307/N4
Niafunké, Mali 106/D5
Niagara (co.), N.Y. 276/C4
Niagara (riv.), N.Y. 276/B4
Niagara, N. Dak. 282/P4
Niagara (reg. munic.), Ontario 177/E4
Niagara (riv.), Ontario 177/E4
Niagara, Wis. 317/K4
Niagara Falls, N.Y. 188/K2
Niagara Falls, N.Y. 276/C4
Niagara Falls, Ont. 162/J7
Niagara Falls, Ontario 177/E4
Niagara-on-the-Lake, Ontario 177/E4
Niamey (cap.), Niger 2/K5
Niamey (cap.), Niger 102/C3
Niamey (cap.), Niger 106/E6
Niangara, Zaire 115/E3
Niangua, Mo. 261/G8
Niantic, Conn. 210/G3
Niantic (riv.), Conn. 210/G3
Niantic, Ill. 222/D4
Niarada, Mont. 262/B3
Niari (riv.), Congo 115/B4
Nias (isl.), Indonesia 54/L9
Nias (isl.), Indonesia 85/B5
Niassa (prov.), Mozambique 118/F2
Nibbe, Mont. 262/H4
Nibe, Denmark 21/C4
Nibe, Denmark 18/F8
Nibley, Utah 304/C2
Nicaragua 2/E5
Nicaragua 146/K8
NICARAGUA 154/E4
Nicaragua (lake), Nic. 146/K8
Nicaragua (lake), Nicaragua 154/E5
Nicaro, Cuba 158/J3
Nicasio, Calif. 204/H1
Nicastro, Italy 34/F5
Nicatous (lake), Maine 243/G5
Nice, France 7/E4
Nice, France 28/G6
Niceville, Fla. 212/C6
Nichinan, Japan 81/E8
Nichol (isl.), Nova Scotia 168/F4
Nicholas (chan.), Cuba 156/B2
Nicholas (chan.), Cuba 158/E1
Nicholas (co.), Ky. 237/N4
Nicholas (co.), W. Va. 312/E6
Nicholas Denys, New Bruns. 170/D1
Nicholasville, Ky. 237/N5
Nicholls, Georgia 217/G7
Nichols, Conn. 210/C4
Nichols, Fla. 212/E4
Nichols, Iowa 229/L6
Nichols, Minn. 255/E4
Nichols, N.Y. 276/H6
Nichols, S.C. 296/J3
Nichols, Wis. 317/K6
Nichols Hills, Okla. 288/L3
Nicholson (riv.), Australia 88/F3
Nicholson, Br. Col. 184/J4
Nicholson, Georgia 217/F2
Nicholson, Miss. 256/E10
Nicholson, Port (inlet), N. Zealand 100/B3
Nicholson (riv.), North. Terr. 93/E5
Nicholson, Pa. 294/L2
Nicholson (riv.), Queensland 95/A3
Nicholson, W. Australia 92/E2
Nicholsville, Ala. 195/C6
Nicholville, N.Y. 276/L1
Nickel Centre, Ontario 175/D3
Nickel Centre, Ontario 177/D1
Nickelsville, Va. 307/D7
Nickerie (dist.), Suriname 131/C3
Nickerie (riv.), Suriname 131/C3
Nickerson, Kansas 232/D3
Nickerson, Minn. 255/F4
Nickerson, Nebr. 264/H3
Nicobar (isls.), India 54/L9
Nicobar (isls.), India 68/G7
Nicodemus, Kansas 232/C2
Nicola, Br. Col. 184/G5
Nicolaus, Calif. 204/B8
Nicolet (co.), Québec 172/E3
Nicolet, Québec 172/E3
Nicolet (lake), Québec 172/F4
Nicolet (riv.), Québec 172/E3
Nicollet (co.), Minn. 255/D6
Nicollet, Minn. 255/D6
Nicoma Park, Okla. 288/M4
Nicomen Island, Br. Col. 184/L3
Nico Pérez, Uruguay 145/D4
Nicosia (cap.), Cyprus 63/E5
Nicosia (cap.), Cyprus 59/B2
Nicosia (cap.), Cyprus 54/E6
Nicosia, Italy 34/E6
Nicoya, C. Rica 154/E5
Nicoya (gulf), C. Rica 154/E6
Nicoya (pen.), C. Rica 154/E6
Nictau, New Bruns. 170/C1
Nictaux, Nova Scotia 168/D4
Nidau, Switzerland 39/D2
Nidd (riv.), England 10/F3
Nidwalden (canton), Switzerland 39/F3
Nidzica, Poland 47/E2
Niebüll, Germany 22/C1
Niederbipp, Switzerland 39/E2
Niedere Tauern (range), Austria 41/B3
Niederurnen, Switzerland 39/G2
Nielsville, Minn. 255/B3
Niemba, Zaire 115/E5
Niemen (riv.), U.S.S.R. 7/G3
Niemen (riv.), U.S.S.R. 52/B4
Niemen (riv.), U.S.S.R. 53/A3
Nienburg, Germany 22/C2
Nieuport (Nieuwpoort), Belgium 27/B6
Nieuw-Amsterdam, Suriname 131/D2
Nieuw-Buinen, Netherlands 27/K3
Nieuwegein, Netherlands 27/G4
Nieuwendam, Netherlands 27/C4
Nieuwe-Pekela, Netherlands 27/L2
Nieuweschans, Netherlands 27/L2
Nieuwkoop, Netherlands 27/F4
Nieuw-Nickerie, Suriname 120/D2
Nieuw-Nickerie, Suriname 131/C2
Nieuwpoort, Belgium 27/B6
Nieuw-Schoonebeek, Netherlands 27/L3
Nieuwveld (range), S. Africa 118/C6
Nieves, Mexico 150/H5
Nièvre (dept.), France 28/E4
Nigadoo, New Bruns. 170/E1
Niğde (prov.), Turkey 63/F4
Niğde, Turkey 59/B2
Niğde, Turkey 63/F4
Nigel, S. Africa 118/J7
Niger 2/K5
Niger 102/C3
NIGER 106/F5
Niger (riv.) 2/K5
Niger (riv.) 102/C4
Niger (riv.), Benin 106/E6
Niger (riv.), Guinea 106/C6
Niger (riv.), Mali 106/D5
Niger (riv.), Niger 106/E6
Niger (state), Nigeria 106/F7
Niger (delta), Nigeria 106/F8
Niger (riv.), Nigeria 106/F7
Nigeria 2/K5
Nigeria 102/C4
NIGERIA 106/F6
Nightcaps, N. Zealand 100/B6
Nighthawk, Wash. 310/F2
Nightingale, Alberta 182/D4
Nightingale (mts.), Nev. 266/B2
Nightingale (Bach Long Vi) (isl.), Vietnam 72/F2
Nightmute, Alaska 196/F2
Nigrita, Greece 45/F5
Nigua (riv.), P. Rico 161/D2
Nihoa (isl.), Hawaii 87/K3
Nihoa (isl.), Hawaii 188/F6
Nihoa (isl.), Hawaii 218/D6
Nii (isl.), Japan 81/J6
Niigata (pref.), Japan 81/J5
Niigata, Japan 54/P6
Niigata, Japan 81/J5
Niihama, Japan 81/F6
Niihau (isl.), Hawaii 87/K3
Niihau (isl.), Hawaii 188/E5
Niihau (isl.), Hawaii 218/A2
Niimi, Japan 81/F6
Niitsu, Japan 81/J5
Níjar, Spain 33/E4
Nijkerk, Netherlands 27/H4
Nijmegen, Netherlands 27/H5
Nijvel (Nivelles), Belgium 27/E7
Nijverdal, Netherlands 27/J4
Nikel', U.S.S.R. 52/C1
Nikep, Md. 245/C2
Nikki, Benin 106/E7
Nikko National Park, Japan 81/J5
Nikolai, Alaska 196/H2
Nikolayev, U.S.S.R. 7/H4
Nikolayev, U.S.S.R. 48/D5
Nikolayev, U.S.S.R. 52/D5
Nikolayevsk, U.S.S.R. 2/S3
Nikolayevsk, U.S.S.R. 48/Q4
Nikolayevsk, U.S.S.R. 54/P4
Nikolayevsk, U.S.S.R. 52/G4
Nikolayevsk-na-Amure, U.S.S.R. 48/P4
Nikol'sk, U.S.S.R. 52/G3
Nikol'sk, U.S.S.R. 52/G4
Nikolski, Alaska 196/E4
Nikol'skoye, U.S.S.R. 48/R4
Nikopol, Bulgaria 45/G4
Nikopol', U.S.S.R. 52/D5
Niksar, Turkey 63/G2
Nikshahr, Iran 59/H4
Nikshahr, Iran 66/L7
Nikšić, Yugoslavia 45/D4
Nikumaroro (isl.), Kiribati 87/J6
Nila (isl.), Indonesia 85/H7
Nilahue, Chile 138/E6
Niland, Calif. 204/K10
Nilaveli, Sri Lanka 68/E7
Nile (riv.) 2/L5
Nile (riv.) 102/F2
Nile (riv.), Egypt 111/F2
Nile (riv.), Egypt 59/B4
Nile (prov.), Sudan 111/F4
Nile (riv.), Sudan 59/B6
Nile (riv.), Sudan 111/F4
Niles, Ill. 222/B5
Niles, Kansas 232/E2
Niles, Mich. 250/C7
Niles, Ohio 284/J3
Ni'lin, West Bank 65/C4
Nilópolis, Brazil 135/E3
Nilwood, Ill. 222/D4
Nimach, India 68/D4
Nimba (lag.), Guinea 106/C7
Nimba (lag.), Ivory Coast 106/C7
Nimba (lag.), Liberia 106/C7
Nîmes, France 28/F6
Nîmes, France 7/E4
Nimmitabel, N.S. Wales 97/E5
Nimmons, Ark. 202/K1
Nimnyrskiy, U.S.S.R. 48/N4
Nimrod, Ark. 202/D4
Nimrod (lake), Ark. 202/D4
Nimrod, Minn. 255/D4
Nimule, Sudan 111/F7
Nin (bay), Philippines 82/D4
Nin, Yugoslavia 45/B3
Ninaview, Colo. 208/N7
Ninawa (gov.), Iraq 66/B3
Nine Degree (chan.), India 68/C7
Ninemile (pt.), Mich. 250/E3
Nine Mile (creek), Utah 304/D4
Nine Mile Falls, Wash. 310/H3
Nine Mile River, Nova Scotia 168/E3
Ninepipe (res.), Mont. 262/C3
Nine Times, S.C. 296/B2
Ninette, Manitoba 179/C5
Ninety Mile (beach), N. Zealand 100/D1
Ninety Mile (beach), Victoria 97/D6
Ninety Six, S.C. 296/C3
Ninety Six Nat'l Hist. Site, S.C. 296/C3
Nineveh (ruins), Iraq 66/C2
Nineveh, N.Y. 276/J6
Nineveh, Pa. 294/B6
Ninfas (pt.), Argentina 143/D5
Ninga, Manitoba 179/C5
Ning'an, China 77/L3
Ningbo (Ningpo), China 77/K6
Ningbo, China 54/O7
Ningde, China 77/K6
Ningdu, China 77/J6
Ninghua, China 77/J6
Ningpo (Ningbo), China 77/K6
Ningsia (Yinchuan, Yinchwan), China 77/G4
Ningsia Hui Aut. Reg. (Ningxia Huizu), China 77/F3
Ningwu, China 77/H4
Ningxia Huizu (Ningsia Hui Aut. Reg.), China 77/F3
Ning Xian, China 77/G4
Ninh Binh, Vietnam 72/E3
Ninigo Group (isls.), Papua N.G. 87/E6
Ninilchik, Alaska 196/B1
Ninini (pt.), Hawaii 218/D2
Ninnekah, Okla. 288/L5
Ninnescah (riv.), Kansas 232/E4
Ninnis Glacier Tongue, Antarc. 5/C8
Ninole, Hawaii 218/J4
Ninove, Belgium 27/D7
Nioaque, Brazil 132/C8
Niobe, N.Y. 276/B6
Niobe, N. Dak. 282/F2
Niobrara (riv.), Nebr. 188/F2
Niobrara, Nebr. 264/G2
Niobrara (riv.), Nebr. 264/E2
Niobrara (co.), Wyo. 319/H2
Niobrara (riv.), Wyo. 319/J3
Niono, Mali 106/C6
Nioro, Mali 106/C5
Nioro, Mali 102/B3
Nioro-du-Rip, Senegal 106/A6
Niort, France 28/C4
Niota, Ill. 222/B3
Niota, Tenn. 237/M9
Niotaze, Kansas 232/F4
Nipani, India 68/C5
Nipawin, Sask. 181/H2
Nipawin Prov. Park, Sask. 181/G1
Nipe (bay), Cuba 158/J3
Nipigon, Ont. 162/H6
Nipigon, Ontario 177/H5
Nipigon, Ontario 175/C3
Nipigon (lake), Ont. 146/K5
Nipigon (lake), Ont. 162/H6
Nipigon (lake), Ontario 175/C3
Nipigon (lake), Ontario 177/H5
Nipinnawasee, Calif. 204/F6
Nipishish (lake), Newf. 166/B3
Nipissing (terr. dist.), Ontario 177/F2
Nipissing (terr. dist.), Ontario 175/E3
Nipissing, Ontario 177/E1
Nipissing (lake), Ontario 177/E1
Nipissing (lake), Ontario 175/E3
Nipomo, Calif. 204/E8
Nippers Harbour, Newf. 166/C4
Nipton, Calif. 204/K8
Niquelândia, Brazil 132/D6
Niquén, Chile 138/E1
Niquero, Cuba 158/G4
Niquero, Cuba 156/C2
Niquivil, Argentina 143/C3
Nirgua, Venezuela 124/D2
Nirmal, India 68/D5
Nirvana, Mich. 250/D5
Nir Yitzhaq, Israel 65/A5
Niš, Yugoslavia 7/G4
Niš, Yugoslavia 45/F4
Nisa, Portugal 33/C3
Nisab, Yemen 59/E7
Nisab, Saudi Arabia 59/D4
Nisbet, Pa. 294/H3
Niscemi, Italy 34/E6
Nishapur (Neyshabur), Iran 66/L2
Nishino (isl.), Japan 81/M3
Nishinomiya, Japan 81/H8
Nishinoomote, Japan 81/E8
Nísiros (isl.), Greece 45/H7
Niskayuna, N.Y. 276/N5
Nisko, Poland 47/E3
Nisku, Alberta 182/D3
Nisland, S. Dak. 298/C4
Nisqually, Wash. 310/C3
Nisqually (riv.), Wash. 310/C4
Nisqually Ind. Res., Wash. 310/C4
Nissan (isl.), Papua N.G. 86/C2
Nissum (fjord), Denmark 21/A5
Nisswa, Minn. 255/D4
Niterói, Brazil 132/F8
Niterói, Brazil 120/E5
Niterói, Brazil 135/E3
Nith (riv.), Scotland 15/E5
Nith (riv.), Scotland 10/E3
Nitil, Jordan 65/D4
Nitinat, Br. Col. 184/H3
Nitinat (lake), Br. Col. 184/H3
Niton Junction, Alberta 182/C3
Nitra, Czech. 41/E2
Nitra (riv.), Czech. 41/E2
Nitro, W. Va. 312/C6
Nitta Yuma, Miss. 256/C4
Nittedal, Norway 18/D3
Niuafo'ou (isl.), Tonga 87/J7
Niuatoputapu (isl.), Tonga 87/J7
Niue (isl.) 87/K7
Niue (isl.), N. Zealand 2/A6
Niutao (atoll), Tuvalu 87/H6
Nivala, Finland 18/O5
Nive (riv.), Tasmania 99/C4
Nivelles, Belgium 27/E7
Nivernais (trad. prov.), France 29
Niverville, Manitoba 179/F5
Niwot, Colo. 208/J2
Nixa, Mo. 261/F8
Nixburg, Ala. 195/F5
Nixon, Nev. 266/B3
Nixon, N.J. 273/E2
Nixon, Texas 303/G8
Nixonville, S.C. 296/K4
Niya (Minfeng), China 77/B4
Nizamabad, India 68/D5
Nizao, Dom. Rep. 158/E6
Nizhnekamsk, U.S.S.R. 7/K3
Nizhnekamsk, U.S.S.R. 52/H3
Nizhneudinsk, U.S.S.R. 48/K4
Nizhnevartovsk, U.S.S.R. 48/H3
Nizhneyansk, U.S.S.R. 48/O3
Nizhniy Lomov, U.S.S.R. 52/F4
Nizhniy Novgorod (Gor'kiy), U.S.S.R. 48/E4
Nizhniy Novgorod (Gor'kiy), U.S.S.R. 52/F3
Nizhniy Tagil, U.S.S.R. 54/H4
Nizhniy Tagil, U.S.S.R. 48/G4
Nizhnyaya Pesha, U.S.S.R. 52/G1
Nizina, Alaska 196/K2
Nizip, Turkey 63/G4
Nizwa, Oman 59/G5
Nizza Monferrato, Italy 34/B2
Nizzanim, Israel 65/B4
Njazidja (isl.), Comoros 118/G2
Njazidja (isl.), Comoros 102/G6
Njombe, Tanzania 115/F5
Njombe (riv.), Tanzania 115/F5
Nkambe, Cameroon 115/B2
Nkayi, Congo 115/B4
Nkhata Bay, Malawi 115/F6
Nkhotakota, Malawi 115/F6
N'Komi (lag.), Gabon 115/A4
Nkongsamba, Cameroon 115/B3
Nkongsamba, Cameroon 102/D4
Nkurenkuru, Namibia 118/B3
Nkurenkuru, Namibia 115/C7
Nmai (riv.), Burma 72/C1
Nnewi, Nigeria 106/F7
Noah, Tenn. 237/J9
Noakhali, Bangladesh 68/G4
Noank, Conn. 210/G3
Noatak, Alaska 196/F1
Noatak (riv.), Alaska 196/F1
Noatak Nat'l Preserve, Alaska 196/F1
Nobel, Ontario 177/D2
Nobeoka, Japan 81/E7
Noble, Georgia 217/B1
Noble, Ill. 222/E5
Noble (co.), Ind. 227/G2
Noble, Iowa 229/K6
Noble, La. 238/C3
Noble, Mo. 261/G9
Noble (co.), Ohio 284/G6
Noble (co.), Okla. 288/M2
Noble, Okla. 288/M4
Nobleboro•, Maine 243/D7
Nobleford, Alberta 182/D5
Noble Lake, Ark. 202/G5
Nobles (co.), Minn. 255/C7
Noblesville, Ind. 227/F4
Nobleton, Fla. 212/D3
Nobleton, Ontario 177/J3
Noboribetsu, Japan 81/K2
Nocatee, Fla. 212/E4
Noccundra, Queensland 95/B5
Nocera Inferiore, Italy 34/E4
Nochistlán, Mexico 150/H6
Nocona, Texas 303/G4
Noctor, Ky. 237/P5
Noda, Japan 81/P2
Nodaway, Iowa 229/D7
Nodaway (riv.), Iowa 229/D7
Nodaway (co.), Mo. 261/C2
Nodaway, Mo. 261/C3
Node, Wyo. 319/H3
Nodine, Minn. 255/G7
Noel, Mo. 261/D9
Noel, Nova Scotia 168/E3
Noel Road, Nova Scotia 168/E3
Noelville, Ontario 177/D1
Nogal, N. Mex. 274/D5
Nogal (reg.), Somalia 115/J2
Nogales, Ariz. 188/D4
Nogales, Ariz. 198/E7
Nogales, Chile 138/F2
Nogales, Mexico 150/P2
Nogamut, Alaska 196/G2
Nogata, Japan 81/E7
Nogent-le-Rotrou, France 28/D3
Nogent-sur-Seine, France 28/E3
Nogoa (riv.), Queensland 88/H4
Nogoa (riv.), Queensland 95/C5
Nogoyá, Argentina 143/F6
Nógrád (co.), Hungary 41/E3
Nohili (pt.), Hawaii 218/B1
Nohkū (pt.), Mexico 150/Q7
Noinville, New Bruns. 170/E2
Noir (isl.), Chile 138/E11
Noires (mts.), Dom. Rep. 158/C5
Noires (mts.), Haiti 158/C5
Noirmont (mt.), Switzerland 39/B4
Noirmoutier (isl.), France 28/B4
Noisy-le-Sec, France 28/B1
Nojima (cape), Japan 81/K6
Nokesville, Va. 307/N3
Nokhowch, Kuh-e (mt.), Iran 66/M7
Nokia, Finland 18/N6
Nok Kundi, Pakistan 68/A3
Nok Kundi, Pakistan 59/H4
Nokomis, Ala. 195/D8
Nokomis, Fla. 212/D4
Nokomis, Ill. 222/D4
Nokomis, Sask. 181/F4
Nokou, Chad 111/B5
Nola, Ark. 202/C4
Nola, Cent. Afr. Rep. 115/C3
Nola, Miss. 256/D7
Nolan (co.), Texas 303/D5
Nolan, W. Va. 312/B7
Nolichucky (riv.), N.C. 281/E2
Nolichucky (riv.), Tenn. 237/R8
Nolin, Ky. 237/K5
Nolin (lake), Ky. 237/K6
Nolin (riv.), Ky. 237/J6
Nolinsk, U.S.S.R. 52/H3
Nollesemic (lake), Maine 243/F4
Noma, Fla. 212/C5
Nomans Land (isl.), Mass. 249/L7
Nombre de Dios, Mexico 150/G5
Nome, Alaska 146/B3
Nome, Alaska 196/E2
Nome, Alaska 188/C5
Nome, Alaska 2/A2
Nome, N. Dak. 282/P6
Nome, U.S. 4/C18
Nomgon, Mongolia 77/G3
Nomininque, Québec 172/B3
Nomininque (lake), Québec 172/B3
Nomoi (isls.), Micronesia 87/F5
Nonacho (lake), N.W.T. 162/F3
Nonacho (lake), N.W. Terr. 187/H3

onamesset (isl.), Mass. 249/M6
ondalton, Alaska 196/G2
ong Het, Laos 72/E3
ong Khai, Thailand 72/D3
ong Lahan (lake), Thailand 72/D3
onoava, Mexico 150/F3
onouti (atoll), Kiribati 87/H6
onquitt, Mass. 249/L6
onsan, S. Korea 81/C5
ontron, France 28/D5
ooksack, Wash. 310/C2
ooksack (riv.), Wash. 310/C2
oonan, S. Dak. 298/C2
oord (pt.), Neth. Ant. 161/F8
oord (pt.), Neth. Ant. 161/D8
oord di Salinja, Neth. Ant. 161/E8
oordwijk, Netherlands 27/E4
oorvik, Alaska 196/F1
ootka, Br. Col. 184/D5
ootka (isl.), Br. Col. 184/D5
ootka (sound), Br. Col. 184/D5
opalucan de la Granja, Mexico 150/O1
opeming, Minn. 255/F4
opiming Prov. Park, Manitoba 179/G4
óqui, Angola 115/B5
oquochoke P.O. (Westport), Mass. 249/K6
Jora, Ill. 222/D1
Jora, Nebr. 264/G4
Jora, Sask. 181/H3
ora, S. Dak. 298/R8
ora, Sweden 18/J7
ora, Va. 307/D6
oranda, Québec 162/J6
oranda, Québec 174/K3
oranside, Queensland 95/A4
ora Springs, Iowa 229/H2
orbeck, S. Dak. 298/L3
orberto de la Riestra, Argentina 143/G7
orbertville, Québec 172/F3
orberg, Sweden 18/K6
orborne, Mo. 261/E4
orcatur, Kansas 232/B2
orco, Calif. 204/E11
orco, La. 238/N3
orcross, Georgia 217/D3
orcross, Maine 243/F4
orcross, Minn. 255/B5
ord (dept.), France 28/E2
ord (pt.), Guadeloupe 161/B7
ord (dept.), Haiti 158/C5
ord (riv.), Québec 172/C4
ordaustlandet (isl.), Norway 18/D1
Jordborg, Denmark 21/C7
Jordby, Århus, Denmark 21/D5
Jordby, Ribe, Denmark 21/B7
orddeich, Germany 22/B2
Jordegg, Alberta 182/B3
Jordegg (riv.), Alberta 182/C3
Jorden, Nebr. 264/G4
Jorden, Germany 22/B2
Jordenham, Germany 22/C2
Jorderney, Germany 22/B2
Jorderney (isl.), Germany 22/B2
Jorderstedt, Germany 22/D2
ord-Est (pt.), Guadeloupe 161/B6
Jordfjord (fjord), Norway 18/E6
Jordhausen, Germany 22/D3
Jordheim, Texas 303/G9
Jordhorn, Germany 22/B2
Jordin, New Bruns. 170/E1
Jordjylland (co.), Denmark 21/D4
Jordkapp (cape), Norway 7/G1
Jordkapp (pt.), Norway 18/Q1
Jordkinn (headland), Norway 18/Q1
Jordkinn (pen.), Norway 18/P1
Jordland (co.), Norway 18/J3
Jordland, Wash. 310/C2
Jordli, Norway 18/H4
Jördlingen, Germany 22/D4
Jordmaling, Sweden 18/L5
Jordman, Idaho 220/B1
Jord-Ostsee (canal), Germany 22/C1
Jord-Ouest (dept.), Haiti 158/B5
Jordstrand (isl.), Germany 22/C1
Jord-Trøndelag (co.), Norway 18/H4
Jordvik-Ugol'naya, U.S.S.R. 4/B4
Jordvik-Ugol'naya, U.S.S.R. 48/M2
Jore (riv.), Ireland 10/C4
Jore (riv.), Ireland 17/G7
Jorene, Tenn. 237/J8
Jorfield, Miss. 256/C8
Jorfolk (isl.), Australia 2/T7
Jorfolk, Conn. 210/C1
Jorfolk (co.), England 13/H5
Jorfolk (co.), Mass. 249/K4
Jorfolk●, Mass. 249/J4
Jorfolk, Nebr. 188/G2
Jorfolk, Nebr. 264/G2
Jorfolk, N.Y. 276/K1
Jorfolk (bay), Tasmania 99/D4
Jorfolk, Va. 188/L3
Jorfolk, Va. 146/L6
Jorfolk (I.C.), Va. 307/R7
Jorfolk Island (terr.), Australia 88/L5
Jorfolk Island (terr.), Australia 87/G8
Jorfork, Ark. 202/F1
Jorfork (lake), Ark. 202/F1
Jorfork (lake), Mo. 261/H10
Jorg, Netherlands 27/J4
Jorge, Okla. 288/K4
Jorge, Va. 307/P6
Jorglenwold, Alberta 182/C3
Jorilsk, U.S.S.R. 2/P2
Noril'sk, U.S.S.R. 54/L3
Noril'sk, U.S.S.R. 4/B5
Norland, Fla. 212/D6
Norland, Ontario 177/F3
Norlina, N.C. 281/N2
Norma, N.J. 273/C4

Norma, N. Dak. 282/G2
Norma, Tenn. 237/N8
Normal, Ill. 222/E3
Normalville, Pa. 294/D5
Norman, Ark. 202/C5
Norman, Ind. 227/E7
Norman (co.), Minn. 255/B3
Norman, Nebr. 264/F4
Norman (cape), Newf. 166/C3
Norman, N.C. 281/K4
Norman (lake), N.C. 281/H3
Norman, Okla. 288/M4
Norman (riv.), Queensland 88/G3
Norman (creek), Queensland 95/D3
Norman (riv.), Queensland 95/B3
Norman (isl.), Virgin Is. (U.K.) 161/D4
Normanby, Queensland 88/K2
Normand (lake), Québec 172/D2
Normandale, Ontario 177/D5
Normandin, Québec 172/E1
Normandy (trad. prov.), France 29
Normandy, Mo. 261/R2
Normandy (riv.), Queensland 95/C2
Normandy, Tenn. 237/J10
Normandy, Texas 303/D9
Normandy Beach, N.J. 273/E3
Normandy Park, Wash. 310/A2
Normangee, Texas 303/H6
Norman Park, Georgia 217/E8
Norman's Cove, Newf. 166/D2
Normanton, Australia 87/F7
Normanton, Queensland 95/B3
Normanton, Queensland 88/G3
Normantown, Georgia 217/H6
Normantown, W. Va. 312/F5
Norman Wells, Canada 4/C16
Norman Wells, N.W.T. 146/F3
Norman Wells, N.W.T. 162/D2
Norman Wells, N.W. Terr. 187/F3
Normétal, Québec 174/B3
Noroton, Conn. 210/B4
Noroton Heights, Conn. 210/B4
Norphlet, Ark. 202/E7
Norquay, Sask. 181/J4
Norquincó, Argentina 143/B5
Norrbotten (co.), Sweden 18/L3
Nørre Åby, Denmark 21/C7
Nørre Alslev, Denmark 21/E8
Nørre Broby, Denmark 21/D7
Nørre Nebel, Denmark 21/B6
Nørre Snede, Denmark 21/C6
Nørre Vorupør, Denmark 21/B4
Norridge, Ill. 222/B5
Norridgewock, Maine 243/D6
Norridgewock●, Maine 243/D6
Norrie, Wis. 317/H6
Norris, Ill. 222/C3
Norris, Miss. 256/F6
Norris, Mont. 262/E5
Norris, S.C. 296/B2
Norris, S. Dak. 298/G7
Norris, Tenn. 237/N8
Norris (dam), Tenn. 237/N8
Norris (lake), Tenn. 188/C3
Norris (lake), Tenn. 237/O8
Norris, Wyo. 319/B1
Norris Arm, Newf. 166/C4
Norris City, Ill. 222/E6
Norris Point, Newf. 166/C4
Norristown, Georgia 217/H5
Norristown, Ind. 227/F6
Norristown, Pa. 294/M5
Norrisville, Md. 245/N2
Norrköping, Sweden 7/F3
Norrköping, Sweden 18/K7
Norrsundet, Sweden 18/K6
Norrtälje, Sweden 18/L7
Norseland, Minn. 255/D6
Norseman, W. Australia 88/C6
Norseman, W. Australia 92/C6
Norsjö, Sweden 8/L4
Norte (pt.), Argentina 143/D5
Norte (chan.), Brazil 120/E2
Norte, Serra do (range), Brazil 132/B5
Norte del Cabo San Antonio (pt.), Argentina 143/E4
Norte de Santander (dept.), Colombia 126/D3
North (sea) 2/K3
North (sea) 7/E3
North (cape), Alaska 196/L4
North (pt.), Barbados 161/B8
North (sea), Belgium 27/D4
North (rocks), Bermuda 156/H2
North (sea), Denmark 21/B9
North (sea), England 13/J4
North (sea), France 28/E1
North (sea), Germany 22/B2
North (cape), Ice. 4/C11
North (Horn) (cape), Iceland 21/B1
North (sound), Ireland 17/B5
North (isls.), La. 238/M7
North (pass), La. 238/N8
North (pt.), La. 238/M7
North (pt.), Md. 245/N4
North (pt.), Mich. 250/F2
North (pt.), Mich. 250/F3
North (lake), Minn. 255/F1
North (sea), Netherlands 27/E3
North (lake), New Bruns. 170/C3
North (riv.), Newf. 166/C3
North (pt.), Newf. 166/B2
North (isl.), N. Zealand 87/H9
North (cape), N. Zealand 87/H9
North (cape), N. Zealand 100/D1
North (isl.), N. Zealand 100/F1
North (lake), N. Dak. 282/J3
North (chan.), N. Ireland 10/D3
North (chan.), N. Ireland 17/K1
North (Nordkapo) (cape), Norway 7/G1
North (cape), Norway 4/B8

North (cape), Nova Scotia 162/K6
North (cape), Nova Scotia 168/H1
North (mt.), Nova Scotia 168/H2
North (chan.), Ontario 177/A1
North (chan.), Ontario 175/D3
North (mt.), Pa. 294/K3
North (pt.), Pr. Edward I. 168/E1
North (chan.), Scotland 10/D3
North (chan.), Scotland 15/F1
North (sound), Scotland 15/G4
North (sound), Scotland 15/F1
North (isl.), Seychelles 118/H5
North, S.C. 296/E4
North (inlet), S.C. 296/J5
North (inlet), S.C. 296/J5
North (pt.), Tasmania 99/E1
North (creek), Utah 304/C6
North (lake), Utah 304/B2
North (riv.), W. Va. 312/J4
North (riv.), Wash. 310/B4
North (lake), Wis. 317/J1
North Abington, Mass. 249/L4
North Acton, Mass. 249/J2
North Adams, Mass. 249/B2
North Adams, Mich. 250/E7
North Amity, Maine 243/H4
North Amherst, Mass. 249/E3
North America 2/C4
NORTH AMERICA 146
North Andaman (isl.), India 68/G6
North Andover●, Mass. 249/K2
North Anna (riv.), Va. 307/M4
North Anson, Maine 243/D6
North Apollo, Pa. 294/D4
North Arlington, N.J. 273/B2
North Arm (inlet), N.W. Terr. 187/G3
North Ashford, Conn. 210/G1
North Aspy (riv.), Nova Scotia 168/H2
North Atlantic Ocean 2/H3
North Attleboro●, Mass. 249/J5
North Augusta, Ontario 177/J3
North Augusta, S.C. 296/C5
North Aulatsivik (isl.), Newf. 166/B2
North Aurora, Ill. 222/E2
North Avondale, Colo. 208/L6
North Ballachulish, Scotland 15/C4
North Baltimore, Ohio 284/C3
North Bangor, N.Y. 276/M1
North Barrington, Ill. 222/B5
North Bass (isl.), Ohio 284/E2
North Battleford, Sask. 146/F4
North Battleford, Sask. 162/F5
North Battleford, Sask. 181/C3
North Bay, N.Y. 276/J4
North Bay, Ont. 146/L5
North Bay, Ont. 162/J6
North Bay, Ontario 177/E1
North Bay, Ontario 175/E3
North Bay, Wis. 317/M3
North Bay Ingonish (bay), Nova Scotia 168/H2
North Bay Village, Fla. 212/B4
North Beach, Md. 245/N6
North Belgrade, Maine 243/D7
North Bellingham, Mass. 249/J4
North Bend, Br. Col. 184/G5
North Bend, Nebr. 264/H3
North Bend, Ohio 284/B9
North Bend, Oreg. 291/C4
North Bend, Pa. 294/K3
North Bend, Wash. 310/D3
North Bend, Wis. 317/D7
North Bennington, Vt. 268/A6
North Bergen●, N.J. 273/B2
North Berwick, Maine 243/B9
North Berwick●, Maine 243/B9
North Berwick, Scotland 15/F4
North Berwick, Scotland 15/F1
North Beveland (isl.), Netherlands 27/D5
North Billerica, Mass. 249/J2
North Bloomfield, Conn. 210/E1
North Bloomfield, Ohio 284/J3
North Bonneville, Wash. 310/C5
North Borneo (Sabah) (state), Malaysia 85/F3
Northboro, Iowa 229/C7
Northborough, Mass. 249/H3
Northborough●, Mass. 249/H3
North Boston, N.Y. 276/C5
North Bourke, N.S. Wales 97/C2
North Brabant (prov.), Netherlands 27/F5
North Braddock, Pa. 294/C7
North Bradford, Maine 243/F5
North Bradley, Mich. 250/E5
Northbranch, Kansas 232/D2
North Branch, Md. 245/D2
North Branch, Mich. 250/F5
North Branch, Minn. 255/E5
North Branch, N.H. 268/D5
North Branch Oromocto (riv.), New Bruns. 170/D3
North Branford●, Conn. 210/E3
North Brentwood, Md. 245/F4
Northbridge●, Mass. 249/H4
North Bridgton, Maine 243/B7
Northbrook, Ill. 222/B5
North Brook, Ontario 177/G3

North Brookfield, Mass. 249/F3
North Brookfield●, Mass. 249/F3
North Brooksville, Maine 243/F7
North Brunswick●, N.J. 273/D3
North Bruny (isl.), Tasmania 99/D5
North Buena Vista, Iowa 229/L3
North Calais, Vt. 268/C3
North Caldwell, N.J. 273/B2
North Calling Lake, Alberta 182/D2
North Canadian (riv.) 188/G3
North Canadian (riv.), Okla. 288/K3
North Canton, Conn. 210/D1
North Canton, Georgia 217/C2
North Canton, Ohio 284/H4
North Cape (Nordkapp) (pt.), Norway 18/P1
North Cape May, N.J. 273/C6
North Caribou (lake), Ontario 175/B2
North Carolina 188/L3
NORTH CAROLINA 281
North Carolina (state), U.S. 146/K6
North Carrizo (creek), Colo. 208/N8
North Carrizo (riv.), Okla. 288/A1
North Carrollton, Miss. 256/E3
North Carter (mt.), N.H. 268/E3
North Carver, Mass. 249/L5
North Cascades Nat'l Park, Wash. 310/D2
North Catasauqua, Pa. 294/L4
North Charleston, S.C. 296/G6
North Charlestown, N.H. 268/C5
North Chatham, Mass. 249/O6
North Chatham, N.H. 268/E5
North Chelmsford, Mass. 249/J2
North Chesterville, Maine 243/C6
North Chicago, Ill. 222/B4
North Chichester, N.H. 268/E5
North Chili, N.Y. 276/E4
North City (Coello), Ill. 222/E5
North Clarendon, Vt. 268/B4
North Cohasset, Mass. 249/F7
North Colebrook, Conn. 210/C1
North College Hill, Ohio 284/B9
Northcliffe, W. Australia 92/B6
North Collins, N.Y. 276/C5
North Concho (riv.), Texas 303/C6
North Concord, Vt. 268/D3
North Conway, N.H. 268/E5
North Cooking Lake, Alberta 182/D3
North Cotabato (prov.), Philippines 82/E7
Northcote, Minn. 255/A2
Northcote, N. Zealand 100/B1
Northcote, Victoria 88/L7
Northcote, Victoria 97/J5
North Cove, N.C. 281/F3
North Cove, Wash. 310/A4
North Cowichan, Br. Col. 184/J3
North Creek, N.Y. 276/M3
North Crossett, Ark. 202/G7
North Cutler, Maine 243/J6
North Dakota 188/F1
NORTH DAKOTA 282
North Dakota (state), U.S. 146/H5
North Dandalup, W. Australia 88/B3
North Danger (reef), Philippines 85/E3
North Danville, Vt. 268/C3
North Dartmouth, Mass. 249/K6
North Dexter, Maine 243/E5
North Dighton, Mass. 249/K5
North Dixmont, Maine 243/E6
North Down (dist.), N. Ireland 17/K2
North Downs (hills), England 13/G6
North Eagle Butte, S. Dak. 298/G4
Northeast (cape), Alaska 196/E2
Northeast (pt.), Jamaica 158/K6
Northeast (pass.), La. 238/M8
North East, Md. 245/P2
North East, Pa. 294/B1
North East Breakers, Bermuda 156/H2
North East Cape Fear (riv.), N.C. 281/O4
North East Carry, Maine 243/D4
North-Eastern (prov.), Kenya 115/G3
Northeast Foreland (pen.), Greenl. 4/A10
North Eastham, Mass. 249/O5
Northeast Harbor, Maine 243/G7
Northeast Land I., Norway 4/B8
Northeast Margaree (riv.), Nova Scotia 168/H2
North Easton, Mass. 249/K4
North East Providence (chan.), Bahamas 159/C1
North Edisto (riv.), S.C. 296/G6
North Edwards, Calif. 204/H8
North Egremont, Mass. 249/A4
Northeim, Germany 22/C3
North English, Iowa 229/J5
North Enid, Okla. 288/L2
Northern (dist.), Israel 65/C2
Northern (head), New Bruns. 170/D4
Northern (prov.), Sudan 111/E3
Northern Cheyenne Ind. Res., Mont. 262/K5
Northern Dvina (riv.), U.S.S.R. 52/F2
Northern Dvina (riv.), U.S.S.R. 48/E3
Northern Indian (lake), Manitoba 179/J2
NORTHERN IRELAND 17
NORTHERN IRELAND 17
Northern Ireland, U.K. 7/D3
Northern Marianas 87/E4
Northern Marianas, U.S. 2/S5
Northern Peninsula Aboriginal Reserve, Queensland 88/G2
Northern Peninsula Aboriginal Res., Queensland 95/B1
Northern Samar (prov.), Philippines 82/E4
Northern Sporades (isls.), Greece 45/F6
Northern Territory, 88/E3
NORTHERN TERRITORY 93
Northern Territory (terr.), Australia 87/D7

Northern Yukon Nat'l Park, Yukon 162/R2
Northern Yukon Nat'l Park, Yukon 187/D3
North Esk (riv.), Scotland 15/F4
North Esk (riv.), Tasmania 99/D3
North Fairfield, Ohio 284/F3
North Falmouth, Mass. 249/M6
North Ferrisburg, Vt. 268/A3
Northfield, Conn. 210/C2
Northfield, Ill. 222/B5
Northfield, Ky. 237/K1
Northfield●, Maine 243/H6
Northfield, Mass. 249/E2
Northfield●, Mass. 249/E2
Northfield, Minn. 255/D5
Northfield●, N.H. 268/D5
Northfield, N.J. 273/D5
Northfield, Ohio 284/J10
Northfield, Texas 303/D3
Northfield●, Vt. 268/B3
Northfield, Wis. 317/D7
Northfield Falls, Vt. 268/B3
Northfield Farms, Mass. 249/E2
Northfield-Tilton, N.H. 268/D5
Northfleet, England 10/G5
Northfleet, England 13/J8
North Fond du Lac, Wis. 317/J8
Northford, Conn. 210/D3
North Foreland (prom.), England 10/G5
North Foreland (prom.), England 13/J6
North Fork, Calif. 204/F6
North Fork, Gunnison (riv.), Colo. 208/D5
North Fork, Smoky Hill (riv.), Colo. 208/P4
North Fork, Idaho 220/D4
North Fork (riv.), Idaho 220/B7
North Fork, Flathead (riv.), Mont. 262/B2
North Fork, Little Humboldt (riv.), Nev. 266/D1
North Fork, Grand (riv.), N. Dak. 282/E8
Northfork, W. Va. 312/D8
North Fork, Powder (riv.), Wyo. 319/F2
North Fork, Wind (riv.), Wyo. 319/C2
North Fork, Shoshone (riv.), Wyo. 319/C1
North Fort Myers, Fla. 212/E5
North Fourchu, Nova Scotia 168/H3
North Fox (isl.), Mich. 250/D3
North Franklin, Conn. 210/G2
North Freedom, Wis. 317/G9
North Friars (bay), St. Kitts and Nevis 161/D10
North Friesland (reg.), German 22/C1
North Frisian (isls.), Denmark 21/B7
North Frisian (isls.), Germany 22/B1
North Fryeburg, Maine 243/B7
North Galiano, Br. Col. 184/K3
North Garden, Va. 307/L5
Northgate, N. Dak. 282/F2
Northgate, Sask. 181/J6
Northglenn, Colo. 208/K3
North Gorham, Maine 243/B8
North Gosforth, England 13/J3
North Gower, Ontario 177/J2
North Grafton, Mass. 249/H4
North Granby, Conn. 210/D1
North Grant, Nova Scotia 168/G3
North Grosvenor Dale, Conn. 210/H1
North Groton, N.H. 268/D4
North Grove, Ind. 227/F3
North Guilford, Conn. 210/E3
North Gulfport, Miss. 256/F10
North Hadley, Mass. 249/D3
North Haledon, N.J. 273/B2
North Hampton●, N.H. 268/F6
North Hampton, Ohio 284/B6
North Hanover, Mass. 249/L4
North Hansel (mts.), Utah 304/B2
North Harbour, Newf. 166/D2
North Harlowe, N.C. 281/R5
North Hartland, Vt. 268/C4
North Hartsville, S.C. 296/G3
North Harwich, Mass. 249/O6
North Hatfield, Mass. 249/D3
North Hatley, Québec 172/F4
North Haven●, Conn. 210/D3
North Haven, Maine 243/F7
North Haven●, Maine 243/F7
North Haverhill, N.H. 268/D3
North Havre, Mont. 262/G2
North Hayden, Ind. 227/B2
North Head, New Bruns. 170/D4
North Henderson, Ill. 222/C2
North Hero, Vt. 268/A2
North Hero●, Vt. 268/A2
North Highlands, Calif. 204/B8
North High Shoals, Georgia 217/F3
North Hills, W. Va. 312/D4
North Hodge, La. 238/E2
North Holland (prov.), Netherlands 27/F3
North Holland (canal), Netherlands 27/C4
North Hollywood, Calif. 204/B10
North Hornell, N.Y. 276/E6
North Horr, Kenya 115/G3
North Hudson, N.Y. 276/N3
North Hudson, Wis. 317/A5
North Hyde Park, Vt. 268/B2
North Hykeham, England 13/G4
North Industry, Ohio 284/H4
North Inishkea (isl.), Ireland 17/A3
North Java, N.Y. 276/D5
North Jay, Maine 243/C6
North Johns, Ala. 195/D4
North Judson, Ind. 227/D2

North Kansas City, Mo. 261/P5
North Kedgwick (riv.), New Bruns. 170/C1
North Kent, Conn. 210/B1
North Kent (isl.), N.W. Terr. 187/J2
North Kingstown●, R.I. 249/J6
North Kingsville, Ohio 284/J2
North Knife (lake), Manitoba 179/J2
North Knife (riv.), Manitoba 179/J2
North Korea 54/O5
North La Junta, Colo. 208/N7
Northlake, Ill. 222/B5
Northlake, Texas 303/F1
North Lake, Wis. 317/J1
North Lakhimpur, India 68/G3
Northland, Wis. 317/H6
Northland, Wis. 317/H6
North Laramie (riv.), Wyo. 319/G3
North Las Vegas, Nev. 266/F6
North Lauderdale, Fla. 212/B3
North Lawrence, N.Y. 276/L1
North Lawrence, Ohio 284/G4
North Leeds, Maine 243/C7
North Lewisburg, Ohio 284/C6
North Liberty, Ind. 227/E1
North Liberty, Iowa 229/K5
North Lima, Ohio 284/J4
North Limington, Maine 243/B8
North Little Rock, Ark. 202/F4
North Livermore, Maine 243/C7
North Loup, Nebr. 264/F3
North Loup (riv.), Nebr. 264/E3
North Lovell, Maine 243/B7
North Lubec, Maine 243/J6
North Luconia (shoals), Philippines 85/F4
North Madison, Conn. 210/E3
North Madison, Ohio 284/H2
North Magnetic Pole (dist.) 162/F1
North Magnetic Pole, Canada 4/B15
North Magnetic Pole, N.W. Terr. 187/H2
North Manchester, Ind. 227/F3
North Manitou (isl.), Mich. 250/C3
North Mankato, Minn. 255/D6
North Marshfield, Mass. 249/M4
North Merritt (isl.), Fla. 212/F4
North Miami, Fla. 212/B4
North Miami, Okla. 288/R1
North Miami Beach, Fla. 212/C4
North Middleboro, Mass. 249/L5
North Middletown, Ky. 237/N4
North Minch (sound), Scotland 10/D1
North Minch (sound), Scotland 15/B3
North Montpelier, Vt. 268/C3
Northmoor, Mo. 261/P5
North Motton, Tasmania 99/C3
North Mountain, W. Va. 312/K3
North Muskegon, Mich. 250/C5
North Myrtle Beach, S.C. 296/K4
North Naples, Fla. 212/E5
North Natuna (isl.), Indonesia 85/D4
North Negril (pt.), Jamaica 158/G6
North Newport, N.H. 268/C5
North New Portland, Maine 243/C6
North New River (canal), Fla. 212/F5
North Newry, Maine 243/B6
North Newton, Kansas 232/E3
North Oaks, Minn. 255/G5
North Ogden, Utah 304/C2
North Olmsted, Ohio 284/G9
Northome, Minn. 255/D3
North Ossetian A.S.S.R., U.S.S.R. 48/C15
North Ossetian A.S.S.R., U.S.S.R. 52/F2
North Oxford, Mass. 249/G4
North Pacific (ocean) 87/F4
North Pacific Ocean 2/B5
North Pacific Ocean 2/T4
North Pagai (isl.), Indonesia 85/C6
North Palm Beach, Fla. 212/F5
North Parsonfield, Maine 243/A8
North Pease (riv.), Texas 303/D3
North Pekin, Ill. 222/D3
North Pembroke, Mass. 249/M4
North Pender Island, Br. Col. 184/K3
North Penobscot, Maine 243/F7
North Perry, Maine 243/J5
North Perry, Ohio 284/H2
North Petherton, England 13/D6
North Pine, Br. Col. 184/G2
North Plain, Conn. 210/F3
North Plainfield, N.J. 273/E2
North Plains, Oreg. 291/A2
North Platte 188/F2
North Platte (riv.), Colo. 208/G1
North Platte, Nebr. 188/F2
North Platte, Nebr. 264/D3
North Platte (riv.), Nebr. 264/B3
North Platte (riv.), U.S. 146/H5
North Platte (riv.), Wyo. 319/H3
North Plymouth, Mass. 249/L5
North Pole 4/A1
North Pole 2/F1
North Pole, Alaska 196/J2
North Pole (brook), New Bruns. 170/D1
North Pomfret, Vt. 268/B4
Northport, Ala. 195/C4
North Port, Fla. 212/D4
Northport●, Maine 243/E7
Northport, Mich. 250/D3
Northport, Nebr. 264/B3
Northport, N.Y. 276/O9
Northport, Nova Scotia 168/E3
Northport, Wash. 310/H2
North Portal, Sask. 181/J6
North Potomac, Md. 245/K4
North Pownal, Vt. 268/A6
North Powder, Oreg. 291/K2
North Prairie, Wis. 317/J2
North Providence●, R.I. 249/J5
North Pulaski, Va. 307/G6
North Randall, Ohio 284/H9

North Randolph, Vt. 268/B4
North Raymond, Maine 243/C8
North Reading•, Mass. 249/C5
North Redington Beach, Fla. 212/B3
North Redwood, Minn. 255/D6
North Renous (riv.), New Bruns. 170/D2
North Rhine-Westphalia (state), Germany 22/B3
North Richland Hills, Texas 303/F2
Northridge, Ohio 284/B6
North Ridgeville, Ohio 284/F3
North Rim, Ariz. 198/C2
North River, Newf. 166/D2
North River, N.Y. 276/M3
North River, N. Dak. 282/S6
North River, Nova Scotia 168/D4
North Riverside, Ill. 222/K4
North Robinson, Ohio 284/E4
North Ronaldsay (firth), Scotland 15/F1
North Ronaldsay (isl.), Scotland 15/F1
North Ronaldsay (isl.), Scotland 10/E1
Northrop, Minn. 255/D7
North Rose, N.Y. 276/G4
North Roxbury, N.C. 281/L2
North Royalton, Ohio 284/H10
North Saanich, Br. Col. 184/K3
North Saint Paul, Minn. 255/G5
North Salem, Ind. 227/D5
North Salem, N.H. 268/E6
North Salt Lake, Utah 304/E3
North Sandwich, N.H. 268/E4
North San Juan, Calif. 204/E4
North Santiam (riv.), Oreg. 291/E3
North Saskatchewan (riv.) 162/E5
North Saskatchewan (riv.), Alberta 182/E3
North Saskatchewan (riv.), Canada 146/G4
North Saskatchewan (riv.), Sask. 181/D3
North Scituate, Mass. 249/F8
North Scituate, R.I. 249/H5
North Sea (canal), Netherlands 27/F4
North Seal (riv.), Manitoba 179/H2
North Searsmont, Maine 243/F7
North Sentinel (isl.), India 68/G6
North Sevogle (riv.), New Bruns. 170/D1
North Shapleigh, Maine 243/B8
North Shoal (lake), Manitoba 179/E4
Northside, N.C. 281/M2
Northside, Sask. 181/F2
North Sioux City, S. Dak. 298/R8
North Skunk (riv.), Iowa 229/H5
North Somercotes, England 13/H4
North Somercotes (canal), England 10/H4
North Somers, Conn. 210/F1
North Spectacle (lake), Conn. 210/B2
North Spirit Lake, Ontario 175/B2
North Springfield, Pa. 294/A1
North Springfield, Vt. 268/B5
North Springfield, Va. 307/S3
North Star, Alberta 182/B1
North Star, Mich. 250/E5
North Star, Ohio 284/A5
North Stonington•, Conn. 210/H3
North Stratford, N.H. 268/D2
North Sunderland, England 13/F2
North Sutton, N.H. 268/D5
North Swansea, Mass. 249/K5
North Sydney, N.S. Wales 88/L4
North Sydney, N.S. Wales 97/J3
North Sydney, Nova Scotia 168/H2
North Syracuse, N.Y. 276/H4
North Taranaki (bight), N. Zealand 100/D3
North Tarrytown, N.Y. 276/O6
North Terre Haute, Ind. 227/C5
North Thetford, Vt. 268/C4
North Thompson (riv.), Br. Col. 184/G4
North Tidworth, England 13/F6
North Tiverton, R.I. 249/K6
North Tolsta, Scotland 15/B2
Northton, Scotland 15/B3
North Tonawanda, N.Y. 276/C4
North Trap (isl.), N. Zealand 100/B7
North Troy, Vt. 268/C2
North Truchas (peak), N. Mex. 274/F2
North Truro, Mass. 249/O4
North Tunbridge, Vt. 268/C4
North Turner, Maine 243/C7
North Twin (mt.), N.H. 268/D3
North Tyne (riv.), England 13/E2
North Uist (isl.), Scotland 15/A3
North Uist (isl.), Scotland 10/C2
Northumberland (co.), England 13/E2
Northumberland (co.), New Bruns. 170/D2
Northumberland (str.), New Bruns. 170/F2
Northumberland•, N.H. 268/D2
Northumberland (str.), Nova Scotia 168/E2
Northumberland (county), Ontario 177/G3
Northumberland (co.), Pa. 294/J4
Northumberland, Pa. 294/J4
Northumberland (str.), Pr. Edward I. 168/D2
Northumberland (isls.), Queensland 95/D4
Northumberland (cape), S. Australia 94/F8
Northumberland National Park, England 13/E2
North Umpqua (riv.), Oreg. 291/E4

North Ural (mts.), U.S.S.R. 52/K1
North Utica (Utica), Ill. 222/E2
North Uxbridge, Mass. 249/H4
Northvale, N.J. 273/F1
North Vancouver, Br. Col. 162/D6
North Vancouver, Br. Col. 184/K3
North Vassalboro, Maine 243/D7
North Vernon, Ind. 227/F6
Northview, Mo. 261/G8
North Wabasca (lake), Alberta 182/D1
North Wakefield, N.H. 268/E4
North Waldoboro, Maine 243/E7
North Wales, Pa. 294/M5
North Walpole, N.H. 268/C5
North Walsham, England 13/J5
North Walsham, England 10/G4
North Waltham, Mass. 249/B6
North Warren, Pa. 294/D2
North Washington, Iowa 229/J2
North Waterboro, Maine 243/B8
North Waterford, Maine 243/B7
Northway, Alaska 196/K2
North Wayne, Maine 243/C7
North Weare, N.H. 268/D5
North Webster, Ind. 227/F2
Northwest (pt.), Fla. 212/E6
North West (dist.), Guyana 131/A2
North West (pt.), Jamaica 158/B6
North West (cape), Australia 87/B8
North West (cape), W. Australia 88/A4
North West (cape), W. Australia 92/A3
North-West Aboriginal Reserve, S. Australia 88/E5
North-West Aboriginal Res., W. Australia 92/E4
North West Arm (inlet), Newf. 166/D2
North West Brook, Newf. 166/C2
North West Brook (riv.), Newf. 166/D2
North Westchester, Conn. 210/F2
North-West Frontier (prov.), Pakistan 68/C3
North West Gander (riv.), Newf. 166/C4
North Westminster, Vt. 268/B5
Northwest Miramichi (riv.), New Bruns. 170/D1
Northwest Oromocto (riv.), New Bruns. 170/D3
North Westport, Mass. 249/K6
North West Providence (chan.), Bahamas 156/B1
North West River, Newf. 166/B3
Northwest Territories 162/E2
NORTHWEST TERRITORIES 187
Northwest Territories (prov.), Canada 146/G3
Northwest Upsalquitch (riv.), New Bruns. 170/D1
North Weymouth, Mass. 249/D8
North Whitefield, Maine 243/D7
Northwich, England 13/H2
Northwich, England 10/G2
North Wilbraham, Mass. 249/E4
North Wildwood, N.J. 273/B6
North Wilkesboro, N.C. 281/G2
North Williston, Vt. 268/A3
North Wilton, Conn. 210/B4
North Windham, Conn. 210/G1
North Windham, Maine 243/C8
North Wolcott, Vt. 268/B2
Northwood, Iowa 229/G2
Northwood•, N.H. 268/E5
Northwood, N. Dak. 282/P4
Northwood, Ohio 284/D2
North Woodbury, Conn. 210/C2
Northwood Center, N.H. 268/E5
Northwood Narrows (Northwood P.O.), N.H. 268/E5
Northwoods, Mo. 261/H2
North Woodstock, Conn. 210/G1
North Woodstock, Maine 243/B7
North Woodstock, N.H. 268/D3
Northwye, Mo. 261/J7
North Yarmouth, Maine 243/C8
North Yarmouth•, Maine 243/C8
North York, Ontario 177/J4
North York Moors National Park, England 13/G3
North Yorkshire (co.), England 13/F3
North Zanesville, Ohio 284/G6
Norton (bay), Alaska 196/C2
Norton (sound), Alaska 146/B3
Norton (sound), Alaska 188/C5
Norton (sound), Alaska 196/E2
Norton, England 13/G3
Norton (peak), Idaho 220/D6
Norton (co.), Kansas 232/C2
Norton (res.), Kansas 232/C2
Norton, Mass. 249/H5
Norton•, Mass. 249/K5
Norton, New Bruns. 170/E3
Norton, Ohio 284/G3
Norton, Texas 303/E6
Norton (sound), U.S. 4/C18
Norton•, Vt. 268/D2
Norton (pond), Vt. 268/D2
Norton (I.C.), Va. 307/C7
Norton, W. Va. 312/G5
Norton A.F.B., Calif. 204/F10
Norton-Radstock, England 13/E6
Norton Shores, Mich. 250/C5
Nortonville, Kansas 232/G2
Nortonville, Ky. 237/G6
Nortonville, N. Dak. 282/N6
Norumbega, Argentina 143/F7
Norvegia (cape) 5/B18
Norvell, Ark. 202/K3
Norvelt, Pa. 294/D5
Norwalk, Calif. 204/C11
Norwalk, Conn. 210/B4
Norwalk (isls.), Conn. 210/B4

Norwalk (riv.), Conn. 210/B4
Norwalk, Iowa 229/F6
Norwalk, Mich. 250/C4
Norwalk, Ohio 284/E3
Norwalk, Wis. 317/E8
Norway 2/K2
Norway 4/C9
NORWAY 18
Norway 7/E2
Norway (head), Scotland 15/E1
Norway, Ind. 227/D3
Norway, Iowa 229/K5
Norway, Kansas 232/E2
Norway, Maine 243/B7
Norway, Mich. 250/B3
Norway (bay), N.W. Terr. 187/H2
Norway, Oreg. 291/C4
Norway, S.C. 296/E5
Norway House, Man. 162/G5
Norway House, Manitoba 179/J3
Norway Lake, Maine 243/B7
Norwegian (sea) 4/C10
Norwegian (sea) 7/D2
Norwegian (bay), N.W. Terr. 187/J2
Norwegian (sea), Norway 18/F3
Norwell•, Mass. 249/F8
Norwich, Conn. 210/G2
Norwich, England 13/J5
Norwich, England 10/G4
Norwich, Kansas 232/E4
Norwich, N.Y. 276/J5
Norwich, N. Dak. 282/J3
Norwich, Ohio 284/G6
Norwich, Ontario 177/E4
Norwich•, Vt. 268/C4
Norwichtown, Conn. 210/G2
Norwood, Colo. 208/C6
Norwood, Georgia 217/G4
Norwood, La. 238/H5
Norwood•, Mass. 249/B8
Norwood, Minn. 255/E6
Norwood, Mo. 261/H8
Norwood, N.J. 273/C1
Norwood, N.Y. 276/L1
Norwood, N.C. 281/J4
Norwood, Ohio 284/C9
Norwood, Ontario 177/F3
Norwood, Pa. 294/M7
Norwood, R.I. 249/J6
Norwood, Va. 307/L5
Nosappu (pt.), Japan 81/N2
Nosbonsing (lake), Ontario 177/E1
Nose, Japan 81/J7
Noshiro, Japan 81/J3
Nosovka, U.S.S.R. 52/D4
Nosratabad, Iran 66/L6
Noss (head), Scotland 15/F2
Nossa Senhora do Livramento, Brazil 132/B6
Nossob (riv.), Botswana 118/B4
Nossob (riv.), Namibia 118/B4
Nosy Be (isl.), Madagascar 118/H2
Nosy Boraha (isl.), Madagascar 118/J3
Nosy-Varika, Madagascar 118/H4
Notakwanon (riv.), Newf. 166/B2
Notasulga, Ala. 195/G5
Noteć (riv.), Poland 47/B2
Notikewin, Alberta 182/B1
Notikewin (riv.), Alberta 182/A1
Noto, Italy 34/E6
Noto, Japan 81/H5
Noto (pen.), Japan 81/H5
Notodden, Norway 18/F7
Notre Dame, Ind. 227/E1
Notre Dame, New Bruns. 170/F2
Notre Dame (bay), Newf. 166/C4
Notre-Dame-de-Ham, Québec 172/F4
Notre-Dame-de-la-Doré, Québec 172/E1
Notre-Dame-de-la-Paix, Québec 172/C2
Notre-Dame-de-la-Salette, Québec 172/B4
Notre Dame de Lourdes, Manitoba 179/D5
Notre-Dame-de-Pierreville, Québec 172/D3
Notre-Dame-des-Anges, Québec 172/E3
vNotre-Dame-des-Bois, Québec 172/G4
Notre-Dame-des-Laurentides, Québec 172/H3
Notre-Dame-des-Monts, Québec 172/G2
Notre-Dame-des-Prairies, Québec 172/D3
Notre-Dame-de-Stanbridge, Québec 172/C4
Notre-Dame-du-Bon-Conseil, Québec 172/E4
Notre-Dame-du-Lac, Québec 172/J2
Notre-Dame-du-Laus, Québec 172/B3
Notre-Dame-du-Portage, Québec 172/H2
Notre-Dame-du-Rosaire, Québec 172/F1
Nottawa, Ontario 177/D3
Nottawasaga (bay), Ontario 177/D3
Nottawasaga (riv.), Ontario 177/E3
Nottaway (riv.), Que. 162/J5
Nottaway (riv.), Québec 174/B2
Nottely (lake), Georgia 217/D1
Nottingham, Ala. 195/F4
Nottingham, England 13/F5
Nottingham, England 10/F4
Nottingham•, N.H. 268/E5
Nottingham (isl.), N.W.T. 162/H3
Nottingham (isl.), N.W.T. 187/L3
Nottinghamshire (co.), England 13/F4
Nottinghill, Mo. 261/G9
Nottoway (riv.), Va. 307/M6
Nottoway, Va. 307/M6
Nottoway (riv.), Va. 307/O7
Notukeu (creek), Sask. 181/D6

Notus, Idaho 220/B6
Nouadhibou, Mauritania 106/A4
Nouadhibou, Mauritania 102/A2
Nouakchott (cap.), Mauritania 106/A5
Nouakchott (cap.), Mauritania 102/A3
Nouakchott (cap.), Mauritania 2/J5
Nouméa (cap.), New Caled. 87/G8
Nouméa (cap.), New Caledonia 2/T7
Nouméa (cap.), New Caled. 86/H5
Nounan, Idaho 220/H5
Noup (head), Scotland 15/E1
Noupoort, S. Africa 118/C6
Nouveau-Québec (terr.), Québec 174/E1
Nouveau-Québec (crater), Québec 174/F1
Nouvelle, Québec 172/C2
Nouvelle (riv.), Québec 172/C2
Nouvelle-France (cape), Québec 174/F1
Nouvelle-Ouest, Québec 172/C2
Nova, Hungary 41/D3
Nova, Ohio 284/F3
Nová Baña, Czech. 41/E2
Nová Bystrica, Czech. 41/E2
Nová Bystřice, Czech. 41/C2
Nova Cruz, Brazil 132/H4
Nova Era, Brazil 135/E1
Nova Friburgo, Brazil 132/F8
Nova Friburgo, Brazil 135/E3
Nova Goa (Panaji), India 68/C5
Nova Gorizia, Yugoslavia 45/A2
Nova Gradiška, Yugoslavia 45/C3
Nova Granada, Brazil 135/B2
Nova Iguaçu, Brazil 120/E5
Nova Iguaçu, Brazil 135/E3
Nova Iguaçu, Brazil 132/F8
Nova Iorque, Brazil 132/E4
Nova Lima, Brazil 135/E2
Nova Lusitânia, Mozambique 118/E3
Nova Mambone, Mozambique 118/F4
Novar, Ontario 177/E2
Novara (prov.), Italy 34/B2
Novara, Italy 34/B2
Nova Russas, Brazil 132/F4
Nova Scotia (prov.) 162/K7
Nova Scotia (prov.), Canada 146/M5
NOVA SCOTIA 168
Nova Sofala, Mozambique 118/F4
Novato, Calif. 204/H1
Novaya Kakhovka, U.S.S.R. 52/D5
Novaya Kazanka, U.S.S.R. 48/F5
Novaya Sibir' (isl.), U.S.S.R. 4/B2
Novaya Sibir' (isl.), U.S.S.R. 48/Q2
Novaya Zemlya (isl.), U.S.S.R. 2/L2
Novaya Zemlya (isl.), U.S.S.R. 4/B7
Novaya Zemlya (isls.), U.S.S.R. 48/F2
Novaya Zemlya (isls.), U.S.S.R. 52/H1
Nova Zagora, Bulgaria 45/H4
Nové Hrady, Czech. 41/C2
Novelda, Spain 33/F3
Novelty, Mo. 261/H2
Nové Město nad Váhom, Czech. 41/D2
Nové Město na Moravě, Czech. 41/D2
Nové Strašecí, Czech. 41/B1
Nové Zámky, Czech. 41/D3
Novgorod, U.S.S.R. 7/H3
Novgorod, U.S.S.R. 52/D3
Novgorod, U.S.S.R. 52/D3
Novgorod-Severskiy, U.S.S.R. 52/D4
Novi, Mich. 250/F6
Novi, Yugoslavia 45/B3
Novi Ligure, Italy 34/B4
Novinger, Mo. 261/G2
Novi Pazar, Bulgaria 45/H4
Novi Pazar, Yugoslavia 45/E4
Novi Sad, Yugoslavia 45/D3
Novi Sad, Yugoslavia 7/F4
Nóvita, Colombia 126/B5
Novo Aripuaná, Brazil 120/D3
Novocherkassk, U.S.S.R. 7/J4
Novocherkassk, U.S.S.R. 52/F5
Novodvinsk, U.S.S.R. 52/F2
Novograd-Volynskiy, U.S.S.R. 52/C4
Novogrudok, U.S.S.R. 52/C4
Novo Hamburgo, Brazil 132/D10
Novo Horizonte, Brazil 135/B2
Novokazalinsk, U.S.S.R. 48/G5
Novokuybyshevsk, U.S.S.R. 7/K3
Novokuybyshevsk, U.S.S.R. 52/G4
Novokuznetsk, U.S.S.R. 54/K4
Novokuznetsk, U.S.S.R. 48/J4
Novo Mesto, Yugoslavia 45/B3
Novomoskovsk, U.S.S.R. 7/H3
Novomoskovsk, U.S.S.R. 52/E4
Novomoskovsk, U.S.S.R. 48/E4
Novopolotsk, U.S.S.R. 52/C3
Novorossiysk, U.S.S.R. 7/H4
Novorossiysk, U.S.S.R. 48/D5
Novorossiysk, U.S.S.R. 52/E6
Novosergiyevka, U.S.S.R. 52/H4
Novoshakhtinsk, U.S.S.R. 52/E5
Novosibirsk, U.S.S.R. 54/J4
Novosibirsk, U.S.S.R. 2/P3
Novosibirsk, U.S.S.R. 48/J4
Novotroitsk, U.S.S.R. 52/J4
Novoukrainka, U.S.S.R. 52/D5
Novouzensk, U.S.S.R. 52/G4
Novovolynsk, U.S.S.R. 52/B4
Novovyatsk, U.S.S.R. 52/G3
Novozybkov, U.S.S.R. 48/D4
Novozybkov, U.S.S.R. 52/D4
Novra, Manitoba 179/B2
Novska, U.S.S.R. 45/C3
Nový Bohumín, Czech. 41/E2
Nový Bor, Czech. 41/C1
Nový Bydžov, Czech. 41/C1
Nový Hrozenkov, Czech. 41/E2
Nový Jičín, Czech. 41/E2
Novyy Bug, U.S.S.R. 52/D5
Novyy Port, U.S.S.R. 4/C6
Novyy Port, U.S.S.R. 48/G3
Novyy Urengoy, U.S.S.R. 48/H3
Novyy Uzen', U.S.S.R. 48/F5

Nowa Dęba, Poland 47/E3
Nowa Nowa, Victoria 97/F5
Nowa Ruda, Poland 47/C3
Nowa Sól, Poland 47/B3
Nowata (co.), Okla. 288/P1
Nowata, Okla. 288/P1
Nowe, Poland 47/D2
Nowendoc, N.S. Wales 97/F2
Nowgong, Assam, India 68/G3
Nowgong, Madhya Pradesh, India 68/D3
Nowitna (riv.), Alaska 196/H2
Nowogard, Poland 47/B2
Nowood (riv.), Wyo. 319/E1
Nowra-Bomaderry, N.S. Wales 88/J6
Nowra-Bomaderry, N.S. Wales 97/F4
Now Shahr, Iran 66/G2
Nowshera, Pakistan 59/K3
Nowshera, Pakistan 68/C2
Nowy Dwór Gdański, Poland 47/D1
Nowy Dwór Mazowiecki, Poland 47/E2
Nowy Sącz (prov.), Poland 47/E4
Nowy Sącz, Poland 47/E4
Nowy Staw, Poland 47/D1
Nowy Targ, Poland 47/E4
Nowy Tomyśl, Poland 47/C2
Now Zad, Afghanistan 68/A2
Now Zad, Afghanistan 59/H3
Noxapater, Miss. 256/F5
Noxen, Pa. 294/F7
Noxon, Mont. 262/A3
Noxubee (co.), Miss. 256/G4
Noxubee (riv.), Miss. 256/G4
Noya, Spain 33/B1
Noyes (isl.), Alaska 196/M2
Noyes, Minn. 255/A2
Noyes (pt.), R.I. 249/H7
Noyo (riv.), Calif. 204/B4
Noyon, France 28/E3
Noyon, Mongolia 77/F3
Nsanje, Malawi 115/G7
Nsawam, Ghana 106/D7
Nsukka, Nigeria 106/F7
Nsuta, Ghana 106/D7
Nuba (mts.), Sudan 111/E5
Nubanusit (lake), N.H. 268/C5
Nubeena, Tasmania 99/D5
Nuberg, Georgia 217/G9
Nubia (lake), Sudan 111/F3
Nubian (des.), Sudan 102/F2
Nubian (des.), Sudan 111/F3
Nubian (des.), Sudan 59/B5
Nubieber, Calif. 204/D2
Nuckols (co.), Nebr. 264/F4
Nuckols, Ky. 237/J5
Nucla, Colo. 208/B6
Nudgee, Queensland 88/K2
Nueces (co.), Texas 303/G10
Nueces (riv.), Texas 188/G5
Nueces (riv.), Texas 303/F9
Nueltin (lake) 162/G3
Nueltin (lake), Manitoba 179/H1
Nueltin (lake), N.W. Terr. 187/H3
Nuestra Señora (bay), Chile 138/A5
Nueva (isl.), Argentina 143/C8
Nueva (isl.), Chile 138/F11
Nueva Alejandría, Peru 128/F5
Nueva Antioquia, Colombia 126/F5
Nueva Armenia, Honduras 154/D4
Nueva Asunción, Paraguay 144/B2
Nueva Casas Grandes, Mexico 150/F1
Nueva Ciudad Guerrero, Mexico 150/K3
Nueva Colombia, Paraguay 144/B4
Nueva Ecija (prov.), Philippines 82/C3
Nueva Esparta (state), Venezuela 124/C2
Nueva Germania, Paraguay 144/D3
Nueva Gerona, Cuba 156/C2
Nueva Gerona, Cuba 158/B2
Nueva Helvecia, Uruguay 145/B5
Nueva Imperial, Chile 138/D2
Nueva Italia, Paraguay 144/B5
Nueva Italia de Ruiz, Mexico 150/J7
Nueva Ocotepeque, Honduras 154/C3
Nueva Palmira, Uruguay 145/A4
Nueva Rosita, Mexico 150/J3
Nueva San Salvador, El Salvador 154/C4
Nueva Vizcaya (prov.), Philippines 82/C2
Nueve de Julio, Argentina 143/F7
Nuevitas, Cuba 156/C2
Nuevitas, Cuba 158/D2
Nuevitas (bay), Cuba 158/H2
Nuevo (gulf), Argentina 143/D5
Nuevo Berlín, Uruguay 145/B3
Nuevo Chagres, Panama 154/G6
Nuevo Ideal, Mexico 150/H4
Nuevo Juncal, Chile 138/B5
Nuevo Laredo, Mexico 146/H7
Nuevo Laredo, Mexico 150/J3
Nuevo León (state), Mexico 150/K4
Nuevo Mamo, Venezuela 124/D3
Nuevo Rocafuerte, Ecuador 128/E3
Nufenen, Switzerland 39/H3
Nugaal (prov.), Somalia 115/J2
Nugget (pt.), N. Zealand 100/C7
Nugrus, Jebel (mt.), Egypt 59/B4
Nui (atoll), Tuvalu 87/H6
Nuiqsut, Alaska 196/H1
Nu Jiang (riv.), China 77/E6
Nuka (bay), Alaska 196/C2
Nukey Bluff (mt.), S. Australia 94/D5
Nukheila (oasis), Sudan 111/E4
Nuku'alofa (cap.), Tonga 87/J8
Nukuhiva (isl.), Fr. Poly. 87/M6
Nukulaelae (atoll), Tuvalu 87/H6
Nukumanu (atoll), Papua N.G. 87/F6
Nukumanu (isls.), Papua N.G. 86/E5
Nukunonu (atoll), Tokelau Is. 87/J6

Nukuoro (atoll), Micronesia 87/F5
Nukus, U.S.S.R. 54/H5
Nukus, U.S.S.R. 48/G5
Nulato, Alaska 196/G2
Nules, Spain 33/F3
Nulhegan (riv.), Vt. 268/D2
Nulhegan, East Branch (riv.), Vt. 268/D2
Nullagine, W. Australia 87/C4
Nullagine, W. Australia 92/C3
Nullarbor (plain), Australia 88/D6
Nullarbor (plain), Australia 87/C9
Nullarbor, S. Australia 94/B4
Nullarbor (plain), S. Australia 94/A4
Nullarbor (plain), W. Australia 92/D5
Nulliberg (mt.), Virgin Is. (U.S.) 161/A4
Nulltown, Ind. 227/G5
Numa, Iowa 229/G7
Numan, Nigeria 106/G7
Numancia, Philippines 82/D5
Numansdorp, Netherlands 27/E5
Numata, Japan 81/J5
Numazu, Japan 81/J6
Numbulwar, North. Terr. 88/F2
Numbulwar, North. Terr. 93/D3
Numfoor (isl.), Indonesia 85/J6
Numí, Paraguay 144/D4
Nu Mine, Pa. 294/D4
Numurkah, Victoria 97/C5
Nunaksaluk (isl.), Newf. 166/B2
Nunapitchuk, Alaska 196/F2
Nunawading, Victoria 88/L7
Nunawading, Victoria 97/J3
Nunchia, Colombia 126/D5
Nunda, N.Y. 276/E5
Nunda, S. Dak. 298/P5
Nundah, Queensland 88/K2
Nundah, Queensland 95/E2
Nundle, N.S. Wales 97/F2
Nuneaton, England 13/F5
Nuneaton, England 10/F4
Núñez (isl.), Chile 138/D10
Nunez, Georgia 217/H5
Nungarin, W. Australia 92/B5
Nungesser (lake), Ontario 175/B2
Nunivak (isl.), Alaska 146/B4
Nunivak (isl.), Alaska 188/C6
Nunivak (isl.), Alaska 196/E2
Nunivak (isl.), U.S. 4/D18
Nunley, Ark. 202/B4
Nunn, Colo. 208/K1
Nunnelly, Tenn. 237/G9
Nunningen, Switzerland 39/E2
Nuñoa, Peru 128/G10
Nunspeet, Netherlands 27/H4
Nuoro (prov.), Italy 34/B4
Nuoro, Italy 34/B4
Nuqub, Yemen 59/E6
Nuquí, Colombia 126/B5
Nuremberg, Germany 7/F4
Nuremberg, Germany 22/D4
Nuremberg, Pa. 294/K4
Nurestan (reg.), Afghanistan 59/K2
Nurhak (river), Turkey 63/G4
Nuri, Mexico 150/E3
Nuri (ruins), Sudan 111/F4
Nuria, Sierra de (mts.), Venezuela 124/H4
Nuriootpa, S. Australia 94/F6
Nuristan (reg.), Afghanistan 68/C1
Nurlat, U.S.S.R. 52/H4
Nurmes, Finland 18/Q5
Nürnberg (Nuremberg), Germany 22/D4
Nurrari (lakes), S. Australia 94/B3
Nursery, Texas 303/H9
Nürtingen, Germany 22/C4
Nuruhak Dağı (mt.), Turkey 63/G3
Nus, Ras (cape), Oman 59/G6
Nusa Barung (isl.), Indonesia 85/K3
Nusaybin, Turkey 63/J4
Nushagak (bay), Alaska 196/G3
Nushagak (riv.), Alaska 196/G2
Nushki, Pakistan 68/B3
Nushki, Pakistan 59/J4
Nussaq, Greenland 4/B12
Nutimik, Manitoba 179/G5
Nutley, N.J. 273/B2
Nut Mountain, Sask. 181/H3
Nutrioso, Ariz. 198/F5
Nuttby (mt.), Nova Scotia 168/F3
Nutter Fort, W. Va. 312/F4
Nutting Lake, Mass. 249/B5
Nutwood Downs, North. Terr. 93/D3
Nuuanu (stream), Hawaii 218/C4
Nuuk (cap.), Greenland 4/C12
Nuuk (cap.), Greenland 146/N3
Nuuk (cap.), Greenland 2/G2
Nuupere (pt.), Fr. Poly. 86/S13
Nuwara Eliya, Sri Lanka 68/E7
Nuweiba, Egypt 111/F2
Nuyakuk (lake), Alaska 196/F3
Nuyts (arch.), S. Australia 94/C5
Nuyts (cape), S. Australia 94/C5
Nyabing, W. Australia 88/B6
Nyabisindu, Rwanda 115/F2
Nyack, Mont. 262/C2
Nyack, N.Y. 276/K8
Nyah, Victoria 97/B4
Nyah West, Victoria 97/B4
Nyainqêntanglha Shan (range), China 77/D5
Nyainrong, China 77/D5
Nyala, Sudan 111/E5
Nyala, Sudan 102/E3
Ny-Ålesund, Norway 18/C2
Nyamlell, Sudan 111/E6
Nyandoma, U.S.S.R. 7/J2
Nyandoma, U.S.S.R. 48/E3
Nyandoma, U.S.S.R. 52/F2
Nyanga, Gabon 115/A4
Nyanga, S. Africa 118/F6
Nyanza (prov.), Kenya 115/F2
Nyasa (lake) 102/F6
Nyasa (lake) 2/L6
Nyasa (lake), Malawi 115/F6

Iyasa (lake), Mozambique 118/E2
Iyasa (lake), Tanzania 115/F6
Iyborg, Denmark 21/D7
Iyborg, Denmark 18/G9
Iybro, Sweden 18/J8
Iye, Mont. 262/G5
Iyeri, Kenya 115/G4
Iyerol, Sudan 111/F6
Iyima, China 77/C5
Iyingchi, China 77/D6
Iyirábrány, Hungary 41/G3
Iyiradony, Hungary 41/G3
Iyirbátor, Hungary 41/G3
Iyiregyháza, Hungary 41/F3
Iyirmada, Hungary 41/F2
Iyiru (mt.), Kenya 115/G3
Iykarleby, Finland 18/N5
Iyköbing, Denmark 18/H9
Iyköbing, Denmark 18/G9
Iyköbing, Denmark 18/F8
Iyköbing, Storstrøm, Denmark 21/F8
Iyköbing, Vestsjaelland, Denmark 21/E
Iyköbing, Viborg, Denmark 21/B4
Iyköping, Sweden 18/K7
Iylstroom, S. Africa 118/D4
Iymagee, N.S. Wales 97/D3
Iymboida, N.S. Wales 97/G1
Iymboida (riv.), N.S. Wales 97/G1
Iymburk, Czech. 41/C1
Iynäshamn, Sweden 18/L7
Iyngan, N. S. Wales 88/H6
Iyngan, N. S. Wales 97/D2
Iyon, Switzerland 39/B4
Iyons, France 28/F5
Iyrany, Czech. 41/B2
Iyrob, U.S.S.R. 52/J2
Iyrsko, Czech. 41/B2
Iysa, Poland 47/C3
Iysa Kłodzka (riv.), Poland 47/C3
Iysa Łużycka (Neisse) (riv.), Poland 47/B3
Iyssa, Oreg. 291/K4
Iysted, Denmark 21/E8
Iytva, U.S.S.R. 52/H3
Iyudo (cape), Japan 81/J4
Iyukhcha, U.S.S.R. 52/G2
Iyunzu, Zaire 115/F5
Iyurba, U.S.S.R. 48/M3
Iyuvchim, U.S.S.R. 52/H2
Izega, Tanzania 115/F4
'Zérékoré, Guinea 106/C7
'zeto, Angola 115/B5
Izwani (isl.), Comoros 118/G2
Izwani (isl.), Comoros 102/G6

O

a, Mull of (prom.), Scotland 10/C3
a, Mull of (prom.), Scotland 15/B5
acoma, S. Dak. 298/L6
adby, England 13/F5
ahe (lake), N. Dak. 282/J7
ahe (dam), S. Dak. 298/J5
ahe (lake), S. Dak. 188/F1
ahe (lake), S. Dak. 298/J1
ahe (lake), U.S. 146/J5
ahu (isl.), Hawaii 87/L3
ahu (isl.), Hawaii 188/F3
ahu (isl.), Hawaii 218/E2
ak (lake), Manitoba 179/B5
ak (pt.), Mich. 250/F5
ak, Nebr. 264/G4
ak (creek), N. Dak. 282/J8
ak (isl.), Nova Scotia 168/E3
ak (creek), S. Dak. 298/H2
ak (isl.), Wis. 317/E2
akbank, Manitoba 179/F5
ak Bay, Br. Col. 184/K4
ak Bay, New Bruns. 170/C3
ak Bluffs, Mass. 249/M7
ak Bluffs •, Mass. 249/M7
ak Bluff Station, Manitoba 179/E5
akboro, N.C. 281/J4
ak Brae, Manitoba 179/C3
ak Brook, Ill. 222/B6
akbrook Terrace, Ill. 222/B5
akburn, Manitoba 179/B4
ak Center, Minn. 255/F6
ak City, N.C. 281/P3
ak City, Utah 304/B4
ak Creek, Colo. 208/F2
ak Creek, Wis. 317/M2
akdale, Calif. 204/E6
akdale, Conn. 210/G3
akdale, Ill. 222/D5
akdale, Iowa 229/K5
akdale, La. 238/E5
akdale, Mass. 249/G3
akdale, Minn. 255/F6
akdale, Nebr. 264/F2
akdale, Pa. 294/B5
akdale, Tenn. 237/M9
akdale, Wash. 310/H3
akes, N. Dak. 282/O7
akfield, Georgia 217/E7
akfield •, Maine 243/G3
akfield, N.Y. 276/D4
akfield, Tenn. 237/D9
akfield, Wis. 317/J8
akford, Ill. 222/D3
akford, Ind. 227/C4
ak Forest, Ill. 222/B6
ak Grove, Ala. 195/B9
ak Grove, Ala. 195/F4
ak Grove, Ark. 202/C1
ak Grove, Del. 245/R6
ak Grove, Ill. 222/C2
ak Grove, Ky. 237/G7
ak Grove, La. 238/H1

Oak Grove, Mich. 250/F6
Oak Grove, Mo. 261/S6
Oak Grove, Mo. 261/K6
Oak Grove, Oreg. 291/B2
Oak Grove, Va. 307/O4
Oak Grove Fork, Clackamas (riv.), Oreg. 291/F2
Oak Hall, Pa. 294/C4
Oak Hall, Va. 307/S5
Oakham, England 13/G5
Oakham, England 10/F4
Oakham •, Mass. 249/F3
Oak Harbor, Ohio 284/D2
Oak Harbor, Wash. 310/C2
Oak Harbor Naval Air Sta., Wash. 310/C2
Oakhaven, Ark. 202/C6
Oak Hill, Ala. 195/D7
Oak Hill, Fla. 212/F3
Oak Hill, Ill. 222/D3
Oakhill, Kansas 232/E2
Oak Hill, Mo. 261/K6
Oak Hill, Ohio 284/E8
Oak Hill, Tenn. 237/H8
Oak Hill, W. Va. 312/D6
Oakhurst, Calif. 204/F6
Oakhurst, N.J. 273/E3
Oakhurst, Okla. 288/P2
Oakhurst, Texas 303/J7
Oak Island, Minn. 255/D1
Oak Lake, Manitoba 179/B5
Oakland, Calif. 14/F6
Oakland, Calif. 18/E3
Oakland, Calif. 204/J2
Oakland, Conn. 210/E1
Oakland, Fla. 212/E3
Oakland, Iowa 229/C6
Oakland, Ky. 237/L6
Oakland, La. 238/F1
Oakland, Maine 243/D6
Oakland •, Maine 243/D6
Oakland, Md. 245/L3
Oakland, Md. 245/A3
Oakland (co.), Mich. 250/F6
Oakland, Miss. 256/E2
Oakland, Mo. 261/P3
Oakland, Mo. 261/G7
Oakland, Nebr. 264/H3
Oakland, N.J. 273/J1
Oakland, Okla. 288/N6
Oakland, Ontario 177/D4
Oakland, Oreg. 291/D4
Oakland, Pa. 294/L2
Oakland, R.I. 249/H5
Oakland, Tenn. 237/B10
Oakland Acres, Iowa 229/H5
Oakland Army Base, Calif. 204/J2
Oakland Beach, R.I. 249/J6
Oakland City, Ind. 227/C8
Oakland Mills, Iowa 229/K7
Oakland Park, Fla. 212/E6
Oaklands, N.S. Wales 97/D4
Oak Lawn, Ill. 222/B6
Oakleigh, Victoria 88/L7
Oakleigh, Victoria 97/J5
Oakley, Calif. 204/L1
Oakley, Idaho 220/D7
Oakley, Ill. 222/E4
Oakley, Iowa 229/G6
Oakley, Kansas 232/B2
Oakley, Mich. 250/E5
Oakley, Miss. 256/D6
Oakley, N.C. 281/P3
Oakley, Scotland 5/C1
Oakley, S.C. 296/E5
Oakley, Tenn. 237/L8
Oakley, Utah 304/C3
Oaklyn, N.J. 273/B3
Oakman, Ala. 195/D3
Oakman, Georgia 217/C1
Oakmont, Pa. 294/C6
Oakmulgee (creek), Ala. 195/D5
Oakner, Manitoba 179/B4
Oak Orchard, Del. 245/T6
Oakover (riv.), W. Australia 88/C4
Oakover (riv.), W. Australia 92/C3
Oak Park, Georgia 217/H6
Oak Park, Ill. 222/B5
Oak Park, Mich. 250/B6
Oak Park, Minn. 255/E5
Oakpark, Va. 307/M4
Oak Point, Manitoba 179/B5
Oak Point, New Bruns. 170/D3
Oak Ridge, La. 238/G1
Oak Ridge, Miss. 256/C6
Oak Ridge, Mo. 261/N7
Oak Ridge, N.J. 273/E1
Oak Ridge (res.), N.J. 273/D1
Oak Ridge, Oreg. 291/E4
Oak Ridge, Tenn. 254/D3
Oak Ridge, Tenn. 188/J3
Oak Ridge, Tenn. 237/N8
Oak River, Manitoba 179/D4
Oaks, Mo. 261/P5
Oaks, Okla. 288/S2
Oakshela, Sask. 181/J5
Oakton, Ky. 237/C7
Oakton, Va. 307/N3
Oaktown, Ind. 227/C7
Oak Vale, Miss. 256/D7
Oak Valley, Kansas 232/G4
Oak View, Calif. 204/F9
Oakview, Manitoba 179/D3
Oakview, Mo. 261/P5
Oakville, Conn. 210/C2
Oakville, Ind. 227/G4
Oakville, Iowa 229/L6
Oakville, Ky. 237/H7
Oakville, Manitoba 179/D5
Oakville, Ontario 177/E4
Oakville, Pa. 294/H5
Oakville, Texas 303/G9
Oakville, Wash. 310/D4
Oakway, S.C. 296/A2

Oakwood, Georgia 217/E2
Oakwood, Ill. 222/F3
Oakwood, Mo. 261/P5
Oakwood, N. Dak. 282/R3
Oakwood, Ohio 284/H9
Oakwood, Ohio 284/B6
Oakwood, Ohio 284/B3
Oakwood, Okla. 288/J3
Oakwood, Ontario 177/F3
Oakwood, Texas 303/J6
Oakwood, Va. 307/E6
Oakwood Heights, Ill. 222/B2
Oakwood Manor, Mo. 261/P5
Oakwood Park, Mo. 261/P5
Oamaru, N. Zealand 100/C6
Oani (riv.), Japan 81/K3
Oasis, Nev. 266/G1
Oasis, Utah 304/B4
Oates, Coast (reg.) 5/B8
Oatlands, Tasmania 99/D4
Oatman, Ariz. 198/A3
Oatsville, Ind. 227/C8
Oaxaca (state), Mexico 150/L8
Oaxaca, Mexico 146/J8
Oaxaca de Juárez, Mexico 150/L8
Ob' (gulf), U.S.S.R. 4/B6
Ob' (gulf), U.S.S.R. 48/H3
Ob' (gulf), U.S.S.R. 54/J3
Ob' (riv.), U.S.S.R. 2/N2
Ob' (riv.), U.S.S.R. 4/C6
Ob' (riv.), U.S.S.R. 48/G3
Ob' (riv.), U.S.S.R. 54/H3
Oba, Ont. 162/H6
Oba, Ontario 177/J5
Oba, Ontario 175/D3
Obama, Japan 81/G6
Oban (Half Moon Bay), N. Zealand 100/B7
Oban, Sask. 181/C3
Oban, Scotland 15/C4
Oban, Scotland 10/D2
Obbia, Somalia 115/J2
Obed, Alberta 182/B3
Obed (riv.), Tenn. 237/M8
Ober, Ind. 227/C6
Oberá, Argentina 143/F2
Oberägeri, Switzerland 39/G2
Oberalp (pass), Switzerland 39/G3
Oberalpstock (mt.), Switzerland 39/G3
Oberammergau, Germany 22/D5
Oberburg, Switzerland 39/E2
Oberdiessbach, Switzerland 39/E3
Oberdorf, Switzerland 39/E2
Ober Grafendorf, Austria 41/C2
Oberhausen, Germany 22/B3
Oberhof, Germany 22/D3
Oberlin, Kansas 232/B2
Oberlin, La. 238/E5
Oberlin, Mich. 250/E4
Oberlin, Ohio 284/F3
Oberndorf bei Salzburg, Austria 41/B3
Oberon, Manitoba 179/C4
Oberon, N.S. Wales 97/E3
Oberon, N. Dak. 282/M4
Oberpfälzer Wald (for.), Germany 22/E4
Oberriet, Switzerland 39/J2
Obersaxen, Switzerland 39/H3
Obersiggenthal, Switzerland 39/F1
Oberstammheim, Switzerland 39/G1
Oberstdorf, Germany 22/D5
Obert, Nebr. 264/G3
Oberursel, Germany 22/C3
Obervellach, Austria 41/B3
Oberwald, Switzerland 39/F3
Oberwart, Austria 41/D3
Oberwil, Switzerland 39/D3
Oberwölz, Austria 41/C3
Oberzwil, Switzerland 39/H2
Obetz, Ohio 284/E6
Obi (isl.), Indonesia 85/H6
Obi (isls.), Indonesia 85/H6
Óbidos, Brazil 120/D3
Óbidos, Brazil 132/C3
Óbidos, Portugal 33/B3
Obihiro, Japan 81/L2
Obion (riv.), Ky. 237/C7
Obion (co.), Tenn. 237/C8
Obion, Tenn. 237/C8
Obion, South Fork (riv.), Tenn. 237/C8
Obion, Middle Fork (riv.), Tenn. 237/D8
Obion (riv.), Tenn. 237/C8
Obion, North Fork (riv.), Tenn. 237/D8
Obispos, Venezuela 124/D3
Obitsu (riv.), Japan 81/P3
Oblong, Ill. 222/F5
Obluch'ye, U.S.S.R. 48/N5
Obninsk, U.S.S.R. 52/E3
Obo, Cent. Afr. Rep. 115/E2
Obock, Djibouti 111/H5
Oborniki, Poland 47/C2
Oboyan', U.S.S.R. 52/E4
Obozerskiy, U.S.S.R. 52/E2
O'Brien, Fla. 212/D1
O'Brien (co.), Iowa 229/B2
O'Brien, Oreg. 291/C5
O'Brien, Texas 303/E4
O'Briensbridge-Montpelier, Ireland 17/D6
Observatory (inlet), Br. Col. 184/C2
Obsidian, Idaho 220/D6
Obuasi, Ghana 106/D7
Obukowin (lake), Manitoba 179/G3
Obwalden (canton), Switzerland 39/F3
Ocala, Fla. 212/D2
Ocamo (riv.), Venezuela 124/F6
Ocampo, Chihuahua, Mexico 150/E2
Ocampo, Coahuila, Mexico 150/H3
Ocampo, Tamaulipas, Mexico 150/K5
Ocaña, Colombia 126/D3
Ocaña, Spain 33/E3

Ocate, N. Mex. 274/E2
Ocate (creek), N. Mex. 274/E2
Occidental, Cordillera (range), Bolivia 136/A6
Occidental, Cordillera (range), Colombia 126/B5
Occidental, Cordillera (range), Peru 128/F10
Occidental Mindoro (prov.), Philippines 82/C4
Occoquan, Va. 307/O3
Occum, Conn. 210/G2
Ocean (cape), Alaska 196/K3
Ocean (pond), Fla. 212/D1
Ocean (Banaba) (isl.), Kiribati 87/G6
Ocean (co.), N.J. 273/E1
Ocean (lake), Nova Scotia 168/G3
Ocean (lake), Wyo. 319/D2
Oceana (co.), Mich. 250/C5
Oceana, W. Va. 312/C7
Oceana N.A.S., Va. 307/S7
Ocean Beach, N.Y. 276/O9
Ocean Bluff-Brant Rock, Mass. 249/M4
Ocean Breeze Park, Fla. 212/F4
Ocean City, Md. 245/T7
Ocean City, N.J. 273/D5
Ocean City, Wash. 310/A3
Ocean Falls, Br. Col. 184/D4
Ocean Gate, N.J. 273/D5
Ocean Grove, Mass. 249/K6
Ocean Grove, N.J. 273/F3
Ocean Isle Beach, N.C. 281/N7
Oceano, Calif. 204/F8
Oceanographic Office, Md. 245/F5
Ocean Park, Maine 243/C9
Ocean Park, Wash. 310/A4
Oceanport, N.J. 273/F3
Ocean Ridge, Fla. 212/F5
Ocean Shores, Wash. 310/A3
Oceanside, Calif. 204/H10
Oceanside, N.Y. 276/R7
Oceanside, Oreg. 291/C2
Ocean Springs, Miss. 256/G10
Ocean View, Del. 245/T6
Ocean View, N.J. 273/D5
Oceanville, N.J. 273/E4
Ocelota, Ohio 284/D4
Ochamchira, U.S.S.R. 52/F6
Ochelata, Okla. 288/P1
Ocheyedan, Iowa 229/B2
Ochil (hills), Scotland 15/E4
Ochiltree (co.), Texas 303/D1
Ochlocknee, Georgia 217/E9
Ochlockonee (riv.), Fla. 212/B1
Ochlockonee (riv.), Georgia 217/C10
Ochoco (creek), Oreg. 291/G3
Ochopee, Fla. 212/E6
Ocho Rios, Jamaica 158/J6
Ochre River, Manitoba 179/C3
Ochsen (mt.), Switzerland 39/D3
Ochsenfurt, Germany 22/D4
Ochsenkopf (mt.), Liecht. 39/J2
Ocie, Mo. 261/G9
Ocilla, Georgia 217/F7
Ockelbo, Sweden 18/K6
Ocklawaha (lake), Fla. 212/E2
Ockley, Ind. 227/D4
Ocmulgee (riv.), Georgia 217/E5
Ocmulgee Nat'l Mon., Georgia 217/F5
Ocna Mureş, Romania 45/G2
Ocoa, Chile 138/G2
Ocoa (bay), Dom. Rep. 158/D6
Ocoee, Fla. 212/E3
Ocoee (riv.), Tenn. 237/M10
Ocoña, Peru 128/F11
Ocoña (riv.), Peru 128/F11
Oconee (co.), Georgia 217/F4
Oconee, Georgia 217/G5
Oconee (riv.), Georgia 217/F5
Oconee, Ill. 222/D4
Oconee (co.), S.C. 296/A2
Oconomowoc, Wis. 317/H1
Oconomowoc Lake, Wis. 317/H1
Oconto, Nebr. 264/E4
Oconto (co.), Wis. 317/K6
Oconto, Wis. 317/L6
Oconto (riv.), Wis. 317/K6
Oconto Falls, Wis. 317/K5
Ocós, Guatemala 154/B3
Ocosingo, Mexico 150/O8
Ocosta, Wash. 310/B4
Ocotal, Segovia, Nicaragua 154/D4
Ocotal, Zelaya, Nicaragua 154/E4
Ocotlán, Mexico 150/H6
Ocotlán de Morelos, Mexico 150/L8
Ocqueoc, Mich. 250/F3
Ocracoke, N.C. 281/T4
Ocracoke (inlet), N.C. 281/T5
Ocracoke (isl.), N.C. 281/T4
Ocre, Ala. 195/H4
Ocros, Peru 128/D8
Octa, Mo. 261/M10
Octa, Ohio 284/D6
Octagon, Ala. 195/C6
Octavia, Nebr. 264/G3
Octavia, Okla. 288/S5
October Revolution (isl.), U.S.S.R. 54/K2
October Revolution (isl.), U.S.S.R. 4/B5
October Revolution (isl.), U.S.S.R. 48/L2
Ocú, Panama 154/G7
Ocumare de la Costa, Venezuela 124/E2
Ocumare del Tuy, Venezuela 124/E2
Ocuri, Bolivia 136/C6
Oda, Japan 81/F6
Oda, Jebel (mt.), Sudan 59/C5
Oda, Jebel (mt.), Sudan 111/G3
Odanah, Wis. 317/E3
Odate, Japan 81/K3
Odawara, Japan 81/J6
Odd, W. Va. 312/D7
Odda, Norway 18/E6

Odder, Denmark 21/D6
Oddur, Somalia 115/H3
Odebolt, Iowa 229/C4
Odell, Ill. 222/E2
Odell, Ind. 227/C4
Odell, Nebr. 264/H4
Odell, Oreg. 291/F2
Odell (lake), Oreg. 291/E4
Odell, Texas 303/E2
Odell River, New Bruns. 170/C2
Odemira, Portugal 33/B4
Ödemiş, Turkey 63/C3
Oden, Ark. 202/C4
Odenburg, La. 238/G5
Odendaalsrus, S. Africa 118/D5
Odense, Denmark 7/F3
Odense, Denmark 18/G9
Odense, Denmark 21/D7
Odense (fjord), Denmark 21/D7
Odenton, Md. 245/M4
Odenville, Ala. 195/F4
Odenwald (for.), Germany 22/C4
Oder (riv.) 7/F3
Oder (riv.), Germany 22/F2
Oder (riv.), Poland 47/B2
Oder-Haff (mts.), Germany 22/F2
Oder-Haff (lag.), Poland 47/B2
Odessa, Md. 245/T7
Odessa, Fla. 212/D3
Odessa, Minn. 255/B5
Odessa, Mo. 261/L5
Odessa, Nebr. 264/E4
Odessa, N.Y. 276/G4
Odessa, Ontario 177/H3
Odessa, Sask. 181/H5
Odessa, Tex. 188/F4
Odessa, Texas 146/H6
Odessa, Texas 303/B6
Odessa, U.S.S.R. 2/L3
Odessa, U.S.S.R. 7/H4
Odessa, U.S.S.R. 48/D5
Odessa, U.S.S.R. 52/D5
Odessa, Wash. 310/G3
Odessadale, Georgia 217/C5
Odgen, Utah 188/D2
Odiel (riv.), Spain 33/C4
Odienne, Ivory Coast 106/C7
Odin, Ill. 222/D5
Odin, Kansas 232/E2
Odin, Minn. 255/D7
Odin, Nova Scotia 168/F3
Odin (riv.), Nova Scotia 168/D4
Odin (riv.), Ohio 284/B8
Odin (riv.), Pa. 294/A4
Odin (state), U.S. 146/K5
Odin, Ind. 227/F7
Odiongan, Philippines 82/C4
Odivelas, Portugal 33/A1
Odobeşti, Romania 45/H3
Odon, Ind. 227/C7
Odongk, Cambodia 72/E5
O'Donnell, Texas 303/C5
O'Donnells, Newf. 166/D2
Odoorn, Netherlands 27/K3
Odorheiu Secuiesc, Romania 45/G2
Odra (Oder) (riv.), Poland 47/B2
Odry, Czech. 41/D2
Odum, Georgia 217/H7
Odweina, Somalia 115/J2
Oebisfelde, Germany 22/D2
Oeiras, Brazil 132/F4
Oeiras, Portugal 33/B3
Oelemari (riv.), Suriname 131/D4
Oella, Md. 245/L3
Oelrichs, S. Dak. 298/C7
Oelsnitz, Germany 22/E3
Oelsnitz im Erzgebirge, Germany 22/E3
Oelwein, Iowa 229/K3
Oeno (isl.), Pitcairn Is. 87/O8
Oenpelli, North. Terr. 93/C2
Oensingen, Switzerland 39/E2
Of, Turkey 63/J2
Ofahoma, Miss. 256/E5
O'Fallon, Ill. 222/B2
O'Fallon, Mo. 261/L5
O'Fallon (creek), Mont. 262/L4
Ofanto (riv.), Italy 34/E4
Ofaqim, Israel 65/B5
Ofen (pass), Switzerland 39/K3
Ofenhorn (mt.), Switzerland 39/F4
Offa, Nigeria 106/F7
Offenbach am Main, Germany 22/C3
Offenburg, Germany 22/B4
Offerle, Kansas 232/C4
Offerman, Georgia 217/H8
Offutt, Ky. 237/R5
Offutt A.F.B., Nebr. 264/J3
Oftenfjorden (fjord), Norway 18/K2
Oftringen, Switzerland 39/E2
Ofunato, Japan 81/K4
Oga, Calif. 204/F9
Oga, Japan 81/J4
Oga (pen.), Japan 81/J4
Ogaden (reg.), Ethiopia 102/G4
Ogaden (reg.), Ethiopia 111/H6
Ogaki, Japan 81/H6
Ogallah, Kansas 232/C3
Ogallala, Nebr. 264/D3
Ogasawara-gunto (Bonin) (isls.), Japan 81/M3
Ogbomosho, Nigeria 102/E6
Ogbomosho, Nigeria 106/E7
Ogden, Ark. 202/B4
Ogden, Ill. 222/F3
Ogden, Iowa 229/E4
Ogden, Kansas 232/F2
Ogden (bay), N.W. Terr. 187/H3
Ogden, Utah 146/G5
Ogden, Utah 304/C2
Ogden Dunes, Ind. 227/C1
Ogdensburg, N.J. 273/D1
Ogdensburg, N.Y. 276/K1
Ogdensburg, Wis. 317/J7
Ogeechee (riv.), Georgia 217/J5
Ogema, Minn. 255/C3
Ogema, Sask. 181/G6
Ogema, Wis. 317/F5
Ogemaw, Ark. 202/E7

Ogemaw (co.), Mich. 250/E4
Ogi, Japan 81/J5
Ogidaki (mt.), Ontario 175/D3
Ogidaki (mt.), Ontario 177/J5
Ogilvie, Manitoba 179/D4
Ogilvie, Minn. 255/F5
Ogilvie (mts.), Yukon 187/E3
Ogilvie (riv.), Yukon 187/E3
Oglala, S. Dak. 298/D7
Ogle (co.), Ill. 222/D1
Ogle, Ky. 237/O6
Oglesby, Ill. 222/D2
Oglesby, Texas 303/G6
Oglethorpe (co.), Georgia 217/F3
Oglethorpe, Georgia 217/D6
Oglio (riv.), Italy 34/C2
Ogmore, Queensland 88/J4
Ogmore and Garw, Wales 13/A6
Ogoja, Nigeria 106/F7
Ogoki (riv.), Ont. 162/H5
Ogoki (riv.), Ontario 175/C2
Ogooué (riv.), Congo 115/A4
Ogooué (riv.), Gabon 115/A4
Ogre, U.S.S.R. 53/C2
Ogulin, Yugoslavia 45/B3
Ogun (state), Nigeria 106/E7
Ogunquit, Maine 243/D10
Ohai, N. Zealand 100/A6
Ohakune, N. Zealand 100/E3
O'Hare Field-Chicago International Airport, Ill. 222/B5
Ohariu (stream), N. Zealand 100/B2
Ohata, Japan 81/K3
Ohatchee, Ala. 195/G3
Ohaton, Alberta 182/D3
Ohau (lake), N. Zealand 100/B6
Ohaupo, N. Zealand 100/E2
Ohey, Belgium 27/G8
O'Higgins (lake), Chile 138/D7
OHIO 284
Ohio 118/K2
Ohio (riv.) 188/J3
Ohio, Colo. 208/F5
Ohio, Ill. 222/D2
Ohio (riv.), Ill. 222/E6
Ohio (co.), Ind. 227/H7
Ohio (co.), Ind. 227/B9
Ohio (co.), Ky. 237/H6
Ohio (riv.), Ky. 237/F5
Ohio, Nova Scotia 168/F3
Ohio (riv.), Nova Scotia 168/D4
Ohio (riv.), Ohio 284/B8
Ohio (riv.), Pa. 294/A4
Ohio (state), U.S. 146/K5
Ohio (riv.), U.S. 146/K6
Ohio (riv.), U.S. 2/E4
Ohio (co.), W. Va. 312/E2
Ohio (riv.), W. Va. 312/B5
Ohio Brush (creek), Ohio 284/D8
Ohio City, Ohio 284/H4
Ohiopyle, Pa. 294/E4
Ohioville, Pa. 294/B4
Ohiowa, Nebr. 264/G4
Ohley, W. Va. 312/D6
Ohlman, Ill. 222/D4
Ohoopee, Georgia 217/H6
Ohře (riv.), Czech. 41/B1
Ohrid (lake), Albania 45/E5
Ohrid, Yugoslavia 45/E5
Ohrid (lake), Yugoslavia 45/E5
Ohura, N. Zealand 100/E3
Oiapoque (Oyapock) (riv.), Brazil 132/C2
Oich, Loch (lake), Scotland 15/D3
Oich (riv.), Scotland 15/D3
Oies (isl.), Québec 172/G2
Oil (creek), Pa. 294/C2
Oil Center, N. Mex. 274/F6
Oil City, La. 238/C1
Oil City, Ontario 177/B5
Oil City, Pa. 188/L2
Oil City, Pa. 294/C3
Oildale, Calif. 204/F8
Oilmont, Mont. 262/F2
Oil Spring Ind. Res., N.Y. 276/D6
Oil Springs, Ky. 237/P5
Oil Springs, Ontario 177/B5
Oilton, Okla. 288/N2
Oilton, Texas 303/F10
Oil Trough, Ark. 202/G2
Oinoi, Greece 45/F6
Oinoússai (isl.), Greece 45/G4
Oirschot, Netherlands 27/G6
Oise (dept.), France 28/E3
Oise (riv.), France 28/E3
Oiseau (lake), Manitoba 179/G4
Oiseau (riv.), Manitoba 179/G4
Oisterwijk, Netherlands 27/G5
Oistins, Barbados 161/B9
Oistins (bay), Barbados 161/B9
Oita (pref.), Japan 81/E7
Oita, Japan 81/E7
Ojai, Calif. 204/F9
Ojibwa, Wis. 317/D4
Ojinaga, Mexico 150/G2
Ojiya, Japan 81/J5
Ojocaliente, Mexico 150/H5
Ojo Caliente, N. Mex. 274/D2
Ojo del Toro (mt.), Cuba 158/G4
Ojo Feliz, N. Mex. 274/E2
Ojo Sarco, N. Mex. 274/D2
Ojos del Salado (mt.) 120/C5
Ojos del Salado, Cerro (mt.), Argentina 143/C3
Ojos del Salado, Nevado (mt.), Chile 138/B6
Ojos Negros, Spain 33/F2
Ojus, Fla. 212/B4
Oka, Québec 172/C4
Oka (riv.), U.S.S.R. 7/J3
Oka (riv.), U.S.S.R. 48/L4
Oka (riv.), U.S.S.R. 52/F4
Okaba, Indonesia 85/K7
Okabena, Minn. 255/C7
Okahandja, Namibia 102/D7
Okahandja, Namibia 118/B4
Okahumpka, Fla. 212/D3
Okak (bay), Newf. 166/B2
Okak (isls.), Newf. 166/B2

422 Okaloacoochee Slough

Okaloacoochee Slough (swamp), Fla. 212/E5
Okaloosa (co.), Fla. 212/C6
Okamanpeedan (lake), Iowa 229/D2
Okanagan (lake), Br. Col. 162/D6
Okanagan (lake), Br. Col. 184/H5
Okanagan Centre, Br. Col. 184/H5
Okanagan Falls, Br. Col. 184/H5
Okanagan Landing, Br. Col. 184/H5
Okanagan Mission, Br. Col. 184/H5
Okanagan Mtn. Prov. Park, Br. Col. 184/G5
Okanogan (riv.), Br. Col. 184/H6
Okanogan (co.), Wash. 310/F2
Okanogan, Wash. 310/F2
Okanogan (riv.), Wash. 310/F2
Okarche, Okla. 288/L3
Okatibbee (creek), Miss. 256/G5
Okatibbee (lake), Miss. 256/G5
Okato, N. Zealand 100/D3
Okaton, S. Dak. 298/H6
Okauchee, Wis. 317/J1
Okauchee (lake), Wis. 317/J1
Okaukuejo, Namibia 118/B3
Okawa, Japan 81/E7
Okawville, Ill. 222/D5
Okay, Okla. 288/R3
Okaya, Japan 81/H5
Okayama (pref.), Japan 81/F6
Okayama, Japan 81/F6
Okazaki, Japan 81/H6
O'Kean, Ark. 202/J1
Okeana, Ohio 284/A7
Okee, Wis. 317/H9
Okeechobee (co.), Fla. 212/F4
Okeechobee, Fla. 212/F4
Okeechobee (lake), Fla. 188/K5
Okeechobee (lake), Fla. 212/F5
O'Keeffe Nat'l Hist. Site, N. Mex. 274/C2
Okeene, Okla. 288/K2
Okefenokee (swamp), Fla. 212/D1
Okefenokee (swamp), Georgia 217/H9
Okehampton, England 13/D7
Okehampton, England 10/D5
Okemah, Okla. 288/O4
Okemo (Ludlow) (mt.), Vt. 268/B5
Okemos, Mich. 250/E6
Okene, Nigeria 106/F7
Oker (riv.), Germany 22/D2
Okesa, Okla. 288/O1
Oketo, Kansas 232/F2
Okfuskee (co.), Okla. 288/O3
Okha, U.S.S.R. 54/R4
Okha, U.S.S.R. 48/P4
Okha Port, India 68/B4
Okhotsk (sea) 2/S3
Okhotsk (sea), Japan 81/M1
Okhotsk, U.S.S.R. 48/P4
Okhotsk, U.S.S.R. 54/R4
Okhotsk (sea), U.S.S.R. 48/P4
Okhotsk (sea), U.S.S.R. 54/R4
Oki (isls.), Japan 81/F5
Okiep, S. Africa 118/B5
Okinawa (pref.), Japan 81/N6
Okinawa (isls.), Japan 54/O7
Okinawa (isl.), Japan 81/N6
Okinawa (isls.), Japan 81/N6
Okinoerabu (isl.), Japan 81/N5
Okino-Tori-Shima (Parace Vela) (isls.), Japan 85/D3
Okkan, Burma 72/B3
Okla, Sask. 181/H3
Oklahoma 188/G3
OKLAHOMA 288
Oklahoma (co.), Okla. 288/M3
Oklahoma (state), U.S. 146/J6
Oklahoma City (cap.), Okla. 146/J6
Oklahoma City (cap.), Okla. 188/G3
Oklahoma City (cap.), Okla. 288/L4
Oklaunion, Texas 303/F3
Oklawaha, Fla. 212/E2
Oklawaha (riv.), Fla. 212/E2
Oklee, Minn. 255/C3
Okmulgee, Okla. 188/G3
Okmulgee (co.), Okla. 288/P3
Okmulgee, Okla. 288/O3
Okoboji, Iowa 229/C2
Okobojo (creek), S. Dak. 298/J4
Okolona, Ark. 202/D5
Okolona, Ky. 237/K4
Okolona, Miss. 256/G2
Okolona, Ohio 284/B3
Okondja, Gabon 115/B4
Okotoks, Alberta 182/C4
Okovango (riv.) 102/D6
Okovango (riv.), Botswana 118/C3
Okovango (swamps), Botswana 118/C3
Okovango (riv.), Namibia 118/C3
Okoyo, Congo 115/C4
Okpo, Burma 72/C3
Okreek, S. Dak. 298/J7
Oksino, U.S.S.R. 52/H1
Oktaha, Okla. 288/R3
Oktibbeha (co.), Miss. 256/G4
Oktyabr'sk, U.S.S.R. 52/G4
Oktyabr'skiy, U.S.S.R. 52/H4
Okulovka, U.S.S.R. 52/D3
Okushiri (isl.), Japan 81/J2
Ola, Ark. 202/D3
Ola, Georgia 217/E4
Ola, Idaho 220/B5
Olá, Panama 154/G6
Ólafsfjördhur, Iceland 21/C1
Ola Grande (pt.), P. Rico 161/D3
Olalla, Br. Col. 184/H5
Olalla, Wash. 310/A2
Olamon, Maine 243/F5
Olancha, Calif. 204/H7
Olanchito, Honduras 154/D3
Öland (isl.), Sweden 7/F3
Öland (isl.), Sweden 18/K8
Olanta, Pa. 294/F4
Olanta, S.C. 296/H4
Olar, S.C. 296/E5
Olary, S. Australia 94/G5
Olathe, Colo. 208/D5
Olathe, Kansas 232/H3
Olathe Nav. Air Sta., Kansas 232/H3
Olavarría, Argentina 143/D4
Olavarría, Argentina 120/C6
Oława, Poland 47/C3
Olberg, Ariz. 198/D5
Olbernhau, Germany 22/E3
Olbia, Italy 34/B4
Olcott, N.Y. 276/C4
Old (riv.), Calif. 204/L1
Old (riv.), La. 238/G5
Old (stream), Maine 243/H6
Oldany (isl.), Scotland 15/C2
Old Appleton, Mo. 261/N7
Old Bahama (chan.), Bahamas 156/B2
Old Bahama (chan.), Cuba 158/G1
Old Bahama (chan.), Cuba 156/B2
Old Bar, N.S. Wales 97/G2
Old Barkerville, Br. Col. 184/G3
Old Bennington, Vt. 268/A6
Old Bonaventure, Newf. 166/D2
Old Bridge, N.J. 273/E3
Old Castile (reg.), Spain 33/D2
Oldcastle, Ireland 10/C4
Oldcastle, Ireland 17/G4
Old Crow, Yukon 187/E3
Oldemarkt, Netherlands 27/J3
Olden, Mo. 261/J9
Olden, Norway 18/E6
Olden, Texas 303/F5
Oldenburg, Germany 22/C2
Oldenburg, Ind. 227/G6
Oldenburg, Miss. 256/C7
Oldenburg in Holstein, Germany 22/D1
Old England, Jamaica 158/H6
Old Entrance, Alberta 182/B3
Oldenzaal, Netherlands 27/K4
Old Faithful, Wyo. 319/B1
Oldfield, La. 238/L1
Old Fields, W. Va. 312/J4
Old Forge, N.Y. 276/L3
Old Forge, Pa. 294/F7
Old Fort, N.C. 281/E3
Old Fort, Ohio 284/D3
Oldfort, Tenn. 237/M10
Old Glory, Texas 303/D4
Old Greenwich, Conn. 210/A4
Oldham, England 13/H2
Oldham, England 10/G2
Oldham (co.), Ky. 237/L4
Oldham, S. Dak. 298/P5
Oldham (co.), Texas 303/B2
Old Harbor, Alaska 196/H3
Old Harbour, Jamaica 158/J6
Old Harbour (bay), Jamaica 158/J6
Old Harbour Bay, Jamaica 158/J6
Old Hickory (dam), Tenn. 237/H8
Old Hickory (lake), Tenn. 237/J8
Old Kilpatrick, Scotland 15/B2
Old Landing, Ky. 237/O5
Old Leighlin, Ireland 17/G6
Old Lyme•, Conn. 210/F3
Old Main Centre, Sask. 181/D5
Oldman (riv.), Alberta 182/D5
Oldman (riv.), Sask. 181/L2
Oldmans (creek), N.J. 273/C4
Old Marsh Bed, North. Terr. 93/B6
Oldmeldrum, Scotland 15/F3
Oldmeldrum, Scotland 10/E2
Old Mill Creek, Ill. 222/B4
Old Mission, Mich. 250/D4
Old Monroe, Mo. 261/L5
Old Mystic, Conn. 210/H3
Old Orchard Beach, Maine 243/C9
Old Orchard Beach•, Maine 243/C9
Old Perlican, Newf. 166/D2
Old Rhine (riv.), Netherlands 27/E4
Old Rhodes (key), Fla. 212/F6
Old Ripley, Ill. 222/D5
Old Road, Ant. & Bar. 161/D11
Old Road Town, St. Kitts & Nevis 161/C10
Olds, Alberta 182/D4
Olds, Iowa 229/K6
Old Saybrook, Conn. 210/F3
Old Saybrook•, Conn. 210/F3
Old Shawneetown, Ill. 222/E6
Oldsmar, Fla. 212/B2
Old Spring Hill, Ala. 195/C6
Old Sturbridge Village, Mass. 249/F4
Old Tampa (bay), Fla. 212/B3
Old Tappan, N.J. 273/C1
Old Town, Fla. 212/C2
Oldtown, Idaho 220/A1
Oldtown, Ky. 237/R4
Old Town, Maine 243/F6
Oldtown, Md. 245/D2
Old Trap, N.C. 281/T2
Olduvai Gorge (canyon), Tanzania 115/G4
Old Washington, Ohio 284/H5
Oldwick, N.J. 273/D2
Old Wives, Sask. 181/E5
Old Wives (lake), Sask. 181/E5
Old Woman (creek), Wyo. 319/H3
Olean, Mo. 261/G6
Olean, N.Y. 276/D6
O'Leary (peak), Ariz. 198/D3
O'Leary, Pr. Edward I. 168/D2
Olecko, Poland 47/F1
Oleiros, Portugal 33/B3
Olëkma (riv.), U.S.S.R. 48/N4
Olëkminsk, U.S.S.R. 48/N3
Olema, Calif. 204/H1
Olenegorsk, U.S.S.R. 52/D1
Olenek, U.S.S.R. 4/C4
Olenëk (riv.), U.S.S.R. 54/N3
Olënek, U.S.S.R. 48/M3
Olënek (bay), U.S.S.R. 48/N2
Olënek (riv.), U.S.S.R. 48/M3
Olentangy (riv.), Ohio 284/D4
Oléron (isl.), France 28/C5
Oleśnica, Poland 47/C3
Olesno, Poland 47/D3
Oleta, Okla. 288/R6
Olex, Oreg. 291/G2
Oley, Pa. 294/L5
Olga, N. Dak. 282/O2
Olga (Kata Tjuta) (mt.), North. Terr. 93/B8
Olga, Wash. 310/C2
Ölgiy (Ulegei), Mongolia 77/C2
Ølgod, Denmark 21/B6
Olha, Manitoba 179/B4
Olhão, Portugal 33/C4
Oliena, Italy 34/B4
Olifants (riv.), Mozambique 118/D4
Olifants (riv.), S. Africa 118/D4
Olimar, Uruguay 145/E3
Olimar Grande (riv.), Uruguay 145/E4
Olímpia, Brazil 135/B2
Olin, Iowa 229/L5
Olin, Ky. 237/N6
Olin, N.C. 281/H3
Olinda, Brazil 120/F3
Olinda, Brazil 132/H4
Olinda, Calif. 204/C3
Olinda, Victoria 97/K5
Oliva, Argentina 143/D3
Oliva, Spain 33/F3
Oliva de la Frontera, Spain 33/C3
Olivais, Portugal 33/A1
Olivar Alto, Chile 138/G5
Olivares, Cerro de (mt.), Argentina 143/B3
Olivares, Cerro de (mt.), Chile 138/B8
Olive, Mont. 262/L5
Olive, Okla. 288/O2
Olive Branch, Ill. 222/D6
Olive Branch, Miss. 256/E1
Olive Branch, Ohio 284/D10
Olive Hill, Ky. 237/P4
Olivehill, Tenn. 237/E10
Oliveira, Brazil 135/D2
Olivenza, Spain 33/C3
Oliver (dam), Ala. 195/J5
Oliver, Br. Col. 184/H5
Oliver, Georgia 217/J5
Oliver (dam), Georgia 217/B6
Oliver (lake), Georgia 217/B5
Oliver, Ind. 227/B8
Oliver (co.), N. Dak. 282/H5
Oliver, Pa. 294/C6
Oliver, Wis. 317/B2
Oliver Springs, Tenn. 237/N8
Olivet, Ill. 222/F4
Olivet, Kansas 232/G3
Olivet, Md. 245/N7
Olivet, Mich. 250/E6
Olivet, S. Dak. 298/O7
Olivet, Wis. 317/B6
Olivette, Mo. 261/O2
Olivia, Minn. 255/C6
Olivia, N.C. 281/L4
Olivier, La. 238/G7
Olivone, Switzerland 39/G3
Olkusz, Poland 47/D3
Olla, La. 238/F3
Ollachea, Peru 128/G9
Ollagüe (vol.), Bolivia 136/B7
Ollagüe, Chile 120/C5
Ollagüe, Chile 138/B3
Ollantaytambo, Peru 128/F9
Ollie, Iowa 229/J6
Ollon, Switzerland 39/D4
Olmedo, Spain 33/D2
Olmitz, Kansas 232/D3
Olmos, Peru 128/C5
Olmos Park, Texas 303/F8
Olmstead, Ky. 237/H7
Olmsted, Ill. 222/D6
Olmsted (co.), Minn. 255/F7
Olmsted Falls, Ohio 284/G9
Olmstedville, N.Y. 276/N3
Olmué, Chile 138/F2
Olney, Ill. 222/E5
Olney, Md. 245/K4
Olney, Mo. 261/K4
Olney, Mont. 262/B2
Olney, Okla. 288/O6
Olney, Oreg. 291/D1
Olney, Texas 303/F4
Olney Springs, Colo. 208/M6
Olofström, Sweden 18/J8
Oloh, Miss. 256/E8
Olomouc, Czech. 7/F4
Olomouc, Czech. 41/D2
Olonets, U.S.S.R. 52/D2
Olongapo, Philippines 82/C3
Oloron-Sainte-Marie, France 28/C6
Olot, Spain 33/H1
Olowalu, Hawaii 218/H2
Oloy (range), U.S.S.R. 48/R3
Olpe, Kansas 232/F3
Olsa (riv.), Austria 41/C3
Olsburg, Kansas 232/F2
Olst, Netherlands 27/J4
Olsztyn (prov.), Poland 47/E2
Olsztyn, Poland 7/G3
Olsztyn, Poland 4//E2
Olsztynek, Poland 47/E2
Olt (riv.), Romania 7/G4
Olt (riv.), Romania 45/G3
Olta, Argentina 143/C3
Olten, Switzerland 39/E2
Oltenița, Romania 45/H3
Olton, Texas 303/B3
Oltu, Turkey 63/J2
Olur, Turkey 63/K2
Olustee, Fla. 212/D1
Olustee (riv.), Fla. 212/D1
Olustee, Okla. 288/H5
Olutanga (isl.), Philippines 82/D7
Olutanga (isl.), Philippines 85/G4
Olvera, Spain 33/D4
Olvey, Ark. 202/E1
Olwampi (cape), China 77/K7
Olympia (isls.), Greece 45/E7
Olympia, Ky. 237/O4
Olympia (cap.), Wash. 146/F5
Olympia (cap.), Wash. 188/B1
Olympia (cap.), Wash. 310/C3
Olympia Fields, Ill. 222/B6
Olympian Village, Mo. 261/M6
Olympic (mts.), Wash. 310/B3
Olympic Nat'l Park, Wash. 188/A1
Olympic Nat'l Park, Wash. 310/B3
Olympic Valley, Calif. 204/E4
Olympus (mt.), Greece 45/F5
Olympus (mt.), Wash. 310/B3
Olyphant, Ark. 202/H3
Olyphant, Pa. 294/F7
Olyphic, N.C. 281/M7
Olyutorskiy (cape), U.S.S.R. 54/U4
Olyutorskiy (cape), U.S.S.R. 48/S4
Oma (cape), Japan 81/K3
Oma, Miss. 256/D7
Omagari, Japan 81/K4
Omagh (dist.), N. Ireland 17/G2
Omagh, N. Ireland 10/C3
Omagh, N. Ireland 17/G2
Omaguas, Peru 128/F5
Omaha, Ala. 195/H4
Omaha, Ark. 202/D1
Omaha (beach), France 28/C3
Omaha, Georgia 217/C6
Omaha, Ill. 222/E6
Omaha, Nebr. 188/G2
Omaha, Nebr. 146/J5
Omaha, Nebr. 264/J3
Omaha Ind. Res., Nebr. 264/H2
Omak, Wash. 310/F2
Omak (lake), Wash. 310/F2
Oman 2/M5
Oman 54/G8
OMAN 59/G6
Oman (gulf) 54/G7
Oman (gulf), Iran 59/G5
Oman (gulf), Iran 66/M8
Oman (gulf), Oman 59/G5
Oman (reg.), Oman 59/G5
Oman (gulf), U.A.E. 59/G5
Omar, W. Va. 312/C7
Omaruru, Namibia 118/B4
Omas, Peru 128/D9
Omatako (riv.), Namibia 118/B3
Omate, Peru 128/G11
Ombai (str.), Indonesia 85/H7
Omboué, Gabon 115/A4
Ombrone (riv.), Italy 34/C3
Ombúes de Lavalle, Uruguay 145/B4
Ombúes de Oribe, Uruguay 145/C4
Omdurman, Sudan 102/F3
Omdurman, Sudan 59/B6
Omdurman, Sudan 111/F4
Omega, Georgia 217/E8
Omega, Ind. 227/F4
Omega, Ohio 284/E7
Omega, Okla. 288/K3
Omemee, N. Dak. 282/K2
Omemee, Ontario 177/F3
Omena, Mich. 250/D3
Omeo, Victoria 97/D5
'Omer, Israel 65/B5
Omer, Mich. 250/F4
Ömerli, Turkey 63/J4
Omerville, Québec 172/E4
Ometepe (isl.), Nicaragua 154/E5
Ometepec, Mexico 150/K8
Omey (isl.), Ireland 17/A5
Omineca (mts.), Br. Col. 184/E2
Omineca (riv.), Br. Col. 184/E2
Omiš, Yugoslavia 45/C4
Omiya, Japan 81/O2
Ommaney (cape), Alaska 196/M2
Ommanney (bay), N.W. Terr. 187/H2
Omme (riv.), Denmark 21/B6
Ommen, Netherlands 27/J3
Ömnögovĭ, Mongolia 77/F3
Omø (isl.), Denmark 21/E7
Omo (riv.), Ethiopia 111/G6
Omoa, Honduras 154/C3
Omolon (riv.), U.S.S.R. 54/S3
Omolon (riv.), U.S.S.R. 4/C1
Omolon (riv.), U.S.S.R. 48/Q3
Omoloy (riv.), U.S.S.R. 48/O3
Omono (riv.), Japan 81/J4
Ompah, Ontario 177/H2
Omps, W. Va. 312/K4
Omro, Wis. 317/J7
Omsk, U.S.S.R. 54/J4
Omsk, U.S.S.R. 2/N3
Omsk, U.S.S.R. 48/H4
Omsukchan, U.S.S.R. 48/Q3
Omu, Japan 81/L1
Omura, Bonin Is., Japan 81/M3
Omura, Nagasaki, Japan 81/E7
Omurtag, Bulgaria 45/H4
Omuta, Japan 81/E7
Omutninsk, U.S.S.R. 48/F4
Omutninsk, U.S.S.R. 52/H3
Ona, Fla. 212/E4
Ona, W. Va. 312/B6
Onaga, Kansas 232/F2
Onagawa, Japan 81/K4
Onaka, S. Dak. 298/L3
Onalaska, Texas 303/J7
Onalaska, Wash. 310/C4
Onalaska, Wis. 317/D8
Onaman (lake), Ontario 177/H4
Onamia, Minn. 255/E4
Onancock, Va. 307/S5
Onangué (lake), Gabon 115/A4
Onanole, Manitoba 179/C4
Onaping Falls, Ontario 177/J5
Onaping Falls, Ontario 175/D3
Onaqui, Utah 304/B3
Onarga, Ill. 222/E3
Onawa, Iowa 229/A4
Onawa, Maine 243/E5
Onawa (lake), Maine 243/E5
Onaway, Idaho 220/B3
Onaway, Mich. 250/E3
Onchan, I. of Man 13/C3
Onchiota, N.Y. 276/M2
Oncócua, Angola 115/B7
Onda, Spain 33/F3
Ondangwa, Namibia 118/B3
Ondava (riv.), Czech. 41/F2
Ondjiva, Angola 102/D6
Ondjiva, Angola 114/C7
Ondo (state), Nigeria 106/F7
Ondo, Nigeria 106/F7
Öndörhaan (Undur Khan), Mongolia 77/G2
Öndörhaan, Mongolia 54/N5
Öndverdharnes (mt.), Iceland 21/A1
O'Neals, Calif. 204/F6
Oneco, Conn. 210/H2
Oneco, Fla. 212/D4
Onefour, Alberta 182/E5
Onega, U.S.S.R. 7/H2
Onega (lake), U.S.S.R. 7/H2
Onega (riv.), U.S.S.R. 7/H2
Onega, U.S.S.R. 52/E2
Onega, U.S.S.R. 48/D3
Onega (bay), U.S.S.R. 52/E2
Onega (lake), U.S.S.R. 48/D3
Onega (lake), U.S.S.R. 52/E2
Onega (riv.), U.S.S.R. 48/D3
Onega (riv.), U.S.S.R. 52/E2
Onego, W. Va. 312/H5
One Hundred and Fifty Mile House, Br. Col. 184/G4
One Hundred Mile House, Br. Col. 184/G4
Onehunga, N. Zealand 100/B1
Oneida, Ark. 202/J5
Oneida (co.), Idaho 220/F7
Oneida, Ill. 222/C2
Oneida, Iowa 229/L3
Oneida, Kansas 232/G2
Oneida, Ky. 237/O6
Oneida (co.), N.Y. 276/J4
Oneida, N.Y. 276/J4
Oneida (lake), N.Y. 276/J4
Oneida, Pa. 294/K4
Oneida, Tenn. 237/N7
Oneida (co.), Wis. 317/G4
Oneida, Wis. 317/K7
O'Neill, Nebr. 264/F2
Onekama, Mich. 250/C4
Oneonta, Ala. 195/E3
Oneonta, N.Y. 276/K6
One Tree Hill, N. Zealand 100/B1
Ong, Nebr. 264/G4
Ongjin, N. Korea 81/B5
Ongniud, China 77/J3
Ongole, India 68/E5
Onhaye, Belgium 27/F8
Oni, U.S.S.R. 52/F6
Onida, S. Dak. 298/K4
Onilahy (riv.), Madagascar 118/G4
Onima, Neth. Ant. 161/E8
Onion Lake, Sask. 181/B2
Onitsha, Nigeria 106/F7
Onitsha, Nigeria 102/C4
Onkaparinga (riv.), S. Australia 88/D8
Onkaparinga (riv.), S. Australia 94/B8
Onkivesi (lake), Finland 18/P5
Onley, Va. 307/S5
Only, Tenn. 237/F9
Ono, Calif. 204/C3
Ono, Japan 81/H6
Ono (riv.), Japan 81/E7
Ono, Pa. 294/J5
Onoda, Japan 81/E6
Onomea, Hawaii 218/J4
Onomichi, Japan 81/F6
Onon, Mongolia 77/H2
Onondaga, Mich. 250/E6
Onondaga (co.), N.Y. 276/H5
Onondaga Ind. Res., N.Y. 276/H5
Onota (lake), Mass. 249/A3
Onoto, Venezuela 124/F3
Onotoa (atoll), Kiribati 87/H6
Onoway, Alberta 182/C3
Onrusrivier, S. Africa 118/G7
Onset, Mass. 249/M6
Onslow, Australia 87/B8
Onslow, Iowa 229/M4
Onslow (co.), N.C. 281/P5
Onslow (bay), N.C. 281/P6
Onslow, W. Australia 88/B4
Onslow, W. Australia 92/A3
Onsŏng, N. Korea 81/E2
Onsted, Mich. 250/E6
Onstwedde, Netherlands 27/K2
Ontake (mt.), Japan 81/H6
ONTARIO 177
ONTARIO, NORTHERN 175
Ontario (prov.) 162/H5
Ontario (lake) 146/L5
Ontario (lake) 162/J7
Ontario, Calif. 204/D10
Ontario (prov.), Canada 146/K4
Ontario, Ind. 227/G1
Ontario, Iowa 229/F4
Ontario (lake), N.Y. 188/L2
Ontario (co.), N.Y. 276/F5
Ontario, N.Y. 276/F4
Ontario (lake), N.Y. 276/F3
Ontario, Ohio 284/E4
Ontario (lake), Ontario 177/G4
Ontario, Oreg. 291/K3
Ontario, Wis. 317/E8
Onteniente, Spain 33/F3
Onton, Ky. 237/G5
Ontonagon (co.), Mich. 250/F1
Ontonagon, Mich. 250/F1
Ontonagon (riv.), Mich. 250/G1
Ontonagon Ind. Res., Mich. 250/F1
Ontong Java (isl.), Solomon Is. 87/G6
Ontong Java (isls.), Solomon Is. 86/D2
Onverwacht, Suriname 131/D3
Onward, Ind. 227/E3
Onward, Miss. 256/C5
Onycha, Ala. 195/F8
Onyx, Ark. 202/D4
Onyx, Calif. 204/G8
Oobagooma, W. Australia 92/D2
Oodnadatta, Australia 87/D8
Oodnadatta, S. Australia 88/E5
Oodnadatta, S. Australia 94/D2
Ookala, Hawaii 218/J4
Oola, Ireland 17/E6
Ooldea, S. Australia 94/B4
Oolitic, Ind. 227/E7
Oologah, Okla. 288/P2
Oologah (lake), Okla. 288/P1
Ooltewah, Tenn. 237/M10
Oona River, Br. Col. 184/C3
Oosterwolde, Netherlands 27/J2
Oostanaula, Georgia 217/B1
Oostanaula (riv.), Georgia 217/B2
Oostburg, Netherlands 27/C6
Oostburg, Wis. 317/L8
Oostende (Ostend), Belgium 27/B6
Oosterend, Netherlands 27/G2
Oosterhout, Netherlands 27/F5
Oostkamp, Belgium 27/C6
Oostmahorn, Netherlands 27/J2
Oost-Vlieland, Netherlands 27/F2
Oostzaan, Netherlands 27/C4
Oostzaan Polder, Netherlands 27/B4
Ootacamund, India 68/D6
Ootmarsum, Netherlands 27/K4
Ootsa (lake), Br. Col. 184/D3
Ootsa Lake, Br. Col. 184/E3
Oozewekwun, Manitoba 179/B5
Opal, Alberta 182/D3
Opal, S. Dak. 298/D4
Opal, Wyo. 319/B4
Opala, Zaire 115/D4
Opal Cliffs, Calif. 204/K4
Opa Locka, Fla. 212/B4
Opalton, Queensland 95/B4
Opari, Sudan 111/F7
Oparino, U.S.S.R. 52/G3
Opasatika, Ontario 177/J5
Opasatika, Ontario 175/D3
Opasatika (riv.), Ontario 175/D3
Opatija, Yugoslavia 45/A3
Opatów, Poland 47/E3
Opava, Czech. 41/E2
Opdyke, Ill. 222/E5
Opelika, Ala. 195/H5
Opelousas, La. 238/G5
Opeongo (lake), Ontario 177/F2
Opfikon, Switzerland 39/G2
Opheim, Ill. 222/C2
Opheim, Mont. 262/K2
Ophir, Alaska 196/G2
Ophir, Colo. 208/D7
Ophir, Oreg. 291/C5
Ophir, Utah 304/B3
Opihikao, Hawaii 218/K6
Opinaca (riv.), Que. 162/J5
Opinaca (riv.), Québec 174/B2
Opine, Ala. 195/C7
Opinnagau (riv.), Ontario 175/D2
Opiscotéo (lake), Québec 174/D2
Opochka, U.S.S.R. 52/C3
Opoco, Bolivia 136/B6
Opoczno, Poland 47/E3
Opole, Minn. 255/D5
Opole (prov.), Poland 47/C3
Opole, Poland 47/C3
Opolis, Kansas 232/H4
Oporto (Porto) (dist.), Portugal 33/B2
Oporto (Porto), Portugal 33/B2
Opotiki, N. Zealand 100/F3
Opp, Ala. 195/F8
Oppdal, Norway 18/F5
Oppeln, Poland 47/C3
Oppelo, Ark. 202/E3
Oppenheim, Germany 22/C4
Oppland (co.), Norway 18/F6
Opportunity, Wash. 310/H3
Oppy, Ky. 237/S5
Optima, Okla. 288/D1
Optima (lake), Okla. 288/D1
Opua, N. Zealand 100/D1
Opunake, N. Zealand 100/D3
Opuntia (lake), Sask. 181/C4
Opwijk, Belgium 27/E7
Opuwo, Namibia 118/A3
'Oqair, Saudi Arabia 59/E4
Oquawka, Ill. 222/C3
Oquossoc, Maine 243/B6
Ora, Ind. 227/D2
Ora, Miss. 256/E7
Ora, S.C. 296/D2
Oracabessa, Jamaica 158/J5
Oracle, Ariz. 198/E6
Oradea, Romania 7/G4
Oradea, Romania 45/E2
Oradell, N.J. 273/B1
Oradell (res.), N.J. 273/B1
Orai, India 68/D3
Oraibi Wash (dry riv.), Ariz. 198/E3
Oral, S. Dak. 298/C7
Oran, Algeria 106/D1
Oran, Algeria 102/B1
Oran, Iowa 229/J3
Oran, Mo. 261/N8
Orange (riv.) 2/K7
Orange (riv.) 102/D7
Orange, Australia 87/E9
Orange (riv.), Botswana 118/B5
Orange (cape), Brazil 132/D1
Orange (co.), Calif. 204/H10
Orange, Calif. 204/D11
Orange•, Conn. 210/C3
Orange (co.), Fla. 212/E3
Orange, Fla. 212/B1
Orange (lake), Fla. 212/D2
Orange, France 28/F5
Orange, Georgia 217/D2
Orange (co.), Ind. 227/E7
Orange, Ind. 227/G5
Orange, Mass. 249/E2
Orange•, Mass. 249/E2
Orange (canal), Netherlands 27/K3
Orange•, N.H. 268/D4
Orange, N.J. 273/B2
Orange, N.S. Wales 88/H6

nge, N.S. Wales 97/E3
nge (co.), N.Y. 276/M8
nge (co.), N.C. 281/L2
nge, Ohio 284/J9
nge (riv.), S. Africa 118/B5
nge (mts.), Suriname 131/D4
nge, Texas 303/L7
nge (butte), Utah 304/D5
nge (co.), Vt. 268/C3
nge •, Vt. 268/C3
nge (co.), Va. 307/M4
nge, Va. 307/M4
nge Beach, Ala. 195/C10
ngeburg, N.Y. 276/K8
ngeburg (co.), S.C. 296/F5
ngeburg, S.C. 296/F4
nge City, Fla. 212/D2
nge City, Iowa 229/A2
nge Cove, Calif. 204/F7
ngedale, Nova Scotia 168/G3
nge Free State (prov.), S. Africa 102/E7
nge Free State (prov.), S. Africa 118/D5
nge Grove, Miss. 256/H10
nge Grove, Texas 303/F10
nge Hill, St. Vin. & Grens. 161/A8
nge Lake, Fla. 212/D2
nge Park, Fla. 212/E1
nge Springs, Fla. 212/E2
ngeville, Ill. 222/D1
ngeville, Ind. 227/D7
ngeville, Mich. 250/D6
ngeville, Ohio 284/J3
ngeville, Ontario 177/D4
ngeville, Pa. 294/K3
ngeville, Utah 304/C4
anienburg, Germany 22/E2
anjemund, Namibia 102/D7
anjemund, Namibia 118/B5
anjestad (cap.), Aruba, Neth. Ant. 161/D10
anjestad, Neth. Ant. 156/D4
anmore, Ireland 17/D5
apa, Botswana 118/D4
as, Philippines 82/E4
astie, Romania 45/F3
ava (res.), Czech. 41/E2
ava (riv.), Czech. 41/E2
ava (res.), Poland 47/D4
aville, Ill. 222/D6
avita, Romania 45/E3
(riv.), France 28/E6
e, Switzerland 39/C3
e (riv.), Switzerland 39/C3
etello, Italy 34/C3
isonia, Pa. 294/C6
igo (riv.), Spain 33/D1
ost, Victoria 88/H7
ost, Victoria 97/E5
byhus, Sweden 18/K6
ca, Alaska 196/J2
cadia, Sask. 181/J4
cas (isl.), Wash. 310/C2
cera, Spain 33/E3
chard, Colo. 208/L2
chard, Iowa 229/H2
chard, Nebr. 264/F2
chard Beach, Md. 245/M4
chard Hill, Georgia 217/D4
chard Lake, Mich. 250/F6
chard Mesa, Colo. 208/C4
chard Park, N.Y. 276/C5
chards, Wash. 310/C5
chard Valley, Wyo. 319/H4
chid, Fla. 212/F4
chid, Va. 307/N5
chy (mt.), Scotland 15/D4
cotuna, Peru 128/E8
cutt, Calif. 204/E9
cuttville, Conn. 210/F1
d (mt.), Ariz. 198/D5
d (riv.), Australia 87/C7
d, Nebr. 264/F3
d (riv.), W. Australia 88/D3
d (mt.), W. Australia 92/D2
d (riv.), W. Australia 92/E2
denes, Spain 33/B1
derville, Utah 304/B6
doqui, Argentina 143/F7
dos (mt.), China 77/G4
d River, W. Australia 92/E2
du (prov.), Turkey 63/G2
du, Turkey 59/C1
du, Turkey 63/G2
dway, Iowa 229/J6
dway, S. Dak. 298/N2
e City, Texas 303/K5
AEGON 291
egon 188/B2
egon (co.), Mo. 261/K9
egon, Mo. 261/B2
egon (inlet), N.C. 281/U3
egon, Ohio 284/D2
egon Canyon (creek), Oreg. 291/K5
egon City, Calif. US 146/F5
egon, Wis. 317/H10
egon Caves Nat'l Mon., Oreg. 291/C6
egon City, Oreg. 188/B1

Oregon City, Oreg. 291/B2
Oregon Dunes Nat'l Rec. Area, Oreg. 291/C4
Oregonia, Ohio 284/B7
Öregrund, Sweden 13/L6
Orel, U.S.S.R. 7/H3
Orel, U.S.S.R. 52/E4
Orel, U.S.S.R. 48/D4
Orellana, Peru 128/E3
Orellana la Vieja, Spain 33/D3
Orem, Utah 304/C3
Orenburg, U.S.S.R. 7/K3
Orenburg, U.S.S.R. 8/F4
Orenburg, U.S.S.R. 52/J4
Orenco, Oreg. 291/A2
Orense (prov.), Spain 33/C1
Orense, Spain 33/C1
Orense, Spain 7/D4
Orestes, Ind. 227/F4
Orestías, Greece 45/H5
Øresund (sound), Denmark 21/F6
Øresund (sound), Denmark 18/H9
Øresund (sound), Sweden 18/H9
Oreti (riv.), N. Zealand 100/B6
Oretta, La. 238/D5
Orewa, N. Zealand 100/E2
Orford •, N.H. 268/C4
Orford, Tasmania 99/D4
Orford Ness (prom.), England 13/J5
Orfordville, N.H. 268/C4
Orfordville, Wis. 317/H10
Organ, N. Mex. 274/C6
Organabo, Fr. Guiana 131/E3
Organ Pipe Cactus Nat'l Mon., Ariz. 198/C6
Órgãos (range), Brazil 135/E3
Orgas, W. Va. 312/C6
Orgaz, Spain 33/E3
Orgeyev, U.S.S.R. 52/C5
Orhaneli, Turkey 63/C3
Orhangazi, Turkey 63/C2
Orhon Gol (riv.), Mongolia 77/F2
Oria, Spain 33/E4
Orick, Calif. 204/A2
Orient, Ill. 222/E6
Orient, Iowa 229/E6
Orient •, Maine 243/H4
Orient, N.Y. 276/R8
Orient (pt.), N.Y. 275/R8
Orient, Ohio 284/D7
Orient, S. Dak. 298/L4
Orient, Wash. 310/C2
Orienta, Okla. 288/J2
Oriental, Cordillera (range), Bolivia 136/C5
Oriental, Cordillera (range), Colombia 126/D5
Oriental, Cordillera (range), Dom. Rep. 158/F6
Oriental, Mexico 150/O1
Oriental, N.C. 281/R4
Oriental, Cordillera (range), Peru 128/H10
Oriental Mindoro (prov.), Philippines 82/C4
Orihuela, Spain 33/F3
Orihvesi (lake), Finland 18/Q5
Orillia, Ontario 177/F3
Orin, Wash. 310/H2
Orin, Wyo. 319/G3
Orinda, Calif. 204/J3
Orinoca, Bolivia 136/B6
Orinoco (riv.) 120/C3
Orinoco (riv.) 2/F5
Orinoco (riv.), Colombia 126/G5
Orinoco (delta), Venezuela 120/C2
Orinoco (delta), Venezuela 124/H3
Orinoco (riv.), Venezuela 124/G3
Oriole, Md. 245/P8
Orion, Ala. 195/F7
Orion, Alberta 182/E5
Orion, Ill. 222/C2
Oriska, N. Dak. 282/P6
Oriskany, N.Y. 276/K4
Oriskany, Va. 307/L5
Oriskany Falls, N.Y. 276/J5
Orissa (state), India 68/E5
Oristano, Italy 34/B5
Oristano (gulf), Italy 34/B5
Orituco (riv.), Venezuela 124/E3
Oriximiná, Brazil 132/C3
Orizaba, Mexico 145/J8
Orizaba, Mexico 150/P2
Orizaba (Citlaltépet) (mt.), Mexico 150/O2
Órjiva, Spain 33/E4
Orkanger, Norway 8/F5
Orkény, Hungary 41/E3
Orkney, Sask. 181/J6
Orkney (islands area), Scotland 15/E1
Orkney (isls.), Scotland 7/D3
Orkney (isls.), Scotland 15/F1
Orkney (isls.), Scotland 10/E1
Orkney (trad. co.), Scotland 15/B4
Orla, Texas 303/D10
Orland, Calif. 204/C4
Orland, Ind. 227/G
Orland, Maine 243/F6
Orland •, Maine 243/F6
Orland Hills, Ill. 222/B6
Orlândia, Brazil 135/C2
Orlando, Fla. 146/H7
Orlando, Fla. 188/H5
Orlando, Fla. 212/E3
Orlando, Ky. 237/J6
Orlando, Okla. 288/M2
Orlando, W. Va. 312/E5
Orland Park, Ill. 222/B6
Orleães, Brazil 132/D10
Orléanais (trad. prov.), France 29
Orleans, Calif. 204/B2
Orléans, France 7/E4
Orléans, France 28/D3
Orleans, Ind. 227/D7
Orleans, Iowa 229/C2
Orleans (par.), La. 238/L6

Orleans, Mass. 249/O5
Orleans •, Mass. 249/O5
Orleans, Minn. 255/B2
Orleans, Nebr. 264/E4
Orleans (co.), N.Y. 276/D4
Orleans, Ontario 177/J3
Orléans (isl.), Québec 172/F3
Orleans (co.), Vt. 268/C2
Orleans, Vt. 268/C2
Orleans Cross Roads, W. Va. 312/K3
Orléansville (El Asnam), Algeria 106/E1
Orlice (riv.), Czech. 41/D1
Orlická (res.), Czech. 41/C2
Orlinda, Tenn. 237/H7
Orlová, Czech. 41/E2
Orly, France 28/B2
Orma, W. Va. 312/D5
Ormara, Pakistan 59/J4
Ormara, Pakistan 68/A3
Orme, Tenn. 237/K10
Ormea, Italy 34/A2
Ormiston, Sask. 181/F6
Ormoc, Philippines 82/E5
Ormoc (bay), Philippines 82/E5
Ormond Beach, Fla. 212/E2
Ormond-by-the-Sea, Fla. 212/E2
Ormont-Dessus, Switzerland 39/D4
Ormsby, Minn. 255/D7
Ormsby, Pa. 294/E2
Ormskirk, England 10/F2
Ormskirk, England 13/G2
Ormstown, Québec 172/D4
Orne (dept.), France 28/C3
Orne (riv.), France 28/C3
Orneta, Poland 47/E1
Ornö (isl.), Sweden 18/J2
Örnsköldsvik, Sweden 18/L5
Orobayaya, Bolivia 136/D3
Orocovis, P. Rico 161/C2
Orocué, Colombia 126/E5
Orofino, Idaho 220/B3
Orofino (creek), Idaho 220/C3
Oro Grande, Calif. 204/H9
Orogrande, Idaho 220/C4
Orogrande, N. Mex. 274/D6
Orohena (mt.), Fr. Poly. 86/T13
Oro Ingenio, Bolivia 136/C7
Oroluk (atoll), Micronesia 87/F5
Oromocto, New Bruns. 170/D3
Oromocto (lake), New Bruns. 170/C3
Oromocto (riv.), New Bruns. 170/D3
Oron, Israel 65/C6
Oron, Nigeria 106/F8
Orona (Hull) (isl.), Kiribati 87/J6
Orondo, Wash. 310/E3
Orongorongo (riv.), N. Zealand 100/B3
Oron-la-Ville, Switzerland 39/C3
Orono (isl.), Kiribati 87/L5
Orono, Maine 243/F6
Orono •, Maine 243/F6
Orono, Minn. 255/F5
Oronoco, Minn. 255/F6
Oronogo, Mo. 261/D8
Oronsay (isl.), Scotland 15/B4
Orontes (riv.), Syria 59/C2
Orontes (riv.), Syria 63/G5
Oropesa, Spain 33/D3
Oropuche (riv.), Trin. & Tob. 161/N12
Oroqen, China 77/K1
Oroquieta, Philippines 85/G4
Oroquieta, Philippines 82/D6
Orosei (gulf), Italy 34/B4
Orosháza, Hungary 41/F3
Orosi, Calif. 204/F7
Oroszlány, Hungary 41/E3
Orote (pen.), Guam 86/K7
Orotina, C. Rica 154/E6
Orotukan, U.S.S.R. 48/O3
Orovada, Nev. 266/D1
Oro Valley, Ariz. 198/E6
Oroville, Calif. 204/D4
Oroville (lake), Calif. 204/D4
Oroville, Wash. 310/F2
Orozco, Cuba 158/B1
Orpha, Wyo. 319/G3
Orr, Minn. 255/F2
Orr, N. Dak. 282/P3
Orr, Okla. 288/M6
Orrefors, Sweden 18/J8
Orrick, Mo. 261/D4
Orrin, N. Dak. 282/K3
Orrin (riv.), Scotland 15/D3
Orrington •, Maine 243/F6
Orroroo, S. Australia 94/F5
Orrs Island, Maine 243/D8
Orrstown, Pa. 294/G5
Orrtanna, Pa. 294/G5
Orrum, N.C. 281/L6
Orrville, Ala. 195/D6
Orrville, Ohio 284/G4
Orrville, Ontario 177/E2
Orsa, Sweden 18/J6
Orsainville, Québec 172/H3
Orsha, U.S.S.R. 7/G3
Orsha, U.S.S.R. 52/C4
Orsières, Switzerland 39/D4
Orsk, U.S.S.R. 7/K3
Orsk, U.S.S.R. 48/F4
Orsk, U.S.S.R. 52/J4
Orson, Pa. 294/M2
Orsonnens, Switzerland 39/D3
Orşova, Romania 45/F3
Ørsted, Denmark 21/D5
Orta, Turkey 63/E2
Ortaca, Turkey 63/C4
Ortakaraviran, Turkey 63/E4
Ortaköy, Çorum, Turkey 63/F2
Ortaköy, Niğde, Turkey 63/F3
Ortega, Colombia 126/C6
Ortegal (cape), Spain 33/B1
Orteguaza (riv.), Colombia 126/C7
Orthez, France 28/C6
Ortigueira, Spain 33/C1
Orting, Wash. 310/C3

Ortiz, Colo. 208/H8
Ortiz, Mexico 150/D2
Ortiz, Venezuela 124/E3
Ortles (range), Italy 34/C1
Ortley, S. Dak. 298/P3
Ortoire (riv.), Trin. & Tob. 161/B11
Ortón (riv.), Bolivia 136/B2
Ortona, Italy 34/E3
Ortonville, Mich. 250/F6
Ortonville, Minn. 255/B5
Oruro (dept.), Bolivia 136/A6
Oruro, Bolivia 120/B7
Oruro, Bolivia 136/B5
Oruzgan (Hazar Qadam), Afghanistan 68/B2
Orvieto, Italy 34/D3
Orville, Ky. 237/M4
Orviston, Pa. 294/H3
Orwell, N.Y. 276/J3
Orwell, Ohio 284/J2
Orwell •, Vt. 268/A4
Orwigsburg, Pa. 294/K4
Oryakhovo, Bulgaria 45/F4
Or Yehuda, Israel 65/B4
Orzesze, Poland 47/A4
Orzysz, Poland 47/E2
Osa (riv.), Nigeria 106/F7
Osa, U.S.S.R. 52/J3
Osage (riv.) 188/H3
Osage, Ark. 202/D1
Osage, Iowa 229/H2
Osage (co.), Kansas 232/G3
Osage, Minn. 255/C4
Osage (co.), Mo. 261/J6
Osage (co.), Mo. 261/J6
Osage (co.), Okla. 288/O1
Osage, Okla. 288/O2
Osage, Sask. 181/H6
Osage, W. Va. 312/F3
Osage, Wyo. 319/H2
Osage Beach, Mo. 261/G6
Osage City, Kansas 232/G3
Osage Ind. Res., Okla. 288/O1
Osaka (pref.), Japan 81/J8
Osaka, Japan 2/R4
Osaka, Japan 54/P6
Osaka, Japan 81/J8
Osaka (bay), Japan 81/H8
Osakis, Minn. 255/C5
Osasco, Brazil 135/C3
Osawatomie, Kansas 232/H3
Osborn, Miss. 256/G3
Osborn, Mo. 261/D3
Osborn, S.C. 296/G6
Osborne (co.), Kansas 232/D2
Osborne, Kansas 232/D2
Osborne, Pa. 294/B4
Osbornsville, N.J. 273/E3
Osburn, Idaho 220/B2
Oscar, Fr. Guiana 131/E4
Oscar, La. 238/H5
Oscar, Okla. 288/L7
Oscarville, Alaska 196/F2
Osceola (co.), Fla. 212/E3
Osceola, Ind. 227/E1
Osceola, Iowa 229/B2
Osceola, Iowa 229/F6
Osceola (co.), Mich. 250/D5
Osceola, Mo. 261/E6
Osceola, Nebr. 264/G3
Osceola (mt.), N.H. 268/E3
Osceola, N.Y. 276/J3
Osceola, Pa. 294/H2
Osceola, S. Dak. 298/O5
Osceola, Wis. 317/A5
Osceola Mills, Pa. 294/H4
Oschatz, Germany 22/E3
Oschersleben, Germany 22/D2
Oscoda (co.), Mich. 250/E4
Oscoda, Mich. 250/F4
Oscura (mts.), N. Mex. 274/C5
Oscuro, N. Mex. 274/C5
Osel (Saaremaa) (isl.), U.S.S.R. 52/B3
Osgood, Ind. 227/G6
Osgood, Mo. 261/F2
Osgood, Ohio 284/A5
Osgoode, Ontario 177/J2
Osh, U.S.S.R. 54/J5
Osh, U.S.S.R. 48/H5
Osha (peak), N. Mex. 274/C4
Oshakat, Namibia 118/B3
Oshawa, Ontario 177/F4
Oshikango, Namibia 118/A3
O-Shima (isl.), Japan 81/J6
Oshkosh, Nebr. 264/B3
Oshkosh, Wis. 188/J2
Oshkosh, Wis. 317/J8
Oshnoviyeh, Iran 66/D2
Oshogbo, Nigeria 102/C4
Oshogbo, Nigeria 100/C1
Oshoto, Wyo. 319/G1
Oshtoran Kuh (mt.), Iran 66/F4
Oshwe, Zaire 115/C4
Osierfield, Georgia 217/F7
Osijek, Yugoslavia 7/F4
Osijek, Yugoslavia 45/D3
Osimo, Italy 34/D3
Osipenko (Berdyansk), U.S.S.R. 52/E5
Osipovichi, U.S.S.R. 52/C4
Oskaloosa, Iowa 229/H6
Oskaloosa, Iowa 188/H2
Oskaloosa, Kansas 232/G2
Oskaloosa, Mo. 261/D7
Oskarshamn, Sweden 18/K8
Oskélanéo, Québec 174/C3
Oslany, Czech. 41/D2
Osler, Sask. 181/E3
Oslo, Minn. 255/A2
Oslo (city county), Norway 18/D3
Oslo (cap.), Norway 2/K2
Oslo (cap.), Norway 18/D3
Oslofjord (fjord), Norway 18/D4
Osmanabad, India 68/D5
Osmancık, Turkey 63/F2

Osmaneli, Turkey 63/D2
Osmaniye, Turkey 63/G4
Osmond, Nebr. 264/G2
Osnabrock, N. Dak. 282/O2
Osnabrück, Germany 22/C2
Osnaburgh House, Ontario 175/B2
Oso, Wash. 310/D2
Osogna, Switzerland 39/H4
Osorno, Chile 120/B7
Osorno, Chile 138/D3
Osorno, Spain 33/D1
Osoyoos, Br. Col. 184/H5
Osoyoos (lake), Wash. 310/F1
Ospino, Venezuela 124/D3
Osprey (reef), 95/C2
Osprey, Fla. 212/D4
Osprey (reef), Queensland 88/H2
Oss, Netherlands 27/H5
Ossa, Serra da (mts.), Portugal 33/C3
Ossa (mt.), Tasmania 88/H8
Ossa (mt.), Tasmania 99/C3
Ossabaw (isl.), Georgia 217/K7
Ossabaw (sound), Georgia 217/K7
Osse (riv.), Nigeria 106/F7
Osseo, Mich. 250/E7
Osseo, Minn. 255/G5
Osseo, Wis. 317/D6
Ossian, Ind. 227/G3
Ossian, Iowa 229/K2
Ossineke, Mich. 250/F4
Ossining, N.Y. 276/N8
Ossipee, N.H. 268/E4
Ossipee (lake), N.H. 268/E4
Ossipee (mts.), N.H. 268/E4
Ossipee (riv.), N.H. 268/F4
Ossokmanuan (res.), Newf. 166/B3
Ostashkov, U.S.S.R. 52/D3
Oste (riv.), Germany 22/C2
Osteen, Fla. 212/E3
Ostend, Belgium 27/B6
Osterburg, Pa. 294/E5
Österdalälven (riv.), Sweden 18/H6
Osterdock, Iowa 229/L3
Östergötland (co.), Sweden 18/J7
Osterholz-Scharmbeck, Germany 22/C2
Osterode am Harz, Germany 22/D3
Östersund, Sweden 7/F2
Östersund, Sweden 18/J5
Osterville, Mass. 249/N6
Øster Vrå, Denmark 21/D3
Osterwick, Manitoba 179/D5
Østfold (co.), Norway 18/G7
Osthammar, Sweden 18/L6
Ostia Antica, Italy 34/F7
Ostrander, Minn. 255/F7
Ostrander, Ohio 284/D5
Ostrava, Czech. 7/F4
Ostrava, Czech. 41/E2
Ostróda, Poland 47/D2
Ostrogozhsk, U.S.S.R. 48/D4
Ostrogozhsk, U.S.S.R. 52/E4
Ostroł eka (prov.), Poland 47/E2
Ostroł eka, Poland 47/E2
Ostrov, Czech. 41/B1
Ostrov, U.S.S.R. 52/C3
Ostrowiec Świę tokrzyski, Poland 47/E3
Ostrów Mazowiecka, Poland 47/E2
Ostrów Wielkopolski, Poland 47/C3
Ostrzeszów, Poland 47/C3
Ostuni, Italy 34/F4
O'Sullivan (dam), Wash. 310/F4
Osům (riv.), Bulgaria 45/G4
Osumi (isls.), Japan 81/E8
Osumi (pen.), Japan 81/E8
Osumi (str.), Japan 81/E8
Osuna, Spain 33/D4
Oswaldtwistle, England 13/H1
Oswayo, Pa. 294/G2
Oswegatchie, N.Y. 276/K2
Oswegatchie (riv.), N.Y. 276/K2
Oswego, Ill. 222/E2
Oswego, Ind. 227/F2
Oswego, Kansas 232/G4
Oswego, Mont. 262/L2
Oswego (co.), N.J. 273/E4
Oswego (co.), N.Y. 276/H4
Oswego, N.Y. 276/G4
Oswego, N.Y. 276/H4
Oswego, N.Y. 188/L2
Oswego, S.C. 296/G3
Oswestry, England 10/E4
Oswestry, England 13/E5
Oświę cim, Poland 47/D3
Osyka, Miss. 256/D8
Ota, Japan 81/J5
Otago (harb.), N. Zealand 100/C6
Otago (pen.), N. Zealand 100/C6
Otahuhu, N. Zealand 100/C1
Otaki, N. Zealand 100/E3
Otakine (mt.), Japan 81/K5
Otaru, Japan 81/K2
Otautau, N. Zealand 100/B7
Otava (riv.), Czech. 41/B2
Otavalo, Ecuador 128/C2
Otavi, Namibia 118/B3
Otawara, Japan 81/K5
O. T. Downs, North. Terr. 93/D4
Oteen, N.C. 281/E3
Otego, N.Y. 276/K6
Otematata, N. Zealand 100/B6
Otero (co.), Colo. 208/M7
Otero (co.), N. Mex. 274/D6
Othello, Wash. 310/F4
Otho, Iowa 229/E4
Oti (riv.), Ghana 106/E7
Oti (riv.), Togo 106/E7
Oti (riv.), Burkina Faso 106/E7
Otira, N. Zealand 100/C5
Otis, Colo. 208/O2
Otis, Ind. 227/D1
Otis, Kansas 232/C3
Otis, La. 238/E4
Otis •, Mass. 249/B4
Otis (res.), Mass. 249/B4

Otis, N. Mex. 274/E6
Otis, Oreg. 291/D2
Otis, Québec 172/G1
Otis A.F.B., Mass. 249/M6
Otisco, Ind. 227/F7
Otisco, Minn. 255/E7
Otisco (lake), N.Y. 276/H5
Otisfield, Maine 243/B7
Otisfield •, Maine 243/B7
Otish (mts.), Québec 174/C2
Otis Orchards-East Farms, Wash. 310/H3
Otisville, Mich. 250/F5
Otisville, N.Y. 276/L8
Otjiwarongo, Namibia 102/D7
Otjiwarongo, Namibia 118/B4
Otley, Iowa 229/G6
Oto, Iowa 229/B4
Otoe (co.), Nebr. 264/H4
Otoe, Nebr. 264/H4
Otofuke, Japan 81/L2
Otog, China 77/G4
Otorohanga, N. Zealand 100/E3
Otoskwin (riv.), Ontario 175/B2
Otra (riv.), Norway 18/E7
Otrabanda, Neth. Ant. 161/F9
Otradnyy, U.S.S.R. 52/H4
Otranto (str.), Albania 45/D5
Otranto, Iowa 229/H2
Otranto, Italy 34/G4
Otranto (str.), Italy 34/G5
Otsego (co.), Mich. 250/E3
Otsego, Mich. 250/D6
Otsego (lake), Mich. 250/E4
Otsego (co.), N.Y. 276/L5
Otsego (lake), N.Y. 276/L5
Otsego, Ohio 284/G5
Otsego Lake, Mich. 250/E4
Otselic, N.Y. 276/J5
Otsu, Japan 81/J7
Otta, Norway 18/F6
Ottauquechee (riv.), Vt. 268/C4
Ottawa (cap.), Canada 2/F3
Ottawa (cap.), Canada 146/L5
Ottawa (cap.), Canada 162/J6
Ottawa (riv.), Canada 146/L5
Ottawa (riv.), Canada 162/J6
Ottawa, Ill. 222/E2
Ottawa (co.), Kansas 232/E2
Ottawa, Kansas 232/G3
Ottawa (co.), Mich. 250/C6
Ottawa, Minn. 255/E6
Ottawa (isls.), N.W.T. 146/K4
Ottawa (isls.), N.W.T. 162/H4
Ottawa (isls.), N.W. Terr. 187/K4
Ottawa (co.), Ohio 284/D3
Ottawa, Ohio 284/B3
Ottawa (co.), Okla. 288/S1
Ottawa (cap.), Canada, Ontario 177/J2
Ottawa (riv.), Ontario 175/E3
Ottawa (riv.), Ontario 177/H2
Ottawa (riv.), Québec 172/J3
Ottawa (riv.), Québec 174/B3
Ottawa Beach, Mich. 250/C6
Ottawa-Carleton (reg. munic.), Ontario 177/J2
Ottawa Hills, Ohio 284/C2
Ottawa Lake, Mich. 250/F7
Otter (isl.), Alaska 196/D3
Otter (isl.), Alberta 182/B1
Otter, Mont. 262/K5
Otter (creek), Utah 304/C2
Otter (creek), Utah 304/C2
Otter (creek), Vt. 268/A3
Otterbein, Ind. 227/C4
Otterburne, Manitoba 179/E5
Otterburn Park, Québec 172/D4
Otter Creek, Fla. 212/D2
Otter Creek, Maine 243/G7
Otter Creek (riv.), Utah 304/C5
Otter Lake, Mich. 250/F5
Otterlo, Netherlands 27/H4
Otterøya (isl.), Norway 18/E5
Otter River, Mass. 249/F2
Otter Rock, Oreg. 291/C3
Otter Tail (co.), Minn. 255/C4
Ottertail, Minn. 255/C4
Otter Tail (lake), Minn. 255/C4
Otter Tail (riv.), Minn. 255/B4
Otterup, Denmark 21/D7
Otterville, Ill. 222/C4
Otterville, Iowa 229/K3
Otterville, Mo. 261/G5
Otterville, Ontario 177/D5
Ottery Saint Mary, England 13/D7
Ottery Saint Mary, England 10/E5
Otthon, Sask. 181/J4
Ottleys (creek), N.S. Wales 97/F1
Otto, Ind. 227/G7
Otto, Mo. 261/M6
Otto, N.Y. 276/C6
Otto, N.C. 281/C4
Otto (fjord), N.W. Terr. 187/K1
Otto, Wyo. 319/D1
Ottosen, Iowa 229/E3
Ottoville, Ohio 284/B4
Ottsville, Pa. 294/M5
Ottumwa, Iowa 188/H2
Ottumwa, Iowa 229/J6
Ottumwa, S. Dak. 298/G5
Otumba de Gómez Farías, Mexico 150/M1
Otuquis (riv.), Bolivia 136/F6
Otuzco, Peru 128/C5
Otway (bay), Chile 138/D10
Otway (sound), Chile 138/E10
Otway (riv.), Victoria 88/G7
Otway (cape), Victoria 88/G7
Otwell, Ind. 227/C8
Otwell, Ind. 227/C8
Otwock, Poland 47/E2
Ötztal Alps (mts.), Austria 41/A3
Ötztal Alps (range), Italy 34/C1
Ou, Nam (riv.), Laos 72/D2
Ouachita (riv.) 188/H4
Ouachita (co.), Ark. 202/E6

Ouachita, Ark. 202/E6
Ouachita (lake), Ark. 202/C4
Ouachita (mts.), Ark. 202/B4
Ouachita (riv.), Ark. 202/E7
Ouachita (par.), La. 238/F2
Ouachita (riv.), La. 238/F1
Ouachita (mts.), Okla. 288/R5
Ouadane, Mauritania 106/B4
Ouadda, Cent. Afr. Rep. 115/D2
Ouagadougou (cap.), Burkina Faso 106/D6
Ouagadougou (cap.), Burkina Faso 102/B3
Ouahigouya, Burkina Faso 106/D6
Ouahigouya, Burkina Faso 102/B3
Oualata, Mauritania 106/C5
Ouallene, Algeria 106/E4
Ouanaminthe, Haiti 158/C5
Ouanary, Fr. Guiana 131/F3
Ouanda Djalle, Cent. Afr. Rep. 115/D2
Ouango, Cent. Afr. Rep. 115/D3
Ouaqui, Fr. Guiana 131/D4
Ouarane (reg.), Mauritania 106/B4
Ouareau (lake), Québec 172/D3
Ouareau (riv.), Québec 172/D3
Ouargla, Algeria 106/F2
Ouargla, Algeria 102/C1
Ouarzazate, Morocco 106/C2
Ouchy, Switzerland 39/C4
Oud-Beijerland, Netherlands 27/E5
Ouddorp, Netherlands 27/D5
Oudenaarde, Belgium 27/D7
Oudenbosch, Netherlands 27/E5
Oudenburg, Belgium 27/B6
Oude-Pekela, Netherlands 27/K2
Oudeschild, Netherlands 27/F2
Oude-Tonge, Netherlands 27/E5
Oudewater, Netherlands 27/F4
Oudtshoorn, S. Africa 102/E8
Oudtshoorn, S. Africa 118/E6
Oud-Turnhout, Belgium 27/F6
Oued Zem, Morocco 106/C2
Ouelle (riv.), Québec 172/H2
Ouellette, Maine 243/G1
Ouémé (riv.), Benin 106/E7
Ouessant (isl.), France 28/A3
Ouesso, Congo 115/C3
Ouest (dept.), Haiti 158/C6
Ouest (pt.), Haiti 158/B4
Ouest (pt.), Haiti 158/B6
Ouezzane, Morocco 106/C2
Oughter (lake), Ireland 17/G3
Oughterard, Ireland 17/C5
Ouham (riv.), Cent. Afr. Rep. 115/C2
Ouham (riv.), Chad 111/C6
Ouidah, Benin 106/E7
Oujda, Morocco 106/D2
Oujda, Morocco 102/B1
Oujeft, Mauritania 106/B4
Oulainen, Finland 18/04
Ouled Djellal, Algeria 106/F2
Oullins, France 28/F5
Oulu (prov.), Finland 18/P4
Oulu, Finland 7/G2
Oulu, Finland 18/04
Oulu (lake), Finland 7/G2
Oulujärvi (lake), Finland 18/P4
Oulujoki (riv.), Finland 18/04
Oum Chalouba, Chad 111/D4
Oum el Asel (well), Mali 106/D4
Oum Hadjer, Chad 102/E3
Oum Hadjer, Chad 111/D5
Ounas (riv.), Finland 7/F2
Ounasjoki (riv.), Finland 18/03
Oundle, England 13/G5
Oungre, Sask. 181/H6
Ounianga-Kébir, Chad 111/D4
Oupeye, Belgium 27/H7
Oupu, China 77/L1
Our (riv.), Germany 22/B3
Our (riv.), Luxembourg 27/J9
Ouray (co.), Colo. 208/D6
Ouray, Colo. 208/D6
Ouray (peak), Colo. 208/G6
Ouray, Utah 304/E3
Ourinhos, Brazil 132/D8
Ourinhos, Brazil 135/B3
Ourique, Portugal 33/B4
Ouro Fino, Brazil 132/E8
Ouro Fino, Brazil 135/C3
Ouro Preto, Brazil 132/F8
Ouro Preto, Brazil 135/E2
Ourthe (riv.), Belgium 27/G8
Ouse (riv.), England 13/G6
Ouse (riv.), England 13/J6
Ouse, Tasmania 99/C4
Ouse (riv.), Tasmania 99/C4
Ousley, Georgia 217/F9
Outagamie (co.), Wis. 317/K7
Outardes (riv.), Québec 174/D2
Outer (isl.), Wis. 317/F1
Outer Harbor, S. Australia 94/A7
Outer Hebrides (isls.), Scotland 15/A3
Outer Santa Barbara (passage), Calif. 204/G10
Outing, Minn. 255/E4
Outjo, Namibia 118/B4
Outjo, Namibia 102/D7
Outlook, Mont. 262/M2
Outlook, Sask. 181/E4
Outlook, Wash. 310/E4
Outokumpu, Finland 18/Q5
Outram, Sask. 181/H6
Outremont, Québec 172/H4
Ouyen, Victoria 88/G7
Ouyen, Victoria 97/B4
Ouzinkie, Alaska 196/H3
Ovacık, Çankırı, Turkey 63/E2
Ovacık, İçel, Turkey 63/E4
Ovacık, Tunceli, Turkey 63/H3
Ovalau, Fiji 86/Q10
Ovalle, Chile 120/B6
Ovalle, Chile 138/A8
Ovamboland (reg.), Namibia 118/B3
Ovando, Mont. 262/C3

Ovar, Portugal 33/B2
Ovens (riv.), Victoria 97/D5
Overall, Tenn. 237/J9
Overbrook, Kansas 232/G3
Overbrook, Okla. 288/M6
Overflakkee (isl.), Netherlands 27/E5
Overflow (bay), Manitoba 179/A1
Overflowing (riv.), Manitoba 179/A1
Overflowing (riv.), Sask. 181/K2
Overflowing River, Manitoba 179/A1
Overgaard, Ariz. 198/E4
Overhills, N.C. 281/L4
Overijse, Belgium 27/F7
Overijssel (prov.), Netherlands 27/J4
Overisel, Mich. 250/C6
Överkalix, Sweden 18/N3
Overland, Mo. 261/Q2
Overland Park, Kansas 232/H3
Overlea, Md. 245/N3
Overloon, Netherlands 27/H5
Overly, N. Dak. 282/K2
Overpelt, Belgium 27/G6
Overstreet, Fla. 212/D6
Overton, Nebr. 264/E4
Overton, Nev. 266/G6
Overton, Pa. 294/K2
Overton, Texas 303/K5
Övertorneå, Sweden 18/N3
Överum, Sweden 18/K7
Ovett, Miss. 256/F8
Ovid, Colo. 208/P1
Ovid, Idaho 220/G7
Ovid, Mich. 250/E5
Ovid, N.Y. 276/G5
Oviedo, Dom. Rep. 158/D7
Oviedo, Fla. 212/E4
Oviedo (prov.), Spain 33/C1
Oviedo, Spain 33/C1
Oviedo, Spain 7/D4
Ovilla, Texas 303/G2
Ovoca (riv.), Ireland 17/J6
Övörhangay, Mongolia 77/F2
Øvre-Sirdal, Norway 18/E7
Ovruch, U.S.S.R. 52/C4
Owaka, N. Zealand 100/B7
Owando, Congo 115/C3
Owando, Congo 102/D5
Owaneco, Ill. 222/D4
Owanka, S. Dak. 298/D5
Owasa, Iowa 229/G4
Owasco, N.Y. 276/G5
Owasco (lake), N.Y. 276/G5
Owase, Japan 81/H6
Owassa, Ala. 195/E8
Owassa (lake), N.J. 273/D1
Owasso, Okla. 288/P2
Owatonna, Minn. 255/E6
Owbeh, Afghanistan 68/A2
Owbeh, Afghanistan 59/H3
Owego, N.Y. 276/H6
Owell (lake), Ireland 17/G4
Owen (co.), Ind. 227/D6
Owen (co.), Ky. 237/M3
Owen (mt.), N. Zealand 100/D4
Owen (chan.), Ontario 177/C2
Owen (sound), Ontario 177/D3
Owen, Wis. 317/F6
Owen (lake), Wis. 317/D3
Owendale, Alberta 182/D5
Owendale, Mich. 250/F5
Owendo, Gabon 115/A3
Owen Falls (dam), Uganda 115/F3
Owenga, N. Zealand 100/T7
Owenkillew (riv.), N. Ireland 17/G2
Owenmore (riv.), Ireland 17/B3
Owenmore (riv.), Ireland 17/B3
Owens (lake), Calif. 188/C3
Owens (lake), Calif. 204/H7
Owens (peak), Calif. 204/H8
Owens (riv.), Calif. 204/G6
Owensboro, Ky. 237/G5
Owensboro, Ky. 188/J3
Owensburg, Ind. 227/D7
Owens Cross Roads, Ala. 195/E1
Owen Sound, Ont. 162/H7
Owen Sound, Ontario 177/D3
Owensville, Ark. 202/C4
Owensville, Ind. 227/B8
Owensville, Mo. 261/K6
Owensville, Ohio 284/B7
Owenton, Ky. 237/M3
Owenton, Va. 307/O5
Owerri, Nigeria 106/F7
Owey (isl.), Ireland 17/D1
Owia (bay), St. Vin. & Grens. 161/A8
Owikeno (lake), Br. Col. 184/D4
Owings, Md. 245/M6
Owings, S.C. 296/C2
Owings Mills, Md. 245/L3
Owingsville, Ky. 237/O4
Owl (creek), Colo. 208/K1
Owl (riv.), Manitoba 179/K2
Owl (creek), S. Dak. 298/B4
Owl, North Fork (creek), Wyo. 319/D2
Owl Creek (mts.), Wyo. 319/D2
Owl River (lake), Alberta 182/E2
Owlseye, Alberta 182/E2
Owls Head •, Maine 243/F7
Owo, Nigeria 106/F7
Owosso, Mich. 250/E5
Owraman, Iran 66/E3
Owsley (co.), Ky. 237/O6
Owyhee (riv.), Idaho 220/B7
Owyhee (co.), Idaho 220/B7
Owyhee (mts.), Idaho 220/B6
Owyhee, East Fork (riv.), Idaho 220/B7
Owyhee, Nev. 266/F1
Owyhee (riv.), Nev. 266/E1
Owyhee (dam), Oreg. 291/K4
Owyhee (lake), Oreg. 291/K4
Owyhee (mts.), Oreg. 291/K4
Owyhee, North Fork (riv.), Oreg. 291/K5

Owyhee (riv.), Oreg. 291/K5
Ox (Slieve Gamph) (mts.), Ireland 17/D3
Oxapampa, Peru 128/E8
Oxbow (dam), Idaho 220/B5
Oxbow •, Maine 243/G3
Oxbow (isl.), Scotland 15/A3
Oxbow, Oreg. 291/L2
Oxbow (riv.), Oreg. 291/L3
Oxbow, Sask. 181/J6
Oxelösund, Sweden 18/K7
Oxford, Ala. 195/G3
Oxford, Ark. 202/G1
Oxford •, Conn. 210/C3
Oxford, England 13/F6
Oxford, England 10/F5
Oxford, Fla. 212/D3
Oxford, Georgia 217/E3
Oxford, Idaho 220/F7
Oxford, Ind. 227/C3
Oxford, Iowa 229/K5
Oxford, Kansas 232/E4
Oxford, La. 238/C3
Oxford (co.), Maine 243/B7
Oxford, Maine 243/B7
Oxford •, Maine 243/B7
Oxford (isl.), Manitoba 179/J3
Oxford, Md. 245/06
Oxford, Mass. 249/G4
Oxford •, Mass. 249/G4
Oxford, Mich. 250/F6
Oxford, Miss. 256/F2
Oxford, Nebr. 264/E4
Oxford, N.J. 273/C2
Oxford, N.Y. 276/J6
Oxford, N. Zealand 100/D5
Oxford, N.C. 281/M2
Oxford, Nova Scotia 168/E3
Oxford, Ohio 284/A5
Oxford, Pa. 294/K6
Oxford, W. Va. 312/E4
Oxford, Wis. 317/H8
Oxford House, Manitoba 179/J3
Oxford Junction, Iowa 229/M4
Oxford Junction, Nova Scotia 168/E3
Oxford Mills, Iowa 229/L5
Oxford Mills, Ontario 177/J3
Oxfordshire (co.), England 13/F6
Oxkutzcab, Mexico 150/P6
Oxley, N.S. Wales 97/C2
Oxley (creek), Queensland 95/D3
Oxly, Mo. 261/L9
Oxnard, Calif. 204/F9
Oxnard A.F.B., Calif. 204/F9
Oxon Hill, Md. 245/F6
Oxon Run (riv.), Md. 245/F5
Oxton, Scotland 15/F5
Oxtongue Lake, Ontario 177/E2
Oyabe, Japan 81/H5
Oyahue (vol.), Chile 138/C3
Oyama, Br. Col. 184/H5
Oyama, Japan 81/J5
Oyapock (riv.), 120/D2
Oyapock (riv.), Brazil 132/C2
Oyapock (riv.), Fr. Guiana 131/F2
Oyem, Gabon 102/D4
Oyem, Gabon 115/B3
Oyen, Alberta 182/E4
Oyens, Iowa 229/A3
Oykel (riv.), Scotland 15/D3
Oykel Bridge, Scotland 15/D3
Oylen, Minn. 255/D4
Oymyakon, U.S.S.R. 4/C3
Oymyakon, U.S.S.R. 48/Q3
Oyo, Congo 115/C4
Oyo (state), Nigeria 106/E7
Oyo, Nigeria 106/E7
Oyón, Peru 128/D8
Oyonnax, France 28/F4
Oyster (bay), Tasmania 88/H8
Oyster (bay), Tasmania 99/E4
Oyster, Va. 307/S6
Oyster Bay, N.Y. 276/R6
Oyster River (pt.), Conn. 210/D4
Oysterville, Wash. 310/A4
Özalp, Turkey 63/K3
Ozamis, Philippines 82/D6
Ozan, Ark. 202/C6
Ozark (mts.) 188/H3
Ozark, Ala. 195/G8
Ozark, Ark. 202/C3
Ozark (lake), Ark. 202/C3
Ozark (plat.), Ark. 202/C1
Ozark (res.), Ark. 202/C3
Ozark, Ill. 222/E6
Ozark (co.), Mo. 261/H9
Ozark, Mo. 261/F8
Ozark (plat.), Mo. 261/F9
Ozark Nat'l Scenic Riverways, Mo. 261/K8
Ozarks, Lake of the (lake), Mo. 261/F6
Ozaukee (co.), Wis. 317/L9
Ozawkie, Kansas 232/G2
Özd, Hungary 41/F2
Ozernovskiy, U.S.S.R. 48/Q4
Ozernoy (cape), U.S.S.R. 48/R4
Ozette, Wash. 310/A2
Ozette (lake), Wash. 310/A2
Ozette Ind. Res., Wash. 310/A2
Ozieri, Italy 34/B4
Ozona, Fla. 212/D3
Ozona, Texas 303/C7
Ozone, Ark. 202/D2
Ozone, Tenn. 237/M9
Ozorków, Poland 47/D3
Ozu, Japan 81/F7
Ozuluama, Mexico 150/L6
Ozumba de Alzate, Mexico 150/M1

P

Paamiut, Greenland 4/C12
Pa-an, Burma 72/C3
Paarden (bay), Neth. Ant. 161/D10
Paarl, S. Africa 102/D8

Paarl, S. Africa 118/F6
Paauhau, Hawaii 218/H4
Paauilo, Hawaii 218/H4
Paavola, Finland 18/04
Pabbay (isl.), Scotland 15/A4
Pabbay (isl.), Scotland 15/A3
Pabianice, Poland 47/D3
Pabna, Bangladesh 68/F4
Pablo, Mont. 262/B3
Pabos, Québec 172/D2
Pabos-Mills, Québec 172/D2
Pabradė, U.S.S.R. 53/C3
Pacajá Grande (riv.), Brazil 132/D4
Pacaraimã, Serra da (mts.), Brazil 132/H8
Pacaraima, Sierra (mts.), Venezuela 124/C5
Pacasmayo, Peru 128/C6
Pachaug, Conn. 210/H2
Pachaug (pond), Conn. 210/H2
Pachaug (riv.), Conn. 210/H2
Pacheco, Calif. 204/K1
Pachino, Italy 34/E6
Pachitea (riv.), Peru 128/E7
Pachiza, Peru 128/D6
Pachmarhi, India 68/D4
Pacho, Colombia 126/C5
Pachuca de Soto, Mexico 150/K6
Pachuta, Miss. 256/G6
Pacific (ocean) 54/T5
Pacific (ocean) 146/E6
Pacific, Mo. 261/N7
Pacific (co.), Wash. 310/B4
Pacific, Wash. 310/C3
Pacifica, Calif. 204/H2
Pacific Beach, Calif. 204/H11
Pacific Beach, Wash. 310/A3
Pacific City, Oreg. 291/C2
Pacific Grove, Calif. 204/C7
Pacific Heights, Hawaii 218/H1
Pacific Junction, Iowa 229/B6
Pacific Palisades, Hawaii 218/E2
Pacific Rim Nat'l Park, Br. Col. 184/E6
Pacitan, Indonesia 85/J2
Pack (riv.), Idaho 220/B1
Pack (creek), Utah 304/E5
Packanack Lake, N.J. 273/B1
Packertown, Ind. 227/F2
Packerville, Conn. 210/H2
Packington, Québec 172/J2
Packsville, W. Va. 312/C7
Packwaukee, Wis. 317/G8
Packwood, Iowa 229/J6
Packwood, Wash. 310/D4
Paco, Philippines 82/C2
Pacoa, Colombia 126/E7
Paço de Arcos, Portugal 33/A1
Pacoima, Calif. 204/B10
Pacolet, S.C. 296/D2
Pacolet (riv.), S.C. 296/D1
Pacolet Mills, S.C. 296/D2
Pacov, Czech. 41/C2
Pacsa, Hungary 41/D3
Pacsan (mt.), Philippines 82/C2
Pactolus, N.C. 281/P3
Padada, Philippines 82/E7
Padang, Indonesia 54/L10
Padang, Indonesia 85/B6
Padangpanjang, Indonesia 85/B6
Padangsidempuan, Indonesia 85/B5
Padany, U.S.S.R. 52/D2
Padborg, Denmark 21/C8
Padcaya, Bolivia 136/C7
Paddle Prairie, Alberta 182/A5
Paddock Lake, Wis. 317/K10
Paddockwood, Sask. 181/F2
Paden, Miss. 256/H1
Paden, Okla. 288/N3
Paden City, W. Va. 312/D3
Paderborn, Germany 22/C3
Padgett, S.C. 296/F5
Padiham, England 13/H1
Padilla, Bolivia 136/C6
Padilla, Mexico 150/K5
Padilla (creek), N. Mex. 274/D5
Padilla (bay), Wash. 310/C2
Padloping (isl.), N.W.T. 162/K2
Padloping (isl.), N.W.T. 187/M3
Padre (isl.), Texas 188/G5
Padre (isl.), Texas 303/G10
Padre Island Nat'l Seashore, Texas 303/G11
Padre Las Casas, Dom. Rep. 158/D6
Padrón, Spain 33/B1
Padroni, Colo. 208/N1
Padstow, England 10/D5
Padstow, England 13/B7
Padua (prov.), Italy 34/C2
Padua, Italy 7/F4
Padua, Italy 34/C2
Padua, Minn. 255/C5
Paducah, Ky. 237/C9
Paducah, Ky. 146/K6
Paducah, Ky. 188/J3
Paducah, Texas 303/D4
Padul, Spain 33/H4
Paekam, N. Korea 81/D3
Paektu (mt.), N. Korea 81/C3
Paeroa, N. Zealand 100/E2
Páez, Colombia 126/C6
Pafúri, Mozambique 118/E4
Pag, Yugoslavia 45/B3
Pag (isl.), Yugoslavia 45/B3
Pagadian, Philippines 82/D7
Pagalungan, Philippines 82/E7
Pagan, Burma 72/B2
Pagan (isl.), No. Marianas 87/E4
Page, Ariz. 198/D2
Page (co.), Iowa 229/C7
Page, Nebr. 264/F2
Page, N. Dak. 282/P5
Page, Okla. 288/S5
Page, Va. 307/M3
Page, W. Va. 312/D6

Page City, Kansas 232/A2
Pagedale, Mo. 261/P2
Pageland, S.C. 296/G2
Pago (bay), Guam 86/K7
Pago Pago (cap.), Amer. Samoa 86/N9
Pago Pago (cap.), Amer. Samoa 87/J7
Pagosa Junction, Colo. 208/E8
Pagosa Springs, Colo. 208/E8
Pagoua (bay), Dominica 161/F6
Paguate, N. Mex. 274/B3
Pagwa River, Ontario 177/J5
Pagwa River, Ontario 175/D3
Pahala, Hawaii 188/G6
Pahala, Hawaii 218/H6
Pahang (state), Malaysia 72/D7
Pahang, Sungai (riv.), Malaysia 72/D7
Pahaska, Wyo. 319/C1
Pahiatua, N. Zealand 100/F4
Pahlevi (Enzeli), Iran 59/E2
Pahlevi (Enzeli), Iran 66/F2
Pahoa, Hawaii 218/J5
Pahokee, Fla. 212/F5
Pahranagat (range), Nev. 266/F5
Pahrock (range), Nev. 266/F5
Pah-rum (peak), Nev. 266/B2
Pahrump, Nev. 266/E6
Pahrump (valley), Nev. 266/F6
Pahsimeroi (riv.), Idaho 220/E5
Pahute (mesa), Nev. 266/E5
Pahvant (range), Utah 304/B5
Paia, Hawaii 218/J2
Paicheng (Baicheng), China 77/K2
Paicines, Calif. 204/D7
Paide, U.S.S.R. 53/C1
Paige, Texas 303/G7
Paihia, N. Zealand 100/D1
Paihuano, Chile 138/B8
Paiján, Peru 128/C6
Päijänne (lake), Finland 18/06
Pailin, Cambodia 72/D4
Paillaco, Chile 138/D3
Paine, Chile 138/G4
Paine, Cerro (mt.), Chile 138/D9
Painesdale, Mich. 250/G1
Painesville, Ohio 284/H2
Painswick, Ontario 177/D3
Paint (lake), Manitoba 179/J2
Paint (riv.), Mich. 250/A2
Paint (creek), Ohio 284/D7
Paint, Pa. 294/E5
Paint Bank, Va. 307/H5
Paint Branch (riv.), Md. 245/F4
Painted (des.), Ariz. 198/D2
Painted Desert Section (Petrified Forest), Ariz. 198/F3
Painted Post, N.Y. 276/F6
Painted Rock (dam), Ariz. 198/C5
Painter, Ala. 195/F2
Painter, Va. 307/S5
Painter Ridge (hills), Conn. 210/B2
Paintersville, Ohio 284/C6
Paint Lick, Ky. 237/N5
Paint Lick (riv.), Ky. 237/M5
Paint Rock, Ala. 195/F1
Paint Rock (riv.), Ala. 195/F1
Paint Rock, Texas 303/E6
Paintsville, Ky. 237/R5
Paipa, Colombia 126/C4
Paipote, Chile 138/A7
Paipote, Quebrada de (riv.), Chile 138/B6
Paisley, Ontario 177/C3
Paisley, Oreg. 291/G5
Paisley, Scotland 10/A1
Paisley, Scotland 15/B2
Paita, Peru 128/B5
Paita (bay), Peru 128/B5
Paiute Ind. Res., Calif. 204/G6
Pajala, Sweden 18/N3
Paján, Ecuador 128/B3
Pajarito (creek), N. Mex. 274/A2
Pajaro, Calif. 204/D7
Pájaros (isls.), Chile 138/A7
Pakanbaru, Indonesia 54/M9
Pakanbaru, Indonesia 85/C5
Pakaraima (mts.), Guyana 131/A3
Pakawau, N. Zealand 100/D4
Pakchan (riv.), Burma 72/C5
Pakch'ŏn, N. Korea 81/B4
Pakenham, Ontario 177/H2
Pakhoi (Beihai), China 77/G7
Pakistan 2/N4
Pakistan 54/H7
PAKISTAN 59/J4
PAKISTAN 68/B3
Pakokku, Burma 72/B2
Pakowki (lake), Alberta 182/E5
Paks, Hungary 41/E3
Pakwach, Uganda 115/F3
Pakxé, Laos 72/E4
Pala, Chad 111/B6
Pala Ind. Res., Calif. 204/H10
Palacios, Texas 303/H9
Palafrugell, Spain 33/H2
Palagruža (Pelagosa) (isl.), Yugoslavia 45/C4
Palamós, Spain 33/H2
Palana, U.S.S.R. 54/S4
Palana, U.S.S.R. 48/R4
Palanan, Philippines 82/D2
Palanan, Philippines 85/G2
Palanan (bay), Philippines 82/D2
Palanda, Ecuador 128/C3
Palanga, U.S.S.R. 53/A3
Palangkaraya, Indonesia 85/E6

Palanpur, India 68/C4
Palaoa (pt.), Hawaii 218/G4
Palapag, Philippines 82/E4
Palapye, Botswana 118/D4
Palas de Rey, Spain 33/C1
Palatine, Ill. 222/E5
Palatka, Ark. 202/J1
Palatka, Fla. 212/E2
Palau 87/D5
Palauli (bay), W. Samoa 86/L8
Palaumerak, Indonesia 85/G1
Palaw, Burma 72/C4
Palawan (prov.), Philippines 82/B6
Palawan (isl.), Philippines 2/Q5
Palawan (isl.), Philippines 82/B6
Palawan (isl.), Philippines 85/F4
Palawan (isl.), Philippines 82/B6
Palawan (passage), Philippines 85/F4
Palawan (passage), Philippines 82/A6
Palaya, Bolivia 136/A6
Palayan, Philippines 82/C3
Palayankottai, India 68/D7
Palazzolo Acreide, Italy 34/E6
Palca, Bolivia 136/A5
Palco, Kansas 232/C2
Paldiski, U.S.S.R. 53/B1
Paldiski, U.S.S.R. 52/B3
Paleleh, Indonesia 85/G5
Palembang, Indonesia 54/M10
Palembang, Indonesia 85/D6
Palena, Chile 138/E5
Palena (lake), Chile 138/E5
Palena (riv.), Chile 138/E5
Palencia (prov.), Spain 33/D1
Palencia, Spain 33/D2
Palenque (pt.), Dom. Rep. 158/D6
Palenque, Mexico 150/08
Palenque (ruin), Mexico 150/08
Palenville, N.Y. 276/M6
Palermo, Calif. 204/D4
Palermo (prov.), Italy 34/D5
Palermo, Italy 7/F5
Palermo, Italy 34/D5
Palermo •, Maine 243/F7
Palermo, N.J. 273/C5
Palermo, N. Dak. 282/F3
Palermo, Uruguay 145/D4
Palestina, Chile 138/B4
Palestine, Ala. 195/H3
Palestine, Ark. 202/J4
Palestine, Ill. 222/F5
Palestine, Ind. 227/F2
Palestine, Ohio 284/A5
Palestine, Texas 188/H4
Palestine, Texas 303/K6
Palestine, W. Va. 312/D4
Palestrina, Italy 34/F7
Paletwa, Burma 72/B2
Palghat, India 68/D6
Palha, Mar da (bay), Portugal 33/A1
Pali, India 68/C3
Palidoro, Italy 34/F6
Paliocabe (Payocabe), Chile 138/F4
Palisade, Colo. 208/C4
Palisade, Minn. 255/E4
Palisade, Nebr. 264/C4
Palisade, Nev. 266/E2
Palisades, Idaho 220/G6
Palisades (res.), Idaho 220/G6
Palisades, N.J. 273/C1
Palisades, N.Y. 276/K8
Palisades, Wash. 310/E3
Palisades (res.), Wyo. 319/A2
Palisades Park, N.J. 273/C2
Paliseul, Belgium 27/G9
Palizada, Mexico 150/07
Palk (str.), India 68/D7
Palk (str.), Sri Lanka 68/D7
Pallamallawa, N.S. Wales 97/F1
Palling, Br. Col. 184/D3
Palliser (bay), N. Zealand 100/C3
Palliser (cape), N. Zealand 100/E4
Pall Mall, Tenn. 237/M7
Palm (beach), Neth. Ant. 161/D10
Palma (bay), Alaska 196/L1
Palma, Mozambique 118/G2
Palma, Spain 7/E5
Palma, Spain 33/H3
Palma, Spain 33/H3
Palma del Río, Spain 33/D4
Palma di Montechiaro, Italy 34/D6
Palmarejo, Venezuela 124/C2
Palmares, Brazil 132/H5
Palmares, C. Rica 154/F6
Palmarito, Apure, Venezuela 124/D4
Palmarito, Guárico, Venezuela 124/D3
Palmarola (isl.), Italy 34/D4
Palmas (cape) 102/B2
Palmas, Brazil 132/C9
Palmas (cape), Liberia 106/C8
Palmas Altas (pt.), P. Rico 161/C12
Palma Soriano, Cuba 158/L4
Palm Bay, Fla. 212/F4
Palm Beach, Fla. 188/L5
Palm Beach (co.), Fla. 212/F5
Palm Beach, Fla. 212/G4
Palm Beach Gardens, Fla. 212/F5
Palm Beach Shores, Fla. 212/G5
Palm City, Fla. 212/F4
Palm Coast, Fla. 212/E2
Palmdale, Calif. 204/G9
Palmdale, Fla. 212/E5
Palm Desert, Calif. 204/J10
Palmeira, Brazil 132/D9
Palmeira, Brazil 135/B4
Palmeira das Missões, Brazil 132/C9
Palmeiras, Brazil 132/F6
Palmeirinhas (pt.), Angola 115/B5
Palmer, Alaska 196/C1
Palmer, Alaska 188/D5
Palmer (arch.), Ant. 5/C15

Parry Sound 425

lmer, Ill. 222/D4
lmer, Ind. 227/C2
lmer, Iowa 229/D3
lmer, Kansas 232/E2
lmer, Mass. 249/E4
lmer•, Mass. 249/E4
lmer, Mich. 250/B2
lmer, Nebr. 264/F3
lmer (head), N. Zealand 100/B3
lmer, P. Rico 161/F1
lmer (riv.), Queensland 95/B2
lmer, Sask. 181/E6
lmer, Tenn. 237/K10
lmer, Wash. 310/D3
lmer (lake), Wash. 310/F2
lmer Lake, Colo. 208/J4
lmer Land (reg.), Ant. 2/F9
lmer Land (reg.), Ant. 5/B15
lmer Rapids, Ontario 177/G2
lmers, Minn. 255/G4
lmers Crossing, Miss. 256/F8
lmer Station, Ant. 5/C15
lmerston (atoll), Cook Is. 87/K7
lmerston, N. Zealand 100/C6
lmerston, Ontario 177/D4
lmerston North, N. Zealand 87/H10
lmerston North, N. Zealand 100/E4
lmersville, Tenn. 237/D8
lmerton, Pa. 294/L4
lmerville, Queensland 95/B3
lmetto, Fla. 212/D4
lmetto, Georgia 217/C3
lmetto, La. 238/G5
lmetto (pt.), St. Kitts & Nevis 161/C10
lm Harbor, Fla. 212/D3
lmi, Italy 34/E5
lmiet (riv.), S. Africa 118/F7
milla, Chile 138/F6
lmillas (pt.), Dom. Rep. 158/F6
lmillas, Mexico 150/K5
lmira, Colombia 120/B2
lmira, Colombia 126/B6
lmira, Cuba 158/E2
lmitas, Uruguay 145/B4
lmito de la Virgen (isl.), Mexico 150/F5
lmito del Verde (isl.), Mexico 150/F5
lm River-Clair Mel, Fla. 212/C3
lms, Mich. 250/G5
lms, Isle of (isl.), S.C. 296/H6
lm Shores, Fla. 212/F3
lm Springs, Calif. 188/C4
lm Springs, Calif. 204/J10
lm Springs, Fla. 212/F5
myra, Ill. 222/C4
lmyra, Ind. 227/E8
lmyra•, Maine 243/E6
myra, Mich. 250/E7
myra, Mo. 261/J3
myra, Nebr. 264/H4
myra, N.J. 273/B3
lmyra, N.Y. 276/F4
lmyra (atoll), Pacific 87/K5
lmyra, Pa. 294/J5
lmyra (ruin), Syria 59/C3
lmyra (Tadmor) (ruins), Syria 63/H5
myra, Tenn. 237/G8
myra (isl.), U.S. 2/A5
myra, Va. 307/M5
myra, Wis. 317/H2
myras (pt.), India 68/F4
nackie, Scotland 15/E6
ni, India 68/D6
o, Iowa 229/K4
o, Mich. 250/E5
o, Minn. 255/F3
lo, Philippines 82/E5
lo Alto, Calif. 188/B3
lo Alto, Calif. 204/K3
o Alto, Cuba 158/F3
o Alto (co.), Iowa 229/D2
o Alto (lake), Iowa 229/D2
lo Bola, Mexico 150/D4
lo Duro (creek), Texas 303/B2
lo Duro (creek), Texas 303/C1
loemeu (riv.), Suriname 131/D4
olo (stream), Hawaii 218/D4
oma, Ill. 222/B3
lomar (mt.), Calif. 204/J10
lomas, Mexico 150/F1
lomas, Uruguay 145/B2
lombara Sabina, Italy 34/F6
lometas, Bolivia 136/D5
ompon, Philippines 82/E5
lo Pinto (co.), Texas 303/F5
lo Pinto, Texas 303/F5
lopo, Indonesia 85/F6
los (cape), Spain 33/F4
lo Santo, Argentina 143/E2
lo Seco, P. Rico 161/D1
lo Seco, Trin. & Tob. 161/A11
los Heights, Ill. 222/B6
los Hills, Ill. 222/B6
los Park, Ill. 222/B6
los Verdes Estates, Calif. 204/B11
lotás, Hungary 41/E3
lourde (lake), La. 238/H7
louse (riv.), Idaho 220/B3
louse, Wash. 310/H4
louse (riv.), Wash. 310/G4
lo Verde, Ariz. 198/C5
lo Verde, Calif. 204/L10
lpa, Nepal 68/E3
lpa, Peru 128/E10
lsagua, Nicaragua 154/E4
lsen (riv.), Manitoba 179/G2
lu, Indonesia 85/F6
lu, Turkey 63/H3
luan, Philippines 82/C4
ma, Burkina Faso 106/E6
mangkat, Indonesia 85/D5
mar, Colombia 126/E8
mbrun, Sask. 181/D6
Pambula, N.S. Wales 97/E5
Pamekasan, Indonesia 85/L2
Pameungpeuk, Indonesia 85/H2
Pamiers, France 28/D6
Pamir (plat.) 54/J6
Pamlico (sound), N.C. 188/L3
Pamlico (co.), N.C. 281/R4
Pamlico (riv.), N.C. 281/R4
Pamlico (sound), N.C. 281/S4
Pampa, Texas 188/F3
Pampa, Texas 303/D2
Pampa Aullagas, Bolivia 136/B6
Pampachiri, Peru 128/F10
Pampacolca, Peru 128/F10
Pampa de la Salina (salt dep.), Argentina 143/C3
Pampa de las Salinas, Argentina 143/C3
Pampa de la Tres Hermanas (plain), Argentina 143/C6
Pampa del Infierno, Argentina 143/D2
Pampa Grande, Bolivia 136/D5
Pampanga (prov.), Philippines 82/C3
Pampas (plain), Argentina 120/C6
Pampas (plain), Argentina 143/D4
Pampas, Peru 128/E9
Pampas (riv.), Peru 128/E9
Pampilhosa da Serra, Portugal 33/C3
Pamplico, S.C. 296/H4
Pamplin, Va. 307/L6
Pamplona, Colombia 126/D4
Pamplona, Spain 33/F1
Pamplona, Spain 7/D4
Pamunkey (riv.), Va. 307/O5
Pamunkey Ind. Res., Va. 307/P5
Pana, Ill. 222/D4
Panabá, Mexico 150/P6
Panabo, Philippines 82/E7
Panaca, Nev. 266/G5
Panacachi, Bolivia 136/B6
Panacea, Fla. 212/B1
Panache (lake), Ontario 177/C1
Panagyurishte, Bulgaria 45/F4
Panaitan (isl.), Indonesia 85/C7
Panaji, India 68/C5
Panama 2/E5
Panama 146/K9
PANAMA 154/G6
Panama (canal) 2/E5
Panama, Ill. 222/D4
Panama, Iowa 229/B5
Panama, Nebr. 264/H4
Panama, N.Y. 276/A6
Panama, Okla. 288/S4
Panamá (cap.), Pan. 146/L9
Panamá (cap.), Panama 154/H6
Panama (canal), Pan. 146/L8
Panamá (gulf), Pan. 146/L9
Panamá (gulf), Panama 154/H7
Panama City, Fla. 188/K4
Panama City, Fla. 212/C6
Panama City Beach, Fla. 212/C6
Panamint (range), Calif. 204/H7
Panamint (valley), Calif. 204/H7
Panao, Peru 128/E7
Panaon (isl.), Philippines 82/E5
Panarea (isl.), Italy 34/E5
Panaro (riv.), Italy 34/C2
Panarukan, Indonesia 85/K2
Panay (isl.), Philippines 54/O8
Panay (isl.), Philippines 85/G3
Panay (isl.), Philippines 82/D5
Pancake (range), Nev. 266/F4
Pančevo, Yugoslavia 45/E3
Panchor, Malaysia 72/F5
Panchur, India 68/F2
Panciu, Romania 45/H3
Panda, Mozambique 118/E4
Pandale, Texas 303/C7
Panda-Likasi, Zaire 115/E6
Panda-Likasi, Zaire 102/E6
Pandan, Antique, Philippines 82/C5
Pandan, Catanduanes, Philippines 82/E3
Pan de Azúcar, Quebrado (riv.), Chile 138/B5
Pan de Azúcar, Uruguay 145/D5
Pandeglang, Indonesia 85/G1
Pandharpur, India 68/D5
Pandi Pandi, S. Australia 94/F2
Pando (dept.), Bolivia 136/B2
Pando, Cerro (mt.), Panama 154/F6
Pando, Uruguay 145/B6
Pando (riv.), Uruguay 145/B6
Pandora, Ohio 284/C4
Pandrup, Denmark 21/C3
Panevėžys, U.S.S.R. 52/B3
Panevėžys, U.S.S.R. 53/C3
Panfilov, U.S.S.R. 48/H5
Pangai, Tonga 87/J7
Pangala, Congo 115/B4
Pangalanes (canal), Madagascar 118/H4
Pangani, Tanzania 115/G5
Pangani (riv.), Tanzania 115/G4
Panganiban, Philippines 82/E4
Pangasinan (prov.), Philippines 82/C3
Pangburn, Ark. 202/G3
Pangi, Zaire 115/E4
Pangkalanberandan, Indonesia 85/B5
Pangkalanbuun, Indonesia 85/E6
Pangkalpinang, Indonesia 85/D6
Pangkor, Pulau (isl.), Malaysia 72/D6
Panglao (isl.), Philippines 82/D6
Pangman, Sask. 181/G6
Pangnirtung, Canada 4/C13
Pangnirtung, N.W.T. 162/K2
Pangnirtung, N.W.T. 187/M3
Pangong Tso (lake), India 68/D2
Pangsau (pass), Burma 72/C1
Panguipulli, Chile 138/E2
Panguitch, Utah 304/B6
Panguitch (creek), Utah 304/B6
Pangutaran, Philippines 82/C7
Pangutaran (isl.), Philippines 82/C7
Pangutaran Group (isls.), Philippines 82/C7
Pangutaran Group (isls.), Philippines 85/G4
Panhandle, Texas 303/C2
Paniau (peak), Hawaii 218/A2
Panié (mt.), New Caled. 86/G4
Panihati, India 68/F1
Panipat, India 68/D3
Paniqui, Philippines 82/C3
Panj (riv.), Afghanistan 68/C1
Panjab, Afghanistan 68/B2
Panjab, Afghanistan 59/J3
Panjang, Hon (Hon Tho Chau) (isl.), Vietnam 72/D5
Panjgur, Pakistan 68/A3
Panjgur, Pakistan 59/H4
Panjim (Panaji), India 54/J8
Panjim (Panaji), India 68/C5
Pankow, Germany 22/F3
Pankshin, Nigeria 106/F7
P'anmunjŏm, N. Korea 81/C5
P'anmunjŏm, S. Korea 81/C5
Panmure (riv.), Pr. Edward I. 168/F2
Panna, India 68/E4
Pannawonica, W. Australia 92/B3
Pannonhalma, Hungary 41/D3
Panny (riv.), Alberta 182/C1
Panola, Ala. 195/B5
Panola, Ill. 222/E3
Panola (co.), Miss. 256/E2
Panola, Okla. 288/R5
Panola (co.), Texas 303/K5
Panora, Iowa 229/E5
Panorama Park, Iowa 229/N5
Panquehue, Chile 138/G2
Panruti, India 68/D6
Pansey, Ala. 195/H8
Pantanal (reg.), Brazil 120/D4
Pantar (isl.), Indonesia 85/G7
Pantego, N.C. 281/R3
Pantego, Texas 303/F2
Pantelleria, Italy 34/C6
Pantelleria (isl.), Italy 7/F5
Pantelleria (isl.), Italy 34/D6
Pantha, Burma 72/B2
Panther (creek), Idaho 220/D4
Panther (creek), Ky. 237/G5
Panther, W. Va. 312/C8
Panther Burn, Miss. 256/C4
Panthersville, Georgia 217/L1
Pantin, France 28/B1
Pantoja, Peru 128/E3
Panton•, Vt. 268/A3
Pánuco, Mexico 150/K6
Pánuco (riv.), Mexico 150/K5
Panuke (lake), Nova Scotia 168/D4
Pan Xian, China 77/G6
Panyam, Nigeria 106/F7
Panzós, Guatemala 154/C3
Pao (riv.), Venezuela 124/D3
Pao (riv.), Venezuela 124/F3
Paoki (Baoji), China 77/G5
Paola, Italy 34/E5
Paola, Kansas 232/H3
Paoli, Colo. 208/P1
Paoli, Ind. 227/E7
Paoli, Okla. 288/M5
Paoli, Pa. 294/M5
Paoli, Wis. 317/G10
Paonia, Colo. 208/D5
Paopao (bay), Fr. Poly. 86/S12
Paoting (Baoding), China 77/J4
Paotow (Baotou), China 77/G3
Paoua, Cent. Afr. Rep. 115/C2
Paoy Pet, Cambodia 72/D4
Papa, Hawaii 218/G6
Pápa, Hungary 41/D3
Papaaloa, Hawaii 218/J4
Papagaio (riv.), Brazil 132/B6
Papagayo (gulf), C. Rica 154/E5
Papago Ind. Res., Ariz. 198/C6
Papaikou, Hawaii 188/G6
Papaikou, Hawaii 218/J5
Papakura, N. Zealand 100/E2
Papallacta, Ecuador 128/D3
Papanoa, Mexico 150/J8
Papantla de Olarte, Mexico 150/L6
Papar, Malaysia 85/F4
Papara, Fr. Poly. 86/S13
Papa Stour (isl.), Scotland 10/G1
Papa Stour (isl.), Scotland 15/F2
Papatoetoe, N. Zealand 100/C1
Papa Westray (isl.), Scotland 15/F1
Papa Westray (isl.), Scotland 10/E1
Papeete (cap.), Fr. Polynesia 2/B6
Papeete (cap.), Fr. Poly. 86/S13
Papeete (cap.), Fr. Poly. 87/M7
Papelón, Venezuela 124/D3
Papenburg, Germany 22/B2
Papenoo, Fr. Poly. 86/T12
Papetoai, Fr. Poly. 86/S12
Paphos, Cyprus 63/E5
Papillion, Nebr. 264/J3
Papineau, Ill. 222/F3
Papineau (lake), Ontario 177/G2
Papineau (co.), Québec 172/B4
Papineau (lake), Québec 172/C4
Papineauville, Québec 172/C4
Paposo, Chile 138/A5
Papradno, Czech. 41/E2
Paps, The (mt.), Ireland 17/C7
Paps of Jura (mt.), Scotland 15/C5
Papua (gulf), Papua N.G. 87/E6
Papua New Guinea 2/S6
PAPUA NEW GUINEA 86/B1
PAPUA NEW GUINEA 85/B7
Papua New Guinea 87/E6
Papudo, Chile 138/A9
Papun, Burma 72/C3
Papunáua (riv.), Colombia 126/E6
Papunya, North. Terr. 93/B7
Papurí (riv.), Colombia 126/F7
Paquera, C. Rica 154/E6
Paquette, Québec 172/F4
Paquetville, New Bruns. 170/E1
Pará (state), Brazil 132/C4
Pará (Belém), Brazil 132/E3
Pará (est.), Brazil 120/E3
Pará (riv.), Brazil 132/D3
Para (dist.), Suriname 131/D3
Paraburdoo, W. Australia 88/B4
Paraburdoo, W. Australia 92/B3
Paracale, Philippines 82/D3
Paracas (pen.), Peru 128/D9
Paracatu, Brazil 132/E7
Paracatu (riv.), Brazil 132/E7
Paracel (isls.), China 85/E2
Parachilna, S. Australia 88/F6
Parachilna, S. Australia 94/F4
Parachute, Colo. 208/C4
Paraćin, Yugoslavia 45/E4
Parada Esperanza, Uruguay 145/B3
Parada Liebigs, Uruguay 145/A4
Parada Rivas, Uruguay 145/B2
Parade, S. Dak. 298/G3
Pará de Minas, Brazil 132/E7
Pará de Minas, Brazil 135/D1
Paradip, India 68/F4
Paradis, La. 238/M4
Paradise, Ariz. 198/F7
Paradise, Calif. 204/D4
Paradise, Guyana 131/C3
Paradise, Kansas 232/D2
Paradise, Mich. 250/D2
Paradise (lake), Mich. 250/E3
Paradise, Mo. 261/D4
Paradise, Mont. 262/B3
Paradise, Newf. 166/D2
Paradise (riv.), Newf. 166/C3
Paradise, Nova Scotia 168/C4
Paradise (lake), Nova Scotia 168/C4
Paradise, Pa. 294/K5
Paradise, Texas 303/G5
Paradise, Utah 304/C2
Paradise, W. Va. 312/C5
Paradise Hill, Okla. 288/R3
Paradise Hill, Sask. 181/B2
Paradise Inn, Wash. 310/D4
Paradise River, Newf. 166/C3
Paradise Valley, Alberta 182/E3
Paradise Valley, Ariz. 198/D5
Paradise Valley, Nev. 266/F6
Paradise Valley, Nev. 266/D1
Paradise Valley, Wyo. 319/F3
Paradisino (peak), Switzerland 39/K4
Paradiso, Switzerland 39/G5
Paradox, Colo. 208/B6
Paragon, Ind. 227/D6
Paragonah, Utah 304/B6
Paragould, Ark. 202/J1
Paraguá (riv.), Bolivia 136/E4
Paragua (riv.), Venezuela 124/G4
Paraguaçu (riv.), Brazil 120/F4
Paraguaçu (riv.), Brazil 132/F6
Paraguaçu Paulista, Brazil 132/D8
Paraguai (riv.) 120/D4
Paraguai (riv.), Brazil 132/B8
Paraguaipoa, Venezuela 124/C2
Paraguaná (pen.), Venezuela 124/C1
Paraguarí (dept.), Paraguay 144/D4-5
Paraguay 2/F7
Paraguay 120/D5
PARAGUAY 144
Paraguay (riv.), Argentina 143/E1
Paraguay (riv.), Bolivia 136/F7
Paraguay (riv.), Paraguay 144/D4
Paraíba (state), Brazil 132/G4
Paraíba (riv.), Brazil 120/E5
Paraíba (riv.), Brazil 135/E2
Paraíba do Sul, Brazil 135/E3
Parainen, Finland 18/M6
Paraíso, C. Rica 154/F6
Paraíso, Dom. Rep. 158/D7
Paraíso, Mexico 150/N7
Paraíso de Chabasquén, Venezuela 124/D3
Parakou, Benin 106/E7
Parallel, Kansas 232/F2
Paraloma, Ark. 202/B6
Paramaribo (dist.), Suriname 131/D2
Paramaribo (cap.), Suriname 131/D2
Paramaribo (cap.), Suriname 2/G5
Paramaribo (cap.), Suriname 120/D2
Paramithía, Greece 45/E6
Paramonga, Peru 128/C8
Paramount, Calif. 204/C11
Paramus, N.J. 273/B1
Paramushir (isl.) 54/S5
Paramushir (isl.), U.S.S.R. 48/Q4
Paran (dry riv.), Israel 65/D5
Paraná (riv.) 2/G7
Paraná (riv.) 120/D5
Paraná, Argentina 143/F5
Paraná, Argentina 120/D6
Paraná (riv.), Argentina 143/E2
Paraná (state), Brazil 132/D9
Paraná (state), Brazil 135/B4
Paranã, Brazil 132/E6
Paraná (riv.), Brazil 132/C8
Paranã (riv.), Brazil 132/E6
Paranaguá, Brazil 120/E5
Paranaguá, Brazil 132/E9
Paranaguá, Brazil 135/B4
Paranaíba, Brazil 132/D7
Paranam, Suriname 131/D3
Paranapanema (riv.), Brazil 132/C8
Paranapanema (riv.), Brazil 135/B3
Paranapiacaba (range), Brazil 135/B4
Paranatinga (riv.), Brazil 120/D4
Paranatinga (riv.), Brazil 132/C6
Parang, Maguindanao, Philippines 82/E7
Parang, Sulu, Philippines 82/C8
Parao (riv.), Uruguay 145/E3
Paraparaumu, N. Zealand 100/E4
Parapetí (riv.), Bolivia 136/D6
Para Station, N.S. Wales 97/B3
Parati, Brazil 135/D3
Paratinga, Brazil 132/F6
Paray-le-Monial, France 28/F4
Parbhani, India 68/D5
Parchim, Germany 22/D2
Parchman, Miss. 256/D3
Parchment, Mich. 250/D6
Parczew, Poland 47/F3
Pardee (res.), Calif. 204/C9
Pardee, Va. 307/C6
Pardeeville, Wis. 317/H8
Pardes Hanna-Karkur, Israel 65/B2
Parding, China 77/C5
Pardo (riv.), Brazil 132/D8
Pardo (riv.), Brazil 132/F6
Pardo (riv.), Brazil 135/B2
Pardo (riv.), Brazil 132/C8
Pardoe, Pa. 294/B3
Pardoo, W. Australia 92/B3
Pardubice, Czech. 41/C1
Pare, Indonesia 85/K2
Parece Vela (isl.), Japan 54/P7
Parece Vela (isl.), Japan 87/D3
Parecis (mts.), Brazil 120/C4
Parecis, Serra dos (range), Brazil 132/B6
Paredes de Nava, Spain 33/D1
Paredones, Chile 138/A10
Parent, Québec 174/C3
Pareora, N. Zealand 100/C6
Parepare, Indonesia 85/F6
Parguera, P. Rico 161/A3
Parham, Ant. & Bar. 161/E11
Parham, Ontario 177/H3
Parhams, La. 238/G4
Paria (gulf) 120/C1
Paria (plat.), Ariz. 198/D2
Paria (riv.), Ariz. 198/D1
Paria, Bolivia 136/B5
Paria (gulf), Trin. & Tob. 156/G5
Paria (gulf), Trin. & Tob. 161/A11
Paria (riv.), Utah 304/B6
Paria (gulf), Venezuela 124/H2
Paria (pen.), Venezuela 124/G2
Pariaguán, Venezuela 124/F3
Pariaman, Indonesia 85/B6
Paricutín (vol.), Mexico 150/H7
Parida (isl.), Panama 154/F6
Parika, Guyana 131/B2
Parikkala, Finland 18/Q6
Parima, Sierra (mts.), Venezuela 124/F6
Parinacochas (lake), Peru 128/F10
Parinacota, Cerro (mt.), Chile 138/B1
Parinari, Peru 128/E5
Pariñas (pt.), Peru 128/B5
Parintins, Brazil 120/D3
Parintins, Brazil 132/B3
Paris, Ark. 202/C3
Paris (city) (dept.), France 28/B2
Paris (cap.), France 2/J3
Paris (cap.), France 7/E4
Paris (cap.), France 28/B2
Paris, Idaho 220/G7
Paris, Ill. 222/F4
Paris, Iowa 229/K4
Paris, Ky. 237/N4
Paris•, Maine 243/B7
Paris, Mich. 250/D5
Paris, Miss. 256/F2
Paris, Mo. 261/J4
Paris, Ohio 284/H4
Paris, Ontario 177/D4
Paris, Tenn. 237/E8
Paris, Texas 303/J4
Paris, Texas 188/G4
Paris, Va. 307/N3
Paris Crossing, Ind. 227/F7
Parish, N.Y. 276/H4
Parish, Uruguay 145/C3
Parishville, N.Y. 276/L1
Parisville, Mich. 250/G5
Parisville, Québec 172/F3
Parita, Panama 154/G6
Parita (bay), Panama 154/G6
Park (co.), Colo. 208/H4
Park (range), Colo. 208/F1
Park (riv.), Conn. 210/E2
Park, Kansas 232/B2
Park (co.), Mont. 262/F5
Park (riv.), N. Dak. 282/R3
Park (dist.), Scotland 15/B2
Park (co.), Wyo. 319/C1
Parkano, Finland 18/N6
Parkbeg, Sask. 181/E5
Park City, Ill. 222/B4
Park City, Kansas 232/E4
Park City, Ky. 237/J6
Park City, Mont. 262/H5
Park City, Utah 304/C3
Parkdale, Ark. 202/H7
Parkdale, Colo. 208/H6
Parkdale, Oreg. 291/F2
Parkdale, Pr. Edward I. 168/E2
Parke (co.), Ind. 227/C5
Parker, Ariz. 198/A4
Parker (dam), Ariz. 198/A4
Parker, Colo. 208/K4
Parker, Fla. 212/C6
Parker, Idaho 220/G6
Parker, Kansas 232/H3
Parker, Pa. 294/C3
Parker, S. Dak. 298/P7
Parker (lake), S. Dak. 298/P3
Parker (co.), Texas 303/G5
Parker, Texas 303/H1
Parker, Wash. 310/E4
Parker City, Ind. 227/G4
Parker Dam, Calif. 204/L9
Parkersburg, Ill. 222/F5
Parkersburg, Ind. 227/D5
Parkersburg, Iowa 229/H3
Parkersburg, W. Va. 188/K3
Parkersburg, W. Va. 312/D4
Parkers Cove, Newf. 166/D4
Parkers Cove, Nova Scotia 168/C4
Parkers Lake, Ky. 237/M7
Parkers Prairie, Minn. 255/C4
Parkertown, N.J. 273/E4
Parkerview, Sask. 181/H4
Parkerville, Kansas 232/F3
Parkes, N.S. Wales 88/H6
Parkes, N.S. Wales 97/E3
Parkesburg, Pa. 294/L6
Park Falls, Wis. 317/F4
Park Forest, Ill. 222/B6
Park Forest South, Ill. 222/F2
Park Hall, Md. 245/N8
Park Hill, Okla. 288/R3
Parkhill, Ontario 177/C4
Park Hills, Ky. 237/S2
Parkin, Ark. 202/J3
Parkland, Alberta 182/D4
Parkland, Fla. 212/F5
Parkland, Okla. 288/N3
Parkland, Wash. 310/C3
Parkman•, Maine 243/D5
Parkman, Ohio 284/H3
Parkman, Sask. 181/K6
Parkman, Wyo. 319/E1
Park Place, Oreg. 291/B2
Park Rapids, Minn. 255/D4
Park Rapids, Wash. 310/H2
Park Ridge, Ill. 222/B5
Park Ridge, N.J. 273/B1
Park Ridge, Wis. 317/H6
Park River, N. Dak. 282/P3
Parks, Ariz. 198/C3
Parks, Ark. 202/B4
Parks, La. 238/G6
Parks, Nebr. 264/C4
Parksdale, Mo. 261/L6
Parkside, Pa. 294/M7
Parkside, Sask. 181/E2
Parksley, Va. 307/S5
Parkston, S. Dak. 298/O7
Parksville, Br. Col. 184/J3
Parksville, Ky. 237/M5
Parksville, N.Y. 276/L7
Parksville, S.C. 296/C4
Parkton, Md. 245/M2
Parkton, N.C. 281/M5
Park Valley, Utah 304/A2
Parkview (mt.), Colo. 208/G2
Parkville, Md. 245/M3
Parkville, Mo. 261/O5
Parkville, Pa. 294/J6
Parkville, Victoria 97/H5
Parkway, Mo. 261/L6
Parkway Village, Ky. 237/J2
Parkwood, N.C. 281/M3
Parlakhemundi, India 68/E5
Parlier, Calif. 204/F7
Parlin, Colo. 208/F6
Parlin (pond), Maine 243/C4
Parma, Idaho 220/B6
Parma (prov.), Italy 34/C2
Parma, Italy 7/E4
Parma, Italy 34/C2
Parma (riv.), Italy 34/C2
Parma, Mich. 250/E6
Parma, Mo. 261/N9
Parma, Ohio 284/H9
Parmachenee (lake), Maine 243/B5
Parma Heights, Ohio 284/G9
Parmana, Venezuela 124/F4
Parmele, N.C. 281/P3
Parmelee, S. Dak. 298/G7
Parmer (co.), Texas 303/B3
Parnaguá, Brazil 132/E5
Parnaíba, Brazil 132/F3
Parnaíba, Brazil 120/E3
Parnaíba (riv.), Brazil 120/E3
Parnaíba (riv.), Brazil 132/F3
Parnamirim, Brazil 132/F4
Parnassus (mt.), Greece 45/F6
Parnassus, N. Zealand 100/D5
Parndana, S. Australia 94/E6
Parnell, Iowa 229/J5
Parnell, Mo. 261/C2
Pärnu, U.S.S.R. 7/G3
Pärnu, U.S.S.R. 53/C1
Pärnu, U.S.S.R. 52/C3
Pärnu, U.S.S.R. 48/C4
Paro, Bhutan 68/F3
Paron, Ark. 202/E4
Paroo (chan.), N.S. Wales 97/B2
Paroo (riv.), N. S. Wales 88/G5
Paroo (riv.), N.S. Wales 97/C1
Paroo (riv.), Queensland 95/C6
Paropamisus (mts.), Afghanistan 59/H3
Paropamisus (range), Afghanistan 68/A2
Páros (isl.), Greece 45/G7
Parow, S. Africa 118/F6
Parowan, Utah 304/B6
Parpan, Switzerland 39/J3
Parr, Ind. 227/C2
Parr, S.C. 296/E3
Parral, Chile 138/A11
Parral, Mexico 150/G3
Parral, Ohio 284/G4
Parramatta, N.S. Wales 88/K4
Parramatta, N.S. Wales 97/H3
Parramatta (riv.), N.S. Wales 88/K4
Parramatta (riv.), N.S. Wales 97/J3
Parramore (isl.), Va. 307/S5
Parran, Md. 245/M6
Parras de la Fuente, Mexico 150/H4
Parratah, Tasmania 99/D4
Parrett (riv.), England 13/E6
Parrish, Ala. 195/D3
Parrish, Fla. 212/D4
Parrish, Wis. 317/H5
Parris Island Marine Base, S.C. 296/F7
Parrotsville, Tenn. 237/P8
Parrott, Georgia 217/D7
Parrott, Va. 307/G6
Parrsboro, Nova Scotia 168/D3
Parry (bay), N.W.T. 187/K3
Parry (cape), N.W.T. 187/F2
Parry (chan.), N.W.T. 187/G2
Parry (chan.), N.W.T. 146/G2
Parry (chan.), N.W.T. 162/E-H1
Parry (isls.), N.W.T. 146/G2
Parry (isls.), N.W.T. 187/G2
Parry (pen.), N.W.T. 187/F2
Parry (isl.), Ontario 177/D2
Parry (sound), Ontario 177/D2
Parry, Sask. 181/G6
Parry Sound, Ont. 162/J6

Parry Sound (terr. dist.), Ontario 175/E3
Parry Sound, Ontario 175/D3
Parry Sound, Ontario 177/E2
Parseierspitze (mt.), Austria 41/A3
Parshall, Colo. 208/G2
Parshall, N. Dak. 282/F4
Parsippany-Troy Hills•, N.J. 273/E2
Parsnip (riv.), Br. Col. 184/F3
Parson, Br. Col. 184/J4
Parsons, Kans. 188/G3
Parsons, Kansas 232/G4
Parsons, Tenn. 237/E9
Parsons, W. Va. 312/G4
Parsonsburg, Md. 245/R7
Parson's Pond, Newf. 166/C3
Partanna, Italy 34/D6
Partapgarh, India 68/C4
Parthenay, France 28/C4
Partinico, Italy 34/D6
Partizansk, U.S.S.R. 48/O5
Partizánske, Czech. 41/E2
Partlow, Va. 307/N4
Partridge, Kansas 232/D4
Partridge (riv.), Minn. 255/G3
Partridge (bay), Newf. 166/C3
Partridge (pt.), Newf. 166/C3
Partry (mts.), Ireland 17/C4
Paru (riv.), Brazil 132/C3
Paru de Oeste (riv.), Brazil 120/D3
Paru de Oeste (riv.), Brazil 132/B3
Paruro, Peru 128/F9
Parvatipuram, India 68/E5
Parys, S. Africa 118/D5
Pas, De (riv.), Québec 174/D1
Pasadena, Calif. 188/C4
Pasadena, Calif. 204/C10
Pasadena, Md. 245/M4
Pasadena, Newf. 166/C4
Pasadena, Texas 303/J2
Pasado (cape), Ecuador 128/B3
Pasaje, Ecuador 128/C4
Pasawng, Burma 72/C3
Pasayten (riv.), Wash. 310/E2
Pascagoula, Miss. 256/G10
Pascagoula (riv.), Miss. 256/G9
Pascalis, Québec 174/B3
Paşcani, Romania 45/H2
Paschall, N.C. 281/N1
Pasco (dept.), Peru 128/E8
Pasco, Wash. 310/F4
Pascoag, R.I. 249/H5
Pascola, Mo. 261/N10
Pascua (riv.), Chile 138/C7
Pas-de-Calais (dept.), France 28/E2
Pasewalk, Germany 22/F2
Pasighat, India 68/G3
Pasinler, Turkey 63/J3
Pasión (riv.), Guatemala 154/B2
Paskenta, Calif. 204/C4
Pasłek, Poland 47/D1
Pasley (bay), N.W.T. 187/J2
Pasni, Pakistan 68/A3
Pasni, Pakistan 54/H7
Pasni, Pakistan 59/H4
Paso Ataques, Uruguay 145/D2
Paso Barreto, Paraguay 144/D3
Paso de Andrés Pérez, Uruguay 145/B3
Paso de Indios, Argentina 143/C5
Paso de la Laguna, Salto, Uruguay 145/B2
Paso de la Laguna, Tacuarembó, Uruguay 145/D3
Paso de las Piedras, Uruguay 145/C2
Paso del Borracho, Uruguay 145/D2
Paso del Cerro, Uruguay 145/C2
Paso de León, Uruguay 145/B1
Paso del Horno, Uruguay 145/C2
Paso de Los Libres, Argentina 143/E2
Paso de los Toros, Uruguay 145/C3
Paso del Parque, Uruguay 145/B2
Paso de Ovejas, Mexico 150/Q2
Paso de Patria, Paraguay 144/C5
Paso de Ramos, Uruguay 145/C1
Paso de Uleste, Uruguay 145/B3
Paso Flores, Argentina 143/C5
Paso Hondo, Uruguay 145/B4
Paso Potrero, Uruguay 145/C2
Pasorapa, Bolivia 136/C6
Paso Real, Honduras 154/E3
Paso Robles, Calif. 204/E8
Paspébiac, Québec 172/D2
Pasqua, Sask. 181/F5
Pasque (isl.), Mass. 249/L7
Pasquia (hills), Sask. 181/J2
Pasquia (riv.), Sask. 181/K2
Pasquotank (co.), N.C. 281/S2
Pass (creek), Wyo. 319/F5
Passaconaway (mt.), N.H. 268/E4
Passadumkeag•, Maine 243/F5
Passage (isl.), Mich. 250/E1
Passage East, Ireland 17/G7
Passagem Franca, Brazil 132/E4
Passage West, Ireland 17/E8
Passage West, Ireland 10/B5
Passaic, Md. 261/D6
Passaic (co.), N.J. 273/E1
Passaic, N.J. 273/E2
Passaic (riv.), N.J. 273/E2
Passamaquoddy (bay), Maine 243/J5
Passamaquoddy (bay), New Bruns. 170/C3
Passamaquoddy Ind. Res., Maine 243/J6
Passau, Germany 22/E4
Pass Christian, Miss. 256/F10
Passero (cape), Italy 7/F5
Passero (cape), Italy 34/E6
Passes (lake), Québec 172/F2

Passi, Philippines 82/D5
Passo Fundo, Brazil 120/D5
Passo Fundo, Brazil 132/D10
Passos, Brazil 132/E8
Passos, Brazil 135/C2
Passumpsic, Vt. 268/D3
Passumpsic (riv.), Vt. 268/D2
Pastaza (riv.) 120/B3
Pastaza (prov.), Ecuador 128/D3
Pastaza (riv.), Ecuador 128/D4
Pastaza (riv.), Peru 128/D5
Pasto, Colombia 120/B2
Pasto, Colombia 126/B7
Pastol (bay), Alaska 196/F2
Pastora (peak), Ariz. 198/F2
Pastrana, Spain 33/E2
Pastura, N. Mex. 274/E4
Pasuquin, Philippines 82/C1
Pasuruan, Indonesia 85/K2
Pasvalys, U.S.S.R. 53/C2
Pasvikelv (riv.), Norway 18/Q2
Pásztó, Hungary 41/E3
Pata, Bolivia 136/A4
Patacamaya, Bolivia 136/B5
Patagonia (reg.), Argentina 120/C7
Patagonia (reg.), Argentina 143/C5
Patagonia, Ariz. 198/E7
Pataguanset (lake), Conn. 210/G3
Pataha, Wash. 310/H4
Pataha (creek), Wash. 310/H4
Patan, India 68/C4
Patapédia (riv.), New Bruns. 170/C1
Patapédia (riv.), Québec 172/B2
Patapsco, Md. 245/L2
Patapsco (riv.), Md. 245/M4
Pataskala, Ohio 284/E5
Pataz, Peru 128/D6
Patchewollock, Victoria 97/A4
Patch Grove, Wis. 317/D10
Patchogue, N.Y. 276/P9
Patea, N. Zealand 100/E3
Paternion, Austria 41/B3
Pateros, Wash. 310/E2
Pateros (lake), Wash. 310/F2
Paterson, N.J. 188/M2
Paterson, N.J. 273/E2
Paterson, Wash. 310/F5
Patesville, Ky. 237/H5
Pathankot, India 68/D2
Pathfinder (res.), Wyo. 188/E2
Pathfinder (res.), Wyo. 319/F3
Pathiu, Thailand 72/C5
Pathlow, Sask. 181/G3
Pati (pt.), Guam 86/K6
Pati, Indonesia 85/J2
Patía, Colombia 126/B6
Patía (riv.), Colombia 126/B6
Patiala, India 68/D2
Patillas, P. Rico 161/E2
Patillas (lake), P. Rico 161/E2
Pativilca (riv.), Peru 128/D8
Patmos, Ark. 202/C7
Pátmos (isl.), Greece 45/H7
Patna, India 68/F3
Patna, India 54/K7
Patna, Scotland 15/D5
Patnanongan (isl.), Philippines 82/D3
Patnos, Turkey 63/K3
Patoka, Ill. 222/D5
Patoka, Ind. 227/B8
Patoka (riv.), Ind. 227/C8
Paton, Iowa 229/E4
Patos, Brazil 120/F3
Patos, Brazil 132/G4
Patos (lake), Brazil 120/D6
Patos (lake), Brazil 132/D10
Patos (lag.), Brazil 132/D10
Patos de Minas, Brazil 120/E4
Patos de Minas, Brazil 132/E7
Patoutville, La. 238/G7
Patquía, Argentina 143/C3
Pátrai, Greece 7/G5
Pátrai, Greece 45/E6
Patricia, Alberta 182/E4
Patricia, S. Dak. 298/G7
Patricia, Texas 303/B5
Patricio Lynch (isl.), Chile 138/D7
Patrick, Neth. Ant. 161/F8
Patrick, S.C. 296/G2
Patrick (co.), Va. 307/H7
Patrick A.F.B., Fla. 212/F3
Patricksburg, Ind. 227/D6
Patrick's Cove, Newf. 166/C4
Patrick Springs, Va. 307/H7
Patrickswell, Ireland 17/D6
Patriot, Ind. 227/H7
Patriot, Ohio 284/F8
Patrocínio, Brazil 132/E7
Patronville, Ind. 227/C9
Patsaliga (creek), Ala. 195/F7
Patsburg, Ala. 195/F7
Patta (isl.), Kenya 115/H4
Pattani, Thailand 72/D6
Patten, Maine 243/H4
Patten•, Maine 243/F4
Pattenburg, N.J. 273/C2
Patterson, Ark. 202/H3
Patterson, Calif. 204/D6
Patterson, Georgia 217/H8
Patterson, Ill. 222/C4
Patterson, Iowa 229/F6
Patterson, La. 238/H7
Patterson (pt.), Mich. 250/D3
Patterson, Mo. 261/L8
Patterson, N.Y. 276/N7
Patterson, N.C. 281/F3
Patterson, Edward A. (lake), N. Dak. 282/E6
Patterson, Ohio 284/C4
Patterson, Va. 307/D6
Patterson (creek), W. Va. 312/J4
Patterson Creek, W. Va. 312/J3
Pattersonville, N.Y. 276/M5

Patti, Italy 34/E5
Pattison, Miss. 256/C7
Patton, Mo. 261/M8
Patton, Pa. 294/E4
Pattonsburg, Mo. 261/D2
Patuanak, Sask. 181/L3
Patuca, Honduras 154/E3
Patuca (pt.), Honduras 154/E3
Patuca (riv.), Honduras 154/E3
Patuha (mt.), Indonesia 85/H2
Patutahi, N. Zealand 100/F3
Patuxent (riv.), Md. 245/M7
Patuxent River Nav. Air Test Ctr., Md. 245/N7
Patzau, Wis. 317/B3
Pátzcuaro, Mexico 150/J7
Pátzcuaro (lake), Mexico 150/J7
Pau, France 28/C6
Pau, France 7/D4
Paucarbamba, Peru 128/E9
Paucartambo, Cuzco, Peru 128/G9
Paucartambo, Pasco, Peru 128/E8
Paudash (lake), Ontario 177/F3
Pau dos Ferros, Brazil 132/G4
Pauillac, France 28/C5
Paukaa, Hawaii 218/J5
Paul, Ala. 195/E8
Paul, Idaho 220/E7
Paul (isl.), Newf. 166/B2
Paul (stream), Vt. 268/D2
Paulatuk, N.W.T. 162/D2
Paulatuk, N.W.T. 187/F3
Paulaya (riv.), Honduras 154/E3
Paulden, Ariz. 198/C4
Paulding (co.), Georgia 217/C3
Paulding, Miss. 256/F6
Paulding (co.), Ohio 284/A3
Paulding, Ohio 284/A3
Paulette, Miss. 256/H4
Paulina, La. 238/L3
Paulina, Oreg. 291/G3
Paulina (lake), Oreg. 291/F4
Pauline, Kansas 232/G3
Pauline, Nebr. 264/F4
Pauline, S.C. 296/D2
Paulins Kill (riv.), N.J. 273/D1
Paul Isnard, Fr. Guiana 131/D3
Paulistana, Brazil 132/F4
Paullina, Iowa 229/B3
Paulo Afonso, Brazil 120/F3
Paulo Afonso, Brazil 132/G5
Paulo Afonso (falls), Brazil 120/F3
Paulo de Faria, Brazil 135/B2
Paulsboro, N.J. 273/C4
Paul Smiths, N.Y. 276/M2
Paul Spur, Ariz. 198/F7
Pauls Valley, Okla. 288/M5
Paungassi, Manitoba 179/G2
Paungde, Burma 72/B3
Pauni, India 68/E4
Paunsaugunt (plat.), Utah 304/B6
Paupack, Pa. 294/M3
Paute, Ecuador 128/C4
Pauto (riv.), Colombia 126/E5
Pauwalu (pt.), Hawaii 218/K2
Pauwela, Hawaii 218/K2
Pavia (prov.), Italy 34/B2
Pavia, Italy 34/B2
Pavilion (key), Fla. 212/E6
Pavilion, N.Y. 276/D5
Pavillion, Wyo. 319/D2
Pãvilosta, U.S.S.R. 53/A2
Pãvilosta, U.S.S.R. 52/B3
Pavlodar, U.S.S.R. 54/J4
Pavlodar, U.S.S.R. 48/H4
Pavlof (bay), Alaska 196/F3
Pavlof (vol.), Alaska 196/F3
Pavlograd, U.S.S.R. 52/E5
Pavlovo, U.S.S.R. 52/F3
Pavo, Georgia 217/E9
Pavón, Colombia 126/D6
Pavullo nel Frignano, Italy 34/C2
Pawcatuck, Conn. 210/H3
Pawcatuck (riv.), Conn. 210/H3
Pawcatuck (riv.), R.I. 249/G7
Pawhuska, Okla. 288/N1
Pawling, N.Y. 276/N7
Pawleys Island, S.C. 296/J5
Pawn, Nam (riv.), Burma 72/C2
Pawnee (creek), Colo. 208/M1
Pawnee, Ill. 222/D4
Pawnee (co.), Kansas 232/C3
Pawnee (co.), Kansas 232/B3
Pawnee (co.), Nebr. 264/H4
Pawnee (co.), Okla. 288/N2
Pawnee, Okla. 288/N2
Pawnee City, Nebr. 264/H4
Pawnee Rock, Kansas 232/D3
Pawpaw, Ill. 222/E2
Paw Paw, Mich. 250/D6
Paw Paw (riv.), Mich. 250/C6
Paw Paw, W. Va. 312/K3
Paw Paw Lake, Mich. 250/C6
Pawtuckaway (pond), N.H. 268/E5
Pawtucket, R.I. 249/J5
Pax, W. Va. 312/D7
Paxico, Kansas 232/F2
Paxoí (isl.), Greece 45/D6
Paxson, Alaska 196/J2
Paxton, Fla. 212/C5
Paxton, Ill. 222/E3
Paxton, Ind. 227/C6
Paxton•, Mass. 249/G3
Paxton, Nebr. 264/C3
Paxville, S.C. 296/G4
Payakumbuh, Indonesia 85/C6
Paya Lebar, Singapore 72/F6
Payerne, Switzerland 39/C3
Payette (co.), Idaho 220/B5
Payette, Idaho 220/B5
Payette (lake), Idaho 220/C4
Payette (mts.), Idaho 220/C4
Payette (riv.), Idaho 220/B6
Payne, Georgia 217/E5
Payne, Minn. 255/F9
Payne, Ohio 284/A3

Payne (co.), Okla. 288/N2
Payne (lake),Que. 162/J4
Payne (lake), Québec 174/E1
Payneham, S. Australia 88/E8
Payneham, S. Australia 94/B7
Paynes, Miss. 256/D3
Paynes Creek, Calif. 204/D3
Payne's Find, W. Australia 92/B5
Payneville, Ind. 227/F7
Paynesville, Mich. 250/C2
Paynesville, Minn. 255/D5
Paynesville, Mo. 261/L4
Paynton, Sask. 181/B2
Paysandú (dept.), Uruguay 145/B3
Paysandú, Uruguay 145/A3
Paysandú, Uruguay 120/D6
Payson, Ariz. 198/D4
Payson, Ill. 222/B4
Payson, Utah 304/C3
Pay-Yer (mt.), U.S.S.R. 52/K1
Pazanan, Iran 66/F5
Pazar, Rize, Turkey 63/J2
Pazar, Tokat, Turkey 63/G2
Pazarcık, Turkey 63/G4
Pazardzhik, Bulgaria 45/G4
Pazaryeri, Turkey 63/C3
Paz de Ariporo, Colombia 126/E5
Paz de Río, Colombia 126/D4
Pazña, Bolivia 136/B6
Pea (riv.), Ala. 195/F8
Peabody, Kansas 232/E3
Peabody, Ky. 237/O6
Peabody, Mass. 249/E5
Peace (riv.), Alberta 182/B1
Peace (riv.), Alta. 162/E4
Peace (riv.), Br. Col. 162/D4
Peace (riv.), Br. Col. 184/G2
Peace (riv.), Canada 146/G4
Peace (riv.), Fla. 212/E4
Peace Dale-Wakefield, R.I. 249/J7
Peace Garden, Manitoba 179/C5
Peace River, Alberta 182/B1
Peace River, Alta. 146/G4
Peace River, Alta. 162/E4
Peace Valley, Mo. 261/J9
Peach (co.), Georgia 217/E5
Peacham•, Vt. 268/C3
Peach Bottom, Pa. 294/K6
Peachland, Br. Col. 184/G5
Peachland, N.C. 281/J5
Peach Orchard, Ark. 202/J1
Peach Springs, Ariz. 198/B3
Peachtree (creek), Georgia 217/K1
Peachtree, North Fork (creek), Georgia 217/L1
Peachtree City, Georgia 217/C4
Peacock, Alberta 182/D4
Peacock, Mich. 250/D4
Peacock, Texas 303/D4
Peahi, Hawaii 218/K2
Peak, The (mt.), England 13/J2
Peak (range), Queensland 95/C4
Peak, S.C. 296/E3
Peak District National Park, England 13/F4
Peak Hill, N.S. Wales 97/E3
Peak Hill, W. Australia 92/B4
Peaks, Va. 307/O5
Peale (mts.), Idaho 220/G7
Peale (mt.), Utah 304/E5
Peapack-Gladstone, N.J. 273/D2
Pear, W. Va. 312/E7
Pearblossom, Calif. 204/H9
Pearce, Alberta 182/D5
Pearce, Ariz. 198/F7
Pearcy, Ark. 202/D5
Peard (bay), Alaska 196/G1
Pea Ridge, Ark. 202/B1
Pea Ridge Nat'l Mil. Park, Ark. 202/B1
Pearisburg, Va. 307/G6
Pearl (harb.), Hawaii 188/F5
Pearl (harb.), Hawaii 218/A3
Pearl, Ill. 222/C4
Pearl (riv.), La. 238/L5
Pearl (riv.), Miss. 256/D6
Pearl (cays), Nicaragua 154/F4
Pearl (cays), S. Dak. 298/N5
Pearl, Texas 303/F6
Pearland, Texas 303/J2
Pearl and Hermes (reef), Hawaii 188/E5
Pearl and Hermes (atoll), Hawaii 218/B5
Pearl Beach, Mich. 250/G6
Pearl City, Hawaii 218/B3
Pearl City, Ill. 222/D1
Pearl Harbor Naval Station, Hawaii 218/B3
Pearlington, Miss. 256/E10
Pearl Lake, Québec 172/E2
Pearl River, La. 238/L6
Pearl River (co.), Miss. 256/E9
Pearl River, N.Y. 276/K8
Pearsall, Texas 303/E9
Pearse (canal), Alaska 196/N2
Pearson, Ark. 202/F3
Pearson, Georgia 217/G8
Pearson, Okla. 288/N4
Pearson, Wis. 317/H5
Peary (chan.), N.W.T. 162/M3
Peary (chan.), N.W.T. 187/H2
Peary Land (reg.), Greenl. 4/A11
Peary Land (reg.), Greenland 146/Q1
Pease, Minn. 255/E5
Pease (riv.), Texas 303/D3
Pease A.F.B., N.H. 268/F5
Peasleeville, N.Y. 276/N1
Peason, La. 238/D4
Pebane, Mozambique 118/F3
Pebble, Idaho 220/G7
Pebble Beach, Calif. 204/C7
Pebworth, Ky. 237/O5
Pecan, Yugoslavia 45/E4

Peçanha, Brazil 132/F7
Pecan Island, La. 238/F7
Pecan Point, Ark. 202/L3
Pecatonica, Ill. 222/D1
Pecatonica (riv.), Wis. 317/H11
Peccia, Switzerland 39/G4
Pechea, Romania 45/H3
Pechenga, U.S.S.R. 4/C8
Pechenga, U.S.S.R. 52/D1
Pechora, U.S.S.R. 7/K2
Pechora, U.S.S.R. 48/D2
Pechora, U.S.S.R. 4/C7
Pechora, U.S.S.R. 7/K2
Pechora, U.S.S.R. 48/F3
Pechora (bay), U.S.S.R. 52/H1
Pechora (riv.), U.S.S.R. 48/F3
Pechora (riv.), U.S.S.R. 48/C4
Pechora (sea), U.S.S.R. 52/H1
Pecica, Romania 45/E2
Peck, Idaho 220/B3
Peck, Kansas 232/E4
Peck, La. 238/G5
Peck, Mich. 250/G5
Peckerwood (lake), Ark. 202/G4
Peckham, Okla. 288/M1
Pecks Mill, W. Va. 312/B7
Peconic, N.Y. 276/P8
Peconic (bay), N.Y. 276/R9
Pecos (riv.), N. Mex. 274/E5
Pecos (co.), Texas 303/B7
Pecos (riv.), Texas 303/C7
Pecos, Texas 303/D10
Pecos (riv.), U.S. 146/H6
Pecos Nat'l Mon., N. Mex. 274/D3
Pécs, Hungary 7/F3
Pécs, Hungary 41/E3
Pécsvárad, Hungary 41/E3
Peculiar, Mo. 261/D5
Pedasi, Panama 154/G7
Pedder (lake), Tasmania 99/B4
Pedee, Oreg. 291/D3
Pedernal, Argentina 143/G5
Pedernales, Salar de (salt dep.), Chile 138/D3
Pedernales (prov.), Dom. Rep. 158/D7
Pedernales, Dom. Rep. 158/C7
Pedernales, Ecuador 128/B2
Pedernales, Texas 303/F7
Pedernales, Venezuela 124/G3
Pederneiras, Brazil 135/B3
Pedlar Mills, Va. 307/K5
Pedley, Alberta 182/B3
Pedley, Calif. 204/E10
Pedra Azul, Brazil 132/F6
Pedraza, Colombia 126/C2
Pedregal, Venezuela 124/C2
Pedreiras, Brazil 132/E4
Pedrera, Uruguay 145/C6
Pedricktown, N.J. 273/C4
Pedrika, S. Australia 94/D2
Pedro (bank), Jamaica 156/B3
Pedro (cays), Jamaica 156/C3
Pedro, Ohio 284/E8
Pedro, S. Dak. 298/E5
Pedro (pt.), Sri Lanka 68/E6
Pedro Afonso, Brazil 132/E5
Pedro Antonio de los Santos, Mexico 150/Q7
Pedro Bay, Alaska 196/H3
Pedro Betancourt, Cuba 158/D1
Pedro Chico, Colombia 126/E7
Pedro de Valdivia, Chile 138/B4
Pedro Díaz Colodrero, Argentina 143/G5
Pedro Juan Caballero, Argentina 120/D5
Pedro Juan Cabellero, Paraguay 144/F3
Pedro Luro, Argentina 143/D4
Pedro Montoya, Mexico 150/K6
Pedro Segundo, Brazil 132/F4
Peduyim, Israel 65/B5
Peebles, Ohio 284/D6
Peebles, Sask. 181/J5
Peebles (trad. co.), Scotland 15/B5
Peebles, S. Dak. 298/N5
Peebles, Scotland 15/E5
Peebles, Scotland 15/E5
Pee Dee, N.C. 281/K5
Pee Dee (riv.), N.C. 281/J2
Peedee, S.C. 296/H3
Pee Dee (riv.), S.C. 296/H2
Peekskill, N.Y. 276/N8
Peeksville, Wis. 317/E3
Peel (riv.) 162/C2
Peel, I. of Man 10/D3
Peel, I. of Man 13/C3
Peel, New Bruns. 170/C2
Peel (sound), N.W.T. 162/G1
Peel (sound), N.W.T. 187/J2
Peel (reg. munic.), Ontario 177/E4
Peel (inlet), W. Australia 92/A2
Peel (riv.), Yukon 187/E3
Peel (riv.), Yukon 187/E3
Peel Fell (mt.), England 13/E2
Peel Fell (mt.), Scotland 15/F5
Pe Ell, Wash. 310/B4
Peene (riv.), Germany 22/E2
Peenemünde, Germany 22/E1
Peer, Belgium 27/G6
Peera Peera Poolanna (lake), S. Australia 94/F2
Peerless (lake), Alberta 182/C1
Peerless, Mont. 262/L2
Peerless, Mont. 146/H3
Peerless Lake, Alberta 182/C1
Peerless Park, Mo. 261/N4
Peers, Alberta 182/B3
Peers, Mo. 261/K5
Peery (lake), N.S. Wales 97/B2
Peesane, Sask. 181/H3
Peetz, Colo. 208/N1
Peever, S. Dak. 298/R2
Pefferlaw, Ontario 177/E3
Pegarah, Tasmania 99/B1
Pegasus (bay), N. Zealand 100/D5

Pegasus, Port (inlet), N. Zealand 100/B7
Peggs, Okla. 288/R2
Pegnitz, Germany 22/D4
Pego, Spain 33/F3
Pegram, Tenn. 237/H8
Pegu (div.), Burma 72/C3
Pegu, Burma 54/L8
Pegu, Burma 72/C3
Pegun (isl.), Indonesia 85/J5
Pegu Yoma (mts.), Burma 72/B3
Pehan (Bei'an), China 77/L2
Pehuajó, Argentina 143/D4
Pehuajó, Argentina 120/C6
Peine, Germany 22/D2
Peiping, Poland 47/D2
Peipus (lake), U.S.S.R. 7/G3
Peipus (lake), U.S.S.R. 53/D1
Peipus (lake), U.S.S.R. 48/C4
Peipus (lake), U.S.S.R. 52/C3
Peixe, Brazil 132/D6
Pei Xian, China 77/J5
Pejepscot, Maine 243/D8
Pejivalle, C. Rica 154/F6
Pekalongan, Indonesia 85/J2
Pekan, Malaysia 72/D7
Pekan Nanas, Malaysia 72/E5
Pekelmeer (lake), Neth. Ant. 161/G2
Pekin, Ill. 222/D3
Pekin, Ind. 227/E7
Pekin, N. Dak. 282/O4
Peking (Beijing) (cap.), China 54/N5
Peking (Beijing) (cap.), China 22/O3
Peking (Beijing) (cap.), China 77/J3
Pekisko, Alberta 182/C4
Pelabuhan Ratu (bay), Indonesia 85/G2
Pelagie (isls.), Italy 34/D7
Pelagosa (Palagruža) (isl.), Yugoslavia 45/C4
Pelahatchie, Miss. 256/E6
Peleaga (mt.), Romania 45/F3
Pelechuco, Bolivia 136/A4
Peleduy, U.S.S.R. 48/M4
Pelée (vol.), Martinique 161/C5
Pelée (vol.), Martinique 156/F4
Pelee (pt.), Ontario 177/B6
Peleihari, Indonesia 85/F4
Peleliu (isl.), Belau 87/D5
Peleng (isl.), Indonesia 85/G6
Pelequén, Chile 138/G5
Pelham, Ala. 195/E4
Pelham, Georgia 217/E8
Pelham•, Mass. 249/E3
Pelham•, N.H. 268/E5
Pelham, N.Y. 276/O7
Pelham, N.C. 281/L1
Pelham, Ontario 177/E4
Pelham, Queensland 95/B3
Pelham, Tenn. 237/K10
Pelham Manor, N.Y. 276/O7
Pelhřimov, Czech. 41/C2
Pelican, Alaska 196/M1
Pelican (lake), Alberta 182/D2
Pelican (mt.), Alberta 182/D2
Pelican (mts.), Alberta 182/D2
Pelican (lake), Barbados 161/B9
Pelican, La. 238/C3
Pelican (bay), Manitoba 179/B2
Pelican (lake), Manitoba 179/C5
Pelican (lake), Minn. 255/C4
Pelican (lake), Minn. 255/B5
Pelican (lake), Minn. 255/F2
Pelican (riv.), Minn. 255/B4
Pelican (riv.), Minn. 255/F2
Pelican (lake), Nebr. 264/E2
Pelican (lake), Sask. 181/E5
Pelican, Wis. 317/H4
Pelican Lake, Wis. 317/H4
Pelican Lakes (Breezy Point), Minn. 255/C4
Pelican Narrows, Sask. 181/N3
Pelican Portage, Alberta 182/D2
Pelican Rapids, Manitoba 179/B2
Pelican Rapids, Minn. 255/B4
Pelileo, Ecuador 128/C3
Pelion, S.C. 296/E4
Pelkie, Mich. 250/G1
Pelkosenniemi, Finland 18/P3
Pella, Iowa 229/H4
Pella, Wis. 317/J6
Pell City, Ala. 195/F3
Pellegrini, Argentina 143/D4
Pelletier Mills, New Bruns. 170/B1
Pell Lake, Wis. 317/K10
Pello, Finland 18/O3
Pellston, Mich. 250/E3
Pellville, Ky. 237/H5
Pellworm (isl.), Germany 22/C1
Pelly (bay), N.W. Terr. 187/J3
Pelly (lake), N.W. Terr. 187/H3
Pelly, Sask. 181/K4
Pelly (riv.), Yukon 162/C3
Pelly (mts.), Yukon 187/E3
Pelly (riv.), Yukon 187/E3
Pelly Bay, N.W.T. 162/G2
Pelly Bay, N.W.T. 187/K3
Pelly Crossing, Yukon 187/E3
Peloncillo (mts.), Ariz. 198/G5
Peloncillo (mts.), N. Mex. 274/A6
Pelopónnisos (reg.), Greece 45/F7
Pelotas, Brazil 120/D6
Pelotas, Brazil 132/C10
Pelsart (isl.), W. Australia 92/A5
Pelzer, S.C. 296/B2
Pelzer, Ind. 227/C8
Pemadumcook (lake), Maine 243/F4
Pemalang, Indonesia 85/J2
Pemaquid, Maine 243/E8
Pematangsiantar, Indonesia 54/L9
Pematangsiantar, Indonesia 85/B5
Pemba, Mozambique 118/G2
Pemba, Mozambique 102/F6
Pemba (reg.), Tanzania 115/H5
Pemba (isl.), Tanzania 102/G5
Pemba (isl.), Tanzania 115/H5
Pemberton, Br. Col. 184/F5

mberton, Minn. 255/E7
mberton, N.J. 273/D4
mberton, Ohio 284/B5
mberton, W. Australia 92/A6
mberton, W. Va. 312/D7
mberville, Ohio 284/C3
mbina (riv.), Alberta 182/C3
mbina (hills), Manitoba 179/D5
mbina (riv.), Manitoba 179/C5
mbina (co.), N. Dak. 282/P2
mbina, N. Dak. 282/R2
mbina (riv.), N. Dak. 282/O1
mbine, Wis. 317/L4
mbrey, Wales 13/C6
mbroke, Georgia 217/J6
mbroke, Ky. 237/D7
mbroke, Maine 243/J6
mbroke •, Mass. 249/L4
mbroke •, Maine 243/J6
mbroke •, N.H. 268/E5
mbroke, N.C. 281/L5
mbroke, Ont. 162/J6
mbroke, Ontario 177/G2
mbroke, Ontario 175/E3
mbroke, Va. 307/G6
mbroke, Wales 13/C6
mbroke, Wales 10/D5
mbroke Park, Fla. 212/B4
mbroke Pines, Fla. 212/B4
mbrokeshire Coast National Park,
  Wales 13/C6
mbuang (riv.), Indonesia 85/E6
migewasset, East Branch (riv.),
  N.H. 268/D3
migewasset (riv.), N.H. 268/D4
miscot (co.), Mo. 261/N10
muco, Chile 138/E1
ñablanca, Chile 138/F2
na Blanca, N. Mex. 274/C3
nafiel, Portugal 33/B2
ñaflor, Chile 138/D7
ñal, Trin. & Tob. 161/B11
ñalara (mts.), Spain 33/E2
nalosa, Kansas 232/D4
nalva, Brazil 132/E3
namacor, Portugal 33/C2
nápolis, Brazil 135/A2
ñaranda de Bracamonte, Spain
  33/D2
n Argyl, Pa. 294/M4
ñarroya (peak), Spain 33/F2
ñarroya-Pueblonuevo, Spain
  33/D3
narth, Wales 13/B7
nas (gulf), Chile 120/B7
nas (gulf), Chile 138/D7
ñas (cape), Spain 33/D1
nasco, N. Mex. 274/C2
ña Vieja (mt.), Spain 33/D1
nbrook, Pa. 294/J5
ncarrow (head), N. Zealand
  100/B3
nce, Ind. 227/C4
nce, Wis. 317/F3
ncer, Minn. 255/C2
nce Springs, W. Va. 307/J7
ncil Bluff, Ark. 202/C4
nco, Chile 138/D1
ndant d'Oreille, Alberta 182/E5
ndé (riv.), Cent. Afr. Rep. 115/C2
ndé (riv.), Chad 111/C6
ndembu, S. Leone 106/B7
nder, Nebr. 264/H2
nder (co.), N.C. 281/O5
ndergrass, Georgia 217/E2
ndleton, Camp, Calif. 204/H10
ndleton, Ind. 227/F5
ndleton (co.), Ky. 237/N3
ndleton, N.Y. 276/C4
ndleton, N.C. 281/P2
ndleton, Oreg. 188/C1
ndleton, Oreg. 291/J2
ndleton, S.C. 296/B2
ndleton (co.), W. Va. 312/H5
ndletons, Va. 307/N5
nd Oreille (riv.), Br. Col. 184/D3
nd Oreille (lake), Idaho 188/C1
nd Oreille (lake), Idaho 220/B1
nd Oreille (lake), Idaho 220/B1
nd Oreille (mt.), Idaho 220/B1
nd Oreille (riv.), Idaho 220/A1
nd Oreille (co.), Wash. 310/H2
nd Oreille (riv.), Wash. 310/H2
ndroy, Mont. 262/D2
ndryl, Alberta 182/C3
nedo, Brazil 132/G5
netanguishene, Ontario 177/D3
nfield, Georgia 217/F3
nfield, Ill. 222/F3
nfield, N.Y. 276/F4
nfield, Pa. 294/E3
nganga (riv.), India 68/D5
nge, Zaire 115/D5
nghu (Pescadores) (isls.),
  China 77/J7
ngilly, Minn. 255/E3
nglai, China 77/K4
ngpu (Bengbu), China 77/J5
ngshui, China 77/G6
nguin, Tasmania 99/C3
njamo, Mexico 150/J6
nk (riv.), England 10/G2
nki (Benxi), China 77/K3
nmaenmawr, Wales 13/C4

Penmarch (pt.), France 28/A4
Penn, N. Dak. 282/N3
Penn, Pa. 294/C5
Pennant (pt.), Nova Scotia 168/E4
Pennant, Sask. 181/C5
Penndel, Pa. 294/NE
Penne, Italy 34/D3
Pennell (mt.), Utah 304/D6
Penner (riv.), India 68/D6
Penney Farms, Fla. 212/E2
Pennfield, New Bruns. 170/D3
Penn Hills •, Pa. 294/C7
Penniac, New Bruns. 170/D2
Pennine Alps (range), Italy 34/A2
Pennine Alps (range), Switzerland
  39/D5
Pennine Chain (range), England
  13/E3
Pennington, Ala. 195/B6
Pennington, Minn. 255/B2
Pennington, Minn. 255/D3
Pennington, N.J. 273/D3
Pennington (co.), S. Dak. 298/C6
Pennington, Texas 303/J6
Pennington Gap, Va. 307/C7
Pennline, Pa. 294/A2
Pennock, Minn. 255/C5
Penn Run, Pa. 294/L4
Pennsauken •, N.J. 273/B3
Pennsauken (creek), N.J. 273/B3
Pennsboro, Mo. 261/E8
Pennsboro, W. Va. 312/E4
Pennsburg, Pa. 294/M5
Pennsdale, Pa. 294/L3
Penns Grove, N.J. 273/C4
Penns Park, Pa. 294 N5
Pennsuco, Fla. 212/E4
Pennsville, N.J. 273/C4
Pennsville, Ohio 284/G6
Pennsylvania 188/L2
PENNSYLVANIA 294
Pennsylvania (state), U.S. 146/L5
Pennsylvania Furnace, Pa. 294/G4
Pennville, Ind. 227/G4
Pennville, Pa. 294/J6
Penn Wynne, Pa. 294/M6
Penny, Br. Col. 184/G3
Penny (str.), N.W. Terr. 187/J2
Penn Yan, N.Y. 276/F3
Penobscot (co.), Maine 243/F5
Penobscot •, Maine 243/F7
Penobscot (bay), Maine 243/F7
Penobscot (lake), Maine 243/C4
Penobscot (riv.), Maine 243/F6
Penobscot Ind. Res., Maine 243/F6
Penobsquis, New Bruns. 170/E3
Penokee, Kansas 232/C2
Penola, S. Australia E8/G7
Penola, S. Australia 94/G7
Peñón (pt.), P. Rico 161/B1
Peñón Blanco, Mexico 150/H4
Penong, S. Australia 38/C5
Penong, S. Australia 94/C4
Penonomé, Panama 54/G6
Penpont, Scotland 15/E5
Penrhyn (Tongareva) (atoll), Cook Is.
  87/L6
Penrith, England 10/E3
Penrith, England 13/E3
Penrith, N. S. Wales 98/J6
Penrith, N.S. Wales 97/F3
Penrod, Ky. 237/G6
Penrose, Colo. 208/K3
Penrose, N.C. 281/D5
Penryn, Calif. 204/C8
Penryn, England 13/E7
Pensacola, Fla. 146/K3
Pensacola, Fla. 188/J1
Pensacola, Fla. 212/B6
Pensacola (bay), Fla. 212/B6
Pensacola, Okla. 288/R2
Pensacola, Mexico 150/F4
Pensacola N.A.S., Fla. 212/B6
Pensamiento, Bolivia 136/E4
Pensaukee, Wis. 317/L6
Pense, Sask. 181/G5
Penshurst, Victoria 97/B5
Pentagon, Va. 307/T3
Penthalaz, Switzerland 39/C3
Penticton, Br. Col. 184/H5
Pentland (firth), Scotland 10/E1
Pentland (firth), Scotland 15/E2
Pentland (hills), Scotland 15/D2
Penton, Miss. 256/D1
Pentress, W. Va. 312/F3
Pentwater, Mich. 250/C5
Peñuelas, Chile 138/F3
Peñuelas (lake), Chile 138/F2
Peñuelas, P. Rico 161/B2
Penwell, Texas 303/B6
Penyu (isls.), Indonesia 85/H7
Penza, U.S.S.R. 7/J3
Penza, U.S.S.R. 52/G4
Penza, U.S.S.R. 48/E4
Penzance, England 10/D5
Penzance, England 13/B7
Penzance, Sask. 181/H4
Penzberg, Germany 22/D5
Penzhina (bay), U.S.S.R. 48/R3
Peoa, Utah 304/D3
Peonan (pt.), Manitoba 179/D3
Peoples, Ky. 237/N6
Peoria, Alberta 182/A2
Peoria, Ariz. 198/C5
Peoria, Ill. 188/J2
Peoria, Ill. 146/K5
Peoria (co.), Ill. 222/D8
Peoria, Ill. 222/D3
Peoria, Iowa 229/H6
Peoria, Kansas 232/G2
Peoria, Miss. 256/C8
Peoria, Ohio 284/B5
Peoria, Okla. 288/S1
Peoria Heights, Ill. 222/D3
Peosta, Iowa 229/M4
Peotone, Ill. 222/F2
Pep, N. Mex. 274/F5
Pepacton (res.), N.Y. 276/L6

Pepe (cape), Cuba 158/B3
Pepeekeo, Hawaii 218/J4
Pepeekeo (pt.), Hawaii 218/J4
Pepel, S. Leone 106/B7
Pepin (lake), Minn. 255/F6
Pepin (co.), Wis. 317/C6
Pepin, Wis. 317/E7
Pepin (lake), Wis. 317/B7
Pepperell, Mass. 249/H2
Pepperell •, Mass. 249/H2
Pepper Pike, Ohio 284/J9
Pepperwood, Calif. 204/A3
Peqin, Albania 45/D5
Peqin, Albania 45/D5
Peque, Mexico 150/O1
Pequabuck, Conn. 210/C2
Pequabuck (riv.), Conn. 210/D2
Pequaming, Mich. 250/A2
Pequannock •, N.J. 273/B1
Pequea, Pa. 294/K6
Pequest (riv.), N.J. 273/D2
Pequonnock (riv.), Conn. 210/C3
Pequop (mts.), Nev. 266/F2
Pequot Lakes, Minn. 255/D4
Pera (head), Queensland 88/G2
Pera (head), Queensland 95/B2
Pera (Beyoğlu), Turkey 63/D6
Perabumulih, Indonesia 85/C6
Peraitepuí, Venezuela 124/H5
Perak (state), Malaysia 72/D6
Perak, Gunong (mt.), Malaysia 72/D6
Perales (riv.), Spain 33/F4
Peralta, Dom. Rep. 158/D6
Peralta, N. Mex. 274/C4
Peralta, Spain 33/F1
Peralta, Uruguay 145/C3
Peravia (prov.), Dom. Rep. 158/E6
Percé (cape), Nova Scotia 168/J2
Percé, Québec 172/D1
Percé, Québec 174/F2
Perch (lake), Mich. 250/G2
Perch (riv.), Mich. 250/G2
Perche (reg.), France 28/D3
Percival, Iowa 229/B7
Percival, Sask. 181/J5
Percival (lakes), W. Australia 88/C4
Percival (lakes), W. Australia 92/D3
Percy, Ill. 222/D5
Percy, Miss. 256/C4
Percy, N.H. 268/E2
Perdido, Ala. 195/C8
Perdido (bay), Ala. 195/D10
Perdido, Ala. 195/C9
Perdido (riv.), Fla. 212/B6
Perdido (mt.), Spain 33/G1
Perdido Beach, Ala. 195/C10
Pérdika, Greece 45/E6
Perdue, Sask. 181/D3
Perdue Hill, Ala. 195/C8
Pereira, Colombia 126/C5
Pereira, Colombia 120/B2
Perelló, Spain 33/G2
Pere Marquette (riv.), Mich. 250/D5
Perené (riv.), Peru 128/E8
Perenjori, W. Australia 92/B5
Pérez, Argentina 143/F6
Pérez (isl.), Mexico 150/P5
Perg, Austria 41/C2
Pergamino, Argentina 143/F6
Pergamino, Argentina 120/C6
Pergine Valsugana, Italy 34/C1
Pergola, Italy 34/D3
Perham •, Maine 243/G2
Perham, Minn. 255/C4
Perhentian, Kepulauan (isls.),
  Malaysia 72/D6
Periam, Romania 45/E2
Péribonca (riv.), Que. 162/J5
Péribonca (riv.), Québec 174/C3
Péribonca (riv.), Québec 172/F1
Péribonka, Québec 172/E1
Perico, Cuba 158/D1
Perico, Texas 303/B1
Pericos, Mexico 150/F4
Peridot, Ariz. 198/E5
Perigord, Sask. 181/H3
Périgueux, France 28/D5
Perijá, Serranía de (mts.), Colombia
  126/D2
Perijá, Sierra de (mts.), Venezuela
  124/B7
Perim (isl.), Yemen 59/D7
Perintown, Ohio 284/B6
Perito F.P. Moreno Nat'l Park,
  Argentina 143/B6
Perito Moreno, Argentina 143/B6
Periyar (lake), India 68/D7
Perkam (cape), Indonesia 85/K6
Perkasie, Pa. 294/M5
Perkatkin, U.S.S.R. 48/T2
Perkins (mt.), Conn. 210/F1
Perkins, Georgia 217/J5
Perkins, Iowa 229/A2
Perkins, Mich. 250/B3
Perkins, Mo. 261/N8
Perkins (co.), Nebr. 264/C4
Perkins, Okla. 288/M3
Perkins, Québec 172/B4
Perkins (co.), S. Dak. 298/D3
Perkins, S. Dak. 298/O8
Perkins, W. Va. 312/E5
Perkinsfield, Ontario 177/E3
Perkinston, Miss. 256/F9
Perkinstown, Wis. 317/E5
Perkinsville, Ind. 227/F4
Perkinsville, N.Y. 276/E5
Perkinsville, Vt. 268/B5
Perks, Ill. 222/D6
Perla, Ark. 202/E5
Perlas (lag.), Nicaragua 154/F4
Perlas (pt.), Nicaragua 154/F4
Perlas (arch.), Panama 154/H6
Perleberg, Germany 22/D2
Perley, Minn. 255/B3
Perlis (state), Malaysia 72/D6
Perm', U.S.S.R. 7/K3
Perm', U.S.S.R. 7/K3
Perm', U.S.S.R. 52/J3
Perm', U.S.S.R. 48/F4
Perma, Mont. 262/B3

Përmet, Albania 45/E5
Pernambuco (state), Brazil 132/G5
Pernambuco (Recife), Brazil 132/H5
Pernell, Okla. 288/M5
Pernik, Bulgaria 45/F4
Peron (isls.), North. Terr. 88/D2
Peron (isls.), North. Terr. 93/A2
Peron (cape), Tasmania 99/E4
Peron (cape), W. Australia 88/A2
Peron (pen.), W. Australia 92/A4
Péronne, France 28/E3
Perote, Ala. 195/G7 .
Perote, Mexico 150/O1
Perow, Br. Col. 184/D3
Perpetua (cape), Oreg. 291/C3
Perpignan, France 7/E4
Perpignan, France 28/E6
Perquilauquén (riv.), Chile 138/A11
Perquimans (co.), N.C. 281/S2
Perrin, Mo. 261/D3
Perrin, Texas 303/G5
Perrine, Fla. 212/F6
Perrineville, N.J. 273/E3
Perrinton, Mich. 250/E5
Perris, Calif. 204/F11
Perro (mts.), N. Mex. 274/D4
Perronville, Mich. 250/B3
Perros (bay), Cuba 158/D1
Perry (co.), Ala. 195/D5
Perry (isl.), Alaska 196/C1
Perry (co.), Ark. 202/E4
Perry, Ark. 202/E3
Perry, Fla. 212/C1
Perry, Georgia 217/E6
Perry (co.), Ill. 222/D5
Perry, Ill. 222/C4
Perry (co.), Ind. 227/D7
Perry, Iowa 229/E5
Perry, Kansas 232/G2
Perry (lake), Kansas 232/G2
Perry (co.), Ky. 237/P6
Perry (isl.), Ky. 237/P6
Perry, La. 238/F7
Perry •, Maine 243/J6
Perry, Mich. 250/E6
Perry (co.), Miss. 256/G8
Perry (co.), Mo. 261/N7
Perry, Mo. 261/J4
Perry (stream), N.H. 268/E1
Perry, N.Y. 276/D5
Perry (co.), Ohio 284/F6
Perry, Ohio 284/H2
Perry (co.), Pa. 294/H5
Perry, S.C. 296/E4
Perry (co.), Tenn. 237/F9
Perry, Utah 304/D2
Perry, W. Va. 312/J5
Perrydale, Oreg. 291/D2
Perrygo Place, Wis. 317/J10
Perry Hall, Md. 245/N3
Perryman, Md. 245/O3
Perryopolis, Pa. 294/C5
Perrysburg, Ind. 227/E4
Perrysburg, N.Y. 276/B6
Perrysburg, Ohio 284/C2
Perry's Cove, Newf. 166/D2
Perry's Victory and Int'l Peace Mem.,
  Ohio 284/E2
Perrysville, Ind. 227/C4
Perrysville, Ohio 284/F4
Perrysville, Pa. 294/B6
Perryton, Ohio 284/F5
Perryton, Texas 303/D1
Perrytown, Ark. 202/C6
Perryvale, Alberta 182/D2
Perryville, Alaska 196/G3
Perryville, Ark. 202/E3
Perryville, Ky. 237/M5
Perryville, La. 238/G1
Perryville, Md. 245/O2
Perryville, Mo. 261/N7
Perryville, Tenn. 237/F9
Persembe, Turkey 63/G6
Persepolis (ruins), Iran 66/H6
Perseverance (bay), Virgin Is.
  (U.S.) 161/A4
Perseverancia, Bolivia 136/D4
Pershing, Ind. 227/E6
Pershing, Ind. 227/G5
Pershing, Iowa 229/G6
Pershing (co.), Nev. 266/C2
Pershing, Okla. 288/O1
Pershore, England 13/E5
Persia, Iowa 229/B5
Persia, Tenn. 237/P8
Persian (gulf) 54/G7
Persian (gulf), Bahrain 59/F4
Persian (gulf), Iran 66/F6
Persian (gulf), Iran 59/F4
Persian (gulf), Iraq 59/F4
Persian (gulf), Kuwait 59/F4
Persian (gulf), Qatar 59/F4
Persian (gulf), Saudi Arabia 59/F4
Persinger, W. Va. 312/E6
Person (co.), N.C. 281/M2
Pertek, Turkey 63/H3
Perth, Australia 2/Q7
Perth, Kansas 232/E4
Perth, N. Dak. 282/M2
Perth (county), Ontario 177/C4
Perth-Andover, New Bruns. 170/C2
Perthshire, Miss. 256/C3
Perth (trad. co.), Scotland 15/A5
Perth, Scotland 10/E2
Perth, Scotland 15/E4
Perth, Tasmania 99/D3
Perth (cap.), W. Australia 88/B2
Perth Airport, W. Australia 88/B2
Perth Amboy, N.J. 273/E2
Perth, Ontario 177/C4
Peru (cap.), W. Australia 88/A2
Pertominsk, U.S.S.R. 48/E2
Peru 120/B4
Peru 128
PERU 128

Peru, Ill. 222/D2
Peru, Ind. 227/E3
Peru, Iowa 229/F6
Peru, Kansas 232/F4
Peru, Maine 243/C6
Peru •, Maine 243/C6
Peru, Nebr. 264/J4
Peru, N.Y. 276/N1
Peru •, Vt. 268/B5
Perugia (prov.), Italy 34/D3
Perugia, Italy 34/D3
Perugia, Italy 7/F4
Perugorría, Argentina 143/G4
Péruwelz, Belgium 27/D8
Pervari, Turkey 63/K4
Pervomaysk, U.S.S.R. 52/F3
Pervomaysk, U.S.S.R. 52/D5
Pervoural'sk, U.S.S.R. 48/F4
Perwez, Belgium 27/F7
Pesaro (prov.), Italy 34/D3
Pesaro, Italy 34/D3
Pesaro e Urbino (prov.), Italy 34/D3
Pescadero, Calif. 204/J4
Pescadero (creek), Calif. 204/J3
Pescadero (pt.), Calif. 204/J3
Pescadero, Mexico 150/D5
Pescadores (Penghu) (isls.), China
  77/J7
Pescara (prov.), Italy 34/E3
Pescara, Italy 34/E3
Pescara, Italy 7/F4
Pescara (riv.), Italy 34/D3
Pescia, Italy 34/C3
Peseux, Switzerland 39/C2
Peshastin, Wash. 310/E3
Peshawar, Pakistan 54/H6
Peshawar, Pakistan 59/K3
Peshawar, Pakistan 68/C2
Peshkopi, Albania 45/E5
Peshtera, Bulgaria 45/G4
Peshtigo, Wis. 317/L5
Peshtigo (riv.), Wis. 317/K5
Peski, U.S.S.R. 52/D3
Peso da Régua, Portugal 33/C2
Pesotum, Ill. 222/E4
Pespire, Honduras 154/D4
Pessac, France 28/C5
Pest (co.), Hungary 41/E3
Pestel, Haiti 158/A6
Pestovo, U.S.S.R. 52/D3
Péta, Greece 45/E6
Petacalco (bay), Mexico 150/H8
Petah Tiqwa, Israel 65/B3
Petal, Miss. 256/F8
Petaluma, Calif. 204/H1
Pétange, Luxembourg 27/H9
Petas, Las (riv.), Bolivia 136/F5
Petatlán, Mexico 150/J8
Petauke, Zambia 115/F6
Petawaga (lake), Québec 172/A2
Petawawa, Ontario 177/G2
Petawawa (riv.), Ontario 177/G2
Petén-Itzá (lake), Guatemala 154/B2
Petenwell (lake), Wis. 317/G7
Peter (isl.), Virgin Is. (U.K.) 156/H1
Peter (isl.), Virgin Is. (U.K.) 161/F4
Peterborough, England 13/G5
Peterborough, England 10/F4
Peterborough, N.H. 268/D6
Peterborough •, N.H. 268/D6
Peterborough, Ont. 162/J7
Peterborough (county), Ontario
  177/F3
Peterborough, Ontario 177/F3
Peterborough, S. Australia 88/F6
Peterborough, S. Australia 94/F5
Peterculter, Scotland 15/F3
Peterhead, Scotland 15/G3
Peterhead, Scotland 10/F2
Peter I (isl.), Ant. 5/B14
Peter I (isl.), Norway 2/E9
Peterlee, England 13/J3
Peterman, Ala. 195/D7
Petermann (ranges), North. Terr.
  93/A8
Petermann (ranges), W. Australia
  92/E4
Petermann Ranges Aboriginal Res.,
  North. Terr. 88/D4
Petermann Ranges Aboriginal Res.,
  North. Terr. 93/A8
Peteroa (vol.), Argentina 143/B4
Peteroa (vol.), Chile 138/B10
Peter Pond (lake), Sask. 181/L3
Peter's (riv.), Newf. 166/D2
Petersburg, Alaska 188/E6
Petersburg, Alaska 196/N1
Petersburg, Ill. 222/D4
Petersburg, Ind. 227/C7
Petersburg, Ky. 237/M2
Petersburg, Mich. 250/E8
Petersburg, Minn. 255/C7
Petersburg, Nebr. 264/G2
Petersburg, N.J. 273/D5
Petersburg, N.Y. 276/O5
Petersburg, N. Dak. 282/P3
Petersburg, Pa. 294/G4
Petersburg, Tenn. 237/H10
Petersburg, Texas 303/C4
Petersburg, Va. 188/L3
Petersburg (I.C.), Va. 307/N6
Petersburg, W. Va. 312/H3
Petersburg Nat'l Battlefield, Va.
  307/O6
Petersfield, England 13/F6
Petersfield, Jamaica 158/G6
Petersfield, Manitoba 179/G4
Petersham •, Mass. 249/H3
Peterson, Ala. 195/D4
Peterson, Iowa 229/C3
Peterson, Minn. 255/G7
Peterson, Sask. 181/F3
Peterson Air Force Base, Colo.
  208/K5

Petersville, Ind. 227/F6
Petersville, Ky. 237/P4
Petersville, Md. 245/H3
Pétervására, Hungary 41/F3
Peterview, Newf. 166/C4
Pétionville, Haiti 158/C6
Petit Bois (isl.), Miss. 256/H10
Petit-Bourg, Guadeloupe 161/A6
Petit-Canal, Guadeloupe 161/A6
Petit Cap, Québec 172/D1
Petitcodiac, New Bruns. 170/E3
Petitcodiac (riv.), New Bruns.
  170/F3
Petit Cul-de-Sac Marin (bay),
  Guadeloupe 161/A6
Petit-de-Grat, Nova Scotia 168/H3
Petit-de-Grat (isl.), Nova Scotia
  168/H3
Petite Cascapédia (riv.), Québec
  172/C1
Petite-Matane, Québec 172/B1
Petite Nation (riv.), Québec 172/B4
Petite Riviere Bridge, Nova Scotia
  168/D4
Petite Rivière de l'Artibonite, Haiti
  158/B5
Petite-Rivière-de-l'Île, New Bruns.
  170/F1
Petites, Newf. 166/C4
Petit-Étang, Nova Scotia 168/G2
Petite-Terre (isls.), Guadeloupe
  161/B6
Petite-Vallée, Québec 172/D1
Petit-Goâve, Haiti 156/D3
Petit Goâve, Haiti 158/B6
Petit Jean (mt.), Ark. 202/C3
Petit Jean (riv.), Ark. 202/C3
Petitjean (Sidi-Kacem), Morocco
  106/C2
Petit Mécatina (isl.), Québec 174/F2
Petit Mécatina (riv.), Québec 174/E2
Petitot (riv.), Br. Col. 184/M2
Petitot (riv.), N.W. Terr. 187/F4
Petit Piton (mt.), St. Lucia 161/G6
Petit Rocher, New Bruns. 170/E1
Petit Rocher Sud, New Bruns. 170/E1
Petit-Saguenay (Saint-François-
  d'Assise), Québec 172/G1
Petitsikapau (lake), Newf. 166/A3
Petit Soufrière, Dominica 161/F6
Petley, Newf. 166/D2
Peto, Mexico 150/P6
Petone, N. Zealand 100/B2
Petorca, Chile 138/A9
Petoskey, Mich. 250/E4
Petpeswick (head), Nova Scotia
  168/F4
Petra (ruins), Jordan 65/D5
Petre (bay), N. Zealand 100/D7
Petre (pt.), Ontario 177/G4
Petrey, Ala. 195/F7
Petrich, Bulgaria 45/F5
Petrified Forest, Ariz. 198/F3
Petrified Forest Nat'l Park, Ariz.
  198/F4
Petrila, Romania 45/F3
Petrinja, Yugoslavia 45/B3
Petrohué, Chile 138/E3
Petrokrepost', U.S.S.R. 52/D3
Petrólea, Colombia 126/D3
Petróleo, Ind. 227/G3
Petroleum, Ky. 237/G7
Petroleum (co.), Mont. 262/H3
Petroleum, W. Va. 312/D4
Petrolia, Kansas 232/G4
Petrolia, Ontario 177/B5
Petrolia, Pa. 294/C3
Petrolia, Texas 303/F4
Petrolina, Brazil 120/D4
Petrolina, Brazil 132/G5
Petrona (pt.), P. Rico 161/D3
Petrópolis, Brazil 132/F8
Petrópolis, Brazil 135/E3
Petros, Tenn. 237/M8
Petroşeni, Romania 45/F3
Petrovsk, U.S.S.R. 52/G4
Petrovsk-Zabaykal'skiy, U.S.S.R.
  48/L4
Petrozavodsk, U.S.S.R. 7/H2
Petrozavodsk, U.S.S.R. 48/D3
Petrozavodsk, U.S.S.R. 52/D2
Petsamo (Pechenga), U.S.S.R.
  52/D1
Pettibone, N. Dak. 282/L5
Pettigo, Ireland 17/F2
Pettigo, N. Ireland 17/F2
Pettigrew, Ark. 202/C2
Pettis (co.), Mo. 261/F5
Pettisville, Ohio 284/B2
Pettus, Texas 303/G9
Petty Harbour, Newf. 166/D2
Petworth, D.C. 245/F4
Peu, Solomon Is. 87/G7
Peuco, Chile 138/G4
Peuerbach, Austria 41/B2
Peumo, Chile 138/F5
Pevas, Peru 128/G4
Pevek, U.S.S.R. 54/U3
Pevek, U.S.S.R. 48/S3
Pevely, Mo. 261/M6
Pewamo, Mich. 250/E6
Pewaukee, Wis. 317/K1
Pewaukee (lake), Wis. 317/K1
Pewee Valley, Ky. 237/L4
Peyrano, Argentina 143/F6
Peyton, Colo. 208/K4
Peytona, W. Va. 312/E6
Pézenas, France 28/E6
Pezinok, Czech. 41/D2

Pfaffenhofen an der Ilm, Germany 22/D4
Pfaffnau, Switzerland 39/E2
Pfarrkirchen, Germany 22/E4
Pfeifer, Kansas 232/C3
Pflugerville, Texas 303/G7
Pforzheim, Germany 22/C4
Pfronten, Germany 22/D5
Pfullingen, Germany 22/C4
Pfunds, Austria 41/A3
Pha Hom Pok, Doi (mt.), Thailand 72/C2
Phalaborwa, S. Africa 118/E4
Phalodi, India 68/C3
Phanat Nikhom, Thailand 72/D4
Phangan, Ko (isl.), Thailand 72/D5
Phangnga, Thailand 72/C5
Phan Rang, Vietnam 72/F5
Phan Thiet, Vietnam 72/F5
Phan Thiet, Vietnam 54/M8
Phantom (lake), Wis. 317/J2
Pharoah, Okla. 288/O4
Pharr, Texas 303/F11
Phatthalung, Thailand 72/D6
Phayao, Thailand 72/C3
Pheasant (hills), Sask. 181/J5
Pheba, Miss. 256/G3
Phelps (mt.) 120/C2
Phelps, Ky. 237/S6
Phelps (co.), Mo. 261/J7
Phelps (co.), Nebr. 264/E4
Phelps, N.Y. 276/F5
Phelps (lake), N.C. 281/S3
Phelps (peak), Venezuela 124/E7
Phelps, Wis. 317/H3
Phelps City, Mo. 261/A2
Phenix, Va. 307/L6
Phenix City, Ala. 188/J4
Phenix City, Ala. 195/H6
Phet Buri, Thailand 72/C4
Phetchabun, Thailand 72/D3
Phiafai, Laos 72/E4
Phichai, Thailand 72/D3
Phichit, Thailand 72/D3
Phil, Ky. 237/M6
Philadelphia, Ill. 222/C4
Philadelphia, Miss. 256/F5
Philadelphia, Mo. 261/J3
Philadelphia, N.Y. 276/J2
Philadelphia, Pa. 188/M2
Philadelphia, Pa. 146/L6
Philadelphia (city county), Pa. 294/M6
Philadelphia, Pa. 294/N6
Philadelphia, Tenn. 237/M9
Philadelphia, U.S. 2/F4
Philbrook, Minn. 255/D4
Phil Campbell, Ala. 195/C2
Philip (riv.), Nova Scotia 168/E3
Philip, S. Dak. 298/F5
Philipp, Miss. 256/D3
Philippeville (Skikda), Algeria 106/F1
Philippeville, Belgium 27/E8
Philippi, W. Va. 312/G4
Philippine (sea) 54/O8
Philippine (sea), Guam 86/K6
Philippine (sea), N. Mex. 274/D5
Philippine (sea), Philippines 85/G2
Philippine (sea), Philippines 82/D3
Philippines 2/R5
Philippines 54/O8
PHILIPPINES 82
PHILIPPINES 85/H4
Philipsburg, Mont. 262/C4
Philipsburg, Pa. 294/F4
Philipsburg, Québec 172/D4
Philip Smith (mts.), Alaska 196/J1
Phillip (pt.), N.S. Wales 97/J2
Phillip (isl.), Victoria 97/C6
Phillippy, Tenn. 237/C8
Phillips (co.), Ark. 202/J5
Phillips (co.), Colo. 208/P1
Phillips (co.), Kansas 232/C2
Phillips•, Maine 243/C6
Phillips (co.), Mont. 262/J2
Phillips, Nebr. 264/F4
Phillips (bay), N.W. Terr. 187/J1
Phillips, Okla. 288/O6
Phillips, Texas 303/C2
Phillips, Wis. 317/E4
Phillipsburg, Georgia 217/E8
Phillipsburg, Kansas 232/C2
Phillipsburg, Mo. 261/G7
Phillipsburg, N.J. 273/C2
Phillipsburg, Ohio 284/B6
Phillipston•, Mass. 249/F2
Phillipstown, Ill. 222/F4
Phillipsville, N.C. 281/D3
Philmont, N.Y. 276/N6
Philo, Calif. 204/B4
Philo, Ill. 222/E3
Philo, Ohio 284/G6
Philomath, Georgia 217/G3
Philomath, Oreg. 291/D3
Philomont, Va. 307/N2
Philpot, Ky. 237/M6
Philpots (isl.), N.W. Terr. 187/L2
Philpott (lake), Va. 307/H7
Phippen, Sask. 181/C3
Phippsburg, Colo. 208/F2
Phippsburg, Maine 243/D8
Phippsburg•, Maine 243/D8
Phitsanulok, Thailand 72/D3
Phlox, Wis. 317/J5
Phnom Penh (cap.), Cambodia 54/M8
Phnom Penh (cap.), Cambodia 72/E5
Phnum Tbeng Meanchey, Cambodia 72/E4
Phoenix (cap.), Ariz. 146/G6
Phoenix (cap.), Ariz. 188/D4
Phoenix (cap.), Ariz. 198/C5
Phoenix, Ill. 222/C6
Phoenix (isls.), Kiribati 87/J6
Phoenix, La. 238/L7
Phoenix, Md. 245/M2
Phoenix, N.Y. 276/H4
Phoenix, Oreg. 291/E5

Phoenixville, Conn. 210/G1
Phoenixville, Pa. 294/L5
Phôngsali, Laos 72/D2
Phon Phisai, Thailand 72/D3
Phoques (bay), Tasmania 99/A1
Phou Bia (mt.), Laos 72/D3
Phou Cô Pi (mt.), Laos 72/E3
Phou Loi (mt.), Laos 72/D2
Phou San (mt.), Laos 72/D3
Phrae, Thailand 72/D3
Phra Nakhon Si Ayutthaya, Thailand 72/D4
Phsar Ream, Cambodia 72/D5
Phuc Loi, Vietnam 72/E3
Phu Cuong, Vietnam 72/E5
Phu Dien, Vietnam 72/E3
Phuket, Thailand 54/L9
Phuket, Thailand 72/C6
Phuket, Ko (isl.), Thailand 72/C5
Phu Lang Thuong (Bac Giang), Vietnam 72/E2
Phulbani, India 68/E4
Phu Ly, Vietnam 72/E2
Phumi Banam, Cambodia 72/E5
Phumi Phsar, Cambodia 72/E4
Phumi Prek Kak, Cambodia 72/E4
Phumi Samraong, Cambodia 72/D4
Phu My, Vietnam 72/F4
Phu Qui, Vietnam 72/E3
Phu Quoc, Dao (isl.), Vietnam 72/D5
Phu Rieng, Vietnam 72/E5
Phu Tho, Vietnam 72/E2
Phutthaisong, Thailand 72/D4
Phu Vinh, Vietnam 72/E5
Piaçabuçu, Brazil 132/H5
Piacenza (prov.), Italy 34/B2
Piacenza, Italy 34/B2
Piacoa, Venezuela 124/H3
Pia Fai, Doi (mt.), Thailand 72/D4
Piai, Tanjong (pt.), Malaysia 72/E6
Pian (creek), N.S. Wales 97/E1
Piankatank (riv.), Va. 307/R5
Pianosa (isl.), Italy 34/C4
Pianosa (isl.), Italy 34/E3
Piapoco, Colombia 126/F6
Piapot, Sask. 181/B6
Piarco, Trin. & Tob. 161/B10
Piat, Philippines 82/C2
Piatra Neamţ, Romania 45/G2
Piatt (co.), Ill. 222/E4
Piauí (state), Brazil 132/F4
Piauí, Serra do (range), Brazil 132/F5
Piauí (riv.), Brazil 132/F5
Piave (riv.), Italy 34/D2
Piave, Miss. 256/G8
Piazza Armerina, Italy 34/E6
Piazzi (isl.), Chile 138/D9
Pibor (riv.), Sudan 111/F6
Pibor Post, Sudan 111/F6
Pibrac, Québec 172/F1
Pibroch, Alberta 182/D2
Pica, Chile 138/B2
Picabo, Idaho 220/D6
Picacho, Ariz. 198/D6
Picacho, N. Mex. 274/D5
Picadilly, Newf. 166/C4
Picara (pt.), Virgin Is. (U.S.) 161/B4
Picard (lake), Québec 172/D2
Picardville, Alberta 182/D2
Picardy (trad. prov.), France 29
Picatinny Arsenal, N.J. 273/D2
Picayune, Miss. 256/F9
Piceance (creek), Colo. 208/C3
Picher, Okla. 288/S1
Pichidegua, Chile 138/F5
Pichilemu, Chile 138/A10
Pichincha (prov.), Ecuador 128/C3
Pichis (riv.), Peru 128/E8
Pichones (cays), Honduras 154/F3
Pichucalco, Mexico 150/N8
Pickard, Ind. 227/E4
Pickaway (co.), Ohio 284/D6
Pickaway, W. Va. 312/E7
Pick City, N. Dak. 282/G5
Pickens (co.), Ala. 195/B4
Pickens, Ark. 202/H6
Pickens (co.), Georgia 217/D2
Pickens, Miss. 256/E5
Pickens, Okla. 288/S6
Pickens (co.), S.C. 296/B2
Pickens, S.C. 296/B2
Pickens, W. Va. 312/F5
Pickensville, Ala. 195/B4
Pickerel (lake), Conn. 210/F2
Pickerel (lake), Manitoba 179/C2
Pickerel, Wis. 317/J5
Pickering, England 13/G3
Pickering, Mo. 261/C2
Pickering, Ontario 177/K4
Pickerington, Ohio 284/E6
Pickersgill, Guyana 131/B2
Pickert, N. Dak. 282/P5
Pickett (co.), Tenn. 237/M7
Pickett, Wis. 317/J8
Pickford, Mich. 250/E2
Pickle Lake, Ontario 175/C2
Pickrell, Nebr. 264/H4
Pickstown, S. Dak. 298/M7
Pickton, Texas 303/J5
Pickwick (lake), Ala. 195/B1
Pickwick, Minn. 255/G7
Pickwick (lake), Miss. 256/H1
Pickwick (lake), Tenn. 237/E11
Pickwick Dam, Tenn. 237/E10
Pico (isl.), Portugal 33/C1
Pico (peak), Vt. 268/B4
Pico Rivera, Calif. 204/C10
Picos, Brazil 132/F4
Picos, Brazil 120/E3
Picota, Peru 128/D6
Pico Truncado, Argentina 143/C6
Pictograph (rocks), Ariz. 198/B5
Picton (isl.), Argentina 143/C8
Picton (isl.), Chile 138/F11
Picton, N.S. Wales 98/H4
Picton, N. Zealand 100/D4
Picton, Ontario 177/G3

Picton (mt.), Tasmania 99/C5
Pictou (co.), Nova Scotia 168/F3
Pictou, Nova Scotia 168/F3
Pictou (harb.), Nova Scotia 168/F3
Pictou Landing, Nova Scotia 168/F3
Picture Butte, Alberta 182/D3
Pictured Rocks (cliff), Mich. 250/C2
Pictured Rocks Nat'l Lakeshore, Mich. 250/C2
Picture Rocks, Pa. 294/J3
Pidurutalagala (mt.), Sri Lanka 68/E7
Pie, W. Va. 312/B7
Piedade, Brazil 135/C3
Piedade do Rio Grande, Brazil 135/D2
Piedecuesta, Colombia 126/D4
Piedmont, Ala. 195/G3
Piedmont, Calif. 204/J2
Piedmont, Georgia 217/D4
Piedmont (reg.), Italy 34/A2
Piedmont, Kansas 232/F4
Piedmont, Mo. 261/L8
Piedmont, Ohio 284/H5
Piedmont (lake), Ohio 284/H5
Piedmont, Okla. 288/L3
Piedmont, S.C. 296/C2
Piedmont, S. Dak. 298/C5
Piedmont, W. Va. 312/H4
Piedmont, Wyo. 319/B4
Piedra, Calif. 204/F7
Piedra (riv.), Colo. 208/E8
Piedra Blanca, Dom. Rep. 158/E6
Piedrabuena, Spain 33/D3
Piedrahita, Spain 33/D2
Piedras, Las (riv.), Peru 128/G8
Piedras Blancas (pt.), Calif. 204/D8
Piedras Coloradas, Uruguay 145/B3
Piedras Negras, Mexico 146/H7
Piedras Negras, Coahuila, Mexico 150/J2
Piedras Negras, Veracruz, Mexico 150/J2
Piedra Sola, Uruguay 145/C3
Piekary Śląskie, Poland 47/B4
Pieksämäki, Finland 18/P5
Pielinen (lake), Finland 18/Q5
Pieman (riv.), Tasmania 99/B3
Piendamó, Colombia 126/B6
Pierce, Colo. 208/K1
Pierce, Fla. 212/E4
Pierce (co.), Georgia 217/H8
Pierce, Idaho 220/D3
Pierce, Ky. 237/K6
Pierce (pond), Maine 243/C5
Pierce (co.), Nebr. 264/G2
Pierce, Nebr. 264/G2
Pierce (co.), N. Dak. 282/K3
Pierce (co.), Wash. 310/C3
Pierce, W. Va. 312/H4
Pierce (co.), Wis. 317/B6
Pierce City, Mo. 261/E8
Piercefield, N.Y. 276/L2
Pierceland, Sask. 181/K4
Pierceton, Ind. 227/F2
Pierceville, Ind. 227/G6
Pierceville, Kansas 232/B4
Piermont•, N.H. 268/C4
Piermont, N.Y. 276/K8
Pierowall, Scotland 15/E1
Pierpont, Ohio 284/J2
Pierpont, S. Dak. 298/O3
Pierre (bayou), Miss. 256/C7
Pierre (cap.), S. Dak. 146/J5
Pierre (cap.), S. Dak. 188/F2
Pierre (cap.), S. Dak. 298/J5
Pierrefonds, Québec 172/H4
Pierrepont Manor, N.Y. 276/J3
Pierreville, Québec 172/E3
Pierron, Ill. 222/D5
Pierson, Fla. 212/E2
Pierson, Iowa 229/B3
Pierson, Manitoba 179/A5
Pierson, Mich. 250/D5
Pierson Station, Ill. 222/E4
Pierz, Minn. 255/D5
Pieśť any, Czech. 41/D2
Pietarsaari (Jakobstad), Finland 18/N5
Pieterlen, Switzerland 39/D2
Pietermaritzburg (cap.), Natal, S. Africa 102/F7
Pietermaritzburg, S. Africa 118/E6
Pietersburg, S. Africa 102/F7
Pietersburg, S. Africa 118/D4
Pie Town, N. Mex. 274/A4
Pietrasanta, Italy 34/B3
Piet Retief, S. Africa 118/D5
Pietrosul (mt.), Romania 45/G2
Pigeon (lake), Alberta 182/D3
Pigeon, Ala. 195/E7
Pigeon (lake), Alberta 182/D3
Pigeon, Guadeloupe 161/A6
Pigeon (creek), Ind. 227/C8
Pigeon (riv.), Ind. 227/F1
Pigeon (riv.), Manitoba 179/F2
Pigeon, Mich. 250/F5
Pigeon (riv.), Mich. 250/D7
Pigeon (riv.), Mich. 250/E3
Pigeon (riv.), Minn. 255/G2
Pigeon (riv.), N.C. 281/C3
Pigeon (isl.), St. Lucia 161/G5
Pigeon, W. Va. 312/D5
Pigeon (creek), W. Va. 312/B7
Pigeon Cove, Mass. 249/M2
Pigeon Creek, Ala. 195/E7
Pigeon Falls, Wis. 317/D7
Pigeon Forge, Tenn. 237/O9
Pigeon Hill, New Bruns. 170/F1
Pigeonroost, Ky. 237/O6
Pigg (riv.), Va. 307/J7
Piggott, Ark. 202/K1
Pignon, Haiti 158/C5
Pigs (Cochinos) (bay), Cuba 158/D2
Pigüé, Argentina 143/D4
Piippola, Finland 18/P4
Pija, Sierra de (mts.), Honduras 154/D3

Pijijiapan, Mexico 150/N9
Pik, Iran 66/G3
Pike (co.), Ala. 195/G7
Pike (co.), Ark. 202/C5
Pike (co.), Georgia 217/D4
Pike (co.), Ill. 222/C4
Pike (co.), Ind. 227/C8
Pike (co.), Ky. 237/S6
Pike (riv.), Minn. 255/F3
Pike (co.), Miss. 256/D8
Pike (co.), Mo. 261/K4
Pike, N.H. 268/C3
Pike, N.Y. 276/D5
Pike (co.), Ohio 284/D7
Pike (co.), Pa. 294/M3
Pike, W. Va. 312/D4
Pike Bay, Ontario 177/C3
Pike Lake, Sask. 181/E4
Pike Road, Ala. 195/F6
Pike Road, N.C. 281/R3
Pikes (peak), Colo. 188/E3
Pikes Peak, Ind. 227/E6
Pikesville, Md. 245/M3
Piketberg, S. Africa 118/B6
Piketon, Ohio 284/E7
Pike View, W. Va. 237/K6
Pikeville, Ind. 227/C8
Pikeville, Ky. 237/S6
Pikeville, N.C. 281/N4
Pikeville, Tenn. 237/L9
Pikwitonei, Manitoba 179/J3
Pila, Argentina 143/H7
Piła (prov.), Poland 47/C2
Piła, Poland 47/C2
Pilão Arcado, Brazil 132/F5
Pilar, Argentina 143/F5
Pilar, Brazil 132/H5
Pilar, Paraguay 120/D5
Pilar, Paraguay 144/C5
Pilas (isl.), Philippines 82/C7
Pilate, Haiti 158/C5
Pilatus (mt.), Switzerland 39/F2
Pilaya (riv.), Bolivia 136/C7
Pilcomayo (riv.) 120/C5
Pilcomayo (riv.), Argentina 143/E1
Pilcomayo (riv.), Bolivia 136/D7
Pilcomayo (riv.), Paraguay 144/C4
Pilger, Nebr. 264/G2
Pilger, Sask. 181/F3
Pilgrim, Ky. 237/S5
Pili, Philippines 82/D4
Pilibhit, India 68/D3
Pilica (riv.), Poland 47/D3
Pilis, Hungary 41/E3
Pilisvörösvár, Hungary 41/E3
Pillager, Minn. 255/D4
Pillar (pt.), Calif. 204/H3
Pillar (cape), Tasmania 88/H8
Pillar (cape), Tasmania 99/E5
Pillar (pt.), Wash. 310/A2
Pillaro, Ecuador 128/C3
Pilliga, N.S. Wales 97/E2
Pillow, Pa. 294/J4
Pillsbury (lake), Calif. 204/C4
Pillsbury, N. Dak. 282/P5
Pillsbury (sound), Virgin Is. (U.S.) 161/B4
Pilmaiquén (riv.), Chile 138/D3
Pilón, Cuba 158/H4
Pílos, Greece 45/E7
Pilot (peak), Idaho 220/C6
Pilot (peak), Idaho 220/C4
Pilot, Ky. 237/O5
Pilot (peak), Nev. 266/C4
Pilot, Va. 307/H6
Pilot Butte, Sask. 181/G5
Pilot Butte (res.), Wyo. 319/D2
Pilote (riv.), Martinique 161/D7
Pilot Grove, Iowa 229/L7
Pilot Grove, Mo. 261/G5
Pilot Knob (mt.), Idaho 220/C4
Pilot Knob, Ind. 227/E8
Pilot Knob, Mo. 261/L7
Pilot Mound, Iowa 229/F4
Pilot Mound, Manitoba 179/D5
Pilot Mound, Minn. 255/F7
Pilot Mountain, N.C. 281/J2
Pilot Point, Alaska 196/G3
Pilot Point, Texas 303/H4
Pilot Rock, Oreg. 291/J2
Pilot Station, Alaska 196/F2
Pilottown, La. 238/M8
Pilsen, Wis. 317/L7
Pilsen, U.S.S.R. 53/A2
Piltene, U.S.S.R. 53/A2
Pima (co.), Ariz. 198/D7
Pima, Ariz. 198/F6
Pimenta, Brazil 135/D2
Pimental, Dom. Rep. 158/E5
Pimental, Peru 128/B6
Pimento, Ind. 227/C6
Pimichín, Venezuela 124/E6
Pimmit, W. 307/S2
Pina, Spain 33/F2
Pinal (co.), Ariz. 198/D6
Pinal (peak), Ariz. 198/E5
Pinaleno (mts.), Ariz. 198/F6
Pinamalayan, Philippines 82/C4
Pinang (Penang) (state), Malaysia 72/D6
Pinang (George Town), Malaysia 72/D6
Pinang, Pulau (isl.), Malaysia 72/C6
Pınarbaşı, Turkey 63/G3
Pınarhisar, Turkey 63/B2
Piñas, Ecuador 128/C3
Piñas (pt.), Panama 154/H7
Pinatubo (mt.), Philippines 82/C3
Pinawa, Manitoba 179/G4
Pinch, W. Va. 312/D6

Pinchbeck, England 13/G5
Pincher Creek, Alberta 182/D5
Pincher Creek, Br. Col. 162/E6
Pincher Station, Alberta 182/C5
Pinchi (lake), Br. Col. 184/E3
Pinckard, Ala. 195/G6
Pinckney, Mich. 250/F6
Pinckneyville, Ill. 222/D5
Pinckneyville, Mich. 256/B8
Pinconning, Mich. 250/F5
Pincota, Romania 45/E2
Pincourt, Québec 172/D4
Pińczów, Poland 47/E3
Pindall, Ark. 202/E1
Pindamonhangaba, Brazil 135/D3
Pindi Gheb, Pakistan 68/C2
Pindo (riv.), Ecuador 128/D3
Pindus (mts.), Greece 45/E6
Pine, Ariz. 198/D4
Pine (riv.), Br. Col. 184/G2
Pine (creek), Calif. 204/D3
Pine, Colo. 208/J4
Pine (creek), Colo. 188/E3
Pine (riv.), Fla. 212/D5
Pine (pt.), Fla. 212/C2
Pine, Idaho 220/D6
Pine (riv.), Ky. 237/O7
Pine (lake), Mich. 250/F4
Pine (riv.), Mich. 250/D4
Pine (riv.), Mich. 250/E5
Pine (co.), Minn. 255/F4
Pine, Mo. 261/K9
Pine (creek), Nev. 266/E2
Pine (cape), Newf. 166/D2
Pine (riv.), N.H. 268/E4
Pine (creek), Oreg. 291/J4
Pine (creek), Pa. 294/H2
Pine (creek), Utah 304/C6
Pine (creek), Wis. 317/J1
Pine (lake), Wis. 317/J1
Pine Alcove (creek), Utah 304/D6
Pine Apple, Ala. 195/E7
Pine Beach, N.J. 273/E4
Pine Bluff, Ark. 188/H4
Pine Bluff, Ark. 202/F5
Pinebluff, N.C. 281/K4
Pine Bluff Arsenal, Ark. 202/F5
Pine Bluffs, Wyo. 319/H4
Pine Brook, N.J. 273/E2
Pine Bush, N.Y. 276/M7
Pine City, Ark. 202/H4
Pine City, Minn. 255/F5
Pine City, Wash. 310/H3
Pinecliffe, Colo. 208/J3
Pine Creek (pt.), Conn. 210/C4
Pine Creek, Minn. 255/C2
Pine Creek, North. Terr. 88/E2
Pine Creek, North. Terr. 93/C2
Pine Creek (lake), Okla. 288/R6
Pinecrest, Calif. 204/F5
Pinedale, Ariz. 198/E4
Pinedale, Calif. 204/F7
Pinedale, Wyo. 319/C3
Pine Dock, Manitoba 179/F3
Pine Falls, Manitoba 179/F4
Pine Flat (lake), Calif. 204/F7
Pine Forest (range), Nev. 266/C1
Pinega, U.S.S.R. 52/F2
Pinega (riv.), U.S.S.R. 52/G2
Pine Grove, Ark. 202/E6
Pine Grove, Georgia 217/H7
Pine Grove, Ky. 237/N5
Pine Grove, La. 238/J5
Pine Grove, Pa. 294/K4
Pine Grove (res.), Pa. 294/K6
Pine Grove, W. Va. 312/E3
Pine Grove Furnace, Pa. 294/H5
Pine Grove Mills, Pa. 294/G4
Pine Hall, N.C. 281/K2
Pine Hill, Ala. 195/C7
Pine Hill, Ky. 237/N6
Pine Hill, N.J. 273/D4
Pine Hill, N.Y. 276/M6
Pine Hills, Fla. 212/E3
Pine House, Sask. 181/M3
Pine Island (sound), Fla. 212/D5
Pine Island, Minn. 255/F6
Pine Island, N.Y. 276/L8
Pine Knoll Shores, N.C. 281/R5
Pine Knot, Ky. 237/M7
Pine Lake, Alberta 182/B4
Pine Lake, Georgia 217/D3
Pine Lake, Ind. 227/D2
Pine Lake Prov. Park, Sask. 181/E4
Pineland, Fla. 212/D5
Pineland, S.C. 296/E6
Pineland, Texas 303/L6
Pinelands, S. Africa 118/F6
Pine Lawn, Mo. 261/R2
Pine Level, Ala. 195/F6
Pine Level, N.C. 281/N4
Pinellas (co.), Fla. 212/C3
Pinellas (pt.), Fla. 212/C3
Pinellas Park, Fla. 212/C3
Pine Log (creek), Fla. 212/C6
Pine Log, Georgia 217/C2
Pine Meadow, Conn. 210/D1
Pine Mountain, Georgia 217/C5
Pineola, N.C. 281/F2
Pineora, Georgia 217/K6
Pine Orchard, Conn. 210/D3
Pine Park, Georgia 217/D9
Pine Plains, N.Y. 276/N7
Pine Point, Maine 243/C8
Pine Point, N.W. Terr. 187/G3
Pine Prairie, La. 238/F5
Piñera, Uruguay 145/D3
Pine Ridge, Ark. 202/C4
Pine Ridge, Miss. 256/B7

Pineridge, S.C. 296/E4
Pine Ridge, S. Dak. 298/E7
Pine Ridge Ind. Res., S. Dak. 298/D7
Pine River, Manitoba 179/B3
Pine River, Minn. 255/D4
Pine River, Wis. 317/H7
Pinerolo, Italy 34/A2
Pines (Isla de la Juventud) (isl.), Cuba 158/B3
Pines (isl.), New Caled. 87/G8
Pines (isl.), New Caled. 86/H5
Pines, New Caled. 86/H5
Pines (lake), N.J. 273/B1
Pine Springs, Texas 303/C10
Pinetop, Ariz. 198/F4
Pinetops, N.C. 281/Q3
Pinetown, N.C. 281/R3
Pinetown, S. Africa 118/E6
Pinetta, Fla. 212/C1
Pine Valley, Br. Col. 184/F2
Pine Valley, Calif. 204/J11
Pine Valley, N.J. 273/C4
Pine Valley, N.Y. 276/G6
Pine Valley, Utah 304/A6
Pineview, Georgia 217/F6
Pineview, N.C. 281/L4
Pine Village, Ind. 227/C4
Pineville, Ark. 202/F1
Pineville, Ky. 237/O7
Pineville, La. 238/F4
Pineville, Miss. 256/F6
Pineville, Mo. 261/D9
Pineville, N.C. 281/H4
Pineville, S.C. 296/H5
Pineville, W. Va. 312/C7
Pinewood, Minn. 255/C3
Pinewood, S.C. 296/G4
Piney, Ark. 202/D3
Piney (isl.), Fla. 212/B1
Piney (pt.), Fla. 212/C2
Piney, Manitoba 179/F5
Piney Flats, Tenn. 237/S8
Piney Fork, Ohio 284/J5
Piney Park, Mo. 261/L6
Piney Point, Md. 245/M8
Piney River, Va. 307/L5
Piney Woods, Miss. 256/D6
Ping, Mae Nam (riv.), Thailand 72/C3
Pingdingshan, China 77/H5
Pingelap (atoll), Micronesia 87/G5
Pingelly, W. Australia 88/B6
Pingelly, W. Australia 92/B2
Pingelly West, W. Australia 92/B2
Pinger (pt.), N.W. Terr. 187/K3
Pingguo, China 77/G7
Pingjiang, China 77/H6
Pingle, China 77/H7
Pingliang, China 77/F4
Pingluo, China 77/G4
Pingquan, China 77/J2
Pingree, N. Dak. 282/N5
Pingree, N. Dak. 282/N5
Pingtan (isl.), China 77/K6
Pingtung, China 77/K7
Pingwu, China 77/F5
Pingxiang, Guangxi Zhuangzu, China 77/G7
Pingxiang, Jiangxi, China 77/H6
Pingyang, China 77/K6
Pinhal, Brazil 135/C3
Pinheiro, Brazil 132/E3
Pinheiro, Brazil 120/E3
Pinhel, Portugal 33/C2
Piniós (riv.), Greece 45/E6
Pinjarra, W. Australia 88/B6
Pinjarra, W. Australia 92/B2
Pink (cliffs), Ariz. 198/E4
Pink, Okla. 288/M4
Pinkafeld, Austria 41/C3
Pinke Gat (chan.), Netherlands 27/H2
Pinkham, Sask. 181/B4
Pinkham Notch (pass), N.H. 268/E3
Pink Hill, N.C. 281/O4
Pink Mountain, Br. Col. 184/F1
Pinkstaff, Ill. 222/F5
Pinnacle, N.C. 281/J2
Pinnacles Nat'l Mon., Calif. 204/D7
Pinnaroo, S. Australia 88/G7
Pinnaroo, S. Australia 94/G6
Pinneberg, Germany 22/C2
Pinnebog, Mich. 250/F5
Pinney's (beach), St. Kitts & Nevis 161/D11
Pinola, Miss. 256/E7
Pinole, Calif. 204/J1
Pinon, Ariz. 198/E2
Pinon, Colo. 208/K6
Pinopolis, S.C. 296/G5
Pinos (riv.), Colo. 208/D8
Pinos, Rio de los (riv.), N. Mex. 274/B2
Pinos Altos, N. Mex. 274/A6
Pinos-Puente, Spain 33/E4
Pinquén, Peru 128/G9
Pinrang, Indonesia 85/F6
Pins (pt.), Ontario 177/C5
Pinsk, U.S.S.R. 48/C1
Pinsk, U.S.S.R. 52/C4
Pinson, Ala. 195/E4
Pinson, Tenn. 237/D10
Pinta (isl.), Ecuador 128/B9
Pintada, N. Mex. 274/D4
Pintada Arroyo (creek), N. Mex. 274/E4
Pintado, Artigas, Uruguay 145/C1
Pintado, Florida, Uruguay 145/C4
Pintados, Chile 138/B2
Pintados, Salar de (salt dep.), Chile 138/B2
Pintendre, Québec 172/J3
Pinto, Chile 138/A11
Pinto, Md. 245/C2
Pinto (creek), Sask. 181/D6

Pintura, Utah 304/A6
Pintuyan, Philippines 82/E6
Pintwater (range), Nev. 266/F6
Pinware (riv.), Newf. 166/C3
Pinware River, Newf. 166/C3
Pinyon (peak), Idaho 220/C5
Pinzón (isl.), Ecuador 128/B9
Pioche, Nev. 266/G5
Piombino, Italy 34/C3
Pioneer (mts.), Idaho 220/D6
Pioneer, Iowa 229/E3
Pioneer, La. 238/H1
Pioneer, Mo. 261/E9
Pioneer, Ohio 284/A2
Pioneer, Tenn. 237/N8
Pioneer (isl.), U.S.S.R. 48/J2
Pionerskiy, U.S.S.R. 48/G3
Pionki, Poland 47/E3
Piopio, N. Zealand 100/E3
Piopolis, Québec 172/F4
Piotrków (prov.), Poland 47/D3
Piotrków Trybunalski, Poland 47/D3
Piove di Sacco, Italy 34/C2
Pipe (creek), Ind. 227/F4
Piper (peak), Nev. 266/D5
Piper City, Ill. 222/E3
Pipersville, Pa. 294/M5
Piperton, Tenn. 237/B10
Pipe Spring Nat'l Mon., Ariz. 198/C2
Pipestem (riv.), N. Dak. 282/M5
Pipestem, W. Va. 312/E7
Pipestone, Manitoba 179/B5
Pipestone (creek), Manitoba 179/A5
Pipestone (co.), Minn. 255/B6
Pipestone, Minn. 255/B7
Pipestone (riv.), Ontario 175/B2
Pipestone (creek), Sask. 181/K6
Pipestone (riv.), Sask. 181/L2
Pipestone Nat'l Mon., Minn. 255/B6
Pipinas, Argentina 143/H7
Pipinui (pt.), N. Zealand 100/B2
Pipmuacan (res.), Québec 174/D3
Piqan (Shanshan), China 77/D3
Piqua, Kansas 232/H2
Piqua, Ohio 284/B5
Piquete, Brazil 135/D3
Piquiri (riv.), Brazil 132/C7
Piquiri (riv.), Brazil 132/C9
Piracanjuba, Brazil 132/D7
Piracicaba, Brazil 120/E5
Piracicaba, Brazil 135/C3
Piracicaba, Brazil 132/E8
Piracuruca, Brazil 132/F3
Piraí do Sul, Brazil 132/D9
Piraí do Sul, Brazil 135/B4
Piraiévs, Greece 7/G5
Piraiévs (Piraeus), Greece
  45/F7
Piraju, Brazil 135/B3
Pirajuba, Brazil 135/B1
Pirajuí, Brazil 135/B2
Pirámide, Cerro (mt.), Chile
  138/D8
Piran, Yugoslavia 45/A3
Pirané, Argentina 143/E2
Pirapora, Brazil 120/E4
Pirapora, Brazil 132/E7
Piraraja, Uruguay 145/E4
Pirassununga, Brazil 135/C2
Pirata (mt.), P. Rico 161/F2
Piraúba, Brazil 135/E2
Piray (riv.), Bolivia 136/D5
Pirayú, Paraguay 144/B5
Pirdop, Bulgaria 45/G4
Pirenópolis, Brazil 132/D6
Pires do Rio, Brazil 132/D7
Pírgos, Greece 45/E7
Piriápolis, Uruguay 145/D5
Piribebuy, Paraguay 144/B5
Piribebuy (riv.), Paraguay 144/B4
Piripiri, Brazil 132/F4
Píritu, Anzoátegui, Venezuela
  124/F2
Píritu, Falcón, Venezuela 124/D2
Píritu, Portuguesa, Venezuela
  124/D3
Pirmasens, Germany 22/B4
Pirna, Germany 22/E3
Pirongia (mt.), N. Zealand 100/E3
Pirot, Yugoslavia 45/F4
Piru, Calif. 204/G9
Piru, Indonesia 85/H6
Piryatin, U.S.S.R. 52/D4
Piryí, Greece 45/G6
Pisa (prov.), Italy 34/C3
Pisa, Italy 34/C3
Pisac, Peru 128/G9
Pisagua, Chile 138/A2
Piscadera (bay), Neth. Ant. 161/F9
Piscataqua (riv.), Maine 243/B9
Piscataqua (riv.), N.H. 268/F5
Piscataquis (co.), Maine 243/E4
Piscataquis (riv.), Maine 243/E5
Piscataquog (riv.), N.H. 268/D5
Piscataway, Md. 245/L6
Piscataway •, N.J. 273/D2
Piscataway Park, Md. 245/K6
Piscatosine (lake), Québec 172/B3
Pisco, Peru 128/D9
Pisco, Peru 120/B4
Pisco (bay), Peru 128/D9
Pisco (riv.), Peru 128/D9
Piseco, Peru 128/D9
Piseco (lake), N.Y. 276/M4
Pišek, Czech. 41/C2
Pišek, N. Dak. 282/P3
Pisgah, Ala. 195/G1
Pisgah, Iowa 229/B5
Pisgah, Md. 245/K6
Pisgah Forest, N.C. 281/D4
Pishan (Guma), China 77/A4
Pishin, Iran 66/M7
Pishin, Pakistan 68/B2
Pishin, Pakistan 59/J3
Pishkun (res.), Mont. 262/D3
Pisinimo, Ariz. 198/C6

Pismo Beach, Calif. 204/E8
Piso Firme, Bolivia 136/D3
Pisoniano, Italy 34/F6
Pissis (mt.), Argentina 143/C2
Pistakee (lake), Ill. 222/A4
Pistapaug (pond) Conn. 210/E3
Pistoia (prov.), Italy 34/C2
Pistoia, Italy 34/C2
Pistolet (bay), Newf. 166/C3
Pistol River, Oreg. 291/C5
Pisz, Poland 47/E2
Pit (riv.), Calif. 204/D2
Pitalito, Colombia 126/B7
Pitangui, Brazil 135/D1
Pitarpunga (lake), N.S. Wales 97/B4
Pitcairn (isl.) 87/C8
Pitcairn (isl.), (U.K.) 2/C7
Pitcairn, Pa. 294/C5
Pitch (lake), Trin. & Tob. 161/A11
Piteå, Sweden 18/M4
Piteälv (riv.), Sweden 18/M4
Pitești, Romania 45/G3
Pitești, Romania 7/G4
Píthion, Greece 45/H5
Pithiviers, France 28/E3
Pitiquito, Mexico 50/D1
Pitkas Point, Alaska 196/F2
Pitkin (co.), Colo. 208/F4
Pitkin, Colo. 208/F5
Pitkin, La. 238/E5
Pitlochry, Scotland 15/E4
Pitlochry, Scotland 10/E2
Pitman, N.J. 273/C4
Pitman, Sask. 181/G5
Pitmedden, Scotland 15/F3
Pitogo, Philippines 82/C4
Piton des Neiges (mt.), Réunion
  118/G5
Pitrufquén, Chile 138/D2
Pitsburg, Ohio 284/A6
Pitt (isl.), Br. Col. 184/C3
Pitt (lake), Br. Col. 184/L2
Pitt, Minn. 255/D2
Pitt (isl.), N. Zealand 100/E7
Pitt (str.), N. Zealand 100/E7
Pitt (co.), N.C. 281/P3
Pittenweem, Scotland 15/F4
Pitti (isl.), India 68/C6
Pittman Center, Tenn. 237/P9
Pitt Meadows, Br. Col. 184/L3
Pitts, Ark. 202/J2
Pitts, Georgia 217/E7
Pittsboro, Ind. 227/D5
Pittsboro, Miss. 256/F3
Pittsboro, N.C. 28 /L3
Pittsburg, Calif. 2C4/L1
Pittsburg, Georgia 217/L1
Pittsburg, Ill. 222/C6
Pittsburg, Ind. 227/D3
Pittsburg, Kansas 232/H4
Pittsburg, Ky. 237/N6
Pittsburg, Mo. 261/F7
Pittsburg •, N.H. 258/E1
Pittsburg (co.), Okla. 288/P5
Pittsburg, Okla. 288/P5
Pittsburg, Texas 303/J4
Pittsburgh, Pa. 294/K5
Pittsburgh, Pa. 184/L2
Pittsburgh, Pa. 29−/B7
Pittsfield, Ill. 222/C4
Pittsfield, Maine 2−3/E6
Pittsfield •, Maine 243/E6
Pittsfield, Mass. 188/M2
Pittsfield, Mass. 249/A3
Pittsfield, N.H. 268/E5
Pittsfield •, N.H. 268/E5
Pittsfield, Pa. 294/D2
Pittsfield •, Vt. 268/B4
Pittsford, Mich. 250/E7
Pittsford, N.Y. 276 E4
Pittsford, Vt. 268/F4
Pittsford •, Vt. 268/A4
Pittston •, Maine 243/D7
Pittston, Pa. 294/F
Pittstown, N.J. 273/C2
Pittsview, Ala. 195/H6
Pittsville, Md. 245/S7
Pittsville, Mo. 261/F5
Pittsville, W. Va. 307/H7
Pittsville, Wis. 317/F7
Pittsylvania (co.), Va. 307/K7
Pittville, Calif. 204/D2
Pittwood, Ill. 222/F3
Piuí, Brazil 132/E8
Piuí, Brazil 135/D2
Piura (dept.), Peru 128/B5
Piura, Peru 120/A3
Piura, Peru 128/B5
Piura (riv.), Peru 128/B5
Piute (co.), Utah 304/B5
Piute (res.), Utah 304/B5
Pivijay, Colombia 126/D1
Pixley, Calif. 204/F8
Piyas (lake), S. Dak. 298/P2
Pizacoma, Peru 128/H11
Pizarro, Colombia 126/B5
Pizol (peak), Switzerland 39/H3
Place, Ky. 237/N7
Placentia, Calif. 204/D11
Placentia, Newf. 166/C2
Placentia (bay), Newf. 166/C2
Placentia (sound), Newf. 166/C2
Placer (co.), Calif. 204/F4
Placer, Philippines 82/E6
Placerville, Calif. 204/F4
Placerville, Colo. 208/D6
Placerville, Idaho 220/C6
Placetas, Cuba 158/E2
Placid (lake), Fla. 212/E4
Placid (lake), N.Y. 276/N2
Placida, Fla. 212/D5
Placilla, Chile 138/F3
Placilla de Caracoles, Chile 138/B4
Placilla de Peñuelas, Chile 138/F2
Placitas, N. Mex. 274/C3
Plad, Mo. 261/G7

Pladda (isl.), Scotland 15/C5
Plaffeien, Switzerland 39/D3
Plain, Wash. 310/E3
Plain, Wis. 317/F9
Plain City, Ohio 284/D5
Plain City, Utah 304/B2
Plain Dealing, La. 238/C1
Plainfield, Ark. 202/D7
Plainfield, Conn. 210/H2
Plainfield •, Conn. 210/H2
Plainfield, Georgia 217/F6
Plainfield, Ill. 222/A6
Plainfield, Ind. 227/E5
Plainfield, Iowa 229/J3
Plainfield •, Mass. 249/C2
Plainfield •, N.H. 268/C4
Plainfield, N.J. 273/E2
Plainfield, Ohio 284/G2
Plainfield, Colo. 268/C3
Plainfield •, Vt. 268/C3
Plainfield, Wis. 317/G7
Plains, Georgia 217/D6
Plains, Kansas 232/B4
Plains, Mont. 262/B3
Plains, Pa. 294/F7
Plains, Texas 303/B4
Plainsboro, N.J. 273/D3
Plainview, Ark. 202/D4
Plainview, Nebr. 264/G2
Plainview, N.Y. 276/R7
Plainview, S. Dak. 298/M2
Plainview, Texas 303/C3
Plainville •, Conn. 210/D2
Plainville, Georgia 217/C2
Plainville, Ill. 222/C4
Plainville, Ind. 227/C7
Plainville, Kansas 232/C2
Plainville •, Mass. 249/J4
Plainwell, Mich. 250/D6
Plaisance, Haiti 158/C5
Plaisance (riv.), Québec 172/B4
Plaisted, Maine 243/F1
Plaistow •, N.H. 268/E6
Plaju, Indonesia 85/D6
Plamondon, Alberta 182/D2
Plana (cays), Bahamas 156/D2
Planá, Czech. 41/B2
Planada, Calif. 204/E6
Planeta Rica, Colombia 126/C3
Plánice, Czech. 41/B2
Plankinton, S. Dak. 298/N6
Plano, Ill. 222/E2
Plano, Iowa 229/J7
Plano, Texas 303/G1
Plant, Tenn. 237/F9
Plantagenet, Ontario 177/K2
Plantation, Fla. 212/B4
Plantation (key), Fla. 212/F7
Plantation, Ky. 237/K1
Plant City, Fla. 212/D3
Plantersville, Ala. 195/E5
Plantersville, Miss. 256/G2
Plantersville, S.C. 296/J4
Plantsite, Ariz. 198/F5
Plantsville, Conn. 210/D2
Plaquemine, La. 238/J2
Plaquemines (par.), La. 238/L8
Plasencia, Spain 33/C2
Plaster City, Calif. 204/K11
Plaster Rock, New Bruns. 170/C2
Plastun, U.S.S.R. 48/O5
Plasy, Czech. 41/B2
Plat, Wis. 317/K1
Plata (riv.), 2/G7
Plata, Río de la (est.), Argentina
  143/E4
Plata (riv.), P. Rico 161/D2
Plata, La (riv.), Uruguay 145/B5
Platanal, Venezuela 124/F6
Platanilla, C. Rica 154/F6
Platea, Pa. 294/B2
Plateau (creek), Colo. 208/C4
Plateau (state), Nigeria 106/F7
Plateau, Nova Scotia 168/H2
Plateau City, Colo. 208/D4
Plateau, Nova Scotia 168/H2
Plate Cove, Newf. 166/D2
Platen, Kapp (pt.), Norway
  18/D1
Platina, Calif. 204/B3
Platinum, Alaska 196/F3
Platner, Colo. 208/N2
Plato, Colombia 126/D3
Plato, Minn. 255/D6
Plato, Mo. 261/H8
Plato, Sask. 181/C4
Platoro (res.), Colo. 208/F8
Platte (riv.), Iowa 229/D8
Platte (riv.), Mich. 250/C4
Platte (riv.), Mo. 261/C3
Platte (co.), Nebr. 264/G3
Platte (riv.), Nebr. 146/J5
Platte (riv.), Nebr. 188/G2
Platte (riv.), Nebr. 264/E4
Platte, S. Dak. 298/N6
Platte (lake), S. Dak. 298/M6
Platte (co.), Wyo. 319/H4
Platte Center, Nebr. 264/G3
Platte City, Mo. 261/C4
Platten (lake), La. 238/K4
Platter, Okla. 288/O7
Platteville, Colo. 208/M2
Platteville, Wis. 317/F10
Platte Woods, Mo. 261/O5
Plattsburg, Mo. 261/D3
Plattsburg, N.Y. 276/O1
Plattsburgh A.F.B., N.Y. 276/N1
Plattsmouth, Nebr. 264/J3
Plattsville, Ontario 177/D4
Plau, Germany 22/E2
Plaucheville, La. 238/G5
Placida, Fla. 212/D5
Plauen, Germany 22/E3
Plauersee (lake), Germany 22/E2
Plav, Yugoslavia 45/D4
Plavinas, U.S.S.R. 53/C2
Playa (pt.), Guyana 131/B1
Playa Azul, Mexico 150/H7

Playa Bonita, C. Rica 154/E6
Playa de Fajardo, P. Rico 161/F1
Playa de Humacao, P. Rico 161/F2
Playa Grande, Nicaragua 154/D4
Playas, Ecuador 128/B4
Playas (lake), N. Mex. 274/A7
Playón Chico, Panama 154/H6
Playón Grande, Panama 154/H6
Plaza, N. Dak. 282/G3
Plaza, Wash. 310/H3
Plaza Huincul, Argentina 143/B4
Pleasant (isl.), Alaska 196/M1
Pleasant (lake), Ariz. 198/C5
Pleasant (lake), Maine 243/H5
Pleasant (lake), Maine 243/H5
Pleasant (lake), Maine 243/H6
Pleasant (riv.), Maine 243/H6
Pleasant (mt.), New Bruns. 170/D3
Pleasant (riv.), Maine 243/H6
Pleasant (bay), Nova Scotia
  168/H2
Pleasant Bay, Nova Scotia 168/H2
Pleasant City, Ohio 284/G6
Pleasant Dale, Nebr. 264/G4
Pleasantdale, Sask. 181/G3
Pleasant Gap, Ala. 195/H3
Pleasant Gap, Pa. 294/H4
Pleasant Green, Mo. 261/F5
Pleasant Grove, Ala. 195/D4
Pleasant Grove, Calif. 204/B8
Pleasant Grove, Miss. 256/D2
Pleasant Grove, N.J. 273/D2
Pleasant Grove, Utah 304/C3
Pleasant Hill, Ala. 195/E6
Pleasant Hill, Calif. 204/K2
Pleasant Hill, Ill. 222/C4
Pleasant Hill, La. 238/D3
Pleasant Hill, Miss. 256/E1
Pleasant Hill, Mo. 261/D5
Pleasant Hill, N.C. 281/O1
Pleasant Hill, Ohio 284/B5
Pleasant Hill, S.C. 296/F2
Pleasant Hill, Tenn. 237/L9
Pleasant Hills, Md. 245/N3
Pleasant Hope, Mo. 261/F8
Pleasant Island, Maine 243/B5
Pleasant Lake, Ind. 227/H1
Pleasant Lake, Mass. 249/O6
Pleasant Lake, Minn. 255/D5
Pleasant Lake, N. Dak. 282/L3
Pleasant Lane, S.C. 296/D4
Pleasant Mills, Ind. 227/H3
Pleasant Mound, Ill. 222/D5
Pleasant Mount, Pa. 294/M2
Pleasanton, Calif. 204/L2
Pleasanton, Iowa 229/J7
Pleasanton, Kansas 232/H3
Pleasanton, Nebr. 264/E4
Pleasanton, N. Mex. 274/A5
Pleasanton, Texas 303/F9
Pleasant Plain, Iowa 229/K6
Pleasant Plain, Ohio 284/B7
Pleasant Plains, Ark. 202/G2
Pleasant Plains, Ill. 222/D4
Pleasant Point, N. Zealand 100/C6
Pleasant Pond, Maine 243/D5
Pleasant Prairie, Wis. 317/L10
Pleasant Ridge, Mich. 250/B6
Pleasants (co.), W. Va. 312/D4
Pleasant Shade, Tenn. 237/K8
Pleasant Valley, Conn. 210/C1
Pleasant Valley, Md. 245/L2
Pleasant Valley, Mich. 250/B6
Pleasant Valley, Mo. 261/R5
Pleasant Valley, Oreg. 291/K3
Pleasant Valley (creek), S. Dak.
  298/B6
Pleasant Valley, Va. 307/L4
Pleasant View, Colo. 208/B7
Pleasant View, Ill. 222/C3
Pleasant View, Ky. 237/M7
Pleasant View, Tenn. 237/G8
Pleasantville, Ind. 227/C7
Pleasantville, Iowa 229/G6
Pleasantville, N.J. 273/D5
Pleasantville, N.Y. 276/N8
Pleasantville, Ohio 284/F6
Pleasantville (Alum Bank), Pa.
  294/E5
Pleasantville, Pa. 294/C2
Pleasantville, Tenn. 237/F9
Pleasure Beach, Conn. 210/G3
Pleasure Ridge Park, Ky. 237/J4
Pleasureville, Ky. 237/L4
Pleiku, Vietnam 72/E4
Plenița, Romania 45/F3
Plenty (bay), N. Zealand 100/F2
Plenty, Sask. 181/C4
Plenty (riv.), Victoria 97/J4
Plenty (riv.), Victoria 88/L6
Plenty River Mine, North. Terr.
  93/D7
Plentywood, Mont. 262/M2
Plesetsk, U.S.S.R. 52/F2
Plessis, N.Y. 276/J2
Plessisville, Québec 172/F3
Plessur (riv.), Switzerland 39/J3
Pletcher, Ala. 195/E5
Plétipi (lake), Que. 162/J5
Plétipi (lake), Québec 174/C2
Plettenberg, Germany 22/C3
Plettenberg (bay), S. Africa 118/C6
Pleven, Bulgaria 7/G4
Pleven, Bulgaria 45/G4
Plevna, Ala. 195/F1
Plevna, Ind. 227/E3
Plevna, Kansas 232/D4
Plevna, Mo. 261/H3
Plevna, Mont. 262/M4
Plevna, Ontario 177/H3
Pliny, W. Va. 312/B5
Pljevlja, Yugoslavia 45/D4
Plöce, Yugoslavia 45/D4
Plavinas, U.S.S.R. 53/C2
Playa (pt.), Guyana 131/B1
Płock (prov.), Poland 47/D2
Płock, Poland 47/D2

Plockton, Scotland 15/C3
Ploërmel, France 28/B4
Ploiești, Romania 45/H3
Ploiești, Romania 7/G4
Plomárion, Greece 45/H6
Plomb du Cantal (mt.), France
  28/C5
Plombières, Belgium 27/H7
Plomer (pt.), N.S. Wales 97/G2
Plomosa (mts.), Ariz. 198/A5
Plön, Germany 22/D1
Płonia (riv.), Poland 47/B2
Płońsk, Poland 47/E2
Plovdiv, Bulgaria 7/G4
Plovdiv, Bulgaria 45/G4
Plover, Iowa 229/D3
Plover, Wis. 317/G7
Pluckemin, N.J. 273/D2
Plum (creek), Manitoba 179/B5
Plum (lake), Manitoba 179/B5
Plum (isl.), Mass. 249/L2
Plum (isl.), N.Y. 276/R8
Plum, Pa. 294/C5
Plumas (co.), Calif. 204/E4
Plumas, Manitoba 179/D4
Plumber (creek), Utah 304/D2
Plum Branch, S.C. 296/C4
Plum City, Wis. 317/B6
Plum Coulee, Manitoba 179/E5
Plumerville, Ark. 202/E3
Plummer, Idaho 220/B2
Plummer, Ind. 227/C7
Plummer, Minn. 255/B3
Plummers Landing, Ky. 237/P4
Plum Point, Md. 245/N6
Plum Springs, Ky. 237/J7
Plumsteadville, Pa. 294/M5
Plum Tree, Ind. 227/G3
Plumtree, Zimbabwe 118/D4
Plumville, Pa. 294/D4
Plumwood, Ohio 284/D6
Plunge, U.S.S.R. 53/B3
Plunkett, Sask. 181/F4
Plunkettville, Okla. 288/S6
Plush, Oreg. 291/H5
Plymouth (cap.), 156/F3
Plymouth, Calif. 204/C8
Plymouth •, Conn. 210/C2
Plymouth, England 7/D3
Plymouth, England 10/E5
Plymouth, England 13/C7
Plymouth (sound), England 13/C7
Plymouth, Fla. 212/E3
Plymouth, Ill. 222/C3
Plymouth, Ind. 227/E2
Plymouth (co.), Iowa 229/A3
Plymouth, Iowa 229/G2
Plymouth •, Maine 243/E6
Plymouth (co.), Mass. 249/L5
Plymouth, Mass. 249/M5
Plymouth •, Mass. 249/M5
Plymouth (bay), Mass. 249/M5
Plymouth, Mich. 250/F6
Plymouth, Minn. 255/D6
Plymouth, Nebr. 264/H4
Plymouth, N.H. 268/D4
Plymouth •, N.H. 268/D4
Plymouth, N.C. 281/R3
Plymouth, Ohio 284/E4
Plymouth, Pa. 294/E7
Plymouth, Utah 304/B2
Plymouth •, Vt. 268/B4
Plymouth, Wash. 310/F5
Plymouth, W. Va. 312/C6
Plymouth, Wis. 317/L8
Plymouth Valley (creek), S. Dak.
  298/B6
Plymouth Union, Vt. 268/B4
Plympton •, Mass. 249/L5
Plympton, Nova Scotia 168/C4
Plynlimon (mt.), Wales 13/D5
Plzeň, Czech. 7/F4
Plzeň, Czech. 41/B2
Pniel, S. Africa 118/F6
Pniewy, Poland 47/C2
Po, Burkina Faso 106/D6
Po (riv.), Italy 7/E4
Po (riv.), Italy 34/C2
Po (riv.), W. Va. 307/N4
Poá, Brazil 135/C3
Poatina, Tasmania 99/C3
Pobeda (peak), China 77/A3
Pobeda (peak), U.S.S.R. 48/J5
Población, Chile 138/F5
Pobla de Segur, Spain 33/G1
Poca, W. Va. 312/C6
Pocahontas, Alberta 182/B3
Pocahontas, Ark. 202/H1
Pocahontas, Ill. 222/D5
Pocahontas (co.), Iowa 229/D3
Pocahontas, Iowa 229/D3
Pocahontas, Miss. 256/D6
Pocahontas, Mo. 261/N8
Pocahontas, Tenn. 237/D10
Pocahontas, Va. 307/F6
Pocahontas (co.), W. Va. 312/F6
Pocasset, Mass. 249/M6
Pocasset, Okla. 288/L4
Pocatalico (riv.), W. Va. 312/C6
Pocatello, Idaho 146/G5
Pocatello, Idaho 220/F7
Pocatello, Idaho 188/D2
Počátky, Czech. 41/C2
Pochep, U.S.S.R. 52/D4
Pöchlarn, Austria 41/C2
Pocklington, England 13/G4
Pocoata, Bolivia 136/B6
Poções, Brazil 132/F6
Pocola, Okla. 288/T4
Pocologan, New Bruns. 170/D3
Pocomoke (riv.), Md. 245/S8
Pocomoke (sound), Md. 245/P9
Pocomoke, Mont. 307/S5
Pocomoke City, Md. 245/R8
Pocomoonshine (lake), Maine 243/H5
Pocona, Bolivia 136/C5
Poconé, Brazil 132/B7
Pocono (mts.), Pa. 294/M3
Pocono Lake, Pa. 294/L3

Pocono Pines, Pa. 294/M3
Poços de Caldas, Brazil 120/E5
Poços de Caldas, Brazil 135/C2
Poços de Caldas, Brazil 132/E8
Pocotalago, Georgia 217/F2
Pocotalico, W. Va. 312/C6
Pocotaligo (riv.), S.C. 296/F5
Pocotopaug (lake), Conn. 210/E2
Pocpo, Bolivia 136/C6
Podbořany, Czech. 41/B1
Poděbrady, Czech. 41/C1
Podol'sk, U.S.S.R. 7/H3
Podol'sk, U.S.S.R. 52/E3
Podol'sk, U.S.S.R. 48/D4
Podor, Senegal 106/B5
Podorozh'ye, U.S.S.R. 52/D2
Podunk (riv.), Conn. 210/E1
Poe, Alberta 182/D3
Poe, Ind. 227/G3
Poel (isl.), Germany 22/D1
Poenari Burchi, Romania 45/G3
Poge (cape), Mass. 249/N7
Poggibonsi, Italy 34/C3
Pogradec, Albania 45/E5
Pohakuloa (pt.), Hawaii 218/H2
P'ohang, S. Korea 81/D5
Pohatcong (creek), N.J. 273/C2
Pohénégamooke, Québec 172/H2
Pohjois-Karjala (prov.), Finland
  18/Q5
Pohnpei (isl.), Micronesia 87/F5
Pohořelice, Czech. 41/D2
Pohsien (Bo Xian), China 77/J5
Poiana Mare, Romania 45/F4
Poigan (lake), Québec 172/A2
Poinsett (co.), Ark. 202/J2
Poinsett (lake), Fla. 212/F3
Poinsett (lake), S. Dak. 298/P4
Point, La. 238/F4
Point (lake), N.W. Terr. 187/G3
Point, Texas 303/J5
Point Alexander, Ontario 177/G1
Point Arena, Calif. 204/B5
Point au Fer (isl.), La. 238/H8
Point au Fer (pt.), La. 238/H8
Point Baker, Alaska 196/M2
Point Cedar, Ark. 202/C5
Point Clear, Ala. 195/C10
Point Comfort, Texas 303/H9
Point Cross, Nova Scotia 168/G2
Point de Bute, New Bruns. 170/F3
Point du Bois, Manitoba 179/G4
Pointe-à-la-Croix, Québec 172/C2
Pointe-à-la-Frégate, Québec 172/D1
Pointe-à-la-Garde, Québec 172/B2
Pointe a la Hache, La. 238/L7
Pointe-à-Pitre, Guadeloupe 161/B6
Pointe-à-Pitre, Guadeloupe 156/G3
Pointe à Raquette, Haiti 158/B6
Pointe au Baril Station, Ontario
  177/D2
Pointe-au-Chêne, Québec 172/C4
Pointe-au-Père, Québec 172/J1
Pointe-au-Pic, Québec 172/G2
Pointe Aux Barques, Mich. 250/G4
Pointe-aux-Outardes, Québec 172/A1
Pointe Aux Pins, Mich. 250/E3
Pointe-aux-Trembles, Québec 172/J4
Pointe-Bleue, Québec 172/E1
Pointe-Calumet, Québec 172/G4
Pointe-Claire, Québec 172/J4
Pointe Coupee (par.), La. 238/G5
Pointe du Bout, Martinique 161/C6
Pointe-du-Chêne, New Bruns. 170/F2
Pointe-du-Lac, Québec 172/E3
Pointe-du-Moulin, Québec 172/H4
Point Edward, Ontario 177/B4
Pointe-Gatineau, Québec 172/B4
Pointe-Lebel, Québec 172/A1
Pointe-Noire, Congo 102/D5
Pointe-Noire, Congo 115/B4
Pointe-Noire, Guadeloupe 161/A6
Pointe-Sapin, New Bruns. 170/F2
Pointe-Verte, New Bruns. 170/E1
Point Fortin, Trin. & Tob. 161/A11
Point Harbor, N.C. 281/T2
Point Hope, Alaska 188/C5
Point Hope, Alaska 196/C1
Point Isabel, Ind. 227/F4
Point La Haye, Newf. 166/D2
Point Lance, Newf. 166/D2
Point Lay, Alaska 196/F1
Point Leamington, Newf. 166/C4
Point Marion, Pa. 294/C6
Point Mugu Pacific Missile Test Center,
  Calif. 204/F9
Point of Rocks, Md. 245/J3
Point of Rocks, Wyo. 319/D4
Point Pelee, Ontario 177/B6
Point Pelee Nat'l Park, Ontario 177/B5
Point Pleasant, Mo. 261/O10
Point Pleasant, N.J. 273/E3
Point Pleasant, Ohio 284/B8
Point Pleasant, Pa. 294/N5
Point Pleasant, W. Va. 312/B5
Point Pleasant Beach, N.J. 273/E3
Point Reyes Nat'l Seashore, Calif.
  204/H1
Point Reyes Station, Calif. 204/H1
Point Roberts, Wash. 310/B2
Points, W. Va. 312/J4
Point Salvation Aboriginal Reserve,
  W. Australia 88/C5
Point Salvation Aboriginal Res.,
  W. Australia 92/D5
Point Tupper, Nova Scotia 168/G3
Point Verde, Newf. 166/C2
Point Washington, Fla. 212/C6
Poipu, Hawaii 218/C2
Poison (creek), Wyo. 319/E2
Poison Spider (creek), Wyo. 319/F3
Poisson Blanc (lake), Québec 172/B4
Poissons (riv.), Newf. 166/A3
Poitiers, France 7/E4
Poitiers, France 28/D4
Poitou (trad. region), France 29
Pojo, Bolivia 136/C5
Pojoaque, N. Mex. 274/C3

Pokaran, India 68/C3
Pokataroo, N.S. Wales 97/E1
Pokegama (lake), Minn. 255/E3
Pokemouche (riv.), New Bruns. 170/E1
Pokesudie (isl.), New Bruns. 170/F1
Pokhara, Nepal 68/E3
Pokhvistnevo, U.S.S.R. 52/H4
Poko, Zaire 115/E3
Pokrovsk, U.S.S.R. 48/N3
Pola, Philippines 82/C4
Pola (Pula), Yugoslavia 45/A3
Polacca, Ariz. 198/E3
Polacca Wash (dry riv.), Ariz. 198/E3
Pola de Lena, Spain 33/C1
Pola de Siero, Spain 33/D1
Polanco del Yi, Uruguay 145/D4
Poland 2/K3
Poland 7/F3
POLAND 47
Poland (riv.), Conn. 210/C2
Poland, Ind. 227/C6
Poland, Maine 243/C7
Poland •, Maine 243/C7
Poland, N.Y. 276/L4
Poland, Ohio 284/J3
Poland Spring, Maine 243/C7
Polar, Wis. 317/H5
Polar Bear Prov. Park, Ontario 175/D2
Polaris, Mont. 262/C5
Polatlı, Turkey 63/E3
Polatlı, Turkey 59/B2
Połczyn-Zdroj, Poland 47/C2
Polebridge, Mont. 262/B2
Pol-e Khomri, Afghanistan 68/B1
Pol-e Khomri, Afghanistan 59/J2
Polgár, Hungary 41/F3
Polgárdi, Hungary 41/E3
Poli, Cameroon 115/B2
Policastro (gulf), Italy 34/E5
Police, Poland 47/B2
Polička, Czech. 41/D2
Poligny, France 28/F4
Poligus, U.S.S.R. 48/K3
Polikastron, Greece 45/F5
Políkhnitos, Greece 45/G6
Polillo, Philippines 82/D3
Polillo (isl.), Philippines 85/G3
Polillo (isl.), Philippines 82/C3
Polillo (str.), Philippines 82/C3
Polis, Cyprus 63/E5
Políyiros, Greece 45/F5
Polk (co.), Ark. 202/B5
Polk (co.), Fla. 212/E4
Polk (co.), Georgia 217/B3
Polk (co.), Iowa 229/F5
Polk (co.), Minn. 255/B3
Polk (co.), Mo. 261/F7
Polk, Mo. 261/F7
Polk (co.), Nebr. 264/G3
Polk, Nebr. 264/G3
Polk (co.), N.C. 281/E4
Polk, Ohio 284/F4
Polk (co.), Oreg. 291/D3
Polk, Pa. 294/C2
Polk (co.), Tenn. 237/N10
Polk (co.), Texas 303/K7
Polk (co.), Wis. 317/B5
Polk City, Fla. 212/E4
Polk City, Iowa 229/F5
Polkowice, Poland 47/C3
Polkton, N.C. 281/J4
Polkville, Miss. 256/E6
Polkville, N.C. 281/F4
Pollaphuca (res.), Ireland 17/J5
Pollard, Ala. 195/D8
Pollard, Ark. 202/K1
Pollards Point, Newf. 166/C4
Põllau, Austria 41/C3
Pollensa, Spain 33/H3
Pollett (riv.), New Bruns. 170/E3
Pollett River, New Bruns. 170/E3
Pollock, Idaho 220/B4
Pollock, La. 238/F3
Pollock, Mo. 261/F2
Pollock, S. Dak. 298/J2
Pollock Pines, Calif. 204/E5
Pollocksville, N.C. 281/P5
Pollockville, Alberta 182/E4
Polmak, Norway 18/O2
Polná, Czech. 41/C2
Polo, Dom. Rep. 158/D6
Polo, Ill. 222/D1
Polo, Mo. 261/D3
Polomka, Czech. 41/E2
Polonia, Chile 138/G6
Polonia, Wis. 317/H6
Polonio (cape), Uruguay 145/F5
Polonnaruwa, Sri Lanka 68/E7
Polonnoye, U.S.S.R. 52/C4
Polotsk, U.S.S.R. 52/C3
Polperro, England 13/C7
Polson, Mont. 262/B3
Poltava, U.S.S.R. 7/H4
Poltava, U.S.S.R. 52/D5
Poltava, U.S.S.R. 48/D5
Poltimore, Québec 172/B4
Põltsamaa, U.S.S.R. 53/D1
Polvadera, N. Mex. 274/B4
Polyarnyy, U.S.S.R. 52/D1
Polyarnyy, U.S.S.R. 48/D3
Polynesia (reg.), Pacific 87/K7
Pomabamba, Peru 128/D7
Pomaire, Chile 138/F4
Román, Argentina 143/C2
Pomaria, S.C. 296/F3
Pombal, Brazil 132/G4
Pombal, Portugal 33/B3
Pomeranian (bay), Germany 22/F1
Pomeranian (bay), Poland 47/B1
Pomerene, Ariz. 198/E6
Pomeroon (riv.), Guyana 131/B2
Pomeroy, Iowa 229/D3
Pomeroy, N. Ireland 17/H2
Pomeroy, Ohio 284/D7
Pomeroy, Wash. 310/H4
Pomezia, Italy 34/F7

Pomfret •, Conn. 210/H1
Pomfret, Md. 245/L6
Pomfret •, Vt. 268/B4
Pomfret Center, Conn. 210/H1
Pomme de Terre (riv.), Minn. 255/C5
Pomme de Terre (lake), Mo. 261/E7
Pomona, Calif. 188/C4
Pomona, Calif. 204/D10
Pomona, Kansas 232/G3
Pomona (lake), Kansas 232/G3
Pomona, Md. 245/O4
Pomona, Mo. 261/J9
Pomona, N.J. 273/D5
Pomona Park, Fla. 212/E2
Pomonkey, Md. 245/K6
Pomorie, Bulgaria 45/H4
Pompano Beach, Fla. 212/F5
Pompanoosuc, Vt. 268/C4
Pompéia, Brazil 135/B2
Pompeii (ruins), Italy 34/E4
Pompeii, Mich. 250/E6
Pomperaug, Conn. 210/C2
Pomperaug (riv.), Conn. 210/C3
Pompey, N.Y. 276/J5
Pompeys Pillar, Mont. 262/J5
Pompton (lake), N.J. 273/B1
Pompton Lakes, N.J. 273/A1
Pompton Plains, N.J. 273/B1
Pomquet, Nova Scotia 168/G3
Pomy, Switzerland 39/C3
Ponape (Pohnpei) (isl.), Micronesia 87/F5
Ponass (lakes), Sask. 181/H3
Ponca, Ark. 202/D1
Ponca, Nebr. 264/H2
Ponca (creek), S. Dak. 298/L7
Ponca City, Okla. 188/G3
Ponca City, Okla. 288/M1
Ponce (dist.), P. Rico 161/C2
Ponce, P. Rico 161/C3
Ponce, P. Rico 156/F1
Ponce de Leon, Fla. 212/C6
Ponce de Leon (bay), Fla. 212/E6
Ponce Inlet, Fla. 212/F2
Poncha Springs, Colo. 208/G6
Ponchatoula, La. 238/N2
Pond (pt.), Conn. 210/C4
Pond, Miss. 256/B8
Pond, Mo. 261/M3
Pond (inlet), N.W. Terr. 187/L2
Pond Creek, Okla. 288/L1
Pond Eddy, Pa. 294/N3
Pondera (co.), Mont. 262/D2
Ponderay, Idaho 220/B1
Ponderosa, N. Mex. 274/C3
Pond Fork (riv.), W. Va. 312/C6
Pondicherry (terr.), India 68/E6
Pondicherry, India 68/E6
Pond Inlet, Canada 4/B13
Pond Inlet, N.W.T. 162/J1
Pond Inlet, N.W.T. 187/L2
Pondoland (reg.), S. Africa 118/D6
Pondosa, Calif. 204/D2
Ponds (isl.), Newf. 166/D2
Poneloya, Nicaragua 154/D4
Ponemah, Minn. 255/D2
Ponemah, N.H. 268/D6
Poneto, Ind. 227/G4
Ponferrada, Spain 33/C1
Pongara (pt.), Gabon 115/A3
Ponhook (lake), Nova Scotia 168/D4
Poniatowa, Poland 47/E3
Ponnani, India 68/D6
Ponoka, Alberta 182/D3
Ponomarevka, U.S.S.R. 52/H4
Ponoy, U.S.S.R. 48/E3
Ponoy, U.S.S.R. 52/F1
Ponoy (riv.), U.S.S.R. 52/E1
Pons, France 28/C5
Ponset, Conn. 210/E3
Ponsford, Minn. 255/C4
Pont-à-Celles, Belgium 27/E8
Ponta Delgada (dist.), Portugal 33/D2
Ponta Delgada, Portugal 33/C2
Ponta de Pedras, Brazil 132/D3
Ponta do Sol, Portugal 33/A2
Ponta Grossa, Brazil 120/D5
Ponta Grossa, Brazil 132/D9
Ponta Grossa, Brazil 135/B4
Pont-à-Mousson, France 28/G3
Ponta Porã, Brazil 132/C8
Ponta Porã, Paraguay 144/A3
Pontarlier, France 28/G4
Pontbriand, Québec 172/F3
Pont Canavese, Italy 34/A2
Pontchartrain (lake), La. 188/J5
Pontchartrain (lake), La. 238/O3
Pontchartrain Causeway, La. 238/O3
Pontecorvo, Italy 34/D4
Ponte de Sor, Portugal 33/C3
Ponte do Lima, Portugal 33/B2
Ponteix, Sask. 181/D6
Ponteland, England 13/H3
Ponte Nova, Brazil 132/F8
Ponte Nova, Brazil 135/E2
Pontevedra, Philippines 82/C3
Pontevedra (prov.), Spain 33/B1
Pontevedra, Spain 33/B1
Ponte Vedra Beach, Fla. 212/E1
Pontgrave, New Bruns. 170/F1
Pontiac, Ill. 222/D3
Pontiac, Mich. 188/K2
Pontiac, Mich. 250/F6
Pontiac, Mo. 261/G9
Pontiac (co.), Québec 172/A3
Pontiac, R.I. 249/J6
Pontiac, S.C. 296/F3
Pontianak, Indonesia 85/D6
Pontianak, Indonesia 54/N10
Pontian Kechil, Malaysia 72/E5
Pontic (mts.), Turkey 59/C1
Pontic (mts.), Turkey 63/H2
Pontine (isls.), Italy 34/D4

Pontinia, Italy 34/D4
Pontivy, France 28/B3
Pont-l'Abbe, France 28/A4
Pont-Lafrance, New Bruns. 170/E1
Pont-Landry, New Bruns. 170/F1
Pont-l'Évêque, France 28/D3
Ponto da Divisão, Brazil 132/B5
Pontoise, France 28/E3
Pontoon Beach, Ill. 222/A2
Pontoosuc, Ill. 222/B3
Pontoosuc (lake), Mass. 249/A3
Pontorson, France 28/C3
Pontotoc (co.), Miss. 256/F2
Pontotoc, Miss. 256/G2
Pontotoc (co.), Okla. 288/N5
Pontotoc, Okla. 288/N6
Pontotoc, Texas 303/E7
Pontremoli, Italy 34/B2
Pontresina, Switzerland 39/J3
Pontrilas, Sask. 181/H2
Pont-Rouge, Québec 172/F3
Pontypool, Ontario 177/F3
Pontypool, Wales 13/B6
Pontypridd, Wales 13/A6
Pontypridd, Wales 10/E5
Pony, Mont. 262/E5
Pony (creek), Okla. 288/C1
Ponza (isl.), Italy 34/D4
Ponzer, N.C. 281/S3
Poole, England 13/E7
Poole, England 10/E5
Poole (bay), England 13/F7
Poole, Ky. 237/F5
Poole, Nebr. 264/F4
Pooler, Georgia 217/K6
Pooles (isl.), Md. 245/O3
Poolesville, Md. 245/J4
Pooleville, Okla. 288/M6
Poolewe, Scotland 15/C3
Poolville, N.Y. 276/K5
Poona, India 54/J8
Pooncarie, N.S. Wales 97/B3
Poopeloe (lake), N.S. Wales 97/C2
Poopó, Bolivia 136/C6
Poopó, Bolivia 136/B6
Poopó (lake), Bolivia 136/B6
Poor Knights (isls.), N. Zealand 100/E1
Poorman, Alaska 196/G2
Poosepatuck Ind. Res., N.Y. 276/P9
Popa Hill (mt.), Burma 72/B2
Popayán, Colombia 120/B2
Popayán, Colombia 126/B6
Pope (co.), Ark. 202/D3
Pope (co.), Ill. 222/E6
Pope (creek), Ill. 222/C2
Pope, Manitoba 179/B5
Pope (co.), Minn. 255/C5
Popes, Miss. 256/E2
Pope A.F.B., N.C. 281/L4
Popejoy, Iowa 229/G3
Poperinge, Belgium 27/B7
Popes Creek, Md. 245/L7
Popham Beach, Maine 243/D8
Popilta (lake), N.S. Wales 97/A3
Popiltah, N.S. Wales 97/A3
Popina, Bulgaria 45/H3
Popkum, Br. Col. 184/M3
Poplar, Calif. 204/F7
Poplar (pt.), Manitoba 179/E2
Poplar (riv.), Manitoba 179/E2
Poplar (isl.), Md. 245/N5
Poplar (riv.), Minn. 255/C3
Poplar, Mont. 262/L2
Poplar (riv.), Mont. 262/L2
Poplar (riv.), Sask. 181/E6
Poplar, Wis. 317/C2
Poplar Bluff, Mo. 261/L9
Poplar Branch, N.C. 281/T2
Poplar Creek, Br. Col. 184/J5
Poplar Creek, Miss. 256/E4
Poplarfield, Manitoba 179/E4
Poplar Grove, Ark. 202/J4
Poplar Grove, Ill. 222/E1
Poplar Hill, Ontario 175/B2
Poplar Point, Manitoba 179/D4
Poplarville, Ky. 237/N6
Poplarville, Miss. 256/E9
Popo Agie (riv.), Wyo. 319/D3
Popocatépetl (mt.), Mexico 150/M1
Popokabaka, Zaire 115/C5
Popoli, Italy 34/E4
Popomanatseu (mt.), Solomon Is. 86/E3
Popondetta, Papua N.G. 85/C7
Popondetta, Papua N.G. 87/E6
Popovo, Bulgaria 45/H4
Poprad, Czech. 41/F2
Poprad (riv.), Czech. 41/F2
Poquetanuck, Conn. 210/G2
Poquis, Nevados de (mt.), Chile 138/C4
Poquonock, Conn. 210/E1
Poquonock Bridge, Conn. 210/G3
Poquoson (I.C.), Va. 307/R6
Porangahau, N. Zealand 100/F4
Porangatu, Brazil 132/D6
Porangatu, Brazil 120/E4
Porbandar, India 68/B4
Porcher (isl.), Br. Col. 184/B3
Porciúncula, Brazil 135/E2
Porco, Bolivia 136/B6
Porcuna, Spain 33/D4
Porcupine (riv.) 146/D3
Porcupine (riv.), Alaska 196/K1
Porcupine (hills), Alberta 182/C4
Porcupine (hills), Manitoba 179/A2
Porcupine (mts.), Mich. 250/F1
Porcupine (creek), Mont. 262/K2
Porcupine (cape), Newf. 166/C4
Porcupine (creek), N. Dak. 282/J7
Porcupine, S. Dak. 298/E7
Porcupine (creek), Wyo. 319/G2
Porcupine (riv.), Yukon 187/E3
Porcupine Plain, Sask. 181/H3
Pordenone (prov.), Italy 34/D2

Pordenone, Italy 34/D2
Pore, Colombia 126/D5
Poreč, Yugoslavia 45/A3
Porepunkah, Victoria 97/H6
Pori, Finland 18/M6
Pori, Finland 7/G2
Porirua, N. Zealand 100/B2
Porirua (harb.), N. Zealand 100/B2
Porjus, Sweden 18/M3
Porkhov, U.S.S.R. 52/C3
Porkkala (pen.), Finland 18/O7
Porlamar, Venezuela 124/E2
Porlock, England 13/D6
Pornic, France 28/C4
Poroma, Bolivia 136/C6
Poronaysk, U.S.S.R. 54/R5
Poronaysk, U.S.S.R. 48/P5
Póros, Greece 45/F7
Poroto (pt.), Chile 138/A7
Porrentruy, Switzerland 39/C2
Porsangen (fjord), Norway 18/O1
Porsgrunn, Norway 18/G7
Porsuk (riv.), Turkey 63/D3
Portachuelo, Bolivia 136/D5
Portadown, N. Ireland 17/H3
Portaferry, N. Ireland 17/K3
Portage, Ind. 227/C1
Portage •, Maine 243/G2
Portage (bay), Maine 243/F2
Portage (bay), Manitoba 179/D3
Portage, Mich. 250/D6
Portage (isl.), New Bruns. 170/F1
Portage (co.), Ohio 284/H3
Portage, Ohio 284/C3
Portage (riv.), Ohio 284/D3
Portage, Pa. 294/E5
Portage, Utah 304/B2
Portage (co.), Wis. 317/G6
Portage, Wis. 317/G6
Portage-des-Roches, Québec 172/F1
Portage Des Sioux, Mo. 261/M5
Portage la Prairie, Man. 162/G5
Portage la Prairie, Manitoba 179/D4
Portageville, Mo. 261/N10
Portageville, N.Y. 276/D5
Portal, Ariz. 198/F7
Portal, Georgia 217/J5
Portal, N. Dak. 282/E2
Portalban, Switzerland 39/C3
Port Alberni, Br. Col. 184/H3
Port Albert, Ontario 177/C4
Port Albert, Victoria 97/H6
Port Albion, Br. Col. 184/E6
Portalegre (dist.), Portugal 33/C3
Portalegre, Portugal 33/C3
Portales, N. Mex. 188/F4
Portales, N. Mex. 274/F4
Port Alexander, Alaska 196/M2
Port-Alfred, Québec 172/G1
Port Alfred, S. Africa 118/D6
Port Alice, Br. Col. 184/D5
Port Allegany, Pa. 294/F2
Port Allen, La. 238/J2
Port Alma, Ontario 177/B5
Port Angeles, Wash. 188/B1
Port Angeles, Wash. 310/B2
Port Angeles Ind. Res., Wash. 310/B2
Port Antonio, Jamaica 158/K6
Port Antonio, Jamaica 156/C3
Port-à-Piment, Haiti 158/A6
Port Appin, Scotland 15/D3
Port Aransas, Texas 303/H10
Portarlington, Ireland 17/G5
Portarlington, Ireland 10/C4
Port Arthur, Texas 146/J7
Port Arthur, Texas 188/H5
Port Arthur, Texas 303/K8
Port Askaig, Scotland 15/B5
Port au Bras, Newf. 166/D4
Port au Choix, Newf. 166/B3
Port Augusta, Australia 87/D9
Port Augusta, S. Australia 88/F6
Port Augusta, S. Australia 94/E5
Port-au-Persil, Québec 172/G2
Port au Port, Newf. 166/C4
Port au Port (bay), Newf. 166/C4
Port au Port (pen.), Newf. 166/C4
Port-au-Prince (cap.), Haiti 156/D3
Port-au-Prince (cap.), Haiti 146/L8
Port-au-Prince (cap.), Haiti 158/C5
Port Austin, Mich. 250/F4
Portavogie, N. Ireland 17/K3
Port Bannatyne, Scotland 15/A2
Port Barre, La. 238/G5
Port-Bergé, Madagascar 118/H3
Portis, Kansas 232/D2
Port Isabel, Texas 303/G11
Portishead, England 13/E6
Port Blair, India 54/L8
Port Blair, India 68/G6
Port Blakely, Wash. 310/A2
Port Blandford, Newf. 166/C2
Port Bolivar, Texas 303/L3
Port-Bou, Spain 33/H1
Port-Bouet, Ivory Coast 106/D7
Port Broughton, S. Australia 94/F5
Port Bruce, Ontario 177/D5
Port Burwell, N.W. Terr. 187/M3
Port Burwell, Ontario 177/D5
Port Byron, Ill. 222/C2
Port Byron, N.Y. 276/G4

Port Clinton, Pa. 294/K4
Port Clyde, Maine 243/E8
Port Clyde, Nova Scotia 168/C5
Port Colborne, Ontario 177/E5
Port Coquitlam, Br. Col. 184/L3
Port Costa, Calif. 204/J1
Port Darwin (inlet), North. Terr. 93/B2
Port Davey (inlet), Tasmania 88/G8
Port Davey (inlet), Tasmania 99/B5
Port-de-Bouc, France 28/F6
Port-de-Paix, Haiti 156/D3
Port-de-Paix, Haiti 158/B5
Port Deposit, Md. 245/O2
Port Dickinson, N.Y. 276/J6
Port Dickson, Malaysia 72/D7
Port Dufferin, Nova Scotia 168/F4
Porte des Morts (str.), Wis. 317/N5
Port Edward, Br. Col. 184/B3
Port Edwards, Wis. 317/G7
Port Elgin, New Bruns. 170/F2
Port Elgin, Ontario 177/D3
Port Elizabeth, N.J. 273/D5
Port Elizabeth, S. Africa 102/E8
Port Elizabeth, S. Africa 118/D6
Port Ellen, Scotland 15/B5
Porter (co.), Ind. 227/C2
Porter, Ind. 227/C1
Porter, Maine 243/B8
Porter •, Maine 243/B8
Porter, Minn. 255/B6
Porter, Ohio 284/F8
Porter, Okla. 288/R3
Porter (pt.), St. Vin. & Grens. 161/A8
Porter, Texas 303/J3
Porter, Wash. 310/B4
Porterdale, Georgia 217/E3
Porterfield, Wis. 317/L5
Port Erin, I. of Man 13/C3
Porters (lake), Nova Scotia 168/E4
Porters Lake, Nova Scotia 168/E4
Portersville, Ala. 195/G2
Portersville, Ind. 227/C8
Portersville, Pa. 294/B4
Porterville, Calif. 204/G7
Porterville, Miss. 256/G5
Porterwood, W. Va. 312/G4
Port Everglades (harb.), Fla. 212/C4
Port Ewen, N.Y. 276/N7
Port Fairy, Victoria 97/F7
Port Felix, Nova Scotia 168/G3
Port Franks, Ontario 177/C4
Port Fuad, Egypt 111/K3
Port Gamble, Wash. 310/C3
Port Gamble Ind. Res., Wash. 310/C3
Port-Gentil, Gabon 115/A4
Port-Gentil, Gabon 102/C5
Port Gibson, Miss. 256/B7
Port Glasgow, Scotland 10/A1
Port Glasgow, Scotland 15/F3
Portglenone, N. Ireland 17/H2
Portgordon, Scotland 15/F3
Port Graham, Alaska 196/H2
Port Greville, Nova Scotia 168/D3
Port Hamilton (So) (isl.), S. Korea 81/C4
Port Hammond, Br. Col. 184/M3
Port Harcourt, Nigeria 106/F8
Port Harcourt, Nigeria 102/C4
Port Hardy, Br. Col. 184/D5
Port Hastings, Nova Scotia 168/G3
Port Hawkesbury, Nova Scotia 168/G3
Porthcawl, Wales 13/D6
Port Hebert (harb.), Nova Scotia 168/D5
Port Hedland, Australia 2/R7
Port Hedland, Australia 87/B7
Port Hedland, W. Australia 88/B3
Port Hedland, W. Australia 92/B3
Port Heiden, Alaska 196/G3
Port Heiden (inlet), Alaska 196/G3
Port Henry, N.Y. 276/O2
Porthill, Idaho 220/B1
Port Hood, Nova Scotia 168/G2
Port Hood (isl.), Nova Scotia 168/G2
Port Hope, Mich. 250/G5
Port Hope, Ontario 177/F4
Port Hope Simpson, Newf. 166/C3
Port Houghton (inlet), Alaska 196/N1
Port Howe, Nova Scotia 168/E3
Port Hudson, La. 238/J1
Port Hueneme, Calif. 204/F9
Port Huron, Mich. 188/K2
Port Huron, Mich. 250/G6
Portia, Ark. 202/H1
Portimão, Portugal 33/B4
Port Isabel, Texas 303/G11
Port Jackson (inlet), N.S. Wales 88/L4
Port Jackson (inlet), N.S. Wales 97/J3
Port Jefferson, N.Y. 276/P9
Port Jefferson, Ohio 284/C4
Port Jervis, N.Y. 276/L8
Port Joli, Nova Scotia 168/D5
Port Joli (harb.), Nova Scotia 168/D5
Port Kaiser, Jamaica 158/H7
Port Kaituma, Guyana 131/A2
Port Keats, North. Terr. 93/A3
Port Keats Mission, North. Terr. 88/D2
Port Kelang, Malaysia 72/D7
Port Kembla, N.S. Wales 97/F4
Port Kenny, S. Australia 94/D5
Port Kent, N.Y. 276/O1
Port Kindu, Zaire 115/E4
Port Kindu, Zaire 102/E5
Port Kirwan, Newf. 166/D2
Portknockie, Scotland 15/F3
Port Lambton, Ontario 177/B5
Portland, Ark. 202/H7

Portland, Barbados 161/B8
Portland (canal), Br. Col. 162/C4
Portland (canal), Br. Col. 184/B2
Portland (inlet), Br. Col. 184/C3
Portland, Colo. 208/K6
Portland, Colo. 208/D6
Portland, Conn. 210/E2
Portland •, Conn. 210/E2
Portland, England 13/E7
Portland, Bill of (prom.), England 10/E5
Portland, Bill of (prom.), England 13/E7
Portland, Fla. 212/C6
Portland, Ind. 227/H4
Portland (pt.), Jamaica 156/C3
Portland (pt.), Jamaica 158/J7
Portland, Maine 188/N2
Portland, Maine 146/M5
Portland, Maine 243/C8
Portland, Mich. 250/E6
Portland, Mo. 261/J5
Portland, N.S. Wales 97/E3
Portland, N.Y. 276/B6
Portland, N. Zealand 100/E1
Portland (isl.), N. Zealand 100/G3
Portland, N. Dak. 282/R5
Portland, Ohio 284/G7
Portland, Ontario 177/H3
Portland, Oreg. 146/F5
Portland, Oreg. 188/B1
Portland, Oreg. 291/B2
Portland, Pa. 294/M4
Portland (cape), Tasmania 99/D2
Portland, Tenn. 237/H7
Portland, Texas 303/G10
Portland, U.S. 2/C3
Portland, Victoria 88/G7
Portland, Victoria 97/E7
Portland (bay), Victoria 97/A6
Portland (bay), Victoria 88/G7
Portland Canal (inlet), Alaska 196/N2
Portland Creek (pond), Newf. 166/C3
Portland Int'l Airport, Oreg. 291/B2
Portlaoise, Ireland 17/G5
Portlaoise, Ireland 10/C4
Port Latta, Tasmania 99/B5
Port Lavaca, Texas 303/H9
Portlaw, Ireland 17/G7
Port Leyden, N.Y. 276/K3
Port Lincoln, Australia 87/D9
Port Lincoln, S. Australia 88/E6
Port Lincoln, S. Australia 94/E6
Port Lions, Alaska 196/H3
Portlock, Alaska 196/C2
Port Loko, S. Leone 106/B7
Port Loring, Ontario 177/E2
Port Lorne, Nova Scotia 168/C4
Port-Louis, France 28/B4
Port-Louis, Guadeloupe 161/B5
Port-Louis, Guadeloupe 156/C3
Port Louis (cap.), Mauritius 118/G5
Port Ludlow, Wash. 310/C3
Port-Lyautey (Kénitra), Morocco 106/C2
Port Macquarie, N. S. Wales 88/J5
Port Macquarie, N.S. Wales 97/G2
Port Madison Ind. Res., Wash. 310/A1
Portmadog (Porthmadog), Wales 10/D4
Portmahomack, Scotland 15/E3
Port Maitland, Nova Scotia 168/B5
Port Manvers (harb.), Newf. 166/B2
Port Margot, Haiti 158/C5
Port Maria, Jamaica 158/J6
Port Maria, Jamaica 156/C3
Portmarnock, Ireland 17/J5
Port Matilda, Pa. 294/F4
Port Mayaca, Fla. 212/F5
Port McNeill, Br. Col. 184/D5
Port McNicoll, Ontario 177/E3
Port Medway, Nova Scotia 168/D4
Port Melbourne, Victoria 88/K7
Port Melbourne, Victoria 97/H5
Port Mellon, Br. Col. 184/K2
Port-Menier, Que. 162/E4
Port-Menier, Québec 174/E3
Port Moller (inlet), Alaska 196/F3
Port Monmouth, N.J. 273/E3
Port Moody, Br. Col. 184/L3
Port Morant, Jamaica 158/K6
Port Moresby (cap.), Papua N.G. 87/E6
Port Moresby (cap.), Papua N.G. 85/B7
Port Morien, Nova Scotia 168/J2
Port Morris, N.J. 273/D2
Port Mouton, Nova Scotia 168/D5
Port Mouton (harb.), Nova Scotia 168/D5
Port Murray, N.J. 273/D2
Port Neches, Texas 303/K7
Port Nellie Juan, Alaska 196/C1
Portneuf (riv.), Idaho 220/F7
Portneuf (county), Québec 174/C3
Portneuf (co.), Québec 172/E3
Portneuf, Québec 172/E3
Portneuf (riv.), Québec 172/H1
Portneuf-sur-Mer, Québec 172/H1
Port Neville, Br. Col. 184/E5
Port Nicholson (inlet), N. Zealand 100/B3
Port Nolloth, S. Africa 102/D7
Port Nolloth, S. Africa 118/B5
Port Norris, N.J. 273/C5
Porto, Brazil 132/F3
Porto (dist.), Portugal 33/B2
Porto, Portugal 7/D4
Porto, Portugal 33/B2
Porto Alegre, Brazil 132/D10
Porto Alegre, Brazil 120/D6
Porto Alegre, Brazil 2/G7
Porto Amboim, Angola 115/B6
Porto Amboim, Angola 102/D6
Portobelo, Panama 154/H6
Portocivitanova, Italy 34/D3
Porto Colômbia (res.), Brazil 135/D2

Port O'Connor, Texas 303/H9
Porto de Mós, Portugal 33/B3
Porto de Moz, Brazil 132/D3
Portu Empedocle, Italy 34/D6
Porto Esperança, Brazil 132/B7
Porto Feliz, Brazil 135/C3
Portoferraio, Italy 34/C3
Portofino, Italy 34/B2
Porto Franco, Brazil 132/E4
Port-of-Spain (cap.), Trin. & Tob. 161/A10
Port-of-Spain (cap.), Trin. & Tob. 156/G5
Portogruaro, Italy 34/D2
Portola, Calif. 204/E4
Pôrto La Cruz, Venezuela 120/C1
Portola Valley, Calif. 204/J3
Portomaggiore, Italy 34/C2
Porto Moniz, Portugal 33/A2
Porto Moroco, Brazil 132/C6
Porto Murtinho do Sul, Brazil 132/B8
Porto Nacional, Brazil 120/E4
Porto Nacional, Brazil 132/E5
Porto-Novo (cap.), Benin 106/E7
Porto-Novo (cap.), Benin 102/C4
Porto Novo, India 68/E6
Porto Poet, Brazil 132/C2
Port Orange, Fla. 212/F2
Porto Recanati, Italy 34/D3
Port Orchard, Wash. 310/A2
Port Orford, Oreg. 291/C5
Porto Santo, Portugal 33/A2
Pôrto Santo (isl.), Portugal 102/A1
Pôrto Santo (isl.), Portugal 106/A2
Pôrto Santo (isl.), Brazil 33/B2
Porto Seguro, Brazil 132/G7
Porto Tolle, Italy 34/D2
Porto Torres, Italy 34/B4
Porto União, Brazil 132/D9
Porto Velho, Brazil 132/H10
Porto Velho, Brazil 120/C3
Portoviejo, Ecuador 120/A3
Portoviejo, Ecuador 128/B3
Portpatrick, Scotland 15/C6
Portpatrick, Scotland 10/D3
Port Pegasus (inlet), N. Zealand 100/B7
Port Penn, Del. 245/R2
Port Perry, Ontario 177/E3
Port Phaeton (bay), Fr. Poly. 86/T13
Port Phillip (bay), Victoria 97/C6
Port Phillip (bay), Victoria 88/K7
Port Pirie, Australia 87/D9
Port Pirie, S. Australia 88/F6
Port Pirie, S. Australia 94/E5
Port Praslin (bay), St. Lucia 161/G6
Port Reading, N.J. 273/E2
Portree, Scotland 10/C2
Portree, Scotland 15/B3
Portreeve, Sask. 181/B5
Port Renfrew, Br. Col. 184/J3
Port Republic, Md. 245/N6
Port Republic, N.J. 273/D4
Port Republic, Va. 307/L4
Port Rexton, Newf. 166/D2
Port Rhoades, Jamaica 158/H5
Port Richey, Fla. 212/D3
Port Rowan, Ontario 177/D5
Port Royal, Jamaica 158/J6
Port Royal, Ky. 237/L3
Port Royal, Nova Scotia 168/H4
Port Royal, Pa. 294/H4
Port Royal, S.C. 296/F7
Port Royal (sound), S.C. 296/F7
Port Royal, Va. 307/O4
Portrush, N. Ireland 10/C3
Portrush, N. Ireland 17/H1
Port Safâga, Egypt 59/B4
Port Safâga, Egypt 111/F2
Port Said, Egypt 102/F1
Port Said, Egypt 59/B3
Port Said, Egypt 111/K2
Port Saint Joe, Fla. 212/D6
Port Saint Johns (Umzimbuvu), S. Africa 118/D6
Port-Saint-Louis-du-Rhône, France 28/F6
Port Saint Lucie, Fla. 212/F4
Port Saint Mary, I. of Man 13/C3
Port Salerno, Fla. 212/F4
Port-Salut, Haiti 158/A6
Port Sanilac, Mich. 250/G5
Port Saunders, Newf. 166/C3
Pörtschach am Wörthersee, Austria 41/C3
Port Severn, Ontario 177/E3
Port Severn, Ontario 175/C1
Port Shepstone, S. Africa 102/F8
Port Shepstone, S. Africa 118/E6
Port Simpson, Br. Col. 184/D3
Portslade-by-Sea, England 13/G7
Portsmouth, Dominica 156/G4
Portsmouth, Dominica 161/E5
Portsmouth, England 10/F5
Portsmouth, England 7/D3
Portsmouth, England 13/F7
Portsmouth, Iowa 229/C5
Portsmouth, N.H. 188/N2
Portsmouth, N.H. 268/F5
Portsmouth, N.C. 281/S4
Portsmouth (isl.), N.C. 281/T5
Portsmouth, Ohio 188/K3
Portsmouth, Ohio 284/D6
Portsmouth •, R.I. 249/J6
Portsmouth, Va. 188/N4
Portsmouth (I.C.), Va. 307/R7
Port Sorell, Tasmania 99/C3
Portsoy, Scotland 15/F3
Port Stanley, Ontario 177/C5
Port Stephens (inlet), N.S. Wales 97/G3
Portstewart, N. Ireland 17/H1
Port Sudan, Sudan 111/G4
Port Sudan, Sudan 102/F3
Port Sudan, Sudan 59/G4
Port Sulphur, La. 238/L8

Port Talbot, Wales 10/E5
Port Talbot, Wales 13/D6
Port Tampa (harb.), Fla. 212/B3
Port Taufiq, Egypt 111/K3
Port Tobacco, Md. 245/K6
Port Townsend, Wash. 310/C2
Port Trevorton, Pa. 294/J4
Portugal 2/J3
Portugal 7/D5
PORTUGAL 33/B3
Portugal Cove, Newf. 166/D2
Portugal Cove South, Newf. 166/D2
Portugalete, Bolivia 136/B7
Portugalete, Spain 33/E1
Portuguesa (state), Venezuela 124/D3
Portuguesa (riv.), Venezuela 124/D3
Portuguese Cove, Nova Scotia 168/E4
Portumna, Ireland 17/E5
Port Union, Newf. 166/D2
Port-Valais, Switzerland 39/C4
Port-Vendres, France 28/E6
Portville, Pa. 294/B2
Port Vincent, La. 238/L2
Port Vue, Pa. 294/C7
Port Washington, N.Y. 276/R6
Port Washington, Ohio 284/G5
Port Washington, Wis. 317/L9
Port Weld, Malaysia 72/D6
Port Wells (inlet), Alaska 196/C1
Port Wentworth, Georgia 217/K6
Port William, Ohio 284/C6
Port William, Scotland 15/D6
Port Williams, Nova Scotia 168/D3
Port Wing, Wis. 317/D2
Porum, Okla. 288/R4
Porus, Jamaica 158/H6
Porvenir, Santa Cruz, Bolivia 136/E4
Porvenir, Pando, Bolivia 136/A2
Porvenir, Chile 133/E10
Porvenir, Peru 128/E5
Porvenir, Uruguay 145/B3
Porz am Rhein, Germany 22/B3
Posadas, Argentina 143/E2
Posadas, Argentina 120/D5
Posadas, Paraguay 144/E5
Posadas, Spain 33/D4
Poschiavo, Switzerland 39/J4
Poschiavo (riv.), Switzerland 39/K4
Poschiavo (valley), Switzerland 39/K4
Posen, Ill. 222/B6
Posen, Mich. 250/F3
Posey (co.), Ind. 227/B8
Poseyville, Ind. 227/B8
Posio, Finland 18/D3
Poskin, Wis. 317/C5
Poso, Indonesia 83/G6
Posof, Turkey 63/E2
Posong, S. Korea 31/C6
Poscrja, Ecuador 128/B4
Posse, Brazil 132/E6
Possel, Cent. Afr. Rep. 115/C2
Pössneck, Germany 22/D3
Possum Kingdom (lake), Texas 3C3/F5
Post, Oreg. 291/G3
Post, Texas 303/C6
Postavy, U.S.S.R. 52/C3
Poste (riv.), Québec 172/D3
Postelle, Ark. 202/H1
Postelle, Tenn. 237/N10
Poste Maurice Cortier, Algeria 106/E4
Poste Weygand, Algeria 106/D4
Post Falls, Idaho 220/A2
Postmasburg, S. Africa 118/C5
Post Mills, Vt. 268 C4
Postoak, Mo. 261/L5
Postoak, Texas 303/F4
Postojna, Yugoslavia 45/B3
Poston, Ariz. 198/A4
Poston, S.C. 296/J4
Postrervalle, Bolivia 136/D6
Postville, Iowa 229/K2
Postville, Newf. 166/B3
Pot (creek), Colo. 208/A1
Pot (mt.), Idaho 220/C3
Pot (creek), Utah 304/D4
Potagannissing (bay), Mich. 250/F2
Potam, Mexico 150/C3
Potaro (riv.), Guyana 131/B3
Potato Creek, S. Dak. 298/F6
Potawatomi Ind. Res., Kansas 232/G2
Potchefstroom, S. Africa 118/D5
Poteau (mt.), Ark. 202/B4
Poteau, Okla. 288/S4
Poteau (riv.), Okla. 288/S5
Poteca, Nicaragua 154/E4
Poteet, Texas 303/F8
Potenza (prov.), Italy 34/E4
Potenza, Italy 34/E4
Potes, Spain 33/D1
Potgietersrus, S. Africa 118/D4
Poth, Texas 303/F8
Potholes (res.), Wash. 310/F3
Potiskum, Nigeria 107/J3
Potlatch, Idaho 22C/A3
Potlatch (riv.), Idaho 220/B3
Potlatch, Wash. 310/B3
Potomac (riv.) 188/L3
Potomac, Ill. 222/F3
Potomac (riv.), Md 245/M8
Potomac (riv.), Mont. 262/C4
Potomac (riv.), Va. 307/O4
Potomac, South Branch (riv.), W. Va. 312/J4
Potomac (riv.), W. Va. 312/L3
Potomac, North Branch (riv.), W. Va. 312/J4
Potomac Beach, Va. 307/P4
Potomac Heights, Md. 245/K6
Potomac Park-Bowling Green, Md. 245/C2
Potomac Valley, Md. 245/E4
Potosí (dept.), Bolivia 136/B7
Potosí, Bolivia 136/C6
Potosí, Bolivia 120/C4

Potosí, Colombia 126/C7
Potosi, Mo. 261/L7
Potosi (mt.), Nev. 266/F7
Potosi, Wis. 317/E10
Potrerillo (peak), Cuba 158/E2
Potrerillos, Chile 138/B6
Potrero, Calif. 204/J11
Potrillo (mts.), N. Mex. 274/B7
Potro, Cerro del (mt.), Argentina 143/C2
Potro, Cerro del (mt.), Chile 138/B7
Potsdam, Germany 22/E2
Potsdam, Minn. 255/F6
Potsdam, N.Y. 276/K1
Potsdam, Ohio 284/B6
Pottageville, Ontario 177/J3
Pottawatomie (co.), Kansas 232/F2
Pottawatomie (co.), Okla. 288/N4
Pottawattamie (co.), Iowa 229/B6
Pottawattomie Park, Ind. 227/C1
Potter, Kansas 232/G2
Potter, Nebr. 264/A3
Potter (co.), Pa. 294/G2
Potter (co.), S. Dak. 298/J3
Potter (co.), Texas 303/C2
Potter, Wis. 317/K7
Potter Hill, R.I. 249/H7
Potters Bar, England 13/H7
Potters Bar, England 10/B5
Pottersdale, Pa. 294/F3
Pottersville, Mo. 261/H9
Pottersville, N.J. 273/D2
Pottersville, N.Y. 276/N3
Potterville, Mich. 250/E6
Potts (creek), W. Va. 312/F7
Pottsboro, Texas 303/H4
Potts Camp, Miss. 256/F1
Pottstown, Pa. 294/L5
Pottsville, Ark. 202/D3
Pottsville, Pa. 294/K4
Pottsville, Texas 303/F6
Potwin, Kansas 232/F4
Pouce-Coupé, Br. Col. 184/G2
Pouch Cove, Newf. 166/D2
Poudre d'Or, Mauritius 118/G5
Poughkeepsie, Ark. 202/H1
Poughkeepsie, N.Y. 276/N7
Pouillon, France 28/C6
Poulan, Georgia 217/E8
Poulet Cove (bay), Nova Scotia 168/H2
Poulo Wai (isls.), Cambodia 72/D5
Poulsbo, Wash. 310/A1
Poultney, Vt. 268/A4
Poultney •, Vt. 268/A4
Poultney (riv.), Vt. 268/A4
Poulton le Fylde, England 10/F1
Poulton-le-Fylde, England 13/G1
Pound, Va. 307/C6
Pound, Wis. 317/L5
Pounding Mill, Va. 307/E6
Pouso Alegre, Brazil 135/D3
Pouthisat, Cambodia 72/D4
Považská Bystrica, Czech. 41/E2
Povenets, U.S.S.R. 52/E2
Poverty Point Nat'l Monument, La. 238/L1
Poverty (isl.), Mich. 250/C3
Poverty (bay), N. Zealand 100/G3
Póvoa de Varzim, Portugal 33/B3
Povorino, U.S.S.R. 52/F4
Povungnituk, Que. 162/J3
Povungnituk, Québec 174/E1
Powassan, Ontario 177/E1
Poway, Calif. 204/J11
Powder (riv.) 188/E2
Powder (riv.), Mont. 262/L4
Powder (riv.), Oreg. 291/K3
Powder (riv.), Wyo. 319/F2
Powderhorn, Colo. 208/E6
Powderly, Ky. 237/G6
Powderly, Texas 303/J4
Powder River, Wyo. 319/F2
Powder Springs, Georgia 217/C3
Powder Springs, Tenn. 237/O8
Powderville, Mont. 262/L5
Powe, Mo. 261/M9
Powell (lake) 188/D3
Powell (lake), Ariz. 198/E1
Powell (co.), Ky. 237/O5
Powell, Manitoba 179/A2
Powell (co.), Mont. 262/D4
Powell, Nebr. 264/G4
Powell, Ohio 284/D5
Powell, Pa. 294/J2
Powell, Tenn. 237/N8
Powell (riv.), Tenn. 237/P8
Powell (lake), U.S. 146/G3
Powell (lake), Utah 304/D6
Powell (riv.), Va. 307/B7
Powell, Wyo. 319/F1
Powell Butte, Oreg. 291/G3
Powell Creek, North. Terr. 93/C5
Powell River, Br. Col. 184/E5
Powell's Crossroads, Ala. 195/G1
Powells Crossroads, Tenn. 237/L10
Powells Point, N.C. 281/T1
Powellsville, N.C. 281/R2
Powellton, W. Va. 312/D6
Powellville, Md. 245/S7
Poweleton, Georgia 217/E5
Power (co.), Idaho 220/F7
Power, Mont. 262/E3
Powers (lake), Conn. 210/G3
Powers, Mich. 250/B3
Powers, Oreg. 291/D5
Powers Lake, N. Dak. 282/E2
Powersville, Georgia 217/E5
Powersville, Iowa 229/H3
Powersville, Mo. 261/F1
Powerview, Manitoba 179/F4
Poweshiek (co.), Iowa 229/H5
Powhatan, Ark. 202/H1

Powhatan, La. 238/D3
Powhatan (co.), Va. 307/N5
Powhatan, Va. 307/N5
Powhatan, W. Va. 312/D8
Powhatan Point, Ohio 284/J6
Powhattan, Kansas 232/G2
Pownal •, Maine 243/A4
Pownal •, Vt. 268/A6
Pownal Center, Vt. 268/A6
Powys (co.), Wales 13/D5
Poxoréo, Brazil 132/C6
Poyang (lake), China 54/N7
Poyang Hu (lake), China 77/J6
Poyen, Ark. 202/E5
Poygan (lake), Wis. 317/J7
Poynette, Wis. 317/G9
Poynor, Mo. 261/L9
Poynor, Texas 303/J6
Poysdorf, Austria 41/D2
Poy Sippi, Wis. 317/J7
Pozanti, Turkey 63/F4
Požarevac, Yugoslavia 45/E3
Poza Rica de Hidalgo, Mexico 150/L6
Poznań (prov.), Poland 47/C2
Poznań, Poland 47/C2
Poznań, Poland 7/F3
Pozo Almonte, Chile 138/B2
Pozoblanco, Spain 33/D3
Pozo Colorado, Paraguay 144/C3
Pozo Hondo, Argentina 143/D2
Pozohondo, Spain 33/F3
Pozuelo de Alarcón, Spain 33/D2
Pozuelos, Venezuela 124/F2
Pozuzo, Peru 128/E8
Pozzallo, Italy 34/E6
Pozzuoli, Italy 34/D4
Prabuty, Poland 47/D2
Prachatice, Czech. 41/B2
Prachin Buri, Thailand 72/D4
Prachuap Khiri Khan, Thailand 72/D5
Pradera, Colombia 126/B6
Prades, France 28/E6
Prado (dam), Calif. 204/E11
Praestø, Denmark 21/F7
Pragel (pass), Switzerland 39/G2
Prague (cap.), Czech. 7/F3
Prague (Praha) (cap.), Czech. 41/C1
Prague, Nebr. 264/H3
Prague, Okla. 288/N4
Praha (city) (reg.), Czech. 41/C1
Prahan, Victoria 88/L7
Prahran, Victoria 97/J4
Praia (cap.), C. Verde 106/B8
Prainha, Amazonas, Brazil 132/A4
Prainha, Pará, Brazil 132/C3
Prairie, Ala. 195/D6
Prairie (co.), Ark. 202/G4
Prairie (creek), Ind. 227/C7
Prairie (riv.), Mich. 250/D7
Prairie (riv.), Minn. 255/E3
Prairie, Miss. 256/G3
Prairie (co.), Mont. 262/L4
Prairie, Queensland 95/C4
Prairie (lake), S. Dak. 298/P3
Prairieburg, Iowa 229/L4
Prairie City, Iowa 229/G5
Prairie City, S. Dak. 298/D2
Prairie City, Oreg. 291/J3
Prairie Creek, Ind. 227/C7
Prairie Dog Town Fork, Red (riv.), Okla. 288/C3
Prairie Dog Town Fork, Red (riv.), Texas 303/C3
Prairie du Chien, Wis. 317/D9
Prairie du Rocher, Ill. 222/C5
Prairie du Sac, Wis. 317/G9
Prairie Farm, Wis. 317/C5
Prairie Grove, Ark. 202/B2
Prairie Grove, Ill. 222/E1
Prairie Home, Mo. 261/G5
Prairie Point, Miss. 256/H4
Prairie River, Sask. 181/J3
Prairies (riv.), Québec 172/H4
Prairieton, Ind. 227/B6
Prairietown, Ill. 222/B2
Prairie View, Ark. 202/C3
Prairie View, Kansas 232/C2
Prairie View, Texas 303/J7
Prairie Village, Kansas 232/H2
Prairieville, La. 238/K2
Pran Buri, Thailand 72/D4
Prangins, Switzerland 39/B4
Prapat, Indonesia 85/B5
Praslin, St. Lucia 161/G6
Praslin (isl.), Seychelles 118/H5
Prat (isl.), Chile 138/D7
Pratas (Dongsha) (isl.), China 77/J7
Prathersville, Mo. 261/R4
Prato, Italy 34/C3
Prato-Sornico, Switzerland 39/G4
Pratt (co.), Kansas 232/D4
Pratt, Kansas 232/D4
Pratt, Manitoba 179/D5
Pratt, Minn. 255/E6
Pratt, W. Va. 312/D6
Pratteln, Switzerland 39/E1
Prattsburg, Georgia 217/D5
Prattsburg •, N.Y. 276/F5
Prattsville, Ark. 202/F5
Prattsville, N.Y. 276/M6
Prattville, Ala. 195/E6
Pratum, Oreg. 291/A3
Pravia, Spain 33/C1
Prawda, Manitoba 179/G5
Prawle (pt.), England 13/D7
Prawle (pt.), England 10/E5
Praxedis G. Guerrero, Mexico 150/G1
Pray, Mont. 262/F5
Praya, Indonesia 85/F7
Preble, Ind. 227/H3
Preble, N.Y. 276/J5
Preble (co.), Ohio 284/A6
Preeceville, Sask. 181/J4

Preemption, Ill. 222/C2
Preesall, England 13/E4
Preetz, Germany 22/D1
Pregarten, Austria 41/C2
Pregnall, S.C. 296/G5
Pregonero, Venezuela 124/C3
Preiji, U.S.S.R. 53/D2
Prek Po, Cambodia 72/E5
Prelate, Sask. 181/B5
Premier, W. Va. 312/C8
Premium, Ky. 237/R6
Premont, Texas 303/F10
Prentice, Ill. 222/C4
Prentice, Wis. 317/F4
Prentiss •, Maine 243/G5
Prentiss (co.), Miss. 256/G1
Prentiss, Miss. 256/E7
Prentiss, N.C. 281/C4
Prenzlau, Germany 22/E2
Preparis (isl.), Burma 72/B4
Preparis North (chan.), Burma 72/B4
Preparis South (chan.), Burma 72/B4
Přerov, Czech. 41/D2
Presanella (mt.), Italy 34/C1
Prescott, Ariz. 188/D4
Prescott, Ariz. 198/C4
Prescott, Ark. 202/D6
Prescott, Ind. 227/F8
Prescott, Iowa 229/D6
Prescott, Kansas 232/H3
Prescott, Mich. 250/F4
Prescott (county), Ontario 177/K2
Prescott, Ontario 177/J3
Prescott, Oreg. 291/D1
Prescott, Wash. 310/G4
Prescott, Wis. 317/A6
Prescott Valley, Ariz. 198/C4
Preseli (mts.), Wales 13/C6
Preševo, Yugoslavia 45/E4
Presho, S. Dak. 298/J6
Presidencia de la Plaza, Argentina 143/D2
Presidencia R. Sáenz Peña, Argentina 120/C5
Presidencia Roque Sáenz Peña, Argentina 143/D2
President, Pa. 294/C3
Presidente Dutra, Brazil 132/E4
Presidente Hayes, Paraguay 144/C3
Presidente Prudente, Brazil 132/D8
Presidente Prudente, Brazil 120/D5
Presidente Ríos (lake), Chile 138/D6
Presidente Venceslau, Brazil 132/D8
Presidential (range), N.H. 268/E3
Presidio, Calif. 204/J2
Presidio (co.), Texas 303/C12
Presidio, Texas 303/C12
Presidio Modelo, Cuba 158/C4
Prešov, Czech. 41/F2
Prespa (lake), Albania 45/E5
Prespa (lake), Greece 45/E5
Prespa (lake), Yugoslavia 45/E5
Presque Isle, Maine 243/H2
Presque Isle (co.), Mich. 250/F3
Presque Isle, Mich. 250/F3
Presque Isle (riv.), Mich. 250/F1
Presque Isle, Wis. 317/G3
Presque Isle A.F.B., Maine 243/G2
Presqu'Ile Prov. Park, Ontario 177/G4
Prestatyn, Wales 13/D4
Prestea, Ghana 106/D7
Presteigne, Wales 10/E4
Presteigne, Wales 13/D5
Přeštice, Czech. 41/B2
Presto, Bolivia 136/C6
Preston •, Conn. 210/H2
Preston, England 10/F1
Preston, England 13/G1
Preston, Georgia 217/C6
Preston, Idaho 220/G7
Preston, Ill. 222/D5
Preston, Iowa 229/N4
Preston, Ky. 237/O4
Preston, Md. 245/P6
Preston, Minn. 255/F7
Preston, Miss. 256/G5
Preston, Mo. 261/F7
Preston, Nebr. 264/J4
Preston, Nev. 266/G4
Preston (co.), W. Va. 312/G4
Preston City, Conn. 210/H2
Preston Hollow, N.Y. 276/M6
Prestonburg, Ky. 237/R5
Prestonpans, Scotland 15/D1
Prestonville, Ky. 237/L3
Prestwich, England 13/G2
Prestwick, Scotland 10/D3
Prestwick, Scotland 15/D5
Prêto (riv.), Brazil 132/E5
Preto (riv.), Brazil 135/E3
Preto (riv.), Brazil 132/A4
Pretoria (cap.), S. Africa 2/L7
Pretoria (cap.), S. Africa 102/E7
Pretoria (cap.), S. Africa 118/D5
Prettyboy (res.), Md. 245/M2
Pretty Prairie, Kansas 232/D4
Préveza, Greece 45/E6
Prévost, Québec 172/C4
Prevost, Wash. 310/B2
Prewitt (res.), Colo. 208/N2
Prewitt, N. Mex. 274/B3
Prey Veng, Cambodia 72/E5
Pribilof (isls.), Alaska 188/C6
Pribilof (isls.), Alaska 196/C6
Pribilof (isls.), U.S. 4/D18
Priboj, Yugoslavia 45/D4
Příbor, Czech. 41/E2
Preble, Ind. 227/H3
Příbram, Czech. 41/B2
Price (isl.), Br. Col. 184/C4
Price, Md. 245/P4

Price, N. Dak. 282/H5
Price, Québec 172/A1
Price, Utah 304/D4
Price, Utah 188/D3
Price (riv.), Utah 304/D4
Price (co.), Wis. 317/F4
Price, Wis. 317/E6
Pricedale, Miss. 256/D8
Priceville, Ala. 195/E1
Priceville, Ky. 237/K6
Priceville, Ontario 177/D3
Prichard, Ala. 195/B9
Prichard, Miss. 256/D1
Prichard, W. Va. 312/A6
Prickly (isl.), Grenada 161/C9
Priddis, Alberta 182/C4
Priddy, Texas 303/F6
Pride, Ky. 237/F5
Pride, La. 238/K1
Pridgen, Georgia 217/G7
Priego, Spain 33/E2
Priego de Córdoba, Spain 33/D4
Priekule, U.S.S.R. 53/A2
Priekulė, U.S.S.R. 53/A3
Prien am Chiemsee, Germany 22/E5
Prieska, S. Africa 118/C5
Priest (lake), Idaho 220/B1
Priest (riv.), Idaho 220/B1
Priest, J. Percy (lake), Tenn. 237/J8
Priestly (lake), Maine 243/F2
Priest Rapids (dam), Wash. 310/F4
Priest Rapids (lake), Wash. 310/F4
Priest River, Idaho 220/A1
Prievidza, Czech. 41/E2
Prijedor, Yugoslavia 45/C3
Prijepolje, Yugoslavia 45/D4
Prikumsk, U.S.S.R. 52/F6
Prikumsk, U.S.S.R. 48/E5
Prilep, Yugoslavia 45/E5
Priluki, U.S.S.R. 52/D4
Prim (pt.), Nova Scotia 168/C4
Prim (pt.), Pr. Edward I. 168/E2
Prima Porta, Italy 34/F6
Primate, Sask. 181/B3
Prime, New Bruns. 170/B1
Primero de Marzo, Paraguay 144/B4
Primero Enero, Cuba 158/F2
Primghar, Iowa 229/B2
Primm Springs, Tenn. 237/G9
Primorsk, U.S.S.R. 52/C2
Primorsko-Akhtarsk, U.S.S.R. 52/E5
Primos, Pa. 294/M7
Primrose (lake), Alberta 182/E2
Primrose, Georgia 217/C4
Primrose, Iowa 229/K7
Primrose, Nebr. 264/F3
Primrose (lake), Sask. 181/L3
Primrose Lake Air Weapons Range, Sask. 181/L3
Prince (co.), Pr. Edward I. 168/D2
Prince, Sask. 181/C3
Prince Albert (pen.), N.W.T. 162/E1
Prince Albert (pen.), N.W.T. 187/G2
Prince Albert (sound), N.W.T. 162/E1
Prince Albert (sound), N.W.T. 187/G2
Prince Albert, Sask. 162/F5
Prince Albert, Sask. 164/F5
Prince Albert, Sask. 181/F2
Prince Albert, S. Africa 118/C6
Prince Albert Nat'l Park, Sask. 162/F5
Prince Albert Nat'l Park, Sask. 181/N10
Prince Alfred (cape), N.W.T. 187/F2
Prince Charles (isl.), Canada 4/C13
Prince Charles (isl.), N.W.T. 162/J2
Prince Charles (isl.), N.W.T. 187/L3
Prince Edward (isls.) Ant. 5/E2
Prince Edward (county), Ontario 177/G3
Prince Edward (isls.), S. Africa 2/L8
Prince Edward (co.), Va. 307/M6
Prince Edward Island (prov.) 162/K6
PRINCE EDWARD ISLAND 168
Prince Edward Island (prov.), Canada 146/M5
Prince Edward Island Nat'l Park, Pr. Edward I. 168/E2
Prince Frederick, Md. 245/M6
Prince George, Br. Col. 146/F4
Prince George, Br. Col. 184/F3
Prince George (co.), Md. 245/L5
Prince George, Va. 307/O6
Princes (gorges (co.), Md. 245/L5
Prince Gustav Adolf (sea), N.W.T. 187/H2
Prince of Wales (cape), Alaska 196/E1
Prince of Wales (isl.), Alaska 196/N2
Prince of Wales (isl.), Canada 4/B14
Prince of Wales, New Bruns. 170/D3
Prince of Wales (str.), N.W.T. 162/D1
Prince of Wales (isl.), N.W.T. 162/F1
Prince of Wales (isl.), N.W.T. 146/J2
Prince of Wales (isl.), N.W.T. 187/J2
Prince of Wales (isl.), Queensland 88/G2
Prince of Wales (isl.), Queensland 95/B1
Prince of Wales (cape), U.S. 4/C18
Prince Olav Coast (reg.) 5/C3
Prince Patrick (isl.), Canada 4/B16
Prince Patrick (isl.), N.W.T. 146/F2
Prince Patrick (isl.), N.W.T. 162/M3
Prince Patrick (isl.), N.W.T. 187/F2
Prince Regent (inlet), N.W.T. 162/G1
Prince Regent (inlet), N.W.T. 187/J2
Prévost, Québec 172/C4
Prevost, Wash. 310/B2
Prince Rupert, Br. Col. 162/C5
Prince Rupert, Br. Col. 146/F4
Prince Rupert, Br. Col. 184/B3
Prince Rupert (bay), Dominica 161/E5
Princes Lakes, Ind. 227/E6
Princess Anne, Md. 245/P8
Princess Astrid Coast (reg.) 5/B1
Princess Charlotte (bay), Queensland 88/G2
Princess Charlotte (bay), Queensland 95/C2
Princess Harbour, Manitoba 179/F3

Princess Martha Coast (reg.) 5/B18
Princess Ragnhild Coast (reg.) 5/B2
Princess Royal (isl.), Br. Col. 184/C3
Princes Town, Trin. & Tob. 161/B11
Princeton, Ala. 195/F1
Princeton, Ark. 202/E6
Princeton, Br. Col. 184/G5
Princeton, Calif. 204/C4
Princeton (mt.), Colo. 208/G5
Princeton, Fla. 212/F6
Princeton, Idaho 220/B3
Princeton, Ill. 222/D2
Princeton, Ind. 227/B8
Princeton, Iowa 229/N5
Princeton, Kansas 232/G3
Princeton, Ky. 237/F6
Princeton, La. 238/C1
Princeton •, Maine 243/H5
Princeton •, Mass. 249/G3
Princeton, Mich. 250/B2
Princeton, Minn. 255/E5
Princeton, Mo. 261/E2
Princeton, N.J. 273/D3
Princeton, N.C. 281/N4
Princeton, Ontario 177/D4
Princeton, Oreg. 291/J4
Princeton, S.C. 296/D3
Princeton, W. Va. 312/D8
Princeton, Wis. 317/H8
Princeton Junction, N.J. 273/D3
Princeville, Hawaii 218/C1
Princeville, Ill. 222/D3
Princeville, N.C. 281/P3
Princeville, Québec 172/E3
Prince William (sound), Alaska 196/D1
Prince William, New Bruns. 170/C3
Prince William (co.), Va. 307/O3
Principe (chan.), Br. Col. 184/C3
Príncipe (isl.), S. Tomé & Pr. 106/F8
Principio Furnace, Md. 245/P2
Prineville, Oreg. 291/G3
Prineville (res.), Oreg. 291/G3
Pringle, S. Dak. 298/B6
Prinkipo (Adalar) (isl.), Turkey 63/D6
Prinsburg, Minn. 255/C6
Prins Karls Forland (isl.), Norway 18/B2
Prinzapolca (riv.), Nicaragua 154/F4
Prinzapolka, Nicaragua 154/F4
Prior (cape), Spain 33/B1
Prior Lake, Minn. 255/E6
Priozersk, U.S.S.R. 52/C4
Pripet (marshes), U.S.S.R. 52/C4
Pripyat' (riv.), U.S.S.R. 7/G3
Pripyat' (riv.), U.S.S.R. 52/C4
Priština, Yugoslavia 45/E4
Pritchards (isl.), S.C. 296/G7
Pritchardville, S.C. 296/E7
Pritchett, Colo. 208/O8
Pritzwalk, Germany 22/E2
Privas, France 28/F5
Privateer (pt.), Virgin Is. (U.S.) 161/D4
Priverno, Italy 34/D4
Privolzhskiy, U.S.S.R. 52/G4
Priyutnoye, U.S.S.R. 52/F5
Priyutovo, U.S.S.R. 52/H4
Prizren, Yugoslavia 45/E4
Probolinggo, Indonesia 85/K2
Procious, W. Va. 312/D5
Procter, Br. Col. 184/J5
Proctor, Ark. 202/K3
Proctor, Colo. 208/N1
Proctor, Minn. 255/F4
Proctor, Mont. 262/B3
Proctor, Okla. 288/S3
Proctor, Pa. 294/J3
Proctor, Texas 303/F3
Proctor •, Vt. 268/A4
Proctor, W. Va. 312/E3
Proctorsville, Vt. 268/B5
Proctorville, N.C. 281/M6
Proctorville, Ohio 284/F9
Proddatur, India 68/D6
Proença-a-Nova, Portugal 33/B3
Profesor Rafael Ramírez, Mexico 150/O1
Profondeville, Belgium 27/F8
Progreso, Mexico 150/P6
Progreso, Uruguay 145/B6
Progress, Br. Col. 184/G2
Progress, Oreg. 291/A2
Progress, U.S.S.R. 48/O5
Progress Village, Fla. 212/C3
Project City, Calif. 204/C3
Prokhladnyy, U.S.S.R. 52/F6
Prokop'yevsk, U.S.S.R. 54/K4
Prokop'yevsk, U.S.S.R. 48/J4
Prokuplje, Yugoslavia 45/E4
Prole, Iowa 229/F6
Prome (Pye), Burma 72/B3
Promise City, Iowa 229/G7
Promissão, Brazil 135/B2
Promontory, Utah 304/B2
Prompton, Pa. 294/M2
Prongua, Sask. 181/C3
Prony (bay), New Caled. 86/H5
Prophet (riv.), Br. Col. 184/M2
Prophetstown, Ill. 222/D2
Propriá, Brazil 132/G5
Proserpine, Queensland 88/H4
Proserpine, Queensland 95/D4
Prosit, Minn. 255/F4
Prosna (riv.), Poland 47/C3
Prospect, Ala. 195/D3
Prospect •, Conn. 210/D2
Prospect, Ky. 237/K4
Prospect •, Maine 243/F6
Prospect (res.), N. S. Wales 88/K4
Prospect (res.), N.S. Wales 97/H3
Prospect, N.Y. 276/K4
Prospect, Nova Scotia 168/E4
Prospect, Ohio 284/C5
Prospect, Oreg. 291/E5
Prospect, Pa. 294/B4

Prospect, S. Australia 88/D8
Prospect, S. Australia 94/B7
Prospect, Tenn. 237/G10
Prospect, Va. 307/L6
Prospect (lake), Wis. 317/H8
Prospect Harbor, Maine 243/H7
Prospect Heights, Ill. 222/B5
Prospect Hill, N.C. 281/L2
Prospect Park, N.J. 273/B1
Prospect Park, Pa. 294/M7
Prosper, Mich. 250/E4
Prosper, Minn. 255/G7
Prosper, N. Dak. 282/R6
Prosper, Oreg. 291/C4
Prosperidad, Philippines 82/F6
Prosperity, Pa. 294/B5
Prosperity, S.C. 296/D3
Prosser, Nebr. 264/F4
Prosser, Wash. 310/F4
Prostějov, Czech. 41/D2
Protection, Kansas 232/C4
Protem, Mo. 261/G9
Protivín, Czech. 41/C2
Protivin, Iowa 229/J2
Proulxville, Québec 172/E3
Prouts Neck, Maine 243/C8
Provadiya, Bulgaria 45/H4
Provencal, La. 238/D3
Provence (trad. prov.), France 29
Provence (mts.), Calif. 204/K8
Providence, Ala. 195/C6
Providence (mts.), Calif. 204/K8
Providence, Fla. 212/D2
Providence, Grenada 161/D9
Providence, Ind. 227/F6
Providence, Ky. 237/F6
Providence (cape), N. Zealand 100/A7
Providence (cap.), R.I. 188/M2
Providence (cap.), R.I. 146/L5
Providence (co.), R.I. 249/H5
Providence (cap.), R.I. 249/H5
Providence, Utah 304/C2
Providence Bay, Ontario 177/B2
Providence Forge, Va. 307/P6
Providencia (isl.), Colombia 126/B9
Providenciales (isl.), Turks & Caicos 156/D2
Provideniya, U.S.S.R. 4/C18
Provideniya, U.S.S.R. 48/T3
Province Lake, N.H. 268/E4
Provincetown, Mass. 249/O4
Provincetown •, Mass. 249/O4
Provins, France 28/E3
Provo, Ark. 202/B5
Provo, S. Dak. 298/B7
Provo, Utah 146/G6
Provo, Utah 304/C3
Provo, Utah 188/D2
Provo (peak), Utah 304/C3
Provo (riv.), Utah 304/C3
Provost, Alberta 182/E3
Prowers (co.), Colo. 208/P7
Prozor, Yugoslavia 45/C4
Pruden, Tenn. 237/O7
Prudence (isl.), R.I. 249/J6
Prudence Island, R.I. 249/J6
Prudentópolis, Brazil 132/D9
Prudenville, Mich. 250/E4
Prudhoe (bay), Alaska 146/D2
Prudhoe (bay), Alaska 196/J1
Prudhoe, England 13/H3
Prudhoe Bay, Alaska 196/J1
Prud'homme, Sask. 181/F3
Prudnik, Poland 47/C3
Prue, Okla. 288/O2
Pruitt, Ark. 202/D1
Prüm, Germany 22/B3
Pruntytown, W. Va. 312/F4
Pruszcz Gdanski, Poland 47/D1
Pruszków, Poland 47/E2
Prut (riv.), 7/G4
Prut (riv.), Romania 45/J2
Prut (riv.), U.S.S.R. 52/C5
Prydz (bay), 5/C4
Pryor, Colo. 208/K8
Pryor, Mont. 262/H5
Pryor, Okla. 288/R2
Pryorsburg, Ky. 237/D7
Pryse, Ky. 237/O5
Przasnysz, Poland 47/E2
Przemkow, Poland 47/B2
Przemsza (riv.), Poland 47/B4
Przemyśl (prov.), Poland 47/F4
Przemyśl, Poland 47/F4
Przemyśl, Poland 7/G4
Przeworsk, Poland 47/F3
Przheval'sk, U.S.S.R. 48/H5
Psakhná, Greece 45/F6
Psará (isl.), Greece 45/G6
Psári, Greece 45/E7
Psel (riv.), U.S.S.R. 52/D4
Psevdhókavos (cape), Greece 45/G6
Pskov, U.S.S.R. 7/G3
Pskov, U.S.S.R. 48/C4
Pskov, U.S.S.R. 52/C3
Pskov (lake), U.S.S.R. 53/D1
Ptolemaís, Greece 45/E5
Ptuj, Yugoslavia 45/C2
Puako, Hawaii 218/G4
Puán, Argentina 143/D4
Puangue, Chile 138/F4
Puangue, Estero de (riv.), Chile 138/F3
Pubnico, Nova Scotia 168/C5
Pubnico (harb.), Nova Scotia 168/C5
Puca Barranca, Peru 128/E4
Pucallpa, Peru 128/E7
Pucallpa, Peru 120/B3
Pucara, Bolivia 136/C6
Pucará, Peru 128/G10
Pucarani, Bolivia 136/A5
Pucatrihue, Chile 138/D3
Pucaurco, Peru 128/G4
Puce, Ontario 177/B5
Pucheng, China 77/J6
Púchov, Czech. 41/E2
Puchuncaví, Chile 138/F2

Pucio (pt.), Philippines 82/C5
Pucioasa, Romania 45/G3
Puck, Poland 47/D1
Puckaway (lake), Wis. 317/H8
Puckett, Miss. 256/E6
Pucón, Chile 138/E2
Pucusana, Peru 128/D9
Pudahuel, Chile 138/G3
Pudasjärvi, Finland 18/P4
Pudding (riv.), Oreg. 291/A3
Puduchcheri (Pondicherry), India 68/D6
Pudukkottai, India 68/D6
Pudozh, U.S.S.R. 52/E2
Puebla (state), Mexico 150/L7
Puebla, Mexico 146/J8
Puebla de Alcocer, Spain 33/D3
Puebla de Don Fadrique, Spain 33/E4
Puebla del Caramiñal, Spain 33/B1
Puebla de Sanabria, Spain 33/C1
Puebla de Trives, Spain 33/C1
Puebla de Zaragoza, Mexico 150/N2
Pueblo, Colo. 146/H6
Pueblo, Colo. 188/F3
Pueblo (co.), Colo. 208/K6
Pueblo (res.), Colo. 208/K6
Pueblo (mts.), Oreg. 291/J5
Pueblo Army Depot, Colo. 208/L6
Pueblo Colorado Wash (dry riv.), Ariz. 198/F3
Pueblo del Sauce, Uruguay 145/E4
Pueblo Hondo, Venezuela 124/B3
Pueblo Hundido, Chile 138/B6
Pueblo Ind. Res., N. Mex. 274/B4
Pueblo Ind. Res., N. Mex. 274/B3
Pueblo Ind. Res., N. Mex. 274/D3
Pueblo Ind. Res., N. Mex. 274/C3
Pueblo La Paloma, Uruguay 145/D3
Pueblo Nuevo, Uruguay 145/B2
Pueblo Nuevo, Venezuela 124/D1
Pueblo of Acoma, N. Mex. 274/B3
Puebloviejo, Colombia 126/D5
Puelches, Argentina 143/C4
Puelén, Argentina 143/C4
Puelo (riv.), Chile 138/E4
Puenteareas, Spain 33/B1
Puente de Ixtla, Mexico 150/K8
Puente del Inca, Argentina 143/B3
Puentedeume, Spain 33/C1
Puente-Genil, Spain 33/D4
Puente Nacional, Colombia 126/D5
Pueo (pt.), Hawaii 218/A2
Pu'er, China 77/F7
Puerca (pt.), P. Rico 161/F2
Puerco (riv.), Ariz. 198/F3
Puerco (riv.), N. Mex. 274/A3
Puercos, Morro de (head), Panama 154/H7
Puerto Acosta, Bolivia 136/A4
Puerto Aisén, Chile 138/E6
Puerto Aisén, Chile 120/B7
Puerto Alegre, Bolivia 136/E3
Puerto Alianza, Peru 128/D5
Puerto Almacen, Bolivia 136/C4
Puerto Amaro, Uruguay 145/F3
Puerto América, Peru 128/D5
Puerto Ángel, Mexico 150/L9
Puerto Antioquia, Colombia 126/C4
Puerto Arazatí, Uruguay 145/C5
Puerto Argentina, Colombia 126/C7
Puerto Armuelles, Panama 154/F6
Puerto Arturo, Peru 128/F3
Puerto Asís, Colombia 126/C6
Puerto Ayacucho, Venezuela 120/C2
Puerto Ayacucho, Venezuela 124/E5
Puerto Ayora, Ecuador 128/B9
Puerto Bahía Negra, Paraguay 144/C2
Puerto Ballivián, Bolivia 136/C4
Puerto Barrios, Guatemala 154/C3
Puerto Bermúdez, Peru 128/E8
Puerto Berrío, Colombia 126/C4
Puerto Bertrand, Chile 138/E7
Puerto Boy, Colombia 126/C7
Puerto Caballas, Peru 128/E10
Puerto Caballo, Paraguay 144/C2
Puerto Cabello, Venezuela 124/E4
Puerto Cabello, Venezuela 120/C1
Puerto Cabezas, Nicaragua 154/F3
Puerto Calvimonte, Bolivia 136/C4
Puerto Carlos Pfannl, Paraguay 144/C4
Puerto Carranza, Colombia 126/F9
Puerto Carreño, Colombia 120/C2
Puerto Carreño, Colombia 126/G4
Puerto Casado, Paraguay 144/C3
Puerto Castilla, Honduras 154/D3
Puerto Chacabuco, Chile 138/D6
Puerto Chicama, Peru 128/C6
Puerto Cisnes, Chile 138/E5
Puerto Coig, Argentina 143/C7
Puerto Colombia, Colombia 126/C2
Puerto Colón, Paraguay 144/C3
Puerto Cooper, Paraguay 144/C3
Puerto Córdoba, Colombia 126/E8
Puerto Cortés, C. Rica 154/F6
Puerto Cortés, Honduras 154/D2
Puerto Cortés, Mexico 150/D4
Puerto Crevaux, Colombia 126/C6
Puerto Cristal, Chile 138/E6
Puerto Cumarebo, Venezuela 124/C2
Puerto de Cayo, Ecuador 128/B3
Puerto de la Concordia, El Salvador 154/C4
Puerto de Lunas, N. Mex. 274/E4
Puerto de Nutrias, Venezuela 124/D3
Puerto Deseado, Argentina 143/D6
Puerto Deseado, Argentina 120/C7
Puerto El Carmen, Ecuador 128/E3
Puerto Escondido, Colombia 126/B3
Puerto Escondido, Mexico 150/L9
Puerto Esperanza, Cuba 158/A1
Puerto Esperanza, Paraguay 144/C2
Puerto Estrella, Colombia 126/E1
Puerto Eten, Peru 128/B6
Puerto Foncière, Paraguay 144/D3

Puerto Frey, Bolivia 136/E4
Puerto Galileo, Paraguay 144/C4
Puerto General Busch, Bolivia 136/G7
Puerto General Ovando, Bolivia 136/50
Puerto Grether, Bolivia 136/C5
Puerto Guachalla, Bolivia 136/F6
Puerto Guaraní, Paraguay 144/C2
Puerto Harberton, Argentina 143/C7
Puerto Heath, Bolivia 136/A3
Puerto Hierro, Venezuela 124/H2
Puerto Huitoto, Colombia 126/D7
Puerto Iguazú, Argentina 143/F2
Puerto Inca, Peru 128/E7
Puerto Ingeniero Ibáñez, Chile 138/E6
Puerto Inírida, Colombia 126/G6
Puerto Irigoyen, Argentina 143/D1
Puerto Isabel, Bolivia 136/F6
Puerto Izozog, Bolivia 136/D6
Puerto José Pardo, Peru 128/D4
Puerto Juárez, Mexico 150/Q6
Puerto La Concordia, Colombia 126/D6
Puerto La Cruz, Venezuela 124/F2
Puerto Leguía, Loreto, Peru 128/D4
Puerto Leguía, Puno, Peru 128/G9
Puerto Leguízamo, Colombia 126/C8
Puerto Lempira, Honduras 154/F3
Puerto Liberador General San Martín, Argentina 143/D2
Puerto Limón, Colombia 126/B7
Puerto López, La Guajira, Colombia 126/E2
Puerto López, Meta, Colombia 126/D5
Puerto López, Colombia 126/D6
Puerto Madero, Mexico 150/N9
Puerto Madryn, Argentina 143/C5
Puerto Madryn, Argentina 120/C7
Puerto Maldonado, Peru 128/H9
Puerto Maldonado, Peru 120/B4
Puerto Mamoré, Bolivia 136/C5
Puerto Manglares, Colombia 126/B5
Puerto María, Paraguay 144/C2
Puerto Max, Paraguay 144/D3
Puerto Mayor Otaño, Paraguay 144/E5
Puerto Medio Mundo (bay), P. Rico 161/F2
Puerto Mercedes, Colombia 126/D7
Puerto Mihanovich, Paraguay 144/C2
Puerto Miranda, Venezuela 124/E4
Puerto Montt, Chile 120/B7
Puerto Montt, Chile 138/E4
Puerto Morelos, Mexico 150/Q6
Puerto Morín, Peru 128/C7
Puerto Mosquito, Colombia 126/C3
Puerto Murillo, Colombia 126/G4
Puerto Mutis, Colombia 126/B4
Puerto Napo, Ecuador 128/D3
Puerto Nare, Colombia 126/D7
Puerto Nariño, Colombia 126/F5
Puerto Natales, Chile 120/B8
Puerto Natales, Chile 138/E9
Puerto Niño, Colombia 126/C5
Puerto Nuevo, Colombia 126/F5
Puerto Nuevo, Paraguay 144/C2
Puerto Nuevo, P. Rico 161/D1
Puerto Nuevo (pt.), P. Rico 161/C1
Puerto Obaldía, Panama 154/J4
Puerto Ocopa, Peru 128/E8
Puerto Olaya, Colombia 126/C4
Puerto Ospina, Colombia 126/C7
Puerto Padre, Cuba 158/H3
Puerto Padre, Cuba 156/C2
Puerto Páez, Venezuela 124/E4
Puerto Palena, Chile 138/D5
Puerto Pando, Bolivia 136/B4
Puerto Paraíso, Paraguay 144/A5
Puerto Pardo, Peru 128/F7
Puerto Patiño, Bolivia 136/C5
Puerto Paulina, Colombia 126/D7
Puerto Peñasco, Mexico 150/C1
Puerto Pinasco, Paraguay 144/C3
Puerto Pirámides, Argentina 143/D5
Puerto Piritu, Venezuela 124/F2
Puerto Pizarro, Colombia 126/D8
Puerto Pizarro, Peru 128/B4
Puerto Plata (prov.), Dom. Rep. 158/D1
Puerto Plata, Dom. Rep. 156/D3
Puerto Plata, Dom. Rep. 158/D5
Puerto Portillo, Peru 128/F7
Puerto Prado, Peru 128/E8
Puerto Presidente Franco, Paraguay 144/E4
Puerto Princesa, Philippines 85/E3
Puerto Princesa, Philippines 82/B6
Puerto Quellón, Chile 138/D4
Puerto Quijarro, Bolivia 136/G5
Puerto Ramírez, Chile 138/E5
Puerto Real, P. Rico 161/A2
Puerto Real (Playa de Fajardo), P. Rico 161/F1
Puerto Real, Spain 33/D4
Puerto Reyes, Colombia 126/B5
Puerto Rico 2/F5
Puerto Rico 146/M8
PUERTO RICO 161
PUERTO RICO 156/G1
Puerto Rico, Argentina 143/D1
Puerto Rico, Bolivia 136/B2
Puerto Rico, Caquetá, Colombia 126/C7
Puerto Rico, Meta, Colombia 126/C6
Puerto Rondón, Colombia 126/E5
Puerto Rosario, Paraguay 144/D4
Puerto Ruiz, Argentina 143/G6
Puerto Saavedra, Chile 138/D2
Puerto Salgar, Colombia 126/C5
Puerto Samanco, Peru 128/C7
Puerto San Francisco, Bolivia 136/C5
Puerto San José, Paraguay 144/E5
Puerto San Rafael, Paraguay 144/E5
Puerto Sastre, Paraguay 144/C3
Puerto Saucedo, Bolivia 136/D3

Puerto Siles, Bolivia 136/C3
Puerto Suárez, Bolivia 136/F6
Puerto Tacurú Pytá, Paraguay 144/D3
Puerto Tahuantinsuyo, Peru 128/G9
Puerto Tarafa, Cuba 158/H3
Puerto Tejada, Colombia 126/B6
Puerto Toledo, Colombia 126/C8
Puerto Torno, Bolivia 136/C5
Puerto Tres Palmas, Paraguay 144/C2
Puerto Vallarta, Mexico 150/G6
Puerto Varas, Chile 138/E3
Puerto Velarde, Bolivia 136/D5
Puerto Victoria, Peru 128/E7
Puerto Villarroel, Bolivia 136/C5
Puerto Villazón, Bolivia 136/D3
Puerto Wilches, Colombia 126/D4
Puerto Williams, Chile 138/F11
Puerto Yartou, Chile 138/E10
Puerto Ybapobó, Paraguay 144/D3
Pueyrredón (lake), Argentina 143/B6
Puffin (isl.), Ireland 17/A8
Pugachev, U.S.S.R. 52/G4
Puget (isl.), Wash. 310/B4
Puget (sound), Wash. 310/C3
Puget Sound Navy Yard, Wash. 310/A2
Pugwash, Nova Scotia 168/E3
Pugwash (harb.), Nova Scotia 168/E3
Puha, N. Zealand 100/F3
Puhi, Hawaii 218/C2
Puigcerdá, Spain 33/G1
Puina, Bolivia 136/A4
Puinagua, Canal de (riv.), Peru 128/E5
Puinahuén, S. Leone 106/B7
Pujilí, Ecuador 128/C3
Pujut (pt.), Indonesia 85/G1
Pukaki (lake), N. Zealand 100/B6
Pukalani, Hawaii 218/J2
Puka-Puka (atoll), Fr. Poly. 87/N7
Pukapuka (atoll), Cook Is. 87/K7
Pukaskwa Nat'l Park, Ont. 162/H6
Pukaskwa Prov. Park, Ontario 175/C3
Pukaskwa Prov. Park, Ontario 177/H5
Pukch'ŏng, N. Korea 81/C3
Puké, Albania 45/D3
Pukekohe, N. Zealand 100/E2
Pukoo, Hawaii 218/H1
Puksubaek (mt.), N. Korea 81/C3
Pukwana, S. Dak. 298/L6
Pula, Yugoslavia 45/A3
Pulacayo, Bolivia 120/C5
Pulacayo, Bolivia 136/B7
Pulai, Sungai (riv.), Malaysia 82/F5
Pulanduta (pt.), Philippines 82/D5
Pulangi (riv.), Philippines 82/E7
Pulap (atoll), Micronesia 87/F5
Púlar, Cerro (mt.), Chile 138/B4
Pulaski (co.), Ark. 202/F4
Pulaski (co.), Georgia 217/E6
Pulaski, Georgia 217/J6
Pulaski (co.), Ill. 222/D6
Pulaski, Ill. 222/D6
Pulaski, Ind. 227/D3
Pulaski (co.), Ind. 227/D2
Pulaski, Iowa 229/J7
Pulaski (co.), Ky. 237/M6
Pulaski, Ky. 237/M6
Pulaski, Miss. 256/E6
Pulaski (co.), Mo. 261/H7
Pulaski, N.Y. 276/H3
Pulaski, Ohio 284/A2
Pulaski, Pa. 294/B3
Pulaski, Tenn. 237/G10
Pulaski (co.), Va. 307/G6
Pulaski, Va. 307/G6
Pulaski, Wis. 317/K6
Pulehu, Hawaii 218/J2
Pulicat (lake), India 68/E6
Pull (pt.), Virgin Is. (U.S.) 161/F3
Pullman, Mich. 250/C6
Pullman, Wash. 310/H4
Pullman, W. Va. 312/D4
Pully, Switzerland 39/C4
Pulo Anna (isl.), Belau 87/D5
Pulog (mt.), Philippines 82/C1
Pulpit Harbor, Maine 243/F7
Pulteney, Alberta 182/D4
Pulteney, N.Y. 276/F5
Pulteneyville, N.Y. 276/F4
Pułtusk, Poland 47/E2
Pülümür, Turkey 63/H3
Pulusuk (atoll), Micronesia 87/F5
Puluwat (atoll), Micronesia 87/E5
Pumanque, Chile 138/F6
Pumphrey, Md. 245/M4
Pumpkin (creek), Nebr. 264/A3
Pumpville, Texas 303/C8
Puna, Bolivia 136/C6
Puná (isl.), Ecuador 128/B4
Punakaiki, N. Zealand 100/B5
Punakha, Bhutan 68/G3
Punaluu, Hawaii 218/H7
Punaluu (harb.), Hawaii 218/H7
Punata, Bolivia 136/C5
Punchaw, Br. Col. 184/F3
Punchbowl (hill), Hawaii 218/C4
Punchestown, Ireland 17/H5
Pune, India 68/C5
Pungo, N.C. 281/R3
Pungo (lake), N.C. 281/S3
Pungo (riv.), N.C. 281/R4
Pungoteague, Va. 307/S5
P'ungsan, N. Korea 81/D3
Punia, Zaire 115/C4
Punitaqui, Chile 138/A8
Punjab (state), India 68/D2
Punjab (prov.), Pakistan 68/C2
Punk (isl.), Manitoba 179/F3
Punnichy, Sask. 181/G4
Puno (dept.), Peru 128/G10
Puno, Peru 128/G10
Puno, Peru 120/B4

Punta, Cerro de (mt.), P. Rico 161/C2
Punta Abreojos, Mexico 150/C3
Punta Alta, Argentina 143/D4
Punta Alta, Argentina 120/C6
Punta Arenas, Chile 120/B8
Punta Arenas, Chile 138/E10
Punta Cardón, Venezuela 124/C2
Punta de Bombón, Peru 128/F11
Punta de Díaz, Chile 138/B7
Punta del Este, Uruguay 145/E6
Punta de Mata, Venezuela 124/G3
Punta de Piedras, Venezuela 124/F2
Punta Gorda, Belize 154/C2
Punta Gorda (pt.), Calif. 204/A3
Punta Gorda, Fla. 212/E5
Punta Medanosa, Argentina 143/C6
Punta Moreno, Peru 128/C6
Punta Negra, Salar de (salt dep.), Chile 138/B5
Puntarenas, C. Rica 154/E6
Punta Santiago (Playa de Humacao), P. Rico 161/F2
Puntas de Maciel, Uruguay 145/C4
Punto Fijo, Venezuela 120/C1
Punto Fijo, Venezuela 124/D2
Punxsutawney, Pa. 294/E4
Puolanka, Finland 18/P4
Puolo (pt.), Hawaii 218/C2
Pupiales, Colombia 126/B7
Puposky, Minn. 255/C3
Pupuke (lake), N. Zealand 100/B1
Pupuya, Nevada (mt.), Bolivia 136/A4
Puqi, China 77/H6
Puquina, Peru 128/G11
Puquintica, Nevado (mt.), Bolivia 136/A6
Puquintica, Cerro (mt.), Chile 138/B1
Puquio, Peru 128/F10
Puquios, Chile 138/B1
Pur (riv.), U.S.S.R. 48/H3
Puracé (vol.), Colombia 126/B6
Purbeck, Isle of (pen.), England 13/F7
Purbolinggo, Indonesia 85/J2
Purcell (mts.), Br. Col. 184/J5
Purcell (mts.), Idaho 220/B1
Purcell, Kansas 232/G2
Purcell, Mo. 261/D8
Purcell (mts.), Mont. 262/A2
Purcell, Okla. 288/M4
Purcellville, Va. 307/N2
Purchase, N.Y. 276/P6
Purdin, Mo. 261/F3
Purdum, Nebr. 264/D2
Purdy, Mo. 261/E8
Purdy, Va. 307/N7
Pure Air, Mo. 261/G2
Purén, Chile 138/D2
Purgatoire (riv.), Colo. 208/M8
Purgitsville, W. Va. 312/J4
Puri, India 68/F5
Purial, Sierra de (mts.), Cuba 158/A4
Purificación, Colombia 126/C5
Purificación, Mexico 150/G7
Purli, India 68/D5
Purmerend, Netherlands 27/F4
Purnea, India 68/F3
Purple Springs, Alberta 182/E5
Purple Valley, Ontario 177/C3
Purranque, Chile 138/D3
Pursat (Pouthisat), Cambodia 72/C3
Puruándiro, Mexico 150/J7
Puruey, Venezuela 124/F4
Purukcahu, Indonesia 85/E6
Purulia, India 68/F4
Puruname, Venezuela 124/F4
Puruni (riv.), Guyana 131/B2
Purus (riv.), Brazil 120/C3
Purus (riv.), Brazil 132/H9
Purús (riv.), Peru 128/G8
Puruvesi (lake), Finland 18/Q6
Purves, Manitoba 179/D5
Purvis, Miss. 256/F6
Purwakarta, Indonesia 85/H2
Purwodadi, Indonesia 85/J2
Purwokerto, Indonesia 85/H2
Purworejo, Indonesia 85/J2
Puryear, Tenn. 237/E6
Pusan, S. Korea 54/O6
Pusan, S. Korea 81/D6
Pushaw (lake), Maine 243/F6
Pushkin, U.S.S.R. 48/C4
Pushkin, U.S.S.R. 52/C3
Pushmataha, Ala. 195/B6
Pushmataha (co.), Okla. 288/R6
Püspökladány, Hungary 41/F3
Pustunich, Mexico 150/O7
Püsztaszabolcs, Hungary 41/E3
Pützstaszabolcs, Hungary 41/E3
Putaendo, Chile 138/A9
Putao, Burma 72/C1
Putararu, N. Zealand 100/F3
Putbus, Germany 22/E1
Puteau, France 28/A2
Putian, China 77/J6
Putignano, Italy 34/F4
Put-in-Bay, Ohio 284/E2
Puting, Borneo (cape), Indonesia 85/E6
Puting, Sumatra (cape), Indonesia 85/C7
Putla de Guerrero, Mexico 150/L8
Putnam, Ala. 195/B6
Putnam, Conn. 210/H1
Putnam •, Conn. 210/H1
Putnam (co.), Fla. 212/E2
Putnam (co.), Georgia 217/F4
Putnam, Georgia 217/D6
Putnam (co.), Ill. 222/D2
Putnam, Ill. 222/D2
Putnam (co.), Ind. 227/D5
Putnam (co.), Mo. 261/F2
Putnam (co.), N.Y. 276/N8
Putnam (co.), Ohio 284/C3
Putnam, Okla. 288/J3

Putnam (co.), Tenn. 237/K8
Putnam, Texas 303/E5
Putnam (co.), W. Va. 312/C6
Putnam Heights, Conn. 210/H1
Putnam Valley •, N.Y. 276/N8
Putnamville, Ind. 227/D6
Putney, Georgia 217/D8
Putney, S. Dak. 298/N2
Putney •, Vt. 268/B6
Putnok, Hungary 41/F2
Putre, Chile 138/B1
Putten, Belgium 27/F6
Putten, Netherlands 27/H4
Puttgarden, Germany 22/D1
Puttur, India 68/D6
Putumayo (riv.) 120/B3
Putumayo (inten.), Colombia 126/C7
Putumayo (riv.), Colombia 126/E9
Putumayo, Ecuador 128/E3
Putumayo (riv.), Ecuador 128/E2
Putumayo (riv.), Peru 128/G4
Pütürge, Turkey 63/H3
Putussibau, Indonesia 85/E5
Puuanahulu, Hawaii 218/G4
Puuhonua O Honaunau Nat'l Hist.
  Park, Hawaii 218/G4
Puuiki, Hawaii 218/K2
Puu Keahiakahoe (mt.), Hawaii
  218/D3
Puu Kukui (mt.), Hawaii 218/J2
Puu Lanihuli (mt.), Hawaii 218/D3
Puulavesi (lake), Finland 18/P5
Puu Moaularui (mt.), Hawaii 218/H3
Puunene, Hawaii 218/J2
Puunui, Hawaii 218/A2
Puuwai, Hawaii 218/A2
Puuwaawaa, Hawaii 218/G5
Puxico, Mo. 261/M9
Puyallup, Wash. 188/B1
Puyallup, Wash. 310/C3
Puyallup (riv.) Wash. 310/C4
Puy-de-Dôme (dept.), France 28/E5
Puy-de-Dôme (mt.), France 28/E5
Puyehue, Chile 138/E3
Puyehue (lake), Chile 138/E2
Puyo, Ecuador 128/D3
Puysegur (pt.), New Zealand 100/A7
Pwani (Coast) (reg.), Tanzania 115/G5
Pweto, Zaire 115/E5
Pwllheli, Wales 10/D4
Pwllheli, Wales 13/C5
Pyapon, Burma 72/B3
Pyasina (riv.), U.S.S.R. 48/J2
Pyatigorsk, U.S.S.R. 52/F6
Pyatt, Ark. 202/E1
Pye (isls.), Alaska 196/C2
Pye, Burma 72/B3
Pye, Burma 54/L8
Pyengana, Tasmania 99/E3
Pygmalion (Indira) (pt.), India
  68/G7
Pyhäjärvi (lake), Finland 18/M6
Pyhäjärvi (lake), Finland 18/O5
Pyinmana, Burma 72/C3
Pyland, Miss. 256/F3
Pymatuning (res.), Ohio 284/J2
Pymatuning (res.), Pa. 294/A2
P'yŏnggang, N. Korea 81/C4
P'yŏngyang, N. Korea 81/C4
P'yŏngyang, Jiangxi, China 77/J6
P'yŏngyang (cap.), N. Korea 54/O6
P'yŏngyang (cap.), N. Korea 81/C4
Pyote, Texas 303/A6
Pyramid (peak), Idaho 220/E4
Pyramid, Ky. 237/R5
Pyramid (lake), Nev. 266/C2
Pyramid (isl.), N. Zealand 100/E7
Pyramid Lake Ind. Res., Nev. 266/B2
Pyramids (ruins), Egypt 111/J3
Pyrenees (mts.) 7/D4
Pyrenees (range), France 28/C6
Pyrenees (range), Spain 33/F1
Pyrénées-Atlantiques (dept.), France
  28/C6
Pyrénées-Orientales (dept.), France
  28/E6
Pyrites, N.Y. 276/K1
Pyriton, Ala. 195/G4
Pyrzyce, Poland 47/B2
Pytalovo, U.S.S.R. 52/C3
Pyu, Burma 72/C3
Pyuthan, Nepal 68/E3

Q

Qaanaq, Greenland 4/B13
Qabalan, West Bank 65/C3
Qabatiya, West Bank 65/C3
Qabr Hud, Yemen 59/E6
Qadhima, Saudi Arabia 59/C5
Qadima, Israel 65/B3
Qadisiya (heads), Iraq 66/D4
Qafar, Saudi Arabia 59/D4
Qaffin, West Bank 65/C3
Qagan Nur, China 77/H3
Qâhira, El (Cairo) (cap.), Egypt
  111/J3
Qaidam (basin), China 54/L6
Qaidam Pendi (basin) (swamp),
  China 77/D3
Qala'en Nahl, Sudan 59/C7
Qala'en Nahl, Sudan 111/F5
Qalansuwa, Israel 65/B3
Qal'a Sharqat, Iraq 59/D2
Qal'a Sharqat, Iraq 66/C3
Qalat, Afghanistan 68/B2
Qalat, Afghanistan 59/J3
Qal'at Diza, Iraq 66/D2
Qal'at es Salihiye, Syria 63/J5
Qal'eh Mureh (riv.), Iran 66/G3
Qal'eh-ye Now, Afghanistan 68/A1
Qal'eh-ye Now, Afghanistan 59/H3

Qal'eh-ye Panjeh, Afghanistan 59/K2
Qal'eh-ye Panjeh, Afghanistan 68/C1
Qalqiliya, West Bank 65/C3
Qalyub, Egypt 111/J3
Qamdo, China 77/E5
Qamdo, China 54/L6
Qamishliye, Syria 63/J4
Qamr (bay), Yemen 59/F6
Qandahar, Afghanistan 54/H6
Qandahar, Afghanistan 68/B2
Qandahar, Afghanistan 59/J3
Qantara, El, Egypt 111/K3
Qaqortoq, Greenland 4/D12
Qaranqu (riv.), Iran 66/E2
Qareh Dagh (mts.), Iran 66/E1
Qareh Su (riv.), Iran 66/E1
Qareh Su (riv.), Iran 66/G3
Qarkilik (Ruoqiang), China 77/C4
Qarqan (Qiemo), China 77/C4
Qarqan He (riv.), China 77/C4
Qarn (riv.), Israel 65/C1
Qasr al Haiyanya, Saudi Arabia
  59/D4
Qasr al Khubbaz, Iraq 66/B4
Qasr-e Qand, Iran 59/H4
Qasr-e Qand, Iran 68/A2
Qasr-e-Shirin, Iran 66/E3
Qasr Farâfra, Egypt 111/E2
Qasr Farâfra, Egypt 102/F2
Qasr Farâfra, Egypt 59/A4
Qatar 2/M4
Qatar 54/G7
QATAR 59/F4
Qatif, Saudi Arabia 59/E4
Qattara (depr.), Egypt 59/A4
Qattara (depr.), Egypt 102/F2
Qattara (depr.), Egypt 111/E2
Qayen, Iran 66/L4
Qayen, Iran 59/G3
Qazvin, Iran 54/F6
Qazvin, Iran 59/E2
Qazvin, Iran 66/F2
Qedma, Israel 65/B3
Qena, Egypt 111/F2
Qena, Egypt 102/F2
Qena, Egypt 59/B4
Qeqertarsuaq, Greenland 4/C12
Qeshm (isl.), Iran 59/G4
Qeshm (isl.), Iran 66/J7
Qeys (isl.), Iran 59/F4
Qeys (isl.), Iran 66/J7
Qezel Owzan (riv.), Iran 66/F2
Qezel Owzan (riv.), Iran 59/E2
Qianyang (Kienyang), China 77/H6
Qiaowan, China 77/E3
Qibya, West Bank 65/C4
Qiebei, China 77/F7
Qiema, China 54/K3
Qiemo (Qarqan), China 77/C4
Qijiang, China 77/C6
Qila Ladgasht, Pakistan 68/A3
Qila Ladgasht, Pakistan 59/H4
Qilian, China 77/E4
Qilian Shan (range), China 54/L6
Qilian Shan (range), China 77/C4
Qimen, China 77/J5
Qina (Qena), Egypt 59/B4
Qingdao (Tsingtao), China 77/K4
Qingdao, China 54/O6
Qinghai (Tsinghai) (prov.), China
  77/E4
Qinghai (lake), China 54/L6
Qinghai Hu (lake), China 77/E4
Qinghe (Qinggil), China 77/C2
Qingjiang, Jiangxi, China 77/J6
Qingjiang, Anhui, China 77/J5
Qingtongxia, China 77/F4
Qingyuan, China 77/H7
Qinhuangdao (Chinwangtao), China
  77/K4
Qinzhou, China 77/G7
Qionghai, China 77/H8
Qiongshan, China 77/H8
Qiongzhou Haixia (str.), China
  77/G7
Qiqihar (Tsitsihar), China 77/K2
Qiqihar, China 54/O5
Qira, China 77/B4
Qiryat Atta, Israel 65/C2
Qiryat Bialik, Israel 65/C2
Qiryat Gat, Israel 65/B4
Qiryat Mal'akhi, Israel 65/B4
Qiryat Motzkin, Israel 65/C2
Qiryat Shemona, Israel 65/C1
Qiryat Tiv'on, Israel 65/C2
Qiryat Yam, Israel 65/C2
Qishn, Yemen 59/F6
Qishon (riv.), Israel 65/C2
Qitai, China 77/C3
Qitaihe, China 77/M2
Qizan, Saudi Arabia 59/D6
Qog, China 77/G3
Qom (Qum), Iran 54/G6
Qom, Iran 59/F3
Qom, Iran 66/G3
Qonduz (Konduz), Afghanistan 68/B1
Qonduz (Konduz), Afghanistan 59/J2
Qonduz (Konduz) (riv.), Afghanistan
  68/B1
Qonduz (Konduz) (riv.), Afghanistan
  59/J2
Qorveh, Iran 66/E3
Qotur, Iran 66/D1
Quabbin (res.), Mass. 249/E3
Quaboag (riv.), Mass. 249/F4
Quaco (head), New Bruns. 170/E3
Quaddick (res.), Conn. 210/H1
Quadeville, Ontario 177/G2
Quail, Texas 303/D3
Quairading, W. Australia 92/B1
Quajote Wash (dry riv.), Ariz. 198/D6
Quakenbrück, Germany 22/C2
Quaker City, Ohio 284/H6
Quaker Farms, Conn. 210/C3
Quakertown, N.J. 273/D2
Quaker Hill, Conn. 210/G3
Quakertown, Pa. 294/M5
Qualicum Beach, Br. Col. 184/J3

Quality, Ky. 237/H6
Quallam, Niger 106/E6
Quamba, Minn. 255/E5
Quambatook, Victoria 97/B4
Quambone, N.S. Wales 97/E2
Quanah, Texas 303/E3
Quan Dao Nam Du (isls.), Vietnam
  72/D5
Quandary (peak), Colo. 208/G4
Quandialla, N.S. Wales 97/D4
Quanduck (brook), Conn. 210/H1
Quang Nam, Vietnam 72/E4
Quang Ngai, Vietnam 72/F3
Quang Tri, Vietnam 72/E3
Quang Yen, Vietnam 72/E2
Quan Long, Vietnam 72/E5
Quantico, Okla. 288/J2
Quantico, Va. 307/O3
Quantico Marine Corps Air Sta., Va.
  307/O4
Quanzhou, China 77/H6
Quanzhou (Chüanchow), China
  77/J7
Quapaw, Okla. 288/S1
Qu'Appelle, Sask. 181/H5
Qu'Appelle (riv.), Sask. 181/J5
Quaqtaq, Québec 174/F1
Quaraí, Brazil 132/C10
Quaregnon, Belgium 27/D8
Quarryville, New Bruns. 170/E2
Quarryville, Pa. 294/K6
Quartu Sant'Elena, Italy 34/B5
Quartz (peak), Calif. 204/L11
Quartz Hill, Calif. 204/G9
Quartz Mountain, Oreg. 291/G5
Quartzsite, Ariz. 198/A5
Quasqueton, Iowa 229/K4
Quassapaug (pond), Conn. 210/C2
Quatervals (peak), Switzerland
  39/K3
Quathiaski Cove, Br. Col. 184/E5
Quatre Bornes, Mauritius 118/F5
Quatsino (sound), Br. Col. 184/C5
Quay (co.), N. Mex. 274/F3
Quay, N. Mex. 274/F3
Quay, Okla. 288/N2
Quchan, Iran 66/L2
Quchan, Iran 59/G2
Quealy, Wyo. 319/C4
Queanbeyan, N. S. Wales 88/H7
Queanbeyan, N.S. Wales 97/E4
QUÉBEC 172
QUÉBEC, NORTHERN 174
Québec (prov.) 162/J5
Québec, Canada 2/F3
Québec (prov.), Canada 146/L4
Québec (co.), Québec 172/F3
Québec (county), Québec 174/C3
Québec (cap.), Que. 146/L5
Québec (cap.), Que. 162/J6
Québec (cap.), Québec 172/H3
Québec (cap.), Québec 174/C3
Quebeck, Tenn. 237/K9
Quebracho, Uruguay 145/B2
Quebracho Coto, Argentina 143/D2
Quebrada de Alvarado, Chile
  138/F2
Quebradillas, P. Rico 161/B1
Quechee, Vt. 268/C4
Quechisla, Bolivia 136/C7
Quecholac, Mexico 150/O2
Quecreek, Pa. 294/D5
Quedlinburg, Germany 22/D3
Queen (cape), N.W. Terr. 187/L3
Queen, Pa. 294/E5
Queen Anne, Md. 245/O5
Queen Annes (co.), Md. 245/P4
Queen Charlotte (isls.), Br. Col.
  146/E4
Queen Charlotte (isls.), Br. Col.
  162/C5
Queen Charlotte, Br. Col. 184/A3
Queen Charlotte (isls.), Br. Col.
  184/B3
Queen Charlotte (sound), Br. Col.
  184/C4
Queen Charlotte (str.), Br. Col.
  184/D5
Queen Charlotte (sound), N.W.T.
  162/D5
Queen City, Mo. 261/H2
Queen City, Texas 303/L4
Queen Creek, Ariz. 198/D5
Queen Elizabeth (isls.), Canada 2/C2
Queen Elizabeth (isls.), Canada 4/B15
Queen Elizabeth (isls.), N.W.T. 146/G2
Queen Elizabeth (isls.), N.W.T. 162/M3
Queen Elizabeth (isls.), N.W.T. 187/H1
Queen Mary Coast (reg.) 5/C5
Queen Maud (mts.) 5/A12
Queen Maud (gulf), N.W.T. 162/F2
Queen Maud (gulf), N.W.T. 187/H3
Queen Maud Land (reg.), Ant. 2/K10
Queen Maud Land (reg.) 5/B1
Queens (sound), Br. Col. 184/C4
Queen's (co.), New Bruns. 170/D3
Queens (co.), N.Y. 276/N9
Queens (borough), N.Y. 276/N9
Queens (chan.), N.W.T. 187/J2
Queens (co.), Nova Scotia 168/C4
Queens (co.), Pr. Edward I. 168/E2
Queens, W. Va. 312/F5
Queensberry (mt.), Scotland 15/E5
Queenscliff, Victoria 97/C6
Queensferry, Scotland 10/C1
Queensferry, Scotland 15/D1
Queen Shoals, W. Va. 312/D6
QUEENSLAND 95
Queensland (state), Australia 88/G4
Queensland (state), Australia 87/E8
Queensport, Nova Scotia 168/G3
Queenstown, Alberta 182/D4
Queenstown, Guyana 131/B2
Queenstown (Cóbh), Ireland 10/B5
Queenstown (Cóbh), Ireland 17/E8
Queenstown, Md. 245/O5

Queenstown, New Bruns. 170/D3
Queenstown, N. Zealand 100/B6
Queenstown, S. Africa 102/E3
Queenstown, S. Africa 118/D9
Queenstown, Tasmania 99/B4
Queenstown, Tasmania 88/H8
Queensville, Ind. 227/F6
Queets, Wash. 310/A3
Queets (riv.), Wash. 310/A3
Queilén, Chile 138/D4
Queimadas, Brazil 132/N6
Queimadas, Mozambique 118/F3
Quela, Angola 115/C5
Quelimane, Mozambique 118/F3
Quelimane, Mozambique 102/F6
Quelpart (Cheju) (isl.), S. Korea
  81/C7
Queluz, Portugal 33/A1
Quemado (pt.), Cuba 158/K4
Quemado, N. Mex. 274/A4
Quemado, Texas 303/D9
Quemado de Güines, Cuba 158/E1
Quemchi, Chile 138/D4
Quemoy (Jinmen) (isl.), China 77/J7
Quemú-Quemú, Argentina 143/D4
Quenemo, Kansas 232/G3
Quentin, Miss. 256/D2
Quepos, C. Rica 154/E6
Quequay Chico (riv.), Uruguay 145/B3
Quequay Grande (riv.), Uruguay
  145/B3
Que Que (Kwekwe), Zimbabwe 118/D3
Que Que (Kwekwe), Zimbabwe 102/E6
Quequén, Argentina 143/E4
Querecotillo, Peru 128/B4
Querétaro, Mexico 146/J7
Querétaro, Mexico 150/J6
Querétaro, Mexico 150/J6
Quesada, Spain 33/E4
Queshan, China 77/H5
Quesnel, Br. Col. 162/D5
Quesnel, Br. Col. 184/G4
Quesnel (lake), Br. Col. 184/G4
Quesnel (riv.), Br. Col. 184/F4
Quesnel (lake), Manitoba 179/G4
Questa, N. Mex. 274/D2
Queteña, Bolivia 136/B8
Quetico Prov. Park, Ontario 175/B3
Quetico Prov. Park, Ontario 177/G5
Quetta, Pakistan 54/H6
Quetta, Pakistan 59/J3
Quetta, Pakistan 68/B2
Queule, Chile 138/D2
Quevedo, Ecuador 128/C3
Quévy, Belgium 27/D8
Quezaltenango, Guatemala 154/B3
Quezaltepeque, Guatemala 154/C3
Quezon (prov.), Philippines 82/C3
Quezon City, Philippines 82/C3
Quibala, Angola 115/C6
Quibaxe, Angola 115/C5
Quibdó, Colombia 126/B5
Quiberon, France 28/B4
Quibor, Venezuela 124/D2
Quicacha, Peru 128/F10
Quick, Br. Col. 184/D3
Quick, W. Va. 312/D6
Quicksand, Ky. 237/P5
Quicksburg, Va. 307/L3
Quiebra Hacha, Cuba 158/B1
Quiévrain, Belgium 27/D8
Quigley, Alberta 182/E1
Quiindy, Paraguay 144/B5
Quijotoa, Ariz. 198/C6
Quilalí, Nicaragua 154/E4
Quilán (cape), Chile 138/D4
Quilán (isl.), Chile 138/D5
Quilca, Peru 128/F11
Quilcene, Wash. 310/B3
Quilchena, Br. Col. 184/H4
Quilengues, Angola 115/B6
Quilicura, Chile 138/F2
Quill (lakes), Sask. 181/G4
Quillabamba, Peru 128/G8
Quillacas, Bolivia 136/B6
Quillacollo, Bolivia 136/B5
Quillacollo, Bolivia 120/C5
Quillagua, Chile 138/D4
Quillaicillo, Chile 138/A8
Quillan, France 28/E6
Quilla.yute Ind. Res., Wash. 310/A3
Quilleco, Chile 138/E1
Quill Lake, Sask. 181/G4
Quillon, India 68/D7
Quilpie, Queensland 88/G5
Quilpué, Chile 138/F2
Quimby, Iowa 229/B3
Quimby, Maine 243/F2
Quime, Bolivia 136/B5
Quimili, Argentina 143/D2
Quimper, France 28/A4
Quimperlé, France 28/B4
Quinault, Wash. 310/B3
Quinault (lake), Wash. 310/B3
Quinault (riv.), Wash. 310/A3
Quinault Ind. Res., Wash. 310/A3
Quinby, S.C. 296/H3
Quinby, Va. 307/S5
Quinby (inlet), Va. 307/S6
Quince Mil, Peru 128/G9
Quincy, Calif. 204/E4
Quincy, Fla. 212/B1
Quincy, Ill. 188/F6
Quincy, Ill. 222/B4
Quincy, Ind. 227/D6
Quincy, Kansas 232/F4
Quincy, Ky. 237/P3
Quincy, Mass. 249/D7
Quincy (bay), Mass. 249/D7
Quincy, Mich. 250/E7
Quincy, Miss. 256/H3
Quincy, Mo. 261/F6
Quincy, N.H. 268/C4
Quincy, Ohio 284/C5
Quincy, Wash. 310/F3
Quincy, W. Va. 312/C6

Quindío (dept.), Colombia 126/C5
Quinebaug, Conn. 210/H1
Quinebaug (riv.), Conn. 210/H2
Quinebaug (riv.), Mass. 249/F4
Quines, Argentina 143/C3
Quinhagak, Alaska 196/F3
Qui Nhon, Vietnam 72/F4
Qui Nhon, Vietnam 54/M8
Quiniluban (isls.), Philippines
  82/C5
Quinlan, Okla. 288/J2
Quinlan, Texas 303/H5
Quinn (riv.), Nev. 266/D1
Quinn, S. Dak. 298/E5
Quinn Canyon (range), Nev. 266/F4
Quinnesec, Mich. 250/A3
Quinnimont, W. Va. 312/D7
Quinnipiac, Conn. 210/D3
Quinnipiac (riv.), Conn. 210/D3
Quinta de Tilcoco, Chile 138/G5
Quintana de la Serena, Spain 33/D3
Quintanar de la Orden, Spain 33/E3
Quintana Roo (state), Mexico 150/P7
Quintay, Chile 138/F3
Quinter, Kansas 232/B2
Quintero, Chile 138/F2
Quinto (riv.), Argentina 143/D3
Quinto, Spain 33/F2
Quinto, Switzerland 39/G3
Quinton, Ky. 237/M7
Quinton, N.J. 273/C4
Quinton, Okla. 288/R4
Quinton, Sask. 181/G4
Quinton, Va. 307/O5
Quinwood, W. Va. 312/E6
Quinzau, Angola 115/B5
Quionga, Mozambique 118/G2
Quipapá, Brazil 132/G5
Quipungo, Angola 115/B6
Quirey, Colombia 126/F5
Quirihue, Chile 138/E1
Quirindi, N.S. Wales 97/F3
Quirino (prov.), Philippines 82/C2
Quirino, Philippines 82/C2
Quiriquire, Venezuela 124/G3
Quirke (lake), Ontario 177/B1
Quiroga, Argentina 143/F7
Quiroga, Bolivia 136/C6
Quiroga, Spain 33/C1
Quirusillas, Bolivia 136/D6
Quisiro, Venezuela 124/C2
Quispamsis, New Bruns. 170/E3
Quissanga, Mozambique 118/G2
Quissett, Mass. 249/M6
Quissico, Mozambique 118/F4
Quitaque, Texas 303/C3
Quitasueño (bank), Colombia
  126/A8
Quitilipi, Argentina 143/D2
Quitman, Ark. 202/F3
Quitman (co.), Georgia 217/B8
Quitman, Georgia 217/E9
Quitman, La. 238/E2
Quitman (co.), Miss. 256/D2
Quitman, Miss. 256/D2
Quitman, Miss. 256/H3
Quitman, Mo. 261/C2
Quitman, Texas 303/J5
Quitman (mts.), Texas 303/B11
Quito (cap.), Ecuador 2/F6
Quito (cap.), Ecuador 128/C3
Quito (cap.), Ecuador 120/B2
Quixadá, Brazil 120/F3
Quixadá, Brazil 132/F4
Quixeramobim, Brazil 132/F4
Qujing, China 77/F6
Qulin, Mo. 261/M9
Qum, Iran 54/G6
Qum (Qom), Iran 59/F3
Qum (Qom), Iran 66/G3
Qumar He (riv.), China 77/D4
Qumarlêb, China 77/D5
Qumeim, Jordan 65/D2
Qunfidha, Saudi Arabia 59/D6
Quogue, N.Y. 276/P9
Quoich (riv.), N.W. Terr. 187/J3
Quoich, Loch (lake), Scotland 15/C3
Quonnipaug (lake), Conn. 210/D3
Quorn, S. Australia 88/F6
Quorn, S. Australia 94/F5
Quryat, Oman 59/G5
Qusaiba, Saudi Arabia 59/D4
Quteife, Syria 63/G6
Qu Xian, Sichuan, China 77/G5
Qüxü, China 77/D6
Quyon, Québec 172/A4
Quyuquyó, Paraguay 144/D5
Quzhou, China 77/J6

R

Raab (riv.), Austria 41/C3
Raabs an der Thaya, Austria 41/C2
Raahe, Finland 18/O4
Raalte, Netherlands 27/J4
Ra'anana, Israel 65/B3
Raanes (pen.), N.W. Terr. 187/K2
Raasay (isl.), Scotland 15/C3
Raasay (sound), Scotland 15/B3
Rab, Yugoslavia 45/B3
Rab (isl.), Yugoslavia 45/B3
Rába (riv.), Hungary 41/D3
Raba, Indonesia 85/F7
Rabat (cap.), Morocco 2/J4
Rabat (cap.), Morocco 106/C2
Rabat (cap.), Morocco 102/B1
Rabaul, Papua N.G. 87/E4
Rabaul, Papua N.G. 86/B2
Rabbit (riv.), Mich. 250/D6
Rabbit (isl.), N.S. Wales 97/J2
Rabbit (creek), S. Dak. 298/E3
Rabbit Ears (pass), Colo. 208/G2
Rabbit Ears (range), Colo. 208/F2
Rabbithash, Ky. 237/M3
Rabbit Lake, Sask. 181/G2
Rabbit Lake, Sask. 181/M2

Rabigh, Saudi Arabia 59/C5
Rabinal, Guatemala 154/B3
Rabka, Poland 47/D4
Rabocheostrovsk, U.S.S.R. 52/D1
Rabun, Ala. 195/C6
Rabun (co.), Georgia 217/F1
Rabun (lake), Georgia 217/E1
Rabun Gap, Georgia 217/F1
Raccoon (pt.), Fla. 212/D3
Raccoon, Ind. 227/D5
Raccoon (riv.), Iowa 229/D4
Raccoon (riv.), La. 238/H8
Raccoon (creek), N.J. 273/C4
Raccoon (creek), Ohio 284/F8
Race (pt.), Mass. 249/M4
Race (cape), Newf. 166/D2
Race (cape), Newf. 146/N5
Race (cape), Newf. 162/L6
Raceland, Ky. 237/R3
Raceland, La. 238/G7
Racepond, Georgia 217/H8
Rachel, W. Va. 312/F3
Rach Gia, Vietnam 72/E5
Racibórz, Poland 47/C3
Racine, Minn. 255/F5
Racine, Mo. 261/C9
Racine, Ohio 284/F8
Racine, Québec 172/E4
Racine, W. Va. 312/C6
Racine (co.), Wis. 317/K10
Racine, Wis. 188/J2
Racine, Wis. 317/M3
Räckeve, Hungary 41/E3
Rackham, Manitoba 179/B4
Raco, Mich. 250/E2
Racola, Mo. 261/L6
Radama (isls.), Madagascar
  118/H2
Rădăuţi, Romania 45/G2
Radbuza (riv.), Czech. 41/B2
Radcliff, Ky. 237/K5
Radcliff, Ohio 284/F7
Radcliffe, England 13/H2
Radcliffe, Iowa 229/G4
Radeberg, Germany 22/E3
Radebeul, Germany 22/E3
Radenthein, Austria 41/B3
Rader, Tenn. 237/R8
Radersburg, Mont. 262/E4
Radford (I.C.), Va. 307/G6
Radhanpur, India 68/C4
Radiant, Va. 307/M4
Radisson, Québec 174/B2
Radisson, Sask. 181/D3
Radisson, Wis. 317/D4
Radium, Colo. 208/G3
Radium, Kansas 232/D3
Radium, Minn. 255/B2
Radium Hill, S. Australia 88/G6
Radium Hill, S. Australia 94/G5
Radium Hot Springs, Br. Col. 184/J5
Radium Springs, N. Mex. 274/B6
Radkersburg, Austria 41/C3
Radley, Ind. 227/F4
Radnice, Czech. 41/B2
Radnor, Ind. 227/D3
Radnor, Ohio 284/D5
Radnor (for.), Wales 13/D5
Radnor, W. Va. 312/A6
Radolfzell, Germany 22/C5
Radom, Ill. 222/D5
Radom (prov.), Poland 47/E3
Radom, Poland 7/G3
Radom, Poland 47/E3
Radomir, Bulgaria 45/F4
Radomsko, Poland 47/D3
Radovišt, Yugoslavia 45/F5
Radstadt, Austria 41/B3
Radviliškis, U.S.S.R. 53/B3
Radville, Sask. 162/F6
Radville, Sask. 181/G6
Radway, Alberta 182/D2
Radziejów, Poland 47/D2
Radzyń Podlaski, Poland 47/F3
Rae (isth.), N.W.T. 162/H2
Rae (isth.), N.W.T. 187/K3
Rae (riv.), N.W.T. 187/G3
Rae (isr.), N.W.T. 187/J3
Rae-Edzo, N.W.T. 162/E4
Rae-Edzo, N.W.T. 187/G3
Raeford, N.C. 281/L5
Rae Lake, N.W.T. 187/G3
Raeren, Belgium 27/M7
Raeside (lake), W. Australia 88/C5
Raeside (lake), W. Australia 92/C5
Raetihi, N. Zealand 100/E3
Raeville, Nebr. 264/F3
Rafaela, Argentina 143/F5
Rafaela, Argentina 120/C6
Rafah, Gaza Strip 65/A5
Rafai, Cent. Afr. Rep. 115/D2
Rafidiya, West Bank 65/C3
Rafsanjan, Iran 59/G3
Rafsanjan, Iran 54/G6
Raft (riv.), Idaho 220/E7
Raft (riv.), Utah 304/A1
Raft River (mts.), Utah 304/A2
Rafz, Switzerland 39/G1
Raga, Sudan 111/E6
Ragang (vol.), Philippines 82/E7
Ragay (gulf), Philippines 82/D4
Ragged (isl.), Bahamas 159/D2
Ragged (pt.), Barbados 161/C8
Ragged (isl.), Maine 243/G3
Ragged (lake), Maine 243/E4
Ragged (isl.), Newf. 166/C2
Raglan, N. Zealand 100/E4
Raglan (harb.), N. Zealand 100/E2
Ragland, Ala. 195/G4
Ragley, La. 238/D5
Rago, Kansas 232/D4
Ragsdale, Ind. 227/C7
Ragusa (prov.), Italy 34/E6
Ragusa, Italy 34/E6
Ragusa (Dubrovnik), Yugoslavia
  45/C4
Raha, Indonesia 85/G6

Rahaeng (Tak), Thailand 72/C3
Rahan, Ireland 17/F5
Rahimyar Khan, Pakistan 68/C3
Rahotu, N. Zealand 100/D3
Rahue (riv.), Chile 138/D3
Rahway, N.J. 273/E2
Raiatea (isl.), Fr. Poly. 87/L7
Raíces, Argentina 143/G6
Raichur, India 68/D5
Raiford, Fla. 212/D1
Raigarh, India 68/E4
Railley (mt.), Mont. 262/C3
Railroad (valley), Nev. 266/F4
Railroad, Pa. 294/J6
Railroad Canyon (res.), Calif. 204/E11
Railton, Tasmania 99/C3
Rainbow (riv.), Chile 138/D3
Rainbow, Conn. 210/E1
Rainbow (mt.), Idaho 220/C4
Rainbow (plat.), Ariz. 198/D2
Rainbow, Conn. 210/E1
Rainbow (mt.), Idaho 220/C4
Rainbow (lake), Maine 243/E4
Rainbow, Victoria 97/A4
Rainbow Bridge Nat'l Mon., Utah 304/C6
Rainbow City, Ala. 195/F3
Rainbow Lake, Alberta 182/A5
Rainelle, W. Va. 312/E7
Rainier, Alberta 182/D4
Rainier, Oreg. 291/E1
Rainier (mt.), Wash. 188/B1
Rainier, Wash. 310/C4
Rainier (mt.), Wash. 310/D4
Rains, S.C. 296/J3
Rains (co.), Texas 303/J5
Rainsboro, Ohio 284/C7
Rainsburg, Pa. 294/F6
Rainsville, Ala. 195/G2
Rainsville, Ind. 227/C4
Rainsville, N. Mex. 274/D2
Rainy (riv.), Minn. 188/H1
Rainy (lake), Minn. 188/H1
Rainy (lake), Minn. 255/E2
Rainy (riv.), Minn. 255/D2
Rainy (lake), Ont. 162/G6
Rainy (lake), Ontario 177/G5
Rainy (lake), Ontario 175/B3
Rainy River, Ont. 162/G6
Rainy River (terr. dist.), Ontario 177/G5
Rainy River (terr. dist.), Ontario 175/B3
Rainy River, Ontario 175/A3
Rainy River, Ontario 177/F5
Raipur, India 54/K7
Raipur, India 68/E4
Raisin, Calif. 204/E4
Raisin (riv.), Mich. 250/F7
Raisio, Finland 18/M8
Raith, Ontario 175/C3
Raith, Ontario 177/G5
Raivavae (isl.), Fr. Poly. 87/M8
Raja Ampat Group (isls.), Indonesia 85/H6
Rajahmundry, India 68/E5
Rajang (riv.), Malaysia 85/E5
Rajapalaiyam, India 68/D7
Rajapur, India 68/C5
Rajasthan (state), India 68/C3
Rajec, Czech. 41/E2
Rajgarh, India 68/D4
Rajka, Hungary 41/D3
Rajkot, India 54/H7
Rajkot, India 68/C4
Rajnandgaon, India 68/E4
Rajpipla, India 68/C4
Rajpur, India 68/F2
Rajpura, India 68/D2
Rajshahi, Bangladesh 68/F4
Rakahanga (atoll), Cook Is. 87/K7
Rakaia, N. Zealand 100/C5
Rakaia (riv.), N. Zealand 100/C5
Rakamaz, Hungary 41/F2
Rakan, Ras (cape), Qatar 59/F4
Rakaposhi (mt.), Pakistan 68/C1
Rakaposhi (mt.), Pakistan 59/K2
Rakata (isl.), Indonesia 85/C7
Rake, Iowa 229/F2
Rakhine (state), Burma 72/B3
Rakhov, U.S.S.R. 52/B5
Rakino (isl.), N. Zealand 100/C1
Rakitu (isl.), N. Zealand 100/E2
Rakkestad, Norway 18/G7
Rakof (isls.), Alaska 196/M1
Rákospalota, Hungary 41/E3
Rakovník, Czech. 41/B1
Rakvere, U.S.S.R. 53/D1
Rakvere, U.S.S.R. 52/C3
Raleigh, Fla. 212/D1
Raleigh, Georgia 217/C5
Raleigh, Ill. 222/E6
Raleigh, Ind. 227/G5
Raleigh, Miss. 256/F6
Raleigh, Newf. 166/C4
Raleigh (cap.), N.C. 146/L6
Raleigh (cap.), N.C. 188/L3
Raleigh (cap.), N.C. 281/M3
Raleigh (bay), N.C. 281/S5
Raleigh, N. Dak. 282/H7
Raleigh, Tenn. 237/B10
Raleigh (co.), W. Va. 312/D7
Raleigh, W. Va. 312/D7
Ralik Chain (isls.), Marshall Is. 87/G5
Ralls (co.), Mo. 261/J3
Ralls, Texas 303/C4
Ralph, Ala. 195/D4
Ralph, Mich. 250/B2
Ralph, Sask. 181/H6
Ralph, S. Dak. 298/C2
Ralphton, Pa. 294/D5
Ralston, Alberta 182/A4
Ralston, Iowa 229/D4
Ralston, Nebr. 264/J3
Ralston, N.J. 273/D2
Ralston, Okla. 288/N2
Ralston, Pa. 294/H2
Ralston, Tenn. 237/D8
Ralston, Wash. 310/G4

Ralston, Wyo. 319/D1
Ram (head), Virgin Is. (U.S.) 161/C5
Rama, Nicaragua 154/E4
Rama, Sask. 181/H4
Ramadi, Iraq 59/D3
Ramadi, Iraq 66/C4
Ramage, W. Va. 312/C7
Ramah (bay), Newf. 166/B2
Ramah, N. Mex. 274/A3
Ramallah, West Bank 65/C4
Ramallo, Argentina 143/F6
Ramapo (riv.), N.J. 273/E1
Ramat Gan, Israel 65/B3
Ramat Hasharon, Israel 65/B3
Rambi (isl.), Fiji 86/R10
Ramblewood, N.J. 273/D4
Rambouillet, France 28/D3
Rame, Israel 65/C2
Ramea, Newf. 166/C4
Ramea (isls.), Newf. 166/C4
Ramechhap, Nepal 68/F3
Ramelton, Ireland 17/F1
Ramer, Ala. 195/F6
Ramer, Tenn. 237/D10
Rameswaram, India 68/D7
Ramey, Minn. 255/E6
Ramey, Pa. 294/F4
Ramey A.F.B., P. Rico 161/A1
Ramhormoz, Iran 66/F5
Ramhurst, Georgia 217/C1
Ramières (isl.), Martinique 161/C6
Ramla, Israel 65/B4
Ramm, Jebel (mt.), Jordan 65/D5
Ramme, Denmark 21/B4
Rammun, West Bank 65/C4
Ramnäs, Sweden 18/J7
Ramon (mt.), Israel 65/D5
Ramon, N. Mex. 274/D4
Ramona, Calif. 204/J10
Ramona, Kansas 232/E3
Ramona, Okla. 288/P1
Ramona, S. Dak. 298/P5
Ramón Castilla, Peru 128/G5
Ramón de las Yaguas, Cuba 158/J4
Ramón Santana, Dom. Rep. 158/F6
Ramón Trigo, Uruguay 145/E3
Ramore, Ontario 177/K5
Ramore, Ontario 177/K5
Ramos (riv.), Mexico 150/G4
Ramos Árizpe, Mexico 150/J4
Ramosch, Switzerland 39/K3
Ramotswa, Botswana 118/H1
Rampart, Alaska 196/H1
Ramparts (riv.), N.W.T. 187/E3
Rampur, Him. Pradesh, India 68/D2
Rampur, Uttar Pradesh, India 68/D3
Ramree (isl.), Burma 72/B3
Ramsay, Mich. 250/F2
Ramsay, Mont. 262/D4
Ramsay, Ontario 177/J5
Ramsbottom, England 13/H2
Ramsele, Sweden 18/K5
Ramsen, Switzerland 39/G1
Ramseur, N.C. 281/K3
Ramsey, England 10/F4
Ramsey, England 13/G5
Ramsey, Ill. 222/D4
Ramsey, Ind. 227/E8
Ramsey, I. of Man 13/C3
Ramsey, I. of Man 13/C3
Ramsey (bay), I. of Man 13/C3
Ramsey (co.), Minn. 255/E5
Ramsey, Minn. 255/E5
Ramsey, N.J. 273/B1
Ramsey (co.), N. Dak. 282/N3
Ramsey (mt.), Tasmania 99/B3
Ramsey (isl.), Wales 13/B6
Ramsgate, England 13/G5
Ramsgate, England 13/G6
Ramsjö, Sweden 18/J5
Ramu (riv.), Papua N.G. 85/B7
Ramunia, Tanjong (pt.), Malaysia 72/F6
Ramville (isl.), Martinique 161/D6
Rana (fjord), Norway 18/H3
Rana (riv.), Norway 18/J3
Ranau, Malaysia 85/F4
Ranburne, Ala. 195/H3
Rancagua, Chile 138/D5
Rancagua, Chile 120/B6
Ranchester, Wyo. 319/E1
Ranchi, India 68/F4
Rancho Cordova, Calif. 204/C8
Rancho Cucamonga, Calif. 204/E10
Rancho Mirage, Calif. 204/J10
Rancho Palos Verdes, Calif. 204/B11
Rancho Santa Fe, Calif. 204/H10
Ranchos de Taos, N. Mex. 274/D4
Rancho Veloz, Cuba 158/D1
Ranchuelo, Cuba 158/E4
Ranchwood Manor, Okla. 288/L4
Ranco (lake), Chile 138/E3
Rancocas, N.J. 273/D3
Rancocas (creek), N.J. 273/D3
Rand, Colo. 208/G2
Randalia, Iowa 229/K3
Randall, Iowa 229/F4
Randall, Kansas 232/D2
Randall, Minn. 255/D5
Randall (co.), Texas 303/C2
Randall (mt.), W. Australia 88/B3
Randallstown, N. Ireland 17/J2
Randburg, S. Africa 118/H6
Randers, Denmark 18/G8
Randers, Denmark 21/C5
Randfontein, S. Africa 118/G6
Randle, Wash. 310/D4
Randleman, N.C. 281/K3
Randles, Mo. 261/N8
Randlett, Okla. 288/K6
Randlett, Utah 304/E3
Randolph (co.), Ala. 195/H4
Randolph, Ala. 195/E5
Randolph, Ariz. 198/D6
Randolph (co.), Ark. 202/H1

Randolph (co.), Georgia 217/C7
Randolph (co.), Ill. 222/D5
Randolph (co.), Ind. 227/G4
Randolph, Iowa 229/B7
Randolph, Kansas 232/F2
Randolph •, Maine 243/D7
Randolph, Md. 245/K4
Randolph •, Mass. 249/D8
Randolph, Minn. 255/E6
Randolph, Miss. 256/F2
Randolph (co.), Mo. 261/G3
Randolph, Mo. 261/P5
Randolph, Nebr. 264/G2
Randolph •, N.H. 268/E3
Randolph •, N.J. 273/D2
Randolph, N.Y. 276/C6
Randolph (co.), N.C. 281/K3
Randolph, Ohio 284/H3
Randolph, Utah 304/D8
Randolph, Vt. 268/B4
Randolph •, Vt. 268/B4
Randolph, Va. 307/L7
Randolph, Wis. 317/H8
Randolph A.F.B., Texas 303/K10
Randolph Center, Vt. 268/B4
Random (isl.), Newf. 166/D2
Random (sound), Newf. 166/D2
Random Lake, 317/K8
Randsburg, Calif. 204/H8
Randwick, N. S. Wales 88/L4
Randwick, N.S. Wales 97/J3
Ranelagh, Tasmania 99/C4
Ranfurly, Alberta 182/E3
Ranfurly, N. Zealand 100/B6
Rangamati, Bangladesh 68/G4
Rangasa (cape), Indonesia 85/F6
Rangatira (isl.), N. Zealand 100/E7
Range, Ala. 195/D8
Range (creek), Utah 304/D4
Rangeley, Maine 243/B6
Rangeley •, Maine 243/B6
Rangeley (lake), Maine 243/B6
Rangely, Colo. 208/B2
Ranger, Georgia 217/C2
Ranger (peak), Idaho 220/D3
Ranger, N.C. 281/A4
Ranger, Sask. 181/D2
Ranger, Texas 303/F5
Ranger, W. Va. 312/B6
Rangiauria (Pitt) (isl.), N. Zealand 100/E7
Rangiora, N. Zealand 100/D5
Rangiroa (atoll), Fr. Poly. 87/M7
Rangitaiki (riv.), N. Zealand 100/E4
Rangitata (riv.), N. Zealand 100/C5
Rangitikei (riv.), N. Zealand 100/D5
Rangitoto (isl.), N. Zealand 100/C1
Rangkasbitung, Indonesia 85/G2
Rangoon (div.), Burma 72/C3
Rangoon (cap.), Burma 2/P5
Rangoon (cap.), Burma 54/L8
Rangoon (cap.), Burma 72/C3
Rangoon, W. Va. 312/C7
Rangpur, Bangladesh 68/F3
Rania, Iraq 66/D2
Ranier, Minn. 255/E2
Ranken (riv.), North. Terr. 93/E6
Rankin, Ill. 222/F3
Rankin (co.), Miss. 256/E6
Rankin, Pa. 294/C7
Rankin, Texas 303/B6
Rankine Store, North. Terr. 93/E5
Rankin Inlet, N.W. Terr. 187/J3
Rankins Springs, N.S. Wales 97/J3
Rankweil, Austria 41/A3
Ranlo, N.C. 281/G4
Rannoch (dist.), Scotland 15/D4
Rannoch, Loch (lake), Scotland 10/D2
Rannoch, Loch (lake), Scotland 15/D4
Ranong, Thailand 72/C5
Ransiki, Indonesia 85/J6
Ransom, Il!. 222/E2
Ransom, Kansas 232/C3
Ransom (co.), N. Dak. 282/P7
Ransom, Pa. 294/F7
Ransomville, N.Y. 276/C4
Ranson, W. Va. 312/L4
Rantauprapat, Indonesia 85/C5
Rantekombola (mt.), Indonesia 85/F6
Rantis, West Bank 65/C3
Rantoul, Ill. 222/E4
Rantoul, Kansas 232/G3
Ranua, Finland 18/P4
Ranui, N. Zealand 100/B1
Ranum, Denmark 21/C4
Ranya, Wadi (dry riv.), Saudi Arabia 59/D5
Rao Co (mt.), Laos 72/E3
Rao Co (mt.), Vietnam 72/E3
Raohe, China 77/M2
Raoui, Erg er (des.), Algeria 106/D3
Raoul (isl.), N. Zealand 87/K8
Raoul (cape), Tasmania 99/D5
Rapa (isl.), Fr. Poly. 87/M8
Rapa Nui (Easter) (isl.), Chile 87/Q8
Rapch (riv.), Iran 66/L8
Rapel, Chile 138/F4
Rapel (riv.), Chile 138/F4
Rapelje, Mont. 262/G6
Raper (cape), N.W.T. 162/K2
Raper (cape), N.W.T. 187/M3·
Raphine, W. Va. 307/K5
Raphoe, Ireland 17/F2
Rapid (riv.), Mich. 250/B2
Rapid (riv.), Minn. 255/D2
Rapidan, Va. 307/M4
Rapidan (riv.), Va. 307/M4
Rapid City, Manitoba 179/B4
Rapid City, Mich. 250/D4
Rapid City, S. Dak. 146/H5
Rapid City, S. Dak. 188/F2
Rapid City, S. Dak. 298/C5
Rapide-Blanc, Québec 174/C3

Rapides (par.), La. 238/E4
Rapide Taureau (dam), Québec 172/D3
Rapid River, Mich. 250/C3
Rapids City, Ill. 222/C2
Rapid View, Sask. 181/C1
Räpina, U.S.S.R. 53/D1
Raposos, Brazil 135/E2
Rappahannock (co.), Va. 307/M3
Rappahannock (riv.), Va. 307/P4
Rapperswil, Switzerland 39/G2
Rápulo (riv.), Bolivia 136/C4
Rapti (riv.), Bolivia 136/C4
Raqqa (El Rashid), Syria 63/H5
Rarají (atoll), Fr. Poly. 87/M7
Raron, Switzerland 39/E4
Rarotonga (isl.), Cook Is. 87/K8
Rasa (isl.), Philippines 82/B6
Ra's al Khafji, Saudi Arabia 59/E4
Ras al Khaimah, U.A.E. 59/G4
Ras Asēr (cape), Somalia 102/H3
Ras Asēr (cape), Somalia 115/K1
Ras Dashan (mt.), Ethiopia 102/F3
Ras Dashan (mt.), Ethiopia 111/G5
Raseiniai, U.S.S.R. 53/B3
Ra's en Naqb, Jordan 65/E5
Ras Ghârib, Egypt 111/F2
Rashad, Sudan 111/F5
Ras Hafun (cape), Somalia 102/H3
Ras Hafun (cape), Somalia 115/K1
Rasharkin, N. Ireland 17/J2
Rasheiya, Lebanon 63/F6
Rashid (Rosetta), Egypt 111/J2
Rashid (Rosetta), Egypt 59/B3
Rashid (prov.), Syria 63/H5
Rasht, Iran 59/E2
Rasht, Iran 66/F2
Rask, Iran 66/M7
Rask, Ko (isl.), Thailand 72/C6
Rasmark, N. Dak. 282/C4
Rason (lake), W. Australia 88/C5
Rason (lake), W. Australia 92/D5
Rasskazovo, U.S.S.R. 52/F4
Ras Tanura, Saudi Arabia 59/F4
Rastatt, Germany 22/C4
Rastede, Germany 22/C2
Rat (isls.), Alaska 196/K4
Rat (riv.), Manitoba 179/F5
Ratak Chain (isls.), Marshall Is. 87/G5
Ratangarh, India 68/C3
Rat Buri, Thailand 72/C4
Ratcliff, Ark. 202/C3
Ratcliff, Texas 303/J6
Ratcliffe, Sask. 181/G6
Rathangan, Ireland 17/G5
Rathbun, Iowa 229/H7
Rathbun (lake), Iowa 229/G7
Rathcoole, Ireland 17/F7
Rathcormac, Ireland 17/E7
Rathdowney, Ireland 17/F6
Rathdrum, Idaho 220/A2
Rathdrum, Ireland 17/J6
Rathedaung, Burma 72/B2
Rathenow, Germany 22/E2
Rathfriland, N. Ireland 17/J3
Rathgormuck, Ireland 17/F7
Rathkeale, Ireland 17/D7
Rathkeale, Ireland 17/D6
Rathlin (isl.), N. Ireland 10/C3
Rathlin (isl.), N. Ireland 17/J1
Rathlin (sound), N. Ireland 17/J1
Rathlin O'Birne (isl.), Ireland 17/C2
Rathluirc, Ireland 10/B4
Rathluirc, Ireland 17/D7
Rathmore, Ireland 17/J5
Rathmullen, Ireland 17/F1
Rathnew-Merrymeeting, Ireland 17/J6
Rathowen, Ireland 17/F4
Rathvilly, Ireland 17/H6
Rathwell, Manitoba 179/D5
Ratibor (Racibórz), Poland 47/C3
Ratingen, Germany 22/B3
Ratio, Ark. 202/C6
Ratlam, India 68/C4
Ratliff City, Okla. 288/M6
Ratnagiri, India 68/C5
Ratnapura, Sri Lanka 68/E7
Ratoath, Ireland 17/J5
Raton, N. Mex. 188/F3
Raton, N. Mex. 274/E2
Rats (riv.), Québec 172/D2
Rattan, China 288/R6
Ratten, Austria 41/C3
Rattlesnake (creek), Kansas 232/D4
Rattlesnake (creek), Ohio 284/C7
Rattlesnake (creek), Oreg. 291/K5
Rattlesnake (hills), Wyo. 319/E3
Rattlesnake (range), Wyo. 319/E3
Rattray (head), Scotland 15/G3
Rättvik, Sweden 18/J6
Ratzeburg, Germany 22/D2
Raub, Ind. 227/C3
Raub, Malaysia 72/D7
Raub, N. Dak. 282/H4
Rauch, Argentina 143/E4
Rauch, Minn. 255/E3
Raukumara (range), N. Zealand 100/F3
Raul Leoni (dam), Venezuela 124/G4
Raul Soares, Brazil 135/E2
Rauma, Finland 18/M6
Rauma (riv.), Norway 18/F5
Raunds, England 13/G5
Raung (mt.), Indonesia 85/L2

Raurkela, India 68/F4
Rausu, Japan 81/M1
Rauville, S. Dak. 298/P3
Ravalli (co.), Mont. 262/B4
Ravalli, Mont. 262/C7
Ravanna, Ark. 202/C7
Ravanna, Mo. 261/E2
Ravar, Iran 59/G3
Ravar, Iran 66/K5
Ravelo, Bolivia 136/C6
Ravels, Belgium 27/G6
Raven, Va. 307/E6
Ravena, N.Y. 276/N6
Ravendale, Calif. 204/E3
Ravenden, Ark. 202/H1
Ravenden Springs, Ark. 202/H1
Ravenel, S.C. 296/J6
Ravenna (prov.), Italy 34/D2
Ravenna, Ky. 237/D5
Ravenna, Italy 34/D2
Ravenna, Nebr. 264/F4
Ravenna, Ohio 284/H3
Ravenna, Texas 303/H4
Raven Rock, W. Va. 312/D4
Ravenscrag, Sask. 181/C6
Ravensdale, Wash. 310/D3
Ravenshoe, Queensland 88/H3
Ravenshoe, Queensland 95/C3
Ravensthorpe, W. Australia 88/C6
Ravensthorpe, W. Australia 92/B6
Ravenswood, W. Va. 312/C5
Ravenwood, Mo. 261/C2
Ravi (riv.), Pakistan 68/C2
Ravia, Okla. 288/N6
Ravine, Pa. 294/K4
Ravinia, S. Dak. 298/N7
Ravne na Koroškem, Yugoslavia 45/B2
Rawalpindi, Pakistan 54/J6
Rawalpindi, Pakistan 68/C2
Rawalpindi, Pakistan 59/K3
Rawa Mazowiecka, Poland 47/E3
Rawdon, Québec 172/D3
Rawene, N. Zealand 100/D2
Rawhide (creek), Wyo. 319/G1
Rawhide (creek), Wyo. 319/G1
Rawi, Ko (isl.), Thailand 72/C6
Rawicz, Poland 47/C3
Rawlings, Md. 245/C2
Rawlings, Va. 307/N7
Rawlina, W. Australia 88/C6
Rawlina, W. Australia 92/D5
Rawlins (co.), Kansas 232/A2
Rawlins, Wyo. 188/E2
Rawlins, Wyo. 319/E4
Rawson, Argentina 120/C7
Rawson, N. Dak. 282/D3
Rawson, Buenos Aires, Argentina 143/F7
Rawson, Chubut, Argentina 143/D5
Rawson, N. Dak. 282/C4
Rawson, Ohio 284/C4
Rawtenstall, England 13/H1
Rawtenstall, England 10/G2
Raxaul, India 68/E3
Ray (mts.), Alaska 196/H1
Ray, Ill. 222/C3
Ray, Minn. 255/E2
Ray (co.), Mo. 261/E4
Ray (cape), Newf. 166/C4
Ray (cape), Newf. 162/K6
Ray, N. Dak. 282/D3
Ray, Ohio 284/E7
Raya (mt.), Indonesia 85/E6
Rayagada, India 68/E5
Rayborn, Mo. 261/H8
Raychikhinsk, U.S.S.R. 48/N5
Ray City, Georgia 217/F8
Ray Hubbard (lake), Texas 303/H2
Rayland, Ohio 284/J5
Rayle, Georgia 217/G3
Rayleigh, Br. Col. 184/G5
Rayleigh, England 13/J8
Raymer (New Raymer), Colo. 208/M1
Raymond, Alberta 182/D5
Raymond, Calif. 204/F6
Raymond, Idaho 220/G7
Raymond, Ill. 222/D4
Raymond, Ind. 227/E6
Raymond, Iowa 229/J4
Raymond, Kansas 232/D3
Raymond, Maine 243/B8
Raymond •, Maine 243/B8
Raymond, Minn. 255/C5
Raymond, Miss. 256/D6
Raymond, Mont. 262/P2
Raymond, Nebr. 264/H4
Raymond •, N.H. 268/E5
Raymond, Ohio 284/E5
Raymond, S. Dak. 298/N5
Raymond, Wash. 310/C4
Raymond, Wis. 317/L2
Raymond City, W. Va. 312/C6
Raymond Terrace, N.S. Wales 97/F3
Raymondville, Mo. 261/J8
Raymondville, N.Y. 276/L1
Raymondville, Texas 303/G11
Raymore, Mo. 261/D5
Raymore, Sask. 181/G4
Rayne, La. 238/F6
Raynesford, Mont. 262/F3
Raynham •, Mass. 249/K5
Raynham, N.C. 281/L5
Raynham Center, Mass. 249/K5
Rayón, San Luis Potosí, Mexico 150/K6
Rayón, Sonora, Mexico 150/D2
Rayong, Thailand 72/D4

Rays (lake), Idaho 220/F6
Rays Crossing, Ind. 227/F5
Rayside-Balfour, Ontario 177/K5
Raystown (lake), Pa. 294/F5
Raystown Branch, Juniata (riv.), Pa. 294/F5
Raysut (Risut), Oman 59/F6
Raytown, Mo. 261/P6
Raytown, Mo. 261/P6
Rayville, La. 238/G2
Rayville, Mo. 261/E4
Raywick, Ky. 237/L5
Razan, Iran 66/F3
Razaza (res.), Iraq 66/C4
Razdan, U.S.S.R. 52/G6
Razgrad, Bulgaria 45/H4
Razlog, Bulgaria 45/F5
Ré (isl.), France 28/C4
Rea, Mo. 261/C2
Reader, Ark. 202/C5
Reader, W. Va. 312/D5
Readfield •, Maine 243/D7
Readfield, Maine 243/D7
Readfield, Wis. 317/J7
Reading, England 10/F5
Reading, England 13/F8
Reading, England 13/G8
Reading •, Mass. 249/C5
Reading, Mich. 250/E7
Reading, Minn. 255/C7
Reading, Ohio 284/C9
Reading, Pa. 188/L2
Reading, Pa. 294/L5
Reading •, Vt. 268/B5
Readington, N.J. 273/D2
Readland, Ark. 202/H7
Readlyn, Iowa 229/J3
Readlyn, Sask. 181/F6
Readsboro, Vt. 268/B6
Readsboro •, Vt. 268/B6
Reads Landing, Minn. 255/F6
Reads Mill, Ala. 195/G3
Readstown, Wis. 317/E9
Readsville, Mo. 261/J5
Readville, Mass. 249/C8
Ready, Ky. 237/J6
Readyville, Tenn. 237/J9
Reagan, Okla. 288/N6
Reagan, Tenn. 237/E9
Reagan (co.), Texas 303/C6
Reagan, Texas 303/H6
Real, Cordillera (range), Bolivia 136/A5
Real (co.), Texas 303/E8
Real de San Carlos, Uruguay 145/A5
Realitos, Texas 303/F10
Realp, Switzerland 39/F4
Reamstown, Pa. 294/K5
Reao (atoll), Fr. Poly. 87/N7
Reardan, Wash. 310/H3
Reasnor, Iowa 229/G5
Reaville, N.J. 273/D3
Reay, Scotland 15/E2
Rebecca, Georgia 217/E7
Rebecca (lake), W. Australia 88/C5
Rebecca (lake), W. Australia 92/C5
Rebecq, Belgium 27/E7
Rebersburg, Pa. 294/H4
Rebiana (oasis), Libya 111/D3
Rebiana Sand Sea (des.), Libya 111/D3
Reboledo, Uruguay 145/D4
Rebun (isl.), Japan 81/K1
Recanati, Italy 34/D3
Recherche (arch.), Australia 87/C9
Recherche (arch.), W. Australia 88/C6
Recherche (arch.), W. Australia 92/C6
Rechitsa, U.S.S.R. 52/C4
Rechnitz, Austria 41/D3
Rechthalten, Switzerland 39/D3
Recife, Brazil 132/H5
Recife, Brazil 120/H3
Recife, Brazil 2/H6
Reckingen, Switzerland 39/F4
Recklinghausen, Germany 22/B5
Recluse, Wyo. 319/G1
Reconquista, Argentina 143/F4
Recreo, Argentina 143/C2
Rector, Ark. 202/K1
Rectortown, Va. 307/N3
Recuay, Peru 128/D7
Red (riv.) 146/J3
Red (riv.) 188/H4
Red (sea) 2/L4
Red (sea) 54/E7
Red (riv.) 54/M7
Red (sea) 102/F2
Red (riv.), Ark. 202/C6
Red (mt.), Conn. 210/B1
Red (sea), Egypt 111/G3
Red (riv.), Idaho 220/C4
Red (riv.), Ky. 237/G7
Red (riv.), Ky. 237/O5
Red (riv.), La. 238/G4
Red (riv.), Manitoba 179/F4
Red (lake), Minn. 188/H1
Red (isl.), Newf. 166/C4
Red (bay), N. Ireland 17/J1
Red, North Fork (riv.), Okla. 288/H4
Red (riv.), Okla. 288/R7
Red (lake), Ontario 175/D3
Red (sea), Saudi Arabia 59/C5
Red (lake), S. Dak. 298/L6
Red (sea), Sudan 111/G3
Red (riv.), Tenn. 237/G7
Red (riv.), Texas 303/F3
Red (riv.), U.S.J. 146/J6
Red (riv.), Utah 304/D3
Red (riv.), Vietnam 72/E2
Red (sea), Yemen 59/D5
Reda, Poland 47/D1
Redang, Pulau (isl.), Malaysia 72/D6
Redange, Luxembourg 27/H9
Red Ash, Va. 307/E6
Red Bank, New Bruns. 170/G2
Red Bank, N.J. 273/E3
Redbank (creek), Pa. 294/E3

Red Bank, Tenn. 237/L10
Red Banks, Miss. 256/F1
Red Bay, Ala. 195/B2
Red Bay, Fla. 212/C6
Red Bay, Newf. 166/C3
Red Bay, Ontario 177/C3
Red Beach, Maine 243/J5
Red Bird, Mo. 261/J6
Redbird, Okla. 288/P3
Red Bluff, Calif. 204/C3
Red Bluff (lake), N. Mex. 274/E7
Red Bluff (lake), Texas 188/F4
Red Bluff (lake), Texas 303/A6
Red Boiling Springs, Tenn. 237/K7
Redbridge, England 13/H8
Redbridge, England 10/C5
Red Bud, Ill. 222/D5
Redbush, Ky. 237/P5
Redby, Minn. 255/D3
Redcar, England 10/F3
Redcar, England 13/F3
Red Cedar (riv.), Wis. 317/C5
Red Chute (bayou), La. 238/C1
Redcliff, Alberta 182/E4
Red Cliff, Colo. 208/G4
Red Cliff, Wis. 317/E2
Redcliffe, Queensland 95/E5
Red Cliffe, Queensland 88/J5
Red Cliff Ind. Res., Wis. 317/E2
Red Cliffs, Victoria 97/B4
Redcloud (peak), Colo. 208/E6
Red Cloud, Nebr. 264/F4
Red Creek, N.Y. 276/G4
Red Creek, W. Va. 312/H4
Redcrest, Calif. 204/A3
Red Deer, Alberta 182/D3
Red Deer (lake), Alberta 182/D3
Red Deer (riv.), Alberta 182/D4
Red Deer, Alta. 146/G4
Red Deer, Alta. 162/E5
Red Deer (lake), Manitoba 179/A2
Red Deer (riv.), Manitoba 179/A2
Red Deer (riv.), Sask. 181/K3
Red Deer (riv.), Sask. 181/A5
Red Deer Hill, Sask. 181/J5
Reddell, La. 238/F2
Redden, Del. 245/S5
Red Devil, Alaska 196/G2
Reddick, Fla. 212/D4
Reddick, Ill. 222/E2
Redding, Calif. 146/F5
Redding, Calif. 188/B2
Redding, Calif. 204/C3
Redding •, Calif. 204/80
Redding •, Conn. 210/B3
Redding, Iowa 229/E7
Redding Ridge, Conn. 210/B3
Reddington, Ind. 227/F6
Redditch, England 13/E5
Redditch, England 10/G3
Red Earth Creek, Alberta 182/C1
Red Elm, S. Dak. 298/F3
Redeye (riv.), Minn. 255/D4
Red Feather Lakes, Colo. 208/H1
Redfield, Ark. 202/F5
Redfield, Iowa 229/E5
Redfield, Kansas 232/H4
Redfield, N.Y. 276/J3
Redfield, Sask. 181/D2
Redfield, S. Dak. 298/O3
Redfish (lake), Idaho 220/D5
Redford, Mo. 261/L8
Redford, Texas 303/C12
Red Fork, Powder (riv.), Wyo. 319/F2
Redgranite, Wis. 317/J7
Redhead, Trin. & Tob. 161/B10
Red Head Cove, Newf. 166/D2
Red Hill (mt.), Hawaii 218/K2
Red Hill, Pa. 294/L5
Red Hill Patrick Henry Nat'l Mem., Va. 306/L6
Red Hook, N.Y. 276/N7
Redhouse, Ky. 237/N5
Red House, Nev. 266/D2
Red House, W. Va. 307/L6
Red House, W. Va. 312/C5
Redig, S. Dak. 298/C2
Red Indian (lake), Newf. 166/C4
Redington, Nebr. 264/A3
Redington Beach, Fla. 212/B3
Redington Shores, Fla. 212/B3
Red Jacket, W. Va. 312/B7
Redkey, Ind. 227/G4
Red Lake (co.), Minn. 255/B3
Redlake, Minn. 255/C3
Red Lake (riv.), Minn. 255/B2
Red Lake, Ont. 162/G4
Red Lake, Ontario 175/B2
Red Lake Falls, Minn. 255/B3
Red Lake Ind. Res., Minn. 255/C2
Red Lake Road, Ontario 177/G5
Red Lake Road, Ontario 175/B2
Redland, Alberta 182/D4
Redland, Oreg. 291/B2
Redlands, Calif. 204/H9
Red Level, Ala. 195/E8
Red Lick, Miss. 256/B7
Red Lion, Del. 245/R2
Red Lion, N.J. 273/D4
Red Lion, Ohio 284/B7
Red Lion, Pa. 294/J6
Red Lodge, Mont. 262/G5
Redman, Mich. 250/G5
Red Mesa, Colo. 208/C8
Redmon, Ill. 222/F4
Redmond, Oreg. 291/F3
Redmond, Utah 304/C4
Redmond, Wash. 310/H1
Red Mountain, Calif. 204/H8
Red Oak, Georgia 217/J2
Red Oak, Iowa 229/C6
Red Oak, Mich. 250/E4
Red Oak, N.C. 281/N2
Red Oak, Okla. 288/R5
Red Oak, Texas 303/H5
Red Oak, Va. 307/L7
Red Oaks Mill, N.Y. 276/N7

Redon, France 28/C4
Redonda (isl.), Ant. & Bar. 156/F3
Redondela, Spain 33/B1
Redondo, Portugal 33/C3
Redondo, Wash. 310/C3
Redondo Beach, Calif. 204/B11
Redoubt (vol.), Alaska 196/H2
Redowl, S. Dak. 298/D4
Red Owl (creek), S. Dak. 298/E4
Redpa, Tasmania 99/A2
Regeneração, Brazil 132/F4
Redridge, Mich. 250/G1
Red River (par.), La. 238/D2
Red River, N. Mex. 274/D2
Red River, Nova Scotia 168/H2
Red River, S.C. 296/F2
Red River (co.), Texas 303/G9
Red River Hot Springs, Idaho 220/C4
Red River of the North (riv.) 188/G1
Red River of the North (riv.), Minn. 255/A2
Red River of the North (riv.), N. Dak. 282/S4
Red Rock, Ariz. 198/D6
Red Rock, Br. Col. 184/F3
Red Rock (lake), Iowa 229/G6
Red Rock (lakes), Mont. 262/E6
Red Rock (riv.), Mont. 262/D6
Redrock, N. Mex. 274/A6
Red Rock, Okla. 288/M2
Red Rock, Ontario 177/H5
Red Rock, Ontario 175/C3
Red Rock, Texas 303/G8
Red Scaffold (creek), S. Dak. 298/F4
Red Sea (prov.), Sudan 111/G4
Red Sea Hills (mts.), Sudan 59/C5
Red Springs, N.C. 281/L5
Red Springs, Texas 303/E4
Redstar, W. Va. 312/D7
Redstone, Br. Col. 184/F4
Redstone, Colo. 208/E4
Redstone, Mont. 262/M2
Redstone (riv.), N.W. Terr. 187/F3
Redstone (lake), Ontario 177/F2
Redstone (creek), S. Dak. 298/O5
Redstone Arsenal, Ala. 195/E1
Red Sucker Lake, Manitoba 179/K3
Red Sulphur Springs, W. Va. 312/E7
Redtop, Minn. 255/E4
Redvale, Colo. 208/B6
Redvers, Sask. 181/K6
Red Volta (riv.), Ghana 106/D6
Red Volta (Nazinon) (riv.), Burkina Faso 106/D6
Redwater, Alberta 182/D3
Redwater (riv.), Mont. 262/L3
Redwater (creek), S. Dak. 298/A4
Redway, Calif. 204/B3
Red Willow, Alberta 182/D3
Red Willow (co.), Nebr. 264/D4
Redwine, Ky. 237/P4
Red Wine (riv.), Newf. 166/B3
Red Wing, Colo. 208/J7
Redwing, Kansas 232/D3
Red Wing, Minn. 255/F6
Redwood (co.), Minn. 255/C6
Redwood (riv.), Minn. 255/C6
Redwood, Miss. 256/C6
Redwood, N.Y. 276/J2
Redwood City, Calif. 204/J3
Redwood Estates-Chemeketa Park, Calif. 204/K4
Redwood Falls, Minn. 255/C6
Redwood Nat'l Park, Calif. 204/A2
Redwood Valley, Calif. 204/B4
Ree, Lough (lake), Ireland 10/B4
Ree (lake), Ireland 17/C5
Reece, Kansas 232/F4
Reece City, Ala. 195/G2
Reed, Ark. 202/H6
Reed, Ky. 237/G5
Reed, Okla. 288/G5
Reed (mt.), Québec 174/D2
Reed City, Mich. 250/D5
Reeder, Manitoba 179/A4
Reeder, N. Dak. 282/E7
Reedley, Calif. 204/F7
Reedpoint, Mont. 262/G5
Reeds, Mo. 261/D8
Reedsburg (res.), Mich. 250/E4
Reedsburg, Ohio 284/F4
Reedsburg, Wis. 317/G8
Reeds Ferry, N.H. 268/D6
Reedsport, Oreg. 291/C4
Reeds Spring, Mo. 261/F9
Reedsville, Ohio 284/G7
Reedsville, Pa. 294/G4
Reedsville, W. Va. 312/G4
Reedsville, Wis. 317/L7
Reedville, Oreg. 291/A2
Reedville, Va. 307/R5
Reedy (lake), Fla. 212/E4
Reedy (riv.), S.C. 296/C2
Reedy, W. Va. 312/D5
Reedy (creek), W. Va. 312/D5
Reedyville, Ky. 237/H6
Reef (bay), Virgin Is. (U.S.) 161/C4
Reefton, N. Zealand 100/C5
Ree Heights, S. Dak. 298/L4
Reelfoot (lake), Tenn. 237/C8
Reelsville, Ind. 227/D6
Reeman, Mich. 250/D5
Reese, Mich. 250/F5
Reese (riv.), Nev. 266/D3
Reese A.F.B., Texas 303/B4
Reeseville, Wis. 317/J9
Reesville, Ohio 284/C6
Reeves, La. 238/C5
Reeves (co.), Texas 303/D11
Reeves Knob (mt.), Ark. 202/E2
Reevesville, Ill. 222/E6
Reevesville, S.C. 296/E5
Refahiye, Turkey 63/H3
Refa'i, Iraq 66/E5
Reform, Ala. 195/C4
Reform, Miss. 256/F4

Refton, Pa. 294/K6
Refuge Cove, Br. Col. 184/E5
Refugio (isl.), Chile 138/D5
Refugio (co.), Texas 303/G9
Refugio, Texas 303/G9
Rega (riv.), Poland 47/B2
Regal, Minn. 255/D5
Regan, N. Dak. 282/K5
Regen (riv.), Germany 22/E4
Regen, Germany 22/E4
Regensburg, Germany 7/F4
Regensburg, Germany 22/E4
Regensdorf, Switzerland 39/F2
Regent, Belgium 27/D7
Regent, N. Dak. 282/E7
Reger, Mo. 261/F2
Reggane, Algeria 106/D3
Regge (riv.), Netherlands 27/K4
Reggio, La. 238/L7
Reggio di Calabria (prov.), Italy 34/E5
Reggio di Calabria, Italy 7/F5
Reggio di Calabria, Italy 34/E5
Reggio nell'Emilia (prov.), Italy 34/C2
Reggio nell'Emilia, Italy 34/C2
Reghin, Romania 45/G2
Régina, Fr. Guiana 131/E3
Regina, Mont. 262/J3
Regina, N. Mex. 274/B2
Regina (cap.), Sask. 162/F5
Regina (cap.), Sask. 146/H4
Regina (cap.), Sask. 181/G5
Regina Beach, Sask. 181/F5
Register, Georgia 217/J6
Registro, Brazil 135/C4
Regla, Cuba 158/C1
Regnitz (riv.), Germany 22/D4
Reguengos de Monsaraz, Portugal 33/C3
Regway, Sask. 181/G6
Rehau, Germany 22/D3
Rehoboth, Ala. 195/D6
Rehoboth, Namibia 118/B4
Rehoboth, Namibia 102/D7
Rehoboth, N. Mex. 274/A3
Rehoboth, Va. 307/M7
Rehoboth Beach, Del. 245/T6
Rehovot, Israel 65/B4
Rehrersburg, Pa. 294/K5
Reichenau an der Rax, Austria 41/C3
Reichenbach, Germany 22/E3
Reichenbach im Kandertal, Switzerland 39/E3
Reid, Md. 245/H2
Reid (lake), S. Dak. 298/O3
Reid (rocks), Tasmania 99/B1
Reid, W. Australia 92/E5
Reiden, Switzerland 39/F2
Reids Grove, Md. 245/P6
Reidsville, Georgia 217/H6
Reidsville, N.C. 281/K2
Reidville, S.C. 296/C2
Reily, Ohio 284/A7
Re'im, Israel 65/A5
Reims, France 7/E4
Reims, France 28/E3
Reina Adelaida (arch.), Chile 120/B8
Reina Adelaida (arch.), Chile 138/D9
Reinach in Aargau, Switzerland 39/F2
Reinach in Baselland, Switzerland 39/E2
Reinbeck, Iowa 229/H4
Reindeer (lake) 162/F4
Reindeer (lake), Canada 146/H4
Reindeer (isl.), Manitoba 179/E2
Reindeer (lake), Manitoba 179/H2
Reindeer (lake), Sask. 181/N3
Reindeer (riv.), Sask. 181/M3
Reinersville, Ohio 284/G6
Reinfeld, Germany 22/D2
Reinga (cape), N. Zealand 100/D1
Reinland, Manitoba 179/E5
Reisaelv (riv.), Norway 18/M2
Reisduoddarhal'di (Haltiatunturi), Norway 18/M2
Reiss, Scotland 15/E2
Reisterstown, Md. 245/L3
Reitz, S. Africa 118/D5
Rejaf, Sudan 111/F7
Rejowiec, Poland 47/F3
Répcelak, 41/D3
Repentigny, Québec 172/J4
Replete, W. Va. 312/F5
Repos (lake), Québec 172/C2
Repton, Ala. 195/D8
Republic (co.), Kansas 232/E2
Republic, Kansas 232/E2
Republic, Mich. 250/B2
Republic, Mo. 261/E8
Republic, Ohio 284/D3
Republic, Wash. 310/M2
República Dominicana, Cuba 158/F2
Republican (riv.) 188/F2
Republican (riv.), Colo. 208/P3
Republican (riv.), Kansas 232/E2
Republican (riv.), Nebr. 264/G5
Republican City, Nebr. 264/F4
Republican Grove, Va. 307/K7
Repulse (bay), Queensland 88/H4
Repulse Bay, Canada 4/C14
Repulse Bay, N.W.T. 146/F2
Repulse Bay, N.W.T. 187/K3
Requa, Calif. 204/A2
Requena, Peru 128/F5
Requena, Spain 33/F3
Requína, Chile 138/G5
Rera, Brazil 132/A1

Resaca, Georgia 217/C1
Reşadiye, Turkey 63/G2
Research, Victoria 97/J4
Reseda, Calif. 204/B10
Resende, Brazil 135/D3
Resende, Portugal 33/B2
Reserve, Kansas 232/G2
Reserve, La. 238/M3
Reserve, Mont. 262/M3
Reserve, N. Mex. 274/A5
Reserve, Sask. 181/J3
Reserve, Wis. 317/D4
Reserve Mines, Nova Scotia 168/H2
Resht (Rasht), Iran 66/F2
Reshui, China 77/F4
Resistencia, Argentina 143/E2
Resistencia, Argentina 120/D5
Reşiţa, Romania 45/E3
Resolute, Canada 4/B14
Resolute, N.W.T. 162/G1
Resolute, N.W.T. 187/J2
Resolution (isl.), N. Zealand 100/A6
Resolution (isl.), N.W.T. 146/M3
Resolution (isl.), N.W.T. 162/K3
Resolution (isl.), N.W.T. 187/M3
Resolution Island, N.W.T. 187/M3
Resort, Loch (inlet), Scotland 15/A2
Resource, Sask. 181/G3
Respenda de la Peña, Spain 33/D1
Restauración, Dom. Rep. 158/D5
Rest Haven, Georgia 217/E2
Restigouche (co.), New Bruns. 170/C1
Restigouche (riv.), New Bruns. 170/C1
Restigouche, Québec 172/C2
Reston, Manitoba 179/A5
Reston, Va. 307/R2
Restoule, Ontario 177/E1
Restoule (lake), Ontario 177/E1
Restrepo, Colombia 126/D5
Reszel, Poland 47/E1
Retalhuleu, Guatemala 154/B3
Retamosa, Uruguay 145/E4
Rethel, France 28/F3
Réthimnon, Greece 45/G8
Retie, Belgium 27/G6
Retiro, Chile 138/A11
Retlaw, Alberta 182/D4
Rétság, Hungary 41/E3
Retsil, Wash. 310/A2
Retsof, N.Y. 276/F5
Retz, Austria 41/D2
Reubens, Idaho 220/B5
Réunion (isl.), (Fr.) 2/M7
RÉUNION 118/F5
Reus, Spain 33/G2
Reusel, Netherlands 27/G6
Reuss (riv.), Switzerland 39/F2
Reutlingen, Germany 22/C4
Reutte, Austria 41/A3
Reva, S. Dak. 298/C2
Revadim, Israel 65/B4
Reveille (peak), Nev. 266/E5
Reveille (range), Nev. 266/E4
Revel, France 28/E6
Revel (Tallinn), U.S.S.R. 52/B3
Revelo, Ky. 237/N7
Revelstoke, Br. Col. 162/E5
Revelstoke, Br. Col. 184/J5
Revenue, Sask. 181/B3
Revenue, Sask. 181/D3
Revere, Mass. 249/D6
Revere, Minn. 255/C6
Revere, Mo. 261/J2
Revere, N. Dak. 282/O5
Revere, W. Va. 312/F6
Reverie, Tenn. 237/A9
Revillagigedo (chan.), Alaska 196/N2
Revillagigedo (isl.), Alaska 196/N2
Revillagigedo (isl.), Mexico 146/G8
Revillagigedo (isls.), Mexico 2/D5
Revillagigedo (isls.), Mexico 150/C5
Revillo, S. Dak. 298/R3
Révin, France 28/F3
Revivim, Israel 65/D5
Revúca, Czech. 41/F2
Revuelto (creek), N. Mex. 274/F3
Rew, Pa. 294/F2
Rewa, India 68/E4
Reward, Sask. 181/B3
Rewataya (reef), Indonesia 85/F7
Rewey, Wis. 317/F10
Rex, N.C. 281/M5
Rex, Oreg. 291/A2
Rexburg, Idaho 220/G6
Rexford, Kansas 232/B2
Rexford, Mont. 262/B2
Rexton, Mich. 250/D2
Rexton, New Bruns. 170/F2
Rexville, Ind. 227/G7
Rexville, N.Y. 276/E6
Rey, Iran 59/F2
Rey, Iran 66/G3
Rey (isl.), Panama 154/H6
Rey Bouba, Cameroon 115/B2
Reydell, Ark. 202/G5
Reydon, Okla. 288/G3
Reyes, Bolivia 136/B4
Reyes (pt.), Calif. 204/B6
Reyhanlı, Turkey 63/G5
Reykjanestá (cape), Iceland 7/B2
Reykjanestá (cape), Iceland 21/A2
Reykjavík (cap.), Iceland 4/C11
Reykjavík (cap.), Iceland 7/B2
Reykjavík (cap.), Iceland 21/B1
Reykjavík (cap.), Iceland 18/C1
Reynaud, Sask. 181/F3
Reyno, Ark. 202/J1
Reynolds, Georgia 217/D5
Reynolds (creek), Idaho 220/B6
Reynolds, Ill. 222/C3
Reynolds, Ind. 227/D3
Reynolds (co.), Mo. 261/L8
Reynolds, Mo. 261/K8
Reynolds, Nebr. 264/G4

Reynolds, N. Dak. 282/R4
Reynolds Bridge, Conn. 210/C2
Reynoldsburg, Ohio 284/E6
Reynolds Station, Ky. 237/H5
Reynoldsville, Pa. 294/F3
Reynosa, Mexico 150/K3
Rezaiyeh (Urmia), Iran 66/D2
Reza'iyeh (Urmia), Iran 59/D2
Rezé, France 28/C4
Rēzekne, U.S.S.R. 52/C3
Rēzekne, U.S.S.R. 53/D2
Rhaetian Alps (range), Switzerland 39/J3
Rhame, N. Dak. 282/C7
Rhätikon (mts.), Liecht. 39/J2
Rhätikon (mts.), Switzerland 39/J2
Rhayader, Wales 13/D5
Rhea (creek), Oreg. 291/H2
Rhea (co.), Tenn. 237/M9
Rheatown, Tenn. 237/R8
Rheda-Wiedenbrück, Germany 22/C3
Rheden, Netherlands 27/J4
Rheims (Reims), France 28/E4
Rhein, Sask. 181/J4
Rheinau, Switzerland 39/G1
Rheine, Germany 22/B3
Rheineck, Switzerland 39/J2
Rheinfeld, Sask. 181/D5
Rheinfelden, Switzerland 39/E1
Rheinfelden, Germany 22/B5
Rheinsberg, Germany 22/E2
Rheinwaldhorn (mt.), Switzerland 39/G4
Rhems, S.C. 296/H4
Rhenen, Netherlands 27/H5
Rhéris, Wadi (dry riv.), Morocco 106/D2
Rhine (riv.) 7/E4
Rhine (riv.), Austria 41/A3
Rhine (riv.), France 28/G3
Rhine, Georgia 217/F7
Rhine (riv.), Liecht. 39/J2
Rhine (riv.), Netherlands 27/J5
Rhine (riv.), Germany 22/B3
Rhine (riv.), Switzerland 39/J2
Rhinebeck, N.Y. 276/N7
Rhinecliff, N.Y. 276/N7
Rhineland, Mo. 261/J5
Rhineland, Sask. 181/D5
Rhinelander, Wis. 317/H4
Rhineland-Palatinate (state), Germany 22/B4
Rhinns, The (pen.), Scotland 15/C6
Rhinns (pt.), Scotland 15/B5
Rhino Camp, Uganda 115/F3
Rhir, Wadi (dry riv.), Algeria 106/F2
Rhir (cape), Morocco 106/B2
Rho, Italy 34/B2
Rhode Island 188/M2
RHODE ISLAND 249
Rhode Island (isl.), R.I. 249/J6
Rhode Island (sound), R.I. 249/J7
Rhode Island (state), U.S. 146/M5
Rhodell, W. Va. 312/D7
Rhodes (Ródhos), Greece 45/J7
Rhodes (isl.), Greece 7/G5
Rhodes (isl.), Greece 45/H7
Rhodes (peak), Idaho 220/D3
Rhodes, Iowa 229/G5
Rhodes, Mich. 250/E5
Rhodes Point, Md. 245/O9
Rhodhiss, N.C. 281/F3
Rhododendron, Oreg. 291/F2
Rhodope (mts.), Bulgaria 45/G5
Rhodope (mts.), Greece 45/G5
Rhome, Texas 303/E1
Rhön (mts.), Germany 22/D3
Rhön (mts.), Germany 22/D3
Rhondda, Wales 13/A6
Rhondda, Wales 10/C5
Rhône (dept.), France 28/F5
Rhône (riv.), France 7/E4
Rhône (riv.), France 28/F5
Rhône (riv.), Switzerland 39/D4
Rhosllanerchrugog, Wales 13/D4
Rhu, Scotland 15/A1
Rhu Coigeach (cape), Scotland 15/C2
Rhyl, Wales 13/D4
Rhymney, Wales 13/A6
Rhymney (riv.), Wales 13/B6
Rhynie, Scotland 15/F3
Rhyolite (Ghost Town), Nev. 266/E6
Riachão, Brazil 132/E4
Riachuelo, Uruguay 145/B5
Rialto, Calif. 204/E10
Riana, Tasmania 99/B3
Riaño, Spain 33/D1
Riau (arch.), Indonesia 85/C5
Riau, Spain 33/E2
Riaza, Spain 33/E2
Rib (mt.), Wis. 317/G6
Ribadavia, Spain 33/B1
Ribadeo, Spain 33/C1
Ribamar, Brazil 132/F3
Ribas do Rio Pardo, Brazil 132/C8
Ribat Qila, Pakistan 68/A3
Ribat Qila, Pakistan 59/H4
Ribáuè, Mozambique 118/F3
Ribble (riv.), England 10/E4
Ribble (riv.), England 13/E4
Ribe (co.), Denmark 21/B7
Ribe, Denmark 21/B7
Ribe, Denmark 18/F9
Ribeira, Brazil 135/B4
Ribeira, Brazil 135/B4
Ribeira Brava, Portugal 33/A2
Ribeira de Iguape, Brazil 135/C4
Ribeira de Pena, Portugal 33/C2
Ribeira Grande, C. Verde 106/B7
Ribeirão Preto, Brazil 120/E5
Ribeirão Preto, Brazil 135/C2
Ribeirão Preto, Brazil 132/E8
Ribera, N. Mex. 274/D3
Ribérac, France 28/D5
Riberach an der Riss, Germany 22/C4
Riberalta, Bolivia 136/C2
Riberalta, Bolivia 120/C4

Rib Falls, Wis. 317/G6
Ribla, Kuh-e (riv.), Iran 66/J6
Rib Lake, Wis. 317/F5
Ribnitz-Damgarten, Germany 22/E1
Ribstone, Alberta 182/E3
Říčany u Prahy, Czech. 41/C2
Ricaurte, Colombia 126/A7
Riccarton, N. Zealand 100/D5
Rice, Calif. 204/L9
Rice (co.), Kansas 232/D3
Rice, Kansas 232/E2
Rice (co.), Minn. 255/E6
Rice, Minn. 255/D5
Rice (lake), Minn. 255/E4
Rice (mt.), N.H. 268/E2
Rice (lake), Ontario 177/F3
Rice, Texas 303/H5
Rice, Va. 307/M6
Rice, Wash. 310/G2
Riceboro, Georgia 217/K7
Rice Lake, Wis. 317/F5
Rices Landing, Pa. 294/C6
Riceton, Sask. 181/G5
Ricetown, Ky. 237/O5
Riceville, Iowa 229/H2
Riceville, Pa. 294/C2
Riceville, Tenn. 237/M10
Rich, Miss. 256/D2
Rich (cape), Ontario 177/D3
Rich (co.), Utah 304/C2
Richard, Sask. 181/D3
Richard City, Tenn. 237/K11
Richard Collinson (inlet), N.W. Terr.
   187/G2
Richards, Iowa 229/D4
Richards, Mo. 261/D7
Richards (isl.), N.W. Terr. 187/E3
Richards Bay, S. Africa 118/E5
Richards Gebaur A.F.B., Mo. 261/P6
Richards Landing, Ontario 177/J5
Richardson (riv.), Alberta 182/C5
Richardson, Ky. 237/R5
Richardson (lakes), Maine 243/B6
Richardson (co.), Nebr. 264/J4
Richardson (isls.), N.W. Terr. 187/G3
Richardson, Texas 303/G2
Richardson, W. Va. 312/D5
Richardson (mts.), Yukon 187/E3
Richardsons Landing, Tenn. 237/B10
Richardsville, Ky. 237/J6
Richardsville, New Bruns. 170/D1
Richard Toll, Senegal 106/A5
Richardton, N. Dak. 282/F6
Richburg, N.Y. 276/D6
Richburg, S.C. 296/E2
Rich Creek, Va. 307/G6
Richdale, Alberta 182/E4
Riche (pt.), Newf. 166/C3
Richelieu, Ky. 237/H7
Richelieu (co.), Québec 172/D4
Richelieu (riv.), Québec 172/D4
Richer, Manitoba 179/F5
Richey, Mont. 262/L3
Richfield, Idaho 220/D6
Richfield, Kansas 232/A4
Richfield, Minn. 255/G6
Richfield, N.C. 281/J4
Richfield, Nova Scotia 168/C4
Richfield, Ohio 284/G3
Richfield, Pa. 294/H4
Richfield, Utah 304/B5
Richfield, Wis. 317/K1
Richfield Springs, N.Y. 276/K5
Richford, N.Y. 276/H6
Richford, Vt. 268/B2
Richford•, Vt. 268/B2
Richford, Wis. 317/H7
Rich Fountain, Mo. 261/J6
Richgrove, Calif. 204/F8
Rich Hill, Mo. 261/D6
Richhill, N. Ireland 17/H3
Richibucto, New Bruns. 170/E2
Richibucto (harb.), New Bruns.
   170/F2
Richibucto (riv.), New Bruns.
   170/F2
Richibucto Village, New Bruns.
   170/F2
Rich Lake, Alberta 182/E2
Richland, Fla. 212/D3
Richland, Georgia 217/C6
Richland (co.), Ill. 222/E5
Richland, Ind. 227/C9
Richland (creek), Ind. 227/D6
Richland, Iowa 229/K6
Richland, Kansas 232/G3
Richland (par.), La. 238/G2
Richland, Mich. 250/D4
Richland, Miss. 256/D6
Richland, Mo. 261/H7
Richland (co.), Mont. 262/M3
Richland, Mont. 262/J4
Richland, Nebr. 264/G3
Richland, N.J. 273/D5
Richland, N.Y. 276/H3
Richland (co.), N. Dak. 282/R7
Richland (co.), Ohio 284/E4
Richland, Oreg. 291/K3
Richland, Pa. 294/K5
Richland (co.), S.C. 296/F4
Richland, S.C. 296/E2
Richland, S. Dak. 298/R5
Richland (creek), Tenn. 237/G10
Richland, Texas 303/H6
Richland, Wash. 188/B1
Richland, Wash. 310/F4
Richland (co.), Wis. 317/F9
Richland Balsam (mt.), N.C.
   281/D4
Richland Center, Wis. 317/F9
Richland Hills, Texas 303/F2
Richland-Kennewick, Wash. 310/80
Richlands, N.C. 281/O5
Richlands, Va. 307/E6
Richland Springs, Texas 303/F6
Richlandtown, Pa. 294/M5

Richlea, Sask. 181/C4
Richmond, Ala. 195/D6
Richmond, Ark. 202/B6
Richmond, Br. Col. 184/K3
Richmond, Calif. 204/J1
Richmond, England 13/F3
Richmond, England 10/E3
Richmond (co.), Georgia 217/H4
Richmond, Ill. 222/E1
Richmond, Ind. 227/H5
Richmond, Iowa 229/K6
Richmond, Jamaica 158/J6
Richmond, Kansas 232/G3
Richmond, Ky. 237/N5
Richmond, La. 238/H2
Richmond, Maine 243/D7
Richmond•, Maine 243/D7
Richmond•, Mass. 249/A3
Richmond, Mich. 250/G6
Richmond, Minn. 255/D5
Richmond, Mo. 261/D4
Richmond•, N.H. 268/C6
Richmond (range), N.S. Wales 97/G1
Richmond (riv.), N.S. Wales 97/G1
Richmond (co.), N.Y. 276/M9
Richmond (Staten Island) (borough),
   N.Y. 276/M9
Richmond, N. Zealand 100/D4
Richmond (range), N. Zealand 100/D4
Richmond (co.), N.C. 281/H4
Richmond (co.), Nova Scotia 168/H3
Richmond (Grand River), Ohio 284/H2
Richmond, Ohio 284/J5
Richmond, Ontario 177/J2
Richmond (co.), Québec 172/E4
Richmond, Québec 172/E4
Richmond, Queensland 88/G4
Richmond, Queensland 95/B4
Richmond (peak), St. Vin. & Grens.
   161/A8
Richmond, S. Africa 118/C6
Richmond, Tasmania 99/D3
Richmond, Texas 303/J8
Richmond, Utah 304/C2
Richmond, Vt. 268/A3
Richmond•, Vt. 268/A3
Richmond, Victoria 88/L7
Richmond, Victoria 97/J5
Richmond (co.), Va. 307/M9
Richmond (cap.), Va. 188/L3
Richmond (cap.), Va. 146/L6
Richmond (cap.) (I.C.), Va. 307/O5
Richmond Beach-Innis Arden, Wash.
   310/A1
Richmond Corner, Maine 243/D7
Richmond Corner, New Bruns.
   170/C2
Richmond Dale, Ohio 284/E7
Richmond Furnace, Mass. 249/A3
Richmond Heights, Fla. 212/F6
Richmond Heights, Mo. 261/P3
Richmond Heights, Ohio 284/H9
Richmond Highlands, Wash. 310/A1
Richmond Hill, Georgia 217/K7
Richmond Hill, Ontario 177/J4
Richmond Nat'l Battlefield Park,
   Va. 307/O6
Richmond upon Thames, England
   10/B5
Richmond upon Thames, England
   13/H8
Richmondville, N.Y. 276/M5
Richmond-Windsor, N.S. Wales
   97/F3
Richmound, Sask. 181/B5
Rich Mountain, Ark. 202/B4
Rich Square, N.C. 281/P2
Richterswil, Switzerland 39/G2
Richthofen (mt.), Colo. 208/G2
Richton, Miss. 256/G8
Richton Park, Ill. 222/B6
Richvale, Calif. 204/D4
Richvalley, Ind. 227/F3
Richview, Ill. 222/D5
Richville, Mich. 250/F5
Richville, Minn. 255/C4
Richville, N.Y. 276/K2
Richwood, La. 238/G2
Richwood, Minn. 255/C4
Richwood, N.J. 273/B2
Richwood, Ohio 284/D5
Richwood, W. Va. 312/F6
Richwood, Wis. 317/J9
Richwoods, Mo. 261/L6
Rickardsville, Iowa 229/M3
Rickenbacker Air Force Base,
   Ohio 284/E6
Ricketts, Iowa 229/B4
Ricketts (pt.), Victoria 97/J6
Ricketts (pt.), Victoria 88/L8
Rickman, Tenn. 237/L8
Rickmansworth, England 13/G8
Rickmansworth, England 10/A5
Rickreall, Oreg. 291/D3
Ricla, Spain 33/F2
Rico, Colo. 208/C7
Ricobayo (res.), Spain 33/D2
Ricse, Hungary 41/G2
Ridderkerk, Netherlands 27/F5
Riddle, Idaho 220/B7
Riddle, Oreg. 291/D5
Riddlesburg, Pa. 294/F5
Riddleton, Tenn. 237/J8
Riddleville, Georgia 217/G5
Riddon, Loch (inlet), Scotland
   15/C5
Rideau (lake), Ontario 177/H3
Riderwood, Ala. 195/B6
Ridge, Md. 245/N8
Ridge, Mont. 262/M5
Ridgecrest, Calif. 204/H8
Ridgecrest, La. 238/G2
Ridgedale, Mo. 261/F9
Ridgedale, Sask. 181/H2
Ridge Farm, Ill. 222/F4
Ridgefield, Conn. 210/B3
Ridgefield•, Conn. 210/B3
Ridgefield, N.J. 273/B2

Ridgefield, Wash. 310/C5
Ridgefield Park, N.J. 273/B2
Ridgeland, Miss. 256/D6
Ridgeland, S.C. 296/E7
Ridgeland, Wis. 317/B5
Ridgeley, W. Va. 312/J3
Ridgely, Md. 245/P5
Ridgely, Mo. 261/C4
Ridgely, Tenn. 237/B8
Ridgeside, Tenn. 237/L10
Ridge Spring, S.C. 296/D4
Ridgetop, Tenn. 237/H8
Ridgetown, Ontario 177/C5
Ridgeview, S. Dak. 298/H3
Ridgeville, Georgia 217/K8
Ridgeville, Ind. 227/G4
Ridgeville, Manitoba 179/E5
Ridgeville, S.C. 296/G5
Ridgeville Corners, Ohio 284/B3
Ridgeway, Iowa 229/K2
Ridgeway, Minn. 255/H2
Ridgeway, Mo. 261/D2
Ridgeway, N.C. 281/N2
Ridgeway, Ohio 284/C4
Ridgeway, S.C. 296/F3
Ridgeway, Va. 307/J7
Ridgeway, W. Va. 312/K4
Ridgeway, Wis. 317/F10
Ridgeway Branch, Toms (riv.), N.J.
   273/E3
Ridgewood, N.J. 273/B1
Ridgléy, Tasmania 99/B3
Ridgway, Colo. 208/D6
Ridgway, Ill. 222/E6
Ridgway, Pa. 294/E3
Ridi, Nepal 68/E3
Riding (mt.), Manitoba 179/B4
Riding Mountain, Manitoba 179/C4
Riding Mountain Nat'l Park, Manitoba
   162/F5
Riding Mountain Nat'l Park, Manitoba
   179/B4
Ridley, Tenn. 237/G9
Ridley Park, Pa. 294/M7
Ridott, Ill. 222/D1
Ridotto, Iowa 229/D3
Ried im Innkreis, Austria 41/B2
Riegelsville, N.J. 273/C2
Riegelsville, Pa. 294/M4
Riegelwood, N.C. 281/N6
Riehen, Switzerland 39/E1
Rienzi, Miss. 256/G1
Riesa, Germany 22/E3
Riesco (isl.), Chile 138/E10
Riesel, Texas 303/H6
Riesi, Italy 34/E6
Rietavas, U.S.S.R. 53/A3
Rietberg, Germany 22/C3
Rietfontein, Namibia 118/C4
Rieth, Oreg. 291/J2
Rieti (prov.), Italy 34/D3
Rieti, Italy 34/D3
Rif, Er (range), Morocco 106/D2
Riffelalp, Switzerland 39/E5
Rifle, Colo. 208/D3
Rifle (creek), Colo. 208/D3
Rifle (riv.), Mich. 250/E4
Rifle (lake), Wash. 310/C4
Rifstangi (cape), Iceland 21/C1
Rift Valley (prov.), Kenya 115/G3
Riga (cap.), Conn. 210/B1
Riga, U.S.S.R. 2/L3
Riga, U.S.S.R. 7/G3
Riga, U.S.S.R. 48/C4
Riga, U.S.S.R. 52/B3
Riga (cap.), Latvian S.S.R., U.S.S.R.
   53/C2
Riga (gulf), U.S.S.R. 7/G3
Riga (gulf), U.S.S.R. 52/B3
Riga (gulf), U.S.S.R. 53/B2
Riga (gulf), U.S.S.R. 48/C4
Rigan, Iran 66/L6
Rigaud, Québec 172/C4
Rigby, Idaho 220/F6
Rigdon, Ind. 227/F4
Rigestan (reg.), Afghanistan 59/H3
Riggins, Idaho 220/B4
Riggisberg, Switzerland 39/E3
Rigi (mt.), Switzerland 39/F2
Rigo, Papua N.G. 85/C7
Rigolet, Newf. 166/C4
Rigolet, Newf. 162/L5
Rig Rig, Chad 111/B5
Rigside, Scotland 15/E5
Riihimäki, Finland 18/O6
Riiser-Larsen (pen.), Ant. 2/L9
Riiser-Larsen (pen.) 5/C2
Rijeka, Yugoslavia 45/B3
Rijeka, Yugoslavia 7/F4
Rijen, Netherlands 27/F5
Rijnsburg, Netherlands 27/F4
Rijssen, Netherlands 27/J4
Rijswijk, Netherlands 27/E4
Rikitea, Fr. Poly. 87/N8
Rikuchu-Kaigan National Park, Japan
   81/L4
Rikuzentakata, Japan 81/K4
Riley, Ind. 227/C6
Riley (co.), Kansas 232/F2
Riley, Kansas 232/F2
Riley, Ky. 237/L5
Riley, Maine 243/A2
Riley, Oreg. 291/H4
Riley Brook, New Bruns. 170/C1
Rileysburg, Ind. 227/B4
Rillito, Ariz. 198/D6
Rillton, Pa. 294/C5
Rima (riv.), Niger 106/F6
Rima (riv.), Nigeria 106/F6
Rima, Wadi (dry riv.), Saudi Arabia
   59/D4
Rimac (riv.), Peru 128/D9
Rimal, Ar (des.), Saudi Arabia 59/F5
Rimatara (isl.), Fr. Poly. 87/L8
Rimavská Sobota, Czech. 41/E2
Rimbey, Alberta 182/C3
Rimbo, Sweden 18/L7
Rimersburg, Pa. 294/D3

Rimini, Italy 34/D2
Rimini, S.C. 296/G4
Rîmnicu Sărat, Romania 45/H3
Rîmnicu Vîlcea, Romania 45/G3
Rimouski (co.), Québec 172/J1
Rimouski (county), Québec
   174/D3
Rimouski, Québec 172/J1
Rimouski, Québec 172/J1
Rimouski (riv.), Québec 172/J1
Rimouski-Est, Québec 172/J1
Rimpfischhorn (mt.), Switzerland
   39/E4
Rimrock, Ariz. 198/D4
Rimrock (lake), Wash. 310/D4
Rimutaka (range), N. Zealand
   100/B3
Rinard, Ill. 222/E5
Rinard, Iowa 229/D4
Rincón, Cerro (mt.), Argentina
   143/C1
Rincon (peak), Ariz. 198/E6
Rincón, Cerro (mt.), Chile 138/C4
Rincón, Dom. Rep. 158/E5
Rincón (bay), Dom. Rep. 158/F5
Rincon, Georgia 217/K6
Rincon, Neth. Ant. 161/E8
Rincon, N. Mex. 274/C6
Rincón (pt.), Panama 154/G6
Rincón, P. Rico 161/A1
Rincón (bay), P. Rico 161/D3
Rinconada, Argentina 143/C1
Rinconada San Martín, Chile
   138/G2
Rincón de Romos, Mexico 150/H5
Rindge•, N.H. 268/C6
Riner, Va. 307/H6
Rineyville, Ky. 237/K5
Ringarooma, Tasmania 99/D3
Ringarooma (bay), Tasmania 99/D2
Ringe, Denmark 21/D7
Ringebu, Norway 18/G6
Ringgold, Georgia 217/B1
Ringgold (co.), Iowa 229/E7
Ringgold, La. 238/D2
Ringgold, Md. 245/H2
Ringgold, Nebr. 264/D3
Ringgold, Texas 303/G4
Ringgold, Va. 307/K7
Ringim, Nigeria 106/F6
Ringkøbing (co.), Denmark 21/B5
Ringkøbing, Denmark 18/E8
Ringkøbing, Denmark 21/A5
Ringkøbing (fjord), Denmark
   21/B6
Ringling, Mont. 262/F4
Ringling, Okla. 288/L6
Ringmer, England 13/H7
Ringoes, N.J. 273/D3
Ringold, Okla. 288/R6
Ringsted, Denmark 21/E7
Ringsted, Iowa 229/D2
Ringtown, Pa. 294/K4
Ringvassøy (isl.), Norway 18/L2
Ringwood, England 13/F7
Ringwood, Ill. 222/E1
Ringwood, N.J. 273/E1
Ringwood, N.C. 281/O2
Ringwood, North. Terr. 93/D7
Ringwood, Okla. 288/K2
Ringwood, Victoria 88/M7
Ringwood, Victoria 97/K5
Rinn (lake), Ireland 17/F4
Rinteln, Germany 22/C2
Rio, Ill. 222/C2
Rio, La. 238/L5
Rio, W. Va. 312/J4
Rio, Wis. 317/H9
Rio Arriba (co.), N. Mex. 274/B2
Riobamba, Ecuador 128/C3
Riobamba, Ecuador 120/B3
Rio Blanco, Chile 138/B9
Rio Blanco (co.), Colo. 208/C3
Rio Blanco, Colo. 208/C3
Río Blanco, P. Rico 161/F2
Rio Bonito, Brazil 135/E3
Rio Branco, Brazil 120/C3
Rio Branco, Brazil 132/G10
Río Branco, Uruguay 145/F3
Rio Brazos (riv.), N. Mex. 274/C2
Rio Brilhante, Brazil 132/C8
Rio Bueno, Chile 138/D3
Rio Bueno, Jamaica 158/H5
Río Caribe, Venezuela 124/G2
Rio Cauto, Cuba 158/H4
Rio Chama (riv.), N. Mex. 274/C2
Río Chico, Venezuela 124/F2
Río Cisnes, Chile 138/E5
Rio Claro, Brazil 132/E8
Rio Claro, Brazil 135/C3
Rio Claro, Trin. & Tob. 161/B11
Río Claro, Venezuela 124/D3
Río Colorado, Argentina 120/C6
Río Colorado, La Pampa, Argentina
   143/D4
Río Colorado, Río Negro, Argentina
   143/D4
Río Creek, Wis. 317/L6
Río Cuarto, Argentina 143/D3
Río Cuarto, Argentina 120/C6
Rio de Janeiro (state), Brazil 135/E3
Rio de Janeiro (state), Brazil 132/F8
Rio de Janeiro, Brazil 2/G7
Rio de Janeiro, Brazil 120/E5
Rio de Janeiro, Brazil 135/E3
Rio de Janeiro, Brazil 132/G9
Rio Dell, Calif. 204/A3
Rio de Oro, Colombia 126/D3
Rio do Sul, Brazil 132/D9
Río Felix (riv.), N. Mex. 274/E5
Río Gallegos, Argentina 120/C8
Río Gallegos, Argentina 143/C7
Rio Grande (riv.) 2/D4
Rio Grande (riv.) 146/H7
Rio Grande (riv.) 188/F5

Rio Grande, Argentina 143/C7
Rio Grande, Bolivia 136/B7
Rio Grande, Brazil 120/D6
Rio Grande, Brazil 132/D11
Rio Grande (co.), Colo. 208/G7
Rio Grande (res.), Colo. 208/E7
Rio Grande (riv.), Colo. 208/H8
Rio Grande, N.J. 273/D5
Rio Grande, Ohio 284/F8
Rio Grande, P. Rico 161/E1
Rio Grande (riv.), Texas 303/D9
Rio Grande, Ohio 284/F8
Rio Grande City, Texas 303/F11
Rio Grande do Norte (state), Brazil
   132/G4
Rio Grande do Sul (state), Brazil
   132/D10
Rio Grande Pyramid (mt.), Colo.
   208/E7
Rio Grande Wild and Scenic River,
   Texas 303/B8
Riohacha, Colombia 120/B1
Riohacha, Colombia 126/D2
Río Hondo, Guatemala 154/C3
Río Hondo (riv.), N. Mex. 274/E5
Rio Hondo, Texas 303/G11
Rioja, Peru 128/C3
Río Lagartos, Mexico 150/P6
Rio Linda, Calif. 204/B8
Río Maior, Portugal 33/B3
Río Mulato, Bolivia 136/B6
Río Muni (terr.), Equat. Guinea
   115/B3
Rion, S.C. 296/E3
Riondel, Br. Col. 184/J5
Río Negro (prov.), Argentina
   143/C5
Río Negro, Brazil 132/D9
Río Negro, Chile 138/D3
Rionegro, Antioquia, Colombia
   126/C4
Rionegro, Santander, Colombia
   126/D3
Río Negro (dept.), Uruguay 145/B3
Río Negro (res.), Uruguay 145/D3
Rionero in Vulture, Italy 34/E4
Rio Pardo, Brazil 132/C10
Rio Pardo de Minas, Brazil 132/F6
Río Penasco (riv.), N. Mex. 274/E6
Río Piedras, P. Rico 161/E1
Rio Pomba, Brazil 135/E2
Río Puerco (riv.), N. Mex. 274/C4
Rio Rancho, N. Mex. 274/C3
Rio Real, Brazil 132/G5
Río Rico, Ariz. 198/E7
Rio Salado (riv.), N. Mex. 274/B4
Río San Juan, Dom. Rep. 158/E5
Río Seco, Cuba 158/A2
Río Segundo, Argentina 143/D3
Ríosucio, Caldas, Colombia 126/C5
Ríosucio, Chocó, Colombia 126/B4
Río Tercero, Argentina 143/D3
Río Tigre, Ecuador 128/D4
Rio Tinto, Brazil 132/H4
Río Tocuyo, Venezuela 124/C2
Riou (lake), Sask. 181/M2
Rio Verde, Brazil 132/D7
Rio Verde, Brazil 120/D4
Río Verde, Chile 138/E10
Ríoverde, Mexico 150/J6
Rio Verde de Mato Grosso, Brazil
   132/C7
Rio Vista, Calif. 204/L1
Riparia, Wash. 310/G4
Riparius, N.Y. 276/M3
Ripley, Calif. 204/L10
Ripley, England 13/F4
Ripley, Ill. 222/C3
Ripley (co.), Ind. 227/G6
Ripley•, Maine 243/E5
Ripley, Miss. 256/G1
Ripley (co.), Mo. 261/L9
Ripley, N.Y. 276/A6
Ripley, Ohio 284/C8
Ripley, Okla. 288/N2
Ripley, Ontario 177/C3
Ripley, Tenn. 237/B9
Ripley, W. Va. 312/E4
Riplinger, Wis. 317/E6
Ripoll, Spain 33/H1
Ripon, Calif. 204/D6
Ripon, England 10/F3
Ripon, England 13/F3
Ripon, Québec 172/B4
Ripon, Wis. 317/J8
Rippey, Iowa 229/E5
Ripplemead, Va. 307/G6
Ripples, New Bruns. 170/D3
Rippon, W. Va. 312/L4
Rippowam (riv.), Conn. 210/A4
Ripton•, Vt. 268/A3
Ririe, Idaho 220/G6
Risafe, Syria 63/H5
Risalpur Cantonment, Pakistan
   68/C2
Risaralda (dept.), Colombia
   126/B5
Risca, Wales 13/B6
Risco, Mo. 261/N9
Rishiri (isl.), Japan 81/K1
Rishon Le Ziyyon, Israel 65/B4
Rishra, India 68/F1
Rising City, Nebr. 264/G3
Rising Fawn, Georgia 217/A1
Rising Star, Texas 303/F5
Rising Sun, Ind. 227/H7
Rising Sun, Md. 245/O2
Risingsun, Ohio 284/C5
Rising Sun, Wis. 317/J8
Risle (riv.), France 28/D3
Rison, Ark. 202/F6
Risør, Norway 18/F7
Risoux (mt.), Switzerland 39/B3
Ristigouche (riv.), Québec 172/B2
Ristijärvi, Finland 18/O4
Rita Blanca (creek), Texas 303/B2
Ritchey, Mo. 261/D9
Ritchie, Md. 245/G5

Ritchie (co.), W. Va. 312/D4
Ritchies (arch.), India 68/G6
Ritidian (pt.), Guam 86/K6
Ritner, Ky. 237/M7
Ritter, Oreg. 291/H3
Ritter, S.C. 296/F6
Rittman, Ohio 284/G4
Ritzville, Wash. 310/G3
Riva (riv.), Va. 307/M5
Rivadavia, Salta, Argentina
   143/D1
Rivadavia, San Juan, Argentina
   143/C3
Rivadavia, Mendoza, Argentina
   143/C3
Rivadavia, Chile 138/A7
Riva del Garda, Italy 34/C2
Rivanna (riv.), Va. 307/M5
Rivas, Nicaragua 154/E5
Riva San Vitale, Switzerland
   39/G5
Rive-de-Gier, France 28/F5
Rivera, Switzerland 39/G4
Rivera (dept.), Uruguay 145/D2
Rivera, Uruguay 145/D1
Rivera, Uruguay 120/D6
Riverbank, Calif. 204/E6
River Bourgeois, Nova Scotia
   168/H3
River Cess, Liberia 106/C7
Rivercourse, Alberta 182/E3
Riverdale, Calif. 204/E7
Riverdale, Georgia 217/K2
Riverdale, Ill. 222/C6
Riverdale, Iowa 229/N5
Riverdale, Kansas 232/E4
Riverdale, Md. 245/G5
Riverdale, Mich. 250/E4
Riverdale, Nebr. 264/E4
Riverdale, N.H. 268/D5
Riverdale, N.J. 273/A1
Riverdale, N. Dak. 282/H4
River de Chute, New Bruns.
   170/C2
River Denys, Nova Scotia
   168/G3
River Edge, N.J. 273/B1
River Falls, Ala. 195/E8
River Falls, Wis. 317/A6
River Forest, Ill. 222/B6
River Forest, Ind. 227/F4
River Glade, New Bruns. 170/E3
River Grove, Ill. 222/B5
River Grove, Oreg. 291/B2
Riverhead, Newf. 166/D2
Riverhead, Newf. 276/P9
Riverhead, N. Zealand 100/B1
River Hébert, Nova Scotia 168/D3
River Heights, Utah 304/C2
River Hills, Manitoba 179/G4
River Hills, Wis. 317/M1
Riverhurst, Sask. 181/E5
Riverina (reg.), N. S. Wales 88/H7
Riverina (reg.), N.S. Wales 97/J4
River John, Nova Scotia 168/E3
River Jordan, Br. Col. 184/J3
Riverland, Fla. 212/B4
Riverlea, Ohio 284/D5
Rivermines, Mo. 261/L7
Rivero (isl.), Chile 138/D6
River Oaks, Texas 303/E2
River of Ponds, Newf. 166/C3
River of Ponds (lake), Newf.
   166/C3
Riverport, Nova Scotia 168/D4
River Rouge, Mich. 250/D4
Rivers (inlet), Br. Col. 184/D4
Rivers, Manitoba 179/B4
Rivers (state), Nigeria 106/F8
Rivers (lake), Sask. 181/F6
Riversdale, Jamaica 158/J6
Riversdale, S. Africa 118/H7
Riverdale, S. Africa 118/C6
Riverside, Ala. 195/F3
Riverside (co.), Calif. 204/J10
Riverside, Calif. 188/C2
Riverside, Calif. 204/E11
Riverside (res.), Colo. 208/L2
Riverside, Conn. 210/A4
Riverside, Georgia 217/B2
Riverside, Georgia 217/E8
Riverside, Ill. 222/B6
Riverside, Ind. 227/C4
Riverside, Iowa 229/K6
Riverside, Ky. 237/J6
Riverside, Md. 245/K7
Riverside, Mass. 249/D2
Riverside, Mich. 250/O5
Riverside, Mo. 261/O5
Riverside•, N.J. 273/B3
Riverside, N.Y. 276/F6
Riverside, N. Dak. 282/S6
Riverside, Oreg. 291/J4
Riverside, Pa. 294/J4
Riverside, R.I. 249/J5
Riverside, Sask. 181/G6
Riverside, Texas 303/J7
Riverside, Utah 304/B2
Riverside, Wash. 310/E2
Riverside, Wyo. 319/F4
Riverside-Albert, New Bruns.
   170/F3
Riverside Stage Stop, Ariz.
   198/D5
Rivers Inlet, Br. Col. 184/D4
River Sioux, Iowa 229/B5
Riverstown, Ireland 17/E3
Riverton, Conn. 210/D1
Riverton, Ill. 222/D4
Riverton, Ind. 227/B6
Riverton, Iowa 229/B7
Riverton, Kansas 232/H4
Riverton, La. 238/F2
Riverton, Man. 162/G5
Riverton, Manitoba 179/E3
Riverton, Minn. 255/D4
Riverton, N.J. 273/B3
Riverton, N. Zealand 100/B7

Roseau 437

Riverton, Nova Scotia 168/F3
Riverton, Oreg. 291/C4
Riverton, Utah 304/B3
Riverton, Vt. 268/B3
Riverton, Va. 307/M3
Riverton, Wash. 310/B2
Riverton, W. Va. 312/H5
Riverton, Wyo. 319/D2
Riverton Heights, Wash. 310/B2
Rivervale, Ark. 202/K2
River Vale•, N.J. 273/B1
River Valley, Ontario 177/D1
Riverview, Ala. 195/D8
Riverview, Fla. 212/D4
Riverview, Mich. 250/B7
Riverview, Mo. 261/R2
Riverview, New Bruns. 170/F2
Riverville, Va. 307/L5
Riverwood, Ky. 237/K1
Riverwoods, Ill. 222/B5
Rives, Mo. 261/M10
Rives, Tenn. 237/C8
Rives Junction, Mich. 250/E6
Rivesville, W. Va. 312/F3
Riviera (reg.), France 28/G6
Riviera, Texas 303/G10
Riviera Beach, Fla. 212/G5
Riviera Beach, Md. 245/N4
Riviera-Bullhead, Ariz. 198/A3
Rivière-à-Claude, Québec 172/C1
Rivière-à-Pierre, Québec 172/E3
Rivière-au-Renard, Québec 172/D1
Rivière-au-Tonnerre, Québec 174/D2
Rivière-Bleue, Québec 172/J2
Rivière-Bois-Clair, Québec 172/F3
Rivière-du-Loup (co.), Québec 172/H2
Rivière-du-Loup, Québec 172/H2
Rivière-du-Loup, Québec 174/D3
Rivière-du-Loup, Québec 172/H2
Rivière-du-Moulin, Québec 172/G1
Rivière-du-Portage, New Bruns. 170/F1
Rivière-Éternité, Québec 172/G1
Rivière-la-Madeleine, Québec 172/C1
Rivière-Matawin, Québec 172/E3
Rivière-Ouelle, Québec 172/G2
Rivière-Pentecôte, Québec 174/D3
Rivière-Pilote, Martinique 161/D7
Rivière-Port-Daniel, Québec 172/D2
Rivière-Portneuf, Québec 172/H1
Rivière-Saint-Paul, Québec 174/F2
Rivière-Salée, Martinique 161/D7
Rivière-Trois-Pistoles, Québec 172/J1
Rivière Verte, New Bruns. 170/B1
Rivière-Verte, Québec 172/H2
Riwaka, N. Zealand 100/D4
Riwoqê, China 77/E5
Rixeyville, Va. 307/M3
Rixford, Pa. 294/F2
Riyadh (cap.), Saudi Arabia 2/M4
Riyadh (cap.), Saudi Arabia 54/F7
Riyadh (cap.), Saudi Arabia 59/E5
Riyan, Yemen 59/E7
Rizal (prov.), Philippines 82/C3
Rize (prov.), Turkey 63/J2
Rize, Turkey 59/D1
Rize, Turkey 63/J2
Rizokarpasso, Cyprus 63/F5
Rjukan, Norway 18/F7
Roa, Norway 18/G6
Roa, Spain 33/E2
Roachdale, Ind. 227/D5
Road (bay), Virgin Is. (U.K.) 161/D3
Roadside, Scotland 15/F4
Roadstown, N.J. 273/C5
Road Town (cap.), Virgin Is. (U.K.) 161/D3
Road Town (cap.), Virgin Is. (U.K.) 156/H1
Roag, Loch (inlet), Scotland 15/B2
Roan (creek), Colo. 208/C4
Roan (plat.), Colo. 208/B3
Roan, Norway 18/G4
Roan (isl.), Scotland 15/D2
Roan (cliffs), Utah 304/E4
Roane (co.), Tenn. 237/M9
Roane (co.), W. Va. 312/D5
Roan Mountain, Tenn. 237/S8
Roann, Ind. 227/F3
Roanne, France 28/E4
Roanoke (riv.) 188/L3
Roanoke, Ala. 195/H4
Roanoke, Ill. 222/D3
Roanoke, Ind. 227/G3
Roanoke, La. 238/E6
Roanoke, Mo. 261/G4
Roanoke (isl.), N.C. 281/T3
Roanoke (riv.), N.C. 281/P2
Roanoke, Texas 303/F1
Roanoke, Va. 146/L6
Roanoke, Va. 188/K3
Roanoke (co.), Va. 307/H6
Roanoke (I.C.), Va. 307/H6
Roanoke (riv.), Va. 307/N8
Roanoke, W. Va. 312/F5
Roanoke Rapids, N.C. 281/O2
Roaring (brook), Conn. 210/F1
Roaring (brook), Conn. 210/E2
Roaring Branch, Pa. 294/J2
Roaring Fork, Colorado (riv.), Colo. 208/E4
Roaring Gap, N.C. 281/H2
Roaring River, N.C. 281/G2
Roaring Spring, Pa. 294/F5
Roaring Springs, Texas 303/D4
Roaringwater (bay), Ireland 17/B9
Roark, Ky. 237/P6
Roatán, Honduras 154/D2
Roatán (isl.), Honduras 154/D2
Roba, Ala. 195/G6
Robards, Ky. 237/F5
Robat Karim, Iran 66/G3
Robb, Alberta 182/B3
Robben (isl.), S. Africa 118/E6
Robbins, Calif. 204/B8
Robbins, Ill. 222/B6
Robbins, N.C. 281/K4
Robbins (isl.), Tasmania 99/B2
Robbins, Tenn. 237/M8
Robbinsdale, Minn. 255/G5
Robbinston, Maine 243/J5
Robbinston•, Maine 243/J5
Robbinsville, N.J. 273/D3
Robbinsville, N.C. 281/B4
Robe (mt.), N.S. Wales 97/A2
Robe, S. Australia 94/F7
Robe, Wash. 310/D2
Robeline, La. 238/D3
Roberdel, N.C. 281/K5
Robersonville, N.C. 281/P3
Robert (isl.), China 85/E2
Robert, La. 238/N1
Robert (harb.), Martinique 161/D6
Roberta, Georgia 217/D5
Roberta, Okla. 288/K7
Robert Lee, Texas 303/D6
Roberto Payán, Colombia 126/A7
Roberts, Idaho 220/F6
Roberts, Ill. 222/E3
Roberts, Mont. 262/G5
Roberts (co.), S. Dak. 298/P2
Roberts (co.), Texas 303/D2
Roberts, Wis. 317/A6
Robert's Arm, Newf. 166/C4
Robertsburg, W. Va. 312/C5
Roberts Creek, Br. Col. 184/J3
Robertsdale, Ala. 195/C9
Robertsdale, Pa. 294/F5
Roberts Field Int'l Airport, Liberia 106/C7
Robertsfors, Sweden 18/M4
Robertsganj, India 68/E4
Robertson (co.), Ky. 237/N3
Robertson, S. Africa 118/C6
Robertson (co.), Tenn. 237/H7
Robertson (co.), Texas 303/H6
Robertson, Wyo. 319/B4
Robertsonville, Québec 172/F3
Robertsport, Liberia 102/A4
Robertsport, Liberia 106/B7
Robertstown, Georgia 217/E1
Robertsville, Conn. 210/C1
Robertsville, Ohio 284/H4
Robertville, New Bruns. 170/E1
Roberval, Québec 162/J6
Roberval, Québec 174/C3
Roberval, Québec 172/E1
Robeson (co.), N.C. 281/L5
Robeson (chan.), N.W. Terr. 187/M1
Robesonia, Pa. 294/K5
Robichaud, New Bruns. 170/F2
Robinhood, Sask. 181/C2
Robins, Iowa 229/K4
Robins, Ohio 284/H6
Robins A.F.B., Georgia 217/F5
Robinson, Ill. 222/F5
Robinson, Iowa 229/K4
Robinson, Kansas 232/G2
Robinson, Ky. 237/N4
Robinson, N. Dak. 282/L5
Robinson (riv.), North. Terr. 93/E4
Robinson, Pa. 294/D5
Robinson (lake), S.C. 296/G3
Robinson (ranges), W. Australia 92/B4
Robinson Creek, Ky. 237/S6
Robinson Crusoe (isl.), Chile 120/B6
Robinson River, North. Terr. 93/E4
Robinsons, Maine 243/H3
Robinsonville, Miss. 256/D1
Robinsonville, New Bruns. 170/C1
Robinvale, Victoria 97/B4
Robles, Colombia 126/D2
Roblin, Manitoba 179/A3
Roblin, Ontario 177/G3
Roboré, Bolivia 136/F6
Roboré, Bolivia 120/D4
Rob Roy, Ind. 227/C4
Robsart, Sask. 181/B6
Robson, Br. Col. 184/J5
Robson (mt.), Br. Col. 162/D5
Robson (mt.), Br. Col. 184/H3
Robstown, Texas 303/G10
Roby, Mo. 261/H7
Roby, Texas 303/D5
Roca, Nebr. 264/H4
Roca (cape), Portugal 33/B3
Rocafuerte, Ecuador 128/B3
Rocanville, Sask. 181/K5
Roca Partida (isl.), Mexico 150/C7
Roca que Vela (cay), Colombia 126/B8
Rocas (isl.), Brazil 120/F3
Rocas de Santo Domingo, Chile 138/F4
Roccastrada, Italy 34/C3
Rocha (dept.), Uruguay 145/E4
Rocha, Uruguay 145/E5
Rocha (lag.), Uruguay 145/E5
Rochdale, England 13/H2
Rochdale, England 10/G2
Rochdale, Mass. 249/G4
Roche, Switzerland 39/C4
Rochechouart, France 28/D5
Rochefort, Belgium 27/G8
Rochefort, France 28/C4
Roche Harbor, Wash. 310/B2
Rochelle, Georgia 217/F7
Rochelle, Ill. 222/D2
Rochelle, Texas 303/E6
Rochelle, Wyo. 319/H2
Rochelle Park•, N.J. 273/B2
Roche Percé, Sask. 181/J6
Rocheport, Mo. 261/H5
Rocher River, N.W.T. 162/E3
Rocher River, N.W.T. 187/G3
Rochert, Minn. 255/C4
Rochester, Alberta 182/D2
Rochester, England 13/J8
Rochester, England 10/G5
Rochester, Ill. 222/D4
Rochester, Ind. 227/E2
Rochester, Iowa 229/L5
Rochester, Ky. 237/H6
Rochester•, Mass. 249/L6
Rochester, Mich. 250/F6
Rochester, Minn. 188/H2
Rochester, Minn. 255/F6
Rochester, N.H. 268/E5
Rochester, N.Y. 188/L2
Rochester, N.Y. 146/L5
Rochester, N.Y. 276/E4
Rochester, Ohio 284/F3
Rochester, Pa. 294/B4
Rochester, Texas 303/E4
Rochester•, Vt. 268/B4
Rochester, Victoria 97/C5
Rochester, Wash. 310/C4
Rochester, Wis. 317/K3
Rochester Mills, Pa. 294/D4
Rochford, S. Dak. 298/B5
Rochfort Bridge, Alberta 182/C3
Rochon Sands, Alberta 182/D3
Rociada, N. Mex. 274/D3
Rock (creek), Idaho 220/F7
Rock (creek), Ill. 222/D2
Rock (riv.), Ill. 222/C2
Rock (riv.), Iowa 229/A2
Rock, Kansas 232/F4
Rock (lake), Manitoba 179/C5
Rock (creek), Md. 245/K4
Rock, Mass. 249/L5
Rock, Mich. 250/B2
Rock (co.), Minn. 255/B7
Rock (riv.), Minn. 255/B7
Rock (creek), Mont. 262/C4
Rock (co.), Nebr. 264/E2
Rock (creek), Nev. 266/E2
Rock (creek), Oreg. 291/E2
Rock (creek), Oreg. 291/G2
Rock (creek), Oreg. 291/H3
Rock (creek), S. Dak. 298/O6
Rock (creek), Wash. 310/H3
Rock (lake), Wash. 310/H3
Rock (co.), Wis. 317/H10
Rock (riv.), Wis. 317/J9
Rockall (isl.), Scotland 7/C3
Rockaway, N.J. 273/D2
Rockaway, Oreg. 291/C2
Rockaway Beach, Mo. 261/F9
Rock Bluff, Fla. 212/B1
Rockbridge, Ill. 222/C4
Rockbridge, Mo. 261/H9
Rockbridge, Ohio 284/E6
Rockbridge (co.), Va. 307/K5
Rockbridge, Wis. 317/F9
Rockcastle (co.), Ky. 237/N6
Rockcastle (riv.), Ky. 237/N6
Rock Castle, W. Va. 312/C5
Rock Cave, W. Va. 312/F5
Rock City, Ill. 222/D1
Rockcliffe Park, Ontario 177/J2
Rockcorry, Ireland 17/H3
Rock Creek, Br. Col. 184/H6
Rock Creek, Kansas 232/G2
Rock Creek, Minn. 255/F5
Rock Creek, Ohio 284/J2
Rock Creek, Yukon 187/E3
Rockdale (co.), Georgia 217/D3
Rockdale, Ill. 222/E2
Rockdale, N. S. Wales 88/K4
Rockdale, N.S. Wales 97/J4
Rockdale, Texas 303/G7
Rockdale, Wis. 317/J10
Rock Dell, Minn. 255/F7
Rockerville, S. Dak. 298/C6
Rockfall, Conn. 210/E2
Rock Falls, Ill. 222/D2
Rock Falls, Iowa 229/G2
Rock Falls, Wis. 317/C6
Rockfield, Ind. 227/D3
Rockfield, Ky. 237/J7
Rockfield, Wis. 317/L1
Rockfish, N.C. 281/L5
Rockford, Ala. 195/F5
Rockford, Idaho 220/F6
Rockford, Ill. 146/K5
Rockford, Ill. 188/J2
Rockford, Ill. 222/D1
Rockford, Iowa 229/H2
Rockford, Mich. 250/D5
Rockford, Minn. 255/F5
Rockford, N.C. 281/H2
Rockford, Ohio 284/A4
Rockford, Sask. 181/J3
Rockford, Tenn. 237/O9
Rockford, Wash. 310/H3
Rock Forest, Québec 172/F4
Rock Glen, Pa. 294/K4
Rockglen, Sask. 181/F6
Rock Grove, Ill. 222/D1
Rock Hall, Md. 245/O4
Rockham, S. Dak. 298/M4
Rockhampton, Australia 2/S7
Rockhampton, Australia 87/F8
Rockhampton, Queensland 88/H4
Rockhampton, Queensland 95/D4
Rockhampton Downs, North. Terr. 93/D5
Rockhaven, Sask. 181/B3
Rock Hill, Mo. 261/P3
Rock Hill, S.C. 188/K4
Rock Hill, S.C. 296/E2
Rockholds, Ky. 237/N7
Rockingham, Georgia 217/H7
Rockingham (co.), N.H. 268/E5
Rockingham (co.), N.C. 281 208/H2
Rocky Point, N.C. 281/O6
Rocky Point, Wash. 310/A2
Rockypoint, Wyo. 319/G1
Rocky Rapids, Alberta 182/C3
Rocky Reach (dam), Wash. 310/E3
Rocky Ridge (mt.), Idaho 220/C3
Rocky Ridge, Ohio 284/D2
Rocky River, Ohio 284/G9
Rodanthe, N.C. 281/U3
Rodarte, N. Mex. 274/D2
Rodas, Cuba 158/E2
Rødby, Denmark 21/E8
Rødby, Denmark 18/G9
Roddickton, Newf. 166/C3
Rødding, Denmark 21/B7
Roddy, Tenn. 237/M9
Rødekro, Denmark 21/C7
Roden, Netherlands 27/J2
Rodeo, Calif. 204/J1
Rodeo, Mexico 150/G4
Rodeo, N. Mex. 274/A7
Roderfield, W. Va. 312/C8
Roderick (isl.), Br. Col. 184/C4
Rodessa, La. 238/B1
Rodez, France 28/E5
Ródhos, Greece 45/J7
Roding (riv.), England 13/J7
Rodinga, North. Terr. 93/D8
Rødkaersbro, Denmark 21/C5
Rodman, Iowa 229/D2
Rodman, N.Y. 276/J3
Rodman, S.C. 296/E2
Rodney, Iowa 229/A4
Rodney, Mich. 250/D5
Rodney, Miss. 256/B7
Rodney, Ontario 177/C5
Rodney Village, Del. 245/R4
Rodrigues, Brazil 132/F10
Rodríguez, Uruguay 145/C5
Rødvig, Denmark 21/F7
Roe, Ark. 202/H4
Roe (riv.), N. Ireland 17/H1
Roebling-Florence, N.J. 273/D3
Roebourne, W. Australia 88/B4
Roebourne, W. Australia 92/B3
Roebuck (bay), W. Australia 88/C3
Roebuck (bay), W. Australia 92/C2
Roebuck Plains, W. Australia 92/C2
Roeland Park, Kansas 232/H2
Roer (riv.), Netherlands 27/J6
Roermond, Netherlands 27/J6
Roeselare, Belgium 27/C7
Roes Welcome (sound), N.W.T. 162/H2
Roes Welcome (sound), N.W.T. 187/K3
Roff, Okla. 288/N5
Rogachev, U.S.S.R. 52/D4
Rogagua (lake), Bolivia 136/B3
Rogaguado (lake), Bolivia 136/C3
Rogaland (co.), Norway 18/E7
Rogatica, Yugoslavia 45/D4
Roger Mills (co.), Okla. 288/G3
Rogers, Ark. 202/B1
Rogers, Br. Col. 184/J4
Rogers (lake), Calif. 204/H9
Rogers, Conn. 210/H1
Rogers (lake), Conn. 210/F3
Rogers, La. 238/F3
Rogers, Minn. 255/E5
Rogers, Nebr. 264/H3
Rogers, N. Mex. 274/F5
Rogers, N. Dak. 282/O5
Rogers, Ohio 284/J4
Rogers (co.), Okla. 288/P2
Rogers, Texas 303/G7
Rogers (mt.), Va. 307/E7
Rogers City, Mich. 250/F3
Rogerson, Idaho 220/D7
Rogers Springs, Tenn. 237/D10
Rogersville, Ala. 195/D1
Rogersville, Mo. 261/G8
Rogersville, New Bruns. 170/E2
Rogersville, Pa. 294/B6
Rogersville, Tenn. 237/P8
Roger Williams Nat'l Mem., R.I. 249/J5
Roggen, Colo. 208/L2
Roggwil, Switzerland 39/E2
Rogliano, France 28/B6
Rogozno, Poland 47/C2
Rogue (riv.), Oreg. 291/C5
Rogue River, Oreg. 291/D5
Roha, India 68/C5
Rohnert Park, Calif. 204/C5
Rohnerville, Calif. 204/B3
Rohrbach in Oberüsterreich, Austria 41/B2
Rohrersville, Md. 245/H3
Rohri, Pakistan 68/B3
Rohtak, India 68/C3
Rohwer, Ark. 202/H6
Roi Et, Thailand 72/D4
Roja, U.S.S.R. 53/B2
Rojas, Argentina 143/F7
Rojo (cape), Mexico 150/L6
Rojo (cape), P. Rico 161/A3
Rojo (cape), P. Rico 156/F1
Rokan (riv.), Indonesia 85/C5
Rokeby, Sask. 181/J4
Rokiškis, U.S.S.R. 53/C2
Rokycany, Czech. 41/B2
Rokytnice nad Jizerou, Czech. 41/C1
Rola Co (lake), China 77/C4
Roland, Ark. 202/E4
Roland, Iowa 229/F4
Roland, Manitoba 179/D5
Roland, Okla. 288/S4
Røldal, Norway 18/E7
Roldán, Argentina 143/F6
Rolecha, Chile 138/D4
Rolesville, N.C. 281/N3
Rolette (co.), N. Dak. 282/L2
Rolette, N. Dak. 282/L2
Roleystone, W. Australia 88/B2
Rolfe, Iowa 229/D3
Roll, Ariz. 198/A6
Rolla, Ark. 202/E5
Rolla, Br. Col. 184/G2
Rolla, Kansas 232/A4
Rolla, Mo. 261/J7
Rolla, N. Dak. 282/L2
Rollag, Minn. 255/B4
Rolle, Switzerland 39/B4
Rollingbay, Wash. 310/A2
Rollingdam, New Bruns. 170/C3
Rolling Fields, Ky. 237/K2
Rolling Fork (riv.), Ky. 237/L5
Rolling Fork, Miss. 256/C5
Rolling Hills, Alberta 182/E4
Rolling Hills, Calif. 204/B11
Rolling Hills, Ky. 237/L1
Rolling Hills Estates, Calif. 204/B11
Rolling Meadows, Ill. 222/A5
Rolling Prairie, Ind. 227/D1
Rollingstone, Minn. 255/G6
Rollins, Mont. 262/B3
Rollo (bay), Pr. Edward I. 168/F2
Rolphton, Ontario 177/G1
Roma, Australia 87/E8
Roma (Rome) (cap.), Italy 34/F6
Roma, Queensland 88/H5
Roma, Queensland 95/D5
Roma, Sweden 18/L8
Romain (cape), S.C. 296/J6
Romaine (riv.), Newf. 166/B3
Romaine (riv.), Que. 162/K5
Romaine, Québec 174/E2
Romaine (riv.), Québec 174/E2
Roma-Los Saenz, Texas 303/E11
Roman, Romania 45/H2
Romance, Ark. 202/F3
Romance, Sask. 181/G3
Romance, W. Va. 312/C5
Romang, Argentina 143/F4
Romang (isl.), Indonesia 85/H7
Romania 2/L3
Romania 7/G4
ROMANIA 45/F3
Romano (cay), Cuba 158/G2
Romano (cay), Cuba 156/C2
Romano (cape), Fla. 212/E6
Romanshorn, Switzerland 39/H1
Romans-sur-Isère, France 28/F5
Romanzof (cape), Alaska 196/E2
Rombauer, Mo. 261/M9
Romblon (prov.), Philippines 82/D4
Romblon, Philippines 82/D4
Romblon (isl.), Philippines 82/D4
Rome, Ga. 188/K4
Rome, Georgia 217/B2
Rome, Ill. 222/D3
Rome, Ind. 227/D9
Rome, Iowa 229/K7
Rome (prov.), Italy 34/F6
Rome (cap.), Italy 7/F4
Rome (cap.), Italy 34/F6
Rome (cap.), Italy 2/L3
Rome•, Maine 243/D6
Rome, Miss. 256/C3
Rome, N.Y. 188/M2
Rome, N.Y. 276/J4
Rome (Stout), Ohio 284/D8
Rome, Ohio 284/J2
Rome, Oreg. 291/K5
Rome, Pa. 294/K2
Rome, Wis. 317/H1
Rome City, Ind. 227/G1
Romeo, Colo. 208/G8
Romeo, Mich. 250/F6
Romeoville, Ill. 222/B6
Romeroville, N. Mex. 274/D3
Romeville, La. 238/L3
Romilly-sur-Seine, France 28/F3
Romney, Ind. 227/D4
Romney, W. Va. 312/J4
Romny, U.S.S.R. 52/D4
Rømø, Denmark 21/B7
Rømø (isl.), Denmark 21/B7
Rømø (isl.), Denmark 18/F9
Romont, Switzerland 39/C3
Romorantin-Lanthenay, France 28/D4
Romsdalsfjorden (fjord), Norway 18/E5
Romsey, England 10/F5
Romsey, England 13/F6
Romulus, Mich. 250/F6
Romulus, N.Y. 276/G5
Ron, Vietnam 72/E3
Ron, Mui (cape), Vietnam 72/E3
Rona (isl.), Scotland 15/B3
Ronald, Wash. 310/E3
Ronan, Mont. 262/C3
Ronay (isl.), Scotland 15/A3
Roncador, Serra do (range), Brazil 132/D5
Roncador (cays), Colombia 126/B9
Ronceverte, W. Va. 312/F7
Ronciglione, Italy 34/C3
Ronda, N.C. 281/H2
Ronda, Spain 33/D4
Rønde, Denmark 21/D5
Ronde (isl.), Grenada 161/D7
Rondeau Prov. Park, Ontario 177/C5
Rondo, Ark. 202/J4
Rondônia (state), Brazil 132/H10
Rondônia, Brazil 132/H10
Rondonópolis, Brazil 120/D4
Rondout (res.), N.Y. 276/M7
Rondu, Pakistan 68/D1
Rong, Koh (isl.), Cambodia 72/D5
Rong'an, China 77/G6
Ronge, Lac La (lake), Sask. 162/F4
Ronge, La (lake), Sask. 181/M3
Rongelap (atoll), Marshall Is. 87/G4
Rongjiang, China 77/G6
Rong Kwang, Thailand 72/D3
Rong Xian, China 77/H7
Ronju (mt.), Fr. Poly. 86/T13
Ronkonkoma, N.Y. 276/O9
Rønne, Denmark 21/F9
Rønne, Denmark 18/J9
Ronneby, Minn. 255/E5
Ronneby, Sweden 18/J8
Ronne Entrance (inlet), Ant. 5/B15
Ronne Ice Shelf, Ant. 2/F10
Ronne Ice Shelf, Ant. 5/B15
Ronse, Belgium 27/D7
Ronuro (riv.), Brazil 132/C6
Roodeport, S. Africa 118/H6
Roodhouse, Ill. 222/C4
Roof Butte (mt.), Ariz. 198/F2
Rooi, Neth. Ant. 161/E8
Rooks (co.), Kansas 232/C2
Roopville, Georgia 217/B4
Roosendaal, Netherlands 27/F5
Roosevelt (isl.), Ant. 2/A10
Roosevelt (isl.), Ant. 5/A10
Roosevelt (res.), Ariz. 188/D4
Roosevelt, Ariz. 198/D5
Roosevelt (riv.), Brazil 120/C3
Roosevelt (riv.), Brazil 132/A5
Roosevelt, La. 238/H1
Roosevelt, Minn. 255/C2
Roosevelt (co.), Mont. 262/L2
Roosevelt, N.J. 273/E3
Roosevelt (co.), N. Mex. 274/F4
Roosevelt, N.Y. 276/R7
Roosevelt, Okla. 288/J5
Roosevelt, Texas 303/D7
Roosevelt, Utah 304/D3
Roosevelt, Wash. 310/E5
Roosevelt Campobello Int'l Park, New Bruns. 170/D4
Roosevelt City, Ala. 195/E4
Roosevelt Park, Mich. 250/C5
Roosevelt Road Naval Res., P. Rico 161/F2
Roosville, Br. Col. 184/K5
Root (riv.), Minn. 255/G7
Rootstown, Ohio 284/H3
Roper, N.C. 281/R3
Roper (riv.), North. Terr. 88/E3
Roper (riv.), North. Terr. 93/C3
Roper River, North. Terr. 93/D3
Roper River Mission, North. Terr. 88/E2
Roper Valley, North. Terr. 93/D3
Ropesville, Texas 303/B4
Roque Bluffs•, Maine 243/H6
Roque González de Santa Cruz, Paraguay 144/B5
Roque Pérez, Argentina 143/G7
Roquetas, Spain 33/G2
Rora (head), Scotland 15/E2
Roraima (mt.) 120/C2
Roraima (terr.), Brazil 132/H8
Roraima (mt.), Guyana 131/A3
Roraima (mt.), Venezuela 124/H5
Rørby, Denmark 21/E6
Rorketon, Manitoba 179/C3
Røros, Norway 18/G5
Rorschach, Switzerland 39/H2
Rosa, Ala. 195/E3
Rosa (cape), Ecuador 128/B10
Rosa (mt.), Italy 34/A1
Rosa, La. 238/G5
Rosa, Manitoba 179/F5
Rosa (mt.), Switzerland 39/E5
Rosaire, Québec 172/G3
Rosaireville, New Bruns. 170/E2
Rosalia, Kansas 232/F4
Rosalia, Wash. 310/H3
Rosalie, Dominica 161/F6
Rosalie, Nebr. 264/H2
Rosalina, Paraguay 144/D3
Rosalind, Alberta 182/D3
Rosamond, Calif. 204/G9
Rosamond (lake), Calif. 204/G9
Rosamond, Ill. 222/D4
Rosamorada, Mexico 150/G5
Rosapenna, Ireland 17/F1
Rosario, Argentina 143/F6
Rosario, Argentina 120/C6
Rosário, Brazil 132/F3
Rosario, Chile 138/F5
Rosario (cay), Cuba 158/C2
Rosario, Sinaloa, Mexico 150/G5
Rosario, Sonora, Mexico 150/E3
Rosario, Paraguay 144/D4
Rosario, P. Rico 161/A2
Rosario, Uruguay 145/B5
Rosario, Venezuela 124/B2
Rosario (str.), Wash. 310/C2
Rosario de la Frontera, Argentina 143/D2
Rosario de Lerma, Argentina 143/C1
Rosario del Tala, Argentina 143/G6
Rosáriodo Sul, Brazil 132/C10
Rosário Oeste, Brazil 132/C6
Rosas, Spain 33/H1
Rosas (gulf), Spain 33/H1
Rosati, Mo. 261/J6
Rosa Zárate, Ecuador 128/C2
Rosburg, Wash. 310/B4
Rosbys Rock, W. Va. 312/E3
Roscoe, Ill. 222/D1
Roscoe, Minn. 255/D5
Roscoe, Mo. 261/E7
Roscoe, Mont. 262/G5
Roscoe, Nebr. 264/C3
Roscoe, N.Y. 276/L7
Roscoe, Pa. 294/C5
Roscoe, S. Dak. 298/L3
Roscoe, Texas 303/D5
Roscoff, France 28/A3
Roscommon (co.), Ireland 17/E4
Roscommon, Ireland 10/B4
Roscommon, Ireland 17/E4
Roscommon (co.), Mich. 250/E4
Roscommon, Mich. 250/E4
Roscrea, Ireland 10/B4
Roscrea, Ireland 17/F6
Rose (peak), Ariz. 198/F5
Rose (pt.), Br. Col. 184/B3
Rose (pt.), Martinique 161/D6
Rose, Nebr. 264/E2
Rose, N.Y. 276/G4
Rose (riv.), North. Terr. 93/D2
Rose, Okla. 288/R2
Roseau (cap.), Dominica 156/G4
Roseau (cap.), Dominica 161/E7
Roseau (riv.), Dominica 161/E7
Roseau (co.), Minn. 255/C2
Roseau, Minn. 255/C2
Roseau (riv.), Minn. 255/B2

Roseau (riv.), St. Lucia 161/G6
Roseau River, Manitoba 179/F5
Roseaux, Haiti 158/A6
Rosebank, Manitoba 179/D5
Roseberry, Br. Col. 184/J5
Rosebery, Tasmania 99/B3
Rose Blanche, Newf. 166/C4
Roseboom, N.Y. 276/L5
Roseboro, N.C. 281/N5
Rosebud, Alberta 182/D4
Rosebud (riv.), Alberta 182/D4
Rose Bud, Ark. 202/F3
Rosebud, Mo. 261/K6
Rosebud (co.), Mont. 262/K4
Rosebud, Mont. 262/K4
Rosebud (creek), Mont. 262/K4
Rosebud, S. Dak. 298/H7
Rosebud, Texas 303/G7
Rosebud (creek), Utah 304/A2
Rosebud Ind. Res., S. Dak. 298/H7
Roseburg, Oreg. 291/D4
Rosebush, Mich. 250/E5
Rose City, Mich. 250/E4
Rose Creek, Minn. 255/F7
Rosedale, Ind. 227/C5
Rosedale, La. 238/G6
Rosedale, Md. 245/M3
Rosedale, Miss. 256/B3
Rosedale, Okla. 288/M5
Rosedale, Tenn. 237/N8
Rosedale, Va. 307/E7
Rosedale, W. Va. 312/E5
Rosefield, La. 238/F5
Roseglen, N. Dak. 282/G4
Rosehearty, Scotland 15/F3
Rosehill, Ala. 195/F8
Rose Hill, Barbados 161/B8
Rose Hill, N.C. 222/E4
Rose Hill, Iowa 229/J6
Rose Hill, Kansas 232/E4
Rose Hill, Ky. 237/M5
Rose Hill, Miss. 256/F6
Rose Hill, N.C. 281/N5
Rose Hill, Va. 307/B7
Roseisle, Manitoba 179/D5
Rose Lake, Br. Col. 184/E3
Roseland, Ark. 202/K2
Roseland, Fla. 212/F4
Roseland, Ind. 227/E1
Roseland, Kansas 232/H4
Roseland, La. 238/J5
Roseland, Minn. 255/C6
Roseland, Nebr. 264/F4
Roseland, N.J. 273/A2
Roseland, Va. 307/K5
Roselawn, Ind. 227/C2
Roselle, Ill. 222/A5
Roselle, N.J. 273/B2
Roselle Park, N.J. 273/A2
Rose Lodge, Oreg. 291/D3
Rose Lynn, Alberta 182/E4
Rosemark, Tenn. 237/B10
Rosemary, Alberta 182/E4
Rosemead, Calif. 204/C10
Rosemère, Québec 172/H4
Rosemont, Ill. 222/B5
Rosemont, Md. 245/H3
Rosemont, N.J. 273/D3
Rosemont, Pa. 294/M5
Rosemount, Minn. 255/E6
Rosemount, Ohio 284/D8
Rosen, Minn. 255/B5
Rosenberg, Texas 303/J8
Rosendale, Minn. 255/D5
Rosendale, Mo. 261/C2
Rosendale, N.Y. 276/M7
Rosendale, Wis. 317/J8
Rosenfeld, Manitoba 179/E5
Rosengart, Manitoba 179/E5
Rosenhayn, N.J. 273/C5
Rosenheim, Germany 22/D5
Rosenhof, Sask. 181/D5
Rosenlaui, Switzerland 39/F3
Rosenort, Manitoba 179/E5
Rosepine, La. 238/D5
Rose Prairie, Br. Col. 184/G2
Roseray, Sask. 181/C5
Roseto, Pa. 294/M4
Rosetown, Sask. 162/F5
Rosetown, Sask. 181/D4
Rosetta, Egypt 111/J2
Rosetta, Egypt 59/B3
Rosetta, Miss. 256/B8
Rosette, Utah 304/A2
Rose Valley, Pa. 294/L7
Rose Valley, Sask. 181/H3
Roseville, Calif. 204/B8
Roseville, Ill. 222/C3
Roseville, Ind. 227/D4
Roseville, Mich. 250/B6
Roseville, Minn. 255/G5
Roseville, Ohio 284/F6
Roseville, Pa. 294/H2
Roseway (riv.), Nova Scotia 168/C4
Rosewood, North. Terr. 93/A4
Rosewood, Ohio 284/C5
Rosewood Heights, Ill. 222/B2
Roshage (cape), Denmark 18/F8
Rosharon, Texas 303/J3
Rosh Ha 'Ayin, Israel 65/B3
Rosholt, S. Dak. 298/R2
Rosholt, Wis. 317/H6
Rosh Pinna, Israel 65/D2
Rosice, Czech. 41/D2
Rosiclare, Ill. 222/E6
Rosie, Ark. 202/G2
Rosier, Georgia 217/H5
Rosignano Marittimo, Italy 34/C3
Rosignol, Guyana 131/C2
Rosine, Ky. 237/H6
Roşiori de Vede, Romania 45/G3
Rositsa, Bulgaria 45/H4
Roskilde (co.), Denmark 21/E6
Roskilde, Denmark 21/E6
Roskilde, Denmark 18/G9

Roslavl', U.S.S.R. 52/D4
Roslev, Denmark 21/B4
Roslin, Ontario 177/G3
Roslin, Tenn. 237/M8
Roslyn, N.Y. 276/R6
Roslyn, S. Dak. 298/P2
Roslyn, Wash. 310/E3
Rosman, N.Y. 281/K4
Rosmaninhal, Portugal 33/C3
Røsnaes (pen.), Denmark 21/D6
Rosneath, Scotland 15/A1
Rosneath, Scotland 10/A1
Ross (isl.), Ant. 2/T10
Ross (isl.), Ant. 5/B9
Ross (sea), Ant. 2/A10
Ross (sea), Ant. 5/B10
Ross, Calif. 204/H1
Ross, Iowa 229/D5
Ross, Manitoba 179/J3
Ross (isl.), Manitoba 179/J3
Ross, Minn. 255/C2
Ross (isl.), New Bruns. 170/D4
Ross, N. Zealand 100/C5
Ross (pt.), Norfolk I. 88/L6
Ross, N. Dak. 282/E3
Ross (co.), Ohio 284/D7
Ross, Ohio 284/B9
Ross, Tasmania 99/D4
Ross (dam), Wash. 310/D2
Ross (lake), Wash. 310/D2
Rossa, Switzerland 39/H4
Rossall (pt.), England 13/D4
Rossan (pt.), Ireland 10/B3
Ross and Cromarty (trad. co.), Scotland 15/A5
Rossano, Italy 34/F5
Rossarden, Tasmania 99/D3
Ross Barnett (res.), Miss. 256/D6
Ross Bay Junction, Newf. 166/A3
Rossbear (lake), Alberta 182/C1
Rossburg, Ohio 284/A5
Rossburn, Manitoba 179/B4
Rosscarbery (bay), Ireland 10/B5
Rosscarbery, Ireland 17/C8
Rosscarbery (bay), Ireland 17/D9
Rosseau, Ontario 177/E2
Rosseau (lake), Ontario 177/E2
Rossel (isl.), Papua N.G. 85/D8
Rossendale, Manitoba 179/D5
Rosser, Manitoba 179/E4
Rosses (bay), Ireland 17/D1
Rosses Point, Ireland 17/D3
Rossford, Ohio 284/C2
Ross Fork, Mont. 262/G3
Ross Ice Shelf, Ant. 2/A11
Ross Ice Shelf, Ant. 5/A10
Rossie, Iowa 229/C3
Rossie, N.Y. 276/J2
Rossignol (lake), Nova Scotia 168/C4
Rossing, Namibia 118/B4
Rossiter, Pa. 294/E4
Rosskeeragh (pt.), Ireland 17/D3
Ross Lake Nat'l Rec. Area, Wash. 310/E2
Rossland, Br. Col. 162/E6
Rossland, Br. Col. 184/H6
Rosslare, Ireland 10/C4
Rosslare, Ireland 17/J7
Rosslare (bay), Ireland 17/J7
Rosslare Harbour (Ballygeary), Ireland 17/J7
Rosslau, Germany 22/E3
Rosslyn Farms, Pa. 294/B7
Rosslyn Village, Ontario 177/G5
Rosslyn Village, Ontario 175/C3
Rossmore, W. Va. 312/C7
Rossmoyne, Ohio 284/C9
Rosso, Mauritania 106/B5
Rosso, Mauritania 102/A3
Ross of Mull (pen.), Scotland 15/B4
Ross-on-Wye, England 10/E5
Ross-on-Wye, England 13/E6
Rossosh', U.S.S.R. 52/E4
Rossport, Ontario 177/H5
Ross River, Yukon 187/E3
Rosston, Ark. 202/D6
Rosston, Ind. 227/E4
Rosston, Okla. 288/G1
Rossville, Georgia 217/B1
Rossville, Ill. 222/F3
Rossville, Ind. 227/D4
Rossville, Iowa 229/L2
Rossville, Kansas 232/G2
Rossville, Tenn. 237/B10
Rosswein, Germany 22/E3
Rostaq, Afghanistan 68/B1
Rostaq, Afghanistan 59/J2
Rosthern, Sask. 162/F5
Rosthern, Sask. 181/E3
Rostock, Germany 7/F3
Rostock, Germany 22/E1
Rostov, U.S.S.R. 2/M3
Rostov, U.S.S.R. 7/J4
Rostov, U.S.S.R. 52/E3
Rostov-na-Donu, U.S.S.R. 48/E5
Rostov-na-Donu, U.S.S.R. 52/F5
Rostrevor, N. Ireland 17/J3
Røsvatn (lake), Norway 18/H4
Roswell, Georgia 217/D2
Roswell, Idaho 220/A6
Roswell, N. Mex. 146/H6
Roswell, N. Mex. 188/E4
Roswell, N. Mex. 274/E5
Roswell, Ohio 284/H5
Roswell, S. Dak. 298/O6
Rosyth, Scotland 15/D2
Rota (isl.), No. Marianas 87/E4
Rota, Spain 33/C4
Rotan, Texas 303/D5
Rotenburg, Germany 22/C2
Rotenburg an der Fulda, Germany 22/C3
Roth, N. Dak. 282/J2
Roth bei Nürnberg, Germany 22/D4
Rothbury, England 10/E3

Rothbury, England 13/E2
Rothbury, Mich. 250/C5
Rothenburg ob der Tauber, Germany 22/D4
Rotherham, England 13/K2
Rotherham, England 10/F4
Rothes, Scotland 10/E2
Rothes, Scotland 15/E3
Rothesay, New Bruns. 170/E3
Rothesay, Scotland 10/D3
Rothesay, Scotland 15/A2
Rothorn (mt.), Switzerland 39/D4
Rothrist, Switzerland 39/E2
Rothsay, Minn. 255/B4
Rothschild, Wis. 317/G6
Rothville, Mo. 261/F3
Roti (isl.), Indonesia 85/G8
Roto, N.S. Wales 97/C3
Rotoroa (lake), N. Zealand 100/D4
Rotorua, N. Zealand 100/F3
Rotorua (lake), N. Zealand 100/F3
Rottenburg am Neckar, Germany 22/C4
Rottenmann, Austria 41/C3
Rotterdam, Netherlands 27/E5
Rotterdam, Netherlands 7/E3
Rotterdam Junction, N.Y. 276/N5
Rottnest (isl.), W. Australia 92/A1
Rottumeplaat (isl.), Netherlands 27/J1
Rottumeroog (isl.), Netherlands 27/J1
Rottweil, Germany 22/C4
Rotuma (isl.), Fiji 87/H7
Roubaix, France 28/E2
Roudnice nad Labem, Czech. 41/C1
Rouen, France 28/D3
Rouen, France 7/E4
Rouge (riv.), Québec 172/C3
Rougemont, N.C. 281/L2
Rougemont, Québec 172/D4
Rougemont, Switzerland 39/D4
Rough (riv.), Ky. 237/H5
Rough River (lake), Ky. 237/J5
Rouka, Papua N.G. 85/B7
Rouleau, Sask. 181/G5
Roulers (Roeselare), Belgium 27/C7
Roulette, Pa. 294/F2
Roumania (Romania) 45
Round (pond), Maine 243/E2
Round (isl.), Miss. 256/G10
Round (pond), Newf. 166/B4
Round, The (mt.), N.S. Wales 97/G2
Round (lake), N.Y. 276/L7
Round (lake), N. Dak. 282/K3
Round (lake), Ontario 177/G2
Round (lake), Wis. 317/F4
Round (lake), Wis. 317/D3
Roundaway, Miss. 256/C2
Round Grove, Ill. 222/D2
Round Grove, Mo. 261/E8
Roundhead, Ohio 284/C4
Round Hill, Alberta 182/D3
Round Hill, Conn. 210/A4
Round Hill, Nova Scotia 168/C4
Round Hill, Va. 307/N2
Round Lake, Fla. 212/D6
Round Lake, Ill. 222/A4
Round Lake, Minn. 255/C7
Roundlake, Miss. 256/C2
Round Lake, N.Y. 276/N5
Round Lake Beach, Ill. 222/A4
Round Lake Centre, Ontario 177/G2
Round Lake Heights, Ill. 222/E1
Round Lake Park, Ill. 222/A4
Round Mountain, Ala. 195/G2
Round Mountain, Calif. 204/D3
Round Mountain, Nev. 266/E4
Round O, S.C. 296/F6
Round Oak, Georgia 217/E4
Round Pond, Ark. 202/J3
Round Pond, Maine 243/E8
Round Prairie, Minn. 255/D5
Round Rock, Texas 303/G7
Round Spring, Mo. 261/J8
Roundstone, Ireland 17/A5
Roundtop (mt.), Hawaii 218/C4
Round Top, Texas 303/H7
Roundup, Mont. 262/H4
Round Valley (res.), N.J. 273/D2
Round Valley Ind. Res., Calif. 204/B4
Roundwood, Ireland 17/J5
Rounthwaite, Manitoba 179/C5
Roura, Fr. Guiana 131/E3
Rousay (isl.), Scotland 10/E1
Rousay (isl.), Scotland 15/E1
Rouses Point, N.Y. 276/O1
Rouseville, Pa. 294/C3
Roussillion (trad. prov.), France 29
Routhierville, Québec 172/B2
Routt (co.), Colo. 208/E1
Rouville (co.), Québec 172/D4
Rouvroy, Belgium 27/G9
Rouyn, Que. 162/J6
Rouyn, Québec 174/B3
Rouzerville, Pa. 294/G6
Rovaniemi, Finland 18/O3
Rover, Ark. 202/D4
Rover, Mo. 261/J9
Roveredo, Switzerland 39/H4
Rovereto, Italy 34/C2
Roviana, Italy 34/H1
Rovieng Tbong, Cambodia 72/E4
Rovigo (prov.), Italy 34/C2
Rovigo, Italy 34/C2
Rovinj, Yugoslavia 45/A3
Rovira, Colombia 126/C5
Rovno, U.S.S.R. 2/L4
Rovno, U.S.S.R. 48/C4
Rovno, U.S.S.R. 52/C4
Rovuma (riv.) 102/F6
Rovuma (riv.), Mozambique 118/F2
Rovuma (riv.), Tanzania 115/G6
Rowan, Iowa 229/H4
Rowan (co.), Ky. 237/P4

Rowan (co.), N.C. 281/H3
Rowans Ravine Prov. Park, Sask. 181/F4
Rowatt, Sask. 181/G5
Rowayton, Conn. 210/B4
Rowe (lake), Maine 243/F2
Rowe •, Mass. 249/C2
Rowe, N. Mex. 274/D3
Rowell, Ark. 202/F6
Rowena, Georgia 217/C8
Rowena, Ky. 237/L7
Rowena, New Bruns. 170/C2
Rowena, N.S. Wales 97/E1
Rowena, S. Dak. 298/R6
Rowena, Texas 303/D6
Rowesville, S.C. 296/F5
Rowland, Ky. 237/M5
Rowland, Nev. 266/F1
Rowland, N.C. 281/L5
Rowlesburg, W. Va. 312/G4
Rowlett, Texas 303/H2
Rowletta, Sask. 181/F5
Rowletts, Ky. 237/K6
Rowley, Alberta 182/D4
Rowley, Iowa 229/K4
Rowley, Mass. 249/L2
Rowley •, Mass. 249/L2
Rowley (isl.), N.W. Terr. 187/K3
Rowley (shoals), W. Australia 92/B2
Roxana, Del. 245/T6
Roxana, Ill. 222/B2
Roxas, Capiz, Philippines 82/D5
Roxas, Isabela, Philippines 82/C2
Roxas, Or. Mindoro, Philippines 82/C4
Roxas, Palawan, Philippines 82/B5
Roxboro, N.C. 281/M2
Roxboro, Québec 172/H4
Roxburgh, N. Zealand 100/B6
Roxburgh (trad. co.), Scotland 15/B5
Roxbury •, Conn. 210/B2
Roxbury, Kansas 232/E3
Roxbury, Maine 243/B6
Roxbury •, Maine 243/B6
Roxbury, Mass. 249/L1
Roxbury •, N.H. 268/C6
Roxbury •, N.J. 273/D2
Roxbury, N.Y. 276/L6
Roxbury, Pa. 294/G5
Roxbury •, Vt. 268/B3
Roxbury, Wis. 317/G9
Roxbury Center, N.H. 268/C6
Roxbury Falls, Conn. 210/B2
Roxbury Station, Conn. 210/B2
Roxie, Miss. 256/B8
Roxobel, N.C. 281/P2
Roxton, Texas 303/J4
Roxton Falls, Québec 172/E4
Roxton Pond, Québec 172/E4
Roy, Georgia 217/D1
Roy, Idaho 220/E7
Roy, Mont. 262/H3
Roy, New Bruns. 170/F2
Roy, N. Mex. 274/E3
Roy, Oreg. 291/A2
Roy, Utah 304/C4
Roy, Wash. 310/C4
Royal, Ill. 222/F3
Royal, Iowa 229/C2
Royal, Nebr. 264/F2
Royal, N.C. 281/R4
Royal Center, Ind. 227/E3
Royal City, Wash. 310/F4
Royale (isl.), Mich. 188/J1
Royale (isl.), Mich. 250/F1
Royal Geographical Society (isls.), N.W. Terr. 187/J3
Royal Gorge (canyon), Colo. 208/J6
Royal Lakes, Ill. 222/C4
Royal Natal Nat'l Park, S. Africa 118/D3
Royal Oak, Md. 245/O6
Royal Oak, Mich. 250/B6
Royal Park, Alberta 182/D3
Royal Pines, N.C. 281/D4
Royal Road, New Bruns. 170/D2
Royalston •, Mass. 249/F2
Royalties, Alberta 182/C4
Royalton, Ill. 222/D6
Royalton, Ind. 227/E5
Royalton, Ky. 237/R5
Royalton, Minn. 255/D5
Royalton, Ohio 284/E6
Royalton, Pa. 294/J5
Royalton •, Vt. 268/B4
Royalton, Wis. 317/J7
Royal Tunbridge Wells, England 13/H6
Royal Tunbridge Wells, England 10/G5
Royalty, Texas 303/B6
Royan, France 28/C5
Royersford, Pa. 294/L5
Royerton, Ind. 227/E4
Roy Hill, W. Australia 92/B3
Royse City, Texas 303/H4
Royston, Br. Col. 184/F7
Royston, England 10/F4
Royston, England 13/G5
Royston, Georgia 217/F2
Rožaj, Yugoslavia 45/E4
Rozel, Kansas 232/C3
Rozet, Wyo. 319/G1
Rožňava, Czech. 41/F2
Rožnov pod Radhoštěm, Czech. 41/E2
Rtishchevo, U.S.S.R. 52/F4
Ruacana Falls (dam), Angola 115/B7
Ruacana (falls), Namibia 118/A3
Ruaha Nat'l Park, Tanzania 115/F5
Ruahine (range), N. Zealand 100/F4

Ruapehu (mt.), N. Zealand 100/E3
Ruapuke (isl.), N. Zealand 100/B7
Ruatapu, N. Zealand 100/C5
Ruawai, N. Zealand 100/D2
Rub al Khali (des.), Saudi Arabia 54/G7
Rub al Khali (des.), Saudi Arabia 59/F5
Rubezhnoye, U.S.S.R. 52/E5
Rubicon, Wis. 317/K9
Rubidoux, Calif. 204/E10
Rubin (dry riv.), Israel 65/B4
Rubio, Venezuela 124/C4
Rubio, Venezuela 124/B4
Rubottom, Okla. 288/M7
Rubtsovsk, U.S.S.R. 54/K4
Rubtsovsk, U.S.S.R. 48/J4
Ruby, Alaska 196/G2
Ruby, La. 238/F4
Ruby (riv.), Mont. 262/D5
Ruby (lake), Nev. 266/F2
Ruby (mts.), Nev. 266/F2
Ruby, S.C. 296/G2
Ruby, Va. 307/N3
Ruby, Wash. 310/H3
Ruby Creek, Br. Col. 184/M3
Ruby Lake, Sask. 181/J3
Ruby River (res.), Mont. 262/D5
Ruby Valley, Nev. 266/F2
Rucava, U.S.S.R. 53/A2
Ruch, Oreg. 291/E5
Ruch'i, U.S.S.R. 48/E3
Ruch'i, U.S.S.R. 52/F1
Rucia (pt.), Dom. Rep. 158/D5
Ruckersville, Georgia 217/G2
Ruda Śląska, Poland 47/B4
Rudbar, Afghanistan 59/H3
Rudbar, Afghanistan 68/A2
Rudd, Iowa 229/H2
Ruddell, Sask. 181/D3
Ruddle, W. Va. 312/H5
Rudeis, Egypt 111/F2
Rüdersdorf bei Berlin, Germany 22/F2
Rüdesheim am Rhein, Germany 22/B3
Rudha Hunish (cape), Scotland 15/B3
Rudh Re (cape), Scotland 15/C3
Rudkøbing, Denmark 18/G9
Rudkøbing, Denmark 21/D8
Rudnik, Poland 47/F3
Rudnyy, U.S.S.R. 48/G4
Rudolf (Turkana) (lake), Ethiopia 111/G7
Rudolf (Turkana) (lake), Kenya 115/G3
Rudolf (isl.), U.S.S.R. 4/A7
Rudolph, Ohio 284/C3
Rudolph, Wis. 317/G7
Rudolstadt, Germany 22/D3
Rud Sar, Iran 66/G2
Ruds Vedby, Denmark 21/E7
Rudy, Ark. 202/B2
Rudyard, Mich. 250/E2
Rudyard, Mont. 262/F2
Rue, France 28/C2
Rueda, Spain 33/D2
Ruedi (res.), Colo. 208/F4
Rüeggisberg, Switzerland 39/E3
Rueil-Malmaison, France 28/A2
Ruen, Switzerland 39/H3
Ruern, Switzerland 39/H3
Rufa'a, Sudan 102/F5
Rufa'a, Sudan 59/B7
Rufa'a, Sudan 111/F5
Rufe, Okla. 288/R6
Ruff, Wash. 310/F3
Ruffec, France 28/D5
Ruffin, N.C. 281/K2
Ruffin, S.C. 296/F6
Rufiji (riv.), Tanzania 102/F6
Rufiji (riv.), Tanzania 115/G5
Rufino, Argentina 143/D3
Rufisque, Senegal 106/A6
Rufus, Oreg. 291/G2
Rufus Woods (lake), Wash. 310/F2
Rugby, England 13/F5
Rugby, England 10/F4
Rugby, N. Dak. 282/L3
Rugby, Tenn. 237/M8
Rugeley, England 13/E5
Rugeley, England 10/F2
Rügen (isl.), Germany 7/F3
Rügen (isl.), Germany 22/E1
Rugless, Ky. 237/P3
Ruhama, Israel 65/B4
Ruhnu (isl.), U.S.S.R. 53/B2
Ruhr (riv.), Germany 22/B3
Ruhtuk (riv.), Iran 66/M7
Ruidosa, Texas 303/C12
Ruidoso, N. Mex. 274/D5
Ruidoso Downs, N. Mex. 274/D5
Ruijin (Juichin), China 77/J6
Ruili, China 77/E7
Ruiselede, Belgium 27/C6
Ruiz, Mexico 150/G6
Rujen (mt.), Bulgaria 45/F4
Rujen (mt.), Yugoslavia 45/F4
Rūjiena, U.S.S.R. 53/C2
Rukwa (reg.), Tanzania 115/F5
Rukwa (lake), Tanzania 102/F6
Rukwa (lake), Tanzania 115/F5
Rule (creek), Colo. 208/N7
Rule, Texas 303/D5
Ruleton, Kansas 232/A2
Ruleville, Miss. 256/C4
Rulhieres (cape), W. Australia 88/D2
Rulhieres (cape), W. Australia 92/D1
Rulo, Nebr. 264/J4

Ruma, Ill. 222/C5
Ruma, Yugoslavia 45/D3
Rumah, Saudi Arabia 59/E4
Rumaitha, Iraq 66/D3
Ruman, Venezuela 124/H5
Rumania (Romania) 45
Rumbek, Sudan 111/E6
Rumble, Md. 245/P8
Rumburk, Czech. 41/C1
Rumelifeneri, Turkey 63/D5
Rumford, Maine 188/M2
Rumford, Maine 243/B6
Rumford •, Maine 243/B6
Rumford, R.I. 249/J5
Rumford, S. Dak. 298/B7
Rumford Center, Maine 243/B7
Rumford Point, Maine 243/B6
Rumia, Poland 47/D1
Rum Jungle, North. Terr. 88/E2
Rum Jungle, North. Terr. 93/B2
Rumlang, Switzerland 39/G2
Rummerfeld, Pa. 294/K2
Rumney •, N.H. 268/D4
Rumoi, Japan 81/K2
Rumphi, Malawi 115/F6
Rumsey, Alberta 182/D4
Rumsey, Ky. 237/G5
Rumson, N.J. 273/F3
Rumuruti, Kenya 115/G3
Runa, W. Va. 312/E6
Runanga, N. Zealand 100/C5
Runaway (cape), N. Zealand 100/G2
Runaway Bay, Jamaica 158/J5
Runcorn, England 10/G2
Runcorn, England 13/G2
Rundu, Namibia 118/B3
Runge, Texas 303/G8
Rungue, Chile 138/G2
Rungwa, Tanzania 115/F5
Rungwa (riv.), Tanzania 115/F5
Rungwe (mt.), Tanzania 115/F5
Runnells, Iowa 229/G5
Runnels (co.), Texas 303/E6
Runnelstown, Miss. 256/F8
Runnemede, N.J. 273/B3
Running Water, S. Dak. 298/N8
Runnymede, Sask. 181/K4
Ruoqiang (Qarkilik), China 77/C4
Rupanco (lake), Chile 138/D3
Rupat (isl.), Indonesia 85/C5
Rupel (riv.), Belgium 27/F7
Rupert, Georgia 217/D6
Rupert, Idaho 220/E7
Rupert (riv.), Québec 174/B2
Rupert •, Vt. 268/A5
Rupert, W. Va. 312/E7
Rupununi (dist.), Guyana 131/B4
Rupununi (riv.), Guyana 131/B4
Rural Hall, N.C. 281/J2
Rural Hill, Miss. 256/F4
Rural Retreat, Va. 307/F7
Rural Valley, Pa. 294/D4
Rurrenabaque, Bolivia 136/B4
Rurutu (isl.), Fr. Poly. 87/L8
Rusagonis, New Bruns. 170/D3
Rusanovo, U.S.S.R. 52/J1
Rusape, Zimbabwe 118/E3
Rüschegg, Switzerland 39/D3
Ruse, Bulgaria 7/G4
Ruse, Bulgaria 45/H4
Rush, Colo. 208/L5
Rush (creek), Colo. 208/N5
Rush (co.), Ind. 227/G5
Rush, Ireland 10/C4
Rush, Ireland 17/J4
Rush (co.), Kansas 232/C3
Rush, Ky. 237/R4
Rush, N.Y. 276/F5
Rush (lake), N. Dak. 282/J4
Rush (riv.), N. Dak. 282/R5
Rush Center, Kansas 232/C3
Rush City, Minn. 255/F5
Rushden, England 13/G5
Rushden, England 10/F4
Rushford, Minn. 255/G7
Rushford, N.Y. 276/D6
Rush Hill, Mo. 261/J4
Rush Lake, Sask. 181/D5
Rush Lake, Wis. 317/J8
Rushmere, Va. 307/P6
Rushmore, Minn. 255/C7
Rushoon, Newf. 166/D4
Rush River, Minn. 255/D6
Rush Run, Ohio 284/J5
Rushsylvania, Ohio 284/C5
Rushville, Ill. 222/C3
Rushville, Ind. 227/G5
Rushville, Mo. 261/B3
Rushville, Nebr. 264/B2
Rushville, N.Y. 276/F5
Rushville, Ohio 284/F6
Rushworth, Victoria 97/C5
Rusk, Ind. 227/D7
Rusk (co.), Texas 303/K5
Rusk, Texas 303/J6
Rusk (co.), Wis. 317/D5
Ruskin, Fla. 212/C3
Ruskin, Nebr. 264/F4
Ruskington, England 13/G4
Ruso, N. Dak. 282/J4
Russas, Brazil 132/G4
Russell (lake), Alberta 182/C1
Russell, Ark. 202/G3
Russell, Georgia 217/E3
Russell, Iowa 229/G7
Russell (co.), Kansas 232/D3
Russell, Kansas 232/D3
Russell (co.), Ky. 237/L7
Russell, Ky. 237/R3
Russell, Manitoba 179/A4
Russell •, Mass. 249/C4
Russell, Minn. 255/C6

Saint Charles 439

Russell, Miss. 256/G6
Russell, N.Y. 276/K2
Russell, N. Zealand 100/E1
Russell, N. Dak. 282/J2
Russell (cape), N.W. Terr. 187/G2
Russell (isl.), N.W. Terr. 187/J2
Russell (pt.), N.W. Terr. 187/G2
Russell (county), Ontario 177/J2
Russell, Ontario 177/J2
Russell, Pa. 294/D2
Russell (isls.), Solomon Is. 86/D3
Russell (co.), Va. 307/D7
Russell Cave Nat'l Mon., Ala. 195/G1
Russell Fork (riv.), Va. 307/C5
Russells Point, Ohio 284/C5
Russell Springs, Kansas 232/A3
Russell Springs, Ky. 237/L6
Russellton, Pa. 294/C4
Russellville, Ala. 195/C2
Russellville, Ark. 202/D3
Russellville, Ill. 222/F5
Russellville, Ind. 227/D5
Russellville, Ky. 237/H7
Russellville, Mo. 261/H6
Russellville, Ohio 284/C8
Russellville, S.C. 296/H5
Russellville, Tenn. 237/P8
Russellville, W. Va. 312/E6
Rüsselsheim, Germany 22/C4
Russia, Ohio 284/B5
Russian (riv.), Calif. 204/B4
Russian Mission, Alaska 196/F2
Russian S.F.S.R., U.S.S.R. 7/H3
Russian S.F.S.R., U.S.S.R. 52/F3
Russian S.F.S.R., U.S.S.R. 48/D4
Russian Soviet Federated Socialist Republic, U.S.S.R. 54/L3
Russiaville, Ind. 227/E4
Russkiy Zavorot (cape), U.S.S.R. 52/H1
Russum, Miss. 256/B7
Rust, Austria 41/D3
Rustad, Minn. 255/B4
Rustavi, U.S.S.R. 52/G6
Rustburg, Va. 307/K6
Rustenburg, S. Africa 118/D5
Ruston, La. 238/E1
Ruston, Wash. 310/C3
Ruswil, Switzerland 39/F2
Rutan, Sask. 181/F3
Rutba, Iraq 59/D3
Rutba, Iraq 66/B4
Rute, Spain 33/D4
Ruteng, Indonesia 85/G7
Ruth, Mich. 250/G5
Ruth, Miss. 256/D8
Ruth, Nev. 266/F3
Ruth, N.C. 281/E4
Rutherford, Ala. 195/H6
Rutherford, N.J. 273/B2
Rutherford (co.), N.C. 281/E4
Rutherford (co.), Tenn. 237/J9
Rutherford, Tenn. 237/C8
Rutherford College, N.C. 281/F3
Rutherford Fork, Obion (riv.), Tenn. 237/D8
Rutherfordton, N.C. 281/E4
Rutherglen, Ontario 177/F1
Rutherglen, Scotland 15/B2
Rutherglen, Scotland 10/B1
Rutherglen, Victoria 97/D5
Ruther Glen, Va. 307/O5
Rutheron, N. Mex. 274/C2
Rüthi, Switzerland 39/J2
Ruthilda, Sask. 181/C4
Ruthin, Wales 10/E4
Ruthin, Wales 13/D4
Ruthsburg, Md. 245/P4
Ruthton, Minn. 255/B6
Ruthven, Iowa 229/D2
Ruthven, Ontario 177/B6
Ruthville, Va. 307/P6
Rüti, Zürich, Switzerland 39/G2
Rüti, Glarus, Switzerland 39/H3
Rutland, Br. Col. 184/H5
Rutland, Ill. 222/D3
Rutland (isl.), India 68/G6
Rutland, Iowa 229/E3
Rutland, Mass. 249/G3
Rutland•, Mass. 249/G3
Rutland, N. Dak. 282/P7
Rutland, Ohio 284/F7
Rutland, Sask. 181/B3
Rutland, S. Dak. 298/P5
Rutland (co.), Vt. 268/A4
Rutland, Vt. 268/B4
Rutland•, Vt. 268/B4
Rutland, Vt. 188/M2
Rutland Plains, Queensland 95/B2
Rutledge, Ala. 195/F7
Rutledge, Georgia 217/E3
Rutledge, Minn. 255/F4
Rutledge, Mo. 261/H2
Rutledge, Pa. 294/M7
Rutledge, Tenn. 237/P8
Rutog, China 77/A5
Rutshuru, Zaire 115/E4
Rutten, Netherlands 27/H3
Ruurlo, Netherlands 27/J4
Ruus al Jibal (dist.), Oman 59/G4
Ruvo di Puglia, Italy 34/F4
Ruvuma (reg.), Tanzania 115/G6
Ruwais, U.A.E. 59/F5
Ruwandiz, Iraq 66/D2
Ruwaq, Jebel er (mts.), Syria 63/G5
Ruwenzori (range), Uganda 115/E3
Ruwenzori (range), Zaire 115/E3
Ruzayevka, U.S.S.R. 52/F4
Ruzizi (riv.), Burundi 115/E4
Ruzizi (riv.), Rwanda 115/E4
Ruzizi (riv.), Zaire 115/E4
Ružomberok, Czech. 41/E2
Rwanda 2/L6
Rwanda 102/F5
RWANDA 115/E4
Ry, Denmark 21/C5
Ryan (peak), Idaho 220/D6
Ryan, Iowa 229/K4
Ryan, Okla. 288/L6
Ryan, Loch (inlet), Scotland 15/C5
Ryan Park, Wyo. 319/F4
Ryans (bay), Newf. 166/B2
Ryazan', U.S.S.R. 7/H3
Ryazan', U.S.S.R. 48/E4
Ryazan', U.S.S.R. 52/E4
Ryazhsk, U.S.S.R. 52/F4
Rybachiy (pen.), U.S.S.R. 48/D2
Rybachiy (pen.), U.S.S.R. 52/D1
Rybach'ye, U.S.S.R. 48/H5
Rybinsk, U.S.S.R. 7/H3
Rybinsk, U.S.S.R. 52/E3
Rybinsk, U.S.S.R. 48/D4
Rybinsk (res.), U.S.S.R. 7/H3
Rybinsk (res.), U.S.S.R. 52/E3
Rybinsk (res.), U.S.S.R. 48/D4
Rybnik, Poland 47/D3
Rybnitsa, U.S.S.R. 52/C5
Rychnov nad Kněžnou, Czech. 41/D1
Rycroft, Alberta 182/A2
Rydal, Georgia 217/C2
Ryde, Calif. 204/B9
Ryde, England 10/F5
Ryde, England 13/F7
Ryde, N.S. Wales 88/K4
Ryde, N.S. Wales 97/J3
Ryder, N. Dak. 282/G4
Ryderwood, Wash. 310/B4
Rye, Ark. 202/F6
Rye, Colo. 208/K7
Rye, England 13/H7
Rye, England 10/G5
Rye (bay), England 13/H7
Rye•, N.H. 268/F5
Rye, N.Y. 276/P6
Rye, Texas 303/K7
Rye Beach, N.H. 268/F6
Ryegate, Mont. 262/G4
Ryegate•, Vt. 268/C3
Rye North Beach, N.H. 268/F5
Rye Patch (res.), Nev. 266/C2
Ryerson, Sask. 181/K6
Rye Valley, Oreg. 291/K3
Ryggebyen, Norway 18/D4
Ryki, Poland 47/F3
Ryland, Ala. 195/F1
Ryland, N.C. 281/R2
Ryland Heights, Ky. 237/M3
Ryley, Alberta 182/D3
Rylstone, N.S. Wales 97/E3
Rýmařov, Czech. 41/D2
Ryomgård, Denmark 21/D5
Ryotsu, Japan 81/J4
Rypin, Poland 47/D2
Rysy (mt.), Poland 47/D4
Ryton, England 13/H3
Ryugasaki, Japan 81/P2
Ryukyu (isls.), Japan 54/O7
Ryukyu (isls.), Japan 2/R4
Ryukyu (isls.), Japan 81/L7
Rzepin, Poland 47/B2
Rzeszów (prov.), Poland 47/F4
Rzeszów, Poland 47/F4
Rzhev, U.S.S.R. 7/H3
Rzhev, U.S.S.R. 48/D4
Rzhev, U.S.S.R. 52/D3

S

Sa'ad, Israel 65/B5
Sa'ada, Yemen 59/D6
Saale (riv.), Germany 22/D3
Saalfeld, Germany 22/D3
Saalfelden am Steinernen Meer, Austria 41/B3
Saane (Sarine) (riv.), Switzerland 39/D3
Saanen, Switzerland 39/D4
Saanich, Br. Col. 184/K3
Saar (riv.), France 28/G3
Saar (riv.), Germany 22/B4
Saarbrücken, Germany 7/E4
Saarbrücken, Germany 22/B4
Saarburg, Germany 22/B4
Saaremaa (isl.), U.S.S.R. 7/G3
Saaremaa (isl.), U.S.S.R. 53/B1
Saaremaa (isl.), U.S.S.R. 52/B3
Saaremaa (isl.), U.S.S.R. 48/B4
Saarijärvi, Finland 18/O5
Saarland (state), Germany 22/B4
Saarlouis, Germany 22/B4
Saas, Switzerland 39/J3
Saas Fee, Switzerland 39/E4
Saba (isl.), Neth. Ant. 156/F3
Saba (isl.), Virgin Is. (U.S.) 161/A4
Šabac, Yugoslavia 45/D3
Sabadell, Spain 7/E4
Sabadell, Spain 33/H2
Sabae, Japan 81/H5
Sabah (reg.), Malaysia 54/N9
Sabah (state), Malaysia 2/Q5
Sabah (state), Malaysia 85/F4
Sábalo, Cuba 158/A2
Sabana, Cuba 158/K4
Sabana (arch.) Cuba 158/E1
Sabana de la Mar, Dom. Rep. 156/E3
Sabana de la Mar, Dom. Rep. 158/F5
Sabana Grande, Dom. Rep. 158/E6
Sabanagrande, Honduras 154/D4
Sabana Grande, P. Rico 161/B2
Sabanalarga, Colombia 126/C2
Sabana Seca, P. Rico 161/D1
Sabancuy, Mexico 150/O7
Sabaneta, Dom. Rep. 158/D5
Sabaneta, Barinas, Venezuela 124/D3
Sabaneta, Falcón, Venezuela 124/D2
Sabang, Celebes, Indonesia 85/F5
Sabang, Weh, Indonesia 85/B4
Şabanözü, Turkey 63/E2
Sabará, Brazil 135/E1
Sabattus, Maine 243/C7
Sabattus•, Maine 243/C7
Sabaudia, Italy 34/D4
Sabaya, Bolivia 136/A6
Saberi, Hamun-e (lake), Iran 66/M5
Sabetha, Kansas 232/G2
Sabi (riv.), Zimbabwe 118/E3
Sabile, U.S.S.R. 53/B2
Sabillasville, Md. 245/J2
Sabin, Minn. 255/B4
Sabina, Ohio 284/C7
Sabinal (cay), Cuba 158/H2
Sabinal, Texas 303/E8
Sabinas, Mexico 150/J3
Sabinas (riv.), Mexico 150/J3
Sabinas Hidalgo, Mexico 150/J3
Sabine (riv.) 188/H4
Sabine (mt.) 5/B9
Sabine (par.), La. 238/C3
Sabine (lake), La. 238/C7
Sabine (passage), La. 238/C7
Sabine (riv.), La. 238/C5
Sabine (pen.), N.W.T. 187/H2
Sabine (co.), Texas 303/L6
Sabine, Texas 303/L8
Sabine (lake), Texas 303/L8
Sabine (riv.), Texas 303/L7
Sabine Pass, Texas 303/L8
Sabinópolis, Brazil 132/F7
Sabinoso, N. Mex. 274/E3
Sabinov, Czech. 41/F2
Sabinsville, Pa. 294/G2
Sabir, Jebel (mt.), Yemen 59/D7
Sabirabad, U.S.S.R. 52/G6
Sabkha, Syria 63/H5
Sablayan, Philippines 82/C4
Sable (cape), Fla. 188/K5
Sable (cape), Fla. 212/E6
Sable (cape), N.S. 146/M5
Sable (isl.), N.S. 146/N5
Sable (cape), N.S. 162/K7
Sable (isl.), N.S. 162/L7
Sable (cape), Nova Scotia 168/C5
Sable (isl.), Nova Scotia 168/J5
Sable (riv.), Ontario 177/B1
Sable (riv.), Québec 174/D1
Sable River, Nova Scotia 168/C5
Sables (lake), Québec 172/B3
Sables (lake), Québec 172/H1
Sablé-sur-Sarthe, France 28/C4
Sabougla, Miss. 256/F3
Sabra (cape), Indonesia 85/J6
Sabrathaa, Libya 111/B1
Sabrina Coast (reg.) 5/C6
Sabtang, Philippines 82/B2
Sabtang (isl.), Philippines 82/B2
Sabugal, Portugal 33/C2
Sabula, Iowa 229/N4
Sabula, Mo. 261/L8
Sabula, Pa. 294/E3
Sabya, Saudi Arabia 59/D6
Sabzevar, Iran 54/G6
Sabzevar, Iran 59/G2
Sabzevar, Iran 66/K2
Sabzvaran, Iran 66/K6
Sabzvaran, Iran 59/G4
Sac (co.), Iowa 229/C4
Sac (riv.), Mo. 261/E7
Sacaba, Bolivia 136/C5
Sacaca, Bolivia 136/B6
Sacajawea (peak), Oreg. 291/K2
Sacajawea (lake), Wash. 310/G4
Sácama, Colombia 126/D4
Sacandaga (lake), N.Y. 276/L3
Sac and Fox Ind. Res., Iowa 229/H5
Sacapulas, Guatemala 154/B3
Sacaton, Ariz. 198/D5
Sacavém, Portugal 33/A1
Sac City, Iowa 229/C4
Sacedón, Spain 33/E2
Săcele, Romania 45/G3
Sac-Fox-Iowa Ind. Res., Kansas 232/G2
Sacheen (lake), Wash. 310/H2
Sachem (head), Conn. 210/E4
Sachem Head, Conn. 210/E3
Sachigo (riv.), Ont. 162/G5
Sachigo (riv.), Ontario 175/B2
Sachojere, Bolivia 136/C4
Sachse, Texas 303/H2
Sachseln, Switzerland 39/F3
Sachs Harbour, Canada 4/B16
Sachs Harbour, N.W.T. 162/D1
Sachs Harbour, N.W.T. 187/F2
Sackets (harb.), N.Y. 276/H3
Sackets Harbor, N.Y. 276/H3
Säckingen, Germany 22/C5
Sackville, New Bruns. 170/F3
Sackville, Nova Scotia 168/E4
Saco, Ala. 195/G7
Saco, Maine 243/C8
Saco (riv.), Maine 243/B8
Saco, Mo. 261/M8
Saco, Mont. 262/J2
Saco (riv.), N.H. 268/E3
Sacol (isl.), Philippines 82/D7
Sacramento, Brazil 132/D7
Sacramento, Brazil 135/C1
Sacramento (co.), Calif. 204/D5
Sacramento (cap.), Calif. 146/F6
Sacramento (cap.), Calif. 188/B3
Sacramento (cap.), Calif. 204/B8
Sacramento (riv.), Calif. 188/B3
Sacramento (riv.), Calif. 204/D5
Sacramento, Ky. 237/G6
Sacramento, N. Mex. 274/D6
Sacramento (mts.), N. Mex. 274/D6
Sacramento Army Depot, Calif. 204/B8
Sacramento Wash (dry riv.), Ariz. 198/A4
Sacratif (cape), Spain 33/E4
Sacré-Coeur-de-Saguenay, Québec 172/H1
Sacred Heart, Minn. 255/C6
Sacul, Texas 303/K6
Sádaba, Spain 33/F1
Sadani, Tanzania 115/G5
Saddle (hills), Alberta 182/A2
Saddle, Ark. 202/G1
Saddle (mt.), Idaho 220/F6
Saddle (mt.), Idaho 220/D3
Saddle (riv.), N.J. 273/B1
Saddle (mts.), Wash. 310/E4
Saddle Brook•, N.J. 273/B1
Saddle Mountain, Okla. 288/J5
Saddle River, N.J. 273/B1
Saddlestring, Wyo. 319/F1
Saddleworth, England 13/J2
Saddleworth, England 10/G2
Sa Dec, Vietnam 72/E5
Sadhoowa, Trin. & Tob. 161/B11
Sadieville, Ky. 237/M4
Sadij (riv.), Iran 66/L8
Sadiya, India 68/H3
Sa'diya, Iraq 66/D3
Sa'diya, Hor (lake), Iraq 66/E4
Sadlers Village, St. Kitts & Nevis 161/C10
Sadlersville, Tenn. 237/G7
Sado (isl.), Japan 81/J4
Sado (riv.), Portugal 33/B3
Sadon, Burma 72/C1
Sadorus, Ill. 222/E4
Saeby, Denmark 18/G8
Saeby, Denmark 21/D3
Saeendey, Iran 66/E2
Saegertown, Pa. 294/B2
Saetermoen, Norway 18/L2
Safad (Zefat), Israel 65/C2
Safaniya, Ras (cape), Saudi Arabia 59/E4
Šafárikovo, Czech. 41/F2
Safata (bay), W. Samoa 86/M9
Safe, Mo. 261/J6
Safety Harbor, Fla. 212/B2
Säffle, Sweden 18/H7
Safford, Ala. 195/D6
Safford, Ariz. 198/F6
Saffordville, Kansas 232/F3
Saffron Walden, England 10/G4
Saffron Walden, England 13/H5
Safi, Jordan 65/E5
Safi, Morocco 102/B1
Safi, Morocco 106/C2
Safidar, Kuh-e (mt.), Iran 59/F4
Safidar, Kuh-e (mt.), Iran 66/H6
Safid Rud (riv.), Iran 66/F2
Safien, Switzerland 39/H3
Safita, Syria 63/G5
Safonovo, U.S.S.R. 52/D3
Safranbolu, Turkey 63/E2
Safut, Jordan 65/D3
Saga, China 77/B6
Saga (pref.), Japan 81/E7
Saga, Japan 81/E7
Sagadahoc (co.), Maine 243/D7
Sagaing (div.), Burma 72/B1
Sagaing, Burma 72/B2
Sagami (bay), Japan 81/O3
Sagami (riv.), Japan 81/O2
Sagami (sea), Japan 81/J6
Sagamihara, Japan 81/O2
Sagamore, Mass. 249/M5
Sagamore, Pa. 294/D4
Sagamore Hill Nat'l Hist. Site, N.Y. 276/R6
Sagamore Hills, Ohio 284/J10
Saganaga (lake), Minn. 255/H2
Saganaga (lake), Ontario 175/B3
Sagar, India 68/D4
Sagavanirktok (riv.), Alaska 196/J1
Sagay, Camiguin, Philippines 82/E6
Sagay, Negros Occ., Philippines 82/D5
Sage, Ark. 202/G1
Sage (creek), Mont. 262/F2
Sage (mt.), Virgin Is. (U.K.) 161/D4
Sage, Wyo. 319/B4
Sagemace (bay), Manitoba 179/B3
Sagerton, Texas 303/E4
Sageville, Iowa 229/M3
Sag Harbor, N.Y. 276/R8
Saginaw, Ala. 195/E4
Saginaw, Mich. 188/K2
Saginaw (bay), Mich. 188/K2
Saginaw (co.), Mich. 250/E5
Saginaw, Mich. 250/F5
Saginaw (bay), Mich. 250/F5
Saginaw (riv.), Mich. 250/F5
Saginaw, Minn. 255/F4
Saginaw, Mo. 261/C8
Saginaw, Oreg. 291/E4
Saginaw, Texas 303/E2
Sagle, Idaho 220/B1
Saglek (bay), Newf. 166/B2
Saglek (fjord), Newf. 166/B2
Sagnay, Philippines 82/D4
Sagola, Mich. 250/B2
Saguache (co.), Colo. 208/G6
Saguache, Colo. 208/G6
Saguache (creek), Colo. 208/F6
Sagua de Tánamo, Cuba 158/K3
Sagua la Grande, Cuba 156/B2
Sagua la Grande, Cuba 158/E1
Sagua la Grande (riv.), Cuba 158/E1
Saguaro (lake), Ariz. 198/D5
Saguaro Nat'l Mon., Ariz. 198/E6
Saguenay (county), Québec 174/D2
Saguenay (co.), Québec 172/H1
Saguenay (riv.), Québec 174/C3
Saguenay (riv.), Québec 172/G1
Saguia el Hamra (dry riv.), Western Sahara 106/B3
Sagunto, Spain 33/F3
Sa'gya, China 77/C6
Sahagún, Colombia 126/C3
Sahagún, Spain 33/D1
Sahand, Kuh-e (mt.), Iran 66/E2
Sahara (desert) 2/J4
Sahara (des.) 102/C2
Sahara (des.), Algeria 106/E4
Sahara (des.), Chad 111/C3
Sahara (des.), Egypt 111/E3
Sahara (des.), Libya 111/C3
Sahara (des.), Mali 106/D4
Sahara (des.), Mauritania 106/C4
Sahara (des.), Niger 106/F4
Sahara (des.), Sudan 111/E3
Saharan Atlas (ranges), Algeria 106/E2
Saharanpur, India 68/D3
Saharsa, India 68/F3
Şahinli, Turkey 63/C6
Sahiwal, Pakistan 68/C2
Sahiwal, Pakistan 59/K3
Sahuaripa, Mexico 150/E2
Sahuarita, Ariz. 198/E7
Sahuayo de Díaz, Mexico 150/H7
Šahy, Czech. 41/E2
Saïda, Algeria 106/E2
Saida, Lebanon 63/F6
Sa'idabad, Iran 66/J6
Sa'idabad, Iran 59/G4
Saïdia, Morocco 106/D2
Saidor, Papua N.G. 85/B7
Saidu, Pakistan 68/C2
Saignelégier, Switzerland 39/D2
Saigo, Japan 81/F5
Saigon (Ho Chi Minh City), Vietnam 54/M8
Saigon (Ho Chi Minh City), Vietnam 72/E5
Saihut, Yemen 54/G8
Saihut, Yemen 59/F6
Saikai Nat'l Park, Japan 81/D7
Saiki, Japan 81/E7
Sailes, La. 238/D2
Sailor (creek), Idaho 220/C7
Sailor Springs, Ill. 222/E5
Saimaa (lake), Finland 18/Q6
Saimbeyli, Turkey 63/G4
Sain Alto, Mexico 150/H5
Sain-ni, N. Korea 81/B4
Saint Abbs, Scotland 15/F5
Saint Abbs (head), Scotland 15/F5
Saint-Adalbert, Québec 172/H3
Saint-Adelme, Québec 172/B1
Saint-Adelphe, Québec 172/E3
Saint Adolphe, Manitoba 179/E5
Saint-Adolphe, Québec 172/F2
Saint-Adolphe-d'Howard, Québec 172/C4
Saint-Adrien, Québec 172/F4
Saint-Affrique, France 28/E6
Saint-Agapitville, Québec 172/F3
Saint Agatha•, Maine 243/G1
Saint Agnes, England 13/B7
Saint-Aimé-des-Lacs, Québec 172/G2
Saint-Alban, Québec 172/E3
Saint Albans, England 13/H7
Saint Albans, England 10/F5
Saint Alban's (head), England 13/F7
Saint Albans•, Maine 243/E6
Saint Albans, Mo. 261/L5
Saint Alban's, Newf. 166/C4
Saint Albans, Vt. 268/A2
Saint Albans•, Vt. 268/A2
Saint Albans, W. Va. 312/C6
Saint Albans Bay, Vt. 268/A2
Saint Albert, Alberta 182/D3
Saint Albert, Ontario 177/J2
Saint-Albert, Québec 172/E3
Saint-Alexandre, Québec 172/D4
Saint-Alexandre-de-Kamouraska, Québec 172/H2
Saint-Alexis, Québec 172/D4
Saint-Alexis-de-Matapédia, Québec 172/B2
Saint-Alexis-des-Monts, Québec 172/D3
Saint Almo, New Bruns. 170/C2
Saint Alphonse, Manitoba 179/C5
Saint-Alphonse, Québec 172/D3
Saint Alphonse de Clare, Nova Scotia 168/B4
Saint-Alphonse-de-Caplan, Québec 172/C2
Saint-Amable, Québec 172/J4
Saint-Amand-Mont-Rond, France 28/E4
Saint Amant, La. 238/L2
Saint Ambroise, Manitoba 179/E4
Saint-Ambroise, Québec 172/F1
Saint-Anaclet, Québec 172/J1
Saint-André (cape), Madagascar 118/G3
Saint-André, New Bruns. 170/C1
Saint-André, Québec 172/B2
Saint-André, Réunion 118/G5
Saint-André-Avellin, Québec 172/B4
Saint-André-de-Kamouraska, Québec 172/H2
Saint-André-du-Lac-Saint-Jean, Québec 172/E1
Saint-André-Est, Québec 172/C4
Saint Andrew (pt.), Fla. 212/D6
Saint Andrew (sound), Georgia 217/K9
Saint Andrew (lake), Manitoba 179/E3
Saint Andrew (mt.), St. Vin. & Grens. 161/A9
Saint Andrews, New Bruns. 170/C3
Saint Andrew's, Newf. 166/C4
Saint Andrews, Nova Scotia 168/F3
Saint Andrews (chan.), Nova Scotia 168/H2
Saint Andrews, Scotland 15/F4
Saint Andrews, Scotland 10/E2
Saint Andrews (bay), Scotland 15/F4
Saint Andrews, S.C. 296/G6
Saint Andrews, Tenn. 237/K10
Saint-Anicet, Québec 172/C4
Saint Ann, Mo. 261/O2
Saint Anne, Chan. Is. 13/E8
Saint Anne, Ill. 222/F2
Saint Anns (bay), Nova Scotia 168/H2
Saint Anns, Ontario 177/E4
Saint Ann's Bay, Jamaica 156/C3
Saint Ann's Bay, Jamaica 158/J5
Saint-Anselme, Québec 172/F3
Saint Ansgar, Iowa 229/H2
Saint Anthony, Idaho 220/G6
Saint Anthony, Ind. 227/D8
Saint Anthony, Iowa 229/G4
Saint Anthony, Minn. 255/D5
Saint Anthony, Minn. 255/G5
Saint Anthony, Newf. 166/C3
Saint Anthony, N. Dak. 282/H6
Saint-Antoine, New Bruns. 170/F2
Saint-Antoine, Québec 172/H4
Saint-Antoine-Abbé, Québec 172/D4
Saint-Antoine-sur-Richelieu, Québec 172/D4
Saint-Antonin, Québec 172/H2
Saint-Antonin-Noble-Val, France 28/D5
Saint Arnaud, Victoria 97/B5
Saint-Arsène, Québec 172/H2
Saint Arthur, New Bruns. 170/D1
Saint-Astier, France 28/D5
Saint-Athanase, Québec 172/H2
Saint-Aubert, Québec 172/G2
Saint Aubin, Chan. Is. 13/E8
Saint-Aubin-Sauges, Switzerland 39/C3
Saint Augustin (riv.), Newf. 166/C3
Saint-Augustin, Québec 172/G4
Saint-Augustin, Québec 174/F2
Saint-Augustin (riv.), Québec 174/F2
Saint-Augustin-de-Québec, Québec 172/E3
Saint Augustine, Fla. 188/K5
Saint Augustine, Fla. 146/K7
Saint Augustine, Fla. 212/E2
Saint Augustine, Ill. 222/C3
Saint Augustine, Md. 245/P3
Saint Augustine Beach, Fla. 212/E2
Saint Austell (bay), England 13/C7
Saint Austell-with-Fowey, England 13/C7
Saint Austell with Fowey, England 10/D5
Saint-Barnabé, Québec 172/D4
Saint-Barthélemy (isl.), Guadeloupe 156/F3
Saint-Barthélemy, Québec 172/D3
Saint Basile, New Bruns. 170/B1
Saint-Basile-le-Grand, Québec 172/J4
Saint-Basile-Sud, Québec 172/F3
Saint Bees (head), England 13/D3
Saint Benedict, Kansas 232/F2
Saint Benedict, La. 238/K5
Saint Benedict, Oreg. 291/B3
Saint Benedict, Pa. 294/E4
Saint Benedict, Sask. 181/F3
Saint-Benjamin, Québec 172/G3
Saint-Benoît, Réunion 118/G5
Saint-Benoît-Labre, Québec 172/G3
Saint Bernard, Ala. 195/E2
Saint Bernard (par.), La. 238/L7
Saint Bernard, La. 238/L7
Saint Bernard, Nova Scotia 168/B4
Saint Bernard, Ohio 284/B9
Saint-Bernard, Québec 172/F3
Saint Bernard, Great (pass), Switzerland 39/D5
Saint-Bernard-sur-Mer, Québec 172/G2
Saint Bernice, Ind. 227/C5
Saint Bethlehem, Tenn. 237/G7
Saint Blaise, Québec 172/E4
Saint-Blaise, Switzerland 39/D2
Saint-Bonaventure-de-Yamaska, Québec 172/E4
Saint-Boniface-de-Shawinigan, Québec 172/D3
Saint Bonifacius, Minn. 255/F5
Saint Brendan's, Newf. 166/D4
Saint Brides, Alberta 182/E2
Saint Bride's, Newf. 166/C2
Saint Brides (bay), Wales 10/D5
Saint Brides (bay), Wales 13/B6
Saint-Brieuc, France 28/B3
Saint Brieux, Sask. 181/G3
Saint-Bruno, Québec 172/F1
Saint-Bruno-de-Montarville, Québec 172/J4
Saint-Calais, France 28/D4
Saint-Calixte-de-Kilkenny, Québec 172/D4
Saint-Camille, Québec 172/F4
Saint-Camille-de-Bellechasse, Québec 172/G3
Saint-Casimir, Québec 172/E3
Saint Catharine, Mo. 261/G3
Saint Catharines, Ontario 177/E4
Saint Catherine, Fla. 212/D3
Saint Catherine (mt.), Grenada 161/D8
Saint Catherine (lake), Vt. 268/A5
Saint Catherines (isl.), Georgia 217/K7
Saint Catherines (sound), Georgia 217/K7
Saint-Céré, France 28/D5
Saint-Cergue, Switzerland 39/B4
Saint-Césaire, Québec 172/D4
Saint-Chamond, France 28/F5
Saint Charles, Ark. 202/H5
Saint Charles, Idaho 220/G7
Saint Charles, Ill. 222/E2
Saint Charles, Iowa 229/F6
Saint Charles, Ky. 237/G6
Saint Charles (par.), La. 238/K7
Saint Charles, Mich. 250/E5
Saint Charles, Minn. 255/F7
Saint Charles (co.), Mo. 261/M2
Saint Charles, Mo. 261/N1
Saint-Charles, New Bruns. 170/F2
Saint Charles, Ontario 177/D1
Saint-Charles, Bellechasse, Québec 172/G3
Saint Charles, S.C. 296/G3
Saint Charles, S. Dak. 298/L7

Saint Charles, Va. 307/B7
Saint-Charles-de-Mandeville, Québec 172/D3
Saint-Charles-Garnier, Québec 172/J1
Saint-Charles-sur-Richelieu, Québec 172/D4
Saint Christopher (Saint Kitts) (isl.), St. Kitts & Nevis 156/F3
Saint Christopher (Saint Kitts) (isl.), St. Kitts & Nevis 161/D10
Saint Chrysostom, Pr. Edward I. 168/E2
Saint-Chrysostome, Québec 172/D4
Saint Clair (co.), Ala. 195/F3
Saint Clair, Ala. 195/E6
Saint Clair, Georgia 217/H4
Saint Clair (co.), Ill. 222/D5
Saint Clair (lake), Mich. 188/K2
Saint Clair (co.), Mich. 250/G6
Saint Clair, Mich. 250/G6
Saint Clair (lake), Mich. 250/G6
Saint Clair (riv.), Mich. 250/G6
Saint Clair, Minn. 255/E6
Saint Clair (co.), Mo. 261/E6
Saint Clair, Mo. 261/K6
Saint Clair (lake), Ontario 177/B5
Saint Clair (riv.), Ontario 177/B5
Saint Clair, Pa. 294/K4
Saint Clair (lake), Tasmania 99/C4
Saint Clair Beach, Ontario 177/B5
Saint Clair Shores, Mich. 250/B6
Saint Clair Springs, Ala. 195/F3
Saint Clairsville, Ohio 284/J5
Saint Clairsville, Pa. 294/F5
Saint-Claude, France 28/F4
Saint-Claude, Guadeloupe 161/A7
Saint-Claude, Manitoba 179/D5
Saint-Claude, Québec 172/F3
Saint Clears, Wales 13/C6
Saint-Clément, Québec 172/H2
Saint Clements, Ontario 177/D4
Saint-Cléophas, Québec 172/D3
Saint-Clet, Québec 172/C4
Saint Cloud, Fla. 212/E4
Saint-Cloud, France 28/A2
Saint Cloud, Minn. 188/H1
Saint Cloud, Minn. 255/D5
Saint Cloud, Wis. 317/K8
Saint Columb Major, England 13/B7
Saint Combs, Scotland 15/G3
Saint-Côme, Québec 172/D3
Saint-Constant, Québec 172/H4
Saint Croix (riv.) 188/H1
Saint Croix, Ind. 227/D8
Saint Croix (riv.), Maine 243/J5
Saint Croix (riv.), Minn. 255/F5
Saint Croix, New Bruns. 170/C3
Saint Croix (riv.), New Bruns. 170/C3
Saint Croix, Nova Scotia 168/E4
Saint Croix (isl.), Virgin Is. (U.S.) 156/H2
Saint Croix (isl.), Virgin Is. (U.S.) 161/G4
Saint Croix (co.), Wis. 317/B5
Saint Croix (lake), Wis. 317/A6
Saint Croix (riv.), Wis. 317/A4
Saint Croix Falls, Wis. 317/A5
Saint Croix Flowage (res.), Wis. 317/C3
Saint Croix Isl. Nat'l Mon., Maine 243/J5
Saint-Cuthbert, Québec 172/D3
Saint-Cyprien, Québec 172/J2
Saint-Cyrille, Québec 172/E4
Saint-Cyrille-de-L'Islet, Québec 172/G3
Saint Cyrus, Scotland 15/F4
Saint-Damase, Québec 172/B1
Saint-Damase-des-Aulnaies, Québec 172/C2
Saint-Damien-de-Brandon, Québec 172/D3
Saint-Damien-de-Buckland, Québec 172/G3
Saint David, Ariz. 198/E7
Saint David, Ill. 222/C3
Saint David, Maine 243/J1
Saint-David, Québec 172/J3
Saint-David-de-Falardeau, Québec 172/F1
Saint-David-d'Yamaska, Québec 172/E4
Saint Davids (isl.), Bermuda 156/H2
Saint David's, Wales 13/B6
Saint David's (head), Wales 10/D5
Saint David's (head), Wales 13/B6
Saint-Denis, France 28/B1
Saint-Denis, France 28/B4
Saint-Denis (cap.), Réunion 118/F5
Saint Denis, Sask. 181/B3
Saint-Denis-de-la-Bouteillerie, Québec 172/G2
Saint-Didace, Québec 172/D3
Saint-Dié, France 28/G3
Saint-Dizier, France 28/F3
Saint-Dominique, Québec 172/E4
Saint-Donat-de-Montcalm, Québec 172/D3
Saint-Donat-de-Rimouski, Québec 172/J1
Saint Donatus, Iowa 229/M4
Sainte-Adèle, Québec 172/C4
Sainte Agathe, Manitoba 179/E5
Sainte-Agathe, Québec 172/D3
Sainte-Agathe-des-Monts, Québec 172/C3
Sainte-Agnès-de-Charlevoix, Québec 172/G2
Sainte Amélie, Manitoba 179/C4
Sainte-Anastasie, Québec 172/F3
Sainte-Angèle-de-Mérici, Québec 172/J1
Sainte Anne (lake), Alberta 182/C3
Sainte-Anne, Guadeloupe 161/B6
Sainte Anne, Manitoba 179/F5

Sainte-Anne, Martinique 161/D7
Sainte-Anne, New Bruns. 170/E1
Sainte-Anne (lake), Québec 172/H2
Sainte-Anne (riv.), Québec 172/C1
Sainte-Anne (riv.), Québec 172/G2
Sainte-Anne (riv.), Québec 172/F3
Sainte Anne (isl.), Seychelles 118/H5
Sainte-Anne-de-Beaupré, Québec 172/F2
Sainte-Anne-de-Bellevue, Québec 172/H4
Sainte-Anne-de-Kent, New Bruns. 170/F2
Sainte-Anne-de-Madawaska, New Bruns. 170/B1
Sainte-Anne-des-Monts, Québec 172/C1
Sainte-Anne-des-Plaines, Québec 172/H4
Sainte-Anne-du-Lac, Québec 172/B3
Sainte-Apolline, Québec 172/G3
Sainte-Aurélie, Québec 172/G3
Sainte-Béatrix, Québec 172/D3
Sainte-Bernadette, Québec 172/G1
Sainte-Blandine, Québec 172/J1
Sainte-Brigide, Québec 172/D4
Sainte-Catherine, Québec 172/F3
Sainte-Cécile-de-Frontenac, Québec 172/G4
Sainte-Cécile-de-Masham, Québec 172/A4
Sainte-Claire, Québec 172/G3
Sainte-Clothilde-de-Horton, Québec 172/E4
Sainte-Croix, Québec 172/F3
Sainte-Croix, Switzerland 39/B3
Saint-Édouard-de-Kent, New Bruns. 170/F2
Saint-Édouard-de-Maskinongé, Québec 172/D3
Saint-Édouard-de-Napierville, Québec 172/D4
Saint Edward, Nebr. 264/G3
Saint Edward, Pr. Edward I. 168/D2
Sainte-Edwidge, Québec 172/F4
Sainte-Élisabeth, Québec 172/D3
Sainte-Émélie-de-l'Énergie, Québec 172/D3
Sainte-Eulalie, Québec 172/E3
Sainte-Euphémie, Québec 172/G3
Sainte-Famille-d'Aumond, Québec 172/B3
Sainte-Famille-d'Orléans, Québec 172/G3
Sainte-Félicité, Québec 172/B1
Sainte-Flavie, Québec 172/J1
Sainte-Florence, Québec 172/B2
Sainte-Foy, Québec 172/H3
Sainte-Françoise, Québec 172/H1
Sainte-Geneviève, Manitoba 179/F5
Sainte Genevieve (co.), Mo. 261/M7
Sainte Genevieve, Mo. 261/M6
Sainte-Geneviève, Québec 172/H4
Sainte-Geneviève-de-Batiscan, Québec 172/E3
Sainte-Hedwidge-de-Roberval, Québec 172/E1
Sainte-Hélène-de-Bagot, Québec 172/E4
Sainte-Hélène-de-Kamouraska, Québec 172/H2
Sainte-Hénédine, Québec 172/F3
Sainte-Julie-de-Verchères, Québec 172/J4
Sainte-Julienne, Québec 172/D4
Sainte-Julie-Station, Québec 172/F3
Sainte-Justine, Québec 172/G3
Sainte-Justine-de-Newton, Québec 172/C4
Saint Eleanors, Pr. Edward I. 168/E2
Saint-Éleuthère, Québec 172/H2
Saint Elias (cape), Alaska 196/K3
Saint Elias (mt.), Alaska 188/D5
Saint Elias (mt.), Alaska 196/K2
Saint Elias (mts.), Alaska 196/L2
Saint Elias (mt.), Yukon 162/B3
Saint Elias (mt.), Yukon 187/E3
Saint Elias (mts.), Yukon 187/E3
Saint-Élie, Fr. Guiana 131/D3
Sainte-Élie, Québec 172/E3
Saint Elizabeth, Mo. 261/H6
Saint Elmo, Ala. 195/B10
Saint Elmo, Colo. 208/G5
Saint Elmo, Ill. 222/E4
Saint-Éloi, Québec 172/H1
Sainte-Louise, Québec 172/G2
Sainte-Luce, Martinique 161/D7
Sainte-Luce, Québec 172/J1
Sainte-Lucie-de-Beauregard, Québec 172/H3
Sainte-Lucie-de-Doncaster, Québec 172/C3
Saint-Elzéar, Québec 172/F3
Saint-Elzéar-de-Bonaventure, Québec 172/C2
Sainte-Marguerite, Guadeloupe 161/B6
Sainte-Marguerite-de-Dorchester, Québec 172/G3
Sainte-Marguerite-Marie, Québec 172/B2
Sainte-Marguerite (riv.), Québec 172/G1
Sainte-Marguerite (riv.), Québec 174/D2
Sainte-Marguerite Nord-Est (riv.), Québec 172/H1
Sainte-Marie, Guadeloupe 161/A6
Sainte-Marie, Ill. 222/E5
Sainte-Marie (cape), Madagascar 2/M4
Sainte-Marie (Vohimena) (cape), Madagascar 118/G5
Sainte-Marie (Nosy Boraha) (isl.), Madagascar 118/J3
Sainte-Marie, Martinique 161/D5

Sainte-Marie, Beauce, Québec 172/G3
Sainte-Marie, Nicolet, Québec 172/E3
Sainte-Marie (lake), Québec 172/B4
Sainte-Marie-de-Kent, New Bruns. 170/F2
Sainte-Marie-sur-Mer, New Bruns. 170/F1
Sainte-Marthe-de-Gaspé, Québec 172/C1
Sainte-Martine, Québec 172/D4
Sainte-Menehould, France 28/F3
Sainte-Mère-Église, France 28/C3
Saint-Émile, Québec 172/H3
Saint-Émile-de-Suffolk, Québec 172/B4
Sainte-Monique, Nicolet, Québec 172/E3
Sainte-Monique, Lac-St-Jean-E., Québec 172/F1
Sainte-Ode, Belgium 27/H8
Sainte-Perpétue, Québec 172/E3
Sainte-Perpétue-de-L'Islet, Québec 172/H2
Saint-Éphrem-de-Tring, Québec 172/G3
Saint-Épiphane, Québec 172/H2
Sainte-Pudentienne, Québec 172/F4
Sainte Rita, Manitoba 179/F5
Sainte-Rosalie, Québec 172/E4
Sainte-Rose, Guadeloupe 161/A6
Sainte-Rose-de-Watford, Québec 172/G3
Sainte Rose du Lac, Manitoba 179/C3
Sainte-Rose-du-Nord, Québec 172/G1
Sainte-Rose-Gloucester, New Bruns. 170/F1
Saintes, France 28/C5
Saintes (chan.), Guadeloupe 161/A7
Saintes (isls.), Guadeloupe 161/A7
Sainte-Sabine-de-Bellechasse, Québec 172/G3
Sainte-Savine, France 28/E3
Sainte-Sophie-de-Lévrard, Québec 172/E3
Sainte-Sophie-de-Mégantic, Québec 172/F3
Saint-Esprit, Québec 172/D4
Sainte-Thècle, Québec 172/E3
Sainte-Thérèse, Québec 172/H4
Sainte-Thérèse (isl.), Québec 172/J4
Sainte-Thérèse-de-L'Enfant-Jésus, Québec 172/D2
Sainte-Thérèse-Ouest, Québec 172/H4
Saint-Étienne, France 7/E4
Saint-Étienne, France 28/F5
Saint-Étienne-de-Grès, Québec 172/E3
Saint-Étienne-de-Lauzon, Québec 172/J3
Saint-Eugène, Ontario 177/K2
Saint-Eugène-de-Grantham, Québec 172/E4
Sainte-Ursule, Québec 172/D3
Sainte-Eusèbe, Québec 172/J2
Saint Eustache, Manitoba 179/E5
Saint Eustache, Québec 172/H4
Saint Eustatius (isl.), Neth. Ant. 156/F1
Saint-Évariste-de-Forsyth, Québec 172/F4
Sainte-Véronique, Québec 172/C3
Sainte-Victoire, Québec 172/D4
Saint-Fabien, Québec 172/J1
Saint-Fabien-de-Panet, Québec 172/G3
Saint-Félicien, Québec 172/E1
Saint-Félicien, Québec 174/C3
Saint-Félix-de-Valois, Québec 172/D3
Saint Fergus, Scotland 15/G3
Saint-Fidèle, Québec 172/H2
Saintfield, N. Ireland 17/K3
Saint Finan's (bay), Ireland 17/A8
Saint-Flavien, Québec 172/F3
Saint-Florent (gulf), France 28/B6
Saint-Florent-sur-Cher, France 28/E4
Saint Florian, Ala. 195/C1
Saint-Flour, France 28/E5
Saint-Fortunat, Québec 172/F4
Saint Francis (co.), Ark. 202/J3
Saint Francis, Ark. 202/K1
Saint Francis (riv.), Ark. 202/J4
Saint Francis, Kansas 232/A2
Saint Francis, Ky. 237/L5
Saint Francis•, Maine 243/E1
Saint Francis (riv.), Maine 243/E1
Saint Francis, Minn. 255/E6
Saint Francis (riv.), Mo. 261/M9
Saint Francis (riv.), New Bruns. 170/A1
Saint Francis (cape), Newf. 166/D2
Saint Francis (bay), S. Africa 118/D6
Saint Francis, S. Dak. 298/H7
Saint Francis, Wis. 317/M2
Saint Francis Harbour, Nova Scotia 168/G3
Saint Francisville, Ill. 222/F5
Saint Francisville, La. 238/H5
Saint Francisville, Mo. 261/J2
Saint-François, Guadeloupe 161/B6
Saint François (co.), Mo. 261/M7
Saint-François (mts.), Mo. 261/L7
Saint-François (lake), Québec 172/F4
Saint-François (riv.), Québec 172/E4
Saint-François-d'Assise, Québec 172/C1
Saint François de Madawaska, New Bruns. 170/B1
Saint-François-de-Montmagny, Québec 172/G3
Saint-François-de-Sales, Québec 172/E1
Saint-François-du-Lac, Québec 172/E3
Saint-Frédéric, Québec 172/G3

Saint Froid (lake), Maine 243/F2
Saint Front, Sask. 181/G3
Saint-Fulgence, Québec 172/G1
Saint Gabriel, La. 238/K2
Saint-Gabriel, Québec 172/D3
Saint-Gabriel-de-Rimouski, Québec 172/J1
Saint Gall (Sankt Gallen), Switzerland 39/H2
Saint-Gaudens, France 28/D6
Saint-Gaudens Nat'l Hist. Site, N.H. 268/B4
Saint-Gédéon, Frontenac, Québec 172/G4
Saint-Gédéon, Lac-St-Jean-E., Québec 172/F1
Saint George, Alaska 196/E3
Saint George (isl.), Alaska 196/D3
Saint George (head), Aust. Cap. Terr. 97/F4
Saint George, Bermuda 156/H2
Saint George (pt.), Calif. 204/A2
Saint George (cape), Fla. 212/A2
Saint George (isl.), Fla. 212/B2
Saint George (sound), Fla. 212/B2
Saint George, Georgia 217/H9
Saint George, Kansas 232/F2
Saint George, Maine 243/E7
Saint George•, Maine 243/E7
Saint George, Manitoba 179/F3
Saint George (lake), Manitoba 179/E3
Saint George (isl.), Md. 245/M8
Saint George, Minn. 255/D6
Saint George, Mo. 261/P4
Saint George, New Bruns. 170/D3
Saint George (cape), Newf. 166/C4
Saint George, N.Y. 276/M9
Saint George, Ontario 177/D4
Saint George (cape), Papua N.G. 86/C2
Saint George, Queensland 95/D5
Saint George, Queensland 88/H5
Saint George, S.C. 296/F5
Saint George, Utah 304/A6
Saint George, Utah 188/D3
Saint George•, Vt. 268/A2
Saint George, W. Va. 312/G4
Saint George's (chan.) 7/D3
Saint George's (isl.), Bermuda 156/H2
Saint Georges, Del. 245/R2
Saint-Georges, Fr. Guiana 131/H4
Saint George's (cap.), Grenada 156/F5
Saint George's (cap.), Grenada 161/C9
Saint George's (chan.), Ireland 10/D4
Saint George's (chan.), Ireland 17/K7
Saint George's, Newf. 166/C4
Saint George's (bay), Newf. 166/C4
Saint Georges (bay), Nova Scotia 168/G3
Saint George's (chan.), Papua N.G. 86/C2
Saint-Georges, Beauce, Québec 172/G3
Saint-Georges, Champlain, Québec 172/E3
Saint George's (chan.), Wales 13/B5
Saint George's (chan.), Wales 10/D4
Saint-Georges-de-Malbaie, Québec 172/D1
Saint-Georges-de-Windsor, Québec 172/F4
Saint-Georges-Ouest, Québec 172/G3
Saint-Georges-sur-Meuse, Belgium 27/G7
Saint-Gérard, Québec 172/F4
Saint-Germain-de-Grantham, Québec 172/E4
Saint-Germain-de-Kamouraska, Québec 172/H2
Saint-Germain-en-Laye, France 28/A2
Saint-Gervais, Québec 172/G3
Saint-Gilles, Belgium 27/B9
Saint-Gilles-Croix-de-Vie, France 28/B4
Saint-Gingolph, Switzerland 39/C4
Saint-Girons, France 28/D6
Saint-Godefroi, Québec 172/D2
Saint Gotthard (pass), Switzerland 39/G3
Saint Gotthard (tunnel), Switzerland 39/G3
Saint Gowans (head), Wales 13/C6
Saint-Grégoire-de-Greenlay, Québec 172/E4
Saint Gregor, Sask. 181/G3
Saint Gregory (cape), Newf. 166/C4
Saint-Guillaume-Nord, Québec 172/D3
Saint Hedwig, Texas 303/K11
Saint Helen, Mich. 250/E4
Saint Helena (isl.) (U.K.) 2/J6
Saint Helena, Calif. 204/C5
Saint Helena (par.), La. 238/J5
Saint Helena, Nebr. 264/G2
Saint Helena (bay), S. Africa 118/B6
Saint Helena (isl.), S.C. 296/F7
Saint Helena (sound), S.C. 296/G7
Saint Helena Island, S.C. 296/F7
Saint Helens, England 10/F2
Saint Helens, England 13/G2
Saint Helens, Ky. 237/O5
Saint Helens, Oreg. 291/E2
Saint Helens, Tasmania 99/E3
Saint Helens (pt.), Tasmania 99/E3
Saint Helens (mt.), Tasmania 188/B1
Saint Helens (mt.), Wash. 310/C4
Saint Helier (cap.), Jersey, Chan. Is. 13/E8
Saint Helier (cap.), Jersey, Chan. Is. 10/E6
Saint-Henri, Québec 172/J3
Saint Henry, Ind. 227/D8

Saint Henry, Ohio 284/A5
Saint-Herménégilde, Québec 172/F4
Saint Hilaire, Minn. 255/B2
Saint-Hilaire, New Bruns. 170/B1
Saint-Hilarion, Québec 172/G2
Saint Hippolyte, Sask. 181/C2
Saint-Honoré, Beauce, Québec 172/G4
Saint-Honoré, Chicoutimi, Québec 172/F1
Saint-Honoré-de-Témiscouata, Québec 172/H2
Saint-Hubert, Belgium 27/G8
Saint-Hubert, Québec 172/J4
Saint-Hubert-de-Témiscouata, Québec 172/J2
Saint Hubert Mission, Sask. 181/J5
Saint-Hugues, Québec 172/E4
Saint-Hyacinthe (co.), Québec 172/D4
Saint-Hyacinthe, Québec 172/E4
Saint Ignace, Mich. 250/F3
Saint-Ignace, New Bruns. 170/F2
Saint Ignace (isl.), Ontario 177/H5
Saint Ignace (isl.), Ontario 175/C3
Saint Ignatius, Mont. 262/C3
Saint-Imier, Switzerland 39/D2
Saint Inigoes, Md. 245/N8
Saint-Irénée, Québec 172/G2
Saint-Isidore, Alberta 182/B1
Saint-Isidore, New Bruns. 170/F1
Saint-Isidore, Québec 172/G3
Saint-Isidore-d'Auckland, Québec 172/F4
Saint-Isidore-de-Gaspé, Québec 172/D1
Saint-Isidore-de-Laprairie, Québec 172/H4
Saint Isidore de Prescott, Ontario 177/K2
Saint Issells, Wales 13/C6
Saint Ives, Cornwall, England 13/B7
Saint Ives, England 10/D5
Saint Ives, Cambs., England 13/G5
Saint Ives (bay), England 13/B7
Saint Jacob, Ill. 222/D5
Saint Jacobs, Ontario 177/D4
Saint-Jacques, New Bruns. 170/B1
Saint-Jacques, Québec 172/D4
Saint-Jacques-le-Mineur, Québec 172/H4
Saint James, Ark. 202/F2
Saint James (cape), Br. Col. 184/B4
Saint James, Ill. 222/E5
Saint James (par.), La. 238/L3
Saint James, La. 238/L3
Saint James, Md. 245/G2
Saint James, Mich. 250/D3
Saint James, Minn. 255/D7
Saint James, Mo. 261/J6
Saint James, N.Y. 276/D9
Saint James (isls.), Virgin Is. (U.S.) 161/BA4
Saint James City, Fla. 212/D5
Saint-Jean, Fr. Guiana 131/D3
Saint-Jean (lake), Que. 162/J6
Saint-Jean (co.), Québec 172/D4
Saint-Jean, Québec 172/D4
Saint-Jean (lake), Québec 172/E1
Saint-Jean (lake), Québec 174/C3
Saint-Jean (riv.), Québec 172/D1
Saint Jean Baptiste, Manitoba 179/E5
Saint-Jean-Baptiste-de-Restigouche, New Bruns. 170/C1
Saint-Jean-Chrysostome, Québec 172/J3
Saint-Jean-de-Dieu, Québec 172/J1
Saint-Jean-de-Luz, France 28/C6
Saint-Jean-de-Matha, Québec 172/D3
Saint-Jean-de-Maurienne, France 28/G5
Saint-Jean-des-Monts, France 28/B4
Saint-Jean-des-Piles, Québec 172/E3
Saint-Jean-d'Orléans, Québec 172/G3
Saint-Jean du Sud, Haiti 158/B6
Saint-Jean-Pied-de-Port, France 28/C6
Saint-Jean-Port-Joli, Québec 172/G2
Saint-Jean-sur-le-Lac, Québec 172/B3
Saint-Jérôme, Terrebonne, Québec 172/H4
Saint Jo, Texas 303/G4
Saint-Joachim, Québec 172/G2
Saint Joe, Ark. 202/E1
Saint Joe, Idaho 220/B2
Saint Joe (riv.), Idaho 220/B2
Saint Joe, Ind. 227/D2
Saint John, Kansas 232/D3
Saint John, Ind. 227/C2
Saint John•, Maine 243/F1
Saint John (pond), Maine 188/N1
Saint John (riv.), Maine 188/N1
Saint John (riv.), Maine 243/G1
Saint John, Mo. 261/P2
Saint John (co.), New Bruns. 170/E3
Saint John (cap.), New Bruns. 170/E3
Saint John (cap.), N. Br. 146/M5
Saint John, N. Br. 162/K6
Saint John (harb.), New Bruns. 170/E3
Saint John (riv.), New Bruns. 170/C2
Saint John (bay), Newf. 166/C3
Saint John (cape), Newf. 166/C3
Saint John (isl.), Newf. 166/C3
Saint John, N. Dak. 282/L2
Saint John, Utah 304/B3
Saint John (isl.), Virgin Is. (U.S.) 161/C4
Saint John (isl.), Virgin Is. (U.S.) 156/H1
Saint John, Wash. 310/H3
Saint John's (cap.), Ant. & Bar. 161/E11
Saint John's, Ant. & Bar. 156/G3
Saint John's (harb.), Ant. & Bar. 161/C11
Saint Johns, Ariz. 198/F4
Saint John's, Canada 2/G3

Saint Johns (co.), Fla. 212/E2
Saint Johns (riv.), Fla. 212/E2
Saint Johns, Ill. 222/D5
Saint John's (riv.), Ireland 17/D2
Saint Johns, Mich. 250/E6
Saint John's (cap.), Newf. 166/D2
Saint John's (cap.), Newf. 146/N5
Saint John's (cap.), Newf. 162/L6
Saint John's (pt.), N. Ireland 17/K3
Saint Johns, Ohio 284/B4
Saint John's (head), Scotland 15/E2
Saint Johns Branch, Nanticoke (riv.), Del. 245/R6
Saint Johnsbury, Vt. 268/D3
Saint Johnsbury•, Vt. 268/D3
Saint Johnsbury Center, Vt. 268/D3
Saint Johnston, Ireland 17/F2
Saint Johnsville, N.Y. 276/L5
Saint John the Baptist (par.), La. 238/M3
Saint Jones (riv.), Del. 245/R4
Saint Joseph, Dominica 161/E6
Saint Joseph (bay), Fla. 212/D6
Saint Joseph (pen.), Fla. 212/D7
Saint Joseph (pt.), Fla. 212/D6
Saint Joseph, Ill. 222/E3
Saint Joseph (co.), Ind. 227/E1
Saint Joseph (riv.), Ind. 227/E1
Saint Joseph (riv.), Ind. 227/E1
Saint Joseph, Kansas 232/E2
Saint Joseph, Ky. 237/G5
Saint Joseph, La. 238/H3
Saint Joseph, Manitoba 179/E5
Saint-Joseph, Martinique 161/D6
Saint Joseph (co.), Mich. 250/D7
Saint-Joseph (co.), Mich. 250/C6
Saint Joseph (riv.), Mich. 250/C7
Saint Joseph, Minn. 255/D5
Saint Joseph, Mo. 261/C3
Saint-Joseph, Mo. 188/H3
Saint-Joseph, Mo. 146/J6
Saint-Joseph, New Bruns. 170/F3
Saint Joseph (riv.), Ohio 284/A3
Saint Joseph (lake), Ont. 162/G5
Saint Joseph (isl.), Ontario 175/B2
Saint-Joseph, Réunion 118/G6
Saint Joseph, Tenn. 237/G10
Saint Joseph, Trin. & Tob. 161/B10
Saint Joseph, Trin. & Tob. 161/B11
Saint-Joseph-de-Beauce, Québec 172/G3
Saint-Joseph-de-Kamouraska, Québec 172/H2
Saint-Joseph-de-la-Rive, Québec 172/G2
Saint-Joseph-de-Madawaska, New Bruns. 170/B1
Saint-Joseph-de-Mékinac, Québec 172/E3
Saint-Joseph-de-Sorel, Québec 172/D3
Saint-Joseph-du-Lac, Québec 172/C4
Saint-Joseph-du-Moine, Nova Scotia 168/G2
Saint Joseph Ridge, Wis. 317/D8
Saint Joseph's, Newf. 166/D2
Saint-Josse-ten-Noode, Belgium 27/C9
Saint-Jovite, Québec 172/C3
Saint-Jude, Québec 172/E4
Saint-Junien, France 28/D5
Saint Just, England 13/B7
Saint-Justin, Québec 172/D3
Saint Kilda, N. Zealand 100/C7
Saint Kilda (isl.), Scotland 15/A2
Saint Kilda, Victoria 88/L7
Saint Kilda, Victoria 97/J5
Saint Kilian, Minn. 255/C7
Saint Kitts (isl.), St. Kitts & Nevis 156/F3
Saint Kitts (isl.), St. Kitts & Nevis 161/D10
SAINT KITTS AND NEVIS 156/F3
SAINT KITTS AND NEVIS 161/D11
Saint-Lambert, Québec 172/J4
Saint Landry (par.), La. 238/F5
Saint Landry, La. 238/F5
Saint Laurent, Manitoba 179/D4
Saint-Laurent, Québec 172/H4
Saint-Laurent-de-la-Salanque, France 28/E6
Saint-Laurent-d'Orléans, Québec 172/G3
Saint-Laurent-du-Maroni, Fr. Guiana 120/D2
Saint-Laurent du Maroni (dist.), Fr. Guiana 131/D3
Saint-Laurent du Maroni, Fr. Guiana 131/E3
Saint Lawrence (gulf) 146/M5
Saint Lawrence (riv.) 162/K6
Saint Lawrence (riv.) 146/L5
Saint Lawrence (isl.), Alaska 146/A3
Saint Lawrence (isl.), Alaska 196/D2
Saint Lawrence, Barbados 161/B9
Saint Lawrence (gulf), Canada 2/G3
Saint Lawrence (gulf), N.Y. 188/D1
Saint Lawrence (gulf), N.Y. 276/K1
Saint Lawrence (gulf), New Bruns. 170/F1
Saint Lawrence, Newf. 166/C4
Saint Lawrence, Newf. 166/B4
Saint Lawrence (co.), N.Y. 276/K2
Saint Lawrence (lake), N.Y. 276/K1
Saint Lawrence (riv.), N.Y. 276/K2
Saint Lawrence (bay), Nova Scotia 168/H1
Saint Lawrence (cape), Nova Scotia 168/H1
Saint Lawrence (lake), Ontario 177/K3
Saint Lawrence (riv.), Ontario 177/K3
Saint Lawrence (gulf), Pr. Edward I. 168/F2
Saint Lawrence (gulf), Que. 162/K6
Saint Lawrence (gulf), Québec 172/D2
Saint Lawrence (gulf), Québec 174/D3
Saint Lawrence (riv.), Québec 172/H1

Saint Lawrence, Queensland 95/D4
Saint Lawrence, S. Dak. 298/M4
Saint Lawrence (isl.), U.S. 4/C18
Saint Lawrence Is. Nat'l Park, Ontario 177/J3
Saint-Lazare, Manitoba 179/A4
Saint-Lazare, Québec 172/G3
Saint-Léandre, Québec 172/B1
Saint-Léger, Belgium 27/H9
Saint-Léger-La Chiésaz, Switzerland 39/C4
Saint Leo, Fla. 212/D3
Saint Leo, Minn. 255/C6
Saint-Léolin, New Bruns. 170/E1
Saint Leon, Ind. 227/H6
Saint Leon, Manitoba 179/D5
Saint-Léon, Québec 172/D3
Saint Leonard, Md. 245/N7
Saint Leonard, New Bruns. 170/C1
Saint-Léonard, Québec 172/H4
Saint-Léonard-d'Aston, Québec 172/E3
Saint-Léonard-de-Noblat, France 28/D5
Saint-Léonard-de-Portneuf, Québec 172/E3
Saint-Léon-de-Chicoutimi, Québec 172/F1
Saint-Léon-de-Standon, Québec 172/G3
Saint-Léon-le-Grand, Québec 172/B2
Saint Lewis (cape), Newf. 166/C3
Saint Lewis (riv.), Newf. 166/C3
Saint-Liboire, Québec 172/E4
Saint Libory, Ill. 222/D5
Saint Libory, Nebr. 264/F3
Saint Lina, Alberta 182/E2
Saint-Lô, France 28/C3
Saint-Louis, Guadeloupe 161/B7
Saint Louis (lake). Minn. 255/F3
Saint Louis (riv.), Minn. 255/F4
Saint Louis (bay), Miss. 256/F10
Saint Louis (co.), Mo. 261/O3
Saint Louis (city county), Mo. 261/P3
Saint Louis, Mo. 261/R3
Saint Louis, Mo. 146/K6
Saint Louis, Mo. 188/H3
Saint Louis, Okla. 288/N4
Saint Louis, Oreg. 291/A3
Saint Louis, Pr. Edward I. 168/D2
Saint-Louis (lake), Québec 172/H4
Saint-Louis, Réunion 118/F5
Saint Louis, Sask. 181/F3
Saint-Louis, Senegal 102/A3
Saint-Louis, Senegal 106/A5
Saint Louis, U.S. 2/E4
Saint Louis (riv.), Wis. 317/A2
Saint Louis Crossing, Ind. 227/F6
Saint-Louis-de-Gonzague, Québec 172/D4
Saint-Louis-de-Kent, New Bruns. 170/F2
Saint-Louis-de-Terrebonne, Québec 172/H4
Saint-Louis-du-Ha! Ha!, Québec 172/H2
Saint-Louis du Nord, Haiti 158/B5
Saint-Louis du Sud, Haiti 158/B6
Saint Louis Park, Minn. 255/G5
Saint Louisville, Ohio 284/F5
Saint-Luc, Québec 172/D4
Saint Lucas, Iowa 229/K2
Saint-Luc-de-Matane, Québec 172/B1
Saint Lucia 2/G5
Saint Lucia 146/M8
SAINT LUCIA 161/G5
SAINT LUCIA 156/G4
Saint Lucia, Queensland 88/K3
Saint Lucia, Queensland 95/D3
Saint Lucia (chan.), St. Lucia 156/G4
Saint Lucia (chan.), St. Lucia 161/G5
Saint Lucia (cape), S. Africa 118/E5
Saint Lucia (lake), S. Africa 118/E5
Saint Lucie (co.), Fla. 212/F4
Saint Lucie, Fla. 212/F4
Saint Lucie (canal), Fla. 212/F4
Saint Lucie (inlet), Fla. 212/F4
Saint-Ludger, Québec 172/G4
Saint Luminie-Griquet, Newf. 166/C3
Saint-Magloire, Québec 172/G3
Saint Magnus (bay), Scotland 10/G1
Saint Magnus (bay), Scotland 15/F2
Saint-Malachie, Québec 172/G3
Saint-Malo, France 28/B3
Saint-Malo (gulf), France 28/B3
Saint Malo, Manitoba 179/F5
Saint-Malo, Québec 172/F4
Saint-Mandé, France 28/B2
Saint-Marc, Haiti 158/B5
Saint-Marc, Haiti 156/B5
Saint-Marc (chan.), Haiti 158/B6
Saint-Marc (pt.), Haiti 158/B5
Saint-Marc, Québec 172/D4
Saint-Marc-des-Carrières, Québec 172/E3
Saint-Marcel (mt.), Fr. Guiana 131/E4
Saint-Marcel-de-L'Islet, Québec 172/G3
Saint-Marcellin, France 28/F5
Saint Margarets, New Bruns. 170/E2
Saint Margarets (bay), Nova Scotia 168/E4
Saint Margaret's Bay, Jamaica 158/K6
Saint Margaret's Hope, Scotland 15/F2
Saint Margaret Village, Nova Scotia 168/H2
Saint Maries, Idaho 220/B2
Saint Maries (riv.), Idaho 220/B2
Saint Marks, Fla. 212/B1
Saint Marks, Georgia 217/C4
Saint Marks, Manitoba 179/E4
Saint Martin (isl.), Guadeloupe 156/F3
Saint Martin (par.), La. 238/G6
Saint Martin (lake), Manitoba 179/D3
Saint-Martin (cape), Martinique 161/C5

Saint Martin, Md. 245/T7
Saint Martin (bay), Mich. 250/E3
Saint Martin (isl.), Mich. 250/C3
Saint Martin, Minn. 255/D5
Saint Martin (Sint Maarten) (isl.), Neth. Ant. 156/F3
Saint Martin, Ohio 284/C7
Saint-Martin, Switzerland 39/E4
Saint Martin de Restigouche, New Bruns. 170/C1
Saint Martins, Barbados 161/C9
Saint Martin's (isl.), England 13/A8
Saint Martins, Mo. 261/H5
Saint Martins, New Bruns. 170/E3
Saint Martin Station, Manitoba 179/D3
Saint Martinville, La. 238/G6
Saint Mary (res.), Alberta 182/D5
Saint Mary (riv.), Alberta 182/D5
Saint Mary, Ky. 237/L5
Saint Mary (par.), La. 238/H7
Saint Mary (lake), Mont. 262/C2
Saint Mary (riv.), Mont. 262/C1
Saint Mary, Nebr. 264/H4
Saint Mary (cape), Nova Scotia 168/B4
Saint Mary (peak), S. Australia 94/F4
Saint Mary-of-the-Woods, Ind. 227/B6
Saint Marys, Alaska 196/F2
Saint Mary's (isl.), England 13/A8
Saint Marys (riv.), Fla. 212/D1
Saint Marys, Georgia 217/J9
Saint Marys (riv.), Georgia 217/J9
Saint Marys, Ind. 227/E1
Saint Marys (lake), Ind. 227/H3
Saint Marys (riv.), Ind. 227/H3
Saint Marys, Iowa 229/F6
Saint Marys, Kansas 232/G2
Saint Marys (co.), Md. 245/M7
Saint Marys (riv.), Md. 245/N8
Saint Marys (riv.), Mich. 250/E2
Saint Marys, Mo. 261/M7
Saint Mary's, Newf. 166/D2
Saint Mary's (bay), Newf. 166/C2
Saint Mary's (cape), Newf. 166/C2
Saint Mary's (bay), Nova Scotia 168/B4
Saint Mary's (riv.), Nova Scotia 168/F3
Saint Marys, Ohio 284/B4
Saint Marys (lake), Ohio 284/A4
Saint Marys (riv.), Ohio 284/A4
Saint Marys, Ontario 177/C4
Saint Marys, Pa. 294/E3
Saint Mary's, Scotland 15/F2
Saint Mary's (lake), Scotland 15/E5
Saint Marys, Tasmania 99/E3
Saint Marys, W. Va. 312/D4
Saint Marys (peak), Wyo. 319/D3
Saint Marys City, Md. 245/N8
Saint Marys Entrance (inlet), Fla. 212/F1
Saint-Mathieu, Québec 172/J1
Saint-Mathieu (lake), Québec 172/J1
Saint Matthew (sl.), Alaska 188/C5
Saint Matthew (sl.), Alaska 146/A4
Saint Matthew (sl.), Alaska 196/D2
Saint Matthew (sl.), U.S. 4/C18
Saint Matthews, Ky. 237/K2
Saint Matthews, S.C. 296/F4
Saint Matthias Group (isls.), Papua N.G. 86/B1
Saint-Maur-des-Fossés, France 28/B2
Saint Maurice, Ind. 227/G6
Saint Maurice, La. 238/E3
Saint-Maurice (co.), Québec 172/D3
Saint-Maurice (county), Québec 174/C2
Saint-Maurice (riv.), Québec 172/E2
Saint-Maurice, Switzerland 39/C4
Saint-Médard, Québec 172/J1
Saint Meinrad, Ind. 227/D8
Saint-Méthode, Québec 172/E1
Saint-Méthode-de-Frontenac, Québec 172/F3
Saint Michael, Alaska 196/F2
Saint Michael, Alberta 182/D3
Saint Michael, Minn. 255/E5
Saint Michael, N. Dak. 282/M4
Saint Michael, Pa. 294/E5
Saint Michaels, Ariz. 198/F3
Saint Michaels, Md. 245/N5
Saint Michaels (bay), Newf. 166/C3
Saint-Michel-de-Bellechasse, Québec 172/G3
Saint-Michel de l'Atalaye, Haiti 158/C5
Saint-Michel-des-Saints, Québec 172/D3
Saint-Michel du Sud, Haiti 158/B6
Saint-Mihiel, France 28/F3
Saint-Modeste, Québec 172/H2
Saint-Moïse, Québec 172/B1
Saint Monance, Scotland 15/F4
Saint Moritz, Switzerland 39/J3
Saint-Narcisse-de-Rimouski, Québec 172/J1
Saint-Nazaire, France 28/B4
Saint-Nazaire, France 28/B4
Saint-Nazaire, Fr. Guiana 131/E3
Saint-Nazaire, Québec 172/E4
Saint-Nazaire-de-Buckland, Québec 172/G3
Saint-Nazaire-de-Chicoutimi, Québec 172/F1
Saint Nazianz, Wis. 317/L7
Saint Neots, England 13/G5
Saint Neots, England 10/F4
Saint-Nérée, Québec 172/G3
Saint-Nicolas, Belgium 27/G7
Saint Niklaus, Switzerland 39/E4
Saint-Noël, Québec 172/B1
Saint-Octave, Québec 172/B1
Saint-Odilon, Québec 172/G3
Saint Olaf, Iowa 229/L3
Saint-Omer, France 28/E2
Saint-Omer, France 28/E2
Saint-Omer, Québec 172/C2

Saint-Onésime, Québec 172/H2
Saintonge (trad. prov.), France 29
Saint Onge, S. Dak. 298/B4
Saint-Ouen, France 28/B1
Saint-Ours, Québec 172/D4
Saint-Pacôme, Québec 172/G2
Saint-Pamphile, Québec 172/H3
Saint Paris, Ohio 284/C5
Saint-Pascal, Québec 174/D3
Saint-Pascal, Québec 172/H2
Saint-Patrice-de-Beaurivage, Québec 172/F3
Saint Patrick (lake), Manitoba 179/E3
Saint Patrick, Mo. 261/J2
Saint Patrick (chan.), Nova Scotia 168/G3
Saint Paul (isl.), (Fr.) 2/P7
Saint Paul (isl.), Alaska 196/D3
Saint Paul, Alberta 182/E4
Saint Paul, Alta. 162/E5
Saint Paul, Ark. 202/C2
Saint Paul (cape), Ghana 106/E7
Saint Paul, Ind. 227/F6
Saint Paul, Iowa 229/L7
Saint Paul, Kansas 232/G4
Saint Paul (cap.), Minn. 188/H1
Saint Paul (cap.), Minn. 146/J5
Saint Paul (cap.), Minn. 255/G6
Saint Paul, Mo. 261/L5
Saint Paul, Nebr. 264/F3
Saint Paul (isl.), Nova Scotia 168/H1
Saint Paul, Oreg. 291/A3
Saint Paul, Québec 172/E4
Saint Paul (riv.), Québec 174/F2
Saint Paul, S.C. 296/G4
Saint Paul, Texas 303/H1
Saint Paul, Va. 307/D7
Saint-Paul-de-Montminy, Québec 172/G3
Saint-Paul-du-Nord, Québec 172/H1
Saint-Paulin, Québec 172/D3
Saint Paul Island, Alaska 196/D3
Saint-Paul-l'Ermite, Québec 172/J4
Saint Paul Park, Minn. 255/G6
Saint Paul's, Newf. 166/C4
Saint Pauls, N.C. 281/M5
Saint Peter, Ill. 222/E5
Saint Peter, Ind. 227/H6
Saint Peter, Kansas 232/C2
Saint Peter, Minn. 255/E6
Saint Peter Port (cap.), Guernsey, Chan. Is. 13/B7
Saint Peter Port (cap.), Guernsey, Chan. Is. 10/E6
Saint Peters, Mo. 261/M1
Saint Peters, Nova Scotia 168/H3
Saint Peters (bay), Nova Scotia 168/H3
Saint Peters, Pr. Edward I. 168/F2
Saint Peters (bay), Pr. Edward I. 168/F2
Saint Peters (isl.), Pr. Edward I. 168/E2
Saint Peters, S. Australia 88/E8
Saint Petersburg, Fla. 188/K5
Saint Petersburg, Fla. 146/K7
Saint Petersburg, Fla. 212/B3
Saint Petersburg, Pa. 294/C3
Saint Petersburg Beach, Fla. 212/B3
Saint-Petronille, Québec 172/J3
Saint-Philémon, Québec 172/G3
Saint Philip, Ind. 227/B9
Saint-Philippe-de-Laprairie, Québec 172/J4
Saint-Philippe-de-Néri, Québec 172/H2
Saint Philips, Sask. 181/K4
Saint Phillips, Mont. 262/M4
Saint Phillips, Newf. 166/D2
Saint-Pie, Québec 172/E4
Saint-Pierre, Martinique 161/C6
Saint-Pierre, Martinique 156/G4
Saint-Pierre (bay), Martinique 161/C6
Saint-Pierre, Ile-de-Mont., Québec 172/H4
Saint-Pierre, Joliette, Québec 172/E3
Saint-Pierre (lake), Québec 172/E3
Saint-Pierre (pt.), Québec 172/D1
Saint-Pierre, Réunion 118/F5
Saint-Pierre (cap.), Saint Pierre & Miquelon 166/C4
Saint-Pierre (isl.), Saint-Pierre & Miquelon 166/C4
SAINT PIERRE AND MIQUELON 166/C4
Saint Pierre & Miquelon (isls.) (Fr.) 162/L8
Saint Pierre and Miquelon (isls.) (Fr.) 146/N5
Saint-Pierre-Baptiste, Québec 172/F3
Saint-Pierre-de-Broughton, Québec 172/F3
Saint-Pierre-d'Orléans, Québec · 172/G3
Saint-Pierre-Jolys, Manitoba 179/F5
Saint-Pierre-Montmagny, Québec 172/G3
Saint-Placide, Québec 172/C4
Saint-Pol-de-Léon, France 28/A3
Saint-Pol-sur-Ternoise, France 28/E2
Saint-Polycarpe, Québec 172/C4
Saint-Pons, France 28/E6
Saint-Prex, Switzerland 39/B4
Saint-Prime, Québec 172/E1
Saint-Prosper-de-Dorchester, Québec 172/G3
Saint-Quentin, France 28/E3
Saint-Quentin, New Bruns. 170/C1
Saint-Raphaël, France 28/G6
Saint-Raphaël, Haiti 158/C5
Saint-Raphaël, Québec 172/G3
Saint-Raphaël-sur-Mer, New Bruns. 170/F1
Saint-Raymond, Québec 172/F3
Saint-Rédempteur, Québec 172/J3
Saint Regis, Mont. 262/A3

Saint Regis (riv.) N.Y. 276/L1
Saint-Régis, Québec 172/C4
Saint Regis Falls, N.Y. 276/M1
Saint Regis Ind. Res., N.Y. 276/M1
Saint Regis Park, Ky. 237/K2
Saint-Rémi, Québec 172/D4
Saint-Rémi-d'Amherst, Québec 172/C3
Saint-Rémi-de-Tingwick, Québec 172/F4
Saint-René-de-Matane, Québec 172/B1
Saint Robert, Mo. 261/H7
Saint-Roch-de-l'Achigan, Québec 172/D4
Saint-Roch-de-Mékinac, Québec 172/E2
Saint-Roch-de-Richelieu, Québec 172/D4
Saint-Romain, Québec 172/F4
Saint-Romuald-d'Etchemin, Québec 172/J3
Saint Rosa, Minn. 255/D5
Saint Rose, Ill. 222/D5
Saint Rose, La. 238/N4
Saint Sampson's, Chan. Is. 13/E8
Saints-Anges, Québec 172/G3
Saint Sauveur, New Bruns. 170/E1
Saint-Sauveur-des-Monts, Québec 172/C4
Saint-Sébastien (cape), Madagascar 118/H2
Saint-Sébastien, Frontenac, Québec 172/F4
Saint-Sébastien, Iberville, Québec 172/D4
Saint-Sever, France 28/C6
Saint-Séverin-de-Beaurivage, Québec 172/F3
Saint Shotts, Newf. 166/D2
Saint-Siméon, Québec 172/G2
Saint-Siméon-de-Bonaventure, Québec 172/C2
Saint-Simon, Québec 172/H1
Saint-Simon-de-Bagot, Québec 172/E4
Saint Simons, Georgia 217/K8
Saint Simons Island, Georgia 217/K8
Saint-Stanislas, Québec 172/E3
Saint Stephan, Switzerland 39/D3
Saint Stephen, Minn. 255/D5
Saint Stephen, N. Brunswick 162/K6
Saint Stephen, New Bruns. 170/C3
Saint Stephen, S.C. 296/H5
Saint Stephen-in-Brannel, England 13/B7
Saint Stephens, Ala. 195/B7
Saint Stephens, Wyo. 319/D3
Saint Stephens Church, Va. 307/O5
Saint-Sylvère, Québec 172/E3
Saint-Sylvestre, Québec 172/F3
Saint Tammany (par.), La. 238/L6
Saint Tammany, La. 238/L6
Saint Teresa, Fla. 212/B2
Saint-Théodore, Québec 172/D3
Saint-Théodore-d'Acton, Québec 172/E4
Saint-Théophile, Québec 172/G4
Saint Theresa Point, Manitoba 179/J3
Saint Thomas, Mo. 261/H6
Saint Thomas, N. Dak. 282/R2
Saint Thomas, Ontario 177/C5
Saint Thomas, Pa. 294/E6
Saint Thomas (harb.), Virgin Is. (U.S.) 161/B4
Saint Thomas (isl.), Virgin Is. (U.S.) 156/G1
Saint Thomas (isl.), Virgin Is. (U.S.) 161/A4
Saint-Thomas-de-Joliette, Québec 172/D3
Saint-Thuribe, Québec 172/E3
Saint-Timothée, Québec 172/C4
Saint-Tite, Québec 172/E3
Saint-Tite-des-Caps, Québec 172/G2
Saint-Trond (Sint-Truiden), Belgium 27/G7
Saint-Tropez, France 28/G6
Saint-Ubald, Québec 172/E3
Saint-Ulric, Québec 172/B1
Saint-Urbain-de-Charlevoix, Québec 172/G2
Saint-Ursanne, Switzerland 39/D2
Saint-Valentin, Québec 172/D4
Saint-Valère-de-Bulstrode, Québec 172/F3
Saint-Valérien, Québec 172/E4
Saint-Valérien-de-Rimouski, Québec 172/J1
Saint-Valéry-sur-Somme, France 28/D2
Saint-Vallier, France 28/F5
Saint-Vallier, Québec 172/G3
Saint-Victor, Québec 172/G3
Saint Victor, Sask. 181/F6
Saint Victor Petroglyphs Hist. Park, Sask. 181/F6
Saint Vincent, Alberta 182/E2
Saint Vincent (isl.), Fla. 212/D4
Saint Vincent, Italy 34/A2
Saint Vincent, Minn. 255/A2
Saint Vincent (São Vincente) (cape), Portugal 33/B4
Saint Vincent (chan.), St. Lucia 161/G7
SAINT VINCENT & THE GRENADINES 161/A8
Saint Vincent (isl.), St. Vin. & Grens. 156/G4
Saint Vincent (passage), St. Vin. & Grens. 156/G4
Saint Vincent (passage), St. Vin. & Grens. 161/A8
Saint Vincent (gulf), S. Australia 88/D8
Saint Vincent (gulf), S. Australia 94/F6
Saint Vincent (cape), Tasmania 99/B5
Saint Vincent and The Grenadines 2/F5
Saint Vincent and the Grenadines 146/M8

SAINT VINCENT AND THE GRENADINES 156/G4
SAINT VINCENT AND THE GRENADINES 161/A8
Saint Vincent's, Newf. 166/D2
Saint-Vith (Sankt Vith), Belgium 27/J8
Saint Vrain, N. Mex. 274/F4
Saint Walburg, Sask. 162/F5
Saint Walburg, Sask. 181/B2
Saint-Wenceslas, Québec 172/E3
Saint Wendel, Ind. 227/B8
Saint Wilfred, New Bruns. 170/E1
Saint Williams, Ontario 177/D5
Saint Xavier, Mont. 262/J5
Saint-Yrieix-la-Perche, France 28/D5
Saint-Yvon, Québec 172/D1
Saint-Zacharie, Québec 172/G3
Saint-Zénon, Québec 172/D3
Saint-Zéphirin, Québec 172/E3
Saint-Zotique, Québec 172/C4
Saio (Dembidollo), Ethiopia 111/F6
Saipan (isl.), No. Marianas 87/E4
Saipina, Bolivia 136/C6
Saitama (pref.), Japan 81/O2
Saito, Japan 81/E7
Sajama, Bolivia 136/A6
Sajama, Nevada (mt.), Bolivia 136/A6
Sajó (riv.), Hungary 41/F2
Sajószentpéter, Hungary 41/F2
Sak (riv.), S. Africa 118/C6
Sakado, Japan 81/O2
Sakai, Ibaraki, Japan 81/P1
Sakai, Osaka, Japan 81/J8
Sakaide, Japan 81/G6
Sakaiminato, Japan 81/F6
Sakaka, Saudi Arabia 59/D4
Sakakawea (lake), N. Dak. 146/H5
Sakakawea (lake), N. Dak. 188/F1
Sakakawea (lake), N. Dak. 282/G5
Sakami (lake), Québec 174/B2
Sakami (riv.), Québec 174/B2
Sakania, Zaire 115/E6
Sakarya (prov.), Turkey 63/D2
Sakarya (Adapazarī), Turkey 63/D2
Sakarya (riv.), Turkey 59/B1
Sakarya (riv.), Turkey 63/D2
Sakata, Japan 81/J5
Sakhalin (gulf), U.S.S.R. 48/P4
Sakhalin (isl.), U.S.S.R. 2/S3
Sakhalin (isl.), U.S.S.R. 54/R4
Sakhalin (isl.), U.S.S.R. 48/P4
Sakhar, Afghanistan 68/B2
Sakhar, Afghanistan 59/J3
Sakht-Sar, Iran 66/G2
Sakhnin, Israel 65/C2
Saki, U.S.S.R. 52/D5
Sakiai, U.S.S.R. 53/B3
Sakishima (isls.) Japan 54/O7
Sakishima (isls.), Japan 81/K7
Sakon Nakhon, Thailand 72/E3
Sakonnet (pt.), R.I. 249/K7
Sakonnet (riv.), R.I. 249/K7
Sakrivier, S. Africa 118/C6
Saksaul'skiy, U.S.S.R. 48/F5
Sakskøbing, Denmark 21/E8
Saku, Japan 81/J5
Sakurai, Japan 81/J8
Sakwatamau (riv.), Alberta 182/C2
Sal (isl.), C. Verde 106/B7
Šal'a, Czech. 41/D2
Sala, Sweden 18/K7
Salabangka (isls.), Indonesia 85/G6
Salacgrīva, U.S.S.R. 53/C2
Sala Consilina, Italy 34/E4
Saladas, Argentina 143/E2
Saladillo (riv.), Argentina 143/D2
Saladillo, Bolivia 136/D7
Salado (riv.), Argentina 120/C6
Salado (riv.), Argentina 143/H7
Salado (riv.), Argentina 143/C4
Salado, Ark. 202/G2
Salado, Chile 138/B4
Salado, Quebrado del (riv.), Chile 138/B6
Salado, Cuba 158/H3
Salado, Honduras 154/D3
Salado del Norte (riv.), Argentina 120/C5
Salado del Norte (riv.), Argentina 143/D2
Salaga, Ghana 106/D7
Salahuddin (gov.), Iraq 66/C3
Sala'ilua, W. Samoa 86/L8
Salala, Oman 59/F6
Salala, Oman 54/G8
Salamá, Guatemala 154/B3
Salamanca, Mexico 150/J6
Salamanca, N.Y. 276/C6
Salamanca (prov.), Spain 33/C2
Salamanca, Spain 33/D2
Salamanca, Spain 33/D2
Salamat, Bahr (riv.), Chad 111/C6
Salamina, Colombia 126/C5
Salamis, Greece 45/F4
Salamonia, Ind. 227/H4
Salamonie (lake), Ind. 227/F3
Salamonie (riv.), Ind. 227/G4
Salas, Spain 33/C1
Salas de los Infantes, Spain 33/E2
Salat (riv.), France 28/D6
Salavat, U.S.S.R. 7/K3
Salavat, U.S.S.R. 52/H4
Salawati (isl.), Indonesia 85/J6
Salay, Philippines 82/E6
Sala y Gómez (isl.), Chile 2/D7
Sala y Gómez (isl.), Chile 87/P8
Salazar, Colombia 126/D4
Salcantay (mt.), Peru 128/F9
Salcedo (prov.), Dom. Rep. 158/E5
Salcedo, Dom. Rep. 158/E5
Salcombe, England 13/D7
Salcombe, England 10/D5
Saldaña (riv.), Colombia 126/C6
Saldaña, Spain 33/D1

Saldanha, S. Africa 118/B6
Saldee, Ky. 237/P6
Saldus, U.S.S.R. 53/B2
Sale, England 13/H2
Sale (riv.), Manitoba 179/E5
Sale, Morocco 106/C2
Sale, Victoria 88/H7
Sale, Victoria 97/D6
Sale City, Georgia 217/D8
Sale Creek, Tenn. 237/L10
Salée (riv.), Guadeloupe 161/A6
Salekhard, U.S.S.R. 4/C6
Salekhard, U.S.S.R. 2/N2
Salekhard, U.S.S.R. 48/G3
Salem, Ala. 195/H5
Salem, Ark. 202/G1
Salem •, Conn. 210/F3
Salem, Fla. 212/C2
Salem, Ill. 222/E5
Salem, India 54/J8
Salem, India 68/D6
Salem, Ind. 227/E7
Salem, Ind. 227/H3
Salem, Iowa 229/K7
Salem, Ky. 237/E6
Salem, Maine 243/C6
Salem, Md. 245/P7
Salem, Mass. 249/E5
Salem, Mich. 250/F6
Salem, Mo. 261/J7
Salem, Nebr. 264/J4
Salem •, N.H. 268/E6
Salem (co.), N.J. 273/C4
Salem, N.J. 273/C4
Salem, N.J. 273/C4
Salem, N. Mex. 274/B6
Salem, N.Y. 276/O4
Salem, Ohio 284/J4
Salem, Ontario 177/D4
Salem (cap.), Oreg. 146/F5
Salem (cap.), Oreg. 188/B1
Salem (cap.), Oreg. 291/A3
Salem, S.C. 296/A2
Salem, S. Dak. 298/P6
Salem, Utah 304/C3
Salem (lake), Vt. 268/C2
Salem (I.C.), Va. 307/H6
Salem, W. Va. 312/E4
Salemburg, N.C. 281/N4
Salem Center, Ind. 227/G1
Salem Depot, N.H. 268/E6
Salemi, Italy 34/D6
Salem Maritime Nat'l Hist. Site, Mass. 249/E5
Salen, Scotland 15/C4
Saleratus Wash (creek), Utah 304/D4
Salernes, France 28/G6
Salerno (prov.), Italy 34/E4
Salerno, Italy 7/F4
Salerno, Italy 34/E4
Salerno (gulf), Italy 34/E4
Salesville, Ark. 202/F1
Salesville, Ohio 284/H6
Salfit, West Bank 65/C3
Salford, England 13/H2
Salford, England 10/G2
Salgótarján, Hungary 41/E2
Salgueiro, Brazil 132/G5
Sali (riv.), Argentina 143/C2
Salida, Colo. 208/H6
Salies-de-Béarn, France 28/C6
Salihli, Turkey 63/C3
Salima, Malawi 115/F6
Salima, Italy 34/F5
Salina, Kans. 188/G3
Salina, Kansas 232/E3
Salina, Kansas 146/J6
Salina, Okla. 288/R2
Salina, Utah 304/C5
Salina (creek), Utah 304/C5
Salina Cruz, Mexico 150/M9
Salinas, Brazil 132/F7
Salinas, Calif. 188/B3
Salinas, Calif. 204/D7
Salinas (riv.), Calif. 204/D7
Salinas, Chile 138/B4
Salinas (bay), C. Rica 154/D5
Salinas (pt.), Dom. Rep. 158/E6
Salinas, Ecuador 128/B3
Salinas (riv.), Guatemala 154/B2
Salinas, Mexico 150/J5
Salinas (riv.), Mexico 150/O8
Salinas (bay), Nicaragua 154/D5
Salinas, P. Rico 156/G1
Salinas, P. Rico 161/D1
Salinas (pt.), P. Rico 161/D1
Salinas (cape), Spain 33/H3
Salinas de Garci Mendoza, Bolivia 136/B6
Salinas de Santiago, Bolivia 136/E6
Salinas Grandes (salt dep.), Argentina 143/D2
Salinas Pueblo Missions Nat'l Mon., N. Mex. 274/C4
Saline (co.), Ark. 202/E4
Saline (riv.), Ark. 202/E5
Saline (riv.), Ark. 202/B6
Saline (pt.), Grenada 161/C9
Saline (co.), Ill. 222/E6
Saline (riv.), Ill. 222/E6
Saline (co.), Kansas 232/E3
Saline (riv.), Kansas 232/D3
Saline, La. 238/E2
Saline (lake), La. 238/E3
Saline, Mich. 250/F6
Saline (co.), Mo. 261/H1
Saline, Mo. 261/E1
Saline (co.), Nebr. 264/H4
Saline, Scotland 15/C1
Saline City, Ind. 227/C6
Salineno, Texas 303/E11
Salines (pt.), Martinique 161/D7
Salineville, Ohio 284/J4
Salinópolis, Brazil 132/E3
Salins-les-Bains, France 28/F4
Salisbury (sound), Alaska 196/M1

Salisbury•, Conn. 210/B1
Salisbury, England 13/F6
Salisbury, England 10/F5
Salisbury, Md. 245/R7
Salisbury, Mass. 249/L1
Salisbury•, Mass. 249/L1
Salisbury, Mo. 261/G4
Salisbury, New Bruns. 170/E2
Salisbury (bay), New Bruns. 170/F3
Salisbury•, N.H. 268/D5
Salisbury, N.C. 281/H3
Salisbury (isl.), N.W.T. 162/J3
Salisbury (isl.), N.W.T. 187/L3
Salisbury, Pa. 294/D6
Salisbury, S. Australia 88/E7
Salisbury, S. Australia 94/B7
Salisbury•, Vt. 268/A4
Salisbury (Harare) (cap.), Zimbabwe 118/E3
Salisbury (Harare) (cap.), Zimbabwe 102/E6
Salisbury Beach, Mass. 249/L1
Salisbury Center, N.Y. 276/L4
Salisbury Downs, N.S. Wales 97/B1
Salitpa, Ala. 195/C7
Salix, Iowa 229/A4
Salkehatchie (riv.), S.C. 296/E5
Salkum, Wash. 310/C4
Salladasburg, Pa. 294/H3
Sallent, Spain 33/H2
Salley, S.C. 296/E4
Salliquelo, Argentina 143/D4
Sallis, Miss. 256/E4
Sallisaw, Okla. 288/S4
Sallyan, Nepal 68/E3
Sally's Cove, Newf. 166/C4
Salma, Jebel (mts.), Saudi Arabia 59/D4
Salmas, Iran 66/D1
Salmo, Br. Col. 184/J5
Salmon (riv.), Br. Col. 184/F3
Salmon (riv.), Calif. 204/B2
Salmon (brook), Conn. 210/D1
Salmon (creek), Conn. 210/B1
Salmon (riv.), Conn. 210/F2
Salmon, Idaho 220/B1
Salmon, Idaho 188/D1
Salmon (riv.), Idaho 188/C1
Salmon (falls), Idaho 220/C7
Salmon (riv.), Idaho 220/B4
Salmon (riv.), New Bruns. 170/C1
Salmon (riv.), New Bruns. 170/E2
Salmon (res.), N.Y. 276/J3
Salmon (riv.), N.Y. 276/H3
Salmon (riv.), N.Y. 276/M1
Salmon (riv.), Nova Scotia 168/G3
Salmon (riv.), Nova Scotia 168/E3
Salmon Arm, Br. Col. 184/H5
Salmon Arm (inlet), Br. Col. 184/J2
Salmon Beach, New Bruns. 170/E1
Salmon Cove, Newf. 166/D2
Salmon Creek, New Bruns. 170/E2
Salmon Falls (creek), Idaho 220/D7
Salmon Falls (riv.), Maine 243/B9
Salmon Falls, N.H. 268/F5
Salmon Falls (riv.), N.H. 268/F5
Salmon Falls Creek (res.), Idaho 220/D7
Salmon Gums, W. Australia 88/C6
Salmon Gums, W. Australia 92/C6
Salmonier (riv.), Newf. 166/D2
Salmon River (mts.), Idaho 220/C5
Salmon River, Colchester, Nova Scotia 168/E3
Salmon River, Digby, Nova Scotia 168/B4
Salmons, Ky. 237/H7
Salmon Valley, Br. Col. 184/F3
Salo, Finland 18/N6
Salobreña, Spain 33/E4
Salol, Minn. 255/C2
Saloma, Ky. 237/L6
Salome, Ariz. 198/B5
Salomon (pt.), Martinique 161/C7
Salona, Pa. 294/H3
Salon-de-Provence, France 28/F6
Salong, Philippines 82/D5
Salonga Nat'l Park, Zaire 115/D4
Salonika (Thessaloniki), Greece 45/F5
Salonika (Thermaic) (gulf), Greece 45/F6
Salonta, Romania 45/E2
Sal Rei, C. Verde 106/B8
Salsette (isl.), India 68/B7
Sal'sk, U.S.S.R. 52/F5
Sal'sk, U.S.S.R. 48/E5
Salso (riv.), Italy 34/D6
Salsomaggiore Terme, Italy 34/B2
Salt (riv.), Ariz. 188/D4
Salt (riv.), Ariz. 198/D5
Salt (creek), Calif. 204/J7
Salt (lake), Hawaii 218/B3
Salt (creek), Ill. 222/D3
Salt (creek), Ind. 227/E6
Salt (riv.), Ky. 237/K5
Salt (riv.), Mo. 261/J3
Salt (pt.), Mich. 250/E2
Salt (creek), N. Mex. 274/E5
Salt (lake), N. Mex. 274/F4
Salt, The (lake), N.S. Wales 97/B2
Salt (creek), Ohio 284/E7
Salt (creek), Oreg. 291/E4
Salt, Spain 33/H1
Salt (cay), Virgin Is. (U.S.) 161/A4
Salt (riv.), Virgin Is. (U.S.) 161/F4
Salt (lake), W. Australia 88/B5
Salt (lake), W. Australia 92/B5
Salt (riv.), Wyo. 319/B3
Salta (prov.), Argentina 143/D1
Salta, Argentina 120/C5
Salta, Argentina 143/C1
Saltair, Br. Col. 184/J3
Saltaire, N.Y. 276/O9
Saltash, England 10/D5
Saltash, England 13/C7

Saltburn and Marske-by-the-Sea, England 13/G3
Saltcoats, Sask. 181/J4
Saltcoats, Scotland 15/D5
Saltcoats, Scotland 10/D3
Saltee (isls.), Ireland 17/H7
Saltelv (riv.), Norway 18/J3
Salters, S.C. 296/H4
Saltese, Mont. 262/A3
Saltfjorden (fjord), Norway 18/J3
Salt Fork (creek), Ohio 284/H5
Salt Fork (lake), Ohio 284/H5
Salt Fork, Okla. 288/L1
Salt Fork, Arkansas (riv.), Okla. 288/J1
Salt Fork, Red (riv.), Okla. 288/G5
Salt Fork, Red (riv.), Texas 303/D3
Saltillo, Ind. 227/E7
Saltillo, Mexico 146/H7
Saltillo, Mexico 150/J4
Saltillo, Miss. 256/G2
Saltillo, Pa. 294/G5
Saltillo, Tenn. 237/E10
Salt Lake (co.), Utah 304/B3
Salt Lake City (cap.), Utah 304/C3
Salt Lake City (cap.), Utah 188/D2
Salt Lake City (cap.), Utah 146/G6
Salt Lick, Ky. 237/O4
Salt Marsh (lake), Utah 304/A4
Salto, Argentina 143/F7
Salto (riv.), Argentina 143/F7
Salto, Brazil 135/C3
Salto (dept.), Uruguay 145/B2
Salto, Uruguay 120/D6
Salto, Uruguay 145/B2
Salto Angel (fall), Venezuela 124/G5
Salto del Guairá, Paraguay 144/E4
Salto Grande (dam), Argentina 143/E3
Salto Grande (falls), Colombia 120/B3
Salto Grande (falls), Colombia 126/B3
Salto Grande, Lago (res.), Brazil 132/B10
Salto Grande (dam), Uruguay 145/B2
Salton Sea (lake), Calif. 188/F5
Salton Sea (lake), Calif. 204/K10
Saltpetre, W. Va. 312/A6
Salt River, N.W. Terr. 187/G3
Salt River (bay), Virgin Is. (U.S.) 161/F3
Salt River (range), Wyo. 319/B3
Salt River Ind. Res., Ariz. 198/D5
Salt Rock, W. Va. 312/B6
Saltsburg, Pa. 294/C4
Saltsjöbaden, Sweden 18/J1
Salt Sulphur Springs, W. Va. 312/E7
Saltville, Va. 307/E7
Salt Wells (creek), Wyo. 319/D4
Saluda, N.C. 281/E4
Saluda (co.), S.C. 296/D3
Saluda, S.C. 296/E4
Saluda (dam), S.C. 296/F3
Saluda (riv.), S.C. 296/D3
Saluda, Va. 307/P5
Salûm, Egypt 102/E1
Salûm, Egypt 111/E1
Salus, Ark. 202/D2
Salut (isls.), Fr. Guiana 131/F3
Saluzzo, Italy 34/A2
Salvador, Brazil 132/G6
Salvador, Brazil 120/F4
Salvador, Brazil 2/H6
Salvador (lake), La. 238/K7
Salvador, Sask. 181/B3
Salvage (isls.), Portugal 106/A2
Salvaterra de Magos, Portugal 33/B3
Salvatierra, Mexico 150/J6
Salvation (creek), Utah 304/C5
Salvisa, Ky. 237/M5
Salvo, N.C. 281/U3
Salwa, Saudi Arabia 59/F5
Salween (riv.) 54/L8
Salween (riv.), Burma.72/C3
Salween (Nu Jiang) (riv.), China 77/E6
Sal'yany, U.S.S.R. 52/G7
Salybia, Dominica 161/F6
Salyer, Calif. 204/B3
Salyersville, Ky. 237/P5
Salzach (riv.), Austria 41/B2
Salzach (riv.), Germany 22/E5
Salzburg (prov.), Austria 41/B3
Salzburg, Austria 7/F4
Salzburg, Austria 41/B3
Salzgitter, Germany 22/D2
Salzkammergut (reg.), Austria 41/B3
Salzwedel, Germany 22/D2
Samá, Cuba 158/J3
Sama (riv.), Peru 128/G11
Sama, Spain 33/D1
Samagaltay, U.S.S.R. 48/K4
Samaipata, Bolivia 136/D6
Samal (isl.), Philippines 82/E7
Samales Group (isls.), Philippines 82/D7
Samalkot, India 68/E5
Samalût, Egypt 111/J4
Samalût, Egypt 59/B4
Samana (cay), Bahamas 156/D2
Samaná (prov.), Dom. Rep. 158/E5
Samaná, Dom. Rep. 158/F5
Samaná, Dom. Rep. 156/E3
Samaná (bay), Dom. Rep. 156/E3
Samaná (bay), Dom. Rep. 158/F5
Samaná (cape), Dom. Rep. 158/F5
Samandağ̃, Turkey 63/F4
Samaniego, Colombia 126/B7
Samantha, Ala. 195/C4
Samar, Jordan 65/D2
Samar (isls.), Philippines 54/O8
Samar (isl.), Philippines 85/H3
Samar (isl.), Philippines 82/E5
Samar (sea), Philippines 82/E4
Samara, U.S.S.R. 48/F4
Samara, U.S.S.R. 52/H4
Samara (riv.), U.S.S.R. 52/H4
Samarai, Papua N.G. 87/F7
Samarai, Papua N.G. 85/C8
Samaria, Idaho 220/F7

Samaria, Ind. 227/E6
Samaria (reg.), Jordan 65/C3
Samariapo, Venezuela 124/E5
Samarinda, Indonesia 85/F6
Samarinda, Indonesia 54/N10
Samarkand, U.S.S.R. 54/H6
Samarkand, U.S.S.R. 48/G6
Samarra, Iraq 59/D3
Samarra, Iraq 66/D3
Samawa, Iraq 66/E3
Samawa, Iraq 59/D3
Samba, Zaire 115/E4
Sambalpur, India 68/E4
Sambas, Indonesia 85/D5
Sambava, Madagascar 118/J2
Sambhal, India 68/D3
Sambhar (lake), India 68/C3
Sambiase, Italy 34/F5
Samboja, Indonesia 85/F6
Sambor, Cambodia 72/E4
Sambor, U.S.S.R. 52/B5
Samborombón (bay), Argentina 143/E4
Sambre (riv.), Belgium 27/D8
Sambre (riv.), France 28/F2
Sambro, Nova Scotia 168/E4
Samburg, Tenn. 237/C8
Samch'ŏk, S. Korea 81/D5
Same, Tanzania 115/G4
Samedan, Switzerland 39/J3
Sámi, Greece 45/D6
Samish (lake), Wash. 310/C2
Samka, Burma 72/C2
Sam Lord's Castle, Barbados 161/C9
Sammamish (lake), Wash. 310/B2
Samnangjin, S. Korea 81/D6
Samnaun, Switzerland 39/K3
Samnorwood, Texas 303/D2
Samoa, Calif. 204/A3
Samoa (falls), Calif. 204/A3
Samoa (isls.), Pacific 87/J7
Samo Alto, Chile 138/A8
Samobor, Yugoslavia 45/B3
Samokov, Bulgaria 45/F4
Samorín, Czech. 41/D2
Sámos (isl.), Greece 45/H7
Sámos, Greece 45/H7
Samoset, Fla. 212/M4
Samothráki, Greece 45/G5
Samothráki (isl.), Greece 45/G5
Sampang, Indonesia 85/K2
Samper de Calanda, Spain 33/F2
Sampit, Indonesia 85/E6
Sampson (co.), N.C. 281/N4
Sam Rayburn (riv.), Tex. 188/G4
Sam Rayburn (res.), Texas 303/K6
Samsang, China 77/B5
Samsat, Turkey 63/H4
Samso (isl.), Denmark 21/D6
Samso Baelt (chan.), Denmark 21/D6
Samson, Ala. 195/F8
Samsula, Fla. 212/E2
Samsun (prov.), Turkey 63/F2
Samsun, Turkey 59/C1
Samsun, Turkey 63/F2
Samsun, Turkey 54/E5
Sams Valley, Oreg. 291/E5
Samtown, La. 238/F4
Samu, West Bank 65/C5
Samuels, Idaho 220/B1
Samuels, Ky. 237/L5
Samui, Ko (isl.), Thailand 72/D5
Samui (str.), Thailand 72/D5
Samut Prakan, Thailand 72/D4
Samut Sakhon, Thailand 72/D4
Samut Songkhram, Thailand 72/C4
San, Se (riv.), Cambodia 72/E4
San, Mali 106/D6
San, Mali 102/B3
San (riv.), Poland 47/F3
Sana, Yemen 59/F6
Saña, Peru 128/C6
San'a (cap.), Yemen 54/F8
San'a (cap.), Yemen 59/D6
Sanaag (prov.), Somalia 115/J1
San Acacia, N. Mex. 274/B4
San Acacio, Colo. 208/J8
Sanae Station, Ant. 5/B18
Sanaga (riv.), Cameroon 115/B3
San Agustín, Bolivia 136/B7
San Agustín, Colombia 126/B7
San Agustin (plains), N. Mex. 274/B5
San Agustin (cape), Philippines 85/H4
San Agustin (cape), Philippines 82/F7
Sanak (isl.), Alaska 196/F4
Sanam, Saudi Arabia 59/D5
San Ambrosio (isl.), Chile 120/B5
Sanana, Indonesia 85/H6
Sanandaj, Iran 59/D3
Sanandaj, Iran 66/E3
Sanandita, Bolivia 136/D7
San Andreas, Calif. 204/E5
San Andreas (lake), Calif. 204/H2
San Andrés, Bolivia 136/C4
San Andrés (riv.), Calif. 204/H1
San Antero, Colombia 126/C3
San Antonio (cape), Argentina 120/D6
San Antonio (cape), Argentina 143/E4
San Antonio, El Beni, Bolivia 136/C4
San Antonio, Chile 138/F3
San Antonio, Colombia 126/B6

San Antonio (cape), Cuba 156/A2
San Antonio (cape), Cuba 158/A2
San Antonio, Fla. 212/D3
San Antonio, Mexico 150/D5
San Antonio (reef), Mexico 150/L4
San Antonio, N. Mex. 274/B5
San Antonio (peak), N. Mex. 274/C3
San Antonio, Paraguay 144/A5
San Antonio, Philippines 82/B3
San Antonio (bay), Philippines 82/A6
San Antonio, P. Rico 161/A1
San Antonio, Texas 146/J7
San Antonio, Texas 303/J11
San Antonio, Texas 188/G5
San Antonio (bay), Texas 303/H9
San Antonio (mt.), Texas 303/B10
San Antonio (riv.), Texas 303/K11
San Antonio, Canelones, Uruguay 145/B6
San Antonio, Salto, Uruguay 145/B2
San Antonio, Amazonas, Venezuela 124/E6
San Antonio, Monagas, Venezuela 124/G2
San Antonio, Zulia, Venezuela 124/C3
San Antonio Abad, Spain 33/G3
San Antonio de Areco, Argentina 143/G7
San Antonio de Caparo, Venezuela 124/C4
San Antonio de Lípez, Bolivia 136/B7
San Antonio de los Baños, Cuba 158/C1
San Antonio de los Baños, Cuba 156/A2
San Antonio de los Cobres, Argentina 143/C1
San Antonio del Parapetí, Bolivia 136/D7
San Antonio del Táchira, Venezuela 124/B4
San Antonio de Tabasca, Venezuela 124/G3
San Antonio Missions Nat'l Hist. Park, Texas 303/J11
San Antonio Oeste, Argentina 120/C7
San Antonio Oeste, Argentina 143/C5
San Ardo, Calif. 204/D7
Sanare, Venezuela 124/D3
Sanator, S. Dak. 298/B6
Sanatorium, Miss. 256/E7
San Augustine (co.), Texas 303/K6
San Augustine, Texas 303/K6
San Bartolomeo in Galdo, Italy 34/E4
San Bautista, Uruguay 145/B6
San Benedetto del Tronto, Italy 34/E3
San Benedicto (isl.), Mexico 150/D7
San Benito (co.), Calif. 204/D7
San Benito (riv.), Calif. 204/D7
San Benito (isl.), Mexico 150/B2
San Benito, Texas 303/G12
San Bernardino, Calif. 146/G6
San Bernardino, Calif. 188/D4
San Bernardino (co.), Calif. 204/J9
San Bernardino, Calif. 204/E10
San Bernardino (mts.), Calif. 204/J10
San Bernardino, Paraguay 144/B4
San Bernardino (str.), Philippines 82/E4
San Bernardino, Switzerland 39/H4
San Bernardino (pass), Switzerland 39/H3
San Bernardo, Chile 138/G4
San Bernardo (isls.), Colombia 126/C3
San Blas (cape), Fla. 212/D7
San Blas, Nayarit, Mexico 150/G6
San Blas, Sinaloa, Mexico 150/E3
San Blas, Archipiélago de (arch.), Panama 154/J7
San Blas, Golfo de (bay), Panama 154/H6
San Blas, Cordillera de (mts.), Panama 154/H6
San Blas, Pta. de (pt.), Panama 154/H6
San Borja, Bolivia 136/B4
Sanborn, Iowa 229/B2
Sanborn, Minn. 255/C6
Sanborn, N.Y. 276/C4
Sanborn, N. Dak. 282/O6
Sanborn (co.), S. Dak. 298/N5
Sanborn, Wis. 317/E3
Sanbornton•, N.H. 268/D5
Sanbornville, N.H. 268/F4
San Bruno, Calif. 204/J2
San Bruno, Mexico 150/D3
San Buenaventura, Bolivia 136/A4
San Buenaventura, Mexico 150/J3
San Carlos, Mendoza, Argentina 143/C3
San Carlos, Santa Fe, Argentina 143/F6
San Carlos, Ariz. 198/E5
San Carlos (lake), Ariz. 188/E4
San Carlos (lake), Ariz. 198/E5
San Carlos (riv.), Ariz. 198/E5
San Carlos, Bolivia 136/D5
San Carlos, Calif. 204/J3
San Carlos, Chile 138/E1
San Carlos, Coahuila, Mexico 150/J2
San Carlos, Tamaulipas, Mexico 150/K4
San Carlos, Nicaragua 154/E5
San Carlos, Panama 154/H6
San Carlos, Paraguay 144/D3
San Carlos, Negros Occ., Philippines 82/D5
San Carlos, Pangasinan, Philippines 82/C3
San Carlos, Uruguay 145/E5
San Carlos, Cojedes, Venezuela 124/D3
San Carlos, Zulia, Venezuela 124/C2
San Carlos de Bariloche, Argentina 143/B5
San Carlos de Bariloche, Argentina 120/B7
San Carlos de la Rápita, Spain 33/G2

San Carlos del Zulia, Venezuela 124/C3
San Carlos de Río Negro, Venezuela 124/E7
San Carlos Ind. Res., Ariz. 198/E5
San Casimiro, Venezuela 124/E3
San Cataldo, Italy 34/D6
San Cayetano, Argentina 143/E4
Sancerre, France 28/E4
Sanchez (res.), Colo. 208/H8
Sánchez, Dom. Rep. 156/E3
Sánchez, Dom. Rep. 158/E5
Sánchez, Uruguay 145/B3
Sánchez Ramírez (prov.), Dom. Rep. 158/E5
San Clara, Manitoba 179/A3
San Clemente (isl.), Calif. 204/G11
San Clemente, Calif. 204/H10
San Clemente, Chile 138/A11
San Clemente, Spain 33/E3
Sancoins, France 28/E4
San Cosme y Damián, Paraguay 144/D5
San Cristóbal, Argentina 143/F5
San Cristóbal, Potosí, Bolivia 136/B7
San Cristóbal, Santa Cruz, Bolivia 136/E3
San Cristóbal, Cuba 158/B1
San Cristóbal (prov.), Dom. Rep. 158/E6
San Cristóbal, Dom. Rep. 158/E6
San Cristóbal (isl.), Ecuador 128/C9
San Cristobal, N. Mex. 274/D2
San Cristóbal, Panama 154/G6
San Cristóbal (isl.), Solomon Is. 87/G7
San Cristobal (isl.), Solomon Is. 86/E3
San Cristóbal, Venezuela 124/B4
San Cristóbal, Venezuela 120/B2
San Cristóbal de las Casas, Mexico 150/N8
Sancti Spíritus (prov.), Cuba 158/E2
Sancti Spíritus, Cuba 156/B2
Sanctuary, Sask. 181/D4
Sand (mt.), Ala. 195/G1
Sand (key), Fla. 212/B3
Sand (isl.), Hawaii 218/B4
Sand (creek), Ind. 227/F6
Sand (pt.), Mich. 250/F5
Sand (creek), Minn. 255/F5
Sand, Norway 18/F7
Sand (isl.), S. Africa 118/D4
Sand (creek), S. Dak. 298/M5
Sand (creek), S. Dak. 298/C2
Sand (isl.), Wash. 310/A2
Sand (isl.), Wis. 317/D2
Sanda, Japan 81/H7
Sanda (isl.), Scotland 15/C5
Sandakan, Malaysia 54/N9
Sandakan, Malaysia 85/F4
Sandalwood (Sumba) (isl.), Indonesia 85/F7
Sandane, Norway 18/D6
Sandanski, Bulgaria 45/F5
Sand Arroyo (dry riv.), Colo. 208/O8
Sanday (isl.), Scotland 10/E1
Sanday (isl.), Scotland 15/B3
Sanday (isl.), Scotland 15/F1
Sanday (sound), Scotland 15/F1
Sandbach, England 10/G2
Sandbach, England 13/H2
Sandbank, Scotland 15/A1
Sandborn, Ind. 227/C7
Sand Brook, N.J. 273/D3
Sand Coulee, Mont. 262/E3
Sand Creek, Wis. 317/C5
Sand Draw, Wyo. 319/D3
Sandefjord, Norway 18/C4
San de Fuca, Wash. 310/C2
Sandel, La. 238/C4
Sanders, Ariz. 198/F3
Sanders, Idaho 220/B2
Sanders, Ind. 227/E6
Sanders, Ky. 237/M3
Sanders (co.), Mont. 262/A3
Sanders, Mont. 262/A3
Sanderson, Fla. 212/D1
Sanderson, Texas 303/B10
Sandersville, Georgia 217/G5
Sandersville, Miss. 256/F7
Sandford, Ind. 227/B5
Sand Fork, W. Va. 312/D6
Sandgap, Ky. 237/N6
Sandgate, Queensland 88/K2
Sandgate, Queensland 95/D2
Sandgate•, Vt. 268/A4
Sandhead, Scotland 15/D6
Sand Hill (riv.), Minn. 255/B3
Sandhill, Miss. 256/E5
Sand Hill (riv.), Newf. 166/C3
Sand Hills, Mass. 249/M4
Sandhurst, England 13/G8
Sandia (peak), N. Mex. 274/C3
Sandia, Peru 128/H10
Sandia, Texas 303/F9
Sandia Park, N. Mex. 274/C3
San Diego (cape), Argentina 120/E8
San Diego (cape), Argentina 143/D7
San Diego, Bolivia 136/D7
San Diego (co.), Calif. 204/J10
San Diego, Calif. 146/F6
San Diego, Calif. 188/C4
San Diego, Calif. 204/H11
San Diego (bay), Calif. 204/H11
San Diego, Texas 303/F10
San Diego de Cabrutica, Venezuela 124/F3
San Diego de los Baños, Cuba 158/B1
Sandıklı, Turkey 63/D3
Sandilands, Manitoba 179/F5
San Dimas, Calif. 204/D10
Sanding (isl.), Indonesia 85/C6
Sandisfield•, Mass. 249/B4
Sand Lake, Mich. 250/D5
Sand Lake, N.Y. 276/O5
Sandnes, Norway 18/D7

Sandoa, Zaire 115/D5
Sandomierz, Poland 47/E3
Sandoná, Colombia 126/B7
Sándorfalva, Hungary 41/F3
Sandoval, Ill. 222/D5
Sandoval (co.), N. Mex. 274/C3
Sandover (riv.), North. Terr. 93/D6
Sandoway, Burma 72/B3
Sandown•, N.H. 268/E6
Sandown (bay), S. Africa 118/D4
Sandown-Shanklin, England 13/F7
Sandoy (isl.), Denmark 21/B3
Sand Point, Alaska 196/G3
Sandpoint, Idaho 220/B1
Sand Point, Okla. 288/N7
Sandray (isl.), Scotland 15/A4
Sandridge, Manitoba 179/F4
Sand Ridge, N.Y. 276/H4
Sandringham, Victoria 88/L7
Sandringham, Victoria 97/J5
Sands (key), Fla. 212/F6
Sands, Mich. 250/B2
Sand Shoal (inlet), Va. 307/S6
Sandspit, Br. Col. 184/B3
Sands Point, N.Y. 276/P6
Sand Springs, Iowa 229/L4
Sand Springs, Ky. 237/N6
Sand Springs, Mont. 262/L3
Sand Springs (salt flat), Nev. 266/C3
Sand Springs, Okla. 288/O2
Sandston, Va. 307/O5
Sandstone, W. Australia 88/B5
Sandstone, W. Australia 92/B4
Sandstone, W. Va. 312/E7
Sand Tank (mt.), Ariz. 198/C6
Sandusky, Ill. 222/D6
Sandusky, Ind. 227/F6
Sandusky, Mich. 250/G5
Sandusky, N.Y. 276/D6
Sandusky (co.), Ohio 284/E3
Sandusky, Ohio 284/E3
Sandusky, Ohio 188/K2
Sandusky (bay), Ohio 284/E3
Sandusky (riv.), Ohio 284/D3
Sandvika, Norway 18/C3
Sandviken, Sweden 18/K6
Sandwich, England 13/J6
Sandwich, Ill. 222/E2
Sandwich, Mass. 249/N5
Sandwich•, Mass. 249/N5
Sandwich•, N.H. 268/E4
Sandwich (inlet), Newf. 166/C3
Sandwich•, N.H. 268/E4
Sandwich (range), N.H. 268/E4
Sandwich, Scotland 15/B2
Sandwith, Sask. 181/C2
Sandy (creek), Ala. 195/H7
Sandy (brook), Conn. 210/C1
Sandy, England 13/G5
Sandy (riv.), Maine 243/C6
Sandy (isls.), Manitoba 179/D2
Sandy (lake), Mont. 262/F2
Sandy (lake), Newf. 166/C3
Sandy (lake), Ont. 162/G5
Sandy (lake), Ontario 175/B2
Sandy, Oreg. 291/E2
Sandy, Pa. 294/E3
Sandy (cape), Queensland 88/J4
Sandy (cape), Queensland 95/E5
Sandy (pt.), R.I. 249/H8
Sandy (pt.), S.C. 296/H6
Sandy (riv.), S.C. 296/E2
Sandy (cape), Tasmania 99/A3
Sandy, Utah 304/C3
Sandy (isl.), Virgin Is. (U.S.) 161/D4
Sandy Bay, Jamaica 158/G5
Sandy Bay, Nicaragua 154/F2
Sandy Bay, Sask. 181/N3
Sandy Beach, Alberta 182/D2
Sandy Beach, Sask. 181/H5
Sandy Cove, Nova Scotia 168/B4
Sandy Creek, Maine 243/B7
Sandy Creek, N.Y. 276/H3
Sandy Hook, Conn. 210/B3
Sandy Hook, Ky. 237/P4
Sandy Hook, Manitoba 179/F4
Sandy Hook, Miss. 256/E8
Sandy Hook (spit), N.J. 273/F3
Sandy Hook, Va. 307/M5
Sandy Lake, Alberta 182/D2
Sandy Lake, Manitoba 179/B4
Sandy Lake, Pa. 294/B3
Sandy Point, Maine 243/F7
Sandy Point, Nova Scotia 168/C5
Sandy Point, St. Kitts & Nevis 161/C12
Sandy Ridge, Ala. 195/E6
Sandy Ridge, N.C. 281/J1
Sandy Ridge, Pa. 294/F4
Sandy Spring-Ashton, Md. 245/K4
Sandy Springs, Georgia 217/K1
Sandy Springs, S.C. 296/B2
Sandyville, Ind. 227/B6
Sandyville, Ohio 284/H4
San Elizario, Texas 303/A10
San Estanislao, Paraguay 144/D4
San Esteban (gulf), Chile 138/D4
San Esteban, Honduras 154/D2
San Esteban de Gormaz, Spain 33/E2
San Felipe, Chile 138/G2
San Felipe, Colombia 126/G7
San Felipe (cays), Cuba 156/A2
San Felipe (cays), Cuba 158/B2
San Felipe, Guatemala 154/B3
San Felipe, Baja California, Mexico 150/B1
San Felipe, Guanajuato, Mexico 150/J6
San Felipe, Philippines 82/B3
San Felipe, Yaracuy, Venezuela 124/D2
San Felipe, Zulia, Venezuela 124/B3
San Felíu de Guíxols, Spain 33/H2
San Félix, Chile 138/A7
San Félix (isl.), Chile 120/A5

Santa Cruz 443

San Félix, Panama 154/G6
San Félix, Venezuela 124/C2
San Fernando, Argentina 143/G7
San Fernando (riv.), Bolivia 136/F5
San Fernando, Calif. 204/C10
San Fernando, Chile 138/G6
San Fernando, Tamaulipas, Mexico 150/L4
San Fernando, La Union, Philippines 82/C2
San Fernando, Masbate, Philippines 82/D4
San Fernando, Pampanga, Philippines 82/C3
San Fernando, Spain 33/C4
San Fernando, Trin. & Tob. 161/A11
San Fernando, Trin. & Tob. 156/G5
San Fernando, Venezuela 120/C2
San Fernando de Apure, Venezuela 124/E4
San Fernando de Atabapo, Venezuela 124/E5
San Fidel, N. Mex. 274/B3
Sanford, Ala. 195/F8
Sanford (mt.), Alaska 196/K2
Sanford, Colo. 208/H8
Sanford, Fla. 188/K5
Sanford, Fla. 212/E3
Sanford, Maine 243/B9
Sanford•, Maine 243/B9
Sanford, Manitoba 179/E5
Sanford, Mich. 250/E5
Sanford, Miss. 256/F8
Sanford, N.C. 281/L4
Sanford, Nova Scotia 168/B5
San Francique, Trin. & Tob. 161/A11
San Francisco, Argentina 120/C6
San Francisco, San Luis, Argentina 143/C3
San Francisco, Córdoba, Argentina 143/D3
San Francisco (riv.), Ariz. 198/F5
San Francisco, Bolivia 136/C4
San Francisco (city county), Calif. 204/J2
San Francisco, Calif. 146/F6
San Francisco, Calif. 188/B3
San Francisco, Calif. 204/H2
San Francisco (bay), Calif. 204/J2
San Francisco, Colombia 126/B7
San Francisco (cape), Ecuador 128/B2
San Francisco, Honduras 154/D3
San Francisco (riv.), N. Mex. 274/A5
San Francisco, Nicaragua 154/E5
San Francisco, Panama 154/G6
San Francisco (creek), Texas 303/B8
San Francisco, U.S. 2/C4
San Francisco, Lara, Venezuela 124/C2
San Francisco de la Paz, Honduras 154/D3
San Francisco del Chañar, Argentina 143/C2
San Francisco del Oro, Mexico 150/F3
San Francisco del Rincón, Mexico 150/H6
San Francisco de Macorís, Dom. Rep. 158/E5
San Francisco de Macorís, Dom. Rep. 156/E3
San Francisco de Mostazal, Chile 138/G4
San Francisco Gotera, El Salvador 154/C4
Sanga (riv.), Cameroon 115/C3
Sanga (riv.), Cent. Afr. Rep. 115/C3
San Gabriel, Calif. 204/C10
San Gabriel (res.), Calif. 204/D10
San Gabriel, Ecuador 128/D2
San Gabriel Chilac, Mexico 150/K7
San Gallán (isl.), Peru 128/D9
Sangamner, India 68/C5
Sangamon (co.), Ill. 222/D4
Sangamon (riv.), Ill. 222/C3
Sangan, Iran 66/M3
Sangar, U.S.S.R. 54/O3
Sangar, U.S.S.R. 48/N3
Sangaredyi, Guinea 106/B6
Sangay (mt.), Ecuador 128/C4
Sangeang (isl.), Indonesia 85/F7
San Genaro, Argentina 143/F6
Sanger, Calif. 204/F7
Sanger, N. Dak. 282/H5
Sanger, Texas 303/G4
Sangerhausen, Germany 22/D3
San Germán, Cuba 158/J3
San Germán, P. Rico 161/A2
San Germán, P. Rico 156/F1
Sangerville•, Maine 243/E5
Sangestan, Kuh-e (mt.), Iran 66/H5
Sanggabuwana (mt.), Indonesia 85/G2
Sanggau, Indonesia 85/E5
Sangha (riv.), Congo 115/C3
Sangihe (isls.), Indonesia 54/O9
Sangihe (isl.), Indonesia 85/H5
Sangihe (isls.), Indonesia 85/G5
San Gil, Colombia 126/D4
San Giovanni in Fiore, Italy 34/F5
San Giovanni in Persiceto, Italy 34/C2
San Giuliano Terme, Italy 34/C3
Sangju, S. Korea 81/D5
Sangkulirang, Indonesia 85/F5
Sangli, India 68/C5
Sangmélima, Cameroon 115/B3
Sangolquí, Ecuador 128/C3
Sangre de Cristo (mts.), Colo. 208/H6
Sangre de Cristo (mts.), N. Mex. 274/D3
San Gregorio, Calif. 204/J3
San Gregorio, San José, Uruguay 145/C4
San Gregorio, Tacuarembó, Uruguay 145/D3
Sangre Grande, Trin. & Tob. 161/B10
Sangre Grande, Trin. & Tob. 156/G5
Sangri, China 77/D6
Sangro (riv.), Italy 34/E4
Sangudo, Alberta 182/C3
Sangue (riv.), Brazil 132/B6
Sangüesa, Spain 33/F1
Sanhe, China 77/E1
Sanibel, Fla. 212/D5
Sanibel (isl.), Fla. 212/D5
San Ignacio, Argentina 143/E2
San Ignacio, Belize 154/C2
San Ignacio, El Beni, Bolivia 136/C4
San Ignacio, Santa Cruz, Bolivia 136/E5
San Ignacio, Chile 138/E1
San Ignacio, C. Rica 154/E6
San Ignacio, Baja California Sur, Mexico 150/C3
San Ignacio, Sinaloa, Mexico 150/F5
San Ignacio, Paraguay 144/D5
San Ignacio, Venezuela 124/B2
Sanilac (co.), Mich. 250/G5
San Ildefonso, N. Mex. 274/C3
San Ildefonso (cape), Philippines 82/D2
San Ildefonso, Spain 33/E2
San'in Kaigan National Park, Japan 81/G6
San Isabel, Colo. 208/K7
Sanish, N. Dak. 282/E4
San Isidro, Argentina 143/C2
San Isidro, Philippines 82/E5
Saniya, Hor (lake), Iraq 66/E5
San Jacinto, Calif. 204/H10
San Jacinto, Colombia 126/C3
San Jacinto, Nev. 266/G1
San Jacinto, Philippines 82/D4
San Jacinto (co.), Texas 303/J7
San Jacinto, Uruguay 145/C6
San Jaime de la Frontera, Argentina 143/G5
San Javier, Río Negro, Argentina 143/D5
San Javier, Santa Fe, Argentina 143/F5
San Javier, Santa Cruz, Bolivia 136/D5
San Javier, El Beni, Bolivia 136/C4
San Javier, Chile 138/A11
San Javier, Uruguay 145/A3
San Jerónimo de Juárez, Mexico 150/J8
Sanjo, Japan 81/J5
San Joaquín, Bolivia 136/C3
San Joaquin (riv.), Calif. 188/C3
San Joaquin (co.), Calif. 204/D6
San Joaquin, Calif. 204/E7
San Joaquin (riv.), Calif. 204/E6
San Joaquin (valley), Calif. 204/D6
San Joaquín, Paraguay 144/E4
San Jon, N. Mex. 274/F3
San Jorge (gulf), Argentina 120/C7
San Jorge (gulf), Argentina 143/C6
San Jorge (riv.), Colombia 126/C3
San Jorge (bay), Mexico 150/C1
San Jorge, Nicaragua 154/E5
San Jorge (gulf), Spain 33/G2
San José, Belize 154/C2
San Jose, Calif. 146/F6
San Jose, Calif. 188/B3
San Jose, Calif. 204/L3
San José, Colombia 126/F6
San José (cap.), C. Rica 146/K9
San José (cap.), C. Rica 154/F5
San José, Guatemala 154/B4
San Jose, Ill. 222/D3
San José (isl.), Mexico 150/D4
San Jose, N. Mex. 274/D3
San Jose (riv.), N. Mex. 274/B3
San José (isl.), Panama 154/H6
San José, Paraguay 144/B5
San José, Peru 128/B6
San Jose, Philippines 85/G3
San Jose, Nueva Ecija, Philippines 82/C3
San Jose, Occ. Mindoro, Philippines 82/C4
San José (lag.), P. Rico 161/E1
San Jose (isl.), Texas 303/H9
San José (dept.), Uruguay 145/C5
San José (riv.), Uruguay 145/C4
San José, Amazonas, Venezuela 124/E5
San José, Zulia, Venezuela 124/B3
San José de Amacuro, Venezuela 124/H3
San José de Areocuar, Venezuela 124/G2
San Jose de Buenavista, Philippines 82/C5
San José de Chiquitos, Bolivia 136/E5
San José de Feliciano, Argentina 143/G5
San José de Guanipa, Venezuela 124/G3
San José de la Costa, Venezuela 124/D2
San José de la Mariquina, Chile 138/D2
San José de las Lajas, Cuba 158/C1
San José de las Matas, Dom. Rep. 158/D5
San José del Cabo, Mexico 150/D5
San José del Guaviare, Colombia 126/D6
San Jose del Monte, Philippines 82/C3
San José del Ocune, Colombia 126/E5
San José de los Ramos, Cuba 158/D1
San José de Maipo, Chile 138/B10
San José de Mayo, Uruguay 145/C5
San José de Ocoa, Dom. Rep. 158/E6
San José de Río Chico, Venezuela 124/F2
San José de Sisa, Peru 128/D6
San José de Tiznados, Venezuela 124/E3
San José de Uchupiamonas, Bolivia 136/A4
San Juan (riv.) 188/E3
San Juan (prov.), Argentina 143/C3
San Juan, Argentina 143/C3
San Juan, Argentina 120/C6
San Juan (riv.), Argentina 143/C3
San Juan, Potosí, Bolivia 136/B7
San Juan, Santa Cruz, Bolivia 136/F5
San Juan (riv.), Bolivia 136/C7
San Juan (riv.), Br. Col. 184/J3
San Juan (creek), Calif. 204/E8
San Juan (riv.), Colombia 126/B5
San Juan (co.), Colo. 208/D7
San Juan (mts.), Colo. 208/F7
San Juan (riv.), Colo. 208/E8
San Juan (riv.), C. Rica 154/E5
San Juan (prov.), Dom. Rep. 158/D6
San Juan, Dom. Rep. 158/D6
San Juan, Mexico 150/K6
San Juan (co.), N. Mex. 274/A2
San Juan (riv.), N. Mex. 274/B2
San Juan (riv.), Nicaragua 154/E5
San Juan, Peru 128/E10
San Juan, Philippines 82/E5
San Juan (dist.), P. Rico 161/D1
San Juan (cap.), P. Rico 146/M8
San Juan (cap.), P. Rico 161/E1
San Juan (cap.), P. Rico 156/G1
San Juan (cape), P. Rico 156/G1
San Juan, Cabezas de (prom.), P. Rico 161/F1
San Juan, Texas 303/F11
San Juan, Trin. & Tob. 161/A10
San Juan (co.), Utah 304/E6
San Juan (riv.), Utah 304/D6
San Juan (co.), Wash. 310/C2
San Juan (isl.), Wash. 310/B2
San Juan Bautista, Calif. 204/D7
San Juan Bautista, Paraguay 144/D5
San Juan Bautista de Neembucú, Paraguay 144/D5
San Juan Capistrano, Calif. 204/H10
San Juan de Colón, Venezuela 124/B3
San Juan de Flores, Honduras 154/D3
San Juan de las Galdonas, Venezuela 124/G2
San Juan del César, Colombia 126/D2
San Juan del Norte, Nicaragua 154/F5
San Juan del Norte (bay), Nicaragua 154/F5
San Juan de los Cayos, Venezuela 124/D2
San Juan de los Lagos, Mexico 150/H6
San Juan de los Morros, Venezuela 124/E3
San Juan de los Planes, Mexico 150/D4
San Juan del Piray, Bolivia 136/C7
San Juan del Potrero, Bolivia 136/C5
San Juan del Sur, Nicaragua 154/D5
San Juan de Manapiare, Venezuela 124/E5
San Juan de Payara, Venezuela 124/E4
San Juan Island Nat'l Hist. Park, Wash. 310/B2
San Juan Nat'l Hist. Site, P. Rico 161/D1
San Juan Nepomuceno, Paraguay 144/E5
San Juan Pueblo, N. Mex. 274/C2
San Juan Xiutetelco, Mexico 150/O1
San Juan y Martínez, Cuba 158/B2
San Julián, Argentina 143/C6
San Julián, Argentina 120/C7
San Justo, Argentina 143/F5
Sankrail, India 68/E2
Sankt Aegyd am Neuwalde, Austria 41/C3
Sankt Anton am Arlberg, Austria 41/A3
Sankt Blasien, Germany 22/C5
Sankt Gallen (canton), Switzerland 39/H2
Sankt Gallen, Switzerland 39/H2
Sankt Goar, Germany 22/B3
Sankt Ingbert, Germany 22/B4
Sankt Johann in Tirol, Austria 41/B3
Sankt Margrethen, Switzerland 39/J2
Sankt Michael im Lungau, Austria 41/B3
Sankt Michael in Obersteiermark, Austria 41/C3
Sankt Paul im Lavanttal, Austria 41/C3
Sankt Peter-Ording, Germany 22/C1
Sankt Pölten, Austria 41/C2
Sankt Valentin, Austria 41/C2
Sankt Veit an der Glan, Austria 41/C3
Sankt Vith, Belgium 27/J8
Sankt Wendel, Germany 22/B4
Sankt Wolfgang im Dalzkammergut, Austria 41/B3
Sankuru (riv.), Zaire 102/E5
Sankuru (riv.), Zaire 115/D4
San Lázaro (cape), Mexico 150/C4
San Lázaro, Paraguay 144/D3
San Leandro, Calif. 204/J2
San Leon, Texas 303/L2
San Lorenzo, Argentina 143/F6
San Lorenzo, Cerro (mt.), Argentina 143/B6
San Lorenzo, El Beni, Bolivia 136/C4
San Lorenzo, Pando, Bolivia 136/B2
San Lorenzo, Tarija, Bolivia 136/C7
San Lorenzo, Serranía (mts.), Bolivia 136/E5
San Lorenzo, Calif. 204/K2
San Lorenzo (riv.), Calif. 204/K4
San Lorenzo, Cerro (Cochrane) (mt.), Chile 138/E7
San Lorenzo, Ecuador 128/C2
San Lorenzo (cape), Ecuador 128/B3
San Lorenzo, N. Mex. 274/B6
San Lorenzo, Paraguay 144/B4
San Lorenzo, Peru 128/H8
San Lorenzo (isl.), Peru 128/D9
San Lorenzo, P. Rico 161/E2
San Lorenzo, P. Rico 156/G1
San Lorenzo, Falcón, Venezuela 124/D2
San Lorenzo, Zulia, Venezuela 124/C3
San Lorenzo de El Escorial, Spain 33/E2
Sanlúcar de Barrameda, Spain 33/C4
Sanlúcar la Mayor, Spain 33/C4
San Lucas, Bolivia 136/C7
San Lucas, Calif. 204/E7
San Lucas (cape), Mexico 146/G7
San Lucas (cape), Mexico 2/D4
San Lucas (cape), Mexico 150/E5
San Luis (prov.), Argentina 143/C3
San Luis, Argentina 143/C3
San Luis, Argentina 120/C6
San Luis, Ariz. 198/A6
San Luis (lake), Bolivia 136/C3
San Luis (res.), Calif. 204/E7
San Luis, Colo. 208/J8
San Luis (creek), Colo. 208/H6
San Luis (lake), Colo. 208/H7
San Luis (peak), Colo. 208/F6
San Luis, Cuba 156/C2
San Luis, Pinar del Río, Cuba 158/B2
San Luis, Santiago de Cuba, Cuba 158/J4
San Luis, Guatemala 154/C2
San Luis, Honduras 154/C3
San Luis, Philippines 82/E6
San Luis (passage), Texas 303/K8
San Luis, Venezuela 124/D2
San Luis de la Paz, Mexico 150/J6
San Luis del Cordero, Mexico 150/H4
San Luis Jilotepeque, Guatemala 154/C3
San Luis Obispo, Calif. 188/B3
San Luis Obispo, Calif. 146/F6
San Luis Obispo (co.), Calif. 204/E8
San Luis Obispo, Calif. 204/E8
San Luis Potosí (state), Mexico 150/J5
San Luis Potosí, Mexico 150/J5
San Luis Potosí, Mexico 146/H7
San Luis Río Colorado, Mexico 150/B1
San Manuel, Ariz. 198/E6
San Marcelino, Philippines 82/B3
San Marco in Lamis, Italy 34/E4
San Marcos, Calif. 204/H10
San Marcos, Colombia 126/C3
San Marcos, C. Rica 154/E6
San Marcos, Guatemala 154/B3
San Marcos, Honduras 154/C3
San Marcos, Mexico 150/K8
San Marcos (isl.), Mexico 150/D3
San Marcos, Texas 303/F8
San Mariano, Philippines 82/D2
San Marino 7/F4
SAN MARINO 34
San Marino, Calif. 204/D10
San Marino (cap.), San Marino 34/D3
San Martín (lake) 120/B7
San Martín, Argentina 143/C3
San Martín (lake), Argentina 143/B6
San Martín (riv.), Bolivia 136/D3
San Martin, Calif. 204/L4
San Martin (cape), Calif. 204/D8
San Martín (lake), Chile 138/E7
San Martín, Colombia 126/D6
San Martín (dept.), Peru 128/D6
San Martín, Peru 128/E3
San Martín de las Pirámides, Mexico 150/M1
San Martín de los Andes, Argentina 143/C5
San Martín de Valdeiglesias, Spain 33/D2
San Martine Draw (dry riv.), Texas 303/C11
San Martín Jilotepeque, Guatemala 154/B3
San Martín Texmelucan, Mexico 150/M1
San Mateo (co.), Calif. 204/C3
San Mateo, Calif. 204/J3
San Mateo, Fla. 212/E2
San Mateo, N. Mex. 274/B3
San Mateo (mts.), N. Mex. 274/B5
San Mateo, Spain 33/F2
San Mateo, Venezuela 124/F3
San Mateo Ixtatán, Guatemala 154/B3
San Matías (gulf), Argentina 120/C7
San Matías (gulf), Argentina 143/D5
San Matías, Bolivia 136/F5
Sanmaur, Québec 174/C3
San Mauricio, Venezuela 124/E3
Sanmenxia, China 77/H5
San Miguel, Argentina 143/E2
San Miguel, Bolivia 136/E5
San Miguel (riv.), Bolivia 136/D4
San Miguel, Calif. 204/E8
San Miguel (isl.), Calif. 204/E9
San Miguel (riv.), Colombia 126/B7
San Miguel (co.), Colo. 208/C6
San Miguel (mts.), Colo. 208/C7
San Miguel (riv.), Colo. 208/B6
San Miguel, Cuba 158/H3
San Miguel, Ecuador 128/C3
San Miguel (riv.), Ecuador 128/D2
San Miguel, El Salvador 154/D4
San Miguel (co.), N. Mex. 274/D3
San Miguel, N. Mex. 274/C6
San Miguel, Golfo de (bay), Panama 154/H6
San Miguel, Paraguay 144/D5
San Miguel, Ayacucho, Peru 128/F9
San Miguel, Cajamarca, Peru 128/C6
San Miguel (bay), Philippines 82/D3
San Miguel (isls.), Philippines 85/F4
San Miguel (isls.), Philippines 82/B7
San Miguel (swamp), Uruguay 145/F4
San Miguel de Allende, Mexico 150/J6
San Miguel de Huachi, Bolivia 136/B4
San Miguel del Monte, Argentina 143/G7
San Miguel de Salcedo, Ecuador 128/C3
San Miguel de Tucumán, Argentina 143/D2
San Miguel de Tucumán, Argentina 120/C5
San Miguelito, Bolivia 136/A2
San Miguelito, Nicaragua 154/E5
San Miguel Nuevo, Colombia 126/B7
Sanming, China 77/J6
San Miniato, Italy 34/C3
San Narciso, Philippines 82/D4
Sannicandro Garganico, Italy 34/E4
San Nicolás, Argentina 143/F6
San Nicolás, Argentina 120/D6
San Nicolas (isl.), Calif. 204/F10
San Nicolás, Cuba 158/C1
San Nicolás (bay), Peru 128/E10
San Nicolás de los Garza, Mexico 150/J3
Sannikova (str.), U.S.S.R. 48/O2
San Nua (Sam Neua), Laos 72/E2
Sano, Ky. 237/L6
Sanok, Poland 47/F4
San Onofre, Colombia 126/C3
San Pablo, Potosí, Bolivia 136/B7
San Pablo, Santa Cruz, Bolivia 136/D4
San Pablo, Calif. 204/J1
San Pablo (bay), Calif. 204/J1
San Pablo, Chile 138/D3
San Pablo, Colombia 126/B7
San Pablo, Colo. 208/J8
San Pablo, Sierra (mts.), Honduras 154/E3
San Pablo, Laguna, Philippines 82/C3
San Pablo, Negros Occ., Philippines 82/D5
San Pascual, Philippines 82/D4
San Patricio, N. Mex. 274/D5
San Patricio, Paraguay 144/D5
San Patricio (co.), Texas 303/G10
San Pedro, Buenos Aires, Argentina 143/F6
San Pedro, Jujuy, Argentina 143/D1
San Pedro (riv.), Ariz. 188/D4
San Pedro (riv.), Ariz. 198/E6
San Pedro, Belize 154/D2
San Pedro, Chuquisaca, Bolivia 136/C6
San Pedro, El Beni, Bolivia 136/C4
San Pedro, Pando, Bolivia 136/B2
San Pedro, Santa Cruz, Bolivia 136/D5
San Pedro, Calif. 204/C11
San Pedro (bay), Calif. 204/C11
San Pedro (chan.), Calif. 204/G10
San Pedro, Santiago, Chile 138/F4
San Pedro, Valparaíso, Chile 138/F2
San Pedro (pt.), Chile 138/A5
San Pedro, Colombia 126/E5
San Pedro, Cuba 158/B2
San Pedro (riv.), Cuba 158/G3
San Pedro (riv.), Guatemala 154/B2
San Pedro, Ivory Coast 106/C8
San Pedro, Nicaragua 154/E4
San Pedro, Paraguay 144/D4-5
San Pedro, Paraguay 144/D3
San Pedro (bay), Philippines 82/E5
San Pedro, Sierra de (range), Spain 33/C3
San Pedro Carchá, Guatemala 154/B3
San Pedro de Arimena, Colombia 126/E5
San Pedro de Atacama, Chile 138/C4
San Pedro de Buena Vista, Bolivia 136/C6
San Pedro de las Bocas, Venezuela 124/G4
San Pedro de las Colonias, Mexico 150/H4
San Pedro del Gallo, Mexico 150/G4
San Pedro de Lloc, Peru 128/C6
San Pedro del Paraná, Paraguay 144/D5
San Pedro de Macorís (prov.), Dom. Rep. 158/F6
San Pedro de Macorís, Dom. Rep. 156/E3
San Pedro de Macorís, Dom. Rep. 158/F6
San Pedro de Quemes, Bolivia 136/A7
San Pedro Pochutla, Mexico 150/L9
San Pedro Sula, Honduras 154/C3
San Pedro Zacapa, Honduras 154/D3
San Perlita, Texas 303/G11
Sanpete (co.), Utah 304/C4
San Pierre, Ind. 227/D2
San Pietro (isl.), Italy 34/B5
San Pitch (riv.), Utah 304/C4
Sanpoil (riv.), Wash. 310/G2
San Quentin, Calif. 204/H1
Sanquhar, Scotland 15/D5
San Quintin, Philippines 82/C3
San Rafael, Argentina 143/C3
San Rafael, Argentina 120/C6
San Rafael, Bolivia 136/E5
San Rafael, Calif. 204/J1
San Rafael (cape), Dom. Rep. 158/F5
San Rafael, Mexico 150/M1
San Rafael (reef), Mexico 150/L4
San Rafael, N. Mex. 274/A3
San Rafael (riv.), Utah 304/D4
San Rafael, Venezuela 124/C2
San Rafael de Atamaica, Venezuela 124/E4
San Rafael del Norte, Nicaragua 154/E4
San Rafael del Sur, Nicaragua 154/D5
San Rafael del Yuma, Dom. Rep. 158/F6
San Rafael de Orituco, Venezuela 124/E3
San Rafael Swell (mts.), Utah 304/D5
San Ramón, El Beni, Bolivia 136/C3
San Ramón, Santa Cruz, Bolivia 136/D5
San Ramon, Calif. 204/K2
San Ramón, C. Rica 154/E5
San Ramón, Cuba 158/H4
San Ramón, Nicaragua 154/E4
San Ramón, Peru 128/E8
San Ramón, Uruguay 145/D5
San Ramon de la Nva. Orán, Argentina 143/D1
San Remo, Italy 34/A3
San Roque, Colombia 126/C4
San Roque, Spain 33/D4
San Rosendo, Chile 138/E1
San Saba (co.), Texas 303/F6
San Saba, Texas 303/F6
San Saba (riv.), Texas 303/D7
San Salvador, Argentina 143/G5
San Salvador (isl.), Bahamas 156/D1
San Salvador (isl.), Ecuador 128/B9
San Salvador (cap.), El Salvador 154/C4
San Salvador (cap.), El Salvador 146/J8
San Salvador, Paraguay 144/C5
San Salvador (riv.), Uruguay 145/B4
San Salvador el Seco, Mexico 150/O1
Sans Bois (mts.), Okla. 288/R4
San Sebastián, Argentina 143/C7
San Sebastián, Chile 138/F3
San Sebastián, P. Rico 161/B1
San Sebastián, Spain 7/D4
San Sebastián, Spain 33/E1
San Sebastián, Venezuela 124/E2
Sansepolcro, Italy 34/C3
San Servando, Uruguay 145/F3
San Severino Marche, Italy 34/D3
San Severo, Italy 34/E4
San Simeon, Calif. 204/D8
San Simon, Ariz. 198/F6
San Simon (riv.), Ariz. 198/F6
San Simón, Serranía (mts.), Bolivia 136/D4
San Simón del Cocuy, Venezuela 124/E3
Sanski Most, Yugoslavia 45/C3
Sansom Park Village, Texas 303/E2
Sans Souci, Trin. & Tob. 161/B10
Sans Toucher (mt.), Guadeloupe 161/A6
Santa, Idaho 220/B2
Santa, Peru 128/C7
Santa (riv.), Peru 128/C7
Santa Ana, El Beni, Bolivia 136/C3
Santa Ana, La Paz, Bolivia 136/B4
Santa Ana, Santa Cruz, Bolivia 136/E5
Santa Ana, Santa Cruz, Bolivia 136/F6
Santa Ana, Calif. 188/C4
Santa Ana, Calif. 204/D11
Santa Ana (riv.), Calif. 204/E11
Santa Ana, Colombia 126/F6
Santa Ana, Ecuador 128/B3
Santa Ana, El Salvador 154/C4
Santa Ana (mt.), El Salvador 154/C4
Santa Ana, Guatemala 154/C2
Santa Ana, Mexico 150/D1
Santa Ana (reef), Mexico 150/N7
Santa Ana, Uruguay 145/B1
Santa Ana (range), Uruguay 145/D2
Santa Ana, Anzoátegui, Venezuela 124/F3
Santa Ana, Táchira, Venezuela 124/B4
Santa Ana Chiautempan (Chiautempan), Mexico 150/N1
Santa Anna, Texas 303/E6
Santa Barbara (co.), Calif. 204/E9
Santa Barbara, Calif. 204/F9
Santa Barbara, Calif. 146/F6
Santa Barbara, Calif. 188/C4
Santa Barbara (chan.), Calif. 204/E9
Santa Barbara (isls.), Calif. 146/F6
Santa Barbara (isls.), Calif. 188/C4
Santa Barbara (isl.), Calif. 204/G10
Santa Barbara (isls.), Calif. 204/F10
Santa Bárbara, Chile 138/E1
Santa Bárbara, Colombia 126/C5
Santa Bárbara, Cuba 158/B2
Santa Bárbara, Honduras 154/C3
Santa Bárbara, Mexico 150/F3
Santa Bárbara, Neth. Ant. 161/G9
Santa Bárbara, Amazonas, Venezuela 124/E6
Santa Bárbara, Barinas, Venezuela 124/C4
Santa Bárbara, Monagas, Venezuela 124/G3
Santa Bárbara, Zulia, Venezuela 124/C3
Santa Catalina, Argentina 143/C1
Santa Catalina (mts.), Ariz. 198/E6
Santa Catalina (gulf), Calif. 204/G11
Santa Catalina (isl.), Calif. 204/G10
Santa Catalina (isl.), Colombia 126/A9
Santa Catalina (isl.), Mexico 150/D4
Santa Catalina, Philippines 82/D6
Santa Catalina, Uruguay 145/B4
Santa Catalina, Delta Amacuro, Venezuela 124/H3
Santa Catalina, Barinas, Venezuela 124/D4
Santa Catarina (state), Brazil 132/D9
Santa Catarina (isl.), Brazil 120/E5
Santa Catarina (isl.), Brazil 132/E9
Santa Catharina, Neth. Ant. 161/G9
Santa Clara (co.), Calif. 204/D6
Santa Clara, Calif. 204/K3
Santa Clara, Colombia 126/F9
Santa Clara, Cuba 158/E2
Santa Clara, Cuba 146/K7
Santa Clara, Cuba 156/B2
Santa Clara (bay), Cuba 158/D1
Santa Clara, Mexico 150/H4
Santa Clara, Utah 304/A6
Santa Clara (riv.), Utah 304/A6
Santa Clara de Olimar, Uruguay 145/D3
Santa Clarita, Calif. 204/G9
Santa Claus, Georgia 217/H6
Santa Claus, Ind. 227/D8
Santa Clotilde, Peru 128/E4
Santa Cruz (prov.), Argentina 143/C6
Santa Cruz, Argentina 120/C8
Santa Cruz, Argentina 143/C7
Santa Cruz (riv.), Argentina 120/B7
Santa Cruz (riv.), Argentina 143/B7
Santa Cruz (co.), Ariz. 198/E7
Santa Cruz (riv.), Ariz. 198/D6
Santa Cruz (dept.), Bolivia 136/E5
Santa Cruz, Bolivia 120/C4
Santa Cruz, Santa Cruz, Bolivia 136/D5
Santa Cruz, Brazil 132/G4
Santa Cruz, Calif. 188/B3
Santa Cruz (co.), Calif. 204/C6
Santa Cruz, Calif. 204/K4
Santa Cruz (chan.), Calif. 204/F10
Santa Cruz (isl.), Calif. 204/F10
Santa Cruz (cap.), Canary Is., Spain 102/A2
Santa Cruz, Chile 138/F6
Santa Cruz, C. Rica 154/E5
Santa Cruz (isl.), Ecuador 128/C9

444 Santa Cruz

Santa Cruz, India 68/B7
Santa Cruz, Jamaica 158/H6
Santa Cruz, Mexico 150/D1
Santa Cruz (isl.), Mexico 150/D4
Santa Cruz, N. Mex. 274/D2
Santa Cruz, Nicaragua 154/E4
Santa Cruz, Cajamarca, Peru 128/C6
Santa Cruz, Loreto, Peru 128/E5
Santa Cruz, Davao del Sur, Philippines 82/E7
Santa Cruz, Laguna, Philippines 82/C3
Santa Cruz, Marinduque, Philippines 82/D4
Santa Cruz, Zambales, Philippines 82/B3
Santa Cruz, Portugal 33/A2
Santa Cruz (isls.), Solomon Is. 87/G6
Santa Cruz, Venezuela 124/C3
Santa Cruz das Flores, Portugal 33/A1
Santa Cruz de Bucaral, Venezuela 124/D2
Santa Cruz de la Palma, Spain 33/B4
Santa Cruz de la Palma, Spain 106/A3
Santa Cruz de la Zarza, Spain 33/E3
Santa Cruz del Norte, Cuba 158/C1
Santa Cruz de los Pinos, Cuba 158/B1
Santa Cruz del Quiché, Guatemala 154/B3
Santa Cruz del Sur, Cuba 158/G3
Santa Cruz del Sur, Cuba 156/B2
Santa Cruz del Valle Ameno, Bolivia 136/A4
Santa Cruz del Zulia, Venezuela 124/B3
Santa Cruz de Mara, Venezuela 124/C2
Santa Cruz de Mudela, Spain 33/E3
Santa Cruz de Orinoco, Venezuela 124/F3
Santa Cruz de Tenerife (prov.), Spain 33/B5
Santa Cruz de Tenerife, Spain 33/B4
Santa Cruz de Tenerife, Spain 106/A3
Santa Cruz de Yojoa, Honduras 154/D3
Santa Cruz do Rio Pardo, Brazil 135/B3
Santa Cruz do Sul, Brazil 132/C10
Santa Elena, Argentina 143/F5
Santa Elena, Bolivia 136/C7
Santa Elena (cape), C. Rica 154/D5
Santa Elena, Ecuador 128/B4
Santa Elena (bay), Ecuador 128/B3
Santa Elena, Paraguay 144/B5
Santa Elena, Peru 128/F5
Santa Elena, Venezuela 124/H5
Santa Eugenia (pt.), Bahamas 156/B1
Santa Eugenia (pt.), Mexico 146/G7
Santa Eugenia (pt.), Mexico 150/B3
Santa Eugenia, Spain 33/B1
Santa Fe (prov.), Argentina 143/D3
Santa Fe, Argentina 120/C6
Santa Fe, Argentina 143/F5
Santa Fe, Bolivia 136/D6
Santa Fe (peak), Colo. 208/H4
Santa Fe, Cuba 158/B2
Santa Fe, Cuba 156/A2
Santa Fe (isl.), Ecuador 128/C9
Santa Fe, Fla. 212/D2
Santa Fe (lake), Fla. 212/D2
Santa Fe (riv.), Fla. 212/D2
Santa Fe, Ind. 227/E3
Santa Fe, Mo. 261/J4
Santa Fe (co.), N. Mex. 274/C3
Santa Fe (cap.), N. Mex. 146/H6
Santa Fe (cap.), N. Mex. 188/E3
Santa Fe (cap.), N. Mex. 274/C3
Santa Fe, Panama 154/G6
Santa Fe, Philippines 82/C2
Santa Fé, Spain 33/E4
Santa Fe, Tenn. 237/G9
Santa Fe, Texas 303/K3
Santa Fe Springs, Calif. 204/C11
Santa Filomena, Brazil 132/E5
Santa Helena de Goiás, Brazil 132/D7
Santai, China 77/G5
Santa Inés (isl.), Chile 120/B8
Santa Inés (isl.), Chile 138/D10
Santa Inés, Anzoátegui, Venezuela 124/F3
Santa Inés, Barinas, Venezuela 124/C3
Santa Isabel, Bolivia 136/B7
Santa Isabel, Brazil 132/B5
Santa Isabel, Colombia 126/B9
Santa Isabel, Ecuador 128/C4
Santa Isabel, P. Rico 161/C3
Santa Isabel (isl.), Solomon Is. 87/G6
Santa Isabel (isl.), Solomon Is. 86/D2
Santa Isabel (creek), Texas 303/E10
Santa Isabel, Venezuela 124/F7
Santa Isabel de las Lajas, Cuba 158/E2
Santa Isabel de Sihuas, Peru 128/F11
Santa Leopoldina, Brazil 132/G7
Santa Lucía, Buenos Aires, Argentina 143/F6
Santa Lucía, Corrientes, Argentina 143/E2
Santa Lucía, Camagüey, Cuba 158/H3
Santa Lucía, Holguín, Cuba 158/J3
Santa Lucía, Pinar del Río, Cuba 158/A1
Santa Lucía, Uruguay 145/B6
Santa Lucía (riv.), Uruguay 145/D5
Santa Lucía, Venezuela 124/D3
Santa Lucía Chico (riv.), Uruguay 145/D4
Santa Luzia, Brazil 135/E1
Santa Luzia (isl.), C. Verde 106/B8
Santa Margarita, Calif. 204/E8
Santa Margarita (isl.), Mexico 150/C4
Santa Maria (cape), Angola 115/B6
Santa María, Argentina 143/C2
Santa Maria (riv.), Ariz. 198/B4
Santa Maria, Brazil 132/C10
Santa Maria, Brazil 120/D5
Santa Maria, Calif. 204/E9
Santa Maria (riv.), Calif. 204/E9
Santa Maria, C. Verde 106/B8
Santa María, Chile 138/G2
Santa María (isl.), Chile 138/D1
Santa María (cay), Cuba 158/F1
Santa María (isl.), Ecuador 128/B10
Santa María (lake), Mexico 150/F1
Santa María (riv.), Mexico 150/F1
Santa María, Paraguay 144/D5
Santa Maria, Philippines 82/C7
Santa Maria (cape), Portugal 33/C4
Santa Maria (isl.), Portugal 33/D2
Santa Maria, Texas 303/F12
Santa María (cape), Uruguay 145/F5
Santa María, Bolívar, Venezuela 124/G3
Santa Maria Capua Vetere, Italy 34/E4
Santa Maria da Vitória, Brazil 132/F6
Santa María de Erebató, Venezuela 124/F5
Santa María de Ipire, Venezuela 124/F3
Santa María del Orinoco, Venezuela 124/E4
Santa María del Oro, Mexico 150/G3
Santa María del Río, Mexico 150/J6
Santa María del Tule, Mexico 150/L8
Santa María de Nanay, Peru 128/F4
Santa Maria di Leuca (cape), Italy 34/G5
Santa Maria im Münstertal, Switzerland 39/K3
Santa Marta, Colombia 126/D2
Santa Marta, Colombia 120/B1
Santa Marta, Sierra Nevada de (range), Colombia 126/D2
Santa Monica, Calif. 204/B10
Santa Monica (bay), Calif. 204/B11
Santana, Brazil 132/E6
Santana, Portugal 33/A2
Santana do Ipanema, Brazil 132/G5
Santana do Jacaré, Brazil 135/D2
Santana do Livramento, Brazil 132/C10
Santana do Livramento, Brazil 120/D6
Santander (dept.), Colombia 126/D4
Santander, Colombia 126/B6
Santander, Philippines 82/D6
Santander (prov.), Spain 33/D1
Santander, Spain 33/D1
Santander, Spain 7/D4
Santander Jiménez, Mexico 150/K4
Santanilla (isls.), Honduras 154/F2
Sant'Antioco (pen.), Italy 34/B5
Santañy, Spain 33/H3
Santa Olalla del Cala, Spain 33/C4
Santa Paula, Calif. 204/F9
Santaquin, Utah 304/C4
Santarém, Brazil 132/C3
Santarém, Brazil 120/D3
Santarém (dist.), Portugal 33/B3
Santarém, Portugal 33/B3
Santarén (chan.), Bahamas 156/B1
Santarén (chan.), Cuba 156/B1
Santa Rita, Cuba 158/H4
Santa Rita, Guam 86/K7
Santa Rita, Honduras 154/D3
Santa Rita, Mont. 262/D2
Santa Rita, N. Mex. 274/B6
Santa Rita, Philippines 82/E5
Santa Rita, Guárico, Venezuela 124/E3
Santa Rita, Zulia, Venezuela 124/C2
Santa Rita do Sapucaí, Brazil 135/D3
Santa Rosa, Argentina 120/C6
Santa Rosa, Córdoba, Argentina 143/D3
Santa Rosa, La Pampa, Argentina 143/C4
Santa Rosa, San Luis, Argentina 143/C3
Santa Rosa, Cochabamba, Bolivia 136/B5
Santa Rosa, Cochabamba, Bolivia 136/C5
Santa Rosa, El Beni, Bolivia 136/B4
Santa Rosa, Pando, Bolivia 136/B2
Santa Rosa, Santa Cruz, Bolivia 136/D5
Santa Rosa, Brazil 132/C4
Santa Rosa, Calif. 188/B3
Santa Rosa, Calif. 204/C5
Santa Rosa (isl.), Calif. 204/E10
Santa Rosa, C. Rica 154/E5
Santa Rosa, Ecuador 128/C4
Santa Rosa (co.), Fla. 212/B6
Santa Rosa (isl.), Fla. 212/B6
Santa Rosa (sound), Fla. 212/B6
Santa Rosa, Mo. 261/D3
Santa Rosa (range), Nev. 266/D1
Santa Rosa, N. Mex. 274/E4
Santa Rosa, Paraguay 144/D5
Santa Rosa, Uruguay 145/B6
Santa Rosa, Anzoátegui, Venezuela 124/F3
Santa Rosa, Apure, Venezuela 124/D4
Santa Rosa, Barinas, Venezuela 124/D3
Santa Rosa Beach, Fla. 212/C6
Santa Rosa de Aguán, Honduras 154/E2
Santa Rosa de Amanadona, Venezuela 124/E7
Santa Rosa de Cabal, Colombia 126/C5
Santa Rosa de Copán, Honduras 154/C3
Santa Rosa de la Mina, Bolivia 136/D5
Santa Rosa de la Roca, Bolivia 136/E5
Santa Rosa de Lima, El Salvador 154/D4
Santa Rosa de Lima, Guatemala 154/B3
Santa Rosa del Palmar, Bolivia 136/E5
Santa Rosa de Osos, Colombia 126/C4
Santa Rosa Ind. Res., Calif. 204/J10
Santa Rosalía, Mexico 150/C3
Santa Rosalía, Venezuela 124/F4
Santa Rosa Wash (dry riv.), Ariz. 198/D6
Santa Teresa, North. Terr. 93/D8
Santa Teresa, Venezuela 124/E2
Santa Venetia, Calif. 204/J1
Santa Victoria, Argentina 143/D1
Santa Vitória do Palmar, Brazil 132/C11
Santa Ynez (riv.), Calif. 204/E9
Santa Ysabel Ind. Res., Calif. 204/J10
Santee, Calif. 204/J11
Santee, Nebr. 264/G2
Santee (riv.), S.C. 188/L4
Santee, S.C. 296/F5
Santee (dam), S.C. 296/G4
Santee (riv.), S.C. 296/H5
Santee Ind. Res., Nebr. 264/G2
Santeetlah (lake), N.C. 281/B4
Sant'Elpidio a Mare, Italy 34/E3
Santeramo in Colle, Italy 34/F4
Sant'Eufemia (gulf), Italy 34/F5
Santiago, Potosí, Bolivia 136/A7
Santiago, Santa Cruz, Bolivia 136/F6
Santiago, Serranía de (mts.), Bolivia 136/F6
Santiago, Brazil 132/C10
Santiago, Región Metropolitana de (Santiago Metropolitan Region) (reg.), Chile 138/A9
Santiago (cap.), Chile 2/F7
Santiago (cap.), Chile 120/B6
Santiago (cap.), Chile 138/G3
Santiago (prov.), Dom. Rep. 158/D5
Santiago, Dom. Rep. 158/D5
Santiago, Dom. Rep. 156/D3
Santiago (San Salvador) (isl.), Ecuador 128/B9
Santiago, Mexico 150/E5
Santiago (riv.), Mexico 146/H7
Santiago, Minn. 255/E5
Santiago, Panama 154/G6
Santiago, Cerro (mt.), Panama 154/G6
Santiago, Paraguay 144/D5
Santiago, Peru 128/E10
Santiago (riv.), Peru 128/D4
Santiago, Philippines 82/C2
Santiago, Spain 33/B1
Santiago (mts.), Texas 303/A8
Santiago (peak), Texas 303/D12
Santiago de Cao, Peru 128/C6
Santiago de Chocorvos, Peru 128/E9
Santiago de Chuco, Peru 128/C7
Santiago de Cuba (prov.), Cuba 158/H4
Santiago de Cuba, Cuba 146/L8
Santiago de Cuba, Cuba 156/C3
Santiago de Cuba, Cuba 158/J4
Santiago de Huata, Bolivia 136/A5
Santiago de las Vegas, Cuba 158/C1
Santiago del Estero (prov.), Argentina 143/D2
Santiago del Estero, Argentina 120/C5
Santiago del Estero, Argentina 143/D2
Santiago de Machaca, Bolivia 136/A5
Santiago de Pacaguaras, Bolivia 136/A3
Santiago do Cacem, Portugal 33/B3
Santiago Ixcuintla, Mexico 150/G6
Santiago Jamiltepec, Mexico 150/K8
Santiago Juxtlahuaca, Mexico 150/K8
Santiago Miahuatlán, Mexico 150/O2
Santiago Papasquiaro, Mexico 150/F4
Santiago Pinotepa Nacional, Mexico 150/K8
Santiago Rodríguez (prov.), Dom. Rep. 158/D5
Santiago Tuxtla, Mexico 150/M7
Santiago Vázquez, Uruguay 145/A7
Santiaguillo (lake), Mexico 150/G4
San Timoteo, Venezuela 124/C3
Santipur, India 68/F4
Säntis (mt.), Switzerland 39/H2
Santo, Texas 303/F5
Santo Amaro, Brazil 132/G6
Santo André, Brazil 135/C3
Santo Ângelo, Brazil 132/C10
Santo Antão (isl.), C. Verde 106/A7
Santo António, São T. & Pr. 106/F8
Santo Antônio da Platina, Brazil 132/D8
Santo Antônio da Platina, Brazil 135/A3
Santo Antônio do Leverger, Brazil 132/C6
Santo Corazón, Bolivia 136/F5
Santo Domingo, C. Rica 154/F6
Santo Domingo, Cuba 158/E1
Santo Domingo (cap.), Dom. Rep. 146/L8
Santo Domingo (cap.), Dom. Rep. 156/E3
Santo Domingo (cap.), Dom. Rep. 158/E6
Santo Domingo, Nicaragua 154/E4
Santo Domingo de la Calzada, Spain 33/E1
Santo Domingo de los Colorados, Ecuador 128/C3
Santo Domingo Pueblo, N. Mex. 274/C3
San Tomé, Venezuela 124/F3
Santoña, Spain 33/E1
Santos, Brazil 2/G7
Santos, Brazil 132/E9
Santos, Brazil 120/E5
Santos, Brazil 135/C3
Santos, Fla. 212/D2
Santos Dumont, Brazil 132/F8
Santos Dumont, Brazil 135/E2
Santos Mercado, Bolivia 136/B1
Santo Tomás, Mexico 150/A1
Santo Tomás, Nicaragua 154/E5
Santo Tomás, Amazonas, Peru 128/C6
Santo Tomás, Cuzco, Peru 128/G10
Santo Tomas, Davao, Philippines 82/E7
Santo Tomas, La Union, Philippines 82/C2
Santo Tomas (mt.), Philippines 82/C2
Santo Tomás de Andoas, Peru 128/D4
Santo Tomás de Castilla, Guatemala 154/C3
Santo Tomé, Corrientes, Argentina 143/E2
Santo Tomé, Santa Fe, Argentina 143/F5
Santuck, S.C. 296/D2
Santuit, Mass. 249/N6
Santurce, P. Rico 161/E1
San Urbano, Argentina 143/F6
San Valentín, Cerro (mt.), Chile 138/D6
San Vicente, Chile 138/F4
San Vicente (San Vicente de Tagua Tagua), Chile 138/F5
San Vicente, El Salvador 154/C4
San Vicente, Mexico 150/B1
San Vicente, Apure, Venezuela 124/D4
San Vicente, Amazonas, Venezuela 124/E5
San Vicente de Alcántara, Spain 33/C3
San Vicente de Cañete, Peru 128/D9
San Vicente del Caguán, Colombia 126/C6
San Vito, Italy 34/B5
San Vito (cape), Italy 34/D5
San Vito al Tagliamento, Italy 34/D2
San Vito dei Normanni, Italy 34/F4
San Vito Romano, Italy 34/F6
San Xavier Ind. Res., Ariz. 198/D6
Sanyati (riv.), Zimbabwe 118/D3
San Ygnacio, Texas 303/E10
San Ysidro, N. Mex. 274/C3
Sanyuan, China 77/G5
Sanza Pombo, Angola 115/C5
São Bento, Brazil 132/E3
São Bernardo do Campo, Brazil 135/C3
São Borja, Brazil 132/C10
São Brás de Alportel (Alportel), Portugal 33/C4
São Carlos, Brazil 135/C3
São Cristóvão, Brazil 132/G5
São Domingos, Brazil 132/E6
São Félix, Brazil 132/G6
São Fidélis, Brazil 132/F8
São Fidélis, Brazil 135/F2
São Francisco, Brazil 132/E6
São Francisco (riv.), Brazil 120/E4
São Francisco (riv.), Brazil 2/G6
São Francisco (riv.), Brazil 132/F5
São Francisco (riv.), Brazil 135/D2
São Francisco do Sul, Brazil 132/E9
São Gabriel, Brazil 132/C10
São Gonçalo, Brazil 132/F8
São Gonçalo, Brazil 135/E3
São Gonçalo do Sapucaí, Brazil 135/D2
São João da Boa Vista, Brazil 132/E8
São João da Boa Vista, Brazil 135/C2
São João da Madeira, Portugal 33/B2
São João da Pesqueira, Portugal 33/C2
São João del Rei, Brazil 132/E8
São João del Rei, Brazil 135/D2
São João de Meriti, Brazil 135/E3
São João do Piauí, Brazil 132/F5
São João dos Patos, Brazil 132/E4
São João Nepomuceno, Brazil 135/E2
São Joaquim da Barra, Brazil 135/C2
São Jorge (isl.), Portugal 33/B1
São José, Brazil 132/D9
São José da Laje, Brazil 132/H5
São José do Gurupi, Brazil 132/E3
São José do Rio Pardo, Brazil 135/C2
São José do Rio Preto, Brazil 120/E5
São José do Rio Preto, Brazil 132/D8
São José do Rio Preto, Brazil 135/B2
São José dos Campos, Brazil 135/D3
São José dos Pinhais, Brazil 132/D9
São Leopoldo, Brazil 132/D10
São Lourenço, Brazil 135/D3
São Lourenço (riv.), Brazil 132/C7
São Lourenço do Sul, Brazil 132/C10
São Luís, Brazil 132/F3
São Luís, Brazil 120/E3
São Luís Gonzaga, Brazil 132/C10
São Manuel, Brazil 135/B3
São Marcos (bay), Brazil 120/E3
São Marcos (bay), Brazil 132/F3
São Martinho do Porto, Portugal 33/B3
São Mateus, Brazil 132/G7
São Miguel (isl.), Portugal 33/D2
São Miguel Arcanjo, Brazil 135/C3
São Miguel do Guamá, Brazil 132/E3
São Miguel dos Campos, Brazil 132/G5
Saona (isl.), Dom. Rep. 156/E3
Saona (isl.), Dom. Rep. 158/F6
Saône (riv.), France 28/F4
Saône-et-Loire (dept.), France 28/F4
Saonek, Indonesia 85/J6
São Nicolau (isl.), C. Verde 106/B8
São Paulo (state), Brazil 135/B3
São Paulo (state), Brazil 132/D8
São Paulo, Brazil 120/E5
São Paulo, Brazil 2/G6
São Paulo, Brazil 132/E8
São Paulo, Brazil 135/C3
São Paulo de Olivença, Brazil 132/G9
São Pedro do Piauí, Brazil 132/F4
São Pedro do Sul, Portugal 33/B2
São Raimundo das Mangabeiras, Brazil 132/E4
São Raimundo Nonato, Brazil 132/F5
São Romão, Brazil 132/E7
São Roque, Brazil 135/C3
São Roque (cape), Brazil 2/H6
São Roque (cape), Brazil 120/F3
São Roque (cape), Brazil 132/H4
São Sebastião, Brazil 135/D3
São Sebastião (isl.), Brazil 120/E5
São Sebastião (isl.), Brazil 135/D3
São Sebastião (isl.), Brazil 132/E8
São Sebastião (pt.), Mozambique 118/F4
São Sebastião do Paraíso, Brazil 135/C2
São Sebastião do Paraíso, Brazil 132/E8
São Simão, Brazil 135/C2
São Teotónio, Portugal 33/B4
São Tiago (isl.), C. Verde 106/B8
São Tomé (cape), Brazil 120/F5
São Tomé (cape), Brazil 132/F8
São Tomé (cap.), São T. & Pr. 106/F8
São Tomé (isl.), São T. & Pr. 106/F8
São Tomé & Príncipe 102/C4
SÃO TOMÉ AND PRÍNCIPE 106/F8
Saoura, Wadi (dry riv.), Algeria 106/D3
São Vicente, Brazil 135/C4
São Vicente (isl.), C. Verde 106/B7
São Vicente, Portugal 33/A2
São Vicente (cape), Portugal 7/C5
São Vicente Ferrer, Brazil 132/E3
São Vincent (cape), Portugal 33/B4
Sapahaqui, Bolivia 136/B5
Sápai, Greece 45/G5
Sapanca, Turkey 63/D2
Saparua, Indonesia 85/H6
Sapawe, Ontario 177/G5
Sapawe, Ontario 175/B3
Sapele, Nigeria 106/F7
Sapello, N. Mex. 274/D3
Sapelo (isl.), Georgia 217/K8
Sapelo (sound), Georgia 217/K7
Sapelo Island, Georgia 217/K8
Şaphane, Turkey 63/C3
Saponac, Maine 243/G5
Saposoa, Peru 128/D6
Sappa (creek), Kansas 232/B2
Sappemeer-Hoogezand, Netherlands 27/K2
Sapphire, N.C. 281/D4
Sappho, Wash. 310/A2
Sappington, Mo. 261/O4
Sapporo, Japan 2/S3
Sapporo, Japan 54/P5
Sapporo, Japan 81/K2
Sapse, Bolivia 136/C6
Sapucaí (riv.), Brazil 135/D2
Sapucaí, Paraguay 144/B5
Sapulpa, Okla. 288/O3
Saqqez, Iran 59/E2
Saqqez, Iran 66/E2
Saquena, Peru 128/F5
Sara (riv.), Cent. Afr. Rep. 115/C2
Sara (riv.), Chad 111/C6
Sara, Philippines 82/D5
Sarab, Iran 66/E2
Sara Buri, Thailand 72/D4
Saragosa, Texas 303/D11
Saragossa, Ala. 195/D3
Saragossa, Spain 7/D4
Saragossa, Spain 33/F2
Saraguro, Ecuador 128/C4
Sarah (lake), Minn. 255/F5
Sarah, Miss. 256/D1
Sarahsville, Ohio 284/H6
Sarajevo, Yugoslavia 7/F4
Sarajevo, Yugoslavia 45/D4
Sarakhs, Iran 66/M2
Saraland, Ala. 195/B9
Saramacca (dist.), Suriname 131/C3
Saramacca (riv.), Suriname 131/D3
Sarampiuni, Bolivia 136/A4
Saran', U.S.S.R. 48/H5
Saranac, Mich. 250/D6
Saranac, N.Y. 276/N1
Saranac (lkes), N.Y. 276/M2
Saranac (riv.), N.Y. 276/N1
Saranac Lake, N.Y. 276/M2
Sarandë, Albania 45/E6
Sarandí del Yi, Uruguay 145/D4
Sarandí de Navarro, Uruguay 145/C3
Sarandí Grande, Uruguay 145/C4
Sarangani (bay), Philippines 82/E8
Sarangani (isls.), Philippines 82/E8
Sarangani (isls.), Philippines 85/G4
Sarangani (str.), Philippines 82/E8
Saransk, U.S.S.R. 7/J3
Saransk, U.S.S.R. 48/E4
Saransk, U.S.S.R. 52/G4
Sarapul, U.S.S.R. 7/K3
Sarapul, U.S.S.R. 48/F4
Sarapul, U.S.S.R. 52/H3
Sarare, Venezuela 124/D3
Sarare (riv.), Venezuela 124/C4
Sarasota, Fla. 188/K5
Sarasota (co.), Fla. 212/D4
Sarasota, Fla. 212/D4
Sarasota (pt.), Fla. 212/D4
Sarasota Springs, Fla. 212/D4
Saraswati (riv.), India 68/F1
Saratoga, Ark. 202/C6
Saratoga, Calif. 204/K4
Saratoga, Ind. 227/H4
Saratoga, Iowa 229/J2
Saratoga, Miss. 256/E7
Saratoga (co.), N.Y. 276/N4
Saratoga (lake), N.Y. 276/N4
Saratoga, Texas 303/K7
Saratoga, Wyo. 319/F4
Saratoga Nat'l Hist. Park, N.Y. 276/N4
Saratoga Springs, N.Y. 276/N4
Saratov, U.S.S.R. 7/J3
Saratov, U.S.S.R. 48/E4
Saratov, U.S.S.R. 52/G4
Saravan, Iran 59/H4
Saravan, Iran 66/N7
Saravan, Laos 72/E4
Sarawak (state), Malaysia 2/Q5
Sarawak (state), Malaysia 85/E5
Sarawak (reg.), Malaysia 54/N9
Sarayacu, Ecuador 128/D3
Sarayköy, Turkey 63/C4
Sarayönü, Turkey 63/E3
Sarbaz, Iran 66/M7
Sarbaz, Iran 59/H4
Sarben, Nebr. 264/C3
Sárbogárd, Hungary 41/E3
Sarco (bay), Chile 138/A7
Sarcoxie, Mo. 261/D8
Sardarshahr, India 68/C3
Sar Dasht, Iran 66/D2
Sardina (pt.), P. Rico 161/A1
Sardinata, Colombia 126/D3
Sardinia, Ind. 227/F6
Sardinia (reg.), Italy 34/B4
Sardinia (isl.), Italy 7/E4
Sardinia (isl.), Italy 34/B4
Sardinia, N.Y. 276/C5
Sardinia, Ohio 284/C7
Sardinia, S.C. 296/G4
Sardis, Ala. 195/E6
Sardis, Ala. 195/F2
Sardis, Br. Col. 184/M3
Sardis, Georgia 217/J5
Sardis, Ky. 237/O3
Sardis (lake), Miss. 188/J4
Sardis, Miss. 256/E2
Sardis (dam), Miss. 256/E2
Sardis (lake), Miss. 256/E2
Sardis, Ohio 284/J6
Sardis, Okla. 288/R5
Sardis, Tenn. 237/E10
Sardis, W. Va. 312/F4
Sar-e Pol, Afghanistan 68/B1
Sar-e Pol, Afghanistan 59/J2
Sarepta, La. 238/D1
Sarepta, Miss. 256/F2
Sargans, Switzerland 39/H2
Sargeant, Minn. 255/F7
Sargent, Georgia 217/C4
Sargent, Nebr. 264/E3
Sargent (co.), N. Dak. 282/P7
Sargents, Colo. 208/F6
Sargodha, Pakistan 59/K3
Sargodha, Pakistan 68/C2
Sarh, Chad 111/C6
Sarh, Chad 102/D4
Sarhro, Jebel (mts.), Morocco 106/C2
Sari, Iran 59/F2
Sari, Iran 66/H2
Saría (isl.), Greece 45/H8
Sarigan (isl.), No. Marianas 87/E4
Sarîgül, Turkey 63/C3
Sarih, Jordan 65/D2
Sarîkamîş, Turkey 63/K2
Sarîkamîş, Turkey 59/D1
Sarîkaya, Turkey 63/F3
Sarîküy, Turkey 63/B2
Sarina, Queensland 88/H4
Sarina, Queensland 95/D4
Sarine (Saane) (riv.), Switzerland 39/D3
Sariñena, Spain 33/F2
Sarîoğlan, Turkey 63/G3
Sarita, Texas 303/G10
Sariwŏn, N. Korea 81/B4
Sarîyer, Turkey 63/D5
Sarîz, Turkey 63/G3
Sark (isl.), Chan. Is. 13/E8
Sark (isl.), Chan. Is. 10/E6
Sarkad, Hungary 41/F3
Sarkand, U.S.S.R. 48/J5
Şarkikaraağaç, Turkey 63/D3
Şarkîşla, Turkey 63/G3
Şarköy, Turkey 63/B2
Sarlat-La-Canéda, France 28/D5
Sarles, N. Dak. 282/N2
Sarmi, Indonesia 85/K6
Sarmiento, Argentina 143/B6
Sarmiento, Argentina 120/C7
Sarmiento, Cerro (mt.), Chile 138/E11
Särna, Sweden 18/H6
Sarnath, India 68/E3
Sarnen, Switzerland 39/F3
Sarnen (lake), Switzerland 39/F3
Sarnia, Ont. 162/H7
Sarnia, Ontario 177/B5
Sarny, U.S.S.R. 52/C4
Sarona, Wis. 317/C4
Saronic (gulf), Greece 45/F7
Saronno, Italy 34/B2
Saronville, Nebr. 264/G4
Saros (gulf), Turkey 63/B2
Sárospatak, Hungary 41/F2
Sarpsborg, Norway 18/D4
Sarpy (co.), Nebr. 264/H3
Sarra (well), Libya 111/D3
Sarralbe, France 28/G3
Sarrebourg, France 28/G3
Sarreguemines, France 28/G3
Sarria, Spain 33/C1
Sarroch, Italy 34/B5
Sarsati (riv.), India 68/F1
Sarstún (riv.), Belize 154/C3
Sarstún (riv.), Guatemala 154/C3
Sartell, Minn. 255/D5
Sartène, France 28/B7
Sarthe (dept.), France 28/D3
Sarthe (riv.), France 28/D4
Sartrouville, France 28/A1
Sarufutsu, Japan 81/L1
Sarur, Oman 59/G5
Sárvár, Hungary 41/D3
Sarver, Pa. 294/C4
Sárviz csatorna (canal), Hungary 41/E3
Saryshagan, U.S.S.R. 48/H5
Sary Su (riv.), U.S.S.R. 48/H5
Sasabe, Ariz. 198/D7
Sasabe, Mexico 150/C1
Sasaginnigak (lake), Manitoba 179/G3
Sasakwa, Okla. 288/N5
Sasaram, India 68/E4
Sasebo, Japan 81/D7
Saseenos, Br. Col. 184/J3
SASKATCHEWAN 181
Saskatchewan (prov.) 162/F5
Saskatchewan (riv.) 162/F5
Saskatchewan (prov.), Canada 146/H4
Saskatchewan (riv.), Canada 2/D3
Saskatchewan (riv.), Sask. 181/H2
Saskatchewan Beach, Sask. 181/G5
Saskatchewan Landing Prov. Park, Sask. 181/C5
Saskatoon, Sask. 162/F5
Saskatoon, Sask. 146/H4
Saskatoon, Sask. 181/E3
Saskeram (riv.), Sask. 181/K2
Sason, Turkey 63/J3
Sasovo, U.S.S.R. 52/F4
Saspamco, Texas 303/K11
Sassafras, Md. 245/P3
Sassafras (riv.), Md. 245/P3
Sassafras (mt.), S.C. 296/B1
Sassafras, Tasmania 99/C3
Sassandra, Ivory Coast 106/C8
Sassandra (riv.), Ivory Coast 106/C7
Sassari (prov.), Italy 34/B4
Sassari, Italy 34/B4
Sassari, Italy 7/E4
Sasseneire (mt.), Switzerland 39/E4
Sasser, Georgia 217/D7

Sassnitz, Germany 22/E1
Sasstown, Liberia 106/C8
Sassuolo, Italy 34/C2
Sástago, Spain 33/F2
Sasu (mt.), N. Korea 81/C4
Sata (cape), Japan 81/E8
Satadougou, Mali 106/B6
Satanta, Kansas 232/B4
Satara, India 68/C5
Satartia, Miss. 256/C5
Satawal (isl.), Micronesia 87/E5
Satellite Beach, Fla. 212/F3
Säter, Sweden 18/J6
Satigny, Switzerland 39/A4
Satilla (riv.), Georgia 217/G8
Satipo, Peru 128/E8
Satluj (Sutlej) (riv.), 68/C3
Satna, India 68/E4
Sátoraljaújhely, Hungary 41/F2
Satpayev, U.S.S.R. 48/G5
Satpayev, U.S.S.R. 52/G5
Satpura (range), India 68/D4
Satsop, Wash. 310/B3
Satsuma, Ala. 195/B9
Satsuma, Fla. 212/E2
Satsuma, La. 238/L1
Satte, Japan 81/O1
Satu Mare, Romania 45/F2
Satu Mare, Romania 7/G4
Satun, Thailand 72/C6
Satupaitea, W. Samoa 86/L8
Saturna Island, Br. Col. 184/K3
Saturnia, Italy 34/C3
Satus (creek), Wash. 310/E4
Sauble Beach, Ontario 177/C3
Sauce, Argentina 143/G5
Sauce, Peru 128/D6
Sauce, Canelones, Uruguay 145/B6
Sauce, Rocha, Uruguay 145/B6
Sauce (lag.), Uruguay 145/D5
Sauceda (mts.), Ariz. 198/C6
Sauce de Luna, Argentina 143/G5
Saucedo, Uruguay 145/B2
Sauce del Yí, Uruguay 145/D4
Sauchie, Scotland 15/C1
Saucier, Miss. 256/F9
Saucillo, Mexico 150/G2
Sauda, Qurnet es (mt.), Lebanon 63/D3
Saudhárkrókur, Iceland 21/B1
Saudi Arabia 2/M4
Saudi Arabia 54/D4
SAUDI ARABIA 59/D4
Sauer (riv.), Germany 22/B4
Sauer (riv.), Luxembourg 27/J9
Sauerland (reg.), Germany 22/B3
Saugatuck, Conn. 210/B4
Saugatuck (res.), Conn. 210/B3
Saugatuck (riv.), Conn. 210/B3
Saugatuck, Mich. 250/C6
Saugeen (riv.), Ontario 177/C3
Saugerties, N.Y. 276/M6
Sauget, Ill. 222/A2
Saugus•, Mass. 249/D6
Saugus Iron Works Nat'l Hist. Site, Mass. 249/D6
Sauiá, Brazil 132/B3
Sauk (riv.), Wash. 310/D2
Sauk (co.), Wis. 317/G9
Sauk Centre, Minn. 255/C5
Sauk City, Wis. 317/G9
Sauk Rapids, Minn. 255/D5
Sauk Village, Ill. 222/C6
Saül, Fr. Guiana 131/E4
Saulgau, Germany 22/C5
Saulkrasti, U.S.S.R. 53/C2
Saulnierville, Nova Scotia 168/B4
Saulsbury, Tenn. 237/C10
Saulsville, W. Va. 312/C7
Sault-au-Mouton, Québec 172/H1
Sault au Mouton (riv.), Québec 172/H1
Saulteaux (riv.), Alberta 182/C2
Sault Sainte Marie, Mich. 188/J1
Sault Sainte Marie, Mich. 250/E2
Sault Sainte Marie, Ont. 162/H6
Sault Sainte Marie, Ontario 177/J5
Sault Sainte Marie, Ontario 175/D3
Sault Ste. Marie, Ont. 146/K5
Saum, Minn. 255/D3
Saumarez (reef) 95/E4
Saumarez (reef), Coral Sea Is. Terr. 88/J4
Saumarez, New Bruns. 170/E1
Saumâtre (lake), Haiti 158/C6
Saumlaki, Indonesia 85/J7
Saumur, France 28/D4
Saunders (isl.), 143/E7
Saunders (co.), Nebr. 264/H3
Saunderstown, R.I. 249/J6
Saundersville, Mass. 249/G4
Saunemin, Ill. 222/E3
Sauqira (bay), Oman 59/G6
Sauqira, Ras (cape), Oman 59/G6
Sauquoit, N.Y. 276/K5
Saurimo, Angola 115/D5
Saurimo, Angola 102/E6
Sausalito, Calif. 204/H2
Sautatá, Colombia 126/B4
Sautee-Nacoochee, Georgia 217/E1
Sauteurs, Grenada 161/G3
Saut-Tigre, Fr. Guiana 131/E3
Sauzal, Chile 138/G5
Sava (riv.) 7/F4
Sava (riv.), Yugoslavia 45/D3
Savage (riv.), Md. 245/B2
Savage, Minn. 255/G6
Savage, Miss. 256/D1
Savage, Mont. 262/M3
Savage (harb.), Pr. Edward I. 168/F2
Savage (riv.), Tasmania 99/B3
Savage-Guilford, Md. 245/B2
Savage River (lake), Md. 245/B2
Savage River, Tasmania 99/B3
Savageton, Wyo. 319/G2
Savah, Ind. 227/B8
Savai'i (isl.), W. Samoa 87/J7

Savai'i (isl.), W. Samoa 86/L8
Savalou, Benin 106/E7
Savana (isl.), Virgin Is. (U.S.) 161/A4
Savanat (Estahbanat), Iran 66/J6
Savaneta, Neth. Ant. 161/E10
Savanette, Haiti 158/C6
Savanna, Ill. 222/C1
Savanna, Okla. 288/P5
Savanna Army Depot, Ill. 222/C1
Savannah (riv.) 188/K4
Savannah, Ga. 146/K6
Savannah, Ga. 188/K4
Savannah, Georgia 217/L6
Savannah (riv.), Georgia 217/K5
Savannah, Mo. 261/C3
Savannah•, N.Y. 276/G4
Savannah, Ohio 284/F4
Savannah (riv.), S.C. 296/E6
Savannah, Tenn. 237/E10
Savannah, U.S. 2/F4
Savannah (riv.), U.S. 146/K6
Savannah River Plant Atomic Energy Commission, S.C. 296/D5
Savannakhét, Laos 72/E3
Savanna-la-Mar, Jamaica 158/G6
Savanna-la-Mar, Jamaica 156/B3
Savannes (bay), St. Lucia 161/G7
Savant (lake), Ontario 177/G4
Savant (lake), Ontario 175/B2
Savant Lake, On ario 177/G4
Savant Lake, Ontario 175/B2
Savantvadi, India 68/C5
Savanur, India 68/D6
Savaştepe, Turkey 63/B3
Save (riv.) 102/F7
Savé, Benin 106/E7
Save (riv.), Mozambique 118/E4
Saveh, Iran 59/F2
Saveh, Iran 66/G3
Săveni, Romania 45/H1
Saverne, France 28/G3
Saverton, Mo. 261/K3
Savery, Wyo. 319/E4
Savery (creek), Wyo. 319/E4
Savièse, Switzerland 39/D4
Savigliano, Italy 34/A2
Savo (isl.), Solomon Is. 86/D3
Savognin, Switzerland 39/J3
Savoie (dept.), France 28/G5
Savona, Br. Col. 184/G5
Savona (prov.), Italy 34/B2
Savona, Italy 34/B2
Savona, N.Y. 276/G6
Savonburg, Kansas 232/G4
Savonet, Neth. Ant. 161/F8
Savonlinna, Finland 18/Q6
Savoonga, Alaska 196/E2
Savoy (isl.), Scotland 15/B4
Savoy, Ill. 222/E5
Savoy, Ky. 237/N7
Savoy•, Mass. 249/B2
Savoy, Mont. 262/H2
Savoy, S. Dak. 258/B5
Savoy, Scotland 15/K2
Şavşat, Turkey 63/K2
Sävsjö, Sweden 18/J8
Savu (sea), Indonesia 54/O10
Savukoski, Finland 18/Q3
Savur, Turkey 63/J4
Savusavu (bay), Fiji 86/Q10
Sawahlunto, Indonesia 85/C6
Sawankhalok, Thailand 72/C3
Sawara, Japan 81/K6
Sawatch (range), Colo. 208/G4
Sawbill, Newf. 163/A3
Sawbill Landing, Minn. 255/G3
Sawbridgeworth, England 13/H7
Saweba (cape), Indonesia 85/J6
Sawi, India 68/G7
Sawmill Bay, N.W.T. 187/G3
Sawpit, Colo. 208/D7
Sawston, England 13/H5
Sawtell, N.S. Wales 97/G2
Sawtooth (range) Idaho 220/C6
Sawtooth (ridge), Wash. 310/E2
Sawtooth Nat'l Rec. Area, Idaho 220/D5
Sawu (isl.), Indonesia 85/G8
Sawu (isls.), Indonesia 85/G8
Sawu (sea), Indonesia 85/G7
Sawyer, Kansas 232/D4
Sawyer, Ky. 237/N7
Sawyer, Mich. 250/C7
Sawyer, Minn. 255/F4
Sawyer, N. Dak. 282/H3
Sawyer, Okla. 288 R7
Sawyer (co.), Wis. 317/D4
Sawyers Bar, Calif. 204/B2
Sawyerville, Ala. 135/C5
Sawyerville, Ill. 222/D4
Sawyerville, Québec 172/F4
Saxapahaw, N.C. 281/L3
Saxe, Va. 307/L7
Saxeville, Wis. 317/H7
Saxis, Va. 307/S5
Saxman, Alaska 196/N2
Saxmundham, England 13/J5
Saxon, S.C. 296/D1
Saxon, Switzerland 39/D4
Saxon, Wis. 317/F3
Saxonburg, Pa. 294/C4
Saxonville, Mass. 249/A7
Saxony (state), Germany 22/E3
Saxony-Anhalt (state), Germany 22/D2
Saxton, Ky. 237/N1
Saxton, Pa. 294/F5
Saxtons River, Vt. 268/B5
Say, Niger 106/E6
Saya, Bolivia 136/E5
Sayabec, Québec 172/B2
Sayaboury (Muang Xaignabouri), Laos 72/D3
Sayama, Japan 81/O2
Sayán, Peru 128/D8
Sayan (mts.), U.S.S.R. 48/K4
Saybrook, Ill. 222/E3
Saybrook, Pa. 294/O2
Saybrook Point, Conn. 210/F3
Sayhan-Ovoo, Mongolia 77/F2
Saylesville, R.I. 249/J5

Saylorsburg, Pa. 294/M4
Saylorville (lake), Iowa 229/F5
Sayner, Wis. 317/H4
Saynshand, Mongolia 77/H3
Saynshand, Mongolia 54/M5
Sayre, Ala. 195/E3
Sayre, Okla. 288/G4
Sayre, Pa. 294/K2
Sayreville, N.J. 273/E3
Sayula, Mexico 150/H7
Sayula de Alemán, Mexico 150/M8
Sayville, N.Y. 276/O9
Sayward, Br. Col. 184/D5
Sazan (isl.), Albania 45/D5
Sázava (riv.), Czech. 41/C2
Sbaa, Algeria 106/D3
Sbeitla, Tunisia 106/H1
Scafell Pike (mt.), England 13/D3
Scafell Pike (mt.), England 10/E3
Scalasaig, Scotland 15/B4
Scalby, England 13/G3
Scales Mound, Ill. 222/C1
Scaletta (pass), Switzerland 39/J3
Scalf, Ky. 237/O7
Scalloway, Scotland 10/G1
Scalloway, Scotland 15/G2
Scalpay (isl.), Scotland 15/B3
Scalpay (isl.), Scotland 15/C3
Scalp Level, Pa. 294/E5
Scaly Mountain, N.C. 281/C4
Scammon, Kansas 232/H4
Scammon Bay, Alaska 196/E2
Scandia, Alberta 182/E4
Scandia, Kansas 232/E2
Scandia, Minn. 255/F5
Scandia, Wash. 310/A1
Scandinavia 18
Scandinavia, Wis. 317/H7
Scanlon, Minn. 255/F4
Scanterbury, Manitoba 179/F4
Scantic, Conn. 210/E1
Scantic (riv.), Conn. 210/E1
Scapa, Alberta 182/D4
Scapa Flow (chan.), Scotland 15/E2
Scapa Flow (chan.), Scotland 10/E1
Scappoose, Oreg. 291/E2
Scarba (isl.), Scotland 15/C4
Scarboro, Barbados 161/B9
Scarboro, Georgia 217/J5
Scarborough, England 10/F3
Scarborough, England 13/G3
Scarborough, Maine 243/C8
Scarborough•, Maine 243/C8
Scarborough, Ontario 177/K4
Scarborough, Trin. & Tob. 156/G5
Scarborough, Tasmania 99/E4
Scarbro, W. Va. 312/D7
Scarinish, Scotland 15/B4
Scarp (isl.), Scotland 15/A2
Scarriff, Ireland 17/E6
Scarriff (isl.), Ireland 17/A8
Scarsdale, N.Y. 276/P6
Scarth, Manitoba 179/B5
Scarville, Iowa 229/F2
Scatarie (isl.), Nova Scotia 168/J2
Scavaig, Loch (inlet), Scotland 15/B3
Sceaux, France 28/A2
Scenic, S. Dak. 298/D6
Scenic, Wash. 310/D3
Sceptre, Sask. 181/B5
Schaal, Ark. 202/C6
Schaalsee (lake), Germany 22/D2
Schaan, Liecht. 39/H2
Schaefferstown, Pa. 294/K5
Schaerbeek, Belgium 27/C9
Schaffer, Mich. 250/B3
Schaffhausen (canton), Switzerland 39/G1
Schaffhausen, Switzerland 39/G1
Schagen, Netherlands 27/F3
Schaghticoke, N.Y. 276/N5
Schaller, Iowa 229/C4
S-chanf, Switzerland 39/J3
Schangnau, Switzerland 39/E3
Schänis, Switzerland 39/H2
Scharans, Switzerland 39/J3
Schärding, Austria 41/B2
Scharhörn (isl.), Germany 22/C2
Schattdorf, Switzerland 39/G3
Schaumburg, Ill. 222/A5
Schawana, Wash. 310/F4
Schefferville, Que. 146/L4
Schefferville, Que. 162/K5
Schefferville, Québec 174/D2
Scheibbs, Austria 41/C2
Scheinfeld, Germany 22/D4
Schelde (Scheldt) (riv.), Belgium 27/C7
Scheldt (riv.), Belgium 27/C7
Schell City, Mo. 261/D6
Schell Creek (range), Nev. 266/G3
Schellsburg, Pa. 294/E5
Schellville, Calif. 204/J1
Schenectady (co.), N.Y. 276/M5
Schenectady, N.Y. 188/M2
Schenectady, N.Y. 276/M5
Schenevus, N.Y. 276/L5
Schererville, Ind. 227/C2
Scherhorn (mt.), Switzerland 39/G3
Schertz, Texas 303/K10
Scherzingen, Switzerland 39/H1
Schesaplana (mt.), Switzerland 39/J2
Scheveningen, Netherlands 27/E4
Schichallion (mt.), Scotland 15/D4
Schiedam, Netherlands 27/E5
Schiermonnikoog, Netherlands 27/J1
Schiermonnikoog (isl.), Netherlands 27/J1
Schijndel, Netherlands 27/G5
Schiller Park, Ill. 222/B5
Schinznach-Dorf, Switzerland 39/F2
Schio, Italy 34/C2
Schiphol, Netherlands 27/B5
Schkeuditz, Germany 22/E3
Schladming, Austria 41/B3
Schlater, Miss. 256/D3
Schlei (inlet), Germany 22/C1
Schleicher (co.), Texas 303/D7

Schleitheim, Switzerland 39/G1
Schleusingen, Germany 22/C1
Schleswig, Iowa 229/B4
Schleswig-Holstein (state), Germany 22/C1
Schley (co.), Georgia 217/D6
Schley, Minn. 255/D3
Schlieren, Switzerland 39/F2
Schliersee, Germany 22/D5
Schlitz, Germany 22/C3
Schlüchtern, Germany 22/C3
Schmalkalden, Germany 22/D3
Schmöllin, Germany 22/E3
Schneckenville, Pa. 294/L4
Schneeberg, Germany 22/E3
Schneeberg (mt.), Germany 22/D3
Schnee Eifel (plat.), Germany 22/B3
Schneidemühl (Piła), Poland 47/C2
Schneider, Ind. 227/C2
Schnellville, Ind. 227/D8
Schoelcher, Martinique 161/C6
Schoenchen, Kansas 232/C3
Schoenfeld, Sask. 181/F5
Schoen Lake Prov. Park, Br. Col. 184/E5
Schofield, Wis. 317/H6
Schofield Barracks, Hawaii 218/E2
Schoharie (co.), N.Y. 276/M5
Schoharie, N.Y. 276/M5
Schoharie (creek), N.Y. 276/M6
Schoharie (res.), N.Y. 276/M6
Scholle, N. Mex. 274/D4
Scholls, Oreg. 291/A2
Schomberg, Ontario 177/J3
Schönberg, Germany 22/D1
Schönberg, Germany 22/E4
Schönebeck, Germany 22/D3
Schöneberg, Germany 22/E4
Schöneiche, Germany 22/F3
Schönenwerd, Switzerland 39/E2
Schongau, Germany 22/D5
Schöningen, Germany 22/D2
Schoodic (lake), Maine 243/F5
Schoolcraft (co.), Mich. 250/C2
Schoolcraft, Mich. 250/C6
Schoolcraft (riv.), Minn. 255/C3
Schooleys Mountain, N.J. 273/D2
School Hill, Wis. 317/L8
Schoonhoven, Netherlands 27/F5
Schoten, Belgium 27/F6
Schottegat (bay), Neth. Ant. 161/G9
Schouten (isls.), Indonesia 85/K6
Schouten (isls.), Papua N.G. 85/B6
Schouten (isl.), Tasmania 99/E4
Schouwen (isl.), Netherlands 27/D5
Schramberg, Germany 22/C4
Schram City, Ill. 222/D4
Schreckhorn (mt.), Switzerland 39/F3
Schreiber, Ontario 177/H5
Schreiber, Ontario 175/D3
Schrems, Austria 41/C2
Schriever, La. 238/J7
Schroeder, Minn. 255/G3
Schroon (lake), N.Y. 276/N3
Schroon (riv.), N.Y. 276/N3
Schroon Lake, N.Y. 276/N3
Schruns, Austria 41/A3
Schübelbach, Switzerland 39/G2
Schulenburg, Texas 303/H8
Schuler, Alberta 182/E5
Schull, Ireland 10/B5
Schull, Ireland 17/B8
Schulter, Okla. 288/P3
Schultz (lake), N.W.T. 187/J3
Schultze, Oreg. 291/B3
Schumacher, Ontario 175/D3
Schüpfheim, Switzerland 39/F3
Schurz, Nev. 266/C4
Schussenried, Germany 22/C4
Schuyler (co.), Ill. 222/C3
Schuyler (co.), Mo. 261/G2
Schuyler, Nebr. 264/G3
Schuyler (co.), N.Y. 276/G6
Schuyler, Va. 307/M6
Schuyler Lake, N.Y. 276/L5
Schuylerville, N.Y. 276/N4
Schuylkill (co.), Pa. 294/K4
Schuylkill (riv.), Pa. 294/M5
Schuylkill Haven, Pa. 294/K4
Schwaan, Germany 22/E2
Schwabach, Germany 22/D4
Schwäbisch Gmünd, Germany 22/C4
Schwäbisch Hall, Germany 22/C4
Schwalmstadt, Germany 22/C3
Schwanden, Switzerland 39/H2
Schwandorf im Bayern, Germany 22/E4
Schwaner (mts.), Indonesia 85/E6
Schwarzach im Pongau, Austria 41/B3
Schwarzenburg, Switzerland 39/D3
Schwarzhorn (mt.), Switzerland 39/E4
Schwarzhorn (mt.), Switzerland 39/F3
Schwarzwald (Black) (for.), Germany 22/C4
Schwatka (mts.), Alaska 196/G1
Schwaz, Austria 41/A3
Schwechat, Austria 41/D2
Schwedt, Germany 22/F2
Schweidnitz (Świdnica), Poland 47/C3
Schweinfurt, Germany 22/D3
Schwelm, Germany 22/B3
Schwenksville, Pa. 294/L5
Schwerin, Germany 22/D2
Schwerinersee (lake), Germany 22/D2
Schwertberg, Austria 41/C2
Schwetzingen, Germany 22/C4
Schwyz (canton), Switzerland 39/G2
Schwyz, Switzerland 39/G2
Sciacca, Italy 34/D6
Scicli, Italy 34/E6
Science Hill, Ky. 237/M6
Scilly, England 13/A7
Scilly (isls.), England 10/C6
Scio, N.Y. 276/E6
Scio, Ohio 284/H5
Scio, Oreg. 291/E3
Sciota, Ill. 222/C3
Sciota, Pa. 294/M4

Scioto (co.), Ohio 284/D8
Scioto (riv.), Ohio 284/D8
Sciotodale, Ohio 284/E8
Scioto Furnace, Ohio 284/E8
Scipio, Ind. 227/F6
Scipio, Ind. 227/H6
Scipio, Okla. 288/P4
Scipio, Utah 304/B4
Scircleville, Ind. 227/E4
Scitico, Conn. 210/E1
Scituate, Mass. 249/F8
Scituate•, Mass. 249/F8
Scituate (res.), R.I. 249/H5
Sclater, Manitoba 179/B3
Scobey, Miss. 256/E3
Scobey, Mont. 262/L2
Scofield, Utah 304/D4
Scofield (res.), Utah 304/C4
Scollard, Alberta 182/D4
Scone, N.S. Wales 97/F3
Scooba, Miss. 256/G5
Scopi (mt.), Switzerland 39/G3
Scopus, Mo. 261/N8
Scoresby (sound), Greenl. 4/B10
Scoresbysund (Ittoqqortoormiit), Greenl. 4/B10
Scotch Grove, Iowa 229/L4
Scotch Plains•, N.J. 273/E2
Scotchtown, Nova Scotia 168/H2
Scotch Village, Nova Scotia 168/E3
Scotfield, Alberta 182/E4
Scotia (sea) 2/G8
Scotia (sea) 5/D16
Scotia, Calif. 204/A3
Scotia, Nebr. 264/F3
Scotia, N.Y. 276/N5
Scotia, S.C. 296/E6
SCOTLAND 10/D2
SCOTLAND 15
Scotland, Ark. 202/E2
Scotland•, Conn. 210/G2
Scotland, Georgia 217/G6
Scotland, Ind. 227/D7
Scotland, Md. 245/N8
Scotland (co.), Mo. 261/H2
Scotland (co.), N.C. 281/L5
Scotland, Ontario 177/D4
Scotland, Pa. 294/G6
Scotland, S. Dak. 298/O7
Scotland, Texas 303/F4
Scotland, U.K. 7/D3
Scotland Neck, N.C. 281/P2
Scotlandville, La. 238/J1
Scots (bay), Nova Scotia 168/D3
Scots Bay, Nova Scotia 168/D3
Scotsburn, Nova Scotia 168/F3
Scotsguard, Sask. 181/C6
Scotstown, Ireland 17/H3
Scotstown, Québec 172/F4
Scotsville, Nova Scotia 168/G2
Scott (isl.), Ant. 2/A9
Scott (isl.) 5/C10
Scott (co.), Ark. 202/B4
Scott, Ark. 202/F4
Scott (cape), Br. Col. 162/D5
Scott (cape), Br. Col. 184/C5
Scott (isls.), Br. Col. 184/C5
Scott (riv.), Calif. 204/B2
Scott, Georgia 217/G5
Scott (co.), Ill. 222/C4
Scott (co.), Ind. 227/F7
Scott (co.), Iowa 229/M5
Scott (co.), Ky. 237/M4
Scott, La. 238/F6
Scott (co.), Minn. 255/E6
Scott (co.), Miss. 256/E6
Scott (co.), Mo. 261/N8
Scott (co.), Okla. 288/K5
Scott (lake), Sask. 181/M4
Scott (co.), Tenn. 237/M8
Scott (co.), Va. 307/D7
Scott A.F.B., Ill. 222/B4
Scott City, Kansas 232/B3
Scott City, Mo. 261/O8
Scottdale, Georgia 217/L1
Scottdale, Pa. 294/C5
Scott-Jonction, Québec 172/F3
Scottland, Ill. 222/G2
Scotts (head), Dominica 161/E7
Scotts, N.C. 281/H3
Scottsbluff, Nebr. 188/F2
Scottsbluff, Nebr. 146/H5
Scotts Bluff (co.), Nebr. 264/A3
Scottsbluff, Nebr. 264/A3
Scotts Bluff Nat'l Mon., Nebr. 264/A3
Scottsboro, Ala. 195/F1
Scottsburg, Ind. 227/F7
Scottsburg, Ky. 237/F6
Scottsburg, Oreg. 291/B3
Scottsburg, Va. 307/L7
Scottsdale, Ariz. 198/D5
Scottsdale, Tasmania 99/D3
Scotts Hill, N.C. 281/O6
Scotts Hill, Tenn. 237/E10
Scotts Mills, Oreg. 291/B3
Scottsmoor, Fla. 212/F3
Scotts Ridge (hills), Conn. 210/A3
Scott Station, Ant. 5/B9
Scotts Valley, Calif. 204/K4
Scottsville, Ky. 237/J7
Scottsville, Kansas 232/D2
Scottsville, N.Y. 276/F4
Scottsville, Va. 307/L5
Scottville, Ill. 222/C4
Scottville, Mich. 250/C5
Scounslow, New Bruns. 170/F2
Scourie, Scotland 15/C2
Scout Lake, Sask. 181/F6
Scrabster, Scotland 15/E2
Scraggly (lake), Maine 243/H5
Scraggly (lake), Maine 243/F5
Scranage, Ala. 195/C8

Scranton, Ark. 202/C3
Scranton, Iowa 229/D4
Scranton, Kansas 232/G3
Scranton, Ky. 237/O5
Scranton, N.C. 281/S4
Scranton, N.Y. 276/C5
Scranton, Pa. 188/L2
Scranton, Pa. 146/L5
Scranton, Pa. 294/F7
Scranton, S.C. 296/H4
Scraper, Okla. 288/S2
Screven (co.), Georgia 217/J5
Screven, Georgia 217/H7
Scriba, N.Y. 276/H4
Scridain, Loch (inlet), Scotland 15/B4
Scugog (lake), Ontario 177/F3
Scullin, Okla. 288/N5
Scunthorpe, England 10/F4
Scunthorpe, England 13/G4
Scuol, Switzerland 39/K3
Scurdie Ness (prom.), Scotland 15/F4
Scurrival (pt.), Scotland 15/A3
Scurry (co.), Texas 303/D5
Scurry, Texas 303/P6
Scusciuban, Somalia 115/J1
Scutari (lake), Albania 45/D4
Scutari (lake), Yugoslavia 45/D4
Scyrene, Ala. 195/C7
Sea (isls.), Georgia 217/K9
Sea (isls.), S.C. 296/G5
Seabeck, Wash. 310/C3
Seaboard, N.C. 281/O1
Seabold, Wash. 310/A1
Sea Breeze, N.Y. 276/F4
Sea Bright, N.J. 273/F3
Seabrook•, N.H. 268/F6
Seabrook, N.J. 273/C5
Seabrook, S.C. 296/F6
Seabrook (isl.), S.C. 296/G6
Seabrook, Texas 303/K2
Seabrook-Lanham, Md. 245/G4
Sea Cliff, N.Y. 276/R6
Seadrift, Texas 303/H9
Seaford, Del. 245/R6
Seaford, England 10/G5
Seaford, England 13/H7
Seaford, N.Y. 276/R7
Seaford, Va. 307/R6
Seaforth, Minn. 255/C6
Seaforth, Ontario 177/C4
Seaforth, Loch (inlet), Scotland 15/B3
Sea Girt, N.J. 273/E3
Seagoville, Texas 303/H3
Seagraves, Texas 303/B5
Seagrove, N.C. 281/K3
Seaham, England 10/F3
Seaham, England 13/J3
Seahorse (lake), Newf. 166/A3
Seahorse (pt.), N.W. Terr. 187/L3
Seahurst, Wash. 310/A2
Sea Island, Georgia 217/K8
Sea Isle City, N.J. 273/D5
Seal (isl.), Maine 243/F8
Seal (riv.), Man. 162/G2
Seal (riv.), Manitoba 179/J2
Seal (lake), Newf. 166/B3
Seal (isl.), Nova Scotia 168/B5
Seal (isl.), S. Africa 118/F7
Sea Lake, Victoria 97/B4
Seal Beach, Calif. 204/C11
Seal Cove, Maine 243/G7
Seal Cove, New Bruns. 170/D4
Seal Cove, Newf. 166/C4
Seal Cove, Newf. 166/C3
Seale, Ala. 195/H6
Sealevel, N.C. 281/S5
Seal Harbor, Maine 243/G7
Seal Rock, Oreg. 291/A3
Sealston, Va. 307/O4
Sealy, Texas 303/H8
Seaman, Ohio 284/C8
Seamer, England 13/G3
Sea Pines, S.C. 296/F7
Sea Ranch Lakes, Fla. 212/C3
Searchlight, Nev. 266/F7
Searchmont, Ontario 177/J5
Searcy (co.), Ark. 202/E2
Searcy, Ark. 202/G3
Searight, Ala. 195/F8
Searles, Ala. 195/D4
Searles (lake), Calif. 204/H8
Searles, Minn. 255/D6
Sears, Mich. 250/D5
Searsboro, Iowa 229/H5
Searsburg•, Vt. 268/A6
Searsmont, Maine 243/E7
Searsmont•, Maine 243/E7
Searsport, Maine 243/F7
Searsport•, Maine 243/F7
Seascale, England 13/D3
Seascale (delta), England 10/E2
Seaside, Calif. 204/D7
Seaside, Oreg. 291/D2
Seaside Heights, N.J. 273/E4
Seaside Park, N.J. 273/E4
Seaton, England 13/D7
Seaton, Ill. 222/C2
Seaton Valley, England 13/J3
Seatonville, Ill. 222/D2
Seat Pleasant, Md. 245/G5
Seattle, U.S. 2/C3
Seattle, Wash. 146/F5
Seattle, Wash. 188/B1
Seattle, Wash. 310/A2
Seaview, Wash. 310/A4
Seaward Kaikouras (range), N. Zealand 100/D5
Seawell, Barbados 161/B9
Seba, Indonesia 85/G8
Seba Beach, Alberta 182/C3
Sebago (lake), Maine 243/B8
Sebago Lake, Maine 243/B8

Sebastian (co.), Ark. 202/B3
Sebastian, Fla. 212/F4
Sebastian (cape), Oreg. 291/C5
Sebastián Vizcaíno (bay), Mexico 150/B2
Sebasticook (lake), Maine 243/E6
Sebastopol, Calif. 204/C5
Sebastopol, Miss. 256/F5
Sebastopol, Victoria 97/B5
Sebatik (isl.), Indonesia 85/F5
Sebatik (isl.), Malaysia 85/F5
Sebec, Maine 243/E5
Sebec•, Maine 243/E5
Sebec Lake, Maine 243/E5
Sebec Station, Maine 243/E5
Sebeka, Minn. 255/C4
Seben, Turkey 63/D2
Sebeş, Romania 45/F3
Sebeş Kürüs (riv.), Hungary 41/F3
Sebewaing, Mich. 250/F5
Sebha, Libya 102/D2
Sebha, Libya 111/B2
Şebinkarahisar, Turkey 63/H2
Sebiş, Romania 45/F2
Sebnitz, Germany 22/F3
Seboeis•, Maine 243/F5
Seboeis (lake), Maine 243/F5
Seboeis (riv.), Maine 243/F3
Seboomook, Maine 243/D4
Seboomook (lake), Maine 243/D4
Seboruco, Venezuela 124/B3
Sebou (riv.), Morocco 106/C2
Seboyeta, N. Mex. 274/B3
Sebree, Ky. 237/F5
Sebrell, Va. 307/O7
Sebring, Fla. 212/E4
Sebring, Ohio 284/H4
Sebringville, Ontario 177/C4
Sebuku (bay), Indonesia 85/F5
Secane, Pa. 294/M7
Secas (isls.), Panama 154/G7
Secaucus, N.J. 273/B2
Secesh (riv.), Idaho 220/C4
Sechelt, Br. Col. 184/J2
Sechura, Peru 128/B5
Sechura (bay), Peru 128/B5
Seco, Ky. 237/R6
Second (lake), N.H. 268/E1
Second Cataract, Sudan 59/B5
Second Cataract, Sudan 111/F3
Secondcreek, W. Va. 312/F7
Second Mesa, Ariz. 198/E3
Secor, Ill. 222/D3
Sečovce, Czech. 41/F2
Secretan, Sask. 181/E5
Secretary, Md. 245/P6
Secretary (isl.), N. Zealand 100/A6
Section, Ala. 195/G1
Secunderabad, India 68/D5
Sécure (riv.), Bolivia 136/C4
Security-Widefield, Colo. 208/K5
Sedalia, Alberta 182/E4
Sedalia, Colo. 208/K4
Sedalia, Ind. 227/E4
Sedalia, Ky. 237/D7
Sedalia, Mo. 261/F5
Sedalia, Mo. 188/H3
Sedalia, Ohio 284/D6
Sedalia, S.C. 296/D2
Sedan, France 28/F4
Sedan, Ind. 227/G2
Sedan, Kansas 232/F4
Sedan, Minn. 255/C6
Sedan, N. Mex. 274/F2
Sedano, Spain 33/E1
Sedbergh (co.), England 10/E3
Sedbergh, England 13/E4
Seddon, N. Zealand 100/E4
Seddonville, N. Zealand 100/C4
Seddülbahir, Turkey 63/B6
Sede Boqer, Israel 65/D5
Sederot, Israel 65/B4
Sedgewick, Alberta 182/E3
Sedgewickville, Mo. 261/N7
Sedgwick, Ark. 202/E5
Sedgwick (co.), Colo. 208/P1
Sedgwick, Colo. 208/O1
Sedgwick (co.), Kansas 232/E4
Sedgwick, Kansas 232/E4
Sedgwick•, Maine 243/F7
Sedhiou, Senegal 106/A6
Sedili Kechil, Tanjong (pt.), Malaysia 72/F5
Sedlčany, Czech. 41/C2
Sedley, Sask. 181/H5
Sedley, Va. 307/P7
Sedom, Israel 65/D5
Sedona, Ariz. 198/D4
Sedot Yam, Israel 65/B3
Sedro-Woolley, Wash. 310/C2
Šeduva, U.S.S.R. 53/B3
Seebe, Alberta 182/C4
Seebert, W. Va. 312/F6
Seechelt (inlet), Br. Col. 184/J2
Seechelt (pen.), Br. Col. 184/J2
Seeheim, Namibia 118/B5
Seeis, Namibia 118/B4
Seekonk•, Mass. 249/J5
Seeley, Calif. 204/K11
Seeley, Wis. 317/D3
Seeley Lake, Mont. 262/C3
Seeleys Bay, Ontario 177/H3
Seelyville, Ind. 227/C6
Seelyville, Pa. 294/M2
Seesen, Germany 22/D3
Seewis im Prättigau, Switzerland 39/J2
Seez (riv.), Switzerland 39/H2
Şefaatlî, Turkey 63/F3
Şeferihisar, Turkey 63/B3
Seffner, Fla. 212/D4
Sefrou, Morocco 106/D2
Sefton, N. Zealand 100/D5
Seg (lake), U.S.S.R. 52/D2
Segamat, Malaysia 72/D7
Segarcea, Romania 45/F3
Segezha, U.S.S.R. 52/D2
Segezha, U.S.S.R. 48/D3

Segnes (pass), Switzerland 39/H3
Segni, Italy 34/F7
Segorbe, Spain 33/F3
Ségou, Mali 106/C6
Ségou, Mali 102/B3
Segovia, Colombia 126/C4
Segovia (Coco) (riv.), Honduras 154/E3
Segovia (Coco) (riv.), Nicaragua 154/E3
Segovia (prov.), Spain 33/D2
Segovia, Spain 33/D2
Segrê, France 28/C4
Segre (riv.), Spain 33/G2
Segreganset, Mass. 249/K5
Seguam (isl.), Alaska 196/D4
Seguam (passage), Alaska 196/D4
Séguéla, Ivory Coast 106/C7
Seguí, Argentina 143/F6
Seguin, Kansas 232/B2
Séguin (lake), Québec 172/B2
Seguin, Texas 303/H5
Segula (isl.), Alaska 196/K4
Segundo, Colo. 208/K8
Segura (riv.), Spain 33/F3
Sehore, India 68/D4
Sehwan, Pakistan 59/J4
Sehwan, Pakistan 68/B3
Seiad Valley, Calif. 204/B2
Seibert (lake), Alberta 182/E2
Seibert, Colo. 208/O4
Seibo, Dom. Rep. 156/E3
Seil (isl.), Scotland 15/E4
Seiland (isl.), Norway 18/N1
Seiling, Okla. 288/J2
Sein (isl.), France 28/A3
Seinäjoki, Finland 18/N5
Seine (riv.), France 7/E4
Seine (bay), France 28/C3
Seine (riv.), France 28/C2
Seine (riv.), Ontario 175/B3
Seine-et-Marne (dept.), France 28/E3
Seine-Saint-Denis (dept.), France 28/C1
Seistan (reg.), Iran 66/M5
Seixal, Portugal 33/A1
Seiyun, Yemen 59/E6
Sejerø (isl.), Denmark 21/E6
Sejny, Poland 47/F1
Se Khong (riv.), Cambodia 72/E4
Se Khong (riv.), Laos 72/E4
Sekiu, Wash. 310/A2
Sekkane, Erg (des.), Mali 106/D4
Sekondi, Ghana 106/D8
Selah, Wash. 310/E4
Selama, Malaysia 72/D6
Selangor (state), Malaysia 72/D7
Selaphum, Thailand 72/E3
Selaru (isl.), Indonesia 85/J7
Selatan (cape), Indonesia 85/E6
Selawik, Alaska 196/G1
Selawik (lake), Alaska 196/F1
Selayar (isl.), Indonesia 85/G7
Selb, Germany 22/E3
Selby, England 13/F4
Selby, S. Dak. 298/J3
Selby, Victoria 97/K5
Selby-on-the-Bay, Md. 245/N5
Selbyville, Del. 245/S7
Selbyville, W. Va. 312/F5
Selçuk, Turkey 63/B3
Selden, Kansas 232/B2
Seldom, Newf. 166/D4
Seldovia, Alaska 196/B2
Sele (riv.), Italy 34/E4
Selebi-Pikwe, Botswana 118/D4
Selemdzha (riv.), U.S.S.R. 48/O4
Selemiya, Syria 63/G5
Selendi, Turkey 63/C3
Selenga (riv.) 54/M5
Selenge, Mongolia 77/G2
Selenge, Mongolia 77/F2
Selenge Mürün (Selenga) (riv.), Mongolia 77/G2
Sélestat, France 28/G3
Selfridge, N. Dak. 282/J7
Sélibaby, Mauritania 106/B5
Seligman, Ariz. 198/B3
Seligman, Mo. 261/D9
Selim, Turkey 63/K2
Selima (oasis), Sudan 111/E3
Selima (oasis), Sudan 59/A5
Selimiye, Turkey 63/B3
Selinsgrove, Pa. 294/J4
Selje, Norway 18/D5
Selkirk (mts.), Br. Col. 184/J4
Selkirk (mts.), Idaho 220/B1
Selkirk, Kansas 232/A3
Selkirk, Man. 162/G5
Selkirk, Manitoba 179/F4
Selkirk (isl.), Manitoba 179/C1
Selkirk, Mich. 250/E4
Selkirk (trad. co.), Scotland 15/B5
Selkirk, Scotland 10/E3
Selkirk, Scotland 15/F5
Sella, Bolivia 136/C7
Selle (peak), Haiti 158/C6
Selleck, Wash. 310/D3
Sellers, Ala. 195/F6
Sellers, S.C. 296/H3
Sellersburg, Ind. 227/F8
Sellersville, Pa. 294/M5
Sells, Ariz. 198/D7
Sells, Georgia 217/E2
Sellye, Hungary 41/D4
Selma, Ala. 188/J4
Selma, Ala. 195/E6
Selma, Ark. 202/G6
Selma, Calif. 204/F7
Selma, Ind. 227/G4
Selma, Iowa 229/J7
Selma, Miss. 256/F5
Selma, N.C. 281/N3
Selma, Ohio 284/C6
Selma, Oreg. 291/D5

Selma, Texas 303/K10
Selma, Va. 307/J5
Selmah, Nova Scotia 168/E3
Selman, Okla. 288/H1
Selmer, Tenn. 237/D10
Selmont, Ala. 195/E6
Selous (mt.), Yukon 187/E3
Selsey, England 13/G7
Selsey Bill (prom.), England 13/G7
Selva, Argentina 143/D2
Selvas (for.), Brazil 120/C3
Sens, France 28/E3
Selway (riv.), Idaho 220/C3
Selwyn (lake), N.W. Terr. 187/H4
Selwyn, Queensland 95/B4
Selwyn (range), Queensland 95/B4
Selwyn (lake), Sask. 181/M2
Selwyn, W. Va. 312/B7
Selwyn (mts.), Yukon 187/E3
Selz, N. Dak. 282/L4
Selz, U.S.S.R. 52/E4
Seman, Ala. 195/F5
Semans, Sask. 181/G4
Semara, W. Sahara 102/A2
Semara, W. Sahara 106/B3
Semarang, Indonesia 54/N10
Semarang, Indonesia 85/J2
Sematan, Malaysia 85/D5
Sembé, Congo 115/B3
Sembrancher, Switzerland 39/D4
Şemdinli, Turkey 63/L4
Semenov, U.S.S.R. 52/F3
Semeru (mt.), Indonesia 85/K2
Semichi (isls.), Alaska 196/J3
Semidi (isls.), Alaska 196/C3
Semiluki, U.S.S.R. 52/E4
Semily, Czech. 41/C1
Seminary, Miss. 256/E7
Seminoe (res.), Wyo. 188/E2
Seminoe (mts.), Wyo. 319/F3
Seminoe (res.), Wyo. 319/F3
Seminoe Dam, Wyo. 319/F3
Seminole, Ala. 195/D10
Seminole (co.), Fla. 212/E3
Seminole, Fla. 212/B3
Seminole (lake), Fla. 212/B1
Seminole (co.), Georgia 217/C9
Seminole (lake), Georgia 217/B9
Seminole (co.), Okla. 288/N4
Seminole, Okla. 288/N4
Seminole, Pa. 294/E4
Seminole, Texas 303/B5
Seminole Ind. Res., Fla. 212/F5
Seminole Ind. Res., Fla. 212/E4
Semipalatinsk, U.S.S.R. 54/K4
Semipalatinsk, U.S.S.R. 48/H4
Semirara (isls.), Philippines 82/C5
Semisopochnoi (isl.), Alaska 196/K4
Semitau, Indonesia 85/E5
Semmering (pass), Austria 41/C3
Semmes, Ala. 195/B9
Semnan (governorate), Iran 66/J3
Semnan, Iran 59/F2
Semnan, Iran 66/H3
Semois (riv.), Belgium 27/G9
Semora, N.C. 281/L2
Sempach, Switzerland 39/F2
Sempach (lake), Switzerland 39/F2
Semporna, Malaysia 85/F5
Semsales, Switzerland 39/C3
Semur-en-Auxois, France 28/F4
Sen, Stoeng (riv.), Cambodia 72/E4
Sena, Bolivia 136/B2
Sena, N. Mex. 274/D3
Senador Pompeu, Brazil 132/G4
Senai, Malaysia 85/G5
Sena Madureira, Brazil 132/G10
Senanga, Zambia 115/D7
Senate, Sask. 181/B6
Senath, Mo. 261/M10
Senatobia, Miss. 256/E1
Sendai, Japan 54/R6
Sendai, Kagoshima, Japan 81/E8
Sendai, Miyagi, Japan 81/K4
Senec, Czech. 41/D2
Seneca, Ill. 222/E2
Seneca, Kansas 232/F2
Seneca, Miss. 256/F8
Seneca, Mo. 261/C9
Seneca, N. Mex. 274/F2
Seneca (co.), N.Y. 276/G5
Seneca (lake), N.Y. 276/G5
Seneca (co.), Ohio 284/D3
Seneca, Oreg. 291/J3
Seneca, S.C. 296/A2
Seneca (riv.), S.C. 296/B2
Seneca, S. Dak. 298/L3
Seneca, Wis. 317/E9
Seneca Falls, N.Y. 276/G5
Seneca Gardens, Ky. 237/K2
Senécal (lake), Newf. 166/B3
Senecaville, Ohio 284/H6
Senecaville (lake), Ohio 284/H6
Senegal 2/J5
Senegal 102/A3
SENEGAL 106/A5
Senegal (riv.) 102/A3
Senegal (riv.), Mali 106/B5
Senegal (riv.), Mauritania 106/B5
Senegal (riv.), Senegal 106/B5
Senekal, S. Africa 118/D5
Seney, Iowa 229/A3
Seney, Mich. 250/C2
Senftenberg, Germany 22/F3
Sengiley, U.S.S.R. 52/G4
Senguerr (riv.), Argentina 143/B6
Senhor do Bonfim, Brazil 120/F4
Senhor do Bonfim, Brazil 132/F5
Senica, Czech. 41/D2
Senigallia, Italy 34/D3
Senirkent, Turkey 63/D3
Senj, Yugoslavia 45/B3
Senja (isl.), Norway 72/E4
Senja (isl.), Norway 18/K2
Şenkaya, Turkey 63/K2
Şenlac, Sask. 181/B3
Senlis, France 28/E3

Senmonoron, Cambodia 72/E4
Sennar, Sudan 59/B7
Sennar, Sudan 111/F5
Sennar, Sudan 102/F3
Sennar (dam), Sudan 59/B7
Sennar (dam), Sudan 111/F5
Senne (riv.), Belgium 27/E7
Senneterre, Québec 174/B3
Senneville, Québec 172/G4
Senoia, Georgia 217/C4
Sens, France 28/E3
Sense (riv.), Switzerland 39/D3
Sensuntepeque, El Salvador 154/C4
Sent, Switzerland 39/K3
Senta, Yugoslavia 45/D3
Sentery, Zaire 115/E5
Sentinel, Alberta 182/C5
Sentinel, Ariz. 198/B6
Sentinel (butte), N. Dak. 282/C6
Sentinel, Okla. 288/H4
Sentinel Butte, N. Dak. 282/C6
Senyavin (isls.), Micronesia 87/F5
Seo de Urgel, Spain 33/G1
Seon, Switzerland 39/F2
Seoni, India 68/D4
Seoul (cap.), S. Korea 77/L4
Seoul (cap.), S. Korea 54/O6
Seoul (cap.), S. Korea 81/C5
Separ, N. Mex. 274/A6
Sepetiba (bay), Brazil 135/D3
Sepik (riv.), Papua N.G. 85/B6
Sepólno Krajenskie, Poland 47/C2
Septentrional, Cordillera (range), Dom. Rep. 158/D2
Sept-Îles, Québec 146/M4
Sept-Îles, Québec 162/K5
Sept-Îles, Québec 174/D2
Septimer (pass), Switzerland 39/J4
Sepulga (riv.), Ala. 195/E7
Sepulveda, Calif. 204/B10
Sequatchie (co.), Tenn. 237/L10
Sequatchie, Tenn. 237/K10
Sequatchie (riv.), Tenn. 237/L10
Sequeira, Uruguay 145/C1
Sequeros, Spain 33/C2
Sequim, Wash. 310/B2
Sequoia Nat'l Park, Calif. 204/G7
Sequoyah (co.), Okla. 288/S3
Sera (isl.), Indonesia 85/J7
Serafimovich, U.S.S.R. 52/F2
Serafina, N. Mex. 274/D3
Seraing, Belgium 27/G7
Serakhs, U.S.S.R. 48/B6
Serampore, India 68/F1
Serang, Indonesia 85/H2
Serangoon, Singapore 72/F6
Serasan (isl.), Indonesia 85/D5
Serbia (rep.), Yugoslavia 45/E3
Serçiler, Turkey 63/C6
Serdobol (Sortavala), U.S.S.R. 52/D2
Serdobsk, U.S.S.R. 52/F4
Sered', Czech. 41/D2
Şereflikoçhisar, Turkey 63/E3
Seremban, Malaysia 72/D7
Serena, Ill. 222/E2
Serengeti Nat'l Park, Tanzania 115/F4
Serenje, Zambia 115/F6
Sergach, U.S.S.R. 52/F3
Sergeant, Pa. 294/E2
Sergeant Bluff, Iowa 229/A4
Sergeantsville, N.J. 273/D3
Sergeya Kirova (isls.), U.S.S.R. 48/J2
Sergipe (state), Brazil 132/G5
Seria, Brunei 85/E5
Serian, Malaysia 85/E5
Sérifos (isl.), Greece 45/G7
Sérigny (riv.), Québec 174/D1
Serik, Turkey 63/D4
Seringapatam, India 68/D6
Sermata (isls.), Indonesia 85/H7
Serón, Spain 33/E4
Serós, Spain 33/G2
Serov, U.S.S.R. 54/H4
Serov, U.S.S.R. 48/G4
Serowe, Botswana 118/D4
Serowe, Botswana 102/E7
Serpa, Portugal 33/C4
Serpentine (lake), New Bruns. 170/D1
Serpentine (lakes), S. Australia 88/D5
Serpentine (lakes), S. Australia 94/A3
Serpentine (riv.), W. Australia 88/B3
Serpents Mouth (passage), Trin. & Tob. 156/G5
Serpents Mouth (passage), Trin. & Tob. 161/A11
Serpents Mouth (passage), Venezuela 124/K3
Serpukhov, U.S.S.R. 7/H3
Serpukhov, U.S.S.R. 48/D5
Serpukhov, U.S.S.R. 52/E4
Serra do Navio, Brazil 132/C2
Sérrai, Greece 7/G4
Sérrai, Greece 45/F5
Serrana (bank), Colombia 126/B9
Serra Namuli (mt.), Mozambique 102/F6
Serranilla (bank), Colombia 126/B8
Serra Talhada, Brazil 132/G4
Serres, France 28/F5
Serrinha, Brazil 120/F4
Serrinha, Brazil 132/G5
Sertã, Portugal 33/B3
Sertânia, Brazil 132/G5
Sertãozinho, Brazil 135/B2
Serua (isl.), Indonesia 85/H7
Serui, Indonesia 85/K6
Serule, Botswana 118/D4
Sérvia, Greece 45/F5
Servia, Ind. 227/F3
Servia, W. Va. 312/E5
Service Creek, Oreg. 291/G3
Serviceton, Victoria 97/A5
Sêrxü, China 77/E5
Se San (riv.), Vietnam 72/E4
Sese (isls.), Uganda 115/F4
Sesegenaga (lake), Ontario 177/G4
Sesfontein, Namibia 118/A3
Sesfontein, S. Africa 118/J6

Sesheke, Zambia 115/D7
Sesimbra, Portugal 33/B3
Sesser, Ill. 222/D5
Sessums, Miss. 256/G4
Sesto Fiorentino, Italy 34/C3
Sestri Levante, Italy 34/B2
Sesvenna (peak), Switzerland 39/K3
Sète, France 28/E6
Sete Lagoas, Brazil 120/E4
Sete Lagoas, Brazil 132/E7
Sete Quedas, (Grande) (isl.), Brazil 132/C8
Seth, W. Va. 312/C6
Sétif, Algeria 106/F1
Sétif, Algeria 102/C1
Seto, Japan 81/H6
Setonaikai National Park, Japan 81/H7
Seton Portage, Br. Col. 184/F5
Setouchi, Japan 81/O5
Settat, Morocco 106/C2
Settebagni, Italy 34/F6
Setté-Cama, Gabon 115/A4
Settecamini, Italy 34/F6
Setting (lake), Manitoba 179/H3
Settle, England 13/E3
Settsu, Japan 81/J8
Sétubal (dist.), Portugal 33/B3
Sétubal, Portugal 7/D5
Sétubal, Portugal 33/B3
Setúbal (bay), Portugal 33/B3
Seul (lake), Ontario 177/G4
Seul (lake), Ontario 175/B2
Seul Choix (pt.), Mich. 250/D3
Seuzach, Switzerland 39/G1
Sevan (lake), U.S.S.R. 7/J4
Sevan (lake), U.S.S.R. 52/G6
Sevaruyo, Bolivia 136/B6
Sevastopol', U.S.S.R. 7/H4
Sevastopol', U.S.S.R. 52/D6
Sevastopol', U.S.S.R. 48/D5
Sevelen, Switzerland 39/H2
Seven (heads), Ireland 17/D7
Seven Corners, Va. 307/S3
Seven Devils (res.), Ark. 202/G6
Seven Devils (mts.), Idaho 220/B4
Seven Hills, Ohio 284/H9
Seven Hogs, The (isls.), Ireland 17/A7
Seven Islands (bay), Newf. 166/B2
Seven Mile, Ohio 284/A7
Sevenmile (creek), Ohio 284/A6
Seven Mile Ford, Va. 307/E7
Sevenoaks, England 13/J8
Sevenoaks, England 10/C6
Seven Persons, Alberta 182/E5
Seven Rivers (riv.), N. Mex. 274/E5
Seven Sisters, Texas 303/F9
Seven Sisters Falls, Manitoba 179/G4
Seven Springs, N.C. 281/O4
Seven Springs, Pa. 294/D6
Seventy Mile House, Br. Col. 184/G4
Seven Valleys, Pa. 294/J6
Severance, Colo. 208/K1
Severance, Kansas 232/G2
Severn (riv.), England 13/E6
Severn (riv.), England 10/E5
Severn, Md. 245/M4
Severn (riv.), Md. 245/N4
Severn (riv.), N.S. Wales 97/F1
Severn, N.C. 281/P2
Severn (riv.), Ont. 146/J4
Severn (riv.), Ont. 162/G5
Severn (lake), Ontario 175/B2
Severn (riv.), Ontario 177/F3
Severn (riv.), Ontario 175/B2
Severn, Mouth of the (est.), Wales 13/B7
Severn (riv.), Wales 13/E5
Severna Park, Md. 245/M4
Severnaya Zemlya (isls.), U.S.S.R. 4/A4
Severnaya Zemlya (isls.), U.S.S.R. 54/M1
Severnaya Zemlya (isls.), U.S.S.R. 2/P1
Severnaya Zemlya (isls.), U.S.S.R. 48/L1
Severnyy, U.S.S.R. 52/K1
Severobaykal'sk, U.S.S.R. 48/M4
Severočeský (reg.), Czech. 41/C1
Severodonetsk, U.S.S.R. 52/E5
Severodvinsk, U.S.S.R. 7/H2
Severodvinsk, U.S.S.R. 48/E3
Severodvinsk, U.S.S.R. 52/E2
Severo-Kuril'sk, U.S.S.R. 48/Q4
Severomoravský (reg.), Czech. 41/D2
Severomorsk, U.S.S.R. 52/D1
Severoural'sk, U.S.S.R. 48/G3
Severo-Yeniseysk, U.S.S.R. 48/K3
Severy, Kansas 232/F4
Sevier (co.), Ark. 202/B6
Sevier, N.C. 281/F3
Sevier (co.), Tenn. 237/O9
Sevier (co.), Utah 304/C5
Sevier, Utah 304/B4
Sevier (des.), Utah 304/B4
Sevier (lake), Utah 188/D3
Sevier (lake), Utah 304/A5
Sevier (riv.), Utah 188/D3
Sevier (riv.), Utah 304/B4
Sevier, East Fork (riv.), Utah 304/B6
Sevier Bridge (res.), Utah 304/C4
Sevierville, Tenn. 237/P9
Sevilla, Colombia 126/C5
Sevilla (prov.), Spain 33/D4
Seville, Fla. 212/E3
Seville, Georgia 217/E7
Seville, Ohio 284/G3
Seville, Spain 7/D5
Seville, Spain 33/D4
Sevlievo, Bulgaria 45/G4
Sèvres, France 28/A2
Sewal, Iowa 229/G7
Sewalls Point, Fla. 212/F5
Sewanee, Tenn. 237/K10
Seward, Alaska 146/C3

Seward, Alaska 188/D6
Seward, Alaska 196/C1
Seward (pen.), Alaska 146/B3
Seward (pen.), Alaska 196/E1
Seward (co.), Kansas 232/B4
Seward, Kansas 232/D3
Seward (co.), Nebr. 264/G4
Seward, Nebr. 264/H4
Seward, Okla. 288/M3
Seward, Pa. 294/E5
Seward, U.S. 4/D17
Seward (pen.), U.S. 4/C18
Swaren, U.S. 4/D17
Sewart A.F.B., Tenn. 237/J8
Sewell, Br. Col. 184/A3
Sewell, Ky. 237/P5
Sewell, N.J. 273/C4
Sewickley, Pa. 294/B4
Sexmith, Alberta 182/A2
Sexton, Ind. 227/G5
Sexton, Iowa 229/E2
Sextons Creek, Ky. 237/O6
Sextonville, Wis. 317/F9
Seybaplaya, Mexico 150/O7
Seychelles 2/M6
SEYCHELLES 118/H5
Seydhisfjördhur, Iceland 21/D1
Seydişehir, Turkey 63/D4
Seyfe (lake), Turkey 63/F3
Seyhan (riv.), Turkey 63/F4
Seyhan (riv.), Turkey 59/C2
Seyitgazi, Turkey 63/D3
Seym (riv.), U.S.S.R. 52/D4
Seymour (canal), Alaska 196/N1
Seymour (inlet), Br. Col. 184/D4
Seymour•, Conn. 210/C3
Seymour, Ill. 222/E3
Seymour, Ind. 227/G7
Seymour, Iowa 229/G7
Seymour, Mo. 261/G8
Seymour, Tenn. 237/O9
Seymour, Texas 303/E4
Seymour (lake), Vt. 268/E2
Seymour, Victoria 88/H7
Seymour, Victoria 97/C5
Seymour, Wis. 317/K6
Seymour Johnson A.F.B., N.C. 281/O4
Seymourville, La. 238/J2
Seymourville, Manitoba 179/F3
Seyppel, Ark. 202/K4
Sézanne, France 28/E3
Sezze, Italy 34/D4
Sfax, Tunisia 106/G2
Sfax, Tunisia 102/D1
Sfíntu Gheorghe, Romania 45/G3
Sfíntu Gheorghe, Romania 45/J3
's-Gravenbrakel (Braine-le-Comte), Belgium 27/D7
's Gravendeel, Netherlands 27/E5
'S Gravenhage (The Hague) (cap.), Netherlands 27/E4
'S Gravenzande, Netherlands 27/E4
Sgurr a Choire Ghlais (mt.), Scotland 15/D3
Sgurr Alasdair (mt.), Scotland 15/B3
Sgurr Mor (mt.), Scotland 15/D3
Sgurr na Ciche (mt.), Scotland 15/C3
Sgurr na Lapaich (mt.), Scotland 15/C3
Shaanxi (Shensi), China 77/H5
Shaba (prov.), Zaire 115/E5
Shabasha, Sudan 59/B7
Shabbona, Ill. 222/E2
Shabeellaha Dhexe (prov.), Somalia 115/J3
Shabeellaha Hoose (prov.), Somalia 115/H3
Shabla, Bulgaria 45/J4
Shabo, Newf. 166/A3
Shabogamo (lake), Newf. 166/A3
Shabunda, Zaire 115/E4
Shabwa, Yemen 59/E6
Shache (Yarkand), China 77/A4
Shache, China 54/J6
Shackelford (co.), Texas 303/E5
Shackleton, Sask. 181/C5
Shackleton Ice Shelf, Ant. 2/P9
Shackleton Ice Shelf, Ant. 5/C5
Shade, Ohio 284/G7
Shadegan, Iran 66/F5
Shade Gap, Pa. 294/G5
Shadehill, S. Dak. 298/E2
Shadehill (res.), S. Dak. 298/E2
Shadeland, Ind. 227/C4
Shader, Scotland 15/B2
Shadrinsk, U.S.S.R. 48/G4
Shady Bend, Kansas 232/D2
Shady Cove, Oreg. 291/E5
Shady Dale, Georgia 217/E4
Shady Grove, Ala. 195/F7
Shady Grove, Fla. 212/C1
Shady Grove, Ky. 237/F5
Shady Grove, Pa. 294/G6
Shady Point, Okla. 288/S4
Shady Side, Md. 245/M5
Shadyside, Ohio 284/J6
Shady Valley, Tenn. 237/T7
Shafer, Minn. 255/F5
Shafter, Calif. 204/F8
Shafter, Nev. 266/G2
Shafter, Texas 303/C12
Shaftesbury, England 13/E7
Shaftesbury, England 10/E5
Shaftsbury•, Vt. 268/A6
Shageluk, Alaska 196/G2
Shag Harbour, Nova Scotia 168/C5
Shahat, Libya 102/E1
Shahat, Libya 111/D1
Shahbandar, Pakistan 68/B4
Shahdad, Iran 59/G3
Shahdad, Iran 66/K5
Shahdol, India 68/E4
Shahistan (Saravan), Iran 66/N7
Shah Jahan, Kuh-e (mts.), Iran 66/L2
Shahjahanpur, India 68/E3
Shah Juy, Afghanistan 59/J3

Shahrakht, Iran 66/M4
Shahreza, Iran 59/F3
Shahreza, Iran 66/H4
Shahr Kord, Iran 66/G4
Shahrud, Iran 59/G2
Shahrud, Iran 66/J2
Shaibara (isl.), Saudi Arabia 59/C4
Sha'ib Hisb, Wadi (dry riv.), Iraq 66/C5
Shaikh Sa'ad, Iraq 66/E4
Shaikh Shu'aib (isl.), Iran 66/H7
Shaikh Shu'aib (isl.), Iran 59/F4
Shailerville, Conn. 210/E3
Shajapur, India 68/D4
Shakawe, Botswana 118/C3
Shaker Heights, Ohio 284/H9
Shakespeare, Ontario 177/D4
Shakhtinsk, U.S.S.R. 48/H5
Shakhty, U.S.S.R. 7/J4
Shakhty, U.S.S.R. 48/E5
Shakhty, U.S.S.R. 52/F5
Shakhun'ya, U.S.S.R. 52/G3
Shaki, Nigeria 106/E7
Shâkir (isl.), Egypt 59/B4
Shakopee, Minn. 255/F6
Shakopee (creek), Minn. 255/C5
Shaktoolik, Alaska 196/F2
Shalalth, Br. Col. 184/F5
Shaler (mts.), N.W. Terr. 187/G2
Shalimar, Fla. 212/C6
Shallala, Wadi esh (dry riv.), Jordan 65/D2
Shallotte, N.C. 281/N7
Shallow (lake), Maine 243/E3
Shallowater, Texas 303/B4
Shallow Lake, Ontario 177/C3
Shallow Water, Kansas 232/B3
Sham, Jebel (mt.), Oman 59/G5
Shamattawa, Manitoba 179/K2
Shamattawa (riv.), Ontario 175/C2
Shambaugh, Iowa 229/D7
Shambe, Sudan 111/F6
Shamil, Iran 66/K7
Shammar, Jebel (plat.), Saudi Arabia 59/D4
Shamokin, Pa. 294/J4
Shamokin Dam, Pa. 294/J4
Shamrock, Okla. 288/N3
Shamrock, Sask. 181/E5
Shamrock, Texas 303/D2
Shamrock Lakes, Ind. 227/G4
Shamva, Zimbabwe 118/E3
Shan (state), Burma 72/C2
Shan (plat.), Burma 72/C2
Shanagolden, Ireland 17/C6
Shandan, China 77/F4
Shandon, Calif. 204/E8
Shandong (Shantung) (prov.), China 77/J4
Shangani (riv.), Zimbabwe 118/D3
Shangdu, China 77/H3
Shanghai, China 2/R4
Shanghai, China 54/O6
Shanghai, China 77/K5
Shanghai, Va. 307/P5
Shanghai, W. Va. 312/K4
Shanghang, China 77/J6
Shangnan, China 77/H5
Shangqui (Shangkiu), China 77/J5
Shangrao (Shangjao), China 77/J6
Shangshui, China 77/J5
Shang Xian, China 77/H5
Shangzhi, China 77/L2
Shaniko, Oreg. 291/G3
Shanks, W. Va. 312/J4
Shanksville, Pa. 294/E5
Shannock, R.I. 249/H7
Shannon, Georgia 217/B2
Shannon (isl.), Greenl. 4/B10
Shannon, Ill. 222/D1
Shannon, Mouth of the (est.), Ireland 17/B6
Shannon (riv.), Ireland 10/B4
Shannon (riv.), Ireland 17/E6
Shannon, Miss. 256/G2
Shannon (co.), Mo. 261/K8
Shannon, New Bruns. 170/E3
Shannon, N. Zealand 100/E4
Shannon, N.C. 281/L5
Shannon, Québec 172/F3
Shannon (co.), S. Dak. 298/D7
Shannon (lake), Wash. 310/D2
Shannon Airport, Ireland 17/D6
Shannon Bridge, Ireland 17/F5
Shannon City, Iowa 229/E7
Shannondale, Ind. 227/D4
Shannon Hills, Ark. 202/F4
Shannontown, S.C. 296/G4
Shannonville, Ontario 177/G3
Shanshan (Piqan), China 77/D3
Shansi (Shanxi) (prov.), China 77/H4
Shantar (isls.), U.S.S.R. 54/P4
Shantar (isls.), U.S.S.R. 48/O4
Shantou (Swatow), China 77/J7
Shantou, China 54/N7
Shantung (Shandong) (prov.), China 77/J4
Shanty Bay, Ontario 177/E3
Shanxi (Shansi) (prov.), China 77/H4
Shanyang, China 77/G5
Shanyin, China 77/H4
Shaoguan (Shiukwan), China 77/H7
Shaowu, China 77/J6
Shaoxing (Shaohing), China 77/K5
Shaoyang, China 77/H6
Shap, England 13/E3
Shapinsay (isl.), Scotland 15/F1
Shapio (lake), Newf. 166/B3
Shapleigh, Maine 243/B8
Shapleigh •, Maine 243/B8
Shaqlawa, Iraq 66/D2
Shaqra, Saudi Arabia 54/F7
Shaqra, Saudi Arabia 59/D4
Sharafkhaneh, Iran 66/D1
Sharbot Lake, Ontario 177/H3
Shari (riv.) 102/G4

Shari (riv.), Chad 111/C5
Shari, Japan 81/M2
Sharifabad, Iran 66/L2
Sharjah, U.A.E. 59/F4
Shark (pt.), Fla. 212/E6
Shark (bay), W. Australia 88/A5
Shark (bay), W. Australia 92/A4
Shark Bay, W. Australia 88/A5
Sharkey (co.), Miss. 256/F5
Sharlyk, U.S.S.R. 52/H4
Sharon •, Conn. 210/B1
Sharon, Georgia 217/G3
Sharon, Kansas 232/D4
Sharon, Mass. 249/K4
Sharon •, Mass. 249/K4
Sharon, Miss. 256/E5
Sharon •, N.H. 268/D6
Sharon, N. Dak. 282/P4
Sharon, Ohio 284/G6
Sharon, Okla. 283/H2
Sharon, Pa. 294/B3
Sharon, S.C. 296/E2
Sharon, Tenn. 237/D8
Sharon •, Vt. 268/C4
Sharon, W. Va. 312/D6
Sharon, Wis. 317/J11
Sharon Center, Ohio 284/G3
Sharon Grove, Ky. 237/G7
Sharon Hill, Pa. 294/N7
Sharon Springs, Kansas 232/A3
Sharon Springs, N.Y. 276/L5
Sharon Valley, Conn. 210/B1
Sharonville, Ohio 284/E9
Sharp (co.), Ark. 202/G1
Sharpe, Kansas 232/G3
Sharpe (lake), S. Dak. 298/J5
Sharpe Army Depot, Calif. 204/D6
Sharpes, Fla. 212/F4
Sharples, W. Va. 312/C7
Sharps (isl.), Md. 245/N6
Sharps, Va. 307/F5
Sharpsburg, Georgia 217/C4
Sharpsburg, Iowa 229/D7
Sharpsburg, Ky. 237/G4
Sharpsburg, Md. 245/G3
Sharpsburg, N.C. 281/O3
Sharpsburg, Pa. 294/B6
Sharps Chapel, Tenn. 237/O8
Sharpsville, Ind. 227/E4
Sharpsville, Pa. 294/A3
Sharptown, Md. 245/R6
Sharptown, N.J. 273/C4
Shar'ya, U.S.S.R. 48/E4
Shar'ya, U.S.S.R. 52/G3
Shashe, Botswana 118/D4
Shashe (riv.), Botswana 118/D4
Shashe (riv.), Zimbabwe 118/D4
Shashi (Shasi), China 77/H5
Shasta, Iraq 66/E5
Shasta, Calif. 204/C3
Shasta (co.), Calif. 204/C3
Shasta (dam), Calif. 204/C3
Shasta (lake), Calif. 204/C3
Shasta (mt.), Calif. 188/B2
Shasta (mt.), Calif. 204/C2
Shasta (res.), Calif. 188/B2
Shasta (riv.), Calif. 204/C2
Shati, Wadi esh (dry riv.), Libya 111/B2
Shatra, Iraq 66/E6
Shattuc, Ill. 222/D5
Shattuck, Okla. 283/G2
Shattuckville, Mass. 249/D2
Shauck, Ohio 284/E4
Shaughnessy, Alberta 182/D5
Shaunavon, Sask. 162/F6
Shaunavon, Sask. 181/C6
Shavano Park, Texas 303/J10
Shaver Lake, Calif. 204/F6
Shavers Fork (riv.), W. Va. 312/G5
Shave Ziyyon, Israel 65/B2
Shaw, Kansas 232/G4
Shaw, La. 238/G4
Shaw, Minn. 255/F3
Shaw, Miss. 256/C3
Shaw (mt.), N.H. 268/E4
Shaw, Oreg. 291/K8
Shaw A.F.B., S.C. 296/F4
Shawan, China 77/33
Shawanese, Pa. 294/E7
Shawano (co.), Wis. 317/J6
Shawano, Wis. 317/J6
Shawano (lake), Wis. 317/K6
Shawboro, N.C. 281/P2
Shawbost, Scotland 15/B2
Shawbridge, Québec 172/C4
Shawinigan, Que. 162/J6
Shawinigan, Québec 172/E3
Shawinigan, Québec 172/E3
Shawinigan (riv.), Québec 172/E3
Shawinigan-Sud, Québec 172/E3
Shaw Island, Wash 310/B2
Shawmut, Maine 243/D6
Shawmut, Mont. 262/G4
Shawmut, Pa. 294/E3
Shawnee, Colo. 208/H4
Shawnee (co.), Kansas 232/G2
Shawnee, Kansas 232/H2
Shawnee, Ohio 284/F6
Shawnee, Okla. 18/G3
Shawnee, Okla. 288/N4
Shawnee, Wyo. 319/G3
Shawnee Hills, Ohio 284/D5
Shawnee on Delaware, Pa. 294/N3
Shawneetown, Ill. 222/E6
Shawinigan Lake, Br. Col. 184/J3
Shawomet, R.I. 249/J6
Shawsheen Village, Mass. 249/K2
Shawshine (riv.), Mass. 249/K2
Shawsville, W. Va. 245/M2
Shawsville, Va. 307/H6
Shawville, Québec 172/A4
Shay Gap, W. Australia 92/C3
Shayib, Jebel (mt.), Egypt 59/B4
Shay Juy, Afghanistan 68/B2
Shchekino, U.S.S.R. 52/E4
Shchel'yayur, U.S.S.R. 52/H1
Shchigry, U.S.S.R. 52/E4
Shchuchinsk, U.S.S.R. 48/H4

Sheakleyville, Pa. 294/B3
Sheaville, Oreg. 291/K4
Shebandowan, Ontario 177/G5
Sheberghan, Afghanistan 54/H6
Sheberghan, Afghanistan 68/B1
Sheberghan, Afghanistan 59/H2
Sheboygan, Wis. 188/J2
Sheboygan (co.), Wis. 317/L8
Sheboygan, Wis. 317/L8
Sheboygan Falls, Wis. 317/L8
Shedd, Oreg. 291/D3
Shedden, Ontario 177/C5
Shediac, New Bruns. 170/F2
Shediac (isl.), New Bruns. 170/F2
Shediac Bridge, New Bruns. 170/F2
Sheeffry (hills), Ireland 17/G4
Sheelin (lake), Ireland 17/G4
Sheenjek (riv.), Alaska 196/K1
Sheep (mt.), Colo. 208/E6
Sheep (mt.), Mont. 262/C2
Sheep (range), Nev. 266/F6
Sheep (creek), Oreg. 291/L2
Sheep (creek), Utah 304/E3
Sheep Creek, Alberta 182/A2
Sheep Haven (harb.), Ireland 17/F1
Sheepscott, Maine 243/D7
Sheeps (head), Ireland 17/B8
Sheepscott, Maine 243/D7
's Heerenberg, Netherlands 27/J5
Sheerness, Alberta 182/E4
Sheet (harb.), Nova Scotia 168/F4
Sheet Harbour, Nova Scotia 168/F4
Shefar'am, Israel 65/C2
Shefayim, Israel 65/B3
Sheffield, Ala. 195/C1
Sheffield, England 7/D3
Sheffield, England 10/F4
Sheffield, England 13/J2
Sheffield, Ill. 222/D2
Sheffield, Iowa 229/G3
Sheffield •, Mass. 249/A4
Sheffield, New Bruns. 170/D3
Sheffield, Ohio 284/F3
Sheffield, Pa. 294/D2
Sheffield, Tasmania 99/C3
Sheffield, Texas 303/B7
Sheffield •, Vt. 268/C2
Sheffield Lake, Ohio 284/F3
Shefford (co.), Québec 172/E4
Sheguiandah, Ontario 177/C2
Sheho, Sask. 181/H4
Shehy (mts.), Ireland 17/C8
Sheikh Sa'id, Yemen 59/D7
Sheila, New Bruns. 170/F1
Sheki, U.S.S.R. 52/G6
Shelagh (riv.), Iran 66/M5
Shelagskiy (cape), U.S.S.R. 48/R2
Shelbiana, Ky. 237/R6
Shelbina, Mo. 261/H3
Shelburn, Ind. 227/C6
Shelburne, N.H. 268/E3
Shelburne •, N.H. 268/E3
Shelburne (co.), Nova Scotia 168/C5
Shelburne, Nova Scotia 168/C5
Shelburne, Ontario 177/D3
Shelburne •, Vt. 268/A3
Shelburne (pond), Vt. 268/A3
Shelburne Falls, Mass. 249/D2
Shelby (co.), Ala. 195/E4
Shelby, Ala. 195/E4
Shelby (co.), Ill. 222/E4
Shelby (co.), Ind. 227/F5
Shelby, Ind. 227/E5
Shelby (co.), Iowa 229/C5
Shelby, Iowa 229/C5
Shelby (co.), Ky. 237/L4
Shelby, Mich. 250/C5
Shelby (co.), Mo. 261/H3
Shelby, Mont. 262/E2
Shelby, Nebr. 264/G3
Shelby, N.C. 281/G4
Shelby (co.), Ohio 284/B5
Shelby, Ohio 284/E4
Shelby (co.), Tenn. 237/B10
Shelby (co.), Texas 303/K6
Shelby Center, N.Y. 276/D4
Shelbyville, Ill. 222/E4
Shelbyville, Ind. 227/F6
Shelbyville (lake), Ill. 222/E4
Shelbyville, Ky. 237/L4
Shelbyville, Mo. 261/H3
Shelbyville, Tenn. 237/H10
Shelbyville, Texas 303/L6
Sheldahl, Iowa 229/F5
Sheldon, Ill. 222/F3
Sheldon, Iowa 229/B2
Sheldon, Minn. 255/G7
Sheldon, Mo. 261/D7
Sheldon, N. Dak. 282/P6
Sheldon, S.C. 296/F6
Sheldon, Texas 303/K1
Sheldon •, Vt. 268/B2
Sheldon, Wis. 317/D5
Sheldon Junction, Vt. 268/B2
Sheldon Point, Alaska 196/E2
Sheldon Springs, Vt. 268/A2
Sheldonville, Mass. 249/K4
Shelekhov (gulf), U.S.S.R. 54/S3
Shelekhov (gulf), U.S.S.R. 48/Q4
Shelikof (str.), Alaska 196/H4
Shell (pt.), Fla. 212/B1
Shell (riv.), Minn. 255/C4
Shell (creek), N. Dak. 282/F3
Shell, Loch (inlet), Scotland 15/B3
Shell (lake), Wis. 317/C4
Shell, Wyo. 319/E1
Shell (creek), Wyo. 319/E1
Shellbrook, Sask. 162/F5
Shellbrook, Sask. 181/E2
Shelldrake (riv.), Mich. 250/D2
Shelley, Br. Col. 184/F3
Shelley, Idaho 220/F6
Shellharbour, N.S. Wales 97/F4
Shell Knob, Mo. 261/E9
Shell Lake, Sask. 181/D2
Shell Lake, Wis. 317/C4
Shellman, Georgia 217/C7

Shellmouth, Manitoba 179/A4
Shell Rock, Iowa 229/H3
Shellsburg, Iowa 229/K4
Shelltown, Md. 245/R9
Shelly, Minn. 255/B3
Shelmerdine, N.C. 281/P4
Shelocta, Pa. 294/D4
Shelter (isl.), N.Y. 276/R8
Shelton, Conn. 210/C3
Shelton, Nebr. 264/F4
Shelton, S.C. 296/E3
Shelton, Wash. 310/B3
Shemakha, U.S.S.R. 52/G6
Shemogue, New Bruns. 170/F2
Shemya (isl.), Alaska 196/J3
Shemya Air Force Base, Alaska 196/J3
Shenandoah, Iowa 229/C7
Shenandoah (co.), Va. 307/L3
Shenandoah, Va. 307/L4
Shenandoah (mt.), Va. 307/K3
Shenandoah (riv.), Va. 307/N2
Shenandoah (riv.), W. Va. 312/K4
Shenandoah Junction, W. Va. 312/L4
Shenandoah Nat'l Park, Va. 307/L3
Shenango, Pa. 294/A3
Shenango River (lake), Pa. 294/B3
Shendam, Nigeria 106/H7
Shendi, Sudan 59/B6
Shendi, Sudan 102/F3
Shendi, Sudan 111/F4
Shèngjin, Albania 45/D5
Sheng Xian, China 77/K6
Sheopur, India 68/D3
Shepard, Alberta 182/D4
Shepardsville, Ind. 227/B5
Shepaug (dam), Conn. 210/B3
Shepaug (riv.), Conn. 210/B2
Shepetovka, U.S.S.R. 52/C4
Shepherd, Mich. 250/E5
Shepherd, Mont. 262/H5
Shepherd (bay), N.W. Terr. 187/J3
Shepherd, Texas 303/K7
Shepherdstown, W. Va. 312/L4
Shepherdsville, Ky. 237/K4
Shepody, New Bruns. 170/F3
Shepody (bay), New Bruns. 170/F3
Sheppard A.F.B., Texas 303/F3
Shepparton, Victoria 88/G7
Shepparton, Victoria 97/C5
Sheppey (isl.), England 13/J6
Sheppton, Pa. 294/K4
Shepshed, England 13/F5
Shepton Mallet, England 13/E6
Shepton Mallet, England 10/E5
Sheqi, China 77/H5
Sherack, Minn. 255/B2
Sherard, Miss. 256/C2
Sherard (cape), N.W. Terr. 187/L2
Sherborn •, Mass. 249/A8
Sherborne, England 10/E6
Sherborne, England 13/E7
Sherbro (isl.), S. Leone 106/B7
Sherbrooke, Nova Scotia 168/G3
Sherbrooke (lake), Nova Scotia 168/D4
Sherbrooke (riv.), Nova Scotia 168/D4
Sherbrooke, Que. 162/J7
Sherbrooke (co.), Québec 172/E4
Sherbrooke, Québec 172/E4
Sherburn, Minn. 255/D7
Sherburne (co.), Minn. 255/E5
Sherburne, W. Va. 276/K5
Shercock, Ireland 17/G4
Shereik, Sudan 111/F4
Sheridan, Ark. 202/F5
Sheridan, Calif. 204/D5
Sheridan, Colo. 208/J3
Sheridan, Ill. 222/E2
Sheridan, Ind. 227/E4
Sheridan (co.), Kansas 232/C2
Sheridan, Maine 243/F2
Sheridan, Mich. 250/D5
Sheridan, Mo. 261/C1
Sheridan (co.), Mont. 262/M2
Sheridan (co.), Nebr. 264/B2
Sheridan, N.Y. 276/B5
Sheridan (co.), N. Dak. 282/K4
Sheridan, Oreg. 291/D2
Sheridan, W. Va. 312/B6
Sheridan, Wis. 317/H7
Sheridan, Wyo. 146/H5
Sheridan (co.), Wyo. 319/F1
Sheridan, Wyo. 319/F1
Sheridan Lake, Colo. 208/P6
Sheridan, Wyo. 319/F1
Shiloh Nat'l Mil. Park, Tenn. 237/E10

Sherman (inlet), N.W. Terr. 187/J3
Sherman (co.), Oreg. 291/G2
Sherman, S. Dak. 298/S6
Sherman (co.), Texas 303/C1
Sherman, Texas 303/H4
Sherman, Texas 188/G4
Sherman, W. Va. 312/D5
Sherman City, Mich. 250/D5
Sherman Mills, Maine 243/G4
Shermans Dale, Pa. 294/H5
Sherman Station, Maine 243/F4
Sherrard, Ill. 222/C2
Sherrard, W. Va. 312/E3
Sherrill, Ark. 202/F5
Sherrill, Iowa 229/M3
Sherrill, N.Y. 276/J4
Sherrington, Québec 172/D4
Sherrodsville, Ohio 284/H4
Sherry, Wis. 317/G6
's Hertogenbosch, Netherlands 27/G5
Sherwood, Ark. 202/F4
Sherwood (pt.), Conn. 210/B4
Sherwood (for.), England 13/F4
Sherwood, Mich. 250/D6
Sherwood, N. Dak. 282/G2
Sherwood, Ohio 284/A3
Sherwood, Okla. 288/S6
Sherwood, Oreg. 291/A3
Sherwood, Pr. Edward I. 168/E2
Sherwood, Tenn. 237/K10
Sherwood, Texas 303/C5
Sherwood, Wis. 317/K7
Sherwood Park, Alberta 182/D3
Sheslay (riv.), Br. Col. 184/J2
Shetek (lake), Minn. 255/C6
Shetland (islands area), Scotland 15/F2
Shetland (isls.), Scotland 7/D2
Shetland (isls.), Scotland 10/G1
Shetland (isls.), Scotland 15/G2
Shetucket (riv.), Conn. 210/G2
Shevchenko, U.S.S.R. 54/G5
Shevchenko, U.S.S.R. 48/F5
Shevlin, Manitoba 179/A3
Shevlin, Minn. 255/C3
Sheyenne, N. Dak. 282/M4
Sheyenne (riv.), N. Dak. 188/G1
Sheyenne (riv.), N. Dak. 282/O6
Sheykh Sho'eyb (isl.), Iran 66/H7
Shiant (isls.), Scotland 15/B3
Shiant (sound), Scotland 15/B3
Shiawassee (co.), Mich. 250/E6
Shiawassee (riv.), Mich. 250/E6
Shibam, Yemen 59/E7
Shibata, Japan 81/J5
Shibetsu, Japan 81/M2
Shibin el Kom, Egypt 111/J3
Shibogama (lake), Ontario 175/C2
Shickley, Nebr. 264/G4
Shickshinny, Pa. 294/K3
Shideler, Ind. 227/G4
Shidler, Okla. 288/N1
Shiel, Loch (lake), Scotland 10/D2
Shiel, Loch (lake), Scotland 15/C4
Shieldaig, Scotland 15/C3
Shields, Kansas 232/B3
Shields (riv.), Mont. 262/F4
Shields, N. Dak. 282/H7
Shieldsville, Minn. 255/E6
Shifnal, England 13/E5
Shiga (pref.), Japan 81/J7
Shigatse (Xigazê), China 77/C6
Shigawake, Québec 172/D2
Shihezi (Shihhotzu), China 77/C3
Shihr, Yemen 59/E7
Shijak, Albania 45/D5
Shijiazhuang (Shihkiachwang), China 77/J4
Shijiazhuang, China 54/N6
Shikarpur, Pakistan 68/B3
Shikarpur, Pakistan 59/J4
Shikoku, Japan 54/P6
Shikoku (isl.), Japan 2/R4
Shikoku (isl.), Japan 81/F7
Shikotan (isl.), Japan 81/N2
Shikotsu (lake), Japan 81/K2
Shikotsu-Toya Nat'l Park, Japan 81/K2
Shilbottle, England 13/F2
Shildon, England 13/F3
Shilka (riv.), U.S.S.R. 54/N4
Shilka, U.S.S.R. 48/N4
Shillelagh, Ireland 17/J6
Shillelagh, Ireland 10/C4
Shillington, Pa. 294/K5
Shillong, India 68/G3
Shilo, Manitoba 179/C5
Shiloh, Ala. 195/G2
Shiloh, Ala. 195/C6
Shiloh, Georgia 217/C5
Shiloh, Ill. 222/B3
Shiloh, N.J. 273/C5
Shiloh, Ohio 284/E4
Shiloh, S.C. 296/F4
Shiloh, Tenn. 237/E10
Shiloh, Va. 307/O4
Shilovo, U.S.S.R. 52/F4
Shimabara, Japan 81/E7
Shimamoto, Japan 81/J7
Shimane (pref.), Japan 81/F6
Shimane (pen.), Japan 81/F6
Shimanovsk, U.S.S.R. 48/N4
Shimbir Berris (mt.), Somalia 115/J1
Shimizu, Japan 81/J6
Shimoda, Japan 81/J6
Shimoga, India 68/D6
Shimokita (pen.), Japan 81/K3
Shimonoseki, Japan 81/E6
Shin (falls), Scotland 15/D3
Shin, Loch (lake), Scotland 10/D1
Shin, Loch (lake), Scotland 15/D3
Shin (riv.), Scotland 15/D3
Shinano (riv.), Japan 81/J5
Shinas, Oman 59/G5
Shindand, Afghanistan 59/H3

Shindand, Afghanistan 68/A2
Shindler, S. Dak. 298/R7
Shiner, Texas 303/G8
Shingbwiyang, Burma 72/B1
Shinglehouse, Pa. 294/F2
Shingler, Georgia 217/E7
Shingle Springs, Calif. 204/C8
Shingleton, Mich. 250/C2
Shingu, Japan 81/H7
Shining Tree, Ontario 177/J5
Shinjo, Japan 81/K4
Shinko (riv.), Cent. Afr. Rep. 115/D2
Shinnecock Ind. Res., N.Y. 276/R9
Shinnston, W. Va. 312/F3
Shin Pond, Maine 243/F3
Shinrone, Ireland 17/F5
Shinyanga (reg.), Tanzania 115/F4
Shinyanga, Tanzania 115/F4
Shinyanga, Tanzania 102/F5
Shiocton, Wis. 317/K7
Shiogama, Japan 81/K4
Shiono (cape), Japan 81/H7
Ship (isl.), Miss. 256/G10
Ship Bottom, N.J. 273/E4
Ship Harbour, Newf. 166/D2
Ship Harbour, Nova Scotia 168/A4
Shiping, China 77/F7
Shipki (pass), India 68/D2
Shipman, Ill. 222/C4
Shipman, Sask. 181/F2
Shipman, Va. 307/L5
Shippan (pt.), Conn. 210/A4
Shippagan, New Bruns. 170/F1
Shippagan (bay), New Bruns. 170/E1
Shippagan (gully), New Bruns. 170/F1
Shippensburg, Pa. 294/H5
Shippenville, Pa. 294/D3
Shiprock, N. Mex. 274/A2
Ship Rock (peak), N. Mex. 274/A2
Shipshaw (riv.), Québec 172/F1
Shipshewana, Ind. 227/F1
Ship Shoal (isl.), Va. 307/S6
Shipston on Stour, England 13/F5
Shiqian, China 77/G6
Shiqma (riv.), Israel 65/B4
Shiquan, China 77/G5
Shiquanhe, China 77/A5
Shiragami (cape), Japan 81/J3
Shirakawa, Japan 81/K5
Shirane (mt.), Japan 81/H6
Shirane (mt.), Japan 81/J5
Shiranuka, Japan 81/M2
Shiraz, Iran 54/G7
Shiraz, Iran 66/H6
Shiraz, Iran 59/F4
Shire (riv.), Malawi 115/G7
Shire (riv.), Mozambique 118/E3
Shiretoko (cape), Japan 81/M1
Shiriya (cape), Japan 81/K3
Shir Kuh (mt.), Iran 59/F3
Shir Kuh (mt.), Iran 66/J5
Shirland, Ill. 222/E1
Shirley, Ark. 202/F2
Shirley, Ill. 222/E3
Shirley, Ind. 227/F5
Shirley, Mass. 249/H2
Shirley •, Mass. 249/H2
Shirley, Mo. 261/L7
Shirley, W. Va. 312/E4
Shirley (basin), Wyo. 319/F3
Shirley Basin, Wyo. 319/F3
Shirley Center, Mass. 249/H2
Shirley City (Woodburn), Ind. 227/H2
Shirley Mills, Maine 243/D5
Shirley Mills •, Maine 243/D5
Shirleysburg, Pa. 294/F5
Shiro, Texas 303/J7
Shiroishi, Japan 81/K4
Shirvan, Iran 59/G2
Shirvan, Iran 66/K2
Shirvan (riv.), Iran 66/E3
Shishaldin (vol.), Alaska 196/G4
Shishmaref, Alaska 196/E1
Shithatha, Iraq 59/D3
Shithatha, Iraq 66/C4
Shitike (creek), Oreg. 291/F3
Shiukwan (Shaoyuan), China 77/H7
Shively, Calif. 204/B3
Shively, Ky. 237/K4
Shivers, Miss. 256/E7
Shivpuri, India 68/D4
Shivwits (plat.), Ariz. 198/B2
Shivwits Ind. Res., Utah 304/A6
Shiyan, China 77/H5
Shizuishan (Shihsuishan), China 77/G4
Shizunai, Japan 81/L2
Shizuoka (pref.), Japan 81/H6
Shizuoka, Japan 54/P6
Shizuoka, Japan 81/H6
Shkodër, Albania 7/F4
Shkodër, Albania 45/D5
Shoa (prov.), Ethiopia 111/G6
Shoal (riv.), Fla. 212/C6
Shoal (creek), Ill. 222/D5
Shoal (lake), Manitoba 179/B4
Shoal (lake), Manitoba 179/G5
Shoal (riv.), Manitoba 179/B2
Shoal (bay), Newf. 166/D2
Shoal (bay), Nova Scotia 168/F4
Shoal (creek), Tenn. 237/F10
Shoal (creek), Utah 304/A6
Shoal Branch, Wading (riv.), N.J. 273/D4
Shoal Cove, Newf. 166/C3
Shoal Harbour, Newf. 166/C2
Shoalhaven (riv.), N.S. Wales 97/E4
Shoal Lake, Manitoba 179/B4
Shoals, Ind. 227/D7
Shoals (isls.), N.H. 268/F4
Shoals, W. Va. 312/B6
Shoals, N.C. 281/J2
Shoals Junction, S.C. 296/C3
Shoalwater (bay), Queensland 88/J4
Shoalwater (cape), Wash. 310/A4

Shoalwater Ind. Res., Wash. 310/B4
Shobara, Japan 81/F6
Shobonier, Ill. 222/D5
Shock, W. Va. 312/D5
Shoemakersville, Pa. 294/K4
Shoffner, Ark. 202/H2
Shohola, Pa. 294/N3
Sholapur, India 54/J8
Sholapur, India 68/D5
Sholes, Nebr. 264/G2
Shona (isl.), Scotland 15/C4
Shongaloo, La. 238/D1
Shonkin, Mont. 262/F3
Shonto, Ariz. 198/E2
Shonto (plat.), Ariz. 198/E2
Shook, Mo. 261/M8
Shooting Creek, N.C. 281/B4
Shopiere, Wis. 317/H10
Shop Springs, Tenn. 237/J8
Shorapur, India 68/D5
Shoreacres, Br. Col. 184/J5
Shore Acres, N.J. 273/E3
Shore Acres, Texas 303/K2
Shoreham, Mich. 250/C6
Shoreham, Minn. 255/C4
Shoreham, N.Y. 276/F8
Shoreham •, Vt. 268/A4
Shoreham-by-Sea, England 13/G7
Shoreham-by-Sea, England 10/F5
Shoreview, Minn. 255/G5
Shorewood, Ill. 222/E2
Shorewood, Mich. 250/C7
Shorewood, Minn. 255/F5
Shorewood, Wis. 317/M1
Shorewood Hills, Wis. 317/G9
Short, Okla. 288/S3
Short Beach, Conn. 210/D3
Short Creek, Ohio 284/J5
Shortdale, Manitoba 179/A3
Shorter, Ala. 195/G6
Shorterville, Ala. 195/H7
Short Falls, N.H. 268/E5
Short Hills, N.J. 273/E2
Shortland (isls.), Solomon Is. 86/D2
Shortleaf, Ala. 195/G6
Shortsville, N.Y. 276/F5
Shoshone (co.), Idaho 220/B2
Shoshone, Idaho 220/D7
Shoshone (falls), Idaho 220/D7
Shoshone (mt.), Nev. 266/E6
Shoshone (mts.), Nev. 266/E2
Shoshone (range), Nev. 266/E2
Shoshone (lake), Wyo. 319/B1
Shoshone (riv.), Wyo. 319/D1
Shoshong, Botswana 118/D4
Shoshoni, Wyo. 319/D2
Shostka, U.S.S.R. 52/D4
Shotley, England 13/J6
Shotts, Scotland 15/C2
Shouldice, Alberta 182/D4
Shouns, Tenn. 237/T8
Shoup, Idaho 220/D4
Shoval, Israel 65/B5
Shovel Lake, Minn. 255/E4
Showak, Sudan 111/G5
Showell, Md. 245/T7
Show Low, Ariz. 198/F4
Shoyna, U.S.S.R. 52/F1
Shpola, U.S.S.R. 52/D5
Shreve, Ohio 284/F4
Shreveport, La. 188/H4
Shreveport, La. 238/C2
Shrewsbury, England 13/E5
Shrewsbury, England 10/E4
Shrewsbury •, Mass. 249/H3
Shrewsbury, Mo. 261/P3
Shrewsbury, N.J. 273/E3
Shrewsbury, Pa. 294/J6
Shrewsbury •, Vt. 268/B4
Shropshire (co.), England 13/E5
Shrule, Ireland 17/C4
Shuangcheng, China 77/L2
Shuangliao, China 77/K3
Shuangyashan, China 77/M2
Shubenacadie, Nova Scotia 168/E3
Shubenacadie (lake), Nova Scotia 168/E4
Shubenacadie (riv.), Nova Scotia 168/E3
Shubert, Nebr. 264/J4
Shubuta, Miss. 256/F6
Shue (creek), S. Dak. 298/N5
Shu'eib, Wadi (dry riv.), Jordan 65/D4
Shueyville, Iowa 229/K5
Shu'fat, West Bank 65/C4
Shuicheng, China 77/G6
Shuksan (mt.), Wash. 310/D2
Shulan, China 77/L3
Shulerville, S.C. 296/H5
Shullsburg, Wis. 317/F10
Shumagin (isls.), Alaska 196/G4
Shumen, Bulgaria 45/H4
Shumerlya, U.S.S.R. 52/G3
Shumway, Ill. 222/E4
Shunat Nimrin, Jordan 65/D4
Shunchang, China 77/J6
Shungnak, Alaska 196/G1
Shungopavy (Shongopovi), Ariz. 198/E3
Shunk, Pa. 294/J2
Shunock (riv.), Conn. 210/H3
Shuo Xian, China 77/H4
Shuqaiq, Saudi Arabia 59/D6
Shuqra, Yemen 59/E7
Shuqualak, Miss. 256/G5
Shur (riv.), Iran 66/J2
Shurugwi, Zimbabwe 118/E3
Shusf, Iran 66/L5
Shush, Iran 66/F4
Shushan, N.Y. 276/O4
Shushenskoye, U.S.S.R. 48/K4
Shushtar, Iran 66/F4
Shustar, Iran 59/E3
Shuswap (lake), Br. Col. 162/E5

Shuswap (lake), Br. Col. 184/H4
Shutesbury•, Mass. 249/E3
Shuttle Meadow (res.), Conn. 210/D2
Shutty Bench, Br. Col. 184/J5
Shuweika, West Bank 65/C3
Shuya, U.S.S.R. 52/F3
Shuyak (isl.), Alaska 196/H3
Shwebo, Burma 72/B2
Shwegyin, Burma 72/C3
Shweli (riv.), Burma 72/C2
Shwenyaung, Burma 72/C2
Shyok, India 68/D2
Si (riv.), China 54/N7
Siahan (mts.), Pakistan 59/H4
Siahan (range), Pakistan 68/A3
Siah Kuh (mt.), Iran 66/L3
Siak (riv.), Indonesia 85/C5
Siaksriinderapura, Indonesia 85/C5
Siakwan (Xiaguan), China 77/E6
Sialkot, Pakistan 68/C2
Sialkot, Pakistan 59/K3
Siam (Thailand) (gulf), Thailand 72/D5
Sian (Xi'an), China 77/G5
Siangfan (Xiangfan), China 77/H5
Siangtan (Xiangtan), China 77/H6
Siapa (riv.), Venezuela 124/E7
Siargao (isl.), Philippines 85/H4
Siargao (isl.), Philippines 82/F6
Siasconset, Mass. 249/P7
Siasi, Philippines 82/C8
Siasi (isl.), Philippines 82/C8
Siátista, Greece 45/E5
Siaton, Philippines 82/D6
Siaton (pt.), Philippines 82/D6
Siau (isl.), Indonesia 85/H5
Šiauliai, U.S.S.R. 7/B4
Šiauliai, U.S.S.R. 53/B3
Šiauliai, U.S.S.R. 52/B3
Šiauliai, U.S.S.R. 48/C4
Sib, Iran 66/N7
Sibalom, Philippines 82/C5
Sibanicú, Cuba 158/G3
Sibay (isl.), Philippines 82/C5
Sibay, U.S.S.R. 52/J4
Sibbald, Alberta 182/E4
Šibenik, Yugoslavia 45/C4
Siberia, Ind. 227/D8
Siberia (reg.), U.S.S.R. 4/C2
Siberia (reg.), U.S.S.R. 2/P2
Siberia (reg.), U.S.S.R. 54/M4
Siberia (reg.), U.S.S.R. 48/M3
Sibert, Ky. 237/O6
Siberut (isl.), Indonesia 54/L10
Siberut (isl.), Indonesia 85/B6
Siberut (str.), Indonesia 85/B6
Sibi, Pakistan 68/B2
Sibi, Pakistan 59/J4
Sibiti, Congo 115/B4
Sibiu, Romania 7/G4
Sibiu, Romania 45/G3
Sibley, Ill. 222/E3
Sibley, Iowa 229/B2
Sibley, La. 238/D1
Sibley (co.), Minn. 255/D6
Sibley, Miss. 256/B8
Sibley, Mo. 261/S5
Sibley, N. Dak. 282/P5
Sibley Prov. Park, Ontario 175/C3
Sibley Prov. Park, Ontario 177/H5
Sibolga, Indonesia 85/B5
Siboney, Cuba 158/J4
Sibsagar, India 68/H3
Sibu, Malaysia 85/E5
Sibu, Malaysia 54/N9
Sibube, C. Rica 154/F6
Sibuco, Philippines 82/C7
Sibuguey (bay), Philippines 82/D7
Sibundoy, Colombia 126/B3
Sibut, Cent. Afr. Rep. 115/C2
Sibutu (passage), Philippines 85/F4
Sibutu (passage), Philippines 82/B8
Sibutu Group (isls.), Philippines 82/B8
Sibuyan (isl.), Philippines 85/G3
Sibuyan (isl.), Philippines 82/D4
Sibuyan (sea), Philippines 82/D4
Sibuyan (sea), Philippines 85/G3
Sicamous, Br. Col. 184/H5
Sicasica, Bolivia 128/B6
Siccus (riv.), S. Australia 88/F6
Sichuan (Szechwan) (prov.), China 77/F5
Sicily (reg.), Italy 34/D6
Sicily (isl.), Italy 7/F5
Sicily (isl.), Italy 34/E6
Sicily (str.), Italy 34/D6
Sicily Island, La. 238/G3
Sicklerville, N.J. 273/D4
Sico (riv.), Honduras 154/E3
Sicuani, Peru 128/G10
Šid, Yugoslavia 45/D3
Sidamo (prov.), Ethiopia 111/G7
Siddipet, India 68/D5
Sideby, Finland 18/M5
Side Lake, Minn. 255/E3
Sidell, Ill. 222/F4
Siderno, Italy 34/F5
Sidewood, Sask. 181/C5
Sídheros (cape), Greece 45/H8
Sidhi, India 68/E4
Sidhirókastron, Greece 45/F5
Sidhpur, India 68/C4
Sidi Barrani, Egypt 111/E1
Sidi Barrani, Egypt 59/A3
Sidi Bel-Abbes, Algeria 106/D1
Sidi Bel-Abbes, Algeria 102/C1
Sidi Ifni, Morocco 106/B3
Sidi Ifni, Morocco 102/B2
Sidi Kacem, Morocco 106/C2
Siding Springs, N.S. Wales 97/E2
Sidlaw (hills), Scotland 15/F4
Sidley (mt.) 5/B12
Sidmouth, England 13/D7
Sidmouth, England 10/E5
Sidmouth (cape), Queensland 95/C2
Sidnaw, Mich. 250/G2
Sidney, Ark. 202/G1

Sidney, Br. Col. 184/K3
Sidney, Ill. 222/E3
Sidney, Ind. 227/F2
Sidney, Iowa 229/B7
Sidney•, Maine 243/D7
Sidney, Manitoba 179/C5
Sidney, Mich. 250/D5
Sidney, Mont. 262/M3
Sidney, N.Y. 276/K6
Sidney, Nebr. 264/B3
Sidney, N.Y. 276/K6
Sidney, Ohio 284/B5
Sidney Center, N.Y. 276/K6
Sidney Lanier (lake), Georgia 217/D2
Sidoharjo, Indonesia 85/K2
Sidon, Ark. 202/G3
Sidon (Saida), Lebanon 63/F6
Sidon, Miss. 256/D4
Sidonia, Tenn. 237/D8
Sidra (gulf) 102/D1
Sidra (gulf), Libya 111/C1
Siedlce (prov.), Poland 47/F2
Siedlce, Poland 47/F2
Siegas, New Bruns. 170/C1
Siegburg, Germany 22/B3
Siegen, Germany 22/C3
Siemianowice Śląskie, Poland 47/B4
Siemiatycze, Poland 47/F2
Siempang, Cambodia 72/E4
Siemreab, Cambodia 72/D4
Siena (prov.), Italy 34/C3
Siena, Italy 34/C3
Sienyang (Xianyang), China 77/G5
Sieper, La. 238/E4
Sieradz (prov.), Poland 47/D3
Sieradz, Poland 47/D3
Sierning, Austria 41/C2
Sierpc, Poland 47/D2
Sierra (co.), Calif. 204/E4
Sierra (co.), N. Mex. 274/B5
Sierra Ancha (mts.), Ariz. 198/D5
Sierra Apache (mts.), Ariz. 198/E5
Sierra Army Depot, Calif. 204/E3
Sierra Blanca (peak), N. Mex. 274/C5
Sierra Blanca, Texas 303/B11
Sierra City, Calif. 204/E4
Sierra Colorada, Argentina 143/C5
Sierra Diablo (mts.), Texas 303/C10
Sierra Gorda, Chile 138/B4
Sierra Grande, Argentina 143/C5
Sierra Leone 2/J5
Sierra Leone 102/A4
SIERRA LEONE 106/B7
Sierra Madre, Calif. 204/D10
Sierra Madre (mts.), Philippines 82/D2
Sierra Madre (mts.), Wyo. 319/E4
Sierra Madre Occidental (mts.), Mexico 146/H7
Sierra Madre Oriental (mts.), Mexico 146/H7
Sierra Mojada, Mexico 150/H3
Sierra Morena (mts.), Spain 7/D5
Sierra Nevada (mts.) 188/B3
Sierra Nevada (range), Calif. 146/F6
Sierra Nevada (mts.), Calif. 204/E4
Sierra Vieja (mts.), Texas 303/C11
Sierraville, Calif. 204/E4
Sierra Vista, Ariz. 198/E7
Sierre, Switzerland 39/D4
Siesta Key, Fla. 212/D4
Siete Cerros, Uruguay 145/E5
Sífnos (isl.), Greece 45/G7
Sifton, Manitoba 179/B3
Sigean, France 28/E6
Sigel, Ill. 222/E4
Sigel, Pa. 294/D3
Sighetu Marmaţiei, Romania 45/F2
Sighişoara, Romania 45/G2
Sigiriya, Sri Lanka 68/E7
Sigli, Indonesia 85/B4
Siglufjürdhur, Iceland 21/C1
Sigmaringen, Germany 22/C4
Sigmundsherberg, Austria 41/C2
Signal Hill, Calif. 204/C11
Signal Mountain, Tenn. 237/L10
Signau, Switzerland 39/E3
Signourney, Iowa 229/J4
Sigiswil, Switzerland 39/E3
Sigsig, Ecuador 128/C4
Sigtuna, Sweden 18/H1
Siguanea (bay), Cuba 158/B2
Siguatepeque, Honduras 154/D3
Sigüe, Ecuador 128/C2
Sigüenza, Spain 33/E2
Siguiri, Guinea 106/C6
Sigulda, U.S.S.R. 53/C2
Sigurd, Utah 304/B5
Sihlsee (lake), Switzerland 39/G2
Sihuas, Peru 128/D7
Siikajoki (riv.), Finland 18/O4
Siipyy (Sideby), Finland 18/M5
Siirt (prov.), Turkey 63/J4
Siirt, Turkey 63/J4
Siirt, Turkey 59/D2
Sikanni Chief (riv.), Br. Col. 184/F1
Sikar, India 68/D3
Sikasso, Mali 106/C6
Sikasso, Mali 102/B3
Sikes, La. 238/F2
Sikeston, Mo. 261/N9
Sikhote-Alin' (range), U.S.S.R. 54/P5
Sikhote-Alin' (range), U.S.S.R. 48/O5
Sikkim (state), India 68/F3
Siklós, Hungary 41/E4
Siktyakh, U.S.S.R. 48/N3
Sil (riv.), Spain 33/C1
Silao, Mexico 150/J6
Silas, Ala. 195/B7
Silat Dhahr, West Bank 65/C3
Silay, Philippines 82/D5
Silchar, India 68/G4
Šile, Turkey 63/C2
Silento, Tenn. 237/D10
Silent City, N.C. 281/L3
Silerton, Tenn. 237/D10
Silesia, Mont. 262/H5
Silet, Algeria 106/E4

Siletz, Oreg. 291/D3
Silex, Mo. 261/K4
Silhouette (isl.), Seychelles 118/H5
Silica, Kansas 232/D3
Silifke, Turkey 59/B2
Silifke, Turkey 63/D4
Siliguri, India 68/F3
Siling Co (lake), China 77/C5
Silinhot (Abnagar), China 77/J3
Silisili (riv.), W. Samoa 86/L8
Silistra, Bulgaria 45/H3
Silivri, Turkey 63/C3
Siljan (lake), Sweden 18/J6
Silkeborg, Denmark 21/C5
Silkeborg, Denmark 18/F8
Sillajguay, Cordillera (mt.), Chile 138/B2
Sillajhuay, Cordillera (mt.), Bolivia 136/A6
Sillamäe, U.S.S.R. 53/D1
Silleda, Spain 33/B1
Sillery, Québec 172/J3
Sillian, Austria 41/B3
Sillikers, New Bruns. 170/E2
Silloth, England 13/D3
Silo, Okla. 288/N6
Siloam, Georgia 217/F3
Siloam, Ky. 237/L3
Siloam, N.C. 281/H2
Siloam Springs, Ark. 202/B1
Siloam Springs, Mo. 261/H9
Silopi, Turkey 63/K4
Silsbee, Texas 303/K7
Silt, Colo. 208/D4
Siltcoos, Oreg. 291/C4
Silton, Sask. 181/H5
Silup (riv.), Iran 66/M8
Šilutè, U.S.S.R. 53/A3
Silva, Mo. 261/M8
Silva, N. Dak. 282/L3
Silvan, Turkey 63/J3
Silvana, Wash. 310/C2
Silvânia, Brazil 132/D7
Silvaplana, Switzerland 39/J4
Silvassa, India 68/C4
Silver (creek), Ariz. 198/E4
Silver (creek), Ill. 222/B2
Silver (creek), Ind. 227/E7
Silver, Manitoba 179/E4
Silver (lake), Mass. 249/L4
Silver, Newf. 166/A3
Silver (lake), N.Y. 276/N1
Silver (creek), Oreg. 291/H4
Silver (creek), Oreg. 291/H4
Silver (lake), Oreg. 291/G3
Silver (lake), Oreg. 291/H4
Silver (bank), Turks & Caicos 156/E2
Silver (lake), Wash. 310/C4
Silverado, Calif. 204/E11
Silver Bank (passage), Turks & Caicos 156/D2
Silver Bay, Minn. 255/G3
Silver Beach, Alberta 182/D3
Silver Bell, Ariz. 198/D6
Silver Bow (co.), Mont. 262/D5
Silver City, Georgia 217/D2
Silver City, Idaho 220/B6
Silver City, Iowa 229/B6
Silver City, Miss. 256/C4
Silver City, Nev. 266/B3
Silver City, N. Mex. 188/E4
Silver City, N. Mex. 274/A6
Silver City, S. Dak. 298/B5
Silver Cliff, Colo. 208/J6
Silver Creek, Georgia 217/B2
Silver Creek, Minn. 255/D5
Silver Creek, Miss. 256/D7
Silver Creek, Nebr. 264/G3
Silver Creek, N.Y. 276/B5
Silver Creek, Wash. 310/C4
Silverdale, Kansas 232/F3
Silverdale, N.C. 281/P5
Silverdale, Wash. 310/A2
Silver Dollar City, Mo. 261/F9
Silver Grove, Ky. 237/T2
Silverhill, Ala. 195/C9
Silverhill, N.J. 273/E3
Silver Hill, W. Va. 312/E3
Silver Hill-Suitland, Md. 245/F5
Silver Island (mts.), Utah 304/A3
Silver Lake, Ind. 227/F2
Silver Lake, Kansas 232/G2
Silver Lake, Mass. 249/C5
Silver Lake, Minn. 255/D6
Silver Lake, Mo. 261/M7
Silver Lake, N.H. 268/E4
Silver Lake, Oreg. 291/F4
Silverlake, Wash. 310/C4
Silver Lake, Wis. 317/K10
Silverleaf, N. Dak. 282/O7
Silvermine (riv.), Conn. 210/B4
Silvermine (mts.), Ireland 17/E6
Silver Park, Sask. 181/G3
Silver Peak, Nev. 266/D5
Silver Peak (range), Nev. 266/D5
Silver Plume, Colo. 208/G5
Silver Point, Tenn. 237/K8
Silver Run, Ala. 195/G3
Silver Run, Md. 245/K2
Silvers Mills, Maine 243/E5
Silver Spring, Md. 245/F4
Silver Springs, Fla. 212/D2
Silver Springs, N.Y. 276/E5
Silver Star, Mont. 262/D5
Silver Star Prov. Park, Br. Col. 184/H5
Silverstreet, S.C. 296/D3
Silverton, Br. Col. 184/J5
Silverton, Colo. 208/D7
Silverton, N.S. Wales 97/A2
Silverton, Ohio 284/C9
Silverton, Oreg. 291/B3
Silverton, Texas 303/C3
Silverton, Wash. 310/D2
Silverton, W. Va. 312/C5

Silverton Station, Manitoba 179/A4
Silver Valley, Alberta 182/A1
Silver Water, Ontario 177/B2
Silverwood, Ind. 227/C5
Silverwood, Mich. 250/F5
Silves, Portugal 33/B4
Silvia, Colombia 126/B6
Silvies, Oreg. 291/H3
Silvies (riv.), Oreg. 291/H4
Silvis, Ill. 222/C2
Silvretta (mts.), Switzerland 39/K3
Sim (cape), Morocco 106/B2
Simanggang, Malaysia 85/E5
Simao (Fusingchen), China 77/F7
Simara (isl.), Philippines 82/D4
Simaraña, Venezuela 124/G5
Simav, Turkey 63/C3
Simav (riv.), Turkey 63/C3
Simcoe, N. Dak. 282/J3
Simcoe (county), Ontario 177/E3
Simcoe, Ontario 177/D5
Simcoe (lake), Ontario 177/E3
Simen (mts.), Ethiopia 111/G5
Simeonovgrad (Maritsa), Bulgaria 45/H4
Simeto (riv.), Italy 34/E6
Simeulue (isl.), Indonesia 54/L9
Simeulue (isl.), Indonesia 85/A5
Simferopol', U.S.S.R. 7/H4
Simferopol', U.S.S.R. 52/D6
Simferopol', U.S.S.R. 48/D5
Símí, Greece 45/H7
Simi (isl.), Greece 45/H7
Simikot, Nepal 68/E3
Similkameen (riv.), Wash. 310/F1
Simití, Colombia 126/C4
Simi Valley, Calif. 204/G9
Simla, Colo. 208/M4
Simla, India 68/D2
Şimleul Silvaniei, Romania 45/F2
Simme (riv.), Switzerland 39/D3
Simmern, Germany 22/B4
Simmesport, La. 238/G5
Simmie, Sask. 181/C6
Simmons, Mo. 261/H8
Simms, Mont. 262/E3
Simnasho, Oreg. 291/F3
Simojärvi (lake), Finland 18/P3
Simojoki (riv.), Finland 18/O4
Simojovel de Allende, Mexico 150/N8
Simon (lake), Québec 172/B4
Simonds, New Bruns. 170/C2
Simonette (riv.), Alberta 182/A2
Simonstown, S. Africa 118/E7
Simonsville, Vt. 268/B5
Simontornya, Hungary 41/E3
Simoom Sound, Br. Col. 184/D5
Simpelveld, Netherlands 27/H7
Simplício Mendes, Brazil 132/F4
Simplon (tunnel), Italy 34/A1
Simplon, Switzerland 39/E4
Simplon (pass), Switzerland 39/F4
Simplon (tunnel), Switzerland 39/F4
Simpson (des.), Australia 87/D8
Simpson (riv.), Chile 138/E6
Simpson, Ill. 222/E6
Simpson, Kansas 232/E2
Simpson (co.), Ky. 237/H7
Simpson, Ky. 237/P5
Simpson, La. 238/D4
Simpson, Minn. 255/F7
Simpson (co.), Miss. 256/E7
Simpson, Mont. 262/F2
Simpson, N.C. 281/P3
Simpson (des.), North. Terr. 88/F4
Simpson (des.), North. Terr. 93/E8
Simpson (des.), N.W. Terr. 187/K3
Simpson, Pa. 294/L2
Simpson (des.), Queensland 95/A5
Simpson, Sask. 181/F4
Simpson (des.), S. Australia 94/E1
Simpson, W. Va. 312/F4
Simpson Park (mts.), Nev. 266/E3
Simpsons, Va. 307/H6
Simpsonville, Ky. 237/L4
Simpsonville, S.C. 296/C2
Simrishamn, Sweden 18/J9
Sims, Ark. 202/C4
Sims, Ill. 222/E5
Sims, Ind. 227/F3
Sims (lake), Newf. 166/A3
Sims, N.C. 281/N3
Simsboro, Ark. 202/K3
Simsboro, La. 238/E1
Simsbury, Conn. 210/D1
Simsbury•, Conn. 210/D1
Sims Chapel, Ala. 195/B8
Simunul (isl.), Philippines 82/B8
Sinabang, Indonesia 85/B5
Sinai (mt.), Egypt 111/F2
Sinai (pen.), Egypt 111/F2
Sinai (pen.), Egypt 59/B4
Sinai (mt.), Grenada 161/D8
Sinai, S. Dak. 298/P5
Sinaia, Romania 45/G3
Sinait, Philippines 82/C2
Sinajana, Guam 86/K7
Sinaloa (state), Mexico 150/F4
Sinaloa de Leyva, Mexico 150/E4
Sinamaica, Venezuela 124/D2
Sinawen, Libya 111/B1
Sincanlı, Turkey 63/C3
Sincé, Colombia 126/C3
Sincelejo, Colombia 126/C3
Sinch'ŏn, N. Korea 81/B4
Sinchu, China 77/K7
Sinclair (lake), Georgia 217/F4
Sinclair, Maine 243/G1
Sinclair (head), N. Zealand 100/A3
Sinclair, Wyo. 319/F4
Sinclair Mills, Br. Col. 184/G3
Sinclair's (bay), Scotland 15/E2
Sinclair Station, Manitoba 179/A5
Sinclairville, N.Y. 276/B6
Sindh (prov.), Pakistan 68/B3
Sindh (reg.), Pakistan 59/J4
Sindal, Denmark 21/D3

Sindangan, Philippines 82/D6
Sindangan (bay), Philippines 82/D6
Sindangbarang, Indonesia 85/D7
Sindelfingen, Germany 22/C4
Sindi, U.S.S.R. 53/C1
Sĭndĭrgĭ, Turkey 63/C3
Sines, Portugal 33/B4
Sines (cape), Portugal 33/B4
Sinewit (mt.), Papua N.G. 86/B2
Sinfra, Ivory Coast 106/C7
Singa, Sudan 111/F5
Singa, Sudan 102/F3
Singa, Sudan 59/B7
Singac, N.J. 273/B2
Singapore 2/Q5
Singapore 72
SINGAPORE 85/C5
Singapore (str.), Malaysia 72/F6
Singapore (cap.), Singapore 85/C6
Singapore (cap.), Singapore 72/F6
Singapore (str.), Singapore 72/F6
Singaraja, Indonesia 85/F7
Sing Buri, Thailand 72/D4
Singen, Germany 22/C5
Singer, La. 238/D5
Singers Glen, Va. 307/K3
Singhampton, Ontario 177/D3
Singida (reg.), Tanzania 115/F5
Singida, Tanzania 115/F4
Singida, Tanzania 102/F5
Singkaling Hkamti, Burma 72/B1
Singkang, Indonesia 85/F6
Singkawang, Indonesia 85/D5
Singkep (isl.), Indonesia 85/D6
Singleton, N.S. Wales 97/F3
Singleton (mt.), North. Terr. 93/B6
Singora (Songkhla), Thailand 72/D6
Singsås, Norway 18/G5
Singtai (Xingtai), China 77/H4
Singu, Burma 72/C2
Singur, India 68/F1
Sinhallen (Lianyungang), China 77/J5
Sining (Xining), China 77/F4
Siniscola, Italy 34/B4
Sinjai, Indonesia 85/G7
Sinjar, Iraq 66/B2
Sinjar, Jebel (mts.), Iraq 66/B2
Sinjar, Jebel (mts.), Syria 63/J4
Sinjil, West Bank 65/C3
Sinkat, Sudan 59/C6
Sinkat, Sudan 111/G4
Sinkiang (reg.), China 54/K5
Sinkiang (reg.), China 2/P3
Sinkiang-Uigur Aut. Reg. (Xinjiang Uygur), China 77/B3
Sinking Spring, Ohio 284/D7
Sinking Spring, Pa. 294/K5
Sinks Grove, W. Va. 312/F7
Sinlumkaba, Burma 72/C1
Sinnai, Italy 34/B6
Sinnamahoning, Pa. 294/G3
Sinnamary, Fr. Guiana 131/E3
Sinnamary (riv.), Fr. Guiana 131/E3
Sinneh (Sanandaj), Iran 66/E3
Sinnemahoning (creek), Pa. 294/F3
Sinnett, Sask. 181/G4
Sinnicolaul Mare, Romania 45/E2
Sinnûris, Egypt 111/J3
Sinoie, La. 238/G5
Sinop (prov.), Turkey 63/F2
Sinop, Turkey 59/C1
Sinop, Turkey 63/F2
Sinop (cape), Turkey 63/F1
Sinp'o, N. Korea 81/D4
Sins, Switzerland 39/F2
Sinsiang (Xinxiang), China 77/H4
Sintaluta, Sask. 181/H5
Sintang, Indonesia 85/E5
Sint Anna, Neth. Ant. 161/D10
Sint Anna (bay), Neth. Ant. 161/G9
Sint Annaland, Netherlands 27/E5
Sint Christoffel (mt.), Neth. Ant. 161/F8
Sint Jacobiparochie, Netherlands 27/H2
Sint Jan, Neth. Ant. 161/D8
Sint Joris (bay), Neth. Ant. 161/G9
Sint Kruis, Neth. Ant. 161/F8
Sint Maarten (Saint Martin) (isl.), Neth. Ant. 156/F3
Sint Martha, Neth. Ant. 161/F8
Sint Michiel, Neth. Ant. 161/F9
Sint Nicolaas, Neth. Ant. 161/E10
Sint-Niklaas, Belgium 27/E6
Sinton, Texas 303/G9
Sint-Pieters-Leeuw, Belgium 27/B9
Sintra, Portugal 33/B3
Sint-Truiden, Belgium 27/G7
Sint Willebrordus, Neth. Ant. 161/F8
Sinú (riv.), Colombia 126/B3
Sinuapa, Honduras 154/C3
Sinŭiju, N. Korea 81/B3
Sinyang (Xinyang), China 77/H5
Siocon, Philippines 82/D7
Siocon (Siokun), Philippines 85/G4
Sió csatorna (canal), Hungary 41/E3
Siófok, Hungary 41/E3
Sion, Switzerland 39/D4
Sion Mills, N. Ireland 17/G2
Sioux (co.), Iowa 229/A2
Sioux (co.), Nebr. 264/A2
Sioux (co.), N. Dak. 282/H7
Sioux Center, Iowa 229/A2
Sioux City, Iowa 146/J5
Sioux City, Iowa 229/A3
Sioux City, Iowa 188/G2
Sioux Falls, S. Dak. 188/G4
Sioux Falls, S. Dak. 146/J5
Sioux Falls, S. Dak. 298/R6
Sioux Lookout, Ont. 162/G5
Sioux Lookout, Ontario 175/G3
Sioux Lookout, Ontario 177/G4
Sioux Narrows, Ontario 177/F5
Sioux Rapids, Iowa 229/C3
Sioux Valley, Minn. 255/C7

Sipacate, Guatemala 154/B4
Sipalay, Philippines 82/D6
Sipaliwini (riv.), Suriname 131/C4
Sipapo (riv.), Venezuela 124/E5
Siparia, Trin. & Tob. 156/G5
Siparia, Trin. & Tob. 161/B11
Sipí, Colombia 126/B5
Siping (Szeping), China 77/K3
Sipiwesk (lake), Manitoba 179/J3
Siple (mt.), Ant. 5/B12
Sipocot, Philippines 82/D4
Sipsey, Ala. 195/D3
Sipsey (riv.), Ala. 195/B4
Sipsey Fork (riv.), Ala. 195/D2
Sip Song Chau Thai (mts.), Vietnam 72/D2
Sipura (isl.), Indonesia 85/B6
Siquijor (prov.), Philippines 82/D6
Siquijor, Philippines 82/D6
Siquijor (isl.), Philippines 82/D6
Siquirres, C. Rica 154/F5
Siquisique, Venezuela 124/D2
Siracusa (Syracuse), Italy 34/E6
Sirajganj, Bangladesh 68/F4
Siran, Turkey 63/H2
Sirdar, Br. Col. 184/J5
Sir Edward Pellew Group (isls.), North. Terr. 88/F3
Sir Edward Pellew Group (isls.), North. Terr. 93/E3
Siren, Wis. 317/B4
Siret (riv.) 7/G4
Siret, Romania 45/G1
Siret (riv.), Romania 45/H2
Sir Francis Drake (chan.), Virgin Is. (U.K.) 161/D4
Sirhan, Wadi (dry riv.), Saudi Arabia 59/C3
Sirik, Iran 66/K7
Sirik (cape), Malaysia 85/E5
Siris, West Bank 65/C3
Sirius (pt.), Alaska 196/J4
Sir James MacBrien (mt.), N.W. Terr. 187/F3
Sirjan (Sa'idabad), Iran 66/J6
Sirjan (Sa'idabad), Iran 59/G4
Sir John's (peak), Jamaica 158/K6
Sir Johns Run, W. Va. 312/K3
Sir Joseph Banks Group (isls.), S. Australia 94/E6
Sirnach, Switzerland 39/G2
Şirnak, Turkey 63/K4
Sirohi, India 68/C4
Sironj, India 68/D4
Síros (isl.), Greece 45/G7
Sirri (isl.), Iran 66/J8
Sirsa, India 68/D3
Sir Sandford (mt.), Br. Col. 184/H5
Sirsi, India 68/D6
Siruma, Philippines 82/D3
Şirvan, Turkey 63/K3
Širvintos, U.S.S.R. 53/C3
Sisak, Yugoslavia 45/C3
Sisaket, Thailand 72/E4
Sisal, Mexico 150/O6
Sishen, S. Africa 118/C5
Sisi (cape), Indonesia 85/F6
Sisib (lake), Manitoba 179/C2
Sisikon, Switzerland 39/G3
Sisimiut, Greenland 4/C12
Siskiwit (bay), Mich. 250/E1
Siskiyou (co.), Calif. 204/C2
Siskiyou (mts.), Calif. 204/C2
Siskiyou (mts.), Oreg. 291/D6
Sisophon, Cambodia 72/D4
Sissach, Switzerland 39/E2
Sisseton, S. Dak. 298/R2
Sissiboo (riv.), Nova Scotia 168/C4
Sisson Branch, Tobique (riv.), New Bruns. 170/C1
Sisson Ridge, New Bruns. 170/C2
Sissonville, W. Va. 312/C3
Sistan and Baluchestan (prov.), Iran 66/M6
Sister Bay, Wis. 317/M5
Sister Lakes, Mich. 250/C6
Sisteron, France 28/F5
Sisters, The (isls.), N. Zealand 100/D6
Sisters, Oreg. 291/F3
Sistersville, W. Va. 312/D3
Sitapur, India 68/E3
Siteki, Swaziland 118/E5
Sites, Calif. 204/C4
Sitges, Spain 33/G2
Sithoniá (pen.), Greece 45/F5
Sitía, Greece 45/H8
Sítio d'Abadia, Brazil 132/E6
Sitionuevo, Colombia 126/C2
Sitka, Alaska 146/E4
Sitka, Alaska 188/D6
Sitka, Alaska 196/M1
Sitka (sound), Alaska 196/M1
Sitka, Ark. 202/H1
Sitka, Kansas 232/C4
Sitka, U.S. 4/D16
Sitkalidak (isl.), Alaska 196/H3
Sitka Nat'l Hist. Park, Alaska 196/M1
Sitkinak (isl.), Alaska 196/H3
Sitkinak (str.), Alaska 196/H3
Sitkum, Oreg. 291/D4
Sittang (riv.), Burma 72/C3
Sittard, Netherlands 27/H6
Sittingbourne and Milton, England 13/H6
Sittwe, Burma 54/L7
Sittwe, Burma 72/B2
Situbondo, Indonesia 85/L2
Siuna, Nicaragua 154/E4
Siuslaw (riv.), Oreg. 291/D4
Sivand, Iran 66/H5
Sivas (prov.), Turkey 63/G3
Sivas, Turkey 54/E5
Sivas, Turkey 63/G3
Sivas, Turkey 59/C1
Sivaslı, Turkey 63/C3
Siverek, Turkey 63/H4

Siviriez, Switzer and 39/C3
Sivrihisar, Turkey 63/D3
Sivry-Rance, Belgium 27/E8
Siwa, Egypt 111/E2
Siwa, Egypt 102/E2
Siwa (oasis), Egypt 111/E2
Sixes, Oreg. 29?/C5
Sixes (riv.), Oreg. 291/C5
Six Flags Over Georgia, Georgia 217/J1
Six Flags Over Mid America, Mo. 261/M4
Six Lakes, Mich 250/D5
Six Mens, Barbados 161/B8
Six Mile, S.C. 296/B2
Sixmilebridge, Ireland 17/D6
Sixmilecross, N Ireland 17/G2
Six Mile Run, Pa. 294/F5
Six Roads, New Bruns. 170/F1
Six Run (creek), N.C. 281/N4
Sixteen, Mont. 262/F2
Sixteen Island Lake, Québec 172/C4
Sixth Cataract, Sudan 111/F4
Sixth Cataract (cam), Sudan 102/F3
Sixth Cataract, Sudan 59/B6
Siyah Kuh (mt.) Iraq 66/D2
Siyeh (mt.), Mont. 262/C2
Sizerock, Ky. 237/P6
Siziwang, China 77/H3
Sjaelland (isl.), Denmark 21/E6
Sjaelland (isl.), Denmark 18/H9
Sjaellands Odde (pen.), Denmark 21/E5
Sjenica, Yugoslavia 45/E4
Skadovsk, U.S.S.R. 52/D5
Skaelskør, Denmark 21/E7
Skaerbaek, Denmark 21/B7
Skagata (cape), Iceland 21/B1
Skagen, Denmark 21/D2
Skagen, Denmark 18/G8
Skagens Odde (cape), Denmark 21/D2
Skagens Odde (cape), Denmark 18/G8
Skagerrak (str.) 7/E3
Skagerrak (str.), Denmark 21/C2
Skagerrak (str.), Denmark 18/F8
Skagerrak (str.), Norway 18/F8
Skagerrak (str.), Sweden 18/F8
Skagit (riv.), Br. Col. 184/G6
Skagit (co.), Wash. 310/D2
Skagit (riv.), Wash. 310/C2
Skagway, Alaska 146/E4
Skagway, Alaska 196/M1
Skalica, Czech. 41/D2
Skals, Denmark 21/C4
Skamania (co.), Wash. 310/D5
Skamania, Wash. 310/C5
Skamokawa, Wash. 310/B4
Skanderborg, Denmark 21/D5
Skanderborg, Denmark 18/F8
Skaneateles, N.Y. 276/H5
Skaneateles (lake), N.Y. 276/H5
Skanee, Mich. 250/A2
Skåneviksjøen, Norway 18/E7
Skanür med Falsterbo, Sweden 18/H9
Skara, Sweden 13/H7
Skaraborg (co.), Sweden 18/H7
Skardu, Pakistan 68/D1
Skårup, Denmark 21/D7
Skarzysko-Kamienna, Poland 47/E3
Skateraw, Scotland 15/F3
Skaudvilė, U.S.S.R. 53/B3
Skaw, The (Skagens Odde) (cape), Denmark 18/G8
Skaw, The (Skagens Odde) (cape), Denmark 21/D2
Skawina, Poland 47/D4
Skedee, Okla. 283/N2
Skeena (mts.), B. Col. 184/C2
Skeena (riv.), Br. Col. 162/D5
Skeena (riv.), Br. Col. 184/C2
Skegness, England 13/H4
Skegness, England 10/G4
Skeleton (lake), Ontario 177/E2
Skeleton Coast (reg.), Namibia 118/A3
Skellefte (riv.), Sweden 7/F2
Skellefteå, Sweden 7/F2
Skellefteå, Sweden 18/M4
Skellefteälv (riv.) Sweden 18/L4
Skellytown, Texas 303/C2
Skelmersdale, England 10/F2
Skelmersdale, England 13/F4
Skelmorlie, Scotland 15/A2
Skelton, Ind. 227/B8
Skelton and Brotton, England 13/G3
Skene, Miss. 256/C3
Skerries, Ireland 17/J4
Skerries, Ireland 10/D4
Skerries, The (isls.), Wales 13/C4
Ski, Norway 18/C4
Skíathos, Greece 45/F6
Skiatook, Okla. 248/O2
Skibbereen, Ireland 10/B5
Skibbereen, Ireland 17/C8
Skibby, Denmark 21/E6
Skidaway (isl.), Georgia 217/L7
Skiddaw (mt.), England 13/D3
Skiddy, Kansas 232/F3
Skidegate, Br. Col. 184/B3
Skidegate (inlet), Br. Col. 184/B3
Skidmore, Mo. 261/A0
Skidmore, Texas 303/G9
Skien, Norway 7/E3
Skien, Norway 18/F7
Skierniewice (prov.), Poland 47/E3
Skierniewice, Poland 47/E2
Skiff, Alberta 182/E5
Skiff (lake), New Bruns. 170/C3
Skikda, Algeria 112/C1
Skikda, Algeria 106/F1
Skilak (lake), Alaska 196/C1
Skillet Fork (riv.), Ill. 222/E5
Skillman, N.J. 273/D3
Skinners Eddy, Pa. 294/K2
Skipness, Scotland 15/C5
Skippack, Pa. 294/M5
Skippers, Va. 307/O7
Skipperville, Ala. 95/G7

Skipsea, England 13/G4
Skipton, England 13/H1
Skipton, England 13/G4
Skipwith, Va. 307/L7
Skir Dhu, Nova Scotia 168/H2
Skíros, Greece 45/G6
Skíros (isl.), Greece 45/G6
Skive, Denmark 18/F8
Skive, Denmark 21/B4
Skive (riv.), Denmark 21/C5
Skjåk, Norway 18/F6
Skjalfandafljót (stream), Iceland 21/C1
Skjern, Denmark 21/B6
Skodborg, Denmark 21/C7
Škofja Loka, Yugoslavia 45/A2
Skokie, Ill. 222/B5
Skokomish (mt.), Wash. 310/B3
Skokomish Ind. Res., Wash. 310/B3
Skomer (isl.), Wales 13/B6
Skookumchuck, Br. Col. 184/K5
Skootamatla (lake), Ontario 177/H3
Skópelos, Greece 45/F6
Skopin, U.S.S.R. 52/F4
Skopje, Yugoslavia 7/G4
Skopje, Yugoslavia 45/E5
Skørping, Denmark 21/C4
Skúvde, Sweden 18/H7
Skovorodino, U.S.S.R. 54/O4
Skovorodino, U.S.S.R. 48/N4
Skowhegan, Maine 243/D6
Skowhegan•, Maine 243/D6
Skownan, Manitoba 179/C3
Skradin, Yugoslavia 45/B4
Skreia, Norway 18/D7
Skudeneshavn, Norway 18/D7
Skull Valley, Ariz. 198/C4
Skull Valley Ind. Res., Utah 304/B3
Skuna (riv.), Miss. 256/F2
Skungamaug (riv.), Conn. 210/F1
Skunk (riv.), Iowa 229/K6
Skuteč, Czech. 41/D2
Skutskär, Sweden 18/K6
Skwentna, Alaska 196/B1
Skwentna (riv.), Alaska 196/A1
Skwierzyna, Poland 47/B2
Skye, Isle of (isl.), Scotland 15/B3
Skye (isl.), Scotland 10/C2
Skykomish, Wash. 310/D3
Skykomish (riv.), Wash. 310/D3
Skyland, N.C. 281/R4
Skylight (mt.), N.Y. 276/M2
Skyline Valley, Ky. 237/N7
Skyline, Minn. 255/D6
Skyring (bay), Chile 138/E10
Skytop, Pa. 294/M3
Sky Valley, Georgia 217/F1
Slab Fork, W. Va. 312/D7
Slade, Ky. 237/O5
Sládečkovce, Czech. 41/D2
Slag (bay), Neth. Ant. 161/D8
Slagelse, Denmark 21/E7
Slagelse, Denmark 18/G9
Slagle, La. 238/D4
Sľakow, Poland 47/B4
Slamannan, Scotland 15/C2
Slamet (mt.), Indonesia 85/J2
Slana, Alaska 196/K2
Slaná (riv.), Czech. 41/F2
Slane, Ireland 17/H4
Slanesville, W. Va. 312/K4
Slaney (riv.), Ireland 17/H7
Slangerup, Denmark 21/E6
Slangkop (pt.), S. Africa 118/E7
Slănic, Romania 45/G3
Slantsy, U.S.S.R. 52/C3
Slaný, Czech. 41/C1
Slate (mt.), Ariz. 198/D3
Slate (riv.), Colo. 208/E5
Slate (creek), Idaho 220/B4
Slate (isls.), Ontario 175/C3
Slate (riv.), Va. 307/L5
Slate, W. Va. 312/D4
Slate (creek), Wyo. 319/C3
Slatedale, Pa. 294/L4
Slater, Colo. 208/E1
Slater, Iowa 229/F5
Slater, Mo. 261/G4
Slater, Wyo. 319/H4
Slater-Marietta, S.C. 296/C4
Slatersville, R.I. 249/H4
Slate Run, Pa. 294/H3
Slaterville Springs, N.Y. 276/H6
Slate Spring, Miss. 256/F3
Slatina, Romania 45/G3
Slatington, Pa. 294/L4
Slaton, Texas 303/C4
Slaughter, La. 238/H5
Slaughter Beach, Del. 245/S5
Slaughters, Ky. 237/F6
Slaughterville, Okla. 288/M4
Slave (riv.) 162/E3
Slave (riv.), Alberta 182/C5
Slave (riv.), Canada 146/G3
Slave (riv.), N.W. Terr. 187/G3
Slave Coast (reg.), Benin 106/E7
Slave Coast (reg.), Nigeria 106/E7
Slave Coast (reg.), Togo 106/E7
Slave Lake, Alberta 182/C2
Slavgorod, U.S.S.R. 48/H4
Slavkov, Czech. 41/D2
Slavonia (reg.), Yugoslavia 45/C3
Slavonska Požega, Yugoslavia 45/C3
Slavonski Brod, Yugoslavia 45/D3
Slavuta, U.S.S.R. 52/C4
Slavyansk, U.S.S.R. 52/E5
Slavyansk-na-Kubani, U.S.S.R. 52/E5
Sľawno, Poland 47/C1
Slayden, Miss. 256/F1
Slayden, Tenn. 237/G8
Slayton, Minn. 255/C7
Sleaford, England 13/G5
Sleaford, England 10/G3
Sleat (dist.), Scotland 15/B3
Sleat (pt.), Scotland 15/B4
Sleat (sound), Scotland 15/C3
Sledge, Miss. 256/D2
Sleeper, Mo. 261/G7

Sleeping Bear Dunes Nat'l Lakeshore, Mich. 250/C4
Sleeping Deer (mt.), Idaho 220/D5
Sleepy Creek, W. Va. 312/K3
Sleepy Eye, Minn. 255/D6
Sleepy Eye (creek), Minn. 255/C6
Sleepy Hollow, Ill. 222/E1
Sleetmute, Alaska 196/G2
Sleeve (lake), Manitoba 179/E3
Slemish (mt.), N. Ireland 17/J2
Slemon (lake), Manitoba 179/G1
Slemp, Ky. 237/P6
Slick, Okla. 288/P3
Slickford, Ky. 237/M7
Slickville, Pa. 294/C5
Slidell, La. 238/L6
Slide (mt.), N.Y. 276/L6
Sliedrecht, Netherlands 27/F5
Sliema, Malta 34/F7
Slieve Anierin (mt.), Ireland 17/F3
Slieve Aughty (mts.), Ireland 17/D5
Slieve Beagh (mt.), N. Ireland 17/G3
Slieve Bernagh (mt.), Ireland 17/D6
Slieve Bloom (mts.), Ireland 17/F5
Slieve Callan (mt.), Ireland 17/C6
Slieve Car (mt.), Ireland 17/B3
Slieve Donard (mt.), Ireland 17/J3
Slieve Donard (mt.), N. Ireland 17/K3
Slieve Elva (mt.), Ireland 17/C5
Slievefelim (mts.), Ireland 17/E6
Slieve Gamph (mts.), Ireland 17/D3
Slieve Gullion (mt.), N. Ireland 17/J3
Slieve League (mt.), Ireland 17/D2
Slieve Mishkish (mts.), Ireland 17/B8
Slievenamon (mt.), Ireland 17/F7
Sligo (co.), Ireland 17/E3
Sligo, Ireland 17/E3
Sligo, Ireland 10/B3
Sligo (bay), Ireland 17/E3
Sligo (bay), Ireland 17/D3
Sligo, La. 238/C2
Sligo, Pa. 294/C3
Slinger, Wis. 317/K9
Slipper (isl.), N. Zealand 100/F2
Slippery Rock, Pa. 294/B3
Slite, Sweden 18/L8
Sliven, Bulgaria 45/H4
Sliven, Bulgaria 7/G4
Sloan, Iowa 229/A4
Sloan, Nev. 266/F7
Sloan, N.Y. 276/C5
Sloans Valley, Ky. 237/N7
Sloat, Calif. 204/E4
Sloatsburg, N.Y. 276/M8
Slobodskoy, U.S.S.R. 48/E4
Slobodskoy, U.S.S.R. 52/H3
Slobozia, Romania 45/H3
Slocan, Br. Col. 184/J5
Slocan (lake), Br. Col. 184/J5
Slocan Park, Br. Col. 184/J5
Slocomb, Ala. 195/G8
Slocum, R.I. 249/H6
Slocum, Texas 303/J6
Slonim, U.S.S.R. 52/B4
Slope (co.), N. Dak. 282/C7
Slot, The (chan.), Solomon Is. 86/D3
Sloten, Friesland, Netherlands 27/H3
Sloten, North Holland, Netherlands 27/B5
Sloterdijk, Netherlands 27/B4
Slotermeer (lake), Netherlands 27/H3
Slough, England 13/G8
Sloughhouse, Calif. 204/C8
Slovak Rep., Czech. 41/E2
Slovenia (rep.), Yugoslavia 45/B2
Slovenské Rudohorie (mts.), Czech. 41/E2
Sľubice, Poland 47/B2
Sluis, Netherlands 27/C6
Sľupca, Poland 47/D2
Sľupia (riv.), Poland 47/C1
Sľupsk (prov.), Poland 47/C1
Sľupsk, Poland 47/C1
Sľupsk, Poland 7/F3
Slutsk, U.S.S.R. 52/B4
Slyne (head), Ireland 10/A4
Slyne (head), Ireland 17/A5
Slyudyanka, U.S.S.R. 48/L4
Smackover, Ark. 202/E7
Smale, Ark. 202/H1
Small, Idaho 220/F5
Small (cape), Maine 243/D8
Small Isles (isls.), Scotland 15/B4
Small Point, Maine 243/D8
Smallwood (res.), Newf. 166/B3
Smallwood (res.), Newf. 146/M5
Smallwood (res.), Newf. 162/K5
Smarr, Georgia 217/E5
Smarts (mt.), N.H. 268/C4
Smartt, Tenn. 237/K9
Smartville, Calif. 204/D4
Smeaton, Sask. 181/G2
Smederevo, Yugoslavia 45/E3
Smederevska Palanka, Yugoslavia 45/E3
Smedjebacken, Sweden 18/J6
Smela, U.S.S.R. 52/D5
Smelterville, Idaho 220/B2
Smerwick (harb.), Ireland 17/A7
Smethport, Pa. 294/F2
Smicksburg, Pa. 294/D4
Smilax, Ky. 237/P6
Smilde, Netherlands 27/K3
Smiley, Sask. 181/B4
Smiley, Texas 303/G8
Smiltene, U.S.S.R. 53/C2
Smith (bay), Alaska 196/H1
Smith, Alberta 182/D2
Smith (riv.), Calif. 204/A2
Smith (creek), Idaho 220/A1
Smith (co.), Kansas 232/D2
Smith (isl.), Md. 245/O8
Smith (co.), Miss. 256/E6
Smith (mt.), Mont. 262/E3
Smith, Nev. 266/E4
Smith (sound), Newf. 166/D2

Smith (isl.), N.C. 281/O7
Smith (basin), N.W.T. 162/N3
Smith (bay), N.W.T. 162/H3
Smith (cape), N.W.T. 162/H3
Smith (cape), N.W.T. 187/L2
Smith (cape), N.W.T. 187/L3
Smith (sound), N.W.T. 187/L3
Smith (riv.), Oreg. 291/C3
Smith (co.), Tenn. 237/J8
Smith (co.), Texas 303/J5
Smith (isl.), Va. 307/S6
Smith (riv.), Va. 307/J7
Smith Arm (inlet), N.W. Terr. 187/F3
Smithboro, Ill. 222/D5
Smithburg, N.J. 273/E3
Smithburg, W. Va. 312/E4
Smith Center, Kansas 232/D2
Smith Creek, W. Va. 312/H3
Smithdale, Miss. 256/C8
Smithers, Br. Col. 146/F4
Smithers, Br. Col. 162/D5
Smithers, Br. Col. 184/D3
Smithers, W. Va. 312/D6
Smithfield, Ill. 222/C3
Smithfield, Ky. 237/L4
Smithfield•, Maine 243/D6
Smithfield, Nebr. 264/E4
Smithfield, N.C. 281/N3
Smithfield, Ohio 284/J5
Smithfield, Ontario 177/H4
Smithfield, Pa. 294/C6
Smithfield, Texas 303/F2
Smithfield, Utah 304/C2
Smithfield, Va. 307/P7
Smithfield, W. Va. 312/E4
Smith Hill, Manitoba 179/C5
Smithland, Iowa 229/B4
Smithland, Ky. 237/E6
Smithmill, Pa. 294/F4
Smith Mills, Ky. 237/E6
Smith Mountain (lake), Va. 307/J6
Smithonia, Georgia 217/F2
Smithport (lake), La. 238/C2
Smith River, Calif. 204/A2
Smiths, Ala. 195/H5
Smithsburg, Md. 245/H2
Smiths Cove, Nova Scotia 168/C4
Smiths Creek, Mich. 250/G6
Smiths Creek, New Bruns. 170/G4
Smiths Falls, Ontario 177/H3
Smiths Ferry, Idaho 220/C5
Smiths Fork (riv.), Wyo. 319/B3
Smiths Grove, Ky. 237/J6
Smithshire, Ill. 222/C3
Smiths Station, Miss. 256/C6
Smithton, Ark. 202/D6
Smithton, Ill. 222/C5
Smithton, Mo. 261/F5
Smithton, Pa. 294/C5
Smithton, Tasmania 99/D5
Smithton, Tasmania 88/H8
Smith Town, Ky. 237/M7
Smithtown, N.H. 268/F6
Smithtown, N.Y. 276/O9
Smithtown-Gladstone, N.S. Wales 97/G2
Smith Valley, Ind. 227/E5
Smithville, Ark. 202/H1
Smithville, Georgia 217/D7
Smithville, Ind. 227/D6
Smithville, Miss. 256/H2
Smithville, Mo. 261/D4
Smithville, N.J. 273/D4
Smithville, N.J. 273/E5
Smithville, Ohio 284/G4
Smithville, Okla. 288/S6
Smithville, Ontario 177/E4
Smithville, Tenn. 237/K9
Smithville, Texas 303/G7
Smithville, W. Va. 312/D4
Smithville Flats, N.Y. 276/J6
Smithwick, S. Dak. 298/C7
Smoaks, S.C. 296/F5
Smoke Bend, La. 238/K3
Smoke Creek (des.), Nev. 266/B2
Smoke Hole, W. Va. 312/H5
Smokey Burn, Sask. 181/H2
Smoky (riv.), Alberta 182/A2
Smoky (riv.), Alta. 162/E5
Smoky (mts.), Idaho 220/D5
Smoky (cape), N.S. Wales 97/G2
Smoky (lake), N. Dak. 282/E3
Smoky (cape), Nova Scotia 168/H2
Smoky Bay, S. Australia 88/E6
Smoky Bay, S. Australia 94/C3
Smoky Hill (riv.) 188/G3
Smoky Hill (riv.), Colo. 208/P5
Smoky Hill, North Fork (riv.), Kansas 232/A2
Smoky Hill (riv.), Kansas 232/C3
Smoky Junction, Tenn. 237/N8
Smoky Lake, Alberta 182/D2
Smøla (isl.), Norway 18/E5
Smolan, Kansas 232/E3
Smolensk, U.S.S.R. 7/H3
Smolensk, U.S.S.R. 48/D4
Smolensk, U.S.S.R. 52/D3
Smolyan, Bulgaria 45/G5
Smoot, W. Va. 312/E7
Smoot, Wyo. 319/B2
Smooth Rock Falls, Ontario 177/D3
Smooth Rock Falls, Ontario 175/D3
Smugglers Notch (pass), Vt. 268/B2
Smuts, Sask. 181/F3
Smyadovo, Bulgaria 45/H4
Smyer, Ala. 195/B7
Smyrna, Del. 245/R3
Smyrna (res.), Del. 245/R3
Smyrna, Georgia 217/K1
Smyrna, Mich. 250/D5
Smyrna, N.Y. 276/J5
Smyrna, N.C. 281/R5
Smyrna, S.C. 296/E2
Smyrna, Tenn. 237/H9
Smyrna (Izmir), Turkey 63/B3

Smyrna, Wash. 310/F4
Smyrna Mills, Maine 243/G3
Smyrna Mills•, Maine 243/G3
Smyth (co.), Va. 307/E7
Snaefell (mts.), I. of Man 13/C3
Snaefell (mt.), I. of Man 10/D3
Snake (riv.) 188/C1
Snake (riv.), Idaho 220/A3
Snake (riv.), Minn. 255/A2
Snake (riv.), Minn. 255/E4
Snake (riv.), Nebr. 264/C2
Snake (mts.), Nev. 266/F1
Snake (range), Nev. 266/G3
Snake (riv.), Oreg. 291/K3
Snake (isl.), Victoria 97/D6
Snake (riv.), Wash. 310/G4
Snake (riv.), Wyo. 319/B2
Snake Creek (canal), Fla. 212/B4
Snake Indian (riv.), Alberta 182/A3
Snake River (plain), Idaho 220/G6
Snake River (range), Idaho 220/G6
Snake River, Wash. 310/G4
Snare (riv.), N.W. Terr. 187/G3
Snare Lake, N.W. Terr. 187/G3
Snares, The (isls.), N. Zealand 100/A7
Snåsa, Norway 18/H4
Snåsavatn (lake), Norway 18/H4
Snead, Ala. 195/F2
Sneads, Fla. 212/B4
Sneads Ferry, N.C. 281/P5
Snedsted, Denmark 21/B4
Sneedville, Tenn. 237/P7
Sneek, Netherlands 27/H2
Sneekermeer (lake), Netherlands 27/H2
Sneem, Ireland 17/B8
Sneeuwkop (mt.), S. Africa 118/F6
Sneffels (mt.), Colo. 208/D7
Snegamook (lake), Newf. 166/B3
Snell, Va. 307/N4
Snelling, Calif. 204/E6
Snelling, S.C. 296/E5
Snellville, Georgia 217/D3
Snezhnogorsk, U.S.S.R. 48/J3
Śniardwy, Jezioro (lake), Poland 47/E2
Sniečkus, U.S.S.R. 53/D3
Snina, Czech. 41/G2
Snipe (lake), Alberta 182/B2
Snipe Lake, Sask. 181/B4
Snizort, Loch (inlet), Scotland 15/B3
Snohomish (co.), Wash. 310/D2
Snohomish, Wash. 310/D3
Snohomish (riv.), Wash. 310/D3
Snoqualmie, Wash. 310/D3
Snoqualmie (pass), Wash. 310/D3
Snoqualmie (riv.), Wash. 310/D3
Snoqualmie Falls, Wash. 310/D3
Snover, Mich. 250/G5
Snow, Okla. 288/R6
Snow (mt.), Vt. 268/B6
Snow (peak), Wash. 310/G2
Snowball, Ark. 202/G2
Snowbird (lake), N.W. Terr. 187/H3
Snow Camp, N.C. 281/L3
Snowden, Sask. 181/H2
Snowdon (mt.), Wales 13/D4
Snowdon (mt.), Wales 10/D4
Snowdonia Nat'l Park, Wales 13/D4
Snowdoun, Ala. 195/F6
Snowdrift, N.W.T. 162/E3
Snowfield (peak), Wash. 310/D2
Snowflake, Ariz. 198/E4
Snowflake, Manitoba 179/D5
Snow Hill, Ala. 195/E7
Snow Hill, Ark. 202/E7
Snow Hill, Md. 245/S8
Snow Hill, N.C. 281/O4
Snow Lake, Ark. 202/H5
Snow Lake, Man. 162/G5
Snow Lake, Manitoba 179/H3
Snowmass, Colo. 208/E4
Snowshoe (lake), Manitoba 179/G4
Snow Shoe, Pa. 294/G3
Snowtown, S. Australia 94/E5
Snowville, N.H. 268/E4
Snowville, Utah 304/B2
Snow Water (lake), Nev. 266/G2
Snowy (mts.), N.S. Wales 97/E5
Snowy (riv.), N.S. Wales 97/E5
Snowy (riv.), Victoria 88/H7
Snug, Tasmania 99/D5
Snyder, Ark. 202/C7
Snyder, Colo. 208/M2
Snyder, Mo. 261/B4
Snyder, Nebr. 264/H3
Snyder, Okla. 288/J5
Snyder (co.), Pa. 294/H4
Snyder, Texas 303/D5
Snydertown, Pa. 294/J4
So (isl.), S. Korea 81/C6
Soalala, Madagascar 118/H3
Soalara, Madagascar 118/G4
Soanierana-Ivongo, Madagascar 118/H3
Soap (lake), Wash. 310/F3
Soap Lake, Wash. 310/F3
Soasiu, Indonesia 85/H5
Soatá, Colombia 126/D4
Soay (isl.), Scotland 15/A2
Soay (isl.), Scotland 15/B3
Sobat (riv.), Sudan 111/F6
Sobeslav, Czech. 41/C2
Soběslav, Czech. 41/C2
Sobieski, Minn. 255/D5
Sobieski, Wis. 317/L6
Sobotka, Czech. 41/C1
Sobradinho (res.), Brazil 120/E3
Sobradinho (res.), Brazil 132/F5
Sobradinho, Brazil 120/E3
Sobral, Brazil 132/G3

Sobrance, Czech. 41/G2
Soca, Uruguay 145/C6
Sochaczew, Poland 47/E2
Soche (Shache), China 77/A4
Sochi, U.S.S.R. 7/H4
Sochi, U.S.S.R. 48/D5
Sochi, U.S.S.R. 52/E6
Social Circle, Georgia 217/E3
Society (isls.), Fr. Poly. 87/L7
Society Hill, Ala. 195/H6
Society Hill, S.C. 296/H2
Socompa (vol.), Chile 138/B4
Socorro, Brazil 135/C3
Socorro, Colombia 126/D4
Socorro (isl.), Mexico 150/C5
Socorro, N. Mex. 188/E4
Socorro (co.), N. Mex. 274/C5
Socorro, N. Mex. 274/E4
Socotra (isl.), Yemen 54/G8
Socotra (isl.), Yemen 2/M5
Socotra (isl.), Yemen 59/F7
Socuéllamos, Spain 33/E3
Soda (lake), Calif. 204/K8
Soda (plains), India 68/D1
Soda Creek, Br. Col. 184/F4
Sodankylä, Finland 18/P3
Soda Plains, Pakistan 68/D1
Soda Springs, Calif. 204/E4
Soda Springs, Idaho 220/G7
Sodaville, Oreg. 291/E3
Soddu, Ethiopia 111/G6
Soddy-Daisy, Tenn. 237/L10
Süderhamn, Sweden 18/K6
Süderküping, Sweden 18/K7
Südermanland (co.), Sweden 18/K7
Südertälje, Sweden 18/G1
Sodiri, Sudan 111/E5
Sodus, Mich. 250/C6
Sodus, N.Y. 276/G4
Sodus Point, N.Y. 276/G4
Soe, Indonesia 85/G7
Soest, Netherlands 27/G4
Soest, Germany 22/C3
Soesterberg, Netherlands 27/G4
Soeurs (isl.), Québec 172/H4
Sofala (prov.), Mozambique 118/E3
Sofia (cap.), Bulgaria 7/G4
Sofia (cap.), Bulgaria 45/F4
Sofia (riv.), Madagascar 118/H3
Sofkee, Georgia 217/G5
Soft Shell, Ky. 237/P6
Sogamoso, Colombia 126/D5
Sogamoso (riv.), Colombia 126/D4
Soğanli (mts.), Turkey 63/H2
Soğanli (riv.), Turkey 63/F2
Sognafjorden (fjord), Norway 18/D6
Sognefjorden (fjord), Norway 7/E2
Sogn og Fjordane (co.), Norway 18/E6
Sogod, Philippines 82/E5
Sogod (bay), Philippines 82/E5
Sogüt, Turkey 63/D3
Süğüt, Turkey 63/D4
Sog (lake), Turkey 63/D4
Sog Xian, China 77/D5
Soh, Iran 66/G4
Sohâg, Egypt 111/F2
Sohâg, Egypt 59/B4
Sohâg, Egypt 102/F2
Soham, N. Mex. 274/D3
Sohar, Oman 59/G5
Söhüng, N. Korea 81/C4
Soignies, Belgium 27/D5
Sointula, Br. Col. 184/D5
Soissons, France 28/E3
Soka, Japan 81/O2
Sokch'o, S. Korea 81/D4
Süke, Turkey 63/B4
Süke, Turkey 59/A2
Sokna, Libya 111/C2
Sokodé, Togo 106/E7
Sokol, U.S.S.R. 52/F3
Sokol, U.S.S.R. 48/E4
Sokólka, Poland 47/F2
Sokolo, Mali 106/C6
Sokolov, Czech. 41/B1
Sokoló w Podlaski, Poland 47/F2
Sokota, Ethiopia 111/G5
Sokoto (state), Nigeria 106/F6
Sokoto, Nigeria 102/C3
Sokoto, Nigeria 106/F6
Sokoto (riv.), Nigeria 106/F6
Sola, Cuba 158/G2
Solana Beach, Calif. 204/H11
Solander (isl.), N. Zealand 100/A7
Solano (co.), Calif. 204/D5
Solano (pt.), Colombia 126/B4
Solano, N. Mex. 274/E2
Solano, Philippines 82/C2
Solano, Venezuela 124/G6
Solbad Hall in Tirol, Austria 41/A3
Solca, Romania 45/G2
Soldado (pt.), P. Rico 161/G2
Soldier, Iowa 229/B5
Soldier, Kansas 232/G2
Soldier, Ky. 237/P4
Soldier Pond, Maine 243/F1
Soldiers Cove, Nova Scotia 168/H3
Soldiers Grove, Wis. 317/F4
Soldier Summit, Utah 304/C4
Soldotna, Alaska 196/J1
Soledad, Argentina 143/F5
Soledad, Calif. 204/D7
Soledad, Colombia 126/C2
Soledad, Venezuela 124/G4
Soledad de Doblado, Mexico 150/Q2
Soledad Díez Gutiérrez, Mexico 150/J5
Soleduck (riv.), Wash. 310/A3
Solen, N. Dak. 282/J7
Solent (chan.), England 13/F5
Solentiname (isls.), Nicaragua 154/E5
Soleure (Solothurn) (canton), Switzerland 39/E2
Solgohachia, Ark. 202/E3
Solhan, Turkey 63/J3
Soligalich, U.S.S.R. 52/F3
Soligorsk, U.S.S.R. 52/C4
Solihull, England 13/F5
Solihull, England 10/G3

Solikamsk, U.S.S.R. 7/K3
Solikamsk, U.S.S.R. 48/F3
Solikamsk, U.S.S.R. 52/J3
Sol'-Iletsk, U.S.S.R. 52/J4
Solingen, Germany 22/B3
Solís, Uruguay 145/D5
Solis de Mataojo, Uruguay 145/D5
Solitary (isl.), N.S. Wales 97/G1
Sollefteå, Sweden 18/K5
Sollentuna, Sweden 18/H1
Sóller, Spain 33/H3
Søllested, Denmark 21/E8
Solna, Sweden 18/H1
Solo (Surakarta), Indonesia 85/J2
Solo, Mo. 261/J8
Sologne (reg.), France 28/E4
Solok, Indonesia 85/C6
Sololá, Guatemala 154/B3
Solomon (sea) 87/F6
Solomon, Alaska 196/F2
Solomon, Ariz. 198/F6
Solomon, Kansas 232/E3
Solomon (riv.), Kansas 232/E2
Solomon (isls.), Pacific 87/F6
Solomon (isls.), Papua N.G. 86/C3
Solomon (sea), Papua N.G. 85/C7
Solomon (isls.), Solomon Is. 86/C3
Solomon (sea), Solomon Is. 86/D3
Solomon Islands 2/T6
SOLOMON ISLANDS 86/D2
Solomon Islands 87/G6
Solomons, Md. 245/N7
Solon, China 77/K2
Solon, Ind. 227/F7
Solon, Iowa 229/L5
Solon•, Maine 243/D6
Solon, Ohio 284/J9
Solon Springs, Wis. 317/C3
Solor (isl.), Indonesia 85/G7
Solothurn (elec. div.), Switzerland 39/E2
Solothurn (Soleure), Switzerland 39/E2
Solovetskiye (isls.), U.S.S.R. 52/E1
Solsberry, Ind. 227/D6
Solsgirth, Manitoba 179/B4
Solsona, Spain 33/G2
Solsona, Spain 33/G2
Solt, Hungary 41/E3
Šolta (isl.), Yugoslavia 45/C4
Soltau, Germany 22/C2
Soltvadkert, Hungary 41/E3
Soluk, Libya 111/D1
Solund, Norway 18/D6
Solvang, Calif. 204/E9
Solvay, N.Y. 276/H4
Sülvesborg, Sweden 18/J9
Solway (firth), England 13/D3
Solway, Minn. 255/C3
Solway (firth), Scotland 10/D3
Solway (firth), Scotland 15/E6
Solwezi, Zambia 115/E6
Soma, Japan 81/K5
Soma, Turkey 63/B3
Somabhula, Zimbabwe 118/D3
Somalia 2/M5
Somalia 102/E2
SOMALIA 115/J2
Sombor, Yugoslavia 45/D3
Sombra, Ontario 177/B5
Sombrerete, Mexico 150/H5
Sombrero (chan.), India 68/G7
Sombrero (isl.), St. Kitts & Nevis 156/F3
Somerdale, N.J. 273/B4
Somers, Conn. 210/F1
Somers•, Conn. 210/F1
Somers, Iowa 229/E4
Somers, Mont. 262/B2
Somers, Wis. 317/M3
Somerset, Va. 307/M4
Somerset (isl.), Bermuda 156/G3
Somerset (isl.), Canada 4/B14
Somerset, Colo. 208/E5
Somerset (co.), England 13/E6
Somerset, Ind. 227/F3
Somerset, Ky. 237/M6
Somerset, La. 238/H2
Somerset (co.), Maine 243/C4
Somerset, Manitoba 179/D5
Somerset (co.), Md. 245/R8
Somerset, Md. 245/E4
Somerset•, Mass. 249/K5
Somerset (co.), N.J. 273/D2
Somerset, N.Y. 276/G4
Somerset (isl.), N.W.T. 146/J2
Somerset (isl.), N.W.T. 162/G1
Somerset (isl.), N.W.T. 187/J2
Somerset, Nova Scotia 168/D3
Somerset, Ohio 284/F6
Somerset (co.), Pa. 294/D6
Somerset, Pa. 294/D6
Somerset, Texas 303/J11
Somerset (res.), Vt. 268/A5
Somerset, Wis. 317/A5
Somerset East, S. Africa 118/D6
Somerset West, S. Africa 118/F6
Somers Point, N.J. 273/E5
Somersville, Conn. 210/F1
Somersworth, N.H. 268/F5
Somerton, Ariz. 198/A6
Somerton, England 13/E6
Somerton, Ohio 284/H6
Somervell (co.), Texas 303/G5
Somerville, Ala. 195/G2
Somerville, Ind. 227/C8
Somerville•, Maine 243/D7
Somerville, Mass. 249/C6
Somerville, New Bruns. 170/C2
Somerville, N.J. 273/D2
Somerville, Ohio 284/A6
Somerville, Tenn. 237/C10
Somerville, Texas 303/H7
Somes (isl.), N. Zealand 100/B2
Someş (riv.), Romania 45/F2
Somesbar, Calif. 204/B2
Somesville (Mount Desert), Maine 243/G7

Somme (dept.), France 28/E3
Somme (riv.), France 28/D2
Somme, Sask. 181/J3
Somme-Leuze, Belgium 27/G8
Sommen (lake), Sweden 18/J8
Sümmerda, Germany 22/D3
Somonauk, Ill. 222/E2
Somonauk, Ill. 222/E2
Somoto, Nicaragua 154/D4
Somotillo, Nicaragua 154/D4
Somovix, Switzerland 39/G3
Son, Norway 18/D4
Son, India 68/E3
Son, Con (isls.), Vietnam 72/E5
Soná, Panama 154/G6
Sonaguera, Honduras 154/D3
Sonaki (cap.), Oman 59/G5
Sonepur, India 68/E4
Sonestown, Pa. 294/K3
Song Ba (riv.), Vietnam 72/F4
Song Ca (riv.), Vietnam 72/E3
Song Cai (riv.), Vietnam 72/F4
Song Cau, Vietnam 72/F4
Song Da (Black) (riv.), Vietnam 72/E2
Songea, Tanzania 115/G6
Songea, Tanzania 102/F6
Song Hong (Red) (riv.), Vietnam 72/F2
Songhua (riv.), China 54/P5
Songhua Hu (lake), China 77/L3
Songhua Jiang (Sungari) (riv.), China 77/M2
Songkhla, Thailand 54/L9
Songkhla, Thailand 72/D6
Songling, China 77/K2
Songnim, N. Korea 81/B4
Songo, Angola 115/C5
Songo, Angola 102/D5
Songo, Mozambique 118/E3
Songololo, Zaire 115/B5
Songololo, Zaire 102/D5
Songpan, China 77/F5
Songxi, China 77/K6
Son Ha, Vietnam 72/F4
Sonid Youqi, China 77/H3
Sonid Zuoqi, China 77/H3
Son La, Vietnam 72/D2
Sonmiani, Pakistan 68/B3
Sonmiani, Pakistan 59/J4
Sonneberg, Germany 22/D3
Sonnenhorn (mt.), Switzerland 39/F4
Sonnette, Mont. 262/L5
Sono (riv.), Brazil 132/E5
Sonobe, Japan 81/J7
Sonoita, Ariz. 198/E7
Sonoma (co.), Calif. 204/C5
Sonoma, Calif. 204/C5
Sonoma (range), Nev. 266/D2
Sonora, Calif. 204/E6
Sonora, Ky. 237/K5
Sonora (state), Mexico 150/D2
Sonora (riv.), Mexico 150/D2
Sonora, Nova Scotia 168/G3
Sonora, Texas 303/D7
Sonoyta, Mexico 150/C1
Sonqor, Iran 66/E3
Sonseca, Spain 33/D3
Sonsón, Colombia 126/C5
Sonsonate, El Salvador 154/C4
Sonsorol (isl.), Belau 87/D5
Sontag, Miss. 256/D7
Son Tay, Vietnam 72/E2
Sonthofen, Germany 22/D5
Sonvico, Switzerland 39/G4
Soochow (Suzhou), China 77/K5
Sooke, Br. Col. 184/J4
Sopachuy, Bolivia 136/C6
Sopas, Arroyo (riv.), Uruguay 145/C2
Sopchoppy, Fla. 212/B1
Soper, Okla. 288/P6
Soperton, Georgia 217/G6
Sopetrán, Colombia 126/C4
Sophia, N.C. 281/K3
Sophia, W. Va. 312/D7
Sophie, Fr. Guiana 131/E4
Sopi (cape), Indonesia 85/H5
Sopot, Poland 47/D1
Sopron, Hungary 41/D3
Soquel, Calif. 204/K4
Sora, Italy 34/C4
Sorah, Pakistan 68/B3
Sorata, Bolivia 136/A4
Sorbas, Spain 33/E4
Sorcière, La (mt.), St. Lucia 161/G6
Sorel, Québec 172/D4
Sorell (cape), Tasmania 99/B4
Sorell (lake), Tasmania 99/D4
Sorell-Midway Point, Tasmania 99/D4
Sorento, Ill. 222/D5
Soresina, Italy 34/C2
Sorgun, Turkey 63/F3
Soria (prov.), Spain 33/E2
Soria, Spain 33/E2
Soriano (dept.), Uruguay 145/B4
Soriano, Uruguay 145/A4
Sorikmerapi (mt.), Indonesia 85/B5
Sørkapp (pt.), Norway 18/C2
Sørø, Denmark 21/E7
Sorocaba, Brazil 132/D8
Sorocaba, Brazil 120/E5
Sorocaba, Brazil 135/C3
Sorochinsk, U.S.S.R. 52/H4
Soroki, U.S.S.R. 52/C5
Sorol (atoll), Micronesia 87/D5
Sorong, Indonesia 54/P10

Sorong, Indonesia 85/J6
Sororieng (mt.), Guyana 131/B2
Soroti, Uganda 115/F3
Sürüya (isl.), Norway 7/G1
Sorøya (isl.), Norway 18/N1
Sorrento, Br. Col. 184/H5
Sorrento, Fla. 212/E3
Sorrento, Italy 34/E4
Sorrento, La. 238/L3
Sorrento•, Maine 243/G7
Sorsele, Sweden 18/K4
Sorso, Italy 34/B4
Sorsogon (prov.), Philippines 82/E4
Sorsogon, Philippines 82/E4
Sorsogon, Philippines 85/G3
Sort, Spain 33/G1
Sortava, U.S.S.R. 48/C3
Sortavala, U.S.S.R. 52/D2
Sør-Trøndelag (co.), Norway 18/G5
Sorum, S. Dak. 298/D3
Sösan, S. Korea 81/C5
Sos del Rey Católico, Spain 33/F1
Sosnogorsk, U.S.S.R. 7/K2
Sosnogorsk, U.S.S.R. 48/F3
Sosnogorsk, U.S.S.R. 52/H2
Sosnovka, U.S.S.R. 52/F4
Sosnovo-Ozerskoye, U.S.S.R. 48/M4
Sosnowiec, Poland 47/B4
Soso, Miss. 256/F7
Sosúa, Dom. Rep. 158/E5
Sotkamo, Finland 18/Q4
Soto la Marina, Mexico 150/L4
Sotomayor, Bolivia 136/C6
Sotrondio, Spain 33/D1
Sotteville-les-Rouen, France 28/D3
Sotuta, Mexico 150/P6
Soubey, Switzerland 39/D2
Soudan, Ark. 202/J4
Soudan, Minn. 255/F3
Soudan, North. Terr. 93/E6
Souderton, Pa. 294/M5
Souf (oasis), Algeria 106/F2
Souflíon, Greece 45/H5
Soufrière, Dominica 161/E7
Soufrière (bay), Dominica 161/E7
Soufrière, Guadeloupe 161/A7
Soufrière, St. Lucia 161/E6
Soufrière, St. Lucia 156/G4
Soufrière (bay), St. Lucia 161/F6
Soufrière•, St. Vin. & Grens. 161/A8
Souhegan (riv.), N.H. 268/D6
Souillac, Mauritius 118/G5
Souk Ahras, Algeria 106/F1
Souk Ahras, Algeria 106/F1
Soulanges (co.), Québec 172/C4
Soul City, N.C. 281/N2
South Branch Oromocto (riv.), New Bruns. 170/D2
Sounding (creek), Alberta 182/E4
Sound View, Conn. 210/F3
Sourdnahunk (lake), Maine 243/F3
Sourdough, Alaska 196/J2
Soure, Brazil 132/D3
Soure, Portugal 33/B2
Souris, Man. 162/F6
Souris, Manitoba 179/B5
Souris (riv.), Manitoba 179/B5
Souris (riv.), N. Dak. 188/F1
Souris, N. Dak. 282/J2
Souris (riv.), N. Dak. 282/J2
Souris, P.E.I. 162/K6
Souris, Pr. Edward I. 168/F2
Souris (riv.), Sask. 181/H6
Sour Lake, Texas 303/K7
Sousa, Brazil 120/F3
Sousel, Portugal 33/C3
Sousse, Tunisia 102/D1
Sousse, Tunisia 106/G1
Soustons, France 28/C6
South, Ala. 195/E8
South (pt.), Barbados 161/B9
South (riv.), Georgia 217/E3
South (Ka Lae) (cape), Hawaii 218/G7
South (sound), Ireland 17/C5
South, Ky. 237/J6
South (pass), La. 238/M8
South (pt.), La. 238/G8
South (riv.), Mass. 249/D2
South (bay), Mich. 250/C2
South (chan.), Mich. 250/E3
South (pt.), Mich. 250/F4
South (isl.), N. Zealand 87/G10
South (isl.), N. Zealand 100/B5
South (isl.), N. Zealand 100/C7
South (bay), N. Terr. 187/K3
South (bay), Ontario 177/C2
South (mt.), Pa. 294/H6
South (isl.), S.C. 296/J5
South (cape), Tasmania 99/C5
South Acton, Maine 243/B8
South Acton, Mass. 249/J3
South Acworth, N.H. 268/C5
South Addison, Maine 243/H6
South Africa 102/E7
South Africa 102/E7
SOUTH AFRICA 118/C5
South Alexandria, N.H. 268/D4
South Allan, Sask. 181/E4
South Alligator (riv.), North. Terr. 88/C2
South Alligator (riv.), North. Terr. 93/C2
Southam, N. Dak. 282/N3
South Amana, Iowa 229/J5
South Amboy, N.J. 273/E3
South America 2/D6
South Amherst, Mass. 249/E3
South Amherst, Ohio 284/F3
Southampton, England 7/D3
Southampton, England 10/F5
Southampton, England 13/F7
Southampton•, Mass. 249/E4
Southampton, N.Y. 276/R9
Southampton (cape), N.W.T. 187/K3
Southampton (isl.), N.W.T. 162/H2
Southampton (isl.), N.W.T. 187/K3

Southampton, Nova Scotia 168/D3
Southampton, Ontario 177/C3
Southampton (co.), Va. 307/O7
South Andaman (isl.), India 68/G6
South Anna (riv.), Va. 307/N5
Southard, Okla. 288/K2
South Ashburnham, Mass. 249/G2
South Athol, Mass. 249/F2
South Atlantic Ocean 2/J6
South Australia 88/F6
SOUTH AUSTRALIA 94
South Australia (state), Australia 87/D8
Southaven, Miss. 256/E1
South Bancroft, Maine 243/G4
South Barre, Mass. 249/F3
South Barre, Vt. 268/B3
South Barrington, Ill. 222/A5
South Barwon, Victoria 97/C6
South Bass (isl.), Ohio 284/E2
South Bay, Fla. 212/F6
South Bay Aqueduct, Calif. 204/L2
South Baymouth, Ontario 177/B2
South Beach, Oreg. 291/C3
South Belmar, N.J. 273/E4
South Beloit, Ill. 222/E1
South Bend, Ind. 188/J2
South Bend, Ind. 227/E1
South Bend, Nebr. 264/H4
South Bend, Wash. 310/B4
South Bennettsville, S.C. 296/H2
South Bentinck Arm (inlet), Br. Col. 184/D4
South Berlin, Mass. 249/H3
South Berwick, Maine 243/B9
South Berwick•, Maine 243/B9
South Bethany, Del. 245/T6
South Bethlehem, N.Y. 276/N5
South Bethlehem, Pa. 294/D4
South Beveland (isl.), Netherlands 27/D6
South Bloomfield, Ohio 284/D6
South Bloomingville, Ohio 284/E7
South Boardman, Mich. 250/D4
South Bolton, Québec 172/E4
Southborough, England 13/J8
Southborough, England 13/J8
Southborough•, Mass. 249/H3
South Boston (I.C.), Va. 307/L7
South Boston, Ind. 227/F7
South Bound Brook, N.J. 273/E2
South Braintree, Mass. 249/D8
South Branch, Mich. 250/E4
South Branch, Minn. 255/D7
South Branch, Newf. 166/C4
South Branch, N.J. 273/D2
South Branch Oromocto (riv.), New Bruns. 170/D2
Southbridge, Mass. 249/G4
Southbridge•, Mass. 249/G4
Southbridge, N. Zealand 100/D5
South Bridgton, Maine 243/B8
South Bristol•, Maine 243/D8
South Britain, Conn. 210/B3
South Broadway, Wash. 310/E4
South Brook, Green Bay Dist., Newf. 166/C4
South Brook, Humber Dist., Newf. 166/C4
South Brookfield, Nova Scotia 168/D4
South Brooksville, Maine 243/F7
South Brunswick•, N.J. 273/E3
South Bruny (isl.), Tasmania 99/D5
South Burlington, Vt. 268/A3
South Burro (mt.), Utah 304/D3
Southbury•, Conn. 210/C3
South Calling Lake, Alberta 182/D2
South Canaan, Conn. 210/B1
South Carolina 188/K4
SOUTH CAROLINA 296
South Carolina (state), U.S. 146/K6
South Carrollton, Ky. 237/G6
South Carthage, Tenn. 237/K8
South Carver, Mass. 249/M5
South Casco, Maine 243/B8
South Charleston, Ohio 284/C6
South Charleston, W. Va. 312/C6
South Chatham, Mass. 249/O6
South Chatham, N.H. 268/E3
South Cheyenne, Wyo. 319/H2
South Chicago Heights, Ill. 222/C6
South China (sea) 54/N8
South China (sea) 2/Q5
South China (sea), China 77/J7
South China (sea), Indonesia 85/D4
South China, Maine 243/D7
South China (sea), Malaysia 85/D4
South China (sea), Philippines 85/D4
South China (sea), Philippines 82/B3
South China (sea), Vietnam 72/F4
South Cle Elum, Wash. 310/D3
South Cleveland, Tenn. 237/M10
South Clinton, Tenn. 237/N8
South Coffeyville, Okla. 288/P1
South Colby, Wash. 310/A2
South Colton, N.Y. 276/L1
South Congaree, S.C. 296/F4
South Connellsville, Pa. 294/C6
South Corning, N.Y. 276/F6
South Cotabato (prov.), Philippines 82/E7
South Coventry (Coventry), Conn. 210/F1
South Cow (creek), Calif. 204/C3
SOUTH DAKOTA 298
South Dakota (state), U.S. 146/H5
South Danbury, N.H. 268/D5
South Danville, N.H. 268/E6
South Dartmouth, Mass. 249/L6
South Dayton, N.Y. 276/C6
South Daytona, Fla. 212/F2
South Deerfield, Mass. 249/E3
South Deerfield, N.H. 268/E5
South Dennis, Mass. 249/O6
South Dennis, N.J. 273/D5

South Dorset, Vt. 268/A5
South Dos Palos, Calif. 204/E7
South Downs (hills), England 13/G7
South Dum Dum, India 68/F2
South Duxbury, Mass. 249/M4
Southeast (cape), Alaska 196/E2
South East (cape), Australia 87/E10
South East (pt.), Jamaica 158/K6
Southeast (pass), La. 238/M8
South East (cape), Tasmania 99/C5
South East (pt.), Victoria 97/D6
SOUTHEAST ASIA 85
Southeast Loch (inlet), Hawaii 218/B3
South Easton, Mass. 249/K4
Southeast Upsalquitch (riv.), New Bruns. 170/D1
South Effingham, N.H. 268/E4
South Egremont, Mass. 249/A4
South Elgin, Ill. 222/B4
South Eliot, Maine 243/B9
South El Monte, Calif. 204/C10
Southend, Scotland 15/C5
Southend-on-Sea, England 10/G5
Southend-on-Sea, England 13/H6
South English, Iowa 229/J6
Southern (dist.), Israel 65/B5
Southern Alps (range), N. Zealand 100/C5
Southern Cross, Mont. 262/C4
Southern Cross, W. Australia 88/E6
Southern Cross, W. Australia 92/B5
Southern Harbour, Newf. 166/C2
Southern Indian (lake), Man. 162/G4
Southern Indian (lake), Man. 146/J4
Southern Indian (lake), Manitoba 179/H2
Southern Leyte (prov.), Philippines 82/E5
Southern Pines, N.C. 281/L4
Southern Ute Ind. Res., Colo. 208/08
South Esk (riv.), Scotland 15/F4
South Esk (riv.), Tasmania 99/D3
Southesk Tablelands, W. Australia 92/D3
South Euclid, Ohio 284/H9
South Exeter, Maine 243/E6
Southey, Sask. 181/G5
South Fallsburg, N.Y. 276/L7
Southfield, Mass. 249/B4
Southfield, Mich. 250/C6
Southfields, N.Y. 276/M8
South Foreland (prom.), England 13/J6
South Fork, Colo. 208/F7
South Fork, Frenchman, Colo. 208/01
South Fork, Mo. 261/J9
South Fork, Flathead (riv.), Mont. 262/C3
South Fork, Humboldt (riv.), Nev. 266/F2
South Fork, Owyhee (riv.), Nev. 266/E1
South Fork, Pa. 294/E5
South Fork, Sask. 181/C6
South Fork, Shoshone (riv.), Wyo. 319/C1
South Fork, Powder (riv.), Wyo. 319/F2
South Foster, R.I. 249/H5
South Fowl (lake), Minn. 255/G4
South Fox (isl.), Mich. 250/D3
South Friars (bay), St. Kitts & Nevis 161/C10
South Fulton, Tenn. 237/D8
South Gate, Calif. 204/C11
Southgate, Ky. 237/T2
South Gate, Md. 245/M4
Southgate, Mich. 250/F6
South Georgia (isl.), Ant. (U.K.) 2/H8
South Georgia (isl.), Ant. 5/D17
South Gifford, Mo. 261/G2
South Glamorgan, Wales 13/A7
South Glastonbury, Conn. 210/E2
South Glens Falls, N.Y. 276/N4
South Goldsboro, N.C. 281/N4
South Grafton, Mass. 249/H4
South Greenfield, Mo. 261/E8
South Groveland, Mass. 249/L2
South Hadley•, Mass. 249/D4
South Hadley Falls, Mass. 249/D4
Southhampton (isl.), N.W.T. 146/K3
South Hampton•, N.H. 268/F6
South Hanover, Mass. 249/L4
South Harbour, Nova Scotia 168/H2
South Harpswell, Maine 243/C8
South Harwich, Mass. 249/O6
South Haven, Kansas 232/E4
South Haven, Mich. 250/C6
South Haven, Minn. 255/D5
South Haven, Nova Scotia 168/H2
South Hazelton, Br. Col. 184/D2
South Heart, N. Dak. 282/D6
South Heights, Pa. 294/B4
South Hero•, Vt. 268/A2
South Hill, Va. 307/M7
South Hiram, Maine 243/B8
South Holland, Ill. 222/C6
South Holland (prov.), Netherlands 27/E5
South Holston (lake), Tenn. 237/S7
South Holston (lake), Va. 307/E7
South Hope, Maine 243/E7
South Horr, Kenya 115/G3
South Houston, Texas 303/J2
South Hutchinson, Kansas 232/D3
South Indian Lake, Manitoba 179/H2
Southington•, Conn. 210/D2
South International Falls, Minn. 255/E2
South Irvine, Ky. 237/N5
South Jacksonville, Ill. 222/C4
South Jordan, Utah 304/B3
South Junction, Manitoba 179/G5
South Junction, Oreg. 291/F3
South Kedgwick (riv.), New Bruns. 170/B1

Squibnocket 451

South Kensington, Md. 245/E4
South Kent, Conn. 210/B2
South Killingly, Conn. 210/H1
South Knife (riv.), Manitoba 179/J2
South Knife Lake, Manitoba 179/J2
South Korea 54/O6
South La Grange, Maine 243/F5
Southlake, Texas 303/F2
South Lake Tahoe, Calif. 204/F5
South Lancaster, Mass. 249/H3
Southland, Texas 303/C4
South Laurel, Md. 245/L4
South Lead Hill, Ark. 202/D1
South Lebanon, Maine 243/A9
South Lebanon, Ohio 284/B7
South Lee, Mass. 249/A3
South Lee, N.H. 268/E5
South Liberty, Maine 243/E7
South Lincoln, Maine 243/F5
South Lincoln, Vt. 268/B3
South Lineville, Mo. 261/E1
South Londonderry, Vt. 268/B5
South Loup (riv.), Nebr. 264/E3
South Luconia (shoal), Philippines 85/E4
South Lunenburg, Vt. 268/D3
South Lyme, Conn. 210/F3
South Lyndeboro, N.H. 268/D6
South Lynnfield, Mass. 249/D5
South Lyon, Mich. 250/F6
South Magnetic Pole, Ant. 2/R9
South Magnetic Pole, Ant. 5/C8
South Maitland, Nova Scotia 168/E3
South Manitou, Mich. 250/C3
South Manitou (isl.), Mich. 250/C3
South Mansfield, La. 238/C3
South Marsh (isl.), Md. 245/O8
South Mayo (riv.), Va. 307/H7
South Medford, Oreg. 291/E5
South Melbourne, Victoria 97/J5
South Melbourne, Victoria 88/K7
South Merrimack, N.H. 268/D6
South Miami, Fla. 212/B5
South Miami Heights, Fla. 212/F6
South Middleboro, Mass. 249/L5
South Milford, Ind. 227/G1
South Mills, N.C. 281/S2
South Milwaukee, Wis. 317/M2
South Molton, England 10/E5
South Molton, England 13/D6
South Monmouth, Maine 243/D7
South Monroe, Mich. 250/F7
Southmont, N.C. 281/J3
South Mound, Kansas 232/G4
South Mountain, Ontario 177/J3
South Mountain, Pa. 294/H6
South Nahanni (riv.), N.W. Terr. 187/F3
South Naknek, Alaska 196/G3
South Natick, Mass. 249/A7
South Natuna (isls.), Indonesia 85/D5
South Negril (pt.), Jamaica 158/G6
South Negril (pt.), Jamaica 156/B3
South New Berlin, N.Y. 276/K5
South Newbury, N.H. 268/D5
South Newbury, Vt. 268/C3
South Newfane, Vt. 268/B6
South Newport, Georgia 217/K7
South New River (canal), Fla. 212/F5
South Norfolk, Conn. 210/C1
South Norwalk, Conn. 210/B4
South Nyack, N.Y. 276/K8
South Ogden, Utah 304/C2
South Ohio, Nova Scotia 168/B5
Southold, N.Y. 276/P8
South Olive, Ohio 284/G6
South Orange•, N.J. 273/A2
South Orkney (isls.), Ant. (U.K.) 2/G9
South Orkney (isls.), Ant. 5/C16
South Orleans, Mass. 249/O5
South Oromocto (lake), New Bruns. 170/D3
South Oroville, Calif. 204/D4
South Orrington, Maine 243/F6
South Ossetian Aut. Obl., U.S.S.R. 48/E5
South Ossetian Aut. Obl., U.S.S.R. 52/F6
South Otselic, N.Y. 276/J5
South Pacific (ocean) 87/H8
South Pacific Ocean 2/C8
South Padre Island, Texas 303/G11
South Pagai (isl.), Indonesia 85/C6
South Para (riv.), S. Australia 94/C7
South Paris, Maine 243/C7
South Pasadena, Calif. 204/C10
South Pasadena, Fla. 212/B3
South Pass City, Wyo. 319/D3
South Patrick Shores, Fla. 212/F3
South Pekin, Ill. 222/D3
South Pender Island, Br. Col. 184/K3
South Penobscot, Maine 243/F7
South Perry, Ohio 284/E6
South Perth, W. Australia 88/B2
South Perth, W. Australia 92/A1
South Philipsburg, Pa. 294/F4
South Piney (creek), Wyo. 319/B3
South Pittsburg, Tenn. 237/K10
South Pittsfield, N.H. 268/E5
South Plainfield, N.J. 273/E2
South Plains, Texas 303/C3
South Platte (riv.) 188/F2
South Platte (riv.), Colo. 208/N1
South Platte (riv.), Nebr. 264/C3
South Platte (riv.), U.S. 146/H6
South Point, Ohio 284/E9
South Polar (plat.), Ant. 5/A1
South Pole 2/E11
South Pole, Ant. 5/A4
South Pomfret, Vt. 268/B4
South Porcupine, Ontario 175/D3
Southport, Conn. 210/B4
Southport, England 10/F2
Southport, England 13/G1
Southport, Fla. 212/C6
Southport, Ind. 227/E5
Southport, Maine 243/D8
Southport•, Maine 243/D8
Southport, N.Y. 276/G6
Southport, N.C. 281/N7
South Portland, Maine 243/C8
South Portsmouth, Ky. 237/P3
South Prairie, Wash. 310/D3
South Pugwash, Nova Scotia 168/E3
South Range, Mich. 250/G1
South Range, Wis. 317/B2
South Renous (riv.), New Bruns. 170/D2
South Renovo, Pa. 294/G3
South River (peak), Colo. 208/F7
South River, Newf. 166/D2
South River, N.J. 273/E3
South River, Ontario 177/E2
South Rockwood, Mich. 250/F7
South Ronaldsay (isl.), Scotland 10/E1
South Ronaldsay (isl.), Scotland 15/F2
South Roxana, Ill. 222/B2
South Royalston, Mass. 249/F2
South Royalton, Vt. 268/C4
South Russell, Ohio 284/H3
South Ryegate, Vt. 268/C3
South Sacramento, Calif. 204/B8
South Saint Paul, Minn. 255/G6
South Salem, Ohio 284/D7
South Salt Lake, Utah 304/C3
South Sandisfield, Mass. 249/B4
South Sandwich (isls.), Ant. (U.K.) 2/H8
South Sandwich (isls.), Ant. 5/D17
South Sanford, Maine 243/B9
South San Francisco, Calif. 204/J2
South Santiam (riv.), Oreg. 291/E3
South Saskatchewan (riv.), Alberta 182/E4
South Saskatchewan (riv.), Canada 146/G4
South Saskatchewan (riv.), Sask. 181/C5
South Seabrook, N.H. 268/F6
South Seal (riv.), Manitoba 179/J2
South Seaville, N.J. 273/D5
South Sevogle (riv.), New Bruns. 170/D1
South Shaftsbury, Vt. 268/A6
South Shetland (isls.) 2/F9
South Shetland (isls.) 5/C15
South Shields, England 13/J3
South Shields, England 10/F3
South Shore, Ky. 237/R3
South Shore, S. Dak. 298/P3
Southside, Ala. 195/F3
Southside, Tenn. 237/G8
Southside Place, Texas 303/J2
South Sioux City, Nebr. 264/H2
South Skunk (riv.), Iowa 229/H6
South Slocan, Br. Col. 184/J5
South Solon, Ohio 284/C6
South Spectacle (lake), Conn. 210/B2
South Stoddard, N.H. 268/C5
South Strafford, Vt. 268/C4
South Suburban, India 68/F2
South Sudbury, Mass. 249/J3
South Superior, Wyo. 319/D4
South Sutton, N.H. 268/D5
South Sydney, N.S. Wales 88/L4
South Sydney, N.S. Wales 97/J3
South Taft, Calif. 204/F8
South Tamworth, N.H. 268/E4
South Taranaki (bight), N. Zealand 100/D3
South Thomaston•, Maine 243/E7
South Toms River, N.J. 273/E4
South Trap (isl.), N. Zealand 100/B7
South Tucson, Ariz. 198/D6
South Tunnel, Tenn. 237/H7
South Twin (mt.), N.H. 268/D3
South Tyne (riv.), England 13/E3
South Uist (isl.), Scotland 10/C2
South Uist (isl.), Scotland 15/A3
South Umpqua (riv.), Oreg. 291/E4
South Union, Ky. 237/H7
South Union, Maine 243/E7
South Ural (mts.), U.S.S.R. 52/J4
South Venice, Fla. 212/D4
South Vienna, Ohio 284/C6
Southville, Mass. 249/H3
South Wabasca (lake), Alberta 182/D2
South Wadesboro, N.C. 281/J5
South Waldoboro, Maine 243/E7
South Wallingford, Vt. 268/A5
South Walpole, Mass. 249/K4
South Wanatah, Ind. 227/D2
Southwark, England 13/H8
Southwark, England 10/B5
South Warren, Maine 243/E7
South Waterford, Maine 243/B7
South Waverly, Pa. 294/J2
South Wayne, Wis. 317/G10
South Weare, N.H. 268/D5
South Webster, Ohio 284/E8
South Weldon, N.C. 281/O2
South Wellfleet, Mass. 249/P5
South Wellington, Br. Col. 184/J3
Southwest (pass), La. 238/L8
Southwest (head), New Bruns. 170/D4
South West (brook), Newf. 166/C2
South West (cape), Tasmania 88/G7
South West (cape), Tasmania 99/B5
Southwest (cape), Virgin Is. (U.S.) 161/E4
South West Arm (inlet), Newf. 166/D2
South West City, Mo. 261/D9
South West Gander (riv.), Newf. 166/C4
Southwest Harbor, Maine 243/G7
Southwest Harbor•, Maine 243/G7
South West Margaree (riv.), Nova Scotia 168/G2
Southwest Miramichi (riv.), New Bruns. 170/D2
South Westport, Mass. 249/K6
South West Port Mouton, Nova Scotia 168/D5
South West Rocks, N.S. Wales 97/G2
South Weymouth, Mass. 249/E8
South Whitley, Ind. 227/F2
Southwick, England 13/G7
Southwick, Idaho 220/B3
Southwick•, Mass. 249/C4
South Williamson, Ky. 237/S5
South Williamsport, Pa. 294/J3
South Willington, Conn. 210/F1
South Wilmington, Ill. 222/E2
South Wilton, Conn. 210/B4
South Windham, Conn. 210/G2
South Windham (Little Falls-South Windham), Maine 243/C8
South Windham, Vt. 268/B5
South Windsor•, Conn. 210/E1
Southwold, England 13/J5
Southwold, England 10/G4
South Wolf (isl.), Newf. 166/C3
South Wolfeboro, N.H. 268/E4
South Woodbury, Vt. 268/C3
South Woodstock, Conn. 210/G1
South Woodstock, Vt. 268/B4
Southworth, Wash. 310/A2
South Worthington, Mass. 249/C3
South Yadkin (riv.), N.C. 281/H3
South Yarmouth, Mass. 249/O6
South Yorkshire (co.), England 13/F4
South Zanesville, Ohio 284/F6
Sovata, Romania 45/G2
Sovereign, Sask. 181/D4
Sovetsk, U.S.S.R. 7/J3
Sovetsk, U.S.S.R. 52/G3
Sovetsk (Tilsit), U.S.S.R. 52/B4
Sovetskaya Gavan', U.S.S.R. 54/R5
Sovetskaya Gavan', U.S.S.R. 48/P5
SOVIET UNION (U.S.S.R.) 48
Sowerby Bridge, England 13/H1
Sowerby Bridge, England 10/G2
Soweto, S. Africa 118/H6
Soya (pt.), Japan 81/L1
Soyhières, Switzerland 39/D2
Soyo, Angola 115/B5
Soyo, Angola 102/D5
Sozopol, Bulgaria 45/H4
Spa, Belgium 27/H8
Spades, Ind. 227/G6
Spain 2/J3
Spain 7/D4
SPAIN 33
SPAIN-Canary Islands, Ceuta and Melilla 106
Spalding, England 13/G5
Spalding, England 10/F4
Spalding (co.), Georgia 217/D4
Spalding, Mich. 250/B3
Spalding, Mo. 261/J3
Spalding, Nebr. 264/F3
Spalding, Sask. 181/G3
Spaldings, Jamaica 158/G6
Spallumcheen, Br. Col. 184/H5
Spanaway, Wash. 310/C3
Spandau, Germany 22/E3
Spangle, Wash. 310/H3
Spangler, Pa. 294/E4
Spaniard's Bay, Newf. 166/D2
Spanish (head), I. of Man 13/C3
Spanish, Ontario 177/J5
Spanish (riv.), Ontario 177/C1
Spanishburg, W. Va. 312/D8
Spanish Fork, Utah 304/C3
Spanish Fork (riv.), Utah 304/C3
Spanish Fort, Ala. 195/C9
Spanish Fort, Texas 303/G4
Spanish Lake, Mo. 261/R1
Spanish Ship Bay, Nova Scotia 168/G4
Spanish Town, Jamaica 158/J6
Spanish Town, Jamaica 156/C3
Sparkill, N.Y. 276/K8
Sparkman, Ark. 202/E6
Sparks, Georgia 217/F8
Sparks, Kansas 232/G2
Sparks, Nebr. 264/D2
Sparks, Nev. 188/C3
Sparks, Nev. 266/B3
Sparks, Okla. 288/N3
Sparks (lake), Oreg. 291/F3
Sparksville, Ky. 237/L6
Sparland, Ill. 222/D2
Sparlingville, Mich. 250/G6
Sparr, Fla. 212/D2
Sparrow Bush, N.Y. 276/L8
Sparrows Point, Md. 245/N4
Sparta, Georgia 217/F4
Sparta, Greece 45/F7
Sparta, Ill. 222/D5
Sparta, Ky. 237/M3
Sparta, Mich. 250/D5
Sparta, Mo. 261/F9
Sparta•, N.J. 273/D1
Sparta, N.C. 281/G1
Sparta, Ohio 284/E5
Sparta, Ontario 177/C5
Sparta, Oreg. 291/K3
Sparta, Tenn. 237/K9
Sparta, Va. 307/O4
Sparta, Wis. 317/E8
Spartanburg, Ind. 227/H4
Spartanburg, S.C. 188/K4
Spartanburg (co.), S.C. 296/D2
Spartanburg, S.C. 296/C1
Spartansburg, Pa. 294/C2
Spartivento (cape), Italy 34/B5
Spartivento (cape), Italy 34/F6
Sparwood, Br. Col. 184/K5
Spassk-Dal'niy, U.S.S.R. 48/O5
Spátha (cape), Greece 45/F8
Spaulding, Ill. 222/D4
Spavinaw, Okla. 288/R2
Spavinaw (lake), Okla. 288/S2
Spean (riv.), Scotland 15/D4
Spean Bridge, Scotland 15/D4
Spear (cape), New Bruns. 170/G2
Spear (cape), Newf. 166/D2
Spearfish, S. Dak. 298/B5
Spearman, Texas 303/C1
Spearsville, Ind. 227/E6
Spearsville, La. 238/E1
Spearville, Kansas 232/C4
Spectacle (lakes), Conn. 210/B2
Specter (range), Nev. 266/E6
Speculator, N.Y. 276/M3
Spedden, Alberta 182/E2
Spednik (lake), New Bruns. 170/C3
Speed, Ind. 227/F8
Speed, Kansas 232/C2
Speed, N.C. 281/P3
Speedway, Ind. 227/E5
Speedwell, Tenn. 237/O8
Speedwell, Va. 307/F8
Speer (mt.), Switzerland 39/H2
Speers, Sask. 181/D3
Speightstown, Barbados 161/B8
Speightstown, Barbados 156/G4
Speigner, Ala. 195/F5
Spelterville, Ind. 227/C5
Spelve, Loch (inlet), Scotland 15/C4
Spenard, Alaska 196/C1
Spenborough, England 13/J1
Spence Bay, N.W. Terr. 187/J3
Spencer (cape), Alaska 196/L1
Spencer (pt.), Alaska 196/E1
Spencer (lake), Alberta 182/E2
Spencer (gulf), Australia 87/D9
Spencer, Idaho 220/F5
Spencer (co.), Ind. 227/C9
Spencer, Ind. 227/D6
Spencer, Iowa 229/C2
Spencer (co.), Ky. 237/L4
Spencer, La. 238/F1
Spencer (pond), Maine 243/D4
Spencer (stream), Maine 243/C5
Spencer, Mass. 249/F3
Spencer•, Mass. 249/F3
Spencer, Nebr. 264/F2
Spencer (cape), New Bruns. 170/E3
Spencer, N.Y. 276/H6
Spencer, N.C. 281/H3
Spencer, Ohio 284/F3
Spencer, Okla. 288/M3
Spencer (creek), Oreg. 291/E5
Spencer (gulf), S. Australia 88/F6
Spencer (cape), S. Australia 88/F7
Spencer (cape), S. Australia 94/E6
Spencer (gulf), S. Australia 94/E6
Spencer, S. Dak. 298/O6
Spencer, Tenn. 237/L9
Spencer, Va. 307/J7
Spencer, W. Va. 312/D5
Spencer, Wis. 317/F6
Spencerburg, Mo. 261/K4
Spencerport, N.Y. 276/E4
Spencers Island, Nova Scotia 168/D3
Spencerville, Ind. 227/G2
Spencerville, Ohio 284/B4
Spencerville, Okla. 288/R6
Spencerville, Ontario 177/J3
Spences Bridge, Br. Col. 184/G5
Spennymoor, England 13/F3
Spennymoor, England 10/F3
Spenser (mts.), N. Zealand 100/D5
Sperling, Manitoba 179/E5
Sperrin (mts.), N. Ireland 17/G2
Sperry, Iowa 229/L7
Sperry, Okla. 288/P2
Sperryville, Va. 307/M3
Spessart (range), Germany 22/C4
Spétsai, Greece 45/F7
Spey (riv.), Scotland 10/E2
Spey (riv.), Scotland 15/E3
Speyer, Germany 22/C4
Sphinx (mt.), Mont. 262/E5
Spiceland, Ind. 227/F5
Spicer, Minn. 255/C5
Spicer (isls.), N.W. Terr. 187/L3
Spicewood, Texas 303/F7
Spickard, Mo. 261/F2
Spiddal, Ireland 17/C5
Spider (lake), Maine 243/E3
Spider (lake), Wis. 317/D3
Spiekeroog (isl.), Germany 22/B2
Spies, N.C. 281/K4
Spiez, Switzerland 39/E3
Spili, Greece 45/G8
Spillimacheen, Br. Col. 184/J5
Spillville, Iowa 229/J2
Spilsby, England 13/H4
Spin Buldak, Afghanistan 68/B2
Spin Buldak, Afghanistan 59/J3
Spindale, N.C. 281/F4
Spink (co.), S. Dak. 298/N4
Spink, S. Dak. 298/R8
Spinnerstown, Pa. 294/M5
Spirit (lake), Idaho 220/B2
Spirit (lake), Iowa 229/C2
Spirit (lake), S. Dak. 298/O4
Spirit (lake), Wash. 310/C4
Spirit, Wis. 317/F5
Spirit Lake, Idaho 220/A2
Spirit Lake, Iowa 229/C2
Spirit River, Alberta 182/A2
Spirit River, Alta. 162/E4
Spiritwood, N. Dak. 282/N6
Spiritwood, Sask. 181/D2
Spiro, Okla. 288/S4
Spišská Belá, Czech. 41/F2
Spišská Nová Ves, Czech. 41/F2
Spital am Pyhrn, Austria 41/C3
Spithead (chan.), England 13/F7
Spitsbergen (isl.), Norway 4/B9
Spitsbergen (isl.), Norway 18/C2
Spittal an der Drau, Austria 41/B3
Spitz, Austria 41/C2
Spivey, Kansas 232/D4
Splendora, Texas 303/J7
Split (lake), Manitoba 179/J2
Split (cape), Nova Scotia 168/D3
Split, Yugoslavia 7/F4
Split, Yugoslavia 45/C4
Split Lake, Manitoba 179/J2
Split Rock, Wis. 317/H6
Splügen (pass), Italy 34/B1
Splügen, Switzerland 39/H3
Splügen (pass), Switzerland 39/H3
Spofford, N.H. 268/C6
Spofford, Texas 303/D8
Spokane, Mo. 261/F9
Spokane (co.), Wash. 310/H3
Spokane, Wash. 146/G5
Spokane, Wash. 188/C1
Spokane, Wash. 310/H3
Spokane (mt.), Wash. 310/H3
Spokane (riv.), Wash. 310/H3
Spokane Ind. Res., Wash. 310/G3
Spöl (riv.), Switzerland 39/F2
Spoleto, Italy 34/D3
Spoon (riv.), Ill. 222/C3
Spooner, Wis. 317/B4
Spot (pond), Mass. 249/C6
Spotswood, N.J. 273/E3
Spotsylvania (co.), Va. 307/N4
Spotsylvania, Va. 307/N4
Spotted (range), Nev. 266/F6
Spotted Horse, Wyo. 319/G1
Spottsville, Ky. 237/G5
Spottswood, Va. 307/K5
Spotville, Ark. 202/D7
Spragge, Ontario 177/J5
Sprague, Ala. 195/F6
Sprague, Manitoba 179/G5
Sprague, Nebr. 264/H4
Sprague (riv.), Oreg. 291/F5
Sprague, Wash. 310/G3
Sprague (lake), Wash. 310/G3
Sprague River, Oreg. 291/F5
Spragueville, Iowa 229/N4
Spratly (isl.), Philippines 85/E4
Spratt, Mich. 250/F3
Spray (mts.), Alberta 182/C4
Spray, Oreg. 291/H3
Spray Lakes, Alberta 182/C4
Spraytown, Ind. 227/E6
Spread Eagle, Wis. 317/K4
Spreckelsville, Hawaii 218/J1
Spree (riv.), Germany 22/F3
Spreewald (for.), Germany 22/F3
Spremberg, Germany 22/F3
Sprent, Tasmania 99/C3
Sprigg, W. Va. 312/B7
Sprimont, Belgium 27/H8
Spring (riv.), Ark. 202/H1
Spring (creek), Nev. 266/D2
Spring (mts.), Nev. 266/F6
Spring (valley), Nev. 266/G3
Spring (creek), N. Dak. 282/E5
Spring (creek), S. Dak. 298/J2
Spring (creek), S. Dak. 298/C6
Spring, Texas 303/J7
Spring Arbor, Mich. 250/E6
Spring Bay, Ill. 222/D3
Spring Bay, Ontario 177/B2
Springbok, S. Africa 118/B5
Springboro, Ohio 284/B6
Springboro, Pa. 294/B2
Springbrook, Iowa 229/N4
Spring Brook, N. Dak. 282/D3
Springbrook, Ontario 177/G3
Springbrook, Oreg. 291/A2
Springbrook, Wis. 317/C4
Spring City, Mo. 261/C9
Spring City, Pa. 294/L5
Spring City, Tenn. 237/M9
Spring City, Utah 304/C4
Spring Coulée, Alberta 182/D5
Spring Creek, Pa. 294/D2
Spring Creek, Tenn. 237/D9
Spring Creek, W. Va. 312/F7
Springdale, Ark. 202/B1
Springdale, Iowa 229/L5
Springdale, Mont. 262/F5
Springdale, Newf. 166/C4
Springdale, Ohio 284/B9
Springdale, Pa. 294/C6
Springdale, S.C. 296/F2
Springdale, S.C. 296/E4
Springdale, Utah 304/B6
Springdale, Wash. 310/H2
Springe, Germany 22/C2
Springer (mt.), Georgia 217/D1
Springer, N. Mex. 274/E2
Springer, Okla. 288/M6
Springerton, Ill. 222/E5
Springerville, Ariz. 198/F4
Springfield, Ark. 202/E3
Springfield, Colo. 208/O8
Springfield, Fla. 212/D6
Springfield, Georgia 217/K6
Springfield, Idaho 220/F6
Springfield (cap.), Ill. 146/J6
Springfield (cap.), Ill. 188/H3
Springfield (cap.), Ill. 222/D4
Springfield (lake), Ill. 222/D4
Springfield, Ind. 227/B8
Springfield, Ky. 237/L5
Springfield, La. 238/M2
Springfield•, Maine 243/G5
Springfield, Mass. 188/M2
Springfield, Mass. 249/D4
Springfield, Mich. 250/D6
Springfield, Minn. 255/C6
Springfield, Mo. 261/F8
Springfield, Mo. 188/H3
Springfield, Mo. 146/J6
Springfield, Nebr. 264/H3
Springfield, King's, New Bruns. 170/E3
Springfield, York, New Bruns. 170/C2
Springfield•, N.H. 268/C4
Springfield•, N.J. 273/E2
Springfield, Nova Scotia 168/D4
Springfield, Ohio 188/K2
Springfield, Ohio 284/C6
Springfield, Ontario 177/C5
Springfield, Oreg. 291/E3
Springfield•, Pa. 294/M7
Springfield, Queensland 88/G5
Springfield, Queensland 95/B5
Springfield, S.C. 296/E4
Springfield, S. Dak. 298/N8
Springfield, Tenn. 237/H8
Springfield, Vt. 268/B5
Springfield•, Vt. 268/B5
Springfield, Va. 307/S3
Springfield, W. Va. 312/J4
Springfield Armory Nat'l Hist. Site, Mass. 249/D4
Springford, Ontario 177/D5
Spring Garden, Ala. 195/G3
Spring Garden, Calif. 204/D4
Spring Garden, Ill. 222/E5
Spring Green, Wis. 317/G9
Spring Grove, Ill. 222/E1
Spring Grove, Ind. 227/H5
Spring Grove, Minn. 255/G7
Spring Grove, Pa. 294/J6
Spring Grove, Va. 307/P6
Spring Hall, Barbados 161/B8
Springhaven, Nova Scotia 168/C5
Spring Hill, Ark. 202/C6
Spring Hill, Iowa 229/F6
Spring Hill, Kansas 232/H3
Springhill, La. 238/D1
Spring Hill, Minn. 255/D5
Springhill, Nova Scotia 168/E3
Spring Hill, Tenn. 237/H9
Springhill Junction, Nova Scotia 168/D3
Springhills, Ohio 284/C5
Springholm, Scotland 15/E5
Spring Hope, N.C. 281/N3
Springhouse, Br. Col. 184/G4
Spring Lake, Ind. 227/F5
Spring Lake, Mich. 250/C5
Spring Lake, Minn. 255/E5
Spring Lake, Minn. 255/E3
Spring Lake, N.J. 273/F3
Spring Lake, N.C. 281/M4
Springlake, Texas 303/B3
Spring Lake, Wis. 317/H8
Spring Lake Heights, N.J. 273/E3
Spring Lake Park, Minn. 255/E5
Springlee, Ky. 237/K2
Spring Lick, Ky. 237/H6
Spring Mills, Pa. 294/G4
Spring Mills, S.C. 296/F2
Spring Park, Minn. 255/F5
Spring Place, Georgia 217/C1
Springport, Ind. 227/G4
Springport, Mich. 250/E6
Spring Ridge, La. 238/B2
Springs, S. Africa 118/J6
Springside, Sask. 181/J4
Springstein, Manitoba 179/E5
Springsure, Queensland 95/D5
Springton (res.), Pa. 294/L6
Springtown, Ark. 202/B1
Springtown, Texas 303/G5
Springvale, Georgia 217/C7
Springvale, Maine 243/B9
Springvale, Victoria 88/L7
Springvale, Victoria 97/J5
Spring Valley, Ala. 195/C1
Spring Valley, Ill. 222/D2
Spring Valley, Minn. 255/F7
Spring Valley, N.Y. 276/K8
Spring Valley, Ohio 284/C6
Spring Valley, Sask. 181/F6
Spring Valley, Texas 303/J1
Spring Valley, Wis. 317/B6
Springview, Nebr. 264/E2
Springville, Ala. 195/E3
Springville, Calif. 204/G7
Springville, Ind. 227/D7
Springville, Iowa 229/L4
Springville, La. 238/L2
Springville, Miss. 256/F2
Springville, N.Y. 276/C5
Springville, Pa. 294/L2
Springville, Tenn. 237/E8
Springville, Utah 304/C3
Springwater, N.Y. 276/E5
Springwater, Sask. 181/C4
Springwood, Va. 307/J5
Sproat Lake, Br. Col. 184/H3
Sprott, Ala. 195/D5
Sprowston, England 13/J5
Spruce (isl.), Manitoba 179/B1
Spruce, Mich. 250/F4
Spruce (mt.), Vt. 268/C3
Spruce Creek, Pa. 294/F4
Sprucedale, Ontario 177/E2
Spruce Grove, Alberta 182/D3
Spruce Home, Sask. 181/F2
Spruce Knob (mt.), W. Va. 312/G5
Spruce Knob-Seneca Rocks Nat'l Rec. Area, W. Va. 312/H5
Spruce Lake, Sask. 181/B2
Spruce Pine, Ala. 195/C2
Spruce Pine, N.C. 281/E3
Spruce Run (res.), N.J. 273/D2
Spruce View, Alberta 182/C3
Spruce Woods, Manitoba 179/C5
Spruce Woods Prov. Park, Manitoba 179/C5
Sprule, Ky. 237/O7
Spry (harb.), Nova Scotia 168/F4
Spry Harbour, Nova Scotia 168/F4
Spur, Texas 303/D4
Spurgeon, Ind. 227/C8
Spurlockville, W. Va. 312/B6
Spurn (head), England 13/H4
Spurn (head), England 10/G4
Spurr (mt.), Alaska 196/B1
Spur Tree, Jamaica 158/H6
Spuzzum, Br. Col. 184/G5
Spy (pond), Mass. 249/C6
Spy Hill, Sask. 181/K5
Squam (lake), N.H. 268/E4
Squamish, Br. Col. 184/F5
Squa Pan, Maine 243/G2
Squa Pan (lake), Maine 243/G2
Square (lake), Maine 243/G1
Square Butte, Mont. 262/F3
Square Islands, Newf. 166/C3
Squatec, Québec 172/J2
Squatec (lake), Québec 172/J2
Squaw (creek), Idaho 220/B5
Squaw (peak), Idaho 220/D4
Squaw (creek), Oreg. 291/F3
Squaw (creek), S. Dak. 298/B3
Squaw Harbor, Alaska 196/F3
Squaw Lake, Minn. 255/D3
Squaw Rapids, Sask. 181/H2
Squibnocket (pt.), Mass. 249/M7

Squillace (gulf), Italy 34/F5
Squinzano, Italy 34/G4
Squire, W. Va. 312/C8
Squires, Mo. 261/G9
Squires Mem. Park, Newf. 166/C4
Squirrel, Idaho 220/G5
Sragen, Indonesia 85/J2
Sre Ambel, Cambodia 72/D5
Srebrenica, Yugoslavia 45/D3
Srednekolymsk, U.S.S.R. 4/C2
Srednekolymsk, U.S.S.R. 48/Q3
Sre Khtum, Cambodia 72/E4
Śrem, Poland 47/C2
Sremska Mitrovica, Yugoslavia 45/D3
Srepok (riv.), Cambodia 72/E4
Sretensk, U.S.S.R. 54/N4
Sretensk, U.S.S.R. 48/M4
Srikakulam, India 68/E5
Sri Lanka 54/K9
SRI LANKA (CEYLON) 68/E7
Srinagar, India 68/D2
Srinagar, India 54/J6
Srivardhan, India 68/C5
Środa Śląska, Poland 47/C3
Środa Wielkopolska, Poland 47/C2
Staaten (riv.), Queensland 88/G3
Staaten (riv.), Queensland 95/B3
Staatsburg, N.Y. 276/N7
Stab, Ky. 237/G5
Stacks (mts.), Ireland 17/B7
Stacy, Minn. 255/E5
Stacy, N.C. 281/S5
Stacy, Va. 307/E6
Stacyville, Iowa 229/H2
Stacyville, Maine 243/F4
Stacyville•, Maine 243/F4
Stade, Germany 22/C2
Staden, Belgium 27/B7
Stadskanaal, Netherlands 27/L3
Stadthagen, Germany 22/C2
Stäfa, Switzerland 39/G2
Staffa (isl.), Scotland 15/B4
Staffelstein, Germany 22/D3
Staffhorst, Germany 22/C2
Stafford•, Conn. 210/F1
Stafford, England 10/G2
Stafford, England 13/E5
Stafford (lake), Fla. 212/D4
Stafford (co.), Kansas 232/D3
Stafford, Kansas 232/D4
Stafford, N.Y. 276/D5
Stafford, Ohio 284/H6
Stafford, Okla. 288/H3
Stafford, Queensland 88/K2
Stafford, Queensland 95/D2
Stafford, Texas 303/J2
Stafford (co.), Va. 307/O4
Stafford, Va. 307/O4
Staffordshire (co.), England 13/E5
Stafford Springs, Conn. 210/F1
Staffordsville, Ky. 237/R5
Staffordville, Conn. 210/G1
Staffordville, N.J. 273/E4
Staines (pen.), Chile 138/D9
Staines, England 10/B5
Staines, England 13/G8
Stainville, Tenn. 237/N8
Staked (Llano Estacado) (plain), N. Mex. 274/D4
Staked (Llano Estacado) (plain), Texas 303/B4
Stakhanov, U.S.S.R. 52/E5
Stalden, Switzerland 39/E4
Staley, N.C. 281/K3
Stalham, England 13/J5
Stalheim, Norway 18/E6
Stalin, Albania 45/D5
Stalingrad (Volgograd), U.S.S.R. 7/J4
Stalingrad (Volgograd), U.S.S.R. 48/E5
Stalingrad (Volgograd), U.S.S.R. 52/F5
Stallings, N.C. 281/H4
Stallo, Miss. 256/F5
Stallworthy (cape), N.W. Terr. 187/J1
Stalowa Wola, Poland 47/F3
Stalwart, Mich. 250/E2
Stalwart, Sask. 181/F4
Stambaugh, Mich. 250/G2
Stamford, Conn. 210/A4
Stamford, England 13/G5
Stamford, England 10/F4
Stamford, Nebr. 264/E4
Stamford, N.Y. 276/L6
Stamford, Queensland 88/G4
Stamford, Texas 303/E5
Stamford (lake), Texas 303/E4
Stamford•, Vt. 268/A6
Stampa, Switzerland 39/J4
Stamping Ground, Ky. 237/M4
Stampriet, Namibia 118/B4
Stamps, Ark. 202/D7
Stanardsville, Va. 307/L4
Stanberry, Mo. 261/C2
Stanbridge-Est, Québec 172/D4
Stanchfield, Minn. 255/E5
Standard, Alberta 182/D4
Standard, Calif. 204/E6
Standard, Ill. 222/D4
Standard, La. 238/F3
Standard City, Ill. 222/D4
Standerton, S. Africa 118/D5
Standfast (pt.), Ant. & Bar. 161/E11
Standing Rock, Ala. 195/H4
Standing Rock Ind. Res.•, N. Dak. 282/J7
Standish, Calif. 204/E3
Standish, Maine 243/B8
Standish•, Maine 243/B8
Standish, Mich. 250/F5
Standish-with-Langtree, England 13/G2
Stand Off, Alberta 182/D5
Stanfield, Ariz. 198/C6
Stanfield, N.C. 281/J4
Stanfield, Oreg. 291/H2
Stanford, Calif. 204/J3
Stanford, Ill. 222/D3
Stanford, Ind. 227/D6
Stanford, Ky. 237/M5

Stanford, Mont. 262/F3
Stanfordville, N.Y. 276/N7
Stangelville, Wis. 317/L7
Stanger, S. Africa 118/E5
Stanhope, England 13/E3
Stanhope, Iowa 229/F4
Stanhope, N.J. 273/D2
Stanhope, Pr. Edward I. 168/E2
Stanhope, Québec 172/F4
Stanislaus (co.), Calif. 204/D6
Stanke Dimitrov, Bulgaria 45/F4
Stanley, England 13/H3
Stanley (cap.), Falk. Is. 143/E7
Stanley (cap.), Falk. Is. 120/D8
Stanley, Idaho 220/D5
Stanley, Iowa 229/K3
Stanley, Kansas 232/H3
Stanley, Ky. 237/G5
Stanley, La. 238/C3
Stanley, New Brans. 170/D2
Stanley, N. Mex. 274/D3
Stanley, N.Y. 276/F5
Stanley, N.C. 281/G4
Stanley, N. Dak. 282/F3
Stanley, Nova Scotia 168/E3
Stanley, Okla. 288/R5
Stanley (co.), S. Dak. 298/H5
Stanley, Tasmania 99/B2
Stanley (mt.), Tasmania 99/A1
Stanley, Va. 307/L3
Stanley, Wis. 317/E6
Stanley (Boyoma) (falls), Zaire 102/E5
Stanley (Boyoma) (falls), Zaire 115/D3
Stanley Pool (lake), Zaire 115/C4
Stanleytown, Va. 307/H7
Stanleyville, N.C. 281/J2
Stanly (co.), N.C. 281/J4
Stanmore, Alberta 182/E4
Stannards, N.Y. 276/E6
Stann Creek Town, Belize 154/C2
Stanovoy (range), U.S.S.R. 54/N4
Stanovoy (range), U.S.S.R. 48/N4
Stans, Switzerland 39/F3
Stanstead (co.), Québec 172/F4
Stanstead Plain, Québec 172/F4
Stanthorpe, Queensland 88/J5
Stanthorpe, Queensland 95/D6
Stanton, Ala. 195/E5
Stanton, Calif. 204/D11
Stanton, England 13/H5
Stanton, Iowa 229/C7
Stanton (co.), Kansas 232/A4
Stanton, Ky. 237/O5
Stanton, Mich. 250/D5
Stanton, Miss. 256/R7
Stanton, Mo. 261/K6
Stanton (co.), Nebr. 264/G3
Stanton, Nebr. 264/G3
Stanton, N.J. 273/D2
Stanton, N. Dak. 282/H5
Stanton, Tenn. 237/C10
Stanton, Texas 303/C5
Stantonsburg, N.C. 281/O3
Stantonville, Tenn. 237/E10
Stanwood, Iowa 229/L5
Stanwood, Mich. 250/D5
Stanwood, Wash. 310/C2
Stanzel, Iowa 229/E6
Staphorst, Netherlands 27/J3
Staplehurst, Nebr. 264/G4
Staples, Minn. 255/D4
Staples, Ontario 177/B5
Stapleton, Ala. 195/C9
Stapleton, Georgia 217/H4
Stapleton, Nebr. 264/D3
Stapylton (bay), N.W. Terr. 187/G3
Star, Alberta 182/D3
Star, Idaho 220/B6
Star (lake), Minn. 255/C4
Star, Miss. 256/D6
Star, N.C. 281/K4
Star, Texas 303/F6
Starachowice, Poland 47/E3
Stará L'ubovňa, Czech. 41/F2
Staraya Russa, U.S.S.R. 52/D3
Stara Zagora, Bulgaria 7/G4
Stara Zagora, Bulgaria 45/G4
Starbuck (isl.), Kiribati 87/L6
Starbuck, Manitoba 179/G5
Starbuck, Minn. 255/C5
Starbuck, Wash. 310/G4
Star City, Ark. 202/G6
Star City, Ind. 227/D3
Star City, Sask. 181/G3
Star City, W. Va. 312/C7
Staré Mĕsto, Czech. 41/D2
Stargard Szczeciński, Poland 47/B2
Stargo, Ariz. 198/F5
Starhill, La. 238/H5
Stark (co.), Ill. 222/D2
Stark, Kansas 232/G4
Stark, Minn. 255/E5
Stark, Mont. 262/B3
Stark•, N.H. 268/E2
Stark (co.), N. Dak. 282/E6
Stark (co.), Ohio 284/J5
Stark City, Mo. 261/D9
Starke, Fla. 212/D2
Starke (co.), Ind. 227/D2
Starkey, Oreg. 291/J2
Star Keys (isls.), N. Zealand 100/E7
Starks, La. 238/C5
Starks•, Maine 243/D6
Starks, Wis. 317/H4
Starksboro•, Vt. 268/A3
Starkville, Colo. 208/L8
Starkville, Miss. 256/G4
Starkweather, N. Dak. 282/N3
Star Lake, N.Y. 276/K2
Star Lake, Wis. 317/G3
Starlight, Ind. 227/F8
Starnberg, Germany 22/D4
Starnbergersee (lake), Germany 22/D5
Starodub, U.S.S.R. 52/D4
Starogard Gdański, Poland 47/D2
Star Prairie, Wis. 317/A5

Starr, S.C. 296/B3
Starr (co.), Texas 303/F11
Starr King (mt.), N.H. 268/E3
Starrucca, Pa. 294/M2
Start, La. 238/G2
Start (pt.), Scotland 15/F1
Start (pt.), England 15/P5
Star Tannery, Va. 307/L2
Startex, S.C. 296/C2
Startup, Wash. 310/D3
Starvation (res.), Utah 304/D3
Stary Sacz, Poland 47/E4
Staryy Oskol, U.S.S.R. 52/E4
Staser, Ind. 227/B8
Stassfurt, Germany 22/D3
Staszów, Poland 47/E3
State Center, Iowa 229/G5
State College, Pa. 294/G4
State Line, Idaho 220/A2
State Line, Ind. 227/A7
State Line, Mass. 249/A3
State Line, Miss. 256/G8
State Line, Pa. 294/G6
Staten (Los Estados) (isl.), Argentina 143/D7
Staten (isl.), N.Y. 276/M9
Staten Island (borough), N.Y. 276/M9
Statenville, Georgia 217/G9
State Road, N.C. 281/H2
Statesboro, Georgia 217/J6
Statesville, N.C. 281/H3
Statesville, Tenn. 237/J8
Statham, Georgia 217/F3
Static, Tenn. 237/L7
Station Camp, Ky. 237/N5
Statts Mills, W. Va. 312/C5
Statue of Liberty Nat'l Mon., N.J. 273/B2
Statue of Liberty Nat'l Mon., N.Y. 276/M9
Staunton, Ill. 222/D5
Staunton, Ind. 227/C6
Staunton (I.C.), Va. 307/K4
Staunton (Roanoke) (riv.), Va. 307/H6
Stavanger, Norway 18/D7
Stavanger, Norway 7/E3
Stave (lake), Br. Col. 184/L3
Staveley, England 13/K2
Stavelot, Belgium 27/H8
Stavely, Alberta 182/D4
Staveren, Netherlands 27/G3
Stavern, Norway 18/D4
Stavropol', U.S.S.R. 7/J4
Stavropol', U.S.S.R. 52/F5
Stavropol', U.S.S.R. 48/E5
Stavrós, Greece 45/F5
Stawell, Victoria 97/B5
Stayner, Ontario 177/E3
Stayton, Oreg. 291/E3
Stead, Manitoba 179/F4
Stead, N. Mex. 274/F2
Steamboat, Ariz. 198/F3
Steamboat (mt.), Idaho 220/C4
Steamboat Rock, Iowa 229/G4
Steamboat Springs, Colo. 208/F2
Steamburg, N.Y. 276/C6
Steamtown Nat'l Historic Site, Pa. 294/F7
Stearns, Ky. 237/N7
Stearns (co.), Minn. 255/D5
Stebbins, Alaska 196/F2
Steckborn, Switzerland 39/G1
Stecoah, N.C. 281/B4
Stedman, N.C. 281/M4
Steedman, S.C. 296/E4
Steeds, N.C. 281/K4
Steel (mt.), Idaho 220/C6
Steele, Ala. 195/F3
Steele (co.), Minn. 255/E7
Steele, Mo. 261/N10
Steele (co.), N. Dak. 282/P4
Steele, N. Dak. 282/L6
Steele City, Nebr. 264/G4
Steele Narrows Hist. Park, Sask. 181/B2
Steeles (pt.), Norfolk I. 88/L5
Steeles Tavern, Va. 307/K5
Steelville, Ill. 222/D6
Steelman, Sask. 181/J6
Steelmanville, N.J. 273/D5
Steelton, Pa. 294/J5
Steelville, Mo. 261/K7
Steen, Minn. 255/B7
Steen, Sask. 181/H3
Steenbergen, Netherlands 27/E5
Steenkool, Indonesia 85/J6
Steenokkerzeel, Belgium 27/C9
Steen River, Alberta 182/B4
Steens, Miss. 256/G4
Steens (mt.), Oreg. 291/J5
Steensby (inlet), N.W. Terr. 187/L2
Steenwijk, Netherlands 27/J3
Steep (pt.), W. Australia 88/A5
Steep (pt.), W. Australia 92/A1
Steep Falls, Maine 243/B8
Steep Rock, Manitoba 179/D3
Stefănești, Romania 45/H2
Stefanie (lake), Ethiopia 111/G7
Stefansson (isl.), N.W.T. 162/F1
Stefansson (isl.), N.W.T. 187/H2
Steffenville, Mo. 261/J3
Steffisburg, Switzerland 39/E3
Stege, Denmark 21/F8
Stege, Denmark 18/H9
Steger, Ill. 222/F2
Stehekin, Wash. 310/E2
Steigerwald (for.), Germany 22/D3
Steilacoom, Wash. 310/C3
Stein, Switzerland 39/E1
Steinach, Germany 22/D3
Stein am Rhein, Switzerland 39/G1
Steinauer, Nebr. 264/H4
Steinbach, Manitoba 179/F5
Steinhatchee, Fla. 212/D4
Steinhausen, Namibia 118/B4
Steinhuder Meer (lake), Germany 22/C2

Steinkjer, Norway 18/G4
Steinneset (cape), Norway 18/E2
Stekene, Belgium 27/E6
Stella, Mo. 261/D9
Stella, Nebr. 264/J4
Stella, N.C. 281/P5
Stella, Wash. 310/B4
Stellarton, Nova Scotia 168/F3
Stellenbosch, S. Africa 118/F6
Steller (mt.), Alaska 196/K2
Stelvio (pass), Switzerland 39/K3
Stem, N.C. 281/M2
Stendal, Germany 22/D2
Stendal, Ind. 227/C8
Stenen, Sask. 181/J4
Stenhousemuir, Scotland 15/C1
Stennett, Iowa 229/C6
Stenness, Denmark 21/E6
Stenstrup, Denmark 21/D7
Stenungsund, Sweden 18/G7
Stepanakert, U.S.S.R. 48/E6
Stepanakert, U.S.S.R. 52/F5
Stepaside, Ireland 17/J5
Stephan, S. Dak. 298/K5
Stephen, Minn. 255/A2
Stephenfield, Manitoba 179/D5
Stephens (passage), Alaska 196/N1
Stephens, Ark. 202/E7
Stephens (co.), Br. Col. 184/B3
Stephens (co.), Georgia 217/F1
Stephens, Georgia 217/F3
Stephens (isl.), N. Zealand 100/D4
Stephens (co.), Okla. 288/L6
Stephens (co.), Texas 303/F5
Stephensburg, Ky. 237/J5
Stephensburg, N.J. 273/D2
Stephens City, Va. 307/M2
Stephen's Creek, N.S. Wales 97/A2
Stephenson (co.), Ill. 222/D1
Stephenson, Mich. 250/D3
Stephensport, Ky. 237/H6
Stephenville, N.Y. 276/O5
Stephenville, Newf. 166/C4
Stephenville, Newf. 162/L6
Stephenville, Texas 303/F5
Stephenville Crossing, Newf. 166/C4
Stepney, Conn. 210/B3
Stepovak (bay), Alaska 196/G3
Steprock, Ark. 202/G3
Steptoe, Wash. 310/H3
Sterling, Alaska 196/B1
Sterling, Colo. 188/F2
Sterling, Colo. 208/N1
Sterling (res.), Colo. 208/N1
Sterling•, Conn. 210/H2
Sterling, Georgia 217/K8
Sterling, Idaho 220/F6
Sterling, Ill. 222/D2
Sterling, Kansas 232/D3
Sterling•, Mass. 249/G3
Sterling, Mich. 250/E4
Sterling, Nebr. 264/H4
Sterling, N. Dak. 282/K6
Sterling, Ohio 284/G4
Sterling, Okla. 288/K5
Sterling, Pa. 294/M3
Sterling (co.), Texas 303/C6
Sterling, Utah 304/C4
Sterling, Va. 307/O2
Sterling City, Texas 303/D6
Sterling Heights, Mich. 250/B6
Sterling Run, Pa. 294/F3
Sterlington, La. 238/F1
Sterlitamak, U.S.S.R. 7/K3
Sterlitamak, U.S.S.R. 48/F4
Sterlitamak, U.S.S.R. 52/J4
Sternberg, Germany 22/D2
Šternberk, Czech. 41/D2
Sterrett, Ala. 195/F4
Stet, Mo. 261/E4
Stetson•, Maine 243/F4
Stetsonville, Wis. 317/F5
Stettin (Szczecin), Poland 47/B2
Stettler, Alberta 182/D3
Stettler, Alta. 162/E5
Stettyn (mt.), S. Africa 118/G6
Steuben (co.), Ind. 227/G1
Steuben, Maine 243/H6
Steuben•, Maine 243/H6
Steuben (co.), N.Y. 276/F6
Steuben, Wis. 317/E9
Steubenville, Ohio 188/K2
Steubenville, Ohio 284/J5
Steve, Ark. 202/D4
Stevenage, England 13/G6
Stevenage, England 10/F5
Stevens (co.), Kansas 232/A4
Stevens (co.), Minn. 255/B5
Stevens (creek), S.C. 296/C4
Stevens (co.), Wash. 310/H2
Stevens (pass), Wash. 310/D3
Stevensburg, Va. 307/N4
Stevenson, Ala. 195/G1
Stevenson (lake), Manitoba 179/J3
Stevenson, The (riv.), S. Australia 94/D2
Stevenson, Wash. 310/C5
Stevenson Entrance (str.), Alaska 196/H3
Stevens Point, Wis. 317/G7
Stevens Pottery, Georgia 217/F5
Stevenston, Scotland 15/D5
Stevenstown, Wis. 317/D7
Stevens Village, Alaska 196/J1
Stevensville, Mich. 250/C6
Stevensville, Mont. 262/C4
Stevns Klint (cliff), Denmark 21/F7
Steward, Ill. 222/D2
Stewardson, Ill. 222/E4
Stewart, Ala. 195/C5
Stewart, Br. Col. 162/D4
Stewart, Br. Col. 184/C2
Stewart (isl.), Chile 138/E11
Stewart (co.), Georgia 217/C6
Stewart, Minn. 255/D6

Stewart, Miss. 256/F4
Stewart (isl.), N. Zealand 87/G10
Stewart (isl.), N. Zealand 100/A7
Stewart (cape), North. Terr. 93/D1
Stewart, Ohio 284/G7
Stewart (co.), Tenn. 237/F7
Stewart, Tenn. 237/F8
Stewart (riv.), Yukon 162/C3
Stewart (mt.), Alaska 196/K2
Stewart Crossing, Yukon 187/E3
Stewarton, Scotland 15/D5
Stewart River, Yukon 187/D3
Stewart River, Yukon 162/B3
Stewarts Point, Calif. 204/B5
Stewartstown•, N.H. 268/E2
Stewartstown, N. Ireland 17/H2
Stewartstown, Pa. 294/K6
Stewartsville, Ind. 227/B8
Stewartsville, Mo. 261/C3
Stewartsville, N.J. 273/C2
Stewartsville, Ohio 284/J6
Stewart Town, Jamaica 158/H6
Stewart Valley, Sask. 181/D5
Stewartville, Ala. 195/F4
Stewartville, Minn. 255/F7
Stewiacke, Nova Scotia 168/E3
Stewiacke (riv.), Nova Scotia 168/E3
Steyer, Mo. 261/C3
Steyr, Austria 41/C2
Stia, Italy 34/C3
Stickney, Ill. 222/B6
Stickney, New Bruns. 170/C2
Stickney, S. Dak. 298/M6
Stickney, W. Va. 312/D7
Stidham, Okla. 288/P4
Stiens, Netherlands 27/H2
Stigler, Okla. 288/R4
Stikine (riv.), Alaska 196/N2
Stikine (str.), Alaska 196/N2
Stikine (riv.), Br. Col. 162/C4
Stikine (riv.), Br. Col. 184/B1
Stiles, Iowa 229/J7
Stiles, Wis. 317/L6
Stilesville, Ind. 227/D5
Stilis, Greece 45/F6
Still (riv.), Conn. 210/B3
Still (riv.), Conn. 210/C1
Still (riv.), Conn. 210/C1
Stillman Valley, Ill. 222/D1
Stillmore, Georgia 217/H6
Still Pond, Md. 245/S8
Still River, Mass. 249/H3
Stillwater, Maine 243/F6
Stillwater (riv.), Mass. 249/G3
Stillwater, Minn. 255/F5
Stillwater (co.), Mont. 262/G5
Stillwater (riv.), Mont. 262/G5
Stillwater, Nev. 266/C3
Stillwater (range), Nev. 266/C3
Stillwater, N.J. 273/D1
Stillwater, N.Y. 276/N5
Stillwater, Ohio 284/H5
Stillwater (riv.), Ohio 284/B5
Stillwater, Okla. 288/N2
Stillwater, Pa. 294/K4
Stillwater (res.), R.I. 249/C2
Stillwell, Ill. 222/D6
Stilwell, Ind. 227/D1
Stilson, Georgia 217/J6
Stilwell, Kansas 232/H3
Stilwell, Okla. 288/S3
Stimson (mt.), Mont. 262/C2
Stinchar (riv.), Scotland 15/D5
Stinesville, Ind. 227/D6
Stinnett, Texas 303/C2
Stinson Beach, Calif. 204/H2
Stinson Lake, N.H. 268/D4
Stintino, Italy 34/B4
Štip, Yugoslavia 45/F5
Stiring-Wendel, France 28/G3
Stirling, Alberta 182/D5
Stirling, N.J. 273/E2
Stirling (creek), North. Terr. 88/D3
Stirling (creek), North. Terr. 93/A4
Stirling, Ontario 177/G3
Stirling, Scotland 15/C1
Stirling (trad. co.), Scotland 15/A5
Stirling, W. Australia 88/B2
Stirling, W. Australia 92/A1
Stirling City, Calif. 204/D4
Stirling North, S. Australia 94/E5
Stirling Station, North. Terr. 93/C6
Stirrat, W. Va. 312/C7
Stirum, N. Dak. 282/P7
Stites, Idaho 220/D3
Stittsville, Ontario 177/J2
Stittville, N.Y. 276/K5
Stitzer, Wis. 317/E10
Stockbridge, Georgia 217/D3
Stockbridge, Mass. 249/A3
Stockbridge•, Mass. 249/A3
Stockbridge, Mich. 250/E6
Stockbridge•, Vt. 268/B4
Stockbridge, Wis. 317/K7
Stockbridge Ind. Res., Wis. 317/J6
Stockdale, Ohio 284/E8
Stockdale, Texas 303/G8
Stockerau, Austria 41/D2
Stockertown, Pa. 294/M4
Stockett, Mont. 262/E3
Stockham, Nebr. 264/F4
Stockholm•, Maine 243/G1
Stockholm, N.J. 273/D1
Stockholm, Sask. 181/J5
Stockholm, S. Dak. 298/R3
Stockholm (co.), Sweden 18/L7
Stockholm (cap.), Sweden 2/F3
Stockholm (cap.), Sweden 18/G1
Stockholm, Wis. 317/B7
Stockhorn (mt.), Switzerland 39/E3
Stockland, Ill. 222/F3
Stockley, Del. 245/S6
Stockport, England 13/H2
Stockport, England 10/G2
Stockport, Iowa 229/K7

Stockport, Ohio 284/G6
Stocksbridge, England 13/J2
Stockton, Ala. 195/C9
Stockton, Calif. 188/B3
Stockton, Calif. 204/D6
Stockton, Georgia 217/G9
Stockton, Ill. 222/C1
Stockton, Iowa 229/M5
Stockton, Kansas 232/C2
Stockton, Manitoba 179/C5
Stockton, Md. 245/S8
Stockton, Minn. 255/G6
Stockton, Mo. 261/E7
Stockton (lake), Mo. 261/E7
Stockton, N.J. 273/D3
Stockton, N.Y. 276/B6
Stockton (plat.), Texas 303/B7
Stockton, Utah 304/B3
Stockton (isl.), Wis. 317/F2
Stockton-on-Tees, England 13/F3
Stockton-on-Tees, England 10/F3
Stockton Springs, Maine 243/F7
Stockton Springs•, Maine 243/F7
Stockville, Nebr. 264/D4
Stockwell, Ind. 227/D4
Stoco, Ontario 177/G3
Stod, Czech. 41/B2
Stoddard (co.), Mo. 261/N9
Stoddard•, N.H. 268/C5
Stoddard, Wis. 317/D8
Stoeng Treng, Cambodia 72/E4
Stoer (pt.), Scotland 15/C2
Stoholm, Denmark 21/C5
Stoke-on-Trent, England 13/E4
Stoke-on-Trent, England 10/E4
Stokes (bay), Chile 138/D10
Stokes (co.), N.C. 281/J2
Stokes, N.C. 281/P5
Stokes (pt.), Tasmania 99/A1
Stokes Bay, Ontario 177/D3
Stokesdale, N.C. 281/K2
Stolac, Yugoslavia 45/D4
Stolberg, Germany 22/B3
Stolp (Słupsk), Poland 47/C1
Ston, Yugoslavia 45/D4
Stone (co.), Ark. 202/F2
Stone, England 10/E4
Stone, England 13/E5
Stone, Idaho 220/G7
Stone, Ky. 237/S5
Stone (co.), Miss. 256/F9
Stone (co.), Mo. 261/F9
Stone (mts.), N.C. 281/F2
Stone (mts.), Tenn. 237/T8
Stone Bank, Wis. 317/J1
Stonebluff, Ind. 227/C4
Stonebluff, Okla. 288/P3
Stoneboro, Pa. 294/B3
Stoneboro, S.C. 296/F2
Stone City, Iowa 229/L4
Stonecliffe, Ontario 177/G1
Stone Creek, Ohio 284/G5
Stonefort, Ill. 222/E6
Stonega, Va. 307/C7
Stoneham•, Mass. 249/C6
Stoneham, Colo. 208/M1
Stoneham, Québec 172/F2
Stone Harbor, N.J. 273/D5
Stonehaven, Scotland 10/E2
Stonehaven, Scotland 15/F4
Stonehenge (ruins), England 13/F6
Stonehenge, Queensland 95/B5
Stonehenge, Queensland 88/G4
Stonehenge, Sask. 181/F6
Stonehouse, Scotland 15/D5
Stone Lake, Wis. 317/C4
Stone Mountain, Georgia 217/D3
Stone Mountain Prov. Park, Br. Col. 184/C2
Stone Park, Ill. 222/B5
Stoner, Br. Col. 184/F3
Stones (riv.), Tenn. 237/H9
Stones River Nat'l Battlefield, Tenn. 237/H9
Stoneville, Miss. 256/C4
Stoneville, N.C. 281/K2
Stoneville, S. Dak. 298/D4
Stonewall•, Ark. 202/J1
Stonewall, Georgia 217/J2
Stonewall, La. 238/C2
Stonewall, Manitoba 179/E4
Stonewall, Miss. 256/G6
Stonewall, N.C. 281/R4
Stonewall, Okla. 288/O5
Stonewall (co.), Texas 303/D4
Stonewall, Texas 303/F7
Stonewood, W. Va. 312/D6
Stoney Creek, Ontario 177/E4
Stoney Point, Ontario 177/B5
Stonington, Colo. 208/P4
Stonington, Conn. 210/H3
Stonington•, Conn. 210/H3
Stonington, Ill. 222/D4
Stonington, Maine 243/F7
Stonington, Mich. 250/C3
Stono (inlet), S.C. 296/H6
Stony (riv.), Alaska 196/G2
Stony (isl.), Newf. 166/C3
Stony (brook), N.J. 273/D3
Stony (ranges), N.S. Wales 97/B2
Stony (pt.), N.Y. 276/H3
Stony (isl.), Ontario 177/E2
Stony (lake), Ontario 177/G3
Stony (head), Tasmania 99/C2
Stony (creek), Va. 307/N5
Stony (riv.), W. Va. 312/H4
Stony Beach, Sask. 181/F5
Stony Bottom, W. Va. 312/F6
Stony Brook, N.Y. 276/G9
Stony Creek, Conn. 210/E3
Stony Creek, N.Y. 276/M4
Stony Creek, Va. 307/N7
Stonyford, Calif. 204/C4
Stony Gorge (res.), Calif. 204/C4
Stony Island, Nova Scotia 168/C5
Stony Lake, Mich. 250/C5
Stony Mountain, Manitoba 179/E4

Stony Plain, Alberta 182/C3
Stony Point, N.Y. 276/M8
Stony Point, N.C. 281/D5
Stony Rapids, Sask. 181/M2
Stony River, Alaska 196/G2
Stony Tunguska (riv.), U.S.S.R. 54/L3
Stony Tunguska (riv.), U.S.S.R. 48/K3
Stony Wold, N.Y. 276/M1
Storå (riv.), Denmark 21/B5
Stora Lulevatten (lake), Sweden 18/L3
Storden, Minn. 255/C6
Store Baelt (chan.), Denmark 18/G9
Store Baelt (chan.), Denmark 21/D6
Store Heddinge, Denmark 21/F7
Store-Heddinge, Denmark 18/H9
Stor-Elvdal, Norway 18/G6
Støren, Norway 18/F5
Storey (co.), Nev. 266/B3
Storeys Creek, Tasmania 99/D3
Storeytown, New Bruns. 170/D2
Storfjorden (fjord), Norway 18/D2
Storjorm (lake), Sweden 18/J4
Storkerson (bay), N.W. Terr. 187/F2
Storla, S. Dak. 298/M6
Storm (lake), Iowa 229/C3
Storm (bay), Tasmania 99/D5
Storm Lake, Iowa 229/C3
Stormont (county), Ontario 177/K2
Stornoway, Québec 172/F4
Stornoway, Sask. 181/K4
Stornoway, Scotland 15/B2
Stornoway, Scotland 10/C1
Stornoway (harb.), Scotland 15/B2
Storøya (isl.), Norway 18/E1
Storozhevsk, U.S.S.R. 52/H2
Storr, The (mt.), Scotland 15/B3
Storrs, Conn. 210/F1
Storsjün (lake), Sweden 18/J5
Storstrøm (co.), Denmark 21/E7
Stort (riv.), England 13/H7
Storthoaks, Sask. 181/K6
Storuman, Sweden 18/K4
Storuman (lake), Sweden 18/K4
Storvik, Sweden 18/K6
Story, Ind. 227/E6
Story (co.), Iowa 229/G4
Story, Wyo. 319/F1
Story City, Iowa 229/F4
Stosch (isl.), Chile 138/C8
Stotesbury, Mo. 261/C7
Stotesbury, W. Va. 312/D7
Stotts City, Mo. 261/E6
Stottville, N.Y. 276/N6
Stoughton ●, Mass. 249/K4
Stoughton, Sask. 181/J6
Stoughton, Wis. 317/H10
Stoumont, Belgium 27/H8
Stour (riv.), England 13/J6
Stour (riv.), England 13/H6
Stour (riv.), England 13/E7
Stour (riv.), England 13/J7
Stourbridge, England 13/E5
Stourbridge, England 10/G3
Stourport-on-Severn, England 10/G3
Stourport-on-Severn, England 13/E5
Stout, Iowa 229/H3
Stout, Ohio 284/D8
Stout (lake), Ontario 175/B2
Stoutland, Mo. 261/G7
Stoutsville, Mo. 261/J3
Stoutsville, Ohio 284/E6
Stovall, Miss. 256/C2
Stovall, N.C. 281/M2
Stover, Mo. 261/G6
Støvring, Denmark 21/C4
Stow ●, Maine 243/A7
Stow ●, Mass. 249/H3
Stow (creek), N.J. 273/C5
Stow, Ohio 284/H3
Stow, Scotland 15/F5
Stowe, Pa. 294/L5
Stowe, Vt. 268/B3
Stowe ●, Vt. 268/B3
Stowmarket, England 13/J5
Stowmarket, England 10/G4
Stowport, Tasmania 99/B3
Stoy, Ill. 222/F5
Stoystown, Pa. 294/E5
Strabane (dist.), N. Ireland 17/G2
Strabane, N. Ireland 17/G2
Strabane, N. Ireland 10/C3
Strachan, Scotland 15/F3
Strachur Bay, Scotland 15/C4
Stradbally, Laois, Ireland 17/G5
Stradbally, Waterford, Ireland 17/F7
Strafford, Mo. 261/F8
Strafford ●, N.H. 268/E5
Strafford ●, N.H. 268/E5
Strafford ●, Vt. 268/C4
Straffordville, Ontario 177/D5
Strahan, Iowa 229/B7
Strahan, Tasmania 99/B4
Strait (butte), Utah 304/C6
Straits, N.C. 281/R5
Straits Pond, Mass. 249/F7
Straitsville, Conn. 210/C3
Strakonice, Czech. 41/B2
Stralsund, Germany 22/E1
Strand, S. Africa 118/F4
Strandburg, S. Dak. 298/R3
Strandby, Denmark 21/D3
Strandquist, Minn. 255/B2
Strang, Nebr. 264/G4
Strang, Okla. 288/R2
Strange Creek, W. Va. 312/E5
Strangford, N. Ireland 17/K3
Strangford (inlet), N. Ireland 17/K3
Strängnäs, Sweden 18/F1
Stranraer, Sask. 181/C4
Stranraer, Scotland 10/D3
Stranraer, Scotland 15/C6
Strasbourg, France 28/H3
Strasbourg, France 7/E4
Strasbourg, Sask. 181/G4
Strasburg, Colo. 208/L3
Strasburg, Ill. 222/E4
Strasburg, Mo. 261/D5
Strasburg, N. Dak. 282/K7

Strasburg, Ohio 284/G4
Strasburg, Pa. 294/K6
Strasburg, Va. 3C7/M3
Strassburg, Austria 41/C4
Stratford, Calif. 204/F7
Stratford ●, Conn. 210/C4
Stratford (pt.), Conn. 210/C4
Stratford, Iowa 229/F4
Stratford ●, N.H. 268/D2
Stratford, N.J. 273/B4
Stratford, N.Y. 276/L4
Stratford, N. Zealand 100/E3
Stratford, Okla. 238/M5
Stratford, Ontario 177/C4
Stratford, S. Dak. 298/N3
Stratford, Texas 303/C1
Stratford, Va. 307/P4
Stratford, Wash. 310/F3
Stratford, Wis. 317/F6
Stratford-Centre, Québec 172/F4
Stratford-upon-Avon, England 13/F5
Stratford-upon-Avon, England 10/F3
Strathalbyn, S. Australia 94/F6
Stratham ●, N.H. 268/F5
Strathaven, Scotland 15/D5
Strathbogie (dist.), Scotland 15/F3
Strathbogie (reg.), Scotland 15/C4
Strathclyde (reg.), Scotland 15/C4
Strathclair, Manitoba 179/B4
Strathcona, Minn 255/B2
Strathcona Prov. Park, Br. Col. 184/E5
Strathfield, N. S. Wales 88/K4
Strathfield, N.S. Wales 97/J3
Strathfoyle, N. Ireland 17/G1
Strathgordon, Tasmania 99/C4
Strathlorne, Nova Scotia 168/G2
Strathmere, N.J. 273/D5
Strathmoor Village, Ky. 237/J2
Strathmore, Alberta 182/D4
Strathmore, Calif. 204/F7
Strathmore, N.J. 273/E3
Strathmore, Scotland 15/E4
Strathnaver, Br. Col. 184/E5
Strathpeffer, Scotland 15/D3
Strathroy, Ontario 177/C5
Strathspey (dist.) Scotland 15/E3
Strathy (pt.), Scotland 15/E2
Strathy (pt.), Scotland 10/D1
Strathyre, Scotland 15/D4
Strattanville, Pa. 294/D3
Stratton, Colo. 203/O4
Stratton, Maine 243/B5
Stratton, Nebr. 264/C4
Stratton, Ohio 284/J4
Stratton, Ontario ●77/F5
Stratton, Ontario 175/B3
Stratton ●, Vt. 268/B5
Stratton (mt.), Vt. 268/B5
Straubing, Germany 22/E4
Straubville, N. Dak. 282/07
Straughn, Ind. 227/G5
Strausberg, Germany 22/F2
Straussstown, Pa. 294/K5
Straw, Mont. 262/G4
Strawberry, Ark. 202/H2
Strawberry (lake), N. Dak. 282/J4
Strawberry (res.), Utah 304/D3
Strawberry (res.), Utah 304/D3
Strawberry Plains, Tenn. 237/08
Strawberry Point, owa 229/K3
Strawn, Ill. 222/E3
Strawn, Kansas 232/G3
Strawn, Texas 303/F5
Strawn, Miss. 256/D1
Stráznice, Czech. 41/D2
Strayhorn, Miss. 256/D1
Streaky (bay), S. Australia 88/E6
Streaky (bay), S. Australia 94/C5
Streaky Bay, S. Australia 88/E6
Streaky Bay, S. Australia 94/C5
Streamstown, Alberta 182/E3
Streamwood, Ill. 222/A5
Streator, Ill. 222/E2
Stredocesky (reg.), Czech. 41/C2
Stredoslovensky (reg.), Czech. 41/E2
Street, England 10/E5
Street, England 13/E6
Street, Md. 245/N2
Streeter, N. Dak. 232/M6
Streeter, Texas 303/E7
Streetman, Texas 303/H6
Streetsboro, Ohio 284/H3
Strehaia, Romania 45/F3
Stresa, Italy 34/B2
Stretford, England 13/H2
Stretford, England 10/G2
Streymoy (isl.), Denmark 21/B3
Strezhevoy, U.S.S.R. 48/H3
Stríbro, Czech. 41/B2
Strichen, Scotland 15/F3
Strickler, Ark. 202/B2
Strike, C.J. (res.), Idaho 220/C7
Strimón (gulf), Greece 45/G5
Stringer, Miss. 256/F7
Stringtown, Miss. 256/C3
Stringtown, Okla. 288/P6
Stripe (lake), Sask. 181/C4
Striven, Loch (inlet), Scotland 15/A2
Stroeder, Argentina 143/D5
Strofádhes (isls.), Greece 45/E7
Stroh, Ind. 227/G1
Strokestown, Ireland 17/E4
Stroma (isl.), Scotland 15/E2
Stromboli (isl.), Italy 34/E5
Strome, Alberta 182/E3
Stromeferry, Scotland 15/C3
Stromness, Scotland 10/E1
Stromness, Scotland 15/E2
Stromsburg, Nebr. 264/G3
Strümstad, Sweden 18/G7
Strümsund, Sweden 18/K5
Strom Thurmond (lake), Georgia 217/H3
Strom Thurmond (dam), S.C. 296/C4
Strom Thurmond (lake), S.C. 296/C4
Stronach, Mich. 250/C4
Strong, Ark. 202/F7
Strong ●, Maine 243/C6
Strong (riv.), Miss. 256/D7
Strong City, Kansas 232/F3

Strong City, Okla. 288/G3
Strongfield, Sask. 181/E4
Stronghurst, Ill. 222/C3
Strongs, Mich. 250/E2
Strongs, Miss. 256/G5
Strongsville, Ohio 284/G10
Stronsay (firth), Scotland 15/F1
Stronsay (isl.), Scotland 10/E1
Stronsay (isl.), Scotland 15/F1
Strontian, Scotland 15/C4
Stropkov, Czech. 41/F2
Stroud, Ala. 195/H4
Stroud, England 13/E6
Stroud, England 10/E5
Stroud, N.S. Wales 97/G3
Stroud, Okla. 288/N3
Stroud, Ontario 177/E3
Stroudsburg, Pa. 294/M4
Struan, Sask. 181/D3
Struan, Scotland 15/B3
Struble, Iowa 229/A3
Struer, Denmark 21/B5
Struer, Denmark 18/F8
Struga, Yugoslavia 45/E5
Struma (riv.), Bulgaria 45/F5
Strumble (head), Wales 13/B5
Strumica, Yugoslavia 45/F5
Strunk, Ky. 237/N7
Struthers, Ohio 284/J3
Stryker, Mont. 262/B2
Stryker, Ohio 284/B3
Strykersville, N.Y. 276/C5
Stuart (isl.), Alaska 196/F2
Stuart (lake), Br. Col. 184/E3
Stuart, Fla. 212/F4
Stuart, Iowa 229/E6
Stuart, Nebr. 264/F2
Stuart, Okla. 288/05
Stuart (range), S. Australia 94/D3
Stuart, Va. 307/H7
Stuart (mt.), Wash. 310/E3
Stuartburn, Manitoba 179/F5
Stuart Island, Br. Col. 184/E5
Stuarts Draft, Va. 307/L4
Stuart Town, N.S. Wales 97/E3
Stubbekøbing, Denmark 21/F8
Stubbenkammer (pt.), Germany 22/E1
Stub Hill (mt.), N.H. 268/E1
Stuckey, S.C. 296/F4
Studénka, Czech. 41/D2
Studley, Kansas 232/B2
Studley, Va. 307/05
Stukely-Sud, Québec 172/E4
Stump (lake), N. Dak. 282/O4
Stumptown, W. Va. 312/E5
Stumpy Point, N.C. 281/T3
Stupino, U.S.S.R. 52/E4
Stura (riv.), Italy 34/A2
Sturbridge, Mass. 249/F4
Sturbridge ●, Mass. 249/F4
Sturdivant, Mo. 261/M8
Sturgeon (lake), Alberta 182/B2
Sturgeon (bay), Manitoba 179/E3
Sturgeon (riv.), Mich. 250/C2
Sturgeon (riv.), Minn. 255/F3
Sturgeon, Mo. 261/H4
Sturgeon (lake), Ontario 177/G5
Sturgeon, Pa. 294/B5
Sturgeon, Pr. Edward I. 168/F2
Sturgeon (riv.), Sask. 181/E2
Sturgeon Bay, Wis. 317/M6
Sturgeon Falls, Ont. 162/H6
Sturgeon Falls, Ontario 175/D3
Sturgeon Falls, Ontario 177/E1
Sturgeon Heights, Alberta 182/B2
Sturgeon Lake, Minn. 255/F4
Sturgeon Point, Ontario 177/F3
Sturgeon Weir, Sask. 181/N4
Sturgis, Ky. 237/F5
Sturgis, Mich. 250/D7
Sturgis, Miss. 256/G4
Sturgis, Sask. 181/J4
Sturgis, S. Dak. 298/B5
Sturovo, Czech. 41/E3
Sturt (mt.), N.S. Wales 97/A1
Sturt (plain), North. Terr. 93/C4
Sturt (des.), Queensland 88/G5
Sturt (des.), Queensland 95/B3
Sturt (riv.), S. Australia 88/D8
Sturt (des.), S. Australia 94/G3
Sturt (riv.), S. Australia 94/B8
Sturt (creek), W. Australia 88/D8
Sturt (creek), W. Australia 92/D2
Sturtevant, Wis. 317/M3
Stutsman (co.), N. Dak. 282/M5
Stutterheim, S. Africa 118/D6
Stuttgart, Ark. 202/H4
Stuttgart, Kansas 232/C2
Stuttgart, Germany 7/E4
Stuttgart, Germany 22/C4
Styria (prov.), Austria 41/C3
Sufian, Iran 66/E1
Sugar (creek), Ind. 227/B3
Sugar (creek), Ind. 227/F5
Sugar (creek), Ind. 227/C5
Sugar (isl.), Mich. 250/E2
Sugar (creek), N.H. 268/C5
Sugar (creek), Pa. 294/J2
Sugar Bush, Wis. 317/J7
Sugarbush Hill (mt.), Wis. 317/J4
Sugar City, Colo. 208/M6
Sugar City, Idaho 220/G6
Sugar Creek, Mo. 261/R5
Sugarcreek, Ohio 284/G5
Sugar Creek, Pa. 294/C3
Sugar Grove, Ark. 202/C3
Sugar Grove, Ill. 222/E2

Subiaco, Ark. 202/C3
Subiaco, W. Australia 88/B2
Subi Besar (isl.), Indonesia 85/D5
Subic (bay), Philippines 82/B3
Sublett (mts.), Idaho 220/E7
Sublett, Ky. 237/P5
Sublette, Ill. 222/D2
Sublette, Kansas 232/B4
Sublette (co.), Wyo. 319/C3
Subligna, Georgia 217/B1
Sublimity, Oreg. 291/E3
Subotica, Yugoslavia 7/F4
Subotica, Yugoslavia 45/D2
Subtle, Ky. 237/L7
Sucarnochee, Miss. 256/H5
Sucarnochee (creek), Miss. 256/G5
Succasunna, N.J. 273/D2
Success, Mo. 261/H8
Success, Sask. 181/D5
Success, Sask. 181/D5
Succor (creek), Oreg. 291/K4
Suceava, Romania 18/F8
Suchedniów, Poland 47/E3
Suches, Bolivia 136/A4
Suches (riv.), Bolivia 136/A4
Suches, Georgia 217/E1
Suchitoto, El Salvador 154/C4
Sucia (bay), Wash. 310/C2
Sucia (isl.), Wash. 310/C2
Sucio (riv.), Colombia 126/B4
Suck (riv.), Ireland 17/E5
Sucre (cap.), Bolivia 2/F6
Sucre (cap.), Bolivia 120/C4
Sucre (cap.), Bolivia 136/C6
Sucre (dept.), Colombia 126/C3
Sucre, Bolívar, Colombia 126/C3
Sucre, Caquetá, Colombia 126/C7
Sucre, Ecuador 128/B3
Sucre (state), Venezuela 124/G2
Sucre, Venezuela 124/D3
Sucúa, Ecuador 128/C4
Sucuriju, Brazil 132/D2
Sud (dept.), Haiti 158/A6
Sud (chan.), Haiti 158/B6
Suda (riv.), U.S.S.R. 52/E3
Sudak, U.S.S.R. 52/E6
Sudan 2/L5
Sudan 102/E3
SUDAN 59/B6
SUDAN 111/E4
Sudan (reg.), Africa 102/D3
Sudan (reg.), Benin 106/E6
Sudan (reg.), Burkina Faso 106/D6
Sudan (reg.), Chad 111/C5
Sudan (reg.), Mali 106/D6
Sudan (reg.), Niger 106/F6
Sudan (reg.), Nigeria 106/F6
Sudan (reg.), Sudan 111/E5
Sudan, Texas 303/B3
Sudbury, England 13/H5
Sudbury, England 10/G4
Sudbury ●, Mass. 249/H3
Sudbury (res.), Mass. 249/H3
Sudbury (riv.), Mass. 249/A6
Sudbury, Ontario 162/G6
Sudbury, Ontario 146/K5
Sudbury, Ontario 177/K5
Sudbury, Ontario 175/D3
Sudbury (reg. munic.), Ontario 175/D3
Sudbury (reg. munic.), Ontario 177/K6
Sudbury (terr. dist.), Ontario 175/D3
Sudbury (terr. dist.), Ontario 177/J5
Sudbury ●, Vt. 268/A4
Sudd (swamp), Sudan 102/F4
Sudd (swamp), Sudan 111/F6
Suddie, Guyana 131/B2
Sudeten (mts.), Czech. 41/C1
Sudeten (range), Poland 47/B3
Sudhuroy (isl.), Denmark 21/B3
Sudirman (range), Indonesia 85/K6
Sudith, Ky. 237/O4
Sudlersville, Md. 245/P4
Sue (riv.), Sudan 111/E6
Sueca, Spain 33/F3
Suemez (isl.), Alaska 196/M2
Suez (canal) 2/L4
Suez, Egypt 111/K3
Suez, Egypt 59/B4
Suez, Egypt 102/F2
Suez (canal), Egypt 102/F1
Suez (canal), Egypt 111/K3
Suez (canal), Egypt 59/B3
Suez (gulf), Egypt 111/F2
Suez (gulf), Egypt 59/B4
Suf, Jordan 65/D3
Sufeina, Saudi Arabia 59/D5
Sufers, Switzerland 39/H4
Suffern, N.Y. 276/J8
Suffield, Alberta 182/E4
Suffield, Conn. 210/E1
Suffield ●, Conn. 210/E1
Suffield, Ohio 284/H3
Suffolk (co.), England 13/H5
Suffolk (co.), Mass. 249/K3
Suffolk, Mont. 262/G3
Suffolk (co.), N.Y. 276/P9
Suffolk (I.C.), Va. 307/P7

Sugar Grove, Ohio 284/E6
Sugar Grove, Pa. 294/D1
Sugar Grove, Va. 307/E7
Sugar Grove, W. Va. 312/H5
Sugar Hill, Georgia 217/E2
Sugar Hill ●, N.H. 268/D3
Sugar Island, Mich. 250/E2
Sugar Land, Texas 303/J8
Sugarloaf (key), Fla. 212/E7
Sugarloaf (hill), Hawaii 218/C4
Sugarloaf (mt.), Ireland 17/B8
Sugarloaf (pt.), N. S. Wales 88/J6
Sugarloaf (passage), N.S. Wales 97/J1
Sugarloaf (pt.), N.S. Wales 97/G3
Sugarloaf P.O. (Big Bear City), Calif. 204/J9
Sugar Notch, Pa. 294/E7
Sugartown, La. 238/D5
Sugar Tree, Tenn. 237/E9
Sugar Tree Ridge, Ohio 284/C7
Sugar Valley, Georgia 217/C1
Sugbai (passage), Philippines 82/C8
Sugden, Okla. 288/L6
Suggsville, Ala. 195/C7
Sühbaatar, Mongolia 77/H2
Sühbaatar (Sukhe Bator), Mongolia 77/G1
Sühbaatar, Mongolia 54/M5
Suheli Par (atoll), India 68/C6
Suhl, Germany 22/D3
Suhr, Switzerland 39/F2
Suhut, Turkey 63/D3
Sui, Pakistan 68/B3
Suiattle (riv.), Wash. 310/D2
Suichang, China 77/J6
Suide, China 77/G4
Suifenhe, China 77/M3
Suihua, China 77/L2
Suijiang, China 77/F6
Suileng, China 77/L2
Suining, China 77/H4
Suipacha, Argentina 143/G7
Suipacha, Bolivia 136/C7
Suir (riv.), Ireland 10/C4
Suir (riv.), Ireland 17/G7
Suisun (bay), Calif. 204/K1
Suisun City, Calif. 204/K1
Suit, N.C. 281/A4
Suita, Japan 81/J7
Suitland-Silver Hill, Md. 245/F5
Sui Xian, China 77/H5
Suizhong, China 77/K3
Sukabumi, Indonesia 85/H2
Sukadana, Indonesia 85/E6
Sukagawa, Japan 81/K5
Sukhana, U.S.S.R. 48/M3
Sukhinichi, U.S.S.R. 52/E4
Sukhona (riv.), U.S.S.R. 52/F2
Sukhothai, Thailand 72/D3
Sukhumi, U.S.S.R. 57/H4
Sukhumi, U.S.S.R. 52/F6
Sukhumi, U.S.S.R. 48/D5
Suki, Sudan 111/F5
Sukkertoppen (Maniitsoq), Greenl. 4/C12
Sukkur, Pakistan 54/H7
Sukkur, Pakistan 59/J4
Sukkur, Pakistan 68/B3
Süküsd, Hungary 41/E3
Sukumo, Japan 81/F7
Sul (chan.), Brazil 120/E2
Sul (chan.), Brazil 132/D2
Sula (isls.), Indonesia 54/O10
Sula (isls.), Indonesia 85/H6
Sula, Mont. 262/B5
Sulaco, Honduras 154/D3
Sulaco (riv.), Honduras 154/D3
Sulaiman (range), Pakistan 68/C3
Sulaimaniya (heads), Iraq 66/D3
Sulaimaniya, Iraq 59/E2
Sulaimaniya, Iraq 66/D3
Sulaiyil, Saudi Arabia 59/E5
Sulakyurt, Turkey 63/E2
Sulanheer, Mongolia 77/G3
Sulawesi (isl.), Indonesia 85/G6
Sulechów, Poland 47/B2
Sulecin, Poland 47/B2
Sulgen, Switzerland 39/H1
Sulina, Romania 45/J3
Sulina, Romania 45/J3
Sulitelma (mt.), Sweden 18/K3
Sulitjelma, Norway 18/K3
Sulitjelma (mt.), Norway 18/J3
Sullana, Peru 128/B5
Sullana, Peru 120/A3
Sulligent, Ala. 195/B3
Sullivan (lake), Alberta 182/D3
Sullivan, Ill. 222/E4
Sullivan (co.), Ind. 227/C6
Sullivan, Ind. 227/C6
Sullivan, Ky. 237/E6
Sullivan, Maine 243/G6
Sullivan (co.), Mo. 261/F2
Sullivan, Mo. 261/K6
Sullivan (co.), N.H. 268/C5
Sullivan ●, N.H. 268/C5
Sullivan, Ohio 284/F3
Sullivan (co.), N.Y. 276/L7
Sullivan (co.), Pa. 294/J3
Sullivan (co.), Tenn. 237/S7
Sullivan (lake), Wash. 310/H2
Sullivan, W. Va. 312/D7
Sullivan, Wis. 317/H1
Sullivan Gardens, Tenn. 237/R8
Sullivan Mines, Québec 174/B3
Sullivans Island, S.C. 296/H6
Sullom Voe, Scotland 15/G2
Sully, Iowa 229/H5
Sully (co.), S. Dak. 298/J4
Sully, Québec 172/F2
Sully (co.), S. Dak. 298/J4
Sulmona, Italy 34/D3
Sulphide, Ontario 177/G3
Sulphur (riv.), Ark. 202/B7
Sulphur, Ind. 227/E6
Sulphur, Ky. 237/L4
Sulphur, La. 238/D6
Sulphur, Nev. 266/C2
Sulphur, Okla. 288/N5

Sulphur (creek), S. Dak. 298/D4
Sulphur (riv.), Texas 303/J4
Sulphur City, Ark. 202/B2
Sulphur Creek, Tasmania 99/C1
Sulphur Draw (dry riv.), Texas 303/B4
Sulphur Fork, Red (riv.), Tenn. 237/H6
Sulphur Rock, Ark. 202/H2
Sulphur Spring (valley), Ariz. 198/F6
Sulphur Spring (range), Nev. 266/E3
Sulphur Springs, Ala. 195/G1
Sulphur Springs, Ark. 202/B1
Sulphur Springs, Ind. 227/G4
Sulphur Springs, Iowa 229/C3
Sulphur Springs, Mo. 261/M6
Sulphur Springs, Ohio 284/E4
Sulphur Springs, Texas 303/J4
Sulphur Springs (creek), Texas 303/B4
Sulphur Well, Ky. 237/K6
Sultan, Ontario 175/D3
Sultan, Ontario 177/J5
Sultan (mts.), Turkey 63/D3
Sultan, Wash. 310/D3
Sultan (riv.), Wash. 310/D3
Sultanabad (Kashmar), Iran 66/L3
Sultandagi, Turkey 63/D3
Sultanhani, Turkey 63/E3
Sultan Kudarat (prov.), Philippines 82/E7
Sulu (prov.), Philippines 82/C7
Sulu (arch.), Philippines 54/N9
Sulu (sea), Philippines 82/B8
Sulu (arch.), Philippines 85/G4
Sulu (sea), Philippines 85/G4
Sulu (sea), Philippines 82/B6
Suluan (isl.), Philippines 82/F5
Suluova, Turkey 63/F2
Sulz, Switzerland 39/F1
Sulzbach, Germany 22/B4
Sulzbach-Rosenberg, Germany 22/D4
Sulzberger (bay), Ant. 5/B11
Sulzflüh (mt.), Switzerland 39/J2
Sumami Auma, Brazil 132/B4
Sumampa, Argentina 143/D2
Sumas, Wash. 310/C2
Sumatra, Fla. 212/B1
Sumatra (isl.), Indonesia 2/P6
Sumatra (isl.), Indonesia 54/L9
Sumatra (isl.), Indonesia 85/B5
Sumatra, Mont. 262/J4
Sumava Resorts, Ind. 227/C2
Sumba (isl.), Indonesia 54/N11
Sumba (isl.), Indonesia 85/F7
Sumba (str.), Indonesia 85/F7
Sumbawa (isl.), Indonesia 54/N11
Sumbawa (isl.), Indonesia 85/F7
Sumbawa Besar, Indonesia 85/F7
Sumbawanga, Tanzania 115/F5
Sumbay, Peru 128/G10
Sumbe, Angola 102/D6
Sumbe, Angola 115/B6
Sumbing (mt.), Indonesia 85/J2
Sumburgh (head), Scotland 15/G2
Sumedang, Indonesia 85/H2
Sümeg, Hungary 41/D3
Sumenep, Indonesia 85/L2
Sumgait, U.S.S.R. 57/J4
Sumgait, U.S.S.R. 52/G6
Sumidero, Cuba 158/A2
Sumiswald, Switzerland 39/E2
Sumiton, Ala. 195/D3
Summan (plat.), Saudi Arabia 59/E4
Summer (lake), Mich. 250/C3
Summer (lake), Oreg. 188/D2
Summer (lake), Oreg. 291/G5
Summerberry, Sask. 181/J5
Summerdale, Ala. 195/C10
Summerfield, Ala. 195/E5
Summerfield, Fla. 212/D2
Summerfield, Ill. 222/D6
Summerfield, Kansas 232/F2
Summerfield, La. 238/E1
Summerfield, Mo. 261/J6
Summerfield, N.C. 281/K2
Summerfield, Ohio 284/H6
Summerfield, Okla. 288/S5
Summerfield, Texas 303/B3
Summerford, Newf. 166/C4
Summerford, Ohio 284/D6
Summer Hill, Ill. 222/C4
Summerhill, Pa. 294/E5
Summer Isles (isls.), Scotland 15/C2
Summer Lake, Oreg. 291/G5
Summerland, Br. Col. 184/G5
Summerland, Calif. 204/F9
Summerland, Miss. 256/F7
Summerland Key, Fla. 212/E7
Summers, Ark. 202/A2
Summers (co.), W. Va. 312/E7
Summerset, Iowa 229/F6
Summer Shade, Ky. 237/K7
Summerside, Pr. Edward I. 168/E2
Summersville, Ky. 237/K6
Summersville, Mo. 261/J8
Summersville, Ohio 284/D5
Summersville, W. Va. 312/E6
Summersville (lake), W. Va. 312/E6
Summerton, S.C. 296/G4
Summertown, Georgia 217/H5
Summertown, Tenn. 237/G10
Summerville, Georgia 217/B2
Summerville, La. 238/F3
Summerville, Newf. 166/D2
Summerville, Oreg. 291/K2
Summerville, Pa. 294/D3
Summerville, S.C. 296/G5
Summerville Centre, Nova Scotia 168/D5
Summit, Ala. 195/F2
Summit, Alaska 196/J2
Summit, Ark. 202/E1
Summit (co.), Colo. 208/G3

Summit (peak), Colo. 208/F8
Summit (lake), Iowa 229/E6
Summit, Miss. 256/D8
Summit (lake), Nev. 266/C1
Summit, N.J. 273/E2
Summit (co.), Ohio 284/G3
Summit (creek), Oreg. 291/J3
Summit, Québec 172/E2
Summit, R.I. 249/H6
Summit, S.C. 296/E4
Summit, S. Dak. 298/P3
Summit (co.), Utah 304/D3
Summit, Utah 304/B6
Summit Bridge, Del. 245/R2
Summit City, Calif. 204/C3
Summit City, Mich. 250/D4
Summit Hill, Pa. 294/L4
Summit Lake, Wis. 317/H5
Summit Lake Ind. Res., Nev. 266/B1
Summit Point, W. Va. 312/K4
Summitville, Ind. 227/F4
Summitville, Iowa 229/K8
Summitville, N.Y. 276/L7
Summitville, Ohio 284/J4
Summitville, Tenn. 237/K9
Summum, Ill. 222/C3
Sumner (str.), Alaska 196/M2
Sumner, Georgia 217/D4
Sumner, Ill. 222/F5
Sumner, Iowa 229/J3
Sumner (co.), Kansas 232/E4
Sumner •, Maine 243/C7
Sumner, Mich. 250/E5
Sumner, Miss. 256/D3
Sumner, Mo. 261/F3
Sumner, Nebr. 264/E4
Sumner (dam), N. Mex. 274/E4
Sumner (lake), N. Mex. 274/E4
Sumner (lake), N. Zealand 100/D5
Sumner, Oreg. 291/C4
Sumner (co.), Tenn. 237/J8
Sumner, Wash. 310/C3
Sumner-East Sumner, Maine 243/C7
Sumoto, Japan 81/G6
Šumperk, Czech. 41/D1
Sumprabum, Burma 72/C1
Sumpter, Ark. 202/F7
Sumpter, Oreg. 291/J3
Sumrall, Miss. 256/D8
Sumter, Ala. 195/D4
Sumter (co.), Fla. 212/D3
Sumter (co.), Georgia 217/D6
Sumter (co.), S.C. 296/G4
Sumter, S.C. 296/G4
Sumterville, Ala. 195/B5
Sumy, U.S.S.R. 7/H3
Sumy, U.S.S.R. 52/E4
Sumy, U.S.S.R. 48/D4
Sun, La. 238/L5
Sun (riv.), Mont. 262/D3
Sunagawa, Japan 81/K2
Sunapee •, N.H. 268/C5
Sunapee (lake), N.H. 268/C5
Sunart, Loch (inlet), Scotland 15/C4
Sunbeam, Colo. 208/C1
Sunbeam, Idaho 220/D5
Sunbright, Tenn. 237/M8
Sunburg, Minn. 255/C5
Sunburst, Mont. 262/E2
Sunbury, Iowa 229/M5
Sunbury (co.), New Bruns. 170/D3
Sunbury, N.C. 281/R2
Sunbury, Ohio 284/E5
Sunbury, Pa. 294/J4
Sunbury, Victoria 97/C5
Sunbury-on-Thames, England 13/G8
Sunbury-on-Thames, England 10/B6
Sunchales, Argentina 143/F5
Suncho Corral, Argentina 143/D2
Sunch'ŏn, N. Korea 81/B4
Sunch'ŏn, S. Korea 81/C6
Sun City, Ariz. 198/C5
Sun City, Calif. 204/F11
Sun City, Fla. 212/D4
Sun City, Kansas 232/D4
Sun City Center, Fla. 212/C3
Suncook, N.H. 268/D5
Suncook (lakes), N.H. 268/E5
Suncook (riv.), N.H. 268/E5
Sunda (isls.), Indonesia 54/L10
Sunda (str.), Indonesia 54/M10
Sunda (str.), Indonesia 85/C7
Sundahl, Minn. 255/B3
Sundance, Wyo. 319/H1
Sundarbans (reg.), Bangladesh 68/F4
Sundarbans (reg.), India 68/F4
Sundargarh, India 68/E4
Sunday (riv.), Maine 243/B6
Sundbyberg, Sweden 18/G1
Sunderland, England 13/J3
Sunderland, England 10/F2
Sunderland •, Mass. 249/D3
Sunderland, Ontario 177/E3
Sunderland •, Vt. 268/A5
Sundown, Manitoba 179/F5
Sundown, Texas 303/B4
Sundra, S. Africa 118/J6
Sundre, Alberta 182/C4
Sundridge, Ontario 177/E2
Sundsvall, Sweden 18/K5
Sundsvall, Sweden 7/F2
Sunfield, Ill. 222/D5
Sunfield, Mich. 250/D6
Sunfish Lake, Minn. 255/E6
Sunflower, Ala. 195/B8
Sunflower (mt.), Kansas 232/A2
Sunflower (co.), Miss. 256/C3
Sunflower, Miss. 256/C3
Sunflower (riv.), Miss. 256/C5
Sungaipenuh, Indonesia 85/C6
Sungai Petani, Malaysia 72/C6
Sungurlu, Turkey 63/F2
Sunland, Calif. 204/C10
Sunland Gardens, Fla. 212/F4
Sunman, Ind. 227/G6
Sunndalsøra, Norway 18/F5

Sunne, Sweden 18/H7
Sunnybrae, Nova Scotia 168/F3
Sunnybrook, Alberta 182/C3
Sunny Corner, New Bruns. 170/E2
Sunnydale, Wash. 310/B2
Sunny Isles, Fla. 212/C4
Sunnynook, Alberta 182/E4
Sunny Point Mil. Ocean Term., N.C. 281/O6
Sunnyside, Fla. 212/C6
Sunny Side, Georgia 217/D4
Sunnyside, Ill. 222/A4
Sunnyside, New Bruns. 170/D1
Sunnyside, Newf. 166/D2
Sunnyside, Utah 304/D4
Sunnyside, Wash. 310/F4
Sunnyslope, Alberta 182/D4
Sunny South, Ala. 195/C7
Sunnyvale, Calif. 204/K3
Sunnyvale, Texas 303/H2
Sunny Valley, Oreg. 291/D5
Sunol, Calif. 204/L2
Sunol, Nebr. 264/B3
Sun Prairie, Wis. 317/H9
Sunray, Texas 303/C1
Sunrise, Fla. 212/B4
Sunrise, Wyo. 319/H3
Sunrise Beach, Mo. 261/G6
Sunrise Manor, Nev. 266/F6
Sunrise Valley, Br. Col. 184/G2
Sun River, Mont. 262/D3
Sunsas, Serranía de (mts.), Bolivia 136/F5
Sunset, Ark. 202/K3
Sunset (peak), Idaho 220/E6
Sunset, La. 238/F6
Sunset, Maine 243/F7
Sunset, S.C. 296/B2
Sunset, Texas 303/G4
Sunset, Utah 304/B2
Sunset Beach, Calif. 204/C11
Sunset Beach, Hawaii 218/E1
Sunset Beach, N.C. 281/N7
Sunset Crater Nat'l Mon., Ariz. 198/D3
Sunset Hills, Mo. 261/O4
Sunset Hills, Va. 307/R2
Sunset House, Alberta 182/B2
Sunset Prairie, Br. Col. 184/G2
Sunshine, La. 238/K2
Sunshine, Maine 243/G7
Sunshine, Victoria 88/K7
Sunshine, Victoria 97/H5
Sunspot, N. Mex. 274/D6
Suntar, U.S.S.R. 48/M3
Suntrana, Alaska 196/J2
Sun Valley, Idaho 220/D6
Sun Valley, Nev. 266/B3
Sun Valley, Sask. 181/F5
Sunyani, Ghana 106/D7
Sunzu (mt.), Zambia 115/F5
Suo (sea), Japan 81/E7
Suolahti, Finland 18/O5
Suomussalmi, Finland 13/Q4
Suonenjoki, Finland 18/P5
Suong, Cambodia 72/E5
Suoyarvi, U.S.S.R. 52/D2
Supai, Ariz. 198/C2
Supe, Peru 128/D8
Superb, Sask. 181/B4
Superior (lake) 162/G-H6
Superior (lake) 188/J1
Superior (lake) 188/J1
Superior, Ariz. 198/D5
Superior, Colo. 208/J3
Superior, Iowa 229/D2
Superior (lag.), Mexico 150/M9
Superior (lake), Mich. 250/C2
Superior (lake), Minn. 255/G3
Superior, Mont. 262/B3
Superior, Nebr. 264/F4
Superior (lake), Ontario 177/H5
Superior (lake), Ontario 175/C3
Superior, Wis. 188/H1
Superior, Wis. 317/H5
Superior (lake), Wis. 317/F1
Superior, Wyo. 319/D4
Superior Village, Wis. 317/B2
Superstition (mts.), Ariz. 198/D5
Suphan Buri, Thailand 72/C4
Süphan Daği (mt.), Turkey 59/D2
Süphan Daği (mt.), Turkey 63/K3
Supiori (isl.), Indonesia 85/K6
Supply, N.C. 281/N6
Supreme, La. 238/K4
Supung (res.), N. Korea 81/B3
Suqian, China 77/J5
Suquamish, Wash. 310/A1
Sur (pt.), Calif. 204/D7
Sur, Lebanon 63/F6
Sur, Oman 59/G5
Sura, Ras (cape), Somalia 115/J1
Sura (riv.), U.S.S.R. 52/G4
Surab, Pakistan 68/B3
Surab, Pakistan 59/J4
Surabaya, Indonesia 54/N10
Surabaya, Indonesia 85/K2
Surada, India 68/E5
Surahammar, Sweden 18/J7
Surakarta, Indonesia 54/N10
Surakarta, Indonesia 85/J2
Surány, Czech. 41/E2
Surat, India 54/J7
Surat, India 68/C4
Surat, Queensland 88/H5
Suratgarh, India 68/C3
Surat Thani, Thailand 72/C5
Sur del Cabo San Antonio (pt.), Argentina 143/E4
Surdulica, Yugoslavia 45/F4
Surendranagar, India 68/C4
Suresnes, France 28/A2
Suretka, C. Rica 154/F6
Surette Island, Nova Scotia 168/B5
Surf, Calif. 204/E9
Surf City, N.J. 273/E4
Surf City, N.C. 281/O6
Surfside, Fla. 212/B4

Surfside Beach, S.C. 296/K4
Surgidero de Batabanó, Cuba 156/A2
Surgidero de Batabanó, Cuba 158/C1
Surgoinsville, Tenn. 237/R8
Surgut, U.S.S.R. 48/H3
Surigao, Philippines 82/E6
Surigao, Philippines 85/H4
Surigao (str.), Philippines 82/E6
Surigao del Norte (prov.), Philippines 82/F5
Surigao del Sur (prov.), Philippines 82/F6
Surimena, Colombia 126/D6
Surin, Thailand 72/D4
Suriname 120/D2
SURINAME 131/C3
Suriname (dist.), Suriname 131/D3
Suriname (riv.), Suriname 131/D3
Suring, Wis. 317/K5
Suripa, Venezuela 124/D4
Suripá (riv.), Venezuela 124/C4
Surire, Salar de (salt dep.), Chile 138/B2
Sürmene, Turkey 63/J2
Surprise, Ariz. 198/C5
Surprise, Ind. 227/E7
Surprise, Nebr. 264/G2
Surrency, Georgia 217/H7
Surrey, Br. Col. 184/F3
Surrey (co.), England 13/G6
Surrey, N. Dak. 282/H3
Surry •, Maine 243/F7
Surry •, N.H. 268/C5
Surry (co.), N.C. 281/H2
Surry (co.), Va. 307/P6
Surry, Va. 307/P6
Surry Mountain (lake), N.H. 268/C5
Sursee, Switzerland 39/F2
Surtsey (isl.), Iceland 21/B2
Sürüç, Turkey 63/H4
Suruga (bay), Japan 81/J6
Surup, Philippines 82/F7
Surveyor, W. Va. 312/D7
Surwakwima (fall), Guyana 131/A2
Susà (riv.), Denmark 21/E7
Susa (ruins), Iran 66/F4
Susa, Italy 34/A2
Susa, Libya 111/D1
Susa Creek, Alberta 182/A3
Susaki, Japan 81/F7
Susan (riv.), Calif. 204/D3
Susan, Va. 307/R6
Susangerd, Iran 59/E3
Susangerd, Iran 66/F5
Susank, Kansas 232/D3
Susanville, Calif. 204/E3
Susch, Switzerland 39/K3
Suşehri, Turkey 63/H2
Sušice, Czech. 41/B2
Susie, Ky. 237/M7
Susitna, Alaska 196/B1
Susitna (riv.), Alaska 196/B1
Susquehanna (riv.), Md. 245/N1
Susquehanna (riv.), N.Y. 276/H6
Susquehanna (co.), Pa. 294/L2
Susquehanna, Pa. 294/L2
Susquehanna (riv.), Pa. 294/K6
Susquehanna, West Branch (riv.), Pa. 294/G3
Susques, Argentina 143/C1
Sussex (co.), Del. 245/S6
Sussex, East (co.), England 13/H7
Sussex, West (co.), England 13/G7
Sussex, New Bruns. 170/D3
Sussex (co.), N.J. 273/D1
Sussex, N.J. 273/D1
Sussex (co.), Va. 307/O7
Sussex, Va. 307/O7
Sussex, Wis. 317/K1
Sussex, Wyo. 319/F5
Sussex Corner, New Bruns. 170/E3
Sussex Inlet, N.S. Wales 97/F4
Susten (pass), Switzerland 39/G3
Sustenhorn (mt.), Switzerland 39/G3
Sustut (riv.), Br. Col. 184/D2
Susuman, U.S.S.R. 4/C2
Susuman, U.S.S.R. 54/R3
Susuman, U.S.S.R. 48/P3
Susurluk, Turkey 63/C3
Susuz, Turkey 63/K2
Sütçüler, Turkey 63/D4
Sutherland, Iowa 229/B3
Sutherland, Nebr. 264/C3
Sutherland (res.), Nebr. 264/C3
Sutherland, N.S. Wales 88/K5
Sutherland, N.S. Wales 97/K4
Sutherland (trad. co.), Scotland 15/A4
Sutherland Springs, Texas 303/K11
Sutherlin, Oreg. 291/D4
Sutherlin, Va. 307/O7
Sutlej (riv.), India 68/C3
Sutlej (riv.), Pakistan 68/C3
Sutlej (riv.), Pakistan 59/K4
Sutter (co.), Calif. 204/D4
Sutter, Calif. 204/D4
Sutter Creek, Calif. 204/C9
Suttle, Ala. 195/D5
Sutton, Alaska 196/C1
Sutton, England 13/H8
Sutton, England 10/B6
Sutton, Mass. 249/G4
Sutton, Nebr. 264/G4
Sutton •, N.H. 268/D5
Sutton, N. Dak. 282/O5
Sutton, Ontario 177/E3
Sutton (lake), Ontario 175/D2
Sutton (riv.), Ontario 175/D2
Sutton, Québec 172/E4
Sutton •, Vt. 268/C2
Sutton, W. Va. 312/E5
Sutton (lake), W. Va. 312/F5
Sutton Bridge, England 13/H5
Sutton in Ashfield, England 10/F4

Sutton in Ashfield, England 13/K2
Suttons Bay, Mich. 250/D3
Suttor (riv.), Queensland 88/H4
Suttor (riv.), Queensland 95/C4
Suttsu, Japan 81/J2
Sutwik (isl.), Alaska 196/G3
Suure-Jaani, U.S.S.R. 53/C1
Suva (cap.), Fiji 87/H7
Suva (cap.), Fiji 2/T6
Suva (Cap.), Fiji 86/Q11
Suwa, Japan 81/H6
Suwaiq, Oman 59/G5
Suwaiqiya, Hor as (lake), Iraq 66/D4
Suwałki (prov.), Poland 47/F1
Suwałki, Poland 47/F1
Suwanee, Georgia 217/D2
Suwannaphum, Thailand 72/D4
Suwannee (co.), Fla. 212/C1
Suwannee, Fla. 212/C2
Suwannee (riv.), Fla. 212/C2
Suwannee (riv.), Georgia 217/G10
Suwanose (isl.), Japan 81/O4
Suwar, Syria 63/J5
Suwarrow (atoll), Cook Is. 87/K7
Suweilih, Jordan 65/D3
Suweima, Jordan 65/D4
Suwŏn, S. Korea 81/C5
Su Xian, China 77/J5
Suzhou (Soochow), China 77/K5
Suzhou, China 54/O6
Suzu, Japan 81/H5
Suzu (pt.), Japan 81/H5
Suzu, Japan 81/H6
Suzzara, Italy 34/C2
Svalbard (isls.), Norway 2/J2
Svalbard (isls.), Norway 4/B9
Svalbard (isls.), Norway 18/C3
Svaneke, Denmark 21/F8
Svanstein, Sweden 18/N3
Svanvik, Norway 18/R2
Svárov, Czech. 41/C1
Svay Rieng, Cambodia 72/E5
Svea, Minn. 255/C6
Sveagruva, Norway 18/D2
Sveg, Sweden 18/J5
Svelvik, Norway 18/D4
Švenčionis, U.S.S.R. 53/D3
Svendborg, Denmark 18/G9
Svendborg, Denmark 21/D7
Svenljunga, Sweden 18/H8
Svensen, Oreg. 291/D1
Svenstavik, Sweden 18/H5
Sverdlovsk, U.S.S.R. 2/N3
Sverdlovsk, U.S.S.R. 54/H4
Sverdlovsk, U.S.S.R. 48/F4
Sverdrup (chan.), N.W.T. 187/J1
Sverdrup (isls.), N.W.T. 187/J2
Sverdrup (isls.), N.W.T. 187/J2
Svetlogorsk, U.S.S.R. 52/C4
Svetlograd, U.S.S.R. 52/F5
Svetlyy, U.S.S.R. 52/K4
Svetozarevo, Yugoslavia 45/E4
Svidnik, Czech. 41/F2
Svilajnac, Yugoslavia 45/E3
Svilengrad, Bulgaria 45/G5
Svinninge, Denmark 21/E6
Svir' (riv.), U.S.S.R. 52/D2
Svishtov, Bulgaria 45/G4
Svitava (riv.), Czech. 41/D2
Svitavy, Czech. 41/D2
Svobodnyy, U.S.S.R. 54/O4
Svobodnyy, U.S.S.R. 48/N4
Svolvaer, Norway 18/J2
Svratka (riv.), Czech. 41/D2
Swabian Jura (range), Germany 22/C4
Swadlincote, England 10/G2
Swadlincote, England 13/F5
Swaffham, England 13/H5
Swaffham, England 10/G4
Swaim, Ala. 195/F1
Swain (co.), N.C. 281/B3
Swain (reefs), Queensland 88/J4
Swain (reefs), Queensland 95/C4
Swains (isl.), Amer. Samoa 87/K7
Swainsboro, Georgia 217/H5
Swakop (riv.), Namibia 118/B4
Swakopmund, Namibia 118/A4
Swakopmund, Namibia 102/D7
Swale (riv.), England 13/F3
Swale (riv.), England 10/F3
Swale (isl.), Newf. 166/D1
Swaledale, Iowa 229/G3
Swalwell, Alberta 182/D4
Swampscott •, Mass. 249/E6
Swan (hills), Alberta 182/C2
Swan (riv.), Alberta 182/C2
Swan (Santanilla) (isls.), Honduras 154/F2
Swan, Iowa 229/G6
Swan (lake), Manitoba 179/B2
Swan (lake), Manitoba 179/D5
Swan (riv.), Manitoba 179/A3
Swan (lake), Minn. 255/D6
Swan (lake), Mont. 262/C2
Swan (lake), Nebr. 264/B3
Swan (riv.), Sask. 181/J3
Swan (creek), S. Dak. 298/J3
Swan (lake), S. Dak. 298/N3
Swan (lake), S. Dak. 298/O3
Swan (isl.), Tasmania 99/E5
Swan (lake), Utah 304/B4
Swan, W. Australia 88/B2
Swanage, England 10/F5
Swanage, England 13/E7
Swan Creek, Ill. 222/C3
Swandale, W. Va. 312/E5
Swan Hill, Victoria 88/G7
Swan Hill, Victoria 97/B4
Swan Hills, Alberta 182/C2
Swanington, Ind. 227/C3
Swanlake, Idaho 220/F7
Swan Lake, Manitoba 179/D5
Swan Lake, Miss. 256/D3
Swan Lake, Mont. 262/C3

Swanlinbar, Ireland 17/F3
Swannanoa, N.C. 281/E3
Swan Plain, Sask. 181/K3
Swanquarter, N.C. 281/S4
Swan River, Man. 162/F5
Swan River, Manitoba 179/A2
Swan River, Minn. 255/E3
Swansboro, N.C. 281/P5
Swanscombe, England 10/C5
Swanscombe, England 13/J8
Swansea, Ill. 222/B3
Swansea •, Mass. 249/K5
Swansea, S.C. 296/E4
Swansea, Tasmania 99/D4
Swansea, Wales 7/D3
Swansea, Wales 13/C6
Swansea, Wales 10/D5
Swansea (bay), Wales 13/D6
Swansea Center, Mass. 249/K5
Swans Island, Maine 243/G7
Swans Island •, Maine 243/G7
Swanson, Nebr. 264/D4
Swanson, Sask. 181/D4
Swanton, Md. 245/A3
Swanton, Nebr. 264/H4
Swanton, Ohio 284/C2
Swanton, Vt. 268/A2
Swanton •, Vt. 268/A2
Swan Valley, Idaho 220/G6
Swan View, W. Australia 88/B2
Swanville •, Maine 243/E6
Swanville, Minn. 255/D5
Swanwick, Ill. 222/D5
Swanzey •, N.H. 268/C6
Swarthmore, Pa. 294/M7
Swartswood, N.J. 273/D1
Swartswood (lake), N.J. 273/D1
Swartz, La. 238/G1
Swartz Creek, Mich. 250/F6
Swarzędz, Poland 47/C2
Swatara, Minn. 255/E4
Swatara, Pa. 294/J5
Swatow (Shantou), China 77/J7
Swayzee, Ind. 227/F4
Swaziland 2/L7
Swaziland 102/F7
SWAZILAND 118/E5
Swea City, Iowa 229/E2
Sweatman, Miss. 256/E3
Swedeborg, Mo. 261/H7
Swedeburg, Nebr. 264/H3
Sweden 2/K2
Sweden 4/D9
Sweden 7/F2
SWEDEN 18
Sweden, Maine 243/B7
Sweden •, Maine 243/B7
Swedesboro, N.J. 273/C4
Swedesburg, Iowa 229/L6
Sweeden, Ky. 237/J6
Sween, Loch (inlet), Scotland 15/C5
Sweeny, Texas 303/J8
Sweet, Idaho 220/B6
Sweet Bay, Newf. 166/D2
Sweet Briar, Va. 307/K5
Sweet Chalybeate, Va. 307/H5
Sweet Grass (co.), Mont. 262/G5
Sweetgrass, Mont. 262/E2
Sweet Home, Ark. 202/L2
Sweet Home, Oreg. 291/E3
Sweet Home, Texas 303/H8
Sweet Lake, La. 238/D7
Sweetser, Ind. 227/F4
Sweet Springs, Mo. 261/F5
Sweet Springs, W. Va. 312/F7
Sweet Valley, Pa. 294/K3
Sweet Water, Ala. 195/C6
Sweetwater, Fla. 212/B5
Sweetwater, Nebr. 264/E3
Sweetwater (lake), N. Dak. 282/N3
Sweetwater, Okla. 288/G4
Sweetwater, Tenn. 237/N9
Sweetwater, Texas 188/F4
Sweetwater, Texas 303/D5
Sweetwater (co.), Wyo. 319/D4
Sweetwater (riv.), Wyo. 319/D3
Swellendam, S. Africa 118/C6
Swenson, Texas 303/E5
Swett, S. Dak. 298/E7
Świdnica, Poland 47/C3
Świdnik, Poland 47/F3
Świdwin, Poland 47/B2
Świebodzice, Poland 47/C3
Świebodzin, Poland 47/B2
Świecie, Poland 47/D2
Świętochłowice, Poland 47/A4
Swift (riv.), Mass. 249/B6
Swift (riv.), Mass. 249/E4
Swift (co.), Minn. 255/C5
Swift, Minn. 255/C2
Swift (creek), Va. 307/O6
Swift Creek (res.), Wash. 310/C4
Swift Current, Newf. 166/C2
Swift Current, Sask. 146/H4
Swift Current, Sask. 162/F5
Swift Current, Sask. 181/D5
Swift Current (creek), Sask. 181/D5
Swifterbant, Netherlands 27/H3
Swift Falls, Minn. 255/C5
Swifton, Ark. 202/H2
Swiftown, Miss. 256/D4
Swift River, Yukon 187/E3
Swifts Creek, Victoria 97/D5
Swiftwater, N.H. 268/D3
Swilly (inlet), Ireland 17/F1
Swilly, Lough (inlet), Ireland 10/C3
Swilly (riv.), Ireland 17/F2
Swinburne (cape), N.W. Terr. 187/J2
Swindon, England 10/E5
Swindon, England 13/F6
Swinemünde (Świnoujście), Poland 47/A2
Swinford, Ireland 17/C4
Swink, Colo. 208/M7
Swink, Okla. 288/R6
Swinomish Ind. Res., Wash. 310/C2
Świnoujście (Swinemünde) Poland 47/B1

Swinton, Scotland 15/F5
Swisher, Iowa 229/K5
Swisher (co.), Texas 303/C3
Swiss, W. Va. 312/D6
Swisshome, Oreg. 291/D3
Swissvale, Pa. 294/C7
Switz City, Ind. 227/C6
Switzer, Ky. 237/M4
Switzer, W. Va. 312/B7
Switzerland 2/K3
Switzerland 7/E4
SWITZERLAND 39
Switzerland, Fla. 212/E1
Switzerland (co.), Ind. 227/G7
Switzerland, S.C. 296/E7
Swona (isl.), Scotland 15/E2
Swords, Ireland 17/J5
Swords Creek, Va. 307/H3
Sybille (creek), Wyo. 319/G4
Sybouts, Sask. 181/J5
Sycamore, Ala. 195/F4
Sycamore, Georgia 217/E7
Sycamore, Ill. 222/E2
Sycamore, Ind. 227/F4
Sycamore, Kansas 232/G4
Sycamore, Mo. 261/H9
Sycamore, Ohio 284/D4
Sycamore, Pa. 294/B6
Sycamore, S.C. 296/E5
Sycan (riv.), Oreg. 291/F5
Syców, Poland 47/C3
Sydenham, Ontario 177/H3
Sydenham (riv.), Ontario 177/B5
Sydney, Australia 2/S7
Sydney, Australia 87/F9
Sydney (Manra) (isl.), Kiribati 87/K6
Sydney (cap.), N.S. Wales 88/L4
Sydney (bay), Norfolk I. 88/L6
Sydney, N. Dak. 282/N6
Sydney, Nova Scotia 168/H2
Sydney, Nova Scotia 162/K6
Sydney, Nova Scotia 146/N5
Sydney (harb.), Nova Scotia 168/H2
Sydney Mines, Nova Scotia 168/H2
Sydney River, Nova Scotia 168/H2
Sykeston, N. Dak. 282/M5
Sykesville, Md. 245/K3
Sykesville, Pa. 294/E3
Syktyvkar, U.S.S.R. 7/K2
Syktyvkar, U.S.S.R. 48/F3
Syktyvkar, U.S.S.R. 52/H2
Sylacauga, Ala. 195/F4
Sylhet, Bangladesh 68/G4
Sylt (isl.), Germany 22/C1
Sylva, N.C. 281/C4
Sylvan, Oreg. 291/B2
Sylvan, Pa. 294/G6
Sylvan (lake), Wash. 310/G3
Sylvan Beach, N.Y. 276/J4
Sylvan Grove, Kansas 232/D2
Sylvania, Ala. 195/G1
Sylvania, Georgia 217/J5
Sylvania, Ind. 227/C5
Sylvania, Ohio 284/C1
Sylvania, Pa. 294/J2
Sylvania, Sask. 181/G3
Sylvan Lake, Alberta 182/C3
Sylvan Lake, Mich. 250/F6
Sylvarena, Miss. 256/F6
Sylvatus, Va. 307/G7
Sylvester, Georgia 217/E7
Sylvester (lake), North. Terr. 93/D5
Sylvester, Texas 303/D5
Sylvester, W. Va. 312/C6
Sylvia, Kansas 232/D4
Sylvia, Tenn. 237/G8
Symco, Wis. 317/J6
Symerton, Ill. 222/F2
Symmes (creek), Ohio 284/F8
Symonds, Miss. 256/C3
Syosset, N.Y. 276/R6
Syracuse, Ind. 227/F2
Syracuse (prov.), Italy 34/E6
Syracuse, Italy 7/G5
Syracuse, Italy 34/E6
Syracuse, Kansas 232/A3
Syracuse, Mo. 261/G5
Syracuse, Nebr. 264/H4
Syracuse, N.Y. 188/L2
Syracuse, N.Y. 276/H4
Syracuse, Ohio 284/G7
Syracuse, Utah 304/B2
Syrdar'ya, U.S.S.R. 2/N3
Syrdar'ya, U.S.S.R. 54/H5
Syrdar'ya, U.S.S.R. 48/G5
Syre, Minn. 255/B3
Syria 2/L4
Syria 54/E6
SYRIA 63/G5
SYRIA 59/C3
Syria, Va. 307/M4
Syriam, Burma 72/C3
Syrian (des.), Iraq 66/B4
Syrian (El Hamad) (des.), Iraq 59/C3
Syrte, Libya 102/D1
Syrte, Libya 111/C1
Sysladobsis, Lower (lake), Maine 243/G5
Sysola (riv.), U.S.S.R. 52/H2
Syssleback, Sweden 18/H6
Syzran', U.S.S.R. 7/J3
Syzran', U.S.S.R. 48/E4
Syzran', U.S.S.R. 52/G4
Szabadszállás, Hungary 41/E3
Szabolcs-Szatmár (co.), Hungary 41/G3
Szamotuły, Poland 47/C2
Szarvas, Hungary 41/F3
Százhalombatta, Hungary 41/E3
Szczebrzeszyn, Poland 47/F3
Szczecin (prov.), Poland 47/B2
Szczecin, Poland 7/F3
Szczecin, Poland 47/B2
Szczecinek, Poland 47/C2
Szczytno, Poland 47/E2

Tarabulus 455

Szechwan (Sichuan) (prov.), China 77/F5
Szécsény, Hungary 41/E2
Szeged, Hungary 41/E3
Szeged, Hungary 7/F4
Szeghalom, Hungary 41/F3
Szegvár, Hungary 41/F3
Székesfehérvár, Hungary 41/E3
Szekszárd, Hungary 41/E3
Szendrű, Hungary 41/F2
Szentendre, Hungary 41/E3
Szentendreisziget (isl.), Hungary 41/E3
Szentes, Hungary 41/F3
Szentgotthárd, Hungary 41/D3
Szentlőrinc, Hungary 41/E3
Szeping (Siping), China 77/K3
Szerencs, Hungary 41/F2
Szigetvár, Hungary 41/D3
Szikszó, Hungary 41/F2
Szil, Hungary 41/D3
Szirák, Hungary 41/E3
Szolnok (co.), Hungary 41/F3
Szolnok, Hungary 41/F3
Szombathely, Hungary 41/D3
Szprotawa, Poland 47/B3
Sztum, Poland 47/D2
Szubin, Poland 47/C2
Szydłowiec, Poland 47/E3

T

Taal (lake), Philippines 82/C4
Tab, Hungary 41/E3
Tab, Ind. 227/C4
Taba, Bir, Egypt 59/B4
Tabacal (pt.), Cuba 158/H4
Tabacundo, Ecuador 128/C2
Tabaquite, Trin. & Tob. 161/B11
Tabar (isls.), Papua N.G. 86/C1
Tabarka, Tunisia 106/F1
Tabas, Iran 59/G3
Tabas, Iran 66/L4
Tabas, Iran 66/K4
Tabasará (mts.), Panama 154/G6
Tabasco (state), Mexico 150/N7
Tabasco, Mexico 150/H6
Tabask, Kuh-e (mt.), Iran 66/G6
Tabas-Masina (Tabas), Iran 59/H3
Tabb, Va. 307/R6
Tabelbala, Algeria 106/D3
Taber, Alberta 182/E5
Taberg, N.Y. 276/J4
Tabernacle, St. Kitts & Nevis 161/C10
Tabernash, Colo. 208/H3
Tabernes de Valldigna, Spain 33/G3
Taberville, Mo. 261/E6
Tabiang, Kiribati 87/G6
Tabiona, Utah 304/D3
Tabiteuea (atoll), Kiribati 87/H6
Tablas (cape), Chile 138/A9
Tablas (isl.), Philippines 82/D4
Tablas (str.), Philippines 82/C4
Table (mt.), Nev. 266/C3
Table (bay), Newf. 166/C3
Table (bay), S. Africa 118/E6
Table (mt.), S. Africa 118/E6
Table (peak), Wyo. 319/B2
Table Grove, Ill. 222/C3
Tableland, Trin. & Tob. 161/B11
Tableland Station, W. Australia 92/D2
Tabler, Okla. 288/L4
Table Rock (riv.), Ark. 202/D1
Table Rock (res.), Mo. 261/E9
Table Rock, Nebr. 264/H4
Tablers Station, W. Va. 312/K4
Taboada, Spain 33/C1
Taboga (isl.), Panama 154/H6
Tábor, Czech. 41/C2
Tabor, Iowa 229/B7
Tabor (mt.), Israel 65/C2
Tabor, Minn. 255/B2
Tabor, S. Dak. 298/O8
Tabor (mt.), Vt. 268/B5
Tabora (reg.), Tanzania 115/F5
Tabora, Tanzania 115/F5
Tabora, Tanzania 102/F5
Tabor City, N.C. 281/M6
Tabou, Ivory Coast 106/C8
Tabriz, Iran 54/F6
Tabriz, Iran 66/D2
Tabriz, Iran 59/E2
Tabuaeran (isl.), Kiribati 87/L5
Tabuk, Philippines 82/C2
Tabusintac, New Bruns. 170/E1
Tabusintac (gully), New Bruns. 170/F1
Tabusintac (riv.), New Bruns. 170/E1
Täby, Sweden 18/H1
Tacajó, Cuba 158/J3
Tacámbaro de Codallos, Mexico 150/J7
Tacaná, Guatemala 154/A3
Tacaná (vol.), Guatemala 154/A3
Tacarigua, Trin. & Tob. 161/B10
Taché (lake), Québec 172/J1
Tachen (Taizhou) (isls.), China 77/K6
Tacheng, China 77/B2
Tachikawa, Japan 81/O2
Tachina, Ecuador 128/C2
Táchira (state), Venezuela 124/C4
Tachov, Czech. 41/B2
Tacloban, Philippines 82/E5
Tacloban, Philippines 85/H3
Tacna, Ariz. 198/B6
Tacna (dept.), Peru 128/G11
Tacna, Peru 128/G11
Tacna, Peru 120/B4
Tacobamba, Bolivia 136/C6
Tacoma, Va. 307/C7
Tacoma, Wash. 146/F5
Tacoma, Wash. 188/B1
Tacoma, Wash. 310/C3
Tacoma Park, S. Dak. 298/N2
Taconic, Conn. 210/B1
Taconic (mts.), Mass. 249/A2
Taconite, Minn. 255/E3
Taconite Harbor, Minn. 255/H3
Tacopaya, Bolivia 136/B5
Tacora (vol.), Chile 138/B1
Tacotalpa, Mexico 150/N8
Tacuaras, Paraguay 144/C5
Tacuarembó (dept.), Uruguay 145/D3
Tacuarembó, Uruguay 145/D2
Tacuarembó (riv.), Uruguay 145/D2
Tacuarí (riv.), Uruguay 145/E3
Tacuatí, Paraguay 144/D3
Tacutu (riv.), Brazil 132/B2
Tadcaster, England 13/K1
Tademaït (plat.), Algeria 102/C2
Tademaït, Plateau du (plat.), Algeria 106/E3
Tadine, New Caled. 86/H4
Tadjnout Hagguerete (well), Mali 106/D4
Tadjoura, Djibouti 111/H5
Tadley, England 13/F6
Tadmor (Palmyra) (ruin), Syria 59/C3
Tadmore, Sask. 181/J4
Tadmur, Syria 59/C3
Tadmur, Syria 63/H5
Tadó, Colombia 126/B5
Tadoule (lake), Manitoba 179/J2
Tadoussac, Que. 162/J6
Tadoussac, Québec 174/C3
Tadoussac, Québec 172/H1
Tadzhik S.S.R., U.S.S.R. 54/H6
Tadzhik S.S.R., U.S.S.R. 48/H6
Taebaek (mt.), S. Korea 81/D5
Taedong (riv.), N. Korea 81/C4
Taegu, S. Korea 54/O6
Taegu, S. Korea 81/D6
Taejŏn, S. Korea 54/O6
Taejŏn, S. Korea 81/C5
Tafalla, Spain 33/F1
Tafassasset, Wadi (dry riv.), Algeria 106/F4
Tafassasset, Wadi (dry riv.), Niger 106/F4
Tafers, Switzerland 39/D3
Taff (riv.), Wales 13/B7
Tafí Viejo, Argentina 120/C5
Tafí Viejo, Argentina 143/C2
Taft, Calif. 204/F8
Taft, Fla. 212/E3
Taft, Iran 66/J5
Taft, La. 238/N4
Taft, Okla. 288/R3
Taft, Philippines 82/E5
Taft, Tenn. 237/H10
Taft, Texas 303/G9
Taftan, Kuh-e (mt.), Iran 66/M6
Taftan, Kuh-e (mt.), Iran 59/H4
Taftsville, Vt. 268/C4
Taftville, Conn. 210/G2
Tagab, Afghanistan 59/J3
Tagab, Afghanistan 68/B2
Taga Dzong, Bhutan 68/G3
Taganrog, U.S.S.R. 7/H4
Taganrog, U.S.S.R. 52/E5
Taganrog, U.S.S.R. 48/D5
Tagant (reg.), Mauritania 106/B5
Tagapula (isl.), Philippines 82/E4
Tagawa, Japan 81/E7
Tagaytay, Philippines 82/C3
Tagbilaran, Philippines 82/E6
Taghit, Algeria 106/D2
Taghmon, Ireland 17/H7
Tagish (lake), Br. Col. 184/J1
Tagish, Yukon 187/E3
Tagliamento (riv.), Italy 34/D1
Tagolo (pt.), Philippines 82/D6
Tagolo (pt.), Philippines 85/G4
Tagoloan, Philippines 82/E6
Tagomago (isl.), Spain 33/G3
Tagounite, Morocco 106/C3
Tagua, Bolivia 136/B6
Taguatinga, Brazil 120/E4
Taguatinga, Goiás, Brazil 132/E6
Taguatinga, Fed. Dist., Brazil 132/D6
Tague (bay), Virgin Is. (U.S.) 161/G4
Tagula (isl.), Papua N.G. 85/C8
Tagum, Philippines 82/E7
Tagus (riv.) 7/D5
Tagus, N. Dak. 282/G3
Tagus (riv.), Portugal 33/B3
Tagus (riv.), Spain 33/D3
Tahaa (isl.), Fr. Poly. 87/L7
Tahakopa, N. Zealand 100/B7
Tahan, Gunong (mt.), Malaysia 72/D6
Tahat (mt.), Algeria 102/C2
Tahat (mt.), Algeria 106/F4
Tahawus, N.Y. 276/M2
Tahiryuak (lake), N.W. Terr. 187/G2
Tahiti (isl.), Fr. Polynesia 2/B6
TAHITI, Fr. Poly. 86/S13
Tahiti (isl.), Fr. Poly. 87/L7
Tahiti (isl.), Fr. Poly. 86/S13
Tahlequah, Okla. 288/R3
Tahma (riv.), Turkey 63/G3
Tahoe (lake) 188/C3
Tahoe (lake), Calif. 204/F4
Tahoe (lake), Nev. 266/B3
Tahoe City, Calif. 204/E4
Tahoka, Texas 303/C4
Taholah, Wash. 310/A3
Tahoma, Calif. 204/E4
Tahoua, Niger 102/C3
Tahoua, Niger 106/F6
Tahquamenon (falls), Mich. 250/D2
Tahquamenon (riv.), Mich. 250/D2
Tahsis, Br. Col. 184/D5
Tahta, Egypt 59/B4
Tahta, Egypt 111/F2
Tahtsa (lake), Br. Col. 184/D3
Tahua, Bolivia 136/E3
Tahuamanu (riv.), Bolivia 136/A2
Tahuamanu, Peru 128/H8
Tahuamanu (riv.), Peru 128/H8
Tahulandang (isl.), Indonesia 85/H5
Tahuna, Indonesia 85/G5
Tahuya, Wash. 310/B3
Tai'an, China 77/J4
Taiarapu (pen.), Fr. Poly. 86/T13
Taiban, N. Mex. 274/F4
Taibus, China 77/J3
Taichow (Taizhou), China 77/K5
Taichung, China 77/K7
Taichung, Taiwan 54/O7
Taieri (riv.), N. Zealand 100/C7
Taif, Saudi Arabia 54/F7
Taif, Saudi Arabia 59/D5
Taigu, China 77/H4
Taihape, N. Zealand 100/E3
Taihe, China 77/J6
Tai Hu (lake), China 77/J5
Tailem Bend, S. Australia 88/F7
Tailem Bend, S. Australia 94/F6
Taima, Saudi Arabia 59/C4
Tain, Scotland 15/D3
Tain, Scotland 10/D2
Tainan, China 77/J7
Tainaron (cape), Greece 7/G5
Tainaron (cape), Greece 45/F7
Taintor, Iowa 229/H6
Taipei, China 77/K7
Taipei (cap.), Taiwan 54/O7
Taipei (cap.), Taiwan 2/R4
Taiping, Malaysia 72/D6
Taitao (pen.), Chile 120/B7
Taitao (cape), Chile 138/D6
Taitao (pen.), Chile 138/D6
Taits Gap, Ala. 195/F3
Taitung, China 77/K7
Taivalkoski, Finland 18/P4
Taiwan 54/N7
Taiwan 2/R4
Taiwan (str.) 54/N7
Taiwan (isl.) 54/N7
TAIWAN, CHINA 77/K7
Taiwan, China 77/K7
Taiwan (Formosa) (isl.), China 77/K7
Taiwan (Formosa) (str.), China 77/J7
Taiyuan, China 77/H4
Taiyuan, China 54/N6
Taizhou (Taichow), China 77/K5
Taizhou (Tachen) (isls.), China 77/K6
Ta'izz, Yemen 54/F8
Ta'izz, Yemen 59/D7
Tajimi, Japan 81/H6
Tajique, N. Mex. 274/C4
Tajo (Tagus) (riv.), Spain 33/D3
Tajrish, Iran 66/G3
Tajumulco (vol.), Guatemala 154/B3
Tak, Thailand 72/C3
Takaishi, Japan 81/H8
Takaka, N. Zealand 100/D4
Takalar, Indonesia 85/F7
Takama, Guyana 131/C3
Takamatsu, Japan 81/F6
Takaoka, Japan 81/H5
Takapau, N. Zealand 100/F4
Takapuna, N. Zealand 100/B1
Takarazuka, Japan 81/H7
Takaroa (atoll), Fr. Poly. 87/M7
Takasaki, Japan 81/J5
Takatsuki, Japan 81/J7
Takayama, Japan 81/H5
Takefu, Japan 81/G6
Takeshima (isls.), Japan 81/F5
Takestan, Iran 66/F2
Takev, Cambodia 72/E5
Takhiatash, U.S.S.R. 48/F5
Takhta-Bazar, U.S.S.R. 48/G6
Takijuq (lake), N.W.T. 186/G3
Takikawa, Japan 81/K2
Takingeun, Indonesia 85/B5
Takitimu (mts.), N. Zealand 100/A6
Takkaze (riv.), Ethiopia 111/G5
Takla (lake), Br. Col. 184/D2
Takla Makan (des.), China 54/K6
Takla Makan (Taklimakan Shamo) (des.), China 77/B4
Taklimakan Shamo (des.), China 77/B4
Tako, Sask. 181/B3
Takoma Park, Md. 245/F4
Takoradi, Ghana 106/D8
Takoradi-Sekondi, Ghana 102/B4
Taksimo, U.S.S.R. 48/M4
Taku (glac.), Alaska 196/N1
Taku (riv.), Alaska 196/N1
Taku (riv.), Br. Col. 184/J2
Takua Pa, Thailand 72/C5
Takutu (riv.), Guyana 131/B4
Tala, Mexico 150/H6
Tala, Uruguay 145/D5
Talab (riv.), Iran 59/H4
Talab (riv.), Iran 66/N6
Talab (riv.), Pakistan 68/A3
Talagante, Chile 138/G4
Talai (Da'an, Dalai), China 77/K2
Talak (reg.), Niger 106/E5
Talala, Okla. 288/P1
Talamanca (range), C. Rica 154/F6
Talangbetutu, Indonesia 85/C6
Talara, Peru 128/B5
Talara, Peru 120/A3
Talaud (isls.), Indonesia 54/O9
Talaud (isls.), Indonesia 85/H5
Talavera de la Reina, Spain 33/D2
Talawe (mt.), Papua N.G. 86/B2
Talbert, Ky. 237/P6
Talbingo, N.S. Wales 97/E4
Talbot, Alberta 182/E3
Talbot (isl.), Fla. 212/E1
Talbot (co.), Georgia 217/C5
Talbot, Ind. 227/C3
Talbot (co.), Md. 245/O5
Talbot (inlet), N.W. Terr. 187/L2
Talbot (cape), W. Australia 88/D2
Talbot (cape), W. Australia 92/D1
Talbott, Tenn. 237/P8
Talbotton, Georgia 217/C5
Talca, Chile 138/A11
Talca, Chile 120/B6
Talca (pt.), Chile 138/E3
Talcahuano, Chile 138/D1
Talcahuano, Chile 120/B6
Talcán (isl.), Chile 138/D4
Talco, Texas 303/K4
Talcott (range), Conn. 210/D1
Talcott, W. Va. 312/E7
Talcottville, Conn. 210/F1
Taldy-Kurgan, U.S.S.R. 54/J5
Taldy-Kurgan, U.S.S.R. 48/H5
Taleh, Somalia 115/J2
Talent, Oreg. 291/E5
Talgar, U.S.S.R. 48/H5
Talgarth, Wales 13/D5
Tali (Dali), China 77/E6
Taliabu (isl.), Indonesia 85/G6
Taliaferro (co.), Georgia 217/G3
Talibon, Philippines 82/E5
Talihina, Okla. 288/S5
Talina, Bolivia 136/B7
Tali Post, Sudan 111/F6
Talisayan, Philippines 82/E6
Talisheek, La. 238/L5
Talita, Uruguay 145/D4
Tal Kaif, Iraq 66/C2
Talkeetna, Alaska 196/B1
Talkeetna (mts.), Alaska 196/J2
Talkheh (riv.), Iran 66/E1
Talking Rock, Georgia 217/D1
Tallaboa, P. Rico 161/B3
Talladega (co.), Ala. 195/F4
Talladega, Ala. 195/F4
Talladega Springs, Ala. 195/F4
Tallaght, Ireland 17/J5
Tallahaga (creek), Miss. 256/F4
Tallahala (creek), Miss. 256/F7
Tallahassee (cap.), Fla. 146/K6
Tallahassee (cap.), Fla. 188/K4
Tallahassee (cap.), Fla. 212/B1
Tallahatchie (co.), Miss. 256/D3
Tallahatchie (riv.), Miss. 256/D3
Tallahatta Springs, Ala. 195/C7
Tallangatta, Victoria 97/D5
Tallant, Okla. 288/O1
Tallapoosa (co.), Ala. 195/G5
Tallapoosa (riv.), Ala. 195/G4
Tallapoosa, Georgia 217/B3
Tallapoosa, Mo. 261/N9
Tallassee, Ala. 195/G5
Tallinn, U.S.S.R. 7/G3
Tallinn (cap.), Estonian S.S.R., U.S.S.R. 53/C1
Tallinn, U.S.S.R. 48/C4
Tallinn, U.S.S.R. 52/B3
Tallmadge, Ohio 284/H3
Tallman, N.Y. 276/J8
Tallman, Sask. 181/E3
Tallmansville, W. Va. 312/F5
Tallow, Ireland 17/F7
Tallula, Ill. 222/D4
Tallulah, La. 238/H2
Tallulah Falls, Georgia 217/F1
Talma, Ind. 227/E2
Talmage, Kansas 232/E2
Talmage, Nebr. 264/H4
Talmage, Sask. 181/H6
Talmage, Utah 304/D3
Talmo, Georgia 217/E2
Talmo, Kansas 232/E2
Talmoon, Minn. 255/E3
Talodi, Sudan 111/F5
Talofofo (bay), Guam 86/K7
Taloga, Okla. 288/J2
Talon (lake), Ontario 177/E1
Taloqan, Afghanistan 68/B1
Taloqan, Afghanistan 59/J2
Talpa, Texas 303/E6
Talpa de Allende, Mexico 150/G6
Talparo, Trin. & Tob. 161/B10
Talquin (lake), Fla. 212/B1
Talsi, U.S.S.R. 53/B2
Taltal, Chile 138/A5
Taltal, Chile 120/B5
Taltal, Quebrada de (riv.), Chile 138/B5
Taltson (riv.), N.W. Terr. 187/G3
Talvik, Norway 18/N2
Talyawalka (creek), N.S. Wales 97/B2
Talyawalka Ana Branch, Darling (riv.), N.S. Wales 97/B3
Tama (co.), Iowa 229/H4
Tama, Iowa 229/H5
Tama (riv.), Japan 81/O2
Tamaha, Okla. 288/S4
Tamaki (str.), N. Zealand 100/C1
Tamale, Ghana 102/B4
Tamale, Ghana 106/D7
Tamalpais (mt.), Calif. 204/H1
Tamana (mt.), Trin. & Tob. 161/B10
Tamanrasset, Algeria 106/F4
Tamanrasset, Algeria 102/C2
Tamanrasset, Wadi (dry riv.), Algeria 106/E4
Tamaqua, Pa. 294/L4
Tamar (riv.), England 13/C7
Tamar (riv.), England 10/D5
Tamar (riv.), Tasmania 99/D3
Támara, Colombia 126/D5
Tamarac, Fla. 212/B3
Tamarac (riv.), Minn. 255/A2
Tamarack, Idaho 220/B5
Tamarack (isl.), Manitoba 179/F3
Tamarack, Minn. 255/E4
Tamarack (riv.), Minn. 255/D2
Tamarack, Pa. 294/G3
Tamarite de Litera, Spain 33/G2
Tamaro (mt.), Switzerland 39/G4
Tamaroa, Ill. 222/D5
Tamarugal, Pampa del (plain), Chile 138/B3
Tamási, Hungary 41/E3
Tamassee, S.C. 296/A2
Tamatama, Venezuela 124/F6
Tamatave (Toamasina), Madagascar 118/H3
Tamaulipas (state), Mexico 150/K4
Tamaya, Chile 138/A8
Tamayo, Dom. Rep. 158/D6
Tamazula, Mexico 150/F4
Tamazulapan del Progreso, Mexico 150/L8
Tamazunchale, Mexico 150/K6
Tambacounda, Senegal 106/B6
Tambar Springs, N.S. Wales 97/E2
Tambelan (isls.), Indonesia 85/D5
Tamberías, Argentina 143/C3
Tambey, U.S.S.R. 48/G2
Tambo (riv.), Peru 128/G11
Tambo, Queensland 88/H4
Tambo, Queensland 95/C5
Tambo de Mora, Peru 128/D9
Tambo Grande, Peru 128/B5
Tambohorano, Madagascar 118/G3
Tambopata (riv.), Peru 128/H9
Tambores, Uruguay 145/C2
Tamboril, Dom. Rep. 158/D5
Tamboritha (mt.), Victoria 97/D5
Tambov, U.S.S.R. 7/J3
Tambov, U.S.S.R. 52/F4
Tambov, U.S.S.R. 48/E4
Tambura, Sudan 111/E6
Tamchakett, Mauritania 106/B5
Tame, Colombia 126/E4
Tame (riv.), England 10/G3
Tâmega (riv.), Portugal 33/C2
Tamentit, Algeria 106/D3
Tamiahua, Mexico 150/L6
Tamiami (canal), Fla. 212/E6
Tamil Nadu (state), India 68/D6
Tamin (gov.), Iraq 66/D3
Tamina (riv.), Switzerland 39/H3
Tamins, Switzerland 39/H3
Tamise (Temse), Belgium 27/E6
Tam Ky, Vietnam 72/F4
Tammisaari (Ekenäs), Finland 18/N6
Tamms, Ill. 222/D6
Tammun, West Bank 65/C3
Tamo, Ark. 202/G5
Tamora, Nebr. 264/G4
Tampa, Fla. 188/K5
Tampa, Fla. 146/K7
Tampa, Fla. 212/C2
Tampa (bay), Fla. 188/K5
Tampa (bay), Fla. 212/D4
Tampa, Kansas 232/E3
Tampere, Finland 7/G2
Tampere, Finland 18/N6
Tampico, Ill. 222/D2
Tampico, Ind. 227/F7
Tampico, Mexico 146/J7
Tampico, Mexico 150/L5
Tampico, Mont. 262/K2
Tampico, Wash. 310/E4
Tampoc (riv.), Fr. Guiana 131/E4
Tam Quan, Vietnam 72/F4
Tamra, Saudi Arabia 59/E5
Tams, W. Va. 312/D7
Tamsagbulag, Mongolia 77/J2
Tamsagout, Mauritania 106/C4
Tamshiyacu, Peru 128/F5
Tamsweg, Austria 41/B3
Tamuín, Mexico 150/K6
Tamuning, Guam 86/K7
Tamworth, Australia 87/E9
Tamworth, England 13/F5
Tamworth, England 10/G3
Tamworth •, N.H. 268/E4
Tamworth, N.S. Wales 88/J6
Tamworth, N.S. Wales 97/F2
Tamworth, Ontario 177/H3
Tamyang, S. Korea 81/C6
Tana (lake), Ethiopia 102/F3
Tana (lake), Ethiopia 111/G5
Tana (riv.), Finland 18/P2
Tana (riv.), Kenya 102/G5
Tana (riv.), Kenya 115/G4
Tana, Norway 18/Q1
Tana (riv.), Norway 18/P1
Tanabe, Kyoto, Japan 81/J7
Tanabe, Wakayama, Japan 81/G7
Tanacross, Alaska 196/K2
Tanafjord (fjord), Norway 18/Q1
Tanaga (isl.), Alaska 196/K4
Tanaga (vol.), Alaska 196/K4
Tanahgrogot, Indonesia 85/F6
Tanahmerah, Indonesia 85/K7
Tanah Merah, Malaysia 72/D6
Tanamá (riv.), P. Rico 161/B1
Tanami (des.), North. Terr. 88/E3
Tanami, North. Terr. 93/A5
Tanami (des.), North. Terr. 93/C5
Tánamo, Cuba 158/J3
Tan An, Vietnam 72/E5
Tanana, Alaska 188/D5
Tanana, Alaska 196/H1
Tanana (riv.), Alaska 146/D3
Tanana (riv.), Alaska 188/D5
Tanana (riv.), Alaska 196/J2
Tananarive (Antananarivo) (cap.), Madagascar 118/H3
Tanaro (riv.), Italy 34/B2
Tanch'ŏn, N. Korea 81/D3
Tancook Island, Nova Scotia 168/D4
Tanda, India 68/E3
Tandag, Philippines 82/F6
Tandil, Argentina 143/E4
Tandil, Argentina 120/D6
Tando Adam, Pakistan 68/B3
Tando Allahyar, Pakistan 68/B3
Tandou (lake), N.S. Wales 97/A3
Tandragee, N. Ireland 17/J3
Tanega (isl.), Japan 81/E8
Taney (co.), Mo. 261/F9
Taneycomo (lake), Mo. 261/F9
Taneytown, Md. 245/J2
Taneyville, Mo. 261/F9
Tanezrouft (des.), Algeria 102/C2
Tanezrouft (des.), Algeria 106/E4
Tang, Kas (isl.), Cambodia 72/D5
Tanga (isls.), Papua N.G. 86/C1
Tanga (reg.), Tanzania 115/G5
Tanga, Tanzania 115/G4
Tanga, Tanzania 102/F5
Tangainony, Madagascar 118/H4
Tangalla, Sri Lanka 68/E7
Tanganyika (lake) 102/F5
Tanganyika (lake), Burundi 115/E5
Tanganyika (lake), Tanzania 115/E5
Tanganyika (lake), Zaire 115/E5
Tanganyika (lake), Zambia 115/E5
Tangent (pt.), Alaska 196/H1
Tangent, Alberta 182/B2
Tangent, Oreg. 291/D3
Tangerang, Indonesia 85/G1
Tangermünde, Germany 22/D2
Tanggula Shan (range), China 77/D5
Tangier, Ind. 227/C5
Tangier (sound), Md. 245/P8
Tangier (Tanger), Morocco 106/C1
Tangier, Morocco 102/B1
Tangier, Nova Scotia 168/F4
Tangier (riv.), Nova Scotia 168/F4
Tangier, Okla. 288/G2
Tangier, Va. 307/R5
Tangier (isl.), Va. 307/R5
Tangier (sound), Va. 307/S5
Tangipahoa (par.), La. 238/K5
Tangipahoa, La. 238/J5
Tangipahoa (riv.), La. 238/N1
Tangra Yumco (lake), China 77/C5
Tangshan, China 77/J4
Tangshan, China 54/N5
Tangub, Philippines 82/D6
Tangyanika (lake) 2/L6
Tangyuan, China 77/L2
Tanimbar (isls.), Indonesia 54/P10
Tanimbar (isls.), Indonesia 85/J7
Tanjay, Philippines 82/D6
Tanjore (Thanjavur), India 68/D6
Tanjungbalai, Indonesia 85/C5
Tanjungkarang, Indonesia 54/M10
Tanjungkarang, Indonesia 85/C7
Tanjungpandan, Indonesia 85/D6
Tanjungpinang, Indonesia 85/C5
Tanjungpriok, Indonesia 85/H1
Tanjungpura, Indonesia 85/B5
Tanjungredeb, Indonesia 85/F5
Tanjungselor, Indonesia 85/F5
Tanna (isl.), Vanuatu 87/H7
Tanner, Ala. 195/E1
Tanner, W. Va. 312/E5
Tannersville, N.Y. 276/M6
Tannersville, Pa. 294/M3
Tannis (bay), Denmark 21/D2
Tannu-Ola (range), Mongolia 77/D1
Tannu-Ola (range), U.S.S.R. 48/K5
Tanon (str.), Philippines 82/D6
Tanout, Niger 106/F6
Tanque Verde, Ariz. 198/E6
Tanta, Egypt 111/J3
Tanta, Egypt 59/B3
Tantallon, Sask. 181/K5
Tantalus (mt.), Hawaii 218/D4
Tan-Tan, Morocco 106/B3
Tantoyuca, Mexico 150/L6
Tantung (Dandong), China 77/K3
Tanumshede, Sweden 18/G7
Tanunda, S. Australia 94/C6
Tanzania 2/L6
Tanzania 102/F5
TANZANIA 115/F5
Tao, Ko (isl.), Thailand 72/C5
Tao'an, China 77/K2
Taole, China 77/G4
Taongi (atoll), Marshall Is. 87/G4
Taopi, Minn. 255/F7
Taormina, Italy 34/E6
Taos, Mo. 261/H5
Taos (co.), N. Mex. 274/D2
Taos, N. Mex. 274/D2
Taos Pueblo, N. Mex. 274/D2
Taoudenni, Mali 106/D4
Taoudenni, Mali 102/B2
Taourirt, Algeria 106/E3
Taourirt, Morocco 106/D2
Taouz, Morocco 106/D2
Taoyuan, China 77/K6
Tapa, U.S.S.R. 53/C1
Tapacarí, Bolivia 136/B5
Tapachula, Mexico 150/N9
Tapajós (riv.), Brazil 2/G6
Tapajós (riv.), Brazil 120/D3
Tapajós (riv.), Brazil 132/B4
Tapaktuan, Indonesia 85/B5
Tapalquén, Argentina 143/E4
Tapanahoni (riv.), Suriname 131/D4
Tapani (lake), Québec 172/B3
Tapanui, N. Zealand 100/B6
Tapaz, Philippines 82/D5
Tapera do Jeronimo, Brazil 132/C2
Tapeta, Liberia 106/C7
Tapi, Mae Nam (riv.), Thailand 72/C5
Tapiantana Group (isls.), Philippines 82/D7
Tapiche (riv.), Peru 128/E6
Taping (riv.), Burma 72/C1
Tápiószele, Hungary 41/E3
Tapirapecó, Sierra (mts.), Venezuela 124/F7
Tapiutan (isl.), Philippines 82/B5
Tapoco, N.C. 281/A4
Tapolca, Hungary 41/D3
Tappahannock, Va. 307/O5
Tappan (lake), N.J. 273/C1
Tappan, N.Y. 276/K8
Tappan (lake), Ohio 284/H5
Tappen, N. Dak. 282/L6
Tappi (cape), Japan 81/K3
Tapti (riv.), India 68/D4
Tapul (isl.), Philippines 82/C8
Tapul Group (isls.), Philippines 85/G4
Tapul Group (isls.), Philippines 82/C8
Taputapu (cape), Amer. Samoa 86/N9
Taquari (riv.), Brazil 132/C7
Taquaritinga, Brazil 132/D8
Taquaritinga, Brazil 135/B2
Tar (riv.), N.C. 281/O3
Tara (hill), Ireland 17/H4
Tara, Ontario 177/C3
Tara (isl.), Philippines 82/C4
Tara, Queensland 95/D5
Tara, Queensland 88/J5
Tara, U.S.S.R. 48/H4
Tara (riv.), Yugoslavia 45/D4
Tarabuco, Bolivia 136/C6
Tarabulus, Lebanon 63/F5
Tarabulus, Lebanon 59/C3

456 Taradale

Taradale, N. Zealand 100/F3
Taraira (riv.), Colombia 126/F8
Tarairí, Bolivia 136/D7
Tarakan, Indonesia 54/N9
Tarakan, Indonesia 85/F5
Taralga, N.S. Wales 97/E4
Tarama (isl.), Japan 81/L7
Tarancón, Spain 33/E3
Tarangire Nat'l Park, Tanzania 115/G4
Taranna, Tasmania 99/D5
Taransay (isl.), Scotland 15/A3
Taranto (prov.), Italy 34/F4
Taranto, Italy 34/F4
Taranto, Italy 7/F4
Taranto (gulf), Italy 7/F5
Taranto (gulf), Italy 34/F5
Tarapacá (reg.), Chile 138/B2
Tarapacá, Chile 138/B2
Tarapacá, Colombia 126/F9
Tarapaya, Bolivia 136/B6
Tarapoto, Peru 120/B3
Tarapoto, Peru 128/D6
Tarare, France 28/F5
Tararua (range), N. Zealand 100/E4
Tarascon, France 28/F6
Tarasp, Switzerland 39/K3
Tarata, Bolivia 136/C5
Tarata, Peru 128/H11
Tarauacá, Brazil 132/G10
Tarauaca, Brazil 120/C3
Taravao (bay), Fr. Poly. 86/T13
Taravao (isth.), Fr. Poly. 86/T13
Tarawa (atoll), Kiribati 87/H5
Tarazona, Spain 33/E2
Tarazona de la Mancha, Spain 33/F3
Tarbat Ness (prom.), Scotland 15/E3
Tarbert, Ireland 17/C6
Tarbert, Strathclyde, Scotland 15/C5
Tarbert, W. Isles, Scotland 15/B3
Tarbert, East Loch (inlet), Scotland 15/B3
Tarbert, Loch (inlet), Scotland 15/B5
Tarbert, West Loch (inlet), Scotland 15/C5
Tarbert, West Loch (inlet), Scotland 15/A3
Tarbes, France 7/E4
Tarbes, France 28/D6
Tarbolton, Scotland 15/D5
Tarboro, Georgia 217/J8
Tarboro, N.C. 281/O3
Tarbot, Nova Scotia 168/H2
Tarcoola, S. Australia 88/E6
Tarcoola, S. Australia 94/D4
Tarcutta, N.S. Wales 97/D4
Tardienta, Spain 33/F2
Tardošked, Czech. 41/E2
Taree, N. S. Wales 88/J6
Taree, N.S. Wales 97/G2
Tärendö, Sweden 18/N3
Tarentum, Pa. 294/C4
Tarfaya, Morocco 106/B3
Tarfaya, Morocco 102/A2
Tar Heel, N.C. 281/M5
Tarhuna, Libya 102/D1
Tarhuna, Libya 111/B1
Tariana, Colombia 126/F7
Táriba, Venezuela 124/B4
Tarifa, Spain 33/D4
Tariff, W. Va. 312/D5
Tariffville, Conn. 210/D1
Tarija (riv.), Argentina 143/D1
Tarija (dept.), Bolivia 136/D7
Tarija, Bolivia 120/C5
Tarija, Bolivia 136/C7
Tarija, Rio Grande de (riv.), Bolivia 136/C8
Tariku (riv.), Indonesia 85/K6
Tarim (riv.), China 54/K5
Tarim, Yemen 59/E6
Tarim He (riv.), China 77/B3
Tarim Pendi (basin), China 77/B4
Tar Island, Alberta 182/E1
Taritatu (riv.), Indonesia 85/K6
Tarkio, Mo. 261/B2
Tarkio, Mont. 262/B4
Tarko-Sale, U.S.S.R. 48/H3
Tarkwa, Ghana 106/D7
Tarlac (prov.), Philippines 82/C3
Tarlac, Philippines 82/C3
Tarlac, Philippines 85/G2
Tarland, Scotland 15/F3
Tarleton (lake), N.H. 268/D4
Tarlton, Ohio 284/E6
Tarlton, Tenn. 237/K9
Tarlton Downs, North. Terr. 93/E7
Tarm, Denmark 21/B6
Tarma, Peru 128/E8
Tarn (dept.), France 28/E6
Tarn (riv.), France 28/E6
Tarna (riv.), Hungary 41/F3
Tärnaby, Sweden 18/J4
Tarnak (riv.), Afghanistan 68/B2
Tårnby, Denmark 21/F6
Tarn-et-Garonne (dept.), France 28/D5
Tarnobrzeg (prov.), Poland 47/E3
Tarnobrzeg, Poland 47/E3
Tarnopol, Sask. 181/F3
Tarnov, Nebr. 264/G3
Tarnów (prov.), Poland 47/E4
Tarnów, Poland 7/G3
Tarnów, Poland 47/E4
Tarnowskie Góry, Poland 47/A3
Tarom, Iran 66/J6
Tarom, Iran 59/G4
Taroom, Queensland 95/D5
Tarouca, Portugal 33/C2
Taroudannt, Morocco 106/C2
Taroudannt, Morocco 102/A2
Tarpa, Hungary 41/G2
Tarpon Springs, Fla. 212/D3
Tarqui, Peru 128/E3
Tarquinia, Italy 34/C3
Tarqumiya, West Bank 65/C4
Tarragona (prov.), Spain 33/G2
Tarragona, Spain 33/G2
Tarragona, Spain 7/E4
Tarraleah, Tasmania 99/C4
Tarrant (co.), Texas 303/G5
Tarrant, Ala. 195/E3
Tarrants, Mo. 261/K4
Tarrasa, Spain 33/G2
Tárrega, Spain 33/G2
Tarryall (creek), Colo. 208/H4
Tarrytown, Georgia 217/H6
Tarrytown, N.Y. 276/O6
Tarsney Lakes, Mo. 261/R6
Tarsus, Turkey 59/C2
Tarsus, Turkey 63/F4
Tart, China 77/D4
Tartagal, Argentina 143/D1
Tartagal, Argentina 120/C5
Tartas, France 28/C6
Tartu, U.S.S.R. 7/G3
Tartu, U.S.S.R. 53/D1
Tartu, U.S.S.R. 48/C4
Tartu, U.S.S.R. 52/C3
Tartus (prov.), Syria 63/G5
Tartus, Syria 63/F5
Tarutung, Indonesia 85/B5
Tarver, Georgia 217/G9
Tarzan, Texas 303/B5
Tarzana, Calif. 204/B10
Täsch, Switzerland 39/E4
Tasco, Kansas 232/B2
Tashauz, U.S.S.R. 48/F5
Tashk (lake), Iran 59/F4
Tashk (lake), Iran 66/J6
Tashkent, U.S.S.R. 54/H5
Tashkent, U.S.S.R. 2/N3
Tashkent, U.S.S.R. 48/G5
Tasikmalaya, Indonesia 85/H2
Tasisuak (lake), Newf. 166/B2
Taşkent, Turkey 63/E4
Taşköprü, Turkey 63/F2
Taşlıçay, Turkey 63/K3
Tasman (sea) 2/S7
Tasman (sea) 87/G9
Tasman (sea) 88/J7
Tasman (sea), N.S. Wales 97/F5
Tasman (bay), N. Zealand 100/D4
Tasman (mt.), N. Zealand 100/C5
Tasman (mts.), N. Zealand 100/D4
Tasman (sea), N. Zealand 100/B4
Tasman (head), Tasmania 99/D5
Tasman (pen.), Tasmania 88/H8
Tasman (pen.), Tasmania 99/E5
Tasman (sea), Tasmania 99/E4
Tasman (sea), Victoria 97/F5
TASMANIA 99
Tasmania, Australia 87/H8
Tasmania (state), Australia 87/E10
Tasmania (isl.), Australia 2/S8
Tăşnad, Romania 45/F2
Taşova, Turkey 63/F4
Tassili N'Ahaggar (plat.), Algeria 106/E4
Tassili N'Ajjer (plat.), Algeria 106/F3
Tåstrup, Denmark 21/F6
Tasu, Br. Col. 184/A4
Taşucu (gulf), Turkey 63/E4
Taswell, Ind. 227/D8
Tata, Hungary 41/E3
Tataa (pt.), Fr. Poly. 86/S13
Tatabánya, Hungary 41/E3
Tatahouine, Tunisia 106/G2
Tatalrose, Br. Col. 184/D3
Tatamagouche, Nova Scotia 168/E3
Tatamba, Solomon Is. 86/D3
Tatamy, Pa. 294/M4
Tatar (str.), U.S.S.R. 54/R5
Tatar (str.), U.S.S.R. 48/P4
Tatar A.S.S.R., U.S.S.R. 52/G3
Tatar A.S.S.R., U.S.S.R. 48/F4
Tatarsk, U.S.S.R. 48/H4
Tate, Georgia 217/D2
Tate (co.), Miss. 256/E1
Tate, Sask. 181/G4
Tateville, Ky. 237/M7
Tateyama, Japan 81/K6
Tathlina (lake), N.W. Terr. 187/G3
Tathlith, Saudi Arabia 59/D6
Tathra, N.S. Wales 97/F5
Tati (riv.), Botswana 118/D4
Tatitlek, Alaska 196/D1
Tatla Lake, Br. Col. 184/E4
Tatlatui (lake), Br. Col. 184/D2
Tatlayoko (lake), Br. Col. 184/E4
Tatnam (cape), Manitoba 179/K2
Tatnum (cape), Man. 162/G4
Tatoosh (isl.), Wash. 310/A2
Tatra, High (mts.), Czech. 41/E2
Tatra, High (range), Poland 47/D4
Tatta, Pakistan 59/J5
Tatta, Pakistan 68/B4
Tattnall (co.), Georgia 217/J6
Tatuí, Brazil 135/C3
Tatum, N. Mex. 274/F5
Tatum, S.C. 296/H2
Tatum, Texas 303/K5
Tatums, Okla. 288/M6
Tatung (Datong), China 77/H3
Tatura, Victoria 97/C5
Tatvan, Turkey 63/K3
Taubaté, Brazil 132/E8
Taubaté, Brazil 135/D3
Tauber (riv.), Germany 22/C4
Täuffelen, Switzerland 39/D2
Taumarunui, N. Zealand 100/E3
Taum Sauk (mt.), Mo. 261/L7
Taung, S. Africa 118/C5
Taungdwingyi, Burma 72/C2
Taunggyi, Burma 72/C2
Taungthonton (mt.), Burma 72/B1
Taungup, Burma 72/B3
Taunton, England 13/D6
Taunton, England 10/E5
Taunton, Mass. 249/K5
Taunton (riv.), Mass. 249/K5
Taunton, Minn. 255/B6
Taunus (range), Germany 22/C3
Taupo, N. Zealand 100/F3
Taupo (lake), N. Zealand 100/F3
Tauq, Iraq 66/D3
Taurage, U.S.S.R. 53/B3
Taurage, U.S.S.R. 52/B3
Tauranga, N. Zealand 100/F2
Taureau (res.), Québec 172/D3
Taurianova, Italy 34/E5
Tauroa (pt.), N. Zealand 100/D1
Taurus (mts.), Turkey 59/B2
Taurus (mts.), Turkey 63/D4
Tauste, Spain 33/F2
Tautira, Fr. Poly. 86/T13
Tautira (pt.), Fr. Poly. 86/T13
Tauu (isls.), Papua N.G. 86/D2
Tavai, Paraguay 144/E5
Tavan Bogd Uul (mt.), Mongolia 77/C2
Tavannes, Switzerland 39/D2
Tavaputs (plat.), Utah 304/D4
Tavares, Fla. 212/E3
Tavas, Turkey 63/C4
Tavda, U.S.S.R. 48/G4
Tavernier, Fla. 212/F6
Taveta, Kenya 115/G4
Tavetsch, Switzerland 39/G3
Taveuni (isl.), Fiji 87/H7
Taveuni (isl.), Fiji 86/R10
Tavignano (riv.), France 28/B6
Tavira, Portugal 33/C4
Tavistock (rock), England 10/D5
Tavistock, England 13/C7
Tavistock, N.J. 273/B3
Tavistock, Ontario 177/D4
Tavoy, Burma 54/L8
Tavoy, Burma 72/C4
Tavoy (pt.), Burma 72/C4
Tavrichanka, U.S.S.R. 48/O5
Tavşanlı, Turkey 63/C3
Taw (riv.), England 13/D7
Taw (riv.), England 10/D5
Tawa, N. Zealand 100/B2
Tawas (lake), Mich. 250/F4
Tawas (pt.), Mich. 250/F4
Tawas City, Mich. 250/F4
Tawatinaw, Alberta 182/D2
Tawau, Malaysia 85/F5
Tawin (isl.), Ireland 17/C5
Tawi-Tawi (prov.), Philippines 82/B8
Tawi-Tawi (isl.), Philippines 82/B8
Tawitawi Group (isls.), Philippines 85/G4
Taxco de Alarcón, Mexico 150/K7
Taxila (ruins), Pakistan 68/C2
Taxis River, New Bruns. 170/D2
Taxkorgan, China 77/A4
Tay (firth), Scotland 15/F4
Tay (firth), Scotland 10/E2
Tay, Loch (lake), Scotland 10/D2
Tay, Loch (lake), Scotland 15/D4
Tay (riv.), Scotland 10/E2
Tay (riv.), Scotland 15/E4
Tay (lake), W. Australia 88/C6
Tayabamba, Peru 128/D7
Tayabas (bay), Philippines 82/C4
Tayasan, Philippines 82/D6
Taycheedah, Wis. 317/K8
Tay Creek, New Bruns. 170/D2
Tayibe, Israel 65/C3
Tayinloan, Scotland 15/C5
Taylor, Ala. 195/H8
Taylor (mts.), Alaska 196/G2
Taylor, Ariz. 198/E4
Taylor, Ark. 202/D7
Taylor, Br. Col. 184/G2
Taylor (peak), Colo. 208/F5
Taylor (riv.), Colo. 208/F5
Taylor (co.), Fla. 212/C1
Taylor (co.), Georgia 217/D5
Taylor (mt.), Idaho 220/D5
Taylor (co.), Iowa 229/D7
Taylor (co.), Ky. 237/L6
Taylor, La. 238/D1
Taylor, Mich. 250/B7
Taylor, Miss. 256/E2
Taylor, Mo. 261/J3
Taylor, Nebr. 264/E3
Taylor (mt.), N. Mex. 274/B3
Taylor, N. Dak. 282/F6
Taylor (head), Nova Scotia 168/F4
Taylor, Pa. 294/F7
Taylor (co.), Texas 303/E5
Taylor, Texas 303/G7
Taylor, Texas 188/G4
Taylor (co.), W. Va. 312/F4
Taylor (co.), Wis. 317/E5
Taylor, Wis. 317/E7
Taylor Lake Village, Texas 303/K2
Taylor Mill, Ky. 237/S2
Taylor Park (res.), Colo. 208/F5
Taylors, S.C. 296/C2
Taylor's Arm, N.S. Wales 97/G2
Taylors Falls, Minn. 255/F5
Taylors Island, Md. 245/N7
Taylorsport, Ky. 237/R2
Taylor Springs, Ill. 222/D4
Taylorstown, Pa. 294/A5
Taylorsville, Calif. 204/E3
Taylorsville, Georgia 217/C2
Taylorsville, Ind. 227/F6
Taylorsville, Ky. 237/L4
Taylorsville, Md. 245/K3
Taylorsville, Miss. 256/F7
Taylorsville, N.C. 281/G3
Taylorsville (Philo), Ohio 284/G6
Taylorsville, Utah 304/B3
Taylortown, La. 238/C2
Taylorville, Ill. 222/D4
Taymouth, New Bruns. 170/D2
Taymyr (lake), U.S.S.R. 4/B5
Taymyr (lake), U.S.S.R. 54/M2
Taymyr (lake), U.S.S.R. 48/K2
Taymyr (pen.), U.S.S.R. 4/B4
Taymyr (pen.), U.S.S.R. 54/L2
Taymyr (pen.), U.S.S.R. 48/L2
Taymyr (riv.), U.S.S.R. 48/K2
Taymyr Aut. Okr., U.S.S.R. 48/K2
Tay Ninh, Vietnam 72/E5
Tayoltita, Mexico 150/G4
Tayport, Scotland 10/E2
Tayport, Scotland 15/F4
Tayshet, U.S.S.R. 48/K4
Tayside (reg.), Scotland 15/E4
Taytay, Philippines 85/G3
Taytay, Philippines 82/B5
Taytay (bay), Philippines 82/B5
Tayyebat, Iran 66/M3
Taz (riv.), U.S.S.R. 54/K3
Taz (riv.), U.S.S.R. 4/C5
Taz (riv.), U.S.S.R. 48/J3
Taza, Morocco 106/D2
Tazadit, Mauritania 106/B4
Taza Khurmatu, Iraq 66/D3
Tazawa (lake), Japan 81/K4
Tazerbo (oasis), Libya 111/D2
Tazewell, Georgia 217/D6
Tazewell (co.), Ill. 222/D3
Tazewell, Tenn. 237/O8
Tazewell (co.), Va. 307/E6
Tazewell, Va. 307/E6
Tazin (lake), Sask. 181/L2
Tazlina (lake), Alaska 196/D1
Tazlina (riv.), Alaska 196/D1
Tazlina Glacier Lodge, Alaska 196/C1
Tazovskiy, U.S.S.R. 48/J3
Tbilisi, U.S.S.R. 7/J4
Tbilisi, U.S.S.R. 2/M3
Tbilisi, U.S.S.R. 52/F6
Tbilisi, U.S.S.R. 48/E5
Tchentlo (lake), Br. Col. 184/E2
Tchibanga, Gabon 115/B4
Tcholliré, Cameroon 115/B2
Tchula, Miss. 256/D4
Tchula (lake), Miss. 256/D4
Tczew, Poland 47/D1
Tea, S. Dak. 298/R7
Teacapán (inlet), Mexico 150/F5
Teachey, N.C. 281/N5
Teague, Texas 303/H6
Te Anau, N. Zealand 100/A6
Te Anau (lake), N. Zealand 100/A6
Teaneck•, N.J. 273/B2
Teapa, Mexico 150/N8
Teapot Dome (mt.), Wyo. 319/F2
Te Araroa, N. Zealand 100/G2
Te Aroha, N. Zealand 100/E2
Teasdale, Utah 304/C5
Te Atatu, N. Zealand 100/B1
Teaticket, Mass. 249/M6
Tea Tree Gully, S. Australia 88/E7
Tea Tree Gully, S. Australia 94/B7
Tea Tree Well, North. Terr. 93/C7
Te Awamutu, N. Zealand 100/E3
Teays, W. Va. 312/B6
Tebenkof (bay), Alaska 196/M2
Tébessa, Algeria 102/C1
Tébessa, Algeria 106/F1
Tebicuary (riv.), Paraguay 144/C5
Tebicuary Mí, Paraguay 144/B5
Tebicuary Mí (riv.), Paraguay 144/C5
Tebingtinggi, Indonesia 85/B5
Tebuk (Tabuk), Saudi Arabia 59/C4
Tecamachalco, Mexico 150/O2
Tecate, Mexico 150/A1
Tecer (mts.), Turkey 63/G3
Techirghiol, Romania 45/J3
Tecka, Argentina 143/B5
Tecolote (creek), N. Mex. 274/D3
Tecomán, Mexico 150/H7
Tecopa, Calif. 204/J8
Tecpan de Galeana, Mexico 150/J8
Tecuala, Mexico 150/G5
Tecuci, Romania 45/H3
Tecumseh, Kansas 232/G2
Tecumseh, Mich. 250/F7
Tecumseh, Mo. 261/H9
Tecumseh, Nebr. 264/H4
Tecumseh (mt.), N.H. 268/D4
Tecumseh, Okla. 288/N4
Tecumseh, Ontario 177/B5
Tedrow, Ohio 284/B2
Teduzara, Bolivia 136/B2
Tedzhen, U.S.S.R. 48/F6
Teec Nos Pos, Ariz. 198/F2
Teeds Grove, Iowa 229/N4
Teegarden, Ind. 227/E2
Teepee Creek, Alberta 182/A2
Tees, Alberta 182/D3
Tees (riv.), England 10/F3
Tees (riv.), England 13/F3
Teeswater, Ontario 177/C3
Teeterville, Ontario 177/D5
Tefé, Brazil 132/G9
Tefé, Brazil 120/C3
Tefé (riv.), Brazil 132/G9
Tefenni, Turkey 63/C4
Tefft, Ind. 227/D2
Tegal, Indonesia 85/J2
Tegel, Germany 22/E3
Tegelen, Netherlands 27/J6
Tegernsee (lake), Germany 22/D5
Tegucigalpa (cap.), Hond. 146/K8
Tegucigalpa (cap.), Honduras 154/D3
Tehachapi, Calif. 204/G8
Tehachapi (mts.), Calif. 204/G9
Tehama (co.), Calif. 204/C3
Tehama, Calif. 204/C3
Tehchow (Dezhou), China 77/J4
Tehek (lake), N.W. Terr. 187/J3
Tehkummah, Ontario 177/B2
Tehran (cap.), Iran 2/M4
Tehran (cap.), Iran 66/G3
Tehran (cap.), Iran 59/F2
Tehran (cap.), Iran 54/G6
Tehri, India 68/D2
Tehuacán, Mexico 150/L7
Tehuantepec, Mexico 146/J8
Tehuantepec, Mexico 150/M8
Tehuantepec (gulf), Mexico 150/M9
Tehuantepec (isth.), Mexico 150/M8
Tehuipango, Mexico 150/P2
Teide, Pico de (peak), Spain 33/B5
Teifi (riv.), Wales 13/C5
Teifi (riv.), Wales 10/D4
Teigen, Mont. 262/H3
Teignmouth, England 10/E5
Teignmouth, England 13/D7
Teith (riv.), Scotland 15/D4
Tejerri, Libya 111/B3
Tejerri, Libya 102/D2
Tejo (Tagus) (riv.), Portugal 33/B3
Tejutla, Guatemala 154/B3
Tekamah, Nebr. 264/H3
Te Kao, N. Zealand 100/D1
Tekapo (lake), N. Zealand 100/C5
Te Karaka, N. Zealand 100/F3
Te Kauwhata, N. Zealand 100/E2
Tekax de álaro Obregón, Mexico 150/P6
Tekeli, U.S.S.R. 48/H5
Tekes, China 77/B3
Tekirdağ (prov.), Turkey 63/B2
Tekirdağ, Turkey 59/A1
Tekirdağ, Turkey 63/B2
Tekman, Turkey 63/J3
Teknaf, Bangladesh 68/G4
Tekoa, Wash. 310/H3
Tekong Besar, Pulau (isl.), Singapore 72/F6
Tekonsha, Mich. 250/E6
Te Kopuru, N. Zealand 100/D2
Te Kuiti, N. Zealand 100/E3
Tel (riv.), India 68/E4
Tela, Honduras 154/D3
Telanaipura, Indonesia 54/M10
Telavi, U.S.S.R. 52/G6
Tel Aviv (dist.), Israel 65/B3
Tel Aviv-Jaffa, Israel 59/B3
Tel Aviv-Jaffa, Israel 65/B3
Tel Aviv-Jaffa, Israel 54/E6
Telč, Czech. 41/C2
Telde, Spain 33/B5
Telefomin, Papua N.G. 85/B7
Telegraph, Texas 303/E7
Telegraph Creek, Br. Col. 184/K2
Telemark (co.), Norway 18/F7
Telephone, Texas 303/J4
Telescope (peak), Calif. 204/H7
Telescope (pt.), Grenada 161/D8
Teles Pires (riv.), Brazil 120/D3
Teles Pires (riv.), Brazil 132/B5
Telfair (co.), Georgia 217/G7
Telford, England 13/E5
Telford, Pa. 294/M5
Telford, Tenn. 237/S8
Telfordville, Alberta 182/C3
Telfs, Austria 41/A3
Telgte, Germany 22/B3
Télimélé, Guinea 106/B6
Telkalakh, Syria 63/F5
Tel Kotchek, Syria 59/D2
Tel Kotchek, Syria 63/K4
Telkwa, Br. Col. 184/D3
Tell, Georgia 217/J2
Tell, Texas 303/D3
Tell 'Asur (mt.), Jordan 65/C4
Tell City, Ind. 227/D9
Teller, Alaska 196/E1
Teller (co.), Colo. 208/J5
Tellicherry, India 68/C6
Tellico (riv.), Tenn. 237/N10
Tellico Plains, Tenn. 237/N10
Tellin, Belgium 27/G8
Telluride, Colo. 208/D7
Telma, Wash. 310/E3
Telocaset, Oreg. 291/K2
Telogia, Fla. 212/B1
Teloloapan, Mexico 150/J7
Telpaneca, Nicaragua 154/D4
Tel'pos-Iz (mt.), U.S.S.R. 52/K2
Telsen, Argentina 143/C5
Telšiai, U.S.S.R. 53/B2
Telšiai, U.S.S.R. 52/B3
Teltow, Germany 22/E4
Teltown, Ireland 17/H4
Telukbayur, Indonesia 85/C6
Teluk Intan, Malaysia 72/D6
Tema, Ghana 106/E7
Tema, Ghana 102/C4
Temacine, Algeria 106/F2
Temae (lake), Fr. Poly. 86/S12
Temagami, Ontario 177/K5
Temagami, Ontario 175/E3
Temagami (lake), Ontario 177/K5
Temagami (lake), Ontario 175/D3
Temanggung, Indonesia 85/J2
Temascalapa, Mexico 150/M1
Tematangi (isl.), Fr. Poly. 87/M8
Temax, Mexico 150/P6
Tembisa, S. Africa 118/H6
Temblador, Venezuela 124/G3
Tembuè, Mozambique 118/E2
Temecula, Calif. 204/H10
Temerloh, Malaysia 72/D7
Temiang, Bukit (mt.), Malaysia 72/D6
Temirtau, U.S.S.R. 54/J4
Temirtau, U.S.S.R. 48/H4
Témiscaming, Québec 174/B3
Témiscamingue (county), Québec 174/B3
Témiscouata (co.), Québec 172/J2
Témiscouata (lake), Québec 172/H2
Temma, Tasmania 99/A3
Temora, N. S. Wales 88/H6
Temora, N.S. Wales 97/D4
Temoris, Mexico 150/E3
Temósachic, Mexico 150/E2
Tempe, Ariz. 198/D5
Tempe Downs, North. Terr. 93/C8
Tempelhof, Germany 22/F4
Temperance, Mich. 250/F7
Temperance Hall, Tenn. 237/K8
Temperance Vale, New Bruns. 170/C2
Temperanceville, Va. 307/T5
Tempio Pausania, Italy 34/B4
Temple (mt.), Alberta 182/B4
Temple, Georgia 217/B3
Temple, La. 238/E4
Temple•, Maine 243/C6
Temple, Mich. 250/E4
Temple•, N.H. 268/D6
Temple, Okla. 288/K6
Temple, Pa. 294/L5
Temple, Texas 303/G6
Temple, Texas 188/G4
Temple Bar, Ariz. 198/A2
Temple City, Calif. 204/D10
Templemore, Ireland 10/C4
Templemore, Ireland 17/F6
Templestowe and Doncaster, Victoria 97/J5
Temple Terrace, Fla. 212/C2
Templeton, Calif. 204/E8
Templeton, Ind. 227/C3
Templeton, Iowa 229/D5
Templeton•, Mass. 249/F2
Templeton, Pa. 294/C4
Templeton, Québec 172/B4
Templetuohy, Ireland 17/F6
Templeville, Md. 245/P4
Templin, Germany 22/E2
Tempo, N. Ireland 17/G3
Temryuk, U.S.S.R. 52/E5
Temse, Belgium 27/E6
Temuco, Chile 120/B6
Temuco, Chile 138/E2
Temuka, N. Zealand 100/C6
Temvik, N. Dak. 282/K7
Ten, Colombia 126/D5
Tena, Ecuador 128/D3
Tenabo, Mexico 150/P6
Tenafly, N.J. 273/C1
Tenaha, Texas 303/K6
Tenakee Springs, Alaska 196/M1
Tenali, India 68/E5
Tenancingo de Degollado, Mexico 150/K7
Tenango de Río Blanco, Mexico 150/O2
Tenants Harbor, Maine 243/E8
Tenares, Dom. Rep. 158/E5
Tenasserim (div.), Burma 72/C4
Tenasserim, Burma 72/C5
Tenasserim (isl.), Burma 72/C4
Tenbury, England 13/E5
Tenby, Manitoba 179/C4
Tenby, Wales 10/D5
Tenby, Wales 13/C6
Tendal, La. 238/H2
Ten Degree (chan.), India 68/G7
Tendelti, Sudan 111/F5
Tendelti, Sudan 102/F3
Tendo, Japan 81/K4
Tendoy, Idaho 220/E5
Tendrara, Morocco 106/D2
Tendre (peak), Switzerland 39/B3
Tenecape, Nova Scotia 168/E3
Ténenkou, Mali 106/C6
Ténéré (des.), Niger 106/G5
Tenerife (isl.), Spain 102/A2
Tenerife (isl.), Spain 106/A3
Tenerife (isl.), Spain 33/B5
Ténès, Algeria 106/E1
Teng, Nam (riv.), Burma 72/C2
Tengchong, China 77/E6
Tenggarong, Indonesia 85/F6
Tenggol, Pulau (isl.), Malaysia 72/D6
Tengiz (lake), U.S.S.R. 48/G4
Teng Xian, China 77/H7
Tenigerbad, Switzerland 39/G3
Tenino, Wash. 310/C4
Tenke, Zaire 115/E6
Tenkiller Ferry (lake), Okla. 288/S3
Tenkodogo, Burkina Faso 106/E6
Tenleytown, D.C. 245/E4
Ten Mile (lake), Newf. 166/C3
Tenmile, Oreg. 291/D4
Tenmile (creek), Oreg. 291/K5
Ten Mile, Tenn. 237/M9
Tenmile (creek), Texas 303/G3
Tennant, Calif. 204/C2
Tennant, Iowa 229/C5
Tennant Creek, Australia 87/D7
Tennant Creek, North. Terr. 88/E3
Tennant Creek, North. Terr. 93/C5
Tennent, N.J. 273/E3
Tennessee 188/J3
TENNESSEE 237
Tennessee (riv.) 188/J3
Tennessee (riv.), Ala. 195/C1
Tennessee, Ill. 222/C3
Tennessee (riv.), Ky. 237/D6
Tennessee (riv.), Tenn. 237/E10
Tennessee (state), U.S. 146/K6
Tennessee City, Tenn. 237/F8
Tennessee Pass, Colo. 208/G4
Tennessee Ridge, Tenn. 237/F8
Tennessee-Tombigbee Waterway, Ala. 195/B4
Tennessee-Tombigbee Waterway, Miss. 256/H2
Tenneville, Belgium 27/H8
Tenney, Minn. 255/B4
Tennga, Georgia 217/C1
Tennille, Ala. 195/G7
Tennille, Georgia 217/G5
Tennyson, Ind. 227/C8
Tennyson, Texas 303/D6
Tennyson, Wis. 317/E10
Teno, Chile 138/A10
Tenosique de Pino Suárez, Mexico 150/O8
Tenquehuen (isl.), Chile 138/D6
Tenri, Japan 81/J8
Tensas (par.), La. 238/H2
Tensas (riv.), La. 238/G3
Tensaw, Ala. 195/C8
Tensaw (riv.), Ala. 195/C9
Tensed, Idaho 220/B2
Ten Sleep, Wyo. 319/E1
Tenstrike, Minn. 255/D3
Tenterden, England 13/H6
Tenterfield, N. S. Wales 88/J5
Tenterfield, N.S. Wales 97/G1
Ten Thousand (isls.), Fla. 188/K5
Ten Thousand (isls.), Fla. 212/E6
Ten Thousand Smokes (valley), Alaska 196/G3
Teocaltiche, Mexico 150/H6
Teocelo, Mexico 150/P1
Teófilo Otoni, Brazil 120/E4
Teófilo Otoni, Brazil 132/F7
Te One, N. Zealand 100/D7
Teotihuacán (ruin), Mexico 150/M1
Teotihuacán de Arista, Mexico 150/L1
Teotitlán del Camino, Mexico 150/L8
Tepa, Indonesia 85/H7
Tepache, Mexico 150/E2
Tepalcingo, Mexico 150/M2

Tepatitlán de Morelos, Mexico 150/H6
Tepeaca, Mexico 150/N2
Tepeapulco, Mexico 150/M1
Tepehuanes, Mexico 150/G4
Tepeji del Río, Mexico 150/L1
Tepelenë, Albania 45/D5
Tepetlán, Mexico 150/P1
Tepexi de Rodríguez, Mexico 150/N2
Tepeyahualco, Mexico 150/O1
Teplá u Toužimě, Czech. 41/B1
Teplice, Czech. 41/B1
Tepoztlán, Mexico 150/L1
Te Puke, N. Zealand 100/F2
Tequendama (falls), Colombia 126/C5
Tequesquite (creek), N. Mex. 274/E2
Tequesta, Fla. 212/F5
Tequixquitla, Mexico 150/O1
Ter (riv.), Spain 33/H1
Ter (riv.), Spain 33/H1
Téra, Niger 106/E6
Teraina (isl.), Kiribati 87/L5
Teramo (prov.), Italy 34/D3
Teramo, Italy 34/D3
Terán, Mexico 150/N8
Terang, Victoria 97/B6
Ter Apel, Netherlands 27/L3
Terawhiti (cape), N. Zealand 100/A3
Tercan, Turkey 63/J3
Terceira (isl.), Portugal 33/C1
Tercero (riv.), Argentina 143/D3
Terchová, Czech. 41/E2
Terempa, Indonesia 85/D5
Terence Bay, Nova Scotia 168/E4
Terengganu (state), Malaysia 72/D6
Teresina, Brazil 120/E3
Teresina, Brazil 132/F4
Teresita, Mo. 261/J9
Teresópolis, Brazil 135/E3
Terespol, Poland 47/F2
Teressa (isl.), India 68/G7
Terevinto, Bolivia 136/H5
Terhazza (ruins), Mali 106/C4
Terhune, Ind. 227/H4
Teriberka, U.S.S.R. 52/E1
Terlingua, Texas 303/D12
Terlingua (creek), Texas 303/D12
Terlton, Okla. 288/O2
Termas de Cauquenes, Chile 138/B10
Terme, Turkey 63/G2
Termez, U.S.S.R. 48/G6
Termini Imerese, Italy 34/D6
Términos (lag.), Mexico 150/O7
Termo, Calif. 204/E3
Termoli, Italy 34/E3
Termonde (Dendermonde), Belgium 27/E6
Termonfeckin, Ireland 17/J4
Termunten, Netherlands 27/K2
Ternate, Indonesia 54/O9
Ternate, Indonesia 85/H5
Terneuzen, Netherlands 27/D6
Terni (prov.), Italy 34/D3
Terni, Italy 34/D3
Terni, Italy 7/F4
Ternitz, Austria 41/D3
Ternopol', U.S.S.R. 48/C5
Ternopol', U.S.S.R. 52/C5
Te Roto, N. Zealand 100/D7
Terowie, S. Australia 94/F5
Terpeniye (cape), U.S.S.R. 48/P5
Terra Alta, W. Va. 312/H4
Terra Bella, Calif. 204/G8
Terrabona, Nicaragua 154/E4
Terrace, Br. Col. 162/D5
Terrace, Br. Col. 184/C3
Terrace, Br. Col. 184/C3
Terrace, Minn. 255/C5
Terrace Bay, Ontario 177/H5
Terrace Bay, Ontario 175/C3
Terrace Heights, Wash. 310/E4
Terra Ceia, Fla. 212/D4
Terrace Park, Ohio 284/D9
Terracina, Italy 34/D4
Terra Corra, Neth. Ant. 161/E8
Terrak, Norway 18/H4
Terral, Okla. 289/L7
Terralba, Italy 34/B5
Terra Nova, Newf. 166/C2
Terra Nova, Newf. 166/C2
Terra Nova Nat'l Park, Newf. 166/D2
Terrebonne (par.), La. 238/J8
Terrebonne (bay), La. 238/J8
Terrebonne, Minn. 255/B3
Terrebonne, Oreg. 291/F3
Terrebonne (co.), Québec 172/H4
Terrebonne, Québec 172/H4
Terre-de-Bas (isl.), Guadeloupe 161/A7
Terre-de-Haut (isl.), Guadeloupe 161/A7
Terre Haute, Ill. 222/C3
Terre Haute, Ind. 188/J3
Terre Haute, Ind. 227/C6
Terre Hill, Pa. 294/L5
Terrell (co.), Georgia 217/D7
Terrell, N.C. 281/G3
Terrell (co.), Texas 303/B7
Terrell, Texas 188/G4
Terrell, Texas 3C3/H5
Terrell Hills, Texas 303/K11
Terrenate, Mexico 150/N1
Terre Neuve, Haiti 158/C5
Terreton, Idaho 220/F6
Terrey Hills, N. S. Wales 88/L3
Terrey Hills, N.S. Wales 97/J3
Terril, Iowa 229/C2
Terrill (mt.), Utah 304/C5
Territouk (cape), Newf. 166/B2
Terry, La. 238/H1
Terry, Miss. 256/D6
Terry, Mont. 262/L4
Terry (co.), Texas 303/B4

Terry Town, La. 238/O4
Terrytown, Nebr. 264/A3
Terryville, Conn. 210/C2
Terschelling (isl.) Netherlands 27/G2
Teruel (prov.), Spain 33/F2
Teruel, Spain 33/F2
Terutao, Ko (isl.), Thailand 72/C6
Tervola, Finland 13/O3
Tesawa, Libya 11-/B2
Tescott, Kansas 232/E2
Teshekpuk (lake), Alaska 196/H1
Teshio, Japan 81/L1
Teshio (mt.), Japan 81/L1
Teshio (riv.), Japan 81/L1
Tesla, W. Va. 312/E5
Teslić, Yugoslavia 45/C3
Teslin (lake) 162/C3
Teslin (lake), Br. Col. 184/K1
Teslin, Yukon 187/E3
Teslin (lake), Yukon 187/E4
Teslin (riv.), Yukon 187/E3
Tessalit, Mali 106/E4
Tessaoua, Niger 106/F6
Tessenderlo, Belgium 27/G6
Tessenei, Ethiopia 59/C6
Tessenei, Ethiopia 111/H4
Tessier, Sask. 181/D4
Test (riv.), England 13/F6
Testa (cape), Italy 34/B4
Testa del Gargano (cape), Italy 34/F4
Tesuque, N. Mex. 274/C3
Tét, Hungary 41/D3
Tetachuck (lake), Br. Col. 184/E3
Tetagouche (riv.), New Bruns. 170/D1
Tetas (pt.), Chile 138/A4
Tete (prov.), Mozambique 118/E3
Tete, Mozambique 102/F6
Tete, Mozambique 118/E3
Tête-à-la-Baleine, Québec 174/E2
Tete Jaune Cache, Br. Col. 184/H4
Te Teko, N. Zealand 100/F3
Teterboro, N.J. 273/B2
Teterow, Germany 22/E2
Teterton, W. Va. 312/H5
Teteven, Bulgaria 45/G4
Tetiaroa (atoll), Fr. Poly. 87/M7
Tetlin, Alaska 196/H2
Teton (co.), Idaho 220/G6
Teton, Idaho 220/G3
Teton (riv.), Idaho 220/G6
Teton (co.), Mont. 262/E3
Teton (riv.), Mont. 262/E3
Teton (co.), Wyo. 319/B2
Teton (range), Wyo. 319/B2
Tetonia, Idaho 220/G6
Teton Village, Wyo. 319/B2
Tetotum, Va. 307/P4
Tétouan, Morocco 106/C1
Tétouan, Morocco 102/B1
Tetovo, Yugoslavia 45/E5
Teuco (riv.), Argentina 143/D1
Teufen, Switzerland 39/H2
Teulada (cape), Italy 7/E5
Teulada (cape), Italy 34/B5
Teulon, Manitoba 179/E4
Teupasenti, Honduras 154/D3
Teustepe, Nicaragua 154/E4
Teutoburger Wald (for.), Germany 22/C2
Teutopolis, Ill. 222/E4
Teuva, Finland 18/M5
Teviot (riv.), Scotland 15/F5
Teviot (riv.), Scotland 10/E3
Te Waewae (bay), N. Zealand 100/A7
Tewantin-Noosa, Queensland 95/E5
Te Whanga (mts.), N. Zealand 100/E7
Tewkesbury, England 10/F5
Tewkesbury, England 13/E6
Tewkesbury, Mass. 249/K2
Texa (isl.), Scotland 15/B5
Texada (isl.), Br. Col. 184/J2
Texarkana, Ark. 188/H4
Texarkana, Ark. 202/C7
Texarkana, Texas 188/H4
Texarkana, Texas 146/J6
Texarkana, Texas 303/L4
TEXAS 188/G4
TEXAS 303
Texas, Georgia 217/E4
Texas, Ky. 237/L5
Texas, Md. 245/M3
Texas (co.), Mo. 261/J8
Texas (co.), Okla. 288/C1
Texas (state), U.S. 146/J6
Texas City, Texas 303/K3
Texas Creek, Colo. 208/H6
Texcoco de Mora, Mexico 150/M1
Texel (isl.), Netherlands 27/F2
Texhoma, Okla. 288/C1
Texhoma, Texas 303/C1
Texico, N. Mex. 274/F4
Texistepeque, El Salvador 154/C3
Texline, Texas 303/B1
Texola, Okla. 288/G4
Texoma (lake), Okla. 288/N7
Texoma (lake), Texas 303/H3
Texon, Texas 303/C6
Teykovo, U.S.S.R. 52/E3
Teyvareh, Afghanistan 68/A2
Teyvareh, Afghanistan 39/H3
Teziutlán, Mexico 150/O1
Tezonapa, Mexico 150/P2
Tezontepec, Mexico 150/M1
Tezpur, India 68/G3
Tezu, India 68/H3
Tezzeron (lake), Br. Col. 184/E3
Tha, Nam (riv.), Laos 72/D2
Tha-anne (riv.), N.W.T. 187/J3
Thabazimbi, S. Africa 118/E3
Thacher (isl.), Mass. 249/M2
Tha Chin, Mae Nam (riv.), Thailand 72/C4
Thacker, W. Va. 312/B7
Thackeray, Ill. 222/E5
Thackeray, Ohio 284/C5
Thackerville, Okla. 288/M7
Thai Binh, Vietnam 72/E2

Thailand 2/Q5
Thailand 54/M8
THAILAND (SIAM) 72
Thailand (gulf) 2/Q5
Thailand (gulf) 54/M9
Thailand (gulf), Cambodia 72/D5
Thailand (gulf), Thailand 72/D5
Thai Nguyen (cliff), Vietnam 72/E2
Thakhek (Muang Khammouan), Laos 72/E3
Thal, Pakistan 59/K3
Thal, Switzerland 39/J2
Thalberg, Manitoba 179/F4
Thale, Germany 22/D3
Thale Luang (lag.), Thailand 72/D6
Thalia, Texas 303/E4
Thalmann, Georgia 217/J8
Thalu, Ko (isl.), Thailand 72/C5
Thalwil, Switzerland 39/G2
Thame, England 13/G6
Thame (riv.), England 13/G7
Thames (riv.), Conn. 210/G2
Thames (riv.), England 10/F5
Thames (riv.), England 13/H6
Thames, N. Zealand 100/E3
Thames (firth), N. Zealand 100/E2
Thames (riv.), Ontario 177/B5
Thamesford, Ontario 177/C4
Thamesville, Conn. 210/G2
Thamesville, Ontario 177/C5
Thana, India 68/B6
Thana (creek), India 68/B7
Thane, Alaska 196/N1
Thangool, Queensland 95/D5
Thanh Hoa, Vietnam 72/E3
Thanh Tri, Vietnam 72/E5
Thanjavur, India 68/D6
Thann, France 28/G4
Thar (des.), Pakistan 68/C3
Thargomindah, Queensland 88/G5
Thargomindah, Queensland 95/C5
Tharrawaddy, Burma 72/C3
Tharthar, Wadi (dry riv.), Iraq 66/C3
Tharthar (res.), Iraq 66/C3
Thásos, Greece 45/G5
Thásos (isl.), Greece 45/G5
Thatch (cay), Virgin Is. (U.S.) 161/B4
Thatcham, England 13/F6
Thatcher, Ariz. 198/F6
Thatcher, Colo. 208/L7
Thatcher, Idaho 220/G7
That Khe, Vietnam 72/E2
Thaton, Burma 72/C3
Thau (mts.), France 28/F6
Thaungdut, Burma 72/B1
Thauville, Ill. 222/E3
Thaxton, Miss. 256/F2
Thaxton, Va. 307/K6
Thaya (riv.), Austria 41/C2
Thayawthadangyi Kyun (isl.), Burma 72/C4
Thayer, Ill. 222/D4
Thayer, Ind. 227/C2
Thayer, Iowa 229/E6
Thayer, Kansas 232/G4
Thayer, Mo. 261/J9
Thayer (co.), Nebr. 264/G4
Thayer, Nebr. 264/G4
Thayer, W. Va. 312/E7
Thayer Junction, Wyo. 319/D4
Thayetmyo, Burma 72/B3
Thayne, Wyo. 319/A3
Thaynes, Switzerland 39/G1
Thazi, Burma 72/C2
The Alberga (riv.), S. Australia 94/D2
Thealka, Ky. 237/N5
Theano (pt.), Ontario 177/J5
THE ANTILLES 156
Thebarton, S. Australia 88/D8
Thebarton, S. Australia 94/A7
The Battlefords Prov. Park, Sask. 181/C2
Thebes, Ill. 222/D6
The Colony, Texas 303/G1
The Coorong (lag.), S. Australia 94/F4
The Dalles, Oreg. 188/B1
The Dalles, Oreg. 291/F2
The Dalles (dam), Oreg. 291/F2
The Dalles (dam), Wash. 310/D5
Thedford, Nebr. 264/D3
Thedford, Ontario 177/C4
The Entrance, N.S. Wales 88/J4
The Entrance, N.S. Wales 97/F3
The Gap, N.S. Wales 97/A2
The Gap, Queensland 88/J2
The Glen, N.Y. 276/N3
The Granites, North. Terr. 93/B6
The Hamilton (riv.), S. Australia 94/D2
The Hawk, Nova Scotia 168/C5
The Heads (prom.), Oreg. 291/C5
The Hermitage, N. Zealand 100/C5
Theilman, Minn. 255/F5
Thelon (riv.), N.W.T. 146/H3
Thelon (riv.), N.W.T. 162/F3
Thelon (riv.), N.W. Terr. 187/H3
Them, Denmark 21/C5
The Macumba (riv.), S. Australia 94/C2
The Narrows (str.), N.J. 273/E2
Thendara, N.Y. 276/K3
The Neales (riv.), S. Australia 94/E3
Theodore, Ala. 195/B9
Theodore, Queensland 95/D5
Theodore, Sask. 181/J4
Theodore Roosevelt (dam), Ariz. 198/D5
Theodore Roosevelt (lake), Ariz. 198/D5
Theodore Roosevelt Nat'l Mem. Park, N. Dak. 282/D4
Theodore Roosevelt Nat'l Mem. Park, N. Dak. 282/C5
Theodore Roosevelt Nat'l Mem. Park, N. Dak. 282/D6
Theodosia, Mo. 261/G9
The Pas (lake), Man. 162/F5
The Pas, Manitoba 179/H3

The Plains, Ohio 284/F7
The Plains, Va. 307/N3
The Range, New Bruns. 170/E2
Theresa, N.Y. 276/J2
Theresa, Wis. 317/K8
Therien, Alberta 182/E2
Theriot, La. 238/J8
Thermaic (gulf), Greece 45/F6
Thermal, Calif. 204/J10
Thermalito, Calif. 204/D4
Thermopolis, Wyo. 319/D2
The Rock, Georgia 217/D5
The Rock, N.S. Wales 97/D4
The Round (mt.), N.S. Wales 97/G2
Therwil, Switzerland 39/E1
The Salt (lake), N.S. Wales 97/B2
The Skaw (Skagens Odde) (cape), Denmark 21/D2
Thessalia (riv.), N.W. Terr. 187/G2
Thessalon, Ont. 162/H6
Thessalon, Ontario 177/J5
Thessalon, Ontario 175/D3
Thessaloníki, Greece 7/G4
Thessaloníki, Greece 45/F5
Thessaly (reg.), Greece 45/F6
The Stevenson (riv.), S. Australia 94/D2
Thetford, England 13/H5
Thetford, England 10/G5
Thetford •, Vt. 268/C4
Thetford Center, Vt. 268/C4
Thetford Mines, Québec 172/F3
Thetis Island, Br. Col. 184/J3
The Twins (mt.), Alberta 182/B3
Theux, Belgium 27/H8
Thibault, New Bruns. 170/C1
Thibodaux, La. 238/J7
Thicket Portage, Manitoba 179/J3
Thickwood (hills), Alberta 182/D1
Thickwood (hills), Sask. 181/D1
Thida, Ark. 202/H2
Thief (lake), Minn. 255/C2
Thief (riv.), Minn. 255/B2
Thief River Falls, Minn. 255/B2
Thielsen (mt.), Oreg. 291/F4
Thiells, N.Y. 276/C1
Thiensville, Wis. 317/L1
Thiers, France 28/E5
Thiès, Senegal 106/A5
Thiès, Senegal 102/A3
Thika, Kenya 102/F5
Thika, Kenya 115/G4
Thimphu (cap.), Bhutan 54/L7
Thimphu (cap.), Bhutan 68/G3
Thio, Ethiopia 111/H5
Thio, New Caled. 86/H4
Thion ville, France 28/G3
Thíra, Greece 45/G7
Thíra (isl.), Greece 45/G7
Third (lake), Maine 243/H5
Third (lake), N.H. 268/E1
Third Cataract, Sudan 111/E4
Third Cataract (dam), Sudan 102/E3
Third Cataract, Sudan 59/B6
Third Lake, Ill. 222/H4
Thirsk, England 13/F3
Thirty Mile (creek), N. Dak. 282/F6
Thirtymile (creek), Oreg. 291/G2
Thisted, Denmark 21/B4
Thisted, Denmark 18/F8
Thistle (isl.), S. Australia 94/E6
Thistle, Utah 304/C4
Thithia (isl.), Fiji 86/R10
Thívai, Greece 45/G6
Thiviers, France 28/D5
Thjórsá (riv.), Iceland 21/C1
Thlewiaza (riv.), N.W. Terr. 187/J3
Thoa (riv.), N.W. Terr. 187/H3
Tho Chau, Hon (isl.), Vietnam 72/D5
Thoen, Thailand 72/C3
Thohoyandou, S. Africa 118/E4
Thohoyandou (cap.), Venda, S. Africa 102/F7
Tholen, Netherlands 27/E5
Thomas (co.), Georgia 217/E8
Thomas (co.), Kansas 232/A2
Thomas, Md. 245/N6
Thomas (co.), Nebr. 264/D3
Thomas, Okla. 288/J3
Thomas (creek), Oreg. 291/G5
Thomas, S. Dak. 298/P4
Thomas (lake), Texas 303/C5
Thomas (range), Utah 304/A4
Thomas, W. Va. 312/H4
Thomasboro, Ill. 222/E3
Thomas Stone Nat'l Hist. Site, Md. 245/K6
Thomaston •, Conn. 210/C2
Thomaston, Conn. 210/C2
Thomaston, Georgia 217/D5
Thomaston, Maine 243/E7
Thomaston •, Maine 243/E7
Thomaston, N.Y. 276/P7
Thomastown, Ireland 10/C4
Thomastown, Ireland 17/G7
Thomastown, La. 238/H4
Thomastown, Miss. 256/E5
Thomastown, Victoria 97/J4
Thomasville, Ala. 195/C7
Thomasville, Ga. 188/K4
Thomasville, Georgia 217/E9
Thomasville, Miss. 256/E6
Thomasville, Mo. 261/J9
Thomasville, N.C. 281/J1
Thomasville, Pa. 294/J6
Thomonde, Haiti 158/C6
Thompson, Ala. 195/G6
Thompson (riv.), Br. Col. 184/G5
Thompson •, Conn. 210/H1
Thompson (peak), Idaho 220/C5
Thompson (riv.), Iowa 229/E7
Thompson (riv.), Iowa 229/E7
Thompson, Man. 162/G4
Thompson, Man. 146/J4
Thompson, Manitoba 179/J2
Thompson (isl.), Mass. 249/D7
Thompson, Mich. 250/C3

Thompson (creek), Miss. 256/G8
Thompson, Mo. 261/J4
Thompson (peak), N. Mex. 274/D3
Thompson, N. Dak. 282/R4
Thompson, Ohio 284/H2
Thompson, Pa. 294/L2
Thompson (riv.), Queensland 95/B5
Thompson (lake), S. Dak. 298/O5
Thompson (mt.), Wyo. 319/B3
Thompson Falls, Mont. 262/A3
Thompsons (creek), S.C. 296/G2
Thompson Springs, Utah 304/E5
Thompsons Station, Tenn. 237/H9
Thompsontown, Pa. 294/H4
Thompson Valley (res.), Oreg. 291/F5
Thompsonville, Conn. 210/E1
Thompsonville, Ill. 222/E6
Thompsonville, Mich. 250/D3
Thomsen (riv.), N.W. Terr. 187/G2
Thomson, Georgia 217/H4
Thomson, Ill. 222/C2
Thomson, Minn. 255/F4
Thomson (riv.), Queensland 88/G4
Thomson's Falls, Kenya 115/G3
Thon Buri, Thailand 72/D4
Thongwa, Burma 72/C3
Thonon-les-Bains, France 28/G4
Thonotosassa, Fla. 212/D3
Thor, Iowa 229/E3
Thorburn, Nova Scotia 168/F3
Thoreau, N. Mex. 274/A3
Thoresby (mt.), Newf. 166/F3
Thorhild, Alberta 182/D2
Thorn, Miss. 256/F3
Thornaby-on-Tees (hill), England 10/F3
Thornaby-on-Tees, England 13/F3
Thornburg, Iowa 229/J6
Thornburg, Va. 307/N4
Thornbury, England 13/E6
Thornbury, Ontario 177/D3
Thorndale, Ontario 177/C4
Thorndale, Texas 303/G7
Thorndike •, Maine 243/E6
Thorndike, Mass. 249/E4
Thorne, England 13/F4
Thorne, N. Dak. 282/L2
Thorne, Ontario 177/E5
Thorne Bay, Alaska 196/M2
Thornfield, Mo. 261/H9
Thornhill, Br. Col. 184/C3
Thornhill, Manitoba 179/D5
Thornhill, Central, Scotland 15/D4
Thornhill, Dumf. & Gall., Scotland 15/D5
Thorn Hill, Tenn. 237/P8
Thornhurst, Pa. 294/L3
Thornley, England 13/J4
Thornloe, Ontario 175/E3
Thornloe, Ontario 177/K5
Thornton, Ark. 202/F6
Thornton, Calif. 204/B9
Thornton, Colo. 208/K3
Thornton, Idaho 220/G6
Thornton, Ill. 222/C6
Thornton, Iowa 229/G3
Thornton, Miss. 256/D4
Thornton •, N.H. 268/D4
Thornton, Ontario 177/E3
Thornton, Texas 303/H6
Thornton, Wash. 310/H3
Thornton, W. Va. 312/G4
Thornton Cleveleys, England 13/G1
Thornton Cleveleys, England 10/F1
Thornton, Ind. 227/D4
Thornville, Ohio 284/F6
Thornwell, La. 238/E6
Thornwood, W. Va. 312/G5
Thorofare, N.J. 273/B4
Thorold, Ontario 177/E4
Thorp (lake), N.C. 281/C4
Thorpe, W. Va. 312/D8
Thorp Spring, Texas 303/F5
Thorsby, Ala. 195/E5
Thorsby, Alberta 182/C3
Thouars, France 28/D4
Thouin (pt.), W. Australia 88/B4
Thouin (pt.), W. Australia 92/B3
Thousand (isls.) N.Y. 276/G2
Thousand (isls.), Ontario 177/H3
Thousand Island Park, N.Y. 276/J2
Thousand Lake (mt.), Utah 304/C5
Thousand Oaks, Calif. 204/G9
Thousand Spring (creek), Nev. 266/G1
Thousand Springs, Nev. 266/G1
Thrace (reg.), Greece 45/G5
Thrall, Kansas 232/F3
Thrasher, Miss. 256/G1
Three (isls.), New Bruns. 170/D4
Three Bridges, N.J. 273/D2
Three Churches, W. Va. 312/J4
Three Creek, Idaho 220/C7
Three Creeks, Alberta 182/B1
Three Creeks, Ark. 202/F7
Three Forks, Mont. 262/E5
Three Guardsmen (mt.), Br. Col. 184/H1
Three Hills, Alberta 182/D4
Three Hummock (isl.), Tasmania 89/F8
Three Kings (isls.), N. Zealand 100/D1
Three Lakes, Wis. 317/J4
Three Mile Bay, N.Y. 276/H2
Three Mile Plains, Nova Scotia 168/D4
Three Notch, Ala. 195/G6
Three Oaks, Mich. 250/C7
Three Pagodas (pass), Burma 72/C4
Three Pagodas (pass), Thailand 72/C4
Three Points (pass), Ghana 106/D8
Three Rivers, Mass. 249/E4
Three Rivers, Mich. 250/D7
Three Rivers, N. Mex. 274/C4
Three Rivers (Trois-Rivières), Québec 172/F3
Three Rivers, Texas 303/F9

Three Rivers, W. Australia 92/B4
Three Sisters (mt.), Oreg. 291/F3
Three Springs, Pa. 294/G5
Three Springs, W. Australia 88/B5
Three Springs, W. Australia 92/A5
Throckmorton (co.), Texas 303/E4
Throckmorton, Texas 303/F4
Throne, Alberta 182/E3
Throop, Pa. 294/F7
Thrums, Br. Col. 184/J5
Thrumster, Scotland 15/E2
Thuin, Belgium 27/E8
Thule Air Base, Greenland 2/F2
Thule Air Base, Greenland 4/B13
Thule Air Base, Greenland 146/M2
Thumail, Iraq 66/C4
Thun, Switzerland 39/E3
Thunder (bay), Mich. 250/F4
Thunder (bay), Sask. 181/L4
Thunder (creek), S. Dak. 298/N4
Thunder (creek), S. Dak. 298/N6
Thunder (lake), Wis. 317/H4
Thunder Bay (riv.), Mich. 250/F3
Thunder Bay, Ont. 162/H6
Thunder Bay, Ont. 146/K5
Thunder Bay (terr. dist.), Ontario 175/C3
Thunder Bay (terr. dist.), Ontario 177/H5
Thunder Bay, Ontario 175/C3
Thunder Bay, Ontario 177/H5
Thunderbird (lake), Okla. 288/M4
Thunderbolt, Georgia 217/K6
Thunder Butte (creek), S. Dak. 298/E3
Thunder Hawk, S. Dak. 298/F2
Thunder Lake, Alberta 182/C2
Thunersee (lake), Switzerland 39/E3
Thunstetten, Switzerland 39/E2
Thur (riv.), Switzerland 39/G1
Thurgau (canton), Switzerland 39/H1
Thüringer Wald (for.), Germany 22/D3
Thuringia (state), Germany 22/D3
Thurles, Ireland 10/B4
Thurles, Ireland 17/F6
Thurloo Downs, N.S. Wales 97/B1
Thurlow (dam), Ala. 195/G6
Thurlow, Mont. 262/K4
Thurman, Iowa 229/B7
Thurman, N.Y. 276/M3
Thurman, Ohio 284/F8
Thurmond, W. Va. 312/D7
Thurmont, Md. 245/J2
Thurrock, England 13/J8
Thurrock, England 10/G8
Thursday Island, Queensland 88/G2
Thursday Island, Queensland 95/B1
Thurso, Québec 172/G4
Thurso, Scotland 10/E1
Thurso (riv.), Scotland 15/E2
Thurso, Scotland 15/E2
Thurston (isl.), 5/C14
Thurston (co.), Nebr. 264/H2
Thurston, Nebr. 264/H2
Thurston, Ohio 284/E6
Thurston (co.), Wash. 310/C4
Thusis, Switzerland 39/H3
Thutade (lake), Br. Col. 184/D2
Thyatira, Miss. 256/E1
Thyborøn, Denmark 21/A4
Thyolo, Malawi 115/F7
Thyregod, Denmark 21/C6
Tia, N.S. Wales 97/F2
Tiahuanaco, Bolivia 136/A5
Tia Juana, Venezuela 124/C2
Tiandong, China 77/G7
Tianjin, China 2/Q4
Tianjin (Tientsin), China 77/J4
Tianjun, China 77/E4
Tianlin, China 77/F3
Tian Shan (range), China 77/C3
Tianshui, China 77/F5
Tianzhu, China 77/F4
Tiaret, Algeria 106/F1
Tiatucurá, Uruguay 145/C3
Tiavea, W. Samoa 86/M8
Tib, Ras el (Bon) (cape), Tunisia 106/G1
Tibagi, Brazil 135/A4
Tibagi (riv.), Brazil 135/A4
Tibaná, Colombia 126/D5
Tibati, Cameroon 115/B2
Tibbie, Ala. 195/B8
Tiber (riv.), Italy 7/F4
Tiber (riv.), Italy 34/C3
Tiberias, Israel 65/D2
Tiberias (lake), Israel 65/D2
Tibesti (mts.) 102/2
Tibesti, Serir (des.), Chad 111/C3
Tibesti (mts.), Chad 111/C3
Tibesti, Serir (des.), Libya 111/C3
Tibet (reg.), China 2/P4
Tibet (reg.), China 54/K6
Tibet (reg.), China 77/B5
Tibet Aut. Reg. (Xizang), China 77/B5
Tibooburra, N.S. Wales 88/G5
Tibooburra, N.S. Wales 97/B1
Tibro, Sweden 18/J7
Tibugá (gulf), Colombia 126/B5
Tiburon, Calif. 204/J2
Tiburón, Haiti 158/A6
Tiburon (cape), Haiti 156/C3
Tiburon (cape), Haiti 158/A6
Tiburón (isl.), Mexico 150/C2
Tiburón (cape), Panama 154/J6
Ticaco, Peru 128/H11
Ticao (isl.), Philippines 82/D4
Tice, Fla. 212/E5
Ticehurst, England 13/H6
Tichfield, Sask. 181/D4
Tichigan (lake), Wis. 317/K2
Tichigan Lake, Wis. 317/K2
Tichitt, Mauritania 106/C5
Tichlá (well), Western Sahara 106/B4

Tichnor, Ark. 202/H5
Ticino (canton), Switzerland 39/G4
Ticino (riv.), Switzerland 39/G4
Tickfaw, La. 238/M1
Tickfaw (riv.), La. 238/M1
Tickle (bay), Newf. 166/D2
Ticonderoga, N.Y. 276/N3
Ticonic, Iowa 229/B4
Ticul, Mexico 150/P6
Tidaholm, Sweden 18/J7
Tide Head, New Bruns. 170/D1
Tidewater, Oreg. 291/D3
Tidikelt (oasis), Algeria 106/E3
Tidioute, Pa. 294/D2
Tidjikja, Mauritania 102/A3
Tidjikja, Mauritania 106/B5
Tidnish, Nova Scotia 168/E3
Tidore (isl.), Indonesia 85/H5
Tidra (isl.), Mauritania 106/A5
Tiedemann (mt.), Br. Col. 184/E4
Tiefencastel, Switzerland 39/J3
Tiel, Netherlands 27/G5
Tieling, China 77/K3
Tielt, Belgium 27/C7
Tielt-Winge, Belgium 27/F7
Tienen, Belgium 27/F7
Tien Shan (range) 54/K5
Tienshui (Tianshui), China 77/F5
Tientsin (Tianjin), China 77/J4
Tien Yen, Vietnam 72/E2
Tie Plant, Miss. 256/E3
Tiernan, Oreg. 291/C3
Tierp, Sweden 18/K6
Tierra Amarilla, Chile 138/A6
Tierra Amarilla, N. Mex. 274/C2
Tierra Blanca, Mexico 150/A2
Tierra Blanca (creek), N. Mex. 274/B6
Tierra Blanca (creek), Texas 303/B3
Tierra del Fuego (isl.) 2/F8
Tierra del Fuego (isl.) 120/C8
Tierra del Fuego, Antártida e Islas del Atlán (prov.), Argentina 143/C7
Tierra del Fuego, Grande de (isl.), Argentina 143/C7
Tierra del Fuego, Grande de (isl.), Chile 138/E11
Tierralta, Colombia 126/C3
Tie Siding, Wyo. 319/G4
Tietê, Brazil 135/C3
Tietê (riv.), Brazil 120/E5
Tietê (riv.), Brazil 132/D8
Tietê (riv.), Brazil 135/B2
Tieton, Wash. 310/E4
Tieton (riv.), Wash. 310/D4
Tieyon, S. Australia 94/C2
Tiff, Mo. 261/L6
Tiffany, Colo. 208/D8
Tiffany (mt.), Wash. 310/F2
Tiff City, Mo. 261/C9
Tiffin, Iowa 229/K5
Tiffin, Mo. 261/E7
Tiffin, Ohio 284/D3
Tiffin (riv.), Ohio 284/B3
Tiflis (Tbilisi), U.S.S.R. 52/F6
Tift (co.), Georgia 217/E7
Tifton, Georgia 217/F8
Tiftona, Tenn. 237/L11
Tigalda (isl.), Alaska 196/F4
Tigard, Oreg. 291/A2
Tiger, Georgia 217/F1
Tiger (falls), Guyana 131/C4
Tiger (Macan) (isls.), Indonesia 85/G7
Tiger (falls), Suriname 131/C4
Tiger, Wash. 310/H2
Tiger Lily, Alberta 182/C2
Tigerton, Wis. 317/H6
Tigerville, S.C. 296/C1
Tighina (Bendery), U.S.S.R. 52/C5
Tigieglo, Somalia 115/H3
Tignall, Georgia 217/G3
Tignamar, Chile 138/B1
Tignéré, Cameroon 115/B2
Tignish, Pr. Edward I. 168/D2
Tigre, Argentina 143/G7
Tigre (prov.), Ethiopia 111/H5
Tigre (riv.), Peru 128/E4
Tigre (isl.), Uruguay 145/A7
Tigre (riv.), Venezuela 124/G3
Tigrett, Tenn. 237/C9
Tigris (riv.) 54/F6
Tigris (riv.), Iran 59/E3
Tigris (riv.), Iraq 59/E3
Tigris (riv.), Iraq 66/E4
Tigris (riv.), Syria 59/E3
Tigris (riv.), Syria 63/K4
Tigris (Dicle) (riv.), Turkey 63/J4
Tigris (riv.), Turkey 59/E3
Tiguentourine, Algeria 106/F3
Tihama (reg.), Saudi Arabia 59/C5
Tihama (reg.), Yemen 59/C5
Tihany, Hungary 41/D3
Tijamuchi (riv.), Bolivia 136/C4
Tijeras, N. Mex. 274/C4
Tijuana, Mexico 150/A1
Tijuana, Mexico 146/G6
Tijucas, Brazil 132/D4
Tikal, Guatemala 154/C2
Tikamgarh, India 68/D4
Tikchik (Ikes), Alaska 196/G2
Tikhoretsk, U.S.S.R. 52/F5
Tikhvin, U.S.S.R. 52/D3
Tiko, Cameroon 102/C4
Tiko, Cameroon 115/A3
Tikopia (isl.), Solomon Is. 87/G7
Tikrit, Iraq 59/D3
Tikrit, Iraq 66/E3
Tiksi, U.S.S.R. 4/B3
Tiksi, U.S.S.R. 54/P2
Tiksi, U.S.S.R. 48/N2
Tila, Mexico 150/N8
Tilburg, Netherlands 27/G5
Tilbury, Ontario 177/B5
Tilcara, Argentina 143/C1
Tilcha, S. Australia 94/G3
Tilden, Ill. 222/D5
Tilden, Ky. 237/F5
Tilden, Miss. 256/H4
Tilden, Nebr. 264/G2

Tilden, Texas 303/F9
Tilehurst, England 13/F6
Tilemsi (valley), Mali 106/E5
Tilford, S. Dak. 298/C5
Tilghman, Md. 245/N6
Tilin, Burma 72/B2
Tiline, Ky. 237/E6
Tillabéry, Niger 106/E6
Tillamook (co.), Oreg. 291/D2
Tillamook, Oreg. 291/D2
Tillamook (head), Oreg. 291/C2
Tillanchong (isl.), India 68/G7
Tillar, Ark. 202/H6
Tillatoba, Miss. 256/E3
Tilleda, Wis. 317/J6
Tiller, Oreg. 291/E5
Tillery, N.C. 281/O2
Tillery (lake), N.C. 281/J4
Tilley, Alberta 182/E4
Tilley, New Bruns. 170/C2
Tillicoultry, Scotland 10/B1
Tillicoultry, Scotland 15/C1
Tillicum, Wash. 310/C3
Tillman, Miss. 256/C7
Tillman (co.), Okla. 288/J6
Tillman, S.C. 296/E7
Tillson, N.Y. 276/M7
Tillsonburg, Ontario 177/D5
Tilney, Sask. 181/F5
Tilomonte, Chile 138/B4
Tílos (isl.), Greece 45/H7
Tilpa, N.S. Wales 97/C2
Tilsit (Sovetsk), U.S.S.R. 52/B4
Tilston, Manitoba 179/A5
Tilt (riv.), Scotland 15/E4
Tiltagara, N.S. Wales 97/C2
Tiltil, Chile 138/G2
Tilting, Newf. 166/D4
Tilton, Ark. 202/J3
Tilton, Georgia 217/B1
Tilton, Ill. 222/F3
Tilton •, N.H. 268/D5
Tilton-Northfield, N.H. 268/D5
Tiltonsville, Ohio 284/J5
Tim, Denmark 21/B5
Timan (ridge), U.S.S.R. 52/G1
Timaná, Colombia 126/C7
Timane (riv.), Paraguay 144/B2
Timaru, N. Zealand 100/C6
Timashevsk, U.S.S.R. 52/E5
Timbákion, Greece 45/G8
Timbalier (bay), La. 238/K8
Timbalier (isl.), La. 238/K8
Timbarra (riv.), N.S. Wales 97/G1
Timbédra, Mauritania 106/C5
Timber (mt.), Nev. 266/E5
Timber (mt.), Nev. 266/F4
Timber, Oreg. 291/D2
Timber Bay, Sask. 181/F1
Timber Creek, North. Terr. 88/E3
Timberlake, N.C. 281/M2
Timberlake, Ohio 284/J8
Timber Lake, S. Dak. 298/H3
Timberlea, Nova Scotia 168/E4
Timberville, Va. 307/J3
Timbío, Colombia 126/B6
Timbiquí, Colombia 126/B6
Timblin, Pa. 294/D4
Timbo, Ark. 202/F2
Timboulaga (well), Niger 106/F5
Timbuktu (Tombouctou), Mali 106/D5
Timbuktu, Mali 102/B3
Time, Ill. 222/C4
Timehri Airport, Guyana 130/B2
Timewell, Ill. 222/C3
Timgad, Algeria 106/F1
Timia, Niger 106/F4
Timia, Niger 102/C2
Timimoun, Algeria 102/C2
Timimoun, Algeria 106/E3
Timiris (cape), Mauritania 106/A5
Timiş (riv.), Romania 45/F3
Timişkaming (lake) 162/J6
Timiskaming (terr. dist.), Ontario 177/K5
Timiskaming (terr. dist.), Ontario 175/D3
Timiskaming (lake), Ontario 175/E3
Timişoara, Romania 7/G4
Timişoara, Romania 45/E3
Timken, Kansas 232/D2
Timmendorfer Strand, Germany 22/D1
Timmiarmiut, Greenland 4/C12
Timmins, Ont. 146/K5
Timmins, Ont. 162/H6
Timmins, Ontario 177/J5
Timmins, Ontario 175/D3
Timmissao (well), Algeria 106/E4
Timmonsville, S.C. 296/H3
Timms Hill (mt.), Wis. 317/F5
Timnath, Colo. 208/J2
Timok (riv.), Bulgaria 45/F3
Timok (riv.), Yugoslavia 45/F3
Timoleague, Ireland 17/D8
Timon, Brazil 132/F4
Timonium-Lutherville, Md. 245/M3
Timor (sea) 54/O11
Timor (sea) 88/D2
Timor (isl.), Indonesia 54/O10
Timor (isl.), Indonesia 2/R6
Timor (reg.), Indonesia 85/H7
Timor (sea), Indonesia 85/H7
Timor (sea), North. Terr. 93/A2
Timor (sea), W. Australia 92/D1
Timote, Uruguay 145/D4
Timotes, Venezuela 124/C3
Timothy, Tenn. 237/H2
Timpahute (range), Nev. 266/F5
Timpanogos Cave Nat'l Mon., Utah 304/C3
Timpas, Colo. 208/M7
Timpas (creek), Colo. 208/M7
Timpson, Texas 303/N6
Timrå, Sweden 18/K5
Tims Ford (lake), Tenn. 237/J10
Timucuan Ecological and Historical Preserve, Fla. 212/E1

Tina (mt.), Dom. Rep. 158/D6
Tina, Mo. 261/F3
Tinaca (pt.), Philippines 54/O9
Tinaca (pt.), Philippines 85/H4
Tinaca (pt.), Philippines 82/E8
Tinaco, Venezuela 124/D3
Tinahely, Ireland 17/H6
Tinaquillo, Venezuela 124/D3
Tinca, Romania 45/F2
Tin City, Alaska 196/E1
Tincup, Colo. 208/F5
Tindall, Mo. 261/E2
Tindouf, Algeria 102/B2
Tindouf, Algeria 106/C3
Tindouf, Sebkha de (salt lake), Algeria 106/C3
Tinela, Ala. 195/D7
Tineo, Spain 33/C1
Tinggi, Pulau (isl.), Malaysia 72/E7
Tingha, N.S. Wales 97/F1
Tinghert Hamada (Tinrhert) (des.), Libya 111/B2
Tinglev, Denmark 21/C8
Tingley, Iowa 229/E7
Tingmerkpuk (mt.), Alaska 196/F1
Tingo María, Peru 128/D7
Tingri, China 77/C6
Tinguipaya, Bolivia 136/C6
Tinguiririca, Chile 138/G6
Tinguiririca (riv.), Chile 138/F5
Tingwick, Québec 172/F4
Tinian (isl.), No. Marianas 87/E4
Tinjoub, Algeria 106/C3
Tinker A.F.B., Okla. 288/M4
Tinkers (creek), Md. 245/F6
Tinley Park, Ill. 222/B6
Tinmouth •, Vt. 268/A5
Tinnie, N. Mex. 274/D5
Tinogasta, Argentina 143/C2
Tínos, Greece 45/G7
Tínos (isl.), Greece 45/G7
Tinrhert, Hamada de (des.), Algeria 106/F3
Tinrhert Hamada (Tinghert) (des.), Libya 111/B2
Tinsley, Ky. 237/O7
Tinsman, Ark. 202/F6
Tinsukia, India 68/H3
Tintagel, Br. Col. 184/E3
Tintagel (head), England 13/C7
Tintah, Minn. 255/B5
Tintigny, Belgium 27/G9
Tintina, Argentina 143/D2
Tinto (riv.), Spain 33/C4
Tinton Falls, N.J. 273/E3
Tinui, N. Zealand 100/F4
Tiny, Sask. 181/J4
Tin-Zaouatene, Algeria 106/E5
Tioga, Ill. 222/B3
Tioga, La. 238/F4
Tioga (co.), N.Y. 276/H6
Tioga, N. Dak. 282/E2
Tioga (co.), Pa. 294/H2
Tioga, Pa. 294/H2
Tioga (riv.), Pa. 294/H1
Tioga, W. Va. 312/E6
Tioman, Pulau (isl.), Malaysia 72/E7
Tiona, Pa. 294/D2
Tionesta, Pa. 294/C2
Tionesta Creek (lake), Pa. 294/D3
Tiosa, Ind. 227/E2
Tioughnioga (riv.), N.Y. 276/H6
Tipitapa, Nicaragua 154/E4
Tipler, Wis. 317/J4
Tiplersville, Miss. 256/G1
Tippah (co.), Miss. 256/G1
Tipp City, Ohio 284/B6
Tippecanoe (co.), Ind. 227/D4
Tippecanoe, Ind. 227/E2
Tippecanoe (riv.), Ind. 227/E2
Tippecanoe, Ohio 284/H5
Tipperary (co.), Ireland 17/F6
Tipperary, Ireland 10/B4
Tipperary, Ireland 17/E7
Tippettville, Georgia 217/E6
Tippo, Miss. 256/E3
Tipton, Calif. 204/F7
Tipton (co.), Ind. 227/E4
Tipton, Ind. 227/E4
Tipton, Iowa 229/L5
Tipton, Kansas 232/D2
Tipton, Mo. 261/G5
Tipton, Okla. 288/H6
Tipton, Pa. 294/F4
Tipton (co.), Tenn. 237/B9
Tipton, Tenn. 237/B10
Tiptonville, Tenn. 237/B8
Tiptop, Ky. 237/P5
Tiptop, Va. 307/F6
Tiptree, England 13/H6
Tipuani, Bolivia 136/B4
Tiracambu, Serra (range), Brazil 132/E4
Tiran (str.), Egypt 111/F2
Tiran (str.), Egypt 59/C4
Tiran (isl.), Saudi Arabia 59/C4
Tiran (str.), Saudi Arabia 59/C4
Tirana (Tiranë) (cap.), Albania 45/E5
Tiranë (Tirana) (cap.), Albania 45/E5
Tiranë (cap.), Albania 7/F4
Tirano, Italy 34/C1
Tiraque, Bolivia 136/C5
Tiraspol', U.S.S.R. 7/G4
Tiraspol', U.S.S.R. 52/C5
Tirat Hakarmel, Israel 65/B2
Tirat Zevi, Israel 65/D3
Tire, Turkey 59/A2
Tire, Turkey 63/B3
Tirebolu, Turkey 63/H2
Tiree (isl.), Scotland 15/B4
Tiree (isl.), Scotland 10/C2
Tîrgovişte, Romania 45/G3
Tîrgu Cărbuneşti, Romania 45/F3
Tîrgu Frumos, Romania 45/H2
Tîrgu Jiu, Romania 45/F3
Tîrgu Mureş, Romania 7/G4
Tîrgu Mureş, Romania 45/G2
Tîrgu Neamţ, Romania 45/G2
Tîrgu Ocna, Romania 45/H2

Tîrgu Secuiesc, Romania 45/H2
Tirich Mir (mt.), Pakistan 68/C1
Tirich Mir (mt.), Pakistan 59/K2
Tirlemont (Tienen), Belgium 27/F7
Tîrnăveni, Romania 45/F2
Tîrnavos, Greece 45/F6
Tiro, Ohio 284/E4
Tirol (prov.), Austria 41/A3
Tirso (riv.), Italy 34/B4
Tiruchchirappalli, India 54/J8
Tiruchchirappalli, India 68/D6
Tiruchendur, India 68/D7
Tirunelveli, India 68/D7
Tiruntán, Peru 128/E6
Tirupati, India 68/D6
Tiruppattur, India 68/D6
Tiruppur, India 68/D6
Tiruvannamalai, India 68/D6
Tirzah, S.C. 296/E2
Tisa (riv.), Yugoslavia 45/E3
Tisbury, England 13/E6
Tisch Mills, Wis. 317/L7
Tisdale, Sask. 162/F5
Tisdale, Sask. 181/H3
Tishomingo (co.), Miss. 256/H1
Tishomingo, Miss. 256/H1
Tishomingo, Okla. 288/N6
Tisisat (fall), Ethiopia 111/H6
Tiskilwa, Ill. 222/D2
Tisnov, Czech. 41/D2
Tisovec, Czech. 41/E2
Tistrup, Denmark 21/B6
Tisza (riv.), Hungary 41/F3
Tiszacsege, Hungary 41/F3
Tiszaföldvár, Hungary 41/F3
Tiszafüred, Hungary 41/F3
Tiszakécske, Hungary 41/F3
Tiszalük, Hungary 41/F3
Tiszavasvári, Hungary 41/F3
Titagarh, India 68/F1
Titicaca (lake) 2/F6
Titicaca (lake) 120/C4
Titicaca (lake), Bolivia 136/A4
Titicaca (lake), Peru 128/H10
Titicus, Conn. 210/A3
Titicus (riv.), Conn. 210/A3
Titicus (riv.), Conn. 210/A3
Titihira (head), N. Zealand 100/B5
Titirangi, N. Zealand 100/B1
Titistee-Neustadt, Germany 22/C5
Titlagarh, India 68/E4
Titlis (mt.), Switzerland 39/F3
Titograd, Yugoslavia 7/F4
Titograd, Yugoslavia 45/D4
Titonka, Iowa 229/E2
Titovo Užice, Yugoslavia 45/D4
Titov Veles, Yugoslavia 45/E5
Tittabawassee (riv.), Mich. 250/E5
Titule, Zaire 115/D2
Titus, Ala. 195/F5
Titus, Georgia 217/E1
Titus (lake), N.Y. 276/M1
Titus (co.), Texas 303/K4
Titusville, Fla. 188/K5
Titusville, Fla. 212/F3
Titusville, N.J. 273/D3
Titusville, Pa. 294/C2
Tiumpan (head), Scotland 15/B2
Tivaouane, Senegal 106/A5
Tiverton, England 10/D5
Tiverton, England 13/D7
Tiverton, Nova Scotia 168/B4
Tiverton, Ontario 177/C3
Tiverton, R.I. 249/K6
Tiverton •, R.I. 249/K6
Tiverton Four Corners, R.I. 249/K6
Tivoli, Italy 34/D3
Tivoli, N.Y. 276/N6
Tivoli, Texas 303/G9
Tiwi, Philippines 82/D4
Tixtla de Guerrero, Mexico 150/K8
Tizard (bank), Philippines 85/E3
Tizayuca, Mexico 150/L1
Tizimín, Mexico 150/Q6
Tizi Ouzou, Algeria 106/E1
Tiznit, Morocco 106/B3
Tjeukemeer (lake), Netherlands 27/H3
Tjilatjap (Cilacap), Indonesia 85/H2
Tjirebon (Cirebon), Indonesia 85/H2
Tjonger (riv.), Netherlands 27/J3
Tjuvfjorden (fjord), Norway 18/D2
Tlachichuca, Mexico 150/O1
Tlacolula de Matamoros, Mexico 150/L8
Tlacotepec de Mejiá, Mexico 150/P1
Tlahualilo de Zaragoza, Mexico 150/H3
Tlalancaneca, Mexico 150/M1
Tlalixcoyan, Mexico 150/Q2
Tlalmanalco de Velásquez, Mexico 150/L1
Tlalnepantla de Comonfort, Mexico 150/L1
Tlalpan, Mexico 150/L1
Tlaltenango de Sánchez Román, Mexico 150/H6
Tlaltizapan, Mexico 150/L2
Tlapacoyan, Mexico 150/P1
Tlapa de Comonfort, Mexico 150/K8
Tlaquepaque, Mexico 150/G6
Tlaquiltenango, Mexico 150/L2
Tlatlauquitepec, Mexico 150/O1
Tlaxcala (state), Mexico 150/N1
Tlaxcala de Xicotencatl, Mexico 150/M1
Tlaxco, Mexico 150/N1
Tlaxiaco, Mexico 150/L8
Tlayacapan, Mexico 150/L1
Tlell, Br. Col. 184/B3
Tlemcen, Algeria 106/D2
Tlemcen, Algeria 102/B1
Tmessa, Libya 111/C2
Tmessa, Libya 102/D2
Tni Haïa (well), Algeria 106/D4
Toa, Cuchillas de (mts.), Cuba 158/K4
Toa Alta, P. Rico 161/D1
Toa Baja, P. Rico 161/D1
Toad (riv.), Br. Col. 184/L2

Toadlena, N. Mex. 274/A2
Toamasina (prov.), Madagascar 118/H3
Toamasina, Madagascar 118/H3
Toamasina, Madagascar 102/G6
Toana (range), Nev. 266/G2
Toano, Va. 307/P6
Toast, N.C. 281/H2
Toba (inlet), Br. Col. 184/E5
Toba (isl.), Indonesia 85/B5
Toba, Japan 81/H6
Tobago (isl.), Trin. & Tob. 156/G5
Tobarra, Spain 33/F3
Tobasco, Ohio 284/C10
Tobatí, Paraguay 144/B4
Tobeatic (lake), Nova Scotia 168/C4
Tobelo, Indonesia 85/H5
Tobermory, Ontario 177/C2
Tobermory, Scotland 10/C2
Tobermory, Scotland 15/B4
Tobetsu, Japan 81/K2
Tobi (isl.), Belau 87/D5
Tobi (isl.), Japan 81/J4
Tobias, Nebr. 264/G4
Tobin (lake), Sask. 181/H2
Tobin (lake), W. Australia 88/D4
Tobin Lake, Sask. 181/H2
Tobinsport, Ind. 227/D9
Tobique (riv.), New Bruns. 170/C2
Tobique Narrows, New Bruns. 170/C2
Tobol (riv.), U.S.S.R. 54/H4
Tobol (riv.), U.S.S.R. 48/G4
Tobol'sk, U.S.S.R. 54/J4
Tobol'sk, U.S.S.R. 48/G4
Tobruk, Libya 102/E1
Tobruk, Libya 111/D1
Tobseda, U.S.S.R. 52/H1
Toby (mt.), Mass. 249/E3
Tobyhanna, Pa. 294/M3
Tocache, Peru 128/D7
Tocantínia, Brazil 136/B6
Tocantinópolis, Brazil 120/E3
Tocantinópolis, Brazil 132/D8
Tocantins (state), Brazil 132/D5
Tocantins (riv.), Brazil 2/G6
Tocantins (riv.), Brazil 120/E4
Tocantins (riv.), Brazil 132/D4
Toccoa, Georgia 217/F1
Toccopola, Miss. 256/F2
Tochcha (lake), Br. Col. 184/E3
Tochigi (pref.), Japan 81/K5
Tochimilco, Mexico 150/M2
Toco, Chile 138/A3
Toco, Trin. & Tob. 161/B10
Tocoa, Honduras 154/D2
Toco Hills, Georgia 217/K1
Tocomechi, Bolivia 136/D5
Toconao, Chile 138/C4
Tocópero, Venezuela 124/D2
Tocopilla, Chile 138/A3
Tocopilla, Chile 120/B5
Tocorpuri, Cerros de (mt.), Bolivia 136/A8
Tocorpuri, Cerro de (mts.), Chile 138/B3
Tocsin, Ind. 227/G3
Tocuco (riv.), Venezuela 124/B3
Tocumen (head), Scotland 15/D2
Tocumwal, N.S. Wales 97/C4
Tocuyo (riv.), Venezuela 124/D2
Tocuyo de la Costa, Venezuela 124/D2
Todd (co.), Ky. 237/G7
Todd (co.), Minn. 255/D4
Todd (mt.), New Bruns. 170/D2
Todd, N.C. 281/F2
Todd (co.), North. Terr. 93/D8
Todd (co.), S. Dak. 298/H7
Toddville, Iowa 229/K4
Toddville, Md. 245/O7
Toddville, S.C. 296/E4
Todenyang, Kenya 115/G3
Todi, Italy 34/D3
Tüdi (mt.), Switzerland 39/G3
Todmorden, England 13/H1
Todmorden, England 10/G2
Todos Santos, Cochabamba, Bolivia 136/C5
Todos Santos, La Paz, Bolivia 136/B3
Todos Santos, Oruro, Bolivia 136/A6
Todos Santos, Mexico 150/D5
Toe (head), Ireland 17/C9
Toe (head), Scotland 15/A3
Toekomstig (res.), Suriname 131/C3
Toeterville, Iowa 229/H2
Tofield, Alberta 182/D3
Tofino, Br. Col. 184/E5
Tofte, Minn. 255/H3
Toftlund, Denmark 21/B7
Togane, Japan 81/K6
Togdheer (prov.), Somalia 115/J2
Toggenburg (dist.), Switzerland 39/H2
Togiak, Alaska 196/H3
Togiak (bay), Alaska 196/F3
Togian (isls.), Indonesia 85/G6
Togliatti (Tol'yatti), U.S.S.R. 52/G4
Togliatti (Tol'yatti), U.S.S.R. 48/F4
Togo 102/C4
TOGO 106/E7
Togo, Minn. 255/E3
Togo, Sask. 181/K4
Togtoh, China 77/H3
Tohamiyam, Sudan 59/C6
Tohatchi, N. Mex. 274/A3
Tohivea (mt.), Fr. Poly. 86/S13
Toi, Japan 81/K7
Toibalawe, India 68/G6
Toijala, Finland 18/N6
Toimi, Minn. 255/G3
Toivola, Minn. 255/F3
Toiyabe (range), Nev. 266/D3
Tojo, Japan 81/G6
Tok, Alaska 196/K2
Tokachi (mt.), Japan 81/L2
Tokachi (riv.), Japan 81/L2
Tokaj, Hungary 41/F2

Tokamachi, Japan 81/J5
Tokanui, N. Zealand 100/B7
Tokar, Sudan 111/G4
Tokar, Sudan 102/F3
Tokar, Sudan 59/C6
Tokara (isls.), Japan 81/O5
Tokat (prov.), Turkey 63/G3
Tokat, Turkey 59/C1
Tokat, Turkey 63/G2
Tokeen, Alaska 196/M2
Tokeland, Wash. 310/A4
Tokelau (isls.) 87/J6
Tokewamna (peak), Utah 304/D3
Tokio, N. Dak. 282/N4
Tokio, Texas 303/B4
Tokke (riv.), Norway 18/F7
Tokmak, U.S.S.R. 48/H5
Tokmak, U.S.S.R. 52/E5
Toko, N. Zealand 100/E3
Tokomaru Bay, N. Zealand 100/G3
Tokoroa, N. Zealand 100/F3
Tokorozawa, Japan 81/O2
Tokra, Libya 111/D1
Toksook Bay, Alaska 196/E2
Toksu (Xinhe), China 77/B3
Toksun, China 77/C3
Tokuno (isl.), Japan 81/O5
Tokunoshima, Japan 81/O5
Tokushima (pref.), Japan 81/G7
Tokushima, Japan 81/F6
Tokuyama, Japan 81/F6
Tokyo (pref.), Japan 81/O2
Tokyo (cap.), Japan 2/R4
Tokyo (cap.), Japan 81/K6
Tokyo (cap.), Japan 54/R6
Tokyo (cap.), Japan 81/O2
Tokyo (bay), Japan 81/O2
Tolaga Bay, N. Zealand 100/G3
Tolar, Texas 303/B4
Tolbukhin, Bulgaria 45/H4
Tolchester Beach, Md. 245/N4
Tolé, Panama 154/F7
Toledo, Bolivia 136/B6
Toledo, Colombia 126/C3
Toledo, Ill. 222/E4
Toledo, Iowa 229/H4
Toledo, Ohio 146/K5
Toledo, Ohio 284/D2
Toledo, Ohio 188/K2
Toledo, Ontario 177/H3
Toledo, Oreg. 291/D3
Toledo, Philippines 82/D5
Toledo, Spain 7/D5
Toledo (prov.), Spain 33/D3
Toledo, Spain 33/E3
Toledo (mts.), Spain 33/E3
Toledo, Uruguay 145/B6
Toledo, Wash. 310/C4
Toledo Bend (lake) 188/H4
Toledo Bend (dam), La. 238/C4
Toledo Bend (lake), La. 238/C3
Toledo Bend (dam), Texas 303/L6
Toledo Bend (res.), Texas 303/L6
Tolentino, Italy 34/D3
Toli, China 77/B2
Toliara (prov.), Madagascar 118/G4
Toliara, Madagascar 118/G4
Toliara, Madagascar 102/G7
Tolima (dept.), Colombia 126/C5
Tolima, Colombia 126/B8
Tolima (mt.), Colombia 120/B2
Tolima, Nevada del (mt.), Colombia 126/C5
Tolimán, Mexico 150/K6
Tolitoli, Indonesia 85/G6
Tolland, Alberta 182/E3
Tolland (co.), Conn. 210/F1
Tolland •, Conn. 210/F1
Tolland •, Mass. 249/B4
Tollensee (lake), Germany 22/E2
Tollesboro, Ky. 237/O3
Tolleson, Ariz. 198/C5
Tollette, Ark. 202/C6
Tolley, N. Dak. 282/G2
Toll Gate, W. Va. 312/E4
Tollose, Denmark 21/E6
Tollville, Ark. 202/G4
Tollygunge, India 68/F2
Tolna (co.), Hungary 41/E3
Tolna, Hungary 41/E3
Tolna, N. Dak. 282/O4
Tolo (gulf), Indonesia 85/G6
Tolob, Scotland 15/G2
Tolona, Mo. 261/J2
Tolong (bay), Philippines 82/D6
Tolono, Ill. 222/E4
Tolosa, Spain 33/F1
Tolovana Park, Oreg. 291/C2
Tolsta (head), Scotland 15/B2
Tolstoi, Manitoba 179/F5
Tolstoy, S. Dak. 298/K3
Toltén, Chile 138/D2
Toltén (riv.), Chile 138/D2
Tolt River (res.), Wash. 310/D3
Tolú, Colombia 126/B4
Tolu, Ky. 237/E6
Toluca, Ill. 222/D2
Toluca, Mexico 146/H8
Toluca de Lerdo, Mexico 150/K7
Tom (mt.), Conn. 210/B1
Tom (mt.), Mass. 249/E3
Tom (mt.), N.H. 268/C3
Tom, Okla. 288/S7
Tomah, Wis. 317/F6
Tomahawk, Alberta 182/C3
Tomahawk, N.C. 281/N5
Tomahawk, Wis. 317/G5
Tomakomai, Japan 81/K2
Tomales, Calif. 204/C5
Tomales (pt.), Calif. 204/B5
Tomanao, Philippines 82/E4
Tomaniivi (mt.), Fiji 86/Q10
Tomar, Portugal 33/B3
Tomarza, Turkey 63/F3
Tomasaki (mt.), Utah 304/E5
Tomás Barrón, Bolivia 136/B5
Tomás Gomensoro, Uruguay 145/B1
Tomaszów Lubelski, Poland 47/F3

Tres Palmas 459

Tomaszów Mazowiecki, Poland 47/E3
Tomatin, Scotland 15/D3
Tomatlán, Mexico 150/G6
Tomave, Bolivia 136/B7
Tombador, Serra do (range), Brazil 132/B6
Tomball, Texas 303/J7
Tombe, Sudan 111/F6
Tombigbee (riv.) 188/J4
Tombigbee (riv.), Ala. 195/B7
Tombigbee (riv.), Miss. 256/H4
Tombstone, Ariz. 198/F7
Tombua, Angola 115/B7
Tomé, Chile 138/D1
Tome, N. Mex. 274/C4
Tomelilla, Sweden 18/J9
Tomelloso, Spain 33/E3
Tom Green (co.), Texas 303/D6
Tomhannock (res.), N.Y. 276/O5
Tomichi (creek), Colo. 208/F5
Tomifobia, Québec 172/E4
Tomina, Bolivia 136/C6
Tomingley, N.S. Wales 97/E3
Tomini (gulf), Indonesia 54/O10
Tomini (gulf), Indonesia 85/G6
Tomintoul, Scotland 15/E3
Tomiyama, Japan 81/O3
Tomkinson (ranges), W. Australia 92/E4
Tommerup, Denmark 21/D7
Tommot, U.S.S.R. 48/N4
Tomnolen, Miss. 256/F4
Tomo (riv.), Colombia 126/F5
To Mo, Thailand 72/D6
Tompa, Hungary 41/E3
Tompkins (co.), N.Y. 276/H6
Tompkins, Sask. 181/C5
Tompkinsville, Ky. 237/K7
Tompkinsville, Md. 245/L7
Tom Price, W. Australia 88/B4
Tom Price, W. Australia 92/B3
Toms (riv.), N.J. 273/E3
Toms Brook, Va. 307/L3
Toms Creek, Va. 307/D7
Tomsk, U.S.S.R. 54/K4
Tomsk, U.S.S.R. 48/J4
Tomslake, Br. Col. 184/H2
Toms River, N.J. 273/E4
Tom Steed (res.), Okla. 288/J5
Tümük, Turkey 63/F4
Tonalá, Mexico 150/N8
Tonalea, Ariz. 198/E2
Tonasket, Wash. 310/F2
Tonate, Fr. Guiana 131/E3
Tonawanda, N.Y. 276/B4
Tonawanda Ind. Res., N.Y. 276/D4
Tonbridge, England 13/H8
Tonckens (falls), Suriname 131/C3
Tondabayashi, Japan 81/J8
Tondano, Indonesia 85/H5
Tønder, Denmark 21/B8
Tønder, Denmark 18/F9
Tone (riv.), Japan 81/K6
Tonegrama, Peru 128/D4
Tonekabon, Iran 59/F2
Tonekabon, Iran 66/G2
Toney, Ala. 195/E1
Toney River, Nova Scotia 168/F3
Tonga 2/A6
Tonga 87/J8
Tonga, Sudan 111/F6
Tongala, Victoria 97/C5
Tonganoxie, Kansas 232/G2
Tongareva (atoll), Cook Is. 87/L6
Tongatapu (isls.), Tonga 87/J8
Tongcheng, China 77/J5
T'ongch'ŏn, N. Korea 81/D4
Tongchuan (Tungchwan), China 77/G5
Tongde, China 77/F4
Tongeren, Belgium 27/G7
Tonghai, China 77/F7
Tonghe, China 77/L2
Tonghua (Tunghwa), China 77/L3
Tongjiang (Tungkiang), China 77/M2
Tongliao, China 77/K3
Tongling, China 77/J5
Tongo, N.S. Wales 97/B2
Tongo (lake), N.S. Wales 97/B2
Tongoy, Chile 138/A8
Tongoy (bay), Chile 138/A8
Tongquil (isl.), Philippines 82/D8
Tongren, Qinghai, China 77/F4
Tongren, Guizhou, China 77/G6
Tongres (Tongeren), Belgium 27/G7
Tongs, Ky. 237/R3
Tongsa Dzong, Bhutan 68/G3
Tongtian He (Zhi Qu) (riv.), China 77/E5
Tongue (riv.), Mont. 262/K5
Tongue (pt.), N. Zealand 100/A3
Tongue (riv.), N. Dak. 282/P2
Tongue, Scotland 15/D2
Tongue (riv.), Wyo. 319/E1
Tongue of the Ocean (chan.), Bahamas 156/C1
Tongxin, China 77/G4
Tongyu, China 77/K3
Tongzi, China 77/G6
Tonica, Ill. 222/E2
Tonj, Sudan 111/E6
Tonk, India 68/D3
Tonka Bay, Minn. 255/F5
Tonkawa, Okla. 288/M1
Tonkin (gulf) 54/M8
Tonkin (gulf), China 77/G7
Tonkin, Sask. 181/J4
Tonkin (gulf), Vietnam 72/E3
Tonle Sap (lake), Cambodia 72/D4
Ton Mhor (pt.), Scotland 15/B5
Tonneins, France 28/D5
Tonnerre, France 28/E4
Tünning, Germany 22/C1
Tonopah, Ariz. 198/B5
Tonopah, Nev. 188/C3
Tonopah, Nev. 266/D4
Tonosí, Panama 154/G7
Tonota, Botswana 118/D4
Tonota, Botswana 102/E7
Tønsberg, Norway 18/D4
Tonsina, Alaska 196/J2
Tontitown, Ark. 202/B1
Tonto (basin), Ariz. 198/D4
Tonto (creek), Ariz. 198/D4
Tonto Basin, Ariz. 198/D5
Tontogany, Ohio 284/C3
Tonto Nat'l Mon., Ariz. 198/D5
Tony, Wis. 317/E5
Tonya, Turkey 63/H2
Toodyay, W. Australia 88/B2
Toodyay, W. Australia 92/B1
Tooele (co.), Utah 304/A3
Tooele, Utah 304/B3
Tooele, Utah 188/D2
Tooele Army Depot, Utah 304/B3
Toole (co.), Mont. 262/E2
Tooleybuc, N.S. Wales 97/B4
Toombs (co.), Georgia 217/H6
Toomevara, Ireland 17/E6
Tooms (lake), Tasmania 99/D4
Toomsboro, Georgia 217/F5
Toomsuba, Miss. 256/G6
Toone, Tenn. 237/D10
Tooraweenah, N.S. Wales 97/E2
Toowoomba, Australia 87/F8
Toowoomba, Queensland 88/J5
Toowoomba, Queensland 95/D5
Top (lake), U.S.S.R. 52/D1
Topador, Uruguay 145/C1
Topanga, Calif. 204/B10
Topanga Beach, Calif. 204/B10
Topawa, Ariz. 198/D7
Topaz (lake), Nev. 266/B4
Topeka, Ill. 222/D3
Topeka, Ind. 227/F1
Topeka (cap.), Kans. 188/G3
Topeka (cap.), Kansas 146/J6
Topeka (cap.), Kansas 232/G2
Topia, Mexico 150/F4
Topinabee, Mich. 250/E3
Topl'a (riv.), Czech. 41/F2
Topley, Br. Col. 184/D3
Toplița, Romania 45/G2
Topocalma (pt.), Chile 138/A10
Topock, Ariz. 198/A4
Top Of The World Prov. Park, Br. Col. 184/K5
Topographic Center, Md. 245/E4
Topol'čany, Czech. 41/D2
Topolobampo, Mexico 150/E4
Topolovgrad, Bulgaria 45/H4
Toponas, Colo. 208/F2
Toppenish, Wash. 310/E4
Toppenish (creek), Wash. 310/E4
Topsail Beach, N.C. 281/O6
Topsfield•, Maine 243/H5
Topsfield, Mass. 249/L2
Topsfield•, Mass. 249/L2
Topsham, Maine 243/D8
Topsham•, Maine 243/D8
Topsham•, Vt. 268/C3
Top Springs, North. Terr. 93/C4
Topton, N.C. 281/B4
Topton, Pa. 294/L5
Toquepala, Peru 128/G11
Toquerville, Utah 304/A6
Toquima (range), Nev. 266/E4
Tor (bay), Nova Scotia 168/G3
Torata, Peru 128/G11
Torawitan (cape), Indonesia 85/G5
Torbalı, Turkey 63/B3
Torbat-e-Heydariyeh, Iran 66/L3
Torbat-e Heydariyeh, Iran 59/G2
Torbat-e Jam, Iran 66/M3
Torbat-e Jam, Iran 59/H2
Torbay, England 10/E5
Torbay, England 13/D7
Torbay, Newf. 166/D2
Torbay (pt.), Newf. 166/D2
Torbeck, Haiti 158/A6
Torch (key), Fla. 212/E7
Torch (lake), Mich. 250/D3
Torch, Ohio 284/G7
Torch (riv.), Sask. 181/H2
Torch River, Sask. 181/G2
Tordesillas, Spain 33/D2
Torgau, Germany 22/E3
Torgelow, Germany 22/F2
Torhout, Belgium 27/C6
Tori, Ethiopia 111/F6
Torino (Turin), Italy 34/A2
Torit, Sudan 111/F7
Torne (riv.) 7/G2
Torneälv (riv.), Sweden 18/M3
Tor Ness (prom.), Scotland 15/E2
Torneträsk (lake), Sweden 18/L2
Torngat (mts.), Newf. 166/B2
Tornillo, Texas 303/A10
Tornio, Finland 18/O4
Tornionjoki (riv.), Finland 18/O3
Tornquist, Argentina 143/D4
Toro, Cerro del (mt.), Argentina 143/B2
Toro (lake), Chile 138/D9
Toro, Cerro del (mt.), Chile 138/B7
Toro (pt.), Chile 138/A10
Toro, La. 238/C4
Toro, El (mt.), P. Rico 161/F2
Toro, Spain 33/D2
Türükszentmiklós, Hungary 41/F3
Toronaic (gulf), Greece 45/F5
Toronto, Canada 2/F3
Toronto, Iowa 229/M5
Toronto, Kansas 232/G4
Toronto (lake), Kansas 232/F4
Toronto (res.), N.Y. 276/L7
Toronto, Ohio 284/J5
Toronto (cap.), Ont. 146/K5
Toronto (cap.), Ont. 162/H7
Toronto (metro. munic.), Ontario 177/K4
Toronto (cap.), Ontario 177/K4
Toronto, S. Dak. 298/R4
Toropalca, Bolivia 136/B7
Toropets, U.S.S.R. 52/D3
Tororo, Uganda 115/F3
Torote (riv.), Spain 33/G4
Torotoro, Bolivia 136/C6
Torpedo, Pa. 294/D2
Torphins, Scotland 15/F3
Torpoint, England 13/C7
Torquay, Sask. 181/H6
Torquemada, Spain 33/D1
Torr (head), N. Ireland 17/K1
Torrance, Calif. 188/C4
Torrance, Calif. 204/C11
Torrance (co.), N. Mex. 274/D4
Torrance, Ontario 177/E3
Torrance, Pa. 294/D5
Torre, Cerro de la (mt.), Chile 138/E4
Torre Annunziata, Italy 34/E4
Torreblanca, Spain 33/G2
Torrecilla (lag.), P. Rico 161/E1
Torre del Greco, Italy 34/E4
Torre de Moncorvo, Portugal 33/C2
Torredonjimeno, Spain 33/D4
Torre Gaia, Italy 34/F6
Torrejón (res.), Spain 33/D3
Torrejoncillo, Spain 33/C3
Torrejón de Ardoz, Spain 33/G4
Torrelaguna, Spain 33/E2
Torrelavega, Spain 33/D1
Torremaggiore, Italy 34/E4
Torremolinos, Spain 33/D4
Torrens (riv.) 88/E7
Torrens (lake), Australia 87/D9
Torrens (isl.), S. Australia 88/D7
Torrens (lake), S. Australia 88/F6
Torrens (lake), S. Australia 94/E4
Torrens (riv.), S. Australia 94/C7
Torrente, Spain 33/F3
Torreón, Mexico 146/H7
Torreón, Mexico 150/H4
Torreon, N. Mex. 274/C4
Torre-Pacheco, Spain 33/F4
Torres (strait) 87/E7
Torres (str.), Papua N.G. 85/A7
Torres (str.), Queensland 88/G2
Torres (str.), Queensland 95/B1
Torres (isls.), Vanuatu 87/G7
Torres Martinez Ind. Res., Calif. 204/J10
Torres Novas, Portugal 33/B3
Torres Vedras, Portugal 33/B3
Torrevieja, Spain 33/F4
Torrey, Utah 304/C5
Torridge (riv.), England 13/C7
Torridon, Loch (inlet), Scotland 15/C3
Torriente, Cuba 158/D1
Torrijos, Philippines 82/D4
Torrijos, Spain 33/D2
Torring, Denmark 21/C6
Torringford, Conn. 210/C1
Torrington, Alberta 182/D4
Torrington, Conn. 210/C1
Torrington, Wyo. 319/H3
Torroella de Montgrí, Spain 33/H1
Torrowangee, N.S. Wales 97/A2
Torrox, Spain 33/E4
Torsby, Sweden 18/H6
Tors Cove, Newf. 166/D2
Torshälla, Sweden 18/K7
Tórshavn, Denmark 7/D2
Tórshavn (cap.), Faroe Is., Denmark 21/A3
Tortilla Flat, Ariz. 198/D5
Tortola (isl.), Virgin Is. (U.K.) 161/D3
Tortola (isl.), Virgin Is. (U.K.) 156/H1
Tórtolas, Cerro de las (mt.), Chile 138/B8
Tortona, Italy 34/B2
Tortorici, Italy 34/E6
Tortosa, Spain 33/G2
Tortosa (cape), Spain 33/G2
Tortue (chan.), Haiti 158/C5
Tortue (Tortuga) (isl.), Haiti 156/D2
Tortue (Tortuga) (isl.), Haiti 158/C4
Tortuga (isl.), Haiti 158/C4
Tortuga (isl.), Haiti 156/D2
Tortugas (gulf), Colombia 126/B6
Tortuguero (lag.), P. Rico 161/D1
Tortuguilla (pt.), Cuba 158/K4
Tortum, Turkey 63/J2
Torud, Iran 59/F2
Torud, Iran 66/J3
Torul, Turkey 63/H2
Toruń (prov.), Poland 47/D2
Toruń, Poland 7/F3
Toruń, Poland 47/D2
Torunos, Venezuela 124/C3
Türva, U.S.S.R. 53/C1
Tory (isl.), Ireland 17/E1
Tory (isl.), Ireland 10/B3
Tory (sound), Ireland 17/E1
Torysa (riv.), Czech. 41/F2
Torzhok, U.S.S.R. 52/D3
Tosa, Japan 81/F7
Tosa (bay), Japan 81/F7
Tosashimizu, Japan 81/F7
Toson Hu (lake), China 77/E4
Tüss (riv.), Switzerland 39/G1
Tostado, Argentina 143/D2
Toston, Mont. 262/E4
Tosu, Japan 81/E7
Tosya, Turkey 63/F2
Tota, Laguna de (lake), Colombia 126/D5
Totana, Spain 33/F4
Tótkomlós, Hungary 41/F3
Tot'ma, U.S.S.R. 48/E4
Tot'ma, U.S.S.R. 52/F3
Totnes, England 13/D7
Totnes, England 10/E5
Totnes, Sask. 181/C4
Totness, Suriname 131/C3
Toto, Ind. 227/D2
Totoket, Conn. 210/D3
Totonicapán, Guatemala 154/B3
Totora, Cochabamba, Bolivia 136/C5
Totora, Oruro, Bolivia 136/A5
Totoral, Chile 138/A6
Totoral, Quebrada (riv.), Chile 138/A6
Totoral, Uruguay 145/C3
Totowa, N.J. 273/B1
Totoya (isl.), Fiji 86/R11
Tottenham, N.S. Wales 97/D3
Tottenham, Ontario 177/E3
Tottori (pref.), Japan 81/G6
Tottori, Japan 81/G6
Touat (oasis), Algeria 106/E3
Touba, Ivory Coast 106/C7
Touba, Senegal 106/A6
Toubkal, Jebel (mt.), Morocco 102/B1
Toubkal, Jebel (mt.), Morocco 106/C2
Touchet, Wash. 310/G4
Touchet (riv.), Wash. 310/G4
Touchwood (lake), Alberta 182/E2
Touchwood (hills), Sask. 181/G4
Toufourine (well), Mali 106/C4
Tougaloo, Miss. 256/D6
Tougan, Burkina Faso 106/D6
Touggourt, Algeria 106/F2
Touggourt, Algeria 102/C1
Toughkenamon, Pa. 294/L6
Tougué, Guinea 106/B6
Touila (well), Algeria 106/C3
Touila (well), Mauritania 106/C3
Toukoto, Mali 106/C6
Toul, France 28/F3
Touladi, Grand Lac (lake), Québec 172/J1
Toulnustouc (riv.), Québec 174/D2
Toulon, France 7/E4
Toulon, France 28/F6
Toulon, Ill. 222/D2
Toulouse, France 7/E4
Toulouse, France 28/D6
Toumodi, Ivory Coast 106/D7
Toungo, Nigeria 106/G7
Toungoo, Burma 72/C3
Touraine (trad. prov.), France 29
Tourakom, Laos 72/D3
Tourbis (lake), Québec 172/C2
Tourcoing, France 28/E2
Tour d'Ai (mt.), Switzerland 39/C4
Tourelle, Québec 172/C1
Tournai, Belgium 27/C7
Tournavista, Peru 128/E7
Tournon, France 28/F5
Tournus, France 28/F4
Touros, Brazil 132/H4
Touro Synagogue Nat'l Hist. Site, R.I. 249/J7
Tours, France 28/D4
Tours, France 7/E4
Tourville, Québec 172/H2
Toutes Aides, Manitoba 179/C3
Toutle, Wash. 310/C4
Toutle, South Fork (riv.), Wash. 310/C4
Toutle, North Fork (riv.), Wash. 310/C4
Toužim, Czech. 41/B1
Tüv, Mongolia 77/G2
Tovar, Venezuela 124/C3
Tovey, Ill. 222/D4
Towaco, N.J. 273/E2
Towada, Japan 81/K3
Towada (lake), Japan 81/K3
Towada-Hachimantai National Park, Japan 81/K3
Towakaima, Guyana 131/B2
Towanda, Ill. 222/D3
Towanda, Kansas 232/E4
Towanda, Pa. 294/J2
Towanda (creek), Pa. 294/J2
Towaoc, Colo. 208/B8
Towcester, England 13/F5
Tower, Mich. 250/E3
Tower, Minn. 255/F3
Tower, Wyo. 319/B1
Tower City, N. Dak. 282/P6
Tower City, Pa. 294/J4
Tower Hamlets, England 13/H8
Tower Hill, Ill. 222/E4
Tower Lakes, Ill. 222/A4
Towers of Silence, India 68/B7
Tow Law, England 13/H4
Town (creek), Ala. 195/C1
Town (creek), Md. 245/E2
Town and Country, Mo. 261/O3
Town and Country, Wash. 310/H3
Town Creek, Ala. 195/D1
Towner, Colo. 208/P6
Towner (co.), N. Dak. 282/M2
Towner, N. Dak. 282/K3
Townley, Ala. 195/D3
Town 'n Country, Fla. 212/C2
Town of Pines, Ind. 227/D1
Town Point, Md. 245/P3
Towns (co.), Georgia 217/E1
Towns, Georgia 217/G7
Townsend, Del. 245/R3
Townsend, Georgia 217/J7
Townsend, Mass. 249/H2
Townsend•, Mass. 249/H2
Townsend, Mont. 262/E4
Townsend (inlet), N.J. 273/D5
Townsend, Tenn. 237/O9
Townsend, Va. 307/R6
Townsend, Wis. 317/K5
Townsend Harbor, Mass. 249/G2
Townsends Inlet, N.J. 273/D5
Townshend•, Vt. 268/B5
Townsville, Australia 2/S6
Townsville, Australia 87/E7
Townsville, N.C. 281/N1
Townsville, Queensland 88/H3
Townsville, Queensland 95/C3
Townville, Pa. 294/C2
Townville, S.C. 296/B2
Towot, Sudan 111/F6
Towraghondi, Afghanistan 68/A1
Towson, Md. 245/M3
Towuti (lake), Indonesia 85/G6
Towy (riv.), Wales 13/D6
Towy (riv.), Wales 10/E5
Toxey, Ala. 195/B7
Toya (lake), Japan 81/K2
Toyah, Texas 303/D11
Toyah (creek), Texas 303/D11
Toyah (lake), Texas 303/D11
Toyahvale, Texas 303/D11
Toyama (pref.), Japan 81/H5
Toyama, Japan 81/H5
Toyama (bay), Japan 81/H5
Toyohashi, Japan 81/H6
Toyonaka, Japan 81/J7
Toyooka, Japan 81/G6
Toyota, Japan 81/H6
Tozeur, Tunisia 106/F2
Trabzon (prov.), Turkey 63/H2
Trabzon, Turkey 54/E5
Trabzon, Turkey 63/H2
Trabzon, Turkey 59/C1
Tracadie, New Bruns. 170/F1
Tracadie, Nova Scotia 168/G3
Tracadie (bay), Pr. Edward I. 168/F2
Trachselwald, Switzerland 39/E2
Tracy, Calif. 204/D6
Tracy, Conn. 210/D2
Tracy, Iowa 229/H6
Tracy, Ky. 237/K7
Tracy, Minn. 255/C6
Tracy, Mo. 261/C4
Tracy, New Bruns. 170/D3
Tracy, Québec 172/D3
Tracy Arm (inlet), Alaska 196/N1
Tracy City, Tenn. 237/K10
Tracyton, Wash. 310/A2
Trade, Tenn. 237/T8
Trade Lake, Wis. 317/A4
Tradespark, Scotland 15/E3
Tradesville, S.C. 296/F2
Tradewater (riv.), Ky. 237/F6
Trading (bay), Alaska 196/B1
Trading Post, Kansas 232/H3
Traer, Iowa 229/J4
Traer, Kansas 232/B2
Trafalgar, Ind. 227/E6
Trafalgar, Nova Scotia 168/F3
Trafalgar (cape), Spain 33/C4
Trafaria, Portugal 33/A1
Trafford, Ala. 195/E3
Trafford, Pa. 294/C5
Traghen, Libya 111/B2
Traiguén, Chile 138/D2
Traiguén (isl.), Chile 138/D6
Trail, Br. Col. 162/E6
Trail, Br. Col. 146/G4
Trail, Br. Col. 184/J6
Trail, Minn. 255/C3
Trail, Oreg. 291/E5
Trail City, S. Dak. 298/H3
Trail Creek, Ind. 227/D1
Traill (isl.), Greenl. 4/B10
Traill (co.), N. Dak. 282/R5
Traîne (lake), Québec 172/D2
Trainer, Pa. 294/L7
Traiskirchen, Austria 41/D2
Trakai, U.S.S.R. 53/C3
Tralake, Miss. 256/C4
Tralee, Ireland 10/B4
Tralee, Ireland 17/B7
Tralee (bay), Ireland 17/B7
Tramán-tepuí (mt.), Venezuela 124/G5
Tramelan, Switzerland 39/D2
Trammel, Va. 307/D6
Tramore, Ireland 10/C4
Tramore, Ireland 17/G7
Tramore (bay), Ireland 17/G7
Trampas, N. Mex. 274/D2
Tramperos (creek), N. Mex. 274/F2
Tramping (lake), Sask. 181/C3
Tramping Lake, Sask. 181/B3
Tranås, Sweden 18/J7
Trancoso, Portugal 33/C2
Tranebjerg, Denmark 21/D6
Tranebjerg (mt.), Denmark 21/C6
Tranent, Scotland 15/F5
Trang, Thailand 72/C6
Trangan (isl.), Indonesia 85/J7
Trangie, N.S. Wales 97/D3
Trani, Italy 34/F4
Tranquebar, India 68/E6
Tranqueras, Uruguay 145/D2
Tranqui (isl.), Chile 138/D4
Tranquility, N.J. 273/D2
Tranquillity, Calif. 204/E7
Transantarctic (mts.) 5/B17
Trans-Carpathian Oblast, U.S.S.R. 52/B5
Transfer, Pa. 294/A3
Transkei (bantustan), S. Africa 102/E8
Transkei (rep.), S. Africa 118/D6
Transquaking (riv.), Md. 245/P7
Transvaal (prov.), S. Africa 102/E7
Transvaal (prov.), S. Africa 118/D4
Transylvania, La. 238/H1
Transylvania (co.), N.C. 281/D4
Transylvanian Alps (mts.), Romania 45/G3
Trapani (prov.), Italy 34/D5
Trapani, Italy 7/F5
Trapani, Italy 34/D5
Trap Falls (res.), Conn. 210/C3
Traphill, N.C. 281/H2
Trappe, Md. 245/O6
Trappers (lake), Colo. 208/E3
Traralgon, Victoria 97/D6
Traralgon, Victoria 88/H7
Trarza (reg.), Mauritania 106/A5
Trasimeno (lake), Italy 34/D3
Traskwood, Ark. 202/E5
Trat, Thailand 72/D4
Traun, Austria 41/C2
Traun (riv.), Austria 41/C2
Traun See (lake), Austria 41/B3
Traunstein, Germany 22/E5
Travancore (reg.), India 68/D7
Travelers Rest, S.C. 296/C2
Travellers (lake), N.S. Wales 97/B3
Travellers Rest, Ky. 237/O6
Travemünde, Germany 22/D2
Travers, Alberta 182/D4
Travers (res.), Alberta 182/D4
Traverse (bay), Manitoba 179/F4
Traverse (isl.), Mich. 250/A1
Traverse (pt.), Mich. 250/A1
Traverse (co.), Minn. 255/B5
Traverse, Minn. 255/D6
Traverse (lake), Minn. 255/B5
Traverse (lake), S. Dak. 298/R2
Traverse City, Mich. 188/K2
Traverse City, Mich. 250/D4
Tra Vinh (Phu Vinh), Vietnam 72/E5
Travis (co.), Texas 303/G7
Travis (lake), Texas 303/G7
Travis A.F.B., Calif. 204/L1
Travnik, Yugoslavia 45/C3
Trawbreaga (bay), Ireland 17/F1
Traynor, Sask. 181/C3
Traytown, Newf. 166/D1
Trbovlje, Yugoslavia 45/B2
Treadway, Tenn. 237/P8
Treasure (isl.), Fla. 212/B3
Treasure (co.), Mont. 262/J4
Treasure Island, Fla. 212/B3
Treasury (isls.), Solomon Is. 86/C2
Treaty, Ind. 227/F3
Trebbia (riv.), Italy 34/B2
Třebíč, Czech. 41/C2
Trebinje, Yugoslavia 45/D4
Trebišov, Czech. 41/F2
Trebizond (Trabzon), Turkey 63/H2
Trebloc, Miss. 256/G3
Třeboň, Czech. 41/C2
Trece Martires, Philippines 82/C3
Tredegar, Wales 13/B6
Treece, Kansas 232/H4
Treelon, Sask. 181/C6
Trees, La. 238/B1
Treesbank, Manitoba 179/C5
Tregaron, Wales 13/D5
Tregaron, Wales 10/E4
Tregarva, Sask. 181/G5
Trego (co.), Kansas 232/C3
Trego, Mont. 262/B2
Trego, Wis. 317/C4
Treherne, Manitoba 179/D5
Treig, Loch (lake), Scotland 15/D4
Treinta y Tres (dept.), Uruguay 145/E4
Treinta y Tres, Uruguay 145/E4
Trelew, Argentina 143/C5
Trelleborg, Sweden 18/H9
Tremadoc (bay), Wales 10/D4
Tremadoc (prom.), Wales 13/C5
Tremblant (lake), Québec 172/C3
Trembleur (lake), Br. Col. 184/E3
Trementina, N. Mex. 274/E3
Tremiti (isls.), Italy 34/E3
Tremont, Ill. 222/D3
Tremont, Maine 243/G7
Tremont•, Maine 243/G7
Tremont, Miss. 256/H2
Tremont, Pa. 294/K4
Tremont City, Ohio 284/C5
Tremonton, Utah 304/B2
Tremp, Spain 33/G1
Trempealeau (co.), Wis. 317/D7
Trempealeau, Wis. 317/C8
Trempealeau (riv.), Wis. 317/C7
Trenary, Mich. 250/C2
Trenčín, Czech. 41/E2
Trenel, Argentina 143/D4
Trenggalek, Indonesia 85/K2
Trenque Lauquen, Argentina 143/D4
Trent (riv.), England 13/G4
Trent (riv.), England 10/F4
Trent (riv.), N.C. 281/P4
Trent, Oreg. 291/E4
Trent, S. Dak. 298/R6
Trent, Texas 303/D5
Trente et un Milles (lake), Québec 172/B3
Trentham, Manitoba 179/F5
Trentham Cliffs, N.S. Wales 97/B4
Trentino-Alto Adige (reg.), Italy 34/C1
Trento (prov.) Italy 34/C1
Trento, Italy 34/C1
Trenton, Ala. 195/F1
Trenton, Ark. 202/J5
Trenton, Fla. 212/D2
Trenton, Georgia 217/A1
Trenton, Ill. 222/D5
Trenton, Iowa 229/K6
Trenton, Ky. 237/G7
Trenton, Maine 243/G7
Trenton•, Maine 243/G7
Trenton, Md. 245/L2
Trenton, Mich. 250/B7
Trenton, Miss. 256/E6
Trenton, Mo. 261/E2
Trenton, Nebr. 264/D4
Trenton (cap.), N.J. 146/L5
Trenton (cap.), N.J. 188/M2
Trenton (cap.), N.J. 273/D3
Trenton, N.C. 281/P4
Trenton, N. Dak. 282/C3
Trenton, Nova Scotia 168/F3
Trenton, Ohio 284/B7
Trenton, Ontario 177/G3
Trenton, S.C. 296/D4
Trenton, Tenn. 237/D9
Trenton, Texas 303/H4
Trenton, Utah 304/B2
Trent Woods, N.C. 281/P4
Trepassey, Newf. 166/D2
Treptow, Germany 22/F4
Tres Arboles, Uruguay 145/C3
Tres Arroyos, Argentina 143/D4
Tres Arroyos, Argentina 120/C6
Tres Bocas, Uruguay 145/B2
Tresckow, Pa. 294/K4
Tresco (isl.), England 13/A8
Três Corações, Brazil 132/E8
Três Corações, Brazil 135/D2
Tres Cruces, Nevada (mt.), Chile 138/B6
Tres Esquinas, Colombia 126/C7
Treshnish (isls.), Scotland 15/B4
Tres Islas, Uruguay 145/E3
Três Lagoas, Brazil 120/D5
Três Lagoas, Brazil 132/C8
Três Marias (res.), Brazil 120/E4
Tres Montes (cape), Chile 120/B7
Tres Montes (cape), Chile 138/C7
Tres Montes (gulf), Chile 138/D6
Tres Montes (pen.), Chile 138/C6
Tres Palmas, Colombia 126/B3

Trespassey (bay), Newf. 166/D2
Tres Picos, Cerro (mt.), Argentina 143/B5
Tres Piedras, N. Mex. 274/D2
Tres Pinos, Calif. 204/D7
Três Pontas, Brazil 135/D2
Tres Puntas (cape), Argentina 120/C7
Tres Puntas (cape), Argentina 143/D6
Tres Puntas (cape), Guatemala 154/C3
Três Rios, Brazil 135/E3
Três Rios, Brazil 132/F8
Tres Ritos, N. Mex. 274/D2
Třešt', Czech. 41/C2
Treuchtlingen, Germany 22/D4
Treungen, Norway 18/F7
Treutlen (co.), Georgia 217/G6
Trevelin, Argentina 143/B5
Trevett, Maine 243/D8
Treviglio, Italy 34/B2
Treviño, Spain 33/E1
Treviso, Italy 34/D2
Treviso (prov.), Italy 34/D2
Trevlac, Ind. 227/E6
Trevorton, Pa. 294/J4
Trevose (head), England 13/B7
Trévoux, France 28/F5
Treynor, Iowa 229/B6
Treyvaux, Switzerland 39/D3
Trezevant, Tenn. 237/D8
Trhové Sviny, Czech. 41/C2
Triabunna, Tasmania 99/H4
Triadelphia (lake), Md. 245/L4
Triadelphia, W. Va. 312/E2
Triana, Ala. 195/E1
Triangle, Alberta 182/B2
Triangle, Va. 307/O3
Triángulo Este (isl.), Mexico 150/N6
Triángulo Oeste (isl.), Mexico 150/N6
Tribbett, Miss. 256/C4
Tribbey, Okla. 288/M4
Triberg im Schwarzwald, Germany 22/C4
Tribune, Kansas 232/A3
Tribune, Sask. 181/H6
Tricase, Italy 34/G5
Trichur, India 68/D6
Trida, N.S. Wales 97/C3
Tridell, Utah 304/E5
Trident, Mont. 262/E5
Trident (peak), Nev. 266/C1
Trieben, Austria 41/C3
Trier, Germany 22/B4
Triesen, Liecht. 39/H2
Trieste (prov.), Italy 34/E2
Trieste, Italy 34/E2
Trieste, Italy 7/F4
Trieste (gulf), Italy 34/D2
Trigal, Bolivia 136/C6
Trigg (co.), Ky. 237/F7
Triglav (mt.), Yugoslavia 45/A2
Trigueros, Spain 33/C4
Tríkkala, Greece 45/E6
Tri Lakes, Ind. 227/G2
Trilby, Fla. 212/D3
Trilla, Ill. 222/E4
Trillick, N. Ireland 17/G3
Trim, Ireland 17/H4
Trim, Ireland 10/C4
Trimble, Ill. 222/F4
Trimble (co.), Ky. 237/L3
Trimble, Ky. 237/M6
Trimble, Mo. 261/D4
Trimble, Ohio 284/F7
Trimble, Tenn. 237/C8
Trim Cane (creek), Miss. 256/G4
Trimmis, Switzerland 39/J3
Trimont, Minn. 255/D7
Trin, Switzerland 39/H3
Trinchera, Colo. 208/M8
Trinchera (peak), Colo. 208/J8
Trinchera (riv.), Colo. 208/H8
Trincheras, Mexico 150/D1
Trincomalee, Sri Lanka 54/K9
Trincomalee, Sri Lanka 68/E7
Trindade, Brazil 132/D7
Třinec, Czech. 41/E2
Tring, England 13/G7
Tring, England 10/F5
Tring-Jonction, Québec 172/F3
Trinidad (isl.), Argentina 143/D4
Trinidad, Bolivia 120/C4
Trinidad, Bolivia 136/C4
Trinidad, Calif. 204/A2
Trinidad (head), Calif. 204/A2
Trinidad (gulf), Chile 138/D8
Trinidad, Colombia 126/C5
Trinidad, Colo. 146/H6
Trinidad, Colo. 188/F3
Trinidad, Colo. 208/L8
Trinidad, Cuba 158/E2
Trinidad, Cuba 156/B2
Trinidad, Honduras 154/C3
Trinidad, Paraguay 144/E5
Trinidad, Texas 303/J5
Trinidad (isl.), Trin. & Tob. 156/G5
Trinidad (isl.), Trin. & Tob. 161/A9
Trinidad, Uruguay 145/E3
Trinidad, Wash. 310/F3
Trinidad and Tobago 2/G5
Trinidad and Tobago 146/N8
TRINIDAD AND TOBAGO 161
TRINIDAD AND TOBAGO 156/G5
Trinity, Ala. 195/D1
Trinity (isls.), Alaska 196/H3
Trinity (co.), Calif. 204/B3
Trinity (riv.), Calif. 204/B3
Trinity (riv.), Idaho 220/C6
Trinity, Ky. 237/O3
Trinity (range), Nev. 266/C2
Trinity, Newf. 166/D2
Trinity, Newf. 166/D2
Trinity (bay), Newf. 166/D2
Trinity (bay), Queensland 88/H3
Trinity (bay), Queensland 95/C3
Trinity (co.), Texas 303/J6
Trinity, Texas 303/J7
Trinity (bay), Texas 303/L2
Trinity (riv.), Texas 188/G4

Trinity (riv.), Texas 303/H5
Trinity, West Fork (riv.), Texas 303/G2
Trinity Center, Calif. 204/C2
Trinity Springs, Ind. 227/D7
Trinity Ville, Jamaica 158/K6
Trinkitat, Sudan 111/G4
Trinkitat, Sudan 59/C6
Trino, Italy 34/B2
Trinway, Ohio 284/F5
Trio, S.C. 296/H5
Trion, Georgia 217/B1
Triplet, Va. 307/N7
Triplett, Mo. 261/F4
Triplett, Va. 307/N7
Tripoli (Tarabulus), Lebanon 59/C3
Tripoli (Tarabulus), Lebanon 63/F5
Tripoli (cap.), Libya 2/K4
Tripoli (cap.), Libya 102/D1
Tripoli (cap.), Libya 111/B1
Tripoli, Wis. 317/G4
Trípolis, Greece 45/F7
Tripolitania (reg.), Libya 102/D1
Tripolitania (reg.), Libya 111/B1
Tripp (co.), S. Dak. 298/K7
Tripp, S. Dak. 298/N7
Tripura (state), India 68/G4
Trischen (isl.), Germany 22/C1
Tristan da Cunha (isl.), St. Helena 2/J7
Triste (gulf), Venezuela 124/D2
Triton (isl.), China 85/E2
Triumph, Ill. 222/E2
Triumph-Buras, La. 238/L8
Triune, Tenn. 237/H9
Trivandrum, India 54/J9
Trivandrum, India 68/D7
Trivoli, Ill. 222/D4
Trnava, Czech. 41/D2
Trobriand (isls.), Papua N.G. 87/F6
Trobriand (isls.), Papua N.G. 85/C7
Trochu, Alberta 182/D4
Troense, Denmark 21/D7
Trofaiach, Austria 41/C3
Trogir, Yugoslavia 45/C4
Troisdorf, Germany 22/B3
Trois-Pistoles, Québec 172/H1
Trois Pitons, Morne (mt.), Dominica 161/E2
Trois-Ponts, Belgium 27/H8
Trois-Rivières, Guadeloupe 161/A7
Trois-Rivières (riv.), Haiti 158/C3
Trois-Rivières, Que. 162/J6
Trois-Rivières, Que. 146/L5
Trois-Rivières, Québec 172/E3
Trois-Rivières-Ouest, Québec 172/E3
Trois-Saumons, Québec 172/G2
Troistorrents, Switzerland 39/C4
Troisvierges, Luxembourg 27/J9
Troitsa (lake), Br. Col. 184/D3
Troitsk, U.S.S.R. 48/G4
Troitsko-Pechorsk, U.S.S.R. 52/J2
Trojan, S. Dak. 298/B5
Trollhättan, Sweden 18/H7
Trombay, India 68/B7
Trombetas (riv.), Brazil 132/B3
Tromie (riv.), Scotland 15/D4
Trommald, Minn. 255/D4
Troms (co.), Norway 18/L2
Tromsø, Norway 4/B9
Tromsø, Norway 7/F2
Tromsø, Norway 18/L2
Trona, Calif. 204/H8
Tronador (mt.), Argentina 143/B5
Tronador, Cerro (mt.), Chile 138/E3
Trondheim, Norway 7/F2
Trondheim, Norway 18/F5
Trondheimsfjorden (fjord), Norway 7/F2
Trondheimsfjorden (fjord), Norway 18/G5
Troodos (mt.), Cyprus 63/E5
Troon, Scotland 10/D3
Troon, Scotland 15/D5
Tropic, Utah 304/B6
Trosa, Sweden 18/K7
Trosky, Minn. 255/B7
Trossachs, Sask. 181/G6
Trossachs, The, Scotland 15/D4
Trostan (mt.), N. Ireland 17/J1
Trotternish (dist.), Scotland 15/B3
Trotters, N. Dak. 282/C5
Trotwood, Ohio 284/B6
Trou Bonbon, Haiti 158/A6
Trou du Nord, Haiti 158/C5
Troup (co.), Georgia 217/B4
Troup (head), Scotland 15/F3
Troup, Texas 303/J5
Troupsburg, N.Y. 276/F6
Trousdale, Kansas 232/C4
Trousdale, Okla. 288/M4
Trousdale (co.), Tenn. 237/J8
Trousers (lake), New Bruns. 170/C1
Trout (mt.), Alberta 182/C1
Trout (riv.), Alberta 182/C1
Trout (creek), Ariz. 198/B3
Trout (lake), Colo. 208/E2
Trout (creek), Idaho 220/B1
Trout, La. 238/F2
Trout (lake), Minn. 255/F2
Trout (lake), Mich. 250/G2
Trout (lake), N.W. Terr. 162/D3
Trout (lake), N.W. Terr. 187/F3
Trout (lake), Ontario 177/F1
Trout (lake), Ontario 177/F1
Trout (creek), Ontario 177/E1
Trout (creek), Oreg. 291/F3
Trout (creek), Oreg. 291/J5
Trout (riv.), Sask. 181/L2
Trout (riv.), Vt. 268/B2
Trout, W. Va. 312/F6
Trout (lake), Wis. 317/G3
Trout Creek, Mich. 250/G2
Trout Creek, Mont. 262/A3
Trout Creek, Utah 304/A4
Troutdale, Maine 243/D5
Troutdale, Oreg. 291/E2
Trout Dale, Va. 307/F7
Trout Hall, Jamaica 158/J6
Trout Lake, Alberta 182/C1

Trout Lake, Br. Col. 184/J5
Trout Lake, Mich. 250/E2
Trout Lake, N.W. Terr. 187/F3
Trout Lake, Wash. 310/D5
Troutman, Georgia 217/C7
Troutman, N.C. 281/H3
Trout River, Newf. 166/C4
Trout Run, Pa. 294/H3
Troutville, Pa. 294/E3
Troutville, Va. 307/J6
Trowbridge, England 13/E6
Trowbridge, England 10/E5
Trowutta, Tasmania 99/B3
Troxelville, Pa. 294/H4
Troy, Ala. 195/G7
Troy, Idaho 220/B3
Troy, Ill. 222/B2
Troy, Ind. 227/D9
Troy, Iowa 229/J7
Troy, Kansas 232/G2
Troy, Maine 243/E6
Troy, Mich. 250/B6
Troy, Miss. 256/G2
Troy, Mo. 261/L5
Troy, Mont. 262/A2
Troy, N.H. 268/C6
Troy•, N.H. 268/C6
Troy, N.Y. 188/M2
Troy, N.Y. 276/N5
Troy, N.C. 281/K4
Troy, Nova Scotia 168/G3
Troy, Ohio 284/B5
Troy, Okla. 288/N6
Troy, Oreg. 291/K2
Troy, Pa. 294/J2
Troy, S.C. 296/C4
Troy, S. Dak. 298/R3
Troy, Tenn. 237/C8
Troy (Ilium) (ruins), Turkey 63/B6
Troy•, Vt. 268/C2
Troy, W. Va. 312/E4
Troyan, Bulgaria 45/G4
Troyes, France 7/E4
Troyes, France 28/F3
Troyes (lake), Québec 172/C2
Troy Grove, Ill. 222/E2
Troy Mills, Iowa 229/K4
Trstená, Czech. 41/E2
Trstenik, Yugoslavia 45/E4
Truandó (riv.), Colombia 126/B4
Truax, Sask. 181/G6
Trub, Switzerland 39/E3
Truba, Saudi Arabia 59/D3
Truc Giang, Vietnam 72/E5
Truchas, N. Mex. 274/D2
Truckee, Calif. 204/E4
Truckee (riv.), Calif. 204/F4
Truckee (riv.), Nev. 266/B3
Truckton, Colo. 208/L5
Truesdale, Iowa 229/C3
Truesdale, Mo. 261/K5
Trufant, Mich. 250/D5
Truganina, Victoria 97/H5
Trujillo, Honduras 154/E3
Trujillo, N. Mex. 274/F3
Trujillo, Peru 120/B3
Trujillo, Peru 128/B3
Trujillo, Spain 33/D3
Trujillo (creek), Texas 303/A2
Trujillo (state), Venezuela 124/C3
Trujillo, Venezuela 124/C2
Trujillo, Venezuela 124/C3
Trujillo Alto, P. Rico 161/E1
Truk (isls.), Micronesia 87/F5
Truman, Minn. 255/D7
Trumann, Ark. 202/J2
Trumansburg, N.Y. 276/G5
Trumbauersville, Pa. 294/M5
Trumbull (mt.), Ariz. 198/B2
Trumbull•, Conn. 210/C4
Trumbull (lake), Iowa 229/C2
Trumbull, Nebr. 264/F4
Trumbull (co.), Ohio 284/J3
Trün, Bulgaria 45/F4
Trun, Switzerland 39/G3
Trundle, N.S. Wales 97/D3
Trung Khanh Phu, Vietnam 72/E2
Truro, England 13/B7
Truro, England 10/D5
Truro, Iowa 229/F6
Truro•, Mass. 249/O5
Truro, N.S. 162/K6
Truro, Nova Scotia 168/G3
Truscott, Texas 303/E4
Truskmore (mt.), Ireland 17/E3
Trussville, Ala. 195/E3
Trustrup, Denmark 21/D5
Trutch, Br. Col. 184/F1
Truth or Consequences, N. Mex. 274/B5
Trutnov, Czech. 41/D1
Truxno, La. 238/F1
Truxton, Mo. 261/K4
Truxton, N.Y. 276/H5
Trwyn Cilan (prom.), Wales 13/C5
Tryon, Nebr. 264/C3
Tryon, N.C. 281/E4
Tryon, Okla. 288/N3
Tryonville, Pa. 294/C2
Trysil, Norway 18/H6
Trysilelv (riv.), Norway 18/H6
Trzcianka, Poland 47/C2
Trzebiatów, Poland 47/B1
Trzebinia-Siersza, Poland 47/C4
Tržič, Yugoslavia 45/B2
Tsagaannuur, Mongolia 77/C2
Tsagaan-Ovoo, Mongolia 77/H2
Tsagaan-Uul, Mongolia 77/F2
Tsaile, Ariz. 198/F2
Tsala Apopka (lake), Fla. 212/D3
Tsamkong (Zhanjiang), China 77/H7
Tsangchow (Cangzhou), China 77/J4
Tsau, Botswana 118/C4
Tsavo, Kenya 115/G4
Tsavo Nat'l Park, Kenya 115/G4
Tschida (lake), N. Dak. 282/G6

Tschierv, Switzerland 39/K3
Tschlin, Switzerland 39/K3
Tseelim (dry riv.), Israel 65/C5
Tselinograd, U.S.S.R. 54/J4
Tselinograd, U.S.S.R. 48/H4
Tsenhermandal, Mongolia 77/H2
Tses, Namibia 118/B5
Tsetseg, Mongolia 77/D3
Tsetserleg, Mongolia 77/F2
Tsetserleg, Mongolia 54/L5
Tshabong, Botswana 118/C5
Tshane, Botswana 118/C4
Tshela, Zaire 115/B4
Tshikapa, Zaire 115/D5
Tshofa, Zaire 115/D5
Tshuapa (riv.), Zaire 115/D4
Tsiáfajavona (mt.), Madagascar 102/G6
Tsiáfajavona (mt.), Madagascar 118/H3
Tsiaotso (Jiaozuo), China 77/H4
Tsihombe, Madagascar 118/H5
Tsil'ma (riv.), U.S.S.R. 52/H1
Tsimlyansk (res.), U.S.S.R. 7/J8
Tsimlyansk (res.), U.S.S.R. 52/F5
Tsimlyansk (res.), U.S.S.R. 48/E5
Tsin (dry riv.), Israel 65/D5
Tsinan (Jinan), China 77/J4
Tsinghai (Qinghai), China 77/E4
Tsingkiang (Qingjiang), China 77/J5
Tsingshih (Jinshi), China 77/H6
Tsingtao (Qingdao), China 77/K4
Tsining (Jining), Nei Monggol, China 77/H3
Tsining (Jining), Shandong, China 77/J4
Tsiribihina (riv.), Madagascar 118/G3
Tsiroanomandidy, Madagascar 118/H3
Tsitsihar (Qiqihar), China 77/K2
Tsivory, Madagascar 118/H4
Tskhinvali, U.S.S.R. 48/E5
Tskhinvali, U.S.S.R. 52/C5
Tsodilo Hill (mt.), Botswana 118/C3
Tsu, Japan 81/H6
Tsu (isls.), Japan 81/D6
Tsubame, Japan 81/J5
Tsuchiura, Japan 81/J5
Tsugaru (str.), Japan 81/K3
Tsumeb, Namibia 118/B3
Tsumeb, Namibia 102/D6
Tsunyi (Zunyi), China 77/G6
Tsuruga, Japan 81/G6
Tsurugi (mt.), Japan 81/G7
Tsuruoka, Japan 81/J4
Tsushima (str.), Japan 81/D7
Tsuyama, Japan 81/F6
Tuadook (lake), New Bruns. 170/D2
Tuakau, N. Zealand 100/E2
Tual, Indonesia 85/J7
Tualatin, Oreg. 291/A2
Tualatin (riv.), Oreg. 291/A2
Tuam, Ireland 10/B4
Tuam, Ireland 17/D4
Tuamotu (arch.), Fr. Polynesia 2/C6
Tuamotu (arch.), Fr. Poly. 87/M7
Tuapse, U.S.S.R. 52/E6
Tuatapere, N. Zealand 100/A7
Tuath, Loch (inlet), Scotland 15/B4
Tubac, Ariz. 198/E7
Tuba City, Ariz. 198/D2
Tubal, Wadi al (dry riv.), Iraq 66/B4
Tuban, Indonesia 85/K2
Tubarão, Brazil 120/E5
Tubarão, Brazil 132/D10
Tubarão, Brazil 132/G8
Tubas, West Bank 65/C3
Tubbataha (reefs), Philippines 85/G4
Tubbataha (reefs), Philippines 82/B6
Tubbercurry, Ireland 17/D3
Tubeke (Tubize), Belgium 27/E7
Tuberose, Sask. 181/C5
Tubigon, Philippines 82/D6
Tübingen, Germany 22/C4
Tubize, Belgium 27/E7
Tubmanburg, Liberia 106/B7
Tubuai (Austral) (isls.), Fr. Poly. 87/M8
Tubuai (isl.), Fr. Poly. 87/M8
Tuburan, Philippines 82/D5
Tucacas, Venezuela 124/D1
Tucannon (riv.), Wash. 310/G4
Tucano, Brazil 132/G5
Tucavaca, Bolivia 136/F6
Tucavaca (riv.), Bolivia 136/F6
Tuchola, Poland 47/C2
Tuckahoe (creek), Md. 245/P5
Tuckahoe, N.J. 273/D5
Tuckahoe (riv.), N.J. 273/D5
Tuckahoe, N.Y. 276/O7
Tucker, Ark. 202/G5
Tucker (co.), W. Va. 312/F4
Tuckerman, Ark. 202/H2
Tuckernuck (isl.), Mass. 249/N7
Tuckerton, N.J. 273/E4
Tucson, Ariz. 188/D4
Tucson, Ariz. 146/G6
Tucson, Ariz. 198/D6
Tucumán (prov.), Argentina 143/C2
Tucumcari, N. Mex. 188/F3
Tucumcari, N. Mex. 274/F3
Tucupido, Venezuela 124/F3
Tucupita, Venezuela 124/F2
Tucuruí, Brazil 132/D3
Tucuruí (res.), Brazil 120/E3
Tucuruí (res.), Brazil 132/D4
Tudela, Spain 33/F1
Tudela de Duero, Spain 33/D2
Tudor (lake), Québec 172/H1
Tudor, Alberta 182/D3
Tuena, N.S. Wales 97/E3
Tuffnell, Sask. 181/H4
Tufi, Papua N.G. 85/C7
Tuftonboro•, N.H. 268/E4
Tugaloo (riv.), Georgia 217/F1
Tugaloo (riv.), S.C. 296/A2
Tugaske, Sask. 181/E5
Tug Fork (riv.), Ky. 237/S5
Tug Fork (riv.), Va. 307/D5
Tug Fork (riv.), W. Va. 312/E7
Tuggerah (lake), N.S. Wales 97/F3
Tugidak (isl.), Alaska 196/G3

Tugnug (pt.), Philippines 82/E5
Tuguegarao, Philippines 85/G2
Tuguegarao, Philippines 82/C2
Tuichi (riv.), Bolivia 136/A4
Tujunga, Calif. 204/C10
Tuktoyaktuk, Canada 4/C16
Tuktoyaktuk, N.W.T. 162/C2
Tuktoyaktuk, N.W. Terr. 187/E3
Tukuhnikivatz (mt.), Utah 304/E5
Tukums, U.S.S.R. 53/B2
Tukums, U.S.S.R. 52/B3
Tukuran, Philippines 82/D7
Tukuyu, Tanzania 115/F5
Tukwila, Wash. 310/B2
Tula, Tamaulipas, Mexico 150/K5
Tula (riv.), Mexico 150/L1
Tula, Miss. 256/F2
Tula, U.S.S.R. 7/H3
Tula, U.S.S.R. 48/D4
Tula, U.S.S.R. 52/D3
Tula de Allende, Mexico 150/K6
Tulagi, Solomon Is. 86/E3
Tulak, Afghanistan 68/A2
Tulak, Afghanistan 59/H3
Tulalip, Wash. 310/C2
Tulalip Ind. Res., Wash. 310/C2
Tulameen, Br. Col. 184/G5
Tulancingo, Mexico 150/K7
Tulare (lake), Calif. 188/B3
Tulare (lake), Calif. 204/G7
Tulare, Calif. 204/F7
Tulare, S. Dak. 298/N4
Tularosa, N. Mex. 274/C5
Tularosa (valley), N. Mex. 274/C6
Tulcán, Ecuador 128/D2
Tulcea, Romania 45/J3
Tulcingo del Valle, Mexico 150/M2
Tule (lake), Calif. 204/D2
Tule (des.), Nev. 266/G5
Tule (lake), Wash. 310/G3
Tulelake, Calif. 204/D2
Tule River Ind. Res., Calif. 204/G7
Tuli, Zimbabwe 118/D4
Tulia, Texas 303/C3
Tulip, Ark. 202/E5
Tulip, Ind. 227/D6
Tulkarm, West Bank 65/C3
Tull, Ark. 202/E5
Tulla, Ireland 17/D6
Tullahan, Tasmania 99/B3
Tullahassee, Okla. 288/P3
Tullahoma, Tenn. 237/J10
Tullamore, Ireland 10/C4
Tullamore, Ireland 17/G5
Tullamore, N.S. Wales 97/D3
Tullaroan, Ireland 17/G6
Tullibee, France 28/D5
Tullibigeal, N.S. Wales 97/D3
Tullibody, Scotland 15/C1
Tulliby Lake, Alberta 182/E3
Tullis, Sask. 181/D4
Tulln, Austria 41/D2
Tullos, La. 238/F3
Tullow, Ireland 10/C4
Tullow, Ireland 17/H6
Tully, Mass. 249/E2
Tully, N.Y. 276/H5
Tully, Queensland 88/H3
Tully, Queensland 95/C3
Tully (falls), Queensland 95/C3
Tullytown, Pa. 294/N5
Tuloma (riv.), U.S.S.R. 52/D1
Tulot, Ark. 202/K2
Tulsa, Okla. 188/G3
Tulsa, Okla. 146/J6
Tulsa (co.), Okla. 288/P2
Tulsa, Okla. 288/O5
Tulsi (lake), India 68/B6
Tultepec, Mexico 150/L1
Tuluá, Colombia 126/B5
Tuluksak, Alaska 196/D2
Tulun, U.S.S.R. 54/M4
Tulun, U.S.S.R. 48/L4
Tulungagung, Indonesia 85/K2
Tuma (riv.), Nicaragua 154/E4
Tumacacori, Ariz. 198/E7
Tumacacori Nat'l Mon., Ariz. 198/E7
Tumaco, Colombia 120/B2
Tumaco, Colombia 126/A7
Tumaco, Rada de (bay), Colombia 126/A6
Tumalo, Oreg. 291/F3
Tumalo (creek), Oreg. 291/F3
Tumatumari, Guyana 131/J3
Tumba (lake), Zaire 115/C4
Tumbarumba, N.S. Wales 97/D4
Tumbes (riv.), Ecuador 128/B4
Tumbes (dept.), Peru 128/B4
Tumbes, Peru 120/A3
Tumbes, Peru 128/B4
Tumbes•, Peru 128/B4
Tumbong, N.S. Wales 97/E4
Tumby Bay, S. Australia 88/E6
Tumby Bay, S. Australia 94/E6
Tumd Youqi, China 77/H3
Tumd Zuoqi, China 77/H3
Tumen, China 77/M3
Tumen, China 54/O5
Tumen (riv.), China 77/N3
Tumen (riv.), N. Korea 81/D2
Tumeremo, Venezuela 124/H4
Tumereng, Guyana 131/H3
Tumindao (isl.), Philippines 82/B8
Tumkur, India 68/D6
Tummel (lake), Scotland 15/E4
Tummo (El War) (well), Niger 106/H6
Tump, Pakistan 68/A3
Tump, Pakistan 59/H4
Tumpat, Malaysia 72/D6
Tumtum (lake), Oreg. 291/J5

Tumtum, Wash. 310/H3
Tumu, Ghana 106/D6
Tumuc-Humac (mts.), Fr. Guiana 131/D3
Tumuc-Humac (mts.), Suriname 131/D4
Tumucumaque, Serra de (range), Brazil 132/C2
Tumupasa, Bolivia 136/B4
Tumusla, Bolivia 136/C7
Tumut, N.S. Wales 88/H7
Tumuţ, N.S. Wales 97/E4
Tumwater, Wash. 310/B3
Tun (Ferdows), Iran 66/K3
Tuna (pt.), P. Rico 161/E3
Tunahí, Sierra (mts.), Colombia 126/E7
Tunapuna, Trin. & Tob. 161/B10
Tunas, Mo. 261/F7
Tunas de Zaza, Cuba 158/E2
Tunas de Zaza, Cuba 156/B2
Tunbridge, N. Dak. 282/K3
Tunbridge•, Vt. 268/C4
Tunceli (prov.), Turkey 63/H3
Tunceli (Kalan), Turkey 63/H3
Tunduru, Tanzania 115/G6
Tundzha (riv.), Bulgaria 45/H4
Tungabhadra (riv.), India 68/D5
Tungchwan (Tongchuan), China 77/G5
Tunghwa (Tonghua), China 77/L3
Tungkiang (Tongjiang), China 77/M2
Tungliao (Tongliao), China 77/K3
Tungsten, N.W. Terr. 187/F3
Tungurahua (prov.), Ecuador 128/C3
Tunhwa (Dunhua), China 77/L3
Tuni, India 68/E5
Tunica, La. 238/G5
Tunica (co.), Miss. 256/D1
Tunica, Miss. 256/D1
Tunis, N.C. 281/R2
Tunis (cap.), Tunisia 102/D1
Tunis (cap.), Tunisia 106/G1
Tunis (cap.), Tunisia 2/K4
Tunis (gulf), Tunisia 106/G1
Tunisia 2/K4
Tunisia 102/C1
TUNISIA 106/F1
Tunis Mills, Md. 245/O5
Tunja, Colombia 120/B3
Tunja, Colombia 126/D5
Tunker, Ind. 227/F2
Tunkhannock, Pa. 294/L2
Tunki, Nicaragua 154/E4
Tunnack, Tasmania 99/D4
Tunnel, Alaska 196/H1
Tunnel City, Wis. 317/E7
Tunnel Hill, Georgia 217/C1
Tunnel Springs, Ala. 195/D7
Tunnelton, Ind. 227/E7
Tunnelton, W. Va. 312/G4
Tunnsjøen (lake), Norway 18/H4
Tunstall, Va. 307/O5
Tuntutuliak, Alaska 196/F2
Tununak, Alaska 196/D2
Tunungayualok (isl.), Newf. 166/B2
Tunuyán, Argentina 143/B3
Tunuyán (riv.), Argentina 143/C3
Tunxi (Tunki), China 77/J6
Tuolumne (co.), Calif. 204/F5
Tuolumne, Calif. 204/E6
Tuotuo He (riv.), China 77/D5
Tupã, Brazil 132/D8
Tupã, Brazil 135/A2
Tupambaé, Uruguay 145/E3
Tupanciretã, Brazil 132/C10
Tupelo, Ark. 202/H3
Tupelo, Miss. 256/G2
Tupelo, Okla. 288/O5
Tupelo Nat'l Battlefield, Miss. 256/G2
Tupi, Venezuela 124/F2
Tupiza, Bolivia 120/C5
Tupiza, Bolivia 136/C7
Tupman, Calif. 204/F8
Tupper, Br. Col. 184/G2
Tupper (lake), N.Y. 276/M2
Tupper (lake), Nova Scotia 168/D4
Tupper Lake, N.Y. 276/M2
Tuppers Plains, Ohio 284/G7
Tupungato, Cerro (mt.), Argentina 143/B3
Tupungato, Cerro (mt.), Chile 138/B9
Tuquan, China 77/K2
Túquerres, Colombia 126/B7
Tur, West Bank 65/C4
Tura, Hungary 41/E3
Tura, India 68/G3
Tura, U.S.S.R. 54/M3
Tura, U.S.S.R. 48/L3
Turaba, Saudi Arabia 59/D5
Turagua, Serranía (mts.), Venezuela 124/F4
Turakina, N. Zealand 100/E4
Turakirae (head), N. Zealand 100/B3
Turan, Iran 66/J2
Turan, Iran 66/K3
Tur'an, Israel 65/C2
Turan, U.S.S.R. 48/K4
Turangi, N. Zealand 100/E3
Turbaco, Colombia 126/B3
Turbat, Pakistan 59/H4
Turbat-i-Shaikh Jam, Iran 59/H2
Turbat-i-Shaikh Jam, Iran 66/H3
Turbenthal, Switzerland 39/G2
Turbeville, S.C. 296/G4
Turbeville, Va. 307/K7
Turbo, Colombia 126/B3
Turbotville, Pa. 294/J3
Turčianske Teplice, Czech. 41/E2
Turco, Bolivia 136/A6
Turda, Romania 45/G2
Tureia (atoll), Fr. Poly. 87/N8
Turek, Indonesia 85/K2
Turek, Poland 47/D2
Turén, Venezuela 124/D3
Turfan (Turpan), China 77/C3

Union 461

Turgay, U.S.S.R. 48/G5
Türgovishte, Bulgaria 45/H4
Turgutlu, Turkey 63/B3
Turhal, Turkey 63/F2
Türi, U.S.S.R. 53/C1
Turia (riv.), Spain 33/F3
Turiaçu, Brazil 132/E3
Turiaçu (riv.), Brazil 132/E3
Turiamo, Venezuela 124/E2
Turin, Alberta 182/D5
Turin, Georgia 217/C4
Turin, Iowa 229/B4
Turin (prov.), Italy 34/A2
Turin, Italy 34/A2
Turin, Italy 7/E4
Turin, N.Y. 276/K3
Turkana (lake), Ethiopia 111/G7
Turkana (lake), Kenya 102/F4
Turkana (lake), Kenya 115/G3
Türkeli, Turkey 63/F2
Turkestan, U.S.S.R. 48/G5
Túrkeve, Hungary 41/F3
Turkey 2/L4
Turkey 7/H5
Turkey 54/E6
TURKEY 59/B2
TURKEY 63/D3
Turkey (riv.), Iowa 229/K2
Turkey, Ky. 237/P6
Turkey, N.C. 281/N4
Turkey (creek), Okla. 288/L2
Turkey (creek), S.C. 296/E2
Turkey, Texas 303/D3
Turkey Creek, La. 238/F5
Turkey Creek (lake), La. 238/G3
Turkey Creek, W. Australia 92/E2
Turkey Point, Ontario 177/D5
Türkmen Dağı (mt.), Turkey 63/D3
Turkmen S.S.R., U.S.S.R. 54/G6
Turkmen S.S.R., U.S.S.R. 48/F6
Türkoğlu, Turkey 63/G4
Turks (isls.), Turks & Caicos 156/D2
Turks and Caicos (isls.) 146/L7
TURKS AND CAICOS ISLANDS 156/D2
Turks Island (passage), Turks & Caicos 156/D2
Turku, Finland 7/G2
Turku, Finland 18/N6
Turku ja Pori (prov.), Finland 18/N6
Turlock, Calif. 204/E6
Turmero, Venezuela 124/E2
Turnagain (riv.), Br. Col. 184/K2
Turnagain (cape), N. Zealand 100/F4
Turnagain Arm (inlet), Alaska 196/B1
Turnavik (isls.), Newf. 166/C2
Turnberry, Scotland 15/D5
Turneffe (isls.), Belize 154/D2
Turnen (mt.), Switzerland 39/D3
Turner, Ark. 202/H5
Turner (co.), Georgia 217/E7
Turner, Maine 243/C7
Turner•, Maine 243/C7
Turner, Mich. 250/F4
Turner, Mont. 262/H2
Turner, Oreg. 291/E3
Turner (co.), S. Dak. 298/P7
Turner, Wash. 310/H4
Turner Center, Maine 243/C7
Turner Hole (bay), Virgin Is. (U.S.) 161/G4
Turners, Mo. 261/F8
Turnersburg, N.C. 281/H3
Turners Falls, Mass. 249/D2
Turners Station, Ky. 237/L3
Turnersville, N.J. 273/C4
Turnersville, Texas 303/G6
Turner Valley, Alberta 182/C4
Turnerville, Wyo. 319/A3
Turney, Mo. 261/D3
Turnhout, Belgium 27/F6
Turnor Lake, Sask. 181/L3
Turnov, Czech. 41/C1
Turnu Măgurele, Romania 45/G4
Turon, Kansas 232/D4
Turpan (Turfan), China 77/C3
Turpan, China 54/L5
Turpin, Okla. 288/E1
Turquino (peak), Cuba 158/H4
Turrell, Ark. 202/K3
Turrialba, C. Rica 154/F6
Turriff, Scotland 10/E2
Turriff, Scotland 15/F3
Turtle (Penju) (isls.), Indonesia 85/H7
Turtle (mts.), Manitoba 179/B5
Turtle (riv.), Manitoba 179/C3
Turtle (lake), Mich. 250/F4
Turtle (lake), N. Dak. 282/H4
Turtle (mts.), N. Dak. 282/K2
Turtle (isls.), Philippines 82/B7
Turtle (lake), Sask. 181/C2
Turtle (creek), S. Dak. 298/M4
Turtle Creek, New Bruns. 170/F3
Turtle Creek, Pa. 294/C7
Turtle Creek, W. Va. 312/C6
Turtleford, Sask. 181/B2
Turtle Lake, N. Dak. 282/J4
Turtle Lake, Wis. 317/B5
Turtle Mountain Ind. Res., N. Dak. 282/L2
Turtle Mountain Prov. Park, Manitoba 179/B5
Turtlepoint, Pa. 294/F2
Turtle River, Minn. 255/D3
Turtletown, Tenn. 237/N10
Turtola, Finland 18/O3
Turton, England 13/H2
Turton, S. Dak. 298/N3
Turukhansk, U.S.S.R. 48/J3
Turvo (riv.), Brazil 135/B2
Turzovka, Czech. 41/E2
Tuscaloosa, Ala. 188/J4
Tuscaloosa (co.), Ala. 195/C4
Tuscaloosa, Ala. 195/C4
Tuscaloosa (lake), Ala. 195/D4
Tuscan (arch.), Italy 34/B3
Tuscany (reg.), Italy 34/C3
Tuscarawas (co.), Ohio 284/H5
Tuscarawas, Ohio 284/H5
Tuscarawas (riv.), Ohio 284/H5
Tuscarora, Nev. 266/E1
Tuscarora (mts.), Nev. 266/E1
Tuscarora (mt.), Pa. 294/G5
Tuscarora Ind. Res., N.Y. 276/B4
Tuscola, Ill. 222/E4
Tuscola (co.), Mich. 250/F5
Tuscola, Mich. 250/F5
Tuscola, Texas 303/E5
Tuscor, Mont. 262/A3
Tusculum, Georgia 217/K6
Tusculum, Tenn. 237/R8
Tuscumbia, Ala. 195/C1
Tuscumbia, Mo. 261/H6
Tushar (mts.), Utah 304/B5
Tushka, Okla. 288/O6
Tuskahoma, Okla. 288/R5
Tuskegee, Ala. 195/G6
Tuskegee Institute, Ala. 195/G6
Tuskegee Institute Nat'l Hist. Park, Ala. 195/G6
Tusket, Nova Scotia 168/C5
Tusket (isl.), Nova Scotia 168/B5
Tusket (riv.), Nova Scotia 168/C4
Tussy, Okla. 288/L6
Tustin, Calif. 204/D11
Tustin, Mich. 250/D4
Tustin, Wis. 317/J7
Tustumena (lake), Alaska 196/C1
Tutak, Turkey 63/K3
Tutamoe (range), N. Zealand 100/D1
Tutayev, U.S.S.R. 52/E3
Tuthill, S. Dak. 298/G7
Tuticorin, India 68/D7
Tutóia, Brazil 132/F3
Tutrakan, Bulgaria 45/H4
Tuttle, Idaho 220/D7
Tuttle, N. Dak. 282/L5
Tuttle, Okla. 288/L4
Tuttle Creek (lake), Kansas 232/F2
Tuttlingen, Germany 22/C5
Tutuila (isl.), Amer. Samoa 87/J7
Tutuila (isl.), Amer. Samoa 86/N9
Tutwiler, Miss. 256/D2
Tuun (mt.), N. Korea 81/C3
Tuvalu 2/T6
Tuvalu 87/H6
Tuvinian A.S.S.R., U.S.S.R. 48/K4
Tuwaiq, Jebel (range), Saudi Arabia 59/E5
Tuxedo, Md. 245/G5
Tuxedo Park, N.Y. 276/M8
Tuxford, Sask. 181/F5
Tuxpan, Nayarit, Mexico 150/G6
Tuxpan, Jalisco, Mexico 150/H7
Tuxpan de Rodríguez Cano, Mexico 150/L6
Tuxtepec, Mexico 150/L7
Tuxtla Gutiérrez, Mexico 146/J8
Tuxtla Gutiérrez, Mexico 150/N8
Túy, Spain 33/B1
Tuy (riv.), Venezuela 124/E2
Tuya (riv.), Br. Col. 184/K2
Tuyen Quang, Vietnam 72/E2
Tuy Hoa, Vietnam 72/F4
Tuymazy, U.S.S.R. 52/H4
Tuysarkan, Iran 66/F3
Tuyün (Duyun), China 77/G6
Tuz (lake), Turkey 63/E3
Tuz (lake), Turkey 59/B2
Tuzigoot Nat'l Mon., Ariz. 198/D4
Tuz Khurmatu, Iraq 66/D3
Tuzla, Yugoslavia 7/F4
Tuzla, Yugoslavia 45/D3
Tuzluca, Turkey 63/K3
Tuzlukçu, Turkey 63/D3
Tvedestrand, Norway 18/F7
Tver', U.S.S.R. 48/D4
Tver', U.S.S.R. 52/E3
Tversted, Denmark 21/D2
Twain, Calif. 204/D4
Twain Harte, Calif. 204/E6
Tway, Sask. 181/F3
Tweed (riv.), England 13/E2
Tweed, Ontario 177/G3
Tweed (riv.), Scotland 15/F5
Tweed (riv.), Scotland 10/E3
Tweed Heads, N.S. Wales 97/G1
Tweedie, Alberta 182/E2
Tweedside, New Bruns. 170/C3
Tweedsmuir, Sask. 181/F2
Tweedsmuir, Scotland 15/E5
Tweedsmuir Prov. Park, Br. Col. 184/D3
Twello, Netherlands 27/J4
Twelve Mile, Ind. 227/E3
Twelvemile (lake), Sask. 181/E6
Twelve Mile (creek), Utah 304/C2
Twelve Pins (mt.), Ireland 17/B4
Twelvepole (creek), W. Va. 312/A6
Twentynine Palms, Calif. 204/K9
Twentynine Palms Marine Base, Calif. 204/J9
Twig, Minn. 255/F4
Twiggs (co.), Georgia 217/F5
Twila, Ky. 237/P7
Twillingate, Newf. 166/C4
Twin (lakes), Conn. 210/B1
Twin (falls), Idaho 220/D7
Twin (lakes), Maine 243/F4
Twin (lakes), Wash. 310/G2
Twin Bridges, Mont. 262/D5
Twin Brooks, S. Dak. 298/R3
Twin City, Georgia 217/H5
Twin Falls (co.), Idaho 220/D7
Twin Falls, Idaho 220/D7
Twin Falls, Idaho 188/C2
Twin Falls, Idaho 146/G5
Twin Falls, Newf. 166/B3
Twin Hills, Alaska 196/F3
Twining, Mich. 250/F4
Twin Lake, Mich. 250/C5
Twin Lakes, Calif. 204/K4
Twin Lakes, Colo. 208/G4
Twin Lakes (res.), Colo. 208/G4
Twin Lakes, Minn. 255/E7
Twin Lakes, Wis. 317/K11
Twin Mountain, N.H. 268/D3
Twin Oaks, Mo. 261/N3
Twin Peaks, Calif. 204/H9
Twin Peaks (mt.), Idaho 220/D5
Twin Rocks, Oreg. 291/C2
Twin Rocks, Pa. 294/E4
Twinsburg, Ohio 284/J10
Twin Sisters (mt.), Wash. 310/D2
Twin Valley, Minn. 255/B3
Twisp, Wash. 310/E2
Twisp (pass), Wash. 310/E2
Twisp (riv.), Wash. 310/E2
Twitchell (res.), Calif. 204/E9
Two Arm (bay), Alaska 196/C2
Two Butte (creek), Colo. 208/N7
Two Buttes, Colo. 208/P7
Two Buttes (res.), Colo. 208/O7
Twodot, Mont. 262/F4
Twofold (bay), N.S. Wales 97/F5
Two Harbors, Minn. 255/G3
Two Hearted (riv.), Mich. 250/D2
Two Hills, Alberta 182/E3
Two Rivers (riv.), Minn. 255/A1
Two Rivers (res.), N. Mex. 274/E5
Two Rivers, Wis. 317/M7
Two Water (creek), Utah 304/E4
Twynholm, Scotland 15/D6
Tyaskin, Md. 245/P7
Tybee Island, Georgia 217/L6
Tybee Roads (chan.), S.C. 296/F7
Tychy, Poland 47/B4
Tye, Texas 303/E5
Tye River, Va. 307/L5
Tygart (lake), W. Va. 312/G4
Tygart Valley (riv.), W. Va. 312/F5
Tyger (riv.), S.C. 296/D2
Tygh Valley, Oreg. 291/F2
Tyler, Ala. 195/E6
Tyler (lake), Conn. 210/B1
Tyler, Minn. 255/B6
Tyler, Mo. 261/N10
Tyler, N. Dak. 282/S7
Tyler, Pa. 294/F3
Tyler (co.), Texas 303/K7
Tyler, Texas 188/H4
Tyler, Texas 303/J5
Tyler, Wash. 310/H3
Tyler (co.), W. Va. 312/E4
Tylersburg, Pa. 294/D3
Tylersville, Pa. 294/G4
Tylertown, Miss. 256/D8
Tylerville, Conn. 210/F3
Tym (riv.), U.S.S.R. 48/J3
Tymovskoye, U.S.S.R. 48/P4
Týn, Czech. 41/C2
Tynagh, Ireland 17/E5
Tynan, Texas 303/G9
Tynda, U.S.S.R. 48/N4
Tyndall, Manitoba 179/F4
Tyndall, S. Dak. 298/O8
Tyndall A.F.B., Fla. 212/C6
Tyndrum, Scotland 15/D4
Tyne (riv.), England 13/F3
Tyne (riv.), England 10/F3
Tyne (riv.), Scotland 15/F5
Tyne and Wear (co.), England 13/H3
Tynemouth, England 13/J3
Tynemouth, England 10/F3
Tyner, Ind. 227/E2
Tyner, Ky. 237/O6
Tyner, N.C. 281/R2
Tyner, Sask. 181/C4
Tyne Valley, Pr. Edward I. 168/E2
Tyngsboro•, Mass. 249/J2
Tynset, Norway 18/G5
Tyntynder South, Victoria 97/B4
Tyonek, Alaska 196/B1
Tyra (cays), Nicaragua 154/F4
Tyre (Sur), Lebanon 63/F6
Tyrifjord (lake), Norway 18/C3
Tyringham•, Mass. 249/A4
Tyrnyauz, U.S.S.R. 52/F6
Tyro, Kansas 232/G4
Tyro, Miss. 256/E1
Tyro, Va. 307/K5
Tyrol (Tirol) (prov.), Austria 41/A3
Tyrone, Colo. 208/L8
Tyrone, Georgia 217/C4
Tyrone, Ky. 237/M4
Tyrone, Mo. 261/J8
Tyrone, N. Mex. 274/A6
Tyrone, Okla. 288/D1
Tyrone, Pa. 294/F4
Tyronza, Ark. 202/K3
Tyronza (riv.), Ark. 202/K2
Tyrrell (co.), N.C. 281/S3
Tyrrell (lake), Victoria 97/B4
Tyrrellspass, Ireland 17/G5
Tyrrhenian (sea) 7/F4
Tyrrhenian (sea), Italy 34/C4
Tysnes, Norway 18/D6
Tyson, Vt. 268/B5
Tyson Wash (dry riv.), Ariz. 198/A5
Ty Ty, Georgia 217/E8
Tyumen, U.S.S.R. 54/H4
Tyumen', U.S.S.R. 48/G4
Tyung (riv.), U.S.S.R. 48/M3
Tyvan, Sask. 181/H5
Tywyn, Wales 13/C5
Tywyn, Wales 10/D4
Tzaneen, S. Africa 118/E4
Tzekung (Zigong), China 77/F6
Tzepo (Zibo), China 77/J4
Tzucabab, Mexico 150/P7

U

Uahuka, Fr. Poly. 87/N6
Uanda, Queensland 95/C4
Uanle Uen, Somalia 115/H3
Uanle Uen, Somalia 102/G4
Uapou (isl.), Fr. Poly. 87/M6
Uatumã (riv.), Brazil 132/B3
Uaupés (riv.), Brazil 132/G9
Ub, Yugoslavia 45/E3
Ubá, Brazil 135/E2
Ubá, Brazil 132/F8
Übach-Palenberg, Germany 22/B3
Ubaíra, Brazil 132/G6
Ubaitaba, Brazil 132/G6
Ubaiyidh, Wadi (dry riv.), Iraq 66/B5
Ubangi (riv.) 102/D4
Ubangi (riv.), Cent. Afr. Rep. 115/C3
Ubangi (riv.), Congo 115/C3
Ubangi (riv.), Zaire 115/C3
Ubari, Libya 102/D2
Ubari, Libya 111/B2
Ubaté, Colombia 126/D5
Ubatuba, Brazil 135/D3
Ubay, Philippines 82/E5
Ube, Japan 81/E6
Úbeda, Spain 33/E3
Uberaba (lag.), Bolivia 136/G5
Uberaba, Brazil 120/E4
Uberaba, Brazil 132/D7
Uberaba, Brazil 135/C1
Uberlândia, Brazil 120/E4
Uberlândia, Brazil 132/E7
Überlingen, Germany 22/C5
Ubina, Bolivia 136/B7
Ubinas, Peru 128/G11
Ubly, Mich. 250/G5
Ubombo, S. Africa 118/E5
Ubon, Thailand 54/M8
Ubon, Thailand 72/E4
Ubrique, Spain 33/D4
Ubundu, Zaire 115/E4
Ucayali (dept.), Peru 128/E6
Ucayali (riv.), Peru 2/F6
Ucayali (riv.), Peru 120/B3
Ucayali (riv.), Peru 128/F5
Uccle, Belgium 27/B9
Uch, Pakistan 68/B3
Uchaly, U.S.S.R. 7/K3
Uchaly, U.S.S.R. 52/J4
Ucharonidge, North. Terr. 93/D4
Uchee, Ala. 195/H6
Uchiura (bay), Japan 81/K2
Uchiza, Peru 128/D7
Uch Turfan (Wushi), China 77/A3
Uckange, France 28/G3
Ücker (riv.), Germany 22/E2
Uckfield (forests), England 10/G5
Uckfield, England 13/H7
Ucluelet, Br. Col. 184/E6
Ucon, Idaho 220/F6
Ucross, Wyo. 319/F1
Ucumasi, Bolivia 136/B6
Uda (riv.), U.S.S.R. 48/O4
Udaipur, India 68/C4
Udall, Kansas 232/E4
Udaypur, India 54/J7
Uddevalla, Sweden 18/G7
Uddingston, Scotland 15/B2
Uddjaur (lake), Sweden 18/L4
Udell, Iowa 229/H7
Uden, Netherlands 27/H5
Udhampur, India 68/D2
Udine (prov.), Italy 34/D1
Udine, Italy 34/D2
Udine, Italy 7/F4
Udipi, India 68/C6
Udmurt A.S.S.R., U.S.S.R. 48/F4
Udmurt A.S.S.R., U.S.S.R. 52/H3
Udon Thani, Thailand 54/M8
Udon Thani, Thailand 72/D3
Udora, Ontario 177/E3
Ueckermünde, Germany 22/F2
Ueda, Japan 81/J5
Uehling, Nebr. 264/H3
Uele (riv.) 102/E4
Uele (riv.), Zaire 115/E3
Uelen, U.S.S.R. 54/V3
Uelen, U.S.S.R. 4/C18
Uelen, U.S.S.R. 48/T3
Uelzen, Germany 22/D2
Uen (isl.), New Caled. 86/H5
Uetendorf, Switzerland 39/E3
Uetersen, Germany 22/C2
Ufa, U.S.S.R. 2/M3
Ufa, U.S.S.R. 7/K3
Ufa, U.S.S.R. 48/F4
Ufa, U.S.S.R. 52/J4
Ufa (riv.), U.S.S.R. 52/J3
Ugab (riv.), Namibia 118/A4
Uganda 2/L5
Uganda 102/F4
UGANDA 115/F3
Ugashik, Alaska 196/G3
Ugashik (lakes), Alaska 196/G3
Ugie (riv.), Scotland 15/G3
Ugíjar, Spain 33/E4
Ugjoktok (bay), Newf. 166/B2
Uglegorsk, U.S.S.R. 48/P5
Uglich, U.S.S.R. 52/E3
Ugo, Japan 81/K4
Ugod, Hungary 41/D3
Uherské Hradiště, Czech. 41/D2
Uherský Brod, Czech. 41/D2
Uhlava (riv.), Czech. 41/B2
Uhlířské Janovice, Czech. 41/C2
Uhrichsville, Ohio 284/H5
Uig, Scotland 10/C2
Uig, Highland, Scotland 15/B3
Uig, W. Isles, Scotland 15/A2
Uige (prov.), Angola 115/B5
Uige, Angola 115/C5
Uiju, N. Korea 81/B3
Uinkaret (plat.), Ariz. 198/B2
Uinta (mts.), Utah 304/D3
Uinta (riv.), Utah 304/D3
Uinta (co.), Wyo. 319/B4
Uintah (co.), Utah 304/E3
Uintah, Utah 304/C2
Uintah and Ouray Ind. Res., Utah 304/D3
Uisŏng, S. Korea 81/D5
Uitenhage, S. Africa 102/E8
Uitenhage, S. Africa 118/C6
Uithoorn, Netherlands 27/F4
Uithuizen, Netherlands 27/K2
Uitkijk, Suriname 131/D3
Uivak (cape), Newf. 166/B2
Ujelang (atoll), Marshall Is. 87/F5
Újfehértó, Hungary 41/F3
Uji, Honduras 154/F3
Uji, Japan 81/J7
Ujjain, India 68/D4
Ujiji (Kigoma-Ujiji), Tanzania 115/E4
Újpest, Hungary 41/E3
Újszász, Hungary 41/F2
Ujung Pandang, Indonesia 54/N10
Ujung Pandang, Indonesia 85/F7
Ukasiksalik (isl.), Newf. 166/B2
Ukhta, U.S.S.R. 48/F3
Ukiah, Calif. 204/B4
Ukiah, Oreg. 291/J2
Ukkel (Uccle), Belgium 27/B9
Ukmergė, U.S.S.R. 53/C3
Ukmergė, U.S.S.R. 52/C3
Ukrainian S.S.R., U.S.S.R. 7/G4
Ukrainian S.S.R., U.S.S.R. 48/C5
Ukrainian S.S.R., U.S.S.R. 52/D5
Uku, Angola 115/B6
Ula, Turkey 63/C4
Ulaanbaatar (Ulan Bator) (cap.), Mongolia 77/G2
Ulaanbaatar (cap.), Mongolia 54/M5
Ulaanbaatar (cap.), Mongolia 2/Q3
Ulaangom (Ulangom), Mongolia 77/D2
Ulaangom, Mongolia 54/L5
Ulah, N.C. 281/K3
Ulak (isl.), Alaska 196/K4
Ulan, China 77/E4
Ulanhot (Horquin Youyi Qianqi), China 77/K2
Ulan-Ude, U.S.S.R. 54/M4
Ulan-Ude, U.S.S.R. 2/Q3
Ulan-Ude, U.S.S.R. 48/L4
Ulapes, Argentina 143/C3
Ulaş, Turkey 63/G3
Ulchin, S. Korea 81/D5
Ulcinj, Yugoslavia 45/D5
Uldum, Denmark 21/C6
Ulegei (Ulgiy), Mongolia 77/C2
Ulen, Ind. 227/E4
Ulen, Minn. 255/B3
Uler, W. Va. 312/D5
Ulfborg, Denmark 21/B5
Ulhasnagar, India 68/C5
Uliastay (Jibhalanta), Mongolia 77/E2
Uliastay, Mongolia 54/L5
Ulindi (riv.), Zaire 115/E4
Ulithi (atoll), Micronesia 87/D4
Ulla (riv.), Spain 33/B1
Ulladulla, N.S. Wales 97/F4
Ullapool, Scotland 10/D2
Ullapool, Scotland 15/C3
Ulla Ulla, Bolivia 136/A4
Ulldecona, Spain 33/G2
Ullensvang, Norway 18/E6
Ullin, Ill. 222/D6
Ulloma, Bolivia 136/A5
Ullŭng (isl.), S. Korea 81/E5
Ulm, Ark. 202/H4
Ulm, Mont. 262/E3
Ulm, Germany 22/C4
Ulm, Wyo. 319/F1
Ulman, Mo. 261/H6
Ulmarra, N.S. Wales 97/G1
Ulmer, Iowa 229/D4
Ulmer, S.C. 296/E5
Ulongue, Mozambique 118/E2
Ulricehamn, Sweden 18/H8
Ulrichen, Switzerland 39/F3
Ulriksfors, Sweden 18/K5
Ulrum, Netherlands 27/J2
Ulsan, S. Korea 81/D6
Ulster (part) (trad. prov.), Ireland 17/G2
Ulster (co.), N.Y. 276/M7
Ulster (part) (trad. prov.), N. Ireland 17/G2
Ulster, Pa. 294/J2
Ulster Spring, Jamaica 158/H6
Ultima Esperanza (sound), Chile 138/E9
Ulúa (riv.), Honduras 154/D3
Ulubat (lake), Turkey 63/C2
Ulubey, Turkey 63/C3
Uluborlu, Turkey 63/D3
Uludağ (mt.), Turkey 63/C3
Uludere, Turkey 63/K4
Ulugan (bay), Philippines 82/B5
Ulughchat (Wuqia), China 77/A4
Ulukışla, Turkey 63/F4
Ulumalu, Hawaii 218/K2
Ulu Muztag (mt.), China 77/C4
Ulundi, S. Africa 118/E5
Ulungur He (riv.), China 77/C2
Ulungur Hu (lake), China 77/C2
Ulupalakua, Hawaii 218/J2
Uluru (Ayers Rock) (mt.), North. Terr. 88/E5
Uluru Nat'l Park, North. Terr. 88/E5
Uluru Nat'l Park, North. Terr. 93/B8
Ulus, Turkey 63/E2
Ulutau (mts.), U.S.S.R. 48/G5
Ulu Tiram, Malaysia 72/F5
Ulva (isl.), Scotland 15/B4
Ulverston, England 13/D3
Ulverston, England 10/E3
Ulverstone, Tasmania 99/C3
Ulvik, Norway 18/E6
Ulvila, Finland 18/N6
Ul'yanovsk, U.S.S.R. 7/J3
Ul'yanovsk, U.S.S.R. 48/E4
Ul'yanovsk, U.S.S.R. 52/G4
Ulysses, Kansas 232/A4
Ulysses, Ky. 237/R5
Ulysses, Nebr. 264/G3
Ulysses, Pa. 294/G2
Umag, Yugoslavia 45/A3
Umala, Bolivia 136/B5
Umán, Mexico 150/P6
Uman', U.S.S.R. 52/D5
Umanun (pt.), Philippines 82/F6
Umapine, Oreg. 291/J2
Umarkot, Pakistan 59/J4
Umatilla, Fla. 212/E3
Umatilla (co.), Oreg. 291/J2
Umatilla, Oreg. 291/H2
Umatilla (lake), Oreg. 291/G2
Umatilla (riv.), Oreg. 291/H2
Umatilla (lake), Wash. 310/E5
Umatilla Army Depot, Oreg. 291/H2
Umatilla Ind. Res., Oreg. 291/J2
Umba, U.S.S.R. 52/D1
Umbagog (lake), Maine 243/A6
Umbagog (lake), N.H. 268/E2
Umbakumba, North. Terr. 93/E3
Umbarger, Texas 303/B3
Umbeara, North. Terr. 93/C8
Umbertide, Italy 34/D3
Umboi (isl.), Papua N.G. 86/A2
Umbrail (peak), Switzerland 39/K3
Umbría, Colombia 126/B7
Umbria (reg.), Italy 34/D3
Umcalcus (lake), Maine 243/G3
Ume (riv.), Sweden 7/F2
Umeå, Sweden 7/F2
Umeå, Sweden 18/M5
Umeälv (riv.), Sweden 18/L4
Umiakovik (lake), Newf. 166/B2
Umiat, Alaska 196/H1
Umikoa, Hawaii 218/H4
Umingmatok, N.W.T. 187/H3
Um Jauza, Jordan 65/D3
Umm al Qaiwain, U.A.E. 59/G4
Umm el Abid, Libya 111/C2
Umm el Fahm, Israel 65/C2
Umm Hajar, Ethiopia 111/G5
Umm Keddada, Sudan 111/E5
Umm Lajj, Saudi Arabia 59/C4
Umm Qasr, Iraq 66/E5
Umm Ruwaba, Sudan 111/F5
Umm Ruwaba, Sudan 102/F3
Umm Ruwaba, Sudan 59/B7
Umm Sa'id, Qatar 59/F5
Umnak (isl.), Alaska 196/E4
Umnak (passage), Alaska 196/E4
Umnak (isl.), U.S. 4/D18
Umpire, Ark. 202/B5
Umpqua, Oreg. 291/D4
Umpqua (riv.), Oreg. 291/D4
Umrer, India 68/D4
Umsaskis (lake), Maine 243/E2
Umtata, S. Africa 118/D6
Umtata (cap.), Transkei, S. Africa 102/E8
Umurbey, Turkey 63/C6
Umvukwe (range), Zimbabwe 118/E3
Umzimbuvu, S. Africa 118/D6
Umzinto, S. Africa 118/E6
Una (mt.), N. Zealand 100/D5
Una (riv.), Yugoslavia 45/C3
Unadilla, Georgia 217/E6
Unadilla, Nebr. 264/H4
Unadilla, N.Y. 276/K6
Unadilla (riv.), N.Y. 276/K5
Unaí, Brazil 132/E7
Unaka, N.C. 281/A4
Unaka (mts.), N.C. 281/E2
Unaka (mts.), Tenn. 237/S8
Unalakleet, Alaska 196/G2
Unalakleet, Alaska 188/C5
Unalaska, Alaska 188/C6
Unalaska, Alaska 196/E4
Unalaska (isl.), Alaska 196/E4
Unalaska (isl.), U.S. 4/D18
Unare (riv.), Venezuela 124/F3
Un Azaou (well), Niger 106/F4
Uncastillo, Spain 33/F1
Uncasville, Conn. 210/G3
Uncertain, Texas 303/K5
Uncía, Bolivia 136/B6
Uncompahgre (peak), Colo. 208/E6
Uncompahgre (plat.), Colo. 208/B5
Uncompahgre (riv.), Colo. 208/D5
Underbool, Victoria 97/A4
Underhill, Manitoba 179/B5
Underhill•, Vt. 268/B2
Underhill, Wis. 317/K6
Underhill Center, Vt. 268/B2
Underwood, Ind. 227/F7
Underwood, Iowa 229/B6
Underwood, Minn. 255/C4
Underwood, N. Dak. 282/H5
Underwood, Ontario 177/C3
Underwood, Wash. 310/D5
Undu (pt.), Fiji 86/R10
Undzha (riv.), U.S.S.R. 52/F3
Unecha, U.S.S.R. 52/D4
Uneeda, W. Va. 312/C6
Unga (isl.), Alaska 196/F3
Ungalik, Alaska 196/F2
Ungarie, N.S. Wales 97/D3
Ungava (bay), Canada 146/M4
Ungava (bay), N.W.T. 162/K4
Ungava (bay), N.W. Terr. 187/M4
Ungava (bay), Québec 174/F1
Ungava (pen.), Que. 146/L3
Ungava (pen.), Que. 162/J3
Ungava (pen.), Que. 174/E1
Ungeny, U.S.S.R. 52/C5
Unger, W. Va. 312/K4
Unggi, N. Korea 81/E2
União, Brazil 132/F4
União da Vitória, Brazil 132/D9
União dos Palmares, Brazil 132/H5
Unicoi (mts.), N.C. 281/A4
Unicoi (co.), Tenn. 237/S8
Unicoi, Tenn. 237/S8
Unicoi (mts.), Tenn. 237/N10
Uničov, Czech. 41/D2
Unimak (bight), Alaska 196/F4
Unimak (isl.), Alaska 188/C6
Unimak (isl.), Alaska 196/E4
Unimak (passage), Alaska 196/F4
Unimak (isl.), U.S. 4/D18
Unini, Peru 128/F8
Union, Ala. 195/C5
Union (mt.), Ariz. 198/C4
Union (co.), Ark. 202/E7
Union, Ark. 202/G1
Union•, Conn. 210/G1
Union (co.), Fla. 212/D1
Union (co.), Georgia 217/E1
Union, Grenada 161/D8
Union (co.), Ill. 222/D6

Union, Ill. 222/E1
Union (co.), Ind. 227/H5
Union (co.), Iowa 229/E7
Union, Iowa 229/G4
Union (co.), Ky. 237/F5
Union, Ky. 237/M3
Union (par.), La. 238/F1
Union, La. 238/L3
Union, Maine 243/E7
Union•, Maine 243/E7
Union, West Branch (riv.), Maine 243/G6
Union (co.), Miss. 256/F2
Union, Miss. 256/F5
Union, Mo. 261/L6
Union, Nebr. 264/J4
Union, N.H. 268/E5
Union (co.), N.J. 273/E2
Union•, N.J. 273/A2
Union (co.), N. Mex. 274/F2
Union (co.), N.C. 281/H4
Union, N. Dak. 282/D2
Union (co.), Ohio 284/D5
Union, Ohio 284/B6
Union, Ontario 177/C5
Union (co.), Oreg. 291/J2
Union, Oreg. 291/K2
Unión, Paraguay 144/D4
Union (co.), Pa. 294/K2
Union (isl.), St. Vin. & Grens. 156/G4
Union (co.), S.C. 296/D2
Union, S.C. 296/D2
Union (co.), S. Dak. 298/R8
Union (co.), Tenn. 237/O8
Union, Uruguay 145/B7
Union, Wash. 310/B3
Union (lake), Wash. 310/B2
Union, W. Va. 312/E7
Union Bay, Br. Col. 184/H2
Union Beach, N.J. 273/E3
Union Bridge, Md. 245/K2
Union Center, S. Dak. 298/D4
Union Center, Wis. 317/F8
Union Church, Miss. 256/C7
Union City, Calif. 204/K2
Union City, Conn. 210/C2
Union City, Georgia 217/J2
Union City, Ind. 227/H4
Union City, Mich. 250/D6
Union City, N.J. 273/C2
Union City, Ohio 284/A5
Union City, Okla. 288/L4
Union City, Pa. 294/C2
Union City, Tenn. 237/C8
Union Creek, Oreg. 291/E5
Uniondale, Ind. 227/G3
Uniondale, N.Y. 276/R7
Union Dale, Pa. 294/M2
Unión de Reyes, Cuba 158/C1
Unión de Tula, Mexico 150/G7
Union Furnace, Ohio 284/F7
Union Gap, Wash. 310/E4
Union Grove, Ala. 195/E2
Union Grove, N.C. 281/H2
Union Grove, Wis. 317/L3
Union Hall, Va. 307/J6
Unión Hidalgo, Mexico 150/M8
Union Hill, Ill. 222/E2
Union Hill, N.Y. 276/F4
Union Level, Va. 307/M7
Union Mills, Ind. 227/D2
Union Mills, Md. 245/K2
Union Mills, N.C. 281/F3
Union of Soviet Socialist Republics 2/L2
Union of Soviet Socialist Republics 4/C2
Union of Soviet Socialist Republics 7/H2
Union of Soviet Socialist Republics 54/L3
Union of Soviet Socialist Republics 48
Union of Soviet Socialist Republics 52
Union Pier, Mich. 250/C7
Union Point, Georgia 217/F3
Unionport, Ind. 227/G4
Unionport, Ohio 284/J5
Union Springs, Ala. 195/G6
Union Springs, N.Y. 276/G5
Union Star, Ky. 237/H5
Union Star, Mo. 261/C2
Uniontown, Ala. 195/D6
Uniontown, Ark. 202/B2
Uniontown, Ind. 227/D8
Uniontown, Kansas 232/G4
Uniontown, Ky. 237/F5
Uniontown, Md. 245/K2
Uniontown, Mo. 261/N7
Uniontown, Ohio 284/H4
Uniontown, Pa. 294/C6
Uniontown, Wash. 310/H4
Union Village, Vt. 268/C4
Unionville, Conn. 210/D1
Unionville, Georgia 217/F8
Unionville, Ill. 222/E6
Unionville, Ind. 227/E6
Unionville, Iowa 229/H7
Unionville, Maine 243/H6
Unionville, Md. 245/K3
Unionville, Mich. 250/F5
Unionville, Mo. 261/G2
Unionville, Nev. 266/C2
Unionville, N.C. 281/J4
Unionville, Ohio 284/D2
Unionville (Fleming), Pa. 294/G4
Unionville, Tenn. 237/H9
Unionville, Va. 307/N4
Unionville Center, Ohio 284/D5
Uniopolis, Ohio 284/B4
United, Pa. 294/D5
United Arab Emirates 2/M4
United Arab Emirates 54/G7
UNITED ARAB EMIRATES 59/F5
United Kingdom 2/J3
United Kingdom 7/D3

UNITED KINGDOM 10
United States 2/D4
United States 146/H5
United States 4/C17
UNITED STATES 188
U.S. Capitol, D.C. 245/F5
U.S. Nav. Air Sta., Virgin Is. (U.S.) 161/A4
U.S. Naval Base, Va. 307/R7
U.S.S. Arizona Memorial, Hawaii 218/B3
Unity•, Maine 243/E6
Unity, Md. 245/K4
Unity•, N.H. 268/C5
Unity, Ohio 284/J4
Unity, Oreg. 291/J3
Unity, Sask. 181/B3
Unity, Wis. 317/F6
Unity Village, Mo. 261/R6
Unityville, Pa. 294/K3
Unityville, S. Dak. 298/P6
Universal, Ind. 227/C5
Universal City, Texas 303/K10
University, Fla. 212/C2
University, N.C. 281/L2
University City, Mo. 261/P3
University City, Mo. 188/H3
University Heights, Iowa 229/K5
University Heights, Ohio 284/H9
University Park, Iowa 229/K6
University Park, Md. 245/F4
University Park, N. Mex. 274/C6
University Park, Texas 303/G2
Unley, S. Australia 88/D8
Unley, S. Australia 94/B8
Unnao, India 68/E3
Uno, Manitoba 179/B4
Unsan, N. Korea 81/C4
Unst (isl.), Scotland 15/G2
Unst (isl.), Scotland 10/H1
Unstrut (riv.), Germany 22/D3
Unterägeri, Switzerland 39/G2
Unteriberg, Switzerland 39/G3
Unterkulm, Switzerland 39/F2
Untermann (mt.), Utah 304/E3
Untersee (lake), Switzerland 39/H1
Unterseen, Switzerland 39/E3
Untervaz, Switzerland 39/H3
Unterwalden (reg.), Switzerland 39/F3
Unuk (riv.), Alaska 196/N2
Unuk (riv.), Br. Col. 184/B2
Ünye, Turkey 59/C1
Ünye, Turkey 63/G2
Unzen (vol.), Japan 81/D7
Unzen-Amakusa National Park, Japan 81/D7
Uozu, Japan 81/H5
Upalco, Utah 304/D3
Upata, Venezuela 124/G3
Upemba (lake), Zaire 115/E5
Upemba Nat'l Park, Zaire 115/E5
Upernavik, Greenl. 4/B12
Uphall, Scotland 15/C1
Upham, New Bruns. 170/E3
Upham, N. Dak. 282/J2
Upía (riv.), Colombia 126/D5
Upice, Czech. 41/C1
Upington, S. Africa 102/E7
Upington, S. Africa 118/C5
Upland, Calif. 204/E10
Upland, Ind. 227/F4
Upland, Kansas 232/E2
Upland, Nebr. 264/F4
Upland, Pa. 294/L7
Upolu (pt.), Hawaii 218/G3
Upolu (isl.), W. Samoa 87/J7
Upolu (isl.), W. Samoa 86/M8
Upper Alkali (lake), Calif. 204/E2
Upper Amherst Cove, Newf. 166/D2
Upper Ammonoosuc (riv.), N.H. 268/E2
Upper Arlington, Ohio 284/D4
Upper Arrow (lake), Br. Col. 184/H5
Upper Austria (prov.), Austria 41/B2
Upper Black Eddy, Pa. 294/N4
Upper Blackville, New Bruns. 170/E2
Upper Buctouche, New Bruns. 170/F2
Upper Chateaugay (lake), N.Y. 276/M1
Upperco, Md. 245/L2
Upper Dam, Maine 243/B6
Upper Darby•, Pa. 294/M6
Upper Des Lacs (lake), N. Dak. 282/F2
Upper Engadine (valley), Switzerland 39/J4
Upper Fairmount, Md. 245/P8
Upper Falls, Md. 245/N3
Upper Fraser, Br. Col. 184/G3
Upper Frenchville, Maine 243/G1
Upper Gagetown, New Bruns. 170/D3
Upper Glade, W. Va. 312/F6
Upper Greenwood Lake, N.J. 273/E1
Upper Hainesville, New Bruns. 170/C2
Upper Horton, N.S. Wales 97/F2
Upper Hutt, N. Zealand 100/D2
Upper Iowa (riv.), Iowa 229/K2
Upper Island Cove, Newf. 166/D2
Upper Jay, N.Y. 276/N2
Upper Kennetcook, Nova Scotia 168/E3
Upper Kent, New Bruns. 170/C2
Upper Klamath (lake), Oreg. 188/B2
Upper Klamath (lake), Oreg. 291/E5
Upper Lake, Calif. 204/C4
Upper Liard, Yukon 187/F3
Upper Lough Erne (lake), N. Ireland 17/F3
Upper Lough Erne (lake), N. Ireland 10/C3
Upper Macopin, N.J. 273/E1
Upper Manzanilla, Trin. & Tob. 161/B10
Upper Marlboro, Md. 245/M5
Upper Matecumbe (key), Fla. 212/F7
Upper Maugerville, New Bruns. 170/D3
Upper Mills, New Bruns. 170/C3
Upper Musquodoboit, Nova Scotia 168/F3
Upper New York (bay), N.J. 273/E2
Upper Nile (prov.), Sudan 111/F6
Upper Rawdon, Nova Scotia 168/E3

Upper Red (lake), 255/D2
Upper Red Rock (lake), Mont. 262/E6
Upper Rockport, New Bruns. 170/F3
Upper Saddle River, N.J. 273/B1
Upper Saint Claire•, Pa. 294/B7
Upper Sandusky, Ohio 284/D4
Upper Saranac (lake), N.Y. 276/M2
Upper Seven Sisters, Manitoba 179/J4
Upper Sheikh, Somalia.115/J2
Upper Sheila, New Bruns. 170/E1
Upper South River, Nova Scotia 168/G3
Upper Stepney, Conn. 210/B3
Upper Stewiacke, Nova Scotia 168/F3
Upperstrasburg, Pa. 294/G5
Upper Tract, W. Va. 312/H5
Upper Tygart, Ky. 237/P4
Upper Vaughan, Nova Scotia 168/D4
Upperville, N.S. Wales 97/G2
Upper Volta (Burkina Faso) 102/B3
Upper Woodstock, New Bruns. 170/C2
Uppingham, England 13/E5
Uppsala (co.), Sweden 18/K7
Uppsala, Sweden 7/F3
Uppsala, Sweden 18/K7
Upright (cape), Alaska 196/D2
Upsala, Minn. 255/D5
Upsala, Ontario 177/G5
Upsala, Ontario 175/B3
Upsalquitch, New Bruns. 170/D1
Upsalquitch (riv.), New Bruns. 170/D1
Upshaw (co.), Texas 303/K5
Upshur (co.), W. Va. 312/F5
Upson (co.), Georgia 217/D5
Upson, Wis. 317/F3
Upton, Ky. 237/K6
Upton•, Maine 243/B6
Upton•, Mass. 249/H4
Upton, Québec 172/E4
Upton (co.), Texas 303/B6
Upton, Wyo. 319/H1
Upton upon Severn, England 13/E5
Upton-West Upton, Mass. 249/H4
Ur (ruins), Iraq 66/E5
Urabá (gulf), Colombia 126/B3
Urachiche, Venezuela 124/C4
Uracoa, Venezuela 124/G3
Urad Qianqi, China 77/G3
Urad Zhonghou Lianheqi, China 77/G3
Uraidla, S. Australia 94/B8
Urakawa, Japan 81/L2
Ural (mts.), U.S.S.R. 54/C6
Ural (riv.), U.S.S.R. 54/G5
Ural (mts.), U.S.S.R. 54/G4
Ural (mts.), U.S.S.R. 7/L2
Ural (mts.), U.S.S.R. 52/J2
Ural (riv.), U.S.S.R. 48/F5
Ural (riv.), U.S.S.R. 52/J4
Uralla, N.S. Wales 97/F2
Ural'sk, U.S.S.R. 54/G4
Ural'sk, U.S.S.R. 48/F4
Urambo, Tanzania 115/F4
Uran, India 68/B7
Urana, N.S. Wales 97/D4
Urana (lake), N.S. Wales 97/D4
Urania, La. 238/F3
Uranium City, Sask. 162/F4
Uranium City, Sask. 146/H4
Uranium City, Sask. 181/L2
Urapunga, North. Terr. 93/D3
Uraricoera, Brazil 132/H8
Uraricoera (riv.), Brazil 132/H8
Uravan, Colo. 208/B6
Urawa, Japan 81/O2
Uray, U.S.S.R. 48/G3
Urban, Ky. 237/N6
Urban, Pa. 294/J4
Urban, Wash. 310/C2
Urbana, Ark. 202/E7
Urbana, Ill. 222/E3
Urbana, Ind. 227/F3
Urbana, Iowa 229/K4
Urbana, Md. 245/J3
Urbana, Mo. 261/F7
Urbana, Ohio 284/C5
Urbancrest, Ohio 284/D6
Urbandale, Iowa 229/F5
Urbank, Minn. 255/C4
Urbanna, Va. 307/P5
Urbenville, N.S. Wales 97/G1
Urbino, Italy 34/D3
Urcos, Peru 128/G9
Urda, Spain 33/E3
Urdinarrain, Argentina 143/G6
Ure (riv.), England 13/F3
Uren, Sask. 181/E5
Urenui, N. Zealand 100/E3
Ures, Mexico 150/D2
Urfa (prov.), Turkey 63/H4
Urfa, Turkey 59/C2
Urfa, Turkey 63/H4
Urga (Ulaanbaatar) (cap.), Mongolia 77/G2
Urgel, Llanos de (plain), Spain 33/G2
Urgench, U.S.S.R. 54/G5
Urgench, U.S.S.R. 48/G5
Ürgüp, Turkey 63/F3
Uri (canton), Switzerland 39/G3
Uriah, Ala. 195/D8
Uribe, Colombia 126/C6
Uribia, Colombia 126/D2
Urica, Venezuela 124/F3
Urich, Mo. 261/E6
Urim, Israel 65/B5
Urimán, Venezuela 124/G5
Uriondo, Bolivia 136/C7
Urique (riv.), Mexico 150/F3
Urirotstock (mt.), Switzerland 39/G3
Urituyacu (riv.), Peru 128/D5
Urk, Netherlands 27/H3
Urla, Turkey 63/B3
Urlaţa, Romania 45/H3
Urlingford, Ireland 17/F6
Urmia, Iran 59/D2
Urmia (Orumiyah), Iran 66/D2

Urmia (lake), Iran 54/F6
Urmia (lake), Iran 59/E2
Urmia (lake), Iran 66/D2
Urmston, England 13/H2
Urnäsch, Switzerland 39/H2
Uromi, Nigeria 106/F7
Urošević, Yugoslavia 45/E4
Urrao, Colombia 126/B4
Ursa, Ill. 222/B3
Ursina, Pa. 294/D6
Ursine, Nev. 266/G5
Úrsulo Galván, Mexico 150/Q1
Uruáchic, Mexico 150/E3
Uruaçu, Brazil 132/D6
Uruaçu, Brazil 120/E4
Uruana, Brazil 132/D5
Uruapan del Progreso, Mexico 150/H7
Urubamba, Peru 128/F9
Urubamba (riv.), Peru 128/F8
Urubichá, Bolivia 136/D4
Urubu (riv.), Brazil 132/A3
Urubupungá (dam), Brazil 132/C8
Urubupungá (dam), Brazil 120/D5
Urucará, Brazil 132/B3
Uruçuí, Brazil 132/E4
Urucún, Morro do (mt.), Brazil 132/B7
Urucurituba, Brazil 132/B3
Uruguai (riv.), Brazil 132/C9
Uruguaiana, Brazil 120/D5
Uruguaiana, Brazil 132/B10
Uruguay 2/G7
Uruguay 120/D6
URUGUAY 145
Uruguay (riv.) 120/D5
Uruguay (riv.), Argentina 143/E3
Uruguay (riv.), Uruguay 145/A3
Urumaco, Venezuela 124/C2
Ürümqi, China 2/P3
Ürümqi, China 54/K5
Ürümqi (Urumchi), China 77/C3
Urunga, N.S. Wales 97/G2
Urup (isl.), U.S.S.R. 54/S5
Urup (isl.), U.S.S.R. 48/Q5
Uruyén, Venezuela 124/G5
Uryupinsk, U.S.S.R. 52/F4
Urzhum, U.S.S.R. 52/G3
Urziceni, Romania 45/H3
Usa (riv.), U.S.S.R. 7/K2
Usa (riv.), U.S.S.R. 52/K1
Uşak (prov.), Turkey 63/C3
Uşak, Turkey 59/B2
Uşak, Turkey 63/C3
Usakos, Namibia 118/B4
Usakos, Namibia 102/D7
Usedom (isl.), Germany 22/F1
Usedom (Uznam), Poland 47/B1
Ushakov (isl.), U.S.S.R. 4/B5
Ushant (isl.), France 7/D4
Ushant (Ouessant) (isl.), France 28/A3
Usherville, Sask. 181/J3
Ushibuka, Japan 81/D7
Ushtobe, U.S.S.R. 48/H5
Ushuaia, Argentina 143/C7
Ushuaia, Argentina 120/C8
Usibelli, Alaska 196/J2
Usinsk, U.S.S.R. 52/J1
Usk, Br. Col. 184/C3
Usk, Wales 13/B6
Usk (riv.), Wales 10/E5
Usk (riv.), Wales 13/B6
Usk, Wash. 310/H2
Üsküdar, Turkey 63/D6
Uslar, Germany 22/C3
Usman', U.S.S.R. 52/E4
Usol'ye-Sibirskoye, U.S.S.R. 48/L4
Usquepaug, R.I. 249/H6
Ussel, France 28/E5
Ussuri (riv.) 54/P5
Ussuri (Wusuli Jiang) (riv.), China 77/M2
Ussuri, U.S.S.R. 48/O5
Ussuriysk, U.S.S.R. 54/P5
Ussuriysk, U.S.S.R. 48/O5
Ústěk, Czech. 41/C1
Uster, Switzerland 39/G2
Ustica (isl.), Italy 34/D5
Ust'-Ilimsk, U.S.S.R. 48/L4
Ústí nad Labem, Czech. 41/C1
Ústí nad Orlicí, Czech. 41/D2
Ustka, Poland 47/C1
Ust'-Kamchatsk, U.S.S.R. 54/T4
Ust'-Kamchatsk, U.S.S.R. 48/R4
Ust'-Kamenogorsk, U.S.S.R. 54/J5
Ust'-Kamenogorsk, U.S.S.R. 48/J5
Ust'-Kulom, U.S.S.R. 52/H2
Ust'-Kut, U.S.S.R. 54/M4
Ust'-Kut, U.S.S.R. 48/L4
Ust'-Kuyga, U.S.S.R. 4/C3
Ust'-Kuyga, U.S.S.R. 48/O3
Ust'-Maya, U.S.S.R. 54/P3
Ust'-Nera, U.S.S.R. 54/R3
Ust'-Nera, U.S.S.R. 48/P3
Ust'-Olenëk, U.S.S.R. 48/M2
Ust'-Omchug, U.S.S.R. 48/P3
Ust'-Ordynskiy, U.S.S.R. 48/L4
Ust'-Ordynskiy Buryat Aut. Okr., U.S.S.R. 48/L4
Ust'-Pinega, U.S.S.R. 52/F2
Ust'-Port, U.S.S.R. 48/J2
Ustrzyki Dolne, Poland 47/F4
Ust'-Tsil'ma, U.S.S.R. 52/H1
Ust'-Urt (plat.), U.S.S.R. 54/G5
Ust'-Urt (plat.), U.S.S.R. 48/F5
Ustyuzhna, U.S.S.R. 52/E3
Usu, China 77/B3
Usuki, Japan 81/F7
Usulután, El Salvador 154/C4
Usumacinta (riv.), Guatemala 154/B2
Usumacinta (riv.), Mexico 150/O8
Utah 10/D3
UTAH 304
Utah (beach), France 28/C3
Utah (state), U.S. 146/G6
Utah (co.), Utah 304/D3
Utah (lake), Utah 188/D2
Utah (lake), Utah 304/C3
Utajärvi, Finland 18/P4
Ute, Iowa 229/B4

Ute (creek), N. Mex. 274/F3
Ute (peak), N. Mex. 274/D2
Ute (res.), N. Mex. 274/F3
Ute Mountain Ind. Res., Colo. 208/B8
Ute Mountain Ind. Res., N. Mex. 274/A1
Utena, U.S.S.R. 53/C3
Utena, U.S.S.R. 52/C3
Ute Park, N. Mex. 274/D2
Utete, Tanzania 115/G5
Uthai Thani, Thailand 72/C4
Uthal, Pakistan 68/B3
Uthal, Pakistan 59/J4
Utica, Ill. 222/E2
Utica, Ind. 227/F8
Utica, Kansas 232/B3
Utica, Ky. 237/G5
Utica, Mich. 250/F6
Utica, Minn. 255/G7
Utica, Miss. 256/C6
Utica, Mo. 261/E3
Utica, Mont. 262/F4
Utica, N.Y. 188/M2
Utica, Nebr. 264/G4
Utica, N.Y. 276/K4
Utica, Ohio 284/F5
Utica, Okla. 288/O7
Utica, Pa. 294/C3
Utica, S.C. 296/B2
Utica, S. Dak. 298/P8
Utica, Wis. 317/H10
Utica Junior College, Miss. 256/C6
Utiel, Spain 33/F3
Utikuma (lake), Alberta 182/C2
Utikuma (riv.), Alberta 182/C1
Utikumasis (lake), Alberta 182/C2
Utila, Honduras 154/D2
Utila (isl.), Honduras 154/D2
Utleyville, Colo. 208/O8
Utopia, Alaska 196/H1
Utopia (lake), New Bruns. 170/D3
Utopia, North. Terr. 93/D7
Utopia, Texas 303/E8
Utrecht (prov.), Netherlands 27/G4
Utrecht, Netherlands 27/G4
Utrecht, Netherlands 7/E3
Utrera, Spain 33/D4
Utsjoki, Finland 18/P2
Utsunomiya, Japan 81/K5
Uttaradit, Thailand 72/C3
Uttarpara-Kotrung, India 68/F1
Uttar Pradesh (state), India 68/D3
Uttoxeter, England 13/F5
Uttoxeter, England 10/F4
Utuado, P. Rico 156/F1
Utuado, P. Rico 161/B2
Utukok (riv.), Alaska 196/F1
Uturoa, Fr. Poly. 87/L7
Utzenstorf, Switzerland 39/E2
Uusikaarlepyy (Nykarleby), Finland 18/N5
Uusikaupunki, Finland 18/M6
Uusimaa (prov.), Finland 18/O6
Uva, Laguna (lake), Colombia 126/E6
Uva (riv.), Colombia 126/E6
Uvalda, Georgia 217/H6
Uvalde (co.), Texas 303/E8
Uvalde, Texas 303/E8
Uvarovo, U.S.S.R. 52/F4
Uvéa (isl.), New Caled. 87/G7
Uvéa (isl.), New Caled. 86/H4
Uvéa (bay), New Caled. 86/H4
Uverito, Venezuela 124/F3
Uvinza, Tanzania 115/F5
Uvira, Zaire 115/E4
Uvs, Mongolia 77/D2
Uvs Nuur (lake), Mongolia 54/L4
Uvs Nuur (lake), Mongolia 77/D1
Uwajima, Japan 81/F7
Uwchland, Pa. 294/L5
'Uweinat, Jebel (mt.), Egypt 111/E3
'Uweinat, Jebel (mt.), Libya 111/E3
'Uweinat, Jebel (mt.), Sudan 111/E3
Uxbridge•, Mass. 249/H4
Uxbridge, Ontario 177/E3
Uxin, China 77/G4
Uxmal (ruins), Mexico 150/P6
Uyak, Alaska 196/H3
Uyo, Nigeria 106/F8
Uyuni, Bolivia 120/C5
Uyuni, Bolivia 136/C6
Uyuni (salt dep.), Bolivia 136/B7
Už (riv.), Czech. 41/G2
Uzbek (S.S.R.), U.S.S.R. 54/H5
Uzbek S.S.R., U.S.S.R. 48/G5
Uzès, France 28/F5
Uzhgorod, U.S.S.R. 7/G4
Uzhgorod, U.S.S.R. 52/B4
Uzlovaya, U.S.S.R. 52/E4
Uznach, Switzerland 39/H2
Uznam (Usedom) (isl.), Poland 47/B1
Uzümlü, Turkey 63/D4
Uzunköprü, Turkey 63/B2
Uzwil, Switzerland 39/H2
Uzza, Israel 65/B4

V

Vaaifetu (mt.), W. Samoa 86/M8
Vaal (riv.), S. Africa 102/E7
Vaal (riv.), S. Africa 118/D5
Vaala, Finland 18/P4
Vaals, Netherlands 27/H7
Vaalsberg (mt.), Belgium 27/J7
Vaalserberg (mt.), Netherlands 27/J7
Vaalspan, S. Africa 118/C5
Vaasa, Finland 7/E3
Vaasa (prov.), Finland 18/N5
Vaasa, Finland 18/M5
Vác, Hungary 41/E3
Vaca (key), Fla. 212/E7
Vacaria, Brazil 132/D10
Vacaville, Calif. 204/D5
Vaccarès (lag.), France 28/F6

Vache (isl.), Haiti 158/B6
Vache (isl.), Haiti 156/D3
Vacherie, La. 238/L3
Vacía Talega (pt.), P. Rico 161/E1
Vada, Ky. 237/O5
Vaden, Ark. 202/E6
Vader, Wash. 310/C4
Vadis, W. Va. 312/E4
Vadito, N. Mex. 274/D2
Vadnais Heights, Minn. 255/G5
Vado, N. Mex. 274/C6
Vadodara, India 68/C4
Vadret (peak), Switzerland 39/J3
Vadsø, Norway 7/H1
Vadsø, Norway 18/Q1
Vadstena, Sweden 18/J7
Vaduz (cap.), Liecht. 39/H2
Vaea (mt.), W. Samoa 86/M8
Vaerøy (isl.), Norway 18/H3
Vaga (riv.), U.S.S.R. 52/F2
Vagåvatn (lake), Norway 18/F6
Vaggeryd, Sweden 18/J8
Vagos, Portugal 33/B2
Vagthus (pt.), Virgin Is. (U.S.) 161/F4
Váh (riv.), Czech. 41/D2
Vahitahi (atoll), Fr. Poly. 87/N7
Vaiden, Miss. 256/E4
Vaihiria (lake), Fr. Poly. 86/T13
Vail, Ariz. 198/E6
Vail, Colo. 208/G3
Vail, Iowa 229/C4
Vails, U.S.S.R. 52/D3
Vaitupu (atoll), Tuvalu 87/H6
Vakfıkebir, Turkey 63/H2
Vakh (riv.), U.S.S.R. 48/J3
Vakhan (reg.), Afghanistan 59/K2
Vakhtan, U.S.S.R. 52/G3
Vál, Hungary 41/E3
Valais (canton), Switzerland 39/D4
Valašské Meziříčí, Czech. 41/D2
Valatie, N.Y. 276/N6
Val-Barrette, Québec 172/B3
Val-Brillant, Québec 172/B1
Valcheta, Argentina 143/C5
Val-Comeau, New Bruns. 170/E1
Valcour (isl.), N.Y. 276/N1
Valcourt, Québec 172/E4
Valday, U.S.S.R. 52/D3
Valday (hills), U.S.S.R. 52/D3
Valdagno, Italy 34/C2
Val d'Amour, New Bruns. 170/D1
Val-David, Québec 172/C3
Valday, U.S.S.R. 52/D3
Valdecañas (res.), Spain 33/D3
Val-de-Marne (dept.), France 28/C1
Valdemarsvik, Sweden 18/K7
Valdemoro, Spain 33/F4
Valdepeñas, Spain 33/E3
Valderas, Spain 33/D2
Valderrobres, Spain 33/F2
Valders, Wis. 317/L7
Valdés, Argentina 143/C3
Valdés (pen.), Argentina 120/C7
Valdés (pen.), Argentina 143/C5
Valdes (isl.), Br. Col. 184/K3
Val-des-Bois, Québec 172/B4
Valdese, N.C. 281/F3
Valdeverdeja, Spain 33/D3
Valdez, Alaska 196/D1
Valdez, Colo. 208/K8
Valdez, Ecuador 128/C2
Valdez, N. Mex. 274/D2
Valdivia, Chile 2/F7
Valdivia, Chile 118/D3
Valdivia, Chile 120/B6
Valdivia, Colombia 126/C3
Val-d'Oise (dept.), France 28/E3
Val-d'Or, Que. 162/J6
Val d'Or, Québec 174/B3
Valdosta, Ga. 188/K4
Valdosta, Georgia 217/F9
Val Doucet, New Bruns. 170/E1
Vale, N.C. 281/G3
Vale, Oreg. 291/K4
Vale, S. Dak. 298/C4
Vale, Tenn. 237/E8
Valeda, Kansas 232/G4
Valeene, Ind. 227/E8
Valemount, Br. Col. 184/H4
Valença, Brazil 120/B8
Valença, Brazil 135/E3
Valença, Brazil 132/G6
Valença, Portugal 33/B2
Valença do Piauí, Brazil 132/F4
Valence, France 7/E4
Valence, France 28/F5
Valencia, Calif. 204/G9
Valencia (Valentia) (isl.), Ireland 10/A5
Valencia (isl.), Ireland 17/A8
Valencia (co.), N. Mex. 274/C4
Valencia, N. Mex. 274/C4
Valencia, Pa. 294/C4
Valencia, Philippines 82/E7
Valencia (prov.), Spain 33/F3
Valencia, Spain 7/D5
Valencia, Spain 33/F3
Valencia (gulf), Spain 33/G3
Valencia, Albufera de (lag.), Spain 33/G3
Valencia (reg.), Spain 33/F3
Valencia, Trin. & Tob. 161/B10
Valencia, Venezuela 120/C2
Valencia (lake), Venezuela 124/D2
Valencia (lake), Venezuela 124/E2
Valencia de Alcántara, Spain 33/C3
Valencia de Don Juan, Spain 33/D1
Valenciennes, France 28/E2
Valentia (isl.), Ireland 10/A5
Valentine, Ariz. 198/B3
Valentine, Ind. 227/G1
Valentine, Nebr. 264/D2
Valentine, Texas 303/C11
Valentines, Uruguay 145/G4
Valentines, Va. 307/N7
Valenza, Italy 34/B2
Valenzuela, Paraguay 144/B5

Verona 463

Valera, Texas 303/E6
Valera, Venezuela 124/C3
Valera, Venezuela 120/B2
Valeria, Iowa 229/G5
Vale Summit, Md. 245/C2
Valga, U.S.S.R. 52/C3
Valga, U.S.S.R. 53/D2
Valhalla, Alberta 182/A2
Valhalla, N.Y. 276/P6
Valhalla Centre, Alberta 182/A2
Valhermoso Springs, Ala. 195/E2
Valiente (pen.), Panama 154/G6
Valier, Ill. 222/D5
Valier, Mont. 262/D2
Valier, Pa. 294/D4
Valjean, Sask. 181/E5
Valjevo, Yugoslavia 45/D3
Valka, U.S.S.R. 53/C2
Valkeakoski, Finland 18/N6
Valkenswaard, Netherlands 27/H6
Valladolid, Mexico 146/K7
Valladolid, Mexico 150/P6
Valladolid (prov.), Spain 33/D2
Valladolid, Spain 33/D2
Valladolid, Spain 7/E4
Vallay (isl.), Scotland 15/A3
Vall de Uxó, Spain 33/F3
Valle, Norway 18/E7
Valle Alegre, Chile 138/F2
Vallecas, Spain 33/G4
Vallecito (res.), Colo. 208/D8
Vallecitos, N. Mex. 274/C2
Valle de Allende, Mexico 150/G3
Valle de Bravo, Mexico 150/J7
Valle de Guanape, Venezuela 124/F3
Valle de la Pascua, Venezuela 124/F3
Valle del Cauca (dept.), Colombia 126/B6
Valledupar, Colombia 120/B1
Valledupar, Colombia 126/D2
Vallée-Jonction, Québec 172/G3
Vallegrande, Bolivia 120/C4
Vallegrande, Bolivia 136/C6
Valle Hermoso, Mexico 150/L4
Vallehermoso, Spain 33/A5
Vallejo, Calif. 188/B3
Vallejo, Calif. 204/J1
Valle Mí, Paraguay 144/D3
Vallenar, Chile 138/A7
Vallentuna, Sweden 18/H1
Valle San Telmo, Mexico 150/A1
Valles Mines, Mo. 261/L6
Valletta (cap.), Malta 7/F5
Valletta (cap.), Malta 34/E7
Valley, Ala. 195/H5
Valley (co.), Idaho 220/C5
Valley (riv.), Manitoba 179/B3
Valley (co.), Mont. 262/K2
Valley (co.), Nebr. 264/E3
Valley, Nebr. 264/H3
Valley, Nova Scotia 168/E3
Valley, Wash. 310/H2
Valley, Wis. 317/F8
Valley, Wyo. 319/C1
Valley Bend, W. Va. 312/F5
Valley Brook, Okla. 288/M4
Valley Center, Kansas 232/E4
Valley Centre, Sask. 181/D4
Valley City, Ill. 222/C4
Valley City, N. Dak. 282/P6
Valley City, Ohio 284/G3
Valley Cottage, N.Y. 276/K8
Valley East, Ontario 177/J5
Valley East, Ontario 175/D3
Valley Falls, Kansas 232/G2
Valley Falls, N.Y. 276/N5
Valley Falls, Oreg. 291/G5
Valley Falls, R.I. 249/J5
Valley Farms, Ariz. 198/D6
Valleyfield, Québec 172/C4
Valleyford, Wash. 310/H3
Valley Forge, Pa. 294/L5
Valley Grove, W. Va. 312/E2
Valley Head, Ala. 195/G1
Valley Head, W. Va. 312/G5
Valley Hi, Ohio 284/C5
Valley Lee, Md. 245/M8
Valley Mills, Texas 303/G6
Valley Park, Miss. 256/C5
Valley Park, Mo. 261/O3
Valley Point, W. Va. 312/G3
Valley River, Manitoba 179/B3
Valley Spring, Texas 303/F7
Valley Springs, Ark. 202/D1
Valley Springs, Calif. 204/C9
Valley Springs, S. Dak. 298/S6
Valley Station, Ky. 237/K4
Valley Stream, N.Y. 276/P7
Valleyview, Alberta 182/B2
Valley View, Ky. 237/N5
Valley View, Ohio 284/D6
Valley View, Ohio 284/H9
Valley View, Pa. 294/J4
Valley View, Texas 303/H4
Vallgrund (isl.), Finland 18/M5
Valliant, Okla. 288/R6
Vallières, Haiti 158/C5
Vallimanca (riv.), Argentina 143/F7
Vallonia, Ind. 227/E7
Vallon-Pont-d'Arc, France 28/F5
Vallorbe, Switzerland 39/B3
Valls, Spain 33/G2
Val Marie, Sask. 181/D6
Valmeyer, Ill. 222/C5
Valmiera, U.S.S.R. 53/C2
Valmiera, U.S.S.R. 52/C3
Valmont, Québec 172/E3
Valmontone, Italy 34/F7
Valmora, N. Mex. 274/D3
Valmy, Nev. 266/D2
Valmy, Wis. 317/M6
Valognes, France 28/C3
Valona, Georgia 217/K8
Valor, Sask. 181/E6
Valpaços, Portugal 33/C2
Valparaíso (reg.), Chile 138/A9
Valparaíso, Chile 2/F7
Valparaíso, Chile 120/B6
Valparaíso, Chile 138/E2
Valparaiso, Fla. 212/C6
Valparaiso, Ind. 227/C2
Valparaiso, Nebr. 264/H3
Valparaiso, Sask. 181/G3
Val-Racine, Québec 172/G4
Vals (cape), Indonesia 85/K7
Vals, Switzerland 39/H3
Valsad, India 68/C4
Valsequillo (res.), Mexico 150/N2
Valserrhein (riv.), Switzerland 39/H3
Valsetz, Oreg. 291/D3
Value, Miss. 256/D6
Valuyki, U.S.S.R. 52/E4
Valverda, La. 238/G5
Valverde (prov.), Dom. Rep. 158/D5
Valverde, Dom. Rep. 158/D5
Val Verde (co.), Texas 303/C8
Valverde del Camino, Spain 33/C4
Vamdrup, Denmark 21/C7
Vammala, Finland 18/N6
Vámos, Greece 45/F8
Vámospércs, Hungary 41/F3
Van, Ky. 237/R6
Van (lake), N. Dak. 282/L5
Van, Oreg. 291/J4
Van, Pa. 294/C3
Van, Texas 303/J5
Van (prov.), Turkey 63/K3
Van, Turkey 59/D2
Van, Turkey 63/K3
Van (lake), Turkey 54/F6
Van (lake), Turkey 59/D2
Van (lake), Turkey 63/K3
Van, W. Va. 312/D7
Vanadium, N. Mex. 274/A6
Van Alstyne, Texas 303/H4
Vananda, Br. Col. 184/E5
Vananda, Mont. 262/K4
Vanatta, Ohio 284/E5
Vanavara, U.S.S.R. 48/L3
Van Blommenstein (lake), Suriname 120/D2
Van Blommesteir (lake), Suriname 131/D3
Van Bruyssel, Québec 172/E2
Van Buren (co.), Ark. 202/E2
Van Buren, Ark. 202/B3
Van Buren, Ind. 227/F3
Van Buren (co.), Iowa 229/K7
Van Buren, Maine 243/G1
Van Buren•, Maine 243/G1
Van Buren (co.), Mich. 250/C6
Van Buren, Mo. 261/L8
Van Buren, Ohio 284/C3
Van Buren (co.), Tenn. 237/L9
Vance, Ala. 195/D4
Vance, Miss. 256/D2
Vance (co.), N.C. 281/N2
Vance, S.C. 296/G5
Vance A.F.B., Okla. 288/K2
Vanceboro•, Maine 243/J4
Vanceboro, N.C. 281/P4
Vanceburg, Ky. 237/P3
Vancleave, Miss. 256/G9
Van Cleve, Iowa 229/G5
Vancourt, Texas 303/D6
Vancouver (mt.), Alaska 196/L2
Vancouver, Br. Col. 146/F4
Vancouver, Br. Col. 162/D6
Vancouver (Greater), Br. Col. 184/K3
Vancouver (isl.), Br. Col. 146/F5
Vancouver (isl.), Br. Col. 162/D6
Vancouver, Br. Col. 184/K3
Vancouver (isl.), Br. Col. 184/D5
Vancouver, Canada 2/C3
Vancouver (isl.), Canada 2/C3
Vancouver, Wash. 188/B1
Vancouver, Wash. 310/C5
Vancouver (lake), Wash. 310/C5
Vandalia, Ill. 222/D5
Vandalia, Mich. 250/D7
Vandalia, Mo. 261/J4
Vandalia, Mont. 262/J2
Vandalia, Ohio 284/B6
Vandalia, W. Va. 312/F5
Vandemere, N.C. 281/R4
Vandenberg A.F.B., Calif. 204/E9
Vanderbijl Park, S. Africa 118/D5
Vanderbilt, Mich. 250/E3
Vanderbilt, Pa. 294/C5
Vanderbilt, Texas 303/H9
Vanderburgh (co.), Ind. 227/B8
Vandergrift, Pa. 294/D4
Vanderhoof, Br. Col. 162/D5
Vanderhoof, Br. Col. 184/E3
Vanderlin (isl.), North. Terr. 88/F3
Vanderlin (isl.), North. Terr. 93/E3
Vanderpool, Texas 303/E8
Vanderpool, Va. 307/J4
Vandervoort, Ark. 202/B5
Van Diemen (cape), North. Terr 88/D2
Van Diemen (cape), North. Terr 93/A1
Van Diemen (gulf), North. Terr 88/E2
Van Diemen (gulf), North. Terr 93/B1
Vandiver, Ala. 195/F4
Vandiver, Mo. 261/J4
Vandling, Pa. 294/M2
Vändra, U.S.S.R. 53 C1
Vandura, Sask. 181/K5
Vanduser, Mo. 261/N9
Vanegas, Mexico 150/J5
Vänern (lake), Sweden 7/F3
Vänern (lake), Sweden 18/H7
Vänersborg, Sweden 18/G7
Van Etten, N.Y. 276/G6
Vanga, Kenya 115/G4
Vangaindrano, Madagascar 118/H4
Vanguard, Sask. 181/D6
Vangunu (isl.), Solomon Is. 86/D3
Van Hoa, Vietnam 72/E2
Van Horn, Texas 303/C11
Van Horne, Iowa 229/J4
Van Hornesville, N.Y. 276/L5
Vanier, Ontario 177/J2
Vanier, Québec 172/J3
Vanikoro (isl.), Solomon Is. 87/G7
Vanil Noir (mt.), Switzerland 39/D3
Vanimo, Papua N.G. 87/E6
Vanimo, Papua N.G. 85/B6
Vanino, U.S.S.R. 48/P5
Vaniyambadi, India 68/D6
Vankleek Hill, Ontario 177/K2
Van Lear, Ky. 237/R5
Vanleer, Tenn. 237/G8
Vanlue, Ohio 284/C4
Van Meter, Iowa 229/E5
Vanna, Georgia 217/F2
Vännäs, Sweden 18/L5
Vanndale, Ark. 202/J3
Vannes, France 28/B4
Van Ninh, Vietnam 72/F4
Vannøy (isl.), Norway 18/L1
Van Nuys, Calif. 204/B10
Van Orin, Ill. 222/D2
Vanoss, Okla. 288/N5
Vanrhynsdorp, S. Africa 118/B6
Van Rook, Queensland 95/B3
Vansant, Va. 307/D6
Vansbro, Sweden 18/H6
Vanscoy, Sask. 181/D4
Vansittart (isl.), N.W. Terr. 187/K3
Vansittart (isl.), Tasmania 99/E2
Vantaa, Finland 18/O6
Vantage, Sask. 181/F6
Vantage, Wash. 310/E4
Van Tassell, Wyo. 319/H3
Vanua Levu (isl.), Fiji 87/H7
Vanua Levu (isl.), Fiji 86/Q10
Vanuatu 2/T6
Vanuatu 87/G7
VANUATU 87/G7
Van Vleet, Miss. 256/G3
Vanvoorhis, W. Va. 312/G3
Van Wert, Georgia 217/B3
Van Wert, Iowa 229/F7
Van Wert (co.), Ohio 284/A4
Van Wert, Ohio 284/A4
Van Wyck, S.C. 296/F2
Van Yen, Vietnam 72/E2
Vanylven, Norway 18/E5
Van Zandt (co.), Texas 303/J5
Van Zandt, Wash. 310/C2
Vanzant, Mo. 261/H9
Var (dept.), France 28/G6
Vara, Sweden 18/H7
Vara de María, Venezuela 124/C4
Varadero, Cuba 158/D1
Varakļāni, U.S.S.R. 53/D2
Varallo Pombia, Italy 34/B2
Varamin, Iran 66/G3
Varanasi, India 54/K7
Varanasi, India 68/E3
Varangerfjord (fjord), Norway 18/Q2
Varangerfjorden (fjord), Norway 7/H1
Varangerhalvøya (pen.), Norway 18/Q1
Varano (lake), Italy 34/F3
Varaždin, Yugoslavia 45/B2
Varazze, Italy 34/B2
Varberg, Sweden 18/G8
Vardaman, Miss. 256/F3
Vardar (riv.), Greece 45/E5
Vardar (riv.), Yugoslavia 45/E5
Varde, Denmark 18/F9
Varde, Denmark 21/B6
Varde (riv.), Denmark 21/B6
Vardø, Norway 18/R1
Varel, Germany 22/C2
Varella, Mui (cape), Vietnam 72/F4
Varėna, U.S.S.R. 53/C3
Varennes, Québec 172/J4
Vareš, Yugoslavia 45/D3
Varese (prov.), Italy 34/B2
Varese, Italy 34/B2
Vargem Bonita, Brazil 135/E3
Varginha, Brazil 135/D2
Varginha, Brazil 132/E8
Varina, Iowa 229/D3
Varkaus, Finland 18/Q5
Värmland (co.), Sweden 18/H7
Varna, Bulgaria 7/G4
Varna, Bulgaria 45/J4
Varna, Ill. 222/D2
Varnado, La. 238/L5
Värnamo, Sweden 18/J8
Varnek, U.S.S.R. 52/J1
Varnell, Georgia 217/C1
Varner, Kansas 232/D4
Varney, Ontario 177/D3
Varney, W. Va. 312/B7
Varnsdorf, Czech. 41/C1
Varnville, S.C. 296/E6
Várpalota, Hungary 41/E3
Vars, Ontario 177/J2
Vartholomión, Greece 45/E7
Varto, Turkey 63/J3
Varysburg, N.Y. 276/D5
Varzarin, Kuh-e (mt.), Iran 59/E3
Varzarin, Kuh-e (mt.), Iran 66/E4
Vas (co.), Hungary 41/D3
Vasa (Vaasa), Finland 18/M5
Vasa, Minn. 255/F6
Vasa Barris (riv.), Brazil 132/G5
Vásárosnamény, Hungary 41/G2
Vascongadas (reg.), Spain 33/E1
Vashi, India 68/B7
Vashka (riv.), U.S.S.R. 52/G2
Vashon, Wash. 310/A2
Vasile Roaită, Romania 45/J3
Vasil'kov, U.S.S.R. 52/D4
Vaslui, Romania 45/H2
Vass, N.C. 281/L4
Vassalboro, Maine 243/D7
Vassalboro•, Maine 243/D7
Vassar, Kansas 232/G3
Vassar, Manitoba 179/G5
Vassar, Mich. 250/F5
Vassouras, Brazil 135/E3
Vastenjaure (lake), Sweden 18/K3
Västerås, Sweden 7/F3
Västerås, Sweden 18/K7
Västerbotten (co.), Sweden 18/K4
Västerdalälven (riv.), Sweden 18/H6
Västerhaninge, Sweden 18/H1
Västernorrland (co.), Sweden 18/K5
Västervik, Sweden 18/K8
Västmanland (co.), Sweden 18/K7
Vasto, Italy 34/E3
Vasvár, Hungary 41/D3
Vaternish (dist.), Scotland 15/B3
Vaternish (pt.), Scotland 15/B3
Vatersay (isl.), Scotland 15/A4
Vathí, Greece 45/H7
Vatican City 7/F4
VATICAN CITY 34
Vatican City, Vatican City 34/B6
Vaticano (cape), Italy 34/E5
Vatnajökull (glac.), Iceland 21/C1
Vatomandry, Madagascar 118/H3
Vatra Dornei, Romania 45/G2
Vättern (lake), Sweden 7/F3
Vättern (lake), Sweden 18/J7
Vatukoula, Fiji 86/P10
Vatulele (isl.), Fiji 86/P11
Vauclin (mt.), Martinique 161/D6
Vaucluse (dept.), France 28/F6
Vaucluse, S.C. 296/D4
Vaud (canton), Switzerland 39/B3
Vaudreuil (co.), Québec 172/C4
Vaudreuil, Québec 172/C4
Vaughan, Miss. 256/D5
Vaughan, N.C. 281/N2
Vaughan, Ontario 177/J4
Vaughan, W. Va. 310/D6
Vaughn, Mont. 262/E3
Vaughn, N. Mex. 274/D4
Vaughn, Wash. 310/C3
Vaughnsville, Ohio 284/B4
Vaupés (comm.), Colombia 126/E7
Vaupés (riv.), Colombia 120/B2
Vaupés (riv.), Colombia 126/E7
Vauxhall, Alberta 182/D4
Vauxhall, N.J. 273/A2
Vaux-sur-Sûre, Belgium 27/H9
Vava'u Group (isls.), Tonga 87/J7
Vavenby, Br. Col. 184/H4
Vavuniya, Sri Lanka 68/E7
Vawn, Sask. 181/C2
Vaxholm, Sweden 18/J1
Växjö, Sweden 7/F3
Växjö, Sweden 18/J8
Vaygach (isl.), U.S.S.R. 4/C6
Vaygach (isl.), U.S.S.R. 52/K1
Vayland, S. Dak. 298/M5
Važec, Czech. 41/E2
Vazhgort, U.S.S.R. 52/G2
Vaz-Obervaz, Switzerland 39/J3
Vázquez, Cuba 158/H3
Veagh (lake), Ireland 17/F1
Vealmoor, Texas 303/C5
Veazie•, Maine 243/F6
Veblen, S. Dak. 298/P2
Vechigen, Switzerland 39/E3
Vecht (riv.), Netherlands 27/F4
Vechta, Germany 22/C2
Vechte (riv.), Germany 22/B2
Vechte (riv.), Netherlands 27/J3
Vecsés, Hungary 41/E3
Vedaranniyam, India 68/E6
Vedia, Argentina 143/F7
Veedersburg, Ind. 227/C4
Veendam, Netherlands 27/K2
Veenendaal, Netherlands 27/G4
Veenhuizen, Netherlands 27/J2
Veere, Netherlands 27/D5
Veersche Meer (lake), Netherlands 27/D5
Vega (pt.), Alaska 196/J4
Vega, Alberta 182/C2
Vega (isl.), Norway 18/G4
Vega, Texas 303/B2
Vega Alta, P. Rico 161/D1
Vega Baja, P. Rico 161/D1
Vegafjorden (fjord), Norway 18/G4
Vegas Creek, Nev. 266/G6
Veghel, Netherlands 27/H5
Vegreville, Alberta 182/E3
Vègreville, Alta. 162/E5
Veguita, N. Mex. 274/C4
Vehar (lake), India 68/B7
Veinticinco de Agosto, Uruguay 145/A6
Veinticinco de Diciembre, Paraguay 144/D4
Veinticinco de Mayo, Argentina 143/F7
Veinticinco de Mayo, Ecuador 128/C4
Veinticinco de Mayo, Uruguay 145/C5
Veintiocho de Noviembre, Argentina 143/B7
Vejen, Denmark 21/C7
Vejer de la Frontera, Spain 33/C4
Vejle (co.), Denmark 21/C6
Vejle, Denmark 21/C6
Vejle, Denmark 18/F9
Vejle (fjord), Denmark 21/C6
Vejprty, Czech. 41/B1
Vela, La (cape), Colombia 126/D1
Vela, Roca que (cay), Colombia 126/B8
Vélan (mt.), Switzerland 39/D5
Velarde, N. Mex. 274/C2
Velas (cape), C. Rica 154/D5
Velasco, Ciego de Ávila, Cuba 158/G2
Velasco, Holguín, Cuba 158/H3
Velázquez, Uruguay 145/E5
Velda, Mo. 261/P2
Velden am Würthersee, Austria 41/C3
Veldhoven, Netherlands 27/G6
Veldrif, S. Africa 118/B6
Velence, Hungary 41/E3
Velenje, Yugoslavia 45/B2
Vélez, Colombia 126/D4
Vélez-Blanco, Spain 33/E4
Vélez-Málaga, Spain 33/E4
Vélez-Rubio, Spain 33/E4
Velhas (riv.), Brazil 132/E7
Velika Plana, Yugoslavia 45/E3
Velikaya (riv.), U.S.S.R. 48/S3
Velikaya (riv.), U.S.S.R. 52/C3
Veliki Bečkerek (Zrenjanin), Yugoslavia 45/E3
Velikiye Luki, U.S.S.R. 7/H3
Velikiye Luki, U.S.S.R. 52/D3
Velikiye Luki, U.S.S.R. 48/D4
Velikiy Ustyug, U.S.S.R. 7/J2
Velikiy Ustyug, U.S.S.R. 48/E3
Velikiy Ustyug, U.S.S.R. 52/F2
Veliko Tŭrnovo, Bulgaria 45/G4
Velikovisochnoye, U.S.S.R. 52/H1
Velizh, U.S.S.R. 52/D3
Velká Bíteš, Czech. 41/D2
Velká Bystřice, Czech. 41/D2
Vel'ké Kapušany, Czech. 41/G2
Velké Meziříčí, Czech. 41/D2
Vel'ké Rovné, Czech. 41/E2
Vella Lavella (isl.), Solomon Is. 86/D2
Velletri, Italy 34/F7
Vellore, India 68/D6
Velluda, Sierra (mt.), Chile 138/E1
Velma, Okla. 288/L6
Velp, Netherlands 27/J5
Velpen, Ind. 227/C8
Velsen, Netherlands 27/F4
Vel'sk, U.S.S.R. 52/F2
Vel'sk, U.S.S.R. 48/E3
Velten, Germany 22/E2
Veluwe (reg.), Netherlands 27/H4
Velva, N. Dak. 282/J3
Velvendós, Greece 45/F5
Vemb, Denmark 21/B5
Véménd, Hungary 41/E3
Venadillo, Colombia 126/C5
Venado, Mexico 150/J5
Venado Tuerto, Argentina 143/D3
Venafro, Italy 34/E4
Venaissin (trad. prov.), France 29
Venamo (mt.), Guyana 131/A3
Venamo, Cerro (mt.), Venezuela 124/H4
Venamo (riv.), Venezuela 124/H4
Venango, Nebr. 264/C4
Venango (co.), Pa. 294/C3
Venango, Pa. 294/B2
Vena Park, Queensland 95/B3
Vence, France 28/G6
Venda (bantustan), S. Africa 102/F7
Venda (rep.), S. Africa 118/E4
Vendas Novas, Portugal 33/B3
Vendée (dept.), France 28/C4
Vendôme, France 28/D4
Vendrell, Spain 33/G2
Venedocia, Ohio 284/B4
Venedy, Ill. 222/D5
Veneta, Oreg. 291/D3
Venetie, Alaska 196/J1
Veneto (reg.), Italy 34/D3
Venezia (Venice), Italy 34/D2
Venezuela 2/F5
Venezuela 120/C2
VENEZUELA 124
Venezuela, Cuba 158/F2
Venezuela (gulf), Venezuela 120/B1
Venezuela (gulf), Venezuela 124/C2
Vengurla, India 68/C5
Veniaminof (crater), Alaska 196/F3
Venice, Alberta 182/E2
Venice, Calif. 204/B11
Venice, Fla. 212/D4
Venice, Ill. 222/A2
Venice (prov.), Italy 34/D2
Venice, Italy 7/F4
Venice, Italy 34/D2
Venice (gulf), Italy 34/D2
Venice, La. 238/M8
Venice, Utah 304/C5
Vénissieux, France 28/F5
Venkatagiri, India 68/D6
Venlo, Netherlands 27/J6
Venn, Sask. 181/E4
Venosa, Italy 34/E4
Venraij, Netherlands 27/H6
Venta (riv.), U.S.S.R. 53/B2
Ventersposs, S. Africa 118/G6
Ventimiglia, Italy 34/A3
Ventnor, England 10/F5
Ventnor, England 13/F7
Ventnor City, N.J. 273/E5
Ventotene (isl.), Italy 34/D4
Ventspils, U.S.S.R. 48/B4
Ventspils, U.S.S.R. 53/A2
Ventspils, U.S.S.R. 52/B3
Ventuari (riv.), Venezuela 124/E5
Ventura (co.), Calif. 204/F9
Ventura, Calif. 204/F9
Ventura, Iowa 229/F2
Venturia, N. Dak. 282/L7
Venus, Fla. 212/E4
Venus (pt.), Fr. Poly. 86/T12
Venus, Pa. 294/C3
Venus (bay), Victoria 97/C6
Venustiano Carranza, Mexico 150/N8
Venustiano Carranza (res.), Mexico 150/J3
Ver (riv.), England 13/H7
Vera, Argentina 143/F5
Vera, Ill. 222/D4
Vera, Okla. 288/P2
Vera (lag.), Paraguay 144/D5
Vera, Spain 33/F4
Vera, Texas 303/E4
Vera, Va. 307/L6
Vera Cruz, Brazil 135/B3
Vera Cruz, Ind. 227/G3
Veracruz (state), Mexico 150/L7
Veracruz, Mexico 150/Q1
Veracruz, Mexico 2/E5
Veracruz, Mexico 146/J8
Veradale, Wash. 310/H3
Veragua Abajo, Dom. Rep. 158/E5
Veras, Uruguay 145/C2
Veraval, India 68/C4
Verbania, Italy 34/B2
Verbena, Ala. 195/E5
Verboort, Oreg. 291/A2
Vercelli (prov.), Italy 34/B2
Vercelli, Italy 34/B2
Verchères (co.), Québec 172/J4
Verchères, Québec 172/J4
Verçinin Tepesi (mt.), Turkey 63/J2
Verda, Ky. 237/P7
Verda, La. 238/E3
Verde (riv.), Ariz. 188/D4
Verde (riv.), Ariz. 198/D5
Verde (cay), Bahamas 156/C2
Verde (riv.), Brazil 132/C7
Verde (riv.), Mexico 150/F3
Verde (riv.), Mexico 150/L8
Verde (riv.), Paraguay 144/C3
Verde (cape), Senegal 102/A3
Verde (cape), Senegal 106/A6
Verde Island (passage), Philippines 82/C4
Verdel, Nebr. 264/F2
Verden, Okla. 288/K4
Verden, Germany 22/C2
Verdery, S.C. 296/C3
Verdi, Minn. 255/B6
Verdi, Nev. 266/B3
Verdigre, Nebr. 264/F2
Verdigris (riv.), Kansas 232/G5
Verdigris, Okla. 288/P2
Verdigris (riv.), Okla. 288/P2
Verdinho (riv.), Brazil 132/D7
Verdon, Nebr. 264/J4
Verdon, S. Dak. 298/N3
Verdun, Québec 172/H4
Verdún, Uruguay 145/D5
Verdun-sur-Meuse, France 28/F3
Verdunville, W. Va. 312/B7
Vereeniging, S. Africa 102/E7
Vereeniging, S. Africa 118/D5
Veregin, Sask. 181/K4
Verendrye, N. Dak. 282/J3
Vereshchagino, U.S.S.R. 52/H3
Verga (cape), Guinea 106/B6
Vergara, Argentina 143/H7
Vergara, Spain 33/E1
Vergara, Uruguay 145/E3
Vergas, Minn. 255/C4
Vergeletto, Switzerland 39/G4
Vergennes, Ill. 222/D6
Vergennes, Vt. 268/A3
Veribest, Texas 303/D6
Verín, Spain 33/C2
Veríssimo, Brazil 135/B1
Verkhnevilyuysk, U.S.S.R. 48/N3
Verkhnyaya Toyma, U.S.S.R. 52/G2
Verkhoyansk, U.S.S.R. 2/R2
Verkhoyansk, U.S.S.R. 4/C3
Verkhoyansk, U.S.S.R. 48/N3
Verkhoyansk, U.S.S.R. 54/P3
Verkhoyansk (range), U.S.S.R. 4/C3
Verkhoyansk (range), U.S.S.R. 48/N3
Verkhoyansk (range), U.S.S.R. 54/O3
Verkniy At-Uryakh, U.S.S.R. 48/Q3
Verlo, Sask. 181/C5
Vermejo (riv.), N. Mex. 274/E2
Vermejo Park, N. Mex. 274/D2
Vermilion, Alberta 182/E3
Vermilion (riv.), Alberta 182/E3
Vermilion (cliffs), Ariz. 198/D2
Vermilion (co.), Ill. 222/F3
Vermilion, Ill. 222/F4
Vermilion (riv.), Ind. 227/B4
Vermilion (par.), La. 238/F7
Vermilion (bay), La. 238/F7
Vermilion (lake), Minn. 188/H1
Vermilion (lake), Minn. 255/F3
Vermilion (range), Minn. 255/F3
Vermilion (riv.), Minn. 255/F2
Vermilion, Ohio 284/F3
Vermilion (riv.), Ohio 284/F3
Vermilion (hills), Sask. 181/E5
Vermilion (cliffs), Utah 304/B6
Vermilion Bay, Ontario 177/G4
Vermilion Bay, Ontario 175/B3
Vermilion Grove, Ill. 222/F4
Vermillion (co.), Ind. 227/C5
Vermillion, Kansas 232/F2
Vermillion, Minn. 255/F6
Vermillion, S. Dak. 298/R8
Vermillion (riv.), S. Dak. 298/P6
Vermillion (riv.), Québec 172/D2
Vermont 188/M2
VERMONT 268
Vermont, Ill. 222/C3
Vermont (state), U.S. 146/L5
Vermontville, Mich. 250/E6
Vernal, Utah 304/E3
Vernayaz, Switzerland 39/D4
Verndale, Minn. 255/C4
Verndon, Minn 255/E4
Verner, Ontario 177/D1
Verneuil-sur-Avre, France 28/D3
Vernon, Ala. 195/B3
Vernon, Ariz. 198/F4
Vernon, Br. Col. 162/E5
Vernon, Br. Col. 184/H5
Vernon, Colo. 208/P3
Vernon•, Conn. 210/F1
Vernon, Fla. 212/C6
Vernon, France 28/D3
Vernon, Ill. 222/D5
Vernon, Ind. 227/F7
Vernon, Ky. 237/L7
Vernon (par.), La. 238/D4
Vernon, La. 238/E2
Vernon (lake), La. 238/D4
Vernon, Mich. 250/F6
Vernon (co.), Mo. 261/D7
Vernon, N.J. 273/E1
Vernon, Okla. 288/P4
Vernon, Ontario 177/J2
Vernon (lake), Ontario 177/E2
Vernon, Pr. Edward I. 168/E2
Vernon, Texas 303/E3
Vernon, Utah 304/B3
Vernon•, Vt. 268/B6
Vernon (co.), Wis. 317/E8
Vernonburg, Georgia 217/K7
Vernon Center, Conn. 210/F1
Vernon Center, Minn. 255/D7
Vernon Fork (creek), Ind. 227/F7
Vernon Hill, Va. 307/K7
Vernon Hills, Ill. 222/B4
Vernonia, Oreg. 291/D2
Vero Beach, Fla. 212/F4
Veroli, Italy 34/D4
Verona, Ill. 222/E2
Verona (prov.), Italy 34/C2
Verona, Italy 34/C2

Verona, Italy 7/F4
Verona, Ky. 237/M3
Verona, Miss. 256/G2
Verona, Mo. 261/E9
Verona, N.J. 273/B2
Verona, N. Dak. 282/O7
Verona, Ohio 284/A6
Verona, Ontario 177/H3
Verona, Pa. 294/C6
Verona, Va. 307/K4
Verona, Wis. 317/G9
Verónica, Argentina 143/H7
Verpelét, Hungary 41/F2
Verret (lake), La. 238/H7
Verret, New Bruns. 170/B1
Verrettes, Haiti 158/C6
Vérroia, Greece 45/F5
Versailles, Conn. 210/G2
Versailles, France 28/A2
Versailles, France 7/E4
Versailles, Ill. 222/C4
Versailles, Ind. 227/G6
Versailles, Ky. 237/M4
Versailles, Mo. 261/G6
Versailles, N.Y. 276/B6
Versailles, Ohio 284/A5
Versailles, Pa. 294/C7
Versalles, Bolivia 136/D3
Vershire •, Vt. 268/C4
Versoix, Switzerland 39/B4
Verte (bay), New Bruns. 170/G2
Verte (bay), Nova Scotia 168/D2
Verte (isl.), Québec 172/H1
Vertientes, Cuba 158/G3
Vert-Pré, Martinique 161/D6
Vertus, France 28/E3
Verviers, Belgium 27/H7
Verwoerd, Hendrik (dam), S. Africa 118/D6
Verwood, Sask. 181/F6
Vesava, India 68/B7
Vesdre (riv.), Belgium 27/H7
Veseleyville, N. Dak. 282/R3
Veseli, Minn. 255/E6
Veseli nad Lužnicí, Czech. 41/C2
Veseli nad Moravou, Czech. 41/D2
Vesoul, France 28/F4
Vesper, Kansas 232/D2
Vesper, Sask. 181/D5
Vesper, Wis. 317/F7
Vesta, C. Rica 154/F6
Vesta, Minn. 255/C6
Vesta, Va. 307/H7
Vestaburg, Mich. 250/E5
Vest-Agder (co.), Norway 18/E7
Vestal •, N.Y. 276/H6
Vestavia Hills, Ala. 195/E4
Vesterålen (isls.), Norway 7/F2
Vesterålen (isls.), Norway 18/J2
Vester Skerninge, Denmark 21/D7
Vestervig, Denmark 21/B4
Vestfjord (fjord), Norway 18/F2
Vestfjorden (fjord), Norway 7/F2
Vestfold (co.), Norway 18/F2
Vestmannaeyjar, Iceland 7/C2
Vestmannaeyjar, Iceland 7/C2
Vestsjaelland (co.), Denmark 21/E6
Vestvågøya (isl.), Norway 18/H3
Vesuvius (vol.), Italy 34/E4
Vesuvius, Va. 307/K5
Veszprém (co.), Hungary 41/D3
Veszprém, Hungary 41/D3
Vésztő, Hungary 41/F3
Vetal, S. Dak. 298/G7
Veteran, Alberta 182/E3
Veteran, Wyo. 319/H4
Vetlanda, Sweden 18/J8
Vetluga (riv.), U.S.S.R. 52/G3
Veurne, Belgium 27/B6
Vevay, Ind. 227/G7
Vevey, Switzerland 39/C4
Vex, Switzerland 39/D4
Veyo, Utah 304/A6
Veys, Iran 66/F5
Veytaux, Switzerland 39/C4
Vezirköprü, Turkey 63/F2
Viacha, Bolivia 120/C4
Viacha, Bolivia 136/A5
Viadana, Italy 34/C2
Viale, Argentina 143/F5
Vian, Okla. 288/S4
Viana, Brazil 132/E3
Viana do Bollo, Spain 33/C1
Viana do Alentejo, Spain 33/C3
Viana do Castelo, Portugal 33/B2
Vianden, Luxembourg 27/J9
Vianen, Netherlands 27/G5
Viangchan (Vientiane), Laos 72/D3
Viangphoukha, Laos 72/D2
Viano do Castelo (dist.), Portugal 33/B2
Viareggio, Italy 34/C3
Vibank, Sask. 181/H5
Viborg (co.), Denmark 21/C4
Viborg, Denmark 18/F8
Viborg, Denmark 21/C5
Viborg, S. Dak. 298/P7
Vibo Valentia, Italy 34/F5
Viburnum, Mo. 261/K7
Viby, Denmark 21/F6
Vicálvaro, Spain 33/G4
Vicco, Ky. 237/P6
Vicam, Mexico 150/D3
Vicente Guerrero, Baja California, Mexico 150/A1
Vicente Guerrero, Durango, Mexico 150/G5
Vicente López, Argentina 143/G7
Vicenza (prov.), Italy 34/C2
Vicenza, Italy 34/C2
Viceroy, Sask. 181/F6
Vich, Spain 33/H2
Vichacla, Bolivia 136/C7
Vichada (comm.), Colombia 126/F5
Vichada (riv.), Colombia 126/F5
Vichadero, Uruguay 145/E2
Vichaya, Bolivia 136/A5
Viche, Ecuador 128/C2

Vichuga, U.S.S.R. 52/F3
Vichy, France 28/E4
Vichy, Mo. 261/J6
Vici, Okla. 288/H2
Vick, Ark. 202/F7
Vick, La. 238/F4
Vickers (lake), Manitoba 179/F3
Vickery, Ohio 284/D3
Vicksburg, Ariz. 198/B5
Vicksburg, Ind. 227/C6
Vicksburg, Mich. 250/D6
Vicksburg, Miss. 188/H4
Vicksburg, Miss. 256/C6
Vicksburg Nat'l Mil. Park, Miss. 256/C6
Viçosa, Brazil 135/E2
Viçosa, Brazil 132/E3
Vicosoprano, Switzerland 39/J4
Vicovaro, Italy 34/F6
Victoire, Sask. 181/D2
Victor, Calif. 204/C9
Victor, Colo. 208/J5
Victor, Idaho 220/G6
Victor, Iowa 229/J5
Victor, Mont. 262/B4
Victor, N.Y. 276/F5
Victor, S. Dak. 298/R2
Victor, W. Va. 312/D6
Victor Harbor, S. Australia 88/F7
Victor Harbor, S. Australia 94/F6
Victoria 88/G7
VICTORIA 97
Victoria (lake) 2/L6
Victoria (lake), Africa 102/F5
Victoria (Mosi-Oa-Tunya) (falls), Africa 102/E6
Victoria, Argentina 143/F6
Victoria, Ark. 202/K2
Victoria (state), Australia 87/E9
Victoria (cap.), Br. Col. 146/F5
Victoria (cap.), Br. Col. 162/D6
Victoria (cap.), Br. Col. 184/K4
Victoria (mt.), Burma 72/B2
Victoria (Limbe), Cameroon 115/A3
Victoria (isl.), Canada 2/D2
Victoria (isl.), Canada 4/B15
Victoria, Malleco, Chile 138/D2
Victoria, Tarapacá, Chile 138/A3
Victoria, Grenada 161/B7
Victoria, Guinea 106/B6
Victoria, Ill. 222/C2
Victoria, Kansas 232/C3
Victoria (lake), Kenya 115/F4
Victoria, Malta 34/E6
Victoria, Minn. 255/F6
Victoria, Miss. 256/E1
Victoria, Mo. 261/M6
Victoria (co.), New Bruns. 170/C1
Victoria, Newf. 166/D2
Victoria (lake), Newf. 166/C4
Victoria (lake), N.S. Wales 97/A3
Victoria (riv.), North. Terr. 88/E3
Victoria (riv.), North. Terr. 93/B3
Victoria (isl.), N.W.T. 146/G1
Victoria (isl.), N.W.T. 162/E1
Victoria (isl.), N.W.T. 187/G2
Victoria (str.), N.W.T. 162/F2
Victoria (str.), N.W.T. 187/H1
Victoria (co.), Nova Scotia 168/H2
Victoria (county), Ontario 177/F3
Victoria (lake), Ontario 177/F2
Victoria (peaks), Philippines 82/B6
Victoria, Pr. Edward I. 168/F2
Victoria (cap.), Seychelles 118/H5
Victoria (lake), Tanzania 115/F4
Victoria, Tenn. 237/K10
Victoria (co.), Texas 303/H9
Victoria, Texas 188/G5
Victoria, Texas 303/H9
Victoria (lake), Uganda 115/F4
Victoria, Va. 307/M6
Victoria (falls), Zambia 115/E7
Victoria (falls), Zimbabwe 118/C3
Victoria Beach, Manitoba 179/F4
Victoria Beach, Nova Scotia 168/C4
Victoria de las Tunas, Cuba 158/H3
Victoria Harbour, Ontario 177/F3
Victoria Land (reg.), Ant. 2/T10
Victoria Land (reg.), Ant. 5/B8
Victoria River Downs, North. Terr 88/E3
Victoria River Downs, North. Terr. 93/B4
Victoria Road, Ontario 177/F3
Victorias, Philippines 82/D5
Victoriaville, Québec 172/F3
Victoria West, S. Africa 118/C6
Victorica, Argentina 143/C4
Victorino, Colombia 126/F6
Victorino, Venezuela 124/E6
Victor Rosales, Mexico 150/H5
Victorville, Calif. 204/H9
Victory, Ky. 237/N6
Victory, Wis. 317/D9
Victory Mills (Victory), N.Y. 276/N4
Vicuña, Chile 138/A8
Vicuña Mackenna, Argentina 143/D3
Vida, Mo. 261/J7
Vida, Mont. 262/L3
Vida, Oreg. 291/E3
Vidal, Calif. 204/L9
Vidal Gormaz (isl.), Chile 138/D9
Vidalia, Georgia 217/H6
Vidalia, La. 238/G5
Videbaek, Denmark 21/B5
Videle, Romania 45/G3
Vidette, Georgia 217/H4
Vidigueira, Portugal 33/C3
Vidin, Bulgaria 45/F4
Vidisha, India 68/D4
Vidor, Texas 303/L7
Vidora, Sask. 181/B6
Vidrine, La. 238/F5
Viechtach, Germany 22/E4
Viedma, Argentina 143/D5
Viedma, Argentina 120/C7
Viedma (lake), Argentina 120/B7
Viedma (lake), Argentina 143/B6

Vieille Case, Dominica 161/E5
Vieira de Leiria, Portugal 33/B3
Vieja, Sierra (mts.), Texas 303/C11
Viella, Spain 33/G1
Vielsalm, Belgium 27/H8
Vienna (city prov.), Austria 41/D2
Vienna (cap.), Austria 41/D2
Vienna (cap.), Austria 7/F4
Vienna, Georgia 217/E6
Vienna, Ill. 222/E6
Vienna, Ind. 227/F7
Vienna, La. 238/E1
Vienna •, Maine 243/D4
Vienna, Md. 245/P7
Vienna, Mo. 261/H6
Vienna, N.J. 273/D2
Vienna, Ohio 284/J3
Vienna, Ontario 177/D5
Vienna, S. Dak. 298/O4
Vienna, Va. 307/R2
Vienna, W. Va. 312/D4
Vienne (dept.), France 28/D4
Vienne, France 28/F5
Vienne (riv.), France 28/D4
Vientiane (cap.), Laos 72/D3
Vientiane (cap.), Laos 54/M8
Viento (pt.), P. Rico 161/E3
Vieques, P. Rico 156/G1
Vieques (Isabel Segunda), P. Rico 161/G2
Vieques (isl.), P. Rico 161/G2
Vieques (isl.), P. Rico 156/G1
Vieques (passage), P. Rico 161/F2
Vieques (sound), P. Rico 161/G2
Vierge (pt.), St. Lucia 161/G6
Vierkant (pt.), Neth. Ant. 161/E8
Viersen, Germany 22/B3
Vierzon, France 28/D4
Viesca, Mexico 150/H4
Vietnam 2/Q5
Vietnam 54/M8
VIETNAM 72
Vieux Desert (lake), Mich. 250/G2
Vieux Desert (lake), Wis. 317/J3
Vieux-Fort, Guadeloupe 161/B7
Vieux-Fort (pt.), Guadeloupe 161/A7
Vieux Fort, St. Lucia 156/G8
Vieux Fort, St. Lucia 161/G7
Vieux Fort (riv.), St. Lucia 161/G6
Vieux-Habitants, Guadeloupe 161/A7
Vievis, U.S.S.R. 53/C3
Viewpark, Scotland 15/C2
Vieytes, Argentina 143/H7
Vig, Denmark 21/E6
Viga, Philippines 82/E4
Vigan, Philippines 85/F2
Vigan, Philippines 82/C2
Vigevano, Italy 34/B2
Vigia, Brazil 132/E3
Vigía (cay), Colombia 126/A10
Vignemale (mt.), France 28/C6
Vigo (co.), Ind. 227/C6
Vigo, Spain 7/D4
Vigo, Spain 33/B1
Vigrestad, Norway 18/D7
Vigsø (bay), Denmark 21/B3
Viiala, Argentina 143/G5
Viipuri (Vyborg), U.S.S.R. 52/C2
Vijayawada, India 54/K8
Vijayawada, India 68/D5
Vijosë (riv.), Albania 45/D5
Vik, Norway 18/E6
Vikeke, Indonesia 85/H7
Viking, Alberta 182/E3
Viking (lake), Manitoba 179/G3
Viking, Minn. 255/B2
Vikna (isl.), Norway 18/G4
Vilacaya, Bolivia 136/C6
Vila de Maganja, Mozambique 118/F3
Vila de Sena, Mozambique 118/E3
Vila do Bispo, Portugal 33/B4
Vila do Conde, Portugal 33/B2
Vila do Porto, Portugal 33/D2
Vilafranca del Penedés, Spain 33/G2
Vila Franca de Xira, Portugal 33/B3
Vila Guilherme Capelo, Angola 115/B5
Vilaine (riv.), France 28/C4
Vilaka, U.S.S.R. 53/D2
Vilanculos, Mozambique 118/E4
Vila Nova de Foz Côa, Portugal 33/C2
Vila Nova de Gaia, Portugal 33/B2
Vila Nova de Milfontes, Portugal 33/B4
Vila Pouca de Aguiar, Portugal 33/C2
Vila Real (dist.), Portugal 33/C2
Vila Real, Portugal 33/C2
Vila Real de Santo António, Portugal 33/C4
Vilar Formoso, Portugal 33/C2
Vilas, Colo. 208/P8
Vilas, N.C. 281/F2
Vilas, S. Dak. 298/O6
Vilas (co.), Wis. 317/G3
Vila Velha, Brazil 132/D2
Vila Velha Argolas, Brazil 132/F8
Vila Velha de Ródão, Portugal 33/C3
Vila Verde, Portugal 33/B2
Vila Viçosa, Portugal 33/C3
Vilcabamba, Cordillera (mts.), Peru 128/F9
Vilcanota (mt.), Peru 128/G10
Vildbjerg, Denmark 21/B5
Vildo, Tenn. 237/C10
Vileyka, U.S.S.R. 52/C4
Vilhelmina, Sweden 18/K4
Vilhena, Brazil 132/H10
Viliya (riv.), U.S.S.R. 53/C3
Viljandi, U.S.S.R. 53/B3
Vilkija, U.S.S.R. 53/B3
Vil'kitskogo (str.), U.S.S.R. 4/B4
Vil'kitskogo (str.), U.S.S.R. 48/L2
Villa, Switzerland 39/H3
Vilela Abecia, Bolivia 136/C7
Villa Acuña, Mexico 150/J2
Villa Alemana, Chile 138/F2
Villa Alhué, Chile 138/G4
Villa Altagracia, Dom. Rep. 158/E6
Villa Amazónica, Colombia 126/B7
Villa Ana, Argentina 143/E2

Villa Ángela, Argentina 143/D2
Villa Atamisqui, Argentina 143/D2
Villa Atuel, Argentina 143/C3
Villa Bella, Bolivia 136/C2
Villablino, Spain 33/C1
Villa Bruzual, Venezuela 124/D3
Villabruzzi (Johar), Somalia 115/J3
Villa Bustos, Argentina 143/C2
Villa Cañas, Argentina 143/F6
Villacañas, Spain 33/E3
Villacarriedo, Spain 33/D1
Villacarrillo, Spain 33/E3
Villach, Austria 41/B3
Villacidro, Italy 34/B5
Villa Cisneros (Dakhla), W. Sahara 102/A2
Villa Cisneros (Dakhla), Western Sahara 106/A4
Villa Clara, Argentina 143/G5
Villa Clara (prov.), Cuba 158/E1
Villa Constitución, Argentina 143/F6
Villa Cuauhtémoc, Mexico 150/L5
Villada, Spain 33/D1
Villa Darwin, Uruguay 145/B4
Villa de Cos, Mexico 150/H5
Villa de Cura, Venezuela 124/E2
Villa de Guadelupe Hidalgo, Mexico 150/L1
Villa del Cerro, Uruguay 145/A7
Villa del Rosario, Argentina 143/D3
Villa de María, Argentina 143/D2
Villa de San Antonio, Honduras 154/D3
Villa Diego, Argentina 143/F6
Villadiego, Spain 33/D1
Villa Dolores, Argentina 143/C3
Villa E. Viscarra, Bolivia 136/C6
Villa Elisa, Argentina 143/G6
Villafamés, Spain 33/G2
Villa Federal, Argentina 143/F5
Villa Florida, Paraguay 144/D5
Villa Franca, Paraguay 144/C5
Villafranca, Spain 33/F1
Villafranca del Bierzo, Spain 33/C1
Villafranca del Cid, Spain 33/F2
Villafranca de los Barros, Spain 33/C3
Villafranca di Verona, Italy 34/C2
Villa Frontado, Venezuela 124/G2
Villa Frontera, Mexico 150/J3
Villa García, Mexico 150/J5
Villagarcía, Spain 33/B1
Village, Ark. 202/D7
Village, N.S. Wales 97/J2
Village-Blier, Québec 172/H2
Village-des-Aulnaies, Québec 172/G2
Village Mills, Texas 303/K7
Villa General Pérez, Bolivia 136/A4
Villa General Ramírez, Argentina 143/F6
Villa General Roca, Argentina 143/C3
Village-Saint-Laurent, New Bruns. 170/E1
Villagran, Mexico 150/K4
Villa Grove, Colo. 208/G6
Villa Grove, Ill. 222/E4
Villaguay, Argentina 143/G5
Villa Guillermina, Argentina 143/D2
Villa Hayes, Paraguay 144/A4
Villahermosa, Mexico 146/J8
Villahermosa, Mexico 150/N8
Villahermosa, Spain 33/E3
Villa Hidalgo, Durango, Mexico 150/G3
Villa Hidalgo, Sonora, Mexico 150/E1
Villa Hills, Ky. 237/F2
Villa Huidobro, Argentina 143/D3
Villa Industrial, Chile 138/B1
Villa Ingavi, Bolivia 136/D7
Villajoyosa, Spain 33/F3
Villalba, P. Rico 161/C2
Villalba, Spain 33/C1
Villalbín, Paraguay 144/C5
Villaldama, Mexico 150/J3
Villalon, Philippines 82/E5
Villalón de Campos, Spain 33/D1
Villalpando, Spain 33/D2
Villa Mantero, Argentina 143/G6
Villa María, Argentina 143/D3
Villa María, Argentina 120/C6
Villa María Grande, Argentina 143/F5
Villa Martín, Bolivia 136/B7
Villa Matamoros, Mexico 150/G3
Villamil, Ecuador 128/B9
Villa Montes, Bolivia 120/C5
Villa Montes, Bolivia 136/D7
Villanova, Pa. 294/M6
Villanow, Georgia 217/B1
Villa Nueva, Argentina 143/D3
Villanueva, Colombia 126/D2
Villanueva, Mexico 150/H5
Villanueva, N. Mex. 274/D4
Villanueva de Córdoba, Spain 33/D3
Villanueva del Arzobispo, Spain 33/E3
Villanueva de la Serena, Spain 33/D3
Villanueva de los Infantes, Spain 33/E3
Villanueva y Geltrú, Spain 33/G2
Villány, Hungary 41/E4
Villa Ocampo, Argentina 143/D2
Villa Oliva, Paraguay 144/C5
Villa Orías, Bolivia 136/D5
Villa Park, Calif. 204/D11
Villa Park, Ill. 222/B5
Villar, Bolivia 136/C6
Villarcayo, Spain 33/E1
Villard, Minn. 255/C5
Villar del Arzobispo, Spain 33/F3
Villareal, Philippines 82/E5
Villa Regina, Argentina 143/C4
Villa Rica, Georgia 217/C3
Villa Ridge, Ill. 222/D6
Villa Riva, Dom. Rep. 158/E5
Villa Rosario, Colombia 126/D4
Villarreal de los Infantes, Spain 33/F3
Villarrica, Chile 138/E2
Villarrica (lake), Chile 138/E2
Villarrica, Paraguay 120/D5

Villarrica, Paraguay 144/C5
Villarrobledo, Spain 33/E3
Villarrubia de los Ojos, Spain 33/E3
Villas, N.J. 273/D5
Villasana de Mena, Spain 33/E1
Villa San Agustín, Argentina 143/C3
Villa San José, Argentina 143/G6
Villa San Martín, Argentina 143/D2
Villa Serrano, Bolivia 136/C6
Villa Tasso, Fla. 212/C6
Villa Tunari, Bolivia 136/C5
Villa Unión, Argentina 143/C2
Villa Unión, Coahuila, Mexico 150/J2
Villa Unión, Durango, Mexico 150/H5
Villa Unión, Sinaloa, Mexico 150/F5
Villa Vaca Guzmán, Bolivia 136/D6
Villaverde, Spain 33/F4
Villavicencio, Colombia 120/B2
Villavicencio, Colombia 126/D5
Villa Vicente Guerrero, Mexico 150/N1
Villaviciosa, Spain 33/D1
Villawood, N.S. Wales 88/K4
Villawood, N.S. Wales 97/H3
Villa y Puerto del Son, Spain 33/B1
Villazón, Bolivia 120/C5
Villazón, Bolivia 136/C7
Ville Bonheur, Haiti 158/C6
Villefranche, France 28/G6
Villefranche-de-Lauragais, France 28/D6
Villefranche-de-Rouergue, France 28/E5
Villefranche-sur-Saône, France 28/F4
Villegreen, Colo. 208/M8
Villejuif, France 28/B2
Ville-Marie, Québec 174/B3
Villemomble, France 28/C1
Villena, Spain 33/F3
Villeneuve, Québec 172/J3
Villeneuve, Switzerland 39/C4
Villeneuve-Saint-Georges, France 28/E3
Villeneuve-sur-Lot, France 28/D5
Ville Platte, La. 238/F6
Villeroy, Québec 172/F3
Villeta, Colombia 126/C5
Villeta, Paraguay 144/A5
Villeta (lake), Québec 172/C2
Villeurbanne, France 28/F5
Villiers (lake), Québec 172/G2
Villiersdorp, S. Africa 118/D6
Villingen-Schwenningen, Germany 22/C4
Villisca, Iowa 229/C7
Villupuram, India 68/D6
Vilna, Alberta 182/E2
Vilnius (Vilna), U.S.S.R. 7/G3
Vilnius (Vilna), U.S.S.R. 48/C4
Vilnius (Vilna), U.S.S.R. 52/C4
Vilnius (Vilna) (cap.), Lithuanian S.S.R., U.S.S.R. 53/C3
Vilonia, Ark. 202/F3
Vils, Austria 41/A3
Vilvoorde, Belgium 27/F7
Vilvorde (Vilvoorde), Belgium 27/F7
Vilyuy (riv.), U.S.S.R. 54/N3
Vilyuy (range), U.S.S.R. 48/M3
Vilyuy (res.), U.S.S.R. 48/M3
Vilyuy (riv.), U.S.S.R. 48/L3
Vilyuysk, U.S.S.R. 48/N3
Vimianzo, Spain 33/B1
Vimioso, Portugal 33/C2
Vimmerby, Sweden 18/J8
Vimperk, Czech. 41/B2
Vimy, Alberta 182/D2
Vimy Ridge, Ark. 202/F4
Vina, Ala. 195/B2
Vina, Calif. 204/D4
Viña del Mar, Chile 120/B8
Viña del Mar, Chile 138/F2
Viñales, Cuba 156/A2
Viñales, Cuba 158/A1
Vinalhaven •, Maine 243/F7
Vinalhaven (isl.), Maine 243/F7
Vinaroz, Spain 33/G2
Vincennes (bay) 5/C6
Vincennes, France 28/B2
Vincennes, Ind. 227/C7
Vincennes, Iowa 229/K7
Vincent, Ala. 195/F4
Vincent, Ark. 202/K3
Vincent, Iowa 229/F4
Vincent (pt.), Norfolk I. 88/K6
Vincent, Ohio 284/F5
Vincentown, N.J. 273/D4
Vinces, Ecuador 128/C3
Vinchina, Argentina 143/C2
Vinchos, Peru 128/E9
Vindelälven (riv.), Sweden 18/L4
Vindeln, Sweden 18/L4
Vinderup, Denmark 21/B5
Vindhya (range), India 68/D4
Vinegar Bend, Ala. 195/B8
Vine Grove, Ky. 237/K5
Vineland, Colo. 208/K6
Vineland, N.J. 273/C5
Vinemont, Ala. 195/E2
Vineyard (sound), Mass. 249/L7
Vineyard Haven, Mass. 249/M7
Vinh, Vietnam 72/E3
Vinh, Vietnam 54/M8
Vinhais, Portugal 33/C2
Vinh Long, Vietnam 72/E5
Vinh Yen, Vietnam 72/E2
Vining, Iowa 229/J5
Vining, Kansas 232/E2
Vining, Minn. 255/C4
Vinings, Georgia 217/K1
Vinita, Okla. 288/E1
Vinita Park, Mo. 261/P2
Vinkovci, Yugoslavia 45/D3
Vinland, Kansas 232/G3
Vinnitsa, U.S.S.R. 7/G4
Vinnitsa, U.S.S.R. 52/C5
Vinnitsa, U.S.S.R. 48/C5
Vinohene, S. Africa 118/E7
Vinson, Okla. 288/G3
Vinson Massif (mt.), Ant. 5/B14
Vinsulla, Br. Col. 184/G5

Vint Hill Farms Mil. Res., Va. 307/N3
Vinton, Iowa 229/J4
Vinton, La. 238/C6
Vinton (co.), Ohio 284/E7
Vinton, Ohio 284/F8
Vinton, Va. 307/J6
Vintondale, Pa. 294/E5
Vinukonda, India 68/D5
Viola, Ark. 202/G1
Viola, Del. 245/R4
Viola, Idaho 220/B3
Viola, Ill. 222/C2
Viola, Iowa 229/L4
Viola, Kansas 232/E4
Viola, Ky. 237/D7
Viola, Minn. 255/F6
Viola, Mo. 261/E9
Viola, N.Y. 276/J8
Viola, Tenn. 237/K9
Viola, Wis. 317/E8
Violet, La. 238/P4
Violet Grove, Alberta 182/C3
Violet Hill, Ark. 202/G1
Violette Brook, New Bruns. 170/C1
Violet Valley Aboriginal Res., W. Australia 88/D3
Virac, Philippines 82/E4
Virago (sound), Br. Col. 184/A3
Virajpet, India 68/D6
Viramgam, India 68/C4
Viranşehir, Turkey 63/H4
Virden, Ill. 222/D4
Virden, Manitoba 179/A5
Virden, N. Mex. 274/A6
Vire, France 28/C3
Virgelle, Mont. 262/F2
Virgie, Ky. 237/R6
Virgil, Kansas 232/F4
Virgil, S. Dak. 298/N5
Virgilina, Va. 307/L7
Virgin (mts.), Ariz. 198/B2
Virgin (riv.), Ariz. 198/B2
Virgin (mts.), Nev. 266/G6
Virgin (peak), Nev. 266/G6
Virgin (riv.), Nev. 266/G6
Virgin (creek), S. Dak. 298/H3
Virgin, Utah 304/A6
Virgin, East Fork (riv.), Utah 304/B6
Virgin (riv.), Utah 304/A6
Virgin (str.), Virgin Is. (U.S.) 161/A4
Virgin Gorda (isl.), Virgin Is. (U.K.) 156/H1
Virginia 188/L3
VIRGINIA 307
Virginia (key), Fla. 212/B5
Virginia, Idaho 220/F7
Virginia, Ill. 222/C4
Virginia, Ireland 17/G2
Virginia, Minn. 188/H1
Virginia, Minn. 255/J3
Virginia, Nebr. 264/H4
Virginia (range), Nev. 266/B3
Virginia, S. Australia 94/B7
Virginia (state), U.S. 146/L6
Virginia Beach, Va. 188/L3
Virginia Beach (I.C.), Va. 307/S7
Virginia City, Mont. 262/E5
Virginia City, Nev. 266/B3
Virginia Dale, Colo. 208/J1
Virginia Gardens, Fla. 212/B5
Virginiatown, Ontario 177/K5
Virginiatown, Ontario 175/E3
VIRGIN ISLANDS (U.K.) 156/H1
VIRGIN ISLANDS (U.K.) 161
VIRGIN ISLANDS (U.S.) 156/H1
VIRGIN ISLANDS (U.S.) 161
Virgin Isls. Nat'l Park, Virgin Is. (U.S.) 161/C4
Virginville, W. Va. 312/F2
Virochey, Cambodia 72/E4
Viroinval, Belgium 27/F8
Viroqua, Wis. 317/D8
Virovitica, Yugoslavia 45/C3
Virrat, Finland 18/N5
Virserum, Sweden 18/J8
Virton, Belgium 27/H9
Virtsu, U.S.S.R. 53/B1
Virú, Peru 128/D7
Virunga (range), Rwanda 115/E4
Virunga (range), Uganda 115/E4
Virunga (range), Zaire 115/E4
Virunga Nat'l Park, Uganda 115/E4
Virunga Nat'l Park, Zaire 115/E4
Vis (isl.), Yugoslavia 45/C4
Visakhapatnam, India 54/K8
Visakhapatnam, India 68/E5
Visalia, Calif. 188/C3
Visalia, Calif. 204/F7
Visalia, Ky. 237/N3
Visayan (sea), Philippines 82/D5
Visayan (sea), Philippines 85/G3
Visby, Sweden 18/L8
Visby, Sweden 7/F3
Visconde dos Rio Branco, Brazil 135/E2
Viscount, Sask. 181/F4
Viscount Melville (sound), Canada 4/B15
Viscount Melville (sound), N.W.T. 162/E1
Viscount Melville (sound), N.W.T. 146/H2
Viscount Melville (sound), N.W.T. 187/G2
Visé, Belgium 27/H7
Višegrad, Yugoslavia 45/D4
Viseu, Brazil 132/E3
Viseu (dist.), Portugal 33/C2
Viseu, Portugal 33/C2
Viseu de Sus, Romania 45/F2
Vishera (riv.), U.S.S.R. 52/J2
Vishoek, S. Africa 118/E7
Vislanda, Sweden 18/H8
Visnagar, India 68/C4
Viso (mt.), Italy 34/A2
Visoko, Yugoslavia 45/D4

Wallace 465

Visp, Switzerland 39/E4
Visp (riv.), Switzerland 39/E4
Vissoie, Switzerland 39/E4
Vista, Calif. 204/H10
Vista, Manitoba 179/B4
Vista, Mo. 261/E7
Vista Hermosa, Cuba 158/G3
Vistula, Ind. 227/F1
Vistula (riv.), Poland 7/F3
Vistula (riv.), Poland 47/D2
Vistula (spit), Poland 47/D1
Vit (riv.), Bulgaria 45/G4
Vita, Manitoba 179/F5
Vitali (isl.), Philippines 82/D7
Vitebsk, U.S.S.R. 7/H3
Vitebsk, U.S.S.R. 52/C3
Vitebsk, U.S.S.R. 48/D4
Viterbo (prov.), Italy 34/C3
Viterbo, Italy 34/C3
Vitiaz (str.), Papua N.G. 85/B7
Vitiaz (str.), Papua N.G. 86/A2
Vitichi, Bolivia 136/C7
Vitigudino, Spain 33/C2
Viti Levu (isl.), Fiji 87/H7
Viti Levu (isl.), Fiji 86/P11
Vitim (riv.), U.S.S.R. 54/N4
Vitim (riv.), U.S.S.R. 48/M4
Vitimskiy, U.S.S.R. 48/M4
Vitkov, Czech. 41/D2
Vitor, Quebrado (riv.), Chile 138/A1
Vitor, Peru 128/G11
Vitor (riv.), Peru 128/F11
Vitória, Brazil 120/F5
Vitória, Brazil 132/G8
Vitoria, Spain 33/E1
Vitoria, Spain 7/D4
Vitória da Conquista, Brazil 120/E4
Vitória da Conquista, Brazil 132/F6
Vitória de Santo Antão, Brazil 132/G4
Vitória de Santo Antão, Brazil 120/F3
Vitré, France 28/C3
Vitry-le-François, France 28/F3
Vitry-sur-Seine, France 28/B2
Vittangi, Sweden 18/M3
Vittel, France 28/F3
Vittoria, Italy 34/E6
Vittoria, Ontario 177/D5
Vittorio Veneto, Italy 34/D1
Vitu (isls.), Papua N.G. 86/B2
Vivero, Spain 33/C1
Vivian, La. 238/B1
Vivian, S. Dak. 298/J6
Vivian, W. Va. 312/D8
Vivorillo (cays), Honduras 154/F3
Vixen, La. 238/F2
Vizagapatam (Visakhapatnam), India 68/E5
Vizcaino (cape), Calif. 204/B4
Vizcaya (prov.), Spain 33/E1
Vize, Turkey 63/B2
Vizianagaram, India 68/E5
Vizille, France 28/F5
Vizinga, U.S.S.R. 52/G2
Viziru, Romania 45/H3
Vizovice, Czech. 41/D2
Vizzini, Italy 34/E6
Vlaardingen, Netherlands 27/E5
Vladimir, U.S.S.R. 7/J3
Vladimir, U.S.S.R. 48/D4
Vladimir, U.S.S.R. 52/F3
Vladimir-Volynskiy, U.S.S.R. 52/B4
Vladivostok, U.S.S.R. 54/P5
Vladivostok, U.S.S.R. 2/R3
Vladivostok, U.S.S.R. 48/O5
Vlagtwedde, Netherlands 27/L3
Vlasenica, Yugoslavia 45/D3
Vlašim, Czech. 41/C2
Vleteren, Belgium 27/B7
Vlieland (isl.), Netherlands 27/F2
Vliestroom (str.), Netherlands 27/G2
Vliets, Kansas 232/F2
Vlijmen, Netherlands 27/G5
Vlissingen (Flushing), Netherlands 27/C6
Vlorë, Albania 45/D5
Vltava (riv.), Czech. 41/C2
Voca, Texas 303/E7
Vöcklabruck, Austria 41/B2
Voda, Kansas 232/C2
Vodl (lake), U.S.S.R. 52/E2
Vodňany, Czech. 41/C2
Vogar, Manitoba 179/D4
Vogel Center, Mich. 250/E4
Vogelkop (Doberai) (pen.), Indonesia 85/J6
Vogelsberg (mts.), Germany 22/C3
Voghera, Italy 34/B2
Voglers Cove, Nova Scotia 168/D4
Voh, New Caled. 86/G4
Vohibinany, Madagascar 118/H3
Vohimarina (Vohémar), Madagascar 118/J2
Vohimena (cape), Madagascar 102/G7
Vohimena (cape), Madagascar 118/G5
Vohipeno, Madagascar 118/H4
Voi, Kenya 115/G4
Voi, Kenya 102/F5
Voil, Loch (lake), Scotland 15/D4
Voiron, France 28/F5
Voisey (bay), Newf. 166/B2
Voitsberg, Austria 41/C3
Voïviïs (lake), Greece 45/F6
Vojens, Denmark 21/C7
Vojmsjön (lake), Sweden 18/J4
Vojnice, Czech. 41/E3
Vojvodina (aut. prov.), Yugoslavia 45/D3
Volador, Colombia 126/C3
Volant, Pa. 294/B3
Volary, Czech. 41/B2
Volborg, Mont. 262/L5
Volcano, Calif. 204/E5
Volcano, Hawaii 218/J6
Volcano (isls.), Japan 87/E3
Volcano (isls.), Japan 81/M4
Volda, Norway 18/E5
Volendam-Edam, Netherlands 27/G4
Volga, Iowa 229/L3
Volga, S. Dak. 298/R5
Volga (riv.), U.S.S.R. 7/J4
Volga (riv.), U.S.S.R. 2/M3
Volga (riv.), U.S.S.R. 48/E5
Volga (riv.), U.S.S.R. 52/G5
Volga, W. Va. 312/F4
Volga-Don (canal), U.S.S.R. 52/F5
Volgodonsk, U.S.S.R. 52/F5
Volgograd, U.S.S.R. 2/M3
Volgograd, U.S.S.R. 7/J4
Volgograd, U.S.S.R. 48/E5
Volgograd, U.S.S.R. 52/F5
Volgograd (res.), U.S.S.R. 52/G5
Volin, S. Dak. 298/P8
Völkermarkt, Austria 41/C3
Volkhov, U.S.S.R. 52/D3
Volkhov (riv.), U.S.S.R. 52/D3
Völklingen, Germany 22/B4
Volkovysk, U.S.S.R. 52/B4
Volksrust, S. Africa 118/D5
Volney, Mich. 250/D5
Volney, Va. 307/F7
Volochanka, U.S.S.R. 48/K2
Vologda, U.S.S.R. 7/J3
Vologda, U.S.S.R. 48/E4
Vologda, U.S.S.R. 52/F3
Vólos, Greece 7/G5
Vólos, Greece 45/F6
Vol'sk, U.S.S.R. 7/J3
Vol'sk, U.S.S.R. 52/G4
Volta (lake), Ghana 102/B4
Volta (riv.), Ghana 102/C4
Volta (lake), Ghana 106/D7
Volta (riv.), Ghana 106/E7
Volta Grande (res.), Brazil 135/B1
Voltaire, N. Dak. 282/J3
Volta Redonda, Brazil 120/E5
Volta Redonda, Brazil 132/E8
Volta Redonda, Brazil 135/D3
Volterra, Italy 34/C3
Volturno (riv.), Italy 34/E4
Voluntown•, Conn. 210/H2
Volusia (co.), Fla. 212/E2
Vólvi (lake), Greece 45/F5
Volyně, Czech. 41/B2
Volyn Oblast, U.S.S.R. 52/C4
Volzhsk, U.S.S.R. 52/G3
Volzhskiy, U.S.S.R. 7/J4
Volzhskiy, U.S.S.R. 52/G5
Vom, Nigeria 106/F7
Vona, Colo. 208/O4
Vonda, Sask. 181/F3
Vónitsa, Greece 45/E6
Vonore, Tenn. 237/N9
Von Ormy, Texas 303/J11
Voorburg, Netherlands 27/E4
Voorhees•, N.J. 273/B3
Voorheesville, N.Y. 276/M5
Voorhies, Iowa 229/J4
Voorne (isl.), Netherlands 27/D5
Voorst, Netherlands 27/J4
Vopnafjördhur (fjord), Iceland 21/D1
Vorab (mt.), Switzerland 39/H3
Vorarlberg (prov.), Austria 41/A3
Vorbasse, Denmark 21/B6
Vorden, Netherlands 27/J4
Vordernberg, Austria 41/C3
Vorderrhein (riv.), Switzerland 39/G3
Vordingborg, Denmark 21/E7
Vordingborg, Denmark 18/G9
Vorgod (riv.), Denmark 21/B6
Vorkuta, U.S.S.R. 4/C6
Vorkuta, U.S.S.R. 7/L2
Vorkuta, U.S.S.R. 52/K1
Vorkuta, U.S.S.R. 48/G3
Vormsi (isl.), U.S.S.R. 53/B1
Vorona (riv.), U.S.S.R. 52/F4
Voronezh, U.S.S.R. 7/H3
Voronezh, U.S.S.R. 52/E4
Voronezh, U.S.S.R. 48/E4
Voroshilovgrad (Lugansk), U.S.S.R. 7/H4
Voroshilovgrad (Lugansk), U.S.S.R. 52/E5
Voroshilovgrad (Lugansk), U.S.S.R. 48/E5
Vorskla (riv.), U.S.S.R. 52/E4
Vorst (Forest), Belgium 27/B9
Võrtsjärv (lake), U.S.S.R. 53/D1
Võru, U.S.S.R. 52/C2
Võru, U.S.S.R. 53/D2
Vosges (dept.), France 28/G3
Vosges (mts.), France 28/G3
Voskresensk, U.S.S.R. 52/E3
Voss, N. Dak. 282/R3
Voss, Norway 18/E6
Vossburg, Miss. 256/F7
Vostochnyy, U.S.S.R. 48/O5
Vostok (isl.), Kiribati 2/B6
Vostok (isl.), Kiribati 87/L7
Votamo (riv.), Venezuela 124/F6
Votice, Czech. 41/C2
Votkinsk, U.S.S.R. 48/F4
Votkinsk, U.S.S.R. 52/H3
Votuporanga, Brazil 135/B2
Vouvry, Switzerland 39/C4
Voúxa (cape), Greece 45/F8
Vouziers, France 28/F3
Voyageurs Nat'l Park, Minn. 255/F2
Voy-Vozh, U.S.S.R. 48/F3
Voy-Vozh, U.S.S.R. 52/H2
Vozhe (lake), U.S.S.R. 52/F2
Vozhega, U.S.S.R. 52/F2
Vozhma, U.S.S.R. 52/G3
Voznesensk, U.S.S.R. 52/D5
Vrå, Denmark 21/C3
Vráble, Czech. 41/E2
Vracov, Czech. 41/D2
Vrangelya (isl.), U.S.S.R. 54/U2
Vranje, Yugoslavia 45/F4
Vranov nad Teplou, Czech. 41/F2
Vratsa, Bulgaria 45/F4
Vrbas, Yugoslavia 45/D3
Vrbas (riv.), Yugoslavia 45/C3
Vrbno pod Pradědem, Czech. 41/D1
Vrbovce, Czech. 41/D1
Vrbové, Czech. 41/D2
Vrchlabí, Czech. 41/C1
Vrede, S. Africa 118/D5
Vredenburg, S. Africa 118/B6
Vredenburgh, Ala. 195/D7
Vredendal, S. Africa 118/B6
Vreed-en-Hoop, Guyana 131/B2
Vresse-sur-Semois, Belgium 27/F9
Vriezenveen, Netherlands 27/K4
Vrondádhes, Greece 45/G6
Vršac, Yugoslavia 45/E3
Vrútky, Czech. 41/E2
Vryburg, S. Africa 118/C5
Vryheid, S. Africa 118/E5
Vsetín, Czech. 41/D2
Vsevidof (mt.), Alaska 196/E4
Vuadens, Switzerland 39/C3
Vučitrn, Yugoslavia 45/E4
Vught, Netherlands 27/G5
Vukovar, Yugoslavia 45/D3
Vulcan, Alberta 182/D4
Vulcan, Mich. 250/B3
Vulcan, Mo. 261/L8
Vulcan, W. Va. 312/B7
Vulcano (isl.), Italy 34/E5
Vu Liet, Vietnam 72/E3
Vung Tau, Vietnam 72/E5
Vuollerim, Sweden 18/M3
Vuolvojaure (lake), Sweden 18/L3
Vuotso, Finland 18/P2
Vya, Nev. 266/B1
Vyatka (riv.), U.S.S.R. 52/H3
Vyatskiye Polyany, U.S.S.R. 52/H3
Vyazemskiy, U.S.S.R. 48/O5
Vyaz'ma, U.S.S.R. 52/D3
Vyborg, U.S.S.R. 7/G2
Vyborg, U.S.S.R. 52/C2
Vyborg, U.S.S.R. 48/C3
Vychegda (riv.), U.S.S.R. 52/G2
Východočeský (reg.), Czech. 41/C1
Východoslovenský (reg.), Czech. 41/F2
Vyg (lake), U.S.S.R. 52/E2
Vyksa, U.S.S.R. 52/F3
Vym' (riv.), U.S.S.R. 52/H2
Vyshniy Volochek, U.S.S.R. 7/H2
Vyshniy Volochek, U.S.S.R. 52/D3
Vyshniy Volochek, U.S.S.R. 48/D4
Vysoké, Czech. 41/D2
Vysoké Mýto, Czech. 41/D2
Vysoké Tatry, Czech. 41/F2
Vyšší Brod, Czech. 41/C2
Vytegra, U.S.S.R. 52/E2

W

Wa, Ghana 106/D6
Waal (riv.), Netherlands 27/G5
Waalre, Netherlands 27/G6
Waalwijk, Netherlands 27/F5
Waarschoot, Belgium 27/D6
Waas (mt.), Utah 304/E5
Waasis, New Bruns. 170/D3
Wabamun, Alberta 182/C3
Waban, Mass. 249/B7
Wabana, Newf. 166/D2
Wabaningo, Mich. 250/C5
Wabasca, Alberta 182/D2
Wabasca (riv.), Alberta 182/C1
Wabasca (riv.), Alta. 162/E4
Wabash (riv.) 188/J3
Wabash, Ark. 202/J5
Wabash (co.), Ill. 222/F5
Wabash (riv.), Ill. 222/F5
Wabash (co.), Ind. 227/F3
Wabash, Ind. 227/F3
Wabash (riv.), Ind. 227/B7
Wabash, Ohio 284/A4
Wabash (riv.), Ohio 284/A5
Wabasha (co.), Minn. 255/F6
Wabasha, Minn. 255/G6
Wabasso, Fla. 212/F4
Wabasso, Minn. 255/C6
Wabatawangang (lake), Minn. 255/D3
Wabaunsee (co.), Kansas 232/F3
Wabaunsee, Kansas 232/F2
Wabbaseka, Ark. 202/G5
Wabeno, Wis. 317/J5
Wabi (riv.), Ethiopia 111/H6
Wabigoon, Ontario 175/B3
Wabigoon, Ontario 177/G5
Wabi Shebelle (riv.) 102/G4
Wabi Shebelle (riv.), Ethiopia 111/H6
Wabowden, Manitoba 179/J3
Wąbrzeźno, Poland 47/D2
Wabuk (pt.), Ontario 175/D1
Wabush, Newf. 166/A3
Wabush, Newf. 162/K5
Wabuska, Nev. 266/B3
Waccamaw (lake), N.C. 281/N6
Waccamaw (riv.), N.C. 281/M7
Waccamaw (riv.), S.C. 296/J5
Waccasassa (bay), Fla. 212/D2
Waccasassa (riv.), Fla. 212/D2
Wachapreague, Va. 307/S5
Wachapreague (inlet), Va. 307/T6
Wachtebeke, Belgium 27/D6
Wachusett (mt.), Mass. 249/G3
Wachusett (res.), Mass. 249/G3
Wacissa, Fla. 212/B1
Waco, Georgia 217/B3
Waco, Ky. 237/N5
Waco, Mo. 261/C8
Waco, Nebr. 264/G4
Waco, N.C. 281/G4
Waco, Texas 188/G4
Waco, Texas 146/J6
Waco, Texas 303/G6
Waconda (lake), Kansas 232/D2
Waconia, Minn. 255/E6
Wadai (reg.), Chad 111/D5
Waddamana, Tasmania 99/C4
Waddan, Libya 102/D2
Waddan, Libya 111/C2
Waddell, Ariz. 198/C5
Waddenzee (sound), Netherlands 27/G2
Waddington (mt.), Br. Col. 162/D5
Waddington (mt.), Br. Col. 184/E4
Waddington, N.Y. 276/K1
Waddy, Ky. 237/L4
Wade, Miss. 256/G9
Wade (lake), Newf. 166/A3
Wade, N.C. 281/M4
Wade, Okla. 288/O7
Wadebridge, England 13/C7
Wade-Hampton, S.C. 296/C2
Wadena, Ind. 227/C3
Wadena, Iowa 229/K3
Wadena (co.), Minn. 255/D4
Wadena, Minn. 255/C4
Wadena, Sask. 181/H4
Wädenswil, Switzerland 39/G2
Wadesboro, La. 238/M2
Wadesboro, N.C. 281/J5
Wadestown, W. Va. 312/F3
Wadesville, Ind. 227/B8
Wadeville, N.C. 281/J4
Wadhams, N.Y. 276/N2
Wadi Dra, Morocco 102/B2
Wadi es Sir, Jordan 65/D4
Wadi Halfa, Sudan 111/F3
Wadi Musa, Jordan 65/E5
Wading (riv.), N.J. 273/D4
Wading River, N.Y. 276/P9
Wadley, Ala. 195/G4
Wadley, Georgia 217/H5
Wadmalaw (isl.), S.C. 296/G6
Wad Medani, Sudan 111/F5
Wad Medani, Sudan 59/B7
Wad Medani, Sudan 102/F3
Wadowice, Poland 47/D4
Wadsworth, Ala. 195/E5
Wadsworth, Ill. 222/B4
Wadsworth, Nev. 266/B3
Wadsworth, Ohio 284/G3
Wadsworth, Texas 303/J9
Waelder, Texas 303/G8
Wagait Aboriginal Res., North. Terr. 93/B2
Wagarville, Ala. 195/B8
Wagener, S.C. 296/E4
Wageningen, Netherlands 27/H5
Wageningen, Suriname 131/C3
Wager (bay), N.W.T. 146/J3
Wager (bay), N.W.T. 162/G2
Wager (bay), N.W.T. 187/K3
Wagga Wagga, Australia 87/E9
Wagga Wagga, N.S. Wales 88/H7
Wagga Wagga, N.S. Wales 97/D4
Waggoner, Ill. 222/D4
Waggrakine, W. Australia 92/A5
Wagin, W. Australia 88/B6
Wagin, W. Australia 92/B2
Wagner, Alberta 182/C2
Wagner, Mont. 262/H2
Wagner, S. Dak. 298/N7
Wagoner (co.), Okla. 288/P3
Wagoner, Okla. 288/R3
Wagon Mound, N. Mex. 274/E2
Wagontire, Oreg. 291/H4
Wagon Wheel Gap, Colo. 208/F7
Wagram, N.C. 281/L5
Wągrowiec, Poland 47/C2
Wah, Pakistan 68/C2
Wahai, Indonesia 85/H6
Wahalak, Miss. 256/G5
Wahiawa, Hawaii 218/E2
Wahiawa, Hawaii 188/F5
Wahkiacus, Wash. 310/D5
Wahkiakum (co.), Wash. 310/B4
Wahkon, Minn. 255/E4
Wahlern, Switzerland 39/D3
Wahoo, Nebr. 264/H3
Wahpeton, Iowa 229/C2
Wahpeton, N. Dak. 188/G1
Wahpeton, N. Dak. 282/S7
Wahsatch, Utah 304/C2
Wah Wah (mts.), Utah 304/A5
Wahwashkesh (lake), Ontario 177/D2
Wahweap (creek), Utah 304/C6
Wai, Poulo (isls.), Vietnam 72/E4
Waiakoa, Hawaii 218/J2
Waialae, Hawaii 218/D4
Waialeale (mt.), Hawaii 218/C1
Waialee, Hawaii 218/E1
Waialua, Hawaii 188/F5
Waialua, Molokai, Hawaii 218/H1
Waialua, Oahu, Hawaii 218/E1
Waianae, Hawaii 218/D2
Waiau, N. Zealand 100/D5
Waiau (riv.), N. Zealand 100/A6
Waidhofen an der Thaya, Austria 41/C2
Waidhofen an der Ybbs, Austria 41/C3
Waidsboro, Va. 307/J7
Waigama, Indonesia 85/H6
Waigeo (isl.), Indonesia 85/J5
Waihee, Hawaii 218/J2
Waiheke (isl.), N. Zealand 100/E2
Waihi, N. Zealand 100/E2
Waikabubak, Indonesia 85/F7
Waikanae, N. Zealand 100/E4
Waikane, Hawaii 218/F2
Waikapu, Hawaii 218/J2
Waikaremoana (lake), N. Zealand 100/F3
Waikari, N. Zealand 100/D5
Waikato (riv.), N. Zealand 100/E2
Waikawa, N. Zealand 100/B7
Waikerie, S. Australia 94/F6
Waikii, Hawaii 218/H4
Waikiki, Hawaii 218/C4
Waikiki (beach), Hawaii 218/C4
Waikouaiti, N. Zealand 100/C6
Wailau, Hawaii 218/H1
Wailea, Hawaii 218/J4
Wailea, Maui, Hawaii 218/J2
Wailua, Hawaii 218/D2
Wailuku, Hawaii 218/J2
Wailuku, Hawaii 188/F5
Wailuku (riv.), Hawaii 218/J5
Waimakariri (riv.), N. Zealand 100/D5
Waimalu, Hawaii 218/B3
Waimanalo, Hawaii 218/F2
Waimanalo Beach., Hawaii 218/F2
Waimangaroa, N. Zealand 100/C4
Waimate, N. Zealand 100/C6
Waimea (Kamuela), Hawaii 218/G3
Waimea, Kauai, Hawaii 218/B2
Waimea, Oahu, Hawaii 218/E1
Waimea (bay), Hawaii 218/B2
Waimea (riv.), Hawaii 218/C2
Waimes, Belgium 27/J8
Wainaku, Hawaii 218/J5
Wainfleet, Ontario 177/E4
Wainfleet All Saints, England 13/H4
Waingapu, Indonesia 85/G7
Waini (riv.), Guyana 131/B2
Wainiha, Hawaii 218/C1
Wainiha (riv.), Hawaii 218/C1
Wainuiomata, N. Zealand 100/B3
Wainui-o-mata (riv.), N. Zealand 100/B3
Wainwright, Alaska 196/F1
Wainwright, Alberta 182/E3
Wainwright, Ohio 284/G5
Wainwright, Okla. 288/R3
Wainwright, U.S. 4/B18
Waiohinu, Hawaii 218/G7
Waipa (riv.), N. Zealand 100/E2
Waipahu, Hawaii 188/F5
Waipahu, Hawaii 218/A3
Waipara, N. Zealand 100/D5
Waipawa, N. Zealand 100/F3
Waipio, Hawaii 218/H3
Waipio (bay), Hawaii 218/H3
Waipio (pen.), Hawaii 218/A3
Waipio (pt.), Hawaii 218/A4
Waipio Acres, Hawaii 218/E2
Waipiro Bay, N. Zealand 100/G3
Waipukurau, N. Zealand 100/F4
Wairau (riv.), N. Zealand 100/D4
Wairoa, N. Zealand 100/F3
Wairoa (riv.), N. Zealand 100/E1
Waitakere, N. Zealand 100/B1
Waitakere (range), N. Zealand 100/A1
Waitaki (riv.), N. Zealand 100/C6
Waitangi, N. Zealand 100/D7
Waitara, N. Zealand 100/E3
Waite•, Maine 243/H5
Waite Hill, Ohio 284/H2
Waitemata, N. Zealand 100/B1
Waitemata (harb.), N. Zealand 100/B1
Waite Park, Minn. 255/D5
Waiteville, W. Va. 312/F8
Waitotara, N. Zealand 100/E3
Waits (riv.), Vt. 268/C3
Waitsburg, Wash. 310/G4
Waitsfield•, Vt. 268/B3
Waits River, Vt. 268/C3
Waitville, Sask. 181/F3
Waiuku, N. Zealand 100/E2
Waiyevu, Fiji 86/R10
Wajabula, Indonesia 85/H5
Wajima, Japan 81/H5
Wajir, Kenya 115/H3
Wajir, Kenya 102/F4
Waka, Ethiopia 111/G6
Waka, Texas 303/D1
Waka, Zaire 115/D3
Wakarusa, Ind. 227/F1
Wakarusa, Kansas 232/G3
Wakasa, Japan 81/G6
Wakasa (bay), Japan 81/G6
Wakatipu (lake), N. Zealand 100/B6
Wakaw, Sask. 181/F3
Wakaw Lake, Sask. 181/F3
Wakayama (pref.), Japan 81/G6
Wakayama, Japan 54/P6
Wakayama, Japan 81/G6
Wakde (isl.), Indonesia 85/K6
Wake (co.), N.C. 281/M3
Wake (isl.), Pacific 87/G4
WaKeeney, Kansas 232/C2
Wakefield, England 10/F4
Wakefield, England 13/J2
Wakefield, Kansas 232/E2
Wakefield, La. 238/H5
Wakefield•, Mass. 249/C5
Wakefield, Mich. 250/F2
Wakefield, Nebr. 264/H2
Wakefield•, N.H. 268/F4
Wakefield, Ohio 284/E8
Wakefield, Va. 307/O7
Wakefield-Peace Dale, R.I. 249/J7
Wake Forest, N.C. 281/M3
Wakema, Burma 72/B3
Wakeman, Ohio 284/F3
Wakenda, Mo. 261/F4
Wake Village, Texas 303/K4
Wakita, Okla. 288/L1
Wakkanai, Japan 81/K1
Wakonda, S. Dak. 298/P7
Wakool, N.S. Wales 97/C4
Wakopa, Manitoba 179/C5
Wakpala, S. Dak. 298/H2
Waku Kungo, Angola 115/C6
Wakulla (co.), Fla. 212/B1
Wakulla, Fla. 212/B1
Wakwekobi (lake), Ontario 177/A1
Wala, Kuh-i- (mt.), Afghanistan 59/H3
Walbridge, Ohio 284/C2
Wałbrzych (prov.), Poland 47/C3
Wałbrzych, Poland 47/C3
Walcha, N.S. Wales 97/F2
Walchensee (lake), Germany 22/D5
Walcheren (isl.), Netherlands 27/C5
Walcott, Ark. 202/J1
Walcott, Br. Col. 184/D3
Walcott (lake), Idaho 220/E7
Walcott, Iowa 229/M5
Walcott, N. Dak. 282/R6
Walcott, Wyo. 319/F4
Walcourt, Belgium 27/F8
Wałcz, Poland 47/C2
Wald, Switzerland 39/G2
Waldeck, Sask. 181/D5
Walden, Colo. 208/G1
Walden, Georgia 217/E5
Walden, Ky. 237/N7
Walden (pond), Mass. 249/A6
Walden, N.Y. 276/M7
Walden, Ontario 175/D3
Walden, Ontario 177/J5
Walden, Tenn. 237/L10
Walden•, Vt. 268/C3
Waldenburg, Ark. 202/J2
Waldenburg (Wałbrzych), Poland 47/C3
Waldenburg, Switzerland 39/E2
Walden Heights, Vt. 268/C3
Waldersee, Manitoba 179/D4
Waldheim, Germany 22/E3
Waldheim, La. 238/L5
Waldheim, Sask. 181/E3
Waldia, Ethiopia 111/G5
Waldkirch, Switzerland 39/H2
Waldkirch, Germany 22/B4
Waldkraiburg, Germany 22/E4
Waldo, Ala. 195/F4
Waldo, Ark. 202/D7
Waldo, Br. Col. 184/K5
Waldo, Fla. 212/D2
Waldo, Kansas 232/D2
Waldo (co.), Maine 243/E6
Waldo•, Maine 243/E7
Waldo, Ohio 284/D5
Waldo (lake), Oreg. 291/E4
Waldo, Wis. 317/L8
Waldoboro, Maine 243/E7
Waldoboro•, Maine 243/E7
Waldorf, Md. 245/L6
Waldorf, Minn. 255/E7
Waldport, Oreg. 291/C3
Waldron, Ark. 202/B4
Waldron, Ind. 227/F6
Waldron, Kansas 232/D4
Waldron, Mich. 250/E7
Waldron, Mo. 261/O5
Waldron, Sask. 181/J5
Waldron, Wash. 310/B2
Waldrup, Miss. 256/F7
Waldsassen, Germany 22/E3
Waldshut-Tiengen, Germany 22/C5
Waldwick, N.J. 273/B1
Waldwick, Wis. 317/G10
Walensee (lake), Switzerland 39/H2
Walenstadt, Switzerland 39/H2
Wales, Alaska 196/E1
Wales, Alaska 188/C5
Wales•, Mass. 249/F4
Wales, Minn. 255/G3
Wales, N. Dak. 282/N2
Wales (isl.), N.W. Terr. 187/K3
Wales, Tenn. 237/G10
Wales, U.K. 7/D3
Wales, Utah 304/C4
WALES 13
WALES 10/E4
Wales, Wis. 317/J1
Walesboro, Ind. 227/F6
Waleska, Georgia 217/D2
Walford, Iowa 229/K5
Walford, Ontario 177/B1
Walgett, N.S. Wales 88/H6
Walgett, N.S. Wales 97/E2
Walgreen Coast (reg.) 5/B13
Walhachin, Br. Col. 184/G5
Walhalla, Mich. 250/C5
Walhalla, N. Dak. 282/P2
Walhalla, S.C. 296/A2
Walhonding, Ohio 284/F5
Walikale, Zaire 115/E4
Walker (co.), Ala. 195/D3
Walker (creek), Ariz. 198/F2
Walker (mt.), Ark. 202/E2
Walker (co.), Georgia 217/B1
Walker, Iowa 229/K4
Walker, Kansas 232/C3
Walker, Ky. 237/O7
Walker, La. 238/L1
Walker, Mich. 250/D6
Walker, Minn. 255/D3
Walker, Mo. 261/D7
Walker (lake), Nev. 188/C3
Walker (lake), Nev. 266/C4
Walker (riv.), Nev. 266/C3
Walker, N.Y. 276/E4
Walker (bay), N.W. Terr. 187/G2
Walker, Oreg. 291/D4
Walker, S. Dak. 298/G2
Walker (isl.), Tasmania 99/B2
Walker (co.), Texas 303/J7
Walker (creek), Va. 307/F6
Walker, W. Va. 312/D4
Walkerburn, Scotland 15/F5
Walker Mill, Md. 245/F5
Walker River Ind. Res., Nev. 266/C3
Walker Springs, Ala. 195/C7
Walkerston, Queensland 88/H4
Walkerston, Queensland 95/D4
Walkersville, Md. 245/J3
Walkersville, W. Va. 312/F5
Walkerton, Ind. 227/E2
Walkerton, Ontario 177/C3
Walkerton, Va. 307/O5
Walkertown, N.C. 281/J2
Walkerville, Mich. 250/C5
Walkerville, Mont. 262/D4
Walkerville, S. Australia 88/E8
Wall•, N.J. 273/E3
Wall, Pa. 294/C5
Wall, S. Dak. 298/E6
Wall, Texas 303/D6
Wallace, Ala. 195/D8
Wallace (mt.), Alberta 182/C2
Wallace, Calif. 204/C9
Wallace, Idaho 220/C2
Wallace, Ind. 227/C5
Wallace (co.), Kansas 232/A3
Wallace, Kansas 232/A3
Wallace, La. 238/M3
Wallace (lake), La. 238/C2
Wallace, Mich. 250/B3
Wallace, Nebr. 264/C4
Wallace, N.Y. 276/E6
Wallace, N.C. 281/N5

466 Wallace

Wallace, Nova Scotia 168/E3
Wallace (harb.), Nova Scotia 168/E3
Wallace, S.C. 296/H2
Wallace, S. Dak. 298/P3
Wallace, W. Va. 312/E4
Wallaceburg, Ontario 177/B5
Wallace Lake, Manitoba 179/G3
Wallaceton, Pa. 294/F4
Wallacetown, Ontario 177/C5
Wallaga (prov.), Ethiopia 111/G6
Wallal Station, W. Australia 92/C2
Walland, Tenn. 237/O9
Wallaroo, S. Australia 94/E5
Wallasey, England 13/G2
Wallasey, England 10/F2
Walla Walla, N.S. Wales 97/D4
Walla Walla (riv.), Oreg. 291/J1
Walla Walla, Wash. 188/C1
Walla Walla (co.), Wash. 310/G4
Walla Walla, Wash. 310/G4
Walla Walla (riv.), Wash. 310/G4
Wallback, W. Va. 312/D5
Wallburg, N.C. 281/J3
Walldürn, Germany 22/C4
Walled Lake, Mich. 250/F6
Wallen, Ind. 227/G2
Wallendbeen, N.S. Wales 97/E4
Wallenpaupack (lake), Pa. 294/M3
Waller (co.), Texas 303/J8
Wallerawang, N.S. Wales 97/F3
Wallerville, Miss. 256/G2
Wallibu, St. Vin. & Grens. 161/A8
Walling, Tenn. 237/K9
Wallingford, Conn. 210/D3
Wallingford•, Conn. 210/D3
Wallingford, England 13/F6
Wallingford, Iowa 229/D2
Wallingford, Ky. 237/O4
Wallingford, Pa. 294/L7
Wallingford, Vt. 268/B5
Wallingford•, Vt. 268/B5
Wallington, N.J. 273/B2
Wallins Creek, Ky. 237/O7
Wallis (lake), N.S. Wales 97/G3
Wallis, Texas 303/H8
Wallis (isls.), Wallis and Futuna 87/J7
Wallis and Futuna 87/J7
Wallisellen, Switzerland 39/G2
Wallisville, Texas 303/L1
Wallkill (riv.), N.J. 273/D1
Wallkill, N.Y. 276/M7
Wallkill (riv.), N.Y. 276/L8
Wall Lake, Iowa 229/C4
Wallo (prov.), Ethiopia 111/H5
Wallonia, Ky. 237/F7
Walloon (lake), Mich. 250/E3
Walloon Lake, Mich. 250/E3
Wallops (isl.), Va. 307/T5
Wallowa (co.), Oreg. 291/K2
Wallowa, Oreg. 291/K2
Wallowa (mts.), Oreg. 291/K2
Wallowa (riv.), Oreg. 291/K2
Wallpack Center, N.J. 273/D1
Walls, Miss. 256/D1
Walls, Scotland 15/G2
Wallsburg, Utah 304/C3
Wallsend, England 13/J3
Wallula (lake), Oreg. 291/H1
Wallula, Wash. 310/G4
Wallula (lake), Wash. 310/F4
Walney, Isle of (isl.), England 13/D3
Walney, Isle of (isl.), England 10/E3
Walnut, Calif. 204/D10
Walnut (creek), Calif. 204/K1
Walnut, Ill. 222/D2
Walnut, Iowa 229/C6
Walnut, Kansas 232/G4
Walnut (creek), Kansas 232/B3
Walnut (riv.), Kansas 232/E4
Walnut, Miss. 256/G1
Walnut, N.C. 281/D3
Walnut, Pa. 294/G4
Walnut (creek), Texas 303/F3
Walnut Bottom, Pa. 294/H5
Walnut Canyon Nat'l Mon., Ariz. 198/D3
Walnut Cove, N.C. 281/J2
Walnut Creek, Calif. 204/K2
Walnut Creek, N.C. 281/O4
Walnut Creek, Ohio 284/G4
Walnut Grove, Ala. 195/F2
Walnut Grove, Calif. 204/B9
Walnut Grove, Georgia 217/E3
Walnut Grove, Ill. 222/C3
Walnut Grove, Ky. 237/M6
Walnut Grove, Minn. 255/C6
Walnut Grove, Miss. 256/F5
Walnut Grove, Mo. 261/F8
Walnut Hill, Ark. 202/C7
Walnut Hill, Fla. 212/B5
Walnut Hill, Ill. 222/E5
Walnut Hill, Maine 243/C8
Walnutport, Pa. 294/L4
Walnut Ridge, Ark. 202/J1
Walnut Springs, Texas 303/G5
Walpole, Mass. 249/B8
Walpole•, Mass. 249/B8
Walpole•, N.H. 268/C5
Walpole (isl.), Ontario 177/B5
Walpole, Sask. 181/K6
Walpole, W. Australia 92/B6
Walrus (isl.), Alaska 196/E3
Walrus (isls.), Alaska 196/F3
Walsall, England 10/G3
Walsall, England 13/E5
Walsenburg, Colo. 208/K7
Walsh, Alberta 182/E5
Walsh, Colo. 208/P8
Walsh (co.), N. Dak. 282/P3
Walsh, Queensland 95/B3
Walshville, Ill. 222/D4
Walsingham, England 13/H5
Walsingham (cape), N.W.T. 162/K2
Walsingham (cape), N.W.T. 187/M3
Walsrode, Germany 22/C2
Walston, Pa. 294/D4
Walstonburg, N.C. 281/O3
Walterboro, S.C. 296/F6
Walter F. George (dam), Ala. 195/H7
Walter F. George (res.), Ala. 195/H7
Walter F. George (dam), Georgia 217/B7
Walter F. George (res.), Georgia 217/B7
Walterhill, Tenn. 237/J9
Walter Reed Army Med. Ctr., D.C. 245/E4
Walter Reed Army Med. Ctr. Annex, Md. 245/E4
Walters, La. 238/G3
Walters, Minn. 255/E7
Walters, Okla. 288/K6
Walters Falls, Ontario 177/D3
Waltershausen, Germany 22/D3
Waltersville, Ky. 237/N5
Waltersville, Miss. 256/C6
Walterville, Oreg. 291/E3
Walthall (co.), Miss. 256/D8
Walthall, Miss. 256/F3
Waltham•, Maine 243/G6
Waltham, Mass. 249/B6
Waltham, Minn. 255/F7
Waltham•, Vt. 268/A3
Waltham Forest, England 13/H8
Waltham Forest, England 10/B5
Waltham Holy Cross, England 13/H7
Waltham Holy Cross, England 10/B5
Walthill, Nebr. 264/H2
Walthourville, Georgia 217/J7
Waltman, Wyo. 319/E2
Walton (co.), Fla. 212/C6
Walton, Fla. 212/F4
Walton (co.), Georgia 217/E3
Walton, Ind. 227/E3
Walton, Kansas 232/E3
Walton, Ky. 237/M3
Walton, Nebr. 264/H4
Walton, N.Y. 276/K6
Walton, Nova Scotia 168/E3
Walton, Ontario 177/C4
Walton, Oreg. 291/D3
Walton, W. Va. 312/D5
Walton and Weybridge, England 13/G8
Walton and Weybridge, England 10/B6
Walton Hills, Ohio 284/J10
Walton-le-Dale, England 13/G1
Walton-le-Dale, England 10/F1
Waltonville, Ill. 222/D5
Waltreak, Ark. 202/C4
Waltz, Mich. 250/F6
Walum, N. Dak. 282/O5
Walupt (lake), Wash. 310/D4
Walvis (bay), S. Africa 118/A4
Walvis Bay, S. Africa 2/K7
Walvis Bay, S. Africa 102/D7
Walvis Bay, S. Africa 118/A4
Walworth, N.Y. 276/F4
Walworth (co.), S. Dak. 298/J3
Walworth (co.), Wis. 317/J10
Walworth, Wis. 317/J10
Walzenhausen, Switzerland 39/J2
Wamac, Ill. 222/D5
Wamba, Kenya 115/G3
Wamba, Nigeria 106/F7
Wamba, Zaire 115/E3
Wamego, Kansas 232/F2
Wamel, Netherlands 27/H5
Wamena, Indonesia 85/K6
Wamgumbaug (lake), Conn. 210/F1
Wami (riv.), Tanzania 115/G5
Wamic, Oreg. 291/F2
Wampee, S.C. 296/K4
Wampsville, N.Y. 276/J4
Wampum, Manitoba 179/G5
Wampum, Pa. 294/B4
Wamsutter, Wyo. 319/E4
Wana, Pakistan 68/C2
Wana, Pakistan 59/J3
Wana, W. Va. 312/F3
Wanaaring, N.S. Wales 97/B1
Wanaka, N. Zealand 100/B6
Wanaka (lake), N. Zealand 100/B6
Wanakah, N.Y. 276/C5
Wanakena, N.Y. 276/K2
Wanamassa, N.J. 273/E3
Wanamingo, Minn. 255/F6
Wan'an, China 77/H6
Wanapitei (riv.), Ontario 177/D1
Wanapum (dam), Wash. 310/E4
Wanapum (lake), Wash. 310/E3
Wanaque, N.J. 273/B1
Wanaque (res.), N.J. 273/E1
Wanatah, Ind. 227/D2
Wanblee, S. Dak. 298/F6
Wanchese, N.C. 281/T3
Wanda, Minn. 255/C6
Wandel (sea), Greenl. 4/A10
Wandering, W. Australia 92/B2
Wandering River, Alberta 182/D2
Wanderoos, Wis. 317/B5
Wandfluhhorn (mt.), Switzerland 39/G4
Wando, S.C. 296/H6
Wando (riv.), S.C. 296/H6
Wandoan, Queensland 95/D5
Wandsworth, England 13/H8
Wandsworth, England 10/B5
Wanette, Okla. 288/M5
Wang, Mae Nam (riv.), Thailand 72/C3
Wanganella, N.S. Wales 97/C4
Wangahui, N. Zealand 87/H9
Wanganui, N. Zealand 100/E3
Wanganui (riv.), N. Zealand 100/E3
Wangaratta, Victoria 88/H7
Wangaratta, Victoria 97/D5
Wangen an der Aare, Switzerland 39/E2
Wangen im Allgäu, Germany 22/C5
Wangerooge (isl.), Germany 22/B2
Wängi, Switzerland 39/H1
Wangi-Rathmines, N.S. Wales 97/F3
Wangiwangi (isl.), Indonesia 85/G7
Wangqing, China 77/M3
Wangum (lake), Conn. 210/B1
Wanham, Alberta 182/A2
Wanhsien (Wanxian), China 77/G5
Wanilla, S. Australia 94/D6
Wanipigow, Manitoba 179/F3
Wanipigow (riv.), Manitoba 179/G3
Wankai, Sudan 111/E6
Wankie (Hwange), Zimbabwe 118/D3
Wankie (Hwange), Zimbabwe 102/E6
Wanks (Coco) (riv.), Honduras 154/E3
Wanks (Coco) (riv.), Nicaragua 154/E3
Wanless, Manitoba 179/H3
Wann, Okla. 288/P1
Wanna (lakes), W. Australia 92/E5
Wannaska, Minn. 255/C2
Wanneroo, W. Australia 88/B2
Wanneroo, W. Australia 92/A1
Wanning, China 77/H8
Wanship, Utah 304/C3
Wantage, England 13/F6
Wantage, England 10/F5
Wantagh, N.Y. 276/R7
Wanxian (Wanhsien), China 77/G5
Wanzai, China 77/H6
Wao, Philippines 82/E7
Wapakoneta, Ohio 284/B4
Wapanucka, Okla. 288/N6
Wapato, Wash. 310/E4
Wapawekka (hills), Sask. 181/M4
Wapella, Ill. 222/E3
Wapella, Sask. 181/K5
Wapello (co.), Iowa 229/J6
Wapello, Iowa 229/L6
Wapinitia, Oreg. 291/F2
Wapiti (riv.), Alberta 182/A2
Wapiti (riv.), Br. Col. 184/H3
Wapiti, Wyo. 319/C1
Wappapello, Mo. 261/M9
Wappapello (lake), Mo. 261/L8
Wappau (lake), Alberta 182/E2
Wappingers Falls, N.Y. 276/N7
Wapsipinicon (riv.), Iowa 229/J3
Wapske, New Bruns. 170/C2
Wapwallopen, Pa. 294/K3
Waqqas, Jordan 65/D2
Waquoit, Mass. 249/M6
War, W. Va. 312/C8
Warabi, Japan 81/O2
Waramaug (lake), Conn. 210/B2
Waranga (res.), Victoria 97/C5
Warangal, India 54/J8
Warangal, India 68/D5
Waratah, Tasmania 99/B3
Waratah (bay), Victoria 97/C6
Warba, Minn. 255/E3
Warburg, Alberta 182/C3
Warburg, Germany 22/C3
Warburton, The (riv.), S. Australia 94/F2
Warburton, The (riv.), S. Australia 88/F5
Warburton, Victoria 97/C5
Warburton Aboriginal Reserve, W. Australia 88/D5
Warburton Aboriginal Res., W. Australia 92/D4
Ward, Ala. 195/B6
Ward, Ark. 202/F3
Ward, Colo. 208/H2
Ward (peak), Mont. 262/A3
Ward, N. Zealand 100/E4
Ward (co.), N. Dak. 282/G3
Ward, S.C. 296/D4
Ward, S. Dak. 298/R5
Ward (co.), Texas 303/A6
Ward, W. Va. 312/D6
Ward Cove, Alaska 196/N2
Wardell, Mo. 261/N10
Warden, La. 238/H1
Warden, Québec 172/E4
Warden, Wash. 310/F4
Wardensville, W. Va. 312/J4
Wardere, Ethiopia 111/J6
Wardha, India 68/D4
Wardha (riv.), India 68/D4
Wardlow, Alberta 182/E4
Wardner, Br. Col. 184/K5
Wardner, Idaho 220/B2
Ward Ridge, Fla. 212/D6
Wardsboro•, Vt. 268/B5
Ward Springs, Minn. 255/D5
Wardsville, Mo. 261/H6
Wardsville, Ontario 177/C5
Wardville, La. 238/F4
Wardville, Okla. 288/P5
Ware, Br. Col. 184/E1
Ware, England 13/H7
Ware, England 10/F5
Ware (co.), Georgia 217/H8
Ware, Mass. 249/E3
Ware•, Mass. 249/E3
Ware (riv.), Mass. 249/F3
War Eagle, Ark. 202/C1
War Eagle, W. Va. 312/C7
Waregem, Belgium 27/C7
Wareham, England 13/E7
Wareham, England 10/E5
Wareham, Mass. 249/L5
Wareham•, Mass. 249/L5
Wareham Center, Mass. 249/L5
Warehouse Point, Conn. 210/E1
Waremme, Belgium 27/G7
Waren, Germany 22/E2
Waren, Indonesia 85/K6
Warenda, Queensland 95/B4
Warendorf, Germany 22/B3
Ware Neck, Va. 307/R6
Waresboro, Georgia 217/H8
Ware Shoals, S.C. 296/C3
Waretown, N.J. 273/E4
Warfield, Br. Col. 184/J5
Warfield, Ky. 237/S5
Warfield, Va. 307/N7
Warfordsburg, Pa. 294/F6
Warialda, N.S. Wales 97/F1
Warin Chamrap, Thailand 72/E4
Waring (mts.), Alaska 196/G1
Waring, Texas 303/F8
Warka, Poland 47/E3
Warkworth, N. Zealand 100/E2
Warkworth, Ontario 177/G3
Warley, England 13/E5
Warley, England 10/G3
Warm (creek), Utah 304/C6
Warman, Sask. 181/E3
Warmbad, Namibia 118/B5
Warmbad, S. Africa 118/D5
Warm Beach, Wash. 310/C2
Warmenhuizen, Netherlands 27/F3
Warmia (reg.), Poland 47/D1
Warminster, England 10/E5
Warminster, England 13/E6
Warminster, Pa. 294/M5
Warm Lake, Idaho 220/C5
Warm River, Idaho 220/G5
Warm Springs, Ark. 202/H1
Warm Springs, Georgia 217/C5
Warmsprings, Mont. 262/D4
Warm Springs, Oreg. 291/F3
Warm Springs (res.), Oreg. 291/J4
Warm Springs, Va. 307/J4
Warm Springs Ind. Res., Oreg. 291/F3
Warne, N.C. 281/B5
Warner, Alberta 182/D5
Warner•, N.H. 268/D5
Warner (riv.), N.H. 268/D5
Warner, Ohio 284/H6
Warner, Okla. 288/R4
Warner, S. Dak. 298/M3
Warner Robins, Georgia 217/E5
Warners, N.Y. 276/H4
Warnerton, La. 238/K5
Warnes, Bolivia 136/D5
Warnow (riv.), Germany 22/D2
Waroona, W. Australia 92/A2
Warrabri, North. Terr. 93/D6
Warrabri Aboriginal Reserve, North. Terr. 88/E4
Warracknabeal, Victoria 97/B5
Warracknabeal, Victoria 88/G7
Warr Acres, Okla. 288/L3
Warragamba, N.S. Wales 97/F3
Warragul, Victoria 97/D6
Warrandyte, Victoria 97/J4
Warrandyte, Victoria 88/M6
Warrego (riv.), N.S. Wales 97/C1
Warrego, North. Terr. 93/C5
Warrego (range), Queensland 88/H5
Warrego (range), Queensland 95/C5
Warrego (riv.), Queensland 88/H5
Warrego (riv.), Queensland 95/C5
Warren, Ark. 202/F6
Warren•, Conn. 210/B2
Warren (co.), Georgia 217/G4
Warren, Idaho 220/C4
Warren (co.), Ill. 222/C3
Warren, Ill. 222/C1
Warren (co.), Ind. 227/C4
Warren, Ind. 227/G3
Warren (co.), Iowa 229/F6
Warren (co.), Ky. 237/H6
Warren, Maine 243/E7
Warren•, Maine 243/E7
Warren, Manitoba 179/E4
Warren, Mass. 249/F4
Warren•, Mass. 249/F4
Warren, Mich. 250/B6
Warren, Minn. 255/B2
Warren (co.), Miss. 256/C6
Warren (co.), Mo. 261/K5
Warren, Mo. 261/J3
Warren, N. S. Wales 88/H6
Warren•, N.H. 268/D4
Warren (co.), N.J. 273/C2
Warren•, N.J. 273/D2
Warren, N.S. Wales 97/D2
Warren (co.), N.Y. 276/N3
Warren (co.), N.C. 281/N2
Warren, Nova Scotia 168/D3
Warren (co.), Ohio 284/B7
Warren, Ohio 284/J3
Warren, Ontario 177/D1
Warren, Oreg. 291/E2
Warren (co.), Pa. 294/D2
Warren, Pa. 294/D2
Warren•, R.I. 249/J6
Warren (res.), S. Australia 94/C7
Warren (co.), Tenn. 237/K9
Warren•, Vt. 268/B3
Warren (co.), Va. 307/M3
Warren Center, Pa. 294/K2
Warrenpoint, N. Ireland 17/J3
Warrens, Wis. 317/E7
Warrensburg, Ill. 222/D4
Warrensburg, Mo. 261/E5
Warrensburg, N.Y. 276/N3
Warrensville, Alberta 182/B1
Warrensville, N.C. 281/F2
Warrensville, Pa. 294/J3
Warrensville Heights, Ohio 284/H9
Warrenton, Georgia 217/G4
Warrenton, Ind. 227/B8
Warrenton, Mo. 261/K5
Warrenton, N.C. 281/N2
Warrenton, Oreg. 291/C1
Warrenton, S. Africa 118/C5
Warrenton, Va. 307/N3
Warrenville, Conn. 210/G1
Warrenville, Ill. 222/A6
Warrenville, S.C. 296/D4
Warri, Nigeria 106/F7
Warrick (co.), Ind. 227/C8
Warrick, Mont. 262/G2
Warrina, S. Australia 94/D3
Warringah, N.S. Wales 97/K3
Warrington, England 13/G2
Warrington, England 10/F2
Warrington, Fla. 212/B6
Warrington, Ind. 227/F5
Warrior, Ala. 195/E3
Warrior (dam), Ala. 195/C5
Warrior Run, Pa. 294/E7
Warriors Mark, Pa. 294/F4
Warrnambool, Australia 87/D9
Warrnambool, Victoria 97/B6
Warrnambool, Victoria 88/G7
Warroad, Minn. 255/C2
Warrumbungle (range), N. S. Wales 88/H6
Warsaw, Ill. 222/B3
Warsaw, Ind. 227/F2
Warsaw, Ky. 237/M3
Warsaw, Minn. 255/E6
Warsaw, Mo. 261/F6
Warsaw, N.Y. 276/D5
Warsaw, N.C. 281/N4
Warsaw, N. Dak. 282/R3
Warsaw, Ohio 284/G5
Warsaw, Ontario 177/F3
Warsaw (city prov.), Poland 47/E2
Warsaw (prov.), Poland 47/E2
Warsaw (cap.), Poland 7/G3
Warsaw (cap.), Poland 2/L3
Warsaw (Warszawa) (cap.), Poland 47/E2
Warsaw, Va. 307/P5
Warson Woods, Mo. 261/O3
Warsop, England 13/F4
Warspite, Alberta 182/D2
Warta (riv.), Poland 7/F3
Warta (riv.), Poland 47/B2
Wartau, Switzerland 39/H2
Wartburg, Tenn. 237/M8
Warthen, Georgia 217/G4
Wartime, Sask. 181/C4
Wartrace, Tenn. 237/J9
Warwick, Alberta 182/D3
Warwick, England 10/F4
Warwick, England 13/F5
Warwick, Georgia 217/E7
Warwick, Md. 245/P3
Warwick•, Mass. 249/E2
Warwick, N.Y. 276/M8
Warwick, N. Dak. 282/N4
Warwick (chan.), North. Terr. 93/E3
Warwick, Okla. 288/M3
Warwick, Québec 172/F4
Warwick, Queensland 88/J5
Warwick, Queensland 95/D6
Warwick, R.I. 249/J6
Warwickshire (co.), England 13/F5
Wasa, Br. Col. 184/K5
Wasaga Beach, Ontario 177/D3
Wasagaming, Manitoba 179/C4
Wasatch (co.), Utah 304/C3
Wasatch (plat.), Utah 304/C4
Wasatch (range), Utah 304/C3
Wasco, Calif. 204/F8
Wasco (co.), Oreg. 291/F2
Wasco, Oreg. 291/G2
Wascott, Wis. 317/C3
Waseca (co.), Minn. 255/E6
Waseca, Minn. 255/E6
Waseca, Sask. 181/B2
Wasen, Switzerland 39/E2
Wash, The (bay), England 13/H5
Wash, The (bay), England 10/G4
Washademoak (lake), New Bruns. 170/E3
Washago, Ontario 177/E3
Washakie (co.), Wyo. 319/E2
Washakie Ind. Res., Utah 304/B2
Washburn, Ark. 202/B3
Washburn, Ill. 222/D3
Washburn, Iowa 229/J4
Washburn, Maine 243/G2
Washburn•, Maine 243/G2
Washburn, Mo. 261/E9
Washburn, N. Dak. 282/J5
Washburn (co.), Pakistan 317/C4
Washburn, Tenn. 237/O8
Washburn, W. Va. 312/D4
Washburn, Wis. 317/D2
Washburn (mt.), Wyo. 319/B1
Washdyke, N. Zealand 100/C6
Washington 188/B1
WASHINGTON 310
Washington (co.), Ala. 195/B8
Washington (co.), Ark. 202/B2
Washington, Ark. 202/C6
Washington (co.), Colo. 208/N3
Washington•, Conn. 210/B2
Washington, D.C. (cap.), U.S. 146/L6
Washington, D.C. (cap.), U.S. 188/L3
Washington, D.C. (cap.), U.S. 245/F5
Washington, England 13/J3
Washington (co.), Fla. 212/C6
Washington (lake), Fla. 212/F3
Washington (co.), Georgia 217/G4
Washington, Georgia 217/G3
Washington (co.), Idaho 220/B5
Washington (co.), Ill. 222/D5
Washington, Ill. 222/D3
Washington (co.), Ind. 227/E7
Washington, Ind. 227/C7
Washington (co.), Iowa 229/K6
Washington, Iowa 229/K6
Washington (co.), Kansas 232/E2
Washington, Kansas 232/F2
Washington (co.), Ky. 237/L5
Washington, Ky. 237/O3
Washington (Teraina) (isl.), Kiribati 87/L5
Washington (par.), La. 238/K5
Washington, La. 238/G5
Washington (co.), Maine 243/H6
Washington•, Maine 243/E7
Washington (co.), Md. 245/G2
Washington•, Mass. 249/B3
Washington (co.), Minn. 255/F5
Washington (co.), Miss. 256/C4
Washington, Miss. 256/B7
Washington (co.), Mo. 261/L7
Washington, Mo. 261/K5
Washington (co.), Nebr. 264/H3
Washington, Nebr. 264/H3
Washington•, N.H. 268/C5
Washington (mt.), N.H. 268/E3
Washington, N.J. 273/D2
Washington (co.), N.Y. 276/O4
Washington (co.), N.C. 281/R3
Washington, N.C. 281/R3
Washington (co.), Ohio 284/H7
Washington (Old Washington), Ohio 284/H5
Washington (co.), Okla. 288/P1
Washington, Okla. 288/L4
Washington (co.), Oreg. 291/D2
Washington (co.), Pa. 294/B5
Washington, Pa. 294/B5
Washington (co.), R.I. 249/H7
Washington (Coventry), R.I. 249/H6
Washington (co.), Tenn. 237/R8
Washington (co.), Texas 303/H7
Washington, Texas 303/J7
Washington (state), U.S. 146/F5
Washington, D.C. (cap.), U.S. 2/F4
Washington (co.), Utah 304/A6
Washington, Utah 304/A6
Washington (co.), Vt. 268/B3
Washington•, Vt. 268/C3
Washington (co.), Va. 307/D7
Washington, Va. 307/M3
Washington (lake), Wash. 310/B2
Washington, W. Va. 312/C4
Washington (co.), Wis. 317/K9
Washington (isl.), Wis. 317/M5
Washington Court House, Ohio 284/D6
Washington Crossing, N.J. 273/D3
Washington Crossing, Pa. 294/N5
Washington Depot, Conn. 210/B2
Washington Grove, Md. 245/K4
Washington Island, Wis. 317/M5
Washington Lands, W. Va. 312/E3
Washington Park, Ill. 222/B2
Washington Park, N.C. 281/R3
Washington Terrace, Utah 304/B2
Washingtonville, N.Y. 276/M8
Washingtonville, Ohio 284/J4
Washingtonville, Pa. 294/J3
Washita, Ark. 202/C4
Washita (co.), Okla. 288/J4
Washita, Okla. 288/K4
Washita (riv.), Okla. 288/M5
Washita (riv.), Texas 303/D2
Washoe, Mont. 262/G5
Washoe (co.), Nev. 266/B2
Washoe (lake), Nev. 266/B3
Washougal, Wash. 310/C5
Washow (bay), Manitoba 179/F3
Washta, Iowa 229/B3
Washtenaw (co.), Mich. 250/F6
Washtucna, Wash. 310/G4
Wasilkow, Poland 47/F2
Wasilla, Alaska 196/B1
Wasior, Indonesia 85/K6
Wasit (heads), Iraq 66/D4
Waskada, Manitoba 179/B5
Waskaganish (Rupert House), Québec 174/B2
Waskaganish (Rupert House), Québec 162/J5
Waskana (creek), Sask. 181/G5
Waskatenau, Alberta 182/D2
Waskesiu (lake), Sask. 181/E2
Waskesiu Lake, Sask. 181/E2
Waskigomog (lake), Ontario 177/F2
Waskish, Minn. 255/D2
Waskom, Texas 303/L5
Waspán, Nicaragua 154/E3
Waspuk (riv.), Nicaragua 154/E3
Wassataquoik (stream), Maine 243/F4
Wassaw (sound), Georgia 217/L7
Wassen, Switzerland 39/G3
Wasser, Namibia 118/B5
Wasserbillig, Luxembourg 27/J9
Wasserburg am Inn, Germany 22/E4
Wasserkuppe (mt.), Germany 22/C3
Wasson, Ill. 222/E6
Wassuk (range), Nev. 266/C4
Wassy, France 28/F3
Wasta, S. Dak. 298/D5
Wataga, Ill. 222/C2
Watampone, Indonesia 85/G6
Watauga (co.), N.C. 281/F2
Watauga, S. Dak. 298/F2
Watauga, Tenn. 237/S8
Watauga (lake), Tenn. 237/T8
Watauga, Texas 303/F2
Watauga Valley, Tenn. 237/S8
Watchet, England 13/D6
Watch Hill, R.I. 249/G7
Watch Hill (pt.), R.I. 249/G7
Watchman (isl.), Newf. 166/B2
Watchung, N.J. 273/E2
Watchusk (lake), Alberta 182/E1
Water (isl.), Virgin Is. (U.S.) 161/A4
Waterberg, Namibia 118/B4
Waterboro, Maine 243/B8
Waterboro•, Maine 243/B8
Waterbury, Conn. 188/M2
Waterbury, Conn. 210/C2
Waterbury, Nebr. 264/H2
Waterbury, Vt. 268/B3
Waterbury•, Vt. 268/B3
Waterbury (res.), Vt. 268/B3
Waterbury Center, Vt. 268/B3
Waterdown, Ontario 177/D4
Wateree, S.C. 296/F4
Wateree (lake), S.C. 296/F3
Wateree (riv.), S.C. 296/F3
Waterflow, N. Mex. 274/A2
Waterford, Calif. 204/E6
Waterford, Conn. 210/G3
Waterford•, Conn. 210/G3
Waterford (co.), Ireland 17/F7
Waterford, Ireland 17/G7
Waterford, Ireland 10/C4
Waterford (harb.), Ireland 10/C4
Waterford (harb.), Ireland 17/G7
Waterford, Maine 243/B7
Waterford•, Maine 243/B7
Waterford, Miss. 256/E1
Waterford, New Bruns. 170/E3
Waterford, N.Y. 276/N5
Waterford, Ohio 284/G6
Waterford, Pa. 294/B2
Waterford, Va. 307/N2
Waterford, Wis. 317/K3
Waterford Works, N.J. 273/D4
Watergap, Ky. 237/R5
Waterhen (lake), Manitoba 179/C2
Waterhouse (isl.), Tasmania 99/D2
Waterloo, Ala. 195/B1
Waterloo, Ark. 202/D6
Waterloo, Belgium 27/E7
Waterloo, Ill. 222/C5

West Alton 467

Waterloo, Ind. 227/G2
Waterloo, Iowa 188/H2
Waterloo, Iowa 146/J5
Waterloo, Iowa 229/J4
Waterloo, Kansas 232/E4
Waterloo, Mont. 262/D5
Waterloo, Nebr. 264/H3
Waterloo, N.Y. 276/G5
Waterloo, North. Terr. 93/A4
Waterloo, Ohio 284/F8
Waterloo (reg. munic.), Ontario 177/D4
Waterloo, Ontario 177/D4
Waterloo, Oreg. 291/E3
Waterloo, Québec 172/E4
Waterloo, S.C. 296/C3
Waterloo, Trin. & Tob. 161/A10
Waterloo, Wis. 317/J9
Watermaal-Bosvoorde (Watermael Boitsfort), Belgium 27/C9
Watermael-Boitsfort, Belgium 27/C9
Waterman, Ill. 222/E2
Waterman, Ind. 227/C5
Waterpocket Fold (cliffs), Utah 304/D6
Waterport, N.Y. 276/D4
Waterproof, La. 238/H3
Waters, Mich. 250/E4
Watersmeet, Mich. 250/G2
Waterton-Glacier Int'l Peace Park, Alberta 182/C5
Waterton-Glacier International Peace Park, Alta. 162/E6
Waterton-Glacier Int'l Peace Park, Mont. 262/C2
Waterton Lakes Nat'l Park, Alberta 182/C5
Waterton Park, Alberta 182/D5
Watertown•, Conn. 210/C2
Watertown, Fla. 212/D1
Watertown•, Mass. 249/C6
Watertown, Minn. 255/E6
Watertown, N.Y. 188/M2
Watertown, N.Y. 276/J3
Watertown, Ohio 284/G7
Watertown, S. Dak. 188/G1
Watertown, S. Dak. 298/P4
Watertown, Tenn. 237/J8
Watertown, Wis. 317/J9
Waterval-Bo, S. Africa 118/D5
Water Valley, Ala. 195/B7
Water Valley, Alberta 182/C4
Water Valley, Ky. 237/D7
Water Valley, Miss. 256/E2
Water Valley, Texas 303/C6
Waterview, Ky. 237/L7
Waterview, Md. 245/P8
Water View, Va. 307/P5
Waterville, Iowa 229/L2
Waterville, Ireland 17/A8
Waterville, Kansas 232/F2
Waterville, Maine 188/N2
Waterville, Maine 243/D6
Waterville, Mass. 249/F2
Waterville, Minn. 255/E6
Waterville, New Bruns. 170/C2
Waterville, N.Y. 276/K5
Waterville, Nova Scotia 168/D3
Waterville, Ohio 284/C3
Waterville, Québec 172/F4
Waterville•, Vt. 268/B2
Waterville, Wash. 310/E3
Waterville Valley•, N.H. 268/D4
Watervliet, Mich. 250/C6
Watervliet, N.Y. 276/N5
Waterways, Alberta 182/E1
Watford, England 10/B5
Watford, England 13/H7
Watford, Ontario 177/C5
Watford City, N. Dak. 282/D4
Watha, N.C. 281/O5
Wathaman (riv.), Sask. 181/M3
Wathena, Kansas 232/H2
Watheroo, W. Australia 92/A5
Watino, Alberta 182/B2
Watkins, Iowa 229/J5
Watkins, Minn. 255/D5
Watkins Glen, N.Y. 276/G6
Watkinsville, Georgia 217/E3
Watling (San Salvador) (isl.), Bahamas 156/C1
Watonga, Okla. 288/K3
Watonwan (co.), Minn. 255/D7
Watova, Okla. 288/P1
Watrous, N. Mex. 274/D3
Watrous, Sask. 162/F5
Watrous, Sask. 181/F4
Watsa, Zaire 115/E3
Watseka, Ill. 222/F3
Watson, Ark. 202/H6
Watson, Ill. 222/E4
Watson, Ind. 227/F8
Watson, La. 238/L1
Watson, Minn. 255/C5
Watson, Mo. 261/A1
Watson, Okla. 288/S6
Watson, Sask. 181/G3
Watson (mt.), Utah 304/C3
Watson Lake, Yukon 187/F3
Watson Lake, Yukon 162/D3
Watsontown, Pa. 294/J3
Watsonville, Calif. 204/D7
Watten, Scotland 15/E2
Watten, Loch (lake), Scotland 15/E2
Wattensaw (bayou), Ark. 202/G4
Watton, England 13/H5
Watton, Mich. 250/G2
Watts, Okla. 288/S2
Watts Bar (dam), Tenn. 237/M9
Watts Bar (lake), Tenn. 237/M9
Watts Bar Dam, Tenn. 237/M9
Wattsburg, Pa. 294/C1
Watt Section Sheet Harbour, Nova Scotia 168/F4
Watts Mills, S.C. 296/D2
Wattsview, Manitoba 179/A4
Wattsville, Ala. 195/F3
Wattwil, Switzerland 39/H2
Watubela (isls.), Indonesia 85/J6
Watuppa (pond), Mass. 249/K6
Watzmann (mt.), Germany 22/E5
Wau, Papua N.G. 85/B7
Wau, Papua N.G. 87/E6
Wau, Sudan 111/E6
Wau, Sudan 102/E4
Waubamik, Ontario 177/E2
Waubaushene, Ontario 177/E3
Waubay, S. Dak. 298/P3
Waubay (lake), S. Dak. 298/O3
Waubeek, Iowa 229/K4
Waubeka, Wis. 317/L9
Waubun, Minn. 255/C3
Waucedah, Mich. 250/B3
Wauchope, N.S. Wales 97/G2
Wauchope, Sask. 181/K6
Wauchula, Fla. 212/E4
Waucoma, Iowa 229/J2
Wauconda, Ill. 222/A4
Wauconda, Wash. 310/F2
Wau el Kebir, Libya 111/C2
Waugh, Ala. 195/F6
Waugh (mt.), Idaho 220/D4
Waugh, Manitoba 179/G5
Waukarlyearly (lake), W. Australia 88/C4
Waukee, Iowa 229/F5
Waukeenah, Fla. 212/C1
Waukegan, Ill. 222/B4
Waukesha (co.), Wis. 317/K9
Waukesha, Wis. 317/K1
Waukomis, Okla. 288/K2
Waukon, Iowa 229/L2
Waukon, Wash. 310/H3
Waukon Junction, Iowa 229/L2
Waumandee, Wis. 317/C7
Waumbek (mt.), N.H. 268/E3
Wauna, Oreg. 291/D1
Wauna, Wash. 310/C3
Waunakee, Wis. 317/G9
Wauneta, Kansas 232/F4
Wauneta, Nebr. 264/C4
Waupaca (co.), Wis. 317/J6
Waupaca, Wis. 317/H7
Waupun, Wis. 317/J8
Wauregan, Conn. 210/H2
Waurika, Okla. 288/L6
Waurika (lake), Okla. 288/K6
Wausa, Nebr. 264/G2
Wausau, Fla. 212/D6
Wausau, Wis. 188/J2
Wausau, Wis. 317/G6
Wausau•, Wis. 317/80
Wausaukee, Wis. 317/K5
Wauseon, Ohio 284/B2
Waushara (co.), Wis. 317/H7
Wautoma, Wis. 317/H7
Wauwatosa, Wis. 317/L1
Wauzeka, Wis. 317/E9
Wave Hill, North. Terr. 88/E3
Wave Hill, North. Terr. 93/B4
Waveland, Ark. 202/C3
Waveland, Ind. 227/D5
Waveland, Miss. 256/F10
Waver (Wavre), Belgium 27/F7
Waverley, Mass. 249/B6
Waverley, N.S. Wales 88/L4
Waverley, N.S. Wales 97/K3
Waverley, N. Zealand 100/E3
Waverley, Nova Scotia 168/E4
Waverley, Ontario 177/E3
Waverley, Victoria 97/J5
Waverley, Victoria 88/L7
Waverley Downs, N.S. Wales 97/B1
Waverly, Ala. 195/G5
Waverly, Fla. 212/E4
Waverly, Georgia 217/J8
Waverly, Ill. 222/D4
Waverly, Iowa 229/J3
Waverly, Kansas 232/G3
Waverly, Ky. 237/F5
Waverly, La. 238/H2
Waverly, Minn. 255/E5
Waverly, Mo. 261/E4
Waverly, Nebr. 264/H4
Waverly, N.Y. 276/G7
Waverly, Ohio 284/D7
Waverly, S. Dak. 298/R3
Waverly, Tenn. 237/F8
Waverly, Va. 307/O6
Waverly, Wash. 310/H3
Waverly, W. Va. 312/D4
Waverly Hall, Georgia 217/C5
Waves, N.C. 281/J3
Wavre, Belgium 27/F7
Wawa (riv.), Nicaragua 154/E3
Wawa, Ontario 175/C3
Wawa, Ontario 177/J5
Wawaka, Ind. 227/F2
Wawanesa, Manitoba 179/C5
Wawasee, Ind. 227/F2
Wawasee (lake), Ind. 227/F2
Wawayanda (lake), N.J. 273/E1
Waweig, New Bruns. 170/C3
Wawina, Minn. 255/E3
Wawota, Sask. 181/J6
Wawpecong, Ind. 227/F3
Wax, Ky. 237/J6
Waxahachie, Texas 303/H5
Waxhaw, N.C. 281/H5
Way, Miss. 256/E5
Way (lake), W. Australia 88/C5
Way (lake), W. Australia 92/C4
Wayagamac (lake), Québec 172/E2
Wayan, Idaho 220/G7
Wayatinah, Tasmania 99/C4
Waycross, Ga. 188/K4
Waycross, Georgia 217/H8
Wayerton, New Bruns. 170/E1
Wayland, Iowa 229/K6
Wayland, Ky. 237/R6
Wayland•, Mass. 249/A7
Wayland, Mich. 250/D6
Wayland, Mo. 261/J2
Wayland, N.Y. 276/E5
Wayland, Ohio 284/H3
Waymansville, Ind. 227/E6
Waymart, Pa. 294/M2
Wayne, Ala. 195/C6
Wayne, Alberta 182/D4
Wayne (co.), Georgia 217/J7
Wayne (co.), Ill. 222/E5
Wayne, Ill. 222/E2
Wayne (co.), Ind. 227/G5
Wayne (co.), Iowa 229/G7
Wayne, Kansas 232/E2
Wayne (co.), Ky. 237/M7
Wayne, Maine 243/D7
Wayne•, Maine 243/D7
Wayne (co.), Mich. 250/F6
Wayne, Mich. 250/F6
Wayne (co.), Miss. 256/G7
Wayne (co.), Mo. 261/L8
Wayne (co.), Nebr. 264/G2
Wayne, Nebr. 264/G2
Wayne•, N.J. 273/A1
Wayne (co.), N.Y. 276/F4
Wayne, N.Y. 276/F6
Wayne (co.), N.C. 281/N4
Wayne (co.), Ohio 284/G4
Wayne, Ohio 284/C3
Wayne, Okla. 288/M5
Wayne (co.), Pa. 294/M2
Wayne, Pa. 294/M6
Wayne (co.), Tenn. 237/F10
Wayne (co.), Utah 304/C5
Wayne (co.), W. Va. 312/B6
Wayne, W. Va. 312/B6
Wayne City, Ill. 222/E5
Waynesboro, Georgia 217/J4
Waynesboro, Miss. 256/G7
Waynesboro, Pa. 294/G6
Waynesboro, Tenn. 237/F10
Waynesboro (I.C.), Va. 307/K4
Waynesburg, Ky. 237/M6
Waynesburg, Ohio 284/H4
Waynesburg, Pa. 294/B6
Waynesfield, Ohio 284/C4
Waynesville, Georgia 217/J8
Waynesville, Ill. 222/D3
Waynesville, Ind. 227/F6
Waynesville, Mo. 261/H7
Waynesville, N.C. 281/D4
Waynesville, Ohio 284/B6
Waynetown, Ind. 227/C4
Waynoka, Okla. 288/J1
Wayside, Georgia 217/E4
Wayside, Kansas 232/G4
Wayside, Miss. 256/C4
Wayside, Texas 303/C3
Wayside, Wis. 317/L7
Wayzata, Minn. 255/G5
Wazirabad, Pakistan 59/K3
We (isl.), Indonesia 85/B4
Wé, New Caled. 86/H4
Weagamow Lake, Ontario 175/B2
Weakley (co.), Tenn. 237/D8
Weald, The (reg.), England 13/H6
Wear (riv.), England 13/F3
Wear (riv.), England 10/F3
Weare•, N.H. 268/D5
Weare P.O. (North Weare), N.H. 268/D5
Weatherby, Mo. 261/D3
Weatherby Lake, Mo. 261/O5
Weatherford, Okla. 288/J4
Weatherford, Texas 303/G5
Weatherly, Pa. 294/L4
Weathers, Okla. 288/P5
Weathersby, Miss. 256/E7
Weatogue, Conn. 210/D1
Weaubleau, Mo. 261/F7
Weaver, Ala. 195/G3
Weaver (riv.), England 13/G2
Weaver (lake), Manitoba 179/F2
Weaver, Minn. 255/G6
Weaver, New Bruns. 170/E2
Weaver, N. Dak. 282/N2
Weaverville, Calif. 204/B3
Weaverville, N.C. 281/D3
Webb, Ala. 195/H8
Webb, Iowa 229/D3
Webb (lake), Maine 243/C6
Webb, Miss. 256/D3
Webb (bay), Newf. 166/B2
Webb, Sask. 181/C5
Webb (co.), Texas 303/E10
Webb, Texas 303/F3
Webb City, Ark. 202/C3
Webb City, Mo. 261/C8
Webb City, Okla. 288/N1
Webber, Kansas 232/D2
Webbers Falls, Okla. 288/R3
Webbers Falls (res.), Okla. 288/R3
Webberville, Mich. 250/E6
Webb Lake, Wis. 317/B3
Webbs Cross Roads, Ky. 237/L6
Webbville, Ky. 237/R4
Webbwood, Ontario 177/C1
Webequie, Ontario 175/C2
Weber (co.), Utah 304/B2
Weber (riv.), Utah 304/C3
Weber City, Va. 307/C7
Webi Shabelle (riv.), Somalia 115/H3
Webster, Fla. 212/D3
Webster (co.), Georgia 217/C6
Webster, Ind. 227/H5
Webster (co.), Iowa 229/E4
Webster, Iowa 229/J6
Webster (res.), Kansas 232/C2
Webster (co.), Ky. 237/F5
Webster, Ky. 237/J5
Webster (par.), La. 238/D1
Webster (brook), Maine 243/E3
Webster, Mass. 249/G4
Webster•, Mass. 249/G4
Webster (lake), Mass. 249/G4
Webster, Minn. 255/E6
Webster (co.), Miss. 256/F3
Webster (co.), Mo. 261/G8
Webster (co.), Nebr. 264/F4
Webster•, N.H. 268/D5
Webster, N.Y. 276/F4
Webster, N.C. 281/C4
Webster, N. Dak. 282/N3
Webster, Pa. 294/C5
Webster, S. Dak. 298/P3
Webster, Texas 303/K2
Webster (co.), W. Va. 312/F6
Webster, Wis. 317/B4
Webster City, Iowa 229/F4
Webster Groves, Mo. 261/P3
Webster Mills, Pa. 294/F6
Webster Springs, W. Va. 312/F6
Websterville, Vt. 268/B3
Wecota, S. Dak. 298/L3
Weda, Indonesia 85/H5
Wedau, Papua N.G. 85/C7
Weddel (isl.) 143/D7
Weddell (sea), Ant. 2/H10
Weddell (sea), Ant. 5/C16
Wedderburn, Oreg. 291/C5
Wedderburn, Victoria 97/B5
Weddington, Ark. 202/B1
Wedel, Germany 22/C2
Wedgefield, S.C. 296/F4
Wedgeport, Nova Scotia 168/C5
Wedgeworth, Ala. 195/C5
Wedowee, Ala. 195/H4
Weed, Calif. 204/C2
Weed, N. Mex. 274/D6
Weed (hills), Sask. 181/J5
Weed Heights, Nev. 266/B4
Weedon-Centre, Québec 172/F4
Weedsport, N.Y. 276/G4
Weedville, Pa. 294/F3
Weehawken•, N.J. 273/C2
Week (isls.), Chile 138/D10
Weekapaug, R.I. 249/G7
Weekes, Sask. 181/J3
Weeki Wachee, Fla. 212/D3
Weeks, La. 238/G7
Weeks, Nev. 266/B3
Weeks (isl.), N. Zealand 100/B1
Weeksbury, Ky. 237/R6
Weeks Mills, Maine 243/E7
Weeksville, N.C. 281/S2
Weems, Va. 307/P5
Weeping Water, Nebr. 264/J4
Weert, Netherlands 27/H6
Weesatche, Texas 303/G9
Weesen, Switzerland 39/H2
Weesp, Netherlands 27/C5
Weethalle, N.S. Wales 97/D3
Wee Waa, N.S. Wales 97/E2
Wegdahl, Minn. 255/C6
Weggis, Switzerland 39/F2
Węgorzewo, Poland 47/E1
Wegra-Flat Creek, Ala. 195/D3
Węgrów, Poland 47/E2
Weichang, China 77/J3
Weida, Germany 22/D3
Weiden in der Oberpfalz, Germany 22/D4
Weidman, Mich. 250/D5
Weifang, China 77/J4
Weihai (Weihaiwei), China 77/K4
Wei He (riv.), China 77/G5
Weilburg, Germany 22/C3
Weilheim im Oberbayern, Germany 22/D5
Weimar, Germany 22/D3
Weimar, Texas 303/H8
Weinan, China 77/H5
Weiner, Ark. 202/J2
Weinert, Texas 303/E4
Weinfelden, Switzerland 39/H1
Weingarten, Germany 22/C5
Weinheim, Germany 22/C4
Weining, China 77/F6
Weinsberg, Germany 22/C4
Weipa, Queensland 88/G1
Weipa, Queensland 95/B2
Weippe, Idaho 220/C3
Weir (lake), Fla. 212/E2
Weir, Kansas 232/H4
Weir, Miss. 256/F4
Weirdale, Sask. 181/F2
Weirgor, Wis. 317/D4
Weir River, Manitoba 179/J2
Weirsdale, Fla. 212/D3
Weirton, W. Va. 312/E2
Weirwood, Va. 307/S6
Weisburg, Ind. 227/H6
Weiser, Idaho 220/B5
Weiser (riv.), Idaho 220/B5
Weishan, China 77/F6
Weismes (Waimes), Belgium 27/J8
Weiss (lake), Ala. 195/G2
Weiss (lake), Georgia 217/A2
Weissenburg im Bayern, Germany 22/D4
Weissenfels, Germany 22/D3
Weissensee, Germany 22/F3
Weissenstein (mts.), Switzerland 39/D2
Weisserstein (mt.), Belgium 27/J8
Weissert, Nebr. 264/E3
Weisshorn (mt.), Switzerland 39/J3
Weisshorn (mt.), Switzerland 39/E4
Weissmies (mt.), Switzerland 39/F4
Weisswasser, Germany 22/F3
Weitchpec, Calif. 204/B2
Weitensfeld-Flattnitz, Austria 41/B3
Weitra, Austria 41/C2
Weixi, China 77/E6
Weixin, China 77/F6
Weiz, Austria 41/C3
Wejh, Saudi Arabia 59/C4
Wejh, Saudi Arabia 54/E7
Wejherowo, Poland 47/D1
Welaka, Fla. 212/E2
Welbekend, S. Africa 118/J6
Welch, Okla. 288/R1
Welch, Texas 303/B5
Welch, W. Va. 312/C8
Welches, Oreg. 291/E2
Welchman Hall, Barbados 161/B8
Welchville, Maine 243/C7
Welcome, La. 238/L3
Welcome, Md. 245/K7
Welcome, Minn. 255/D7
Welcome, N.C. 281/J3
Welcome, Ontario 177/F4
Welcome All, Georgia 217/J2
Weld (co.), Colo. 208/L1
Weld•, Maine 243/C6
Weld (range), W. Australia 92/B4
Welda, Kansas 232/G3
Weldon, Ark. 202/H3
Weldon, Calif. 204/G8
Weldon, Ill. 222/E3
Weldon, Iowa 229/F7
Weldon, New Bruns. 170/F3
Weldon, N.C. 281/O2
Weldon, Sask. 181/F2
Weldon, Texas 303/J6
Weldona, Colo. 208/M2
Weldon Spring Heights, Mo. 261/M2
Weleetka, Okla. 288/O4
Welford, Queensland 95/C5
Welkom, S. Africa 102/E7
Welkom, S. Africa 118/D5
Welland (riv.), England 13/G5
Welland (riv.), England 10/F4
Welland, Ontario 177/E5
Welland (canal), Ontario 177/E5
Wellandport, Ontario 177/E4
Wellborn, Fla. 212/D1
Wellersburg, Pa. 294/E6
Wellesley (isls.), Australia 87/D7
Wellesley•, Mass. 249/B7
Wellesley, Ontario 177/D4
Wellesley (isls.), Queensland 88/F3
Wellesley (isls.), Queensland 95/A3
Wellesley Hills, Mass. 249/B7
Wellfleet•, Mass. 249/O5
Wellfleet (harb.), Mass. 249/O5
Wellfleet, Nebr. 264/D4
Wellford, S.C. 296/C2
Wellin, Belgium 27/G8
Welling, Alberta 182/D5
Welling, Okla. 288/S3
Wellingborough, England 13/G5
Wellingborough, England 10/F4
Wellington, Ala. 195/G3
Wellington (isl.), Chile 120/B7
Wellington (isl.), Chile 138/D8
Wellington, Colo. 208/K1
Wellington, England 13/D7
Wellington, England 10/E5
Wellington, Ill. 222/F3
Wellington, Kansas 232/E4
Wellington, Ky. 237/K2
Wellington, Ky. 237/O5
Wellington•, Maine 243/D5
Wellington, Mo. 261/E4
Wellington, Nev. 266/B4
Wellington, N.S. Wales 97/E3
Wellington (cap.), N. Zealand 2/T8
Wellington (cap.), N. Zealand 100/A3
Wellington (bay), N.W.T. 187/H3
Wellington (chan.), N.W.T. 162/G1
Wellington (chan.), N.W.T. 187/J2
Wellington, Nova Scotia 168/E4
Wellington, Ohio 284/F3
Wellington (co.), Ontario 177/D4
Wellington, Ontario 177/G4
Wellington, Pr. Edward I. 168/D2
Wellington, S. Africa 118/B6
Wellington, Texas 303/D3
Wellington, Utah 304/D4
Wellington (lake), Victoria 97/D6
Wellington, Va. 307/T3
Wellman, Iowa 229/K6
Wellman (lake), Manitoba 179/B3
Wellman, Texas 303/B5
Wellpinit, Wash. 310/G3
Wells, Br. Col. 184/G3
Wells, England 13/E6
Wells, England 10/E5
Wells (co.), Ind. 227/G3
Wells, Kansas 232/E2
Wells, Maine 243/B9
Wells•, Maine 243/B9
Wells, Mich. 250/B3
Wells, Minn. 255/E7
Wells, Nev. 266/G1
Wells, N.Y. 276/M4
Wells (co.), N. Dak. 282/L4
Wells, Texas 303/J6
Wells•, Vt. 268/A5
Wells (riv.), Vt. 268/C3
Wells (lake), W. Australia 88/C5
Wells (dam), Wash. 310/F3
Wells (lake), W. Australia 92/C4
Wells Beach, Maine 243/B9
Wellsboro, Ind. 227/D1
Wellsboro, Pa. 294/H2
Wells Bridge, N.Y. 276/K6
Wellsburg, Iowa 229/G4
Wellsburg, N.Y. 276/G6
Wellsburg, N. Dak. 282/L4
Wellsburg, W. Va. 312/E2
Wellsford, N. Zealand 100/E2
Wells Gray Prov. Park, Br. Col. 184/H4
Wells-next-the-Sea, England 13/H5
Wells-next-the-Sea, England 10/G4
Wells River, Vt. 268/C3
Wellston, Mich. 250/D4
Wellston, Mo. 261/R2
Wellston, Ohio 284/F7
Wellston, Okla. 288/M3
Wellsville, Kansas 232/G3
Wellsville, Mo. 261/K4
Wellsville, N.Y. 276/E6
Wellsville, Ohio 284/J4
Wellsville, Pa. 294/J5
Wellsville, Utah 304/C2
Wellton, Ariz. 198/A6
Wellwood, Manitoba 179/C4
Wels, Austria 41/C2
Welsford, New Bruns. 170/D3
Welsford, Nova Scotia 168/E3
Welsh, La. 238/E6
Welshfield, Ohio 284/H3
Welshpool, New Bruns. 170/D4
Welshpool, Wales 10/E4
Welshpool, Wales 13/D5
Welton, Iowa 229/M5
Welty, Okla. 288/O3
Welwyn, England 13/H7
Welwyn, England 10/F5
Welwyn, Sask. 181/K5
Wem, England 13/E5
Wembere (riv.), Tanzania 115/F4
Wembley, Alberta 182/A2
Wemindji, Québec 174/B2
Wemmel, Belgium 27/B9
Wemyss Bay, Scotland 15/A2
Wenamu (riv.), Guyana 131/A2
Wenas (creek), Wash. 310/E4
Wenasoga, Miss. 256/G1
Wenatchee, Wash. 188/B1
Wenatchee, Wash. 310/E3
Wenatchee (lake), Wash. 310/E3
Wenatchee (mts.), Wash. 310/E3
Wenatchee (riv.), Wash. 310/E3
Wenchi, Ghana 106/D7
Wenchow (Wenzhou), China 77/J6
Wendel, Calif. 204/E3
Wendel, W. Va. 312/F4
Wendell, Idaho 220/D7
Wendell•, Mass. 249/E2
Wendell, Minn. 255/B4
Wendell, N.H. 268/C5
Wendell, N.C. 281/N3
Wendell Depot, Mass. 249/E2
Wenden, Ariz. 198/B5
Wendeng, China 77/K4
Wendover, England 13/G7
Wendover, Ontario 177/J2
Wendover, Utah 304/A3
Wendover, Wyo. 319/H3
Wendron, England 13/B7
Wendte, S. Dak. 298/H5
Wenham•, Mass. 249/L2
Wenling, China 77/K6
Wenlock (riv.), Queensland 88/G2
Wenman (isl.), Ecuador 128/B8
Wenona, Georgia 217/E7
Wenona, Ill. 222/E2
Wenona, Md. 245/P8
Wenona, N.C. 281/R3
Wenonah, Ill. 222/D4
Wenonah, N.J. 273/C4
Wenquan, Qinghai, China 77/D5
Wenquan, Xinjiang Uygur, China 77/B3
Wenshan, China 77/F7
Wensu, China 77/B3
Wensum (riv.), England 13/J5
Wentworth, Mo. 261/D8
Wentworth•, N.H. 268/D4
Wentworth (lake), N.H. 268/E4
Wentworth, N.S. Wales 97/B4
Wentworth, N.C. 281/K2
Wentworth, Nova Scotia 168/E3
Wentworth, S. Dak. 298/R6
Wentworth, Wis. 317/C2
Wentworths Location•, N.H. 268/E2
Wentzville, Mo. 261/L5
Wen Xian, China 77/G5
Wenzhou (Wenchow), China 77/J6
Wenzhou, China 54/N7
Weogufka, Ala. 195/F4
Weohyakapka (lake), Fla. 212/E4
Weott, Calif. 204/A3
Wepawaug (riv.), Conn. 210/C3
Wequetequock, Conn. 210/H3
Werdau, Germany 22/E3
Werder, Germany 22/E2
Werner Lake, Ontario 175/A2
Wernersville, Pa. 294/K5
Wernigerode, Germany 22/D3
Werra (riv.), Germany 22/D3
Werra (riv.), Germany 22/D3
Werribee, Victoria 88/G7
Werrimull, Victoria 97/A4
Werris Creek, N.S. Wales 97/F2
Wertheim, Germany 22/C4
Wervik, Belgium 27/B7
Wesco, Mo. 261/K7
Wesel, Germany 22/B3
Weser (riv.), Germany 7/E3
Weser (riv.), Germany 22/C2
Weskan, Kansas 232/A3
Weslaco, Texas 303/F11
Weslemkoon (lake), Ontario 177/G2
Wesley, Ark. 202/C1
Wesley, Dominica 161/F5
Wesley, Georgia 217/H6
Wesley, Iowa 229/E2
Wesley, Maine 243/H6
Wesley•, Maine 243/H6
Wesley Vale, Tasmania 99/C3
Wesleyville, Newf. 166/D4
Wesleyville, Pa. 294/C1
Wes-Rand, S. Africa 118/G6
Wessel (isls.), Australia 87/D7
Wessel (cape), North. Terr. 88/F2
Wessel (cape), North. Terr. 93/E1
Wessel (isls.), North. Terr. 88/F2
Wessel (isls.), North. Terr. 93/E1
Wessington, S. Dak. 298/M5
Wessington Springs, S. Dak. 298/M5
Wesson, Ark. 202/E7
Wesson, Miss. 256/D7
West (riv.), Conn. 210/D3
West (riv.), Conn. 210/E3
West, Iowa 229/J5
West (bay), La. 238/M8
West (isl.), Mass. 249/L6
West (riv.), Mass. 249/H4
West, Miss. 256/E4
West (isls.), New Bruns. 170/D4
West (cape), N. Zealand 100/A6
West (bay), Nova Scotia 168/G3
West (pt.), Nova Scotia 168/H5
West (riv.), Nova Scotia 168/F3
West (pt.), Pr. Edward I. 168/D2
West (pt.), Tasmania 99/A2
West, Texas 303/G6
West (bay), Texas 303/K3
West (riv.), Vt. 268/B5
West Acton, Mass. 249/H3
West Alexander, Pa. 294/B5
West Alexandria, Ohio 284/A6
West Allis, Wis. 317/L1
West Alton, Mo. 261/M5

468 West Alton

West Alton, N.H. 268/E4
West Amboy, N.Y. 276/J4
West Arichat, Nova Scotia 168/G3
West Ashford, Conn. 210/G1
West Aspetuck (riv.), Conn. 210/B2
West Athens, Maine 243/D6
West Augusta, Va. 307/K4
West Avon, Conn. 210/D1
West Baden Springs, Ind. 227/D7
West Baines (riv.), North. Terr. 93/A4
West Baldwin, Maine 243/B8
Westbank, Br. Col. 184/H5
WEST BANK 59/C3
WEST BANK 65/C3
West Bank (reg.), West Bank 65/C3
West Baraboo, Wis. 317/G9
West Barnet, Vt. 268/C3
West Barns, Scotland 15/F5
West Barnstable, Mass. 249/N6
West Barrington, R.I. 249/J5
West Bath•, Maine 243/D8
West Baton Rouge (par.), La. 238/H6
West Bay, Fla. 212/C6
West Bay, Nova Scotia 168/G3
West Bay Road, Nova Scotia 168/G3
West Bend, Iowa 229/D3
Westbend, Ky. 237/N5
West Bend, Sask. 181/H4
West Bend, Wis. 317/K9
West Bengal (state), India 68/F4
West Berkshire, Vt. 268/B2
West Berlin, Mass. 249/H3
West Berlin, N.J. 273/D4
West Bethel, Maine 243/B7
West Blocton, Ala. 195/D4
West Bloomfield, Wis. 317/J7
Westboro, Mo. 261/B1
Westboro, Ohio 284/C7
Westboro, Wis. 317/F5
Westborough, Mass. 249/H3
Westborough•, Mass. 249/H3
West Bountiful, Utah 304/B3
Westbourne, Manitoba 179/D4
Westbourne, Tenn. 237/O7
West Boxford, Mass. 249/K2
West Boylston•, Mass. 249/G3
West Braintree, Vt. 268/B4
West Branch (res.), Conn. 210/C1
West Branch, Iowa 229/L5
West Branch, Farmington (riv.), Mass. 249/B4
West Branch, Mich. 250/E4
West Branch, Rocky (riv.), Ohio 284/G10
West Brattleboro, Vt. 268/B6
West Brentwood, N.H. 268/E6
West Brewster, Mass. 249/O5
Westbridge, Br. Col. 184/H5
West Bridgewater•, Mass. 249/K4
West Bridgewater, Vt. 268/B4
West Bridgford, England 13/F5
West Bromwich, England 13/F5
West Bromwich, England 10/G3
Westbrook, Conn. 210/F3
Westbrook•, Conn. 210/F3
Westbrook, Maine 243/C8
Westbrook, Minn. 255/C6
West Brook, Nova Scotia 168/D3
Westbrook, Texas 303/C5
West Brookfield, Mass. 249/F4
West Brookfield•, Mass. 249/F4
West Brooklyn, Ill. 222/D2
West Brooksville, Maine 243/F7
West Brownsville, Pa. 294/C5
West Buechel, Ky. 237/K2
West Burke, Vt. 268/C2
West Burlington, Iowa 229/L7
West Burra (isl.), Scotland 15/G2
Westbury, England 10/E5
Westbury, England 13/E6
Westbury, N.Y. 276/R7
Westbury, Tasmania 99/C3
West Buxton, Maine 243/B8
Westby, Mont. 262/M2
Westby, Wis. 317/E8
West Calder, Scotland 15/C2
West Caldwell, N.J. 273/A2
West Campton, N.H. 268/D4
West Canaan, N.H. 268/C4
West Cape May, N.J. 273/D6
West Carroll (par.), La. 238/H1
West Carrollton, Ohio 284/B6
West Carthage, N.Y. 276/J3
West Charleston, Vt. 268/C2
West Chatham, Mass. 249/O6
West Chazy, N.Y. 276/N1
West Chelmsford, Mass. 249/J2
Westchester, Conn. 210/F2
Westchester, Ill. 222/B5
West Chester, Iowa 229/K6
Westchester (co.), N.Y. 276/N8
West Chester, Ohio 284/C9
West Chester, Pa. 294/L6
West Chesterfield, Mass. 249/C3
Westchester Station, Nova Scotia 168/E3
West Chicago, Ill. 222/A5
West Chop (pt.), Mass. 249/M7
West City, Ill. 222/E5
Westcliffe, Colo. 208/H6
West College Corner, Ind. 227/H5
West Columbia, S.C. 296/E4
West Columbia, Texas 303/J8
West Columbia, W. Va. 312/B5
West Concord, Mass. 249/A6
West Concord, Minn. 255/F6
West Corinth, Vt. 268/C3
West Cornwall, Conn. 210/B1
West Cornwall, Vt. 268/A4
West Cote Blanche (bay), La. 238/G7
Westcott, Alberta 182/C4
Westcott Cove (bay), Conn. 210/A4
West Covina, Calif. 204/D10
Westcreek, Colo. 208/J4
West Creek, N.J. 273/E4
West Crossett, Ark. 202/F7
West Cummington, Mass. 249/B3
West Danville, Vt. 268/C3
West Dean, England 13/E6
West Demerara-Essequibo Coast (dist.), Guyana 131/B2
West Dennis, Mass. 249/O6
West Deptford•, N.J. 273/B3
West Des Moines, Iowa 229/F5
West Dover, Nova Scotia 168/E4
West Dover, Vt. 268/B6
West Dublin, Nova Scotia 168/D4
West Dudley, Mass. 249/F4
West Dummerston, Vt. 268/B6
West Dundee (Dundee), Ill. 222/E1
West Eau Gallie, Fla. 212/F3
West Elizabeth, Pa. 294/C5
West Elkton, Ohio 284/A6
West Elmira, N.Y. 276/G6
West Eminence, Mo. 261/J8
Westend, Calif. 204/H8
West End, N.C. 281/K4
West End, Sask. 181/J5
West End, Virgin Is. (U.K.) 161/C4
West End-Cobb Town, Ala. 195/G3
Westend Saltpond (lag.), Virgin Is. (U.S.) 161/E4
West Enfield, Maine 243/F5
West Epping, N.H. 268/E5
Wester Eems (chan.), Netherlands 27/K1
Westerland, Germany 22/C1
Westerlo, Belgium 27/F6
Westerlo, N.Y. 276/M6
Westerly, R.I. 249/G7
Westerly•, R.I. 249/G7
Western (prov.), Kenya 115/G3
Western, Nebr. 264/G4
Western (head), Nova Scotia 168/D5
Western Australia 88/B5
WESTERN AUSTRALIA 92
Western Australia (state), Australia 87/C8
Western Bay, Newf. 166/D2
Western Channel (str.), Japan 81/D6
Western Dvina (riv.), U.S.S.R. 53/C2
Western Dvina (riv.), U.S.S.R. 52/C3
Western Dvina (riv.), U.S.S.R. 48/C4
Western Ghats (mts.), India 68/C5
Western Grove, Ark. 202/D1
Western Institute, Tenn. 237/C10
Western Isles (islands area), Scotland 15/A3
Westernport, Md. 245/B3
Western Port (inlet), Victoria 97/C6
Western Sahara 2/J4
Western Sahara 102/A2
WESTERN SAHARA 106/A4
Western Samar (prov.), Philippines 82/E5
Western Samoa 2/A6
Western Samoa 87/J7
WESTERN SAMOA 86/M8
Western Scheldt (De Honte) (bay), Netherlands 27/D6
Western Shore, Nova Scotia 168/D4
Western Springs, Ill. 222/B6
Westernville, N.Y. 276/K4
Westerose, Alberta 182/C3
Westerstede, Germany 22/B2
Westervelt, Ill. 222/E4
Westerville, Nebr. 264/E3
Westerville, Ohio 284/D5
Westerville, S. Dak. 298/P8
Westerwald (for.), Germany 22/B3
West Fairlee•, Vt. 268/C4
West Falkland (isl.), Falk. Is. 120/C8
West Falkland (isl.), Falk. Is. 143/D7
Westfall, Kansas 232/D3
Westfall, Oreg. 291/K3
West Falmouth, Mass. 249/M6
West Fargo, N. Dak. 282/S6
West Farmington, Maine 243/C6
West Farmington, Ohio 284/J3
West Feliciana (par.), La. 238/H5
Westfield, Conn. 210/E2
Westfield, Ill. 222/F4
Westfield, Ind. 227/E4
Westfield, Iowa 229/A3
Westfield•, Maine 243/G2
Westfield, Mass. 249/D4
Westfield (riv.), Mass. 249/C3
Westfield, New Bruns. 170/D3
Westfield, N.J. 273/E2
Westfield, N.Y. 276/A6
Westfield, N.C. 281/H2
Westfield, N. Dak. 282/K7
Westfield, Nova Scotia 168/C4
Westfield, Pa. 294/H2
Westfield•, Vt. 268/C2
Westfield, Wis. 317/H8
Westfield Center, Ohio 284/G3
West Finley, Pa. 294/B5
Westfir, Oreg. 291/E4
West Flanders (prov.), Belgium 27/B7
Westford, Conn. 210/G1
Westford•, Mass. 249/J2
Westford, Pa. 294/A2
Westford•, Vt. 268/A2
West Fork, Ark. 202/B2
West Fork, Ind. 227/D8
West Fork, Bruneau (riv.), Nev. 266/F1
West Fork (riv.), W. Va. 312/E5
West Forks•, Maine 243/D5
West Frankfort, Ill. 222/E6
West Franklin, Ind. 227/B9
West Franklin, Maine 243/G6
West Frisian (isls.), Netherlands 27/F2
Westgat (chan.), Netherlands 27/F3
Westgate, Iowa 229/K3
Westgate, Manitoba 179/A2
West Glacier, Mont. 262/C2
West Glamorgan, Wales 13/D6
West Glens Falls, N.Y. 276/N4
West Glocester, R.I. 249/G5
West Glover, Vt. 268/C2
West Gorham, Maine 243/C8
West Goshen, Conn. 210/B1
West Gouldsboro, Maine 243/G7
West Granby, Conn. 210/D1
West Grand (lake), Maine 243/H5
West Granville, Mass. 249/C4
West Green, Georgia 217/G7
West Greene, Ala. 195/B5
West Green Harbour, Nova Scotia 168/C5
West Groton, Mass. 249/H2
West Grove, Iowa 229/J7
West Grove, Pa. 294/L6
West Halifax, Vt. 268/B6
West Hamlin, W. Va. 312/B6
West Hampstead, N.H. 268/E6
Westhampton•, Mass. 249/C3
Westhampton, N.Y. 276/P9
Westhampton Beach, N.Y. 276/P9
West Hanover, Mass. 249/L4
West Harrison, Ind. 227/H6
West Hartford•, Conn. 210/D1
West Hartford, Vt. 268/C4
West Hartland, Conn. 210/D1
West Harwich, Mass. 249/O6
West Haven, Conn. 210/D3
West Haven•, Vt. 268/A4
West Hawk (lake), Manitoba 179/G5
Westhawk Lake, Manitoba 179/G5
West Hawley, Mass. 249/C2
West Hazleton, Pa. 294/K4
West Helena, Ark. 202/J4
West Henniker, N.H. 268/D5
West Hickory, Pa. 294/C2
West Hill (pond), Conn. 210/C1
Westhoff, Texas 303/G8
West Hollywood, Calif. 204/B10
Westholme, Br. Col. 184/J3
Westhope, N. Dak. 282/H2
West Hopkinton, N.H. 268/D5
West Hurley, N.Y. 276/M6
West Ice Shelf, Antarc. 5/C5
West Indies (isls.) 2/G5
West Indies (isls.) 146/M7
WEST INDIES 156
West Irvine, Ky. 237/N5
West Jefferson, Ala. 195/D4
West Jefferson, N.C. 281/F2
West Jefferson, Ohio 284/D6
West Jersey, Ill. 222/D2
West Jonesport, Maine 243/H6
West Jordan, Utah 304/B3
Westkapelle, Netherlands 27/C5
West Kennebunk, Maine 243/B9
West Kilbride, Scotland 15/D5
West Kingston, R.I. 249/H7
West Kittanning, Pa. 294/C4
West Lafayette, Ind. 227/D4
West Lafayette, Ohio 284/G5
Westlake, La. 238/D6
Westlake, Ohio 284/G9
Westlake (Dunes City), Oreg. 291/C4
Westlake, Texas 303/F1
Westland, Mich. 250/F6
Westland, Pa. 294/B5
West Lanham Hills, Md. 245/G4
West Laurel, Md. 245/L4
West Lawn, Pa. 294/K5
West Lebanon, Ind. 227/C4
West Lebanon, Maine 243/B9
West Lebanon, N.H. 268/C4
West Ledge, Bermuda 156/G3
West Leechburg, Pa. 294/C4
West Leipsic, Ohio 284/B3
West Leyden, N.Y. 276/J4
West Liberty, Ill. 222/E5
West Liberty, Iowa 229/L5
West Liberty, Ky. 237/P5
West Liberty, Ohio 284/C5
West Liberty, Pa. 294/B4
West Liberty, W. Va. 312/E2
West Lima, Wis. 317/E8
West Line, Mo. 261/C5
Westline, Pa. 294/E2
West Linn, Oreg. 291/B2
West Linton, Scotland 15/D2
West Liscomb (riv.), Nova Scotia 168/F3
West Little Owyhee (riv.), Oreg. 291/K5
West Loch (inlet), Hawaii 218/A3
West Loch Tarbert (inlet), Scotland 15/A3
West Loch Tarbert (inlet), Scotland 15/C5
Westlock, Alberta 182/C2
West Logan, W. Va. 312/C7
West Long (lake), New Bruns. 170/D3
West Long Branch, N.J. 273/F3
West Lorne, Ontario 177/C5
West Los Angeles, Calif. 204/B10
West Lothian (trad. co.), Scotland 15/B5
West Louisville, Ky. 237/G5
West Lubec, Maine 243/J6
Westmalle, Belgium 27/F6
West Manchester, Ohio 284/A6
West Mansfield, Mass. 249/K5
West Mansfield, Ohio 284/C5
West Maui (mts.), Hawaii 218/H2
Westmeath (co.), Ireland 17/G5
Westmeath, Ontario 177/H2
West Medway, Mass. 249/J4
West Melbourne, Fla. 212/F3
West Memphis, Ark. 202/K3
West Mersea, England 13/H6
West Mersea, England 10/G5
West Miami, Fla. 212/B5
West Middlesex, Pa. 294/B3
West Middleton, Ind. 227/E4
West Middletown, Pa. 294/A5
West Midlands (co.), England 13/F5
West Mifflin, Pa. 294/C7
West Milan, N.H. 268/E2
West Milford, N.J. 273/E1
West Milford, W. Va. 312/F4
West Millbury, Mass. 249/G4
West Millgrove, Ohio 284/C3
West Mills, Maine 243/C6
West Milton, Ohio 284/B6
West Milton, Pa. 294/J3
West Milwaukee, Wis. 317/L1
West Mineral, Kansas 232/H4
West Minot, Maine 243/C7
Westminster, Calif. 204/D11
Westminster, Colo. 208/J3
Westminster, Conn. 210/G2
Westminster, England 10/B5
Westminster, England 13/H8
Westminster, Md. 245/L2
Westminster•, Mass. 249/G2
Westminster, S.C. 296/A2
Westminster, Vt. 268/C5
Westminster•, Vt. 268/C5
Westminster Station, Vt. 268/B5
Westminster West, Vt. 268/B5
West Monroe, La. 238/F1
Westmont, Calif. 204/C11
Westmont, Ill. 222/B6
Westmont, N.J. 273/B3
Westmont, Pa. 294/D5
West Monterey, Pa. 294/C3
Westmore•, Vt. 268/C2
Westmoreland, Kansas 232/F2
Westmoreland•, N.H. 268/C6
Westmoreland (co.), Pa. 294/D5
Westmoreland, Queensland 95/A3
Westmoreland, Tenn. 237/J7
Westmoreland (co.), Va. 307/P4
Westmorland, Calif. 204/K10
Westmorland (co.), New Bruns. 170/F2
Westmount, Nova Scotia 168/H2
Westmount, Québec 172/H4
Westmuir, Scotland 15/E4
West Musquash (lake), Maine 243/H5
West Mystic, Conn. 210/H3
West Newbury•, Mass. 249/L1
West Newbury, Vt. 268/C3
West Newfield, Maine 243/B8
West Newton, Mass. 249/B7
West Newton, Pa. 294/C5
West New York, N.J. 273/C2
West Nicholson, Zimbabwe 118/D4
West Nishnabotna (riv.), Iowa 229/C6
West Norwalk, Conn. 210/B4
West Nottingham, N.H. 268/E5
West Nyack, N.Y. 276/K8
West Okoboji, Iowa 229/C2
West Olive, Mich. 250/C6
Weston, Ala. 195/B2
Weston, Colo. 208/K8
Weston•, Conn. 210/B4
Weston, Georgia 217/C7
Weston, Idaho 220/F7
Weston, Ill. 222/E3
Weston, Iowa 229/B6
Weston•, Maine 243/H4
Weston, Malaysia 85/F4
Weston•, Mass. 249/B6
Weston, Mich. 250/E7
Weston, Mo. 261/C4
Weston, Nebr. 264/H3
Weston, Ohio 284/C3
Weston, Oreg. 291/J2
Weston, Pa. 294/K4
Weston•, Vt. 268/B5
Weston, W. Va. 312/F4
Weston, Wis. 317/C6
Weston, Wis. 317/G6
Weston (co.), Wyo. 319/H2
Weston, Wyo. 319/G1
Westonaria, S. Africa 118/H7
Westons Mills, N.Y. 276/D6
Weston-super-Mare, England 13/D6
Weston-super-Mare, England 10/E5
West Orange, N.J. 273/A2
West Orange, Texas 303/L7
West Ossipee, N.H. 268/E4
Westover, Ala. 195/E4
Westover, Md. 245/R8
Westover, Pa. 294/E4
Westover, S. Dak. 298/H6
Westover, W. Va. 312/G3
Westover A.F.B., Mass. 249/D4
Westover Hills, Texas 303/E2
West Paducah, Ky. 237/D6
West Palm Beach, Fla. 188/K5
West Palm Beach, Fla. 146/K7
West Palm Beach, Fla. 212/F5
West Palm Beach (canal), Fla. 212/F5
West Paris•, Maine 243/B7
West Paterson, N.J. 273/B2
West Pawlet, Vt. 268/A5
West Pelzer, S.C. 296/B2
West Pembroke, Maine 243/J6
West Pensacola, Fla. 212/B6
West Peru, Maine 243/C7
West Peterborough, N.H. 268/C6
Westphalia, Ind. 227/C7
Westphalia, Iowa 229/C5
Westphalia, Kansas 232/G3
Westphalia, Mich. 250/E6
Westphalia, Mo. 261/J6
West Pittsburg, Calif. 204/K1
West Pittsburg, Pa. 294/B4
West Pittston, Pa. 294/F7
West Plains (Plains), Kansas 232/B4
West Plains, Mo. 261/J9
West Point, Ala. 195/D2
West Point (lake), Ala. 195/H4
West Point (mt.), Alaska 196/K2
West Point, Ark. 202/G3
West Point, Calif. 204/E5
West Point, Georgia 217/B5
West Point (lake), Georgia 217/B4
West Point, Ill. 222/B3
Westpoint, Ind. 227/C4
West Point, Iowa 229/K7
West Point, Ky. 237/J4
West Point, Miss. 256/G3
West Point, Nebr. 264/H3
West Point, N.Y. 276/M8
West Point, Ohio 284/J4
Westpoint, Tenn. 237/G10
West Point, Va. 307/P5
West Pointe a la Hache, La. 238/L7
West Poland, Maine 243/C7
West Poplar, Sask. 181/E6
Westport, Calif. 204/B4
Westport•, Conn. 210/B4
Westport, Ind. 227/F6
Westport, Ireland 17/C4
Westport, Ireland 10/B4
Westport, Ky. 237/K4
Westport•, Mass. 249/K6
Westport, Minn. 255/C5
Westport, N.H. 268/C6
Westport, N.Y. 276/N2
Westport, N. Zealand 100/C4
Westport, Nova Scotia 168/B4
Westport, Okla. 288/O2
Westport, Ontario 177/H3
Westport, Oreg. 291/D1
Westport, Pa. 294/G3
Westport, S. Dak. 298/M2
Westport, Tenn. 237/E9
Westport, Wash. 310/A4
West Portal, N.J. 273/D2
Westport Point, Mass. 249/K6
West Portsmouth, Ohio 284/D8
West Pubnico, Nova Scotia 168/C5
Westpunt, Aruba 161/D10
Westpunt, Curaçao, Neth. Ant. 161/F8
West Quaco, New Bruns. 170/E3
West Quoddy (head), Maine 243/K6
Westray (firth), Scotland 15/E1
Westray (isl.), Scotland 15/E1
Westray (isl.), Scotland 10/E1
West Redding, Conn. 210/B3
West Richland, Wash. 310/F4
West Ridge, Ark. 202/K2
West Rindge, N.H. 268/C6
West River, Md. 245/M5
West Road (riv.), Br. Col. 184/E3
West Rockport, Maine 243/E7
West Rock Ridge (hills), Conn. 210/D3
West Rumney, N.H. 268/D4
West Rupert, Vt. 268/A5
West Rushville, Ohio 284/E6
West Rutland, Vt. 268/A4
West Rutland•, Vt. 268/A4
West Rye, N.H. 268/F6
West Sacramento, Calif. 204/B8
West Saint Mary's (riv.), Nova Scotia 168/F3
West Saint Modeste, Newf. 166/C3
West Saint Paul, Minn. 255/G5
West Salem, Ill. 222/F5
West Salem, Ohio 284/F4
West Salem, Wis. 317/D8
West Salisbury, Pa. 294/D6
West Salisbury, Vt. 268/A4
West Sayville, N.Y. 276/O9
West Scarborough, Maine 243/C8
West Seboois, Maine 243/F4
West Seneca, N.Y. 276/C5
West Shoal (lake), Manitoba 179/E4
Westside, Iowa 229/C4
West Side, Oreg. 291/G5
West Siloam Springs, Okla. 288/S2
West Simsbury, Conn. 210/D1
West Sister (isl.), Ohio 284/D2
West Sister (isl.), Tasmania 99/D1
West Somerset, Ky. 237/M6
West Springfield•, Mass. 249/D4
West Springfield, N.H. 268/C5
West Springfield, Pa. 294/B2
West Springfield, Va. 307/S3
West Springs, S.C. 296/D2
West Stafford, Conn. 210/F1
West Statesville, N.C. 281/G3
West Stewartstown, N.H. 268/E2
West Stockbridge•, Mass. 249/A3
West Stockholm, N.Y. 276/K1
West Suffield, Conn. 210/E1
West Sullivan, Maine 243/G6
West Sumner, Maine 243/B7
West Sunbury, Pa. 294/C3
West Sussex (co.), England 13/G7
West Swan (riv.), Minn. 255/F3
West Swanzey, N.H. 268/C6
West Terre Haute, Ind. 227/B6
West-Terschelling, Netherlands 27/G2
West Thompson, Conn. 210/H1
West Thornton, N.H. 268/D4
West Thumb-Grant Village, Wyo. 319/B1
West Tisbury•, Mass. 249/M7
West Torrens, S. Australia 88/D8
West Torrens, S. Australia 94/A8
West Torrington, Conn. 210/C1
West Townsend, Mass. 249/H2
West Townshend, Vt. 268/B5
West Tremont, Maine 243/G7
West Trenton, N.J. 273/D3
West Union, Ill. 222/F4
West Union, Iowa 229/K3
West Union, Minn. 255/C5
West Union, Ohio 284/C8
West Union, S.C. 296/B2
West Union, W. Va. 312/E4
West Unity, Ohio 284/B2
West University Place, Texas 303/J2
West Upton-Upton, Mass. 249/H4
West Valley, N.Y. 276/C6
West Vancouver, Br. Col. 184/K3
West Van Lear, Ky. 237/R5
West View, Pa. 294/B6
West View, Sask. 181/J5
Westview, S.C. 296/C2
Westville, Fla. 212/C6
Westville, Ill. 222/F3
Westville, Ind. 227/D1
Westville, N.H. 268/E6
Westville, N.J. 273/B3
Westville, Nova Scotia 168/F3
Westville, Okla. 288/S2
Westville, Pa. 294/E3
Westville, S.C. 296/F3
West Virginia 188/K3
WEST VIRGINIA 313
West Virginia (state), U.S. 146/K6
Westward Ho, Alberta 182/C4
West Wardsboro, Vt. 268/B5
West Wareham, Mass. 249/L5
West Warren, Mass. 249/F4
West Warwick, R.I. 249/H6
West Weber, Utah 304/B2
Westwego, La. 238/O4
West Wenatchee, Wash. 310/E3
West Wildwood, N.J. 273/D6
West Willington, Conn. 210/F1
West Windham, N.H. 268/E6
West Winfield, N.Y. 276/K5
West Winterport, Maine 243/E6
Westwold, Br. Col. 184/G5
Westwood, Lassen, Calif. 204/D3
Westwood, Ky. 237/R4
Westwood, Ky. 237/L1
Westwood•, Mass. 249/B8
Westwood, Mo. 261/O3
Westwood, N.J. 273/B1
West Woodburn, Oreg. 291/A3
Westwood Lakes, Fla. 212/B5
West Woodstock, Conn. 210/G1
West Woodstock, Vt. 268/B4
Westwood Village, Los Angeles, Calif. 204/B10
Westworth, Texas 303/E2
West Wyalong, N. S. Wales 88/H6
West Wyalong, N.S. Wales 97/D3
West Wyoming, Pa. 294/E7
West Yarmouth, Mass. 249/N6
West Yellowstone, Mont. 262/E6
West York, Ill. 222/F4
West York, Pa. 294/J6
West Yorkshire (co.), England 13/J1
West Yuma, Ariz. 198/A6
Westzaan, Netherlands 27/A4
Wet (mts.), Colo. 208/J6
Wetar (isl.), Indonesia 54/O10
Wetar (isl.), Indonesia 85/H7
Wetaskiwin, Alberta 182/D3
Wetaskiwin, Alta. 162/E5
Wete, Tanzania 115/G4
Wetheral, England 13/E3
Wethersfield•, Conn. 210/E2
Wetipquin, Md. 245/P7
Wetmore, Colo. 208/J6
Wetmore, Kansas 232/G2
Wetmore, Mich. 250/C2
Wetmore, Tenn. 237/N10
Wetmore, Texas 303/K10
Wetonka, S. Dak. 298/M2
Wetteren, Belgium 27/D7
Wetterhorn (peak), Colo. 208/D6
Wetterhorn (mt.), Switzerland 39/F3
Wettingen, Switzerland 39/F2
Wetumka, Okla. 288/O4
Wetumpka, Ala. 195/F5
Wetuppa, N.S. Wales 97/B4
Wetzel (co.), W. Va. 312/E3
Wetzikon, Switzerland 39/G2
Wetzlar, Germany 22/C3
Wever, Iowa 229/L7
Weverton, Md. 245/H3
Wewahitchka, Fla. 212/D6
Wewak, Papua N.G. 87/E6
Wewak, Papua N.G. 85/B6
Weweantic (riv.), Mass. 249/L5
Wewela, S. Dak. 298/K7
Wewoka, Okla. 288/O4
Wexford (co.), Ireland 17/H7
Wexford, Ireland 17/H7
Wexford, Ireland 10/C4
Wexford (bay), Ireland 17/J7
Wexford (harb.), Ireland 17/J7
Wexford (harb.), Ireland 10/C4
Wexford (co.), Mich. 250/D4
Wey (riv.), England 13/G6
Weyanoke, La. 238/H5
Weyauwega, Wis. 317/H7
Weybridge•, Vt. 268/A3
Weyburn, Sask. 162/F6
Weyburn, Sask. 181/H6
Weyerhaeuser, Wis. 317/D5
Weyer Markt, Austria 41/C3
Weyers Cave, Va. 307/L4
Weymouth (bay), England 13/E7
Weymouth, Mass. 249/D8
Weymouth, Nova Scotia 168/C4
Weymouth and Melcombe Regis, England 13/E7
Weymouth and Melcombe Regis, England 10/E5
Weymouth North, Nova Scotia 168/C4
Wezembeek-Oppem, Belgium 27/D9
Wezet (Visé), Belgium 27/H7
Whakatane, N. Zealand 100/F2
Whalan, Minn. 255/G7
Whalan (creek), N.S. Wales 97/E1
Whale (bay), Alaska 196/M1
Whaleback (mt.), W. Australia 92/B3
Whale Cove, N.W. Terr. 187/J3
Whaletown, Br. Col. 184/E5
Whaley Bridge, England 13/J2
Whaley Bridge, England 10/G2
Whaleysville, Md. 245/S7
Whallonsburg, N.Y. 276/O2
Whalsay (isl.), Scotland 10/H1
Whalsay (isl.), Scotland 15/G2
Whangamata, N. Zealand 100/F2
Whangarei, N. Zealand 100/E1
Whangarei, N. Zealand 87/H9
Wharfe (riv.), England 13/E3
Wharfe (riv.), England 10/F3
Wharncliffe, W. Va. 312/C7
Wharton (pen.), Chile 138/D8
Wharton, N.J. 273/D2
Wharton (lake), N.W. Terr. 187/H3
Wharton, Ohio 284/D4
Wharton, Pa. 294/G2
Wharton (co.), Texas 303/H8
Wharton, Texas 303/J8
Wharton, W. Va. 312/C7
Whataroa, N. Zealand 100/C5
Whatatutu, N. Zealand 100/F3
What Cheer, Iowa 229/J6
Whatcom (co.), Wash. 310/D2
Whatcom (lake), Wash. 310/C2
Whately•, Mass. 249/D3
Whatley, Ala. 195/C7
Wheatcroft, Ky. 237/F5
Wheatfield, Ind. 227/C2
Wheatland, Calif. 204/D4
Wheatland, Ind. 227/C7
Wheatland, Iowa 229/M5

Wheatland, Manitoba 179/B4
Wheatland, Mo. 261/F7
Wheatland (co.), Mont. 262/G4
Wheatland, N. Mex. 274/F4
Wheatland, Pa. 294/B3
Wheatland, Wyo. 319/H3
Wheatland (res.), Wyo. 319/G4
Wheatley, Ark. 202/H4
Wheatley, Ky. 237/M3
Wheatley, Ontario 177/B5
Wheaton, Ill. 222/A5
Wheaton, Kansas 232/F2
Wheaton, Minn. 255/B5
Wheaton, Mo. 261/E9
Wheaton-Glenmont, Md. 245/E3
Wheeler, Ala. 195/D1
Wheeler (dam), Ala. 195/D1
Wheeler (lake), Ala. 188/J4
Wheeler (lake), Ala. 195/D1
Wheeler (peak), Calif. 204/F5
Wheeler (co.), Georgia 217/G6
Wheeler, Ill. 222/E4
Wheeler, Ind. 227/C1
Wheeler, Kansas 232/A2
Wheeler, Ky. 237/O7
Wheeler, Mich. 250/E5
Wheeler, Miss. 256/G1
Wheeler (co.), Nebr. 264/F3
Wheeler (peak), Nev. 266/G4
Wheeler (peak), N. Mex. 188/F3
Wheeler (peak), N. Mex. 274/D2
Wheeler (co.), Oreg. 291/G3
Wheeler, Oreg. 291/D2
Wheeler (riv.), Québec 174/D1
Wheeler (co.) Texas 303/D2
Wheeler, Texas 303/D2
Wheeler, Wash. 310/F3
Wheeler, Wis. 317/C5
Wheeler A.F.B., Hawaii 218/E1
Wheelersburg, Ohio 284/F6
Wheeless, Okla. 288/A1
Wheeling, Ill. 222/B5
Wheeling, Ind. 227/G4
Wheeling, Ind. 227/C8
Wheeling, Mo. 261/F3
Wheeling, W. Va. 188/K2
Wheeling, W. Va. 312/E2
Wheelock•, Vt. 268/C2
Wheelock, N. Dak. 282/D3
Wheelwright, Ky. 237/R6
Wheelwright, Mass. 249/F3
Whelen Springs, Ark. 202/D6
Whetstone (buttes), N. Dak. 282/E7
Whetstone (creek), S. Dak. 298/R3
Whick, Ky. 237/P6
Whickham, England 13/J3
Whidbey (isls.), S. Australia 94/D6
Whidbey (isl.), Wash. 310/C2
Whigham, Georgia 217/D9
Whigville, Conn. 210/D2
Whipholt, Minn. 255/D3
Whippany, N.J. 273/E2
Whipple (mts.), Calif. 204/L9
Whipple, Ohio 284/H6
Whiskeytown-Shasta-Trinity Nat'l Rec.
   Area, Calif. 204/C3
Whispering Pines, N.C. 281/L4
Whistler, Br. Col. 184/C4
Whitaker, Ind. 227/D6
Whitaker, Pa. 294/C7
Whitakers, N.C. 281/O2
Whitbourne, Newf. 166/D2
Whitburn, Scotland 10/C1
Whitburn, Scotland 15/C2
Whitby, England 13/G3
Whitby, England 10/F3
Whitby, Ontario 177/F4
Whitchurch, England 13/E5
Whitchurch-Stouffville, Ontario 177/J3
Whitcomb, Ind. 227/H6
Whitcombe (mt.), N. Zealand 100/C5
White (mts.), Alaska 196/J1
White (pass), Alaska 196/N1
White (riv.), Alaska 196/K2
White (riv.), Ariz. 198/E5
White (co.), Ark. 202/G3
White, Ark. 202/G7
White (riv.), Ark. 188/H3
White (riv.), Ark. 202/H5
White (riv.), Colo. 208/B2
White (co.), Georgia 217/E1
White, Georgia 217/C2
White (co.), Ill. 222/E5
White (co.), Ind. 227/D3
White, East Fork (riv.), Ind. 227/C7
White, West Fork (riv.), Ind. 227/C7
White (riv.), Ind. 227/B8
White (lake), La. 238/E7
White (riv.), Mich. 250/C5
White (riv.), Mo. 261/G10
White (riv.), Nebr. 264/C3
White (riv.), Nev. 266/F4
White (bay), Newf. 162/L5
White (bay), Newf. 166/C3
White (riv.), N.H. 268/F6
White (mts.), N.H. 268/E3
White (isl.), N. Zealand 100/F2
White (butte), N. Dak. 282/D7
White (lake), North. Terr. 93/A6
White (riv.), N.W. Terr. 187/K3
White, Ontario 177/G2
White (riv.), Ontario 177/H2
White (riv.), Oreg. 291/F2
White, S. Dak. 298/R5
White (riv.), S. Dak. 298/D7
White (co.), Tenn. 237/L9
White (riv.), Texas 303/C3
White (sea), U.S.S.R. 4/C8
White (sea), U.S.S.R. 7/H2
White (sea), U.S.S.R. 48/D3
White (sea), U.S.S.R. 52/E1
White (riv.), Utah 304/E3
White (riv.), Vt. 268/C4
White, First Branch (riv.), Vt. 268/B4

White, Second Branch (riv.), Vt. 268/B4
White (pass), Wash. 310/D4
White (riv.), Wash 310/D3
White (riv.), Yukor 187/D3
White Bear (isl.), Newf. 166/B2
White Bear (lake), Newf. 166/C4
White Bear (riv.), Newf. 166/C4
White Bear, Sask. 81/C5
White Bear Lake, Minn. 255/G5
Whitebeech, Sask. 181/K3
White Bird, Idaho 220/B4
White Bluff, Tenn. 237/G8
White Butte (mt.), N. Dak. 282/D7
White Butte, S. Dak. 298/E2
White Carpathians (mts.), Czech. 41/E2
White Castle, La. 238/J3
White Center-Shorewood, Wash. 310/A2
White City, Fla. 212/F4
White City, Ill. 222/D4
White City, Kansas 232/F3
White City, Oreg. 291/E5
White City, Sask. 131/G5
Whiteclay, Nebr. 264/B2
White Cliffs, N.S. Wales 97/B2
White Cloud, Kansas 232/H2
White Cloud, Kansas 232/G2
White Cloud, Mich. 250/D5
White Coomb (mt.) Scotland 15/E5
White Cottage, Ohio 284/F6
Whitecourt, Alberta 182/C2
White Deer, Pa. 29~/J3
White Deer, Texas 303/C2
White Earth, Minn. 255/C3
White Earth, N. Dak. 282/E3
White Earth (riv.), N. Dak. 282/E3
White Earth Ind. Res., Minn. 255/C3
White Elster (riv.), Germany 22/E3
Whiteface (riv.), Minn. 255/F3
Whiteface (mt.), N.H. 268/E4
Whiteface (mt.), N.Y. 268/B4
Whiteface (mt.), N.Y. 276/N2
Whiteface, Texas 303/C4
White Face (mt.), Vt. 268/B2
Whitefield, Maine 243/D7
Whitefield•, Maine 243/D7
Whitefield, N.H. 268/D3
Whitefield•, N.H. 268/D3
Whitefield, Okla. 288/R4
Whitefish (bay), Mich. 250/E2
Whitefish (pt.), Mich. 250/E2
Whitefish (riv.), Mich. 250/C2
Whitefish (lake), Minn. 255/D4
Whitefish, Mont. 262/B2
Whitefish (lake), Mont. 262/B2
White Fish Falls, Ontario 177/C1
Whitefish Point, Mich. 250/E2
Whiteflat, Texas 303/D3
Whiteford, Md. 245/N2
White Fox, Sask. 181/G2
White Fox (riv.), Sask. 181/G2
Whitegate, Ireland 17/E8
White Gull (creek), Sask. 181/G2
White Hall, Ala. 195/E6
Whitehall, Ark. 202/L3
White Hall, Ark. 202/F5
White Hall, Georgia 217/F3
White Hall, Ill. 222/C4
Whitehall, Ill. 222/C6
Whitehall, La. 238/M2
White Hall, Md. 245/M2
Whitehall, Mich. 250/C5
Whitehall, Mont. 262/D5
Whitehall, N.Y. 276/N3
Whitehall, Ohio 284/E6
Whitehall, Pa. 294/B7
Whitehall, Scotland 15/F1
White Hall, S.C. 296/F6
White Hall, Va. 307/L4
Whitehall, Wis. 317/D7
White Handkerchief (cape), Newf. 166/B2
Whitehaven, England 13/D3
Whitehaven, England 10/E3
Whitehaven, Md. 245/P7
Whitehaven (harb.), Nova Scotia 168/G3
White Haven, Pa. 294/L3
White Head, New Bruns. 170/D4
White Head (isl.), New Bruns. 170/D4
Whitehead, N. Ireland 17/K2
Whitehead, Nova Scotia 168/G3
White Heath, Ill. 222/E3
Whitehills, Scotland 15/F3
White Horn, Tenn. 237/R8
Whitehorse, Canada 4/C16
Whitehorse, Canada 5/C3
Whitehorse, S. Dak. 298/H3
Whitehorse (cap.), Yukon 187/E3
Whitehorse (cap.), Yukon 162/C3
Whitehorse (cap.), Yukon 146/E3
White Horse Lake, N. Mex. 274/B3
Whitehouse, Ky. 237/R5
Whitehouse, N.J. 273/D2
Whitehouse, Ohio 284/C2
White House, Tenn. 237/H8
White House Station, N.J. 273/D2
White Iron (lake), Minn. 255/G3
White Knob (mts.), Idaho 220/E6
White Lake, N.C. 281/M5
White Lake, Ontario 177/H2
White Lake, S. Dak. 298/M6
White Lake, Wis. 317/J5
Whiteland, Ind. 227/E4
Whitelaw, Alberta 182/A1
Whitelaw, Wis. 317/L7
Whiteman A.F.B., Mo. 261/E5
Whitemark, Tasmania 99/D2
White Marsh, Md. 245/N3
White Meadow Lake, N.J. 273/D2
White Mills, Ky. 237/J3
White Mills, Pa. 294/N2
White Mountain, Alaska 196/F2
White Mountains Nat'l Rec. Area,
   Alaska 196/J1
Whitemouth, Manitoba 179/G5
Whitemouth (lake), Manitoba 179/G5

Whitemouth (riv.), Manitoba 179/G5
Whitemud (riv.), Alberta 182/A1
Whiten (head), Scotland 15/D2
White Nile (riv.) 2/L5
White Nile (riv.) 102/F4
White Nile (prov.), Sudan 111/F5
White Nile (riv.), Sudan 111/F5
White Nile (riv.), Sudan 59/B7
White Oak (lake), Ark. 202/D6
White Oak, Georgia 217/J8
White Oak, Md. 245/F3
Whiteoak, Mo. 261/M10
White Oak, N.C. 281/M5
Whiteoak (swamp), N.C. 281/P5
Whiteoak (creek), Ohio 284/C7
White Oak, Okla. 288/R1
White Oak, Pa. 294/C7
White Oak, S.C. 296/E3
Whiteoak (creek), Tenn. 237/F8
White Oak, Texas 303/K5
White Oaks, Conn. 210/C2
White Oaks, N. Mex. 274/C5
White Owl, S. Dak. 298/E4
White Partridge (lake), Ontario 177/G2
White Pass, Wash. 310/D4
White Pigeon, Mich. 250/D7
White Pine, Mich. 250/F1
White Pine (co.), Nev. 266/F3
White Pine (range), Nev. 266/F3
White Pine, Tenn. 237/P8
White Pines, Calif. 204/E5
White Plains, Ala. 195/G3
White Plains, Georgia 217/F4
White Plains, Ky. 237/D6
White Plains, Md. 245/L6
White Plains, N.Y. 276/P6
White Plains, N.C. 281/H1
White Plains, Va. 307/N7
White Pond, S.C. 296/D5
White Post, Va. 307/M2
White Quartz Hill, North. Terr. 93/D7
White Rapids, New Bruns. 170/E2
Whiteriver, Ariz. 198/E5
White River, Ont. 162/H6
White River, Ontario 175/C3
White River, Ontario 177/J5
White River, S. Dak. 298/H6
White River (lake), Texas 303/C4
White River Junction, Vt. 268/C4
White Rock, Br. Col. 184/K3
White Rock, N. Mex. 274/C3
White Rock, S.C. 296/E3
White Rock, S. Dak. 298/R2
Whiterock, N.C. 281/D3
White Rock (creek), Texas 303/G2
Whiterocks, Utah 304/E3
Whites, Wash. 310/B3
Whitesail (lake), Br. Col. 184/D3
White Salmon, Wash. 310/D5
White Salmon (riv.), Wash. 310/D4
White Sands (des.), N. Mex. 274/C5
White Sands Missile Range, N. Mex.
   274/C6
White Sands Missile Range, N. Mex.
   274/C5
White Sands Nat'l Mon., N. Mex.
   274/C6
Whitesbog, N.J. 273/E4
Whitesboro, N.J. 273/D5
Whitesboro, N.Y. 276/K4
Whitesboro, Okla. 288/S5
Whitesboro, Texas 303/H4
Whitesburg, Georgia 217/B4
Whitesburg, Ky. 237/R6
Whitesburg, Tenn. 237/P8
Whites Chapel, Ala. 195/F3
Whites City, N. Mex. 274/E6
Whites Creek, W. Va. 312/A6
White Settlement, Texas 303/E2
Whiteshell Prov. Park, Manitoba
   179/G4
White Shield, N. Dak. 282/G4
Whiteshore (lake), Sask. 181/C3
Whiteside (chan.), Chile 138/E10
Whiteside (co.), Ill. 222/D2
Whiteside, Mo. 261/K4
Whiteside, Tenn. 237/K10
Whites Lake, Nova Scotia 168/E4
Whiteson, Oreg. 291/D2
White Springs, Fla. 212/D1
Whitestone, Georgia 217/C1
White Stone, Va. 307/R5
Whitestown, Ind. 227/D4
White Sulphur Springs, Georgia
   217/C5
White Sulphur Springs, La. 238/F3
White Sulphur Springs, Mont. 262/E4
White Sulphur Springs, W. Va. 312/F7
Whitesville, Georgia 217/C5
Whitesville, Ky. 237/H5
Whitesville, Mo. 261/C2
Whitesville, N.J. 273/E3
Whitesville, N.Y. 276/E6
Whitesville, W. Va. 312/C6
Whiteswan (lakes), Sask. 181/F1
White Swan, Wash. 310/E4
Whitetail, Mont. 262/L2
Whitetop, Va. 307/E7
Whiteville, La. 238/F5
Whiteville, N.C. 281/M6
Whiteville, Tenn. 237/C10
White Volta (riv.) 102/B4
White Volta (riv.), Ghana 106/D6
White Volta (Nakane) (riv.), Burkina
   Faso 106/D6
Whitewater, Colo. 208/C5
Whitewater (bay), Fla. 212/F6
Whitewater, Ind. 227/H5
Whitewater (riv.), Ind. 227/H6
Whitewater, Kansas 232/G4
Whitewater, Manitoba 179/B5
Whitewater (lake), Manitoba 179/B5
Whitewater, Mo. 261/N8
Whitewater, Mont. 262/J2
Whitewater, Wis. 317/J10
Whitewater Baldy (mt.), N. Mex. 274/A5

Whitewood, Sask. 181/J5
Whitewood, S. Dak. 298/B5
Whitewood (creek), S. Dak. 298/B4
Whitewood, Va. 307/E6
Whitewright, Texas 303/H4
Whitfield, Ala. 195/B6
Whitfield (co.), Georgia 217/B1
Whitfield, Miss. 256/E6
Whitford, Alberta 182/D3
Whithorn, Scotland 10/D3
Whithorn, Scotland 15/D6
Whitianga, N. Zealand 100/E2
Whiting, Ind. 227/C1
Whiting, Iowa 229/J6
Whiting, Kansas 232/G2
Whiting•, Maine 243/J6
Whiting, Mo. 261/O9
Whiting, N.J. 273/E4
Whiting•, Vt. 268/A4
Whiting, Wis. 317/H7
Whiting Bay, Scotland 15/C5
Whiting Field Naval Air Sta., Fla. 212/B6
Whitingham•, Vt. 268/B6
Whitinsville, Mass. 249/H4
Whitkow, Sask. 181/D3
Whitla, Alberta 182/E5
Whitlash, Mont. 262/E2
Whitley (co.), Ind. 227/F2
Whitley (co.), Ky. 237/N7
Whitley Bay, England 13/J3
Whitley City, Ky. 237/N7
Whitleyville, Tenn. 237/K8
Whitlock, Tenn. 237/E8
Whitman•, Mass. 249/L4
Whitman (riv.), Mass. 249/L4
Whitman, Nebr. 264/C2
Whitman, N. Dak. 282/O3
Whitman (co.), Wash. 310/H4
Whitman Mission Nat'l Hist. Site,
   Wash. 310/G4
Whitmer, W. Va. 312/G5
Whitmire, S.C. 296/D3
Whitmore, Calif. 204/D3
Whitmore Lake, Mich. 250/F6
Whitmore Village, Hawaii 218/E1
Whitnel, N.C. 281/F5
Whitney (mt.), Calif. 188/C5
Whitney (mt.), Calif. 204/G7
Whitney (lake), Conn. 210/D3
Whitney, Nebr. 264/A2
Whitney, New Bruns. 170/E2
Whitney, Ontario 177/F2
Whitney, Pa. 294/D5
Whitney, S.C. 296/D3
Whitney, Texas 303/G6
Whitney Point, N.Y. 276/J6
Whitney Point (lake), N.Y. 276/J6
Whitneyville, Conn. 210/D3
Whitneyville•, Maine 243/J6
Whitsett, Texas 303/F9
Whitsunday (isl.), Queensland 88/H4
Whitsunday (isl.), Queensland 95/D4
Whitt, Texas 303/E2
Whittaker, Mich. 250/F6
Whittemore, Iowa 229/E2
Whittemore, Mich. 250/F4
Whitten, Iowa 229/H4
Whittier, Alaska 196/C1
Whittier, Calif. 204/D11
Whittier, Iowa 229/K4
Whittier, N.C. 281/C4
Whittle (cape), Québec 174/F2
Whittlesea, Victoria 97/C5
Whittlesey, England 13/G5
Whittlesey, Wis. 317/F5
Whitton, N.S. Wales 97/D4
Whitwell, Tenn. 237/K10
Wholdaia (lake), N.W. Terr. 187/H3
Why, Ariz. 198/C6
Whyalla, Australia 87/D9
Whyalla, S. Australia 94/E5
Whycocomagh, Nova Scotia 168/G3
Whyjonta, N.S. Wales 97/B1
Whyte Yarcowie, S. Australia 94/E4
Wiarton, Ontario 177/C3
Wiau (lake), Alberta 182/F7
Wiawso, Ghana 106/D7
Wiay (isl.), Scotland 15/A3
Wibaux (co.), Mont. 262/M4
Wibaux, Mont. 262/M3
Wichabai, Guyana 131/B4
Wichita (co.), Kansas 232/A3
Wichita, Kans. 188/G3
Wichita, Kansas 146/J6
Wichita, Kansas 232/E4
Wichita (mts.), Okla. 288/J5
Wichita (co.), Texas 303/F3
Wichita (riv.), Texas 303/F4
Wichita Falls, Texas 146/H6
Wichita Falls, Texas 303/F4
Wichita Falls, Texas 188/G4
Wick, Iowa 229/F6
Wick, Scotland 10/E1
Wick, Scotland 15/E2
Wick (riv.), Scotland 15/E2
Wick, W. Va. 312/E4
Wickahoney (creek), Idaho 220/C7
Wickatunk, N.J. 273/D2
Wicked (pt.), Manitoba 179/D2
Wickenburg, Ariz. 198/C5
Wickepin, W. Australia 92/B2
Wickersham, Wash. 310/C2
Wickes, Ark. 202/B5
Wickes, Mont. 262/D4
Wickett, Texas 303/C6
Wickham, New Bruns. 170/D3
Wickham, Québec 172/E4
Wickham (cape), Tasmania 99/A1
Wickham, W. Australia 92/B3
Wickiup (res.), Oreg. 291/F4
Wickliffe, Ky. 237/C7
Wickliffe, Ohio 284/J9
Wicklow (co.), Ireland 17/J5
Wicklow, Ireland 17/K6
Wicklow, Ireland 17/K6
Wicklow (head), Ireland 17/K6
Wicklow (head), Ireland 10/D4
Wicklow (mts.), Ireland 17/J6

Wicklow, New Bruns. 170/C2
Wicksburg, Ala. 195/G4
Wicomico (co.), Md. 245/R7
Wicomico, Md. 245/L7
Wicomico (co.), Md. 245/R7
Wicomico (riv.), Md. 245/L7
Wicomico Church, Va. 307/R5
Wiconisco, Pa. 294/J4
Wide (chan.), Chile 138/D8
Wide (bay), Papua N.G. 86/C2
Wide (bay), Queensland 95/E5
Wideman, Ark. 202/G1
Widemouth, W. Va. 312/D8
Widen, W. Va. 312/E6
Widener, Ark. 202/J3
Widewater, Alberta 182/C2
Widgiemooltha, W. Australia 88/C6
Widgiemooltha, W. Australia 92/C5
Widnes, England 10/F2
Widnes, England 13/G2
Widnoon, Pa. 294/D4
Wiebork, Poland 47/C2
Wiederkehr Village, Ark. 202/C3
Wiehl, Germany 22/B3
Wiek, Germany 22/E1
Wieliczka, Poland 47/E3
Wieluń, Poland 47/D3
Wien (Vienna) (cap.), Austria 41/D2
Wiener Neustadt, Austria 41/D3
Wieprz (riv.), Poland 47/F3
Wierden, Netherlands 27/K4
Wieringermeer Polder, Netherlands
   27/G3
Wierum, Netherlands 27/H2
Wieruszów, Poland 47/D3
Wiesbaden, Germany 7/E3
Wiesbaden, Germany 22/B3
Wiese (isl.), U.S.S.R. 4/B6
Wiese (isl.), U.S.S.R. 48/H2
Wiesmoor, Germany 22/B2
Wigan, England 13/G2
Wigan, England 10/G2
Wiggins, Colo. 208/L2
Wiggins, Miss. 256/F9
Wiggins, S.C. 296/F6
Wight (isl.), England 13/F7
Wight (isl.), England 10/F5
Wigston, England 13/F5
Wigton, England 13/D3
Wigtown (trad. co.), Scotland 15/A5
Wigtown, Scotland 10/D3
Wigtown, Scotland 15/D6
Wigtown (bay), Scotland 10/D3
Wigtown (bay), Scotland 15/D6
Wijhe, Netherlands 27/J4
Wijk bij Duurstede, Netherlands
   27/G5
Wijk en Aalburg, Netherlands 27/F5
Wikel, W. Va. 312/E7
Wikieup, Ariz. 198/B4
Wikwemikong, Ontario 177/C2
Wil, Switzerland 39/H2
Wilawana, Pa. 294/J2
Wilbarger (co.), Texas 303/E3
Wilber, Nebr. 264/G4
Wilberforce, Ontario 177/F3
Wilbert, Minn. 255/D7
Wilbraham, Mass. 249/E4
Wilbraham•, Mass. 249/E4
Wilbur, Ind. 227/D5
Wilbur, Ky. 237/R5
Wilbur, Oreg. 291/D4
Wilbur, Wash. 310/G3
Wilbur, W. Va. 312/E4
Wilbur Park, Mo. 261/P9
Wilburton, Kansas 232/A4
Wilburton, Okla. 288/R5
Wilcannia, N.S. Wales 88/G6
Wilcannia, N.S. Wales 97/B2
Wilchingen, Switzerland 39/F1
Wilcox (co.), Ala. 195/D7
Wilcox, Fla. 212/D2
Wilcox (co.), Georgia 217/F7
Wilcox, Mo. 261/C2
Wilcox, Nebr. 264/E4
Wilcox, Pa. 294/E2
Wilcox, Sask. 181/G5
Wilczek Land (isl.), U.S.S.R. 4/B6
Wilczek Land (isl.), U.S.S.R. 48/G1
Wild Ammonoosuc (riv.), N.H.
   268/D3
Wildbad im Schwarzwald, Germany
   22/C4
Wildcat (creek), Ind. 227/E4
Wild Cat, Ky. 237/O6
Wild Cherry, Ark. 202/F1
Wild Cove, Newf. 166/C3
Wilder, Idaho 220/A6
Wilder, Minn. 255/C7
Wilder (dam), N.H. 268/C4
Wilder, Tenn. 237/L8
Wilder, Vt. 268/C4
Wilder (dam), Vt. 268/C4
Wilderness, Va. 307/N4
Wilders, Ky. 237/S2
Wildersville, Tenn. 237/E9
Wilderswil, Switzerland 39/E3
Wildervank, Netherlands 27/K2
Wilderville, Oreg. 291/D5
Wildeshausen, Germany 22/C2
Wild Goose, Ontario 177/H5
Wild Goose, Ontario 175/C3
Wildhaus, Switzerland 39/H2
Wildhay (riv.), Alberta 182/B3
Wildhorn (mt.), Switzerland 39/D4
Wild Horse, Colo. 208/N5
Wild Horse (res.), Nev. 266/F1
Wildhorse (creek), Okla. 288/L5
Wildie, Ky. 237/N6
Wildorado, Texas 303/B2
Wild Rice (lake), Minn. 255/F4
Wild Rice (riv.), Minn. 255/B3
Wild Rice, N. Dak. 282/S6
Wild Rice (riv.), N. Dak. 282/R7
Wildrose, N. Dak. 282/D2
Wild Rose, Wis. 317/H7

Wildspitze (mt.), Austria 41/A3
Wildstrubel (mt.), Switzerland
   39/E4
Wildsville, La. 238/G3
Wildwood, Alberta 182/C3
Wildwood, Fla. 212/D3
Wildwood, Minn. 255/E3
Wildwood, N.J. 273/D6
Wildwood Crest, N.J. 273/D6
Wileville, Nova Scotia 168/D4
Wiley, Colo. 208/O6
Wiley, Georgia 217/F1
Wiley (creek), Oreg. 291/E3
Wiley City, Wash. 310/E4
Wiley Ford, W. Va. 312/J3
Wileyville, W. Va. 312/E3
Wilfred, Ind. 227/C6
Wilhelm (mt.), Papua N.G. 85/B7
Wilhelm II Coast (reg.), Ant. 2/C10
Wilhelmina (canal), Netherlands
   27/G6
Wilhelmina (mts.), Surinam 131/C4
Wilhelmsburg, Austria 41/C2
Wilhelmshaven, Germany 22/B2
Wilkes (co.), Georgia 217/G3
Wilkes (co.), N.C. 281/G2
Wilkes (lake), Ontario 177/F1
Wilkes-Barre, Pa. 188/L2
Wilkes-Barre, Pa. 294/F7
Wilkesboro, N.C. 281/G2
Wilkes Land (reg.), Ant. 2/R10
Wilkes Land (reg.), Ant. 5/B7
Wilkeson, Wash. 310/D3
Wilkesville, Ohio 284/F7
Wilkie, Sask. 181/C3
Wilkin (co.), Minn. 255/B4
Wilkins, Nev. 266/G1
Wilkins (lakes), S. Australia
   94/C3
Wilkinson, W. Va. 312/B7
Wilkinsonville, Mass. 249/G4
Will (co.), Ill. 222/F2
Willacoochee, Georgia 217/G8
Willacy (co.), Texas 303/G11
Willamette (riv.), Oreg. 291/A3
Willamette, Middle Fork (riv.), Oreg.
   291/F4
Willamina, Oreg. 291/D2
Willandra Billabong (creek),
   N.S. Wales 97/C3
Willapa, Wash. 310/B4
Willapa (bay), Wash. 310/A4
Willard, Kansas 232/G2
Willard, Mich. 250/E5
Willard, Mo. 261/F8
Willard, Mont. 262/M4
Willard, N. Mex. 274/D4
Willard, N.Y. 276/J5
Willard, N.C. 281/O5
Willard, Ohio 284/E3
Willard, Utah 304/C2
Willard, Wis. 317/E6
Willards, Md. 245/S7
Willaumez (pen.), Papua N.G. 86/B2
Willaura, Victoria 97/B5
Willcox, Ariz. 198/F6
Willebroek, Belgium 27/E6
Willems (canal), Netherlands 27/G5
Willemstad, Netherlands 27/F5
Willemstad (cap.), Neth. Ant. 156/E4
Willemstad (cap.), Neth. Ant. 161/F9
Willen, Manitoba 179/A4
Willernie, Minn. 255/G5
Willeroo, North. Terr. 93/B3
Willette, Tenn. 237/K8
Willey, Iowa 229/D5
Willey House, N.H. 268/E3
William (riv.), Sask. 181/L2
William Creek, S. Australia 94/E3
William H. Taft Nat'l Hist. Site, Ohio
   284/C10
William L. Springer (lake), Ill. 222/E4
Williams, Ariz. 198/C4
Williams, Calif. 204/C4
Williams, Ind. 227/D7
Williams, Iowa 229/F3
Williams, Minn. 255/D2
Williams (co.), N. Dak. 282/C3
Williams (co.), Ohio 284/A2
Williams, Okla. 238/T4
Williams, Oreg. 291/D5
Williams, S.C. 296/F5
Williams, W. Australia 92/B2
Williams (riv.), W. Va. 312/F6
Williams A.F.B., Ariz. 198/D5
Williams Bay, Wis. 317/J10
Williamsboro, N.C. 281/M2
Williamsburg, Colo. 208/J6
Williamsburg, Iowa 229/J5
Williamsburg, Kansas 232/G3
Williamsburg, Ky. 237/N7
Williamsburg, Md. 245/P6
Williamsburg•, Mass. 249/E4
Williamsburg, Mich. 250/D4
Williamsburg, Mo. 261/J5
Williamsburg, New Bruns. 170/D2
Williamsburg, N. Mex. 274/B5
Williamsburg, Ohio 284/B7
Williamsburg, Pa. 294/F5
Williamsburg (co.), S.C. 296/H4
Williamsburg (I.C.), Va. 307/P6
Williamsburg, W. Va. 312/F7
Williamsfield, Ill. 222/D3
Williamsfield, Jamaica 158/H6
Williamsfield, Ohio 284/J2
Williamsford, Ontario 177/D3
Williamsford, Tasmania 99/B3
Williams Fork, Colorado 208/G3
Williams Fork, Yampa (riv.), Colo.
   208/E2

Williams Harbour, Newf. 166/C3
Williams Lake, Br. Col. 162/D5
Williams Lake, Br. Col. 184/F4
Williamson, Georgia 217/D4
Williamson (co.), Ill. 222/E6
Williamson, Ill. 222/D5
Williamson, Iowa 229/G6
Williamson, N.Y. 276/F4
Williamson (riv.), Oreg. 291/F5
Williamson (co.), Tenn. 237/H9
Williamson (co.), Texas 303/G7
Williamson, W. Va. 312/B7
Williamsport, Ind. 227/C4
Williamsport, Ky. 237/R5
Williamsport, Md. 245/G2
Williamsport, Newf. 166/C3
Williamsport, Ohio 284/D6
Williamsport, Pa. 188/L2
Williamsport, Pa. 294/H3
Williamsport, Tenn. 237/G9
Williamston, Mich. 250/E6
Williamston, N.C. 281/R3
Williamston, S.C. 296/B2
Williamstown, Kansas 232/G2
Williamstown, Ky. 237/M3
Williamstown, Mass. 249/B2
Williamstown•, Mass. 249/B2
Williamstown, Mo. 261/J2
Williamstown, New Bruns. 170/C2
Williamstown, N.J. 273/D4
Williamstown, N.Y. 276/J4
Williamstown, Ontario 177/K2
Williamstown, Pa. 294/J4
Williamstown, S. Australia 94/C7
Williamstown•, Vt. 268/B3
Williamstown, Victoria 88/K7
Williamstown, Victoria 97/H5
Williamstown, W. Va. 312/C4
Williamsville, Ill. 222/D4
Williamsville, Miss. 256/F4
Williamsville, Mo. 261/L9
Williamsville, N.Y. 276/C5
Williamsville, Vt. 268/B6
Williamsville, Va. 307/J4
Willies (range), Queensland 95/C6
Williford, Ark. 202/H1
Willimantic, Conn. 210/G2
Willimantic (riv.), Conn. 210/F1
Willimantic, Maine 243/E5
Willimantic•, Maine 243/E5
Willingboro•, N.J. 273/D4
Willingdon, Alberta 182/E3
Willington•, Conn. 210/F1
Willington, S.C. 296/C4
Willis (islets), Australia 87/F7
Willis (isls.), Coral Sea Is. Terr. 88/J3
Willis, Kansas 232/G2
Willis, Mich. 250/F6
Willis, Okla. 288/N7
Willis, Texas 303/J7
Willis, Va. 307/H7
Willis (riv.), Va. 307/M5
Willisau, Switzerland 39/F2
Willisburg, Ky. 237/L5
Williston (lake), Br. Col. 162/D4
Williston (lake), Br. Col. 184/F2
Williston, Fla. 212/D2
Williston, N. Dak. 188/F1
Williston, N. Dak. 282/C3
Williston, S.C. 296/E5
Williston, Tenn. 237/C10
Williston•, Vt. 268/A3
Williston Park, N.Y. 276/R7
Willisville, Ark. 202/D6
Willisville, Ill. 222/D6
Willisville, Ontario 177/C1
Willis Wharf, Va. 307/S5
Williton, England 13/D6
Willits, Calif. 204/B4
Willmar, Minn. 255/C5
Willmar, Sask. 181/J6
Willmathsville, Mo. 261/G2
Willmore Wilderness Prov. Park, Alberta 182/A3
Willoughby (bay), Ant. & Bar. 161/E11
Willoughby, N.S. Wales 88/K3
Willoughby, N.S. Wales 97/J3
Willoughby, Ohio 284/J4
Willoughby, Vt. 268/C2
Willoughby (lake), Vt. 268/D2
Willoughby Hills, Ohio 284/J9
Willow, Alaska 196/B1
Willow, Ark. 202/E5
Willow (creek), Calif. 204/E3
Willow (creek), Idaho 220/G6
Willow (riv.), Minn. 255/E4
Willow (creek), Mont. 262/E2
Willow, Okla. 288/G4
Willow (creek), Oreg. 291/H2
Willow (creek), Oreg. 291/K3
Willow (creek), S. Dak. 298/C4
Willow (creek), Utah 304/C4
Willow (res.), Wis. 317/F4
Willow (creek), Wyo. 319/F2
Willow (lake), Wyo. 319/C2
Willow Bend, W. Va. 312/F7
Willow Branch, Ind. 227/F5
Willowbrook, Ill. 222/B6
Willowbrook, Kansas 232/D3
Willowbrook, Sask. 181/J4
Willow Bunch, Sask. 181/F6
Willow Bunch (lake), Sask. 181/F6
Willow City, N. Dak. 282/K2
Willow City, Texas 303/F7
Willow Creek, Calif. 204/B3
Willow Creek, Mont. 262/E5
Willow Creek (res.), Mont. 262/D3
Willowcreek, Oreg. 291/K3
Willow Creek, Sask. 181/B6
Willowdale, Oreg. 291/G3
Willow Grove, Del. 245/R4
Willow Grove, New Bruns. 170/E3
Willow Grove, Pa. 294/M5
Willow Hill, Ill. 222/E5
Willow Hill, Pa. 294/G5
Willowick, Ohio 284/J8
Willow Island, Nebr. 264/D4
Willowlake (riv.), N.W. Terr. 187/F3

Willow Lake, S. Dak. 298/O4
Willowmore, S. Africa 118/C6
Willowra, North. Terr. 93/C6
Willow Ranch, Calif. 204/E2
Willow River, Br. Col. 184/F3
Willow River, Minn. 255/F4
Willows, Calif. 204/C4
Willows, Md. 245/M6
Willows, Sask. 181/F6
Willow Springs, Ill. 222/B6
Willow Springs, Mo. 261/H9
Willowton, W. Va. 312/E8
Willow Tree, N.S. Wales 97/F2
Wills (creek), Ohio 284/G5
Wills (lake), W. Australia 88/D4
Willsboro, N.Y. 276/N2
Wills Creek (lake), Ohio 284/G5
Willshire, Ohio 284/A4
Wills Point, La. 238/L7
Wills Point, Texas 303/J5
Willunga, S. Australia 94/F6
Wilma, Fla. 212/B1
Wilmar, Ark. 202/G6
Wilmer, Ala. 195/B9
Wilmer, Br. Col. 184/J5
Wilmer, La. 238/K5
Wilmer, Texas 303/H3
Wilmerding, Pa. 294/C5
Wilmette, Ill. 222/B5
Wilmington, Calif. 204/C11
Wilmington, Del. 188/M3
Wilmington, Del. 245/R2
Wilmington, Ill. 222/E2
Wilmington (Patterson), Ill. 222/C4
Wilmington, Ind. 227/H6
Wilmington•, Mass. 249/C5
Wilmington, N.Y. 276/N2
Wilmington, N.C. 188/L4
Wilmington, N.C. 146/L6
Wilmington, N.C. 281/N6
Wilmington, Ohio 284/C7
Wilmington, S. Australia 94/F6
Wilmington•, Vt. 268/B6
Wilmington Island, Georgia 217/L7
Wilmont, Minn. 255/C7
Wilmore, Kansas 232/C4
Wilmore, Ky. 237/M5
Wilmore, Pa. 294/E5
Wilmot, Ark. 202/G7
Wilmot, Ind. 227/F2
Wilmot, Kansas 232/F4
Wilmot, New Bruns. 170/C3
Wilmot•, N.H. 268/D5
Wilmot, Ohio 284/G4
Wilmot, Pr. Edward I. 168/E2
Wilmot, S. Dak. 298/R3
Wilmot, Tasmania 99/C3
Wilmot Flat, N.H. 268/D5
Wilmot Station, Nova Scotia 168/D4
Wilmslow, England 10/G2
Wilmslow, England 13/H2
Wilno, Ontario 177/G2
Wilpen, Pa. 294/D5
Wilrijk, Belgium 27/E6
Wilsall, Mont. 262/F5
Wilsey, Kansas 232/F3
Wilson (dam), Ala. 195/C1
Wilson, Ark. 202/K2
Wilson (mt.), Calif. 204/D10
Wilson (mt.), Colo. 188/E3
Wilson (mt.), Colo. 208/C7
Wilson, Conn. 210/E1
Wilson (co.), Kansas 232/G4
Wilson, Kansas 232/D3
Wilson (lake), Kansas 232/D3
Wilson, La. 238/H5
Wilson, Maine 243/E3
Wilson, Mich. 250/B3
Wilson, Minn. 255/G7
Wilson, N.Y. 276/C4
Wilson (co.), N.C. 281/O3
Wilson, N.C. 281/O3
Wilson (cape), N.W. Terr. 187/K3
Wilson, Ohio 284/H6
Wilson (riv.), Oreg. 291/D2
Wilson, Pa. 294/M4
Wilson (riv.), Queensland 95/B5
Wilson, S.C. 296/G4
Wilson (co.), Tenn. 237/J8
Wilson (co.), Texas 303/F8
Wilson, Texas 303/C4
Wilson (creek), Wash. 310/F3
Wilson, W. Va. 312/H4
Wilson, Wis. 317/B6
Wilson, Wyo. 319/B2
Wilson Bluff (prom.), S. Australia 94/A4
Wilsonburg, W. Va. 312/F4
Wilson City, Mo. 261/O9
Wilson Creek, Br. Col. 184/J2
Wilson Creek, Wash. 310/E1
Wilsondale, W. Va. 312/B7
Wilson Lake (res.), Idaho 220/D7
Wilson Landing, Br. Col. 184/H5
Wilson Point, New Bruns. 170/F1
Wilsons (prom.), Victoria 88/H7
Wilsons (prom.), Victoria 97/D6
Wilsons, Va. 307/N6
Wilsons Beach, New Bruns. 170/D4
Wilson's Creek Nat'l Battlefield, Mo. 261/F8
Wilsons Mills, Maine 243/B6
Wilsons Mills, N.C. 281/M3
Wilsonville, Ala. 195/E4
Wilsonville, Conn. 210/H1
Wilsonville, Ill. 222/D4
Wilsonville, Nebr. 264/D4
Wilsonville, Oreg. 291/A2
Wilton, Ala. 195/E4
Wilton, Ark. 202/B6
Wilton, Calif. 204/C9
Wilton•, Conn. 210/B4
Wilton, England 13/E6
Wilton, Iowa 229/M5
Wilton•, Maine 243/C6
Wilton•, Maine 243/C6
Wilton•, Minn. 255/C3

Wilton, N.H. 268/D6
Wilton•, N.H. 268/D6
Wilton, N.Y. 276/N4
Wilton, N. Dak. 282/J5
Wilton, Wis. 317/F8
Wilton Manors, Fla. 212/B3
Wiltshire (co.), England 13/E6
Wiltz, Luxembourg 27/H9
Wiluna, Australia 87/C8
Wiluna, W. Australia 88/C5
Wiluna, W. Australia 92/C4
Wimauma, Fla. 212/D4
Wimbledon, N. Dak. 282/O5
Wimborne, Alberta 182/D4
Wimborne Minster, England 13/E7
Wimico (lake), Fla. 212/A2
Wimmer, Sask. 181/B3
Wimmera (riv.), Victoria 97/A5
Wimmis, Switzerland 39/E3
Winagami (lake), Alberta 182/B2
Winam (bay), Kenya 115/F4
Winamac, Ind. 227/D2
Winborn, Miss. 256/F1
Winburg, S. Africa 118/D5
Winburne, Pa. 294/F4
Wincanton, England 13/E6
Winchburgh, Scotland 15/D1
Winchelsea, Victoria 97/B6
Winchendon, Mass. 249/F2
Winchendon•, Mass. 249/F2
Winchendon Springs, Mass. 249/G2
Winchester•, Conn. 210/C1
Winchester, Ark. 202/G6
Winchester, England 13/F6
Winchester, England 10/F5
Winchester, Idaho 220/B3
Winchester, Ill. 222/C4
Winchester, Ind. 227/G4
Winchester, Kansas 232/G2
Winchester, Ky. 237/N5
Winchester•, Mass. 249/C6
Winchester, Mo. 261/N3
Winchester, Nev. 266/F5
Winchester•, N.H. 268/C6
Winchester, N. Zealand 100/C6
Winchester, Ohio 284/C8
Winchester, Ontario 177/J2
Winchester, Oreg. 291/D4
Winchester (bay), Oreg. 291/C4
Winchester, Tenn. 237/J10
Winchester (I.C.), Va. 307/M2
Winchester, Wash. 310/F3
Winchester, Wis. 317/G3
Winchester Bay, Oreg. 291/C4
Winchester Center, Conn. 210/C1
Wind (riv.), Wash. 310/D5
Wind (lake), Wis. 317/K2
Wind (riv.), Wyo. 319/C2
Wind Cave Nat'l Park, S. Dak. 298/B6
Windcrest, Texas 303/K11
Windermere, Conn. 210/F1
Winder (lake), Fla. 212/F3
Winder, Georgia 217/E3
Windermere, Br. Col. 184/K5
Windermere, England 13/E3
Windermere, England 10/E3
Windermere, Fla. 212/E3
Windermere, Ontario 177/E2
Windfall, Ind. 227/F4
Windgap, Pa. 294/M4
Windham (co.), Conn. 210/H1
Windham•, Conn. 210/G2
Windham, Mont. 262/F3
Windham•, N.H. 268/D4
Windham, N.Y. 276/M6
Windham, Ohio 284/H3
Windham (co.), Vt. 268/B5
Windham•, Vt. 268/B5
Windham Depot, N.H. 268/E6
Windhoek (cap.), Namibia 102/D7
Windhoek (cap.), Namibia 118/B4
Windhoek (cap.), Namibia 2/K7
Winding Gulf, W. Va. 312/D7
Windisch, Switzerland 39/F1
Windischgarsten, Austria 41/C3
Wind Lake, Wis. 317/J8
Windom (peak), Colo. 208/D7
Windom, Ind. 227/D7
Windom, Kansas 232/E3
Windom, Minn. 255/C7
Windorah, Queensland 88/G5
Windorah, Queensland 95/B5
Window Rock, Ariz. 198/F3
Wind Point, Wis. 317/M2
Wind River (canyon), Wyo. 319/D2
Wind River (range), Wyo. 319/C2
Wind River Ind. Res., Wyo. 319/C2
Windsor, Calif. 204/C5
Windsor, Colo. 208/J2
Windsor, Conn. 210/E1
Windsor•, Conn. 210/E1
Windsor (New Windsor), Ill. 222/C2
Windsor, Ill. 222/E4
Windsor, Ind. 227/G4
Windsor•, Maine 243/D7
Windsor•, Mass. 249/B2
Windsor, Mo. 261/F5
Windsor, New Bruns. 170/C2
Windsor, Newf. 166/C4
Windsor, N.J. 273/D3
Windsor, N.Y. 276/J6
Windsor, N.C. 281/P2
Windsor, N. Dak. 282/N6
Windsor, Nova Scotia 162/K7
Windsor, Nova Scotia 168/D3
Windsor, Ohio 284/J2
Windsor, Ont. 162/H7
Windsor, Ontario 177/B5
Windsor, Pa. 294/J6
Windsor, Québec 172/F4
Windsor, Queensland 88/K2
Windsor, Queensland 95/D2
Windsor, S.C. 296/E5
Windsor (co.), Vt. 268/B4
Windsor, Vt. 268/C5
Windsor•, Vt. 268/C5

Windsor, Va. 307/P7
Windsor, Wis. 317/H9
Windsor Heights, Iowa 229/F5
Windsor Heights, W. Va. 312/E2
Windsor Locks•, Conn. 210/E1
Windsorville, Conn. 210/E1
Windthorst, Sask. 181/J5
Windthorst, Texas 303/F4
Winagami (passg.) 146/L8
Windward (passage), Cuba 156/C3
Windward (passage), Grenada 156/C3
Windward (passage), Haiti 158/A5
Windward (isls.), W. Indies 156/G4
Windy, W. Va. 312/B5
Windy Hill, S.C. 296/H3
Windy Hills, Ky. 237/K1
Windyville, Mo. 261/F7
Winefred (lake), Alberta 182/E2
Winefred (riv.), Alberta 182/E2
Winesburg, Ohio 284/G4
Winfall, N.C. 281/S2
Winfield, Ala. 195/C3
Winfield, Alberta 182/C3
Winfield, Ark. 202/B4
Winfield, Br. Col. 184/H5
Winfield, Ill. 222/A5
Winfield, Iowa 229/L6
Winfield, Kansas 232/F4
Winfield, Md. 245/K3
Winfield, Mo. 261/L5
Winfield•, N.J. 273/B2
Winfield, Pa. 294/J4
Winfield, Tenn. 237/M7
Winfield, W. Va. 312/C5
Winfred, S. Dak. 298/P6
Wing, Ala. 195/E8
Wing, Ill. 222/E3
Wing, N. Dak. 282/K5
Wingard, Sask. 181/E3
Wingate, England 13/J4
Wingate, Ind. 227/C4
Wingate, Md. 245/O7
Wingate, N.C. 281/J5
Wingate, Pa. 294/G4
Wingate, Texas 303/D5
Wingate Army Depot, N. Mex. 274/A3
Wingdale, N.Y. 276/N7
Wingene, Belgium 27/C6
Winger, Minn. 255/B9
Winger, Ontario 177/E5
Wingham, N.S. Wales 97/G2
Wingham, Ontario 177/C4
Wingo, Ky. 237/D7
Winifred, Kansas 232/G1
Winifred, Ky. 237/R5
Winifred, Mont. 262/G3
Winifreda, Argentina 143/D4
Winifrede, W. Va. 312/C6
Winigan, Mo. 261/G2
Winisk, Ontario 175/C1
Winisk (lake), Ontario 175/C2
Winisk (riv.), Ontario 162/H5
Winisk (riv.), Ontario 175/C2
Wink, Texas 303/A6
Winkel, Netherlands 27/F3
Winkelman, Ariz. 198/E6
Winkle, Ill. 222/D5
Winkler, Manitoba 179/E5
Winkler (co.), Texas 303/A6
Winlaw, Br. Col. 184/J5
Winlock, Oreg. 291/H3
Winlock, Wash. 310/C4
Winn, Ala. 195/C7
Winn (par.), La. 238/E3
Winn, Maine 243/G5
Winn•, Maine 243/G5
Winn, Mich. 250/E5
Winnaboro, N.C. 281/N6
Winnaleah, Tasmania 99/D3
Winneba, Ghana 106/D7
Winnebago (cap.), Ill. 222/D1
Winnebago (lake), Iowa 229/F2
Winnebago, Minn. 255/D7
Winnebago, Nebr. 264/H2
Winnebago, Wis. 317/J8
Winnebago, Wis. 317/J8
Winnebago (lake), Wis. 317/K7
Winnebago Ind. Res., Nebr. 264/H2
Winnecke (creek), North. Terr. 93/B5
Winneconne, Wis. 317/J7
Winnecook (lake), Maine 243/E6
Winnemaug (lake), Conn. 210/C2
Winnemucca, Nev. 188/C2
Winnemucca (lake), Nev. 188/C2
Winnemucca, Nev. 266/B2
Winnemucca (lake), Nev. 266/B2
Winnemucca Ind. Res., Nev. 266/D2
Winner, S. Dak. 298/K7
Winneshiek (co.), Iowa 229/K2
Winnetka, Ill. 222/B5
Winnetoon, Nebr. 264/F2
Winnett, Mont. 262/H4
Winnfield, La. 238/E3
Winnibigoshish (lake), Minn. 255/D3
Winnie, Texas 303/K8
Winnifred, Alberta 182/E5
Winning Pool, W. Australia 92/A3
Winnipauk, Conn. 210/B4
Winnipeg, Canada 2/E3
Winnipeg (cap.), Manitoba 146/J5
Winnipeg (cap.), Manitoba 179/G6
Winnipeg (cap.), Manitoba 179/E5
Winnipeg (lake), Manitoba 162/G5
Winnipeg (lake), Manitoba 179/G3
Winnipeg (lake), Manitoba 146/J4
Winnipeg (riv.), Manitoba 179/G4
Winnipeg (riv.), Ontario 175/A2
Winnipeg Beach, Manitoba 179/F4
Winnipegosis, Man. 162/F5
Winnipegosis (lake), Man. 146/H4
Winnipegosis (lake), Man. 162/F5
Winnipegosis (lake), Manitoba 179/B3
Winnipegosis (lake), Manitoba 179/C2
Winnipesaukee, N.H. 268/E4
Winnipesaukee (lake), N.H. 268/E4

Winnipesaukee (riv.), N.H. 268/D5
Winnisquam, N.H. 268/E5
Winnisquam (lake), N.H. 268/D4
Winnsboro, La. 238/G2
Winnsboro, S.C. 296/E3
Winnsboro, Texas 303/J5
Winnsboro Mills, S.C. 296/E3
Winokapau (lake), Newf. 166/B3
Winokur, Georgia 217/H8
Winona, Ariz. 198/D3
Winona (lake), Ark. 202/E4
Winona, Kansas 232/A2
Winona, Mich. 250/G1
Winona (co.), Minn. 255/G6
Winona, Minn. 188/H2
Winona, Miss. 256/E4
Winona, Mo. 261/K8
Winona, Ohio 284/J4
Winona, Tenn. 237/M8
Winona, Texas 303/J5
Winona, Wash. 310/H4
Winona Lake, Ind. 227/E2
Winooski, Vt. 268/A2
Winooski (riv.), Vt. 268/B3
Winschoten, Netherlands 27/L2
Winscombe, England 13/D6
Winsen, Germany 22/D2
Winsford, England 13/G2
Winsford, England 10/G2
Winside, Nebr. 264/G2
Winslow, Ariz. 198/E3
Winslow, Ark. 202/B2
Winslow, Ill. 222/D1
Winslow, Ind. 227/C8
Winslow, Maine 243/D6
Winslow•, Maine 243/D6
Winslow, Nebr. 264/H3
Winslow, N.J. 273/D4
Winslow (Bainbridge Island-Winslow), Wash. 310/A2
Winslows Mills, Maine 243/E7
Winsted, Conn. 210/C1
Winsted, Minn. 255/D6
Winston (co.), Ala. 195/D2
Winston, Georgia 217/C3
Winston, Ky. 237/N5
Winston (co.), Miss. 256/F4
Winston, Mo. 261/D3
Winston, Mont. 262/F3
Winston, N. Mex. 274/B5
Winston, Oreg. 291/D4
Winston Park, Ky. 237/S2
Winston-Salem, N.C. 188/K3
Winston-Salem, N.C. 281/J2
Winstonville, Miss. 256/D3
Winsum, Netherlands 27/K2
Winter (harb.), N.W. Terr. 187/H2
Winter (isl.), N.W. Terr. 187/K3
Winter, Sask. 181/B3
Winter, Wis. 317/E4
Winter Beach, Fla. 212/F4
Winterdale, Pa. 294/M2
Winter Garden, Fla. 212/E3
Winter Harbour•, Maine 243/G7
Winterhaven, Calif. 204/L11
Winter Haven, Fla. 212/E3
Winter I. Coast Guard Air Sta., Mass. 249/E3
Winter Park, Colo. 208/H3
Winter Park, Fla. 212/E3
Winterpock, Va. 307/N6
Winterport, Maine 243/F6
Winterport•, Maine 243/F6
Winters, Calif. 204/D5
Winters, Texas 303/E6
Wintersburg, Ariz. 198/C5
Winterset, Iowa 229/E6
Winterset, Ohio 284/H5
Winter Springs, Fla. 212/E3
Winters Run (creek), Md. 245/N2
Wintersville, Ohio 284/J5
Winterswijk, Netherlands 27/K5
Winterthur, Switzerland 39/G1
Winterton, Newf. 166/D2
Winterville, Georgia 217/F3
Winterville, Maine 243/F2
Winterville•, Maine 243/F2
Winterville, Miss. 256/D3
Winterville, N.C. 281/P3
Winthrop, Ark. 202/B6
Winthrop, Conn. 210/E3
Winthrop, Iowa 229/K4
Winthrop, Maine 243/C7
Winthrop•, Maine 243/C7
Winthrop•, Mass. 249/C6
Winthrop, Minn. 255/D6
Winthrop, Wash. 310/E2
Winthrop-Brasher Falls, N.Y. 276/L1
Winthrop Harbor, Ill. 222/F1
Winton, Calif. 204/E6
Winton, Minn. 255/G3
Winton, N.C. 281/P2
Winton, Queensland 88/G4
Winton, Queensland 95/B4
Winton, Wash. 310/E3
Winyah (bay), S.C. 296/J5
Wiota, Iowa 229/D6
Wiota, Wis. 317/G10
Wirksworth, England 13/F4
Wirral, England 13/G2
Wirral, England 10/F2
Wirral (pen.), England 13/G2
Wirral, New Bruns. 170/D3
Wirrulla, S. Australia 94/D5
Wisacky, S.C. 296/G3
Wisbech, England 10/G4
Wisbech, England 13/H5

Wiscasset, Maine 243/D7
Wiscasset•, Maine 243/D7
Wisconsin 188/J2
WISCONSIN 317
Wisconsin (state), U.S. 146/K5
Wisconsin (riv.), Wis. 188/H2
Wisconsin (riv.), Wis. 317/E9
Wisconsin Dells, Wis. 317/G8
Wisconsin Rapids, Wis. 317/G7
Wisdom, Ky. 237/K7
Wisdom, Mont. 262/C5
Wise, N.C. 281/N2
Wise (co.), Texas 303/G4
Wise (co.), Va. 307/C6
Wise, Va. 307/C7
Wiseman, Alaska 196/H1
Wiseman, Ark. 202/G1
Wise River, Mont. 262/C5
Wiseton, Sask. 181/D4
Wishart, Mo. 261/F7
Wishart, Sask. 181/H4
Wishek, N. Dak. 282/L7
Wishram, Wash. 310/D5
Wisła, Poland 47/D4
Wisła (Vistula) (riv.), Poland 47/D2
Wismar, Germany 22/D2
Wisner, La. 238/G3
Wisner, Mich. 250/F5
Wisner, Nebr. 264/H3
Wissembourg, France 28/G3
Wistaria, Br. Col. 184/D3
Wister, Okla. 288/S5
Wister (lake), Okla. 288/S5
Witbank, S. Africa 118/D5
Witchekan (lake), Sask. 181/D2
Witham, England 13/H6
Witham (riv.), England 10/F4
Witham (riv.), England 13/G4
Withamsville, Ohio 284/C10
Witherbee-Mineville, N.Y. 276/N2
Withernsea, England 13/H4
Withernsea, England 10/G4
Witherspoon (mt.), Alaska 196/C1
Withlacoochee (riv.), Fla. 212/C1
Withlacoochee (riv.), Fla. 212/D2
Withrow, Wash. 310/F3
Witkowo, Poland 47/C2
Witless Bay, Newf. 166/D2
Witney, England 13/F6
Witnica, Poland 47/B2
Witoka, Minn. 255/G7
Witt, Ill. 222/D4
Witten, Germany 22/B3
Witten, S. Dak. 298/J7
Wittenberg, Germany 22/E3
Wittenberg, Mo. 261/O7
Wittenberg, Wis. 317/H6
Wittenberge, Germany 22/D2
Wittenoom, W. Australia 88/B4
Wittenoom, W. Australia 92/B3
Witter, Ark. 202/C2
Wittingen, Germany 22/D2
Wittlich, Germany 22/B3
Wittman, Md. 245/N5
Wittmann, Ariz. 198/C5
Witts Springs, Ark. 202/E2
Wittstock, Germany 22/E2
Witu, Kenya 115/H4
Witvlei, Namibia 118/B4
Witwatersberg (range), S. Africa 118/G••
Witwatersrand (reg.), S. Africa 118/D5
Witzenhausen, Germany 22/C3
Wivenhoe, England 13/J6
Wivenhoe, Manitoba 179/K2
Wiville, Ark. 202/H3
Wixom, Mich. 250/F6
Wkra (riv.), Poland 47/E2
Władysławowo, Poland 47/D1
Włocławek (prov.), Poland 47/D2
Włocławek, Poland 47/D2
Włocławskie (lake), Poland 47/D2
Włodawa, Poland 47/F3
Woszczowa, Poland 47/D3
Woburn, Grenada 161/C9
Woburn, Mass. 249/C6
Woburn, Québec 172/G4
Woden, Iowa 229/F2
Wodonga, Victoria 88/H7
Wodonga, Victoria 97/D5
Wodzisław Śląski, Poland 47/D4
Woensdrecht, Netherlands 27/E6
Woerden, Netherlands 27/F4
Wohlen, Switzerland 39/F2
Wohlen bei Bern, Switzerland 39/D3
Wojkowice, Poland 47/B3
Wokam (isl.), Indonesia 85/K7
Woking, Alberta 182/A2
Woking, England 13/G8
Woking, England 10/B6
Wokingham, England 13/G8
Wokingham, England 10/F5
Wolbach, Nebr. 264/F3
Wolbrom, Poland 47/D3
Wolco, Okla. 288/O1
Wolcott, Colo. 208/F3
Wolcott•, Conn. 210/D2
Wolcott, Ind. 227/C3
Wolcott, N.Y. 276/F4
Wolcott•, Vt. 268/C2
Wolcottsville, N.Y. 276/C4
Wolcottville, Ind. 227/G1
Wolds, The (hills), England 13/G4
Woleai (atoll), Micronesia 87/E5
Wolf (lake), Alberta 182/E2
Wolf (Wenman) (isl.), Ecuador 128/B8
Wolf (lake), Ill. 222/B7
Wolf (riv.), Miss. 256/F9
Wolf, Okla. 288/N4
Wolf (creek), Okla. 288/G2
Wolf (creek), S. Dak. 298/L4
Wolf (riv.), Tenn. 237/B10
Wolf (creek), Texas 303/D1
Wolf (riv.), Va. 307/F6
Wolf (riv.), Wis. 317/J5
Wolf, Wyo. 319/E1
Wolf Creek, Alberta 182/B3
Wolf Creek, Ky. 237/J4

Yabebyry 471

Wolf Creek, Mont. 262/D3
Wolf Creek, Oreg. 291/D5
Wolf Creek, Wis. 317/A4
Wolfdale, Pa. 294/B5
Wolfe (co.), Ky. 237/O5
Wolfe (co.), Québec 172/F4
Wolfeboro, N.H. 268/E4
Wolfeboro•, N.H. 268/E4
Wolfeboro Falls, N.H. 268/E4
Wolfe City, Texas 303/J4
Wolfe Island, Ontario 177/H3
Wolfen, Germany 22/E3
Wolfenbüttel, Germany 22/D2
Wolfenschiessen, Switzerland 39/F3
Wolfforth, Texas 303/C4
Wolf Island, Mo. 261/O9
Wolf Lake, Ill. 222/D6
Wolflake, Ind. 227/F2
Wolf Lake, Mich. 250/D5
Wolf Lake, Minn. 255/C4
Wolford, N. Dak. 282/L3
Wolf Pen, W. Va. 312/C7
Wolf Point, Mont. 262/L2
Wolfsberg, Austria 41/C3
Wolfsburg, Germany 22/D2
Wolf Summit, W. Va. 312/F4
Wolfsville, Md. 245/H2
Wolfton, S.C. 296/E4
Wolftown, Va. 307/M4
Wolf Trap Farm Park, Va. 307/S2
Wolfville, Nova Scotia 168/D3
Wolgast, Germany 22/E1
Wolhusen, Switzerland 39/F2
Wolin, Poland 47/B2
Wolin (Wollin) (isl.), Poland 47/B2
Wollaston (isls.), Chile 138/F11
Wollaston (pen.), N.W. Terr. 187/G3
Wollaston (lake), Sask. 162/F4
Wollaston (lake), Sask. 146/H4
Wollaston (lake), Sask. 181/N2
Wollaston Lake, Sask. 181/N2
Wollogorang, North. Terr. 88/F3
Wollogorang, North. Terr. 93/F4
Wollomombi, N.S. Wales 97/G2
Wollondilly (riv.), N.S. Wales 97/F4
Wollongong, Australia 87/F9
Wollongong, N.S. Wales 88/J6
Wollongong, N.S. Wales 97/F4
Wolmaransstad, S. Africa 118/D5
Wołomin, Poland 47/E2
Wołów, Poland 47/C3
Wolseley, Sask. 181/H5
Wolseth, N. Dak. 282/H3
Wolsey, S. Dak. 298/N5
Wolstenholme (cape), Québec 174/E1
Wolsztyn, Poland 47/B2
Wolta, Ethiopia 111/G6
Woluwe-Saint-Lambert, Belgium 27/C9
Woluwe-Saint-Pierre, Belgium 27/C9
Wolvega, Netherlands 27/J3
Wolverhampton, England 13/E5
Wolverhampton, England 10/G3
Wolverine (riv.), Alberta 182/B1
Wolverine, Ky. 237/P5
Wolverine, Mich. 250/E3
Wolverton, Minn. 255/B4
Wolves, The (isls.), New Bruns. 170/D4
Womack, Mo. 261/M7
Womack Hill, Ala. 195/B7
Womboota, N.S. Wales 97/C4
Wombwell, England 13/K2
Womelsdorf, Pa. 294/K5
Womelsdorf (Coalton), W. Va. 312/G5
Womer, Kansas 232/D2
Wonalancet, N.H. 268/E4
Wonder, Oreg. 291/D5
Wonder Lake, Ill. 222/E1
Wonewoc, Wis. 317/F8
Wongallarra (lake), N.S. Wales 97/C2
Wongan Hills, W. Australia 92/B5
Wŏnju, S. Korea 81/D5
Wonogiri, Indonesia 85/J2
Wononpakook (lake), Conn. 210/B1
Wononskopomuc (lake), Conn.
210/B1
Wonosobo, Indonesia 85/J2
Wonowon, Br. Col. 184/G2
Wonreli, Indonesia 85/H7
Wŏnsan, N. Korea 54/O6
Wŏnsan, N. Korea 81/C4
Wonthaggi, Australia 87/E9
Wonthaggi, Victoria 97/C6
Wonthaggi, Victoria 88/G7
Wood (isls.), Chile 138/E11
Wood (isl.), Mich. 250/C2
Wood, N.C. 281/N2
Wood (co.), Ohio 284/C3
Wood (isls.), Pr. Edward I. 168/F3
Wood (mt.), Sask. 181/E6
Wood (riv.), Sask. 181/E6
Wood, S. Dak. 298/J6
Wood (co.), Texas 303/J5
Wood (co.), W. Va. 312/D4
Wood (co.), Wis. 317/F7
Wood (riv.), Wyo. 319/C2
Woodall (mt.), Miss. 256/H1
Woodberry, Ark. 202/E6
Woodberry Forest, Va. 307/M4
Woodbine, Georgia 217/J9
Woodbine, Ill. 222/C1
Woodbine, Iowa 229/B5
Woodbine, Kansas 232/E3
Woodbine, Ky. 237/N7
Woodbine, Md. 245/K3
Woodbine, N.J. 273/D5
Woodbourne, N.Y. 276/M7
Woodbridge, Calif. 204/B9
Woodbridge•, Conn. 210/D3
Woodbridge, England 13/J5
Woodbridge, England 10/G4
Woodbridge•, N.J. 273/E2
Woodbridge, Tasmania 99/D5
Woodbridge, Va. 307/O3
Wood Buffalo Nat'l Park, Alberta
182/B5
Wood Buffalo Nat'l Park, Alta. 162/E4
Wood Buffalo Nat'l Park, N.W. Terr.
187/G3
Woodburn, Ind. 227/H2
Woodburn, Iowa 229/F7
Woodburn, Ky. 237/J7
Woodburn, N.S. Wales 97/G1
Woodburn, Oreg. 291/A3
Woodbury, Conn. 210/C2
Woodbury•, Conn. 210/C2
Woodbury, Georgia 217/C5
Woodbury (co.), Iowa 229/B4
Woodbury, Ky. 237/H6
Woodbury, Minn. 255/F6
Woodbury, N.J. 273/B4
Woodbury, Pa. 294/F5
Woodbury, Tenn. 237/J9
Woodbury•, Vt. 268/C3
Woodbury Heights, N.J. 273/B4
Woodbury P.O. (North Woodbury),
Conn. 210/C2
Woodchopper, Alaska 196/K1
Woodcliff, Georgia 217/J5
Woodcliff Lake, N.J. 273/B1
Woodcock, Pa. 294/B2
Woodcrest, Calif. 204/E11
Wood Dale, Ill. 222/B5
Wooden Ball (isl.), Maine 243/F8
Woodenbong, N.S. Wales 97/G1
Woodenbridge, Ireland 17/J6
Woodend, Victoria 97/C5
Woodfibre, Br. Col. 184/K2
Woodfin, N.C. 281/D3
Woodford, Grenada 161/C8
Woodford (co.), Ill. 222/D3
Woodford, Ireland 17/E5
Woodford (co.), Ky. 237/M4
Woodford, Okla. 288/M6
Woodford, S.C. 296/E4
Woodford•, Vt. 268/A6
Woodford, Wis. 317/G10
Woodgate, N.Y. 276/K3
Woodhall Spa, England 13/G4
Woodhaven, La. 238/M1
Woodhaven, Mich. 250/F6
Woodhouse, Alberta 182/D5
Woodhull, Ill. 222/C2
Woodhull, N.Y. 276/F6
Woodhull (lake), N.Y. 276/L3
Woodington, Ohio 284/A5
Woodinville, Wash. 310/B1
Wood Islands, Pr. Edward I. 168/F2
Woodlake, Calif. 204/G7
Wood Lake, Minn. 255/C6
Wood Lake, Nebr. 264/D2
Woodland, Ala. 195/H4
Woodland, Calif. 204/B8
Woodland, Georgia 217/D5
Woodland, Ill. 222/F3
Woodland, Ind. 227/E1
Woodland, La. 238/J5
Woodland•, Maine 243/H5
Woodland, Mich. 250/D6
Woodland, Miss. 256/F3
Woodland, N.C. 281/P2
Woodland, Pa. 294/F4
Woodland, Utah 304/C3
Woodland, Wash. 310/C5
Woodland Hills, Calif. 204/B10
Woodland Hills, Ky. 237/L2
Woodland Mills, Tenn. 237/C8
Woodland Park, Colo. 208/J4
Woodlands, Manitoba 179/E4
Woodlands, Singapore 72/F6
Woodlands, W. Va. 312/E3
Woodlark (isl.), Papua N.G. 85/C7
Woodlawn, Hawaii 218/D4
Woodlawn, Ill. 222/D5
Woodlawn, Ky. 237/T2
Woodlawn, La. 238/E6
Woodlawn, Md. 245/M3
Woodlawn, Ohio 284/C9
Woodlawn, Tenn. 237/G7
Woodlawn, Va. 307/G7
Woodlawn Heights, Ind. 227/F4
Woodlawn-Oakdale, Ky. 237/D6
Woodlawn Park, Ky. 237/K2
Woodleaf, N.C. 281/H3
Woodley, Sask. 181/J6
Woodley and Sandford, England 13/G8
Woodlyn, Pa. 294/M7
Wood-Lynne, N.J. 273/B3
Woodman, Wis. 317/E9
Woodmere, N.Y. 276/P7
Woodmere, Ohio 284/J9
Woodmont, Conn. 210/D4
Woodmoor, Md. 245/L3
Wood Mountain, Sask. 181/E6
Wood Mountain Hist. Park, Sask.
181/E6
Woodnorth, Manitoba 179/A5
Woodport, N.J. 273/D2
Woodridge, Ill. 222/B6
Woodridge, Manitoba 179/G5
Wood-Ridge, N.J. 273/B2
Woodridge, N.Y. 276/L7
Wood River, Ill. 222/B2
Wood River, Nebr. 264/F4
Wood River Junction, R.I. 249/H7
Woodroffe (mt.), S. Australia 88/E5
Woodroffe (mt.), S. Australia 94/B2
Woodrow, Colo. 208/M3
Woodrow, Sask. 181/E6
Woodruff, Ariz. 198/E4
Woodruff (co.), Ark. 202/H3
Woodruff, Kansas 232/C2
Woodruff, S.C. 296/D2
Woodruff, Utah 304/C2
Woodruff, Wis. 317/G4
Woods (lake) 146/J5
Woods (lake) 162/G6
Woods (lake), Ind. 227/E2
Woods (lake), Manitoba 179/H5
Woods (lake), Minn. 188/G1
Woods (lake), Minn. 255/D1
Woods (lake), Newf. 166/B3
Woods (lake), North. Terr. 88/E3
Woods (lake), North. Terr. 93/C4
Woods (co.), Okla. 288/K1
Woods (lake), Ontario 177/F5
Woods (lake), Ontario 175/B3
Woods (res.), Tenn. 237/J10
Woodsbend, Ky. 237/P5
Woodsboro, Md. 245/J2
Woodsboro, Texas 303/G9
Woods Cross, Utah 304/B3
Woodsdale, N.C. 281/M2
Woodsfield, Ohio 284/H6
Woods Heights, Mo. 261/S4
Woods Hole, Mass. 249/M6
Woodside, Calif. 204/J3
Woodside, Del. 245/R4
Woodside, Manitoba 179/D4
Woodside, Mont. 262/B4
Woodside, S. Australia 94/C8
Woodside, Utah 304/D4
Woodson, Ark. 202/F4
Woodson, Ill. 222/C4
Woodson (co.), Kansas 232/G4
Woodson, Texas 303/E5
Woodson Terrace, Mo. 261/P2
Wood's Point, Victoria 97/D5
Woodstock, Ala. 195/D4
Woodstock•, Conn. 210/H1
Woodstock, England 13/F6
Woodstock, England 10/F5
Woodstock, Georgia 217/D2
Woodstock, Ill. 222/E1
Woodstock, Md. 245/L3
Woodstock, Minn. 255/B7
Woodstock, N. Br. 162/K6
Woodstock, New Bruns. 170/C2
Woodstock•, N.H. 268/D4
Woodstock, N.S. Wales 97/E3
Woodstock, N.Y. 276/M6
Woodstock, Ohio 284/C5
Woodstock, Ontario 177/D4
Woodstock, Vt. 268/B4
Woodstock•, Vt. 268/B4
Woodstock, Va. 307/L3
Woodstock Valley, Conn. 210/G1
Woodston, Kansas 232/C2
Woodstown, N.J. 273/C4
Woodsville, N.H. 268/C3
Wood Village, Oreg. 291/B2
Woodville, Ala. 195/F1
Woodville, Conn. 210/B2
Woodville, Fla. 212/B1
Woodville, Georgia 217/F3
Woodville, Mass. 249/H4
Woodville, Miss. 256/B8
Woodville, N.Y. 276/H3
Woodville, N. Zealand 100/F4
Woodville, Ohio 284/D3
Woodville, Okla. 288/N7
Woodville, Ontario 177/F3
Woodville, Pa. 294/B7
Woodville, S. Australia 88/D7
Woodville, S. Australia 94/A7
Woodville, S.C. 296/C2
Woodville, Texas 303/K7
Woodville, Va. 307/M3
Woodville, W. Va. 312/C6
Woodville, Wis. 317/B6
Woodward, Iowa 229/E5
Woodward (co.), Okla. 288/H2
Woodward, Okla. 288/H2
Woodward, S.C. 296/E2
Woodwards Cove, New Bruns. 170/D4
Woodway, Va. 307/C7
Woodway, Wash. 310/C3
Woodworth, Ill. 222/F3
Woodworth, La. 238/E4
Woodworth, N. Dak. 282/M5
Woody (mt.), Ariz. 198/D3
Woody, Calif. 204/G8
Woody (isl.), China 85/E2
Woody Creek, Colo. 208/F4
Woody Island, Alaska 196/H3
Woody Island, Newf. 166/C2
Woody Point, Newf. 166/C4
Wool, England 13/E7
Wooldridge, Mo. 261/G5
Wooler, England 13/F2
Woolford, Alberta 182/D5
Woolford, Md. 245/O7
Woolgar, Queensland 95/B3
Woolgoolga, N.S. Wales 97/G2
Wooli, N.S. Wales 97/G1
Woollahra, N.S. Wales 88/L4
Woollahra, N.S. Wales 97/K3
Woollum, Ky. 237/O6
Woolrich, Pa. 294/H3
Woolsey, Georgia 217/D4
Woolsington, England 13/H3
Woolstock, Iowa 229/F3
Wooltana, S. Australia 88/F6
Wooltana, S. Australia 94/F4
Woolwich•, Maine 243/D8
Woolwine, Va. 307/H7
Woomera, Australia 87/D9
Woomera, S. Australia 88/F6
Woomera, S. Australia 94/E4
Woonsocket, R.I. 249/J4
Woonsocket, S. Dak. 298/N5
Wooramel, W. Australia 92/A4
Wooramel (riv.), W. Australia 88/A5
Wooramel (riv.), W. Australia 92/A4
Wooroloo, W. Australia 88/B2
Wooster, Ark. 202/F3
Wooster, Ohio 284/G4
Woosung, Ill. 222/D2
Wooton, Ky. 237/P6
Wootton Basset, England 13/E6
Woqooyi Galbeed (prov.), Somalia
115/H1
Worb, Switzerland 39/E3
Worcester, England 13/E5
Worcester, England 10/E4
Worcester (co.), Md. 245/S8
Worcester, Mass. 188/M2
Worcester (co.), Mass. 249/G3
Worcester, Mass. 249/H3
Worcester, N.Y. 276/L5
Worcester, S. Africa 102/D8
Worcester, S. Africa 118/B6
Worcester•, Vt. 268/B3
Worden, Ark. 202/H3
Worden, Ill. 222/B2
Worden, Kansas 232/G3
Worden, Mont. 262/H5
Worden, Oreg. 291/F5
Wordsworth, Sask. 181/J6
Würgl, Austria 41/A3
Work (chan.), Br. Col. 184/C3
Workai (isl.), Indonesia 85/K7
Workington, England 13/D3
Workington, England 10/E3
Worksop, England 10/F4
Worksop, England 13/F4
Workum, Netherlands 27/G3
Worland, Mo. 261/C6
Worland, Wyo. 319/E1
WORLD 2
Worley, Idaho 220/B2
Wormerveer, Netherlands 27/F4
Worms, Germany 22/C4
Woronoco, Mass. 249/C4
Woronora (riv.), N.S. Wales 88/K5
Woronora (riv.), N.S. Wales 97/J4
Worpswede, Germany 22/C2
Worsbrough, England 13/J2
Worsley, Alberta 182/A1
Worsley, England 13/H2
Worth (co.), Georgia 217/E8
Worth, Georgia 217/E7
Worth, Ill. 222/B6
Worth (co.), Iowa 229/G2
Worth (co.), Mo. 261/D2
Worth, Mo. 261/C2
Worth (lake), Texas 303/E2
Wortham, Texas 303/H6
Worthing, England 13/G7
Worthing, England 10/F5
Worthing, S. Dak. 298/R7
Worthington, Ind. 227/C6
Worthington, Iowa 229/L4
Worthington, Ky. 237/R3
Worthington•, Mass. 249/C3
Worthington, Minn. 255/C7
Worthington, Mo. 261/G2
Worthington, Ohio 284/E5
Worthington, Pa. 294/C4
Worthington, W. Va. 312/F4
Worthington Springs, Fla. 212/D2
Worthville, Ky. 237/L3
Worthville, N.C. 281/K3
Worthville, Pa. 294/D3
Worton, Md. 245/O3
Woss Lake, Br. Col. 184/D5
Wostok, Alberta 182/D3
Wotje (atoll), Marshall Is. 87/H5
Wottonville, Québec 172/F4
Wounded Knee, S. Dak. 298/D7
Wounded Knee (creek), S. Dak. 298/E7
Wour, Chad 111/C3
Wowoni (isl.), Indonesia 85/G6
Wragby, England 13/G4
Wrangel (isl.), U.S.S.R. 4/B18
Wrangel (isl.), U.S.S.R. 48/T2
Wrangell, Alaska 196/N2
Wrangell (cape), Alaska 196/H3
Wrangell (isl.), Alaska 196/N2
Wrangell (mts.), Alaska 196/K2
Wrangell-St. Elias Nat'l Park, Alaska
196/K2
Wrangell-St. Elias Nat'l Preserve,
Alaska196/K2
Wrangle, England 13/H4
Wrath (cape), Scotland 15/C2
Wrath (cape), Scotland 10/D1
Wray, Colo. 208/P2
Wray, Georgia 217/F7
Wreck Cove, Nova Scotia 168/H2
Wren, Ala. 195/D2
Wren, Miss. 256/G3
Wren, Ohio 284/A4
Wrens, Georgia 217/H4
Wrenshall, Minn. 255/F4
Wrentham, Alberta 182/D5
Wrentham•, Mass. 249/J4
Wrexham, Wales 13/E4
Wrexham, Wales 10/E4
Wright, Ala. 195/C1
Wright, Ark. 202/F5
Wright (co.), Iowa 229/F3
Wright, Kansas 232/C4
Wright, La. 238/F6
Wright (co.), Minn. 255/D5
Wright, Minn. 255/E4
Wright (co.), Mo. 261/H8
Wright (mt.), Québec 174/D2
Wright (lake), S. Australia 94/A2
Wright, Wyo. 319/G2
Wright Brothers Nat'l Mem., N.C.
281/T2
Wright City, Mo. 261/K5
Wright City, Okla. 288/R6
Wright Patman (lake), Texas 303/K4
Wright-Patterson Air Force Base, Ohio
284/B6
Wrights, Ill. 222/C4
Wrights, Pa. 294/F2
Wrightstown, Minn. 255/C4
Wrightstown, N.J. 273/D3
Wrightstown, Wis. 317/K7
Wrightsville, Ark. 202/G4
Wrightsville, Georgia 217/G5
Wrightsville, Pa. 294/J5
Wrightsville Beach, N.C. 281/O6
Wrightwood, Calif. 204/D10
Wrigley, Ky. 237/P4
Wrigley, N.W.T. 162/D3
Wrigley, N.W.T. 187/F3
Wrigley, Tenn. 237/G9
Wrocław (prov.), Poland 47/C3
Wrocław, Poland 47/C3
Wrocław, Poland 7/F3
Wrong (lake), Manitoba 179/F2
Wroughton, England 13/F6
Wroxeter, Ontario 177/C4
Wroxton, Sask. 181/K4
Września, Poland 47/C2
Wschowa, Poland 47/C3
W. Scott Kerr (res.), N.C. 281/G2
Wuchang, China 77/L3
Wuchow (Wuzhou), China 77/H7
Wuchuan, Guizhou, China 77/G6
Wuchuan, Nei Monggol, China 77/H3
Wuchung (Wuzhong), China 77/G4
Wuda, China 77/G4
Wudaoliang, China 77/D5
Wuding, China 77/F6
Wudinna, S. Australia 88/E6
Wudinna, S. Australia 94/D5
Wudu, China 77/F5
Wugang, China 77/H6
Wuhai, China 77/G4
Wuhan, China 77/H5
Wuhan, China 54/N6
Wuhan, China 2/Q4
Wuhing (Wuxing), China 77/K5
Wuhu, China 77/J5
Wuhu, China 54/N6
Wu Jiang (riv.), China 77/G6
Wukari, Nigeria 106/F7
Wum, Cameroon 115/A2
Wun, India 68/D5
Wundowie, W. Australia 88/C2
Wundowie, W. Australia 92/B1
Wünnewil, Switzerland 39/D3
Wunnummin Lake, Ontario 175/C2
Wunsiedel, Germany 22/E3
Wunstorf, Germany 22/C2
Wupatki Nat'l Mon., Ariz. 198/D3
Wuppertal, Germany 22/B3
Wuqi, China 77/G4
Wuqia, China 77/A4
Würmsee (Starnbergersee) (lake),
Germany 22/D5
Wurong, Queensland 95/B3
Wurtland, Ky. 237/R3
Wurtsboro, N.Y. 276/L7
Wurtsmith A.F.B., Mich. 250/F4
Würzburg, Germany 22/C4
Wurzen, Germany 22/E3
Wushi, China 77/A3
Wusih (Wuxi), China 77/J5
Wusuli Jiang (Ussuri) (riv.), China
77/M2
Wutai, China 77/H4
Wuwei, China 77/F4
Wuxi (Wusih), China 77/K5
Wuxi, China 54/O6
Wuyang, China 77/H4
Wuyiling, China 77/L2
Wuyi Shan (range), China 77/J6
Wuyuan, China 77/G3
Wuzhong (Wuchung), China 77/G4
Wuzhou (Wuchow), China 77/H7
Wyaconda, Mo. 261/J2
Wyalkatchem, W. Australia 88/B6
Wyalkatchem, W. Australia 92/B5
Wyalla, S. Australia 88/F6
Wyalusing, Pa. 294/K2
Wyalusing, Wis. 317/D10
Wyandanch, N.Y. 276/N9
Wyandot (co.), Ohio 284/D4
Wyandotte, Ind. 227/E8
Wyandotte (co.), Kansas 232/H2
Wyandotte, Mich. 250/B7
Wyandotte, Okla. 288/S1
Wyandra, Queensland 95/C5
Wyanet, Ill. 222/D2
Wyangala (res.), N.S. Wales 97/E3
Wyarno, Wyo. 319/G2
Wyassup (lake), Conn. 210/H3
Wyatt, Ind. 227/E1
Wyatt, La. 238/E2
Wyatt, Mo. 261/O9
Wycheproof, Victoria 97/B5
Wyckoff•, N.J. 273/B1
Wye (riv.), England 13/J2
Wye (riv.), England 13/D5
Wye (riv.), Wales 13/D5
Wye (riv.), Wales 10/E4
Wye Mills, Md. 245/O5
Wyeville, Wis. 317/F7
Wyk auf Föhr, Germany 22/C1
Wykoff, Minn. 255/F7
Wylie, Minn. 255/B3
Wylie (lake), S.C. 296/E1
Wylie, Texas 303/H1
Wylliesburg, Va. 307/L7
Wyman, Iowa 229/L6
Wyman (lake), Maine 243/C5
Wyman Dam, Maine 243/D5
Wymark, Sask. 181/D5
Wymer, W. Va. 312/G5
Wymondham, England 13/J5
Wymore, Nebr. 264/H4
Wynberg, S. Africa 118/E6
Wynbring, S. Australia 94/C4
Wyndham, Australia 87/C7
Wyndham, N. Zealand 100/B7
Wyndham, W. Australia 88/D3
Wyndham, W. Australia 92/E1
Wyndmere, N. Dak. 282/R7
Wynigen, Switzerland 39/E2
Wynnburg, Tenn. 237/C8
Wynndel, Br. Col. 184/J5
Wynne, Ark. 202/J3
Wynne, Md. 245/N8
Wynnewood, Okla. 288/M5
Wynnewood, Pa. 294/M6
Wynniatt (bay), N.W. Terr. 187/G2
Wynnum, Queensland 95/E5
Wynnum, Queensland 88/L2
Wynona, Okla. 288/O1
Wynoochee (lake), Wash. 310/B3
Wynoochee (riv.), Wash. 310/B3
Wynot, Nebr. 264/G2
Wynyard, Sask. 162/F5
Wynyard, Sask. 181/G4
Wynyard, Tasmania 88/H8
Wynyard, Tasmania 99/B3
Wyocena, Wis. 317/H9
Wyola, Mont. 262/J5
Wyoming 188/E2
WYOMING 319
Wyoming, Del. 245/R4
Wyoming, Ill. 222/D2
Wyoming, Iowa 229/L4
Wyoming, Mich. 250/D6
Wyoming, Minn. 255/F5
Wyoming (co.), N.Y. 276/D5
Wyoming, N.Y. 276/D5
Wyoming, Ohio 284/C9
Wyoming, Ontario 177/B5
Wyoming (co.), Pa. 294/K2
Wyoming, Pa. 294/E7
Wyoming, R.I. 249/H6
Wyoming (state), U.S. 146/H5
Wyoming (co.), W. Va. 312/C7
Wyoming (peak), Wyo. 319/B3
Wyoming (range), Wyo. 319/B2
Wyomissing, Pa. 294/K5
Wyong, N.S. Wales 97/F3
Wyre (riv.), England 13/G1
Wyre (isl.), Scotland 15/F1
Wyrzysk, Poland 47/C2
Wysokie Mazowieckie, Poland 47/F2
Wysox, Pa. 294/K2
Wyszków, Poland 47/E2
Wythe (co.), Va. 307/F7
Wytheville, Va. 307/G7
Wytopitlock, Maine 243/G4
Wytopitlock (lake), Maine 243/G4

X

Xainza, China 77/C5
Xaitongmoin, China 77/C6
Xai-Xai, Mozambique 118/E5
Xai-Xai, Mozambique 102/F7
Xaltocan, Mexico 150/N1
Xangongo, Angola 115/C7
Xanten, Germany 22/B3
Xánthi, Greece 45/G5
Xapuri, Brazil 132/G10
Xar Moron He (riv.), China 77/J3
Xarrama (riv.), Portugal 33/B3
Xau (lake), Botswana 118/C4
Xavantina, Brazil 132/C6
Xcalak, Mexico 150/Q7
Xenia, Ill. 222/E5
Xenia, Ohio 284/C6
Xiadong, China 77/E3
Xiaguan (Siakwan), China 77/E6
Xiamen (Amoy), China 77/J7
Xiamen, China 54/N7
Xi'an (Sian), China 77/G5
Xi'an, China 54/M6
Xi'an, China 2/Q4
Xianfeng, China 77/G6
Xiangfan (Siangfan), China 77/H5
Xianghoang (plat.), Laos 72/D3
Xiang Jiang (riv.), China 77/H6
Xiangkhoang, Laos 72/D3
Xiangshan, China 77/K6
Xiangtan (Siangtan), China 77/H6
Xiangtan, China 54/N7
Xianyang (Sienyang), China 77/G5
Xiaogan, China 77/H5
Xiapu (Siapu), China 77/K6
Xichang (Sichang), China 77/F6
Xicoténcatl, Mexico 150/K5
Xicotepec de Juárez, Mexico 150/L6
Xicute, Colombia 126/E7
Xigazê (Shigatse), China 77/C6
Xigazê, China 54/K7
Xiji, China 77/G4
Xi Jiang (riv.), China 77/H7
Xilin, China 77/G7
Ximiao, China 77/F3
Xin Barag Zuoqi, China 77/J2
Xinghai, China 77/E4
Xingren, China 77/G6
Xingtai (Singtai), China 77/H4
Xingu (riv.), Brazil 120/D3
Xingu (riv.), Brazil 132/C3
Xingyi, China 77/G6
Xinhe (Toksu), China 77/B3
Xinhui, China 77/H7
Xining (Sining), China 77/F4
Xining, China 54/M6
Xinjiang Uygur (Sinkiang-Uigur
Aut. Reg.), China 77/B3
Xinjin, China 77/K4
Xintai, China 77/J4
Xin Xian, China 77/H4
Xinxiang (Sinsiang), China 77/H4
Xinyang (Sinyang), China 77/H5
Xinyi, China 77/J5
Xinyi He (riv.), China 77/J5
Xinyuan (Künes), China 77/B3
Xique-Xique, Brazil 132/F5
Xisha (isls.), China 85/E2
Xishui, China 77/G6
Xi Ujimqin, China 77/J3
Xiushui, China 77/H6
Xiuyan, China 77/K3
Xixia, China 77/H5
Xizang (Tibet Aut. Reg.), China 77/B5
Xochihuehuetlán, Mexico 150/K8
Xochimilco, Mexico 150/L1
Xochitlán, Mexico 150/N2
Xpujil, Mexico 150/P7
Xuanhan, China 77/G5
Xuan Loc, Vietnam 72/E5
Xuanwei, China 77/F6
Xuchang (Hsüchang), China 77/H5
Xuguit, China 77/K2
Xunke, China 77/L2
Xuwen, China 77/H7
Xuzhou (Süchow), China 77/J5
Xuzhou, China 54/N6

Y

Yaak, Mont. 262/A2
Ya'an, China 77/F6
Yaapeet, Victoria 97/B4
Ya'bad, West Bank 65/C3
Yaballo, Ethiopia 111/G6
Yabassi, Cameroon 115/B3
Yabebyry, Paraguay 144/D5

Yabis, Wadi el (dry riv.), Jordan 65/D3
Yablis, Nicaragua 154/F4
Yablonovyy (range), U.S.S.R. 54/N4
Yablonovyy (range), U.S.S.R. 48/M4
Yabrud, West Bank 65/C4
Yabucoa, P. Rico 161/E2
Yachats, Oreg. 291/C3
Yacimientos de Río Turbio, Argentina 120/B8
Yaco, Bolivia 136/B5
Yacolt, Wash. 310/C5
Yacuiba, Bolivia 120/C5
Yacuiba, Bolivia 136/D7
Yacuma (riv.), Bolivia 136/B3
Yadgir, India 68/D5
Yadkin (co.), N.C. 281/H2
Yadkin (riv.), N.C. 281/J3
Yadkinville, N.C. 281/H2
Yad Mordekhai, Israel 65/A4
Yadong, China 77/C6
Yaeyama (isls.), Japan 81/K7
Yagra, China 77/B5
Yagradagzê Shan (mt.), China 77/D4
Yaguachi Nuevo, Ecuador 128/B4
Yaguajay, Cuba 158/F2
Yaguaraparo, Venezuela 124/G2
Yaguarí, Uruguay 145/G2
Yaguarón, Paraguay 144/B5
Yaguarón (riv.), Uruguay 145/F3
Yaguarú, Bolivia 136/D4
Yaguas (riv.), Peru 128/G4
Yaguate, Dom. Rep. 158/E6
Yagüez (riv.), P. Rico 161/A2
Yagur, Israel 65/C2
Yahav, Israel 65/D5
Yahk, Br. Col. 184/J5
Yahuma, Zaire 115/D3
Yahyalî, Turkey 63/F3
Yaizu, Japan 81/J6
Yajalón, Mexico 150/N8
Yakima (co.), Wash. 310/E4
Yakima, Wash. 146/F5
Yakima, Wash. 188/B1
Yakima, Wash. 310/E4
Yakima (ridge), Wash. 310/E4
Yakima (riv.), Wash. 310/F4
Yakima Ind. Res., Wash. 310/E4
Yako, Burkina Faso 106/D6
Yakobi (isl.), Alaska 196/M1
Yakoma, Zaire 115/D3
Yaku (isl.), Japan 81/E8
Yakumo, Japan 81/J2
Yakut A.S.S.R., U.S.S.R. 48/N3
Yakutat, Alaska 188/D6
Yakutat, Alaska 196/K3
Yakutat (bay), Alaska 196/K3
Yakutsk, U.S.S.R. 54/O3
Yakutsk, U.S.S.R. 2/R2
Yakutsk, U.S.S.R. 48/N3
Yala, Thailand 72/D6
Yalaha, Fla. 212/E3
Yalata Aboriginal Res., S. Australia 88/E6
Yalata Aboriginal Res., S. Australia 94/B4
Yale (mt.), Colo. 208/G5
Yale, Br. Col. 184/M2
Yale, Colo. 208/G5
Yale (lake), Fla. 212/E3
Yale, Ill. 222/E4
Yale, Iowa 229/E5
Yale, Mich. 250/G5
Yale, Okla. 288/N2
Yale, S. Dak. 298/O5
Yale, Va. 307/O7
Yale (lake), Wash. 310/C4
Yalesville, Conn. 210/D3
Yalgoo, W. Australia 92/B5
Yali, Estero (riv.), Chile 138/F4
Yalinga, Cent. Afr. Rep. 115/D2
Yallahs, Jamaica 158/K6
Yallock, N.S. Wales 97/C3
Yallourn, Victoria 97/O6
Yalmer, Mich. 250/M4
Yalobusha (co.), Miss. 256/E2
Yalobusha (riv.), Miss. 256/E3
Yalong (riv.), China 54/M7
Yalong Jiang (riv.), China 77/F6
Yalova, Çanakkale, Turkey 63/B6
Yalova, İstanbul, Turkey 63/C2
Yalpunga, N.S. Wales 97/A1
Yalta, U.S.S.R. 7/H4
Yalta, U.S.S.R. 52/D6
Yalu (riv.), 54/O5
Yalu (riv.), China 77/L3
Yalu (riv.), N. Korea 81/C3
Yalutorsk, U.S.S.R. 48/G4
Yalvaç, Turkey 63/D3
Yalvaç, Turkey 59/E2
Yamachiche, Québec 172/E3
Yamagata (pref.), Japan 81/K4
Yamagata, Japan 81/K4
Yamaguchi (pref.), Japan 81/E6
Yamaguchi, Japan 81/E6
Yamal (pen.), U.S.S.R. 54/H2
Yamal (pen.), U.S.S.R. 4/B6
Yamal (pen.), U.S.S.R. 48/G2
Yamal-Nenets Aut. Okr., U.S.S.R. 48/H3
Yamama, Saudi Arabia 59/E5
Yamanashi (pref.), Japan 81/J6
Yamantau (mt.), U.S.S.R. 52/J4
Yamarna Aboriginal Reserve, W. Australia 88/C5
Yamarna Aboriginal Res., W. Australia 92/D4
Yamasá, Dom. Rep. 158/E6
Yamaska (co.), Québec 172/E3
Yamaska, Québec 172/E4
Yamaska (riv.), Québec 172/E4
Yamaska-Est, Québec 172/E4
Yamato, Japan 81/O2
Yamatokoriyama, Japan 81/J8
Yamatotakada, Japan 81/J8
Yamba, N.S. Wales 97/G1
Yambah, North. Terr. 93/C7
Yambio, Sudan 111/E7
Yambio, Sudan 102/E4
Yambol, Bulgaria 45/H4

Yambou (head), St. Vin. & Grens. 161/A9
Yambrasbamba, Peru 128/D5
Yamdena (isl.), Indonesia 85/J7
Yamethin, Burma 72/C2
Yamhill (co.), Oreg. 291/D2
Yamhill, Oreg. 291/D2
Y'Ami (isl.), Philippines 82/B2
Yamma Yamma (lake), Queensland 88/F5
Yamma Yamma (lake), Queensland 95/B5
Yamoussoukro (cap.), Ivory Coast 102/B4
Yamoussoukro (cap.), Ivory Coast 106/C7
Yampa, Colo. 208/F2
Yampa (riv.), Colo. 208/B2
Yamparáez, Bolivia 136/C6
Yampi Sound, W. Australia 88/C3
Yampi Sound, W. Australia 92/C2
Yamsk, U.S.S.R. 48/Q4
Yamun, West Bank 65/C3
Yamuna (Jumna) (riv.), Pakistan 68/E3
Yamzho Yumco (lake), China 77/C6
Yan, Nigeria 106/G7
Yana (riv.), U.S.S.R. 4/C3
Yana (riv.), U.S.S.R. 48/O3
Yanac, Victoria 97/A5
Yanacachi, Bolivia 136/B5
Yanahuanca, Peru 128/D8
Yanam, India 68/E5
Yan'an (Yenan), China 77/G4
Yanaoca, Peru 128/G10
Yanaul, U.S.S.R. 52/J3
Yancannia, N.S. Wales 97/B2
Yancey, Ky. 237/P7
Yancey (co.), N.C. 281/E3
Yanceyville, N.C. 281/L2
Yancheng, China 77/K5
Yanchi, China 77/G4
Yanco, N.S. Wales 97/D4
Yandé (isl.), New Caled. 86/F4
Yandeyarra Aboriginal Reserve, W. Australia 88/B4
Yandina, Solomon Is. 86/D3
Yandoon, Burma 72/B3
Yanfolila, Mali 106/C6
Yanga, Mexico 150/P2
Yangambi, Zaire 115/D3
Yangambi, Zaire 102/E4
Yangcheng, China 77/H4
Yangchow (Yangzhou), China 77/J5
Yangchüan (Yangquan), China 77/H4
Yangchun, China 77/H7
Yangdök, N. Korea 81/C4
Yanggao, China 77/H3
Yanggu, S. Korea 81/C4
Yangjiang, China 77/H7
Yangquan (Yangchüan), China 77/H4
Yangshan, China 77/H7
Yang Sin, Chu (mt.), Vietnam 72/F4
Yangtze (riv.), China 54/N6
Yangtze (riv.), China 2/Q4
Yangtze (Chang Jiang) (riv.), China 77/K5
Yangyang, S. Korea 81/D4
Yangzhou (Yangchow), China 77/J5
Yanhuqu, China 77/B5
Yanji (Yenki), China 77/L3
Yankee Fork, Salmon (riv.), Idaho 220/C5
Yankee Lake, Ohio 284/J3
Yankeetown, Fla. 212/D2
Yankeetown, Ind. 227/C9
Yanko (creek), N.S. Wales 97/C4
Yankton, S. Dak. 188/G2
Yankton (co.), S. Dak. 298/P7
Yankton, S. Dak. 298/P8
Yanqi, China 77/C3
Yanrey, W. Australia 92/A3
Yantabulla, N.S. Wales 97/C1
Yantai (Chefoo), China 77/K4
Yantai, China 54/O6
Yantara, N.S. Wales 97/B1
Yantara (lake), N.S. Wales 97/B1
Yantic, Conn. 210/G2
Yantic (riv.), Conn. 210/G2
Yantis, Texas 303/J5
Yantley, Ala. 288/R5
Yanush, Okla. 288/R5
Yao, Japan 81/J8
Yaoundé (cap.), Cameroon 2/K5
Yaoundé (cap.), Cameroon 102/D4
Yaoundé (cap.), Cameroon 115/B3
Yap (isl.), Micronesia 87/D5
Yapacani (riv.), Bolivia 136/C5
Yapei, Ghana 106/D7
Yapen (isl.), Indonesia 85/K6
Yapen (str.), Indonesia 85/K6
Yapraklî, Turkey 63/E2
Yaque del Norte (riv.), Dom. Rep. 158/D5
Yaque del Sur (riv.), Dom. Rep. 158/D6
Yaqui, Mexico 150/D3
Yaqui (riv.), Mexico 146/H7
Yaqui (riv.), Mexico 150/E2
Yaquina, Oreg. 237/P6
Yara, Cuba 158/H4
Yaracuy (state), Venezuela 124/D2
Yaraka, Queensland 95/C5
Yaralïgüz Dağï (mt.), Turkey 59/B1
Yaralïgüz Dağï (mt.), Turkey 63/F2
Yaransk, U.S.S.R. 52/G3
Yarbo, Ala. 195/B7
Yarbo, Sask. 181/K5
Yarda, Chad 111/C4
Yardley, Pa. 294/N5
Yardville, N.J. 273/D3
Yare (riv.), England 13/J5
Yare (riv.), England 10/G4
Yarega, U.S.S.R. 52/H2
Yaretas de Vizcachas, Cerro (mt.), Chile 138/C5
Yari, Colombia 126/D7
Yarí (riv.), Colombia 126/D8

Yarim, Yemen 59/D7
Yaritagua, Venezuela 124/D2
Yarkand (Shache), China 77/A4
Yarkant, China 54/K6
Yarkant He (riv.), China 77/A4
Yarker, Ontario 177/H3
Yarle (lkes), S. Australia 94/B4
Yarmouth, Iowa 229/L6
Yarmouth, Maine 243/C8
Yarmouth•, Maine 243/C8
Yarmouth•, Mass. 249/O6
Yarmouth (co.), Nova Scotia 168/C5
Yarmouth, Nova Scotia 162/K7
Yarmouth, Nova Scotia 168/B5
Yarmouth (sound), Nova Scotia 168/B5
Yarmouth Port, Mass. 249/N6
Yarmuk (riv.), Israel 65/D2
Yarnell, Ariz. 198/C4
Yaroslavl', U.S.S.R. 7/H3
Yaroslavl', U.S.S.R. 48/D4
Yaroslavl', U.S.S.R. 52/E4
Yarqon (riv.), Israel 65/B3
Yarra (riv.), Victoria 97/C5
Yarra (riv.), Victoria 88/L6
Yarram, Victoria 97/D6
Yarrawonga, Victoria 97/C5
Yarrow, Br. Col. 184/M3
Yarrow, Mo. 261/G2
Yarrow (riv.), Scotland 15/E5
Yarrowitch, N.S. Wales 97/F2
Yarrow Point, Wash. 310/B2
Yartsevo, U.S.S.R. 48/J4
Yartsevo, U.S.S.R. 52/D3
Yarumal, Colombia 126/C4
Yaruu, Mongolia 77/E2
Yas (isl.), U.A.E. 59/F5
Yasawa Group (isls.), Fiji 86/P10
Yásica Abajo, Dom. Rep. 158/E5
Yasin, Pakistan 59/K2
Yasin, Pakistan 68/C1
Yasnyy, U.S.S.R. 52/J4
Yasothon, Thailand 72/D4
Yass, N.S. Wales 97/E4
Yasuj, Iran 66/G5
Yata (riv.), Bolivia 136/C3
Yatabe, Japan 81/P2
Yatağan, Turkey 63/C4
Yataity, Paraguay 144/C5
Yateley, England 13/G8
Yates (dam), Ala. 195/G5
Yates, N.Y. 276/F5
Yates Center, Kansas 232/G4
Yates City, Ill. 222/C3
Yatesville, Georgia 217/D5
Yathkyed (lake), N.W.T. 162/F3
Yathkyed (lake), N.W.T. 187/J3
Yatina, Bolivia 136/C7
Yatsushiro, Japan 81/E7
Yatta, West Bank 65/C5
Yatton, England 13/E6
Yatua (riv.), Venezuela 124/E7
Yauca, N.Y. 128/E10
Yauco, P. Rico 161/B2
Yauco, P. Rico 156/F1
Yauco (lake), P. Rico 161/B2
Yauli, Peru 128/D8
Yaupon Beach, N.C. 281/N7
Yauri (Espinar), Peru 128/G10
Yautepec, Mexico 150/K7
Yauyos, Peru 128/E9
Yava, Ariz. 198/C4
Yavapai (co.), Ariz. 198/C4
Yavapai Ind. Res., Ariz. 198/C4
Yavaraté, Colombia 126/F7
Yavarí (riv.), 120/B3
Yavarí (riv.), Peru 128/G5
Yavaros, Mexico 150/E3
Yavero (riv.), Peru 128/F9
Yavita, Venezuela 124/E6
Yavne, Israel 65/B4
Yavne'el, Israel 65/D2
Yawata, Japan 81/J7
Yawatahama, Japan 81/F7
Yawkey, W. Va. 312/C6
Yawri (bay), S. Leone 106/B7
Ya Xian, China 77/G8
Yaxley, England 13/G5
Yayladağï, Turkey 63/F5
Yazd (governorate), Iran 66/J5
Yazd (Yezd), Iran 66/J5
Yazd, Iran 59/F3
Yazd, Iran 54/G6
Yazdan, Iran 66/M4
Yazdan, Iran 59/H3
Yazd-e Khvasat, Iran 66/H5
Yazoo (co.), Miss. 256/D5
Yazoo (riv.), Miss. 188/H4
Yazoo (riv.), Miss. 256/C5
Yazoo City, Miss. 256/D5
Ybbs an der Donau, Austria 41/C2
Ybycuí, Paraguay 144/B5
Ybytymí, Paraguay 144/B5
Yding Skovhøj (mt.), Denmark 21/C6
Ye, Burma 72/C4
Yea, Victoria 97/C5
Yeaddiss, Ky. 237/P6
Yeadon, Pa. 294/N7
Yeager, Okla. 288/O4
Yeagertown, Pa. 294/G4
Yebbi-Bou, Chad 111/C3
Yecheng, China 77/A4
Yecla, Spain 33/F3
Yécora, Mexico 150/E2
Yecuatla, Mexico 150/P1
Yeddo, Ind. 227/C4
Yeeda River, W. Australia 92/C2
Yeelirrie, W. Australia 92/C4
Yefremov, U.S.S.R. 52/E14
Yegros, Paraguay 144/D5
Yeguas (isl.), P. Rico 161/F3
Yehualtepec, Mexico 150/O2
Yehud, Israel 65/B3
Yeï, Sudan 111/F7
Yelabuga, U.S.S.R. 52/H3

Yelan', U.S.S.R. 52/F4
Yelcho (lake), Chile 138/E4
Yelets, U.S.S.R. 7/H3
Yelets, U.S.S.R. 48/D4
Yelets, U.S.S.R. 52/E4
Yelimané, Mali 106/B5
Yelizaveta (cape), U.S.S.R. 54/R4
Yelizaveta (cape), U.S.S.R. 48/P4
Yelizovo, U.S.S.R. 48/Q4
Yell (co.), Ark. 202/D3
Yell (isl.), Scotland 15/G2
Yell (isl.), Scotland 10/G1
Yell (sound), Scotland 15/G2
Yellamanchili, India 68/E5
Yelleg, Jebel (mt.), Egypt 59/B3
Yellow (sea) 54/O6
Yellow (Huang He) (riv.), China 77/J4
Yellow (sea), China 77/K4
Yellow (creek), Colo. 208/C3
Yellow (riv.), Fla. 212/B6
Yellow (riv.), Ind. 227/D2
Yellow (sea), N. Korea 81/B6
Yellow (creek), Ohio 284/J4
Yellow (sea), S. Korea 81/B6
Yellow (creek), Tenn. 237/F8
Yellow (creek), W. Va. 312/E1
Yellow (lake), Wis. 317/B4
Yellow (riv.), Wis. 317/F7
Yellow Bluff, Ala. 195/C7
Yellowbud, Ohio 284/D7
Yellowcreek, N.C. 281/A4
Yellow Creek, Sask. 181/H6
Yellow Grass, Sask. 181/H6
Yellow Dog (riv.), Mich. 250/B2
Yellowhead (pass), Alberta 182/A3
Yellowhead (pass), Br. Col. 184/H4
Yellow Jacket, Colo. 208/B7
Yellowknife, Canada 4/C15
Yellowknife, Canada 2/D2
Yellowknife, N.W.T. 146/G3
Yellowknife, Canada 2/D2
Yellowknife (cap.), N.W.T. 162/E3
Yellowknife (cap.), N.W.T. 187/G3
Yellowknife (riv.), N.W.T. 187/G3
Yellow Medicine (co.), Minn. 255/B6
Yellow Pine, Ala. 195/B8
Yellow Pine, Idaho 220/C4
Yellow Pine, La. 238/D2
Yellow Spring, W. Va. 312/J4
Yellow Springs, Md. 245/H3
Yellow Springs, Ohio 284/C5
Yellowstone (riv.) 188/E1
Yellowstone (co.), Mont. 262/H4
Yellowstone (co.), Mont. 262/M3
Yellowstone (riv.), N. Dak. 282/B4
Yellowstone (riv.), U.S. 146/H5
Yellowstone (lake), Wyo. 188/E2
Yellowstone (lake), Wyo. 319/B1
Yellowstone (riv.), Wyo. 319/B1
Yellowstone Nat'l Park, Idaho 220/G5
Yellowstone Nat'l Park, Mont. 262/F6
Yellowstone Nat'l Park, Wyo. 188/E2
Yellowstone Nat'l Park, Wyo. 319/B1
Yellville, Ark. 202/E1
Yelm, Wash. 310/C4
Yelverton (bay), N.W.T. 187/K1
Yelwa, Nigeria 106/F6
Yemassee, S.C. 296/F6
Yemen 2/M5
Yemen 54/F8
YEMEN 59/D-E7
Yemetsk, U.S.S.R. 52/F2
Yenakiyevo, U.S.S.R. 52/E5
Yenan (Yan'an), China 77/G4
Yenangyaung, Burma 72/B2
Yen Bai, Vietnam 72/E2
Yenbo, Saudi Arabia 54/E7
Yenbo, Saudi Arabia 59/C5
Yenda, N.S. Wales 97/D4
Yendi, Ghana 106/D7
Yengisar, China 77/A4
Yenice (riv.), Çanakkale, Turkey 63/B3
Yenice, İçel, Turkey 63/F4
Yenice, Zonguldak, Turkey 63/E2
Yeniceoba, Turkey 63/E3
Yenikūy, Çanakkale, Turkey 63/B6
Yenikūy, Çanakkale, Turkey 63/C5
Yenikūy, İstanbul, Turkey 63/D6
Yenimahalle, Turkey 63/E3
Yenişehir, Turkey 63/C2
Yenisey (riv.), U.S.S.R. 4/C5
Yenisey (riv.), U.S.S.R. 2/P2
Yenisey (riv.), U.S.S.R. 54/K3
Yenisey (riv.), U.S.S.R. 48/J3
Yeniseysk, U.S.S.R. 54/L4
Yeniseysk, U.S.S.R. 48/K4
Yenki (Yanji), China 77/L3
Yen Minh, Vietnam 72/E2
Yentai (Yantai), China 77/K4
Yentna (riv.), Alaska 196/A1
Yeo (lake), W. Australia 88/D5
Yeo (lake), W. Australia 92/D5
Yeola, India 68/C4
Yeoman, Ind. 227/D3
Yeotmal, India 68/D4
Yeoval, N.S. Wales 97/E3
Yeovil, England 10/E5
Yeovil, England 13/E7
Yeppoon, Queensland 95/D4
Yeppoon, Queensland 88/J4
Yerevan, U.S.S.R. 48/E6
Yerevan, U.S.S.R. 52/F6
Yerichaña, Venezuela 124/F5
Yerington, Nev. 266/B4
Yerington Ind. Res., Nev. 266/B3
Yerkesik, Turkey 63/C4
Yerküy, Turkey 63/F3
Yerlisu, Turkey 63/C5
Yermak, U.S.S.R. 48/H4
Yermentau, U.S.S.R. 48/H4
Yermo, Calif. 204/J9
Yeroham, Israel 65/B6
Yerolimin, Greece 45/F7
Yeronga, Queensland 95/D3
Yeronga, Queensland 88/K3
Yerseke, Netherlands 27/E6
Yershov, U.S.S.R. 52/G4
Yesagyo, Burma 72/B2

Yeshbum, Yemen 59/E7
Yesil', U.S.S.R. 48/G4
Yeşilhisar, Turkey 63/F3
Yeşilırmak (riv.), Turkey 63/G2
Yeşilırmak (riv.), Turkey 63/G2
Yeşilküy, Turkey 63/D6
Yeşilova, Niğde, Turkey 63/E3
Yeşilova, Burdur, Turkey 63/C4
Yeşilyurt, Turkey 63/H3
Yeso, N. Mex. 274/E4
Yeso (creek), N. Mex. 274/E4
Yesodot, Israel 65/B4
Yessentuki, U.S.S.R. 52/F6
Yessey, U.S.S.R. 48/L3
Yeste, Spain 33/E3
Yesud Hama'ala, Israel 65/D1
Yetholm, Scotland 15/F5
Yetman, N.S. Wales 97/F1
Yettem, Calif. 204/F7
Yetter, Iowa 229/D4
Ye-u, Burma 72/B2
Yeu (isl.), France 28/B4
Yevlakh, U.S.S.R. 52/G6
Yevpatoria, U.S.S.R. 52/D5
Ye Xian, China 77/K4
Yeysk, U.S.S.R. 52/E5
Ygatimí, Paraguay 144/E4
Yhú, Paraguay 144/D5
Yi (riv.), Uruguay 145/B4
Yialousa, Cyprus 63/E5
Yiannitsá, Greece 45/F5
Yibin (Ipin), China 77/F6
Yibin, China 54/M7
Yibug Caka (lake), China 77/C5
Yichang (Ichang), China 77/H5
Yichun, Heilongjiang, China 77/L2
Yichun, Jiangxi, China 77/H6
Yidu, Hubei, China 77/H5
Yidu, Shandong, China 77/J4
Yiftah, Israel 65/D1
Yiğilca, Turkey 63/D2
Yildizeli, Turkey 63/G3
Yiliang, China 77/F7
Yinchuan (Ningsia, Yinchwan), China 77/G4
Yinchuan, China 54/M6
Yingjiang, China 77/E7
Yingkou (Yinkow), China 77/K3
Yingshan, Hubei, China 77/H5
Yingshan, Sichuan, China 77/G5
Yining, China 77/B3
Yining, China 54/K5
Yinjiang, China 77/G6
Yin Shan (mts.), China 77/G3
Yirka, Israel 65/C2
Yirol, Sudan 111/F6
Yirrkala, North. Terr. 93/E2
Yishan, China 77/G7
Yithion, Greece 45/F7
Yiwu (Aratürük), China 77/D3
Yiyang, China 77/H6
Ylikitka (lake), Finland 18/Q3
Ylitornio, Finland 18/O3
Ylivieska, Finland 18/O4
Ymir, Br. Col. 184/J5
Ynys Môn (Anglesey) (isl.), Wales 10/D7
Ynys Môn (Anglesey) (isl.), Wales 13/C4
Yoakum (co.), Texas 303/B4
Yoakum, Texas'303/G8
Yocalla, Bolivia 136/B6
Yocemento, Kansas 232/C3
Yockanookany (riv.), Miss. 256/E5
Yoco, Venezuela 124/G2
Yocón, Honduras 154/D3
Yocum, Ky. 237/P5
Yoder, Colo. 208/L5
Yoder, Ind. 227/G3
Yoder, Kansas 232/E4
Yoder, Wyo. 319/H4
Yodo (riv.), Japan 81/J7
Yog (pt.), Philippines 82/E3
Yogodor Nat'l Park, Br. Col. 162/E5
Yoho Nat'l Park, Br. Col. 184/J4
Yojoa (lake), Honduras 154/D3
Yokadouma, Cameroon 115/B3
Yokawa, Japan 81/H7
Yokena, Miss. 256/C6
Yokkaichi, Japan 81/H6
Yoko, Cameroon 115/B2
Yokohama, Japan 2/R4
Yokohama, Japan 81/O3
Yokohama, Japan 54/P6
Yokosuka, Japan 81/O3
Yokote, Japan 81/K4
Yola, Nigeria 106/G7
Yola, Nigeria 102/D4
Yolla, Tasmania 99/B3
Yolo (co.), Calif. 204/C5
Yolo, Calif. 204/B8
Yolyn, W. Va. 312/C7
Yona, Guam 86/K7
Yonago, Japan 81/F6
Yonaguni (isl.), Japan 81/K7
Yoncalla, Oreg. 291/D4
Yonezawa, Japan 81/K5
Yongam'p'o, N. Korea 81/B4
Yongchang, China 77/F4
Yongchuan, China 77/G6
Yŏngch'ŏn, S. Korea 81/D6
Yongdeng, China 77/F4
Yŏngdŏk, S. Korea 81/D5
Yonghe, China 77/G4
Yŏnghŭng, N. Korea 81/C4
Yongju, S. Korea 81/D5
Yongren, China 77/F6
Yongxin, China 77/H6
Yongxing, China 77/H6
Yonkers, Georgia 217/F6
Yonkers, N.Y. 276/D6
Yonne (dept.), France 28/E4
Yonne (riv.), France 28/E4
Yono, Japan 81/O2

Yopal, Colombia 126/D5
Yorba Linda, Calif. 204/D11
Yorito, Honduras 154/D3
York, Ala. 195/B6
York (cape), Australia 2/S6
York (cape), Australia 87/E7
York, England 13/F4
York, England 10/F4
York (cape), Greenl. 4/B13
York, Ky. 237/P3
York (co.), Maine 243/B9
York, Maine 243/B9
York•, Maine 243/B9
York (co.), Nebr. 264/G4
York, Nebr. 264/G4
York (co.), New Bruns. 170/C3
York, N.Y. 276/E5
York (reg. munic.), Ontario 177/E4
York, Ontario 177/J4
York (co.), Pa. 294/J6
York, Pa. 188/L3
York, Pa. 294/J6
York (riv.), Québec 172/D1
York (cape), Queensland 88/G2
York (cape), Queensland 95/B1
York (co.), S.C. 296/E2
York, S.C. 296/E1
York (co.), Va. 307/P6
York (riv.), Va. 307/P6
York, W. Australia 88/B6
York, W. Australia 92/B1
York (sound), W. Australia 88/C2
York (sound), W. Australia 92/D1
York, Wis. 317/D7
York Beach, Maine 243/B9
Yorke (pen.), S. Australia 88/F7
Yorke (pen.), S. Australia 94/E6
Yorketown, S. Australia 88/F6
Yorketown, S. Australia 94/E6
York Factory, Man. 162/G4
York Factory, Manitoba 179/K2
York Harbor, Maine 243/B9
York Haven, Pa. 294/J5
York Landing, Man. 146/J4
York Landing, Manitoba 179/J2
Yorklyn, Del. 245/R1
Yorkshire, North (co.), England 13/F3
Yorkshire, South (co.), England 13/F4
Yorkshire, West (co.), England 13/J1
Yorkshire, N.Y. 276/D5
Yorkshire, Ohio 284/B5
Yorkshire Dales Nat'l Park, England 13/E3
York Springs, Pa. 294/H4
Yorkton, Sask. 146/H4
Yorkton, Sask. 162/F5
Yorkton, Sask. 181/J4
Yorktown, Ark. 202/G5
Yorktown, Ind. 227/G4
Yorktown, Iowa 229/C7
Yorktown, N.J. 273/C4
Yorktown, Texas 303/G9
Yorktown, Va. 307/R6
Yorktown Heights, N.Y. 276/N8
Yorkville, Ill. 222/E2
Yorkville, N.Y. 276/K4
Yorkville, Ohio 284/J5
Yorkville, Tenn. 237/C8
Yoro, Honduras 154/D3
Yoron (isl.), Japan 81/N6
Yorosso, Mali 106/C6
Yosemite National Park, Calif. 204/F6
Yosemite Nat'l Park, Calif. 188/C3
Yosemite Nat'l Park, Calif. 204/F6
Yoshino (riv.), Japan 81/G6
Yoshino-Kumano Nat'l Park, Japan 81/H7
Yoshkar-Ola, U.S.S.R. 7/J3
Yoshkar-Ola, U.S.S.R. 52/G3
Yoshkar-Ola, U.S.S.R. 48/E4
Yost, Utah 304/A2
Yōsu, S. Korea 81/C6
Yotala, Bolivia 136/C6
Yotaú, Bolivia 136/D5
Yotvata, Israel 65/D5
Youanmi, W. Australia 92/B5
Youbou, Br. Col. 184/J3
Youghal, Ireland 17/F8
Youghal (bay), Ireland 10/C5
Youghal (bay), Ireland 17/F8
Youghiogheny (riv.), Md. 245/B3
Youghiogheny (dam), Pa. 294/D6
Youghiogheny River (lake), Md. 245/A2
Youghiogheny River (lake), Pa. 294/D6
Young, Ariz. 198/D4
Young, N.S. Wales 88/H6
Young, N.S. Wales 97/E4
Young (cape), N. Zealand 100/D7
Young (riv.), North. Terr. 93/D3
Young, Sask. 181/H4
Young, Uruguay 145/B3
Young America, Ind. 227/E3
Young America, Minn. 255/E6
Youngcane, Georgia 217/D1
Young Cove, Nova Scotia 168/C4
Young Harris, Georgia 217/E1
Youngs Cove, New Bruns. 170/E3
Youngs Creek, Ind. 227/D8
Youngs Creek, Ky. 237/N7
Youngstown, Alberta 182/E4
Youngstown, Fla. 212/D6
Youngstown, Ind. 227/C6
Youngstown, N.Y. 276/C4
Youngstown, Ohio 284/J3
Youngstown, Ohio 188/K2
Youngsville, La. 238/G6
Youngsville, N. Mex. 274/C2
Youngsville, N.C. 281/N2
Youngsville, Pa. 294/D2
Youngtown, Ariz. 198/C5
Youngwood, Pa. 294/D5
Yountville, Calif. 204/C5

Zzyzx 473

Youshashan, China 77/D4
Youssoufia, Morocco 106/C2
Youyang, China 77/G6
Yozgat (prov.), Turkey 63/F3
Yozgat, Turkey 59/B2
Yozgat, Turkey 63/F3
Ypacaraí, Paraguay 144/B5
Ypané, Paraguay 144/B5
Ypané (riv.), Paraguay 144/D3
Ypé Jhú, Paraguay 144/E3
Ypoá (lake), Paraguay 144/B5
Ypres (Ieper), Belgium 27/B7
Ypsilanti, Georgia 217/D5
Ypsilanti, Mich. 250/F6
Ypsilanti, N. Dak. 282/N6
Yreka, Calif. 188/B2
Yreka, Calif. 204/C2
Yser (riv.), Belgium 27/B7
Yssingeaux, France 28/F5
Ystad, Sweden 18/H9
Ystradgynlais, Wales 13/D6
Ythan (riv.), Scotland 15/F3
Yuan (riv.), China 54/M7
Yuan Jiang (riv.), China 77/H6
Yuanling, China 77/G6
Yuanmou, China 77/F6
Yuanping, China 77/H4
Yuba (co.), Calif. 204/D4
Yuba (riv.), Calif. 204/D4
Yuba, Okla. 288/O7
Yuba, Wis. 317/F8
Yuba City, Calif. 204/D4
Yubari, Japan 81/L2
Yubetsu, Japan 81/L1
Yucaipa, Calif. 204/J9
Yucatán (chan.) 146/K7
Yucatán (state), Mexico 150/P6
Yucatán (pen.), Mexico 146/K7
Yucatán (pen.), Mexico 150/P7
Yucca, Ariz. 198/A4
Yucca Flat (basin), Nev. 266/E6
Yucca House Nat'l Mon., Colo. 208/B8
Yucca Valley, Calif. 204/J9
Yuci (Yütze), China 77/H4
Yudu, China 77/J6
Yuendumu, North. Terr. 93/B7
Yuexi, China 77/F6
Yueyang, China 77/H6
Yug (riv.), U.S.S.R. 52/G2
Yugorskiy (pen.), U.S.S.R. 52/K1
Yugoslavia 2/K3
Yugoslavia 7/F4
YUGOSLAVIA 45/C3
Yuhuan (isl.), China 77/K6
Yukon (riv.) 2/B2
Yukon (riv.) 146/C3
Yukon (riv.) 4/C17
Yukon (riv.), Alaska 188/C5
Yukon (riv.), Alaska 196/F2
Yukon, Mo. 261/J8
Yukon, Okla. 288/L3
Yukon, Pa. 294/C5
Yukon (riv.), Yukon 162/C3
Yukon (riv.), Yukon 187/E3
Yukon-Charley Rivers Nat'l Preserve, Alaska 196/K2
Yukon Territory 162/C3
YUKON TERRITORY 187
Yukon Territory (terr.), Canada 146/E3
Yüksekova, Turkey 63/L4
Yukuhashi, Japan 81/E7
Yule (riv.), W. Australia 92/B3
Yulee, Fla. 212/E1
Yuli (Lopnur), China 77/C3
Yulin, Guangxi Zhuangzu, China 77/G7
Yulin, Shanxi, China 77/G4
Yuma (co.), Ariz. 198/A5
Yuma, Ariz. 188/D4
Yuma, Ariz. 146/G6
Yuma, Ariz. 198/A6
Yuma (des.), Ariz. 198/A6
Yuma (co.), Colo. 208/P2
Yuma, Colo. 208/O2
Yuma (bay), Dom. Rep. 158/F6
Yuma, Tenn. 237/E9
Yuma Ind. Res., Calif. 204/L11
Yuma Marine Corps Air Sta., Ariz. 198/A6
Yuma Proving Ground, Ariz. 198/A6
Yumbel, Chile 138/E1
Yumbo, Colombia 126/B6
Yumen, China 77/E4
Yumen, China 54/L6
Yumenzhen, China 77/E3
Yumin, China 77/B2
Yumurtalık, Turkey 63/F4
Yuna (riv.), Dom. Rep. 158/E5
Yuna, W. Australia 92/A5
Yunak, Turkey 63/D3
Yunan, China 77/H7
Yunaska (isl.), Alaska 196/D4
Yuncheng, China 77/H4
Yungas, Las (reg.), Bolivia 136/B5
Yungay, Chile 138/E1
Yungkia (Wenzhou), China 77/J6
Yunguyo, Peru 128/H11
Yunnan, China 77/F7
Yunta, S. Australia 94/F5
Yunxi, China 77/G5
Yunxiao, China 77/J7
Yunyang, China 77/G5
Yupukari, Guyana 131/B4
Yura, Bolivia 136/B7
Yuraguanal, Cuba 158/G2
Yurga, U.S.S.R. 48/J4
Yurimaguas, Peru 128/E5
Yuruá (riv.), Peru 128/F7
Yuruari (riv.), Venezuela 124/H4
Yurungkax He (riv.), China 77/A4
Yur'yevets, U.S.S.R. 52/F3
Yuscarán, Honduras 154/D4
Yushan (isls.), China 77/K6
Yü Shan (mt.), China 77/K7
Yushu, Jilin, China 77/L3
Yushu, Qinghai, China 77/E5
Yusufeli, Turkey 63/J2
Yutan, Nebr. 264/H3
Yutian, Xinjiang Uygur, China 77/B4
Yutian, Hebei, China 77/J4
Yuty, Paraguay 144/D5
Yütze (Yuci), China 77/H4
Yuxi, China 77/F7
Yu Xian, China 77/H4
Yuzawa, Japan 81/K4
Yuzhno-Sakhalinsk, U.S.S.R. 54/R5
Yuzhno-Sakhalinsk, U.S.S.R. 48/P5
Yvelines (dept.), France 28/D3
Yverdon, Switzerland 39/C3
Yvetot, France 28/D3
Yvoir, Belgium 27/F8
Yvonand, Switzerland 39/C3
Ywathit, Burma 72/C3

Z

Zaachila, Mexico 150/L8
Zaandam (Zaanstad), Netherlands 27/B4
Zaandijk, Netherlands 27/B4
Zabaykal'sk, U.S.S.R. 48/M5
Zabid, Yemen 59/D7
Ząbki, Poland 47/E2
Ząbkowice, Poland 47/B3
Ząbkowice Śląskie, Poland 47/C3
Žabljak, Yugoslavia 45/D4
Zabol, Iran 59/H3
Zabol, Iran 66/M5
Zabré, Burkina Faso 106/D6
Zábřeh, Czech. 41/D2
Zabrze, Poland 7/F3
Zabrze, Poland 47/A4
Zacapa, Guatemala 154/C3
Zacapoaxtla, Mexico 150/O1
Zacapu, Mexico 150/J7
Zacatecas (state), Mexico 150/H5
Zacatecas, Mexico 150/H5
Zacatecoluca, El Salvador 154/C4
Zacatelco, Mexico 150/N1
Zacatepec, Mexico 150/L2
Zacatlán, Mexico 150/N1
Zach, Tenn. 237/E3
Zachariah, Ky. 237/O5
Zachary, La. 238/K1
Zachow, Wis. 317/K6
Zacoalco de Torres, Mexico 150/H6
Zadar, Yugoslavia 45/B3
Zadetkyi Kyun (isl.), Burma 72/C5
Zadi, Burma 72/C4
Zadoi, China 77/E5
Zafra, Spain 33/C3
Żagań, Poland 47/B3
Žagarė, U.S.S.R. 53/B2
Zagarolo, Italy 34/F7
Zagazig, Egypt 59/B3
Zagazig, Egypt 111/K3
Zagheh, Iran 66/F4
Zagora, Morocco 106/C2
Zagorsk, U.S.S.R. 7/H3
Zagorsk, U.S.S.R. 52/E3
Zagreb, Yugoslavia 7/F4
Zagreb, Yugoslavia 45/C3
Zagros (mts.), Iran 59/E3
Zagros (mts.), Iran 66/E4
Zagyva (riv.), Hungary 41/F3
Zahedan, Iran 59/H4
Zahedan, Iran 66/M6
Zahedan, Iran 54/G7
Zahl, N. Dak. 282/C2
Zahle, Lebanon 63/F6
Záhony, Hungary 41/G2
Zahran, Saudi Arabia 59/D6
Zaidín, Spain 33/G2
Zaire 2/K6
Zaire 102/E5
ZAIRE 115/D4
Zaire (prov.), Angola 115/B5
Zaire (Congo) (riv.) 102/E4
Zaire (Congo) (riv.) Zaire 115/C4
Zaječar, Yugoslavia 45/E4
Zakamensk, U.S.S.R. 48/L4
Zakho, Iraq 66/C2
Zákinthos, Greece 45/E7
Zákinthos (Zante) (isl.), Greece 45/E7
Zako, Cent. Afr. Rep. 115/D2
Zakopane, Poland 47/D4
Zala (co.), Hungary 41/D3
Zala (riv.), Hungary 41/D3
Zalaegerszeg, Hungary 41/D3
Zalamea de la Serena, Spain 33/D3
Zalamea la Real, Spain 33/C4
Zalaszentgrót, Hungary 41/D3
Zalău, Romania 45/F2
Zaleski, Ohio 284/F7
Zalim, Saudi Arabia 59/D5
Zalingei, Sudan 111 D5
Zalma, Mo. 261/N8
Zaltbommel, Netherlands 27/G5
Zalun, Burma 72/B3
Zama (lake), Alberta 182/A5
Zama, Miss. 256/F5
Zambales (prov.), Philippines 82/C3
Zamberk, Czech. 41/D1
Zambezi (riv.) 2/L6
Zambezi (riv.) 102/E6
Zambezi (riv.), Angola 115/D6
Zambezi (riv.), Mozambique 118/E3
Zambezi (riv.), Namibia 118/C3
Zambezi, Zambia 115/D6
Zambezi (riv.), Zambia 115/D7
Zambezi (riv.), Zimbabwe 118/E3
Zambézia (prov.), Mozambique 118/F3
Zambia 2/L6
Zambia 102/E6
ZAMBIA 115/E7
Zamboanga, Philippines 85/G4
Zamboanga, Philippines 82/C7
Zamboanga, Philippines 54/N9
Zamboanga del Norte (prov.), Philippines 82/D6
Zamboanga del Sur (prov.), Philippines 82/D7
Zambrów, Poland 47/E2
Zamora, Calif. 204/C5
Zamora, Ecuador 128/C5
Zamora (riv.), Ecuador 128/B4
Zamora (prov.), Spain 33/D2
Zamora, Spain 33/D2
Zamora-Chinchipe (prov.), Ecuador 128/C5
Zamora de Hidalgo, Mexico 150/H7
Zamość (prov.), Poland 47/F3
Zamość, Poland 47/F3
Zams, Austria 41/A3
Zamtang, China 77/F5
Zanaga, Congo 115/B4
Zanda, China 77/A5
Zanderij, Suriname 131/D3
Zanderij, Suriname 120/D2
Zandvoort, Netherlands 27/E4
Zanesfield, Ohio 284/C5
Zanesville, Ind. 227/G3
Zanesville, Ohio 188/K3
Zanesville, Ohio 284/G6
Zanja de Lira, Venezuela 124/E3
Zanjan (governorate), Iran 66/F2
Zanjan, Iran 59/E2
Zanjan, Iran 66/K5
Zanjan (riv.), Iran 66/F2
Zanoni, Mo. 261/H9
Zante (Zákinthos), Greece 45/E7
Zanthus, W. Australia 92/C5
Zanzibar, Tanzania 102/F5
Zanzibar, Tanzania 115/G5
Zanzibar (isl.), Tanzania 2/M6
Zanzibar (isl.), Tanzania 102/F5
Zanzibar (isl.), Tanzania 115/G5
Zanzibar Mjini (reg.), Tanzania 115/G5
Zanzibar Shambani North (reg.), Tanzania 115/G5
Zanzibar Shambani South (reg.), Tanzania 115/G5
Zao (mt.), Japan 81/K5
Zaouiet Kounta, Algeria 106/D3
Zaoyang, China 77/H5
Zaozernyy, U.S.S.R. 48/K4
Zaozhuang, China 77/J5
Zap, N. Dak. 282/G5
Západočeský (reg.), Czech. 41/B2
Západoslovenský (reg.), Czech. 41/D2
Zapala, Argentina 143/B4
Zapala, Argentina 120/B6
Zapaleri, Cerro (mt.), Argentina 143/C1
Zapaleri, Cerro (mt.), Bolivia 136/B8
Zapaleri, Cerro (mt.), Chile 138/C4
Zapallar, Chile 138/A9
Zapata (pen.), Cuba 158/C2
Zapata (co.), Texas 303/E11
Zapata, Texas 303/E11
Zapata Occidental (swamp), Cuba 158/D2
Zapata Oriental (swamp), Cuba 158/D2
Zapatera (isl.), Nicaragua 154/E5
Zapatoca, Colombia 126/D4
Zapatosa, Ciénaga de (swamp), Colombia 126/D3
Zapicán, Uruguay 145/E4
Zapiga, Chile 138/B2
Zapolyarnyy, U.S.S.R. 52/D1
Zaporozh'ye, U.S.S.R. 7/H4
Zaporozh'ye, U.S.S.R. 48/D5
Zaporozh'ye, U.S.S.R. 52/E5
Zapotillo, Ecuador 128/B5
Zapucay, Uruguay 145/D2
Zapug, China 77/B5
Za Qu (riv.), China 77/E5
Zara, Turkey 59/C1
Zara, Turkey 63/G3
Zara (Zadar), Yugoslavia 45/B3
Zarafshan, 48/G5
Zaragoza, Colombia 126/C4
Zaragoza, Chihuahua, Mexico 150/F1
Zaragoza, Coahuila, Mexico 150/J2
Zaragoza, Puebla, Mexico 150/O1
Zaragoza (prov.), Spain 33/F2
Zaragoza (Saragossa), Spain 33/F2
Zarand, Iran 59/G3
Zarand, Iran 66/H6
Zaranj, Afghanistan 68/A2
Zaranj, Afghanistan 59/H3
Zarasai, U.S.S.R. 53/C3
Zárate, Argentina 143/G6
Zaraza, Venezuela 124/F3
Zard Kuh (mt.), Iran 66/F4
Zarembo (isl.), Alaska 196/N2
Zarephath, N.J. 273/D2
Zaria, Nigeria 106/F6
Zaria, Nigeria 102/D3
Zarineh (riv.), Iran 66/E2
Zărneşti, Romania 45/G3
Zarqa' (riv.), Jordan 65/D3
Zarqam, Iran 66/H6
Zaruma, Ecuador 128/C4
Zarumilla, Peru 128/B4
Żary, Poland 47/B3
Zarzal, Colombia 126/B5
Zarza la Mayor, Spain 33/C3
Zarzis, Tunisia 106/G2
Zarzis, Tunisia 102/D1
Zaskar (mts.), India 68/D2
Zastron, S. Africa 118/D6
Žatec, Czech. 41/B1
Zavala (co.), Texas 303/E9
Zavalla, Argentina 143/F6
Zavalla, Texas 303/K6
Zavdi'el, Israel 65/B4
Zaventem, Belgium 27/C9
Zavitinsk, U.S.S.R. 48/O4
Zawi, Zimbabwe 118/D3
Zawia, Libya 102/D1
Zawia, Libya 111/B1
Zawiercie, Poland 47/D3
Zayandeh (riv.), Iran 66/H4
Zayar, China 77/B3
Zaysan (lake), U.S.S.R. 54/K5
Zaysan, U.S.S.R. 48/J5
Zaysan (lake), U.S.S.R. 48/J5
Zayü, China 77/E6
Zaza del Medio, Cuba 158/F2
Zázrivá, Czech. 41/E2
Zbąszyń, Poland 47/B2
Zbiroh, Czech. 41/B2
Zborov, Czech. 41/F2
Žďár nad Sázavou, Czech. 41/C2
Zduńska Wola, Poland 47/D3
Zeaand (Sjaelland) (isl.), Den. 21/E6
Zealand, New Bruns. 170/D2
Zealandia, Sask. 181/D4
Zearing, Iowa 229/G4
Zeballos, Br. Col. 184/D5
Zebdani, Syria 63/G6
Zebirget (isl.), Egypt 59/C5
Zebulon, Georgia 217/D4
Zebulon, Ky. 237/S5
Zebulon, N.C. 281/N3
Zedelgem, Belgium 27/C6
Zeebrugge, Belgium 27/C6
Zeehan, Tasmania 99/B3
Zeeland, Mich. 250/D6
Zeeland (prov.), Netherlands 27/D6
Zeeland, N. Dak. 282/L8
Ze'elim, Israel 65/A5
Zeerust, S. Africa 118/D5
Zeewolde, Netherlands 27/G4
Zefat, Israel 65/C2
Zegharta, Lebanon 63/G5
Zegrzyńskie (lake), Poland 47/E2
Zehdenick, Germany 22/E2
Zehner, Sask. 181/G5
Zeigler, Ill. 222/D6
Zeila, Somalia 115/H1
Zeil am Main, Germany 22/D4
Zeist, Netherlands 27/G4
Zeitz, Germany 22/E3
Zekiah Swamp (riv.), Md. 245/L7
Zêkog, China 77/F5
Zele, Belgium 27/E6
Zelenoborskiy, U.S.S.R. 52/D1
Zelenodol'sk, U.S.S.R. 52/G3
Zelenokumsk, U.S.S.R. 52/F6
Zelienople, Pa. 294/B4
Želiezovce, Czech. 41/E2
Zell, S. Dak. 298/M4
Zell, Luzern, Switzerland 39/E2
Zell, Zürich, Switzerland 39/G2
Zell, Germany 22/B4
Zella, Libya 102/D2
Zella, Libya 111/C2
Zella-Mehlis, Germany 22/D3
Zell am See, Austria 41/B3
Zell am Ziller, Austria 41/A3
Zellersee (lake), Switzerland 39/G1
Zellwood, Fla. 212/E3
Zelma, Sask. 181/F4
Zelow, Poland 47/D3
Zelten, Jebel (mts.), Libya 111/D2
Zeltweg, Austria 41/C3
Zelzate, Belgium 27/D6
Zemio, Cent. Afr. Rep. 115/D2
Zemongo, Cent. Afr. Rep. 115/E2
Zemple, Minn. 255/E3
Zempoala, Mexico 150/Q1
Zemst, Belgium 27/E7
Zenas, Ind. 227/G6
Zenda, Kansas 232/D4
Zeneta, Sask. 181/J5
Zenia, Calif. 204/B3
Zenica, Yugoslavia 45/C3
Zenith, Ill. 222/E5
Zenith, Kansas 232/D4
Zenith, W. Va. 312/F7
Zenith-Saltwater, Wash. 310/C3
Zenjan (Zanjan), Iran 66/F2
Zenobia (peak), Colo. 208/B1
Zenon Park, Sask. 181/H2
Zenoria, La. 238/F3
Zent, Ark. 202/H4
Zenta (Senta), Yugo. 45/D3
Zeona, S. Dak. 298/D3
Žepče, Yugoslavia 45/D3
Zepernick, Germany 22/F3
Zephyr, Ontario 177/E3
Zephyr, Texas 303/F6
Zephyr Cove, Nev. 266/A3
Zephyrhills, Fla. 212/D3
Zepp, Va. 307/L3
Zerbst, Germany 22/E3
Zereh, Gowd-e (depr.), Afghanistan 68/A3
Zermatt, Switzerland 39/E4
Zernez, Switzerland 39/K3
Zernograd, U.S.S.R. 52/F5
Zêtang, China 77/D6
Zetland (trad. co.), Scotland 15/B4
Zeulenroda, Germany 22/D3
Zeven, Germany 22/C2
Zevenaar, Netherlands 27/J5
Zevenbergen, Netherlands 27/E5
Zeya, U.S.S.R. 48/N4
Zeya (riv.), U.S.S.R. 48/N4
Zeytinburnu, Turkey 63/D6
Zeytindağ, Turkey 63/B3
Zgierz, Poland 47/D3
Zgorzelec, Poland 47/B3
Zhanang, China 77/D6
Zhangbei, China 77/J3
Zhangjiakou (Kalgan), China 77/J3
Zhangjiakou, China 54/N5
Zhangping, China 77/J6
Zhangye (Changyeh), China 77/F4
Zhangye, China 54/M6
Zhangzhou (Changchow), China 77/J7
Zhanjiang (Chankiang), China 77/H7
Zhanjiang, China 54/N7
Zhanyi, China 77/F6
Zhaodong, China 77/K2
Zhaojue, China 77/F6
Zhaoqing, China 77/H7
Zhaosu, China 77/B3
Zhaotong (Chaotung), China 77/F6
Zhari Namco (lake), China 77/C5
Zhashui, China 77/G5
Zhatay, U.S.S.R. 48/O3
Zhaxi Co (lake), China 77/C5
Zhejiang (Chekiang), China 77/K6
Zhelaniye (cape), U.S.S.R. 48/H2
Zheleznodorozhnyy, U.S.S.R. 52/H2
Zheleznogorsk, U.S.S.R. 52/E4
Zheleznogorsk-Ilimskiy, U.S.S.R. 48/L4
Zhenba, China 77/G5
Zheng'an, China 77/G6
Zhenglan, China 77/J3
Zhengzhou (Chengchow), China 77/H5
Zhengzhou, China 54/N6
Zhenjiang (Chinkiang), China 77/J5
Zhenxiong, China 77/F6
Zhenyuan, China 77/G6
Zhidoi, China 77/E5
Zhigalovo, U.S.S.R. 48/L4
Zhigansk, U.S.S.R. 4/C3
Zhigansk, U.S.S.R. 54/N3
Zhigansk, U.S.S.R. 48/N3
Zhigulevsk, U.S.S.R. 52/G4
Zhi Qu (Tongtian He) (riv.), China 77/E5
Zhirnovsk, U.S.S.R. 52/G4
Zhitomir, U.S.S.R. 7/G3
Zhitomir, U.S.S.R. 48/C4
Zhitomir, U.S.S.R. 52/C4
Zhlobin, U.S.S.R. 52/D4
Zhmerinka, U.S.S.R. 52/C5
Zhob (riv.), Pakistan 59/J3
Zhob (riv.), Pakistan 68/B2
Zhodino, U.S.S.R. 52/C4
Zhongba, China 77/B6
Zhongdian, China 77/F6
Zhongning, China 77/G4
Zhongshan (Chungshan), China 77/H7
Zhongwei, China 77/F4
Zhoushan (arch.), China 77/K5
Zhovtnevoye, U.S.S.R. 52/D5
Zhuanghe, China 77/K4
Zhucheng, China 77/J4
Zhukovka, U.S.S.R. 52/D4
Zhumadian (Chumatien), China 77/H5
Zhushan, China 77/G5
Zhuzhou (Chuchow), China 77/H6
Zhuzhou, China 54/N7
Zia Pueblo, N. Mex. 274/C3
Žiar nad Hronom, Czech. 41/E2
Zibak, Afghanistan 59/K2
Zibak, Afghanistan 68/C1
Zibo (Tzepo), China 77/J4
Zibo, China 54/N6
Zichang, China 77/G4
Židlochovice, Czech. 41/D2
Ziebach (co.), S. Dak. 298/F4
Zięblce, Poland 47/C3
Ziel (mt.), North. Terr. 88/E4
Ziel (mt.), North. Terr. 93/C7
Zielona Góra (prov.), Poland 47/B3
Zielona Góra, Poland 47/B3
Zierikzee, Netherlands 27/D5
Zifta, Egypt 111/J3
Zigong (Tzekung), China 77/F6
Ziguei, Chad 111/C5
Zigui, China 77/H5
Ziguinchor, Senegal 106/A6
Ziguinchor, Senegal 102/A3
Zihuantanejo, Mexico 150/J8
Zikhron Ya'aqov, Israel 65/B2
Zilbir (riv.), Iran 66/D1
Zile, Turkey 59/C1
Zile, Turkey 63/G2
Zilfi, Saudi Arabia 59/E4
Žilina, Czech. 41/E2
Zillah, Wash. 310/E4
Zillis-Reischen, Switzerland 39/H3
Zilupe, U.S.S.R. 53/D2
Zilwaukee, Mich. 250/F5
Zim, Minn. 255/F3
Zima, U.S.S.R. 48/L4
Zimatlán de Álvarez, Mexico 150/L8
Zimbabwe 2/L6
Zimbabwe 102/E6
ZIMBABWE 118/D4
Zimbabwe Nat'l Park, Zimbabwe 118/E4
Zimmerdale, Kansas 232/E3
Zimmerman, La. 238/E4
Zimmerman, Minn. 255/E5
Zimnicea, Romania 45/G4
Zimnitsa, Bulgaria 45/H4
Zinal, Switzerland 39/E4
Zinc, Ark. 202/E1
Zinder, Niger 106/F6
Zinder, Niger 102/C3
Zingst, Germany 22/E1
Zinjibar, Yemen 59/E7
Zinnik (Soignies), Belgium 27/D7
Zion, Ark. 202/G1
Zion, Ill. 222/F1
Zion, Md. 245/P2
Zion, Mo. 261/M8
Zion, N.J. 273/D3
Zion, S.C. 296/J3
Zion Hill, St. Kitts & Nevis 161/D11
Zion National Park, Utah 304/B6
Zion Nat'l Park, Utah 304/A6
Zionsville, Ind. 227/E5
Zionville, N.C. 281/F2
Zipaquirá, Colombia 126/D5
Zippori, Israel 65/C2
Zirc, Hungary 41/D3
Žirje (isl.), Yugoslavia 45/B4
Zirkel (mt.), Colo. 208/F1
Zirko (isl.), U.A.E. 59/F5
Zirl, Austria 41/A3
Zirndorf, Germany 22/D4
Zistersdorf, Austria 41/D2
Zitácuaro, Mexico 150/J7
Zittau, Germany 22/F3
Zitterwald (plat.), Belgium 27/J8
Zivarık, Turkey 63/E3
Ziyang, China 77/F5
Ziz, Wadi (dry riv.), Morocco 106/D2
Zizers, Switzerland 39/J3
Zlaté Moravce, Czech. 41/E2
Zlatograd, Bulgaria 45/G5
Zlatoust, U.S.S.R. 54/G4
Zlatoust, U.S.S.R. 48/F4
Zlín (Gottwaldov), Czech. 41/D2
Zliten, Libya 111/C1
Złocieniec, Poland 47/C2
Złotoryja, Poland 47/C3
Złotów, Poland 47/C2
Žlutice, Czech. 41/B1
Znamenka, U.S.S.R. 52/D5
Żnin, Poland 47/C2
Znojmo, Czech. 41/D2
Zoar (lake), Conn. 210/C3
Zoar, Ohio 284/H4
Zoarville, Ohio 284/H4
Zofingen, Switzerland 39/F2
Zogang, China 77/E5
Zohreh (riv.), Iran 66/F5
Zoigê, China 77/F5
Zolfo Springs, Fla. 212/E4
Zollikofen, Switzerland 39/E3
Zollikon, Switzerland 39/G2
Zolotonosha, U.S.S.R. 52/D5
Zomba, Malawi 115/G7
Zomba, Malawi 102/F6
Zonderend (riv.), S. Africa 118/G6
Zongo, Bolivia 136/B5
Zongo, Zaire 115/C3
Zongolica, Mexico 150/P2
Zonguldak (prov.), Turkey 63/D2
Zonguldak, Turkey 63/D2
Zonguldak, Turkey 59/B1
Zonhoven, Belgium 27/G6
Zoo Baba (well), Niger 106/G5
Zook, Kansas 232/C3
Zorbatiya, Iraq 66/D4
Zorita, Spain 33/D3
Zorritos, Peru 128/B4
Zortman, Mont. 262/H3
Zottegem, Belgium 27/D7
Zouar, Chad 111/C3
Zouîrât, Mauritania 106/B4
Zoutkamp, Netherlands 27/J2
Zrenjanin, Yugoslavia 45/E3
Zuata, Venezuela 124/F3
Zuata (riv.), Venezuela 124/F3
Zububa, West Bank 65/C2
Zucchero (mt.), Switzerland 39/G4
Zudáñez, Bolivia 136/C6
Zug (canton), Switzerland 39/G2
Zug, Switzerland 39/G2
Zugdidi, U.S.S.R. 52/F6
Zugersee (lake), Switzerland 39/F2
Zugspitze (mt.), Austria 41/A3
Zugspitze (mt.), Germany 22/D5
Zuienkerke, Belgium 27/C6
Zuila, Libya 111/C2
Zújar, Spain 33/E4
Zújar (res.), Spain 33/D3
Zula, Ethiopia 111/G4
Zula, Ethiopia 59/C6
Zula, Ky. 237/M7
Zulia (state), Venezuela 124/B2
Zulia (riv.), Venezuela 124/B3
Zülpich, Germany 22/B3
Zulu, Ind. 227/H2
Zulueta, Cuba 158/E2
Zululand (reg.), S. Africa 118/E5
Zumba, Ecuador 128/C5
Zumbo, Mozambique 118/E3
Zumbro (riv.), Minn. 255/F6
Zumbro Falls, Minn. 255/F6
Zumbrota, Minn. 255/F6
Zumpango del Río, Mexico 150/J8
Zumpango de Ocampo, Mexico 150/L1
Zundert, Netherlands 27/F6
Zungeru, Nigeria 106/F7
Zunhua, China 77/J3
Zuni (riv.), Ariz. 198/F4
Zuni, N. Mex. 274/A3
Zuni (mts.), N. Mex. 274/A3
Zuni (riv.), N. Mex. 274/A3
Zuni, Va. 307/P7
Zuni-Cibola Nat'l Historic Park, N. Mex. 274/A3
Zuni Ind. Res., N. Mex. 274/A3
Zunyi (Tsunyi), China 77/G6
Zunyi, China 54/M7
Zuoz, Switzerland 39/J3
Zuqar (isl.), Yemen 59/D7
Zurabad, Iran 66/M3
Zurich, Kansas 232/C2
Zurich, Mont. 262/G2
Zurich, Ontario 177/C4
Zürich (canton), Switzerland 39/G2
Zürich, Switzerland 39/F2
Zürich, Switzerland 7/E4
Zürichsee (lake), Switzerland 39/G2
Zuromin, Poland 47/E2
Zurzach, Switzerland 39/F1
Zushi, Japan 81/O3
Zutphen, Netherlands 27/J4
Zuweiza, Jordan 65/D4
Zuyevka, U.S.S.R. 52/H3
Zvishavana, Zimbabwe 102/E7
Zvishavana, Zimbabwe 118/E4
Zvolen, Czech. 41/E2
Zvornik, Yugoslavia 45/D3
Zwai (lake), Ethiopia 111/G6
Zwanenburg, Netherlands 27/A4
Zwara, Libya 111/B1
Zwart (riv.), S. Africa 118/G7
Zwartsluis, Netherlands 27/H3
Zwedru, Liberia 106/C7
Zweibrücken, Germany 22/B4
Zweisimmen, Switzerland 39/D3
Zwelitsha, S. Africa 118/D6
Zwenkau, Germany 22/E3
Zwettl-Niederösterreich, Austria 41/C2
Zwickau, Germany 22/E3
Zwijndrecht, Netherlands 27/E5
Zwingle, Iowa 229/M4
Zwischenahn, Germany 22/B2
Zwoleń, Poland 47/E3
Zwolle, La. 238/C3
Zwolle, Netherlands 27/J3
Żychlin, Poland 47/D2
Żyrardów, Poland 47/E2
Zyryanka, U.S.S.R. 4/C2
Zyryanka, U.S.S.R. 54/S3
Zyryanka, U.S.S.R. 48/Q3
Zyryanovsk, U.S.S.R. 48/J5
Żywiec, Poland 47/D4
Zzyzx, Calif. 204/J8

GEOGRAPHICAL TERMS

A. = Arabic Burm. = Burmese Camb. = Cambodian Ch. = Chinese Czech. = Czechoslovakian Dan. = Danish Du. = Dutch Finn. = Finnish Fr. = French Ger. = German Ice. = Icelandic It. = Italian Jap. = Japanese Mong. = Mongol Nor. = Norwegian Per. = Persian Port. = Portuguese Russ. = Russian Sp. = Spanish Sw. = Swedish Turk. = Turkish

Å	Nor., Sw.	Stream
Aas	Dan., Nor.	Hills
Abajo	Sp.	Lower
Ada, Adasi	Turk.	Island
Altipiano	It.	Plateau
Altiplano	Sp.	Plateau
Alv, Alf, Elf	Sw.	River
Arrecife	Sp.	Reef
Asa	Nor., Sw.	Hill
Asaga	Turk.	Lower
Austral	Sp.	Southern
Baai	Du.	Bay
Bab	Arabic	Gate or Strait
Bahia	Sp.	Bay
Bahr	Arabic	Marsh, Lake, Sea, River
Baia	Port.	Bay
Baie	Fr.	Bay, Gulf
Baizo	Port.	Low
Bakke	Dan.	Hill
Bana	Jap.	Cape
Bañados	Sp.	Marshes
Band	Per.	Mt. Range
Bandao	Ch.	Peninsula
Bandar	Per.	Harbor
Barra	Sp.	Reef
Bel	Turk.	Pass
Belt	Ger.	Strait
Ben	Gaelic	Mountain
Bera	Du.	Mountain
Berg	Ger., Du.	Mountain
Bir	Arabic	Well
Boca	Sp.	Gulf, Inlet
Boğhaz	Turk.	Strait
Bolshoi, Bolshaya	Russ.	Big
Bolson	Sp.	Depression
Bong	Korean	Mountain
Boreal	Sp.	Northern
Breen	Nor.	Glacier
Bro	Dan., Nor., Sw.	Bridge
Bucht	Ger.	Bay
Bugt	Dan.	Bay
Bukhta	Russ.	Bay
Bukit	Malay	Hill, Mountain
Bukt	Nor., Sw.	Bay, Gulf
Burnu, Burun	Turk.	Cape, Point
By	Dan., Nor., Sw.	Town
Cabo	Port., Sp.	Cape
Campos	Port.	Plains
Canal	Port., Sp.	Channel
Cap, Capo	Fr., It.	Cape
Cataratas	Sp.	Falls
Catena	It.	Mt. Range
Catingas	Port.	Open Woodlands
Cayos	Sp.	Islands
Central, Centrale	Fr., It.	Middle
Cerrito, Cerro	Sp.	Hill
Cerros	Sp.	Hills, Mountains
Chai	Turk.	River
Chott	Arabic	Salt Lake
Ciénaga	Sp.	Swamp
Ciudad	Sp.	City
Col	Fr.	Pass
Cordillera	Sp.	Mt. Range, Mts.
Côte	Fr.	Coast
Csatoria	Magyar	Canal
Cuchilla	Sp.	Mt. Range
Curiche	Sp.	Swamp
Dağ, Dağı	Turk.	Mountain, Peak
Dağlari	Turk.	Mt. Range
Dal	Nor., Sw.	Valley
Dar	Arabic	Land
Dar'ya	Russ.	River
Daryacheh	Per.	Marshy Lake
Dasht	Per.	Desert, Plain
Deniz, Denizi	Turk.	Sea, Lake
Desierto	Sp.	Desert
Détroit	Fr.	Strait
Djeziret	Arabic, Turk.	Island
Do	Korean	Island
Doi	Thai	Mountain
Eiland	Du.	Island
Elv	Dan., Nor.	River
Embalse	Sp.	Reservoir
Emi	Berber	Mountain
Erg	Arabic	Dune, Desert
Eski	Turk.	Old
Est, Este	Fr., Port., Sp.	East
Estero	Sp.	Estuary, Creek
Estrecho, Estreito	Sp., Port.	Strait
Etang	Fr.	Pond, Lagoon, Lake
Feng	Ch.	Mountain
Fiume	It.	River
Fjäll	Sw.	Mountain
Fjeld, Fjell	Nor.	Hills, Mountain
Fjord	Dan., Nor., Sw.	Fiord
Fleuve	Fr.	River
Fljót	Ice.	Stream
Fluss	Ger.	River
Fors	Sw.	Waterfall
Fos, Foss	Dan., Nor.	Waterfall
Gamla	Nor.	Old
Gamle	Dan.	Old
Gata	Jap.	Lake
Gawa	Jap.	River
Gebel	Arabic	Mountain
Gebergte	Du.	Mt. Range
Gebirge	Ger.	Mt. Range
Gobi	Mongol	Desert
Goe	Jap.	Pass
Gol	Mongol, Turk.	Lake, Stream
Golf	Ger., Du.	Gulf
Golfe	Fr.	Gulf
Golfo	Sp., It., Port.	Gulf
Gölü	Turk.	Lake
Gora	Russ.	Mountain
Grand, Grande	Fr., Sp.	Big
Groot	Du.	Big
Gross	Ger.	Big
Grosso	It., Port.	Big
Guba	Russ.	Bay, Gulf
Gunto	Jap.	Archipelago
Gunung	Malay	Mountain
Hai	Ch.	Sea
Haixia	Ch.	Strait
Halbinsel	Ger.	Peninsula
Hamáda, Hammada	Arabic	Rocky Plateau
Hamn	Sw.	Harbor
Hamún	Per.	Marsh
Hanto	Jap.	Peninsula
Has, Hassi	Arabic	Well
Hav	Dan., Nor., Sw.	Sea, Ocean
Havet	Nor.	Bay
Havn	Dan., Nor.	Harbor
Havre	Fr.	Harbor
He	Ch.	River, Stream
Higashi, Higasi	Jap.	East
Hochebene	Ger.	Plateau
Hoek	Du.	Cape
Hoku	Jap.	North
Holm	Dan., Nor., Sw.	Island
Hory	Czech	Mountains
Hoved	Dan., Nor.	Cape, Promontory
Hu	Ch.	Lake
Huang	Ch.	Yellow
Huk	Dan., Nor., Sw.	Point
Hus, Huus	Dan., Nor., Sw.	House
Idehan	Arabic	Desert
Ile	Fr.	Island
Ilet	Fr.	Islet
Ilot	Fr.	Islet
Indre	Dan., Nor.	Inner
Inferieur, Inferiore	Fr., It.	Lower
Inner, Inre	Sw.	Inner
Insel	Ger.	Island
Irmak	Turk.	River
Isla	Sp.	Island
Isola	It.	Island
Jabal, Jebel	Arabic	Mountains
Järvi	Finn.	Lake
Jaure	Sw.	Lake
Jiang	Ch.	River, Stream
Jima	Jap.	Island
Joki	Finn.	River
Kaap	Du.	Cape
Kabir, Kebir	Arabic	Big
Kai	Jap.	Sea
Kaikyo	Jap.	Strait
Kami	Turk.	Upper
Kanaal	Du.	Canal
Kanal	Russ., Ger.	Canal, Channel
Kao	Thai	Mountain
Kap, Kapp	Nor., Sw., Ice.	Cape
Kaupunki	Finn.	Town
Kawa	Jap.	River
Khao	Thai	Mountain
Khrebet	Russ.	Mt. Range
Kita	Jap.	North
Klein	Du., Ger.	Small
Klint	Dan.	Promontory
Kô	Jap.	Lake
Ko	Thai	Island
Koh	Camb., Khmer	Island
Kop	Du.	Peak, Head
Köping	Sw.	Market, Borough
Körfez, Körfezi	Turk.	Gulf
Kosa	Russ.	Spit
Kosui	Jap.	Lake
Kraal	Du.	Native Village
Kuchuk	Turk.	Small
Kuh, Kuhha	Per.	Mt. Range, Mts.
Kul	Sinkiang Turki	Lake
Kum	Turk.	Desert
Kuro	Jap.	Black
Laag	Du.	Low
Lac	Fr.	Lake
Lago	Port., Sp., It.	Lake
Lagoa	Port.	Lagoon
Laguna	Sp.	Lagoon
Lagune	Fr.	Lagoon
Lahti	Finn.	Bay, Bight
Län	Sw.	County
Liedao	Ch.	Islands, Archipelago
Lilla	Sw.	Small
Lille	Dan., Nor.	Small
Ling	Ch.	Mountain
Llanos	Sp.	Plains
Mae Nam	Thai	River
Mali, Malaya	Russ.	Small
Man	Korean	Bay
Mar	Sp., Port.	Sea
Mare	It.	Sea
Medio	Sp.	Middle
Meer	Du.	Lake
Meer	Ger.	Sea
Mer	Fr.	Sea
Meridionale	It.	Southern
Meseta	Sp.	Plateau
Middelst, Midden	Du.	Middle
Minami	Jap.	Southern
Mis	Russ.	Cape
Misaki	Jap.	Cape
Mittel	Ger.	Middle
Mont	Fr.	Mountain
Montagne	Fr.	Mountain
Montaña	Sp.	Mountains
Monte	Sp., It., Port.	Mountain
More	Russ.	Sea
Mörön	Mong.	Stream
Morro	Port., Sp.	Mountain, Promontory
Morue	Fr.	Hill
Moyen	Fr.	Middle
Muang	Siamese	Town
Mui	Vietnamese	Cape, Point
Mys	Russ.	Cape
Nada	Jap.	Sea
Naka	Jap.	Middle
Nam	Burm., Lao	River
Namakzar	Per.	Salt Waste
Nan	Jap.	South
Nes	Nor.	Cape, Point
Nevado	Sp.	Snow-covered Peak
Nieder	Ger.	Lower
Nishi, Nisi	Jap.	West
Nizhni, Nizhnyaya	Russ.	Lower
Njarga	Finn.	Peninsula, Promontory
Nong	Thai	Lake
Noord	Du.	North
Nord	Fr., Ger.	North
Norte	Sp., It., Port.	North
Nos	Russ.	Cape
Novi, Novaya	Russ.	New
Nur, Nuur	Ch., Mong.	Lake
Nuruu	Mong.	Mountains
Nusa	Malay	Island
Ny, Nya	Nor., Sw.	New
O	Jap.	Big
Ö	Nor., Sw.	Island
Ober	Ger.	Upper
Occidental, Occidentale	Sp., It.	Western
Odde	Dan.	Point
Oeste	Port.	West
Ooster	Du.	Eastern
Opper, Over	Du.	Upper
Oriental	Sp., Fr.	Eastern
Orientale	It.	Eastern
Orta	Turk.	Middle
Ost	Ger.	East
Ostrov	Russ.	Island
Ouest	Fr.	West
Öy	Nor.	Island
Ozero	Russ.	Lake
Pampa	Sp.	Plain
Pas	Fr.	Channel, Strait
Paso	Sp.	Pass
Passo	It., Port.	Pass
Peña	Sp.	Rock, Mountain
Pendi	Ch.	Basin
Penisola	It.	Peninsula
Pequeño	Sp.	Small
Pereval	Russ.	Pass
Peski	Russ.	Desert
Petit, Petite	Fr.	Small
Phu	Lao, Annamese	Mtn.
Pic	Fr.	Mountain
Piccolo	It.	Small
Pico	Port., Sp.	Mountain, Peak
Pik	Russ.	Mountain, Peak
Piton	Fr.	Mountain, Peak
Planalto	Port.	Plateau
Plato	Russ.	Plateau
Pointe	Fr.	Point
Poluostrov	Russ.	Peninsula
Ponta	Port.	Point
Presa	Sp.	Reservoir
Presqu'île	Fr.	Peninsula
Proliv	Russ.	Strait
Pulou, Pulo	Malay	Island
Punt	Du.	Point
Punta	Sp., It., Port.	Point
Qiryat	Hebrew	City, Settlement
Qum	Turk.	Desert
Qundao	Ch.	Islands
Rada	Sp.	Inlet
Rade	Fr.	Bay, Inlet
Ras	Arabic	Cape
Reka	Russ.	River
Retto	Jap.	Archipelago
Ria	Sp.	Estuary
Río	Sp.	River
Rivier, Rivière	Du., Fr.	River
Rud	Per.	River
Sai	Jap.	West
Saki	Jap.	Cape
Salar, Salina	Sp.	Salt Deposit
Salto	Sp., Port.	Falls
San	Jap., Korean	Hill
Sanmaek	Korean	Mt. Range
Schiereiland	Du.	Peninsula
Se	Camb., Khmer	River
See	Ger.	Sea, Lake
Selvas	Sp., Port.	Woods, Forest
Seno	Sp.	Bay, Gulf
Serra	Port.	Mts.
Serranía	Sp.	Mts.
Seto	Jap.	Strait
Settentrionale	It.	Northern
Severni, Severnaya	Russ.	North
Shamo	Ch.	Desert
Shan	Ch., Jap.	Hill, Mts.
Shankou	Ch.	Pass
Shatt	Arabic	River
Shima	Jap.	Island
Shimo	Jap.	Lower
Shin	Jap.	Land
Shiro	Jap.	White
Shoto	Jap.	Islands
Si	Ch.	West
Sierra	Sp.	Mt. Range, Mts.
Sjö	Nor., Sw.	Lake, Sea
Sok, Suk, Souk	Arabic	Market
Song	Annamese	River
Sopka	Russ.	Volcano
Spitze	Ger.	Mt. Peak
Sredni, Srednyaya	Russ.	Middle
Stad	Dan., Nor., Sw.	City
Stari, Staraya	Russ.	Old
Step	Russ.	Treeless Plain
Straat	Du.	Strait
Strasse	Ger.	Strait
Stretto	It.	Strait
Ström	Dan., Nor., Sw.	Sound
Stung	Camb., Khmer	River
Su	Turk.	River
Sud, Süd	Sp., Fr., Ger.	South
Suido	Jap.	Strait, Channel
Sul	Port.	South
Sund	Dan., Nor., Sw.	Sound
Sungei	Malay	River
Supérieur	Fr.	Upper
Superior, Superiore	Sp., It.	Upper
Sur	Sp.	South
Suyu	Turk.	River
Ta	Ch.	Big
Tafelland	Du.	Plateau
Tagh	Turk.	Mt. Range
Take	Jap.	Peak, Ridge
Takht	Arabic	Lower
Tal	Ger.	Valley
Tanjung	Malay	Cape, Point
Tell	Arabic	Hill
Thale	Thai	Sea, Lake
Tind	Nor.	Peak
Tō	Jap.	East
To	Jap.	Island
Toge	Jap.	Pass
Trask	Finn.	Lake
Tugh	Somali	Dry River
Ujung	Malay	Point
Umi	Jap.	Bay
Unter	Ger.	Lower
Ura	Jap.	Inlet
Uul	Mong.	Mountain
Val	Fr.	Valley
Vatn	Nor.	Lake
Vecchio	It.	Old
Veld	Du.	Plain, Field
Velho	Port.	Old
Verkhni	Russ.	Upper
Vesi	Finn.	Lake
Viejo	Sp.	Old
Vik	Nor., Sw.	Bay
Vishni, Vishnyaya	Russ.	High
Vodokhranilishche	Russ.	Reservoir
Volcán	Sp.	Volcano
Vostochni, Vostochnaya	Russ.	East, Eastern
Wadi	Arabic	Dry River
Wald	Ger.	Forest
Wan	Jap.	Bay
Westersch	Du.	Western
Wüste	Ger.	Desert
Yama	Jap.	Mountain
Yug, Yuzhni, Yuzhnaya	Russ.	South, Southern
Zaki	Jap.	Cape
Zaliv	Russ.	Bay, Gulf
Zangbo	Tibetan	River, Stream
Zapadni, Zapadnaya	Russ.	Western
Zee	Du.	Sea
Zemlya	Russ.	Land
Zizhiqu	Ch.	Autonomous Region
Zuid	Du.	South

MAP PROJECTIONS
by Erwin Raisz

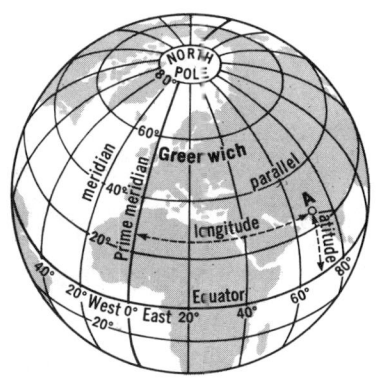

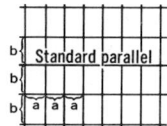

Rectangular Projection

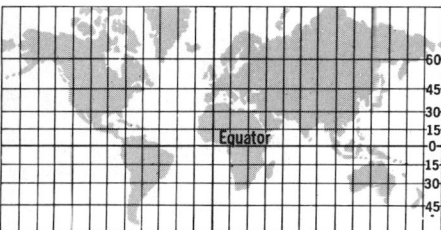

Mercator Projection

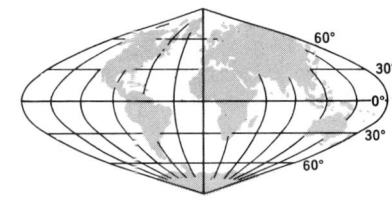

Sinusoidal Projection

Our earth is rotating around its *axis* once a day. The two end points of its axis are the *poles;* the line circling the earth midway between the poles is the *equator.* The arc from either of the poles to the equator is divided into 90 *degrees.* The distance, expressed in degrees, from the equator to any point is its *latitude* and circles of equal latitude are the *parallels.* On maps it is customary to show parallels of evenly-spaced degrees such as every fifth or every tenth.

The equator is divided into 360 degrees. Lines circling from pole to pole through the degree points on the equator are called *meridians.* They are all equal in length but by international agreement the meridian passing through the Greenwich Observatory in London has been chosen as *prime meridian.* The distance, expressed in degrees, from the prime meridian to any point is its *longitude.* While meridians are all equal in length, parallels become shorter and shorter as they approach the poles. Whereas one degree of latitude represents everywhere approximately 69 miles, one degree of longitude varies from 69 miles at the equator to nothing at the poles.

Each degree is divided into 60 minutes and each minute into 60 seconds. One minute of latitude equals a nautical mile.

The map is flat but the earth is nearly spherical. Neither a rubber ball nor any part of a rubber ball may be flattened without stretching or tearing unless the part is very small. To present the curved surface of the earth on a flat map is not difficult as long as the areas under consideration are small, but the mapping of countries, continents, or the whole earth requires some kind of *projection.* Any regular set of parallels and meridians upon which a map can be drawn makes a map projection. Many systems are used.

In any projection only the parallels or the meridians or some other set of lines can be *true* (the same length as on the globe of corresponding scale); all other lines are too long or too short. Only on a globe is it possible to have both the parallels and the meridians true. The scale given on a flat map cannot be true everywhere. The construction of the various projections begins usually with laying out the parallels or meridians which have true lengths.

RECTANGULAR PROJECTION — This is a set of evenly-placed meridians and horizontal parallels. The central or *standard parallel* and all meridians are true. All other parallels are either too long or too short. The projection is used for simple maps of small areas, as city plans, etc.

MERCATOR PROJECTION — In this projection the meridians are evenly-spaced vertical lines. The parallels are horizontal, spaced so that their length has the same relation to the meridians as on a globe. As the meridians converge at higher latitudes on the globe, while on the map they do not, the parallels have to be drawn also farther and farther apart to maintain the correct relationship. When every very small area has the same shape as on a globe we call the projection *conformal.* The most interesting quality of this projection is that all *compass directions* appear as straight lines. For this reason it is generally used for marine charts. It is also frequently used for world maps in spite of the fact that the high latitudes are very much exaggerated in size. Only the equator is true to scale; all other parallels and meridians are too long. The Mercator projection did *not* derive from projecting a globe upon a cylinder.

SINUSOIDAL PROJECTION — The parallels are truly-spaced horizontal lines. They are divided truly and the connecting curves make the meridians. It does not make a good world map because the outer regions are distorted, but the

central portion is good and this part is often used for maps of Africa and South America. Every part of the map has the same area as the corresponding area on the globe. It is an *equal-area* projection.

MOLLWEIDE PROJECTION — The meridians are equally-spaced ellipses; the parallels are horizontal lines spaced so that every belt of latitude should have the same area as on a globe. This projection is popular for world maps, especially in European atlases.

Mollweide Projection

GOODE'S INTERRUPTED PROJECTIONS—Only the good central part of the Mollweide or sinusoidal (or both) projection is used and the oceans are cut. This makes an equal-area map with little distortion of shape. It is commonly used for world maps.

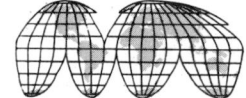
Goode's Interrupted Projection

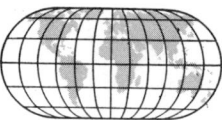
Eckert Projection

ECKERT PROJECTIONS — These are similar to the sinusoidal or the Mollweide projections, but the poles are shown as lines half the length of the equator. There are several variants; the meridians are either sine curves or ellipses; the parallels are horizontal and spaced either evenly or so as to make the projection equal area. Their use for world maps is increasing. The figure shows the elliptical equal-area variant.

CONIC PROJECTION — The original idea of the conic projection is that of capping the globe by a cone upon which both the parallels and meridians are projected from the center of the globe. The cone is then cut open and laid flat. A cone can be made tangent to any chosen *standard parallel.*

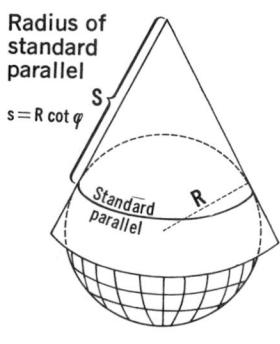

Radius of standard parallel

$s = R \cot \varphi$

Standard parallel

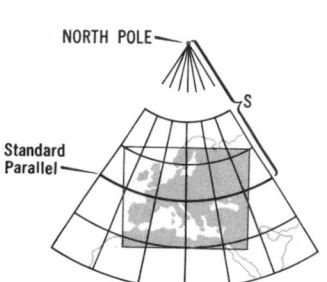
Conic Projection

The actually-used conic projection is a modification of this idea. The radius of the standard parallel is obtained as above. The meridians are straight radiating lines spaced truly on the standard parallel. The parallels are concentric circles spaced at true distances. All parallels except the standard are too long. The projection is used for maps of countries in middle latitudes, as it presents good shapes with small scale error.

There are several variants: The use of *two standard parallels,* one near the top, the other near the bottom of the map, reduces the scale error. In the *Albers projection* the parallels are spaced unevenly, to make the projection equal-area. This is a good projection for the United States. In the *Lambert conformal conic projection* the parallels are spaced so that any small quadrangle of the grid should have the same shape as on the globe. This is the best projection for air-navigation charts as it has relatively straight azimuths.

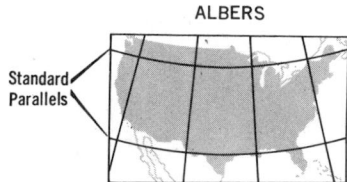
Albers Projection

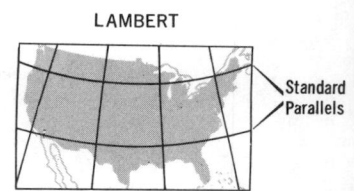
Lambert Conformal Conic Projection

An *azimuth* is a great-circle direction reckoned clockwise from north. A *great-circle direction* points to a place along the shortest line on the earth's surface. This is not the same as compass direction. The center of a great circle is the center of the globe.

BONNE PROJECTION — The parallels are laid out exactly as in the conic projection. All parallels are divided truly and the connecting curves make the meridians. It is an equal-area projection. It is used for maps of the northern continents, as Asia, Europe, and North America.

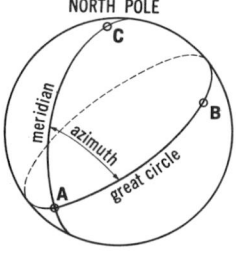

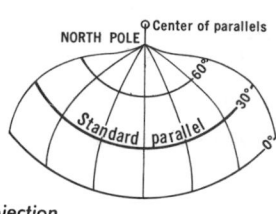
Bonne Projection

POLYCONIC PROJECTION — The central meridian is divided truly. The parallels are non-concentric circles, the radii of which are obtained by drawing tangents to the globe as though the globe were covered by several cones rather than by only one. Each parallel is divided truly and the connecting curves make the meridians. All meridians except the central one are too long. This projection is used for large-scale topographic sheets — less often for countries or continents.

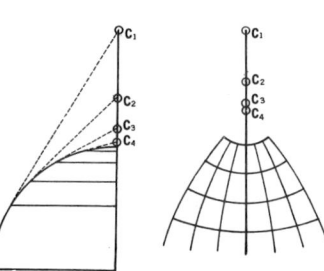
Polyconic Projection

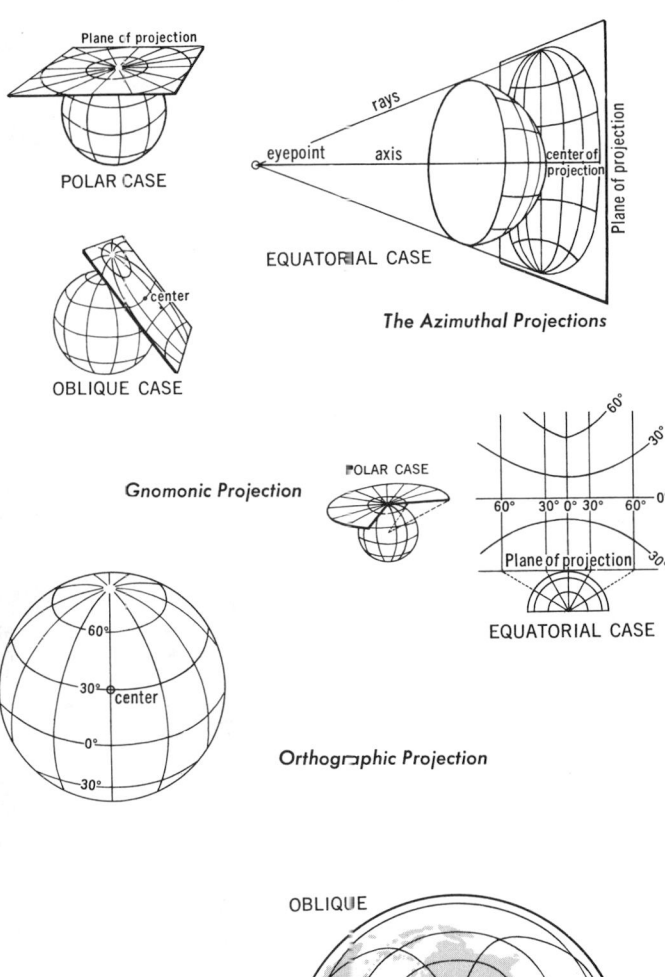

The Azimuthal Projections

Gnomonic Projection

Orthographic Projection

Azimuthal Equidistant Projection

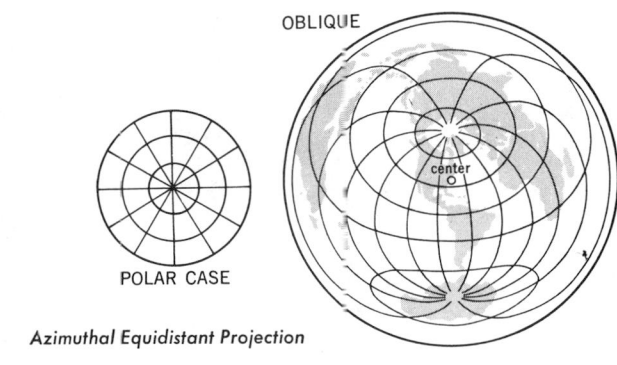

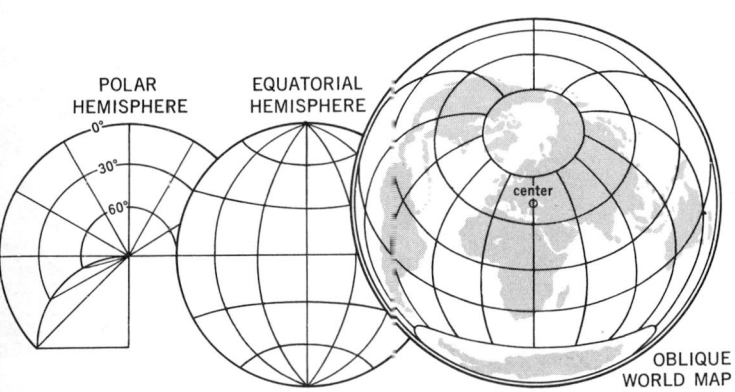

Lambert Azimuthal Equal-Area Projection

THE AZIMUTHAL PROJECTIONS

In this group a part of the globe is projected from an eyepoint onto a plane. The eyepoint can be at different distances, making different projections. The plane of projection can be tangent at the equator, at a pole, or at any other point on which we want to focus attention. The most important quality of all azimuthal projections is that they show every point at its true direction (azimuth) from the center point, and all points equally distant from the center point will be equally distant on the map also.

GNOMONIC PROJECTION

This projection has the eyepoint at the center of the globe Only the central part is good; the outer regions are badly distorted. Yet the projection has one important quality, all great circles being shown as straight lines. For this reason it is used for laying out the routes for long range flying or trans-oceanic navigation.

ORTHOGRAPHIC PROJECTION

This projection has the eyepoint at infinite distance and the projecting rays are parallel. The polar or equatorial varieties are rare but the oblique case became very popular on account of its visual quality. It looks like a picture of a globe. Although the distortion on the peripheries is extreme, we see it correctly because the eye perceives it not as a map but as a picture of a three-dimensional globe. Obviously only a hemisphere (half globe) can be shown.

Some azimuthal projections do not derive from the actual process of projecting from an eyepoint, but are arrived at by other means:

AZIMUTHAL EQUIDISTANT PROJECTION

This is the only projection in which every point is shown both at true great-circle direction and at true distance from the center point, but all other directions and distances are distorted. The principle of the projection can best be understood from the polar case. Most polar maps are in this projection. The oblique case is used for radio direction finding, for earthquake research, and in long-distance flying. A separate map has to be constructed for each central point selected.

LAMBERT AZIMUTHAL EQUAL-AREA PROJECTION

The construction of this projection can best be understood from the polar case. All three cases are widely used. It makes a good polar map and it is often extended to include the southern continents. It is the most common projection used for maps of the Eastern and Western Hemispheres, and it is a good projection for continents as it shows correct areas with relatively little distortion of shape. Most of the continent maps in this atlas are in this projection.

IN THIS ATLAS, on almost all maps, parallels and meridians have been marked because they are useful for the following:

(a) They show the north-south and east-west directions which appear on many maps at oblique angles especially near the margins.

(b) With the help of parallels and meridians every place can be exactly located; for instance, New York City is at 41° N and 74° W on any map.

(c) They help to measure distances even in the distorted parts of the map. The scale given on each map is true only along certain lines which are specified in the foregoing discussion for each projection. One degree of latitude equals nearly 69 statute miles or 60 nautical miles. The length of one degree of longitude varies (1° long. = 1° lat. × cos lat.).

WORLD STATISTICAL TABLES

Elements of the Solar System

	Mean Distance from Sun: in Miles	in Kilometers	Period of Revolution around Sun	Period of Rotation on Axis	Equatorial Diameter: in Miles	in Kilometers	Surface Gravity (Earth = 1)	Mass (Earth = 1)	Mean Density (Water = 1)	Number of Satellites
MERCURY	35,990,000	57,900,000	87.97 days	59 days	3,032	4,880	0.38	0.055	5.5	0
VENUS	67,240,000	108,200,000	224.70 days	243 days†	7,523	12,106	0.90	0.815	5.25	0
EARTH	93,000,000	149,700,000	365.26 days	23h 56m	7,926	12,755	1.00	1.00	5.5	1
MARS	141,730,000	228,100,000	687.00 days	24h 37m	4,220	6,790	0.38	0.107	4.0	2
JUPITER	483,880,000	778,700,000	11.86 years	9h 50m	88,750	142,800	2.87	317.9	1.3	16
SATURN	887,130,000	1,427,700,000	29.46 years	10h 14m	74,580	120,020	1.32	95.2	0.7	17
URANUS	1,783,700,000	2,870,500,000	84.01 years	10h 49m†	31,600	50,900	0.93	14.6	1.3	5
NEPTUNE	2,795,500,000	4,498,800,000	164.79 years	15h 48m	30,200	48,600	1.23	17.2	1.8	3
PLUTO	3,667,900,000	5,902,800,000	247.70 years	6.39 days (?)	1,500	2,400	0.03 (?)	0.01(?)	0.7(?)	1

†Retrograde motion

Facts About the Sun

Equatorial diameter	865,000 miles	1,392,000 kilometers
Period of rotation on axis	25-35 days*	
Orbit of galaxy	every 225 million years	
Surface gravity (Earth = 1)	27.8	
Mass (Earth = 1)	333,000	
Density (Water = 1)	1.4	
Mean distance from Earth	93,000,000 miles	149,700,000 kilometers

*Rotation of 25 days at Equator, decreasing to about 35 days at the poles.

Facts About the Moon

Equatorial diameter	2,160 miles	3,476 kilometers
Period of rotation on axis	27 days, 7 hours, 43 minutes	
Period of revolution around Earth (sidereal month)	27 days, 7 hours, 43 minutes	
Phase period between new moons (synodic month)	29 days, 12 hours, 44 minutes	
Surface gravity (Earth = 1)	0.16	
Mass (Earth = 1)	0.0123	
Density (Water = 1)	3.34	
Maximum distance from Earth	252,710 miles	406,690 kilometers
Minimum distance from Earth	221,460 miles	356,400 kilometers
Mean distance from Earth	238,860 miles	384,400 kilometers

Dimensions of the Earth

	Area in Sq. Miles	Sq. Kilometers
Superficial area	196,939,000	510,073,000
Land surface	57,506,000	148,941,000
Water surface	139,433,000	361,132,000

	Miles	Kilometers
Equatorial circumference	24,902	40,075
Polar circumference	24,860	40,008
Equatorial diameter	7,926.4	12,756.4
Polar diameter	7,899.8	12,713.6
Equatorial radius	3,963.2	6,378.2
Polar radius	3,949.9	6,356.8
Volume of the Earth	2.6×10^{11} cubic miles	10.84×10^{11} cubic kilometers
Mass or weight	6.6×10^{21} short tons	6.0×10^{21} metric tons
Maximum distance from Sun	94,600,000 miles	152,000,000 kilometers
Minimum distance from Sun	91,300,000 miles	147,000,000 kilometers

The Continents

	Area in: Sq. Miles	Sq. Km.	Percent of World's Land
Asia	17,128,500	44,362,815	29.5
Africa	11,707,000	30,321,130	20.2
North America	9,363,000	24,250,170	16.2
South America	6,875,000	17,806,250	11.8
Antarctica	5,500,000	14,245,000	9.5
Europe	4,057,000	10,507,630	7.0
Australia	2,966,136	7,682,300	5.1

Oceans and Major Seas

	Area in: Sq. Miles	Sq. Km.	Greatest Depth in: Feet	Meters
Pacific Ocean	64,186,000	166,241,700	36,198	11,033
Atlantic Ocean	31,862,000	82,522,600	28,374	8,648
Indian Ocean	28,350,000	73,426,500	25,344	7,725
Arctic Ocean	5,427,000	14,056,000	17,880	5,450
Caribbean Sea	970,000	2,512,300	24,720	7,535
Mediterranean Sea	969,000	2,509,700	16,896	5,150
Bering Sea	875,000	2,266,250	15,800	4,800
Gulf of Mexico	600,000	1,554,000	12,300	3,750
Sea of Okhotsk	590,000	1,528,100	11,070	3,370
East China Sea	482,000	1,248,400	9,500	2,900
Sea of Japan	389,000	1,007,500	12,280	3,743
Hudson Bay	317,500	822,300	846	258
North Sea	222,000	575,000	2,200	670
Black Sea	185,000	479,150	7,365	2,245
Red Sea	169,000	437,700	7,200	2,195
Baltic Sea	163,000	422,170	1,506	459

Major Ship Canals

	Length in: Miles	Kms.	Minimum Depth in: Feet	Meters
Volga-Baltic, U.S.S.R.	225	362	—	—
Baltic-White Sea, U.S.S.R.	140	225	16	5
Suez, Egypt	100.76	162	42	13
Albert, Belgium	80	129	16.5	5
Moscow-Volga, U.S.S.R.	80	129	18	6
Volga-Don, U.S.S.R.	62	100	—	—
Göta, Sweden	54	87	10	3
Kiel (Nord-Ostsee), Ger.	53.2	86	38	12
Panama Canal, Panama	50.72	82	41.6	13
Houston Ship, U.S.A.	50	81	36	11

Largest Islands

	Area in: Sq. Mi.	Sq. Km.		Area in: Sq. Mi.	Sq. Km.		Area in: Sq. Mi.	Sq. Km.
Greenland	840,000	2,175,600	South I., New Zealand	58,393	151,238	Hokkaido, Japan	28,983	75,066
New Guinea	305,000	789,950	Java, Indonesia	48,842	126,501	Banks, Canada	27,038	70,028
Borneo	290,000	751,100	North I., New Zealand	44,187	114,444	Ceylon, Sri Lanka	25,332	65,610
Madagascar	226,400	586,376	Newfoundland, Canada	42,031	108,860	Tasmania, Australia	24,600	63,710
Baffin, Canada	195,928	507,454	Cuba	40,533	104,981	Svalbard, Norway	23,957	62,049
Sumatra, Indonesia	164,000	424,760	Luzon, Philippines	40,420	104,688	Devon, Canada	21,331	55,247
Honshu, Japan	88,000	227,920	Iceland	39,768	103,000	Novaya Zemlya (north isl.), U.S.S.R.	18,600	48,200
Great Britain	84,400	218,896	Mindanao, Philippines	36,537	94,631	Marajó, Brazil	17,991	46,597
Victoria, Canada	83,896	217,290	Ireland	31,743	82,214	Tierra del Fuego, Chile & Argentina	17,900	46,360
Ellesmere, Canada	75,767	196,236	Sakhalin, U.S.S.R.	29,500	76,405	Alexander, Antarctica	16,700	43,250
Celebes, Indonesia	72,986	189,034	Hispaniola, Haiti & Dom. Rep.	29,399	76,143			

Principal Mountains of the World

Mountain	Feet	Meters
Everest, Nepal-China	29,028	8,848
Godwin Austen (K2), Pakistan-China	28,250	8,611
Kanchenjunga, Nepal-India	28,208	8,598
Lhotse, Nepal-China	27,923	8,511
Makalu, Nepal-China	27,824	8,481
Dhaulagiri, Nepal	26,810	8,172
Nanga Parbat, Pakistan	26,660	8,126
Annapurna, Nepal	26,504	8,078
Gasherbrum, Pakistan-China	26,740	8,068
Nanda Devi, India	25,645	7,817
Rakaposhi, Pakistan	25,550	7,788
Kamet, India	25,447	7,756
Gurla Mandhada, China	25,355	7,728
Kongur Shan, China	25,325	7,719
Tirich Mir, Pakistan	25,230	7,690
Gongga Shan, China	24,790	7,556
Muztagata, China	24,757	7,546
Communism Peak, U.S.S.R.	24,599	7,498
Pobeda Peak, U.S.S.R.	24,406	7,439
Chomo Lhari, Bhutan-China	23,997	7,314
Muztag, China	23,891	7,282
Cerro Aconcagua, Argentina	22,831	6,959
Ojos del Salado, Chile-Argentina	22,572	6,880
Bonete, Chile-Argentina	22,541	6,870
Tupungato, Chile-Argentina	22,310	6,800
Pissis, Argentina	22,241	6,779
Mercedario, Argentina	22,211	6,770
Huascarán, Peru	22,205	6,768
Llullaillaco, Chile-Argentina	22,057	6,723
Nevada Ancohuma, Bolivia	21,489	6,550
Illampu, Bolivia	21,276	6,485
Chimborazo, Ecuador	20,561	6,267
McKinley, Alaska	20,320	6,194
Logan, Canada (Yukon)	19,524	5,951
Cotopaxi, Ecuador	19,347	5,897
Kilimanjaro, Tanzania	19,340	5,895
El Misti, Peru	19,101	5,822
Pico Cristóbal Colón, Colombia	19,029	5,800
Huila, Colombia	18,865	5,750
Citlaltépetl (Orizaba), Mexico	18,855	5,747
El'brus, U.S.S.R.	18,510	5,642
Damavand, Iran	18,376	5,601
St. Elias, Alaska-Canada (Yukon)	18,008	5,489
Vilcanota, Peru	17,999	5,486
Popocatépetl, Mexico	17,887	5,452
Dykhtau, U.S.S.R.	17,070	5,203
Kenya, Kenya	17,058	5,199
Ararat, Turkey	16,946	5,165
Vinson Massif, Antarctica	16,864	5,140
Margherita (Ruwenzori), Africa	16,795	5,119
Kazbek, U.S.S.R.	16,512	5,033
Puncak Jaya, Indonesia	16,503	5,030
Tyree, Antarctica	16,289	4,965
Blanc, France	15,771	4,807
Klyuchevskaya Sopka, U.S.S.R.	15,584	4,750
Fairweather (Br. Col., Canada)	15,300	4,663
Dufourspitze (Mte. Rosa), Italy-Switzerland	15,203	4,634
Ras Dashan, Ethiopia	15,157	4,620
Matterhorn, Switzerland	14,691	4,478
Whitney, California, U.S.A.	14,494	4,418
Elbert, Colorado, U.S.A.	14,433	4,399
Rainier, Washington, U.S.A.	14,410	4,392
Shasta, California, U.S.A.	14,162	4,350
Pikes Peak, Colorado, U.S.A.	14,110	4,301
Finsteraarhorn, Switzerland	14,022	4,274
Mauna Kea, Hawaii, U.S.A.	13,796	4,205
Mauna Loa, Hawaii, U.S.A.	13,677	4,169
Jungfrau, Switzerland	13,642	4,158
Cameroon, Cameroon	13,350	4,069
Grossglockner, Austria	12,457	3,797
Fuji, Japan	12,389	3,776
Cook, New Zealand	12,349	3,764
Etna, Italy	11,053	3,369
Kosciusko, Australia	7,310	2,228
Mitchell, North Carolina, U.S.A.	6,684	2,037

Longest Rivers of the World

River	Miles	Kms.
Nile, Africa	4,145	6,671
Amazon, S. Amer.	3,915	6,300
Chang Jiang (Yangtze), China	3,900	6,276
Mississippi-Missouri-Red Rock, U.S.A.	3,741	6,019
Ob'Irtysh-Black Irtysh, U.S.S.R.	3,362	5,411
Yenisey-Angara, U.S.S.R.	3,100	4,989
Huang He (Yellow), China	2,877	4,630
Amur-Shilka-Onon, Asia	2,744	4,416
Lena, U.S.S.R.	2,734	4,400
Congo (Zaire), Africa	2,718	4,374
Mackenzie-Peace-Finlay, Canada	2,635	4,241
Mekong, Asia	2,610	4,200
Missouri-Red Rock, U.S.A.	2,564	4,125
Niger, Africa	2,548	4,101
Paraná-La Plata, S. Amer.	2,450	3,943
Mississippi, U.S.A.	2,348	3,778
Murray-Darling, Australia	2,310	3,718
Volga, U.S.S.R.	2,194	3,531
Madeira, S. Amer.	2,013	3,240
Purus, S. Amer.	1,995	3,211
Yukon, Alaska-Canada	1,979	3,185
St. Lawrence, Canada-U.S.A.	1,900	3,058
Rio Grande, Mexico-U.S.A.	1,885	3,034
Syrdar'ya-Naryn, U.S.S.R.	1,859	2,992
São Francisco, Brazil	1,811	2,914
Indus, Asia	1,800	2,897
Danube, Europe	1,775	2,857
Salween, Asia	1,770	2,849
Brahmaputra, Asia	1,700	2,736
Euphrates, Asia	1,700	2,736
Tocantins, Brazil	1,677	2,699
Xi (Si), China	1,650	2,655
Amudar'ya, Asia	1,616	2,601
Nelson-Saskatchewan, Canada	1,600	2,575
Orinoco, S. Amer.	1,600	2,575
Zambezi, Africa	1,600	2,575
Paraguay, S. Amer.	1,584	2,549
Kolyma, U.S.S.R.	1,562	2,514
Ganges, Asia	1,550	2,494
Ural, U.S.S.R.	1,509	2,428
Japurá, S. Amer.	1,500	2,414
Arkansas, U.S.A.	1,450	2,334
Colorado, U.S.A.-Mexico	1,450	2,334
Negro, S. Amer.	1,400	2,253
Dnieper, U.S.S.R.	1,368	2,202
Orange, Africa	1,350	2,173
Irrawaddy, Burma	1,325	2,132
Brazos, U.S.A.	1,309	2,107
Ohio-Allegheny, U.S.A.	1,306	2,102
Kama, U.S.S.R.	1,262	2,031
Red, U.S.A.	1,222	1,966
Don, U.S.S.R.	1,222	1,967
Columbia, U.S.A.-Canada	1,214	1,953
Saskatchewan, Canada	1,205	1,939
Peace-Finlay, Canada	1,195	1,923
Tigris, Asia	1,181	1,901
Darling, Australia	1,160	1,867
Angara, U.S.S.R.	1,135	1,827
Sungari, Asia	1,130	1,819
Pechora, U.S.S.R.	1,124	1,809
Snake, U.S.A.	1,000	1,609
Churchill, Canada	1,000	1,609
Pilcomayo, S. Amer.	1,000	1,609
Magdalena, Colombia	1,000	1,609
Uruguay, S. Amer.	994	1,600
Platte-N. Platte, U.S.A.	990	1,593
Ohio, U.S.A.	981	1,578
Pecos, U.S.A.	926	1,490
Oka, U.S.S.R.	918	1,477
Canadian, U.S.A.	906	1,458
Colorado, Texas, U.S.A.	894	1,439
Dniester, U.S.S.R.	876	1,410

Principal Natural Lakes

Lake	Area Sq. Miles	Area Sq. Km.	Max. Depth Feet	Max. Depth Meters
Caspian Sea, U.S.S.R.-Iran	143,243	370,999	3,264	995
Lake Superior, U.S.A.-Canada	31,820	82,414	1,329	405
Lake Victoria, Africa	26,724	69,215	270	82
Lake Huron, U.S.A.-Canada	23,010	59,596	748	228
Lake Michigan, U.S.A.	22,400	58,016	923	281
Aral Sea, U.S.S.R.	15,830	41,000	213	65
Lake Tanganyika, Africa	12,650	32,764	4,700	1,433
Lake Baykal, U.S.S.R.	12,162	31,500	5,316	1,620
Great Bear Lake, Canada	12,096	31,328	1,356	413
Lake Nyasa (Malawi), Africa	11,555	29,928	2,320	707
Great Slave Lake, Canada	11,031	28,570	2,015	614
Lake Erie, U.S.A.-Canada	9,940	25,745	210	64
Lake Winnipeg, Canada	9,417	24,390	60	18
Lake Ontario, U.S.A.-Canada	7,540	19,529	775	244
Lake Ladoga, U.S.S.R.	7,104	18,399	738	225
Lake Balkhash, U.S.S.R.	7,027	18,200	87	27
Lake Maracaibo, Venezuela	5,120	13,261	100	31
Lake Chad, Africa	4,000-10,000	10,360-25,900	25	8
Lake Onega, U.S.S.R.	3,710	9,609	377	115
Lake Eyre, Australia	3,500-0	9,000-0	—	—
Lake Titicaca, Peru-Bolivia	3,200	8,288	1,000	305
Lake Nicaragua, Nicaragua	3,100	8,029	230	70
Lake Athabasca, Canada	3,064	7,936	400	122
Reindeer Lake, Canada	2,568	6,651	—	—
Lake Turkana (Rudolf), Africa	2,463	6,379	240	73
Issyk-Kul', U.S.S.R.	2,425	6,281	2,303	702
Lake Torrens, Australia	2,230	5,776	—	—
Vänern, Sweden	2,156	5,584	328	100
Nettilling Lake, Canada	2,140	5,543	—	—
Lake Winnipegosis, Canada	2,075	5,374	38	12
Lake Mobutu Sese Seko (Albert), Africa	2,075	5,374	160	49
Kariba Lake, Zambia-Zimbabwe	2,050	5,310	295	90
Lake Nipigon, Canada	1,872	4,848	540	165
Lake Mweru, Zaire-Zambia	1,800	4,662	60	18
Lake Manitoba, Canada	1,799	4,659	12	4
Lake Taymyr, U.S.S.R.	1,737	4,499	85	26
Lake Khanka, China-U.S.S.R.	1,700	4,403	33	10
Lake Kioga, Uganda	1,700	4,403	25	8

Foreign City Weather

Two figures are given for each of the months, thus 88/73. The first figure is the average daily high temperature (°F) and the second is the average daily low temperature (°F) for the month. The **boldface** figures indicate the average number of days with rain for each month.

City	January	February	March	April	May	June	July	August	September	October	November	December
ABIDJAN, Ivory Coast	88/73 **3**	90/75 **4**	90/75 **6**	90/75 **9**	88/75 **16**	85/73 **18**	83/73 **8**	82/71 **7**	83/73 **8**	85/74 **13**	87/74 **13**	88/74 **6**
ACAPULCO, Mexico	85/70 **0**	87/70 **0**	87/70 **0**	87/71 **1**	89/74 **4**	89/76 **15**	89/75 **11**	89/75 **14**	88/75 **18**	88/74 **12**	88/72 **4**	87/70 **1**
ACCRA, Ghana	87/73 **1**	88/75 **2**	88/76 **4**	88/76 **6**	87/75 **9**	84/74 **10**	81/73 **4**	80/71 **3**	81/73 **4**	85/74 **6**	87/75 **3**	88/75 **2**
ADDIS ABABA, Ethiopia	75/43 **2**	76/47 **5**	77/49 **8**	77/50 **10**	77/50 **10**	74/49 **20**	69/50 **28**	69/50 **27**	72/49 **21**	75/45 **3**	75/45 **3**	73/41 **2**
ALGIERS, Algeria	59/49 **11**	61/49 **9**	63/52 **9**	68/55 **5**	73/59 **5**	78/65 **4**	83/70 **1**	85/71 **1**	81/69 **4**	74/63 **7**	66/56 **11**	60/51 **12**
AMSTERDAM, Netherlands	40/34 **19**	41/34 **15**	46/37 **13**	52/43 **14**	60/50 **12**	65/55 **12**	69/59 **14**	68/59 **14**	64/56 **15**	56/48 **18**	47/41 **19**	41/35 **19**
ANKARA, Turkey	39/24 **8**	42/26 **8**	51/31 **7**	63/40 **7**	73/49 **7**	78/53 **5**	86/59 **2**	87/59 **1**	78/52 **3**	69/44 **5**	57/37 **6**	43/29 **9**
APIA, Western Samoa	86/75 **22**	85/76 **19**	86/74 **18**	86/75 **14**	85/74 **12**	85/74 **7**	85/74 **9**	84/75 **9**	84/74 **11**	85/75 **14**	86/74 **16**	85/74 **19**
ATHENS, Greece	54/42 **7**	55/43 **9**	60/46 **5**	67/52 **3**	77/60 **3**	85/67 **2**	90/72 **1**	90/72 **1**	83/66 **2**	74/60 **4**	64/52 **6**	57/46 **7**
BAGHDAD, Iraq	60/39 **4**	64/42 **3**	71/48 **4**	85/57 **3**	97/67 **1**	105/73 **0**	110/76 **0**	110/76 **0**	104/70 **0**	92/61 **1**	77/51 **3**	64/42 **5**
BALI, Indonesia	88/74 **19**	88/74 **14**	88/74 **13**	88/74 **7**	88/73 **5**	87/71 **3**	87/70 **1**	87/70 **1**	89/71 **0**	90/73 **2**	90/75 **6**	88/74 **14**
BANGKOK, Thailand	89/68 **1**	91/72 **1**	93/75 **3**	95/77 **3**	93/77 **9**	91/76 **10**	90/76 **13**	90/76 **13**	89/76 **15**	88/75 **14**	87/72 **5**	87/68 **1**
BARCELONA, Spain	56/42 **5**	57/44 **4**	61/47 **7**	64/51 **8**	71/57 **8**	77/63 **5**	81/69 **4**	82/69 **5**	78/65 **7**	71/58 **8**	62/50 **7**	57/44 **6**
BEIRUT, Lebanon	62/51 **15**	63/51 **12**	66/54 **9**	72/58 **5**	78/64 **2**	84/71 **0**	83/73 **0**	85/74 **0**	84/74 **1**	85/74 **4**	85/73 **12**	85/73 **15**
BELFAST, Northern Ireland	45/34 **22**	47/34 **18**	49/35 **20**	53/39 **18**	59/43 **17**	64/49 **10**	66/51 **18**	65/51 **20**	62/48 **17**	55/42 **19**	50/37 **21**	46/35 **25**
BELGRADE, Yugoslavia	37/27 **8**	41/27 **6**	53/35 **7**	64/45 **9**	74/53 **9**	79/58 **9**	84/61 **6**	83/60 **7**	76/55 **6**	65/47 **8**	52/39 **7**	40/30 **9**
BERLIN, Germany	35/26 **10**	38/27 **8**	46/32 **9**	55/38 **9**	65/46 **8**	70/51 **9**	74/55 **10**	72/54 **10**	66/48 **8**	55/41 **8**	43/33 **8**	37/29 **11**
BIARRITZ, France	54/40 **10**	52/38 **11**	63/43 **11**	63/44 **11**	69/53 **11**	72/56 **10**	74/55 **10**	77/61 **7**	77/58 **9**	74/55 **11**	58/44 **12**	53/41 **14**
BOGOTA, Colombia	67/48 **6**	68/49 **7**	67/50 **13**	67/51 **20**	66/51 **17**	65/51 **16**	64/50 **18**	65/50 **16**	66/49 **13**	66/50 **20**	66/50 **16**	66/49 **15**
BOMBAY, India	83/67 **1**	83/67 **1**	86/72 **1**	89/76 **1**	91/80 **1**	89/79 **14**	85/77 **21**	85/76 **19**	85/76 **13**	89/76 **3**	89/73 **1**	87/69 **1**
BONN, Germany	39/30 **7**	37/26 **6**	50/35 **7**	58/39 **14**	67/46 **13**	69/52 **19**	73/56 **16**	72/55 **17**	67/50 **16**	58/45 **16**	47/37 **15**	44/36 **15**
BRASILIA, Brazil	80/65 **17**	81/64 **20**	82/64 **7**	82/62 **10**	79/56 **5**	77/52 **2**	78/51 **2**	82/55 **0**	87/60 **2**	82/64 **16**	82/66 **17**	78/64 **16**
BRINDISI, Italy	55/43 **10**	57/43 **6**	60/45 **5**	65/50 **5**	73/57 **5**	80/64 **2**	84/68 **1**	84/69 **3**	80/65 **4**	70/58 **8**	64/52 **10**	58/46 **8**
BUCHAREST, Romania	33/20 **6**	38/24 **5**	51/33 **6**	63/41 **6**	74/51 **8**	81/58 **9**	86/61 **7**	86/60 **5**	76/53 **5**	65/44 **5**	49/35 **6**	37/26 **6**
BUDAPEST, Hungary	35/26 **7**	40/28 **6**	51/36 **7**	62/44 **8**	72/52 **9**	78/57 **7**	82/61 **7**	81/59 **6**	74/53 **7**	61/45 **8**	47/37 **8**	38/31 **9**
BUENOS AIRES, Argentina	85/63 **7**	83/63 **6**	79/60 **7**	72/53 **8**	64/47 **7**	57/41 **7**	57/42 **8**	60/43 **8**	64/46 **8**	69/50 **7**	76/56 **9**	82/61 **8**
CAIRO, Egypt	65/47 **1**	69/48 **1**	75/52 **1**	83/57 **1**	91/63 **1**	95/68 **0**	96/70 **0**	95/71 **0**	90/68 **0**	86/65 **1**	78/58 **1**	68/50 **1**
CALCUTTA, India	80/55 **1**	84/59 **2**	93/69 **2**	97/75 **3**	96/77 **7**	92/79 **13**	89/79 **18**	89/78 **18**	90/78 **13**	89/74 **6**	84/64 **1**	79/55 **1**
CAPE TOWN, South Africa	78/60 **3**	79/60 **2**	77/58 **3**	72/53 **6**	67/49 **9**	65/46 **9**	63/45 **10**	64/46 **9**	65/49 **7**	70/52 **5**	73/55 **3**	76/58 **3**
CARACAS, Venezuela	75/56 **6**	77/56 **2**	79/58 **3**	81/60 **4**	80/62 **9**	78/62 **14**	78/61 **15**	79/61 **15**	80/61 **13**	79/61 **12**	77/60 **13**	78/58 **10**
CHARLOTTE AMALIE, Virgin Islands	82/73 **18**	81/72 **13**	82/73 **12**	88/74 **13**	85/76 **15**	86/77 **15**	87/78 **16**	88/78 **19**	87/77 **17**	87/77 **18**	85/76 **19**	83/77 **18**
COLOMBO, Sri Lanka	86/72 **7**	87/72 **6**	88/74 **8**	88/76 **14**	87/78 **19**	85/77 **18**	85/77 **12**	85/77 **11**	85/77 **13**	85/75 **19**	85/73 **16**	85/72 **10**
COPENHAGEN, Denmark	36/29 **9**	36/28 **7**	41/31 **8**	50/37 **9**	61/44 **8**	67/51 **8**	72/55 **9**	69/54 **12**	63/49 **8**	53/42 **9**	43/35 **10**	38/32 **11**
DARWIN, Australia	90/77 **20**	90/77 **18**	91/77 **17**	92/76 **6**	91/73 **1**	88/69 **1**	87/67 **0**	89/70 **0**	91/74 **2**	93/77 **5**	94/78 **10**	92/78 **15**
DJAKARTA, Indonesia	84/74 **18**	84/74 **17**	86/74 **15**	87/75 **11**	87/75 **9**	87/74 **7**	87/73 **5**	87/73 **4**	88/74 **5**	87/74 **8**	86/74 **12**	85/74 **14**
DUBLIN, Ireland	47/35 **13**	47/35 **11**	51/36 **10**	54/38 **11**	59/42 **11**	65/48 **11**	67/51 **13**	67/51 **13**	63/47 **12**	57/43 **12**	51/38 **12**	47/36 **13**
EDINBURGH, Scotland	43/35 **18**	43/35 **15**	47/36 **15**	50/39 **16**	55/43 **15**	62/48 **15**	65/52 **17**	64/52 **17**	60/48 **16**	53/44 **18**	47/39 **18**	44/36 **17**
FLORENCE, Italy	49/35 **9**	53/36 **9**	60/40 **7**	68/46 **7**	75/53 **9**	84/58 **5**	89/63 **4**	88/62 **4**	81/58 **6**	69/51 **9**	58/42 **10**	50/37 **9**
GENEVA, Switzerland	39/29 **10**	43/30 **9**	51/35 **10**	58/41 **11**	66/48 **12**	73/55 **11**	77/58 **9**	76/57 **10**	69/52 **10**	58/44 **11**	47/37 **11**	40/31 **10**
GUAYAQUIL, Ecuador	88/70 **20**	87/71 **25**	88/72 **24**	89/71 **14**	88/68 **9**	87/68 **4**	84/67 **2**	86/65 **0**	87/66 **2**	86/68 **3**	88/68 **4**	88/70 **10**
HAMBURG, Germany	35/28 **12**	37/30 **10**	42/33 **10**	51/39 **11**	60/47 **9**	67/53 **10**	69/56 **12**	67/55 **13**	63/51 **10**	53/44 **11**	44/36 **11**	38/31 **12**
HAMILTON, Bermuda	68/58 **14**	68/57 **13**	68/57 **12**	71/59 **9**	76/64 **7**	81/69 **9**	85/73 **10**	86/74 **13**	84/72 **10**	79/69 **12**	74/63 **13**	70/60 **15**
HAVANA, Cuba	79/65 **6**	79/65 **4**	81/67 **4**	84/69 **4**	86/72 **7**	88/74 **10**	89/75 **9**	89/75 **10**	88/75 **11**	85/73 **11**	81/69 **7**	79/67 **6**
HELSINKI, Finland	27/17 **11**	26/15 **8**	32/22 **8**	43/31 **8**	55/41 **8**	63/49 **9**	71/57 **8**	66/55 **12**	57/46 **11**	45/37 **12**	37/30 **11**	31/22 **11**
HONG KONG	64/56 **4**	63/55 **5**	67/60 **7**	75/67 **8**	82/74 **13**	85/78 **18**	87/78 **17**	87/78 **15**	85/77 **12**	81/73 **6**	74/65 **2**	68/59 **3**
JERUSALEM, Israel	55/41 **9**	56/42 **11**	65/46 **3**	73/50 **3**	81/57 **1**	85/60 **1**	87/63 **0**	87/64 **0**	85/62 **1**	81/59 **1**	70/53 **4**	59/45 **7**
JOHANNESBURG, South Africa	78/58 **12**	77/58 **9**	75/55 **9**	72/50 **4**	66/43 **3**	62/39 **1**	63/39 **1**	68/43 **1**	73/48 **2**	77/53 **7**	77/55 **10**	78/57 **11**
KARACHI, Pakistan	77/55 **1**	79/58 **1**	85/67 **1**	90/73 **1**	93/79 **1**	93/82 **1**	91/81 **2**	88/79 **2**	88/77 **1**	91/72 **1**	87/64 **1**	80/57 **1**
KINGSTON, Jamaica	86/67 **3**	86/67 **3**	86/68 **2**	87/70 **3**	87/72 **4**	89/74 **5**	90/73 **4**	90/73 **7**	89/73 **6**	88/73 **9**	87/71 **5**	87/69 **4**
LAGOS, Nigeria	88/74 **2**	89/77 **3**	89/78 **7**	89/77 **10**	87/76 **16**	85/74 **20**	83/74 **16**	82/73 **10**	83/74 **14**	85/74 **16**	88/75 **7**	88/75 **2**
LA PAZ, Bolivia	63/43 **21**	63/43 **18**	64/42 **16**	65/40 **9**	64/37 **5**	62/34 **2**	62/33 **2**	63/35 **4**	64/38 **9**	66/40 **9**	67/42 **11**	65/42 **18**

Foreign City Weather

	January	February	March	April	May	June	July	August	September	October	November	December
LAS PALMAS, Canary Is.	70/58 8	71/58 5	71/59 5	71/61 3	73/62 1	75/65 1	77/67 1	79/70 1	79/69 1	79/67 5	76/64 7	72/60 8
LENINGRAD, USSR	23/12 17	24/12 15	33/18 13	45/31 11	58/42 12	66/51 12	71/57 13	66/53 15	57/45 14	45/37 15	34/27 17	26/18 18
LIMA, Peru	82/66 1	83/67 1	83/66 1	80/63 1	74/60 1	68/58 1	67/57 1	66/56 2	68/57 1	71/58 1	74/60 1	78/62 1
LISBON, Portugal	56/46 9	58/47 8	61/49 10	64/52 7	69/56 6	75/60 2	79/63 1	80/64 1	76/62 4	69/57 7	62/52 10	57/47 10
LIVERPOOL, England	44/36 18	44/36 13	48/38 13	52/41 14	58/46 14	63/51 13	66/55 15	65/55 16	61/51 15	55/46 17	48/41 17	45/37 18
LONDON, England	44/35 17	45/35 13	51/47 11	56/40 14	63/45 13	69/51 11	73/55 13	72/54 13	67/51 13	58/44 14	49/39 16	45/36 16
MADRID, Spain	47/33 9	51/35 9	57/40 11	64/44 9	71/50 9	80/57 6	87/62 3	86/62 2	77/56 6	66/48 8	54/40 10	48/35 9
MANILA, Philippines	86/69 6	88/69 3	91/71 4	93/73 4	93/75 12	91/75 17	88/75 24	87/75 23	88/75 22	88/74 19	87/72 14	86/70 11
MARACAIBO, Venezuela	90/73 1	90/73 1	91/74 1	92/76 1	92/77 0	93/77 0	94/70 5	94/77 7	94/77 8	92/76 9	91/76 8	91/75 2
MARSEILLE, France	53/38 10	52/37 9	55/38 8	59/41 10	65/46 10	72/52 9	78/58 6	83/61 4	82/61 5	76/57 7	67/50 10	59/43 11
MELBOURNE, Australia	78/57 9	78/57 8	75/55 9	68/51 13	62/47 14	57/44 16	56/42 17	59/43 17	63/46 15	67/48 14	71/51 13	75/54 11
MEXICO CITY, Mexico	66/42 4	69/43 5	75/47 9	77/51 14	78/54 17	76/55 21	73/53 27	73/54 27	74/53 23	70/50 13	68/46 6	66/43 4
MILAN, Italy	40/29 7	47/33 6	56/38 6	66/46 6	72/54 9	80/61 6	84/64 6	82/63 6	76/58 6	64/49 6	51/39 7	42/33 7
MONTEVIDEO, Uruguay	83/62 6	82/61 5	78/59 5	71/53 6	64/48 6	59/43 5	58/43 6	59/43 7	63/46 6	68/49 6	74/54 6	79/59 7
MOSCOW, USSR	21/9 11	23/10 9	32/17 8	47/31 9	65/44 9	73/51 10	76/55 12	72/52 12	61/43 9	46/34 11	31/23 10	23/13 9
MUNICH, Germany	33/23 10	37/25 9	45/31 10	54/37 13	63/45 13	69/51 14	72/54 14	71/53 13	64/48 11	53/40 10	42/31 9	36/26 11
NAIROBI, Kenya	77/54 5	79/55 6	77/57 11	75/58 16	72/56 17	70/53 9	69/51 6	70/52 7	75/52 6	76/55 8	74/56 15	74/55 11
NAPLES, Italy	54/42 11	55/43 11	60/46 6	67/50 6	73/56 6	81/62 3	86/67 1	86/67 3	81/63 6	72/56 9	63/49 11	57/45 11
NASSAU, Bahamas	77/65 6	77/64 5	79/66 5	81/69 6	84/71 9	87/74 12	88/75 14	89/76 14	88/75 15	85/73 13	81/70 9	79/67 6
NEW DELHI, India	70/44 2	75/49 2	87/58 1	97/68 1	105/79 2	102/83 4	96/81 8	93/79 8	93/75 4	93/65 1	84/52 1	73/46 1
NICE, France	56/40 8	56/41 8	59/45 8	64/49 7	69/56 8	76/62 5	81/66 2	81/66 5	77/62 6	70/55 9	62/48 7	58/43 8
NOUMEA, New Caledonia	86/72 10	85/73 12	85/72 16	83/70 13	79/66 15	77/64 13	76/62 13	76/61 12	78/63 8	80/65 7	83/68 7	86/70 6
ODESSA, USSR	28/22 7	31/26 4	39/32 5	52/41 6	67/55 6	74/62 7	79/65 3	78/65 5	68/56 4	57/47 5	43/35 5	33/27 6
OSLO, Norway	30/20 8	32/20 7	40/25 7	50/34 7	62/43 7	69/51 8	73/56 10	69/53 11	60/45 8	49/37 10	37/29 9	31/24 10
PALERMO, Sicily, Italy	58/47 14	60/47 10	62/49 7	67/53 5	73/59 5	82/66 1	86/71 1	87/72 1	83/69 4	75/62 10	67/55 9	61/50 11
PALMA, Majorca, Spain	57/42 8	59/43 8	62/45 8	66/49 5	73/55 5	80/61 3	84/66 1	86/67 2	81/64 6	74/57 8	65/50 9	59/44 10
PAPEETE, Tahiti	89/72 16	89/72 16	89/72 17	89/72 10	87/70 10	86/69 8	86/68 5	86/68 6	86/69 6	87/70 9	88/71 13	88/72 14
PARIS, France	42/32 15	45/33 13	52/36 15	60/41 14	67/47 13	73/52 11	76/55 12	75/55 12	69/50 11	59/44 14	49/38 15	43/33 17
PEKING, China	35/15 3	41/20 3	53/30 3	68/44 4	80/56 6	88/65 9	89/71 13	87/69 11	80/58 7	69/44 4	50/30 2	37/19 2
PHNOM PENH, Cambodia	87/70 1	90/72 1	93/74 3	94/76 6	92/76 14	91/76 15	89/75 16	89/76 17	88/76 19	87/76 17	86/74 9	86/71 4
PORT-AU-PRINCE, Haiti	87/68 3	88/68 5	89/69 7	89/71 11	90/72 13	92/73 8	94/74 7	93/73 11	91/73 12	90/72 12	88/71 7	87/69 3
PORT OF SPAIN, Trinidad	85/67 14	86/67 8	87/67 8	89/69 7	89/70 10	87/71 17	87/70 20	87/71 21	88/71 18	88/71 16	88/71 17	86/69 16
PRAGUE, Czechoslovakia	34/25 12	38/28 11	45/33 13	55/40 12	65/49 13	72/55 14	74/58 14	73/57 12	65/52 11	54/44 11	41/35 12	34/29 13
RANGOON, Burma	89/65 1	92/67 1	96/71 1	97/76 2	92/77 14	86/76 23	85/76 26	85/76 25	86/76 20	88/76 10	88/73 3	88/67 1
RIO DE JANEIRO, Brazil	84/73 13	85/73 11	83/72 12	80/69 10	77/66 10	76/64 7	75/63 7	76/64 7	75/65 11	77/66 13	79/68 13	82/71 14
ROME, Italy	54/39 8	56/39 11	62/42 5	68/46 6	74/55 6	82/60 3	88/64 2	88/64 3	83/61 6	73/53 9	63/46 8	56/41 9
SAIGON (HO CHI MINH CITY), Vietnam	89/70 2	91/71 1	93/74 2	95/76 4	92/76 16	89/75 21	88/75 23	88/75 21	88/74 21	88/74 20	87/73 11	87/71 7
SAN JUAN, Puerto Rico	80/70 20	80/70 15	81/70 15	82/72 14	84/74 16	85/75 17	85/75 17	85/75 18	86/75 18	85/75 18	84/73 19	81/72 21
SANTIAGO, Chile	85/53 0	84/52 0	80/49 1	74/45 1	65/41 5	58/37 6	59/37 6	62/39 5	66/42 3	72/45 3	78/48 1	83/51 0
SÃO PAULO, Brazil	81/63 19	82/64 17	81/62 15	78/58 10	73/54 10	71/51 8	71/49 6	73/51 8	74/54 11	76/57 13	79/59 14	80/61 13
SEOUL, South Korea	32/15 8	37/20 6	47/29 7	62/41 8	72/51 10	80/61 10	84/70 16	87/71 13	78/59 9	67/45 7	51/32 9	37/20 9
SEVILLE, Spain	59/41 8	62/44 9	67/48 9	73/51 8	80/57 5	89/63 2	96/67 1	97/68 1	89/64 3	78/57 7	67/49 6	60/44 8
SHANGHAI, China	46/33 6	47/34 9	55/40 9	66/50 9	77/59 9	82/67 11	90/74 9	90/74 8	82/66 11	74/57 4	63/45 6	53/36 6
SINGAPORE, Singapore	86/73 17	88/73 11	88/75 14	88/75 15	89/75 15	88/75 13	88/75 13	87/75 14	87/75 14	87/74 16	87/74 18	87/74 19
SOFIA, Bulgaria	34/22 6	39/25 6	51/32 8	62/41 8	70/49 11	76/54 9	82/57 7	82/56 6	74/50 6	63/42 7	50/35 7	37/26 7
STOCKHOLM, Sweden	31/23 8	31/22 7	37/26 7	45/32 6	57/41 8	65/49 7	70/55 9	66/53 10	58/46 8	48/39 9	38/31 9	33/26 9
SYDNEY, Australia	78/65 14	78/65 13	76/63 14	71/58 14	66/52 13	61/48 12	60/46 12	63/48 11	67/51 12	71/56 12	74/60 12	77/63 13
TAIPEI, Taiwan, China	66/54 9	65/53 13	70/57 12	77/63 14	83/69 12	89/73 13	92/76 10	91/75 12	88/73 10	81/67 9	75/62 7	69/57 8
TEHRAN, Iran	45/27 4	50/32 4	59/39 5	71/49 3	82/58 2	93/66 1	99/72 1	97/71 1	90/64 1	76/53 1	63/43 3	51/33 4
TEL AVIV, Israel	63/48 10	65/48 6	67/50 9	74/54 2	81/60 1	84/65 0	87/69 0	87/70 0	86/68 1	84/64 2	77/59 7	66/52 11
TOKYO, Japan	47/29 5	48/31 6	54/36 10	63/46 10	71/54 10	76/63 12	83/70 10	86/72 9	79/66 12	69/55 11	60/43 7	52/33 5
VALPARAISO, Chile	72/56 1	72/56 1	70/54 1	67/52 1	63/50 5	60/48 7	60/47 8	61/47 5	62/48 2	65/50 2	69/52 7	71/54 1
VENICE, Italy	43/33 6	46/35 5	54/41 6	63/49 5	71/57 8	78/64 8	82/67 8	82/67 5	78/62 5	65/52 5	54/43 7	46/37 7
VIENNA, Austria	34/26 8	38/28 7	47/34 7	57/41 9	66/50 9	71/56 9	75/59 9	73/58 10	66/52 7	55/44 8	44/36 8	37/30 9
WELLINGTON, New Zealand	69/56 10	69/56 9	67/54 11	63/51 13	58/47 16	55/44 17	53/42 18	54/43 17	57/46 15	60/48 14	63/50 13	67/54 12
ZURICH, Switzerland	48/14 11	52/15 11	62/22 14	70/32 14	77/39 14	83/47 15	86/51 15	84/49 14	78/42 11	68/32 14	57/25 12	49/16 13

U.S. City Weather

City	Record Temperature High (F°)	Record Temperature Low (F°)	Annual Average: Precip. (Water equiv.) (in.)	Annual Average: Snow and Sleet (in.)	Wind Speed (mph)	First Freeze Date 32 F° or less Average	First Freeze Date 32 F° or less Earliest on record	Last Freeze Date 32 F° or less Average	Last Freeze Date 32 F° or less Latest on record	Elevation of Station (feet)
Albany	104	—28	36.46	65.7	8.8	Oct. 13	Sept. 23	Apr. 27	May 20	292
Albuquerque	105	—17	8.33	10.7	9.0	Oct. 29	Oct. 11	Apr. 16	May 18	5,314
Atlanta	103	— 9	48.66	1.5	9.1	Nov. 12	Oct. 24	Mar. 24	Apr. 15	1,034
Baltimore	107	— 7	41.62	21.9	9.5	Oct. 26	Oct. 8	Apr. 15	May 11	155
Birmingham	107	—10	53.46	1.2	7.4	Nov. 10	Oct. 17	Mar. 17	Apr. 21	630
Bismarck	114	—45	16.15	38.4	10.6	Sept. 22	Sept. 6	May 11	May 30	1,660
Boise	111	—23	11.97	21.7	9.0	Oct. 12	Sept. 9	May 6	May 31	2,868
Boston	104	—18	41.55	41.9	12.6	Nov. 7	Oct. 5	Apr. 8	May 3	29
Buffalo	99	—21	35.19	88.6	12.3	Oct. 25	Sept. 23	Apr. 30	May 24	706
Burlington, Vt.	101	—30	32.54	78.4	8.8	Oct. 3	Sept. 13	May 10	May 24	340
Charleston, W. Va.	108	—24	43.66	28.8	6.5	Oct. 28	Sept. 29	Apr. 18	May 11	951
Charlotte	104	— 5	45.00	5.6	7.6	Nov. 4	Oct. 15	Apr. 2	Apr. 16	769
Cheyenne	100	—38	14.48	52.0	13.3	Sept. 27	Aug. 25	May 18	June 18	6,141
Chicago	105	—23	33.47	40.7	10.3	Oct. 26	Sept. 25	Apr. 20	May 14	623
Cincinnati	102	—19	40.40	23.2	9.1	Oct. 25	Sept. 28	Apr. 15	May 25	877
Cleveland	103	—19	34.15	51.5	10.8	Nov. 2	Sept. 29	Apr. 21	May 14	805
Columbia, S.C.	107	— 2	45.23	1.8	6.9	Nov. 3	Oct. 4	Mar. 30	Apr. 21	225
Columbus, Ohio	106	—20	36.98	27.7	8.7	Oct. 31	Oct. 7	Apr. 16	May 9	833
Concord, N.H.	102	—37	38.13	64.1	6.7	Sept. 24	Sept. 13	May 17	June 6	346
Dallas-Ft. Worth, Tex.	112	— 8	32.11	2.7	11.1	Nov. 21	Oct. 27	Mar. 16	Apr. 13	596
Denver	105	—30	14.60	60.1	9.0	Oct. 14	Sept. 16	May 2	May 28	5,332
Des Moines	110	—30	31.49	33.2	11.1	Oct. 10	Sept. 28	Apr. 20	May 11	963
Detroit	105	—24	31.49	31.7	10.2	Oct. 21	Sept. 23	Apr. 23	May 12	626
El Paso	109	— 8	8.47	4.4	9.6	Nov. 11	Oct. 31	Mar. 13	Apr. 11	3,916
Great Falls	107	—49	14.83	57.7	13.1	Sept. 26	Sept. 7	May 14	June 8	3,657
Hartford	102	—26	43.00	53.1	9.0	Oct. 15	Sept. 27	Apr. 22	May 10	179
Houston	108	5	47.07	0.4	7.6	Dec. 11	Oct. 25	Feb. 5	Mar. 27	108
Indianapolis	107	—25	39.98	21.3	9.7	Oct. 22	Sept. 27	Apr. 23	May 27	808
Jackson	107	— 5	50.96	0.8	7.7	Nov. 8	Oct. 9	Mar. 18	Apr. 25	331
Jacksonville	105	10	51.75	Trace	8.6	Dec. 16	Nov. 3	Feb. 6	Mar. 31	31
Juneau	90	—22	53.95	109.1	8.5	Oct. 21	Sept. 9	Apr. 22	June 8	24
Kansas City, Mo.	113	—22	36.66	19.7	10.2	Oct. 26	Sept. 30	Apr. 7	May 6	1,025
Little Rock	110	—13	48.17	5.3	8.2	Nov. 15	Oct. 23	Mar. 16	Apr. 13	265
Los Angeles	110	23	11.94	Trace	7.4	—	Dec. 9	—	Jan. 21	104
Louisville	107	—20	42.94	17.3	8.4	Oct. 25	Oct. 15	Apr. 10	Apr. 19	488
Memphis	106	—13	48.74	5.7	9.2	Nov. 5	Oct. 17	Mar. 20	Apr. 15	284
Miami	100	26	59.21	—	9.1	—	—	—	Feb. 6	12
Milwaukee	105	—25	30.18	45.2	11.8	Oct. 23	Sept. 20	Apr. 25	May 27	693
Minneapolis-St. Paul	108	—34	26.62	45.8	10.6	Oct. 13	Sept. 3	Apr. 29	May 24	838
Mobile	104	— 1	63.26	0.4	9.3	Dec. 12	Nov. 15	Feb. 17	Mar. 20	221
Nashville	107	—15	46.61	10.9	7.9	Oct. 31	Oct. 7	Apr. 3	Apr. 24	605
New Orleans	102	7	58.93	0.2	8.4	Dec. 3	Nov. 11	Feb. 15	Apr. 8	30
New York City	106	—15	43.56	29.1	9.4	Nov. 12	Oct. 19	Apr. 7	Apr. 24	87
Norfolk	105	2	45.22	7.2	10.6	Nov. 21	Nov. 7	Mar. 22	Apr. 14	30
Oklahoma City	113	—17	31.71	9.2	12.9	Nov. 7	Oct. 7	Apr. 1	May 3	1,304
Omaha	114	—32	28.48	32.5	10.9	Oct. 20	Sept. 24	Apr. 14	May 11	982
Philadelphia	106	—11	41.18	20.3	9.6	Nov. 17	Oct. 19	Mar. 30	Apr. 20	28
Phoenix	118	16	7.41	Trace	6.1	Dec. 11	Nov. 4	Jan. 27	Mar. 3	1,107
Pittsburgh	103	—20	36.21	45.5	9.4	Oct. 20	Oct. 10	Apr. 21	May 4	1,225
Portland, Me.	103	—39	42.15	74.3	8.8	Sept. 27	Sept. 17	May 12	May 31	63
Portland, Ore.	107	— 3	37.98	7.5	7.8	Dec. 1	Oct. 26	Feb. 25	May 4	39
Providence	104	—17	40.90	37.8	10.8	Oct. 26	Oct. 3	Apr. 14	Apr. 24	62
Reno	106	—19	7.65	26.8	6.4	Oct. 2	Aug. 30	May 14	June 25	4,400
Richmond	107	—12	43.77	14.3	7.6	Nov. 8	Oct. 5	Apr. 2	May 11	177
Sacramento	115	17	17.33	Trace	8.3	Dec. 11	Nov. 4	Jan. 24	Mar. 14	25
St. Louis	115	—23	36.70	17.8	9.5	Oct. 20	Sept. 28	Apr. 15	May 10	564
Salt Lake City	107	—30	15.63	58.1	8.7	Nov. 1	Sept. 25	Apr. 12	Apr. 30	4,227
San Francisco	106	20	18.88	Trace	10.5	—	Dec. 11	—	Jan. 21	18
Seattle	100	0	40.30	15.2	9.3	Dec. 1	Oct. 19	Feb. 23	Apr. 3	450
Spokane	108	—30	16.19	54.0	8.7	Oct. 12	Sept. 13	Apr. 20	May 16	2,365
Washington, D.C.	106	—15	40.00	16.8	9.2	Nov. 10	Oct. 2	Mar. 29	May 12	65
Wichita	114	—22	30.06	16.3	12.6	Nov. 1	Sept. 27	Apr. 5	Apr. 21	1,340
Wilmington, Del.	107	—15	43.63	20.1	9.1	Oct. 26	Sept. 27	Apr. 18	May 9	80

SOURCE: National Climatic Center

U.S. City Weather

City	Jan.	Feb.	Mar.	April	May	June	July	Aug.	Sept.	Oct.	Nov.	Dec.	ANNUAL
Albany	23.0°	23.7°	33.5°	46.5°	58.4°	67.7°	72.5°	70.2°	62.7°	51.4°	39.7°	27.7°	48.1°
Albuquerque	34.5	39.5	46.3	54.8	63.8	73.3	77.1	75.1	68.4	56.8	43.9	35.1	55.7
Atlanta	43.5	45.6	52.6	61.3	69.6	76.4	78.5	77.8	73.1	62.9	52.0	44.7	61.5
Baltimore	33.2	35.0	42.6	53.6	63.1	72.1	76.8	75.3	68.5	57.3	46.0	36.4	55.0
Birmingham	45.6	47.1	55.0	62.9	70.7	77.8	79.9	79.6	75.2	64.6	53.4	46.3	63.2
Bismarck	8.1	12.2	25.3	42.9	54.6	64.1	70.6	68.5	57.9	45.7	28.6	15.4	41.1
Boise	29.9	35.5	42.3	49.6	57.8	65.4	74.5	72.5	62.7	52.3	40.6	32.1	51.3
Boston	28.9	29.1	36.9	46.9	57.7	67.0	72.6	70.7	64.0	54.2	43.5	32.6	50.3
Buffalo	25.1	24.5	32.3	43.3	54.6	64.7	70.3	68.9	62.6	51.8	40.0	29.5	47.3
Burlington, Vt.	18.0	18.4	29.3	42.6	55.2	64.8	69.7	67.3	59.6	48.8	36.6	23.3	44.5
Charleston, W. Va.	36.6	38.0	46.0	56.0	64.8	72.3	76.0	74.8	69.3	58.0	46.7	38.2	56.4
Charlotte	42.0	43.9	51.0	60.0	68.9	76.0	78.7	77.4	72.2	61.6	50.9	43.1	60.5
Cheyenne	26.1	27.7	32.4	41.4	51.0	61.0	67.7	66.4	57.3	46.4	35.2	28.6	45.1
Chicago	24.7	27.1	36.4	47.8	58.2	68.4	73.8	72.5	65.6	54.5	40.4	29.4	49.9
Cincinnati	30.8	33.6	41.7	53.5	63.3	71.9	75.5	74.2	67.3	56.3	43.6	34.4	53.9
Cleveland	27.5	27.8	35.9	47.0	58.3	67.9	72.2	70.6	64.6	53.8	41.6	31.3	49.9
Columbia, S.C.	46.6	48.1	55.1	63.5	71.9	78.5	80.8	79.9	75.1	64.5	54.4	47.2	63.8
Columbus, Ohio	29.4	30.8	40.0	51.1	61.9	70.9	74.8	72.9	66.6	55.0	42.3	32.4	52.3
Concord, N.H.	21.3	22.8	31.9	44.4	56.2	64.9	70.0	67.3	59.7	49.2	37.5	25.6	45.9
Dallas-Ft. Worth, Tex.	45.6	48.8	56.9	65.2	72.7	80.9	84.5	84.6	77.8	67.8	56.1	47.7	65.7
Denver	30.1	32.8	38.7	47.4	56.7	66.6	72.6	71.3	62.6	51.6	39.6	32.3	50.2
Des Moines	20.8	24.7	36.3	50.4	61.5	71.1	76.1	73.7	65.3	54.2	38.5	26.1	49.9
Detroit	25.3	25.8	34.5	46.7	58.1	68.2	73.0	71.1	64.2	53.1	40.1	29.5	49.2
El Paso	44.7	49.3	55.6	63.8	72.2	80.8	81.9	80.2	74.8	64.7	52.5	45.2	63.8
Great Falls	21.2	26.1	31.4	43.3	53.3	60.9	69.7	67.9	57.6	48.3	34.8	27.1	45.1
Hartford	27.1	27.7	36.9	47.9	59.0	67.9	73.1	70.9	63.7	53.3	42.1	30.4	50.0
Houston	53.2	54.6	62.0	67.9	74.3	79.8	82.4	81.3	77.5	70.2	59.6	55.5	68.2
Indianapolis	28.5	30.8	40.1	52.0	62.5	71.8	75.7	73.7	66.9	55.5	42.0	31.9	52.6
Jackson	48.4	50.9	57.3	65.3	72.6	79.6	81.8	81.5	76.9	66.5	55.7	49.5	65.5
Jacksonville	55.0	56.6	61.8	67.5	73.7	78.5	80.4	80.1	77.1	68.9	60.6	54.9	67.9
Juneau	22.2	27.3	31.2	38.4	46.4	52.8	55.5	54.1	49.0	41.5	32.0	26.9	39.8
Kansas City, Mo.	29.7	33.1	43.2	55.5	65.3	74.7	79.5	78.0	70.0	59.1	44.7	33.6	55.6
Little Rock	41.7	44.8	52.9	62.5	70.1	78.2	81.3	80.5	74.1	63.8	51.9	43.8	62.1
Los Angeles	54.6	55.9	56.9	59.3	62.1	64.9	68.3	69.5	68.5	65.2	60.4	56.4	61.8
Louisville	34.7	36.8	45.6	56.3	66.0	74.6	78.3	76.8	70.4	58.9	46.4	37.2	56.9
Memphis	41.3	44.1	52.2	62.1	70.5	78.2	81.2	80.0	74.1	63.5	51.6	43.6	61.9
Miami	67.5	68.0	71.3	74.9	78.0	80.9	82.2	82.7	81.6	77.8	72.3	68.5	75.5
Milwaukee	20.9	23.2	32.6	44.3	54.3	64.5	70.7	69.7	62.5	51.5	37.7	26.1	46.5
Minneapolis-St. Paul	13.2	16.7	29.6	45.7	57.9	67.8	73.1	70.7	61.5	50.0	33.0	19.5	44.9
Mobile	51.9	54.4	60.1	67.1	74.3	80.3	81.8	81.5	78.1	68.9	58.9	53.1	67.6
Nashville	39.1	41.0	49.5	59.5	68.2	76.3	79.4	78.3	72.2	61.1	48.9	41.1	59.6
New Orleans	54.3	56.5	61.7	68.9	75.4	80.8	82.2	82.0	78.8	70.7	60.7	55.6	69.0
New York City	32.3	32.7	40.6	51.1	61.9	70.9	76.1	74.6	68.0	58.0	46.7	35.7	54.1
Norfolk	41.6	42.3	48.8	57.4	66.7	74.7	78.6	77.5	72.4	62.2	52.1	43.6	59.8
Oklahoma City	37.2	40.8	49.8	60.2	68.2	77.0	81.4	81.1	73.7	62.7	49.4	39.9	60.1
Omaha	22.0	26.5	37.5	51.7	62.7	72.3	77.4	75.1	66.3	55.0	39.3	27.5	51.1
Philadelphia	33.1	33.8	41.6	52.2	63.0	71.8	76.6	74.7	68.4	57.5	46.2	36.2	54.6
Phoenix	51.6	55.4	60.5	67.7	76.0	85.2	90.8	89.0	83.6	71.7	59.8	52.4	70.3
Pittsburgh	30.7	31.3	39.9	51.1	62.0	70.6	74.6	72.8	66.6	55.2	43.2	33.6	52.7
Portland, Me.	22.4	23.4	32.3	42.8	53.2	62.4	68.2	66.6	59.6	49.6	38.6	26.9	45.5
Portland, Ore.	38.5	43.0	45.9	50.6	57.0	60.2	65.8	65.3	62.7	54.0	45.7	41.1	52.5
Providence	29.4	29.3	37.6	47.5	57.8	66.9	72.7	71.0	63.9	54.0	43.4	32.6	50.5
Reno	31.8	36.6	41.2	47.4	54.9	62.5	70.2	68.5	60.7	50.9	41.0	33.4	49.9
Richmond	38.0	39.4	46.9	56.9	66.1	74.0	77.6	76.1	69.9	58.9	48.7	39.7	57.7
Sacramento	44.9	49.8	53.1	58.1	64.5	70.8	75.4	74.3	71.6	63.4	52.9	45.7	60.4
St. Louis	31.7	34.8	44.3	56.1	65.9	75.1	79.3	77.5	70.1	59.0	45.3	35.3	56.2
Salt Lake City	28.0	33.2	40.7	49.0	58.3	68.1	77.2	75.4	65.1	53.1	40.5	31.4	51.7
San Francisco	48.0	50.9	52.9	54.6	57.3	60.3	61.5	62.0	62.9	60.0	54.3	49.3	56.2
Seattle	38.2	42.2	43.9	48.1	55.0	59.9	64.4	63.8	59.6	51.8	44.6	40.5	51.0
Spokane	26.8	31.7	39.4	47.6	55.8	62.5	70.2	68.7	59.5	48.7	37.0	30.4	48.2
Washington, D.C.	36.1	37.7	45.7	56.1	65.8	74.3	78.4	76.9	70.3	59.6	48.4	38.4	57.3
Wichita	31.6	35.2	44.7	56.3	65.4	75.3	80.3	79.3	70.9	59.6	45.2	35.0	56.5
Wilmington, Del.	32.6	33.1	41.9	52.2	62.7	71.4	76.0	74.1	67.9	56.8	45.7	35.2	54.2

SOURCE: National Climatic Center (data based on normals for 1936-1975)

TABLES OF AIRLINE DISTANCES

All Distances in Statute Miles

Between Principal Cities of the World

FROM/TO	Azores	Bagdad	Berlin	Bombay	Buenos Aires	Callao	Cairo	Cape Town	Chicago	Istanbul	Guam	Honolulu	Juneau	London	Los Angeles	Melbourne	Mexico City	Montreal	New Orleans	New York	Panama	Paris	Rio de Janeiro	San Francisco	Santiago	Seattle	Shanghai	Singapore	Tokyo	Wellington
Azores	....	3906	2148	5930	5385	4825	3325	5670	3305	2880	8985	7421	4715	1562	5034	12190	4584	2548	3718	2604	3918	1617	4312	5114	5718	4720	7324	8338	7370	11475
Bagdad	3906	....	2040	2022	8215	8618	785	4923	6490	1085	6380	8445	6180	2568	7695	8150	8155	5814	7212	6066	7807	2385	7012	7521	8876	6848	4468	4443	5242	9782
Berlin	2148	2040	....	3947	7411	6937	1823	5949	4458	1068	7158	7384	4638	575	5849	9992	6119	3776	5182	4026	5902	540	6246	5744	7842	5121	5323	6226	5623	11384
Bombay	5930	2022	3947	....	9380	10530	2698	5133	8144	3043	4831	8172	6992	4526	8810	6140	9818	7582	8952	7875	9832	4391	8438	8523	10127	7830	3219	2425	4247	7752
Buenos Aires	5385	8215	7411	9380	....	1982	7428	4332	5598	7638	10516	7653	7964	6919	6148	7336	4609	5619	4902	5295	3319	6891	1230	6487	731	6956	12295	9940	11601	6341
Callao	4825	8618	6937	10530	1982	....	7870	6195	3765	7666	9760	5993	5806	6376	4155	8196	2619	3954	2990	3633	1450	6455	2400	4500	1548	4964	10760	11700	9740	6696
Cairo	3325	785	1823	2698	7428	7870	....	4476	6231	780	7175	8925	6352	2218	7675	8720	7807	5502	6862	5701	7230	2020	6242	7554	8100	6915	5290	5152	6005	10360
Cape Town	5670	4923	5949	5133	4332	6195	4476	....	8551	5210	8918	11655	10382	5975	10165	6510	8620	7975	8390	7845	7090	5732	3850	10340	5080	10305	8179	6025	9234	7149
Chicago	3305	6490	4458	8144	5598	3765	6231	8551	....	5530	7510	4315	2310	4015	1741	9837	1690	750	827	727	2320	4219	5320	1875	5325	1753	7155	9475	6410	8465
Istanbul	2880	1085	1068	3043	7638	7666	780	5210	5530	....	7015	8200	5665	1540	6895	9189	7160	4825	6220	5060	6797	1390	6420	6770	8230	6124	5084	5440	5649	10790
Guam	8985	6380	7158	4831	10516	9760	7175	8918	7510	7015	....	3896	5225	7605	6255	3497	7690	7840	7895	8115	9220	7675	11710	5952	9946	5785	1945	2990	1596	4206
Honolulu	7421	8445	7384	8172	7653	5993	8925	11655	4315	8200	3896	....	2825	7320	2620	5581	3846	4992	4305	5051	5347	7525	8400	2407	6935	2707	5009	6874	3940	4676
Juneau	4715	6180	4638	6992	7964	5806	6352	10382	2310	5665	5225	2825	....	4496	1835	8162	3210	2647	2860	2874	4456	4700	7611	1530	7320	870	4968	7375	4117	7501
London	1562	2568	575	4526	6919	6376	2218	5975	4015	1540	7605	7320	4496	....	5496	10590	5605	3370	4656	3500	5310	210	5747	5440	7275	4850	5841	6818	6050	11790
Los Angeles	5034	7695	5849	8810	6148	4155	7675	10165	1741	6895	6255	2620	1835	5496	....	8098	1445	2468	1695	2466	3025	5711	6330	345	5595	961	6598	8955	5600	6806
Melbourne	12190	8150	9992	6140	7336	8196	8720	6510	9837	9189	3497	5581	8162	10590	8098	....	8599	10553	9455	10541	9211	10500	8340	7970	7130	8330	4967	3768	5172	1655
Mexico City	4584	8155	6119	9818	4609	2619	7807	8620	1690	7160	7690	3846	3210	5605	1445	8599	....	2247	940	2110	1532	5800	4810	1870	4122	2339	8120	10495	7190	7003
Montreal	2548	5814	3776	7582	5619	3954	5502	7975	750	4825	7840	4992	2647	3370	2468	10553	2247	....	1390	340	2545	3490	5110	2557	5461	2309	7141	9280	6546	9206
New Orleans	3718	7212	5182	8952	4902	2990	6862	8390	827	6220	7895	4305	2860	4656	1695	9455	940	1390	....	1161	1600	4846	4798	1960	4553	2137	7830	10255	6993	7950
New York	2604	6066	4025	7875	5295	3633	5701	7845	727	5060	8115	5051	2874	3500	2466	10541	2110	340	1161	....	2211	3600	4810	2606	5134	2440	7460	9617	6846	9067
Panama	3918	7807	5902	9832	3319	1450	7230	7090	2320	6797	9220	5347	4456	5310	3025	9211	1532	2545	1600	2211	....	5440	3311	3349	3000	3680	9430	11800	8560	7580
Paris	1617	2385	540	4391	6891	6455	2020	5762	4219	1390	7675	7525	4700	210	5711	10500	5800	3490	4846	3600	5440	....	5710	5680	7300	5080	5855	6730	6132	11865
Rio de Janeiro	4312	7012	6246	8438	1230	2400	6242	3850	5320	6420	11710	8400	7611	5747	6330	8340	4810	5110	4798	4810	3311	5710	....	6655	1852	6945	11510	9875	11600	7510
San Francisco	5114	7521	5744	8523	6487	4500	7554	10340	1875	6770	5952	2407	1530	5440	345	7970	1870	2557	1960	2606	3349	5680	6655	....	5960	692	6245	8440	5250	6800
Santiago	5718	8876	7842	10127	731	1548	8100	5080	5325	8230	9946	6935	7320	7275	5595	7130	4122	5461	4553	5134	3000	7300	1852	5960	....	6466	11850	10270	10850	5925
Seattle	4720	6848	5121	7830	6956	4964	6915	10305	1753	6124	5785	2707	870	4850	961	8330	2339	2309	2137	2440	3680	5080	6945	692	6466	....	5780	8200	4863	7310
Shanghai	7324	4468	5323	3219	12295	10760	5290	8179	7155	5084	1945	5009	4968	5841	6598	4967	8120	7141	7830	7460	9430	5855	11510	6245	11850	5780	....	2395	1095	6080
Singapore	8338	4443	6226	2425	9940	11700	5152	6025	9475	5440	2990	6874	7375	6818	8955	3768	10495	9280	10255	9617	11800	6730	9875	8440	10270	8200	2395	....	3350	5360
Tokyo	7370	5242	5623	4247	11601	9740	6005	9234	6410	5649	1596	3940	4117	6050	5600	5172	7190	6546	6993	6846	8560	6132	11600	5250	10850	4863	1095	3350	....	5730
Wellington	11475	9782	11384	7752	6341	6696	10360	7149	8465	10790	4206	4676	7501	11790	6806	1655	7003	9206	7950	9067	7580	11865	7510	6800	5925	7310	6080	5360	5730	.....

Between Principal Cities of Europe

	Amsterdam	Athens	Baku	Barcelona	Belgrade	Berlin	Brussels	Bucharest	Budapest	Cologne	Copenhagen	Istanbul	Dresden	Dublin	Frankfort	Hamburg	Leningrad	Lisbon	London	Lyon	Madrid	Marseilles	Milan	Moscow	Munich	Oslo	Paris	Riga	Rome	Sofia	Stockholm	Toulouse	Warsaw	Vienna	Zurich
Amsterdam	....	1340	2218	770	875	365	105	1100	710	128	381	1360	385	468	228	232	1090	1140	220	458	912	627	517	1325	415	568	257	820	808	1073	695	625	673	580	375
Athens	1340	....	1395	1160	500	1112	1292	460	698	1200	1320	350	1022	1765	1113	1250	1535	1770	1476	1100	1463	1025	900	1388	925	1610	1300	1310	650	335	1495	1215	990	795	1000
Baku	2218	1395	....	2427	1487	1867	2240	1220	1562	2127	1980	1070	1837	2490	2055	2020	1570	3050	2435	2238	2742	2238	2028	1175	1912	2118	2335	1590	1900	1360	1862	2425	1555	1700	2050
Barcelona	770	1160	2427	....	998	925	658	1210	924	692	1085	1380	860	919	665	910	1740	610	707	327	316	211	450	1852	648	1330	518	1440	530	1072	1410	156	1150	830	513
Belgrade	875	500	1487	998	....	618	850	295	205	750	840	502	530	1327	652	760	1165	1555	1040	752	1235	750	540	1160	475	1112	890	855	440	231	1005	930	510	300	590
Berlin	365	1112	1867	925	618	....	401	798	425	300	225	1068	95	815	268	165	815	1410	575	601	1149	730	570	995	310	520	540	520	730	810	503	815	320	322	410
Brussels	105	1292	2240	658	850	401	....	1110	700	110	475	1345	407	480	198	301	1175	998	202	352	807	521	435	1392	372	672	170	900	730	945	793	515	720	568	312
Bucharest	1100	460	1220	1210	295	798	1110	....	295	982	970	272	725	1560	890	950	1080	1842	1285	1025	1518	1020	819	920	725	1245	1152	870	700	194	1080	1210	580	520	855
Budapest	710	698	1562	924	205	425	700	295	....	590	629	650	345	1176	504	572	965	1515	900	680	1214	718	476	965	350	920	770	685	500	395	820	883	342	128	498
Cologne	128	1200	2127	692	750	300	110	982	590	....	400	1240	292	585	93	228	1090	1126	308	370	875	528	390	1285	282	635	250	805	675	945	722	875	602	460	259
Copenhagen	381	1320	1960	1085	840	225	475	970	629	400	....	1240	315	768	412	180	708	1520	590	760	1272	906	720	970	520	303	634	453	948	1010	330	962	415	538	595
Istanbul	1360	350	1070	1380	502	1068	1345	272	650	1240	1240	....	995	1830	1150	1222	1292	2005	1540	1238	1690	1205	1030	1180	975	1505	1390	1115	840	315	1340	1400	852	790	1090
Dresden	385	1022	1837	860	530	95	407	725	345	292	315	995	....	852	236	238	885	1380	592	540	1100	655	435	1200	227	620	523	585	630	730	598	762	325	235	342
Dublin	468	1765	2490	919	1327	815	480	1560	1176	585	768	1830	852	....	671	668	1440	1015	300	720	902	875	880	1728	855	786	480	1210	1175	1525	1010	761	1130	1040	768
Frankfort	228	1113	2055	665	652	268	198	890	504	93	412	1150	236	671	....	250	1075	1160	392	350	888	492	323	1240	193	675	295	780	698	860	730	560	550	370	193
Hamburg	232	1250	2020	910	760	165	301	950	572	228	180	1222	238	668	250	....	880	1301	448	580	1098	730	570	1100	378	445	459	600	810	954	502	780	462	460	432
Leningrad	1090	1535	1570	1740	1165	815	1175	1080	965	1090	708	1292	885	1440	1075	880	....	2235	1300	1420	1980	1540	1315	391	1100	670	1335	300	1440	1218	435	1635	640	975	1225
Lisbon	1140	1770	3050	610	1555	1410	998	1842	1515	1126	1520	2005	1380	1015	1160	1301	2235	....	975	850	313	810	1350	430	1208	1690	890	1940	1150	1685	1848	640	1700	1415	1058
London	220	1476	2435	707	1040	575	202	1285	900	308	590	1540	592	300	392	448	1300	975	....	455	777	620	595	1540	526	720	210	1035	890	1235	885	550	890	762	480
Lyon	458	1100	2238	327	752	601	352	1025	680	370	760	1238	540	720	350	580	1420	850	455	....	577	170	210	1560	352	1005	248	1122	462	928	1080	228	850	562	206
Madrid	912	1463	2742	316	1235	1149	807	1518	1214	875	1272	1690	1100	902	888	1098	1980	313	777	557	....	394	728	2120	910	1474	645	1670	840	1385	1598	344	1410	1110	765
Marseilles	627	1025	2238	211	750	730	521	1020	718	528	906	1205	655	875	492	730	1540	810	620	170	394	....	238	1642	445	1165	410	1238	372	895	1225	196	950	620	318
Milan	517	900	2028	450	540	570	435	819	476	390	720	1030	435	880	323	570	1315	1350	595	210	728	238	....	1408	215	1000	400	1010	295	715	1020	400	705	385	137
Moscow	1325	1388	1175	1852	1160	995	1392	920	965	1285	970	1180	1200	1728	1240	1100	391	430	1540	1560	2120	1642	1408	....	1220	1030	1538	520	1462	1100	770	1770	710	1028	1350
Munich	415	925	1912	648	475	310	372	725	350	282	520	975	227	855	193	378	1100	1208	526	352	910	445	215	1220	....	810	425	800	430	672	811	570	500	222	158
Oslo	568	1610	2118	1330	1112	520	672	1245	920	635	303	1505	620	786	675	445	670	1690	720	1005	1474	1165	1000	1030	810	....	830	531	1242	1295	267	1140	653	835	869
Paris	257	1300	2335	518	890	540	170	1152	770	250	634	1390	523	480	295	459	1335	890	210	248	645	410	400	1538	425	830	....	1050	690	1080	950	431	845	770	295
Riga	820	1310	1590	1440	855	520	900	870	685	805	453	1115	585	1210	780	600	300	1940	1035	1122	1670	1238	1010	520	800	531	1050	....	1155	985	276	1335	350	685	930
Rome	808	650	1900	530	440	730	730	700	500	675	948	840	630	1175	698	810	1440	1150	890	462	840	372	295	1462	430	1242	690	1155	....	545	1220	569	810	470	421
Sofia	1073	335	1360	1072	231	810	945	194	395	945	1010	315	730	1525	860	954	1218	1685	1235	928	1385	895	715	1100	672	1295	1080	985	545	....	1170	1080	662	500	780
Stockholm	695	1495	1862	1410	1005	503	793	1080	820	722	330	1340	598	1010	730	502	435	1848	885	1080	1598	1225	1020	770	811	267	950	276	1220	1170	....	1281	500	770	908
Toulouse	625	1215	2425	156	930	815	515	1210	883	875	962	1400	762	761	560	780	1635	640	550	228	344	196	400	1770	570	1140	431	1335	569	1080	1281	....	1062	725	425
Warsaw	673	990	1555	1150	510	320	720	580	342	602	415	852	325	1130	550	462	640	1700	890	850	1410	950	705	710	500	653	845	350	810	662	500	1062	....	345	640
Vienna	580	795	1700	830	300	322	568	520	128	460	538	790	235	1040	370	460	975	1415	762	562	1110	620	385	1028	222	835	770	685	470	500	770	725	345	....	365
Zurich	375	1000	2050	513	590	410	312	855	498	259	595	1090	342	768	193	432	1225	1058	480	206	765	318	137	1350	158	869	295	930	421	780	908	425	640	365	....

WORLD
Page 1, 2, 3

ARCTIC OCEAN
Page 4

GREENLAND
146

EURO
Page

ALASKA
197

YUKON
TERRITORY
186

NORTHWEST   TERRITORIES
187

21
ICELAND

UNITED
KINGDOM

CANADA
Page 162

BRITISH
COLUMBIA
185

ALBERTA
182

SASKATCH-
EWAN
181

MANITOBA
178

174

166

QUEBEC

NEWFOUNDLAND

IRELAND   17   10

FRA

NORTH AMERICA
Page 146

175

ONTARIO

176

173

166

N.B. P.E.I.
170

168
NOVA SCOTIA

PORTUGAL
32

SPAIN
33

UNITED   STATES
188

AZORES
32

MADEIRA
32

MOROCCO
106

BERMUDA
157

CANARY IS.
33

MEXICO
151

BAHAMAS
157

WEST INDIES
Page 157

W. SAHARA
106

AL

CUBA
158

HAITI
DOM. REP.
158

PUERTO RICO 161

CAPE
VERDE
106

MAURITANIA
106

MALI
106

HAWAII
219

BELIZE
154
HON.

JAM.
158

161

SENEGAL
106

GAMBIA

BURK-FASO
106

GUATEMALA
154   EL SAL.

NICARAGUA
154

GUINEA-BISSAU
106

GUINEA

PACIFIC OCEAN
Page 87

COSTA RICA
154

PANAMA
154

VENEZUELA
124

GUYANA
SURINAME
131
FR. GUIANA

SIERRA LEONE
106

IVORY
COAST
106

GHANA
106

TO

COLOMBIA
126

LIBERIA
106

EQUA

ECUADOR
128

GALÁPAGOS IS.
128

AFRICA
Page 10

PERU
128

BRAZIL
132

SOUTH AMERICA
Page 120

BOLIVIA
136

TAHITI
86

PARAGUAY
144

135

CHILE
138

ARGENTINA
143

145
URUGUAY

ANTARCTIC
Page 5

BR. COLUMBIA 185	ALBERTA 182	SASK. 181	MANITOBA 178	175 ONTARIO		174 QUEBEC	
WASH. 310	MONTANA 262	N. DAKOTA 282	MINN. 255		176	173	MAINE 243
OREGON 290	IDAHO 220	WYOMING 318	S. DAKOTA 298	WIS. 317	MICH. 250	N.Y. 276	
204	NEVADA 266	UTAH 304	COLORADO 209	NEBRASKA 265	IOWA 228	ILL. 222	IND. 227	OHIO 284	PA. 294	
CALIFORNIA				KANSAS 232	MO. 261	KY. 237	W.VA. 312	VA. 307	VT. 268

ALASKA
197

HAWAII
219

MEXICO
151

UNITED STATES
Page 188

ARIZONA
198

NEW MEX.
274

OKLA.
289

ARK.
203

TENN. 237

N.C.
281

S.C.
296

TEXAS
303

MISS.
256

ALA.
195

GA.
217

LA.
239

FLORIDA
212

N.H.   268
MASS.   248
R.I.   248
CONN.   210
N.J.   273
MD.   245
DEL.   245

PAGE LOCATION KEY TO ATLAS MAPS